THE CHRISTIAN LIFE BIBLE

PRESENTED TO

_____

OCCASION

_____

_____

DATE

_____

BY

_____

THE CHRISTIAN LIFE BIBLE

with Old and New Testaments

The New King James Version

with Master Outlines and Study Notes

references, book introductions,
concordance, subject index,
study helps
words of Christ in red

THOMAS NELSON PUBLISHERS
Nashville

A Word to the Reader about...

THE CHRISTIAN LIFE BIBLE

The Christian life is designed to be a life lived to the fullest, shaped and energized by one's relationship with God. The Genesis account of the creation of man and woman and their roles in the garden of Eden tells us that human life is complete only insofar as it enters into that relationship. God desires this completeness for us, and nowhere is His desire more clearly evident than in His incarnation in Jesus Christ—that event when God took upon Himself human flesh in order that men and women "may have life, and that they may have it more abundantly" (John 10:10). Through the birth, life, death and resurrection of Jesus, He who is the Source of life opened the way for us to join our lives with Him.

The Scriptures describe this relationship as "grow [ing] in the grace and knowledge of our Lord and Savior Jesus Christ" (2 Pet. 3:17, 18). The Christian Life Bible is presented as one source of nurture for that relationship between God and you. It makes available in one volume a wealth of biblical guidance.

The prominent feature of The Christian Life Bible is the *Master Outlines and Study Notes*, written by Dr. Porter L. Barrington, for fifty-seven years a noted pastor and evangelist. In fifty-two easy-to-understand outlines, Dr. Barrington identifies and explains the cornerstone theological truths of Christianity. They are arranged in an orderly fashion so that you can proceed step by step through your study, building a solid foundation for your Christian life. By taking one outline each week, you will gain in one year a thorough knowledge of the Bible. But you will also gain an ability to apply that knowledge in your daily life, because the Master Outlines and Study Notes were prepared with the goal of grounding and establishing the believer in practical Christian truth.

Additional helps and study aids in this edition supplement the Master Outlines and Study Notes to make this Bible a complete, well-rounded study tool. Sixty-six *Book Introductions* were penned by pastors, scholars, and lay workers. These introductions emphasize putting biblical knowledge into everyday practice. The *Subject Index* following the Bible text alphabetically arranges the major topics discussed in the Master Outlines and Study Notes and in the book introductions. With the Index you can identify and search out the subject you want to study. The Index even gives you the number of the page on which the subject is found.

Three informative and practical articles round out the study material. "*The Intertestamental Period*" sets the stage for sound New Testament study. "*Backsliding: Its Cause and Cure*" summarizes the warning signs of regressing in the Christian faith and tells us what to do about it. "*New Testament Evangelism*" reminds us of our role as Christians and our responsibility to carry out Christ's commission.

The 123-page *Concordance* enables you to locate key verses throughout the Bible. Each Bible reference in the Concordance was individually selected by Bible scholars on the basis of familiarity and significance.

The Bible text of The New King James Version is highly readable and excelling in accuracy. *Read-along References*™, denoted by the symbol "R", are provided to help tie together related passages of text. *Read-along Translations*™, identified by the symbol "T", explain or give alternate meanings to words and phrases in the

translation. *Textual footnotes* make available additional information on the biblical manuscripts. These aids complement the other helps in The Christian Life Bible to produce an invaluable edition of the Bible for both the layperson and the scholar.

The Christian Life Bible with Master Outlines and Study Notes is published with the confidence that it will serve you well as you grow in your relationship and commitment to God, so that "you may be filled with all the fullness of God" (Eph. 3:19), living abundantly for this glory.

—The Publishers

HOW TO USE
The Christian Life Bible

The Christian Life Master Outlines and Study Notes utilize a simple outline system to approach the study of fifty-two biblical doctrines. Each area of study is named and numbered, and all have been carefully arranged to give the Bible student a logical progression of study.

Each Master Outline contains from four to eight specific points of study. Each point is the source for a Study Note found at the foot of a page containing related Bible scripture. The outlines are designed so that once you are inside, the system will guide you throughout each new phase of the outlines. Familiarize yourself with how to use the Master Outlines before you begin your study. The example page shown below and those on pages six and seven will walk you through portions of an outline.

1. Begin your study of the Christian Life Master Outlines with Master Outline Number One and read a new one each week. It is best to study each outline in order, since they have been carefully positioned to offer the soundest Bible study. For an overview of the arrangement of the Master Outlines, see the Index of Master Outlines on page 21.

2. Introductions to the Master Outlines briefly capsulize the topic of study you will undertake. Begin each Master Outline by reading the Introduction.

3. After reading the Master Outline Introduction, proceed with the first point in the outline. Each point will direct you to a scripture passage. Find the first point by looking up the scripture cited in parentheses. Page numbers for the scripture references are supplied for your convenience.

4. To get maximum benefit from your study, be sure to follow the points in the order they appear here.

MASTER OUTLINE NUMBER ONE

Inerrancy of the Scriptures

For centuries the vast majority of people in the Christian world accepted Holy Bible, and believed it to be God's revealed written message to mankind was free of mistakes (inerrant), that it could not be wrong on any subject (i words came from God Himself through specially chosen prophets (inspired) held this same opinion for centuries before, with respect to the Old Testam Jews still hold this view today. The belief that the Bible was God's written Wo was seen to be the Bible's own claim for itself (2 Tim. 3:16, page 1227), as w claim of Christ Himself (John 10:35, page 1068).

Thus, orthodox Christians today, whatever their denominational label, still the Holy Scriptures (both Old and New Testaments) are God's actual words Him and communicated by His Holy Spirit's guidance through chosen, ho 1:20, 21, page 1273), and are thus verbally (the written words, not merely the fallible, and inspired, as they were originally written in the autographs—that ments penned by the prophets and apostles, or by their secretaries when dicta 1146).

In contrast to the orthodox position, men have periodically risen who have racy. In unbelief they have rejected the Creation account, miracles, the deity of great and eternal truths, expounding theories which attack the inerrancy of

During the past two centuries there has been an increase of negative cri schools of learning, and it has filtered down to our public education system

In light of this, we invite the reader to consider carefully the following rea Bible itself—for believing in the inerrancy of the Scriptures.

1-A.	The Bible Declares Itself to Be the Word of God (2 Timothy 3:16, page 1227)
1-B.	Christ Taught the Inerrancy of the Bible (John 10:35, page 1068)
1-C.	The Prophets of the Old Testament Received the Scriptures as Iner (2 Chronicles 36:20, 21, page 442)
1-D.	Christ and the Apostles Authenticated the New Testament as Inerra (2 Peter 1:21, page 1273)
1-E.	Christ and the Apostles Accepted Genesis as a Factual Account (Matthew 19:4, page 965)
1-F.	Christ and the Apostles Accepted the Books Most Attacked by Criti (Matthew 12:40, 41, page 954)
1-G.	Fulfilled Prophecy Shows the Inerrancy of the Bible (Psalm 119:89, page 583)

5. To understand how to progress to the final point in one of the Master Outlines, turn to the next page (page 6), and find Matthew 12:40, 41, for "Point 1-F. Christ and the Apostles Accepted the Books Most Attacked by Critics." Continue following the "How to Use" steps.

How To Use The Christian Life Bible

6. Matthew 12:40, 41 is the scripture passage to read for Point 1-F in Master Outline Number One. Always look for the bold face point number and name (in this case, "1-F: Christ and the Apostles Accepted the Books Most Attacked by Critics") and a solid black triangle with its point facing downward. These features are placed at the beginning of the scripture reading for each Study Note.

7. An outline triangle at the top of a column indicates that these verses continue to be part of the reading for your Study Note.

8. A solid triangle with its point facing upward indicates you have reached the final verse to be covered in the Study Note.

9. Underscored passages emphasize a theme or concept to be analyzed in the Study Note.

10. Once you have completed the scripture reading, you are ready to begin the Study Note. Read it carefully. You are benefitting from fourteen years of biblical research as you read the Christian Life Master Outlines and Study Notes.

A Tree Known by Its Fruit

33 "Either make the tree good and *its* fruit good, or else make the tree bad and its fruit bad; for a tree is known by *its* fruit.

34 "Brood of vipers! How can you, being evil, speak good things? For out of the abundance of the heart the mouth speaks.

35 "A good man out of the good treasure *of his heart brings forth good things, and an evil man out of the evil treasure brings forth evil things.

36 "But I say to you that for every idle word men may speak, they will give account of it in the day of judgment.

37 "For by your words you will be justified, and by your words you will be condemned."

The Scribes and Pharisees Ask for a Sign

38 Then some of the scribes and Pharisees answered, saying, "Teacher, we want to see a sign from You."   Mark 8:11

39 But He answered and said to them, "An evil and *adulterous generation seeks after a sign, and no sign will be given to it except the sign of the prophet Jonah.   Matt. 16:4

▼ **1-F. Christ and the Apostles Accepted the Books Most Attacked by Critics**

40 "For as Jonah was three days and three nights in the belly of the great fish, so will the

12:35 NU, M omit *of his heart*

Son of Man be three days and three nights in the heart of the earth.   Jon. 1:17

41 "The men of Nineveh will rise up in the judgment with this generation and *condemn it, *because they repented at the preaching of Jonah; and indeed a greater than Jonah *is* here.   Luke 11:32 · Jer. 3:11 · Jon. 3:5

42 "The queen of the South will rise up in the judgment with this generation and condemn it, for she came from the ends of the earth to hear the wisdom of Solomon; and indeed a greater than Solomon *is* here.

An Unclean Spirit Returns

43 *"When an unclean spirit goes out of a man, *he goes through dry places, seeking rest, and finds none.   Luke 11:24-26 · [1 Pet. 5:8]

44 "Then he says, 'I will return to my house from which I came.' And when he comes, he finds *it* empty, swept, and put in order.

45 "Then he goes and takes with him seven other spirits more wicked than himself, and they enter and dwell there; and the last *state* of that man is worse than the first. So shall it also be with this wicked generation."

Jesus' Mother and Brothers Send for Him

46 While He was still talking to the multitudes, behold, His mother and brothers stood outside, seeking to speak with Him.

47 Then one said to Him, "Look, *Your mother and Your brothers are standing outside, seeking to speak with You."   Matt. 13:55, 56

48 But He answered and said to the one

1-F. Christ and the Apostles Accepted the Books Most Attacked by Critics (Matthew 12:40, 41)—The book of Jonah, claimed by some to be fiction, was personally authorized by the all-knowing Christ. Nor is this the only disputed book He attested:

(1) The Pentateuch (the first five Old Testament books) was written by Moses. (Moses' final death account [Deut. 34, page 213] was probably added by Joshua.) Note that in Matthew 4:4, 7, 10 (page 934), Christ defeats Satan by quoting from Deuteronomy 6:16 (page 187); 8:3 (page 189); and 10:20 (page 191). Next to Genesis, Deuteronomy is the book most attacked by critics. Yet it was Christ's first choice in fighting Satan. Our conclusion: Deuteronomy was authenticated as inerrant Scripture, once and forever, by the all-knowing Christ.

(2) The book of Daniel was written by Daniel, about 600–550 B.C., although critics say that it was written four hundred years later at about 168 B.C. They allege this because Daniel's prophecies in chapters 2 (page 632), 7 (page 844), and 8 (page 846) seem to extend this far into history (although, indeed, they extend much farther). These critics do not believe it possible that God's prophets could miraculously predict the future. Jesus, however, quotes Daniel as a God-inspired foreteller of the future (Matt. 24:15, page 973; also Mark 13:14, page 1002). To Christ, and therefore to us, the book of Daniel came from God, was written by Daniel, foretells the future, and is inerrant in all of its words.

(3) Some scholars divide Isaiah into three sections: "First Isaiah," chapters 1—39 (page 642); "Second Isaiah," chapters 40—55 (page 679); "Third Isaiah," chapters 56—66 (page 696). Because of the three divisions of subject matter, different emphases, and alleged variations in style, some maintain that different authors wrote each section. However, Isaiah is mentioned by name in the New Testament seven twenty-one times. For example:

    (a) Matthew 15:7-9 (page 960; cf. Is. 29:13, page 669)
    (b) Mark 3:3 (page 933; cf. Is. 40:3, page 679)
    (c) Acts 8:28-33 (page 1099; cf. Is. 53:7, 8, page 693)

Along with these three quotations (one of which was spoken by the Lord Jesus Christ) from the three different sections of Isaiah, there are at least eighteen others from Matthew through Romans. All New Testament writers accept the unity of the book and that it is the work of one prophet.

See Psalm 119:89, page 583, for Point 1-G: Fulfilled Prophecy Shows the Inerrancy of the Bible.

---

11. The last line of the Study Note will direct you to the scripture and page number of the next point in the Master Outline. In this case, your study is presently on example page 954 of the Gospel of Matthew in the New Testament, and you are being directed to example page 583 of the Book of Psalms in the Old Testament. Now look at the next page (page 7) to find Point 1-G.

▼ **1-G. Fulfilled Prophecy Shows the Inerrancy of the Bible**

89 ᴿForever, O Lᴏʀᴅ,   Matt. 24:35
▲   Your word is settled in heaven.
90 Your faithfulness *endures* to all
    generations;
    You established the earth, and it
    ᵀabides.   Lit. *stands*
91 They continue this day according to
    ᴿYour ordinances,
    For all *are* Your servants.   Jer. 33:25
92 Unless Your law *had been* my delight,
    I would then have perished in my
    affliction.
93 I will never forget Your precepts,
    For by them You have given me life.
94 I *am* Yours, save me;
    For I have sought Your precepts.
95 The wicked wait for me to destroy me,
    But I will consider Your testimonies.
96 ᴿI have seen the consummation of all
    perfection,
    But Your commandment *is* exceedingly
    broad.   Matt. 5:18

ᴋ MEM
97 Oh, how I love Your law!
    ᴿIt *is* my meditation all the day.   Ps. 1:2

98 You, through Your commandments,
    make me ᴿwiser than my enemies;
    For they are ever with me.   Deut. 4:6
99 I have more understanding than all my
    teachers,
    ᴿFor Your testimonies *are* my
    meditation.   [2 Tim. 3:15]
100 I understand more than the ᵀancients,
    Because I keep Your precepts.   *aged*
101 I have restrained my feet from every
    evil way,
    That I may keep Your word.
102 I have not departed from Your
    judgments,
    For You Yourself have taught me.
103 How sweet are Your words to my taste,
    Sweeter than honey to my mouth!
104 Through Your precepts I get
    understanding;
    Therefore I hate every false way.

ᴋ NUN
105 ᴿYour word is a lamp to my feet
    And a light to my path.   Prov. 6:23
106 ᴿI have sworn and confirmed   Neh. 10:29
    That I will keep Your righteous
    judgments.
107 I am afflicted very much;
    Revive me, O Lᴏʀᴅ, according to Your
    word.

1-G. Fulfilled Prophecy Shows the Inerrancy of the Bible (Psalm 119:89)—Jesus said, "Heaven and earth will pass away, but My words will by no means pass away" (Matt. 24:35, page 974). He was speaking in a context of prophetic predictions. He insisted that every predictive word would find its fulfillment because it comes from God, who knows and controls the future. Other prophets have spoken throughout world history; it is apparent that none of them really knew the future, especially the distant future. Only the prophecies of the Bible have been and will be fulfilled in every detail. These prophecies come to us in the exact words of Scripture. Their past fulfillment is a proof that the Bible is God's book—true, as it claims for itself, and inerrant even in its prophetic words. For example:

(1) Prophecies of past history have come true. Amos, in 760 B.C., prophesied judgment on various nations (Amos 1:2, page 874). All of these dire words have come to pass in history, one by one.

(2) Prophecies of the moral nature of man have come true. Christ said that wars would continue (Matt. 24:5–12, page 973) and poverty would continue (Matt. 26:11, page 977); Paul prophesied the future moral corruption of the world (1 Tim. 4:1–3, page 1220). Sadly, these words have stood the test of time.

(3) Prophecies concerning Israel's survival and restoration have come true. The Bible has predicted in many verses the survival of the Hebrew people and their eventual return to the land as survivors from many nations (Jer. 30:1–11, page 743; 31:1–11, page 744; Rom. 11:25, 27, page 1141). The ancient Moabites, Ammonites, Canaanites, and countless others have passed away, but the lasting endurance of Israel stands as a mark of prophetic fulfillment and truth.

(4) Prophecies concerning the coming, the life, and the death of Christ have come true in hundreds of details. Micah 5:2 (page 890), Isaiah 52:13—53:12 (page 693), Psalm 22 (page 522), Zechariah 12:10 (page 918), and other passages describe in minute detail Christ's birth in Bethlehem and His death by crucifixion. The accurate fulfillment of so many predictions, centuries in advance, demonstrates the divine origin of the Scriptures (Luke 24:27, 44, page 1047).

(5) Prophecies came true even when they ran counter to historical trends. Christ said that not one stone of the temple would remain standing upon another (Matt. 24:1, 2, page 972), and today not one does. By contrast, ancient temples still remain today in Persia, Babylon, Athens, Corinth, Ephesus, Egypt, and Rome; their stones, walls, and columns stand nobly after 2000 years.

(6) Prophecies of the end of the age are today coming into focus in the world. In our century several nations, including Russia, Iran, Ethiopia, and Libya, have opposed the new nation of Israel (Ezek. 38:2, 5, page 816).

(7) The prophecies of Christ's Second Coming will yet come to pass. Armies will come to Armageddon (Rev. 16:16, page 1310; 19:19, page 1313) and Christ will return to rescue Israel and put the world in order (Rev. 19:11–16, page 1312). The Word of God is, and shall be, true and inerrant in its every word.

See Index, page 21, for your next study.

---

12. Psalm 119:89 is the scripture passage to read for "Point 1-G: Fulfilled Prophecy Shows the Inerrancy of the Bible." After reading the passage, which is again indicated by solid black triangles, you are ready to study the note at the bottom of the page.

13. To enrich your study and broaden your knowledge of Scripture, the Study Notes contain a total of more than three thousand related biblical references. Take time to look these up. Your study is incomplete without knowledge of the groundwork these Scriptures provide.

14. The Study Notes utilize a format which organizes the content into major and subordinate points for smooth study and quick reference. You will refer to these notes often even long after you have completed your studies of the Christian Life Master Outlines.

15. The last line of the final point you are studying will lead you back to the Index of Master Outlines where you will find the page number for the next Master Outline, which in this case is Master Outline Number Two: "Foundations for Bible Study". Repeat the same steps to walk yourself through the remaining Master Outlines.

16. You are now ready to use the Christian Life Master Outlines and Study Notes. However, it will help to be familiar with how to use the translation features of the New King James Bible. Example pages immediately following this page will illustrate the textual notes, cross-references and other features of the New King James Version.

CONTRIBUTORS
to The Christian Life Bible

In addition to the names mentioned here, two people deserve special recognition. The first is my wife, Dottie, who has patiently stood by me in prayer and encouragement throughout my work on The Christian Life Bible. The second is my friend and colleague, Dr. Gary G. Cohen, for his valuable assistance in researching, writing, and critiquing portions of the Master Outlines and Study Notes.

—Dr. Porter L. Barrington

Porter L. Barrington
Master Outlines and Study Notes
President
Christian Life Ministries
Thousand Oaks, CA

M.A.   **Moody Adams**
Introduction to Third John
Evangelist
Baker, LA

H.A.   **Hyman Appleman** (Deceased)
Introduction to Zechariah
Evangelist
Kansas City, MO

M.R.B.   **Marvin R. Beachy**
Introduction to First Thessalonians
Executive Director
Gospel Echoes Team
Prison Ministry
Goshen, IN

M.M.B.   **Manley M. Beasley**
Introduction to Titus
President
Gospel Harvesters
    Foundation
Euless, TX

R.B.   **Dr. Royal Blue**
Introduction to First Timothy
Senior Pastor
North Valley Baptist Church
Redding, CA

C.W.B.   **Clifton W. Brannon, J.D.**
Introduction to Ezra
Evangelist
Longview, TX

J.W.B.   **Dr. James W. Bryant**
Introduction to John
Pastor
Grand Avenue Baptist Church
Fort Smith, AR

P.W.C.   **Dr. Paul W. Carlin**
Introduction to Leviticus
Prisoner's Bible Institute
Houston, TX

T.J.C.   **Tommy J. Carney**
Introducton to Hosea
Pastor
Mountain Home Baptist Church
Mountain Home, AR

N.B.C.   **N. Bob Carpenter**
Introduction to Lamentations
Pastor
Cherry Road Baptist Church
Memphis, TN

H.F.C.   **H. Frank Collins, D.D.: LITT.D.**
Introduction to Second Chronicles
Pastor
Bellflower, CA

E.J.D.   **Dr. E. J. Daniels**
Introduction to Mark
General Director
Christ for the World, Inc.
Orlando, FL

J.F.D.   **Dr. J. Frank Davis**
Introduction to First Samuel
Pastor
Orchard Hills Baptist Church
Garland, TX

J.J.D.   **Dr. John J. Davis**
Introduction to Obadiah
Professor of Old Testament
Grace Theological Seminary
Winona Lake, IN

E.D.   **Emmett Douglas**
Introduction to Ezekiel
Attorney at Law
Phoenix, AZ

J.D.   **Jimmy Draper**
Introduction to Second Samuel
Pastor
Euless, TX

J.W.D.   **John W. Dungey**
Introduction to Hebrews
Pastor
Central Point, OR

J.R.D.   **John R. Dunkin**
Introduction to Daniel
President
Los Angeles Baptist College
Newhall, CA

R.E.D.   **Dr. Richard E. Dwyer**
Introduction to Deuteronomy
Pastor
First Baptist Church
Fair Oaks, CA

J.E.   **Jim Eller, Jr.**
Introduction to Psalms
Senior Pastor
Grace Baptist Church
Riverside, CA

D.E. **Dr. Don Ellis**
Introduction to Second Corinthians
Vice President of Academic Affairs
East Texas Baptist University
Marshall, TX

J.D.E. **Joyce Donath Ellis**
Introduction to Second Corinthians
Assistant Director of Admissions
East Texas Baptist University
Marshall, TX

A.L.F. **Dr. Arthur L. Farstad**
Introduction to Song of Solomon
Executive Editor, NKJV
Thomas Nelson Publishers
Nashville, TN

H.L.F. **Harold L. Fickett, Jr.**
Introduction to James
Pastor Emeritus
Faith Evangelical Church
Chatsworth, CA

P.R.F. **Paul R. Fink, Th.D.**
Introduction to Second Peter
Professor of Pastoral Ministries
Liberty University
Lynchburg, VA

L.F. **Dr. Lewis Foster**
Introduction to Philippians
Professor of New Testament
Cincinnati Christian Seminary
Cincinnati, OH

J.H.G. **Dr. Jacob H. Gamble**
New Testament Evangelism
Pastor
First Baptist Church
Winter Haven, FL

G.G. **Dr. George Golden**
Introduction to First Corinthians
Senior Pastor
Ventura Baptist Temple
Ventura, CA

J.H. **John Haggai**
Introduction to Haggai
President
Haggai Institute
Atlanta, GA

K.G.H. **Dr. Kenneth G. Hanna**
Introductions to Genesis and Exodus
Vice President and Dean of Education
Moody Bible Institute
Chicago, IL

W.R.H. **W. Robert Harris**
Introduction to Malachi
President
Indepth Ministries, Inc.
Houston, TX

J.W.H. **Dr. Jack W. Hayford**
Introduction to Romans
Senior Pastor
'Church on the Way'
Van Nuys, CA

H.B.H. **Hollis B. Hendon**
Introduction to Second Timothy
Evangelist
Helena, AL

R.H. **Ron Herrod**
Introduction to Acts
Pastor
First Baptist Church
Kenner, LA

W.H.H. **Walter H. Hostettler**
Introduction to Colossians
Reverend, B.A.; M.A.; B.D.
Magalia, CA

C.G.H. **Dr. Clark G. Hutchinson**
Introduction to Esther
Pastor
Eastside Baptist Church
Marietta, GA

J.E.J. **Jimmy E. Jackson, Th.D.**
Intertestamental Period
Huntsville, AL

J.M.L. **Dr. James M. Latimer**
*Introductions to Ephesians and
Second Thessalonians*
Senior Pastor
Central Church
Memphis, TN

G.H.L. **George Herbert Livingston, Ph.D.**
Introduction to First Chronicles
Professor of Old Testament
Asbury Theological Seminary
Wilmore, KY

B.L. **Ben Loveless**
Introduction to Joshua
Missions Coordinator
World Witness Evangelism, Inc.
Thousand Oaks, CA

W.P.L. **Wendell P. Loveless**
Introduction to Numbers
Pastor Emeritus
First Chinese Church of Christ
Honolulu, HI

W.H.M. **Dr. William H. McDowell**
English Editor
Thomas Nelson Publishers
Nashville, TN

A.M. **Dr. Angel Martinez**
Introduction to Matthew
Fort Smith, AR

J.J.M. **Jim J. Merriman**
Backsliding: Its Cause and Cure
Pastor
First Baptist Church
Abbeville, LA

G.M. **Dr. Gene Miller**
Introduction to Jude
Professor of New Testament
Anderson School of Theology
Daleville, IN

J.M. Jess Moody
Introduction to Galatians
Pastor
First Baptist Church
Van Nuys, CA

R.C.M. Robert C. Moore
Introduction to Judges
Pastor
Broadway Baptist Church
Memphis, TN

C.R.N. Curtis R. Nims
Introduction to Joel
Director
F.R.I.E.N.D. Foundation
Atlanta, GA

J.C.N. Dr. Jerry C. Nims
Introduction to Joel
Chairman of the Board
Republic Broadcasting Systems, Inc.
Atlanta, GA

F.W.O. Floyd W. Overstreet
Introduction to Jeremiah
Pastor
Calvary Baptist Church
Manteca, CA

J.A.P. Dr. Jerry A. Passmore
Introduction to Luke
Pastor
Olive Baptist Church
Pensacola, FL

J.R. Dr. Jerry Richardson
Introduction to Jonah
President
Christian Growth Ministries
Northridge, CA

D.W.R. Dr. Darrell W. Robinson
Introduction to First Peter
Pastor
Dauphin Way Baptist Church
Mobile, AL

A.R. Dr. Adrian Rogers
Introduction to First Kings
Bellevue Baptist Church
Memphis, TN

A.P.R. Allen P. Ross, Th.D., Ph.D.
Introduction to Job
Professor and Chairman
Department of Old
  Testament and
  Semitic Languages
Dallas Theological Seminary
Dallas, TX

C.S. Dr. Clarence Sands
Introduction to Amos
Minister at Large
San Jose, CA

J.R.S. J. Roger Skelton, ED.D.
Introduction to Philemon
Professor of Religious Education (Ret.)
Golden Gate Baptist Theological
  Seminary
Mill Valley, CA

J.H.S. J. Harold Smith
Introduction to Revelation
President
Radio Bible Hour
Orlando, FL

J.S. Dr. Jerry Spencer
Introduction to Nahum
Evangelist, U.S.A.

G.C.S. Dr. Gary C. Stafford
Introducton to Second Kings
Regional Director
Southern California Christian
  Nationals
Evangelism Commission
Yorba Linda, CA

B.W. Bill Weber
Introduction to Micah
Pastor
Prestonwood Baptist Church
Dallas, TX

J.W. Dr. Jaroy Weber (Deceased)
Introduction to Ruth
Former President
Southern Baptist Convention
Dallas, TX

R.J.W. Robert J. Wells
Introduction to Zephaniah
Pastor
Anaheim, CA

J.R.W. Rev. James R. White
Introduction to Proverbs
Pastor
Capitol Hill Baptist Church
Oklahoma City, OK

R.E.W. Ron E. Wilson
Introduction to Habakkuk
Pastor
First Baptist Church
Thousand Oaks, CA

M.W. Melvin Wise
Introduction to Isaiah
Evangelist
Atlanta, GA

S.W. Sam Wolfe
Introduction to Ecclesiastes
Evangelist
Huntsville, AL

D.W. Dr. Don Womack
Introduction to First John
Evangelist
Memphis, TN

W.B.Y. Wm. B. Young
Introduction to Nehemiah
President
World-Wide Keswick, Inc.
Palm Bay, FL

T.F.Z. Dr. Thos. F. Zimmerman
Introduction to Second John
General Superintendent
Assemblies of God
Springfield, MO

CONTENTS
of The Christian Life Bible

Preface

Purpose

In the preface to the 1611 edition, the translators of the Authorized Version, known popularly as the King James Bible, state that it was not their purpose "to make a new translation...but to make a good one better." Indebted to the earlier work of William Tyndale and others, they saw their best contribution to consist in revising and enhancing the excellence of the English versions which had sprung from the Reformation of the sixteenth century. In harmony with the purpose of the King James scholars, the translators and editors of the present work have not pursued a goal of innovation. They have perceived the Holy Bible, New King James Version, as a continuation of the labors of the earlier translators, thus unlocking for today's readers the spiritual treasures found especially in the Authorized Version of the Holy Scriptures.

A Living Legacy

For nearly four hundred years, and throughout several revisions of its English form, the King James Bible has been deeply revered among the English-speaking peoples of the world. The precision of translation for which it is historically renowned, and its majesty of style, have enabled that monumental version of the Word of God to become the mainspring of the religion, language, and legal foundations of our civilization.

Although the Elizabethan period and our own era share in zeal for technical advance, the former period was more aggressively devoted to classical learning. Along with this awakened concern for the classics came a flourishing companion interest in the Scriptures, an interest that was enlivened by the conviction that the manuscripts were providentially handed down and were a trustworthy record of the inspired Word of God. The King James translators were committed to producing an English Bible that would be a precise translation, and by no means a paraphrase or a broadly approximate rendering. On the one hand, the scholars were almost as familiar with the original languages of the Bible as with their native English. On the other hand, their reverence for the divine Author and His Word assured a translation of the Scriptures in which only a principle of utmost accuracy could be accepted.

In 1786 Catholic scholar Alexander Geddes said of the King James Bible, "If accuracy and strictest attention to the letter of the text be supposed to constitute an excellent version, this is of all versions the most excellent." George Bernard Shaw became a literary legend in our century because of his severe and often humorous criticisms of our most cherished values. Surprisingly, however, Shaw pays the following tribute to the scholars commissioned by King James: "The translation was extraordinarily well done because to the translators what they were translating was not merely a curious collection of ancient books written by different authors in different stages of culture, but the Word of God divinely revealed through His chosen and expressly inspired scribes. In this conviction they carried out their work with boundless reverence and care and achieved a beautifully artistic result." History agrees with these estimates. Therefore, while seeking to unveil the excellent *form* of the traditional English Bible, special care has also been taken in the present edition to preserve the work of *precision* which is the legacy of the 1611 translators.

Complete Equivalence in Translation

Where new translation has been necessary in the New King James Version, the most complete representation of the original has been rendered by considering the history of usage and etymology of words in their contexts. This principle of complete equivalence seeks to preserve *all* of the information in the text, while presenting it in good literary form. Dynamic equivalence, a recent procedure in Bible translation, commonly results in paraphrasing where a more literal rendering is needed to reflect a specific and vital sense. For example, a completely equivalent rendering of 1 Samuel 15:33 would read, "and Samuel hacked [or hewed] Agag in pieces...." However, one contemporary translation needlessly softens the statement: "and Samuel put Agag to death...." The latter rendering does not accurately translate the language of the text, following the principle of dynamic equivalence, the procedure rather widely followed throughout that version.

In keeping with the principle of complete equivalence, it is the policy to translate interjections which are commonly omitted in modern language renderings of the Bible. As an example, the interjection *behold,* in the older King James editions, continues to have a place in English usage, especially in dramatically calling attention to a spectacular

scene, or an event of profound importance such as the Immanuel prophecy of Isaiah 7:14. Consequently, *behold* is retained for these occasions in the present edition. However, the Hebrew and Greek originals for this word can be translated variously, depending on the circumstances in the passage. Therefore, in addition to *behold*, words such as *indeed, look, see,* and *surely* are also rendered to convey the appropriate sense suggested by the context in each case.

In faithfulness to God and to our readers, it was deemed appropriate that all participating scholars sign a statement affirming their belief in the verbal and plenary inspiration of Scripture, and in the inerrancy of the original autographs.

Devotional Quality

The King James scholars readily appreciated the intrinsic beauty of divine revelation. They accordingly disciplined their talents to render well-chosen English words of their time, as well as a graceful, often musical arrangement of language, which has stirred the hearts of Bible readers through the years. The translators, the committees, and the editors of the present edition, while sensitive to the late-twentieth-century English idiom, and while adhering faithfully to the Hebrew, Aramaic, and Greek texts, have sought to maintain those lyrical and devotional qualities that are so highly regarded in the Authorized Version. This devotional quality is especially apparent in the poetic and prophetic books, although even the relatively plain style of the Gospels and Epistles cannot strictly be likened, as sometimes suggested, to modern newspaper style. The Koine Greek of the New Testament is influenced by the Hebrew background of the writers, for whom even the Gospel narratives were not merely flat utterance, but often song in various degrees of rhythm.

The Style

Students of the Bible applaud the timeless devotional character of our historic Bible. Yet it is also universally understood that our language, like all living languages, has undergone profound change since 1611. Subsequent revisions of the King James Bible have sought to keep abreast of changes in English speech. The present work is a further step toward this objective. Where obsolescence and other reading difficulties exist, present-day vocabulary, punctuation, and grammar have been carefully integrated. Words representing ancient objects, such as *chariot* and *phylactery,* have no modern substitutes and are therefore retained.

A special feature of the New King James Version is its conformity to the thought flow of the 1611 Bible. The reader discovers that the sequence and selection of words, phrases, and clauses of the new edition, while much clearer, are so close to the traditional that there is remarkable ease in listening to the reading of either edition while following with the other.

In the discipline of translating biblical and other ancient languages, a standard method of transliteration, that is, the English spelling of untranslated words, such as names of persons and places, has never been commonly adopted. In keeping with the design of the present work, the King James spelling of untranslated words is retained, although made uniform throughout. For example, instead of the spellings *Isaiah* and *Elijah* in the Old Testament, and *Esaias* and *Elias* in the New Testament, *Isaiah* and *Elijah* now appear in both Testaments.

King James doctrinal and theological terms, for example, *propitiation, justification,* and *sanctification,* are generally familiar to English-speaking peoples. Such terms have been retained except where the original language indicates need for a more precise translation.

Readers of the Authorized Version will immediately be struck by the absence of several pronouns: *thee, thou,* and *ye* are replaced by the simple *you,* while *your* and *yours* are substituted for *thy* and *thine* as applicable. *Thee, thou, thy,* and *thine* were once forms of address to express a special relationship to human as well as divine persons. These pronouns are no longer part of our language. However, reverence for God in the present work is preserved by capitalizing pronouns, including *You, Your,* and *Yours,* which refer to Him. Additionally, capitalization of these pronouns benefits the reader by clearly distinguishing divine and human persons referred to in a passage. Without such capitalization the distinction is often obscure, because the antecedent of a pronoun is not always clear in the English translation.

In addition to the pronoun usages of the seventeenth century, the *-eth* and *-est* verb endings, so familiar in the earlier King James editions, are now obsolete. Unless a speaker is schooled in these verb endings, there is common difficulty in selecting the correct form to be used with a given subject of the verb in vocal prayer. That is, should we use *love, loveth,* or *lovest*? *do, doeth, doest,* or *dost*? *have, hath,* or *hast*? Because these forms are obsolete, contemporary English

usage has been substituted for the previous verb endings.

In older editions of the King James Version, the frequency of the connective *and* far exceeded the limits of present English usage. Also, biblical linguists agree that the Hebrew and Greek original words for this conjunction may commonly be translated otherwise, depending on the immediate context. Therefore, instead of *and*, alternatives such as *also, but, however, now, so, then*, and *thus* are accordingly rendered in the present edition, when the original language permits.

The real character of the Authorized Version does not reside in its archaic pronouns or verbs or other grammatical forms of the seventeenth century, but rather in the care taken by its scholars to impart the letter and spirit of the original text in a majestic and reverent style.

The Format

The format of the New King James Version is designed to enhance the vividness and devotional quality of the Holy Scriptures:

—Subject headings assist the reader to identify topics and transitions in the biblical content.

—Words or phrases in *italics* indicate expressions in the original language which require clarification by additional English words, as also done throughout the history of the King James Bible.

—Verse numbers in bold type indicate the beginning of a paragraph.

—*Oblique type* in the New Testament indicates a quotation from the Old Testament.

—Poetry is structured as contemporary verse to reflect the poetic form and beauty of the passage in the original language.

—The covenant name of God was usually translated from the Hebrew as "LORD" or "GOD" (using capital letters as shown) in the King James Old Testament. This tradition is maintained. In the present edition the name is so capitalized whenever the covenant name is quoted in the New Testament from a passage in the Old Testament.

The Old Testament Text

The Hebrew Bible has come down to us through the scrupulous care of ancient scribes who copied the original text in successive generations. By the sixth century A.D. the scribes were succeeded by a group known as the Masoretes, who continued to preserve the sacred Scriptures for another five hundred years in a form known as the Masoretic Text. Babylonia, Palestine, and Tiberias were the main centers of Masoretic activity; but by the tenth century A.D. the Masoretes of Tiberias, led by the family of ben Asher, gained the ascendancy. Through subsequent editions, the ben Asher text became in the twelfth century the only recognized form of the Hebrew Scriptures.

Daniel Bomberg printed the first Rabbinic Bible in 1516-17; that work was followed in 1524-25 by a second edition prepared by Jacob ben Chayyim and also published by Bomberg. The text of ben Chayyim was adopted in most subsequent Hebrew bibles, including those used by the King James translators. The ben Chayyim text was also used for the first two editions of Rudolph Kittel's Biblia Hebraica of 1906 and 1912. In 1937 Paul Kahle published a third edition of *Biblia Hebraica*. This edition was based on the oldest dated manuscript of the ben Asher text, the Leningrad Manuscript B19a (A.D. 1008), which Kahle regarded as superior to that used by ben Chayyim.

For the New King James Version the text used was the 1967/1977 Stuttgart edition of the *Biblia Hebraica*, with frequent comparisons being made with the Bomberg edition of 1524-25. The Septuagint (Greek) Version of the Old Testament and the Latin Vulgate also were consulted. In addition to referring to a variety of ancient versions of the Hebrew Scriptures, the New King James Version draws on the resources of relevant manuscripts from the Dead Sea caves. In the few places where the Hebrew was so obscure that the 1611 King James was compelled to follow one of the versions, but where information is now available to resolve the problems, the New King James Version follows the Hebrew text. Significant variations are recorded in footnotes.

The New Testament Text

There is more manuscript support for the New Testament than for any other body of ancient literature. Over five thousand Greek, eight thousand Latin, and many more manuscripts in other languages attest the integrity of the New Testament. There is only one basic New Testament used by Protestants, Roman Catholics, and Orthodox, by conservatives and liberals. Minor variations in hand copying have appeared through the centuries, before mechanical printing began about A.D. 1450.

Some variations exist in the spelling of Greek words, in word order, and in similar de-

tails. These ordinarily do not show up in translation and do not affect the sense of the text in any way.

Other manuscript differences such as omission or inclusion of a word or a clause, and two paragraphs in the Gospels, should not overshadow the overwhelming degree of *agreement* which exists among the ancient records. Bible readers may be assured that the most important differences in English New Testaments of today are due, not to manuscript divergence, but to the way in which translators view the task of translation: How literally should the text be rendered? How does the translator view the matter of biblical inspiration? Does the translator adopt a paraphrase when a literal rendering would be quite clear and more to the point? The New King James Version follows the historic precedent of the Authorized Version in maintaining a literal approach to translation, except where the idiom of the original language cannot be translated directly into our tongue.

The King James New Testament was based on the traditional text of the Greek-speaking churches, first published in 1516, and later called the Textus Receptus or Received Text. Although based on the relatively few available manuscripts, these were representative of many more which existed at the time but only became known later. In the late nineteenth century, B. Westcott and F. Hort taught that this text had been officially edited by the fourth-century church, but a total lack of historical evidence for this event has forced a revision of the theory. It is now widely held that the Byzantine Text that largely supports the Textus Receptus has as much right as the Alexandrian or any other tradition to be weighed in determining the text of the New Testament. Those readings in the Textus Receptus which have weak support are indicated in footnotes as being opposed by both Critical and Majority Texts (see "Footnotes," below).

Since the 1880's most contemporary translations of the New Testament have relied upon a relatively few manuscripts discovered chiefly in the late nineteenth and early twentieth centuries. Such translations depend primarily on two manuscripts, Codex Vaticanus and Codex Sinaiticus, because of their greater age. The Greek text obtained by using these sources and the related papyri (our most ancient manuscripts) is known as the Alexandrian Text. However, some scholars have grounds for doubting the faithfulness of Vaticanus and Sinaiticus, since they often disagree with one another, and Sinaiticus exhibits excessive omission.

A third viewpoint of New Testament scholarship holds that the best text is based on the consensus of the majority of existing Greek manuscripts. This text is called the Majority Text. Most of these manuscripts are in substantial agreement. Even though many are late, and none is earlier than the fifth century, usually their readings are verified by papyri, ancient versions, quotations from the early church fathers, or a combination of these. The Majority Text is similar to the Textus Receptus, but it corrects those readings which have little or no support in the Greek manuscript tradition.

Today, scholars agree that the science of New Testament textual criticism is in a state of flux. Very few scholars still favor the Textus Receptus as such, and then often for its historical prestige as the text of Luther, Calvin, Tyndale, and the King James Version. For about a century most have followed a Critical Text—so called because it is edited according to specific principles of textual criticism—which depends heavily upon the Alexandrian type of text. More recently many have abandoned this Critical Text (which is quite similar to the one edited by Westcott and Hort) for one that is more eclectic. Finally, a small but growing number of scholars prefer the Majority Text, which is close to the traditional text except in the Revelation.

In light of these facts, and also because the New King James Version is the fifth revision of an historic document translated from specific Greek texts, the editors decided to retain the traditional text in the body of the New Testament and to indicate major Critical and Majority Text variant readings in footnotes. Although these variations are duly indicated in the footnotes of the present edition, it is most important to emphasize that fully eighty-five percent of the New Testament text is the same in the Textus Receptus, the Alexandrian Text, and the Majority Text.

Footnotes

Significant variations from the texts used in the New King James Version are supplied in footnotes. Also given in footnotes, wherever space does not permit them to be placed at the ends of the relevant verses, are explanatory notes, alternate translations, cross-references, and New Testament citations of Old Testament passages.

Important textual variants in the Old Testament are footnoted in a standard form.

The textual notes in the present edition of the New Testament make no evaluation of

readings, but do clearly indicate the manuscript sources of readings. They objectively present the facts without such tendentious remarks as "the best manuscripts omit" or "the most reliable manuscripts read." Such notes are value judgments that differ according to varying viewpoints on the text. By giving a clearly defined set of variants the New King James Version benefits readers of all textual persuasions.

Where significant variations occur in the New Testament Greek manuscripts, textual notes are classified as follows:

1. NU-Text
   These variations from the traditional text generally represent the Alexandrian or Egyptian type of text described previously in "The New Testament Text." They are found in the Critical Text published in the twenty-sixth edition of the Nestle-Aland Greek New Testament (N) and

in the United Bible Societies' third edition (U), hence the acronym, "NU-Text."

2. M-Text
   This symbol indicates points of variation in the Majority Text from the traditional text, as also previously discussed in "The New Testament Text." It should be noted that M stands for whatever reading is printed in the published *Greek New Testament According to the Majority Text*, whether supported by overwhelming, strong, or only a divided majority textual tradition.

The textual notes reflect the scholarship of the past 150 years and will assist the reader to observe the variations between the different manuscript traditions of the New Testament. Such information is generally not available in English translations of the New Testament.

Special Abbreviations

Arab.	Arabic
Aram.	Aramaic
Bg.	The 1524-25 edition of the Hebrew Old Testament published by Daniel Bomberg (see NKJV Preface, "The Old Testament Text")
cf.	compare
ch., chs.	chapter, chapters
DSS	Dead Sea Scrolls
fem.	feminine
f., ff.	following verse, following verses.
Gr.	Greek
Heb.	Hebrew
i.e.	that is
Kt.	Kethib (literally, in Aramaic, "written")—the written words of the Hebrew Old Testament preserved by the Masoretes (see "Qr." below)
Lat.	Latin
Lit.	Literally
LXX	Septuagint—an ancient translation of the Old Testament into Greek
M	Majority Text (see NKJV Preface, "The New Testament Text")
ms., mss.	manuscript, manuscripts
masc.	masculine
MT	Masoretic Text—the traditional Hebrew Old Testament (see NKJV Preface, "The Old Testament Text")
NU	the modern eclectic, or "critical," text of the Greek New Testament, published in the twenty-sixth edition of the Nestle-Aland Greek New Testament (N) and in the third edition of the United Bible Societies' Greek New Testament (U)
pl.	plural
Qr.	Qere (literally, in Aramaic, "read")—certain words read aloud, differing from the written words, in the Masoretic tradition of the Hebrew Old Testament (see "Kt." above)
Sam.	Samaritan Pentateuch—a variant Hebrew edition of the books of Moses, used by the Samaritan community
sing.	singular
Syr.	Syriac
Tg.	Targum—an Aramaic paraphrase of the Old Testament
TR	*Textus Receptus* or Received Text (see NKJV Preface, "The New Testament Text")
v., vv.	verse, verses
vss.	versions—ancient translations of the Bible
Vg.	Vulgate—an ancient translation of the Bible into Latin, translated and edited by Jerome

The
Christian Life Master
Outlines
and Study Notes

MASTER OUTLINE NUMBER ONE

Inerrancy of the Scriptures

For centuries the vast majority of people in the Christian world accepted the Scriptures as The Holy Bible, and believed it to be God's revealed written message to mankind. They believed that it was free of mistakes (inerrant), that it could not be wrong on any subject (infallible), and that its words came from God Himself through specially chosen prophets (inspired). Jewish believers had held this same opinion for centuries before, with respect to the Old Testament, and the orthodox Jews still hold this view today. The belief that the Bible was God's written Word and free from error was seen to be the Bible's own claim for itself (2 Tim. 3:16, page 1227), as well as the authoritative claim of Christ Himself (John 10:35, page 1068).

Thus, orthodox Christians today, whatever their denominational label, still hold the doctrine that the Holy Scriptures (both Old and New Testaments) are God's actual words to man (originated by Him and communicated by His Holy Spirit's guidance through chosen, holy messengers—2 Pet. 1:20, 21, page 1273), and are thus verbally (the written words, not merely the thoughts) inerrant, infallible, and inspired, as they were originally written in the autographs—that is, in the actual documents penned by the prophets and apostles, or by their secretaries when dictated (Rom. 16:22, page 1146).

In contrast to the orthodox position, men have periodically risen who have attacked biblical accuracy. In unbelief they have rejected the Creation account, miracles, the deity of Jesus, and many other great and eternal truths, expounding theories which attack the inerrancy of the Holy Scriptures.

During the past two centuries there has been an increase of negative criticism of the Bible in schools of learning, and it has filtered down to our public education system.

In light of this, we invite the reader to consider carefully the following reasons—drawn from the Bible itself—for believing in the inerrancy of the Scriptures.

1-A.   The Bible Declares Itself to Be the Word of God
        (2 Timothy 3:16, page 1227)

1-B.   Christ Taught the Inerrancy of the Bible
        (John 10:35, page 1068)

1-C.   The Prophets of the Old Testament Received the Scriptures as Inerrant
        (2 Chronicles 36:20, 21, page 442)

1-D.   Christ and the Apostles Authenticated the New Testament as Inerrant
        (2 Peter 1:21, page 1273)

1-E.   Christ and the Apostles Accepted Genesis as a Factual Account
        (Matthew 19:4, page 965)

1-F.   Christ and the Apostles Accepted the Books Most Attacked by Critics
        (Matthew 12:40, 41, page 954)

1-G.   Fulfilled Prophecy Shows the Inerrancy of the Bible
        (Psalm 119:89, page 583)

MASTER OUTLINE NUMBER TWO

Foundations for Bible Study

Born-again Christians believe the Bible to be God's very own Word. For a discussion of this subject, see Master Outline Number One, "Inerrancy of the Scriptures" (see above). Nevertheless, many sincerely professing Christians are spiritually starving, or spiritually ill, because they have never thought seriously about the quality of their Bible study.

If our physical diet is not well balanced, or if our digestive systems are not functioning properly, our bodies will decline in health. Similarly, if we do not or cannot take in the full value of the spiritual diet offered to us in the Scriptures, we will become spiritually disabled (1 Cor. 3:1, 2, page 1149).

This lesson will help you understand some of the difficulties you may be having with the Bible and your study of it. If you are resolved to persevere in Bible study, the following foundations will be of help. But our lesson will not be a substitute for your own regular Bible study. If you detect that your interest in Bible study is low, you apparently have *deeper* problems. You need to be in prayer, and

seek help from God and mature Christians about this matter. Someone who is starving spiritually must regularly eat nourishing spiritual food, which is the Word of God.

Now let us look at six important foundations for effective Bible study.

2-A.   Know What the Bible Says About Itself
        (Psalm 19:7, page 520)

2-B.   Know What God Intended the Bible to Do for You
        (Genesis 1:1, page 2)

2-C.   Know That the Bible Stands Above All Human Opinions
        (John 10:4, 5, page 1067)

2-D.   Know That the Bible Deals in Facts
        (Colossians 2:8, page 1203)

2-E.   Know the Correct Methods of Bible Study
        (2 Timothy 2:15, page 1226)

2-F.   Know How to Use Bible Helps and Commentaries
        (2 Timothy 2:2, page 1225)

MASTER OUTLINE NUMBER THREE

The Doctrine of God

"He who comes to God must believe that He is." The only way that man can approach God is by faith. "He who comes to God must believe that He is [no one has ever honestly sought after God by faith and failed to find Him], and that He is a rewarder of those who diligently seek Him." Enoch sought God by faith, found God by faith, walked with God by faith, escaped death by faith, and was rewarded by faith. "For before he was taken he had this testimony, that he pleased God. But without faith it is impossible to please Him"—and without faith it is impossible to know Him (Heb. 11:5, 6, page 1247).

None of the patriarchs, prophets, or writers of the Scriptures attempted to prove or argue the existence of God. It is a fact taken by faith by those who wrote and spoke as they were moved by the Holy Spirit, who is the one and only author of the Holy Bible (2 Pet. 1:21, page 1273; 2 Tim. 3:16, 17, page 1227).

Although the Holy Spirit did not move the writers of Scripture to argue the existence of God, He did present some clear facts that will strengthen faith:

(1) *Creation*. This fact demands a living personal Creator. Every effect must be traceable to an adequate cause. For example, if there is a building, there must be a builder. If there is an automobile, boat, or airplane, there must be a mechanical engineer. If there is a watch, there must be a watchmaker. There are thousands of "effects" in the world, such as electric typewriters, cameras of all kinds, power tools, television, radio, computers, word processors, and so on. And not one of them evolved; all had an intelligent, adequate cause. We have a creation; therefore, we must have an adequate, personal Creator. "The heavens declare the glory of God; and the firmament shows His handiwork. Day unto day utters speech, and night unto night reveals knowledge" (Ps. 19:1, 2, page 520).

(2) *The written Word, the Bible*. "All Scripture [all sixty-six books of the Bible] is given by inspiration of God, and is profitable for doctrine, for reproof, for correction, for instruction in righteousness" (2 Tim. 3:16, page 1227). God the Holy Spirit is the Author of the Scriptures; therefore they are inerrant (2 Pet. 1:21, page 1273).

(3) *The living Word, Jesus Christ the Son of God and God the Son*. "In the beginning was the Word [Jesus Christ], and the Word was with God, and the Word was God" (John 1:1, page 1049). The Word did not have a beginning because He is "the same yesterday, today, and forever" (Heb. 13:8, 9, page 1252).

3-A.   God Is a Personal Being
        (Jeremiah 10:10-16, page 722)

3-B.   God Is a Trinity
        (Luke 3:21, 22, page 1014)

3-C.   God Is Light
        (1 John 1:5, page 1278)

3-D.   God Is Immutable
        (Numbers 23:19, page 164)

3-E.   God Is Eternal
        (Psalm 102:24-27, page 569)

MASTER OUTLINE NUMBER FOUR

The Names of God

Jehovah was the sacred name of the God of Israel, used especially with reference to His being the covenant God of His people. The name itself is spelled by only four letters in Hebrew, YHWH. The Canaanites and other nations never used this name for their gods. Due to the holy awe connected with the name from antiquity, both the Bible copiers and readers refrained from even speaking it aloud; therefore its exact pronunciation has been lost to us. Today, most prefer the form Yahweh over Jehovah.

The literal meaning of the name seems to be "He Is." It is similar to the "I AM" name by which God calls Himself when speaking to Moses (Ex. 3:14, page 61). It thus conveys the fact that "He Is"—the eternal, personal, first-causal, self-existing Being. Added to this, the Bible reveals His attributes of holiness, goodness, justice, love, and mercy, as well as His omnipotence (He is all-powerful), omniscience (He is all-knowing), and omnipresence (He is everywhere). The New King James Version consistently translates YHWH as "the LORD" or "GOD," using small capital letters.

So sacred was the name YHWH that when the Hebrews used letters representing numbers to number the Psalms, since the number 15 was made by YH (Y = 10, H = 5), they preferred to use the letters TV (9 + 6) for Psalm 15. They gladly named their children for Jehovah, but out of respect used only the abbreviation, never the full spelling, in such names—e.g., Adon-i-jah, "Lord-my-(is)-Jah" (1 Kin. 1:25, page 326).

Exodus 6:3 (page 64) has puzzled some—"I appeared to Abraham, to Isaac, and to Jacob, as God Almighty, but by My name LORD [Jehovah] I was not known to them"—because of Abraham's use of the name Jehovah in Genesis 22:14 (page 27). This Exodus verse, however, speaks not of simple identification but of the attributes by which these patriarchs knew their God. To Abraham, God appeared as El Shaddai, "the Almighty God," working powerfully in His individual and family affairs. Now in Exodus 6:3 (page 64), to Moses and to the nation of Israel, God was about to reveal Himself as Jehovah, the self-existing covenant God of the nation, unbounded and unfettered by all earthly limitations; about to work mighty miracle after miracle for those who trusted Him.

The compound names of Jehovah are especially revealing as they wonderfully show to us

(1) how God intervened to aid His Old Testament people at crucial moments of need;
(2) the various covenant benefits that we, His people, today derive from our faith relationship to Him;
(3) character traits of God which are revealed in Christ our Lord and in the eternal Jehovah, who would save His people from their Egypt of sin, and then make with them a New Testament even more wonderful than the testament made at Sinai (1 Cor. 11:25, page 1156).

4-A.   Jehovah-Jireh: The LORD Will Provide
        (Genesis 22:14, page 27)

4-B.   Jehovah-Ropheka: The LORD Your Healer
        (Exodus 15:26, page 75)

4-C.   Jehovah-Nissi: The LORD Is My Banner
        (Exodus 17:15, page 77)

4-D.   Jehovah-Shalom: The LORD Is Peace
        (Judges 6:24, page 246)

4-E.   Jehovah-Tsidkenu: The LORD Our Righteousness
        (Jeremiah 23:6, page 735)

4-F.   Jehovah-Rohi: The LORD My Shepherd
        (Psalm 23:1, page 524)

MASTER OUTLINE NUMBER FIVE

The Sovereignty of God

The sovereignty of God is a theological term well established in the Bible and confirmed in all His works. "Known to God from eternity are all His works" (Acts 15:18, page 1109). His sovereignty is not only an attribute, but His prerogative grounded upon His eternal Godhead. This means that our sovereign God has absolute authority and right of dominion over all of His creation, because He is the self-existent Creator (Gen. 1:1, page 2). He has the sovereign right to do whatever pleases Him (Ps. 115:3, page 578). It may not look as though God is in charge of all nations at all times, but He is; and He will remain in sovereign power throughout all time and eternity (Ps. 22:28, page 523; cf. 50:1, page 540). God is both sovereign Creator (He made all things) and Sustainer (He keeps all things functioning) of His creation. "The heavens declare the glory of God; and the firmament shows His handiwork. Day unto day utters speech, and night unto night reveals knowledge" (Ps. 19:1, 2, page 520). Our God never sleeps.

(1) He is in absolute control of all things and all people.

(2) "And we know that all things work together for good to those who love God, to those who are the called according to His purpose" (Rom. 8:28, page 1137).

(3) All of the powers of darkness, sin, Satan, demons, and the wickedness of mankind cannot alter the purpose of our sovereign God.

5-A.   The Sovereignty of God Defined
        (Genesis 17:1, page 21)

5-B.   The Sovereignty of God at Work
        (Habakkuk 1:1-11, page 899)

5-C.   The Sovereignty of God Illustrated
        (Jeremiah 18:1-12, page 730)

5-D.   The Sovereignty of God and Salvation
        (Romans 8:29, 30, page 1137)

5-E.   The Sovereignty of God and the Responsibility of Mankind
        (Romans 9:1-24, page 1139)

MASTER OUTLINE NUMBER SIX

The Unique Jesus

When, at the close of the third year of Christ's ministry, the chief priests and Pharisees sent their soldiers to arrest Christ, they came back empty-handed. Their testimony showed that they had been emotionally, morally, and spiritually stunned. They reported, "No man ever spoke like this Man!" (John 7:46, page 1062). Upon hearing Christ for themselves and being overpowered by His words and His ethical fortitude, such an awe of Him was felt that these temple guards could not bring themselves to apprehend Him, either as a common criminal or as a false Christ.

He possessed qualities of moral integrity and divine righteousness that marked Him as different from all men—different from the rabbis—and indeed a Prophet sent from God. His claims went beyond those made by any rabbi; His teachings sparkled with the luster of truth and godliness; His holiness was unremitting; yet His compassion for the fallen was genuine and offered the forgiveness of the Lord. His understanding of the Law, even at the age of twelve, "astonished" the rabbis, already caught in their own web of self-righteous legalism (Luke 2:42, 46, 47, page 1013). His prayer life quietly and modestly surpassed that of Hezekiah. He did signs and miracles beyond those of both Elijah and Elisha, miracles such as had not been seen in Israel in the fifteen centuries since the Exodus. Yet He called Himself "meek" and was not boastful.

Although He was a Man, He was unique and set apart from all others. He alone possessed and displayed the credentials of the promised Messiah that was to come into the world. These credentials were the outworkings of His perfect moral character. He was the Messiah, and He was in the world; His words, deeds, and manner of life authenticated His divine mission and office (John 1:10-12, 14, page 1049; 7:46, page 1062; Mark 1:22, page 985).

Let us examine some of the ways in which Jesus was unique, which set Him apart and above all other possible messianic claimants (Matt. 24:4, 5, page 973).

6-A. He Was Unique in His Person
      (Hebrews 1:1-13, page 1236)

6-B. He Was Unique in His Birth
      (Luke 1:26-35, page 1010)

6-C. He Was Unique in His Ministry
      (Mark 1:21-28, page 984)

6-D. He Was Unique in His Death
      (John 19:16-30, page 1080)

6-E. He Was Unique in His Resurrection
      (John 20:1-31, page 1082)

6-F. He Was Unique in His Ascension
      (Acts 1:1-9, page 1086)

6-G. He Will Be Unique in His Second Coming
      (Matthew 16:27, page 963)

MASTER OUTLINE NUMBER SEVEN
The Deity of Christ: His Person

If Jesus is God, and you believe with your understanding that He is the God-Man, and you have truly, purposefully, by an act of decision committed your life to Him as Lord and Savior, then everything is settled forever. But if Jesus is not God, then nothing is settled, and we are lost in sin, without hope.

Now the question is, do we have biblical evidence that Jesus is the God-Man, God in the flesh? The answer is a joyful yes! Throughout Christ's ministry His enemies made every effort to disprove His messianic claims and expose Him as a deceiver. They failed completely.

On one occasion the Pharisees, Sadducees, and Herodians, who had nothing in common but a religious hatred for Jesus, came to Him with questions designed to entangle Him in His teaching and to expose Him as a fraud (Matt. 22:15-40, page 970). The omniscient God-Man, Jesus, answered all their questions without getting caught in their web of deceit. Then He asked the Pharisees a question, in order to give them evidence from the Scriptures that He was the Messiah. His question was, "What do you think about the Christ [Messiah]? Whose Son is He?" They answered, "The Son of David." Their reply was correct, but they were not ready for the next question. Jesus continued, "'How then does David in the Spirit call Him "Lord," saying: "The LORD said to my Lord, 'Sit at My right hand, till I make Your enemies Your footstool' "? If David then calls him "Lord," how is He his Son?' " (Matt. 22:41-46, page 971; cf. Ps. 110:1, page 576). They had no answer to this profound question because they did not know, or would not accept, the biblical teaching about the Messiah.

How could King David refer to his own Son as his Lord? Was it illogical? Not in this case. Jesus is David's Son according to the flesh (Rom. 1:3, page 1128), as attested by the genealogies of Matthew and Luke. He is also David's Lord according to His God deity. He is the God-Man, "the only begotten of the Father, full of grace and truth" (John 1:14, page 1049). Jesus is unique in that He is both David's Son and David's God. His humanity began with His conception by the Holy Spirit in the womb of Mary, but His deity is from all eternity. Jesus is God manifested in the flesh (Rom. 8:3, page 1136).

Jesus, as God, is David's Lord. Jesus, as man, is David's Son. Again Jesus said, "I am the Root and the Offspring of David" (Rev. 22:16, page 1316). Jesus was saying, as it were, "Since I am David's God, I am His Root; he is My son spiritually. But in the flesh I am David's offspring. David is My son, and I am David's Son." He is the God-Man.

7-A. Jesus Is the "I AM" of the Old Testament
      (Exodus 3:13-15, page 60)

7-B. Jesus Is the "I AM" of the New Testament
      (John 8:56-59, page 1064)

7-C. Jesus Is Immanuel
      (Isaiah 7:14-16, page 649)

7-D.   Jesus Is the Father's Gift to Us
         (Isaiah 9:6, 7, page 651)

7-E.   Jesus Is God, According to God the Father
         (Psalm 45:6, 7, page 538)

7-F.   Jesus Is the God-Man
         (John 1:14, page 1049)

7-G.   Jesus Is Sovereign
         (Luke 4:31, 32, page 1017)

MASTER OUTLINE NUMBER EIGHT

The Deity of Christ: His Signs

John's Gospel is the Good News of the deity of Jesus Christ. In John 20:30, 31 (page 1084), John interprets his own writings. If we are to comprehend the primary teachings of this book, we must give our undivided attention to his interpretation.

"And truly Jesus did many other signs in the presence of His disciples, which are not written in this book; but these are written that you may believe that Jesus is the Christ, the Son of God, and that believing you may have life in His name" (John 20:30, 31, page 1084).

The Gospel of John is systematic in structure and poetic in tone. In the systematic structure, under the guidance of the Holy Spirit, John selects seven signs or miracles that prove the deity of Jesus Christ. The word "signs" in this gospel is the key that unlocks the door to its essential doctrine, indispensable to the body of theological truth. Here in the Gospel of John there are signs in the form of miracles, of powers, of wonders, and of words. Miracles are manifested in signs. These powers and wonders are supernatural events, in which God transcends the natural laws of His universe, exercising His authority over His creation.

To establish the fact that Jesus is God, John, guided by the Holy Spirit, selected seven signs from the many miracles that Jesus performed. His purpose was twofold:

First, "that you may believe that Jesus is the Christ, the Son of God." The word "Christ" (Greek *Christos*) means the same as "Messiah" in Hebrew, i.e., "Anointed." Jesus is God's anointed Prophet, Priest, and King.

Second, "that believing you may have life in His name." This saving faith is illustrated when unbelieving Thomas saw the risen Lord Jesus and confessed, "My Lord and my God!" (John 20:28, page 1083). This is the greatest confession of faith ever uttered or written. The words "my Lord" are indicative of his volitional commitment to Jesus as Lord and Master. It is a recognition of the lordship of Jesus and the servanthood of the believer (Matt. 6:24, page 943). The words "my God" are indicative of his intellectual conviction that Jesus is God. Saving faith involves volitional commitment to Christ as Lord and Master, as well as an intellectual conviction that He is the God-Man.

Now let us examine the seven signs, or miracles, that prove the deity of Jesus Christ.

8-A.   Jesus Turned Water into Wine, Proving His Deity in His Power to Create
         (John 2:1-11, page 1050)

8-B.   Jesus Healed the Nobleman's Son, Proving His Deity in His Power to Prolong Life
         (John 4:46-54, page 1055)

8-C.   Jesus Healed a Sick Man at the Pool of Bethesda, Proving His Deity in His Power to
         Give Life
         (John 5:1-18, page 1056)

8-D.   Jesus Fed Five Thousand with a Lad's Lunch, Proving His Deity in His Power to
         Supply the Necessities of Life
         (John 6:1-14, page 1058)

8-E.   Jesus Walked on the Water, Proving His Deity in His Power to Protect Life
         (John 6:15-21, page 1059)

8-F.   Jesus Gave Sight to a Blind Beggar, Proving His Deity in His Power to Illuminate Life
         (John 9:1-41, page 1065)

8-G.   Jesus Raised Lazarus from the Dead, Proving His Deity in His Power to Re-create Life
         (John 11:38-44, page 1070)

MASTER OUTLINE NUMBER NINE

Messianic Psalms

"You search the Scriptures, for in them you think you have eternal life; and these are they which testify of Me" (John 5:39, page 1057). In the King James Version this verse reads like a command, "Search the Scriptures"; in the New King James Version and other versions it reads like a statement of fact, "You search the Scriptures." Both translations are valid. We may perceive it as both a command and a statement of fact. We are to search the Old Testament books; for in them Christ is revealed unto us in type and prophecy. He is the theme of the Old Testament from Genesis to Malachi.

It is a fact that the Jews, scribes, and Pharisees searched the Scriptures; they pored over them, they diligently investigated them. However, they were spiritually blind to the Messiah; they saw only the Law, as they wrongly construed it. They were so legalistic that they searched the old Scriptures for but one purpose: to interpret the Law. But they were so blinded by the Law that they did not recognize the Lawgiver, who came to fulfill the Law. "Do not think that I came to destroy the Law or the Prophets. I did not come to destroy but to fulfill" (Matt. 5:17, page 939). In this verse Jesus speaks of the Law and the Prophets; the reference is not just to specific laws, but rather to the whole of the Old Testament books. He fulfilled all the ceremonial laws relative to the atoning sacrifices, as well as the moral laws, both positive and negative. He fulfilled all the types (biblical objects, persons, and events that illustrate what is to come) and all the prophecies that pertained to His first coming. When He returns, He will fulfill all those related to His Second Coming.

If the Jewish rulers had truly understood the types and prophecies of the Old Testament books, they would have recognized the Christ early in His ministry, and accepted Him as their Messiah. May God open our eyes to the Messiah as He is revealed to us in these messianic psalms.

9-A.   The Messiah Exalted
        (Psalm 8:1-9, page 514)

9-B.   The Messiah Rejected
        (Psalm 118:22-29, page 580)

9-C.   The Messiah Forsaken
        (Psalm 69:1-21, page 550)

9-D.   The Messiah Crucified
        (Psalm 22:1-31, page 522)

9-E.   The Messiah Resurrected
        (Psalm 16:1-11, page 517)

9-F.   The Messiah as High Priest
        (Psalm 110:1-7, page 576)

9-G.   The Messiah as King of Kings
        (Psalm 2:1-12, page 509)

MASTER OUTLINE NUMBER TEN

The Holy Spirit: His Ministry

Christians have great and many privileges as children of God because of who the Holy Spirit is, and what He can do in the life of every believer. It is most important to realize that the Holy Spirit is fully God. The deity of the Holy Spirit is affirmed in the Scriptures. He is declared to be God:

(1) By Peter, when Ananias and Sapphira tried to deceive God by bringing a portion of an offering, pretending to bring all of it. "But Peter said, 'Ananias, why has Satan filled your heart to lie to the Holy Spirit and keep back part of the price of the land for yourself?...You have not lied to men but to God' " (Acts 5:1-4, page 1093). When Ananias lied to the Holy Spirit, he therefore lied to God. The Holy Spirit is God, according to the Scriptures.

(2) By the apostle Paul, when he wrote to "the church of God which is at Corinth" (1 Cor. 1:2, page 1148), asking them a most important question: "Do you not know that you are the temple of God and that the Spirit of God dwells in you?" (1 Cor. 3:16, page 1149). Every New Testament church is composed of born-again, Spirit-baptized believers. The building is not the church, it is the sanctuary where the church meets to worship; and God the Holy Spirit indwells each believer in the

church. "Or do you not know that your body is the temple of the Holy Spirit who is in you, whom you have from God, and you are not your own?" (1 Cor. 6:19, 20, page 1152). Yes, your physical body is the temple of God, the Holy Spirit.

(3) By attributes ascribed to the Holy Spirit that are also ascribed to God the Father and God the Son:

(a) *Omnipresence*—He is everywhere present in God's universe (Ps. 139:7-10, page 590).

(b) *Omnipotence*—He has all power in God's universe (Luke 1:35, page 1010).

(c) *Omniscience*—He has all knowledge in God's universe (John 14:26, page 1075; cf. 1 Cor. 2:10, 11, page 1149).

Yes, the Holy Spirit is God, and we should desire everything He has for us.

This study on the Holy Spirit and His ministry will help you recognize your great need of His Christ-exalting presence in your life. Jesus said, "He [the Holy Spirit] will glorify Me, for He will take of what is Mine [receive My teaching] and declare it to you" (John 16:14, page 1077). The Holy Spirit came to glorify Christ in and through every child of God. If He is not exalting Christ in your life, it is because He is "grieved." Paul said, "And do not grieve the Holy Spirit of God, by whom you were sealed for the day of redemption" (Eph. 4:30, page 1191). God the Holy Spirit is grieved by sin in the life of the believer. You are to put off the life-style of the old man (the flesh) and put on the life-style of the new man. Jesus said, "That which is born of the flesh is flesh [first birth], and that which is born of the Spirit is spirit [new spiritual birth]" (John 3:6, page 1052). Paul lists some of the sins that grieve the Holy Spirit in the lives of believers (Eph. 4:22-32, page 1191). Search your life and, if you find any sin therein, practice 1 John 1:9 (page 1278). As you confess your sins, call them by name; repent and forsake them, that you may be filled with the Holy Spirit of power and joy (Acts 1:8, page 1086).

10-A.   The Ministry of the Holy Spirit Before Pentecost
         (Judges 14:5, 6, page 255)

10-B.   The Ministry of the Holy Spirit on the Day of Pentecost and After
         (Acts 2:1-21, page 1088)

10-C.   The Ministry of the Holy Spirit: The Evangelist
         (Acts 5:29-32, page 1094)

10-D.   The Ministry of the Holy Spirit: The Helper
         (John 14:15-17, page 1075)

10-E.   The Ministry of the Holy Spirit: The Giver of Spiritual Gifts
         (1 Corinthians 12:1-31, page 1157)

MASTER OUTLINE NUMBER ELEVEN

Angels

Man is not the highest form of God's created beings. David said, "For You have made him [man] a little lower than the angels" (Ps. 8:5, page 514).

(1) Angels are greater in power and might (2 Pet. 2:11, page 1274) and in strength (Ps. 103:20, page 570).

(2) They are superior in wisdom and knowledge (2 Sam. 14:20, page 311).

(3) Their knowledge of the future often exceeds that of man (Rev. 21:9-27, page 1315). "The Lord God of the holy prophets sent His angel to show His servants the things which must shortly take place" (Rev. 22:6-11, page 1316).

Angels are superior to man in his fallen state, and yet they are in no way equal to the God-Man, Christ Jesus. Jesus is "so much better than the angels" (Heb. 1:4-14, page 1236). He is better

(1) *in name:* "He has on His robe and on His thigh a name written: KING OF KINGS AND LORD OF LORDS" (Rev. 19:16, page 1313; cf. Heb. 1:4, page 1236);

(2) *in His relationship with God the Father:* "I will be to Him a Father, and He shall be to Me a Son" (Heb. 1:5, page 1236);

(3) *in rank:* "Let all the angels of God worship Him" (Heb. 1:6, page 1236);

(4) *in position:* Angels are created beings, but Jesus is the eternal God.

Of His Son, God said, "Your throne, O God, is forever and ever; a scepter of righteousness is the scepter of Your kingdom" (Heb. 1:8, page 1236).

The study and understanding of the doctrine of angels is a vital force in the spiritual life of the believer. Angels are very prominent in fifty-nine books of the Bible. They are not mentioned in Ruth, Nehemiah, Esther, John's epistles, or James. A biblical understanding of angels, Satan, and demons (fallen angels) will equip you with power and knowledge to cope with many of the personal problems of the Christian life.

11-A.   Angels: Their Identity
         (Colossians 1:16, page 1202)

11-B.   Angels: Their Kinds and Ranks
         (Hebrews 12:22, page 1251)

11-C.   Angels: Their Nature
         (Psalm 103:19-21, page 570)

11-D.   Angels: Their Ministry in Heaven and on Earth
         (Revelation 5:11-14, page 1298)

11-E.   Angels: Their Part in the Second Coming of Christ
         (Mark 13:26, 27, page 1002)

MASTER OUTLINE NUMBER TWELVE

Satan

Satan is a person. Yes, there is a personal devil. In this study you will see him appear before God and talk with Him. Only a person can take part in an intelligent dialogue (Job 1:6-12, page 479). He reasoned with Eve in the Garden; only a personal, intelligent being can reason (Gen. 3:1-7, page 5). He quoted Scripture when he tempted Jesus (Matt. 4:1-11, page 934). He accuses the brethren before God (Rev. 12:9, 10, page 1305). He performs miracles—signs (2 Thess. 2:9, page 1215). He tempts both saved and unsaved to commit sin. He makes war (Rev. 20:7-9, page 1313).

He has been given many names and titles in the Scriptures. Some of them are:

(1) *Satan*—"Adversary." He does not have the capacity to love or to show mercy. He is called Satan fifty times in the Bible.
(2) *Devil*—"Slanderer." This title is used over a hundred times in the New Testament.
(3) *Abaddon*—"Destruction."
(4) *Apollyon*—"Destroyer" (Rev. 9:11, page 1303).
(5) *Beelzebub*—"Lord of Flies." He is the god of all the demons (Matt. 12:24, page 953).
(6) *The anointed cherub*—An angel (Ezek. 28:14, page 806).
(7) *Lucifer*—"Day Star" or "Morning Star" (Is. 14:12, page 657). He can transform himself into an angel of light (2 Cor. 11:14, page 1174).

He is called "the god of this age" (2 Cor. 4:4, page 1167), "the prince of the power of the air" (Eph. 2:2, page 1187), "the great dragon" (Rev. 12:9, page 1305), and "that serpent of old" (Rev. 20:2, page 1313). Jesus called him "the ruler of this world" (John 12:31, page 1072). He is not the ruler of creation; he is the ruler of this world system. Therefore, God warns us, "Do not love the world [world system] or the things in the world....For all that is in the world—the lust of the flesh, the lust of the eyes, and the pride of life—is not of the Father" (1 John 2:15-17, page 1279). Satan desires that all be caught up in his system and be lost. God desires that all accept Jesus Christ and be saved.

12-A.   Satan: His Origin
         (Ezekiel 28:11-19, page 805)

12-B.   Satan: His Fall
         (Isaiah 14:12-15, page 657)

12-C.   Satan: The God of This World
         (2 Corinthians 4:3, 4, page 1167)

12-D.   Satan: The Original Manslayer and Father of Lies
        (John 8:44, page 1063)

12-E.   Satan: The Tempter
        (Matthew 4:1-11, page 934)

12-F.   Satan: His Work
        (1 Peter 5:8, page 1269)

12-G.   Satan: His Present and Eternal Abodes
        (Job 1:6-12, page 479)

12-H.   Satan and the Death of Christ
        (John 12:31, page 1072)

MASTER OUTLINE NUMBER THIRTEEN

Demons

Demonology is clearly set forth in the Bible. Jesus spoke to demons and commanded them to come out of the possessed. Demons are disembodied spirits, fallen angels. They belong to Satan, who is the ruler of the demons. In the King James Version *diabolos, daimon,* and *daimonion* are translated "devil" or "devils." *Diabolos* (devil), meaning "accuser" or "slanderer," is always used in the singular in the New Testament. The words *daimon* and *daimonion* are used both in the singular and the plural and are not interchangeable with *diabolos,* since there is but one *diabolos,* the Devil, but many *daimonion* or *daimon,* demons. This distinction has been made in the New King James and other versions. To illustrate, the King James Version reads, "And when he went forth to land, there met him out of the city a certain man, which had devils long time." Now the New King James reads, "And when He stepped out on the land, there met Him a certain man from the city who had demons for a long time" (Luke 8:27, page 1023). The word *diabolos* is used thirty-five times in the New Testament, meaning "devil." *Daimonion* and *daimon* are used sixty-one times, meaning "demon" or "demons."

Paul wrote to the church at Corinth, "We are not ignorant of his [Satan's] devices" (2 Cor. 2:11, page 1166). Are you ignorant of Satan's devices? He would like to keep you in total ignorance of himself, his powers, and his demons who serve him. If you believe in Jesus Christ, that He is the Son of God and God the Son, if you love Him and serve Him, you can be sure of one thing: Satan and his demons are going to buffet you. Take your "stand against the wiles of the devil." He performs spiritual trickery, called "spiritual hosts of wickedness in the heavenly places" (Eph. 6:10-12, page 1192). This spiritual wickedness is found in all religions that deny that Jesus is God. It is also found in witchcraft, fortune-telling, astrology, mediums, the occult, and so on. God calls on all believers to "come out from among them and be separate" (2 Cor. 6:17, page 1169). Satan's strategy is intended to beguile, ensnare, or deceive all who are "ignorant of his devices" (2 Cor. 2:11, page 1166).

Therefore, our greatest defense is knowledge of God's Word. Jesus defeated Satan when He was tempted in the wilderness. After each temptation He said, "It is written"; then He quoted God's Word (Matt. 4:4, see also Point 12-E, "Satan: The Tempter," page 934).

13-A.   Demons: Their Identity
        (Jude 6, page 1289)

13-B.   Demons: Servants of Satan
        (Matthew 12:24, page 953)

13-C.   Demons: Their Work
        (2 Corinthians 12:7-10, page 1175)

13-D.   Demons: Their Power
        (Mark 5:1-20, page 989)

13-E.   Demons: Their Judgment
        (1 Corinthians 6:3, page 1151)

MASTER OUTLINE NUMBER FOURTEEN

What the Bible Teaches About Man

Through the ages philosophers and historians have attempted to understand the nature of our race—its origins, psychological makeup, the purpose of man, why man cannot live in peace, and humanity's final destiny. Biblical theologians have an infinite advantage in this quest, as the Bible alone supplies the answers. David asked the question, "What is man that You are mindful of him, and the son of man that You visit him?" (Ps. 8:4, page 514). This question by David sums up the many questions which man has concerning his position on earth. Man perceives himself as a higher form of life than the animals, but we are below God in our limited control over events and life span. What is our place and function in the universe? In the following outline studies, we will examine the Bible's answers to some of these profound questions.

14-A.   How Did Mankind Appear on This Planet?
         (Psalm 144:3, page 592)

14-B.   How Did Mankind Fall, and What Were the Effects?
         (Romans 3:23, page 1131)

14-C.   What Is God's Purpose for Mankind?
         (Deuteronomy 6:5, page 187)

14-D.   What Does the Bible Teach About Race?
         (Genesis 10:1-5, page 15)

14-E.   What Are the Various States of Man with God?
         (Ecclesiastes 7:29, page 630)

14-F.   What Is the Final Destiny of Man?
         (Proverbs 14:11, 12, page 608)

MASTER OUTLINE NUMBER FIFTEEN

The Doctrine of Sin

The doctrine of sin encompasses the whole Bible from Genesis to Revelation. When the first man and woman sinned against God in the Garden of Eden, their relationship and fellowship with God was broken. Thus began the suffering of the race. Mankind will continue to reap the wages of sin, which are physical and spiritual death (Rom. 6:23, page 1134), until the Lord Jesus Christ returns to this planet to put an end to sin and death forever (1 Cor. 15:20-26, 51-58, page 1161). The only hope for the sinner to escape the wages of sin—death, which is eternal separation from God's mercy—is to accept by faith the Lord Jesus Christ as personal Savior, thus escaping the second death, which includes the lake of fire (Rev. 21:8, page 1315). Faith in His atoning death on Calvary, His burial, and bodily resurrection will robe the believer in the righteousness of God the Son (2 Cor. 5:21, page 1169). Then the sinner will be changed because he is in Christ. "Therefore, if anyone [any sinner] is in Christ, he [or she] is a new creation; old things have passed away [old beliefs, old desires, old ways, old deeds, old plans]; behold, all things have become new" (2 Cor. 5:17, page 1169). God longs to make the sinner a new person in Jesus Christ, His only begotten Son. All sins of those who believe will be cleansed by the blood of God the Son (Rev. 1:5, page 1293; cf. 1 Pet. 1:18, 19, page 1263).

The question is often asked, "What is sin?" God answers this question in clear and simple language. According to the Word of God, sin is

(1) going our own way (doing our will), although "the LORD has laid on Him [the Messiah-Savior Jesus Christ] the iniquity of us all" (Is. 53:6, page 693);
(2) transgression, overstepping God's holy law (1 John 3:4, page 1280);
(3) unbelief—calling God a liar (1 John 5:10, page 1282);
(4) falling short of God's glory (Rom. 3:23, page 1131), when we ought always to glory in the Lord (1 Cor. 1:31, page 1148). Paul tells us in Colossians 3:16, 17 (page 1206) how to glory in the Lord.

Jeremiah also tells us how to glory in the Lord, but first he lists some things we are not to glory in:

(1) "Let not the wise man glory in his wisdom."
(2) "Let not the mighty man glory in his might."
(3) "Nor let the rich man glory in his riches."

Then he writes, " 'But let him who glories glory in this,'

(1) 'That he understands and knows Me,'
(2) 'That I am the LORD, exercising lovingkindness, judgment, and righteousness in the earth.'

" 'For in these I delight,' says the LORD" (Jer. 9:23, 24, page 721). In these things we should delight also, and not permit sin to have dominion over us (Rom. 6:11-18, page 1134), for when we allow sin to have dominion over us we are incapable of glorying in the Lord.

15-A.   The Origin of Sin
         (Genesis 2:15-18, page 4)

15-B.   The Effects of Sin: Immediate and Lasting
         (Genesis 3:7-24, page 6)

15-C.   The Effects of Sin in Human Character
         (Romans 3:9-18, page 1130)

15-D.   The Effects of Sin in Human History
         (James 4:1-5, page 1259)

15-E.   The End of Sin
         (Revelation 14:13, page 1307)

MASTER OUTLINE NUMBER SIXTEEN

Consequences of Sin

There is a general confusion about which type of sin leads to death and which sin does *not* lead to death, as mentioned in 1 John 5:16, 17 (page 1283). In this epistle, John is writing to the saved. He wrote, "If anyone sees his brother [in Christ] sinning a sin which does not lead to death" (1 John 5:16, page 1283), he can pray for forgiveness and God will forgive (1 John 1:9, page 1278) and not chasten him to the point of physical death. But if the believer commits sin leading to physical death, and God so judges him, prayer cannot change God's verdict. Not all sins committed by believers lead to death, but some do (1 John 5:17, page 1283). Also, not all who die before they reach old age die a premature death.

The day that Adam and Eve ate the forbidden fruit they died. They committed the sin unto death in the Garden of Eden. God said to Adam, "Of every tree of the garden you may freely eat; but of the tree of the knowledge of good and evil you shall not eat, for in the day that you eat of it you shall surely die" (Gen. 2:16, 17, page 5). When Adam, the head of our race, sinned, he died and all of the human race died in his loins; his sin corrupted his seed (1 Pet. 1:23, page 1264). "For as in Adam all die" (1 Cor. 15:22, page 1161). Since then, with one exception, every human being that has been or will be born of woman is born in sin (Ps. 51:5, page 541). The one exception is Jesus Christ, who was born of the Virgin Mary, who remained a virgin until after the birth of God the Son (Luke 1:26-38, page 1010). In the first Adam all died, but in the last Adam (Christ), all believers are given eternal life (1 Cor. 15:45-49, page 1162). One represented us unto death, the other unto life eternal.

A sin that leads to physical death can be committed by the saved or the unsaved. Even though all have an appointment with death, because of the original sin (Heb. 9:27, page 1244), it is possible for the saved or unsaved to so sin that the Lord will take them out of this life before their otherwise appointed time.

There are many consequences of sin. Following are but a few of them.

16-A.   Consequences of Sin in the Days of Noah
         (Genesis 6–8, page 11)

16-B.   Consequences of Sin at Kadesh Barnea
         (Numbers 32:6-13, page 174)

16-C.   Consequences of Sin: The Fiery Serpents
         (Numbers 21:4-9, page 161)

16-D.   Consequences of Sin Committed by Nadab and Abihu
         (Leviticus 10:1-10, page 115)

16-E.   Consequences of Sin Committed by Moses and Aaron
         (Numbers 20:1-13, page 159)

16-F.   Consequences of Sin Committed by Ananias and Sapphira
         (Acts 5:1-11, page 1093)

16-G.   Consequences of Sin in the Corinthian Church
         (1 Corinthians 11:17-34, page 1156)

MASTER OUTLINE NUMBER SEVENTEEN

Heaven and Hell

According to the Scriptures there are three heavens. The apostle Paul said, "I know a man in Christ who fourteen years ago…such a one was caught up to the third heaven…he was caught up into Paradise and heard inexpressible words, which it is not lawful for a man to utter" (2 Cor. 12:2-4, page 1175). Since there is a third heaven, it stands to reason that there is also a first and second heaven. The plural for heaven is used more than one hundred times in the Bible.

(1) It is very clear in the Scriptures that the first heaven is the atmospheric heaven. "Thus the heavens and the earth, and all the host of them, were finished" (Gen. 2:1, page 4).

(2) Since heaven is "up," or out beyond the atmosphere, the second heaven would be the stellar heaven, or outer space—reaching up to the heaven of heavens—the very throne of God.

(3) *Paradise* is the same as the third heaven or the heaven of heavens, and is mentioned three times in the Bible:

(a) By Paul when he was caught up to the third heaven (2 Cor. 12:2-4, page 1175).

(b) Jesus said to the thief on the cross, "Today you will be with Me in Paradise" (Luke 23:43, page 1046). This meant that the thief would go immediately to heaven because he had repented and believed.

(c) In our Lord's letter to the church at Ephesus, He said, "He who has an ear, let him hear what the Spirit says to the churches. To him who overcomes I will give to eat from the tree of life, which is in the midst of the Paradise of God" (Rev. 2:7, page 1294). Paradise is also called the heaven of heavens. "But will God indeed dwell on the earth? Behold, heaven and the heaven of heavens cannot contain You. How much less this temple which I have built!" (1 Kin. 8:27, page 335).

The Bible has more to say about hell than it does about heaven. To deny the fact of hell is to deny that the Bible is the infallible Word of God. That there is an eternal hell where the wicked will be tormented forever and ever is not a religious fable used to scare the wicked into becoming good religious citizens. Hell is a biblical fact. There are three words in the Hebrew and Greek that are translated "hell:"

(1) *Sheol* (Hebrew)—generally the temporary abode of the wicked, sometimes *grave* (O.T.);

(2) *Hades* (Greek)—generally the temporary abode of the wicked (N.T.); agrees with O.T. *Sheol*;

(3) *Gehenna* (Greek, based on a Hebrew name)—the eternal abode of the wicked (N.T.).

Sheol and *Hades* are the two names for the intermediate state of the wicked dead. *Gehenna* is the future abode of the lost. *Gehenna* will be occupied by the unsaved after the last resurrection and the Great White Throne judgment; "The sea gave up the dead who were in it, and Death [the last enemy—1 Cor. 15:26, page 1162] and Hades delivered up the dead who were in them. And they were judged, each one according to his works. Then Death [the last enemy] and Hades were cast into the lake of fire. This is the second death" (Rev. 20:13, 14, page 1314).

Gehenna, the eternal abode of the wicked, is found twelve times in the New Testament and is translated "hell" in each case—denoting the eternal torments of the wicked after the last resurrection.

The Lord Jesus used the word *Gehenna* to warn the wicked of their wicked ways. He said:

(1) "And do not fear those who kill the body but cannot kill the soul. But rather fear Him who is able to destroy both soul and body in hell [*Gehenna*]" (Matt. 10:28, page 950).

(2) "But I will show you whom you should fear: Fear Him who, after He has killed, has power to cast into hell [*Gehenna*]; yes, I say to you, fear Him!" (Luke 12:5, page 1029).

To deny that there is an eternal hell is to deny the deity of Christ. If we cannot believe what He

said about hell, then how can we believe anything He taught? If there is no hell, then Christ is not "the way, the truth, and the life" (John 14:6, page 1074).

"Lord, I believe!" (John 9:38, page 1066).

17-A.   Heaven Is a Place
         (John 14:1-6, page 1074)

17-B.   Heaven Is the Saint's Place
         (Colossians 3:1-4, page 1205)

17-C.   Heaven Is an Eternal Place
         (Isaiah 65:17, page 704)

17-D.   Hell Is a Place
         (Psalm 9:17, page 515)

17-E.   Hell Is the Sinner's Place
         (Acts 1:25, page 1087)

17-F.   Hell Is an Eternal Place
         (Matthew 25:41, page 976)

17-G.   You Must Choose: Heaven or Hell
         (Luke 16:19-31, page 1035)

MASTER OUTLINE NUMBER EIGHTEEN

The Judgments

In the Scriptures, we are instructed to rightly divide the word of truth (2 Tim. 2:15, page 1226). This is most essential when studying the judgments. Do not endeavor to make all the judgments conform to the theory of one "general judgment." The "general judgment" theory is the invention of early medieval religion and is not taught in the Word of God.

There are at least five separate judgments revealed in the Bible, and they differ as to time, place, and purpose. Yet, they all have one thing in common: the Lord Jesus Christ is the Judge (John 5:22, page 1057).

Everyone, from Adam to the last man to be born on this earth, will stand before the Lord Jesus Christ to be judged. In the first judgment, the sins of the believer have already been judged in Christ on the cross. In the second judgment, the believer is to judge self or be judged and disciplined by the Lord Jesus Christ. In the third judgment, all believers must appear at the "judgment seat of Christ" (2 Cor. 5:10, page 1168) where their works are to be judged. In the fourth judgment, all nations are to be judged at the second coming of Christ. In the fifth judgment, the wicked dead are to be judged at the Great White Throne.

18-A.   The Judgment of the Believer's Sins
         (John 5:24, page 1057)

18-B.   The Judgment of the Believer's Self
         (1 Corinthians 11:31, 32, page 1157)

18-C.   The Judgment of the Believer's Works
         (2 Corinthians 5:10, page 1168)

18-D.   The Judgment of the Nations
         (Matthew 25:31-46, page 976)

18-E.   The Judgment of the Wicked
         (Revelation 20:11-15, page 1313)

MASTER OUTLINE NUMBER NINETEEN

Man's Ruin—God's Remedy

Out of the millions of books in print, only the Bible, according to Jesus, is the Word of God. Paul said, "All Scripture is given by inspiration of God" (2 Tim. 3:16, page 1227), which means that all Scripture is God-breathed—that it is spoken by the mouth of God, who cannot lie (Titus 1:2, page 1230). The Bible is the only book that reveals God's remedy for man's ruin.

Man would have to be spiritually blind, deaf, and mute not to know that "the whole world lies under the sway of the wicked one" (1 John 5:19, page 1283). In this verse, God reveals two classes of people. First are those who are no longer spiritually blind, deaf, or mute to God's message; they are saved by the grace of God and know it. "[They] know that [they] are of God," and they also know that "the whole world lies under the sway of the wicked one." The whole world of unsaved souls lies in the Evil One, Satan. Now Satan is the father of the wicked (John 8:44, page 1063). The wicked murder because their father is a murderer and the motivator of all murders. He motivated Cain (who was religious) to murder Abel, who was righteous (Gen. 4:8, page 8). He is a liar, and the father of all liars, who will "have their part in the lake which burns with fire and brimstone, which is the second death" (Rev. 21:8, page 1315).

Have you ever wondered why every nation, every tribe, every family, the rich and the poor, the educated and the uneducated, all participate in the ruin of man? We all have a common origin in Adam.

All share a common heritage—the fall of the human race. All share a common legacy, the ruin of man. "The wages of sin is death, but the gift of God is eternal life in Christ Jesus our Lord" (Rom. 6:23, page 1134). Death is the wages of sin, and death is universal, because the ruin is universal. But "the gift of God is eternal life in Christ Jesus our Lord," who is God's remedy for man's ruin.

19-A.   The Ruin of Man
         (Romans 5:12-14, page 1133)

19-B.   The Nature of Man's Ruin
         (Romans 1:18-32, page 1128)

19-C.   The Results of Man's Ruin
         (1 Corinthians 15:22, page 1161)

19-D.   God's Remedy for Man's Ruin
         (Mark 10:45, page 997)

19-E.   The Results of God's Remedy for Man's Ruin
         (1 Peter 1:18, 19, page 1263)

MASTER OUTLINE NUMBER TWENTY

The Blood of Jesus Christ from Genesis to Revelation

"The life of the flesh is in the blood, and I have given it to you upon the altar to make atonement for your souls; for it is the blood that makes atonement for the soul" (Lev. 17:11, page 126). Just as "the life of the flesh is in the blood," so the life of Christianity is in the atoning, life-giving blood of the Lord Jesus Christ. Jesus said, "I am…the life" (John 14:6, page 1074). He is the life of God, made living in the believer. Paul said, "Christ lives in me" (Gal. 2:20, page 1180). Christ lives in every born-again believer because the believer, by faith, is a partaker of the life-giving blood of Jesus. We are children of God by the blood. Therefore, we are "blood relatives" of God through the living blood of Jesus the Son of God, who is God the Son.

If the atoning blood of Jesus is rejected, and the rejecter continues willfully to reject eternal life through the blood, after knowing the truth that "the blood of Jesus Christ His Son cleanses us from all sin" (1 John 1:7, page 1278), for that person "there no longer remains a sacrifice for sins" (Heb. 10:26-28, page 1246). Christ atoned for our sins in His own body on the tree. Therefore, the person who rejects salvation by the blood of Jesus is guilty of a threefold sin:

(1) He has "trampled the Son of God underfoot" (Heb. 10:29, page 1246; 6:6, page 1241).

(2) He has "counted the blood of the covenant by which he was sanctified a common thing" (Heb. 10:29, page 1246).

(3) He has "insulted the Spirit of grace" (Heb. 10:29, page 1246).

This threefold sin is committed by many church members who profess to know Christ as personal Savior, but deny salvation by the precious blood of Jesus. Jesus warned them in His Sermon on the Mount, when He said, "Not everyone who says to Me, 'Lord, Lord,' shall enter the kingdom of heaven, but he who does the will of My Father in heaven" (Matt. 7:21, page 946). In that day they will point to their church membership, baptism, self-righteous life, and all manner of religious works; but Jesus will declare to them, "I never knew you; depart from Me, you who practice lawlessness!" (Matt. 7:23, page 946). Thank God He will never say this to those who, by faith, have "washed their robes and made them white in the blood of the Lamb" (Rev. 7:14, page 1301).

Before you proceed with this study, read God's warning to those who deny the validity of the atoning blood of Jesus (Heb. 10:26-31, page 1246). Now examine your faith: Have you neglected or belittled the doctrine of salvation by the precious blood of Jesus? Have you committed the threefold sin against the saving blood of Christ? (Heb. 10:29, page 1246). If you have, it is not too late to repent and by faith claim salvation through the shed blood of Jesus, and escape the Great White Throne of judgment (Rev. 20:11-15, page 1313). God summed up His warning in Hebrews 10:31 (page 1246): "It is a fearful thing to fall into the hands of the living God."

20-A.	The First Shedding of Blood	(Genesis 3:21, page 7)
20-B.	Abel's Blood Offering	(Genesis 4:3-7, page 7)
20-C.	The Offering of Isaac	(Genesis 22:1-19, page 26)
20-D.	The Passover Blood	(Exodus 12:1-36, page 69)
20-E.	The Day of Atonement in the Old Testament	(Leviticus 16:1-34, page 123)
20-F.	The Day of Atonement in the New Testament	(John 20:17, page 1083)
20-G.	Without the Shedding of Blood	(Hebrews 9:22, page 1244)

MASTER OUTLINE NUMBER TWENTY-ONE

So Great Salvation

Jesus' ministry began with the marvelous message, "Repent, for the kingdom of heaven is at hand" (Matt. 4:17, page 936). In Hebrews 2:3 (page 1237) we have a question that no one can answer: "How shall we escape if we neglect so great a salvation?" The Philippian jailer asked Paul and Silas, "Sirs, what must I do to be saved?" They had the answer: "Believe on the Lord Jesus Christ, and you will be saved" (Acts 16:30, 31, page 1111). Had the jailer asked, "What must I do to be lost?" they would have replied, "Nothing, because you are already lost." Jesus said, "For God did not send His Son into the world to condemn the world, but that the world through Him might be saved. He who believes in Him is not condemned [judged]; but he who does not believe is condemned [judged] already, because he has not believed in the name of the only begotten Son of God" (John 3:17, 18, page 1053).

Salvation is more than "great;" it is "so great" for the following reasons:

(1) It was first preached by the Lord Jesus Christ. He said to Zacchaeus, "Today salvation has come to this house, because he also is a son of Abraham; for the Son of Man has come to seek and to save that which was lost" (Luke 19:9, 10, page 1038).

(2) After His death, burial, resurrection, and ascension, the Lord Jesus sent the Holy Spirit to proclaim salvation to the lost through the apostles and all believers (John 16:7-15, page 1077; Acts 1:8, page 1086).

(3) This salvation is the only salvation. "Nor is there salvation in any other, for there is no other name under heaven given among men by which we must be saved" (Acts 4:12, page 1091).

Christ, in His humiliation, was nailed to the cross for our salvation. But He was resurrected, ex-

alted, and given a name above all names. When He comes in judgment, every knee will bow—in heaven, on earth, and in hell. And every tongue will confess that He is Lord. Those who did not neglect "so great a salvation" (Heb. 2:3, page 1237) will bow the knee and confess His name with great joy; but those who neglected "so great a salvation" will bow the knee and confess His name—but it will be too late (Phil. 2:5-11, page 1197; cf. Matt. 7:21-23, page 946). You will bow the knee now and accept Christ as your personal Savior, or you will bow the knee at the Great White Throne judgment and be lost forever (Rev. 20:11-15, page 1313). If you are not saved—before you read any further—will you stop and ask God to open your eyes to the truth, and make salvation plain, so that you can be saved and know it?

21-A.   So Great in Love
         (1 John 4:8, page 1281)

21-B.   So Great in Giving
         (2 Corinthians 8:9, page 1171)

21-C.   So Great in Power
         (Acts 4:12, page 1091)

21-D.   So Great in Grace
         (Ephesians 2:8, 9, page 1187)

21-E.   So Great in Invitation
         (Revelation 22:17, page 1316)

21-F.   So Great in Assurance
         (2 Timothy 1:12, page 1224)

MASTER OUTLINE NUMBER TWENTY-TWO

Repentance

"He who covers his sins will not prosper, but whoever confesses and forsakes them will have mercy" (Prov. 28:13, page 621).

God desires truth in the inward parts (Ps. 51:6, page 541) and commands all men everywhere to repent (Acts 17:30, page 1112).

(1) The sinner must repent before he can become the recipient of salvation by grace through faith (Eph. 2:8, 9, page 1187).

(2) The Christian must practice daily repentance if he is to enjoy unbroken fellowship with God (Job 42:1-6, page 506). Someone said, "I repented at conversion, before I understood the meaning of repentance, but since then as a Christian I have repented many times."

Repentance is a gift of God (Acts 5:31, page 1094; 11:18, page 1104); "the goodness of God leads you to repentance" (Rom. 2:4, page 1129). The goodness of God is not merited by the act of repentance. Repentance, like faith, is a gift. This gift of repentance is an inward change produced by the convicting power of the Holy Spirit as the Word of God is proclaimed (Acts 2:37, 38, page 1089; cf. John 16:7, 11, page 1077). The results are "repentance toward God and faith toward our Lord Jesus Christ" (Acts 20:21, page 1115); also faith that Christ died for our sins, that He was buried, and that He rose from the dead (1 Cor. 15:1-4, page 1161).

Repentance alone does not qualify a sinner for salvation; faith is also necessary in the death, burial, and resurrection of Christ. True repentance is always coupled with faith. It is impossible to have saving faith and not repent. "Repentance toward God and faith toward our Lord Jesus Christ" are essential and inseparable in salvation.

Faith without repentance is the ultimate of hypocrisy, and repentance without faith in the death, burial, and resurrection of Christ is futile.

22-A.   Repentance Defined
         (2 Peter 3:9, page 1275)

22-B.   Repentance Preached
         (Mark 1:1-4, page 983)

22-C.   Repentance from Dead Works
         (Hebrews 6:1, page 1240)

22-D.   Repentance and God
         (Hebrews 7:21, page 1242)

22-E.   Repentance, Impossible to Renew To
         (Hebrews 6:4-6, page 1240)

22-F.   Repentance: Its Importance
         (Acts 17:30, page 1112)

22-G.   Repentance: The Evidence
         (Acts 26:19, 20, page 1122)

MASTER OUTLINE NUMBER TWENTY-THREE

The Spiritual Birth

The Scriptures clearly teach that there are two births (John 3:6, page 1052).

(1) "That which is born of the flesh is flesh." This birth relates you to the human race—the family of Adam. The only way you can become a member of the human race is to be born of the flesh.

(2) "That which is born of the Spirit is spirit." This birth relates you to the spiritual race—the family of God. The only way you can become a member of God's family is to be born of the Spirit.

Spiritual birth is as real as physical birth. In fact, it is more real than that first birth. Paul said, "We do not look at the things which are seen [first birth], but at the things which are not seen [second birth]. For the things which are seen are temporary [the flesh will die—come to an end], but the things which are not seen are eternal [that which is born of the Spirit will never die]" (2 Cor. 4:18, page 1168).

When Nicodemus came to Jesus Christ, he said, "Rabbi, we know that You are a teacher come from God" (John 3:2, page 1051). When Nicodemus said, "we know," he was speaking for himself and others—perhaps his religious peers. He may have been sent as a delegation of one to learn more about Jesus. What he learned about the Lord Jesus was that He was more than a "teacher," more than a man "come from God." He learned that the Lord Jesus Christ was the God-Man, come down to a lost world as a baby, through the womb of the Virgin Mary. Jesus said, "The Son of Man has come to seek and to save that which was lost" (Luke 19:10, page 1038). Jesus knew the heart of Nicodemus, the Pharisee, teacher, and leader of Israel. In love, the Lord Jesus reached out to him with the gospel that saves to the uttermost. Nicodemus was a devoutly religious man, a teacher, and a keeper of the law; but he was lost.

The New Birth chapter (John 3:1-21, page 1051) contains:

(1) The miracle of spiritual birth (vv. 1-7). Jesus said, "You must be born again [or, from above]."

(2) The mystery of spiritual birth (v. 8). It is like the wind, you cannot understand it, but you know that it is real.

(3) The mentor of spiritual birth (vv. 9-13). Nicodemus said, "We know that You are a teacher come from God" (v. 2). Jesus was a God-sent mentor.

(4) The means of spiritual birth (v. 14). The vicarious death of Christ on Calvary is the only means of salvation.

(5) The message of spiritual birth (vv. 15, 16). The Lord Jesus Christ is God's message of love to a lost world.

(6) The magnitude of spiritual birth (vv. 17, 18). "That the world through Him might be saved."

(7) The manifestation of spiritual birth (vv. 19-21). "And this is the condemnation, that the light has come into the world, and men loved darkness rather than light, because their deeds were evil.

For everyone practicing evil hates the light and does not come to the light, lest his deeds should be exposed. But he who does the truth comes to the light, that his deeds [evidence of spiritual birth] may be clearly seen, that they have been done in God."

23-A.   The Spiritual Birth
         (John 3:1-8, page 1051)

23-B.   The Spiritual Birth and the Natural Birth
         (1 Peter 1:23, page 1264)

23-C.   The Spiritual Birth Is the Washing of Regeneration
         (Titus 3:5, page 1231)

23-D.   The Spiritual Birth: Its Evidence
         (1 John 4:7-21, page 1280)

MASTER OUTLINE NUMBER TWENTY-FOUR

What Is Faith?

"Now faith is the substance [assurance, title-deed] of things [seen and unseen] hoped for, the evidence [proof, conviction] of things not seen" (Heb. 11:1, page 1247; cf. 2 Cor. 4:18, page 1168). This is the only definition of faith found in the Bible, and it is not complete. Faith reaches beyond the natural realm of man's ability to possess. For example, "that Christ may dwell in your hearts through faith…to know the love of Christ which passes knowledge" (Eph. 3:17-20, page 1190). The love of Christ in its fullness is beyond all human comprehension; it is unknown and unknowable by the greatest minds of mankind. Yet, by faith, the most humble believer can begin to know the love of Christ, which cannot intellectually be understood.

(1) "For by it [faith] the elders obtained a good testimony" (Heb. 11:2, page 1247). The biblical heroes of faith pleased God by means of their faith (Heb. 11:5, 6, page 1247).

(2) "By faith we understand that the worlds were framed by the word of God, so that the things which are seen were not made of things which are visible" (Heb. 11:3, page 1247). Without faith you will fail to see the plan and purpose of God in His creation—"For since the creation of the world His invisible attributes are clearly seen, being understood by the things that are made, even His eternal power and Godhead, so that they [the disobedient] are without excuse" (Rom. 1:20, page 1128). To reject the revelation of God in the creation of the heavens and the earth is to be without excuse in the Day of Judgment. "The heavens declare the glory of God; and the firmament shows His handiwork" (Ps. 19:1-3, page 520).

(3) "By faith Abel offered to God a more excellent [acceptable] sacrifice than Cain" (Heb. 11:4, page 1247). Abel's blood sacrifice was acceptable to God because it was a type of the shed blood of Jesus "that speaks better things than that of Abel" (Heb. 12:24, page 1251; cf. Gen. 4:3-13, page 7). Abel, by faith, looked ahead to the day that Jesus Christ, our High Priest, would enter the holy place and sprinkle His blood upon the eternal mercy seat, and obtain everlasting salvation for all believers (Heb. 9:11, 15, page 1243; cf. 1 Pet. 1:18, 19, page 1263).

(4) "By faith Enoch" accomplished three things (Heb. 11:5, 6, page 1247):

(a) He walked with God (see Master Outline Number Forty-Four, "Enoch, a Man Who Walked With God," page 56).

(b) He pleased God.

(c) He was translated, taken up to heaven in his body of flesh and bones. Therefore, he did not experience physical death. He is thus a type of all born-again believers who will be living when Jesus comes again (1 Thess. 4:13-18, page 1211).

(5) "By faith Noah" built the ark (Heb. 11:7, page 1247). Noah did not have a dead faith (James 2:20, page 1257). Had Noah's faith been "dead," there would not be a human being upon the face of the earth today. For the seven elements that embodied Noah's perfect faith, see Hebrews 11:7 (page 1247) and Point 45-E, "Noah: A Man of Faith" (page 1247).

(6) "By faith Abraham" obeyed (Heb. 11:8, page 1248). He sought a country whose location was unknown to him, but God led him. He looked for an eternal city, built by Almighty God (Heb. 11:8, 10, page 1248). "By faith Abraham, when he was tested [God tested his faith], offered up Isaac" (Heb. 11:17-19, page 1249; see also Point 20-C, "The Offering of Isaac," page 26).

(7) By faith Sarah conceived after she had passed the age of childbearing (Heb. 11:11, 12, page 1248; cf. Gen. 17:15-19, page 22; 21:1-8, page 25).

(8) "By faith Isaac blessed Jacob and Esau" (Heb. 11:20, page 1249).

(9) "By faith Jacob, when he was dying, blessed each of the sons of Joseph" (Heb. 11:21, page 1249).

(10) "By faith Joseph" prophesied the return of the children of Israel to the Promised Land and commanded them to take his bones with them (Heb. 11:22, page 1249; Gen. 50:22-26, page 56; Ex. 13:19, page 73; Josh. 24:32, page 239).

(11) By faith Moses' parents were not afraid of the ruler of Egypt who had commanded that all male

children be put to death (Ex. 2:1-10, page 59). By faith Moses refused an Egyptian heritage, choosing to suffer affliction with his own people, esteeming the reproach of Christ to be of greater value than all the riches of Egypt. "By faith he forsook Egypt, not fearing the wrath of the king." For forty years he was a shepherd in the desert. By faith he returned to Egypt and kept the Passover. "By faith they [Moses and Israel] passed through the Red Sea as by dry land" (Heb. 11:23-29, page 1249).

(12) "By faith the walls of Jericho fell down after they were encircled for seven days" (Heb. 11:30, page 1249).

(13) Between verses 29 and 30 there are nearly forty years when the nation of Israel wandered in the wilderness in punishment for their unbelief. Moses and others had faith during that period, but the nation of Israel murmured against God and against Moses (Heb. 3:7-19, page 1238; cf. Num. 14:34, page 154). This is a condition which is repeated when any congregation no longer believes the promises of God.

(14) "By faith the harlot Rahab did not perish with those who did not believe" (Heb. 11:31, page 1249).

Other heroes in God's gallery of faith are mentioned in verses 32-40 (page 1249). Many of them died violent deaths—persecuted, imprisoned, and stoned. Some were slain by the sword and others torn apart by wild beasts. Many of them died, not yet having received by faith the promises of God. Four times the people were told that "the just shall live by faith" (Heb. 10:38, page 1247). In this eleventh chapter of Hebrews we see a great host who were justified by faith and learned the secret of how to live by faith. Like the Tribulation saints, "they did not love their lives to the death" (Rev. 12:11, page 1305).

24-A.   Faith Is a Mystery
         (1 Timothy 3:8, 9, page 1219)

24-B.   The Just Shall Live by Faith
         (Galatians 3:11, page 1181)

24-C.   Faith Is Joyful in Tribulation
         (2 Corinthians 7:4, 5, page 1169)

24-D.   Faith Without Works Is Dead
         (James 2:14-26, page 1257)

24-E.   Saving Faith Is in Christ
         (Hebrews 12:1, 2, page 1249)

MASTER OUTLINE NUMBER TWENTY-FIVE

The Christian Life

"And the disciples were first called Christians in Antioch" (Acts 11:26, page 1104). It was during the year that Barnabas and Paul ministered to the church in Antioch when they were first called Christians. The name "Christian" began to spread as the gospel was preached in that part of the world, and in time it became a title of honor. The name "Christian" is found only three times in the Bible:

(1) "And the disciples were first called Christians in Antioch" (Acts 11:26, page 1104).
(2) "Then Agrippa said to Paul, 'You almost persuade me to become a Christian' " (Acts 26:28, page 1122).
(3) "If anyone suffers as a Christian, let him not be ashamed" (1 Pet. 4:16, page 1267). According to this verse it is evident that the name added to their persecution.

What is a Christian? A Christian is a miracle, unless he is a Christian in name only. Remember Jesus said, "Not everyone who says to Me, 'Lord, Lord,' shall enter the kingdom of heaven" (Matt. 7:21-23, page 946). In other words, not everyone who claims to be a Christian is a born-again believer. All Christians are miracles because:

(1) They have been born from above. They have been born into the family of God by a spiritual birth (John 3:1-8, page 1051).
(2) They are a new creation in Christ (2 Cor. 5:17, page 1169).
(3) They have been made the righteousness of God in Christ (2 Cor. 5:21, page 1169).

(4) They have been declared just because they live by faith (Rom. 5:1, page 1133).

(5) They have accepted God's gift of eternal life in Jesus Christ, and God has canceled their wages of sin, which is death (Rom. 6:23, page 1134).

(6) They have been baptized by the Holy Spirit into the body of Christ (1 Cor. 12:13, page 1158).

(7) They are the sons of God (1 John 3:2, page 1279).

(8) They are ambassadors for Christ (2 Cor. 5:20, page 1169).

(9) They are strangers and pilgrims on the earth because heaven is their home (Heb. 11:13, page 1249).

A Christian is all of these and much, much more.

25-A.   The Christian Life Is an Eternal Life
         (Romans 6:23, page 1134)

25-B.   The Christian Life Is a Faith Life
         (1 Peter 5:5-9, page 1268)

25-C.   The Christian Life Is a Service Life
         (Colossians 3:16, 17, page 1206)

25-D.   The Christian Life Is a Warring Life
         (2 Corinthians 10:3-5, page 1173)

25-E.   The Christian Life Is a Successful Life
         (Joshua 1:1-8, page 215)

MASTER OUTLINE NUMBER TWENTY-SIX

As a Man Thinks

To help overcome the fear that results from an inferior feeling due to sin and to develop a positive, godly mental attitude, study this lesson every day until it becomes part of your daily thinking. It will motivate a change in your attitude from fear to faith. In order to apply these principles to yourself, personally, the following is written in the first person: God said, "As he thinks in his heart, so is he" (Prov. 23:7, page 616).

- Therefore, today I will think like a dynamic servant of God because I am what I think.
- I am not always what I think I am; I am what I think.
- I am not what I eat; I am what I think.
- Clothes do not make the man; thinking makes the man.
- Therefore, I will keep my thought processes active and open to the voice of God.
- God did not call me to a life of failure, but to a life of success.
- This being so, I cannot fail as long as I do His will, allowing Him to work in and through me, motivating my every thought.
- Because my God is a great God, I will think with confidence, knowing my thoughts can never be greater than my God. Today I will think like the apostle Paul, when he said, "I can do all things through Christ who strengthens me" (Phil. 4:13, page 1198).

26-A.   Think like a Dynamic Servant of God
         (Proverbs 23:7, page 616)

26-B.   You Are What You Think
         (Romans 12:3, page 1142)

26-C.   Thinking Makes the Person
         (Isaiah 55:7-9, page 695)

26-D.   Keep Your Thought Processes Active and Open to the Voice of God
         (Hebrews 3:7, page 1238)

26-E.   Think Great Thoughts, Because You Serve a Great God
         (Ephesians 3:20, page 1190)

MASTER OUTLINE NUMBER TWENTY-SEVEN

Fear

The subject of fear is one of the most awesome studies found in God's Word. There are constructive and destructive fears. Some fears are so evil that one can be momentarily paralyzed by them. One can become physically ill through fear. Therefore, it is so important that we give ourselves over to the Lord as we study this important subject. All of the spiritual qualifications and tools necessary to combat the evil fears that may come upon us are found in the Word of God. We can overcome bad fears, be victorious, live happy and joyful Christian lives, and be of greater service and value to our Master.

The following are fears that can keep us from knowing the Lord and doing His will, and that may condemn some to eternal hell:

(1) The fear that you will fail;
(2) The fear that you can't live up to God's standards;
(3) The fear that you can't obey God's Word.

Forms of the words *fear* and *afraid* are found over seven hundred times in the Bible; this should cause us to realize the importance of fear in our lives. Over eighty times we have the words, "Do not fear," or "Fear not."

27-A.   Fear, Constructive and Destructive
        (Matthew 10:24-31, page 950)

27-B.   Fear, Godly
        (Psalm 33:8, page 529)

27-C.   Fear Not: God Is Your Protector
        (Genesis 15:1, page 20)

27-D.   Fear Not: God Is Your Power
        (2 Kings 6:16, page 360)

27-E.   Fear: Its Objects
        (Psalm 34:4, page 530)

MASTER OUTLINE NUMBER TWENTY-EIGHT

Worship

"Worship at the church of your choice" has become a common sign in North America, and believers and unbelievers alike are urged to join in a public service in a specially designed building called a church or synagogue. But is this worship? Can a person who does not believe in Christ join in? No. If we go to the average church, including the average Bible-believing church, we will see a sign, "WORSHIP 11:00 A.M." We will find that the main part of the service is a sermon. But is a sermon worship? No, listening to a sermon, or even preaching one, is not worship. It can, should, and often does draw forth worship, but a sermon is not worship.

But what about prayers? Are they not worship? No, most prayers are petitions and are meant to be that. Some prayers are filled with worship, and most good prayers certainly include worship, but a prayer itself is not necessarily worship. Surely the church music—the anthems of the choir and solos, as well as the hearty congregational singing—is worship. Here we are getting closer to worship, especially when the music is addressed to God in adoration. But music itself is not worship. Some of the most beautiful church music is performed and enjoyed by people who make no profession of Christianity at all. Is the collection of tithes and offerings worship? Giving is a good work, and giving back to God some of what He has blessed us with can be an act of worship.

A beautiful example of worship by a former pagan Gentile is recorded in the book of Daniel. Consider the words of Nebuchadnezzar, as he worshiped the Most High God, after he came to know Him as his God and Savior: "I, Nebuchadnezzar, lifted my eyes to heaven, and my understanding returned to me; and I blessed the Most High and praised and honored Him who lives forever: For His dominion is an everlasting dominion, and His kingdom is from generation to generation. All the inhabitants of the earth are reputed as nothing [compared to His greatness]; He does according to His will in the army of heaven and among the inhabitants of the earth. No one can restrain His hand or

say to Him, 'What have You done?'…Now I, Nebuchadnezzar, praise and extol and honor the King of heaven, all of whose works are truth, and His ways justice. And those who walk in pride He is able to put down" (Dan. 4:34-37, page 840). This is pure worship. He certainly was not preaching; he was not even praying, but was praising the Most High God in worship. His heart was overflowing, bubbling over with a consciousness of the greatness, love, and goodness of the sovereign God.

We also are told to "exalt the LORD our God, and worship at His footstool—He is holy" (Ps. 99:5, page 567). Worship exalts God and humbles man; there is no room for pride, arrogance, or hypocrisy in worship. "God is Spirit, and those who worship Him must worship in spirit and truth" (John 4:24, page 1054).

28-A.   Worship: Some Fundamentals
         (Psalm 29:2, page 526)

28-B.   Worship in the Old Testament
         (Psalm 5:7, page 512)

28-C.   Worship in the New Testament
         (John 4:23, 24, page 1054)

28-D.   Worship: Its Importance
         (Luke 2:13, 14, page 1012)

MASTER OUTLINE NUMBER TWENTY-NINE

God's Will

Although this world system is presently an organized kingdom of evil, ruled and motivated by the will of Satan, who is "the prince of the power of the air, the spirit who now works in the sons of disobedience" (Eph. 2:1-3, page 1187), it must be remembered that Satan is not all-powerful. Only God has all authority over all power. God spoke to Isaiah saying, "I am God, and there is no other; I am God, and there is none like Me, declaring the end from the beginning…'My counsel shall stand, and I will do all My pleasure' " (Is. 46:9, 10, page 686). It is God's pleasure to reveal His will (plan for your life) to all believers. Jesus told His disciples to get into a boat and go to the other side of Galilee. Being omniscient (all-knowing), He knew they would encounter a storm; being omnipotent (all-powerful), He knew that He would save them from the storm. This was His specific will for His disciples (Matt. 14:22-33, page 959). In the will of God they were

(1) Sent into a storm. The will of God is filled with storms. Every believer who walks in God's will encounters contrary winds. Paul faced opposing winds throughout his ministry (2 Cor. 11:24-33, page 1175).

(2) In no danger, because Jesus was in prayer (Heb. 7:25, page 1242).

(3) In darkness. No believer, who is in the will of God, will remain in darkness (John 12:46, page 1072).

(4) Rowing with all their might against contrary winds. Nevertheless, they were making no progress (Mark 6:48, page 992).

When God puts it in your heart to do His will and you face contrary winds, remember that He will direct your path (Prov. 3:5, 6, page 599).

29-A.   God's Will Is Sovereign
         (Isaiah 46:9-11, page 686)

29-B.   God's Will Is Immutable
         (Malachi 3:6, page 924)

29-C.   God's Will Is Good, Acceptable, and Perfect
         (Romans 12:1, 2, page 1142)

29-D.   God's Will Can Be Known
         (Hebrews 13:20, 21, page 1252)

29-E.   God's Will for Individuals
         (Colossians 1:9, 10, page 1201)

MASTER OUTLINE NUMBER THIRTY

Lessons on Prayer

Prayer is one of the pillars of the Christian life. It is a privilege to take all our burdens, requests, and praise to Almighty God in prayer. When we pray, we communicate with our heavenly Father. Jesus taught His disciples to begin their prayer with "Our Father in heaven, hallowed be Your name" (Matt. 6:9, page 943). In prayer we praise Him, thank Him—"Be anxious for nothing, but in everything by prayer and supplication, with thanksgiving, let your requests be made known to God" (Phil. 4:6, page 1198)—and worship Him—"So the people believed; and when they heard that the LORD had visited the children of Israel and that He had looked on their affliction, then they bowed their heads and worshiped" (Ex. 4:31, page 63). If we make our requests known to our Father, with thanksgiving, the indwelling Holy Spirit will guide us into all truth as we pray (John 16:13, page 1077). He will comfort us, strengthen us, and encourage us in the way of righteousness. How shall we pray and for what shall we ask? In this outline we will examine some of the great biblical passages on prayer, from which we will learn six vital lessons.

30-A.   Pray As the Lord Prayed
         (Luke 11:1-4, page 1027)

30-B.   Pray in the Spirit
         (Jude 20, page 1290)

30-C.   Pray According to God's Will
         (1 John 5:14, 15, page 1283)

30-D.   Pray Without Ceasing
         (1 Thessalonians 5:17, 18, page 1213)

30-E.   Pray Believing
         (Matthew 21:21, 22, page 968)

30-F.   Pray in His Name
         (John 16:23, 24, page 1077)

MASTER OUTLINE NUMBER THIRTY-ONE

Prayers of Moses

Moses, a man whom we can emulate, was not merely a great person and servant of God; he was also one who suffered under great human pressures. Torn between the pleasures and glories of Pharaoh's court and the lowliness of the slavery of God's people, he chose to be with the latter, possibly forsaking the opportunity of becoming a Pharaoh someday (Heb. 11:25, page 1249). Through the years ahead he was faced with adversity after adversity. When the children of Israel did not want his help or leadership, he was forced to flee Egypt and go into the desert as a fugitive. For the time being, his potential career in royalty, or as a saving leader of his people, was over. Consequently, he had to resort to the role of a lowly shepherd with foreigners in a strange land. His hopes and dreams were gone. Then, when God called him to rebuke Pharaoh and lead Israel out of Egypt, he felt totally inadequate.

Soon the children of Israel, including his own brother and sister, were complaining about his leadership and their plight during their wandering in the wilderness. He labored all day for them, and still they vacillated between trust and unbelief in the Lord. They wanted to stone Moses every time a new problem arose; nevertheless, he triumphed and grew stronger in daily dependence on the Lord. How did he survive, while dealing with external enemies, internal complainers, and his own doubts, to finish the work for which the Lord had called him? Prayer was the answer.

Thus, this study of the prayers of Moses can become a great inspiration and force in our own lives, to help us keep on marching when difficulty arises in our own life situations. Are things going wrong? Are people complaining? Have obstacles risen in your path? Do doubts about yourself or your future voice themselves in your mind? If so, you would do well to march for a while with Moses through the barren wilderness, sharing his prayer life, so that you may be strengthened for your own walk through crisis times and waterless days. Let Moses teach you, by his prayers, how God's resources and strength can win your battles and provide sweet water in a desert for you and yours.

31-A.   A Prayer That Angered God
(Exodus 4:10-17, page 62)

31-B.   A Prayer of Impatience
(Exodus 5:22, 23, page 63)

31-C.   A Prayer of Intercession
(Exodus 32:11-14, page 92)

31-D.   A Prayer of Compassion
(Exodus 32:30-32, page 93)

31-E.   A Prayer for Fellowship
(Exodus 33:12-23, page 94)

31-F.   A Prayer for a Successor
(Numbers 27:12-19, page 169)

MASTER OUTLINE NUMBER THIRTY-TWO

Prayers of the Prophets

The Hebrew word for prophet is *nabi*, derived from a word which literally means "to bubble forth." Hence, the Old Testament prophets were the spokesmen for God, and like a bubbling brook they gave the message which God put within them. This is further illustrated in Exodus 4:16 (page 62) where God tells a hesitant Moses that Aaron "shall be your spokesman to the people...and you shall be to him as God." Thus Aaron was Moses' prophet; he announced to the multitudes the words that Moses gave him. This prophetic task of uttering God's Word to the populace included varied messages:

(1) Giving general sermons;
(2) Foretelling future events;
(3) Announcing God's will on a particular question;
(4) Encouraging the people to stand fast in the faith;
(5) Issuing warnings;
(6) Rebuking a king or nation for sin;
(7) Proclaiming judgment or doom on nations, peoples, and kings.

The announcements of God's rebuke and judgment were often received by the people with hatred which was directed toward God's prophets; hence, many prophets experienced unhappy periods in their lives (Jer. 20:1, 2, 7, 8, page 732). The prophets lived in trying times. Added to this general difficulty, their individual unpopularity led them—rather, forced them—to become men of prayer. The outline studies that follow focus on their great prayers, which can teach us how to deal with our own days of trial. These prayers, uttered during various types of personal and national difficulties, are even more helpful to the believer of today, who is faced with an array of the old problems in new forms. Let us quietly listen to the prayers of God's prophets as they burst forth from holy lips. Let us hear and share in their anguish and blessing.

32-A.   The Prayer of the Penitent Prophet
(Isaiah 6:5, page 648)

32-B.   Kingdom Prayer and Praise
(Isaiah 25:1-9, page 665)

32-C.   The Prayer of an Inadequate Man
(Jeremiah 1:6, page 710)

32-D.   The Prayer of a Puzzled Prophet
(Jeremiah 12:1-4, page 724)

32-E.   The Prayer of a Backslidden Prophet
(Jonah 2:1-9, page 885)

32-F.   The Prayer of a Prophet at the Crossroads
(1 Kings 18:36, 37, page 348)

32-G.   A Prayer for Revival
         (Habakkuk 3:1-19, page 901)

MASTER OUTLINE NUMBER THIRTY-THREE

For the Jew First

True Christians love the Jewish people. There has been, however, a great deal of confusion about this subject owing to the fact that such a large number of people have persecuted the Jews. For centuries many of these tormentors have invoked God's name to condone their acts of persecution. These outlines will endeavor to state a Christian position on the issues as taught in the Bible.

On the other hand, many believers have a sincere desire to share their faith in Christ with the Jewish people, and have often asked how this might be done. The following outlines will offer some help, using biblical guidelines.

33-A.   The Permanence of God's Love to Israel
         (Jeremiah 31:1-40, page 744)

33-B.   The Prophecies of Israel's Messiah
         (Micah 5:2, page 890)

33-C.   The Plan of Salvation: "For the Jew First"
         (Isaiah 1:16-19, page 643)

33-D.   The Parties to the Crucifixion of Christ
         (Isaiah 53:10, page 693)

33-E.   The Barrier to Evangelism: Persecution of the Jewish People
         (Luke 23:34, page 1045)

33-F.   The Peace That Someday Will Be Israel's
         (Isaiah 11:6-12, page 654)

MASTER OUTLINE NUMBER THIRTY-FOUR

The Birth and History of the Hebrew Nation

Abraham, the father of the Hebrew nation, was born about 2000 B.C., in southern Babylon, in or near Ur of the Chaldeans. Babylon was filled with idolatry. Joshua tells us that Terah, Abraham's father, served other gods (Josh. 24:2, page 238). In this idolatrous climate "the God of glory" (Acts 7:2, page 1096), by His sovereign will, called Abraham to be the father of a chosen race, the Hebrew nation (Gen. 12:2, page 17; 21:12, page 25). God also promised Abraham that he would be the father of many nations (Gen. 17:4, 5, page 22), and that his name would be great. After four thousand years his name is still great in a large number of nations, as well as among his descendants in all nations around the world.

The descendants of Ishmael, the descendants of Jacob, and the descendants of Esau all call him "Father Abraham" (Gen. 32:9, page 39). The apostle Paul told us that because he was "strengthened in faith" (Rom. 4:20, page 1133), he is "the father of all those who believe" (Rom. 4:11, page 1132). Hebrews, Muslims, and Christians all look to him as their spiritual father.

The Bible says four things about Abraham that were never spoken of any other man. He is called:

(1) God's friend by the Lord Himself (Is. 41:8, page 680).
(2) The father of the Hebrew nation (John 8:53, page 1064).
(3) The "father of many nations" (Gen. 17:4, 5, page 22).
(4) "The father of all those who believe" (Rom. 4:11, page 1132).

Millions of the world's population trace their lineage, either physically, spiritually, or both, to our father Abraham.

God called Abraham and commanded him to

(1) leave his country
(2) leave his family

(3) leave his father's house
(4) go "by faith" into a land that the Lord would show him (Gen. 12:1, page 17; Heb. 11:8-19, page 1248).

The Lord also promised Abraham that He would

(1) make of him a great nation
(2) bless him
(3) make his name great
(4) make him a blessing
(5) bless those who bless him
(6) curse those who curse him
(7) through him bless all the families of the earth (Gen. 12:2, 3, page 17)

This last part of God's promise began to be fulfilled in Christ at His first coming, but will not be completely fulfilled until the Lord Jesus Christ returns to this earth as "Lord of lords and King of kings" (Rev. 17:14, page 1311) to sit on the throne of His father David and reign in righteousness (Is. 9:6, 7, page 651; cf. Matt. 25:31-46, page 976).

34-A.   From Ur of the Chaldeans to the Exodus (about 600 years)
         (Genesis 11:31—12:9, page 17)

34-B.   From the Exodus to the Crossing of Jordan (40 years)
         (Exodus 12:37-51, page 71)

34-C.   From the Crossing of Jordan to the Babylonian Captivity (about 830 years)
         (Joshua 3:14-17, page 218)

34-D.   From the Babylonian Captivity to the Crucifixion (over 600 years)
         (Ezra 1:1-11, page 444)

34-E.   From the Crucifixion to the Fall of Jerusalem (about 40 years)
         (Luke 21:20-24, page 1041)

34-F.   From the Fall of Jerusalem to the Millennium (to date, over 1,900 years)
         (Matthew 23:37—24:2, page 972)

34-G.   From the Millennium to the New Heaven and the New Earth (1,000 years)
         (Isaiah 66:22, 23, page 707)

MASTER OUTLINE NUMBER THIRTY-FIVE

The Tabernacle

The Exodus tabernacle was "the dwelling place" of God for almost five centuries, 1450—960 B.C. It was built a few years after the Exodus from Egypt and was the central place of worship until it was replaced by Solomon's temple (Ex. 26:1, page 85; cf. 1 Kin. 6:1, 38, page 331). It was the portable, sacred-tent-dwelling-place of God, where the holy God

(1) manifested His special glorious presence with the children of Israel, while at the same time maintaining barriers and separating Himself from sinful defilements;
(2) provided a sacrificial ritual for individual and national cleansing from sin;
(3) taught His people theological lessons and truths concerning sin, forgiveness, and His will;
(4) prefigured the person and work of the Messiah to come, namely, concerning Christ and His atoning death on the cross for sinners.

The tabernacle's unique design and exact dimensions, as well as the choice of materials to be used, were completely dictated and specified by God to Moses, while he met with God for the forty days and nights on Mount Sinai (Ex. 24:18—31:18, page 83). The specifications for the tabernacle are found in seven Old Testament chapters (Ex. 25—31, page 83), and its construction is described in six additional chapters (Ex. 35—40, page 96). One chapter (Num. 4, page 142) deals with transporting the tabernacle. The epistle to the Hebrews further devotes three New Testament chapters to the tabernacle (Heb. 8—10, page 1242). The book of Hebrews further clarifies that the earthly tabernacle built by Moses, and its service and ritual, were copies of heavenly things (Heb. 9:23, 24, page 1244).

That is, the Mosaic tent-dwelling-place of God represented visually, to the children of Israel, the unseen, heavenly tabernacle, wherein God truly manifested His glorious, divine presence and remained totally apart from sin, and wherein He later received the blood of Christ as the everlasting sacrifice for sin. Therein Christ, as the eternal High Priest, sits at the right hand of the Father and always lives to make intercession for believers (Heb. 7:25, page 1242; 9:11, page 1243). When we study the tabernacle, even today, we are studying the holy and heavenly unseen realities it represents.

Therefore, let us remember that we are about to enter holy ground, and let us proceed slowly with prayer and reverence. (The offerings receive separate treatment in Master Outline Number Thirty-Six).

35-A.   The History of the Tabernacle
         (Exodus 25:1-9, page 83)

35-B.   The Pattern of the Tabernacle
         (Hebrews 9:23, 24, page 1244)

35-C.   The Furniture of the Tabernacle
         (Exodus 35:30-35, page 96)

35-D.   The Priesthood of the Tabernacle
         (Exodus 40:13-15, page 102)

MASTER OUTLINE NUMBER THIRTY-SIX

Old Testament Sacrifices

The sacrificial order was instituted by God as a means whereby He could

(1) preserve His absolute holiness, which required that all sin be punished;
(2) show loving mercy to man—His beloved, fallen creation.

In the Old Testament order, God made the shedding of animal blood a picture of Christ's New Testament payment for man's sins. Only Christ's unique sacrifice would be sufficient to pay the penalty for the sins of all who trust Him through the ages (Heb. 9:11-14, page 1243).

After Adam and Eve had sinned, they made aprons of fig leaves to cover the shame of their sin (Gen. 3:7, page 6; cf. Gal. 6:7, page 1184). However, God replaced those aprons with coats of skins (Gen. 3:21, page 7). It is thus shown that human works are not an acceptable covering for sin; blood must be shed, and that blood eventually would be Christ's.

Cain and Abel also brought their sacrificial offerings; but Cain's self-grown vegetables were unacceptable, while Abel's offering of a lamb was accepted (Gen. 4:1-7, page 7). All of this pointed to the coming of Christ who would give His life and shed His blood for the sins of the world, inviting all to partake, by faith, in the benefits of this offering. John the Baptist saw and understood this when he said, pointing to Jesus, "Behold! The Lamb of God who takes away the sin of the world!" (John 1:29, page 1050).

God's laws pertaining to the offerings are filled with spiritual lessons and benefits for the believer. These lessons and the patterns of the offerings constantly point to Christ and His offering of Himself on the cross (1 Pet. 1:18-20, page 1263).

36-A.   Offerings to the Lord
         (Leviticus 17:1-12, page 125)

36-B.   Whole Burnt Offerings: Devotion
         (Leviticus 1:3-17, page 105)

36-C.   Grain and Drink Offerings: Thanksgiving
         (Leviticus 2:1-16, page 106)

36-D.   Peace Offerings: Fellowship
         (Leviticus 3:1-17, page 107)

36-E.   Sin of Ignorance Offerings: Righting Wrongs
         (Leviticus 4:1-35, page 108)

36-F.   Trespass Offerings: Forgiveness
         (Leviticus 6:1-7, page 111)

36-G.   Special Offerings
         (Leviticus 12:6-8, page 118)

MASTER OUTLINE NUMBER THIRTY-SEVEN

The Beginning of the Church

When Malachi, the last of the Old Testament prophets, put down his pen in 420 B.C., the Old Testament Canon was closed. As the centuries rolled by, the Holy Land was conquered by the Persians, then by the Greeks, later by the Syrians, and finally by Rome. Suddenly, after four hundred silent years, when there had been no prophet in the land, astonishing news began to spread. There was talk of a prophet whom the Lord had raised up. He was preaching in the wilderness of Judea and was called "John the Baptist" (Matt. 3:1-12, page 932).

Thus, after the four hundred years of intertestamental silence (see article "The Intertestamental Period," page 1334), the New Testament period had at last begun. Approximately one hundred years elapsed between Christ's birth and John the apostle's writing of the book of Revelation. During this period the Savior came and died on the cross for man's sins. The church was formed and began to spread the gospel message throughout the world. The momentous events of the New Testament period are worthy of the most careful study for their historic, exemplary, and spiritual lessons. They include:

37-A.   The World into Which Christ Came
         (Matthew 2:1-12, page 931)

37-B.   The Earthly Ministry of Jesus
         (Mark 11:7-11, page 998)

37-C.   The Church: Its Beginning and Development
         (Acts 8:1-8, page 1098)

37-D.   The Evangelistic Missionary Journeys of Paul
         (Acts 13:1-3, page 1105)

37-E.   The Fall of Jerusalem and the End of the First Century
         (Hebrews 3:12-19, page 1238)

MASTER OUTLINE NUMBER THIRTY-EIGHT

The Nature of the Church

The church was to the Old Testament prophets a mystery; but in the beginning of the dispensation of grace, the mystery was made known "by the Spirit to His holy apostles and prophets" (Eph. 3:3-6, page 1189). It was first revealed to the apostles after Christ rose from the dead and appeared to them in a mountain in Galilee, and commissioned them to "Go...and make disciples of all the nations" (Matt. 28:19, 20, page 982). The Holy Spirit chose Peter to be the first to take the gospel to the Gentiles (Acts 10:1-48, page 1102). Next Paul and Barnabas were chosen by the Holy Spirit to be the first evangelistic missionaries to the Gentiles. On their first missionary journey, they went first to the Jews (Rom. 1:16, page 1128). But when the Jews rejected the gospel (Acts 13:1-5, page 1105), "Paul and Barnabas grew bold and said, 'It was necessary that the word of God should be spoken to you first; but since you reject it, and judge yourselves unworthy of everlasting life, behold, we turn to the Gentiles' " (Acts 13:46-49, page 1107). The mystery that God revealed to Paul was that a Gentile did not have to become a Jew to be in the church. In Christ there is neither Jew nor Gentile, "for you are all one in Christ Jesus" (Gal. 3:28, page 1182). This is the mystery that was hidden from the men of the Old Testament.

To help us understand the doctrine of the church, the Holy Spirit, who is the author of the Word of God (2 Pet. 1:21, page 1273; 2 Tim. 3:16, 17, page 1227), has given us seven metaphors or illustrations to help us understand the eternal relationship of Christ and His church. They are:

(1) *Christ the Bridegroom, the church His bride*. The bride, in the resurrection, will have an incor-

ruptible glorified body (1 Cor. 15:51-58, page 1163), and she will be presented to Him as a pure virgin (2 Cor. 11:2, page 1174; Eph. 5:25-27, page 1192).

(2) *Christ the Good Shepherd, the church His sheep.* The Shepherd leads, protects, and feeds His sheep (Ps. 23:1-6, page 524). When sheep are slaughtered, they never fight back; they are always dependent on the shepherd. When lost, they cannot find their way back to the sheepfold; they must be sought and found by the shepherd (Luke 15:3-7, page 1033; John 10:11-16, page 1067).

(3) *Christ the Head, the church His body.* Christ is the "head of the body, the church" (Col. 1:18, page 1202). Nobody can have more than one head; therefore it is wrong for any man, other than the Lord Jesus Christ, to claim to be the head of the church on earth or in heaven. His body has many members, and they are all equal in His sight. His church is one body with only one head, Christ, who has all authority over each member of His body (1 Cor. 12:12-26, page 1158).

(4) *Christ the Foundation and Cornerstone, the church His building.* This building is made of "living stones," alive with the life of Christ (1 Pet. 2:5, page 1265). We are built upon Christ, through the teachings of the apostles and prophets (Eph. 2:19, 20, page 1188).

(5) *Christ Our High Priest, the church His temple.* The church is called a "holy temple in the Lord, in whom you also are being built together for a dwelling place of God in the Spirit" (Eph. 2:21, 22, page 1188). Each member of the church is His temple, and is indwelt by God the Holy Spirit (1 Cor. 6:19, 20, page 1152). A temple is a place of worship—we are to worship our God when alone or with others, who are a part of the holy temple (Matt. 28:16, 17, page 982). The most important thing we can do is to worship God (see Master Outline Number Twenty-Eight, "Worship," page 44).

(6) *Christ the Vine, the church His branches.* Jesus said, "I am the vine, you are the branches" (John 15:5, page 1076). In this church age, from Pentecost to the Rapture, every branch is to bear fruit. There are three stages of fruit bearing:

    (a) Fruit
    (b) More fruit
    (c) Much fruit (John 15:1-5, page 1076)

One of the fruits of a Christian is more Christians. You can be a fruit-bearing, soul-winning branch and be rewarded with the joy of the Lord in this life and in the life to come (John 15:11, page 1076; 1 Thess. 2:19, 20, page 1210).

(7) *Christ the Last Adam, the church His new creation.* The first Adam was given life; the last Adam is the life-giver (John 1:4, page 1049). "Therefore, if anyone is in Christ, he is a new creation; old things have passed away; behold, all things have become new" (2 Cor. 5:17, page 1169). The church is the Lord's; it is in the world, but not of it. For almost two thousand years Satan has tried to destroy the church and failed, because Jesus said, "The gates of Hades shall not prevail against it" (Matt. 16:18, page 962).

38-A.   The Church: A Holy Temple
        (Ephesians 2:19-22, page 1188)

38-B.   The Church: A Body
        (1 Corinthians 12:12-31, page 1158)

38-C.   The Church: Its Mission
        (Matthew 28:16-20, page 982)

38-D.   The Church: A Mystery
        (Ephesians 3:1-11, page 1188)

38-E.   The Church: Its Builder
        (Matthew 16:13-20, page 961)

MASTER OUTLINE NUMBER THIRTY-NINE

The Ordinances of the Church

The old covenant given to the nation of Israel through Moses, in the words of the writer of the book of Hebrews, "had ordinances of divine service and the earthly sanctuary [the tabernacle]...various washings, and fleshly ordinances" (Heb. 9:1, 2, 10, page 1243). But Christ, "after He had offered one sacrifice for sins forever, sat down at the right hand of God" (Heb. 10:12, page 1246). Thus (with the penalty of sin having been forever paid) Christ did not perpetuate the Old Testament

system of countless ceremonies, but established only two ordinances for His church—baptism and the Lord's Supper. These are called ordinances because Christ Himself ordained them.

Unlike those manifold ordinances given to Israel many of which could only find their fulfillment with that nation when it was in the land and possessed its own tabernacle or temple, the two given to the church by Christ are simple and adaptable to multiplied millions of new believers. They provide

(1) an entry rite—rich in the symbolism of the great Christian truths, which would symbolize the entrance of a person into the church;

(2) a fellowship rite—which would regularly call to the believer's mind the essentials of the faith, his ongoing fellowship with Christ, and one which would challenge the believer to reconsecrate himself to his Lord with renewed service and devotion.

39-A.   The Baptism of John the Baptist
(Matthew 3:1-12, page 932)

39-B.   The Baptism of Jesus
(Matthew 3:13-17, page 934)

39-C.   The Baptism of the Believer
(Acts 2:41, 42, page 1090)

39-D.   The Lord's Supper
(Mark 14:12-26, page 1003)

MASTER OUTLINE NUMBER FORTY

Citizens of the Kingdom

The Sermon on the Mount is the King's manifesto of His kingdom principles, as taught by our coming King. When the King delivered this, the greatest of all sermons, His words must have been strange in the ears of His disciples, and amazing to the listening multitudes.

Many believed that John the Baptist was the forerunner of the Messiah. They had heard him declare, "I am 'The voice of one crying in the wilderness: "Make straight the way of the LORD," ' as the prophet Isaiah said" (John 1:23, page 1049; Is. 40:3, page 679). To prepare the way for the coming of the King, John preached repentance. He said, "Repent, for the kingdom of heaven is at hand!" (Matt. 3:2, page 932). After the Lord's baptism by John (in the river Jordan), His temptation in the wilderness, and the imprisonment of John the Baptist, Jesus began His public ministry (Mark 1:14, 15, page 984). He preached repentance, saying, "Repent, for the kingdom of heaven is at hand" (Matt. 4:17, page 936). The King could not set up His kingdom on earth because national Israel would not repent and believe the good news of the kingdom.

John the apostle said, "He came to His own [Israel], and His own did not receive Him. But as many as received Him, to them He gave the right to become children of God, to those who believe in His name" (John 1:11, 12, page 1049). Some did repent and receive Him by faith, as their Messiah. But the national leaders of Israel, and the Romans, nailed Him to the cross. Jesus, knowing that He was to die for the sins of the world, promised to come again and establish God's kingdom on earth, and to sit on the throne of His glory (Matt. 25:31, page 976), which is the throne of His father David, according to the flesh.

God made an unconditional promise to King David when He said, "I will set upon your throne the fruit [descendants] of your body" (Ps. 132:11, page 588). God promised King David that He would be born of His descending line according to the flesh (Rom. 1:3, page 1128). He, the God-Man, would be seated on the throne of David (Acts 2:30, page 1089; cf. Is. 9:6, 7, page 651).

The King could not establish His kingdom on earth because Israel would not repent and accept the Messiah as their King. We do not have the kingdom of heaven on earth, but we do have the King's manifesto. Even though we are not living in the kingdom, we are to practice kingdom life in this corrupt world system. The Beatitudes reveal the secret of true happiness. Study them with an open heart, a receptive mind, and a humble spirit, praying always. Remember that happiness is not found in the things you have, but in what you are in Christ Jesus. "Therefore, if anyone is in Christ, he is a new creation; old things have passed away; behold, all things have become new" (2 Cor. 5:17, page 1169). In this verse we have old things and new things. The old things are the fruits of the natural man (1 Cor. 2:14, page 1149); the new things are the fruits of the new man in Christ.

Happiness is one of the new things we find in Christ our King when we practice daily His kingdom manifesto.

40-A.   The Poor in Spirit
         (Matthew 5:1-3, page 936)

40-B.   The Mourners
         (Matthew 5:4, page 936)

40-C.   The Meek
         (Matthew 5:5, page 936)

40-D.   The Hungry and Thirsty
         (Matthew 5:6, page 937)

40-E.   The Merciful
         (Matthew 5:7, page 937)

40-F.   The Pure in Heart
         (Matthew 5:8, page 938)

40-G.   The Peacemakers
         (Matthew 5:9, page 938)

40-H.   The Persecuted
         (Matthew 5:10-12, page 938)

MASTER OUTLINE NUMBER FORTY-ONE

Manifesting Kingdom Principles

We now come to the second section of the King's manifesto. In the Beatitudes we have seen what the Christian is; now we are told how to manifest kingdom principles. As the King's subjects, we are not to withdraw from the world; we are in the world, but not of it. Jesus said, "You are the salt of the earth" (Matt. 5:13, page 938); but if you lose your saltiness (tang), you are good for nothing. Again He said, "You are the light of the world" (Matt. 5:14, page 939). But if you put your light under a bushel, you will not expel darkness in others around you. Your light does not shine to be seen, but that others may see Christ in you, and hunger and thirst after His righteousness.

When you are abused, turn the other cheek; go the second mile; pray for and love your enemies. Why? Because "you are a chosen generation, a royal priesthood, a holy nation, His own special people, that you may proclaim the praises of Him who called you out of darkness into His marvelous light" (1 Pet. 2:9, page 1265).

Yes, we are the aristocracy of heaven, children of the King of kings and Lord of lords. Don't lose your saltiness or dim your light. The world is in spiritual darkness, blinded by the power of Satan, the prince of darkness (2 Cor. 4:4, page 1167). Live close to Christ and reflect His light; He is the Light of the World (John 8:12, page 1062).

41-A.   Believers Are Salt and Light
         (Matthew 5:13-16, page 938)

41-B.   Christ, the Law, and the Prophets
         (Matthew 5:17-20, page 939)

41-C.   The King's Moral Requirements
         (Matthew 5:21-32, page 939)

41-D.   Christ Speaks on Oaths
         (Matthew 5:33-37, page 941)

41-E.   Turn the Other Cheek, Go the Second Mile, and Love Your Enemy
         (Matthew 5:38-48, page 941)

MASTER OUTLINE NUMBER FORTY-TWO
Making Kingdom Choices

We now come to the third section of the King's manifesto. In the first section we studied the Beatitudes, and saw what a believer in Christ is. In the second section we saw how the believer is to manifest the kingdom principles. Now, in the third section we see:

(1) The right and wrong way to give alms and practice charitable deeds (Matt. 6:1-4, page 942).
(2) The right and wrong way to pray (Matt. 6:5-15, page 942).
(3) The right and wrong way to fast (Matt. 6:16-18, page 943).
(4) The right and wrong place to lay up treasures (Matt. 6:19-21, page 943).
(5) The right and wrong vision (Matt. 6:22, 23, page 943).
(6) The right and wrong master (Matt. 6:24, page 943).
(7) The right and wrong way to think (Matt. 6:25-34, page 944).
(8) The right and wrong way to judge (Matt. 7:1-6, page 944).

42-A.   A Threefold Hypocrite
        (Matthew 6:1-18, page 942)

42-B.   Where Is Your Heart?
        (Matthew 6:19-21, page 943)

42-C.   Do You Have a Good or Evil Eye?
        (Matthew 6:22, 23, page 943)

42-D.   Who Is Your Master?
        (Matthew 6:24, page 943)

42-E.   A Good or Bad Sphere
        (Matthew 6:25-34, page 944)

42-F.   Judge Not
        (Matthew 7:1-6, page 944)

MASTER OUTLINE NUMBER FORTY-THREE
Entering the Kingdom

Now we come to the fourth and concluding section of the King's manifesto. In this part we have the Golden Rule, the key that unlocks the treasure chest of the Sermon on the Mount. It is the essence of His kingdom principles. "Therefore, whatever you want men to do to you, do also to them, for this is the Law and the Prophets" (Matt. 7:12, page 945). Jesus was saying that when you practice the Golden Rule, you are fulfilling the Law and the Prophets.

On a later occasion, a certain lawyer tested Jesus by asking Him this question, "Teacher, which is the great commandment in the law?" (Matt. 22:36, page 970). Jesus knew that the intent of the lawyer was to trap Him and destroy his influence with the masses. He had taught earlier in His ministry, "Do not think that I came to destroy the Law or the Prophets. I did not come to destroy but to fulfill" (Matt. 5:17, page 939). Had Jesus named any one of the laws as the greatest, He would have degraded the other nine commandments. They could then have accused Him of being an unreliable teacher of the law. However, they were not ready for His answer. He did not name just one law as the greatest, but He divided the ten laws into two sections and answered them by saying, " 'You shall love the LORD your God with all your heart, with all your soul, and with all your mind.' This is the first and great commandment" (Matt. 22:37, 38, page 971). He then went on to say, "And the second is like it: 'You shall love your neighbor as yourself.' On these two commandments hang all the Law and the Prophets" (Matt. 22:39, 40, page 971).

When you love God with all your heart, all your soul, and all your mind, you are obeying the first four of the ten commandments; and when you love your neighbor as yourself, you are obeying the last six of the ten commandments (Ex. 20:1-17, page 79). When you reach that spiritual plateau where you truly love your neighbor as you love yourself, you are practicing the Golden Rule. It will be a joy, day after day, to do unto others as you would have others do unto you (Matt. 7:12, page 945).

At the conclusion of the King's manifesto, the multitudes were astonished at His teaching; it is no wonder that they were amazed, for He taught them as one having authority (Matt. 7:28, 29, page 947). He contradicted almost all the traditional interpretations of the scribes and Pharisees, while in

His life and teachings He fulfilled all the Law and the Prophets.

43-A.   Prayer Is Asking, Seeking, and Knocking
         (Matthew 7:7-11, page 945)

43-B.   The Key to the Kingdom
         (Matthew 7:12, page 945)

43-C.   Two Ways: The Broad and the Narrow
         (Matthew 7:13, 14, page 945)

43-D.   Two Prophets: The False and the True
         (Matthew 7:15-20, page 946)

43-E.   Religious but Lost
         (Matthew 7:21-23, page 946)

43-F.   Two Builders: The Wise and the Foolish
         (Matthew 7:24-27, page 946)

43-G.   Two Authorities: Sovereign and Human
         (Matthew 7:28, 29, page 947)

MASTER OUTLINE NUMBER FORTY-FOUR

Enoch, a Man Who Walked with God

The biography of Enoch is brief, only nine verses in all: five verses in Genesis, two in Hebrews, and two in Jude. Yet this remarkable biography points the Bible student to a man who was unique among all men of all generations. For three hundred years Enoch put God first in his life. The Lord was preeminent in everything: in his thinking, in his ways, and in his walk. He was first in his love, in his service, and the only One whom he worshiped. Following are some of the ways in which Enoch was unique:

(1) He was one of two men of whom the Scripture says that he "walked with God." The other was Noah (Gen. 6:9, page 12). We are not told how long Noah walked with God; however, we are told that Enoch "walked with God three hundred years" (Gen. 5:22, page 9).

(2) He was the first of two men who were taken to heaven without experiencing physical death. Elijah was the other (2 Kin. 2:11, page 356).

(3) Enoch was the seventh generation from Adam. Of all the generations before Enoch we read, "And he died;" but with Enoch it was changed, for we read, "And he was not, for God took him" (Gen. 5:24, page 10).

(4) He became the father of the oldest man who ever lived, Methuselah, who lived 969 years (Gen. 5:21, page 9).

(5) He walked with God three hundred years. During those years he was a family man; he was the father of sons and daughters.

(6) Enoch was justified by faith; therefore he lived by faith (Heb. 10:38, page 1247).

(7) Enoch prophesied that the Lord would come and execute judgment on the ungodly (Jude 14, 15, page 1290).

The remainder of the biography of Enoch will not be known until we, too, put on immortality and continue our walk with God in eternity.

44-A.   Enoch Walked with God
         (Genesis 5:21-23, page 9)

44-B.   Enoch Walked by Faith with God
         (Hebrews 11:5, 6, page 1247)

44-C.   Enoch Walked Humbly with God
         (Micah 6:8, page 892)

44-D.   Enoch Walked in Agreement with God
         (Amos 3:3, page 875)

44-E.   Enoch Walked All the Way to Heaven with God
(Genesis 5:24, page 10)

MASTER OUTLINE NUMBER FORTY-FIVE

Noah, the Man Who Built the Ark

The apostle Peter said, "God has spoken by the mouth of all His holy prophets since the world began" (Acts 3:20-22, page 1091). In these verses Peter said that all of God's prophets preached the first and second coming of Jesus Christ "since the world began." According to this Scripture, Adam was God's first prophet to proclaim the gospel of the grace of God by faith in the Lord Jesus Christ.

Adam and Eve experienced the grace of God in the Garden of Eden, when God shed the blood of innocent animals to cover their nakedness, and promised them that the "Seed of the woman," the virgin-born God-Man (a biological miracle), Jesus Christ, would crush the head of Satan and provide salvation by grace through faith for all believers (Gen. 3:15, 21, page 7). Now we know that the people who lived before the Flood, the antediluvians, had the grace of God preached to them from Adam to Noah.

There are three ways in which God revealed to Noah the gospel of the grace of God and His will for Noah's life.

(1) *By word of mouth.* "God has spoken by the mouth of all His holy prophets" (Acts 3:21, page 1091). And God continues to speak to the lost by word of mouth, person to person. It is the most effective way to take the gospel of the grace of God to a lost world (Rom. 10:13-17, page 1140). It is very evident that Adam preached the gospel to his descendants. Consider Cain and Abel; they came at the same time, to the same place, for the same purpose—to worship God (Gen. 4:1-5, page 7). Who taught them to worship God? It was Adam, God's first preacher. We know that Cain killed Abel and that another son was born to Adam and Eve, whose name was Seth. Seth had a son whose name was Enosh. "Then men began to call on the name of the LORD" (Gen. 4:25, 26, page 9). Who taught Seth and Enosh to call on the name of Jehovah? God's first prophet, Adam.

Noah could have received God's Word from Methuselah, who could have been taught by Adam. When Adam died, Methuselah was 253 years old. This means that Adam, God's first prophet, had 253 years in which to indoctrinate Methuselah. Methuselah lived 600 years after Noah was born; he was Noah's grandfather. He had 600 years in which to teach Noah, his grandson. By word of mouth Adam taught Methuselah, and Methuselah taught Noah. So Noah found grace in the eyes of the Lord.

(2) *By written records.* Who is to say that Noah, who descended from Adam through Seth, Enosh, Cainan, Mahalalel, Jared, Enoch, Methuselah, and Lamech, was not heir to all the records from Adam to Lamech? Jude tells us that Enoch prophesied, saying, "Behold, the Lord comes with ten thousands of His saints, to execute judgment on all" (Jude 14, 15, page 1290). This prophecy was written in the days of Enoch, who was born 622 years after the creation of Adam. When God created Adam, he was perfect in every way—spirit, soul, and body. This means that Adam, though never having learned, had perfect knowledge of all things related to this creation (Gen. 2:18-20, page 5). In this he is a type of Christ, the last Adam (1 Cor. 15:45, page 1162). When God created all the birds of the air and the beasts of the field, he brought them to Adam, who gave each of them their names. Adam did not memorize their names, he named them. He was created with a language and a vocabulary to express his every thought.

Therefore, it does not take a great faith to believe that Adam could have invented an alphabet of letters or other characters with which his spoken language could be written. Or God could have given him the alphabet of letters or characters when He created him. The people who lived before the Flood must have had a system of keeping written records. Noah must have had some of the written records from Adam to Lamech.

(3) *By revelation.* God revealed His will to Noah. He said to Noah, "Make yourself an ark of gopherwood" (Gen. 6:14, page 12). When the ark was ready, He spoke to Noah and told him to enter the ark. When the Flood ended and the land was dry, God told Noah to come out of the ark. God speaks in many different ways to man.

Today, He speaks to us through the Holy Spirit and His written Word. However, in the past six thousand years, He spoke to man through dreams, or a voice from heaven. He often revealed Himself to man in the form of a man, or as the Angel of the Lord. We are not told how He spoke to Noah; all we know is that He revealed His will for Noah's life. Noah obeyed all of God's commandments, "Noah walked with God" (Gen. 6:9, page 12). God, knowing that Noah and his family would be the

only survivors of the Flood, entrusted Noah with the knowledge of all of His acts from Creation to the Flood. In so doing, Noah was able to pass these truths on to his descendants down to Moses, who wrote under the inspiration of God the first five books of the Bible.

45-A.   Noah: A Man Convicted
         (Matthew 24:37-39, page 974)

45-B.   Noah: A Man of Vision
         (Proverbs 29:18, page 622)

45-C.   Noah: A Preacher of Righteousness
         (2 Peter 2:5, page 1274)

45-D.   Noah: A Man of Action
         (Genesis 6:22, page 12)

45-E.   Noah: A Man of Faith
         (Hebrews 11:7, page 1247)

MASTER OUTLINE NUMBER FORTY-SIX

Paul, an Apostle

The Lord Jesus Christ personally called Paul to faith and service. From that point on it was Paul whom Christ used to:

(1) Write thirteen of the New Testament books.
(2) Win the first European convert to Christianity (Acts 16:14, 15, page 1110).
(3) Become the great missionary founder of churches abroad.
(4) Win many Jewish and countless Gentile people (he became "an apostle to the Gentiles"— Rom. 11:13, page 1141).
(5) Explain the doctrines of the new faith by his many letters to the churches.
(6) Suffer many things for Christ's sake.

Many lessons can be learned from the life of Paul in the New Testament. Paul said of himself:

(1) "I am a debtor both to Greeks and to barbarians, both to wise and to unwise" (Rom. 1:14, page 1128).
(2) "I am ready to preach the gospel" (Rom. 1:15, page 1128).
(3) "I am not ashamed of the gospel" (Rom. 1:16, page 1128).
(4) "I am appointed for the defense of the gospel" (Phil. 1:17, page 1196).
(5) "I labored more abundantly than they all" (1 Cor. 15:10, page 1161).

The above texts give us some concept of the apostle Paul's commitment to Christ. Note that Paul was a tireless worker for his Lord and Savior, a fervent preacher of the gospel, a great apostle and teacher, and a courageous spiritual warrior (2 Cor. 4:6-8, page 1167).

46-A.   Paul's Early Life
         (Acts 22:1-5, page 1117)

46-B.   Paul's Conversion
         (Acts 9:1-18, page 1100)

46-C.   Paul's Early Ministry
         (Acts 9:19-31, page 1101)

46-D.   Paul's Evangelistic Missionary Ministry to the Gentiles
         (Galatians 2:7-10, page 1179)

46-E.   Paul's Letters
         (2 Thessalonians 3:17, page 1216)

46-F.   Paul's Imprisonments and Final Journeys
         (Philippians 1:12-14, page 1195)

MASTER OUTLINE NUMBER FORTY-SEVEN

Seven Parables of the Kingdom of Heaven

The kingdom of heaven is God's rule during this present age and after. The expression, "kingdom of heaven," used over and over by Matthew, comes by implication from Daniel where the messianic "Son of Man" came in "the clouds of heaven" to God the Father, "Then to Him was given…a kingdom" (Dan. 7:13, 14, page 845). A basic theme of the kingdom of heaven parables involves a king giving a marriage feast or taking a journey, followed by a long period in which some come to the marriage feast or work diligently for the king; then comes the king's surprise return, his reward of the faithful, and his punishment of the wicked. Thus these parables show how Christ will administer the church and the world during this present age, and how He will judge all upon His return.

A New Testament parable is an earthly story that parallels a scriptural truth. Why did Christ teach in parables? He explained part of the answer in Matthew 13:10-17 (page 955). Parables vividly communicated from the known (earthly) to the unknown—unseen (spiritual), and providentially discriminated among the hearers. Those whose ears had been opened by God would understand (Matt. 13:9, page 955) and be blessed (Matt. 13:16, 17, page 956), while the unsaved and uninterested would hear but not comprehend (Matt. 13:13-15, page 955; cf. 1 Cor. 2:14, page 1149). Today these parables still help our understanding of what is going on in the world, what God is accomplishing, how He is working, how different segments of mankind will react to the gospel message during our age, and what God will do when Christ returns to set up His earthly kingdom. Each one is a rare beauty capable of unending study and admiration.

47-A.   The Sower
(Matthew 13:3-9, 18-23, page 955)

47-B.   The Tares
(Matthew 13:24-30, 36-43, page 956)

47-C.   The Mustard Seed
(Matthew 13:31, 32, page 956)

47-D.   The Leaven
(Matthew 13:33, page 957)

47-E.   The Hidden Treasure
(Matthew 13:44, page 957)

47-F.   The Pearl of Great Price
(Matthew 13:45, 46, page 958)

47-G.   The Net
(Matthew 13:47-50, page 958)

MASTER OUTLINE NUMBER FORTY-EIGHT

Crowns for Christians

There is a vast difference in the doctrine of salvation for the lost, and the doctrine of rewards for the saved. Salvation is "the gift of God, not of works" (Eph. 2:8, 9, page 1187). Salvation is received by faith in the finished work of the Lord Jesus Christ (John 3:36, page 1053). Rewards are according to the works of the believer (Matt. 16:27, page 963).

A most revealing Scripture concerning rewards is found in 1 Corinthians 3:8-15 (page 1149).

(1) Every believer will be rewarded according to his own labor (v. 8). We do not labor for salvation.

(2) "We are God's fellow workers" (v. 9)—not for salvation, but for rewards.

(3) The believer is to build on the Lord Jesus Christ, the only foundation (v. 11).

(4) The believer has a choice of two main types of building materials: "gold, silver, precious stones"—eternal materials; or "wood, hay, straw"—temporal materials (v. 12; cf. 2 Cor. 4:18, page 1168).

The believer who builds on Christ with eternal materials, "gold, silver, precious stones," will receive a reward. Those who build on Christ with temporal materials, "wood, hay, straw," will receive no reward. The "wood, hay, straw" works will be destroyed at the "judgment seat of Christ" (2 Cor.

5:10, page 1168), and the believer will suffer loss—not the loss of salvation, but the loss of eternal rewards.

Some believers will be ashamed at the judgment seat of Christ (1 John 2:28, page 1279)—ashamed of their works of "wood, hay, straw."

In the first year of his ministry, a pastor sat at the bedside of a dying friend. As they talked of the home-going of the dying man, tears filled his eyes. The pastor thought his friend was afraid to die, and attempted to speak words of encouragement to him. But the man said, "I am not *afraid* to die; I am *ashamed* to die." He went on to say that Christ was his Savior, but that he had lived for himself, and now had to meet the Lord Jesus Christ empty-handed. His life loomed up before him as "wood, hay, straw." He was saved but he had few works of apparent eternal value to offer the Lord (1 Cor. 3:15, page 1149).

48-A.   The Crown of Life
         (James 1:12, page 1255)

48-B.   The Crown Imperishable
         (1 Corinthians 9:24-27, page 1154)

48-C.   The Crown of Rejoicing
         (1 Thessalonians 2:19, 20, page 1210)

48-D.   The Crown of Righteousness
         (2 Timothy 4:5-8, page 1228)

48-E.   The Crown of Glory
         (1 Peter 5:2-4, page 1268)

MASTER OUTLINE NUMBER FORTY-NINE

The Four Phases of the Second Coming

Many events will occur in connection with Christ's second coming to earth. This has caused some to wonder if there are a number of second comings. That such questions are asked should not surprise us. Before His first coming, rabbis, as later recorded in the Jewish Talmud, wondered if the Messiah might have two comings: one to suffer (Is. 53:3-9, page 693), and again to reign (Is. 9:6, 7, page 651). The purpose of this outline is to clarify the four major phases of Christ's second coming.

The Bible clearly teaches certain great prophetic truths concerning the future; the doctrine of Christ's second coming is one of these. Many facts of what will then occur are given to us; they should not be obscured because we do not know *every* detail, nor should the truths that we *do* know be clouded or made questionable by speculative guesses that are without clear scriptural basis. Some subtract from the body of truth by forever doubting even what is plainly told us. Others enthusiastically add their own brand of "icing" to the top of the layers of truth. Let us rather stand firmly on the biblical statements of prophecy, and hesitantly advance our own between-the-lines commentary in order to have eschatological clarity and also some silence concerning details of the future that are not given to us. Also, let us note clearly that God's Word concerning the Second Coming does not emphasize getting our prophetical chart one hundred percent straight, but rather to "Watch...you also be ready" (Matt. 24:42, 44, page 975).

49-A.   The Rapture of the Church
         (1 Thessalonians 4:13-18, page 1211)

49-B.   The Tribulation on the Earth
         (Matthew 24:9-30, page 973)

49-C.   The Battle of Armageddon
         (Revelation 16:13-16, page 1309)

49-D.   The Establishment of the Millennial Kingdom
         (Joel 3:11-17, page 871)

MASTER OUTLINE NUMBER FIFTY

Daniel, the Prophet: His Life

In the first six chapters of Daniel we have history, biography, prophecy, and typology. Daniel, Hananiah, Mishael, and Azariah were believed to be in their teens when taken captive to Babylon in 606 B.C. They were of the "king's descendants" of the tribe of Judah (Dan. 1:3-6, page 830), and descendants of godly King Hezekiah (Is. 39:1-7, page 678). They were turned over to the prince of the eunuchs, who changed their names and had supervision over them for three years. The name of Daniel was changed to Belteshazzar, Hananiah to Shadrach, Mishael to Meshach, and Azariah to Abed-Nego. The apparent purpose for this was to draw them away from their own land and religion, and induce them to accept the religion and habits of Babylon.

Daniel was a man of purpose, prayer, power, and faith. If he had a flaw in his character, it is not revealed in the Scriptures. Even his enemies could not find a blemish, a defect, or weakness in him (Dan. 6:4, page 843).

(1) *Daniel was a man of purpose.* In the hour of testing "Daniel purposed in his heart that he would not defile himself with the portion of the king's delicacies, nor with the wine which he drank" (Dan. 1:8, page 831; cf. 1 Sam. 16:7, page 283). Daniel and his Hebrew friends were not tempted with the meat and wine of the king, because it was an offering to Babylon's false gods. God gave them the wisdom and spiritual strength to say "No" (1 Cor. 10:13, 14, page 1155).

(2) *Daniel was a man of prayer.* In the hour of trouble Daniel sought his three Hebrew companions, and they went to God in prayer; and the God of mercy saved them from the wrath of the king (Dan. 2:17-20, page 833). Daniel not only prayed when he was in trouble, but he prayed three times a day; this was his prayer pattern (Dan. 6:10, page 843).

(3) *Daniel was a man of power.* In the hour of responsibility Daniel was a man of power. Nebuchadnezzar bestowed honor, gifts, and great power on Daniel. Now Daniel requested of the king that his three companions in prayer share his good fortune with him (Dan. 2:46-49, page 835). Daniel received power from the king, but the source of his real power was God (Dan. 2:27-30, page 834; Eph. 3:20, page 1190).

(4) *Daniel was a man of faith.* In the hour of need, Daniel was a man of faith. He was forced to spend a night in a den of hungry lions. Early in the morning, anxious King Darius came to the den and found Daniel alive and well, "and no injury whatever was found on him, because he believed in his God" (Dan. 6:23, page 844). Daniel's faith is also included in the eleventh chapter of Hebrews, without identifying him by name: "who through faith...stopped the mouths of lions" (Heb. 11:33, page 1249).

Daniel was truly a man of purpose, prayer, power, and faith. We would do well to emulate this great and godly man.

MASTER OUTLINE NUMBER FIFTY-ONE

Daniel, the Prophet: His Visions

In the second six chapters of Daniel, we have what could be called "The Old Testament Book of Revelation." Here we discover vision after vision which God showed to Daniel, so that His people might have the security and stability of knowing, through dark times, that:

(1) Their God knows all that will come to pass;
(2) He has control of coming events;
(3) In the end His righteousness will triumph over evil.

The two biblical prophets to whom God revealed the future most plainly were Daniel (in the Old Testament book of Daniel) and John (in the New Testament book of Revelation). Both men were described as being especially beloved of God. Daniel is called by the angel, "O man greatly beloved" (Dan. 10:19, page 853); and of John we read, "The other disciple, whom Jesus loved" (John 20:2, page 1082). Seeing these visions was a great privilege withheld from ordinary men, "but holy men of God spoke as they were moved by the Holy Spirit" (2 Pet. 1:21, page 1273).

The visions appeared to Daniel between 606 B.C., when Nebuchadnezzar conquered Jerusalem the first time, and 536 B.C., which was the third year of Cyrus the Persian (Dan. 10:1, page 851), and the first year of Darius the Mede (Dan. 11:1, page 853). Why, then, do some critics date the book of Daniel in the second century B.C., or more specifically, in 168 B.C.? The answer is threefold:

(1) Some critics simply reject the idea from the start that God can enable men to prophesy the future in such accurate detail.
(2) Daniel 8:11 (page 847) seems to be a reference to King Antiochus IV of Syria's desecration of the temple in Jerusalem in 168 B.C.
(3) Since this seems to be the last predicted item before the New Testament era, they date the book of Daniel at this time, 168 B.C.

There is evidence, however, that at least by the year 270 B.C., when the Old Testament was translated into Greek in the Septuagint, that the book of Daniel was totally accepted as an unquestioned part of the Old Testament on the grounds of its having been written long before by Daniel, the prophet of God. Dead Sea Scroll manuscripts of Daniel show the book was revered and popular in the second century B.C.

Daniel 2:4–7:28 (page 832) is written in Aramaic, a Semitic language related to Hebrew, quite possibly because Nebuchadnezzar, in one of his typical fits, ruled that during this period all writing would be in the leading world language of the day. Thus, as John wrote the New Testament book of Revelation with its many visions for God's people, in Greek, the common language of his day, so also Daniel wrote the Old Testament book of visions at least partially in the common language of Daniel's day, as a foretaste of what was to come.

The last six chapters contain so magnificent an array of visions that have already come true, that this section of the Bible alone proves that God indeed knows the future and has declared it to us through His servants the prophets.

51-A.   The Vision of the Four Beasts
         (Daniel 7:1-28, page 844)

51-B.   The Vision of the Ram and Goat
         (Daniel 8:1-27, page 846)

51-C.   The Vision of the Seventy Weeks
         (Daniel 9:1-27, page 848)

51-D.   The Vision of the Angel in Linen
         (Daniel 10:1-21, page 851)

51-E.   The Vision of the Struggling Kings
         (Daniel 11:1-45, page 853)

51-F.   The Vision of the Angel's Oath
         (Daniel 12:1-13, page 856)

MASTER OUTLINE NUMBER FIFTY-TWO

The Seven Sevens of the Revelation

The number "seven" is often used symbolically in the Bible to signify completeness. This usage is partly derived from the Genesis account of God having created all things in six days and resting on the seventh. In other words, at the end of the seventh day, the work and rest cycle of Creation was complete. Similarly, from biblical antiquity, the week has been fitted into a cycle of seven days, ending with the day of rest—the Sabbath.

Since the book of Revelation, the Apocalypse, is the closing book of the Bible, proclaiming God's end of this present age (an age of sin growing rampant, and Satan seemingly triumphant for a season), it is not surprising that the book's imagery is presented in stages of sevens. The end of all things tainted by sin lies before us. The age is viewed through the telescope of prophecy as having run its course, and, in sets of seven after seven, the conclusion is breathtakingly displayed before us. The revelation of God's total victory and triumph, in every area of the spiritual battle of the universe, is outlined for us by the book itself in the Seven Sevens of Revelation.

The seven letters were written to actual historical assemblies of believers that existed at the close of the first century in the province of Asia—today's western Turkey. The letters were delivered to the seven churches. They were real cities and real churches. There were, of course, at that time many other Christian churches at such cities as Rome, Corinth, Colosse, and so on.

These seven, in the providence of God, provide for us a microcosm of all churches of every age, and thus they are representative. Likewise, the problems that these seven churches faced are today faced by churches in varying degrees. From the letters we can learn what qualities displease God, and what Christ advocates for their remedy.

Some have also seen in these churches a prophetic quality, i.e., that in this book of prophecy they foreshadow the seven dominant characteristics of the entire church on earth through the various eras until the Lord comes. The suggested eras, looking back from the present, are as follows:

(1) Ephesus—apostolic church (A.D. 30—100)
(2) Smyrna—persecuted church (A.D. 100—313)
(3) Pergamos—state church (A.D. 313—590)
(4) Thyatira—papal church (A.D. 590—1517)
(5) Sardis—reformation church (A.D. 1517—1730)
(6) Philadelphia—evangelistic church (A.D. 1730—until the Rapture)
(7) Laodicea—apostate church (A.D. 1900—until Second Coming)

Christ wrote to the seven local churches because each congregation was a self-governing body. A local church may be affiliated with a fellowship, a denomination, or a larger, corporate society, but God holds the leadership responsible for the teaching of his congregation.

The secret to the study of each letter is to recognize the chief problem of each church, as identified by the Lord, and then to see how everything in the letter—Christ's appearance, warnings, and promises of reward—relates to this problem.

Before you begin the study of the Seven Sevens, read God's introduction to the study of the seven churches, in the first chapter of Revelation (page 1293).

52-A.   The Seven Churches
         (Revelation 2:1—3:22, page 1294)

52-B.   The Seven Seals
         (Revelation 6:1-17; 8:1, page 1299)

52-C.   The Seven Trumpets
         (Revelation 8:2—9:21; 11:15-19, page 1301)

52-D.   The Seven Personages
         (Revelation 11:3—13:18, page 1303)

52-E.   The Seven Bowls
         (Revelation 16:1-21, page 1308)

52-F.   The Seven Dooms
         (Revelation 17:1—20:15, page 1310)

52-G.   The Seven New Wonders
         (Revelation 21:1—22:7, page 1314)

The
Old Testament

The New King James Version

THE FIRST BOOK OF MOSES CALLED

Genesis

Origins are important, whether of products or people. Each item we buy is identified by its country of origin and its manufacturer. People likewise trace their family tree in order to establish their roots.

Genesis is the book of ultimate origins. Appropriately it stands first in the Bible because it explains the origin of all that the other sixty-five books develop. It is the seed-plot of Scripture, the foundation on which the whole Bible is built.

The title of the book, *Genesis*, comes to us from the Septuagint, a translation of the Old Testament from Hebrew into Greek completed about 150 years before Christ. Genesis means "Beginning." The Hebrew title, *Bereshith*, follows the Jewish custom of using the first word of a book as a title. It means "in the beginning."

AUTHORSHIP. Genesis is the first of five books written by Moses, often called the Pentateuch or the Law. The authorship by Moses is indicated by numerous references within the books themselves (Ex. 17:14; 24:4, 7; 34:27; Num. 33:2; Deut. 31:9). Other Old Testament books also speak of Moses as the writer (Josh. 1:7, 8; 8:32–35; 1 Kin. 2:3; Ezra 6:18; Dan. 9:11, 13). In the New Testament, Jesus emphatically credited the writing of the first five books to Moses (Luke 20:37; John 5:45–47). These statements are supported by the historical accuracy and eyewitness quality of the other four books. For the writing of Genesis, Moses likely had both oral and written records. Some things, such as creation, could have been known only as God Himself revealed them (Job 38:1–7). Moses was educated in Egypt and ideally suited for the task of writing (Acts 7:22). Furthermore, his writing was inspired by the Holy Spirit (2 Tim. 3:16, 17; 2 Pet. 1:20, 21).

In no book of the Bible are authorship and historical authenticity as important as in Genesis. From before the time of Christ to the present, Genesis has been viewed as inspired by God through the human authorship of Moses. Indeed, until 150 years ago there were few who questioned the Mosaic authorship or the historical and literal character of Genesis. As in the origin of man, so in the development of Israel's religion and the authorship of the Pentateuch, some critics have tried to replace divine creation and direct revelation with natural evolution. According to such a view, Genesis and the following four books were written not by Moses but by four or more editors writing over many years and at a much later time. Though carefully studied and frequently discussed, their view has not been supported by historical and archaeological evidence. It also stands in contrast to the evidence of the Bible itself and seriously undermines the nature and value of the book of Genesis. We may confidently affirm with Christ that Moses wrote the first five books of our Bible. These books are Mosaic, not a mosaic pieced together by anonymous editors. Genesis represents origination, not imagination. It is a historical account, not a religious myth.

CONTEXT. Although written during the forty years immediately following the Exodus (1445–1405 B.C.), the events of Genesis cover a much longer, earlier time period. Before creation there was no time, no matter, and no being apart from God Himself. The universe, including earth, and all of life, including man, began when God spoke them into existence (Gen. 1:3, 6, 11, 14, 20, 24, 26). They appeared complete and mature. Although it is difficult to establish an exact date for creation, such a date is certainly recent.

The period of history recorded in Genesis begins with Adam and Eve in paradise and ends with the death of Joseph in Egypt. The history of the human race in general occupies only the first eleven chapters. The last thirty-nine chapters are devoted to redemptive history as the nation Israel grows out of the faith of one man, Abraham. Thus almost eighty percent of the book is devoted to the 365 years from the birth of Abraham to the death of Joseph (2165 B.C. to about 1800 B.C.).

HOW GENESIS FITS INTO THE BIBLE. Genesis is the first book of the Bible in location and in importance. It begins what the last book of the Bible, Revelation, concludes. Genesis explains man's origin; Revelation explains man's destiny. In between, God's love for a rebellious world dramatically unfolds. Without apology, Genesis begins with God. God is not introduced or explained. No effort is made to prove His existence. The Bible is God's revelation to man. It simply asserts, "In the beginning God." What follows is the creation of the universe, of man, of marriage and family life, of love, and so forth. We are told that God pronounced His creative

work "good." But not all of human experience recorded in Genesis or experienced today is good. Sin has marred the perfection of God's creation.

Genesis documents man's sinful rebellion and the tragic consequences. Sin, death, hatred, jealousy, murder, war, hunger, and ultimately judgment find their beginning in Genesis. So too does redemption. Satan tempted Eve and brought about the downfall of Adam and Eve (3:1-8). The result was physical and spiritual death (2:17; 3:8; Rom. 5:12). Even as God announced the consequences of sin, He promised a Redeemer who would ultimately destroy Satan and defeat sin (3:15). The story of redemption develops throughout the rest of the Old Testament and climaxes in the coming of Jesus Christ, God's Son and the Savior of sinners (Rom. 5).

How Genesis Fits Together. Genesis can be outlined by the genealogies it contains. The phrase "this is the genealogy of . . ." occurs ten times (5:1; 6:9; 10:1; 11:10; 11:27; 25:12, 19; 36:1, 9; 37:2). However, it is best seen in light of its two major histories. Chapters 1—11 provide a general history of mankind. They highlight events, including creation (1, 2), the fall of man (3), the spread of sin (4, 5), the Flood (6—10), and the dispersal of mankind from Babel (11). The key verse in the first eleven chapters is 1:1, "In the beginning God created the heavens and the earth."

Chapters 12—50 provide a special history of Israel. They highlight people. The faith of Abraham, the friend of God, fills chapters 12—25. Abraham was to be God's instrument for blessing all mankind (12:1-3). The key thought in these thirty-nine chapters is 12:3, "And in you all the families of the earth shall be blessed." By virtue of his faith Abraham became the father of all who believe (Gen. 15:6; Rom. 4:3, 16; Gal. 3:6-9). He also became the one through whom God sent His Son. The New Testament opens in Matthew 1:1 by linking Abraham to the birth of Jesus Christ, "The book of the genealogy of Jesus Christ, the Son of David, the Son of Abraham." Although Isaac was Abraham's promised son, chapters 26—35 really dwell on Abraham's grandson, Jacob. Jacob had twelve sons; the eleventh was Joseph. Because of jealousy, Joseph's older brothers sold him into slavery in Egypt. Chapters 36—50 show how God preserved Abraham's great-grandson, Joseph, and prepared the way for the family of Jacob (renamed Israel) to become a nation. Exodus continues the national history of Israel. As a dictionary provides the words with which other books are written, so Genesis provides the people and themes from which all other Bible books are drawn. If we would understand the Bible, or ourselves and our world, we must first master Genesis.

—K.G.H.

The History of Creation

▼ 2-B. **Know What God Intended the Bible to Do for You**

▲ I N the ^Rbeginning ^RGod created the heavens and the earth.   [John 1:1-3] · Acts 17:24

2 The earth was ^Rwithout form, and void; and darkness *was* on the face of the deep. ^RAnd the Spirit of God was hovering over the face of the waters.   Jer. 4:23 · Is. 40:13, 14

3 Then God said, ^R"Let there be ^Rlight"; and there was light.   2 Cor. 4:6 · [Heb. 11:3]

4 And God saw the light, that it *was* good;

1:2 Words in italic type have been added for clarity. They are not found in the original Hebrew or Aramaic.

and God divided the light from the darkness.

5 God called the light Day, and the ^Rdarkness He called Night. So the evening and the morning were the first day.   Ps. 19:2; 33:6

6 Then God said, "Let there be a ^Tfirmament in the midst of the waters, and let it divide the waters from the waters."   expanse

7 Thus God made the firmament, and divided the waters which *were* under the firmament from the waters which *were* above the firmament; and it was so.

8 And God called the firmament Heaven. So the evening and the morning were the second day.

9 Then God said, ^R"Let the waters under the heavens be gathered together into one

2-B. **Know What God Intended the Bible to Do for You (Genesis 1:1)**—"In the beginning God . . . " Effective Bible study must be guided by a clear understanding of the general and specific purposes of biblical revelation. At the apex of this revelation is the revealed One Himself. At the very outset of our journey into the Bible we are placed on notice that we will encounter the self-existent, preexistent God everywhere along the way. This is because the Bible is not only the book *from* God, it is the book *about* God. In it He vividly reveals Himself as the God we will everywhere have to face and deal with. As such, He is our Creator, our Sustainer, our Judge, and our Hope in this world and for eternity.

(1) "I am the LORD your God. . . . You shall have no other gods before Me" (Ex. 20:2, 3, page 79). We must be controlled in our Bible study by the primary fact that our lives are not our own, but we belong to

(Point 2-B continued on next page)

place, and ᴿlet the dry *land* appear"; and it was so.   Job 26:10 • Ps. 24:1, 2; 33:7; 95:5

10 And God called the dry *land* Earth, and the gathering together of the waters He called Seas. And God saw that *it was* good.

11 Then God said, "Let the earth ᴿbring forth grass, the herb *that* yields seed, *and* the ᴿfruit tree *that* yields fruit according to its kind, whose seed *is* in itself, on the earth"; and it was so.   Heb. 6:7 • 2 Sam. 16:1

12 And the earth brought forth grass, the herb *that* yields seed according to its kind, and the tree *that* yields fruit, whose seed *is* in itself according to its kind. And God saw that *it was* good.

13 So the evening and the morning were the third day.

14 Then God said, "Let there be lights in the firmament of the heavens to divide the day from the night; and let them be for signs and seasons, and for days and years;

15 "and let them be for lights in the firma-ment of the heavens to give light on the earth"; and it was so.

16 Then God made two great ᵀlights: the ᴿgreater light to rule the day, and the ᴿlesser light to rule the night. *He made* ᴿthe stars also.   luminaries • Ps. 136:8 • Ps. 8:3 • Job 38:7

17 God set them in the firmament of the ᴿheavens to give light on the earth,   Gen. 15:5

18 and to ᴿrule over the day and over the night, and to divide the light from the darkness. And God saw that *it was* good.   Jer. 31:35

19 So the evening and the morning were the fourth day.

20 Then God said, "Let the waters abound with an abundance of living creatures, and let birds fly above the earth across the face of the ᵀfirmament of the heavens."   expanse

21 So ᴿGod created great sea creatures and every living thing that moves, with which the waters abounded, according to their kind, and every winged bird according to its kind. And God saw that *it was* good.   Ps. 104:25-28

(Point 2-B continued from previous page)
the Creator of heaven and earth (Gen. 1:27, page 4; 1 Cor. 6:19, 20, page 1152). This fact should abruptly awaken us to our need to draw near to God in serious Bible study. Surely, if we belong to someone else and are not masters of our own fate, it is more than wise to seek all we can obtain of the knowledge of that One, for it is He who, by the utterance of His Word, created the universe (Ps. 19:1–5, page 520; Is. 42:5, page 681). "Where were you when I laid the foundations of the earth? Tell Me, if you have understanding" (Job 38:4, page 503). Unfortunately, we have no such understanding. We must be thankful and glad for the opportunity to listen in the Word of this One who calls Himself "I AM" (Ex. 3:14, page 61).

(2) This God is also our Sustainer. "Even the youths shall faint and be weary, and the young men shall utterly fall, but those who wait on the LORD shall renew their strength" (Is. 40:30, 31, page 680). Life is too much for us. We faint and are weary, and the best of us "utterly fall." Was this all there was to God's plan in creating mankind in His own image? Surely He had something nobler in mind in creation than such frail creatures as we! But if so, how shall we gain an understanding of that more excellent design that God had for man before the Fall? (Gen. 3:17–19, page 7). Certainly the answer is in the study of His Word. Then we will know how "those who wait on the LORD shall renew their strength."

(3) Without careful Bible study, inadequate images and misrepresentations of God's character form in our minds. For example, the Bible is given to show us that God is Judge of all the earth. "When I say to the righteous that he shall surely live, but he trusts in his own righteousness and commits iniquity . . . he shall die. Again, when I say to the wicked, 'You shall surely die,' if he turns from his sin and does what is lawful and right . . . he shall surely live" (Ezek. 33:13–15, page 812). It is important that we have no illusions about the perfect justice of God. Through superficial Bible study we can be misled by the false, popular image of God as an easygoing, indulgent uncle who regards sin as a mere minor flaw to be "brushed off."

Only by careful attention to the whole counsel of God in the Bible do we come to realize that God's standards of righteousness are very much higher than ours: "The LORD, the LORD God, merciful and gracious, longsuffering, and abounding in goodness and truth, keeping mercy for thousands, . . . by no means clearing the guilty" (Ex. 34:6, 7, page 95). God's just requirements normally terrify the conscience awakened by the study of His Word.

Until the conscience is thus truly aroused to a full sense of responsibility before the Judge, there can be no hope for the sinner. Careless study produces a deficient picture of God's holiness, leading to the peril of presumed self-righteousness. As we meditate on God's Word we must be like Isaiah coming into the temple of God, where he "saw the Lord sitting on a throne, high and lifted up" (Is. 6:1, page 647).

(4) But the Bible, above all, is a book of hope. This is the great reason countless millions have turned to the world's most popular book, the Holy Bible. We must come to our study of the Bible fully confident that the Lord has "no pleasure in the death of the wicked, but that the wicked turn from his way and live" (Ezek. 33:11, page 811). In that same Bible Jesus describes Himself as the gracious Host, who urgently desires to "dine" with those who open their hearts to Him (Rev. 3:20, page 1297). Truly, the Bible throughout presents *Christ* to its readers, who has offered His own body for our sins, and who has said, "My flesh is food indeed, and My blood is drink indeed" (John 6:55, page 1060). Therefore, come to the Word of God with your heart prepared to dine with the risen Christ, who is the living Word (John 1:14, page 1049). As you dine with Him you shall be nourished on the Bread of heaven, and live with Him forever.

See John 10:4, 5, page 1067, for **Point 2-C: Know That the Bible Stands Above All Human Opinions.**

22 And God blessed them, saying, "Be fruitful and multiply, and fill the waters in the seas, and let birds multiply on the earth."

23 So the evening and the morning were the fifth day.

24 Then God said, "Let the earth bring forth the living creature according to its kind: cattle and creeping thing and beast of the earth, *each* according to its kind"; and it was so.

25 And God made the beast of the earth according to its kind, cattle according to its kind, and everything that creeps on the earth according to its kind. And God saw that *it was* good.

26 Then God said, R"Let Us make man in Our image, according to Our likeness; let them have dominion over the fish of the sea, over the birds of the air, and over the cattle, over all the earth and over every creeping thing that creeps on the earth."   [Eph. 4:24]

27 So God created man Rin His *own* image; in the image of God He created him; Rmale and female He created them.   Gen. 5:2 · Matt. 19:4

28 Then God blessed them, and God said to them, "Be fruitful and multiply; fill the earth and subdue it; have dominion over the fish of the sea, over the birds of the air, and over every living thing that moves on the earth."

29 And God said, "See, I have given you every herb *that* yields seed which *is* on the face of all the earth, and every tree whose fruit yields seed; to you it shall be for food.

30 "Also, to Revery beast of the earth, to every Rbird of the air, and to everything that creeps on the earth, in which *there is* Rlife, I *have given* every green herb for food"; and it was so.   Ps. 145:15 · Job 38:41 · *a living soul*

31 Then God saw everything that He had made, and indeed *it was* very good. So the evening and the morning were the sixth day.

2 Thus the heavens and the earth, and Rall the host of them, were finished.   Ps. 33:6

2 RAnd on the seventh day God ended His work which He had done, and He rested on the seventh day from all His work which He had done.   Ex. 20:9-11; 31:17

3 Then God blessed the seventh day and sanctified it, because in it He rested from all His work which God had created and made.

4 This *is* the Thistory of the heavens and the earth when they were created, in the day that the LORD God made the earth and the heavens,   Heb. *toledoth,* lit. *generations*

5 before any Rplant of the field was in the earth and before any herb of the field had grown. For the LORD God had not Rcaused it to rain on the earth, and *there was* no man Rto till the ground;   Gen. 1:11, 12 · Gen. 7:4 · Gen. 3:23

6 but a mist went up from the earth and watered the whole face of the ground.

7 And the LORD God formed man *of* the dust of the ground, and Rbreathed into his Rnostrils the breath of life; and Rman became a living being.   Job 33:4 · Gen. 7:22 · 1 Cor. 15:45

Life in God's Garden

8 The LORD God planted a garden Reastward in REden, and there He put the man whom He had formed.   Gen. 3:23, 24 · Gen. 4:16

9 And out of the ground the LORD God made every tree grow that is pleasant to the sight and good for food. The tree of life *was* also in the midst of the garden, and the tree of the knowledge of good and evil.

10 Now a river went out of Eden to water the garden, and from there it parted and became four riverheads.

11 The name of the first *is* Pishon; it *is* the one which skirts Rthe whole land of Havilah, where *there is* gold.   Gen. 25:18

12 And the gold of that land *is* good. RBdellium and the onyx stone *are* there.   Num. 11:7

13 The name of the second river *is* Gihon; it *is* the one which goes around the whole land of Cush.

14 The name of the third river *is* *Hiddekel; it *is* the one which goes toward the east of Assyria. The fourth river *is* the Euphrates.

15-A. The Origin of Sin

15 Then the LORD God took Tthe man and put him in the garden of Eden to Ttend and keep it.   Or *Adam* · *cultivate*

2:14 Or *Tigris*

15-A. The Origin of Sin (Genesis 2:15-18)—Sin is rebellion against God, doing evil, violating His will, breaking His law. Many ask how sin first gained entrance into the world. When God created Adam and Eve, He gave them the power of choice. They could choose to obey their holy and righteous Creator or they could choose to disobey. They both ate the forbidden fruit, disobeying God's explicit instructions and His perfect will for their lives (Gen. 3:6, page 5; cf. 1 Tim. 2:14, page 1219).

(1) Before the fall of man, Satan and his angels had already fallen:

(a) Satan's fall is described in Isaiah 14:12-17 (page 657) as the prophet gazed past the wicked king of Babylon to Satan who indwelt him. He fell because of pride, and his desire to be equal to God. Later he enticed Eve with this same desire: "You will be like God" (Gen. 3:5, page 5).

(b) Satan's fall is further described in Ezekiel 28:12-19 (page 805) as the prophet considered the evil

(Point 15-A continued on next page)

▽ 16 And the LORD God commanded the man, saying, "Of every tree of the garden you may freely eat;

17 "but of the tree of the knowledge of good and evil you shall not eat, for in the day that you eat of it you shall surely die."

18 And the LORD God said, "It is not good that man should be alone; ᴿI will make him a

▲ helper comparable to him."   1 Cor. 11:8, 9

19 Out of the ground the LORD God formed every beast of the field and every bird of the air, and brought them to Adam to see what he would call them. And whatever Adam called each living creature, that was its name.

20 So Adam gave names to all cattle, to the birds of the air, and to every beast of the field. But for Adam there was not found a helper comparable to him.

21 And the LORD God caused a ᴿdeep sleep to fall on Adam, and he slept; and He took one of his ribs, and closed up the flesh in its place.   1 Sam. 26:12

22 Then the rib which the LORD God had taken from man He ᵀmade into a woman, and He brought her to the man.   Lit. built

23 And Adam said:

"This is now ᴿbone of my bones
And flesh of my flesh;

She shall be called Woman,   Gen. 29:14
Because she was taken out of Man."

24 Therefore a man shall leave his father and mother and ᵀbe joined to his wife, and they shall become one flesh.   Lit. cling

25 And they were both naked, the man and his wife, and were not ᴿashamed.   Is. 47:3

The Temptation and Fall of Man

3 Now the serpent was ᴿmore cunning than any beast of the field which the LORD God had made. And he said to the woman, "Has God indeed said, 'You shall not eat of every tree of the garden'?"   2 Cor. 11:3

2 And the woman said to the serpent, "We may eat the fruit of the trees of the garden;

3 "but of the fruit of the tree which is in the midst of the garden, God has said, 'You shall not eat it, nor shall you ᴿtouch it, lest you die.'"   Ex. 19:12, 13

4 ᴿThen the serpent said to the woman, "You will not surely die.   [2 Cor. 11:3]

5 "For God knows that in the day you eat of it your eyes will be opened, and you will be like God, knowing good and evil."

6 So when the woman saw that the tree was good for food, that it was pleasant to the

(Point 15-A continued from previous page)
personality who indwelt the wicked king of Tyre. Satan is described as "the anointed cherub" who had been in Eden, "the garden of God." He was created as a perfect being, but he fell into iniquity. Pride in his own beauty was the source of his fall.

(c) The book of Revelation indicates that a third of the angels also fell with Satan—"His tail drew a third of the stars of heaven" (Rev. 12:3, 4, 9, page 1305). Angels are at times represented by "stars" (Rev. 1:20, page 1294).

(2) Adam and Eve fell by breaking a clear command of God:

(a) *The clear command* (vv. 16, 17). Adam and Eve were commanded by God not to eat of the tree of the knowledge of good and evil. They were told that "in the day that you eat of it you shall surely die" (v. 17).

(b) *The tempter's lies* (Gen. 3:1-5). Satan, the already fallen being, used the body of a serpent to speak to Eve, enticing her to sin. He denied that she would die for her sin, and he told her that she would have a new freedom and knowledge, and thus be like God.

(c) *Lingering with temptation* (Gen. 3:4-6). Eve listened to Satan's lies and was attracted by the fruit. Her taste anticipated that it "was good for food" and she desired to be made wise.

(d) *The Fall* (Gen. 3:6; cf. 1 Tim. 2:12-14, page 1219). Eve ate the forbidden fruit and gave it to Adam, and "he ate." It was a test of simple obedience. They had the fruit of all of the other trees, and there was no need for them to eat of the forbidden tree (vv. 15, 16).

There are still many lessons in this account for us today:

(1) Satan's lies are the same.
(2) He uses nearby temptations to lure us.
(3) There is danger in lingering or toying with sin.
(4) The Fall has had death-dealing effects.
(5) God had foreknowledge of Adam's fall, and from the beginning of creation He made provision for it:

(a) Christ's death was "foreordained before the foundation of the world" (1 Pet. 1:20, page 1264). Before He created the world God had determined to create mankind and allow the test in Eden (knowing that man would fall), and He had determined already to send Christ to die for man's sin.

(b) God in no way compelled Adam and Eve to sin, nor is God ever the chargeable cause of sin. James, using the word *tempt,* meaning to entice to sin, tells us God does this to no one (James 1:13-15, page 1256).

See Genesis 3:7-24, page 6, for **Point 15-B: The Effects of Sin: Immediate and Lasting.**

eyes, and a tree desirable to make one wise, she took of its fruit and ate. She also gave to her husband with her, and he ate.

▼ 15-B. The Effects of Sin: Immediate and Lasting

7 Then the eyes of both of them were opened, ᴿand they knew that they were naked; and they sewed fig leaves together and made themselves coverings.   Gen. 2:25

8 And they heard the sound of the LORD God walking in the garden in the ᵀcool of the day, and Adam and his wife hid themselves from the presence of the LORD God among the trees of the garden.   ▽ Or wind, breeze

9 Then the LORD God called to Adam and said to him, "Where are you?"

10 So he said, "I heard Your voice in the garden, ᴿand I was afraid because I was naked; and I hid myself."   Gen. 2:25

11 And He said, "Who told you that you were naked? Have you eaten from the tree of which I commanded you that you should not eat?"

12 Then the man said, ᴿ"The woman whom

15-B. The Effects of Sin: Immediate and Lasting (Genesis 3:7–24)—Satan's lie to Adam and Eve encouraged them to rebel against God's goodness by violating His commandment, suggesting that they would not really suffer for breaking God's law. No lie was ever farther from the truth. All of this planet's ills—physical, psychological, political, economic, social, medical, religious, and spiritual (Eph. 6:12, page 1192)—can be traced to the entrance of sin into the world (Eph. 2:1–3, page 1187).

(1) Adam and Eve's sin had immediate effects:

(a) They experienced an inner agony of guilt. "They knew that they were naked" (v. 7).

(b) They made a futile attempt at self-righteousness. "They sewed fig leaves together and made themselves coverings" (v. 7).

(c) Fellowship with God was broken. They "hid themselves from the presence of the LORD God" (v. 8).

(d) They feared sin's punishment. "I was afraid . . . I hid myself" (v. 10).

(e) Fellowship with other humans was broken. "The woman . . . gave me of the tree" (v. 12).

(f) Harmony with the creatures of the earth was also broken. "The serpent deceived me" (v. 13).

(g) Part of the animal creation was "cursed more than all cattle . . . on your belly you shall go" (v. 14).

(h) Part of the animal creation became hostile to mankind. "I will put enmity between you [the serpent] and the woman" (v. 15).

(i) Physical pain became a part of human life, especially pain in childbirth. "I will greatly multiply your sorrow and your conception; in pain you shall bring forth children" (v. 16).

(j) Authority, rank, and tension appeared in marriage. "Your desire shall be for your husband, and he shall rule over you" (v. 16).

(k) The ground was cursed and became hostile to mankind in bringing forth weeds. "Cursed is the ground for your sake. . . . Both thorns and thistles it shall bring forth" (vv. 17, 18).

(l) Human physical death began. "To dust you shall return" (v. 19).

(m) Mankind was driven out of the garden. "God sent him out of the garden of Eden to till the ground" (v. 23).

(n) Mankind was denied the Tree of Life. God "placed cherubim . . . and a flaming sword" to keep man from eating from the Tree of Life (vv. 22, 24).

(2) Adam and Eve's sin also had wider effects:

(a) Mankind was separated from God. "So He drove out the man" (v. 24; cf. Eph. 2:12, page 1187).

(b) Sin was brought into the human race. "Through one man sin entered the world" (Rom. 5:12, page 1133).

(c) Death was brought into the human race. "Through one man sin entered the world, and death through sin" (Rom. 5:12, page 1133).

(d) All mankind inherited death. "And thus death spread to all men" (Rom. 5:12, page 1133).

(e) All inherited Adam's guilt. "All sinned" (Rom. 5:12, page 1133).

(f) All became condemned in Adam, and by their own sins. "For all have sinned [broken God's laws] and fall short of the glory of God"—fall short of His requirements (Rom. 3:23, page 1131).

(g) All died spiritually. "For to be carnally minded is death" (Rom. 8:6–9, page 1137).

(h) All bore the penalty. "For the wages of sin is death"—physical and spiritual (Rom. 6:23, page 1134).

(i) All unbelievers will be judged after death at the Great White Throne (Rev. 20:11–13, page 1313).

(j) All unbelievers will spend eternity, separated from God, in the lake of fire (Rev. 20:14, 15, page 1314).

Original sin clearly affected our entire race. Newborn infants do not start anew as did Adam and Eve in the Garden; they enter with an already formed sin nature and a limited life span. To all this we can only shout with glad hearts that God has provided a remedy for sin and death—through Christ.

See Romans 3:9–18, page 1130, for **Point 15-C: The Effects of Sin in Human Character.**

∇ You gave *to be* with me, she gave me of the tree, and I ate." [Prov. 28:13]

13 And the LORD God said to the woman, "What *is* this you have done?" The woman said, "The serpent deceived me, and I ate."

14 So the LORD God said to the serpent:

"Because you have done this,
You *are* cursed more than all cattle,
And more than every beast of the field;
On your belly you shall go,
And RYou shall eat dust
All the days of your life.   Deut. 28:15–20

15 And I will put enmity
Between you and the woman,
And between your seed and her Seed;
RHe shall bruise your head,   Rom. 16:20
And you shall bruise His heel."

16 To the woman He said:

"I will greatly multiply your sorrow and
your conception;
In pain you shall bring forth children;
Your desire *shall be* Tfor your husband,
And he shall rule over you."   Lit. *toward*

17 Then to Adam He said, "Because you have heeded the voice of your wife, and have eaten from the tree of which I commanded you, saying, 'You shall not eat of it':

"Cursed is the ground for your sake;
RIn toil you shall eat *of* it
All the days of your life.   Eccl. 2:23

18 Both thorns and thistles it shall Tbring
forth for you,   *cause to grow*
And you shall eat the herb of the field.

19 RIn the sweat of your face you shall eat
bread   2 Thess. 3:10

Till you return to the ground,   ∇
For out of it you were taken;
RFor dust you *are*,   Gen. 2:7; 5:5
And Rto dust you shall return."   Job 21:26

20 And Adam called his wife's name Eve, because she was the mother of all living.

20–A. The First Shedding of Blood   ▼

21 Also for Adam and his wife the LORD God made tunics of skin, and clothed them.   ▲

22 Then the LORD God said, "Behold, the man has become like one of Us, to know good and evil. And now, lest he put out his hand and take also of the tree of life, and eat, and live forever"—

23 therefore the LORD God sent him out of the garden of Eden Rto till the ground from which he was taken.   Gen. 4:2; 9:20

24 So He drove out the man; and He placed cherubim at the east of the garden of Eden, and a flaming sword which turned every way, to guard the way to the tree of life.   ▲

Cain Murders Abel

4 Now Adam knew Eve his wife, and she conceived and bore Cain, and said, "I have acquired a man from the LORD."

2 Then she bore again, this time his brother Abel. Now Abel was a keeper of sheep, but Cain was a tiller of the ground.

20–B. Abel's Blood Offering   ▼

3 And in the process of time it came to pass that Cain brought an offering of the fruit Rof the ground to the LORD.   Num. 18:12

20–A. The First Shedding of Blood (Genesis 3:21)—"The LORD God made tunics of skin, and clothed them" (v. 21). When the first man and woman sinned, God did not drive them from the garden robed in their manmade, bloodless religion. The Word says, "Then the eyes of both of them were opened, and they knew that they were naked; and they sewed fig leaves together and made themselves coverings" (v. 7). Adam and Eve experienced a new feeling; for the first time they felt guilt, which caused them to fear God and to hide.

God judged the man and the woman, and before He drove them from the garden He sacrificed animals; the innocent shed their blood for the guilty. What an excellent *type*, or illustration, of the Lord Jesus "who Himself bore our sins in His own body on the tree" (1 Pet. 2:24, page 1266). Peter also tells us that we have been redeemed "with the precious blood of Christ, as of a lamb without blemish and without spot" (1 Pet. 1:18, 19, page 1263).

Adam and Eve must have watched as God selected the animals; and so they witnessed the first shedding of innocent blood, knowing that it was because Adam had failed God (1 Cor. 15:45–49, page 1162). As they watched, they learned that God in His sovereign grace provided a covering, a propitiation for their sins. Not a cover-up, but a *cover*—a promise of payment in full to blot out sin and to make atonement for mankind (Lev. 17:11, page 126). They departed from the garden knowing that "without shedding of blood there is no remission"—no forgiveness of sin (Heb. 9:22, page 1244).

Verse 21 gives us a perfect picture of salvation by the grace of God apart from works (Eph. 2:8, 9, page 1187). Just as the animals shed their blood in Eden, to provide a covering for the nakedness of Adam and Eve, so the blood of Jesus Christ covers the sins of the believer and robes him in the righteousness of Christ (Rom. 10:1–4, page 1140).

See Genesis 4:3–7, above, for **Point 20-B: Abel's Blood Offering.**

20-B. Abel's Blood Offering (Genesis 4:3–7)—Why did God reject Cain's offering and accept Abel's? A careful examination of the two brothers and their offerings will answer this question, and will give you a fresh glimpse of "the Lamb of God who takes away the sin of the world" (John 1:29, page 1050).

(Point 20-B continued on next page)

▽ 4 Abel also brought of the firstborn of his flock and of their fat. And the LORD ᴿrespected Abel and his offering,   Heb. 11:4

5 but He did not respect Cain and his offering. And Cain was very angry, and his countenance fell.

6 So the LORD said to Cain, "Why are you angry? And why has your countenance fallen?

7 "If you do well, will you not be accepted? And if you do not do well, sin lies at the door. And its desire is ᵀfor you, but you
▲ should rule over it."   Lit. toward

8 Now Cain ᵀtalked with Abel his *brother; and it came to pass, when they were in the field, that Cain rose up against Abel his brother and killed him.   Lit. said to

9 Then the LORD said to Cain, "Where is Abel your brother?" He said, "I do not know. Am I my brother's keeper?"

10 And He said, "What have you done? The voice of your brother's blood ᴿcries out to Me from the ground.   Heb. 12:24

11 "So now ᴿyou are cursed from the earth, which has opened its mouth to receive your brother's blood from your hand.   Gen. 3:14

12 "When you till the ground, it shall no longer yield its strength to you. A fugitive and a vagabond you shall be on the earth."

13 And Cain said to the LORD, "My ᵀpunishment is greater than I can bear!   iniquity

14 "Surely You have driven me out this day from the face of the ground; ᴿI shall be ᴿhidden from Your face; I shall be a fugitive and a vagabond on the earth, and it will happen that ᴿanyone who finds me will kill me."   Ps. 51:11 · Is. 1:15 · Num. 35:19, 21, 27

15 And the LORD said to him, *"Therefore, whoever kills Cain, vengeance shall be taken on him ᴿsevenfold." And the LORD set a ᴿmark on Cain, lest anyone finding him should kill him.   Gen. 4:24 · Ezek. 9:4, 6

The Family of Cain

16 Then Cain went out from the ᴿpresence of the LORD and dwelt in the land of ᵀNod on the east of Eden.   Jon. 1:3 · Lit. Wandering

17 And Cain knew his wife, and she conceived and bore Enoch. And he built a city, ᴿand called the name of the city after the name of his son—Enoch.   Ps. 49:11

18 To Enoch was born Irad; and Irad begot Mehujael, and Mehujael begot Methushael, and Methushael begot Lamech.

19 Then Lamech took for himself ᴿtwo wives: the name of one was Adah, and the name of the second was Zillah.   Gen. 2:24; 16:3

20 And Adah bore Jabal. He was the father of those who dwell in tents and have livestock.

21 His brother's name was Jubal. He was the father of all those who play the harp and ᵀflute.   pipe

22 And as for Zillah, she also bore Tubal-Cain, an instructor of every craftsman in bronze and iron. And the sister of Tubal-Cain was Naamah.

23 Then Lamech said to his wives:

"Adah and Zillah, hear my voice;
Wives of Lamech, listen to my speech!
For I have killed a man for wounding me,
Even a young man for hurting me.

4:8 Sam., LXX, Syr., Vg. add *"Let us go out to the field."*   4:15 So with MT, Tg.; LXX, Syr., Vg. *Not so*

(Point 20-B continued from previous page)

(1) Cain's offering was not an act of saving faith. He believed that God existed, and had come to worship Him. But he had the wrong offering, the wrong attitude, and the wrong motive (Matt. 7:21-23, page 946). Cain did not do the will of God; he acted according to his own will. He had "a form of godliness but denying its power" (2 Tim. 3:5, page 1227). Abel's offering, on the other hand, was an act of saving faith (Eph. 2:8, 9, page 1187). "By faith Abel offered to God a more excellent sacrifice than Cain, through which he obtained witness [from God] that he was righteous" (Heb. 11:4, page 1247). By faith Abel offered a lamb for the remission of sins, and God declared him righteous.

(2) Cain's offering was bloodless; it may have been equal in cost to Abel's, but it was without the shedding of blood (Heb. 9:22, page 1244). Abel's offering was a blood sacrifice; it was a type of the Lamb of God who shed His blood to redeem lost souls (1 Pet. 1:18, 19, page 1263).

(3) Cain's offering was a type of salvation by works (Titus 3:5, page 1231). Abel's offering was a type of salvation by grace (Eph. 1:7, page 1186).

(4) Cain's offering was a type of dead religion. Abel's offering was a type of life: "The life of the flesh is in the blood [the life of Christianity is in the blood of Christ], and I have given it to you upon the altar to make atonement for your souls; for it is the blood that makes atonement for the soul" (Lev. 17:11, page 126).

(5) Cain's bloodless offering was rejected by God. Abel's blood offering was accepted by God, and Abel was made righteous with the righteousness of Jesus who would atone for his sins (2 Cor. 5:21, page 1169).

See Genesis 22:1-19, page 26, for **Point 20-C: The Offering of Isaac.**

24 If Cain shall be avenged sevenfold,
Then Lamech seventy-sevenfold."

A New Son

25 And Adam knew his wife again, and she bore a son and ^Rnamed him ^TSeth, "For God has appointed another seed for me instead of Abel, whom Cain killed."   Gen. 5:3 · Lit. *Appointed*
26 And as for Seth, to him also a son was born; and he named him *Enosh. Then *men* began to call on the name of the LORD.

The Family of Adam

5 This is the book of the genealogy of Adam. In the day that God created man, He made him in the likeness of God.
2 He created them male and female, and ^Rblessed them and called them Mankind in the day they were created.   Gen. 1:28; 9:1
3 And Adam lived one hundred and thirty years, and begot *a son* in his own likeness, after his image, and named him Seth.
4 After he begot Seth, ^Rthe days of Adam were eight hundred years; ^Rand he had sons and daughters.   Luke 3:36-38 · Gen. 1:28; 4:25
5 So all the days that Adam lived were nine hundred and thirty years; and he died.
6 Seth lived one hundred and five years, and begot ^REnosh.   Gen. 4:26
7 After he begot Enosh, Seth lived eight hundred and seven years, and had sons and daughters.
8 So all the days of Seth were nine hundred and twelve years; and he died.

4:26 Gr. *Enos*, Luke 3:38

9 Enosh lived ninety years, and begot ^TCainan.   Heb. *Qenan*
10 After he begot Cainan, Enosh lived eight hundred and fifteen years, and had sons and daughters.
11 So all the days of Enosh were nine hundred and five years; and he died.
12 Cainan lived seventy years, and begot Mahalalel.
13 After he begot Mahalalel, Cainan lived eight hundred and forty years, and had sons and daughters.
14 So all the days of Cainan were nine hundred and ten years; and he died.
15 Mahalalel lived sixty-five years, and begot Jared.
16 After he begot Jared, Mahalalel lived eight hundred and thirty years, and had sons and daughters.
17 So all the days of Mahalalel were eight hundred and ninety-five years; and he died.
18 Jared lived one hundred and sixty-two years, and begot ^REnoch.   Jude 14, 15
19 After he begot Enoch, Jared lived eight hundred years, and had sons and daughters.
20 So all the days of Jared were nine hundred and sixty-two years; and he died.

44-A. Enoch Walked with God   ▼

21 Enoch lived sixty-five years, and begot Methuselah.
22 After he begot Methuselah, Enoch ^Rwalked with God three hundred years, and had sons and daughters.   Gen. 6:9; 17:1; 24:40
23 So all the days of Enoch were three hundred and sixty-five years.   ▲

44-A. Enoch Walked with God (Genesis 5:21-23)—"Enoch walked with God three hundred years" (v. 22). One day, as they walked together, it was as though the Lord said, "Enoch, come home and let us continue our walk in heaven." This is the way it might have happened, for the Scripture says, "Enoch walked with God; and he was not, for God took him" (v. 24). Enoch continued his "walk with God" in glory, a walk that will never end. And all this began when, one day during his life on earth, Enoch got in step with God, walking with Him for three hundred years thereafter, without interruption.

(1) To walk with God requires five things:

(a) *Righteousness.* This is not self-righteousness, which Isaiah calls "filthy rags" (Is. 64:6, page 703), but the imputed righteousness of God (Rom. 10:1-4, page 1140). Enoch was a righteous man, "strong in the Lord and in the power of His might" (Eph. 6:10, page 1192). He was "like a tree planted by the rivers of water" (Ps. 1:3, page 509), rooted and grounded in the truth (John 8:32, page 1063). "The LORD knows the way of the righteous" (Ps. 1:6, page 509), because they walk with Him in righteousness. But it is not so with the ungodly. They cannot walk with God; they are unstable in all their ways; they are like chaff in a windstorm, driven about by the doctrines of this world system, which are promulgated by the servants of Satan (John 8:44, page 1063; 2 Cor. 4:4, page 1167).

(b) *Faith.* Faith is required in the fact that God does exist and that He is the sovereign, almighty, eternal God. "For he who comes to God must believe that He is, and that He is a rewarder of those who diligently seek Him" (Heb. 11:6, page 1247). Enoch sought the Lord by faith, found Him, and walked with Him by faith (Rom. 1:17, page 1128).

(c) *Uprightness.* Enoch was governed by high moral principles and adhered to all the virtues of a true believer. "For the LORD God is a sun and shield; the LORD will give grace and glory; no good thing will He withhold from those who walk uprightly" (Ps. 84:11, page 561). Enoch walked with God uprightly and lived life abundantly (John 10:10, page 1067).

(d) *Humility.* A truly humble person will not be afflicted with that common disease known as
(Point 44-A continued on next page)

▼ **44–E. Enoch Walked All the Way to Heaven with God**

24 And ᴿEnoch walked with God; and he ▲ was not, for God ᴿtook him. 2 Kin. 2:11 • Heb. 11:5

25 Methuselah lived one hundred and eighty-seven years, and begot Lamech.

26 After he begot Lamech, Methuselah lived seven hundred and eighty-two years, and had sons and daughters.

27 So all the days of Methuselah were nine hundred and sixty-nine years; and he died.

28 Lamech lived one hundred and eighty-two years, and had a son.

29 And he called his name ᵀNoah, saying, "This one will comfort us concerning our work and the toil of our hands, because of the ground which the LORD has cursed." Lit. Rest

30 After he begot Noah, Lamech lived five hundred and ninety-five years, and had sons and daughters.

31 So all the days of Lamech were seven hundred and seventy-seven years; and he died.

32 And Noah was five hundred years old, and Noah begot Shem, Ham, and Japheth.

(Point 44-A continued from previous page)
"inflated ego." John the Baptist said of Jesus, "He must increase, but I must decrease" (John 3:30, page 1053). When you walk with God, the "I" (ego) will diminish to its proper limits and then the words of Paul will be understood: "If anyone thinks himself to be something, when he is nothing, he deceives himself" (Gal. 6:3, page 1184).

(e) *Commitment.* Total commitment is called for. This means that the whole person—spirit, soul, and body—is placed figuratively on the altar of God as a burnt sacrifice (a burnt sacrifice was completely consumed by fire). You are to be a "living sacrifice . . . that you may prove what is that good and acceptable and perfect will of God" (Rom. 12:1, 2, page 1142). Enoch knew what it meant to commit his way to the Lord (Ps. 37:5, page 533).

(2) When you walk with God:

(a) You will "fear no evil," even when He leads you through "the valley of the shadow of death" (Ps. 23:4, page 524). You will not be afraid, because you know that He is with you, and that His grace is sufficient for all of life's events (2 Cor. 12:9, page 1175).

(b) You will never walk in darkness, because "God is light and in Him is no darkness at all . . . if we walk in the light as He is in the light, we have fellowship with one another" (1 John 1:5-7, page 1278). When we walk with God, as Enoch did, we have fellowship with the Father, Son, and Holy Spirit—and all the saints of God who are walking with Him. This is heavenly fellowship, and it is forever and ever.

(c) "If you abide in My word, you are My disciples indeed. And you shall know the truth, and the truth shall make you free" (John 8:31, 32, page 1063). The Truth that sets you free is the Lord Jesus Christ (John 14:6, page 1074). To walk with God is to walk with the Lord Jesus Christ, who is the Living Word. John said, "The Word was with God, and the Word was God" (John 1:1, page 1049). Enoch walked with the Living Word.

See Hebrews 11:5, 6, page 1247, for **Point 44-B: Enoch Walked by Faith with God.**

44-E. Enoch Walked All the Way to Heaven with God (Genesis 5:24)—"Enoch walked with God; and he was not, for God took him" (v. 24). This verse says three things about Enoch that deserve our attention. Each statement is brief, direct, simple, and yet profound. To discover the depth of this verse and the riches of its simplicity, we go to the New Testament.

(1) "Enoch walked with God." As he walked by faith "he had this testimony, that he pleased God" (Heb. 11:5, page 1247). Enoch's walk with God was no secret; all who knew him must have said, "There goes a man who pleases God." He prophesied the second coming of Christ, and the judgments of God upon the ungodly in the last days (Jude 14, 15, page 1290). First, he lived his testimony; and second, he preached the good news of the coming of the Lord. What is meant when it is said that Enoch walked with God by faith?

(a) It means that he got in step with God, and made spiritual progress one step at a time; he grew in the grace and knowledge of God (2 Pet. 3:17, 18, page 1276). He was steadfast in his walk with God, all the way to heaven.

(b) It means that he could no longer go in his own way (Is. 53:6, page 693), or walk according to the course of this world system, which is satanic (Eph. 2:1, 2, page 1187). If he would walk with God, he must seek God's way and walk in it (Matt. 6:33, page 944).

(c) It implies total commitment to the revealed will of God (Rom. 12:1, 2, page 1142). Enoch's life demonstrates the good and perfect will of God. He could say with David, "I delight to do Your will, O my God" (Ps. 40:8, page 535).

(2) "Enoch walked with God; and he was not." One day Enoch vanished, disappeared, and was taken up into heaven in the presence of witnesses. When Elijah was taken up in a whirlwind, Elisha witnessed his translation (2 Kin. 2:1-13, page 355). When Jesus was taken up, the disciples were witnesses (Acts 1:9-11,

(Point 44-E continued on next page)

The Wickedness and Judgment of Man

▼ **16–A. Consequences of Sin in the Days of Noah**

6 Now it came to pass, ᴿwhen men began to multiply on the face of the earth, and daughters were born to them, *Gen. 1:28*

2 that the sons of God saw the daughters ▽ of men, that they *were* beautiful; and they ᴿtook wives for themselves of all whom they chose. *Deut. 7:3, 4*

3 And the LORD said, ᴿ"My Spirit shall not ᴿstrive* with man forever, ᴿfor he *is* indeed

6:3 LXX, Syr., Tg., Vg. *abide*

(Point 44-E continued from previous page)
page 1087). Enoch had his ungodly critics, as does anyone who walks with God. Because of them, had there been no witnesses when he was translated, there would probably have been no record of his translation. Further proof of witnesses is found in the New Testament. "By faith Enoch was taken away so that he did not see death, 'and was not found'" (Heb. 11:5, page 1247). Unbelievers may have searched for him to prove that his translation was a religious hoax. When Elisha brought word to the school of the prophets that Elijah had been translated, they doubted Elisha and formed search parties and looked in vain for him. People searched for Enoch, but he "was not found, because God had taken him."

(3) "Enoch walked with God; and he was not, for God took him." Again we go to the New Testament for a better understanding of this brief and beautiful statement, "for God took him." And we read, "By faith Enoch was taken away so that he did not see death" (Heb. 11:5, page 1247). His spirit and soul were not separated from his body of flesh. Had he died physically, his spirit and soul would have left his body, and search parties could have found it and buried it. Enoch was taken up (translated) because he pleased God by faith. Now all who please God by faith will be resurrected and caught up like Enoch at the Rapture, and will be given glorified bodies (1 Thess. 4:16, 17, page 1212). "Amen. Even so, come, Lord Jesus!" (Rev. 22:20, page 1317).

See Index, page 17, for your next study.

16-A. Consequences of Sin in the Days of Noah (Genesis 6—8)—Those who committed the sin that leads to physical death in the antediluvian age were unsaved. The whole human race, apart from Noah and his family, died prematurely. God in His grace gave them 120 years to repent, but they rejected God's message and His messenger. Therefore, when the judgment of God fell upon them they were "without excuse" (Rom. 1:20, page 1128). They committed the sin that leads to eternal separation from the mercy of God (1 Pet. 3:18-20, page 1267). The sovereign purpose of God, in the days of Noah, is clearly seen to have been twofold: first, judgment upon those who, by choice, followed a life of sin that led to eternal death; second, salvation for Noah and his family, whom God found righteous. Now let us observe

(1) What the Lord saw in the days of Noah:

(a) "The wickedness of man was great in the earth" (6:5).
(b) "The earth was filled with violence" (6:11).
(c) "All flesh had corrupted their way [life-style] on the earth" (6:12). Just before the Lord Jesus comes back to set up His kingdom, the earth will be filled with violence and moral corruption will prevail "as in the days before the flood" (Matt. 24:38, 39, page 975).

(2) How the Lord felt in the days of Noah: "And the LORD was sorry that He had made man on the earth." God felt a sense of loss because "God is love" (1 John 4:8, page 1281). "He was grieved in His heart" (6:6).

(3) What the Lord said in the days of Noah:

(a) "My Spirit shall not strive with man forever" (6:3). He was long-suffering (1 Pet. 3:20, page 1267).
(b) "I will destroy man whom I have created from the face of the earth" (6:7).
(c) "The end of all flesh has come before Me" (6:13).
(d) "Come into the ark, you and all your household" (7:1).

(4) What the Lord did in the days of Noah:

(a) God gave Noah the plans for the ark (6:14-16).
(b) God established His covenant with Noah (6:18). To accomplish His perfect will, God always chooses a person and works through him for the good of all.
(c) God filled the ark with Noah and his family, the beasts of the field, and the birds of the air (7:1-3).
(d) God shut the door of the ark. The world was shut out when Noah and his family were shut in (7:16).
(e) God sent the Flood and destroyed every living thing that was not in the ark (7:21-24).
(f) "God remembered Noah" (8:1). The Lord will never forget His own.

There is a sin that leads to eternal separation from God, His love, and His mercy. The way of sin seems right to man, but the end is death (Prov. 14:12, page 608).

See Numbers 32:6-13, page 174, for **Point 16-B: Consequences of Sin at Kadesh Barnea.**

▽ flesh; yet his days shall be one hundred and twenty years." [Gal. 5:16, 17] · 2 Thess. 2:7 · Ps. 78:39

4 There were giants on the earth in those days, and also afterward, when the sons of God came in to the daughters of men and they bore *children* to them. Those *were* the mighty men who *were* of old, men of renown.

5 Then *the LORD saw that the wickedness of man *was* great in the earth, and *that* every Rintent of the thoughts of his heart *was* only evil continually.   Gen. 8:21 · thought · all the day

6 And Rthe LORD was sorry that He had made man on the earth, and RHe was grieved in His Rheart.   1 Sam. 15:11, 29 · Is. 63:10 · Mark 3:5

7 So the LORD said, "I will Rdestroy man whom I have created from the face of the earth, both man and beast, creeping thing and birds of the air, for I am sorry that I have made them."   Gen. 7:4, 23

8 But Noah Rfound grace in the eyes of the LORD.   Gen. 19:19

Noah Pleases God

9 This is the genealogy of Noah. RNoah was a just man, Tperfect in his generations. Noah walked with God.   2 Pet. 2:5 · blameless

10 And Noah begot three sons: RShem, Ham, and Japheth.   Gen. 5:32; 7:13

11 The earth also was corrupt before God, and the earth was filled with violence.

12 So God looked upon the earth, and indeed it was corrupt; for Rall flesh had corrupted their way on the earth.   Ps. 14:1-3

13 And God said to Noah, "The end of all flesh has come before Me, for the earth is filled with violence through them; and behold, I will destroy them with the earth.

The Ark Prepared

14 "Make yourself an ark of gopherwood; make Trooms in the ark, and cover it inside and outside with pitch.   Lit. compartments or nests

6:5 So with MT, Tg.; Vg. *God;* LXX *LORD God*

15 "And this is how you shall make it: The ▽ length of the ark *shall be* Tthree hundred cubits, its width Tfifty cubits, and its height Tthirty cubits.   450 ft. · 75 ft. · 45 ft.

16 "You shall make a window for the ark, and you shall finish it to a Tcubit from above; and set the door of the ark in its side. You shall make it *with* lower, second, and third *decks.*   18 in.

17 R"And behold, I Myself am bringing Rfloodwaters on the earth, to destroy from under heaven all flesh in which *is* the breath of life; everything that *is* on the earth shall Rdie.   2 Pet. 2:5 · 2 Pet. 3:6 · Luke 16:22

18 "But I will establish My Rcovenant with you; and Ryou shall go into the ark—you, your sons, your wife, and your sons' wives with you.   Gen. 8:20—9:17; 17:7 · Gen. 7:1, 7, 13

19 "And of every living thing of all flesh you shall bring Rtwo of every *sort* into the ark, to keep *them* alive with you; they shall be male and female.   Gen. 7:2, 8, 9, 14-16

20 "Of the birds after their kind, of animals after their kind, and of every creeping thing of the earth after its kind, two of every *kind* will come to you to keep *them* alive.

21 "And you shall take for yourself of all food that is eaten, and you shall gather *it* to yourself; and it shall be food for you and for them."

45-D. Noah: A Man of Action   ▼

22 Thus Noah did; according to all that RGod commanded him, so he did.   [1 John 5:3] ▲

The Great Flood

7 Then the LORD said to Noah, "Come into the ark, you and all your household, because I have seen *that* Ryou *are* righteous before Me in this generation.   Gen. 6:9

2 "You shall take with you seven each of every Rclean animal, a male and his female;

45-D. Noah: A Man of Action (Genesis 6:22)—"Thus Noah did; according to all that God commanded him, so he did" (v. 22). Noah was a man of action—God commanded, Noah acted! (Ps. 37:5, page 533). Once he knew the will of God for his life, he obeyed. In the Genesis account of the Flood, we learn of Noah's ingrained, unwavering, active obedience to God's revealed will. He was conformed to the purpose of God (Rom. 12:1, 2, page 1142), but not to the ways of the pre-Flood world system; for he had nothing in common with that wicked generation (2 Cor. 6:14–18, page 1169). "Noah walked with God" (Gen. 6:9, above). He walked in fellowship with God and found the spiritual strength to resist the temptations of that day.

Paul tells us that all temptations are common to man; so don't think that you are the only believer that has been overtaken by temptation. You may live in a situation where there is obviously much to tempt you, or you may live where there is apparently little to tempt you. Regardless of your circumstances, you will be tempted; there is no escape. But we have good news: God has promised that He will not allow us to be tempted above our spiritual capacity to resist, and that He will make "the way of escape" (1 Cor. 10:13, page 1155). "He [the Holy Spirit] who is in you is greater than he [Satan] who is in the world" (1 John 4:4, page 1280).

Noah, a man of action, resisted the temptations of that age as he walked with God. He found:

(1) Saving grace through faith (Eph. 2:8, 9, page 1187).
(2) Justification by faith (Rom. 5:1, page 1133).
(3) Peace with God by faith (Rom. 5:1, page 1133).

(Point 45-D continued on next page)

▽ R two each of animals that *are* unclean, a male and his female;   Lev. 11 • Lev. 10:10

3 "also seven each of birds of the air, male and female, to keep T the species alive on the face of all the earth.   Lit. *seed*

4 "For after seven more days I will cause it to rain on the earth forty days and forty nights, and I will destroy from the face of the earth all living things that I have made."

5 R And Noah did according to all that the LORD commanded him.   Gen. 6:22

6 Noah *was* six hundred years old when the floodwaters were on the earth.

7 R So Noah, with his sons, his wife, and his sons' wives, went into the ark because of the waters of the flood.   Matt. 24:38

8 Of clean animals, of animals that *are* unclean, of birds, and of everything that creeps on the earth,

9 two by two they went into the ark to Noah, male and female, as God had commanded Noah.

10 And it came to pass after seven days that the waters of the flood were on the earth.

11 In the six hundredth year of Noah's life, in the second month, the seventeenth day of the month, on that day all the fountains of the great deep were broken up, and the R windows of heaven were opened.   Ps. 78:23

12 R And the rain was on the earth forty days and forty nights.   Gen. 7:4, 17

13 On the very same day Noah and Noah's sons, Shem, Ham, and Japheth, and Noah's wife and the three wives of his sons with them, entered the ark—

14 R they and every beast after its kind, all cattle after their kind, every creeping thing that creeps on the earth after its kind, and ▽ every bird after its kind, every bird of every R sort.   Gen. 6:19 • Gen. 1:21

15 And they R went into the ark to Noah, two by two, of all flesh in which *is* the breath of life.   Gen. 6:19, 20; 7:9

16 So those that entered, male and female of all flesh, went in R as God had commanded him; and the LORD shut him in.   Gen. 7:2, 3

17 Now the flood was on the earth forty days. The waters increased and lifted up the ark, and it rose high above the earth.

18 The waters prevailed and greatly increased on the earth, R and the ark moved about on the surface of the waters.   Ps. 104:26

19 And the waters prevailed exceedingly on the earth, and all the high hills under the whole heaven were covered.

20 The waters prevailed fifteen cubits upward, and the mountains were covered.

21 R And all flesh died that moved on the earth: birds and cattle and beasts and every creeping thing that creeps on the earth, and every man.   Gen. 6:7, 13, 17; 7:4

22 All in R whose nostrils *was* the breath *of the spirit of life, all that *was* on the dry *land*, died.   Gen. 2:7

23 So He destroyed all living things which were on the face of the ground: both man and cattle, creeping thing and bird of the air. They were destroyed from the earth. Only R Noah and those who *were* with him in the ark remained *alive*.   2 Pet. 2:5

24 R And the waters prevailed on the earth one hundred and fifty days.   Gen. 8:3, 4

7:22 LXX, Vg. omit *of the spirit*

(Point 45-D continued from previous page)
(4) The righteousness of God, which he preached by faith (2 Pet. 2:5, page 1274).
(5) Perfection in his generation, because he found it by faith in God (Col. 1:28, page 1203).

God commanded Noah, saying, "Make yourself an ark of gopherwood" (v. 14). He gave Noah the plans for the ark, and Noah went to work. It was a monumental undertaking in many ways:

(1) Consider the size of the ark—300 cubits long, 50 cubits wide, and 30 cubits high. But how long is a cubit? The Hebrews, Egyptians, Babylonians, Greeks, and Romans defined it differently, from 17.5 inches to 24 inches. Using an 18-inch cubit, we see that Noah's ark was 450 feet long, 75 feet wide, and 45 feet high. It has been calculated that the ark had the cubic capacity of more than 500 freight cars. It was three stories high and was divided throughout into rooms, or dens.

(2) Noah and his sons needed skilled help to build the ark. The trees had to be felled, sawn into thick boards, and dried in the sun or in a kiln. For that huge amount of lumber, much of it must have been transported many miles. The ark was covered with pitch inside and out to make it waterproof; this must have taken tons of pitch.

(3) Noah took enough supplies to last a year and ten days for his family and all the animals while in the ark, as well as enough to last until first harvest (Gen. 7:11, above; 8:13-19, page 14).

(4) Noah assumed the total cost of the ark and all the supplies. He must have been a wealthy man. Yes, it cost Noah dearly to build the ark; but consider what it would have cost him if he had not built the ark. If your faith has never cost you anything, you have faith that is dead (James 2:17, 18, page 1257). When King David wanted to buy Araunah's threshing floor to build an altar to the Lord, Araunah offered to give it to the king, and David said, "No, but I will surely buy it from you for a price; nor will I offer burnt offerings to the LORD my God with that which costs me nothing" (2 Sam. 24:24, page 323). Noah had faith that cost him every material thing, but it also gave him and his family every eternal thing—salvation by grace through faith (2 Cor. 4:18, page 1168).

See Hebrews 11:7, page 1247, for **Point 45-E: Noah: A Man of Faith.**

▽ *Noah's Deliverance*

8 Then God ᴿremembered Noah, and every living thing, and all the animals that *were* with him in the ark. ᴿAnd God made a wind to pass over the earth, and the waters subsided. Gen. 19:29 · Ex. 14:21; 15:10

2 The fountains of the deep and the windows of heaven were also stopped, and ᴿthe rain from heaven was restrained. Job 38:37

3 And the waters receded continually from the earth. At the end ᴿof the hundred and fifty days the waters decreased. Gen. 7:24

4 Then the ark rested in the seventh month, the seventeenth day of the month, on the mountains of Ararat.

5 And the waters decreased continually until the tenth month. In the tenth *month*, on the first *day* of the month, the tops of the mountains were seen.

6 So it came to pass, at the end of forty days, that Noah opened ᴿthe window of the ark which he had made. Gen. 6:16

7 Then he sent out a raven, which kept going to and fro until the waters had dried up from the earth.

8 He also sent out from himself a dove, to see if the waters had receded from the face of the ground.

9 But the dove found no resting place for the sole of her foot, and she returned into the ark to him, for the waters *were* on the face of the whole earth. So he put out his hand and took her, and drew her into the ark to himself.

10 And he waited yet another seven days, and again he sent the dove out from the ark.

11 Then the dove came to him in the evening, and behold, a freshly plucked olive leaf *was* in her mouth; and Noah knew that the waters had receded from the earth.

12 So he waited yet another seven days and sent out the dove, which did not return again to him anymore.

13 And it came to pass in the six hundred and first year, in the first *month*, the first *day* of the month, that the waters were dried up from the earth; and Noah removed the covering of the ark and looked, and indeed the surface of the ground was dry.

14 And in the second month, on the twenty-seventh day of the month, the earth was dried.

15 Then God spoke to Noah, saying,

16 "Go out of the ark, you and your wife, and your sons and your sons' wives with you.

17 "Bring out with you every living thing of all flesh that *is* with you: birds and cattle and every creeping thing that creeps on the earth, so that they may abound on the earth, and be fruitful and multiply on the earth."

18 So Noah went out, and his sons and his wife and his sons' wives with him.

19 Every animal, every creeping thing, every bird, *and* whatever creeps on the earth, according to their families, went out of the ark.

God's Covenant with Creation

20 Then Noah built an ᴿaltar to the LORD, and took of ᴿevery clean animal and of every clean bird, and offered ᴿburnt offerings on the altar. Gen. 12:7 · Lev. 11 · Ex. 10:25

21 And the LORD smelled a soothing aroma. Then the LORD said in His heart, "I will never again curse the ground for man's sake, although the imagination of man's heart *is* evil from his youth; nor will I again destroy every living thing as I have done.

22 "While the earth ᴿremains,
Seedtime and harvest,
Cold and heat,
Winter and summer,
And ᴿday and night
Shall not cease." Is. 54:9 · Jer. 33:20, 25 ▲

9 So God blessed Noah and his sons, and said to them: ᴿ"Be fruitful and multiply, and fill the earth. Gen. 1:28, 29; 8:17; 9:7, 19; 10:32

2 ᴿ"And the fear of you and the dread of you shall be on every beast of the earth, on every bird of the air, on all that move *on* the earth, and on all the fish of the sea. They are given into your hand. Ps. 8:6

3 "Every moving thing that lives shall be food for you. I have given you ᴿall things, even as the ᴿgreen herbs. Rom. 14:14, 20 · Gen. 1:29

4 ᴿ"But you shall not eat flesh with its life, *that is*, its blood. 1 Sam. 14:33, 34

5 "Surely for your lifeblood I will demand *a reckoning*; from the hand of every beast I will require it, and ᴿfrom the hand of man. From the hand of every ᴿman's brother I will require the life of man. Gen. 4:9, 10 · Acts 17:26

6 "Whoever ᴿsheds man's blood,
By man his blood shall be shed;
ᴿFor in the image of God
He made man. Lev. 24:17 · Gen. 1:26, 27

7 And as for you, ᴿbe fruitful and multiply;
Bring forth abundantly in the earth
And multiply in it." Gen. 9:1, 19

8 Then God spoke to Noah and to his sons with him, saying:

9 "And as for Me, ᴿbehold, I establish ᴿMy covenant with you and with your ᵀdescendants after you, Gen. 6:18 · Is. 54:9 · Lit. *seed*

10 ᴿ"and with every living creature that *is* with you: the birds, the cattle, and every beast of the earth with you, of all that go out of the ark, every beast of the earth. Ps. 145:9

11 "Thus ᴿI establish My covenant with you: Never again shall all flesh be cut off by the waters of the flood; never again shall there be a flood to destroy the earth." Is. 54:9

12 And God said: ᴿ"This *is* the sign of the covenant which I make between Me and you,

and every living creature that is with you, for perpetual generations: Gen. 9:13, 17; 17:11

13 "I set ᴿMy rainbow in the cloud, and it shall be for the sign of the covenant between Me and the earth.   Ezek. 1:28

14 "It shall be, when I bring a cloud over the earth, that the rainbow shall be seen in the cloud;

15 "and ᴿI will remember My covenant which is between Me and you and every living creature of all flesh; the waters shall never again become a flood to destroy all flesh.   Lev. 26:42, 45

16 "The rainbow shall be in the cloud, and I will look on it to remember the everlasting covenant between God and every living creature of all flesh that is on the earth."

17 And God said to Noah, "This is the sign of the covenant which I have established between Me and all flesh that is on the earth."

Noah and His Sons

18 Now the sons of Noah who went out of the ark were Shem, Ham, and Japheth. ᴿAnd Ham was the father of Canaan.   Gen. 9:25-27

19 These three were the sons of Noah, and from these the whole earth was populated.

20 And Noah began to be ᴿa farmer, and he planted a vineyard.   Gen. 3:19, 23; 4:2

21 Then he drank of the wine and was drunk, and became uncovered in his tent.

22 And Ham, the father of Canaan, saw the nakedness of his father, and told his two brothers outside.

23 But Shem and Japheth took a garment, laid it on both their shoulders, and went backward and covered the nakedness of their father. Their faces were turned away, and they did not see their father's nakedness.

24 So Noah awoke from his wine, and knew what his younger son had done to him.

25 Then he said:

ᴿ"Cursed be Canaan;   Deut. 27:16
A ᴿservant of servants   Josh. 9:23
He shall be to his brethren."

26 And he said:

ᴿ"Blessed be the LORD,   Gen. 14:20; 24:27
The God of Shem,
And may Canaan be his servant.

27 May God enlarge Japheth,
And may he dwell in the tents of Shem;
And may Canaan be his servant."

28 And Noah lived after the flood three hundred and fifty years.

29 So all the days of Noah were nine hundred and fifty years; and he died.

Nations Descended from Noah

14-D. What Does the Bible Teach About ▼ Race?

10 Now this is the genealogy of the sons of Noah: Shem, Ham, and Japheth. And sons were born to them after the flood.

2 ᴿThe sons of Japheth were Gomer, Magog, Madai, Javan, Tubal, Meshech, and Tiras.   1 Chr. 1:5-7

3 The sons of Gomer were Ashkenaz, *Riphath, and Togarmah.

10:3 Diphath, 1 Chr. 1:6

14-D. What Does the Bible Teach About Race? (Genesis 10:1-5)—"From these the coastland peoples of the Gentiles were separated into their lands" (v. 5). The gradual spread of humanity over the globe, and its division into races, is shown in its major parts by the Bible. Other questions remain for us to search out. Through the centuries some persons have uttered both unbiblical and frequently hate-filled declarations on racial issues. The believer must, however, seek the light of Christ and the Bible as his or her guide, and reject the false pronouncements of all others.

(1) All mankind originated from a single God-created pair. "Eve . . . was the mother of all living" (Gen. 3:20, page 7). Some anthropologists today, although not Bible-believers, acknowledge that all humans are derived from an original pair. The Bible clearly states that this is so. Man did not evolve originally on different continents from separate, related human couples, thus producing the races. Neither did the races originate by interbreeding between human and animal. No, all people, according to the Scriptures, came from our first parents.

(2) Early men lived long lives and had many children. Genesis 5 (page 9) and 11 (page 16) supply the early genealogy lists, which very likely are purposely abbreviated, as is the genealogy in Matthew 1:1 (page 930): "Jesus Christ, the Son of David [1000 B.C.], the Son of Abraham [2000 B.C.]." Note that in Genesis 5, from Adam to the Flood, many men were commonly living 900 years. In Genesis 11, after the Flood, until Abraham (2000 B.C.), life spans are shown declining steadily from 600 to 150 years.

(3) After the Flood, migrations populated the world. "For in his days the earth was divided" (Gen. 10:25, page 16). The above verse may speak of a period of great human migration, or of a period of geologic-type changes on the land masses of the earth. If all humans could descend from one original pair, then they could also descend after the Flood from three pairs—the sons of Noah and their wives. Genesis 10 and 11 record these early migrations.

See Ecclesiastes 7:29, page 630, for **Point 14-E: What Are the Various States of Man with God?**

▽ 4 The sons of Javan were Elishah, Tarshish, Kittim, and *Dodanim.

5 From these the coastland peoples of the Gentiles were separated into their lands, everyone according to his language, accord-
▲ ing to their families, into their nations.

6 RThe sons of Ham were Cush, Mizraim, TPut, and Canaan.   1 Chr. 1:8-16 • Or Phut

7 The sons of Cush were Seba, Havilah, Sabtah, Raamah, and Sabtechah; and the sons of Raamah were Sheba and Dedan.

8 Cush begot RNimrod; he began to be a mighty one on the earth.   Mic. 5:6

9 He was a mighty hunter Rbefore the LORD; therefore it is said, "Like Nimrod the mighty hunter before the LORD."   Gen. 21:20

10 RAnd the beginning of his kingdom was RBabel, Erech, Accad, and Calneh, in the land of Shinar.   Mic. 5:6 • Gen. 11:9

11 From that land he went Rto Assyria and built Nineveh, Rehoboth Ir, Calah,   Mic. 5:6

12 and Resen between Nineveh and Calah (that is the principal city).

13 Mizraim begot Ludim, Anamim, Lehabim, Naphtuhim,

14 Pathrusim, and Casluhim (from whom came the Philistines and Caphtorim).

15 Canaan begot Sidon his firstborn, and RHeth;   Gen. 23:3

16 Rthe Jebusite, the Amorite, and the Girgashite;   Gen. 14:7; 15:19-21

17 the Hivite, the Arkite, and the Sinite;

18 the Arvadite, the Zemarite, and the Hamathite. Afterward the families of the Canaanites were dispersed.

19 And the border of the Canaanites was from Sidon as you go toward Gerar, as far as Gaza; then as you go toward Sodom, Gomorrah, Admah, and Zeboiim, as far as Lasha.

20 These were the sons of Ham, according to their families, according to their languages, in their lands and in their nations.

21 And children were born also to Shem, the father of all the children of Eber, the brother of Japheth the elder.

22 The sons of Shem were Elam, Asshur, RArphaxad, Lud, and Aram.   Luke 3:36

23 The sons of Aram were Uz, Hul, Gether, and *Mash.

24 *Arphaxad begot RSalah, and Salah begot Eber.   Gen. 11:12

25 RTo Eber were born two sons: the name of one was TPeleg, for in his days the earth was divided; and his brother's name was Joktan.   1 Chr. 1:19 • Lit. Division

26 Joktan begot Almodad, Sheleph, Hazarmaveth, Jerah,

27 Hadoram, Uzal, Diklah,

28 TObal, Abimael, Sheba,   Ebal, 1 Chr. 1:22

10:4 Sam. Rodanim and 1 Chr. 1:7
10:23 LXX Meshech and 1 Chr. 1:17
10:24 So with MT, Vg., Tg.; LXX Arphaxad begot Cainan, and Cainan begot Salah (cf. Luke 3:35, 36)

29 Ophir, Havilah, and Jobab. All these were the sons of Joktan.

30 And their dwelling place was from Mesha as you go toward Sephar, the mountain of the east.

31 These were the sons of Shem, according to their families, according to their languages, in their lands, according to their nations.

32 These were the families of the sons of Noah, according to their generations, in their nations; and from these the nations were divided on the earth after the flood.

The Tower of Babel

11 Now the whole earth had one language and one Tspeech.   Lit. lip

2 And it came to pass, as they journeyed from the east, that they found a plain in the land of Shinar, and they dwelt there.

3 Then they said to one another, "Come, let us make bricks and Tbake them thoroughly." They had brick for stone, and they had asphalt for mortar.   Lit. burn

4 And they said, "Come, let us build ourselves a city, and a tower whose top is in the heavens; let us make a Rname for ourselves, lest we Rbe scattered abroad over the face of the whole earth."   Gen. 6:4 • Deut. 4:27

5 RBut the LORD came down to see the city and the tower which the sons of men had built.   Gen. 18:21

6 And the LORD said, "Indeed Rthe people are one and they all have Rone language, and this is what they begin to do; now nothing that they Rpropose to do will be withheld from them.   Gen. 9:19 • Gen. 11:1 • Ps. 2:1

7 "Come, Rlet Us go down and there Rconfuse their language, that they may not understand one another's speech."   Gen. 1:26 • Ex. 4:11

8 So Rthe LORD scattered them abroad from there over the face of all the earth, and they ceased building the city.   [Luke 1:51]

9 Therefore its name is called TBabel, Rbecause there the LORD confused the language of all the earth; and from there the LORD scattered them abroad over the face of all the earth.   Lit. Confusion, Babylon • 1 Cor. 14:23

Shem's Descendants

10 RThis is the genealogy of Shem: Shem was one hundred years old, and begot Arphaxad two years after the flood.   Gen. 10:22-25

11 After he begot Arphaxad, Shem lived five hundred years, and begot sons and daughters.

12 Arphaxad lived thirty-five years, Rand begot Salah.   Luke 3:35

13 After he begot Salah, Arphaxad lived four hundred and three years, and begot sons and daughters.

14 Salah lived thirty years, and begot Eber.

15 After he begot Eber, Salah lived four

hundred and three years, and begot sons and daughters.

16 ᴿEber lived thirty-four years, and begot ᴿPeleg.   1 Chr. 1:19 • Luke 3:35

17 After he begot Peleg, Eber lived four hundred and thirty years, and begot sons and daughters.

18 Peleg lived thirty years, and begot Reu.

19 After he begot Reu, Peleg lived two hundred and nine years, and begot sons and daughters.

20 Reu lived thirty-two years, and begot ᴿSerug.   Luke 3:35

21 After he begot Serug, Reu lived two hundred and seven years, and begot sons and daughters.

22 Serug lived thirty years, and begot Nahor.

23 After he begot Nahor, Serug lived two hundred years, and begot sons and daughters.

24 Nahor lived twenty-nine years, and begot ᴿTerah.   Josh. 24:2

25 After he begot Terah, Nahor lived one hundred and nineteen years, and begot sons and daughters.

26 Now Terah lived seventy years, and begot ᴿAbram, Nahor, and Haran.   Gen. 17:5

Terah's Descendants

27 This *is* the genealogy of Terah: Terah begot ᴿAbram, Nahor, and Haran. Haran begot Lot.   Gen. 11:31; 17:5

28 And Haran died before his father Terah in his native land, in Ur of the Chaldeans.

29 Then Abram and Nahor took wives: the name of Abram's wife *was* ᴿSarai, and the name of Nahor's wife, ᴿMilcah, the daughter of Haran the father of Milcah and the father of Iscah.   Gen. 17:15; 20:12 • Gen. 22:20, 23; 24:15

30 But Sarai was barren; she had no child.

▼ 34-A. From Ur of the Chaldeans to the Exodus

31 And Terah took his son Abram and his grandson Lot, the son of Haran, and his daughter-in-law Sarai, his son Abram's wife, and they went out with them from Ur of the Chaldeans to go to the land of Canaan; and they came to Haran and dwelt there.

32 So the days of Terah were two hundred and five years, and Terah died in Haran.

Promises to Abram   ▽

12 Now the ᴿLᴏʀᴅ had said to Abram:

"Get ᴿout of your country,
From your family   Acts 7:2, 3 • Gen. 13:9
And from your father's house,
To a land that I will show you.
2 ᴿI will make you a great nation;   Deut. 26:5
ᴿI will bless you   Gen. 22:17; 24:35
And make your name great;
ᴿAnd you shall be a blessing.   Gen. 28:4
3 I will bless those who bless you,
And I will curse him who curses you;
And in ᴿyou all the families of the earth
shall be ᴿblessed."   Gal. 3:8 • Is. 41:27

4 So Abram departed as the Lᴏʀᴅ had spoken to him, and Lot went with him. And Abram *was* seventy-five years old when he departed from Haran.

5 Then Abram took Sarai his wife and Lot his brother's son, and all their possessions that they had gathered, and the ᵀpeople whom they had acquired in Haran, and they departed to go to the land of Canaan. So they came to the land of Canaan.   Lit. *souls*

6 Abram passed through the land to the place of Shechem, as far as ᵀthe terebinth tree of Moreh. ᴿAnd the Canaanites *were* then in the land.   Or *Alon Moreh* • Gen. 10:18, 19

7 Then the Lᴏʀᴅ appeared to Abram and said, "To your descendants I will give this land." And there he built an altar to the Lᴏʀᴅ, who had appeared to him.

8 And he moved from there to the mountain east of Bethel, and he pitched his tent *with* Bethel on the west and Ai on the east; there he built an altar to the Lᴏʀᴅ and ᴿcalled on the name of the Lᴏʀᴅ.   Gen. 4:26; 13:4; 21:33

9 So Abram journeyed, going on still toward the ᵀSouth.   Heb. *Negev* ▲

Abram in Egypt

10 Now there was a famine in the land, and Abram went down to Egypt to dwell there, for the famine *was* severe in the land.

11 And it came to pass, when he was close to entering Egypt, that he said to Sarai his wife, "Indeed I know that you *are* ᴿa woman of beautiful countenance.   Gen. 12:14; 26:7; 29:17

12 "Therefore it will happen, when the Egyptians see you, that they will say, 'This *is*

34-A. From Ur of the Chaldeans to the Exodus (about 600 years) (Genesis 11:31—12:9)—There were six stages of Abraham's journeys that show his growth in obedience to God's will:

(1) From Ur of the Chaldeans to Haran. His father Terah and his nephew Lot traveled with him. He thus left his father's house, but not his father (11:31, 32).

(2) From Haran to Shechem, the center of Canaan. Terah died in Haran, but Lot continued on with Abraham, who thus had left his country but not his family. At Shechem the Lord appeared to Abraham and promised that He would give the land of Canaan to Abraham's children. There Abraham built his first altar to the Lord (12:7).

(Point 34-A continued on next page)

his wife'; and they ^Rwill kill me, but they will let you live. Gen. 20:11; 26:7

13 "Please say you *are* my sister, that it may be well with me for your sake, and that ^TI may live because of you." Lit. *my soul*

14 So it was, when Abram came into Egypt, that the Egyptians saw the woman, that she *was* very beautiful.

15 The princes of Pharaoh also saw her and commended her to Pharaoh. And the woman was taken to Pharaoh's house.

16 He treated Abram well for her sake. He had sheep, oxen, male donkeys, male and female servants, female donkeys, and camels.

17 But the LORD ^Rplagued Pharaoh and his house with great plagues because of Sarai, Abram's wife. 1 Chr. 16:21

18 And Pharaoh called Abram and said, "What *is* this you have done to me? Why did you not tell me that she *was* your wife?

19 "Why did you say, 'She *is* my sister'? I might have taken her as my wife. Now therefore, here is your wife; take *her* and go your way."

20 ^RSo Pharaoh commanded *his* men concerning him; and they sent him away, with his wife and all that he had. [Prov. 21:1]

Abram Inherits Canaan

13 Then Abram went up from Egypt, he and his wife and all that he had, and Lot with him, ^Rto the ^TSouth. Gen. 12:9 · Heb. *Negev*

2 ^RAbram *was* very rich in livestock, in silver, and in gold. Gen. 24:35; 26:14

3 And he went on his journey ^Rfrom the South as far as Bethel, to the place where his tent had been at the beginning, between Bethel and Ai, Gen. 12:8, 9

4 to the ^Rplace of the altar which he had made there at first. And there Abram called on the name of the LORD. Gen. 12:7, 8; 21:33

5 Lot also, who went with Abram, had flocks and herds and tents.

6 Now ^Rthe land was not able to ^Tsupport them, that they might dwell together, for their possessions were so great that they could not dwell together. Gen. 36:7 · Lit. *bear*

7 And there was ^Rstrife between the herdsmen of Abram's livestock and the herdsmen of Lot's livestock. The Canaanites and the Perizzites then dwelt in the land. Gen. 26:20

8 So Abram said to Lot, ^R"Please let there be no strife between you and me, and between my herdsmen and your herdsmen; for we *are* brethren. 1 Cor. 6:7

(Point 34-A continued from previous page)

(3) From Shechem to Bethel ("house of God"). Here Abraham built his second altar and called upon the name of the Lord (12:8).

(4) From Bethel to Egypt, because there was a famine in the land of Canaan. This was God's way of testing Abraham's faith. He failed the test by going into Egypt, in disobedience to God. He built no altar in Egypt or Babylonia. For Abraham to be out of Canaan was to be in disobedience, out of the will of God. Only in the perfect will of God can man truly worship the Lord (Rom. 12:1, 2, page 1142). It is better to endure trials, accepting God's will, than to attempt our own limited solution (Gen. 12:10–20, page 17).

(5) From Egypt back to Bethel. Abraham went back to the house of God, back to worshiping at the altar of God, and back to obeying the will of God. At Bethel Lot was separated from Abraham. For the first time since the Lord called Abraham out of Ur of the Chaldeans, he fully obeyed the Lord. He was separated from his country and his family, and from his father and his father's house (Gen. 13:1–18, page 18; cf. Rom. 12:1, 2, page 1142).

(6) From Bethel to Hebron. Here he established roots, and Hebron became home. He made short journeys away, but always returned. Ten important events occurred in or near Hebron:

(a) Ishmael, his first son, was born to Hagar, Sarah's maid, in disregard of God's intention to provide a son by Sarah (Gen. 16:1–16, page 21).

(b) Isaac, his second son, was born to Sarah. God chose Isaac over Ishmael to be Abraham's heir (Gen. 17:15–19, page 22; 21:1–8, page 25). This meant that the line of Christ would run through Isaac.

(c) Isaac was presented for offering on an altar of sacrifice. This was Abraham's greatest test of faith, and he did not fail (Gen. 22:1–14, page 26; Heb. 11:17–19, page 1249). Positive, unwavering, active, obedient faith always honors God, and God in turn honors that quality of faith. The lesson is wonderful: when you are tested, and there seems to be no way out, obey God and He will make a way.

(d) Sarah died and was buried in Hebron (Gen. 23:1–20, page 28).

(e) Isaac married Rebekah (Gen. 24:1–67, page 29).

(f) Abraham married Keturah, who bore him six sons (Gen. 25:1–6, page 31).

(g) Abraham, at 175 years of age, died and was buried beside Sarah (Gen. 25:7–11, page 31).

(h) Esau and Jacob were born to Isaac and Rebekah (Gen. 25:24–26, page 31). The line of Christ was to run through Jacob (Gen. 27:1–40, page 33; Heb. 12:16, 17, page 1250).

(i) To Jacob were born twelve sons, from whom came the twelve tribes of Israel (Gen. 29:31—30:24, page 36).

(j) Jacob's family obeyed the Lord and departed for Egypt (Gen. 46:1–7, page 52). With him went his twelve sons and their families, seventy in all. In Egypt they and their offspring remained for 430 years (Ex. 12:40, page 71), most of it in slavery. But in Egypt God blessed them, and they became a great nation (Ex. 1:1–22, page 59).

See Exodus 12:37–51, page 71, for **Point 34-B: From the Exodus to the Crossing of Jordan.**

9 "Is not the whole land before you? Please separate from me. If you take the left, then I will go to the right; or, if you go to the right, then I will go to the left."

10 And Lot lifted his eyes and saw all the plain of Jordan, that it was well watered everywhere (before the LORD ᴿdestroyed Sodom and Gomorrah) ᴿlike the garden of the LORD, like the land of Egypt as you go toward ᴿZoar.   Gen. 19:24 · Gen. 2:8, 10 · Deut. 34:3

11 Then Lot chose for himself all the plain of Jordan, and Lot journeyed east. And they separated from each other.

12 Abram dwelt in the land of Canaan, and Lot dwelt in the cities of the plain and pitched his tent even as far as Sodom.

13 But the men of Sodom were exceedingly wicked and sinful against the LORD.

14 And the LORD said to Abram, after Lot ᴿhad separated from him: "Lift your eyes now and look from the place where you are— ᴿnorthward, southward, eastward, and westward;   Gen. 13:11 · Gen. 28:14

15 "for all the land which you see I give to you and your *descendants forever.

16 "And I will make your descendants as the dust of the earth; so that if a man could number the dust of the earth, then your descendants also could be numbered.

17 "Arise, walk in the land through its length and its width, for I give it to you."

18 Then Abram moved his tent, and went and ᴿdwelt by ᵀthe terebinth trees of Mamre, which are in Hebron, and built an altar there to the LORD.   Gen. 14:13 · Or Alon Mamre

Lot's Captivity and Rescue

14 And it came to pass in the days of Amraphel king of Shinar, Arioch king of Ellasar, Chedorlaomer king of Elam, and Tidal king of ᵀnations,   Heb. goyim

2 that they made war with Bera king of Sodom, Birsha king of Gomorrah, Shinab king of Admah, Shemeber king of Zeboiim, and the king of Bela (that is, Zoar).

3 All these joined together in the Valley of Siddim ᴿ(that is, the Salt Sea).   Num. 34:12

4 Twelve years they served Chedorlaomer, and in the thirteenth year they rebelled.

5 In the fourteenth year Chedorlaomer and the kings that were with him came and attacked the Rephaim in Ashteroth Karnaim, ᴿthe Zuzim in Ham, ᴿthe Emim in Shaveh Kiriathaim,   Deut. 2:20 · Deut. 2:10

6 ᴿand the Horites in their mountain of Seir, as far as El Paran, which is by the wilderness.   Deut. 2:12, 22

7 Then they turned back and came to En Mishpat (that is, Kadesh), and attacked all the country of the Amalekites, and also the Amorites who dwelt in Hazezon Tamar.

8 And the king of Sodom, the king of

13:15 Lit. seed

Gomorrah, the king of Admah, the king of Zeboiim, and the king of Bela (that is, Zoar) went out and joined together in battle in the Valley of Siddim

9 against Chedorlaomer king of Elam, Tidal king of ᵀnations, Amraphel king of Shinar, and Arioch king of Ellasar—four kings against five.   Heb. goyim

10 Now the Valley of Siddim was full of ᴿasphalt pits; and the kings of Sodom and Gomorrah fled; some fell there, and the remainder fled to the mountains.   Gen. 11:3

11 Then they took ᴿall the goods of Sodom and Gomorrah, and all their provisions, and went their way.   Gen. 14:16, 21

12 They also took Lot, Abram's ᴿbrother's son ᴿwho dwelt in Sodom, and his goods, and departed.   Gen. 11:27; 12:5 · Gen. 13:12

13 Then one who had escaped came and told Abram the Hebrew, for he dwelt by ᵀthe terebinth trees of Mamre the Amorite, brother of Eshcol and brother of Aner; and they were allies with Abram.   Or Alon Mamre

14 Now when Abram heard that ᴿhis brother was taken captive, he armed his three hundred and eighteen trained servants who were born in his own house, and went in pursuit as far as Dan.   Gen. 13:8; 14:12

15 He divided his forces against them by night, and he and his servants attacked them and pursued them as far as Hobah, which is ᵀnorth of Damascus.   to the left of

16 So he brought back all the goods, and also brought back his brother Lot and his goods, as well as the women and the people.

17 And the king of Sodom went out to meet him at the Valley of Shaveh (that is, the ᴿKing's Valley), ᴿafter his return from ᵀthe defeat of Chedorlaomer and the kings who were with him.   2 Sam. 18:18 · Heb. 7:1 · Lit. striking

Abram and Melchizedek

18 Then Melchizedek king of Salem brought out bread and wine; he was ᴿthe priest of ᴿGod Most High.   Ps. 110:4 · Acts 16:17

19 And he blessed him and said:

"Blessed be Abram of God Most High,
    ᴿPossessor of heaven and earth;   Gen. 14:22
20 And ᴿblessed be God Most High,
    Who has delivered your enemies into
        your hand."   Gen. 24:27

And he ᴿgave him a tithe of all.   Heb. 7:4

21 Now the king of Sodom said to Abram, "Give me the ᵀpersons, and take the goods for yourself."   Lit. souls

22 But Abram said to the king of Sodom, "I have raised my hand to the LORD, God Most High, the Possessor of heaven and earth,

23 "that ᴿI will take nothing, from a thread to a sandal strap, and that I will not take anything that is yours, lest you should say, 'I have made Abram rich'—   2 Kin. 5:16

24 "except only what the young men have

eaten, and the portion of the men who went with me: Aner, Eshcol, and Mamre; let them take their portion."

God's Covenant with Abram

▼ 27-C. Fear Not: God Is Your Protector

15 After these things the word of the LORD came to Abram in a vision, saying, "Do not be afraid, Abram. I *am* your ▲ shield, your exceedingly great reward."

2 But Abram said, "Lord GOD, what will You give me, seeing I go childless, and the heir of my house *is* Eliezer of Damascus?"

3 Then Abram said, "Look, You have given me no offspring; indeed ᵀone born in my house is my heir!"   *a servant, Gen. 14:14*

4 And behold, the word of the LORD *came* to him, saying, "This one shall not be your heir, but one who ᴿwill come from your own body shall be your heir."   2 Sam. 7:12

5 Then He brought him outside and said, "Look now toward heaven, and ᴿcount the ᴿstars if you are able to number them." And

He said to him, ᴿ"So shall your ᴿdescendants be."   Ps. 147:4 · Jer. 33:22 · Ex. 32:13 · Gen. 17:19

6 And he believed in the LORD, and He accounted it to him for righteousness.

7 Then He said to him, "I *am* the LORD, who brought you out of Ur of the Chaldeans, to give you this land to inherit it."

8 And he said, "Lord GOD, ᴿhow shall I know that I will inherit it?"   Luke 1:18

9 So He said to him, "Bring Me a three-year-old heifer, a three-year-old female goat, a three-year-old ram, a turtledove, and a young pigeon."

10 Then he brought all these to Him and ᴿcut them in two, down the middle, and placed each piece opposite the other; but he did not cut ᴿthe birds in two. Jer. 34:18 · Lev. 1:17

11 And when the vultures came down on the carcasses, Abram drove them away.

12 Now when the sun was going down, a deep sleep fell upon Abram; and behold, horror *and* great darkness fell upon him.

13 Then He said to Abram: "Know certainly

27-C. Fear Not: God Is Your Protector (Genesis 15:1)—"After these things the word of the LORD came to Abram in a vision" (v. 1). This was the fifth time the Lord manifested Himself to Abram—later named Abraham (Gen. 17:5, page 22).

(1) The first manifestation was in Ur of the Chaldeans (Gen. 11:31, page 17; cf. Acts 7:1-4, page 1096).

(2) The second manifestation was in Haran where the Lord reaffirmed His call and promise to Abram (Gen. 12:1-4, page 17).

(3) The third manifestation was in Canaan, the promised land (Gen. 12:7, page 17).

(4) The fourth manifestation was in Canaan, after Lot was separated from him (Gen. 13:14, 15, page 19).

(5) The fifth manifestation was in Hebron. After Lot was separated from Abram, the latter moved his herd and all his servants away to Hebron, which became home to this pilgrim. Because this great man of faith was now experiencing fear, the Lord appeared to Abram, saying, "Do not be afraid, Abram. I am your shield, your exceedingly great reward" (v. 1). Why was Abram afraid? What did he fear? Abram was the friend of God. He talked with God person-to-person, as the Lord manifested Himself to him, but he still was afraid. He is the only man in the Bible called God's friend, yet he was afraid.

We must go back to chapter 14 (page 19), to understand Abram's fear. Chedorlaomer was king of Elam, a country east of Babylon. He was allied with three other ruthless kings. Five other kings of the Jordan valley, including the kings of Sodom and Gomorrah, had paid tribute to Chedorlaomer for twelve years. In the thirteenth year they rebelled (Gen. 14:1-4, page 19). In the fourteenth year these four kings, with their armies, invaded the Jordan valley, sacked Sodom and Gomorrah, defeated their armies, took all their wealth, and captured women and men, including Abram's nephew Lot. When the news reached Abram, he armed his 318 servants and pursued the numerically superior army into Dan. By night he divided his 318 men, then attacked the army while they were sleeping and defeated them. The Word of God tells us that when he returned from the slaughter, he brought back the captives and all the wealth they had taken.

Now we can answer the question, "What did Abram fear?" Most likely he feared reprisal. He had defeated an army; he had humiliated them with 318 servants—perhaps men without experience in battle. He feared that these four vanquished kings would return and invade Hebron. He was afraid, and rightly so, from the human standpoint. But God appeared to him and said, "Do not be afraid, Abram. I am your shield." In effect, God was saying, "I am your protector. Abram, you don't have to fear those barbarians, those wicked, ruthless kings. I am God Almighty; I will shield you; I will keep My promises and make you a great nation; I will give this land to your descendants. Abram, don't fear!"

Then the Lord said, "[I am] your exceedingly great reward." Abram, returning from the battle, was approached by the king of Sodom, who came out and told Abram to keep all the wealth that he had recovered—leaving him only with the people he had rescued. Abram replied that he would not take even a shoelace "lest you should say, 'I have made Abram rich'" (Gen. 14:23, page 19). Abram would not give anyone the opportunity to take credit for the way in which God had blessed him. God had blessed Abram and made him one of the richest men of all times. Abram honored God and sought only His glory. For Abram's faithfulness God rewarded him with heaven's highest honor: "I am your shield, your exceedingly great reward."

See 2 Kings 6:16, page 360, for **Point 27-D: Fear Not: God Is Your Power.**

Rthat your descendants will be strangers in a land *that is* not theirs, and will serve them, and Rthey will afflict them four hundred years.   Ex. 1:11 · Ex. 12:40

14 "And also the nation whom they serve RI will judge; afterward Rthey shall come out with great possessions.   Ex. 6:6 · Ex. 12:36

15 "Now as for you, you shall Tgo to your fathers in peace; you shall be buried at a good old age.   Die and join your ancestors

16 "But Rin the fourth generation they shall return here, for the iniquity Rof the Amorites *is* not yet complete."   Ex. 12:41 · 1 Kin. 21:26

17 And it came to pass, when the sun went down and it was dark, that behold, there appeared a smoking oven and a burning torch that passed between those pieces.

18 On the same day the LORD Rmade a covenant with Abram, saying: Gen. 24:7

R"To your descendants I have given this land, from the river of Egypt to the great river, the River Euphrates—   Gen. 12:7; 17:8

19 "the Kenites, the Kenezzites, the Kadmonites,

20 "the Hittites, the Perizzites, the Rephaim,

21 "the Amorites, the Canaanites, the Girgashites, and the Jebusites."

Hagar and Ishmael

16 Now Sarai, Abram's wife, had borne him no *children.* And she had an Egyptian maidservant whose name was Hagar.

2 So Sarai said to Abram, "See now, the LORD has restrained me from bearing *children.* Please, go in to my maid; perhaps I shall Tobtain children by her." And Abram heeded the voice of Sarai.   Lit. *be built up from*

3 Then Sarai, Abram's wife, took Hagar her maid, the Egyptian, and gave her to her husband Abram to be his wife, after Abram had dwelt ten years in the land of Canaan.

4 So he went in to Hagar, and she conceived. And when she saw that she had conceived, her mistress became Rdespised in her eyes.   [Prov. 30:21, 23]

5 Then Sarai said to Abram, "My wrong *be* upon you! I gave my maid into your embrace; and when she saw that she had conceived, I became despised in her eyes. The LORD judge between you and me."

6 So Abram said to Sarai, "Indeed your maid *is* in your hand; do to her as you please." And when Sarai dealt harshly with her, Rshe fled from her presence.   Ex. 2:15

7 Now the Angel of the LORD found her by a spring of water in the wilderness, by the spring on the way to RShur.   Ex. 15:22

8 And He said, "Hagar, Sarai's maid, where have you come from, and where are you going?" She said, "I am fleeing from the presence of my mistress Sarai."

9 The Angel of the LORD said to her, "Return to your mistress, and Rsubmit yourself under her hand."   [Titus 2:9]

10 Then the Angel of the LORD said to her, R"I will multiply your descendants exceedingly, so that they shall not be counted for multitude."   Gen. 17:20

11 And the Angel of the LORD said to her:

"Behold, you *are* with child,
And you shall bear a son.
You shall call his name TIshmael,
Because the LORD has heard your
    affliction.   Lit. *God Hears*

12 RHe shall be a wild man;
His hand *shall be* against every man,
And every man's hand against him.
RAnd he shall dwell in the presence of all
    his brethren."   Gen. 21:20 · Gen. 25:18

13 Then she called the name of the LORD who spoke to her, You-Are-Tthe-God-Who-Sees; for she said, "Have I also here seen Him Rwho sees me?"   Heb. *El Roi* · Gen. 31:42

14 Therefore the well was called T Beer Lahai Roi; observe, *it is* between Kadesh and Bered.   Lit. *Well of the One Who Lives and Sees Me*

15 So Hagar bore Abram a son; and Abram named his son, whom Hagar bore, Ishmael.

16 Abram *was* eighty-six years old when Hagar bore Ishmael to Abram.

The Sign of the Covenant

5-A. The Sovereignty of God Defined   ▼

17 When Abram was ninety-nine years old, the LORD appeared to Abram and said to him, "I am TAlmighty God; walk before Me and be blameless.   Heb. *El Shaddai* ▲

2 "And I will make My Rcovenant between Me and you, and Rwill multiply you exceedingly."   Gen. 15:18 · Gen. 12:2; 13:16; 15:5; 18:18

5-A. The Sovereignty of God Defined (Genesis 17:1)—It is impossible for the finite mind to fully comprehend the sovereignty of God. When He appeared to Abraham He said, "I am Almighty God" (v. 1). We can only know Almighty God as He is revealed to us in His infallible Word. Moses said, "The secret things belong to the LORD our God, but those things which are revealed belong to us and to our children forever, that we may do all the words of this law" (Deut. 29:29, page 208). Only eternity will be long enough for us to understand all there is to know about our sovereign God. Until then, we must be satisfied with "those things which are revealed" and wait for the complete revelation of His glory when He returns to this planet.

Therefore, to attempt to explain the sovereignty of God is an attempt to put into words the inexplicable. We must search God's Word for "those things which are revealed" that will help us to begin to grasp His

(Point 5-A continued on next page)

3 Then Abram fell on his face, and God talked with him, saying:

4 "As for Me, behold, My covenant is with you, and you shall be ᴿa father of ᵀmany nations.   [Rom. 4:11, 12, 16] • Lit. *multitude of nations*

5 "No longer shall your name be called Abram, but your name shall be Abraham; for I have made you a father of many nations.

6 "I will make you exceedingly fruitful; and I will make ᴿnations of you, and ᴿkings shall come from you.   Gen. 17:16; 35:11 • Matt. 1:6

7 "And I will ᴿestablish My covenant between Me and you and your descendants after you in their generations, for an everlasting covenant, to be God to you and ᴿyour descendants after you.   [Gal. 3:17] • Rom. 9:8

8 "Also I give to you and your descendants after you the land in which you are a stranger, all the land of Canaan, as an everlasting possession; and I will be their God."

9 And God said to Abraham: "As for you, ᴿyou shall keep My covenant, you and your descendants after you throughout their generations.   Ex. 19:5

10 "This is My covenant which you shall keep, between Me and you and your descendants after you: ᴿEvery male child among you shall be circumcised;   Acts 7:8

11 "and you shall be circumcised in the flesh of your foreskins, and it shall be a sign of the covenant between Me and you.

12 "He who is eight days old among you ᴿshall be circumcised, every male child in your generations, he who is born in your house or bought with money from any foreigner who is not your descendant.   Lev. 12:3

13 "He who is born in your house and he who is bought with your money must be circumcised, and My covenant shall be in your flesh for an everlasting covenant.

14 "And the uncircumcised male child, who is not circumcised in the flesh of his foreskin, that person ᴿshall be cut off from his people; he has broken My covenant."   Ex. 4:24–26

15 Then God said to Abraham, "As for Sarai your wife, you shall not call her name Sarai, but ᵀSarah *shall be* her name.   Lit. *Princess*

16 "And I will bless her and also give you a son by her; then I will bless her, and she shall be *a mother* ᴿof nations; ᴿkings of peoples shall be from her."   Gen. 35:11 • Gen. 17:6; 36:31

17 Then Abraham fell on his face ᴿand laughed, and said in his heart, "Shall *a child* be born to a man who is one hundred years old? And shall Sarah, who is ninety years old, bear *a child?*"   Gen. 17:3; 18:12; 21:6

18 And Abraham ᴿsaid to God, "Oh, that Ishmael might live before You!"   Gen. 18:23

19 Then God said: "No, ᴿSarah your wife shall bear you a son, and you shall call his name Isaac; I will establish My covenant with him for an everlasting covenant, *and* with his descendants after him.   [Gal. 4:28]

20 "And as for Ishmael, I have heard you. Behold, I have blessed him, and will make him fruitful, and will multiply him exceedingly. He shall beget twelve princes, ᴿand I will make him a great nation.   Gen. 21:13, 18

21 "But My covenant I will establish with Isaac, ᴿwhom Sarah shall bear to you at this ᴿset time next year."   Gen. 21:2 • Gen. 18:14

22 Then He finished talking with him, and God went up from Abraham.

23 So Abraham took Ishmael his son, all who were born in his house and all who were bought with his money, every male among the men of Abraham's house, and circumcised the flesh of their foreskins that very same day, as God had said to him.

24 Abraham *was* ninety-nine years old when he was circumcised in the flesh of his foreskin.

25 And Ishmael his son *was* thirteen years old when he was circumcised in the flesh of his foreskin.

26 That very same day Abraham was circumcised, and his son Ishmael;

27 and ᴿall the men of his house, born in the house or bought with money from a foreigner, were circumcised with him.   Gen. 18:19

The Son of Promise

18 Then the LORD appeared to him by *the terebinth trees of Mamre, as he was sitting in the tent door in the heat of the day.

18:1 Or *Alon Mamre*

(Point 5-A continued from previous page)
sovereignty. Sovereignty means that God has supreme authority and power over the universe. All other authority is delegated. It means that He has all power over, and absolute control of, all things in heaven and all things on earth (Matt. 28:18, page 982).

Writing of the sovereignty of God, the apostle Paul must have recorded these profound words in a state of awe and worship: "Oh, the depth of the riches both of the wisdom and knowledge of God! How unsearchable are His judgments and His ways past finding out! 'For who has known the mind of the LORD? Or who has become His counselor?' " (Rom. 11:33, 34, page 1142). When the prophet Isaiah compared the sovereignty of nations with the sovereignty of God, he said, "Behold, the nations are as a drop in a bucket, and are counted as the small dust on the scales" (Is. 40:15, page 679). Sovereign nations have boundaries, but the sovereignty of God knows no boundaries and is under no external restraints. It is immeasurable, without limits of any kind.

See Habakkuk 1:1–11, page 899, for **Point 5-B: The Sovereignty of God at Work.**

2 ᴿSo he lifted his eyes and looked, and behold, three men were standing by him; ᴿand when he saw *them*, he ran from the tent door to meet them, and bowed himself to the ground,   Heb. 13:2 · Gen. 19:1

3 and said, "My Lord, if I have now found favor in Your sight, do not pass on by Your servant.

4 "Please let ᴿa little water be brought, and wash your feet, and rest yourselves under the tree.   Gen. 19:2; 24:32; 43:24

5 "And I will bring a morsel of bread, that ᴿyou may refresh your hearts. After that you may pass by, ᴿinasmuch as you have come to your servant." They said, "Do as you have said."   Judg. 19:5 · Gen. 19:8; 33:10

6 So Abraham hurried into the tent to Sarah and said, "Quickly, make ready ᵀthree measures of fine meal; knead *it* and make cakes."   6.524 bu.

7 And Abraham ran to the herd, took a tender and good calf, gave *it* to a young man, and he hastened to prepare it.

8 So ᴿhe took butter and milk and the calf which he had prepared, and set *it* before them; and he stood by them under the tree as they ate.   Gen. 19:3

9 Then they said to him, "Where *is* Sarah your wife?" So he said, "Here, in the tent."

10 And He said, "I will certainly return to you ᴿaccording to the time of life, and behold, ᴿSarah your wife shall have a son." (Sarah was listening in the tent door which *was* behind him.)   2 Kin. 4:16 · Rom. 9:9

11 Now ᴿAbraham and Sarah were old, well advanced in age; *and* ᴿSarah had passed the age of childbearing.   Gen. 17:17 · Gen. 31:35

12 Therefore Sarah laughed within herself, saying, "After I have grown old, shall I have pleasure, my ᴿlord being old also?"   1 Pet. 3:6

13 And the Lᴏʀᴅ said to Abraham, "Why did Sarah laugh, saying, 'Shall I surely bear *a child*, since I am old?'

14 ᴿ"Is anything too hard for the Lᴏʀᴅ? ᴿAt the appointed time I will return to you, according to the time of life, and Sarah shall have a son."   Jer. 32:17 · Gen. 17:21; 18:10

15 But Sarah denied *it*, saying, "I did not laugh," for she was afraid. And He said, "No, but you did laugh!"

Abraham Intercedes for Sodom

16 Then the men rose from there and looked toward Sodom, and Abraham went with them to send them on the way.

17 And the Lᴏʀᴅ said, ᴿ"Shall I hide from Abraham what I am doing,   Ps. 25:14

18 "since Abraham shall surely become a great and mighty nation, and all the nations of the earth shall be blessed in him?

19 "For I have known him, in order ᴿthat he may command his children and his household after him, that they keep the way of the Lᴏʀᴅ, to do righteousness and justice, that

the Lᴏʀᴅ may bring to Abraham what He has spoken to him."   [Deut. 4:9, 10; 6:6, 7]

20 And the Lᴏʀᴅ said, "Because the outcry against Sodom and Gomorrah is great, and because their sin is very grave,

21 ᴿ"I will go down now and see whether they have done altogether according to the outcry against it that has come to Me; and if not, ᴿI will know."   Gen. 11:5 · Deut. 8:2; 13:3

22 Then the men turned away from there ᴿand went toward Sodom, but Abraham still stood before the Lᴏʀᴅ.   Gen. 18:16; 19:1

23 And Abraham ᴿcame near and said, ᴿ"Would You also destroy the righteous with the wicked?   [Heb. 10:22] · Num. 16:22

24 "Suppose there were fifty righteous within the city; would You also destroy the place and not spare *it* for the fifty righteous that were in it?

25 "Far be it from You to do such a thing as this, to slay the righteous with the wicked, so ᴿthat the righteous should be as the wicked; far be it from You! ᴿShall not the Judge of all the earth do right?"   Is. 3:10, 11 · Deut. 1:16, 17; 32:4

26 So the Lᴏʀᴅ said, ᴿ"If I find in Sodom fifty righteous within the city, then I will spare all the place for their sakes."   Jer. 5:1

27 Then Abraham answered and said, "Indeed now, I who *am* but dust and ashes have taken it upon myself to speak to the Lord:

28 "Suppose there were five less than the fifty righteous; would You destroy all of the city for *lack of* five?" So He said, "If I find there forty-five, I will not destroy *it*."

29 And he spoke to Him yet again and said, "Suppose there should be forty found there?" So He said, "I will not do *it* for the sake of forty."

30 Then he said, "Let not the Lord be angry, and I will speak: Suppose thirty should be found there?" So He said, "I will not do *it* if I find thirty there."

31 And he said, "Indeed now, I have taken it upon myself to speak to the Lord: Suppose twenty should be found there?" So He said, "I will not destroy *it* for the sake of twenty."

32 Then he said, "Let not the Lord be angry, and I will speak but once more: Suppose ten should be found there?" And He said, "I will not destroy *it* for the sake of ten."

33 So the Lᴏʀᴅ went His way as soon as He had finished speaking with Abraham; and Abraham returned to his place.

Sodom's Depravity

19 Now the two angels came to Sodom in the evening, and ᴿLot was sitting in the gate of Sodom. When Lot saw *them*, he rose to meet them, and he bowed himself with his face toward the ground.   Gen. 18:1-5

2 And he said, "Here now, my lords, please ᴿturn in to your servant's house and spend the night, and ᴿwash your feet; then you may rise early and go on your way." And they

said, "No, but we will spend the night in the open square."   [Heb. 13:2] • Gen. 18:4; 24:32

3 But he insisted strongly; so they turned in to him and entered his house. ᴿThen he made them a feast, and baked ᴿunleavened bread, and they ate.   Gen. 18:6–8 • Ex. 12:8

4 Now before they lay down, the men of the city, the men of Sodom, both old and young, all the people from every quarter, surrounded the house.

5 ᴿAnd they called to Lot and said to him, "Where are the men who came to you tonight? ᴿBring them out to us that we ᴿmay know them *carnally*."   Is. 3:9 • Judg. 19:22 • Gen. 4:1

6 So ᴿLot went out to them through the doorway, shut the door behind him,   Judg. 19:23

7 and said, "Please, my brethren, do not do so wickedly!

8 ᴿ"See now, I have two daughters who have not known a man; please, let me bring them out to you, and you may do to them as you wish; only do nothing to these men, since this is the reason they have come under the shadow of my roof."   Judg. 19:24

9 And they said, "Stand back!" Then they said, "This one came in to stay *here*, ᴿand he keeps acting as a judge; now we will deal worse with you than with them." So they pressed hard against the man Lot, and came near to break down the door.   Ex. 2:14

10 But the men reached out their hands and pulled Lot into the house with them, and shut the door.

11 And they ᴿstruck the men who *were* at the doorway of the house with blindness, both small and great, so that they became weary *trying* to find the door.   Gen. 20:17

Sodom and Gomorrah Destroyed

12 Then the men said to Lot, "Have you anyone else here? Son-in-law, your sons, your daughters, and whomever you have in the city—take *them* out of this place!

13 "For we will destroy this place, because the ᴿoutcry against them has grown great before the face of the LORD, and ᴿthe LORD has sent us to destroy it."   Gen. 18:20 • 1 Chr. 21:15

14 So Lot went out and spoke to his sons-in-law, who had married his daughters, and said, "Get up, get out of this place; for the LORD will destroy this city!" ᴿBut to his sons-in-law he seemed to be joking.   Ex. 9:21

15 When the morning dawned, the angels urged Lot to hurry, saying, ᴿ"Arise, take your wife and your two daughters who are here, lest you be consumed in the punishment of the city."   Rev. 18:4

16 And while he lingered, the men took hold of his hand, his wife's hand, and the hands of his two daughters, the LORD being merciful to him, ᴿand they brought him out and set him outside the city.   Ps. 34:22

17 So it came to pass, when they had brought them outside, that *he said, "Escape for your life! Do not look behind you nor stay anywhere in the plain. Escape ᴿto the mountains, lest you be destroyed."   Gen. 14:10

18 Then Lot said to them, "Please, ᴿno, my lords!   Acts 10:14

19 "Indeed now, your servant has found favor in your sight, and you have increased your mercy which you have shown me by saving my life; but I cannot escape to the mountains, lest some evil overtake me and I die.

20 "See now, this city *is* near *enough* to flee to, and it *is* a little one; please let me escape there (*is* it not a little one?) and my soul shall live."

21 And he said to him, "See, ᴿI have favored you concerning this thing also, in that I will not overthrow this city for which you have spoken.   Job 42:8, 9

22 "Hurry, escape there. For I cannot do anything until you arrive there." Therefore the name of the city was called Zoar.

23 The sun had risen upon the earth when Lot entered Zoar.

24 Then the LORD rained ᴿbrimstone and ᴿfire on Sodom and Gomorrah, from the LORD out of the heavens.   Deut. 29:23 • Lev. 10:2

25 So He ᵀoverthrew those cities, all the plain, all the inhabitants of the cities, and ᴿwhat grew on the ground.   devastated • Ps. 107:34

26 But his wife looked back behind him, and she became ᴿa pillar of salt.   Luke 17:32

27 And Abraham went early in the morning to the place where ᴿhe had stood before the LORD.   Gen. 18:22

28 Then he looked toward Sodom and Gomorrah, and toward all the land of the plain; and he saw, and behold, ᴿthe smoke of the land which went up like the smoke of a furnace.   Rev. 9:2; 18:9

29 And it came to pass, when God destroyed the cities of the plain, that God remembered Abraham, and sent Lot out of the midst of the overthrow, when He overthrew the cities in which Lot had dwelt.

The Descendants of Lot

30 Then Lot went up out of Zoar and ᴿdwelt in the mountains, and his two daughters were with him; for he was afraid to dwell in Zoar. And he and his two daughters dwelt in a cave.   Gen. 19:17, 19

31 Now the firstborn said to the younger, "Our father *is* old, and *there is* no man on the earth ᴿto come in to us as is the custom of all the earth.   Gen. 16:2, 4; 38:8, 9

32 "Come, let us make our father drink wine, and we will lie with him, that we may preserve the ᵀlineage of our father."   Lit. *seed*

33 So they made their father drink wine that night. And the firstborn went in and lay with her father, and he did not know when she lay down or when she arose.

19:17 LXX, Syr., Vg. *they*

34 It happened on the next day that the firstborn said to the younger, "Indeed I lay with my father last night; let us make him drink wine tonight also, and you go in *and* lie with him, that we may preserve the ᵀlineage of our father."   Lit. *seed*
35 Then they made their father drink wine that night also. And the younger arose and lay with him, and he did not know when she lay down or when she arose.
36 Thus both the daughters of Lot were with child by their father.
37 The firstborn bore a son and called his name Moab; ᴿhe *is* the father of the Moabites to this day.   Deut. 2:9
38 And the younger, she also bore a son and called his name Ben-Ammi; ᴿhe *is* the father of the people of Ammon to this day. Deut. 2:19

Abraham and Abimelech

20 And Abraham journeyed from ᴿthere to the South, and dwelt between Kadesh and Shur, and stayed in Gerar. Gen. 18:1
2 Now Abraham said of Sarah his wife, "She *is* my sister." And Abimelech king of Gerar sent and ᴿtook Sarah.   Gen. 12:15
3 But God came to Abimelech in a dream by night, and said to him, "Indeed you *are* a dead man because of the woman whom you have taken, for she *is* a man's wife."
4 But Abimelech had not come near her; and he said, "Lord, ᴿwill You slay a righteous nation also?   Gen. 18:23-25
5 "Did he not say to me, 'She *is* my sister'? And she, even she herself said, 'He *is* my brother.' In the integrity of my heart and innocence of my hands I have done this."
6 And God said to him in a dream, "Yes, I know that you did this in the integrity of your heart. For ᴿI also withheld you from sinning ᴿagainst Me; therefore I did not let you touch her.   1 Sam. 25:26, 34 • Gen. 39:9
7 "Now therefore, restore the man's wife; for he *is* a prophet, and he will pray for you and you shall live. But if you do not restore her, ᴿknow that you shall surely die, you ᴿand all who *are* yours."   Gen. 2:17 • Num. 16:32, 33
8 So Abimelech rose early in the morning, called all his servants, and told all these things in their hearing; and the men were very much afraid.
9 And Abimelech called Abraham and said to him, "What have you done to us? How have I ᵀoffended you, ᴿthat you have brought on me and on my kingdom a great sin? You have done deeds to me ᴿthat ought not to be done."   sinned against • Gen. 26:10; 39:9 • Gen. 34:7
10 Then Abimelech said to Abraham, "What did you have in view, that you have done this thing?"
11 And Abraham said, "Because I thought, surely the fear of God *is* not in this place; and they will kill me on account of my wife.
12 "But indeed she *is* truly my sister. She *is*

the daughter of my father, but not the daughter of my mother; and she became my wife.
13 "And it came to pass, when God caused me to wander from my father's house, that I said to her, 'This *is* your kindness that you should do for me: in every place, wherever we go, say of me, "He *is* my brother." ' "
14 Then Abimelech ᴿtook sheep, oxen, and male and female servants, and gave *them* to Abraham; and he restored Sarah his wife to him.   Gen. 12:16
15 And Abimelech said, "See, my land *is* before you; dwell where it pleases you."
16 Then to Sarah he said, "Behold, I have given your brother a ᵀthousand *pieces* of silver; indeed *this vindicates you ᴿbefore all who *are* with you and before everybody." Thus she was rebuked. $128,000 • Gen. 24:65
17 So Abraham prayed to God; and God ᴿhealed Abimelech, his wife, and his female servants. Then they bore *children*; Gen. 21:2
18 for the Lord ᴿhad closed up all the wombs of the house of Abimelech because of Sarah, Abraham's wife.   Gen. 12:17

Isaac Is Born

21 And the Lord ᴿvisited Sarah as He had said, and the Lord did for Sarah ᴿas He had spoken.   1 Sam. 2:21 • [Gal. 4:23, 28]
2 For Sarah conceived and bore Abraham a son in his old age, ᴿat the set time of which God had spoken to him. Gen. 17:21; 18:10, 14
3 And Abraham called the name of his son who was born to him—whom Sarah bore to him—ᴿIsaac.ᵀ   Gen. 17:19, 21 • Lit. *Laughter*
4 Then Abraham ᴿcircumcised his son Isaac when he was eight days old, ᴿas God had commanded him.   Acts 7:8 • Gen. 17:10, 12
5 Now Abraham was one hundred years old when his son Isaac was born to him.
6 And Sarah said, "God has made me laugh, *and* all who hear will laugh with me."
7 She also said, "Who would have said to Abraham that Sarah would nurse children? For I have borne *him* a son in his old age."

Hagar and Ishmael Depart

8 So the child grew and was weaned. And Abraham made a great feast on the same day that Isaac was weaned.
9 And Sarah saw the son of Hagar ᴿthe Egyptian, whom she had borne to Abraham, ᴿscoffing.ᵀ   Gen. 16:1, 4, 15 • [Gal. 4:29] • Lit. *laughing*
10 Therefore she said to Abraham, ᴿ"Cast out this bondwoman and her son; for the son of this bondwoman shall not be heir with my son, *namely* with Isaac."   Gal. 3:18; 4:30
11 And the matter was very ᵀdispleasing in Abraham's sight because of his son. bad
12 But God said to Abraham, "Do not let it be displeasing in your sight because of the lad or because of your bondwoman. Whatever

20:16 Lit. *is a covering of the eyes for you to all*

Sarah has said to you, listen to her voice; for ^Rin Isaac your seed shall be called. [Rom. 9:7, 8]

13 "Yet I will also make a nation of the son of the bondwoman, because he *is* your seed."

14 So Abraham rose early in the morning, and took bread and ^Ta skin of water; and putting *it* on her shoulder, he gave *it* and the boy to Hagar, and ^Rsent her away. Then she departed and wandered in the Wilderness of Beersheba.   A water bottle made of skins • John 8:35

15 And the water in the skin was used up, and she placed the boy under one of the shrubs.

16 Then she went and sat down across from *him* at a distance of about a bowshot; for she said to herself, "Let me not see the death of the boy." So she sat opposite *him*, and lifted her voice and wept.

17 And ^RGod heard the voice of the lad. Then the ^Rangel of God called to Hagar out of heaven, and said to her, "What ails you, Hagar? Fear not, for God has heard the voice of the lad where he *is*.   Ex. 3:7 • Gen. 22:11

18 "Arise, lift up the lad and hold him with your hand, for ^RI will make him a great nation."   Gen. 16:10; 21:13; 25:12-16

19 Then God opened her eyes, and she saw a well of water. And she went and filled the skin with water, and gave the lad a drink.

20 So God ^Rwas with the lad; and he grew and dwelt in the wilderness, ^Rand became an archer.   Gen. 28:15; 39:2, 3, 21 • Gen. 16:12

21 He dwelt in the Wilderness of Paran; and his mother ^Rtook a wife for him from the land of Egypt.   Gen. 24:4

A Covenant with Abimelech

22 And it came to pass at that time that Abimelech and Phichol, the commander of his army, spoke to Abraham, saying, ^R"God *is* with you in all that you do.   Gen. 26:28

23 "Now therefore, ^Tswear to me by God that you will not deal falsely with me, with my offspring, or with my posterity; but that according to the kindness that I have done to you, you will do to me and to the land in which you have dwelt."   take an oath

24 And Abraham said, "I will swear."

25 Then Abraham rebuked Abimelech because of a well of water which Abimelech's servants ^Rhad seized.   Gen. 26:15, 18, 20-22

26 And Abimelech said, "I do not know who has done this thing; you did not tell me, nor had I heard *of it* until today."

27 So Abraham took sheep and oxen and gave them to Abimelech, and the two of them ^Rmade a ^Tcovenant.   Gen. 26:31; 31:44 • treaty

28 And Abraham set seven ewe lambs of the flock by themselves.

29 Then Abimelech asked Abraham, "What *is the meaning of* these seven ewe lambs which you have set by themselves?"

30 And he said, "You will take *these* seven ewe lambs from my hand, that they may be my witness that I have dug this well."

31 Therefore he called that place ^TBeersheba, because the two of them swore an oath there.   Lit. *Well of the Oath* or *Well of the Seven*

32 Thus they made a covenant at Beersheba. So Abimelech rose with Phichol, the commander of his army, and they returned to the land of the Philistines.

33 Then *Abraham* planted a tamarisk tree in Beersheba, and there called on the name of the LORD, the Everlasting God.

34 And Abraham stayed in the land of the Philistines many days.

Abraham's Faith Confirmed

20-C. The Offering of Isaac   ▼

22 Now it came to pass after these things that God tested Abraham, and said to him, "Abraham!" And he said, "Here I am."

2 Then he said, "Take now your son, your

20-C. The Offering of Isaac (Genesis 22:1–19)—This chapter is a treasure of spiritual wealth, and awesome in many ways. We can never reach its height or depth, nor exhaust its spiritual significance. Gradually we see beneath the surface, and slowly begin to discern the purpose of God in this unique picture of Jesus Christ, our substitute. When Abraham and Isaac left the land of Moriah, after seeing God provide a ram to take the place of Isaac, they knew that "the eternal God is your refuge, and underneath are the everlasting arms" (Deut. 33:27, page 213). How can anyone read of this amazing event and not stand in awe of Jehovah-Jireh. "And Abraham called the name of the place, The-LORD-Will-Provide" (v. 14). And God did provide a ram to take the place of Isaac, because Abraham believed God and obeyed Him without asking, "Why, Lord?"

Verse 1 tells us that "God tested Abraham." God did not tempt him toward evil in the sense of luring him to fall, because "God cannot be tempted by evil, nor does He Himself tempt anyone" (James 1:13, page 1256). Rather, He tested Abraham to show the quality of this man who was His friend. In this chapter God put Abraham's faith to the supreme test. He said to Abraham, "Take now your son, your only son Isaac, whom you love, and go to the land of Moriah, and offer him there as a burnt offering on one of the mountains of which I shall tell you" (v. 2). The mountain in the land of Moriah, where Abraham built the altar to sacrifice Isaac, is believed to be the plateau on which Solomon built the temple. Some believe that the Most Holy Place stood over the exact spot where Abraham built his altar. This chapter is also rich in typology; in it we have Abraham as a twofold type, Isaac as a twofold type, and the ram as a single type. Abraham is a type of:

(1) All who are justified by faith (Rom. 5:1, page 1133). Abraham lived by faith (Gal. 3:11, page 1181), and his faith was "accounted . . . to him for righteousness" (Gen. 15:6, page 20; cf. Gal. 3:6, 7, page 1181).

(Point 20-C continued on next page)

▽ only *son* Isaac, whom you love, and go to the land of Moriah, and offer him there as a ᴿburnt offering on one of the mountains of which I shall tell you." Gen. 8:20; 31:54

3 So Abraham rose early in the morning and saddled his donkey, and took two of his young men with him, and Isaac his son; and he split the wood for the burnt offering, and arose and went to the place of which God had told him.

4 Then on the third day Abraham lifted his eyes and saw the place afar off.

5 And Abraham said to his young men, "Stay here with the donkey; the ᵀlad and I will go yonder and worship, and we will ᴿcome back to you." Lit. *young man* • [Heb. 11:19]

6 So Abraham took the wood of the burnt offering and ᴿlaid *it* on Isaac his son; and he took the fire in his hand, and a knife, and the two of them went together. John 19:17

7 But Isaac spoke to Abraham his father and said, "My father!" And he said, "Here I am, my son." Then he said, "Look, the fire and the wood, but where *is* the ᵀlamb for a burnt offering?" Or *goat*

8 And Abraham said, "My son, God will provide for Himself the lamb for a burnt offering." So the two of them went together.

9 Then they came to the place of which ▽ God had told him. And Abraham built an altar there and placed the wood in order; and he bound Isaac his son and ᴿlaid him on the altar, upon the wood. [Heb. 11:17-19]

10 And Abraham stretched out his hand and took the knife to slay his son.

11 But the ᴿAngel of the LORD called to him from heaven and said, "Abraham, Abraham!" So he said, "Here I am." Gen. 16:7-11; 21:17, 18

12 And He said, ᴿ"Do not lay your hand on the lad, or do anything to him; for ᴿnow I know that you fear God, since you have not ᴿwithheld your son, your only *son*, from Me." 1 Sam. 15:22 • James 2:21, 22 • Gen. 22:2, 16

13 Then Abraham lifted his eyes and looked, and there behind *him was* a ram caught in a thicket by its horns. So Abraham went and took the ram, and offered it up for a burnt offering instead of his son.

4-A. Jehovah-Jireh: The LORD Will Provide ▼

14 And Abraham called the name of the place, ᵀThe-LORD-Will-Provide; as it is said *to* this day, "In the Mount of the LORD it shall be provided." Heb. *YHWH Yireh* ▲

(Point 20-C continued from previous page)
God tested Abraham's faith in four great personal crises. In each crisis God called on him to surrender by faith something or someone whom he loved. If faith is to grow to greatness, it always requires sacrifice.

(a) *The first crisis.* God called on Abraham to leave his country and relatives and to go by faith, "not knowing where he was going" (Heb. 11:8, page 1248; cf. Gen. 12:1, page 17).

(b) *The second crisis.* God called on him to separate himself from Lot, his brother's son. Abraham had no heir but Lot. Then, "after Lot had separated from him," God promised him the land, and "your descendants as the dust of the earth" (Gen. 13:1-18, page 18).

(c) *The third crisis.* God called on him to abandon all plans for his firstborn son Ishmael. Abraham pleaded with God to make Ishmael his heir: "Oh, that Ishmael might live before You!" (Gen. 17:18, 19, page 22).

(d) *The fourth crisis.* In his greatest crisis of faith, Abraham was commanded by God to offer up Isaac, his God-appointed heir, as a burnt offering (Heb. 11:17-19, page 1249). Abraham's faith stood the test, and God gave him the victory. Anyone who lives by faith will be tested many times, because it is only through discipline that Christian character is developed.

(2) God the Father (John 3:16, page 1052). Abraham was told, "Take now your son, your only son Isaac, whom you love . . . and offer him there as a burnt offering" (v. 2). This type was fulfilled when God the Father gave His only Son to become our sin offering. "For He [God the Father] made Him [God the Son] who knew no sin to be sin for us, that we might become the righteousness of God in Him" (2 Cor. 5:21, page 1169).

Isaac is a type of:

(1) The Lord Jesus Christ, God's only begotten Son, who came into the world to do the will of His Father. Just as Isaac obeyed his father, and was willing to become a burnt offering, so the Lord Jesus obeyed His Father, and "humbled Himself and became obedient to the point of death, even the death of the cross" (Phil. 2:8, page 1197).

(2) The whole human race, which is born in sin (Ps. 51:5, page 541; Rom. 3:23-25, page 1131). Isaac needed a substitute to take his place on the altar of sacrifice, and God provided a ram. The ram is a type of Christ, who became our substitute. This type was fulfilled in Christ almost two thousand years later, when He freed us from sin's penalty and power (Rom. 8:1-3, page 1136).

See Exodus 12:1-36, page 69, for **Point 20-D: The Passover Blood.**

4-A. Jehovah-Jireh: The LORD Will Provide (Genesis 22:14)—God promised Abraham that from him He would make a great nation; and He ordered Abraham to leave his homeland, the ancient moon-god city of

(Point 4-A continued on next page)

▽ **15** Then the Angel of the Lord called to Abraham a second time out of heaven,
16 and said: ᴿ"By Myself I have sworn, says the Lord, because you have done this thing, and have not withheld your son, your only son—   Ps. 105:9
17 "in blessing I will bless you, and multiplying I will multiply your descendants as the stars of the heaven and as the sand which *is* on the seashore; and your descendants shall possess the gate of their enemies.
18 "In your seed ᴿall the nations of the earth shall be blessed, because you have obeyed My voice."   Gal. 3:16
19 So Abraham returned to his young men, and they rose and went together to Beer-
▲ sheba; and Abraham dwelt at Beersheba.

The Family of Nahor

20 Now it came to pass after these things that it was told Abraham, saying, "Indeed ᴿMilcah also has borne children to your brother Nahor: Gen. 11:29; 24:15
21 ᴿ"Huz his firstborn, Buz his brother, Kemuel the father ᴿof Aram,   Job 1:1 · Job 32:2
22 "Chesed, Hazo, Pildash, Jidlaph, and Bethuel."
23 And ᴿBethuel begot ᵀRebekah. These eight Milcah bore to Nahor, Abraham's brother.   Gen. 24:15 · *Rebecca*, Rom. 9:10

24 His concubine, whose name was Reumah, also bore Tebah, Gaham, Thahash, and Maachah.

Sarah's Death and Burial

23 Sarah lived one hundred and twenty-seven years; *these were* the years of the life of Sarah.
2 So Sarah died in ᴿKirjath Arba (that *is,* ᴿHebron) in the land of Canaan, and Abraham came to mourn for Sarah and to weep for her.   Josh. 14:15; 15:13; 21:11 · Gen. 13:18; 23:19
3 Then Abraham stood up from before his dead, and spoke to the sons of Heth, saying,
4 ᴿ"I *am* a foreigner and a visitor among you. ᴿGive me property for a burial place among you, that I may bury my dead out of my sight."   [Gen. 17:8] · Acts 7:5, 16
5 And the sons of Heth answered Abraham, saying to him,
6 "Hear us, my lord: You *are* a ᵀmighty prince among us; bury your dead in the choicest of our burial places. None of us will withhold from you his burial place, that you may bury your dead."   Lit. *prince of God*
7 Then Abraham stood up and bowed himself to the people of the land, the sons of Heth.
8 And he spoke with them, saying, "If it is your wish that I bury my dead out of my

---

(Point 4-A continued from previous page)
Ur (Gen. 12:1, 2, page 17). Abraham was 75 and Sarah 65 at this time, already old for moving and pioneering. Yet by faith they obeyed God, packed up, and struck out for faraway Canaan.

Twenty-four years later, when Abraham was 99 and Sarah 89, God promised that they would soon have a son named Isaac, who would be Abraham's covenant heir (Gen. 17:19, page 22). Months later, when Abraham was 100 and Sarah 90, by a miracle of Almighty God, Sarah gave birth to Isaac (Gen. 21:1–7, page 25).

Then the great test came some years later. God commanded Abraham to take the young Isaac (his only child by Sarah, his heir, his sole hope of the future fulfillment of God's promise that Abraham would be a father of many nations) and offer him as a burnt offering on Mt. Moriah, later the site of Jerusalem (Gen. 22:2, page 26). In trust and innocence Isaac asked his father, "But where is the lamb for a burnt offering?" Abraham's classic reply of faith and compassion was simply, "God will provide for Himself the lamb for a burnt offering" (Gen. 22:7, 8, page 27).

One of the most moving moments in Bible history occurred when God's call stopped Abraham's hand from slaying his son, and a ram for the sacrifice was seen caught by his horns in a nearby thicket. Abraham called that place *Jehovah-Jireh*, "The-Lord-Will-Provide" (Gen. 22:9–14, page 27).

Note that:

(1) Abraham trusted God. He considered "that God was able to raise him [Isaac] up, even from the dead" (Heb. 11:19, page 1249). He believed that God, who had miraculously brought Isaac into the world, would raise him from the dead, even if the boy was sacrificed.

(2) God did not fail Abraham. He restrained Abraham's hand and provided a ram instead.

(3) Isaac, as a *type*, or illustration, of the submissive Christ, went to this same Moriah—the site of the temple and near to Calvary—in obedience to the Father's will.

(4) Christ was the true Lamb of God provided by Jehovah (John 1:29, 36, page 1050; cf. Rev. 5:6, page 1297; 6:1, page 1299). In this instance the Father did not stop the sacrifice at Calvary; but in His love for us and desire for our salvation, He allowed His only Son's life to be taken. Christ's coming and His atoning death were the fulfillment of the name Jehovah-Jireh (John 3:14–18, page 1052).

(5) Jesus said, "Your father Abraham rejoiced to see My day, and he saw it and was glad" (John 8:56, page 1064). Jesus was referring to the day that Abraham offered Isaac and saw, in a typical way, "the Lamb of God who takes away the sin of the world" (John 1:29, page 1050; cf. 1 Pet. 1:18, 19, page 1263).

This great episode should teach us to trust God daily for His provision in every test of life. God is Jehovah-Jireh, "The-Lord-Will-Provide."

See Exodus 15:26, page 75, for **Point 4-B: Jehovah-Ropheka: The Lord Your Healer.**

sight, hear me, and [T]meet with Ephron the son of Zohar for me,   approach

9 "that he may give me the cave of Machpelah which he has, which is at the end of his field. Let him give it to me at the full price, as property for a burial place among you."

10 Now Ephron dwelt among the sons of Heth; and Ephron the Hittite answered Abraham in the presence of the sons of Heth, all who entered at the gate of his city, saying,

11 [R]"No, my lord, hear me: I give you the field and the cave that is in it; I give it to you in the presence of the sons of my people. I give it to you. Bury your dead!"   2 Sam. 24:21-24

12 Then Abraham bowed himself down before the people of the land;

13 and he spoke to Ephron in the hearing of the people of the land, saying, "If you will give it, please hear me. I will give you money for the field; take it from me and I will bury my dead there."

14 And Ephron answered Abraham, saying to him,

15 "My lord, listen to me; the land is worth four hundred shekels of silver. What is that between you and me? So bury your dead."

16 And Abraham listened to Ephron; and Abraham [R]weighed out the silver for Ephron which he had named in the hearing of the sons of Heth, [T]four hundred shekels of silver, currency of the merchants.   Jer. 32:9, 10 • $51,200

17 So [R]the field of Ephron which was in Machpelah, which was before Mamre, the field and the cave which was in it, and all the trees that were in the field, which were within all the surrounding borders, were deeded   Gen. 25:9; 49:29-32; 50:13

18 to Abraham as a possession in the presence of the sons of Heth, before all who went in at the gate of his city.

19 And after this, Abraham buried Sarah his wife in the cave of the field of Machpelah, before Mamre (that is, Hebron) in the land of Canaan.

20 So the field and the cave that is in it [R]were deeded to Abraham by the sons of Heth as property for a burial place. Jer. 32:10, 11

A Bride for Isaac

24 Now Abraham was old, well advanced in age; and the LORD [R]had blessed Abraham in all things.   Gen. 12:2; 13:2; 24:35

2 So Abraham said to the oldest servant of his house, who ruled over all that he had, "Please, put your hand under my thigh,

3 "and I will make you [T]swear by the LORD, the God of heaven and the God of the earth, that [R]you will not take a wife for my son from the daughters of the Canaanites, among whom I dwell;   take an oath • Deut. 7:3

4 "but you shall go to my country and to my family, and take a wife for my son Isaac."

5 And the servant said to him, "Perhaps the woman will not be willing to follow me to this land. Must I take your son back to the land from which you came?"

6 But Abraham said to him, "Beware that you do not take my son back there.

7 "The LORD God of heaven, who [R]took me from my father's house and from the land of my family, and who spoke to me and swore to me, saying, [R]'To your descendants I give this land,' He will send His angel before you, and you shall take a wife for my son from there.   Gen. 12:1; 24:3 • Gen. 12:7; 13:15; 15:18; 17:8

8 "And if the woman is not willing to follow you, then [R]you will be released from this oath; only do not take my son back there."   Josh. 2:17-20

9 So the servant put his hand under the thigh of Abraham his master, and swore to him concerning this matter.

10 Then the servant took ten of his master's camels and departed, for all his master's goods were in his hand. And he arose and went to Mesopotamia, to the city of Nahor.

11 And he made his camels kneel down outside the city by a well of water at evening time, the time [R]when women go out to draw water.   Ex. 2:16

12 Then he [R]said, "O LORD God of my master Abraham, please [R]give me success this day, and show kindness to my master Abraham.   Ex. 3:6, 15 • Neh. 1:11

13 "Behold, here I stand by the well of water, and [R]the daughters of the men of the city are coming out to draw water.   Ex. 2:16

14 "Now let it be that the young woman to whom I say, 'Please let down your pitcher that I may drink,' and she says, 'Drink, and I will also give your camels a drink'—let her be the one You have appointed for Your servant Isaac. And by this I will know that You have shown kindness to my master."

15 And it happened, before he had finished speaking, that behold, [T]Rebekah, who was born to Bethuel, son of Milcah, the wife of Nahor, Abraham's brother, came out with her pitcher on her shoulder.   Rebecca, Rom. 9:10

16 Now the young woman [R]was very beautiful to behold, a virgin; no man had known her. And she went down to the well, filled her pitcher, and came up.   Gen. 12:11; 26:7; 29:17

17 And the servant ran to meet her and said, "Please let me drink a little water from your pitcher."

18 [R]So she said, "Drink, my lord." Then she quickly let her pitcher down to her hand, and gave him a drink.   [1 Pet. 3:8, 9]

19 And when she had finished giving him a drink, she said, "I will draw water for your camels also, until they have finished drinking."

20 Then she quickly emptied her pitcher into the trough, ran back to the well to draw water, and drew for all his camels.

21 And the man, wondering at her, remained silent so as to know whether [R]the

LORD had made his journey prosperous or not.   Gen. 24:12-14, 27, 52

22 So it was, when the camels had finished drinking, that the man took a golden nose ring weighing half a shekel, and two bracelets for her wrists weighing ten *shekels* of gold, **23** and said, "Whose daughter *are* you? Tell me, please, is there room *in* your father's house for us ᵀto lodge?"   *to spend the night*

24 So she said to him, ᴿ"I *am* the daughter of Bethuel, Milcah's son, whom she bore to Nahor."   Gen. 22:23; 24:15

25 Moreover she said to him, "We have both straw and feed enough, and room to lodge."

26 Then the man ᴿbowed down his head and worshiped the LORD.   Ex. 4:31

27 And he said, ᴿ"Blessed *be* the LORD God of my master Abraham, who has not forsaken ᴿHis mercy and His truth toward my master. As for me, being on the way, the LORD ᴿled me to the house of my master's brethren."   Ex. 18:10 · Gen. 32:10 · Gen. 24:21, 48

28 So the young woman ran and told her mother's household these things.

29 Now Rebekah had a brother whose name *was* ᴿLaban, and Laban ran out to the man by the well.   Gen. 29:5, 13

30 So it came to pass, when he saw the nose ring, and the bracelets on his sister's wrists, and when he heard the words of his sister Rebekah, saying, "Thus the man spoke to me," that he went to the man. And there he stood by the camels at the well.

31 And he said, "Come in, ᴿO blessed of the LORD! Why do you stand outside? For I have prepared the house, and a place for the camels."   Judg. 17:2

32 Then the man came to the house. And he unloaded the camels, and ᴿprovided straw and feed for the camels, and water to ᴿwash his feet and the feet of the men who *were* with him.   Gen. 43:24 · Gen. 19:2

33 *Food* was set before him to eat, but he said, ᴿ"I will not eat until I have told about my errand." And he said, "Speak on." John 4:34

34 So he said, "I *am* Abraham's servant.

35 "The LORD ᴿhas blessed my master greatly, and he has become great; and He has given him flocks and herds, silver and gold, male and female servants, and camels and donkeys.   Gen. 13:2; 24:1

36 "And Sarah my master's wife bore a son to my master when she was old; and ᴿto him he has given all that he has.   Gen. 21:10; 25:5

37 "Now my master ᴿmade me swear, saying, 'You shall not take a wife for my son from the daughters of the Canaanites, in whose land I dwell;   Gen. 24:2-4

38 'but you shall go to my father's house and to my family, and take a wife for my son.'

39 ᴿ"And I said to my master, 'Perhaps the woman will not follow me.'   Gen. 24:5

40 "But he said to me, 'The LORD, before whom I walk, will send His angel with you and ᵀprosper your way; and you shall take a wife for my son from my family and from my father's house.   *make your way successful*

41 ᴿ"You will be clear from this oath when you arrive among my family; for if they will not give *her* to you, then you will be released from my oath.'   Gen. 24:8

42 "And this day I came to the well and said, 'O LORD God of my master Abraham, if You will now prosper the way in which I go, **43** ᴿbehold, I stand by the well of water; and it shall come to pass that when the virgin comes out to draw *water*, and I say to her, "Please give me a little water from your pitcher to drink,"   Gen. 24:13

44 'and she says to me, "Drink, and I will draw for your camels also,"—*let* her *be* the woman whom the LORD has appointed for my master's son.'

45 "But before I had finished speaking in my heart, there was Rebekah, coming out with her pitcher on her shoulder; and she went down to the well and drew *water*. And I said to her, 'Please let me drink.'

46 "And she made haste and let her pitcher down from her *shoulder*, and said, 'Drink, and I will give your camels a drink also.' So I drank, and she gave the camels a drink also.

47 "Then I asked her, and said, 'Whose daughter *are* you?' And she said, 'The daughter of Bethuel, Nahor's son, whom Milcah bore to him.' So I put the nose ring on her nose and the bracelets on her wrists.

48 ᴿ"And I bowed my head and worshiped the LORD, and blessed the LORD God of my master Abraham, who had led me in the way of truth to ᴿtake the daughter of my master's brother for his son.   Gen. 24:26, 52 · Gen. 22:23; 24:27

49 "Now if you will ᴿdeal kindly and truly with my master, tell me. And if not, tell me, that I may turn to the right hand or to the left."   Josh. 2:14

50 Then Laban and Bethuel answered and said, "The thing comes from the LORD; we cannot speak to you either bad or good.

51 ᴿ"Here *is* Rebekah before you; take *her* and go, and let her be your master's son's wife, as the LORD has spoken."   Gen. 20:15

52 And it came to pass, when Abraham's servant heard their words, that he worshiped the LORD, *bowing himself* to the earth.

53 Then the servant brought out jewelry of silver, jewelry of gold, and clothing, and gave *them* to Rebekah. He also gave precious things to her brother and to her mother.

54 And he and the men who *were* with him ate and drank and stayed all night. Then they arose in the morning; and he said, "Send me away to my master."

55 But her brother and her mother said, "Let the young woman stay with us *a few* days, at least ten; after that she may go."

56 And he said to them, "Do not hinder me,

since the LORD has prospered my way; send me away so that I may go to my master." 57 So they said, "We will call the young woman and ask her personally." 58 Then they called Rebekah and said to her, "Will you go with this man?" And she said, "I will go." 59 So they sent away Rebekah their sister Rand her nurse, and Abraham's servant and his men.   Gen. 35:8 60 And they blessed Rebekah and said to her:

"Our sister, may you become
RThe mother of thousands of ten
   thousands;   Gen. 17:16
And may your descendants possess
The gates of those who hate them."

61 Then Rebekah and her maids arose, and they rode on the camels and followed the man. So the servant took Rebekah and departed. 62 Now Isaac came from the way of Beer Lahai Roi, for he dwelt in the South. 63 And Isaac went out to meditate in the field in the evening; and he lifted his eyes and looked, and there, the camels were coming. 64 Then Rebekah lifted her eyes, and when she saw Isaac Rshe dismounted from her camel;   Josh. 15:18 65 for she had said to the servant, "Who is this man walking in the field to meet us?" The servant said, "It is my master." So she took a veil and covered herself. 66 And the servant told Isaac all the things that he had done. 67 Then Isaac brought her into his mother Sarah's tent; and he took Rebekah and she became his wife, and he loved her. So Isaac was comforted after his mother's death.

Abraham and Keturah

25 Abraham again took a wife, and her name was RKeturah.   1 Chr. 1:32, 33 2 And she bore him Zimran, Jokshan, Medan, Midian, Ishbak, and Shuah. 3 Jokshan begot Sheba and Dedan. And the sons of Dedan were Asshurim, Letushim, and Leummim. 4 And the sons of Midian were Ephah, Epher, Hanoch, Abidah, and Eldaah. All these were the children of Keturah. 5 And RAbraham gave all that he had to Isaac.   Gen. 24:35, 36 6 But Abraham gave gifts to the sons of the concubines which Abraham had; and while he was still living he Rsent them eastward, away from Isaac his son, to Rthe country of the east.   Gen. 21:14 • Judg. 6:3

Abraham's Death and Burial

7 This is the sum of the years of Abraham's life which he lived: one hundred and seventy-five years.

8 Then Abraham breathed his last and died in a good old age, an old man and full of years, and was gathered to his people. 9 And his sons Isaac and Ishmael buried him in the cave of RMachpelah, which is before Mamre, in the field of Ephron the son of Zohar the Hittite,   Gen. 23:9, 17; 49:30 10 the field which Abraham purchased from the sons of Heth. RThere Abraham was buried, and Sarah his wife.   Gen. 49:31 11 And it came to pass, after the death of Abraham, that God blessed his son Isaac. And Isaac dwelt at RBeer Lahai Roi. Gen. 16:14

The Families of Ishmael and Isaac

12 Now this is the genealogy of Ishmael, Abraham's son, whom Hagar the Egyptian, Sarah's maidservant, bore to Abraham. 13 And Rthese were the names of the sons of Ishmael, by their names, according to their generations: The firstborn of Ishmael, Nebajoth; then Kedar, Adbeel, Mibsam, 1 Chr. 1:29-31 14 Mishma, Dumah, Massa, 15 *Hadar, Tema, Jetur, Naphish, and Kedemah. 16 These were the sons of Ishmael and these were their names, by their towns and their Tsettlements, Rtwelve princes according to their nations.   camps • Gen. 17:20 17 These were the years of the life of Ishmael: one hundred and thirty-seven years; and Rhe breathed his last and died, and was gathered to his people.   Gen. 25:8; 49:33 18 (They dwelt from Havilah as far as Shur, which is east of Egypt as you go toward Assyria.) He Tdied in the presence of all his brethren.   fell 19 This is the genealogy of Isaac, Abraham's son. RAbraham begot Isaac.   Matt. 1:2 20 Isaac was forty years old when he took Rebekah as wife, Rthe daughter of Bethuel the Syrian of Padan Aram, the sister of Laban the Syrian.   Gen. 22:23; 24:15, 29, 67 21 Now Isaac pleaded with the LORD for his wife, because she was barren; Rand the LORD granted his plea, Rand Rebekah his wife conceived.   1 Chr. 5:20 • Rom. 9:10-13 22 But the children struggled together within her; and she said, "If all is well, why am I like this?" RSo she went to inquire of the LORD.   1 Sam. 1:15; 9:9; 10:22 23 And the LORD said to her:

R"Two nations are in your womb,
Two peoples shall be separated from
   your body;   Gen. 17:4-6, 16; 24:60
One people shall be stronger than Rthe
   other,   2 Sam. 8:14
And the older shall serve the younger."

24 So when her days were fulfilled for her to give birth, indeed there were twins in her womb.

25:15 MT Hadad

25 And the first came out red. *He was* ᴿlike a hairy garment all over; so they called his name ᵀEsau.   Gen. 27:11, 16, 23 · Lit. *Hairy*
26 Afterward his brother came out, and his hand took hold of Esau's heel; so his name was called ᵀJacob. Isaac *was* sixty years old when she bore them.   Lit. *Supplanter* or *Deceitful*
27 So the boys grew. And Esau was a skillful hunter, a man of the field; but Jacob was a mild man, dwelling in tents.
28 And Isaac loved Esau because he ate *of his* game, but Rebekah loved Jacob.

Esau Sells His Birthright

29 Now Jacob cooked a stew; and Esau came in from the field, and he *was* weary.
30 And Esau said to Jacob, "Please feed me with that same red *stew,* for I *am* weary." Therefore his name was called ᵀEdom. Lit. *Red*
31 But Jacob said, "Sell me your birthright as of this day."
32 And Esau said, "Look, I *am* about to die; so what *is* this birthright to me?"
33 Then Jacob said, ᵀ"Swear to me as of this day." So he swore to him, and ᴿsold his birthright to Jacob.   Take an oath · Heb. 12:16
34 And Jacob gave Esau bread and stew of lentils; then ᴿhe ate and drank, arose, and went his way. Thus Esau ᴿdespised *his* birthright.   Eccl. 8:15 · Heb. 12:16, 17

Isaac and Abimelech

26 There was a famine in the land, besides the first famine that was in the days of Abraham. And Isaac went to Abimelech king of the Philistines, in Gerar.
2 Then the Lᴏʀᴅ appeared to him and said: "Do not go down to Egypt; live in ᴿthe land of which I shall tell you.   Gen. 12:1
3 "Dwell in this land, and I will be with you and bless you; for to you and your descendants I give all these lands, and I will perform the oath which I swore to Abraham your father.
4 "And ᴿI will make your descendants multiply as the stars of heaven; I will give to your descendants all these lands; ᴿand in your seed all the nations of the earth shall be blessed;   Gal. 3:8 · Gen. 12:3; 22:18
5 ᴿ"because Abraham obeyed My voice and kept My charge, My commandments, My statutes, and My laws."   Gen. 22:16, 18
6 So Isaac dwelt in Gerar.
7 And the men of the place asked about his wife. And he said, "She *is* my sister"; for ᴿhe was afraid to say, "She *is* my wife," *because he thought,* "lest the men of the place kill me for Rebekah, because she *is* beautiful to behold."   Prov. 29:25
8 Now it came to pass, when he had been there a long time, that Abimelech king of the Philistines looked through a window, and saw, and there was Isaac, ᵀshowing endearment to Rebekah his wife.   *caressing*
9 Then Abimelech called Isaac and said,

"Quite obviously she *is* your wife; so how could you say, 'She *is* my sister'?" Isaac said to him, "Because I said, 'Lest I die on account of her.'"
10 And Abimelech said, "What *is* this you have done to us? One of the people might soon have lain with your wife, and ᴿyou would have brought guilt on us."   Gen. 20:9
11 So Abimelech charged all *his* people, saying, "He who ᴿtouches this man or his wife shall surely be put to death."   Ps. 105:15
12 Then Isaac sowed in that land, and reaped in the same year a hundredfold; and the Lᴏʀᴅ ᴿblessed him.   Gen. 24:1; 25:3, 11; 26:3
13 The man ᴿbegan to prosper, and continued prospering until he became very prosperous;   [Prov. 10:22]
14 for he had possessions of flocks and possessions of herds and a great number of servants. So the Philistines envied him.
15 Now the Philistines had stopped up all the wells ᴿwhich his father's servants had dug in the days of Abraham his father, and they had filled them with earth.   Gen. 21:25, 30
16 And Abimelech said to Isaac, "Go away from us, for ᴿyou are much mightier than we."   Ex. 1:9
17 Then Isaac departed from there and ᵀpitched his tent in the Valley of Gerar, and dwelt there.   *camped*
18 And Isaac dug again the wells of water which they had dug in the days of Abraham his father, for the Philistines had stopped them up after the death of Abraham. ᴿHe called them by the names which his father had called them.   Gen. 21:31
19 Also Isaac's servants dug in the valley, and found a well of running water there.
20 But the herdsmen of Gerar quarreled with Isaac's herdsmen, saying, "The water *is* ours." So he called the name of the well *Esek, because they quarreled with him.
21 Then they dug another well, and they quarreled over that *one* also. So he called its name ᵀSitnah.   Lit. *Enmity*
22 And he moved from there and dug another well, and they did not quarrel over it. So he called its name *Rehoboth, because he said, "For now the Lᴏʀᴅ has made room for us, and we shall be fruitful in the land."
23 Then he went up from there to Beersheba.
24 And the Lᴏʀᴅ appeared to him the same night and said, "I *am* the God of your father Abraham; do not fear, for ᴿI *am* with you. I will bless you and multiply your descendants for My servant Abraham's sake."   Gen. 26:3, 4
25 So he built an altar there and called on the name of the Lᴏʀᴅ, and he pitched his tent there; and there Isaac's servants dug a well.
26 Then Abimelech came to him from Gerar

26:20 Lit. *Quarrel*
26:22 Lit. *Spaciousness*

with Ahuzzath, one of his friends, ^Rand Phichol the commander of his army. Gen. 21:22

27 And Isaac said to them, "Why have you come to me, ^Rsince you hate me and have ^Rsent me away from you?" Judg. 11:7 • Gen. 26:16

28 But they said, "We have certainly seen that the LORD ^Ris with you. So we said, 'Let there now be an oath between us, between you and us; and let us make a ^Tcovenant with you, Gen. 21:22, 23 • treaty

29 'that you will do us no harm, since we have not touched you, and since we have done nothing to you but good and have sent you away in peace. ^RYou are now the blessed of the LORD.' " Gen. 24:31

30 ^RSo he made them a feast, and they ate and drank. Gen. 19:3

31 Then they arose early in the morning and ^Rswore an oath with one another; and Isaac sent them away, and they departed from him in peace. Gen. 21:31

32 It came to pass the same day that Isaac's servants came and told him about the well which they had dug, and said to him, "We have found water."

33 So he called it *Shebah. Therefore the name of the city is *Beersheba to this day.

34 ^RWhen Esau was forty years old, he took as wives Judith the daughter of Beeri the Hittite, and Basemath the daughter of Elon the Hittite. Gen. 28:8; 36:2

35 And ^Rthey were a grief of mind to Isaac and Rebekah. Gen. 27:46; 28:1, 8

Isaac Blesses Jacob

27 Now it came to pass, when Isaac was ^Rold and ^Rhis eyes were so dim that he could not see, that he called Esau his older son and said to him, "My son." And he answered him, "Here I am." Gen. 35:28 • Gen. 48:10

2 Then he said, "Behold now, I am old. I ^Rdo not know the day of my death. [Prov. 27:1]

3 ^R"Now therefore, please take your weapons, your quiver and your bow, and go out to the field and hunt game for me. Gen. 25:27, 28

4 "And make me savory food, such as I love, and bring it to me that I may eat, that my soul may bless you before I die."

5 Now Rebekah was listening when Isaac spoke to Esau his son. And Esau went to the field to hunt game and to bring it.

6 So Rebekah spoke to Jacob her son, saying, "Indeed I heard your father speak to Esau your brother, saying,

7 'Bring me game and make savory food for me, that I may eat it and bless you in the presence of the LORD before my death.'

8 "Now therefore, my son, obey my voice according to what I command you.

9 "Go now to the flock and bring me from there two choice kids of the goats, and I will

make ^Rsavory food from them for your father, such as he loves. Gen. 27:4

10 "Then you shall take it to your father, that he may eat it, and that he ^Rmay bless you before his death." Gen. 27:4; 48:16

11 And Jacob said to Rebekah his mother, "Look, ^REsau my brother is a hairy man, and I am a smooth-skinned man. Gen. 25:25

12 "Perhaps my father will feel me, and I shall seem to be a deceiver to him; and I shall bring a curse on myself and not a blessing."

13 But his mother said to him, ^R"Let your curse be on me, my son; only obey my voice, and go, get them for me." Gen. 43:9

14 And he went and got them and brought them to his mother, and his mother made savory food, such as his father loved.

15 Then Rebekah took ^Rthe choice clothes of her elder son Esau, which were with her in the house, and put them on Jacob her younger son. Gen. 27:27

16 And she put the skins of the kids of the goats on his hands and on the smooth part of his neck.

17 Then she gave the savory food and the bread, which she had prepared, into the hand of her son Jacob.

18 So he went to his father and said, "My father." And he said, "Here I am. Who are you, my son?"

19 Jacob said to his father, "I am Esau your firstborn; I have done just as you told me; please arise, sit and eat of my game, ^Rthat your soul may bless me." Gen. 27:4

20 But Isaac said to his son, "How is it that you have found it so quickly, my son?" And he said, "Because the LORD your God brought it to me."

21 Then Isaac said to Jacob, "Please come near, that I ^Rmay feel you, my son, whether you are really my son Esau or not." Gen. 27:12

22 So Jacob went near to Isaac his father, and he felt him and said, "The voice is Jacob's voice, but the hands are the hands of Esau."

23 And he did not recognize him, because ^Rhis hands were hairy like his brother Esau's hands; so he blessed him. Gen. 27:16

24 Then he said, "Are you really my son Esau?" He said, "I am."

25 He said, "Bring it near to me, and I will eat of my son's game, so ^Rthat my soul may bless you." So he brought it near to him, and he ate; and he brought him wine, and he drank. Gen. 27:4, 10, 19, 31

26 Then his father Isaac said to him, "Come near now and kiss me, my son."

27 And he came near and ^Rkissed him; and he smelled the smell of his clothing, and blessed him and said: Gen. 29:13

"Surely, ^Rthe smell of my son Song 4:11
Is like the smell of a field
Which the LORD has blessed.

26:33 Lit. *Oath* or *Seven* • Lit. *Well of the Oath* or *Well of the Seven*

28 Therefore may ^RGod give you   Heb. 11:20
Of ^Rthe dew of heaven,   Deut. 33:13, 28
Of ^Rthe fatness of the earth,   Gen. 45:18
And plenty of grain and wine.
29 ^RLet peoples serve you,   Gen. 9:25; 25:23
And nations bow down to you.
Be master over your brethren,
And ^Rlet your mother's sons bow down
   to you.   Gen. 37:7, 10; 49:8
Cursed *be* everyone who curses you,
And blessed *be* those who bless you!"

Esau's Lost Hope

30 Now it happened, as soon as Isaac had
finished blessing Jacob, and Jacob had
scarcely gone out from the presence of Isaac
his father, that Esau his brother came in from
his hunting.
31 He also had made savory food, and
brought it to his father, and said to his father,
"Let my father arise and eat of his son's
game, that your soul may bless me."
32 And his father Isaac said to him, "Who
are you?" So he said, "I *am* your son, your
firstborn, Esau."
33 Then Isaac trembled exceedingly, and
said, "Who? Where *is* the one who hunted
game and brought *it* to me? I ate all *of it*
before you came, and I have blessed him—
^R*and* indeed he shall be blessed."   Gen. 25:23
34 When Esau heard the words of his fa-
ther, ^Rhe cried with an exceedingly great and
bitter cry, and said to his father, "Bless me—
me also, O my father!"   [Heb. 12:17]
35 But he said, "Your brother came with
deceit and has taken away your blessing."
36 And *Esau* said, "Is he not rightly named
^TJacob? For he has supplanted me these two
times. He took away my birthright, and now
look, he has taken away my blessing!" And
he said, "Have you not reserved a blessing for
me?"   Lit. *Supplanter* or *Deceitful*
37 Then Isaac answered and said to Esau,
"Indeed I have made him your master, and all
his brethren I have given to him as servants;
with grain and wine I have sustained him.
What shall I do now for you, my son?"
38 And Esau said to his father, "Have you
only one blessing, my father? Bless me—me
also, O my father!" And Esau lifted up his
voice ^Rand wept.   Heb. 12:17
39 Then Isaac his father answered and said
to him:

"Behold, ^Ryour dwelling shall be of the
^Tfatness of the earth,   Heb. 11:20 • *fertility*
And of the dew of heaven from above.
40 By your sword you shall live,
And ^Ryou shall serve your brother;
And ^Rit shall come to pass, when you
   become restless,
That you shall break his yoke from
   your neck."   Gen. 25:23; 27:29 • 2 Kin. 8:20-22

Jacob Escapes from Esau

41 So Esau hated Jacob because of the
blessing with which his father blessed him,
and Esau said in his heart, ^R"The days of
mourning for my father are at hand; then I
will kill my brother Jacob."   Gen. 50:2-4, 10
42 And the words of Esau her older son
were told to Rebekah. So she sent and called
Jacob her younger son, and said to him,
"Surely your brother Esau comforts himself
concerning you *by intending* to kill you.
43 "Now therefore, my son, obey my voice:
arise, flee to my brother Laban in Haran.
44 "And stay with him a ^Rfew days, until
your brother's fury turns away,   Gen. 31:41
45 "until your brother's anger turns away
from you, and he forgets what you have done
to him; then I will send and bring you from
there. Why should I be bereaved also of you
both in one day?"
46 And Rebekah said to Isaac, "I am weary
of my life because of the daughters of Heth; if
Jacob takes a wife of the daughters of Heth,
like these *who are* the daughters of the land,
what good will my life be to me?"

28 Then Isaac called Jacob and blessed
him, and ^Tcharged him, and said to
him: ^R"You shall not take a wife from the
daughters of Canaan.   commanded • Gen. 24:3
2 "Arise, go to Padan Aram, to the house
of ^RBethuel your mother's father; and take
yourself a wife from there of the daughters of
Laban your mother's brother.   Gen. 22:23

3 "May ^RGod Almighty bless you,
And make you ^Rfruitful and multiply
   you,   Gen. 17:16; 35:11; 48:3 • Gen. 26:4, 24
That you may be an assembly of
   peoples;
4 And give you the blessing of Abraham,
To you and your descendants with you,
That you may inherit the land
In which you are a stranger,
Which God gave to Abraham."

5 So Isaac sent Jacob away, and he went
to Padan Aram, to Laban the son of Bethuel
the Syrian, the brother of Rebekah, the
mother of Jacob and Esau.

Esau Marries Mahalath

6 Esau saw that Isaac had blessed Jacob
and sent him away to Padan Aram to take
himself a wife from there, *and that* as he
blessed him he gave him a charge, saying,
"You shall not take a wife from the daughters of Canaan,"
7 and that Jacob had obeyed his father and
his mother and had gone to Padan Aram.
8 Also Esau saw that the daughters of
Canaan did not please his father Isaac.
9 So Esau went to Ishmael and took
Mahalath the daughter of Ishmael, Abra-
ham's son, ^Rthe sister of Nebajoth, to be his
wife in addition to the wives he had.   Gen. 25:13

Jacob's Vow at Bethel

10 Now Jacob ᴿwent out from Beersheba and went toward Haran.   Hos. 12:12

11 So he came to a certain place and stayed there all night, because the sun had set. And he took one of the stones of that place and put it at his head, and he lay down in that place to sleep.

12 Then he dreamed, and behold, a ladder *was* set up on the earth, and its top reached to heaven; and there ᴿthe angels of God were ascending and descending on it.   John 1:51

13 And behold, the LORD stood above it and said: ᴿ"I *am* the LORD God of Abraham your father and the God of Isaac; ᴿthe land on which you lie I will give to you and your descendants.   Gen. 26:24 • Gen. 13:15, 17; 26:3; 35:12

14 "Also your descendants shall be as the dust of the earth; you shall spread abroad to the west and the east, to the north and the south; and in you and in your seed all the families of the earth shall be blessed.

15 "Behold, I *am* with you and will keep you wherever you go, and will bring you back to this land; for I will not leave you until I have done what I have spoken to you."

16 Then Jacob awoke from his sleep and said, "Surely the LORD is in ᴿthis place, and I did not know *it*."   Ex. 3:5

17 And he was afraid and said, "How awesome *is* this place! This *is* none other than the house of God, and this *is* the gate of heaven!"

18 Then Jacob rose early in the morning, and took the stone that he had put at his head, ᴿset it up as a pillar, ᴿand poured oil on top of it.   Gen. 31:13, 45 • Lev. 8:10–12

19 And he called the name of ᴿthat place ᵀBethel; but the name of that city had been Luz previously.   Judg. 1:23, 26 • Lit. *House of God*

20 Then Jacob made a vow, saying, "If God will be with me, and keep me in this way that I am going, and give me ᴿbread to eat and clothing to put on,   1 Tim. 6:8

21 "so that ᴿI come back to my father's house in peace, ᴿthen the LORD shall be my God.   Judg. 11:31 • Deut. 26:17

22 "And this stone which I have set as a pillar ᴿshall be God's house, ᴿand of all that You give me I will surely give a ᵀtenth to You."   Gen. 35:7, 14 • Gen. 14:20 • *tithe*

Jacob Meets Rachel

29 So Jacob went on his journey and came to the land of the people of the East.

2 And he looked, and saw a ᴿwell in the field; and behold, there *were* three flocks of sheep lying by it; for out of that well they watered the flocks. A large stone *was* on the well's mouth.   Gen. 24:10, 11

3 Now all the flocks would be gathered there; and they would roll the stone from the well's mouth, water the sheep, and put the stone back in its place on the well's mouth.

4 And Jacob said to them, "My brethren, where *are* you from?" And they said, "We *are* from ᴿHaran."   Gen. 11:31; 28:10

5 Then he said to them, "Do you know ᴿLaban the son of Nahor?" And they said, "We know him."   Gen. 24:24, 29; 28:2

6 So he said to them, ᴿ"Is he well?" And they said, "*He is* well. And look, his daughter Rachel is coming with the sheep."   Gen. 43:27

7 Then he said, "Look, *it is* still ᵀhigh day; *it is* not time for the cattle to be gathered together. Water the sheep, and go and feed *them*."   *early in the day*

8 But they said, "We cannot until all the flocks are gathered together, and they have rolled the stone from the well's mouth; then we water the sheep."

9 Now while he was still speaking with them, ᴿRachel came with her father's sheep, for she was a shepherdess.   Ex. 2:16

10 And it came to pass, when Jacob saw Rachel the daughter of Laban his mother's brother, and the sheep of Laban his mother's brother, that Jacob went near and ᴿrolled the stone from the well's mouth, and watered the flock of Laban his mother's brother.   Ex. 2:17

11 Then Jacob ᴿkissed Rachel, and lifted up his voice and wept.   Gen. 33:4; 45:14, 15

12 And Jacob told Rachel that he *was* her father's relative and that he *was* Rebekah's son. So she ran and told her father.

13 Then it came to pass, when Laban heard the report about Jacob his sister's son, that ᴿhe ran to meet him, and embraced him and kissed him, and brought him to his house. So he told Laban all these things.   Gen. 24:29–31

14 And Laban said to him, ᴿ"Surely you *are* my bone and my flesh." And he stayed with him for a month.   Gen. 2:23; 37:27

Jacob Marries Leah and Rachel

15 Then Laban said to Jacob, "Because you *are* my relative, should you therefore serve me for nothing? Tell me, ᴿwhat *should* your wages *be*?"   Gen. 30:28; 31:41

16 Now Laban had two daughters: the name of the elder *was* Leah, and the name of the younger *was* Rachel.

17 Leah's eyes *were* ᵀdelicate, but Rachel was beautiful of form and appearance.   Or *weak*

18 Now Jacob loved Rachel; so he said, ᴿ"I will serve you seven years for Rachel your younger daughter."   Gen. 31:41

19 And Laban said, "*It is* better that I give her to you than that I should give her to another man. Stay with me."

20 So Jacob ᴿserved seven years for Rachel, and they seemed *only* a few days to him because of the love he had for her.   Gen. 30:26

21 Then Jacob said to Laban, "Give me my wife, for my days are fulfilled, that I may ᴿgo in to her."   Judg. 15:1

22 And Laban gathered together all the men of the place and ᴿmade a feast.   John 2:1, 2

23 Now it came to pass in the evening, that he took Leah his daughter and brought her to Jacob; and he went in to her.

24 And Laban gave his maid ᴿZilpah to his daughter Leah *as* a maid.   Gen. 30:9, 10

25 So it came to pass in the morning, that behold, it *was* Leah. And he said to Laban, "What is this you have done to me? Was it not for Rachel that I served you? Why then have you ᴿdeceived me?"   1 Sam. 28:12

26 And Laban said, "It must not be done so in our ᵀcountry, to give the younger before the firstborn.   Lit. *place*

27 "Fulfill her week, and we will give you this one also for the service which you will serve with me still another seven years."

28 Then Jacob did so and fulfilled her week. So he gave him his daughter Rachel as wife also.

29 And Laban gave his maid ᴿBilhah to his daughter Rachel as a maid.   Gen. 30:3-5

30 Then *Jacob* also went in to Rachel, and he also ᴿloved Rachel more than Leah. And he served with Laban ᴿstill another seven years.   Deut. 21:15-17 • Gen. 30:26; 31:41

The Children of Jacob

31 When the Lᴏʀᴅ ᴿsaw that Leah *was* ᵀunloved, He ᴿopened her womb; but Rachel *was* barren.   Ps. 127:3 • Lit. *hated* • Gen. 30:1

32 So Leah conceived and bore a son, and she called his name ᵀReuben; for she said, "The Lᴏʀᴅ has surely ᴿlooked on my affliction. Now therefore, my husband will love me."   Lit. *See, a Son* • Deut. 26:7

33 Then she conceived again and bore a son, and said, "Because the Lᴏʀᴅ has heard that I *am* ᵀunloved, He has therefore given me this *son* also." And she called his name ᵀSimeon.   Lit. *hated* • Lit. *Heard*

34 She conceived again and bore a son, and said, "Now this time my husband will become attached to me, because I have borne him three sons." Therefore his name was called ᵀLevi.   Lit. *Attached*

35 And she conceived again and bore a son, and said, "Now I will praise the Lᴏʀᴅ." Therefore she called his name ᴿJudah.ᵀ Then she stopped bearing.   Matt. 1:2 • Lit. *Praise*

30 Now when Rachel saw that she bore Jacob no children, Rachel ᴿenvied her sister, and said to Jacob, "Give me children, ᴿor else I die!"   Gen. 37:11 • [Job 5:2]

2 And Jacob's anger was aroused against Rachel, and he said, ᴿ"*Am* I in the place of God, who has withheld from you the fruit of the womb?"   1 Sam. 1:5

3 So she said, "Here is my maid Bilhah; go in to her, ᴿand she will bear *a child* on my knees, ᴿthat I also may ᵀhave children by her."   Gen. 50:23 • Gen. 16:2, 3 • Lit. *be built up by her*

4 Then she gave him Bilhah her maid ᴿas wife, and Jacob went in to her.   Gen. 16:3, 4

5 And Bilhah conceived and bore Jacob a son.

6 Then Rachel said, "God has ᴿjudged my case; and He has also heard my voice and given me a son." Therefore she called his name ᵀDan.   Lam. 3:59 • Lit. *Judge*

7 And Rachel's maid Bilhah conceived again and bore Jacob a second son.

8 Then Rachel said, "With ᵀgreat wrestlings I have wrestled with my sister, *and* indeed I have prevailed." So she called his name *Naphtali.   Lit. *wrestlings of God*

9 When Leah saw that she had stopped bearing, she took Zilpah her maid and ᴿgave her to Jacob as wife.   Gen. 30:4

10 And Leah's maid Zilpah bore Jacob a son.

11 Then Leah said, "A troop comes!" So she called his name *Gad.

12 And Leah's maid Zilpah bore Jacob a second son.

13 Then Leah said, "I am happy, for the daughters ᴿwill call me blessed." So she called his name ᵀAsher.   Luke 1:48 • Lit. *Happy*

14 Now Reuben went in the days of wheat harvest and found mandrakes in the field, and brought them to his mother Leah. Then Rachel said to Leah, ᴿ"Please give me *some* of your son's mandrakes."   Gen. 25:30

15 But she said to her, "*Is it* a small matter that you have taken away my husband? Would you take away my son's mandrakes also?" And Rachel said, "Therefore he will lie with you tonight for your son's mandrakes."

16 When Jacob came out of the field in the evening, Leah went out to meet him and said, "You must come in to me, for I have surely hired you with my son's mandrakes." And he lay with her that night.

17 And God listened to Leah, and she conceived and bore Jacob a fifth son.

18 Leah said, "God has given me my wages, because I have given my maid to my husband." So she called his name *Issachar.

19 Then Leah conceived again and bore Jacob a sixth son.

20 And Leah said, "God has endowed me *with* a good endowment; now my husband will dwell with me, because I have borne him six sons." So she called his name *Zebulun.

21 Afterward she bore a ᴿdaughter, and called her name ᵀDinah.   Gen. 34:1 • Lit. *Judgment*

22 Then God remembered Rachel, and God listened to her and opened her womb.

23 And she conceived and bore a son, and said, "God has taken away my reproach."

24 So she called his name *Joseph, and said, "The Lᴏʀᴅ shall add to me another son."

30:8 Lit. *My Wrestling*
30:11 So with Qr., Syr., Tg.; Kt., LXX, Vg. *in fortune*
30:18 Lit. *Hire*
30:20 Lit. *Dwelling*
30:24 Lit. *He Will Add*

Jacob's Agreement with Laban

25 And it came to pass, when Rachel had borne Joseph, that Jacob said to Laban, "Send me away, that I may go to ᴿmy own place and to my country. Gen. 18:33

26 "Give me my wives and my children ᴿfor whom I have served you, and let me go; for you know my service which I have done for you." Gen. 29:18–20, 27, 30

27 And Laban said to him, "Please stay, if I have found favor in your eyes, for ᴿI have learned by experience that the Lᴏʀᴅ has blessed me for your sake." Gen. 26:24; 39:3

28 Then he said, ᴿ"Name me your wages, and I will give it." Gen. 29:15; 31:7, 41

29 So Jacob said to him, ᴿ"You know how I have served you and how your livestock has been with me. Gen. 31:6, 38–40

30 "For what you had before I came was little, and it has increased to a great amount; the Lᴏʀᴅ has blessed you ᵀsince my coming. And now, when shall I also ᴿprovide for my own house?" Lit. at my foot • [1 Tim. 5:8]

31 So he said, "What shall I give you?" And Jacob said, "You shall not give me anything. If you will do this thing for me, I will again feed and keep your flocks:

32 "Let me pass through all your flock today, removing from there all the speckled and spotted sheep, and all the brown ones among the lambs, and the spotted and speckled among the goats; and ᴿthese shall be my wages. Gen. 31:8

33 "So my ᴿrighteousness will answer for me in time to come, when the subject of my wages comes before you: every one that is not speckled and spotted among the goats, and brown among the lambs, will be considered stolen, if it is with me." Ps. 37:6

34 And Laban said, "Oh, that it were according to your word!"

35 So he removed that day the male goats that were ᴿspeckled and spotted, all the female goats that were speckled and spotted, every one that had some white in it, and all the brown ones among the lambs, and gave them into the hand of his sons. Gen. 31:9–12

36 Then he put ᵀthree days' journey between himself and Jacob, and Jacob fed the rest of Laban's flocks. 60 mi.

37 Now Jacob took for himself rods of green poplar and of the almond and chestnut trees, peeled white strips in them, and exposed the white which was in the rods.

38 And the rods which he had peeled, he set before the flocks in the gutters, in the watering troughs where the flocks came to drink, so that they should conceive when they came to drink.

39 So the flocks conceived before the rods, and the flocks brought forth streaked, speckled, and spotted.

40 Then Jacob separated the lambs, and made the flocks face toward the streaked and all the brown in the flock of Laban; but he put his own flocks by themselves and did not put them with Laban's flock.

41 And it came to pass, whenever the stronger livestock conceived, that Jacob placed the rods before the eyes of the livestock in the gutters, that they might conceive among the rods.

42 But when the flocks were feeble, he did not put them in; so the feebler were Laban's and the stronger Jacob's.

43 Thus the man became exceedingly prosperous, and had large flocks, female and male servants, and camels and donkeys.

Jacob Flees from Laban

31 Now Jacob heard the words of Laban's sons, saying, "Jacob has taken away all that was our father's, and from what was our father's he has acquired all this wealth."

2 And Jacob saw the ᴿcountenance of Laban, and indeed it was not ᴿfavorable toward him as before. Gen. 4:5 • Deut. 28:54

3 Then the Lᴏʀᴅ said to Jacob, "Return to the land of your fathers and to your family, and I will ᴿbe with you." Gen. 46:4

4 So Jacob sent and called Rachel and Leah to the field, to his flock,

5 and said to them, ᴿ"I see your father's ᵀcountenance, that it is not favorable toward me as before; but the God of my father ᴿhas been with me. Gen. 31:2, 3 • Lit. face • Is. 41:10

6 "And ᴿyou know that with all my might I have served your father. Gen. 30:29; 31:38–41

7 "Yet your father has deceived me and changed my wages ᴿten times, but God ᴿdid not allow him to hurt me. Num. 14:22 • Job 1:10

8 "If he said thus: 'The speckled shall be your wages,' then all the flocks bore speckled. And if he said thus: 'The streaked shall be your wages,' then all the flocks bore streaked.

9 "So God has taken away the livestock of your father and given them to me.

10 "And it happened, at the time when the flocks conceived, that I lifted my eyes and saw in a dream, and behold, the rams which leaped upon the flocks were streaked, speckled, and gray-spotted.

11 "Then ᴿthe Angel of God spoke to me in a dream, saying, 'Jacob.' And I said, 'Here I am.' Gen. 16:7–11; 22:11, 15; 31:13; 48:16

12 "And He said, 'Lift your eyes now and see, all the rams which leap on the flocks are streaked, speckled, and gray-spotted; for I have seen all that Laban is doing to you.

13 'I am the God of Bethel, where you anointed the pillar and where you made a vow to Me. Now arise, get out of this land, and return to the land of your family.' "

14 Then Rachel and Leah answered and said to him, "Is there still any portion or inheritance for us in our father's house?

15 "Are we not considered strangers by

him? For ᴿhe has sold us, and also completely consumed our money.   Gen. 29:15, 20, 23, 27

16 "For all these riches which God has taken from our father are *really* ours and our children's; now then, whatever God has said to you, do it."

17 Then Jacob rose and set his sons and his wives on camels.

18 And he carried away all his livestock and all his possessions which he had gained, his acquired livestock which he had gained in Padan Aram, to go to his father Isaac in the land of ᴿCanaan.   Gen. 17:8; 33:18; 35:27

19 Now Laban had gone to shear his sheep, and Rachel had stolen the ᴿhouseholdᵀ idols that were her father's.   Judg. 17:5 • Heb. teraphim

20 And Jacob stole away, unknown to Laban the Syrian, in that he did not tell him that he intended to flee.

21 So he fled with all that he had. He arose and crossed the river, and ᵀheaded toward the mountains of Gilead.   Lit. set his face toward

Laban Pursues Jacob

22 And Laban was told on the third day that Jacob had fled.

23 Then he took his brethren with him and pursued him for seven days' journey, and he overtook him in the mountains of Gilead.

24 But God ᴿhad come to Laban the Syrian in a dream by night, and said to him, "Be careful that you ᴿspeak to Jacob neither good nor bad."   Gen. 20:3; 31:29; 46:2-4 • Gen. 24:50; 31:7, 29

25 So Laban overtook Jacob. Now Jacob had pitched his tent in the mountains, and Laban with his brethren pitched in the mountains of Gilead.

26 And Laban said to Jacob: "What have you done, that you have stolen away unknown to me, and carried away my daughters like captives *taken* with the sword?

27 "Why did you flee away secretly, and steal away from me, and not tell me; for I might have sent you away with joy and songs, with timbrel and harp?

28 "And you did not allow me ᴿto kiss my sons and my daughters. Now ᴿyou have done foolishly in *so* doing.   Gen. 31:55 • 1 Sam. 13:13

29 "It is in my power to do you harm, but the God of your father spoke to me ᴿlast night, saying, 'Be careful that you speak to Jacob neither good nor bad.'   Gen. 31:24

30 "And now you have surely gone because you greatly long for your father's house, *but* why did you ᴿsteal my gods?"   Judg. 17:5; 18:24

31 Then Jacob answered and said to Laban, "Because I was ᴿafraid, for I said, 'Perhaps you would take your daughters from me by force.'   Gen. 26:7; 32:7, 11

32 "With whomever you find your gods, ᴿdo not let him live. In the presence of our brethren, identify what I have of yours and take *it* with you." For Jacob did not know that Rachel had stolen them.   Gen. 44:9

33 And Laban went into Jacob's tent, into Leah's tent, and into the two maids' tents, but he did not find *them*. Then he went out of Leah's tent and entered Rachel's tent.

34 Now Rachel had taken the ᵀhousehold idols, put them in the camel's saddle, and sat on them. And Laban ᵀsearched all about the tent but did not find *them*.   Heb. teraphim • Lit. felt

35 And she said to her father, "Let it not displease my lord that I cannot ᴿrise before you, for the manner of women *is* with me." And he searched but did not find the ᵀhousehold idols.   Lev. 19:32 • Heb. teraphim

36 Then Jacob was angry and rebuked Laban, and Jacob answered and said to Laban: "What *is* my ᵀtrespass? What *is* my sin, that you have so hotly pursued me?   transgression

37 "Although you have searched all my things, what part of your household things have you found? Set *it* here before my brethren and your brethren, that they may judge between us both!

38 "These twenty years I *have been* with you; your ewes and your female goats have not miscarried their young, and I have not eaten the rams of your flock.

39 ᴿ"That which was torn *by beasts* I did not bring to you; I bore the loss of it. ᴿYou required it from my hand, *whether* stolen by day or stolen by night.   Ex. 22:10 • Ex. 22:10-13

40 "*There* I was! In the day the drought consumed me, and the frost by night, and my sleep departed from my eyes.

41 "Thus I have been in your house twenty years; I served you fourteen years for your two daughters, and six years for your flock, and you have changed my wages ten times.

42 "Unless the God of my father, the God of Abraham and the Fear of Isaac, had been with me, surely now you would have sent me away empty-handed. ᴿGod has seen my affliction and the labor of my hands, and ᴿrebuked *you* last night."   Ex. 3:7 • 1 Chr. 12:17

Laban's Covenant with Jacob

43 And Laban answered and said to Jacob, "*These* daughters *are* my daughters, and *these* children *are* my children, and *this* flock *is* my flock; all that you see *is* mine. But what can I do this day to these my daughters or to their children whom they have borne?

44 "Now therefore, come, let us make a ᵀcovenant, ᴿyou and I, and let it be a witness between you and me."   treaty • Josh. 24:27

45 So Jacob ᴿtook a stone and set it up *as* a pillar.   Gen. 28:18; 35:14

46 Then Jacob said to his brethren, "Gather stones." And they took stones and made a heap, and they ate there on the heap.

47 Laban called it ᵀJegar Sahadutha, but Jacob called it ᵀGaleed.   Both mean Heap of Witness

48 And Laban said, ᴿ"This heap *is* a witness between you and me this day." Therefore its name was called Galeed,   Josh. 24:27

49 also ᵀMizpah, because he said, "May the

LORD watch between you and me when we are absent one from another. Lit. *Watch*

50 "If you afflict my daughters, or if you take *other* wives besides my daughters, although no man *is* with us—see, God *is* witness between you and me!"

51 Then Laban said to Jacob, "Here is this heap and here is *this* pillar, which I have placed between you and me.

52 "This heap *is* a witness, and *this* pillar *is* a witness, that I will not pass beyond this heap to you, and you will not pass beyond this heap and this pillar to me, for harm.

53 "The God of Abraham, the God of Nahor, and the God of their father judge between us." And Jacob swore by Rthe TFear of his father Isaac.   Gen. 31:42 · A reference to God

54 Then Jacob offered a sacrifice on the mountain, and called his brethren to eat bread. And they ate bread and stayed all night on the mountain.

55 And early in the morning Laban arose, and kissed his sons and daughters and Rblessed them. Then Laban departed and Rreturned to his place.   Gen. 28:1 · Num. 24:25

Esau Comes to Meet Jacob

32 So Jacob went on his way, and Rthe angels of God met him.   Num. 22:31

2 When Jacob saw them, he said, "This *is* God's Rcamp." And he called the name of that place TMahanaim.   Josh. 5:14 · Lit. *Double Camp*

3 Then Jacob sent messengers before him to Esau his brother in the land of Seir, Rthe Tcountry of Edom.   Gen. 25:30; 36:6-9 · Lit. *field*

4 And he commanded them, saying, R"Speak thus to my lord Esau, 'Thus your servant Jacob says: "I have dwelt with Laban and stayed there until now.   Prov. 15:1

5 R"I have oxen, donkeys, flocks, and male and female servants; and I have sent to tell my lord, that RI may find favor in your sight." ' "   Gen. 30:43 · Gen. 33:8, 15

6 Then the messengers returned to Jacob, saying, "We came to your brother Esau, and Rhe also is coming to meet you, and four hundred men *are* with him."   Gen. 33:1

7 So Jacob was greatly afraid and Rdistressed; and he divided the people that *were* with him, and the flocks and herds and camels, into two companies.   Gen. 32:11; 35:3

8 And he said, "If Esau comes to the one company and Tattacks it, then the other company which is left will escape." Lit. *strikes*

9 RThen Jacob said, R"O God of my father Abraham and God of my father Isaac, the LORD Rwho said to me, 'Return to your country and to your family, and I will deal well with you':   [Ps. 50:15] · Gen. 28:13; 31:42 · Gen. 31:3, 13

10 "I am not worthy of the least of all the Rmercies and of all the truth which You have shown Your servant; for I crossed over this Jordan with Rmy staff, and now I have become two companies.   Gen. 24:27 · Job 8:7

11 "Deliver me, I pray, from the hand of my brother, from the hand of Esau; for I fear him, lest he come and Tattack me *and* Rthe mother with the children. Lit. *strike* · Hos. 10:14

12 "For RYou said, 'I will surely treat you well, and make your descendants as the Rsand of the sea, which cannot be numbered for multitude.' "   Gen. 28:13-15 · Gen. 22:17

13 So he lodged there that same night, and took what came to his hand as Ra present for Esau his brother: Gen. 43:11

14 two hundred female goats and twenty male goats, two hundred ewes and twenty rams,

15 thirty milk camels with their colts, forty cows and ten bulls, twenty female donkeys and ten foals.

16 Then he delivered *them* to the hand of his servants, every drove by itself, and said to his servants, "Pass over before me, and put some distance between successive droves."

17 And he commanded the first one, saying, "When Esau my brother meets you and asks you, saying, 'To whom do you belong, and where are you going? Whose *are* these in front of you?'

18 "then you shall say, 'They *are* your servant Jacob's. It *is* a present sent to my lord Esau; and behold, he also *is* behind us.' "

19 So he commanded the second, the third, and all who followed the droves, saying, "In this manner you shall speak to Esau when you find him;

20 "and also say, 'Behold, your servant Jacob *is* behind us.' " For he said, "I will Rappease him with the present that goes before me, and afterward I will see his face; perhaps he will accept me."   [Prov. 21:14]

21 So the present went on over before him, but he himself lodged that night in the camp.

Wrestling with God

22 And he arose that night and took his two wives, his two female servants, and his eleven sons, and crossed over the ford of Jabbok.

23 He took them, sent them over the brook, and sent over what he had.

24 Then Jacob was left alone; and a Man wrestled with him until the breaking of day.

25 Now when He saw that He did not prevail against him, He Ttouched the socket of his hip; and the socket of Jacob's hip was out of joint as He wrestled with him.   struck

26 And RHe said, "Let Me go, for the day breaks." But he said, R"I will not let You go unless You bless me!"   Luke 24:28 · Hos. 12:4

27 So He said to him, "What *is* your name?" He said, "Jacob."

28 And He said, R"Your name shall no longer be called Jacob, but TIsrael; for you have struggled with God and with men, and have prevailed."   Gen. 35:10 · Lit. *Prince with God*

29 Then Jacob asked, saying, "Tell *me* Your name, I pray." And He said, R"Why *is* it *that*

you ask about My name?" And He ^Rblessed him there.   Judg. 13:17, 18 • Gen. 35:9

30 So Jacob called the name of the place ^TPeniel: "For I have seen God face to face, and my life is preserved."   Lit. Face of God

31 Just as he crossed over *Penuel the sun rose on him, and he limped on his hip.

32 Therefore to this day the children of Israel do not eat the muscle that shrank, which is on the hip socket, because He ^Ttouched the socket of Jacob's hip in the muscle that shrank.   Or struck

Jacob and Esau Meet

33 Now Jacob lifted his eyes and looked, and there, ^REsau was coming, and with him were four hundred men. So he divided the children among Leah, Rachel, and the two maidservants.   Gen. 32:6

2 And he put the maidservants and their children in front, Leah and her children behind, and Rachel and Joseph last.

3 Then he crossed over before them and ^Rbowed himself to the ground seven times, until he came near to his brother. Gen. 18:2; 42:6

4 ^RBut Esau ran to meet him, and embraced him, ^Rand fell on his neck and kissed him, and they wept.   Gen. 32:28 • Gen. 45:14, 15

5 And he lifted his eyes and saw the women and children, and said, "Who are these with you?" So he said, "The children ^Rwhom God has graciously given your servant."   Gen. 48:9

6 Then the maidservants came near, they and their children, and bowed down.

7 And Leah also came near with her children, and they bowed down. Afterward Joseph and Rachel came near, and they bowed down.

8 Then Esau said, "What do you mean by ^Rall this company which I met?" And he said, "These are ^Rto find favor in the sight of my lord."   Gen. 32:13–16 • Gen. 32:5

9 But Esau said, "I have enough, my brother; keep what you have for yourself."

10 And Jacob said, "No, please, if I have now found favor in your sight, then receive my present from my hand, inasmuch as I ^Rhave seen your face as though I had seen the face of God, and you were pleased with me.   Gen. 43:3

11 "Please, take my blessing that is brought to you, because God has dealt graciously with me, and because I have enough." So he urged him, and he took it.

12 Then Esau said, "Let us take our journey; let us go, and I will go before you."

13 But Jacob said to him, "My lord knows that the children are weak, and the flocks and herds which are nursing are with me. And if the men should drive them hard one day, all the flock will die.

14 "Please let my lord go on ahead before his servant. I will lead on slowly at a pace which the livestock that go before me, and the children, are able to endure, until I come to my lord ^Rin Seir."   Gen. 32:3; 36:8

15 And Esau said, "Now let me leave with you some of the people who are with me." But he said, "What need is there? ^RLet me find favor in the sight of my lord."   Ruth 2:13

16 So Esau returned that day on his way to Seir.

17 And Jacob journeyed to ^RSuccoth, built himself a house, and made ^Tbooths for his livestock. Therefore the name of the place is called ^TSuccoth.   Josh. 13:27 • shelters • Lit. Booths

Jacob Comes to Canaan

18 Then Jacob came safely to the city of ^RShechem, which is in the land of Canaan, when he came from Padan Aram; and he pitched his tent before the city.   Josh. 24:1

19 And ^Rhe bought the parcel of ^Tland, where he had pitched his tent, from the children of Hamor, Shechem's father, for one hundred pieces of money.   John 4:5 • Lit. the field

20 Then he erected an altar there and called it ^TEl Elohe Israel.   Lit. God, the God of Israel

The Dinah Incident

34 Now ^RDinah the daughter of Leah, whom she had borne to Jacob, went out to see the daughters of the land. Gen. 30:21

2 And when Shechem the son of Hamor the Hivite, prince of the country, saw her, he took her and lay with her, and violated her.

3 His soul ^Twas strongly attracted to Dinah the daughter of Jacob, and he loved the young woman and spoke ^Tkindly to the young woman.   Lit. clung to • tenderly

4 So Shechem ^Rspoke to his father Hamor, saying, "Get me this young woman as a wife."   Judg. 14:2

5 And Jacob heard that he had defiled Dinah his daughter. Now his sons were with his livestock in the field; so Jacob ^Rheld^T his peace until they came.   2 Sam. 13:22 • kept silent

6 Then Hamor the father of Shechem went out to Jacob to speak with him.

7 And the sons of Jacob came in from the field when they heard it; and the men were grieved and very angry, because he ^Rhad done a disgraceful thing in Israel by lying with Jacob's daughter, ^Ra thing which ought not to be done.   Judg. 20:6 • 2 Sam. 13:12

8 But Hamor spoke with them, saying, "The soul of my son Shechem longs for your daughter. Please give her to him as a wife.

9 "And make marriages with us; give your daughters to us, and take our daughters to yourselves.

10 "So you shall dwell with us, and the land shall be before you. Dwell and trade in it, and acquire possessions for yourselves in it."

11 Then Shechem said to her father and her

32:31 Lit. Face of God; same as Peniel, v. 30

brothers, "Let me find favor in your eyes, and whatever you say to me I will give.

12 "Ask me ever so much dowry and gift, and I will give according to what you say to me; but give me the young woman as a wife."

13 But the sons of Jacob answered Shechem and Hamor his father, and spoke deceitfully, because he had defiled Dinah their sister.

14 And they said to them, "We cannot do this thing, to give our sister to one who is ᴿuncircumcised, for ᴿthat *would be* a reproach to us.   Ex. 12:48 • Josh. 5:2-9

15 "But on this *condition* we will consent to you: If you will become as we *are*, if every male of you is circumcised,

16 "then we will give our daughters to you, and we will take your daughters to us; and we will dwell with you, and we will become one people.

17 "But if you will not heed us and be circumcised, then we will take our daughter and be gone."

18 And their words pleased Hamor and Shechem, Hamor's son.

19 So the young man did not delay to do the thing, because he delighted in Jacob's daughter. He *was* ᴿmore honorable than all the household of his father.   1 Chr. 4:9

20 And Hamor and Shechem his son came to the ᴿgate of their city, and spoke with the men of their city, saying: Ruth 4:1, 11

21 "These men *are* at peace with us. Therefore let them dwell in the land and trade in it. For indeed the land *is* large enough for them. Let us take their daughters to us as wives, and let us give them our daughters.

22 "Only on this *condition* will the men consent to dwell with us, to be one people: if every male among us is circumcised as they *are* circumcised.

23 "*Will* not their livestock, their property, and every animal of theirs *be* ours? Only let us consent to them, and they will dwell with us."

24 And all who went out of the gate of his city heeded Hamor and Shechem his son; every male was circumcised, all who ᴿwent out of the gate of his city.   Gen. 23:10, 18

25 Now it came to pass on the third day, when they were in pain, that two of the sons of Jacob, Simeon and Levi, Dinah's brothers, each took his sword and came boldly upon the city and killed all the males.

26 And they killed Hamor and Shechem his son with the edge of the sword, and took Dinah from Shechem's house, and went out.

27 The sons of Jacob came upon the slain, and plundered the city, because their sister had been defiled.

28 They took their sheep, their oxen, and their donkeys, what *was* in the city and what *was* in the field,

29 and all their wealth. All their little ones and their wives they took captive; and they plundered even all that *was* in the houses.

30 Then Jacob said to Simeon and Levi, ᴿ"You have ᴿtroubled me ᴿby making me obnoxious among the inhabitants of the land, among the Canaanites and the Perizzites; ᴿand since I *am* few in number, they will gather themselves together against me and kill me. I shall be destroyed, my household and I."   Gen. 49:6 • Josh. 7:25 • Ex. 5:21 • Deut. 4:27

31 But they said, "Should he treat our sister like a harlot?"

Jacob's Return to Bethel

35 Then God said to Jacob, "Arise, go up to ᴿBethel and dwell there; and make an altar there to God, ᴿwho appeared to you ᴿwhen you fled from the face of Esau your brother."   Gen. 28:19; 31:13 • Gen. 28:13 • Gen. 27:43

2 And Jacob said to his ᴿhousehold and to all who *were* with him, "Put away the foreign gods that *are* among you, purify yourselves, and change your garments.   Josh. 24:15

3 "Then let us arise and go up to Bethel; and I will make an altar there to God, ᴿwho answered me in the day of my distress ᴿand has been with me in the way which I have gone."   Gen. 32:7, 24 • Gen. 28:15, 20; 31:3, 42

4 So they gave Jacob all the foreign ᵀgods which *were* in their hands, and all the ᴿearrings which *were* in their ears; and Jacob hid them under ᴿthe terebinth tree which *was* by Shechem.   idols • Hos. 2:13 • Josh. 24:26

5 And they journeyed, and ᴿthe terror of God was upon the cities that *were* all around them, and they did not pursue the sons of Jacob.   Ex. 15:16; 23:27

6 So Jacob came to ᴿLuz (that *is*, Bethel), which *is* in the land of Canaan, he and all the people who *were* with him.   Gen. 28:19, 22; 48:3

7 And he built an altar there and called the place ᵀEl Bethel, because there God appeared to him when he fled from the face of his brother.   Lit. *God of the House of God*

8 Now ᴿDeborah, Rebekah's nurse, died, and she was buried below Bethel under the terebinth tree. So the name of it was called ᵀAllon Bachuth.   Gen. 24:59 • Lit. *Terebinth of Weeping*

9 Then ᴿGod appeared to Jacob again, when he came from Padan Aram, and ᴿblessed him.   Josh. 5:13 • Gen. 32:29

10 And God said to him, "Your name *is* Jacob; ᴿyour name shall not be called Jacob anymore, ᴿbut Israel shall be your name." So He called his name Israel.   Gen. 17:5 • Gen. 32:28

11 Also God said to him: "I *am* God Almighty. Be fruitful and multiply; a nation and a company of nations shall proceed from you, and kings shall come from your body.

12 "The ᴿland which I gave Abraham and Isaac I give to you; and to your descendants after you I give this land."   Gen. 12:7; 13:15

13 Then God ᵀwent up from him in the place where He talked with him.   *departed*

14 So Jacob ᴿset up a pillar in the place where He talked with him, a pillar of stone; and he poured a drink offering on it, and he poured oil on it.   Gen. 28:18, 19; 31:45
15 And Jacob called the name of the place where God spoke with him, ᴿBethel. Gen. 28:19

Death of Rachel

16 Then they journeyed from Bethel. And when there was but a ᵀlittle distance to go to Ephrath, Rachel labored *in childbirth,* and she had hard labor.   5 mi.
17 Now it came to pass, when she was in hard labor, that the midwife said to her, "Do not fear; you will have this son also."
18 And so it was, as her soul was departing (for she died), that she called his name *Ben-Oni; but his father called him *Benjamin.
19 So Rachel died and was buried on the way to Ephrath (that *is,* Bethlehem).
20 And Jacob set a pillar on her grave, which *is* the pillar of Rachel's grave ᴿto this day.   1 Sam. 10:2
21 Then Israel journeyed and pitched his tent beyond ᴿthe tower of Eder.   Mic. 4:8
22 And it happened, when Israel dwelt in that land, that Reuben went and ᴿlay with Bilhah his father's concubine; and Israel heard *about* it.   Gen. 49:4

Jacob's Twelve Sons

Now the sons of Jacob were twelve:
23 the sons of Leah *were* ᴿReuben, Jacob's firstborn, and Simeon, Levi, Judah, Issachar, and Zebulun;   Ex. 1:1-4
24 the sons of Rachel *were* Joseph and Benjamin;
25 the sons of Bilhah, Rachel's maidservant, *were* Dan and Naphtali;
26 and the sons of Zilpah, Leah's maidservant, *were* Gad and Asher. These *were* the sons of Jacob who were born to him in Padan Aram.

Death of Isaac

27 Then Jacob came to his father Isaac at Mamre, or *Kirjath Arba (that *is,* Hebron), where Abraham and Isaac had dwelt.
28 Now the days of Isaac were one hundred and eighty years.
29 So Isaac breathed his last and died, and was ᵀgathered to his people, *being* old and full of days. And ᴿhis sons Esau and Jacob buried him.   Joined his ancestors · Gen. 25:9; 49:31

The Family of Esau

36 Now this *is* the genealogy of Esau, ᴿwho is Edom.   Gen. 25:30
2 Esau took his wives from the daughters of Canaan: Adah the daughter of Elon the ᴿHittite; Aholibamah the daughter of Anah, the daughter of Zibeon the Hivite;   2 Kin. 7:6

3 and ᴿBasemath, Ishmael's daughter, sister of Nebajoth.   Gen. 28:9
4 Now ᴿAdah bore Eliphaz to Esau, and Basemath bore Reuel.   1 Chr. 1:35
5 And Aholibamah bore Jeush, Jaalam, and Korah. These *were* the sons of Esau who were born to him in the land of Canaan.
6 Then Esau took his wives, his sons, his daughters, and all the persons of his household, his cattle and all his animals, and all his goods which he had gained in the land of Canaan, and went to a country away from the presence of his brother Jacob.
7 For their possessions were too great for them to dwell together, and ᴿthe land where they were strangers could not support them because of their livestock.   Gen. 17:8; 28:4
8 So Esau dwelt in ᴿMount Seir. ᴿEsau *is* Edom.   Gen. 32:3 · Gen. 36:1, 19
9 And this *is* the genealogy of Esau, father of the Edomites in Mount Seir.
10 These *were* the names of Esau's sons: ᴿEliphaz the son of Adah the wife of Esau, and Reuel the son of Basemath the wife of Esau.   1 Chr. 1:35
11 And the sons of Eliphaz were Teman, Omar, *Zepho, Gatam, and Kenaz.
12 Now Timna was the concubine of Eliphaz, Esau's son, and she bore ᴿAmalek to Eliphaz. These *were* the sons of Adah, Esau's wife.   Num. 24:20
13 These *were* the sons of Reuel: Nahath, Zerah, Shammah, and Mizzah. These *were* the sons of Basemath, Esau's wife.
14 These were the sons of ᵀAholibamah, Esau's wife, the daughter of Anah, the daughter of Zibeon. And she bore to Esau: Jeush, Jaalam, and Korah.   Or *Oholibamah*

The Chiefs of Edom

15 These *were* the chiefs of the sons of Esau. The sons of Eliphaz, the firstborn *son* of Esau, were Chief Teman, Chief Omar, Chief Zepho, Chief Kenaz,
16 *Chief Korah, Chief Gatam, *and* Chief Amalek. These *were* the chiefs of Eliphaz in the land of Edom. They *were* the sons of Adah.
17 These *were* the sons of Reuel, Esau's son: Chief Nahath, Chief Zerah, Chief Shammah, and Chief Mizzah. These *were* the chiefs of Reuel in the land of Edom. These *were* the sons of Basemath, Esau's wife.
18 And these *were* the sons of ᵀAholibamah, Esau's wife: Chief Jeush, Chief Jaalam, and Chief Korah. These *were* the chiefs *who* descended from Aholibamah, Esau's wife, the daughter of Anah.   Or *Oholibamah*
19 These *were* the sons of Esau, who is Edom, and these *were* their chiefs.

35:18 Lit. *Son of My Sorrow* • Lit. *Son of the Right Hand*
35:27 Lit. *Town or City of Arba*

36:11 *Zephi,* 1 Chr. 1:36
36:16 Sam. omits *Chief Korah*

The Sons of Seir

20 ᴿThese were the sons of Seir ᴿthe Horite who inhabited the land: Lotan, Shobal, Zibeon, Anah,   1 Chr. 1:38–42 • Gen. 14:6
21 Dishon, Ezer, and Dishan. These were the chiefs of the Horites, the sons of Seir, in the land of Edom.
22 And the sons of Lotan were Hori and *Hemam. Lotan's sister was Timna.
23 These were the sons of Shobal: *Alvan, Manahath, Ebal, *Shepho, and Onam.
24 These were the sons of Zibeon: both Ajah and Anah. This was the Anah who found the *water in the wilderness as he pastured the *donkeys of his father Zibeon.
25 These were the children of Anah: Dishon and Aholibamah the daughter of Anah.
26 These were the sons of ᵀDishon: *Hemdan, Eshban, Ithran, and Cheran.   Heb. Dishan
27 These were the sons of Ezer: Bilhan, Zaavan, and Akan.
28 These were the sons of Dishan: ᴿUz and Aran.   Job 1:1
29 These were the chiefs of the Horites: Chief Lotan, Chief Shobal, Chief Zibeon, Chief Anah,
30 Chief Dishon, Chief Ezer, and Chief Dishan. These were the chiefs of the Horites, according to their chiefs in the land of Seir.

The Kings of Edom

31 ᴿNow these were the kings who reigned in the land of Edom before any king reigned over the children of Israel: 1 Chr. 1:43
32 Bela the son of Beor reigned in Edom, and the name of his city was Dinhabah.
33 And when Bela died, Jobab the son of Zerah of Bozrah reigned in his place.
34 When Jobab died, Husham of the land of the Temanites reigned in his place.
35 And when Husham died, Hadad the son of Bedad, who attacked Midian in the field of Moab, reigned in his place. And the name of his city was Avith.
36 When Hadad died, Samlah of Masrekah reigned in his place.
37 And when Samlah died, Saul of Rehoboth-by-the-River reigned in his place.
38 When Saul died, Baal-Hanan the son of Achbor reigned in his place.
39 And when Baal-Hanan the son of Achbor died, *Hadar reigned in his place; and the name of his city was *Pau. His wife's name was Mehetabel, the daughter of Matred, the daughter of Mezahab.

The Chiefs of Esau

40 And these were the names of the chiefs of Esau, according to their families and their

36:22 Homam, 1 Chr. 1:39
36:23 Alian, 1 Chr. 1:40 • Shephi, 1 Chr. 1:40
36:24 So with MT, Vg. (hot springs); LXX Jamin; Tg. mighty men; Talmud mules
36:26 Hamran, 1 Chr. 1:41
36:39 Sam., Syr. Hadad and 1 Chr. 1:50 • Pai, 1 Chr. 1:50

places, by their names: Chief Timnah, Chief ᵀAlvah, Chief Jetheth,   Aliah, 1 Chr. 1:51
41 Chief ᵀAholibamah, Chief Elah, Chief Pinon,   Or Oholibamah
42 Chief Kenaz, Chief Teman, Chief Mibzar,
43 Chief Magdiel, and Chief Iram. These were the chiefs of Edom, according to their dwelling places in the land of their possession. Esau was the father of the Edomites.

Joseph Dreams of Greatness

37 Now Jacob dwelt in the land ᴿwhere his father was a ᵀstranger, in the land of Canaan.   Gen. 17:8; 23:4 • sojourner, temporary resident
2 This is the history of Jacob. Joseph, being seventeen years old, was feeding the flock with his brothers. And the lad was with the sons of Bilhah and the sons of Zilpah, his father's wives; and Joseph brought ᴿa bad report of them to his father.   1 Sam. 2:22–24
3 Now Israel loved Joseph more than all his children, because he was ᴿthe son of his old age. Also he ᴿmade him a tunic of many colors.   Gen. 44:20 • Gen. 37:23, 32
4 But when his brothers saw that their father loved him more than all his brothers, they ᴿhated him and could not speak peaceably to him.   Gen. 27:41; 49:23
5 Now Joseph had a dream, and he told it to his brothers; and they hated him even more.
6 So he said to them, "Please hear this dream which I have dreamed:
7 "There we were, binding sheaves in the field. Then behold, my sheaf arose and also stood upright; and indeed your sheaves stood all around and bowed down to my sheaf."
8 And his brothers said to him, "Shall you indeed reign over us? Or shall you indeed have dominion over us?" So they hated him even more for his dreams and for his words.
9 Then he dreamed still another dream and told it to his brothers, and said, "Look, I have dreamed another dream. And this time, ᴿthe sun, the moon, and the eleven stars bowed down to me."   Gen. 46:29; 47:25
10 So he told it to his father and his brothers; and his father rebuked him and said to him, "What is this dream that you have dreamed? Shall your mother and I and ᴿyour brothers indeed come to bow down to the earth before you?"   Gen. 27:29
11 And his brothers envied him, but his father ᴿkept the matter in mind.   Dan. 7:28

Joseph Sold by His Brothers

12 Then his brothers went to feed their father's flock in ᴿShechem.   Gen. 33:18–20
13 And Israel said to Joseph, "Are not your brothers feeding the flock in Shechem? Come, I will send you to them." So he said to him, "Here I am."
14 Then he said to him, "Please go and see

if it is well with your brothers and well with the flocks, and bring back word to me." So he sent him out of the Valley of ᴿHebron, and he went to Shechem. Gen. 13:18; 23:2, 19; 35:27

15 Now a certain man found him, and there he was, wandering in the field. And the man asked him, saying, "What are you seeking?"

16 So he said, "I am seeking my brothers. ᴿPlease tell me where they are feeding their flocks." Song 1:7

17 And the man said, "They have departed from here, for I heard them say, 'Let us go to Dothan.' " So Joseph went after his brothers and found them in ᴿDothan. 2 Kin. 6:13

18 Now when they saw him afar off, even before he came near them, ᴿthey conspired against him to kill him. Mark 14:1

19 Then they said to one another, "Look, this ᵀdreamer is coming! Lit. master of dreams

20 "Come therefore, let us now kill him and cast him into some pit; and we shall say, 'Some wild beast has devoured him.' We shall see what will become of his dreams!"

21 But ᴿReuben heard it, and he delivered him out of their hands, and said, "Let us not kill him." Gen. 42:22

22 And Reuben said to them, "Shed no blood, but cast him into this pit which is in the wilderness, and do not lay a hand on him"—that he might deliver him out of their hands, and bring him back to his father.

23 So it came to pass, when Joseph had come to his brothers, that they ᴿstripped Joseph of his tunic, the tunic of many colors that was on him. Matt. 27:28

24 Then they took him and cast him into a pit. And the pit was empty; there was no water in it.

25 ᴿAnd they sat down to eat a meal. Then they lifted their eyes and looked, and there was a company of Ishmaelites, coming from Gilead with their camels, bearing spices, ᴿbalm, and myrrh, on their way to carry them down to Egypt. Prov. 30:20 • Jer. 8:22

26 So Judah said to his brothers, "What profit is there if we kill our brother and ᴿconceal his blood? Gen. 37:20

27 "Come and let us sell him to the Ishmaelites, and let not our hand be upon him, for he is ᴿour brother and ᴿour flesh." And his brothers listened. Gen. 42:21 • Gen. 29:14

28 Then Midianite traders passed by; so the brothers pulled Joseph up and lifted him out of the pit, ᴿand sold him to the Ishmaelites for ᴿtwentyᵀ shekels of silver. And they took Joseph to Egypt. Ps. 105:17 • Matt. 27:9 • $2,560

29 Then Reuben returned to the pit, and indeed Joseph was not in the pit; and he ᴿtore his clothes. Job 1:20

30 And he returned to his brothers and said, "The lad ᴿis no more; and I, where shall I go?" Gen. 42:13, 36

31 So they took ᴿJoseph's tunic, killed a kid of the goats, and dipped the tunic in the blood. Gen. 37:3, 23

32 Then they sent the tunic of many colors, and they brought it to their father and said, "We have found this. Do you know whether it is your son's tunic or not?"

33 And he recognized it and said, "It is my son's tunic. A wild beast has devoured him. Without doubt Joseph is torn to pieces."

34 Then Jacob ᴿtore his clothes, put sackcloth on his waist, and ᴿmourned for his son many days. 2 Sam. 3:31 • Gen. 50:10

35 And all his sons and all his daughters ᴿarose to comfort him; but he refused to be comforted, and he said, "For ᴿI shall go down into the grave to my son in mourning." Thus his father wept for him. 2 Sam. 12:17 • Gen. 25:8

36 Now ᴿthe *Midianites had sold him in Egypt to Potiphar, an officer of Pharaoh and captain of the guard. Gen. 39:1

Judah and Tamar

38 It came to pass at that time that Judah departed from his brothers, and visited a certain Adullamite whose name was Hirah.

2 And Judah saw there a daughter of a certain Canaanite whose name was Shua, and he married her and went in to her.

3 So she conceived and bore a son, and he called his name ᴿEr. Gen. 46:12

4 She conceived again and bore a son, and she called his name ᴿOnan. Num. 26:19

5 And she conceived yet again and bore a son, and called his name ᴿShelah. He was at Chezib when she bore him. Num. 26:20

6 Then Judah took a wife for Er his firstborn, and her name was ᴿTamar. Ruth 4:12

7 But ᴿEr, Judah's firstborn, was wicked in the sight of the Lᴏʀᴅ, ᴿand the Lᴏʀᴅ killed him. Gen. 46:12 • 1 Chr. 2:3

8 And Judah said to Onan, "Go in to ᴿyour brother's wife and marry her, and raise up an heir to your brother." Deut. 25:5, 6

9 But Onan knew that the heir would not be ᴿhis; and it came to pass, when he went in to his brother's wife, that he emitted on the ground, lest he should give an heir to his brother. Deut. 25:6

10 And the thing which he did displeased the Lᴏʀᴅ; therefore He killed him also.

11 Then Judah said to Tamar his daughter-in-law, "Remain a widow in your father's house till my son Shelah is grown." For he said, "Lest he also die like his brothers." And Tamar went and dwelt in her father's house.

12 Now in the process of time the daughter of Shua, Judah's wife, died; and Judah ᴿwas comforted, and went up to his sheepshearers at Timnah, he and his friend Hirah the Adullamite. 2 Sam. 13:39

13 And it was told Tamar, saying, "Look, your father-in-law is going up ᴿto Timnah to shear his sheep." Josh. 15:10, 57

37:36 MT Medanites

14 So she took off her widow's garments, covered *herself* with a veil and wrapped herself, and ᴿsat in an open place which *was* on the way to Timnah; for she saw ᴿthat Shelah was grown, and she was not given to him as a wife. Prov. 7:12 • Gen. 38:11, 26

15 When Judah saw her, he thought she *was* a harlot, because she had covered her face.

16 Then he turned to her by the way, and said, "Please let me come in to you"; for he did not know that she *was* his daughter-in-law. So she said, "What will you give me, that you may come in to me?"

17 And he said, "I will send a young goat from the flock." So she said, "Will you give *me* a pledge till you send *it*?"

18 Then he said, "What pledge shall I give you?" So she said, ᴿ"Your signet and cord, and your staff that *is* in your hand." Then he gave *them* to her, and went in to her, and she conceived by him. Gen. 38:25; 41:42

19 So she arose and went away, and ᴿlaid aside her veil and put on the garments of her widowhood. Gen. 38:14

20 And Judah sent the young goat by the hand of his friend the Adullamite, to receive *his* pledge from the woman's hand, but he did not find her.

21 Then he asked the men of that place, saying, "Where is the harlot who *was* openly by the roadside?" And they said, "There was no harlot in this *place*."

22 So he returned to Judah and said, "I cannot find her. Also, the men of the place said there was no harlot in this *place*."

23 Then Judah said, "Let her take *them* for herself, lest we be shamed; for I sent this young goat and you have not found her."

24 And it came to pass, about three months after, that Judah was told, saying, "Tamar your daughter-in-law has ᴿplayed the harlot; furthermore she *is* ᵀwith child by harlotry." So Judah said, "Bring her out ᴿand let her be burned!" Judg. 19:2 • pregnant • Lev. 20:14; 21:9

25 When she *was* brought out, she sent to her father-in-law, saying, "By the man to whom these belong, I *am* with child." And she said, "Please determine whose these *are*—the signet and cord, and staff."

26 So Judah acknowledged *them* and said, "She has been more righteous than I, because I did not give her to Shelah my son." And he ᴿnever knew her again. Job 34:31, 32

27 Now it came to pass, at the time for giving birth, that behold, twins *were* in her womb.

28 And so it was, when she was giving birth, that the one put out *his* hand; and the midwife took a scarlet *thread* and bound it on his hand, saying, "This one came out first."

29 Then it happened, as he drew back his hand, that his brother came out unexpectedly; and she said, "How did you break through? *This* breach *be* upon you!" Therefore his name was called ᴿPerez*. Gen. 46:12

30 Afterward his brother came out who had the scarlet *thread* on his hand. And his name was called ᴿZerah. 1 Chr. 2:4

Joseph a Slave in Egypt

39 Now Joseph had been taken down to Egypt. And Potiphar, an officer of Pharaoh, captain of the guard, an Egyptian, ᴿbought him from the Ishmaelites who had taken him down there. Gen. 37:28; 45:4

2 ᴿThe LORD was with Joseph, and he was a successful man; and he was in the house of his master the Egyptian. Acts 7:9

3 And his master saw that the LORD *was* with him and that the LORD ᴿmade all he did ᵀto prosper in his hand. Ps. 1:3 • *to be a success*

4 So Joseph ᴿfound favor in his sight, and served him. Then he made him overseer of his house, and all *that* he had he put under his authority. Gen. 18:3; 19:19; 39:21

5 So it was, from the time *that* he had made him overseer of his house and all that he had, that ᴿthe LORD blessed the Egyptian's house for Joseph's sake; and the blessing of the LORD was on all that he had in the house and in the field. Gen. 18:26; 30:27

6 Thus he left all that he had in Joseph's ᵀhand, and he did not know what he had except for the ᵀbread which he ate. Now Joseph ᴿwas handsome in form and appearance. Care • Food • 1 Sam. 16:12

7 And it came to pass after these things that his master's wife cast longing eyes on Joseph, and she said, "Lie with me."

8 But he refused and said to his master's wife, "Look, my master does not know what *is* with me in the house, and he has committed all that he has to my hand.

9 "*There is* no one greater in this house than I, nor has he kept back anything from me but you, because you *are* his wife. ᴿHow then can I do this great wickedness, and ᴿsin against God?" Prov. 6:29, 32 • Ps. 51:4

10 So it was, as she spoke to Joseph day by day, that he ᴿdid not heed her, to lie with her or to be with her. Prov. 1:10

11 But it happened about this time, when Joseph went into the house to do his work, and none of the men of the house *was* inside,

12 that she caught him by his garment, saying, "Lie with me." But he left his garment in her hand, and fled and ran outside.

13 And so it was, when she saw that he had left his garment in her hand and fled outside,

14 that she called to the men of her house and spoke to them, saying, "See, he has brought in to us a ᴿHebrew to ᵀmock us. He came in to me to lie with me, and I cried out with a loud voice. Gen. 14:13; 41:12 • *laugh at*

38:29 Lit. *Breach* or *Breakthrough*

15 "And it happened, when he heard that I lifted my voice and cried out, that he left his garment with me, and fled and went outside."
16 So she kept his garment with her until his master came home.
17 Then she spoke to him with words like these, saying, "The Hebrew servant whom you brought to us came in to me to mock me;
18 "so it happened, as I lifted my voice and cried out, that he left his garment with me and fled outside."
19 So it was, when his master heard the words which his wife spoke to him, saying, "Your servant did to me after this manner," that his ᴿanger was aroused.   Prov. 6:34, 35
20 Then Joseph's master took him and ᴿput him into the ᴿprison, a place where the king's prisoners were confined. And he was there in the prison.   Ps. 105:18 • Gen. 40:3, 15; 41:14
21 But the LORD was with Joseph and showed him mercy, and He gave him favor in the sight of the keeper of the prison.
22 And the keeper of the prison ᴿcommitted to Joseph's hand all the prisoners who were in the prison; whatever they did there, it was his doing.   Gen. 39:4; 40:3, 4
23 The keeper of the prison did not look into anything that was under *Joseph's authority, because the LORD was with him; and whatever he did, the LORD made it prosper.

The Prisoners' Dreams

40 It came to pass after these things that the butler and the baker of the king of Egypt offended their lord, the king of Egypt.
2 And Pharaoh was angry with his two officers, the chief butler and the chief baker.
3 So he put them in custody in the house of the captain of the guard, in the prison, the place where Joseph was confined.
4 And the captain of the guard charged Joseph with them, and he served them; so they were in custody for a while.
5 Then the butler and the baker of the king of Egypt, who were confined in the prison, ᴿhad a dream, both of them, each man's dream in one night and each man's dream with its own interpretation.   Gen. 37:5; 41:1
6 And Joseph came in to them in the morning and looked at them, and saw that they were sad.
7 So he asked Pharaoh's officers who were with him in the custody of his lord's house, saying, "Why do you look so sad today?"
8 And they said to him, ᴿ"We each have had a dream, and there is no interpreter of it." So Joseph said to them, ᴿ"Do not interpretations belong to God? Tell them to me, please."   Gen. 41:15 • [Dan. 2:11, 20–22, 27, 28, 47]
9 Then the chief butler told his dream to Joseph, and said to him, "Behold, in my dream a vine was before me,

10 "and in the vine were three branches; it was as though it budded, its blossoms shot forth, and its clusters brought forth ripe grapes.
11 "Then Pharaoh's cup was in my hand; and I took the grapes and pressed them into Pharaoh's cup, and placed the cup in Pharaoh's hand."
12 And Joseph said to him, ᴿ"This is the interpretation of it: The three branches ᴿare three days.   Dan. 2:36; 4:18, 19 • Gen. 40:18; 42:17
13 "Now within three days Pharaoh will ᴿlift up your head and restore you to your ᵀplace, and you will put Pharaoh's cup in his hand according to the former manner, when you were his butler.   2 Kin. 25:27 • position
14 "But ᴿremember me when it is well with you, and ᴿplease show kindness to me; make mention of me to Pharaoh, and get me out of this house.   Luke 23:42 • Josh. 2:12
15 "For indeed I was ᴿstolen away from the land of the Hebrews; ᴿand also I have done nothing here that they should put me into the dungeon."   Gen. 37:26–28 • Gen. 39:20
16 When the chief baker saw that the interpretation was good, he said to Joseph, "I also was in my dream, and there were three white baskets on my head.
17 "In the uppermost basket were all kinds of baked goods for Pharaoh, and the birds ate them out of the basket on my head."
18 So Joseph answered and said, ᴿ"This is the interpretation of it: The three baskets are three days.   Gen. 40:12
19 "Within three days Pharaoh will lift off your head from you and hang you on a tree; and the birds will eat your flesh from you."
20 Now it came to pass on the third day, which was Pharaoh's birthday, that he made a feast for all his servants; and he lifted up the head of the chief butler and of the chief baker among his servants.
21 Then he ᴿrestored the chief butler to his butlership again, and ᴿhe placed the cup in Pharaoh's hand.   Gen. 40:13 • Neh. 2:1
22 But he ᴿhanged the chief baker, as Joseph had interpreted to them.   Gen. 40:19
23 Yet the chief butler did not remember Joseph, but ᴿforgot him.   Eccl. 9:15, 16

Pharaoh's Dreams

41 Then it came to pass, at the end of two full years, that ᴿPharaoh had a dream; and behold, he stood by the river.   Gen. 40:5
2 Suddenly there came up out of the river seven cows, fine looking and fat; and they fed in the meadow.
3 Then behold, seven other cows came up after them out of the river, ugly and gaunt, and stood by the other cows on the bank of the river.
4 And the ugly and gaunt cows ate up the

39:23 Lit. his hand

seven fine looking and fat cows. So Pharaoh awoke.

5 He slept and dreamed a second time; and suddenly seven heads of grain came up on one stalk, plump and good.

6 Then behold, seven thin heads, blighted by the east wind, sprang up after them.

7 And the seven thin heads devoured the seven plump and full heads. So Pharaoh awoke, and indeed, *it was* a dream.

8 Now it came to pass in the morning that his spirit was troubled, and he sent and called for all the magicians of Egypt and all its ᴿwise men. And Pharaoh told them his dreams, but *there was* no one who could interpret them for Pharaoh.   Matt. 2:1

9 Then the chief butler spoke to Pharaoh, saying: "I remember my faults this day.

10 "When Pharaoh was ᴿangry with his servants, ᴿand put me in custody in the house of the captain of the guard, *both* me and the chief baker,   Gen. 40:2, 3 · Gen. 39:20

11 ᴿ"we each had a dream in one night, he and I. Each of us dreamed according to the interpretation of his *own* dream.   Gen. 40:5

12 "Now there *was* a young Hebrew man with us there, a servant of the captain of the guard. And we told him, and he ᴿinterpreted our dreams for us; to each man he interpreted according to his *own* dream.   Gen. 40:12

13 "And it came to pass, just ᴿas he interpreted for us, so it happened. He restored me to my office, and he hanged him."   Gen. 40:21, 22

14 Then Pharaoh sent and called Joseph, and they brought him quickly ᴿout of the dungeon; and he shaved, changed his clothing, and came to Pharaoh.   [1 Sam. 2:8]

15 And Pharaoh said to Joseph, "I have had a dream, and *there is* no one who can interpret it. But I have heard it said of you *that* you can understand a dream, to interpret it."

16 So Joseph answered Pharaoh, saying, ᴿ"*It is* not in me; ᴿGod will give Pharaoh an answer of peace."   Dan. 2:30 · Dan. 2:22, 28, 47

17 Then Pharaoh said to Joseph: "Behold, in my dream I stood on the bank of the river.

18 "Suddenly seven cows came up out of the river, fine looking and fat; and they fed in the meadow.

19 "Then behold, seven other cows came up after them, poor and very ugly and gaunt, such ugliness as I have never seen in all the land of Egypt.

20 "And the gaunt and ugly cows ate up the first seven, the fat cows.

21 "When they had eaten them up, no one would have known that they had eaten them, for they *were* just as ugly as at the beginning. So I awoke.

22 "Also I saw in my dream, and suddenly seven ᵀheads came up on one stalk, full and good.   Heads of grain

23 "Then behold, seven heads, withered, thin, *and* blighted by the east wind, sprang up after them.

24 "And the thin heads devoured the seven good heads. So ᴿI told *this* to the magicians, but *there was* no one who could explain *it* to me."   Is. 8:19

25 Then Joseph said to Pharaoh, "The dreams of Pharaoh *are* one; ᴿGod has shown Pharaoh what He *is* about to do: Dan. 2:28, 29, 45

26 "The seven good cows *are* seven years, and the seven good ᵀheads *are* seven years; the dreams *are* one.   Heads of grain

27 "And the seven thin and ugly cows which came up after them *are* seven years, and the seven empty heads blighted by the east wind are ᴿseven years of famine. 2 Kin. 8:1

28 ᴿ"This *is* the thing which I have spoken to Pharaoh. God has shown Pharaoh what He *is* about to do.   [Gen. 41:25, 32]

29 "Indeed seven years of great plenty will come throughout all the land of Egypt;

30 "but after them seven years of famine will ᴿarise, and all the plenty will be forgotten in the land of Egypt; and the famine ᴿwill deplete the land.   Gen. 41:54, 56 · Gen. 47:13

31 "So the plenty will not be known in the land because of the famine following, for it *will be* very severe.

32 "And the dream was repeated to Pharaoh twice because the thing *is* established by God, and God will shortly bring it to pass.

33 "Now therefore, let Pharaoh select a discerning and wise man, and set him over the land of Egypt.

34 "Let Pharaoh do *this*, and let him appoint ᵀofficers over the land, ᴿto collect one-fifth *of the produce* of the land of Egypt in the seven plentiful years.   overseers · [Prov. 6:6–8]

35 "And let them gather all the food of those good years that are coming, and store up grain under the authority of Pharaoh, and let them keep food in the cities.

36 "Then that food shall be as a reserve for the land for the seven years of famine which shall be in the land of Egypt, that the land may not perish during the famine."

Joseph's Rise to Power

37 So the advice was good in the eyes of Pharaoh and in the eyes of all his servants.

38 And Pharaoh said to his servants, "Can we find *such a one* as this, a man ᴿin whom *is* the Spirit of God?"   Num. 27:18

39 Then Pharaoh said to Joseph, "Inasmuch as God has shown you all this, *there is* no one as discerning and wise as you.

40 ᴿ"You shall be ᵀover my house, and all my people shall be ruled according to your word; only in regard to the throne will I be greater than you."   Ps. 105:21 · In charge of

41 And Pharaoh said to Joseph, "See, I have ᴿset you over all the land of Egypt."   Dan. 6:3

42 Then Pharaoh ᴿtook his signet ring off his hand and put it on Joseph's hand; and he

clothed him in garments of fine linen and put a gold chain around his neck.   Esth. 3:10

43 And he had him ride in the second chariot which he had; ^Rand they cried out before him, "Bow the knee!" So he set him ^Rover all the land of Egypt.   Esth. 6:9 · Gen. 42:6

44 Pharaoh also said to Joseph, "I *am* Pharaoh, and without your consent no man may lift his hand or foot in all the land of Egypt."

45 And Pharaoh called Joseph's name ^TZaphnath-Paaneah. And he gave him as a wife Asenath, the daughter of Poti-Pherah priest of On. So Joseph went out over *all* the land of Egypt. Probably means *God Speaks and He Lives*

46 Joseph was thirty years old when he ^Rstood before Pharaoh king of Egypt. And Joseph went out from the presence of Pharaoh, and went throughout all the land of Egypt.   1 Sam. 16:21

47 Now in the seven plentiful years the ground brought forth abundantly.

48 So he gathered up all the food of the seven years which were in the land of Egypt, and laid up the food in the cities; he laid up in every city the food of the fields which surrounded them.

49 Joseph gathered very much grain, ^Ras the sand of the sea, until he stopped counting, for *it was* immeasurable.   Gen. 22:17

50 ^RAnd to Joseph were born two sons before the years of famine came, whom Asenath, the daughter of Poti-Pherah priest of On, bore to him.   Gen. 46:20; 48:5

51 Joseph called the name of the firstborn *Manasseh: "For God has made me forget all my toil and all my ^Rfather's house."   Ps. 45:10

52 And the name of the second he called *Ephraim: "For God has caused me to be fruitful in the land of my affliction."

53 Then the seven years of plenty which were in the land of Egypt ended,

54 ^Rand the seven years of famine began to come, ^Ras Joseph had said. The famine was in all lands, but in all the land of Egypt there was bread.   Acts 7:11 · Gen. 41:30

55 So when all the land of Egypt was famished, the people cried to Pharaoh for bread. Then Pharaoh said to all the Egyptians, "Go to Joseph; whatever he says to you, do."

56 The famine was over all the face of the earth, and Joseph opened *all the storehouses and ^Rsold to the Egyptians. And the famine became severe in the land of Egypt.   Gen. 42:6

57 ^RSo all countries came to Joseph in Egypt to ^Rbuy *grain*, because the famine was severe in all lands.   Ezek. 29:12 · Gen. 27:28, 37; 42:3

Joseph's Brothers Go to Egypt

42 When ^RJacob saw that there was grain in Egypt, Jacob said to his sons, "Why do you look at one another?"   Acts 7:12

2 And he said, "Indeed I have heard that there is grain in Egypt; go down to that place and buy for us there, that we may ^Rlive and not die."   Gen. 43:8

3 So Joseph's ten brothers went down to buy grain in Egypt.

4 But Jacob did not send Joseph's brother Benjamin with his brothers, for he said, ^R"Lest some calamity befall him."   Gen. 42:38

5 And the sons of Israel went to buy *grain* among those who journeyed, for the famine was ^Rin the land of Canaan.   Acts 7:11

6 Now Joseph *was* governor ^Rover the land; and it was he who sold to all the people of the land. And Joseph's brothers came and ^Rbowed down before him with *their* faces to the earth.   Gen. 41:41, 55 · Gen. 37:7-10; 41:43

7 Joseph saw his brothers and recognized them, but he acted as a stranger to them and spoke roughly to them. Then he said to them, "Where do you come from?" And they said, "From the land of Canaan to buy food."

8 So Joseph recognized his brothers, but they did not recognize him.

9 Then Joseph remembered the dreams which he had dreamed about them, and said to them, "You *are* spies! You have come to see the ^Tnakedness of the land!"   Exposed parts

10 And they said to him, "No, my lord, but your servants have come to buy food.

11 "We *are* all one man's sons; we *are* honest *men*; your servants are not spies."

12 But he said to them, "No, but you have come to see the nakedness of the land."

13 And they said, "Your servants *are* twelve brothers, the sons of one man in the land of Canaan; and in fact, the youngest *is* with our father today, and one *is* no more."

14 But Joseph said to them, "It *is* as I spoke to you, saying, 'You *are* spies!'

15 "In this *manner* you shall be tested: ^RBy the life of Pharaoh, you shall not leave this place unless your youngest brother comes here.   1 Sam. 1:26; 17:55

16 "Send one of you, and let him bring your brother; and you shall be ^Tkept in prison, that your words may be tested to see whether *there is* any truth in you; or else, by the life of Pharaoh, surely you *are* spies!"   Lit. *bound*

17 So he ^Tput them all together in prison ^Rthree days.   Lit. *gathered* · Gen. 40:4, 7, 12

18 Then Joseph said to them the third day, "Do this and live, ^R*for* I fear God: Lev. 25:43

19 "If you *are* honest *men*, let one of your brothers be confined to your prison house; but you, you go and carry grain for the famine of your houses.

20 "And ^Rbring your youngest brother to me; so your words will be verified, and you shall not die." And they did so.   Gen. 44:18-34

21 Then they said to one another, "We *are* truly guilty concerning our brother, for we saw the anguish of his soul when he pleaded

41:51 Lit. *Making Forgetful*
41:52 Lit. *Fruitfulness*
41:56 Lit. *all that was in them*

with us, and we would not hear; ^Rtherefore
this distress has come upon us."　　Prov. 21:13
22 And Reuben answered them, saying,
^R"Did I not speak to you, saying, 'Do not sin
against the boy'; and you would not listen?
Therefore behold, his blood is now ^Rrequired
of us."　　　　Gen. 37:21, 22, 29 · Gen. 9:5, 6
23 But they did not know that Joseph understood *them*, for he spoke to them through
an interpreter.
24 And he turned himself away from them
and wept. Then he returned to them again,
and talked with them. And he took Simeon
from them and bound him before their eyes.

The Brothers Return to Canaan

25 Then Joseph ^Rgave a command to fill
their sacks with grain, to ^Rrestore every
man's money to his sack, and to give them
provisions for the journey. ^RThus he did for
them.　　Gen. 44:1 · Gen. 43:12 · [Rom. 12:17, 20, 21]
26 So they loaded their donkeys with the
grain and departed from there.
27 But as ^Rone *of them* opened his sack to
give his donkey feed at the encampment, he
saw his money; and there it was, in the
mouth of his sack.　　　　　Gen. 43:21, 22
28 So he said to his brothers, "My money
has been restored, and there it is, in my
sack!" Then their hearts ^Tfailed *them* and
they were afraid, saying to one another,
"What *is* this *that* God has done to us?"　sank
29 Then they went to Jacob their father in
the land of Canaan and told him all that had
happened to them, saying:
30 "The man *who is* lord of the land ^Rspoke
roughly to us, and took us for spies of the
country.　　　　　　　　　　　Gen. 42:7
31 "But we said to him, 'We *are* honest
men; we are not spies.
32 'We *are* twelve brothers, sons of our
father; one *is* no *more*, and the youngest *is*
with our father this day in the land of Canaan.'
33 "Then the man, the lord of the country,
said to us, ^R'By this I will know that you *are*
honest *men*: Leave one of your brothers *here*
with me, take *food for* the famine of your
households, and be gone.　　Gen. 42:15, 19, 20
34 'And bring your ^Ryoungest brother to
me; so I shall know that you *are* not spies,
but *that* you *are* honest *men*. I will grant
your brother to you, and you may ^Rtrade in
the land.' "　　Gen. 42:20; 43:3, 5 · Gen. 34:10
35 Then it happened as they emptied their
sacks, that surprisingly ^Reach man's bundle of
money *was* in his sack; and when they and
their father saw the bundles of money, they
were afraid.　　　　　　　　　Gen. 43:12, 18
36 And Jacob their father said to them,
"You have bereaved me: Joseph is no *more*,
Simeon is no *more*, and you want to take
Benjamin. All these things are against me."
37 Then Reuben spoke to his father, saying,

"Kill my two sons if I do not bring him *back*
to you; put him in my hands, and I will bring
him back to you."
38 But he said, "My son shall not go down
with you, for his brother is dead, and he is left
alone. ^RIf any calamity should befall him
along the way in which you go, then you
would ^Rbring down my gray hair with sorrow
to the grave."　　Gen. 42:4; 44:29 · Gen. 37:35; 44:31

Joseph's Brothers Return with Benjamin

43 Now the famine *was* severe in the
land.
2 And it came to pass, when they had eaten
up the grain which they had brought from
Egypt, that their father said to them, "Go
^Rback, buy us a little food."　　Gen. 42:2; 44:25
3 But Judah spoke to him, saying, "The
man solemnly warned us, saying, 'You shall
not see my face unless your ^Rbrother *is* with
you.' "　　　　　　　　Gen. 42:20; 43:5; 44:23
4 "If you send our brother with us, we will
go down and buy you food.
5 "But if you will not send *him*, we will not
go down; for the man said to us, 'You shall
not see my face unless your brother *is* with
you.' "
6 And Israel said, "Why did you deal *so*
wrongfully with me *as* to tell the man
whether you had still *another* brother?"
7 But they said, "The man asked us point-
edly about ourselves and our family, saying,
'Is your father still alive? Have you *another*
brother?' And we told him according to these
words. Could we possibly have known that
he would say, 'Bring your brother down'?"
8 Then Judah said to Israel his father,
"Send the lad with me, and we will arise and
go, that we may ^Rlive and not die, both we
and you *and* also our little ones.　Gen. 42:2; 47:19
9 "I myself will be surety for him; from my
hand you shall require him. ^RIf I do not bring
him *back* to you and set him before you, then
let me bear the blame forever.　Gen. 42:37; 44:32
10 "For if we had not lingered, surely by
now we would have returned this second
time."
11 And their father Israel said to them, "If
it must be so, then do this: Take some of the
best fruits of the land in your vessels and
carry down a present for the man—a little
^Rbalm and a little honey, spices and myrrh,
pistachio nuts and almonds.　　　　Jer. 8:22
12 "Take double money in your hand, and
take back in your hand the money ^Rthat was
returned in the mouth of your sacks; perhaps
it was an oversight.　　　Gen. 42:25, 35; 43:21, 22
13 "Take your brother also, and arise, go
back to the man.
14 "And may God Almighty ^Rgive you
mercy before the man, that he may release
your other brother and Benjamin. ^RIf I am
bereaved, I am bereaved!"　Ps. 106:46 · Esth. 4:16
15 So the men took that present and Benja-

min, and they took double money in their hand, and arose and went ᴿdown to Egypt; and they stood before Joseph.   Gen. 39:1; 46:3, 6

16 When Joseph saw Benjamin with them, he said to the steward of his house, "Take *these* men to my home, and slaughter ᵀan animal and make ready; for *these* men will dine with me at noon."   Lit. *a slaughter*

17 Then the man did as Joseph ordered, and the man brought the men into Joseph's house.

18 Now the men were ᴿafraid because they were brought into Joseph's house; and they said, "*It is* because of the money, which was returned in our sacks the first time, that we are brought in, so that he may make a case against us and seize us, to take us as slaves with our donkeys."   Gen. 42:28

19 When they drew near to the steward of Joseph's house, they talked with him at the door of the house,

20 and said, "O sir, ᴿwe indeed came down the first time to buy food;   Gen. 42:3, 10

21 "but ᴿit happened, when we came to the encampment, that we opened our sacks, and there, *each* man's money *was* in the mouth of his sack, our money in full weight; so we have brought it back in our hand.   Gen. 42:27, 35

22 "And we have brought down other money in our hands to buy food. We do not know who put our money in our sacks."

23 But he said, "Peace *be* with you, do not be afraid. Your God and the God of your father has given you treasure in your sacks; I had your money." Then he brought ᴿSimeon out to them.   Gen. 42:24

24 So the man brought the men into Joseph's house and ᴿgave *them* water, and they washed their feet; and he gave their donkeys feed.   Gen. 18:4; 19:2; 24:32

25 Then they made the present ready for Joseph's coming at noon, for they heard that they would eat bread there.

26 And when Joseph came home, they brought him the present which *was* in their hand into the house, and ᴿbowed down before him to the earth.   Gen. 37:7, 10; 42:6; 44:14

27 Then he asked them about *their* well-being, and said, "*Is* your father well, the old man of whom you spoke? *Is* he still alive?"

28 And they answered, "Your servant our father *is* in good health; he *is* still alive." ᴿAnd they bowed their heads down and prostrated themselves.   Gen. 37:7, 10

29 Then he lifted his eyes and saw his brother Benjamin, his mother's son, and said, "*Is* this your younger brother ᴿof whom you spoke to me?" And he said, "God be gracious to you, my son."   Gen. 42:13

30 Now ᴿhis heart yearned for his brother; so Joseph made haste and sought *somewhere* to weep. And he went into *his* chamber and ᴿwept there.   1 Kin. 3:26 · Gen. 42:24; 45:2, 14, 15; 46:29

31 Then he washed his face and came out; and he restrained himself, and said, "Serve the ᴿbread."   Gen. 43:25

32 So they set him a place by himself, and them by themselves, and the Egyptians who ate with him by themselves; because the Egyptians could not eat food with the ᴿHebrews, for that *is* ᴿan abomination to the Egyptians.   Gen. 41:12 · Gen. 46:34

33 And they sat before him, the firstborn according to his ᴿbirthright and the youngest according to his youth; and the men looked in astonishment at one another.   Gen. 27:36; 42:7

34 Then he took servings to them from before him, but Benjamin's serving was ᴿfive times as much as any of theirs. So they drank and were merry with him.   Gen. 45:22

Joseph's Cup

44 And he commanded the steward of his house, saying, "Fill the men's sacks with food, as much as they can carry, and put each man's money in the mouth of his sack.

2 "Also put my cup, the silver cup, in the mouth of the sack of the youngest, and his grain money." So he did according to the word that Joseph had spoken.

3 As soon as the morning dawned, the men were sent away, they and their donkeys.

4 When they had gone out of the city, *and* were not *yet* far off, Joseph said to his steward, "Get up, follow the men; and when you overtake them, say to them, 'Why have you ᴿrepaid evil for good?   1 Sam. 25:21

5 '*Is* not this *the one* from which my lord drinks, and with which he indeed practices divination? You have done evil in so doing.' "

6 So he overtook them, and he spoke to them these same words.

7 And they said to him, "Why does my lord say these words? Far be it from us that your servants should do such a thing.

8 "Look, we brought back to you from the land of Canaan the money which we found in the mouth of our sacks. How then could we steal silver or gold from your lord's house?

9 "With whomever of your servants it is found, ᴿlet him die, and we also will be my lord's slaves."   Gen. 31:32

10 And he said, "Now also let it *be* according to your words; he with whom it is found shall be my slave, and you shall be blameless."

11 Then each man speedily let down his sack to the ground, and each opened his sack.

12 So he searched. He began with the oldest and ᵀleft off with the youngest; and the cup was found in Benjamin's sack.   finished with

13 Then they ᴿtore their clothes, and each man loaded his donkey and returned to the city.   2 Sam. 1:11

14 So Judah and his brothers came to Joseph's house, and he *was* still there; and they ᴿfell before him on the ground.   Gen. 37:7, 10

15 And Joseph said to them, "What deed *is* this you have done? Did you not know that such a man as I can certainly practice divination?"

16 Then Judah said, "What shall we say to my lord? What shall we speak? Or how shall we clear ourselves? God has ᴿfound out the iniquity of your servants; here ᴿwe are, my lord's slaves, both we and *he* also with whom the cup was found."   [Num. 32:23] • Gen. 44:9

17 But he said, "Far be it from me that I should do so; the man in whose hand the cup was found, he shall be my slave. And as for you, go up in peace to your father."

Judah Intercedes for Benjamin

18 Then Judah came near to him and said: "O my lord, please let your servant speak a word in my lord's hearing, and ᴿdo not let your anger burn against your servant; for you *are* even like Pharaoh.   Ex. 32:22

19 "My lord asked his servants, saying, 'Have you a father or a brother?'

20 "And we said to my lord, 'We have a father, an old man, and a child of *his* old age, *who is* young; his brother is dead, and he ᴿalone is left of his mother's children, and his ᴿfather loves him.'   Gen. 46:19 • Gen. 42:4

21 "Then you said to your servants, ᴿ'Bring him down to me, that I may set my eyes on him.'   Gen. 42:15, 20

22 "And we said to my lord, 'The lad cannot leave his father, for *if* he should leave his father, *his father* would die.'

23 "But you said to your servants, ᴿ'Unless your youngest brother comes down with you, you shall see my face no more.'   Gen. 43:3, 5

24 "So it was, when we went up to your servant my father, that we told him the words of my lord.

25 "And ᴿour father said, 'Go back *and* buy us a little food.'   Gen. 43:2

26 "But we said, 'We cannot go down; if our youngest brother is with us, then we will go down; for we may not see the man's face unless our youngest brother *is* with us.'

27 "Then your servant my father said to us, 'You know that my wife bore me two sons;

28 'and the one went out from me, and I said, ᴿ"Surely he is torn to pieces"; and I have not seen him since.   Gen. 37:31-35

29 'But if you take this one also from me, and calamity befalls him, you shall bring down my gray hair with sorrow to the grave.

30 "Now therefore, when I come to your servant my father, and the lad *is* not with us, since his life is bound up in the lad's life,

31 "it will happen, when he sees that the lad *is* not *with us*, that he will die. So your servants will bring down the gray hair of your servant our father with sorrow to the grave.

32 "For your servant became surety for the lad to my father, saying, ᴿ'If I do not bring

him *back* to you, then I shall bear the blame before my father forever.'   Gen. 43:9

33 "Now therefore, please let your servant remain instead of the lad as a slave to my lord, and let the lad go up with his brothers.

34 "For how shall I go up to my father if the lad *is* not with me, lest perhaps I see the evil that would ᵀcome upon my father?"   Lit. *find*

Joseph Revealed to His Brothers

45 Then Joseph could not restrain himself before all those who stood by him, and he cried out, "Make everyone go out from me!" So no one stood with him ᴿwhile Joseph made himself known to his brothers. Acts 7:13

2 And he wept aloud, and the Egyptians and the house of Pharaoh heard *it.*

3 Then Joseph said to his brothers, ᴿ"I *am* Joseph; does my father still live?" But his brothers could not answer him, for they were dismayed in his presence.   Acts 7:13

4 And Joseph said to his brothers, "Please come near to me." So they came near. Then he said: "I *am* Joseph your brother, ᴿwhom you sold into Egypt.   Gen. 37:28; 39:1

5 "But now, do not therefore be grieved or angry with yourselves because you sold me here; ᴿfor God sent me before you to preserve life.   Gen. 45:7, 8; 50:20

6 "For these two years the ᴿfamine *has been* in the land, and *there are* still five years in which *there will be* neither plowing nor harvesting.   Gen. 43:1; 47:4, 13

7 "And God sent me before you to preserve a posterity for you in the earth, and to save your lives by a great deliverance.

8 "So now *it was* not you *who* sent me here, but God; and He has made me a father to Pharaoh, and lord of all his house, and a ruler throughout all the land of Egypt.

9 "Hurry and go up to my father, and say to him, 'Thus says your son Joseph: "God has made me lord of all Egypt; come down to me, do not ᵀtarry.   *delay*

10 "You shall dwell in the land of Goshen, and you shall be near to me, you and your children, your children's children, your flocks and your herds, and all that you have.

11 "There I will ᴿprovide for you, lest you and your household, and all that you have, come to poverty; for *there are* still five years of famine." '   Gen. 47:12

12 "And behold, your eyes and the eyes of my brother Benjamin see that *it is* ᴿmy mouth that speaks to you.   Gen. 42:23

13 "So you shall tell my father of all my glory in Egypt, and of all that you have seen; and you shall hurry and ᴿbring my father down here."   Acts 7:14

14 Then he fell on his brother Benjamin's neck and wept, and Benjamin wept on his neck.

15 Moreover he ᴿkissed all his brothers and wept over them, and after that his brothers talked with him.   Gen. 48:10

16 Now the report of it was heard in Pharaoh's house, saying, "Joseph's brothers have come." So it pleased Pharaoh and his servants well.

17 And Pharaoh said to Joseph, "Say to your brothers, 'Do this: Load your animals and depart; go to the land of Canaan.

18 'Bring your father and your households and come to me; I will give you the best of the land of Egypt, and you will eat ᴿthe ᵀfat of the land.   Gen. 27:28; 47:6 • The choicest produce

19 'Now you are commanded—do this: Take carts out of the land of Egypt for your little ones and your wives; bring your father and come.

20 'Also do not be concerned about your goods, for the best of all the land of Egypt is yours.' "

21 Then the sons of Israel did so; and Joseph gave them ᴿcarts, according to the command of Pharaoh, and he gave them provisions for the journey.   Gen. 45:19; 46:5

22 He gave to all of them, to each man, ᴿchanges of garments; but to Benjamin he gave three hundred pieces of silver and ᴿfive changes of garments.   2 Kin. 5:5 • Gen. 43:34

23 And he sent to his father these things: ten donkeys loaded with the good things of Egypt, and ten female donkeys loaded with grain, bread, and food for his father for the journey.

24 So he sent his brothers away, and they departed; and he said to them, "See that you do not become troubled along the way."

25 Then they went up out of Egypt, and came to the land of Canaan to Jacob their father.

26 And they told him, saying, "Joseph is still alive, and he is governor over all the land of Egypt." ᴿAnd Jacob's heart stood still, because he did not believe them.   Job 29:24

27 But when they told him all the words which Joseph had said to them, and when he saw the carts which Joseph had sent to carry him, the spirit of Jacob their father revived.

28 Then Israel said, "It is enough. Joseph my son is still alive. I will go and see him before I die."

Jacob's Journey to Egypt

46 So Israel took his journey with all that he had, and came to ᴿBeersheba, and offered sacrifices to the God of his father Isaac.   Gen. 21:31, 33; 26:32, 33; 28:10

2 Then God spoke to Israel ᴿin the visions of the night, and said, "Jacob, Jacob!" And he said, "Here I am."   Gen. 15:1; 22:11; 31:11

3 So He said, "I am God, the God of your father; do not fear to go down to Egypt, for I will make of you a great nation there.

4 "I will go down with you to Egypt, and I will also surely bring you up again; and Joseph *will put his hand on your eyes."

46:4 Will close your eyes when you die

5 Then Jacob arose from Beersheba; and the sons of Israel carried their father Jacob, their little ones, and their wives, in the carts which Pharaoh had sent to carry him.

6 So they took their livestock and their goods, which they had acquired in the land of Canaan, and went to Egypt, ᴿJacob and all his descendants with him.   Deut. 26:5

7 His sons and his sons' sons, his daughters and his sons' daughters, and all his descendants he brought with him to Egypt.

8 Now these were the names of the children of Israel, Jacob and his sons, who went to Egypt: Reuben was Jacob's firstborn.

9 The ᴿsons of Reuben were Hanoch, Pallu, Hezron, and Carmi.   Ex. 6:14

10 ᴿThe sons of Simeon were *Jemuel, Jamin, Ohad, *Jachin, *Zohar, and Shaul, the son of a Canaanite woman.   Ex. 6:15

11 The sons of ᴿLevi were Gershon, Kohath, and Merari.   1 Chr. 6:1, 16

12 The sons of Judah were Er, Onan, Shelah, Perez, and Zerah (but Er and Onan died in the land of Canaan). ᴿThe sons of Perez were Hezron and Hamul.   Gen. 38:29

13 The sons of Issachar were Tola, ᵀPuvah, *Job, and Shimron.   Puah, 1 Chr. 7:1

14 The ᴿsons of Zebulun were Sered, Elon, and Jahleel.   Num. 26:26

15 These were the ᴿsons of Leah, whom she bore to Jacob in Padan Aram, with his daughter Dinah. All the persons, his sons and his daughters, were thirty-three.   Gen. 35:23; 49:31

16 The sons of Gad were *Ziphion, Haggi, Shuni, *Ezbon, Eri, *Arodi, and Areli.

17 The sons of Asher were Jimnah, Ishuah, Isui, Beriah, and Serah, their sister. And the sons of Beriah were Heber and Malchiel.

18 These were the sons of Zilpah, ᴿwhom Laban gave to Leah his daughter; and these she bore to Jacob: sixteen persons.   Gen. 29:24

19 The ᴿsons of Rachel, ᴿJacob's wife, were Joseph and Benjamin.   Gen. 35:24 • Gen. 44:27

20 ᴿAnd to Joseph in the land of Egypt were born Manasseh and Ephraim, whom Asenath, the daughter of Poti-Pherah priest of On, bore to him.   Gen. 41:45, 50–52; 48:1

21 The sons of Benjamin were Belah, Becher, Ashbel, Gera, Naaman, Ehi, Rosh, ᴿMuppim, *Huppim, and Ard.   Num. 26:38, 39

22 These were the sons of Rachel, who were born to Jacob: fourteen persons in all.

23 The son of Dan was *Hushim.

24 ᴿThe sons of Naphtali were *Jahzeel, Guni, Jezer, and *Shillem.   Num. 26:48

46:10 Nemuel, 1 Chr. 4:24 • Jarib, 1 Chr. 4:24 • Zerah, 1 Chr. 4:24
46:13 Jashub, Num. 26:24; 1 Chr. 7:1
46:16 Sam., LXX Zephon and Num. 26:15 • Ozni, Num. 26:16 • Arod, Num. 26:17
46:21 Hupham, Num. 26:39
46:23 Shuham, Num. 26:42
46:24 Jahziel, 1 Chr. 7:13 • Shallum, 1 Chr. 7:13

25 These *were* the sons of Bilhah, whom Laban gave to Rachel his daughter, and she bore these to Jacob: seven persons in all.

26 ᴿAll the persons who went with Jacob to Egypt, who came from his body, ᴿbesides Jacob's sons' wives, *were* sixty-six persons in all.   Ex. 1:5 · Gen. 35:11

27 And the sons of Joseph who were born to him in Egypt *were* two persons. ᴿAll the persons of the house of Jacob who went to Egypt were seventy.   Deut. 10:22

Jacob Settles in Goshen

28 Then he sent Judah before him to Joseph, ᴿto point out before him *the way* to Goshen. And they came ᴿto the land of Goshen.   Gen. 31:21 · Gen. 47:1

29 So Joseph made ready his chariot and went up to Goshen to meet his father Israel; and he presented himself to him, and fell on his neck and wept on his neck a good while.

30 And Israel said to Joseph, ᴿ"Now let me die, since I have seen your face, because you *are* still alive."   Luke 2:29, 30

31 Then Joseph said to his brothers and to his father's household, ᴿ"I will go up and tell Pharaoh, and say to him, 'My brothers and those of my father's house, who *were* in the land of Canaan, have come to me.   Gen. 47:1

32 'And the men *are* ᴿshepherds, for their occupation has been to feed livestock; and they have brought their flocks, their herds, and all that they have.'   Gen. 47:3

33 "So it shall be, when Pharaoh calls you and says, 'What is your occupation?'

34 "that you shall say, 'Your servants' ᴿoccupation has been with livestock from our youth even till now, both we *and* also our fathers,' that you may dwell in the land of Goshen; for every shepherd *is* ᴿan abomination to the Egyptians."   Gen. 47:3 · Gen. 43:32

47 Then Joseph went and told Pharaoh, and said, "My father and my brothers, their flocks and their herds and all that they possess, have come from the land of Canaan; and indeed they *are* in the land of Goshen."

2 And he took five men from among his brothers and presented them to Pharaoh.

3 Then Pharaoh said to his brothers, "What *is* your occupation?" And they said to Pharaoh, ᴿ"Your servants *are* shepherds, both we *and* also our fathers."   Gen. 46:32, 34

4 And they said to Pharaoh, ᴿ"We have come to dwell in the land, because your servants have no pasture for their flocks, for the famine *is* severe in the land of Canaan. Now therefore, please let your servants dwell in the land of Goshen."   Deut. 26:5

5 Then Pharaoh spoke to Joseph, saying, "Your father and your brothers have come to you.

6 "The land of Egypt *is* before you. Have your father and brothers dwell in the best of the land; let them dwell ᴿin the land of Goshen. And if you know *any* competent men among them, then make them chief herdsmen over my livestock."   Gen. 47:4

7 Then Joseph brought in his father Jacob and set him before Pharaoh; and Jacob ᴿblessed Pharaoh.   Gen. 47:10; 48:15, 20

8 Pharaoh said to Jacob, "How old *are* you?"

9 And Jacob said to Pharaoh, "The days of the years of my ᵀpilgrimage *are* one hundred and thirty years; ᴿfew and evil have been the days of the years of my life, and they have not attained to the days of the years of the life of my fathers in the days of their pilgrimage."   Lit. *sojourning* · [Job 14:1]

10 So Jacob ᴿblessed Pharaoh, and went out from before Pharaoh.   Gen. 47:7

11 And Joseph situated his father and his brothers, and gave them a possession in the land of Egypt, in the best of the land, in the land of ᴿRameses, ᴿas Pharaoh had commanded.   Ex. 1:11; 12:37 · Gen. 47:6, 27

12 Then Joseph provided ᴿhis father, his brothers, and all his father's household with bread, according to the number in *their* families.   Gen. 45:11; 50:21

Joseph Deals with the Famine

13 Now *there was* no bread in all the land; for the famine *was* very severe, ᴿso that the land of Egypt and the land of Canaan languished because of the famine.   Gen. 41:30

14 ᴿAnd Joseph gathered up all the money that was found in the land of Egypt and in the land of Canaan, for the grain which they bought; and Joseph brought the money into Pharaoh's house.   Gen. 41:56; 42:6

15 So when the money failed in the land of Egypt and in the land of Canaan, all the Egyptians came to Joseph and said, "Give us bread, for ᴿwhy should we die in your presence? For the money has failed."   Gen. 47:19

16 Then Joseph said, "Give your livestock, and I will give you *bread* for your livestock, if the money is gone."

17 So they brought their livestock to Joseph, and Joseph gave them bread in *exchange* for the horses, the flocks, the cattle of the herds, and for the donkeys. Thus he ᵀfed them with bread in *exchange* for all their livestock that year.   supplied

18 When that year had ended, they came to him the next year and said to him, "We will not hide from my lord that our money is gone; my lord also has our herds of livestock. There is nothing left in the sight of my lord but our bodies and our lands.

19 "Why should we die before your eyes, both we and our land? Buy us and our land for bread, and we and our land will be servants of Pharaoh; give *us* seed, that we may ᴿlive and not die, that the land may not be desolate."   Gen. 43:8

20 Then Joseph ᴿbought all the land of Egypt for Pharaoh; for every man of the Egyptians sold his field, because the famine was severe upon them. So the land became Pharaoh's.   Jer. 32:43

21 And as for the people, he *moved them into the cities, from one end of the borders of Egypt to the other end.

22 ᴿOnly the land of the ᴿpriests he did not buy; for the priests had rations allotted to them by Pharaoh, and they ate their rations which Pharaoh gave them; therefore they did not sell their lands.   Ezra 7:24 · Gen. 41:45

23 Then Joseph said to the people, "Indeed I have bought you and your land this day for Pharaoh. Look, here is seed for you, and you shall sow the land.

24 "And it shall come to pass in the harvest that you shall give one-fifth to Pharaoh. Four-fifths shall be your own, as seed for the field and for your food, for those of your households and as food for your little ones."

25 So they said, "You have saved ᴿour lives; let us find favor in the sight of my lord, and we will be Pharaoh's servants."   Gen. 33:15

26 And Joseph made it a law over the land of Egypt to this day, that Pharaoh should have one-fifth, except for the land of the priests only, which did not become Pharaoh's.

Joseph's Vow to Jacob

27 So Israel ᴿdwelt in the land of Egypt, in the country of Goshen; and they had possessions there and ᴿgrew and multiplied exceedingly.   Gen. 47:11 · Gen. 17:6; 26:4; 35:11; 46:3

28 And Jacob lived in the land of Egypt seventeen years. So the length of Jacob's life was one hundred and forty-seven years.

29 When the time drew near that Israel must die, he called his son Joseph and said to him, "Now if I have found favor in your sight, please put your hand under my thigh, and ᴿdeal kindly and truly with me. ᴿPlease do not bury me in Egypt,   Gen. 24:49 · Gen. 50:25

30 "but ᴿlet me lie with my fathers; you shall carry me out of Egypt and ᴿbury me in their burial place." And he said, "I will do as you have said."   2 Sam. 19:37 · Gen. 49:29; 50:5-13

31 Then he said, "Swear to me." And he swore to him. So ᴿIsrael bowed himself on the head of the bed.   1 Kin. 1:47

Jacob Blesses Joseph's Sons

48 Now it came to pass after these things that Joseph was told, "Indeed your father is sick"; and he took with him his two sons, ᴿManasseh and Ephraim.   Gen. 41:51, 52

2 And Jacob was told, "Look, your son Joseph is coming to you"; and Israel strengthened himself and sat up on the bed.

3 Then Jacob said to Joseph: "God Almighty appeared to me at ᴿLuz in the land of Canaan and blessed me,   Gen. 28:13, 19; 35:6, 9

4 "and said to me, 'Behold, I will make you fruitful and multiply you, and I will make of you a multitude of people, and ᴿgive this land to your descendants after you ᴿas an everlasting possession.'   Ex. 6:8 · Gen. 17:8

5 "And now your ᴿtwo sons, Ephraim and Manasseh, who were born to you in the land of Egypt before I came to you in Egypt, are mine; as Reuben and Simeon, they shall be mine.   Josh. 13:7; 14:4

6 "Your offspring whom you beget after them shall be yours; they will be called by the name of their brothers in their inheritance.

7 "But as for me, when I came from Padan, ᴿRachel died beside me in the land of Canaan on the way, when there was but a ᵀlittle distance to go to Ephrath; and I buried her there on the way to Ephrath (that is, Bethlehem)."   Gen. 35:9, 16, 19, 20 · 5 mi.

8 Then Israel saw Joseph's sons, and said, "Who are these?"

9 And Joseph said to his father, "They are my sons, whom God has given me in this place." And he said, "Please bring them to me, and ᴿI will bless them."   Gen. 27:4; 47:15

10 Now the eyes of Israel were dim with age, so that he could not see. Then Joseph brought them near him, and he ᴷkissed them and embraced them.   Gen. 27:27; 45:15; 50:1

11 And Israel said to Joseph, ᴿ"I had not thought to see your face; but in fact, God has also shown me your offspring!"   Gen. 45:26

12 So Joseph brought them from beside his knees, and he bowed down with his face to the earth.

13 And Joseph took them both, Ephraim with his right hand toward Israel's left hand, and Manasseh with his left hand toward Israel's right hand, and brought them near him.

14 Then Israel stretched out his right hand and laid it on Ephraim's head, who was the younger, and his left hand on Manasseh's head, ᴿguiding his hands knowingly, for Manasseh was the ᴿfirstborn.   Gen. 48:19 · Josh. 17:1

15 And ᴿhe blessed Joseph, and said:

"God, before whom my fathers Abraham
     and Isaac walked,
The God who has fed me all my life
     long to this day,   [Heb. 1|:21]

16 The Angel ᴿwho has redeemed me from
     all evil,   Gen. 22:11, 15-18; 28:13-15; 31:11
Bless the lads;
Let ᴿmy name be named upon them,
And the name of my fathers Abraham
     and Isaac;   Amos 9:12
And let them ᴿgrow into a multitude in
     the midst of the earth."   Num. 26:34, 37

17 Now when Joseph saw that his father ᴿlaid his right hand on the head of Ephraim, it displeased him; so he took hold of his father's hand to remove it from Ephraim's head to Manasseh's head.   Gen. 48:14

47:21 So with MT, Tg.; Sam., LXX made the people virtual slaves (cf. Vg.)

18 And Joseph said to his father, "Not so, my father, for this one is the firstborn; put your right hand on his head."

19 But his father refused and said, R"I know, my son, I know. He also shall become a people, and he also shall be great; but truly Rhis younger brother shall be greater than he, and his descendants shall become a multitude of nations."   Gen. 48:14 • Num. 1:33, 35

20 So he blessed them that day, saying, "By you Israel will bless, saying, 'May God make you as Ephraim and as Manasseh!'" And thus he set Ephraim before Manasseh.

21 Then Israel said to Joseph, "Behold, I am dying, but God will be with you and bring you back to the land of your fathers.

22 "Moreover I have given to you one Tportion above your brothers, which I took from the hand of the Amorite with my sword and my bow."   Lit. shoulder, ridge

Jacob's Last Words to His Sons

49 And Jacob called his sons and said, "Gather together, that I may tell you what shall befall you in the last days:

2 "Gather together and hear, you sons of Jacob,
   And listen to Israel your father.

3 "Reuben, you are Rmy firstborn,
   My might and the beginning of my strength,
   The excellency of dignity and the excellency of power.   Gen. 29:32

4 Unstable as water, you shall not excel,
   Because you Rwent up to your father's bed;
   Then you defiled it—
   He went up to my couch.   Gen. 35:22

5 "Simeon and Levi are brothers;
   Instruments of Tcruelty are in their dwelling place.   violence

6 RLet not my soul enter their council;
   Let not my honor be united Rto their assembly;   Prov. 1:15, 16 • Ps. 26:9
   RFor in their anger they slew a man,
   And in their self-will they Thamstrung an ox.   Gen. 34:26 • lamed

7 Cursed be their anger, for it is fierce;
   And their wrath, for it is cruel!
   RI will divide them in Jacob
   And scatter them in Israel.   Josh. 19:1, 9

8 "Judah,R you are he whom your brothers shall praise;   Deut. 33:7
   RYour hand shall be on the neck of your enemies;   Ps. 18:40
   RYour father's children shall bow down before you.   1 Chr. 5:2

9 Judah is Ra lion's whelp;   [Rev. 5:5]
   From the prey, my son, you have gone up.
   He bows down, he lies down as a lion;
   And as a lion, who shall rouse him?

10 RThe *scepter shall not depart from Judah,   Ps. 60:7; Rev. 5:5
   Nor Ra lawgiver from between his feet,
   RUntil Shiloh comes;   Ps. 60:7 • Is. 11:1
   RAnd to Him shall be the obedience of the people.   Ps. 2:6-9; 72:8-11

11 Binding his donkey to the vine,
   And his donkey's colt to the choice vine,
   He washed his garments in wine,
   And his clothes in the blood of grapes.

12 His eyes are darker than wine,
   And his teeth whiter than milk.

13 "ZebulunR shall dwell by the haven of the sea;   Deut. 33:18, 19
   He shall become a haven for ships,
   And his border shall adjoin Sidon.

14 "IssacharR is a strong donkey,   1 Chr. 12:32
   Lying down between two burdens;

15 He saw that rest was good,
   And that the land was pleasant;
   He bowed Rhis shoulder to bear a burden,   1 Sam. 10:9
   And became a band of slaves.

16 "DanR shall judge his people
   As one of the tribes of Israel.   Deut. 33:22

17 RDan shall be a serpent by the way,
   A viper by the path,   Judg. 18:27
   That bites the horse's heels
   So that its rider shall fall backward.

18 RI have waited for your salvation, O LORD!   Is. 25:9

19 "Gad,R a troop shall tramp upon him,
   But he shall triumph at last.   Deut. 33:20

20 "Bread from Asher shall be rich,
   And he shall yield royal dainties.

21 "NaphtaliR is a deer let loose;
   He uses beautiful words.   Deut. 33:23

22 "Joseph is a fruitful bough,
   A fruitful bough by a well;
   His branches run over the wall.

23 The archers have Rbitterly grieved him,
   Shot at him and hated him.   Gen. 37:4, 24

24 But his Rbow remained in strength,
   And the arms of his hands were Tmade strong   Job 29:20 • Or supple
   By the hands of Rthe Mighty God of Jacob   Ps. 132:2, 5
   (From there Ris the Shepherd, Rthe Stone of Israel),   [Ps. 23:1; 80:1] • Is. 28:16

25 RBy the God of your father who will help you,   Gen. 28:13; 32:9; 35:3; 43:23; 50:17
   RAnd by the Almighty Rwho will bless you   Gen. 17:1; 35:11 • Deut. 33:13
   With blessings of heaven above,
   Blessings of the deep that lies beneath,
   Blessings of the breasts and of the womb.

26 The blessings of your father

49:10 A symbol of kingship

Have excelled the blessings of my
ancestors,
^RUp to the utmost bound of the
everlasting hills.   Deut. 33:15
They shall be on the head of Joseph,
And on the crown of the head of him
who was separate from his brothers.

27 "Benjamin is a ^Rravenous wolf;
In the morning he shall devour the
prey,   Judg. 20:21, 25
And at night he shall divide the spoil."

28 All these are the twelve tribes of Israel,
and this is what their father spoke to them.
And he blessed them; he blessed each one
according to his own blessing.

Jacob's Death and Burial

29 Then he charged them and said to them:
"I am to be gathered to my people; bury me
with my fathers ^Rin the cave that is in the
field of Ephron the Hittite,   Gen. 23:16–20; 50:13
30 "in the cave that is in the field of Machpelah, which is before Mamre in the land of
Canaan, ^Rwhich Abraham bought with the
field of Ephron the Hittite as a possession for
a burial place.   Gen. 23:3–20
31 "There they buried Abraham and Sarah
his wife, there they buried Isaac and Rebekah
his wife, and there I buried Leah.
32 "The field and the cave that is there
were purchased from the sons of Heth."
33 And when Jacob had finished commanding his sons, he drew his feet up into the bed
and breathed his last, and was gathered to his
people.

50 Then Joseph fell on his father's face,
and wept over him, and kissed him.
2 And Joseph commanded his servants the
physicians to ^Rembalm his father. So the
physicians embalmed Israel.   Gen. 50:26
3 Forty days were required for him, for
such are the days required for those who are
embalmed; and the Egyptians ^Rmourned^T for
him seventy days.   Deut. 34:8 · Lit. wept
4 Now when the days of his mourning
were past, Joseph spoke to ^Rthe household of
Pharaoh, saying, "If now I have found favor
in your eyes, please speak in the hearing of
Pharaoh, saying,   Esth. 4:2
5 ^R'My father made me swear, saying,
"Behold, I am dying; in my grave ^Rwhich I
dug for myself in the land of Canaan, there
you shall bury me." Now therefore, please let
me go up and bury my father, and I will come
back.' "   Gen. 47:29–31 · Is. 22:16
6 And Pharaoh said, "Go up and bury your
father, as he made you swear."
7 So Joseph went up to bury his father;
and with him went up all the servants of
Pharaoh, the elders of his house, and all the
elders of the land of Egypt,
8 as well as all the house of Joseph, his
brothers, and his father's house. Only their

little ones, their flocks, and their herds they
left in the land of Goshen.
9 And there went up with him both chariots and horsemen, and it was a very great
gathering.
10 Then they came to the threshing floor of
Atad, which is beyond the Jordan, and they
^Rmourned there with a great and very solemn
lamentation. ^RHe observed seven days of
mourning for his father.   Acts 8:2 · 1 Sam. 31:13
11 And when the inhabitants of the land,
the Canaanites, saw the mourning at the
threshing floor of Atad, they said, "This is a
deep mourning of the Egyptians." Therefore
its name was called ^TAbel Mizraim, which is
beyond the Jordan.   Mourning of Egypt
12 So his sons did for him just as he had
commanded them.
13 For his sons carried him to the land of
Canaan, and buried him in the cave of the
field of Machpelah, before Mamre, which
Abraham bought with the field from Ephron
the Hittite as property for a burial place.
14 And after he had buried his father,
Joseph returned to Egypt, he and his brothers
and all who went up with him to bury his
father.

Joseph Reassures His Brothers

15 When Joseph's brothers saw that their
father was dead, they said, "Perhaps Joseph
will hate us, and may ^Tactually repay us for
all the evil which we did to him."   fully
16 So they sent messengers to Joseph, saying, "Before your father died he commanded,
saying,
17 'Thus you shall say to Joseph: "I beg
you, please forgive the trespass of your brothers and their sin; for they did evil to you." '
Now, please, forgive the trespass of the servants of the God of your father." And Joseph
wept when they spoke to him.
18 Then his brothers also went and ^Rfell
down before his face, and they said, "Behold,
we are your servants."   Gen. 37:7–10; 41:43; 44:14
19 Joseph said to them, "Do not be afraid,
^Rfor am I in the place of God?   2 Kin. 5:7
20 ^R"But as for you, you meant evil against
me; but ^RGod meant it for good, in order to
bring it about as it is this day, to save many
people alive.   Ps. 56:5 · [Acts 3:13–15]
21 "Now therefore, do not be afraid; I will
provide for you and your little ones." And he
comforted them and spoke kindly to them.

Death of Joseph

22 So Joseph dwelt in Egypt, he and his
father's household. And Joseph lived one
hundred and ten years.
23 Joseph saw Ephraim's children to the
third generation. ^RThe children of Machir, the
son of Manasseh, ^Rwere also brought up on
Joseph's knees.   Num. 26:29; 32:39 · Gen. 30:3

24 And Joseph said to his brethren, "I am dying; but ᴿGod will surely visit you, and bring you out of this land to the land ᴿof which He swore to Abraham, to Isaac, and to Jacob." Ex. 3:16, 17 · Gen. 26:3; 35:12; 46:4

25 Then Joseph took an oath from the children of Israel, saying, "God will surely ᵀvisit you, and ᴿyou shall carry up my ᴿbones from here." *help* · Deut. 1:8; 30:1-8 · Ex. 13:19

26 So Joseph died, *being* one hundred and ten years old; and they embalmed him, and he was put in a coffin in Egypt.

THE SECOND BOOK OF MOSES CALLED

Exodus

The book of Exodus finds its counterpart in all our public buildings today. Exit signs proclaim *the way out,* the exact meaning of *Exodus.* It is the book that describes how God brought Israel out of slavery and established them as a nation. It derives its name from the event which dominates the book.

AUTHORSHIP. Moses is both the principal character and the author of Exodus. The book contains direct references to Moses' writing (17:14; 24:4). The book bears the stamp of a man of Moses' caliber. The vivid descriptions of geography and events are those of an eyewitness. The historical detail and literary quality point to a well-educated author. From the earliest times, Jewish tradition has recognized the unity and harmony of the book as coming from Moses' authorship. Christ specifically refers to Exodus and to Moses as author (John 5:45-47; 7:19-24). The New Testament writers likewise declare Moses to be the author (John 1:17; Rom. 10:5; 2 Cor. 3:15). No other person in Jewish history was so gifted to have his writing accepted as the truth. Exodus was inspired by God through the human authorship of Moses.

CONTEXT. Exodus follows the book of Genesis both logically and chronologically. Genesis closes with Abraham's family numbering seventy people and enjoying prominence in Egypt. Exodus opens with the family now grown to a nation of almost three million people. They are no longer high in society; they have become slaves. Four hundred years have passed in comparative silence but not without significance. God informed Abraham ahead of time about the four hundred years of suffering and the great deliverance that would follow (Gen. 15:13-21). The Exodus occurred in 1447 B.C. (cf. 1 Kin. 6:1). That date fits what we know of Egyptian history and continues to be supported by archaeological findings.

HOW EXODUS FITS INTO THE BIBLE. Exodus is the Magna Charta of Israel, the indispensable link between Abraham, the individual, and the great nation of Jews who claim him as their founding father. Historically it marks the founding or establishing of Israel as a nation. When Exodus opens, they are an unorganized, enslaved people. When Exodus closes, they are a cohesive nation with central leadership and both religious and civil law. No nation in all of human history has been so dramatically transformed or so rapidly established. The exodus out of Egypt was Israel's birth as a nation. The law, the statutes, and the ordinances were Israel's constitution. Just as we cannot understand human history without the record of Genesis, so we cannot understand Jewish history without Exodus.

Theologically Exodus is the book of redemption. It is the Romans of the Old Testament. The nation is redeemed out of spiritual bondage as well as physical slavery. The Passover marked Israel's departure from Egypt (Ex. 12:13, 14). The Passover lamb whose blood was shed is a type of Jesus Christ, the Lamb of God, who takes away the sin of the world (John 1:29; 1 Cor. 5:7).

HOW EXODUS FITS TOGETHER. The content of the book can best be divided by its geographic location or its activity. In chapters 1—12 we find Israel in Egypt. Moses' birth is recorded in chapters 1 and 2, and his call in chapters 3 and 4. Chapters 5—11 record the contest between Moses as God's representative and Pharaoh. Chapter 12 records the Passover and the tenth and final plague brought against Egypt.

Chapters 13—18 describe Israel's experience in the wilderness. It is dominated by their miraculous crossing of the Red Sea and God's provision of manna.

Chapters 19—40 find Israel at Mount Sinai. There God gives the Ten Commandments and the civil law (chs. 19—24). The nation needs a place to worship and God gives a detailed pattern for the tabernacle and its furnishings in chapters 25—40.

KEY VERSES: 3:7, 8—"And the LORD said: 'I have surely seen the oppression of My people who are in Egypt, and have heard their cry because of their taskmasters, for I know their sorrows. So I have come down to deliver them out of the hand of the Egyptians, and to bring them up from that land to a good and large land, to a land flowing with milk and honey, to the place of the Canaanites and the Hittites and the Amorites and the Perizzites and the Hivites and the Jebusites.'" Here Israel's past, present, and future are stated. The turning point is God's redemption of Israel out of bondage.

—K.G.H.

Israel's Suffering in Egypt

NOW these *are* the names of the children of Israel who came to Egypt; each man and his household came with Jacob:

2 Reuben, Simeon, Levi, and Judah;
3 Issachar, Zebulun, and Benjamin;
4 Dan, Naphtali, Gad, and Asher.
5 All those ᵀwho were descendants of Jacob were *seventy persons (for Joseph was in Egypt *already*).   Lit. *who came from the loins of*
6 And ᴿJoseph died, all his brothers, and all that generation.   Gen. 50:26
7 ᴿBut the children of Israel were fruitful and increased abundantly, multiplied and ᵀgrew exceedingly mighty; and the land was filled with them.   Acts 7:17 • *became very numerous*
8 Now there arose a new king over Egypt, ᴿwho did not know Joseph.   Acts 7:18, 19
9 And he said to his people, "Look, the people of the children of Israel *are* more and ᴿmightier than we;   Gen. 26:16
10 ᴿ"come, let us ᴿdeal shrewdly with them, lest they multiply, and it happen, in the event of war, that they also join our enemies and fight against us, and *so* go up out of the land."   Ps. 83:3, 4 • Acts 7:19
11 Therefore they set taskmasters over them to afflict them with their burdens. And they built for Pharaoh ᴿsupply cities, Pithom ᴿand Raamses.   1 Kin. 9:19 • Gen. 47:11
12 But the more they afflicted them, the more they multiplied and grew. And they were in dread of the children of Israel.
13 So the Egyptians made the children of Israel ᴿserve with ᵀrigor.   Gen. 15:13 • *harshness*
14 And they ᴿmade their lives bitter with hard bondage—ᴿin mortar, in brick, and in all manner of service in the field. All their service in which they made them serve *was* with rigor.   Num. 20:15 • Ps. 81:6
15 Then the king of Egypt spoke to the ᴿHebrew midwives, of whom the name of one *was* Shiphrah and the name of the other Puah;   Ex. 2:6
16 and he said, "When you do the duties of a midwife for the Hebrew women, and see *them* on the birthstools, if it *is* a ᴿson, then you shall kill him; but if it *is* a daughter, then she shall live."   Acts 7:19
17 But the midwives feared God, and did not do as the king of Egypt commanded them, but saved the male children alive.
18 So the king of Egypt called for the midwives and said to them, "Why have you done this thing, and saved the male children alive?"
19 And the midwives said to Pharaoh, "Because the Hebrew women *are* not like the Egyptian women; for they *are* lively and give birth before the midwives come to them."

20 ᴿTherefore God dealt well with the midwives, and the people multiplied and ᵀgrew very mighty.   [Prov. 11:18] • *became very numerous*
21 And so it was, because the midwives feared God, ᴿthat He ᵀprovided households for them.   1 Sam. 2:35 • *gave them families*
22 So Pharaoh commanded all his people, saying, ᴿ"Every son who is *born you shall cast into the river, and every *daughter you shall save alive."   Acts 7:19

Moses Is Born

2 And a man of the house of Levi went and took *as wife* a daughter of Levi.
2 So the woman conceived and bore a son. And ᴿwhen she saw that he *was* a beautiful *child*, she hid him three months.   Acts 7:20
3 But when she could no longer hide him, she took an ark of bulrushes for him, daubed it with asphalt and pitch, put the child in it, and laid *it* in the reeds by the river's bank.
4 ᴿAnd his sister stood afar off, to know what would be done to him.   Num. 26:59
5 Then the ᴿdaughter of Pharaoh came down to bathe at the river. And her maidens walked along the riverside; and when she saw the ark among the reeds, she sent her maid to get it.   Acts 7:21
6 And when she opened *it*, she saw the child, and behold, the baby wept. So she had compassion on him, and said, "This is one of the Hebrews' children."
7 Then his sister said to Pharaoh's daughter, "Shall I go and call a nurse for you from the Hebrew women, that she may nurse the child for you?"
8 And Pharaoh's daughter said to her, "Go." So the maiden went and called the child's mother.
9 Then Pharaoh's daughter said to her, "Take this child away and nurse him for me, and I will give you your wages." So the woman took the child and nursed him.
10 And the child grew, and she brought him to Pharaoh's daughter, and he became her son. So she called his name *Moses, saying, "Because I drew him out of the water."

Moses Flees to Midian

11 Now it came to pass in those days, ᴿwhen Moses was grown, that he went out to his brethren and looked at their burdens. And he saw an Egyptian beating a Hebrew, one of his brethren.   Heb. 11:24-26
12 So he looked this way and that way, and when he saw no one, he ᴿkilled the Egyptian and hid him in the sand.   Acts 7:24, 25
13 And when he went out the second day, behold, two Hebrew men ᴿwere fighting, and he said to the one who did the wrong, "Why are you striking your companion?"   Prov. 25:8

1:22 Sam., LXX, Tg. add *to the Hebrews*
2:10 Heb. *Mosheh*, lit. *Drawn Out*

1:5 DSS, LXX *seventy-five;* cf. Acts 7:14

14 Then he said, R"Who made you a prince and a judge over us? Do you intend to kill me as you killed the Egyptian?" So Moses Rfeared and said, "Surely this thing is known!"   Acts 7:27, 28 · Judg. 6:27

15 When Pharaoh heard of this matter, he sought to kill Moses. But Moses fled from the face of Pharaoh and dwelt in the land of RMidian; and he sat down by a well.   Ex. 3:1

16 Now the priest of Midian had seven daughters. RAnd they came and drew water, and they filled the Rtroughs to water their father's flock.   Gen. 24:11, 13, 19; 29:6-10 · Gen. 30:38

17 Then the shepherds came and drove them away; but Moses stood up and helped them, and Rwatered their flock.   Gen. 29:3, 10

18 When they came to RReuelT their father, Rhe said, "How is it that you have come so soon today?"   Num. 10:29 · Jethro, Ex. 3:1 · Ex. 3:1; 4:18

19 And they said, "An Egyptian delivered us from the hand of the shepherds, and he also drew enough water for us and watered the flock."

20 So he said to his daughters, "And where is he? Why is it that you have left the man? Call him, that he may eat bread."

21 Then Moses was content to live with the man, and he gave RZipporah his daughter to Moses.   Ex. 4:25; 18:2

22 And she bore him a son. He called his name TGershom, for he said, "I have been a stranger in a foreign land."   Lit. Stranger There

23 Now it happened in the process of time that the king of Egypt died. Then the children of Israel groaned because of the bondage, and they cried out; and Rtheir cry came up to God because of the bondage.   James 5:4

24 So God Rheard their groaning, and God Rremembered His covenant with Abraham, with Isaac, and with Jacob.   Ex. 6:5 · Gen. 15:13

25 And God looked upon the children of Israel, and God Racknowledged them.   Ex. 3:7

Moses at the Burning Bush

3 Now Moses was tending the flock of Jethro his father-in-law, the priest of Midian. And he led the flock to the back of the desert, and came to Horeb, the mountain of God.

2 And Rthe Angel of the LORD appeared to him in a flame of fire from the midst of a bush. So he looked, and behold, the bush was burning with fire, but the bush was not consumed.   Deut. 33:16

3 Then Moses said, "I will now turn aside and see this Rgreat sight, why the bush does not burn."   Acts 7:31

4 So when the LORD saw that he turned aside to look, God called Rto him from the midst of the bush and said, "Moses, Moses!" And he said, "Here I am."   Deut. 33:16

5 Then He said, "Do not draw near this place. Take your sandals off your feet, for the place where you stand is holy ground."

6 Moreover He said, R"I am the God of your father—the God of Abraham, the God of Isaac, and the God of Jacob." And Moses hid his face, for Rhe was afraid to look upon God.   [Matt. 22:32] · 1 Kin. 19:13

7 And the LORD said: "I have surely seen the oppression of My people who are in Egypt, and have heard their cry because of their taskmasters, for I know their sorrows.

8 "So I have come down to deliver them out of the hand of the Egyptians, and to bring them up from that land Rto a good and large land, to a land flowing with milk and honey, to the place of the Canaanites and the Hittites and the Amorites and the Perizzites and the Hivites and the Jebusites.   Deut. 1:25

9 "Now therefore, behold, Rthe cry of the children of Israel has come to Me, and I have also seen the Roppression with which the Egyptians oppress them.   Ex. 2:23 · Ex. 1:11, 13, 14

10 "Come now, therefore, and I will send you to Pharaoh that you may bring My people, the children of Israel, out of Egypt."

11 But Moses said to God, "Who am I that I should go to Pharaoh, and that I should bring the children of Israel out of Egypt?"

12 So He said, R"I will certainly be with you. And this shall be a Rsign to you that I have sent you: When you have brought the people out of Egypt, you shall serve God on this mountain."   Gen. 31:3 · Ex. 4:8; 19:3

7-A. Jesus Is the "I AM" of the Old Testament   ▼

13 Then Moses said to God, "Indeed, when I come to the children of Israel and say to them, 'The God of your fathers has sent me to you,' and they say to me, 'What is His name?' what shall I say to them?"

7-A. Jesus Is the "I AM" of the Old Testament (Exodus 3:13-15)—Moses led his father-in-law's flock to the "back of the desert, and came to Horeb, the mountain of God" (vv. 1-6). There he saw an unusual sight, a desert bush enveloped in flames but not consumed. In his curiosity he turned aside to see this phenomenon; "and the Angel of the LORD appeared to him in a flame of fire from the midst of a bush" (v. 2), saying, "Do not draw near this place. Take your sandals off your feet, for the place where you stand is holy ground" (v. 5). Then the Angel of the LORD revealed His identity: "I am the God of your father—the God of Abraham, the God of Isaac, and the God of Jacob" (v. 6). In John 8:58 (page 1064), Jesus looked back in time to this event and identified Himself as the great "I AM." Jesus did not say, "Before Abraham was, I was." He said, "Before Abraham was, I AM." When Jesus said, "I AM," He made the following claims:

(Point 7-A continued on next page)

▽ 14 And God said to Moses, "I AM WHO I AM." And He said, "Thus you shall say to the children of Israel, ᴿ'I AM has sent me to you.'"   [John 8:24, 28, 58]

15 Moreover God said to Moses, "Thus you shall say to the children of Israel: 'The LORD God of your fathers, the God of Abraham, the God of Isaac, and the God of Jacob, has sent me to you. This *is* My name forever, and this
▲ *is* My memorial to all generations.'

16 "Go and ᴿgather the elders of Israel together, and say to them, 'The LORD God of your fathers, the God of Abraham, of Isaac, and of Jacob, appeared to me, saying, ᴿ"I have surely visited you and *seen* what is done to you in Egypt;   Ex. 4:29 • Ex. 2:25; 4:31

17 "and I have said ᴿI will bring you up out of the affliction of Egypt to the land of the Canaanites and the Hittites and the Amorites and the Perizzites and the Hivites and the Jebusites, to a land flowing with milk and honey." '   Gen. 15:13-21; 46:4; 50:24, 25

18 "Then they will heed your voice; and you shall come, you and the elders of Israel, to the king of Egypt; and you shall say to him, 'The LORD God of the Hebrews has met with us; and now, please, let us go ᵀthree days' journey into the wilderness, that we may sacrifice to the LORD our God.'   60 mi.

19 "But I am sure that the king of Egypt ᴿwill not let you go, no, not even by a mighty hand.   Ex. 5:2

20 "So I will ᴿstretch out My hand and strike Egypt with ᴿall My wonders which I will do in its midst; and ᴿafter that he will let you go.   Ex. 6:6; 9:15 • Deut. 6:22 • Ex. 11:1; 12:31-37

21 "And I will give this people favor in the sight of the Egyptians; and it shall be, when you go, that you shall not go empty-handed.

22 ᴿ"But every woman shall ask of her neighbor, namely, of her who dwells near her house, ᴿarticles of silver, articles of gold, and

clothing; and you shall put *them* on your sons and on your daughters. So ᴿyou shall plunder the Egyptians."   Ex. 11:2 • Ex. 33:6 • Job 27:17

Miraculous Signs for Pharaoh

4 Then Moses answered and said, "But suppose they will not believe me or listen to my voice; suppose they say, 'The LORD has not appeared to you.'"

2 So the LORD said to him, "What *is* that in your hand?" He said, "A rod."

3 And He said, "Cast it on the ground." So he cast it on the ground, and it became a serpent; and Moses fled from it.

4 Then the LORD said to Moses, "Reach out your hand and take *it* by the tail" (and he reached out his hand and caught it, and it became a rod in his hand),

5 "that they may ᴿbelieve that the ᴿLORD God of their fathers, the God of Abraham, the God of Isaac, and the God of Jacob, has appeared to you."   Ex. 4:31; 19:9 • Ex. 3:6, 15

6 Furthermore the LORD said to him, "Now put your hand in your bosom." And he put his hand in his bosom, and when he took it out, behold, his hand *was* leprous, like snow.

7 And He said, "Put your hand in your bosom again." So he put his hand in his bosom again, and drew it out of his bosom, and behold, ᴿit was restored like his *other* flesh.   Deut. 32:39

8 "Then it will be, if they do not believe you, nor heed the message of the ᴿfirst sign, that they may believe the message of the latter sign.   Ex. 7:6-13

9 "And it shall be, if they do not believe even these two signs, or listen to your voice, that you shall take water from ᵀthe river and pour *it* on the dry *land*. ᴿThe water which you take from the river will become blood on the dry *land*."   The Nile • Ex. 7:19, 20

(Point 7-A continued from previous page)

(1) He claimed more than prior existence to Abraham; He declared Himself to be the eternally self-existing One.

(2) He claimed to antedate everything that had a beginning. He antedates the multiplied thousands of galaxies that make up the universe.

(3) He claimed to be the Creator of everything in God's universe. "For by Him [the I AM] all things were created that are in heaven and that are on earth, visible and invisible, whether thrones or dominions or principalities or powers. All things were created through Him and for Him" (Col. 1:16, page 1202).

Moses said to God, "Indeed, when I come to the children of Israel and say to them, 'The God of your fathers has sent me to you,' and they say to me, 'What is His name?' what shall I say to them?" Then God said to Moses, "I AM WHO I AM . . . say to the children of Israel, 'I AM has sent me to you'" (vv. 13, 14). What is the meaning of "I AM WHO I AM"? God is saying, I am self-existent, eternal Jehovah God. I am immutable, I do not change (Mal. 3:6, page 924). There are only two ways to change—for better or for worse; God cannot do either, because this would be inconsistent with His absolutely perfect character. He is infallible; He errs not; He is incapable of sin (James 1:13, page 1256). He is the great I AM.

See John 8:56-59, page 1064, for **Point 7-B: Jesus Is the "I AM" of the New Testament.**

▼ 31-A. A Prayer That Angered God

10 Then Moses said to the LORD, "O my Lord, I *am* not eloquent, neither before nor since You have spoken to Your servant; but I *am* slow of speech and slow of tongue."

11 So the LORD said to him, R"Who has made man's mouth? Or who makes the mute, the deaf, the seeing, or the blind? *Have* not I, the LORD?   Ps. 94:9; 146:8

12 "Now therefore, go, and I will be Rwith your mouth and teach you what you shall say."   Is. 50:4

13 But he said, "O my Lord, please send by the hand of whomever *else* You may send."

14 So the anger of the LORD was kindled against Moses, and He said: "Is not Aaron the Levite your Rbrother? I know that he can speak well. And look, Rhe is also coming out to meet you. When he sees you, he will be glad in his heart.   Num. 26:59 • Ex. 4:27

15 "Now you shall speak to him and put the words in his mouth. And I will be with your mouth and with his mouth, and RI will teach you what you shall do.   Deut. 5:31

16 "So he shall be your spokesman to the people. And he himself shall be as a mouth for you, and you shall be to him as God.

17 "And you shall take this rod in your
▲ hand, with which you shall do the signs."

Moses Goes to Egypt

18 So Moses went and returned to Jethro his father-in-law, and said to him, "Please let me go and return to my brethren who *are* in Egypt, and see whether they are still alive." And Jethro said to Moses, "Go in peace."

19 Now the LORD said to Moses in Midian, "Go, return to Egypt; for Rall the men who sought your life are dead."   Ex. 2:15, 23

20 Then Moses Rtook his wife and his sons and set them on a donkey, and he returned to the land of Egypt. And Moses took Rthe rod of God in his hand.   Ex. 18:2–5 • Num. 20:8, 9, 11

21 And the LORD said to Moses, "When you go back to Egypt, see that you do all those wonders before Pharaoh which I have put in your hand. But RI will harden his heart, so that he will not let the people go.   John 12:40

22 "Then you shall Rsay to Pharaoh, 'Thus says the LORD: R"Israel *is* My son, RMy first-born.   Ex. 5:1 • Hos. 11:1 • Jer. 31:9

23 "So I say to you, let My son go that he may serve Me. But if you refuse to let him go, indeed I will kill your son, your firstborn." ' "

24 And it came to pass on the way, at the encampment, that the LORD Rmet him and sought to Rkill him.   Num. 22:22 • Gen. 17:14

25 Then Zipporah took a sharp stone and cut off the foreskin of her son and Tcast *it* at *Moses' feet, and said, "Surely you *are* a husband of blood to me!"   Lit. *made it touch*

26 So He let him go. Then she said, "*You are* a Thusband of blood!"—because of the circumcision.   *bridegroom*

27 And the LORD said to Aaron, "Go into the wilderness Rto meet Moses." So he went and met him on Rthe mountain of God, and kissed him.   Ex. 4:14 • Ex. 3:1; 18:5; 24:13

4:25 Lit. *his*

31-A. A Prayer That Angered God (Exodus 4:10–17)—Some forty years earlier, Moses, in his own strength, had attempted to aid the Hebrew people. He had failed. Now, four decades later, God called upon the older and wiser Moses to be His spokesman in leading Israel out of Egypt, their land of bondage (Ex. 3:10, page 60). At the holy scene of the burning bush, Moses spoke with God—and in that sense, he was praying. Moses raised certain objections to serving God, and God answered them all:

(1) Moses: "Who am I that I should go to Pharaoh?" (Ex. 3:11, page 60). God: "I will certainly be with you" (3:12).

(2) Moses: "What shall I say to them" when they ask me Your name? (3:13). God: "Say to the children of Israel, 'I AM has sent me to you'" (3:14).

(3) Moses: "They will not believe me" (4:1). God, paraphrased: "I will use what you already have—your simple shepherd's rod—for a sign to the people" (4:2–5).

(4) Moses: "O my Lord, I am not eloquent . . . I am slow of speech and slow of tongue" (4:10). God: "Who has made man's mouth? . . . Now therefore, go, and I will be with your mouth and teach you what you shall say" (4:11, 12).

(5) Moses: "O my Lord, please send by the hand of whomever else You may send" (4:13). Paraphrased, Moses was saying, "Lord, send anyone, but not me." God: "Is not Aaron the Levite your brother? . . . he shall be your spokesman . . . and you shall be to him as God" (4:14–16).

God finally became angry with Moses' many objections to serving Him. These five objections, or fearful hesitations, each reflect the older Moses' recollection of his youthful failure and realization of his present weaknesses and limitations. All of God's replies, however, stress His

(1) divine power;
(2) presence with His servant;
(3) provision of everything and everyone necessary for the ministry ahead.

The God who calls is the God who will supply. Let us hear God and have this faith; to doubt angers God (4:14–18, above).

See Exodus 5:22, 23, page 63, for **Point 31-B: A Prayer of Impatience.**

28 So Moses told Aaron all the words of the LORD who had sent him, and all the ᴿsigns which He had commanded him.   Ex. 4:8, 9

29 Then Moses and Aaron ᴿwent and gathered together all the elders of the children of Israel.   Ex. 3:16; 12:21

30 ᴿAnd Aaron spoke all the words which the LORD had spoken to Moses. Then he did the signs in the sight of the people.   Ex. 4:15, 16

31 So the people believed; and when they heard that the LORD had ᴿvisited the children of Israel and that He ᴿhad looked on their affliction, then ᴿthey bowed their heads and worshiped.   Gen. 50:24 • Ex. 2:25; 3:7 • Gen. 24:26

First Encounter with Pharaoh

5 Afterward Moses and Aaron went in and told Pharaoh, "Thus says the LORD God of Israel: 'Let My people go, that they may hold a feast to Me in the wilderness.' "

2 And Pharaoh said, ᴿ"Who is the LORD, that I should obey His voice to let Israel go? I do not know the LORD, ᴿnor will I let Israel go."   2 Kin. 18:35 • Ex. 3:19; 7:14

3 So they said, "The God of the Hebrews has met with us. Please, let us go ᵀthree days' journey into the desert and sacrifice to the LORD our God, lest He fall upon us with ᴿpestilence or with the sword."   60 mi. • Ex. 9:15

4 Then the king of Egypt said to them, "Moses and Aaron, why do you take the people from their work? Get back to your ᴿlabor."   Ex. 1:11; 2:11; 6:6

5 And Pharaoh said, "Look, the people of the land are ᴿmany now, and you make them rest from their labor!"   Ex. 1:7, 9

6 So the same day Pharaoh commanded the ᴿtaskmasters of the people and their officers, saying,   Ex. 1:11; 3:7; 5:10, 13, 14

7 "You shall no longer give the people straw to make ᴿbrick as before. Let them go and gather straw for themselves.   Ex. 1:14

8 "And you shall lay on them the quota of bricks which they made before. You shall not reduce it. For they are idle; therefore they cry out, saying, 'Let us go and sacrifice to our God.'

9 "Let more work be laid on the men, that they may labor in it, and let them not regard false words."

10 And the taskmasters of the people and their officers went out and spoke to the people, saying, "Thus says Pharaoh: 'I will not give you straw.

11 'Go, get yourselves straw where you can find it; yet none of your work will be reduced.' "

12 So the people were scattered abroad throughout all the land of Egypt to gather stubble instead of straw.

13 And the taskmasters forced them to hurry, saying, "Fulfill your work, your daily quota, as when there was straw."

14 Also the ᴿofficers of the children of Israel, whom Pharaoh's taskmasters had set over them, were ᴿbeaten and were asked, "Why have you not fulfilled your task in making brick both yesterday and today, as before?"   Ex. 5:6 • Is. 10:24

15 Then the officers of the children of Israel came and cried out to Pharaoh, saying, "Why are you dealing thus with your servants?

16 "There is no straw given to your servants, and they say to us, 'Make brick!' And indeed your servants are beaten, but the fault is in your own people."

17 But he said, "You are idle! Idle! Therefore you say, 'Let us go and sacrifice to the LORD.'

18 "Therefore go now and work; for no straw shall be given you, yet you shall deliver the quota of bricks."

19 And the officers of the children of Israel saw that they were in trouble after it was said, "You shall not reduce any bricks from your daily quota."

20 Then, as they came out from Pharaoh, they met Moses and Aaron who stood there to meet them.

21 And they said to them, "Let the LORD look on you and judge, because you have made us ᵀabhorrent in the sight of Pharaoh and in the sight of his servants, to put a sword in their hand to kill us."   Lit. stink

Israel's Deliverance Assured

31-B. A Prayer of Impatience   ▼

22 So Moses returned to the LORD and said, "Lord, why have You brought trouble on this people? Why is it You have sent me?

23 "For since I came to Pharaoh to speak in Your name, he has done evil to this people; neither have You delivered Your people at all."   ▲

31-B. A Prayer of Impatience (Exodus 5:22, 23)—Moses and Aaron obeyed the Lord and went to Pharaoh. In the Lord's name they demanded that he let the children of Israel go. At this time, however, they asked only for permission to go into the desert to worship God in a feast (Ex. 5:1–3, above). This would be like asking for a holy week (the first in four centuries) to worship God. Pharaoh not only refused, but to spite their God and Moses, he commanded that from that time forward they were to gather straw for their bricks at night, during their only free time (vv. 4–19). Angry, the leaders of the Israelite work crews came to Moses and Aaron, and in bitterness called upon God to bring judgment on Moses and Aaron because they had angered Pharaoh with hopeless requests for release (vv. 20, 21, above).

(Point 31-B continued on next page)

6 Then the LORD said to Moses, "Now you shall see what I will do to Pharaoh. For [R]with a strong hand he will let them go, and with a strong hand [R]he will drive them out of his land."   Ex. 3:19 • Ex. 12:31, 33, 39

2 And God spoke to Moses and said to him: "I *am* the LORD.

3 "I appeared to Abraham, to Isaac, and to Jacob, as God Almighty, but *by* My name [T]LORD I was not known to them.   Heb. *YHWH*

4 "I have also established My covenant with them, to give them the land of Canaan, the land of their [T]pilgrimage, in which they were [T]strangers.   *sojournings* • Temporary residents

5 "And [R]I have also heard the groaning of the children of Israel whom the Egyptians keep in bondage, and I have remembered My covenant.   Ex. 2:24

6 "Therefore say to the children of Israel: 'I *am* the LORD; I will bring you out from under the burdens of the Egyptians, I will [R]rescue you from their bondage, and I will redeem you with [T]an outstretched arm and with great judgments.   Deut. 7:8 • Mighty power

7 'I will take you as My people, and I will be your God. Then you shall know that I *am* the LORD your God who brings you out from under the burdens of the Egyptians.

8 'And I will bring you into the land which I [T]swore to give to Abraham, Isaac, and Jacob; and I will give it to you *as* a heritage: I *am* the LORD.' "   *promised,* lit. *lifted up my hand*

9 So Moses spoke to the children of Israel; but they did not heed Moses, because of anguish of spirit and cruel bondage.

10 And the LORD spoke to Moses, saying,

11 "Go in, tell Pharaoh king of Egypt to let the children of Israel go out of his land."

12 And Moses spoke before the LORD, saying, "The children of Israel have not heeded me. How then shall Pharaoh heed me, for I *am* [T]of uncircumcised lips?"   A poor speaker

13 Then the LORD spoke to Moses and Aaron, and gave them a [R]command[T] for the children of Israel and for Pharaoh king of Egypt, to bring the children of Israel out of the land of Egypt.   Deut. 31:14 • *charge*

The Family of Moses and Aaron

14 These *are* the heads of their fathers' houses: The sons of Reuben, the firstborn of Israel, *were* Hanoch, Pallu, Hezron, and Carmi. These are the families of Reuben.

15 [R]And the sons of Simeon *were* [T]Jemuel, Jamin, Ohad, Jachin, Zohar, and Shaul the son of a Canaanite woman. These *are* the families of Simeon.   Gen. 46:10 • *Nemuel,* Num. 26:12

16 These *are* the names of the sons of Levi according to their generations: Gershon, Kohath, and Merari. And the years of the life of Levi *were* one hundred and thirty-seven.

17 [R]The sons of Gershon *were* Libni and Shimi according to their families.   1 Chr. 6:17

18 And [R]the sons of Kohath *were* Amram, Izhar, Hebron, and Uzziel. And the years of the life of Kohath *were* one hundred and thirty-three.   1 Chr. 6:2, 18

19 [R]The sons of Merari *were* Mahli and Mushi. These *are* the families of Levi according to their generations.   1 Chr. 6:19; 23:21

20 Now [R]Amram took for himself [R]Jochebed, his father's sister, as wife; and she bore him [R]Aaron and Moses. And the years of the life of Amram *were* one hundred and thirty-seven.   Ex. 2:1, 2 • Num. 26:59 • Num. 26:59

21 [R]The sons of Izhar *were* Korah, Nepheg, and Zichri.   1 Chr. 6:37, 38

22 And [R]the sons of Uzziel *were* Mishael, Elzaphan, and Zithri.   Lev. 10:4

23 Aaron took to himself Elisheba, daughter of [R]Amminadab, sister of Nahshon, as wife; and she bore him [R]Nadab, Abihu, [R]Eleazar, and Ithamar.   Ruth 4:19, 20 • Lev. 10:1 • Ex. 28:1

24 And [R]the sons of Korah *were* Assir, Elkanah, and Abiasaph. These are the families of the Korahites.   Num. 26:11

(Point 31-B continued from previous page)

At this, Moses became despondent, and uttered this prayer of impatience, complaining to God:

(1) You have made the condition of the people worse, not better;
(2) You should not have sent me to do this job;
(3) since we started, things have only worsened;
(4) You still have not delivered Your people (vv. 22, 23).

Soon Moses would see that

(1) God would, in His time, greatly better their condition;
(2) God's choice of Moses as His servant would prove to be correct, as impatient Moses developed into a man of giant faith and patience;
(3) the temporary troubles which were brought by Moses and Aaron would yet achieve benefits that would endure;
(4) God, in the end, would mightily deliver His people.

In your life, do you ever speak or pray in impatience? If so, learn a lesson from God's dealing with Moses, and wait patiently on the Lord. "Be anxious for nothing" (Phil. 4:6, page 1198; cf. Is. 40:31, page 680).

See Exodus 32:11-14, page 92, for **Point 31-C: A Prayer of Intercession.**

25 Eleazar, Aaron's son, took for himself one of the daughters of Putiel as wife; and ᴿshe bore him Phinehas. These *are* the heads of the fathers' houses of the Levites according to their families. Num. 25:7, 11

26 These *are the same* Aaron and Moses to whom the LORD said, "Bring out the children of Israel from the land of Egypt according to their ᴿarmies."ᵀ Ex. 7:4; 12:17, 51 • *hosts*

27 These *are* the ones who spoke to Pharaoh king of Egypt, ᴿto bring out the children of Israel from Egypt. These *are the same* Moses and Aaron. Ps. 77:20

Aaron Is Moses' Spokesman

28 And it came to pass, on the day the LORD spoke to Moses in the land of Egypt,

29 that the LORD spoke to Moses, saying, "I *am* the LORD. ᴿSpeak to Pharaoh king of Egypt all that I say to you." Ex. 6:11; 7:2

30 But Moses said before the LORD, "Behold, ᴿI *am* of uncircumcised lips, and how shall Pharaoh heed me?" Ex. 4:10; 6:12

7 So the LORD said to Moses: "See, I have made you *as* God to Pharaoh, and Aaron your brother shall be your prophet.

2 "You ᴿshall speak all that I command you. And Aaron your brother shall tell Pharaoh to send the children of Israel out of his land. Ex. 4:15

3 "And ᴿI will harden Pharaoh's heart, and ᴿmultiply My ᴿsigns and My wonders in the land of Egypt. Ex. 4:21; 9:12 • Ex. 11:9 • Deut. 4:34

4 "But Pharaoh will not heed you, so that I may lay My hand on Egypt and bring My armies *and* My people, the children of Israel, out of the land of Egypt by great judgments.

5 "And the Egyptians shall know that I *am* the LORD, when I ᴿstretch out My hand on Egypt and ᴿbring out the children of Israel from among them." Ex. 9:15 • Ex. 3:20; 6:6; 12:51

6 Then Moses and Aaron did so; just as the LORD commanded them, so they did.

7 And Moses *was* ᴿeighty years old and ᴿAaron eighty-three years old when they spoke to Pharaoh. Deut. 29:5; 31:2; 34:7 • Num. 33:39

Aaron's Miraculous Rod

8 Then the LORD spoke to Moses and Aaron, saying,

9 "When Pharaoh speaks to you, saying, ᴿ'Show a miracle for yourselves,' then you shall say to Aaron, ᴿ'Take your rod and cast *it* before Pharaoh, *and* let it become a serpent.'" Is. 7:11 • Ex. 4:2, 3, 17

10 So Moses and Aaron went in to Pharaoh, and they did so, just ᴿas the LORD commanded. And Aaron cast down his rod before Pharaoh and before his servants, and it ᴿbecame a serpent. Ex. 7:9 • Ex. 4:3

11 But Pharaoh also called the wise men and ᴿthe sorcerers; so the magicians of Egypt, they also ᴿdid in like manner with their enchantments. 2 Tim. 3:8 • Ex. 7:22; 8:7, 18

12 For every man threw down his rod, and they became serpents. But Aaron's rod swallowed up their rods.

13 And Pharaoh's heart grew hard, and he did not heed them, as the LORD had said.

The First Plague: Waters Become Blood

14 So the LORD said to Moses: ᴿ"Pharaoh's heart is hard; he refuses to let the people go. Ex. 8:15; 10:1, 20, 27

15 "Go to Pharaoh in the morning, when he goes out to the ᴿwater, and you shall stand by the river's bank to meet him; and ᴿthe rod which was turned to a serpent you shall take in your hand. Ex. 2:5; 8:20 • Ex. 4:2, 3; 7:10

16 "And you shall say to him, 'The LORD God of the Hebrews has sent me to you, saying, "Let My people go, that they may ᵀserve Me in the wilderness"; but indeed, until now you would not hear! *worship*

17 'Thus says the LORD: "By this you shall know that I *am* the LORD. Behold, I will strike the waters which *are* in the river with the rod that *is* in my hand, and ᴿthey shall be turned ᴿto blood. Ex. 4:9; 7:20 • Rev. 11:6; 16:4, 6

18 "And the fish that *are* in the river shall die, the river shall stink, and the Egyptians will ᴿloathe to drink the water of the river." ' " Ex. 7:24

19 Then the LORD spoke to Moses, "Say to Aaron, 'Take your rod and stretch out your hand over the waters of Egypt, over their streams, over their rivers, over their ponds, and over all their pools of water, that they may become blood. And there shall be blood throughout all the land of Egypt, both in *buckets of* wood and *pitchers of* stone.' "

20 And Moses and Aaron did so, just as the LORD commanded. So he lifted up the rod and struck the waters that *were* in the river, in the sight of Pharaoh and in the sight of his servants. And all the ᴿwaters that *were* in the river were turned to blood. Ps. 78:44; 105:29, 30

21 The fish that *were* in the river died, the river stank, and the Egyptians could not drink the water of the river. So there was blood throughout all the land of Egypt.

22 Then the magicians of Egypt did ᴿso with their enchantments; and Pharaoh's heart grew hard, and he did not heed them, ᴿas the LORD had said. Ex. 8:7 • Ex. 3:19; 7:3

23 And Pharaoh turned and went into his house. Neither was his heart moved by this.

24 So all the Egyptians dug all around the river for water to drink, because they could not drink the water of the river.

25 And seven days passed after the LORD had struck the river.

The Second Plague: Frogs

8 And the LORD spoke to Moses, "Go to Pharaoh and say to him, 'Thus says the LORD: "Let My people go, ᴿthat they may serve Me. Ex. 3:12, 18; 4:23; 5:1, 3

2 "But if you ᴿrefuse to let *them* go, behold, I will smite all your territory with ᴿfrogs.   Ex. 7:14; 9:2 · Rev. 16:13

3 "So the river shall bring forth frogs abundantly, which shall go up and come into your house, into your ᴿbedroom, on your bed, into the houses of your servants, on your people, into your ovens, and into your kneading bowls.   Ps. 105:30

4 "And the frogs shall come up on you, on your people, and on all your servants."' "

5 Then the LORD spoke to Moses, "Say to Aaron, ᴿ'Stretch out your hand with your rod over the streams, over the rivers, and over the ponds, and cause frogs to come up on the land of Egypt.' "   Ex. 7:19

6 So Aaron stretched out his hand over the waters of Egypt, and ᴿthe frogs came up and covered the land of Egypt.   Ps. 78:45; 105:30

7 ᴿAnd the magicians did so with their ᵀenchantments, and brought up frogs on the land of Egypt.   Ex. 7:11, 22 · *secret arts*

8 Then Pharaoh called for Moses and Aaron, and said, ᵀ"Entreat the LORD that He may take away the frogs from me and from my people; and I will let the people go, that they may sacrifice to the LORD."   *Pray to*

9 And Moses said to Pharaoh, "Accept the honor of saying when I shall intercede for you, for your servants, and for your people, to destroy the frogs from you and your houses, *that* they may remain in the river only."

10 So he said, "Tomorrow." And he said, "*Let it be* according to your word, that you may know that ᴿ*there is* no one like the LORD our God.   Ex. 9:14; 15:11

11 "And the frogs shall depart from you, from your houses, from your servants, and from your people. They shall remain in the river only."

12 Then Moses and Aaron went out from Pharaoh. And Moses ᴿcried out to the LORD concerning the frogs which He had brought against Pharaoh.   Ex. 8:30; 9:33; 10:18; 32:11

13 So the LORD did according to the word of Moses. And the frogs died out of the houses, out of the courtyards, and out of the fields.

14 They gathered them together in heaps, and the land stank.

15 But when Pharaoh saw that there was ᴿrelief, he hardened his heart and did not heed them, as the LORD had said.   Eccl. 8:11

The Third Plague: Lice

16 So the LORD said to Moses, "Say to Aaron, 'Stretch out your rod, and strike the dust of the land, so that it may become ᵀlice throughout all the land of Egypt.' "   *Or gnats*

17 And they did so. For Aaron stretched out his hand with his rod and struck the dust of the earth, and ᴿit became lice on man and beast. All the dust of the land became lice throughout all the land of Egypt.   Ps. 105:31

18 Now ᴿthe magicians so worked with their ᵀenchantments to bring forth lice, but they ᴿcould not. So there were lice on man and beast.   Ex. 7:11, 12; 8:7 · *secret arts* · Dan. 5:8

19 Then the magicians said to Pharaoh, "This *is* ᵀthe finger of God." But Pharaoh's heart grew hard, and he did not heed them, just as the LORD had said.   *An act of God*

The Fourth Plague: Flies

20 And the LORD said to Moses, "Rise early in the morning and stand before Pharaoh as he comes out to the water. Then say to him, 'Thus says the LORD: ᴿ"Let My people go, that they may serve Me.   Ex. 3:18; 4:23; 5:1, 3; 8:1

21 "Or else, if you will not let My people go, behold, I will send swarms *of flies* on you and your servants, on your people and into your houses. The houses of the Egyptians shall be full of swarms *of flies*, and also the ground on which they *stand*.

22 "And in that day I will set apart the land of ᴿGoshen, in which My people dwell, that no swarms *of flies* shall be there, in order that you may ᴿknow that I *am* the LORD in the midst of the land.   Gen. 50:8 · Ex. 7:5, 17; 10:2

23 "I will ᵀmake a difference between My people and your people. Tomorrow this ᴿsign shall be."' "   Lit. *set a ransom*, Ex. 9:4; 11:7 · Ex. 4:8

24 And the LORD did so. ᴿThick swarms *of flies* came into the house of Pharaoh, *into* his servants' houses, and into all the land of Egypt. The land was corrupted because of the swarms *of flies*.   Ps. 78:45; 105:31

25 Then Pharaoh called for Moses and Aaron, and said, "Go, sacrifice to your God in the land."

26 And Moses said, "It is not right to do so, for we would be sacrificing ᴿthe abomination of the Egyptians to the LORD our God. If we sacrifice the abomination of the Egyptians before their eyes, then will they not ᵀstone us?   Gen. 43:32; 46:34 · Put us to death by stoning

27 "We will go ᴿthree days' journey into the wilderness and sacrifice to the LORD our God as ᴿHe will command us."   Ex. 3:18; 5:3 · Ex. 3:12

28 So Pharaoh said, "I will let you go, that you may sacrifice to the LORD your God in the wilderness; only you shall not go very far away. ᴿIntercede for me."   Ex. 8:8, 15, 29, 32; 9:28

29 Then Moses said, "Indeed I am going out from you, and I will entreat the LORD, that the swarms *of flies* may depart tomorrow from Pharaoh, from his servants, and from his people. But let Pharaoh not ᴿdeal deceitfully anymore in not letting the people go to sacrifice to the LORD."   Ex. 8:8, 15

30 So Moses went out from Pharaoh and ᴿentreated the LORD.   Ex. 8:12

31 And the LORD did according to the word of Moses; He removed the swarms *of flies* from Pharaoh, from his servants, and from his people. Not one remained.

32 But Pharaoh hardened his heart at this time also; neither would he let the people go.

The Fifth Plague: Livestock Diseased

9 Then the LORD said to Moses, "Go in to Pharaoh and tell him, 'Thus says the LORD God of the Hebrews: "Let My people go, that they may ^Rserve Me.   Ex. 7:16

2 "For if you ^Rrefuse to let *them* go, and still hold them,   Ex. 8:2

3 "behold, the ^Rhand of the LORD will be on your cattle in the field, on the horses, on the donkeys, on the camels, on the oxen, and on the sheep—a very severe pestilence.   Ex. 7:4

4 "And the LORD will make a difference between the livestock of Israel and the livestock of Egypt. So nothing shall die of all *that* belongs to the children of Israel." ' "

5 Then the LORD appointed a set time, saying, "Tomorrow the LORD will do this thing in the land."

6 So the LORD did this thing on the next day, and ^Rall the livestock of Egypt died; but of the livestock of the children of Israel, not one died.   Ps. 78:48, 50

7 Then Pharaoh sent, and indeed, not even one of the livestock of the Israelites was dead. But the heart of Pharaoh became hard, and he did not let the people go.

The Sixth Plague: Boils

8 So the LORD said to Moses and Aaron, "Take for yourselves handfuls of ashes from a furnace, and let Moses scatter it toward the heavens in the sight of Pharaoh.

9 "And it will become fine dust in all the land of Egypt, and it will cause ^Rboils that break out in sores on man and beast throughout all the land of Egypt."   Rev. 16:2

10 Then they took ashes from the furnace and stood before Pharaoh, and Moses scattered *them* toward heaven. And *they* caused ^Rboils that break out in sores on man and beast.   Deut. 28:27

11 And the ^Rmagicians could not stand before Moses because of the ^Rboils, for the boils were on the magicians and on all the Egyptians.   [Ex. 8:18, 19] • Job 2:7

12 But the LORD hardened the heart of Pharaoh; and he did not heed them, just ^Ras the LORD had spoken to Moses.   Ex. 4:21

The Seventh Plague: Hail

13 Then the LORD said to Moses, ^R"Rise early in the morning and stand before Pharaoh, and say to him, 'Thus says the LORD God of the Hebrews: "Let My people go, that they may ^Rserve Me,   Ex. 8:20 • Ex. 9:1

14 "for at this time I will send all My plagues to your very heart, and on your servants and on your people, ^Rthat you may know that *there is* none like Me in all the earth.   Ex. 8:10

15 "Now if I had ^Rstretched out My hand and struck you and your people with ^Rpestilence, then you would have been cut off from the earth.   Ex. 3:20; 7:5 • Ex. 5:3

16 "But indeed for ^Rthis *purpose* I have raised you up, that I may show My power *in* you, and that My ^Rname may be declared in all the earth.   [Rom. 9:17, 18] • 1 Kin. 8:43

17 "As yet you exalt yourself against My people in that you will not let them go.

18 "Behold, tomorrow about this time I will cause very heavy hail to rain down, such as has not been in Egypt since its founding until now.

19 "Therefore send now *and* gather your livestock and all that you have in the field, for the hail shall come down on every man and every animal which is found in the field and is not brought home; and they shall die." ' "

20 He who feared the word of the LORD among the servants of Pharaoh made his servants and his livestock flee to the houses.

21 But he who did not regard the word of the LORD left his servants and his livestock in the field.

22 Then the LORD said to Moses, "Stretch out your hand toward heaven, that there may be ^Rhail in all the land of Egypt—on man, on beast, and on every herb of the field, throughout the land of Egypt."   Rev. 16:21

23 And Moses stretched out his rod toward heaven; and ^Rthe LORD sent thunder and hail, and fire darted to the ground. And the LORD rained hail on the land of Egypt.   Josh. 10:11

24 So there was hail, and fire mingled with the hail, so very heavy that there was none like it in all the land of Egypt since it became a nation.

25 And the ^Rhail struck throughout the whole land of Egypt, all that *was* in the field, both man and beast; and the hail struck every herb of the field and broke every tree of the field.   Ps. 78:47, 48; 105:32, 33

26 Only in the land of Goshen, where the children of Israel *were*, there was no hail.

27 And Pharaoh sent and ^Rcalled for Moses and Aaron, and said to them, "I have sinned this time. ^RThe LORD *is* righteous, and my people and I *are* wicked.   Ex. 8:8 • 2 Chr. 12:6

28 ^T"Entreat the LORD, that there may be no more ^Tmighty thundering and hail, for *it is* enough. I will let you go, and you shall stay no longer."   *Pray to* • Lit. *sounds of God*

29 So Moses said to him, "As soon as I have gone out of the city, I will spread out my hands to the LORD; the thunder will cease, and there will be no more hail, that you may know that the ^Rearth *is* the LORD's.   Ps. 24:1

30 "But as for you and your servants, ^RI know that you will not yet fear the LORD God."   [Is. 26:10]

31 Now the flax and the barley were struck, ^Rfor the barley *was* in the head and the flax *was* in bud.   Ruth 1:22; 2:23

32 But the wheat and the spelt were not struck, for they *are* late crops.

33 So Moses went out of the city from

Pharaoh and spread out his hands to the Lord; then the thunder and the hail ceased, and the rain was not poured on the earth.

34 And when Pharaoh saw that the rain, the hail, and the thunder had ceased, he sinned yet more; and he hardened his heart, he and his servants.

35 So ᴿthe heart of Pharaoh was hard; neither would he let the children of Israel go, as the Lord had spoken by Moses.   Ex. 4:21

The Eighth Plague: Locusts

10 Now the Lord said to Moses, "Go in to Pharaoh; for I have hardened his heart and the hearts of his servants, that I may show these signs of Mine before him,

2 "and that ᴿyou may tell in the hearing of your son and your son's son the mighty things I have done in Egypt, and My signs which I have done among them, that you may know that I am the Lord."   Joel 1:3

3 So Moses and Aaron came in to Pharaoh and said to him, "Thus says the Lord God of the Hebrews: 'How long will you refuse to ᴿhumble yourself before Me? Let My people go, that they may serve Me.   [1 Kin. 21:29]

4 'Or else, if you refuse to let My people go, behold, tomorrow I will bring ᴿlocusts into your territory.   Rev. 9:3

5 'And they shall cover the face of the earth, so that no one will be able to see the earth; and ᴿthey shall eat the residue of what is left, which remains to you from the hail, and they shall eat every tree which grows up for you out of the field.   Ex. 9:32

6 'They shall fill your houses, the houses of all your servants, and the houses of all the Egyptians—which neither your fathers nor your fathers' fathers have seen, since the day that they were on the earth to this day.' " And he turned and went out from Pharaoh.

7 Then Pharaoh's ᴿservants said to him, "How long shall this man be ᴿa snare to us? Let the men go, that they may serve the Lord their God. Do you not yet know that Egypt is destroyed?"   Ex. 7:5; 8:19; 9:20; 12:33 • Ex. 23:33

8 So Moses and Aaron were brought again to Pharaoh, and he said to them, "Go, serve the Lord your God. Who are the ones that are going?"

9 And Moses said, "We will go with our young and our old; with our sons and our daughters, with our flocks and our herds we will go, for ᴿwe must hold a feast to the Lord."   Ex. 5:1; 7:16

10 Then he said to them, "The Lord had better be with you when I let you and your little ones go! Beware, for evil is ahead of you.

11 "Not so! Go now, you who are men, and serve the Lord, for that is what you desired." And they were driven ᴿout from Pharaoh's presence.   Ex. 10:28

12 Then the Lord said to Moses, ᴿ"Stretch out your hand over the land of Egypt for the locusts, that they may come upon the land of Egypt, and ᴿeat every herb of the land—all that the hail has left."   Ex. 7:19 • Ex. 10:5, 15

13 So Moses stretched out his rod over the land of Egypt, and the Lord brought an east wind on the land all that day and all that night. When it was morning, the east wind brought the locusts.

14 And the locusts went up over all the land of Egypt and rested on all the territory of Egypt. They were very severe; ᴿpreviously there had been no such locusts as they, nor shall there be such after them.   Joel 2:1-11

15 For they ᴿcovered the face of the whole earth, so that the land was darkened; and they ᴿate every herb of the land and all the fruit of the trees which the hail had left. So there remained nothing green on the trees or on the plants of the field throughout all the land of Egypt.   Ex. 10:5 • Ps. 105:35

16 Then Pharaoh called for Moses and Aaron in haste, and said, "I have sinned against the Lord your God and against you.

17 "Now therefore, please forgive my sin only this once, and ᴿentreatᵀ the Lord your God, that He may take away from me this death only."   1 Kin. 13:6 • make supplication to

18 So he ᴿwent out from Pharaoh and entreated the Lord.   Ex. 8:30

19 And the Lord turned a very strong west wind, which took the locusts away and blew them ᴿinto the Red Sea. There remained not one locust in all the territory of Egypt.   Joel 2:20

20 But the Lord hardened Pharaoh's heart, and he did not let the children of Israel go.

The Ninth Plague: Darkness

21 Then the Lord said to Moses, ᴿ"Stretch out your hand toward heaven, that there may be darkness over the land of Egypt, darkness which may even be felt."   Ex. 9:22

22 So Moses stretched out his hand toward heaven, and there was thick darkness in all the land of Egypt ᴿthree days.   Ex. 3:18

23 They did not see one another; nor did anyone rise from his place for three days. ᴿBut all the children of Israel had light in their dwellings.   Ex. 8:22, 23

24 Then Pharaoh called to Moses and ᴿsaid, "Go, serve the Lord; only let your flocks and your herds be kept back. Let your ᴿlittle ones also go with you."   Ex. 8:8, 25; 10:8 • Ex. 10:10

25 But Moses said, "You must also give ᵀus sacrifices and burnt offerings, that we may sacrifice to the Lord our God.   Lit. into our hands

26 "Our ᴿlivestock also shall go with us; not a hoof shall be left behind. For we must take some of them to serve the Lord our God, and even we do not know with what we must serve the Lord until we arrive there."   Ex. 10:9

27 But the Lord ᴿhardened Pharaoh's heart, and he would not let them go.   Ex. 4:21

28 Then Pharaoh said to him, ᴿ"Get away from me! Take heed to yourself and see my

face no more! For in the day you see my face you shall die!"   Ex. 10:11

29 So Moses said, "You have spoken well. ᴿI will never see your face again."   Heb. 11:27

Death of the Firstborn Announced

11 And the Lᴏʀᴅ said to Moses, "I will bring one more plague on Pharaoh and on Egypt. Afterward he will let you go from here. ᴿWhen he lets *you* go, he will surely drive you out of here altogether.   Ex. 6:1; 12:39

2 "Speak now in the hearing of the people, and let every man ask from his neighbor and every woman from her neighbor, ᴿarticles of silver and articles of gold."   Ex. 3:22; 12:35, 36

3 And the Lᴏʀᴅ gave the people favor in the sight of the Egyptians. Moreover the man ᴿMoses *was* very great in the land of Egypt, in the sight of Pharaoh's servants and in the sight of the people.   Deut. 34:10-12

4 Then Moses said, "Thus says the Lᴏʀᴅ: ᴿ'About midnight I will go out into the midst of Egypt;   Ex. 12:12, 23, 29

5 'and all the firstborn in the land of Egypt shall die, from the firstborn of Pharaoh who sits on his throne, even to the firstborn of the female servant who *is* behind the handmill, and all the firstborn of the animals.

6 'Then there shall be a great cry throughout all the land of Egypt, such as was not like it *before*, nor shall be like it again.

7 ᴿ'But against none of the children of Israel ᴿshall a dog ᵀmove its tongue, against man or beast, that you may know that the Lᴏʀᴅ does make a difference between the Egyptians and Israel.'   Ex. 8:22 • Josh. 10:21 • *sharpen*

8 "And all these your servants shall come down to me and bow down to me, saying, 'Get out, and all the people who follow you!' After that I will go out." ᴿThen he went out from Pharaoh in great anger.   Heb. 11:27

9 But the Lᴏʀᴅ said to Moses, "Pharaoh will not heed you, so that My wonders may be multiplied in the land of Egypt."

10 So Moses and Aaron did all these wonders before Pharaoh; ᴿand the Lᴏʀᴅ hardened Pharaoh's heart, and he did not let the children of Israel go out of his land.   Rom. 2:5

The Passover Instituted

20-D. The Passover Blood   ▼

12 Now the Lᴏʀᴅ spoke to Moses and Aaron in the land of Egypt, saying,

2 ᴿ"This month *shall be* your beginning of months; it *shall be* the first month of the year to you.   Deut. 16:1

3 "Speak to all the congregation of Israel, saying: 'On the ᴿtenth of this month every man shall take for himself a lamb, according to the house of *his* father, a lamb for a household.   Josh. 4:19

4 'And if the household is too small for the lamb, let him and his neighbor next to his house take *it* according to the number of the persons; according to each man's need you shall make your count for the lamb.

5 'Your lamb shall be ᴿwithout blemish, a male of the first year. You may take *it* from the sheep or from the goats.   [1 Pet. 1:19]

6 'Now you shall keep it until the ᴿfourteenth day of the same month. Then the

20-D. The Passover Blood (Exodus 12:1-36)—The twelfth chapter of Exodus is one of the great chapters of the Bible. It displays deliverance from slavery for Israel, but judgment for Pharaoh and all Egypt. The Lord said to Moses, "I will bring one more plague on Pharaoh and on Egypt" (Ex. 11:1). The "one more plague" was death for the firstborn, wherever there was no Passover blood on the doorpost and the lintel.

(1) The Passover lamb is a type of the Lord Jesus Christ, who redeems, not with silver or gold, but with His own life-giving blood (1 Pet. 1:18, 19, page 1263). Paul reminds the Corinthian church that Christ is our Passover Lamb who was sacrificed for us (1 Cor. 5:7, page 1150).

(a) The Passover lamb "shall be without blemish, a male of the first year" (v. 5). The Passover lamb is a type of Jesus, "who knew no sin." He was without blemish (2 Cor. 5:21, page 1169), and even challenged His enemies to find sin in Him: "Which of you convicts Me of sin?" (John 8:46, page 1063).

(b) The Passover lamb was to be separated from the sheep or goats, from the tenth to the fourteenth day. This separation period was a time of examination, to make certain that the Passover lamb was without blemish. The Passover lamb is a type of Jesus, "who is holy, harmless, undefiled, separate from sinners, and has become higher than the heavens" (Heb. 7:25-28, page 1242).

(c) The Passover lamb was to be killed: "And you shall take a bunch of hyssop, dip it in the blood that is in the basin, and strike the lintel [the crossbeam] and the two doorposts with the blood that is in the basin" (v. 22). The blood of the Passover lamb is a type of the blood of Jesus, who hung upon the cross and shed His precious blood for the remission of our sins (John 19:28-37, page 1081). The blood on the crossbeam and on the two doorposts is a picture of the bloodstained cross.

(2) God said to Israel, "The blood shall be a sign for you on the houses where you are. And when I see the blood, I will pass over you" (v. 13). Now God did not say, when I see your good works, or your moral character, or your self-righteousness, or your religion, or the laws you keep, I will pass over you. No! He said, "When I see the blood, I will pass over you" (v. 13). Remember, without the blood of Jesus there is no forgiveness of sin (Heb. 9:22, page 1244).

See Leviticus 16:1-34, page 123, for **Point 20-E: The Day of Atonement in the Old Testament.**

▽ whole assembly of the congregation of Israel shall kill it at twilight. Lev. 23:5

7 'And they shall take *some* of the blood and put *it* on the two doorposts and on the lintel of the houses where they eat it.

8 'Then they shall eat the flesh on that ᴿnight; ᴿroasted in fire, with ᴿunleavened bread *and* with bitter *herbs* they shall eat it. Num. 9:12 • Deut. 16:7 • 1 Cor. 5:8

9 'Do not eat it raw, nor boiled at all with water, but ᴿroasted in fire—its head with its legs and its entrails. Deut. 16:7

10 ᴿ'You shall let none of it remain until morning, and what remains of it until morning you shall burn with fire. Ex. 16:19; 23:18; 34:25

11 'And thus you shall eat it: *with* a belt on your waist, your sandals on your feet, and your staff in your hand. So you shall eat it in haste. ᴿIt *is* the LORD's Passover. Ex. 12:13

12 'For I will pass through the land of Egypt on that night, and will strike all the firstborn in the land of Egypt, both man and beast; and against all the gods of Egypt I will execute judgment: ᴿI *am* the LORD. Ex. 6:2

13 'Now the blood shall be a sign for you on the houses where you *are*. And when I see the blood, I will pass over you; and the plague shall not be on you to destroy *you* when I strike the land of Egypt.

14 'So this day shall be to you a memorial; and you shall keep it as a feast to the LORD throughout your generations. You shall keep it as a feast by an everlasting ordinance.

15 ᴿ'Seven days you shall eat unleavened bread. On the first day you shall remove leaven from your houses. For whoever eats leavened bread from the first day until the seventh day, ᴿthat ᵀperson shall be ᵀcut off from Israel. Lev. 23:6 • Gen. 17:14 • *soul* • Put to death

16 'On the first day *there shall be* ᴿa holy convocation, and on the seventh day there shall be a holy convocation for you. No manner of work shall be done on them; but *that* which everyone must eat—that only may be prepared by you. Lev. 23:2, 7, 8

17 'So you shall observe the Feast of Unleavened Bread, for on this same day I will have brought your ᵀarmies ᴿout of the land of Egypt. Therefore you shall observe this day throughout your generations as an everlasting ordinance. *hosts* • Num. 33:1

18 ᴿ'In the first *month*, on the fourteenth day of the month at evening, you shall eat unleavened bread, until the twenty-first day of the month at evening. Lev. 23:5-8

19 'For ᴿseven days no leaven shall be found in your houses, since whoever eats what is leavened, that same person shall be cut off from the congregation of Israel, whether *he is* a stranger or a native of the land. Ex. 12:15

20 'You shall eat nothing leavened; in all your dwellings you shall eat unleavened bread.' "

21 Then ᴿMoses called for all the elders of ▽ Israel and said to them, "Pick out and take lambs for yourselves according to your families, and kill the Passover *lamb.* [Heb. 11:28]

22 ᴿ'And you shall take a bunch of hyssop, dip *it* in the blood that *is* in the basin, and ᴿstrike the lintel and the two doorposts with the blood that *is* in the basin. And none of you shall go out of the door of his house until morning. Heb. 11:28 • Ex. 12:7

23 "For the LORD will pass through to strike the Egyptians; and when He sees the blood on the lintel and on the two doorposts, the LORD will pass over the door and ᴿnot allow ᴿthe destroyer to come into your houses to strike *you.* Rev. 7:3; 9:4 • Heb. 11:28

24 "And you shall observe this thing as an ordinance for you and your sons forever.

25 "It will come to pass when you come to the land which the LORD will give you, ᴿjust as He promised, that you shall keep this service. Ex. 3:8, 17

26 "And it shall be, when your children say to you, 'What do you mean by this service?'

27 "that you shall say, ᴿ'It *is* the Passover sacrifice of the LORD, who passed over the houses of the children of Israel in Egypt when He struck the Egyptians and delivered our households.' " So the people ᴿbowed their heads and worshiped. Ex. 12:11 • Ex. 4:31

28 Then the children of Israel went away and ᴿdid *so;* just as the LORD had commanded Moses and Aaron, so they did. [Heb. 11:28]

The Tenth Plague: Death of the Firstborn

29 And it came to pass at midnight that ᴿthe LORD struck all the firstborn in the land of Egypt, from the firstborn of Pharaoh who sat on his throne to the firstborn of the captive who *was* in the dungeon, and all the firstborn of ᴿlivestock. Num. 8:17; 33:4 • Ex. 9:6

30 So Pharaoh rose in the night, he, all his servants, and all the Egyptians; and there was a great cry in Egypt, for *there was* not a house where *there was* not one dead.

The Exodus

31 Then he called for Moses and Aaron by night, and said, "Rise, go out from among my people, both you and the children of Israel. And go, serve the LORD as you have said.

32 ᴿ'Also take your flocks and your herds, as you have said, and be gone; and bless me also." Ex. 10:9, 26

33 And the Egyptians urged the people, that they might send them out of the land in haste. For they said, "We *shall* all *be* dead."

34 So the people took their dough before it was leavened, having their kneading bowls bound up in their clothes on their shoulders.

35 Now the children of Israel had done according to the word of Moses, and they had asked from the Egyptians ᴿarticles of silver, articles of gold, and clothing. Ex. 3:21, 22; 11:2, 3

▽ 36 ᴿAnd the LORD had given the people favor in the sight of the Egyptians, so that they granted them *what they requested.* ▲ Thus they plundered the Egyptians.   Ex. 3:21

▼ 34–B. From the Exodus to the Crossing of Jordan

37 Then the children of Israel journeyed from Rameses to Succoth, about six hundred thousand men on foot, besides children.

38 A ᴿmixed multitude went up with them also, and flocks and herds—a great deal of ᴿlivestock.   Num. 11:4 · Deut. 3:19

39 And they baked unleavened cakes of the dough which they had brought out of Egypt; for it was not leavened, because they were driven out of Egypt and could not wait, nor had they prepared provisions for themselves.

40 Now the ᵀsojourn of the children of Israel who lived in Egypt *was* ᴿfour hundred and thirty years.   Length of the stay · Acts 7:6

41 And it came to pass at the end of the four hundred and thirty years—on that very same day—it came to pass that all the armies of the LORD went out from the land of Egypt.

42 It *is* a ᵀnight of solemn observance to the LORD for bringing them out of the land of Egypt. This *is* that night of the LORD, a solemn observance for all the children of Israel throughout their generations.   *vigil*

Passover Regulations

43 And the LORD said to Moses and Aaron, "This *is* ᴿthe ordinance of the Passover: No foreigner shall eat it.   Num. 9:14

44 "But every man's servant who is bought for money, when you have ᴿcircumcised him, then he may eat it.   Gen. 17:12, 13

45 ᴿ"A sojourner and a hired servant shall not eat it.   Lev. 22:10

46 "In one house it shall be eaten; you shall not carry any of the flesh outside the house, nor shall you break one of its bones.

47 ᴿ"All the congregation of Israel shall keep it.   Ex. 12:6

48 "And ᴿwhen a stranger dwells with you *and wants* to keep the Passover to the LORD, let all his males be circumcised, and then let him come near and keep it; and he shall be as a native of the land. For no uncircumcised person shall eat it.   Num. 9:14

49 "One law shall be for the native-born and for the stranger who dwells among you."

34-B. From the Exodus to the Crossing of Jordan (40 years) (Exodus 12:37–51)—Begin this study by reading 1 Corinthians 10:1-15 (page 1154). The Hebrews originally were not a slave people. In fact, Abraham, the father of the Hebrew nation, possessed great wealth (Gen. 13:2, 14-18, page 18). After the death of Joseph, however, "there arose a new king over Egypt, who did not know Joseph" (Ex. 1:8, page 59). Fearing the children of Israel because they were multiplying rapidly, he enslaved them, and they remained slaves until God raised up Moses to deliver them from bondage (Ex. 1—3, page 59).

From Egypt to Canaan, in a period of forty years, the children of Israel made forty-two camps (Num. 33:1-49, page 176). Let us look at some of the most important camps and consider some of the miracles, successes, and failures of this young nation. Led out by Moses, the children of Israel began their journey after observing the Passover (Ex. 12:1-28, page 69). The young and the old were in good health; "there was none feeble among His tribes" (Ps. 105:37, page 572).

(1) The first three stages of their march took them from Rameses to Succoth, to Etham, and to the Red Sea. The Lord appeared to them in a pillar of cloud by day and in a pillar of fire by night. This was the first miracle of their journey. The pillar led them for forty years by day and by night (Ex. 13:21, 22, page 73; Num. 14:14, page 153).

(2) The next stage of their journey saw God open the Red Sea. Israel marched through on dry land, with walls of water on the right and on the left. Pharaoh's army pursued Israel into the Red Sea. In the morning watch God "troubled the army of the Egyptians," and "took off their chariot wheels" (Ex. 14:24-31, page 74). God stopped them and destroyed them.

(3) The next stage of their march took them three days into the wilderness of Shur, and they came to the waters of Marah (bitter waters). They complained against Moses because they had no water to drink. God showed Moses a tree, and when he had it cast into the waters, the waters were made sweet (Ex. 15:22-26, page 75).

(4) From Elim they journeyed to the wilderness of Sin. Because they missed the food of Egypt, they murmured against Moses and Aaron. God sent great flocks of quail in the evening and manna in the morning (Ex. 16:1-36, page 75; Num. 11:31, 32, page 151). The manna continued for forty years, every day except the Sabbath.

(5) The next stage of their march went as far as Rephidim, where once again they found no water. Here they accused Moses of bringing them into the wilderness to kill them with thirst. The Lord instructed Moses to move on to Horeb, and to take his rod and strike the rock (Ex. 17:1-7, page 77; cf. 1 Cor. 10:4, page 1154). The Lord gave them water from the rock. Then Amalek came and fought with Israel. As long as Moses held up his arms in prayer, Israel prevailed. This was Israel's first war, and God gave them victory (Ex. 17:8-16, page 77).

(6) The next stage of their march took them to the mountain of God, which is Sinai (Ex. 19:1-7, page 78). Here they camped for about one year (Ex. 18—40, page 78). Here a number of events took place:

(Point 34-B continued on next page)

▽ **50** Thus all the children of Israel did; as the LORD commanded Moses and Aaron, so they did.

51 ᴿAnd it came to pass, on that very same day, that the LORD brought the children of Israel out of the land of Egypt ᴿaccording to ▲ their armies.   Ex. 12:41; 20:2 • Ex. 6:26

The Firstborn Consecrated

13 Then the LORD spoke to Moses, saying, **2** ᴿ"Consecrate to Me all the firstborn, whatever opens the womb among the children of Israel, *both* of man and beast; it is Mine."   Deut. 15:19; Luke 2:23

The Feast of Unleavened Bread

3 And Moses said to the people: "Remember this day in which you went out of Egypt, out of the house of bondage; for by strength of hand the LORD brought you out of this *place*. No leavened bread shall be eaten. **4** ᴿ"On this day you are going out, in the month Abib.   Ex. 12:2; 23:15; 34:18

5 "And it shall be, when the LORD brings you into the ᴿland of the Canaanites and the Hittites and the Amorites and the Hivites and the Jebusites, which He ᴿswore to your fathers to give you, a land flowing with milk and honey, ᴿthat you shall keep this service in this month.   Gen. 17:8 • Ex. 6:8 • Ex. 12:25, 26

6 ᴿ"Seven days you shall eat unleavened bread, and on the seventh day *there shall be* a feast to the LORD.   Ex. 12:15–20

7 "Unleavened bread shall be eaten seven days. And ᴿno leavened bread shall be seen among you, nor shall leaven be seen among you in all your quarters.   Ex. 12:19

8 "And you shall tell your son in that day, saying, 'This *is* done because of what the LORD did for me when I came up from Egypt.'

9 "It shall be as ᴿa sign to you on your hand and as a memorial between your eyes, that the LORD's law may be in your mouth; for with a strong hand the LORD has brought you out of Egypt.   Deut. 6:8; 11:18

10 "You shall therefore keep this ordinance in its season from year to year.

The Law of the Firstborn

11 "And it shall be, when the LORD ᴿbrings you into the land of the ᴿCanaanites, as He swore to you and your fathers, and gives it to you,   Ex. 13:5 • Num. 21:3

12 ᴿ"that you shall set apart to the LORD all that open the womb, that is, every firstborn that comes from an animal which you have; the males *shall be* the LORD's.   Lev. 27:26

13 "But ᴿevery firstborn of a donkey you shall redeem with a lamb; and if you will not

---

(Point 34-B continued from previous page)

(a) Jethro, Moses' father-in-law, brought to him his Midianite wife and two sons (Ex. 18:1–12, page 78).

(b) At Sinai God gave to Moses

    (i) the moral, civil, and ceremonial laws—a new covenant for Israel;
    (ii) the plan and direction for building the tabernacle;
    (iii) the order of the priesthood;
    (iv) the order of the camp and the march.

While Moses was on the mount of God for forty days receiving the law, the children of Israel persuaded Aaron to make an idol of gold, which would lead them out of the wilderness. This idolatry ended in the judgment of God upon the people (Ex. 32:1–35, page 91).

(7) The next stage of their march took them to Kadesh Barnea. The Israelites had then spent two years of preparation in the wilderness. After one more test of their faith, they were ready to possess the Promised Land. Moses sent twelve spies to search out the land. They were gone forty days and returned with evidence of the fruitfulness of the land. But ten of the spies had no faith, and reported that the land would be impossible to conquer. The people turned on Moses and Aaron, and called for a captain to lead them back to Egypt (Num. 14:1–39, page 153). God judged Israel because of their unbelief (Heb. 3:7–12, page 1238; Jude 5, page 1289). All who were twenty years and over died during the next thirty-eight years in the wilderness—all except Caleb and Joshua, the two spies who did not sin through unbelief (Num. 14:37, 38, page 154). The spies who brought the evil report of unbelief were the first to die. When Israel heard that judgment had come upon the ten spies, they tried to repent and take the land. Moses said, "Do not go up . . . for the LORD is not among you" (Num. 14:39–45, page 154). They were presumptuous, went against the will of the Lord, and suffered bitter defeat. Thus began the premature deaths of over one million Israelites.

(8) In the next stage of their march they circled Mount Seir for many days (Deut. 2:1, page 182). Continuing their wilderness journey for thirty-eight more years, they made about twenty-three camps. The last station of their long forty-year march brought them to the plains of Moab, by the Jordan near Jericho (Num. 33:47–49, page 177). Moses and Aaron also died in the wilderness because they sinned against the Lord (Num. 20:1–13, 22–29, page 159; Deut. 34:1–8, page 213). Joshua was chosen to lead Israel into the Promised Land. Just as God had opened the Red Sea to lead Israel out of Egypt into the wilderness, so after forty years He parted the waters of the Jordan to lead them out of the wilderness into the land of Canaan (Josh. 1—3, page 215).

See Joshua 3:14–17, page 218, for **Point 34-C: From the Crossing of Jordan to the Babylonian Captivity.**

redeem *it*, then you shall break its neck. And all the firstborn of man among your sons ᴿyou shall redeem.   Ex. 34:20 • Num. 3:46, 47; 18:15, 16

14 ᴿ"So it shall be, when your son asks you in time to come, saying, 'What *is* this?' that you shall say to him, ᴿ'By strength of hand the Lᴏʀᴅ brought us out of Egypt, out of the house of bondage.   Deut. 6:20 • Ex. 13:3, 9

15 'And it came to pass, when Pharaoh was stubborn about letting us go, that ᴿthe Lᴏʀᴅ killed all the firstborn in the land of Egypt, both the firstborn of man and the firstborn of beast. Therefore I sacrifice to the Lᴏʀᴅ all males that open the womb, but all the firstborn of my sons I redeem.'   Ex. 12:29

16 "It shall be as ᴿa sign on your hand and as frontlets between your eyes, for by strength of hand the Lᴏʀᴅ brought us out of Egypt."   Ex. 13:9

The Wilderness Way

17 Then it came to pass, when Pharaoh had let the people go, that God did not lead them *by* way of the land of the Philistines, although that *was* near; for God said, "Lest perhaps the people change their minds when they see war, and return to Egypt."

18 So God ᴿled the people around *by* way of the wilderness of the Red Sea. And the children of Israel went up in orderly ranks out of the land of Egypt.   Num. 33:6

19 And Moses took the bones of Joseph with him, for he had placed the children of Israel under solemn oath, saying, ᴿ"God will surely ᵀvisit you, and you shall carry up my bones from here with you."   Gen. 50:25 • *help*

20 So ᴿthey took their journey from ᴿSuccoth and camped in Etham at the edge of the wilderness.   Num. 33:6–8 • Ex. 12:37

21 And ᴿthe Lᴏʀᴅ went before them by day in a pillar of cloud to lead the way, and by night in a pillar of fire to give them light, so as to go by day and night.   Deut. 1:33

22 He did not take away the pillar of cloud by day or the pillar of fire by night *from* before the people.

The Red Sea Crossing

14 Now the Lᴏʀᴅ spoke to Moses, saying: 2 "Speak to the children of Israel, that they turn and camp before Pi Hahiroth, between Migdol and the sea, opposite Baal Zephon; you shall camp before it by the sea. 3 "For Pharaoh will say of the children of Israel, ᴿ'They *are* bewildered by the land; the wilderness has closed them in.'   Ps. 71:11

4 "Then I will harden Pharaoh's heart, so that he will pursue them; and I ᴿwill gain honor over Pharaoh and over all his army, ᴿthat the Egyptians may know that I *am* the Lᴏʀᴅ." And they did so.   Ex. 9:16 • Ex. 7:5; 14:25

5 Now it was told the king of Egypt that the people had fled, and ᴿthe heart of Pharaoh and his servants was turned against the

people; and they said, "Why have we done this, that we have let Israel go from serving us?"   Ps. 105:25

6 So he ᵀmade ready his chariot and took his people with him.   *harnessed*

7 Also, he took ᴿsix hundred choice chariots, and all the chariots of Egypt with captains over every one of them.   Ex. 15:4

8 And the Lᴏʀᴅ ᴿhardened the heart of Pharaoh king of Egypt, and he pursued the children of Israel; and ᴿthe children of Israel went out with boldness.   Ex. 14:4 • Num. 33:3

9 So the ᴿEgyptians pursued them, all the horses *and* chariots of Pharaoh, his horsemen and his army, and overtook them camping by the sea beside Pi Hahiroth, before Baal Zephon.   Josh. 24:6

10 And when Pharaoh drew near, the children of Israel lifted their eyes, and behold, the Egyptians marched after them. So they were very afraid, and the children of Israel ᴿcried out to the Lᴏʀᴅ.   Neh. 9:9

11 ᴿThen they said to Moses, "Because *there were* no graves in Egypt, have you taken us away to die in the wilderness? Why have you so dealt with us, to bring us up out of Egypt?   Ps. 106:7, 8

12 ᴿ"*Is* this not the word that we told you in Egypt, saying, 'Let us alone that we may serve the Egyptians?' For *it would have been* better for us to serve the Egyptians than that we should die in the wilderness."   Ex. 5:21; 6:9

13 And Moses said to the people, "Do not be afraid. Stand still, and see the salvation of the Lᴏʀᴅ, which He will accomplish for you today. For the Egyptians whom you see today, you shall see again no more forever.

14 "The Lᴏʀᴅ will fight for you, and you shall ᴿholdᵀ your peace."   [Is. 30:15] • *Lit. be quiet*

15 And the Lᴏʀᴅ said to Moses, "Why do you cry to Me? Tell the children of Israel to go forward.

16 "But ᴿlift up your rod, and stretch out your hand over the sea and divide it. And the children of Israel shall go on dry *ground* through the midst of the sea.   Num. 20:8, 9, 11

17 "And I indeed will harden the hearts of the Egyptians, and they shall follow them. So I will gain honor over Pharaoh and over all his army, his chariots, and his horsemen.

18 "Then the Egyptians shall know that I *am* the Lᴏʀᴅ, when I have gained honor for Myself over Pharaoh, his chariots, and his horsemen."

19 And the Angel of God, ᴿwho went before the camp of Israel, moved and went behind them; and the pillar of cloud went from before them and stood behind them.   [Is. 63:9]

20 So it came between the camp of the Egyptians and the camp of Israel. Thus it was a cloud and darkness *to the one*, and it gave light by night *to the other*, so that the one did not come near the other all that night.

21 Then Moses stretched out his hand over the sea; and the LORD caused the sea to go *back* by a strong east wind all that night, and ᴿmade the sea into dry *land,* and the waters were ᴿdivided.   Ps. 66:6; 106:9; 136:13, 14 · Is. 63:12, 13

22 So ᴿthe children of Israel went into the midst of the sea on the dry *ground,* and the waters *were* ᴿa wall to them on their right hand and on their left.   Ex. 15:19 · Ex. 14:29; 15:8

23 And the Egyptians pursued and went after them into the midst of the sea, all Pharaoh's horses, his chariots, and his horsemen.

24 Now it came to pass, in the morning ᴿwatch, that ᴿthe LORD looked down upon the army of the Egyptians through the pillar of fire and cloud, and He ᵀtroubled the army of the Egyptians.   Judg. 7:19 · Ex. 13:21 · *confused*

25 And He *took off their chariot wheels, so that they drove them with difficulty; and the Egyptians said, "Let us flee from the face of Israel, for the LORD ᴿfights for them against the Egyptians."   Ex. 7:5; 14:4, 14, 18

26 Then the LORD said to Moses, "Stretch out your hand over the sea, that the waters may come back upon the Egyptians, on their chariots, and on their horsemen."

27 And Moses stretched out his hand over the sea; and when the morning appeared, the sea ᴿreturned to its full depth, while the Egyptians were fleeing into it. So the LORD ᴿoverthrewᵀ the Egyptians in the midst of the sea.   Josh. 4:18 · Ex. 15:1, 7 · Lit. *shook off*

28 Then the waters returned and covered the chariots, the horsemen, *and* all the army of Pharaoh that came into the sea after them. Not so much as one of them remained.

29 But ᴿthe children of Israel had walked on dry *land* in the midst of the sea, and the waters *were* a wall to them on their right hand and on their left.   Ps. 66:6; 78:52, 53

30 So the LORD saved Israel that day out of the hand of the Egyptians, and Israel ᴿsaw the Egyptians dead on the seashore.   Ps. 59:10

31 Thus Israel saw the great work which the LORD had done in Egypt; so the people feared the LORD, and ᴿbelieved the LORD and His servant Moses.   John 2:11; 11:45

The Song of Moses

15 Then ᴿMoses and the children of Israel sang this song to the LORD, and spoke, saying: Ps. 106:12

"I will ᴿsing to the LORD,   Is. 12:1-6
For He has triumphed gloriously!
The horse and its rider
He has thrown into the sea!
2 The LORD *is* my strength and song,
And He has become my salvation;
He *is* my God, and I will praise Him;
My father's God, and I will exalt Him.

3 The LORD *is* a man of ᴿwar;   Rev. 19:11
The LORD *is* His ᴿname.   Ps. 24:8; 83:18
4 ᴿPharaoh's chariots and his army He has cast into the sea;   Ex. 14:28
ᴿHis chosen captains also are drowned in the Red Sea.   Ex. 14:7
5 The depths have covered them;
They sank to the bottom like a stone.

6 "Your ᴿright hand, O LORD, has become glorious in power;   Ps. 17:7; 118:15
Your right hand, O LORD, has dashed the enemy in pieces.
7 And in the greatness of Your ᴿexcellence   Deut. 33:26
You have overthrown those who rose against You;
You sent forth Your wrath;
It consumed them ᴿlike stubble.   Is. 5:24
8 And with the blast of Your nostrils
The waters were gathered together;
ᴿThe floods stood upright like a heap;
The depths ᵀcongealed in the heart of the sea.   Ps. 78:13 · *became firm*
9 ᴿThe enemy said, 'I will pursue,
I will overtake,   Judg. 5:30
I will ᴿdivide the spoil;   Is. 53:12
My desire shall be satisfied on them.
I will draw my sword,
My hand shall destroy them.'
10 You blew with Your wind,
The sea covered them;
They sank like lead in the mighty waters.

11 "Whoᴿ *is* like You, O LORD, among the gods?   1 Kin. 8:23
Who *is* like You, glorious in holiness,
Fearful in praises, doing wonders?
12 You stretched out Your right hand;
The earth swallowed them.
13 You in Your mercy have ᴿled forth
The people whom You have redeemed;
You have guided *them* in Your strength
To Your holy habitation.   [Ps. 77:20]

14 "The people will hear *and* be afraid;
ᴿSorrow will take hold of the inhabitants of Philistia.   Ps. 48:6
15 ᴿThen ᴿthe chiefs of Edom will be dismayed;   Gen. 36:15, 40 · Deut. 2:4
ᴿThe mighty men of Moab,   Num. 22:3, 4
Trembling will take hold of them;
ᴿAll the inhabitants of Canaan will ᴿmelt away.   Josh. 5:1 · Josh. 2:9-11, 24
16 Fear and dread will fall on them;
By the greatness of Your arm
They will be ᴿas still as a stone,
Till Your people pass over, O LORD,
Till the people pass over   1 Sam. 25:37
ᴿWhom You have purchased.   Jer. 31:11
17 You will bring them in and ᴿplant them
In the ᴿmountain of Your inheritance,
In the place, O LORD, *which* You have made   Ps. 44:2; 80:8, 15 · Ps. 2:6; 78:54, 68

14:25 Sam., LXX, Syr. *bound*

For Your own dwelling,
The ᴿsanctuary, O LORD, *which* Your
hands have established.   Ps. 68:16; 76:2

18 "The LORD shall reign forever and ever."

19 For the horses of Pharaoh went with his chariots and his horsemen into the sea, and the LORD brought back the waters of the sea upon them. But the children of Israel went on dry *land* in the midst of the sea.

The Song of Miriam

20 Then Miriam the prophetess, the sister of Aaron, took the timbrel in her hand; and all the women went out after her ᴿwith timbrels and with dances.   Judg. 11:34; 21:21

21 And Miriam ᴿanswered them:

ᴿ"Sing to the LORD,   1 Sam. 18:7 • Ex. 15:1
For He has triumphed gloriously!
The horse and its rider
He has thrown into the sea!"

Bitter Waters Made Sweet

22 So Moses brought Israel from the Red Sea; then they went out into the Wilderness of Shur. And they went three days in the wilderness and found no ᴿwater.   Num. 20:2

23 Now when they came to ᴿMarah, they could not drink the waters of Marah, for they *were* bitter. Therefore the name of it was called ᵀMarah.   Num. 33:8 • Lit. *Bitter*

24 And the people ᴿcomplained against Moses, saying, "What shall we drink?"   Ex. 14:11

25 So he cried out to the LORD, and the LORD showed him a tree. When he cast *it* into the waters, the waters were made sweet. There He made a statute and an ᵀordinance for them, and there He tested them,   *law*

4-B. Jehovah-Ropheka: The LORD Your Healer   ▼

26 and said, "If you diligently heed the voice of the LORD your God and do what is right in His sight, give ear to His commandments and keep all His statutes, I will put none of the ᴿdiseases on you which I have brought on the Egyptians. For I *am* the LORD ᴿwho heals you."   Deut. 28:27, 58, 60 • Ex. 23:25 ▲

27 Then they came to Elim, where there *were* twelve wells of water and seventy palm trees; so they camped there by the waters.

Bread from Heaven

16 And they ᴿjourneyed from Elim, and all the congregation of the children of Israel came to the Wilderness of Sin, which is between Elim and ᴿSinai, on the fifteenth day of the second month after they departed from the land of Egypt.   Num. 33:10, 11 • Ex. 12:6, 51; 19:1

2 Then the whole congregation of the children of Israel ᴿcomplained against Moses and Aaron in the wilderness.   1 Cor. 10:10

3 And the children of Israel said to them, ᴿ"Oh, that we had died by the hand of the LORD in the land of Egypt, ᴿwhen we sat by the pots of meat *and* when we ate bread to

---

4-B. Jehovah-Ropheka: The LORD Your Healer (Exodus 15:26)—God delivered the children of Israel from Pharaoh, took them dryshod through the Red Sea, and there drowned their wicked pursuers in their own chariots (Ex. 14:1–31, page 73). Israel then entered the wilderness and for three days found no water. On the fourth day they reached the waters of Marah, but the water was bitter and they could not drink (Ex. 15:22, 23, above). They complained to Moses, and the Lord showed him a tree which, when cast into the water, made it sweet and drinkable (Ex. 15:25, above). At this wonderful event, a miracle of instantaneous chemical purification, the Lord revealed His name as *Jehovah-Ropheka*, "The LORD Who Heals You" (v. 26).

From this come the following lessons:

(1) God is the great healer. He "healed" the bitter waters so that Israel could drink and live.

(2) God is also the healer of the body, soul, and spirit of man (Is. 53:5, page 693; cf. 1 Pet. 2:24, page 1266).

(3) Man can wound his fellow man, and he can clean and sew a wound; but true healing comes from Jehovah-Ropheka. God can use any means to heal, as He did here, calling upon Moses to cast a tree into the waters.

(4) It is important to note that just as God turned bitter water into the sweet water of life for God's people by means of a tree, so also Christ turned the bitter wages of sin into sweet life by His death for us on "a tree" (Acts 5:30, page 1094). God cast this "tree" (the cross) into the midst of a bitter world, and gave life and joy to all who by faith will receive Christ as personal Savior (John 1:12, page 1049; cf. 2 Pet. 1:4, page 1272).

(5) When Jehovah-Ropheka returns to the earth at Christ's second coming, He will again heal the bitter waters of this world (1 Thess. 4:13–18, page 1211).

(6) When Jesus changed the water into wine at Cana (John 2:1–11, page 1050), He showed the same ability to instantaneously and miraculously work a great chemical change among liquids. Similarly, Jesus' touch healed His people, showing that He, as Messiah, possessed the power of Jehovah-Ropheka (Matt. 8:1–4, page 947).

This particular episode should teach us not to complain so quickly, as did the children of Israel. We are to trust God, who will turn our bitter trials to sweetness by means of a tree, the Cross. He is Jehovah-Ropheka: "The LORD Who Heals You."

See Exodus 17:15, page 77, for **Point 4-C: Jehovah-Nissi: The LORD Is My Banner.**

the full! For you have brought us out into this wilderness to kill this whole assembly with hunger." Lam. 4:9 • Num. 11:4, 5

4 Then the LORD said to Moses, "Behold, I will rain bread from heaven for you. And the people shall go out and gather a certain quota every day, that I may test them, whether they will walk in My law or not.

5 "And it shall be on the sixth day that they shall prepare what they bring in, and it shall be twice as much as they gather daily."

6 Then Moses and Aaron said to all the children of Israel, R"At evening you shall know that the LORD has brought you out of the land of Egypt. Ex. 6:7

7 "And in the morning you shall see the glory of the LORD; for He hears your complaints against the LORD. But Rwhat are we, that you complain against us?" Num. 16:11

8 Also Moses said, "This shall be seen when the LORD gives you meat to eat in the evening, and in the morning bread to the full; for the LORD hears your complaints which you make against Him. And what are we? Your complaints are not against us but Ragainst the LORD." 1 Sam. 8:7

9 Then Moses spoke to Aaron, "Say to all the congregation of the children of Israel, R'Come near before the LORD, for He has heard your complaints.' " Num. 16:16

10 Now it came to pass, as Aaron spoke to the whole congregation of the children of Israel, that they looked toward the wilderness, and behold, the glory of the LORD Rappeared in the cloud. Num. 16:19

11 And the LORD spoke to Moses, saying,

12 R"I have heard the complaints of the children of Israel. Speak to them, saying, R'At twilight you shall eat meat, and Rin the morning you shall be filled with bread. And you shall know that I am the LORD your God.' " Ex. 16:8 • Ex. 16:6 • Ex. 16:7

13 So it was that quails came up at evening and covered the camp, and in the morning Rthe dew lay all around the camp. Num. 11:9

14 And when the layer of dew lifted, there, on the surface of the wilderness, was a small round Rsubstance, as fine as Rfrost on the ground. Num. 11:7, 8 • Ps. 147:16

15 So when the children of Israel saw it, they said to one another, "What is it?" For they did not know what it was. And Moses said to them, R"This is the bread which the LORD has given you to eat. 1 Cor. 10:3

16 "This is the thing which the LORD has commanded: 'Let every man gather it Raccording to each one's need, one RomerT for each person, according to the number of persons; let every man take for those who are in his tent.' " Ex. 12:4 • Ex. 16:32, 36 • 2.087 qt.

17 Then the children of Israel did so and gathered, some more, some less.

18 So when they measured it by omers, he who gathered much had nothing left over, and he who gathered little had no lack. Every man had gathered according to each one's need.

19 And Moses said, "Let no one Rleave any of it till morning." Ex. 12:10; 16:23; 23:18

20 Notwithstanding they did not Theed Moses. But some of them left part of it until morning, and it bred worms and stank. And Moses was angry with them. listen to

21 So they gathered it every morning, every man according to his need. And when the sun became hot, it melted.

22 And so it was, on the sixth day, that they gathered twice as much bread, Ttwo omers for each one. And all the rulers of the congregation came and told Moses. 4.174 qt.

23 Then he said to them, "This is what the LORD has said: 'Tomorrow is Ra Sabbath rest, a holy Sabbath to the LORD. Bake what you will bake today, and boil what you will boil; and lay up for yourselves all that remains, to be kept until morning.' " Gen. 2:3

24 So they laid it up till morning, as Moses commanded; and it did not Rstink, nor were there any worms in it. Ex. 16:20

25 Then Moses said, "Eat that today, for today is a Sabbath to the LORD; today you will not find it in the field.

26 R"Six days you shall gather it, but on the seventh day, the Sabbath, there will be none." Ex. 20:9, 10

27 Now it happened that some of the people went out on the seventh day to gather, but they found none.

28 And the LORD said to Moses, "How long Rdo you refuse to keep My commandments and My laws? 2 Kin. 17:14

29 "See! For the LORD has given you the Sabbath; therefore He gives you on the sixth day bread for two days. Let every man remain in his place; let no man go out of his place on the seventh day."

30 So the people rested on the seventh day.

31 And the house of Israel called its name TManna. And Rit was like white coriander seed, and the taste of it was like wafers made with honey. Lit. What? cf. Ex. 16:15 • Num. 11:7-9

32 Then Moses said, "This is the thing which the LORD has commanded: 'Fill an Tomer with it, to be kept for your generations, that they may see the bread with which I fed you in the wilderness, when I brought you out of the land of Egypt.' " 2.087 qt.

33 And Moses said to Aaron, R"Take a pot and put an omer of manna in it, and lay it up before the LORD, to be kept for your generations." Heb. 9:4

34 As the LORD commanded Moses, so Aaron laid it up Rbefore the Testimony, to be kept. Num. 17:10

35 And the children of Israel ate manna forty years, Runtil they came to an inhabited

land; they ate manna until they came to the border of the land of Canaan.   Josh. 5:12

36 Now an omer *is* one-tenth of an ephah.

Water from the Rock

17 Then ᴿall the congregation of the children of Israel set out on their journey from the Wilderness of ᴿSin, according to the commandment of the LORD, and camped in Rephidim; but *there was* no water for the people to ᴿdrink.   Ex. 16:1 · Num. 33:11-15 · Ex. 15:22

2 ᴿTherefore the people contended with Moses, and said, "Give us water, that we may drink." So Moses said to them, "Why do you contend with me? Why do you ᴿtempt the LORD?"   Num. 20:2, 3, 13 · [Deut. 6:16]

3 And the people thirsted there for water, and the people ᴿcomplained against Moses, and said, "Why *is* it you have brought us up out of Egypt, to kill us and our children and our ᴿlivestock with thirst?"   Ex. 16:2, 3 · Ex. 12:38

4 So Moses cried out to the LORD, saying, "What shall I do with this people? They are almost ready to ᴿstone me!"   John 8:59; 10:31

5 And the LORD said to Moses, ᴿ"Go on before the people, and take with you some of the elders of Israel. Also take in your hand your rod with which ᴿyou struck the river, and go.   Ezek. 2:6 · Num. 20:8

6 ᴿ"Behold, I will stand before you there on the rock in Horeb; and you shall strike the rock, and water will come out of it, that the people may drink." And Moses did so in the sight of the elders of Israel.   Num. 20:10, 11

7 So he called the name of the place ᵀMassah and ᵀMeribah, because of the contention of the children of Israel, and because they ᵀtempted the LORD, saying, "Is the LORD among us or not?"   Lit. *Tempted · Contention · tested*

Victory over the Amalekites

8 ᴿNow Amalek came and fought with Israel in Rephidim.   Gen. 36:12

9 And Moses said to Joshua, "Choose us some men and go out, fight with Amalek. Tomorrow I will stand on the top of the hill with ᴿthe rod of God in my hand."   Ex. 4:20

10 So Joshua did as Moses said to him, and fought with Amalek. And Moses, Aaron, and Hur went up to the top of the hill.

11 And so it was, when Moses ᴿheld up his hand, that Israel prevailed; and when he let down his hand, Amalek prevailed.   [James 5:16]

12 But Moses' hands *became* ᵀheavy; so they took a stone and put *it* under him, and he sat on it. And Aaron and Hur supported his hands, one on one side, and the other on the other side; and his hands were steady until the going down of the sun.   *tired*

13 So Joshua defeated Amalek and his people with the edge of the sword.

14 Then the LORD said to Moses, ᴿ"Write this *for* a memorial in the book and recount *it* in the hearing of Joshua, that ᴿI will utterly blot out the remembrance of Amalek from under heaven."   Ex. 24:4; 34:27 · 1 Sam. 15:3

4–C. Jehovah-Nissi: The LORD Is My Banner   ▼

15 And Moses built an altar and called its name, *The-LORD-Is-My-Banner;   ▲

16 for he said, "Because the LORD has ᴿsworn: the LORD *will have* war with Amalek from generation to generation."   Gen. 22:14-16

17:15 Heb. *YHWH Nissi*

4–C. Jehovah-Nissi: The LORD Is My Banner (Exodus 17:15)—After the Israelites had been delivered from Egypt and Pharaoh, during their wilderness journey a new enemy, the Amalekites, arose "and fought with Israel in Rephidim" (Ex. 17:8, above). At Moses' command Joshua formed an army and led it against Amalek, while on a nearby hill Moses held the staff of God over his head. So long as Moses held up the staff of God, Joshua prevailed; when his arms grew heavy and he lowered the rod, Amalek would prevail. Aaron and Hur held up Moses' hands until Israel was victorious. Joshua defeated Amalek, and the Lord announced that He would "have war with Amalek from generation to generation" (vv. 9–16). Moses built an altar there and called it *Jehovah-Nissi*, "The-LORD-Is-My-Banner" (v. 15).

From this incident we may observe the following:

(1) Like Aaron and Hur, we should hold up the tiring hands of our pastors, teachers, evangelists, missionaries, and all who fight the good fight of faith (2 Tim. 4:1–8, page 1228; cf. Eph. 4:11, 12, page 1191).

(2) Amalek is an illustration of the flesh to the Christian. After leaving Egypt and crossing the Red Sea, Israel encountered a new enemy—Amalek—who is a picture of the flesh (the old sinful nature of man). The war between Amalek (the flesh) and the believer has raged on for almost two thousand years, and will continue until Jesus comes. This warfare with the flesh is perpetual, but will be won as long as we look to Jehovah with uplifted arms, seeking His strength. Paul speaks of this war against the flesh and warns the believer (Gal. 5:16, 24, page 1184).

(3) Isaiah 11:12 (page 654) looks prophetically into the future millennial age, following Christ's return, and gloriously announces, "He [God] will set up a banner for the nations, and will assemble the outcasts of Israel." This standard to which both the nations and Israel will flock will be the Lord Jesus Christ.

(4) The cross of Christ is our banner, and we must hold it high (John 12:32, 33, page 1072; cf. 1 Cor. 2:2, page 1148).

(5) Christ is ashamed of those who fail to hold Him high before a lost world (Mark 8:38, page 994).

We learn from this incident that, in the battles of life, the believer's strength comes not from himself but from Jehovah-Nissi, "The-LORD-Is-My-Banner."

See Judges 6:24, page 246, for **Point 4-D: Jehovah-Shalom: The LORD Is Peace.**

Jethro's Advice

18 And ^RJethro, the priest of Midian, Moses' father-in-law, heard of all that ^RGod had done for Moses and for Israel His people—that the LORD had brought Israel out of Egypt.   Ex. 2:16, 18; 3:1 • [Ps. 106:2, 8]

2 Then Jethro, Moses' father-in-law, took ^RZipporah, Moses' wife, after he had sent her back,   Ex. 2:21; 4:20-26

3 with her two sons, of whom the ^Rname of one *was* Gershom (for he said, "I have been a stranger in a foreign land")   Ex. 2:22

4 and the name of the other *was* ^TEliezer (for *he* said, "The God of my father *was* my ^Rhelp, and delivered me from the sword of Pharaoh");   Lit. *My God Is Help* • Gen. 49:25

5 and Jethro, Moses' father-in-law, came with his sons and his wife to Moses in the wilderness, where he was encamped at ^Rthe mountain of God.   Ex. 3:1, 12; 4:27; 24:13

6 Now he had said to Moses, "I, your father-in-law Jethro, am coming to you with your wife and her two sons with her."

7 So Moses ^Rwent out to meet his father-in-law, bowed down, and ^Rkissed him. And they asked each other about *their* well-being, and they went into the tent.   Gen. 18:2 • Ex. 4:27

8 And Moses told his father-in-law all that the LORD had done to Pharaoh and to the Egyptians for Israel's sake, all the hardship that had come upon them on the way, and *how* the LORD had ^Rdelivered them.   Ex. 15:6, 16

9 Then Jethro rejoiced for all the ^Rgood which the LORD had done for Israel, whom He had delivered out of the hand of the Egyptians.   [Is. 63:7-14]

10 And Jethro said, ^R"Blessed *be* the LORD, who has delivered you out of the hand of the Egyptians and out of the hand of Pharaoh, *and* who has delivered the people from under the hand of the Egyptians.   Gen. 14:20

11 "Now I know that the LORD is ^Rgreater than all the gods; for in the very thing in which they ^Tbehaved ^Rproudly, *He was* above them."   2 Chr. 2:5 • *acted presumptuously* • Luke 1:51

12 Then Jethro, Moses' father-in-law, *took a burnt ^Roffering and *other* sacrifices *to offer* to God. And Aaron came with all the elders of Israel ^Rto eat bread with Moses' father-in-law before God.   Ex. 24:5 • Deut. 12:7

13 And so it was, on the next day, that Moses ^Rsat to judge the people; and the people stood before Moses from morning until evening.   Matt. 23:2

14 So when Moses' father-in-law saw all that he did for the people, he said, "What *is* this thing that you are doing for the people? Why do you alone ^Tsit, and all the people stand before you from morning until evening?"   Sit as judge

15 And Moses said to his father-in-law,

18:12 So with MT, LXX; Syr., Tg., Vg. *offered*

"Because ^Rthe people come to me to inquire of God.   Lev. 24:12

16 "When they have ^Ra ^Tdifficulty, they come to me, and I judge between one and another; and I make known the statutes of God and His laws."   Ex. 24:14 • *dispute*, lit. *matter*

17 So Moses' father-in-law said to him, "The thing that you do is not good.

18 "Both you and these people who *are* with you will surely wear yourselves out. For this thing *is* too much for you; ^Ryou are not able to perform it by yourself.   Num. 11:14, 17

19 "Listen now to my voice; I will give you counsel, and God will be with you: Stand before God for the people, so that you may ^Rbring the difficulties to God.   Num. 9:8; 27:5

20 "And you shall ^Rteach them the statutes and the laws, and show them the way in which they must walk and ^Rthe work they must do.   Deut. 5:1 • Deut. 1:18

21 "Moreover you shall select from all the people ^Rable men, such as ^Rfear God, ^Rmen of truth, ^Rhating covetousness; and place *such* over them *to be* rulers of thousands, rulers of hundreds, rulers of fifties, and rulers of tens.   Acts 6:3 • 2 Sam. 23:3 • Ezek. 18:8 • Deut. 16:19

22 "And let them judge the people at all times. ^RThen it will be *that* every great matter they shall bring to you, but every small matter they themselves shall judge. So it will be easier for you, for ^Rthey will bear *the burden* with you.   Deut. 1:17 • Num. 11:17

23 "If you do this thing, and God *so* commands you, then you will be able to endure, and all this people will also go to their ^Rplace in peace."   Ex. 16:29

24 So Moses heeded the voice of his father-in-law and did all that he had said.

25 And ^RMoses chose able men out of all Israel, and made them heads over the people: rulers of thousands, rulers of hundreds, rulers of fifties, and rulers of tens.   Deut. 1:15

26 So they judged the people at all times; the hard cases they brought to Moses, but they judged every small case themselves.

27 Then Moses let his father-in-law depart, and he went his way to his own land.

Israel at Mount Sinai

19 In the third month after the children of Israel had gone out of the land of Egypt, on the same day, ^Rthey came *to* the Wilderness of Sinai.   Num. 33:15

2 For they had departed from ^RRephidim, had come *to* the Wilderness of Sinai, and camped in the wilderness. So Israel camped there before ^Rthe mountain. Ex. 17:1 • Ex. 3:1, 12; 18:5

3 And Moses went up to God, and the LORD ^Rcalled to him from the mountain, saying, "Thus you shall say to the house of Jacob, and tell the children of Israel: Ex. 3:4

4 'You have seen what I did to the Egyptians, and *how* ^RI bore you on eagles' wings and brought you to Myself.   Is. 63:9

5 'Now therefore, if you will indeed obey My voice and keep My covenant, then you shall be a special treasure to Me above all people; for all the earth is ᴿMine.   Ex. 9:29

6 'And you shall be to Me a ᴿkingdom of priests and a ᴿholy nation.' These *are* the words which you shall speak to the children of Israel."   [1 Pet. 2:5, 9] • Deut. 7:6; 14:21; 26:19

7 So Moses came and called for the elders of the people, and ᵀlaid before them all these words which the Lᴏʀᴅ commanded him.   *set*

8 Then ᴿall the people answered together and said, "All that the Lᴏʀᴅ has spoken we will do." So Moses brought back the words of the people to the Lᴏʀᴅ.   Deut. 5:27; 26:17

9 And the Lᴏʀᴅ said to Moses, "Behold, I come to you in the thick cloud, ᴿthat the people may hear when I speak with you, and believe you forever." So Moses told the words of the people to the Lᴏʀᴅ.   Deut. 4:12

10 Then the Lᴏʀᴅ said to Moses, "Go to the people and consecrete them today and tomorrow, and let them wash their clothes.

11 "And let them be ready for the third day. For on the third day the Lᴏʀᴅ will come down upon Mount Sinai in the sight of all the people.

12 "You shall set bounds for the people all around, saying, 'Take heed to yourselves *that* you do *not* go up to the mountain or touch its base. ᴿWhoever touches the mountain shall surely be put to death.   Heb. 12:20

13 'Not a hand shall touch him, but he shall surely be stoned or shot *with an arrow;* whether man or beast, he shall not live.' When the trumpet sounds long, they shall come near the mountain."

14 So Moses went down from the mountain to the people and sanctified the people, and they washed their clothes.

15 And he said to the people, "Be ready for the third day; do not come near *your* wives."

16 Then it came to pass on the third day, in the morning, that there were ᴿthunderings and lightnings, and a thick cloud on the mountain; and the sound of the trumpet was very loud, so that all the people who *were* in the camp ᴿtrembled.   Heb. 12:18, 19 • Heb. 12:21

17 And ᴿMoses brought the people out of the camp to meet with God, and they stood at the foot of the mountain.   Deut. 4:10

18 Now ᴿMount Sinai *was* completely in smoke, because the Lᴏʀᴅ descended upon ᴿit in fire. ᴿIts smoke ascended like the smoke of a furnace, and the whole mountain quaked greatly.   Deut. 4:11 • Ex. 3:2; 24:17 • Gen. 15:17; 19:28

19 And when the blast of the trumpet sounded long and became louder and louder, ᴿMoses spoke, and ᴿGod answered him by voice.   Heb. 12:21 • Ps. 81:7

20 Then the Lᴏʀᴅ came down upon Mount Sinai, on the top of the mountain. And the Lᴏʀᴅ called Moses to the top of the mountain, and Moses went up.

21 And the Lᴏʀᴅ said to Moses, "Go down and warn the people, lest they break through ᴿto gaze at the Lᴏʀᴅ, and many of them perish.   1 Sam. 6:19

22 "Also let the priests who come near the Lᴏʀᴅ ᴿconsecrate themselves, lest the Lᴏʀᴅ break out against them."   Lev. 21:6–8

23 But Moses said to the Lᴏʀᴅ, "The people cannot come up to Mount Sinai; for You warned us, saying, ᴿ'Set bounds around the mountain and consecrate it.' "   Ex. 19:12

24 Then the Lᴏʀᴅ said to him, "Away! Get down and then come up, you and Aaron with you. But do not let the priests and the people break through to come up to the Lᴏʀᴅ, lest He break out against them."

25 So Moses went down to the people and spoke to them.

The Ten Commandments

20 And God spoke all these words, saying:

2 "I *am* the Lᴏʀᴅ your God, who brought you out of the land of Egypt, out of the house of bondage.

3 "Youᴿ shall have no other gods before Me.   Jer. 25:6; 35:15

4 "You shall not make for yourself a carved image—any likeness *of anything* that *is* in heaven above, or that *is* in the earth beneath, or that *is* in the water under the earth;

5 you shall not bow down to them nor serve them. For I, the Lᴏʀᴅ your God, *am* a jealous God, visiting the iniquity of the fathers upon the children to the third and fourth *generations* of those who hate Me,

6 but ᴿshowing mercy to thousands, to those who love Me and keep My commandments.   Deut. 7:9

7 "You shall not take the name of the Lᴏʀᴅ your God in vain, for the Lᴏʀᴅ ᴿwill not hold *him* guiltless who takes His name in vain.   Mic. 6:11

8 "Rememberᴿ the Sabbath day, to keep it holy.   Lev. 26:2

9 ᴿSix days you shall labor and do all your work,   Luke 13:14

10 but the seventh day *is* the Sabbath of the Lᴏʀᴅ your God. *In it* you shall do no work: you, nor your son, nor your daughter, nor your male servant, nor your female servant, nor your cattle, ᴿnor your stranger who *is* within your gates.   Neh. 13:16–19

11 For ᴿin six days the Lᴏʀᴅ made the heavens and the earth, the sea, and all that *is* in them, and rested the seventh day. Therefore the Lᴏʀᴅ blessed the Sabbath day and hallowed it.   Ex. 31:17

12 "Honor your father and your mother, that your days may be ᴿlong upon the land which the Lᴏʀᴅ your God is giving you.   Deut. 5:16, 33; 6:2; 11:8, 9
13 "Youᴿ shall not murder.   Rom. 13:9
14 "You shall not commit adultery.
15 "Youᴿ shall not steal.   Lev. 19:11, 13
16 "Youᴿ shall not bear false witness against your neighbor.   Deut. 5:20
17 "You shall not covet your neighbor's house; ᴿyou shall not covet your neighbor's wife, nor his male servant, nor his female servant, nor his ox, nor his donkey, nor anything that *is* your neighbor's."   [Matt. 5:28]

The People Afraid of God's Presence

18 Now all the people ᴿwitnessed the thunderings, the lightning flashes, the sound of the trumpet, and the mountain ᴿsmoking; and when the people saw *it,* they trembled and stood afar off.   Rev. 1:10, 12 • Ex. 19:16, 18
19 Then they said to Moses, "You speak with us, and we will hear; but ᴿlet not God speak with us, lest we die."   Deut. 5:5, 23–27
20 And Moses said to the people, ᴿ"Do not fear; ᴿfor God has come to test you, and ᴿthat His fear may be before you, so that you may not sin."   [Is. 41:10, 13] • [Deut. 13:3] • Is. 8:13
21 So the people stood afar off, but Moses drew near ᴿthe thick darkness where God *was.*   Ex. 19:16

The Law of the Altar

22 Then the Lᴏʀᴅ said to Moses, "Thus you shall say to the children of Israel: 'You have seen that I have talked with you ᴿfrom heaven.   Deut. 4:36; 5:24, 26
23 'You shall not make *anything* to be ᴿwith Me—gods of silver or gods of gold you shall not make for yourselves.   Ex. 32:1, 2, 4
24 'An altar of earth you shall make for Me, and you shall sacrifice on it your burnt offerings and your peace offerings, your sheep and your oxen. In every place where I ᵀrecord My name I will come to you, and I will bless you.   *cause My name to be remembered*
25 'And if you make Me an altar of stone, you shall not build it of hewn stone; for if you use your tool on it, you have profaned it.
26 'Nor shall you go up by steps to My altar, that your nakedness may not be exposed on it.'

The Law Concerning Servants

21 "Now these *are* the ᵀjudgments which you shall set before them: *ordinances*
2 ᴿ"If you buy a Hebrew servant, he shall serve six years; and in the seventh he shall go out free and pay nothing.   Jer. 34:14
3 "If he comes in by himself, he shall go out by himself; if he *comes in* married, then his wife shall go out with him.
4 "If his master has given him a wife, and

she has borne him sons or daughters, the wife and her children shall be her master's, and he shall go out by himself.
5 ᴿ"But if the servant plainly says, 'I love my master, my wife, and my children; I will not go out free,'   Deut. 15:16, 17
6 "then his master shall bring him to the ᴿjudges. He shall also bring him to the door, or to the doorpost, and his master shall pierce his ear with an awl; and he shall serve him forever.   Ex. 12:12; 22:8, 9
7 "And if a man ᴿsells his daughter to be a female servant, she shall not go out as the male servants do.   Neh. 5:5
8 "If she ᵀdoes not please her master, who has betrothed her to himself, then he shall let her be redeemed. He shall have no right to sell her to a foreign people, since he has dealt deceitfully with her.   Lit. *is evil in the eyes of*
9 "And if he has betrothed her to his son, he shall deal with her according to the custom of daughters.
10 "If he takes another *wife,* he shall not diminish her food, her clothing, ᴿand her marriage rights.   [1 Cor. 7:3, 5]
11 "And if he does not do these three for her, then she shall go out free, without *paying* money.

The Law Concerning Violence

12 ᴿ"He who strikes a man so that he dies shall surely be put to death.   [Matt. 26:52]
13 "However, if he did not lie in wait, but God delivered *him* into his hand, then I will appoint for you a place where he may flee.
14 "But if a man acts with ᴿpremeditation against his neighbor, to kill him by treachery, ᴿyou shall take him from My altar, that he may die.   Deut. 19:11, 12 • 1 Kin. 2:28–34
15 "And he who strikes his father or his mother shall surely be put to death.
16 ᴿ"He who kidnaps a man and ᴿsells him, or if he is ᴿfound in his hand, shall surely be put to death.   Deut. 24:7 • Gen. 37:28 • Ex. 22:4
17 "And ᴿhe who curses his father or his mother shall surely be put to death.   Mark 7:10
18 "If men contend with each other, and one strikes the other with a stone or with *his* fist, and he does not die but is confined to *his* bed,
19 "if he rises again and walks about outside with his staff, then he who struck *him* shall be ᵀacquitted. He shall only pay *for* the loss of his time, and shall provide *for him* to be thoroughly healed.   *exempt from punishment*
20 "And if a man beats his male or female servant with a rod, so that he dies under his hand, he shall surely be punished.
21 "Notwithstanding, if he remains alive a day or two, he shall not be punished; for he *is* his ᴿproperty.   Lev. 25:44–46
22 "If men fight, and hurt a woman with child, so that ᵀshe gives birth prematurely, yet no harm follows, he shall surely be pun-

ished accordingly as the woman's husband imposes on him; and he shall pay as the judges *determine*. _{Lit. *her children come out*}

23 "But if *any* harm follows, then you shall give life for life,

24 ᴿ"eye for eye, tooth for tooth, hand for hand, foot for foot, _{Lev. 24:20}

25 "burn for burn, wound for wound, stripe for stripe.

26 "If a man strikes the eye of his male or female servant, and destroys it, he shall let him go free for the sake of his eye.

27 "And if he knocks out the tooth of his male or female servant, he shall let him go free for the sake of his tooth.

Animal Control Laws

28 "If an ox gores a man or a woman to death, then ᴿthe ox shall surely be stoned, and its flesh shall not be eaten; but the owner of the ox *shall be* acquitted. _{Gen. 9:5}

29 "But if the ox ᵀtended to thrust with its horn in times past, and it has been made known to his owner, and he has not kept it confined, so that it has killed a man or a woman, the ox shall be stoned and its owner also shall be put to death. _{was inclined}

30 "If there is imposed on him a sum of money, then he shall pay ᴿto redeem his life, whatever is imposed on him. _{Num. 35:31}

31 "Whether it has gored a son or gored a daughter, according to this judgment it shall be done to him.

32 "If the ox gores a male or female servant, he shall give to their master thirty shekels of silver, and the ox shall be stoned.

33 "And if a man opens a pit, or if a man digs a pit and does not cover it, and an ox or a donkey falls in it,

34 "the owner of the pit shall make *it* good; he shall give money to their owner, but the dead *animal* shall be his.

35 "If one man's ox hurts another's, so that it dies, then they shall sell the live ox and divide the money from it; and the dead ox they shall also divide.

36 "Or if it was known that the ox tended to thrust in time past, and its owner has not kept it confined, he shall surely pay ox for ox, and the dead animal shall be his own.

Responsibility for Property

22 "If a man steals an ox or a sheep, and slaughters it or sells it, he shall ᴿrestore five oxen for an ox and four sheep for a sheep. _{2 Sam. 12:6}

2 "If the thief is found ᴿbreaking in, and he is struck so that he dies, *there shall be* no guilt for his bloodshed. _{Matt. 6:19; 24:43}

3 "If the sun has risen on him, *there shall be* guilt for his bloodshed. He should make full restitution; if he has nothing, then he shall be ᴿsoldᵀ for his theft. _{Ex. 21:2 • Sold as a slave}

4 "If the theft is certainly found alive in his hand, whether it is an ox or donkey or sheep, he shall ᴿrestore double. _{Prov. 6:31}

5 "If a man causes a field or vineyard to be grazed, and lets loose his animal, and it feeds in another man's field, he shall make restitution from the best of his own field and the best of his own vineyard.

6 "If fire breaks out and catches in thorns, so that stacked grain, standing grain, or the field is consumed, he who kindled the fire shall surely make restitution.

7 "If a man ᴿdelivers to his neighbor money or articles to keep, and it is stolen out of the man's house, ᴿif the thief is found, he shall pay double. _{Lev. 6:1–7 • Ex. 22:4}

8 "If the thief is not found, then the master of the house shall be brought to the ᴿjudges *to see* whether he has put his hand into his neighbor's goods. _{Ex. 21:6, 22; 22:28}

9 "For any kind of trespass, *whether it concerns* an ox, a donkey, a sheep, or clothing, *or* for any kind of lost thing which *another* claims to be his, the ᴿcause of both parties shall come before the judges; *and* whomever the judges condemn shall pay double to his neighbor. _{Deut. 25:1}

10 "If a man delivers to his neighbor a donkey, an ox, a sheep, or any animal to keep, and it dies, is hurt, or driven away, no one seeing *it*,

11 "then an ᴿoath of the Lᴏʀᴅ shall be between them both, that he has not put his hand into his neighbor's goods; and the owner of it shall accept *that*, and he shall not make *it* good. _{Heb. 6:16}

12 "But if, in fact, it is stolen from him, he shall make restitution to the owner of it.

13 "If it is ᴿtorn to pieces *by a beast, then* he shall bring it as evidence, *and* he shall not make good what was torn. _{Gen. 31:39}

14 "And if a man borrows *anything* from his neighbor, and it becomes injured or dies, the owner of it not *being* with it, he shall surely make *it* good.

15 "If its owner *was* with it, he shall not make *it* good; if it *was* hired, it came for its hire.

Moral and Ceremonial Principles

16 "If a man entices a virgin who is not betrothed, and lies with her, he shall surely pay the bride-price for her *to be* his wife.

17 "If her father utterly refuses to give her to him, he shall pay money according to the ᴿbride-price of virgins. _{Gen. 34:12}

18 "You shall not permit a sorceress to live.

19 ᴿ"Whoever lies with an animal shall surely be put to death. _{Lev. 18:23; 20:15, 16}

20 "He who sacrifices to *any* god, except to the Lᴏʀᴅ only, he shall be utterly destroyed.

21 ᴿ"You shall neither mistreat a ᵀstranger nor oppress him, for you were strangers in the land of Egypt. _{Deut. 10:19 • *sojourner*}

22 R"You shall not afflict any widow or fatherless child. [James 1:27]

23 "If you afflict them in any way, *and* they cry at all to Me, I will surely hear their cry;

24 "and My wrath will become hot, and I will kill you with the sword; your wives shall be widows, and your children fatherless.

25 R"If you lend money to *any of* My people *who are* poor among you, you shall not be like a moneylender to him; you shall not charge him Rinterest. Lev. 25:35–37 • Ps. 15:5

26 R"If you ever take your neighbor's garment as a pledge, you shall return it to him before the sun goes down. Deut. 24:6, 10–13

27 "For that *is* his only covering, it *is* his garment for his skin. What will he sleep in? And it will be that when he cries to Me, I will hear, for I *am* Rgracious. Ex. 34:6, 7

28 R"You shall not revile God, nor curse a Rruler of your people. Eccl. 10:20 • Acts 23:5

29 "You shall not delay *to offer* the first of your ripe produce and your juices. The firstborn of your sons you shall give to Me.

30 R"Likewise you shall do with your oxen *and* your sheep. It shall be with its mother Rseven days; on the eighth day you shall give it to Me. Deut. 15:19 • Lev. 22:27

31 "And you shall be holy men to Me: Ryou shall not eat meat torn *by beasts* in the field; you shall throw it to the dogs. Ezek. 4:14

Justice for All

23 "You shall not circulate a false report. Do not put your hand with the wicked to be an Runrighteous witness. Deut. 19:16–21

2 "You shall not follow a crowd to do evil; nor shall you testify in a dispute so as to turn aside after many to pervert *justice.*

3 "You shall not show partiality to a Rpoor man in his dispute. Deut. 1:17; 16:19

4 R"If you meet your enemy's ox or his donkey going astray, you shall surely bring it back to him again. [Rom. 12:20]

5 R"If you see the donkey of one who hates you lying under its burden, and you would refrain from helping it, you shall surely help him with it. Deut. 22:4

6 R"You shall not pervert the judgment of your poor in his dispute. Eccl. 5:8

7 "Keep yourself far from a false matter; do not kill the innocent and righteous. For RI will not justify the wicked. Rom. 1:18

8 "And Ryou shall take no bribe, for a bribe blinds the discerning and perverts the words of the righteous. Prov. 15:27; 17:8, 23

9 "Also you shall not oppress a stranger, for you know the heart of a stranger, because you were strangers in the land of Egypt.

The Law of Sabbaths

10 R"Six years you shall sow your land and gather in its produce, Lev. 25:1–7

11 "but the seventh *year* you shall let it rest and lie fallow, that the poor of your people may eat; and what they leave, the beasts of the field may eat. In like manner you shall do with your vineyard *and* your olive grove.

12 R"Six days you shall do your work, and on the seventh day you shall rest, that your ox and your donkey may rest, and the son of your female servant and the stranger may be refreshed. Luke 13:14

13 "And in all that I have said to you, Rbe circumspect and Rmake no mention of the name of other gods, nor let it be heard from your mouth. 1 Tim. 4:16 • Josh. 23:7

Three Annual Feasts

14 R"Three times you shall keep a feast to Me in the year: Ex. 23:17; 34:22–24

15 R"You shall keep the Feast of Unleavened Bread (you shall eat unleavened bread seven days, as I commanded you, at the time appointed in the month of Abib, for in it you came out of Egypt; Rnone shall appear before Me empty); Ex. 12:14–20 • Ex. 22:29; 34:20

16 "and the Feast of Harvest, the firstfruits of your labors which you have sown in the field; and the Feast of Ingathering at the end of the year, when you have gathered in *the fruit of* your labors from the field.

17 "Three times in the year all your males shall appear before the Lord *GOD.

18 "You shall not offer the blood of My sacrifice with leavened bread; nor shall the fat of My sacrifice remain until morning.

19 R"The first of the firstfruits of your land you shall bring into the house of the LORD your God. RYou shall not boil a young goat in its mother's milk. Deut. 26:2, 10 • Deut. 14:21

The Angel and the Promises

20 R"Behold, I send an Angel before you to keep you in the way and to bring you into the place which I have prepared. Ex. 3:2; 13:15; 14:19

21 "Beware of Him and obey His voice; do not provoke Him, for He will not pardon your transgressions; for My name is in Him.

22 "But if you indeed obey His voice and do all that I speak, then RI will be an enemy to your enemies and an adversary to your adversaries. Deut. 30:7

23 R"For My Angel will go before you and Rbring you in to the Amorites and the Hittites and the Perizzites and the Canaanites and the Hivites and the Jebusites; and I will Tcut them off. Ex. 23:20 • Josh. 24:8, 11 • *annihilate them*

24 "You shall not Rbow down to their gods, nor serve them, Rnor do according to their works; Rbut you shall utterly overthrow them and completely break down their *sacred* pillars. Ex. 20:5; 23:13, 33 • Deut. 12:30, 31 • Num. 33:52

25 "So you shall Rserve the LORD your God, and RHe will bless your bread and your water. And RI will take sickness away from the midst of you. Deut. 6:13 • Deut. 28:5 • Ex. 15:26

23:17 Heb. *YHWH,* usually translated *LORD*

26 R"No one shall suffer miscarriage or be barren in your land; I will Rfulfill the number of your days.   Deut. 7:14; 28:4 • 1 Chr. 23:1

27 "I will send My fear before you, I will Rcause confusion among all the people to whom you come, and will make all your enemies turn *their* backs to you.   Deut. 7:23

28 "And RI will send hornets before you, which shall drive out the Hivite, the Canaanite, and the Hittite from before you.   Josh. 24:12

29 R"I will not drive them out from before you in one year, lest the land become desolate and the beasts of the field become too numerous for you.   Deut. 7:22

30 "Little by little I will drive them out from before you, until you have increased, and you inherit the land.

31 "And I will set your bounds from the Red Sea to the sea, Philistia, and from the desert to the *River. For I will deliver the inhabitants of the land into your hand, and you shall drive them out before you.

32 R"You shall make no Tcovenant with them, nor with their gods.   Ex. 34:12, 15 • *treaty*

33 "They shall not dwell in your land, lest they make you sin against Me. For *if* you serve their gods, Rit will surely be a snare to you."   Ps. 106:36

Israel Affirms the Covenant

24 Now He said to Moses, "Come up to the LORD, you and Aaron, RNadab and Abihu, Rand seventy of the elders of Israel, and worship from afar.   Lev. 10:1 • Num. 11:16

2 "And Moses alone shall come near the LORD, but they shall not come near; nor shall the people go up with him."

3 So Moses came and told the people all the words of the LORD and all the Tjudgments. And all the people answered with one voice and said, R"'All the words which the LORD has said we will do."   *ordinances* • Ex. 19:8; 24:7

4 And Moses Rwrote all the words of the LORD. And he rose early in the morning, and built an altar at the foot of the mountain, and twelve Rpillars according to the twelve tribes of Israel.   Deut. 31:9 • Gen. 28:18

5 Then he sent young men of the children of Israel, who offered Rburnt offerings and sacrificed peace offerings of oxen to the LORD.   Ex. 18:12; 20:24

6 And Moses Rtook half the blood and put *it* in basins, and half the blood he sprinkled on the altar.   Heb. 9:18

23:31 The Euphrates

7 Then he Rtook the Book of the Covenant and read in the hearing of the people. And they said, "All that the LORD has said we will do, and be obedient."   Heb. 9:19

8 And Moses took the blood, sprinkled *it* on the people, and said, "This is the blood of the covenant which the LORD has made with you according to all these words."

On the Mountain with God

9 Then Moses went up, also Aaron, Nadab, and Abihu, and seventy of the elders of Israel,

10 and they saw the God of Israel. And *there was* under His feet as it were a paved work of sapphire stone, and it was like the Tvery heavens in *its* clarity.   Lit. *substance of sky*

11 But on the nobles of the children of Israel He did not Tlay His hand. So they saw God, and they ate and drank.   stretch out

12 Then the LORD said to Moses, "Come up to Me on the mountain and be there; and I will give you Rtablets of stone, and the law and commandments which I have written, that you may teach them."   Ex. 31:18; 32:15

13 So Moses arose with Rhis assistant Joshua, and Moses went up to the mountain of God.   Ex. 32:17

14 And he said to the elders, "Wait here for us until we come back to you. Indeed, Aaron and RHur *are* with you. If any man has a difficulty, let him go to them."   Ex. 17:10, 12

15 Then Moses went up into the mountain, and Ra cloud covered the mountain.   Ex. 19:9

16 Now the glory of the LORD rested on Mount Sinai, and the cloud covered it six days. And on the seventh day He called to Moses out of the midst of the cloud.

17 The sight of the glory of the LORD *was* like a consuming fire on the top of the mountain in the eyes of the children of Israel.

18 So Moses went into the midst of the cloud and went up into the mountain. And RMoses was on the mountain forty days and forty nights.   Ex. 34:28

Offerings for the Sanctuary

35-A. The History of the Tabernacle   ▼

25 Then the LORD spoke to Moses, saying:

2 "Speak to the children of Israel, that they bring Me an offering. RFrom everyone who gives it willingly with his heart you shall take My offering.   Ex. 35:4-9, 21

3 "And this *is* the offering which you shall take from them: gold, silver, and bronze;

35-A. The History of the Tabernacle (Exodus 25:1-9)—It is an astounding fact that the tabernacle was God's center of Israel's worship for nearly five hundred years, from the time Moses met with God on Mt. Sinai, just after the exodus from Egypt, until the completion of the temple by Solomon. The gold covering of the ark and other furnishings lasted, untarnished, through the centuries. The tent, unless supernaturally preserved, *(Point 35-A continued on next page)*

▽ 4 "blue, purple, and scarlet *thread*, fine linen, and goats' *hair*;

5 "ram skins dyed red, ^Tbadger skins, and acacia wood;   Or *dolphin*

6 "oil for the light, and spices for the anointing oil and for the sweet incense;

7 "onyx stones, and stones to be set in the ^Rephod and in the breastplate.   Ex. 28:4, 6–14

8 "And let them make Me a sanctuary, that ^RI may dwell among them.   [2 Cor. 6:16]

9 "According to all that I show you, *that is*, the pattern of the tabernacle and the pattern of all its furnishings, just so you shall

▲ make *it*.

The Ark of the Testimony

10 ^R"And they shall make an ark of acacia wood; ^Ttwo and a half cubits *shall be* its length, a cubit and a half its width, and a cubit and a half its height.   Ex. 37:1-9 • 45 in.

11 "And you shall overlay it with pure gold, inside and out you shall overlay it, and shall make on it a molding of gold all around.

12 "You shall cast four rings of gold for it, and put *them* in its four corners; two rings *shall be* on one side, and two rings on the other side.

13 "And you shall make poles *of* acacia wood, and overlay them with gold.

14 "You shall put the poles into the rings on

(Point 35-A continued from previous page)
would have shown aging as the years went by. Instead, it withstood the passage of time to serve its magnificent and holy purpose. Notice that:

(1) Its plan was given by God, not by men. God specified to Moses not only the exact shape and size of the tabernacle, but also the dimensions and materials for every item of its furniture (Ex. 25:9—27:21, above). He specified the design and materials of the priest's garments (Ex. 28:1-43, page 87). He also detailed the consecration rites of the priests (Ex. 29:1-9, page 88) and the offerings (Ex. 29:38—30:10, page 89). He then chose two main craftsmen—Bezalel of the tribe of Judah, and Aholiab of the tribe of Dan—as well as other workers who were to help build the tabernacle and all of its furnishings (Ex. 31:1-6, page 91; cf. Ex. 36:1—39:4, page 98).

(2) Its materials were secured by an offering (vv. 1-9; cf. Ex. 35:21-29, page 96). God instructed Moses to secure the materials for the tabernacle by appealing to the people, in God's name, to contribute from their substance. Those with willing hearts were privileged to share in this great undertaking. The materials used for the tabernacle and its furniture were

    (a) gold
    (b) silver
    (c) bronze
    (d) linens (dyed and white)
    (e) goat's wool
    (f) skins
    (g) acacia wood (vv. 1-5, page 83)

(3) It was filled with the Lord's glory (Ex. 40:34-38, page 103). When the tabernacle was first erected, the cloud of God's glorious presence came and covered it. Thus, from the very beginning of the tabernacle's service, it became the appointed place where the infinite God, who filled all space with His omnipresence, met with man.

(4) It was carried in front of Israel in the wilderness journey. The ark of the covenant, upon which the mercy seat was placed, led the procession of Israel (Num. 10:33-36, page 150; cf. Josh. 3:3-6, page 218). It showed visually that God's presence goes before His people. This typifies Christ's presence with believers and His going before them (Matt. 28:20, page 982).

(5) It was moved from place to place. It crossed the Jordan with Israel into the Promised Land, and they encamped with it at Gilgal (Josh. 5:10, page 220). It was set up at Shiloh, which became Israel's temporary religious capital (Josh. 18:1, page 232; cf. 1 Sam. 1:3, page 269). This is where Samuel grew up and ministered to the Lord (1 Sam. 3:19-21, page 271). During the reign of Saul, it was located at Nob (1 Sam. 21:1-6, page 288), and later it was moved to Gibeon (1 Kin. 3:4, page 329).

(6) David brought it to Jerusalem about 1000 B.C. He desired the ark of God's covenant to be in his new capital, Jerusalem. It was transported, however, without regard to God's prescribed method (1 Chr. 15:12, 13, page 398). A man named Uzzah died for touching it (Num. 4:15, page 142; cf. 2 Sam. 6:6, 7, page 304). Later it was moved according to God's command, and joy filled the city (1 Chr. 16:1-6, page 398).

(7) It was brought into Solomon's temple about 960 B.C. Solomon moved the ark and vessels of the Lord from the southwest hill of Jerusalem (Zion) to the newly built temple on the western plateau of the city (Mt. Moriah). At this time, only the two tablets of the law were found in the ark. The bowl of manna and Aaron's rod that budded were no longer in it (2 Chr. 5:9, 10, page 414). Probably the remaining articles of the tabernacle—the tentage, poles, loops for carrying, etc.—were at this time sealed inside the temple, perhaps in the 10-cubit-high space between the Holy Place and the roof. God's glory and presence then filled the temple, as it had five centuries before when the tabernacle was filled with the presence of God (1 Kin. 8:10, 11, page 334). The world had to wait almost another thousand years for the promised greater glory of the Messiah to enter the temple (Mal. 3:1, page 924).

See Hebrews 9:23, 24, page 1244, for **Point 35-B: The Pattern of the Tabernacle.**

the sides of the ark, that the ark may be carried by them.

15 R"The poles shall be in the rings of the ark; they shall not be taken from it.   1 Kin. 8:8

16 "And you shall put into the ark Rthe Testimony which I will give you.   Heb. 9:4

17 R"You shall make a mercy seat of pure gold; two and a half cubits *shall be* its length and a cubit and a half its width.   Ex. 37:6

18 "And you shall make two cherubim of gold; of hammered work you shall make them at the two ends of the mercy seat.

19 "Make one cherub at one end, and the other cherub at the other end; you shall make the cherubim at the two ends of it *of one piece* with the mercy seat.

20 "And Rthe cherubim shall stretch out *their* wings above, covering the mercy seat with their wings, and they shall face one another; the faces of the cherubim *shall be* toward the mercy seat.   1 Kin. 8:7

21 "You shall put the mercy seat on top of the ark, and Rin the ark you shall put the Testimony that I will give you.   Ex. 25:16

22 "And there I will meet with you, and I will speak with you from above the mercy seat, from Rbetween the two cherubim which *are* on the ark of the Testimony, about everything which I will give you in commandment to the children of Israel.   Num. 7:89

The Table for the Showbread

23 "You shall also make a table of acacia wood; two cubits *shall be* its length, a cubit its width, and a cubit and a half its height.

24 "And you shall overlay it with pure gold, and make a molding of gold all around.

25 "You shall make for it a frame of a handbreadth all around, and you shall make a gold molding for the frame all around.

26 "And you shall make for it four rings of gold, and put the rings on the four corners that *are* at its four legs.

27 "The rings shall be close to the frame, as holders for the poles to bear the table.

28 "And you shall make the poles of acacia wood, and overlay them with gold, that the table may be carried with them.

29 "You shall make Rits dishes, its pans, its pitchers, and its bowls for pouring. You shall make them of pure gold.   Ex. 37:16

30 "And you shall set the Rshowbread on the table before Me always.   Lev. 24:5-9

The Gold Lampstand

31 R"You shall also make a lampstand of pure gold; the lampstand shall be of hammered work. Its shaft, its branches, its bowls, its *ornamental* knobs, and flowers shall be *of one piece.*   Zech. 4:2

32 "And six branches shall come out of its sides: three branches of the lampstand out of one side, and three branches of the lampstand out of the other side.

33 R"Three bowls *shall be* made like almond *blossoms* on one branch, *with* an *ornamental* knob and a flower, and three bowls made like almond *blossoms* on the other branch, *with* an *ornamental* knob and a flower—and so for the six branches that come out of the lampstand.   Ex. 37:19

34 "On the lampstand itself four bowls *shall be* made like almond *blossoms, each with* its *ornamental* knob and flower.

35 "And *there shall be* a knob under the *first* two branches of the same, a knob under the *second* two branches of the same, and a knob under the *third* two branches of the same, according to the six branches that extend from the lampstand.

36 "Their knobs and their branches *shall be of one piece*; all of it *shall be* one hammered piece of pure gold.

37 "You shall make seven lamps for it, and Rthey shall arrange its lamps so that they Rgive light in front of it.   Lev. 24:3, 4 • Num. 8:2

38 "And its wick-trimmers and their trays *shall be* of pure gold.

39 "It shall be made of a Ttalent of pure gold, with all these utensils. $5,760,000

40 "And Rsee to it that you make *them* according to the pattern which was shown you on the mountain.   [Heb. 8:5]

The Tabernacle

26 "Moreover Ryou shall make the tabernacle *with* ten curtains *of* fine woven linen and blue, purple, and scarlet *thread*; with artistic designs of cherubim you shall weave them.   Ex. 36:8-19

2 "The length of each curtain *shall be* twenty-eight cubits, and the width of each curtain four cubits. And every one of the curtains shall have the same measurements.

3 "Five curtains shall be coupled to one another, and *the other* five curtains *shall be* coupled to one another.

4 "And you shall make loops of blue *yarn* on the edge of the curtain on the selvedge of *one* set, and likewise you shall do on the outer edge of *the other* curtain of the second set.

5 "Fifty loops you shall make in the one curtain, and fifty loops you shall make on the edge of the curtain that *is* on the end of the second set, that the loops may be clasped to one another.

6 "And you shall make fifty clasps of gold, and couple the curtains together with the clasps, so that it may be one tabernacle.

7 R"You shall also make curtains of goats' *hair*, to be a tent over the tabernacle. You shall make eleven curtains.   Ex. 36:14

8 "The length of each curtain *shall be* Tthirty cubits, and the width of each curtain Tfour cubits; and the eleven curtains shall all have the same measurements.   45 ft. • 6 ft.

9 "And you shall couple five curtains by

themselves and six curtains by themselves, and you shall double over the sixth curtain at the forefront of the tent.

10 "You shall make fifty loops on the edge of the curtain that is outermost in *one* set, and fifty loops on the edge of the curtain of the second set.

11 "And you shall make fifty bronze clasps, put the clasps into the loops, and couple the tent together, that it may be one.

12 "The remnant that remains of the curtains of the tent, the half curtain that remains, shall hang over the back of the tabernacle.

13 "And a ᵀcubit on one side and a cubit on the other side, of what remains of the length of the curtains of the tent, shall hang over the sides of the tabernacle, on this side and on that side, to cover it.   18 in.

14 "You shall also make a covering of ram skins dyed red for the tent, and a covering of badger skins above that.

15 "And for the tabernacle you shall make the boards of acacia wood, standing upright.

16 ᵀ"Ten cubits *shall be* the length of a board, and a ᵀcubit and a half *shall be* the width of each board.   15 ft. • 27 in.

17 "Two ᵀtenons *shall be* in each board for binding one to another. Thus you shall make for all the boards of the tabernacle.   tabs

18 "And you shall make the boards for the tabernacle, twenty boards for the south side.

19 "You shall make forty sockets of silver under the twenty boards: two sockets under each of the boards for its two tenons.

20 "And for the second side of the tabernacle, the north side, *there shall be* twenty boards

21 "and their forty sockets of silver: two sockets under each of the boards.

22 "For the far side of the tabernacle, westward, you shall make six boards.

23 "And you shall also make two boards for the two back corners of the tabernacle.

24 "They shall be coupled together at the bottom and they shall be coupled together at the top by one ring. Thus it shall be for both of them. They shall be for the two corners.

25 "So there shall be eight boards with their sockets of silver—sixteen sockets—two sockets under each of the boards.

26 "And you shall make bars of acacia wood: five for the boards on one side of the tabernacle,

27 "five bars for the boards on the other side of the tabernacle, and five bars for the boards of the side of the tabernacle, for the far side westward.

28 "The ᴿmiddle bar shall pass through the midst of the boards from end to end.   Ex. 36:33

29 "You shall overlay the boards with gold, make their rings of gold *as* holders for the bars, and overlay the bars with gold.

30 "And you shall raise up the tabernacle

ᴿaccording to its pattern which you were shown on the mountain.   Acts 7:44

31 ᴿ"You shall make a veil woven of blue, purple, and scarlet *thread*, and fine woven linen. It shall be woven with an artistic design of cherubim.   Matt. 27:51

32 "You shall hang it upon the four pillars of acacia *wood* overlaid with gold. Their hooks *shall be* gold, upon four sockets of silver.

33 "And you shall hang the veil from the clasps. Then you shall bring the ark of the Testimony in there, behind the veil. The veil shall be a divider for you between ᴿthe holy *place* and the Most Holy.   Heb. 9:2, 3

34 "You shall put the mercy seat upon the ark of the Testimony in the Most Holy.

35 "You shall set the table outside the veil, and the lampstand across from the table on the side of the tabernacle toward the south; and you shall put the table on the north side.

36 ᴿ"You shall make a screen for the door of the tabernacle, *woven of* blue, purple, and scarlet *thread*, and fine woven linen, made by a weaver.   Ex. 36:37

37 "And you shall make for the screen five pillars of acacia *wood*, and overlay them with gold; their hooks *shall be* gold, and you shall cast five sockets of bronze for them.

The Altar of Burnt Offering

27 "You shall make ᴿan altar of acacia wood, ᵀfive cubits long and five cubits wide—the altar shall be square—and its height *shall be* three cubits.   Ex. 38:1 • 7.5 ft.

2 "You shall make its horns on its four corners; its horns shall be of one piece with it. And you shall overlay it with bronze.

3 "Also you shall make its pans to receive its ashes, and its shovels and its basins and its forks and its firepans; you shall make all its utensils of bronze.

4 "You shall make a grate for it, a network of bronze; and on the network you shall make four bronze rings at its four corners.

5 "You shall put it under the rim of the altar beneath, that the network may be midway up the altar.

6 "And you shall make poles for the altar, poles of acacia wood, and overlay them with bronze.

7 "The poles shall be put in the rings, and the poles shall be on the two sides of the altar to bear it.

8 "You shall make it hollow with boards; ᴿas it was shown you on the mountain, so shall they make *it*.   Ex. 25:40; 26:30

The Court of the Tabernacle

9 "You shall also make the court of the tabernacle. For the south side *there shall be* hangings for the court *made of* fine woven linen, one hundred cubits long for one side.

10 "And its twenty pillars and their twenty

sockets *shall be* bronze. The hooks of the pillars and their bands *shall be* silver.

11 "Likewise along the length of the north side *there shall be* hangings ᵀone hundred *cubits* long, with its twenty pillars and their twenty sockets of bronze, and the hooks of the pillars and their bands of silver.   150 ft.

12 "And along the width of the court on the west side *shall be* hangings of fifty cubits, with their ten pillars and their ten sockets.

13 "The width of the court on the east side *shall be* ᵀfifty cubits.   75 ft.

14 "The hangings on *one* side *of the gate shall be* ᵀfifteen cubits, *with* their three pillars and their three sockets.   22.5 ft.

15 "And on the other side *shall be* hangings of ᵀfifteen *cubits*, *with* their three pillars and their three sockets.   22.5 ft.

16 "For the gate of the court *there shall be* a screen ᵀtwenty cubits long, *woven of* blue, purple, and scarlet *thread*, and fine woven linen, made by a weaver. It *shall have* four pillars and four sockets.   30 ft.

17 "All the pillars around the court shall have bands of silver; their ᴿhooks *shall be* of silver and their sockets of bronze.   Ex. 38:19

18 "The length of the court *shall be* one hundred cubits, the width fifty throughout, and the height five cubits, *woven of* fine linen thread, and its sockets of bronze.

19 "All the utensils of the tabernacle for all its service, all its pegs, and all the pegs of the court, *shall be* of bronze.

The Care of the Lampstand

20 "And ᴿyou shall command the children of Israel that they bring you pure oil of pressed olives for the light, to cause the lamp to ᵀburn continually.   Lev. 24:1-4 • Lit. *ascend*

21 "In the tabernacle of meeting, outside the veil which *is* before the Testimony, ᴿAaron and his sons shall tend it from evening until morning before the Lᴏʀᴅ. *It shall be* a statute forever to their generations on behalf of the children of Israel.   Ex. 30:8

Garments for the Priesthood

28 "Now take Aaron your brother, and his sons with him, from among the children of Israel, that he may minister to Me as priest, Aaron *and* Aaron's sons: Nadab, Abihu, ᴿEleazar, and Ithamar.   Ex. 6:23

2 "And you shall make holy garments for Aaron your brother, for glory and for beauty.

3 "So ᴿyou shall speak to all *who are* gifted artisans, ᴿwhom I have filled with the spirit of wisdom, that they may make Aaron's garments, to consecrate him, that he may minister to Me as priest.   Ex. 31:6; 36:1 • Ex. 31:3; 35:30, 31

4 "And these *are* the garments which they shall make: a breastplate, an ᵀephod, a robe, a skillfully woven tunic, a turban, and a sash. So they shall make holy garments for Aaron

your brother and his sons, that he may minister to Me as priest.   An ornamented vest

The Ephod

5 "They shall take the gold, blue, purple, and scarlet *thread*, and the fine linen,

6 ᴿ"and they shall make the ephod of gold, blue, purple, *and* scarlet *thread*, and fine woven linen, artistically worked.   Ex. 39:2-7

7 "It shall have two shoulder straps joined at its two edges, and *so* it shall be joined together.

8 "And the intricately woven band of the ephod, which *is* on it, shall be of the same workmanship, *made of* gold, blue, purple, and scarlet *thread*, and fine woven linen.

9 "Then you shall take two onyx ᴿstones and engrave on them the names of the sons of Israel: Ex. 35:27

10 "six of their names on one stone and six names on the other stone, in order of their ᴿbirth.   Gen. 29:31—30:24

11 "With the work of an ᴿengraver in stone, *like* the engravings of a signet, you shall engrave the two stones with the names of the sons of Israel. You shall set them in settings of gold.   Ex. 35:35

12 "And you shall put the two stones on the shoulders of the ephod *as* memorial stones for the sons of Israel. So Aaron shall bear their names before the Lᴏʀᴅ on his two shoulders ᴿas a memorial.   Josh. 4:7

13 "You shall also make settings of gold,

14 "and you shall make two chains of pure gold like braided cords, and fasten the braided chains to the settings.

The Breastplate

15 ᴿ"You shall make the breastplate of judgment. Artistically woven according to the workmanship of the ephod you shall make it: of gold, blue, purple, and scarlet *thread*, and fine woven linen, you shall make it.   Ex. 39:8-21

16 "It shall be doubled into a square: a ᵀspan *shall be* its length, and a span *shall be* its width.   9 in.

17 ᴿ"And you shall put settings of stones in it, four rows of stones: The *first* row *shall be* a ᵀsardius, a topaz, and an emerald; *this shall be* the first row;   Ex. 39:10 • Or *ruby*

18 "the second row *shall be* a turquoise, a sapphire, and a diamond;

19 "the third row, a ᵀjacinth, an agate, and an amethyst;   Or *amber*

20 "and the fourth row, a ᵀberyl, an ᵀonyx, and a jasper. They shall be set in gold settings.   Or *yellow jasper* • Or *carnelian*

21 "And the stones shall have the names of the sons of Israel, twelve according to their names, *like* the engravings of a signet, each one with its own name; they shall be according to the twelve tribes.

22 "You shall make chains for the breastplate at the end, like braided cords of pure gold.

23 "And you shall make two rings of gold for the breastplate, and put the two rings on the two ends of the breastplate.

24 "Then you shall put the two braided *chains* of gold in the two rings which are on the ends of the breastplate;

25 "and the *other* two ends of the two braided *chains* you shall fasten to the two settings, and put them on the shoulder straps of the ephod in the front.

26 "You shall make two rings of gold, and put them on the two ends of the breastplate, on the edge of it, which is on the inner side of the ephod.

27 "And two *other* rings of gold you shall make, and put them on the two shoulder straps, underneath the ephod toward its front, right at the seam above the Tintricately woven band of the ephod.   *ingenious work of*

28 "They shall bind the breastplate by means of its rings to the rings of the ephod, using a blue cord, so that it is above the intricately woven band of the ephod, and so that the breastplate does not come loose from the ephod.

29 "So Aaron shall Rbear the names of the sons of Israel on the breastplate of judgment over his heart, when he goes into the holy *place*, as a memorial before the LORD continually.   Ex. 28:12

30 "And you shall put in the breastplate of judgment the *Urim and the Thummim, and they shall be over Aaron's heart when he goes in before the LORD. So Aaron shall bear the judgment of the children of Israel over his heart before the LORD continually.

Other Priestly Garments

31 R"You shall make the robe of the ephod all of blue.   Ex. 39:22-26

32 "There shall be an opening for his head in the middle of it; it shall have a woven binding all around its opening, like the opening in a coat of mail, so that it does not tear.

33 "And upon its hem you shall make pomegranates of blue, purple, and scarlet, all around its hem, and bells of gold between them all around:

34 "a golden bell and a pomegranate, a golden bell and a pomegranate, upon the hem of the robe all around.

35 "And it shall be upon Aaron when he ministers, and its sound will be heard when he goes into the holy *place* before the LORD and when he comes out, that he may not die.

36 R"You shall also make a plate of pure gold and engrave on it, *like* the engraving of a signet: Ex. 39:30, 31

28:30 Lit. *Lights and the Perfections*

HOLINESS TO THE LORD.

37 "And you shall put it on a blue cord, that it may be on the turban; it shall be on the front of the turban.

38 "So it shall be on Aaron's forehead, that Aaron may Rbear the iniquity of the holy things which the children of Israel hallow in all their Tholy gifts; and it shall always be on his forehead, that they may be accepted before the LORD.   [1 Pet. 2:24] • *sacred*

39 "You shall Rskillfully weave the tunic of fine linen *thread*, you shall make the turban of fine linen, and you shall make the sash of woven work.   Ex. 35:35; 39:27-29

40 R"For Aaron's sons you shall make tunics, and you shall make sashes for them. And you shall make Thats for them, for glory and beauty.   Ezek. 44:17, 18 • *headgear or turbans*

41 "So you shall put them on Aaron your brother and on his sons with him. You shall Ranoint them, Rconsecrate them, and Tsanctify them, that they may minister to Me as priests.   Lev. 10:7 • Lev. 8 • *set them apart*

42 "And you shall make for them linen trousers to cover their nakedness; they shall Treach from the waist to the thighs.   Lit. *be*

43 "They shall be on Aaron and on his sons when they come into the tabernacle of meeting, or when they come near the altar to minister in the holy *place*, that they do not incur iniquity and die. It *shall be* a statute forever to him and his descendants after him.

Aaron and His Sons Consecrated

29 "And this is what you shall do to them to hallow them for ministering to Me as priests: RTake one young bull and two rams without blemish,   [Heb. 7:26-28]

2 "and Runleavened bread, unleavened cakes mixed with oil, and unleavened wafers anointed with oil (you shall make them of wheat flour).   Lev. 2:4; 6:19-23

3 "You shall put them in one basket and bring them in the basket, with the bull and the two rams.

4 "And Aaron and his sons you shall bring to the door of the tabernacle of meeting, Rand you shall wash them with water.   Ex. 40:12

5 R"Then you shall take the garments, put the tunic on Aaron, and the robe of the ephod, the ephod, and the breastplate, and gird him with Rthe intricately woven band of the ephod.   Ex. 28:2 • Ex. 28:8

6 R"You shall put the turban on his head, and put the holy crown on the turban. Lev. 8:9

7 "And you shall take the anointing oil, pour *it* on his head, and anoint him.

8 "Then Ryou shall bring his sons and put tunics on them.   Ex. 28:39, 40

9 "And you shall gird them with sashes, Aaron and his sons, and put the hats on them. RThe priesthood shall be theirs for a

perpetual statute. So you shall ᴿconsecrate Aaron and his sons.   Num. 18:7; 25:13 · Ex. 28:41

10 "You shall also have the bull brought before the tabernacle of meeting, and ᴿAaron and his sons shall put their hands on the head of the bull.   Lev. 1:4; 8:14

11 "Then you shall kill the bull before the LORD, by the door of the tabernacle of meeting.

12 "You shall take some of the blood of the bull and put it on ᴿthe horns of the altar with your finger, and ᴿpour all the blood beside the base of the altar.   Lev. 8:15 · Ex. 27:2; 30:2

13 "And you shall take all the fat that covers the entrails, the fatty lobe attached to the liver, and the two kidneys and the fat that is on them, and burn them on the altar.

14 "But ᴿthe flesh of the bull, with its skin and its offal, you shall burn with fire outside the camp. It is a sin offering.   Lev. 4:11, 12, 21

15 ᴿ"You shall also take one ram, and Aaron and his sons shall ᴿput their hands on the head of the ram;   Lev. 8:18 · Lev. 1:4-9

16 "and you shall kill the ram, and you shall take its blood and ᴿsprinkle it all around on the altar.   Ex. 24:6

17 "Then you shall cut the ram in pieces, wash its entrails and its legs, and put them with its pieces and with its head.

18 "And you shall burn the whole ram on the altar. It is a ᴿburnt offering to the LORD; it is a sweet aroma, an offering made by fire to the LORD.   Ex. 20:24

19 ᴿ"You shall also take the other ram, and Aaron and his sons shall put their hands on the head of the ram.   Lev. 8:22

20 "Then you shall kill the ram, and take some of its blood and put it on the tip of the right ear of Aaron and on the tip of the right ear of his sons, on the thumb of their right hand and on the big toe of their right foot, and sprinkle the blood all around on the altar.

21 "And you shall take some of the blood that is on the altar, and some of ᴿthe anointing oil, and sprinkle it on Aaron and on his garments, on his sons and on the garments of his sons with him; and ᴿhe and his garments shall be hallowed, and his sons and his sons' garments with him.   Ex. 30:25, 31 · [Heb. 9:22]

22 "Also you shall take the fat of the ram, the fat tail, the fat that covers the entrails, the fatty lobe attached to the liver, the two kidneys and the fat on them, the right thigh (for it is a ram of consecration),

23 "one loaf of bread, one cake made with oil, and one wafer from the basket of the unleavened bread that is before the LORD;

24 "and you shall put all these in the hands of Aaron and in the hands of his sons, and you shall ᴿwave them as a wave offering before the LORD.   Lev. 7:30; 10:14

25 "You shall receive them back from their hands and burn them on the altar as a burnt

offering, as a sweet aroma before the LORD. It is an offering made by fire to the LORD.

26 "Then you shall take ᴿthe breast of the ram of Aaron's consecration and wave it as a wave offering before the LORD; and it shall be your portion.   Lev. 7:31, 34; 8:29

27 "And from the ram of the consecration you shall consecrate the breast of the wave offering which is waved, and the thigh of the heave offering which is raised, of that which is for Aaron and of that which is for his sons.

28 "It shall be from the children of Israel for Aaron and his sons ᴿby a statute forever. For it is a heave offering; it shall be a heave offering from the children of Israel from the sacrifices of their peace offerings, that is, their heave offering to the LORD.   Lev. 10:15

29 "And the holy garments of Aaron shall be his sons' after him, ᴿto be anointed in them and to be consecrated in them.   Num. 18:8

30 "That son who becomes priest in his place shall put them on for ᴿseven days, when he enters the tabernacle of meeting to minister in the ᵀholy place.   Lev. 8:35 · sanctuary

31 "And you shall take the ram of the consecration and ᴿboil its flesh in the holy place.   Lev. 8:31

32 "Then Aaron and his sons shall eat the flesh of the ram, and the ᴿbread that is in the basket, by the door of the tabernacle of meeting.   Matt. 12:4

33 "They shall eat those things with which the atonement was made, to consecrate and to sanctify them; ᴿbut an outsider shall not eat them, because they are holy.   Lev. 22:10

34 "And if any of the flesh of the consecration offerings, or of the bread, remains until the morning, then ᴿyou shall burn the remainder with fire. It shall not be eaten, because it is holy.   Lev. 7:18; 8:32

35 "Thus you shall do to Aaron and his sons, according to all that I have commanded you. Seven days you shall consecrate them.

36 "And you shall offer a bull every day as a sin offering for atonement. You shall cleanse the altar when you make atonement for it, and you shall anoint it to sanctify it.

37 "Seven days you shall make atonement for the altar and sanctify it. And the altar shall be most holy. ᴿWhatever touches the altar must be holy.   Num. 4:15, Hag. 2:11-13

The Daily Offerings

38 "Now this is what you shall offer on the altar: ᴿtwo lambs of the first year, ᴿday by day continually.   Num. 28:3-31; 29:6-38 · Dan. 12:11

39 "One lamb you shall offer ᴿin the morning, and the other lamb you shall offer ᵀat twilight.   Ezek. 46:13-15 · Lit. between the two evenings

40 "With the one lamb shall be ᵀone-tenth of an ephah of flour mixed with ᵀone-fourth of a hin of pressed oil, and one-fourth of a hin of wine as a drink offering.   2.087 qt. · 1 qt.

41 "And the other lamb you shall offer ᵀat

twilight; and you shall offer with it the grain offering and the drink offering, as in the morning, for a sweet aroma, an offering made by fire to the LORD.   Lit. *between the two evenings*

42 "This shall be a continual burnt offering throughout your generations *at* the door of the tabernacle of meeting before the LORD, where I will meet you to speak with you.

43 "And there I will meet with the children of Israel, and *the tabernacle* ᴿshall be sanctified by My glory.   1 Kin. 8:11

44 "So I will consecrate the tabernacle of meeting and the altar. I will also ᴿconsecrate both Aaron and his sons to minister to Me as priests.   Lev. 21:15

45 ᴿ"I will dwell among the children of Israel and will be their God.   [Rev. 21:3]

46 "And they shall know that I *am* the LORD their God, who ᴿbrought them up out of the land of Egypt, that I may dwell among them. I *am* the LORD their God.   Lev. 11:45

The Altar of Incense

30 "You shall make ᴿan altar to burn incense on; you shall make it of acacia wood.   Ex. 37:25–29

2 "A ᵀcubit *shall be* its length and a cubit its width—it shall be square—and ᵀtwo cubits *shall be* its height. Its horns *shall be* of one piece with it.   18 in. • 3 ft.

3 "And you shall overlay its top, its sides all around, and its horns with pure gold; and you shall make for it a ᵀmolding of gold all around.   *border*

4 "Two gold rings you shall make for it, under the molding on both its sides. You shall place *them* on its two sides, and they will be holders for the poles with which to bear it.

5 "You shall make the poles of acacia wood, and overlay them with gold.

6 "And you shall put it before the veil that *is* before the ark of the Testimony, before the ᴿmercy seat that *is* over the Testimony, where I will meet with you.   Ex. 25:21, 22

7 "Aaron shall burn on it ᴿsweet incense every morning; when ᴿhe tends the lamps, he shall burn incense on it.   1 Sam. 2:28 • Ex. 27:20, 21

8 "And when Aaron lights the lamps ᵀat twilight, he shall burn incense on it, a perpetual incense before the LORD throughout your generations.   Lit. *between the two evenings*

9 "You shall not offer ᴿstrange incense on it, or a burnt offering, or a grain offering; nor shall you pour a drink offering on it.   Lev. 10:1

10 "And ᴿAaron shall make atonement upon its horns once a year with the blood of the sin offering of atonement; once a year he shall make atonement upon it throughout your generations. It *is* most holy to the LORD."   Lev. 16:3–34

The Ransom Money

11 Then the LORD spoke to Moses, saying:

12 "When you take the census of the chil-dren of Israel for their number, then every man shall give ᴿaᵀ ransom for himself to the LORD, when you number them, that there may be no plague among them when *you* number them.   [1 Pet. 1:18, 19] • *the price of a life*

13 "This is what everyone among those who are numbered shall give: half a shekel according to the shekel of the sanctuary (a shekel *is* twenty gerahs). ᴿThe ᵀhalf-shekel *shall be* an offering to the LORD.   Ex. 38:26 • $64

14 "Everyone included among those who are numbered, from twenty years old and above, shall give an offering to the LORD.

15 "The ᴿrich shall not give more and the poor shall not give less than ᵀhalf a shekel, when *you* give an offering to the LORD, to make atonement for yourselves.   [Eph. 6:9] • $64

16 "And you shall take the atonement money of the children of Israel, and ᴿshall ᵀappoint it for the service of the tabernacle of meeting, that it may be a memorial for the children of Israel before the LORD, to make atonement for yourselves."   Ex. 38:25–31 • *give*

The Bronze Laver

17 Then the LORD spoke to Moses, saying:

18 ᴿ"You shall also make a ᵀlaver of bronze, with its base also of bronze, for washing. You shall ᴿput it between the tabernacle of meeting and the altar. And you shall put water in it,   Ex. 38:8 • *basin* • Ex. 40:30

19 "for Aaron and his sons shall wash their hands and their feet in water from it.

20 "When they go into the tabernacle of meeting, or when they come near the altar to minister, to burn an offering made by fire to the LORD, they shall wash with water, lest they die.

21 "So they shall wash their hands and their feet, lest they die. And it shall be a statute forever to them—to him and his descendants throughout their generations."

The Holy Anointing Oil

22 Moreover the LORD spoke to Moses, saying:

23 "Also take for yourself quality spices—five hundred *shekels* of liquid myrrh, half as much sweet-smelling cinnamon (two hundred and fifty *shekels*), two hundred and fifty *shekels* of sweet-smelling ᴿcane,   Song 4:14

24 ᵀ"five hundred *shekels* of ᴿcassia, according to the shekel of the sanctuary, and a ᴿhinᵀ of olive oil.   12.5 lb • Ps. 45:8 • Ex. 29:40 • 1 gal

25 "And you shall make from these a holy anointing oil, an ointment compounded according to the art of the perfumer. It shall be ᴿa holy anointing oil.   Ex. 37:29; 40:9

26 "With it you shall anoint the tabernacle of meeting and the ark of the Testimony;

27 "the table and all its utensils, the lampstand and its utensils, and the altar of incense;

28 "the altar of burnt offering with all its utensils, and the laver and its base.

29 "You shall consecrate them, that they may be most holy; ᴿwhatever touches them must be holy.   Ex. 29:37; Num. 4:15; Hag. 2:11–13

30 ᴿ"And you shall anoint Aaron and his sons, and consecrate them, that *they* may minister to Me as priests.   Lev. 8:12

31 "And you shall speak to the children of Israel, saying: 'This shall be a holy anointing oil to Me throughout your generations.

32 'It shall not be poured on man's flesh; nor shall you make *any other* like it, according to its composition. ᴿIt *is* holy, *and* it shall be holy to you.   Ex. 30:25, 37

33 'Whoever ᵀcompounds *any* like it, or whoever puts *any* of it on an outsider, ᴿshall be cut off from his people.' "   *mixes* • Gen. 17:14

The Incense

34 And the Lᴏʀᴅ said to Moses: "Take sweet spices, stacte and onycha and galbanum, and pure frankincense with *these* sweet spices; there shall be equal amounts of each.

35 "You shall make of these an incense, a compound ᴿaccording to the art of the perfumer, salted, pure, *and* holy.   Ex. 30:25

36 "And you shall beat *some* of it very fine, and put some of it before the Testimony in the tabernacle of meeting where I will meet with you. It shall be most holy to you.

37 "But *as for* the incense which you shall make, you shall not make any for yourselves, according to its ᵀcomposition. It shall be to you holy for the Lᴏʀᴅ.   Lit. *proportion*

38 ᴿ"Whoever makes *any* like it, to smell it, he shall be cut off from his people."   Ex. 30:33

Artisans for Building the Tabernacle

31 Then the Lᴏʀᴅ spoke to Moses, saying:

2 ᴿ"See, I have called by name Bezalel the ᴿson of Uri, the son of Hur, of the tribe of Judah.   Ex. 35:30—36:1 • 1 Chr. 2:20

3 "And I have filled him with the Spirit of God, in wisdom, in understanding, in knowledge, and in all *manner of* workmanship,

4 "to design artistic works, to work in gold, in silver, in bronze,

5 "in cutting jewels for setting, in carving wood, and to work in all *manner of* workmanship.

6 "And I, indeed I, have appointed with him Aholiab the son of Ahisamach, of the tribe of Dan; and I have put wisdom in the hearts of all the gifted artisans, that they may make all that I have commanded you:

7 "the tabernacle of meeting, the ark of the Testimony and the mercy seat that *is* on it, and all the furniture of the tabernacle—

8 ᴿ"the table and its utensils, ᴿthe pure *gold* lampstand with all its utensils, the altar of incense,   Ex. 37:10–16 • Ex. 37:17–24

9 "the altar of burnt offering with all its utensils, and the laver and its base—

10 "the *garments of ministry, the holy garments for Aaron the priest and the garments of his sons, to minister as priests,

11 "and the anointing oil and sweet incense for the holy *place*. According to all that I have commanded you they shall do."

The Sabbath Law

12 And the Lᴏʀᴅ spoke to Moses, saying,

13 "Speak also to the children of Israel, saying: 'Surely My Sabbaths you shall keep, for it *is* a sign between Me and you throughout your generations, that *you* may know that I *am* the Lᴏʀᴅ who sanctifies you.

14 'You shall keep the Sabbath, therefore, for *it is* holy to you. Everyone who profanes it shall surely be put to death; for ᴿwhoever does *any* work on it, that person shall be cut off from among his people.   Num. 15:32–36

15 'Work shall be done for six days, but the seventh *is* the Sabbath of rest, holy to the Lᴏʀᴅ. Whoever does *any* work on the Sabbath day, he shall surely be put to death.

16 'Therefore the children of Israel shall keep the Sabbath, to observe the Sabbath throughout their generations *as* a perpetual covenant.

17 'It *is* ᴿa sign between Me and the children of Israel forever; for ᴿin six days the Lᴏʀᴅ made the heavens and the earth, and on the seventh day He rested and was refreshed.' "   Ex. 31:13 • Gen. 1:31; 2:2, 3

18 And when He had made an end of speaking with him on Mount Sinai, He gave Moses two tablets of the Testimony, tablets of stone, written with the finger of God.

The Gold Calf

32 Now when the people saw that Moses delayed coming down from the mountain, the people ᴿgathered together to Aaron, and said to him, ᴿ"Come, make us gods that shall go before us; for *as for* this Moses, the man who brought us up out of the land of Egypt, we do not know what has become of him."   Ex. 17:1-3 • Acts 7:40

2 And Aaron said to them, "Break off the ᴿgolden earrings which *are* in the ears of your wives, your sons, and your daughters, and bring *them* to me."   Ex. 11:2; 35:22

3 So all the people broke off the golden earrings which *were* in their ears, and brought *them* to Aaron.

4 And he received *the* gold from their hand, and he fashioned it with an engraving tool, and made a molded calf. Then they said, "This *is* your god, O Israel, that ᴿbrought you out of the land of Egypt!"   Ex. 29:45, 46

5 So when Aaron saw *it*, he built an altar

31:10 Or *woven garments*

before it. And Aaron made a proclamation and said, "Tomorrow is a feast to the LORD."

6 Then they rose early on the next day, offered burnt offerings, and brought peace offerings; and the people ᴿsat down to eat and drink, and rose up to play.　　Num. 25:2

7 And the LORD said to Moses, ᴿ"Go, get down! For your people whom you brought out of the land of Egypt ᴿhave corrupted themselves.　　Deut. 9:8-21 • Gen. 6:11, 12

8 "They have turned aside quickly out of the way which I commanded them. They have made themselves a molded calf, and worshiped it and sacrificed to it, and said, ᴿ'This is your god, O Israel, that brought you out of the land of Egypt!' "　　1 Kin. 12:28

9 And the LORD said to Moses, ᴿ"I have seen this people, and indeed it is a ᵀstiff-necked people!　　[Acts 7:51] • stubborn

10 "Now therefore, let Me alone, that ᴿMy wrath may burn hot against them and I may ᵀconsume them. And ᴿI will make of you a great nation."　　Ex. 22:24 • destroy • Num. 14:12

▼ 31-C. A Prayer of Intercession

11 Then Moses pleaded with the LORD his God, and said: "LORD, why does Your wrath burn hot against Your people whom You have brought out of the land of Egypt with great power and with a mighty hand?

12 ᴿ"Why should the Egyptians speak, and say, 'He brought them out to harm them, to kill them in the mountains, and to consume them from the face of the earth'? Turn from Your fierce wrath, and ᴿrelent from this harm to Your people.　　Num. 14:13-19 • Ex. 32:14

13 "Remember Abraham, Isaac, and Israel, Your servants, to whom You ᴿswore by Your own self, and said to them, ᴿ'I will multiply your descendants as the stars of heaven; and all this land that I have spoken of I give to your descendants, and they shall inherit it forever.' "　　[Heb. 6:13] • Gen. 12:7; 13:15; 15:7, 18; 22:17

▲ 14 So the LORD relented from the harm which He said He would do to His people.

15 And ᴿMoses turned and went down from the mountain, and the two tablets of the Testimony were in his hand. The tablets were written on both sides; on the one side and on the other they were written.　　Deut. 9:15

16 Now the ᴿtablets were the work of God, and the writing was the writing of God engraved on the tablets.　　Ex. 31:18

17 And when Joshua heard the noise of the people as they shouted, he said to Moses, "There is a noise of war in the camp."

18 But he said:

"It is not the noise of the shout of
　victory,
Nor the noise of the cry of defeat,
But the sound of singing I hear."

19 So it was, as soon as he came near the camp, that ᴿhe saw the calf and the dancing. So Moses' anger became hot, and he cast the tablets out of his hands and broke them at the foot of the mountain.　　Deut. 9:16, 17

20 ᴿThen he took the calf which they had made, burned it in the fire, and ground it to powder; and he scattered it on the water and made the children of Israel drink it.　　Deut. 9:21

21 And Moses said to Aaron, ᴿ"What did this people do to you that you have brought so great a sin upon them?"　　Gen. 26:10

22 So Aaron said, "Do not let the anger of my lord become hot. ᴿYou know the people, that they are set on evil.　　Deut. 9:24

23 "For they said to me, 'Make us gods that shall go before us; as for this Moses, the man who brought us out of the land of Egypt, we do not know what has become of him.'

24 "And I said to them, 'Whoever has any gold, let them break it off.' So they gave it to me, and I cast it into the fire, and this calf came out."

25 Now when Moses saw that the people were ᴿunrestrained (for Aaron ᴿhad not restrained them, to their shame among their enemies),　　Ex. 33:4, 5 • 2 Chr. 28:19

26 then Moses stood in the entrance of the

31-C. A Prayer of Intercession (Exodus 32:11–14)—When Moses lingered with the Lord on Mt. Sinai for days, the children of Israel grew impatient and had Aaron build them a golden calf, which they worshiped as a god (Ex. 32:1-6, page 91). In reaction, God offered to destroy these obstinate people for Moses and to build a new nation from the line of Moses, just as the present one had descended from Abraham (vv. 9, 10, above).

To this, Moses responded with this wonderful prayer of intercession, a prayer to God on behalf of another. He pleaded with God in the following three appeals:

(1) Please do not destroy these people, because You are their Savior (v. 11). Paul also prayed for backslidden Israel (Rom. 10:1-4, page 1140).

(2) If Your people are allowed to perish, the pagans will blaspheme Your name and reputation (v. 12). (This was God's argument in Ezekiel 36:16–24, page 814; cf. Ex. 32:16, above.)

(3) You cannot go back on Your promises to bless them and to give them the land You promised to Abraham, Isaac and Jacob (v. 13). Paul used the same argument in Romans 11:26, 29 (page 1141).

This prayer of Moses (and God knew that Moses would respond in this way) was indeed effective, and the nation was spared (v. 14). No wonder James declared, "The effective, fervent prayer of a righteous man avails much" (James 5:16, page 1261). Let us also pray in intercession for one another.

See Exodus 32:30–32, page 93, for **Point 31-D: A Prayer of Compassion.**

camp, and said, "Whoever *is* on the LORD's side—*come* to me!" And all the sons of Levi gathered themselves together to him.

27 And he said to them, "Thus says the LORD God of Israel: 'Let every man put his sword on his side, and go in and out from entrance to entrance throughout the camp, and ᴿlet every man kill his brother, every man his companion, and every man his neighbor.' " Num. 25:5-13

28 So the sons of Levi did according to the word of Moses. And about three thousand men of the people fell that day.

29 ᴿThen Moses said, "Consecrate yourselves today to the LORD, that He may bestow on you a blessing this day, for every man has opposed his son and his brother." Ex. 28:41

▼ **31-D. A Prayer of Compassion**

30 Now it came to pass on the next day that Moses said to the people, ᴿ"You have committed a great sin. So now I will go up to the LORD; ᴿperhaps I can ᴿmake atonement for your sin." 1 Sam. 12:20, 23 • 2 Sam. 16:12 • Num. 25:13

31 Then Moses ᴿreturned to the LORD and said, "Oh, these people have committed a great sin, and have ᴿmade for themselves a god of gold! Deut. 9:18 • Ex. 20:23

32 "Yet now, if You will forgive their sin— but if not, I pray, ᴿblot me ᴿout of Your book
▲ which You have written." Ps. 69:28 • Dan. 12:1

33 And the LORD said to Moses, ᴿ"Whoever has sinned against Me, I will ᴿblot him out of My book. [Ezek. 18:4; 33:2, 14, 15] • Ex. 17:14

34 "Now therefore, go, lead the people to *the place* of which I have ᴿspoken to you. ᴿBehold, My Angel shall go before you. Nevertheless, ᴿin the day when I ᴿvisit for punishment, I will visit punishment upon them for their sin." Ex. 3:17 • Ex. 23:20 • Deut. 32:35 • Ps. 89:32

35 So the LORD plagued the people because of ᴿwhat they did with the calf which Aaron made. Neh. 9:18

The Command to Leave Sinai

33 Then the LORD said to Moses, "Depart *and* go up from here, you and the people whom you have brought out of the land of Egypt, to the land of which I swore to Abraham, Isaac, and Jacob, saying, ᴿ'To your descendants I will give it.' Gen. 12:7

2 ᴿ"And I will send *My* Angel before you, ᴿand I will drive out the Canaanite and the Amorite and the Hittite and the Perizzite and the Hivite and the Jebusite. Ex. 32:34 • Josh. 24:11

3 *"Go up* ᴿto a land flowing with milk and honey; for I will not go up in your midst, lest I ᵀconsume you on the way, for you *are* a ᵀstiff-necked people." Ex. 3:8 • *destroy* • *stubborn*

4 And when the people heard this bad news, ᴿthey mourned, ᴿand no one put on his ornaments. Num. 14:1, 39 • Ezra 9:3

5 For the LORD had said to Moses, "Say to the children of Israel, 'You *are* a stiff-necked people. I could come up into your midst in one moment and consume you. Now therefore, take off your ᵀornaments, that I may ᴿknow what to do to you.' " *jewelry* • [Ps. 139:23]

6 So the children of Israel stripped themselves of their ornaments by Mount Horeb.

Moses Meets with the LORD

7 Moses took his tent and pitched it outside the camp, far from the camp, and ᴿcalled it the tabernacle of meeting. And it came to pass *that* everyone who ᴿsought the LORD went out to the tabernacle of meeting which *was* outside the camp. Ex. 29:42, 43 • Deut. 4:29

8 So it was, whenever Moses went out to the tabernacle, *that* all the people rose, and each man stood ᴿat his tent door and

---

31-D. A Prayer of Compassion (Exodus 32:30-32)—After the golden calf had been destroyed, and those who worshiped it were slain, Moses again addressed the people of Israel. He announced that he was about to "go up to the LORD," to ask that their sin of making the golden calf might be forgiven and that an atonement might be accepted for them (v. 30).

His prayer of compassion on behalf of his fellow sojourners contained a most touching element. He said that if their sin of making the calf could not be forgiven, then, "I pray, blot me out of Your book which You have written"—the Book of Life (v. 32; cf. Rev. 3:5, page 1296). Moses did not want to go on living if those whom he loved could find no forgiveness.

God's holiness and justice comes forth with His reply, "Whoever has sinned against Me, I will blot him out of My book" (v. 33). That this eternal judgment refers only to those who remained impenitent is made clear from Scripture by the fact that God did not destroy the nation. Also, Aaron continued to serve as high priest.

Although God did not accept Moses' offer to die for those at Sinai, nor for those in Israel who would sin some fourteen hundred years later, God the Father *did* accept the death of Christ for the sins of those who were to become His people, even two thousand years after that death (Mark 10:45, page 997).

Like Moses, Paul said, "I could wish that I myself were accursed from Christ for my brethren, my countrymen according to the flesh" (Rom. 9:1-4, page 1139).

Such examples show so clearly the attitude true Christians should have toward their brothers in Christ. Too many appoint themselves as judges, as those who would condemn their fellow believers (Matt. 7:1-5, page 944; cf. Rom. 14:4, 12, page 1144). At the same time such people abandon their God-ordained role of offering prayers of compassion and intercession. Without this Moses-like compassion, the church becomes a one-sided grand jury, rather than a haven of rescue and rest for lost souls (Matt. 11:28-30, page 952).

See Exodus 33:12-23, page 94, for **Point 31-E: A Prayer for Fellowship.**

watched Moses until he had gone into the tabernacle. Num. 16:27

9 And it came to pass, when Moses entered the tabernacle, that the pillar of cloud descended and stood *at* the door of the tabernacle, and *the* LORD talked with Moses.

10 All the people saw the pillar of cloud standing *at* the tabernacle door, and all the people rose and ᴿworshiped, each man *in* his tent door. Ex. 4:31

11 So ᴿthe LORD spoke to Moses face to face, as a man speaks to his friend. And he would return to the camp, but ᴿhis servant Joshua the son of Nun, a young man, did not depart from the tabernacle. Num. 12:8 • Ex. 24:13

The Promise of God's Presence

▼ **31–E. A Prayer for Fellowship**

12 Then Moses said to the LORD, "See, ᴿYou say to me, 'Bring up this people.' But You have not let me know whom You will send with me. Yet You have said, ᴿ'I know you by name, and you have also found grace in My sight.' Ex. 3:10; 32:34 • Ex. 33:17

13 "Now therefore, I pray, if I have found grace in Your sight, show me now Your way, that I may know You and that I may find grace is Your sight. And consider that this nation is ᴿYour people." Deut. 9:26, 29

14 And He said, ᴿ"My Presence will go *with you*, and I will give you rest." Is. 63:9

15 Then he said to Him, ᴿ"If Your Presence does not go *with us*, do not bring us up from here. Ex. 33:3

16 "For how then will it be known that Your people and I have found grace in Your sight, except You go with us? So we shall be separate, Your people and I, from all the people who *are* upon the face of the earth."

17 So the LORD said to Moses, ᴿ"I will also △ do this thing that you have spoken; for you have found grace in My sight, and I know you by name." [James 5:16]

18 And he said, "Please, show me ᴿYour glory." [1 Tim. 6:16]

19 Then He said, "I will make all My goodness pass before you, and I will proclaim the name of the LORD before you. ᴿI will be gracious to whom I will be ᴿgracious, and I will have compassion on whom I will have compassion." [Rom. 9:15, 16, 18] • [Rom. 4:4, 16]

20 But He said, "You cannot see My face; for ᴿno man shall see Me, and live." [Gen. 32:30]

21 And the LORD said, "Here is a place by Me, and you shall stand on the rock.

22 "So it shall be, while My glory passes by, that I will put you ᴿin the cleft of the rock, and will ᴿcover you with My hand while I pass by. Is. 2:21 • Ps. 91:1, 4

23 "Then I will take away My hand, and you shall see My back; but My face shall ᴿnot be seen." [John 1:18] ▲

Moses Makes New Tablets

34 And the LORD said to Moses, "Cut two tablets of stone like the first *ones*, and I will write on *these* tablets the words that were on the first tablets which you broke.

2 "So be ready in the morning, and come up in the morning to Mount Sinai, and present yourself to Me there ᴿon the top of the mountain. Ex. 19:11, 18, 20

3 "And no man shall ᴿcome up with you, and let no man be seen throughout all the mountain; let neither flocks nor herds feed before that mountain." Ex. 19:12, 13; 24:9-11

4 So he cut two tablets of stone like the first *ones*. Then Moses rose early in the morning and went up Mount Sinai, as the

---

31-E. A Prayer for Fellowship (Exodus 33:12-23)—

(1) Moses, in contemplating the journey before the children of Israel, asked God to tell him "whom You will send with me" (v. 12). God answered reassuringly, "My Presence will go with you, and I will give you rest" (v. 14). In other words, Moses was saying, "I am going to need some more help and some comfort for the long march ahead." God's reply assured him that the Lord Himself would continue with Moses and the nation in their journey. He would carry the burden of the trials ahead, and give Moses rest.

Moses prayerfully reminded God that

(a) He had said that Moses had "found grace" (favor) in His sight (v. 12);
(b) this was His nation (v. 13).

In effect, Moses was begging:

(a) "If You love me, then help me";
(b) "They are Your people, so You will have to take care of them—I can't." Moses was crying out, "I need You."

What an example this is for each of us—and especially to those whom God has called to some special work for Himself!

(2) Next Moses asks, "Please, show me Your glory" (v. 18). Now that he was sure that God would accompany him in the work ahead, he wanted to know God even better. This was also the outcry of Paul's heart: "That I may know Him" (Phil. 3:10, 12, page 1198).

Surely these impassioned prayers for fellowship (outcries for more of God's presence), which were on the lips of Moses and Paul, should also be on our own lips today.

See Numbers 27:12-19, page 169, for **Point 31-F: A Prayer for a Successor.**

Lord had commanded him; and he took in his hand the two tablets of stone.

5 Now the Lord descended in the ᴿcloud and stood with him there, and ᴿproclaimed the name of the Lord. Ex. 19:9 · Ex. 33:19

6 And the Lord passed before him and proclaimed, "The Lord, the Lord God, merciful and gracious, longsuffering, and abounding in goodness and ᴿtruth, Ps. 108:4

7 ᴿ"keeping mercy for thousands, ᴿforgiving iniquity and transgression and sin, ᴿby no means clearing the guilty, visiting the iniquity of the fathers upon the children and the children's children to the third and the fourth generation." Ex. 20:6 · Ps. 103:3, 4 · Job 10:14

8 So Moses made haste and ᴿbowed his head toward the earth, and worshiped. Ex. 4:31

9 Then he said, "If now I have found grace in Your sight, O Lord, let my Lord, I pray, go among us, even though we are a stiff-necked people; and pardon our iniquity and our sin, and take us as Your inheritance."

The Covenant Renewed

10 And He said: "Behold, I make a covenant. Before all your people I will do marvels such as have not been done in all the earth, nor in any nation; and all the people among whom you are shall see the work of the Lord. For it is ᴿan awesome thing that I will do with you. Ps. 145:6

11 ᴿ"Observe what I command you this day. Behold, ᴿI am driving out from before you the Amorite and the Canaanite and the Hittite and the Perizzite and the Hivite and the Jebusite. Deut. 6:25 · Ex. 23:20-33; 33:2

12 ᴿ"Take heed to yourself, lest you make a covenant with the inhabitants of the land where you are going, lest it be a snare in your midst. Ex. 23:32, 33

13 "But you shall ᴿdestroy their altars, break their sacred pillars, and ᴿcut down their wooden images Deut. 12:3 · 2 Kin. 18:4

14 "(for you shall worship ᴿno other god, for the Lord, whose ᴿname is Jealous, is a ᴿjealous God), [Ex. 20:3-5] · [Is. 9:6; 57:15] · [Deut. 4:24]

15 "lest you make a covenant with the inhabitants of the land, and they play the harlot with their gods and make sacrifice to their gods, and one of them invites you and you ᴿeat of his sacrifice, 1 Cor. 8:4, 7, 10

16 "and you take of ᴿhis daughters for your sons, and his daughters ᴿplay the harlot with their gods and make your sons play the harlot with their gods. Gen. 28:1 · Num. 25:1, 2

17 ᴿ"You shall make no molded gods for yourselves. Ex. 20:4, 23; 32:8

18 "The Feast of ᴿUnleavened Bread you shall keep. Seven days you shall eat unleavened bread, as I commanded you, in the appointed time of the month of Abib; for in the ᴿmonth of Abib you came out from Egypt. Ex. 12:15, 16 · Ex. 12:2; 13:4

19 ᴿ"All ᵀthat open the womb are Mine, and every male firstborn among your livestock, whether ox or sheep. Ex. 13:2; 22:29 · the firstborn

20 "But ᴿthe firstborn of a donkey you shall redeem with a lamb. And if you will not redeem him, then you shall break his neck. All the firstborn of your sons you shall redeem. And none shall appear before Me ᴿempty-handed. Ex. 13:13 · Ex. 22:29; 23:15

21 ᴿ"Six days you shall work, but on the seventh day you shall rest; in plowing time and in harvest you shall rest. Ex. 20:8-11

22 "And you shall observe the Feast of Weeks, of the firstfruits of wheat harvest, and the Feast of Ingathering at the year's end.

23 ᴿ"Three times in the year all your men shall appear before the Lord, the Lord God of Israel. Ex. 23:14-17

24 "For I will ᴿcast out the nations before you and enlarge your borders; neither will any man covet your land when you go up to appear before the Lord your God three times in the year. [Ex. 33:2]

25 "You shall not offer the blood of My sacrifice with leaven, ᴿnor shall the sacrifice of the Feast of the Passover be left until morning. Ex. 12:10

26 ᴿ"The first of the firstfruits of your land you shall bring to the house of the Lord your God. You shall not boil a young goat in its mother's milk." Ex. 23:19

27 Then the Lord said to Moses, "Write ᴿthese words, for according to the tenor of these words I have made a covenant with you and with Israel." Deut. 31:9

28 ᴿSo he was there with the Lord forty days and forty nights; he neither ate bread nor drank water. And ᴿHe wrote on the tablets the words of the covenant, the Ten ᵀCommandments. Ex. 24:18 · Ex. 34:1, 4 · Lit. Words

The Shining Face of Moses

29 Now it was so, when Moses came down from Mount Sinai (and the ᴿtwo tablets of the Testimony were in Moses' hand when he came down from the mountain), that Moses did not know that ᴿthe skin of his face shone while he talked with Him. Ex. 32:15 · 2 Cor. 3:7

30 So when Aaron and all the children of Israel saw Moses, behold, the skin of his face shone, and they were afraid to come near him.

31 Then Moses called to them, and Aaron and all the rulers of the congregation returned to him; and Moses talked with them.

32 Afterward all the children of Israel came near, ᴿand he gave them as commandments all that the Lord had spoken with him on Mount Sinai. Ex. 24:3

33 And when Moses had finished speaking with them, he put a veil on his face.

34 But ᴿwhenever Moses went in before the Lord to speak with Him, he would take the

veil off until he came out; and he would come out and speak to the children of Israel whatever he had been commanded.   [2 Cor. 3:13-16]

35 And whenever the children of Israel saw the face of Moses, that the skin of Moses' face shone, then Moses would put the veil on his face again, until he went in to speak with Him.

Sabbath Regulations

35 Then Moses gathered all the congregation of the children of Israel together, and said to them, "These *are* the words which the LORD has commanded *you* to do:

2 "Work shall be done for six days, but the seventh day shall be a holy day for you, a Sabbath of rest to the LORD. Whoever does any work on it shall be put to death.

3 "You shall kindle no fire throughout your dwellings on the Sabbath day."

Offerings for the Tabernacle

4 And Moses spoke to all the congregation of the children of Israel, saying, "This *is* the thing which the LORD commanded, saying:

5 'Take from among you an offering to the LORD. ^RWhoever *is* of a willing heart, let him bring it as an offering to the LORD: ^Rgold, silver, and bronze;   Ex. 25:2 · Ex. 38:24

6 ^R'blue, purple, and scarlet *thread*, fine linen, and ^Rgoats' *hair*;   Ex. 36:8 · Ex. 36:14

7 'ram skins dyed red, badger skins, and acacia wood;

8 'oil for the light, and spices for the anointing oil and for the sweet incense;

9 'onyx stones, and stones to be set in the ephod and in the breastplate.

Articles of the Tabernacle

10 ^R'All *who are* gifted artisans among you shall come and make all that the LORD has commanded: Ex. 31:2-6; 36:1, 2

11 ^R'the tabernacle, its tent, its covering, its clasps, its boards, its bars, its pillars, and its sockets;   Ex. 26:1, 2; 36:14

12 ^R'the ark and its poles, *with* the mercy seat, and the veil of the covering;   Ex. 25:10-22

13 'the ^Rtable and its poles, all its utensils, ^Rand the showbread;   Ex. 25:23 · Ex. 25:30

14 'also the lampstand for the light, its utensils, its lamps, and the oil for the light;

15 'the incense altar, its poles, the anointing oil, the sweet incense, and the screen for the door at the entrance of the tabernacle;

16 ^R'the altar of burnt offering with its bronze grating, its poles, all its utensils, *and* the laver and its base;   Ex. 27:1-8

17 ^R'the hangings of the court, its pillars, their sockets, and the screen for the gate of the court;   Ex. 27:9-18

18 'the pegs of the tabernacle, the pegs of the court, and their cords;

19 'the ^Tgarments of ministry, for ministering in the holy *place*—the holy garments for Aaron the priest and the garments of his sons, to minister as priests.' "   Or *woven garments*

The Tabernacle Offerings Presented

20 And all the congregation of the children of Israel departed from the presence of Moses.

21 Then everyone came whose heart was stirred, and everyone whose spirit was willing, *and* they brought the LORD's offering for the work of the tabernacle of meeting, for all its service, and for the holy garments.

22 They came, both men and women, as many as had a willing heart, *and* brought earrings and nose rings, rings and necklaces, all jewelry of gold, that is, every man who *made* an offering of gold to the LORD.

23 And ^Revery man, with whom was found blue, purple, and scarlet *thread*, fine linen, goats' *hair*, red skins of rams, and ^Tbadger skins, brought *them*.   1 Chr. 29:8 · Or *dolphin*

24 Everyone who offered an offering of silver or bronze brought the LORD's offering. And everyone with whom was found acacia wood for any work of the service, brought *it*.

25 All the women *who were* ^Rgifted artisans spun yarn with their hands, and brought what they had spun, of blue, purple, *and* scarlet, and fine linen.   Ex. 28:3; 31:6; 36:1

26 And all the women whose hearts stirred with wisdom spun yarn of goats' *hair*.

27 ^RThe rulers brought onyx stones, and the stones to be set in the ephod and in the breastplate,   Ezra 2:68

28 and spices and oil for the light, for the anointing oil, and for the sweet incense.

29 The children of Israel brought a freewill offering to the LORD, all the men and women whose hearts were willing to bring *material* for all kinds of work which the LORD, by the hand of Moses, had commanded to be done.

The Artisans Called by God

35-C. The Furniture of the Tabernacle   ▼

30 And Moses said to the children of Israel, "See, ^Rthe LORD has called by name Bezalel the son of Uri, the son of Hur, of the tribe of Judah;   Ex. 31:1-6

31 "and He has filled him with the Spirit of

35-C. The Furniture of the Tabernacle (Exodus 35:30–35)—Each of the four sacred items in the tabernacle had its own special significance and use. In those early five hundred years, from the Exodus to Solomon's temple, the priests saw these sacred items of furniture and no doubt meditated deeply upon what they represented. It is only in this age, however, after Christ has come and the New Testament has been written,

(Point 35-C continued on next page)

(Point 35-C continued from previous page)
that we can see more fully what God was symbolizing in these holy patterns and types of heavenly realities (Heb. 9:23, 24, page 1244).

(1) *The table and the showbread—Christ, our Sustainer* (Ex. 25:23-30, page 85; cf. Lev. 24:5-9, page 132). The gold-covered table had the showbread placed upon it every Sabbath—two rows of six pieces of bread, sprinkled with frankincense. They remained for the week and then were eaten there in the Holy Place by Aaron, the high priest, and his priest-sons. This was a sign to Israel that it was God who fed and sustained His people, that is, that He kept them alive. It symbolized both His physical and His spiritual feeding. Christ, in Matthew 4:3, 4 (page 934), reminded us that God feeds us in both of these ways. Christ Himself is the fulfillment of God's provision for our spiritual life. We see Him in the showbread as the true bread from heaven (John 6:32-35, page 1059) unifying God's people into one body.

(2) *The menorah (candelabrum)—Christ, our Light* (Ex. 25:31-37, page 85; 27:20, 21, page 87). The number seven, in the Bible, often symbolizes totality and completeness, after the seven days of the creation of the world and the rest which followed. The golden candelabrum burned olive oil, which represented God's Holy Spirit, and had seven lights which represented

(a) God's all-seeing, omniscient capacity;
(b) the illumination which His Spirit gives to His people.

Christ declared that He was the light of the world. We should see Him symbolized in the candelabrum (John 8:12, page 1062). In Revelation 1:20 and 2:1 (page 1294) the seven churches are represented as seven lampstands, giving off the light of God by the Spirit. Christ is seen walking among them.

(3) *The altar of incense—Christ, our Intercessor* (Ex. 35:15, page 96). The great sacrifices, including those during the Day of Atonement, took place upon the bronze altar outside the tabernacle itself, just as Christ was later to suffer outside Jerusalem's gates. Here, however, in the Holy Place before the veil, stood this smaller altar of incense. Upon this altar, morning and evening, the priest daily offered incense which would give a pleasant aroma to the Holy Place. This spoke to Israel of the daily prayers of those who loved God, prayers that rose to Him as a "soothing aroma" (Gen. 8:21, page 14; cf. Eph. 5:2, page 1191).

(4) *The ark of the covenant—Christ, our divine Savior* (Ex. 25:10-22, page 84). This was the sacred chest of Israel, made of acacia wood overlaid with gold: "two and a half cubits shall be its length, a cubit and a half its width, and a cubit and a half its height." It consisted of

(a) the ark itself;
(b) the golden lid called the mercy seat;
(c) two winged cherubs—the cherubim—attached to the mercy seat;
(d) its contents (see below);
(e) the two staves which fitted through the loops on the side of the ark to transport it by porters.

Its very name, "the ark of the covenant" or "the ark of the testimony," witnesses to its unique position as the primary emblem of God's covenant with Israel, where He promised that He would be their God and they would be His special people. Note that:

(a) Of the tabernacle furniture, the ark alone stood behind the veil in the Most Holy Place. It was here, with the mercy seat, golden lid, and two winged cherubs, that God manifested His presence with Israel in a special, localized sense. His holy presence was sealed off from sin and sinners by the veil.
(b) The contents of the ark consisted of three items (Heb. 9:4, page 1243):

(i) The two stone tablets of the covenant of the law—one for our duties to God, the other for our duties to man. Christ is our law-keeper, having paid the penalty for our disobedience of the law (Gal. 3:13, page 1181; cf. Heb. 5:1, 5, page 1239).
(ii) Aaron's almond rod that budded, which signified to a complaining Israel that Aaron was indeed chosen by God to be high priest (Num. 17:8, page 157). Christ is our High Priest. Like Aaron, He was chosen by God (John 8:18, page 1062).
(iii) The pot of manna—that special food provided by God to sustain His people in their journey through the wilderness. Christ is our manna from heaven. He daily feeds His own, physically and spiritually (John 6:1-14, 31-35, page 1058).

(c) The top of the ark, overlaid with gold, formed the mercy seat. The mercy seat was sprinkled with blood once a year, on the Day of Atonement. Thus, the requirements of the law were covered by the blood, typifying the covering of Christ's blood for us.
(d) The ark accompanied and led the hosts of Israel on the march (Num. 10:35, 36, page 150). It led them into the Jordan River which God divided (Josh. 3:8-11, page 218), and around the mighty fortress of Jericho, which God's power pulled down (Josh. 6:6-9, page 221). It thus typifies Christ's presence with us daily. His great power is available to rescue us by dividing rivers which block our path to

(i) safety and hope
(ii) His holy presence near us
(iii) His daily guidance for our lives (Matt. 28:18-20, page 982)

See Exodus 40:13-15, page 102, for **Point 35-D: The Priesthood of the Tabernacle.**

▽ God, in wisdom and understanding, in knowledge and all manner of workmanship,

32 "to design artistic works, to work in gold and silver and bronze,

33 "in cutting jewels for setting, in carving wood, and to work in all manner of artistic workmanship.

34 "And He has put in his heart the ability to teach, in him and ᴿAholiab the son of Ahisamach, of the tribe of Dan.   Ex. 31:6

35 "He has ᴿfilled them with skill to do all manner of work of the engraver and the designer and the tapestry maker, in blue, purple, and scarlet thread, and fine linen, and of the weaver—those who do every work and ▲ those who design artistic works.   1 Kin. 7:14

36 "And Bezalel and Aholiab, and every gifted artisan in whom the Lᴏʀᴅ has put wisdom and understanding, to know how to do all manner of work for the service of the ᴿsanctuary,ᵀ shall do according to all that the Lᴏʀᴅ has commanded."   Ex. 25:8 · holy place

The People Give More than Enough

2 Then Moses called Bezalel and Aholiab, and every gifted artisan in whose heart the Lᴏʀᴅ had put wisdom, everyone whose heart was stirred, to come and do the work.

3 And they received from Moses all the ᴿoffering which the children of Israel had brought for the work of the service of making the sanctuary. So they continued bringing to him freewill offerings every morning.   Ex. 35:5

4 Then all the craftsmen who were doing all the work of the sanctuary came, each from the work he was doing,

5 and they spoke to Moses, saying, ᴿ"The people bring much more than enough for the service of the work which the Lᴏʀᴅ commanded us to do."   [2 Cor. 8:2, 3]

6 So Moses gave a commandment, and they caused it to be proclaimed throughout the camp, saying, "Let neither man nor woman do any more work for the offering of the sanctuary." And the people were restrained from bringing,

7 for the material they had was sufficient for all the work to be done—indeed too ᴿmuch.   1 Kin. 8:64

Building the Tabernacle

8 Then all the gifted artisans among them who worked on the tabernacle made ten curtains woven of fine linen, and of blue, purple, and scarlet thread; with artistic designs of cherubim they made them.

9 The length of each curtain was ᵀtwenty-eight cubits, and the width of each curtain ᵀfour cubits; the curtains were all the same size.   42 ft. · 6 ft.

10 And he coupled five curtains to one another, and the other five curtains he coupled to one another.

11 He made loops of blue yarn on the edge

of the curtain on the selvedge of one set; likewise he did on the outer edge of the other curtain of the second set.

12 ᴿFifty loops he made on one curtain, and fifty loops he made on the edge of the curtain on the end of the second set; the loops held one curtain to another.   Ex. 26:5

13 And he made fifty clasps of gold, and coupled the curtains to one another with the clasps, that it might be one tabernacle.

14 ᴿHe made curtains of goats' hair for the tent over the tabernacle; he made eleven curtains.   Ex. 26:7

15 The length of each curtain was ᵀthirty cubits, and the width of each curtain ᵀfour cubits; the eleven curtains were the same size.   45 ft. · 6 ft.

16 He coupled five curtains by themselves and six curtains by themselves.

17 And he made fifty loops on the edge of the curtain that is outermost in one set, and fifty loops he made on the edge of the curtain of the second set.

18 He also made fifty bronze clasps to couple the tent together, that it might be one.

19 ᴿThen he made a covering for the tent of ram skins dyed red, and a covering of ᵀbadger skins above that.   Ex. 26:14 · Or dolphin

20 For the tabernacle ᴿhe made boards of acacia wood, standing upright.   Ex. 26:15-29

21 The length of each board was ᵀten cubits, and the width of each board a ᵀcubit and a half.   15 ft. · 27 in.

22 Each board had two ᵀtenons ᴿfor binding one to another. Thus he made for all the boards of the tabernacle.   tabs · Ex. 26:17

23 And he made boards for the tabernacle, twenty boards for the south side.

24 Forty sockets of silver he made to go under the twenty boards: two sockets under each of the boards for its two tenons.

25 And for the other side of the tabernacle, the north side, he made twenty boards

26 and their forty sockets of silver: two sockets under each of the boards.

27 For the west side of the tabernacle he made six boards.

28 He also made two boards for the two back corners of the tabernacle.

29 And they were coupled at the bottom and ᵀcoupled together at the top by one ring. Thus he made both of them for the two corners.   Lit. doubled

30 So there were eight boards and their sockets—sixteen sockets of silver—two sockets under each of the boards.

31 And he made bars of acacia wood: five for the boards on one side of the tabernacle,

32 five bars for the boards on the other side of the tabernacle, and five bars for the boards of the tabernacle on the far side westward.

33 And he made the middle bar to pass through the boards from one end to the other.

34 He overlaid the boards with gold, made their rings of gold *to be* holders for the bars, and overlaid the bars with gold.

35 And he made a veil of blue, purple, and scarlet *thread*, and fine woven linen; it was worked *with* an artistic design of cherubim.

36 He made for it four pillars of acacia *wood*, and overlaid them with gold, with their hooks of gold; and he cast four sockets of silver for them.

37 He also made a screen for the tabernacle door, of blue, purple, and scarlet *thread*, and fine woven linen, made by a weaver,

38 and its five pillars with their hooks. And he overlaid their capitals and their rings with gold, but their five sockets *were* bronze.

Making the Ark of the Testimony

37 Then Bezalel made ᴿthe ark of acacia wood; ᵀtwo and a half cubits *was* its length, a cubit and a half its width, and a cubit and a half its height.   Ex. 25:10-20 • 45 in.

2 He overlaid it with pure gold inside and outside, and made a molding of gold all around it.

3 And he cast for it four rings of gold *to be* set in its four corners: two rings on one side, and two rings on the other side of it.

4 He made poles of acacia wood, and overlaid them with gold.

5 And he put the poles into the rings at the sides of the ark, to bear the ark.

6 He also made the ᴿmercy seat of pure gold; two and a half cubits *was* its length and a cubit and a half its width.   Ex. 25:17

7 He made two cherubim of beaten gold; he made them of one piece at the two ends of the mercy seat:

8 one cherub at one end on this side, and the other cherub at the *other* end on that side. He made the cherubim at the two ends *of one piece* with the mercy seat.

9 The cherubim spread out *their* wings above, *and* covered the ᴿmercy seat with their wings. They faced one another; the faces of the cherubim were toward the mercy seat.   Ex. 25:20

Making the Table for the Showbread

10 He made ᴿthe table of acacia wood; two cubits *was* its length, a cubit its width, and a ᵀcubit and a half its height.   Ex. 25:23-29 • 27 in.

11 And he overlaid it with pure gold, and made a molding of gold all around it.

12 Also he made a frame of a ᵀhandbreadth all around it, and made a molding of gold for the frame all around it.   3 in.

13 And he cast for it four rings of gold, and put the rings on the four corners that *were* at its four legs.

14 The rings were close to the frame, as holders for the poles to bear the table.

15 And he made the poles of acacia wood to bear the table, and overlaid them with gold.

16 He made of pure gold the utensils which were on the table: its ᴿdishes, its cups, its bowls, and its pitchers for pouring.   Ex. 25:29

Making the Gold Lampstand

17 He also made the ᴿlampstand of pure gold; of hammered work he made the lampstand. Its shaft, its branches, its bowls, its ornamental knobs, and its flowers were of the same piece.   Ex. 25:31-39

18 And six branches came out of its sides: three branches of the lampstand out of one side, and three branches of the lampstand out of the other side.

19 There were three bowls made like almond *blossoms* on one branch, with an *ornamental* knob and a flower, and three bowls made like almond *blossoms* on the other branch, with an *ornamental* knob and a flower—and so for the six branches coming out of the lampstand.

20 And on the lampstand itself *were* four bowls made like almond *blossoms, each with* its *ornamental* knob and flower.

21 *There was* a knob under the *first* two branches of the same, a knob under the *second* two branches of the same, and a knob under the *third* two branches of the same, according to the six branches extending from it.

22 Their knobs and their branches were of one piece; all of it *was* one hammered piece of pure gold.

23 And he made its seven lamps, its ᴿwick-trimmers, and its trays of pure gold.   Num. 4:9

24 Of a ᵀtalent of pure gold he made it, with all its utensils. $5,760,000

Making the Altar of Incense

25 He made the incense altar of acacia wood. Its length *was* a cubit and its width a cubit—*it was* square—and two cubits *was* its height. Its horns were *of one piece* with it.

26 And he overlaid it with pure gold: its top, its sides all around, and its horns. He also made for it a molding of gold all around it.

27 He made two rings of gold for it under its molding, by its two corners on both sides, as holders for the poles with which to bear it.

28 And he ᴿmade the poles of acacia wood, and overlaid them with gold.   Ex. 30:5

Making the Anointing Oil and the Incense

29 He also made ᴿthe holy anointing oil and the pure incense of sweet spices, according to the work of the perfumer.   Ex. 30:23-25

Making the Altar of Burnt Offering

38 He made the altar of burnt offering of acacia wood; five cubits *was* its length and five cubits its width—*it was* square—and its height *was* three cubits.

2 He made its horns on its four corners; the horns were *of one piece* with it. And he overlaid it with bronze.

3 He made all the utensils for the altar: the pans, the shovels, the basins, the forks, and the firepans; all its utensils he made of bronze.

4 And he made a grate of bronze network for the altar, under its rim, midway from the bottom.

5 He cast four rings for the four corners of the bronze grating, *as* holders for the poles.

6 And he made the poles of acacia wood, and overlaid them with bronze.

7 Then he put the poles into the rings on the sides of the altar, with which to bear it. He made the altar hollow with boards.

Making the Bronze Laver

8 He made ᴿthe laver of bronze and its base of bronze, from the bronze mirrors of the serving women who assembled at the door of the tabernacle of meeting.   Ex. 30:18

Making the Court of the Tabernacle

9 Then he made the court on the south side; the hangings of the court *were of* fine woven linen, one hundred cubits long.

10 There *were* twenty pillars for them, with twenty bronze sockets. The hooks of the pillars and their bands *were* silver.

11 On the north side *the hangings were* one hundred cubits *long,* with twenty pillars and their twenty bronze sockets. The hooks of the pillars and their bands *were* silver.

12 And on the west side *there were* hangings of ᵀfifty cubits, with ten pillars and their ten sockets. The hooks of the pillars and their bands *were* silver.   75 ft.

13 For the east side *the hangings were* ᵀfifty cubits.   75 ft.

14 The hangings of one side *of the gate were* ᵀfifteen cubits long, *with* their three pillars and their three sockets,   22.5 ft.

15 and the same for the other side of the court gate; on this side and that *were* hangings of ᵀfifteen cubits, *with* their three pillars and their three sockets.   22.5 ft.

16 All the hangings of the court all around *were of* fine woven linen.

17 The sockets for the pillars *were* bronze, the hooks of the pillars and their bands *were* silver, and the overlay of their capitals *was* silver; and all the pillars of the court had bands of silver.

18 The screen for the gate of the court *was* woven of blue, purple, and scarlet *thread,* and of fine woven linen. The length *was* ᵀtwenty cubits, and the height along its width *was* ᵀfive cubits, corresponding to the hangings of the court.   30 ft. • 7.5 ft.

19 And *there were* four pillars *with* their four sockets of bronze; their hooks *were*

silver, and the overlay of their capitals and their bands *was* silver.

20 All the ᴿpegs of the tabernacle, and of the court all around, *were* bronze.   Ex. 27:19

Materials of the Tabernacle

21 This is the inventory of the tabernacle, the tabernacle of the Testimony, which was counted according to the commandment of Moses, for the service of the Levites, by the hand of Ithamar, son of Aaron the priest.

22 ᴿBezalel the son of Uri, the son of Hur, of the tribe of Judah, made all that the Lᴏʀᴅ had commanded Moses.   Ex. 31:2, 6

23 And with him *was* Aholiab the son of Ahisamach, of the tribe of Dan, an engraver and designer, a weaver of blue, purple, and scarlet thread, and of fine linen.

24 All the gold that was used in all the work of the holy *place,* that is, the gold of the ᴿoffering, was twenty-nine talents and seven hundred and thirty shekels, according to ᴿthe shekel of the sanctuary.   Ex. 35:5, 22 • Ex. 30:13, 24

25 And the silver from those who were ᴿnumbered of the congregation *was* one hundred talents and one thousand seven hundred and seventy-five shekels, according to the shekel of the sanctuary: Ex. 30:11–16

26 ᴿa ᵀbekah for ᵀeach man (*that is,* half a shekel, according to the shekel of the sanctuary), for everyone included in the numbering from twenty years and above, for six hundred and three thousand, five hundred and fifty *men.*   Ex. 30:13, 15 • $64 • Lit. *a head*

27 And from the ᵀhundred talents of silver were cast ᴿthe sockets of the sanctuary and the bases of the veil: one hundred sockets from the hundred talents, one talent for each socket. $38,400,000 • Ex. 26:19, 21, 25, 32

28 Then from the one thousand seven hundred and seventy-five *shekels* he made hooks for the pillars, overlaid their capitals, and ᴿmade bands for them.   Ex. 27:17

29 The offering of bronze *was* seventy talents and two thousand four hundred shekels.

30 And with it he made the sockets for the door of the tabernacle of meeting, the bronze altar, the bronze grating for it, and all the utensils for the altar,

31 the sockets for the court all around, the bases for the court gate, all the pegs for the tabernacle, and all the pegs for the court all around.

Making the Garments of the Priesthood

39 Of the blue, purple, and scarlet *thread* they made ᵀgarments of ministry, for ministering in the holy *place,* and made the holy garments for Aaron, ᴿas the Lᴏʀᴅ had commanded Moses.   Or *woven garments* • Ex. 28:4

Making the Ephod

2 ᴿHe made the ᴿephod of gold, blue, purple, and scarlet *thread,* and of fine woven linen.   Ex. 28:6–14 • Lev. 8:7

3 And they beat the gold into thin sheets and cut it into threads, to work it in with the blue, purple, and scarlet thread, and the fine linen, into artistic designs.

4 They made shoulder straps for it to couple it together; it was coupled together at its two edges.

5 And the intricately woven band of his ephod that was on it was of the same workmanship, woven of gold, blue, purple, and scarlet thread, and of fine woven linen, as the LORD had commanded Moses.

6 RAnd they set onyx stones, enclosed in Tsettings of gold; they were engraved, as signets are engraved, with the names of the sons of Israel.   Ex. 28:9-11 · filigrees

7 He put them on the shoulders of the ephod as memorial stones for the sons of Israel, as the LORD had commanded Moses.

Making the Breastplate

8 RAnd he made the breastplate, artistically woven like the workmanship of the ephod, of gold, blue, purple, and scarlet thread, and of fine woven linen.   Ex. 28:15-30

9 They made the breastplate square by doubling it; a Tspan was its length and a span its width when doubled.   9 in.

10 RAnd they set in it four rows of stones: a row with a sardius, a topaz, and an emerald was the first row;   Ex. 28:17

11 the second row, a turquoise, a sapphire, and a diamond;

12 the third row, a jacinth, an agate, and an amethyst;

13 the fourth row, a beryl, an onyx, and a jasper. They were enclosed in settings of gold in their mountings.

14 There were Rtwelve stones according to the names of the sons of Israel: according to their names, engraved like a signet, each one with its own name according to the twelve tribes.   Rev. 21:12

15 And they made chains for the breastplate at the ends, like braided cords of pure gold.

16 They also made two settings of gold and two gold rings, and put the two rings on the two ends of the breastplate.

17 And they put the two braided chains of gold in the two rings on the ends of the breastplate.

18 The two ends of the two braided chains they fastened in the two settings, and put them on the shoulder straps of the ephod in the front.

19 And they made two rings of gold and put them on the two ends of the breastplate, on the edge of it, which was on the inward side of the ephod.

20 They made two other gold rings and put them on the two shoulder straps, underneath the ephod toward its front, right at the seam above the intricately woven band of the ephod.

21 And they bound the breastplate by means of its rings to the rings of the ephod with a blue cord, so that it would be above the intricately woven band of the ephod, and that the breastplate would not come loose from the ephod, as the LORD had commanded Moses.

Making the Other Priestly Garments

22 RHe made the Rrobe of the ephod of woven work, all of blue.   Ex. 28:31-35 · Ex. 29:5

23 And there was an opening in the middle of the robe, like the opening in a coat of mail, with a woven binding all around the opening, so that it would not tear.

24 They made on the hem of the robe pomegranates of blue, purple, and scarlet, and of fine woven linen.

25 And they made Rbells of pure gold, and put the bells between the pomegranates on the hem of the robe all around between the pomegranates: Ex. 28:33

26 a bell and a pomegranate, a bell and a pomegranate, all around the hem of the robe to Tminister in, as the LORD had commanded Moses.   serve

27 RThey made tunics, artistically woven of fine linen, for Aaron and his sons, Ex. 28:39, 40

28 a turban of fine linen, exquisite hats of fine linen, short trousers of fine woven linen,

29 and a sash of fine woven linen with blue, purple, and scarlet thread, made by a weaver, as the LORD had commanded Moses.

30 Then they made the plate of the holy crown of pure gold, and wrote on it an inscription like the engraving of a signet:

HOLINESS TO THE LORD.

31 And they tied to it a blue cord, to fasten it above on the turban, as the LORD had commanded Moses.

The Work Completed

32 Thus all the work of the tabernacle of the tent of meeting was finished. And the children of Israel did according to all that the LORD had commanded Moses; so they did.

33 And they brought the tabernacle to Moses, the tent and all its furnishings: its clasps, its boards, its bars, its pillars, and its sockets;

34 the covering of ram skins dyed red, the covering of badger skins, and the veil of the covering;

35 the ark of the Testimony with its poles, and the mercy seat;

36 the table, all its utensils, and the Rshowbread;   Ex. 25:23-30

37 the pure gold lampstand with its lamps (the lamps set in order), all its utensils, and the oil for light;

38 the gold altar, the anointing oil, and the sweet incense; the screen for the tabernacle door;

39 the bronze altar, its grate of bronze, its poles, and all its utensils; the laver with its base;

40 the hangings of the court, its pillars and its sockets, the screen for the court gate, its cords, and its pegs; all the utensils for the service of the tabernacle, for the tent of meeting;

41 and the ᵀgarments of ministry, to ᵀminister in the holy *place*: the holy garments for Aaron the priest, and his sons' garments, to minister as priests.   Or *woven garments • serve*

42 According to all that the Lord had commanded Moses, so the children of Israel ᴿdid all the work.   Ex. 35:10

43 Then Moses looked over all the work, and indeed they had done it; as the Lord had commanded, just so they had done it. And Moses ᴿblessed them.   Lev. 9:22, 23

The Tabernacle Erected and Arranged

40 Then the Lord spoke to Moses, saying:

2 "On the first day of the ᴿfirst month you shall set up ᴿthe tabernacle of the tent of meeting.   Ex. 12:2; 13:4 • Ex. 26:1, 30; 40:17

3 ᴿ"You shall put in it the ark of the Testimony, and ᵀpartition off the ark with the veil.   Num. 4:5 • *screen*

4 "You shall bring in the table and ᴿarrange the things that are to be set in order on it; ᴿand you shall bring in the lampstand and ᵀlight its lamps.   Ex. 25:30; 40:23 • Ex. 40:24, 25 • *set up*

5 ᴿ"You shall also set the altar of gold for the incense before the ark of the Testimony, and put up the screen for the door of the tabernacle.   Ex. 40:26

6 "Then you shall set the ᴿaltar of the burnt offering before the door of the tabernacle of the tent of meeting.   Ex. 39:39

7 "And ᴿyou shall set the laver between the tabernacle of meeting and the altar, and put water in it.   Ex. 30:18; 40:30

8 "You shall set up the court all around, and hang up the screen at the court gate.

9 "And you shall take the anointing oil, and ᴿanoint the tabernacle and all that *is* in it; and you shall hallow it and all its utensils, and it shall be holy.   Ex. 30:26

10 "You shall anoint the altar of the burnt offering and all its utensils, and consecrate the altar. The altar shall be most holy.

11 "And you shall anoint the laver and its base, and consecrate it.

12 ᴿ"Then you shall bring Aaron and his sons to the door of the tabernacle of meeting and wash them with water.   Lev. 8:1-13

35-D. The Priesthood of the Tabernacle ▼

13 "You shall put the holy garments on Aaron, and anoint him and consecrate him, that he may minister to Me as priest.

14 "And you shall bring his sons and clothe them with tunics.

15 "You shall anoint them, as you anointed their father, that they may minister to Me as priests; for their anointing shall surely be ᴿan everlasting priesthood throughout their generations."   Num. 25:13 ▲

35-D. The Priesthood of the Tabernacle (Exodus 40:13-15)—Christ is indeed the High Priest of God in the true heavenly tabernacle, of which the earthly tabernacle is only a model. The book of Hebrews plainly declares this to be so (Heb. 9:11-14, 24-26, page 1243). Although He was not from the tribe of Levi like Aaron, Christ (of Judah) was independently appointed by God as our High Priest; and He was so anointed, as was Melchizedek to whom Abraham gave tithes (Heb. 7:11-17, page 1241; cf. Gen. 14:18-20, page 19). See Christ here as our true eternal High Priest.

(1) The priesthood consisted of one high priest, Aaron, the brother of Moses, and Aaron's sons (Ex. 29:1-9, page 88). It was a hereditary office.

(2) Aaron was consecrated as high priest by pouring olive oil on his head (Ex. 29:7, page 88). This signified God's Spirit upon him. See Psalm 133 (page 588), celebrating this joyous event.

(3) Even Aaron's sons, though priests, were not permitted to invent their own ceremonies. Because Nadab and Abihu disobeyed this principle, they were struck down (Lev. 10:1-3, page 115). True religion came from God and was not invented by man.

(4) The high priest wore special clothes, including a breastplate (the ephod) bedecked with twelve jeweled stones, representing the twelve tribes, and a turban (the miter) which had upon it a gold plate with the engraved words, "HOLINESS TO THE LORD" (Ex. 39:8-14, 30, 31, page 101).

(5) The high priest alone (with the goat's blood to be sprinkled on the mercy seat) could enter the Most Holy Place and then only on the Day of Atonement (Lev. 16:15, page 124).

(6) The Levites (tribe of Levi) were appointed ministers of the tabernacle service, under the authority of the priests, who also were of the family of Levi (Num. 8:5-26, page 148). The transporting of the tabernacle was divided among the Levite clans: Gershon, Merari, and Kohath (Num. 10:17-21, page 150; cf. 1 Chr. 15:2, page 397).

(7) Some murmured against God's chosen high priest and rejected him in favor of others of their own choosing. But God caused only Aaron's rod to bud, authenticating Aaron as His choice (Num. 16:1-3, page 155; cf. 17:1-11, page 157). In the same way they murmured against Christ (Is. 53:1-3, page 693). But God has chosen Him, and His almond rod alone has budded and blossomed (Is. 53:10-12, page 693).

See Index, page 17, for your next study.

16 Thus Moses did; according to all that the LORD had commanded him, so he did.

17 And it came to pass in the first month of the second year, on the first *day* of the month, *that* the tabernacle was raised up.

18 So Moses raised up the tabernacle, fastened its sockets, set up its boards, put in its bars, and raised up its pillars.

19 And he spread out the tent over the tabernacle and put the covering of the tent on top of it, as the LORD had commanded Moses.

20 He took ^Rthe Testimony and put *it* into the ark, inserted the poles through the rings of the ark, and put the mercy seat on top of the ark.   Ex. 25:16

21 And he brought the ark into the tabernacle, ^Rhung up the veil of the covering, and partitioned off the ark of the Testimony, as the LORD had commanded Moses.   Ex. 26:33

22 ^RHe put the table in the tabernacle of meeting, on the north side of the tabernacle, outside the veil;   Ex. 26:35

23 ^Rand he set the bread in order upon it before the LORD, as the LORD had commanded Moses.   Ex. 40:4

24 ^RHe put the lampstand in the tabernacle of meeting, across from the table, on the south side of the tabernacle;   Ex. 26:35

25 and ^Rhe lit the lamps before the LORD, as the LORD had commanded Moses.   Ex. 40:4

26 ^RHe put the gold altar in the tabernacle of meeting in front of the veil;   Ex. 30:1, 6; 40:5

27 ^Rand he burned sweet incense on it, as the LORD had commanded Moses.   Ex. 30:7

28 ^RHe hung up the screen *at* the door of the tabernacle.   Ex. 26:36; 40:5

29 ^RAnd he put the altar of burnt offering *before* the door of the tabernacle of the tent of meeting, and ^Roffered upon it the burnt offering and the grain offering, as the LORD had commanded Moses.   Ex. 40:6 • Ex. 29:38–42

30 ^RHe set the laver between the tabernacle of meeting and the altar, and put water there for washing;   Ex. 30:18; 40:7

31 and Moses, Aaron, and his sons would wash their hands and their feet *with water* from it.

32 Whenever they went into the tabernacle of meeting, and when they came near the altar, they washed, ^Ras the LORD had commanded Moses.   Ex. 30:19

33 ^RAnd he raised up the court all around the tabernacle and the altar, and hung up the screen of the court gate. So Moses ^Rfinished the work.   Ex. 27:9–18; 40:8 • [Heb. 3:2–5]

The Cloud and the Glory

34 Then the ^Rcloud covered the tabernacle of meeting, and the ^Rglory of the LORD filled the tabernacle.   1 Kin. 8:10, 11 • Lev. 9:6, 23

35 And Moses ^Rwas not able to enter the tabernacle of meeting, because the cloud rested above it, and the glory of the LORD filled the tabernacle.   1 Kin. 8:11

36 ^RWhenever the cloud was taken up from above the tabernacle, the children of Israel would go onward in all their journeys. Num. 9:17

37 But ^Rif the cloud was not taken up, then they did not journey till the day that it was taken up.   Num. 9:19–22

38 For ^Rthe cloud of the LORD *was* above the tabernacle by day, and fire was over it by night, in the sight of all the house of Israel, throughout all their journeys.   Ex. 13:21

THE THIRD BOOK OF MOSES CALLED
Leviticus

The book of Leviticus reveals the Lord Jesus Christ like the dazzle of a many-faceted diamond. Were it possible for all men to grasp the full beauty, truth, and meaning of its powerful message (considered by many as "the Gospel in Leviticus"), religions, cults, and sects would fade into obscurity. For hidden in the types and shadows of this book is the Son of God Himself (Rom. 15:4; 2 Cor. 10:11).

AUTHORSHIP. Our LORD Himself attests that Moses wrote Leviticus by ascribing the priestly ritual in Leviticus 13 to him (Mark 1:44). Within the book itself over fifty times it is said that it was *to Moses* that the Lord spoke the words he recorded.

Therefore, Leviticus holds some wonderful instructions for the modern Bible student. The book begins with, "Now the LORD called to Moses, and spoke to him from the tabernacle of meeting." Prior to this a distant God spoke from "the mountain that . . . burned with fire" (Heb. 12:18). Now a tabernacle has been erected according to a divine plan and God dwells among His people in fellowship, speaking to them "from the tabernacle." On the grounds of a covenant of blood the people of Leviticus are brought into a new relationship, namely fellowship with the holy God.

In keeping with this, the sacrifices of Leviticus do not set forth how the people may be redeemed. Redemption has already been established by the Passover lamb in Exodus and is memorialized in the Passover Feast.

Leviticus reveals how the new relationship with God may be maintained; it is, therefore, *a book about worship*.

In the beauty of the types recorded in Leviticus we see the many-sided work of Christ concerning all who have already entered into a new relationship with God (justification by faith).

HOW LEVITICUS FITS INTO THE BIBLE. In Genesis we see God's answer to man's sin—the Seed of woman. In Exodus, we see God's answer to man's helplessness—the blood of the Lamb. In Leviticus we see God's provision for man's need—a sacrifice, and an altar and a priest. In Leviticus we have the picture of forgiveness through a sacrifice, reconciliation at an altar, and communion and worship through a priest (a type of Christ).

HOW LEVITICUS FITS TOGETHER. The sacrifices mentioned in Leviticus are perhaps the most complete description of our Savior's atoning work anywhere recorded. As we study these sacrifices we gain a greater appreciation of what the Lord Jesus Christ accomplished on Calvary. God's grace is seen as all-sufficient.

(1) Christ is the *burnt offering*, "offering Himself without spot to God." The New Testament sees Christ as the sinner's substitute (Eph. 5:2). He is the acceptable offering to God, a lamb without blemish and without spot (1 John 3:5; also 2 Cor. 5:21; Heb. 7:26; 1 Pet. 2:22). He is seen not only as the acceptable offering but also as the One who accomplishes the will of God.

(2) Christ is the *grain offering*, an offering that foreshadows His perfect humanity. The point here is that the *life* was offered. The burnt offering relates to our *justification*; the meal offering relates to our *sanctification*. Over the grain offering was poured a specially prepared holy oil—not common oil, but oil of unction. This is a picture of the Holy Spirit and His ministry of setting apart whom He pleases. Christ was thus anointed, again setting the example for us; likewise we are to offer our bodies as a living sacrifice to God, holy and acceptable to Him.

(3) Christ is the *peace offering*. The emphasis here is not on justification or sanctification, but rather on restored communion. It is not the peace of Colossians 1:20–22, but the peace of Ephesians 2:13–22. The peace offering brings unity among God's people and among the various peoples of the world.

(4) Christ is the *sin offering*. The sin offering addresses itself to the problem of our sinful nature (Rom. 7). In the sin offering we see Christ meeting man's deepest human need—the need to be saved from the penalty, power, and presence of sin. The sin offering is a type of Christ as the Bearer of sin (2 Cor. 5:21). The sin offering tells us what Christ did on the cross (Heb. 10:19–22). He bore our sin.

(5) Christ is the *trespass offering*. Whereas the sin offering speaks of Christ as the Sin-Bearer, the trespass offering speaks of "sins"—plural (1 John 1:9). The sin offering typifies Christ as meeting the sin problem, while the trespass offering typifies Christ as meeting the problem of

"sins"—one the nature and the other the acts, one the root and the other the fruit. Christ died not only for our *sin* (our sinful nature) but also for our *sins* (our sinful acts).

Christ Jesus our Lord is all the sacrifices in one person. The book of Hebrews expresses this truth succinctly: "For by one offering He has perfected forever those who are being sanctified" (Heb. 10:14).

In Leviticus the priests hold a prominent place (chs. 8—10). If there is to be fellowship between the holy God and sinful man, there must be not only *sacrifice* (chs. 1—7) but also *a priest* (chs. 8—10). The Lord Jesus is both sacrifice and priest (Heb. 8:1, 2). He appeared once on the cross *for us;* He now is seated at the right hand of the Father *for us* (Heb. 9:24). Only by His ever living intercession are we sustained (Heb. 7:25). We have access to God by "a new and living way" (Heb. 10:20). The way is *new* because it is the way of the *cross;* the way is *living* because of the resurrection of Christ, our faithful High Priest.

KEY WORD AND KEY VERSE. Many key words in Leviticus describe priesthood and worship, but perhaps the most expressive word is *holy* (used eighty-seven times). The key verse is 19:2— "You shall be holy, for I the LORD your God am holy."

—P.W.C.

The Burnt Offering

NOW the LORD [R]called to Moses, and spoke to him [R]from the tabernacle of meeting, saying,   Ex. 19:3; 25:22 · Ex. 40:34

2 "Speak to the children of Israel, and say to them: [R]When any one of you brings an offering to the LORD, you shall bring your offering of the livestock—of the herd and of the flock.   Lev. 22:18, 19

▼ 36-B. Whole Burnt Offerings: Devotion

3 'If his offering *is* a burnt sacrifice of the herd, let him offer a male [R]without blemish; he shall offer it of his own free will at the door of the tabernacle of meeting before the LORD.   Eph. 5:27

4 'Then he shall put his hand on the head ▽ of the burnt offering, and it will be accepted on his behalf to make atonement for him.

5 'He shall kill the [R]bull before the LORD; [R]and the priests, Aaron's sons, shall bring the blood [R]and sprinkle the blood all around on the altar that *is* by the door of the tabernacle of meeting.   Mic. 6:6 · 2 Chr. 35:11 · [Heb. 12:24]

6 'And he shall [R]skin the burnt offering and cut it into its pieces.   Lev. 7:8

7 'The sons of Aaron the priest shall put [R]fire on the altar, and [R]lay the wood in order on the fire.   Mal. 1:10 · Gen. 22:9

8 'Then the priests, Aaron's sons, shall lay the parts, the head, and the fat in order on the wood that *is* on the fire upon the altar;

36-B. Whole Burnt Offerings: Devotion (Leviticus 1:3–17)—The Hebrew words for the whole burnt offering (v. 3) are *olah* and *kalil* (Deut. 33:10, page 212). The former means "that which goes up," and signifies the burnt offering entirely ascended up to God, except for the skin of a bull or the discarded crop and feathers of a bird (vv. 6, 16). The latter means "that which is complete or perfect," and speaks of this offering as being devoted wholly to God. In the case of other sacrifices, the meat went to the priests and Levites. This offering thus represented complete devotion.

(1) God clearly prescribed that even this whole burnt offering must be offered only at His tabernacle, by His priests, and in accordance with His instructions (vv. 3–9). True religion cannot be invented by man.

(2) The offering of a male without defect reminds us that we ought to give our best to God. The perfect male represents Christ (v. 3).

(3) The offerer laid his hand on the head of the sacrifice and it became an atonement on his behalf (v. 4). The Hebrew word *kippur,* "covering" or "atonement," shows that here too there is a covering of sin by the sacrifice of the animal. The atonement of Christ for the believer was vicarious—one suffering in another's place (2 Cor. 5:21, page 1169).

(4) The blood was offered up to God by sprinkling it around the altar (v. 5). The blood was not to be thought of as discarded, for it made the atonement for sin (Lev. 17:11, page 126). Thus, Christ saw His own bleeding at Calvary as "the new covenant in My blood" (1 Cor. 11:25, page 1156).

(5) The burnt offering, by being consumed entirely, symbolized one who desired to be entirely consecrated or rededicated to the Lord (vv. 7–9; cf. Rom. 12:1, 2, page 1142). It reminds us of this goal and need in our lives to be wholly His.

(6) Every morning and evening a whole burnt offering of a lamb was to be offered up to the Lord for the congregation (Num. 28:1–4, page 170). This speaks of our need to rekindle daily our devotion to the Lord.

(7) A choice of burnt offerings could be made—bull, sheep, goat, turtledoves, or pigeons (vv. 2, 5, 10, 14). Here we remember that God sees our limitations, and provides for the lowly and the one too poor to bring a great gift. Whatever we give, however, it is to be wholly given to the Lord.

See Leviticus 2:1–16, page 106, for **Point 36-C: Grain and Drink Offerings: Thanksgiving.**

▽ 9 'but he shall wash its entrails and its legs with water. And the priest shall burn all on the altar as a burnt sacrifice, an offering made by fire, a sweet aroma to the LORD.

10 'If his offering *is* of the flocks—of the sheep or of the goats—as a burnt sacrifice, he shall bring a male without blemish.

11 ᴿ'He shall kill it on the north side of the altar before the LORD; and the priests, Aaron's sons, shall sprinkle its blood all around on the altar.   Lev. 1:5

12 'And he shall cut it into its pieces, with its head and its fat; and the priest shall lay them in order on the wood that *is* on the fire upon the altar;

13 'but he shall wash the entrails and the legs with water. Then the priest shall bring *it* all and burn *it* on the altar; it *is* a burnt sacrifice, an ᴿoffering made by fire, a sweet aroma to the LORD.   Num. 15:4–7; 28:12–14

14 'And if the burnt sacrifice of his offering to the LORD *is* of birds, then he shall bring his offering of turtledoves or young pigeons.

15 'The priest shall bring it to the altar, ▽ ᵀwring off its head, and burn *it* on the altar; its blood shall be drained out at the side of the altar.   Lit. *nip* or *chop off*

16 'And he shall remove its crop with its feathers and cast it ᴿbeside the altar on the east side, into the place for ashes.   Lev. 6:10

17 'Then he shall split it at its wings, *but* shall not divide *it* completely; and the priest shall burn it on the altar, on the wood that *is* on the fire. It *is* a burnt sacrifice, an offering made by fire, a sweet aroma to the LORD. ▲

The Grain Offering

36-C. Grain and Drink Offerings: Thanksgiving ▼

2 'When anyone offers ᴿa grain offering to the LORD, his offering shall be *of* fine flour. And he shall pour oil on it, and put ᴿfrankincense on it.   Num. 15:4 · Lev. 5:11

2 'He shall bring it to Aaron's sons, the priests, one of whom shall take from it his

---

36-C. Grain and Drink Offerings: Thanksgiving (Leviticus 2:1-16)—Grain and drink offerings expressed gratitude to God for His life-giving provision for His people. The Hebrew word *minchah* is best translated "grain offering." The King James Version rendered it "meat offering," meaning "food offering." Today people may inadvertently take this to be animal's flesh, which it is not. This offering consisted of flour, usually baked into unleavened cakes with olive oil, incense, salt, and wine added. Psalm 104:15 (page 571) singles out these three items in singing praise to the Lord's bounteous and all-wise provision for mankind's needs and refreshment.

(1) The grain was the staff of life for nourishment.

(2) The olive oil had many uses, including fuel for light and use in cooking.

(3) The juice of the grape provided a pleasant, sweet drink.

We could have survived on grain and water, but God in His kindness ordered a better menu for His human creatures. These sacrifices thank Him for this.

Cain's vegetable offering was refused as an atonement for sin, while Abel's sacrifice, in which the blood was shed for sin was accepted (Gen. 4:2–5, page 7). Thus, it is here also demonstrated that grain and drink offerings were not given as atonement for sin, but as an expression of gratitude by the people for God's provision of food.

The three national annual grain offerings were:

(1) *The showbread.* Twelve cakes representing the unity of the tribes were baked fresh each week and placed in the tabernacle (Lev. 24:5–9, page 132).

(2) *The firstfruits.* The first sheaf of the early barley was waved before the Lord on the second day of Passover. The Feast of Pentecost was celebrated on the fiftieth day after the second day of the Feast of Passover (Lev. 23:10–14, page 130).

(3) *Two baked loaves.* At Pentecost they gave thanks to God for the full and now complete harvest (Lev. 23:15–18, page 131).

Note the following lessons for our time:

(1) The oil on the flour symbolizes the Holy Spirit giving unity; the frankincense imparts a pleasing aroma to it (vv. 1, 2). Such unity in His children is indeed a pleasing aroma to the Lord.

(2) This gift from God's people provided the physical food for God's servants to live (v. 3). Such provision is still made today.

(3) That it was to be unleavened (vv. 4, 11) spoke of separation from sin, which characterized all that was done on behalf of God.

(4) Man himself was forbidden to offer up his own gift at the tabernacle; it had to be offered by the priests (vv. 8, 9). Even to thank God properly a mediator is necessary, and that Mediator is Christ (1 Tim. 2:5, page 1219).

(5) Note that even the portion that went to the priests is called "most holy" (v. 10). It would have been easy for the donor to think that this portion, not offered by fire to the Lord, was a wasted portion. Thus we learn that what we give to His servants is given as if to Him directly (Matt. 25:40, page 976).

(Point 36-C continued on next page)

▽ handful of fine flour and oil with all the frankincense. And the priest shall burn ᴿ*it as a memorial* on the altar, an offering made by fire, a sweet aroma to the LORD.   Lev. 2:9

3 ᴿ'The rest of the grain offering *shall be* Aaron's and his sons'. *It is* most holy of the offerings to the LORD made by fire.   Lev. 7:9

4 'And if you bring as an offering a grain offering baked in the oven, *it shall be* unleavened cakes of fine flour mixed with oil, or unleavened wafers anointed with oil.

5 'But if your offering *is* a grain offering *baked* in a ᵀpan, *it shall be of* fine flour, unleavened, mixed with oil.   *flat plate or griddle*

6 'You shall break it in pieces and pour oil on it; it *is* a grain offering.

7 'If your offering *is* a grain offering *baked* in a ᴿcovered pan, it shall be made *of* fine flour with oil.   Lev. 7:9

8 'You shall bring the grain offering that is made of these things to the LORD. And when it is presented to the priest, he shall bring it to the altar.

9 'Then the priest shall take from the grain offering ᴿa memorial portion, and burn *it* on the altar. *It is* an ᴿoffering made by fire, a sweet aroma to the LORD.   Lev. 2:2, 16 · Ex. 29:18

10 'And what is left of the grain offering *shall be* Aaron's and his sons'. *It is* most holy of the offerings to the LORD made by fire.

11 'No grain offering which you bring to the LORD shall be made with ᴿleaven, for you shall burn no leaven nor any honey in any offering to the LORD made by fire.   Lev. 6:16, 17

12 'As for the offering of the firstfruits, you ▽ shall offer them to the LORD, but they shall not be burned on the altar for a sweet aroma.

13 'And every offering of your grain offering ᴿyou shall season with salt; you shall not allow the salt of the covenant of your God to be lacking from your grain offering. With all your offerings you shall offer salt.   [Col. 4:6]

14 'If you offer a grain offering of your firstfruits to the LORD, ᴿyou shall offer for the grain offering of your firstfruits green heads of grain roasted on the fire, grain beaten from ᴿfull heads.   Lev. 23:10, 14 · 2 Kin. 4:42

15 'And you shall put oil on it, and lay frankincense on it. It *is* a grain offering.

16 'Then the priest shall burn ᴿthe memorial portion: *part* of its beaten grain and *part* of its oil, with all the frankincense, as an offering made by fire to the LORD.   Lev. 2:2 ▲

The Peace Offering

36-D. Peace Offerings: Fellowship   ▼

3 'When his offering *is* a sacrifice of a peace offering, if he offers *it* of the herd, whether male or female, he shall offer it without ᵀblemish before the LORD.   *defect*

2 'And ᴿhe shall lay his hand on the head of his offering, and kill it *at* the door of the tabernacle of meeting; and Aaron's sons, the priests, shall ᴿsprinkle the blood all around on the altar.   Lev. 1:4, 5; 16:21 · Lev. 1:5

3 'Then he shall offer from the sacrifice of the peace offering an offering made by fire to

---

(Point 36-C continued from previous page)

(6) The salt is said to be "the salt of the covenant" (v. 13), a reminder that thanksgiving to God, merely for His bounty in rains and harvests, is not enough. Thanksgiving to God must be connected always with heart-felt gratitude for God's deliverance from sin, and for His taking those who are forgiven into covenant relationship as His people (1 Cor. 11:25, page 1156).

See Leviticus 3:1–17, above, for **Point 36-D: Peace Offerings: Fellowship.**

36-D. Peace Offerings: Fellowship (Leviticus 3:1–17)—"Sacrifice of peace," *zebach shalomim* (v. 1), literally "sacrifice [singular] of peaces [plural]," refers to various offerings presented by loving and thankful hearts, grateful for the peace and blessing that God has bestowed upon individuals and families. The blood was sprinkled around the altar, and the fat and entrails were burned for the sacrifice. Then the meat was shared by priests and the family of the one making the offering, as a love feast of contentment for the Lord's blessing. It expressed the believer's fellowship with God. Peace offerings could be of several types:

(1) *Thanksgiving* (Lev. 7:12, page 112). Gratitude to God was expressed for some recent blessings.

(2) *Vow* (Lev. 7:16, page 112). This offering commemorated the making or completion of a vow made to Jehovah.

(3) *Freewill* (Lev. 7:16, page 112). The offering was without any specific reason, but out of the sheer delight in being in fellowship with the Lord and knowing His peace.

Lessons which can be applied to the New Testament believer include the following:

(1) The sacrifice of joy was not restricted to a male animal, since it did not directly portray Christ on the cross (v. 1).

(2) The blood sprinkled around the altar signifies today that even our peace and prosperity in daily life depend first on Christ's blood having been shed for our sins (v. 2).

(3) God, who demanded a sacrifice without defect (v. 1), called for the burning of only the inedible

(Point 36-D continued on next page)

▽ the LORD. The fat that covers the entrails and all the fat that is on the entrails,

4 'the two kidneys and the fat that is on them by the flanks, and the fatty lobe attached to the liver above the kidneys, he shall remove;

5 'and Aaron's sons shall burn it on the altar upon the burnt sacrifice, which is on the wood that is on the fire, as an offering made by fire, a sweet aroma to the LORD.

6 'If his offering as a sacrifice of a peace offering to the LORD is of the flock, whether male or female, ᴿhe shall offer it without blemish.   Lev. 3:1; 22:20-24

7 'If he offers a lamb as his offering, then he shall offer it ᴿbefore the LORD.   Lev. 17:8, 9

8 'And he shall lay his hand on the head of his offering, and kill it before the tabernacle of meeting; and Aaron's sons shall sprinkle its blood all around on the altar.

9 'Then he shall offer from the sacrifice of the peace offering, as an offering made by fire to the LORD, its fat and the whole fat tail which he shall remove close to the backbone. And the fat that covers the entrails and all the fat that is on the entrails,

10 'the two kidneys and the fat that is on them by the flanks, and the fatty lobe attached to the liver above the kidneys, he shall remove;

11 'and the priest shall burn them on the altar as ᴿfood, an offering made by fire to the LORD.   Num. 28:2

12 'And if his offering is a goat, then ᴿhe ▽ shall offer it before the LORD.   Lev. 3:1, 7

13 'He shall lay his hand on its head and kill it before the tabernacle of meeting; and the sons of Aaron shall sprinkle its blood all around on the altar.

14 'Then he shall offer from it his offering, as an offering made by fire to the LORD. The fat that covers the entrails and all the fat that is on the entrails,

15 'the two kidneys and the fat that is on them by the flanks, and the fatty lobe attached to the liver above the kidneys, he shall remove;

16 'and the priest shall burn them on the altar as food, an offering made by fire for a sweet aroma; all the fat is the LORD's.

17 'This shall be a perpetual statute throughout your generations in all your dwellings: you shall eat neither fat nor ᴿblood.' "   Lev. 7:23, 26; 17:10, 14 ▲

The Sin Offering

36-E. Sin of Ignorance Offerings: ▼
Righting Wrongs

4 Now the LORD spoke to Moses, saying,
2 "Speak to the children of Israel, saying:
ᴿ'If a person sins ᵀunintentionally against any of the commandments of the LORD in anything which ought not to be done, and does any of them,   Lev. 5:15-18 · through error

3 'if the anointed priest sins, bringing guilt

(Point 36-D continued from previous page)
portion, and left the good meat to be eaten by His people. This shows that peace and fellowship here flow two ways. God is good (Lev. 2:3, page 107).

(4) "A sweet aroma to the LORD" shows that the Lord delights in the well-being of His people, and in their proper expression of love and gratitude to Him for His care (v. 5).

(5) "Male or female . . . without blemish" (v. 6) demonstrates that, despite certain sacrifices specified as male, femaleness was never regarded by God as a defect.

See Leviticus 4:1-35, above, for **Point 36-E: Sin of Ignorance Offerings: Righting Wrongs.**

36-E. Sin of Ignorance Offerings: Righting Wrongs (Leviticus 4:1-35)—The Mosaic Law consisted of both moral commandments and ceremonial directions, which were often given in great detail. It was not difficult for even the sincerest of God's followers to violate one of these ceremonial laws occasionally. In lovingkindness God made special provision for the forgiveness, cleansing, and restoration of one who inadvertently broke His law.

Lessons to be learned include the following:

(1) God, the moral Judge of the universe, makes a distinction between those who unintentionally violate His statutes and those who intentionally trample them (v. 2). Thus, the one who willfully gathered sticks on the Sabbath, who defied God openly soon after the commandment was issued, was stoned (Num. 15:25-36, page 155). By grace, however, in the trespass offering (see Point 36-F, "Trespass Offerings: Forgiveness," page 111) there is mercy for the penitent (Heb. 12:5-11, page 1250).

(2) Even unintentional violations of God's law are still regarded as sin, for which there must be atonement.

(3) Even God's faithful people sin, whether intentionally or unintentionally (v. 3). God knows their limitations, but does not lower His holy standards. Nor does He make exceptions for His specially anointed people. On the contrary, their liability is greater (James 3:1, page 1258); but He provides for their cleansing and restoration (1 John 1:9, page 1278).

(4) The requirement to sprinkle the blood seven times before the veil, and to place blood on the horns
(Point 36-E continued on next page)

▽ on the people, then let him offer to the LORD for his sin which he has sinned a young bull without blemish as a ᴿsin offering.   Lev. 9:7

4 'He shall bring the bull ᴿto the door of the tabernacle of meeting before the LORD, lay his hand on the bull's head, and kill the bull before the LORD.   Lev. 1:3, 4; 4:15

5 'Then the anointed priest ᴿshall take some of the bull's blood and bring it to the tabernacle of meeting.   Lev. 16:14

6 'The priest shall dip his finger in the blood and sprinkle some of the blood seven times before the LORD, in front of the ᴿveil of the sanctuary.   Ex. 40:21, 26

7 'And the priest shall put some of the blood on the horns of the altar of sweet incense before the LORD, which is in the tabernacle of meeting; and he shall pour the remaining blood of the bull at the base of the altar of the burnt offering, which is at the door of the tabernacle of meeting.

8 'He shall take from it all the fat of the bull as the sin offering. The fat that covers the entrails and all the fat which is on the entrails,

9 'the two kidneys and the fat that is on them by the flanks, and the fatty lobe attached to the liver above the kidneys, he shall remove,

10 ᴿ'as it was taken from the bull of the sacrifice of the peace offering; and the priest shall burn them on the altar of the burnt offering.   Lev. 3:3-5

11 'But the bull's hide and all its flesh, with its head and legs, its entrails and offal—

12 'the whole bull he shall carry outside the camp to a clean place, ᴿwhere the ashes are poured out, and ᴿburn it on wood with fire; where the ashes are poured out it shall be burned.   Lev. 4:21; 6:10, 11; 16:27 · [Heb. 13:11, 12]

13 'Now if the whole congregation of Israel sins unintentionally, ᴿand the thing is hidden from the eyes of the assembly, and they have done something against any of the commandments of the LORD in anything which should not be done, and are guilty;   Lev. 5:2-4, 17

14 'when the sin which they have committed becomes known, then the assembly shall offer a young bull for the sin, and bring it before the tabernacle of meeting.

15 'And the elders of the congregation ᴿshall lay their hands on the head of the bull before the LORD. Then the bull shall be killed before the LORD.   Lev. 1:3, 4

16 'The anointed priest shall bring some of the bull's blood to the tabernacle of meeting.

17 'Then the priest shall dip his finger in the blood and sprinkle it seven times before the LORD, in front of the veil.

18 'And he shall put some of the blood on the horns of the altar which is before the LORD, which is in the tabernacle of meeting; and he shall pour the remaining blood at the base of the altar of burnt offering, which is at the door of the tabernacle of meeting.

19 'He shall take all the fat from it and burn it on the altar.

20 'And he shall do with the bull as he did with the bull as a sin offering; thus he shall do with it. So the priest shall make atonement for them, and it shall be forgiven them.

21 'Then he shall carry the bull outside the camp, and burn it as he burned the first bull. It is a sin offering for the assembly.

22 'When a ruler has sinned, and done something unintentionally against any of the commandments of the LORD his God in anything which should not be done, and is guilty,

23 'or ᴿif his sin which he has committed ᵀcomes to his knowledge, he shall bring as his offering a kid of the goats, a male without blemish.   Lev. 4:14; 5:4 · is made known to him

24 'And ᴿhe shall lay his hand on the head of the goat, and kill it at the place where they kill the burnt offering before the LORD. It is a sin offering.   [Is. 53:6]

25 ᴿ'The priest shall take some of the blood of the sin offering with his finger, put it on the horns of the altar of burnt offering, and pour its blood at the base of the altar of burnt offering.   Lev. 4:7; 18, 30, 34

26 'And he shall burn all its fat on the altar, ▽

(Point 36-E continued from previous page)
of the altar of incense referred particularly to a sacrifice for an unintentional sin of the high priest—for example, if he defiled himself by touching a dead body or by eating an unclean item. The mediator-priest of the people had to be cleansed before he could serve.

   (5) The enormity of the sin of the high priest would be dramatized to the people by requiring that the flesh, head, legs, and entrails be burned outside the camp (vv. 11, 12). These were totally unclean, and, as a symbol of sin, had to be utterly removed from the presence of God and His people. Thus Christ our High Priest carried our sins outside the camp (Jerusalem) at Calvary. Unlike the Old Testament high priest, He was without sin, but He was made "to be sin for us, that we might become the righteousness of God in Him" (2 Cor. 5:21, page 1169; cf. Heb. 13:11-13, page 1252).

   (6) A whole congregation could sin corporately (vv. 13-21). When this was discovered—looking back over the past year or years—the elders had to take the necessary steps for forgiveness, and right the wrong.

   (7) Leaders (v. 22) and common people (v. 27) were not exempt from the consequences of unintentional sins. It is not enough merely to forget about it, and turn over a new leaf; forgiveness must be sought, and amends must be made.

See Leviticus 6:1-7, page 111, for **Point 36-F: Trespass Offerings: Forgiveness.**

▽ like ᴿthe fat of the sacrifice of the peace offering. ᴿSo the priest shall make atonement for him concerning his sin, and it shall be forgiven him.   Lev. 3:3-5 · Lev. 4:20

27 ᴿ'If ᵀanyone of the ᵀcommon people sins unintentionally by doing *something against* any of the commandments of the LORD *in anything* which ought not to be done, and is guilty,   Num. 15:27 · Lit. *any soul* · Lit. *people of the land*

28 'or if his sin which he has committed comes to his knowledge, then he shall bring as his offering a kid of the goats, a female without blemish, for his sin which he has committed.

29 ᴿ'And he shall lay his hand on the head of the sin offering, and kill the sin offering at the place of the burnt offering.   Lev. 1:4; 4:4, 24

30 'Then the priest shall take *some* of its blood with his finger, put *it* on the horns of the altar of burnt offering, and pour all *the remaining* blood at the base of the altar.

31 'He shall remove all its fat, ᴿas fat is removed from the sacrifice of the peace offering; and the priest shall burn it on the altar for a ᴿsweet aroma to the LORD. ᴿSo the priest shall make atonement for him, and it shall be forgiven him.   Lev. 3:3, 4 · Ex. 29:18 · Lev. 4:26

32 'If he brings a lamb as his sin offering, he shall bring a female without blemish.

33 'Then he shall ᴿlay his hand on the head of the sin offering, and kill it as a sin offering at the place where they kill the burnt offering.   Num. 8:12

34 'The priest shall take *some* of the blood of the sin offering with his finger, put *it* on the horns of the altar of burnt offering, and pour all *the remaining* blood at the base of the altar.

35 'He shall remove all its fat, as the fat of the lamb is removed from the sacrifice of the peace offering. Then the priest shall burn it on the altar, according to the offerings made by fire to the LORD. ᴿSo the priest shall make atonement for his sin that he has committed,
▲ and it shall be forgiven him.   Lev. 4:26, 31

The Trespass Offering

5 'If a person sins in hearing the utterance of an oath, and *is* a witness, whether he has seen or known *of the matter*—if he does not tell *it*, he bears guilt.

2 'Or ᴿif a person touches any unclean thing, whether *it is* the carcass of an unclean beast, or the carcass of unclean livestock, or the carcass of unclean creeping things, and he is unaware of it, he also shall be unclean and ᴿguilty.   Num. 19:11-16 · Lev. 5:17

3 'Or if he touches ᴿhuman uncleanness—whatever uncleanness with which a man may be defiled, and he is unaware of it—when he realizes *it*, then he shall be guilty.   Lev. 5:12, 13, 15

4 'Or if a person swears, speaking thoughtlessly with *his* lips to do evil or ᴿto do good, whatever *it is* that a man may pronounce by

an oath, and he is unaware of it—when he realizes *it*, then he shall be guilty in any of these *matters*.   [James 5:12]

5 'And it shall be, when he is guilty in any of these *matters*, that he shall ᴿconfess that he has sinned in that *thing*;   Prov. 28:13

6 'and he shall bring his trespass offering to the LORD for his sin which he has committed, a female from the flock, a lamb or a kid of the goats as a sin offering. So the priest shall make atonement for him concerning his sin.

7 ᴿ'If he is not able to bring a lamb, then he shall bring to the LORD, for his trespass which he has committed, two ᴿturtledoves or two young pigeons: one as a sin offering and the other as a burnt offering.   Lev. 12:6 · Lev. 1:14

8 'And he shall bring them to the priest, who shall offer *that* which *is* for the sin offering first, and wring off its head from its neck, but shall not divide *it* completely.

9 'Then he shall sprinkle *some* of the blood of the sin offering on the side of the altar, and the rest of the blood shall be drained out at the base of the altar. It *is* a sin offering.

10 'And he shall offer the second *as* a burnt offering according to the prescribed manner. So ᴿthe priest shall make atonement on his behalf for his sin which he has committed, and it shall be forgiven him.   Lev. 4:20, 26; 5:13, 16

11 'But if he is not able to bring two turtledoves or two young pigeons, then he who sinned shall bring for his offering one-tenth of an ephah of fine flour as a sin offering. He shall put no oil on it, nor shall he put frankincense on it, for it *is* a sin offering.

12 'Then he shall bring it to the priest, and the priest shall take his handful of it ᴿas a memorial portion, and burn *it* on the altar ᴿaccording to the offerings made by fire to the LORD. It *is* a sin offering.   Lev. 2:2 · Lev. 4:35

13 'The priest shall make atonement for him, ᴿfor his sin that he has committed in any of these matters; and it shall be forgiven him. ᴿ*The rest* shall be the priest's as a grain offering.' "   *concerning his sin* · Lev. 2:3; 6:17, 26

Offerings with Restitution

14 Then the LORD spoke to Moses, saying:

15 "If a person commits a trespass, and sins unintentionally in regard to the holy things of the LORD, then he shall bring to the LORD as his trespass offering a ram without blemish from the flocks, with your valuation in ᵀshekels of silver according to the shekel of the sanctuary, as a trespass offering. $128 each

16 "And he shall make restitution for the harm that he has done in regard to the holy thing, and shall add one-fifth to it and give it to the priest. So the priest shall make atonement for him with the ram of the trespass offering, and it shall be forgiven him.

17 "If a person sins, and commits any of

these things which are forbidden to be done by the commandments of the LORD, though he does not know *it*, yet he is ᴿguilty and shall bear his ᵀiniquity.   Lev. 5:1, 2 • *punishment*

18 ᴿ"And he shall bring to the priest a ram without blemish from the flock, with your valuation, as a trespass offering. So the priest shall make atonement for him regarding his ignorance in which he erred and did not know *it*, and it shall be forgiven him. Lev. 5:15

19 "It is a trespass offering; ᴿhe has certainly trespassed against the LORD."   Ezra 10:2

▼ 36–F. Trespass Offerings: Forgiveness

6 And the LORD spoke to Moses, saying:
2 "If a person sins and commits a trespass against the LORD by lying to his neighbor about what was delivered to him for safekeeping, or about a pledge, or about a robbery, or if he has extorted from his neighbor,

3 "or if he ᴿhas found what was lost and lies concerning it, and ᴿswears falsely—in any one of these things that a man may do in which he sins: Deut. 22:1–4 • Ex. 22:11

4 "then it shall be, because he has sinned and is guilty, that he shall restore what he has stolen, or the thing which he has extorted, or what was delivered to him for safekeeping, or the lost thing which he found,

5 "or all that about which he has sworn falsely. He shall restore its full value, add one-fifth more to it, *and* give it to whomever it belongs, on the day of his trespass offering.

6 "And he shall bring his trespass offering to the LORD, ᴿa ram without blemish from the flock, with your ᵀvaluation, as a trespass offering, to the priest.   Lev. 1:3; 5:15 • *appraisal*

7 ᴿ"So the priest shall make atonement for him before the LORD, and he shall be forgiven

for any one of these things that he may have done in which he trespasses."   Lev. 4:26 ▲

The Law of the Burnt Offering

8 Then the LORD spoke to Moses, saying,

9 "Command Aaron and his sons, saying, 'This *is* the law of the burnt offering: The burnt offering *shall be* on the hearth upon the altar all night until morning, and the fire of the altar shall be kept burning on it.

10 ᴿ'And the priest shall put on his linen garment, and his linen trousers he shall put on his body, and take up the ashes of the burnt offering which the fire has consumed on the altar, and he shall put them ᴿbeside the altar.   Ex. 28:39-43 • Lev. 1:16

11 'Then he shall take off his garments, put on other garments, and carry the ashes outside the camp ᴿto a clean place.   Lev. 4:12

12 'And the fire on the altar shall be kept burning on it; it shall not be put out. And the priest shall burn wood on it every morning, and lay the burnt offering in order on it; and he shall burn on it ᴿthe fat of the peace offerings.   Lev. 3:3, 5, 9, 14

13 'A fire shall always be burning on the ᴿaltar; it shall never go out.   Lev. 1:7

The Law of the Grain Offering

14 'This *is* the law of the grain offering: The sons of Aaron shall offer it on the altar before the LORD.

15 'He shall take from it his handful of the fine flour of the grain offering, with its oil, and all the frankincense which *is* on the grain offering, and shall burn *it* on the altar *for* a sweet aroma, as a memorial to the LORD.

16 'And the remainder of it Aaron and his sons shall eat; with unleavened bread it shall

36–F. Trespass Offerings: Forgiveness (Leviticus 6:1–7)—Trespass offerings pertain to acts committed willfully against one's fellow man, which are also sins against the Lord—such as robbery, fraud, embezzlement, theft, extortion, or retaining property unlawfully. All of these sins involve apparent guilt—plainly breaking God's law, whether willfully or through yielding to temptation. Observe also:

(1) Sins of cheating one's spiritual brother are also trespasses against God (vv. 2, 6).

(2) Not only must divine pardon be sought, but God demands that restitution be made, plus one-fifth interest and penalty (vv. 4, 5).

(3) From the dual requirements here presented, that is, to seek forgiveness from both God and man, we conclude:

(a) One who makes restitution to one's neighbor, and who does not make peace with God, remains unforgiven.

(b) One who offers sacrifice to God, but fails to restore the loss to his brother, remains unforgiven.

(4) True inward conversion, such as in the case of Zacchaeus, is expressed by a sincere outward effort to make amends for wrongs (Luke 19:8–10, page 1038).

(5) Having made restitution and sought God's forgiveness, one must then by faith accept God's forgiveness, and should no longer harbor feelings of guilt (Eph. 1:7, page 1186).

(6) How kind God is to His people to provide for forgiveness of even willful sins! Therefore we also are to forgive one another (Eph. 4:32, page 1191).

(7) How available Christ is today to forgive, cleanse, and give a new life and new direction to those who flee to Him for forgiveness of their trespasses and guilt (Rom. 4:5–8, page 1132; cf. Ps. 32:1, 2, page 528).

See Leviticus 12:6–8, page 118, for **Point 36–G: Special Offerings.**

be eaten in a holy place; in the court of the tabernacle of meeting they shall eat it.

17 'It shall not be baked with leaven. I have given it *as* their ᵀportion of My offerings made by fire; it *is* most holy, like the sin offering and the trespass offering.   *share*

18 'All the males among the children of Aaron may eat it. *It shall be* a statute forever in your generations concerning the offerings made by fire to the LORD. Everyone who touches them must be holy.' "

19 And the LORD spoke to Moses, saying,

20 ᴿ"This *is* the offering of Aaron and his sons, which they shall offer to the LORD, *beginning* on the day when he is anointed: ᵀone-tenth of an ᴿephah of fine flour as a daily grain offering, half of it in the morning and half of it at night.   Ex. 29:2 · 2.1 qt. · Ex. 16:36

21 "It shall be made in a pan with oil. *When it is* mixed, you shall bring it in. The baked pieces of the grain offering you shall offer *for* a sweet aroma to the LORD.

22 "The priest from among his sons, ᴿwho is anointed in his place, shall offer it. *It is* a statute forever to the LORD. ᴿIt shall be ᵀwholly burned.   Lev. 4:3 · Ex. 29:25 · *completely*

23 "For every grain offering for the priest shall be wholly burned. It shall not be eaten."

The Law of the Sin Offering

24 Also the LORD spoke to Moses, saying,

25 "Speak to Aaron and to his sons, saying, 'This *is* the law of the sin offering: ᴿIn the place where the burnt offering is killed, the sin offering shall be killed before the LORD. It *is* most holy.   Lev. 1:1, 3, 5, 11

26 'The priest who offers it for sin shall eat it. In a holy place it shall be eaten, in the court of the tabernacle of meeting.

27 ᴿ'Everyone who touches its flesh must be holy. And when its blood is sprinkled on any garment, you shall wash that on which it was sprinkled, in a holy place.   Num. 4:15; Hag. 2:11–13

28 'But the earthen vessel in which it is boiled ᴿshall be broken. And if it is boiled in a bronze pot, it shall be both scoured and rinsed in water.   Lev. 11:33; 15:12

29 'All the males among the priests may eat it. It *is* most holy.

30 ᴿ'But no sin offering from which *any* of the blood is brought into the tabernacle of meeting, to make atonement in *the holy ᴿplace, shall be eaten. It shall be burned in the fire.   Lev. 4:7, 11, 12, 18, 21; 10:18; 16:27 · Ex. 26:33

The Law of the Trespass Offering

7 'Likewise ᴿthis *is* the law of the trespass offering (it *is* most holy):   Lev. 5:14—6:7

2 'In the place where they kill the burnt offering they shall kill the trespass offering. And its blood he shall sprinkle all around on the altar.

3 'And he shall offer from it all its fat. The fat tail and the fat that covers the entrails,

4 'the two kidneys and the fat that *is* on them by the flanks, and the fatty lobe *attached* to the liver above the kidneys, he shall remove;

5 'and the priest shall burn them on the altar *as* an offering made by fire to the LORD. It *is* a trespass offering.

6 ᴿ'Every male among the priests may eat it. It shall be eaten in a holy place. ᴿIt *is* most holy.   Lev. 6:16–18, 29 · Lev. 2:3

7 ᴿ'The trespass offering is like the sin offering; *there is* one law for them both: the priest who makes atonement with it shall have *it*.   Lev. 6:24–30; 14:13

8 'And the priest who offers anyone's burnt offering, that priest shall have for himself the skin of the burnt offering which he has offered.

9 'Also ᴿevery grain offering that is baked in the oven and all that is prepared in the covered pan, or ᵀin a pan, shall be the priest's who offers it.   Lev. 2:3, 10 · *on a griddle*

10 'Every grain offering, *whether* mixed with oil or dry, shall belong to all the sons of Aaron, to one *as much* as the other.

The Law of Peace Offerings

11 'This *is* the law of the sacrifice of peace offerings which he shall offer to the LORD:

12 'If he offers it for a thanksgiving, then he shall offer, with the sacrifice of thanksgiving, unleavened cakes mixed with oil, unleavened wafers ᴿanointed with oil, or cakes of blended flour mixed with oil.   Num. 6:15

13 'Besides the cakes, *as* his offering he shall offer ᴿleavened bread with the sacrifice of thanksgiving of his peace offering.   Amos 4:5

14 'And from it he shall offer one cake from each offering *as* a heave offering to the LORD. ᴿIt shall belong to the priest who sprinkles the blood of the peace offering.   Num. 18:8, 11, 19

15 ᴿ'The flesh of the sacrifice of his peace offering for thanksgiving shall be eaten the same day it is offered. He shall not leave any of it until morning.   Lev. 22:29, 30

16 'But ᴿif the sacrifice of his offering *is* a vow or a voluntary offering, it shall be eaten the same day that he offers his sacrifice; but on the next day the remainder of it also may be eaten;   Lev. 19:5–8

17 'the remainder of the flesh of the sacrifice on the third day must be burned with fire.

18 'And if *any* of the flesh of the sacrifice of his peace offering is eaten at all on the third day, it shall not be accepted, nor shall it be imputed to him; it shall be an ᴿabomination to him who offers it, and the person who eats of it shall bear ᵀguilt.   Lev. 11:10, 41; 19:7 · *his iniquity*

19 'The flesh that touches any unclean thing shall not be eaten. It shall be burned

with fire. And as for the *clean* flesh, all who are clean may eat of it.

20 'But the person who eats the flesh of the sacrifice of the peace offering that *belongs* to the ^RLORD, while he is unclean, that person shall be cut off from his people. [Heb. 2:17]

21 'Moreover the person who touches any unclean thing, *such as* human uncleanness, an ^Runclean animal, or any ^Rabominable* unclean thing, and who eats the flesh of the sacrifice of the peace offering that *belongs* to the LORD, that person ^Rshall be cut off from his people.' " Lev. 11:24, 28 · Ezek. 4:14 · Lev. 7:20

Fat and Blood May Not Be Eaten

22 And the LORD spoke to Moses, saying,

23 "Speak to the children of Israel, saying: ^R'You shall not eat any fat, of ox or sheep or goat. Lev. 3:17; 17:10-15

24 'And the fat of an animal that dies *naturally*, and the fat of what is torn by wild beasts, may be used in any other way; but you shall by no means eat it.

25 'For whoever eats the fat of the animal of which men offer an offering made by fire to the LORD, the person who eats *it* shall be cut off from his people.

26 ^R'Moreover you shall not eat any blood in any of your dwellings, *whether* of bird or beast. Acts 15:20, 29

27 'Whoever eats any blood, that person shall be cut off from his people.' "

The Portion of Aaron and His Sons

28 Then the LORD spoke to Moses, saying,

29 "Speak to the children of Israel, saying: ^RHe who offers the sacrifice of his peace offering to the LORD shall bring his offering to the LORD from the sacrifice of his peace offering. Lev. 3:1; 22:21

30 'His own hands shall bring the offerings made by fire to the LORD. The fat with the breast he shall bring, that the breast may be waved *as* a wave offering before the LORD.

31 ^R'And the priest shall burn the fat on the altar, but the ^Rbreast shall be Aaron's and his sons'. Lev. 3:5, 11, 16 · Deut. 18:3

32 ^R'Also the right thigh you shall give to the priest *as* a heave offering from the sacrifices of your peace offerings. Num. 6:20

33 'He among the sons of Aaron, who offers the blood of the peace offering and the fat, shall have the right thigh for *his* part.

34 'For the breast of the wave offering and the thigh of the heave offering I have taken from the children of Israel, from the sacrifices of their peace offerings, and I have given them to Aaron the priest and to his sons from the children of Israel by a statute forever.' "

35 This *is* the consecrated portion for Aaron and his sons, from the offerings made by fire to the LORD, on the day when *Moses* pre-

sented them to ^Tminister to the LORD as priests. *serve as priests to the* LORD

36 The LORD commanded this to be given to them by the children of Israel, ^Ron the day that He anointed them, *by* a statute forever throughout their generations. Lev. 8:12, 30

37 This *is* the law of the burnt offering, the grain offering, the sin offering, the trespass offering, ^Rthe consecrations, and the sacrifice of the peace offering, Ex. 29:1

38 which the LORD commanded Moses on Mount Sinai, on the day when He commanded the children of Israel ^Rto offer their offerings to the LORD in the Wilderness of Sinai. Lev. 1:1, 2

Aaron and His Sons Consecrated

8 And the LORD spoke to Moses, saying:

2 "Take Aaron and his sons with him, and the garments, ^Rthe anointing oil, a ^Rbull as the sin offering, two rams, and a basket of unleavened bread; Ex. 30:24, 25 · Ex. 29:10

3 "and gather all the congregation together at the door of the tabernacle of meeting."

4 So Moses did as the LORD commanded him. And the congregation was gathered together at the door of the tabernacle of meeting.

5 And Moses said to the congregation, "This *is* what the LORD commanded to be done."

6 Then Moses brought Aaron and his sons and ^Rwashed them with water. Heb. 10:22

7 And he ^Rput the tunic on him, girded him with the sash, clothed him with the robe, and put the ephod on him; and he girded him with the intricately woven band of the ephod, and with it tied *the ephod* on him. Ex. 39:1-31

8 Then he put the breastplate on him, and he put the ^TUrim and the Thummim in the breastplate. Lit. *Lights and the Perfections,* Ex. 28:30

9 ^RAnd he put the turban on his head. Also on the turban, on its front, he put the golden plate, the holy crown, as the LORD had commanded Moses. Ex. 28:36, 37; 29:6

10 ^RAlso Moses took the anointing oil, and anointed the tabernacle and all that *was* in it, and consecrated them. Ex. 30:26-29; 40:10, 11

11 He sprinkled some of it on the altar seven times, anointed the altar and all its utensils, and the laver and its base, to ^Tconsecrate them. *set them apart* for the LORD

12 And he ^Rpoured some of the anointing oil on Aaron's head and anointed him, to consecrate him. Ps. 133:2

13 Then Moses brought Aaron's sons and put tunics on them, girded them with sashes, and put ^Thats on them, as the LORD had commanded Moses. *headgear or caps*

14 ^RAnd he brought the bull for the sin offering. Then Aaron and his sons ^Rlaid their hands on the head of the bull for the sin offering, Ezek. 43:19 · Lev. 4:4

7:21 So with MT, LXX, Vg.; Sam., Syr., Tg. *swarming thing* (5:2)

15 and Moses killed *it*. ᴿThen he took the blood, and put *some* on the horns of the altar all around with his finger, and purified the altar. And he poured the blood at the base of the altar, and consecrated it, to make atonement for it.   Lev. 4:7

16 ᴿThen he took all the fat that *was* on the entrails, the fatty lobe *attached to* the liver, and the two kidneys with their fat, and Moses burned *them* on the altar.   Ex. 29:13

17 But the bull, its hide, its flesh, and its offal, he burned with fire outside the camp, as the Lᴏʀᴅ ᴿhad commanded Moses.   Lev. 4:11, 12

18 ᴿThen he brought the ram as the burnt offering. And Aaron and his sons laid their hands on the head of the ram,   Ex. 29:15

19 and Moses killed *it*. Then he sprinkled the blood all around on the altar.

20 And he cut the ram into pieces; and Moses ᴿburned the head, the pieces, and the fat.   Lev. 1:8

21 Then he washed the entrails and the legs in water. And Moses burned the whole ram on the altar. It *was* a burnt sacrifice for a ᵀsweet aroma, an offering made by fire to the Lᴏʀᴅ, ᴿas the Lᴏʀᴅ had commanded Moses.   *pleasing* • Ex. 29:18

22 And he brought the second ram, the ram of consecration. Then Aaron and his sons laid their hands on the head of the ram,

23 and Moses killed *it*. Also he took *some* of ᴿits blood and put it on the tip of Aaron's right ear, on the thumb of his right hand, and on the big toe of his right foot.   Lev. 14:14

24 Then he brought Aaron's sons. And Moses put *some* of the ᴿblood on the tips of their right ears, on the thumbs of their right hands, and on the big toes of their right feet. And Moses sprinkled the blood all around on the altar.   [Heb. 9:13, 14, 18–23]

25 ᴿThen he took the fat and the fat tail, all the fat that *was* on the entrails, the fatty lobe *attached to* the liver, the two kidneys and their fat, and the right thigh;   Ex. 29:22

26 ᴿand from the basket of unleavened bread that was before the Lᴏʀᴅ he took one unleavened cake, a cake of bread *anointed with* oil, and one wafer, and put *them* on the fat and on the right thigh;   Ex. 29:23

27 and he put all *these* ᴿin Aaron's hands and in his sons' hands, and waved them *as* a wave offering before the Lᴏʀᴅ.   Ex. 29:24

28 ᴿThen Moses took them from their hands and burned *them* on the altar, on the burnt offering. They *were* consecration offerings for a sweet aroma. That *was* an offering made by fire to the Lᴏʀᴅ.   Ex. 29:25

29 And Moses took the breast and waved it *as* a wave offering before the Lᴏʀᴅ. It was Moses' ᴿpart of the ram of consecration, as the Lᴏʀᴅ had commanded Moses.   Ex. 29:26

30 Then ᴿMoses took some of the anointing oil and some of the blood which *was* on the altar, and sprinkled *it* on Aaron, on his garments, on his sons, and on the garments of his sons with him; and he consecrated Aaron, his garments, his sons, and the garments of his sons with him.   Ex. 29:21; 30:30

31 And Moses said to Aaron and his sons, ᴿ"Boil the flesh *at* the door of the tabernacle of meeting, and eat it there with the bread that *is* in the basket of consecration offerings, as I commanded, saying, 'Aaron and his sons shall eat it.'   Ex. 29:31, 32

32 ᴿ"What remains of the flesh and of the bread you shall burn with fire.   Ex. 29:34

33 "And you shall not go outside the door of the tabernacle of meeting *for* seven days, until the days of your consecration are ended. For seven days he shall consecrate you.

34 ᴿ"As he has done this day, *so* the Lᴏʀᴅ has commanded to do, to make atonement for you.   [Heb. 7:16]

35 "Therefore you shall stay *at* the door of the tabernacle of meeting day and night for seven days, and ᴿkeep the charge of the Lᴏʀᴅ, so that you may not die; for so I have been commanded."   Deut. 11:1

36 So Aaron and his sons did all the things that the Lᴏʀᴅ had commanded by the hand of Moses.

The Priestly Ministry Begins

9 It came to pass on the ᴿeighth day that Moses called Aaron and his sons and the elders of Israel.   Ezek. 43:27

2 And he said to Aaron, "Take for yourself a young ᴿbull as a sin offering and a ram as a burnt offering, without blemish, and offer *them* before the Lᴏʀᴅ.   Lev. 4:1–12

3 "And to the children of Israel you shall speak, saying, ᴿ"Take a kid of the goats as a sin offering, and a calf and a lamb, *both* of the first year, without blemish, as a burnt offering,   Lev. 4:23, 28

4 'also a bull and a ram as peace offerings, to sacrifice before the Lᴏʀᴅ, and ᴿa grain offering mixed with oil; for ᴿtoday the Lᴏʀᴅ will appear to you.' "   Lev. 2:4 • Ex. 29:43

5 So they brought what Moses commanded before the tabernacle of meeting. And all the congregation drew near and stood ᵀbefore the Lᴏʀᴅ.   *in the presence of*

6 Then Moses said, "This *is* the thing which the Lᴏʀᴅ commanded you to do, and the glory of the Lᴏʀᴅ will appear to you."

7 And Moses said to Aaron, "Go to the altar, ᴿoffer your sin offering and your burnt offering, and make atonement for yourself and for the people. ᴿOffer the offering of the people, and make atonement for them, as the Lᴏʀᴅ commanded."   [Heb. 5:3–5; 7:27] • Lev. 4:16, 20

8 Aaron therefore went to the altar and killed the calf of the sin offering, which *was* for himself.

9 Then the sons of Aaron brought the blood to him. And he dipped his finger in the

blood, put *it* on the horns of the altar, and poured the blood at the base of the altar.

10 ^RBut the fat, the kidneys, and the fatty lobe from the liver of the sin offering he burned on the altar, as the LORD had commanded Moses.   Lev. 8:16

11 ^RThe flesh and the hide he burned with fire outside the camp.   Lev. 4:11, 12; 8:17

12 And he killed the burnt offering; and Aaron's sons presented to him the blood, which he sprinkled all around on the altar.

13 ^RThen they presented the burnt offering to him, with its pieces and head, and he burned *them* on the altar.   Lev. 8:20

14 ^RAnd he washed the entrails and the legs, and burned *them* with the burnt offering on the altar.   Lev. 8:21

15 ^RThen he brought the people's offering, and took the goat, which *was* the sin offering for the people, and killed it and offered it for sin, like the first one.   [Is. 53:10]

16 And he brought the burnt offering and offered it ^Raccording to the ^Tprescribed manner.   Lev. 1:1–13 • *ordinance*

17 Then he brought the grain offering, took a handful of it, and burned *it* on the altar, besides the burnt sacrifice of the morning.

18 He also killed the bull and the ram *as* ^Rsacrifices of peace offerings, which *were* for the people. And Aaron's sons presented to him the blood, which he sprinkled all around on the altar,   Lev. 3:1–11

19 and the fat from the bull and the ram— the fatty tail, what covers *the entrails* and the

kidneys, and the fatty lobe *attached to* the liver;

20 and they put the fat on the breasts. Then he burned the fat on the altar;

21 but the breasts and the right thigh Aaron waved ^R*as* a wave offering before the LORD, as Moses had commanded.   Lev. 7:30–34

22 Then Aaron lifted his hand toward the people, ^Rblessed them, and came down from offering the sin offering, the burnt offering, and peace offerings.   Luke 24:50

23 And Moses and Aaron went into the tabernacle of meeting, and came out and blessed the people. Then the glory of the LORD appeared to all the people,

24 and fire came out from before the LORD and consumed the burnt offering and the fat on the altar. When all the people saw *it*, they ^Rshouted and fell on their faces.   Ezra 3:11

The Profane Fire of Nadab and Abihu

16-D. Consequences of Sin Committed by Nadab and Abihu ▼

10 Nadab^R and Abihu, the sons of Aaron, ^Reach took his censer and put fire in it, put incense on it, and offered ^Rprofane fire before the LORD, which He had not commanded them.   Num. 3:2–4 • Lev. 16:12 • Ex. 30:9

2 So ^Rfire went out from the LORD and devoured them, and they died before the LORD.   Num. 11:1; 16:35

3 And Moses said to Aaron, "This is what the LORD spoke, saying:

16-D. Consequences of Sin Committed by Nadab and Abihu (Leviticus 10:1-10)—The sin unto death committed by Nadab and Abihu is difficult to define because there is so much involved. Their sin was so heinous that the fire of God fell upon them and they died instantly, yet their bodies and clothing were not consumed. The fire that fell upon them was God's holiness manifested in judgment on two of His carnal servants (Heb. 12:29, page 1251). They were:

(1) *Privileged young priests.* What an honor to be called of God to the priesthood, to be a mediator between God and men! In this they were a type of Christ (1 Tim. 2:5, page 1219). Aaron, the high priest, was their father; they were in line for the office of the high priest. Moses, one of the truly great men of all times, was their uncle. Yet, privileged as they were, God judged them severely.

(2) *Presumptuous young priests.* They were unstable in spiritual things. They may have acted in ignorance, and under the influence of wine or strong drink (v. 9). Yet they were without excuse (Rom. 1:20, page 1128). The sin of Nadab and Abihu was committed when they performed a holy act of worship in the energy of the flesh. They offered profane fire before the Lord in the Most Holy Place, as a substitute for the fire on the brazen altar (Lev. 6:12, 13, page 111; 16:12, page 124). It was "will worship," by carnal means, in the presence of almighty God in His shekinah glory (Ex. 40:34-38, page 103). It is possible that when they entered the Holy Place to worship, they were carried away with a combination of religious enthusiasm and jealousy against Moses and Aaron. Whatever their reasons, they did the right thing (worship) the wrong way—in the wrong spirit, using the wrong method, at the wrong time, moved by the wrong motive. They broke God's commandments and offered the wrong fire before the Lord.

(3) *Perishable young priests.* They may have thought themselves immune to the judgments of God because of who they were. If so, they soon learned that "God shows no partiality" (Acts 10:34, page 1103). "Therefore let him who thinks he stands take heed lest he fall" (1 Cor. 10:12, 13, page 1155). We are all perishable as long as we are in this body of flesh. The great apostle Paul knew that he was perishable, and he feared, lest he should become unfit for the ministry, becoming one of God's rejects (1 Cor. 9:25-27, page 1154).

We have often heard it said that "the end justifies the means." The judgment of Nadab and Abihu brands this notion as a big lie. The truth is, the right end is never reached by the wrong means. The wrong means will always bring you to the wrong end.

See Numbers 20:1-13, page 159, for **Point 16-E: Consequences of Sin Committed by Moses and Aaron.**

▽   'By those ᴿwho come near Me
I must be regarded as holy;
And before all the people
I must be glorified.' "

So Aaron held his peace.   Ex. 19:22

4 Then Moses called Mishael and Elzaphan, the sons of Uzziel the uncle of Aaron, and said to them, "Come near, ᴿcarry your brethren from ᵀbefore the sanctuary out of the camp."   Acts 5:6, 10 · *in front of*

5 So they went near and carried them by their tunics out of the camp, as Moses had said.

6 And Moses said to Aaron, and to Eleazar and Ithamar, his sons, "Do not ᵀuncover your heads nor tear your clothes, lest you die, and ᴿwrath come upon all the people. But let your brethren, the whole house of Israel, ᵀbewail the burning which the LORD has kindled.   An act of mourning · 2 Sam. 24:1 · *weep bitterly*

7 "You shall not go out from the door of the tabernacle of meeting, lest you die, for the anointing oil of the LORD is upon you." And they did according to the word of Moses.

Conduct Prescribed for Priests

8 Then the LORD spoke to Aaron, saying:
9 ᴿ"Do not drink wine or intoxicating drink, you, nor your sons with you, when you go into the tabernacle of meeting, lest you die. It shall be a statute forever throughout your generations,   Ezek. 44:21

10 "that you may distinguish between holy
▲ and unholy, and between unclean and clean,
11 "and that you may teach the children of Israel all the statutes which the LORD has spoken to them by the hand of Moses."

12 And Moses spoke to Aaron, and to Eleazar and Ithamar, his sons who were left: ᴿ"Take the grain offering that remains of the offerings made by fire to the LORD, and eat it without leaven beside the altar; ᴿfor it is most holy.   Num. 18:9 · Lev. 21:22

13 "You shall eat it in a holy place, because it is your ᵀdue and your sons' due, of the sacrifices made by fire to the LORD; for so I have been commanded.   *portion*

14 ᴿ"The breast of the wave offering and the thigh of the heave offering you shall eat in a clean place, you, your sons, and your ᴿdaughters with you; for *they are* your due and your sons' ᴿdue, *which* are given from the sacrifices of peace offerings of the children of Israel.   Num. 18:11 · Lev. 22:13 · Num. 18:10

15 ᴿ"The thigh of the heave offering and the breast of the wave offering they shall bring with the offerings of fat made by fire, to offer *as* a wave offering before the LORD. And it shall be yours and your sons' with you, by a statute forever, as the LORD has commanded."   Lev. 7:29, 30, 34

16 Then Moses made careful inquiry about ᴿthe goat of the sin offering, and there it was—burned up. And he was angry with

Eleazar and Ithamar, the sons of Aaron *who were* left, saying,   Lev. 9:3, 15

17 ᴿ"Why have you not eaten the sin offering in a holy place, since it *is* most holy, and God has given it to you to bear ᴿthe guilt of the congregation, to make atonement for them before the LORD?   Lev. 6:24–30 · Ex. 28:38

18 "See! Its blood was not brought inside the holy *place*; indeed you should have eaten it in a holy *place*, as I commanded."

19 And Aaron said to Moses, "Look, this day they have offered their sin offering and their burnt offering before the LORD, and such things have befallen me! *If* I had eaten the sin offering today, would it have been accepted in the sight of the LORD?"

20 So when Moses heard *that*, he was content.

Foods Permitted and Forbidden

11 Now the LORD spoke to Moses and Aaron, saying to them,

2 "Speak to the children of Israel, saying, 'These *are* the animals which you may eat among all the animals that *are* on the earth:

3 'Among the animals, whatever divides the hoof, having cloven hooves *and* chewing the cud—that you may eat.

4 'Nevertheless these you shall ᴿnot eat among those that chew the cud or those that have cloven hooves: the camel, because it chews the cud but does not have cloven hooves, is unclean to you;   Acts 10:14

5 'the ᵀrock hyrax, because it chews the cud but does not have cloven hooves, is unclean to you;   *rock badger*

6 'the hare, because it chews the cud but does not have cloven hooves, *is* unclean to you;

7 'and the swine, though it divides the hoof, having cloven hooves, yet does not chew the cud, ᴿ*is* unclean to you.   Is. 66:3, 17

8 'Their flesh you shall not eat, and their carcasses you shall not touch. ᴿThey *are* unclean to you.   Is. 52:11

9 ᴿ'These you may eat of all that *are* in the water: whatever in the water has fins and scales, whether in the seas or in the rivers— that you may eat.   Deut. 14:9

10 'But all in the seas or in the rivers that do not have fins and scales, all that move in the water or any living thing which *is* in the water, they *are* an abomination to you.

11 'They shall be an abomination to you; you shall not eat their flesh, but you shall regard their carcasses as an abomination.

12 'Whatever in the water does not have fins or scales—that *shall be* an abomination to you.

13 ᴿ'And these you shall regard as an abomination among the birds; they shall not be eaten, they *are* an abomination: the eagle, the vulture, the buzzard,   Is. 66:17

14 'the kite, and the falcon after its kind;

15 'every raven after its kind,

16 'the ostrich, the short-eared owl, the seagull, and the hawk after its kind;

17 'the little owl, the fisher owl, and the screech owl;

18 'the white owl, the jackdaw, and the carrion vulture;

19 'the stork, the heron after its kind, the hoopoe, and the bat.

20 'All flying insects that creep on *all* fours *shall be* an abomination to you.

21 'Yet these you may eat of every flying insect that creeps on *all* fours: those which have jointed legs above their feet with which to leap on the earth.

22 'These you may eat: ᴿthe locust after its kind, the destroying locust after its kind, the cricket after its kind, and the grasshopper after its kind.   Matt. 3:4

23 'But all *other* flying insects which have four feet *shall be* an abomination to you.

Unclean Animals

24 'By these you shall become unclean; whoever touches the carcass of any of them shall be unclean until evening;

25 'whoever carries part of the carcass of any of them ᴿshall wash his clothes and be unclean until evening: Num. 19:10, 21, 22; 31:24

26 'The *carcass* of any animal which divides the foot, but is not cloven-hoofed or does not chew the cud, *is* unclean to you. Everyone who touches it shall be unclean.

27 'And whatever goes on its paws, among all kinds of animals that go on *all* fours, those *are* unclean to you. Whoever touches any such carcass shall be unclean until evening.

28 'Whoever carries *any such* carcass shall wash his clothes and be unclean until evening. It *is* unclean to you.

29 'These also *shall be* unclean to you among the creeping things that creep on the earth: the mole, ᴿthe mouse, and the large lizard after its kind;   Is. 66:17

30 'the gecko, the monitor lizard, the sand reptile, the sand lizard, and the chameleon.

31 'These *are* unclean to you among all that creep. Whoever touches them when they are dead shall be unclean until evening.

32 'Anything on which *any* of them falls, when they are dead shall be unclean, whether *it is* any item of wood or clothing or skin or sack, whatever item *it is,* in which *any* work is done, ᴿit must be put in water. And it shall be unclean until evening; then it shall be clean.   Lev. 15:12

33 'Any ᴿearthen vessel into which *any* of them falls ᴿyou shall break; and whatever *is* in it shall be unclean: Lev. 6:28 • Lev. 15:12

34 'in such a vessel, any edible food upon which water falls becomes unclean, and any drink that may be drunk from it becomes unclean.

35 'And everything on which *a part* of *any* such carcass falls shall be unclean; *whether it is* an oven or cooking stove, it shall be broken down; *for* they *are* unclean, and shall be unclean to you.

36 'Nevertheless a spring or a cistern, *in which there is* plenty of water, shall be clean, but whatever touches any such carcass becomes unclean.

37 'And if a part of *any such* carcass falls on any planting seed which is to be sown, it *remains* clean.

38 'But if water is put on the seed, and if *a part* of *any such* carcass falls on it, it *becomes* unclean to you.

39 'And if any animal which you may eat dies, he who touches its carcass shall be ᴿunclean until evening.   Hag. 2:11-13

40 'He who eats of its carcass shall wash his clothes and be unclean until evening. He also who carries its carcass shall wash his clothes and be unclean until evening.

41 'And every creeping thing that creeps on the earth *shall be* ᵀan abomination. It shall not be eaten.   detestable

42 'Whatever crawls on its belly, whatever goes on *all* fours, or whatever has many feet among all creeping things that creep on the earth—these you shall not eat, for they *are* an abomination.

43 'You shall not make ᵀyourselves abominable with any creeping thing that creeps; nor shall you make yourselves unclean with them, lest you be defiled by them. Lit. *your souls*

44 'For I *am* the LORD your ᴿGod. You shall therefore consecrate yourselves, and ᴿyou shall be holy; for I *am* holy. Neither shall you defile yourselves with any creeping thing that creeps on the earth.   Ex. 6:7 • 1 Pet. 1:15, 16

45 'For I *am* the LORD who brings you up out of the land of Egypt, to be your God. You shall therefore be holy, for I *am* holy.

46 'This *is* the law ᵀof the animals and the birds and every living creature that moves in the waters, and of every creature that creeps on the earth,   concerning

47 ᴿᵗto distinguish between the unclean and the clean, and between the animal that may be eaten and the animal that may not be eaten.' "   Ezek. 44:23

The Ritual After Childbirth

12 Then the LORD spoke to Moses, saying, 2 "Speak to the children of Israel, saying: 'If a woman has conceived, and borne a male child, then she shall be unclean seven days; as in the days of her customary impurity she shall be unclean.

3 'And on the ᴿeighth day the flesh of his foreskin shall be circumcised.   Gen. 17:12

4 'She shall then continue in the blood of *her* purification thirty-three days. She shall not touch any ᵀhallowed thing, nor come into the sanctuary until the days of her purification are fulfilled.   consecrated

5 'But if she bears a female child, then she shall be unclean two weeks, as in her customary impurity, and she shall continue in the blood of her purification sixty-six days.

▼ **36–G. Special Offerings**

6 'When the days of her purification are fulfilled, whether for a son or a daughter, she shall bring to the priest a ᴿlamb of the first year as a burnt offering, and a young pigeon or a turtledove as a sin offering, to the door of the tabernacle of meeting.   [John 1:29]

7 'Then he shall offer it before the LORD, and make atonement for her. And she shall be clean from the flow of her blood. This is the law for her who has borne a male or a female.

8 ᴿ'And if she is not able to bring a lamb, then she may bring two turtledoves or two young pigeons—one as a burnt offering and the other as a sin offering. ᴿSo the priest shall make atonement for her, and she will be

▲ ᵀclean.' "   Lev. 5:7 · Lev. 4:26 · pure

The Law Concerning Leprosy

13 And the LORD spoke to Moses and Aaron, saying:

2 "When a man has on the skin of his body a swelling, a scab, or a bright spot, and it becomes on the skin of his body like a *leprous sore, then he shall be brought to Aaron the priest or to one of his sons the priests.

3 "The priest shall examine the sore on the skin of the body; and if the hair on the sore

13:2 Heb. *saraath*, disfiguring skin diseases, including leprosy, and so in vv. 2–46 and 14:1–32

has turned white, and the sore appears to be deeper than the skin of his body, it is a leprous sore. Then the priest shall examine him, and pronounce him unclean.

4 "But if the bright spot is white on the skin of his body, and does not appear to be deeper than the skin, and its hair has not turned white, then the priest shall isolate the one who has the sore ᴿseven days.   Lev. 14:8

5 "And the priest shall examine him on the seventh day; and indeed if the sore appears to be as it was, and the sore has not spread on the skin, then the priest shall isolate him another seven days.

6 "Then the priest shall examine him again on the seventh day; and indeed if the sore has faded, and the sore has not spread on the skin, then the priest shall pronounce him clean; it is only a scab, and he ᴿshall wash his clothes and be clean.   Lev. 11:25; 14:8

7 "But if the scab should at all spread over the skin, after he has been seen by the priest for his cleansing, he shall be seen by the priest again.

8 "And if the priest sees that the scab has indeed spread on the skin, then the priest shall pronounce him unclean. It is leprosy.

9 "When the leprous sore is on a person, then he shall be brought to the priest.

10 ᴿ"And the priest shall examine him; and indeed if the swelling on the skin is white, and it has turned the hair white, and there is a spot of raw flesh in the swelling,   Num. 12:10, 12

11 "it is an old leprosy on the skin of his body. The priest shall pronounce him unclean, and shall not isolate him, for he is unclean.

36-G. Special Offerings (Leviticus 12:6–8)—The following special sacrifices are of particular interest, and convey vital and touching lessons to the believer:

(1) Mary and Joseph, according to Luke 2:22–24 (page 1013), offered a pair of turtledoves or pigeons, after the birth of Jesus, to comply with verse 6. While in Leviticus both a lamb and a bird (turtledove or pigeon) are commanded, if one had no lamb or could not afford one, one could instead bring a second bird. This was the case with Mary and Joseph, as described by Luke. Their poverty was evident in that they were only able and required to bring turtledoves.

(2) The sacrifice of the red heifer, a female cow (Num. 19:1–13, page 159), required that the ashes of this offering be placed in water. This water then became the water of cleansing, and was sprinkled on anyone who became ceremonially defiled by touching a dead body. We note that even cleansing by water must be based on prior sacrifice of blood (Heb. 9:22, page 1244).

(3) The Passover sacrifice, on the fourteenth day of the first month of the religious calendar—March/April (Lev. 23:5, page 130)—was to be a lamb for a household (Ex. 12:3, page 69). This was a family sacrifice. The blood of the lamb was applied to the doorposts of each family dwelling to save the firstborn from the plague (Ex. 12:7–13, page 70). This slain lamb was a type of Christ (Rev. 5:5–13, page 1297).

(4) The Day of Atonement (*Yom Kippur*, "Day of Covering") occurs on the tenth day of the seventh month of the sacred calendar—September/October (Lev. 23:27, page 131). On this day two goats were brought before the high priest and the congregation.

(a) One was selected, by lot, for death. Its blood was sprinkled within the veil, upon the ark, as an atonement for the sins of the people.

(b) The second was the "scapegoat." The sins of the people were confessed over it. It was then led off to be lost in the wilderness, showing that sins confessed and atoned for were now removed from God's sight (Lev. 16:7–10, page 123; cf. Ps. 103:12, page 570).

See Index, page 17, for your next study.

12 "And if leprosy breaks out all over the skin, and the leprosy covers all the skin of *the one who has* the sore, from his head to his foot, wherever the priest looks,

13 "then the priest shall consider; and indeed *if* the leprosy has covered all his body, he shall pronounce *him* clean *who has* the sore. It has all turned white. He *is* clean.

14 "But when raw flesh appears on him, he shall be unclean.

15 "And the priest shall examine the raw flesh and pronounce him to be unclean; *for* the raw flesh *is* unclean. It *is* leprosy.

16 "Or if the raw flesh changes and turns white again, he shall come to the priest.

17 "And the priest shall examine him; and indeed *if* the sore has turned white, then the priest shall pronounce *him* clean *who has* the sore. He *is* clean.

18 "If the body develops a ᴿboil in the skin, and it is healed,   Ex. 9:9; 15:26

19 "and in the place of the boil there comes a white swelling or a bright spot, reddish-white, then it shall be shown to the priest;

20 "and if, when the priest sees it, it indeed *appears* deeper than the skin, and its hair has turned white, the priest shall pronounce him unclean. It *is* a leprous sore which has broken out of the boil.

21 "But if the priest examines it, and indeed *there are* no white hairs in it, and it *is* not deeper than the skin, but has faded, then the priest shall isolate him seven days;

22 "and if it should at all spread over the skin, then the priest shall pronounce him unclean. It *is* a ᵀleprous sore.   *infectious*

23 "But if the bright spot stays in one place, *and* has not spread, it *is* the scar of the boil; and the priest shall pronounce him clean.

24 "Or if the body receives a ᴿburn on its skin by fire, and the raw *flesh* of the burn becomes a bright spot, reddish-white or white,   Is. 3:24

25 "then the priest shall examine it; and indeed *if* the hair of the bright spot has turned white, and it appears deeper than the skin, it *is* leprosy broken out in the burn. Therefore the priest shall pronounce him unclean. It *is* a leprous sore.

26 "But if the priest examines it, and indeed *there are* no white hairs in the bright spot, and it *is* not deeper than the skin, but has faded, then the priest shall isolate him seven days.

27 "And the priest shall examine him on the seventh day. If it has at all spread over the skin, then the priest shall pronounce him unclean. It *is* a leprous sore.

28 "But if the bright spot stays in one place, *and* has not spread on the skin, but has faded, it *is* a swelling from the burn. The priest shall pronounce him clean, for it *is* the scar from the burn.

29 "If a man or woman has a sore on the head or the beard,

30 "then the priest shall examine the sore; and indeed if it appears deeper than the skin, *and there is* in it thin yellow hair, then the priest shall pronounce him unclean. It *is* a scaly leprosy of the head or beard.

31 "But if the priest examines the scaly sore, and indeed it does not appear deeper than the skin, and *there is* no black hair in it, then the priest shall isolate *the one who has* the scale seven days.

32 "And on the seventh day the priest shall examine the sore; and indeed *if* the scale has not spread, and there is no yellow hair in it, and the scale does not appear deeper than the skin,

33 "he shall shave himself, but the scale he shall not shave. And the priest shall isolate *the one who has* the scale another seven days.

34 "On the seventh day the priest shall examine the scale; and indeed *if* the scale has not spread over the skin, and does not appear deeper than the skin, then the priest shall pronounce him clean. He shall wash his clothes and be clean.

35 "But if the scale should at all spread over the skin after his cleansing,

36 "then the priest shall examine him; and indeed *if* the scale has spread over the skin, the priest need not seek for yellow hair. He *is* unclean.

37 "But if the scale appears to be at a standstill, and there is black hair grown up in it, the scale has healed. He *is* clean, and the priest shall pronounce him clean.

38 "If a man or a woman has bright spots on the skin of the body, *specifically* white bright spots,

39 "then the priest shall look; and indeed *if* the bright spots on the skin of the body *are* dull white, it *is* a white spot *that* grows on the skin. He *is* clean.

40 "As for the man whose hair has fallen from his head, he *is* bald, *but* he *is* clean.

41 "He whose hair has fallen from his forehead, he *is* bald on the forehead, *but* he *is* clean.

42 "And if there is on the bald head or bald ᴿforehead a reddish-white sore, it *is* leprosy breaking out on his bald head or his bald forehead.   2 Chr. 26:19

43 "Then the priest shall examine it; and indeed *if* the swelling of the sore *is* reddish-white on his bald head or on his bald forehead, as the appearance of leprosy on the skin of the body,

44 "he is a leprous man. He *is* unclean. The priest shall surely pronounce him ᵀunclean; his sore *is* on his ᴿhead.   *altogether defiled* • Is. 1:5

45 "Now the leper on whom the sore *is*, his clothes shall be torn and his head bare; and

he shall ᴿcover his mustache, and cry, ᴿ'Unclean! Unclean!' Ezek. 24:17, 22 • Lam. 4:15
46 "He shall be unclean. All the days he has the sore he shall be unclean. He is unclean, and he shall ᵀdwell alone; his dwelling shall be ᴿoutside the camp. live alone • Num. 5:1–4; 12:14

The Law Concerning Leprous Garments

47 "Also, if a garment has a *leprous plague in it, whether it is a woolen garment or a linen garment,
48 "whether it is in the warp or woof of linen or wool, whether in leather or in anything made of leather,
49 "and if the plague is greenish or reddish in the garment or in the leather, whether in the warp or in the woof, or in anything made of leather, it is a leprous ᵀplague and shall be shown to the priest. mark
50 "The priest shall examine the plague and isolate that which has the plague seven days.
51 "And he shall examine the plague on the seventh day. If the plague has spread in the garment, either in the warp or in the woof, in the leather or in anything made of leather, the plague is an active leprosy. It is unclean.
52 "He shall therefore burn that garment in which is the plague, whether warp or woof, in wool or in linen, or anything of leather, for it is an active leprosy; the garment shall be burned in the fire.
53 "But if the priest examines it, and indeed the plague has not spread in the garment, either in the warp or in the woof, or in anything made of leather,
54 "then the priest shall command that they wash the thing in which is the plague; and he shall isolate it another seven days.
55 "Then the priest shall examine the plague after it has been washed; and indeed if the plague has not changed its color, though the plague has not spread, it is unclean, and you shall burn it in the fire; it continues eating away, whether the damage is outside or inside.
56 "If the priest examines it, and indeed the plague has faded after washing it, then he shall tear it out of the garment, whether out of the warp or out of the woof, or out of the leather.
57 "But if it appears again in the garment, either in the warp or in the woof, or in anything made of leather, it is a spreading plague; you shall burn with fire that in which is the plague.
58 "And if you wash the garment, either warp or woof, or whatever is made of leather, if the plague has disappeared from it, then it shall be washed a second time, and shall be clean.
59 "This is the law of the leprous plague in

a garment of wool or linen, either in the warp or woof, or in anything made of leather, to pronounce it clean or to pronounce it unclean."

The Ritual for Cleansing Healed Lepers

14 Then the LORD spoke to Moses, saying, 2 "This shall be the law of the ᵀleper for the day of his cleansing: He ᴿshall be brought to the priest. Heb. sora • Matt. 8:2, 4
3 "And the priest shall go out of the camp, and the priest shall examine him; and indeed, if the *leprosy is healed in the leper,
4 "then the priest shall command to take for him who is to be cleansed two living and clean birds, ᴿcedar wood, ᴿscarlet, and ᴿhyssop. Num. 19:6 • Ex. 25:4 • Ps. 51:7
5 "And the priest shall command that one of the birds be killed in an earthen vessel over running water.
6 "As for the living bird, he shall take it, the cedar wood and the scarlet and the hyssop, and dip them and the living bird in the blood of the bird that was killed over the running water.
7 "And he shall sprinkle it seven times on him who is to be cleansed from the leprosy, and shall pronounce him clean, and shall let the living bird loose in the open field.
8 "He who is to be cleansed shall wash his clothes, shave off all his hair, and ᴿwash himself in water, that he may be clean. After that he shall come into the camp, and shall stay outside his tent seven days. [Heb. 10:22]
9 "But on the ᴿseventh day he shall shave all the hair off his head and his beard and his eyebrows—all his hair he shall shave off. He shall wash his clothes and wash his body in water, and he shall be clean. Num. 19:19
10 "And on the eighth day he shall take two male lambs without blemish, one ewe lamb of the first year without blemish, three-tenths of an ephah of fine flour mixed with oil as ᴿa grain offering, and one log of oil. Lev. 2:1
11 "Then the priest who makes him clean shall present the man who is to be made clean, and those things, before the LORD, at the door of the tabernacle of meeting.
12 "And the priest shall take one male lamb and ᴿoffer it as a trespass offering, and the log of oil, and ᴿwave them as a wave offering before the LORD. Lev. 5:6, 18 • Ex. 29:22–24, 26
13 "Then he shall kill the lamb in the place where he kills the sin offering and the burnt offering, in a holy place; for as the sin offering is the priest's, so is the trespass offering. ᴿIt is most holy. Lev. 2:3; 7:6; 21:22
14 "The priest shall take some of the blood of the trespass offering, and the priest shall put it on the tip of the right ear of him who is

---

13:47 A mold, fungus, or similar infestation, and so in vv. 47–59

14:3 Heb. saraath, disfiguring skin diseases, including leprosy, and so in vv. 2–46 and 14:1–32

to be cleansed, on the thumb of his right hand, and on the big toe of his right foot.

15 "And the priest shall take *some* of the ᵀlog of oil, and pour *it* into the palm of his own left hand.   1 pt.

16 "Then the priest shall dip his right finger in the oil that *is* in his left hand, and shall ᴿsprinkle some of the oil with his finger seven times before the LORD.   Lev. 4:6

17 "And of the rest of the oil in his hand, the priest shall put *some* on the tip of the right ear of him who is to be cleansed, on the thumb of his right hand, and on the big toe of his right foot, on the blood of the trespass offering.

18 "The rest of the oil that *is* in the priest's hand he shall put on the head of him who is to be cleansed. So the priest shall make atonement for him before the LORD.

19 "Then the priest shall offer the sin offering, and make atonement for him who is to be cleansed from his uncleanness. Afterward he shall kill the burnt offering.

20 "And the priest shall offer the burnt offering and the grain offering on the altar. So the priest shall make atonement for him, and he shall be ᴿclean.   Lev. 14:8, 9

21 "But ᴿif he *is* poor and cannot afford it, then he shall take one male lamb *as* a trespass offering to be waved, to make atonement for him, ᵀone-tenth *of an ephah* of fine flour mixed with oil as a grain offering, a log of oil,   Lev. 5:7, 11; 12:8; 27:8 · 2.087 qt.

22 ᴿ"and two turtledoves or two young pigeons, such as he is able to afford: one shall be a sin offering and the other a burnt offering.   Lev. 12:8; 15:14, 15

23 "He shall bring them to the priest on the eighth day for his cleansing, to the door of the tabernacle of meeting, before the LORD.

24 ᴿ"And the priest shall take the lamb of the trespass offering and the ᵀlog of oil, and the priest shall wave them *as* a wave offering before the LORD.   Lev. 14:12 · 1 pt.

25 "Then he shall kill the lamb of the trespass offering, ᴿand the priest shall take *some* of the blood of the trespass offering and put *it* on the tip of the right ear of him who is to be cleansed, on the thumb of his right hand, and on the big toe of his right foot.   Lev. 14:14, 17

26 "And the priest shall pour some of the oil into the palm of his own left hand.

27 "Then the priest shall sprinkle with his right finger *some* of the oil that *is* in his left hand seven times before the LORD.

28 "And the priest shall put *some* of the oil that *is* in his hand on the tip of the right ear of him who is to be cleansed, on the thumb of the right hand, and on the big toe of his right foot, on the place of the blood of the trespass offering.

29 "The rest of the oil that *is* in the priest's hand he shall put on the head of him who is

to be cleansed, to make atonement for him before the LORD.

30 "And he shall offer one of ᴿthe turtledoves or young pigeons, such as he can afford—   Lev. 14:22; 15:14, 15

31 "such as he is able to afford, the one *as* a sin offering and the other *as* a burnt offering, with the grain offering. So the priest shall make atonement for him who is to be cleansed before the LORD.

32 "This *is* the law *for one* who had a leprous sore, who cannot afford ᴿthe usual cleansing."   Lev. 14:10

The Law Concerning Leprous Houses

33 And the LORD spoke to Moses and Aaron, saying:

34 "When you have come into the land of Canaan, which I give you as a possession, and ᴿI put the *leprous plague in a house in the land of your possession,   [Prov. 3:33]

35 "and he who owns the house comes and tells the priest, saying, 'It seems to me that *there is* ᴿsome plague in the house,' [Ps. 91:9, 10]

36 "then the priest shall command that they empty the house, before the priest goes *into it* to examine the plague, that all that *is* in the house may not be made unclean; and afterward the priest shall go in to examine the house.

37 "And he shall examine the plague; and indeed *if* the plague *is* on the walls of the house with ingrained streaks, greenish or reddish, which appear to be deep in the wall,

38 "then the priest shall go out of the house, to the door of the house, and ᵀshut up the house seven days.   *quarantine*

39 "And the priest shall come again on the seventh day and look; and indeed *if* the plague has spread on the walls of the house,

40 "then the priest shall command that they take away the stones in which *is* the plague, and they shall cast them into an unclean place outside the city.

41 "And he shall cause the house to be scraped inside, all around, and the dust that they scrape off they shall pour out in an unclean place outside the city.

42 "Then they shall take other stones and put *them* in the place of *those* stones, and he shall take other mortar and plaster the house.

43 "Now if the plague comes back and breaks out in the house, after he has taken away the stones, after he has scraped the house, and after it is plastered,

44 "then the priest shall come and look; and indeed *if* the plague has spread in the house, it *is* ᴿan active leprosy in the house. It *is* unclean.   Lev. 13:51

45 "And he shall break down the house, its stones, its timber, and all the plaster of the

14:34 Decomposition by mildew, mold, dry rot, etc., and so in vv. 34-53

house, and he shall carry *them* outside the city to an unclean place.

46 "Moreover he who goes into the house at all while it is shut up shall be unclean ᴿuntil evening.   Lev. 11:24; 15:5

47 "And he who lies down in the house shall ᴿwash his clothes, and he who eats in the house shall wash his clothes.   Lev. 14:8

48 "But if the priest comes in and examines *it*, and indeed the plague has not spread in the house after the house was plastered, then the priest shall pronounce the house clean, because the plague is healed.

49 "And ᴿhe shall take, to cleanse the house, two birds, cedar wood, scarlet, and hyssop.   Lev. 14:4

50 "Then he shall kill one of the birds in an earthen vessel over running water;

51 "and he shall take the cedar wood, the hyssop, the scarlet, and the living bird, and dip them in the blood of the slain bird and in the running water, and sprinkle the house seven times.

52 "And he shall ᵀcleanse the house with the blood of the bird and the running water and the living bird, with the cedar wood, the hyssop, and the scarlet.   Ceremonially cleanse

53 "Then he shall let the living bird loose outside the city in the open field, and ᴿmake atonement for the house, and it shall be clean.   Lev. 14:20

54 "This *is* the law for any ᴿleprous sore and scale,   Lev. 13:30; 26:21

55 "for the ᴿleprosy of a garment ᴿand of a house,   Lev. 13:47-52 • Lev. 14:34

56 ᴿ"for a swelling and a scab and a bright spot,   Lev. 13:2

57 "to teach when *it is* unclean and when *it is* clean. This *is* the law of leprosy."

The Law Concerning Bodily Discharges

15 And the Lᴏʀᴅ spoke to Moses and Aaron, saying,

2 "Speak to the children of Israel, and say to them: 'When any man has a discharge from his body, his discharge *is* unclean.

3 'And this shall be his uncleanness in regard to his discharge—whether his body runs with his discharge, or his body is stopped up by his discharge, it *is* his uncleanness.

4 'Every bed is unclean on which he who has the discharge lies, and everything on which he sits shall be unclean.

5 'And whoever touches his bed shall wash his clothes and ᴿbathe in water, and be unclean until evening.   Lev. 11:25; 17:15

6 'He who sits on anything on which he who has the ᴿdischarge sat shall wash his clothes and bathe in water, and be unclean until evening.   Deut. 23:10

7 'And he who touches the body of him who has the discharge shall wash his clothes

and bathe in water, and be unclean until evening.

8 'If he who has the discharge ᴿspits on him who is clean, then he shall wash his clothes and bathe in water, and be unclean until evening.   Num. 12:14

9 'Any saddle on which he who has the discharge rides shall be unclean.

10 'Whoever touches anything that was under him shall be unclean until evening. He who carries *any of* those things shall wash his clothes and bathe in water, and be unclean until evening.

11 'And whomever the one who has the discharge touches, and has not rinsed his hands in water, he shall wash his clothes and bathe in water, and be unclean until evening.

12 'The vessel of earth that he who has the discharge touches shall be broken, and every vessel of wood shall be rinsed in water.

13 'And when he who has a discharge is cleansed of his discharge, then he shall count for himself seven days for his cleansing, wash his clothes, and bathe his body in running water; then he shall be clean.

14 'On the eighth day he shall take for himself ᴿtwo turtledoves or two young pigeons, and come before the Lᴏʀᴅ, to the door of the tabernacle of meeting, and give them to the priest.   Lev. 14:22, 23, 30, 31

15 'Then the priest shall offer them, ᴿthe one *as* a sin offering and the other *as* a burnt offering. ᴿSo the priest shall make atonement for him before the Lᴏʀᴅ because of his discharge.   Lev. 14:30, 31 • Lev. 14:19, 31

16 ᴿ'If any man has an emission of semen, then he shall wash all his body in water, and be unclean until evening.   Lev. 22:4

17 'And any garment and any leather on which there is semen, it shall be washed with water, and be unclean until evening.

18 'Also, when a woman lies with a man, and *there is* an emission of semen, they shall bathe in water, and ᴿbe unclean until evening.   [1 Sam. 21:4]

19 ᴿ'If a woman has a discharge, *and* the discharge from her body is blood, she shall be set apart seven days; and whoever touches her shall be unclean until evening.   Lev. 12:2

20 'Everything that she lies on during her impurity shall be unclean; also everything that she sits on shall be unclean.

21 'Whoever touches her bed shall wash his clothes and bathe in water, and be unclean until evening.

22 'And whoever touches anything that she sat on shall wash his clothes and bathe in water, and be unclean until evening.

23 'If *anything* is on *her* bed or on anything on which she sits, when he touches it, he shall be unclean until evening.

24 'And ᴿif any man lies with her at all, so that her impurity is on him, he shall be

Tunclean seven days; and every bed on which he lies shall be unclean.   Lev. 18:19; 20:18 · *defiled*

25 'If Ra woman has a discharge of blood for many days, other than at the time of her *customary* impurity, or if it runs beyond her *usual time of* impurity, all the days of her unclean discharge shall be as the days of her *customary* impurity. She *shall be* unclean.   Matt. 9:20

26 'Every bed on which she lies all the days of her discharge shall be to her as the bed of her impurity; and whatever she sits on shall be unclean, as the uncleanness of her impurity.

27 'Whoever touches those things shall be unclean; he shall wash his clothes and bathe in water, and be unclean until evening.

28 'But Rif she is cleansed of her discharge, then she shall count for herself seven days, and after that she shall be clean.   Lev. 15:13-15

29 'And on the eighth day she shall take for herself two turtledoves or two young pigeons, and bring them to the priest, to the door of the tabernacle of meeting.

30 'Then the priest shall offer the one *as* a sin offering and the other *as* a Rburnt offering, and the priest shall make atonement for her before the LORD for the discharge of her uncleanness.   Lev. 5:7

31 'Thus you shall Rseparate the children of Israel from their uncleanness, lest they die in their uncleanness when they defile My tabernacle that *is* among them.   Deut. 24:8

32 R'This *is* the law for one who has a discharge, Rand *for him* who emits semen and is unclean thereby,   Lev. 15:2 · Lev. 15:16

33 'and for her who is indisposed because of her *customary* impurity, and for one who has a discharge, either man or woman, and for him who lies with her who is unclean.' "

The Day of Atonement

20–E. The Day of Atonement in the Old Testament ▼

16 Now the LORD spoke to Moses after Rthe death of the two sons of Aaron, when they offered *profane fire* before the LORD, and died;   Lev. 10:1, 2

2 and the LORD said to Moses: "Tell Aaron your brother not to come at *just* any time into the Holy *Place* inside the veil, before the mercy seat which *is* on the ark, lest he die; for RI will appear in the cloud above the mercy seat.   Ex. 25:21, 22; 40:34

3 "Thus Aaron shall come into the Holy *Place:* with *the blood of* a young bull as a sin offering, and *of* a ram as a burnt offering.

4 "He shall put the Rholy linen tunic and the linen trousers on his body; he shall be girded with a linen sash, and with the linen turban he shall be attired. These *are* holy garments. Therefore he shall wash his body in water, and put them on.   Ex. 28:39, 42, 43

5 "And he shall take from Rthe congregation of the children of Israel two kids of the goats as a sin offering, and one ram as a burnt offering.   Lev. 4:14

6 "Aaron shall offer the bull as a sin offering, which *is* for himself, and make atonement for himself and for his house.

7 "He shall take the two goats and present them before the LORD *at* the door of the tabernacle of meeting.

8 "Then Aaron shall cast lots for the two goats: one lot for the LORD and the other lot for the scapegoat.

9 "And Aaron shall bring the goat on which the LORD's lot fell, and offer it *as* a sin offering.

20–E. The Day of Atonement in the Old Testament (Leviticus 16:1–34)—This chapter is rich in typology, with Christ as the fulfillment of each type. He is our atonement for all our sins. The biblical meaning of the word *atone* is to cover, to expiate, and to pay the penalty for sins. To reconcile, or to achieve "at-one-ment" with God, is a part of the atoning death of Christ. To atone is to bring the sinner from a state of enmity with God to a place of union or oneness in Him (2 Cor. 5:18, page 1169).

The Day of Atonement was to be repeated on the tenth day of the seventh month, year after year. It was a day of rest; the Israelites were to do no work. It was a day of repentance. God said, "You shall afflict your souls" (v. 29). On the Day of Atonement the high priest entered the Most Holy Place and sprinkled the atoning blood upon the mercy seat, to atone for all the sins of the congregation, including those sins committed unintentionally or in ignorance (Lev. 4:1–35, page 108).

Compare the high priest with the Lord Jesus Christ:

(1) He is a type of Christ in his office as mediator. He was the "go-between"; he alone stood between God and man. Once each year he was to go alone before God with atoning blood, while the congregation waited to be reconciled to God (vv. 16, 34). Christ fulfilled this office of the high priest as recorded in Hebrews: "He is the Mediator of the new covenant, by means of death" (Heb. 9:12–15, page 1243). "For there is one God and one Mediator between God and men, the Man Christ Jesus" (1 Tim. 2:5, page 1219).

(2) His priestly garments are a type of the Lord Jesus Christ. God told Moses to "make holy garments for Aaron your brother, for glory and for beauty." The garments were to be made of "gold, blue, purple and scarlet thread, and fine linen" (Ex. 28:1–5, page 87). Christ fulfilled the type of the holy garments. When the angel Gabriel announced the birth of Jesus, he said, "That Holy One who is to be born will be called the Son of God" (Luke 1:35, page 1010). The writer of Hebrews said, He "is holy, harmless, undefiled, separate from

(Point 20-E continued on next page)

▽ 10 "But the goat on which the lot fell to be the scapegoat shall be presented alive before the LORD, to make ᴿatonement upon it, *and* to let it go as the scapegoat into the wilderness.   [1 John 2:2]

11 "And Aaron shall bring the bull of the sin offering, which is for ᴿhimself, and make atonement for himself and for his house, and shall kill the bull as the sin offering which *is* for himself.   [Heb. 7:27; 9:7]

12 "Then he shall take a censer full of burning coals of fire from the altar before the LORD, with his hands full of sweet incense beaten fine, and bring *it* inside the veil.

13 "And he shall put the incense on the fire before the LORD, that the cloud of incense may cover the ᴿmercy seat that *is* on the Testimony, lest he ᴿdie.   Ex. 25:21 • Ex. 28:43

14 "He shall take some of the blood of the bull and sprinkle *it* with his finger on the mercy seat on the east *side*; and before the mercy seat he shall sprinkle some of the blood with his finger seven times.

15 ᴿ"Then he shall kill the goat of the sin offering, which *is* for the people, bring its blood ᴿinside the veil, do with that blood as he did with the blood of the bull, and sprinkle it on the mercy seat and before the mercy seat.   [Heb. 2:17] • [Heb. 6:19; 7:27; 9:3, 7, 12]

16 "So he shall ᴿmake atonement for the Holy *Place*, because of the uncleanness of the children of Israel, and because of their transgressions, for all their sins; and so he shall do for the tabernacle of meeting which remains among them in the midst of their uncleanness.   Ex. 29:36; 30:10

17 "There shall be ᴿno man in the taberna-

cle of meeting when he goes in to make ▽ atonement in the Holy *Place*, until he comes out, that he may make atonement for himself, for his household, and for all the assembly of Israel.   Luke 1:10

18 "And he shall go out to the altar that *is* before the LORD, and make atonement for ᴿit, and shall take some of the blood of the bull and some of the blood of the goat, and put it on the horns of the altar all around.   Ex. 29:36

19 "Then he shall sprinkle some of the blood on it with his finger seven times, cleanse it, and ᴿconsecrate it from the uncleanness of the children of Israel.   Ezek. 43:20

20 "And when he has made an end of atoning for the Holy *Place*, the tabernacle of meeting, and the altar, he shall bring the live goat.

21 "Aaron shall lay both his hands on the head of the live goat, ᴿconfess over it all the iniquities of the children of Israel, and all their transgressions, concerning all their sins, ᴿputting them on the head of the goat, and shall send *it* away into the wilderness by the hand of a suitable man.   Lev. 5:5; 26:40 • [Is. 53:6]

22 "The goat shall bear on itself all their iniquities to an uninhabited land; and he shall release the goat in the wilderness.

23 "Then Aaron shall come into the tabernacle of meeting, shall take off the linen garments which he put on when he went into the Holy *Place*, and shall leave them there.

24 "And he shall wash his body with water in a holy place, put on his garments, come out and offer his burnt offering and the burnt offering of the people, and make atonement for himself and for the people.

(Point 20-E continued from previous page)

sinners" (Heb. 7:26, page 1242). The gold thread speaks of His deity, the blue thread of His heavenly character, the purple thread of His royalty, the scarlet thread of His shed blood, and the fine linen of His righteousness.

(3) The high priest offered the blood of a bull to make atonement for his own sins (v. 6). In this offering he is not a type of Christ; the Lord Jesus Christ did not have to make atonement for His own sins, because He is the sinless One (Heb. 7:27, 28, page 1242). The Scriptures say that He "committed no sin" (1 Pet. 2:22, page 1266), that "in Him there is no sin" (1 John 3:5, page 1280), and that He "knew no sin" (2 Cor. 5:21, page 1169).

(4) Two goats were presented before the Lord at the door of the tabernacle. Aaron was to cast lots for them: one would be sacrificed and the other would be the "scapegoat" (vv. 7, 8).

(a) The atoning blood of the sacrificial goat, which was sprinkled on the mercy seat to cover the sins of the people (vv. 7–9), is a type of Christ, our High Priest, who "entered the Most Holy Place once for all, having obtained eternal redemption" (Heb. 9:11–14, page 1243).

(b) The scapegoat is also a type of Christ. Aaron, after atoning for the sins of the people with the blood of the sacrificed goat, was to take the live goat and lay his hands on its head, confessing all the iniquities and sins of Israel. Then he was to send it into the wilderness (vv. 21, 22), so that those sins might be lost and out of sight forever. Christ bore our sin in His own body on the cross, was placed in the tomb, and rose on the third day. Christ alone will wear the scars of His sacrifice in His holy body. In His resurrection He fulfills the type of the living scapegoat (Matt. 28:1–7, page 981).

(5) On the Day of Atonement the robes of glory and beauty were laid aside, and after the high priest had washed his body, he put on plain linen garments—plain yet "holy" (v. 4). On this day the priest humbled himself and became a servant. This is a type of Christ in His humiliation (Phil. 2:5–8, page 1197; cf. 2 Cor. 8:9, page 1171).

See John 20:17, page 1083, for **Point 20-F: The Day of Atonement in the New Testament.**

▽ 25 ᴿ"The fat of the sin offering he shall burn on the altar. Lev. 1:8; 4:10

26 "And he who released the goat as the scapegoat shall wash his clothes ᴿand bathe his body in water, and afterward he may come into the camp. Lev. 15:5

27 ᴿ"The bull *for* the sin offering and the goat *for* the sin offering, whose blood was brought in to make atonement in the Holy *Place*, shall be carried outside the camp. And they shall burn in the fire their skins, their flesh, and their offal. Heb. 13:11

28 "Then he who burns them shall wash his clothes and bathe his body in water, and afterward he may come into the camp.

29 "*This* shall be a statute forever for you: ᴿIn the seventh month, on the tenth *day* of the month, you shall ᵀafflict your souls, and do no work at all, *whether* a native of your own country or a stranger who dwells among you. Lev. 23:27-32 • *humble yourselves*

30 "For on that day *the priest* shall make atonement for you, to ᴿcleanse you, *that* you may be clean from all your sins before the LORD. Jer. 33:8

31 ᴿ"*It is* a sabbath of solemn rest for you, and you shall afflict your souls. *It is* a statute forever. Lev. 23:27, 32

32 "And the priest, who is anointed and consecrated to minister as priest in his father's place, shall make atonement, and put on the linen clothes, the holy garments;

33 "then he shall make atonement for ᵀthe Holy Sanctuary, and he shall make atonement for the tabernacle of meeting and for the altar, and he shall make atonement for

the priests and for all the people of the assembly. The Most Holy Place

34 "This shall be an everlasting statute for you, to make atonement for the children of Israel, for all their sins, once a year." And he did as the LORD commanded Moses. ▲

The Sanctity of Blood
36-A. Offerings to the LORD ▼

17 And the LORD spoke to Moses, saying, 2 "Speak to Aaron, to his sons, and to all the children of Israel, and say to them, 'This *is* the thing which the LORD has commanded, saying:

3 "Whatever man of the house of Israel, ᴿkills an ox or lamb or goat in the camp, or who kills *it* outside the camp, Deut. 12:5, 15, 21

4 "and does not bring it to the door of the tabernacle of meeting, to offer an offering to the LORD before the tabernacle of the LORD, the guilt of bloodshed shall be imputed to that man. He has shed blood; and that man shall be cut off from among his people,

5 "to the end that the children of Israel may bring their sacrifices ᴿwhich they offer in the open field, that they may bring them to the LORD at the door of the tabernacle of meeting, to the priest, and offer them *as* peace offerings to the LORD. Deut. 12:1-27

6 "And the priest ᴿshall sprinkle the blood on the altar of the LORD *at* the door of the tabernacle of meeting, and ᴿburn the fat for a sweet aroma to the LORD. Lev. 3:2 • Num. 18:17

7 "They shall no more offer their sacrifices to demons, after whom they have played the harlot. This shall be a statute forever for them throughout their generations." '

36-A. Offerings to the LORD (Leviticus 17:1-12)—As we meditate upon the sacrificial order which God laid down in the Old Testament Law, we fall on our knees anew to worship the Lord, to beg His forgiveness, to seek His approval, to await His sending us forth, and to expect His future blessing. We enter the court of His tabernacle, having His praises on our lips and Christ as our Lamb.

(1) God's regulations for worship by sacrifice applied to all members of the covenant community of Israel (vv. 1, 2). The high priest was specifically included, as were the other priests. No one was above God's law in Israel, unlike Egypt, where Pharaoh was a self-declared god. The worship of God is to be performed by all, according to His revealed will.

(2) God's ceremonial worship was coupled with His call for obedience to his law, both ceremonial (Lev. 17, above), and moral (Lev. 18, page 126). The sacrifices, coupled with faith, made atonement for the broken law of God.

(3) Sacrifices had to be made at the tabernacle (vv. 3, 4, 8, 9). God desired that Israel's worship be focused on His requirements for the forgiveness of sins. Their energy was not to be consumed by endless arguments as to where and how they should worship. It was clear that all sacrifices would take place at the tabernacle. This requirement also kept the Israelites from the temptation to join in idolatrous Canaanite sacrifices at the Baal groves.

(4) God's worship system brought peace to the human heart (v. 5).

(5) Those coming to God came through the divinely appointed agent (v. 6). God had appointed a priesthood to sprinkle the blood on the altar and to burn the sacrifice.

(6) Idol worship was forbidden (v. 7). The Lord clearly and forever forbade mixing His sacrifices with sacrifices made to idols, animals, and demons: "You shall have no other gods before Me" (Ex. 20:3, page 79).

(7) The shed blood made the "atonement for the soul" (vv. 10-12). Prefiguring the death of Christ by fourteen centuries, the Mosaic Law made it clear that this life-giving substance was to be the means of man's atonement.

See Leviticus 1:3-17, page 105, for **Point 36-B: Whole Burnt Offerings: Devotion.**

▽ 8 "Also you shall say to them: 'Whatever man of the house of Israel, or of the strangers who dwell among you, ᴿwho offers a burnt offering or sacrifice,   Lev. 1:2, 3; 18:26

9 'and does not ᴿbring it to the door of the tabernacle of meeting, to offer it to the LORD, that man shall be cut off from among his people.   Lev. 14:23

10 ᴿ'And whatever man of the house of Israel, or of the strangers who dwell among you, who eats any blood, I will set My face against that person who eats blood, and will cut him off from among his people.   Gen. 9:4

11 'For the life of the flesh is in the blood, and I have given it to you upon the altar to make atonement for your souls; for it is the blood that makes atonement for the soul.'

12 "Therefore I said to the children of Israel, 'No one among you shall eat blood, nor shall any stranger who dwells among you ▲ eat blood.'

13 "Whatever man of the children of Israel, or of the strangers who dwell among you, who hunts and catches any animal or bird that may be eaten, he shall pour out its blood and ᴿcover it with dust;   Ezek. 24:7

14 ᴿ"for it is the life of all flesh. Its blood sustains its life. Therefore I said to the children of Israel, 'You shall not eat the blood of any flesh, for the life of all flesh is its blood. Whoever eats it shall be cut off.'   Gen. 9:4

15 "And every person who eats what died naturally or what was torn by beasts, whether he is a native of your own country or a stranger, he shall both wash his clothes and ᴿbathe in water, and be unclean until evening. Then he shall be clean.   Lev. 15:5

16 "But if he does not wash them or bathe his body, then he shall bear his ᵀguilt." iniquity

Laws of Sexual Morality

18 Then the LORD spoke to Moses, saying, 2 "Speak to the children of Israel, and say to them: ᴿ'I am the LORD your God. Ex. 6:7

3 'According to the doings of the land of Egypt, where you dwelt, you shall not do; and according to the doings of the land of Canaan, where I am bringing you, you shall not do; nor shall you walk in their ordinances.

4 ᴿ'You shall observe My judgments and keep My ordinances, to walk in them: I am the LORD your God.   Ezek. 20:19

5 'You shall therefore keep My statutes and My judgments, which if a man does, he shall live by them: I am the LORD.

6 'None of you shall approach anyone who is near of kin to him, to uncover his nakedness: I am the LORD.

7 'The nakedness of your father or the nakedness of your mother you shall not uncover. She is your mother; you shall not uncover her nakedness.

8 'The nakedness of your ᴿfather's wife you shall not uncover; it is your father's nakedness.   Gen. 35:22

9 ᴿ'The nakedness of your sister, the daughter of your father, or the daughter of your mother, whether born at home or elsewhere, their nakedness you shall not uncover.   Deut. 27:22

10 'The nakedness of your son's daughter or your daughter's daughter, their nakedness you shall not uncover; for theirs is your own nakedness.

11 'The nakedness of your father's wife's daughter, begotten by your father—she is your sister—you shall not uncover her nakedness.

12 ᴿ'You shall not uncover the nakedness of your father's sister; she is near of kin to your father.   Lev. 20:19

13 'You shall not uncover the nakedness of your mother's sister, for she is near of kin to your mother.

14 ᴿ'You shall not uncover the nakedness of your father's brother. You shall not approach his wife; she is your aunt.   Lev. 20:20

15 'You shall not uncover the nakedness of your daughter-in-law—she is your son's wife—you shall not uncover her nakedness.

16 'You shall not uncover the nakedness of your brother's wife; it is your brother's nakedness.

17 'You shall not uncover the nakedness of a woman and her daughter, nor shall you take her son's daughter or her daughter's daughter, to uncover her nakedness. They are near of kin to her. It is wickedness.

18 'Nor shall you take a woman ᴿas a rival to her sister, to uncover her nakedness while the other is alive.   1 Sam. 1:6, 8

19 'Also you shall not approach a woman to uncover her nakedness as long as she is in her ᴿcustomary impurity.   Lev. 15:24; 20:18

20 ᴿ'Moreover you shall not lie carnally with your ᴿneighbor's wife, to defile yourself with her.   [Prov. 6:25-33] • Lev. 20:10

21 'And you shall not let any of your descendants pass through ᴿthe fire to ᴿMolech, nor shall you profane the name of your God: I am the LORD.   2 Kin. 16:3 • 1 Kin. 11:7, 33

22 'You shall not lie with ᴿa male as with a woman. It is an abomination.   Lev. 20:13

23 'Nor shall you mate with any ᴿanimal to defile yourself with it. Nor shall any woman stand before an animal to mate with it. It is perversion.   Ex. 22:19

24 'Do not defile yourselves with any of these things; for by all these the nations are defiled, which I am casting out before you.

25 'For the land is defiled; therefore I visit the punishment of its iniquity upon it, and the land vomits out its inhabitants.

26 ᴿ'You shall therefore ᵀkeep My statutes and My judgments, and shall not commit any of these abominations, either any of your

own nation or any stranger who dwells among you   Lev. 18:5, 30 • *obey*

27 '(for all these abominations the men of the land have done, who *were* before you, and thus the land is defiled),

28 'lest ᴿthe land vomit you out also when you defile it, as it vomited out the nations that *were* before you.   Jer. 9:19

29 'For whoever commits any of these abominations, the persons who commit *them* shall be cut off from among their people.

30 'Therefore you shall keep My ordinance, so that *you* do not commit *any* of these abominable customs which were committed before you, and that you do not defile yourselves by them: I *am* the LORD your God.' "

Moral and Ceremonial Laws

19 And the LORD spoke to Moses, saying, 2 "Speak to all the congregation of the children of Israel, and say to them: ᴿ'You shall be holy, for I the LORD your God *am* holy.   Lev. 11:44; 20:7, 26

3 ᴿ'Every one of you shall revere his mother and his father, and keep My Sabbaths: I *am* the LORD your God.   Ex. 20:12

4 ᴿ'Do not turn to idols, ᴿnor make for yourselves ᵀmolded gods: I *am* the LORD your God.   Ex. 20:4 • Ex. 34:17 • Cast metal

5 'And ᴿif you offer a sacrifice of a peace offering to the LORD, you shall offer it of your own free will.   Lev. 7:16

6 'It shall be eaten the same day you offer *it*, and on the next day. And if any remains until the third day, it shall be burned in the fire.

7 'And if it is eaten at all on the third day, it *is* an abomination. It shall not be accepted.

8 'Therefore *everyone* who eats it shall bear his iniquity, because he has profaned the hallowed *offering* of the LORD; and that person shall be cut off from his people.

9 ᴿ'When you reap the harvest of your land, you shall not wholly reap the corners of your field, nor shall you gather the gleanings of your harvest.   Deut. 24:19–22

10 'And you shall not glean your vineyard, nor shall you gather *every* grape of your vineyard; you shall leave them for the poor and the stranger: I *am* the LORD your God.

11 ᴿ'You shall not steal, nor deal falsely, ᴿnor lie to one another.   Ex. 20:15, 16 • Eph. 4:25

12 'And you shall not ᴿswear by My name falsely, ᴿnor shall you profane the name of your God: I *am* the LORD.   Deut. 5:11 • Lev. 18:21

13 ᴿ'You shall not cheat your neighbor, nor rob *him*. ᴿThe wages of him who is hired shall not remain with you all night until morning.   Ex. 22:7–15, 21–27 • Deut. 24:15

14 'You shall not curse the deaf, ᴿnor put a stumblingblock before the blind, but shall fear your God: I *am* the LORD.   Deut. 27:18

15 'You shall do no injustice in judgment. You shall not be partial to the poor, nor

honor the person of the mighty. In righteousness you shall judge your neighbor.

16 'You shall not go about *as* a ᴿtalebearer among your people; nor shall you ᴿtake a stand against the life of your neighbor: I *am* the LORD.   Prov. 11:13; 18:8; 20:19 • 1 Kin. 21:7–19

17 'You shall not hate your brother in your heart. You shall surely rebuke your neighbor, and not bear sin because of him.

18 ᴿ'You shall not take vengeance, nor bear any grudge against the children of your people, ᴿbut you shall love your neighbor as yourself: I *am* the LORD.   [Deut. 32:35] • Mark 12:31

19 'You shall keep My statutes. You shall not let your livestock breed with another kind. You shall not sow your field with mixed seed. Nor shall a garment of mixed linen and wool come upon you.

20 'Whoever lies carnally with a woman who *is* betrothed to a man as a concubine, and who has not at all been redeemed nor given her freedom, for this there shall be ᵀscourging; *but* they shall not be put to death, because she was not free.   *punishment*

21 'And he shall bring his trespass offering to the LORD, to the door of the tabernacle of meeting, a ram as a trespass offering.

22 'The priest shall make atonement for him with the ram of the trespass offering before the LORD for his sin which he has committed. And the sin which he has committed shall be forgiven him.

23 'When you come into the land, and have planted all kinds of trees for food, then you shall count their fruit as ᵀuncircumcised. Three years it shall be as uncircumcised to you. *It* shall not be eaten.   *unclean*

24 'But in the fourth year all its fruit shall be holy, a praise to the LORD.

25 'And in the fifth year you may eat its fruit, that it may yield to you its increase: I *am* the LORD your God.

26 'You shall not eat *anything* with the blood, nor shall you practice divination or soothsaying.

27 'You shall not shave around the sides of your head, nor shall you disfigure the edges of your beard.

28 'You shall not ᴿmake any cuttings in your flesh for the dead, nor tattoo any marks on you: I *am* the LORD.   Jer. 16:6

29 ᴿ'Do not prostitute your daughter, to cause her to be a harlot, lest the land fall into harlotry, and the land become full of wickedness.   Deut. 22:21; 23:17, 18

30 'You shall keep My Sabbaths and ᴿreverence My sanctuary: I *am* the LORD.   Lev. 26:2

31 'Give no regard to mediums and familiar spirits; do not seek after ᴿthem, to be defiled by them: I *am* the LORD your God.   Lev. 20:6, 27

32 'You shall ᵀrise before the gray headed and honor the presence of an old man, and fear your God: I *am* the LORD.   *to give honor*

33 'And ^Rif a stranger dwells with you in your land, you shall not mistreat him. Ex. 22:21

34 ^R'The stranger who dwells among you shall be to you as ^Tone born among you, and ^Ryou shall love him as yourself; for you were strangers in the land of Egypt: I *am* the LORD your God.   Ex. 12:48 • *native among you* • Deut. 10:19

35 'You shall do no injustice in judgment, in measurement of length, weight, or volume.

36 'You shall have ^Rhonest scales, honest weights, an honest ephah, and an honest hin: I *am* the LORD your God, who brought you out of the land of Egypt.   Deut. 25:13-15

37 ^R'Therefore you shall observe all My statutes and all My judgments, and perform them: I *am* the LORD.' "   Lev. 18:4, 5

Penalties for Breaking the Law

20 Then the LORD spoke to Moses, saying, 2 "Again, you shall say to the children of Israel: 'Whoever of the children of Israel, or of the strangers who dwell in Israel, who gives *any* of his descendants to Molech, he shall surely be put to death. The people of the land shall stone him with stones.

3 ^R'I will set My face against that man, and will ^Tcut him off from his people, because he has given *some* of his descendants to Molech, to defile My sanctuary and profane My holy name.   Lev. 17:10 • Put him to death

4 'And if the people of the land should in any way ^Thide their eyes from the man, when he gives *some* of his descendants to Molech, and they do not kill him,   *close*

5 'then I will set My face against that man and against his family; and I will cut him off from his people, and all who prostitute themselves with him to commit harlotry with Molech.

6 'And the person who turns to mediums and familiar spirits, to prostitute himself with them, I will set My face against that person and cut him off from his people.

7 ^R'Consecrate yourselves therefore, and be holy, for I *am* the LORD your God. Lev. 19:2

8 'And you shall keep ^RMy statutes, and perform them: ^RI *am* the LORD who ^Tsanctifies you.   Lev. 19:19, 37 • Ex. 31:13 • *sets you apart*

9 'For ^Reveryone who curses his father or his mother shall surely be put to death. He has cursed his father or his mother. ^RHis blood *shall be* upon him.   Ex. 21:17 • 2 Sam. 1:16

10 'The man who commits adultery with *another* man's wife, *he* who commits adultery with his neighbor's wife, the adulterer and the adulteress, shall surely be put to death.

11 'The man who lies with his ^Rfather's wife has uncovered his father's nakedness; both of them shall surely be put to death. Their blood *shall be* upon them.   Lev. 18:7, 8

12 'If a man lies with his ^Rdaughter-in-law, both of them shall surely be put to death.

They have committed perversion. Their blood *shall be* upon them.   Lev. 18:15

13 'If a man lies with a male as he lies with a woman, both of them have committed an abomination. They shall surely be put to death. Their blood *shall be* upon them.

14 'If a man marries a woman and her ^Rmother, it *is* wickedness. They shall be burned with fire, both he and they, that there may be no wickedness among you.   Lev. 18:17

15 'If a man mates with an ^Ranimal, he shall surely be put to death, and you shall kill the animal.   Lev. 18:23

16 'If a woman approaches any animal and mates with it, you shall kill the woman and the animal. They shall surely be put to death. Their blood *is* upon them.

17 'If a man takes his ^Rsister, his father's daughter or his mother's daughter, and sees her nakedness and she sees his nakedness, it *is* a wicked thing. And they shall be cut off in the sight of their people. He has uncovered his sister's nakedness. He shall bear his ^Tguilt.   Lev. 18:9 • *iniquity*

18 'If a man lies with a woman during her ^Tsickness and uncovers her nakedness, he has exposed her flow, and she has uncovered the flow of her blood. Both of them shall be cut off from their people.   Or *customary impurity*

19 'You shall not uncover the nakedness of your ^Rmother's sister nor of your ^Rfather's sister, for that would uncover his near of kin. They shall bear their guilt.   Lev. 18:13 • Lev. 18:12

20 'If a man lies with his uncle's wife, he has uncovered his uncle's nakedness. They shall bear their sin; they shall die childless.

21 'If a man takes his brother's wife, it *is* an unclean thing. He has uncovered his brother's nakedness. They shall be childless.

22 'You shall therefore keep all My statutes and all My judgments, and perform them, that the land where I am bringing you to dwell ^Rmay not vomit you out.   Lev. 18:25

23 ^R'And you shall not walk in the statutes of the nation which I am casting out before you; for they commit all these things, and ^Rtherefore I abhor them.   Lev. 18:3, 24 • Deut. 9:5

24 'But ^RI have said to you, "You shall inherit their land, and I will give it to you to possess, a land flowing with milk and honey." I *am* the LORD your God, who has separated you from the peoples.   Ex. 3:17; 6:8; 13:5; 33:1-3

25 'You shall therefore distinguish between clean animals and unclean, between unclean birds and clean, ^Rand you shall not make yourselves ^Tabominable by beast or by bird, or by any kind of living thing that creeps on the ground, which I have separated from you as unclean.   Lev. 11:43 • *detestable*

26 'And you shall be holy to Me, ^Rfor I the LORD *am* holy, and have separated you from the peoples, that you should be Mine. Lev. 19:2

27 ^R'A man or a woman who is a medium,

or who has familiar spirits, shall surely be put to death; they shall stone them with stones. Their blood *shall be* upon them.' " Lev. 19:31

Regulations for Conduct of Priests

21 And the LORD said to Moses, "Speak to the priests, the sons of Aaron, and say to them: ^R'None shall defile himself for the dead among his people, Ezek. 44:25

2 'except for his relatives who are nearest to him: his mother, his father, his son, his daughter, and his brother;

3 'also his virgin sister who is near to him, who has had no husband, for her he may defile himself.

4 '*Otherwise* he shall not defile himself, *being* a ^Tchief man among his people, to profane himself. Lit. *master or husband*

5 ^R'They shall not make any bald *place* on their heads, nor shall they shave the edges of their beards nor make any cuttings in their flesh. Deut. 14:1

6 'They shall be ^Rholy to their God and not profane the name of their God, for they offer the offerings of the LORD made by fire, *and* the ^Rbread of their God; ^Rtherefore they shall be holy. Ex. 22:31 • Lev. 3:11 • Is. 52:11

7 'They shall not take a wife *who is* a harlot or a defiled woman, nor shall they take a woman divorced from her husband; for ^T*the priest* is holy to his God. Lit. *he*

8 'Therefore you shall ^Tconsecrate him, for he offers the bread of your God. He shall be holy to you, for ^RI the LORD, who ^Rsanctify you, *am* holy. *set him apart* • Lev. 11:44, 45 • Lev. 8:12, 30

9 'The daughter of any priest, if she profanes herself by playing the harlot, she profanes her father. She shall be ^Rburned with fire. Deut. 22:21

10 '*He who is* the high priest among his brethren, on whose head the anointing oil was poured and who is consecrated to wear the garments, shall not ^Runcover^T his head nor tear his clothes; Lev. 10:6, 7 • In mourning

11 'nor shall he go near any dead body, nor defile himself for his father or his mother;

12 ^R'nor shall he go out of the sanctuary, nor profane the sanctuary of his God; for the ^Rconsecration of the anointing oil of his God *is* upon him: I *am* the LORD. Lev. 10:7 • Ex. 29:6, 7

13 'And he shall take a wife in her virginity.

14 'A widow or a divorced woman or a defiled woman *or* a harlot—these he shall not marry; but he shall take a virgin of his own people as wife.

15 'Nor shall he profane his posterity among his people, for I the LORD sanctify him.' "

16 And the LORD spoke to Moses, saying,

17 "Speak to Aaron, saying: 'No man of your descendants in *succeeding* generations, who has *any* defect, may approach to offer the bread of his God.

18 'For any man who has a defect shall not approach: a man blind or lame, who has a marred *face* or any *limb* too long,

19 'a man who has a broken foot or broken hand,

20 'or is a hunchback or a dwarf, or *a man* who has a defect in his eye, or eczema or scab, or is a eunuch.

21 'No man of the descendants of Aaron the priest, who has a defect, shall come near to offer the offerings made by fire to the LORD. He has a defect; he shall not come near to offer the bread of his God.

22 'He may eat the bread of his God, *both* the most holy and the holy;

23 'only he shall not go near the ^Rveil or approach the altar, because he has a defect, lest ^Rhe profane My sanctuaries; for I the LORD sanctify them.' " Lev. 16:2 • Lev. 21:12

24 And Moses told *it* to Aaron and his sons, and to all the children of Israel.

22 Then the LORD spoke to Moses, saying, 2 "Speak to Aaron and his sons, that they separate themselves from the holy things of the children of Israel, and that they do not profane My holy name *by* what they dedicate to Me: I *am* the LORD.

3 "Say to them: 'Whoever of all your descendants throughout your generations, who goes near the holy things which the children of Israel dedicate to the LORD, while he has uncleanness upon him, that person shall be cut off from My presence: I *am* the LORD.

4 'Whatever man of the descendants of Aaron, who *is* a ^Rleper or has a discharge, shall not eat the holy offerings until he is clean. And ^Rwhoever touches anything made unclean by a corpse, or a man who has had an emission of semen, Num. 5:2 • Num. 19:11

5 'or whoever touches any creeping thing by which he would be made unclean, or any person by whom he would become unclean, whatever his uncleanness may be—

6 'the person who has touched any such thing shall be unclean until evening, and shall not eat the holy *offerings* unless he ^Rwashes his body with water. Lev. 15:5

7 'And when the sun goes down he shall be clean; and afterward he may eat the holy *offerings*, because ^Rit *is* his food. Num. 18:11, 13

8 ^R'Whatever dies *naturally* or is torn *by beasts* he shall not eat, to defile himself with it: I *am* the LORD. Lev. 7:24; 11:39, 40; 17:15

9 'They shall therefore keep ^RMy ^Tordinance, ^Rlest they bear sin for it and die thereby, if they profane it: I the LORD sanctify them. Lev. 18:30 • *charge* • Ex. 28:43

10 ^R'No outsider shall eat the holy *offering*; one who dwells with the priest, or a hired servant, shall not eat the holy thing. Ex. 29:33

11 'But if the priest ^Rbuys a person with his money, he may eat it; and one who is born in his house may eat his food. Ex. 12:44

12 'If the priest's daughter is married to an outsider, she may not eat of the holy offerings.

13 'But if the priest's daughter is a widow or divorced, and has no child, and has returned to her father's house as in her youth, she may eat her father's food; but no outsider shall eat it.

14 'And if a man eats the holy *offering* unintentionally, then he shall restore a holy *offering* to the priest, and add one-fifth to it.

15 'They shall not profane the ᴿholy *offerings* of the children of Israel, which they offer to the LORD,   Num. 18:32

16 'or allow them to bear the guilt of trespass when they eat their holy *offerings*; for I the LORD sanctify them.' "

Offerings Accepted and Not Accepted

17 And the LORD spoke to Moses, saying,

18 "Speak to Aaron and his sons, and to all the children of Israel, and say to them: 'Whatever man of the house of Israel, or of the strangers in Israel, who ᵀoffers his sacrifice for any of his vows or for any of his freewill offerings, which they offer to the LORD as a burnt offering—   brings his offering

19 ᴿ'you shall offer of your own free will a male without blemish from the cattle, from the sheep, or from the goats.   Lev. 1:3

20 ᴿ'Whatever has a defect, you shall not offer, for it shall not be acceptable on your behalf.   Deut. 15:21; 17:1

21 'And ᴿwhoever offers a sacrifice of a peace offering to the LORD, ᴿto fulfill *his* vow, or a freewill offering from the cattle or the sheep, it must be perfect to be accepted; there shall be no defect in it.   Lev. 3:1, 6 • Num. 15:3, 8

22 ᴿ'Those *that are* blind or broken or maimed, or have an ᵀulcer or eczema or scabs, you shall not offer to the LORD, nor make ᴿan offering by fire of them on the altar to the LORD.   Mal. 1:8 • running sore • Lev. 1:9, 13; 3:3, 5

23 'Either a bull or a lamb that has any limb ᴿtoo long or too short you may offer *as* a freewill offering, but for a vow it shall not be accepted.   Lev. 21:18

24 'You shall not offer to the LORD what is bruised or crushed, or torn or cut; nor shall you make *any offering of them* in your land.

25 'Nor from a foreigner's hand shall you offer any of these as ᴿthe bread of your God, because their ᴿcorruption *is* in them, *and* defects *are* in them. They shall not be accepted on your behalf.'"   Lev. 21:6, 17 • Mal. 1:14

26 And the LORD spoke to Moses, saying:

27 ᴿ"When a bull or a sheep or a goat is born, it shall be seven days with its mother; and from the eighth day and thereafter it shall be accepted as an offering made by fire to the LORD.   Ex. 22:30

28 "Whether *it is* a cow or ewe, do not kill both her and her young on the same day.

29 "And when you ᴿoffer a sacrifice of thanksgiving to the LORD, offer *it* of your own free will.   Lev. 7:12

30 "On the same day it shall be eaten; you shall leave ᴿnone of it until morning: I *am* the LORD.   Lev. 7:15

31 ᴿ"Therefore you shall keep My commandments, and perform them: I *am* the LORD.   Deut. 4:40

32 "You shall not profane My holy name, but I will be hallowed among the children of Israel. I *am* the LORD who sanctifies you,

33 "who brought you out of the land of Egypt, to be your God: I *am* the LORD."

Feasts of the LORD

23 And the LORD spoke to Moses, saying, 2 "Speak to the children of Israel, and say to them: 'The feasts of the LORD, which you shall proclaim *to be* ᴿholy convocations, these *are* My feasts.   Ex. 12:16

The Sabbath

3 ᴿ'Six days shall work be done, but the seventh day *is* a Sabbath of solemn rest, a holy convocation. You shall do no work *on it*; it *is* the Sabbath of the LORD in all your dwellings.   Luke 13:14

The Passover and Unleavened Bread

4 ᴿ'These *are* the feasts of the LORD, holy convocations which you shall proclaim at their appointed times.   Ex. 23:14-16

5 'On the fourteenth *day* of the first month at twilight *is* the LORD's Passover.

6 'And on the fifteenth day of the same month *is* the Feast of Unleavened Bread to the LORD; seven days you must eat unleavened bread.

7 ᴿ'On the first day you shall have a holy convocation; you shall do no ᵀcustomary work on it.   Ex. 12:16 • occupational

8 'But you shall offer an offering made by fire to the LORD for seven days. The seventh day *shall be* a holy convocation; you shall do no customary work *on it*.' "

The Feast of Firstfruits

9 And the LORD spoke to Moses, saying,

10 "Speak to the children of Israel, and say to them: 'When you come into the land which I give to you, and reap its harvest, then you shall bring a sheaf of ᴿthe firstfruits of your harvest to the priest.   [Rom. 11:16]

11 'He shall wave the sheaf before the LORD, to be accepted on your behalf; on the day after the Sabbath the priest shall wave it.

12 'And you shall offer on that day, when you wave the ᵀsheaf, a male lamb of the first year, without blemish, as a burnt offering to the LORD.   2.087 qt.

13 'Its grain offering *shall be* two-tenths *of an ephah* of fine flour mixed with oil, an offering made by fire to the LORD, for a

ᵀsweet aroma; and its drink offering *shall be* of wine, ᵀone-fourth of a hin.   *pleasing* • 1 qt.

14 'You shall eat neither bread nor parched grain nor fresh grain until the same day that you have brought an offering to your God; *it shall be* a statute forever throughout your generations in all your dwellings.

The Feast of Weeks

15 'And you shall count for yourselves from the day after the Sabbath, from the day that you brought the sheaf of the wave offering: seven Sabbaths shall be completed.

16 'Count ᴿfifty days to the day after the seventh Sabbath; then you shall offer ᴿa new grain offering to the LORD.   Acts 2:1 • Num. 28:26

17 'You shall bring from your dwellings two wave *loaves* of two-tenths *of an ephah.* They shall be of fine flour; they shall be baked with leaven. *They are* the firstfruits to the LORD.

18 'And you shall offer with the bread seven lambs of the first year, without blemish, one young bull, and two rams. They shall be *as* a burnt offering to the LORD, with their grain offering and their drink offerings, an offering made by fire for a sweet aroma to the LORD.

19 'Then you shall sacrifice one kid of the goats as a sin offering, and two male lambs of the first year as a sacrifice of a peace offering.

20 'The priest shall wave them with the bread of the firstfruits *as* a wave offering before the LORD, with the two lambs. They shall be holy to the LORD for the priest.

21 'And you shall proclaim on the same day *that* it is a holy convocation to you. You shall do no customary work on it. *It shall be* a statute forever in all your dwellings throughout your generations.

22 'When you reap the harvest of your land, you shall not wholly reap the corners of your field when you reap, nor shall you gather any gleaning from your harvest. You shall leave them for the poor and for the stranger: I *am* the LORD your God.' "

The Feast of Trumpets

23 Then the LORD spoke to Moses, saying,

24 "Speak to the children of Israel, saying: 'In the ᴿseventh month, on the first *day* of the month, you shall have a sabbath-*rest*, ᴿa memorial of blowing of trumpets, a holy convocation.   Num. 29:1 • Lev. 25:9

25 'You shall do no customary work on *it*; and you shall offer an offering made by fire to the LORD.' "

The Day of Atonement

26 And the LORD spoke to Moses, saying:

27 ᴿ"Also the tenth *day* of this seventh month *shall be* the Day of Atonement. It shall be a holy convocation for you; you shall afflict your souls, and offer an offering made by fire to the LORD.   Num. 29:7

28 "And you shall do no work on that same day, for it *is* the Day of Atonement, to make atonement for you before the LORD your God.

29 "For any person who is not ᴿafflicted *in* soul on that same day ᴿshall be cut off from his people.   Jer. 31:9 • Num. 5:2

30 "And any person who does any work on that same day, ᴿthat person I will destroy from among his people.   Lev. 20:3-6

31 "You shall do no manner of work; *it shall be* a statute forever throughout your generations in all your dwellings.

32 "It *shall be* to you a sabbath of *solemn* rest, and you shall ᵀafflict your souls; on the ninth *day* of the month at evening, from evening to evening, you shall ᵀcelebrate your sabbath."   *humble yourselves • observe*

The Feast of Tabernacles

33 Then the LORD spoke to Moses, saying,

34 "Speak to the children of Israel, saying: ᴿ"The fifteenth day of this seventh month *shall be* the Feast of Tabernacles *for* seven days to the LORD.   Num. 29:12

35 'On the first day *there shall be* a holy convocation. You shall do no customary work *on it.*

36 '*For* seven days you shall offer an offering made by fire to the LORD. On the eighth day you shall have a holy convocation, and you shall offer an offering made by fire to the LORD. It is a ᴿsacredᵀ assembly, *and* you shall do no customary work *on it.*   Deut. 16:8 • *solemn*

37 ᴿ'These *are* the feasts of the LORD which you shall proclaim *to be* holy convocations, to offer an offering made by fire to the LORD, a burnt offering and a grain offering, a sacrifice and drink offerings, everything on its day—   Lev. 23:2, 4

38 ᴿ'besides the Sabbaths of the LORD, besides your gifts, besides all your vows, and besides all your freewill offerings which you give to the LORD.   Num. 29:39

39 'Also on the fifteenth day of the seventh month, when you have ᴿgathered in the fruit of the land, you shall keep the feast of the LORD *for* seven days; on the first day *there shall be* a sabbath-*rest*, and on the eighth day a sabbath-*rest.*   Ex. 23:16

40 'And ᴿyou shall take for yourselves on the first day the ᵀfruit of beautiful trees, branches of palm trees, the boughs of leafy trees, and willows of the brook; ᴿand you shall rejoice before the LORD your God for seven days.   Neh. 8:15 • Or *foliage* • Deut. 12:7; 16:14, 15

41 'You shall keep it as a feast to the LORD for seven days in the year. *It shall be* a statute forever in your generations. You shall celebrate it in the seventh month.

42 ᴿ'You shall dwell in ᵀbooths for seven days. All who are native Israelites shall dwell in booths,   [Is. 4:6] • *Shelters made of boughs*

43 'that your generations may know that I made the children of Israel dwell in booths

when ᴿI brought them out of the land of Egypt: I *am* the LORD your God.' "   Lev. 22:33
44 So Moses ᴿdeclared to the children of Israel the feasts of the LORD.   Lev. 23:2

Care of the Tabernacle Lamps

24 Then the LORD spoke to Moses, saying:
2 "Command the children of Israel that they bring to you pure oil of pressed olives for the light, to make the lamps burn continually.
3 "Outside the veil of the Testimony, in the tabernacle of meeting, Aaron shall be in charge of it from evening until morning before the LORD continually; *it shall be* a statute forever in your generations.
4 "He shall ᵀbe in charge of the lamps on ᴿthe pure *gold* lampstand before the LORD continually.   *arrange* or *set in order* • Ex. 25:31; 31:8; 37:17

The Bread of the Tabernacle

5 "And you shall take fine flour and bake twelve ᴿcakes with it. Two-tenths *of an ephah* shall be in each cake.   Ex. 25:30; 39:36; 40:23
6 "You shall set them in two rows, six in a row, on the pure *gold* table before the LORD.
7 "And you shall put pure frankincense on *each* row, that it may be on the bread for a ᴿmemorial, an offering made by fire to the LORD.   Lev. 2:2, 9, 16
8 ᴿ"Every Sabbath he shall set it in order before the LORD continually, *being taken* from the children of Israel by an everlasting covenant.   1 Chr. 9:32
9 "And it shall be for Aaron and his sons, and they shall eat it in a holy place; for it *is* most holy to him from the offerings of the LORD made by fire, by a perpetual statute."

The Penalty for Blasphemy

10 Now the son of an Israelite woman, whose father *was* an Egyptian, went out among the children of Israel; and this Israelite *woman's* son and a man of Israel fought each other in the camp.
11 And the Israelite woman's son blasphemed the name *of the* LORD and cursed; and so they ᴿbrought him to Moses. (His mother's name *was* Shelomith the daughter of Dibri, of the tribe of Dan.)   Ex. 18:22, 26
12 Then they ᴿput him ᵀin custody, ᴿthat the mind of the LORD might be shown to them.   Num. 15:34 • *under guard* • Num. 27:5
13 And the LORD spoke to Moses, saying,
14 "Take outside the camp him who has cursed; then let all who heard *him* ᴿlay their hands on his head, and let all the congregation stone him.   Deut. 13:9; 17:7
15 "Then you shall speak to the children of Israel, saying: 'Whoever curses his God ᴿshall ᵀbear his sin.   Lev. 20:17 • *be responsible for*
16 'And whoever ᴿblasphemes the name of the LORD shall surely be put to death. All the congregation shall certainly stone him, the

stranger as well as him who is born in the land. When he blasphemes the name *of the* LORD, he shall be put to death.   [Mark 3:28, 29]
17 ᴿ'Whoever kills any man shall surely be put to death.   Ex. 21:12
18 ᴿ'Whoever kills an animal shall make it good, animal for animal.   Lev. 24:21
19 'If a man causes disfigurement of his neighbor, as ᴿhe has done, so shall it be done to him—   Ex. 21:24
20 'fracture for ᴿfracture, eye for eye, tooth for tooth; as he has caused disfigurement of a man, so shall it be done to him.   Ex. 21:23
21 'And whoever kills an animal shall restore it; but whoever kills a man shall be put to death.
22 'You shall have ᴿthe same law for the stranger and for one from your own country; for I *am* the LORD your God.' "   Ex. 12:49
23 Then Moses spoke to the children of Israel; and they took outside the camp him who had cursed, and stoned him with stones. So the children of Israel did as the LORD commanded Moses.

The Sabbath of the Seventh Year

25 And the LORD spoke to Moses on Mount ᴿSinai, saying,   Lev. 26:46
2 "Speak to the children of Israel, and say to them: 'When you come into the land which I give you, then the land shall ᴿkeep a sabbath to the LORD.   Lev. 26:34, 35
3 'Six years you shall sow your field, and six years you shall prune your vineyard, and gather its fruit;
4 'but in the seventh year there shall be a sabbath of solemn ᴿrest for the land, a sabbath to the LORD. You shall neither sow your field nor prune your vineyard.   [Heb. 4:9]
5 ᴿ'What grows of its own accord of your harvest you shall not reap, nor gather the grapes of your untended vine, *for* it is a year of rest for the land.   2 Kin. 19:29
6 'And the sabbath *produce* of the land shall be food for you: for you, your male and female servants, your hired man, and the stranger who dwells with you,
7 'for your livestock and the beasts that *are* in your land—all its produce shall be for food.

The Year of Jubilee

8 'And you shall count seven sabbaths of years for yourself, seven times seven years; and the time of the seven sabbaths of years shall be to you forty-nine years.
9 'Then you shall cause the trumpet of the Jubilee to sound on the tenth *day* of the seventh month; ᴿon the Day of Atonement you shall make the trumpet to sound throughout all your land.   Lev. 23:24, 27
10 'And you shall consecrate the fiftieth year, and ᴿproclaim liberty throughout *all* the land to all its inhabitants. It shall be a Jubilee

for you; ᴿand each of you shall return to his possession, and each of you shall return to his family.   Jer. 34:8, 15, 17 · Num. 36:4

11 'That fiftieth year shall be a Jubilee to you; in it ᴿyou shall neither sow nor reap what grows of its own accord, nor gather *the* grapes of your untended vine.   Lev. 25:5

12 'For it *is* the Jubilee; it shall be holy to you; you shall eat its produce from the field.

13 ᴿ'In this Year of Jubilee, each of you shall return to his possession.   Lev. 25:10; 27:24

14 'And if you sell anything to your neighbor or buy from your neighbor's hand, you shall not ᴿoppress one another.   Lev. 19:13

15 ᴿ'According to the number of years after the Jubilee you shall buy from your neighbor, and according to the number of years of crops he shall sell to you.   Lev. 27:18, 23

16 'According to the multitude of years you shall increase its price, and according to the fewer number of years you shall diminish its price; for he sells to you *according* to the number *of the years* of the crops.

17 'Therefore ᴿyou shall not ᵀoppress one another, but you shall fear your God; for I *am* the LORD your God.   Lev. 25:14 · *mistreat*

Provisions for the Seventh Year

18 'So you shall observe My statutes and keep My judgments, and perform them; and you will dwell in the land in safety.

19 'Then the land will yield its fruit, and ᴿyou will eat your fill, and dwell there in safety.   Lev. 26:5

20 'And if you say, ᴿ"What shall we eat in the seventh year, since ᴿwe shall not sow nor gather in our produce?"   Matt. 6:25, 31 · Lev. 25:4, 5

21 'Then I will command My blessing on you in the ᴿsixth year, and it will bring forth produce enough for three years.   Ex. 16:29

22 ᴿ'And you shall sow in the eighth year, and eat ᴿold produce until the ninth year; until its produce comes in, you shall eat *of* the old *harvest*.   2 Kin. 19:29 · Josh. 5:11

Redemption of Property

23 'The land shall not be sold permanently, for ᴿthe land is Mine; for you *are* ᴿstrangers and sojourners with Me.   Ex. 19:5 · Ps. 39:12

24 'And in all the land of your possession you shall grant redemption of the land.

25 'If one of your brethren becomes poor, and has sold *some* of his possession, and if his redeeming relative comes to redeem it, then he may redeem what his brother sold.

26 'Or if the man has no one to redeem it, but he himself becomes able to redeem it,

27 'then ᴿlet him count the years since its sale, and restore the remainder to the man to whom he sold it, that he may return to his possession.   Lev. 25:50-52

28 'But if he is not able to have *it* restored to himself, then what was sold shall remain in the hand of him who bought it until the Year

of Jubilee; ᴿand in the Jubilee it shall be released, and he shall return to his possession.   Lev. 25:10, 13

29 'If a man sells a house in a walled city, then he may redeem it within a whole year after it is sold; *within* a full year he may redeem it.

30 'But if it is not redeemed within the space of a full year, then the house in the walled city shall belong permanently to him who bought it, throughout his generations. It shall not be released in the Jubilee.

31 'However the houses of villages which have no wall around them shall be counted as the fields of the country. They may be redeemed, and they shall be released in the Jubilee.

32 'Nevertheless the cities of the Levites, *and* the houses in the cities of their possession, the Levites may redeem at any time.

33 'And if a man purchases a house from the Levites, then the house that was sold in the city of his possession shall be released in the Jubilee; for the houses in the cities of the Levites *are* their possession among the children of Israel.

34 'But ᴿthe field of the common-land of their cities may not be ᴿsold, for it *is* their perpetual possession.   Num. 35:2-5 · Acts 4:36, 37

Lending to the Poor

35 'If one of your brethren becomes poor, and falls into poverty among you, then you shall help him, like a stranger or a sojourner, that he may live with you.

36 ᴿ'Take no usury or interest from him; but ᴿfear your God, that your brother may live with you.   Ex. 22:25 · Neh. 5:9

37 'You shall not lend him your money for usury, nor lend him your food at a profit.

38 'I *am* the LORD your God, who brought you out of the land of Egypt, to give you the land of Canaan *and* to be your God.

The Law Concerning Slavery

39 'And if *one of* your brethren *who dwells* by you becomes poor, and sells himself to you, you shall not compel him to serve as a slave.

40 'As a hired servant *and* a sojourner he shall be with you, *and* shall serve you until the Year of Jubilee.

41 'And *then* he shall depart from you—he and his children ᴿwith him—and shall return to his own family. He shall return to the possession of his fathers.   Ex. 21:3

42 'For they *are* ᴿMy servants, whom I brought out of the land of Egypt; they shall not be sold as slaves.   [Rom. 6:22]

43 'You shall not rule over him with ᵀrigor, but you shall fear your God.   *severity*

44 'And as for your male and female slaves whom you may have—from the nations that

are around you, from them you may buy
male and female slaves.

45 'Moreover you may buy ᴿthe children of
the strangers who dwell among you, and
their families who are with you, which they
beget in your land; and they shall become
your property.   [Is. 56:3, 6, 7]

46 'And ᴿyou may take them as an inheritance for your children after you, to inherit
them as a possession; they shall be your
permanent slaves. But regarding your brethren, the children of Israel, you shall not rule
over one another with rigor.   Is. 14:2

47 'Now if a sojourner or stranger close to
you becomes rich, and *one of* your brethren
who dwells by him becomes poor, and sells
himself to the stranger *or* sojourner close to
you, or to a member of the stranger's family,

48 'after he is sold he may be redeemed
again. One of his brothers may redeem him;

49 'or his uncle or his uncle's son may
redeem him; or *anyone* who is near of kin to
him in his family may redeem him; or if he is
able he may redeem himself.

50 'Thus he shall reckon with him who
bought him: The price of his release shall be
according to the number of years, from the
year that he was sold to him until the Year of
Jubilee; *it shall be* ᴿaccording to the time of a
hired servant for him.   Job 7:1

51 'If *there are* still many years *remaining*,
according to them he shall repay the price of
his redemption from the money with which
he was bought.

52 'And if there remain but a few years
until the Year of Jubilee, then he shall reckon
with him, *and* according to his years he shall
repay him the price of his redemption.

53 'He shall be with him as a yearly hired
servant, and he shall not rule with rigor over
him in your sight.

54 'And if he is not redeemed in these *years*,
then he shall be released in the Year of
Jubilee—he and his children with him.

55 'For the children of Israel *are* servants to
Me; they *are* My servants whom I brought
out of the land of Egypt: I *am* the LORD your
God.

Promise of Blessing and Retribution

26 'You shall ᴿnot make idols for yourselves;   Ex. 20:4, 5
neither a carved image nor a *sacred*
pillar shall you rear up for yourselves;
nor shall you set up an engraved stone in
your land, to bow down to it;
for I *am* the LORD your God.

2 ᴿYou shall ᵀkeep My Sabbaths and reverence My sanctuary:
I *am* the LORD.   Lev. 19:30 • *observe*

3 'If ᴿ you walk in My statutes and keep
My commandments, and perform
them,   Deut. 28:1-14

4 ᴿthen I will give you rain in its season,
ᴿthe land shall yield its produce, and
the trees of the field shall yield their
fruit.   Is. 30:23 • Ps. 67:6

5 Your threshing shall last till the time of
vintage, and the vintage shall last till
the time of sowing;
you shall eat your bread to the full, and
dwell in your land safely.

6 ᴿI will give peace in the land, and ᴿyou
shall lie down, and none will make *you*
afraid;   Is. 45:7 • Job 11:19
I will rid the land of ᴿevilᵀ beasts,
and ᴿthe sword will not go through your
land.   2 Kin. 17:25 • *wild* • Ezek. 14:17

7 You will chase your enemies, and they
shall fall by the sword before you.

8 ᴿFive of you shall chase a hundred, and a
hundred of you shall put ten thousand
to flight;   Deut. 32:30
your enemies shall fall by the sword
before you.

9 'For I will look on you favorably and
make you fruitful, multiply you and
confirm My covenant with you.

10 You shall eat the old harvest, and clear
out the old because of the new.

11 I will set My tabernacle among you, and
My soul shall not abhor you.

12 I will walk among you and be your God,
and you shall be My people.

13 I *am* the LORD your God, who brought
you out of the land of Egypt, that *you*
should not be their slaves;
I have broken the bands of your yoke
and made you walk upright.

14 'But if you do not obey Me, and do not
observe all these commandments,

15 and if you despise My statutes, or if your
soul abhors My judgments, so that
you do not perform all My commandments, *but* break My covenant,

16 I also will do this to you:
I will even appoint terror over you,
ᴿwasting disease and fever which shall
ᴿconsume the eyes and cause sorrow
of heart.   Deut. 28:22 • 1 Sam. 2:33
And you shall sow your seed in vain, for
your enemies shall eat it.

17 I will set My face against you, and you
shall be defeated by your enemies.
ᴿThose who hate you shall reign over
you, and you shall ᴿflee when no one
pursues you.   Ps. 106:41 • Prov. 28:1

18 'And after all this, if you do not obey Me,
then I will punish you ᴿseven times
more for your sins.   1 Sam. 2:5

19 I will break the pride of your power;
I will make your heavens like iron and
your earth like bronze.

20 And your ᴿstrength shall be spent in
vain;   Ps. 127:1

for your ᴿland shall not yield its produce,
nor shall the trees of the land yield
their fruit.   Gen. 4:12

21 'Then, if you walk contrary to Me, and
are not willing to obey Me, I will bring
on you seven times more plagues, according to your sins.

22 I will also send wild beasts among you,
which shall rob you of your children,
destroy your livestock, and make you
few in number;
and your highways shall be desolate.

23 'And if ᴿby these things you are not
reformed by Me, but walk contrary to
Me,   Amos 4:6–12

24 ᴿthen I also will walk contrary to you,
and I will punish you yet seven times
for your sins.   Lev. 26:28, 41

25 And ᴿI will bring a sword against you
that will execute the vengeance of the
covenant;   Ezek. 5:17
when you are gathered together within
your cities ᴿI will send pestilence
among you;   Deut. 28:21
and you shall be delivered into the hand
of the enemy.

26 When I have cut off your supply of
bread, ten women shall bake your
bread in one oven, and they shall bring
back your bread by weight, and you
shall eat and not be satisfied.

27 'And after all this, if you do not obey Me,
but walk contrary to Me,

28 then I also will walk contrary to you in
fury;
and I, even I, will chastise you seven
times for your sins.

29 ᵀYou shall eat the flesh of your sons, and
you shall eat the flesh of your daugh-
ters.   In time of famine

30 ᴿI will destroy your high places, cut down
your incense altars, and cast your
carcasses on the lifeless forms of your
idols;   2 Chr. 34:3
and My soul shall abhor you.

31 I will lay your cities waste and bring
your sanctuaries to desolation, and I
will not smell the fragrance of your
sweet aromas.

32 ᴿI will bring the land to desolation, and
your enemies who dwell in it shall be
astonished at it.   Jer. 9:11

33 ᴿI will scatter you among the nations and
draw out a sword after you;
your land shall be desolate and your
cities waste.   Deut. 4:27

34 ᴿThen the land shall enjoy its sabbaths as
long as it lies desolate and you *are* in
your enemies' land;
then the land shall rest and enjoy its
sabbaths.   2 Chr. 36:21

35 As long as *it* lies desolate it shall rest—

for the time it did not rest on your
sabbaths when you dwelt in it.

36 'And as for those of you who are left, I
will send ᴿfaintnessᵀ into their hearts
in the lands of their enemies;
the sound of a shaken leaf shall cause
them to flee;   Ezek. 21:7, 12, 15 • *fear*
they shall flee as though fleeing from a
sword, and they shall fall when no one
pursues.

37 ᴿThey shall stumble over one another, as
it were before a sword, when no one
pursues;   1 Sam. 14:15, 16
and ᴿyou shall have no *power* to stand
before your enemies.   Josh. 7:12, 13

38 You shall ᴿperish among the nations, and
the land of your enemies shall eat you
up.   Deut. 4:26

39 And those of you who are left shall
ᵀwaste away in their iniquity in your
enemies' lands;   *rot*
also in their ᴿfathers' iniquities, which
are with them, they shall waste
away.   Ex. 34:7

40 'But if they confess their iniquity and the
iniquity of their fathers, with their
unfaithfulness in which they were unfaithful to Me, and that they also have
walked contrary to Me,

41 and *that* I also have walked contrary to
them and have brought them into the
land of their enemies;
if their uncircumcised hearts are humbled, and they accept their guilt—

42 then I will remember My covenant with
Jacob, and My covenant with Isaac
and My covenant with Abraham I will
remember;
I will ᴿremember the land.   Ps. 136:23

43 ᴿThe land also shall be left empty by
them, and will enjoy its sabbaths while
it lies desolate without them;
they will accept their guilt, because
they ᴿdespised My judgments and
because their soul abhorred My
statutes.   Lev. 26:34, 35 • Lev. 26:15

44 Yet for all that, when they are in the
land of their enemies, ᴿI will not cast
them away, nor shall I abhor them, to
utterly destroy them and break My
covenant with them;
for I *am* the LORD their God.   Deut. 4:31

45 But ᴿfor their sake I will remember the
covenant of their ancestors, whom I
brought out of the land of Egypt ᴿin
the sight of the nations, that I might
be their God:
I *am* the LORD.' "   [Rom. 11:28] • Ps. 98:2

46 ᴿThese *are* the statutes and judgments
and laws which the LORD made between
Himself and the children of Israel ᴿon Mount
Sinai by the hand of Moses.   [John 1:17] • Lev. 25:1

Redeeming Persons and Property
Dedicated to God

27 Now the LORD spoke to Moses, saying, 2 "Speak to the children of Israel, and say to them: 'When a man ᵀconsecrates by a vow certain persons to the LORD, according to your valuation, Or *makes a difficult vow*

3 'if your valuation is of a male from twenty years old up to sixty years old, then your valuation shall be fifty shekels of silver, according to the shekel of the sanctuary.

4 'If it *is* a female, then your valuation shall be ᵀthirty shekels; $3,840

5 'and if from five years old up to twenty years old, then your valuation for a male shall be ᵀtwenty shekels, and for a female ᵀten shekels; $2,560 · $1,280

6 'and if from a month old up to five years old, then your valuation for a male shall be five shekels of silver, and for a female your valuation shall be three shekels of silver;

7 'and if from sixty years old and above, if it *is* a male, then your valuation shall be fifteen shekels, and for a female ten shekels.

8 'But if he is too poor to pay your valuation, then he shall present himself before the priest, and the priest shall set a value for him; according to the ability of him who vowed, the priest shall value him.

9 'If *it is* an animal that men may bring as an offering to the LORD, all that *anyone* gives to the LORD shall be holy.

10 'He shall not substitute it or exchange it, good for bad or bad for good; and if he at all exchanges animal for animal then both it and the one exchanged for it shall be holy.

11 'If *it is* an unclean animal which they do not offer as a sacrifice to the LORD, then he shall present the animal before the priest;

12 'and the priest shall set a value for it, whether it is good or bad; as you, the priest, value it, so it shall be.

13 'But if he *wants* at all *to* redeem it, then he must add one-fifth to your valuation.

14 'And when a man ᵀdedicates his house *to* be holy to the LORD, then the priest shall set a value for it, whether it is good or bad; as the priest values it, so it shall stand. *sets apart*

15 'If he who dedicated it *wants to* ᵀredeem his house, then he must add one-fifth of the money of your valuation to it, and it shall be his. *buy back*

16 'If a man ᵀdedicates to the LORD *part* of a field of his possession, then your valuation shall be according to the seed for it. A homer of barley seed *shall be valued* at ᵀfifty shekels of silver. *sets apart* · $6,400

17 'If he dedicates his field from the Year of Jubilee, according to your valuation it shall stand.

18 'But if he dedicates his field after the Jubilee, then the priest shall ᴿreckon to him the money due according to the years that remain till the Year of Jubilee, and it shall be deducted from your valuation. Lev. 25:15, 16, 28

19 'And if he who dedicates the field ever wishes to redeem it, then he must add one-fifth of the money of your valuation to it, and it shall belong to him.

20 'But if he does not want to redeem the field, or if he has sold the field to another man, it shall not be redeemed anymore;

21 'but the field, ᴿwhen it is released in the Jubilee, shall be holy to the LORD, as a ᴿdevoted field; it shall be ᴿthe possession of the priest. Lev. 25:10, 28, 31 · Lev. 27:28 · Num. 18:14

22 'And if a man dedicates to the LORD a field which he has bought, which is not the field of ᴿhis possession, Lev. 25:10, 25

23 'then the priest shall reckon to him the worth of your valuation, up to the Year of Jubilee, and he shall give your valuation on that day *as* a holy *offering* to the LORD.

24 'In the Year of Jubilee the field shall return to him from whom it was bought, to the one who *owned* the land as a possession.

25 'And all your valuations shall be according to the ᵀshekel of the sanctuary: ᴿtwenty gerahs to the shekel. $128 · Ex. 30:13

26 'But the ᴿfirstborn of the animals, which should be the LORD's firstborn, no man shall dedicate; whether *it is* an ox or sheep, it *is* the LORD's. Ex. 13:2, 12; 22:30

27 'And if *it is* an unclean animal, then he shall redeem *it* according to your valuation, and ᴿshall add one-fifth to it; or if it is not redeemed, then it shall be sold according to your valuation. Lev. 27:11, 12

28 'Nevertheless no devoted *offering* that a man may devote to the LORD of all that he has, *both* man and beast, or the field of his possession, shall be sold or redeemed; every devoted *offering is* most holy to the LORD.

29 ᴿ'No person under the ban, who may become doomed to destruction among men, shall be redeemed, *but* shall surely be put to death. Num. 21:2

30 'And ᴿall the tithe of the land, *whether* of the seed of the land or of the fruit of the tree, is the LORD's. It *is* holy to the LORD. Gen. 28:22

31 ᴿ'If a man wants at all to redeem any of his tithes, he shall add one-fifth to it. Lev. 27:13

32 'And concerning the tithe of the herd or the flock, of whatever passes under the rod, the tenth one shall be holy to the LORD.

33 'He shall not inquire whether it is good or bad, ᴿnor shall he exchange it; and if he exchanges it at all, then both it and the one exchanged for it shall be holy; it shall not be redeemed.' " Lev. 27:10

34 These *are* the commandments which the LORD commanded Moses for the children of Israel on Mount ᴿSinai. [Heb. 12:18–29]

THE FOURTH BOOK OF MOSES CALLED

Numbers

The name *Numbers* was first used in the Septuagint (*Arithmoi*) because of the many census figures (chs. 1—3, 26). The Hebrew title is "in the wilderness," and is found in the first line of the book. It is most appropriate since the events of the book largely take place in the desert, where the Israelites wandered for forty years.

AUTHORSHIP AND CONTEXT. Numbers is the fourth book of Moses, written about the middle of the fifteenth century B.C. Numbers is a book of history, taking the Israelites through thirty-nine years of wandering, from where they had encamped in Exodus to the plains of Moab across the Jordan from the Promised Land.

HOW NUMBERS FITS INTO THE BIBLE. The history of the Jews in this book is one of dark unbelief, complaint, failure, and rebellion. This stands out even more against the bright backdrop of God's faithfulness and miraculous provision for His people. Christians should not think that they have advanced beyond the problems mentioned in Numbers, since the New Testament uses the book to teach universal spiritual lessons (John 3:14; 1 Cor. 10:5–11; 2 Pet. 2:15, 16; Jude 11; Rev. 2:14).

HOW NUMBERS FITS TOGETHER. How Israel made preparations for their journey to the Promised Land, including the census of the people, is told in 1:1—10:10. As the people march to Kadesh Barnea (10:11—12:16), they complain, as do Miriam and Aaron. In chapters 13—20 Israel is encamped at Kadesh Barnea, where several dramatic events take place, such as Korah's rebellion and Moses' sin. On the way to Moab (chs. 20—21) Aaron dies, the famous incident of the bronze serpent occurs, and the defeat of kings Sihon and Og take place. The rest of the book (chs. 22—36) takes place on the plains of Moab across from the Promised Land. The important accounts of Balak and Balaam are included in this section.

THE TYPOLOGY OF THE BOOK OF NUMBERS. In reading the book of Numbers, one should remember that "all these things happened to them as examples, and they were written for our admonition, on whom the ends of the ages have come" (1 Cor. 10:11). The word *examples* is literally *types* (*tupikos*). A casual reader is likely to miss the beauty and significance of some of these incidents in the book. A *type* is a person or thing in the Old Testament which foreshadows a person or thing in the New Testament. A study of the types is one of the most rewarding and challenging of all phases of Bible study. The reason for this is that, as someone has said, "Christ is the Golden Key that unlocks the Word of God, and He is seen in all Scripture from Genesis to Revelation." The types of Christ, found throughout the Old Testament and revealed in the New Testament, give added clarity to His Person and work. After His resurrection, in His conversation with two disciples near the village of Emmaus (Luke 24:27), "beginning at Moses and all the Prophets, He expounded to them in all the Scriptures the things concerning Himself."

Look for Him in the Nazirite and his vow (6:1–8). How beautifully this typifies the willing, complete dedication and obedience of our blessed Lord to the Father in His earthly walk (John 6:38).

Look for Him in the celebration of the Passover (9:1–14). He is "the Lamb of God who takes away the sin of the world" (John 1:29). He alone is worthy (Rev. 5:12).

Look for Him in the pillar of cloud by day and the pillar of fire by night, guiding the wanderers in the wilderness (John 10:4; 16:13). How wonderful that He is *with* the Christian, and *in* the Christian, and that He is *before* the Christian in his daily walk. Christ is in all our tomorrows. We may proceed with perfect confidence and joyous assurance every step of the way.

See Him typified by the priesthood of Aaron, the God-appointed high priest of Israel, the representative of a sinful people before a Holy God, on the ground of the shed blood of sacrifice. The priesthood of Aaron was only temporary; the high-priestly office of the crucified, buried, risen, ascended, and living Christ is eternal. The Levitical priesthood has been superseded by a "better" priesthood—the eternal priesthood after the order of Melchizedek (Heb. 6:20; 7:21). And, wonder of wonders, when the Father sees His beloved Son at His right hand (Rom. 6:34), the Father sees the Lord Jesus not only *for* us, but *as* us. God sees us, who by His grace have been born again, as having died with Christ at Calvary, as having been buried with Him in the tomb, as risen with Him, ascended with Him, and seated with Him in the

heavenlies, and as having "become the righteousness of God in Him" (2 Cor. 5:21). Oh, the marvels of His grace!

Look for Him in the red heifer (19:1–10). Not only are we saved from the *penalty* of sin through the Person and work of Christ, but also we are delivered from the *power* of sin in our daily walk through the wilderness of the world and its defilement. There must be the daily confession and cleansing (John 13:1–10; 1 John 1:7–9).

See Him as the Rock in 20:7–11 (cf. 1 Cor. 10:4); in the serpent of bronze upon the pole (21:5–9; cf. John 3:14, 15; 2 Cor. 5:21); and in the six cities of refuge (35:6–15; cf. John 10:27–30; Rom. 8:1–4).

What a treasure of doctrinal, practical, glorious, and challenging truth we find in the book of Numbers. As it is read with the mind and heart in dependence on the Holy Spirit, who delights to make the Lord Jesus a living reality to us, we shall find it rich indeed.

SUMMARY STATEMENT. Numbers teaches failure due to unbelief in contrast with the faithfulness of God—a theme well stated in the New Testament: "Without faith it is impossible to please Him" (Heb. 11:6).

—W.P.L.

The First Census of Israel

NOW the LORD spoke to Moses in the Wilderness of Sinai, in the tabernacle of meeting, on the first *day* of the second month, in the second year after they had come out of the land of Egypt, saying:

2 "Take a census of all the congregation of the children of Israel, by their families, by their fathers' houses, according to the number of names, every male individually,

3 "from twenty years old and above—all who *are able to* go to war in Israel. You and Aaron shall number them by their armies.

4 "And with you there shall be a man from every tribe, each one the head of his father's house.

5 "These are the names of the men who shall stand with you: from Reuben, Elizur the son of Shedeur;

6 "from Simeon, Shelumiel the son of Zurishaddai;

7 "from Judah, Nahshon the son of Amminadab;

8 "from Issachar, Nethanel the son of Zuar;

9 "from Zebulun, Eliab the son of Helon;

10 "from the sons of Joseph: from Ephraim, Elishama the son of Ammihud; from Manasseh, Gamaliel the son of Pedahzur;

11 "from Benjamin, Abidan the son of Gideoni;

12 "from Dan, Ahiezer the son of Ammishaddai;

13 "from Asher, Pagiel the son of Ocran;

14 "from Gad, Eliasaph the son of *Deuel;

15 "from Naphtali, Ahira the son of Enan."

16 These were Tchosen from the congregation, leaders of their fathers' tribes, Rheads of the divisions in Israel. called · Ex. 18:21, 25

17 Then Moses and Aaron took these men who had been mentioned Rby name, Is. 43:1

18 and they assembled all the congregation together on the first *day* of the second

month; and they recited their Rancestry by families, by their fathers' houses, according to the number of names, from twenty years old and above, each one individually. Ezra 2:59

19 As the LORD commanded Moses, so he numbered them in the Wilderness of Sinai.

20 Now the Rchildren of Reuben, Israel's oldest son, their genealogies by their families, by their fathers' house, according to the number of names, every male individually, from twenty years old and above, all who *were able to* go to war: Num. 2:10, 11; 26:5–11

21 those who were numbered of the tribe of Reuben *were* forty-six thousand five hundred.

22 From the children of Simeon, their genealogies by their families, by their fathers' house, of those who were numbered, according to the number of names, every male individually, from twenty years old and above, all who *were able to* go to war:

23 those who were numbered of the tribe of Simeon *were* fifty-nine thousand three hundred.

24 From the Rchildren of Gad, their genealogies by their families, by their fathers' house, according to the number of names, from twenty years old and above, all who *were able to* go to war: Num. 26:15–18

25 those who were numbered of the tribe of Gad *were* forty-five thousand six hundred and fifty.

26 From the Rchildren of Judah, their genealogies by their families, by their fathers' house, according to the number of names, from twenty years old and above, all who *were able to* go to war: 2 Sam. 24:9

27 those who were numbered of the tribe of Judah *were* Rseventy-four thousand six hundred. 2 Chr. 17:14

28 From the Rchildren of Issachar, their genealogies by their families, by their fathers' house, according to the number of names, from twenty years old and above, all who *were able to* go to war: Num. 2:5, 6

1:14 *Reuel*, Num. 2:14

29 those who were numbered of the tribe of Issachar *were* fifty-four thousand four hundred.

30 From the ᴿchildren of Zebulun, their genealogies by their families, by their fathers' house, according to the number of names, from twenty years old and above, all who *were able to* go to war: Num. 2:7, 8; 26:26, 27

31 those who were numbered of the tribe of Zebulun *were* fifty-seven thousand four hundred.

32 From the sons of Joseph, the children of Ephraim, their genealogies by their families, by their fathers' house, according to the number of names, from twenty years old and above, all who *were able to* go to war:

33 those who were numbered of the tribe of Ephraim *were* forty thousand five hundred.

34 From the ᴿchildren of Manasseh, their genealogies by their families, by their fathers' house, according to the number of names, from twenty years old and above, all who *were able to* go to war: Num. 2:20, 21; 26:28-34

35 those who were numbered of the tribe of Manasseh *were* thirty-two thousand two hundred.

36 From the ᴿchildren of Benjamin, their genealogies by their families, by their fathers' house, according to the number of names, from twenty years old and above, all who *were able to* go to war: Num. 26:38-41

37 those who were numbered of the tribe of Benjamin *were* thirty-five thousand four hundred.

38 From the ᴿchildren of Dan, their genealogies by their families, by their fathers' house, according to the number of names, from twenty years old and above, all who *were able to* go to war: Gen. 30:6; 46:23

39 those who were numbered of the tribe of Dan *were* sixty-two thousand seven hundred.

40 From the ᴿchildren of Asher, their genealogies by their families, by their fathers' house, according to the number of names, from twenty years old and above, all who *were able to* go to war: Num. 2:27, 28; 26:44-47

41 those who were numbered of the tribe of Asher *were* forty-one thousand five hundred.

42 From the children of Naphtali, their genealogies by their families, by their fathers' house, according to the number of names, from twenty years old and above, all who *were able to* go to war:

43 those who were numbered of the tribe of Naphtali *were* fifty-three thousand four hundred.

44 ᴿThese are the ones who were numbered, whom Moses and Aaron numbered, with the leaders of Israel, twelve men, each one representing his father's house.   Num. 26:64

45 So all who were numbered of the children of Israel, by their fathers' houses, from twenty years old and above, all who *were able to* go to war in Israel—

46 all who were numbered were ᴿsix hundred and three thousand five hundred and fifty.   Ex. 12:37; 38:26

47 But the Levites were not numbered among them by their fathers' tribe;

48 for the LORD had spoken to Moses, saying:

49 ᴿ"Only the tribe of Levi you shall not number, nor take a census of them among the children of Israel;   Num. 2:33; 26:62

50 "but you shall appoint the Levites over the tabernacle of the Testimony, over all its furnishings, and over all things that belong to it; they shall carry the tabernacle and all its furnishings; they shall attend to it ᴿand camp around the tabernacle.   Num. 3:23, 29, 35, 38

51 "And when the tabernacle is to go forward, the Levites shall take it down; and when the tabernacle is to be set up, the Levites shall set it ᴿup. The outsider who comes near shall be put to death.   Num. 10:21

52 "The children of Israel shall pitch their tents, ᴿeveryone by his own camp, everyone by his own standard, according to their armies;   Num. 2:2, 34; 24:2

53 "but the Levites shall camp around the tabernacle of the Testimony, that there may be no wrath on the congregation of the children of Israel; and the Levites shall keep charge of the tabernacle of the Testimony."

54 Thus the children of Israel did; according to all that the LORD commanded Moses, so they did.

The Tribes and Leaders by Armies

2 And the LORD spoke to Moses and Aaron, saying:

2 ᴿ"Everyone of the children of Israel shall camp by his own ᵀstandard, beside the emblems of his father's house; they shall camp ᴿsome distance from the tabernacle of meeting.   Num. 1:52; 24:2 · *banner* · Josh. 3:4

3 "On the east side, toward the rising of the sun, those of the standard of the forces with Judah shall camp according to their armies; and Nahshon the son of Amminadab *shall be* the leader of the children of Judah."

4 And his army was numbered at seventy-four thousand six hundred.

5 "Those who camp next to him *shall be* the tribe of Issachar, and Nethanel the son of Zuar *shall be* the leader of the children of Issachar."

6 And his army was numbered at fifty-four thousand four hundred.

7 "Then *comes* the tribe of Zebulun, and Eliab the son of Helon *shall be* the leader of the children of Zebulun."

8 And his army was numbered at fifty-seven thousand four hundred.

9 "All who were numbered according to their armies of the forces with Judah, one

hundred and eighty-six thousand four hundred—these shall ᵀbreak camp first.   *set forth*

10 "On the south side *shall be* the standard of the forces with Reuben according to their armies, and the leader of the children of Reuben *shall be* Elizur the son of Shedeur."

11 And his army was numbered at forty-six thousand five hundred.

12 "Those who camp next to him *shall be* the tribe of Simeon, and the leader of the children of Simeon *shall be* Shelumiel the son of Zurishaddai."

13 And his army was numbered at fifty-nine thousand three hundred.

14 "Then *comes* the tribe of Gad, and the leader of the children of Gad *shall be* Eliasaph the son of ᵀReuel."   *Deuel, Num. 1:14; 7:42*

15 And his army was numbered at forty-five thousand six hundred and fifty.

16 "All who were numbered according to their armies of the forces with Reuben, one hundred and fifty-one thousand four hundred and fifty—ᴿthey shall ᵀbe the second to break camp.   *Num. 10:18 · set forth second*

17 "And the tabernacle of meeting shall move out with the ᵀcamp of the Levites in the middle of the ᵀcamps; as they camp, so they shall move out, everyone in his place, by their ᵀstandards.   *company · whole company · banners*

18 "On the west side *shall be* the standard of the forces with Ephraim according to their armies, and the leader of the children of Ephraim *shall be* Elishama the son of Ammihud."

19 And his army was numbered at forty thousand five hundred.

20 "Next to him *comes* the tribe of Manasseh, and the leader of the children of Manasseh *shall be* Gamaliel the son of Pedahzur."

21 And his army was numbered at thirty-two thousand two hundred.

22 "Then *comes* the tribe of Benjamin, and the leader of the children of Benjamin *shall be* Abidan the son of Gideoni."

23 And his army was numbered at thirty-five thousand four hundred.

24 "All who were numbered according to their armies of the forces with Ephraim, one hundred and eight thousand one hundred—they shall be the third to break camp.

25 "The standard of the forces with Dan *shall be* on the north side according to their armies, and the leader of the children of Dan *shall be* Ahiezer the son of Ammishaddai."

26 And his army was numbered at sixty-two thousand seven hundred.

27 "Those who camp next to him *shall be* the tribe of Asher, and the leader of the children of Asher *shall be* Pagiel the son of Ocran."

28 And his army was numbered at forty-one thousand five hundred.

29 "Then *comes* the tribe of Naphtali, and

the leader of the children of Naphtali *shall be* Ahira the son of Enan."

30 And his army was numbered at fifty-three thousand four hundred.

31 "All who were numbered of the forces with Dan, one hundred and fifty-seven thousand six hundred—they shall break camp last, with their ᵀstandards."   *banners*

32 These *are* the ones who were numbered of the children of Israel by their fathers' houses. All who were numbered according to their armies of the forces *were* six hundred and three thousand five hundred and fifty.

33 But ᴿthe Levites were not numbered among the children of Israel, just as the LORD commanded Moses.   *Num. 1:47; 26:57-62*

34 Thus the children of Israel did according to all that the LORD commanded Moses; so they camped by their ᵀstandards and so they broke camp, each one by his family, according to their fathers' houses.   *banners*

The Sons of Aaron

3 Now these *are* the ᴿrecordsᵀ of Aaron and Moses when the LORD spoke with Moses on Mount Sinai.   *Ex. 6:16-27 · Lit. generations*

2 And these *are* the names of the sons of Aaron: Nadab, the ᴿfirstborn, and ᴿAbihu, Eleazar, and Ithamar.   *Ex. 6:23 · Num. 26:60, 61*

3 These *are* the names of the sons of Aaron, ᴿthe anointed priests, whom he consecrated to minister as priests.   *Ex. 28:41*

4 ᴿNadab and Abihu had died before the LORD when they offered profane fire before the LORD in the Wilderness of Sinai; and they had no children. So Eleazar and Ithamar ministered as priests in the presence of Aaron their father.   *1 Chr. 24:2*

The Levites Serve in the Tabernacle

5 And the LORD spoke to Moses, saying:

6 ᴿ"Bring the tribe of Levi near, and present them before Aaron the priest, that they may serve him.   *Num. 8:6-22; 18:1-7*

7 "And they shall attend to his needs and the needs of the whole congregation before the tabernacle of meeting, to do ᴿthe work of the tabernacle.   *Num. 1:50; 8:11, 15, 24, 26*

8 "Also they shall attend to all the furnishings of the tabernacle of meeting, and to the needs of the children of Israel, to do the work of the tabernacle.

9 "And you shall give the Levites to Aaron and his sons; they *are* given entirely to *him from among the children of Israel.

10 "So you shall appoint Aaron and his sons, ᴿand they shall attend to their priesthood; ᴿbut the outsider who comes near shall be put to death.   *Ex. 29:9 · Num. 1:51; 3:38; 16:40*

11 Then the LORD spoke to Moses, saying:

12 "Now behold, I Myself have taken the Levites from among the children of Israel

3:9 Sam., LXX Me

instead of every firstborn who opens the womb among the children of Israel. Therefore the Levites shall be ᴿMine,   Num. 3:45

13 "because all the firstborn are Mine. ᴿOn the day that I struck all the firstborn in the land of Egypt, I sanctified to Myself all the firstborn in Israel, both man and beast. They shall be Mine: I am the Lᴏʀᴅ."   Num. 8:17

Census of the Levites Commanded

14 Then the Lᴏʀᴅ spoke to Moses in the Wilderness of Sinai, saying:

15 "Number the children of Levi by their fathers' houses, by their families; you shall number ᴿevery male from a month old and above."   Num. 3:39; 26:62

16 So Moses numbered them according to the ᵀword of the Lᴏʀᴅ, as he was commanded.   Lit. mouth

17 These were the sons of Levi by their names: Gershon, Kohath, and Merari.

18 And these are the names of the sons of Gershon by their families: Libni and Shimei.

19 And the sons of Kohath by their families: Amram, Izehar, Hebron, and Uzziel.

20 ᴿAnd the sons of Merari by their families: Mahli and Mushi. These are the families of the Levites by their fathers' houses.   Ex. 6:19

21 From Gershon came the family of the Libnites and the family of the Shimites; these were the families of the Gershonites.

22 Those who were numbered, according to the number of all the males from a month old and above—of those who were numbered there were seven thousand five hundred.

23 The families of the Gershonites were to camp behind the tabernacle westward.

24 And the leader of the father's house of the Gershonites was Eliasaph the son of Lael.

25 The duties of the children of Gershon in the tabernacle of meeting included ᴿthe tabernacle, ᴿthe tent with ᴿits covering, ᴿthe screen for the door of the tabernacle of meeting,   Ex. 25:9 · Ex. 26:1 · Ex. 26:7, 14 · Ex. 26:36

26 the screen for the door of the court, the hangings of the court which are around the tabernacle and the altar, and their cords, according to all the work relating to them.

27 ᴿFrom Kohath came the family of the Amramites, the family of the Izharites, the family of the Hebronites, and the family of the Uzzielites; these were the families of the Kohathites.   1 Chr. 26:23

28 According to the number of all the males, from a month old and above, there were eight thousand *six hundred ᵀkeeping charge of the sanctuary.   taking care of

29 ᴿThe families of the children of Kohath were to camp on the south side of the tabernacle.   Num. 1:53

30 And the leader of the fathers' house of

the families of the Kohathites was Elizaphan the son of ᴿUzziel.   Lev. 10:4

31 Their duty included the ark, the table, the lampstand, the altars, the utensils of the sanctuary with which they ministered, the screen, and all the work relating to them.

32 And Eleazar the son of Aaron the priest was to be chief over the leaders of the Levites, with oversight of those who kept charge of the sanctuary.

33 From Merari came the family of the Mahlites and the family of the Mushites; these were the families of Merari.

34 And those who were numbered, according to the number of all the males from a month old and above, were six thousand two hundred.

35 The leader of the fathers' house of families of Merari was Zuriel the son of Abihail. ᴿThese were to camp on the north side of the tabernacle.   Num. 1:53; 2:25

36 And ᴿthe appointed duty of the children of Merari included the boards of the tabernacle, its bars, its pillars, its sockets, its utensils, all the work relating to them,   Num. 4:31, 32

37 and the pillars of the court all around, with their sockets, their pegs, and their cords.

38 Moreover those who were to camp before the tabernacle on the east, before the tabernacle of meeting, were Moses, Aaron, and his sons, keeping charge of the sanctuary, ᴿto meet the needs of the children of Israel; but ᴿthe outsider who came near was to be put to death.   Num. 3:7, 8 · Num. 3:10

39 ᴿAll who were numbered of the Levites, whom Moses and Aaron numbered at the commandment of the Lᴏʀᴅ, by their families, all the males from a month old and above, were twenty-two thousand.   Num. 3:43; 4:48; 26:62

Levites Dedicated Instead of the Firstborn

40 Then the Lᴏʀᴅ said to Moses: ᴿ"Numberᵀ all the firstborn males of the children of Israel from a month old and above, and take the number of their names.   Num. 3:15 · Take a census of

41 ᴿ"And you shall take the Levites for Me—I am the Lᴏʀᴅ—instead of all the firstborn among the children of Israel, and the livestock of the Levites instead of all the firstborn among the livestock of the children of Israel."   Num. 3:12, 45

42 So Moses numbered all the firstborn among the children of Israel, as the Lᴏʀᴅ commanded him.

43 And all the firstborn males, according to the number of names from a month old and above, of those who were numbered of them, were twenty-two thousand two hundred and seventy-three.

44 Then the Lᴏʀᴅ spoke to Moses, saying:

45 ᴿ"Take the Levites instead of all the firstborn among the children of Israel, and

3:28 Some LXX mss. three

the livestock of the Levites instead of their livestock. The Levites shall be Mine: I *am* the LORD.   Num. 3:12, 41

46 "And for ᴿthe redemption of the two hundred and seventy-three of the firstborn of the children of Israel, ᴿwho are more than the number of the Levites,   Ex. 13:13, 15 · Num. 3:39, 43

47 "you shall take ᴿfive shekels for each one individually; you shall take *them* in the currency of the shekel of the sanctuary, ᴿthe shekel of twenty gerahs.   Lev. 27:6 · Ex. 30:13

48 "And you shall give the money, with which the excess number of them is redeemed, to Aaron and his sons."

49 So Moses took the redemption money from those who were over and above those who were redeemed by the Levites.

50 From the firstborn of the children of Israel he took the money, ᵀone thousand three hundred and sixty-five *shekels*, according to the shekel of the sanctuary. $174,720

51 And Moses ᴿgave their redemption money to Aaron and his sons, according to the word of the LORD, as the LORD commanded Moses.   Num. 3:48

Duties of the Sons of Kohath

4 Then the LORD spoke to Moses and Aaron, saying:

2 "Take a census of the sons of ᴿKohath from among the children of Levi, by their families, by their fathers' house,   Num. 3:27-32

3 "from thirty years old and above, even to fifty years old, all who enter the service to do the work in the tabernacle of meeting.

4 ᴿ"This *is* the service of the sons of Kohath in the tabernacle of meeting, *relating to* ᴿthe most holy things: Num. 4:15 · Num. 4:19

5 "When the camp prepares to journey, Aaron and his sons shall come, and they shall take down the covering veil and cover the ᴿark of the Testimony with it.   Ex. 25:10, 16

6 "Then they shall put on it a covering of badger skins, and spread over *that* a cloth entirely of ᴿblue; and they shall insert ᴿits poles.   Ex. 39:1 · Ex. 25:13

7 "On the table of showbread they shall spread a blue cloth, and put on it the dishes, the pans, the bowls, and the pitchers for pouring; and the *showbread shall be on it.

8 "They shall spread over them a scarlet cloth, and cover the same with a covering of badger skins; and they shall insert its poles.

9 "And they shall take a blue cloth and cover the lampstand of the light, with its lamps, its wick-trimmers, its trays, and all its oil vessels, with which they service it.

10 "Then they shall put it with all its utensils in a covering of badger skins, and put *it* on a carrying beam.

11 "Over the golden altar they shall spread

a blue cloth, and cover it with a covering of badger skins; and they shall insert its poles.

12 "Then they shall take all the ᴿutensils of service with which they minister in the sanctuary, put *them* in a blue cloth, cover them with a covering of badger skins, and put *them* on a carrying beam.   Ex. 25:9

13 "Also they shall take away the ashes from the altar, and spread a purple cloth over it.

14 "They shall put on it all its implements with which they minister there—the firepans, the forks, the shovels, the ᵀbasins, and all the utensils of the altar—and they shall spread on it a covering of badger skins, and insert its poles.   *bowls*

15 "And when Aaron and his sons have finished covering the sanctuary and all the furnishings of the sanctuary, when the camp is set to go, then the sons of Kohath shall come to carry *them*; but they shall not touch any holy thing, lest they die. ᴿThese *are* the things in the tabernacle of meeting which the sons of Kohath are to carry.   Num. 3:31

16 "The appointed duty of Eleazar the son of Aaron the priest *is* the oil for the light, the sweet incense, ᴿthe daily grain offering, the ᴿanointing oil, the oversight of all the tabernacle, of all that *is* in it, with the sanctuary and its furnishings."   Ex. 29:38 · Ex. 30:23-25

17 Then the LORD spoke to Moses and Aaron, saying:

18 "Do not cut off the tribe of the families of the Kohathites from among the Levites;

19 "but do this in regard to them, that they may live and not die when they approach ᴿthe most holy things: Aaron and his sons shall go in and ᵀappoint each of them to his service and his task.   Num. 4:4 · *assign*

20 ᴿ"But they shall not go in to watch while the holy things are being covered, lest they die."   Ex. 19:21

Duties of the Sons of Gershon

21 Then the LORD spoke to Moses, saying:

22 "Also take a census of the sons of ᴿGershon, by their fathers' house, by their families.   Num. 3:22

23 ᴿ"From thirty years old and above, even to fifty years old, you shall number them, all who enter to perform the service, to do the work in the tabernacle of meeting.   Num. 4:3

24 "This *is* the ᴿservice of the families of the Gershonites, in serving and carrying: Num. 7:7

25 "They shall carry the ᴿcurtains of the tabernacle and the tabernacle of meeting *with* its covering, the covering of ᴿbadger skins that *is* on it, the screen for the door of the tabernacle of meeting,   Ex. 36:8 · Ex. 26:14

26 "the screen for the door of the gate of the court, the hangings of the court which *are* around the tabernacle and altar, and their cords, all the furnishings for their service and

all that is made for these things: so shall they serve.

27 "Aaron and his sons shall assign all the service of the sons of the Gershonites, all their tasks and all their service. And you shall appoint to them all their tasks as their duty.

28 "This is the service of the families of the sons of Gershon in the tabernacle of meeting. And their duties shall be under the authority of Ithamar the son of Aaron the priest.

Duties of the Sons of Merari

29 "As for the sons of ᴿMerari, you shall number them by their families and by their fathers' house.   Num. 3:33-37

30 "From thirty years old and above, even to fifty years old, you shall number them, everyone who enters the service to do the work of the tabernacle of meeting.

31 "And this is ᴿwhat they must carry as all their service for the tabernacle of meeting: ᴿthe boards of the tabernacle, its bars, its pillars, its sockets,   Num. 7:8 • Ex. 26:15

32 "and the pillars around the court with their sockets, pegs, and cords, with all their furnishings and all their service; and you shall ᴿassign to each man by name the items he must carry.   Ex. 25:9; 38:21

33 "This is the service of the families of the sons of Merari, as all their service for the tabernacle of meeting, under the authority of Ithamar the son of Aaron the priest."

Census of the Levites

34 ᴿAnd Moses, Aaron, and the leaders of the congregation numbered the sons of the Kohathites by their families and by their fathers' house,   Num. 4:2

35 from thirty years old and above, even to fifty years old, everyone who entered the service for work in the tabernacle of meeting;

36 and those who were numbered by their families were two thousand seven hundred and fifty.

37 These were the ones who were numbered of the families of the Kohathites, all who might serve in the tabernacle of meeting, whom Moses and Aaron numbered according to the commandment of the LORD by the hand of Moses.

38 And those who were numbered of the sons of Gershon, by their families and by their fathers' house,

39 from thirty years old and above, even to fifty years old, everyone who entered the service for work in the tabernacle of meeting—

40 those who were numbered by their families, by their fathers' house, were two thousand six hundred and thirty.

41 These are the ones who were numbered of the families of the sons of Gershon, of all who might serve in the tabernacle of meet-

ing, whom Moses and Aaron numbered according to the commandment of the LORD.

42 Those of the families of the sons of Merari who were numbered, by their families, by their fathers' ᵀhouse,   household

43 from thirty years old and above, even to fifty years old, everyone who entered the service for work in the tabernacle of meeting—

44 those who were numbered by their families were three thousand two hundred.

45 These are the ones who were numbered of the families of the sons of Merari, whom Moses and Aaron numbered according to the word of the LORD by the hand of Moses.

46 All who were ᴿnumbered of the Levites, whom Moses, Aaron, and the leaders of Israel numbered, by their families and by their fathers' houses,   1 Chr. 23:3-23

47 from thirty years old and above, even to fifty years old, everyone who came to do the work of service and the work of bearing burdens in the tabernacle of meeting—

48 those who were numbered were eight thousand five hundred and eighty.

49 According to the commandment of the LORD they were numbered by the hand of Moses, ᴿeach according to his service and according to his task; thus were they numbered by him, ᴿas the LORD commanded Moses.   Num. 4:15, 24, 31 • Num. 4:1, 21

Ceremonially Unclean Persons Isolated

5 And the LORD spoke to Moses, saying:
2 "Command the children of Israel that they put out of the camp every leper, everyone who has a discharge, and whoever becomes ᴿdefiled by a corpse.   Lev. 21:1

3 "You shall put out both male and female; you shall put them outside the camp, that they may not defile their camps ᴿin the midst of which I dwell."   Lev. 26:11, 12

4 And the children of Israel did so, and put them outside the camp; as the LORD spoke to Moses, so the children of Israel did.

Confession and Restitution

5 Then the LORD spoke to Moses, saying,
6 "Speak to the children of Israel: ᴿWhen a man or woman commits any sin that men commit in unfaithfulness against the LORD, and that person is guilty,   Lev. 5:14—6:7

7 'then he shall confess the sin which he has committed. He shall make restitution for his trespass in full, plus one-fifth of it, and give it to the one he has wronged.

8 'But if the man has no ᵀrelative to whom restitution may be made for the wrong, the restitution for the wrong must go to the LORD for the priest, in addition to ᴿthe ram of the atonement with which atonement is made for him.   Lit. redeemer • Lev. 5:15; 6:6, 7; 7:7

9 'Every ᴿofferingᵀ of all the holy things of

the children of Israel, which they bring to the priest, shall be his.   Ex. 29:28 · *heave offering*

10 'And every man's ᵀholy things shall be his; whatever any man gives the priest shall be ᴿhis.' "   *consecrated* · Lev. 10:13

Concerning Unfaithful Wives

11 And the LORD spoke to Moses, saying, 12 "Speak to the children of Israel, and say to them: 'If any man's wife goes astray and behaves unfaithfully toward him,

13 'and a man ᴿlies with her carnally, and it is hidden from the eyes of her husband, and it is concealed that she has defiled herself, and *there was* no witness against her, nor was she ᴿcaught—   Lev. 18:20; 20:10 · John 8:4

14 'if the spirit of jealousy comes upon him and he becomes ᴿjealous of his wife, who has defiled herself; or if the spirit of jealousy comes upon him and he becomes jealous of his wife, although she has not defiled herself—   Prov. 6:34

15 'then the man shall bring his wife to the priest. He shall ᴿbring the offering required for her, one-tenth of an ephah of barley meal; he shall pour no oil on it and put no frankincense on it, because it *is* a grain offering of jealousy, an offering for remembering, for bringing iniquity to remembrance.   Lev. 5:11

16 'And the priest shall bring her near, and set her before the LORD.

17 'The priest shall take holy water in an earthen vessel, and take some of the dust that is on the floor of the tabernacle and put *it* into the water.

18 'Then the priest shall stand the woman before the ᴿLORD, uncover the woman's head, and put the offering for remembering in her hands, which *is* the grain offering of jealousy. And the priest shall have in his hand the bitter water that brings a curse.   Heb. 13:4

19 'And the priest shall put her under oath, and say to the woman, "If no man has lain with you, and if you have not gone astray to uncleanness *while* under your husband's *authority*, be free from this bitter water that brings a curse.

20 "But if you have gone astray *while* under your husband's *authority*, and if you have defiled yourself and some man other than your husband has lain with you"—

21 'then the priest shall ᴿput the woman under the oath of the curse, and he shall say to the woman—ᴿ"the LORD make you a curse and an oath among your people, when the LORD makes your thigh ᵀrot and your belly swell;   Josh. 6:26 · Jer. 29:22 · Lit. *fall away*

22 "and may this water that causes the curse go into your stomach, and make *your* belly swell and *your* thigh rot." Then the woman shall say, "Amen, so be it."

23 'Then the priest shall write these curses in a book, and he shall scrape *them* off into the bitter water.

24 'And he shall make the woman drink the bitter water that brings a curse, and the water that brings the curse shall enter her *to* become bitter.

25 ᴿ'Then the priest shall take the grain offering of jealousy from the woman's hand, shall ᴿwave the offering before the LORD, and bring it to the altar;   Lev. 8:27 · Lev. 2:2, 9

26 'and the priest shall take a handful of the offering, ᴿas its memorial portion, burn *it* on the altar, and afterward make the woman drink the water.   Lev. 2:2, 9

27 'When he has made her drink the water, then it shall be, if she has defiled herself and behaved unfaithfully toward her husband, that the water that brings a curse will enter her *and become* bitter, and her belly will swell, her thigh will rot, and the woman ᴿwill become a curse among her people.   Num. 5:21

28 'But if the woman has not defiled herself, and is clean, then she shall be free and may conceive children.

29 'This *is* the law of jealousy, when a wife, *while* under her husband's *authority*, ᴿgoes astray and defiles herself,   Num. 5:19

30 'or when the spirit of jealousy comes upon a man, and he becomes jealous of his wife; then he shall stand the woman before the LORD, and the priest shall execute all this law upon her.

31 'Then the man shall be free from iniquity, but that woman shall bear her guilt.' "

The Law of the Nazirite

6 Then the LORD spoke to Moses, saying, 2 "Speak to the children of Israel, and say to them: 'When either a man or woman consecrates an offering to take the vow of a Nazirite, to separate himself to the LORD,

3 'he shall separate himself from wine and *similar* drink; he shall drink neither vinegar made from wine nor vinegar made from *similar* drink; neither shall he drink any grape juice, nor eat fresh grapes or raisins.

4 'All the days of his ᵀseparation he shall eat nothing that is produced by the grapevine, from seed to skin.   Separation as a Nazirite

5 'All the days of the vow of his separation no ᴿrazor shall come upon his head; until the days are fulfilled for which he separated himself to the LORD, he shall be holy. *Then* he shall let the locks of the hair of his head grow.   1 Sam. 1:11

6 'All the days that he separates himself to the LORD he shall not go near a dead body.

7 'He shall not make himself unclean even for his father or his mother, for his brother or his sister, when they die, because his separation to God *is* on his head.

8 ᴿ'All the days of his separation he shall be holy to the LORD.   [2 Cor. 6:17, 18]

9 'And if anyone dies very suddenly beside him, and he defiles his consecrated head, then he shall ᴿshave his head on the day of his cleansing; on the seventh day he shall shave it.   Lev. 14:8, 9

10 'Then ᴿon the eighth day he shall bring two turtledoves or two young pigeons to the priest, to the door of the tabernacle of meeting;   Lev. 5:7; 14:22; 15:14, 29

11 'and the priest shall offer one as a sin offering and *the* other as a burnt offering, and make atonement for him, because he sinned in regard to the corpse; and he shall sanctify his head that same day.

12 'He shall consecrate to the Lᴏʀᴅ the days of his separation, and bring a male lamb in its first year ᴿas a trespass offering; but the former days shall be ᵀlost, because his separation was defiled.   Lev. 5:6 • *void*

13 'Now this *is* the law of the Nazirite: ᴿWhen the days of his separation are fulfilled, he shall be brought to the door of the tabernacle of meeting.   Acts 21:26

14 'And he shall present his offering to the Lᴏʀᴅ: one male lamb in its first year without blemish as a burnt offering, one ewe lamb in its first year without blemish ᴿas a sin offering, one ram without blemish ᴿas a peace offering,   Lev. 4:2, 27, 32 • Lev. 3:6

15 'a basket of unleavened bread, cakes of fine flour mixed with oil, unleavened wafers anointed with oil, and their grain offering with their ᴿdrink offerings.   Num. 15:5, 7, 10

16 'Then the priest shall bring *them* before the Lᴏʀᴅ and offer his sin offering and his burnt offering;

17 'and he shall offer the ram as a sacrifice of a peace offering to the Lᴏʀᴅ, with the basket of unleavened bread; the priest shall also offer its grain offering and its drink offering.

18 'Then the Nazirite shall shave his consecrated head *at* the door of the tabernacle of meeting, and shall take the hair from his consecrated head and put *it* on the fire which is under the sacrifice of the peace offering.

19 'And the priest shall take the boiled shoulder of the ram, one unleavened cake from the basket, and one unleavened wafer, and put *them* upon the hands of the Nazirite after he has shaved his consecrated *hair,*

20 'and the priest shall wave them as a wave offering before the Lᴏʀᴅ; ᴿthey *are* holy for the priest, together with the breast of the wave offering and the thigh of the heave offering. After that the Nazirite may drink wine.'   Ex. 29:27, 28

21 "This is the law of the Nazirite who vows to the Lᴏʀᴅ the offering for his separation, and besides that, whatever else his hand is able to provide; according to the vow which he takes, so he must do according to the law of his separation."

The Priestly Blessing

22 And the Lᴏʀᴅ spoke to Moses, saying:
23 "Speak to Aaron and his sons, saying, 'This is the way you shall bless the children of Israel. Say to them:

24 "The Lᴏʀᴅ bless you and keep you;
25 The Lᴏʀᴅ ᴿmake His face shine upon you,   Dan. 9:17
And ᴿbe gracious to you;   Mal. 1:9
26 ᴿThe Lᴏʀᴅ ᵀlift up His countenance upon you,   Ps. 4:6; 89:15 • Look on with favor
And ᴿgive you peace."'   Lev. 26:6

27 "So they shall put My name on the children of Israel, and I will bless them."

Offerings of the Leaders

7 Now it came to pass, when Moses had finished setting up the tabernacle, that he anointed it and consecrated it and all its furnishings, and the altar and all its utensils; so he anointed them and consecrated them.

2 Then the leaders of Israel, the heads of their fathers' houses, who *were* the leaders of the tribes ᵀand over those who were numbered, made an offering.   Lit. *who stood over*

3 And they brought their offering before the Lᴏʀᴅ, six covered carts and twelve oxen, a cart for *every* two of the leaders, and for each one an ox; and they presented them before the tabernacle.

4 Then the Lᴏʀᴅ spoke to Moses, saying,
5 "Accept *these* from them, that they may be used in doing the work of the tabernacle of meeting; and you shall give them to the Levites, *to* every man according to his service."

6 So Moses took the carts and the oxen, and gave them to the Levites.

7 Two carts and four oxen he gave to the sons of Gershon, according to their service;
8 ᴿand four carts and eight oxen he gave to the sons of Merari, according to their service, under the ᵀauthority of Ithamar the son of Aaron the priest.   Num. 4:29-33 • Lit. *hand*

9 But to the sons of Kohath he gave none, because theirs *was* ᴿthe service of the holy things, ᴿwhich they carried on their shoulders.   Num. 4:15 • Num. 4:6-14

10 Now the leaders offered ᴿthe dedication *offering* for the altar when it was anointed; so the leaders offered their offering before the altar.   2 Chr. 7:5, 9

11 For the Lᴏʀᴅ said to Moses, "They shall offer their offering, one leader each day, for the dedication of the altar."

12 And the one who offered his offering on the first day *was* ᴿNahshon the son of Amminadab, from the tribe of Judah.   Num. 2:3

13 His offering *was* one silver platter, the weight of which *was* ᵀone hundred and thirty *shekels,* and one silver bowl of seventy shekels, according to ᴿthe shekel of the sanctuary,

both of them full of fine flour mixed with oil as a ᴿgrain offering; $16,640 • Ex. 30:13 • Lev. 2:1

14 one gold pan of ᵀten *shekels*, full of ᴿincense; $19,200 • Ex. 30:34

15 one young bull, one ram, and one male lamb in its first year, as a burnt offering;

16 one kid of the goats as a sin offering;

17 and for the sacrifice of peace offerings: two oxen, five rams, five male goats, and five male lambs in their first year. This *was* the offering of Nahshon the son of Amminadab.

18 On the second day Nethanel the son of Zuar, leader of Issachar, presented *an offering*.

19 *For* his offering he offered one silver platter, the weight of which *was* one hundred and thirty *shekels*, and one silver bowl of ᵀseventy shekels, according to the shekel of the sanctuary, both of them full of fine flour mixed with oil as a grain offering; $8,960

20 one gold pan of ᵀten *shekels*, full of incense; $19,200

21 one young bull, one ram, and one male lamb in its first year, as a burnt offering;

22 one kid of the goats as a sin offering;

23 and as the sacrifice of peace offerings: two oxen, five rams, five male goats, and five male lambs in their first year. This *was* the offering of Nethanel the son of Zuar.

24 On the third day Eliab the son of Helon, leader of the children of Zebulun, *presented an offering.*

25 His offering *was* one silver platter, the weight of which *was* ᵀone hundred and thirty *shekels*, and one silver bowl of ᵀseventy shekels, according to the shekel of the sanctuary, both of them full of fine flour mixed with oil as a grain offering; $16,640 • $8,960

26 one gold pan of ᵀten *shekels*, full of incense; $19,200

27 one young bull, one ram, and one male lamb in its first year, as a burnt offering;

28 one kid of the goats as a sin offering;

29 and for the sacrifice of peace offerings: two oxen, five rams, five male goats, and five male lambs in their first year. This *was* the offering of Eliab the son of Helon.

30 On the fourth day ᴿElizur the son of Shedeur, leader of the children of Reuben, *presented an offering.*   Num. 1:5; 2:10

31 His offering *was* one silver platter, the weight of which *was* ᵀone hundred and thirty *shekels*, and one silver bowl of ᵀseventy shekels, according to the shekel of the sanctuary, both of them full of fine flour mixed with oil as a grain offering; $16,640 • $8,960

32 one gold pan of ᵀten *shekels*, full of incense; $19,200

33 one young bull, one ram, and one male lamb in its first year, as a burnt offering;

34 one kid of the goats as a sin offering;

35 and as the sacrifice of peace offerings: two oxen, five rams, five male goats, and five

male lambs in their first year. This *was* the offering of Elizur the son of Shedeur.

36 On the fifth day ᴿShelumiel the son of Zurishaddai, leader of the children of Simeon, *presented an offering.*   Num. 1:6; 2:12; 7:41

37 His offering *was* one silver platter, the weight of which *was* ᵀone hundred and thirty *shekels*, and one silver bowl of ᵀseventy shekels, according to the shekel of the sanctuary, both of them full of fine flour mixed with oil as a grain offering; $16,640 • $8,960

38 one gold pan of ᵀten *shekels*, full of incense; $19,200

39 one young bull, one ram, and one male lamb in its first year, as a burnt offering;

40 one kid of the goats as a sin offering;

41 and as the sacrifice of peace offerings: two oxen, five rams, five male goats, and five male lambs in their first year. This *was* the offering of Shelumiel the son of Zurishaddai.

42 On the sixth day ᴿEliasaph the son of ᵀDeuel, leader of the children of Gad, *presented an offering.*   Num. 1:14 • *Reuel*, Num. 2:14

43 His offering *was* one silver platter, the weight of which *was* one hundred and thirty *shekels*, and one silver bowl of seventy shekels, according to the shekel of the sanctuary, both of them full of fine flour mixed with oil as a grain offering;

44 one gold pan of ten *shekels*, full of incense;

45 one young bull, one ram, and one male lamb in its first year, as a burnt offering;

46 one kid of the goats as a sin offering;

47 and as the sacrifice of peace offerings: two oxen, five rams, five male goats, and five male lambs in their first year. This *was* the offering of Eliasaph the son of Deuel.

48 On the seventh day ᴿElishama the son of Ammihud, leader of the children of Ephraim, *presented an offering.*   Num. 1:10; 2:18

49 His offering *was* one silver platter, the weight of which *was* one hundred and thirty *shekels*, and one silver bowl of seventy shekels, according to the shekel of the sanctuary, both of them full of fine flour mixed with oil as a grain offering;

50 one gold pan of ten *shekels*, full of incense;

51 one young bull, one ram, and one male lamb in its first year, as a burnt offering;

52 one kid of the goats as a sin offering;

53 and as the sacrifice of peace offerings: two oxen, five rams, five male goats, and five male lambs in their first year. This *was* the offering of Elishama the son of Ammihud.

54 On the eighth day ᴿGamaliel the son of Pedahzur, leader of the children of Manasseh, *presented an offering.*   Num. 1:10; 2:20

55 His offering *was* one silver platter, the weight of which *was* one hundred and thirty *shekels*, and one silver bowl of seventy shekels, according to the shekel of the sanctuary,

both of them full of fine flour mixed with oil as a grain offering;

56 one gold pan of ten *shekels*, full of incense;

57 one young bull, one ram, and one male lamb in its first year, as a burnt offering;

58 one kid of the goats as a sin offering;

59 and as the sacrifice of peace offerings: two oxen, five rams, five male goats, and five male lambs in their first year. This *was* the offering of Gamaliel the son of Pedahzur.

60 On the ninth day ᴿAbidan the son of Gideoni, leader of the children of Benjamin, *presented an offering.*   Num. 1:11; 2:22

61 His offering *was* one silver platter, the weight of which *was* ᵀone hundred and thirty *shekels*, and one silver bowl of ᵀseventy shekels, according to the shekel of the sanctuary, both of them full of fine flour mixed with oil as a grain offering; $16,640 • $8,960

62 one gold pan of ᵀten *shekels*, full of incense; $19,200

63 one young bull, one ram, and one male lamb in its first year, as a burnt offering;

64 one kid of the goats as a sin offering;

65 and as the sacrifice of peace offerings: two oxen, five rams, five male goats, and five male lambs in their first year. This *was* the offering of Abidan the son of Gideoni.

66 On the tenth day ᴿAhiezer the son of Ammishaddai, leader of the children of Dan, *presented an offering.*   Num. 1:12; 2:25

67 His offering *was* one silver platter, the weight of which *was* one hundred and thirty *shekels*, and one silver bowl of seventy shekels, according to the shekel of the sanctuary, both of them full of fine flour mixed with oil as a grain offering;

68 one gold pan of ten *shekels*, full of incense;

69 one young bull, one ram, and one male lamb in its first year, as a burnt offering;

70 one kid of the goats as a sin offering;

71 and as the sacrifice of peace offerings: two oxen, five rams, five male goats, and five male lambs in their first year. This *was* the offering of Ahiezer the son of Ammishaddai.

72 On the eleventh day ᴿPagiel the son of Ocran, leader of the children of Asher, *presented an offering.*   Num. 1:13; 2:27

73 His offering *was* one silver platter, the weight of which *was* one hundred and thirty *shekels*, and one silver bowl of seventy shekels, according to the shekel of the sanctuary, both of them full of fine flour mixed with oil as a grain offering;

74 one gold pan of ten *shekels*, full of incense;

75 one young bull, one ram, and one male lamb in its first year, as a burnt offering;

76 one kid of the goats as a sin offering;

77 and as the sacrifice of peace offerings: two oxen, five rams, five male goats, and five

male lambs in their first year. This *was* the offering of Pagiel the son of Ocran.

78 On the twelfth day ᴿAhira the son of Enan, leader of the children of Naphtali, *presented an offering.*   Num. 1:15; 2:29

79 His offering *was* one silver platter, the weight of which *was* one hundred and thirty *shekels*, and one silver bowl of seventy shekels, according to the shekel of the sanctuary, both of them full of fine flour mixed with oil as a grain offering;

80 one gold pan of ten *shekels*, full of incense;

81 one young bull, one ram, and one male lamb in its first year, as a burnt offering;

82 one kid of the goats as a sin offering;

83 and as the sacrifice of peace offerings: two oxen, five rams, five male goats, and five male lambs in their first year. This *was* the offering of Ahira the son of Enan.

84 This *was* ᴿthe dedication *offering* for the altar from the leaders of Israel, when it was anointed: twelve silver platters, twelve silver bowls, and twelve gold pans.   Num. 7:10

85 Each silver platter *weighed* one hundred and thirty *shekels* and each bowl seventy *shekels*. All the silver of the vessels *weighed* ᵀtwo thousand four hundred *shekels*, according to the shekel of the sanctuary. $307,200

86 The twelve gold pans full of incense *weighed* ᵀten *shekels* apiece, according to the shekel of the sanctuary; all the gold of the pans *weighed* ᵀone hundred and twenty *shekels*. $19,200 • $230,400

87 All the oxen for the burnt offering *were* twelve young bulls, the rams twelve, the male lambs in their first year twelve, with their grain offering, and the kids of the goats as a sin offering twelve.

88 And all the oxen for the sacrifice of peace offerings were twenty-four bulls, the rams sixty, the male goats sixty, and the lambs in their first year sixty. This *was* the dedication *offering* for the altar after it was anointed.

89 Now when Moses went into the tabernacle of meeting ᴿto speak with Him, he heard the voice of One speaking to him from above the mercy seat that *was* on the ark of the Testimony, from between the two cherubim; thus He spoke to him.   [Ex. 33:9, 11]

Arrangement of the Lamps

8 And the Lᴏʀᴅ spoke to Moses, saying:

2 "Speak to Aaron, and say to him, 'When you arrange the lamps, the seven lamps shall give light in front of the lampstand.'"

3 And Aaron did so; he arranged the lamps to face toward the front of the lampstand, as the Lᴏʀᴅ commanded Moses.

4 Now this workmanship of the lampstand *was* hammered gold; from its shaft to its

flowers it *was* hammered work. According to the pattern which the Lord had shown Moses, so he made the lampstand.

Cleansing and Dedication of the Levites

5 Then the Lord spoke to Moses, saying:
6 "Take the Levites from among the children of Israel and cleanse them *ceremonially*.
7 "Thus you shall do to them to cleanse them: Sprinkle water of purification on them, and ᴿlet them ᵀshave all their body, and let them wash their clothes, and *so* make themselves clean.   Lev. 14:8, 9 • Heb. *cause a razor to pass over*
8 "Then let them take a young bull with ᴿits grain offering of fine flour mixed with oil, and you shall take another young bull as a sin offering.   Lev. 2:1
9 ᴿ"And you shall bring the Levites before the tabernacle of meeting, ᴿand you shall gather together the whole congregation of the children of Israel.   Ex. 29:4; 40:12 • Lev. 8:3
10 "So you shall bring the Levites before the Lord, and the children of Israel ᴿshall lay their hands on the Levites;   Lev. 1:4
11 "and Aaron shall ᵀoffer the Levites before the Lord *like* a ᴿwave offering from the children of Israel, that they may perform the work of the Lord.   *present* • Num. 18:6
12 ᴿ"Then the Levites shall lay their hands on the heads of the young bulls, and you shall offer one as a sin offering and the other as a burnt offering to the Lord, to make atonement for the Levites.   Ex. 29:10
13 "And you shall stand the Levites before Aaron and his sons, and then offer them *like* a wave offering to the Lord.
14 "Thus you shall separate the Levites from among the children of Israel, and the Levites shall be ᴿMine.   Num. 3:12, 45; 16:9
15 "After that the Levites shall go in to service the tabernacle of meeting. So you shall cleanse them and ᴿoffer them *like* a wave offering.   Num. 8:11, 13
16 "For they *are* ᴿwholly given to Me from among the children of Israel; I have taken them for Myself ᴿinstead of all who open the womb, the firstborn of all the children of Israel.   Num. 3:9 • Num. 3:12, 45
17 ᴿ"For all the firstborn among the children of Israel *are* Mine, *both* man and beast; on the day that I struck all the firstborn in the land of Egypt I ᵀsanctified them to Myself.   Ex. 12:2, 12, 13, 15 • *set them apart*
18 "I have taken the Levites instead of all the firstborn of the children of Israel.
19 "And I have given the Levites as a gift to Aaron and his sons from among the children of Israel, to do the work for the children of Israel in the tabernacle of meeting, and to make atonement for the children of Israel, ᴿthat there be no plague among the children of Israel when the children of Israel come near the sanctuary."   Num. 1:53; 16:46; 18:5

20 Thus Moses and Aaron and all the congregation of the children of Israel did to the Levites; according to all that the Lord commanded Moses concerning the Levites, so the children of Israel did to them.
21 ᴿAnd the Levites purified themselves and washed their clothes; then Aaron presented them *like* a wave offering before the Lord, and Aaron made atonement for them to cleanse them.   Num. 8:7
22 ᴿAfter that the Levites went in to do their work in the tabernacle of meeting before Aaron and his sons; ᴿas the Lord commanded Moses concerning the Levites, so they did to them.   Num. 8:15 • Num. 8:5
23 Then the Lord spoke to Moses, saying,
24 "This *is* what *pertains* to the Levites: ᴿFrom twenty-five years old and above one may enter to perform service in the work of the tabernacle of meeting;   Num. 4:3
25 "and at the age of fifty years they must cease performing this work, and shall work no more.
26 "They may minister with their brethren in the tabernacle of meeting, ᴿto attend to needs, but they *themselves* shall do no work. Thus you shall do to the Levites regarding their duties."   Num. 1:53

The Second Passover

9 Now the Lord spoke to Moses in the Wilderness of Sinai, in the first month of the second year after they had come out of the land of Egypt, saying:
2 "Let the children of Israel keep ᴿthe Passover at its appointed time.   Lev. 23:5
3 "On the fourteenth day of this month, ᵀat twilight, you shall keep it at its appointed time. According to all its rites and ceremonies you shall keep it."   Lit. *between the evenings*
4 So Moses told the children of Israel that they should keep the Passover.
5 And ᴿthey kept the Passover on the fourteenth day of the first month, at twilight, in the Wilderness of Sinai; according to all that the Lord commanded Moses, so the children of Israel did.   Josh. 5:10
6 Now there were *certain* men who were ᴿdefiled by a human corpse, so that they could not keep the Passover on that day; ᴿand they came before Moses and Aaron that day.   Num. 5:2; 19:11-22 • Num. 27:2
7 And those men said to him, "We *became* defiled by a human corpse. Why are we kept from presenting the offering of the Lord at its appointed time among the children of Israel?"
8 And Moses said to them, "Stand still, that ᴿI may hear what the Lord will command concerning you."   Num. 27:5
9 Then the Lord spoke to Moses, saying,
10 "Speak to the children of Israel, saying: 'If anyone of you or your ᵀposterity is un-

clean because of a corpse, or *is* far away on a journey, he may still keep the LORD's Passover. *descendants*

11 'On ᴿthe fourteenth day of the second month, at twilight, they may keep it. They shall ᴿeat it with unleavened bread and bitter herbs. 2 Chr. 30:2, 15 • Ex. 12:8

12 ᴿ'They shall leave none of it until morning, ᴿnor break one of its bones. According to all the ᵀordinances of the Passover they shall keep it. Ex. 12:10 • Ex. 12:46; John 19:36 • *statutes*

13 'But the man who *is* clean and is not on a journey, and ceases to keep the Passover, that same person shall be cut off from among his people, because he did not bring the offering of the LORD at its appointed time; that man shall ᴿbear his sin. Num. 5:31

14 'And if a stranger dwells among you, and would keep the LORD's Passover, he must do so according to the rite of the Passover and according to its ceremony; ᴿyou shall have one ᵀordinance, both for the stranger and the native of the land.' " Ex. 12:49 • *statute*

The Cloud and the Fire

15 Now on the day that the tabernacle was raised up, the cloud covered the tabernacle, the tent of the Testimony; ᴿfrom evening until morning it was above the tabernacle like the appearance of fire. Ex. 13:21, 22; 40:38

16 So it was always: the cloud covered it *by day*, and the appearance of fire by night.

17 Whenever the cloud was ᵀtaken up from above the tabernacle, after that the children of Israel would journey; and in the place where the cloud settled, there the children of Israel would pitch their tents. *lifted up*

18 At the ᵀcommand of the LORD the children of Israel would journey, and at the command of the LORD they would camp; ᴿas long as the cloud stayed above the tabernacle they remained encamped. Lit. *mouth* • 1 Cor. 10:1

19 Even when the cloud continued long, many days above the tabernacle, the children of Israel ᴿkept the charge of the LORD and did not journey. Num. 1:53; 3:8

20 So it was, when the cloud was above the tabernacle a few days: according to the command of the LORD they would remain encamped, and according to the command of the LORD they would journey.

21 So it was, when the cloud remained only from evening until morning: when the cloud was taken up in the morning, then they would journey; whether by day or by night, whenever the cloud was taken up, they would journey.

22 *Whether it was* two days, a month, or a year that the cloud remained above the tabernacle, the children of Israel ᴿwould remain encamped and not journey; but when it was taken up, they would journey. Ex. 40:36, 37

23 At the command of the LORD they remained encamped, and at the command of the LORD they journeyed; they ᴿkept the charge of the LORD, at the command of the LORD by the hand of Moses. Num. 9:19

Two Silver Trumpets

10 And the LORD spoke to Moses, saying: 2 "Make two silver trumpets for yourself; you shall make them of hammered work; you shall use them for calling the congregation and for directing the movement of the camps.

3 "When ᴿthey blow both of them, all the congregation shall gather before you at the door of the tabernacle of meeting. Jer. 4:5

4 "But if they blow *only* one, then the leaders, the ᴿheads of the divisions of Israel, shall gather to you. Ex. 18:21

5 "When you sound the ᴿadvance, ᴿthe camps that lie on the east side shall then begin their journey. Joel 2:1 • Num. 2:3

6 "When you sound the advance the second time, then the camps that lie ᴿon the south side shall begin their journey; they shall sound the call for them to begin their journeys. Num. 2:10

7 "And when the assembly is to be gathered together, ᴿyou shall blow, but not ᴿsound the advance. Num. 10:3 • Joel 2:1

8 ᴿ"The sons of Aaron, the priests, shall blow the trumpets; and these shall be to you as a ᵀordinance forever throughout your generations. Num. 31:6 • *statute*

9 "When you go to war in your land against the enemy who ᴿoppresses you, then you shall sound an alarm with the trumpets, and you will be ᴿremembered before the LORD your God, and you will be saved from your enemies. Judg. 2:18; 4:3; 6:9; 10:8, 12 • Gen. 8:1

10 "Also ᴿin the day of your gladness, in your appointed feasts, and at the beginning of your months, you shall blow the trumpets over your burnt offerings and over the sacrifices of your peace offerings; and they shall be ᴿa memorial for you before your God: I *am* the LORD your God." Lev. 23:24 • Num. 10:9

Departure from Sinai

11 Now it came to pass on the twentieth *day* of the second month, in the second year, that the cloud ᴿwas taken up from above the tabernacle of the Testimony. Num. 9:17

12 And the children of Israel set out from the ᴿWilderness of Sinai on ᴿtheir journeys; then the cloud settled down in the ᴿWilderness of Paran. Ex. 19:1 • Ex. 40:36 • Gen. 21:21

13 So they started out for the first time ᴿaccording to the command of the LORD by the hand of Moses. Num. 10:5, 6

14 The ᵀstandard of the camp of the children of Judah ᴿset out first according to their armies; over their army was ᴿNahshon the son of Amminadab. *banner* • Num. 2:3-9 • Num. 1:7

15 Over the army of the tribe of the children of Issachar *was* Nethanel the son of Zuar.

16 And over the army of the tribe of the children of Zebulun *was* Eliab the son of Helon.

17 Then the tabernacle was taken down; and the sons of Gershon and the sons of Merari set out, carrying the tabernacle.

18 And the standard of the camp of Reuben set out according to their armies; over their army *was* Elizur the son of Shedeur.

19 Over the army of the tribe of the children of Simeon *was* Shelumiel the son of Zurishaddai.

20 And over the army of the tribe of the children of Gad *was* Eliasaph the son of Deuel.

21 Then the Kohathites set out, carrying the ᴿholy things. (The tabernacle would be prepared for their arrival.)   Num. 4:4–20; 7:9

22 And ᴿthe standard of the camp of the children of Ephraim set out according to their armies; over their army *was* Elishama the son of Ammihud.   Num. 2:18–24

23 Over the army of the tribe of the children of Manasseh *was* Gamaliel the son of Pedahzur.

24 And over the army of the tribe of the children of Benjamin *was* Abidan the son of Gideoni.

25 Then ᴿthe standard of the camp of the children of Dan (the rear guard of all the camps) set out according to their armies; over their army *was* Ahiezer the son of Ammishaddai.   Num. 2:25–31

26 Over the army of the tribe of the children of Asher *was* Pagiel the son of Ocran.

27 And over the army of the tribe of the children of Naphtali *was* Ahira the son of Enan.

28 ᴿThus *was* the order of march of the children of Israel, according to their armies, when they began their journey.   Num. 2:34

29 Now Moses said to Hobab the son of *Reuel the Midianite, Moses' father-in-law, "We are setting out for the place of which the Lord said, 'I will give it to you.' Come with us, and we will treat you well; for ᴿthe Lord has promised good things to Israel."   Ex. 3:8

30 And he said to him, "I will not go, but I will depart to my *own* land and to my relatives."

31 So *Moses* said, "Please do not leave, inasmuch as you know how we are to camp in the wilderness, and you can be our eyes.

32 "And it shall be, if you go with us—indeed it shall be—that ᴿwhatever good the Lord will do to us, the same we will do to you."   Judg. 1:16

33 So they departed from ᴿthe mountain of

10:29 *Jethro*, Ex. 3:1; LXX *Raguel*

the Lord on a journey of three days; and the ark of the covenant of the Lord ᴿwent before them for the three days' journey, to search out a resting place for them.   Ex. 3:1 • Deut. 1:33

34 And ᴿthe cloud of the Lord *was* above them by day when they went out from the camp.   Ex. 13:21

35 So it was, whenever the ark set out, that Moses said:

ᴿ"Rise up, O Lord!
Let Your enemies be scattered,
And let those who hate You flee before
You."   Ps. 68:1, 2; 132:8

36 And when it rested, he said:

"Return, O Lord,
To the many thousands of Israel."

The People Complain

11 Now *when* the people complained, it displeased the Lord; for the Lord heard *it*, and His anger was aroused. So the fire of the Lord burned among them, and consumed *some* in the outskirts of the camp.

2 Then the people ᴿcried out to Moses, and when Moses ᴿprayed to the Lord, the fire was ᵀquenched.   Num. 12:11, 13 • [James 5:16] • *extinguished*

3 So he called the name of the place ᵀTaberah, because the fire of the Lord had burned among them.   Lit. *Burning*

4 Now the mixed multitude who were among them yielded to intense craving; so the children of Israel also wept again and said: "Who will give us meat to eat?

5 ᴿ"We remember the fish which we ate freely in Egypt, the cucumbers, the melons, the leeks, the onions, and the garlic;   Ex. 16:3

6 "but now ᴿour whole being *is* dried up; *there is* nothing at all except this manna *before* our eyes!"   Num. 21:5

7 Now the manna *was* like coriander seed, and its color like the color of bdellium.

8 The people went about and gathered *it*, ground *it* on millstones or beat *it* in the mortar, cooked *it* in pans, and made cakes of it; and ᴿits taste was like the taste of pastry prepared with oil.   Ex. 16:31

9 And ᴿwhen the dew fell on the camp in the night, the manna fell on it.   Ex. 16:13, 14

10 Then Moses heard the people weeping throughout their families, everyone at the door of his tent; and ᴿthe anger of the Lord was greatly aroused; Moses also was displeased.   Ps. 78:21

11 So Moses said to the Lord, "Why have You afflicted Your servant? And why have I not found favor in Your sight, that You have laid the burden of all these people on me?

12 "Did I conceive all these people? Did I beget them, that You should say to me, 'Carry them in your bosom, as a ᴿguardian carries a nursing child,' to the land which You ᴿswore to their fathers?   Is. 49:23 • Gen. 26:3

13 "Where am I to get meat to give to all these people? For they weep all over me, saying, 'Give us meat, that we may eat.'

14 ᴿ"I am not able to bear all these people alone, because the burden *is* too heavy for me.   Ex. 18:18

15 "If You treat me like this, please kill me here and now—if I have found favor in Your sight—and ᴿdo not let me see my wretchedness!"   Rev. 3:17

The Seventy Elders

16 So the Lᴏʀᴅ said to Moses: "Gather to Me ᴿseventy men of the elders of Israel, whom you know to be the elders of the people and ᴿofficers over them; bring them to the tabernacle of meeting, that they may stand there with you.   Ex. 18:25; 24:1, 9 · Deut. 16:18

17 "Then I will come down and talk with you there. ᴿI will take of the Spirit that *is* upon you and will put *the same* upon them; and they shall bear the burden of the people with you, that you may not bear *it* yourself alone.   1 Sam. 10:6

18 "Then you shall say to the people, ᵀ'Consecrate yourselves for tomorrow, and you shall eat meat; for you have wept in the hearing of the Lᴏʀᴅ, saying, "Who will give us meat to eat? For *it was* well with us in Egypt." Therefore the Lᴏʀᴅ will give you meat, and you shall eat.   *Set yourselves apart*

19 'You shall eat, not one day, nor two days, nor five days, nor ten days, nor twenty days,

20 ᴿ'but *for* a whole month, until it comes out of your nostrils and becomes loathsome to you, because you have ᴿdespised the Lᴏʀᴅ who is among you, and have wept before Him, saying, ᴿ"Why did we ever come up out of Egypt?" ' "   Ps. 106:15 · 1 Sam. 10:19 · Num. 21:5

21 And Moses said, "The people whom I *am* among *are* six hundred thousand men on foot; yet You have said, 'I will give them meat, that they may eat *for* a whole month.'

22 ᴿ"Shall flocks and herds be slaughtered for them, to provide enough for them? Or shall all the fish of the sea be gathered together for them, to provide enough for them?"   2 Kin. 7:2

23 And the Lᴏʀᴅ said to Moses, "Has the Lᴏʀᴅ's arm been shortened? Now you shall see whether what I say will happen to you or not."

24 So Moses went out and told the people the words of the Lᴏʀᴅ, and he ᴿgathered the seventy men of the elders of the people and placed them around the tabernacle.   Num. 11:16

25 Then the Lᴏʀᴅ came down in the cloud, and spoke to him, and took of the Spirit that *was* upon him, and placed *the same* upon the seventy elders; and it happened, when the

Spirit rested upon them, that they prophesied, *although they never did *so* again.

26 But two men had remained in the camp: the name of one *was* Eldad, and the name of the other Medad. And the Spirit rested upon them. Now they *were* among those listed, but who ᴿhad not gone out to the tabernacle; yet they prophesied in the camp.   Jer. 36:5

27 And a young man ran and told Moses, and said, "Eldad and Medad are prophesying in the camp."

28 So Joshua the son of Nun, Moses' assistant, *one* of his choice men, answered and said, "Moses my lord, forbid them!"

29 Then Moses said to him, "Are you ᵀzealous for my sake? Oh, that all the Lᴏʀᴅ's people were prophets *and* that the Lᴏʀᴅ would put His Spirit upon them!"   *jealous*

30 And Moses returned to the camp, he and the elders of Israel.

The Lᴏʀᴅ Sends Quail

31 Now a ᴿwind went out from the Lᴏʀᴅ, and it brought quail from the sea and left *them* fluttering near the camp, about a ᵀday's journey on this side and about a day's journey on the other side, all around the camp, and about ᵀtwo cubits above the surface of the ground.   Ex. 16:13 · 20 mi. · 3 ft.

32 And the people stayed up all that day, all night, and all the next day, and gathered the quail (he who gathered least gathered ten ᴿhomers); and they spread *them* out for themselves all around the camp.   Ezek. 45:11

33 But while the ᴿmeat *was* still between their teeth, before it was chewed, the wrath of the Lᴏʀᴅ was aroused against the people, and the Lᴏʀᴅ struck the people with a very great plague.   Ps. 78:29–31; 106:15

34 So he called the name of that place *Kibroth Hattaavah, because there they buried the people who had yielded to craving.

35 From Kibroth Hattaavah the people moved to Hazeroth, and camped at Hazeroth.

Dissension of Aaron and Miriam

12 Then Miriam and Aaron spoke against Moses because of the Ethiopian woman whom he had married; for he had married an Ethiopian woman.

2 So they said, "Has the Lᴏʀᴅ indeed spoken only through ᴿMoses? ᴿHas He not spoken through us also?" And the Lᴏʀᴅ ᴿheard *it*.   Num. 16:3 · Mic. 6:4 · Ezek. 35:12, 13

3 (Now the man Moses *was* very humble, more than all men who *were* on the face of the earth.)

4 ᴿSuddenly the Lᴏʀᴅ said to Moses, Aaron, and Miriam, "Come out, you three, to

11:25 Tg., Vg. *and they did not cease*
11:34 Lit. *Graves of Craving*

the tabernacle of meeting!" So the three came out.   [Ps. 76:9]

5 ᴿThen the LORD came down in the pillar of cloud and stood *in* the door of the tabernacle, and called Aaron and Miriam. And they both went forward.   Ex. 19:9; 34:5

6 Then He said, "Hear now My words:

If there is a prophet among you,
I, the LORD, make Myself known to him
ᴿin a vision;
I speak to him in a dream.   Gen. 46:2

7 Not so with My servant Moses;
He *is* faithful in all My house.

8 I speak with him face to face,
Even plainly, and not in dark sayings;
And he sees the form of the LORD.
Why then were you not afraid
To speak against My servant Moses?"

9 So the anger of the LORD was aroused against them, and He departed.

10 And when the cloud departed from above the tabernacle, ᴿsuddenly Miriam *became* ᴿleprous, as *white as* snow. Then Aaron turned toward Miriam, and there she was, a leper.   Deut. 24:9 • 2 Kin. 5:27; 15:5

11 So Aaron said to Moses, "Oh, my lord! Please ᴿdo not lay ᵀ*this* sin on us, in which we have done foolishly and in which we have sinned.   2 Sam. 19:19; 24:10 • *the penalty for this*

12 "Please ᴿdo not let her be as one dead, whose flesh is half consumed when he comes out of his mother's womb!"   Ps. 88:4

13 So Moses cried out to the LORD, saying, "Please ᴿheal her, O God, I pray!"   Ps. 103:3

14 Then the LORD said to Moses, "If her father had but spit in her face, would she not be shamed seven days? Let her be ᴿshutᵀ out of the camp seven days, and afterward she may be received *again*."   Lev. 13:46 • *exiled from*

15 ᴿSo Miriam was shut out of the camp seven days, and the people did not journey till Miriam was brought in *again*.   Deut. 24:9

16 And afterward the people moved from ᴿHazeroth and camped in the Wilderness of Paran.   Num. 11:35; 33:17, 18

Spies Sent into Canaan

13 And the LORD spoke to Moses, saying,
2 ᴿ"Send men to spy out the land of Canaan, which I am giving to the children of Israel; from each tribe of their fathers you shall send a man, every one a leader among them."   Deut. 1:22; 9:23

3 So Moses sent them ᴿfrom the Wilderness of Paran according to the command of the LORD, all of them men who *were* heads of the children of Israel.   Num. 12:16; 32:8

4 Now these *were* their names: from the tribe of Reuben, Shammua the son of Zaccur;

5 from the tribe of Simeon, Shaphat the son of Hori;

6 ᴿfrom the tribe of Judah, ᴿCaleb the son of Jephunneh;   Num. 34:19 • Josh. 14:6, 7

7 from the tribe of Issachar, Igal the son of Joseph;

8 from the tribe of Ephraim, *Hoshea the son of Nun;

9 from the tribe of Benjamin, Palti the son of Raphu;

10 from the tribe of Zebulun, Gaddiel the son of Sodi;

11 from the tribe of Joseph, *that is*, from the tribe of Manasseh, Gaddi the son of Susi;

12 from the tribe of Dan, Ammiel the son of Gemalli;

13 from the tribe of Asher, Sethur the son of Michael;

14 from the tribe of Naphtali, Nahbi the son of Vophsi;

15 from the tribe of Gad, Geuel the son of Machi.

16 These *are* the names of the men whom Moses sent to spy out the land. And Moses called *Hoshea the son of Nun, Joshua.

17 Then Moses sent them to spy out the land of Canaan, and said to them, "Go up this *way* into the South, and go up to the mountains,

18 "and see what the land is like: whether the people who dwell in it *are* strong or weak, few or many;

19 "whether the land they dwell in *is* good or bad; whether the cities they inhabit *are* like camps or strongholds;

20 "whether the land *is* ᵀrich or poor; and whether there are forests there or not. ᴿBe of good courage. And bring some of the fruit of the land." Now the time *was* the season of the first ripe grapes.   *fertile or barren* • Deut. 31:6, 7, 23

21 So they went up and spied out the land from the Wilderness of Zin as far as Rehob, near the entrance of ᴿHamath.   Josh. 13:5

22 And they went up through the South and came to ᴿHebron; Ahiman, Sheshai, and Talmai, the descendants of ᴿAnak, *were* there. (Now Hebron was built seven years before Zoan in Egypt.) Josh. 15:13, 14 • Josh. 11:21, 22

23 ᴿThen they came to the ᵀValley of Eshcol, and there cut down a branch with one cluster of grapes; they carried it between two of them on a pole. *They* also *brought* some of the pomegranates and figs.   Deut. 1:24, 25 • *Wadi*

24 The place was called the Valley of ᵀEshcol, because of the cluster which the men of Israel cut down there.   Lit. *Cluster*

25 And they returned from spying out the land after forty days.

26 Now they departed and came back to Moses and Aaron and all the congregation of the children of Israel in the Wilderness of Paran, at ᴿKadesh; they brought back word to them and to all the congregation, and showed them the fruit of the land.   Deut. 1:19

13:8 LXX, Vg. *Oshea*
13:16 LXX, Vg. *Oshea*

27 Then they told him, and said: "We went to the land where you sent us. It truly flows with milk and honey, and this *is* its fruit.

28 "Nevertheless the people who dwell in the land *are* strong; the cities *are* fortified *and* very large; moreover we saw the descendants of ᴿAnak there.   Josh. 11:21, 22

29 ᴿ"The Amalekites dwell in the land of the South; the Hittites, the Jebusites, and the Amorites dwell in the mountains; and the Canaanites dwell by the sea and along the banks of the Jordan."   Judg. 6:3

30 Then ᴿCaleb quieted the people before Moses, and said, "Let us go up at once and take possession, for we are well able to overcome it."   Num. 14:6, 24

31 But the men who had gone up with him said, "We are not able to go up against the people, for they *are* stronger than we."

32 And they gave the children of Israel a bad report of the land which they had spied out, saying, "The land through which we have gone as spies *is* a land that devours its inhabitants, and ᴿall the people whom we saw in it *are* men of *great* stature.   Amos 2:9

33 "There we saw the ᵀgiants (the descendants of Anak came from the giants); and we were like grasshoppers in our own sight, and so we were in their sight."   Heb. *nephilim*

Israel Refuses to Enter Canaan

14 So all the congregation lifted up their voices and cried, and the people ᴿwept that night.   Deut. 1:45

2 ᴿAnd all the children of Israel complained against Moses and Aaron, and the whole congregation said to them, "If only we had died in the land of Egypt! Or if only we had died in this wilderness!   Ex. 16:2; 17:3

3 "Why has the Lᴏʀᴅ brought us to this land to fall by the sword, that our wives and children should become victims? Would it not be better for us to return to Egypt?"

4 So they said to one another, "Let us select a leader and return to Egypt."

5 Then Moses and Aaron ᵀfell on their faces before all the assembly of the congregation of the children of Israel. *prostrated themselves*

6 But Joshua the son of Nun and Caleb the son of Jephunneh, *who were* among those who had spied out the land, tore their clothes;

7 and they spoke to all the congregation of the children of Israel, saying: ᴿ"The land we passed through to spy out *is* an exceedingly good land.   Num. 13:27

8 "If the Lᴏʀᴅ delights in us, then He will bring us into this land and give it to us, *ᵃ*a land which flows with milk and honey.'

9 "Only do not rebel against the Lᴏʀᴅ, nor fear the people of the land, for ᵀthey *are* our bread; their protection has departed from

14:8 Ex. 3:8; Num. 13:27

them, and the Lᴏʀᴅ *is* with us. Do not fear them."   They shall be as food for our consumption.

10 And all the congregation said to stone them with stones. Now ᴿthe glory of the Lᴏʀᴅ appeared in the tabernacle of meeting before all the children of Israel.   Ex. 16:10

Moses Intercedes for the People

11 Then the Lᴏʀᴅ said to Moses: "How long will these people reject Me? And how long will they not believe Me, with all the signs which I have performed among them?

12 "I will strike them with the pestilence and disinherit them, and I will make of you a nation greater and mightier than they."

13 And Moses said to the Lᴏʀᴅ: "Then the Egyptians will hear *it*, for by Your might You brought these people up from among them,

14 "and they will tell *it* to the inhabitants of this land. They have ᴿheard that You, Lᴏʀᴅ, *are* among these people; that You, Lᴏʀᴅ, are seen face to face and Your cloud stands above them, and You go before them in a pillar of cloud by day and in a pillar of fire by night.   Deut. 2:25

15 "Now *if* You kill these people as one man, then the nations which have heard of Your fame will speak, saying,

16 'Because the Lᴏʀᴅ was not ᴿable to bring this people to the land which He swore to give them, therefore He killed them in the wilderness.'   Deut. 9:28

17 "And now, I pray, let the power of my Lord be great, just as You have spoken, saying,

18 ᴿ'The Lᴏʀᴅ is longsuffering and abundant in mercy, forgiving iniquity and transgression; but He by no means clears *the* guilty, ᴿvisiting the iniquity of the fathers on the children to the third and fourth *generation*.'   Ex. 34:6, 7 • Ex. 20:5

19 "Pardon the iniquity of this people, I pray, according to the greatness of Your mercy, just ᴿas You have forgiven this people, from Egypt even until now."   Ps. 78:38

20 Then the Lᴏʀᴅ said: "I have pardoned, ᴿaccording to your word;   Mic. 7:18-20

21 "but truly, as I live, ᴿall the earth shall be filled with the glory of the Lᴏʀᴅ—   Ps. 72:19

22 ᴿ"because all these men who have seen My glory and the signs which I did in Egypt and in the wilderness, and have put Me to the test now ᴿthese ten times, and have not heeded My voice,   Deut. 1:35 • Gen. 31:7

23 "they certainly shall not ᴿsee the land of which I swore to their fathers, nor shall any of those who rejected Me see it.   Num. 26:65

24 "But My servant Caleb, because he has a different spirit in him and has followed Me fully, I will bring into the land where he went, and his descendants shall inherit it.

25 "Now the Amalekites and the Canaanites dwell in the valley; tomorrow turn and

Rmove out into the wilderness by the Way of the Red Sea."   Deut. 1:40

Death Sentence on the Rebels

26 And the LORD spoke to Moses and Aaron, saying,

27 "How long shall I bear with this evil congregation who complain against Me? RI have heard the complaints which the children of Israel make against Me.   Ex. 16:12

28 "Say to them, R'As I live,' says the LORD, 'just as you have spoken in My hearing, so I will do to you: Heb. 3:16–19

29 'The carcasses of you who have complained against Me shall fall in this wilderness, Rall of you who were numbered, according to your entire number, from twenty years old and above.   Num. 1:45, 46; 26:64

30 RExcept for Caleb the son of Jephunneh and Joshua the son of Nun, you shall by no means enter the land which I swore I would make you dwell in.   Deut. 1:36–38

31 R'But your little ones, whom you said would be victims, I will bring in, and they shall Tknow the land which Ryou have despised.   Deut. 1:39 • be acquainted with • Ps. 106:24

32 'But as for you, RyourT carcasses shall fall in this wilderness.   Num. 26:64, 65; 32:13 • You shall die

33 'And your sons shall be *shepherds in the wilderness forty years, and Rbear the brunt of your infidelity, until your carcasses are consumed in the wilderness.   Ezek. 23:35

34 'According to the number of the days in which you spied out the land, Rforty days, for each day you shall bear your Tguilt one year, namely forty years, Rand you shall know My Trejection.   Ezek. 4:6 • iniquity • [Heb. 4:1] • opposition

35 R'I the LORD have spoken this. I will surely do so to all Rthis evil congregation who are gathered together against Me. In this wilderness they shall be consumed, and there they shall die.' "   Num. 23:19 • 1 Cor. 10:5

36 Now the men whom Moses sent to spy out the land, who returned and made all the congregation complain against him by bringing a bad report of the land,

37 those very men who brought the evil report about the land, Rdied by the plague before the LORD.   [1 Cor. 10:10]

38 RBut Joshua the son of Nun and Caleb the son of Jephunneh remained alive, of the men who went to spy out the land. Josh. 14:6, 10

A Futile Invasion Attempt

39 Then Moses told these words to all the children of Israel, Rand the people mourned greatly.   Ex. 33:4

40 And they rose early in the morning and went up to the top of the mountain, saying, R"Here we are, and we will go up to the place which the LORD has promised, for we have sinned!"   Deut. 1:41–44

14:33 Vg. wanderers

41 And Moses said, "Now why do you Ttransgress the command of the LORD? For this will not succeed.   overstep

42 "Do not go up, lest you be defeated by your enemies, for the LORD is not among you.

43 "For the Amalekites and the Canaanites are there before you, and you shall fall by the sword; because you have turned away from the LORD, the LORD will not be with you."

44 RBut they presumed to go up to the mountaintop. Nevertheless, neither the ark of the covenant of the LORD nor Moses departed from the camp.   Deut. 1:43

45 Then the Amalekites and the Canaanites who dwelt in that mountain came down and attacked them, and drove them back as far as RHormah.   Num. 21:3

Laws of Grain and Drink Offerings

15 And the LORD spoke to Moses, saying,
2 R"Speak to the children of Israel, and say to them: 'When you have come into the land you are to inhabit, which I am giving to you,   Lev. 23:10

3 'and you make an offering by fire to the LORD, a burnt offering or a sacrifice, to fulfill a vow or as a freewill offering or in your appointed feasts, to make a sweet aroma to the LORD, from the herd or the flock,

4 'then he who presents his offering to the LORD shall bring Ra grain offering of one-tenth of an ephah of fine flour mixed Rwith one-fourth of a hin of oil;   Ex. 29:40 • Num. 28:5

5 'and one-fourth of a hin of wine as a drink offering you shall prepare with the burnt offering or the sacrifice, for each lamb.

6 'Or for a ram you shall prepare as a grain offering two-tenths of an ephah of fine flour mixed with one-third of a hin of oil;

7 'and as a drink offering you shall offer Tone-third of a hin of wine as a sweet aroma to the LORD.   42.7 oz.

8 'And when you prepare a young bull as a burnt offering, or as a sacrifice to fulfill a vow, or as a peace offering to the LORD,

9 'then shall be offered Rwith the young bull a grain offering of Tthree-tenths of an ephah of fine flour mixed with Thalf a hin of oil;   Num. 28:12, 14 • 6.261 qt. • .5 gal.

10 'and you shall bring as the drink offering Thalf a hin of wine as an offering made by fire, a sweet aroma to the LORD.   .5 gal.

11 R'Thus it shall be done for each young bull, for each ram, or for each lamb or young goat.   Num. 28

12 'According to the number that you prepare, so you shall do with everyone according to their number.

13 'All who are native-born shall do these things in this manner, in presenting an offering made by fire, a sweet aroma to the LORD.

14 'And if a stranger dwells with you, or whoever is among you throughout your gen-

erations, and would present an offering made by fire, a sweet aroma to the LORD, just as you do, so shall he do.

15 'One ordinance *shall be* for you of the assembly and for the stranger who dwells *with you*, an ordinance forever throughout your generations; as you are, so shall the stranger be before the LORD.

16 ^R'One law and one custom shall be for you and for the stranger who dwells with you.' "   Ex. 12:49

17 Again the LORD spoke to Moses, saying,

18 ^R"Speak to the children of Israel, and say to them: 'When you come into the land to which I bring you,   Deut. 26:1

19 'then it will be, when you eat of ^Rthe bread of the land, that you shall offer up a heave offering to the LORD.   Josh. 5:11, 12

20 ^R'You shall offer up a cake of the first of your ground meal *as* a heave offering; as ^Ra heave offering of the threshing floor, so shall you offer it up.   Lev. 23:10, 14, 17 • Lev. 2:14; 23:10, 16

21 'Of the first of your ground meal you shall give to the LORD a heave offering throughout your generations.

Laws Concerning Unintentional Sin

22 ^R'If you sin unintentionally, and do not observe all these commandments which the LORD has spoken to Moses—   Lev. 4:2

23 'all that the LORD has commanded you by the hand of Moses, from the day the LORD gave commandment and onward throughout your generations—

24 'then it will be, if it is unintentionally committed, ^Twithout the knowledge of the congregation, that the whole congregation shall offer one young bull as a burnt offering, as a sweet aroma to the LORD, with its grain offering and its drink offering, according to the ordinance, and ^Rone kid of the goats as a sin offering.   Lit. *away from the eyes* • Lev. 4:23

25 ^R'So the priest shall make atonement for the whole congregation of the children of Israel, and it shall be forgiven them, for it was unintentional; they shall bring their offering, an offering made by fire to the LORD, and their sin offering before the LORD, for their unintended sin.   [Heb. 2:17]

26 'It shall be forgiven the whole congregation of the children of Israel and the stranger who dwells among them, because all the people *did it* unintentionally.

27 'And ^Rif a person sins unintentionally, then he shall bring a female goat in its first year as a sin offering.   Lev. 4:27–31

28 ^R'So the priest shall make atonement for the person who sins unintentionally, when he sins unintentionally before the LORD, to make atonement for him; and it shall be forgiven him.   Lev. 4:35

29 'You shall have one law for him who sins unintentionally, *for* him who is native-born

among the children of Israel and for the stranger who dwells among them.

Law Concerning Presumptuous Sin

30 'But the person who does *anything* ^Tpresumptuously, *whether he is* native-born or a stranger, that one ^Tbrings reproach on the LORD, and he shall be cut off from among his people.   *defiantly*, lit. *with a high hand* • *blasphemes*

31 'Because he has ^Rdespised the word of the LORD, and has broken His commandment, that person shall be completely cut off; his ^Tguilt *shall be* upon him.' "   Prov. 13:13 • *iniquity*

Penalty for Violating the Sabbath

32 Now while the children of Israel were in the wilderness, ^Rthey found a man gathering sticks on the Sabbath day.   Ex. 31:14, 15; 35:2, 3

33 And those who found him gathering sticks brought him to Moses and Aaron, and to all the congregation.

34 They put him ^Runder guard, because it had not been explained what should be done to him.   Lev. 24:12

35 Then the LORD said to Moses, ^R"The man must surely be put to death; all the congregation shall ^Rstone him with stones outside the camp."   Ex. 31:14, 15 • Lev. 24:14

36 So, as the LORD commanded Moses, all the congregation brought him outside the camp and stoned him with stones, and he died.

Tassels on Garments

37 Again the LORD spoke to Moses, saying,

38 "Speak to the children of Israel: Tell ^Rthem to make tassels on the corners of their garments throughout their generations, and to put a blue thread in the tassels of the corners.   Matt. 23:5

39 "And you shall have the tassel, that you may look upon it and ^Rremember all the commandments of the LORD and do them, and that you ^R*may* not ^Rfollow the harlotry to which your own heart and your own eyes are inclined,   Ps. 103:18 • Deut. 29:19 • James 4:4

40 "and that you may remember and do all My commandments, and be ^Rholy for your God.   [Lev. 11:44, 45]

41 "I am the LORD your God, who brought you out of the land of Egypt, to be your God: I am the LORD your God."

Rebellion Against Moses and Aaron

16 Now Korah the son of Izhar, the son of Kohath, the son of Levi, with Dathan and Abiram the sons of Eliab, and On the son of Peleth, sons of Reuben, took *men*;

2 and they rose up before Moses with some of the children of Israel, two hundred and fifty leaders of the congregation, representatives of the congregation, men of renown.

3 They gathered together against Moses and Aaron, and said to them, *"You* ᵀ*take* too much upon yourselves, for ᴿall the congregation *is* holy, every one of them, ᴿand the LORD *is* among them. Why then do you exalt yourselves above the assembly of the LORD?"   *assume too much for •* Ex. 19:6 • Ex. 29:45

4 So when Moses heard *it,* he ᴿfell on his face;   Num. 14:5; 20:6

5 and he spoke to Korah and all his company, saying, "Tomorrow morning the LORD will show who *is* ᴿHis and *who is* ᵀholy, and will cause *him* to come near to Him. That one whom He chooses He will cause to come near to Him.   [2 Tim. 2:19] • *set aside* for His use only

6 "Do this: Take censers, Korah and all your company;

7 "put fire in them and put incense in them before the LORD tomorrow, and it shall be *that* the man whom the LORD chooses *is* the holy one. *You take* too much upon yourselves, you sons of Levi!"

8 Then Moses said to Korah, "Hear now, you sons of Levi:

9 *"Is it* ᴿa small thing to you that the God of Israel has ᴿseparated you from the congregation of Israel, to bring you near to Himself, to do the work of the tabernacle of the LORD, and to stand before the congregation to serve them;   Is. 7:13 • Deut. 10:8

10 "and that He has brought you near *to Himself,* you and all your brethren, the sons of Levi, with you? And are you seeking the priesthood also?

11 "Therefore you and all your company *are* gathered together against the LORD. ᴿAnd what *is* Aaron that you complain against him?"   Ex. 16:7, 8

12 And Moses sent to call Dathan and Abiram the sons of Eliab, but they said, "We will not come up!

13 *"Is it* a small thing that you have brought us up out of a land flowing with milk and honey, to kill us in the wilderness, that you should keep acting like a prince over us?

14 "Moreover ᴿyou have not brought us into ᴿa land flowing with milk and honey, nor given us inheritance of fields and vineyards. Will you put out the eyes of these men? We will not come up!"   Num. 14:1-4 • Ex. 3:8

15 Then Moses was very angry, and said to the LORD, "Do not ᵀrespect their offering. I have not taken one donkey from them, nor have I hurt one of them."   *graciously regard*

16 And Moses said to Korah, "Tomorrow, you and all your company be present before the LORD—you and they, as well as Aaron.

17 "Let each take his censer and put incense in it, and each of you bring his censer before the LORD, two hundred and fifty censers; both you and Aaron, each *with* his censer."

18 So every man took his censer, put fire in it, laid incense on it, and stood at the door of the tabernacle of meeting with Moses and Aaron.

19 And Korah gathered all the congregation against them at the door of the tabernacle of meeting. Then ᴿthe glory of the LORD appeared to all the congregation.   Num. 14:10

20 And the LORD spoke to Moses and Aaron, saying,

21 ᴿ"Separate yourselves from among this congregation, that I may ᴿconsume them in a moment."   Gen. 19:17 • Ex. 32:10; 33:5

22 Then they ᴿfellᵀ on their faces, and said, "O God, the God of the spirits of all flesh, shall one man sin, and You be angry with all the congregation?"   Num. 14:5 • *prostrated themselves*

23 So the LORD spoke to Moses, saying,

24 "Speak to the congregation, saying, 'Get away from the tents of Korah, Dathan, and Abiram.'"

25 Then Moses rose and went to Dathan and Abiram, and the elders of Israel followed him.

26 And he spoke to the congregation, saying, "Depart now from the tents of these wicked men! Touch nothing of theirs, lest you be consumed in all their sins."

27 So they got away from around the tents of Korah, Dathan, and Abiram; and Dathan and Abiram came out and stood at the door of their tents, with their wives, their sons, and their little ᴿchildren.   Num. 26:11

28 And Moses said: ᴿ"By this you shall know that the LORD has sent me to do all these works, for *I have* not *done them* ᴿof my own will.   John 5:36 • John 5:30

29 "If these men die naturally like all men, or if they are visited by the common fate of all men, *then* the LORD has not sent me.

30 "But if the LORD creates ᴿa new thing, and the earth opens its mouth and swallows them up with all that belongs to them, and they ᴿgo down alive into the pit, then you will understand that these men have rejected the LORD."   Job 31:3 • [Ps. 55:15]

31 ᴿNow it came to pass, as he finished speaking all these words, that the ground split apart under them,   Num. 26:10

32 and the earth opened its mouth and swallowed them up, with their households and ᴿall the men with Korah, with all *their* goods.   Num. 26:11

33 So they and all those with them went down alive into the pit; the earth closed over them, and they perished from among the assembly.

34 Then all Israel who *were* around them fled at their cry, for they said, "Lest the earth swallow us up *also!"*

35 And ᴿa fire came out from the LORD and consumed the two hundred and fifty men who were offering incense.   Num. 11:1-3; 26:10

36 Then the LORD spoke to Moses, saying:

37 "Tell Eleazar, the son of Aaron the priest, to pick up the censers out of the blaze, for ᴿthey are holy, and scatter the fire some distance away.   Lev. 27:28

38 "The censers of these men who sinned against their own souls, let them be made into hammered plates as a covering for the altar. Because they presented them before the Lᴏʀᴅ, therefore they are holy; and they shall be a sign to the children of Israel."

39 So Eleazar the priest took the bronze censers, which those who were burned up had presented, and they were hammered out as a covering on the altar,

40 *to be* a memorial to the children of Israel that no outsider, who *is* not a descendant of Aaron, should come near to offer incense before the Lᴏʀᴅ, that he might not become like Korah and his companions, just as the Lᴏʀᴅ had said to him through Moses.

Complaints of the People

41 On the next day ᴿall the congregation of the children of Israel complained against Moses and Aaron, saying, "You have killed the people of the Lᴏʀᴅ."   Num. 14:2

42 Now it happened, when the congregation had gathered against Moses and Aaron, that they turned toward the tabernacle of meeting; and suddenly ᴿthe cloud covered it, and the glory of the Lᴏʀᴅ appeared.   Ex. 40:34

43 Then Moses and Aaron came before the tabernacle of meeting.

44 And the Lᴏʀᴅ spoke to Moses, saying,

45 "Get away from among this congregation, that I may consume them in a moment." And they fell on their faces.

46 So Moses said to Aaron, "Take a censer and put fire in it from the altar, put incense *on it*, and take it quickly to the congregation and make atonement for them; ᴿfor wrath has gone out from the Lᴏʀᴅ. The plague has begun."   Num. 18:5

47 Then Aaron took *it* as Moses commanded, and ran into the midst of the assembly; and already the plague had begun among the people. So he put in the incense and made atonement for the people.

48 And he stood between the dead and the living; so ᴿthe plague was stopped.   Num. 25:8

49 Now those who died in the plague were fourteen thousand seven hundred, besides those who died in the Korah incident.

50 So Aaron returned to Moses at the door of the tabernacle of meeting, for the plague had stopped.

The Budding of Aaron's Rod

17 And the Lᴏʀᴅ spoke to Moses, saying: 2 "Speak to the children of Israel, and get from them a rod from each father's house, all their leaders according to their fathers'

houses—twelve rods. Write each man's name on his rod.

3 "And you shall write Aaron's name on the rod of Levi. For there shall be one rod for the head of *each* father's house.

4 "Then you shall place them in the tabernacle of meeting before ᴿthe Testimony, ᴿwhere I meet with you.   Ex. 25:16 · Ex. 25:22

5 "And it shall be *that* the rod of the man whom I choose will blossom; thus I will rid Myself of the complaints of the children of Israel, which they make against you."

6 So Moses spoke to the children of Israel, and each of their leaders gave him a rod apiece, for each leader according to their fathers' houses, twelve rods; and the rod of Aaron *was* among their rods.

7 And Moses placed the rods before the Lᴏʀᴅ in ᴿthe tabernacle of witness.   Ex. 38:21

8 Now it came to pass on the next day that Moses went into the tabernacle of witness, and behold, the rod of Aaron, of the house of Levi, had sprouted and put forth buds, had produced blossoms and yielded ripe almonds.

9 Then Moses brought out all the rods from before the Lᴏʀᴅ to all the children of Israel; and they looked, and each man took his rod.

10 And the Lᴏʀᴅ said to Moses, "Bring Aaron's rod back before the Testimony, to be kept ᴿas a sign against the rebels, ᴿthat you may put their complaints away from Me, lest they die."   Deut. 9:7, 24 · Num. 17:5

11 Thus did Moses; just as the Lᴏʀᴅ had commanded him, so he did.

12 So the children of Israel spoke to Moses, saying, "Surely we die, we perish, we all perish!

13 ᴿ"Whoever even comes near the tabernacle of the Lᴏʀᴅ must die. Shall we all utterly die?"   Num. 1:51, 53; 18:4, 7

Duties of Priests and Levites

18 Then the Lᴏʀᴅ said to Aaron: ᴿ"You and your sons and your father's house with you shall ᴿbear the ᵀiniquity *related to* the sanctuary, and you and your sons with you shall bear the iniquity *associated with* your priesthood.   Num. 17:13 · Ex. 28:38 · *guilt*

2 "Also bring with you your brethren of the tribe of Levi, the tribe of your father, that they may be joined with you and serve you while you and your sons *are* with you before the tabernacle of ᵀwitness.   *testimony*

3 "They shall attend to your ᵀneeds and all the needs of the tabernacle; ᴿbut they shall not come near the articles of the sanctuary and the altar, ᴿlest they die—they and you also.   *service* · Num. 16:40 · Num. 4:15

4 "They shall be joined with you and attend to the needs of the tabernacle of meeting, for all the work of the tabernacle; but an outsider shall not come near you.

5 "And you shall attend to ᴿthe duties of the sanctuary and the duties of the altar, ᴿthat there *may* be no more wrath on the children of Israel.   Lev. 24:3 • Num. 8:19; 16:46

6 "Behold, I Myself have ᴿtaken your brethren the Levites from among the children of Israel; ᴿ*they are* a gift to you, given by the LORD, to do the work of the tabernacle of meeting.   Num. 3:12, 45 • Num. 3:9

7 "Therefore you and your sons with you shall attend to your priesthood for everything at the altar and behind the veil; and you shall serve. I give your priesthood *to you* as a ᴿgift for service, but the outsider who comes near shall be put to death."   1 Pet. 5:2, 3

Offerings for Support of the Priests

8 And the LORD spoke to Aaron: "Here, I Myself have also given you ᵀcharge of My heave offerings, all the holy gifts of the children of Israel; I have given them ᴿas a portion to you and your sons, as an ordinance forever.   *custody* • Ex. 29:29; 40:13, 15

9 "This shall be yours of the most holy things *reserved* from the fire: every offering of theirs, every grain offering and every ᴿsin offering and every ᴿtrespass offering which they render to Me, *shall be* most holy for you and your sons.   Lev. 6:25, 26 • Lev. 7:7

10 ᴿ"In a most holy *place* you shall eat it; every male shall eat it. It shall be holy to you.   Lev. 6:16, 26

11 "This also *is* yours: the heave offering of their gift, with all the wave offerings of the children of Israel; I have given them to you, and your sons and daughters with you, as an ordinance forever. ᴿEveryone who is ᵀclean in your house may eat it.   Lev. 22:1–16 • *purified*

12 ᴿ"All the ᵀbest of the oil, all the best of the new wine and the grain, ᴿtheir firstfruits which they offer to the LORD, I have given them to you.   Ex. 23:19 • Lit. *fat* • Ex. 22:29

13 "Whatever first ripe fruit is in their land, ᴿwhich they bring to the LORD, shall be yours. Everyone who is clean in your house may eat it.   Ex. 22:29; 23:19; 34:26

14 ᴿ"Every ᵀdevoted thing in Israel shall be yours.   Lev. 27:1–33 • *consecrated*

15 "Everything that first opens ᴿthe womb of all flesh, which they bring to the LORD, whether man or beast, shall be yours; nevertheless ᴿthe firstborn of man you shall surely redeem, and the firstborn of unclean animals you shall redeem.   Ex. 13:2 • Ex. 13:12–15

16 "And those redeemed of the devoted things you shall redeem when one month old, according to your valuation, for five shekels of silver, according to the shekel of the sanctuary, which *is* ᴿtwenty gerahs.   Ex. 30:13

17 ᴿ"But the firstborn of a cow, the firstborn of a sheep, or the firstborn of a goat you shall not redeem; they *are* holy. ᴿYou shall sprinkle their blood on the altar, and burn their fat *as* an offering made by fire for a sweet aroma to the LORD.   Deut. 15:19 • Lev. 3:2, 5

18 "And their flesh shall be yours, just as the ᴿwaveᵀ breast and the right thigh are yours.   Ex. 29:26–28 • *breast of the wave offering*

19 "All the heave offerings of the holy things, which the children of Israel offer to the LORD, I have given to you and your sons and daughters with you as an ordinance forever; ᴿit *is* a covenant of salt forever before the LORD with you and your descendants with you."   2 Chr. 13:5

20 Then the LORD said to Aaron: "You shall have ᴿno inheritance in their land, nor shall you have any portion among them; ᴿI *am* your portion and your inheritance among the children of Israel.   Josh. 13:14, 33 • Ezek. 44:28

Tithes for Support of the Levites

21 "Behold, I have given the children of Levi all the tithes in Israel as an inheritance in return for the work which they perform, the work of the tabernacle of meeting.

22 ᴿ"Hereafter the children of Israel shall not come near the tabernacle of meeting, ᴿlest they bear sin and die.   Num. 1:51 • Lev. 22:9

23 "But the Levites shall perform the work of the tabernacle of meeting, and they shall bear their iniquity; *it shall be* a statute forever, throughout your generations, that among the children of Israel they shall have no inheritance.

24 "For the tithes of the children of Israel, which they offer up *as* a heave offering to the LORD, I have given to the Levites ᵀas an inheritance; therefore I have said to them, 'Among the children of Israel they shall have no inheritance.' "   *for a possession*

The Tithe of the Levites

25 Then the LORD spoke to Moses, saying,

26 "Speak thus to the Levites, and say to them: 'When you take from the children of Israel the tithes which I have given you from them as your inheritance, then you shall offer up a heave offering of it to the LORD, ᴿa tenth of the tithe.   Neh. 10:38

27 'And your heave offering shall be reckoned to you as though *it were* the grain of the ᴿthreshing floor and as the fullness of the winepress.   Num. 15:20

28 'Thus you shall also offer a heave offering to the LORD from all your tithes which you receive from the children of Israel, and you shall give the LORD's heave offering from it to Aaron the priest.

29 'Of all your gifts you shall offer up every heave offering due to the LORD, from all the best of them, the consecrated part of them.'

30 "Therefore you shall say to them: 'When you have lifted up the best of it, then *the rest* shall be accounted to the Levites as the produce of the threshing floor and as the produce of the winepress.

31 'You may eat it in any place, you and your households, for it *is* your reward for your work in the tabernacle of meeting.

32 'And you shall bear no sin because of it, when you have lifted up the best of it. But you shall not ᴿprofane the holy gifts of the children of Israel, lest you die.' "   Lev. 22:2, 15

Laws of Purification

19 Now the LORD spoke to Moses and Aaron, saying,

2 "This *is* the ᵀordinance of the law which the LORD has commanded, saying: 'Speak to the children of Israel, that they bring you a red heifer without blemish, in which there *is* no ᴿdefect ᴿ*and* on which a yoke has never come.   statute · Lev. 22:20-25 · Deut. 21:3

3 'You shall give it to Eleazar the priest, that he may take it ᴿoutside the camp, and it shall be slaughtered before him;   Lev. 4:12, 21

4 'and Eleazar the priest shall take some of its blood with his finger, and ᴿsprinkle some of its blood seven times directly in front of the tabernacle of meeting.   Lev. 4:6

5 'Then the heifer shall be burned in his sight: ᴿits hide, its flesh, its blood, and its offal shall be burned.   Ex. 29:14

6 'And the priest shall take cedar wood and hyssop and scarlet, and cast *them* into the midst of the fire burning the heifer.

7 ᴿ'Then the priest shall wash his clothes, he shall bathe in water, and afterward he shall come into the camp; the priest shall be unclean until evening.   Lev. 11:25; 15:5; 16:26, 28

8 'And the one who burns it shall wash his clothes in water, bathe in water, and shall be unclean until evening.

9 'Then a man *who is* clean shall gather up the ashes of the heifer, and store *them* outside the camp in a clean place; and they shall be kept for the congregation of the children of Israel for the water of ᵀpurification; it *is* for purifying from sin.   Lit. *impurity*

10 'And the one who gathers the ashes of the heifer shall wash his clothes, and be unclean until evening. It shall be a statute forever to the children of Israel and to the stranger who dwells among them.

11 'He who touches the dead body of anyone shall be unclean seven days.

12 ᴿ'He shall purify himself with the water on the third day and on the seventh day; *then* he will be clean. But if he does not purify

himself on the third day and on the seventh day, he will not be clean.   Num. 19:19; 31:19

13 'Whoever touches the body of anyone who has died, and does not purify himself, defiles the tabernacle of the LORD. That person shall be cut off from Israel. He shall be unclean, because ᴿthe water of purification was not sprinkled on him; ᴿhis uncleanness *is* still on him.   Num. 8:7; 19:9 · Lev. 7:20; 22:3

14 'This *is* the law when a man dies in a tent: All who come into the tent and all who *are* in the tent shall be unclean seven days;

15 'and every ᴿopen vessel, which has no cover fastened on it, *is* unclean.   Num. 31:20

16 ᴿ'Whoever in the open field touches one who is slain by a sword or who has died, or a bone of a man, or a grave, shall be unclean seven days.   Num. 19:11; 31:19

17 'And for an unclean *person* they shall take some of the ashes of the heifer burnt for purification from sin, and ᵀrunning water shall be put on them in a vessel.   Lit. *living*

18 'A clean person shall take ᴿhyssop and dip *it* in the water, sprinkle *it* on the tent, on all the vessels, on the persons who were there, or on the one who touched a bone, the slain, the dead, or a grave.   Ps. 51:7

19 'The clean *person* shall sprinkle the unclean on the third day and on the seventh day; ᴿand on the seventh day he shall purify himself, wash his clothes, and bathe in water; and at evening he shall be clean.   Lev. 14:9

20 'But the man who is unclean and does not purify himself, that person shall be cut off from among the assembly, because he has ᴿdefiled the sanctuary of the LORD. The water of purification has not been sprinkled on him; he *is* unclean.   Num. 19:13

21 'It shall be a perpetual statute for them. He who sprinkles the water of purification shall wash his clothes; and he who touches the water of purification shall be unclean until evening.

22 'Whatever the unclean *person* touches shall be unclean; and the person who touches *it* shall be unclean until evening.' "

Moses' Error at Kadesh

16-E. Consequences of Sin Committed by Moses and Aaron   ▼

20 Then the children of Israel, the whole congregation, came into the Wilder-

---

16-E. Consequences of Sin Committed by Moses and Aaron (Numbers 20:1-13)—For forty years Moses was a tower of spiritual strength to the nation Israel, as he led them through the wilderness. The world has yet to see his equal as a leader and statesman. No servant of God endured more unjust criticism from his congregation than Moses. However, not even Moses and Aaron were exempted from a premature end of life on earth; each committed a sin unto death. During their wanderings, the Israelites went into the desert of Zin where "there was no water for the congregation . . . they gathered together against Moses and Aaron" (vv. 1-5). Then Moses and Aaron left that angry rebellious congregation and "fell on their faces" in the doorway of the tabernacle. Then "the glory of the LORD appeared to them" (v. 6).

(Point 16-E continued on next page)

▽ ness of Zin in the first month, and the people stayed in ᴿKadesh; and ᴿMiriam died there and was buried there.   Num. 13:26 • Ex. 15:20

2 ᴿNow there was no water for the congregation; ᴿso they gathered together against Moses and Aaron.   Ex. 17:1 • Num. 16:19, 42

3 And the people contended with Moses and spoke, saying: "If only we had died when our brethren died before the Lᴏʀᴅ!

4 ᴿ"Why have you brought up the assembly of the Lᴏʀᴅ into this wilderness, that we and our animals should die here?   Ex. 17:3

5 "And why have you made us come up out of Egypt, to bring us to this evil place? It is not a place of grain or figs or vines or pomegranates; nor is there any water to drink."

6 So Moses and Aaron went from the presence of the assembly to the door of the tabernacle of meeting, and they ᵀfell on their faces. And ᴿthe glory of the Lᴏʀᴅ appeared to them.   prostrated themselves • Num. 14:10

7 Then the Lᴏʀᴅ spoke to Moses, saying,

8 "Take the rod; you and your brother Aaron gather the congregation together. Speak to the rock before their eyes, and it will yield its water; thus you shall bring water for them out of the rock, and give drink to the congregation and their animals."

9 So Moses took the rod ᴿfrom before the Lᴏʀᴅ as He commanded him.   Num. 17:10

10 And Moses and Aaron gathered the assembly together before the rock; and he said to them, "Hear now, you rebels! Must we bring water for you out of this rock?"

11 Then Moses lifted his hand and struck the rock twice with his rod; ᴿand water came

out abundantly, and the congregation and ▽ their animals drank.   [1 Cor. 10:4]

12 Then the Lᴏʀᴅ spoke to Moses and Aaron, "Because ᴿyou did not believe Me, to ᴿhallow Me in the eyes of the children of Israel, therefore you shall not bring this assembly into the land which I have given them."   Deut. 1:37; 3:26, 27; 34:5 • Lev. 10:3

13 This was the water of *Meribah, because the children of Israel contended with the Lᴏʀᴅ, and He was hallowed among them.   ▲

Passage Through Edom Refused

14 Now Moses sent messengers from Kadesh to the king of ᴿEdom. ᴿ"Thus says your brother Israel: 'You know all the hardship that has befallen us,   Gen. 36:31-39 • Deut. 2:4

15 'how our fathers went down to Egypt, and we dwelt in Egypt a long time, and the Egyptians afflicted us and our fathers.

16 'When we cried out to the Lᴏʀᴅ, He heard our voice and sent the Angel and brought us up out of Egypt; now here we are in Kadesh, a city on the edge of your border.

17 'Please let us pass through your country. We will not pass through fields or vineyards, nor will we drink water from wells; we will go along the King's Highway; we will not turn aside to the right hand or to the left until we have passed through your territory.' "

18 Then ᴿEdom said to him, "You shall not pass through my land, lest I come out against you with the sword."   Num. 24:18

19 So the children of Israel said to him, "We will go by the Highway, and if I or my

20:13 Lit. Contention

─────────────────────────

(Point 16-E continued from previous page)
(1) The Lord instructed Moses to

    (a) "Take the rod";
    (b) "Gather the congregation together";
    (c) "Speak to the rock."

"Thus [the promised result] you shall bring water for them out of the rock" (v. 8).

Moses and Aaron obeyed the Lord in all that He had commanded, until Moses stood before the people. Then he lost his temper and called them rebels. This was not the sin unto death; it was the truth.

(2) The sin unto death committed by Moses and Aaron was:

    (a) *Presumptuousness.* Moses took liberties and overstepped divine boundaries when he said, "Must we [Moses and Aaron] bring water for you out of this rock?" (v. 10). Moses, in the energy of the flesh, took all the credit for Aaron and himself for the miracle of bringing water from the rock. Aaron's sin was in concurring with Moses. He did not speak, or strike the rock; he stood by Moses and gave silent consent to all that Moses said and did.

    (b) *Disobedience.* God said, "Speak to the rock" (v. 8), but Moses took his rod and "struck the rock twice . . . and water came out abundantly" (v. 11). This is a great lesson; even though Moses and Aaron failed the Lord, their disobedience did not alter the faithfulness of the Lord (2 Tim. 2:13, page 1225). Moses and Aaron failed God, but God did not fail the people.

    (c) *Unbelief.* The Lord said to Moses and Aaron, "Because you did not believe Me . . . therefore you shall not bring this assembly into the land" (v. 12). God told Moses to speak to the rock, but in unbelief Moses struck it instead, giving the appearance that he and Aaron (not God) had the power to bring forth water miraculously.

For the account of Aaron's premature death, see verses 23-29. For the account of Moses' premature death, see Deuteronomy 34:1-12 (page 213).

See Acts 5:1-11, page 1093, for **Point 16-F: Consequences of Sin Committed by Ananias and Sapphira.**

livestock drink any of your water, ᴿthen I will pay for it; let me only pass through on foot, nothing *more*.   Deut. 2:6, 28

20 Then he said, "You shall not pass through." So Edom came out against them with many men and with a strong hand.

21 Thus Edom ᴿrefused to give Israel passage through his territory; so Israel ᴿturned away from him.   Deut. 2:27, 30 • Judg. 11:18

Death of Aaron

22 Now the children of Israel, the whole congregation, journeyed from ᴿKadesh ᴿand came to Mount Hor.   Num. 33:37 • Num. 21:4

23 And the LORD spoke to Moses and Aaron in Mount Hor by the border of the land of Edom, saying:

24 "Aaron shall ᵀbe ᴿgathered to his people, for he shall not enter the land which I have given to the children of Israel, because you rebelled against My word at the water of Meribah.   Die and join his ancestors • Gen. 25:8

25 ᴿ"Take Aaron and Eleazar his son, and bring them up to Mount Hor;   Num. 33:38

26 "and strip Aaron of his garments and put them on Eleazar his son; for Aaron shall be gathered *to his people* and die there."

27 So Moses did just as the LORD commanded, and they went up to Mount Hor in the sight of all the congregation.

28 ᴿMoses stripped Aaron of his garments and put them on Eleazar his son; and ᴿAaron died there on the top of the mountain. Then

Moses and Eleazar came down from the mountain.   Ex. 29:29, 30 • Num. 33:38

29 Now when all the congregation saw that Aaron was dead, all the house of Israel mourned for Aaron ᴿthirty days.   Deut. 34:8

Canaanites Defeated at Hormah

21 The ᴿking of Arad, the Canaanite, who dwelt in the South, heard that Israel was coming on the road to Atharim. Then he fought against Israel and took *some* of them prisoners.   Judg. 1:16

2 ᴿSo Israel made a vow to the LORD, and said, "If You will indeed deliver this people into my hand, then ᴿI will utterly destroy their cities."   Gen. 28:20 • Deut. 2:34

3 And the LORD listened to the voice of Israel and delivered up the Canaanites, and they utterly destroyed them and their cities. So the name of that place was called ᵀHormah.   Lit. *Utter Destruction*

The Bronze Serpent

16–C. Consequences of Sin: The Fiery Serpents   ▼

4 Then they journeyed from Mount Hor by the Way of the Red Sea, to go around the land of Edom; and the soul of the people became very discouraged on the way.

5 And the people spoke against God and against Moses: "Why have you brought us up out of Egypt to die in the wilderness? For

---

16-C. Consequences of Sin: The Fiery Serpents (Numbers 21:4–9)—Near the end of their forty years of wandering in the wilderness, some of the people sinned the sin that leads to death. In unbelief they spoke against God and Moses. "So the LORD sent fiery serpents among the people, and they bit the people; and many of the people of Israel died" (v. 6). Their sin was threefold. It was a sin of unbelief against

(1) *God.* "And the people spoke against God . . . 'Why have you brought us up out of Egypt to die in the wilderness?' " (v. 5). Unbelief always cries, *"WHY?"*

(2) *Moses.* "And the people spoke against God and against Moses" (v. 5). They were discouraged because the way was hard; they spoke against God, blaming Him and Moses. Moses had come to them in Egypt in the name of the Lord, saying, "I AM has sent me to you" (Ex. 3:13–15, page 60). There is always a price to pay when you go forth to do the will of God in the name of the Lord. Moses suffered because he was doing good, but his persecutors suffered to the point of death because they were doing evil (1 Pet. 3:15–17, page 1267).

(3) *God's provision for them.* They said, "There is no food and no water, and our soul loathes this worthless bread"—manna, bread from heaven (v. 5). God in His mercy gave them water from the rock, and for forty years He gave them bread from heaven. Instead of praising the Lord for providing for them, they complained about the menu and accused God and Moses of bringing them there to die.

Many of the Israelites were dying prematurely because they had sinned unto death. The people came to Moses believing, repenting, and confessing, "We have sinned." Then they named their sin: "For we have spoken against the LORD and against you" (v. 7; cf. 1 John 1:9, page 1278). God made the people taste the bitter fruits of their sin. Then they begged Moses to pray that God would take the serpents away. Moses prayed and God answered his prayer, but not according to the wishes of the people. They begged God to take the serpents away. The Lord told Moses to make a serpent of bronze and put it on a pole, so that all who were bitten would live when they looked at it. By faith they must go to the bronze serpent and look at it, believing that God would heal them. This was an act of faith; only those who thus exercised faith lived.

"As Moses lifted up the serpent in the wilderness, even so must the Son of Man be lifted up" (John 3:14–18, page 1052). As we look to Jesus, placing our faith in Him, we can be saved from the fires of eternal hell (John 3:36, page 1053) and live with Him forever and ever (see Master Outline 17, "Heaven and Hell," page 35).

See Leviticus 10:1–10, page 115, for **Point 16-D: Consequences of Sin Committed by Nadab and Abihu.**

▽ *there is* no food and no water, and our soul ᵀloathes this worthless bread."   *detests*

6 So ᴿthe LORD sent ᴿfiery serpents among the people, and they bit the people; and many of the people of Israel died.   1 Cor. 10:9 • Deut. 8:15

7 ᴿTherefore the people came to Moses, and said, "We have ᴿsinned, for we have spoken against the LORD and against you; ᴿpray to the LORD that He take away the serpents from us." So Moses prayed for the people.   Num. 11:2 • Lev. 26:40 • Ex. 8:8

8 Then the LORD said to Moses, ᴿ"Make a ᴿfiery *serpent*, and set it on a pole; and it shall be that everyone who is bitten, when he looks at it, shall live."   [John 3:14, 15] • Is. 14:29; 30:6

9 So ᴿMoses made a bronze serpent, and put it on a pole; and so it was, if a serpent had bitten anyone, when he looked at the bronze
▲ serpent, he lived.   John 3:14, 15

From Mount Hor to Moab

10 Now the children of Israel moved on and ᴿcamped in Oboth.   Num. 33:43, 44

11 And they journeyed from Oboth and camped at Ije Abarim, in the wilderness which *is* east of Moab, toward the sunrise.

12 ᴿFrom there they moved and camped in the Valley of Zered.   Deut. 2:13

13 From there they moved and camped on the other side of the Arnon, which *is* in the wilderness that extends from the border of the Amorites; for the Arnon *is* the border of Moab, between Moab and the Amorites.

14 Therefore it is said in the Book of the Wars of the LORD:

*"Waheb in Suphah,
    The brooks of the Arnon,
15 And the slope of the brooks
    That reaches to the dwelling of Ar,
    And lies on the border of Moab."

16 From there *they went* ᴿto Beer, which *is* the well where the LORD said to Moses, "Gather the people together, and I will give them water."   Judg. 9:21

17 ᴿThen Israel sang this song: Ex. 15:1

"Spring up, O well!
    All of you sing to it—
18 The well the leaders sank,
    Dug by the nation's nobles,
    By the lawgiver, with their staves."

And from the wilderness *they went* to Mattanah,
19 from Mattanah to Nahaliel, from Nahaliel to Bamoth,
20 and from Bamoth, *in* the valley that *is* in the country of Moab, to the top of Pisgah which looks down on *the wasteland.

21:14 Ancient unknown places; Vg. *What He did in the Red Sea*
21:20 Or *Jeshimon*

King Sihon Defeated

21 Then ᴿIsrael sent messengers to Sihon king of the Amorites, saying,   Deut. 2:26–37

22 ᴿ"Let me pass through your land. We will not turn aside into fields or vineyards; we will not drink water from wells. We will go by the King's Highway until we have passed through your territory."   Num. 20:16, 17

23 But Sihon would not allow Israel to pass through his territory. So Sihon gathered all his people together and ᵀwent out against Israel in the wilderness, and he came to Jahaz and fought against Israel.   *attacked*

24 Then ᴿIsrael defeated him with the edge of the sword, and took possession of his land from the Arnon to the Jabbok, as far as the people of Ammon; for the border of the people of Ammon *was* fortified.   Amos 2:9

25 So Israel took all these cities, and Israel ᴿdwelt in all the cities of the Amorites, in Heshbon and in all its villages.   Amos 2:10

26 For Heshbon *was* the city of Sihon king of the Amorites, who had fought against the former king of Moab, and had taken all his land from his hand as far as the Arnon.

27 Therefore those who speak in ᵀproverbs say: *parables*

"Come to Heshbon, let it be built;
    Let the city of Sihon be repaired.

28 "For fire went out from Heshbon,
    A flame from the city of Sihon;
    It consumed ᴿAr of Moab,   Is. 15:1
    The lords of the heights of the Arnon.

29 Woe to you, ᴿMoab!   Jer. 48:46
    You have perished, O people of
        ᴿChemosh!   Judg. 11:24
    He has given his sons as fugitives,
    And his ᴿdaughters into captivity,
    To Sihon king of the Amorites.   Is. 16:2

30 "But we have shot at them;
    Heshbon has perished as far as Dibon.
    Then we laid waste as far as Nophah,
    Which *reaches* to ᴿMedeba."   Is. 15:2

31 Thus Israel dwelt in the land of the Amorites.

32 Then Moses sent to spy out ᴿJazer; and they took its villages and drove out the Amorites who *were* there.   Jer. 48:32

King Og Defeated

33 ᴿAnd they turned and went up by the way to ᴿBashan. So Og king of Bashan went out against them, he and all his people, to battle ᴿat Edrei.   Deut. 29:7 • Deut. 3:1 • Josh. 13:12

34 Then the LORD said to Moses, "Do not fear him, for I have delivered him into your hand, with all his people and his land; and you shall do to him as you did to Sihon king of the Amorites, who dwelt at Heshbon."

35 So they defeated him, his sons, and all his people, until there was no survivor left him; and they took possession of his land.

Balak Sends for Balaam

22 Then the children of Israel moved, and camped in the plains of Moab on the side of the Jordan *across from* Jericho.

2 Now Balak the son of Zippor saw all that Israel had done to the Amorites.

3 And ᴿMoab was exceedingly afraid of the people because they *were* many, and Moab was sick with dread because of the children of Israel.   Ex. 15:15

4 So Moab said to the elders of Midian, "Now this company will ᵀlick up everything around us, as an ox licks up the grass of the field." And Balak the son of Zippor *was* king of the Moabites at that time.   *consume*

5 Then he sent messengers to Balaam the son of Beor at ᴿPethor, which *is* near *the River in the land of *the sons of his people, to call him, saying: "Look, a people has come from Egypt. See, they cover the face of the earth, and are settling next to me!   Deut. 23:4

6 "Therefore please come at once, ᴿcurse this people for me, for they *are* too mighty for me. Perhaps I shall be able to defeat them and drive them out of the land, for I know that he whom you bless *is* blessed, and he whom you curse is cursed."   Num. 22:12; 24:9

7 So the elders of Moab and the elders of Midian departed with ᴿthe diviner's fee in their hand, and they came to Balaam and spoke to him the words of Balak.   1 Sam. 9:7, 8

8 And he said to them, ᴿ"Lodge here tonight, and I will bring back word to you, as the Lᴏʀᴅ speaks to me." So the princes of Moab stayed with Balaam.   Num. 22:19

9 ᴿThen God came to Balaam and said, "Who *are* these men with you?"   Gen. 20:3

10 So Balaam said to God, "Balak the son of Zippor, king of Moab, has sent to me, *saying,*

11 'Look, a people has come out of Egypt, and they cover the face of the earth. Come now, curse them for me; perhaps I shall be able to overpower them and drive them out.' "

12 And God said to Balaam, "You shall not go with them; you shall not curse the people, for ᴿthey *are* blessed."   [Rom. 11:28]

13 So Balaam rose in the morning and said to the princes of Balak, "Go back to your land, for the Lᴏʀᴅ has refused to give me permission to go with you."

14 And the princes of Moab rose and went to Balak, and said, "Balaam refuses to come with us."

15 Then Balak again sent princes, more numerous and more honorable than they.

16 And they came to Balaam and said to him, "Thus says Balak the son of Zippor: 'Please let nothing hinder you from coming to me;

17 'for I will certainly honor you greatly, and I will do whatever you say to me. Therefore please come, curse this people for me.' "

18 Then Balaam answered and said to the servants of Balak, "Though Balak were to give me his house full of silver and gold, ᴿI could not go beyond the word of the Lᴏʀᴅ my God, to do less or more.   1 Kin. 22:14

19 "Now therefore, please, you also ᴿstay here tonight, that I may know what more the Lᴏʀᴅ will say to me."   Num. 22:8

20 ᴿAnd God came to Balaam at night and said to him, "If the men come to call you, rise *and* go with them; but only the word which I speak to you—that you shall do."   Num. 22:9

21 So Balaam rose in the morning, saddled his donkey, and went with the princes of Moab.

Balaam, the Donkey, and the Angel

22 Then God's anger was aroused because he went, ᴿand the Angel of the Lᴏʀᴅ took His stand in the way as an adversary against him. And he was riding on his donkey, and his two servants *were* with him.   Ex. 4:24

23 Now ᴿthe donkey saw the Angel of the Lᴏʀᴅ standing in the way with His drawn sword in His hand, and the donkey turned aside out of the way and went into the field. So Balaam struck the donkey to turn her back onto the road.   Josh. 5:13

24 Then the Angel of the Lᴏʀᴅ stood in a narrow path between the vineyards, *with* a wall on this side and a wall on that side.

25 And when the donkey saw the Angel of the Lᴏʀᴅ, she pushed herself against the wall and crushed Balaam's foot against the wall; so he struck her again.

26 Then the Angel of the Lᴏʀᴅ went further, and stood in a narrow place where there *was* no way to turn either to the right hand or to the left.

27 And when the donkey saw the Angel of the Lᴏʀᴅ, she lay down under Balaam; so Balaam's anger was aroused, and he struck the donkey with his staff.

28 Then the Lᴏʀᴅ ᴿopened the mouth of the donkey, and she said to Balaam, "What have I done to you, that you have struck me these three times?"   2 Pet. 2:16

29 And Balaam said to the donkey, "Because you have ᵀabused me. I wish there were a sword in my hand, ᴿfor now I would kill you!"   *mocked* • [Prov. 12:10]

30 ᴿSo the donkey said to Balaam, "Am I not your donkey on which you have ridden, ever since *I became* yours, to this day? Was I ever ᵀdisposed to do this to you?" And he said, "No."   2 Pet. 2:16 • *accustomed*

31 Then the Lᴏʀᴅ ᴿopened Balaam's eyes, and he saw the Angel of the Lᴏʀᴅ standing in the way with His drawn sword in His hand; and he bowed his head and fell flat on his face.   Gen. 21:19

32 And the Angel of the LORD said to him, "Why have you struck your donkey these three times? Behold, I have come out ᵀto stand against you, because *your* way is ᵀperverse before Me.   *as an adversary · contrary*

33 "The donkey saw Me and turned aside from Me these three times. If she had not turned aside from Me, surely I would also have killed you by now, and let her live."

34 And Balaam said to the Angel of the LORD, "I have sinned, for I did not know You stood in the way against me. Now therefore, if it displeases You, I will turn back."

35 Then the Angel of the LORD said to Balaam, "Go with the men, ᴿbut only the word that I speak to you, that you shall speak." So Balaam went with the princes of Balak.   Num. 22:20

36 Now when Balak heard that Balaam was coming, he went out to meet him at the city of Moab, which *is* on the border at the Arnon, the boundary of the territory.

37 Then Balak said to Balaam, "Did I not earnestly send to you, calling for you? Why did you not come to me? Am I not able ᴿto honor you?"   Num. 22:17; 24:11

38 And Balaam said to Balak, "Look, I have come to you! Now, have I any power at all to say anything? ᴿThe word that God puts in my mouth, that I must speak."   1 Kin. 22:14

39 So Balaam went with Balak, and they came to Kirjath Huzoth.

40 Then Balak offered oxen and sheep, and he sent *some* to Balaam and to the princes who *were* with him.

Balaam's First Prophecy

41 So it was, the next day, that Balak took Balaam and brought him up to the ᴿhigh places of Baal, that from there he might observe the extent of the people.   Num. 21:28

23 Then Balaam said to Balak, "Build seven altars for me here, and prepare for me here seven bulls and seven rams."

2 And Balak did just as Balaam had spoken, and Balak and Balaam ᴿoffered a bull and a ram on *each* altar.   Num. 23:14, 30

3 Then Balaam said to Balak, ᴿ"Stand by your burnt offering, and I will go; perhaps the LORD will come ᴿto meet me, and whatever He shows me I will tell you." So he went to a desolate height.   Num. 23:15 · Num. 23:4, 16

4 And God met Balaam, and he said to Him, "I have prepared the seven altars, and I have offered on *each* altar a bull and a ram."

5 Then the LORD ᴿput a word in Balaam's mouth, and said, "Return to Balak, and thus you shall speak."   Deut. 18:18

6 So he returned to him, and there he was, standing by his burnt offering, he and all the princes of Moab.

7 And he ᴿtook up his ᵀoracle and said:

"Balak the king of Moab has brought me
  from Aram,   Deut. 23:4 · *prophetic discourse*
From the mountains of the east.
ᴿ'Come, curse Jacob for me,   Num. 22:6, 11, 17
  And come, ᴿdenounce Israel!'   1 Sam. 17:10

8 "Howᴿ shall I curse whom God has not
  cursed?   Num. 22:12
And how shall I denounce *whom* the
  LORD has not denounced?

9 For from the top of the rocks I see him,
  And from the hills I behold him;
There! A people dwelling alone,
  Not reckoning itself among the nations.

10 "Who can count the ᵀdust of Jacob,
  Or number one-fourth of Israel?
Let me die the death of the righteous,
  And let my end be like his!"   Or *dust cloud*

11 Then Balak said to Balaam, "What have you done to me? ᴿI took you to curse my enemies, and look, you have blessed *them* bountifully!"   Num. 22:11

12 So he answered and said, ᴿ"Must I not take heed to speak what the LORD has put in my mouth?"   Num. 22:38

Balaam's Second Prophecy

13 Then Balak said to him, "Please come with me to another place from which you may see them; you shall see only the outer part of them, and shall not see them all; curse them for me from there."

14 So he brought him to the field of Zophim, to the top of Pisgah, and built seven altars, and offered a bull and a ram on *each* altar.

15 And he said to Balak, "Stand here by your burnt offering while I *meet the LORD over there."

16 Then the LORD met Balaam, and put a word in his mouth, and said, "Go back to Balak, and thus you shall speak."

17 So he came to him, and there he was, standing by his burnt offering, and the princes of Moab were with him. And Balak said to him, "What has the LORD spoken?"

18 Then he took up his oracle and said:

ᴿ"Rise up, Balak, and hear!
  Listen to me, son of Zippor!   Judg. 3:20

3–D. God Is Immutable   ▼

19 "Godᴿ *is* not a man, that He should lie,
  Nor a son of man, that He should
  repent.   Mal. 3:6

23:15 So with MT, Tg., Vg.; Syr. *call;* LXX *go and ask God*

3–D. God Is Immutable (Numbers 23:19)—"God is not a man, that He should lie, nor a son of man, that He should repent," i.e., change His mind. Indeed, He does not change at all. Immutability—the quality of never changing or being changed—is one of His attributes that relates to all others. The attributes of God are

(Point 3-D continued on next page)

▽ Has He Rsaid, and will He not do?
  Or has He spoken, and will He not
▲   make it good?   1 Kin. 8:56
20 Behold, I have received a command to
   bless;
   He has blessed, and I cannot reverse it.

21 "He has not observed iniquity in Jacob,
   Nor has He seen wickedness in Israel.
   The LORD his God is with him,
   And the shout of a King is among
   them.
22 God brings them out of Egypt;
   He has strength like a wild ox.

23 "For there is no sorcery against Jacob,
   Nor any divination against Israel.
   It now must be said of Jacob

And of Israel, 'Oh, Rwhat God has
   done!'   Ps. 31:19; 44:1
24 Look, a people rises Rlike a lioness,
   And lifts itself up like a lion;
   RIt shall not lie down until it devours the
   prey,   Gen. 49:9 · Gen. 49:27
   And drinks the blood of the slain."

25 Then Balak said to Balaam, "Neither
curse them at all, nor bless them at all!"
26 So Balaam answered and said to Balak,
"Did I not tell you, saying, R'All that the LORD
speaks, that I must do'?"   Num. 22:38

Balaam's Third Prophecy

27 Then Balak said to Balaam, "Please
come, I will take you to another place; per-

(Point 3-D continued from previous page)
characteristics that cannot be attributed to anyone but Jehovah God. They are fundamental powers or
qualities of His eternal being, and because He is immutable, they are always fact. "For I am the LORD
[Jehovah], I do not change" (Mal. 3:6, page 924). Our God is unchangingly

(1) *Omnipotent* (almighty). He has all power in heaven and earth. "Alleluia! For the Lord [Jehovah] God
Omnipotent reigns!" (Rev. 19:6, page 1312). He has all power over all His universe. Jesus said, "With God all
things are possible" (Matt. 19:26, page 966).

(2) *Omniscient* (all-knowing). "His understanding is infinite" (Ps. 147:5, page 594). His knowledge is
perfect (Job 37:16, page 503). He knows every word spoken by man (Ps. 139:4, page 590). He knows all our
thoughts (Ps. 139:2, page 590). He knows all His works from the beginning of the world (Acts 15:18, page
1109). God knows from eternity to eternity. He knows every minute detail of all things. There are no
surprises to our God, who is perfect in knowledge.

(3) *Omnipresent* (everywhere present at the same time). "Where can I go from Your Spirit? Or where
can I flee from Your presence? If I ascend into heaven, You are there; if I make my bed in hell, behold, You
are there. If I take the wings of the morning, and dwell in the uttermost parts of the sea, even there Your
hand shall lead me, and Your right hand shall hold me" (Ps. 139:7–10, page 590). He is omnipresent in His
vision. "'Can anyone hide himself in secret places, so I shall not see him?' says the LORD; 'Do I not fill
heaven and earth?' says the LORD" (Jer. 23:23, 24, page 737).

God is everywhere present in His universe, but He does not "indwell" material things; for if He did, we
could worship sticks, stones, or any man-made idol. Jesus said, "God is Spirit, and those who worship Him
must worship in spirit and truth" (John 4:24, page 1054). God gave Moses the commandments, saying, "I am
the LORD your God, who brought you out of the land of Egypt, out of the house of bondage. You shall have
no other gods before Me. You shall not make for yourself a carved image—any likeness of anything that is
in heaven above, or that is in the earth beneath, or that is in the water under the earth; you shall not bow
down to them nor serve them. For I, the LORD your God, am a jealous God, visiting the iniquity of the fathers
upon the children to the third and fourth generations of those who hate Me, but showing mercy to
thousands, to those who love Me and keep My commandments" (Ex. 20:2–6, page 79).

(4) *Holy.* God is absolutely pure, undefiled, and undefilable. He is eternally free from all impurities (Lev.
11:43–45, page 117). His holiness demands separation from sinners. "Your iniquities have separated you
from your God; and your sins have hidden His face from you, so that He will not hear" (Is. 59:1, 2, page 698).
But "there is one God and one Mediator between God [the Father] and men, the Man Christ Jesus" (1 Tim.
2:5, 6, page 1219). Christ is the mediator of the new covenant (Heb. 8:8, page 1243), which is better than all
previous covenants:

(a) The Edenic covenant (Gen. 2:16, page 5)
(b) The Adamic covenant (Gen. 3:15, page 7)
(c) The Noahic covenant (Gen. 9:16, page 15)
(d) The Abrahamic covenant (Gen. 12:2, page 17)
(e) The Mosaic covenant (Ex. 19:5, page 79)
(f) The Palestinian covenant (Deut. 30:3, page 208)
(g) The Davidic covenant (2 Sam. 7:16, page 305)

This new covenant is better because it is sealed by the blood of the holy mediator, the God-Man, Jesus
Christ, who mediates the eternal rights of all believers who have, by faith, "washed their robes and made
them white in the blood of the Lamb" (Rev. 7:13, 14, page 1301).
See Psalm 102:24–27, page 569, for **Point 3-E: God Is Eternal.**

haps it will please God that you may curse them for me from there."

28 So Balak took Balaam to the top of Peor, that overlooks ᵀthe wasteland. Or *Jeshimon*

29 Then Balaam said to Balak, "Build for me here seven altars, and prepare for me here seven bulls and seven rams."

30 And Balak did as Balaam had said, and offered a bull and a ram on *every* altar.

24 Now when Balaam saw that it pleased the LORD to bless Israel, he did not go as at other times, to seek to use sorcery, but he set his face toward the wilderness.

2 And Balaam raised his eyes, and saw Israel encamped according to their tribes; and the Spirit of God came upon him.

3 ᴿThen he took up his oracle and said:

"The utterance of Balaam the son of
        Beor,
    The utterance of the man whose eyes
        are opened,   Num. 23:7, 18
4   The utterance of him who hears the
        words of God,
    Who sees the vision of the Almighty,
    Who falls down, with eyes wide open:

5 "How lovely are your tents, O Jacob!
        Your dwellings, O Israel!
6   Like valleys that stretch out,
    Like gardens by the riverside,
    Like aloes planted by the LORD,
    Like cedars beside the waters.
7   He shall pour water from his buckets,
    And his seed *shall be* in many waters.

   "His king shall be higher than Agag,
    And his kingdom shall be exalted.

8 "Godᴿ brings him out of Egypt;
    He has strength like a wild ox;
    He shall ᴿconsume the nations, his
        enemies;   Num. 23:22 • Num. 14:9; 23:24
    He shall ᴿbreak their bones   Ps. 2:9
    And pierce *them* with his arrows.
9 'He* bows down, he lies down as a lion;
    And as a lion, who will rouse him?'

   "Blessed *is* he who blesses you,
    And cursed *is* he who curses you."

10 Then Balak's anger was aroused against Balaam, and he struck his hands together; and Balak said to Balaam, "I called you to curse my enemies, and look, you have bountifully blessed *them* these three times!

11 "Now therefore, flee to your place. I said I would greatly honor you, but in fact, the LORD has kept you back from honor."

12 So Balaam said to Balak, "Did I not also speak to your messengers whom you sent to me, saying,

13 'If Balak were to give me his house full of silver and gold, I could not go beyond the word of the LORD, to do good or bad of my

own will. What the LORD says, that I must speak'?

14 "And now, indeed, I am going to my people. Come, ᴿI will advise you what this people will do to your people in the ᴿlatter days."   [Mic. 6:5] • Gen. 49:1

Balaam's Fourth Prophecy

15 So he took up his oracle and said:

"The utterance of Balaam the son of
        Beor,
    And the utterance of the man whose
        eyes are opened;
16 The utterance of him who hears the
        words of God,
    And has the knowledge of the Most
        High,
    Who sees the vision of the Almighty,
    Who falls down, with eyes wide open:

17 "I see Him, but not now;
    I behold Him, but not near;
    ᴿA Star shall come out of Jacob,   Matt. 1:2
    A Scepter shall rise out of Israel,
    And batter the brow of Moab,
    And destroy all the sons of *tumult.
18 "And ᴿEdom shall be a possession;
    Seir also, his enemies, shall be a
        possession,   2 Sam. 8:14
    While Israel does ᵀvaliantly.   *mightily*
19 Out of Jacob One shall have dominion,
    And destroy the remains of the city."

20 Then he looked on Amalek, and he took up his oracle and said:

"Amalek *was* first among the nations,
    But *shall be* last until he perishes."

21 Then he looked on the Kenites, and he took up his oracle and said:

"Firm is your dwelling place,
    And your nest is set in the rock;
22 Nevertheless Kain shall be burned.
    How long until Asshur carries you
        away captive?"

23 Then he took up his oracle and said:

"Alas! Who shall live when God does
        this?
24 But ships *shall come* from the coasts of
        ᴿCyprus,ᵀ   Gen. 10:4 • Heb. *Kittim*
    And they shall afflict Asshur and afflict
        ᴿEber,   Gen. 10:21, 25
    And so shall ᵀAmalek, until he
        perishes."   Lit. *he* or *that one*

25 So Balaam rose and departed and returned to his place; Balak also went his way.

Israel's Harlotry in Moab

25 Now Israel remained in ᵀAcacia Grove, and the people began to commit harlotry with the women of Moab.   Heb. *Shittim*

2 They invited the people to ᴿthe sacrifices of their gods, and the people ate and ᴿbowed down to their gods.   Ex. 34:15 • Ex. 20:5

3 So Israel was joined to Baal of Peor, and ᴿthe anger of the Lᴏʀᴅ was aroused against Israel.   Ps. 106:28, 29

4 Then the Lᴏʀᴅ said to Moses, ᴿ"Take all the leaders of the people and hang the offenders before the Lᴏʀᴅ, out in the sun, ᴿthat the fierce anger of the Lᴏʀᴅ may turn away from Israel."   Deut. 4:3 • Num. 25:11

5 So Moses said to ᴿthe judges of Israel, ᴿ"Every one of you kill his men who were joined to Baal of Peor."   Ex. 18:21 • Deut. 13:6, 9

6 And indeed, one of the children of Israel came and presented to his brethren a Midianite woman in the sight of Moses and in the sight of all the congregation of the children of Israel, ᴿwho *were* weeping at the door of the tabernacle of meeting.   Joel 2:17

7 Now ᴿwhen Phinehas ᴿthe son of Eleazar, the son of Aaron the priest, saw *it*, he rose from among the congregation and took a javelin in his hand;   Ps. 106:30 • Ex. 6:25

8 and he went after the man of Israel into the tent and thrust both of them through, the man of Israel, and the woman through her body. So ᴿthe plague was ᴿstopped among the children of Israel.   Ps. 106:30 • Num. 16:46–48

9 And ᴿthose who died in the plague were twenty-four thousand.   Deut. 4:3

10 Then the Lᴏʀᴅ spoke to Moses, saying:

11 ᴿ"Phinehas the son of Eleazar, the son of Aaron the priest, has turned back My wrath from the children of Israel, because he was zealous with My zeal among them, so that I did not consume the children of Israel in ᴿMy zeal.   Ps. 106:30 • [Ex. 20:5]

12 "Therefore say, ᴿ'Behold, I give to him My ᴿcovenant of peace;   [Mal. 2:4, 5; 3:1] • Is. 54:10

13 'and it shall be to him and his descendants after him a covenant of ᴿan everlasting priesthood, because he was ᴿzealous for his God, and ᴿmade atonement for the children of Israel.' "   Ex. 40:15 • Acts 22:3 • [Heb. 2:17]

14 Now the name of the Israelite who was killed, who was killed with the Midianite woman, *was* Zimri the son of Salu, a leader of a father's house among the Simeonites.

15 And the name of the Midianite woman who was killed *was* Cozbi the daughter of ᴿZur; he *was* head of the people of a father's house in Midian.   Num. 31:8

16 Then the Lᴏʀᴅ spoke to Moses, saying:

17 ᴿ"Harass the Midianites, and ᵀattack them;   Num. 31:1-3 • *be hostile toward*

18 "for they harassed you with their ᴿschemesᵀ by which they seduced you in the matter of Peor and in the matter of Cozbi, the daughter of a leader of Midian, their sister, who was killed in the day of the plague because of Peor."   Rev. 2:14 • *tricks*

The Second Census of Israel

26 And it came to pass, after the plague, that the Lᴏʀᴅ spoke to Moses and Eleazar the son of Aaron the priest, saying:

2 "Take a census of all the congregation of the children of Israel from twenty years old and above, by their fathers' houses, all who are able to go to war in Israel."

3 So Moses and Eleazar the priest spoke with them in the plains of Moab by the Jordan, *across from* Jericho, saying:

4 *"Take a census of the people* from twenty years old and above, just as the Lᴏʀᴅ ᴿcommanded Moses and the children of Israel who came out of the land of Egypt."   Num. 1:1

5 ᴿReuben *was* the firstborn of Israel. The children of Reuben *were*: *of* Hanoch, the family of the Hanochites; *of* Pallu, the family of the Palluites;   Ex. 6:14

6 *of* Hezron, the family of the Hezronites; *of* Carmi, the family of the Carmites.

7 These *are* the families of the Reubenites: those who were numbered of them were forty-three thousand seven hundred and thirty.

8 And the son of Pallu *was* Eliab.

9 The sons of Eliab *were* Nemuel, Dathan, and Abiram. These *are* the Dathan and Abiram, ᴿrepresentatives of the congregation, who contended against Moses and Aaron in the company of Korah, when they contended against the Lᴏʀᴅ;   Num. 1:16; 16:1, 2

10 ᴿand the earth opened its mouth and swallowed them up together with Korah when that company died, when the fire devoured two hundred and fifty men; ᴿand they became a sign.   Num. 16:32-35 • Num. 16:38-40

11 Nevertheless ᴿthe children of Korah did not die.   Ex. 6:24

12 The sons of Simeon according to their families *were*: *of* Nemuel, the family of the Nemuelites; *of* ᵀJamin, the family of the Jaminites; *of* ᵀJachin, the family of the Jachinites;   *Jemuel*, Gen. 46:10; Ex. 6:15 • *Jarib*, 1 Chr. 4:24

13 *of* *Zerah, the family of the Zarhites; *of* Shaul, the family of the Shaulites;

14 These *are* the families of the Simeonites: twenty-two thousand two hundred.

15 The sons of Gad according to their families *were*: *of* *Zephon, the family of the Zephonites; *of* Haggi, the family of the Haggites; *of* Shuni, the family of the Shunites;

16 *of* ᵀOzni, the family of the Oznites; *of* Eri, the family of the Erites;   *Ezbon*, Gen. 46:16

17 *of* *Arod, the family of the Arodites; *of* Areli, the family of the Arelites.

18 These *are* the families of the sons of Gad according to those who were numbered of them: forty thousand five hundred.

26:13 *Zohar*, Gen. 46:10
26:15 *Ziphion*, Gen. 46:16
26:17 Sam., Syr. *Arodi* and Gen. 46:16

19 The sons of Judah were Er and Onan; and Er and Onan died in the land of Canaan.

20 And the sons of Judah according to their families were: of Shelah, the family of the Shelanites; of Perez, the family of the Parzites; of Zerah, the family of the Zarhites.

21 And the sons of Perez were: of Hezron, the family of the Hezronites; of Hamul, the family of the Hamulites.

22 These are the families of Judah according to those who were numbered of them: seventy-six thousand five hundred.

23 The sons of Issachar according to their families were: of Tola, the family of the Tolaites; of *Puah, the family of the *Punites;

24 of Jashub, the family of the Jashubites; of Shimron, the family of the Shimronites.

25 These are the families of Issachar according to those who were numbered of them: sixty-four thousand three hundred.

26 The sons of Zebulun according to their families were: of Sered, the family of the Sardites; of Elon, the family of the Elonites; of Jahleel, the family of the Jahleelites.

27 These are the families of the Zebulunites according to those who were numbered of them: sixty thousand five hundred.

28 The sons of Joseph according to their families, by Manasseh and Ephraim, were:

29 The sons of Manasseh: of Machir, the family of the Machirites; and Machir begot Gilead; of Gilead, the family of the Gileadites.

30 These are the sons of Gilead: of ᵀJeezer, the family of the Jeezerites; of Helek, the family of the Helekites;   Abiezer, Josh. 17:2

31 of Asriel, the family of the Asrielites; of Shechem, the family of the Shechemites;

32 of Shemida, the family of the Shemidaites; of Hepher, the family of the Hepherites.

33 Now Zelophehad the son of Hepher had no sons, but daughters; and the names of the daughters of Zelophehad were Mahlah, Noah, Hoglah, Milcah, and Tirzah.

34 These are the families of Manasseh; and those who were numbered of them were fifty-two thousand seven hundred.

35 These are the sons of Ephraim according to their families: of Shuthelah, the family of the Shuthalhites; of ᵀBecher, the family of the Bachrites; of Tahan, the family of the Tahanites.   Bered, 1 Chr. 7:20

36 And these are the sons of Shuthelah: of Eran, the family of the Eranites.

37 These are the families of the sons of Ephraim according to those who were numbered of them: thirty-two thousand five hundred. These are the sons of Joseph according to their families.

38 The sons of Benjamin according to their families were: of Bela, the family of the

Belaites; of Ashbel, the family of the Ashbelites; of Ahiram, the family of the Ahiramites;

39 of ᴿShupham,* the family of the Shuphamites; of *Hupham, the family of the Huphamites.   1 Chr. 7:12

40 And the sons of Bela were *Ard and Naaman: of Ard, the family of the Ardites; of Naaman, the family of the Naamites.

41 These are the sons of Benjamin according to their families; and those who were numbered of them were forty-five thousand six hundred.

42 These are the sons of Dan according to their families: of ᵀShuham, the family of the Shuhamites. These are the families of Dan according to their families.   Hushim, Gen. 46:23

43 All the families of the Shuhamites, according to those who were numbered of them, were sixty-four thousand four hundred.

44 ᴿThe sons of Asher according to their families were: of Jimna, the family of the Jimnites; of Jesui, the family of the Jesuites; of Beriah, the family of the Beriites.   Gen. 46:17

45 Of the sons of Beriah: of Heber, the family of the Heberites; of Malchiel, the family of the Malchielites.

46 And the name of the daughter of Asher was Serah.

47 These are the families of the sons of Asher according to those who were numbered of them: fifty-three thousand four hundred.

48 ᴿThe sons of Naphtali according to their families were: of *Jahzeel, the family of the Jahzeelites; of Guni, the family of the Gunites;   1 Chr. 7:13

49 of Jezer, the family of the Jezerites; of Shillem, the family of the Shillemites.

50 These are the families of Naphtali according to their families; and those who were numbered of them were forty-five thousand four hundred.

51 These are those who were numbered of the children of Israel: six hundred and one thousand seven hundred and thirty.

52 Then the LORD spoke to Moses, saying:

53 ᴿ"To these the land shall be ᴿdivided as an inheritance, according to the number of names.   Josh. 11:23; 14:1 • Num. 33:54

54 ᴿ"To a large tribe you shall give a larger inheritance, and to a small tribe you shall give a smaller inheritance. Each shall be given its inheritance according to those who were numbered of them.   Num. 33:54

55 "But the land shall be ᴿdivided by lot; they shall inherit according to the names of the tribes of their fathers.   Num. 33:54; 54:13

26:23 So with Sam., LXX, Syr., Vg.; Heb. *Puvah*, Gen. 46:13; 1 Chr. 7:1 • Sam., LXX, Syr., Vg. *Puaites*

26:39 MT *Shephupham; Shephuphan*, 1 Chr. 8:5
• *Huppim*, Gen. 46:21
26:40 *Addar*, 1 Chr. 8:3
26:48 *Jahziel*, 1 Chr. 7:13

56 "According to the lot their inheritance shall be divided between the larger and the smaller."

57 And these *are* those who were numbered of the Levites according to their families: of Gershon, the family of the Gershonites; of Kohath, the family of the Kohathites; of Merari, the family of the Merarites.

58 These *are* the families of the Levites: the family of the Libnites, the family of the Hebronites, the family of the Mahlites, the family of the Mushites, and the family of the Korathites. And Kohath begot Amram.

59 The name of Amram's wife *was* Jochebed the daughter of Levi, who was born to Levi in Egypt; and to Amram she bore Aaron and Moses and their sister Miriam.

60 ᴿTo Aaron were born Nadab and Abihu, Eleazar and Ithamar.   Num. 3:2

61 And Nadab and Abihu died when they offered profane fire before the LORD.

62 Now those who were numbered of them were twenty-three thousand, every male from a month old and above; for they were not numbered among the other children of Israel, because there was no inheritance given to them among the children of Israel.

63 These *are* those who were numbered by Moses and Eleazar the priest, who numbered the children of Israel ᴿin the plains of Moab by the Jordan, *across from* Jericho.   Num. 26:3

64 But among these there was not a man of those who were numbered by Moses and Aaron the priest when they numbered the children of Israel in the Wilderness of Sinai.

65 For the LORD had said of them, "They shall surely die in the wilderness." So there was not left a man of them, except Caleb the son of Jephunneh and Joshua the son of Nun.

Inheritance Laws

27 Then came the daughters of Zelophehad the son of Hepher, the son of Gilead, the son of Machir, the son of Manasseh, from the families of Manasseh the son of Joseph; and these *were* the names of his daughters: Mahlah, Noah, Hoglah, Milcah, and Tirzah.

2 And they stood before Moses, before Eleazar the priest, and before the leaders and all the congregation, *by* the doorway of the tabernacle of meeting, saying:

3 "Our father died in the wilderness; but he was not in the company of those who gathered together against the LORD, ᴿin company with Korah, but he died in his own sin; and he had no sons.   Num. 16:1, 2

4 "Why should the name of our father be removed from among his family because he had no son? Give us a ᵀpossession among our father's brothers."   *inheritance*

5 So Moses ᴿbrought their case before the LORD.   Ex. 18:13–26

6 And the LORD spoke to Moses, saying:

7 "The daughters of Zelophehad speak *what is* right; ᴿyou shall surely give them a possession of inheritance among their father's brothers, and cause the inheritance of their father to pass to them.   Num. 36:2

8 "And you shall speak to the children of Israel, saying: 'If a man dies and has no son, then you shall cause his inheritance to pass to his daughter.

9 'If he has no daughter, then you shall give his inheritance to his brothers.

10 'If he has no brothers, then you shall give his inheritance to his father's brothers.

11 'And if his father has no brothers, then you shall give his inheritance to the relative closest to him in his family, and he shall possess it.' " And it shall be to the children of Israel ᴿa statute of judgment, just as the LORD commanded Moses.   Num. 35:29

Joshua the Next Leader of Israel

31-F. A Prayer for a Successor   ▼

12 Now the LORD said to Moses: "Go up into this Mount Abarim, and see the land which I have given to the children of Israel.

13 "And when you have seen it, you also

31-F. A Prayer for a Successor (Numbers 27:12-19)—After leading the children of Israel out of Egypt, and then for forty years in their wilderness wanderings, the time came for Moses to die (be "gathered to [his] people") (v. 13). After Moses viewed the Promised Land, looking westward from the summit of Mt. Nebo (v. 12; cf. Deut. 34:1, page 213), he prayed one of his final prayers to God (vv. 15–17). He prayed for a successor.

There are many lessons that we can learn from this prayer and from the situation which occasioned it. Among these let us realize that:

(1) In this life the time comes when even the greatest leaders must pass from the scene (Josh. 1:1–9, page 215).

(2) In searching for a new leader, we must seek the one whom God appoints (v. 16), one "in whom is the Spirit" of God (v. 18; cf. Acts 13:1–3, page 1105).

(3) It is best that the new leader be appointed promptly, so that "the congregation of the LORD may not be like sheep which have no shepherd" (v. 17; cf. Ezek. 34:8–12, page 813).

(4) Truly great leaders seek an able replacement. They do not resent the new leader in sinful jealousy (vv. 18, 19).

(Point 31-F continued on next page)

▽ ᴿshall be gathered to your people, as Aaron your brother was gathered.   Deut. 10:6; 34:5, 6

14 "For in the Wilderness of Zin, during the strife of the congregation, you ᴿrebelled against My command to hallow Me at the waters before their eyes." (These *are* the ᴿwaters of Meribah, at Kadesh in the Wilderness of Zin.)   Ps. 106:32, 33 • Ex. 17:7

15 Then Moses spoke to the LORD, saying:

16 "Let the LORD, the God of the spirits of all flesh, set a man over the congregation,

17 ᴿ"who may go out before them and go in before them, who may lead them out and bring them in, that the congregation of the LORD may not be ᴿlike sheep which have no shepherd."   Deut. 31:2 • Zech. 10:2

18 And the LORD said to Moses: "Take Joshua the son of Nun with you, a man ᴿin whom *is* the Spirit, and ᴿlay your hand on him;   Gen. 41:38 • Deut. 34:9

19 "set him before Eleazar the priest and before all the congregation, and ᴿinaugurateᵀ

▲ him in their sight.   Deut. 31:3, 7, 8, 23 • *commission*

20 "And you shall give *some* of your authority to him, that all the congregation of the children of Israel may be obedient.

21 "He shall stand before Eleazar the priest, who shall inquire before the LORD for him by the judgment of the Urim; at his word they shall go out, and at his word they shall come in, *both* he and all the children of Israel with him, all the congregation."

22 So Moses did as the LORD commanded him. He took Joshua and set him before Eleazar the priest and before all the congregation.

23 And he laid his hands on him ᴿand ᵀinaugurated him, just as the LORD commanded by the hand of Moses.   Deut. 3:28; 31:7, 8 • *commissioned*

Daily Offerings

28 Now the LORD spoke to Moses, saying, 2 "Command the children of Israel, and say to them, 'My offering, ᴿMy food for My offerings made by fire as a sweet aroma to Me, you shall be careful to offer to Me at their appointed time.'   Lev. 3:11; 21:6, 8

3 "And you shall say to them, ᴿThis *is* the offering made by fire which you shall offer to the LORD: two male lambs in their first year without blemish, day by day, as a regular burnt offering.   Ex. 29:38-42

4 'The one lamb you shall offer in the morning, the other lamb you shall offer in the evening,

5 'and ᴿone-tenthᵀ of an ephah of fine flour as a ᴿgrain offering mixed with one-fourth of a hin of pressed oil.   Ex. 16:36 • 2.1 qt. • Lev. 2:1

6 'It is ᴿa regular burnt offering which was ordained at Mount Sinai for a sweet aroma, an offering made by fire to the LORD.   Ex. 29:42

7 'And its drink offering *shall be* ᵀone-fourth of a hin for each lamb; ᴿin a holy *place* you shall pour out the drink to the LORD as an offering.   1 qt. • Ex. 29:42

8 'The other lamb you shall offer in the evening; as the morning grain offering and its drink offering, you shall offer *it* as an offering made by fire, a sweet aroma to the LORD.

Sabbath Offerings

9 'And on the Sabbath day two lambs in their first year, without blemish, and two-tenths *of an ephah* of fine flour as a grain offering, mixed with oil, with its drink offering—

10 '*this is* ᴿthe burnt offering for every Sabbath, besides the regular burnt offering with its drink offering.   Ezek. 46:4

Monthly Offerings

11 ᴿ'At the beginnings of your months you shall present a burnt offering to the LORD: two young bulls, one ram, and seven lambs in their first year, without blemish;   Num. 10:10

12 ᴿ'three-tenths *of an ephah* of fine flour as a grain offering, mixed with oil, for each bull; two-tenths *of an ephah* of fine flour as a

---

(Point 31-F continued from previous page)

(5) There are great advantages in having a successor who, like Joshua, has had significant previous leadership experience, especially with the same people. Joshua (Oshea) was the chosen scout from the tribe of Ephraim (Num. 13:8, page 152). He was Moses' assistant and general of the army (Ex. 17:8-10, page 77).

(6) No matter how people say it will work out, it is nearly impossible for the new leader to be effective while the former leader is still present. For example, in God's providence Moses was gone when Joshua took command.

(7) Selecting a disagreeable or demanding leader always leads to trouble (1 Tim. 3:1-7, page 1219). Joshua's loyalty to Moses was a bright star amid a murmuring, complaining nation.

(8) It is proper that the new leader be installed with a fitting ceremony (vv. 18-23; cf. 2 Tim. 4:1-5, page 1228).

(9) God selects different men for different times and needs. With the passing of Moses, God commissioned Joshua for the next phase of the journey. Joshua's responsibility was to follow "the LORD [Jehovah] your God" (Josh. 1:6-9, page 215), not to become a carbon copy of Moses.

The prayer of Moses in the twilight of his life found its answer in God's appointment of Joshua. The work would go on.

See Index, page 17, for your next study.

grain offering, mixed with oil, for the one ram;   Num. 15:4–12

13 'and ᵀone-tenth *of an ephah* of fine flour, mixed with oil, as a grain offering for each lamb, as a burnt offering of sweet aroma, an offering made by fire to the LORD.   2.087 qt.

14 'Their drink offering shall be ᵀhalf a hin of wine for a bull, ᵀone-third of a hin for a ram, and one-fourth of a hin for a lamb; this *is* the burnt offering for each month throughout the months of the year.   .5 gal · 42.7 oz.

15 'Also ᴿone kid of the goats as a sin offering to the LORD shall be offered, besides the regular burnt offering and its drink offering.   Num. 15:24; 28:3, 22

Offerings at Passover

16 ᴿ'On the fourteenth day of the first month is the Passover of the LORD. Lev. 23:5–8

17 ᴿ'And on the fifteenth day of this month *is* the feast; unleavened bread shall be eaten for seven days.   Lev. 23:6

18 'On the ᴿfirst day *you shall have* a holy ᵀconvocation. You shall do no ᵀcustomary work.   Lev. 23:7 · *assembly* or *gathering* · *occupational*

19 'And you shall present an offering made by fire as a burnt offering to the LORD: two young bulls, one ram, and seven lambs in their first year. ᴿBe sure they are without blemish.   Deut. 15:21

20 'Their grain offering shall be of fine flour mixed with oil: three-tenths *of an ephah* you shall offer for a bull, and two-tenths for a ram;

21 'you shall offer ᵀone-tenth *of an ephah* for each of the seven lambs;   2.087 qt.

22 'also ᴿone goat *as* a sin offering, to make atonement for you.   Num. 28:15

23 'You shall offer these besides the burnt offering of the morning, which *is* for a regular burnt offering.

24 'In this manner you shall offer the food of the offering made by fire daily for seven days, as a sweet aroma to the LORD; it shall be offered besides the regular burnt offering and its drink offering.

25 'And ᴿon the seventh day you shall have a holy convocation. You shall do no customary work.   Lev. 23:8

Offerings at the Feast of Weeks

26 'Also ᴿon the day of the firstfruits, when you bring a new grain offering to the LORD at your *Feast of* Weeks, you shall have a holy convocation. You shall do no customary work.   Deut. 16:9–12

27 'You shall present a burnt offering as a sweet aroma to the LORD: two young bulls, one ram, and seven lambs in their first year,

28 'with their grain offering of fine flour mixed with oil: three-tenths *of an ephah* for each bull, two-tenths for the one ram,

29 'and one-tenth for each of the seven lambs;

30 'also one kid of the goats, to make atonement for you.

31 ᴿ'Be sure they are without ᵀblemish. You shall present *them* with their drink offerings, besides the regular burnt offering with its grain offering.   Num. 28:3, 19 · *defect*

Offerings at the Feast of Trumpets

29 'And in the seventh month, on the first day of the month, you shall have a holy convocation. You shall do no customary work. For you ᴿit is a day of blowing the trumpets.   Lev. 23:23–25

2 'You shall offer a burnt offering as a sweet aroma to the LORD: one young bull, one ram, *and* seven lambs in their first year, without blemish.

3 'Their grain offering *shall be* fine flour mixed with oil: ᵀthree-tenths *of an ephah* for the bull, two-tenths for the ram,   6.261 qt.

4 'and ᵀone-tenth for each of the seven lambs;   2.087 qt.

5 'also one kid of the goats *as* a sin offering, to make atonement for you;

6 'besides the burnt offering with its grain offering for the New Moon, the regular burnt offering with its grain offering, and their drink offerings, ᴿaccording to their ordinance, as a sweet aroma, an offering made by fire to the LORD.   Num. 15:11, 12

Offerings on the Day of Atonement

7 'On the tenth *day* of this seventh month you shall have a holy convocation. You shall afflict your souls; you shall not do any work.

8 'You shall present a burnt offering to the LORD *as* a sweet aroma: one young bull, one ram, *and* seven lambs in their first year. ᴿBe sure they are without blemish.   Num. 28:19

9 'Their grain offering *shall be of* fine flour mixed with oil: three-tenths *of an ephah* for the bull, two-tenths for the one ram,

10 'and ᵀone-tenth for each of the seven lambs;   2.087 qt.

11 'also one kid of the goats *as* a sin offering, besides ᴿthe sin offering for atonement, the regular burnt offering with its grain offering, and their drink offerings. Lev. 16:3, 5

Offerings at the Feast of Tabernacles

12 'On the fifteenth day of the seventh month you shall have a holy convocation. You shall do no customary work, and you shall keep a feast to the LORD seven days.

13 ᴿ'You shall present a burnt offering, an offering made by fire as a sweet aroma to the LORD: thirteen young bulls, two rams, *and* fourteen lambs in their first year. They shall be without blemish.   Ezra 3:4

14 'Their grain offering *shall be of* fine flour mixed with oil: three-tenths *of an ephah* for each of the thirteen bulls, two-tenths for each of the two rams,

15 'and ᵀone-tenth for each of the fourteen lambs;   2.087 qt.

16 'also one kid of the goats *as* a sin offering, besides the regular burnt offering, its grain offering, and its drink offering.

17 'On the ᴿsecond day *present* twelve young bulls, two rams, fourteen lambs in their first year without blemish,   Lev. 23:36

18 'and their grain offering and their drink offerings for the bulls, for the rams, and for the lambs, by their number, ᴿaccording to the ordinance;   Num. 15:12; 28:7, 14; 29:3, 4, 9, 10

19 'also one kid of the goats *as* a sin offering, besides the regular burnt offering with its grain offering, and their drink offerings.

20 'On the third day *present* eleven bulls, two rams, fourteen lambs in their first year without blemish,

21 'and their grain offering and their drink offerings for the bulls, for the rams, and for the lambs, by their number, ᴿaccording to the ordinance;   Num. 29:18

22 'also one goat *as* a sin offering, besides the regular burnt offering, its grain offering, and its drink offering.

23 'On the fourth day *present* ten bulls, two rams, *and* fourteen lambs in their first year, without blemish,

24 'and their grain offering and their drink offerings for the bulls, for the rams, and for the lambs, by their number, according to the ordinance;

25 'also one kid of the goats *as* a sin offering, besides the regular burnt offering, its grain offering, and its drink offering.

26 'On the fifth day *present* nine bulls, two rams, *and* fourteen lambs in their first year without blemish,

27 'and their grain offering and their drink offerings for the bulls, for the rams, and for the lambs, by their number, according to the ordinance;

28 'also one goat *as* a sin offering, besides the regular burnt offering, its grain offering, and its drink offering.

29 'On the sixth day *present* eight bulls, two rams, *and* fourteen lambs in their first year without blemish,

30 'and their grain offering and their drink offerings for the bulls, for the rams, and for the lambs, by their number, according to the ordinance;

31 'also one goat *as* a sin offering, besides the regular burnt offering, its grain offering, and its drink offering.

32 'On the seventh day *present* seven bulls, two rams, *and* fourteen lambs in their first year without blemish,

33 'and their grain offering and their drink offerings for the bulls, for the rams, and for the lambs, by their number, according to the ordinance;

34 'also one goat *as* a sin offering, besides

the regular burnt offering, its grain offering, and its drink offering.

35 'On the eighth day you shall have a ᴿsacredᵀ assembly. You shall do no customary work.   Lev. 23:36 • *solemn*

36 'You shall present a burnt offering, an offering made by fire as a sweet aroma to the LORD: one bull, one ram, seven lambs in their first year without blemish,

37 'and their grain offering and their drink offerings for the bull, for the ram, and for the lambs, by their number, according to the ordinance;

38 'also one goat *as* a sin offering, besides the regular burnt offering, its grain offering, and its drink offering.

39 'These you shall present to the LORD at your ᴿappointed feasts (besides your ᴿvowed offerings and your freewill offerings) as your burnt offerings and your grain offerings, as your drink offerings and your peace offerings.' "   Lev. 23:1-44 • Lev. 7:16; 22:18, 21, 23; 23:38

40 So Moses told the children of Israel everything, just as the LORD commanded Moses.

The Law Concerning Vows

30 Then Moses spoke to ᴿthe heads of the tribes concerning the children of Israel, saying, "This *is* the thing which the LORD has commanded: Num. 1:4, 16; 7:2

2 ᴿ"If a man makes a vow to the LORD, or ᴿswears an oath to bind himself by some agreement, he shall not break his word; he shall ᴿdo according to all that proceeds out of his mouth.   Lev. 27:2 • Matt. 14:9 • Job 22:27

3 "Or if a woman makes a vow to the LORD, and binds *herself* by some agreement while in her father's house in her youth,

4 "and her father hears her vow and the agreement by which she has bound herself, and her father holds his peace, then all her vows shall stand, and every agreement with which she has bound herself shall stand.

5 "But if her father overrules her on the day that he hears, then none of her vows nor her agreements by which she has bound herself shall stand; and the LORD will release her, because her father overruled her.

6 "If indeed she takes a husband, while bound by her vows or by a rash utterance from her lips by which she bound herself,

7 "and her husband hears *it*, and makes no response to her on the day that he hears, then her vows shall stand, and her agreements by which she bound herself shall stand.

8 "But if her husband ᴿoverrules her on the day that he hears *it*, he shall make void her vow which she took and what she uttered with her lips, by which she bound herself, and the LORD will release her.   [Gen. 3:16]

9 "Also any vow of a widow or a divorced woman, by which she has bound herself, shall stand against her.

10 "If she vowed in her husband's house, or bound herself by an agreement with an oath,

11 "and her husband heard *it*, and made no response to her *and* did not overrule her, then all her vows shall stand, and every agreement by which she bound herself shall stand.

12 "But if her husband truly made them void on the day he heard *them*, then whatever proceeded from her lips concerning her vows or concerning the agreement binding her, it shall not stand; her husband has made them void, and the LORD will release her.

13 "Every vow and every binding oath to afflict her soul, her husband may confirm it, or her husband may make it void.

14 "Now if her husband makes no response whatever to her from day to day, then he confirms all her vows or all the agreements that bind her; he confirms them, because he made no response to her on the day that he heard *them*.

15 "But if he does make them void after he has heard *them*, then he shall bear her guilt."

16 These *are* the statutes which the LORD commanded Moses, between a man and his wife, and between a father and his daughter in her youth in her father's house.

Vengeance on the Midianites

31 And the LORD spoke to Moses, saying: **2** "Take vengeance on the Midianites for the children of Israel. Afterward you shall ᴿbe gathered to your people."   Num. 25:12, 13

3 So Moses spoke to the people, saying, "Arm some of yourselves for war, and let them go against the Midianites to take vengeance for the LORD on ᴿMidian.   Josh. 13:21

4 "A thousand from each tribe of all the tribes of Israel you shall send to the war."

5 So there were recruited from the divisions of Israel one thousand from *each* tribe, twelve thousand armed for war.

6 Then Moses sent them to the war, one thousand from *each* tribe; he sent them to the war with Phinehas the son of Eleazar the priest, with the holy articles and ᴿthe signal trumpets in his hand.   Num. 10:9

7 And they warred against the Midianites, just as the LORD commanded Moses, and ᴿthey killed all the ᴿmales.   Deut. 20:13 · Gen. 34:25

8 They killed the kings of Midian with *the rest* of those who were killed—Evi, Rekem, ᴿZur, Hur, and Reba, the five kings of Midian. ᴿBalaam the son of Beor they also killed with the sword.   Num. 25:15 · Josh. 13:22

9 And the children of Israel took the women of Midian captive, with their little ones, and took as spoil all their cattle, all their flocks, and all their goods.

10 They also burned with fire all the cities where they dwelt, and all their forts.

11 And ᴿthey took all the spoil and all the booty—of man and beast.   Deut. 20:14

Return from the War

12 Then they brought the captives, the booty, and the spoil to Moses, to Eleazar the priest, and to the congregation of the children of Israel, to the camp in the plains of Moab by the Jordan, *across from* Jericho.

13 And Moses, Eleazar the priest, and all the leaders of the congregation, went to meet them outside the camp.

14 But Moses was angry with the officers of the army, *with* the captains over thousands and captains over hundreds, who had come from the battle.

15 And Moses said to them: "Have you kept ᴿall the women alive?   Deut. 20:14

16 "Look, these *women* caused the children of Israel, through the counsel of Balaam, to trespass against the LORD in the incident of Peor, and there was a plague among the congregation of the LORD.

17 "Now therefore, ᴿkill every male among the little ones, and kill every woman who has known a man intimately.   Deut. 7:2; 20:16-18

18 "But keep alive ᴿfor yourselves all the young girls who have not known a man intimately.   Deut. 21:10-14

19 "And as for you, ᴿremain outside the camp seven days; whoever has killed any person, and whoever has touched any slain, purify yourselves and your captives on the third day and on the seventh day.   Num. 5:2

20 "Purify every garment, everything made of leather, everything woven of goats' *hair*, and everything made of wood."

21 Then Eleazar the priest said to the men of war who had gone to the battle, "This *is* the ᵀordinance of the law which the LORD commanded Moses: statute

22 "Only the gold, the silver, the bronze, the iron, the tin, and the lead,

23 "everything that can endure fire, you shall put through the fire, and it shall be clean; and it shall be purified ᴿwith the water of purification. But all that cannot endure fire you shall put through water.   Num. 19:9, 17

24 ᴿ"And you shall wash your clothes on the seventh day and be clean, and afterward you may come into the camp."   Lev. 11:25

Division of the Plunder

25 Now the LORD spoke to Moses, saying: **26** "Count up the plunder that was ᵀtaken—of man and beast—you and Eleazar the priest and the chief fathers of the congregation;   captured

27 "and divide the plunder into two parts, between those who took part in the war, who went out to battle, and all the congregation.

28 "And levy a ᵀtribute for the LORD on the men of war who went out to battle: ᴿone of every five hundred of the persons, the cattle, the donkeys, and the sheep;   tax · Num. 31:30, 47

29 "take *it* from their half, and ᴿgive *it* to

Eleazar the priest as a heave offering to the LORD.   Deut. 18:1-5

30 "And from the children of Israel's half you shall take one of every fifty, drawn from the persons, the cattle, the donkeys, and the sheep, from all the livestock, and give them to the Levites who ᵀkeep charge of the tabernacle of the LORD."   perform the service

31 So Moses and Eleazar the priest did as the LORD commanded Moses.

32 The booty remaining from the plunder, which the men of war had taken, was six hundred and seventy-five thousand sheep,

33 seventy-two thousand cattle,

34 sixty-one thousand donkeys,

35 and thirty-two thousand persons in all, of women who had not known a man intimately.

36 And the half, the portion for those who had gone out to war, was in number three hundred and thirty-seven thousand five hundred sheep;

37 and the LORD's ᵀtribute of the sheep was six hundred and seventy-five.   tax

38 The cattle *were* thirty-six thousand, of which the LORD's tribute *was* seventy-two.

39 The donkeys *were* thirty thousand five hundred, of which the LORD's tribute *was* sixty-one.

40 The persons *were* sixteen thousand, of which the LORD's tribute *was* thirty-two persons.

41 So Moses gave the tribute *which was* the LORD's heave offering to Eleazar the priest, ᴿas the LORD commanded Moses.   Num. 5:9, 10

42 And from the children of Israel's half, which Moses separated from the men who fought—

43 now the half belonging to the congregation was three hundred and thirty-seven thousand five hundred sheep,

44 thirty-six thousand cattle,

45 thirty thousand five hundred donkeys,

46 and sixteen thousand persons—

47 and from the children of Israel's half Moses took one of every fifty, drawn from man and beast, and gave them to the Levites, who kept charge of the tabernacle of the LORD, as the LORD commanded Moses.

48 Then the officers who *were* over thousands of the army, the captains of thousands and captains of hundreds, came near to Moses;

49 and they said to Moses, "Your servants have taken a count of the men of war who *are* under our command, and not a man of us is missing.

50 "Therefore we have brought an offering for the LORD, what every man found of ornaments of gold: armlets and bracelets and signet rings and earrings and necklaces, ᴿto make atonement for ourselves before the LORD."   Ex. 30:12-16

51 So Moses and Eleazar the priest received the gold from them, all the fashioned ornaments.

52 And all the gold of the offering that they offered to the LORD, from the captains of thousands and captains of hundreds, was ᵀsixteen thousand seven hundred and fifty shekels. $32,160,000

53 ᴿ(The men of war had taken spoil, every man for himself.)   Deut. 20:14

54 And Moses and Eleazar the priest received the gold from the captains of thousands and of hundreds, and brought it into the tabernacle of meeting as a memorial for the children of Israel before the LORD.

The Tribes Settling East of the Jordan

32 Now the children of Reuben and the children of Gad had a very great multitude of livestock; and when they saw the land of Jazer and the land of Gilead, that indeed the region *was* a place for livestock,

2 the children of Gad and the children of Reuben came and spoke to Moses, to Eleazar the priest, and to the leaders of the congregation, saying,

3 "Ataroth, Dibon, Jazer, Nimrah, Heshbon, Elealeh, Shebam, Nebo, and Beon,

4 "the country which the LORD defeated before the congregation of Israel, *is* a land for livestock, and your servants have livestock."

5 Therefore they said, "If we have found favor in your sight, let this land be given to your servants as a possession. Do not take us over the Jordan."

16-B. Consequences of Sin at Kadesh Barnea ▼

6 And Moses said to the children of Gad and to the children of Reuben: "Shall your brethren go to war while you sit here?

7 "Now why will you discourage the heart

16-B. Consequences of Sin at Kadesh Barnea (Numbers 32:6–13)—The nation Israel reached Kadesh Barnea after two years in the wilderness. At Kadesh Barnea they so sinned against the Lord that He passed judgment upon them, saying, "The carcasses of you who have complained against Me shall fall in this wilderness . . . from twenty years old and above" (Num. 14:29–32, page 154; Deut. 1:1—2:1, page 181). They committed the sin that leads to death. For the next thirty-eight years, every adult twenty years old and above died a premature death, except Joshua and Caleb, who believed that God could give them Canaan. During the two years prior to reaching Kadesh Barnea, Israel witnessed many miracles, some in Egypt and some in the wilderness.

The question is, how could Israel witness so many miracles and then turn their backs on God in unbelief?
(Point 16-B continued on next page)

▽ of the children of Israel from going over into the land which the LORD has given them?

8 "Thus your fathers did ᴿwhen I sent them away from Kadesh Barnea ᴿto see the land.   Num. 13:3, 26 • Deut. 1:19-25

9 "For ᴿwhen they went up to the Valley of Eshcol and saw the land, they discouraged the heart of the children of Israel, so that they did not go into the land which the LORD had given them.   Deut. 1:24, 28

10 "So the LORD's anger was aroused on that day, and He swore an oath, saying,

11 'Surely none of the men who came up from Egypt, from twenty years old and above, shall see the land of which I swore to Abraham, Isaac, and Jacob, because ᴿthey have not wholly followed Me,   Num. 14:24, 30

12 'except Caleb the son of Jephunneh, the Kenizzite, and Joshua the son of Nun, for they have wholly followed the LORD.'

13 "So the LORD's anger was aroused against Israel, and He made them ᴿwander in the wilderness forty years, until ᴿall the generation that had done evil in the sight of ▲ the LORD was gone.   Num. 14:33-35 • Num. 26:64, 65

14 "And look! You have risen in your fathers' place, a brood of sinful men, to increase still more the ᴿfierce anger of the LORD against Israel.   Deut. 1:34

15 "For if you ᴿturn away from following Him, He will once again leave them in the wilderness, and you will destroy all these people."   Deut. 30:17, 18

16 Then they came near to him and said: "We will build sheepfolds here for our livestock, and cities for our little ones,

17 "but we ourselves will be armed, ready to go before the children of Israel until we have brought them to their place; and our little ones will dwell in the fortified cities because of the inhabitants of the land.

18 ᴿ"We will not return to our homes until every one of the children of Israel has ᵀreceived his inheritance.   Josh. 22:1-4 • possessed

19 "For we will not inherit with them on the other side of the Jordan and beyond, ᴿbecause our inheritance has fallen to us on this eastern side of the Jordan."   Josh. 12:1; 13:8

20 Then ᴿMoses said to them: "If you do this thing, if you arm yourselves before the LORD for the war,   Deut. 3:18

21 "and all your armed men cross over the Jordan before the LORD until He has driven out His enemies from before Him,

22 "and ᴿthe land is subdued before the

LORD, then afterward ᴿyou may return and be blameless before the LORD and before Israel; and ᴿthis land shall be your possession before the LORD.   Deut. 3:20 • Josh. 22:4 • Deut. 3:12, 15, 16, 18

23 "But if you do not do so, then take note, you have sinned against the LORD; and be sure ᴿyour sin will find you out.   Is. 59:12

24 "Build cities for your little ones and folds for your sheep, and do ᵀwhat has proceeded out of your mouth."   what you said

25 And the children of Gad and the children of Reuben spoke to Moses, saying: "Your servants will do as my lord commands.

26 ᴿ"Our little ones, our wives, our flocks, and all our livestock will be there in the cities of Gilead;   Josh. 1:14

27 ᴿ"but your servants will cross over, every man armed for war, before the LORD to battle, just as my lord says."   Josh. 4:12

28 So Moses gave command ᴿconcerning them to Eleazar the priest, to Joshua the son of Nun, and to the chief fathers of the tribes of the children of Israel.   Josh. 1:13

29 And Moses said to them: "If the children of Gad and the children of Reuben cross over the Jordan with you, every man armed for battle before the LORD, and the land is subdued before you, then you shall give them the land of Gilead as a possession.

30 "But if they do not cross over armed with you, they shall have possessions among you in the land of Canaan."

31 Then the children of Gad and the children of Reuben answered, saying: "As the LORD has said to your servants, so we will do.

32 "We will cross over armed before the LORD into the land of Canaan, but the possession of our inheritance *shall remain* with us on this side of the Jordan."

33 So Moses gave to the children of Gad, to the children of Reuben, and to half the tribe of Manasseh the son of Joseph, ᴿthe kingdom of Sihon king of the Amorites and the kingdom of Og king of Bashan, the land with its cities within the borders, the cities of the surrounding country.   Num. 21:24, 33, 35

34 And the children of Gad built ᴿDibon and Ataroth and ᴿAroer,   Num. 33:45, 46 • Deut. 2:36

35 Atroth and Shophan and ᴿJazer and Jogbehah,   Num. 32:1, 3

36 ᴿBeth Nimrah and Beth Haran, ᴿfortified cities, and folds for sheep.   Num. 32:3 • Num. 32:24

37 And the children of Reuben built ᴿHeshbon and Elealeh and Kirjathaim,   Num. 21:27

38 Nebo and Baal Meon (*their* names being

(Point 16-B continued from previous page)
(Num. 14:11, page 153). They had faith to forsake Egypt and cross the wilderness, but not enough faith to enter God's Promised Land. "So we see that they could not enter in because of unbelief" (Heb. 3:16-19, page 1239). In the book of Hebrews, God warns us—lest we commit the sin that leads to a premature death—" 'Do not harden your hearts as in the rebellion [in the wilderness]' . . . Beware, brethren, lest there be in any of you an evil heart of unbelief in departing from the living God" (Heb. 3:8-12, page 1238).
See Numbers 21:4-9, page 161, for **Point 16-C: Consequences of Sin: The Fiery Serpents.**

changed) and Shibmah; and they gave *other* names to the cities which they built.

39 And the children of Machir the son of Manasseh went to Gilead and took it, and dispossessed the Amorites who *were* in it.

40 So Moses ᴿgave Gilead to Machir the son of Manasseh, and he dwelt in it. Deut. 3:12, 13, 15

41 Also ᴿJair the son of Manasseh went and took its small towns, and called them ᴿHavoth Jair.ᵀ   Deut. 3:14 • Judg. 10:4 • Lit. *Towns of Jair*

42 Then Nobah went and took Kenath and its villages, and he called it Nobah, after his own name.

Israel's Journey from Egypt Reviewed

33 These *are* the journeys of the children of Israel, who went out of the land of Egypt by their armies under the ᴿhand of Moses and Aaron.   Ps. 77:20

2 Now Moses wrote down the starting points of their journeys at the command of the Lᴏʀᴅ. And these *are* their journeys according to their starting points:

3 They departed from Rameses in the first month, on the fifteenth day of the first month; on the day after the Passover the children of Israel went out ᴿwith boldness in the sight of all the Egyptians.   Ex. 14:8

4 For the Egyptians were burying all *their* firstborn, ᴿwhom the Lᴏʀᴅ had killed among them. Also ᴿon their gods the Lᴏʀᴅ had executed judgments.   Ex. 12:29 • Is. 19:1

5 ᴿThen the children of Israel moved from Rameses and camped at Succoth.   Ex. 12:37

6 They departed from ᴿSuccoth and camped at Etham, which *is* on the edge of the wilderness.   Ex. 13:20

7 They moved from Etham and turned back to Pi Hahiroth, which *is* east of Baal Zephon; and they camped near Migdol.

8 They departed *from before Hahiroth and ᴿpassed through the midst of the sea into the wilderness, went ᵀthree days' journey in the Wilderness of Etham, and camped at Marah.   Ex. 14:22; 15:22, 23 • 60 mi.

9 They moved from Marah and ᴿcame to Elim. At Elim *were* twelve springs of water and seventy palm trees; so they camped there.   Ex. 15:27

10 They moved from Elim and camped by the Red Sea.

11 They moved from the Red Sea and camped in the ᴿWilderness of Sin.   Ex. 16:1

12 They journeyed from the Wilderness of Sin and camped at Dophkah.

13 They departed from Dophkah and camped at Alush.

14 They moved from Alush and camped at ᴿRephidim, where there was no water for the people to drink.   Ex. 17:1; 19:2

15 They departed from Rephidim and camped in the Wilderness of Sinai.

16 They moved from the Wilderness of Sinai and camped at Kibroth Hattaavah.

17 They departed from Kibroth Hattaavah and ᴿcamped at Hazeroth.   Num. 11:35

18 They departed from Hazeroth and camped at ᴿRithmah.   Num. 12:16

19 They departed from Rithmah and camped at Rimmon Perez.

20 They departed from Rimmon Perez and camped at Libnah.

21 They moved from Libnah and camped at Rissah.

22 They journeyed from Rissah and camped at Kehelathah.

23 They went from Kehelathah and camped at Mount Shepher.

24 They moved from Mount Shepher and camped at Haradah.

25 They moved from Haradah and camped at Makheloth.

26 They moved from Makheloth and camped at Tahath.

27 They departed from Tahath and camped at Terah.

28 They moved from Terah and camped at Mithkah.

29 They went from Mithkah and camped at Hashmonah.

30 They departed from Hashmonah and ᴿcamped at Moseroth.   Deut. 10:6

31 They departed from Moseroth and camped at Bene Jaakan.

32 They moved from ᴿBene Jaakan and ᴿcamped at Hor Hagidgad.   Deut. 10:6 • Deut. 10:7

33 They went from Hor Hagidgad and camped at Jotbathah.

34 They moved from Jotbathah and camped at Abronah.

35 They departed from Abronah ᴿand camped at Ezion Geber.   Deut. 2:8

36 They moved from Ezion Geber and camped in the ᴿWilderness of Zin, which *is* Kadesh.   Num. 20:1; 27:14

37 They moved from ᴿKadesh and camped at Mount Hor, on the boundary of the land of Edom.   Num. 20:22, 23; 21:4

38 Then Aaron the priest went up to Mount Hor at the command of the Lᴏʀᴅ, and died there in the fortieth year after the children of Israel had come out of the land of Egypt, on the first *day* of the fifth month.

39 Aaron *was* one hundred and twenty-three years old when he died on Mount Hor.

40 Now ᴿthe king of Arad, the Canaanite, who dwelt in the South in the land of Canaan, heard of the coming of the children of Israel.   Num. 21:1

41 So they departed from Mount Hor and camped at Zalmonah.

42 They departed from Zalmonah and camped at Punon.

33:8 Heb. mss., Sam., Syr., Tg., Vg. *from Pi Hahiroth;* cf. Num. 33:7

43 They departed from Punon and [R]camped at Oboth.   Num. 21:10
44 They departed from Oboth and camped at Ije Abarim, at the border of Moab.
45 They departed from [T]Ijim and camped at Dibon Gad.   Same as Ije Abarim, v. 44
46 They moved from Dibon Gad and camped at [R]Almon Diblathaim.   Jer. 48:22
47 They moved from Almon Diblathaim [R]and camped in the mountains of Abarim, before Nebo.   Deut. 32:49
48 They departed from the mountains of Abarim and [R]camped in the plains of Moab by the Jordan, *across from* Jericho.   Num. 22:1
49 They camped by the Jordan, from Beth Jesimoth as far as the [R]Abel[T] Acacia Grove in the plains of Moab.   Num. 25:1 • Heb. *Abel Shittim*

Instructions for the Conquest of Canaan

50 Now the LORD spoke to Moses in the plains of Moab by the Jordan, *across from* Jericho, saying,
51 "Speak to the children of Israel, and say to them: [R]'When you have crossed the Jordan into the land of Canaan,   Josh. 3:17
52 [R]'then you shall drive out all the inhabitants of the land from before you, destroy all their engraved stones, destroy all their molded images, and demolish all their [T]high places;   Deut. 7:2, 5; 12:3 • Places for pagan worship
53 'you shall dispossess *the inhabitants of* the land and dwell in it, for I have given you the land to [R]possess.   Deut. 11:31
54 'And you shall divide the land by lot as an inheritance among your families; to the larger you shall give a larger inheritance, and to the smaller you shall give a smaller inheritance; there everyone's *inheritance* shall be whatever falls to him by lot. You shall inherit according to the tribes of your fathers.
55 'But if you do not drive out the inhabitants of the land from before you, then it shall be that those whom you let remain *shall be* [R]irritants in your eyes and thorns in your sides, and they shall harass you in the land where you dwell.   Josh. 23:13
56 'Moreover it shall be *that* I will do to you as I thought to do to them.'"

The Appointed Boundaries of Canaan

34 Then the LORD spoke to Moses, saying,
2 "Command the children of Israel, and say to them: 'When you come into [R]the land of Canaan, this *is* the land that shall fall to you as an inheritance—the land of Canaan to its boundaries.   Gen. 17:8
3 'Your southern border shall be from the Wilderness of Zin along the border of Edom; then your southern border shall extend eastward to the end of [R]the Salt Sea;   Gen. 14:3
4 'your border shall turn from the southern side of the Ascent of Akrabbim, continue to Zin, and be on the south of [R]Kadesh

Barnea; then it shall go on to [R]Hazar Addar, and continue to Azmon; Num. 13:26; 32:8 • Josh. 15:3, 4
5 'the border shall turn from Azmon [R]to the Brook of Egypt, and it shall end at the Sea.   Josh. 15:4, 47
6 'As for the [R]western border, you shall have the Great Sea for a border; this shall be your western border.   Ezek. 47:20
7 'And this shall be your northern border: From the Great Sea you shall mark out your *border* line to [R]Mount Hor;   Num. 33:37
8 'from Mount Hor you shall mark out *your border* [R]to the entrance of Hamath; then the direction of the border shall be toward [R]Zedad;   Num. 13:21 • Ezek. 47:15
9 'the border shall proceed to Ziphron, and it shall end at [R]Hazar Enan. This shall be your northern border.   Ezek. 47:17
10 'You shall mark out your eastern border from Hazar Enan to Shepham;
11 'the border shall go down from Shepham to Riblah on the east side of Ain; the border shall go down and reach to the eastern [T]side of the Sea of Chinnereth;   ridge, lit. *shoulder*
12 'the border shall go down along the Jordan, and it shall end at [R]the Salt Sea. This shall be your land with its surrounding boundaries.'"   Num. 34:3
13 Then Moses commanded the children of Israel, saying: [R]"This *is* the land which you shall inherit by lot, which the LORD has commanded to give to the nine tribes and to the half-tribe.   Josh. 14:1-5
14 [R]"For the tribe of the children of Reuben according to the house of their fathers, and the tribe of the children of Gad according to the house of their fathers, have received *their inheritance*; and the half-tribe of Manasseh has received its inheritance.   Num. 32:33
15 "The two tribes and the half-tribe have received their inheritance on this side of the Jordan, *across from* Jericho eastward, toward the sunrise."

The Leaders Appointed to Divide the Land

16 And the LORD spoke to Moses, saying,
17 "These *are* the names of the men who shall divide the land among you as an inheritance: [R]Eleazar the priest and Joshua the son of Nun.   Josh. 14:1, 2; 19:51
18 "And you shall take one leader of every tribe to divide the land for the inheritance.
19 "These *are* the names of the men: from the tribe of Judah, Caleb the son of Jephunneh;
20 "from the tribe of the children of Simeon, Shemuel the son of Ammihud;
21 "from the tribe of Benjamin, Elidad the son of Chislon;
22 "a leader from the tribe of the children of Dan, Bukki the son of Jogli;
23 "from the sons of Joseph: a leader from

the tribe of the children of Manasseh, Hanniel the son of Ephod,

24 "and a leader from the tribe of the children of Ephraim, Kemuel the son of Shiphtan;

25 "a leader from the tribe of the children of Zebulun, Elizaphan the son of Parnach;

26 "a leader from the tribe of the children of Issachar, Paltiel the son of Azzan;

27 "a leader from the tribe of the children of Asher, Ahihud the son of Shelomi;

28 "and a leader from the tribe of the children of Naphtali, Pedahel the son of Ammihud."

29 These *are* the ones the LORD commanded to divide the inheritance among the children of Israel in the land of Canaan.

Cities for the Levites

35 And the LORD spoke to Moses in ᴿthe plains of Moab by the Jordan *across from* Jericho, saying: Num. 33:50

2 ᴿ"Command the children of Israel that they give the Levites cities to dwell in from the inheritance of their possession, and you shall *also* give the Levites ᴿcommon-land around the cities.   Josh. 14:3, 4; 21:2, 3 • Lev. 25:22-34

3 "They shall have the cities to dwell in; and their common-land shall be for their cattle, for their herds, and for all their animals.

4 "The common-land of the cities which you will give the Levites *shall extend* from the wall of the city outward a ᵀthousand cubits all around.   1500 ft.

5 "And you shall measure outside the city on the east side ᵀtwo thousand cubits, on the south side two thousand cubits, on the west side two thousand cubits, and on the north side two thousand cubits. The city *shall be* in the middle. This shall belong to them as common-land for the cities.   3000 ft.

6 "Now among the cities which you will give to the Levites *you shall appoint* ᴿsix cities of refuge, to which a manslayer may flee. And to these you shall add forty-two cities.   Josh. 20:2, 7, 8; 21:3, 13

7 "So all the cities you will give to the Levites *shall be* ᴿforty-eight; these *you shall give* with their common-land.   Josh. 21:41

8 "And the cities which you will give *shall be* ᴿfrom the possession of the children of Israel; ᴿfrom the larger *tribe* you shall give many, from the smaller you shall give few. Each shall give some of its cities to the Levites, in proportion to the inheritance that each receives."   Josh. 21:3 • Num. 26:54; 33:54

Cities of Refuge

9 Then the LORD spoke to Moses, saying,

10 "Speak to the children of Israel, and say to them: ᴿ'When you cross the Jordan into the land of Canaan,   Josh. 20:1-9

11 'then you shall appoint cities to be cities of refuge for you, that the manslayer who kills any person accidentally may flee there.

12 ᴿ'They shall be cities of refuge for you from the avenger, that the manslayer may not die until he stands before the congregation in judgment.   Deut. 19:6

13 'And of the cities which you give, you shall have ᴿsix cities of refuge.   Num. 35:6

14 ᴿ'You shall appoint three cities on this side of the Jordan, and three cities you shall appoint in the land of Canaan, *which* will be cities of refuge.   Deut. 4:41

15 'These six cities shall be for refuge for the children of Israel, ᴿfor the stranger, and for the sojourner among them, that anyone who kills a person accidentally may flee there.   Num. 15:16

16 'But if he strikes him with an iron implement, so that he dies, he *is* a murderer; the murderer shall surely be put to death.

17 'And if he strikes him with a stone in the hand, by which one could die, and he does die, he *is* a murderer; the murderer shall surely be put to death.

18 'Or *if* he strikes him with a wooden hand weapon, by which one could die, and he does die, he *is* a murderer; the murderer shall surely be put to death.

19 ᴿ'The avenger of blood himself shall put the murderer to death; when he meets him, he shall put him to death.   Num. 35:21, 24, 27

20 ᴿ'If he pushes him out of hatred or, ᴿwhile lying in wait, hurls something at him so that he dies,   Gen. 4:8 • Ex. 21:14

21 'or in enmity he strikes him with his hand so that he dies, the one who struck *him* shall surely be put to death; he *is* a murderer. The avenger of blood shall put the murderer to death when he meets him.

22 'However if he pushes him suddenly ᴿwithout enmity, or throws anything at him without lying in wait,   Ex. 21:13

23 'or uses a stone, by which a man could die, throwing *it* at him without seeing *him*, so that he dies, while he was not his enemy or seeking his harm,

24 'then ᴿthe congregation shall judge between the manslayer and the avenger of blood according to these judgments.   Josh. 20:6

25 'So the congregation shall deliver the manslayer from the hand of the avenger of blood, and the congregation shall return him to the city of refuge where he had fled, and ᴿhe shall remain there until the death of the high priest ᴿwho was anointed with the holy oil.   Josh. 20:6 • Ex. 29:7

26 'But if the manslayer at any time goes outside the limits of the city of refuge where he fled,

27 'and the avenger of blood finds him outside the limits of his city of refuge, and the avenger of blood kills the manslayer, he shall not be guilty of ᵀblood,   Murder

28 'because he should have remained in his

city of refuge until the death of the high priest. But after the death of the high priest the manslayer may return to the land of his possession.

29 'And these *things* shall be ᴿa statute of judgment to you throughout your generations in all your dwellings. Num. 27:11

30 'Whoever kills a person, the murderer shall be put to death on the ᴿtestimony of witnesses; but one witness is not *sufficient* testimony against a person for the death *penalty*. Deut. 17:6; 19:15

31 'Moreover you shall take no ransom for the life of a murderer who *is* guilty of death, but he shall surely be put to death.

32 'And you shall take no ransom for him who has fled to his city of refuge, that he may return to dwell in the land before the death of the priest.

33 'So you shall not pollute the land where you *are*; for blood ᴿdefiles the land, and no atonement can be made for the land, for the blood that is shed on it, except ᴿby the blood of him who shed it. Ps. 106:38 · Gen. 9:6

34 'Therefore ᴿdo not defile the land which you inhabit, in the midst of which I dwell; for ᴿI the LORD dwell among the children of Israel.' " Lev. 18:24, 25 · Ex. 29:45, 46

Marriage of Female Heirs

36 Now the chief fathers of the families of the children of Gilead the son of Machir, the son of Manasseh, of the families of the sons of Joseph, came near and ᴿspoke before Moses and before the leaders, the chief fathers of the children of Israel. Num. 27:1–11

2 And they said: ᴿ"The LORD commanded my lord *Moses* to give the land as an inheritance by lot to the children of Israel, and ᴿmy lord was commanded by the LORD to give the inheritance of our brother Zelophehad to his daughters. Josh. 17:4 · Num. 27:1, 5–7

3 "Now if they are married to any of the sons of the *other* tribes of the children of Israel, then their inheritance will be ᴿtaken from the inheritance of our fathers, and it will

be added to the inheritance of the tribe into which they marry; so it will be taken from the lot of our inheritance. Num. 27:4

4 "And when ᴿthe Jubilee of the children of Israel comes, then their inheritance will be added to the inheritance of the tribe into which they marry; so their inheritance will be taken away from the inheritance of the tribe of our fathers." Lev. 25:10

5 Then Moses commanded the children of Israel according to the word of the LORD, saying: ᴿ"What the tribe of the sons of Joseph speaks is right. Num. 27:7

6 "This *is* what the LORD commands concerning the daughters of Zelophehad, saying, 'Let them ᵀmarry whom they think best, ᴿbut they may marry only within the family of their father's tribe.' Lit. *be wives to* · Num. 36:11, 12

7 "So the inheritance of the children of Israel shall not change hands from tribe to tribe, for every one of the children of Israel shall ᴿkeep the inheritance of the tribe of his fathers. 1 Kin. 21:3

8 "And ᴿevery daughter who possesses an inheritance in any tribe of the children of Israel shall be the wife of one of the family of her father's tribe, so that the children of Israel each may possess the inheritance of his fathers. 1 Chr. 23:22

9 "Thus no inheritance shall change hands from *one* tribe to another, but every tribe of the children of Israel shall keep its own inheritance."

10 Just as the LORD commanded Moses, so did the daughters of Zelophehad;

11 for Mahlah, Tirzah, Hoglah, Milcah, and Noah, the daughters of Zelophehad, were married to the sons of their father's brothers.

12 They were married into the families of the children of Manasseh the son of Joseph, and their inheritance remained in the tribe of their father's family.

13 These *are* the commandments and the judgments which the LORD commanded the children of Israel by the hand of Moses ᴿin the plains of Moab by the Jordan, *across from* Jericho. Num. 26:3; 33:50

THE FIFTH BOOK OF MOSES CALLED
Deuteronomy

The name *Deuteronomy* comes from the Septuagint and means "second law-giving." The Jewish title, "Words," comes from 1:1 which begins, "these are the words." This name arises from the Jewish practice of using the opening words of a book as its name.

AUTHORSHIP. Moses is the author of Deuteronomy. There is simply no valid reason to deny the unanimous testimony of Scripture on this matter. Deuteronomy contains the farewell address of Moses to the children of Israel.

HOW DEUTERONOMY FITS INTO THE BIBLE. The era of Exodus was coming to a close and Moses had successfully led the children of Israel out of Egypt. The covenant relationship had been established between God and His chosen people. The rebellion at Kadesh Barnea culminated in forty years of wandering in the wilderness. The entire generation that rebelled against God—except Moses, Joshua, and Caleb—was dead.

These sermons were preached by Moses on the plains of Moab to encourage the new generation to learn from their fathers' mistakes. Moses was also preparing the people to accept his impending death and the challenge that awaited them—the challenge of conquering a new land, under the leadership of Moses' successor, Joshua.

SUMMARY STATEMENT. Deuteronomy emphasizes being faithful to Israel's covenant relationship with God and being true to their calling in the future.

CONTEXT. Moses preached these three sermons about 1410 B.C. while that generation of Israelites was facing the same challenge that defeated their now dead parents. They were about to conquer and settle God's promised land, which meant their future was to be filled with war and the ultimate shock of going from being a nomadic people to a people with a settled way of life. To add to their problems, Moses, their charismatic leader and mediator with God, would not be leading them in this great undertaking. Moses was about to die and he was preparing his people for a change in leadership. Joshua was appointed to lead them in the tasks which lay ahead.

The account of Moses' death (ch. 34) was obviously written by someone else. It was customary for someone to add the obituary to an author's work upon his death. In keeping with his following Moses as a leader of Israel, Joshua may have written this obituary.

Deuteronomy is not a legal code as much as it is an exposition of the law. It contains a reaffirmation of Moses' teachings. Moses is expanding and explaining the law that was given in Sinai in order to clarify this law in the minds of the people. This teaching elaborates Israel's responsibility as God's covenant people. Moses is trying to impress on the hearts of the younger generation a deeper sense of their dependence on, and obligation to, God.

Moses asserts that God's relationship to Israel rests on God's holy choice through His act of redemption and not Israel's merits. Once chosen, God honors His people for their obedience and chastens them for their rebellion, or disobedience.

God is depicted in Deuteronomy as a Father who bears up, chastens, and loves a wayward son. He has chosen to set His heart on Israel even though they have sinned against Him. This covenant idea gave Israel a whole new concept of their history. They saw their national life as sacred to the Lord and an expression of His divine purpose. God still demanded Israel's total devotion. They were to serve God with their whole heart. There was no ground for compromise, no extenuating circumstances. God's covenant was to be obeyed.

Deuteronomy is also a book of renewal. Many scholars believe that all or part of Deuteronomy is the Book of the Law found by Hilkiah the priest. This event brought about the reformation of Josiah (2 Kin. 22, 23). In keeping with this theme, Deuteronomy sets the pattern for later renewal ceremonies in which the children of Israel were reminded of their covenant relationship and rededicated themselves to the purpose of God.

This may be a reason why Deuteronomy is one of the Old Testament books quoted most often by the Lord Jesus and the apostles. More than eighty references from this Old Testament book are found in the twenty-seven books of the New Testament. In Matthew 22:37, 38, Jesus approves of the Deuteronomic summary of the law.

A study of Deuteronomy is profitable in helping Christians gain an understanding of Israel's covenant relationship with God. This knowledge is essential for any meaningful study of the New Testament.

—R.E.D.

The Previous Command to Enter Canaan

THESE *are* the words which Moses spoke to all Israel ᴿon this side of the Jordan in the wilderness, in the ᵀplain opposite *Suph, between Paran, Tophel, Laban, Hazeroth, and Dizahab.   Deut. 4:44-46 • Heb. *arabah*
2 *It is* ᵀeleven days' *journey* from Horeb by way of Mount Seir to Kadesh Barnea.   220 mi.
3 Now it came to pass in the fortieth year, in the eleventh month, on the first *day* of the month, *that* Moses spoke to the children of Israel according to all that the Lᴏʀᴅ had given him as commandments to them,
4 ᴿafter he had killed Sihon king of the Amorites, who dwelt in Heshbon, and Og king of Bashan, who dwelt at Ashtaroth ᴿin* Edrei.   Num. 21:23, 24, 33-35 • Josh. 13:12
5 On this side of the Jordan in the land of Moab, Moses began to explain this law, saying,
6 "The Lᴏʀᴅ our God spoke to us ᴿin Horeb, saying: 'You have dwelt long ᴿenough at this mountain.   Ex. 3:1, 12 • Ex. 19:1, 2
7 'Turn and take your journey, and go to the mountains of the Amorites, and to all the neighboring *places* in the ᵀplain, in the mountains and in the lowland, in the South and on the seacoast, to the land of the Canaanites and to Lebanon, as far as the great river, the River Euphrates.   Heb. *arabah*
8 'See, I have set the land before you; go in and possess the land which the Lᴏʀᴅ ᵀswore to your fathers—to ᴿAbraham, Isaac, and Jacob—to give to them and their descendants after them.'   *promised* • Gen. 12:7; 15:5; 22:17; 26:3; 28:13

Tribal Leaders Appointed

9 "And I spoke to you at that time, saying: 'I alone am not able to bear you.
10 'The Lᴏʀᴅ your God has multiplied you, ᴿand here you *are* today, as the stars of heaven in multitude.   Gen. 15:5; 22:17
11 ᴿ'May the Lᴏʀᴅ God of your fathers make you a thousand times more numerous than you are, and bless you ᴿas He has promised you!   2 Sam. 24:3 • Gen. 15:5
12 'How can I alone bear your problems and your burdens and your complaints?
13 'Choose wise, understanding, and knowledgeable men from among your tribes, and I will make ᵀthem heads over you.'   *rulers*
14 "And you answered me and said, 'The thing which you have told *us* to do *is* good.'
15 "So I took ᴿthe heads of your tribes, wise and knowledgeable men, and ᵀmade them heads over you, leaders of thousands, leaders of hundreds, leaders of fifties, leaders of tens, and officers for your tribes.   Ex. 18:25 • *appointed*
16 "Then I commanded your judges at that time, saying, 'Hear *the cases* between your

1:1 LXX ms., Tg., Vg. *Red Sea*
1:4 LXX, Syr., Vg. *and;* cf. Josh. 12:4

brethren, and ᴿjudge righteously between a man and his ᴿbrother or the stranger who is with him.   Deut. 16:18 • Lev. 24:22
17 'You shall not show partiality in judgment; you shall hear the small as well as the great; you shall not be afraid in any man's presence, for ᴿthe judgment *is* God's. The case that is too hard for you, ᴿbring to me, and I will hear it.'   2 Chr. 19:6 • Ex. 18:22, 26
18 "And I commanded you at that time all the things which you should do.

Israel's Refusal to Enter the Land

19 "So we departed from Horeb, ᴿand went through all that great and terrible wilderness which you saw on the way to the mountains of the Amorites, as the Lᴏʀᴅ our God had commanded us. Then ᴿwe came to Kadesh Barnea.   Deut. 2:7; 8:15; 32:10 • Num. 13:26
20 "And I said to you, 'You have come to the mountains of the Amorites, which the Lᴏʀᴅ our God is giving us.
21 'Look, the Lᴏʀᴅ your God has set the land before you; go up *and* possess *it*, as the Lᴏʀᴅ God of your fathers has spoken to you; ᴿdo not fear or be discouraged.'   Josh. 1:6, 9
22 "And every one of you came near to me and said, 'Let us send men before us, and let them search out the land for us, and bring back word to us of the way by which we should go up, and of the cities into which we shall come.'
23 "The plan pleased me well; so I took twelve of your men, one man from *each* tribe.
24 ᴿ"And they departed and went up into the mountains, and came to the Valley of Eshcol, and spied it out.   Num. 13:21-25
25 "They also took *some* of the fruit of the land in their hands and brought *it* down to us; and they brought back word to us, saying, 'It *is* a ᴿgood land which the Lᴏʀᴅ our God is giving us.'   Num. 13:27
26 ᴿ"Nevertheless you would not go up, but rebelled against the command of the Lᴏʀᴅ your God;   Num. 14:1-4
27 "and you ᴿcomplained in your tents, and said, 'Because the Lᴏʀᴅ ᴿhates us, He has brought us out of the land of Egypt to deliver us into the hand of the Amorites, to destroy us.   Ps. 106:25 • Deut. 9:28
28 'Where can we go up? Our brethren have ᵀdiscouraged our hearts, saying, ᴿ"The people *are* greater and taller than we; the cities *are* great and fortified up to heaven; moreover we have seen the sons of the ᴿAnakim there." '   Lit. *melted* • Deut. 9:1, 2 • Num. 13:28
29 "Then I said to you, 'Do not be terrified, ᴿor afraid of them.   Num. 14:9
30 ᴿ"The Lᴏʀᴅ your God, who goes before you, He will fight for you, according to all He did for you in Egypt before your eyes, Ex. 14:14
31 'and in the wilderness where you saw how the Lᴏʀᴅ your God carried you, as a man

carries his son, in all the way that you went until you came to this place.'

32 "Yet, for all that, ^Ryou did not believe the LORD your God,   Jude 5

33 "who went in the way before you to search out a place for you to pitch your tents, to show you the way you should go, in the fire by night and in the cloud by day.

The Penalty for Israel's Rebellion

34 "And the LORD heard the sound of your words, and was angry, ^Rand took an oath, saying,   Deut. 2:14, 15

35 ^R"Surely not one of these men of this evil generation shall see that good land of which I swore to give to your fathers,   Num. 14:22, 23

36 ^Rexcept Caleb the son of Jephunneh; he shall see it, and to him and his children I am giving the land on which he walked, because he wholly followed the LORD.'   [Josh. 14:9]

37 ^R"The LORD was also angry with me for your sakes, saying, 'Even you shall not go in there.   Deut. 3:26; 4:21; 34:4

38 'Joshua the son of Nun, who stands before you, he shall go in there. Encourage him, for he shall cause Israel to inherit it.

39 'Moreover your little ones and your children, who ^Ryou say will be victims, who today ^Rhave no knowledge of good and evil, they shall go in there; to them I will give it, and they shall possess it.   Num. 14:3 • Is. 7:15, 16

40 ^RBut as for you, turn and take your journey into the wilderness by the Way of the Red Sea.'   Num. 14:25

41 "Then you answered and said to me, ^R'We have sinned against the LORD; we will go up and fight, just as the LORD our God commanded us.' And when everyone of you had girded on his weapons of war, you were ready to go up into the mountain.   Num. 14:40

42 "And the LORD said to me, 'Tell them, ^R"Do not go up nor fight, for I am not among you; lest you be defeated before your enemies." '   Num. 14:41-43

43 "So I spoke to you; yet you would not listen, but ^Rrebelled against the command of the LORD, and ^Rpresumptuously^T went up into the mountain.   Num. 14:44 • Deut. 17:12, 13 • willfully

44 "And the Amorites who dwelt in that mountain came out against you and chased you ^Ras bees do, and drove you back from Seir to Hormah.   Ps. 118:12

45 "Then you returned and wept before the LORD, but the LORD would not listen to your voice nor give ear to you.

46 "So you remained in Kadesh many days, according to the days that you spent there.

The Desert Years

2 "Then we turned and journeyed into the wilderness of the Way of the Red Sea, as the LORD spoke to me, and we skirted Mount Seir for many days.

2 "And the LORD spoke to me, saying:

3 'You have skirted this mountain ^Rlong enough; turn northward.   Deut. 2:7, 14

4 'And command the people, saying, "You are about to pass through the territory of your brethren, the descendants of Esau, who live in Seir; and they will be afraid of you. Therefore watch yourselves carefully.

5 'Do not meddle with them, for I will not give you any of their land, no, not so much as one footstep, ^Rbecause I have given Mount Seir to Esau as a possession.   Gen. 36:8

6 'You shall buy food from them with money, that you may eat; and you shall also buy water from them with money, that you may drink.

7 "For the LORD your God has blessed you in all the work of your hand. He knows your trudging through this great wilderness. These forty years the LORD your God has been with you; you have lacked nothing." '

8 "And when we passed beyond our brethren, the descendants of Esau who dwell in Seir, away from the road of the plain, away from Elath and Ezion Geber, we turned and passed by way of the Wilderness of Moab.

9 "Then the LORD said to me, 'Do not harass Moab, nor contend with them in battle, for I will not give you any of their land as a possession, because I have given Ar to the descendants of Lot as a possession.' "

10 ^R(The Emim had dwelt there in times past, a people as great and numerous and tall as ^Rthe Anakim.   Gen. 14:5 • Deut. 9:2

11 They were also regarded as ^Tgiants, like the Anakim, but the Moabites call them Emim.   Heb. rephaim

12 ^RThe Horites formerly dwelt in Seir, but the descendants of Esau dispossessed them and destroyed them from before them, and dwelt in their ^Tplace, just as Israel did to the land of their possession which the LORD gave them.)   Deut. 2:22 • stead

13 " 'Now rise and cross over ^Rthe ^TValley of the Zered.' So we crossed over the Valley of the Zered.   Num. 21:12 • Wadi or Brook

14 "And the time we took to come from Kadesh Barnea until we crossed over the Valley of the Zered was thirty-eight years, until all the generation of the men of war was consumed from the midst of the camp, just as the LORD had sworn to them.

15 "For indeed the hand of the LORD was against them, to destroy them from the midst of the camp until they were consumed.

16 "So it was, when all the men of war had finally perished from among the people,

17 "that the LORD spoke to me, saying:

18 'This day you are to cross over at Ar, the boundary of Moab.

19 'And when you come near the people of Ammon, do not harass them or meddle with them, for I will not give you any of the land

of the people of Ammon *as* a possession, because I have given it to ᴿthe descendants of Lot *as* a possession.' "   Gen. 19:38

20 (That was also regarded as a land of *giants; giants formerly dwelt there. But the Ammonites call them Zamzummim,

21 ᴿa people as great and numerous and tall as the Anakim. But the Lᴏʀᴅ destroyed them before them, and they dispossessed them and dwelt in their place,   Deut. 2:10

22 just as He had done for the descendants of Esau, ᴿwho dwelt in Seir, when He destroyed ᴿthe Horites from before them. They dispossessed them and dwelt in their place, even to this day.   Gen. 36:8 • Gen. 14:6; 36:20-30

23 And ᴿthe Avim, who dwelt in villages as far as Gaza—ᴿthe Caphtorim, who came from Caphtor, destroyed them and dwelt in their place.)   Josh. 13:3 • Gen. 10:14

24 " 'Rise, take your journey, and cross over the River Arnon. Look, I have given into your hand Sihon the Amorite, king of Heshbon, and his land. Begin ᵀto possess *it*, and engage him in battle.   *to take it over*

25 'This day I will begin to put the dread and fear of you upon the nations ᵀunder the whole heaven, who shall hear the report of you, and shall tremble and be in anguish because of you.'   *everywhere under the heavens*

King Sihon Defeated

26 "And I sent messengers from the Wilderness of Kedemoth to Sihon king of Heshbon, with words of peace, saying,

27 ᴿ'Let me pass through your land; I will keep strictly to the road, and I will turn neither to the right nor to the left.   Judg. 11:19

28 'You shall sell me food for money, that I may eat, and give me water for money, that I may drink; only let me pass through on foot,

29 'just as the descendants of Esau who dwell in Seir and the Moabites who dwell in Ar did for me, until I cross the Jordan to the land which the Lᴏʀᴅ our God is giving us.'

30 "But Sihon king of Heshbon would not let us pass through, for ᴿthe Lᴏʀᴅ your God ᴿhardened his spirit and made his heart obstinate, that He might deliver him into your hand, as *it is* this day.   Josh. 11:20 • Ex. 4:21

31 "And the Lᴏʀᴅ said to me, 'See, I have begun to ᴿgive Sihon and his land over to you. Begin to possess *it*, that you may inherit his land.'   Deut. 1:3, 8

32 ᴿ"Then Sihon and all his people came out against us to fight at Jahaz.   Num. 21:23

33 "And ᴿthe Lᴏʀᴅ our God delivered him ᵀover to us; so ᴿwe defeated him, his sons, and all his people.   Deut. 7:2 • Lit. *before us* • Num. 21:24

34 "We took all his cities at that time, and we ᴿutterly destroyed the men, women, and little ones of every city; we left none remaining.   Lev. 27:28

2:20 Heb. *rephaim*

35 "We took only the livestock as plunder for ourselves, with the spoil of the cities which we took.

36 "From Aroer, which *is* on the bank of the River Arnon, and *from* ᴿthe city that *is* in the ravine, as far as Gilead, there was not one city too strong for us; ᴿthe Lᴏʀᴅ our God delivered all to us.   Josh. 13:9, 16 • Ps. 44:3

37 "Only you did not go near the land of the people of Ammon—anywhere along the River ᴿJabbok, or to the cities of the mountains, or ᴿwherever the Lᴏʀᴅ our God had forbidden us.   Gen. 32:22 • Deut. 2:5, 9, 19

King Og Defeated

3 "Then we turned and went up the road to Bashan; and ᴿOg king of Bashan came out against us, he and all his people, to battle ᴿat Edrei.   Num. 21:33-35 • Deut. 1:4

2 "And the Lᴏʀᴅ said to me, 'Do not fear him, for I have delivered him and all his people and his land into your hand; you shall do to him as you did to ᴿSihon king of the Amorites, who dwelt at Heshbon.'   Num. 21:34

3 "So the Lᴏʀᴅ our God also delivered into our hands Og king of Bashan, with all his people, and we ᵀattacked him until he had no survivors remaining.   *struck*

4 "And we took all his cities at that time; there was not a city which we did not take from them: sixty cities, all the region of Argob, the kingdom of Og in Bashan.

5 "All these cities *were* fortified with high walls, gates, and bars, besides a great many rural towns.

6 "And we utterly destroyed them, as we did to Sihon king ᴿof Heshbon, utterly destroying the men, women, and children of every city.   Deut. 2:24, 34, 35

7 "But all the livestock and the spoil of the cities we took as booty for ourselves.

8 "And at that time we took the land from the hand of the two kings of the Amorites who *were* on this side of the Jordan, from the River Arnon to Mount ᴿHermon   Deut. 4:48

9 "(the Sidonians call ᴿHermon Sirion, and the Amorites call it Senir),   1 Chr. 5:23

10 ᴿ"all the cities of the plain, all Gilead, and all Bashan, as far as Salcah and Edrei, cities of the kingdom of Og in Bashan.   Deut. 4:49

11 "For only Og king of Bashan remained of the remnant of the ᵀgiants. Indeed his bedstead *was* an iron bedstead. (*Is it not in* Rabbah of the people of Ammon?) Nine cubits *is* its length and four cubits its width, according to the standard cubit.   Heb. *rephaim*

The Land East of the Jordan Divided

12 "And this ᴿland, *which* we possessed at that time, ᴿfrom Aroer, which *is* by the River Arnon, and half the mountains of Gilead and ᴿits cities, I gave to the Reubenites and the Gadites.   Num. 32:33 • Deut. 2:36 • Num. 34:14

13 "The rest of Gilead, and all Bashan, the kingdom of Og, I gave to half the tribe of Manasseh. (All the region of Argob, with all Bashan, was called the land of the *giants.

14 "Jair the son of Manasseh took all the region of Argob, ᴿas far as the border of the Geshurites and the Maacathites, and ᴿcalled Bashan after his own name, ᵀHavoth Jair, to this day.)   Josh. 13:13 • Num. 32:41 • Lit. *Towns of Jair*

15 "Also I gave Gilead to Machir.

16 "And to the Reubenites ᴿand the Gadites I gave from Gilead as far as the River Arnon, the middle of the river as *the* border, as far as the River Jabbok, ᴿthe border of the people of Ammon;   2 Sam. 24:5 • Num. 21:24

17 "the plain also, with the Jordan as *the* border, from Chinnereth as far as the east side of the Sea of the Arabah ᴿ(the Salt Sea), below the slopes of Pisgah.   Gen. 14:3

18 "Then I commanded you at that time, saying: 'The Lᴏʀᴅ your God has given you this land to possess. ᴿAll you men of valor shall cross over armed before your brethren, the children of Israel.   Num. 32:20

19 'But your wives, your little ones, and your livestock (I know that you have much livestock) shall stay in your cities which I have given you,

20 'until the Lᴏʀᴅ has given ᴿrest to your brethren as to you, and they also possess the land which the Lᴏʀᴅ your God is giving them beyond the Jordan. Then each of you may ᴿreturn to his possession which I have given you.'   Deut. 12:9, 10 • Josh. 22:4

21 "And ᴿI commanded Joshua at that time, saying, 'Your eyes have seen all that the Lᴏʀᴅ your God has done to these two kings; so will the Lᴏʀᴅ do to all the kingdoms through which you pass.   [Num. 27:22, 23]

22 'You must not fear them, for ᴿthe Lᴏʀᴅ your God Himself fights for you.'   Ex. 14:14

Moses Forbidden to Enter the Land

23 "Then ᴿI pleaded with the Lᴏʀᴅ at that time, saying: [2 Cor. 12:8, 9]

24 'O Lord Gᴏᴅ, You have begun to show Your servant Your greatness and Your ᵀmighty hand, for what god *is there* in heaven or on earth who can do *anything* like Your works and Your mighty *deeds*?   *strong*

25 'I pray, let me cross over and see ᴿthe good land beyond the Jordan, those pleasant mountains, and Lebanon.'   Deut. 4:22

26 "But the Lᴏʀᴅ ᴿwas angry with me on your account, and would not listen to me. So the Lᴏʀᴅ said to me: 'Enough of that! Speak no more to Me of this matter.   Num. 20:12; 27:14

27 'Go up to the top of Pisgah, and lift your eyes toward the west, the north, the south, and the east; behold *it* with your eyes, for you shall not cross over this Jordan.

3:13 Heb. *rephaim*

28 'But ᵀcommand Joshua, and encourage him and strengthen him; for he shall go over before this people, and he shall cause them to inherit the land which you will see.'   *charge*

29 "So we stayed in ᴿthe valley opposite Beth Peor.   Deut. 4:46; 34:6

Moses Commands Obedience

4 "Now, O Israel, listen to ᴿthe statutes and the judgments which I teach you to observe, that you may live, and go in and ᵀpossess the land which the Lᴏʀᴅ God of your fathers is giving you.   [Rom. 10:5] • *take over*

2 "You shall not add to the word which I command you, nor take from it, that you may keep the commandments of the Lᴏʀᴅ your God which I command you.

3 "Your eyes have seen what the Lᴏʀᴅ did at ᴿBaal Peor; for the Lᴏʀᴅ your God has destroyed from among you all the men who followed Baal of Peor.   Num. 25:1-9

4 "But you who held fast to the Lᴏʀᴅ your God *are* alive today, every one of you.

5 "Surely I have taught you statutes and judgments, just as the Lᴏʀᴅ my God commanded me, that you should act according to *them* in the land which you go to possess.

6 "Therefore be careful to observe *them*; for this *is* ᴿyour wisdom and your understanding in the sight of the peoples who will hear all these statutes, and say, 'Surely this great nation *is* a wise and understanding people.'   [2 Tim. 3:15]

7 "For ᴿwhat great nation *is there* that has ᴿGodᵀ *so* near to it, as the Lᴏʀᴅ our God *is* to us, for whatever *reason* we may call upon Him?   [2 Sam. 7:23] • [Is. 55:6] • Or *a god*

8 "And what great nation *is there* that has *such* statutes and righteous judgments as are in all this law which I set before you this day?

9 "Only take heed to yourself, and diligently keep yourself, lest you ᴿforget the things your eyes have seen, and lest they depart from your heart all the days of your life. And ᴿteach them to your children and your grandchildren,   Deut. 29:2-8 • Gen. 18:19

10 "*especially concerning* ᴿthe day you stood before the Lᴏʀᴅ your God in Horeb, when the Lᴏʀᴅ said to me, 'Gather the people to Me, and I will let them hear My words, that they may learn to fear Me all the days they live on the earth, and *that* they may teach their children.'   Ex. 19:9, 16, 17

11 "Then you came near and stood at the foot of the mountain, and the mountain burned with fire to the midst of heaven, with darkness, cloud, and thick darkness.

12 ᴿ"And the Lᴏʀᴅ spoke to you out of the midst of the fire. You heard the sound of the words, but saw no ᵀform; ᴿyou only *heard* a voice.   Deut. 5:4, 22 • *similitude* • 1 Kin. 19:11-18

13 "So He declared to you His covenant which He commanded you to perform, the

Ten Commandments; and ᴿHe wrote them on two tablets of stone.   Ex. 24:12

14 "And the LORD commanded me at that time to teach you statutes and judgments, that you might ᵀobserve them in the land which you cross over to possess.   do or perform

Beware of Idolatry

15 "Take careful heed to yourselves, for you saw no form when the LORD spoke to you at Horeb out of the midst of the fire,

16 "lest you act corruptly and make for yourselves a carved image in the form of any figure: the likeness of male or female,

17 "the likeness of any animal that is on the earth or the likeness of any winged bird that flies in the air,

18 "the likeness of anything that creeps on the ground or the likeness of any fish that is in the water beneath the earth.

19 "And take heed, lest you ᴿlift your eyes to heaven, and when you see the sun, the moon, and the stars, ᴿall the host of heaven, you feel driven to ᴿworship them and serve them, which the LORD your God has ᵀgiven to all the peoples under the whole heaven as a heritage.   Deut. 17:3 · 2 Kin. 21:3 · [Rom. 1:25] · divided

20 "But the LORD has taken you and ᴿbrought you out of the iron furnace, out of Egypt, to be ᴿHis people, an inheritance, as you are this day.   Jer. 11:4 · Deut. 7:6; 27:9

21 "Furthermore the LORD was angry with me for your sakes, and swore that I would not cross over the Jordan, and that I would not enter the good land which the LORD your God is giving you as an inheritance.

22 "But I must die in this land, I must not cross over the Jordan; but you shall cross over and ᵀpossess that good land.   take over

23 "Take heed to yourselves, lest you forget the covenant of the LORD your God which He made with you, and make for yourselves a carved image in the form of anything which the LORD your God has forbidden you.

24 "For ᴿthe LORD your God is a consuming fire, ᴿa jealous God.   Deut. 9:3 · Ex. 20:5; 34:14

25 "When you beget children and grandchildren and have grown old in the land, and act corruptly and make a carved image in the form of anything, and do evil in the sight of the LORD your God to provoke Him to anger,

26 ᴿ"I call heaven and earth to witness against you this day, that you will soon utterly perish from the land which you cross over the Jordan to possess; you will not ᵀprolong your days in it, but will be utterly destroyed.   Deut. 30:18, 19 · live long on it

27 "And the LORD ᴿwill scatter you among the peoples, and you will be left few in number among the nations where the LORD will drive you.   Deut. 28:62

28 "And there you will serve gods, the work of men's hands, wood and stone, which neither see nor hear nor eat nor smell.

29 ᴿ"But from there you will seek the LORD your God, and you will find Him if you seek Him with all your heart and with all your soul.   [2 Chr. 15:4]

30 "When you are in ᵀdistress, and all these things come upon you in the ᴿlatter days, when you ᴿturn to the LORD your God and obey His voice   tribulation · Hos. 3:5 · Joel 2:12

31 "(for the LORD your God is a merciful God), He will not forsake you nor ᴿdestroy you, nor forget the covenant of your fathers which He swore to them.   Jer. 30:11

32 "For ask now concerning the days that are past, which were before you, since the day that God created man on the earth, and ask from one end of heaven to the other, whether any great thing like this has happened, or anything like it has been heard.

33 ᴿ"Did any people ever hear the voice of God speaking out of the midst of the fire, as you have heard, and live?   Deut. 5:24-26

34 "Or did God ever try to go and take for Himself a nation from the midst of another nation, by trials, by signs, by wonders, by war, ᴿby a mighty hand and ᴿan outstretched arm, and by great ᵀterrors, according to all that the LORD your God did for you in Egypt before your eyes?   Ex. 13:3 · Ex. 6:6 · calamities

35 "To you it was shown, that you might know that the LORD Himself is God; ᴿthere is none other besides Him.   Mark 12:32

36 "Out of heaven He let you hear His voice, that He might instruct you; on earth He showed you His great fire, and you heard His words out of the midst of the fire.

37 "And because He loved your fathers, therefore He chose their ᵀdescendants after them; and He brought you out of Egypt with His Presence, with His mighty power,   seed

38 ᴿ"driving out from before you nations greater and mightier than you, to bring you in, to give you their land as an inheritance, as it is this day.   Deut. 7:1

39 "Therefore know this day, and consider it in your heart, that ᴿthe LORD Himself is God in heaven above and on the earth beneath; there is no other.   Josh. 2:11

40 "You shall therefore keep His statutes and His commandments which I command you today, that it may go well with you and with your children after you, and that you may prolong your days in the land which the LORD your God is giving you for all time."

Cities of Refuge East of the Jordan

41 Then Moses ᴿset apart three cities on this side of the Jordan, toward the rising of the sun,   Num. 35:6

42 that the manslayer might flee there, who kills his neighbor unintentionally, without

having hated him in time past, and that by fleeing to one of these cities he might live:

43 ^RBezer in the wilderness on the plateau for the Reubenites, Ramoth in Gilead for the Gadites, and Golan in Bashan for the Manassites. Josh. 20:8

Introduction to God's Law

44 Now this *is* the law which Moses set before the children of Israel.

45 These *are* the testimonies, the statutes, and the judgments which Moses spoke to the children of Israel after they came out of Egypt,

46 on this side of the Jordan, in the valley opposite Beth Peor, in the land of Sihon king of the Amorites, who dwelt at Heshbon, whom Moses and the children of Israel ^Tdefeated after they came out of Egypt. *struck*

47 And they took possession of his land and the land of Og king of Bashan, two kings of the Amorites, who *were* on this side of the Jordan, toward the ^Trising of the sun, *east*

48 ^Rfrom Aroer, which *is* on the bank of the River Arnon, even to Mount *Sion (that is, ^RHermon), Deut. 2:36; 3:12 · Deut. 3:9

49 and all the plain on the east side of the Jordan as far as the Sea of the Arabah, below the ^Rslopes of Pisgah. Deut. 3:17

The Ten Commandments Reviewed

5 And Moses called all Israel, and said to them: "Hear, O Israel, the statutes and judgments which I speak in your hearing today, that you may learn them and be careful to observe them.

2 ^R"The LORD our God made a covenant with us in Horeb. Ex. 19:5

3 The LORD ^Rdid not make this covenant with our fathers, but with us, those who *are* here today, all of us who *are* alive. Heb. 8:9

4 "The LORD talked with you face to face on the mountain from the midst of the fire.

5 "I stood between the LORD and you at that time, to declare to you the word of the LORD; for you were afraid because of the fire, and you did not go up the mountain. *He* said:

6 'I *am* the LORD your God who brought you out of the land of Egypt, out of the house of ^Tbondage. *slaves*

7 ^R'You shall have no other gods ^Tbefore Me. Hos. 13:4 · *besides*

8 'You shall not make for yourself a carved image—any likeness of *anything* that *is* in heaven above, or that *is* in the earth beneath, or that *is* in the water under the earth;

9 you shall not bow down to them nor serve them. For I, the LORD your God, *am* a jealous God, visiting the iniquity of the fathers upon the

children to the third and fourth *generations* of those who hate Me,

10 ^Rbut showing mercy to thousands, to those who love Me and ^Tkeep My commandments. Dan. 9:4 · *observe*

11 'You shall not take the name of the LORD your God in vain, for the LORD will not hold *him* ^Tguiltless who takes His name in vain. *innocent*

12 ^R'Observe the Sabbath day, to ^Tkeep it holy, as the LORD your God commanded you. Ex. 20:8 · *sanctify it*

13 ^RSix days you shall labor and do all your work, Ex. 23:12; 35:2

14 but the seventh day *is* the Sabbath of the LORD your God. *In it* you shall do no work: you, nor your son, nor your daughter, nor your male servant, nor your female servant, nor your ox, nor your donkey, nor any of your cattle, nor your stranger who *is* within your gates, that your male servant, and your female servant, may rest as well as you.

15 And remember that you were a slave in the land of Egypt, and the LORD your God brought you out from there ^Rby a mighty hand and by an outstretched arm; therefore the LORD your God commanded you to keep the Sabbath day. Deut. 4:34, 37

16 ^R'Honor your father and your mother, as the LORD your God has commanded you, ^Rthat your days may be long, and that it may be well with ^Ryou in the land which the LORD your God is giving you. Lev. 19:3 · Deut. 6:2 · Deut. 4:40

17 ^R'You shall not murder. Matt. 5:21

18 ^R'You shall not commit adultery. Ex. 20:14

19 ^R'You shall not steal. [Rom. 13:9]

20 ^R'You shall not bear false witness against your neighbor. Ex. 20:16; 23:1

21 ^R'You shall not covet your neighbor's wife; and you shall not desire your neighbor's house, his field, his male servant, his female servant, his ox, his donkey, or anything that *is* your neighbor's.' Ex. 20:17

22 "These words the LORD spoke to all your assembly, in the mountain from the midst of the fire, the cloud, and the thick darkness, with a loud voice; and He added no more. And ^RHe wrote them on two tablets of stone and gave them to me. Deut. 4:13

The People Afraid of God's Presence

23 ^R"So it was, when you heard the voice from the midst of the darkness, while the mountain was burning with fire, that you came near to me, all the heads of your tribes and your elders. Ex. 20:18, 19

4:48 Syr. *Sirion*

24 "And you said: 'Surely the LORD our God has shown us His glory and His greatness, and we have heard His voice from the midst of the fire. We have seen this day that God speaks with man; yet he *still* lives.

25 'Now therefore, why should we die? For this great fire will consume us; ᴿif we hear the voice of the LORD our God anymore, then we shall die. Deut. 18:16

26 ᴿ'For who *is there* of all flesh who has heard the voice of the living God speaking from the midst of the fire, as we *have*, and lived? Deut. 4:33

27 'You go near and hear all that the LORD our God may say, and ᴿtell us all that the LORD our God says to you, and we will hear and do *it*.' Ex. 20:19

28 "Then the LORD heard the voice of your words when you spoke to me, and the LORD said to me: 'I have heard the voice of the words of this people which they have spoken to you. ᴿThey are right *in* all that they have spoken. Deut. 18:17

29 'Oh, that they had such a heart in them that they would fear Me and always keep all My commandments, that it might be well with them and with their children forever!

30 'Go and say to them, "Return to your tents."

31 'But as for you, stand here by Me, and I will speak to you all the commandments, the statutes, and the judgments which you shall teach them, that they may observe *them* in the land which I am giving them to possess.'

32 "Therefore you shall ᵀbe careful to do as the LORD your God has commanded you; ᴿyou shall not turn aside to the right hand or to the left. observe · Deut. 17:20; 28:14

33 "You shall walk in all the ways which the LORD your God has commanded you, that you may live ᴿand *that it may be* well with you, and *that* you may prolong *your* days in the land which you shall possess. Deut. 4:40

The Greatest Commandment

6 "Now this *is* the commandment, *and* these *are* the statutes and judgments which the LORD your God has commanded to teach you, that you may observe *them* in the land which you are crossing over to possess,

2 "that you may fear the LORD your God, to keep all His statutes and His commandments which I command you, you and your son and your grandson, all the days of your life, and that your days may be prolonged.

3 "Therefore hear, O Israel, and be careful to observe *it*, that it may be well with you, and that you may multiply greatly as the LORD God of your fathers has promised you— *'a land flowing with milk and honey.'

4 ᴿ"Hear, O Israel: *The LORD our God, the LORD *is* one! [1 Cor. 8:4, 6]

14–C. What Is God's Purpose for Mankind? ▼

5 ᴿ"You shall love the LORD your God with all your heart, ᴿwith all your soul, and with all your strength. Matt. 22:37 · 2 Kin. 23:25 ▲

6 "And ᴿthese words which I command you today shall be in your heart. Deut. 11:18-20

7 "You shall teach them diligently to your children, and shall talk of them when you sit in your house, when you walk by the way, when you lie down, and when you rise up.

8 ᴿ"You shall bind them as a sign on your hand, and they shall be as frontlets between your eyes. Prov. 3:3; 6:21; 7:3

9 ᴿ"You shall write them on the doorposts of your house and on your gates. Deut. 11:20

Caution Against Disobedience

10 "So it shall be, when the LORD your God brings you into the land of which He swore to your fathers, to Abraham, Isaac, and Jacob, to give you large and beautiful cities ᴿwhich you did not build, Josh. 24:13

11 "houses full of all good things, which you did not fill, hewn-out wells which you did not dig, vineyards and olive trees which you did not plant—ᴿwhen you have eaten and are full— Deut. 8:10; 11:15; 14:29

12 "*then* beware, lest you forget the ᴿLORD who brought you out of the land of Egypt, from the house of bondage. Deut. 8:11-18

13 "You shall fear the LORD your God and serve Him, and shall take oaths in His name.

14 "You shall not go after other gods, the gods of the peoples who *are* all around you,

15 "(for ᴿthe LORD your God *is* a jealous God ᴿamong you), lest the anger of the LORD your God be aroused against you and destroy you from the face of the earth. Ex. 20:5 · Ex. 33:3

16 "You shall not ᵀtempt the LORD your God as you tempted *Him* in Massah. test

17 "You shall ᴿdiligently keep the com-

6:3 Ex. 3:8, 17
6:4 Or *The LORD is our God, the LORD alone*, i.e., the only one

---

14-C. What Is God's Purpose for Mankind? (Deuteronomy 6:5)—God's eternal purposes for His creatures are manifold. Since the fall of man, His redemptive purposes are accomplished primarily in those who have been saved. His purpose for man can be seen often by biblically commanded duties:

(1) *Love God.* Verse 5 sums up man's duty to God in words given the highest reverence through the ages in Scripture: "You shall love the LORD your God with all your heart, with all your soul, and with all your mind" (Matt. 22:37, page 971).

(Point 14-C continued on next page)

mandments of the LORD your God, His testimonies, and His statutes which He has commanded you. Deut. 11:22

18 "And you Rshall do what is right and good in the sight of the LORD, that it may be well with you, and that you may go in and possess the good land of which the LORD swore to your fathers, Ex. 15:26

19 "to cast out all your enemies from before you, as the LORD has spoken.

20 R"When your son asks you in time to come, saying, 'What is the meaning of the testimonies, the statutes, and the judgments which the LORD our God has commanded you?' Ex. 13:8, 14

21 "then you shall say to your son: 'We were slaves of Pharaoh in Egypt, and the LORD brought us out of Egypt Rwith a mighty hand; Ex. 13:3

22 'and the LORD showed signs and wonders before our eyes, great and severe, against Egypt, Pharaoh, and all his household.

23 'Then He brought us out from there, that He might bring us in, to give us the land of which He swore to our fathers.

24 'And the LORD commanded us to observe all these statutes, to fear the LORD our God, Rfor our good always, that He might preserve us alive, as it is this day. Jer. 32:39

25 'Then Rit will be righteousness for us, if we are careful to observe all these commandments before the LORD our God, as He has commanded us.' [Rom. 10:3, 5]

A Chosen People

7 "When the LORD your God brings you into the land which you go to possess, and has cast out many nations before you, the Hittites and the Girgashites and the Amorites and the Canaanites and the Per-

izzites and the Hivites and the Jebusites, seven nations greater and mightier than you,

2 "and when the LORD your God delivers them over to you, you shall conquer them and utterly destroy them. You shall make no covenant with them nor show mercy to them.

3 R"Nor shall you make marriages with them. You shall not give your daughter to their son, nor take their daughter for your son. 1 Kin. 11:2

4 "For they will turn your sons away from following Me, to serve other gods; Rso the anger of the LORD will be aroused against you and destroy you suddenly. Deut. 6:15

5 "But thus you shall deal with them: you shall destroy their altars, and break down their sacred pillars, and cut down their Twooden images, and burn their carved images with fire. Or Asherim, Canaanite deities

6 "For you are a Tholy people to the LORD your God; Rthe LORD your God has chosen you to be a people for Himself, a special treasure above all the peoples on the face of the earth. set apart • Ex. 19:5, 6

7 "The LORD did not set His Rlove on you nor choose you because you were more in number than any other people, for you were Rthe least of all peoples; Deut. 4:37 • Deut. 10:22

8 "but because the LORD loves you, and because He would keep the oath which He swore to your fathers, the LORD has brought you out with a mighty hand, and redeemed you from the house of Tbondage, from the hand of Pharaoh king of Egypt. slaves

9 "Therefore know that the LORD your God, He is God, Rthe faithful God Rwho keeps covenant and mercy for a thousand generations with those who love Him and keep His commandments; 1 Cor. 1:9 • Neh. 1:5

10 "and He repays those who hate Him to

(Point 14-C continued from previous page)

(2) Love one another. Christ endorsed verse 5 as the great commandment of man's duty to God. He also showed that this first great commandment implied a second: "You shall love your neighbor as yourself" (Matt. 22:39, page 971; cf. Lev. 19:18, page 127). This was not a new purpose in the mind of God for mankind, since He had already given the Ten Commandments on two tablets of stone (Deut. 5:22, page 186). While commandments one through four stood for man's duties toward God, commandments five through ten stood for man's duties to his fellowman.

We are also to

(1) Have joy. The psalmist said, "In Your presence is fullness of joy" (Ps. 16:11, page 518). Christ wished for His disciples "that your joy may be full" (John 16:24, page 1077). This joy, however, comes from being in God's place of blessing and in doing His will (Ps. 40:8, page 535).

(2) Glorify God. "And you shall glorify Me" (Ps. 50:15, page 541).

(3) Worship Him in holiness. "All nations . . . shall come and worship before You" (Ps. 86:9, page 561). Worship incorporates adoration, submission, sincere praise, and a concurrence of the heart, soul, and mind of the One being worshiped.

(4) Subdue the earth. "God blessed them, and God said . . . 'Fill the earth and subdue it; have dominion over the fish.' . . . And God said, 'See, I have given you every herb that yields seed which is on the face of all the earth, and every tree whose fruit yields seed; to you it shall be for food' " (Gen. 1:28, 29, page 4).

(5) Love and honor the Son as the Father. "That all should honor the Son just as they honor the Father" (John 5:23, page 1057). "Be filled with the Spirit" (Eph. 5:18, page 1192).

See Genesis 10:1–5, page 15, for Point 14-D: What Does the Bible Teach About Race?

their face, to destroy them. He will not [T]be [R]slack with him who hates Him; He will repay him to his face.   delay • [2 Pet. 3:10]

11 "Therefore you shall keep the commandment, the statutes, and the judgments which I command you today, to observe them.

Blessings of Obedience

12 "Then it shall come to pass, because you listen to these judgments, and keep and do them, that the LORD your God will keep with you the covenant and the mercy which He swore to your fathers.

13 "And He will love you and bless you and [T]multiply you; He will also bless the fruit of your womb and the fruit of your land, your grain and your new wine and your oil, the increase of your cattle and the offspring of your flock, in the land of which He swore to your fathers to give you.   cause you to increase

14 "You shall be blessed above all peoples; there shall not be a male or female [R]barren among you or among your livestock.   Ex. 23:26

15 "And the LORD will take away from you all sickness, and will afflict you with none of the [R]terrible diseases of Egypt which you have known, but will lay them on all those who hate you.   Ex. 9:14; 15:26

16 "Also you shall [T]destroy all the peoples whom the LORD your God delivers over to you; your eye shall have no pity on them; nor shall you serve their gods, for that will [R]be a snare to you.   consume • Judg. 8:27

17 "If you should say in your heart, 'These nations are greater than I; how can I dispossess them?'—

18 "you shall not be afraid of them, but you shall [R]remember well what the LORD your God did to Pharaoh and to all Egypt: Ps. 105:5

19 [R]"the great trials which your eyes saw, the signs and the wonders, the mighty hand and the outstretched arm, by which the LORD your God brought you out. So shall the LORD your God do to all the peoples of whom you are afraid.   Deut. 4:34; 29:3

20 [R]"Moreover the LORD your God will send the hornet among them until those who are left, who hide themselves from you, are destroyed.   Josh. 24:12

21 "You shall not be terrified of them; for the LORD your God, the great and awesome God, is among you.

22 "And the LORD your God will drive out those nations before you [R]little by little; you will be unable to [T]destroy them at once, lest the beasts of the field become too numerous for you.   Ex. 23:29, 30 • consume

23 "But the LORD your God will deliver them over to you, and will inflict defeat upon them until they are destroyed.

24 "And [R]He will deliver their kings into your hand, and you will destroy their name from under heaven; [R]no one shall be able to stand [T]against you until you have destroyed them.   Josh. 10:24, 42; 12:1–24 • Josh. 23:9 • before

25 "You shall burn the carved images of their gods with fire; you shall not covet the silver or gold that is on them, nor take it for yourselves, lest you be snared by it; for it is an abomination to the LORD your God.

26 "Nor shall you bring an abomination into your house, lest you be doomed to destruction like it. You shall utterly detest it and utterly abhor it, for it is an accursed thing.

Remember the LORD Your God

8 "Every commandment which I command you today you must [T]be careful to observe, that you may live and multiply, and go in and possess the land of which the LORD swore to your fathers.   observe to do

2 "And you shall remember that the LORD your God [R]led you all the way these forty years in the wilderness, to humble you and [R]test you, [R]to know what was in your heart, whether you would keep His commandments or not.   Amos 2:10 • Ex. 16:4 • [John 2:25]

3 "So He humbled you, [R]allowed you to hunger, and [R]fed you with manna which you did not know nor did your fathers know, that He might make you know that man shall [R]not live by bread alone; but man lives by every word that proceeds from the mouth of the LORD.   Ex. 16:2, 3 • Ex. 16:12, 14, 35 • Matt. 4:4

4 "Your garments did not wear out on you, nor did your foot swell these forty years.

5 [R]"You should [T]know in your heart that as a man chastens his son, so the LORD your God chastens you.   2 Sam. 7:14 • consider

6 "Therefore you shall keep the commandments of the LORD your God, [R]to walk in His ways and to fear Him.   [Deut. 5:33]

7 "For the LORD your God is bringing you into a good land, [R]a land of brooks of water, of fountains and springs, that flow out of valleys and hills;   Deut. 11:9–12

8 "a land of wheat and barley, of vines and fig trees and pomegranates, a land of olive oil and honey;

9 "a land in which you will eat bread without scarcity, in which you will lack nothing; a land whose stones are iron and out of whose hills you can dig copper.

10 "When you have eaten and are full, then you shall bless the LORD your God for the good land which He has given you.

11 "Beware that you do not forget the LORD your God by not keeping His commandments, His judgments, and His statutes which I command you today,

12 [R]"lest—when you have eaten and are [T]full, and have built beautiful houses and dwell in them;   Hos. 13:6 • satisfied

13 "and when your herds and your flocks multiply, and your silver and your gold are

Tmultiplied, and all that you have is multiplied; *increased*

14 R"when your heart Tis lifted up, and you Rforget the LORD your God who brought you out of the land of Egypt, from the house of bondage; 1 Cor. 4:7 · *becomes proud* · Ps. 106:21

15 "who led you through that great and terrible wilderness, *in which were* fiery serpents and scorpions and thirsty land where there was no water; who brought water for you out of the flinty rock;

16 "who fed you in the wilderness with manna, which your fathers did not know, that He might humble you and that He might test you, to do you good in the end—

17 "then you say in your heart, 'My power and the might of my hand have gained me this wealth.'

18 "And you shall remember the LORD your God, Rfor *it is* He who gives you power to get wealth, Rthat He may Testablish His covenant which He swore to your fathers, as *it is* this day. Hos. 2:8 · Deut. 7:8, 12 · *confirm*

19 "Then it shall be, if you by any means forget the LORD your God, and follow other gods, and serve them and worship them, RI testify against you this day that you shall surely perish. Deut. 4:26; 30:18

20 "As the nations which the LORD destroys before you, Rso you shall perish, because you would not be obedient to the voice of the LORD your God. [Dan. 9:11, 12]

Israel's Rebellions Reviewed

9 "Hear, O Israel: You *are* to cross over the Jordan today, and go in to dispossess nations greater and mightier than yourself, cities great and fortified up to heaven,

2 "a people great and tall, the descendants of the Anakim, whom you know, and *of whom* you heard *it said*, 'Who can stand before the descendants of Anak?'

3 "Therefore understand today that the LORD your God *is* He who goes over before you *as* a consuming fire. He will destroy them and bring them down before you; so you shall drive them out and destroy them quickly, as the LORD has said to you.

4 R"Do not think in your heart, after the LORD your God has cast them out before you, saying, 'Because of my righteousness the LORD has brought me in to possess this land'; but *it is* Rbecause of the wickedness of these nations *that* the LORD is driving them out from before you. Deut. 8:17 · Lev. 18:3, 24-30

5 R"*It is* not because of your righteousness or the uprightness of your heart *that* you go in to possess their land, but because of the wickedness of these nations *that* the LORD your God drives them out from before you, and that He may Tfulfill the Rword which the LORD swore to your fathers, to Abraham, Isaac, and Jacob. [Titus 3:5] · *perform* · Gen. 50:24

6 "Therefore understand that the LORD your God is not giving you this good land to possess because of your righteousness, for you *are* a Tstiff-necked people. *rebellious*

7 "Remember! Do not forget how you Rprovoked the LORD your God to wrath in the wilderness. RFrom the day that you departed from the land of Egypt until you came to this place, you have been rebellious against the LORD. Num. 14:22 · Ex. 14:11

8 "Also Rin Horeb you provoked the LORD to wrath, so that the LORD was angry *enough* with you to have destroyed you. Ex. 32:1-8

9 R"When I went up into the mountain to receive the tablets of stone, the tablets of the covenant which the LORD made with you, then I stayed on the mountain forty days and Rforty nights. I neither ate bread nor drank water. Deut. 5:2-22 · Ex. 24:18

10 "Then the LORD delivered to me two tablets of stone written with the finger of God, and on them *were* all the words which the LORD had spoken to you on the mountain from the midst of the fire RinT the day of the assembly. Ex. 19:17 · *when you were all gathered together*

11 "And it came to pass, at the end of forty days and forty nights, *that* the LORD gave me the two tablets of stone, the tablets of the covenant.

12 "Then the LORD said to me, 'Arise, go down quickly from here, for your people whom you brought out of Egypt have acted corruptly; they have quickly turned aside from the way which I commanded them; they have made themselves a molded image.'

13 "Furthermore the LORD spoke to me, saying, 'I have seen this people, and indeed they are a Tstiff-necked people. *rebellious*

14 'Let Me alone, that I may destroy them and Rblot out their name from under heaven; Rand I will make of you a nation mightier and greater than they.' Deut. 29:20 · Num. 14:12

15 R"So I turned and came down from the mountain, and Rthe mountain burned with fire; and the two tablets of the covenant *were* in my two hands. Ex. 32:15-19 · Ex. 19:18

16 "And RI looked, and behold, you had sinned against the LORD your God—had made for yourselves a molded calf! You had turned aside quickly from the way which the LORD had commanded you. Ex. 32:19

17 "Then I took the two tablets and threw them out of my two hands and Rbroke them before your eyes. Ex. 32:19

18 "And I Rfell T down before the LORD, as at the first, forty days and forty nights; I neither ate bread nor drank water, because of all your sin which you committed in doing wickedly in the sight of the LORD, to provoke Him to anger. Ex. 34:28 · *prostrated myself*

19 "For I was afraid of the anger and hot displeasure with which the LORD was angry

with you, to destroy you. ^RBut the LORD
listened to me at that time also.   Ex. 32:14

20 "And the LORD was very angry with
Aaron *and* would have destroyed him; so I
prayed for Aaron also at the same time.

21 "Then I took your sin, the calf which
you had made, and burned it with fire and
crushed it *and* ground *it* very small, until it
was as fine as dust; and I threw its dust into
the brook that descended from the mountain.

22 "Also at Taberah and Massah and ^RKib-
roth Hattaavah you ^Tprovoked the LORD to
wrath.   Num. 11:4, 34 · *caused the LORD to be angry*

23 "Likewise, when the LORD sent you from
Kadesh Barnea, saying, 'Go up and possess
the land which I have given you,' then you
rebelled against the commandment of the
LORD your God, and ^Ryou did not believe Him
nor obey His voice.   Ps. 106:24, 25

24 "You have been rebellious against the
LORD from the day that I knew you.

25 ^R"Thus I ^Tprostrated myself before the
LORD; forty days and forty nights I kept
prostrating myself, because the LORD had
said He would destroy you.   Deut. 9:18 · *fell down*

26 "Therefore I prayed to the LORD, and
said: 'O Lord GOD, do not destroy Your
people and ^RYour inheritance whom You
have redeemed through Your greatness,
whom You have brought out of Egypt with a
mighty hand.   Deut. 32:9

27 'Remember Your servants, Abraham,
Isaac, and Jacob; do not look on the stubbornness of this people, or on their wickedness or their sin,

28 'lest the land from which You brought us
should say, "Because the LORD was not able
to bring them to the land which He promised
them, and because He hated them, He has
brought them out to kill them in the wilderness."

29 'Yet they *are* Your people and Your
inheritance, whom You brought out by Your
mighty power and by Your outstretched
arm.'

The Second Pair of Tablets

10 "At that time the LORD said to me,
'Hew for yourself two tablets of stone
like the first, and come up to Me on the
mountain and make yourself an ark of wood.

2 'And I will write on the tablets the words
that were on the first tablets, which you
broke; and you shall put them in the ark.'

3 "So I made an ark of acacia wood,
hewed two tablets of stone like the first, and
went up the mountain, having the two tablets
in my hand.

4 "And He wrote on the tablets according
to the first writing, the Ten ^TCommandments,
^Rwhich the LORD had spoken to you in the
mountain from the midst of the fire in the
day of the assembly; and the LORD gave them
to me.   *Words* · Ex. 20:1; 34:28

5 "Then I turned and came down from the
mountain, and put the tablets in the ark
which I had made; ^Rand there they are, just
as the LORD commanded me."   1 Kin. 8:9

6 (Now the children of Israel journeyed
from the wells of Bene Jaakan to Moserah,
where Aaron died, and where he was buried;
and Eleazar his son ministered as priest in his
^Tstead.   *place*

7 ^RFrom there they journeyed to Gudgodah, and from Gudgodah to Jotbathah, a land
of ^Trivers of water.   Num. 33:32–34 · *brooks*

8 At that time the LORD ^Tseparated the
tribe of Levi to bear the ark of the covenant
of the LORD, ^Rto stand before the LORD to
minister to Him and ^Rto bless in His name, to
this day.   *set apart* · Deut. 18:5 · Num. 6:23

9 ^RTherefore Levi has no portion nor inheritance with his brethren; the LORD *is* his
inheritance, just as the LORD your God promised him.)   Deut. 18:1, 2

10 "As at the first time, I stayed in the
mountain forty days and forty nights;
^Rthe LORD also heard me at that time, *and* the
LORD chose not to destroy you.   Ex. 32:14

11 ^R"Then the LORD said to me, 'Arise, begin
your journey before the people, that they
may go in and possess the land which I swore
to their fathers to give them.'   Ex. 33:1

The Essence of the Law

12 "And now, Israel, what does the LORD
your God require of you, but to fear the LORD
your God, to walk in all His ways and to ^Rlove
Him, to serve the LORD your God with all
your heart and with all your soul,   Deut. 6:5

13 "*and* to keep the commandments of the
LORD and His statutes which I command you
today ^Rfor your ^Tgood? Deut. 6:24 · *benefit* or *welfare*

14 "Indeed heaven and the highest heavens
belong to the ^RLORD your God, *also* the earth
with all that *is* in it.   [Neh. 9:6]

15 "The LORD delighted only in your fa-
thers, to love them; and He chose their ^Tde-
scendants after them, you above all peoples,
as *it is* this day.   Lit. *seed*

16 "Therefore circumcise the foreskin of
your heart, and be stiff-necked no longer.

17 "For the LORD your God *is* God of gods
and ^RLord of lords, the great God, ^Rmighty
and awesome, who ^Rshows no partiality nor
takes a bribe.   Rev. 19:16 · Deut. 7:21 · Acts 10:34

18 ^R"He administers justice for the fatherless and the widow, and loves the stranger,
giving him food and clothing.   Ps. 68:5; 146:9

19 "Therefore love the stranger, for you
were strangers in the land of Egypt.

20 ^R"You shall fear the LORD your God; you
shall serve Him, and to Him you shall hold
fast, and take oaths in His name.   Matt. 4:10

21 "He *is* your praise, and He *is* your God,
who has done for you these great and awesome things which your eyes have seen.

22 "Your fathers went down to Egypt with

seventy persons, and now the LORD your God has made you as the stars of heaven in multitude.

Love and Obedience Rewarded

11 "Therefore you shall love the LORD your God, and keep His charge, His statutes, His judgments, and His commandments always.

2 "Know today that *I do* not *speak* with your children, who have not known and who have not seen the ᵀchastening of the LORD your God, His greatness and His mighty hand and His outstretched arm—   *discipline*

3 "His signs and His acts which He did in the midst of Egypt, to Pharaoh king of Egypt, and to all his land;

4 "what He did to the army of Egypt, to their horses and their chariots: ᴿhow He made the waters of the Red Sea overflow them as they pursued you, and *how* the LORD has destroyed them to this day;   Ps. 106:11

5 "what He did for you in the wilderness until you came to this place;

6 "and what He did to Dathan and Abiram the sons of Eliab, the son of Reuben: how the earth opened its mouth and swallowed them up, their households, their tents, and all the substance that *was* ᵀin their possession, in the midst of all Israel—   *at their feet*

7 "but your eyes have seen every great ᵀact of the LORD which He did.   *work*

8 "Therefore you shall keep every commandment which I command you today, that you may be strong, and go in and possess the land which you cross over to possess,

9 "and that you may prolong *your* days in the land which the LORD swore to give your fathers, to them and their descendants, ᴿ'a land flowing with milk and honey.'   Ex. 3:8

10 "For the land which you go to possess *is* not like the land of Egypt from which you have come, where you sowed your seed and watered *it* by foot, as a vegetable garden;

11 ᴿ'but the land which you cross over to possess *is* a land of hills and valleys, which drinks water from the rain of heaven, Deut. 8:7

12 "a land for which the LORD your God cares; ᴿthe eyes of the LORD your God *are* always on it, from the beginning of the year to the very end of the year.   1 Kin. 9:3

13 'And it shall be that if you earnestly ᵀobey My commandments which I command you today, to love the LORD your God and serve Him with all your heart and with all your soul,   *Lit. listen to*

14 'then ᴿI* will give *you* the rain for your land in its season, ᴿthe early rain and the latter rain, that you may gather in your grain, your new wine, and your oil. Deut. 28:12 • Joel 2:23

15 ᴿ'And I will send grass in your fields for your livestock, that you may ᴿeat and be ᵀfilled.'   Ps. 104:14 • Deut. 6:11 • *satisfied*

16 "Take heed to yourselves, lest your heart be deceived, and you turn aside and serve other gods and worship them,

17 "lest the LORD'S anger be aroused against you, and He shut up the heavens so that there be no rain, and the land yield no produce, and you perish quickly from the good land which the LORD is giving you.

18 "Therefore ᴿyou shall ᵀlay up these words of mine in your heart and in your ᴿsoul, and ᴿbind them as a sign on your hand, and they shall be as frontlets between your eyes.   Deut. 6:6–9 • Lit. *put* • Ps. 119:2, 34 • Deut. 6:8

19 ᴿ'You shall teach them to your children, speaking of them when you sit in your house, when you walk by the way, when you lie down, and when you rise up.   Deut. 4:9, 10; 6:7

20 "And you shall write them on the doorposts of your house and on your gates,

21 "that ᴿyour days and the days of your children may be multiplied in the land of which the LORD swore to your fathers to give them, like ᴿthe days of the heavens above the earth.   Deut. 4:40 • Ps. 72:5; 89:29

22 "For if you carefully keep all these commandments which I command you to do—to love the LORD your God, to walk in all His ways, and to hold fast to Him—

23 "then the LORD will ᴿdrive out all these nations from before you, and you will ᴿdispossess greater and mightier nations than yourselves.   Deut. 4:38 • Deut. 9:1

24 "Every place on which the sole of your foot treads shall be yours: ᴿfrom the wilderness and Lebanon, from the river, the River Euphrates, even to the ᵀWestern Sea, shall be your territory.   Gen. 15:18 • Mediterranean

25 "No man shall be able to stand against you; the LORD your God will put the dread of you and the fear of you upon all the land where you tread, just as He has said to you.

26 ᴿ'Behold, I set before you today a blessing and a curse: Deut. 30:1, 15, 19

27 ᴿ'the blessing, if you obey the commandments of the LORD your God which I command you today;   Deut. 28:1–14

28 "and the ᴿcurse, if you do not obey the commandments of the LORD your God, but turn aside from the way which I command you today, to go after other gods which you have not known.   Deut. 28:15–68

29 "Now it shall be, when the LORD your God has brought you into the land which you go to possess, that you shall put the ᴿblessing on Mount Gerizim and the ᴿcurse on Mount Ebal.   Josh. 8:33 • Deut. 27:13–26

30 "*Are* they not on the other side of the Jordan, toward the setting sun, in the land of the Canaanites who dwell in the plain opposite Gilgal, ᴿbeside the terebinth trees of Moreh?   Gen. 12:6

11:14 So with MT, Tg.; Sam., LXX, Vg. *He*

31 "For you will cross over the Jordan and go in to possess the land which the LORD your God is giving you, and you will possess it and dwell in it.

32 "And you shall be careful to observe all the statutes and judgments which I set before you today.

A Prescribed Place of Worship

12 "These ᴿare the statutes and judgments which you shall be careful to observe in the land which the LORD God of your fathers is giving you to possess, all the days that you live on the earth.   Deut. 6:1

2 "You shall utterly destroy all the places where the nations which you shall dispossess served their gods, on the high mountains and on the hills and under every green tree.

3 "And you shall destroy their altars, break their *sacred* pillars, and burn their ᵀwooden images with fire; you shall cut down the carved images of their gods and destroy their names from that place.   Heb. Asherim

4 "You shall not ᴿworship the LORD your God *with* such *things.*   Deut. 12:31

5 "But you shall seek the ᴿplace where the LORD your God chooses, out of all your tribes, to put His name for His ᴿdwelling place; and there you shall go.   Ex. 20:24 · Ex. 15:13

6 ᴿ"There you shall take your burnt offerings, your sacrifices, your tithes, the heave offerings of your hand, your vowed offerings, your freewill offerings, and the ᴿfirstborn of your herds and flocks.   Lev. 17:3, 4 · Deut. 14:23

7 "And there you shall eat before the LORD your God, and you shall rejoice in ᵀall to which you have put your hand, you and your households, in which the LORD your God has blessed you.   all that you undertake

8 "You shall not at all do as we are doing here today—ᴿevery man doing whatever *is* right in his own eyes—   Judg. 17:6; 21:25

9 "for as yet you have not come to the ᵀrest and the inheritance which the LORD your God is giving you.   Or place of rest

10 "But *when* you cross over the Jordan and dwell in the land which the LORD your God is giving you to inherit, and He gives you ᴿrest from all your enemies round about, so that you dwell in safety,   Josh. 11:23

11 "then there will be the place where the LORD your God chooses to make His name abide. There you shall bring all that I command you: your burnt offerings, your sacrifices, your tithes, the heave offerings of your hand, and all your choice offerings which you vow to the LORD.

12 "And ᴿyou shall rejoice before the LORD your God, you and your sons and your daughters, your male and female servants and the ᴿLevite who *is* within your gates,

since he has no portion nor inheritance with you.   Deut. 12:18; 26:11 · Deut. 10:9; 14:29

13 "Take heed to yourself that you do not offer your burnt offerings in every place that you see;

14 "but in the place which the LORD chooses, in one of your tribes, there you shall offer your burnt offerings, and there you shall do all that I command you.

15 "However, you may slaughter and eat meat within all your gates, whatever your heart desires, according to the blessing of the LORD your God which He has given you; the unclean and the clean may eat of it, ᴿof the gazelle and the deer alike.   Deut. 14:5

16 ᴿ"Only you shall not eat the blood; you shall pour it on the earth like water.   Gen. 9:4

17 "You may not eat within your gates the tithe of your grain or your new wine or your oil, of the firstborn of your herd or your flock, of any of your offerings which you vow, of your freewill offerings, or of the ᵀheave offering of your hand.   contribution

18 "But you must eat them before the LORD your God in the place which the LORD your God chooses, you and your son and your daughter, your male servant and your female servant, and the Levite who *is* within your gates; and you shall rejoice before the LORD your God in all to which you put your hands.

19 ᵀ"Take heed to yourself that you do not forsake the Levite as long as you live in your land.   Be careful

20 "When the LORD your God ᴿenlarges your border as He has promised you, and you say, 'Let me eat meat,' because you long to eat meat, you may eat as much meat as your heart desires.   Ex. 34:24

21 "If the place where the LORD your God chooses to put His name is too far from ᴿyou, then you may slaughter from your herd and from your flock which the LORD has given you, just as I have commanded you, and you may eat within your gates as much as your heart desires.   Deut. 14:24

22 "Just as the gazelle and the deer are eaten, so you may eat them; the unclean and the clean alike may eat them.

23 "Only be sure that you do not eat the blood, ᴿfor the blood *is* the life; you may not eat the life with the meat.   Gen. 9:4

24 "You shall not eat it; you shall pour it on the earth like water.

25 "You shall not eat it, that it may go well with you and your children after you, when you do *what is* right in the sight of the LORD.

26 "Only the holy things which you have, and your vowed offerings, you shall take and go to the place which the LORD chooses.

27 "And ᴿyou shall offer your burnt offerings, the meat and the blood, on the altar of the LORD your God; and the blood of your sacrifices shall be poured out on the altar of

the LORD your God, and you shall eat the meat.   Lev. 1:5, 9, 13, 17

28 "Observe and obey all these words which I command you, Rthat it may go well with you and your children after you forever, when you do *what is* good and right in the sight of the LORD your God.   Deut. 12:25

Beware of False Gods

29 "When Rthe LORD your God cuts off from before you the nations which you go to dispossess, and you displace them and dwell in their land,   Ex. 23:23

30 "take heed to yourself that you are not ensnared to follow them, after they are destroyed from before you, and that you do not inquire after their gods, saying, 'How did these nations serve their gods? I also will do likewise.'

31 "You shall not worship the LORD your God in that way; for every abomination to the LORD which He hates they have done to their gods; for they burn even their sons and daughters in the fire to their gods.

32 "Whatever I command you, be careful to observe it; Ryou shall not add to it nor take away from it.   Rev. 22:18, 19

Punishment of Apostates

13 "If there arises among you a prophet or a Rdreamer of dreams, Rand he gives you a sign or a wonder,   Zech. 10:2 • Matt. 24:24

2 "and Rthe sign or the wonder comes to pass, of which he spoke to you, saying, 'Let us go after other gods,' which you have not known—'and let us serve them,'   Deut. 18:22

3 "you shall not listen to the words of that prophet or that dreamer of dreams, for the LORD your God Ris testing you to know whether you love the LORD your God with all your heart and with all your soul.   Deut. 8:2, 16

4 "You shall Rwalkᵀ after the LORD your God and fear Him, and keep His commandments and obey His voice; you shall serve Him and hold fast to Him.   2 Kin. 23:3 • *follow*

5 "But Rthat prophet or that dreamer of dreams shall be put to death, because he has spoken in order to turn *you* away from the LORD your God, who brought you out of the land of Egypt and redeemed you from the house of bondage, to entice you from the way in which the LORD your God commanded you to walk. So you shall ᵀput away the evil from your midst.   Jer. 14:15 • *exterminate*

6 R"If your brother, the son of your mother, your son or your daughter, Rthe wife ᵀof your bosom, or your friend who is as your own soul, secretly entices you, saying, 'Let us go and serve other gods,' which you have not known, neither you nor your fathers,   Deut. 17:2 • Gen. 16:5 • *Whom you cherish*

7 "of the gods of the people which *are* all around you, near to you or far off from you,

from *one* end of the earth to the *other* end of the earth,

8 "you shall Rnot ᵀconsent to him or listen to him, nor shall your eye pity him, nor shall you spare him or conceal him;   Prov. 1:10 • *yield*

9 "but you shall surely kill him; your hand shall be first against him to put him to death, and afterward the hand of all the people.

10 "And you shall stone him with stones until he dies, because he sought to entice you away from the LORD your God, who brought you out of the land of Egypt, from the house of bondage.

11 "So all Israel shall hear and Rfear, and not again do such wickedness as this among you.   Deut. 17:13

12 R"If you hear someone in one of your cities, which the LORD your God gives you to dwell in, saying,   Judg. 20:1–48

13 'Corrupt men have gone out from among you and enticed the inhabitants of their city, saying, "Let us go and serve other gods" '—which you have not known—

14 "then you shall inquire, search out, and ask diligently. And *if it is* indeed true *and* certain *that* such an ᵀabomination was committed among you,   *detestable action*

15 "you shall surely strike the inhabitants of that city with the edge of the sword, utterly destroying it, all that is in it and its livestock—with the edge of the sword.

16 "And you shall gather all its plunder into the middle of the street, and completely Rburn with fire the city and all its plunder, for the LORD your God. It shall be a heap forever; it shall not be built again.   Josh. 6:24

17 R"So none of the accursed things shall remain in your hand, that the LORD may Rturn from the fierceness of His anger and show you mercy, have compassion on you and ᵀmultiply you, just as He swore to your fathers,   Josh. 6:18 • Josh. 7:26 • *increase*

18 "because you have listened to the voice of the LORD your God, Rto keep all His commandments which I command you today, to do *what is* right in the eyes of the LORD your God.   Deut. 12:25, 28, 32

Improper Mourning

14 "You *are* the children of the LORD your God; you shall not cut yourselves nor shave the front of your head for the dead.

2 R"For you *are* a holy people to the LORD your God, and the LORD has chosen you to be a people for Himself, a special treasure above all the peoples who *are* on the face of the earth.   Lev. 20:26

Clean and Unclean Meat

3 "You shall not eat any detestable thing.

4 R"These *are* the animals which you may eat: the ox, the sheep, the goat,   Lev. 11:2–45

5 "the deer, the gazelle, the roe deer, the

wild goat, the ᵀmountain goat, the antelope, and the mountain sheep. Or *addax*

6 "And you may eat every animal with cloven hooves, having the hoof split into two parts, *and that* chews the cud, among the animals.

7 "Nevertheless, of those that chew the cud or have cloven hooves, you shall not eat, *such as* these: the camel, the hare, and the rock hyrax; for they chew the cud but do not have cloven hooves; they *are* unclean for you.

8 "Also the swine is unclean for you, because it has cloven hooves, yet *does* not *chew* the cud; you shall not eat their flesh ᴿor touch their dead carcasses. Lev. 11:26, 27

9 ᴿ"These you may eat of all that *are* in the waters: you may eat all that have fins and scales. Lev. 11:9

10 "And whatever does not have fins and scales you shall not eat; it *is* unclean for you.

11 "All clean birds you may eat.

12 ᴿ"But these you shall not eat: the eagle, the vulture, the buzzard, Lev. 11:13

13 "the red kite, the falcon, and the kite after their kinds;

14 "every raven after its kind;

15 "the ostrich, the short-eared owl, the seagull, and the hawk after their kinds;

16 "the little owl, the screech owl, the white owl,

17 "the jackdaw, the carrion vulture, the fisher owl,

18 "the stork, the heron after its kind, and the hoopoe and the bat.

19 "Also every creeping thing that flies is unclean for you; they shall not be eaten.

20 "You may eat all clean birds.

21 "You shall not eat anything that dies *of itself*; you may give it to the alien who *is* within your gates, that he may eat it, or you may sell it to a foreigner; for you *are* a holy people to the LORD your God. You shall not boil a young goat in its mother's milk.

Tithing Principles

22 ᴿ"You shall truly tithe all the increase of your grain that the field produces year by year. Lev. 27:30

23 "And you shall eat before the LORD your God, in the place where He chooses to make His name abide, the tithe of your grain and your new wine and your oil, of the firstborn of your herds and your flocks, that you may learn to fear the LORD your God always.

24 "But if the journey is too long for you, so that you are not able to carry *the tithe, or* ᴿif the place where the LORD your God chooses to put His name is too far from you, when the LORD your God has blessed you, Deut. 12:5, 21

25 "then you shall exchange *it* for money, take the money in your hand, and go to the place which the LORD your God chooses.

26 "And you shall spend that money for whatever your heart desires: for oxen or sheep, for wine or similar drink, for whatever your heart desires; you shall eat there before the LORD your God, and you shall ᴿrejoice, you and your household. Deut. 12:7

27 "You shall not ᵀforsake the ᴿLevite who *is* within your gates, for he has no part nor inheritance with you. neglect • Deut. 12:12

28 "At the end of *every* third year you shall bring out the tithe of your produce of that year and store *it* up within your gates.

29 "And the Levite, because he has no portion nor inheritance with you, and the stranger and the fatherless and the widow who *are* within your gates, may come and eat and be satisfied, that the LORD your God may bless you in all the work of your hand which you do.

Debts Canceled Every Seven Years

15 "At the end of *every* seven years you shall grant a release *of debts*.

2 "And this *is* the form of the release: Every creditor who has lent *anything* to his neighbor shall release *it*; he shall not ᵀrequire *it* of his neighbor or his brother, because it is called the LORD's release. *exact it*

3 "Of a foreigner you may require *it*; but you shall give up your claim to what is owed by your brother,

4 "except when there may be no poor among you; for the LORD will greatly bless you in the land which the LORD your God is giving you to possess *as* an inheritance—

5 "only if you carefully obey the voice of the LORD your God, to observe with care all these commandments which I command you today.

6 "For the LORD your God will bless you just as He promised you; ᴿyou shall lend to many nations, but you shall not borrow; you shall reign over many nations, but they shall not reign over you. Deut. 28:12, 44

Generosity to the Poor

7 "If there is among you a poor man of your brethren, within any of the gates in your land which the LORD your God is giving you, you shall not harden your heart nor shut your hand from your poor brother,

8 "but ᴿyou shall ᵀopen your hand wide to him and willingly lend him sufficient for his need, whatever he needs. Matt. 5:42 • *freely open*

9 "Beware lest there be a wicked thought in your heart, saying, 'The seventh year, the year of release, is at hand,' and your eye be evil against your poor brother and you give him nothing, and he cry out to the LORD against you, and it become sin among you.

10 "You shall surely give to him, and your heart should not be grieved when you give to him, because ᴿfor this thing the LORD your God will bless you in all your works and in all to which you put your hand. Deut. 14:29

11 "For the poor will never cease from the land; therefore I command you, saying, 'You shall open your hand wide to your brother, to your poor and your needy, in your land.'

The Law Concerning Bondservants

12 "If your brother, a Hebrew man, or a Hebrew woman, is ᴿsold to you and serves you six years, then in the seventh year you shall let him go free from you.   Lev. 25:39-46

13 "And when you ᵀsend him away free from you, you shall not let him go away empty-handed;   *set him free*

14 "you shall supply him liberally from your flock, from your threshing floor, and from your winepress. *From what* the LORD has blessed you with, you shall give to him.

15 ᴿ"You shall remember that you were a slave in the land of Egypt, and the LORD your God redeemed you; therefore I command you this thing today.   Deut. 5:15

16 "And ᴿif it happens that he says to you, 'I will not go away from you,' because he loves you and your house, since he prospers with you,   Ex. 21:5, 6

17 "then you shall take an awl and thrust *it* through his ear to the door, and he shall be your servant forever. Also to your female servant you shall do likewise.

18 "It shall not seem hard to you when you send him away free from you; for he has been worth ᴿa double hired servant in serving you six years. Then the LORD your God will bless you in all that you do.   Is. 16:14

The Law Concerning Firstborn Animals

19 ᴿ"All the firstborn males that come from your herd and your flock you shall ᵀsanctify to the LORD your God; you shall do no work with the firstborn of your herd, nor shear the firstborn of your flock.   Ex. 13:2, 12 • *set apart*

20 ᴿ"You and your household shall eat *it* before the LORD your God year by year in the place which the LORD chooses.   Deut. 12:5; 14:23

21 "But if there is a defect in it, *if it is* lame or blind *or has* any serious defect, you shall not sacrifice it to the LORD your God.

22 "You may eat it within your gates; the unclean and the clean *person* alike *may eat it*, as *if it were* a gazelle or a deer.

23 "Only you shall not eat its blood; you shall pour it on the ground like water.

The Passover Reviewed

16 "Observe the month of Abib, and keep the Passover to the LORD your God, for in the month of Abib the LORD your God brought you out of Egypt by night.

2 "Therefore you shall sacrifice the Passover to the LORD your God, from the flock and the herd, in the ᴿplace where the LORD chooses to put His name.   Deut. 12:5, 26; 15:20

3 "You shall eat no leavened bread with it; ᴿseven days you shall eat unleavened bread

with it, *that is*, the bread of affliction (for you came out of the land of Egypt in haste), that you may ᴿremember the day in which you came out of the land of Egypt all the days of your life.   Num. 29:12 • Ex. 13:3

4 ᴿ"And no leaven shall be seen among you in all your territory for seven days, nor shall *any* of the meat which you sacrifice the first day at twilight remain overnight until ᴿmorning.   Ex. 13:7 • Num. 9:12

5 "You may not sacrifice the Passover within any of your gates which the LORD your God gives you;

6 "but at the place where the LORD your God chooses to make His name abide, there you shall sacrifice the Passover ᴿat twilight, at the going down of the sun, at the time you came out of Egypt.   Ex. 12:7-10

7 "And you shall roast and eat *it* ᴿin the place which the LORD your God chooses, and in the morning you shall turn and go to your tents.   2 Kin. 23:23

8 "Six days you shall eat unleavened bread, and ᴿon the seventh day there *shall be* a sacred assembly to the LORD your God. You shall do no work *on it*.   Lev. 23:8, 36

The Feast of Weeks Reviewed

9 "You shall count seven weeks for yourself; begin to count the seven weeks from *the time* you begin *to put* the sickle to the grain.

10 "Then you shall keep the ᴿFeast of Weeks to the LORD your God with the tribute of a freewill offering from your hand, which you shall give ᴿas the LORD your God blesses you.   Ex. 34:22 • 1 Cor. 16:2

11 "You shall rejoice before the LORD your God, you and your son and your daughter, your male servant and your female servant, the Levite who *is* within your gates, the stranger and the fatherless and the widow who *are* among you, at the place where the LORD your God chooses to make His name abide.

12 ᴿ"And you shall remember that you were a slave in Egypt, and you shall be careful to observe these statutes.   Deut. 15:15

The Feast of Tabernacles Reviewed

13 ᴿ"You shall observe the Feast of Tabernacles seven days, when you have gathered from your threshing floor and from your winepress.   Ex. 23:16

14 "And you shall rejoice in your feast, you and your son and your daughter, your male servant and your female servant and the Levite, the stranger and the fatherless and the widow, who *are* within your ᵀgates.   *towns*

15 ᴿ"Seven days you shall keep a sacred feast to the LORD your God in the place which the LORD chooses, because the LORD your God will bless you in all your produce and in all the work of your hands, so that you surely rejoice.   Lev. 23:39-41

16 "Three times a year all your males shall appear before the LORD your God in the place which He chooses: at the Feast of Unleavened Bread, at the Feast of Weeks, and at the Feast of Tabernacles; and they shall not appear before the LORD empty-handed.

17 "Every man *shall* give as he is able, ^Raccording to the blessing of the LORD your God which He has given you.   Deut. 16:10

Justice Must Be Administered

18 "You shall appoint judges and officers in all your gates, which the LORD your God gives you, according to your tribes, and they shall judge the people with just judgment.

19 "You shall not pervert justice; you shall not show partiality, nor take a bribe, for a bribe blinds the eyes of the wise and ^Ttwists the words of the righteous.   *perverts*

20 "You shall follow what is altogether just, that you may ^Rlive and inherit the land which the LORD your God is giving you.   Ezek. 18:5-9

21 ^R"You shall not plant for yourself any tree, as a ^Twooden image, near the altar which you build for yourself to the LORD your God.   Ex. 34:13 • Or *Asherah*

22 ^R"You shall not set up a sacred pillar, which the LORD your God hates.   Lev. 26:1

17 "You shall not sacrifice to the LORD your God a bull or sheep which has any ^Tblemish *or* defect, for that *is* an abomination to the LORD your God.   Lit. *evil thing*

2 "If there is found among you, within any of your ^Tgates which the LORD your God gives you, a man or a woman who has been wicked in the sight of the LORD your God, ^Rin transgressing His covenant,   *towns* • Josh. 7:11

3 "who has gone and served other gods and worshiped them, either ^Rthe sun or moon or any of the host of heaven, ^Rwhich I have not commanded,   Deut. 4:19 • Jer. 7:22

4 "and it is told you, and you hear *of it,* then you shall inquire diligently. And if *it is* indeed true *and* certain that such an abomination has been committed in Israel,

5 "then you shall bring out to your gates that man or woman who has committed that wicked thing, and stone ^Rto death that man or woman with stones.   Deut. 13:6-11

6 "Whoever is deserving of death shall be put to death on the testimony of two or three ^Rwitnesses; he shall not be put to death on the testimony of one witness.   Num. 35:30

7 "The hands of the witnesses shall be the first against him to put him to death, and afterward the hands of all the people. So you shall put away the evil from among you.

8 "If a matter arises which is too hard for you to judge, between degrees of guilt for bloodshed, between one judgment or another, or between one punishment or another, matters of controversy within your gates, then you shall arise and go up to the place which the LORD your God chooses.

9 "And you shall come to the priests, the Levites, and to the judge *there* in those days, and inquire *of them;* they shall pronounce upon you the sentence of judgment.

10 "You shall do according to the sentence which they pronounce upon you in that place which the LORD chooses. And you shall be careful to do according to all that they order you.

11 "According to the sentence of the law in which they instruct you, according to the judgment which they tell you, you shall do; you shall not turn aside *to* the right hand or *to* the left from the sentence which they pronounce upon you.

12 "Now the man who acts presumptuously and will not heed the priest who stands to minister there before the LORD your God, or the judge, that man shall die. So you shall put away the evil from Israel.

13 ^R"And all the people shall hear and fear, and no longer act presumptuously.   Deut. 13:11

Principles Governing Kings

14 "When you come to the land which the LORD your God is giving you, and possess it and dwell in it, and say, 'I will set a king over me like all the nations that *are* around me,'

15 "you shall surely set a king over you whom the LORD your God chooses; *one* ^Rfrom among your brethren you shall set as king over you; you may not set a foreigner over you, who *is* not your brother.   Jer. 30:21

16 "But he shall not multiply ^Rhorses for himself, nor cause the people ^Rto return to Egypt to multiply horses, for ^Rthe LORD has said to you, 'You shall not return that way again.'   1 Kin. 4:26; 10:26-29 • Ezek. 17:15 • Ex. 13:17, 18

17 "Neither shall he multiply wives for himself, lest his heart turn away; nor shall he greatly multiply silver and gold for himself.

18 "Also it shall be, when he sits on the throne of his kingdom, that he shall write for himself a copy of this law in a book, from *the one* before the priests, the Levites.

19 "And ^Rit shall be with him, and he shall read it all the days of his life, that he may learn to fear the LORD his God and be careful to observe all the words of this law and these statutes,   Ps. 119:97, 98

20 ^R"that his heart may not ^Tbe lifted above his brethren, that he may not turn aside from the commandment *to* the right hand or *to* the left, and that he may prolong *his* days in his kingdom, he and his children in the midst of Israel.   John 1:45 • *become proud*

The Portion of the Priests and Levites

18 "The priests, the Levites—all the tribe of Levi—shall have ^Tno part nor ^Rinheritance with Israel; they shall eat the offerings of the LORD made by fire, and His portion.   *no portion* • Deut. 10:9

2 "Therefore they shall have no inheri-

tance among their brethren; the LORD is their inheritance, as He said to them.

3 "And this shall be the priest's ᴿdueᵀ from the people, from those who offer a sacrifice, whether *it is* bull or sheep: they shall give to the priest the shoulder, the cheeks, and the stomach. _{Lev. 7:32-34 • *right*}

4 "The firstfruits of your grain and your new wine and your oil, and the first of the fleece of your sheep, you shall give him.

5 "For ᴿthe LORD your God has chosen him out of all your tribes ᴿto stand to minister in the name of the LORD, him and his sons forever. _{Ex. 28:1 • Deut. 10:8}

6 "So if a Levite comes from any of your gates, from where he dwells among all Israel, and comes with all the desire of his mind to the place which the LORD chooses,

7 "then he may serve in the name of the LORD his God as all his brethren the Levites *do*, who stand there before the LORD.

8 "They shall have equal ᴿportions to eat, besides what comes from the sale of his inheritance. _{2 Chr. 31:4}

Avoid Wicked Customs

9 "When you come into the land which the LORD your God is giving you, ᴿyou shall not learn to follow the ᵀabominations of those nations. _{Deut. 12:29, 30; 20:16-18 • *detestable acts*}

10 "There shall not be found among you *anyone* who makes his son or his daughter ᵀpass through the fire, *or one* who practices witchcraft, *or* a soothsayer, or one who interprets omens, or a sorcerer, _{Offering to an idol}

11 ᴿ"or one who conjures spells, or a medium, or a spiritist, or ᴿone who calls up the dead. _{Lev. 20:27 • 1 Sam. 28:7}

12 "For all who do these things *are* ᵀan abomination to the LORD, and ᴿbecause of these abominations the LORD your God drives them out from before you. _{detestable • Lev. 18:24}

13 "You shall be ᵀblameless before the LORD your God. _{Lit. *perfect*}

14 "For these nations which you will dispossess listened to soothsayers and diviners; but as for you, the LORD your God has not ᵀappointed such for you. _{allowed you to do so}

A New Prophet Like Moses

15 ᴿ"The LORD your God will raise up for you a Prophet like me from your midst, from your brethren. Him you shall hear, _{Acts 3:22}

16 "according to all you desired of the LORD your God in Horeb in the day of the assembly, saying, ᴿ'Let me not hear again the voice of the LORD my God, nor let me see this great fire anymore, lest I die.' _{Ex. 20:18, 19}

17 "And the LORD said to me: ᴿ'What they have spoken is good. _{Deut. 5:28}

18 'I will raise up for them a Prophet like you from among their brethren, and will put My words in His mouth, ᴿand He shall speak to them all that I command Him. _{John 4:25}

19 ᴿ'And it shall be *that* whoever will not hear My words, which He speaks in My name, I will require *it* of him. _{Acts 3:23}

20 'But the prophet who presumes to speak a word in My name, which I have not commanded him to speak, or who speaks in the name of other gods, that prophet shall die.'

21 "And if you say in your heart, 'How shall we know the word which the LORD has not spoken?'—

22 ᴿ"when a prophet speaks in the name of the LORD, ᴿif the thing does not happen or come to pass, that *is* the thing which the LORD has not spoken; the prophet has spoken it ᴿpresumptuously; you shall not be afraid of him. _{Jer. 28:9 • Deut. 13:2 • Deut. 18:20}

Three Cities of Refuge

19 "When the LORD your God has cut off the nations whose land the LORD your God is giving you, and you dispossess them and dwell in their cities and in their houses,

2 "you shall separate three cities for yourself in the midst of your land which the LORD your God is giving you to possess.

3 "You shall prepare roads for yourself, and divide into three parts the territory of your land which the LORD your God is giving you to inherit, that any manslayer may flee there.

4 "And this *is* the case of the manslayer who flees there, that he may live: Whoever kills his neighbor ᵀunintentionally, not having hated him in time past— _{ignorantly}

5 "as when *a man* goes to the woods with his neighbor to cut timber, and his hand swings a stroke with the ax to cut down the tree, and the head slips from the handle and strikes his neighbor so that he dies—he shall flee to one of these cities and live;

6 ᴿ"lest the avenger of blood, while his anger is hot, pursue the manslayer and overtake him, because the way is long, and kill him, though he *was* not deserving of death, since he had not hated the victim in time past. _{Num. 35:12}

7 "Therefore I command you, saying, 'You shall separate three cities for yourself.'

8 "Now if the LORD your God ᴿenlarges your territory, as He swore to ᴿyour fathers, and gives you the land which He promised to give to your fathers, _{Deut. 12:20 • Gen. 15:18-21}

9 "and if you keep all these commandments and do them, which I command you today, to love the LORD your God and to walk always in His ways, then you shall add three more cities for yourself besides these three,

10 ᴿ"lest innocent blood be shed in the midst of your land which the LORD your God is giving you *as* an inheritance, and *thus* guilt of bloodshed be upon you. _{Deut. 21:1-9}

11 "But ᴿif anyone hates his neighbor, lies in wait for him, rises against him and strikes

him mortally, so that he dies, and he flees to one of these cities,   Num. 35:16, 24

12 "then the elders of his city shall send and bring him from there, and deliver him over to the hand of the avenger of blood, that he may die.

13 "Your eye shall not pity him, but you shall put away the guilt of innocent blood from Israel, that it may go well with you.

Property Boundaries

14 R"You shall not remove your neighbor's landmark, which the men of old have set, in your inheritance which you will inherit in the land that the LORD your God is giving you to possess.   Prov. 22:28

The Law Concerning Witnesses

15 "One witness shall not rise against a man concerning any iniquity or any sin that he commits; by the mouth of two or three witnesses the matter shall be established.

16 "If a false witness Rrises against any man to testify against him of wrongdoing,   Ex. 23:1

17 "then both men in the controversy shall stand before the LORD, before the priests and the judges who serve in those days.

18 "And the judges shall make careful inquiry, and indeed, if the witness is a false witness, who has testified falsely against his brother,

19 "then you shall do to him as he thought to have done to his brother; so you shall put away the evil from among you.

20 R"And those who remain shall hear and fear, and hereafter they shall not again commit such evil among you.   Deut. 17:13; 21:21

21 R"Your eye shall not pity: Rlife shall be for life, eye for eye, tooth for tooth, hand for hand, foot for foot.   Deut. 19:13 • Ex. 21:23, 24

Principles Governing Warfare

20 "When you go out to battle against your enemies, and see horses and chariots and people more numerous than you, do not be afraid of them; for the LORD your God is Rwith you, who brought you up from the land of Egypt.   2 Chr. 13:12; 32:7, 8

2 "So it shall be, when you are on the verge of battle, that the priest shall approach and speak to the people.

3 "And he shall say to them, 'Hear, O Israel: Today you are on the verge of battle with your enemies. Do not let your heart faint, do not be afraid, and do not tremble or be terrified because of them;

4 'for the LORD your God is He who goes with you, Rto fight for you against your enemies, to save you.'   Josh. 23:10

5 "Then the officers shall speak to the people, saying: 'What man is there who has built a new house and has not dedicated it? Let him go and return to his house, lest he die in the battle and another man dedicate it.

6 'Also what man is there who has planted a vineyard and has not eaten of it? Let him go and return to his house, lest he die in the battle and another man eat of it.

7 'And what man is there who is betrothed to a woman and has not married her? Let him go and return to his house, lest he die in the battle and another man marry her.'

8 "The officers shall speak further to the people, and say, R'What man is there who is fearful and fainthearted? Let him go and return to his house, *lest the heart of his brethren faint like his heart.'   Judg. 7:3

9 "And so it shall be, when the officers have finished speaking to the people, that they shall make captains of the armies to lead the people.

10 "When you go near a city to fight against it, then proclaim an offer of peace to it.

11 "And it shall be that if they accept your offer of peace, and open to you, then all the people who are found in it shall be placed under tribute to you, and serve you.

12 "Now if the city will not make peace with you, but war against you, then you shall besiege it.

13 "And when the LORD your God delivers it into your hands, Ryou shall strike every male in it with the edge of the sword.   Num. 31:7

14 "But the women, the little ones, Rthe livestock, and all that is in the city, all its spoil, you shall plunder for yourself; and Ryou shall eat the enemies' plunder which the LORD your God gives you.   Josh. 8:2 • 1 Sam. 14:30

15 "Thus you shall do to all the cities which are very far from you, which are not of the cities of these nations.

16 "But Rof the cities of these peoples which the LORD your God gives you as an inheritance, you shall let nothing that breathes remain alive,   Deut. 7:1–5

17 "but you shall utterly destroy them: the Hittite and the Amorite and the Canaanite and the Perizzite and the Hivite and the Jebusite, just as the LORD your God has commanded you,

18 "lest Rthey teach you to do according to all their Tabominations which they have done for their gods, and you sin against the LORD your God.   Deut. 7:4; 12:30; 18:9 • detestable things

19 "When you besiege a city for a long time, while making war against it to take it, you shall not destroy its trees by wielding an ax against them; if you can eat of them, do not cut them down to use in the siege, for the tree of the field is man's food.

20 "Only the trees which you know are not trees for food you may destroy and cut down,

20:8 So with MT, Tg.; Sam., LXX, Syr., Vg. lest he make his brother's heart faint

to build siegeworks against the city that makes war with you, until it is subdued.

The Law Concerning Unsolved Murder

21 "If *anyone* is found slain, lying in the field in the land which the LORD your God is giving you to possess, *and* it is not known who killed him,

2 "then your elders and your judges shall go out and measure *the distance* from the slain man to the surrounding cities.

3 "And it shall be *that* the elders of the city nearest to the slain man will take a heifer which has not been worked *and* which has not pulled with a ᴿyoke.   Num. 19:2

4 "The elders of that city shall bring the heifer down to a valley with flowing water, which is neither plowed nor sown, and they shall break the heifer's neck there in the valley.

5 "Then the priests, the sons of Levi, shall come near, for ᴿthe LORD your God has chosen them to minister to Him and to bless in the name of the LORD; ᴿby their word every controversy and every ᵀassault shall be *settled*.   1 Chr. 23:13 · Deut. 17:8, 9 · Lit. *stroke*

6 "And all the elders of that city nearest to the slain *man* ᴿshall wash their hands over the heifer whose neck was broken in the valley.   Matt. 27:24

7 "Then they shall answer and say, 'Our hands have not shed this blood, nor have our eyes seen *it*.

8 'Provide atonement, O LORD, for Your people Israel, whom You have redeemed, and do not lay innocent blood to the charge of Your people Israel.' And atonement shall be provided on their behalf for the blood.

9 "So you shall put away the *guilt of* innocent blood from among you when you do *what is* right in the sight of the LORD.

Female Captives

10 "When you go out to war against your enemies, and the LORD your God delivers them into your hand, and you take them captive,

11 "and you see among the captives a beautiful woman, and desire her and would take her for your ᴿwife,   Num. 31:18

12 "then you shall bring her home to your house, and she shall ᴿshave her head and trim her nails.   Lev. 14:8, 9

13 "She shall put off the clothes of her captivity, remain in your house, and ᴿmourn her father and her mother a full month; after that you may go in to her and be her husband, and she shall be your wife.   Ps. 45:10

14 "And it shall be, if you have no delight in her, then you shall set her free, but you certainly shall not sell her for money; you shall not treat her brutally, because you have ᴿhumbled her.   Judg. 19:24

Firstborn Inheritance Rights

15 "If a man has two wives, one loved and the other unloved, and they have borne him children, *both* the loved and the unloved, and *if* the firstborn son is of her who is unloved,

16 "then it shall be, on the day he bequeaths his possessions to his sons, *that* he must not bestow firstborn status on the son of the loved wife in preference to the son of the unloved, the *true* firstborn.

17 "But he shall acknowledge the son of the unloved wife *as* the firstborn ᴿby giving him a double portion of all that he has, for he ᴿ*is* the beginning of his strength; ᴿthe right of the firstborn *is* his.   2 Kin. 2:9 · Gen. 49:3 · Gen. 25:31, 33

The Rebellious Son

18 "If a man has a stubborn and rebellious son who will not obey the voice of his father or the voice of his mother, and *who*, when they have chastened him, will not heed them,

19 "then his father and his mother shall take hold of him and bring him out to the elders of his city, to the gate of his city.

20 "And they shall say to the elders of his city, 'This son of ours is stubborn and rebellious; he will not obey our voice; he is a glutton and a drunkard.'

21 "Then all the men of his city shall stone him to death with stones; so you shall put away the evil from among you, ᴿand all Israel shall hear and fear.   Deut. 13:11

Miscellaneous Laws

22 "If a man has committed a sin ᴿdeserving of death, and he is put to death, and you hang him on a tree,   Acts 23:29

23 ᴿ"his body shall not remain overnight on the tree, but you shall surely bury him that day, so that ᴿyou do not defile the land which the LORD your God is giving you *as* an inheritance; for ᴿhe who is hanged *is* accursed of God.   John 19:31 · Lev. 18:25 · Gal. 3:13

22 "You ᴿshall not see your brother's ox or his sheep going astray, and ᵀhide yourself from them; you shall certainly bring them back to your brother.   Ex. 23:4 · *ignore them*

2 "And if your brother *is* not near you, or if you do not know him, then you shall bring it to your own house, and it shall remain with you until your brother seeks it; then you shall restore it to him.

3 "You shall do the same with his donkey, and so shall you do with his garment; with any lost thing of your brother's, which he has lost and you have found, you shall do likewise; you must not hide yourself.

4 ᴿ"You shall not see your brother's donkey or his ox fall down along the road, and hide yourself from them; you shall surely help him lift *them* up again.   Ex. 23:5

5 "A woman shall not wear anything that pertains to a man, nor shall a man put on a

woman's garment, for all who do so *are* ^Tan abomination to the LORD your God.   detestable

6 "If a bird's nest happens to be before you along the way, in any tree or on the ground, with young ones or eggs, with the mother sitting on the young or on the eggs, you shall not take the mother with the young;

7 "you shall surely let the mother go, and take the young for yourself, ^Rthat it may be well with you and *that* you may prolong *your* days.   Deut. 4:40

8 "When you build a new house, then you shall make a parapet for your roof, that you may not bring guilt of bloodshed on your household if anyone falls from it.

9 ^R"You shall not sow your vineyard with different kinds of seed, lest the yield of the seed which you have sown and the fruit of your vineyard be defiled.   Lev. 19:19

10 ^R"You shall not plow with an ox and a donkey together.   [2 Cor. 6:14–16]

11 ^R"You shall not wear a garment of different sorts, *such as* wool and linen mixed together.   Lev. 19:19

12 "You shall make ^Rtassels on the four corners of the clothing with which you cover *yourself.*   Num. 15:37–41

Laws of Sexual Morality

13 "If any man takes a wife, and goes in to her, and ^Rdetests her,   Deut. 21:15; 24:3

14 "and charges her with shameful conduct, and brings a bad name on her, and says, 'I took this woman, and when I came to her I found she *was* not a virgin,'

15 "then the father and mother of the young woman shall take and bring out *the evidence of* the young woman's virginity to the elders of the city at the gate.

16 "And the young woman's father shall say to the elders, 'I gave my daughter to this man as wife, and he detests her.

17 'Now he has charged her with shameful conduct, saying, "I found your daughter *was* not a virgin," and yet these *are the evidences of* my daughter's virginity.' And they shall spread the cloth before the elders of the city.

18 "Then the elders of that city shall take that man and punish him;

19 "and they shall fine him one hundred *shekels* of silver and give *them* to the father of the young woman, because he has brought a bad name on a virgin of Israel. And she shall be his wife; he cannot divorce her all his days.

20 "But if the thing is true, *and evidences of* virginity are not found for the young woman,

21 "then they shall bring out the young woman to the door of her father's house, and the men of her city shall stone her to death with stones, because she has done a disgraceful thing in Israel, to play the harlot in her father's house. So you shall ^Tput away the evil from among you.   *purge*

22 ^R"If a man is found lying with a woman married to a husband, then both of them shall die—the man that lay with the woman, and the woman; so you shall put away the evil from Israel.   Lev. 20:10

23 "If a young woman *who is* a virgin is ^Rbetrothed to a husband, and a man finds her in the city and lies with her,   Matt. 1:18, 19

24 "then you shall bring them both out to the gate of that city, and you shall stone them to death with stones, the young woman because she did not cry out in the city, and the man because he ^Rhumbled his neighbor's wife; ^Rso you shall put away the evil from among you.   Deut. 21:14 • Deut. 22:21, 22

25 "But if a man finds a betrothed young woman in the countryside, and the man forces her and lies with her, then only the man who lay with her shall die.

26 "But you shall do nothing to the young woman; *there is* in the young woman no sin *deserving* of death, for just as when a man rises against his neighbor and kills him, even so *is* this matter.

27 "For he found her in the countryside, *and* the betrothed young woman cried out, but *there was* no one to save her.

28 "If a man finds a young woman *who is* a virgin, who is not betrothed, and he seizes her and lies with her, and they are found out,

29 "then the man who lay with her shall give to the young woman's father fifty *shekels* of silver, and she shall be his wife because he has humbled her; he shall not be permitted to divorce her all his days.

30 "A man shall not take his father's wife, nor ^Runcover his father's bed.   Ezek. 16:8

Those Excluded from the Congregation

23 "He who is emasculated by crushing or mutilation shall ^Rnot enter the assembly of the LORD.   Lev. 21:20; 22:24

2 "One of illegitimate birth shall not enter the assembly of the LORD; even to the tenth generation none of his *descendants* shall enter the assembly of the LORD.

3 "An Ammonite or Moabite shall not enter the assembly of the LORD; even to the tenth generation none of his *descendants* shall enter the assembly of the LORD forever,

4 "because they did not meet you with bread and water on the road when you came out of Egypt, and because they hired against you Balaam the son of Beor from Pethor of *Mesopotamia, to curse you.

5 "Nevertheless the LORD your God would not listen to Balaam, but the LORD your God turned the curse into a blessing for you, because the LORD your God loves you.

6 ^R"You shall not seek their peace nor their prosperity all your days forever.   Ezra 9:12

23:4 Heb. *Aram Naharaim*

7 "You shall not abhor an Edomite, ᴿfor he *is* your brother. You shall not abhor an Egyptian, because ᴿyou were an alien in his land. Obad. 10, 12 • Deut. 10:19

8 "The children of the third generation born to them may enter the assembly of the LORD.

Cleanliness of the Camp Site

9 "When the army goes out against your enemies, then keep yourself from every wicked thing.

10 ᴿ"If there is any man among you who becomes unclean by some occurrence in the night, then he shall go outside the camp; he shall not come inside the camp. Lev. 15:16

11 "But it shall be, when evening comes, that ᴿhe shall wash with water; and when the sun sets, he may come into the camp. Lev. 15:5

12 "Also you shall have a place outside the camp, where you may go out;

13 "and you shall have an implement among your equipment, and when you sit down outside, you shall dig with it and turn and cover your refuse.

14 "For the LORD your God ᴿwalks in the midst of your camp, to deliver you and give your enemies over to you; therefore your camp shall be holy, that He may see no unclean thing among you, and turn away from you. Lev. 26:12

Miscellaneous Laws

15 ᴿ"You shall not give back to his master the slave who has escaped from his master to you. 1 Sam. 30:15

16 "He may dwell with you in your midst, in the place which he chooses within one of your gates, where it ᵀseems best to him; ᴿyou shall not oppress him. *pleases him best* • Ex. 22:21

17 "There shall be no *ritual* *harlot ᴿof the daughters of Israel, or a *perverted one of the sons of Israel. Lev. 19:29

18 "You shall not bring the wages of a harlot or the price of a dog to the house of the LORD your God for any vowed offering, for both of these *are* ᵀan abomination to the LORD your God. *detestable*

19 ᴿ"You shall not charge interest to your brother—interest on money *or* food *or* anything that is lent out at interest. Ex. 22:25

20 "To a foreigner you may charge interest, but to your brother you shall not charge interest, that the LORD your God may bless you in all to which you set your hand in the land which you are entering to possess.

21 ᴿ"When you make a vow to the LORD your God, you shall not delay to pay it; for the LORD your God will surely require it of you, and it would be sin to you. Eccl. 5:4, 5

23:17 Heb. *gedeshah,* fem. of gedesh (next note) • Heb. *gedesh,* one practicing sodomy and prostitution in religious rituals

22 "But if you abstain from vowing, it shall not be sin to you.

23 ᴿ"That which has gone from your lips you shall keep and perform, for you voluntarily vowed to the LORD your God what you have promised with your mouth. Ps. 66:13, 14

24 "When you come into your neighbor's vineyard, you may eat your fill of grapes at your pleasure, but you shall not put *any* in your container.

25 "When you come into your neighbor's standing grain, ᴿyou may pluck the heads with your hand, but you shall not use a sickle on your neighbor's standing grain. Luke 6:1

Law Concerning Divorce

24 "When a man takes a wife and marries her, and it happens that she finds no favor in his eyes because he has found some uncleanness in her, and he writes her a certificate of divorce, puts *it* in her hand, and sends her out of his house,

2 "when she has departed from his house, and goes and becomes another man's *wife,*

3 "*if* the latter husband detests her and writes her a certificate of divorce, puts *it* in her hand, and sends her out of his house, or if the latter husband dies who took her as his wife,

4 "*then* her former husband who divorced her must not take her back to be his wife after she has been defiled; for that *is* an abomination before the LORD, and you shall not bring sin on the land which the LORD your God is giving you *as* an inheritance.

Miscellaneous Laws

5 ᴿ"When a man has taken a new wife, he shall not go out to war or be charged with any business; he shall be free at home one year, and ᴿbring happiness to his wife whom he has taken. Deut. 20:7 • Prov. 5:18

6 "No man shall take the lower or the upper millstone in pledge, for he takes ᵀone's living in pledge. *life*

7 "If a man is found ᵀkidnapping any of his brethren of the children of Israel, and mistreats him or sells him, then that kidnapper shall die; and you shall put away the evil from among you. Lit. *stealing*

8 "Take heed in ᴿan outbreak of leprosy, that you carefully observe and do according to all that the priests, the Levites, shall teach you; just as I commanded them, so you shall be careful to do. Lev. 13:2; 14:2

9 ᴿ"Remember what the LORD your God did ᴿto Miriam on the way when you came out of Egypt. [1 Cor. 10:6] • Num. 12:10

10 "When you ᴿlend your brother anything, you shall not go into his house to get his pledge. Matt. 5:42

11 "You shall stand outside, and the man to whom you lend shall bring the pledge out to you.

12 "And if the man *is* poor, you shall not ᵀkeep his pledge overnight.　　Lit. *sleep with*

13 "You shall in any case return the pledge to him again when the sun goes down, that he may sleep in his own garment and bless you; and ᴿit shall be righteousness to you before the LORD your God.　　Deut. 6:25

14 "You shall not ᴿoppress a hired servant *who is* poor and needy, *whether* one of your brethren or one of the aliens who *is* in your land within your gates.　　[Mal. 3:5]

15 "Each day ᴿyou shall give *him* his wages, and not let the sun go down on it, for he *is* poor and has set his heart on it; ᴿlest he cry out against you to the LORD, and it be sin to you.　　Lev. 19:13 · James 5:4

16 ᴿ"Fathers shall not be put to death for *their* children, nor shall children be put to death for *their* fathers; a person shall be put to death for his own sin.　　Ezek. 18:20

17 ᴿ"You shall not pervert justice due the stranger or the fatherless, ᴿnor take a widow's garment as a pledge.　　Ex. 23:6 · Ex. 22:26

18 "But ᴿyou shall remember that you were a slave in Egypt, and the LORD your God redeemed you from there; therefore I command you to do this thing.　　Deut. 24:22

19 ᴿ"When you reap your harvest in your field, and forget a sheaf in the field, you shall not go back to get it; it shall be for the stranger, the fatherless, and the widow, that the LORD your God may ᴿbless you in all the work of your hands.　　Lev. 19:9, 10 · Ps. 41:1

20 "When you beat your olive trees, you shall not go over the boughs again; it shall be for the stranger, the fatherless, and the widow.

21 "When you gather the grapes of your vineyard, you shall not glean *it* afterward; it shall be for the stranger, the fatherless, and the widow.

22 "And you shall remember that you were a slave in the land of Egypt; therefore I command you to do this thing.

25 "If there is a dispute between men, and they come to ᵀcourt, that *the judges* may judge them, and they justify the righteous and condemn the wicked, *the judgment*

2 "then it shall be, if the wicked man ᴿdeserves to be beaten, that the judge will cause him to lie down ᴿand be beaten in his presence, according to his guilt, with a certain number of blows.　　Prov. 19:29 · Matt. 10:17

3 "Forty blows he may give *him and* no more, lest he should exceed this and beat him with many blows above these, and your brother ᴿbe humiliated in your sight.　　Job 18:3

4 ᴿ"You shall not muzzle an ox while it ᵀtreads out *the grain*.　　[Prov. 12:10] · *threshes*

Marriage Duty of the Surviving Brother

5 ᴿ"If brothers dwell together, and one of them dies and has no son, the widow of the dead man shall not be *married* to a stranger outside *the family*; her husband's brother shall go in to her, take her as his wife, and perform the duty of a husband's brother to her.　　Matt. 22:24

6 "And it shall be *that* the firstborn son which she bears ᴿwill succeed to the name of his dead brother, that ᴿhis name may not be blotted out of Israel.　　Gen. 38:9 · Ruth 4:5, 10

7 "But if the man does not want to take his brother's wife, then let his brother's wife go up to the ᴿgate to the elders, and say, 'My husband's brother refuses to raise up a name to his brother in Israel; he will not perform the duty of my husband's brother.'　　Ruth 4:1, 2

8 "Then the elders of his city shall call him and speak to him. But *if* he stands firm and says, ᴿ'I do not want to take her,'　　Ruth 4:6

9 "then his brother's wife shall come to him in the presence of the elders, ᴿremove his sandal from his foot, spit in his face, and answer and say, 'So shall it be done to the man who will not ᴿbuild up his brother's house.'　　Ruth 4:7, 8 · Ruth 4:11

10 "And his name shall be called in Israel, 'The house of him who had his sandal removed.'

Miscellaneous Laws

11 "If *two* men fight together, and the wife of one draws near to rescue her husband from the hand of the one attacking him, and puts out her hand and seizes him by the genitals,

12 "then you shall cut off her hand; ᴿyour eye shall not pity *her*.　　Deut. 7:2; 19:13

13 ᴿ"You shall not have in your bag differing weights, a heavy and a light.　　Mic. 6:11

14 "You shall not have in your house differing measures, a large and a small.

15 "You shall have a perfect and just weight, a perfect and just measure, that your days may be lengthened in the land which the LORD your God is giving you.

16 "For ᴿall who do such things, all who behave unrighteously, *are* ᵀan abomination to the LORD your God.　　Prov. 11:1 · *detestable*

Destroy the Amalekites

17 "Remember what Amalek did to you on the way as you were coming out of Egypt,

18 "how he met you on the way and attacked your rear ranks, all the stragglers at your rear, when you *were* tired and weary; and he ᴿdid not fear God.　　Rom. 3:18

19 "Therefore it shall be, ᴿwhen the LORD your God has given you rest from your enemies all around, in the land which the LORD your God is giving you to possess *as* an inheritance, *that* you will ᴿblot out the remembrance of Amalek from under heaven. You shall not forget.　　1 Sam. 15:3 · Ex. 17:14

Offerings of Firstfruits and Tithes

26 "And it shall be, when you come into the land which the LORD your God is giving you as an inheritance, and you possess it and dwell in it,

2 "that you shall take some of the first of all the produce of the ground, which you shall bring from your land that the LORD your God is giving you, and put it in a basket and ᴿgo to the place where the LORD your God chooses to make His name abide.   Deut. 12:5

3 "And you shall go to the one who is priest in those days, and say to him, 'I declare today to the LORD your God that I have come to the country which the LORD swore to our fathers to give us.'

4 "Then the priest shall take the basket out of your hand and set it down before the altar of the LORD your God.

5 "And you shall answer and say before the LORD your God: 'My father was a ᵀSyrian, about to perish, and he went down to Egypt and dwelt there, ᴿfew in number; and there he became a nation, ᴿgreat, mighty, and populous.   Or Aramean · Deut. 10:22 · Deut. 1:10

6 'But the Egyptians mistreated us, afflicted us, and laid hard bondage on us.

7 ᴿ'Then we cried out to the LORD God of our fathers, and the LORD heard our voice and looked on our affliction and our labor and our oppression.   Ex. 2:23–25; 3:9; 4:31

8 'So ᴿthe LORD brought us out of Egypt with a mighty hand and with an outstretched arm, ᴿwith great terror and with signs and wonders.   Deut. 5:15 · Deut. 4:34; 34:11, 12

9 'He has brought us to this place and has given us this land, ᴿ'a land flowing with milk and honey';   Ex. 3:8, 17

10 'and now, behold, I have brought the firstfruits of the land which you, O LORD, have given me.' Then you shall set it before the LORD your God, and worship before the LORD your God.

11 "So ᴿyou shall rejoice in every good thing which the LORD your God has given to you and your house, you and the Levite and the stranger who is among you.   Deut. 12:7; 16:11

12 "When you have finished laying aside all the ᴿtithe of your increase in the third year—ᴿthe year of tithing—and have given it to the Levite, the stranger, the fatherless, and the widow, so that they may eat within your gates and be filled,   Lev. 27:30 · Deut. 14:28, 29

13 "then you shall say before the LORD your God: 'I have removed the ᵀholy tithe from my house, and also have given them to the Levite, the stranger, the fatherless, and the widow, according to all Your commandments which you have commanded me; I have not transgressed Your commandments, ᴿnor have I forgotten them.   hallowed things · Ps. 119:141, 153

14 'I have not eaten any of it when in mourning, nor have I removed any of it ᵀfor an unclean use, nor given any of it for the dead. I have obeyed the voice of the LORD my God, and have done according to all that You have commanded me.   Or while unclean

15 ᴿ'Look down from Your holy ᵀhabitation, from heaven, and bless Your people Israel and the land which You have given us, just as You swore to our fathers, ᴿ'a land flowing with milk and honey." '   Is. 63:15 · abode · Ex. 3:8

A Special People of God

16 "This day the LORD your God commands you to observe these statutes and judgments; therefore you shall be careful to observe them with all your heart and with all your soul.

17 "Today you have ᴿproclaimed the LORD to be your God, and that you will walk in His ways and keep His statutes, His commandments, and His judgments, and that you will ᴿobey His voice.   Ex. 20:19 · Deut. 15:5

18 "Also today ᴿthe LORD has proclaimed you to be His special people, just as He promised you, that you should keep all His commandments,   Ex. 6:7; 19:5

19 "and that He will set you ᴿhigh above all nations which He has made, in praise, in name, and in honor, and that you may be ᴿa ᵀholy people to the LORD your God, just as He has spoken."   Deut. 4:7, 8; 28:1 · [1 Pet. 2:9] · consecrated

The Law Inscribed on Stones

27 Now Moses, with the elders of Israel, commanded the people, saying: "Keep all the commandments which I command you today.

2 "And it shall be, on the day ᴿwhen you cross over the Jordan to the land which the LORD your God is giving you, that ᴿyou shall set up for yourselves large stones, and whitewash them with lime.   Josh. 4:1 · Josh. 8:32

3 "You shall write on them all the words of this law, when you have crossed over, that you may enter the land which the LORD your God is giving you, ᴿ'a land flowing with milk and honey,' just as the LORD God of your fathers promised you.   Ex. 3:8

4 "Therefore it shall be, when you have crossed over the Jordan, that ᴿon Mount Ebal you shall set up these stones, which I command you today, and you shall whitewash them with lime.   Deut. 11:29

5 "And there you shall build an altar to the LORD your God, an altar of stones; ᴿyou shall not use an iron tool on them.   Ex. 20:25

6 "You shall build with ᵀwhole stones the altar of the LORD your God, and offer burnt offerings on it to the LORD your God.   uncut

7 "You shall offer peace offerings, and shall eat there, and ᴿrejoice before the LORD your God.   Deut. 26:11

8 "And you shall ᴿwrite very plainly on the stones all the words of this law."   Josh. 8:32

9 Then Moses and the priests, the Levites,

spoke to all Israel, saying, "Take heed and listen, O Israel: ᴿThis day you have become the people of the LORD your God.   Deut. 26:18

10 "Therefore you shall obey the voice of the LORD your God, and observe His commandments and His statutes which I command you today."

Curses Pronounced from Mount Ebal

11 And Moses commanded the people on the same day, saying,

12 "These shall stand ᴿon Mount Gerizim to bless the people, when you have crossed over the Jordan: Simeon, Levi, Judah, Issachar, Joseph, and Benjamin;   Josh. 8:33

13 "and ᴿthese shall stand on Mount Ebal to curse: Reuben, Gad, Asher, Zebulun, Dan, and Naphtali.   Deut. 11:29

14 "And the Levites shall speak with a loud voice and say to all the men of Israel:

15 'Cursed is the one who makes a carved or molded image, an abomination to the LORD, the work of the hands of the craftsman, and sets it up in secret.'

And all the people shall answer and say, 'Amen!'

16 ᴿ'Cursed is the one who treats his father or his mother with contempt.'   Ezek. 22:7

And all the people shall say, 'Amen!'

17 ᴿ'Cursed is the one who moves his neighbor's landmark.'   Deut. 19:14

And all the people shall say, 'Amen!'

18 ᴿ'Cursed is the one who makes the blind to wander off the road.'   Lev. 19:14

And all the people shall say, 'Amen!'

19 ᴿ'Cursed is the one who perverts the justice due the stranger, the fatherless, and widow.'   Ex. 22:21, 22; 23:9

And all the people shall say, 'Amen!'

20 ᴿ'Cursed is the one who lies with his father's wife, because he has uncovered his father's bed.'   Deut. 22:30

And all the people shall say, 'Amen!'

21 ᴿ'Cursed is the one who lies with any kind of animal.'   Lev. 18:23; 20:15, 16

And all the people shall say, 'Amen!'

22 ᴿ'Cursed is the one who lies with his sister, the daughter of his father or the daughter of his mother.'   Lev. 18:9

And all the people shall say, 'Amen!'

23 ᴿ'Cursed is the one who lies with his mother-in-law.'   Lev. 18:17; 20:14

And all the people shall say, 'Amen!'

24 ᴿ'Cursed is the one who attacks his neighbor secretly.'   Ex. 20:13; 21:12

And all the people shall say, 'Amen!'

25 ᴿ'Cursed is the one who takes a bribe to slay an innocent person.'   Ex. 23:7

And all the people shall say, 'Amen!'

26 ᴿ'Cursed is the one who does not confirm all the words of this law.'   Gal. 3:10

And all the people shall say, 'Amen!'

Blessings on Obedience

28 "Now it shall come to pass, if you diligently obey the voice of the LORD your God, to observe carefully all His commandments which I command you today, that the LORD your God ᴿwill set you high above all nations of the earth.   Deut. 26:19

2 "And all these blessings shall come upon you and ᴿovertake you, because you obey the voice of the LORD your God: Deut. 28:15

3 "Blessed shall you be in the city, and blessed shall you be in the country.

4 "Blessed shall be ᴿthe ᵀfruit of your body, the produce of your ground and the increase of your herds, the increase of your cattle and the offspring of your flocks.   Gen. 22:17 · offspring

5 "Blessed shall be your basket and your kneading bowl.

6 "Blessed shall you be when you come in, and blessed shall you be when you go out.

7 "The LORD will cause your enemies who rise against you to be defeated before your face; they shall come out against you one way and flee before you seven ways.

8 "The LORD will ᴿcommand the blessing on you in your storehouses and in all to which you ᴿset your hand, and He will bless you in the land which the LORD your God is giving you.   Lev. 25:21 · Deut. 15:10

9 "The LORD will establish you as a holy people to Himself, just as He has sworn to you, if you keep the commandments of the LORD your God and walk in His ways.

10 "Then all peoples of the earth shall see that you are called by the name of the LORD, and they shall be ᴿafraid of you.   Deut. 11:25

11 "And the LORD will grant you plenty of goods, in the fruit of your body, in the increase of your livestock, and in the produce of your ground, in the land of which the LORD swore to your fathers to give you.

12 "The LORD will open to you His good ᵀtreasure, the heavens, to give the rain to your land in its season, and to bless all the work of your hand. You shall lend to many nations, but you shall not borrow.   storehouse

13 "And the LORD will make ᴿyou the head and not the tail; you shall be above only, and not be beneath, if you ᵀheed the commandments of the LORD your God, which I command you today, and are careful to observe them.   [Is. 9:14, 15] · listen to

14 ᴿ"So you shall not turn aside from any of the words which I command you this day, to the right or the left, to go after other gods to serve them.   Deut. 5:32

Curses on Disobedience

15 "But it shall come to pass, ᴿif you do not obey the voice of the LORD your God, to observe carefully all His commandments and His statutes which I command you today, that all these curses will come upon you and overtake you: Lev. 26:14-39

16 "Cursed *shall* you *be* in the city, and cursed *shall* you *be* in the country.

17 "Cursed *shall be* your basket and your kneading bowl.

18 "Cursed *shall be* the fruit of your body and the produce of your land, the increase of your cattle and the offspring of your flocks.

19 "Cursed *shall* you *be* when you come in, and cursed *shall* you *be* when you go out.

20 "The Lord will send on you ᴿcursing, ᴿconfusion, and ᴿrebuke in all that you set your hand to do, until you are destroyed and until you perish quickly, because of the wickedness of your doings in which you have forsaken Me.   Mal. 2:2 • Is. 65:14 • Is. 30:17

21 "The Lord will make the ᵀplague cling to you until He has consumed you from the land which you are going to possess.   *pestilence*

22 "The Lord will strike you with consumption, with fever, with inflammation, with severe burning fever, with the sword, with ᴿscorching,ᵀ and with mildew; they shall pursue you until you perish.   Amos 4:9 • *blight*

23 "And ᴿyour heavens which *are* over your head shall be bronze, and the earth which is under you *shall be* iron.   Lev. 26:19

24 "The Lord will change the rain of your land to powder and dust; from the heaven it shall come down on you until you are destroyed.

25 ᴿ"The Lord will cause you to be defeated before your enemies; you shall go out one way against them and flee seven ways before them; and you shall become ᵀtroublesome to all the kingdoms of the earth. Deut. 32:30 • *a terror*

26 "Your carcasses shall be food for all the birds of the air and the beasts of the earth, and no one shall frighten *them* away.

27 "The Lord will strike you with ᴿthe boils of Egypt, with ᴿtumors, with the scab, and with the itch, from which you cannot be healed.   Ex. 15:26 • 1 Sam. 5:6

28 "The Lord will strike you with madness and blindness and ᴿconfusion of heart. Jer. 4:9

29 "And you shall ᴿgrope at noonday, as a blind man gropes in darkness; you shall not prosper in your ways; you shall be only oppressed and plundered continually, and no one shall save *you*.   Job 5:14

30 ᴿ"You shall betroth a wife, but another man shall lie with her; ᴿyou shall build a house, but you shall not dwell in it; ᴿyou shall plant a vineyard, but shall not gather its grapes.   Jer. 8:10 • Amos 5:11 • Deut. 20:6

31 "Your ox *shall be* slaughtered before your eyes, but you shall not eat of it; your donkey *shall be* violently taken away from before you, and shall not be restored to you; your sheep *shall be* given to your enemies, and you shall have no one to rescue *them*.

32 "Your sons and your daughters *shall be* given to another people, and your eyes shall look and ᴿfail *with* longing for them all day

long; and *there shall be* ᵀno strength in your ᴿhand.   Ps. 119:82 • *nothing you can do* • Neh. 5:5

33 "A nation whom you have not known shall eat ᴿthe fruit of your land and the produce of your labor, and you shall be only oppressed and crushed continually. Jer. 5:15, 17

34 "So you shall be driven mad because of the sight which your eyes see.

35 "The Lord will strike you in the knees and on the legs with severe boils which cannot be healed, and from the sole of your foot to the top of your head.

36 "The Lord will ᴿbring you and the king whom you set over you to a nation which neither you nor your fathers have known, and ᴿthere you shall serve other gods—wood and stone.   Jer. 39:1-9 • Deut. 4:28

37 "And you shall become an astonishment, a proverb, and a byword among all nations where the Lord will drive you.

38 ᴿ"You shall carry much seed out to the field but gather little in, for ᴿthe locust shall ᵀconsume it.   Mic. 6:15 • Joel 1:4 • *devour*

39 "You shall plant vineyards and tend *them*, but you shall neither drink *of* the ᴿwine nor gather the *grapes*; for the worms shall eat them.   Zeph. 1:13

40 "You shall have olive trees throughout all your territory, but you shall not anoint *yourself* with the oil; for your olives shall drop off.

41 "You shall beget sons and daughters, but they shall not be yours; for ᴿthey shall go into captivity.   Lam. 1:5

42 "Locusts shall ᵀconsume all your trees and the produce of your land.   *possess*

43 "The alien who *is* among you shall rise higher and higher above you, and you shall come down lower and lower.

44 "He shall lend to you, but you shall not lend to him; he shall be the head, and you shall be the tail.

45 "Moreover all these curses shall come upon you and pursue and overtake you, until you are destroyed, because you ᵀdid not obey the voice of the Lord your God, to keep His commandments and His statutes which He commanded you.   *did not listen to*

46 "And they shall be upon ᴿyou for a sign and a wonder, and on your descendants forever.   Is. 8:18

47 "Because you did not serve the Lord your God with joy and gladness of heart, ᴿfor the abundance of everything,   Deut. 32:15

48 "therefore you shall serve your enemies, whom the Lord will send against you, in hunger, in thirst, in nakedness, and in need of everything; and He will put a yoke of iron on your neck until He has destroyed you.

49 ᴿ"The Lord will bring a nation against you from afar, from the end of the earth, *as* swift as the eagle flies, a nation whose language you will not understand,   Jer. 5:15

50 "a nation of fierce countenance, ᴿwhich

does not respect the elderly nor show favor to the young.   2 Chr. 36:17

51 "And they shall eat the increase of your livestock and the produce of your land, until you are destroyed; they shall not leave you grain or new wine or oil, *or* the increase of your cattle or the offspring of your flocks, until they have destroyed you.

52 "They shall ^Rbesiege you at all your gates until your high and fortified walls, in which you trust, come down throughout all your land; and they shall besiege you at all your gates throughout all your land which the Lord your God has given you. 2 Kin. 25:1, 2, 4

53 "You shall eat the ^Tfruit of your own body, the flesh of your sons and your daughters whom the Lord your God has given you, in the siege and desperate straits in which your enemy shall distress you.   offspring

54 "The ^Tsensitive and very refined man among you ^Twill be hostile toward his brother, toward the wife of his bosom, and toward the rest of his children whom he leaves behind,   tender • Lit. *his eye shall be evil toward*

55 "so that he will not give any of them the flesh of his children whom he will eat, because he has nothing left in the siege and desperate straits in which your enemy shall distress you at all your gates.

56 "The tender and ^Tdelicate woman among you, who would not venture to set the sole of her foot on the ground because of her delicateness and sensitivity, ^Twill refuse to the husband of her bosom, and to her son and her daughter,   refined • Lit. *her eye shall be evil toward*

57 "her ^Tplacenta which comes out ^Rfrom between her feet and her children whom she bears; for she will eat them secretly for lack of everything in the siege and desperate straits in which your enemy shall distress you at all your gates.   afterbirth • Gen. 49:10

58 "If you do not carefully observe all the words of this law that are written in this book, that you may fear this glorious and awesome name, THE LORD YOUR GOD,

59 "then the Lord will bring upon you and your descendants ^Rextraordinary plagues—great and prolonged plagues—and serious and prolonged sicknesses.   Dan. 9:12

60 "Moreover He will bring back on you all ^Rthe diseases of Egypt, of which you were afraid, and they shall cling to you.   Deut. 7:15

61 "Also every sickness and every plague, which *is* not written in this Book of the Law, will the Lord bring upon you until you are destroyed.

62 "You ^Rshall be left few in number, whereas you were ^Ras the stars of heaven in multitude, because you would not obey the voice of the Lord your God. Deut. 4:27 • Neh. 9:23

63 "And it shall be, *that* just as the Lord rejoiced over you to do you good and multiply you, so the Lord will rejoice over you to destroy you and bring you to nothing; and

you shall be ^Rplucked^T from off the land which you go to possess. Jer. 12:14; 45:4 • *torn*

64 "Then the Lord ^Rwill scatter you among all peoples, from one end of the earth to the other, and ^Rthere you shall serve other gods, which neither you nor your fathers have known—wood and stone. Jer. 16:13 • Deut. 28:36

65 "And ^Ramong those nations you shall find no rest, nor shall the sole of your foot have a resting place; ^Rbut there the Lord will give you a ^Ttrembling heart, failing eyes, and anguish of soul. Amos 9:4 • Lev. 26:36 • *anxious*

66 "Your life shall hang in doubt before you; you shall fear day and night, and have no assurance of life.

67 "In the morning you shall say, 'Oh, that it were evening!' And at evening you shall say, 'Oh, that it were morning!' because of the fear which terrifies your heart, and because of the sight which your eyes see.

68 "And the Lord ^Rwill take you back to Egypt in ships, by the way of which I said to you, ^R'You shall never see it again.' And there you shall be offered for sale to your enemies as male and female slaves, but no one will buy *you*." Hos. 8:13 • Deut. 17:16

The Covenant Renewed in Moab

29 These *are* the words of the covenant which the Lord commanded Moses to make with the children of Israel in the land of Moab, besides the ^Rcovenant which He made with them in Horeb. Deut. 5:2, 3

2 Now Moses called all Israel and said to them: ^R"You have seen all that the Lord did before your eyes in the land of Egypt, to Pharaoh and to all his servants and to all his land— Ex. 19:4

3 "the great trials which your eyes have seen, the signs, and those great wonders.

4 "Yet ^Rthe Lord has not given you a heart to perceive and eyes to see and ears to hear, to this *very* day. [Acts 28:26, 27]

5 ^R"And I have led you forty years in the wilderness. ^RYour clothes have not worn out on you, and your sandals have not worn out on your feet. Deut. 1:3; 8:2 • Deut. 8:4

6 "You have not eaten bread, nor have you drunk wine or *similar* drink, that you may know that I *am* the Lord your God.

7 "And when you came to this place, ^RSihon king of Heshbon and Og king of Bashan came out against us to battle, and we conquered them. Num. 21:23, 24

8 "We took their land and ^Rgave it as an inheritance to the Reubenites, to the Gadites, and to half the tribe of Manasseh. Deut. 3:12, 13

9 "Therefore ^Rkeep the words of this covenant, and do them, that you may ^Rprosper in all that you do. Deut. 4:6 • Josh. 1:7

10 "All of you stand today before the Lord your God: your leaders and your tribes and your elders and your officers, all the men of Israel,

11 "your little ones and your wives—also the stranger who is in your camp, from ᴿthe one who cuts your wood to the one who draws your water—   Josh. 9:21, 23, 27

12 "that you may enter into covenant with the Lᴏʀᴅ your God, and into His oath, which the Lᴏʀᴅ your God makes with you today,

13 "that He may establish you today as a people for Himself, and that He may be God to you, just as He has spoken to you, and ᴿjust as He has sworn to your fathers, to Abraham, Isaac, and Jacob.   Gen. 17:7, 8

14 "I make this covenant and this oath, ᴿnot with you alone,   [Jer. 31:31]

15 "but with him who stands here with us today before the Lᴏʀᴅ our God, as well as with him who is not here with us today

16 (for you know that we dwelt in the land of Egypt and that we came through the nations which you passed by,

17 and you saw their ᵀabominations and their idols which were among them—wood and stone and silver and gold);   detestable things

18 "so that there may not be among you man or woman or family or tribe, whose heart turns away today from the Lᴏʀᴅ our God, to go and serve the gods of these nations, and that there may not be among you a root bearing bitterness or wormwood;

19 "and so it may not happen, when he hears the words of this curse, that he blesses himself in his heart, saying, 'I shall have peace, even though I follow the ᵀdictates of my heart'—as though the drunkard could be included with the sober.   Or stubbornness

20 "The Lᴏʀᴅ would not spare him; for then the anger of the Lᴏʀᴅ and ᴿHis jealousy would burn against that man, and every curse that is written in this book would settle on him, and the Lᴏʀᴅ ᴿwould blot out his name from under heaven.   Ps. 79:5 • Deut. 9:14

21 "And the Lᴏʀᴅ would separate him from all the tribes of Israel for adversity, according to all the curses of the covenant that are written in this Book of the Law,

22 "so that the coming generation of your children who rise up after you, and the foreigner who comes from a far land, would say, when they see the plagues of that land and the sicknesses which the Lᴏʀᴅ has laid on it:

23 'The whole land is brimstone, ᴿsalt, and burning; it is not sown, nor does it bear, nor does any grass grow there, ᴿlike the overthrow of Sodom and Gomorrah, Admah, and Zeboiim, which the Lᴏʀᴅ overthrew in His anger and His wrath.'   Zeph. 2:9 • Gen. 19:24, 25

24 "All nations would say, ᴿ'Why has the Lᴏʀᴅ done so to this land? What does the heat of this great anger mean?'   1 Kin. 9:8

25 "Then people would say: 'Because they have forsaken the covenant of the Lᴏʀᴅ God of their fathers, which He made with them when He brought them out of the land of Egypt;

26 'for they went and served other gods and worshiped them, gods that they did not know and that He had not given to them.

27 'Then the anger of the Lᴏʀᴅ was aroused against this land, ᴿto bring on it every curse that is written in this book.   Dan. 9:11

28 'And the Lᴏʀᴅ ᴿuprooted them from their land in anger, in wrath, and in great indignation, and cast them into another land, as it is this day.'   1 Kin. 14:15

29 "The secret things belong to the Lᴏʀᴅ our God, but those things which are revealed belong to us and to our children forever, that we may do all the words of this law.

The Blessing of Returning to God

30 "Now it shall come to pass, when all these things come upon you, the blessing and the curse which I have set before you, and you ᵀcall them to mind among all the nations where the Lᴏʀᴅ your God drives you,   Lit. cause them to return to your heart

2 "and you return to the Lᴏʀᴅ your God and obey His voice, according to all that I command you today, you and your children, with all your heart and with all your soul,

3 ᴿ"that the Lᴏʀᴅ your God will bring you back from captivity, and have compassion on you, and ᴿgather you again from all the nations where the Lᴏʀᴅ your God has scattered you.   Jer. 29:14 • Ezek. 34:13

4 ᴿ"If any of you are driven out to the farthest parts under heaven, from there the Lᴏʀᴅ your God will gather you, and from there He will bring you.   Neh. 1:9

5 "Then the Lᴏʀᴅ your God will bring you to the land which your fathers possessed, and you shall possess it. He will prosper you and multiply you more than your fathers.

6 "And the Lᴏʀᴅ your God will circumcise your heart and the heart of your descendants, to love the Lᴏʀᴅ your God with all your heart and with all your soul, that you may live.

7 "Also the Lᴏʀᴅ your God will put all these curses on your enemies and on those who hate you, who persecuted you.

8 "And you will ᴿagain obey the voice of the Lᴏʀᴅ and do all His commandments which I command you today.   Zeph. 3:20

9 "The Lᴏʀᴅ your God will make you abound in all the work of your hand, in the fruit of your body, in the increase of your livestock, and in the produce of your land for good. For the Lᴏʀᴅ will again rejoice over you for good as He rejoiced over your fathers,

10 "if you obey the voice of the Lᴏʀᴅ your God, to keep His commandments and His statutes which are written in this Book of the Law, and if you turn to the Lᴏʀᴅ your God with all your heart and with all your soul.

The Choice of Life or Death

11 "For this commandment which I command you today ᴿis ᵀnot too mysterious for you, nor is it far off.   Is. 45:19 • not hidden from

12 "It is not in heaven, that you should say, 'Who will ascend into heaven for us and bring it to us, that we may hear it and do it?'

13 "Nor is it beyond the sea, that you should say, 'Who will go over the sea for us and bring it to us, that we may hear it and do it?'

14 "But the word is very near you, in your mouth and in your heart, that you may do it.

15 "See, ᴿI have set before you today life and good, death and evil,   Deut. 30:1, 19

16 "in that I command you today to love the LORD your God, to walk in His ways, and to keep His commandments, His statutes, and His judgments, that you may live and multiply; and the LORD your God will bless you in the land which you go to possess.

17 "But if your heart turns away so that you do not hear, and are drawn away, and worship other gods and serve them,

18 ᴿ"I announce to you today that you shall surely perish; you shall not prolong your days in the land which you cross over the Jordan to go in and possess.   Deut. 4:26; 8:19

19 ᴿ"I call heaven and earth as witnesses today against you, that ᴿI have set before you life and death, blessing and cursing; therefore choose life, that both you and your descendants may live;   Deut. 4:26 • Deut. 30:15

20 "that you may love the LORD your God, that you may obey His voice, and that you may cling to Him, for He is your ᴿlife and the length of your days; and that you may dwell in the land which the LORD swore to your fathers, to Abraham, Isaac, and Jacob, to give them."   [John 11:25; 14:6]

Joshua the New Leader of Israel

31 Then Moses went and spoke these words to all Israel.

2 And he said to them: "I am one hundred and twenty years old today. I can no longer go out and come in. Also the LORD has said to me, 'You shall not cross over this Jordan.'

3 "The LORD your God Himself crosses over before you; He will destroy these nations from before you, and you shall dispossess them. Joshua himself crosses over before you, just ᴿas the LORD has said.   Num. 27:21

4 "And the LORD will do to them as He did to Sihon and Og, the kings of the Amorites and their land, when He destroyed them.

5 "The LORD will give them over to you, that you may do to them according to every commandment which I have commanded you.

6 "Be strong and of good courage, do not fear nor be afraid of them; for the LORD your God, He is the One who goes with you. He will not leave you nor forsake you."

7 Then Moses called Joshua and said to him in the sight of all Israel, ᴿ"Be strong and of good courage, for you must go with this people to the land which the LORD has sworn to their fathers to give them, and you shall cause them to inherit it.   Deut. 31:23

8 "And the LORD, ᴿHe is the One who goes before you. ᴿHe will be with you, He will not leave you nor forsake you; do not fear nor be dismayed."   Ex. 13:21 • Josh. 1:5

The Law to Be Read Every Seven Years

9 So Moses wrote this law ᴿand delivered it to the priests, the sons of Levi, ᴿwho bore the ark of the covenant of the LORD, and to all the elders of Israel.   Deut. 17:18; 31:25, 26 • Josh. 3:3

10 And Moses commanded them, saying: "At the end of every seven years, at the appointed time in the ᴿyear of release, ᴿat the Feast of Tabernacles,   Deut. 15:1, 2 • Lev. 23:34

11 "when all Israel comes to appear before the LORD your God in the ᴿplace which He chooses, ᴿyou shall read this law before all Israel in their hearing.   Deut. 12:5 • Josh. 8:34

12 ᴿ"Gather the people together, men and women and little ones, and the stranger who is within your gates, that they may hear and that they may learn to fear the LORD your God and carefully observe all the words of this law,   Deut. 4:10

13 "and that their children, who have not known it, may hear and learn to fear the LORD your God as long as you live in the land which you cross the Jordan to possess."

Prediction of Israel's Rebellion

14 Then the LORD said to Moses, ᴿ"Behold, the days approach when you must die; call Joshua, and present yourselves in the tabernacle of meeting, that ᴿI may ᵀinaugurate him." So Moses and Joshua went and presented themselves in the tabernacle of meeting.   Num. 27:13 • Deut. 3:28 • commission

15 Now the LORD appeared at the tabernacle in a pillar of cloud, and the pillar of cloud stood above the door of the tabernacle.

16 And the LORD said to Moses: "Behold, you will ᵀrest with your fathers; and this people will rise and play the harlot with the gods of the foreigners of the land, where they go to be among them, and they will forsake Me and break My covenant which I have made with them.   Die and join your ancestors

17 "Then My anger shall be ᴿaroused against them in that day, and ᴿI will forsake them, and I will ᴿhide My face from them, and they shall be ᵀdevoured. And many evils and troubles shall befall them, so that they will say in that day, 'Have not these evils come upon us because our God is not among us?'   Judg. 2:14; 6:13 • 2 Chr. 15:2 • Deut. 32:20 • consumed

18 "And I will surely hide My face in that day because of all the evil which they have done, in that they have turned to other gods.

19 "Now therefore, write down this song for yourselves, and teach it to the children of Israel; put it in their mouths, that this song

may be Ra witness for Me against the children of Israel.   Deut. 31:22, 26

20 "When I have brought them to the land flowing with milk and honey, of which I swore to their fathers, and they have eaten and filled themselves Rand grown fat, Rthen they will turn to other gods and serve them; and they will provoke Me and break My covenant.   Deut. 32:15-17 · Deut. 31:16

21 "Then it shall be, Rwhen many evils and troubles have come upon them, that this song will testify against them as a witness; for it will not be forgotten in the mouths of their descendants, for RI know the inclination Rof their behavior today, even before I have brought them to the land of which I swore to give them."   Deut. 31:17 · Hos. 5:3 · Amos 5:25, 26

22 Therefore Moses wrote this song the same day, and taught it to the children of Israel.

23 RThen He inaugurated Joshua the son of Nun, and said, R"Be strong and of good courage; for you shall bring the children of Israel into the land of which I swore to them, and I will be with you."   Num. 27:23 · Deut. 31:7

24 So it was, when Moses had completed writing the words of this law in a book, when they were finished,

25 that Moses commanded the Levites, who bore the ark of the covenant of the LORD, saying:

26 "Take this Book of the Law, Rand put it beside the ark of the covenant of the LORD your God, that it may be there Ras a witness against you;   2 Kin. 22:8 · Deut. 31:19

27 "for I know your rebellion and your stiff neck. If today, while I am yet alive with you, you have been rebellious against the LORD, then how much more after my death?

28 "Gather to me all the elders of your tribes, and your officers, that I may speak these words in their hearing Rand call heaven and earth to witness against them.   Deut. 30:19

29 "For I know that after my death you will become utterly corrupt, and turn aside from the way which I have commanded you. And Revil will befall you Rin the latter days, because you will do evil in the sight of the LORD, to provoke Him to anger through the work of your hands."   Deut. 28:15 · Gen. 49:1

The Song of Moses

30 Then Moses spoke in the hearing of all the assembly of Israel the words of this song until they were ended:

32 "Give Rear, O heavens, and I will speak;
And hear, O Rearth, the words of my mouth.   Deut. 4:26 · Jer. 6:19

2 Let my Tteaching drop as the rain,
My speech distill as the dew,   *doctrine*
RAs raindrops on the tender herb,
And as showers on the grass.   Ps. 72:6

3 For I proclaim the Rname of the LORD:
Ascribe greatness to our God.   Deut. 28:58

4 *He is* Rthe Rock, His work *is* perfect;
For all His ways *are* justice,   Ps. 18:2
A God of truth and Rwithout injustice;
Righteous and upright *is* He.   Job 34:10

5 "TheyR have corrupted themselves;
They are not His children,   Deut. 4:25; 31:29
Because of their blemish:
A perverse and crooked generation.

6 Do you thus Tdeal with the LORD,
O foolish and unwise people?   *repay the*
Is He not Ryour Father, *who* Rbought
you?   Is. 63:16 · Ps. 74:2
Has He not Rmade you and established
you?   Deut. 32:15

7 "RememberR the days of old,   Ps. 44:1
Consider the years of many generations.
Ask your father, and he will show you;
Your elders, and they will tell you:

8 When the Most High Rdivided their inheritance to the nations,   Acts 17:26
When He Rseparated the sons of Adam,
He set the boundaries of the peoples
According to the number of the children of Israel.   Gen. 11:8

9 For the LORD's portion *is* His people;
Jacob *is* the place of His inheritance.

10 "He found him Rin a desert land
And in the wasteland, a howling wilderness;   Jer. 2:6
He encircled him, He instructed him,
He kept him as the apple of His eye.

11 RAs an eagle stirs up its nest,   Is. 31:5
Hovers over its young,
Spreading out its wings, taking them up,
Carrying them on its wings,

12 *So* the LORD alone led him,
And *there was* no foreign god with him.

13 "HeR made him ride in the heights of the earth,   Is. 58:14
That he might eat the produce of the fields;
He made him draw honey from the rock,
And oil from the flinty rock;

14 Curds from the cattle, and milk of the flock,
RWith fat of lambs;   Ps. 81:16
And rams of the breed of Bashan, and goats,
With the choicest wheat;
And you drank wine, the Rblood of the grapes.   Gen. 49:11

15 "But Jeshurun grew fat and kicked;
RYou grew fat, you grew thick,
You are obese!   Deut. 31:20
Then he Rforsook God *who* Rmade him,
And scornfully esteemed the RRock of his salvation.   Is. 1:4 · Is. 51:13 · Ps. 95:1

16 ᴿThey provoked Him to jealousy with
      foreign *gods*;   1 Cor. 10:22
   With ᵀabominations they provoked Him
      to anger.   *detestable acts*
17 ᴿThey sacrificed to demons, not to God,
   To gods they did not know,
   To new *gods*, new arrivals
   That your fathers did not fear.   Rev. 9:20
18 ᴿOf the Rock *who* begot you, you are
      unmindful,   Is. 17:10
   And have ᴿforgotten the God who
      fathered you.   Jer. 2:32
19 "Andᴿ when the Lᴏʀᴅ saw *it*, He
      spurned *them*,   Judg. 2:14
   Because of the provocation of His sons
      and His daughters.
20 And He said: 'I will hide My face from
      them,
   I will see what their end *will be*,
   For they *are* a perverse generation,
   ᴿChildren in whom *is* no faith.   Matt. 17:17
21 ᴿThey have provoked Me to jealousy by
      what is not God;   Ps. 78:58
   They have moved Me to anger by their
      ᵀfoolish idols.   *foolishness, lit. vanities*
   But ᴿI will provoke them to jealousy by
      those who are not a nation;   Rom. 10:19
   I will move them to anger by a foolish
      nation.
22 For a fire is kindled in My anger,
   And shall burn to the ᵀlowest hell;
   It shall consume the earth with her
      increase,   *lowest part of Sheol*
   And set on fire the foundations of the
      mountains.
23 'I will heap disasters on them;
   I will spend My arrows on them.
24 *They shall be* wasted with hunger,
   Devoured by pestilence and bitter
      destruction;
   I will also send against them the ᴿteeth
      of beasts,   Lev. 26:22
   With the poison of serpents of the dust.
25 The sword shall destroy outside;
   There shall be terror within
   For the young man and virgin,
   The nursing child with the man of gray
      hairs.
26 ᴿI would have said, "I will dash them in
      pieces,   Ezek. 20:23
   I will make the memory of them to
      cease from among men,"
27 Had I not feared the wrath of the
      enemy,
   Lest their adversaries should
      misunderstand,
   Lest they should say, ᴿ"Our hand *is*
      high;   Is. 10:12–15
   And it is not the Lᴏʀᴅ who has done all
      this." '
28 "For they *are* a nation void of counsel,
   Nor *is there any* understanding in
      them.

29 ᴿOh, that they were wise, *that* they
      understood this,   [Luke 19:42]
   That they would consider their ᴿlatter
      end!   Deut. 31:29
30 How could one chase a thousand,
   And two put ten thousand to flight,
   Unless their Rock had sold them,
   And the Lᴏʀᴅ had surrendered them?
31 For their rock *is* not like our Rock,
   ᴿEven our enemies themselves *being*
      judges.   [1 Sam. 4:7, 8]
32 For ᴿtheir vine *is* of the vine of Sodom
   And of the fields of Gomorrah;
   Their grapes *are* grapes of gall,
   Their clusters *are* bitter.   Is. 1:8–10
33 Their wine *is* the poison of serpents,
   And the cruel venom of cobras.

34 'Is this not laid up in store with Me,
   Sealed up among My treasures?
35 ᴿVengeance is Mine, and recompense;
   Their foot shall slip in *due* time;
   ᴿFor the day of their calamity *is* at hand,
   And the things to come hasten upon
      them.'   Heb. 10:30 • 2 Pet. 2:3
36 "Forᴿ the Lᴏʀᴅ will judge His people
   ᴿAnd have compassion on His servants,
   When He sees that *their* power is gone,
   And ᴿ*there is* no one *remaining*, bond
      or free.   Ps. 135:14 • Jer. 31:20 • 2 Kin. 14:26
37 He will say: 'Where *are* their gods,
   The rock in which they sought refuge?
38 Who ate the fat of their sacrifices,
   And drank the wine of their drink
      offering?
   Let them rise and help you,
   And be your refuge.
39 'Now see that ᴿI, *even* I, *am* He,
   And ᴿ*there is* no God besides Me;
   ᴿI kill and I make alive;
   I wound and I heal;
   Nor *is there any* who can deliver from
      My hand.   Is. 41:4; 43:10 • Is. 45:5 • 1 Sam. 2:6
40 For I raise My hand to heaven,
   And say, "*As* I live forever,
41 If I ᵀwhet My glittering sword,   *sharpen*
   And My hand takes hold on judgment,
   I will render vengeance to My enemies,
   And repay those who hate Me.
42 I will make My arrows drunk with
      blood,
   And My sword shall devour flesh,
   With the blood of the slain and the
      captives,
   From the heads of the leaders of the
      enemy." '
43 "Rejoice,ᴿ O Gentiles, *with* His *people;
   For He will ᴿavenge the blood of His
      servants,   Rom. 15:10 • Rev. 6:10; 19:2

32:43 DSS add *And let all the angels worship Him,* see
Heb. 1:6

And render vengeance to His
   adversaries;
He ^Rwill provide atonement for His land
   and His people."   Ps. 65:3; 79:9; 85:1

44 So Moses came with *Joshua the son of
Nun and spoke all the words of this song in
the hearing of the people.

45 Moses finished speaking all these words
to all Israel,

46 and he said to them: ^R"Set your hearts
on all the words which I testify among you
today, which you shall command your ^Rchil-
dren to be careful to observe—all the words
of this law.   Ezek. 40:4; 44:5 • Deut. 11:19

47 "For it *is* not a ^Tfutile thing for you,
because it *is* your life, and by this word you
shall prolong *your* days in the land which
you cross over the Jordan to possess."   *vain*

Moses to Die on Mount Nebo

48 Then the LORD spoke to Moses that very
same day, saying:

49 ^R"Go up this mountain of the Abarim,
Mount Nebo, which *is* in the land of Moab,
across from Jericho; view the land of Canaan,
which I give to the children of Israel as a
possession;   Num. 27:12–14

50 "and die on the mountain which you
ascend, and be gathered to your people, just
as ^RAaron your brother died on Mount Hor
and was gathered to his people;   Num. 20:25, 28

51 "because you trespassed against Me
among the children of Israel at the waters of
^TMeribah Kadesh, in the Wilderness of Zin,
because you did not hallow Me in the midst
of the children of Israel.   *Contention at Kadesh*

52 "Yet you shall see the land before *you*,
though you shall not go there, into the land
which I am giving to the children of Israel."

Moses' Final Blessing on Israel

33 Now this *is* the blessing with which
Moses ^Rthe man of God blessed the
children of Israel before his death.   Ps. 90

2 And he said:

"The LORD came from Sinai,
   And dawned on them from ^RSeir;
He shone forth from ^RMount Paran,
   And He came with ^Rten thousands of
      saints;   Deut. 2:1, 4 • Num. 10:12 • Dan. 7:10
From His right hand
Came a fiery law for them.

3 Yes, ^RHe loves the people;   Hos. 11:1
   All His saints *are* in Your hand;
They ^Rsit down at Your feet;   [Luke 10:39]
Everyone ^Rreceives Your words.   Prov. 2:1

4 Moses commanded a law for us,
   A heritage of the congregation of
      Jacob.

5 And He was King in Jeshurun,

When the leaders of the people were
   gathered,
All the tribes of Israel together.

6 "Let ^RReuben live, and not die,
   Nor let his men be few."   Gen. 49:3, 4

7 And this he said of ^RJudah:

"Hear, LORD, the voice of Judah,
   And bring him to his people;
^RLet his hands be sufficient for him,
   And may You be ^Ra help against his
      enemies."   Gen. 49:8–12 • Gen. 49:8 • Ps. 146:5

8 And of ^RLevi he said: Gen. 49:5

^R"*Let* Your Thummim and Your Urim *be*
   with Your holy one,   Ex. 28:30
^RWhom You tested at Massah,   Ps. 81:7
   And with whom You contended at the
      waters of Meribah,

9 Who says of his father and mother,
   'I have not ^Rseen them';   [Gen. 29:32]
^RNor did he acknowledge his brothers,
   Or know his own children;   Ex. 32:26–28
For ^Rthey have observed Your word
   And kept Your covenant.   Mal. 2:5, 6

10 ^RThey shall teach Jacob Your
      judgments,
   And Israel Your law.   Lev. 10:11
They shall put incense before You,
   ^RAnd a whole burnt sacrifice on Your
      altar.   Ps. 51:19

11 Bless his substance, LORD,
   And ^Raccept the work of his hands;
Strike the loins of those who rise
      against him,   2 Sam. 24:23
   And of those who hate him, that they
      rise not again."

12 Of Benjamin he said:

"The beloved of the LORD shall dwell in
      safety by Him,
   Who shelters him all the day long;
And he shall dwell between His
      shoulders."

13 And of Joseph he said:

^R"Blessed of the LORD *is* his land,
   With the precious things of heaven,
      with the ^Rdew,   Gen. 49:22–26 • Gen. 27:28
   And the deep lying beneath,

14 With the precious fruits of the sun,
   With the precious produce of the
      months,

15 With the best things of ^Rthe ancient
      mountains,   Gen. 49:26
   With the precious things ^Rof the
      everlasting hills,   Hab. 3:6

16 With the precious things of the earth
      and its fullness,
   And the favor of ^RHim who dwelt in the
      bush.   Ex. 3:2–4
Let *the blessing* come ^Ron the head of
      Joseph,   Gen. 49:26

And on the crown of the head of him
who was separate from his brothers.'
17 His glory *is like* a ^Rfirstborn bull,
And his horns *like* the ^Rhorns of the
wild ox;   1 Chr. 5:1 · Num. 23:22
Together with them
^RHe shall push the peoples   Ps. 44:5
To the ends of the earth;
^RThey *are* the ten thousands of Ephraim,
And they *are* the thousands of
Manasseh."   Gen. 48:19
18 And of Zebulun he said:

^R"Rejoice, Zebulun, in your going out,
And Issachar in your tents!   Gen. 49:13–15
19 They shall ^Rcall the peoples *to* the
mountain;   Is. 2:3
There ^Rthey shall offer sacrifices of
righteousness;   Ps. 4:5; 51:19
For they shall partake *of* the abundance
of the seas
And *of* treasures hidden in the sand."

20 And of Gad he said:

"Blessed *is* he who ^Renlarges Gad;
He dwells as a lion,   1 Chr. 12:8
And tears the arm and the crown of his
head.
21 ^RHe provided the first *part* for himself,
Because a lawgiver's portion was
reserved there.   Num. 32:16, 17
He came *with* the heads of the people;
He administered the justice of the
Lord,
And His judgments with Israel."

22 And of Dan he said:

"Dan *is* a lion's whelp;
^RHe shall leap from Bashan."   Josh. 19:47

23 And of Naphtali he said:

"O Naphtali, satisfied with favor,
And full of the blessing of the Lord,
Possess the west and the south."

24 And of Asher he said:

"Asher *is* most blessed of sons;
Let him be favored by his brothers,
And let him ^Rdip his foot in oil.   Job 29:6
25 Your sandals *shall be* iron and bronze;
As your days, *so shall* your strength *be.*

26 "There is ^Rno one like the God of
^RJeshurun,   Ex. 15:11 · Deut. 32:15
Who rides the heavens to help you,
And in His excellency on the clouds.
27 The eternal God *is* your ^Rrefuge,
And underneath *are* the everlasting
arms;   [Ps. 90:1; 91:2, 9]
^RHe will thrust out the enemy from
before you,   Deut. 9:3–5

And will say, 'Destroy!'
28 Then Israel shall dwell in safety,
The fountain of Jacob ^Ralone,   Num. 23:9
In a land of grain and new wine;
His heavens shall also drop dew.
29 ^RHappy *are* you, O Israel!
^RWho *is* like you, a people saved by the
Lord,   Ps. 144:15 · 2 Sam. 7:23
^RThe shield of your help   Ps. 115:9
And the sword of your majesty!
Your enemies shall submit to you,
And ^Ryou shall tread down their ^Thigh
places."   Num. 33:52 · Places for pagan worship

Moses Dies on Mount Nebo

34 Then Moses went up from the plains
of Moab ^Rto Mount Nebo, to the top of
Pisgah, which is across from Jericho. And the
Lord showed him all the land of Gilead as far
as Dan,   Deut. 32:49
2 all Naphtali and the land of Ephraim and
Manasseh, all the land of Judah as far as the
^TWestern Sea,   Mediterranean
3 the South, and the plain of the Valley of
Jericho, the city of palm trees, as far as Zoar.
4 Then the Lord said to him, ^R"This *is* the
land of which I swore to give Abraham,
Isaac, and Jacob, saying, 'I will give it to your
descendants.' ^RI have caused you to see *it*
with your eyes, but you shall not cross over
there."   Gen. 12:7 · Deut. 3:27
5 ^RSo Moses the servant of the Lord died
there in the land of Moab, according to the
word of the Lord.   Deut. 32:50
6 And He buried him in a valley in the land
of Moab, opposite Beth Peor; but ^Rno one
knows his grave to this day.   Jude 9
7 Moses *was* one hundred and twenty
years old when he died. His eyes were not
dim nor his natural vigor ^Tdiminished.   reduced
8 And the children of Israel wept for Mo-
ses in the plains of Moab ^Rthirty days. So the
days of weeping *and* mourning for Moses
ended.   Gen. 50:3, 10
9 Now Joshua the son of Nun was full of
the ^Rspirit of wisdom, for ^RMoses had laid his
hands on him; so the children of Israel
heeded him, and did as the Lord had commanded Moses.   Is. 11:2 · Num. 27:18, 23
10 But since then there ^Rhas not arisen in
Israel a prophet like Moses, ^Rwhom the Lord
knew face to face,   Deut. 18:15, 18 · Ex. 33:11
11 in all ^Rthe signs and wonders which the
Lord sent him to do in the land of Egypt,
before Pharaoh, before all his servants, and in
all his land,   Deut. 7:19
12 and by all that mighty power and all the
great terror which Moses performed in the
sight of all Israel.

THE BOOK OF
Joshua

If the story of Joshua were published separately in documentary-drama form, it would become an overnight best-seller. From the point of history alone, the story of Joshua is one of astounding and unimaginable adventure that captures the reader's attention from the very beginning. In the first two verses of the book, God spoke to Joshua and appointed him commanding general of Israel's army and, under God, sole leader of all the people, who numbered in the millions. At the same time, God ordered Joshua to have everyone move across the overflowing and raging waters of the Jordan River. Although he had neither boat nor bridge and was totally unaware of how God planned to accomplish this feat, he started immediately to prepare the masses for the crossing. This was the beginning of a series of hazardous events which this eighty-five-year-old hero of the faith undertook without question or looking back. God had told Joshua, "the LORD your God is with you wherever you go" (1:9), and he believed God. The same promise is given today to those who likewise trust in His Son as Lord and Savior (Matt. 28:20).

AUTHORSHIP. Although there is no declarative statement in the book identifying the writer, it is generally acknowledged that Joshua was the author (with the possible exception of fewer than a score of verses, such as the last five verses pertaining to his death).

CONTEXT. Joshua was born into slavery in Egypt forty years prior to the Israelites' exodus from that country. He was one of the twelve men sent to spy in Canaan to determine if it was safe for Moses to lead the nation into the land. During the wilderness period he had led an army of Israelites to victory over the Amalekites. Later he was appointed as a servant to Moses. The events in the book seem to have been written in diary form, as they occurred. The time element covers the years from about 1415 to about 1389 B.C.

SUMMARY STATEMENT. In this book God demonstrates that He is in control of everything, everywhere and that all men through the ages are responsible to Him in all things.

KEY VERSE. During his closing days on earth Joshua charged the people to "take diligent heed to yourselves, that you love the LORD your God" (23:11). Surely a deep and abiding love for God was the root of Joshua's faith and action, to God's glory.

HOW JOSHUA FITS TOGETHER. In the opening paragraph, God gives His commission to General Joshua (1:1–9), and this is followed by preparing the people for the crossing of the Jordan (1:10—3:17). The dramatic conquest of Canaan, first by splitting the land of Canaan in half by invasion and then by defeating the South and the North, is dramatically told in chapters 6—12. Once conquered, the land is divided among the various tribes (chs. 13—21). This is followed by dissension among the tribes (ch. 22). The book ends with the last words of Joshua and his death (chs. 23, 24).

In this remarkable book, the Lord Jesus Christ is made evident as the "Commander of the army of the LORD" (5:14), when he spoke to Joshua face to face. He is also represented in typology. The ark of the Lord was a type of Christ in that when it was carried to the edge of the Jordan River, the waters "rose in a heap" (3:16), allowing the Israelites to cross unharmed into the Promised Land.

A type of the Lord's atonement is the scarlet cord that Rahab used to save the lives of the two Hebrew spies and later to save her and her entire family from certain death. (That brave gentile woman, a converted harlot, became a fifth-generation ancestress of David.) Scarlet, the color of the cord, was the color of the shed blood of Jesus by which man finds forgiveness unto salvation, for "without shedding of blood there is no remission" (Heb. 9:22).

The book teaches some valuable lessons to those who will "wholly follow the Lord," as did Joshua—and to those who will not. An example of both, in a single illustration, is the story of how the sin of one Israelite, Achan, brought shame and defeat to Joshua and the whole nation when Joshua's troops were defeated by a numerically inferior army at Ai. God directed the second battle of Ai (Joshua had not sought His counsel before the first battle), and Joshua followed His plan, which was a demonstration of classic military strategy—profound in its simplicity and daring in execution.

Nearing the end of his life on earth Joshua reminded Israel that during some twenty-five years of war "the LORD your God is He who has fought for you" (23:3); he took no credit

himself. Then, in a soul-stirring charge to the people to beware of worshiping false gods as their fathers did, he challenged them with the words, "Choose for yourselves this day whom you will serve . . . But as for me and my house, we will serve the LORD" (24:15).

The book of Joshua presents a humble man who had no personal goal other than to please God. In every successful battle he gave God the glory. When sin was found in Israel he dealt with it immediately and with finality. He was a leader who showed the way without fear of danger or criticism. Joshua determined to "fear [reverence] the LORD, serve Him in sincerity and in truth" (24:14). God is still using men and women who have the heart of Joshua to serve Him.

—B.L.

God's Commission to Joshua

▼ 25-E. The Christian Life Is a Successful Life

AFTER the death of Moses the servant of the LORD, it came to pass that the LORD spoke to Joshua the son of Nun, Moses' ᴿassistant, saying: Ex. 24:13

2 ᴿ"Moses My servant is dead. Now therefore, arise, go over this Jordan, you and all this people, to the land which I am giving to them—the children of Israel.   Deut. 34:5

3 ᴿ"Every place that the sole of your foot will tread upon I have given you, as I said to Moses.   Deut. 11:24

4 ᴿ"From the wilderness and this Lebanon as far as the great river, the River Euphrates, all the land of the Hittites, and to the Great Sea toward the going down of the sun, shall be your territory.   Gen. 15:18

5 "No man shall be able to stand before you all the days of your life; as I was with Moses, so I will be with you. ᴿI will not leave you nor forsake you.   Deut. 31:6, 7

6 ᴿ"Be strong and of good courage, for to this people you shall ᵀdivide as an inheritance the land which I swore to their fathers to give them.   Deut. 31:7, 23 · give as a possession

7 "Only be strong and very courageous, that you may observe to do according to all the law which Moses My servant commanded you; do not turn from it to the right hand or

to the left, that you may ᵀprosper wherever you go.   ▽ have success or act wisely

8 "This Book of the Law shall not depart from your mouth, but you shall ᵀmeditate in it day and night, that you may observe to do according to all that is written in it. For then you will make your way prosperous, and then you will have good success.   ▲ be constantly in

9 ᴿ"Have I not commanded you? Be strong and of good courage; ᴿdo not be afraid, nor be dismayed, for the LORD your God is with you wherever you go."   Deut. 31:7 · Ps. 27:1

The Order to Cross the Jordan

10 Then Joshua commanded the officers of the people, saying,

11 "Pass through the camp and command the people, saying, 'Prepare provisions for yourselves, for ᴿwithin three days you will cross over this Jordan, to go in to possess the land which the LORD your God is giving you to possess.'"   Deut. 9:1

12 And to the Reubenites, the Gadites, and half the tribe of Manasseh Joshua spoke, saying,

13 "Remember ᴿthe word which Moses the servant of the LORD commanded you, saying, 'The LORD your God is giving you rest and is giving you this land.'   Num. 32:20-28

14 "Your wives, your little ones, and your livestock shall remain in the land which Moses gave you on this side of the Jordan. But you shall ᵀpass before your brethren

25-E. The Christian Life Is a Successful Life (Joshua 1:1-8)—Paul tells us that "All Scripture is given by inspiration of God [both the Old and the New Testaments], and is profitable for doctrine, for reproof, for correction, for instruction in righteousness" (2 Tim. 3:16, 17, page 1227). The Scriptures were not given to you carelessly, but deliberately for your edification, and are "profitable" in that they build you up in Christ.

Success according to the Word of God is just the opposite of success according to the world. Most of the men and women of the Bible would be called failures today, by the standards of this world system; but they were successful according to God's standards. We have an example in Hebrews 11:36-39 (page 1249):

(1) "Still others [Old Testament heroes and heroines of faith] had trial of mockings and scourgings, yes, and of chains and imprisonment"—but they were successful.

(2) "They were stoned, they were sawn in two, were tempted, were slain with the sword. They wandered about in sheepskins and goatskins, being destitute, afflicted, tormented"—but they were successful.

(3) "They wandered in deserts and mountains, in dens and caves of the earth"—but they were successful.

"And all these, having obtained a good testimony through faith, did not receive the promise." In other words, even though they remained faithful to God, they did not receive the promise, but they were successful in His eyes.

(Point 25-E continued on next page)

(Point 25-E continued from previous page)
This does not necessarily mean that Christians who have accumulated great wealth are not in the will of God. Abraham was one of the wealthiest men of his day. David and Job also enjoyed great wealth. As you study the Bible, you will see that God has entrusted a comparative few of His children with the wealth of this world.

God gave Joshua a fourfold conditional promise:

(1) *Prosperity.* "Every place that the sole of your foot will tread upon I have given you" (v. 3).
(2) *Victory in battle.* "No man shall be able to stand before you all the days of your life" (v. 5).
(3) *"Good success"* (v. 8). He would be successful in all that God commanded him to do.
(4) *A reward for obedience.* "I will not leave you nor forsake you" (v. 5).

This fourfold promise was given to one man; however, you can claim that promise if you are willing to meet God's conditions and leave the choice to Him. He may choose to bless you with spiritual victories and success, but not prosper you in the wealth of this world. If you seek first the kingdom of God and His righteousness, He has promised to:

(1) Supply all your needs (Matt. 6:25-34, page 944; cf. Phil. 4:19, page 1199).
(2) Open the "windows of heaven and pour out for you such blessing that there will not be room enough to receive it" (Mal. 3:10, page 925).
(3) Bless you in your spiritual and material needs. "Give, and it will be given to you: good measure, pressed down, shaken together, and running over will be put into your bosom. For with the same measure that you use, it will be measured back to you" (Luke 6:38, page 1020).

As you place God first in your life, He will supply all your needs. Therefore, you can concentrate on laying up treasures in heaven "where neither moth nor rust destroys and where thieves do not break in and steal. . . . For where your treasure is, there your heart will be also" (Matt. 6:19-24, page 943).

God promised Joshua all of this before he crossed the Jordan River. The Jordan separates Canaan (the Land of Promise) from the wilderness.

(1) Canaan is not a type of heaven. It is a type of the victorious Christian life; it is living in the will of God (Rom. 12:1, 2, page 1142).
(2) The wilderness is a type of failure and defeat in which the carnal Christian dwells. It is living out of the will of God. The children of Israel wandered there for forty years because of their unbelief at Kadesh Barnea (Deut. 1:19-46, page 181).

Before Joshua could possess Canaan, he had to cross the Jordan and drive out "the Amorites, the Perizzites, the Canaanites, the Hittites, the Girgashites, the Hivites, and the Jebusites" (Josh. 24:11, page 238). Before we can experience success in the Christian life, we must drive out the forces of evil that draw us away from God, and declare war against the works of the flesh—"adultery, fornication, uncleanness, lewdness, idolatry, sorcery, hatred, contentions, jealousies, outbursts of wrath, selfish ambitions, dissensions, heresies, envy, murders, drunkenness, revelries, and the like" (Gal. 5:19-21, page 1184).

God gave Joshua a fourfold condition for a successful Christian life:

(1) Cross your Jordan. "Arise, go over this Jordan" (v. 2). God gave Canaan to Israel, but they had to cross over the Jordan and take it by faith. They had to "possess their possessions" (Obad. 17, page 882). If you are to know true spiritual success, you must cross your Jordan—put your faith into action (John 11:40 page 1070).
(2) Know God's Word. "This Book of the Law shall not depart from your mouth" (v. 8). Joshua was to fill his mouth with God's Word. He was to be ready at all times to proclaim the Word of God. Like Paul, he was not ashamed of it (Rom. 1:15, 16, page 1128). Joshua had only the first five books of the Bible. We have all sixty-six books—the complete Scripture. To fill your mouth with God's Word you must "be diligent to present yourself approved to God, a worker who does not need to be ashamed, rightly dividing the word of truth" (2 Tim. 2:15, page 1226).
(3) Meditate on God's Word. "You shall meditate in it [God's Word] day and night" (v. 8). Joshua was to fill his mind with God's Word. He was to ponder it—turn it over and over in his mind. He was to chew it as a cow chews the cud. He was to meditate on it and keep it on his mind day and night. He was to hide it in his heart (Ps. 119:11, page 581). To be a successful Christian, you must fill your mind with God's Word and meditate (think) on it (Ps. 1:2, page 509).
(4) Apply God's Word. "That you may observe to do according to all that is written in it" (v. 8). Joshua was to fill his time by obeying God's Word. When King Saul was disobedient to God, Samuel said, "Behold, to obey is better than sacrifice" (1 Sam. 15:22, page 282). To be a successful Christian, you must fill your time with deeds to obey God's Word. You must apply His Word to your life in order to "grow in the grace and knowledge of our Lord and Savior Jesus Christ" (2 Pet. 3:18, page 1276).

To be a spiritual success, you must meet God's fourfold condition. As you live your life for Christ day by day, remember to claim the fruit of the Spirit, which is love. Love is manifested through joy, peace, longsuffering, kindness, goodness, faithfulness, gentleness, and self-control. "If we live in the Spirit, let us also walk in the Spirit" (Gal. 5:22-25, page 1184).

See Index, page 17, for your next study.

armed, all your mighty men of valor, and help them,   *cross over ahead of*

15 "until the Lord has given your brethren rest, as He *gave* you, and they also have taken possession of the land which the Lord your God is giving them. ᴿThen you shall return to the land of your possession and enjoy it, which Moses the Lord's servant gave you on this side of the Jordan toward the sunrise."   Josh. 22:1–4

16 So they answered Joshua, saying, "All that you command us we will do, and wherever you send us we will go.

17 "Just as we heeded Moses in all things, so we will heed you. Only the Lord your God be with you, as He was with Moses.

18 "Whoever rebels against your command and does not heed your words, in all that you command him, shall be put to death. Only be strong and of good courage."

Rahab Hides the Spies

2 Now Joshua the son of Nun sent out two men from Acacia Grove to spy secretly, saying, "Go, view the land, especially Jericho." So they went, and came to the house of a harlot named Rahab, and lodged there.

2 And ᴿit was told the king of Jericho, saying, "Behold, men have come here tonight from the children of Israel to search out the country."   Josh. 2:22

3 So the king of Jericho sent to Rahab, saying, "Bring out the men who have come to you, who have entered your house, for they have come to search out all the country."

4 ᴿThen the woman took the two men and hid them. So she said, "Yes, the men came to me, but I did not know where they *were* from.   2 Sam. 17:19, 20

5 "And it happened as the gate was being shut, when it was dark, that the men went out. Where the men went I do not know; pursue them quickly, for you may overtake them."

6 (But she had brought them up to the roof and hidden them with the stalks of flax, which she had laid in order on the roof.)

7 Then the men pursued them by the road to the Jordan, to the fords. And as soon as those who pursued them had gone out, they shut the gate.

8 Now before they lay down, she came up to them on the roof,

9 and said to the men: ᴿ"I know that the Lord has given you the land, that ᴿthe terror of you has fallen on us, and that all the inhabitants of the land ᴿare fainthearted because of you.   Deut. 1:8 · Deut. 2:25; 11:25 · Josh. 5:1

10 "For we have heard how the Lord dried up the water of the Red Sea for you when you came out of Egypt, and what you did to the two kings of the Amorites who *were* on the other side of the Jordan, Sihon and Og, whom you ᴿutterly destroyed.   Josh. 6:21

11 "And as soon as we heard *these things*, our hearts melted; neither did there remain any more courage in anyone because of you, for ᴿthe Lord your God, He *is* God in heaven above and on earth beneath.   Deut. 4:39

12 "Now therefore, I beg you, swear to me by the Lord, since I have shown you kindness, that you also will show kindness to my father's house, and give me a true token,

13 "and ᴿspare my father, my mother, my brothers, my sisters, and all that they have, and deliver our lives from death."   Josh. 6:23–25

14 So the men answered her, "Our lives for yours, if none of you tell this business of ours. And it shall be, when the Lord has given us the land, that ᴿwe will deal kindly and truly with you."   Judg. 1:24

15 Then she ᴿlet them down by a rope through the window, for her house *was* on the city wall; she dwelt on the wall.   Acts 9:25

16 And she said to them, "Get to the mountain, lest the pursuers meet you. Hide there three days, until the pursuers have returned. Afterward you may go your way."

17 So the men said to her: "We *will be* ᵀblameless of this oath of yours which you have made us swear,   *free from obligation to*

18 ᴿ"unless, *when* we come into the land, you bind this line of scarlet cord in the window through which you let us down, ᴿand unless you ᵀbring your father, your mother, your brothers, and all your father's household to your own home.   Josh. 2:12 · Josh. 6:23 · Lit. *gather*

19 "So it shall be *that* whoever goes outside the doors of your house into the street, his blood *shall be* on his own head, and we *will be* guiltless. And whoever is with you in the house, ᴿhis ᵀblood *shall be* on our head if a hand is laid on him.   1 Kin. 2:32 · *guilt of bloodshed*

20 "And if you tell this business of ours, then we will be ᵀfree from your oath which you made us swear."   *free from obligation to*

21 Then she said, "According to your words, so *be* it." And she sent them away, and they departed. And she bound the scarlet cord in the window.

22 They departed and went to the mountain, and stayed there three days until the pursuers returned. The pursuers sought *them* all along the way, but did not find *them*.

23 So the two men returned, descended from the mountain, and crossed over; and they came to Joshua the son of Nun, and told him all that had befallen them.

24 And they said to Joshua, "Truly the Lord has delivered all the land into our hands, for indeed all the inhabitants of the country are fainthearted because of us."

Israel Crosses the Jordan

3 Then Joshua rose early in the morning; and they set out ᴿfrom ᵀAcacia Grove and came to the Jordan, he and all the

children of Israel, and lodged there before they crossed over.   Josh. 2:1 • Heb. *Shittim*

2 So it was, ᴿafter three days, that the officers went through the camp;   Josh. 1:10, 11

3 and they commanded the people, saying, "When you see the ark of the covenant of the LORD your God, and the priests, the Levites, ᵀbearing it, then you shall set out from your place and go after it.   *carrying*

4 ᴿ"Yet there shall be a space between you and it, about two thousand cubits by measure. Do not come near it, that you may know the way by which you must go, for you have not passed *this* way before."   Ex. 19:12

5 And Joshua said to the people, ᴿ"Sanctifyᵀ yourselves, for tomorrow the LORD will do wonders among you."   Josh. 7:13 • *Consecrate*

6 Then Joshua spoke to the priests, saying, ᴿ"Take up the ark of the covenant and cross over before the people." So they took up the ark of the covenant and went before the people.   Num. 4:15

7 And the LORD said to Joshua, "This day I will begin to ᴿexalt you in the sight of all Israel, that they may know that, as I was with Moses, so I will be with you.   Josh. 4:14

8 "You shall command the priests who bear the ark of the covenant, saying, 'When you have come to the edge of the water of the Jordan, you shall stand in the Jordan.'"

9 So Joshua said to the children of Israel, "Come here, and hear the words of the LORD your God."

10 And Joshua said, "By this you shall know that the living God *is* among you, and *that* He will without fail ᴿdrive out from before you the Canaanites and the Hittites and the Hivites and the Perizzites and the Girgashites and the Amorites and the Jebusites: Ex. 33:2

11 "Behold, the ark of the covenant of ᴿthe Lord of all the earth is crossing over before you into the Jordan.   Zech. 4:14; 6:5

12 "Now therefore, ᴿtake for yourselves twelve men from the tribes of Israel, one man from every tribe.   Josh. 4:2, 4

13 "And it shall come to pass, as soon as the soles of the feet of the priests who bear the ark of the LORD, the Lord of all the earth, shall rest in the waters of the Jordan, *that* the waters of the Jordan shall be cut off, the waters that come down from upstream, and they ᴿshall stand as a heap."   Ps. 78:13; 114:3

34-C. From the Crossing of Jordan to the Babylonian Captivity ▼

14 So it was, when the people set out from their camp to cross over the Jordan, with the priests bearing the ᴿark of the covenant before the people,   Acts 7:44, 45

34-C. From the Crossing of Jordan to the Babylonian Captivity (830 years) (Joshua 3:14-17)—This time in the history of Israel spans the period from the crossing of the Jordan under Joshua (about 1415 B.C.) to the Babylonian captivity under Zedekiah (586 B.C.), the last king of Judah. Joshua, under God, led Israel into Canaan and victory. Under Zedekiah, God drove them out in defeat (Jer. 21:1-9, page 733). There were five periods in the history of Israel from Joshua to Zedekiah:

(1) From the crossing of the Jordan to the death of Joshua (Josh. 1—24, page 215). Joshua led Israel for twenty-six years. He followed Moses, "the servant of the LORD" (Josh. 1:1, page 215). This was no easy task, but Joshua proved himself equal to Moses in many ways. As a soldier, he was gifted in strategy, resourcefulness, and courage. He was strong in faith, wholeheartedly committed to God and His law. He conquered the land of Canaan and divided it among the tribes of Israel.

(2) From the death of Joshua to the last judge (see the book of Judges, page 241, and Ruth, page 264). For over three hundred years, the tribes of Israel were unorganized and scattered. Having little basic connection with each other, they lived as separate nations. Over and over we are told that "the children of Israel did evil in the sight of the LORD" (Judg. 2:11, page 242). Because they did evil, the Lord would send ungodly nations to punish them. When they repented and returned to their God, He would raise up judges to deliver them. Their sins, successes, failures, and weaknesses are recorded in God's Word. God never covers up evil in the life of His children. But when they repent and return to the Lord, He will forgive and cleanse them from all unrighteousness (1 John 1:9, page 1278).

The book of Judges ends with this statement, "Everyone did what was right in his own eyes" (Judg. 21:25, page 263). This was a dark age in the history of Israel.

(3) From King Saul to the end of King Solomon's reign we see the Hebrew nation under a united monarchy (1 Sam. 10—1 Kin. 11, page 276). This period covers the reigns of Saul, David, and Solomon. It lasted about 120 years. During this time the Hebrew nation reached its pinnacle as a nation united under God. They became a great and powerful people economically, politically, socially, and religiously. At the beginning of this era, the Hebrew people occupied about 25,000 square miles. At the close of Solomon's reign, they possessed about 50,000 square miles.

(4) Samuel had warned the Hebrew nation, when they demanded a king, saying, "Make us a king to judge us like all the nations" (1 Sam. 8:1-22, page 274). They rejected the theocracy (the reign of the Lord) and demanded a monarchy. This was in disobedience to the revealed will of God. The Lord spoke to Samuel and said, "They have not rejected you, but they have rejected Me, that I should not reign over them" (1 Sam. 8:7, page 274). Everything Samuel prophesied in this chapter had come to pass, but the worst was yet to

(Point 34-C continued on next page)

▽ 15 and as those who bore the ark came to the Jordan, and ᴿthe feet of the priests who bore the ark dipped in the edge of the water (for the Jordan overflows all its banks during the whole time of harvest),   Josh. 3:13

16 that the waters which came down from upstream stood *still, and* rose in a heap very far away *at Adam, the city that *is* beside Zaretan. So the waters that went down into the Sea of the Arabah, ᴿthe Salt Sea, failed, *and* were cut off; and the people crossed over opposite Jericho.   Gen. 14:3

17 Then the priests who bore the ark of the covenant of the Lᴏʀᴅ stood firm on dry ground in the midst of the Jordan; ᴿand all Israel crossed over on dry ground, until all the people had crossed completely over the ▲ Jordan.   Ex. 3:8; 6:1–8; 14:21, 22, 29; 33:1

The Memorial Stones

4 And it came to pass, when all the people had completely crossed over the Jordan, that the Lᴏʀᴅ spoke to Joshua, saying:

2 ᴿ"Take for yourselves twelve men from the people, one man from every tribe, Josh. 3:12

3 "and command them, saying, 'Take for yourselves twelve stones from here, out of the midst of the Jordan, from the place where the priests' feet stood firm. You shall carry them over with you and leave them in the lodging place where you lodge tonight.' "

4 Then Joshua called the twelve men whom he had appointed from the children of Israel, one man from every tribe;

5 and Joshua said to them: "Cross over before the ark of the Lᴏʀᴅ your God into the midst of the Jordan, and each one of you take up a stone on his shoulder, according to the number of the tribes of the children of Israel,

6 "that this may be a sign among you when your children ask in time to come, saying, 'What do these stones *mean* to you?'

7 "Then you shall answer them that ᴿthe waters of the Jordan were cut off before the ark of the covenant of the Lᴏʀᴅ; when it

3:16 Many mss., vss., and Qr. *from Adam*

crossed over the Jordan, the waters of the Jordan were cut off. And these stones shall be for ᴿa memorial to the children of Israel forever."   Josh. 3:13, 16 • Num. 16:40

8 And the children of Israel did so, just as Joshua commanded, and took up twelve stones from the midst of the Jordan, as the Lᴏʀᴅ had spoken to Joshua, according to the number of the tribes of the children of Israel, and carried them over with them to the place where they lodged, and laid them down there.

9 Then Joshua set up twelve stones in the midst of the Jordan, in the place where the feet of the priests who bore the ark of the covenant stood; and they are there to this day.

10 So the priests who bore the ark stood in the midst of the Jordan until everything was finished that the Lᴏʀᴅ had commanded Joshua to speak to the people, according to all that Moses had commanded Joshua; and the people hurried and crossed over.

11 Then it came to pass, when all the people had completely crossed over, that the ᴿark of the Lᴏʀᴅ and the priests crossed over in the presence of the people.   Josh. 3:11; 6:11

12 And ᴿthe men of Reuben, the men of Gad, and half the tribe of Manasseh crossed over armed before the children of Israel, as Moses had spoken to them.   Num. 32:17, 20, 27, 28

13 About forty thousand ᵀprepared for war crossed over before the Lᴏʀᴅ for battle, to the plains of Jericho.   *equipped*

14 On that day the Lᴏʀᴅ ᴿexaltedᵀ Joshua in the sight of all Israel; and they feared him, as they had feared Moses, all the days of his life.   Josh. 3:7 • *made Joshua great*

15 Then the Lᴏʀᴅ spoke to Joshua, saying,

16 "Command the priests who bear ᴿthe ark of the Testimony to come up from the Jordan."   Ex. 25:16, 22

17 Joshua therefore commanded the priests, saying, "Come up from the Jordan."

18 And it came to pass, when the priests who bore the ark of the covenant of the Lᴏʀᴅ had come up from the midst of the Jordan, *and* the soles of the priests' feet touched the dry

(Point 34-C continued from previous page)
come. Under Rehoboam, the kingdom was divided; therefore, it could not stand (Matt. 12:25, page 953). This was the beginning of the end of Israel's monarchy.

(5) Jeroboam became king of Israel (the northern part of the nation). Rehoboam, king of Judah (the southern part), was ready to declare war on Israel, but the Lord stopped him (1 Kin. 12:16–24, page 340).

Israel, the northern nation of ten tribes, lasted about 250 years and had nineteen kings. They were all guilty of idolatry. Israel, whose capital was Samaria, fell before the cruel, conquering Assyrians, who scattered the northern tribes (2 Kin. 17:5, 6, 24, page 372; cf. Deut. 28:63, 64, page 207). Tiglath-pileser, king of Assyria, brought an end to the kingdom of Israel in 721 B.C. During these years God raised up some great prophets in Israel.

Judah, the southern kingdom, with its capital at Jerusalem, lasted about 150 years after the fall of Israel. The demise of the kingdom of Judah was accomplished by Nebuchadnezzar, who conquered the nation in three invasions (606, 597, and 586 B.C.), destroying the temple and deporting the people to Babylon (2 Chr. 36:17–21, page 441).

See Ezra 1:1–11, page 444, for **Point 34-D: From the Babylonian Captivity to the Crucifixion.**

land, that the waters of the Jordan returned to their place ^Rand overflowed all its banks as before.   Josh. 3:15

19 Now the people came up from the Jordan on the tenth *day* of the first month, and they camped ^Rin Gilgal on the east border of Jericho.   Josh. 5:9

20 And ^Rthose twelve stones which they took out of the Jordan, Joshua set up in Gilgal.   Josh. 4:3; 5:9, 10

21 Then he spoke to the children of Israel, saying: ^R"When your children ask their fathers in time to come, saying, 'What *are* these stones?'   Josh. 4:6

22 "then you shall let your children know, saying, ^R'Israel crossed over this Jordan on ^Rdry land';   Deut. 26:5-9 • Josh. 3:17

23 "for the LORD your God dried up the waters of the Jordan before you until you had crossed over, as the LORD your God did to the Red Sea, ^Rwhich He dried up before us until we had crossed over,   Ex. 14:21

24 "that all the peoples of the earth may know the hand of the LORD, that it *is* ^Rmighty, that you may ^Rfear the LORD your God ^Tforever."   1 Chr. 29:12 • Jer. 10:7 • Lit. *all days*

The Second Generation Circumcised

5 So it was, when all the kings of the Amorites who *were* on the west side of the Jordan, and all the kings of the Canaanites ^Rwho *were* by the sea, heard that the LORD had dried up the waters of the Jordan from before the children of Israel until *we had crossed over, that their heart melted; and there was no spirit in them any longer because of the children of Israel.   Num. 13:29

2 At that time the LORD said to Joshua, "Make flint knives for yourself, and circumcise the sons of Israel again the second time."

3 So Joshua made flint knives for himself, and circumcised the sons of Israel at ^Tthe hill of the foreskins.   Or *Gibeath Haaraloth*

4 And this *is* the reason why Joshua circumcised them: ^RAll the people who came out of Egypt who *were* males, all the men of war, had died in the wilderness on the way, after they had come out of Egypt.   Deut. 2:14-16

5 For all the people who came out had been circumcised, but all the people born in the wilderness, on the way as they came out of Egypt, had not been circumcised.

6 For the children of Israel walked forty years in the wilderness, till all the people who *were* men of war, who came out of Egypt, were ^Tconsumed, because they did not obey the voice of the LORD—to whom the LORD swore that He would not show them the land which the LORD had sworn to their fathers that He would give us, ^R"a land flowing with milk and honey."   *destroyed* • Ex. 3:8

7 Then Joshua circumcised ^Rtheir sons

5:1 Many mss., vss., and Qr. *their crossing over*

whom He raised up in their place; for they were uncircumcised, because they had not been circumcised on the way.   Deut. 1:39

8 So it was, when they had finished circumcising all the people, that they stayed in their places in the camp ^Rtill they were healed.   Gen. 34:25

9 Then the LORD said to Joshua, "This day I have rolled away the reproach of Egypt from you." Therefore the name of the place is called ^TGilgal to this day.   Lit. *Rolling*

10 Now the children of Israel camped in Gilgal, and kept the Passover ^Ron the fourteenth day of the month at twilight on the plains of Jericho.   Ex. 12:6

11 And they ate of the produce of the land on the day after the Passover, unleavened bread and ^Tparched grain, on the very same day.   *roasted*

12 Then ^Rthe manna ceased on the day after they had eaten the produce of the land; and the children of Israel no longer had manna, but they ate the food of the land of Canaan that year.   Ex. 16:35

The Commander of the Army of the LORD

13 And it came to pass, when Joshua was by Jericho, that he lifted his eyes and looked, and behold, ^Ra Man stood opposite him ^Rwith His sword drawn in His hand. And Joshua went to Him and said to Him, "*Are* You for us or for our adversaries?"   Gen. 18:1, 2 • Num. 22:23

14 So He said, "No, but *as* Commander of the army of the LORD I have now come." And Joshua ^Rfell on his face to the earth and ^Rworshiped, and said to Him, "What does my Lord say to His servant?"   Gen. 17:3 • Ex. 34:8

15 Then the Commander of the LORD's army said to Joshua, ^R"Take your sandal off your foot, for the place where you stand *is* holy." And Joshua did so.   Ex. 3:5

The Destruction of Jericho

6 Now ^RJericho was securely shut up because of the children of Israel; none went out, and none came in.   Josh. 2:1

2 And the LORD said to Joshua: "See! I have given Jericho into your hand, its *king, and* the mighty men of valor.   Deut. 7:24

3 "You shall march around the city, all *you* men of war; you shall go all around the city once. This you shall do six days.

4 "And seven priests shall bear seven ^Rtrumpets of rams' horns before the ark. But the seventh day you shall march around the city ^Rseven times, and ^Rthe priests shall blow the trumpets.   Lev. 25:9 • 1 Kin. 18:43 • Num. 10:8

5 "It shall come to pass, when they make a long *blast* with the ram's horn, *and* when you hear the sound of the trumpet, that all the people shall shout with a great shout; then the wall of the city will fall down flat. And the

people shall go up every man straight before him."

6 Then Joshua the son of Nun called the priests and said to them, "Take up the ark of the covenant, and let seven priests bear seven trumpets of rams' horns before the ark of the LORD."

7 And he said to the people, "Proceed, and march around the city, and let him who is armed advance before the ark of the LORD."

8 So it was, when Joshua had spoken to the people, that the seven priests bearing the seven trumpets of rams' horns before the LORD advanced and blew the trumpets, and the ark of the covenant of the LORD followed them.

9 The armed men went before the priests who blew the trumpets, ᴿand the rear guard came after the ark, while *the priests* continued blowing the trumpets.   Num. 10:25

10 Now Joshua had commanded the people, saying, "You shall not shout or make any noise with your voice, nor shall a word proceed out of your mouth, until the day I say to you, 'Shout!' Then you shall shout."

11 So he had the ark of the LORD circle the city, going around *it* once. Then they came into the camp and lodged in the camp.

12 And Joshua rose early in the morning, and the priests took up the ark of the LORD.

13 Then seven priests bearing seven trumpets of rams' horns before the ark of the LORD went on continually and blew with the trumpets. And the armed men went before them. But the rear guard came after the ark of the LORD, while *the priests* continued blowing the trumpets.

14 And the second day they marched around the city once and returned to the camp. So they did six days.

15 But it came to pass on the seventh day that they rose early, about the dawning of the day, and marched around the city seven times in the same manner. On that day only they marched around the city seven times.

16 And the seventh time it happened, when the priests blew the trumpets, that Joshua said to the people: "Shout, for the LORD has given you the city!

17 "Now the city shall be doomed by the LORD to destruction, it and all who *are* in it. Only Rahab the harlot shall live, she and all who *are* with her in the house, because ᴿshe hid the messengers that we sent.   Josh. 2:4, 6

18 "And you, ᴿby all means abstain from the accursed things, lest you become accursed when you take of the accursed things, and make the camp of Israel a curse, ᴿand trouble it.   Deut. 7:26 · Josh. 7:1, 12, 25

19 "But all the silver and gold, and vessels of bronze and iron, *are* ᵀconsecrated to the LORD; they ᵀshall come into the treasury of the LORD."   *set apart · shall go*

20 So the people shouted when *the priests* blew the trumpets. And it happened when the people heard the sound of the trumpet, and the people shouted with a great shout, that ᴿthe wall fell down flat. Then the people went up into the city, every man straight before him, and they took the city.   Heb. 11:30

21 And they ᴿutterly destroyed all that *was* in the city, both man and woman, young and old, ox and sheep and donkey, with the edge of the sword.   Deut. 7:2; 20:16, 17

22 But Joshua had said to the two men who had spied out the country, "Go into the harlot's house, and from there bring out the woman and all that she has, ᴿas you swore to her."   Josh. 2:12-19

23 And the young men who had been spies went in and brought out Rahab, ᴿher father, her mother, her brothers, and all that she had. So they brought out all her relatives and left them outside the camp of Israel. Josh. 2:13

24 But they burned the city and all that *was* in it with fire. Only the silver and gold, and the vessels of bronze and iron, they put into the treasury of the house of the LORD.

25 And Joshua spared Rahab the harlot, her father's household, and all that she had. So ᴿshe dwells in Israel to this day, because she hid the messengers whom Joshua sent to spy out Jericho.   [Matt. 1:5]

26 Then Joshua charged *them* at that time, saying, "Cursed *be* the man before the LORD who rises up and builds this city Jericho; he shall lay its foundation with his firstborn, and with his youngest he shall set up its gates."

27 So the LORD was with Joshua, and his fame spread throughout all the country.

Defeat at Ai

7 But the children of Israel ᵀcommitted a trespass regarding the accursed things, for Achan the son of Carmi, the son of ᵀZabdi, the son of Zerah, of the tribe of Judah, took of the accursed things; so the anger of the LORD burned against the children of Israel.   *acted unfaithfully · Zimri,* 1 Chr. 2:6

2 Now Joshua sent men from Jericho to Ai, which *is* beside Beth Aven, on the east side of Bethel, and spoke to them, saying, "Go up and spy out the country." So the men went up and spied out Ai.

3 And they returned to Joshua and said to him, "Do not let all the people go up, but let about two or three thousand men go up and attack Ai. Do not weary all the people there, for *the people of Ai are* few."

4 So about three thousand men went up there from the people, ᴿbut they fled before the men of Ai.   Lev. 26:17

5 And the men of Ai struck down about thirty-six men, for they chased them *from* before the gate as far as Shebarim, and struck them down on the descent; therefore ᴿtheᵀ

hearts of the people melted and became like water. *Lev. 26:36 · the people's courage failed*

6 Then Joshua tore his clothes, and fell to the earth on his face before the ark of the LORD until evening, he and the elders of Israel; and they put dust on their heads.

7 And Joshua said, "Alas, Lord ᵀGOD, ᴿwhy have You brought this people over the Jordan at all—to deliver us into the hand of the Amorites, to destroy us? Oh, that we had been content, and dwelt on the other side of the Jordan! *Heb. YHWH, LORD · Ex. 17:3*

8 "O Lord, what shall I say when Israel turns its ᵀback before its enemies? *Lit. neck*

9 "For the Canaanites and all the inhabitants of the land will hear *it*, and surround us, and cut off our name from the earth. Then what will You do for Your great name?"

The Sin of Achan

10 So the LORD said to Joshua: "Get up! Why do you lie thus on your face?

11 "Israel has sinned, and they have also transgressed My covenant which I commanded them. ᴿFor they have even taken some of the ᵀaccursed things, and have both stolen and deceived; and they have also put *it* among their own stuff. *Josh. 6:17–19 · devoted*

12 "Therefore the children of Israel could not stand before their enemies, *but* turned *their* backs before their enemies, because they have become doomed to destruction. Neither will I be with you anymore, unless you destroy the accursed from among you.

13 "Get up, ᴿsanctifyᵀ the people, and say, ᴿ'Sanctify yourselves for tomorrow, because thus says the LORD God of Israel: "*There is* an accursed thing in your midst, O Israel; you cannot stand before your enemies until you take away the accursed thing from among you."* *Ex. 19:10 · set apart · Josh. 3:5*

14 'In the morning therefore you shall be brought according to your tribes. And it shall be *that* the tribe which ᴿthe LORD takes shall come according to families; and the family which the LORD takes shall come by households; and the household which the LORD takes shall come man by man. *[Prov. 16:33]*

15 'Then it shall be *that* he who is taken with the accursed thing shall be burned with fire, he and all that he has, because he has ᴿtransgressedᵀ the covenant of the LORD, and because he ᴿhas done a disgraceful thing in Israel.'" *Josh. 7:11 · overstepped · Gen. 34:7*

16 So Joshua rose early in the morning and brought Israel by their tribes, and the tribe of Judah was taken.

17 He brought the clan of Judah, and he took the family of the Zarhites; and he brought the family of the Zarhites man by man, and Zabdi was taken.

18 Then he brought his household man by man, and Achan the son of Carmi, the son of Zabdi, the son of Zerah, of the tribe of Judah, ᴿwas taken. *1 Sam. 14:42*

19 Now Joshua said to Achan, "My son, I beg you, ᴿgive glory to the LORD God of Israel, ᴿand make confession to Him, and ᴿtell me now what you have done; do not hide *it* from me." *Jer. 13:16 · Num. 5:6, 7 · 1 Sam. 14:43*

20 And Achan answered Joshua and said, "Indeed I have sinned against the LORD God of Israel, and this is what I have done:

21 "When I saw among the spoils a beautiful Babylonian garment, two hundred shekels of silver, and a wedge of gold weighing fifty shekels, I coveted them and took them. And there they are, hidden in the earth in the midst of my tent, with the silver under it."

22 So Joshua sent messengers, and they ran to the tent; and there it was, hidden in his tent, with the silver under it.

23 And they took them from the midst of the tent, brought them to Joshua and to all the children of Israel, and laid them out before the LORD.

24 Then Joshua, and all Israel with him, took Achan the son of Zerah, the silver, the garment, the wedge of gold, his sons, his daughters, his oxen, his donkeys, his sheep, his tent, and all that he had, and they brought them to the Valley of Achor.

25 And Joshua said, ᴿ"Why have you troubled us? The LORD will trouble you this day." ᴿSo all Israel stoned him with stones; and they burned them with fire after they had stoned them with stones. *Josh. 6:18 · Deut. 17:5*

26 Then they raised over him a great heap of stones, still there to this day. So the LORD turned from the fierceness of His anger. Therefore the name of that place has been called the Valley of *Achor to this day.

The Fall of Ai

8 Now the LORD said to Joshua: "Do not be afraid, nor be dismayed; take all the people of war with you, and arise, go up to Ai. See, I have given into your hand the king of Ai, his people, his city, and his land.

2 "And you shall do to Ai and its king as you did to ᴿJericho and its king. Only ᴿits spoil and its cattle you shall take as booty for yourselves. Lay an ambush for the city behind it." *Josh. 6:21 · Deut. 20:14*

3 So Joshua arose, and all the people of war, to go up against Ai; and Joshua chose thirty thousand mighty men of valor and sent them away by night.

4 And he commanded them, saying: "Behold, ᴿyou shall lie in ambush against the city, behind the city. Do not go very far from the city, but all of you be ready. *Judg. 20:29*

5 "Then I and all the people who *are* with me will approach the city; and it will come about, when they come out against us as at the first, that we shall flee before them.

7:26 Lit. *Trouble*

6 "For they will come out after us till we have drawn them from the city, for they will say, 'They are fleeing before us as at the first.' Therefore we will flee before them.

7 "Then you shall rise from the ambush and seize the city, for the LORD your God will deliver it into your hand.

8 "And it will be, when you have taken the city, that you shall set the city on fire. According to the commandment of the LORD you shall do. See, I have commanded you."

9 Joshua therefore sent them out; and they went to lie in ambush, and stayed between Bethel and Ai, on the west side of Ai; but Joshua lodged that night among the people.

10 Then Joshua rose up early in the morning and mustered the people, and went up, he and the elders of Israel, before the people to Ai.

11 RAnd all the people of war who were with him went up and drew near; and they came before the city and camped on the north side of Ai. Now a valley lay between them and Ai.   Josh. 8:5

12 So he took about five thousand men and set them in ambush between Bethel and Ai, on the west side of Tthe city.   Ai

13 And when they had set the people, all the army that was on the north of the city, and its rear guard on the west of the city, Joshua went that night into the midst of the valley.

14 Now it happened, when the king of Ai saw it, that the men of the city hurried and rose early and went out against Israel to battle, he and all his people, at an appointed place before the plain. But he Rdid not know that there was an ambush against him behind the city.   Judg. 20:34

15 And Joshua and all Israel Rmade as if they were beaten before them, and fled by the way of the wilderness.   Judg. 20:36

16 So all the people who were in Ai were called together to pursue them. And they pursued Joshua and were drawn away from the city.

17 There was not a man left in Ai or Bethel who did not go out after Israel. So they left the city open and pursued Israel.

18 Then the LORD said to Joshua, "Stretch out the spear that is in your hand toward Ai, for I will give it into your hand." And Joshua stretched out the spear that was in his hand toward the city.

19 So those in ambush arose quickly out of their place; they ran as soon as he had stretched out his hand, and they entered the city and took it, and hurried to set the city on fire.

20 And when the men of Ai looked behind them, they saw, and behold, the smoke of the city ascended to heaven. So they had no power to flee this way or that way, and the people who had fled to the wilderness turned back on the pursuers.

21 Now when Joshua and all Israel saw that the ambush had taken the city and that the smoke of the city ascended, they turned back and struck down the men of Ai.

22 Then the others came out of the city against them; so they were caught in the midst of Israel, some on this side and some on that side. And they struck them down, so that they let none of them remain or escape.

23 But the king of Ai they took alive, and brought him to Joshua.

24 And it came to pass when Israel had made an end of slaying all the inhabitants of Ai in the field, in the wilderness where they pursued them, and when they all had fallen by the edge of the sword until they were consumed, that all the Israelites returned to Ai and struck it with the edge of the sword.

25 So it was that all who fell that day, both men and women, were twelve thousand—all the people of Ai.

26 For Joshua did not draw back his hand, with which he stretched out the spear, until he had Rutterly destroyed all the inhabitants of Ai.   Josh. 6:21

27 ROnly the livestock and the spoil of that city Israel took as booty for themselves, according to the word of the LORD which He had Rcommanded Joshua.   Num. 31:22, 26 • Josh. 8:2

28 So Joshua burned Ai and made it Ra heap forever, a desolation to this day.   Deut. 13:16

29 RAnd the king of Ai he hanged on a tree until evening. RAnd as soon as the sun was down, Joshua commanded that they should take his corpse down from the tree, cast it at the entrance of the gate of the city, and Rraise over it a great heap of stones that remains to this day.   Josh. 10:26 • Deut. 21:22, 23 • Josh. 7:26; 10:27

Joshua Renews the Covenant

30 Now Joshua built an altar to the LORD God of Israel Rin Mount Ebal,   Deut. 27:4-8

31 as Moses the servant of the LORD had commanded the children of Israel, as it is written in the Book of the Law of Moses: R"an altar of whole stones over which no man has wielded an Riron tool." And they offered on it burnt offerings to the LORD, and sacrificed peace offerings.   Ex. 20:25 • Deut. 27:5, 6

32 And there, in the presence of the children of Israel, he wrote on the stones a copy of the law of Moses, which he had written.

33 Then all Israel, with their elders and officers and judges, stood on either side of the ark before the priests, the Levites, who bore the ark of the covenant of the LORD, the stranger as well as he who was born among them. Half of them were in front of Mount Gerizim and half of them in front of Mount Ebal, Ras Moses the servant of the LORD had commanded before, that they should bless the people of Israel.   Deut. 11:29; 27:12

34 And afterward he read all the words of the law, ᴿthe blessings and the cursings, according to all that is written in the ᴿBook of the Law.   Deut. 28:2, 15, 45; 29:20, 21; 30:19 • Josh. 1:8

35 There was not a word of all that Moses had commanded which Joshua did not read before all the assembly of Israel, with the women, the little ones, ᴿand the strangers who were living among them.   Josh. 8:33

The Treaty with the Gibeonites

9 And it came to pass when ᴿall the kings who were on this side of the Jordan, in the hills and in the lowland and in all the coasts of ᴿthe Great Sea toward Lebanon— ᴿthe Hittite, the Amorite, the Canaanite, the Perizzite, the Hivite, and the Jebusite—heard about it,   Josh. 3:10 • Num. 34:6 • Ex. 3:17; 23:23

2 that they gathered together to fight with Joshua and Israel with one accord.

3 But when the inhabitants of ᴿGibeon ᴿheard what Joshua had done to Jericho and Ai,   Josh. 9:17, 22; 10:2; 21:17 • Josh. 6:27

4 they worked craftily, and went and ᵀpretended to be ambassadors. And they took old sacks on their donkeys, old wineskins torn and ᵀmended,   acted as envoys • Lit. tied up

5 old and patched sandals on their feet, and old garments on themselves; and all the bread of their provision was dry and moldy.

6 And they went to Joshua, to the camp at Gilgal, and said to him and to the men of Israel, "We have come from a far country; now therefore, make a covenant with us."

7 Then the men of Israel said to the Hivites, "Perhaps you dwell among us; so ᴿhow can we make a covenant with you?"   Ex. 23:32

8 But they said to Joshua, "We are your servants." And Joshua said to them, "Who are you, and where do you come from?"

9 So they said to him: ᴿ"From a very far country your servants have come, because of the name of the LORD your God; for we have ᴿheard of His fame, and all that He did in Egypt,   Deut. 20:15 • Josh. 2:9, 10; 5:1

10 "and ᴿall that He did to the two kings of the Amorites who were beyond the Jordan— to Sihon king of Heshbon, and Og king of Bashan, who was at Ashtaroth.   Num. 21:24, 33

11 "Therefore our elders and all the inhabitants of our country spoke to us, saying, 'Take provisions with you for the journey, and go to meet them, and say to them, "We are your servants; now therefore, make a covenant with us."'

12 "This bread of ours we took hot for our provision from our houses on the day we departed to come to you. But now look, it is dry and moldy.

13 "And these wineskins which we filled were new, and see, they are torn; and these our garments and our sandals have become old because of the very long journey."

14 Then the men of Israel took some of their provisions; but they ᵀdid not ask counsel of the LORD.   Lit. did not inquire at the mouth of

15 So Joshua ᴿmade peace with them, and made a covenant with them to let them live; and the rulers of the congregation swore to them.   2 Sam. 21:2

16 And it happened at the end of three days, after they had made a covenant with them, that they heard that they were their neighbors who dwelt near them.

17 Then the children of Israel journeyed and came to their cities on the third day. Now their cities were ᴿGibeon, Chephirah, Beeroth, and Kirjath Jearim.   Josh. 18:25

18 But the children of Israel did not ᵀattack them, ᴿbecause the rulers of the congregation had sworn to them by the LORD God of Israel. And all the congregation complained against the rulers.   strike • Ps. 15:4

19 Then all the rulers said to all the congregation, "We have sworn to them by the LORD God of Israel; now therefore, we may not touch them.

20 "This we will do to them: We will let them live, lest wrath be upon us because of the oath which we swore to them."

21 And the rulers said to them, "Let them live, but let them be ᴿwoodcutters and water carriers for all the congregation, as the rulers had ᴿpromised them."   Deut. 29:11 • Josh. 9:15

22 Then Joshua called for them, and he spoke to them, saying, "Why have you deceived us, saying, 'We are very far from you,' when ᴿyou dwell near us?   Josh. 9:16

23 "Now therefore, you are ᴿcursed, and none of you shall be freed from being slaves—woodcutters and water carriers for the house of my God."   Gen. 9:25

24 So they answered Joshua and said, "Because your servants were clearly told that the LORD your God ᴿcommanded His servant Moses to give you all the land, and to destroy all the inhabitants of the land from before you; therefore ᴿwe were very much afraid for our lives because of you, and have done this thing.   Deut. 7:1, 2 • Ex. 15:14

25 "And now, here we are, ᴿin your hands; do with us as it seems good and right to do to us."   Gen. 16:6

26 So he did to them, and delivered them out of the hand of the children of Israel, so that they did not kill them.

27 And that day Joshua made them ᴿwoodcutters and water carriers for the congregation and for the altar of the LORD, ᴿin the place which He would choose, even to this day.   Josh. 9:21, 23 • Deut. 12:5

The Sun Stands Still

10 Now it came to pass when Adoni-Zedek king of Jerusalem heard how Joshua had taken Ai and had utterly destroyed it—as he had done to Jericho and its king, so he had done to Ai and its king—and

how the inhabitants of Gibeon had made peace with Israel and were among them,

2 that they ^Rfeared greatly, because Gibeon *was* a great city, like one of the royal cities, and because it *was* greater than Ai, and all its men *were* mighty.   Ex. 15:14-16

3 Therefore Adoni-Zedek king of Jerusalem sent to Hoham king of Hebron, Piram king of Jarmuth, Japhia king of Lachish, and Debir king of Eglon, saying,

4 "Come up to me and help me, that we may attack Gibeon, for it has made peace with Joshua and with the children of Israel."

5 Therefore the five kings of the ^RAmorites, the king of Jerusalem, the king of Hebron, the king of Jarmuth, the king of Lachish, *and* the king of Eglon, ^Rgathered together and went up, they and all their armies, and camped before Gibeon and made war against it.   Num. 13:29 • Josh. 9:2

6 And the men of Gibeon sent to Joshua at the camp ^Rat Gilgal, saying, "Do not forsake your servants; come up to us quickly, save us and help us, for all the kings of the Amorites who dwell in the mountains have gathered together against us."   Josh. 5:10; 9:6

7 So Joshua ascended from Gilgal, he and ^Rall the people of war with him, and all the mighty men of valor.   Josh. 8:1

8 And the LORD said to Joshua, ^R"Do not fear them, for I have delivered them into your hand; ^Rnot a man of them shall ^Rstand before you."   Josh. 11:6 • Josh. 1:5, 9 • Josh. 21:44

9 Joshua therefore came upon them suddenly, having marched all night from Gilgal.

10 So the LORD routed them before Israel, killed them with a great slaughter at Gibeon, chased them along the road that goes ^Rto Beth Horon, and struck them down as far as ^RAzekah and Makkedah.   Josh. 16:3, 5 • Josh. 15:35

11 And it happened, as they fled before Israel *and* were on the descent of Beth Horon, that the LORD cast down large hailstones from heaven on them as far as Azekah, and they died. *There were* more who died from the hailstones than the children of Israel killed with the sword.

12 Then Joshua spoke to the LORD in the day when the LORD delivered up the Amorites before the children of Israel, and he said in the sight of Israel:

^R"Sun, stand still over Gibeon;   Hab. 3:11
And Moon, in the Valley of Aijalon."

13 So the sun stood still,
And the moon stopped,
Till the people had revenge
Upon their enemies.

^R*Is* this not written in the Book of Jasher? So the sun stood still in the midst of heaven, and did not hasten to go down for about a whole day.   2 Sam. 1:18

14 And there has been ^Rno day like that, before it or after it, that the LORD heeded the voice of a man; for ^Rthe LORD fought for Israel.   Is. 38:7, 8 • Deut. 1:30; 20:4

15 ^RThen Joshua returned, and all Israel with him, to the camp at Gilgal.   Josh. 10:43

The Amorite Kings Executed

16 But these five kings had fled and hidden themselves in a cave at Makkedah.

17 And it was told Joshua, saying, "The five kings have been found hidden in the cave at Makkedah."

18 So Joshua said, "Roll large stones against the mouth of the cave, and set men by it to guard them.

19 "And do not stay *there* yourselves, *but* pursue your enemies, and attack their rear guard. Do not allow them to enter their cities, for the LORD your God has delivered them into your hand."

20 Then it happened, while Joshua and the children of Israel made an end of slaying them with a very great slaughter, till they had finished, that those who escaped entered fortified cities.

21 And all the people returned to the camp, to Joshua at Makkedah, in peace. No one ^Tmoved his tongue against any of the children of Israel.   criticized, lit. sharpened his tongue

22 Then Joshua said, "Open the mouth of the cave, and bring out those five kings to me from the cave."

23 And they did so, and brought out those five kings to him from the cave: the king of Jerusalem, the king of Hebron, the king of Jarmuth, the king of Lachish, *and* the king of Eglon.

24 So it was, when they brought out those kings to Joshua, that Joshua called for all the men of Israel, and said to the captains of the men of war who went with him, "Come near, put your feet on the necks of these kings." And they drew near and ^Rput their feet on their necks.   Mal. 4:3

25 Then Joshua said to them, "Do not be afraid, nor be dismayed; be strong and of good courage, for thus the LORD will do to all your enemies against whom you fight."

26 And afterward Joshua struck ^Tthem and killed them, and hanged them on five trees; and they ^Rwere hanging on the trees until evening.   The kings • Josh. 8:29

27 So it was at the time of the going down of the sun *that* Joshua commanded, and they took them down from the trees, cast them into the cave where they had been hidden, and laid large stones against the cave's mouth, *which remain* until this very day.

Conquest of the Southland

28 On that day Joshua took Makkedah, and struck it and its king with the edge of the sword. He utterly destroyed *them*— all the

10:28 So with MT and most authorities; many Heb. mss.,
some mss. of LXX, and some mss. of Tg. *it*

people who *were* in it. He let none remain. He also did to the king of Makkedah ᴿas he had done to the king of Jericho.　　Josh. 6:21

29 Then Joshua passed from Makkedah, and all Israel with him, to ᴿLibnah; and they fought against Libnah.　　Josh. 15:42; 21:13

30 And the Lᴏʀᴅ also delivered it and its king into the hand of Israel; he struck it and all the people who *were* in it with the edge of the sword. He let none remain in it, but did to its king as he had done to the king of Jericho.

31 Then Joshua passed from Libnah, and all Israel with him, to Lachish; and they encamped against it and fought against it.

32 And the Lᴏʀᴅ delivered Lachish into the hand of Israel, who took it on the second day, and struck it and all the people who *were* in it with the edge of the sword, according to all that he had done to Libnah.

33 Then Horam king of Gezer came up to help Lachish; and Joshua struck him and his people, until he left him none remaining.

34 From Lachish Joshua passed to Eglon, and all Israel with him; and they encamped against it and fought against it.

35 They took it on that day and struck it with the edge of the sword; all the people who *were* in it he utterly destroyed that day, according to all that he had done to Lachish.

36 So Joshua went up from Eglon, and all Israel with him, to ᴿHebron; and they fought against it.　　Josh. 14:13–15; 15:13

37 And they took it and struck it with the edge of the sword—its king, all its cities, and all the people who *were* in it; he left none remaining, according to all that he had done to Eglon, but utterly destroyed it and all the people who *were* in it.

38 Then Joshua returned, and all Israel with him, to Debir; and they fought against it.

39 And he took it and its king and all its cities; they struck them with the edge of the sword and utterly destroyed all the people who *were* in it. He left none remaining; as he had done to Hebron, so he did to Debir and its king, as he had done also to Libnah and its king.

40 So Joshua conquered all the land: the mountain country and the *South and the lowland and the wilderness slopes, and all their kings; he left none remaining, but utterly destroyed all that breathed, as the Lᴏʀᴅ God of Israel had commanded.

41 And Joshua conquered them from Kadesh Barnea as far as Gaza, and all the country of Goshen, even as far as Gibeon.

42 All these kings and their land Joshua took at one time, ᴿbecause the Lᴏʀᴅ God of Israel fought for Israel.　　Josh. 10:14

43 Then Joshua returned, and all Israel with him, to the camp at Gilgal.

The Northern Conquest

11 And it came to pass, when Jabin king of Hazor heard *these things*, that he sent to Jobab king of Madon, to the king of Shimron, to the king of Achshaph,

2 and to the kings who *were* from the north, in the mountains, in the plain south of Chinneroth, in the lowland, and in the heights ᴿof Dor on the west,　　Josh. 17:11

3 to the Canaanites in the east and in the west, the Amorite, the Hittite, the Perizzite, the Jebusite in the mountains, and the Hivite below Hermon in the land of Mizpah.

4 So they went out, they and all their armies with them, *as* many people ᴿ*as* the sand that *is* on the seashore in multitude, with very many horses and chariots.　　Judg. 7:12

5 And when all these kings had met together, they came and camped together at the waters of Merom to fight against Israel.

6 But the Lᴏʀᴅ said to Joshua, "Do not be afraid because of them, for tomorrow about this time I will deliver all of them slain before Israel. You shall ᴿhamstring their horses and burn their chariots with fire."　　2 Sam. 8:4

7 So Joshua and all the people of war with him came against them suddenly by the waters of Merom, and they attacked them.

8 And the Lᴏʀᴅ delivered them into the hand of Israel, who defeated them and chased them to Greater Sidon, to the *Brook ᴿMisrephoth, and to the Valley of Mizpah eastward; they attacked them until they left none of them remaining.　　Josh. 13:6

9 So Joshua did to them as the Lᴏʀᴅ had told him: he hamstrung their horses and burned their chariots with fire.

10 Joshua turned back at that time and took Hazor, and struck its king with the sword; for Hazor was formerly the head of all those kingdoms.

11 And they struck all the people who *were* in it with the edge of the sword, utterly destroying *them*. There was none left breathing. Then he burned Hazor with fire.

12 So all the cities of those kings, and all their kings, Joshua took and struck with the edge of the sword. He utterly destroyed them, ᴿas Moses the servant of the Lᴏʀᴅ had commanded.　　Num. 33:50–56

13 But *as for* the cities that stood on their *mounds, Israel burned none of them, except Hazor only, *which* Joshua burned.

14 And all the spoil of these cities and the livestock, the children of Israel took as booty for themselves; but they struck every man with the edge of the sword until they had destroyed them, and they left none breathing.

10:40 Heb. *Negev*

11:8 Heb. *Misrephoth Maim*
11:13 Heb. *tel*, a heap of successive city ruins

15 As the LORD had commanded Moses his servant, so Moses commanded Joshua, and so Joshua did. He left nothing undone of all that the LORD had commanded Moses.

Summary of Joshua's Conquests

16 Thus Joshua took all this land: the mountain country, all the South, all the land of Goshen, the lowland, and the Jordan *plain—the mountains of Israel and its lowlands,

17 from ᵀMount Halak and the ascent to Seir, even as far as Baal Gad in the Valley of Lebanon below Mount Hermon. He captured all their kings, and struck them down and killed them.   Lit. The Smooth or Bald Mountain

18 Joshua made war a long time with all those kings.

19 There was not a city that made peace with the children of Israel, except ᴿthe Hivites, the inhabitants of Gibeon. All the others they took in battle.   Josh. 9:3–7

20 For it was of the LORD ᵀto harden their hearts, that they should come against Israel in battle, that He might utterly destroy them, and that they might receive no mercy, but that He might destroy them, as the LORD had commanded Moses.   Lit. to make strong

21 And at that time Joshua came and cut off ᴿthe Anakim from the mountains: from Hebron, from Debir, from Anab, from all the mountains of Judah, and from all the mountains of Israel; Joshua utterly destroyed them with their cities.   Num. 13:22, 33

22 None of the Anakim were left in the land of the children of Israel; they remained only in Gaza, in Gath, and in Ashdod.

23 So Joshua took the whole land, according to all that the LORD had said to Moses; and Joshua gave it as an inheritance to Israel ᴿaccording to their divisions by their tribes. Then the land rested from war.   Num. 26:53

The Kings Conquered by Moses

12 These *are* the kings of the land whom the children of Israel defeated, and whose land they possessed on the other side of the Jordan toward the rising of the sun, ᴿfrom the River Arnon to Mount Hermon, and all the eastern Jordan plain: Num. 21:24

2 One king was ᴿSihon king of the Amorites, who dwelt in Heshbon *and* ruled half of Gilead, from Aroer, which *is* on the bank of the River Arnon, from the middle of that river, even as far as the River Jabbok, *which is* the border of the Ammonites,   Deut. 2:24–27

3 and the eastern Jordan plain from the Sea of ᵀChinneroth as far as the ᵀSea of the Arabah (the Salt Sea), the road to Beth

11:16 Heb. arabah

Jeshimoth, and ᵀsouthward below the slopes of Pisgah.   Galilee · The Dead Sea · Or Teman

4 *The other king was* Og king of Bashan and his territory, *who was* of the remnant of the giants, ᴿwho dwelt at Ashtaroth and at Edrei,   Deut. 1:4

5 and reigned over Mount Hermon, ᴿover Salcah, over all Bashan, ᴿas far as the border of the Geshurites and the Maachathites, and over half of Gilead *to* the border of Sihon king of Heshbon.   Deut. 3:10 · Deut. 3:14

6 These Moses the servant of the LORD and the children of Israel had conquered; and Moses the servant of the LORD had given it *as* a possession to the Reubenites, the Gadites, and half the tribe of Manasseh.

The Kings Conquered by Joshua

7 And these *are* the kings of the country ᴿwhich Joshua and the children of Israel conquered on this side of the Jordan, on the west, from Baal Gad in the Valley of Lebanon as far as ᵀMount Halak and the ascent to Seir, which Joshua gave to the tribes of Israel *as* a possession according to their divisions,   Josh. 11:17 · Lit. The Bald Mountain

8 in the mountain country, in the lowlands, in the *Jordan* plain, in the slopes, in the wilderness, and in the South—ᴿthe Hittites, the Amorites, the Canaanites, the Perizzites, the Hivites, and the Jebusites: Ex. 3:8; 23:23

9 ᴿthe king of Jericho, one; ᴿthe king of Ai, which *is* beside Bethel, one;   Josh. 6:2 · Josh. 8:29

10 ᴿthe king of Jerusalem, one; the king of Hebron, one;   Josh. 10:23

11 the king of Jarmuth, one; the king of Lachish, one;

12 the king of Eglon, one; ᴿthe king of Gezer, one;   Josh. 10:33

13 ᴿthe king of Debir, one; the king of Geder, one;   Josh. 10:38, 39

14 the king of Hormah, one; the king of Arad, one;

15 ᴿthe king of Libnah, one; the king of Adullam, one;   Josh. 10:29, 30

16 ᴿthe king of Makkedah, one; ᴿthe king of Bethel, one;   Josh. 10:28 · Judg. 1:22

17 the king of Tappuah, one; ᴿthe king of Hepher, one;   1 Kin. 4:10

18 the king of Aphek, one; the king of ᵀLasharon, one;   Or Sharon

19 the king of Madon, one; ᴿthe king of Hazor, one;   Josh. 11:10

20 the king of ᴿShimron Meron, one; the king of Achshaph, one;   Josh. 11:1; 19:15

21 the king of Taanach, one; the king of Megiddo, one;

22 ᴿthe king of Kedesh, one; the king of Jokneam in Carmel, one;   Josh. 19:37; 20:7; 21:32

23 the king of Dor in the heights of Dor, one; the king of the people of Gilgal, one;

24 the king of Tirzah, one—ᴿall the kings, thirty-one.   Deut. 7:24

Remaining Land to Be Conquered

13 Now Joshua was old, advanced in years. And the LORD said to him: "You are old, advanced in years, and there remains very much land yet to be possessed.

2 R"This is the land that yet remains: Rall the territory of the Philistines and all Rthat of the Geshurites,   Judg. 3:1–3 • Joel 3:4 • 2 Sam. 3:3

3 R"from Sihor, which is east of Egypt, as far as the border of Ekron northward (which is counted as Canaanite); the Rfive lords of the Philistines—the Gazites, the Ashdodites, the Ashkelonites, the Gittites, and the Ekronites; also Rthe Avites;   Jer. 2:18 • Judg. 3:3 • Deut. 2:23

4 "from the south, all the land of the Canaanites, and Mearah that belongs to the Sidonians Ras far as Aphek, to the border of Rthe Amorites;   Josh. 12:18; 19:30 • Judg. 1:34

5 "the land of Rthe TGebalites, and all Lebanon, toward the sunrise, Rfrom Baal Gad below Mount Hermon as far as the entrance to Hamath;   1 Kin. 5:18 • Or Giblites • Josh. 12:7

6 "all the inhabitants of the mountains from Lebanon as far as the *Brook Misrephoth, and all the Sidonians—them I will drive out from before the children of Israel; only Tdivide it by lot to Israel as an inheritance, as I have commanded you.   apportion

7 "Now therefore, divide this land as an inheritance to the nine tribes and half the tribe of Manasseh."

The Land Divided East of the Jordan

8 With the other half tribe the Reubenites and the Gadites received their inheritance, Rwhich Moses had given them, Rbeyond the Jordan eastward, as Moses the servant of the LORD had given them: Num. 32:33 • Josh. 12:1–6

9 from Aroer which is on the bank of the River Arnon, and the town that is in the midst of the ravine, Rand all the plain of Medeba as far as Dibon;   Num. 21:30

10 Rall the cities of Sihon king of the Amorites, who reigned in Heshbon, as far as the border of the children of Ammon; Num. 21:24, 25

11 RGilead, and the border of the Geshurites and Maachathites, all Mount Hermon, and all Bashan as far as Salcah;   Josh. 12:5

12 all the kingdom of Og in Bashan, who reigned in Ashtaroth and Edrei, who remained of the remnant of the giants; for Moses had defeated and cast out these.

13 Nevertheless the children of Israel Rdid not drive out the Geshurites or the Maachathites, but the Geshurites and the Maachathites dwell among the Israelites until this day.   Josh. 13:11

14 Only to the tribe of Levi he had given no Tinheritance; the sacrifices of the LORD God

of Israel made by fire are their inheritance, as He said to them.   land as a possession

The Land of Reuben

15 RAnd Moses had given to the tribe of the children of Reuben an inheritance according to their families.   Num. 34:14

16 Their territory was Rfrom Aroer, which is on the bank of the River Arnon, Rand the city that is in the midst of the ravine, Rand all the plain by Medeba;   Josh. 12:2 • Num. 21:28 • Num. 21:30

17 Heshbon and all its cities that are in the plain: Dibon, Bamoth Baal, Beth Baal Meon,

18 RJahaza, Kedemoth, Mephaath, Num. 21:23

19 Kirjathaim, RSibmah, Zereth Shahar on the mountain of the valley,   Num. 32:38

20 Beth Peor, Rthe slopes of Pisgah, and Beth Jeshimoth—   Deut. 3:17

21 all the cities of the plain and all the kingdom of Sihon king of the Amorites, who reigned in Heshbon, whom Moses had struck with the princes of Midian: Evi, Rekem, Zur, Hur, and Reba, who were princes of Sihon dwelling in the country.

22 The children of Israel also killed with the sword Balaam the son of Beor, the soothsayer, among those who were killed by them.

23 And the border of the children of Reuben was the bank of the Jordan. This was the inheritance of the children of Reuben according to their families, the cities and their villages.

The Land of Gad

24 RMoses also had given an inheritance to the tribe of Gad, to the children of Gad according to their families.   Num. 34:14

25 RTheir territory was Jazer, and all the cities of Gilead, Rand half the land of the Ammonites as far as Aroer, which is before RRabbah,   Num. 32:1, 35 • Judg. 11:13, 15 • Deut. 3:11

26 and from Heshbon to Ramath Mizpah and Betonim, and from Mahanaim to the border of Debir,

27 and in the valley Beth Haram, Beth Nimrah, Succoth, and Zaphon, the rest of the kingdom of Sihon king of Heshbon, with the Jordan as its border, as far as the edge Rof the TSea of Chinnereth, on the other side of the Jordan eastward.   Num. 34:11 • Sea of Galilee

28 This is the inheritance of the children of Gad according to their families, the cities and their villages.

Half the Tribe of Manasseh (East)

29 RMoses also had given an inheritance to half the tribe of Manasseh; it was for half the tribe of the children of Manasseh according to their families: Num. 34:14

30 Their territory was from Mahanaim, all Bashan, all the kingdom of Og king of Bashan, and Rall the towns of Jair which are in Bashan, sixty cities;   Num. 32:41

13:6 Heb. Misrephoth Maim

31 half of Gilead, and Ashtaroth and Edrei, cities of the kingdom of Og in Bashan, were for the ᴿchildren of Machir the son of Manasseh, for half of the children of Machir according to their families.   Num. 32:39, 40

32 These are the areas which Moses had ᵀdistributed as an inheritance in the plains of Moab on the other side of the Jordan, by Jericho eastward.   apportioned

33 But to the tribe of Levi Moses had given no inheritance; the Lᴏʀᴅ God of Israel was their inheritance, as He had said to them.

The Land Divided West of the Jordan

14 These are the areas which the children of Israel inherited in the land of Canaan, ᴿwhich Eleazar the priest, Joshua the son of Nun, and the heads of the fathers of the tribes of the children of Israel distributed as an inheritance to them.   Num. 34:16–29

2 Their inheritance was by lot, as the Lᴏʀᴅ had commanded by the hand of Moses, for the nine tribes and the half-tribe.

3 For Moses had given the inheritance of the two tribes and the half-tribe on the other side of the Jordan; but to the Levites he had given no inheritance among them.

4 For the children of Joseph were two tribes: Manasseh and Ephraim. And they gave no part to the Levites in the land, except cities to dwell in, with their common-lands for their livestock and their property.

5 ᴿAs the Lᴏʀᴅ had commanded Moses, so the children of Israel did; and they divided the land.   Josh. 21:2

Caleb Inherits Hebron

6 Then the children of Judah came to Joshua in Gilgal. And Caleb the son of Jephunneh the Kenizzite said to him: "You know ᴿthe word which the Lᴏʀᴅ said to Moses the man of God concerning ᴿyou and me in Kadesh Barnea.   Num. 14:24, 30 · Num. 13:26

7 "I was forty years old when Moses the servant of the Lᴏʀᴅ sent me from Kadesh Barnea to spy out the land, and I brought back word to him as it was in my heart.

8 "Nevertheless ᴿmy brethren who went up with me made the ᵀheart of the people melt, but I wholly followed the Lᴏʀᴅ my God.   Num. 13:31, 32 · courage of the people fail

9 "So Moses swore on that day, saying, 'Surely the land ᴿwhere your foot has trodden shall be your inheritance and your children's forever, because you have wholly followed the Lᴏʀᴅ my God.'   Deut. 1:36

10 "And now, behold, the Lᴏʀᴅ has kept me alive, as He said, these forty-five years, ever since the Lᴏʀᴅ spoke this word to Moses while Israel wandered in the wilderness; and now, here I am this day, eighty-five years old.

11 "As yet I am as strong this day as on the day that Moses sent me; just as my strength was then, so now is my strength for war, both for going out and for coming in.

12 "Now therefore, give me this mountain of which the Lᴏʀᴅ spoke in that day; for you heard in that day how the Anakim were there, and that the cities were great and fortified. ᴿIt may be that the Lᴏʀᴅ will be with me, and ᴿI shall be able to drive them out as the Lᴏʀᴅ said."   Rom. 8:31 · Josh. 15:14

13 And Joshua ᴿblessed him, ᴿand gave Hebron to Caleb the son of Jephunneh as an inheritance.   Josh. 22:6 · Josh. 10:37; 15:13

14 Hebron therefore became the inheritance of Caleb the son of Jephunneh the Kenizzite to this day, because he ᴿwholly followed the Lᴏʀᴅ God of Israel.   Josh. 14:8, 9

15 And ᴿthe name of Hebron formerly was Kirjath Arba (Arba was the greatest man among the Anakim). ᴿThen the land had rest from war.   Gen. 23:2 · Josh. 11:23

The Land of Judah

15 So this was the ᵀlot of the tribe of the children of Judah according to their families: The border of Edom at the ᴿWilderness of Zin southward was the extreme southern boundary.   allotment · Num. 33:36

2 And their ᴿsouthern border began at the shore of the Salt Sea, from the bay that faces southward.   Num. 34:3, 4

3 Then it went out to the southern side of ᴿthe Ascent of Akrabbim, passed along to Zin, ascended on the south side of Kadesh Barnea, passed along to Hezron, went up to Adar, and went around to Karkaa.   Num. 34:4

4 From there it passed ᴿtoward Azmon and went out to the Brook of Egypt; and the border ended at the sea. This shall be your southern border.   Num. 34:5

5 The east border was the Salt Sea as far as the mouth of the Jordan. And the border on the northern quarter began at the bay of the sea at the mouth of the Jordan.

6 The border went up to ᴿBeth Hoglah and passed north of Beth Arabah; and the border went up ᴿto the stone of Bohan the son of Reuben.   Josh. 18:19, 21 · Josh. 18:17

7 Then the border went up toward ᴿDebir from ᴿthe Valley of Achor, and it turned northward toward Gilgal, which is before the Ascent of Adummim, which is on the south side of the valley. The border continued toward the waters of En Shemesh and ended at ᴿEn Rogel.   Josh. 13:26 · Josh. 7:26 · 2 Sam. 17:17

8 And the border went up by the Valley of the Son of Hinnom to the southern slope of the Jebusite city (which is Jerusalem). The border went up to the top of the mountain that lies before the Valley of Hinnom westward, which is at the end of the Valley ᴿof ᵀRephaim northward.   Josh. 18:16 · Lit. Giants

9 Then the border went around from the top of the hill to the fountain of the water of

Nephtoah, and extended to the cities of Mount Ephron. And the border went around to Baalah (which *is* Kirjath Jearim).

10 Then the border ᵀturned westward from Baalah to Mount Seir, passed along to the side of Mount Jearim on the north (which *is* Chesalon), went down to Beth Shemesh, and passed on to ᴿTimnah.   *turned around* · Gen. 38:13

11 And the border went out to the side of ᴿEkron northward. Then the border went around to Shicron, passed along to Mount Baalah, and extended to Jabneel; and the border ended at the sea.   Josh. 19:43

12 The west border *was* ᴿthe coastline of the Great Sea. This *is* the boundary of the children of Judah all around according to their families.   Num. 34:6, 7

Caleb Occupies Hebron and Debir

13 Now to Caleb the son of Jephunneh he gave a share among the children of Judah, according to the commandment of the Lᴏʀᴅ to Joshua, *namely*, Kirjath Arba, which *is* Hebron (*Arba was* the father of Anak).

14 Caleb drove out ᴿthe three sons of Anak from there: ᴿSheshai, Ahiman, and Talmai, the children of Anak.   Judg. 1:10, 20 · Num. 13:22

15 Then ᴿhe went up from there to the inhabitants of Debir (formerly the name of Debir *was* Kirjath Sepher).   Judg. 1:11

16 And Caleb said, "He who ᵀattacks Kirjath Sepher and takes it, to him I will give Achsah my daughter as wife."   Lit. *strikes*

17 So Othniel the son of Kenaz, the brother of Caleb, took it; and he gave him ᴿAchsah his daughter as wife.   Judg. 1:12

18 Now it was so, when she came *to him*, that she persuaded him to ask her father for a field. So she dismounted from *her* donkey, and Caleb said to her, "What do you wish?"

19 She answered, "Give me a blessing; since you have given me land in the South, give me also springs of water." So he gave her the upper springs and the lower springs.

The Cities of Judah

20 This *was* the inheritance of the tribe of the children of Judah according to their families:

21 The cities at the limits of the tribe of the children of Judah, toward the border of Edom in the South, were Kabzeel, Eder, Jagur,

22 Kinah, Dimonah, Adadah,

23 Kedesh, Hazor, Ithnan,

24 ᴿZiph, Telem, Bealoth,   1 Sam. 23:14

25 Hazor, Hadattah, Kerioth, Hezron (which *is* Hazor),

26 Amam, Shema, Moladah,

27 Hazar Gaddah, Heshmon, Beth Pelet,

28 Hazar Shual, Beersheba, Bizjothjah,

29 Baalah, Ijim, Ezem,

30 Eltolad, Chesil, ᴿHormah,   Josh. 19:4

31 Ziklag, Madmannah, Sansannah,

32 Lebaoth, Shilhim, Ain, and Rimmon: all the cities *are* twenty-nine, with their villages.

33 In the lowland: Eshtaol, Zorah, Ashnah,

34 Zanoah, En Gannim, Tappuah, Enam,

35 Jarmuth, Adullam, Socoh, Azekah,

36 Sharaim, Adithaim, Gederah, and Gederothaim: fourteen cities with their villages;

37 Zenan, Hadashah, Migdal Gad,

38 Dilean, Mizpah, ᴿJoktheel,   2 Kin. 14:7

39 Lachish, Bozkath, ᴿEglon,   Josh. 10:3

40 Cabbon, ᵀLahmas, Kithlish,   Or *Lahmam*

41 Gederoth, Beth Dagon, Naamah, and Makkedah: sixteen cities with their villages;

42 ᴿLibnah, Ether, Ashan,   Josh. 21:13

43 Jiphtah, Ashnah, Nezib,

44 Keilah, Achzib, and Mareshah: nine cities with their villages;

45 Ekron, with its towns and villages;

46 from Ekron to the sea, all that *lay* near ᴿAshdod, with their villages;   Josh. 11:22

47 Ashdod with its towns and villages, Gaza with its towns and villages—as far as ᴿthe Brook of Egypt and ᴿthe Great Sea with *its* coastline.   Josh. 15:4 · Num. 34:6

48 And in the mountain country: Shamir, Jattir, Sochoh,

49 Dannah, Kirjath Sannah (which *is* Debir),

50 Anab, Eshtemoh, Anim,

51 ᴿGoshen, Holon, and Giloh: eleven cities with their villages;   Josh. 10:41; 11:16

52 Arab, Dumah, Eshean,

53 Janum, Beth Tappuah, Aphekah,

54 Humtah, Kirjath Arba (which *is* Hebron), and Zior: nine cities with their villages;

55 Maon, Carmel, Ziph, Juttah,

56 Jezreel, Jokdeam, Zanoah,

57 Kain, Gibeah, and Timnah: ten cities with their villages;

58 Halhul, Beth Zur, Gedor,

59 Maarath, Beth Anoth, and Eltekon: six cities with their villages;

60 Kirjath Baal (which *is* Kirjath Jearim) and Rabbah: two cities with their villages.

61 In the wilderness: Beth Arabah, Middin, Secacah,

62 Nibshan, the City of Salt, and ᴿEn Gedi: six cities with their villages.   1 Sam. 23:29

63 As for the Jebusites, the inhabitants of Jerusalem, ᴿthe children of Judah could not drive them out; ᴿbut the Jebusites dwell with the children of Judah at Jerusalem to this day.   2 Sam. 5:6 · Judg. 1:21

Ephraim and West Manasseh

16 The lot ᵀfell to the children of Joseph from the Jordan, by Jericho, to the waters of Jericho on the east, to the ᴿwilderness that goes up from Jericho through the mountains to *Bethel,   Lit. *went out* · Josh. 8:15; 18:12

16:1 LXX *Bethel Luz*

2 then went out *from ᴿBethel to Luz, passed along to the border of the Archites at Ataroth,   Josh. 18:13

3 and went down westward to the boundary of the Japhletites, as far as the boundary of Lower Beth Horon to Gezer; and ᵀit ended at the sea.   Lit. *the goings out of it were at the sea*

4 So the children of Joseph, Manasseh and Ephraim, took their inheritance.

The Land of Ephraim

5 ᴿThe border of the children of Ephraim, according to their families, was *thus:* The border of their inheritance on the east side was ᴿAtaroth Addar ᴿas far as Upper Beth Horon.   Judg. 1:29 • Josh. 18:13 • 2 Chr. 8:5

6 And the border went out toward the sea on the north side of ᴿMichmethath; then the border went around eastward to Taanath Shiloh, and passed by it on the east of Janohah.   Josh. 17:7

7 Then it went down from Janohah to Ataroth and *Naarah, reached to Jericho, and came out at the Jordan.

8 The border went out from Tappuah westward to the Brook Kanah, and ᵀit ended at the sea. This *was* the inheritance of the tribe of the children of Ephraim according to their families.   Lit. *the goings out of it were at the sea*

9 ᴿThe separate cities for the children of Ephraim *were* among the inheritance of the children of Manasseh, all the cities with their villages.   Josh. 17:9

10 ᴿAnd they did not drive out the Canaanites who dwelt in Gezer; but the Canaanites dwell among the Ephraimites to this day and have become forced laborers.   Judg. 1:29

The Other Half-Tribe of Manasseh (West)

17 There was also a lot for the tribe of Manasseh, for he *was* the firstborn of Joseph: namely for ᴿMachir the firstborn of Manasseh, the father of Gilead, because he was a man of war; therefore he was given ᴿGilead and Bashan.   Gen. 50:23 • Deut. 3:15

2 And there was *a* lot for the rest of the children of Manasseh according to their families: for the children of ᵀAbiezer, the children of Helek, the children of Asriel, the children of Shechem, the children of Hepher, and the children of Shemida; these *were* the male children of Manasseh the son of Joseph according to their families.   Jeezer, Num. 26:30

3 But Zelophehad the son of Hepher, the son of Gilead, the son of Machir, the son of Manasseh, had no sons, but only daughters. And these *are* the names of his daughters: Mahlah, Noah, Hoglah, Milcah, and Tirzah.

4 And they came near before Eleazar the

16:2 LXX *to Bethel,* (that is, Luz)
16:7 *Naaran,* 1 Chr. 7:28

priest, before Joshua the son of Nun, and before the rulers, saying, "The Loʀᴅ commanded Moses to give us an inheritance among our brothers." Therefore, according to the commandment of the Loʀᴅ, he gave them an inheritance among their father's brothers.

5 Ten shares fell to ᴿManasseh, besides the land of Gilead and Bashan, which *were* on the other side of the Jordan,   Josh. 22:7

6 because the daughters of Manasseh received an inheritance among his sons; and the rest of Manasseh's sons had the land of Gilead.

7 And the territory of Manasseh was from Asher to ᴿMichmethath, that *lies* east of Shechem; and the border went along south to the inhabitants of En Tappuah.   Josh. 16:6

8 Manasseh had the land of Tappuah, but ᴿTappuah on the border of Manasseh *belonged* to the children of Ephraim.   Josh. 16:8

9 And the border descended to the Brook Kanah, southward to the brook. These cities of Ephraim *are* among the cities of Manasseh. The border of Manasseh *was* on the north side of the brook; and it ended at the sea.

10 Southward *it was* Ephraim's, northward *it was* Manasseh's, and the sea was its border. Manasseh's territory was adjoining Asher on the north and Issachar on the east.

11 And in Issachar and in Asher, Manasseh had ᴿBeth Shean and its towns, Ibleam and its towns, the inhabitants of Dor and its towns, the inhabitants of En Dor and its towns, the inhabitants of Taanach and its towns, and the inhabitants of Megiddo and its towns—three hilly regions.   1 Kin. 4:12

12 Yet ᴿthe children of Manasseh could not drive out *the inhabitants of* those cities, but the Canaanites were determined to dwell in that land.   Judg. 1:19, 27, 28

13 And it happened, when the children of Israel grew strong, that they put the Canaanites to ᴿforced labor, but did not utterly drive them out.   Josh. 16:10

More Land for Ephraim and Manasseh

14 Then the children of Joseph spoke to Joshua, saying, "Why have you given us *only* one ᵀlot and one share to inherit, since we *are* ᴿa great people, inasmuch as the Loʀᴅ has blessed us until now?"   *allotment* • Gen. 48:19

15 So Joshua answered them, "If you *are* a great people, *then* go up to the forest *country* and clear a place for yourself there in the land of the Perizzites and the giants, since the mountains of Ephraim are too confined for you."

16 But the children of Joseph said, "The mountain country is not enough for us; and all the Canaanites who dwell in the land of the valley have chariots of iron, *both* those who *are* of Beth Shean and its towns and *those* who *are* of the Valley of Jezreel."

17 And Joshua spoke to the house of Joseph—to Ephraim and Manasseh—saying, "You *are* a great people and have great power; you shall not have *only* one lot,

18 "but the mountain country shall be yours. Although it *is* wooded, you shall cut it down, and its ^Tfarthest extent shall be yours; for you shall drive out the Canaanites, ^Rthough they have iron chariots *and* are strong."   Lit. *goings out* · Deut. 20:1

The Remainder of the Land Divided

18 Now the whole congregation of the children of Israel assembled together ^Rat Shiloh, and ^Rset up the tabernacle of meeting there. And the land was subdued before them.   Jer. 7:12 · Judg. 18:31

2 But there remained among the children of Israel seven tribes which had not yet received their inheritance.

3 Then Joshua said to the children of Israel: ^R"How long will you neglect to go and possess the land which the LORD God of your fathers has given you?   Judg. 18:9

4 "Pick out from among you three men for *each* tribe, and I will send them; they shall rise and go through the land, survey it according to their inheritance, and come *back* to me.

5 "And they shall divide it into seven parts. ^RJudah shall remain in their territory on the south, and the house of Joseph shall remain in their territory on the north. Josh. 15:1

6 "You shall therefore ^Tsurvey the land in seven parts and bring *the survey* here to me, ^Rthat I may cast lots for you here before the LORD our God.   *describe in writing* · Josh. 14:2; 18:10

7 "But the Levites have no part among you, for the priesthood of the LORD *is* their inheritance. And Gad, Reuben, and half the tribe of Manasseh have received their inheritance beyond the Jordan on the east, which Moses the servant of the LORD gave them."

8 Then the men arose to go away; and Joshua charged those who went to ^Tsurvey the land, saying, "Go, walk ^Rthrough the land, survey it, and come back to me, that I may cast lots for you here before the LORD in Shiloh."   *describe in writing* · Gen. 13:17

9 So the men went, passed through the land, and wrote the survey in a book in seven parts by cities; and they came to Joshua at the camp in Shiloh.

10 Then Joshua cast lots for them in Shiloh before the LORD, and there ^RJoshua divided the land to the children of Israel according to their divisions.   Num. 34:16–29

The Land of Benjamin

11 ^RNow the lot of the tribe of the children of Benjamin came up according to their families, and the territory of their lot came out between the children of Judah and the children of Joseph.   Judg. 1:21

12 ^RTheir border on the north side began at the Jordan, and the border went up to the side of Jericho on the north, and went up through the mountains westward; it ended at the Wilderness of Beth Aven.   Josh. 16:1

13 The border went over from there toward Luz, to the side of Luz (which *is* Bethel) southward; and the border descended to Ataroth Addar, near the hill that *lies* on the south side ^Rof Lower Beth Horon.   Josh. 16:3

14 Then the border extended around the west side to the south, from the hill that *lies* before Beth Horon southward; and it ended at ^RKirjath Baal (which *is* Kirjath Jearim), a city of the children of Judah. This *was* the west side.   Josh. 15:9

15 The south side *began* at the end of Kirjath Jearim, and the border extended on the west and went out to ^Rthe spring of the waters of Nephtoah.   Josh. 15:9

16 Then the border came down to the end of the mountain that *lies* before ^Rthe Valley of the Son of Hinnom, which *is* in the Valley of the ^TRephaim on the north, descended to the Valley of Hinnom, to the side of the Jebusite city on the south, and descended to ^REn Rogel.   Josh. 15:8 · Lit. *Giants* · Josh. 15:8

17 And it went around from the north, went out to En Shemesh, and extended toward Geliloth, which is before the Ascent of Adummim, and descended to ^Rthe stone of Bohan the son of Reuben.   Josh. 15:6

18 Then it passed along toward the north side of *Arabah, and went down to Arabah.

19 And the border passed along to the north side of Beth Hoglah; then ^Tthe border ended at the north bay at the Salt Sea, at the south end of the Jordan. This *was* the southern boundary.   Lit. *the goings out of the border were*

20 The Jordan was its border on the east side. This *was* the inheritance of the children of Benjamin, according to its boundaries all around, according to their families.

21 Now the cities of the tribe of the children of Benjamin, according to their families, were Jericho, Beth Hoglah, Emek Keziz,

22 Beth Arabah, Zemaraim, Bethel,

23 Avim, Parah, Ophrah,

24 Chephar Haammoni, Ophni, and Gaba: twelve cities with their villages;

25 Gibeon, ^RRamah, Beeroth,   Jer. 31:15

26 Mizpah, Chephirah, Mozah,

27 Rekem, Irpeel, Taralah,

28 Zelah, Eleph, ^RJebus (which *is* Jerusalem), Gibeath, *and* Kirjath: fourteen cities with their villages. This *was* the inheritance of the children of Benjamin according to their families.   Josh. 15:8, 63

Simeon's Inheritance with Judah

19 The ^Rsecond lot came out for Simeon, for the tribe of the children of Simeon

18:18 *Beth Arabah,* Josh. 15:6; 18:22

according to their families. [R]And their inheritance was within the inheritance of the children of Judah.   Judg. 1:3 • Josh. 19:9

2 [R]They had in their inheritance Beersheba (Sheba), Moladah,   1 Chr. 4:28

3 Hazar Shual, Balah, Ezem,

4 Eltolad, Bethul, Hormah,

5 Ziklag, Beth Marcaboth, Hazar Susah,

6 Beth Lebaoth, and Sharuhen: thirteen cities and their villages;

7 Ain, Rimmon, Ether, and Ashan: four cities and their villages;

8 and all the villages that were all around these cities as far as Baalath Beer, [R]Ramah of the South. This was the inheritance of the tribe of the children of Simeon according to their families.   1 Sam. 30:27

9 The inheritance of the children of Simeon was included in the share of the children of Judah, for the share of the children of Judah was too much for them. Therefore the children of Simeon had their inheritance within the inheritance of that people.

The Land of Zebulun

10 The third lot came out for the children of Zebulun according to their families, and the border of their inheritance was as far as Sarid.

11 [R]Their border went toward the west and to Maralah, went to Dabbasheth, and extended along the brook that is [R]east of Jokneam.   Gen. 49:13 • Josh. 12:22

12 Then from Sarid it went eastward toward the sunrise along the border of Chisloth Tabor, and went out toward [R]Daberath, bypassing Japhia.   1 Chr. 6:72

13 And from there it passed along on the east of [R]Gath Hepher, toward Eth Kazin, and extended to Rimmon, which borders on Neah.   2 Kin. 14:25

14 Then the border went around it on the north side of Hannathon, and [T]it ended in the Valley of Jiphthah El.   Lit. the goings out of it were

15 Included were Kattath, Nahallal, Shimron, Idalah, and Bethlehem: twelve cities with their villages.

16 This was the inheritance of the children of Zebulun according to their families, these cities with their villages.

The Land of Issachar

17 The fourth lot came out to Issachar, for the children of Issachar according to their families.

18 And their territory went to Jezreel, and included Chesulloth, Shunem,

19 Haphraim, Shion, Anaharath,

20 Rabbith, Kishion, Abez,

21 Remeth, En Gannim, En Haddah, and Beth Pazzez.

22 And the border reached to Tabor, Shahazimah, and [R]Beth Shemesh; their border ended at the Jordan: sixteen cities with their villages.   Josh. 15:10

23 This was the inheritance of the tribe of the children of Issachar according to their families, the cities and their villages.

The Land of Asher

24 [R]The fifth lot came out for the tribe of the children of Asher according to their families.   Judg. 1:31, 32

25 And their territory included Helkath, Hali, Beten, Achshaph,

26 Alammelech, Amad, and Mishal; it reached to [R]Mount Carmel westward, along the Brook Shihor Libnath.   Jer. 46:18

27 It turned toward the sunrise to Beth Dagon; and it reached to Zebulun and to the Valley of Jiphthah El, then northward beyond Beth Emek and Neiel, bypassing [R]Cabul which was on the left,   1 Kin. 9:13

28 including *Ebron, Rehob, Hammon, and Kanah, [R]as far as Greater Sidon.   Judg. 1:31

29 And the border turned to Ramah and to the fortified city of Tyre; then the border turned to Hosah, and ended at the sea by the region of [R]Achzib.   Judg. 1:31

30 Also Ummah, Aphek, and Rehob were included: twenty-two cities with their villages.

31 This was the inheritance of the tribe of the children of Asher according to their families, these cities with their villages.

The Land of Naphtali

32 [R]The sixth lot came out to the children of Naphtali, for the children of Naphtali according to their families.   Judg. 1:33

33 And their border began at Heleph, enclosing the territory from the terebinth tree in Zaanannim, Adami Nekeb, and Jabneel, as far as Lakkum; it ended at the Jordan.

34 [R]From Heleph the border extended westward to Aznoth Tabor, and went out from there toward Hukkok; it adjoined Zebulun on the south side and Asher on the west side, and ended at Judah by the Jordan toward the sunrise.   Deut. 33:23

35 And the fortified cities are Ziddim, Zer, Hammath, Rakkath, Chinnereth,

36 Adamah, Ramah, Hazor,

37 [R]Kedesh, Edrei, En Hazor,   Josh. 20:7

38 Iron, Migdal El, Horem, Beth Anath, and Beth Shemesh: nineteen cities with their villages.

39 This was the inheritance of the tribe of the children of Naphtali according to their families, the cities and their villages.

19:28 So with MT, Tg., Vg.; a few Heb. mss. Abdon (cf. 21:30 and 1 Chr. 6:74)

The Land of Dan

40 ᴿThe seventh lot came out for the tribe of the children of Dan according to their families.   Judg. 1:34–36
41 And the territory of their inheritance was Zorah, ᴿEshtaol, Ir Shemesh,   Josh. 15:33
42 ᴿShaalabbin, Aijalon, Jethlah,   Judg. 1:35
43 Elon, Timnah, ᴿEkron,   Judg. 1:18
44 Eltekeh, Gibbethon, Baalath,
45 Jehud, Bene Berak, Gath Rimmon,
46 Me Jarkon, and Rakkon, with the region ᵀnear ᵀJoppa.   over against • Heb. Japho
47 And the ᴿborder of the children of Dan went beyond these, because the children of Dan went up to fight against Leshem and took it; and they struck it with the edge of the sword, took possession of it, and dwelt in it. They called Leshem, ᴿDan, after the name of Dan their father.   Judg. 18 • Judg. 18:29
48 This is the inheritance of the tribe of the children of Dan according to their families, these cities with their villages.

Joshua's Inheritance

49 When they had made an end of dividing the land as an inheritance according to their borders, the children of Israel gave an inheritance among them to Joshua the son of Nun.
50 According to the word of the LORD they gave him the city which he asked for, Timnath Serah in the mountains of Ephraim; and he built the city and dwelt in it.
51 These were the inheritances which Eleazar the priest, Joshua the son of Nun, and the heads of the fathers of the tribes of the children of Israel divided as an inheritance by lot in Shiloh before the LORD, at the door of the tabernacle of meeting. So they made an end of dividing the country.

The Cities of Refuge

20 The LORD also spoke to Joshua, saying,
2 "Speak to the children of Israel, saying: 'Appoint for yourselves cities of refuge, of which I spoke to you through Moses,
3 'that the slayer who kills a person accidentally or unintentionally may flee there; and they shall be your refuge from the avenger of blood.
4 'And when he flees to one of those cities, and stands at the entrance of the gate of the city, and ᵀdeclares his case in the hearing of the elders of that city, they shall take him into the city as one of them, and give him a place, that he may dwell among them.   states
5 'Then if the avenger of blood pursues him, they shall not deliver the slayer into his hand, because he struck his neighbor unintentionally, but did not hate him beforehand.
6 'And he shall dwell in that city until he stands before the congregation for judgment, and until the death of the one who is high

priest in those days. Then the slayer may return and come to his own city and his own house, to the city from which he fled.' "
7 So they appointed Kedesh in Galilee, in the mountains of Naphtali, ᴿShechem in the mountains of Ephraim, and ᴿKirjath Arba (which is Hebron) in ᴿthe mountains of Judah.   Josh. 21:21 • Josh. 14:15; 21:11, 13 • Luke 1:39
8 And on the other side of the Jordan, by Jericho eastward, they assigned ᴿBezer in the wilderness on the plain, from the tribe of Reuben, ᴿRamoth in Gilead, from the tribe of Gad, and ᴿGolan in Bashan, from the tribe of Manasseh.   Deut. 4:43 • Josh. 21:38 • Josh. 21:27
9 These were the cities appointed for all the children of Israel and for the stranger who dwelt among them, that whoever killed a person accidentally might flee there, and not die by the hand of the avenger of blood until he stood before the congregation.

Cities of the Levites

21 Then the heads of the fathers' houses of the ᴿLevites came near to ᴿEleazar the priest, to Joshua the son of Nun, and to the heads of the fathers' houses of the tribes of the children of Israel.   Num. 35:1–8 • Josh. 14:1; 17:4
2 And they spoke to them at ᴿShiloh in the land of Canaan, saying, ᴿ"The LORD commanded through Moses to give us cities to dwell in, with their common-lands for our livestock."   Josh. 18:1 • Num. 35:2
3 So the children of Israel gave to the Levites from their inheritance, at the commandment of the LORD, these cities and their common-lands:
4 Now the lot came out for the families of the Kohathites. And ᴿthe children of Aaron the priest, who were of the Levites, ᴿhad thirteen cities by lot from the tribe of Judah, from the tribe of Simeon, and from the tribe of Benjamin.   Josh. 21:8, 19 • Josh. 19:51
5 ᴿThe rest of the children of Kohath had ten cities by lot from the families of the tribe of Ephraim, from the tribe of Dan, and from the half-tribe of Manasseh.   Josh. 21:20
6 And ᴿthe children of Gershon had thirteen cities by lot from the families of the tribe of Issachar, from the tribe of Asher, from the tribe of Naphtali, and from the half-tribe of Manasseh in Bashan.   Josh. 21:27
7 ᴿThe children of Merari according to their families had twelve cities from the tribe of Reuben, from the tribe of Gad, and from the tribe of Zebulun.   Josh. 21:34
8 ᴿAnd the children of Israel gave these cities with their common-lands by lot to the Levites, ᴿas the LORD had commanded by the hand of Moses.   Josh. 21:3 • Num. 35:2
9 So they gave from the tribe of the children of Judah and from the tribe of the children of Simeon these cities which are ᵀdesignated by name,   Lit. called

10 which were for the children of Aaron, one of the families of the Kohathites, who were of the children of Levi; for the lot was theirs first.

11 And they gave them ᵀKirjath Arba (*Arba* was the father of Anak), which *is* Hebron, in the mountains of Judah, with the common-land surrounding it.   Lit. *City of Arba*

12 But ᴿthe fields of the city and its villages they gave to Caleb the son of Jephunneh as his possession.   Josh. 14:14

13 Thus to the children of Aaron the priest they gave ᴿHebron with its common-land (a city of refuge for the slayer), ᴿLibnah with its common-land,   Josh. 15:54; 20:2, 7 • Josh. 15:42

14 ᴿJattir with its common-land, ᴿEshtemoa with its common-land,   Josh. 15:48 • Josh. 15:50

15 ᴿHolon with its common-land, ᴿDebir with its common-land,   1 Chr. 6:58 • Josh. 15:49

16 ᴿAin with its common-land, ᴿJuttah with its common-land, and ᴿBeth Shemesh with its common-land: nine cities from those two tribes;   1 Chr. 6:59 • Josh. 15:55 • Josh. 15:10

17 and from the tribe of Benjamin, ᴿGibeon with its common-land, ᴿGeba with its common-land,   Josh. 18:25 • Josh. 18:24

18 Anathoth with its common-land, and Almon with its common-land: four cities.

19 All the cities of the children of Aaron, the priests, *were* thirteen cities with their common-lands.

20 And the families of the children of Kohath, the Levites, the rest of the children of Kohath, even they had the cities of their ᵀlot from the tribe of Ephraim.   *allotment*

21 For they gave them ᴿShechem with its common-land in the mountains of Ephraim (a city of refuge for the slayer), ᴿGezer with its common-land,   Josh. 20:7 • Judg. 1:29

22 Kibzaim with its common-land, and Beth Horon with its common-land: four cities;

23 and from the tribe of Dan, Eltekeh with its common-land, Gibbethon with its common-land,

24 Aijalon with its common-land, *and* Gath Rimmon with its common-land: four cities;

25 and from the half-tribe of Manasseh, Tanach with its common-land and Gath Rimmon with its common-land: two cities.

26 All the ten cities with their common-lands were for the rest of the families of the children of Kohath.

27 ᴿAlso to the children of Gershon, of the families of the Levites, from the *other* half-tribe of Manasseh, *they gave* ᴿGolan in Bashan with its common-land (a city of refuge for the slayer), and Be Eshterah with its common-land: two cities;   1 Chr. 6:71 • Josh. 20:8

28 and from the tribe of Issachar, Kishion with its common-land, Daberath with its common-land,

29 Jarmuth with its common-land, *and* En Gannim with its common-land: four cities;

30 and from the tribe of Asher, Mishal with its common-land, Abdon with its common-land,

31 Helkath with its common-land, and Rehob with its common-land: four cities;

32 and from the tribe of Naphtali, ᴿKedesh in Galilee with its common-land (a city of refuge for the slayer), Hammoth Dor with its common-land, and Kartan with its common-land: three cities.   Josh. 20:7

33 All the cities of the Gershonites according to their families *were* thirteen cities with their common-lands.

34 ᴿAnd to the families of the children of Merari, the rest of the Levites, from the tribe of Zebulun, Jokneam with its common-land, Kartah with its common-land,   1 Chr. 6:77–81

35 Dimnah with its common-land, *and* Nahalal with its common-land: four cities;

36 *and from the tribe of Reuben, ᴿBezer with its common-land, Jahaz with its common-land,   Josh. 20:8

37 Kedemoth with its common-land, and Mephaath with its common-land: four cities;

38 and from the tribe of Gad, ᴿRamoth in Gilead with its common-land (a city of refuge for the slayer), Mahanaim with its common-land,   Josh. 20:8

39 Heshbon with its common-land, *and* Jazer with its common-land: four cities in all.

40 So all the cities for the children of Merari according to their families, the rest of the families of the Levites, were by their lot twelve cities.

41 All the cities of the Levites within the possession of the children of Israel *were* forty-eight cities with their common-lands.

42 Every one of these cities had its common-land surrounding it; thus *were* all these cities.

The Promise Fulfilled

43 So the LORD gave to Israel ᴿall the land of which He had sworn to give to their fathers, and they ᴿtook possession of it and dwelt in it.   Gen. 12:7; 26:3, 4; 28:4, 13, 14 • Num. 33:53

44 The LORD gave them rest all around, according to all that He had sworn to their fathers. And ᴿnot a man of all their enemies stood against them; the LORD delivered all their enemies into their hand.   Deut. 7:24

45 ᴿNot a word failed of any good thing which the LORD had spoken to the house of Israel. All came to pass.   Josh. 23:14

Eastern Tribes Return to Their Lands

22 Then Joshua called the Reubenites, the Gadites, and half the tribe of Manasseh,

2 and said to them: "You have kept all that Moses the servant of the LORD com-

21:36 So with LXX, Vg. (cf. 1 Chr. 6:78, 79); MT, Bg., Tg. omit vv. 36, 37

manded you, ᴿand have obeyed my voice in all that I commanded you.　Josh. 1:12–18

3 "You have not ᵀleft your brethren these many days, up to this day, but have kept the charge of the commandment of the LORD your God.　*forsaken*

4 "And now the LORD your God has given rest to your brethren, as He promised them; now therefore, return and go to your tents *and* to the land of your possession, ᴿwhich Moses the servant of the LORD gave you on the other side of the Jordan.　Num. 32:33

5 "But ᵀtake careful heed to do the commandment and the law which Moses the servant of the LORD commanded you, to love the LORD your God, to walk in all His ways, to keep His commandments, to hold fast to Him, and to serve Him with all your heart and with all your soul."　*be very careful to do*

6 So Joshua ᴿblessed them and sent them away, and they went to their tents.　2 Sam. 6:18

7 Now to half the tribe of Manasseh Moses had given a possession in Bashan, ᴿbut to the *other* half of it Joshua gave *a possession* among their brethren on this side of the Jordan, westward. And indeed, when Joshua sent them away to their tents, he blessed them,　Josh. 17:1–13

8 and spoke to them, saying, "Return with much riches to your tents, with very much livestock, with silver, with gold, with bronze, with iron, and with very much clothing. ᴿDivide the ᵀspoil of your enemies with your brethren."　1 Sam. 30:24 • *plunder*

9 So the children of Reuben, the children of Gad, and half the tribe of Manasseh returned, and departed from the children of Israel at Shiloh, which *is* in the land of Canaan, to go to ᴿthe country of Gilead, to the land of their possession, which they had obtained according to the word of the LORD by the hand of Moses.　Num. 32:1, 26, 29

An Altar by the Jordan

10 And when they came to the region of the Jordan which *is* in the land of Canaan, the children of Reuben, the children of Gad, and half the tribe of Manasseh built an altar there by the Jordan—a great, impressive altar.

11 Now the children of Israel ᴿheard *someone* say, "Behold, the children of Reuben, the children of Gad, and half the tribe of Manasseh have built an altar on the frontier of the land of Canaan, in the region of the Jordan—on the children of Israel's side."　Judg. 20:12, 13

12 And when the children of Israel heard *of* it, ᴿthe whole congregation of the children of Israel gathered together at Shiloh to go to war against them.　Josh. 18:1

13 Then the children of Israel ᴿsent ᴿPhinehas the son of Eleazar the priest to the children of Reuben, to the children of Gad, and to half the tribe of Manasseh, into the land of Gilead,　Deut. 13:14 • Ex. 6:25

14 and with him ten rulers, one ruler each from the chief house of every tribe of Israel; and each one *was* the head of the house of his father among the *divisions of Israel.

15 Then they came to the children of Reuben, to the children of Gad, and to half the tribe of Manasseh, to the land of Gilead, and they spoke with them, saying,

16 "Thus says the whole congregation of the LORD: 'What ᴿtreachery^T *is* this that you have committed against the God of Israel, to turn away this day from following the LORD, in that you have built for yourselves an altar, ᴿthat you might rebel this day against the LORD?　Deut. 12:5–14 • *unfaithful act* • Lev. 17:8, 9

17 'Is the iniquity ᴿof Peor not enough for us, from which we are not cleansed till this day, although there was a plague in the congregation of the LORD,　Num. 25:1-9

18 'but that you must turn away this day from following the LORD? And it shall be, if you rebel today against the LORD, that tomorrow ᴿHe will be angry with the whole congregation of Israel.　Num. 16:22

19 'Nevertheless, if the land of your possession *is* unclean, *then* cross over to the land of the possession of the LORD, ᴿwhere the LORD's tabernacle stands, and take possession among us; but do not rebel against the LORD, nor rebel against us, by building yourselves an altar besides the altar of the LORD our God.　Josh. 18:1

20 ᴿDid not Achan the son of Zerah ᵀcommit a trespass in the ᵀaccursed thing, and wrath fell on all the congregation of Israel? And that man did not perish alone in his iniquity.' "　Josh. 7:1-26 • *act unfaithfully* • *devoted thing*

21 Then the children of Reuben, the children of Gad, and half the tribe of Manasseh answered and said to the heads of the ᵀdivisions of Israel:　Lit. *thousands*

22 "The LORD God of gods, the LORD God of gods, He knows, and let Israel itself know—if *it is* in rebellion, or if in treachery against the LORD, do not save us this day.

23 "If we have built ourselves an altar to turn from following the LORD, or if to offer on it burnt offerings or grain offerings, or if to offer peace offerings on it, let the LORD Himself ᴿrequire *an account*.　1 Sam. 20:16

24 "But in fact we have done it ᵀfor fear, for a reason, saying, 'In time to come your descendants may speak to our descendants, saying, "What have you to do with the LORD God of Israel?　Lit. *from fear*

25 "For the LORD has made the Jordan a border between you and us, *you* children of Reuben and children of Gad. You have no part in the LORD." So your descendants would make our descendants cease fearing the LORD.'

22:14 Lit. *thousands*

26 "Therefore we said, 'Let us now prepare to build ourselves an altar, not for burnt offering nor for sacrifice,

27 'but that it may be ᴿa ᵀwitness between you and us and our generations after us, that we may ᴿperform the service of the LORD before Him with our burnt offerings, with our sacrifices, and with our peace offerings; that your descendants may not say to our descendants in time to come, "You have no part in the LORD." ' Gen. 31:48 · testimony · Deut. 12:5, 14

28 "Therefore we said that it will be, when they say this to us or to our generations in time to come, that we may say, 'Here is the replica of the altar of the LORD which our fathers made, though not for burnt offerings nor for sacrifices; but it is a witness between you and us.'

29 "Far be it from us that we should rebel against the LORD, and turn from following the LORD this day, ᴿto build an altar for burnt offerings, for grain offerings, or for sacrifices, besides the altar of the LORD our God which is before His tabernacle." Deut. 12:13, 14

30 Now when Phinehas the priest and the rulers of the congregation, the heads of the ᵀdivisions of Israel who were with him, heard the words that the children of Reuben, the children of Gad, and the children of Manasseh spoke, it pleased them. Lit. thousands

31 Then Phinehas the son of Eleazar the priest said to the children of Reuben, the children of Gad, and the children of Manasseh, "This day we perceive that the LORD is ᴿamong us, because you have not committed this treachery against the LORD. Now you have delivered the children of Israel out of the hand of the LORD." Lev. 26:11, 12

32 And Phinehas the son of Eleazar the priest, and the rulers, returned from the children of Reuben and the children of Gad, from the land of Gilead to the land of Canaan, to the children of Israel, and brought back word to them.

33 So the thing pleased the children of Israel, and the children of Israel ᴿblessed God; they spoke no more of going against them in battle, to destroy the land where the children of Reuben and Gad dwelt. 1 Chr. 29:20

34 The children of Reuben and the children of *Gad called the altar, Witness, "For it is a witness between us that the LORD is God."

Joshua's Farewell Address

23 Now it came to pass, a long time after the LORD had given rest to Israel from all their enemies round about, that Joshua ᴿwas old, advanced in age. Josh. 13:1; 24:29

2 And Joshua ᴿcalled for all Israel, for their elders, for their heads, for their judges, and for their officers, and said to them: "I am old, advanced in age. Deut. 31:28

22:34 LXX adds and half the tribe of Manasseh

3 "You have seen all that the ᴿLORD your God has done to all these nations because of you, for the ᴿLORD your God is He who has fought for you. Ps. 44:3 · Deut. 1:30

4 "See, ᴿI have divided to you by lot these nations that remain, to be an inheritance for your tribes, from the Jordan, with all the nations that I have cut off, as far as the Great Sea westward. Josh. 13:2, 6; 18:10

5 "And the LORD your God will expel them from before you and drive them out of your sight. So you shall possess their land, as the LORD your God promised you.

6 ᴿ"Therefore be very courageous to keep and to do all that is written in the Book of the Law of Moses, ᴿlest you turn aside from it to the right hand or to the left, Josh. 1:7 · Deut. 5:32

7 "and lest you go among these nations, these who remain among you. You shall not make mention of the name of their gods, nor cause anyone to swear by them; you shall not serve them nor bow down to them,

8 "but you shall hold fast to the LORD your God, as you have done to this day.

9 ᴿ"For the LORD has ᵀdriven out from before you great and strong nations; but as for you, no one has been able to stand against you to this day. Deut. 7:24; 11:23 · dispossessed

10 "One man of you shall chase a thousand, for the LORD your God is He who fights for you, ᴿas He promised you. Ex. 14:14

11 "Therefore take careful heed to yourselves, that you love the LORD your God.

12 "Or else, if indeed you do ᴿgo back, and cling to the remnant of these nations—these that remain among you—and ᴿmake marriages with them, and go in to them and they to you, [2 Pet. 2:20, 21] · Deut. 7:3, 4

13 "know for certain that ᴿthe LORD your God will no longer drive out these nations from before you. ᴿBut they shall be snares and traps to you, and scourges on your sides and thorns in your eyes, until you perish from this good land which the LORD your God has given you. Judg. 2:3 · Ex. 23:33; 34:12

14 "Behold, this day ᵀI am going the way of all the earth. And you know in all your hearts and in all your souls that not one thing has failed of all the good things which the LORD your God spoke concerning you. All have come to pass for you; not one word of them has failed. I am going to die.

15 ᴿ"Therefore it shall come to pass, that as all the good things have come upon you which the LORD your God promised you, so the LORD will bring upon you ᴿall harmful things, until He has destroyed you from this good land which the LORD your God has given you. Deut. 28:63 · Deut. 28:15–68

16 ᵀ"When you have transgressed the covenant of the LORD your God, which He commanded you, and have gone and served other gods, and bowed down to them, then the

Ranger of the LORD will burn against you, and you shall perish quickly from the good land which He has given you." Or *If ever* · Deut. 4:24–28

The Covenant at Shechem

24 Then Joshua gathered all the tribes of Israel to Shechem and called for the elders of Israel, for their heads, for their judges, and for their officers; and they Rpresented themselves before God.   1 Sam. 10:19

2 And Joshua said to all the people, "Thus says the LORD God of Israel: R'Your fathers, *including* Terah, the father of Abraham and the father of Nahor, dwelt on the other side of *the River in old times; and Rthey served other gods.   Gen. 11:7–32 · Josh. 24:14

3 'Then I took your father Abraham from the other side of the River, led him throughout all the land of Canaan, and multiplied his Tdescendants and gave him Isaac.   Lit. *seed*

4 'To Isaac I gave RJacob and Esau. To REsau I gave the mountains of Seir to possess, Rbut Jacob and his children went down to Egypt.   Gen. 25:24–26 · Deut. 2:5 · Gen. 46:1, 3, 6

5 'Also I sent Moses and Aaron, and I plagued Egypt, according to what I did among them. Afterward I brought you out.

6 'Then I Rbrought your fathers out of Egypt, and you came to the sea; and the Egyptians pursued your fathers with chariots and horsemen to the Red Sea.   Ex. 14:2–31

7 'So they cried out to the LORD; and He put Rdarkness between you and the Egyptians, brought the sea upon them, and covered them. And Ryour eyes saw what I did in Egypt. Then you dwelt in the wilderness Ra long time.   Ex. 14:20 · Deut. 4:34 · Josh. 5:6

8 'And I brought you into the land of the Amorites, who dwelt on the other side of the Jordan, Rand they fought with you. But I gave them into your hand, that you might possess their land, and I destroyed them from before you.   Num. 21:21–35

9 'Then RBalak the son of Zippor, king of Moab, arose to make war against Israel, and Rsent and called Balaam the son of Beor to curse you.   Judg. 11:25 · Num. 22:2–14

10 R'But I would not listen to Balaam; therefore he continued to bless you. So I delivered you out of his hand.   Deut. 23:5

11 'Then you went over the Jordan and came to Jericho. And the men of Jericho fought against you—*also* the Amorites, the Perizzites, the Canaanites, the Hittites, the Girgashites, the Hivites, and the Jebusites. But I delivered them into your hand.

12 R'I sent the hornet before you which drove them out from before you, *also* the two kings of the Amorites, *but* Rnot with your sword or with your bow.   Ex. 23:28 · Ps. 44:3

13 'I have given you a land for which you did not labor, and Rcities which you did not

14:2 The Euphrates

build, and you dwell in them; you eat of the vineyards and olive groves which you did not plant.'   Deut. 6:10, 11

14 "Now therefore, fear the LORD, serve Him in sincerity and in truth, and Rput away the gods which your fathers served on the other side of Tthe River and Rin Egypt. Serve the LORD!   Ezek. 20:18 · The Euphrates · Ezek. 20:7, 8

15 "And if it seems evil to you to serve the LORD, choose for yourselves this day whom you will serve, whether the gods which your fathers served that *were* on the other side of the River, or the gods of the Amorites, in whose land you dwell. RBut as for me and my house, we will serve the LORD."   Gen. 18:19

16 So the people answered and said: "Far be it from us that we should forsake the LORD to serve other gods;

17 "for the LORD our God *is* He who brought us and our fathers up out of the land of Egypt, from the house of bondage, who did those great signs in our sight, and preserved us in all the way that we went and among all the people through whom we passed.

18 "And the LORD drove out from before us all the people, including the Amorites who dwelt in the land. RWe also will serve the LORD, for He *is* our God."   Ps. 116:16

19 But Joshua said to the people, "You cannot serve the LORD, for He *is* a holy God. He *is* a jealous God; RHe will not forgive your transgressions nor your sins.   Ex. 23:21

20 "If you forsake the LORD and serve foreign gods, Rthen He will turn and do you harm and consume you, after He has done you good."   Ezra 8:22 · Deut. 4:24–26

21 And the people said to Joshua, "No, but we will serve the LORD!"

22 So Joshua said to the people, "You *are* witnesses against yourselves that you have chosen the LORD for yourselves, to serve Him." And they said, "*We are* witnesses!"

23 "Now therefore," *he said,* R"put away the foreign gods which *are* among you, and Rincline your heart to the LORD God of Israel."   Gen. 35:2 · 1 Kin. 8:57, 58

24 And the people Rsaid to Joshua, "The LORD our God we will serve, and His voice we will obey!"   Deut. 5:24–27

25 So Joshua Tmade a covenant with the people that day, and made for them a statute and an ordinance in Shechem.   Lit. *cut*

26 Then Joshua wrote these words in the Book of the Law of God. And he took a large stone, and set it up there Runder the oak that *was* by the sanctuary of the LORD.   Gen. 35:4

27 And Joshua said to all the people, "Behold, this stone shall be a witness to us, for it has heard all the words of the LORD which He spoke to us. It shall therefore be a witness to you, lest you deny your God."

28 So RJoshua let the people depart, each to his own inheritance.   Judg. 2:6, 7

Death of Joshua and Eleazar

29 ᴿNow it came to pass after these things that Joshua the son of Nun, the servant of the LORD, died, *being* one hundred and ten years old. Judg. 2:8

30 And they buried him within the border of his inheritance at ᴿTimnath Serah, which *is* in the mountains of Ephraim, on the north side of Mount Gaash. Josh. 19:50

31 ᴿIsrael served the LORD all the days of Joshua, and all the days of the elders who outlived Joshua, who had ᴿknown all the works of the LORD which He had done for Israel. Judg. 2:7 · Deut. 11:2

32 The bones of Joseph, which the children of Israel had brought up out of Egypt, they buried at Shechem, in the plot of ground which Jacob had bought from the sons of Hamor the father of Shechem for one hundred pieces of silver, and which had become an inheritance of the children of Joseph.

33 And ᴿEleazar the son of Aaron died. They buried him in a hill *belonging to* ᴿPhinehas his son, which was given to him in the mountains of Ephraim. Ex. 28:1 · Ex. 6:25

THE BOOK OF
Judges

Judges is a historical book of the Old Testament following the book of Joshua. The book presents a series of spiritual relapses into idolatry and ungodly living. It pictures man's weaknesses and God's strength. The judgment of God on His own people is a vital truth in this book, centering on spiritual failure and deliverance (cf. the New Testament book of Galatians).

Judges receives its name from the Hebrew word *Shophetim* (the Hebrew name of the book), which designates the leaders who delivered Israel from foreign oppressors between the death of Joshua and the beginning of the monarchy (under King Saul). The root meaning of *Shophetim* is "to govern" or "to judge"; the "judges" were various "deliverers" or "saviors" who championed their people in time of crisis.

CONTEXT. The book covers the first 350 years of Israel's history in the land of Canaan. A strong centralized government had not yet arisen in Israel. The tribes were disorganized and weak. The statement is twice repeated that "in those days there was no king in Israel; everyone did what was right in his own eyes" (17:6; 21:25). It was a time of chaos and anarchy, when God's people often fell into sin and were judged for their idolatry and immorality, until a "judge" arose to champion their cause.

AUTHORSHIP. Jewish tradition attributes authorship of this book to Samuel. It is evident that this book manifests a unity of thought, and therefore was probably written and arranged by one person. And what could be more probable than that Samuel, who links the two periods of the judges and the kings, should have had a large hand in the writing of the book? The book nowhere names its author, however, and scholars disagree on this question.

THE CYCLE OF REPRESSION. Perhaps the most striking fact about this book is the recurring cycle of sin, suffering, supplication, and salvation that occurs in its pages. For a brief period the people of Israel enjoy a time of peace and prosperity. Instead of glorifying God for His blessings, however, the people fall into the double sin of idolatry and immorality—adopting the worship and pagan life-style of the heathen people in their midst. God's judgment then falls upon the disobedient and rebellious people (3:8, 12; 4:2; 6:1; 10:7; 13:1), who are subjugated by their enemies. Out of the depths of oppression Israel cries to God in repentance, and God sends a judge to free them from bondage, restoring peace and prosperity to the land. Alas, the people again become complacent and self-willed and the vicious cycle of sin-suffering-supplication-salvation is repeated.

HOW JUDGES FITS TOGETHER. The book is divided into three periods:

(1) The period immediately after the death of Joshua (1:1—2:5)
(2) The period of the judges (2:6—16:31)
(3) The period of confusion and anarchy (17:1—21:25)

Twelve judges are listed: Othniel, Ehud, Shamgar, Deborah (with Barak), Gideon, Tola, Jair, Jephthah, Ibzan, Elon, Abdon, and Samson. Of these, six stand out preeminently: Othniel (3:7-11), Ehud (3:12-30), Deborah (4:1—5:31), Gideon (6:11—8:35), Jephthah (11:1—12:7), and Samson (13:1—16:31). These judges were only temporary "saviors"; they were able to deliver their people temporarily from oppression, but the final, once-and-for-all deliverance of God's people awaited the one and only Savior, our Lord Jesus Christ.

The book of Proverbs says, "Righteousness exalts a nation, but sin is a reproach to any people" (Prov. 14:34). This is perhaps the key message of the book of Judges. Without fear (reverence) of the Lord and a faithful keeping of His holy commandments, people become slaves of a vicious cycle of futility and lose the freedom intended for them—the glorious liberty of the children of God. When everyone does what is right in his own eyes, refusing to serve God, the true King of Israel, the way is laid open for confusion, chaos, collapse, and terrible misery.

—R.C.M.

The Continuing Conquest of Canaan

NOW after the death of Joshua it came to pass that the children of Israel asked the LORD, saying, "Who shall be first to go up for us against the ᴿCanaanites to fight against them?" Josh. 17:12, 13
2 And the LORD said, ᴿ"Judah shall go up. Indeed I have delivered the land into his hand." Gen. 49:8, 9
3 So Judah said to ᴿSimeon his brother, "Come up with me to my allotted territory, that we may fight against the Canaanites; and ᴿI will likewise go with you to your allotted territory." And Simeon went with him. Josh. 19:1 • Judg. 1:17
4 Then Judah went up, and the LORD delivered the Canaanites and the Perizzites into their hand; and they killed ten thousand men at ᴿBezek. 1 Sam. 11:8
5 And they found Adoni-Bezek in Bezek, and fought against him; and they defeated the Canaanites and the Perizzites.
6 Then Adoni-Bezek fled, and they pursued him and caught him and cut off his thumbs and big toes.
7 And Adoni-Bezek said, "Seventy kings with their thumbs and big toes cut off used to gather *scraps* under my table; as I have done, so God has repaid me." Then they brought him to Jerusalem, and there he died.
8 Now ᴿthe children of Judah fought against Jerusalem and took it; they struck it with the edge of the sword and set the city on fire. Josh. 15:63
9 ᴿAnd afterward the children of Judah went down to fight against the Canaanites who dwelt in the mountains, in the *South, and in the lowland. Josh. 10:36
10 Then Judah went against the Canaanites who dwelt in Hebron. (Now the name of Hebron *was* formerly Kirjath Arba.) And they killed Sheshai, Ahiman, and Talmai.
11 ᴿFrom there they went against the inhabitants of Debir. (The name of Debir *was* formerly Kirjath Sepher.) Josh. 15:15
12 ᴿThen Caleb said, "Whoever attacks Kirjath Sepher and takes it, to him I will give my daughter Achsah as wife." Josh. 15:16, 17
13 And Othniel the son of Kenaz, ᴿCaleb's younger brother, took it; so he gave him his daughter Achsah as wife. Judg. 3:9
14 Now it happened, when she came *to him*, that *she urged him to ask her father for a field. And she dismounted from *her* donkey, and Caleb said to her, "What do you wish?"
15 So she said to him, ᴿ"Give me a blessing; since you have given me land in the South, give me also springs of water." And Caleb gave her the upper springs and the lower springs. Gen. 33:11

1:9 Heb. *Negev,* and so throughout this book
1:14 LXX, Vg. *he urged her*

16 Now the children of the Kenite, Moses' father-in-law, went up ᴿfrom the City of Palms with the children of Judah into the Wilderness of Judah, which *lies* in the South near ᴿArad; ᴿand they went and dwelt among the people. Deut. 34:3 • Josh. 12:14 • 1 Sam. 15:6
17 And Judah went with his brother Simeon, and they attacked the Canaanites who inhabited Zephath, and utterly destroyed it. So the name of the city was called Hormah.
18 Also Judah took ᴿGaza with its territory, Ashkelon with its territory, and Ekron with its territory. Josh. 11:22
19 So the LORD was with Judah. And they drove out the mountaineers, but they could not drive out the inhabitants of the lowland, because they had ᴿchariots of iron. Josh. 17:16, 18
20 And they gave Hebron to Caleb, as Moses had said. Then he ᵀexpelled from there the three sons of Anak. *drove out*
21 But the children of Benjamin did not drive out the Jebusites who inhabited Jerusalem; so the Jebusites dwell with the children of Benjamin in Jerusalem to this day.
22 And the house of Joseph also went up against Bethel, and the LORD *was* with them.
23 So the ᵀhouse of Joseph ᴿsent men to spy out Bethel. (The name of the city was formerly ᴿLuz.) *family* • Josh. 2:1; 7:2 • Gen. 28:19
24 And when the spies saw a man coming out of the city, they said to him, "Please show us the entrance to the city, and ᴿwe will show you mercy." Josh. 2:12, 14
25 So he showed them the entrance to the city, and they struck the city with the edge of the sword; but they let the man and all his family go.
26 And the man went to the land of the Hittites, built a city, and called its name Luz, which *is* its name to this day.

Incomplete Conquest of the Land

27 ᴿHowever, Manasseh did not drive out *the inhabitants of* Beth Shean and its villages, or ᴿTaanach and its villages, or the inhabitants of ᴿDor and its villages, or the inhabitants of Ibleam and its villages, or the inhabitants of Megiddo and its villages; for the Canaanites were determined to dwell in that land. Josh. 17:11-13 • Josh. 21:25 • Josh. 17:11
28 And it came to pass, when Israel was strong, that they put the Canaanites ᵀunder tribute, but did not completely drive them out. *to forced labor*
29 ᴿNor did Ephraim drive out the Canaanites who dwelt in Gezer; so the Canaanites dwelt in Gezer among them. Josh. 16:10
30 Nor did Zebulun drive out the inhabitants of Kitron or the inhabitants of Nahalol; so the Canaanites dwelt among them, and ᵀwere put under tribute. *became forced laborers*
31 Nor did Asher drive out the inhabitants of Acco or the inhabitants of Sidon, or of Ahlab, Achzib, Helbah, Aphik, or Rehob.

32 So the Asherites ᴿdwelt among the Canaanites, the inhabitants of the land; for they did not drive them out.   Ps. 106:34, 35

33 Nor did Naphtali drive out the inhabitants of Beth Shemesh or the inhabitants of Beth Anath; but they dwelt among the Canaanites, the inhabitants of the land. Nevertheless the inhabitants of Beth Shemesh and Beth Anath were put under tribute to them.

34 And the Amorites forced the children of Dan into the mountains, for they would not allow them to come down to the valley;

35 and the Amorites were determined to dwell in Mount Heres, ᴿin Aijalon, and in *Shaalbim; yet when the strength of the house of Joseph became greater, they ᵀwere put under tribute.   Josh. 19:42 • *became forced laborers*

36 Now the boundary of the Amorites *was* ᴿfrom the Ascent of Akrabbim, from Sela, and upward.   Josh. 15:3

Israel's Disobedience

2 Then the Angel of the Lᴏʀᴅ came up from Gilgal to Bochim, and said: "I led you up from Egypt and brought you to the land of which I swore to your fathers; and I said, 'I will never break My covenant with you.

2 'And you shall make no ᵀcovenant with the inhabitants of this land; you shall tear down their altars.' But you have not obeyed My voice. Why have you done this?   *treaty*

3 "Therefore I also said, 'I will not drive them out before you; but they shall be *thorns in your side, and ᴿtheir gods shall ᵀbe a ᴿsnare to you.'"   Judg. 3:6 • *entrap* • Ps. 106:36

4 So it was, when the Angel of the Lᴏʀᴅ spoke these words to all the children of Israel, that the people lifted up their voices and wept.

5 Then they called the name of that place ᵀBochim; and they sacrificed there to the Lᴏʀᴅ.   Lit. *Weeping*

6 And when Joshua had dismissed the people, the children of Israel went each to his own inheritance to possess the land.

Death of Joshua

7 ᴿSo the people served the Lᴏʀᴅ all the days of Joshua, and all the days of the elders who outlived Joshua, who had seen all the great works of the Lᴏʀᴅ which He had done for Israel.   Josh. 24:31

8 Now ᴿJoshua the son of Nun, the servant of the Lᴏʀᴅ, died *when he was* one hundred and ten years old.   Josh. 24:29

9 ᴿAnd they buried him within the border of his inheritance at ᴿTimnath Heres, in the mountains of Ephraim, on the north side of Mount Gaash.   Josh. 24:30 • Josh. 19:49, 50

1:35 *Shaalabin,* Josh. 19:42
2:3 LXX, Tg., Vg. *enemies to you*

10 When all that generation had been gathered to their fathers, another generation arose after them who did not know the Lᴏʀᴅ nor the work which He had done for Israel.

Israel's Unfaithfulness

11 Then the children of Israel did evil in the sight of the Lᴏʀᴅ, and served the Baals;

12 and they forsook the Lᴏʀᴅ God of their fathers, who had brought them out of the land of Egypt; and they followed other gods from *among* the gods of the people who *were* all around them, and they bowed down to them; and they provoked the Lᴏʀᴅ to anger.

13 They forsook the Lᴏʀᴅ and served Baal and the ᵀAshtoreths.   *Canaanite goddesses*

14 And the anger of the Lᴏʀᴅ was hot against Israel. So He delivered them into the hands of plunderers who despoiled them; and He sold them into the hands of their enemies all around, so that they ᴿcould no longer stand before their enemies.   Lev. 26:37

15 Wherever they went out, the hand of the Lᴏʀᴅ was against them for calamity, as the Lᴏʀᴅ had said, and as the Lᴏʀᴅ had sworn to them. And they were greatly distressed.

16 Nevertheless, ᴿthe Lᴏʀᴅ raised up judges who delivered them out of the hand of those who plundered them.   Ps. 106:43–45

17 Yet they would not listen to their judges, but they ᴿplayed the harlot with other gods, and bowed down to them. They turned quickly from the way in which their fathers walked, in obeying the commandments of the Lᴏʀᴅ; they did not do so.   Ex. 34:15

18 And when the Lᴏʀᴅ raised up judges for them, ᴿthe Lᴏʀᴅ was with the judge and delivered them out of the hand of their enemies all the days of the judge; ᴿfor the Lᴏʀᴅ was moved to pity by their groaning because of those who oppressed them and harassed them.   Josh. 1:5 • Gen. 6:6

19 And it came to pass, ᴿwhen the judge was dead, that they reverted and behaved more corruptly than their fathers, by following other gods, to serve them and bow down to them. They did not cease from their own doings nor from their stubborn way.   Judg. 3:12

20 Then the anger of the Lᴏʀᴅ was hot against Israel; and He said, "Because this nation has ᴿtransgressed My covenant which I commanded their fathers, and has not heeded My voice,   [Josh. 23:16]

21 "I also will no longer drive out before them any of the nations which Joshua ᴿleft when he died,   Josh. 23:4, 5, 13

22 "so ᴿthat through them I may ᴿtest Israel, whether they will keep the ways of the Lᴏʀᴅ, to walk in them as their fathers kept *them,* or not."   Judg. 3:1, 4 • Deut. 8:2, 16; 13:3

23 Therefore the Lᴏʀᴅ left those nations, without driving them out immediately; nor did He deliver them into the hand of Joshua.

The Nations Remaining in the Land

3 Now these *are* ᴿthe nations which the LORD left, that He might test Israel by them, *that is,* all who had not ᵀknown any of the wars in Canaan   Judg. 1:1; 2:21, 22 · *experienced*

2 (*this was* only so that the generations of the children of Israel might be taught to know war, at least those who had not formerly known it),

3 *namely,* ᴿfive lords of the Philistines, all the Canaanites, the Sidonians, and the Hivites who dwelt in Mount Lebanon, from Mount Baal Hermon to the entrance of Hamath.   Josh. 13:3

4 And they were *left, that He might* test Israel by them, to ᵀknow whether they would obey the commandments of the LORD, which He had commanded their fathers by the hand of Moses.   *find out*

5 Thus the children of Israel dwelt among the Canaanites, the Hittites, the Amorites, the Perizzites, the Hivites, and the Jebusites.

6 And ᴿthey took their daughters to be their wives, and gave their daughters to their sons; and they served their gods.   Ex. 34:15, 16

Othniel

7 So the children of Israel did evil in the sight of the LORD. They forgot the LORD their God, and served the Baals and ᵀAsherahs.   Name or symbol for Canaanite goddesses

8 Therefore the anger of the LORD was hot against Israel, and He ᴿsold them into the hand of Cushan-Rishathaim king of Mesopotamia; and the children of Israel served Cushan-Rishathaim eight years.   Judg. 2:14

9 When the children of Israel ᴿcried out to the LORD, the LORD ᴿraised up a deliverer for the children of Israel, who delivered them: ᴿOthniel the son of Kenaz, Caleb's younger brother.   Judg. 3:15 · Judg. 2:16 · Judg. 1:13

10 The Spirit of the LORD came upon him, and he judged Israel. He went out to war, and the LORD delivered Cushan-Rishathaim king of Mesopotamia into his hand; and his hand prevailed over Cushan-Rishathaim.

11 So the land had rest for forty years. Then Othniel the son of Kenaz died.

Ehud

12 ᴿAnd the children of Israel again did evil in the sight of the LORD. So the LORD strengthened ᴿEglon king of Moab against Israel, because they had done evil in the sight of the LORD.   Judg. 2:19 · 1 Sam. 12:9

13 Then he gathered to himself the people of Ammon and ᴿAmalek, went and ᵀdefeated Israel, and took possession of ᴿthe City of Palms.   Judg. 5:14 · *struck* · Judg. 1:16

14 So the children of Israel ᴿserved Eglon king of Moab eighteen years.   Deut. 28:48

15 But when the children of Israel ᴿcried out to the LORD, the LORD raised up a deliverer for them: Ehud the son of Gera, the Benjamite, a ᴿleft-handed man. By him the children of Israel sent tribute to Eglon king of Moab.   Ps. 78:34 · Judg. 20:16

16 Now Ehud made himself a dagger (it was double-edged and a ᵀcubit in length) and fastened it under his clothes on his right thigh.   18 in.

17 So he brought the tribute to Eglon king of Moab. (Now Eglon *was* a very fat man.)

18 And when he had finished presenting the tribute, he sent away the people who had carried the tribute.

19 But he himself turned back ᴿfrom the *stone images that *were* at Gilgal, and said, "I have a secret message for you, O king." He said, "Keep silence!" And all who attended him went out from him.   Josh. 4:20

20 So Ehud came to him (now he was sitting upstairs in his cool private chamber). Then Ehud said, "I have a message from God for you." So he arose from *his* seat.

21 Then Ehud reached with his left hand, took the dagger from his right thigh, and thrust it into his belly.

22 Even the ᵀhilt went in after the blade, and the fat closed over the blade, for he did not draw the dagger out of his belly; and his entrails came out.   *handle*

23 Then Ehud went out through the porch and shut the doors of the upper room behind him and locked them.

24 When he had gone out, ᵀEglon's servants came to look, and *to their* surprise, the doors of the upper room were locked. So they said, "He is probably ᵀattending to his needs in the cool chamber."   Lit. *his* · Lit. *covering his feet*

25 So they waited till they were ᴿembarrassed, and still he had not opened the doors of the upper room. Therefore they took the key and opened *them.* And there was their master, fallen dead on the floor.   2 Kin. 2:17; 8:11

26 But Ehud had escaped while they delayed, and passed beyond the *stone images and escaped to Seirah.

27 And it happened, when he arrived, that he blew the trumpet in the ᴿmountains of Ephraim, and the children of Israel went down with him from the mountains; and ᵀhe led them.   Josh. 17:15 · Lit. *he went before them*

28 Then he said to them, "Follow *me,* for ᴿthe LORD has delivered your enemies the Moabites into your hand." So they went down after him, seized the ᴿfords of the Jordan leading to Moab, and did not allow anyone to cross over.   Judg. 7:9, 15 · Josh. 2:7

29 And at that time they killed about ten thousand men of Moab, all stout men of valor; not a man escaped.

30 So Moab was subdued that day under the hand of Israel. And ᴿthe land had rest for eighty years.   Judg. 3:11

3:19 Tg. *quarries*
3:26 Tg. *quarries*

Shamgar

31 After him was ᴿShamgar the son of Anath, who killed six hundred men of the Philistines with an ox goad; ᴿand he also delivered ᴿIsrael.   Judg. 5:6 · Judg. 2:16 · 1 Sam. 4:1

Deborah

4 When Ehud was dead, ᴿthe children of Israel again did ᴿevil in the sight of the Lᴏʀᴅ.   Judg. 2:19 · Judg. 2:11

2 So the Lᴏʀᴅ sold them into the hand of Jabin king of Canaan, who reigned in Hazor. The commander of his army *was* Sisera, who dwelt in ᴿHarosheth Hagoyim.   Judg. 4:13, 16

3 And the children of Israel cried out to the Lᴏʀᴅ; for Jabin had nine hundred chariots of iron, and for twenty years he had harshly oppressed the children of Israel.

4 Now Deborah, a prophetess, the wife of Lapidoth, was judging Israel at that time.

5 ᴿAnd she would sit under the palm tree of Deborah between Ramah and Bethel in the mountains of Ephraim. And the children of Israel came up to her for judgment.   Gen. 35:8

6 Then she sent and called for Barak the son of Abinoam from Kedesh in Naphtali, and said to him, "Has not the Lᴏʀᴅ God of Israel commanded, 'Go and ᵀdeploy *troops* at Mount ᴿTabor; take with you ten thousand men of the sons of Naphtali and of the sons of Zebulun;   march · Judg. 8:18

7 'and against you I will deploy Sisera, the commander of Jabin's army, with his chariots and his multitude at the River Kishon; and I will ᵀdeliver him into your hand'?"   Lit. *draw*

8 And Barak said to her, "If you will go with me, then I will go; but if you will not go with me, I will not go!"

9 So she said, "I will surely go with you; nevertheless there will be no glory for you in the journey you are taking, for the Lᴏʀᴅ will ᴿsell Sisera into the hand of a woman." Then Deborah arose and went with Barak to Kedesh.   Judg. 2:14

10 And Barak called Zebulun and Naphtali to Kedesh; he went up with ten thousand men ᴿunderᵀ his command, and Deborah went up with him.   1 Kin. 20:10 · Lit. *at his feet*

11 Now Heber the Kenite, of the children of Hobab the father-in-law of Moses, had separated himself from the Kenites and pitched his tent near the terebinth tree at Zaanaim, ᴿwhich *is* beside Kedesh.   Judg. 4:6

12 And they reported to Sisera that Barak the son of Abinoam had gone up to Mount Tabor.

13 So Sisera gathered together all his chariots, nine hundred chariots of iron, and all the people who *were* with him, from Harosheth Hagoyim to the River Kishon.

14 Then Deborah said to Barak, ᵀ"Up! For this *is* the day in which the Lᴏʀᴅ has delivered Sisera into your hand. ᴿHas not the Lᴏʀᴅ gone out before you?" So Barak went down

from Mount Tabor with ten thousand men following him.   *Arise!* · Deut. 9:3; 31:3

15 And the Lᴏʀᴅ routed Sisera and all *his* chariots and all *his* army with the edge of the sword before Barak; and Sisera alighted from *his* chariot and fled away on foot.

16 But Barak pursued the chariots and the army as far as Harosheth Hagoyim, and all the army of Sisera fell by the edge of the sword; not a man was ᴿleft.   Ex. 14:28

17 However, Sisera had fled away on foot to the tent of ᴿJael, the wife of Heber the Kenite; for *there was* peace between Jabin king of Hazor and the house of Heber the Kenite.   Judg. 5:6

18 And Jael went out to meet Sisera, and said to him, "Turn aside, my lord, turn aside to me; do not fear." And when he had turned aside with her into the tent, she covered him with a ᵀblanket.   *rug*

19 Then he said to her, "Please give me a little water to drink, for I am thirsty." So she opened ᴿa jug of milk, gave him a drink, and covered him.   Judg. 5:24–27

20 And he said to her, "Stand at the door of the tent, and if any man comes and inquires of you, and says, 'Is there any man here?' you shall say, 'No.'"

21 Then Jael, Heber's wife, took a tent peg and took a hammer in her hand, and went softly to him and drove the peg into his temple, and it went down into the ground; for he was fast asleep and weary. So he died.

22 And then, as Barak pursued Sisera, Jael came out to meet him, and said to him, "Come, I will show you the man whom you seek." And when he went into her *tent*, there lay Sisera, dead with the peg in his temple.

23 So on that day God subdued Jabin king of Canaan in the presence of the children of Israel.

24 And the hand of the children of Israel grew stronger and stronger against Jabin king of Canaan, until they had destroyed Jabin king of Canaan.

The Song of Deborah

5 Then Deborah and Barak the son of Abinoam sang on that day, saying:

2 "Whenᵀ leaders lead in Israel,
    When the people willingly offer themselves,
    Bless the Lᴏʀᴅ!   Or *When locks are loosed*

3 "Hear,ᴿ O kings! Give ear, O princes!
    I, *even* ᴿI, will sing to the Lᴏʀᴅ;
    I will sing praise to the Lᴏʀᴅ God of Israel.   Deut. 32:1, 3 · Ps. 27:6

4 "Lᴏʀᴅ, ᴿwhen You went out from Seir,
    When You marched from ᴿthe field of Edom,   Deut. 33:2 · Ps. 68:8
    The earth trembled and the heavens poured,
    The clouds also poured water;

5 ᴿThe mountains ᵀgushed before the
  LORD,   Ps. 97:5 · flowed
  ᴿThis Sinai, before the LORD God of
  Israel.   Ex. 19:18

6 "In the days of ᴿShamgar, son of Anath,
  In the days of ᴿJael,   Judg. 3:31 · Judg. 4:17
  ᴿThe highways were deserted,   Is. 33:8
  And the travelers walked along the
  byways.

7 Village life ceased, it ceased in Israel,
  Until I, Deborah, arose,
  Arose a mother in Israel.

8 They chose ᴿnew gods;   Deut. 32:17
  Then there was war in the gates;
  Not a shield or spear was seen among
  forty thousand in Israel.

9 My heart is with the rulers of Israel
  Who offered themselves willingly with
  the people.
  Bless the LORD!

10 "Speak, you who ride on white
   ᴿdonkeys,
   Who sit in judges' attire,   Judg. 10:4; 12:14
   And who walk along the road.

11 Far from the noise of the archers,
   among the watering places,
   There they shall recount the righteous
   acts of the LORD,
   The righteous acts for His villagers in
   Israel;
   Then the people of the LORD shall go
   down to the gates.

12 "Awake,ᴿ awake, Deborah!   Ps. 57:8
   Awake, awake, sing a song!
   Arise, Barak, and lead your captives
   away,
   O son of Abinoam!

13 "Then the survivors came down, the
   people against the nobles;
   The LORD came down for me against
   the mighty.

14 From Ephraim were those whose roots
   were in ᴿAmalek.   Judg. 3:13
   After you, Benjamin, with your peoples,
   From Machir rulers came down,
   And from Zebulun those who bear the
   recruiter's staff.

15 And *the princes of Issachar were with
   Deborah;
   As Issachar, so was Barak
   Sent into the valley ᵀunder his
   command;   Lit. at his feet
   Among the divisions of Reuben
   There were great resolves of heart.

16 Why did you sit among the sheepfolds,
   To hear the pipings for the flocks?
   The divisions of Reuben have great
   searchings of heart.

17 Gilead stayed beyond the Jordan,

And why did Dan remain *on ships?
ᴿAsher continued at the seashore,
And stayed by his inlets.   Josh. 19:29, 31

18 ᴿZebulun is a people who jeopardized
   their lives to the point of death,
   Naphtali also, on the heights of the
   battlefield.   Judg. 4:6, 10

19 "The kings came and fought,
   Then the kings of Canaan fought
   In ᴿTaanach, by the waters of Megiddo;
   They took no spoils of silver.   Judg. 1:27

20 They fought from the heavens;
   The stars from their courses fought
   against Sisera.

21 ᴿThe torrent of Kishon swept them
   away,   Judg. 4:7
   That ancient torrent, the torrent of
   Kishon.
   O my soul, march on in strength!

22 Then the horses' hooves pounded,
   The galloping, galloping of his steeds.

23 'Curse Meroz,' said the ᵀangel of the
   LORD,   Or Angel
   'Curse its inhabitants bitterly,
   Because they did not come to the help
   of the LORD,
   To the help of the LORD against the
   mighty.'

24 "Most blessed among women is Jael,
   The wife of Heber the Kenite;
   Blessed is she among women in tents.

25 He asked for water, she gave milk;
   She brought out cream in a lordly bowl.

26 She stretched her hand to the tent peg,
   Her right hand to the workmen's
   hammer;
   She pounded Sisera, she pierced his
   head,
   She split and struck through his temple.

27 At her feet he sank, he fell, he lay still;
   At her feet he sank, he fell;
   Where he sank, there he fell dead.

28 "The mother of Sisera looked through
   the window,
   And cried out through the lattice,
   'Why is his chariot so long in coming?
   Why tarries the clatter of his chariots?'

29 Her wisest ᵀladies answered her,
   Yes, she answered herself,   princesses

30 'Are they not finding and dividing the
   spoil:
   To every man a girl or two;
   For Sisera, plunder of dyed garments,
   Plunder of garments embroidered and
   dyed,
   Two pieces of dyed embroidery for the
   neck of the looter?'

31 "Thus let all Your enemies ᴿperish, O
   LORD!   Ps. 92:9

5:15 So with LXX, Syr., Tg., Vg.; MT And my princes in
Issachar

5:17 Or at ease

But *let* those who love Him *be* [R]like the
[R]sun
When it comes out in full strength."
2 Sam. 23:4 • Ps. 37:6; 89:36, 37

So the land had rest for forty years.

Midianites Oppress Israel

6 Then the children of Israel did [R]evil in the
sight of the LORD. So the LORD delivered
them into the hand of [R]Midian for seven
years,
Judg. 2:11 • Num. 22:4; 31:1-3

2 and the hand of Midian prevailed against
Israel. Because of the Midianites, the children
of Israel made for themselves the dens, [R]the
caves, and the strongholds which *are* in the
mountains.
1 Sam. 13:6

3 So it was, whenever Israel had sown,
Midianites would come up; also Amalekites
and the [R]people of the East would come up
against them.
Judg. 7:12

4 Then they would encamp against them
and [R]destroy the produce of the earth as far
as Gaza, and leave no sustenance for Israel,
neither sheep nor ox nor donkey.
Lev. 26:16

5 For they would come up with their livestock and their tents, coming in as numerous
as locusts; both they and their camels were
[T]without number; and they would enter the
land to destroy it.
innumerable

6 So Israel was greatly impoverished be-
cause of the Midianites, and the children of
Israel [R]cried out to the LORD.
Hos. 5:15

7 And it came to pass, when the children
of Israel cried out to the LORD because of the
Midianites,

8 that the LORD sent a prophet to the
children of Israel, who said to them, "Thus
says the LORD God of Israel: 'I brought you
up from Egypt and brought you out of the
[R]house of [T]bondage;
Josh. 24:17 • slaves

9 'and I delivered you out of the hand of
the Egyptians and out of the hand of all who
oppressed you, and [R]drove them out before
you and gave you their land.
Ps. 44:2, 3

10 'Also I said to you, "I *am* the LORD your
God; do not fear the gods of the Amorites, in
whose land you dwell. But you have not
obeyed My [R]voice." ' "
Judg. 2:1, 2

Gideon

11 Now the Angel of the LORD came and sat
under the terebinth tree which *was* in Ophrah, which *belonged* to Joash [R]the Abiezrite,
while his son [R]Gideon threshed wheat in the
winepress, in order to hide *it* from the Midianites.
Josh. 17:2 • Heb. 11:32

12 And the [R]Angel of the LORD appeared to

him, and said to him, "The LORD *is* [R]with you,
you mighty man of valor!"
Judg. 13:3 • Josh. 1:5

13 Gideon said to Him, "O my lord, if the
LORD is with us, why then has all this happened to us? And where *are* all His miracles
[R]which our fathers told us about, saying, 'Did
not the LORD bring us up from Egypt?' But
now the LORD has forsaken us and delivered
us into the hands of the Midianites."
Ps. 44:1

14 Then the LORD turned to him and said,
[R]"Go in this might of yours, and you shall
save Israel from the hand of the Midianites.
[R]Have I not sent you?"
1 Sam. 12:11 • Josh. 1:9

15 So he said to Him, "O [T]my Lord, how can
I save Israel? Indeed [R]my clan *is* the weakest
in Manasseh, and I *am* the least in my father's house."
Heb. Adonai, used of God • 1 Sam. 9:21

16 And the LORD said to him, [R]"Surely I will
be with you, and you shall [T]defeat the Midianites as one man."
Ex. 3:12 • Lit. strike

17 Then he said to Him, "If now I have
found favor in Your sight, then show me a
sign that it is You who talk with me.

18 [R]"Do not depart from here, I pray, until I
come to You and bring out my offering and
set *it* before You." And He said, "I will wait
until you come back."
Gen. 18:3, 5

19 [R]So Gideon went in and prepared a
young goat, and unleavened bread from an
[T]ephah of flour. The meat he put in a basket,
and he put the broth in a pot; and he brought
them out to Him under the terebinth tree and
presented *them*.
Gen. 18:6-8 • 20.87 qt.

20 The Angel of God said to him, "Take the
meat and the unleavened bread and [R]lay
them on this rock, and [R]pour out the broth."
And he did so.
Judg. 13:19 • 1 Kin. 18:33, 34

21 Then the Angel of the LORD put out the
end of the staff that *was* in His hand, and
touched the meat and the unleavened bread;
and fire rose out of the rock and consumed
the meat and the unleavened bread. And the
Angel of the LORD departed out of his sight.

22 Now Gideon [R]perceived that He *was* the
Angel of the LORD. So Gideon said, "Alas, O
Lord GOD! [R]For I have seen the Angel of the
LORD face to face."
Judg. 13:21, 22 • Gen. 16:13

23 Then the LORD said to him, "Peace *be*
with you; do not fear, you shall not die."

4-D. Jehovah-Shalom: The LORD Is Peace ▼

24 So Gideon built an altar there to the
LORD, and called it *The-LORD-Is-Peace. To
this day it *is* still in Ophrah of the Abiezrites. ▲

6:24 Heb. YHWH Shalom, Lit. The LORD is Peace

4-D. Jehovah-Shalom: The LORD Is Peace (Judges 6:24)—During part of the period of the judges, the
Midianites held Israel in subjugation and made raids against Israel's farming communities. God, through the
angel of the Lord, called upon Gideon, a seemingly fearful man, to lead the fight against Israel's oppressors
(vv. 1-16). When Gideon, haltingly, asked for a sign—the first of three he would request to confirm his call
(vv. 17, 36-40)—the Angel touched the altar with his staff. Fire at once sprang from the altar, consuming the
(Point 4-D continued on next page)

25 Now it came to pass the same night that the LORD said to him, "Take your father's young bull, the second bull of seven years old, and tear down the altar of Baal that your father has, and ᴿcut down the *wooden image that is beside it;   Ex. 34:13

26 "and build an altar to the LORD your God on top of this ᵀrock in the proper arrangement, and take the second bull and offer a burnt sacrifice with the wood of the image which you shall cut down."   stronghold

27 So Gideon took ten men from among his servants and did as the LORD had said to him. But because he feared his father's household and the men of the city too much to do it by day, he did it by night.

Gideon Destroys the Altar of Baal

28 And when the men of the city arose early in the morning, there was the altar of Baal, torn down; and the wooden image that was beside it was cut down, and the second bull was being offered on the altar which had been built.

29 So they said to one another, "Who has done this thing?" And when they had inquired and asked, they said, "Gideon the son of Joash has done this thing."

30 Then the men of the city said to Joash, "Bring out your son, that he may die, because he has torn down the altar of Baal, and because he has cut down the wooden image that was beside it."

31 But Joash said to all who stood against him, "Would you ᵀplead for Baal? Would you save him? Let the one who would plead for

him be put to death by morning! If he is a god, let him plead for himself, because his altar has been torn down!"   contend

32 Therefore on that day he called him *Jerubbaal, saying, "Let Baal plead against him, because he has torn down his altar."

33 Then all ᴿthe Midianites and Amalekites, the people of the East, gathered together; and they crossed over and encamped in ᴿthe Valley of Jezreel.   Judg. 6:3 · Josh. 17:16

34 But the Spirit of the LORD came upon Gideon; then he ᴿblew the trumpet, and the Abiezrites gathered behind him.   Judg. 3:27

35 And he sent messengers throughout all Manasseh, who also gathered behind him. He also sent messengers to ᴿAsher, ᴿZebulun, and Naphtali; and they came up to meet them.   Judg. 5:17; 7:23 · Judg. 4:6, 10; 5:18

The Sign of the Fleece

36 So Gideon said to God, "If You will save Israel by my hand as You have said—

37 ᴿ"look, I shall put a fleece of wool on the threshing floor; if there is dew on the fleece only, and it is dry on all the ground, then I shall know that You will save Israel by my hand, as You have said."   [Ex. 4:3-7]

38 And it was so. When he rose early the next morning and squeezed the fleece together, he wrung the dew out of the fleece, a bowlful of water.

39 Then Gideon said to God, "Do not be angry with me, but let me speak just once

6:25 Or *Asherah,* a Canaanite goddess
6:32 Lit. *Let Baal Plead*

(Point 4-D continued from previous page)
sacrifice, and the Angel of the Lord suddenly vanished (vv. 17–21). At this miraculous event Gideon was afraid, realizing that he had seen the holy face of the Angel of the Lord, and that he might be about to die (v. 22). God spoke, "Peace be with you; do not fear, you shall not die" (v. 23). Then Gideon built an altar to God and named it *Jehovah-Shalom,* "The LORD Is Peace" (v. 24).

From the above account we observe:

(1) The holy, almighty presence of the Lord can be a fearful sight to any mortal person—whether an angel, archangel, or Christ Himself in a Christophany (an Old Testament appearance of Christ) who appeared to Gideon (Luke 24:13-35, page 1046).

(2) But when God Himself says to us, "Peace be with you; do not fear, you shall not die" (v. 23), then we are safe and secure, and all fear may be dismissed.

(3) Christ, before His death, said to His disciples, "Peace I leave with you, My peace I give to you" (John 14:27, page 1076). He was vitally concerned that His followers have peace

    (a) with God;
    (b) among themselves;
    (c) within their individual souls and minds.

His peace passes all human understanding (Phil. 4:7, page 1198).

(4) Christ's coming kingdom will be a kingdom of peace (Rom. 14:17, page 1144).

(5) His peace is God's gift, to be received when the sinner accepts Christ as personal Savior. He or she is then justified by faith and has "peace with God" (Rom. 5:1, page 1133).

We should learn, as did Gideon, that our true peace can only come from Jehovah-Shalom, "The LORD Is Peace."

See Jeremiah 23:6, page 735, for **Point 4-E: Jehovah-Tsidkenu: The LORD Our Righteousness.**

more: Let me test, I pray, just once more with the fleece; let it now be dry only on the fleece, but on all the ground let there be dew."

40 And God did so that night. It was dry on the fleece only, but there was dew on all the ground.

Gideon's Valiant Three Hundred

7 Then ᴿJerubbaal (that *is*, Gideon) and all the people who *were* with him rose early and encamped beside the well of Harod, so that the camp of the Midianites was on the north side of them by the hill of Moreh in the valley.   Judg. 6:32

2 And the LORD said to Gideon, "The people who *are* with you *are* too many for Me to give the Midianites into their hands, lest Israel ᴿclaim glory for itself against Me, saying, 'My own hand has saved me.'   Deut. 8:17

3 "Now therefore, proclaim in the hearing of the people, saying, ᴿ'Whoever *is* fearful and afraid, let him turn and depart at once from Mount Gilead.' " And twenty-two thousand of the people returned, and ten thousand remained.   Deut. 20:8

4 But the LORD said to Gideon, "The people *are* still *too* many; bring them down to the water, and I will test them for you there. Then it will be, *that* of whom I say to you, 'This one shall go with you,' the same shall go with you; and of whomever I say to you, 'This one shall not go with you,' the same shall not go."

5 So he brought the people down to the water. And the LORD said to Gideon, "Everyone who laps from the water with his tongue, as a dog laps, you shall set apart by himself; likewise everyone who gets down on his knees to drink."

6 And the number of those who lapped, *putting* their hand to their mouth, was three hundred men; but all the rest of the people got down on their knees to drink water.

7 Then the LORD said to Gideon, ᴿ"By the three hundred men who lapped I will save you, and deliver the Midianites into your hand. Let all the *other* people go, every man to his ᵀplace."   1 Sam. 14:6 • home

8 So the people took provisions and their trumpets in their hands. And he sent away all *the rest of* Israel, every man to his tent, and retained those three hundred men. Now the camp of Midian was below him in the valley.

9 It happened on the same night that the LORD said to him, "Arise, go down against the camp, for I have delivered it into your hand.

10 "But if you are afraid to go down, go down to the camp with Purah your servant,

11 "and you shall hear what they say; and afterward your hands shall be strengthened to go down against the camp." Then he went down with Purah his servant to the outpost of the armed men who *were* in the camp.

12 Now the Midianites and Amalekites, all

the people of the East, were lying in the valley ᴿas numerous as locusts; and their camels *were* ᵀwithout number, as the sand by the seashore in multitude.   Judg. 6:5 • innumerable

13 And when Gideon had come, there was a man telling a dream to his companion. He said, "I have had a dream: *To my* surprise, a loaf of barley bread tumbled into the camp of Midian; it came to a tent and struck it so that it fell and overturned, and the tent collapsed."

14 Then his companion answered and said, "This *is* nothing else but the sword of Gideon the son of Joash, a man of Israel! Into his hand ᴿGod has delivered Midian and the whole camp."   Judg. 6:14, 16

15 And so it was, when Gideon heard the telling of the dream and its interpretation, that he worshiped. He returned to the camp of Israel, and said, "Arise, for the LORD has delivered the camp of Midian into your hand."

16 Then he divided the three hundred men *into* three companies, and he put a trumpet into every man's hand, with empty pitchers, and torches inside the pitchers.

17 And he said to them, "Look at me and do likewise; watch, and when I come to the edge of the camp you shall do as I do:

18 "When I blow the trumpet, I and all who *are* with me, then you also blow the trumpets on every side of the whole camp, and say, 'The sword of the LORD and of Gideon!' "

19 So Gideon and the hundred men who *were* with him came to the outpost of the camp at the beginning of the middle watch, just as they had posted the watch; and they blew the trumpets and broke the pitchers that *were* in their hands.

20 Then the three companies blew the trumpets and broke the pitchers—they held the torches in their left hands and the trumpets in their right hands for blowing—and they cried, "The sword of the LORD and of Gideon!"

21 And ᴿevery man stood in his place all around the camp; ᴿand the whole army ran and cried out and fled.   2 Chr. 20:17 • 2 Kin. 7:7

22 When the three hundred blew the trumpets, ᴿthe LORD set every man's sword against his companion throughout the whole camp; and the army fled to ᵀBeth Acacia, toward Zererah, as far as the border of Abel Meholah, by Tabbath.   Is. 9:4 • Heb. *Beth Shittah*

23 And the men of Israel gathered together from ᴿNaphtali, Asher, and all Manasseh, and pursued the Midianites.   Judg. 6:35

24 Then Gideon sent messengers throughout all the mountains of Ephraim, saying, "Come down against the Midianites, and seize from them the watering places as far as Beth Barah and the Jordan." Then all the men of Ephraim gathered together and

ᴿseized the watering places as far as ᴿBeth Barah and the Jordan.   Judg. 3:28 • John 1:28

25 And they captured two princes of the Midianites, Oreb and Zeeb. They killed Oreb at the rock of Oreb, and Zeeb they killed at the winepress of Zeeb. They pursued Midian and brought the heads of Oreb and Zeeb to Gideon on the other side of the Jordan.

Gideon Subdues the Midianites

8 Now ᴿthe men of Ephraim said to him, "Why have you done this to us by not calling us when you went to fight with the Midianites?" And they reprimanded him sharply.   Judg. 12:1

2 So he said to them, "What have I done now in comparison with you? Is not the gleaning of the grapes of Ephraim better than ᵀthe vintage of Abiezer?   The whole harvest

3 ᴿ"God has delivered into your hands the princes of Midian, Oreb and Zeeb. And what was I able to do in comparison with you?" Then their ᴿanger toward him subsided when he said that.   Judg. 7:24, 25 • Prov. 15:1

4 When Gideon came ᴿto the Jordan, he and ᴿthe three hundred men who were with him crossed over, exhausted but still in pursuit.   Judg. 7:25 • Judg. 7:6

5 Then he said to the men of ᴿSuccoth, "Please give loaves of bread to the people who follow me, for they are exhausted, and I am pursuing Zebah and Zalmunna, kings of Midian."   Gen. 33:17

6 And the leaders of Succoth said, ᴿ"Areᵀ the hands of Zebah and Zalmunna now in your hand, that ᴿwe should give bread to your army?"   Judg. 8:15 • Lit. Is the palm • 1 Sam. 25:11

7 So Gideon said, "For this cause, when the LORD has delivered Zebah and Zalmunna into my hand, then I will tear your flesh with the thorns of the wilderness and with briers!"

8 Then he went up from there ᴿto Penuel and spoke to them in the same way. And the men of Penuel answered him as the men of Succoth had answered.   Gen. 32:30, 31

9 So he also spoke to the men of Penuel, saying, "When I ᴿcome back in peace, ᴿI will tear down this tower!"   1 Kin. 22:27 • Judg. 8:17

10 Now Zebah and Zalmunna were at Karkor, and their armies with them, about fifteen thousand, all who were left of ᴿall the army of the people of the East; for ᴿone hundred and twenty thousand men who drew the sword had fallen.   Judg. 7:12 • Judg. 6:5

11 Then Gideon went up by the road of those who dwell in tents on the east of Nobah and Jogbehah; and he ᵀattacked the army while the camp felt secure.   Lit. struck

12 When Zebah and Zalmunna fled, he pursued them; and he ᴿtook the two kings of Midian, Zebah and Zalmunna, and routed the whole army.   Ps. 83:11

13 Then Gideon the son of Joash returned from battle, from the Ascent of Heres.

14 And he caught a young man of the men of Succoth and interrogated him; and he wrote down for him the leaders of Succoth and its elders, seventy-seven men.

15 Then he came to the men of Succoth and said, "Here are Zebah and Zalmunna, about whom you ᴿridiculed me, saying, 'Are the hands of Zebah and Zalmunna now in your hand, that we should give bread to your weary men?'"   Judg. 8:6

16 And he took the elders of the city, and thorns of the wilderness and briers, and with them he taught the men of Succoth.

17 Then he tore down the tower of ᴿPenuel and killed the men of the city.   1 Kin. 12:25

18 And he said to Zebah and Zalmunna, "What kind of men were they whom you killed at ᴿTabor?" So they answered, "As you are, so were they; each one resembled the son of a king."   Judg. 4:6

19 Then he said, "They were my brothers, the sons of my mother. As the LORD lives, if you had let them live, I would not kill you."

20 And he said to Jether his firstborn, "Rise, kill them!" But the youth would not draw his sword; for he was afraid, because he was still a youth.

21 So Zebah and Zalmunna said, "Rise yourself, and kill us; for as a man is, so is his strength." So Gideon arose and killed Zebah and Zalmunna, and took the crescent ornaments that were on their camels' necks.

Gideon's Ephod

22 Then the men of Israel said to Gideon, ᴿ"Rule over us, both you and your son, and your grandson also; for you have delivered us from the hand of Midian."   [Judg. 9:8]

23 But Gideon said to them, "I will not rule over you, nor shall my son rule over you; ᴿthe LORD shall rule over you."   1 Sam. 8:7; 10:19; 12:12

24 Then Gideon said to them, "I would like to make a request of you, that each of you would give me the earrings from his plunder." For they had golden earrings, ᴿbecause they were Ishmaelites.   Gen. 37:25, 28

25 So they answered, "We will gladly give them." And they spread out a garment, and each man threw into it the earrings from his plunder.

26 Now the weight of the gold earrings that he requested was one thousand seven hundred shekels of gold, besides the crescent ornaments, pendants, and purple robes which were on the kings of Midian, and besides the chains that were around their camels' necks.

27 Then Gideon made it into an ephod and set it up in his city, Ophrah. And all Israel ᴿplayed the harlot with it there. It became a snare to Gideon and to his house.   [Ps. 106:39]

28 Thus Midian was subdued before the children of Israel, so that they lifted their

heads no more. ᴿAnd the country was quiet for forty years in the days of Gideon. Judg. 5:31

Death of Gideon

29 Then ᴿJerubbaal the son of Joash went and dwelt in his own house. Judg. 6:32; 7:1
30 Gideon had seventy sons who were his own offspring, for he had many wives.
31 ᴿAnd his concubine who *was* in Shechem also bore him a son, whose name he called Abimelech. Judg. 9:1
32 Now Gideon the son of Joash died at a good old age, and was buried in the tomb of Joash his father, in Ophrah of the Abiezrites.
33 So it was, ᴿas soon as Gideon was dead, that the children of Israel again ᴿplayed the harlot with the Baals, ᴿand made Baal-Berith their god. Judg. 2:19 • Judg. 2:17 • Judg. 9:4, 46
34 Thus the children of Israel ᴿdid not remember the LORD their God, who had delivered them from the hands of all their enemies on every side; Deut. 4:9
35 nor did they show kindness to the house of Jerubbaal (Gideon) in accordance with the good he had done for Israel.

Abimelech's Conspiracy

9 Then Abimelech the son of Jerubbaal went to Shechem, to his mother's brothers, and spoke with them and with all the family of the house of his mother's father, saying,
2 "Please speak in the hearing of all the men of Shechem: 'Which is better for you, that all ᴿseventy of the sons of Jerubbaal reign over you, or that one reign over you?' Remember that I *am* your own flesh and ᴿbone." Judg. 8:30; 9:5, 18 • Gen. 29:14
3 And his mother's brothers spoke all these words concerning him in the hearing of all the men of Shechem; and their heart was inclined to follow Abimelech, for they said, "He is our ᴿbrother." Gen. 29:15
4 So they gave him ᵀseventy *shekels* of silver from the temple of Baal-Berith, with which Abimelech hired worthless and reckless men; and they followed him. $8,960
5 Then he went to his father's house ᴿat Ophrah and ᴿkilled his brothers, the seventy sons of Jerubbaal, on one stone. But Jotham the youngest son of Jerubbaal was left, because he hid himself. Judg. 6:24 • 2 Kin. 11:1, 2
6 And all the men of Shechem gathered together, all of Beth Millo, and they went and made Abimelech king beside the terebinth tree at the pillar that *was* in Shechem.

The Parable of the Trees

7 Now when they told Jotham, he went and stood on top of ᴿMount Gerizim, and lifted his voice and cried out. And he said to them: Deut. 11:29; 27:12

"Listen to me, you men of Shechem,
That God may listen to you!

8 "Theᴿ trees once went forth to anoint a
      king over them. 2 Kin. 14:9
   And they said to the olive tree,
ᴿ'Reign over us!' Judg. 8:22, 23
9 But the olive tree said to them,
   'Should I cease giving my oil,
ᴿWith which they honor God and men,
   And go to sway over trees?' [John 5:23]

10 "Then the trees said to the fig tree,
   'You come *and* reign over us!'
11 But the fig tree said to them,
   'Should I cease my sweetness and my
      good fruit,
   And go to sway over trees?'

12 "Then the trees said to the vine,
   'You come *and* reign over us!'
13 But the vine said to them,
   'Should I cease my new wine,
ᴿWhich cheers *both* God and men,
   And go to sway over trees?' Ps. 104:15

14 "Then all the trees said to the bramble,
   'You come *and* reign over us!'
15 And the bramble said to the trees,
   'If in truth you anoint me as king over
      you,
   Then come *and* take shelter in my
ᴿshade; Is. 30:2
   But if not, ᴿlet fire come out of the
      bramble Num. 21:28
   And devour the cedars of Lebanon!'

16 "Now therefore, if you have acted in truth and sincerity in making Abimelech king, and if you have dealt well with Jerubbaal and his house, and have done to him ᵀas he deserves— Lit. *according to the doing of his hands*
17 "for my ᴿfather fought for you, risked his life, and ᴿdelivered you out of the hand of Midian; Judg. 7 • Judg. 8:22
18 "but you have risen up against my father's house this day, and killed his seventy sons on one stone, and made Abimelech, the son of his female servant, king over the men of Shechem, because he is your brother—
19 "if then you have acted in truth and sincerity with Jerubbaal and with his house this day, *then* ᴿrejoice in Abimelech, and let him also rejoice in you. Is. 8:6
20 "But if not, ᴿlet fire come from Abimelech and devour the men of Shechem and Beth Millo; and let fire come from the men of Shechem and from Beth Millo and devour Abimelech!" Judg. 9:15, 45, 56, 57
21 And Jotham ran away and fled; and he went to ᴿBeer and dwelt there, for fear of Abimelech his brother. Num. 21:16

Downfall of Abimelech

22 After Abimelech had reigned over Israel three years,

23 ᴿGod sent a ᴿspirit of ill will between Abimelech and the men of Shechem; and the men of Shechem ᴿdealt treacherously with Abimelech,   Is. 19:14 • 1 Sam. 16:14; 18:9, 10 • Is. 33:1

24 that the crime *done* to the seventy sons of Jerubbaal might be settled and their ᴿblood be laid on Abimelech their brother, who killed them, and on the men of Shechem, who aided him in the killing of his brothers.   Num. 35:33

25 And the men of Shechem set ᵀmen in ambush against him on the tops of the mountains, and they robbed all who passed by them along that way; and it was told Abimelech.   Lit. *liers-in-wait for*

26 Now Gaal the son of Ebed came with his brothers and went over to Shechem; and the men of Shechem put their confidence in him.

27 So they went out into the fields, and gathered *grapes* from their vineyards and trod *them*, and ᵀmade merry. And they went into ᴿthe house of their god, and ate and drank, and cursed Abimelech.   *rejoiced* • Judg. 9:4

28 Then Gaal the son of Ebed said, "Who *is* Abimelech, and who *is* Shechem, that we should serve him? *Is he* not the son of Jerubbaal, and *is not* Zebul his officer? Serve the men of ᴿHamor the father of Shechem; but why should we serve him?   Gen. 34:2, 6

29 ᴿ"If only this people were under my ᵀauthority! Then I would remove Abimelech." So *he said to Abimelech, "Increase your army and come out!"   2 Sam. 15:4 • Lit. *hand*

30 When Zebul, the ruler of the city, heard the words of Gaal the son of Ebed, his anger was aroused.

31 And he sent messengers to Abimelech secretly, saying, "Take note! Gaal the son of Ebed and his brothers have come to Shechem; and here they are, fortifying the city against you.

32 "Now therefore, get up by night, you and the people who *are* with you, and ᵀlie in wait in the field.   *set up an ambush*

33 "And it shall be, as soon as the sun is up in the morning, *that* you shall rise early and rush upon the city; and *when* he and the people who are with him come out against you, you may then do to them ᵀas you find opportunity."   Lit. *as your hand can find*

34 So Abimelech and all the people who *were* with him rose by night, and lay in wait against Shechem in four companies.

35 When Gaal the son of Ebed went out and stood in the entrance to the city gate, Abimelech and the people who *were* with him rose from lying in wait.

36 And when Gaal saw the people, he said to Zebul, "Look, people are coming down from the tops of the mountains!" But Zebul said to him, "You see the shadows of the mountains as *if they were* men."

37 So Gaal spoke again and said, "See, people are coming down from the center of the land, and another company is coming from the *Diviners' Terebinth Tree."

38 Then Zebul said to him, "Where indeed *is* your mouth now, with which you said, 'Who *is* Abimelech, that we should serve him?' *Are* not these the people whom you despised? Go out, if you will, and fight with them now."

39 So Gaal went out, leading the men of Shechem, and fought with Abimelech.

40 And Abimelech chased him, and he fled from him; and many fell wounded, to the *very* entrance of the gate.

41 Then Abimelech dwelt at Arumah, and Zebul ᵀdrove out Gaal and his brothers, so that they would not dwell in Shechem.   *exiled*

42 And it came about on the next day that the people went out into the field, and they told Abimelech.

43 So he took his people, divided them into three companies, and lay in wait in the field. And he looked, and there were the people, coming out of the city; and he rose against them and attacked them.

44 Then Abimelech and the company that *was* with him rushed forward and stood at the entrance of the gate of the city; and the *other* two companies rushed upon all who *were* in the fields and killed them.

45 So Abimelech fought against the city all that day; he took the city and killed the people who *were* in it; and he ᴿdemolished the city and sowed it with salt.   2 Kin. 3:25

46 Now when all the men of the tower of Shechem had heard *that*, they entered the stronghold of the temple of the god Berith.

47 And it was told Abimelech that all the men of the tower of Shechem were gathered together.

48 Then Abimelech went up to Mount ᴿZalmon, he and all the people who *were* with him. And Abimelech took an ax in his hand and cut down a bough from the trees, and took it and laid *it* on his shoulder; then he said to the people who were with him, "What you have seen me do, make haste *and* do as I have done."   Ps. 68:14

49 So each of the people likewise cut down his own bough and followed Abimelech, put *them* against the ᵀstronghold, and set the stronghold on fire above them, so that all the people of the tower of Shechem died, about a thousand men and women.   *fortified room*

50 Then Abimelech went to Thebez, and he ᵀencamped against Thebez and took it. *besieged*

51 But there was a strong tower in the city, and all the men and women—all the people of the city—fled there and shut themselves in; then they went up to the top of the tower.

52 So Abimelech came as far as the tower and fought against it; and he drew near the door of the tower to burn it with fire.

53 But a certain woman ᴿdropped an upper millstone on Abimelech's head and crushed his skull.   2 Sam. 11:21

54 Then ᴿhe called quickly to the young man, his armorbearer, and said to him, "Draw your sword and kill me, lest men say of me, 'A woman killed him.'" So his young man thrust him through, and he died.   1 Sam. 31:4

55 And when the men of Israel saw that Abimelech was dead, they departed, every man to his ᵀplace.   home

56 ᴿThus God repaid the wickedness of Abimelech, which he had done to his father by killing his seventy brothers.   Job 31:3

57 And all the evil of the men of Shechem God returned on their own heads, and on them came ᴿthe curse of Jotham the son of Jerubbaal.   Judg. 9:20

Tola

10 After Abimelech there ᴿarose to save Israel Tola the son of Puah, the son of Dodo, a man of Issachar; and he dwelt in Shamir in the mountains of Ephraim. Judg. 2:16

2 He judged Israel twenty-three years; and he died and was buried in Shamir.

Jair

3 After him arose Jair, a Gileadite; and he judged Israel twenty-two years.

4 Now he had thirty sons who rode on thirty donkeys; they also had thirty towns, ᴿwhich are called "Havoth Jair" to this day, which are in the land of Gilead.   Deut. 3:14

5 And Jair died and was buried in Camon.

Israel Oppressed Again

6 Then the children of Israel again did evil in the sight of the Lᴏʀᴅ, and served the Baals and the Ashtoreths, ᴿthe gods of Syria, the gods of ᴿSidon, the gods of Moab, the gods of the people of Ammon, and the gods of the Philistines; and they forsook the Lᴏʀᴅ and did not serve Him.   Judg. 2:12 · 1 Kin. 11:33

7 So the anger of the Lᴏʀᴅ was hot against Israel; and He sold them into the hands of the ᴿPhilistines and into the hands of the people of ᴿAmmon.   Judg. 13:1 · Judg. 3:13

8 From that year they ᵀharassed and oppressed the children of Israel for eighteen years—all the children of Israel who were on the other side of the Jordan in the ᴿland of the Amorites, in Gilead.   Lit. shattered · Num. 32:33

9 Moreover the people of Ammon crossed over the Jordan to fight against Judah also, against Benjamin, and against the house of Ephraim, so that Israel was severely distressed.

10 ᴿAnd the children of Israel cried out to the Lᴏʀᴅ, saying, "We have ᴿsinned against You, because we have both forsaken our God and served the Baals!"   1 Sam. 12:10 · Deut. 1:41

11 So the Lᴏʀᴅ said to the children of Israel, "Did I not deliver you from the Egyptians and from the Amorites and from the people of Ammon and from the Philistines?

12 "Also ᴿthe Sidonians ᴿand Amalekites and *Maonites ᴿoppressed you; and you cried out to Me, and I delivered you from their hand.   Judg. 1:31; 5:19 · Judg. 6:3; 7:12 · Ps. 106:42, 43

13 ᴿ"Yet you have forsaken Me and served other gods. Therefore I will deliver you no more.   [Jer. 2:13]

14 "Go and ᴿcry out to the gods which you have chosen; let them deliver you in your time of distress."   Deut. 32:37, 38

15 And the children of Israel said to the Lᴏʀᴅ, "We have sinned! ᴿDo to us whatever seems best to You; only deliver us this day, we pray."   1 Sam. 3:18

16 ᴿSo they put away the foreign gods from among them and served the Lᴏʀᴅ. And ᴿHis soul could no longer endure the misery of Israel.   Jer. 18:7, 8 · Is. 63:9

17 Then the people of Ammon gathered together and encamped in Gilead. And the children of Israel assembled together and encamped in ᴿMizpah.   Judg. 11:11, 29

18 And the people, the leaders of Gilead, said to one another, "Who is the man who will begin the fight against the people of Ammon? He shall ᴿbe head over all the inhabitants of Gilead."   Judg. 11:8, 11

Jephthah

11 Now Jephthah the Gileadite was a mighty man of valor, but he was the son of a harlot; and Gilead begot Jephthah.

2 Gilead's wife bore sons; and when his wife's sons grew up, they drove Jephthah out, and said to him, "You shall have ᴿno inheritance in our father's house, for you are the son of another woman."   Gen. 21:10

3 Then Jephthah fled from his brothers and dwelt in the land of Tob; and ᴿworthless men banded together with Jephthah and went out raiding with him.   1 Sam. 22:2

4 It came to pass after a time that the people of Ammon made war against Israel.

5 And so it was, when the people of Ammon made war against Israel, that the elders of Gilead went to get Jephthah from the land of Tob.

6 Then they said to Jephthah, "Come and be our commander, that we may fight against the people of Ammon."

7 So Jephthah said to the elders of Gilead, "Did you not hate me, and expel me from my father's house? Why have you come to me now when you are in ᵀdistress?"   trouble

8 And the elders of Gilead said to Jephthah, "That is why we have turned again to

10:12 LXX mss. Midianites

you now, that you may go with us and fight against the people of Ammon, and be our head over all the inhabitants of Gilead."

9 So Jephthah said to the elders of Gilead, "If you take me back home to fight against the people of Ammon, and the LORD delivers them to me, shall I be your head?"

10 And the elders of Gilead said to Jephthah, "The LORD will be a witness between us, if we do not do according to your words."

11 Then Jephthah went with the elders of Gilead, and the people made him head and commander over them; and Jephthah spoke all his words before the LORD in Mizpah.

12 Now Jephthah sent messengers to the king of the people of Ammon, saying, ᴿ"What do you have against me, that you have come to fight against me in my land?"   2 Sam. 16:10

13 And the king of the people of Ammon answered the messengers of Jephthah, "Because Israel took away my land when they came up out of Egypt, from the Arnon as far as the Jabbok, and to the Jordan. Now therefore, restore those *lands* peaceably."

14 So Jephthah again sent messengers to the king of the people of Ammon,

15 and said to him, "Thus says Jephthah: 'Israel did not take away the land of Moab, nor the land of the people of Ammon;

16 'for when Israel came up from Egypt, they walked through the wilderness as far as the Red Sea and came to Kadesh.

17 'Then Israel sent messengers to the king of Edom, saying, "Please let me pass through your land." But the king of Edom would not heed. And in like manner they sent to the king of Moab, but he would not *consent*. So Israel ᴿremained in Kadesh.   Num. 20:1

18 'And they ᴿwent along through the wilderness and ᴿbypassed the land of Edom and the land of Moab, came to the east side of the land of Moab, and encamped on the other side of the Arnon. But they did not enter the border of Moab, for the Arnon *was* the border of Moab.   Deut. 2:9, 18, 19 · Num. 21:4

19 'Then Israel sent messengers to Sihon king of the Amorites, king of Heshbon; and Israel said to him, "Please ᴿlet us pass through your land into our place."   Deut. 2:27

20 ᴿ'But Sihon did not trust Israel to pass through his territory. So Sihon gathered all his people together, encamped in Jahaz, and fought against Israel.   Deut. 2:27

21 'And the LORD God of Israel delivered Sihon and all his people into the hand of Israel, and they ᵀdefeated them. Thus Israel gained possession of all the land of the Amorites, who inhabited that country.   Lit. *struck*

22 'They took possession of ᴿall the territory of the Amorites, from the Arnon to the Jabbok and from the wilderness to the Jordan.   Deut. 2:36, 37

23 'And now the LORD God of Israel has dispossessed the Amorites from before His people Israel; should you then possess it?

24 'Will you not possess whatever Chemosh your god gives you to possess? So whatever ᴿthe LORD our God takes possession of before us, we will possess.   [Deut. 9:4, 5]

25 'And now, *are* you any better than ᴿBalak the son of Zippor, king of Moab? Did he ever strive against Israel? Did he ever fight against them?   Num. 22:2

26 'While Israel dwelt in ᴿHeshbon and its villages, in ᴿAroer and its villages, and in all the cities along the banks of the Arnon, for three hundred years, why did you not recover *them* within that time?   Num. 21:25, 26 · Deut. 2:36

27 'Therefore I have not sinned against you, but you wronged me by fighting against me. May the LORD, the Judge, ᴿrender judgment this day between the children of Israel and the people of Ammon.' "   Gen. 16:5; 31:53

28 However, the king of the people of Ammon did not heed the words which Jephthah sent him.

Jephthah's Vow and Victory

29 Then the Spirit of the LORD came upon Jephthah, and he passed through Gilead and Manasseh, and passed through Mizpah of Gilead; and from Mizpah of Gilead he advanced *toward* the people of Ammon.

30 And Jephthah ᴿmade a vow to the LORD, and said, "If You will indeed deliver the people of Ammon into my hands,   Gen. 28:20

31 "then it will be that whatever comes out of the doors of my house to meet me, when I return in peace from the people of Ammon, ᴿshall surely be the LORD's, ᴿand I will offer it up as a burnt offering."   Lev. 27:2, 3, 28 · Ps. 66:13

32 So Jephthah advanced toward the people of Ammon to fight against them, and the LORD delivered them into his hands.

33 And he defeated them from Aroer as far as Minnith—twenty cities—and to ᵀAbel Keramim, with a very great slaughter. Thus the people of Ammon were subdued before the children of Israel.   Lit. *Plain of Vineyards*

Jephthah's Daughter

34 When Jephthah came to his house at Mizpah, there was ᴿhis daughter, coming out to meet him with timbrels and dancing; and she *was his* only child. Besides her he had neither son nor daughter.   Ex. 15:20

35 And it came to pass, when he saw her, that he tore his clothes, and said, "Alas, my daughter! You have brought me very low! You are among those who trouble me! For I have ᵀgiven my word to the LORD, and I cannot go back on it."   Lit. *opened my mouth*

36 So she said to him, "My father, *if* you have given your word to the LORD, do to me according to what has gone out of your

mouth, because the LORD has avenged you of your enemies, the people of Ammon."

37 Then she said to her father, "Let this thing be done for me: let me alone for two months, that I may go and wander on the mountains and ᵀbewail my virginity, my ᵀfriends and I."   lament · companions

38 So he said, "Go." And he sent her away for two months; and she went with her friends, and bewailed her virginity on the mountains.

39 And it was so at the end of two months that she returned to her father, and he ᴿcarried out his vow with her which he had vowed. She ᵀknew no man. And it became a custom in Israel   Judg. 11:31 · Remained a virgin

40 that the daughters of Israel went four days each year to ᵀlament the daughter of Jephthah the Gileadite.   commemorate

Jephthah's Conflict with Ephraim

12 Then the men of Ephraim gathered together, crossed over toward Zaphon, and said to Jephthah, "Why did you cross over to fight against the people of Ammon, and did not call us to go with you? We will burn your house down on you with fire!"

2 And Jephthah said to them, "My people and I were in a great struggle with the people of Ammon; and when I called you, you did not deliver me out of their hands.

3 "So when I saw that you would not deliver me, I ᴿtook my life in my hands and crossed over against the people of Ammon; and the LORD delivered them into my hand. Why then have you come up to me this day to fight against me?"   1 Sam. 19:5; 28:21

4 Now Jephthah gathered together all the men of Gilead and fought against Ephraim. And the men of Gilead defeated Ephraim, because they said, "You Gileadites ᴿare fugitives of Ephraim among the Ephraimites and among the Manassites."   1 Sam. 25:10

5 The Gileadites seized the ᴿfords of the Jordan before the Ephraimites arrived. And when any Ephraimite who escaped said, "Let me cross over," the men of Gilead would say to him, "Are you an Ephraimite?" If he said, "No,"   Josh. 22:11

6 then they would say to him, "Then say, 'Shibboleth'!" And he would say, "Sibboleth," for he could not ᵀpronounce it right. Then they would take him and kill him at the fords of the Jordan. There fell at that time forty-two thousand Ephraimites.   Lit. speak so

7 And Jephthah judged Israel six years. Then Jephthah the Gileadite died and was buried among the cities of Gilead.

Ibzan, Elon, and Abdon

8 After him, Ibzan of Bethlehem judged Israel.

9 He had thirty sons. And he gave away thirty daughters in marriage, and brought in thirty daughters from elsewhere for his sons. He judged Israel seven years.

10 Then Ibzan died and was buried at Bethlehem.

11 After him, Elon the Zebulunite judged Israel. He judged Israel ten years.

12 And Elon the Zebulunite died and was buried at Aijalon in the country of Zebulun.

13 After him, Abdon the son of Hillel the Pirathonite judged Israel.

14 He had forty sons and thirty grandsons, who ᴿrode on seventy young donkeys. He judged Israel eight years.   Judg. 5:10; 10:4

15 Then Abdon the son of Hillel the Pirathonite died and was buried in Pirathon in the land of Ephraim, ᴿin the mountains of the Amalekites.   Judg. 3:13, 27; 5:14

The Birth of Samson

13 Again the children of Israel ᴿdid evil in the sight of the LORD, and the LORD delivered them ᴿinto the hand of the Philistines for forty years.   Judg. 2:11 · 1 Sam. 12:9

2 Now there was a certain man from ᴿZorah, of the family of the Danites, whose name was Manoah; and his wife was barren and had no children.   Josh. 19:41

3 And the ᴿAngel of the LORD appeared to the woman and said to her, "Indeed now, you are barren and have borne no children, but you shall conceive and bear a son.   Judg. 6:12

4 "Now therefore, please be careful ᴿnot to drink wine or similar drink, and not to eat anything unclean.   Num. 6:2, 3, 20

5 "For behold, you shall conceive and bear a son. And no razor shall come upon his head, for the child shall be a Nazirite to God from the womb; and he shall begin to deliver Israel out of the hand of the Philistines."

6 So the woman came and told her husband, saying, "A Man of God came to me, and His ᵀcountenance was like the countenance of the Angel of God, very awesome; but I did not ask Him where He was from, and He did not tell me His name.   appearance

7 "And He said to me, 'Behold, you shall conceive and bear a son. Now drink no wine or similar drink, nor eat anything unclean, for the child shall be a Nazirite to God from the womb to the day of his death.' "

8 Then Manoah prayed to the LORD, and said, "O my Lord, please let the Man of God whom You sent come to us again and teach us what we shall do for the child who will be born."

9 And God listened to the voice of Manoah, and the Angel of God came to the woman again as she was sitting in the field; but Manoah her husband was not with her.

10 Then the woman ran in haste and told her husband, and said to him, "Look, the Man

who came to me the *other* day has just now appeared to me!"

11 So Manoah arose and followed his wife. When he came to the Man, he said to Him, "Are You the Man who spoke to this woman?" And He said, "I *am*."

12 Manoah said, "Now let Your words come *to pass*! What will be the boy's rule of life, and his work?"

13 So the Angel of the LORD said to Manoah, "Of all that I said to the woman let her be careful.

14 "She may not eat anything that comes from the vine, nor may she drink wine or *similar* drink, nor eat anything unclean. All that I commanded her let her observe."

15 Then Manoah said to the Angel of the LORD, "Please ᴿlet us detain You, and we will prepare a young goat for You."   Gen. 18:5

16 And the Angel of the LORD said to Manoah, "Though you detain Me, I will not eat your food. But if you offer a burnt offering, you must offer it to the LORD." (For Manoah did not know He *was* the Angel of the LORD.)

17 Then Manoah said to the Angel of the LORD, "What *is* Your name, that when Your words come *to pass* we may honor You?"

18 And the Angel of the LORD said to him, ᴿ"Why do you ask My name, seeing it *is* wonderful?"   Gen. 32:29

19 So Manoah took the young goat with the grain offering, and offered it upon the rock to the LORD. And He did a wondrous thing while Manoah and his wife looked on—

20 it happened as the flame went up toward heaven from the altar—the Angel of the LORD ascended in the flame of the altar! When Manoah and his wife saw *this*, they ᴿfell on their faces to the ground.   Ezek. 1:28

21 When the Angel of the LORD appeared no more to Manoah and his wife, then Manoah knew that He *was* the Angel of the LORD.

22 And Manoah said to his wife, "We shall surely die, because we have seen God!"

23 But his wife said to him, "If the LORD had desired to kill us, He would not have accepted a burnt offering and a grain offering from our hands, nor would He have shown us all these *things*, nor would He have told us *such things* as these at this time."

24 So the woman bore a son and called his name ᴿSamson; and ᴿthe child grew, and the LORD blessed him.   Heb. 11:32 · 1 Sam. 3:19

25 And the Spirit of the LORD began to move upon him at *Mahaneh Dan between Zorah and ᴿEshtaol.   Judg. 16:31

Samson's Philistine Wife

14 Now Samson went down to Timnah, and ᴿsaw a woman in Timnah of the daughters of the Philistines.   Gen. 34:2

2 So he went up and told his father and mother, saying, "I have seen a woman in Timnah of the daughters of the Philistines; now therefore, get her for me as a wife."

3 Then his father and mother said to him, "*Is there* no woman among the daughters of your brethren, or among all my people, that you must go and get a wife from the ᴿuncircumcised Philistines?" And Samson said to his father, "Get her for me, for ᵀshe pleases me well."   Gen. 34:14 · Lit. *she is right in my eyes*

4 But his father and mother did not know that it was ᴿof the LORD—that He was seeking an occasion to move against the Philistines. For at that time ᴿthe Philistines had dominion over Israel.   Josh. 11:20 · Deut. 28:48

10-A. The Ministry of the Holy Spirit Before Pentecost   ▼

5 So Samson went down to Timnah with his father and mother, and came to the vineyards of Timnah.

Now *to his* surprise, a young lion *came* roaring against him.

6 And ᴿthe Spirit of the LORD came mightily upon him, and he tore the lion apart as one would have torn apart a young goat, though *he had* nothing in his hand. But he did not tell his father or his mother what he had done.   Judg. 3:10 ▲

7 Then he went down and talked with the woman; and she pleased Samson well.

8 After some time, when he returned to get her, he turned aside to see the carcass of the lion. And behold, a swarm of bees and honey *were* in the carcass of the lion.

9 He took some of it in his hands and went along, eating. When he came to his father and mother, he gave *some* to them, and they also ate. But he did not tell them that he had taken the honey out of the ᴿcarcass of the lion.   Lev. 11:27

10 So his father went down to the woman. And Samson gave a feast there, for young men used to do so.

13:25 Lit. *Camp of Dan,* Judg. 18:12

10-A. The Ministry of the Holy Spirit Before Pentecost (Judges 14:5, 6)—"And the Spirit of the LORD came mightily upon him" (v. 6). Samson was a spiritual enigma. Before his birth he was chosen of God to be a "Nazirite to God" (Judg. 13:1–5, page 254). A Nazirite could be either man or woman, set apart from things of the world for the service of God. Some Nazirites were separated unto God for a short period of time, but Samson was set apart by God for life. In failing to live the life of the Nazirite, he trusted Delilah and revealed to her the secret of his great physical strength (Judg. 16:16, 17, page 258). While he slept, with his head in

(Point 10-A continued on next page)

11 And it happened, when they saw him, that they brought thirty companions to be with him.

12 Then Samson said to them, "Let me ᴿpose a riddle to you. If you can correctly solve and explain it to me ᴿwithin the seven days of the feast, then I will give you thirty linen garments and thirty ᴿchanges of clothing.   Ezek. 17:2 • Gen. 29:27 • 2 Kin. 5:22

13 "But if you cannot explain *it* to me, then you shall give me thirty linen garments and thirty changes of clothing." And they said to him, "Pose your riddle, that we may hear it."

14 So he said to them:

"Out of the eater came something to eat,
And out of the strong came something sweet."

Now for three days they could not explain the riddle.

15 But it came to pass on the *seventh day that they said to Samson's wife, "Entice your husband, that he may explain the riddle to us, or else we will burn you and your father's house with fire. Have you invited us in order to take what is ours? *Is that* not *so?*"

16 Then Samson's wife wept on him, and said, ᴿ"You only hate me! You do not love me! You have posed a riddle to the sons of my people, but you have not explained *it* to me." And he said to her, "Look, I have not explained *it* to my father or my mother; so should I explain *it* to you?"   Judg. 16:15

17 Now she had wept on him the seven days while their feast lasted. And it happened

14:15 So with MT, Tg., Vg.; LXX, [Syr.] *fourth*

on the seventh day that he told her, because she pressed him so much. Then she explained the riddle to the sons of her people.

18 So the men of the city said to him on the seventh day before the sun went down:

"What *is* sweeter than honey?
And what *is* stronger than a lion?"

And he said to them:

"If you had not plowed with my heifer,
You would not have solved my riddle!"

19 Then ᴿthe Spirit of the LORD came upon him mightily, and he went down to Ashkelon and killed thirty of their men, took their apparel, and gave the changes *of clothing* to those who had explained the riddle. So his anger was aroused, and he went back up to his father's house.   Judg. 3:10; 13:25

20 And Samson's wife was *given* to his companion, who had been his best man.

Samson Defeats the Philistines

15 After a while, in the time of wheat harvest, it happened that Samson visited his wife with a young goat. And he said, "Let me go in to my wife, into *her* room." But her father would not permit him to go in.

2 Her father said, "I really thought that you thoroughly ᴿhated her; therefore I gave her to your companion. *Is* not her younger sister better than she? Please, take her instead."   Judg. 14:20

3 And Samson said to them, "This time I shall be blameless regarding the Philistines if I harm them!"

4 Then Samson went and caught three hundred foxes; and he took torches, turned

(Point 10-A continued from previous page)
Delilah's lap, she called for a man to cut his hair. When he awoke, Delilah was saying, "The Philistines are upon you, Samson!" He said, "I will go out as before, at other times, and shake myself free!" Then we come to one of the saddest statements in the Bible—"But he did not know that the LORD had departed from him" (Judg. 16:18–21, page 258). When he lost the power of the Holy Spirit, he lost the victory, and the Philistines captured him. Finally, however, the Spirit again came mightily upon him and defeated the Philistines (Judg. 16:29, 30, page 258).

In the Old Testament the Holy Spirit came upon the Lord's servants, but when they continued to disobey God, the Holy Spirit would leave them. For example, Samuel prophesied to Saul saying, "The Spirit of the LORD will come upon you, and you will prophesy with them [the prophets] and be turned into another man" (1 Sam. 10:6–10, page 276). But the time came when Saul, in disobedience to God, sinned so greatly that the Holy Spirit departed from him (1 Sam. 16:14, page 283).

When King David repented of his sin, knowing that the Holy Spirit had abandoned King Saul, he prayed, "Do not cast me away from Your presence, and do not take Your Holy Spirit from me" (Ps. 51:11, page 541). This psalm of repentance should be read often and when necessary practiced by every believer, lest the Holy Spirit be grieved (1 John 1:9, page 1278). The Holy Spirit not only came upon prophets, kings, judges, and priests in the Old Testament, He also filled some for special work. "The LORD spoke to Moses, saying: 'See, I have called by name Bezalel. . . . And I have filled him with the Spirit of God'" (Ex. 31:1–11, page 91). Bezalel was filled with the Spirit of God and given the wisdom, understanding, and knowledge, to be a Spirit-filled craftsman who could supervise the building of the tabernacle, the ark of the covenant, and all the furniture, and who could make all the clothes for the high priest and his sons (Ex. 35:31—36:7, page 96). The Holy Spirit came upon many, but only filled a few; the great outpouring of the Holy Spirit, however, took place at Pentecost.

See Acts 2:1–21, page 1088, for **Point 10-B: The Ministry of the Holy Spirit on the Day of Pentecost and After.**

the foxes tail to tail, and put a torch between each pair of tails.

5 When he had set the torches on fire, he let the foxes go into the standing grain of the Philistines, and burned up both the shocks and the standing grain, as well as the vineyards and olive groves.

6 Then the Philistines said, "Who has done this?" And they answered, "Samson, the son-in-law of the Timnite, because he has taken his wife and given her to his companion." ᴿSo the Philistines came up and burned her and her father with fire.   Judg. 14:15

7 Samson said to them, "Since you would do a thing like this, I will surely take revenge on you, and after that I will cease."

8 So he attacked them hip and thigh with a great slaughter; then he went down and dwelt in the cleft of the rock of Etam.

9 Now the Philistines went up, encamped in Judah, and deployed themselves ᴿagainst Lehi.   Judg. 15:19

10 And the men of Judah said, "Why have you come up against us?" So they answered, "We have come up to ᵀarrest Samson, to do to him as he has done to us."   Lit. bind

11 Then three thousand men of Judah went down to the cleft of the rock of Etam, and said to Samson, "Do you not know that the Philistines rule over us? What is this you have done to us?" And he said to them, "As they did to me, so I have done to them."

12 But they said to him, "We have come down to arrest you, that we may deliver you into the hand of the Philistines." Then Samson said to them, "Swear to me that you will not kill me yourselves."

13 So they spoke to him, saying, "No, but we will tie you securely and deliver you into their hand; but we will surely not kill you." And they bound him with two new ropes and brought him up from the rock.

14 When he came to Lehi, the Philistines came shouting against him. Then the Spirit of the LORD came mightily upon him; and the ropes that were on his arms became like flax that is burned with fire, and his bonds ᵀbroke loose from his hands.   Lit. melted

15 He found a fresh jawbone of a donkey, reached out his hand and took it, and ᴿkilled a thousand men with it.   Lev. 26:8

16 Then Samson said:

"With the jawbone of a donkey,
Heaps upon heaps,
With the jawbone of a donkey
I have slain a thousand men!"

17 And so it was, when he had finished speaking, that he threw the jawbone from his hand, and called that place *Ramath Lehi.

18 Then he became very thirsty; so he cried out to the LORD and said, ᴿ"You have given this great deliverance by the hand of Your servant; and now shall I die of thirst and fall into the hand of the uncircumcised?"   Ps. 3:7

19 So God split the hollow place that is in *Lehi, and water came out, and he drank; and ᴿhis spirit returned, and he revived. Therefore he called its name ᵀEn Hakkore, which is in Lehi to this day.   Is. 40:29 · Lit. Spring of the Caller

20 And he judged Israel twenty years ᴿin the days of the Philistines.   Judg. 13:1

Samson and Delilah

16 Now Samson went to Gaza and saw a harlot there, and went in to her.

2 When the Gazites were told, "Samson has come here!" they ᴿsurrounded the place and lay in wait for him all night at the gate of the city. They were quiet all night, saying, "In the morning, when it is daylight, we will kill him."   1 Sam. 23:26

3 And Samson lay low till midnight; then he arose at midnight, took hold of the doors of the gate of the city and the two gateposts, pulled them up, bar and all, put them on his shoulders, and carried them to the top of the hill that faces Hebron.

4 Afterward it happened that he loved a woman in the Valley of Sorek, whose name was Delilah.

5 And the ᴿlords of the Philistines came up to her and said to her, ᴿ"Entice him, and find out where his great strength lies, and by what means we may overpower him, that we may bind him to afflict him; and every one of us will give you ᵀeleven hundred pieces of silver."   Josh. 13:3 · Judg. 14:15 · $140,800

6 So Delilah said to Samson, "Please tell me where your great strength lies, and with what you may be bound to afflict you."

7 And Samson said to her, "If they bind me with seven fresh bowstrings, not yet dried, then I shall become weak, and be like any other man."

8 So the lords of the Philistines brought up to her seven fresh bowstrings, not yet dried, and she bound him with them.

9 Now men were lying in wait, staying with her in the room. And she said to him, "The Philistines are upon you, Samson!" But he broke the bowstrings as a strand of yarn breaks when it touches fire. So the secret of his strength was not known.

10 Then Delilah said to Samson, "Look, you have mocked me and told me lies. Now, please tell me what you may be bound with."

11 So he said to her, "If they bind me securely with ᴿnew ropes that have never been used, then I shall become weak, and be like any other man."   Judg. 15:13

12 Therefore Delilah took new ropes and bound him with them, and said to him, "The Philistines are upon you, Samson!" And men

were lying in wait, staying in the room. But he broke them off his arms like a thread.

13 Delilah said to Samson, "Until now you have mocked me and told me lies. Tell me what you may be bound with." And he said to her, "If you weave the seven locks of my head into the web of the loom"—

14 So she wove *it* tightly with the batten of the loom, and said to him, "The Philistines *are* upon you, Samson!" But he awoke from his sleep, and pulled out the batten and the web from the loom.

15 Then she said to him, ᴿ"How can you say, 'I love you,' when your heart *is* not with me? You have mocked me these three times, and have not told me where your great strength lies." Judg. 14:16

16 And it came to pass, when she pestered him daily with her words and pressed him, *so* that his soul was vexed to death,

17 that he ᴿtold her all his heart, and said to her, "No razor has ever come upon my head, for I *have been* a Nazirite to God from my mother's womb. If I am shaven, then my strength will leave me, and I shall become weak, and be like any *other* man." [Mic. 7:5]

18 When Delilah saw that he had told her all his heart, she sent and called for the lords of the Philistines, saying, "Come up once more, for he has told me all his heart." So the lords of the Philistines came up to her and brought the money in their hand.

19 ᴿThen she lulled him to sleep on her knees, and called for a man and had him shave off the seven locks of his head. Then *she began to torment him, and his strength left him. Prov. 7:26, 27

20 And she said, "The Philistines *are* upon you, Samson!" So he awoke from his sleep, and said, "I will go out as before, at other times, and shake myself free!" But he did not know that the LORD had departed from him.

21 Then the Philistines took him and ᵀput out his eyes, and brought him down to Gaza. They bound him with bronze fetters, and he became a grinder in the prison. Lit. *bored out*

22 However, the hair of his head began to grow again after it had been shaven.

Samson Dies with the Philistines

23 Now the lords of the Philistines gathered together to offer a great sacrifice to ᴿDagon their god, and to rejoice. And they said:

"Our god has delivered into our hands
    Samson our enemy!"   1 Sam. 5:2

24 When the people saw him, they ᴿpraised their god; for they said: Dan. 5:4

"Our god has delivered into our hands
    our enemy,
The destroyer of our land,
And the one who multiplied our dead."

16:19 So with MT, Tg., Vg.; LXX *he began to be weak*

25 So it happened, when their hearts were ᴿmerry, that they said, "Call for Samson, that he may perform for us." So they called for Samson from the prison, and he performed for them. And they stationed him between the pillars.   Judg. 9:27

26 Then Samson said to the lad who held him by the hand, "Let me feel the pillars which support the temple, so that I can lean on them."

27 Now the temple was full of men and women. All the lords of the Philistines *were* there—about three thousand men and women on the ᴿroof watching while Samson performed.   Deut. 22:8

28 Then Samson called to the LORD, saying, "O Lord GOD, ᴿremember me, I pray! Strengthen me, I pray, just this once, O God, that I may with one *blow* take vengeance on the Philistines for my two eyes!"   Jer. 15:15

29 And Samson took hold of the two middle pillars which supported the temple, and he braced himself against them, one on his right and the other on his left.

30 Then Samson said, "Let me die with the Philistines!" And he pushed with *all his* might, and the temple fell on the lords and all the people who *were* in it. So the dead that he killed at his death were more than he had killed in his life.

31 And his brothers and all his father's household came down and took him, and brought *him* up and buried him between Zorah and Eshtaol in the tomb of his father Manoah. He had judged Israel twenty years.

Micah's Idolatry

17 Now there was a man from the mountains of Ephraim, whose name *was* ᴿMicah.   Judg. 18:2

2 And he said to his mother, "The eleven hundred *shekels* of silver that were taken from you, and on which you put a curse, even saying it in my ears—here *is* the silver with me; I took it." And his mother said, "*May you be blessed by the LORD, my son!*"

3 So when he had returned the eleven hundred *shekels* of silver to his mother, his mother said, "I had wholly dedicated the silver from my hand to the LORD for my son, to make a carved image and a molded image; now therefore, I will return it to you."

4 Thus he returned the silver to his mother. Then his mother ᴿtook two hundred *shekels* of silver and gave them to the silversmith, and he made it into a carved image and a molded image; and they were in the house of Micah.   Is. 46:6

5 The man Micah had a shrine, and made an ᴿephod and ᴿhouseholdᵀ idols; and he consecrated one of his sons, who became his priest.   Judg. 8:27; 18:14 • Gen. 31:19, 30 • Heb. *teraphim*

6 ᴿIn those days *there was* no king in

Israel; [R]everyone did *what was* right in his own eyes.   Judg. 18:1; 19:1 • Deut. 12:8

7 Now there was a young man from Bethlehem in Judah, of the family of Judah; he *was* a Levite, and was staying there.

8 The man departed from the city of Bethlehem in Judah to stay wherever he could find *a place.* Then he came to the mountains of Ephraim, to the house of Micah, as he journeyed.

9 And Micah said to him, "Where do you come from?" So he said to him, "I *am* a Levite from Bethlehem in Judah, and I am on my way to find *a place* to stay."

10 Micah said to him, "Dwell with me, [R]and be a [R]father and a priest to me, and I will give you ten *shekels* of silver per year, a suit of clothes, and your sustenance." So the Levite went in.   Judg. 18:19 • Gen. 45:8

11 Then the Levite was content to dwell with the man; and the young man became like one of his sons to him.

12 So Micah [T]consecrated the Levite, and the young man became his priest, and lived in the house of Micah.   Lit. *filled the hand of*

13 Then Micah said, "Now I know that the LORD will be good to me, since I have a Levite as [R]priest!"   Judg. 18:4

The Danites Adopt Micah's Idolatry

18 In [R]those days *there was* no king in Israel. And in those days [R]the tribe of the Danites was seeking an inheritance for itself to dwell in; for until that day *their* inheritance among the tribes of Israel had not fallen to them.   Judg. 17:6; 19:1; 21:25 • Josh. 19:40-48

2 So the children of Dan sent five men of their family from their territory, men of valor from [R]Zorah and Eshtaol, [R]to spy out the land and search it. They said to them, "Go, search the land." So they went to the mountains of Ephraim, to the [R]house of Micah, and lodged there.   Judg. 13:25 • Num. 13:17 • Judg. 17:1

3 While they *were* at the house of Micah, they recognized the voice of the young Levite. They turned aside and said to him, "Who brought you here? What are you doing in this *place?* What do you have here?"

4 He said to them, "Thus and so Micah did for me. He has [R]hired me, and I have become his priest."   Judg. 17:10, 12

5 So they said to him, "Please inquire of God, that we may know whether the journey on which we go will be prosperous."

6 And the priest said to them, [R]"Go in peace. The presence of the LORD *be* with you on your way."   1 Kin. 22:6

7 So the five men departed and went to Laish. They saw the people who *were* there, how they dwelt safely, in the manner of the Sidonians, quiet and secure. *There were* no rulers in the land who might put *them* to shame for anything. They *were* far from the Sidonians, and they had no ties with anyone.

8 Then *the spies* came back to their brethren at Zorah and Eshtaol, and their brethren said to them, "What *is* your *report?*"

9 So they said, [R]"Arise, let us go up against them. For we have seen the land, and indeed it *is* very good. Would you [R]do nothing? Do not hesitate to go, *and* enter to possess the land.   Num. 13:30 • 1 Kin. 22:3

10 "When you go, you will come to a secure people and a large land. For God has given it into your hands, a place where *there is* no lack of anything that *is* on the earth."

11 And six hundred men of the family of the Danites went from there, from Zorah and Eshtaol, armed with weapons of war.

12 Then they went up and encamped in Kirjath Jearim in Judah. (Therefore they call that place [T]Mahaneh Dan to this day. There *it is,* west of Kirjath Jearim.)   Lit. *Camp of Dan*

13 And they passed from there to the mountains of Ephraim, and came to [R]the house of Micah.   Judg. 18:2

14 Then the five men who had gone to spy out the country of Laish answered and said to their brethren, "Do you know that there are in these houses an ephod, household idols, a carved image, and a molded image? Now therefore, consider what you should do."

15 So they turned aside there, and came to the house of the young Levite man—to the house of Micah—and greeted him.

16 The six hundred men armed with their weapons of war, who *were* of the children of Dan, stood by the entrance of the gate.

17 Then [R]the five men who had gone to spy out the land went up. Entering there, they took [R]the carved image, the ephod, the household idols, and the molded image. The priest stood at the entrance of the gate with the six hundred men *who were* armed with weapons of war.   Judg. 18:2, 14 • Judg. 17:4, 5

18 When these went into Micah's house and took the carved image, the ephod, the household idols, and the molded image, the priest said to them, "What are you doing?"

19 And they said to him, "Be quiet, [R]put your hand over your mouth, and come with us; [R]be a father and a priest to us. *Is it* better for you to be a priest to the household of one man, or that you be a priest to a tribe and a family in Israel?"   Job 21:5; 29:9; 40:4 • Judg. 17:10

20 So the priest's heart was glad; and he took the ephod, the household idols, and the carved image, and took his place among the people.

21 Then they turned and departed, and put the little ones, the livestock, and the goods in front of them.

22 When they were a good way from the house of Micah, the men who *were* in the houses near Micah's house gathered together and overtook the children of Dan.

23 And they called out to the children of Dan. So they turned around and said to Micah, R"What ails you, that you have gathered such a company?"   2 Kin. 6:28

24 So he said, "You have taken away my gods which I made, and the priest, and you have gone away. Now what more do I have? How can you say to me, 'What ails you?' "

25 And the children of Dan said to him, "Do not let your voice be heard among us, lest angry men fall upon you, and you lose your life, with the lives of your household!"

26 Then the children of Dan went their way. And when Micah saw that they were too strong for him, he turned and went back to his house.

Danites Settle in Laish

27 So they took the things Micah had made, and the priest who had belonged to him, and went to Laish, to a people quiet and secure; Rand they struck them with the edge of the sword and burned the city with fire. Josh. 19:47

28 There was no deliverer, because it was Rfar from Sidon, and they had no ties with anyone. It was in the valley that belongs Rto Beth Rehob. So they rebuilt the city and dwelt there.   Judg. 18:7 • 2 Sam. 10:6

29 And Rthey called the name of the city RDan, after the name of Dan their father, who was born to Israel. However, the name of the city formerly was Laish.   Josh. 19:47 • Judg. 20:1

30 Then the children of Dan set up for themselves the carved image; and Jonathan the son of Gershom, the son of *Manasseh, and his sons were priests to the tribe of Dan until the day of the captivity of the land.

31 So they set up for themselves Micah's carved image which he made, all the time that the house of God was in Shiloh.

The Levite's Concubine

19 And it came to pass in those days, when there was no king in Israel, that there was a certain Levite staying in the remote mountains of Ephraim. He took for himself a concubine from Bethlehem in Judah.

2 But his concubine played the harlot against him, and went away from him to her father's house at Bethlehem in Judah, and was there four whole months.

3 Then her husband arose and went after her, to Rspeak Tkindly to her and bring her back, having his servant and a couple of donkeys with him. So she brought him into her father's house; and when the father of the young woman saw him, he was glad to meet him.   Gen. 34:3; 50:21 • Lit. to her heart

4 Now his father-in-law, the young woman's father, detained him; and he stayed with

18:30 LXX, Vg. Moses

him three days. So they ate and drank and lodged there.

5 Then it came to pass on the fourth day that they arose early in the morning, and he stood to depart; but the young woman's father said to his son-in-law, R"Refresh your heart with a morsel of bread, and afterward go your way."   Gen. 18:5

6 So they sat down, and the two of them ate and drank together. Then the young woman's father said to the man, "Please be content to stay all night, and let your heart be merry."

7 And when the man stood to depart, his father-in-law urged him; so he lodged there again.

8 Then he arose early in the morning on the fifth day to depart, but the young woman's father said, "Please refresh your heart." So they delayed until afternoon; and both of them ate.

9 And when the man stood to depart—he and his concubine and his servant—his father-in-law, the young woman's father, said to him, "Look, the day is now drawing toward evening; please spend the night. See, the day is coming to an end; lodge here, that your heart may be merry. Tomorrow go your way early, so that you may get home."

10 However, the man was not willing to spend that night; so he rose and departed, and came opposite Jebus (that is, Jerusalem). With him were the two saddled donkeys; his concubine was also with him.

11 They were near Jebus, and the day was far spent; and the servant said to his master, "Come, please, and let us turn aside into this city of the Jebusites and lodge in it."

12 But his master said to him, "We will not turn aside here into a city of foreigners, who are not of the children of Israel; we will go on Rto Gibeah."   Josh. 18:28

13 So he said to his servant, "Come, let us draw near to one of these places, and spend the night in Gibeah or in RRamah."   Josh. 18:25

14 And they passed by and went their way; and the sun went down on them near Gibeah, which belongs to Benjamin.

15 They turned aside there to go in to lodge in Gibeah. And when he went in, he sat down in the open square of the city, for no one would Rtake them into his house to spend the night.   Matt. 25:43

16 Just then an old man came in from Rhis work in the field at evening, who also was from the mountains of Ephraim; he was staying in Gibeah, whereas the men of the place were Benjamites.   Ps. 104:23

17 And when he raised his eyes, he saw the traveler in the open square of the city; and the old man said, "Where are you going, and where do you come from?"

18 So he said to him, "We are passing from

Bethlehem in Judah toward the remote mountains of Ephraim; I *am* from there. I went to Bethlehem in Judah; *now* I am going to the house of the LORD. But there *is* no one who will take me into his house,

19 "although we have both straw and fodder for our donkeys, and bread and wine for myself, for your female servant, and for the young man *who is* with your servant; *there is* no lack of anything."

20 And the old man said, R"Peace *be* with you! However, *let* all your needs *be* my responsibility; Ronly do not spend the night in the open square."   Gen. 43:23 · Gen. 19:2

21 So he brought him into his house, and gave fodder to the donkeys. And they washed their feet, and ate and drank.

Gibeah's Crime

22 As they were enjoying themselves, suddenly certain men of the city, Tperverted men, surrounded the house *and* beat on the door. They spoke to the master of the house, the old man, saying, R"Bring out the man who came to your house, that we may know him *carnally!*"   Lit. *sons of Belial* · [Rom. 1:26, 27]

23 But Rthe man, the master of the house, went out to them and said to them, "No, my brethren! I beg you, do not act *so* wickedly! Seeing this man has come into my house, Rdo not commit this outrage.   Gen. 19:6, 7 · 2 Sam. 13:12

24 R"Look, *here is* my virgin daughter and T*the man's* concubine; let me bring them out now. RHumble them, and do with them as you please; but to this man do not do such a vile thing!"   Gen. 19:8 · Lit. *his* · Gen. 34:2

25 But the men would not heed him. So the man took his concubine and brought *her* out to them. And they Rknew her and abused her all night until morning; and when the day began to break, they let her go.   Gen. 4:1

26 Then the woman came as the day was dawning, and fell down at the door of the man's house where her master *was*, till it was light.

27 When her master arose in the morning, and opened the doors of the house and went out to go his way, there was his concubine, fallen *at* the door of the house with her hands on the threshold.

28 And he said to her, "Get up and let us be going." But Rthere was no answer. So the man lifted her onto the donkey; and the man got up and went to his place.   Judg. 20:5

29 When he entered his house he took a knife, laid hold of his concubine, and divided her into twelve pieces, limb by limb, and sent her throughout all the territory of Israel.

30 And so it was that all who saw it said, "No such deed has been done or seen from the day that the children of Israel came up from the land of Egypt until this day. Consider it, confer, and speak up!"

Israel's War with the Benjamites

20 So Rall the children of Israel came out, from Dan to RBeersheba, as well as from the land of Gilead, and the congregation gathered together as one man before the LORD Rat Mizpah.   Josh. 22:12 · Josh. 19:2 · 1 Sam. 7:5

2 And the leaders of all the people, all the tribes of Israel, presented themselves in the assembly of the people of God, four hundred thousand foot soldiers who drew the sword.

3 (Now the children of Benjamin heard that the children of Israel had gone up to Mizpah.) Then the children of Israel said, "Tell *us*, how did this wicked deed happen?"

4 So the Levite, the husband of the woman who was murdered, answered and said, "My concubine and I went into Gibeah, which belongs to Benjamin, to spend the night.

5 R"And the men of Gibeah rose against me, and surrounded the house at night because of me. They intended to kill me, Rbut instead they ravished my concubine so that she died.   Judg. 19:22 · Judg. 19:25, 26

6 "So RI took hold of my concubine, cut her in pieces, and sent her throughout all the territory of the inheritance of Israel, because they Rcommitted lewdness and outrage in Israel.   Judg. 19:29 · Josh. 7:15

7 "Look! All of you *are* children of Israel; give your advice and counsel here and now!"

8 So all the people arose as one man, saying, "None *of us* will go to his tent, nor will any turn back to his house;

9 "but now this *is* the thing which we will do to Gibeah: We *will go up* against it by lot.

10 "We will take ten men out of *every* hundred throughout all the tribes of Israel, a hundred out of *every* thousand, and a thousand out of *every* ten thousand, to make provisions for the people, that when they come to Gibeah in Benjamin, they may repay all the vileness that they have done in Israel."

11 So all the men of Israel were gathered against the city, united together as one man.

12 RThen the tribes of Israel sent men through all the tribe of Benjamin, saying, "What *is* this wickedness that has occurred among you?   Deut. 13:14

13 "Now therefore, deliver up the men, the Tperverted men who *are* in Gibeah, that we may put them to death and remove the evil from Israel!" But the children of Benjamin would not listen to the voice of their brethren, the children of Israel.   Lit. *sons of Belial*

14 Instead, the children of Benjamin gathered together from their cities to Gibeah, to go to battle against the children of Israel.

15 And from their cities at that time Rthe children of Benjamin numbered twenty-six thousand men who drew the sword, besides the inhabitants of Gibeah, who numbered seven hundred select men.   Num. 1:36, 37

16 Among all this people *were* seven hun-

dred select men *who were* [R]left-handed; every one could sling a stone at a hair's *breadth* and not miss. 1 Chr. 12:2

17 Now besides Benjamin, the men of Israel numbered four hundred thousand men who drew the sword; all of these *were* men of war.

18 Then the children of Israel arose and went up to the house of God to inquire of God. They said, "Which of us shall go up first to battle against the children of Benjamin?" The LORD said, [R]"Judah first!" Judg. 1:1, 2

19 So the children of Israel rose in the morning and encamped against Gibeah.

20 And the men of Israel went out to battle against Benjamin, and the men of Israel put themselves in battle array to fight against them at Gibeah.

21 Then [R]the children of Benjamin came out of Gibeah, and on that day cut down to the ground twenty-two thousand men of the Israelites. [Gen. 49:27]

22 And the people, that is, the men of Israel, encouraged themselves and again formed the battle line at the place where they had put themselves in array on the first day.

23 [R]Then the children of Israel went up and wept before the LORD until evening, and asked counsel of the LORD, saying, "Shall I again draw near for battle against the children of my brother Benjamin?" And the LORD said, "Go up against him." Judg. 20:26, 27

24 So the children of Israel approached the children of Benjamin on the second day.

25 And [R]Benjamin went out against them from Gibeah on the second day, and cut down to the ground eighteen thousand more of the children of Israel; all these drew the sword. Judg. 20:21

26 Then all the children of Israel, that is, all the people, [R]went up and came to [T]the house of God and wept. They sat there before the LORD and fasted that day until evening; and they offered burnt offerings and peace offerings before the LORD. Judg. 20:18, 23; 21:2 · Or *Bethel*

27 So the children of Israel inquired of the LORD ([R]the ark of the covenant of God *was* there in those days, Josh. 18:1

28 [R]and Phinehas the son of Eleazar, the son of Aaron, [R]stood before it in those days), saying, "Shall I yet again go out to battle against the children of my brother Benjamin, or shall I cease?" And the LORD said, "Go up, for tomorrow I will deliver them into your hand." Josh. 24:33 · Deut. 10:8; 18:5

29 Then Israel [R]set men in ambush all around Gibeah. Josh. 8:4

30 And the children of Israel went up against the children of Benjamin on the third day, and put themselves in battle array against Gibeah as at the other times.

31 So the children of Benjamin went out against the people, *and* were drawn away from the city. They began to strike down *and*

kill some of the people, as at the other times, in the highways [R](one of which goes up to Bethel and the other to Gibeah) and in the field, about thirty men of Israel. Judg. 21:19

32 And the children of Benjamin said, "They *are* defeated before us, as at first." But the children of Israel said, "Let us flee and draw them away from the city to the highways."

33 So all the men of Israel rose from their place and put themselves in battle array at Baal Tamar. Then Israel's men in ambush burst forth from their position in the plain of Geba.

34 And ten thousand select men from all Israel came against Gibeah, and the battle was fierce. But [T]*the Benjamites* did not know that disaster *was* upon them. Lit. *they*

35 The LORD [T]defeated Benjamin before Israel. And the children of Israel destroyed that day twenty-five thousand one hundred Benjamites; all these drew the sword. struck

36 So the children of Benjamin saw that they were defeated. [R]The men of Israel had given ground to the Benjamites, because they relied on the men in ambush whom they had set against Gibeah. Josh. 8:15

37 [R]And the men in ambush quickly rushed upon Gibeah; the men in ambush spread out and struck the whole city with the edge of the sword. Josh. 8:19

38 Now the appointed signal between the men of Israel and the men in ambush was that they would make a great cloud of [R]smoke rise up from the city, Josh. 8:20

39 whereupon the men of Israel would turn in battle. Now Benjamin had begun [T]to strike *and* kill about thirty of the men of Israel. For they said, "Surely they are defeated before us, as *in* the first battle." Lit. *to strike the slain ones*

40 But when the cloud began to rise from the city in a column of smoke, the Benjamites looked behind them, and there was the whole city going up *in smoke* to heaven.

41 And when the men of Israel turned back, the men of Benjamin panicked, for they saw that disaster had come upon them.

42 Therefore they [T]turned *their backs* before the men of Israel in the direction of the wilderness; but the battle overtook them, and whoever *came* out of the cities they destroyed in their midst. fled

43 They surrounded the Benjamites, chased them, *and* easily trampled them down as far as the front of Gibeah toward the east.

44 And eighteen thousand men of Benjamin fell; all these *were* men of valor.

45 Then *they turned and fled toward the wilderness to the rock of [R]Rimmon; and they cut down five thousand of them on the highways. Then they pursued them relentlessly

20:45 LXX *the rest*

up to Gidom, and killed two thousand of them. Josh. 15:32

46 So all who fell of Benjamin that day were twenty-five thousand men who drew the sword; all these *were* men of valor.

47 ᴿBut six hundred men turned and fled toward the wilderness to the rock of Rimmon, and they stayed at the rock of Rimmon for four months. Judg. 21:13

48 And the men of Israel turned back against the children of Benjamin, and struck them down with the edge of the sword—from *every* city, men and beasts, all who were found. They also set fire to all the cities they came to.

Wives Provided for the Benjamites

21 Now ᴿthe men of Israel had sworn an oath at Mizpah, saying, "None of us shall give his daughter to Benjamin as a wife." Judg. 20:1

2 Then the people came ᴿto ᵀthe house of God, and remained there before God till evening. They lifted up their voices and wept bitterly, Judg. 20:18, 26 · Or *Bethel*

3 and said, "O LORD God of Israel, why has this come to pass in Israel, that today there should be one tribe *missing* in Israel?"

4 So it was, on the next morning, that the people rose early and ᴿbuilt an altar there, and offered burnt offerings and peace offerings. 2 Sam. 24:25

5 The children of Israel said, "Who *is there* among all the tribes of Israel who did not come up with the assembly to the LORD?" ᴿFor they had made a great oath concerning anyone who had not come up to the LORD at Mizpah, saying, "He shall surely be put to death." Judg. 20:1-3

6 And the children of Israel grieved for Benjamin their brother, and said, "One tribe is cut off from Israel today.

7 "What shall we do for wives for those who remain, seeing we have sworn by the LORD that we will not give them our daughters as wives?"

8 And they said, "What one *is there* from the tribes of Israel who did not come up to Mizpah to the LORD?" And, in fact, no one had come to the camp from ᴿJabesh Gilead to the assembly. 1 Sam. 11:1; 31:11

9 For when the people were counted, indeed, not one of the inhabitants of Jabesh Gilead *was* there.

10 So the congregation sent out there twelve thousand of their most valiant men, and commanded them, saying, ᴿ"Go and strike the inhabitants of Jabesh Gilead with the edge of the sword, including the women and children. Num. 31:17

11 "And this *is* the thing that you shall do: ᴿYou shall utterly destroy every male, and every woman who has known a man intimately." Num. 31:17

12 So they found among the inhabitants of Jabesh Gilead four hundred young virgins who had not known a man intimately; and they brought them to the camp at ᴿShiloh, which is in the land of Canaan. Josh. 18:1

13 Then the whole congregation sent *word* to the children of Benjamin ᴿwho *were* at the rock of Rimmon, and announced peace to them. Judg. 20:47

14 So Benjamin came back at that time, and they gave them the women whom they had saved alive of the women of Jabesh Gilead; and yet they had not found enough for them.

15 And the people ᴿgrieved for Benjamin, because the LORD had made a void in the tribes of Israel. Judg. 21:6

16 Then the elders of the congregation said, "What shall we do for wives for those who remain, since the women of Benjamin have been destroyed?"

17 And they said, "There *must be* an inheritance for the survivors of Benjamin, that a tribe may not be destroyed from Israel.

18 "However, we cannot give them wives from our daughters, for the children of Israel have sworn an oath, saying, 'Cursed *be* the one who gives a wife to Benjamin.' "

19 Then they said, "In fact, *there is* a yearly feast of the LORD in ᴿShiloh, which is north of Bethel, on the east side of the ᴿhighway that goes up from Bethel to Shechem, and south of Lebonah." 1 Sam. 1:3 · Judg. 20:31

20 Therefore they instructed the children of Benjamin, saying, "Go, lie in wait in the vineyards,

21 "and watch; and just when the daughters of Shiloh come out ᴿto perform their dances, then come out from the vineyards, and every man catch a wife for himself from the daughters of Shiloh; then go to the land of Benjamin. Judg. 11:34

22 "Then it shall be, when their fathers or their brothers come to us to complain, that we will say to them, 'Be kind to them for our sakes, because we did not take a wife for any of them in the war; for *it is* not *as though* you have given the *women* to them at this time, making yourselves guilty of your oath.' "

23 And the children of Benjamin did so; they took enough wives for their number from those who danced, whom they caught. Then they went and returned to their inheritance, and they ᴿrebuilt the cities and dwelt in them. Judg. 20:48

24 So the children of Israel departed from there at that time, every man to his tribe and family; they went out from there, every man to his inheritance.

25 ᴿIn those days *there was* no king in Israel; ᴿeveryone did *what was* right in his own eyes. Judg. 17:6; 18:1; 19:1 · Judg. 17:6

THE BOOK OF
Ruth

The book of Ruth is the romance book of the Bible. It has all the dramatic love and action of a best-seller on the contemporary book list. The love affair in this story, however, is not the relationship of a young man and woman but rather the affection of a young woman, Ruth, and her mother-in-law, Naomi. Ruth and Naomi exemplify the love of kinship which is absent in the typical home of our present-day society. It gives a high ideal of wedlock and a sense of commitment to the family.

AUTHORSHIP. The writer of the book is unknown. It must have been written when the rule of the Judges had ended with the introduction of the monarchy. It came after the birth of David, and some conclude that Samuel wrote it. The book covers about ten years and stands as a kind of appendix to the book of Judges. The book of Ruth is the only one in the canon which is completely devoted to the history of a woman.

SUMMARY STATEMENT. Ruth teaches the loyal love of God to the faithful minority, even in a time of spiritual decline.

THE PURPOSE OF RUTH. The purpose of this book is to trace the genealogy of David and ultimately of our Lord Jesus Christ. Ruth, who was a Gentile, married Boaz, a Jew. This story is a foreshadowing of the calling of the Gentiles to salvation. The Mosaic law shut off the Moabites, who therefore could be admitted only by God's grace. Ruth was related to Boaz by marriage; so are we related to Christ by the "marriage" of our human nature to His divine nature. As Boaz, who is a type of Christ, receives Ruth with love and tenderness, so our Lord receives us to Himself in forgiveness and cleansing so that we may find rest in Him.

KEY WORD AND KEY VERSE. Although the word *rest* is found only twice in the book of Ruth (1:9; 3:18), yet the thought permeates the entire story. In the East the position of the unmarried woman is dangerous; only in the house of a husband can she be sure of respect and protection. Elimelech forsook rest when he left the Promised Land. To leave Moab for Bethlehem seemed an impossible path to rest, as Naomi gravely and tactfully hinted, but God's ways are not man's ways. Ruth found rest through redemption and union with her redeemer. For us there is no rest in the world apart from union with Christ our Divine Redeemer. The key verse of Ruth is 2:12—"The LORD repay your work, and a full reward be given you by the LORD God of Israel, under whose wings you have come for refuge."

The lessons to be learned from the book of Ruth are pronounced. Israel was out of the will of God and thus suffered the punishment of God. God dealt with a Gentile who married a Jew (Boaz) and completed the lineage of Christ, thus showing the universality of God's redemption of men to form His family. Boaz is a picture of Christ who is the Lord of the harvest and who provides spiritual rest and refreshment for all who come to His feet in submission. Naomi had backslid and found the only way to peace was back in the will of God with His people. Thus it is with all of us: the world cannot satisfy the deepest needs of our lives; only in Christ are they met.

Perhaps the best-known passage in Ruth is found in 1:16–17: "Entreat me not to leave you, or to turn back from following after you; for wherever you go, I will go; and wherever you lodge, I will lodge; your people shall be my people, and your God, my God. Where you die, I will die, and there will I be buried. The LORD do so to me, and more also, if anything but death parts you and me."

—J.W.

Elimelech's Family Goes to Moab

NOW it came to pass, in the days when the judges ᵀruled, that there was a famine in the land. And a certain man of Bethlehem, Judah, went to ᵀdwell in the country of ᴿMoab, he and his wife and his two sons.   Lit. *judged* • Reside temporarily • Gen. 19:37

2 The name of the man *was* Elimelech, the name of his wife *was* Naomi, and the names of his two sons *were* Mahlon and Chilion—ᴿEphrathites of Bethlehem, Judah. And they went ᴿto the country of Moab and remained there.   Gen. 35:19 • Judg. 3:30

3 Then Elimelech, Naomi's husband, died; and she was left, and her two sons.

4 Now they took wives of the women of Moab: the name of the one *was* Orpah, and

the name of the other Ruth. And they dwelt there about ten years.

5 Then both Mahlon and Chilion also died; so the woman survived her two sons and her husband.

Naomi Returns with Ruth

6 Then she arose with her daughters-in-law that she might return from the country of Moab, for she had heard in the country of Moab that the LORD had ᵀvisited His people by ᴿgiving them bread.　　　*aided* · Matt. 6:11

7 Therefore she went out from the place where she was, and her two daughters-in-law with her; and they went on the way to return to the land of Judah.

8 And Naomi said to her two daughters-in-law, ᴿ"Go, return each to her mother's house. The LORD deal kindly with you, as you have dealt with the dead and with me.　　Josh. 24:15

9 "The LORD grant that you may find ᴿrest, each in the house of her husband." So she kissed them, and they lifted up their voices and wept.　　　Ruth 3:1

10 And they said to her, "Surely we will return with you to your people."

11 But Naomi said, "Turn back, my daughters; why will you go with me? *Are* there still sons in my womb, ᴿthat they may be your husbands?　　　Deut. 25:5

12 "Turn back, my daughters, go—for I am too old to have a husband. If I should say I have hope, *if* I should have a husband tonight and should also bear sons,

13 "would you wait for them till they were grown? Would you restrain yourselves from having husbands? No, my daughters; for it grieves me very much for your sakes that ᴿthe hand of the LORD has gone out against me!"　　　Judg. 2:15

14 Then they lifted up their voices and wept again; and Orpah kissed her mother-in-law, but Ruth ᴿclung to her.　　　[Prov. 17:17]

15 And she said, "Look, your sister-in-law has gone back to ᴿher people and to her gods; return after your sister-in-law."　　Judg. 11:24

16 But Ruth said:

ᴿ"Entreatᵀ me not to leave you,
    Or to turn back from following after
    you;　　　2 Kin. 2:2, 4, 6 · *Urge*
For wherever you go, I will go;
    And wherever you lodge, I will lodge;
ᴿYour people *shall be* my people,
    And your God, my God.　　Ruth. 2:11, 12
17 Where you die, I will die,
    And there will I be buried.
ᴿThe LORD do so to me, and more also,
    If *anything but* death parts you and
    me."　　　1 Sam. 3:17

18 When she saw that she was determined to go with her, she stopped speaking to her.

19 Now the two of them went until they came to Bethlehem. And it happened, when they had come to Bethlehem, that ᴿall the city was excited because of them; and the women said, "*Is* this Naomi?"　　Matt. 21:10

20 But she said to them, "Do not call me ᵀNaomi; call me ᵀMara, for the Almighty has dealt very bitterly with me.　Lit. *Pleasant* · *Bitter*

21 "I went out full, ᴿand the LORD has brought me home again empty. Why do you call me Naomi, since the LORD has testified against me, and ᵀthe Almighty has afflicted me?"　　Job 1:21 · Heb. *Shaddai*

22 So Naomi returned, and Ruth the Moabitess her daughter-in-law with her, who returned from the country of Moab. Now they came to Bethlehem ᴿat the beginning of barley harvest.　　　2 Sam. 21:9

Ruth Meets Boaz

2 There was a relative of Naomi's husband, a man of great wealth, of the family of Elimelech. His name *was* Boaz.

2 So Ruth the Moabitess said to Naomi, "Please let me go to the ᴿfield, and glean heads of grain after *him* in whose sight I may find favor." And she said to her, "Go, my daughter."　　　Lev. 19:9, 10; 23:22

3 Then she left, and went and gleaned in the field after the reapers. And she happened to come to the part of the field *belonging* to Boaz, who *was* of the family of Elimelech.

4 Now behold, Boaz came from ᴿBethlehem, and said to the reapers, ᴿ"The LORD *be* with you!" And they answered him, "The LORD bless you!"　　　Ruth 1:1 · Ps. 129:7, 8

5 Then Boaz said to his servant who was in charge of the reapers, "Whose young woman *is* this?"

6 So the servant who was in charge of the reapers answered and said, "It *is* the young Moabite woman ᴿwho came back with Naomi from the country of Moab.　　Ruth 1:22

7 "And she said, 'Please let me glean and gather after the reapers among the sheaves.' So she came and has continued from morning until now, though she rested a little in the house."

8 Then Boaz said to Ruth, "You will listen, my daughter, will you not? Do not go to glean in another field, nor go from here, but stay close by my young women.

9 "*Let* your eyes *be* on the field which they reap, and go after them. Have I not commanded the young men not to touch you? And when you are thirsty, go to the vessels and drink from what the young men have drawn."

10 So she fell on her face, bowed down to the ground, and said to him, "Why have I found favor in your eyes, that you should take notice of me, since I *am* a foreigner?"

11 And Boaz answered and said to her, "It has been fully reported to me, ᴿall that you have done for your mother-in-law since the

death of your husband, and *how* you have left your father and your mother and the land of your birth, and have come to a people whom you did not know before.   Ruth 1:14–18

12 ᴿ"The Lᴏʀᴅ repay your work, and a full reward be given you by the Lᴏʀᴅ God of Israel, ᴿunder whose wings you have come for refuge."   1 Sam. 24:19 • Ruth 1:16

13 Then she said, "Let me find favor in your sight, my lord; for you have comforted me, and have spoken ᵀkindly to your maidservant, ᴿthough I am not like one of your maidservants."   Lit. *to the heart of* • 1 Sam. 25:41

14 Now Boaz said to her at mealtime, "Come here, and eat of the bread, and dip your piece of bread in the vinegar." So she sat beside the reapers, and he passed parched *grain* to her; and she ate and ᴿwas satisfied, and kept some back.   Ruth 2:18

15 And when she rose up to ᵀglean, Boaz commanded his young men, saying, "Let her glean even among the sheaves, and do not ᵀreproach her.   Gather after the reapers • *rebuke*

16 "Also let *grain* from the bundles fall purposely for her; leave *it* that she may glean, and do not rebuke her."

17 So she gleaned in the field until evening, and beat out what she had gleaned, and it was about an ᵀephah of ᴿbarley. .65 bu. • Ruth 1:22

18 Then she took *it* up and went into the city, and her mother-in-law saw what she had gleaned. So she brought out and gave to her ᴿwhat she had kept back after she had been satisfied.   Ruth 2:14

19 And her mother-in-law said to her, "Where have you gleaned today? And where did you work? Blessed be the one who ᴿtook notice of you." So she told her mother-in-law with whom she had worked, and said, "The man's name with whom I worked today *is* Boaz."   [Ps. 41:1]

20 Then Naomi said to her daughter-in-law, "Blessed *be* he of the Lᴏʀᴅ, who has not forsaken His kindness to the living and the dead!" And Naomi said to her, "This man *is* a relation of ours, one of our close relatives."

21 Ruth the Moabitess said, "He also said to me, 'You shall stay close by my young men until they have finished all my harvest.' "

22 And Naomi said to Ruth her daughter-in-law, "*It is* good, my daughter, that you go out with his young women, and that people do not ᵀmeet you in any other field."   *encounter*

23 So she stayed close by the young women of Boaz, to glean until the end of barley harvest and wheat harvest; and she dwelt with her mother-in-law.

Ruth's Redemption Assured

3 Then Naomi her mother-in-law said to her, "My daughter, ᴿshall I not seek ᴿsecurityᵀ for you, that it may be well with you?   1 Tim. 5:8 • Ruth 1:9 • *rest*

2 "Now Boaz, ᴿwhose young women you were with, *is he* not our relative? In fact, he is winnowing barley tonight at the threshing floor.   Ruth 2:3, 8

3 "Therefore wash yourself and ᴿanoint yourself, put on your *best* garment and go down to the threshing floor; *but* do not make yourself known to the man until he has finished eating and drinking.   2 Sam. 14:2

4 "Then it shall be, when he lies down, that you shall notice the place where he lies; and you shall go in, uncover his feet, and lie down; and he will tell you what you should do."

5 And she said to her, "All that you say to me I will do."

6 So she went down to the threshing floor and did according to all that her mother-in-law instructed her.

7 And after Boaz had eaten and drunk, and his heart was cheerful, he went to lie down at the end of the heap of grain; and she came softly, uncovered his feet, and lay down.

8 Now it happened at midnight that the man was startled, and turned himself; and there, a woman was lying at his feet.

9 And he said, "Who *are* you?" So she answered, "I *am* Ruth, your maidservant. *Take your maidservant under your wing, for you are a ᵀclose relative."   *redeemer*

10 Then he said, ᴿ"Blessed *are* you of the Lᴏʀᴅ, my daughter! For you have shown more kindness at the end than ᴿat the beginning, in that you did not go after young men, whether poor or rich.   Ruth 2:20 • Ruth 1:8

11 "And now, my daughter, do not fear. I will do for you all that you request, for all the people of my town know that you *are* ᴿa virtuous woman.   Prov. 12:4; 31:10–31

12 "Now it is true that I *am* a ᴿclose relative; however, ᴿthere is a relative closer than I.   Ruth 3:9 • Ruth 4:1

13 "Stay this night, and in the morning it shall be *that* if he will perform the duty of a close relative for you—good; let him do it. But if he does not want to perform the duty for you, then I will perform the duty for you, *as* the Lᴏʀᴅ lives! Lie down until morning."

14 So she lay at his feet until morning, and she arose before one could recognize another. Then he said, "Do not let it be known that the woman came to the threshing floor."

15 Also he said, "Bring the ᵀshawl that *is* on you and hold it." And when she held it, he measured six *ephahs* of barley, and laid *it* on her. Then *she went into the city.   *cloak*

16 When she came to her mother-in-law, she said, "*Is* that you, my daughter?" Then she told her all that the man had done for her.

3:9 Or *Spread the corner of your garment over your maidservant*
3:15 Many Heb. mss., Syr., Vg. *she;* MT, LXX, Tg. *he*

17 And she said, "These six *ephahs* of barley he gave me; for he said to me, 'Do not go empty-handed to your mother-in-law.' "

18 Then she said, R"Sit still, my daughter, until you know how the matter will turn out; for the man will not rest until he has concluded the matter this day." [Ps. 37:3, 5]

Boaz Redeems Ruth

4 Now Boaz went up to the gate and sat down there; and behold, the close relative of whom Boaz had spoken came by. So Boaz said, "Come aside, *friend, sit down here." So he came aside and sat down.

2 And he took ten men of Rthe elders of the city, and said, "Sit down here." So they sat down. 1 Kin. 21:8

3 Then he said to the close relative, "Naomi, who has come back from the country of Moab, sold the piece of land Rwhich *belonged* to our brother Elimelech. Lev. 25:25

4 "And I thought to Tinform you, saying, 'Buy *it* back Rin the presence of the inhabitants and the elders of my people. If you will redeem *it*, redeem *it*; but if *you will not redeem *it*, *then* tell me, that I may know; Rfor *there is* no one but you to redeem *it*, and I *am* next after you.' " And he said, "I will redeem *it*." Lit. *uncover your ear* • Gen. 23:18 • Lev. 25:25

5 Then Boaz said, "On the day you buy the field from the hand of Naomi, you must also buy *it* from Ruth the Moabitess, the wife of the dead, Rto *perpetuate the name of the dead through his inheritance." Matt. 22:24

6 And the close relative said, "I cannot redeem *it* for myself, lest I ruin my own inheritance. You redeem my right of redemption for yourself, for I cannot redeem *it*."

7 Now this *was the custom* in former times in Israel concerning redeeming and exchanging, to confirm anything: one man took off his sandal and gave *it* to the other, and this *was* a confirmation in Israel.

8 Therefore the close relative said to Boaz, "Buy *it* for yourself." So he took off his sandal.

9 And Boaz said to the elders and all the people, "You *are* witnesses this day that I

have bought all that was Elimelech's, and all that *was* Chilion's and Mahlon's, from the hand of Naomi.

10 "Moreover, Ruth the Moabitess, the widow of Mahlon, I have acquired as my wife, to perpetuate the name of the dead through his inheritance, Rthat the name of the dead may not be cut off from among his brethren and from *his position at the gate. You *are* witnesses this day." Deut. 25:6

11 And all the people who *were* at the gate, and the elders, said, "*We are* witnesses. The LORD make the woman who is coming to your house like Rachel and Leah, the two who Rbuilt the house of Israel; and may you prosper in REphrathah and be famous in RBethlehem. Gen. 29:25–30 • Gen. 35:16–18 • Mic. 5:2

12 "May your house be like the house of Perez, whom Tamar bore to Judah, because of Rthe offspring which the LORD will give you from this young woman." 1 Sam. 2:20

Descendants of Boaz and Ruth

13 So Boaz took Ruth and she became his wife; and when he went in to her, the LORD gave her conception, and she bore a son.

14 Then Rthe women said to Naomi, "Blessed *be* the LORD, who has not left you this day without a Tclose relative; and may his name be famous in Israel! Luke 1:58 • *redeemer*

15 "And may he be to you a restorer of life and a nourisher of your old age; for your daughter-in-law, who loves you, who is better to you than seven sons, has borne him."

16 Then Naomi took the child and laid him on her bosom, and became a nurse to him.

17 Also the neighbor women gave him a name, saying, "There is a son born to Naomi." And they called his name Obed. He *is* the father of Jesse, the father of David.

18 RNow this *is* the genealogy of Perez: RPerez begot Hezron; 1 Chr. 2:4, 5 • Num. 26:20, 21

19 Hezron begot Ram, and Ram begot Amminadab;

20 Amminadab begot Nahshon, and Nahshon begot RSalmon;T Matt. 1:4 • Heb. *Salmah*

21 Salmon begot Boaz, and Boaz begot Obed;

22 Obed begot Jesse, and Jesse begot RDavid. Matt. 1:6

4:1 Lit. *so and so,* Heb. *peloni almoni*

4:4 So with many Heb. mss., LXX, Syr., Tg., Vg.; MT *he*

4:5 Lit. *raise up*

4:10 Probably his civic office

THE FIRST BOOK OF

Samuel

The two books of Samuel were originally one volume. Their division into two books, as we know them, originated with the Septuagint, the Greek translation of the Hebrew Scriptures, in the third century B.C.

How 1 SAMUEL FITS INTO THE BIBLE. 1 Samuel is the first of what has been called the three "double books" of the Old Testament—1 and 2 Samuel, 1 and 2 Kings, and 1 and 2 Chronicles. These three "double books" form a complete section of the Scripture. They record the rise and fall of the Israelite monarchy.

The book of 1 Samuel presents the personal history of Samuel, the last of the judges. It clearly marks a definite period running from the birth of Samuel to the death of Saul, the first of the kings of Israel. Interwoven in this remarkable book are the histories of three outstanding personalities: Samuel (chs. 1—7), Saul (chs. 8—15), and David (chs. 16—31). Samuel was the last of the judges, Saul the first of the kings, and David the greatest of the kings of Israel.

AUTHORSHIP. The divine Author is the Holy Spirit, but the human author is anonymous. Although we do not know whether this book was written by one or more persons, the biblical text does indicate that Samuel made some written records (10:25). Nathan, Gad, and David could have chronicled the events of this book. The writer or writers are of lesser importance when we know they were divinely moved to record as God directed.

The events in 1 Samuel cover a period of time between the birth of Samuel and the closing days of the reign of Saul. If the birth of Samuel (1:20) is dated 1100 B.C., and if David ascended the throne of Judah in 1011 B.C., then the book spans a period of more than a century in Hebrew history.

How 1 SAMUEL FITS TOGETHER. The book begins with the beloved story of Hannah's desire for a child and the subsequent birth of Samuel (chs. 1—3). In chapters 4—6 the capture and later return of the ark of the covenant of the Lord is narrated, followed by Israel's demand for a king like all the other nations (ch. 7). Chapters 8—31 tell the story of Saul, the first king of Israel. In the book of 1 Samuel mention of David by name first occurs in 16:13, which records how "Samuel took the horn of oil and anointed him in the midst of his brothers; and the Spirit of the LORD came upon David from that day forward." From this point the story of the beloved shepherd boy David runs concurrently with that of King Saul, up until the time of Saul's death (ch. 31).

SUMMARY STATEMENT. In demanding a king "like all the nations" (8:20), Israel rejected God's rule and moved from a theocratic form of government to a monarchy. Nevertheless, God was still working to accomplish His purpose through His chosen leader.

God's will for the anointed king was to be the spiritual leader who obeyed His law and recognized Him as the true King of the nation. But, due to the influence of the Canaanites and their own carnality, the people of Israel asked for a tyrannical ruler who was answerable to no one. Thus, the king of the "people's choice" was objectionable both to Samuel and to God (8:10-20).

At least one lesson is obvious to the student of Israel's history: "Righteousness exalts a nation, but sin is a reproach to any people" (Prov. 14:34). Whenever the nation exalted God, God exalted the nation; but when rulers, prophets, priests, and people turned from God's law, God removed His blessing.

God's ultimate purpose to reign as King in the person of His Son, Jesus Christ, continues to move toward fulfillment. No matter how many reject His rule, none can dethrone Him. God is sovereign; He is still the "KING OF KINGS AND LORD OF LORDS" (Rev. 19:16; 17:14).

—J.F.D.

The Family of Elkanah

NOW there was a certain man of Ramathaim Zophim, of the mountains of Ephraim, and his name *was* Elkanah the son of Jeroham, the son of *Elihu, the son of *Tohu, the son of Zuph, an Ephraimite.

2 And he had ᴿtwo wives: the name of one *was* Hannah, and the name of the other Peninnah. Peninnah had children, but Hannah had no children.   Deut. 21:15–17

3 This man went up from his city ᴿyearly ᴿto worship and sacrifice to the LORD of hosts in ᴿShiloh. Also the two sons of Eli, Hophni and Phinehas, the priests of the LORD, *were* there.   Luke 2:41 • Deut. 12:5–7; 16:16 • Josh 18:1

4 And whenever the time came for Elkanah to make an ᴿoffering, he would give portions to Peninnah his wife and to all her sons and daughters.   Deut. 12:17, 18

5 But to Hannah he would give a double portion, for he loved Hannah, ᴿalthough the LORD had closed her womb.   Gen. 16:1; 30:1, 2

6 And her rival also ᴿprovoked her severely, to make her miserable, because the LORD had closed her womb.   Job 24:21

7 So it was, year by year, when she went up to the house of the LORD, that she provoked her; therefore she wept and did not eat.

Hannah's Vow

8 Then Elkanah her husband said to her, "Hannah, why do you weep? Why do you not eat? And why is your heart grieved? *Am* I not ᴿbetter to you than ten sons?"   Ruth 4:15

9 So Hannah arose after they had finished eating and drinking in Shiloh. Now Eli the priest was sitting on the seat by the doorpost of ᴿthe *tabernacle of the LORD.   1 Sam. 3:3

10 And she *was* in bitterness of soul, and prayed to the LORD and wept in anguish.

11 Then she made a vow and said, "O LORD of hosts, if You will indeed look on the affliction of your maidservant and remember me, and not forget your maidservant, but will give your maidservant a male child, then I will give him to the LORD all the days of his life, and no razor shall come upon his head."

12 And it happened, as she continued praying before the LORD, that Eli watched her mouth.

13 Now Hannah spoke in her heart; only her lips moved, but her voice was not heard. Therefore Eli thought she was drunk.

14 So Eli said to her, "How long will you be drunk? Put your wine away from you!"

15 But Hannah answered and said, "No, my lord, I *am* a woman of sorrowful spirit. I have drunk neither wine nor intoxicating drink, but have ᴿpoured out my soul before the LORD.   Ps. 42:4; 62:8

16 "Do not consider your maidservant a ᴿwickedᵀ woman, for out of the abundance of my complaint and grief I have spoken until now."   Deut. 13:13 • Lit. *daughter of Belial*

17 Then Eli answered and said, "Go in peace, and the God of Israel grant your petition which you have asked of Him."

18 And she said, ᴿ"Let your maidservant find favor in your sight." So the woman ᴿwent her way and ate, and her face was no longer *sad*.   Ruth 2:13 • Rom. 15:13

Samuel Is Born and Dedicated

19 Then they rose early in the morning and worshiped before the LORD, and returned and came to their house at Ramah. And Elkanah ᴿknew Hannah his wife, and the LORD ᴿremembered her.   Gen. 4:1 • Gen. 21:1; 30:22

20 So it came to pass in the process of time that Hannah conceived and bore a son, and called his name *Samuel, saying, "Because I have asked for him from the LORD."

21 Now the man Elkanah and all his house ᴿwent up to offer to the LORD the yearly sacrifice and his vow.   1 Sam. 1:3

22 But Hannah did not go up, for she said to her husband, "Not until the child is weaned; then I will take him, that he may appear before the LORD and remain there forever."

23 So Elkanah her husband said to her, "Do what seems best to you; wait until you have weaned him. Only let the LORD establish *His word." Then the woman stayed and nursed her son until she had weaned him.

24 Now when she had weaned him, she took him up with her, with *three bulls, one ephah of flour, and a skin of wine, and brought him to ᴿthe house of the LORD in Shiloh. And the child *was* young.   Josh. 18:1

25 Then they slaughtered a bull, and ᴿbrought the child to Eli.   Luke 2:22

26 And she said, "O my lord! ᴿAs your soul lives, my lord, I *am* the woman who stood by you here, praying to the LORD.   2 Kin. 2:2, 4, 6

27 ᴿ"For this child I prayed, and the LORD has granted me my petition which I asked of Him.   [Matt. 7:7]

28 "Therefore I also have lent him to the LORD; as long as he lives he shall be ᵀlent to the LORD." So they ᴿworshiped the LORD there.   granted • Gen. 24:26, 52

Hannah's Prayer

2 And Hannah ᴿprayed and said: Phil. 4:6

"My heart rejoices in the LORD;
My ᵀhorn is exalted in the LORD.

1:1 *Eliel*, 1 Chr. 6:34 • *Toah*, 1 Chr. 6:34
1:9 Heb. *heykal*, palace or temple
1:20 Lit. *Heard by God*
1:23 So with MT, Tg., Vg.; DSS, LXX, Syr. *your*
1:24 DSS, LXX, Syr. *a three-year-old bull*

I smile at my enemies,   Strength
Because I rejoice in Your salvation.

2 "No one is holy like the Lord,
For there is none besides You,
Nor is there any rock like our God.

3 "Talk no more so very proudly;
RLet no arrogance come from your
mouth,   Ps. 94:4
For the Lord is the God of knowledge;
And by Him actions are weighed.

4 "TheR bows of the mighty men are
broken,   Ps. 37:15; 46:9
And those who stumbled are girded
with strength.

5 Those who were full have hired
themselves out for bread,
And the hungry have ceased to hunger.
Even Rthe barren has borne seven,
And Rshe who has many children has
become feeble.   Ps. 113:9 • Is. 54:1

6 "TheR Lord kills and makes alive;
He brings down to the grave and brings
up.   Deut. 32:39

7 The Lord makes poor and makes rich;
RHe brings low and lifts up.   Ps. 75:7

8 RHe raises the poor from the dust
And lifts the beggar from the ash heap,
RTo set them among princes
And make them inherit the throne of
glory.   Luke 1:52 • Job 36:7

R"For the pillars of the earth are the
Lord's,
And He has set the world upon
them.   Job 38:4-6

9 RHe will guard the feet of His saints,
But the Rwicked shall be silent in
darkness.   [1 Pet. 1:5] • Rom. 3:19

"For by strength no man shall prevail.

10 The adversaries of the Lord shall be
Rbroken in pieces;   Ps. 2:9
RFrom heaven He will thunder against
them.   Ps. 18:13, 14
RThe Lord will judge the ends of the
earth.   Ps. 96:13; 98:9

"He will give strength to His king,
And exalt the horn of His anointed."

11 Then Elkanah went to his house at Ramah. But the child Tministered to the Lord
before Eli the priest.   served

The Wicked Sons of Eli

12 Now the sons of Eli were Tcorrupt; they
did not know the Lord.   Lit. sons of Belial

13 And the priests' custom with the people
was that when any man offered a sacrifice,
the priest's servant would come with a three-
pronged fleshhook in his hand while the meat
was boiling.

14 Then he would thrust it into the pan, or
kettle, or caldron, or pot; and the priest
would take for himself all that the fleshhook
brought up. So they did in RShiloh to all the
Israelites who came there.   1 Sam. 1:3

15 Also, before they Rburned the fat, the
priest's servant would come and say to the
man who sacrificed, "Give meat for roasting
to the priest, for he will not take boiled meat
from you, but raw."   Lev. 3:3–5, 16

16 And if the man said to him, "They
should really burn the fat first; then you may
take as much as your heart desires," he
would then answer him, "No, but you must
give it now; and if not, I will take it by force."

17 Therefore the sin of the young men was
very great before the Lord, for men Tab-
horred the offering of the Lord.   despised

Samuel's Childhood Ministry

18 But Samuel ministered before the Lord,
even as a child, wearing a linen ephod.

19 Moreover his mother used to make him a
little robe, and bring it to him year by year
when she Rcame up with her husband to offer
the yearly sacrifice.   1 Sam. 1:3, 21

20 And Eli would bless Elkanah and his
wife, and say, "The Lord give you descendants from this woman for the Tloan that was
Rgiven to the Lord." Then they would go to
their own home.   gift • 1 Sam. 1:11, 27, 28

21 And the Lord Rvisited T Hannah, so that
she conceived and bore three sons and two
daughters. Meanwhile the child Samuel grew
before the Lord.   Gen. 21:1 • aided

Prophecy Against Eli's Household

22 Now Eli was very old; and he heard
everything his sons did to all Israel, *and how
they lay with Rthe women who assembled at
the door of the tabernacle of meeting. Ex. 38:8

23 So he said to them, "Why do you do such
things? For I hear of your evil dealings from
all the people.

24 "No, my sons! For it is not a good report
that I hear. You make the Lord's people
transgress.

25 "If one man sins against another, RGod*
will judge him. But if a man Rsins against the
Lord, who will intercede for him?" Nevertheless they did not heed the voice of their
father, Rbecause the Lord desired to kill
them.   Deut. 1:17; 25:1, 2 • Num. 15:30 • Josh. 11:20

26 And the child Samuel grew in stature,
and in favor both with the Lord and men.

27 Then a Rman of God came to Eli and said
to him, "Thus says the Lord: R'Did I not
clearly reveal Myself to the house of your
father when they were in Egypt in Pharaoh's
house?   1 Kin. 13:1 • Ex. 4:14–16; 12:1

2:22 So with MT, Tg., Vg.; DSS, LXX omit rest of verse
2:25 Tg. the Judge

28 'Did I not choose him out of all the tribes of Israel to be My priest, to offer upon My altar, to burn incense, and to wear an ephod before Me? And ᴿdid I not give to the house of your father all the offerings of the children of Israel made by fire? Num. 5:9

29 'Why do you kick at My sacrifice and My offering which I have commanded in My dwelling place, and honor your sons more than Me, to make yourselves fat with the best of all the offerings of Israel My people?'

30 "Therefore the Lᴏʀᴅ God of Israel says: ᴿ'I said indeed that your house and the house of your father would walk before Me forever.' But now the Lᴏʀᴅ says: ᴿ'Far be it from Me; for those who honor Me I will honor, and ᴿthose who despise Me shall be lightly esteemed. Ex. 29:9 • Jer. 18:9, 10 • Mal. 2:9–12

31 'Behold, ᴿthe days are coming that I will cut off your ᵀarm and the arm of your father's house, so that there will not be an old man in your house. 1 Kin. 2:27, 35 • strength

32 'And you will see an enemy in My dwelling place, despite all the good which God does for Israel. And there shall not be ᴿan old man in your house forever. Zech. 8:4

33 'But any of your men whom I do not cut off from My altar shall consume your eyes and grieve your heart. And all the descendants of your house shall die in the flower of their age.

34 'Now this shall be ᴿa sign to you that will come upon your two sons, on Hophni and Phinehas: ᴿin one day they shall die, both of them. 1 Kin. 13:3 • 1 Sam. 4:11, 17

35 'Then ᴿI will raise up for Myself a faithful priest who shall do according to what is in My heart and in My mind. ᴿI will build him a sure house, and he shall walk before ᴿMy anointed forever. 1 Kin. 2:35 • 1 Kin. 11:38 • Ps. 18:50

36 ᴿ'And it shall come to pass that everyone who is left in your house will come and bow down to him for a piece of silver and a morsel of bread, and say, "Please, ᵀput me in one of the priestly positions, that I may eat a piece of bread." ' " 1 Kin. 2:27 • assign

Samuel's First Prophecy

3 Now ᴿthe boy Samuel ministered to the Lᴏʀᴅ before Eli. And ᴿthe word of the Lᴏʀᴅ was rare in those days; there was no widespread revelation. 1 Sam. 2:11, 18 • Ps. 74:9

2 And it came to pass at that time, while Eli was lying down in his place, and when his eyes had begun to grow ᴿso dim that he could not see, 1 Sam. 4:15

3 and before the lamp of God went out in the tabernacle of the Lᴏʀᴅ where the ark of God was, and while Samuel was lying down,

4 that the Lᴏʀᴅ called Samuel. And he answered, "Here I am!"

5 So he ran to Eli and said, "Here I am, for you called me." And he said, "I did not call; lie down again." And he went and lay down.

6 Then the Lᴏʀᴅ called yet again, "Samuel!" So Samuel arose and went to Eli, and said, "Here I am, for you called me." He answered, "I did not call, my son; lie down again."

7 (Now Samuel ᴿdid not yet know the Lᴏʀᴅ, nor was the word of the Lᴏʀᴅ yet revealed to him.) 1 Sam. 2:12

8 And the Lᴏʀᴅ called Samuel again the third time. So he arose and went to Eli, and said, "Here I am, for you did call me." Then Eli perceived that the Lᴏʀᴅ had called the boy.

9 Therefore Eli said to Samuel, "Go, lie down; and it shall be, if He calls you, that you must say, ᴿ'Speak, Lᴏʀᴅ, for Your servant hears.' " So Samuel went and lay down in his place. 1 Kin. 2:17

10 Now the Lᴏʀᴅ came and stood and called as at other times, "Samuel! Samuel!" And Samuel answered, "Speak, for Your servant hears."

11 Then the Lᴏʀᴅ said to Samuel: "Behold, I will do something in Israel at which both ears of everyone who hears it will tingle.

12 "In that day I will perform against Eli ᴿall that I have spoken concerning his house, from beginning to end. 1 Sam. 2:27–36

13 "For I have told him that I will judge his house forever for the iniquity which he knows, because his sons made themselves vile, and he did not ᵀrestrain them. rebuke

14 "And therefore I have sworn to the house of Eli that the iniquity of Eli's house ᴿshall not be atoned for by sacrifice or offering forever." Num. 15:30, 31

15 So Samuel lay down until *morning, and opened the doors of the house of the Lᴏʀᴅ. And Samuel was afraid to tell Eli the vision.

16 Then Eli called Samuel and said, "Samuel, my son!" He answered, "Here I am."

17 And he said, "What is the word that the Lᴏʀᴅ spoke to you? Please do not hide it from me. ᴿGod do so to you, and more also, if you hide anything from me of all the things that He said to you." Ruth 1:17

18 Then Samuel told him everything, and hid nothing from him. And he said, "It is the Lᴏʀᴅ. Let Him do what seems good to Him."

19 So Samuel ᴿgrew, and the Lᴏʀᴅ was with him ᴿand let none of his words ᵀfall to the ground. 1 Sam. 2:21 • 1 Sam. 9:6 • fail

20 And all Israel ᴿfrom Dan to Beersheba knew that Samuel had been ᵀestablished as a prophet of the Lᴏʀᴅ. Judg. 20:1 • confirmed

21 Then the Lᴏʀᴅ appeared again in Shiloh. For the Lᴏʀᴅ revealed Himself to Samuel in Shiloh by ᴿthe word of the Lᴏʀᴅ. 1 Sam. 3:1, 4

3:15 So with MT, Tg., Vg.; LXX adds and he arose in the morning

4 And the word of Samuel came to all *Israel.

The Ark of God Captured

Now Israel went out to battle against the Philistines, and encamped beside Ebenezer; and the Philistines encamped in Aphek. 2 Then the Philistines put themselves in battle array against Israel. And when they joined battle, Israel was ᵀdefeated by the Philistines, who killed about four thousand men of the army in the field.   Lit. *struck*
3 And when the people had come into the camp, the elders of Israel said, "Why has the Lᴏʀᴅ defeated us today before the Philistines? ᴿLet us bring the ark of the covenant of the Lᴏʀᴅ from Shiloh to us, that when it comes among us it may save us from the hand of our enemies."   Josh. 6:6-21
4 So the people sent to Shiloh, that they might bring from there the ark of the covenant of the Lᴏʀᴅ of hosts, who dwells *between* the cherubim. And the ᴿtwo sons of Eli, Hophni and Phinehas, *were* there with the ark of the covenant of God.   1 Sam. 2:12
5 And when the ark of the covenant of the Lᴏʀᴅ came into the camp, all Israel shouted so loudly that the earth shook.
6 Now when the Philistines heard the noise of the shout, they said, "What *does* the sound of this great shout in the camp of the Hebrews *mean*?" Then they understood that the ark of the Lᴏʀᴅ had come into the camp.
7 So the Philistines were afraid, for they said, "God has come into the camp!" And they said, ᴿ"Woe to us! For such a thing has never happened before.   Ex. 15:14
8 "Woe to us! Who will deliver us from the hand of these mighty gods? These *are* the gods who struck the Egyptians with all the plagues in the wilderness.
9 ᴿ"Be strong and conduct yourselves like men, you Philistines, that you do not become servants of the Hebrews, ᴿas they have been to you. ᵀConduct yourselves like men, and fight!"   1 Cor. 16:13 • Judg. 13:1 • Lit. *Be men*
10 So the Philistines fought, and Israel was defeated, and every man fled to his tent. There was a very great slaughter, and there fell of Israel thirty thousand foot soldiers.
11 Also ᴿthe ark of God was captured; and ᴿthe two sons of Eli, Hophni and Phinehas, died.   Ps. 78:60, 61 • 1 Sam. 2:34

Death of Eli

12 Then a man of Benjamin ran from the battle line the same day, and came to Shiloh with his clothes torn and dirt on his head.

13 Now when he came, there was Eli, sitting on a seat *by the wayside watching, for his heart ᵀtrembled for the ark of God. And when the man came into the city and told *it*, all the city cried out.   *trembled with anxiety*
14 When Eli heard the noise of the outcry, he said, "What *does* the sound of this tumult *mean*?" And the man came quickly and told Eli.
15 Eli was ninety-eight years old, and his eyes were so dim that he could not see.
16 Then the man said to Eli, "I *am* he who came from the battle. And I fled today from the battle line." And he said, ᴿ"What happened, my son?"   2 Sam. 1:4
17 So the messenger answered and said, "Israel has fled before the Philistines, and there has been a great slaughter among the people. Also your two sons, Hophni and Phinehas, are dead; and the ark of God has been captured."
18 Then it happened, when he made mention of the ark of God, that Eli fell off the seat backward by the side of the gate; and his neck was broken and he died, for the man was old and heavy. And he had judged Israel forty years.

Ichabod

19 Now his daughter-in-law, Phinehas' wife, was with child, *due* to be delivered; and when she heard the news that the ark of God was captured, and that her father-in-law and her husband were dead, she bowed herself and gave birth, for her labor pains came upon her.
20 And about the time of her death the women who stood by her said to her, "Do not fear, for you have borne a son." But she did not answer, nor did she regard *it*.
21 Then she named the child ᵀIchabod, saying, ᴿ"The glory has departed from Israel!" because the ark of God had been captured and because of her father-in-law and her husband.   Lit. *Inglorious* • Ps. 26:8; 78:61
22 And she said, "The glory has departed from Israel, for the ark of God has been captured."

The Philistines and the Ark

5 Then the Philistines took the ark of God and brought it from Ebenezer to Ashdod. 2 When the Philistines took the ark of God, they brought it into the house of ᵀDagon and set it by Dagon.   A Philistine idol
3 And when the people of Ashdod arose early in the morning, there was Dagon, ᴿfallen on its face to the earth before the ark of the Lᴏʀᴅ. So they took Dagon and ᴿset it in its place again.   Is. 19:1; 46:1, 2 • Is. 46:7

4:1 So with MT, Tg.; LXX, Vg. add *And it came to pass in those days that the Philistines gathered themselves together to fight;* LXX adds further *against Israel*

4:13 So with MT, Vg.; LXX *beside the gate watching the road* (cf. Tg.)

4 And when they arose early the next morning, there was Dagon, fallen on its face to the ground before the ark of the LORD. ᴿThe head of Dagon and both the palms of its hands were broken off on the threshold; only *Dagon's torso was left of it.   Mic. 1:7

5 Therefore neither the priests of Dagon nor any who come into Dagon's house ᴿtread on the threshold of Dagon in Ashdod to this day.   Zeph. 1:9

6 But the hand of the LORD was heavy on the people of Ashdod, and He ravaged them and struck them with ᴿtumors,* both Ashdod and its territory.   Deut. 28:27

7 And when the men of Ashdod saw how it was, they said, "The ark of the God of Israel must not remain with us, for His hand is harsh toward us and Dagon our god."

8 Therefore they sent and gathered to themselves all the ᴿlords of the Philistines, and said, "What shall we do with the ark of the God of Israel?" And they answered, "Let the ark of the God of Israel be carried away to ᴿGath." So they carried the ark of the God of Israel away.   1 Sam. 6:4 · Josh. 11:22

9 So it was, after they had carried it away, that the hand of the LORD was against the city with a very great destruction; and He struck the men of the city, both small and great, *and tumors broke out on them.

10 Therefore they sent the ark of God to Ekron. So it was, as the ark of God came to Ekron, that the Ekronites cried out, saying, "They have brought the ark of the God of Israel to us, to kill us and our people!"

11 So they sent and gathered together all the lords of the Philistines, and said, "Send away the ark of the God of Israel, and let it go back to its own place, so that it does not kill us and our people." For there was a deadly destruction throughout all the city; the hand of God was very heavy there.

12 And the men who did not die were stricken with the tumors, and the ᴿcry of the city went up to heaven.   Jer. 14:2

The Ark Returned to Israel

6 Now the ark of the LORD was in the country of the Philistines seven months.

2 And the Philistines ᴿcalled for the priests and the diviners, saying, "What shall we do with the ark of the LORD? Tell us how we should send it to its place."   Gen. 41:8

3 So they said, "If you send away the ark of the God of Israel, do not send it ᴿempty; but by all means return it to Him with ᴿa trespass offering. Then you will be healed,

and it will be known to you why His hand is not removed from you."   Deut. 16:16 · Lev. 5:15, 16

4 Then they said, "What is the trespass offering which we shall return to Him?" They answered, "Five golden tumors and five golden rats, according to the number of the lords of the Philistines. For the same plague was on all of you and on your lords.

5 "Therefore you shall make images of your tumors and images of your rats that ravage the land, and you shall ᴿgive glory to the God of Israel; perhaps He will ᴿlightenᵀ His hand from you, from your gods, and from your land.   Josh. 7:19 · 1 Sam. 5:6, 11 · ease

6 "Why then do you harden your hearts ᴿas the Egyptians and Pharaoh hardened their hearts? When He did mighty things among them, ᴿdid they not let the people go, that they might depart?   Ex. 9:34; 14:17 · Ex. 12:31

7 "Now therefore, make a new cart, take two milk cows which have never been yoked, and hitch the cows to the cart; and take their calves home, away from them.

8 "Then take the ark of the LORD and set it on the cart; and put ᴿthe articles of gold which you are returning to Him as a trespass offering in a chest by its side. Then send it away, and let it go.   1 Sam. 6:4, 5

9 "And watch: if it goes up the road to its own territory, to Beth Shemesh, then He has done us this great evil. But if not, then we shall know that it is not His hand that struck us—it happened to us by chance."

10 Then the men did so; they took two milk cows and hitched them to the cart, and shut up their calves at home.

11 And they set the ark of the LORD on the cart, and the chest with the gold rats and images of their tumors.

12 Then the cows headed straight for the road to Beth Shemesh, and went along the ᴿhighway, lowing as they went, and did not turn aside to the right hand or the left. And the lords of the Philistines went after them to the border of Beth Shemesh.   Num. 20:19

13 Now the people of Beth Shemesh were reaping their ᴿwheat harvest in the valley; and they lifted their eyes and saw the ark, and rejoiced to see it.   1 Sam. 12:17

14 Then the cart came into the field of Joshua of Beth Shemesh, and stood there; a large stone was there. So they split the wood of the cart and offered the cows as a burnt offering to the LORD.

15 The Levites took down the ark of the LORD and the chest that was with it, in which were the articles of gold, and put them on the large stone. Then the men of Beth Shemesh offered burnt offerings and made sacrifices the same day to the LORD.

16 So when ᴿthe five lords of the Philistines had seen it, they returned to Ekron the same day.   Josh. 13:3

5:4 So with LXX, Syr., Tg., Vg.; MT Dagon
5:6 Probably bubonic plague. LXX, Vg. add And in the midst of their land rats sprang up, and there was a great death panic in the city
5:9 Vg. and they had tumors in their secret parts

17 These *are* the golden tumors which the Philistines returned *as* a trespass offering to the LORD: one for Ashdod, one for Gaza, one for Ashkelon, one for Gath, one for Ekron; 18 and the golden rats, *according to* the number of all the cities of the Philistines *belonging* to the five lords, *both* fortified cities and country villages, even as far as the large *stone* of Abel on which they set the ark of the LORD, *which stone remains* to this day in the field of Joshua of Beth Shemesh.

19 Then He struck the men of Beth Shemesh, because they had looked into the ark of the LORD. *He ᴿstruck fifty thousand and seventy men of the people, and the people lamented because the LORD had struck the people with a great slaughter.   2 Sam. 6:7

The Ark at Kirjath Jearim

20 And the men of Beth Shemesh said, "Who is able to stand before this holy LORD God? And to whom shall it go up from us?" 21 So they sent messengers to the inhabitants of Kirjath Jearim, saying, "The Philistines have brought back the ark of the LORD; come down *and* take it up with you."

7 Then the men of Kirjath Jearim came and took the ark of the LORD, and brought it into the house of ᴿAbinadab on the hill, and ᴿconsecrated Eleazar his son to keep the ark of the LORD.   2 Sam. 6:3, 4 • Lev. 21:8

Samuel Judges Israel

2 So it was that the ark remained in Kirjath Jearim a long time; it was there twenty years. And all the house of Israel lamented after the LORD.

3 Then Samuel spoke to all the house of Israel, saying, "If you return to the LORD with all your hearts, *then* put away the foreign gods and the *Ashtoreths from among you, and prepare your hearts for the LORD, and serve Him only; and He will deliver you from the hand of the Philistines."

4 So the children of Israel put away the ᴿBaals and the ᵀAshtoreths, and served the LORD only.   Judg. 2:11 • Canaanite goddesses

5 And Samuel said, "Gather all Israel to Mizpah, and I will pray to the LORD for you."

6 So they gathered together at Mizpah, ᴿdrew water, and poured *it* out before the LORD. And they ᴿfasted that day, and said there, ᴿ"We have sinned against the LORD." And Samuel judged the children of Israel at Mizpah.   2 Sam. 14:14 • Neh. 9:1, 2 • 1 Sam. 12:10

7 Now when the Philistines heard that the children of Israel had gathered together at Mizpah, the lords of the Philistines went up against Israel. And when the children of

6:19 Or *He struck seventy men of the people and fifty oxen of a man*
7:3 Images of Canaanite goddesses

Israel heard *of it,* they were afraid of the Philistines.

8 So the children of Israel said to Samuel, ᴿ"Do not cease to cry out to the LORD our God for us, that He may save us from the hand of the Philistines."   Is. 37:4

9 And Samuel took a suckling lamb and offered *it as* a whole burnt offering to the LORD. Then Samuel cried out to the LORD for Israel, and the LORD answered him.

10 Now as Samuel was offering up the burnt offering, the Philistines drew near to battle against Israel. But the LORD thundered with a loud thunder upon the Philistines that day, and so confused them that they were overcome before Israel.

11 And the men of Israel went out of Mizpah and pursued the Philistines, and drove them back as far as below Beth Car.

12 Then Samuel ᴿtook a stone and set *it* up between Mizpah and Shen, and called its name ᵀEbenezer, saying, "Thus far the LORD has helped us."   Josh. 4:9; 24:26 • Lit. *Stone of Help*

13 So the Philistines were subdued, and they did not come anymore into the territory of Israel. And the hand of the LORD was against the Philistines all the days of Samuel. 14 Then the cities which the Philistines had taken from Israel were restored to Israel, from Ekron to Gath; and Israel recovered its territory from the hands of the Philistines. Also there was peace between Israel and the Amorites.

15 And Samuel ᴿjudged Israel all the days of his life.   1 Sam. 12:11

16 He went from year to year on a circuit to Bethel, Gilgal, and Mizpah, and judged Israel in all those places.

17 But he always returned to Ramah, for his home *was* there. There he judged Israel, and there he built an altar to the LORD.

Israel Demands a King

8 Now it came to pass when Samuel was ᴿold that he ᴿmade his ᴿsons judges over Israel.   1 Sam. 12:2 • Deut. 16:18, 19 • Judg. 10:4

2 The name of his firstborn was Joel, and the name of his second, Abijah; *they were* judges in Beersheba.

3 But his sons did not walk in his ways; they turned aside after dishonest gain, ᴿtook bribes, and perverted justice.   Ex. 23:6–8

4 Then all the elders of Israel gathered together and came to Samuel at Ramah,

5 and said to him, "Look, you are old, and your sons do not walk in your ways. Now ᴿmake us a king to judge us like all the nations."   Deut. 17:14, 15

6 But the thing displeased Samuel when they said, "Give us a king to judge us." So Samuel ᴿprayed to the LORD.   1 Sam. 7:9

7 And the LORD said to Samuel, "Heed the voice of the people in all that they say to you;

for ᴿthey have not rejected you, but ᴿthey have rejected Me, that I should not reign over them.   Ex. 16:8 • 1 Sam. 10:19

8 "According to all the works which they have done since the day that I brought them up out of Egypt, even to this day—with which they have forsaken Me and served other gods—so they are doing to you also.

9 "Now therefore, heed their voice. However, you shall solemnly forewarn them, and ᴿshow them the behavior of the king who will reign over them."   1 Sam. 8:11–18

10 So Samuel told all the words of the LORD to the people who asked him for a king.

11 And he said, "This will be the behavior of the king who will reign over you: He will take your sons and appoint *them* for his own ᴿchariots and *to be* his horsemen, and *some* will run before his chariots.   2 Sam. 15:1

12 "He will ᴿappoint captains over his thousands and captains over his fifties, *will set some* to plow his ground and reap his harvest, and *some* to make his weapons of war and equipment for his chariots.   1 Sam. 22:7

13 "He will take your daughters *to be* perfumers, cooks, and bakers.

14 "And ᴿhe will take the best of your fields, your vineyards, and your olive groves, and give *them* to his servants.   1 Kin. 21:7

15 "He will take a tenth of your grain and your vintage, and give it to his officers and servants.

16 "And he will take your male servants, your female servants, your finest *young men, and your donkeys, and put *them* to his work.

17 "He will take a tenth of your sheep. And you will be his servants.

18 "And you will cry out in that day because of your king whom you have chosen for yourselves, and the LORD ᴿwill not hear you in that day."   Is. 1:15

19 Nevertheless the people ᴿrefused to obey the voice of Samuel; and they said, "No, but we will have a king over us,   Jer. 44:16

20 that we also may be ᴿlike all the nations, and that our king may judge us and go out before us and fight our battles."   1 Sam. 8:5

21 And Samuel heard all the words of the people, and he repeated them in the hearing of the LORD.

22 So the LORD said to Samuel, ᴿ"Heed their voice, and make them a king." And Samuel said to the men of Israel, "Every man go to his city."   Hos. 13:11

Saul Chosen to Be King

9 There was a man of Benjamin whose name *was* ᴿKish the son of Abiel, the son of Zeror, the son of Bechorath, the son of Aphiah, a Benjamite, a mighty man of ᵀpower.   1 Chr. 8:33; 9:36–39 • *wealth*

8:16 LXX *cattle*

2 And he had a choice and handsome son whose name *was* Saul. *There was* not a more handsome person than he among the children of Israel. ᴿFrom his shoulders upward *he was* taller than any of the people.   1 Sam. 10:23

3 Now the donkeys of Kish, Saul's father, were lost. And Kish said to his son Saul, "Please take one of the servants with you, and arise, go and look for the donkeys."

4 So he passed through the mountains of Ephraim and through the land of Shalisha, but they did not find *them*. Then they passed through the land of Shaalim, and *they were* not *there*. Then he passed through the land of the Benjamites, but they did not find *them*.

5 When they had come to the land of ᴿZuph, Saul said to his servant who *was* with him, "Come, let ᴿus return, lest my father cease *caring* about the donkeys and become worried about us."   1 Sam. 1:1 • 1 Sam. 10:2

6 And he said to him, "Look now, *there is* in this city a man of God, and *he is* an honorable man; all that he says surely comes to pass. So let us go there; perhaps he can show us the way that we should go."

7 Then Saul said to his servant, "But look, *if* we go, ᴿwhat shall we bring the man? For the bread in our vessels is all gone, and *there is* no present to bring to the man of God. What do we have?"   Judg. 6:18; 13:17

8 And the servant answered Saul again and said, "Look, I have here at hand ᵀone fourth of a shekel of silver. I will give *that* to the man of God, to tell us our way." $32

9 (Formerly in Israel, when a man went to ᵀinquire of God, he spoke thus: "Come, let us go to the seer"; for *he who is* now *called* a prophet was formerly called a seer.)   *seek*

10 Then Saul said to his servant, "Well said; come, let us go." So they went to the city where the man of God *was*.

11 As they went up the hill to the city, they met some young women going out to draw water, and said to them, "Is the seer here?"

12 And they answered them and said, "Yes, there he is, just ahead of you. Hurry now; for today he came to this city, because ᴿthere is a sacrifice of the people today ᴿon the high place.   Gen. 31:54 • 1 Kin. 3:2

13 "As soon as you come into the city, you will surely find him before he goes up to the high place to eat. For the people will not eat until he comes, because he must bless the sacrifice; afterward those who are invited will eat. Now therefore, go up, for about this time you will find him."

14 So they went up to the city. As they were coming into the city, there was Samuel, coming out toward them on his way up to the high place.

15 Now the LORD had told Samuel in his ear the day before Saul came, saying,

16 "Tomorrow about this time I will send you a man from the land of Benjamin, ᴿand you shall anoint him ᵀcommander over My people Israel, that he may save My people from the hand of the Philistines; for I have looked upon My people, because their cry has come to Me."   1 Sam. 10:1 • *prince or ruler*

17 So when Samuel saw Saul, the LORD said to him, ᴿ"There he is, the man of whom I spoke to you. This one shall reign over My people."   1 Sam. 16:12

18 Then Saul drew near to Samuel in the gate, and said, "Please tell me, where *is* the seer's house?"

19 Samuel answered Saul and said, "I *am* the seer. Go up before me to the high place, for you shall eat with me today; and tomorrow I will let you go and will tell you all that *is* in your heart.

20 "But as for your donkeys that were lost three days ago, do not be anxious about them, for they have been found. And ᵀon whom *is* all the desire of Israel? *Is it* not on you and on all your father's house?"   *for*

21 And Saul answered and said, "*Am* I not a Benjamite, of the smallest of the tribes of Israel, and ᴿmy family the least of all the families of the *tribe of Benjamin? Why then do you speak like this to me?"   Judg. 6:15

22 Now Samuel took Saul and his servant and brought them into the hall, and had them sit in the place of honor among those who were invited; there *were* about thirty persons.

23 And Samuel said to the cook, "Bring the portion which I gave you, of which I said to you, 'Set it apart.' "

24 So the cook took up ᴿthe thigh with its upper part and set *it* before Saul. And *Samuel* said, "Here it is, what was kept back. *It* was set apart for you. Eat; for until this time it has been kept for you, since I said I invited the people." So Saul ate with Samuel that day.   Lev. 7:32, 33

25 When they had come down from the high place into the city, *Samuel spoke with Saul on ᴿthe top of the house.   Deut. 22:8

26 They arose early; and it was about the dawning of the day that Samuel called to Saul on the top of the house, saying, "Get up, that I may send you on your way." And Saul arose, and both of them went outside, he and Samuel.

Saul Anointed King

27 As they were going down to the outskirts of the city, Samuel said to Saul, "Tell the servant to go on ahead of us." And he

went on. "But you stand here ᵀawhile, that I may announce to you the word of God."   *now*

10 Then ᴿSamuel took a flask of oil and poured *it* on his head, ᴿand kissed him and said: "*Is it* not because ᴿthe LORD has anointed you commander over ᴿHis *inheritance?   2 Kin. 9:3, 6 • Ps. 2:12 • Acts 13:21 • Deut. 32:9

2 "When you have departed from me today, you will find two men by Rachel's tomb in the territory of Benjamin ᴿat Zelzah; and they will say to you, 'The donkeys which you went to look for have been found. And now your father has ceased caring about the donkeys and is worrying about you, saying, "What shall I do about my son?" '   Josh. 18:28

3 "Then you shall go on forward from there and come to the terebinth tree of Tabor. There three men going up to God at Bethel will meet you, one carrying three young goats, another carrying three loaves of bread, and another carrying a skin of wine.

4 "And they will ᵀgreet you and give you two *loaves* of bread, which you shall receive from their hands.   *ask you about your welfare*

5 "After that you shall come to the hill of God where the Philistine garrison *is*. And it will happen, when you have come there to the city, that you will meet a group of prophets coming down ᴿfrom the high place with a stringed instrument, a tambourine, a flute, and a harp before them; ᴿand they will be prophesying.   1 Sam. 19:12, 20 • 2 Kin. 3:15

6 "Then the Spirit of the LORD will come upon you, and ᴿyou will prophesy with them and be turned into another man.   1 Sam. 10:10

7 "And let it be, when these ᴿsigns come to you, *that* you do as the occasion demands; for ᴿGod *is* with you.   Ex. 4:8 • Judg. 6:12

8 "You shall go down before me ᴿto Gilgal; and surely I will come down to you to offer burnt offerings *and* make sacrifices of peace offerings. ᴿSeven days you shall wait, till I come to you and show you what you should do."   1 Sam. 11:14, 15; 13:8 • 1 Sam. 13:8-10

9 So it was, when he had turned his back to go from Samuel, that God ᵀgave him another heart; and all those signs came to pass that day.   *changed his heart*

10 ᴿWhen they came there to the hill, there was ᴿa group of prophets to meet him; then the Spirit of God came upon him, and he prophesied among them.   1 Sam. 10:5 • 1 Sam. 19:20

11 And it happened, when all who knew him formerly saw that he indeed prophesied among the prophets, that the people said to one another, "What *is* this *that* has come upon the son of Kish? ᴿ*Is* Saul also among the prophets?"   Matt. 13:54-57

9:21 Lit. *tribes*

9:25 So with MT, Tg.; LXX omits *He spoke with Saul on top of the house;* LXX, Vg. afterward add *And he prepared a bed for Saul on top of the house, and he slept*

10:1 So with MT, Tg., Vg.; LXX *people Israel; and you shall rule the people of the Lord;* LXX, Vg. add *And you shall deliver His people from the hands of their enemies all around them. And this shall be a sign to you, that God has anointed you to be a prince*

12 Then a man from there answered and said, "But ᴿwho is their father?" Therefore it became a proverb: "*Is* Saul also among the prophets?" John 5:30, 36

13 And when he had finished prophesying, he went to the high place.

14 Then Saul's ᴿuncle said to him and his servant, "Where did you go?" So he said, "To look for the donkeys. When we saw that *they were* nowhere to be found, we went to Samuel." 1 Sam. 14:50

15 And Saul's uncle said, "Tell me, please, what Samuel said to you."

16 So Saul said to his uncle, "He told us plainly that the donkeys had been ᴿfound." But about the matter of the kingdom, he did not tell him what Samuel had said. 1 Sam. 9:20

Saul Proclaimed King

17 Then Samuel called the people together ᴿto the Lᴏʀᴅ ᴿat Mizpah, Judg. 20:1 • 1 Sam. 7:5, 6

18 and said to the children of Israel, ᴿ"Thus says the Lᴏʀᴅ God of Israel: 'I brought up Israel out of Egypt, and delivered you from the hand of the Egyptians *and* from the hand of all kingdoms and from those who oppressed you.' Judg. 6:8, 9

19 "But you have today rejected your God, who Himself saved you from all your adversities and your tribulations; and you have said to Him, 'No, set a king over us!' Now therefore, present yourselves before the Lᴏʀᴅ by your tribes and by your *clans."

20 And when Samuel had ᴿcaused all the tribes of Israel to come near, the tribe of Benjamin was chosen. Acts 1:24, 26

21 When he had caused the tribe of Benjamin to come near by their families, the family of Matri was chosen. And Saul the son of Kish was chosen. But when they sought him, he could not be found.

22 Therefore they ᴿinquired of the Lᴏʀᴅ further, "Has the man come here yet?" And the Lᴏʀᴅ answered, "There he is, hidden among the equipment." 1 Sam. 23:2, 4, 10, 11

23 So they ran and brought him from there; and when he stood among the people, ᴿhe was taller than any of the people from his shoulders upward. 1 Sam. 9:2

24 And Samuel said to all the people, "Do you see him whom the Lᴏʀᴅ has chosen, that *there is* no one like him among all the people?" So all the people shouted and said, ᵀ"Long live the king!" Lit. *May the king live*

25 Then Samuel explained to the people ᴿthe behavior of royalty, and wrote *it* in a book and laid *it* up before the Lᴏʀᴅ. And Samuel sent all the people away, every man to his house. 1 Sam. 8:11-18

26 And Saul also went home ᴿto Gibeah;

10:19 *thousands*

and valiant *men* went with him, whose hearts God had touched. Judg. 20:14

27 But some ᴿrebels said, "How can this man save us?" So they despised him, ᴿand brought him no presents. But he ᵀheld his peace. Deut. 13:13 • 1 Kin. 4:21; 10:25 • *kept silent*

Saul Saves Jabesh Gilead

11 Then ᴿNahash the Ammonite came up and ᵀencamped against ᴿJabesh Gilead; and all the men of Jabesh said to Nahash, ᴿ"Make a covenant with us, and we will serve you." 1 Sam. 12:12 • *besieged* • Judg. 21:8 • Gen. 26:28

2 And Nahash the Ammonite answered them, "On this condition I will make *a covenant* with you, that I may put out all your right eyes, and bring reproach on all Israel."

3 Then the elders of Jabesh said to him, "Hold off for seven days, that we may send messengers to all the territory of Israel. And then, if *there is* no one to ᵀsave us, we will come out to you." *deliver*

4 So the messengers came to Gibeah of Saul and told the news in the hearing of the people. And ᴿall the people lifted up their voices and wept. Judg. 2:4; 20:23, 26; 21:2

5 Now there was Saul, coming behind the herd from the field; and Saul said, "What troubles the people, that they weep?" And they told him the words of the men of Jabesh.

6 ᴿThen the Spirit of God came upon Saul when he heard this news, and his anger was greatly aroused. Judg. 3:10; 6:34; 11:29; 13:25; 14:6

7 So he took a yoke of oxen and ᴿcut them in pieces, and sent *them* throughout all the territory of Israel by the hands of messengers, saying, ᴿ"Whoever does not go out with Saul and Samuel to battle, so it shall be done to his oxen." And the fear of the Lᴏʀᴅ fell on the people, and they came out ᵀwith one consent. Judg. 19:29 • Judg. 21:5, 8, 10 • Lit. *as one man*

8 When he numbered them in Bezek, the children of Israel were three hundred thousand, and the men of Judah thirty thousand.

9 And they said to the messengers who came, "Thus you shall say to the men of Jabesh Gilead: 'Tomorrow, by *the time* the sun is hot, you shall have help.' " Then the messengers came and reported *it* to the men of Jabesh, and they were glad.

10 Therefore the men of Jabesh said, "Tomorrow we will come out to you, and you may do with us whatever seems good to you."

11 So it was, on the next day, that Saul put the people in three companies; and they came into the midst of the camp in the morning watch, and killed Ammonites until the heat of the day. And it happened that those who survived were scattered, so that no two of them were left together.

12 Then the people said to Samuel, ᴿ"Who is he who said, 'Shall Saul reign over us?'

R Bring the men, that we may put them to death."   1 Sam. 10:27 • Luke 19:27

13 But Saul said, "Not a man shall be put to death this day, for today R the LORD has accomplished salvation in Israel."   Ex. 14:13, 30

14 Then Samuel said to the people, "Come, let us go R to Gilgal and renew the kingdom there."   1 Sam. 7:16; 10:8

15 So all the people went to Gilgal, and there they made Saul king R before the LORD in Gilgal. R There they made sacrifices of peace offerings before the LORD, and there Saul and all the men of Israel rejoiced greatly.   1 Sam. 10:17 • 1 Sam. 10:8

Samuel's Address at Saul's Coronation

12 Now Samuel said to all Israel: "Indeed I have heeded your voice in all that you said to me, and have made a king over you.

2 "And now here is the king, R walking before you; R and I am old and grayheaded, and look, my sons are with you. I have walked before you from my childhood to this day.   Num. 27:17 • 1 Sam. 8:1, 5

3 "Here I am. Witness against me before the LORD and before His anointed: Whose ox have I taken, or whose donkey have I taken, or whom have I cheated? Whom have I oppressed, or from whose hand have I received any bribe with which to R blind my eyes? I will restore it to you."   Deut. 16:19

4 And they said, R "You have not cheated us or oppressed us, nor have you taken anything from any man's hand."   Lev. 19:13

5 Then he said to them, "The LORD is witness against you, and His anointed is witness this day, R that you have not found anything R in my hand." And they answered, "He is witness."   Acts 23:9; 24:20 • Ex. 22:4

6 Then Samuel said to the people, R "It is the LORD who raised up Moses and Aaron, and who brought your fathers up from the land of Egypt.   Mic. 6:4

7 "Now therefore, stand still, that I may R reason with you before the LORD concerning all the R righteous acts of the LORD which He did to you and your fathers: Is. 1:18 • Judg. 5:11

8 "When Jacob had gone into *Egypt, and your fathers R cried out to the LORD, then the LORD R sent Moses and Aaron, who brought your fathers out of Egypt and made them dwell in this place.   Ex. 2:23-25 • Ex. 3:10; 4:14-16

9 "And when they forgot the LORD their God, He sold them into the hand of R Sisera, commander of the army of Hazor, into the hand of the R Philistines, and into the hand of the king of R Moab; and they fought against them.   Judg. 4:2 • Judg. 3:31; 10:7; 13:1 • Judg. 3:12-30

10 "Then they cried out to the LORD, and said, 'We have sinned, because we have forsaken the LORD and served the Baals and *Ashtoreths; but now deliver us from the hand of our enemies, and we will serve You.'

11 "And the LORD sent *Jerubbaal, *Bedan, Jephthah, and *Samuel, and delivered you out of the hand of your enemies on every side; and you dwelt in safety.

12 "And when you saw that Nahash king of the Ammonites came against you, you said to me, 'No, but a king shall reign over us,' when the LORD your God was your king.

13 "Now therefore, here is the king R whom you have chosen and whom you have desired. And take note, R the LORD has set a king over you.   1 Sam. 8:5; 12:17, 19 • Hos. 13:11

14 "If you fear the LORD and serve Him and obey His voice, and do not rebel against the commandment of the LORD, then both you and the king who reigns over you will continue following the LORD your God.

15 "However, if you do R not obey the voice of the LORD, but R rebel against the commandment of the LORD, then the hand of the LORD will be against you, as it was against your fathers.   Deut. 28:15 • Is. 1:20

16 "Now therefore, R stand and see this great thing which the LORD will do before your eyes: Ex. 14:13, 31

17 "Is today not the wheat harvest? R I will call to the LORD, and He will send thunder and R rain, that you may perceive and see that your wickedness is great, which you have done in the sight of the LORD, in asking a king for yourselves."   [James 5:16-18] • Ezra 10:9

18 So Samuel called to the LORD, and the LORD sent thunder and rain that day; and R all the people greatly feared the LORD and Samuel.   Ex. 14:31

19 And all the people said to Samuel, "Pray for your servants to the LORD your God, that we may not die; for we have added to all our sins the evil of asking a king for ourselves."

20 Then Samuel said to the people, "Do not fear. You have done all this wickedness; yet do not turn aside from following the LORD, but serve the LORD with all your heart.

21 "And do not turn aside; for then you would go after empty things which cannot profit or deliver, for they are nothing.

22 "For the LORD will not forsake His people, for His great name's sake, because it has pleased the LORD to make you His people.

23 "Moreover, as for me, far be it from me that I should sin against the LORD in ceasing to pray for you; but R I will teach you the R good and the right way.   Ps. 34:11 • 1 Kin. 8:36

24 "Only fear the LORD, and serve Him in truth with all your heart; for R consider what great things He has done for you.   Is. 5:12

12:10 Images of Canaanite goddesses

12:11 Syr. Deborah; Tg. Gideon • LXX, Syr. Barak; Tg. Simson • Syr. Simson

25 "But if you still do wickedly, you shall be swept away, both you and your king."

Saul's Unlawful Sacrifice

13 Saul *reigned one year; and when he had reigned two years over Israel,
2 Saul chose for himself three thousand *men* of Israel. Two thousand were with Saul in Michmash and in the mountains of Bethel, and a thousand were with Jonathan in Gibeah of Benjamin. The rest of the people he sent away, every man to his tent.
3 And Jonathan attacked ᴿthe garrison of the Philistines that *was* in ᴿGeba, and the Philistines heard *of it*. Then Saul blew the trumpet throughout all the land, saying, "Let the Hebrews hear!"   1 Sam. 10:5 • 2 Sam. 5:25
4 Now all Israel heard it said *that* Saul had attacked a garrison of the Philistines, and *that* Israel had also become ᵀan abomination to the Philistines. And the people were called together to Saul at Gilgal.   *odious*
5 Then the Philistines gathered together to fight with Israel, *thirty thousand chariots and six thousand horsemen, and people as the sand which *is* on the seashore in multitude. And they came up and encamped in Michmash, to the east of ᴿBeth Aven.   Josh. 7:2
6 When the men of Israel saw that they were in danger (for the people were distressed), then the people hid in caves, in thickets, in rocks, in holes, and in pits.
7 And *some of* the Hebrews crossed over the Jordan to the ᴿland of Gad and Gilead. As for Saul, he *was* still in Gilgal, and all the people followed him trembling.   Num. 32:1-42
8 ᴿThen he waited seven days, according to the time set by Samuel. But Samuel did not come to Gilgal; and the people were scattered from him.   1 Sam. 10:8
9 So Saul said, "Bring a burnt offering and peace offerings here to me." And he offered the burnt offering.
10 Now it happened, as soon as he had finished presenting the burnt offering, that Samuel came; and Saul went out to meet him, that he might ᵀgreet him.   Lit. *bless him*
11 And Samuel said, "What have you done?" Saul said, "When I saw that the people were scattered from me, and *that* you did not come within the days appointed, and *that* the Philistines gathered together at Michmash,
12 "then I said, 'The Philistines will now come down on me at Gilgal, and I have not made supplication to the LORD.' Therefore I felt compelled, and offered a burnt offering."
13 And Samuel said to Saul, ᴿ"You have done foolishly. ᴿYou have not kept the com-

mandment of the LORD your God, which He commanded you. For now the LORD would have established your kingdom over Israel forever.   2 Chr. 16:9 • 1 Sam. 5:11, 22, 28
14 "But now your kingdom shall not continue. The LORD has sought for Himself a man ᴿafter His own heart, and the LORD has commanded him *to be* commander over His people, because you have not kept what the LORD commanded you."   Acts 7:46; 13:22
15 Then Samuel arose and went up from Gilgal to *Gibeah of Benjamin. And Saul numbered the people present with him, ᴿabout six hundred men.   1 Sam. 13:2, 6, 7

No Weapons for the Army

16 Saul, Jonathan his son, and the people present with them remained in ᵀGibeah of Benjamin. But the Philistines encamped in Michmash.   Heb. *Geba*
17 Then raiders came out of the camp of the Philistines in three companies. One company turned onto the road to ᴿOphrah, to the land of Shual,   Josh. 18:23
18 another company turned to the road *to* Beth Horon, and another company turned *to* the road of the border that overlooks the Valley of Zeboim toward the wilderness.
19 Now ᴿthere was no blacksmith to be found throughout all the land of Israel, for the Philistines said, "Lest the Hebrews make swords or spears."   Judg. 5:8
20 But all the Israelites would go down to the Philistines to sharpen each man's plowshare, his mattock, his ax, and his sickle;
21 and the charge for a sharpening was a ᵀpim for the plowshares, the mattocks, the forks, and the axes, and to set the points of the goads.   About two-thirds shekel weight
22 So it came about, on the day of battle, that there was neither sword nor spear found in the hand of any of the people who *were* with Saul and Jonathan. But they were found with Saul and Jonathan his son.
23 ᴿAnd the garrison of the Philistines went out to the pass of Michmash.   1 Sam. 14:1, 4

Jonathan Defeats the Philistines

14 Now it happened one day that Jonathan the son of Saul said to the young man who bore his armor, "Come, let us go over to the Philistines' garrison that *is* on the other side." But he did not tell his father.
2 And Saul was sitting in the outskirts of ᴿGibeah under a pomegranate tree which *is* in Migron. The people who *were* with him *were* about six hundred men.   1 Sam. 13:15, 16
3 Ahijah the son of Ahitub, ᴿIchabod's brother, the son of Phinehas, the son of Eli,

---

13:1 Heb. difficult; cf. 2 Sam. 5:4; 1 Kin. 14:2; see also 2 Sam. 2:10; Acts 13:21
13:5 So with MT, LXX, Tg., Vg.; Syr. and some mss. of LXX *three thousand*

13:15 So with MT, Tg.; [LXX], Vg. add *And the rest of the people went up after Saul to meet the people who fought against them, going from Gilgal to Gibeah in the hill of Benjamin.*

the LORD's priest in Shiloh, was ᴿwearing an ephod. But the people did not know that Jonathan had gone.   1 Sam. 4:21 • 1 Sam. 2:28

4 Between the passes, by which Jonathan sought to go over ᴿto the Philistines' garrison, *there was* a sharp rock on one side and a sharp rock on the other side. And the name of one *was* Bozez, and the name of the other Seneh.   1 Sam. 13:23

5 The front of one faced northward opposite Michmash, and the other southward opposite Gibeah.

6 Then Jonathan said to the young man who bore his armor, "Come, let us go over to the garrison of these ᴿuncircumcised; it may be that the LORD will work for us. For nothing restrains the LORD ᴿfrom saving by many or by few."   1 Sam. 17:26, 36 • Judg. 7:4, 7

7 So his armorbearer said to him, "Do all that is in your heart. Go then; here I am with you, according to your heart."

8 Then Jonathan said, "Very well, let us cross over to *these* men, and we will show ourselves to them.

9 "If they say thus to us, 'Wait until we come to you,' then we will stand still in our place and not go up to them.

10 "But if they say thus, 'Come up to us,' then we will go up. For the LORD has delivered them into our hand, and ᴿthis *will be* a sign to us."   Gen. 24:14

11 So both of them showed themselves to the garrison of the Philistines. And the Philistines said, "Look, the Hebrews are coming out of the holes where they have hidden."

12 Then the men of the garrison called to Jonathan and his armorbearer, and said, "Come up to us, and we will ᵀshow you something." Jonathan said to his armorbearer, "Come up after me, for the LORD has delivered them into the hand of Israel."   *teach*

13 And Jonathan climbed up on his hands and knees with his armorbearer after him; and they fell before Jonathan. And as he came after him, his armorbearer killed them.

14 That first slaughter which Jonathan and his armorbearer made was about twenty men within about *half an acre of land.

15 And ᴿthere was ᵀtrembling in the camp, in the field, and among all the people. The garrison and ᴿthe raiders also trembled; and the earth quaked, so that it was ᴿa very great trembling.   Job 18:11 • *terror* • 1 Sam. 13:17 • Gen. 35:5

16 Now the watchmen of Saul in Gibeah of Benjamin looked, and *there* was the multitude, melting away; and they ᴿwent here and there.   1 Sam. 14:20

17 Then Saul said to the people who *were* with him, "Now call the roll and see who has gone from us." And when they had called the

roll, surprisingly, Jonathan and his armorbearer *were* not *there.*

18 And Saul said to Ahijah, "Bring the *ark of God here" (for at that time the *ark of God was with the children of Israel).

19 Now it happened, while Saul ᴿtalked to the priest, that the noise which *was* in the camp of the Philistines continued to increase; so Saul said to the priest, "Withdraw your hand."   Num. 27:21

20 Then Saul and all the people who *were* with him assembled, and they went to the battle; and indeed ᴿevery man's sword was against his neighbor, *and there was* very great confusion.   Judg. 7:22

21 Moreover the Hebrews *who* were with the Philistines before that time, who went up with them into the camp *from the* surrounding *country,* they also joined the Israelites who *were* with Saul and Jonathan.

22 Likewise all the men of Israel who had hidden in the mountains of Ephraim, *when* they heard that the Philistines fled, they also followed hard after them in the battle.

23 So the LORD saved Israel that day, and the battle shifted ᴿto Beth Aven.   1 Sam. 13:5

Saul's Rash Oath

24 And the men of Israel were distressed that day, for Saul had ᴿplaced the people under oath, saying, "Cursed *is* the man who eats *any* food until evening, before I have taken vengeance on my enemies." So none of the people tasted food.   Josh. 6:26

25 Now all *the people* of the land came to a forest; and there was honey on the ground.

26 And when the people had come into the woods, there was the honey, dripping; but no one put his hand to his mouth, for the people feared the oath.

27 But Jonathan had not heard his father charge the people with the oath; therefore he stretched out the end of the rod that *was* in his hand and dipped it in a honeycomb, and put his hand to his mouth; and his ᵀcountenance brightened.   Lit. *eyes*

28 Then one of the people said, "Your father strictly charged the people with an oath, saying, 'Cursed *is* the man who eats food this day.' " And the people were faint.

29 But Jonathan said, "My father has troubled the land. Look now, how my countenance has brightened because I tasted a little of this honey.

30 "How much better if the people had eaten freely today of the spoil of their enemies which they found! For now would there not have been a much greater slaughter among the Philistines?"

31 Now they had ᵀdriven back the Philis-

14:14 Lit. *half the area plowed by a yoke of oxen in a day*

14:18 So with MT, Tg., Vg.; LXX *ephod* • See preceding note

tines that day from Michmash to Aijalon. So the people were very faint.   Lit. *struck*

32 And the people rushed on the ᵀspoil, and took sheep, oxen, and calves, and slaughtered *them* on the ground; and the people ate *them* ᴿwith the blood.   *plunder* • Deut. 12:16, 23, 24

33 Then they told Saul, saying, "Look, the people are sinning against the LORD by eating with the blood!" So he said, "You have dealt treacherously; roll a large stone to me this day."

34 Then Saul said, "Disperse yourselves among the people, and say to them, 'Bring me here every man's ox and every man's sheep, slaughter *them* here, and eat; and do not sin against the LORD by eating with the blood.'" So every one of the people brought his ox with him that night, and slaughtered *it* there.

35 Then Saul ᴿbuilt an altar to the LORD. This was the first altar that he built to the LORD.   1 Sam. 7:12, 17

36 Now Saul said, "Let us go down after the Philistines by night, and plunder them until the morning light; and let us not leave a man of them." And they said, "Do whatever seems good to you." Then the priest said, "Let us draw near to God here."

37 So Saul asked counsel of God, "Shall I go down after the Philistines? Will You deliver them into the hand of Israel?" But ᴿHe did not answer him that day.   1 Sam. 28:6

38 And Saul said, ᴿ"Come over here, all you chiefs of the people, and know and see what this sin was today.   Josh. 7:14

39 "For ᴿas the LORD lives, who saves Israel, though it be in Jonathan my son, he shall surely die." But not a man among all the people answered him.   2 Sam. 12:5

40 Then he said to all Israel, "You be on one side, and my son Jonathan and I will be on the other side." And the people said to Saul, "Do what seems good to you."

41 Therefore Saul said to the LORD God of Israel, *"Give a perfect *lot*." So Saul and Jonathan were taken, but the people escaped.

42 And Saul said, "Cast *lots* between my son Jonathan and me." So Jonathan was taken.

43 Then Saul said to Jonathan, ᴿ"Tell me what you have done." And Jonathan told him, and said, ᴿ"I only tasted a little honey with the end of the rod that *was* in my hand. So now I must die!"   Josh. 7:19 • 1 Sam. 14:27

44 Saul answered, "God do so and more also; for you shall surely die, Jonathan."

45 But the people said to Saul, "Shall Jonathan die, who has accomplished this great deliverance in Israel? Certainly not! ᴿAs the LORD lives, not one hair of his head shall fall

14:41 So with MT, Tg.; LXX, [Vg.] *Why do you not answer Your servant today? If the injustice is with me or Jonathan my son, O LORD God of Israel, give proof; and if You say it is with Your people Israel, give holiness.*

to the ground, for he has worked ᴿwith God this day." So the people rescued Jonathan, and he did not die.   1 Kin. 1:52 • [2 Cor. 6:1]

46 Then Saul returned from pursuing the Philistines, and the Philistines went to their own place.

Saul's Continuing Wars

47 So Saul established his sovereignty over Israel, and fought against all his enemies on every side, against Moab, against the people of Ammon, against Edom, against the kings of ᴿZobah, and against the Philistines. Wherever he turned, he *harassed them*.   2 Sam. 10:6

48 And he gathered an army and ᵀattacked the Amalekites, and delivered Israel from the hands of those who plundered them.   *struck*

49 The sons of Saul were Jonathan, ᵀJishui, and Malchishua. And the names of his two daughters *were these*: the name of the firstborn Merab, and the name of the younger Michal.   *Abinadab*, 1 Chr. 8:33; 9:39

50 The name of Saul's wife *was* Ahinoam the daughter of Ahimaaz. And the name of the commander of his army *was* Abner the son of Ner, Saul's ᴿuncle.   1 Sam. 10:14

51 Kish *was* the father of Saul, and Ner the father of Abner *was* the son of Abiel.

52 Now there was fierce war with the Philistines all the days of Saul. And when Saul saw any strong man or any valiant man, ᴿhe took him for himself.   1 Sam. 8:11

Saul Spares King Agag

15 Samuel also said to Saul, ᴿ"The LORD sent me to anoint you king over His people, over Israel. Now therefore, heed the voice of the words of the LORD.   1 Sam. 9:16; 10:1

2 "Thus says the LORD of hosts: 'I will punish what Amalek did to Israel, ᴿhow he ambushed him on the way when he came up from Egypt.   Deut. 25:17-19

3 'Now go and ᴿattackᵀ Amalek, and ᴿutterly destroy all that they have, and do not spare them. But kill both man and woman, infant and nursing child, ox and sheep, camel and donkey.'"   Deut. 25:19 • Lit. *strike* • Num. 24:20

4 So Saul gathered the people together and numbered them in Telaim, two hundred thousand foot soldiers and ten thousand men of Judah.

5 And Saul came to a city of Amalek, and lay in wait in the valley.

6 Then Saul said to ᴿthe Kenites, ᴿ"Go, depart, get down from among the Amalekites, lest I destroy you with them. For ᴿyou showed kindness to all the children of Israel when they came up out of Egypt." So the Kenites departed from among the Amalekites.   Num. 24:21 • Gen. 18:25; 19:12, 14 • Ex. 18:10, 19

14:47 LXX, [Tg.], Vg. *prospered*

7 ᴿAnd Saul attacked the Amalekites, from ᴿHavilah all the way to ᴿShur, which is east of Egypt.   1 Sam. 14:48 • Gen. 2:11; 25:17, 18 • Gen. 16:7

8 He also took Agag king of the Amalekites alive, and utterly destroyed all the people with the edge of the sword.

9 But Saul and the people ᴿspared Agag and the best of the sheep, the oxen, the fatlings, the lambs, and all *that was* good, and were unwilling to utterly destroy them. But everything despised and worthless, that they utterly destroyed.   1 Sam. 15:3, 15, 19

Saul Rejected as King

10 Now the word of the Lᴏʀᴅ came to Samuel, saying,

11 "I greatly regret that I have set up Saul *as* king, for he has ᴿturned back from following Me, and has not performed My commandments." And it grieved Samuel, and he cried out to the Lᴏʀᴅ all night.   1 Kin. 9:6

12 So when Samuel rose early in the morning to meet Saul, it was told Samuel, saying, "Saul went to Carmel, and indeed, he set up a monument for himself; and he has gone on around, passed by, and gone down to Gilgal."

13 Then Samuel went to Saul, and Saul said to him, "Blessed *are* you of the Lᴏʀᴅ! I have performed the commandment of the Lᴏʀᴅ."

14 But Samuel said, "What then *is* this bleating of the sheep in my ears, and the lowing of the oxen which I hear?"

15 And Saul said, "They have brought them from the Amalekites; ᴿfor the people spared the best of the sheep and the oxen, to sacrifice to the Lᴏʀᴅ your God; and the rest we have utterly destroyed."   Gen. 3:12, 13

16 Then Samuel said to Saul, "Be quiet! And I will tell you what the Lᴏʀᴅ said to me last night." And he said to him, "Speak on."

17 So Samuel said, ᴿ"When you *were* little in your own eyes, *were* you not head of the tribes of Israel? And did not the Lᴏʀᴅ anoint you king over Israel?   1 Sam. 9:21; 10:22

18 "Now the Lᴏʀᴅ sent you on a mission, and said, 'Go, and utterly destroy the sinners, the Amalekites, and fight against them until they are ᵀconsumed.'   *exterminated*

19 "Why then did you not obey the voice of the Lᴏʀᴅ? Why did you swoop down on the spoil, and do evil in the sight of the Lᴏʀᴅ?"

20 And Saul said to Samuel, ᴿ"But I have obeyed the voice of the Lᴏʀᴅ, and gone on the mission on which the Lᴏʀᴅ sent me, and brought back Agag king of Amalek; but I have utterly destroyed the Amalekites.   1 Sam. 15:13

21 "But the people took of the plunder, sheep and oxen, the best of the things which should have been utterly destroyed, to sacrifice to the Lᴏʀᴅ your God in Gilgal."

22 So Samuel said:

ᴿ"Has the Lᴏʀᴅ *as great* delight in burnt offerings and sacrifices,   [Is. 1:11-17]

As in obeying the voice of the Lᴏʀᴅ?
Behold, to obey is better than sacrifice,
And to heed than the fat of rams.

23 For rebellion *is as* the sin of ᵀwitchcraft,
And stubbornness *is as* iniquity and idolatry.   *divination*
Because you have rejected the word of the Lᴏʀᴅ,
ᴿHe also has rejected you from *being* king."   1 Sam. 13:14; 16:1

24 Then Saul said to Samuel, "I have sinned, for I have transgressed the commandment of the Lᴏʀᴅ and your words, because I feared the people and obeyed their voice.

25 "Now therefore, please pardon my sin, and return with me, that I may worship the Lᴏʀᴅ."

26 But Samuel said to Saul, "I will not return with you, ᴿfor you have rejected the word of the Lᴏʀᴅ, and the Lᴏʀᴅ has rejected you from being king over Israel."   1 Sam. 2:30

27 And as Samuel turned around to go away, ᴿ*Saul* seized the edge of his robe, and it tore.   1 Kin. 11:30, 31

28 So Samuel said to him, ᴿ"The Lᴏʀᴅ has torn the kingdom of Israel from you today, and has given it to a neighbor of yours, *who is* better than you.   1 Kin. 11:31

29 "And also the Strength of Israel ᴿwill not lie nor relent. For He *is* not a man, that He should relent."   Num. 23:19

30 Then he said, "I have sinned; *yet* honor me now, please, before the elders of my people and before Israel, and return with me, that I may worship the Lᴏʀᴅ your God."

31 So Samuel turned back after Saul, and Saul worshiped the Lᴏʀᴅ.

32 Then Samuel said, "Bring Agag king of the Amalekites here to me." So Agag came to him cautiously. And Agag said, "Surely the bitterness of death is past."

33 But Samuel said, ᴿ"As your sword has made women childless, so shall your mother be childless among women." And Samuel hacked Agag in pieces before the Lᴏʀᴅ in Gilgal.   [Gen. 9:6]

34 Then Samuel went to Ramah, and Saul went up to his house at Gibeah of Saul.

35 And ᴿSamuel went no more to see Saul until the day of his death. Nevertheless Samuel mourned for Saul, and the Lᴏʀᴅ regretted that He had made Saul king over Israel.   1 Sam. 19:24

David Anointed King

16 Now the Lᴏʀᴅ said to Samuel, "How long will you mourn for Saul, seeing I have rejected him from reigning over Israel? Fill your horn with oil, and go; I am sending you to Jesse the Bethlehemite. For I have provided Myself a king among his sons."

2 And Samuel said, "How can I go? If Saul hears *it*, he will kill me." But the LORD said, "Take a heifer with you, and say, ^R'I have come to sacrifice to the LORD.'   1 Sam. 9:12

3 "Then invite Jesse to the sacrifice, and I will show you what you shall do; you shall anoint for Me the one I name to you."

4 So Samuel did what the LORD said, and went to Bethlehem. And the elders of the town ^Rtrembled at his coming, and said, ^R"Do you come peaceably?"   1 Sam. 21:1 • 1 Kin. 2:13

5 And he said, "Peaceably; I have come to sacrifice to the LORD. ^RSanctify^T yourselves, and come with me to the sacrifice." Then he consecrated Jesse and his sons, and invited them to the sacrifice.   Ex. 19:10 • *Consecrate*

6 So it was, when they came, that he looked at Eliab and ^Rsaid, "Surely the LORD's anointed *is* before Him!"   1 Kin. 12:26

7 But the LORD said to Samuel, "Do not look at his appearance or at his physical stature, because I have ^Trefused him. *For the LORD does not see as man sees; for man looks at the outward appearance, but the LORD looks at the ^Rheart."   *rejected* • 1 Kin. 8:39

8 So Jesse called Abinadab, and made him pass before Samuel. And he said, "Neither has the LORD chosen this one."

9 Then Jesse made Shammah pass by. And he said, "Neither has the LORD chosen this one."

10 Thus Jesse made seven of his sons pass before Samuel. And Samuel said to Jesse, "The LORD has not chosen these."

11 And Samuel said to Jesse, "Are all the young men here?" Then he said, "There remains yet the youngest, and there he is, keeping the ^Rsheep." And Samuel said to Jesse, "Send and bring him. For we will not *sit down till he comes here."   2 Sam. 7:8

12 So he sent and brought him in. Now he *was* ruddy, ^Rwith ^Tbright eyes, and good-looking. And the LORD said, "Arise, anoint him; for this *is* the one!"   Gen. 39:6 • Lit. *beautiful*

13 Then Samuel took the horn of oil and anointed him in the midst of his brothers; and ^Rthe Spirit of the LORD came upon David from that day forward. So Samuel arose and went to Ramah.   Num. 27:18

A Distressing Spirit Troubles Saul

14 ^RBut the Spirit of the LORD departed from Saul, and ^Ra distressing spirit from the LORD troubled him.   Judg. 16:20 • Judg. 9:23

15 And Saul's servants said to him, "Surely, a distressing spirit from God is troubling you.

16 "Let our master now command your servants, *who are* before you, to seek out a

16:7 LXX *For God does not see as man sees;* Tg. *It is not by the appearance of a man;* Vg. *Nor do I judge according to the looks of a man*

16:11 So with LXX, Vg.; MT *turn around;* Tg., Syr. *turn away*

man *who is* a skillful player on the harp. And it shall be that he will play it with his hand when the ^Tdistressing spirit from God is upon you, and you shall be well."   Lit. *evil*

17 So Saul said to his servants, ^T"Provide me now a man who can play well, and bring *him* to me."   Lit. *Look now for a man for me*

18 Then one of the servants answered and said, "Look, I have seen a son of Jesse the Bethlehemite, *who is* skillful in playing, a mighty man of valor, a man of war, prudent in speech, and a handsome person; and ^Rthe LORD *is* with him."   1 Sam. 3:19; 18:12, 14

19 Therefore Saul sent messengers to Jesse, and said, "Send me your son David, who *is* with the sheep."

20 And Jesse took a donkey *loaded with* bread, a skin of wine, and a young goat, and sent *them* by his son David to Saul.

21 So David came to Saul and ^Rstood before him. And he loved him greatly, and he became his armorbearer.   Gen. 41:46

22 Then Saul sent to Jesse, saying, "Please let David stand before me, for he has found favor in my sight."

23 And so it was, whenever the spirit from God was upon Saul, that David would take a harp and play *it* with his hand. Then Saul would become refreshed and well, and the distressing spirit would depart from him.

David and Goliath

17 Now the Philistines gathered their armies together to battle, and were gathered at ^RSochoh, which *belongs* to Judah; they encamped between Sochoh and Azekah, in Ephes Dammim.   Josh. 15:35

2 And Saul and the men of Israel were gathered together, and they encamped in the Valley of Elah, and drew up in battle array against the Philistines.

3 The Philistines stood on a mountain on one side, and Israel stood on a mountain on the other side, with a valley between them.

4 And a champion went out from the camp of the Philistines, named ^RGoliath, from ^RGath, whose height *was* ^Tsix cubits and a span.   2 Sam. 21:19 • Josh. 11:21, 22 • 9.75 ft.

5 *He had* a bronze helmet on his head, and he *was* ^Tarmed with a coat of mail, and the weight of the coat *was* ^Tfive thousand shekels of bronze.   *clothed with scaled body armor* • 125 lb.

6 And *he had* bronze armor on his legs and a bronze javelin between his shoulders.

7 Now the staff of his spear *was* like a weaver's beam, and his iron spearhead *weighed* ^Tsix hundred shekels; and a shield-bearer went before him.   15 lb.

8 Then he stood and cried out to the armies of Israel, and said to them, "Why have you come out to line up for battle? *Am* I not a Philistine, and you the ^Rservants of Saul?

Choose a man for yourselves, and let him come down to me.   1 Sam. 8:17

9 "If he is able to fight with me and kill me, then we will be your servants. But if I prevail against him and kill him, then you shall be our servants and ᴿserve us." 1 Sam. 11:1

10 And the Philistine said, "I ᴿdefy the armies of Israel this day; give me a man, that we may fight together."   1 Sam. 17:26, 36, 45

11 When Saul and all Israel heard these words of the Philistine, they were dismayed and greatly afraid.

12 Now David was ᴿthe son of that ᴿEphrathite of Bethlehem Judah, whose name was Jesse, and who had ᴿeight sons. And the man was old, advanced in years, in the days of Saul.   Ruth 4:22 • Gen. 35:19 • 1 Sam. 16:10, 11

13 The three oldest sons of Jesse had gone to follow Saul to the battle. The ᴿnames of his three sons who went to the battle were Eliab the firstborn, next to him Abinadab, and the third Shammah.   1 Sam. 16:6, 8, 9

14 David was the youngest. And the three oldest followed Saul.

15 But David occasionally went and returned from Saul ᴿto feed his father's sheep at Bethlehem.   1 Sam. 16:11, 19

16 And the Philistine drew near and presented himself forty days, morning and evening.

17 Then Jesse said to his son David, "Take now for your brothers an ᵀephah of this dried grain and these ten loaves, and run to your brothers at the camp.   .65 bu.

18 "And carry these ten cheeses to the captain of their thousand, and see how your brothers fare, and bring back news of them."

19 Now Saul and they and all the men of Israel were in the Valley of Elah, fighting with the Philistines.

20 So David rose early in the morning, left the sheep with a keeper, and took the things and went as Jesse had commanded him. And he came to the camp as the army was going out to the fight and shouting for the battle.

21 For Israel and the Philistines had drawn up in battle array, army against army.

22 And David left his supplies in the hand of the supply keeper, ran to the army, and came and greeted his brothers.

23 Then as he talked with them, there was the champion, the Philistine of Gath, Goliath by name, coming up from the armies of the Philistines; and he spoke according to the same words. So David heard them.

24 And all the men of Israel, when they saw the man, fled from him and were dreadfully afraid.

25 So the men of Israel said, "Have you seen this man who has come up? Surely he has come up to defy Israel; and it shall be that the man who kills him the king will enrich with great riches, ᴿwill give him his

daughter, and give his father's house exemption from taxes in Israel."   Josh. 15:16

26 Then David spoke to the men who stood by him, saying, "What shall be done for the man who kills this Philistine and takes away the reproach from Israel? For who is this uncircumcised Philistine, that he should defy the armies of the living God?"

27 And the people answered him in this manner, saying, ᴿ"So shall it be done for the man who kills him."   1 Sam. 17:25

28 Now Eliab his oldest brother heard when he spoke to the men; and Eliab's ᴿanger was aroused against David, and he said, "Why did you come down here? And with whom have you left those few sheep in the wilderness? I know your pride and the insolence of your heart, for you have come down to see the battle."   [Matt. 10:36]

29 And David said, "What have I done now? ᵀIs there not a cause?"   Lit. Is it not a matter

30 Then he turned from him toward another and said the same thing; and these people answered him as the first ones did.

31 Now when the words which David spoke were heard, they reported them to Saul; and he sent for him.

32 Then David said to Saul, "Let no man's heart fail because of him; ᴿyour servant will go and fight with this Philistine."   1 Sam. 16:18

33 And Saul said to David, ᴿ"You are not able to go against this Philistine to fight with him; for you are a youth, and he a man of war from his youth."   Num. 13:31

34 But David said to Saul, "Your servant used to keep his father's sheep, and when a ᴿlion or a bear came and took a lamb out of the flock,   Judg. 14:5

35 I went out after it and struck it, and delivered the lamb from its mouth; and when it arose against me, I caught it by its beard, and struck and killed it.

36 "Your servant has killed both lion and bear; and this uncircumcised Philistine will be like one of them, seeing he has defied the armies of the living God."

37 Moreover David said, ᴿ"The Lᴏʀᴅ, who delivered me from the paw of the lion and from the paw of the bear, He will deliver me from the hand of this Philistine." And Saul said to David, ᴿ"Go, and the Lᴏʀᴅ be with you!"   [2 Cor. 1:10] • 1 Chr. 22:11, 16

38 So Saul clothed David with his ᵀarmor, and he put a bronze helmet on his head; he also clothed him with a coat of mail.   Lit. clothes

39 David fastened his sword to his armor and tried to walk, for he had not tested them. And David said to Saul, "I cannot walk with these, for I have not tested them." So David took them off.

40 Then he took his staff in his hand; and he chose for himself five smooth stones from the brook, and put them in a shepherd's bag,

in a pouch which he had, and his sling was in his hand. And he drew near to the Philistine.

41 So the Philistine came, and began drawing near to David, and the man who bore the shield *went* before him.

42 And when the Philistine looked about and saw David, he disdained him; for he was *only* a youth, ruddy and good-looking.

43 So the Philistine said to David, "*Am* I a dog, that you come to me with sticks?" And the Philistine cursed David by his gods.

44 And the Philistine said to David, "Come to me, and I will give your flesh to the birds of the air and the beasts of the field!"

45 Then David said to the Philistine, "You come to me with a sword, with a spear, and with a javelin. But I come to you in the name of the LORD of hosts, the God of the armies of Israel, whom you have defied.

46 "This day the LORD will deliver you into my hand, and I will strike you and take your head from you. And this day I will give Rthe carcasses of the camp of the Philistines to the birds of the air and the wild beasts of the earth, Rthat all the earth may know that there is a God in Israel.   Deut. 28:26 • Josh. 4:24

47 "Then all this assembly shall know that the LORD does not save with sword and spear; for Rthe battle *is* the LORD's, and He will give you into our hands."   2 Chr. 20:15

48 So it was, when the Philistine arose and came and drew near to meet David, that David hurried and Rran toward the army to meet the Philistine.   Ps. 27:3

49 Then David put his hand in his bag and took out a stone; and he slung *it* and struck the Philistine in his forehead, so that the stone sank into his forehead, and he fell on his face to the earth.

50 So David prevailed over the Philistine with a Rsling and a stone, and struck the Philistine and killed him. But *there was* no sword in the hand of David.   Judg. 20:16

51 Therefore David ran and stood over the Philistine, took his sword and drew it out of its sheath and killed him, and cut off his head with it. And when the Philistines saw that their champion was dead, they fled.

52 Now the men of Israel and Judah arose and shouted, and pursued the Philistines as far as the entrance of *the valley and to the gates of Ekron. And the wounded of the Philistines fell along the road to RShaaraim, even as far as Gath and Ekron.   Josh. 15:36

53 Then the children of Israel returned from chasing the Philistines, and they plundered their tents.

54 And David took the head of the Philistine and brought it to Jerusalem, but he put his armor in his tent.

55 When Saul saw David going out against the Philistine, he said to Abner, the com-

mander of the army, "Abner, Rwhose son *is* this youth?" And Abner said, "As your soul lives, O king, I do not know."   1 Sam. 16:21, 22

56 So the king said, "Inquire whose son this young man *is.*"

57 Then, as David returned from the slaughter of the Philistine, Abner took him and brought him before Saul Rwith the head of the Philistine in his hand.   1 Sam. 17:54

58 And Saul said to him, "Whose son *are* you, young man?" So David answered, R"*I am* the son of your servant Jesse the Bethlehemite."   1 Sam. 17:12

Saul Resents David

18 Now when he had finished speaking to Saul, the soul of Jonathan was knit to the soul of David, and Jonathan loved him as his own soul.

2 Saul took him that day, Rand would not let him go home to his father's house anymore.   1 Sam. 17:15

3 Then Jonathan and David made a covenant, because he loved him as his own soul.

4 And Jonathan took off the robe that *was* on him and gave it to David, with his armor, even to his sword and his bow and his belt.

5 So David went out wherever Saul sent him, *and* Tbehaved wisely. And Saul set him over the men of war, and he was accepted in the sight of all the people and also in the sight of Saul's servants.   Or *prospered*

6 Now it had happened as they were coming *home,* when David was returning from the slaughter of the TPhilistine, that Rthe women had come out of all the cities of Israel, singing and dancing, to meet King Saul, with tambourines, with joy, and with musical instruments.   *Philistines* • Ex. 15:20, 21

7 So the women Rsang as they danced, and said: Ex. 15:21

"Saul has slain his thousands,
   And David his ten thousands."

8 Then Saul was very angry, and the saying displeased him; and he said, "They have ascribed to David ten thousands, and to me they have ascribed *only* thousands. Now *what* more can he have but the kingdom?"

9 So Saul Teyed David from that day forward.   Viewed with suspicion

10 And it happened on the next day that the distressing spirit from God came upon Saul, Rand he prophesied inside the house. So David Rplayed *music* with his hand, as at other times; Rbut *there was* a spear in Saul's hand.   1 Sam. 19:24 • 1 Sam. 16:23 • 1 Sam. 19:9, 10

11 And Saul Rcast the spear, for he said, "I will pin David to the wall!" But David escaped his presence twice.   1 Sam. 19:10; 20:33

12 Now Saul was afraid of David, because Rthe LORD was with him, but had Rdeparted from Saul.   1 Sam. 16:13, 18 • 1 Sam. 16:14; 28:15

13 Therefore Saul removed him from [T]his presence, and made him his captain over a thousand; and [R]he went out and came in before the people.   Lit. *himself* • Num. 27:17

14 And David behaved wisely in all his ways, and [R]the LORD *was* with him.   Josh. 6:27

15 Therefore, when Saul saw that he behaved very wisely, he was afraid of him.

16 But [R]all Israel and Judah loved David, because he went out and came in before them.   1 Sam. 18:5

David Marries Michal

17 Then Saul said to David, "Here is my older daughter Merab; I will give her to you as a wife. Only be valiant for me, and fight the LORD's battles." For Saul thought, "Let my hand not be against him, but let the hand of the Philistines be against him."

18 So David said to Saul, "Who *am* I, and what *is* my life or my father's family in Israel, that I should be son-in-law to the king?"

19 But it happened at the time when Merab, Saul's daughter, should have been given to David, that she was given to [R]Adriel the [R]Meholathite as a wife.   2 Sam. 21:8 • Judg. 7:22

20 [R]Now Michal, Saul's daughter, loved David. And they told Saul, and the thing pleased him.   1 Sam. 18:28

21 So Saul said, "I will give her to him, that she may be a snare to him, and that the hand of the Philistines may be against him." Therefore Saul said to David a second time, "You shall be my son-in-law today."

22 And Saul commanded his servants, "Communicate with David secretly, and say, 'Look, the king has delight in you, and all his servants love you. Now therefore, become the king's son-in-law.' "

23 So Saul's servants spoke those words in the hearing of David. And David said, "Does it seem to you *a* light *thing* to be a king's son-in-law, seeing I *am* a poor and lightly esteemed man?"

24 And the servants of Saul told him, saying, "In this manner David spoke."

25 Then Saul said, "Thus you shall say to David: 'The king does not desire any [R]dowry but one hundred foreskins of the Philistines, to take vengeance on the king's enemies.' " But Saul [R]thought to make David fall by the hand of the Philistines.   Ex. 22:17 • 1 Sam. 18:17

26 So when his servants told David these words, it pleased David well to become the king's son-in-law. Now [R]the days had not expired;   1 Sam. 18:21

27 therefore David arose and went, he and [R]his men, and killed two hundred men of the Philistines. And [R]David brought their foreskins, and they gave them in full count to the king, that he might become the king's son-in-law. Then Saul gave him Michal his daughter as a wife.   1 Sam. 18:13 • 2 Sam. 3:14

28 Thus Saul saw and knew that the LORD *was* with David, and *that* Michal, Saul's daughter, loved him;

29 and Saul was still more afraid of David. So Saul became David's enemy continually.

30 Then the princes of the Philistines [R]went out *to war*. And so it was, whenever they went out, *that* David [R]behaved more wisely than all the servants of Saul, so that his name became highly esteemed.   2 Sam. 11:1 • 1 Sam. 18:5

Saul Persecutes David

19 Now Saul spoke to Jonathan his son and to all his servants, that they should kill [R]David; but Jonathan, Saul's son, [R]delighted greatly in David. 1 Sam. 8:8, 9 • 1 Sam. 18:1

2 So Jonathan told David, saying, "My father Saul seeks to kill you. Therefore please be on your guard until morning, and stay in a secret *place* and hide.

3 "And I will go out and stand beside my father in the field where you *are*, and I will speak with my father about you. Then what I observe, I will tell [R]you."   1 Sam. 20:8-13

4 Thus Jonathan [R]spoke well of David to Saul his father, and said to him, "Let not the king [R]sin against his servant, against David, because he has not sinned against you, and because his works *have been* very good toward you.   [Prov. 31:8, 9] • [Prov. 17:13]

5 "For he took his life in his hands and killed the Philistine, and [R]the LORD brought about a great deliverance for all Israel. You saw *it* and rejoiced. Why then will you [R]sin against innocent blood, to kill David without a cause?"   1 Sam. 11:13 • [Deut. 19:10-13]

6 So Saul heeded the voice of Jonathan, and Saul swore, "*As* the LORD lives, he shall not be killed."

7 Then Jonathan called David, and Jonathan told him all these things. So Jonathan brought David to Saul, and he was in his presence [R]as in times past.   1 Sam. 16:21

8 And there was war again; and David went out and fought with the Philistines, [R]and struck them with a mighty blow, and they fled from him.   1 Sam. 18:27; 23:5

9 Now [R]the distressing spirit from the LORD came upon Saul as he sat in his house with his spear in his hand. And David was playing *music* with *his* hand.   1 Sam. 16:14

10 Then Saul sought to pin David to the wall with the spear, but he slipped away from Saul's presence; and he drove the spear into the wall. So David fled and escaped that night.

11 [R]Saul also sent messengers to David's house to watch him and to kill him in the morning. And Michal, David's wife, told him, saying, "If you do not save your life tonight, tomorrow you will be killed."   Ps. 59:title

12 So Michal let David down through a window. And he went and fled and escaped.

13 And Michal took ᵀan image and laid *it* in the bed, put a cover of goats' *hair* for his head, and covered *it* with clothes.   *idols*

14 So when Saul sent messengers to take David, she said, "He *is* sick."

15 Then Saul sent the messengers *back* to see David, saying, "Bring him up to me in the bed, that I may kill him."

16 And when the messengers had come in, there was the image in the bed, with a cover of goats' *hair* for his head.

17 Then Saul said to Michal, "Why have you deceived me like this, and sent my enemy away, so that he has escaped?" And Michal answered Saul, "He said to me, 'Let me go! ᴿWhy should I kill you?'"   2 Sam. 2:22

18 So David fled and escaped, and went to Samuel at ᴿRamah, and told him all that Saul had done to him. And he and Samuel went and stayed in Naioth.   1 Sam. 7:17

19 Now it was told Saul, saying, "Take note, David *is* at Naioth in Ramah!"

20 Then ᴿSaul sent messengers to take David. ᴿAnd when they saw the group of prophets prophesying, and Samuel standing *as* leader over them, the Spirit of God came upon the messengers of Saul, and they also ᴿprophesied.   John 7:32 · 1 Sam. 10:5, 6, 10 · Joel 2:28

21 And when Saul was told, he sent other messengers, and they prophesied likewise. Then Saul sent messengers again the third time, and they prophesied also.

22 Then he also went to Ramah, and came to the great well that *is* at Sechu. So he asked, and said, "Where *are* Samuel and David?" And *someone* said, "Indeed *they are* at Naioth in Ramah."

23 So he went there to Naioth in Ramah. Then ᴿthe Spirit of God was upon him also, and he went on and prophesied until he came to Naioth in Ramah.   1 Sam. 10:10

24 And he also stripped off his clothes and prophesied before Samuel in like manner, and lay down ᴿnaked all that day and all that night. Therefore they say, ᴿ"*Is* Saul also among the prophets?"   Mic. 1:8 · 1 Sam. 10:10–12

Jonathan's Loyalty to David

20 Then David fled from Naioth in Ramah, and went and said to Jonathan, "What have I done? What *is* my iniquity, and what *is* my sin before your father, that he seeks my life?"

2 So Jonathan said to him, "By no means! You shall not die! Indeed, my father will do nothing either great or small without first telling me. And why should my father hide this thing from me? It *is* not *so*!"

3 Then David took an oath again, and said, "Your father certainly knows that I have found favor in your eyes, and he has said, 'Do not let Jonathan know this, lest he be grieved.' But ᴿtruly, *as* the LORD lives and *as*

your soul lives, *there is* but a step between me and death."   1 Sam. 27:1

4 So Jonathan said to David, "Whatever you yourself desire, I will do *it* for you."

5 And David said to Jonathan, "Indeed tomorrow *is* the ᴿNew Moon, and I should not fail to sit with the king to eat. But let me go, that I may ᴿhide in the field until the third *day* at evening.   Num. 10:10; 28:11–15 · 1 Sam. 19:2, 3

6 "If your father misses me at all, then say, 'David earnestly asked *permission* of me that he might run over ᴿto Bethlehem, his city, for *there is* a yearly sacrifice there for all the family.'   1 Sam. 16:4; 17:12

7 "If he says thus: '*It is* well,' your servant will be safe. But if he is very angry, be sure that evil is determined by him.

8 "Therefore you shall ᴿdeal kindly with your servant, for you have brought your servant into a covenant of the LORD with you. Nevertheless, ᴿif there is iniquity in me, kill me yourself, for why should you bring me to your father?"   Josh. 2:14 · 2 Sam. 14:32

9 But Jonathan said, "Far be it from you! For if I knew certainly that evil was determined by my father to come upon you, then would I not tell you?"

10 Then David said to Jonathan, "Who will tell me, or what *if* your father answers you roughly?"

11 And Jonathan said to David, "Come, let us go out into the field." So both of them went out into the field.

12 Then Jonathan said to David: "The LORD God of Israel *is witness*! When I have ᵀsounded out my father sometime tomorrow, or the third *day*, and indeed *there is* good toward David, and I do not send to you and tell you,   *searched out*

13 "may ᴿthe LORD do so and much more to Jonathan. But if it pleases my father *to do* you evil, then I will report it to you and send you away, that you may go in safety. And ᴿthe LORD be with you as He has ᴿbeen with my father.   Ruth 1:17 · Josh. 1:5 · 1 Sam. 10:7

14 "And you shall not only show me the kindness of the LORD while I still live, that I may not die;

15 "but you shall not cut off your kindness from my ᵀhouse forever, no, not when the LORD has cut off every one of the enemies of David from the face of the earth."   *family*

16 So Jonathan made *a covenant* with the house of David, *saying*, "Let the LORD require *it* at the hand of David's enemies."

17 Now Jonathan again caused David to vow, because he loved him; ᴿfor he loved him as he loved his own soul.   1 Sam. 18:1

18 Then Jonathan said to David, ᴿ"Tomorrow *is* the New Moon; and you will be missed, because your seat will be empty.   1 Sam. 20:5, 24

19 "And *when* you have stayed three days, go down quickly and come to ᴿthe place

where you hid on the day of the deed; and remain by the stone Ezel.   1 Sam. 19:2

20 "Then I will shoot three arrows to the side, as though I shot at a target;

21 "and there I will send a lad, *saying*, 'Go, find the arrows.' If I expressly say to the lad, 'Look, the arrows *are* on this side of you; get them and come'—then, ᴿas the LORD lives, *there is* safety for you and no harm.   Jer. 4:2

22 "But if I say thus to the young man, 'Look, the arrows *are* beyond you'—go your way, for the LORD has sent you away.

23 "And as for ᴿthe matter which you and I have spoken of, indeed the LORD *be* between you and me forever."   1 Sam. 20:14, 15

24 Then David hid in the field. And when the New Moon had come, the king sat down to eat the feast.

25 Now the king sat on his seat, as at other times, on a seat by the wall. And *Jonathan arose, and Abner sat by Saul's side, but David's place was empty.

26 Nevertheless Saul did not say anything that day, for he thought, "Something has happened to him; he *is* unclean, surely he *is* ᴿunclean."   Lev. 7:20, 21; 15:5

27 And it happened the next day, the second *day* of the month, that David's place was empty. And Saul said to Jonathan his son, "Why has the son of Jesse not come to eat, either yesterday or today?"

28 So Jonathan ᴿanswered Saul, "David earnestly asked *permission* of me *to* go to Bethlehem.   1 Sam. 20:6

29 "And he said, 'Please let me go, for our family has a sacrifice in the city, and my brother has commanded me *to be there*. And now, if I have found favor in your eyes, please let me get away and see my brothers.' Therefore he has not come to the king's table."

30 Then Saul's anger was aroused against Jonathan, and he said to him, "You son of a perverse, rebellious *woman!* Do I not know that you have chosen the son of Jesse to your own shame and to the shame of your mother's nakedness?

31 "For as long as the son of Jesse lives on the earth, you shall not be established, nor your kingdom. Now therefore, send and bring him to me, for he shall surely die."

32 And Jonathan answered Saul his father, and said to him, ᴿ"Why should he be killed? What has he done?"   Gen. 31:36

33 Then Saul cast a spear at him to kill him, by which Jonathan knew that it was determined by his father to kill David.

34 So Jonathan arose from the table in fierce anger, and ate no food the second day of the month, for he was grieved for David,

20:25 So with MT, Syr., Tg., Vg.; LXX *he sat across from Jonathan*

because his father had treated him shamefully.

35 And so it was, in the morning, that Jonathan went out into the field at the time appointed with David, and a little lad *was* with him.

36 Then he said to his lad, "Now run, find the arrows which I shoot." As the lad ran, he shot an arrow beyond him.

37 When the lad had come to the place where the arrow was which Jonathan had shot, Jonathan cried out after the lad and said, "*Is* not the arrow beyond you?"

38 And Jonathan cried out after the lad, "Make haste, hurry, do not delay!" So Jonathan's lad gathered up the arrows and came back to his master.

39 But the lad did not know anything. Only Jonathan and David knew of the matter.

40 Then Jonathan gave his ᵀweapons to his lad, and said to him, "Go, carry *them* to the city."   equipment

41 As soon as the lad had gone, David arose from *a place* toward the south, fell on his face to the ground, and bowed down three times. And they kissed one another; and they wept together, but David more so.

42 Then Jonathan said to David, ᴿ"Go in peace, since we have both sworn in the name of the LORD, saying, 'May the LORD be between you and me, and between your descendants and my descendants, forever.' " So he arose and departed, and Jonathan went into the city.   1 Sam. 1:17

David and the Holy Bread

21 Now David came to Nob, to Ahimelech the priest. And Ahimelech was afraid when he met David, and said to him, "Why *are* you alone, and no one is with you?"

2 So David said to Ahimelech the priest, "The king has ordered me on some business, and said to me, 'Do not let anyone know anything about the business on which I send you, or what I have commanded you.' And I have directed *my* young men to such and such a place.

3 "Now therefore, what have you on hand? Give *me* five *loaves of* bread in my hand, or whatever can be found."

4 And the priest answered David and said, "*There is* no common bread on hand; but there is holy bread, if the young men have at least kept themselves from women."

5 Then David answered the priest, and said to him, "Truly, women *have been* kept from us about three days since I came out. And the vessels of the young men are holy, and *the bread is* in effect common, even though it was consecrated in the vessel this day."

6 So the priest gave him holy *bread*; for there was no bread there but the showbread ᴿwhich had been taken from before the Lᴏʀᴅ, in order to put hot bread *in its place* on the day when it was taken away.   Lev. 24:8, 9

7 Now a certain man of the servants of Saul *was* there that day, detained before the Lᴏʀᴅ. And his name *was* ᴿDoeg, an Edomite, the chief of the herdsmen who *belonged to* Saul.   1 Sam. 14:47; 22:9

8 And David said to Ahimelech, "Is there not here on hand a spear or a sword? For I have brought neither my sword nor my weapons with me, because the king's business required haste."

9 So the priest said, "The sword of Goliath the Philistine, whom you killed in ᴿthe Valley of Elah, ᴿthere it is, wrapped in a cloth behind the ephod. If you will take that, take *it*. For *there is* no other except that one here." And David said, "*There is* none like it; give it to me."   1 Sam. 17:2, 50 • 1 Sam. 31:10

David Flees to Gath

10 Then David arose and fled that day from before Saul, and went to Achish the king of Gath.

11 And ᴿthe servants of Achish said to him, ᴿ"*Is* this not David the king of the land? Did they not sing of him to one another in dances, saying: Ps. 56:title • 1 Sam. 18:6–8; 29:5

ᴿ'Saul has slain his thousands,
And David his ten thousands'?" 1 Sam. 18:7

12 Now David ᴿtook these words ᵀto heart, and was very much afraid of Achish the king of Gath.   Luke 2:19 • Lit. *in his heart*

13 So he changed his behavior before them, pretended madness in their hands, ᵀscratched on the doors of the gate, and let his saliva fall down on his beard.   *scribbled*

14 Then Achish said to his servants, "Look, you see the man is insane. Why have you brought him to me?

15 "Have I need of madmen, that you have brought this *fellow* to play the madman in my presence? Shall this *fellow* come into my house?"

David's Four Hundred Men

22 David therefore departed from there and escaped to the cave of Adullam. So when his brothers and all his father's house heard *it*, they went down there to him.

2 And everyone *who was* in distress, everyone who *was* in debt, and everyone *who was* discontented gathered to him. So he became captain over them. And there were about four hundred men with him.

3 Then David went from there to Mizpah of ᴿMoab; and he said to the king of Moab, "Please let my father and mother come here

with you, till I know what God will do for me."   2 Sam. 8:2

4 So he brought them before the king of Moab, and they dwelt with him all the time that David was in the stronghold.

5 Now the prophet ᴿGad said to David, "Do not stay in the stronghold; depart, and go to the land of Judah." So David departed and went into the forest of Hereth. 2 Sam. 24:11

Saul Murders the Priests

6 When Saul heard that David and the men who *were* with him had been discovered—now Saul was staying in ᴿGibeah under a tamarisk tree in Ramah, with his spear in his hand, and all his servants standing about him—   1 Sam. 15:34

7 then Saul said to his servants who stood about him, "Hear now, you Benjamites! Will the son of Jesse give every one of you fields and vineyards, *and* make you all captains of thousands and captains of hundreds?

8 "All of you have conspired against me, and *there is* no one who reveals to me that ᴿmy son has made a covenant with the son of Jesse; and *there is* not one of you who is sorry for me or reveals to me that my son has stirred up my servant against me, to lie in wait, as *it is* this day." 1 Sam. 18:3; 20:16, 30

9 Then answered Doeg the Edomite, who was set over the servants of Saul, and said, "I saw the son of Jesse going to Nob, to ᴿAhimelech the son of ᴿAhitub. 1 Sam. 21:1 • 1 Sam. 14:3

10 "And he inquired of the Lᴏʀᴅ for him, ᴿgave him provisions, and gave him the sword of Goliath the Philistine." 1 Sam. 21:6, 9

11 So the king sent to call Ahimelech the priest, the son of Ahitub, and all his father's house, the priests who *were* in Nob. And they all came to the king.

12 And Saul said, "Hear now, son of Ahitub!" He answered, "Here I am, my lord."

13 Then Saul said to him, "Why have you conspired against me, you and the son of Jesse, in that you have given him bread and a sword, and have inquired of God for him, that he should rise against me, to lie in wait, as it is this day?"

14 So Ahimelech answered the king and said, "And who among all your servants *is as* ᴿfaithful as David, who is the king's son-in-law, who goes at your bidding, and is honorable in your house? 1 Sam. 19:4, 5; 20:32; 24:11

15 "Did I then begin to inquire of God for him? Far be it from me! Let not the king impute anything to his servant, *or* to any in the house of my father. For your servant knew nothing of all this, little or much."

16 And the king said, "You shall surely die, Ahimelech, you and all your father's house!"

17 Then the king said to the guards who stood about him, "Turn and kill the priests of the Lᴏʀᴅ, because their hand also *is* with

David, and because they knew when he fled and did not tell it to me." But the servants of the king Rwould not lift their hands to strike the priests of the LORD.   Ex. 1:17

18 And the king said to Doeg, "You turn and kill the priests!" So Doeg the Edomite turned and Tstruck the priests, and Rkilled on that day eighty-five men who wore a linen ephod.   *attacked* · 1 Sam. 2:31

19 RAlso Nob, the city of the priests, he struck with the edge of the sword, both men and women, children and nursing infants, oxen and donkeys and sheep—with the edge of the sword.   1 Sam. 22:9, 11

20 RNow one of the sons of Ahimelech the son of Ahitub, named Abiathar, Rescaped and fled after David.   1 Sam. 23:6, 9; 30:7 · 1 Sam. 2:33

21 And Abiathar told David that Saul had killed the LORD's priests.

22 So David said to Abiathar, "I knew that day, when Doeg the Edomite *was* there, that he would surely tell Saul. I have caused *the death* of all the persons of your father's Thouse.   *family*

23 "Stay with me; do not fear. RFor he who seeks my life seeks your life, but with me you *shall be* safe."   1 Kin. 2:26

David Saves the City of Keilah

23 Then they told David, saying, "Look, the Philistines are fighting against Keilah, and they are robbing the threshing floors."

2 Therefore David inquired of the LORD, saying, "Shall I go and attack these Philistines?" And the LORD said to David, "Go and attack the Philistines, and save Keilah."

3 But David's men said to him, "Look, we are afraid here in Judah. How much more then if we go to Keilah against the armies of the Philistines?"

4 Then David inquired of the LORD once again. And the LORD answered him and said, "Arise, go down to Keilah. For I will deliver the Philistines into your hand."

5 And David and his men went to Keilah and Rfought with the Philistines, struck them with a mighty blow, and took away their livestock. So David saved the inhabitants of Keilah.   1 Sam. 19:8

6 Now it happened, when Abiathar the son of Ahimelech fled to David at Keilah, *that* he went down *with* an ephod in his hand.

7 And Saul was told that David had gone to Keilah. So Saul said, "God has delivered him into my hand, for he has shut himself in by entering a town that has gates and bars."

8 Then Saul called all the people together for war, to go down to Keilah to besiege David and his men.

9 When David knew that Saul plotted evil against him, Rhe said to Abiathar the priest, "Bring the ephod here."   1 Sam. 23:6; 30:7

10 Then David said, "O LORD God of Israel, Your servant has certainly heard that Saul seeks to come to Keilah Rto destroy the city for my sake.   1 Sam. 22:19

11 "Will the men of Keilah deliver me into his hand? Will Saul come down, as Your servant has heard? O LORD God of Israel, I pray, tell Your servant." And the LORD said, "He will come down."

12 Then David said, "Will the men of Keilah Tdeliver me and my men into the hand of Saul?" And the LORD said, "They will deliver *you*."   Lit. *shut up*

13 So David and his men, about six hundred, arose and departed from Keilah and went wherever they could go. Then it was told Saul that David had escaped from Keilah; so he halted the expedition.

David in Wilderness Strongholds

14 And David stayed in strongholds in the wilderness, and remained in Rthe mountains in the Wilderness of RZiph. Saul Rsought him every day, but God did not deliver him into his hand.   Ps. 11:1 · Josh. 15:55 · Ps. 32:7; 54:3, 4

15 So David saw that Saul had come out to seek his life. And David *was* in the Wilderness of Ziph Tin a forest.   Or *in Horesh*

16 Then Jonathan, Saul's son, arose and went to David in the woods and Tstrengthened his hand in God.   *encouraged him*

17 And he said to him, R"Do not fear, for the hand of Saul my father shall not find you. You shall be king over Israel, and I shall be next to you. REven my father Saul knows that."   [Heb. 13:6] · 1 Sam. 20:31; 24:20

18 So the two of them made a covenant before the LORD. And David stayed in the woods, and Jonathan went to his own house.

19 Then the Ziphites came up to Saul at Gibeah, saying, "Is David not hiding with us in strongholds in the woods, in the hill of Hachilah, which *is* on the south of Jeshimon?

20 "Now therefore, O king, come down according to all the desire of your soul to come down; and Rour part *shall be* to deliver him into the king's hand."   Ps. 54:3

21 And Saul said, "Blessed *are* you of the LORD, for you have compassion on me.

22 "Please go and find out for sure, and see the place where his hideout is, *and* who has seen him there. For I am told he is very crafty.

23 "See therefore, and take knowledge of all the lurking places where he hides; and come back to me with certainty, and I will go with you. And it shall be, if he is in the land, that I will search for him throughout all the Tclans of Judah."   Lit. *thousands*

24 So they arose and went to Ziph before Saul. But David and his men *were* in the Wilderness Rof Maon, in the plain on the south of Jeshimon.   1 Sam. 25:2

25 When Saul and his men went to seek *him*, they told David. Therefore he went down to the rock, and stayed in the Wilderness of Maon. And when Saul heard *that*, he pursued David in the Wilderness of Maon.

26 Then Saul went on one side of the mountain, and David and his men on the other side of the mountain. ᴿSo David made haste to get away from Saul, for Saul and his men ᴿwere encircling David and his men to take them.   Ps. 31:22 • Ps. 17:9

27 ᴿBut a messenger came to Saul, saying, "Hurry and come, for the Philistines have invaded the land!"   2 Kin. 19:9

28 Therefore Saul returned from pursuing David, and went against the Philistines; so they called that place the *Rock of Escape.

29 Then David went up from there and dwelt in strongholds at ᴿEn Gedi.   2 Chr. 20:2

David Spares Saul

24 Now it happened, when Saul had returned from following the Philistines, that it was told him, saying, "Take note! David *is* in the Wilderness of En Gedi."

2 Then Saul took three thousand chosen men from all Israel, and went to seek David and his men on the Rocks of the Wild Goats.

3 So he came to the sheepfolds by the road, where there *was* a cave; and Saul went in to attend to his needs. (David and his men were staying in the recesses of the cave.)

4 Then the men of David said to him, "This is the day of which the LORD said to you, 'Behold, I will deliver your enemy into your hand, that you may do to him as it seems good to you.'" And David arose and secretly cut off a corner of Saul's robe.

5 Now it happened afterward that ᴿDavid's heart troubled him because he had cut Saul's robe.   2 Sam. 24:10

6 And he said to his men, ᴿ"The LORD forbid that I should do this thing to my master, the LORD's anointed, to stretch out my hand against him, seeing he *is* the anointed of the LORD."   1 Sam. 26:11

7 So David ᴿrestrained his servants with *these* words, and did not allow them to rise against Saul. And Saul got up from the cave and went on *his* way.   [Matt. 5:44]

8 David also arose afterward, went out of the cave, and called out to Saul, saying, "My lord the king!" And when Saul looked behind him, David stooped with his face to the earth, and bowed down.

9 And David said to Saul: ᴿ"Why do you listen to the words of men who say, 'Indeed David seeks your harm'?   Ps. 141:6

10 "Look, this day your eyes have seen that the LORD delivered you today into my hand in the cave, and *someone* urged *me* to kill you.

But *my eye* spared you, and I said, 'I will not stretch out my hand against my lord, for he *is* the LORD's anointed.'

11 "Moreover, my father, see! Yes, see the corner of your robe in my hand! For in that I cut off the corner of your robe, and did not kill you, know and see that there *is* ᴿneither evil nor rebellion in my hand, and I have not sinned against you. Yet you ᴿhunt my life to take it.   Ps. 7:3; 35:7 • 1 Sam. 26:20

12 "Let the LORD judge between you and me, and let the LORD avenge me on you. But my hand shall not be against you.

13 "As the proverb of the ancients says, 'Wickedness proceeds from the wicked.' But my hand shall not be against you.

14 "After whom has the king of Israel come out? Whom do you pursue? ᴿA dead dog? ᴿA flea?   2 Sam. 9:8 • 1 Sam. 26:20

15 "Therefore let the LORD be judge, and judge between you and me, and ᴿsee and ᴿplead my case, and deliver me out of your hand."   2 Chr. 24:22 • Ps. 35:1; 43:1; 119:154

16 So it was, when David had finished speaking these words to Saul, that Saul said, ᴿ"Is this your voice, my son David?" And Saul lifted up his voice and wept.   1 Sam. 26:17

17 ᴿThen he said to David: "You are ᴿmore righteous than I; for ᴿyou have rewarded me with good, whereas I have rewarded you with evil.   1 Sam. 26:21 • Gen. 38:26 • [Matt. 5:44]

18 "And you have shown this day how you have dealt well with me; for when ᴿthe LORD delivered me into your hand, you did not kill me.   1 Sam. 26:23

19 "For if a man finds his enemy, will he let him get away safely? Therefore may the LORD reward you with good for what you have done to me this day.

20 "And now ᴿI know indeed that you shall surely be king, and that the kingdom of Israel shall be established in your hand.   1 Sam. 23:17

21 "Therefore swear now to me by the LORD that you will not cut off my descendants after me, and that you will not destroy my name from my father's house."

22 So David swore to Saul. And Saul went home, but David and his men went up to ᴿthe stronghold.   1 Sam. 23:29

Death of Samuel

25 Then ᴿSamuel died; and the Israelites gathered together and ᴿlamented for him, and buried him at his home in Ramah. And David arose and went down to the Wilderness of *Paran.   1 Sam. 28:3 • Deut. 34:8

David and the Wife of Nabal

2 Now *there was* a man ᴿin Maon whose business *was* in ᴿCarmel, and the man *was* very rich. He had three thousand sheep and a

thousand goats. And he was shearing his sheep in Carmel. 1 Sam. 23:24 • Josh. 15:55

3 The name of the man was Nabal, and the name of his wife Abigail. And she was a woman of good understanding and beautiful appearance; but the man was harsh and evil in his doings. He was of the house of Caleb.

4 When David heard in the wilderness that Nabal was Rshearing his sheep, Gen. 38:13

5 David sent ten young men; and David said to the young men, "Go up to Carmel, go to Nabal, and greet him in my name.

6 "And thus you shall say to him who lives in prosperity: 'Peace be to you, peace to your house, and peace to all that you have!

7 'Now I have heard that you have shearers. Your shepherds were with us, and we did not hurt them, Rnor was there anything missing from them all the while they were in Carmel. 1 Sam. 25:15, 21

8 'Ask your young men, and they will tell you. Therefore let my young men find favor in your eyes, for we come on a feast day. Please give whatever comes to your hand to your servants and to your son David.' "

9 So when David's young men came, they spoke to Nabal according to all these words in the name of David, and waited.

10 Then Nabal answered David's servants, and said, "Who is David, and who is the son of Jesse? There are many servants nowadays who break away each one from his master.

11 "Shall I then take my bread and my water and my Tmeat that I have killed for my shearers, and give it to men when I do not know where they are from?" Lit. slaughter

12 So David's young men turned on their heels and went back; and they came and told him all these words.

13 Then David said to his men, "Every man gird on his sword." So every man girded on his sword, and David also girded on his sword. And about four hundred men went with David, and two hundred Rstayed with the supplies. 1 Sam. 30:24

14 Now one of the young men told Abigail, Nabal's wife, saying, "Look, David sent messengers from the wilderness to greet our master; and he Treviled them. scolded or scorned at

15 "But the men were very good to us, and Rwe were not hurt, nor did we miss anything as long as we accompanied them, when we were in the fields. 1 Sam. 25:7, 21

16 "They were Ra wall to us both by night and day, all the time we were with them keeping the sheep. Ex. 14:22

17 "Now therefore, know and consider what you will do, for harm is determined against our master and against all his household. For he is such a Tscoundrel that one cannot speak to him." Lit. son of Belial

18 Then Abigail made haste and Rtook two hundred loaves of bread, two skins of wine,

five sheep already dressed, Tfive seahs of roasted grain, one hundred clusters of raisins, and two hundred cakes of figs, and loaded them on donkeys. Gen. 32:13 • 10.873 bu.

19 And she said to her servants, "Go on before me; see, I am coming after you." But she did not tell her husband Nabal.

20 So it was, as she rode on the donkey, that she went down under cover of the hill; and there were David and his men, coming down toward her, and she met them.

21 Now David had said, "Surely in vain I have protected all that this fellow has in the wilderness, so that nothing was missed of all that belongs to him. And he has Rrepaid me evil for good. Ps. 109:5

22 "May God do so, and more also, to the enemies of David, if I leave one male of all who belong to him by morning light."

23 Now when Abigail saw David, she Rdismounted quickly from the donkey, fell on her face before David, and bowed down to the ground. Judg. 1:14

24 So she fell at his feet and said: "On me, my lord, on me let this iniquity be! And please let your maidservant Tspeak in your ears, and hear the words of your maidservant. speak to you

25 "Please, let not my lord regard this scoundrel Nabal. For as his name is, so is he: TNabal is his name, and folly is with him! But I, your maidservant, did not see the young men of my lord whom you sent. Lit. Fool

26 "Now therefore, my lord, as the LORD lives and as your soul lives, since the LORD has held you back from coming to bloodshed and from avenging yourself with your own hand, now then, let your enemies and those who seek harm for my lord be as Nabal.

27 "And now this present which your maidservant has brought to my lord, let it be given to the young men who follow my lord.

28 "Please forgive the trespass of your maidservant. For Rthe LORD will certainly make for my lord an enduring house, because my lord Rfights the battles of the LORD, Rand evil is not found in you throughout your days. 2 Sam. 7:11-16, 27 • 1 Sam. 18:17 • 1 Sam. 24:11

29 "Yet a man has risen to pursue you and seek your life, but the life of my lord shall be Rbound in the bundle of the living with the LORD your God; and the lives of your enemies He shall Rsling out, as from the pocket of a sling. [Col. 3:3] • Jer. 10:18

30 "And it shall come to pass, when the LORD has done for my lord according to all the good that He has spoken concerning you, and has appointed you ruler over Israel,

31 "that this will be no grief to you, nor offense of heart to my lord, either that you have shed blood without cause, or that my lord has avenged himself. But when the LORD has dealt well with my lord, then remember your maidservant."

32 Then David said to Abigail: ᴿ"Blessed *is* the LORD God of Israel, who sent you this day to meet me!   Luke 1:68

33 "And blessed *is* your advice and blessed *are* you, because you have ᴿkept me this day from coming to bloodshed and from avenging myself with my own hand.   1 Sam. 25:26

34 "For indeed, *as* the LORD God of Israel lives, who has kept me back from hurting you, unless you had hurried and come to meet me, surely ᴿby morning light no males would have been left to Nabal!"   1 Sam. 25:22

35 So David received from her hand what she had brought him, and said to her, "Go up in peace to your house. See, I have heeded your voice and respected your person."

36 Now Abigail went to Nabal, and there he was, ᴿholding a feast in his house, like the feast of a king. And Nabal's heart *was* merry within him, for he *was* very drunk; therefore she told him nothing, little or much, until morning light.   2 Sam. 13:28

37 So it was, in the morning, when the wine had gone from Nabal, and his wife had told him these things, that his heart died within him, and he became *like* a stone.

38 Then it happened, *after* about ten days, that the LORD struck Nabal, and he died.

39 So when David heard that Nabal was dead, he said, "Blessed *be* the LORD, who has pleaded the cause of my reproach from the hand of Nabal, and has ᴿkept His servant from evil! For the LORD has ᴿreturned the wickedness of Nabal on his own head." And David sent and proposed to Abigail, to take her as his wife.   1 Sam. 25:26, 34 • 1 Kin. 2:44

40 When the servants of David had come to Abigail at Carmel, they spoke to her saying, "David sent us to you, to ask you to become his wife."

41 Then she arose, bowed her face to the earth, and said, "Here is your maidservant, a servant to ᴿwash the feet of the servants of my lord."   Luke 7:38, 44

42 So Abigail rose in haste and rode on a donkey, ᵀattended by five of her maidens; and she followed the messengers of David, and became his wife. Lit. *with five of her maidens at her feet*

43 David also took Ahinoam of Jezreel, and so both of them were his wives.

44 But Saul had given Michal his daughter, David's wife, to ᵀPalti the son of Laish, who *was* from ᴿGallim.   Paltiel, 2 Sam. 3:15 • Is. 10:30

David Spares Saul a Second Time

26 Now the Ziphites came to Saul at Gibeah, saying, "Is David not hiding in the hill of Hachilah, opposite Jeshimon?"

2 Then Saul arose and went down to the Wilderness of Ziph, having ᴿthree thousand chosen men of Israel with him, to seek David in the Wilderness of Ziph.   1 Sam. 13:2; 24:2

3 And Saul encamped in the hill of Hachilah, which *is* opposite Jeshimon, by the road. But David stayed in the wilderness, and he saw that Saul came after him into the wilderness.

4 David therefore sent out spies, and understood that Saul had indeed come.

5 So David arose and came to the place where Saul had encamped. And David saw the place where Saul lay, and ᴿAbner the son of Ner, the commander of his army. Now Saul lay within the camp, with the people encamped all around him.   1 Sam. 14:50, 51; 17:55

6 Then David answered, and said to Ahimelech the Hittite and to Abishai the son of Zeruiah, brother of Joab, saying, "Who will go down with me to Saul in the camp?" And Abishai said, "I will go down with you."

7 So David and Abishai came to the people by night; and there Saul lay sleeping within the camp, with his spear stuck in the ground by his head. And Abner and the people lay all around him.

8 Then Abishai said to David, ᴿ"God has delivered your enemy into your hand this day. Now therefore, please, let me strike him ᵀat once with the spear, right to the earth; and I will not *have* to *strike* him a second time!"   1 Sam. 24:4 • Or *one time*

9 But David said to Abishai, "Do not destroy him; ᴿfor who can stretch out his hand against the LORD's anointed, and be guiltless?"   1 Sam. 24:6, 7

10 David said furthermore, "*As* the LORD lives, ᴿthe LORD shall strike him, or ᴿhis day shall come to die, or he shall ᴿgo out to battle and perish.   1 Sam. 25:26, 38 • [Job 7:1; 14:5] • 1 Sam. 31:6

11 "The LORD forbid that I should stretch out my hand against the LORD's anointed. But please, take now the spear and the jug of water that *are* by his head, and let us go."

12 So David took the spear and the jug of water *by* Saul's head, and they got away; and no man saw or knew *it* or awoke. For they *were* all asleep, because ᴿa deep sleep from the LORD had fallen on them.   Gen. 2:21; 15:12

13 Now David went over to the other side, and stood on the top of a hill afar off, a great distance *being* between them.

14 And David called out to the people and to Abner the son of Ner, saying, "Do you not answer, Abner?" Then Abner answered and said, "Who *are* you, calling out to the king?"

15 So David said to Abner, "*Are* you not a man? And who *is* like you in Israel? Why then have you not guarded your lord the king? For one of the people came in to destroy your lord the king.

16 "This thing that you have done *is* not good. *As* the LORD lives, you deserve to die, because you have not guarded your master, the LORD's anointed. And now see where the

king's spear *is*, and the jug of water that *was* by his head."

17 Then Saul knew David's voice, and said, "*Is* that your voice, my son David?" David said, "*It is* my voice, my lord, O king."

18 And he said, ᴿ"Why does my lord thus pursue his servant? For what have I done, or what evil *is* in my hand?   1 Sam. 24:9, 11-14

19 "Now therefore, please, let my lord the king hear the words of his servant: If the LORD has stirred you up against me, let Him accept an offering. But if *it is* the children of men, *may* they *be* cursed before the LORD, ᴿfor they have driven me out this day from sharing in the inheritance of the LORD, saying, 'Go, serve other gods.'   Deut. 4:27, 28

20 "So now, do not let my blood fall to the earth before the face of the LORD. For the king of Israel has come out to seek ᴿa flea, as when one hunts a partridge in the mountains."   1 Sam. 24:14

21 Then Saul said, ᴿ"I have sinned. Return, my son David. For I will harm you no more, because my life was precious in your eyes this day. Indeed I have played the fool and erred exceedingly."   1 Sam. 15:24, 30; 24:17

22 And David answered and said, "Here is the king's spear. Let one of the young men come over and get it.

23 ᴿ"May the LORD ᴿrepay every man *for* his righteousness and his faithfulness; for the LORD delivered you into *my* hand today, but I would not stretch out my hand against the LORD's anointed.   Ps. 7:8; 18:20; 62:12 • 2 Sam. 22:21

24 "And indeed, as your life was valued much this day in my eyes, so let my life be valued much in the eyes of the LORD, and let Him deliver me out of all tribulation."

25 Then Saul said to David, "*May* you *be* blessed, my son David! You shall both do great things and also still ᴿprevail." So David went on his way, and Saul returned to his place.   Gen. 32:28

David Allied with the Philistines

27 And David said in his heart, "Now I shall perish someday by the hand of Saul. *There is* nothing better for me than that I should speedily escape to the land of the Philistines; and Saul will despair of ᵀme, to seek me anymore in any part of Israel. So I shall escape out of his hand."   Searching for me

2 Then David arose and went over with the six hundred men who *were* with him to Achish the son of Maoch, king of Gath.

3 So David dwelt with Achish at Gath, he and his men, each man with his household, *and* David ᴿwith his two wives, Ahinoam the Jezreelitess, and Abigail the Carmelitess, Nabal's widow.   1 Sam. 25:42, 43

4 And it was told Saul that David had fled to Gath; so he sought him no more.

5 Then David said to Achish, "If I have now found favor in your eyes, let them give me a place in some town in the country, that I may dwell there. For why should your servant dwell in the royal city with you?"

6 So Achish gave him Ziklag that day. Therefore ᴿZiklag has belonged to the kings of Judah to this day.   Josh. 15:31; 19:5

7 Now ᵀthe time that David ᴿdwelt in the country of the Philistines was one full year and four months.   Lit. *the number of days* • 1 Sam. 29:3

8 And David and his men went up and raided the Geshurites, the *Girzites, and the Amalekites. For those nations were the inhabitants of the land from of old, as you go to Shur, even as far as the land of Egypt.

9 Whenever David ᵀattacked the land, he left neither man nor woman alive, but took away the sheep, the oxen, the donkeys, the camels, and the apparel, and returned and came to Achish.   Lit. *struck*

10 Then Achish would say, "Where have you made a raid today?" And David would say, "Against the southern *area* of Judah, or against the southern *area* of ᴿthe Jerahmeelites, or against the southern *area* of ᴿthe Kenites."   1 Chr. 2:9, 25 • Judg. 1:16

11 David would save neither man nor woman alive, to bring *news* to Gath, saying, "Lest they should inform on us, saying, 'Thus David did.' " And thus *was* his behavior all the time he dwelt in the country of the Philistines.

12 So Achish believed David, saying, "He has made his people Israel utterly abhor him; therefore he will be my servant forever."

28 Now ᴿit happened in those days that the Philistines gathered their armies together for war, to fight with Israel. And Achish said to David, "You assuredly know that you will go out with me to battle, you and your men."   1 Sam. 29:1, 2

2 So David said to Achish, "Surely you know what your servant can do." And Achish said to David, "Therefore I will make you one of my chief guardians forever."

Saul Consults a Medium

3 Now Samuel had died, and all Israel had lamented for him and buried him in Ramah, in his own city. And Saul had put the mediums and the spiritists out of the land.

4 Then the Philistines gathered together, and came and encamped at ᴿShunem. So Saul gathered all Israel together, and they encamped at ᴿGilboa.   Josh. 19:18 • 1 Sam. 31:1

5 When Saul saw the army of the Philistines, he was ᴿafraid, and his heart trembled greatly.   Job 18:11

6 And when Saul inquired of the LORD, the LORD did not answer him, either by dreams or by Urim or by the prophets.

7 Then Saul said to his servants, "Find me a woman who is a medium, ᴿthat I may go to

27:8 Or *Gezrites*

her and inquire of her." And his servants said to him, "In fact, *there is* a woman who is a medium at En Dor."   1 Chr. 10:13

8 So Saul disguised himself and put on other clothes, and he went, and two men with him; and they came to the woman by night. And ᴿhe said, "Please conduct a séance for me, and bring up for me the one I shall name to you."   Deut. 18:10, 11

9 Then the woman said to him, "Look, you know what Saul has done, how he has ᴿcut off the mediums and the spiritists from the land. Why then do you lay a snare for my life, to cause me to die?"   1 Sam. 28:3

10 And Saul swore to her by the Lᴏʀᴅ, saying, "*As* the Lᴏʀᴅ lives, no punishment shall come upon you for this thing."

11 Then the woman said, "Whom shall I bring up for you?" And he said, "Bring up Samuel for me."

12 When the woman saw Samuel, she cried out with a loud voice. And the woman spoke to Saul, saying, "Why have you deceived me? For you *are* Saul!"

13 And the king said to her, "Do not be afraid. What did you see?" And the woman said to Saul, "I saw ᴿaᵀ spirit ascending out of the earth."   Ex. 22:28 • Heb. *elohim*

14 So he said to her, "What *is* his form?" And she said, "An old man is coming up, and he *is* covered with a mantle." And Saul perceived that it *was* Samuel, and he stooped with *his* face to the ground and bowed down.

15 Now Samuel said to Saul, "Why have you disturbed me by bringing me up?" And Saul answered, "I am deeply distressed; for the Philistines make war against me, and God has departed from me and does not answer me anymore, neither by prophets nor by dreams. Therefore I have called you, that you may reveal to me what I should do."

16 Then Samuel said: "So why do you ask me, seeing the Lᴏʀᴅ has departed from you and has become your enemy?

17 "And the Lᴏʀᴅ has done for ᵀHimself as He spoke by me. For the Lᴏʀᴅ has torn the kingdom out of your hand and given it to your neighbor, David.   Or *him*, David

18 ᴿ"Because you did not obey the voice of the Lᴏʀᴅ nor execute His fierce wrath upon ᴿAmalek, therefore the Lᴏʀᴅ has done this thing to you this day.   1 Chr. 10:13 • 1 Sam. 15:3-9

19 "Moreover the Lᴏʀᴅ will also deliver Israel with you into the hand of the Philistines. And tomorrow you and your sons *will be* with ᴿme. The Lᴏʀᴅ will also deliver the army of Israel into the hand of the Philistines."   Job 3:17-19

20 Immediately Saul fell full length on the ground, and was dreadfully afraid because of the words of Samuel. And there was no strength in him, for he had eaten no food all day or all night.

21 And the woman came to Saul and saw that he was severely troubled, and said to him, "Look, your maidservant has obeyed your voice, and I have ᴿput my life in my hands and heeded the words which you spoke to me.   Job 13:14

22 "Now therefore, please, heed also the voice of your maidservant, and let me set a piece of bread before you; and eat, that you may have strength when you go on your way."

23 But he refused and said, "I will not eat." So his servants, together with the woman, urged him; and he heeded their voice. Then he arose from the ground and sat on the bed.

24 Now the woman had a fatted calf in the house, and she hastened to kill it. And she took flour and kneaded *it*, and baked unleavened bread from it.

25 So she brought *it* before Saul and his servants, and they ate. Then they rose and went away that night.

The Philistines Reject David

29 Then the Philistines gathered together all their armies at Aphek, and the Israelites encamped by a fountain which *is* in Jezreel.

2 And the lords of the Philistines ᵀpassed in review by hundreds and by thousands, but David and his men passed in review at the rear with Achish.   *passed on in the rear*

3 Then the princes of the Philistines said, "What *are* these Hebrews *doing here?*" And Achish said to the princes of the Philistines, "*Is* this not David, the servant of Saul king of Israel, who has been with me these days, or these years? And to this day I have found no fault in him since he defected *to me.*"

4 But the princes of the Philistines were angry with him; so the princes of the Philistines said to him, "Make this fellow return, that he may go back to the place which you have appointed for him, and do not let him go down with us to battle, lest in the battle he become our adversary. For with what could he reconcile himself to his master, if not with the heads of these ᴿmen?   1 Chr. 12:19, 20

5 "*Is* this not David, ᴿof whom they sang to one another in dances, saying: 1 Sam. 21:11

ᴿ"Saul has slain his thousands,
    And David his ten thousands'?"   1 Sam. 18:7

6 Then Achish called David and said to him, "Surely, *as* the Lᴏʀᴅ lives, you have been upright, and your going out and your coming in with me in the army *is* good in my sight. For to this day I have not found evil in you since the day of your coming to me. Nevertheless the lords do not favor you.

7 "Therefore return now, and go in peace, that you may not displease the lords of the Philistines."

8 So David said to Achish, "But what have I done? And to this day what have you found in your servant as long as I have been with you, that I may not go and fight against the enemies of my lord the king?"

9 Then Achish answered and said to David, "I know that you *are* as good in my sight as an angel of God; nevertheless ᴿthe princes of the Philistines have said, 'He shall not go up with us to the battle.'   1 Sam. 29:4

10 "Now therefore, rise early in the morning with your master's servants who have come with *you. And as soon as you are up early in the morning and have light, depart."

11 So David and his men rose early to depart in the morning, to return to the land of the Philistines. ᴿAnd the Philistines went up to Jezreel.   2 Sam. 4:4

David's Conflict with the Amalekites

30 Now it happened, when David and his men came to ᴿZiklag, on the third day, that the ᴿAmalekites had invaded the South and Ziklag, attacked Ziklag and burned it with fire,   1 Sam. 27:6 • 1 Sam. 15:7; 27:8

2 and had taken captive the ᴿwomen and those who *were* there, from small to great; they did not kill anyone, but carried *them* away and went their way.   1 Sam. 27:2, 3

3 So David and his men came to the city, and there it was, burned with fire; and their wives, their sons, and their daughters had been taken captive.

4 Then David and the people who *were* with him lifted up their voices and wept, until they had no more power to weep.

5 And David's two wives, Ahinoam the Jezreelitess, and Abigail the widow of Nabal the Carmelite, had been taken captive.

6 Now David was greatly distressed, for the people spoke of stoning him, because the soul of all the people was grieved, every man for his sons and his daughters. But David strengthened himself in the Lᴏʀᴅ his God.

7 ᴿThen David said to Abiathar the priest, Ahimelech's son, "Please bring the ephod here to me." And ᴿAbiathar brought the ephod to David.   1 Sam. 23:2-9 • 1 Sam. 23:6

8 ᴿSo David inquired of the Lᴏʀᴅ, saying, "Shall I pursue this troop? Shall I overtake them?" And He answered him, "Pursue, for you shall surely overtake *them* and without fail recover *all*."   1 Sam. 23:2, 4

9 So David went, he and the six hundred men who *were* with him, and came to the Brook Besor, where those stayed who were left behind.

10 But David pursued, he and four hundred men; ᴿfor two hundred stayed *behind*, who

were so weary that they could not cross the Brook Besor.   1 Sam. 30:9, 21

11 Then they found an Egyptian in the field, and brought him to David; and they gave him bread and he ate, and they let him drink water.

12 And they gave him a piece of a cake of figs and two clusters of raisins. So ᴿwhen he had eaten, his strength came back to him; for he had eaten no bread nor drunk water for three days and three nights.   Judg. 15:19

13 Then David said to him, "To whom do you *belong,* and where *are* you from?" And he said, "I *am* a young man from Egypt, servant of an Amalekite; and my master left me behind, because three days ago I fell sick.

14 "We made an invasion of the southern *area* of ᴿthe Cherethites, in the *territory* which *belongs* to Judah, and of the southern *area* ᴿof Caleb; and we burned Ziklag with fire."   2 Sam. 8:18 • Josh. 14:13; 15:13

15 And David said to him, "Can you take me down to this troop?" So he said, "Swear to me by God that you will neither kill me nor deliver me into the hands of my ᴿmaster, and I will take you down to this troop."   Deut. 23:15

16 And when he had brought him down, there they were, spread out over all the land, ᴿeating and drinking and dancing, because of all the great spoil which they had taken from the land of the Philistines and from the land of Judah.   1 Thess. 5:3

17 Then David attacked them from twilight until the evening of the next day. Not a man of them escaped, except four hundred young men who rode on camels and fled.

18 So David recovered all that the Amalekites had carried away, and David rescued his two wives.

19 And nothing of theirs was lacking, either small or great, sons or daughters, spoil or anything which they had taken from them; ᴿDavid recovered all.   1 Sam. 30:8

20 Then David took all the flocks and herds they had driven before those *other* livestock, and said, "This *is* David's spoil."

21 Now David came to the ᴿtwo hundred men who had been so weary that they could not follow David, whom they also had made to stay at the Brook Besor. So they went out to meet David and to meet the people who *were* with him. And when David came near the people, he greeted them.   1 Sam. 30:10

22 Then all the wicked and ᴿworthlessᵀ men of those who went with David answered and said, "Because they did not go with us, we will not give them *any* of the spoil that we have recovered, except for every man's wife and children, that they may lead *them* away and depart."   Deut. 13:13 • Lit. *men of Belial*

23 But David said, "My brethren, you shall not do so with what the Lᴏʀᴅ has given us, who has preserved us and delivered into our hand the troop that came against us.

29:10 So with MT, Tg., Vg.; LXX adds *and go to the place which I have selected for you there; and set no bothersome word in your heart, for you are good before me. And rise on your way*

24 "For who will heed you in this matter? But ^Ras his part *is* who goes down to the battle, so *shall* his part *be* who stays by the supplies; they shall share alike."   Josh. 22:8

25 So it was, from that day forward; he made it a statute and an ordinance for Israel to this day.

26 Now when David came to Ziklag, he sent *some* of the spoil to the elders of Judah, to his friends, saying, "Here is a present for you from the spoil of the enemies of the LORD"—

27 to *those* who *were* in Bethel, *those* who *were* in ^RRamoth of the South, *those* who *were* in ^RJattir,   Josh. 19:8 • Josh. 15:48; 21:14

28 *those* who *were* in ^RAroer, *those* who *were* in ^RSiphmoth, *those* who *were* in ^REshtemoa,   Josh. 13:16 • 1 Chr. 27:27 • Josh. 15:50

29 *those* who *were* in Rachal, *those* who *were* in the cities of the Jerahmeelites, *those* who *were* in the cities of the Kenites,

30 *those* who *were* in ^RHormah, *those* who *were* in ^TChorashan, *those* who *were* in Athach,   Judg. 1:17 • Or *Borashan*

31 *those* who *were* in Hebron, and to all the places where David himself and his men were accustomed to ^Rrove.   1 Sam. 23:22

The Tragic End of Saul and His Sons

31 Now ^Rthe Philistines fought against Israel; and the men of Israel fled from before the Philistines, and fell slain on Mount ^RGilboa.   1 Chr. 10:1–12 • 1 Sam. 28:4

2 Then the Philistines followed hard after Saul and his sons. And the Philistines killed ^RJonathan, Abinadab, and Malchishua, Saul's sons.   1 Sam. 14:49

3 The battle became fierce against Saul. The archers ^Thit him, and he was severely wounded by the archers.   Lit. *found*

4 ^RThen Saul said to his armorbearer, "Draw your sword, and thrust me through

with it, lest ^Rthese uncircumcised men come and thrust me through and ^Tabuse me." But his armorbearer would not, for he was greatly afraid. Therefore Saul took a sword and fell on it.   Judg. 9:54 • 1 Sam. 14:6; 17:26, 36 • *torture*

5 And when his armorbearer saw that Saul was dead, he also fell on his sword, and died with him.

6 So Saul, his three sons, his armorbearer, and all his men died together that same day.

7 And when the men of Israel who *were* on the other side of the valley, and *those* who *were* on the other side of the Jordan, saw that the men of Israel had fled and that Saul and his sons were dead, they forsook the cities and fled; and the Philistines came and dwelt in them.

8 So it happened the next day, when the Philistines came to strip the slain, that they found Saul and his three sons fallen on Mount Gilboa.

9 And they cut off his head and stripped off his armor, and sent *word* throughout the land of the Philistines, to proclaim *it in* the temple of their idols and among the people.

10 Then they put his armor in the temple of the Ashtoreths, and they fastened his body to the wall of ^RBeth* Shan.   Judg. 1:27

11 ^RNow when the inhabitants of Jabesh Gilead heard what the Philistines had done to Saul,   1 Sam. 11:1–13

12 ^Rall the valiant men arose and traveled all night, and took the body of Saul and the bodies of his sons from the wall of Beth Shan; and they came to Jabesh and ^Rburned them there.   2 Sam. 2:4–7 • 2 Chr. 16:14

13 Then they took their bones and ^Rburied *them* under the tamarisk tree at Jabesh, ^Rand fasted seven days.   2 Sam. 2:4, 5; 21:12–14 • Gen. 50:10

31:10 *Beth Shean,* Josh. 17:11

THE SECOND BOOK OF
Samuel

AUTHORSHIP AND CONTEXT. Since 2 Samuel, in the original Hebrew text, is just the second half of the same book called 1 Samuel, the background notes of that book are valid for 2 Samuel as well.

2 Samuel is the fascinating and revealing account which God has given of David's reign as king of Israel. The book covers the forty years of David's rule (2 Sam. 5:4). David is the establisher of the monarchy, the great hero, ruler, and poet of his people. His dynasty continued until the time of the captivity and was the lineage from which the Messiah came. It should come as no surprise that such prominence should be given to his reign.

David reigned for seven years over Judah before he was crowned king over all Israel. This seven-year period was a tragic time of civil war. Opposition and hostilities abounded. David demonstrated such godly and gracious characteristics during this time that he was swept on a wave of popular enthusiasm to become king over a united nation. He captured the city of Jebus, which had been a stronghold of the Jebusites, a people who had defied Israel for centuries. David then made Jebus his capital city and changed its name to Jerusalem. Under his capable leadership a great sweeping revival of Jewish cultural life and religion occurred. He appointed scribes so that national records would be carefully recorded and he conquered all Israel's enemies. These were the "glory days" of Israel.

David was so committed to the centrality of Israel's religion and its faith in the sovereignty of God, that in his heart was born a dream and passion to build the temple. Even though God forbade David to build the temple (cf. 1 Chr. 22:8), he vigorously and carefully planned for its construction by his son, Solomon. The many victories won by David not only strengthened his position, but also allowed him to gather treasure to be used in building the temple.

HOW 2 SAMUEL FITS TOGETHER. The book is divided in half by David's great sin (ch. 11). Up to the point of his great sin everything goes triumphantly for David (chs. 1—10). After his great sin there is an unbroken record of heartache, tragedy, and grievous trials (chs. 12—24). In the first half we rejoice in David's triumphs; in the second half we grieve over David's tragedies.

The overriding theme and message of this book is clearly seen: victory turns to defeat through sin. Sin is the great destroyer of good. All sin, whether by king or commoner, brings bitter returns. At the height of his power David committed adultery with Bathsheba and then had her husband, one of his most faithful officers, murdered. David sought to cover his sin and lived for a year in hypocrisy, having married the "grieving widow" as an act of "compassion" for her sorrow.

In time God sent Nathan the prophet to confront David with his sin. David's repentance was immediate and genuine. The sincerity of his repentance is seen in his worship following the death of Bathsheba's child. Following that his heartache reaches tragic proportions—all the result of his great sin (12:10-12). His sin and its consequences haunted him for the rest of his life.

Nowhere is the honesty and faithfulness of God's Word more clearly seen than in 2 Samuel. How open it is in recording such a dark time in the life of its hero David. Only God's Holy Spirit would have led the author to record such an incident. Notice the lessons from this great sin: (1) David's fall occurred when he was at ease instead of leading his army into battle. Ease and leisure must be carefully guarded or Satan will destroy us with it. Responsibility can never be delegated when God has assigned it to us. Had David been leading his army, his great sin would not have occurred. (2) David's sin led him on to a more premeditated and heinous one. Murder followed immorality. The adulterous act was a spontaneous response to lust; the murder was a carefully calculated rebellion and deliberate disobedience. (3) David's sin brought on years of agony. God's sword of judgment fell heavily upon David's children. What a terrible harvest sin brings! Sin pays in a living hell!

2 Samuel records it all. Through David's repentance (cf. Ps. 51) we see what our response ought to be when confronted with the conviction of God. David's repentance shows why he is described as "a man after [God's] own heart" (1 Sam. 13:14).

2 Samuel also records the giving of the Davidic covenant. Through David God extends His covenant. This covenant is given in 2 Samuel 7:11-16. It has had and will continue to have a tremendous effect on the entire history of mankind—especially the future. Through this covenant God confirmed David's throne forever and unconditionally with Christ as its occupant. The New Testament opens with the announcement that Jesus Christ is the eternal Davidic King.

Punishment would come to David because of his sin, but the throne belonged unequivocably to David's lineage.

2 Samuel is one of the most scintillating, significant, and revealing of all the books in God's Word. The book ends with the account of the altar to God being erected on the threshing floor of Araunah the Jebusite. In that final account (ch. 24) we see the "man after God's own heart" turning the occasion of another sin and its punishment (24:10–17) into one of devotion and worship (24:18–25). The lessons of God in 2 Samuel abound and its study will bring rich rewards to the careful and committed student.

—J.D.

The Report of Saul's Death

NOW it came to pass after the ᴿdeath of Saul, when David had returned from the slaughter of the Amalekites, and David had stayed two days in Ziklag, 1 Sam. 31:6

2 on the third day, behold, it happened that a man came from Saul's camp with his clothes ᵀtorn and dust on his head. So it was, when he came to David, that he fell to the ground and prostrated himself.   To show grief

3 And David said to him, "Where have you come from?" So he said to him, "I have escaped from the camp of Israel."

4 Then David said to him, ᴿ"How did the matter go? Please tell me." And he answered, "The people have fled from the battle, many of the people are fallen and dead, and Saul and ᴿJonathan his son are dead also."   1 Sam. 4:16; 31:3 • 1 Sam. 31:2

5 So David said to the young man who told him, "How do you know that Saul and Jonathan his son are dead?"

6 Then the young man who told him said, "As I happened by chance to be on ᴿMount Gilboa, there was ᴿSaul, leaning on his spear; and indeed the chariots and horsemen followed hard after him.   1 Sam. 31:1 • 1 Sam. 31:2-4

7 "Now when he looked behind him, he saw me and called to me. And I answered, 'Here I am.'

8 "And he said to me, 'Who are you?' So I answered him, 'I am an Amalekite.'

9 "He said to me again, 'Please stand over me and kill me, for ᵀanguish has come upon me, but my life still remains in me.'   agony

10 "So I stood over him and ᴿkilled him, because I was sure that he could not live after he had fallen. And I took the crown that was on his head and the bracelet that was on his arm, and have brought them here to my lord."   Judg. 9:54

11 Therefore David took hold of his own clothes and ᴿtore them, and so did all the men who were with him.   2 Sam. 3:31; 13:31

12 And they ᴿmourned and wept and ᴿfasted until evening for Saul and for Jonathan his son, for the people of the Lᴏʀᴅ and for the house of Israel, because they had fallen by the sword.   2 Sam. 3:31 • 1 Sam. 31:13

13 Then David said to the young man who told him, "Where are you from?" And he answered, "I am the son of an alien, an Amalekite."

14 So David said to him, "How ᴿwas it you were not afraid to put forth your hand to destroy the Lᴏʀᴅ's anointed?"   Num. 12:8

15 Then ᴿDavid called one of the young men and said, "Go near, and execute him!" And he struck him so that he died. 2 Sam. 4:10, 12

16 So David said to him, ᴿ"Your blood is on your own head, for ᴿyour own mouth has testified against you, saying, 'I have killed the Lᴏʀᴅ's anointed.' "   1 Kin. 2:32-37 • Luke 19:22

The Song of the Bow

17 Then David lamented with this lamentation over Saul and over Jonathan his son,

18 and he told them to teach the children of Judah the Song of the Bow; indeed it is written in the Book of ᵀJasher: Lit. Upright

19 "The beauty of Israel is slain on your
        high places!
    How the mighty have fallen!
20 ᴿTell it not in Gath,   Mic. 1:10
    Proclaim it not in the streets of
        ᴿAshkelon—   Jer. 25:20
    Lest ᴿthe daughters of the Philistines
        rejoice,   Ex. 15:20
    Lest the daughters of ᴿthe
        uncircumcised triumph.   1 Sam. 31:4
21 "O ᴿmountains of Gilboa,   1 Sam. 31:1
    Let there be no dew nor rain upon you,
    Nor fields of offerings.
    For the shield of the mighty is ᵀcast
        away there!   Lit. defiled
    The shield of Saul, not ᴿanointed with
        oil.   1 Sam. 10:1
22 From the blood of the slain,
    From the fat of the mighty,
    ᴿThe bow of Jonathan did not turn back,
    And the sword of Saul did not return
        empty.   1 Sam. 18:4
23 "Saul and Jonathan were beloved and
        pleasant in their lives,
    And in their ᴿdeath they were not
        divided;   1 Sam. 31:2-4
    They were swifter than eagles,
    They were ᴿstronger than lions. Judg. 14:18
24 "O daughters of Israel, weep over Saul,
    Who clothed you in scarlet, with
        luxury;

Who put ornaments of gold on your
　　apparel.

25 "How the mighty have fallen in the
　　midst of the battle!
Jonathan *was* slain in your high places.
26 I am distressed for you, my brother
　　Jonathan;
You have been very pleasant to me;
Your love to me was wonderful,
Surpassing the love of women.

27 "How the mighty have fallen,
And the weapons of war perished!"

David Anointed King of Judah

2 It happened after this that David inquired
of the LORD, saying, "Shall I go up to any
of the cities of Judah?" And the LORD said to
him, "Go up." David said, "Where shall I go
up?" And He said, "To Hebron."

2 So David went up there, and his two
wives also, Ahinoam the Jezreelitess, and
Abigail the widow of Nabal the Carmelite.

3 And David brought up the men who
were with him, every man with his household. So they dwelt in the cities of Hebron.

4 Then the men of Judah came, and there
they ᴿanointed David king over the house of
Judah. And they told David, saying, ᴿ"The
men of Jabesh Gilead *were the ones* who
buried Saul."　　　　1 Sam. 16:13 • 1 Sam. 31:11-13

5 So David sent messengers to the men of
Jabesh Gilead, and said to them, ᴿ"You *are*
blessed of the LORD, for you have shown this
kindness to your lord, to Saul, and have
buried him.　　　　Ruth 2:20; 3:10

6 "And now may the LORD show kindness
and truth to you. I also will repay you this
kindness, because you have done this thing.

7 "Now therefore, let your hands be
strengthened, and be valiant; for your master
Saul is dead, and also the house of Judah has
anointed me king over them."

Ishbosheth Made King of Israel

8 But Abner the son of Ner, commander of
Saul's army, took *Ishbosheth the son of Saul
and brought him over to Mahanaim;

9 and he made him king over ᴿGilead, over
the Ashurites, over Jezreel, over Ephraim,
over Benjamin, and over all Israel.　　Josh. 22:9

10 Ishbosheth, Saul's son, *was* forty years
old when he began to reign over Israel, and
he reigned two years. Only the house of
Judah followed David.

11 And the ᵀtime that David was king in
Hebron over the house of Judah was seven
years and six months.　　　Lit. *number of days*

Israel and Judah at War

12 Now Abner the son of Ner, and the
servants of Ishbosheth the son of Saul, went
out from Mahanaim to ᴿGibeon.　　Josh. 10:2-12

13 And ᴿJoab the son of Zeruiah, and the
servants of David, went out and met them by
ᴿthe pool of Gibeon. So they sat down, one on
one side of the pool and the other on the
other side of the pool.　　1 Chr. 2:16; 11:6 • Jer. 41:12

14 Then Abner said to Joab, "Let the young
men now arise and compete before us." And
Joab said, "Let them arise."

15 So they arose and went over by number,
twelve from Benjamin, *followers* of Ishbosheth the son of Saul, and twelve from the
servants of David.

16 And each one grasped his opponent by
the head and *thrust* his sword in his opponent's side; so they fell down together. Therefore that place was called *the Field of Sharp
Swords, which *is* in Gibeon.

17 So there was a very fierce battle that
day, and Abner and the men of Israel were
beaten before the servants of David.

18 Now the three sons of Zeruiah were
there: Joab and Abishai and Asahel. And
Asahel *was* as fleet of foot as a wild gazelle.

19 So Asahel pursued Abner, and in going
he did not turn to the right hand or to the left
from following Abner.

20 Then Abner looked behind him and said,
"*Are* you Asahel?" He answered, "I *am.*"

21 And Abner said to him, "Turn aside to
your right hand or to your left, and lay hold
on one of the young men and take his armor
for yourself." But Asahel would not turn
aside from following him.

22 So Abner said again to Asahel, "Turn
aside from following me. Why should I strike
you to the ground? How then could I face
your brother Joab?"

23 However, he refused to turn aside.
Therefore Abner struck him in the stomach
with the blunt end of the spear, so that the
spear came out of his back; and he fell down
there and died on the spot. So it was *that* as
many as came to the place where Asahel fell
down and died, stood ᴿstill.　　　2 Sam. 20:12

24 Joab and Abishai also pursued Abner.
And the sun was going down when they
came to the hill of Ammah, which *is* before
Giah by the road to the Wilderness of Gibeon.

25 Now the children of Benjamin gathered
together behind Abner and became a unit,
and took their stand on top of a hill.

26 Then Abner called to Joab and said,
"Shall the sword devour forever? Do you not
know that it will be bitter in the latter end?
How long will it be then until you tell the

2:8 *Esh-Baal,* 1 Chr. 8:33; 9:39　　　　2:16 Heb. *Helkath Hazzurim*

people to return from pursuing their brethren?"

27 And Joab said, "As God lives, [T]unless [R]you had spoken, surely then by morning all the people would have given up pursuing their brethren."   *if you had not spoken* • 2 Sam. 2:14

28 So Joab blew a trumpet; and all the people stood still and did not pursue Israel anymore, nor did they fight anymore.

29 Then Abner and his men went on all that night through the plain, crossed over the Jordan, and went through all Bithron; and they came to Mahanaim.

30 So Joab returned from pursuing Abner. And when he had gathered all the people together, there were missing of David's servants nineteen men and Asahel.

31 But the servants of David had struck down, of Benjamin and Abner's men, three hundred and sixty men who died.

32 Then they took up Asahel and buried him in his father's tomb, which *was* in Bethlehem. And Joab and his men went all night, and they came to Hebron at daybreak.

3 Now there was a long war between the house of Saul and the house of David. But David grew stronger and stronger, and the house of Saul grew weaker and weaker.

Sons of David

2 Sons were born [R]to David in Hebron: His firstborn was Amnon [R]by Ahinoam the Jezreelitess;   1 Chr. 3:1–4 • 1 Sam. 25:42, 43

3 his second, [T]Chileab, by Abigail the widow of Nabal the Carmelite; the third, Absalom the son of Maacah, the daughter of Talmai, king of Geshur;   *Daniel,* 1 Chr. 3:1

4 the fourth, Adonijah the son of Haggith; the fifth, Shephatiah the son of Abital;

5 and the sixth, Ithream, by David's wife Eglah. These were born to David in Hebron.

Abner Joins Forces with David

6 Now it was so, while there was war between the house of Saul and the house of David, that Abner was strengthening *his hold* on the house of Saul.

7 And Saul had a concubine, whose name *was* Rizpah, the daughter of Aiah. So Ishbosheth said to Abner, "Why have you [R]gone in to my father's concubine?"   2 Sam. 16:21

8 Then Abner became very angry at the words of Ishbosheth, and said, "Am I [R]a dog's head that belongs to Judah? Today I show loyalty to the house of Saul your father, to his brothers, and to his friends, and have not delivered you into the hand of David; and you charge me today with a fault concerning this woman?   1 Sam. 24:14

9 [R]"May God do so to Abner, and more also, if I do not do for David [R]as the LORD has sworn to him—   1 Kin. 19:2 • 1 Chr. 12:23

10 "to transfer the kingdom from the

[T]house of Saul, and set up the throne of David over Israel and over Judah, [R]from Dan to Beersheba."   *family* • 1 Sam. 3:20

11 And he could not answer Abner another word, because he feared him.

12 Then Abner sent messengers on his behalf to David, saying, "Whose *is* the land?" saying *also,* "Make your covenant with me, and indeed my hand *shall be* with you to bring all Israel to you."

13 And *David* said, "Good, I will make a covenant with you. But one thing I require of you: [R]you shall not see my face unless you first bring Michal, Saul's daughter, when you come to see my face."   Gen. 43:3

14 So David sent messengers to Ishbosheth, Saul's son, saying, "Give *me* my wife Michal, whom I betrothed to myself for a hundred foreskins of the Philistines."

15 And Ishbosheth sent and took her from *her* husband, from *Paltiel the son of Laish.

16 Then her husband went along with her to Bahurim, weeping behind her. So Abner said to him, "Go, return!" And he returned.

17 Now Abner had communicated with the elders of Israel, saying, "In time past you were seeking for David *to be* king over you.

18 "Now then, do *it!* [R]For the LORD has spoken of David, saying, 'By the hand of My servant David, *I will save My people Israel from the hand of the Philistines and the hand of all their enemies.' "   2 Sam. 3:9

19 And Abner also spoke in the hearing of [R]Benjamin. Then Abner also went to speak in the hearing of David in Hebron all that seemed good to Israel and the whole house of Benjamin.   1 Chr. 12:29

20 So Abner and twenty men with him came to David at Hebron. And David made a feast for Abner and the men who *were* with him.

21 Then Abner said to David, "I will arise and go, and gather all Israel to my lord the king, that they may make a covenant with you, and that you may [R]reign over all that your heart desires." So David sent Abner away, and he went in peace.   1 Kin. 11:37

Joab Murders Abner

22 At that moment the servants of David and Joab came from a raid and brought much [T]spoil with them. But Abner *was* not with David in Hebron, for he had sent him away, and he had gone in peace.   *booty*

23 When Joab and all the troops that *were* with him had come, they told Joab, saying, "Abner the son of Ner came to the king, and he sent him away, and he has gone in peace."

24 Then Joab came to the king and said, "What have you done? Look, Abner came to

3:15 *Palti,* 1 Sam. 25:44
3:18 So with many Heb. mss., LXX, Syr., Tg.; MT *he*

you; why is it that you sent him away, and he has already gone?

25 "Surely you realize that Abner the son of Ner came to deceive you, to know ᴿyour going out and your coming in, and to know all that you are doing."   1 Sam. 29:6

26 And when Joab had gone from David's presence, he sent messengers after Abner, who brought him back from the well of Sirah. But David did not know it.

27 Now when Abner had returned to Hebron, Joab took him aside in the gate to speak with him privately, and there ᵀstabbed him in the stomach, so that he died for the blood of Asahel his brother.   Lit. struck

28 Afterward, when David heard it, he said, "My kingdom and I are ᵀguiltless before the LORD forever of the blood of Abner the son of Ner.   innocent

29 "Let it rest on the head of Joab and on all his father's house; and let there never fail to be in the house of Joab one who has a discharge or is a leper, who leans on a staff or falls by the sword, or who lacks bread."

30 So Joab and Abishai his brother killed Abner, because he had killed their brother ᴿAsahel at Gibeon in the battle.   2 Sam. 2:23

David's Mourning for Abner

31 Then David said to Joab and to all the people who were with him, ᴿ"Tear your clothes, ᴿgird yourselves with sackcloth, and mourn for Abner." And King David followed the coffin.   Josh. 7:6 · Gen. 37:34

32 So they buried Abner in Hebron; and the king lifted up his voice and wept at the grave of Abner, and all the people wept.

33 And the king sang a lament over Abner and said:

"Should Abner die as a fool dies?
34   Your hands were not bound
     Nor your feet put into fetters;
     As a man falls before wicked men, so
       you fell."

Then all the people wept over him again.

35 And when all the people came to persuade David to eat food while it was still day, David took an oath, saying, ᴿ"God do so to me, and more also, if I taste bread or anything else till the sun goes down!"   Ruth 1:17

36 Now all the people took note of it, and it pleased them, since whatever the king did pleased all the people.

37 For all the people and all Israel understood that day that it had not been the king's intent to kill Abner the son of Ner.

38 Then the king said to his servants, "Do you not know that a prince and a great man has fallen this day in Israel?

39 "And I am weak today, though anointed king; and these men, the sons of Zeruiah, are too harsh for me. The LORD shall repay the evildoer according to his wickedness."

Ishbosheth Is Murdered

4 When Saul's *son heard that Abner had died in Hebron, he ᵀlost heart, and all Israel was troubled.   Lit. his hands dropped

2 Now Saul's son had two men who were captains of troops. The name of one was Baanah and the name of the other Rechab, the sons of Rimmon the Beerothite, of the children of Benjamin. (For ᴿBeeroth also was ᵀpart of Benjamin,   Josh. 18:25 · considered part of

3 because the Beerothites fled to ᴿGittaim and have been sojourners there until this day.)   Neh. 11:33

4 ᴿJonathan, Saul's son, had a son who was lame in his feet. He was five years old when the news about Saul and Jonathan came from Jezreel; and his nurse took him up and fled. And it happened, as she made haste to flee, that he fell and became lame. His name was *Mephibosheth.   2 Sam. 9:3

5 Then the sons of Rimmon the Beerothite, Rechab and Baanah, set out and came at about the heat of the day to the ᴿhouse of Ishbosheth, who was lying on his bed at noon.   2 Sam. 2:8, 9

6 And they came there, all the way into the house, as though to get wheat, and they ᵀstabbed him in the stomach. Then Rechab and Baanah his brother escaped.   Lit. struck

7 For when they came into the house, he was lying on his bed in his bedroom; then they struck him and killed him, beheaded him and took his head, and were all night escaping through the plain.

8 And they brought the head of Ishbosheth to David at Hebron, and said to the king, "Here is the head of Ishbosheth, the son of Saul your enemy, who sought your life; and the LORD has avenged my lord the king this day of Saul and his descendants."

9 But David answered Rechab and Baanah his brother, the sons of Rimmon the Beerothite, and said to them, "As the LORD lives, who has redeemed my life from all adversity,

10 "when ᴿsomeone told me, saying, 'Look, Saul is dead,' thinking to have brought good news, I arrested him and had him executed in Ziklag—the one who thought I would give him a reward for his news.   2 Sam. 1:2–16

11 "How much more, when wicked men have killed a righteous person in his own house on his bed? Therefore, shall I not now ᴿrequire his blood at your hand and ᵀremove you from the earth?"   [Gen. 9:5, 6] · Lit. consume you

12 So David ᴿcommanded his young men, and they executed them, cut off their hands and feet, and hanged them by the pool in Hebron. But they took the head of Ishbo-

4:1 Ishbosheth
4:4 Merib-Baal, 1 Chr. 8:34; 9:40

sheth and buried *it* in the ᴿtomb of Abner in Hebron.   2 Sam. 1:15 • 2 Sam. 3:32

David Reigns over All Israel

5 Then all the tribes of Israel came to David at Hebron and spoke, saying, "Indeed we *are* your bone and your flesh.

2 "Also, in time past, when Saul was king over us, you were the one who led Israel out and brought them in; and the LORD said to you, ᴿ'You shall shepherd My people Israel, and be ruler over Israel.'"   1 Sam. 16:1

3 ᴿTherefore all the elders of Israel came to the king at Hebron, ᴿand King David made a covenant with them at Hebron ᴿbefore the LORD. And they anointed David king over Israel.   2 Sam. 3:17 • 2 Kin. 11:17 • 1 Sam. 23:18

4 David *was* thirty years old when he began to reign, *and* he reigned forty years.

5 In Hebron he reigned over Judah ᴿseven years and six months, and in Jerusalem he reigned thirty-three years over all Israel and Judah.   2 Sam. 2:11

The Conquest of Jerusalem

6 ᴿAnd the king and his men went to Jerusalem against ᴿthe Jebusites, the inhabitants of the land, who spoke to David, saying, "You shall not come in here; but the blind and the lame will repel you," thinking, "David cannot come in here."   Judg. 1:21 • Josh. 15:63

7 Nevertheless David took the stronghold of Zion (that *is*, the City of David).

8 Now David said on that day, "Whoever climbs up by way of the water shaft and defeats the Jebusites (the lame and the blind, *who are* hated by David's soul), ᴿ*he shall be chief and captain.*" Therefore they say, "The blind and the lame shall not come into the house."   1 Chr. 11:6

9 Then David dwelt in the stronghold, and called it the City of David. And David built all around from *the Millo and inward.

10 So David went on and became great, and the LORD God of hosts *was* with him.

11 Then Hiram king of Tyre sent messengers to David, and cedar trees, and carpenters and masons. And they built David a house.

12 So David knew that the LORD had established him as king over Israel, and that He had ᴿexalted His kingdom ᴿfor the sake of His people Israel.   Num. 24:7 • Is. 45:4

13 And ᴿDavid took more concubines and wives from Jerusalem, after he had come from Hebron. Also more sons and daughters were born to David.   [Deut. 17:17]

14 Now these *are* the names of those who were born to him in Jerusalem: ᵀShammua, Shobab, Nathan, Solomon,   *Shimea,* 1 Chr. 3:5

15 Ibhar, *Elishua, Nepheg, Japhia,

16 Elishama, Eliada, and Eliphelet.

The Philistines Defeated

17 ᴿNow when the Philistines heard that they had anointed David king over Israel, all the Philistines went up to search for David. And David heard of *it* ᴿand went down to the stronghold.   1 Chr. 11:16 • 2 Sam. 23:14

18 The Philistines also went and deployed themselves in the Valley of Rephaim.

19 So David inquired of the LORD, saying, "Shall I go up against the Philistines? Will You deliver them into my hand?" And the LORD said to David, "Go up, for I will doubtless deliver the Philistines into your hand."

20 So David went to ᴿBaal Perazim, and David defeated them there; and he said, "The LORD has broken through my enemies before me, like a breakthrough of water." Therefore he called the name of that place ᵀBaal Perazim.   Is. 28:21 • Lit. *Master of Breakthroughs*

21 And they left their images there, and David and his men carried them away.

22 ᴿThen the Philistines went up once again and deployed themselves in the Valley of Rephaim.   1 Chr. 14:13

23 Therefore ᴿDavid inquired of the LORD, and He said, "You shall not go up; circle around behind them, and come upon them in front of the mulberry trees.   2 Sam. 5:19

24 "And it shall be, when you ᴿhear the sound of marching in the tops of the mulberry trees, then you shall advance quickly. For then the LORD will go out before you to strike the camp of the Philistines."   1 Chr. 14:15

25 And David did so, as the LORD commanded him; and he drove back the Philistines from *Geba as far as ᴿGezer.   Josh. 16:10

The Ark Brought to Jerusalem

6 Again David gathered all *the* choice *men* of Israel, thirty thousand.

2 And David arose and went with all the people who *were* with him from Baale Judah to bring up from there the ark of God, whose name is called *by the Name, the LORD of Hosts, who dwells *between* the cherubim.

3 So they set the ark of God on a new cart, and brought it out of the house of Abinadab, which *was* on the hill; and Uzzah and Ahio, the sons of Abinadab, drove the new *cart.

4 And they brought it out of ᴿthe house of Abinadab, which *was* on the hill, accompanying the ark of God; and Ahio went before the ark.   1 Sam. 7:1

5 Then David and all the house of Israel ᴿplayed *music* before the LORD on all kinds of *instruments of* fir wood, on harps, on stringed instruments, on tambourines, on sistrums, and on cymbals.   1 Sam. 18:6, 7

5:9 Lit. *The Landfill*
5:15 *Elishama,* 1 Chr. 3:6

5:25 So with MT, Tg., Vg.; LXX *Gibeon*
6:2 LXX, Tg., Vg. omit *by the Name;* many Heb. mss., [Syr.] *there*
6:3 LXX adds *with the ark*

6 And when they came to ᴿNachon's threshing floor, Uzzah put out *his* ᴿhand to the ark of God and ᵀtook hold of it, for the oxen stumbled. 1 Chr. 13:9 · Num. 4:15, 19, 20 · *held it*

7 Then the anger of the Lᴏʀᴅ was aroused against Uzzah, and God struck him there for *his* ᵀerror; and he died there by the ark of God. Or *irreverence*

8 And David became angry because of the Lᴏʀᴅ's outbreak against Uzzah; and he called the name of the place ᵀPerez Uzzah to this day. Lit. *Outburst Against Uzzah*

9 ᴿDavid was afraid of the Lᴏʀᴅ that day; and he said, "How can the ark of the Lᴏʀᴅ come to me?" Ps. 119:120

10 So David would not move the ark of the Lᴏʀᴅ with him into the ᴿCity of David; but David took it aside into the house of Obed-Edom the ᴿGittite. 2 Sam. 5:7 · 1 Chr. 13:13; 26:4-8

11 ᴿThe ark of the Lᴏʀᴅ remained in the house of Obed-Edom the Gittite three months. And the Lᴏʀᴅ ᴿblessed Obed-Edom and all his household. 1 Chr. 13:14 · Gen. 30:27; 39:5

12 Now it was told King David, saying, "The Lᴏʀᴅ has blessed the house of Obed-Edom and all that *belongs* to him, because of the ark of God." So David went and brought up the ark of God from the house of Obed-Edom to the City of David with gladness.

13 And so it was, when those bearing the ark of the Lᴏʀᴅ had gone six paces, that he sacrificed ᴿoxen and fatted sheep. 1 Kin. 8:5

14 Then David ᴿdancedᵀ before the Lᴏʀᴅ with all *his* might; and David *was* wearing a linen ephod. Ps. 30:11; 149:3 · *whirled about*

15 ᴿSo David and all the house of Israel brought up the ark of the Lᴏʀᴅ with shouting and with the sound of the trumpet. 1 Chr. 15:28

16 Now as the ark of the Lᴏʀᴅ came into the City of David, ᴿMichal, Saul's daughter, looked through a window and saw King David leaping and whirling before the Lᴏʀᴅ; and she despised him in her heart. 2 Sam. 3:14

17 So they brought the ark of the Lᴏʀᴅ, and set it in ᴿits place in the midst of the tabernacle that David had erected for it. Then David offered burnt offerings and peace offerings before the Lᴏʀᴅ. 1 Chr. 15:1

18 And when David had finished offering burnt offerings and peace offerings, ᴿhe blessed the people in the name of the Lᴏʀᴅ of hosts. 1 Kin. 8:14, 15, 55

19 ᴿThen he distributed among all the people, among the whole multitude of Israel, both the women and the men, to everyone a loaf of bread, a piece *of meat*, and a cake of raisins. So all the people departed, everyone to his house. 1 Chr. 16:3

20 Then David returned to bless his household. And Michal the daughter of Saul came out to meet David, and said, "How glorious was the king of Israel today, uncovering himself today in the eyes of the maids of his servants, as one of the ᴿbase fellows ᵀshamelessly uncovers himself!" Judg. 9:4 · *openly*

21 So David said to Michal, "*It was* before the Lᴏʀᴅ, who chose me instead of your father and all his house, to appoint me ruler over the people of the Lᴏʀᴅ, over Israel. Therefore I will play *music* before the Lᴏʀᴅ.

22 "And I will be even more undignified than this, and will be humble in my own sight. But as for the maidservants of whom you have spoken, by them I will be held in honor."

23 Therefore Michal the daughter of Saul had no children to the day of her death.

God's Covenant with David

7 Now it came to pass ᴿwhen the king was dwelling in his house, and the Lᴏʀᴅ had given him rest from all his enemies all around, 1 Chr. 17:1-27

2 that the king said to Nathan the prophet, "See now, I dwell in a house of cedar, but the ark of God dwells inside tent curtains."

3 Then Nathan said to the king, "Go, do all that *is* in your ᴿheart, for the Lᴏʀᴅ *is* with you." 1 Kin. 8:17, 18

4 But it happened that night that the word of the Lᴏʀᴅ came to Nathan, saying,

5 "Go and tell My servant David, 'Thus says the Lᴏʀᴅ: ᴿ"Would you build a house for Me to dwell in? 1 Kin. 5:3, 4; 8:19

6 "For I have not dwelt in a house since the time that I brought the children of Israel up from Egypt, even to this day, but have moved about in a tent and in a tabernacle.

7 "Wherever I have ᴿmoved about with all the children of Israel, have I ever spoken a word to anyone from the tribes of Israel, whom I commanded ᴿto shepherd My people Israel, saying, 'Why have you not built Me a house of cedar?' " ' Lev. 26:11, 12 · 2 Sam. 5:2

8 "Now therefore, thus shall you say to My servant David, 'Thus says the Lᴏʀᴅ of hosts: ᴿ"I took you from the sheepfold, from following the sheep, to be ruler over My people, over Israel. 1 Sam. 16:11, 12

9 "And I have been with you wherever you have gone, ᴿand have ᵀcut off all your enemies from before you, and have made you a great name, like the name of the great men who *are* on the earth. 1 Sam. 31:6 · *destroyed*

10 "Moreover I will appoint a place for My people Israel, and will plant them, that they may dwell in a place of their own and move no more; nor shall the sons of wickedness oppress them anymore, as previously,

11 ᴿ"since the time that I commanded judges *to be* over My people Israel, and have caused you to rest from all your enemies. Also the Lᴏʀᴅ ᵀtells you ᴿthat He will make you a *house. Judg. 2:14-16 · *declares to you* · 2 Sam. 7:27

7:11 Royal dynasty

12 "When your days are fulfilled and you rest with your fathers, I will set up your seed after you, who will come from your body, and I will establish his kingdom.

13 ^R"He shall build a house for My name, and I will ^Restablish the throne of his kingdom forever.   1 Kin. 5:5; 8:19 • [Is. 9:7; 49:8]

14 ^R"I will be his Father, and he shall be My son. If he commits iniquity, I will chasten him with the rod of men and with the ^Tblows of the sons of men.   [Heb. 1:5] • strokes

15 "But My mercy shall not depart from him, ^Ras I took it from Saul, whom I removed from before you.   1 Sam. 15:23, 28; 16:14

16 "And your house and your kingdom shall be established forever before *you. Your throne shall be established forever." ' "

17 According to all these words and according to all this vision, so Nathan spoke to David.

David's Thanksgiving to God

18 Then King David went in and sat before the LORD; and he said: ^R"Who am I, O Lord GOD? And what is my house, that You have brought me this far?   Ex. 3:11

19 "And yet this was a small thing in Your sight, O Lord GOD; and You have also spoken of Your servant's house for a great while to come. ^RIs this the manner of man, O Lord GOD?   [Is. 55:8, 9]

20 "Now what more can David say to You? For You, Lord GOD, know Your servant.

21 "For Your word's sake, and according to Your own heart, You have done all these great things, to make Your servant know them.

22 "Therefore You are great, *O Lord GOD. For ^Rthere is none like You, nor is there any God besides You, according to all that we have heard with our ^Rears.   Ex. 15:11 • Ex. 10:2

23 "And who is like Your people, like Israel, ^Rthe one nation on the earth whom God went to redeem for Himself as a people, to make for Himself a name—and to do for Yourself great and awesome deeds for Your land— before ^RYour people whom You redeemed for Yourself from Egypt, the nations, and their gods?   Ps. 147:20 • Deut. 9:26; 33:29

24 "For ^RYou have made Your people Israel Your very own people forever; and You, LORD, have become their God.   [Deut. 26:18]

25 ^R"Now, O LORD God, the word which You have spoken concerning Your servant and concerning his house, establish it forever and do as You have said.   Matt. 19:28

26 "So let Your name be magnified forever, saying, 'The LORD of hosts is the God over Israel.' ^RAnd let the house of Your servant David be established before You.   Matt. 25:31

27 "For You, O LORD of hosts, God of Israel, have revealed this to Your servant, saying, 'I will build you a house.' Therefore Your servant has found it in his heart to pray this prayer to You.

28 "And now, O Lord GOD, You are God, and Your words are true, and You have promised this goodness to Your servant.

29 "Now therefore, let it please You to bless the house of Your servant, that it may continue before You forever; for You, O Lord GOD, have spoken it, and with Your blessing let the house of Your servant be blessed ^Rforever."   2 Sam. 22:51

David's Further Conquests

8 After this it came to pass that David ^Tattacked the Philistines and subdued them. And David took Metheg Ammah from the hand of the Philistines.   Lit. struck

2 Then ^Rhe defeated Moab. Forcing them down to the ground, he measured them off with a line. With two lines he measured off those to be put to death, and with one full line those to be kept alive. So the Moabites became David's ^Rservants, and ^Rbrought tribute.   Num. 24:17 • 2 Sam. 12:31 • 1 Kin. 4:21

3 David also defeated Hadadezer the son of Rehob, king of Zobah, as he went to recover his territory at the River Euphrates.

4 David took from him one thousand chariots, *seven hundred horsemen, and twenty thousand foot soldiers. Also David ^Rhamstrung all the chariot horses, except that he spared enough of them for one hundred chariots.   Josh. 11:6, 9

5 When the Syrians of Damascus came to help Hadadezer king of Zobah, David killed twenty-two thousand of the Syrians.

6 Then David put garrisons in Syria of Damascus; and the Syrians became David's servants, and brought tribute. So the LORD preserved David wherever he went.

7 And David took ^Rthe shields of gold that had belonged to the servants of Hadadezer, and brought them to Jerusalem.   1 Kin. 10:16

8 Also from ^TBetah and from ^RBerothai, cities of Hadadezer, King David took a large amount of bronze.   Tibhath, 1 Chr. 18:8 • Ezek. 47:16

9 When ^TToi king of ^RHamath heard that David had defeated all the army of Hadadezer,   Tou, 1 Chr. 18:9 • 1 Kin. 8:65

10 then Toi sent *Joram his son to King David, to greet him and bless him, because he had fought against Hadadezer and defeated him (for Hadadezer had been at war with Toi); and Joram brought with him articles of silver, articles of gold, and articles of bronze.

11 King David also ^Rdedicated these to the LORD, along with the silver and gold that he

had dedicated from all the nations which he had subdued—   1 Kin. 7:51

12 from *Syria, from Moab, from the people of Ammon, from the ᴿPhilistines, from Amalek, and from the spoil of Hadadezer the son of Rehob, king of Zobah.   2 Sam. 5:17-25

13 And David made *himself* a name when he returned from killing eighteen thousand *Syrians in ᴿthe Valley of Salt.   1 Chr. 18:12

14 He also put garrisons in Edom; throughout all Edom he put garrisons, and all the Edomites became David's servants. And the LORD preserved David wherever he went.

David's Administration

15 So David reigned over all Israel; and David administered judgment and justice to all his people.

16 ᴿJoab the son of Zeruiah *was* over the army; ᴿJehoshaphat the son of Ahilud *was* recorder;   2 Sam. 19:13; 20:23 • 1 Kin. 4:3

17 Zadok the son of Ahitub and Ahimelech the son of Abiathar *were* the priests; ᵀSeraiah *was* the ᵀscribe;   Shavsha, 1 Chr. 18:16 • secretary

18 Benaiah the son of Jehoiada *was over* both the Cherethites and the Pelethites; and David's sons were ᵀchief ministers.   Lit. priests

David's Kindness to Mephibosheth

9 Now David said, "Is there still anyone who is left of the house of Saul, that I may ᴿshow him ᵀkindness for Jonathan's sake?"   1 Sam. 18:3; 20:14-16 • covenant faithfulness

2 And *there was* a servant of the house of Saul whose name *was* Ziba. So when they had called him to David, the king said to him, "*Are* you Ziba?" He said, "At your service!"

3 Then the king said, "*Is* there not still someone of the house of Saul, to whom I may show ᴿthe kindness of God?" And Ziba said to the king, "There is still a son of Jonathan *who is* ᴿlame in *his* feet."   1 Sam. 20:14 • 2 Sam. 4:4

4 So the king said to him, "Where *is* he?" And Ziba said to the king, "Indeed he *is* in the house of ᴿMachir the son of Ammiel, in Lo Debar."   2 Sam. 17:27-29

5 Then King David sent and brought him out of the house of Machir the son of Ammiel, from Lo Debar.

6 Now when Mephibosheth the son of Jonathan, the son of Saul, had come to David, he fell on his face and prostrated himself. Then David said, "Mephibosheth?" And he answered, "Here is your servant!"

7 So David said to him, "Do not fear, for I will surely show you kindness for Jonathan your father's sake, and will restore to you all the land of Saul your grandfather; and you shall eat bread at my table continually."

8 Then he bowed himself, and said, "What *is* your servant, that you should look upon such ᴿa dead dog as I?"   2 Sam. 16:9

9 And the king called to Ziba, Saul's servant, and said to him, ᴿ"I have given to your master's son all that belonged to Saul and to all his house.   2 Sam. 16:4; 19:29

10 "You therefore, and your sons and your servants, shall work the land for him, and you shall bring in *the harvest*, that your master's son may have food to eat. But Mephibosheth your master's son ᴿshall eat at my table always." Now Ziba had ᴿfifteen sons and twenty servants.   2 Sam. 9:7, 11, 13 • 2 Sam. 19:17

11 Then Ziba said to the king, "According to all that my lord the king has commanded his servant, so will your servant do." "As for Mephibosheth," *said the king,* "he shall eat at *my table like one of the king's sons."

12 Mephibosheth had a young son ᴿwhose name was Micha. And all who dwelt in the house of Ziba *were* servants of Mephibosheth.   1 Chr. 8:34

13 So Mephibosheth dwelt in Jerusalem, for he ate continually at the king's table. And he was lame in both his feet.

The Ammonites and Syrians Defeated

10 It happened after this that the ᴿking of the people of Ammon died, and Hanun his son reigned in his place.   1 Chr. 19:1

2 Then David said, "I will show kindness to Hanun the son of Nahash, as his father showed kindness to me." So David sent by the hand of his servants to comfort him concerning his father. And David's servants came into the land of the people of Ammon.

3 And the princes of the people of Ammon said to Hanun their lord, "Do you think that David really honors your father because he has sent comforters to you? Has David not *rather* sent his servants to you to search the city, to spy it out, and to overthrow it?"

4 Therefore Hanun took David's servants, shaved off half of their beards, cut off their garments in the middle, ᴿat their buttocks, and sent them away.   Is. 20:4; 47:2

5 When they told David, he sent to meet them, because the men were greatly ᵀashamed. And the king said, "Wait at Jericho until your beards have grown, and *then* return."   humiliated

6 When the people of Ammon saw that they had made themselves repulsive to David, the people of Ammon sent and hired the Syrians of Beth Rehob and the Syrians of Zoba, twenty thousand foot soldiers; and from the king of Maacah one thousand men, and from Ish-Tob twelve thousand men.

7 Now when David heard *of it*, he sent Joab and all the army of the mighty men.

8:12 LXX, Syr., Heb. mss. *Edom*
8:13 LXX, Syr., Heb. mss. *Edomites* and 1 Chr. 18:12

9:11 LXX *David's table*

8 Then the people of Ammon came out and put themselves in battle array at the entrance of the gate. And ᴿthe Syrians of Zoba, Beth Rehob, Ish-Tob, and Maacah were by themselves in the field.   2 Sam. 10:6

9 When Joab saw that the battle line was against him before and behind, he chose some of Israel's best and put them in battle array against the Syrians.

10 And the rest of the people he put under the command of ᴿAbishai his brother, that he might set them in battle array against the people of Ammon.   2 Sam. 3:30

11 Then he said, "If the Syrians are too strong for me, then you shall help me; but if the people of Ammon are too strong for you, then I will come and help you.

12 ᴿ"Be of good courage, and let us ᴿbe strong for our people and for the cities of our God. And may ᴿthe Lᴏʀᴅ do what is good in His sight."   Deut. 31:6 • 1 Cor. 16:13 • 1 Sam. 3:18

13 So Joab and the people who were with him drew near for the battle against the Syrians, and they fled before him.

14 When the people of Ammon saw that the Syrians were fleeing, they also fled before Abishai, and entered the city. So Joab returned from the people of Ammon and went to ᴿJerusalem.   2 Sam. 11:1

15 When the Syrians saw that they had been defeated by Israel, they gathered together.

16 Then *Hadadezer sent and brought out the Syrians who were beyond ᵀthe River, and they came to Helam. And ᵀShobach the commander of Hadadezer's army went before them.   The Euphrates • Shophach, 1 Chr. 19:16

17 When it was told David, he gathered all Israel, crossed over the Jordan, and came to Helam. And the Syrians set themselves in battle array against David and fought with him.

18 Then the Syrians fled before Israel; and David killed seven hundred charioteers and forty thousand ᴿhorsemen of the Syrians, and struck Shobach the commander of their army, who died there.   1 Chr. 19:18

19 And when all the kings who were servants to *Hadadezer saw that they were defeated by Israel, they made peace with Israel and served them. So the Syrians were afraid to help the people of Ammon anymore.

David, Bathsheba, and Uriah

11 It happened in the spring of the year, at the time when kings go out to battle, that ᴿDavid sent Joab and his servants with him, and all Israel; and they destroyed the people of Ammon and besieged Rabbah. But David remained at Jerusalem.   1 Chr. 20:1

2 Then it happened one evening that David arose from his bed and walked on the roof of the king's house. And from the roof he ᴿsaw a woman bathing, and the woman was very beautiful to behold.   Gen. 34:2

3 So David sent and inquired about the woman. And someone said, "Is this not ᵀBathsheba, the daughter of Eliam, the wife of Uriah the Hittite?"   Bathshua, 1 Chr. 3:5

4 Then David sent messengers, and took her; and she came to him, and ᴿhe lay with her, for she was cleansed from her impurity; and she returned to her house.   [James 1:14, 15]

5 And the woman conceived; so she sent and told David, and said, "I am with child."

6 Then David sent to Joab, saying, "Send me Uriah the Hittite." And Joab sent Uriah to David.

7 When Uriah had come to him, David asked how Joab was doing, and how the people were doing, and how the war prospered.

8 And David said to Uriah, "Go down to your house and ᴿwash your feet." So Uriah departed from the king's house, and a gift of food from the king followed him.   Gen. 18:4; 19:2

9 But Uriah slept at the ᴿdoor of the king's house with all the servants of his lord, and did not go down to his house.   1 Kin. 14:27, 28

10 So when they told David, saying, "Uriah did not go down to his house," David said to Uriah, "Did you not come from a journey? Why did you not go down to your house?"

11 And Uriah said to David, "The ark and Israel and Judah are dwelling in tents, and ᴿmy lord Joab and the servants of my lord are encamped in the open fields. Shall I then go to my house to eat and drink, and to lie with my wife? As you live, and as your soul lives, I will not do this thing."   2 Sam. 20:6–22

12 Then David said to Uriah, "Wait here today also, and tomorrow I will let you depart." So Uriah remained in Jerusalem that day and the next.

13 Now when David called him, he ate and drank before him; and he made him ᴿdrunk. And at evening he went out to lie on his bed ᴿwith the servants of his lord, but he did not go down to his house.   Gen. 19:33, 35 • 2 Sam. 11:9

14 In the morning it happened that David ᴿwrote a letter to Joab and sent it by the hand of Uriah.   1 Kin. 21:8, 9

15 And he wrote in the letter, saying, "Set Uriah in the forefront of the ᵀhottest battle, and retreat from him, that he may ᴿbe struck down and die."   fiercest • 2 Sam. 12:9

16 So it was, while Joab besieged the city, that he assigned Uriah to a place where he knew there were valiant men.

17 Then the men of the city came out and fought with Joab. And some of the people of the servants of David fell; and Uriah the Hittite died also.

10:16 Heb. Hadarezer
10:19 Heb. Hadarezer

18 Then Joab sent and told David all the things concerning the war,

19 and charged the messenger, saying, "When you have finished telling the matters of the war to the king,

20 if it happens that the king's wrath rises, and he says to you: 'Why did you approach so near to the city when you fought? Did you not know that they would shoot from the wall?

21 'Who struck Abimelech the son of *Jerubbesheth? Was it not a woman who cast a piece of a millstone on him from the wall, so that he died in Thebez? Why did you go near the wall?'—then you shall say, 'Your servant Uriah the Hittite is dead also.' "

22 So the messenger went, and came and told David all that Joab had sent by him.

23 And the messenger said to David, "Surely the men prevailed against us and came out to us in the field; then we drove them back as far as the entrance of the gate.

24 "The archers shot from the wall at your servants; and some of the king's servants are dead, and your servant Uriah the Hittite is dead also."

25 Then David said to the messenger, "Thus you shall say to Joab: 'Do not let this thing ᵀdisplease you, for the sword devours one as well as another. Strengthen your attack against the city, and overthrow it.' So encourage him."   Lit. be evil in your sight

26 When the wife of Uriah heard that Uriah her husband was dead, she mourned for her husband.

27 And when her mourning was over, David sent and brought her to his house, and she ᴿbecame his wife and bore him a son. But the thing that David had done ᴿdispleasedᵀ the Lᴏʀᴅ. 2 Sam. 12:9 • 1 Chr. 21:7 • Lit. was evil in the eyes of

Nathan's Parable and David's Confession

12 Then the Lᴏʀᴅ sent Nathan to David. And ᴿhe came to him, and ᴿsaid to him: "There were two men in one city, one rich and the other poor.   Ps. 51:title • 1 Kin. 20:35-41

2 "The rich man had exceedingly many flocks and herds.

3 "But the poor man had nothing, except one little ewe lamb which he had bought and nourished; and it grew up together with him and with his children. It ate of his own food and drank from his own cup and lay in his bosom; and it was like a daughter to him.

4 "And a traveler came to the rich man, who refused to take from his own flock and from his own herd to prepare one for the wayfaring man who had come to him; but he took the poor man's lamb and prepared it for the man who had come to him."

5 So David's anger was greatly aroused against the man, and he said to Nathan, "As

11:21 Jerubbaal, Gideon, Judg. 6:32

the Lᴏʀᴅ lives, the man who has done this ᵀshall surely die!   deserves to die, lit. is a son of death

6 "And he shall restore ᴿfourfold for the lamb, because he did this thing and because he had no pity."   [Ex. 22:1]

7 Then Nathan said to David, "You are the man! Thus says the Lᴏʀᴅ God of Israel: 'I ᴿanointed you king over Israel, and I delivered you from the hand of Saul.   1 Sam. 16:13

8 'I gave you your master's house and your master's wives into your keeping, and gave you the house of Israel and Judah. And if that had been too little, I also would have given you much more!

9 'Why have you despised the commandment of the Lᴏʀᴅ, to do evil in His sight? ᴿYou have killed Uriah the Hittite with the sword; you have taken his wife to be your wife, and have killed him with the sword of the people of Ammon.   2 Sam. 11:14-17, 27

10 'Now therefore, ᴿthe sword shall never depart from your house, because you have despised Me, and have taken the wife of Uriah the Hittite to be your wife.'   [Amos 7:9]

11 "Thus says the Lᴏʀᴅ: 'Behold, I will raise up adversity against you from your own house; and I will ᴿtake your wives before your eyes and give them to your neighbor, and he shall lie with your wives in the sight of this sun.   2 Sam. 16:21, 22

12 'For you did it secretly, but I will do this thing before all Israel, before the sun.' "

13 So David said to Nathan, ᴿ"I have sinned against the Lᴏʀᴅ." And Nathan said to David, "The Lᴏʀᴅ also has ᴿput away your sin; you shall not die.   2 Sam. 24:10 • [Mic. 7:18]

14 "However, because by this deed you have given great occasion to the enemies of the Lᴏʀᴅ ᴿto blaspheme, the child also who is born to you shall surely die."   Is. 52:5

15 Then Nathan departed to his house.

The Death of David's Son

And the Lᴏʀᴅ struck the child that Uriah's wife bore to David, and it became ill.

16 David therefore pleaded with God for the child, and David fasted and went in and ᴿlay all night on the ground.   2 Sam. 13:31

17 So the elders of his house arose and went to him, to raise him up from the ground. But he would not, nor did he eat food with them.

18 Then on the seventh day it came to pass that the child died. And the servants of David were afraid to tell him that the child was dead. For they said, "Indeed, while the child was alive, we spoke to him, and he would not heed our voice. How can we tell him that the child is dead? He may do some harm!"

19 When David saw that his servants were whispering, David perceived that the child

was dead. Therefore David said to his servants, "Is the child dead?" And they said, "He is dead."

20 So David arose from the ground, washed and [R]anointed himself, and changed his clothes; and he went into the house of the LORD and [R]worshiped. Then he went to his own house; and when he requested, they set food before him, and he ate.　Ruth 3:3 • Job 1:20

21 Then his servants said to him, "What is this that you have done? You fasted and wept for the child while he was alive, but when the child died, you arose and ate food."

22 And he said, "While the child was alive, I fasted and wept; [R]for I said, 'Who can tell whether *the LORD will be gracious to me, that the child may live?'　Jon. 3:9

23 "But now he is dead; why should I fast? Can I bring him back again? I shall go to him, but he shall not return to me."

Solomon Is Born

24 Then David comforted Bathsheba his wife, and went in to her and lay with her. So [R]she bore a son, and *he called his name Solomon. Now the LORD loved him,　Matt. 1:6

25 and He sent word by the hand of Nathan the prophet: So *he called his name *Jedidiah, because of the LORD.

Rabbah Is Captured

26 Now [R]Joab fought against [R]Rabbah of the people of Ammon, and took the royal city.　1 Chr. 20:1 • Deut. 3:11

27 And Joab sent messengers to David, and said, "I have fought against Rabbah, and I have taken the city's water supply.

28 "Now therefore, gather the rest of the people together and encamp against the city and take it, lest I take the city and it be called after my name."

29 So David gathered all the people together and went to Rabbah, fought against it, and took it.

30 Then he took their king's crown from his head. Its weight was a [T]talent of gold, with precious stones. And it was set on David's head. Also he brought out the spoil of the city in great abundance.　91 lb. or $5,760,000

31 And he brought out the people who were in it, and put them to work with saws and iron picks and iron axes, and made them cross over to the brick works. So he did to all the cities of the people of Ammon. Then David and all the people returned to Jerusalem.

12:22 Heb. mss., Syr. God
12:24 So with Kt., LXX, Vg.; Qr., a few Heb. mss., Syr., Tg. she
12:25 Qr., some Heb. mss., Syr., Tg., she • Lit. Beloved of the LORD

Amnon and Tamar

13 After this Absalom the son of David had a lovely sister, whose name was [R]Tamar; and [R]Amnon the son of David loved her.　1 Chr. 3:9 • 2 Sam. 3:2

2 Amnon was so distressed over his sister Tamar that he became sick; for she was a virgin. And it was improper for Amnon to do anything to her.

3 But Amnon had a friend whose name was Jonadab the son of Shimeah, David's brother. Now Jonadab was a very crafty man.

4 And he said to him, "Why are you, the king's son, becoming thinner day after day? Will you not tell me?" Amnon said to him, "I love Tamar, my brother Absalom's sister."

5 So Jonadab said to him, "Lie down on your bed and pretend to be ill. And when your father comes to see you, say to him, 'Please let my sister Tamar come and give me food, and prepare the food in my sight, that I may see it and eat it from her hand.' "

6 Then Amnon lay down and pretended to be ill; and when the king came to see him, Amnon said to the king, "Please let Tamar my sister come and [R]make a couple of cakes for me in my sight, that I may eat from her hand."　Gen. 18:6

7 And David sent home to Tamar, saying, "Now go to your brother Amnon's house, and prepare food for him."

8 So Tamar went to her brother Amnon's house; and he was lying down. Then she took flour and kneaded it, made cakes in his sight, and baked the cakes.

9 And she took the pan and placed them out before him, but he refused to eat. Then Amnon said, "Have everyone go out from me." And they all went out from him.

10 Then Amnon said to Tamar, "Bring the food into the bedroom, that I may eat from your hand." And Tamar took the cakes which she had made, and brought them to Amnon her brother in the bedroom.

11 Now when she had brought them to him to eat, [R]he took hold of her and said to her, "Come, lie with me, my sister."　Gen. 39:12

12 But she answered him, "No, my brother, do not [T]force me, for [R]no such thing should be done in Israel. Do not do this disgraceful thing!　Lit. humble me • [Lev. 18:9–11; 20:17]

13 "And I, where could I take my shame? And as for you, you would be like one of the fools in Israel. Now therefore, please speak to the king; [R]for he will not withhold me from you."　Gen. 20:12

14 However, he would not heed her voice; and being stronger than she, he [R]forced her and lay with her.　2 Sam. 12:11

15 Then Amnon hated her [T]exceedingly, so that the hatred with which he hated her was greater than the love with which he had

loved her. And Amnon said to her, "Arise, be gone!" *with a very great hatred*
16 So she said to him, "No, indeed! This evil of sending me away *is* worse than the other that you did to me." But he would not listen to her.
17 Then he called his servant who attended him, and said, "Here! Put this *woman* out, away from me, and bolt the door behind her."
18 Now she had on ᴿa robe of many colors, for the king's virgin daughters wore such apparel. And his servant put her out and bolted the door behind her. Gen. 37:3
19 Then Tamar put ᴿashes on her head, and tore her robe of many colors that *was* on her, and ᴿlaid her hand on her head and went away crying bitterly. Josh. 7:6 • Jer. 2:37
20 And Absalom her brother said to her, "Has Amnon your brother been with you? But now hold your peace, my sister. He *is* your brother; do not take this thing to heart." So Tamar remained desolate in her brother Absalom's house.
21 But when King David heard of all these things, he was very angry.
22 And Absalom spoke to his brother Amnon ᴿneither good nor bad. For Absalom ᴿhated Amnon, because he had forced his sister Tamar. Gen. 24:50; 31:24 • [Lev. 19:17, 18]

Absalom Murders Amnon

23 And it came to pass, after two full years, that Absalom ᴿhad sheepshearers in Baal Hazor, which *is* near Ephraim; so Absalom invited all the king's sons. 1 Sam. 25:4
24 Then Absalom came to the king and said, "Kindly note, your servant has sheepshearers; please, let the king and his servants go with your servant."
25 But the king said to Absalom, "No, my son, let us not all go now, lest we be a burden to you." Then he urged him, but he would not go; and he blessed him.
26 Then Absalom said, "If not, please let my brother Amnon go with us." And the king said to him, "Why should he go with you?"
27 But Absalom urged him; so he let Amnon and all the king's sons go with him.
28 Now Absalom had commanded his servants, saying, "Watch now, when Amnon's heart is merry with wine, and when I say to you, 'Strike Amnon!' then kill him. Do not be afraid. Have I not commanded you? Be courageous and ᵀvaliant." Lit. *sons of valor*
29 So the servants of Absalom ᴿdid to Amnon as Absalom had commanded. Then all the king's sons arose, and each one got on ᴿhis mule and fled. 2 Sam. 12:10 • 2 Sam. 18:9
30 And it came to pass, while they were on the way, that news came to David, saying, "Absalom has killed all the king's sons, and not one of them is left!"

31 So the king arose and tore his garments and ᴿlay on the ground, and all his servants stood by with their clothes torn. 2 Sam. 12:16
32 Then ᴿJonadab the son of Shimeah, David's brother, answered and said, "Let not my lord suppose they have killed all the young men, the king's sons, for only Amnon is dead. For by the command of Absalom this has been determined from the day that he forced his sister Tamar. 2 Sam. 13:3–5
33 "Now therefore, ᴿlet not my lord the king take the thing to his heart, to think that all the king's sons are dead. For only Amnon is dead." 2 Sam. 19:19

Absalom Flees to Geshur

34 Then Absalom fled. And the young man who was keeping watch lifted his eyes and looked, and there, many people were coming from the road on the hillside behind *him.
35 And Jonadab said to the king, "Look, the king's sons are coming; as your servant said, so it is."
36 So it was, as soon as he had finished speaking, that the king's sons indeed came, and they lifted up their voice and wept. Also the king and all his servants wept very bitterly.
37 But Absalom fled and went to Talmai the son of Ammihud, king of Geshur. And *David* mourned for his son every day.
38 So Absalom fled and went to ᴿGeshur, and was there three years. 2 Sam. 14:23, 32; 15:8
39 And *King David *longed to go to Absalom. For he had been ᴿcomforted concerning Amnon, because he was dead. 2 Sam. 12:19, 23

Absalom Returns to Jerusalem

14 So Joab the son of Zeruiah perceived that the king's heart *was* concerned ᴿabout Absalom. 2 Sam. 13:39
2 And Joab sent to Tekoa and brought from there a wise woman, and said to her, "Please pretend to be a mourner, ᴿand put on mourning apparel; do not anoint yourself with oil, but act like a woman who has been mourning a long time for the dead. Ruth 3:3
3 "Go to the king and speak to him in this manner." So Joab ᴿput the words in her mouth. 2 Sam. 14:19
4 And when the woman of Tekoa *spoke to the king, she ᴿfell on her face to the ground and prostrated herself, and said, ᴿ"Help, O king!" 1 Sam. 20:41; 25:23 • 2 Kin. 6:26, 28
5 Then the king said to her, "What trou-

13:34 LXX adds *And the watchman went and told the king, and said, "I see men from the way of Horonaim, from the regions of the mountains."*
13:39 So with MT, Syr., Vg.; LXX *the spirit of the king;* Tg. *the soul of King David* • So with MT, Tg.; LXX, Vg. *ceased to pursue after*
14:4 Many Heb. mss., LXX, Syr., Vg. *came*

bles you?" And she answered, R"Indeed I *am*
a widow, my husband is dead.   [Zech. 7:10]

6 "Now your maidservant had two sons;
and the two fought with each other in the
field, and *there was* no one to part them, but
the one struck the other and killed him.

7 "And now the whole family has risen up
against your maidservant, and they said,
'Deliver him who struck his brother, that we
may execute him Rfor the life of his brother
whom he killed; and we will destroy the heir
also.' So they would extinguish my ember
that is left, and leave to my husband *neither*
name nor remnant on the earth." Deut. 19:12, 13

8 Then the king said to the woman, "Go to
your house, and I will give orders concerning
you."

9 And the woman of Tekoa said to the
king, "My lord, O king, *let* the Tiniquity *be* on
me and on my father's house, and the king
and his throne *be* guiltless."   guilt

10 So the king said, "Whoever says *anything* to you, bring him to me, and he shall
not touch you anymore."

11 Then she said, "Please let the king remember the LORD your God, and do not
permit the avenger of blood to destroy anymore, lest they destroy my son." And he said,
R"*As* the LORD lives, not one hair of your son
shall fall to the ground."   1 Sam. 14:45

12 Therefore the woman said, "Please, let
your maidservant speak *another* word to my
lord the king." And he said, "Say on."

13 So the woman said: "Why then have you
schemed such a thing against Rthe people of
God? For the king speaks this thing as one
who is guilty, *in that* the king does not bring
his banished one home again.   Judg. 20:2

14 "For we Rwill surely die and *become* like
water spilled on the ground, which cannot be
gathered up again. Yet God does not Rtake
away a life; but He Rdevises means, so that
His banished ones are not Texpelled from
Him.   [Heb. 9:27] • Job 34:19 • Num. 35:15 • *cast out*

15 "Now therefore, I have come to speak of
this thing to my lord the king because the
people have made me afraid. And your maidservant said, 'I will now speak to the king; it
may be that the king will perform the request
of his maidservant.

16 'For the king will hear and deliver his
maidservant from the hand of the man *who
would* destroy me and my son together from
the Rinheritance of God.'   Deut. 32:9

17 "Your maidservant said, 'The word of
my lord the king will now be comforting; for
Ras the angel of God, so *is* my lord the king in
Rdiscerning good and evil. And may the LORD
your God be with you.'"   2 Sam. 19:27 • 1 Kin. 3:9

18 Then the king answered and said to the
woman, "Please do not hide from me anything that I ask you." And the woman said,
"Please, let my lord the king speak."

19 So the king said, "*Is* the hand of Joab
with you in all this?" And the woman answered and said, "*As* you live, my lord the
king, no one can turn to the right hand or to
the left from anything that my lord the king
has spoken. For your servant Joab commanded me, and Rhe put all these words in
the mouth of your maidservant.   2 Sam. 14:3

20 "To bring about this change of affairs
your servant Joab has done this thing; but
my lord *is* wise, Raccording to the wisdom of
the angel of God, to know everything that *is*
in the earth."   2 Sam. 14:17; 19:27

21 And the king said to Joab, "All right, I
have granted this thing. Go therefore, bring
back the young man Absalom."

22 Then Joab fell to the ground on his face
and bowed himself, and Tthanked the king.
And Joab said, "Today your servant knows
that I have found favor in your sight, my
lord, O king, in that the king has fulfilled the
request of his servant."   Lit. *blessed*

23 So Joab arose Rand went to Geshur, and
brought Absalom to Jerusalem.   2 Sam. 13:37, 38

24 And the king said, "Let him return to his
own house, but Rdo not let him see my face."
So Absalom returned to his own house, but
did not see the king's face.   2 Sam. 3:13

David Forgives Absalom

25 Now in all Israel there was no one who
was praised as much as Absalom for his good
looks. RFrom the sole of his foot to the crown
of his head there was no blemish in him. Is. 1:6

26 And when he cut the hair of his head—at
the end of every year he cut *it* because it was
heavy on him—when he cut it, he weighed
the hair of his head at Ttwo hundred shekels
according to the king's standard.   5 lb.

27 To Absalom were born three sons, and
one daughter whose name *was* Tamar. She
was a woman of beautiful appearance.

28 And Absalom dwelt two full years in
Jerusalem, but did not see the king's face.

29 Therefore Absalom sent for Joab, to send
him to the king, but he would not come to
him. And when he sent again the second
time, he would not come.

30 So he said to his servants, "See, Joab's
field is near mine, and he has barley there; go
and set it on fire." And Absalom's servants
set the field on fire.

31 Then Joab arose and came to Absalom's
house, and said to him, "Why have your
servants set my field on fire?"

32 And Absalom answered Joab, "Look, I
sent to you, saying, 'Come here, so that I may
send you to the king, to say, "Why have I
come from Geshur? *It would be* better for me
to be there still."' Now therefore, let me see
the king's face; but Rif there is iniquity in me,
let him execute me."   1 Sam. 20:8

33 So Joab went to the king and told him. And when he had called for Absalom, he came to the king and bowed himself on his face to the ground before the king. Then the king ᴿkissed Absalom.   Luke 15:20

Absalom's Treason

15 After this it happened that Absalom provided himself with chariots and horses, and fifty men to run before him.

2 Now Absalom would rise early and stand beside the way to the gate. So it was, whenever anyone who had a lawsuitᵀ came to the king for a decision, that Absalom would call to him and say, "What city are you from?" And he would say, "Your servant is from such and such a tribe of Israel."   controversy

3 Then Absalom would say to him, "Look, your case is good and right; but there is no ᵀdeputy of the king to hear you."   Lit. listener

4 Moreover Absalom would say, ᴿ"Oh, that I were made judge in the land, and everyone who has any suit or cause would come to me; then I would give him justice."   Judg. 9:29

5 And so it was, whenever anyone came near to bow down to him, that he would put out his hand and take him and kiss him.

6 In this manner Absalom acted toward all Israel who came to the king for judgment. ᴿSo Absalom stole the hearts of the men of Israel.   [Rom. 16:18]

7 Now it came to pass ᴿafter *forty years that Absalom said to the king, "Please, let me go to ᴿHebron and pay the vow which I made to the Lᴏʀᴅ.   [Deut. 23:21] • 2 Sam. 3:2, 3

8 "For your servant took a vow ᴿwhile I dwelt at Geshur in Syria, saying, 'If the Lᴏʀᴅ indeed brings me back to Jerusalem, then I will serve the Lᴏʀᴅ.' "   2 Sam. 13:38

9 And the king said to him, "Go in peace." So he arose and went to Hebron.

10 Then Absalom sent spies throughout all the tribes of Israel, saying, "As soon as you hear the sound of the trumpet, then you shall say, 'Absalom ᴿreigns in Hebron!' "   1 Kin. 1:34

11 And with Absalom went two hundred men invited from Jerusalem, and they went along innocently and did not know anything.

12 Then Absalom sent for Ahithophel the Gilonite, ᴿDavid's counselor, from his city— from ᴿGiloh—while he offered sacrifices. And the conspiracy grew strong, for the people with Absalom ᴿcontinually increased in number.   1 Chr. 27:33 • Josh. 15:51 • Ps. 3:1

David Escapes from Jerusalem

13 Now a messenger came to David, saying, ᴿ"The hearts of the men of Israel are ᵀwith Absalom."   Judg. 9:3 • Lit. after

14 So David said to all his servants who were with him at Jerusalem, "Arise, and let

15:7 LXX mss., Syr., Josephus four

us flee, or we shall not escape from Absalom. Make haste to depart, lest he overtake us suddenly and bring disaster upon us, and strike the city with the edge of the sword."

15 And the king's servants said to the king, "We are your servants, ready to do whatever my lord the king commands."

16 Then the king went out with all his household after him. But the king left ten women, concubines, to keep the house.

17 And the king went out with all the people after him, and stopped at the outskirts.

18 Then all his servants passed ᵀbefore him; and all the Cherethites, all the Pelethites, and all the Gittites, ᴿsix hundred men who had followed him from Gath, passed before the king.   Lit. by his hand • 1 Sam. 23:13; 25:13; 30:1, 9

19 Then the king said to ᴿIttai the Gittite, "Why are you also going with us? Return and remain with the king. For you are a foreigner and also an exile from your own place.   2 Sam. 18:2

20 "In fact, you came only yesterday. Should I make you wander up and down with us today, since I go ᴿI know not where? Return, and take your brethren back. Mercy and truth be with you."   1 Sam. 23:13

21 But Ittai answered the king and said, ᴿ"As the Lᴏʀᴅ lives, and as my lord the king lives, surely in whatever place my lord the king shall be, whether in death or life, even there also your servant will be."   Ruth 1:16, 17

22 So David said to Ittai, "Go, and cross over." Then Ittai the Gittite and all his men and all the little ones who were with him crossed over.

23 And all the country wept with a loud voice, and all the people crossed over. The king himself also crossed over the Brook Kidron, and all the people crossed over toward the way of the wilderness.

24 There was ᴿZadok also, and all the Levites with him, bearing the ᴿark of the covenant of God. And they set down the ark of God, and ᴿAbiathar went up until all the people had finished crossing over from the city.   2 Sam. 8:17 • Num. 4:15 • 1 Sam. 22:20

25 Then the king said to Zadok, "Carry the ark of God back into the city. If I find favor in the eyes of the Lᴏʀᴅ, He ᴿwill bring me back and show me both it and ᴿHis dwelling place.   [Ps. 43:3] • Ex. 15:13

26 "But if He says thus: 'I have no ᴿdelight in you,' here I am, ᴿlet Him do to me as seems good to Him."   Num. 14:8 • 1 Sam. 3:18

27 The king also said to Zadok the priest, "Are you not a seer? Return to the city in peace, and your two sons with you, Ahimaaz your son, and Jonathan the son of Abiathar.

28 "See, ᴿI will wait in the plains of the wilderness until word comes from you to inform me."   2 Sam. 17:16

29 Therefore Zadok and Abiathar carried the ark of God back to Jerusalem. And they remained there.

30 So David went up by the Ascent of the Mount of Olives, and wept as he went up; and he had his head covered and went ᴿbarefoot. And all the people who were with him ᴿcovered their heads and went up, ᴿweeping as they went up.   Is. 20:2-4 • Jer. 14:3, 4 • [Ps. 126:6]

31 Then someone told David, saying, ᴿ"Ahithophel is among the conspirators with Absalom." And David said, "O LORD, I pray, ᴿturn the counsel of Ahithophel into foolishness!"   Ps. 3:1, 2; 55:12 • 2 Sam. 16:23; 17:14, 23

32 Now it happened when David had come to the top of the mountain, where he worshiped God—there was Hushai the ᴿArchite coming to meet him ᴿwith his robe torn and dust on his head.   Josh. 16:2 • 2 Sam. 1:2

33 David said to him, "If you go on with me, then you will become a burden to me.

34 "But if you return to the city, and say to Absalom, 'I will be your servant, O king; as I was your father's servant previously, so I will now also be your servant,' then you may defeat the counsel of Ahithophel for me.

35 "And do you not have Zadok and Abiathar the priests with you there? Therefore it will be that whatever you hear from the king's house, you shall tell to ᴿZadok and Abiathar the priests.   2 Sam. 17:15, 16

36 "Indeed they have there with them their two sons, Ahimaaz, Zadok's son, and Jonathan, Abiathar's son; and by them you shall send me everything you hear."

37 So Hushai, David's friend, went into the city. And Absalom came into Jerusalem.

Mephibosheth's Servant

16 When David was a little past the top of the mountain, there was ᴿZiba the servant of Mephibosheth, who met him with a couple of saddled donkeys, and on them two hundred loaves of bread, one hundred clusters of raisins, one hundred summer fruits, and a skin of wine.   2 Sam. 9:2; 19:17, 29

2 And the king said to Ziba, "What do you mean to do with these?" So Ziba said, "The donkeys are for the king's household to ride on, the bread and summer fruit for the young men to eat, and the wine for those who are faint in the wilderness to drink."

3 Then the king said, "And where is your master's son?" And Ziba said to the king, "Indeed he is staying in Jerusalem, for he said, 'Today the house of Israel will restore the kingdom of my father to me.' "

4 So the king said to Ziba, "Here, all that belongs to Mephibosheth is yours." And Ziba said, "I humbly bow before you, that I may find favor in your sight, my lord, O king!"

Shimei Curses David

5 Now when King David came to Bahurim, there was a man from the family of the house of Saul, whose name was Shimei the son of Gera, coming from there. He came out, cursing continuously as he came.

6 And he threw stones at David and at all the servants of King David. And all the people and all the mighty men were on his right hand and on his left.

7 Also Shimei said thus when he cursed: "Come out! Come out! You bloodthirsty man, ᴿyou ᵀrogue!   Deut. 13:13 • worthless man

8 "The LORD has ᴿbrought upon you all the blood of the house of Saul, in whose place you have reigned; and the LORD has delivered the kingdom into the hand of Absalom your son. So now you are caught in your own evil, because you are a ᵀbloodthirsty man!"   Judg. 9:24, 56, 57 • Lit. man of bloodshed

9 Then Abishai the son of Zeruiah said to the king, "Why should this ᴿdead dog ᴿcurse my lord the king? Please, let me go over and take off his head!"   2 Sam. 9:8 • Ex. 22:28

10 But the king said, "What have I to do with you, you sons of Zeruiah? So let him curse, because ᴿthe LORD has said to him, 'Curse David.' ᴿWho then shall say, 'Why have you done so?' "   [Lam. 3:38] • [Rom. 9:20]

11 And David said to Abishai and all his servants, "See how ᴿmy son who ᴿcame from my own body seeks my life. How much more now may this Benjamite? Let him alone, and let him curse; for so the LORD has ordered him.   2 Sam. 12:11 • Gen. 15:4

12 "It may be that the LORD will look on *my affliction, and that the LORD will repay me with good for his cursing this day."

13 And as David and his men went along the road, Shimei went along the hillside opposite him and cursed as he went, threw stones at him and kicked up dust.

14 Now the king and all the people who were with him became weary; so they refreshed themselves there.

The Advice of Ahithophel

15 Meanwhile ᴿAbsalom and all the people, the men of Israel, came to Jerusalem; and Ahithophel was with him.   2 Sam. 15:12, 37

16 And so it was, when Hushai the Archite, ᴿDavid's friend, came to Absalom, that ᴿHushai said to Absalom, "Long live the king! Long live the king!"   2 Sam. 15:37 • 2 Sam. 15:34

17 So Absalom said to Hushai, "Is this your loyalty to your friend? ᴿWhy did you not go with your friend?"   2 Sam. 19:25

18 And Hushai said to Absalom, "No, but whom the LORD and this people and all the

16:12 So with Kt., LXX, Syr., Vg.; Qr. my eyes; Tg. tears of my eyes

men of Israel choose, his I will be, and with him I will remain.

19 "Furthermore, ᴿwhom should I serve? *Should I* not *serve* in the presence of his son? As I have served in your father's presence, so will I be in your presence."   2 Sam. 15:34

20 Then Absalom said to Ahithophel, "Give advice as to what we should do."

21 And Ahithophel said to Absalom, "Go in to your father's ᴿconcubines, whom he has left to keep the house; and all Israel will hear that you ᴿare abhorred by your father. Then ᴿthe hands of all who are with you will be strong."   2 Sam. 15:16; 20:3 • Gen. 34:30 • 2 Sam. 2:7

22 So they pitched a tent for Absalom on the top of the house, and Absalom went in to his father's concubines ᴿin the sight of all Israel.   2 Sam. 12:11, 12

23 Now the advice of Ahithophel, which he gave in those days, *was* as if one had inquired at the oracle of God. So *was* all the advice of Ahithophel ᴿboth with David and with Absalom.   2 Sam. 15:12

17 Moreover Ahithophel said to Absalom, "Now let me choose twelve thousand men, and I will arise and pursue David tonight.

2 "I will come upon him while he *is* weary and weak, and make him ᵀafraid. And all the people who *are* with him will flee, and I will ᴿstrike only the king.   *tremble with fear* • Zech. 13:7

3 "Then I will bring back all the people to you. When all return except the man whom you seek, all the people will be at peace."

4 And the saying pleased Absalom and all the ᴿelders of Israel.   2 Sam. 5:3; 19:11

The Advice of Hushai

5 Then Absalom said, "Now call Hushai the Archite also, and let us hear what he ᴿsays too."   2 Sam. 15:32-34

6 And when Hushai came to Absalom, Absalom spoke to him, saying, "Ahithophel has spoken in this manner. Shall we do as he says? If not, speak up."

7 So Hushai said to Absalom: "The advice that Ahithophel has given *is* not good at this time.

8 "For," said Hushai, "you know your father and his men, that they *are* mighty men, and they *are* enraged in their minds, like ᴿa bear robbed of her cubs in the field; and your father *is* a man of war, and will not camp with the people.   Hos. 13:8

9 "Surely by now he is hidden in some pit, or in some *other* place. And it will be, when some of them are overthrown at the first, that whoever hears *it* will say, 'There is a slaughter among the people who follow Absalom.'

10 "And even he *who is* valiant, whose heart *is* like the heart of a lion, will ᴿmelt completely. For all Israel knows that your father *is* a mighty man, and *those* who *are* with him *are* valiant men.   Josh. 2:11

11 "Therefore I advise that all Israel be fully gathered to you, ᴿfrom Dan to Beersheba, ᴿlike the sand that *is* by the sea for multitude, and that you go to battle in person.   2 Sam. 3:10 • Gen. 22:17

12 "So we will come upon him in some place where he may be found, and we will fall on him as the dew falls on the ground. And of him and all the men who *are* with him there shall not be left so much as one.

13 "Moreover, if he has withdrawn into a city, then all Israel shall bring ropes to that city; and we will pull it into the river, until there is not one small stone found there."

14 So Absalom and all the men of Israel said, "The advice of Hushai the Archite *is* better than the advice of Ahithophel." For the LORD had purposed to defeat the good advice of Ahithophel, to the intent that the LORD might bring disaster on Absalom.

Hushai Warns David to Escape

15 Then Hushai said to Zadok and Abiathar the priests, "Thus and so Ahithophel advised Absalom and the elders of Israel, and thus and so I have advised.

16 "Now therefore, send quickly and tell David, saying, 'Do not spend this night in the plains of the wilderness, but speedily cross over, lest the king and all the people who *are* with him be swallowed up.' "

17 Now Jonathan and Ahimaaz ᴿstayed at ᴿEn Rogel, for they dared not be seen coming into the city; so a female servant would come and tell them, and they would go and tell King David.   Josh. 2:4-6 • Josh. 15:7; 18:16

18 Nevertheless a lad saw them, and told Absalom. But both of them went away quickly and came to a man's house ᴿin Bahurim, who had a well in his court; and they went down into it.   2 Sam. 3:16; 16:5

19 ᴿThen the woman took and spread a covering over the well's mouth, and spread ground grain on it; and the thing was not known.   Josh. 2:4-6

20 And when Absalom's servants came to the woman at the house, they said, "Where *are* Ahimaaz and Jonathan?" So ᴿthe woman said to them, "They have gone over the water brook." And when they had searched and could not find *them*, they returned to Jerusalem.   Josh. 2:3-5

21 Now it came to pass, after they had departed, that they came up out of the well and went and told King David, and said to David, ᴿ"Arise and cross over the water quickly. For thus has Ahithophel advised against you."   2 Sam. 17:15, 16

22 So David and all the people who *were* with him arose and crossed over the Jordan.

By morning light not one of them was left who had not gone over the Jordan.

23 Now when Ahithophel saw that his advice was not followed, he saddled a donkey, and arose and went home to his house, to his city. Then he put his household in order, and hanged himself, and died; and he was buried in his father's tomb.

24 Then David went to ᴿMahanaim. And Absalom crossed over the Jordan, he and all the men of Israel with him.   2 Sam. 2:8; 19:32

25 And Absalom made ᴿAmasa captain of the army instead of Joab. This Amasa was the son of a man whose name was *Jithra, an *Israelite, who had gone in to ᴿAbigail the daughter of Nahash, sister of Zeruiah, Joab's mother.   1 Kin. 2:5, 32 • 1 Chr. 2:16

26 So Israel and Absalom encamped in the land of Gilead.

27 Now it happened, when David had come to Mahanaim, that Shobi the son of Nahash from Rabbah of the people of Ammon, Machir the son of Ammiel from Lo Debar, and Barzillai the Gileadite from Rogelim,

28 brought beds and basins, earthen vessels and wheat, barley and flour, parched grain and beans, lentils and parched seeds,

29 honey and curds, sheep and cheese of the herd, for David and the people who were with him to eat. For they said, "The people are hungry and weary and thirsty ᴿin the wilderness."   2 Sam. 16:2, 14

Absalom's Defeat and Death

18 And David ᵀnumbered the people who were with him, and ᴿset captains of thousands and captains of hundreds over them.   Lit. attended to • Ex. 18:25

2 Then David sent out one third of the people under the hand of Joab, ᴿone third under the hand of Abishai the son of Zeruiah, Joab's brother, and one third under the hand of ᴿIttai the Gittite. And the king said to the people, "I also will surely go out with you myself."   Judg. 7:16 • 2 Sam. 15:19-22

3 ᴿBut the people answered, "You shall not go out! For if we flee away, they will not care about us; nor if half of us die, will they care about us. But you are worth ten thousand of us. For you are now more help to us in the city."   2 Sam. 21:17

4 Then the king said to them, "Whatever seems best to you I will do." So the king stood beside the gate, and all the people went out by hundreds and by thousands.

5 Now the king had commanded Joab, Abishai, and Ittai, saying, "Deal gently for my sake with the young man Absalom." And all the people heard when the king gave all the captains orders concerning Absalom.

6 So the people went out into the field of battle against Israel. And the battle was in the ᴿwoods of Ephraim.   Josh. 17:15, 18

7 The people of Israel were overthrown there before the servants of David, and a great slaughter of twenty thousand took place there that day.

8 For the battle there was scattered over the face of the whole countryside, and the woods devoured more people that day than the sword devoured.

9 Then Absalom met the servants of David. Absalom rode on a mule. The mule went under the thick boughs of a great terebinth tree, and ᴿhis head caught in the terebinth; so he was left hanging between heaven and earth. And the mule which was under him went on.   2 Sam. 14:26

10 Now a certain man saw it and told Joab, and said, "I just saw Absalom hanging in a terebinth tree!"

11 So Joab said to the man who told him, "You just saw him! And why did you not strike him there to the ground? I would have given you ten shekels of silver and a belt."

12 But the man said to Joab, "Though I were to receive a thousand shekels of silver in my hand, I would not raise my hand against the king's son. ᴿFor in our hearing the king commanded you and Abishai and Ittai, saying, *'Beware lest anyone touch the young man Absalom!'   2 Sam. 18:5

13 "Otherwise I would have dealt falsely against my own life. For there is nothing hidden from the king, and you yourself would have set yourself against me."

14 Then Joab said, "I cannot linger with you." And he took three spears in his hand and thrust them through Absalom's heart, while he was still alive in the midst of the terebinth tree.

15 And ten young men who bore Joab's armor surrounded Absalom, and struck and killed him.

16 So Joab blew the trumpet, and the people returned from pursuing Israel. For Joab held back the people.

17 And they took Absalom and cast him into a large pit in the woods, and laid a very large heap of stones over him. Then all Israel ᴿfled, everyone to his tent.   2 Sam. 19:8; 20:1, 22

18 Now Absalom in his lifetime had taken and set up a pillar for himself, which is in the King's Valley. For he said, "I have no son to keep my name in remembrance." He called the pillar after his own name. And to this day it is called Absalom's Monument.

David Hears of Absalom's Death

19 Then ᴿAhimaaz the son of Zadok said, "Let me run now and take the news to the

---

17:25 Jether, 1 Chr. 2:17 • So with MT, some mss. of LXX, Tg.; some mss. of LXX Ishmaelite (cf. 1 Chr. 2:17); Vg. of Jezrael

18:12 Vss. 'Protect the young man Absalom for me!'

king, how the LORD has ᵀavenged him of his enemies."   2 Sam. 15:36; 17:17 · *vindicated*

20 And Joab said to him, "You shall not take the news this day, for you shall take the news another day. But today you shall take no news, because the king's son is dead."

21 Then Joab said to the Cushite, "Go, tell the king what you have seen." So the Cushite bowed himself to Joab and ran.

22 And Ahimaaz the son of Zadok said again to Joab, "But ᵀwhatever happens, please let me also run after the Cushite." So Joab said, "Why will you run, my son, since you have no news ready?"   Lit. *be what may*

23 "But whatever happens," *he said*, "let me run." So he said to him, "Run." Then Ahimaaz ran by way of the plain, and outran the Cushite.

24 Now David was sitting between the two gates. And the watchman went up to the roof over the gate, to the wall, lifted his eyes and looked, and there was a man, running alone.

25 Then the watchman cried out and told the king. And the king said, "If he *is* alone, *there is* news in his mouth." And he came rapidly and drew near.

26 Then the watchman saw *another* man running, and the watchman called to the gatekeeper and said, "There is *another* man, running alone!" And the king said, "He also brings news."

27 So the watchman said, ᵀ"I think the running of the first is like the running of Ahimaaz the son of Zadok." And the king said, "He *is* a good man, and comes with ᴿgood news."   Lit. *I see the running* · 1 Kin. 1:42

28 So Ahimaaz called out and said to the king, ᵀ"All is well!" Then he bowed down with his face to the earth before the king, and said, "Blessed *be* the LORD your God, who has delivered up the men who raised their hand against my lord the king!"   *Peace be to you*

29 The king said, "Is the young man Absalom safe?" Ahimaaz answered, "When Joab sent the king's servant and *me* your servant, I saw a great tumult, but I did not know what *it was about*."

30 And the king said, "Turn aside *and* stand here." So he turned aside and stood still.

31 Just then the Cushite came, and the Cushite said, "There is good news, my lord the king! For the LORD has avenged you this day of all those who rose against you."

32 And the king said to the Cushite, "Is the young man Absalom safe?" So the Cushite answered, "May the enemies of my lord the king, and all who rise against you to do harm, be like *that* young man!"

David's Mourning for Absalom

33 Then the king was deeply moved, and went up to the chamber over the gate, and wept. And as he went, he said thus: ᴿ"O my son Absalom—my son, my son Absalom—if only I had died in your place! O Absalom my son, ᴿmy son!"   2 Sam. 12:10 · 2 Sam. 19:4

19 And Joab was told, "Behold, the king is weeping and mourning for Absalom."

2 So the victory that day was *turned* into ᴿmourning for all the people. For the people heard it said that day, "The king is grieved for his son."   Esth. 4:3

3 And the people ᵀstole back into the city that day, as people who are ashamed steal away when they flee in battle.   *went by stealth*

4 But the king covered his face, and the king cried out with a loud voice, "O my son Absalom! O Absalom, my son, my son!"

5 Then ᴿJoab came into the house to the king, and said, "Today you have disgraced all your servants who today have saved your life, the lives of your sons and daughters, the lives of your wives and the lives of your concubines,   2 Sam. 18:14

6 "in that you love your enemies and hate your friends. For you have declared today that you ᵀregard neither princes nor servants; for today I perceive that if Absalom had lived and all of us had died today, then it would have pleased you well.   *have no respect for*

7 "Now therefore, arise, go out and speak ᵀcomfort to your servants. For I swear by the LORD, if you do not go out, not one will stay with you this night. And that will be worse for you than all the evil that has befallen you from your youth until now."   Lit. *to the heart of*

8 Then the king arose and sat in the gate. And they told all the people, saying, "There is the king, sitting in the gate." So all the people came before the king. For everyone of Israel had ᴿfled to his tent.   2 Sam. 18:17

David Returns to Jerusalem

9 Now all the people were in a dispute throughout all the tribes of Israel, saying, "The king saved us from the hand of our enemies, he delivered us from the hand of the Philistines, and now he has ᴿfled from the land because of Absalom.   2 Sam. 15:14

10 "But Absalom, whom we anointed over us, has died in battle. Now therefore, why do you say nothing about bringing back the king?"

11 So King David sent to ᴿZadok and Abiathar the priests, saying, "Speak to the elders of Judah, saying, 'Why are you the last to bring the king back to his house, since the words of all Israel have come to the king, to his *very* house?   2 Sam. 15:24

12 'You *are* my brethren, you *are* ᴿmy bone and my flesh. Why then are you the last to bring back the king?'   2 Sam. 5:1

13 ᴿ"And say to Amasa, 'Are you not my

bone and my flesh? ᴿGod do so to me, and more also, if you are not commander of the army before me ᵀcontinually in place of Joab.' "   2 Sam. 17:25 • Ruth 1:17 • *permanently*

14 So he swayed the hearts of all the men of Judah, ᴿjust as *the heart of* one man, so that they sent *this word* to the king: "Return, you and all your servants!"   Judg. 20:1

15 Then the king returned and came to the Jordan. And Judah came to ᴿGilgal, to go to meet the king, to escort the king ᴿacross the Jordan.   Josh. 5:9 • 2 Sam. 17:22

16 And ᴿShimei the son of Gera, a Benjamite, who *was* from Bahurim, hurried and came down with the men of Judah to meet King David.   2 Sam. 16:5

17 *There were* a thousand men of ᴿBenjamin with him, and Ziba the servant of the house of Saul, and his fifteen sons and his twenty servants with him; and they went over the Jordan before the king.   1 Kin. 12:21

18 Then a ferryboat went across to carry over the king's household, and to do what he thought good.

David's Mercy to Shimei

Now Shimei the son of Gera fell down before the king when he had crossed the Jordan.

19 Then he said to the king, "Do not let my lord ᵀimpute iniquity to me, or remember what wrong your servant did on the day that my lord the king left Jerusalem, that the king should take *it* to heart.   *charge me with iniquity*

20 "For I, your servant, know that I have sinned. Therefore here I am, the first to come today of all ᴿthe house of Joseph to go down to meet my lord the king."   Judg. 1:22

21 But Abishai the son of Zeruiah answered and said, "Shall not Shimei be put to death for this, ᴿbecause he ᴿcursed the LORD's anointed?"   [Ex. 22:28] • [1 Sam. 26:9]

22 And David said, ᴿ"What have I to do with you, you sons of Zeruiah, that you should be adversaries to me today? ᴿShall any man be put to death today in Israel? For do I not know that today I *am* king over Israel?"   2 Sam. 3:39; 16:10 • 1 Sam. 11:13

23 Therefore the king said to Shimei, "You shall not die." And the king swore to him.

David and Mephibosheth Meet

24 Now Mephibosheth the son of Saul came down to meet the king. And he had not cared for his feet, nor trimmed his mustache, nor washed his clothes, from the day the king departed until the day he returned in peace.

25 So it was, when he had come to Jerusalem to meet the king, that the king said to him, ᴿ"Why did you not go with me, Mephibosheth?"   2 Sam. 16:7

26 And he answered, "My lord, O king, my servant deceived me. For your servant said, 'I will saddle a donkey for myself, that I may ride on it and go to the king,' because your servant *is* lame.

27 "And ᴿhe has slandered your servant to my lord the king, ᴿbut my lord the king *is* like the angel of God. Therefore do *what is* good in your eyes.   2 Sam. 16:3, 4 • 2 Sam. 14:17, 20

28 "For all my father's house were but dead men before my lord the king. Yet you set your servant among those who eat at your own table. Therefore what right have I still to cry out anymore to the king?"

29 So the king said to him, "Why do you speak anymore of your matters? I have said, 'You and Ziba divide the land.' "

30 Then Mephibosheth said to the king, "Rather, let him take it all, inasmuch as my lord the king has come back in peace to his own house."

David's Kindness to Barzillai

31 And ᴿBarzillai the Gileadite came down from Rogelim and went across the Jordan with the king, to escort him across the Jordan.   1 Kin. 2:7

32 Now Barzillai was a very aged man, eighty years old. And he had provided the king with supplies while he stayed at Mahanaim, for he *was* a very rich man.

33 And the king said to Barzillai, "Come across with me, and I will provide for you while you are with me in Jerusalem."

34 But Barzillai said to the king, "How long have I to live, that I should go up with the king to Jerusalem?

35 "I *am* today ᴿeighty years old. Can I discern between the good and bad? Can your servant taste what I eat or what I drink? Can I hear any longer the voice of singing men and singing women? Why then should your servant be a further burden to my lord the king?   Ps. 90:10

36 "Your servant will go a little way across the Jordan with the king. And why should the king repay me *with* such a reward?

37 "Please let your servant turn back again, that I may die in my own city, near the grave of my father and mother. But here is your servant ᴿChimham; let him cross over with my lord the king, and do for him what seems good to you."   Jer. 41:17

38 And the king answered, "Chimham shall cross over with me, and I will do for him what seems good to you. Now whatever you request of me, I will do for you."

39 Then all the people went over the Jordan. And when the king had crossed over, the king ᴿkissed Barzillai and blessed him, and he returned to his own place.   Gen. 31:55

The Quarrel About the King

40 Now the king went on to Gilgal, and *Chimham went on with him. And all the people of Judah escorted the king, and also half the people of Israel.

41 Just then all the men of Israel came to the king, and said to the king, "Why have our brethren, the men of Judah, stolen you away and brought the king, his household, and all David's men with him across the Jordan?"

42 So all the men of Judah answered the men of Israel, "Because the king *is* a close relative of ours. Why then are you angry over this matter? Have we ever eaten at the king's *expense?* Or has he given us any gift?"

43 And the men of Israel answered the men of Judah, and said, "We have ᴿten shares in the king; therefore we also have more *right* to David than you. Why then do you despise us—were we not the first to advise bringing back our king?" Yet ᴿthe words of the men of Judah were ᵀfiercer than the words of the men of Israel.   1 Kin. 11:30, 31 • Judg. 8:1; 12:1 • *harsher*

The Rebellion of Sheba

20 And there happened to be there a ᵀrebel, whose name *was* Sheba the son of Bichri, a Benjamite. And he blew a trumpet, and said: Lit. *man of Belial*

"We have no share in David,
  Nor do we have inheritance in the son
    of Jesse;
  Every man to his tents, O Israel!"

2 So every man of Israel deserted David, *and* followed Sheba the son of Bichri. But the men of Judah, from the Jordan as far as Jerusalem, remained loyal to their king.

3 Now David came to his house at Jerusalem. And the king took the ten women, ᴿhis concubines whom he had left to keep the house, and put them in seclusion and supported them, but did not go in to them. So they were shut up to the day of their death, living in widowhood.   2 Sam. 15:16; 16:21, 22

4 And the king said to Amasa, ᴿ"Assemble the men of Judah for me within three days, and be present here yourself."   2 Sam. 17:25; 19:13

5 So Amasa went to assemble *the men of* Judah. But he delayed longer than the set time which David had appointed him.

6 And David said to ᴿAbishai, "Now Sheba the son of Bichri will do us more harm than Absalom. Take ᴿyour lord's servants and pursue him, lest he find for himself fortified cities, and escape us."   2 Sam. 21:17 • 2 Sam. 11:11

7 So Joab's men, with the Cherethites, the Pelethites, and ᴿall the mighty men, went out after him. And they went out of Jerusalem to pursue Sheba the son of Bichri.   2 Sam. 15:18

8 When they *were* at the large stone which *is* in Gibeon, Amasa came before them. Now Joab was dressed in battle armor; on it was a belt *with* a sword fastened in its sheath at his hips; and as he was going forward, it fell out.

9 Then Joab said to Amasa, "*Are* you in health, my brother?" And Joab took Amasa by the beard with his right hand to kiss him.

10 But Amasa did not notice the sword that *was* in Joab's hand. And he struck him with it in the stomach, and his entrails poured out on the ground; and he did not *strike* him again. Thus he died. Then Joab and Abishai his brother pursued Sheba the son of Bichri.

11 Meanwhile one of Joab's men stood near Amasa, and said, "Whoever favors Joab and whoever is for David—follow Joab!"

12 But Amasa wallowed in *his* blood in the middle of the highway. And when the man saw that all the people stood still, he moved Amasa from the highway to the field and threw a garment over him, when he saw that everyone who came upon him halted.

13 When he was removed from the highway, all the people went on after Joab to pursue Sheba the son of Bichri.

14 And he went through all the tribes of Israel to ᴿAbel and Beth Maachah and all the Berites. So they were gathered together and also went after ᵀSheba.   2 Kin. 15:29 • Lit. *him*

15 Then they came and besieged him in Abel of Beth Maachah; and they cast up a siege mound against the city, and it stood by the rampart. And all the people who *were* with Joab battered the wall to throw it down.

16 Then a wise woman cried out from the city, "Hear, hear! Please say to Joab, 'Come nearby, that I may speak with you.' "

17 When he had come near to her, the woman said, "*Are* you Joab?" He answered, "I *am.*" Then she said to him, "Hear the words of your maidservant." And he answered, "I am listening."

18 So she spoke, saying, "They used to talk in former times, saying, 'They shall surely seek *guidance* at Abel,' and so they would end *disputes.*

19 "I *am* among the peaceable *and* faithful in Israel. You seek to destroy a city and a mother in Israel. Why would you swallow up ᴿthe inheritance of the LORD?"   1 Sam. 26:19

20 And Joab answered and said, "Far be it, far be it from me, that I should swallow up or destroy!

21 "That *is* not so. But a man from the mountains of Ephraim, Sheba the son of Bichri by name, has raised his hand against the king, against David. Deliver him only, and I will depart from the city." So the woman said to Joab, "Watch, his head will be thrown to you over the wall."

22 Then the woman ᴿin her wisdom went to all the people. And they cut off the head of Sheba the son of Bichri, and threw it out to Joab. Then he blew a trumpet, and they withdrew from the city, every man to his tent. So Joab returned to the king at Jerusalem.   [Eccl. 9:13–16]

David's Government Officers

23 And Joab was over all the army of Israel; Benaiah the son of Jehoiada was over the Cherethites and the Pelethites;

24 Adoram was in charge of revenue; Jehoshaphat the son of Ahilud was recorder;

25 Sheva was scribe; ᴿZadok and Abiathar were the priests;   1 Kin. 4:4

26 ᴿand Ira the Jairite was ᵀa chief minister under David.   2 Sam. 8:18 • Or David's priest

David Avenges the Gibeonites

21 Now there was a famine in the days of David for three years, year after year; and David ᴿinquired of the LORD. And the LORD answered, "It is because of Saul and his ᵀbloodthirsty house, because he killed the Gibeonites."   Num. 27:21 • Lit. house of bloodshed

2 So the king called the Gibeonites and spoke to them. Now the Gibeonites were not of the children of Israel, but of the remnant of the Amorites; the children of Israel had sworn protection to them, but Saul had sought to kill them ᴿin his zeal for the children of Israel and Judah.   [Ex. 34:11–16]

3 Therefore David said to the Gibeonites, "What shall I do for you? And with what shall I make atonement, that you may bless ᴿthe inheritance of the LORD?"   2 Sam. 20:19

4 And the Gibeonites said to him, "We will have no silver or gold from Saul or from his house, nor shall you kill any man in Israel for us." So he said, "Whatever you say, I will do for you."

5 Then they answered the king, "As for the man who consumed us and plotted against us, that we should be destroyed from remaining in any of the territories of Israel,

6 "let seven men of his descendants be delivered ᴿto us, and we will hang them before the LORD ᴿin Gibeah of Saul, ᴿwhom the LORD chose." And the king said, "I will give them."   Num. 25:4 • 1 Sam. 10:26 • 1 Sam. 10:24

7 But the king spared Mephibosheth the son of Jonathan, the son of Saul, because of the LORD's oath that was between them, between David and Jonathan the son of Saul.

8 So the king took Armoni and Mephibosheth, the two sons of Rizpah the daughter of Aiah, whom she bore to Saul, and the five sons of *Michal the daughter of Saul, whom she ᵀbrought up for Adriel the son of Barzillai the Meholathite;   Lit. bore to Adriel

9 and he delivered them into the hands of the Gibeonites, and they hanged them on the hill ᴿbefore the LORD. So they fell, all seven

together, and were put to death in the days of harvest, in the first days, in the beginning of barley harvest.   2 Sam. 6:17

10 Now ᴿRizpah the daughter of Aiah took sackcloth and spread it for herself on the rock, ᴿfrom the beginning of harvest until the late rains poured on them from heaven. And she did not allow the birds of the air to rest on them by day nor the beasts of the field by night.   2 Sam. 3:7; 21:8 • Deut. 21:23

11 And David was told what Rizpah the daughter of Aiah, the concubine of Saul, had done.

12 Then David went and took the bones of Saul, and the bones of Jonathan his son, from the men of Jabesh Gilead who had stolen them from the street of *Beth Shan, where the Philistines had hung them up, after the Philistines had struck down Saul in Gilboa.

13 So he brought up the bones of Saul and the bones of Jonathan his son from there; and they gathered the bones of those who had been hanged.

14 They buried the bones of Saul and Jonathan his son in the country of Benjamin in ᴿZelah, in the tomb of Kish his father. So they performed all that the king commanded. And after that ᴿGod heeded the prayer for the land.   Josh. 18:28 • 2 Sam. 24:25

Philistine Giants Destroyed

15 When the Philistines were at war again with Israel, David and his servants went down and fought against the Philistines; and David grew faint.

16 Then Ishbi-Benob, who was one of the sons of ᵀthe ᴿgiant, the weight of whose bronze spear was three hundred shekels, who was bearing a new sword, thought he could kill David.   Or Rapha • 2 Sam. 21:18–22

17 But Abishai the son of Zeruiah came to his aid, and struck the Philistine and killed him. Then the men of David swore to him, saying, "You shall go out no more with us to battle, lest you quench the lamp of Israel."

18 Now it happened afterward that there was again a battle with the Philistines at Gob. Then Sibbechai the Hushathite killed *Saph, who was one of the sons of the giant.

19 Again there was war at Gob with the Philistines, where Elhanan the son of ᵀJaare-Oregim the Bethlehemite killed the brother of Goliath the Gittite, the shaft of whose spear was like a weaver's beam.   Jair, 1 Chr. 20:5

20 Yet again ᴿthere was war at Gath, where there was a man of great stature, who had six fingers on each hand and six toes on each foot, twenty-four in number; and he also was born to ᵀthe giant.   1 Chr. 20:6 • Or Rapha

21 So when he defied Israel, Jonathan the son of Shimea, David's brother, killed him.

21:12 Beth Shean, Josh. 17:11
21:18 Sippai, 1 Chr. 20:4

22 ᴿThese four were born to ᵀthe giant in Gath, and fell by the hand of David and by the hand of his servants.   1 Chr. 20:8 · Or *Rapha*

Praise for God's Deliverance

22 Then David spoke to the Lᴏʀᴅ the words of this song, on the day when the Lᴏʀᴅ had delivered him from the hand of all his enemies, and from the hand of Saul.
2 And he ᴿsaid: Ps. 18

ᴿ"The Lᴏʀᴅ *is* my rock and my ᴿfortress
  and my deliverer;   Deut. 32:4 · Ps. 91:2
3 The God of my strength, ᴿin whom I
  will trust;   Heb. 2:13
  My ᴿshield and the ᴿhornᵀ of my
  salvation,   Gen. 15:1 · Luke 1:69 · Strength
  My stronghold and my refuge;
  My Savior, You save me from violence.
4 I will call upon the Lᴏʀᴅ, *who is*
  worthy to be praised;
  So shall I be saved from my enemies.

5 "When the waves of death surrounded
  me,
  The floods of ungodliness ᵀmade me
  afraid.   Or *overwhelmed*
6 The sorrows of Sheol surrounded me;
  The snares of death confronted me.
7 In my distress ᴿI called upon the Lᴏʀᴅ,
  And cried out to my God;   Ps. 116:4; 120:1
  He ᴿheard my voice from His temple,
  And my cry *entered* His ears.   Ex. 3:7

8 "Then ᴿthe earth shook and trembled;
  ᴿThe foundations of *heaven quaked and
  were shaken,   Judg. 5:4 · Job 26:11
  Because He was angry.
9 Smoke went up from His nostrils,
  And devouring ᴿfire from His mouth;
  Coals were kindled by it.   Heb. 12:29
10 He ᴿbowed the heavens also, and came
  down   Is. 64:1
  With ᴿdarkness under His feet.   Ex. 20:21
11 He rode upon a cherub, and flew;
  And He *was seen ᴿupon the wings of
  the wind.   Ps. 104:3
12 He made ᴿdarkness canopies around
  Him,   Job 36:29
  Dark waters *and* thick clouds of the
  skies.
13 From the brightness before Him
  Coals of fire were kindled.

14 "The Lᴏʀᴅ thundered from heaven,
  And the Most High uttered His voice.
15 He sent out ᴿarrows and scattered
  them;   Deut. 32:23
  Lightning bolts, and He vanquished
  them.

22:8 So with MT, LXX, Tg.; Syr., Vg. *hills* (cf. Ps. 18:7)
22:11 So with MT, LXX; many Heb. mss., Syr., Vg. *flew*
(cf. Ps. 18:10); Tg. *spoke with power*

16 Then the channels of the sea ᴿwere
  seen,   Nah. 1:4
  The foundations of the world were
  uncovered,
  At the ᴿrebuke of the Lᴏʀᴅ,   Ex. 15:8
  At the blast of the breath of His
  nostrils.

17 "He sent from above, He took me,
  He drew me out of many waters.
18 He delivered me from my strong
  enemy,
  From those who hated me;
  For they were too strong for me.
19 They confronted me in the day of my
  calamity,
  But the Lᴏʀᴅ was my ᴿsupport.   Is. 10:20
20 ᴿHe also brought me out into a broad
  place;   Ps. 31:8; 118:5
  He delivered me because He ᴿdelighted
  in me.   2 Sam. 15:26

21 "The ᴿ Lᴏʀᴅ rewarded me according to
  my righteousness;   1 Sam. 26:23
  According to the ᴿcleanness of my
  hands   Ps. 24:4
  He has recompensed me.
22 For I have ᴿkept the ways of the Lᴏʀᴅ,
  And have not wickedly departed from
  my God.   Ps. 119:3
23 For all His ᴿjudgments *were* before me;
  And *as for* His statutes, I did not depart
  from them.   [Deut. 6:6–9; 7:12]
24 I was also blameless before Him,
  And I kept myself from my iniquity.
25 Therefore the Lᴏʀᴅ has recompensed
  me according to my righteousness,
  According to *my cleanness in His eyes.

26 "With ᴿthe merciful You will show
  Yourself merciful;   [Matt. 5:7]
  With a blameless man You will show
  Yourself blameless;
27 With the pure You will show Yourself
  pure;
  And ᴿwith the devious You will show
  Yourself shrewd.   [Lev. 26:23, 24]
28 You will save the humble people;
  But Your eyes *are* on the haughty, *that*
  You may bring *them* down.

29 "For You *are* my lamp, O Lᴏʀᴅ;
  The Lᴏʀᴅ shall enlighten my darkness.
30 For by You I can run against a troop;
  By my God I can leap over a wall.
31 *As for* God, ᴿHis way *is* perfect; [Matt. 5:48]
  ᴿThe word of the Lᴏʀᴅ *is* proven;   Ps. 12:6
  He *is* a shield to all who trust in Him.

32 "For who *is* God, except the Lᴏʀᴅ?
  And who *is* a rock, except our God?

22:25 LXX, Syr., Vg. *the cleanness of my hands in His
sight* (cf. Ps. 22:24); Tg. *my cleanness before His word*

33 *God *is* my ᴿstrength *and* power,   Ps. 27:1
   And He makes *my way perfect.
34 He makes *my feet like the *feet* of deer,
   And sets me on my high places.
35 He teaches my hands ᵀto make war,
   So that my arms can bend a bow of
   bronze.   Lit. *for the war*

36 "You have also given me the shield of
   Your salvation;
   Your gentleness has made me great.
37 You ᴿenlarged my path under me;
   So my feet did not slip.   Prov. 4:12

38 "I have pursued my enemies and
   destroyed them;
   Neither did I turn back again till they
   were destroyed.
39 And I have destroyed them and
   wounded them,
   So that they could not rise;
   They have fallen ᴿunder my feet.   Mal. 4:3
40 For You have armed me with strength
   for the battle;
   You have ᵀsubdued under me those
   who rose against me.   *caused to bow down*
41 You have also ᵀgiven me the ᴿnecks of
   my enemies,   *given me victory over* · Gen. 49:8
   So that I destroyed those who hated
   me.
42 They looked, but *there was* none to
   save;
   Even ᴿto the Lᴏʀᴅ, but He did not
   answer them.   1 Sam. 28:6
43 Then I beat them as fine ᴿas the dust of
   the earth;   Ps. 18:42
   I trod them like dirt in the streets,
   And I ᵀspread them out.   *scattered*

44 "You have also delivered me from the
   ᵀstrivings of my people;   *contentions*
   You have kept me as the ᴿhead of the
   nations.   Deut. 28:13
   ᴿA people I have not known shall serve
   me.   [Is. 55:5]
45 The foreigners submit to me;
   As soon as they hear, they obey me.
46 The foreigners fade away,
   And *come frightened ᴿfrom their
   hideouts.   [Mic. 7:17]

47 "The Lᴏʀᴅ lives!
   Blessed *be* my Rock!
   Let God be exalted,
   The ᴿRock of my salvation!   Ps. 89:26
48 *It is* God who avenges me,
   And subdues the peoples under me;

49 He delivers me from my enemies.
   You also lift me up above those who
   rise against me;
   You have delivered me from the
   ᴿviolent man.   Ps. 140:1, 4, 11
50 Therefore I will give thanks to You, O
   Lᴏʀᴅ, among the Gentiles,
   And sing praises to Your name.
51 *He is* the tower of salvation to His king,
   And shows mercy to His ᴿanointed,
   To David and ᴿhis descendants
   forevermore."   Ps. 89:20 · 2 Sam. 7:12-16

David's Last Words

23 Now these *are* the last words of David.

   Thus says David the son of Jesse;
   Thus says the man raised up on high,
   The anointed of the God of Jacob,
   And the sweet psalmist of Israel:

2 "The Spirit of the Lᴏʀᴅ spoke by me,
   And His word *was* on my tongue.
3 The God of Israel said,
   ᴿThe Rock of Israel spoke to me:
   'He who rules over men *must be* just,
   Ruling in the fear of God.   [Deut. 32:4]
4 And ᴿhe *shall be* like the light of the
   morning *when* the sun rises,
   A morning without clouds,   Ps. 89:36
   Like the tender grass *springing* out of
   the earth,
   By clear shining after rain.'

5 "Although my house *is* not so with God,
   ᴿYet He has made with me an
   everlasting covenant,   Ps. 89:29
   Ordered in all *things* and secure.
   For *this is* all my salvation and all *my*
   desire;
   Will He not make *it* increase?
6 But *the* sons of rebellion *shall* all *be* as
   thorns thrust away,
   Because they cannot be taken with
   hands.
7 But the man *who* touches them
   Must be ᵀarmed with iron and the shaft
   of a spear,   Lit. *filled*
   And they shall be utterly burned with
   fire in *their* place."

David's Mighty Men

8 These *are* the names of the mighty men
whom David had: *Josheb-Basshebeth the
Tachmonite, chief among *the captains. He
was called Adino the Eznite, because he had
killed eight hundred men at one time.

9 And after him *was* Eleazar the son of
*Dodo, the Ahohite, *one* of the three mighty
men with David when they defied the Philis-

22:33 DSS, LXX, Syr., Vg. *It is God who arms me with
strength* (cf. Ps. 22:24); Tg. *It is God who sustains me
with strength* • So with Qr., LXX, Syr., Tg., Vg. (cf. Ps.
18:32); Kt. *His*
22:34 So with Qr., LXX, Syr., Tg., Vg. (cf. Ps. 18:33); Kt.
His
22:46 So with LXX, Tg., Vg. (cf. Ps. 18:45); MT *gird
themselves*

23:8 Lit. *One Who Sits in the Seat* (1 Chr. 11:11) • So
with MT, Tg.; LXX, Vg. *the three*
23:9 *Dodai,* 1 Chr. 27:4

tines *who* were gathered there for battle, and the men of Israel had retreated.

10 He arose and attacked the Philistines until his hand was weary, and his hand stuck to the sword. The LORD brought about a great victory that day; and the people returned after him only to plunder.

11 And after him *was* ᴿShammah the son of Agee the Hararite. The Philistines had gathered together into a troop where there was a piece of ground full of lentils. So the people fled from the Philistines. 1 Chr. 11:27

12 But he stationed himself in the middle of the field, defended it, and killed the Philistines. So the LORD brought about a great victory.

13 Then three of the thirty chief men went down at harvest time and came to David at the cave of Adullam. And the troop of Philistines encamped in the Valley of Rephaim.

14 David *was* then in ᴿthe stronghold, and the garrison of the Philistines *was* then *in* Bethlehem. 1 Sam. 22:4, 5

15 And David said with longing, "Oh, that someone would give me a drink of the water from the well of Bethlehem, which *is* by the gate!"

16 So the three mighty men broke through the camp of the Philistines, drew water from the well of Bethlehem that *was* by the gate, and took it and brought *it* to David. Nevertheless he would not drink it, but poured it out to the LORD.

17 And he said, "Far be it from me, O LORD, that I should do this! Is *this not* the blood of the men who went in *jeopardy of* their lives?" Therefore he would not drink it. These things were done by the three mighty men.

18 Now ᴿAbishai the brother of Joab, the son of Zeruiah, was chief of *another three. He lifted his spear against three hundred *men*, killed *them*, and won a name among *these* three. 1 Chr. 11:20

19 Was he not the most honored of three? Therefore he became their captain. However, he did not attain to the *first* three.

20 Benaiah *was* the son of Jehoiada, the son of a valiant man from ᴿKabzeel, ᵀwho had done many deeds. ᴿHe had killed two lion-like heroes of Moab. He also had gone down and killed a lion in the midst of a pit on a snowy day. Josh. 15:21 · Lit. *great of acts* · Ex. 15:15

21 And he killed an Egyptian, a spectacular man. The Egyptian *had* a spear in his hand; so he went down to him with a staff, wrested the spear out of the Egyptian's hand, and killed him with his own spear.

22 These *things* Benaiah the son of Jehoiada did, and won a name among three mighty men.

23 He was more honored than the thirty, but he did not attain to the *first* three. And David appointed him over his guard.

24 ᴿAsahel the brother of Joab *was* one of the thirty; Elhanan the son of Dodo of Bethlehem, 2 Sam. 2:18

25 ᴿShammah the Harodite, Elika the Harodite, 1 Chr. 11:27

26 Helez the Paltite, Ira the son of Ikkesh the Tekoite,

27 Abiezer the Anathothite, Mebunnai the Hushathite,

28 Zalmon the Ahohite, Maharai the Netophathite,

29 Heleb the son of Baanah (the Netophathite), Ittai the son of Ribai from Gibeah of the children of Benjamin,

30 Benaiah a Pirathonite, Hiddai from the brooks of ᴿGaash, Judg. 2:9

31 Abi-Albon the Arbathite, Azmaveth the Barhumite,

32 Eliahba the Shaalbonite (of the sons of Jashen), Jonathan,

33 ᴿShammah the ᵀHararite, Ahiam the son of Sharar the Hararite, 2 Sam. 23:11 · Or *Ararite*

34 Eliphelet the son of Ahasbai, the son of the Maachathite, Eliam the son of ᴿAhithophel the Gilonite, 2 Sam. 15:12

35 *Hezrai the Carmelite, Paarai the Arbite,

36 Igal the son of Nathan of ᴿZobah, Bani the Gadite, 2 Sam. 8:3

37 Zelek the Ammonite, Naharai the Beerothite (armorbearer of Joab the son of Zeruiah),

38 Ira the Ithrite, Gareb the Ithrite,

39 *and* Uriah the Hittite: thirty-seven in all.

David's Census of Israel and Judah

24 Again the anger of the LORD was aroused against Israel, and He moved David against them to say, ᴿ"Go, ᵀnumber Israel and Judah." 1 Chr. 27:23, 24 · *take a census of*

2 So the king said to Joab the commander of the army who *was* with him, "Now go throughout all the tribes of Israel, from Dan to Beersheba, and count the people, that I may know the number of the people."

3 And Joab said to the king, "Now may the LORD your God ᴿadd to the people a hundred times more than there are, and may the eyes of my lord the king see *it*. But why does my lord the king desire this thing?" Deut. 1:11

4 Nevertheless the king's word ᵀprevailed against Joab and against the captains of the army. Therefore Joab and the captains of the army went out from the presence of the king to count the people of Israel. *overruled*

5 And they crossed over the Jordan and camped in ᴿAroer, on the right side of the town which *is* in the midst of the ravine of Gad, and toward ᴿJazer. Deut. 2:36 · Num. 32:1, 3

23:18 So with MT, LXX, Vg.; some Heb. mss., Syr. *thirty;* Tg. *the mighty men*

23:35 *Hezro,* 1 Chr. 11:37

6 Then they came to Gilead and to the land of Tahtim Hodshi; they came to ^RDan Jaan and around to ^RSidon;   Judg. 18:29 • Josh. 19:28

7 and they came to the stronghold of ^RTyre and to all the cities of the ^RHivites and the Canaanites. Then they went out to South Judah *as far as* Beersheba.   Josh. 19:29 • Josh. 11:3

8 So when they had gone through all the land, they came to Jerusalem at the end of nine months and twenty days.

9 Then Joab gave the sum of the number of the people to the king. ^RAnd there were in Israel eight hundred thousand valiant men who drew the sword, and the men of Judah were five hundred thousand men.   1 Chr. 21:5

The Judgment on David's Sin

10 And David's heart condemned him after he had numbered the people. So David said to the LORD, ^R"I have sinned greatly in what I have done; but now, I pray, O LORD, take away the iniquity of Your servant, for I have ^Rdone very foolishly."   2 Sam. 12:13 • 1 Sam. 13:13

11 Now when David arose in the morning, the word of the LORD came to the prophet ^RGad, David's ^Rseer, saying,   1 Sam. 22:5 • 1 Sam. 9:9

12 "Go and tell David, 'Thus says the LORD: "I offer you three *things*; choose one of them for yourself, that I may do *it* to you." ' "

13 So Gad came to David and told him; and he said to him, "Shall ^Rseven* years of famine come to you in your land? Or shall you flee three months before your enemies, while they pursue you? Or shall there be three days' plague in your land? Now consider and see what answer I should take back to Him who sent me."   Ezek. 14:21

14 And David said to Gad, "I am in great distress. Please let us fall into the hand of the LORD, for His mercies *are* great; but ^Rdo not let me fall into the hand of man."   [Is. 47:6]

15 So ^Rthe LORD sent a plague upon Israel from the morning till the appointed time. From Dan to Beersheba seventy thousand men of the people died.   1 Chr. 21:14

16 ^RAnd when the *angel stretched out his

24:13 So with MT, Syr., Tg., Vg.; LXX *three* (1 Chr. 21:12)
24:16 Or *Angel* • *Ornan,* 1 Chr. 21:15

hand over Jerusalem to destroy it, ^Rthe LORD relented from the destruction, and said to the angel who was destroying the people, "It is enough; now restrain your hand." And the angel of the LORD was by the threshing floor of *Araunah the Jebusite.   Ex. 12:23 • Gen. 6:6

17 Then David spoke to the LORD when he saw the angel who was striking the people, and said, "Surely ^RI have sinned, and I have done wickedly; but these sheep, what have they done? Let Your hand, I pray, be against me and against my father's house."   Ps. 74:1

The Altar on the Threshing Floor

18 And Gad came that day to David and said to him, ^R"Go up, erect an altar to the LORD on the threshing floor of Araunah the Jebusite."   1 Chr. 21:18

19 So David, according to the word of Gad, went up as the LORD commanded.

20 Now Araunah looked, and saw the king and his servants coming toward him. So Araunah went out and bowed before the king with his face to the ground.

21 Then Araunah said, "Why has my lord the king come to his servant?" And David said, "To buy the threshing floor from you, to build an altar to the LORD, that the plague may be withdrawn from the people."

22 Now Araunah said to David, "Let my lord the king take and offer up whatever *seems* good to him. ^RLook, *here are* oxen for burnt sacrifice, and threshing implements and the yokes of the oxen for wood. 1 Kin. 19:21

23 "All these, O king, Araunah has given to the king." And Araunah said to the king, "May the LORD your God accept you."

24 Then the king said to Araunah, "No, but I will surely buy *it* from you for a price; nor will I offer burnt offerings to the LORD my God with that which costs me nothing." So David bought the threshing floor and the oxen for ^Tfifty shekels of silver. $6,400

25 And David built there an altar to the LORD, and offered burnt offerings and peace offerings. ^RSo the LORD heeded the prayers for the land, and ^Rthe plague was withdrawn from Israel.   2 Sam. 21:14 • 2 Sam. 24:21

THE FIRST BOOK OF THE

Kings

AUTHORSHIP. No one knows for sure who wrote the books of Kings. Like the books of Samuel, 1 and 2 Kings were one book in the original Hebrew, and may have been separated only by an editorial decision: the translators of the Septuagint (the Greek version of the Old Testament) divided the one book into two, possibly because the Greek translation took up more space on a scroll than the Hebrew original.

Jewish tradition, as recorded in the Talmud, credits the writing of 1 and 2 Kings to the prophet Jeremiah. This is certainly plausible: not only do the books of Kings reflect the God-centered viewpoint of a prophet such as Jeremiah, but the conclusion to 2 Kings (2 Kin. 24:18—25:30) is almost identical to that of the book of Jeremiah (Jer. 52). Furthermore, the chapters in 2 Kings that deal with Josiah and his successors do not mention Jeremiah, which they most likely would have, had the author been anyone else. True, the conclusion to 2 Kings (and to the book of Jeremiah) describes Jehoiachin in Babylon so vividly that it seems the writer was actually there, whereas Jeremiah was in Egypt at the time (Jer. 43:1-8). But someone else may well have added this section to complete the story, as has happened elsewhere in the Word of God (Deut. 34:5-12, for example). Such a possibility in no way detracts from the inspired nature of the books of Kings or Jeremiah. So then, as with the rest of the Scriptures, we accept these books as the inerrant product of "holy men of God" who "spoke as they were moved by the Holy Spirit" (2 Pet. 1:21).

CONTEXT. 1 and 2 Kings were evidently completed just after the fall of Jerusalem, at the beginning of the Babylonian captivity. Their purpose seems to be to teach God's people, especially those in captivity, why they were where they were.

Although the books of Kings read like history, they are actually a divine *interpretation* of history. Detailed accounts of the reigns of Israel's monarchs can be found elsewhere, says the author—in such works as "the book of the acts of Solomon" (1 Kin. 11:41), "the book of the chronicles of the kings of Israel" (14:19), and "the book of the chronicles of the kings of Judah" (14:29). (The latter two are not the biblical Chronicles, but some kind of court annals.)

Instead, the books of Kings give *God's perspective* on those reigns. Thus the account of each king's rule begins by judging whether what he did was righteous or evil in God's sight. Royal flaws and failures are unabashedly reported, which a court historian would likely have suppressed. And some historically significant kings such as Omri are considered very briefly, while other personages such as Elijah (and Elisha and Hezekiah in 2 Kings) receive extensive treatment because of their importance in God's estimation.

Such emphasis on God's relationship to human history—especially that of the southern kingdom, Judah—suggests that the author is teaching Judahites that their captivity in Babylon is merely the last stage in a decline that came about because of disobedience to God, and that they should therefore commit themselves to obeying Him, honoring His holiness and righteousness.

HOW 1 KINGS FITS INTO THE BIBLE. The book picks up the story of the kingdom of Israel right where 2 Samuel leaves off. The books of Samuel show how the twelve tribes became a unified kingdom and prospered under the leadership of David. 1 and 2 Kings describe the decline, division, and eventual captivity of David's kingdom. Following them, the books of Chronicles recount the same history as Samuel and Kings, from the viewpoint of a post-captivity historian.

1 Kings shows how the decline began, with the rise and fall of Solomon and the fracture of the united kingdom into a northern ("Israel") and a southern kingdom ("Judah").

For a while Solomon, like his father David before him, sought to be a man after God's own heart, and so brought his kingdom to prominence in the world. God blessed him with unsurpassed wisdom which brought him great fame, and it was he who built God's temple in Jerusalem. On the surface his reign was one of dazzling splendor, as Israel became a world power and Solomon's achievements became legend.

Beneath the polished surface, however, corruption was steadily growing. Carried away with his success, Solomon turned away from God's law. He sold cities in Galilee to a foreign ruler, he enslaved the native Canaanites instead of exterminating them, he built up his horse troops, he used Israel's international prominence to increase its wealth, he took foreign wives aplenty, and finally he even worshiped idols outright—all of which Moses had strictly forbidden (Lev. 25:23; Deut. 7:2-5; 17:16, 17). Thus Solomon directly disobeyed the Word of God, and thereby brought

disaster on his nation. After his death the disaster struck: his son's heavy-handed rule tore the kingdom asunder.

A succession of kings followed in the northern and southern kingdoms, and with rare exceptions they also defied God. The final result of this downward slide (described in 2 Kings) was the seizure of the northern kingdom by Assyria and the southern by Babylon. All this could have been averted had the rulers determined to obey the Word of God.

How 1 Kings Fits Together. 1 Kings separates naturally into two parts, before and after Solomon's death. Chapters 1—11 tell the story of *The Splendid Kingdom,* relating how Solomon becomes king (1—2), builds the kingdom (3—8), abandons the law and dies (9—11). Chapters 12—22 chronicle *The Sundered Kingdom,* relating the division of the kingdom into Israel under Jeroboam in the north and Judah under Rehoboam in the south (12—14), the reigns of Abijam and Asa in Judah and Nadab through Ahab in Israel (15—16), the ministry of Elijah in Israel (17—19), and the reigns of Ahab in Israel, Jehoshaphat in Judah, and Amaziah in Israel (20—22).

Summary Statement. After a promising beginning as God's chosen ruler, Solomon turns from Him, and the kingdom is consequently split into two kingdoms that are blessed or judged according to whether their kings are righteous or wicked in God's sight.

Key Verse: 11:11—"Therefore the Lord said to Solomon, 'Because you have done this, and have not kept My covenant and My statutes, which I have commanded you, I will surely tear the kingdom away from you and give it to your servant.' "

The Bible declares that the fate of a nation depends on the godliness of its ruler. If disobedience is not checked promptly, it continues into further sin. Sometimes that sin brings judgment from God, but sometimes the increase of sin is *itself* judgment from God (Rom. 1:21-32). Reading 1 Kings should cause us to ponder the state of our own country in the light of the Word of God. First, we should select our leaders wisely, because theirs is an awesome responsibility: God holds them accountable for the future of their country. Second, when we consider the sin rampant around us, we should ask ourselves: How long God will permit such sin to continue—or are we *already* witnessing His judgment? Either way, our nation will ultimately survive only if its people turn to God and receive His righteousness through our Lord Jesus Christ.

—A.R.

Adonijah Presumes to Be King

NOW King David was old, ᵀadvanced in years; and they put covers on him, but he could not get warm.   70 years

2 Therefore his servants said to him, "Let a young woman, a virgin, be sought for our lord the king, and let her ᵀstand before the king, and let her care for him; and let her lie in your bosom, that our lord the king may be warm."   Or *serve*

3 So they sought for a lovely young woman throughout all the territory of Israel, and found ᴿAbishag the ᴿShunammite, and brought her to the king.   1 Kin. 2:17 • Josh. 19:18

4 The young woman *was* very lovely; and she cared for the king, and served him; but the king did not know her.

5 Then Adonijah the son of Haggith exalted himself, saying, "I will be king"; and he prepared for himself chariots and horsemen, and fifty men to run before him.

6 (And his father had not rebuked him at any time by saying, "Why have you done

so?" He *was* also very good-looking. *His* mother had borne him after Absalom.)

7 Then he conferred with Joab the son of Zeruiah and with Abiathar the priest, and they followed and helped Adonijah.

8 But Zadok the priest, Benaiah the son of Jehoiada, Nathan the prophet, ᴿShimei, Rei, and the mighty men who *belonged* to David were not with Adonijah.   1 Kin. 4:18

9 And Adonijah sacrificed sheep and oxen and fattened cattle by the stone of ᵀZoheleth, which *is* by En Rogel; he also invited all his brothers, the king's sons, and all the men of Judah, the king's servants.   Lit. *Serpent*

10 But he did not invite Nathan the prophet, Benaiah, the mighty men, or ᴿSolomon his brother.   2 Sam. 12:24

11 So Nathan spoke to Bathsheba the mother of Solomon, saying, "Have you not heard that Adonijah the son of ᴿHaggith has become king, and David our lord does not know *it*?   2 Sam. 3:4

12 "Come, please, let me now give you

advice, that you may save your own life and the life of your son Solomon.

13 "Go immediately to King David and say to him, 'Did you not, my lord, O king, swear to your maidservant, saying, R"Assuredly your son Solomon shall reign after me, and he shall sit on my throne"? Why then has Adonijah become king?'   1 Chr. 22:9-13

14 "Then, while you are still talking there with the king, I also will come in after you and confirm your words."

15 So Bathsheba went into the chamber to the king. (Now the king was very old, and Abishag the Shunammite was serving the king.)

16 And Bathsheba bowed and did homage to the king. Then the king said, "What is your wish?"

17 Then she said to him, "My lord, Ryou swore by the LORD your God to your maidservant, saying, 'Assuredly Solomon your son shall reign after me, and he shall sit on my throne.'   1 Kin. 1:13, 30

18 "So now, look! Adonijah has become king; and now, my lord the king, you do not know about it.

19 "He has sacrificed oxen and fattened cattle and sheep in abundance, and has invited all the sons of the king, Abiathar the priest, and Joab the commander of the army; but Solomon your servant he has not invited.

20 "And as for you, my lord, O king, the eyes of all Israel are on you, that you should tell them who will sit on the throne of my lord the king after him."

21 "Otherwise it will happen, when my lord the king rests with his fathers, that I and my son Solomon will be counted as offenders."

22 And just then, while she was still talking with the king, Nathan the prophet also came in.

23 So they told the king, saying, "Here is Nathan the prophet." And when he came in before the king, he bowed down before the king with his face to the ground.

24 And Nathan said, "My lord, O king, have you said, 'Adonijah shall reign after me, and he shall sit on my throne'?

25 "For he has gone down today, and has sacrificed oxen and fattened cattle and sheep in abundance, and has invited all the king's sons, and the commanders of the army, and Abiathar the priest; and look! They are eating and drinking before him; and they say, R"Long live King Adonijah!'   1 Sam. 10:24

26 "But he has not invited me—me your servant—nor Zadok the priest, nor Benaiah the son of Jehoiada, nor your servant Solomon.

27 "Has this thing been done by my lord the king, and you have not told your servant who should sit on the throne of my lord the king after him?"

David Proclaims Solomon King

28 Then King David answered and said, "Call Bathsheba to me." So she came into the king's presence and stood before the king.

29 And the king took an oath and said, R"As the LORD lives, who has redeemed my life from every distress,   2 Sam. 4:9; 12:5

30 R"just as I swore to you by the LORD God of Israel, saying, 'Assuredly Solomon your son shall be king after me, and he shall sit on my throne in my place,' so I certainly will do this day."   1 Kin. 1:13, 17

31 Then Bathsheba bowed with her face to the earth, and paid homage to the king, and said, "Let my lord King David live forever!"

32 And King David said, "Call to me Zadok the priest, Nathan the prophet, and Benaiah the son of Jehoiada." So they came before the king.

33 The king also said to them, "Take with you the servants of your lord, and have Solomon my son ride on my own mule, and take him down to TGihon.   Spring east of Jerusalem

34 "There let Zadok the priest and Nathan the prophet anoint him king over Israel; and Rblow the horn, and say, T'Long live King Solomon!'   2 Sam. 15:10 • Lit. Let King Solomon live

35 "Then you shall come up after him, and he shall come and sit on my throne; and he shall be king in my place. For I have appointed him to be ruler over Israel and Judah."

36 Benaiah the son of Jehoiada answered the king and said, "Amen! May the LORD God of my lord the king say so too.

37 R"As the LORD has been with my lord the king, even so may He be with Solomon, and Rmake his throne greater than the throne of my lord King David."   1 Sam. 20:13 • 1 Kin. 1:47

38 So Zadok the priest, Nathan the prophet, RBenaiah the son of Jehoiada, and the RCherethites, and the Pelethites went down and had Solomon ride on King David's mule, and took him to Gihon.   2 Sam. 8:18; 23:20-23 • 2 Sam. 20:7

39 Then Zadok the priest took a horn of Roil from the tabernacle and anointed Solomon. And they blew the horn, and all the people said, "Long live King Solomon!"   Ps. 89:20

40 And all the people went up after him; and the people played the flutes and rejoiced with great joy, so that the earth seemed to split with their sound.

41 Now Adonijah and all the guests who were with him heard it as they finished eating. And when Joab heard the sound of the horn, he said, "Why is the city in such a noisy uproar?"

42 While he was still speaking, there came Jonathan, the son of Abiathar the priest. And Adonijah said to him, "Come in, for you are a prominent man, and bring good news."

43 Then Jonathan answered and said to

Adonijah, "No! Our lord King David has made Solomon king.

44 "The king has sent with him Zadok the priest, Nathan the prophet, Benaiah the son of Jehoiada, the Cherethites, and the Pelethites; and they have made him ride on the king's mule.

45 "So Zadok the priest and Nathan the prophet have anointed him king at Gihon; and they have gone up from there rejoicing, so that the city is in an uproar. This is the noise that you have heard.

46 "Also Solomon ᴿsits on the throne of the kingdom.   1 Chr. 29:23

47 "And moreover the king's servants have gone to bless our lord King David, saying, 'May God make the name of Solomon better than your name, and may He make his throne greater than your throne.' ᴿThen the king bowed himself on the bed.   Gen. 47:31

48 "Also the king said thus, 'Blessed be the LORD God of Israel, who has ᴿgiven one to sit on my throne this day, while my eyes see ᴿit!' "   1 Kin. 3:6 • 2 Sam. 7:12

49 So all the guests who were with Adonijah were afraid, and arose, and each one went his way.

50 Now Adonijah was afraid of Solomon; so he arose, and went and ᴿtook hold of the horns of the altar.   1 Kin. 2:28

51 And it was told Solomon, saying, "Indeed Adonijah is afraid of King Solomon; for look, he has taken hold of the horns of the altar, saying, 'Let King Solomon swear to me today that he will not put his servant to death with the sword.' "

52 Then Solomon said, "If he proves himself a worthy man, ᴿnot one hair of him shall fall to the earth; but if wickedness is found in him, he shall die."   1 Sam. 14:45

53 So King Solomon sent them to bring him down from the altar. And he came and fell down before King Solomon; and Solomon said to him, "Go to your house."

David's Instructions to Solomon

2 Now ᴿthe days of David drew near that he should die, and he ᵀcharged Solomon his son, saying: Gen. 47:29 • commanded

2 "I go the way of all the earth; be strong, therefore, and prove yourself a man.

3 "And keep the charge of the LORD your God: to walk in His ways, to keep His statutes, His commandments, His judgments, and His testimonies, as it is written in the Law of Moses, that you may ᴿprosper in all that you do and wherever you turn;   [Deut. 29:9]

4 "that the LORD may fulfill His word which He spoke concerning me, saying, 'If your sons take heed to their way, to walk before Me in truth with all their heart and

with all their soul,' He said, 'you shall not lack a man on the throne of Israel.'

5 "Moreover you know also what Joab the son of Zeruiah did to me, and what he did to the two commanders of the armies of Israel, to Abner the son of Ner and Amasa the son of Jether, whom he killed. And he shed the blood of war in peacetime, and put the blood of war on his belt that was around his waist, and on his sandals that were on his feet.

6 "Therefore do ᴿaccording to your wisdom, and do not let his gray hair go down to the grave in peace.   1 Kin. 2:9

7 "But show kindness to the sons of Barzillai the Gileadite, and let them be among those who ᴿeat at your table, for so ᴿthey came to me when I fled from Absalom your brother.   2 Sam. 9:7, 10; 19:28 • 2 Sam. 17:17–29

8 "And see, you have with you Shimei the son of Gera, a Benjamite from Bahurim, who cursed me with a malicious curse in the day when I went to Mahanaim. But he came down to meet me at the Jordan, and ᴿI swore to him by the LORD, saying, 'I will not put you to death with the sword.'   2 Sam. 19:23

9 "Now therefore, ᴿdo not hold him guiltless, for you are a wise man and know what you ought to do to him; but bring his gray hair down to the grave with blood."   Ex. 20:7

Death of David

10 So David rested with his fathers, and was buried in ᴿthe City of David.   2 Sam. 5:7

11 The period that David ᴿreigned over Israel was forty years; seven years he reigned in Hebron, and in Jerusalem he reigned thirty-three years.   2 Sam. 5:4, 5

12 ᴿThen Solomon sat on the throne of his father David; and his kingdom was ᴿfirmly established.   1 Chr. 29:23 • 2 Chr. 1:1

Solomon Executes Adonijah

13 Now Adonijah the son of Haggith came to Bathsheba the mother of Solomon. So she said, ᴿ"Do you come peaceably?" And he said, "Peaceably."   1 Sam. 16:4, 5

14 Moreover he said, "I have something to say to you." And she said, "Say it."

15 Then he said, "You know that the kingdom was ᴿmine, and all Israel had set their expectations on me, that I should reign. However, the kingdom has been turned over, and has become my brother's; for ᴿit was his from the LORD.   1 Kin. 1:11, 18 • [Dan. 2:21]

16 "Now I ask one petition of you; do not deny me." And she said to him, "Say it."

17 Then he said, "Please speak to King Solomon, for he will not refuse you, that he may give me ᴿAbishag the Shunammite as wife."   1 Kin. 1:3, 4

18 So Bathsheba said, "Very well, I will speak for you to the king."

19 Bathsheba therefore went to King Solo-

mon, to speak to him for Adonijah. And the king rose up to meet her and ^Rbowed down to her, and sat down on his throne and had a throne set for the king's mother; ^Rso she sat at his right hand.   [Ex. 20:12] • Ps. 45:9

20 Then she said, "I desire one small petition of you; do not ^Trefuse me." And the king said to her, "Ask it, my mother, for I will not refuse you."   Lit. turn away the face

21 So she said, "Let Abishag the Shunammite be given to Adonijah your brother as wife."

22 And King Solomon answered and said to his mother, "Now why do you ask Abishag the Shunammite for Adonijah? Ask for him the kingdom also—for he is my older brother—for him, and for Abiathar the priest, and for Joab the son of Zeruiah."

23 Then King Solomon swore by the LORD, saying, ^R"May God do so to me, and more also, if Adonijah has not spoken this word against his own life!   Ruth 1:17

24 "Now therefore, as the LORD lives, who has confirmed me and set me on the throne of David my father, and who has established a *house for me, as He ^Rpromised, Adonijah shall be put to death today!"   2 Sam. 7:11, 13

25 So King Solomon sent by the hand of ^RBenaiah the son of Jehoiada; and he struck him down, and he died.   2 Sam. 8:18

Abiathar Exiled, Joab Executed

26 And to Abiathar the priest the king said, "Go to Anathoth, to your own fields, for you are deserving of death; but I will not put you to death at this time, because you carried the ark of the Lord GOD before my father David, and because you were afflicted every time my father was afflicted."

27 So Solomon removed Abiathar from being priest to the LORD, that he might fulfill the word of the LORD which He spoke concerning the house of Eli at Shiloh.

28 Then news came to Joab, for Joab ^Rhad defected to Adonijah, though he had not defected to Absalom. So Joab fled to the tabernacle of the LORD, and ^Rtook hold of the horns of the altar.   1 Kin. 1:7 • 1 Kin. 1:50

29 And King Solomon was told, "Joab has fled to the tabernacle of the LORD; there he is, by the altar." Then Solomon sent Benaiah the son of Jehoiada, saying, "Go, ^Rstrike him down."   1 Kin. 2:5, 6

30 So Benaiah went to the tabernacle of the LORD, and said to him, "Thus says the king, ^R'Come out!' " And he said, "No, but I will die here." And Benaiah brought back word to the king, saying, "Thus said Joab, and thus he answered me."   [Ex. 21:14]

31 Then the king said to him, ^R"Do as he has said, and strike him down and bury him,

2:24 Royal dynasty

^Rthat you may take away from me and from the house of my father the innocent blood which Joab shed.   [Ex. 21:14] • [Num. 35:33]

32 "So the LORD will return his ^Tblood on his head, because he struck down two men more righteous and better than he, and killed them with the sword—Abner the son of Ner, the commander of the army of Israel, and Amasa the son of Jether, the commander of the army of Judah—though my father David did not know it.   Or bloodshed

33 "Their blood shall therefore return upon the head of Joab and upon the head of his descendants forever. But upon David and his descendants, upon his house and his throne, there shall be peace forever from the LORD."

34 So Benaiah the son of Jehoiada went up and struck and killed him; and he was buried in his own house in the wilderness.

35 The king put Benaiah the son of Jehoiada in his place over the army, and the king put ^RZadok the priest in the place of ^RAbiathar.   1 Sam. 2:35 • 1 Kin. 2:27

Shimei Executed

36 Then the king sent and called for ^RShimei, and said to him, "Build yourself a house in Jerusalem and dwell there, and do not go out from there anywhere.   1 Kin. 2:8

37 "For it shall be, on the day you go out and cross the Brook Kidron, know for certain you shall surely die; ^Ryour ^Tblood shall be on your own head."   Josh. 2:19 • Or bloodshed

38 And Shimei said to the king, "The saying is good. As my lord the king has said, so your servant will do." So Shimei dwelt in Jerusalem many days.

39 Now it happened at the end of three years, that two slaves of Shimei ran away to ^RAchish the son of Maachah, king of Gath. And they told Shimei, saying, "Look, your slaves are in Gath!"   1 Sam. 27:2

40 So Shimei arose, saddled his donkey, and went to Achish at Gath to seek his slaves. And Shimei went and brought his slaves from Gath.

41 And Solomon was told that Shimei had gone from Jerusalem to Gath and had come back.

42 Then the king sent and called for Shimei, and said to him, "Did I not make you swear by the LORD, and warn you, saying, 'Know for certain that on the day you go out and travel anywhere, you shall surely die'? And you said to me, 'The word I have heard is good.'

43 "Why then have you not kept the oath of the LORD and the commandment that I gave you?"

44 The king said moreover to Shimei, "You know, as your heart acknowledges, all the wickedness that you did to my father David; therefore the LORD will ^Rreturn your wickedness on your own head.   1 Sam. 25:39

45 "But King Solomon *shall be* blessed, and ^Rthe throne of David shall be established before the LORD forever."   [Prov. 25:5]

46 So the king commanded Benaiah the son of Jehoiada; and he went out and struck him down, and he died. Thus the ^Rkingdom was established in the hand of Solomon.   2 Chr. 1:1

Solomon Requests Wisdom

3 Now Solomon made a treaty with Pharaoh king of Egypt, and married Pharaoh's daughter; then he brought her to the City of David until he had finished building his own house, and ^Rthe house of the LORD, and the wall all around Jerusalem.   1 Kin. 6

2 Meanwhile the people sacrificed at the high places, because there was no house built for the name of the LORD until those days.

3 And Solomon ^Rloved the LORD, ^Rwalking in the statutes of his father David, except that he sacrificed and burned incense at the high places.   [Rom. 8:28] • [1 Kin. 3:6, 14]

4 Now ^Rthe king went to Gibeon to sacrifice there, ^Rfor that *was* the great high place: Solomon offered a thousand burnt offerings on that altar.   2 Chr. 1:3 • 1 Chr. 16:39; 21:29

5 At Gibeon the LORD appeared to Solomon ^Rin a dream by night; and God said, "Ask! What shall I give you?"   Num. 12:6

6 And Solomon said: "You have shown great mercy to Your servant David my father, because he walked before You in truth, in righteousness, and in uprightness of heart with You; You have continued this great kindness for him, and You have given him a son to sit on his throne, as *it is* this day.

7 "Now, O LORD my God, You have made Your servant king instead of my father David, but I *am* a ^Rlittle child; I do not know how ^Rto go out or come in.   Jer. 1:6, 7 • Num. 27:17

8 "And Your servant *is* in the midst of Your people whom You ^Rhave chosen, a great people, ^Rtoo numerous to be numbered or counted.   [Deut. 7:6] • Gen. 13:6; 15:5; 22:17

9 "Therefore give to Your servant an ^Tunderstanding heart ^Rto judge Your people, that I may ^Rdiscern between good and evil. For who is able to judge this great people of Yours?"   Lit. *hearing* • Ps. 72:1, 2 • [Heb. 5:14]

10 The speech pleased the LORD, that Solomon had asked this thing.

11 Then God said to him: "Because you have asked this thing, and have ^Rnot asked long life for yourself, nor have asked riches for yourself, nor have asked the life of your enemies, but have asked for yourself understanding to discern justice,   [James 4:3]

12 ^R"behold, I have done according to your words; see, I have given you a wise and understanding heart, so that there has not been anyone like you before you, nor shall any like you arise after you.   [1 John 5:14, 15]

13 "And I have also ^Rgiven you what you have not asked: both riches and honor, so that there shall not be anyone like you among the kings all your days.   [Matt. 6:33]

14 "So ^Rif you walk in My ways, to keep My statutes and My commandments, as your father David walked, then I will ^Rlengthen^T your days."   [1 Kin. 6:12] • Ps. 91:16 • *prolong*

15 Then Solomon ^Rawoke; and indeed it had been a dream. And he came to Jerusalem and stood before the ark of the covenant of the LORD, offered up burnt offerings, offered peace offerings, and ^Rmade a feast for all his servants.   Gen. 41:7 • 1 Kin. 8:65

Solomon's Wise Judgment

16 Now two women *who were* harlots came to the king, and ^Rstood before him.   Num. 27:2

17 And one woman said, "O my lord, this woman and I dwell in the same house; and I gave birth while she *was* in the house.

18 "Then it happened, the third day after I had given birth, that this woman also gave birth. And we *were* together; ^Tno one *was* with us in the house, except the two of us in the house.   Lit. *no stranger*

19 "And this woman's son died in the night, because she lay on him.

20 "So she arose in the middle of the night and took my son from my side, while your maidservant slept, and laid him in her bosom, and laid her dead child in my bosom.

21 "And when I rose in the morning to nurse my son, there he was, dead. But when I had examined him in the morning, indeed, he was not my son whom I had borne."

22 Then the other woman said, "No! But the living one *is* my son, and the dead one *is* your son." And the first woman said, "No! But the dead one *is* your son, and the living one *is* my son." Thus they spoke before the king.

23 And the king said, "The one says, 'This *is* my son, who lives, and your son *is* the dead one'; and the other says, 'No! But your son *is* the dead one, and my son *is* the living one.'"

24 Then the king said, "Bring me a sword." So they brought a sword before the king.

25 And the king said, "Divide the living child in two, and give half to one, and half to the other."

26 Then the woman whose son *was* living spoke to the king, for she yearned with compassion for her son; and she said, "O my lord, give her the living child, and by no means kill him!" But the other said, "Let him be neither mine nor yours, *but* divide *him*."

27 So the king answered and said, "Give the first woman the living child, and by no means kill him; she *is* his mother."

28 And all Israel heard of the judgment which the king had rendered; and they feared the king, for they saw that the wisdom of God *was* in him to administer justice.

Solomon's Administration

4 So King Solomon was king over all Israel. 2 And these *were* his officials: Azariah the son of Zadok, the priest;

3 Elihoreph and Ahijah, the sons of Shisha, ᵀscribes; ᴿJehoshaphat the son of Ahilud, the recorder;   *secretaries* • 2 Sam. 8:16; 20:24

4 Benaiah the son of Jehoiada, over the army; Zadok and Abiathar, the priests;

5 Azariah the son of Nathan, over the officers; Zabud the son of Nathan, a priest *and* ᴿthe king's friend;   2 Sam. 15:37; 16:16

6 Ahishar, over the household; and Adoniram the son of Abda, over the labor force.

7 And Solomon had twelve governors over all Israel, who provided food for the king and his household; each one made provision for one month of the year.

8 These *are* their names: ᵀBen-Hur, in the mountains of Ephraim;   Lit. *Son of Hur*

9 ᵀBen-Deker, in Makaz, Shaalbim, Beth Shemesh, and Elon Beth Hanan; Lit. *Son of Deker*

10 *Ben-Hesed, in Arubboth; to him *belonged* Sochoh and all the land of Hepher;

11 ᵀBen-Abinadab, *in* all the regions of Dor; he had Taphath the daughter of Solomon as wife;   Lit. *Son of Abinadab*

12 Baana the son of Ahilud, *in* Taanach, Megiddo, and all Beth Shean, which *is* beside Zaretan below Jezreel, from Beth Shean to Abel Meholah, as far as the other side of Jokneam;

13 *Ben-Geber, in Ramoth Gilead; to him *belonged* the towns of Jair the son of Manasseh, in Gilead; to him *also belonged* the region of Argob in Bashan—sixty large cities with walls and bronze gate-bars;

14 Ahinadab the son of Iddo, *in* Mahanaim;

15 Ahimaaz, in Naphtali; he also took Basemath the daughter of Solomon as wife;

16 Baanah the son of ᴿHushai, in Asher and Aloth;   1 Chr. 27:33

17 Jehoshaphat the son of Paruah, in Issachar;

18 Shimei the son of Elah, in Benjamin;

19 Geber the son of Uri, in the land of Gilead, *in* the country of Sihon king of the Amorites, and of Og king of Bashan. *He was* the only governor who *was* in the land.

Prosperity and Wisdom of Solomon's Reign

20 Judah and Israel *were* as numerous ᴿas the sand by the sea in multitude, ᴿeating and drinking and rejoicing.   Gen. 22:17; 32:12 • Mic. 4:4

21 So ᴿSolomon reigned over all kingdoms from ᴿtheᵀ River *to* the land of the Philistines, as far as the border of Egypt. ᴿThey brought tribute and served Solomon all the days of his life.   Ps. 72:8 • Gen. 15:18 • The Euphrates • Ps. 68:29

22 ᴿNow Solomon's ᵀprovision for one day was ᵀthirty kors of fine flour, sixty kors of meal,   Neh. 5:18 • Lit. *bread* • 195.72 bu.

23 ten fatted oxen, twenty oxen from the pastures, and one hundred sheep, besides deer, gazelles, roebucks, and fatted fowl.

24 For he had dominion over all *the* region on this side of ᵀthe River from Tiphsah even to Gaza, namely over ᴿall the kings on this side of the River; and he had peace on every side all around him.   The Euphrates • Ps. 72:11

25 And Judah and Israel ᴿdweltᵀ safely, ᴿeach man under his vine and his fig tree, from Dan as far as Beersheba, all the days of Solomon.   [Jer. 23:6] • *lived in safety* • [Mic. 4:4]

26 ᴿSolomon had *forty thousand stalls of ᴿhorses for his chariots, and twelve thousand horsemen.   1 Kin. 10:26 • [Deut. 17:16]

27 And ᴿthese governors, each man in his month, provided food for King Solomon and for all who came to King Solomon's table. There was no lack in their supply.   1 Kin. 4:7

28 They also brought barley and straw to the proper place, for the horses and steeds, each man according to his charge.

29 And God gave Solomon wisdom and exceedingly great understanding, and largeness of heart like the sand on the seashore.

30 Thus Solomon's wisdom excelled the wisdom of all the men ᴿof the East and all ᴿthe wisdom of Egypt.   Gen. 25:6 • Is. 19:11, 12

31 For he was wiser than all men—than Ethan the Ezrahite, ᴿand Heman, Chalcol, and Darda, the sons of Mahol; and his fame was in all the surrounding nations.   1 Chr. 2:6

32 He spoke three thousand proverbs, and his songs were one thousand and five.

33 Also he spoke of trees, from the cedar tree of Lebanon even to the hyssop that springs out of the wall; he spoke also of animals, of birds, of creeping things, and of fish.

34 And men of all nations, from all the kings of the earth who had heard of his wisdom, came to hear the wisdom of Solomon.

Solomon Prepares to Build the Temple

5 Now Hiram king of Tyre sent his servants to Solomon, because he heard that they had anointed him king in place of his father, for Hiram had always loved David.

2 Then Solomon sent to Hiram, saying:

3 You know how my father David could not build a house for the name of the LORD his God because of the wars which were fought against him on

4:10 Lit. *Son of Hesed*
4:13 Lit. *Son of Geber*

4:26 So with MT, most other authorities; some LXX mss. *four thousand* (cf. 2 Chr. 9:25).

every side, until the LORD put *his foes
under the soles of his feet.
4 But now the LORD my God has given
me Trest on every side; there is neither
adversary nor evil occurrence.   peace
5 And behold, I propose to build a house
for the name of the LORD my God, as
the LORD spoke to my father David,
saying, "Your son, whom I will set on
your throne in your place, he shall build
the house for My name."
6 Now therefore, command that they cut
down Rcedars for me from Lebanon;
and my servants will be with your
servants, and I will pay you wages for
your servants according to whatever
you say. For you know there is none
among us who has skill to cut timber
like the Sidonians.   2 Chr. 2:8, 10

7 So it was, when Hiram heard the words
of Solomon, that he rejoiced greatly and said,

Blessed be the LORD this day, for He
has given David a wise son over this
great people!

8 Then Hiram sent to Solomon, saying:

I have considered the message which
you sent me, and I will do all you
desire concerning the cedar and cypress
logs.
9 My servants shall bring them down
from Lebanon to the sea; I will float
them in rafts by sea to the place you
indicate to me, and will have them
broken apart there; then you can take
them away. And you shall fulfill my
desire by giving food for my household.

10 Then Hiram gave Solomon cedar and
cypress logs according to all his desire.
11 And Solomon gave Hiram twenty thousand kors of wheat as food for his household,
and *twenty kors of pressed oil. Thus Solomon gave to Hiram year by year.
12 So the LORD gave Solomon wisdom, Ras
He had promised him; and there was peace
between Hiram and Solomon, and the two of
them made a treaty together.   1 Kin. 3:12
13 Then King Solomon raised up a labor
force out of all Israel; and the labor force was
thirty thousand men.
14 And he sent them to Lebanon, ten thousand a month in shifts: they were one month
in Lebanon and two months at home; Adoniram was in charge of the labor force.
15 RSolomon had seventy thousand who
carried burdens, and eighty thousand who
quarried stone in the mountains,   2 Chr. 2:17, 18

5:3 Lit. them
5:11 So with MT, Tg., Vg.; LXX, [Syr.] twenty thousand
kors

16 besides three thousand *three hundred
from the Rchiefs of Solomon's deputies, who
supervised the people who labored in the
work.   1 Kin. 9:23
17 And the king commanded them to
quarry large stones, costly stones, and hewn
stones, to lay the foundation of the *temple.
18 So Solomon's builders, Hiram's builders,
and the Gebalites quarried them; and they
prepared timber and stones to build the
Ttemple.   Lit. house

Solomon Builds the Temple

6 And it came to pass in the four hundred
and *eightieth year after the children of
Israel had come out of the land of Egypt, in
the fourth year of Solomon's reign over
Israel, in the month of TZiv, which is the
second month, that he began to build the
house of the LORD.   Or Ayyar, April or May
2 Now the house which King Solomon
built for the LORD, its length was sixty cubits,
its width twenty, and its height thirty cubits.
3 The vestibule in front of the Rsanctuary*
of the house was Ttwenty cubits long across
the width of the house, and the width of *the
vestibule extended Tten cubits from the front
of the house.   Ex. 26:33; Ezek. 41:1 · 30 ft. · 15 ft.
4 And he made for the house Rwindows
with beveled frames.   Ezek. 40:16; 41:16
5 Against the wall of the Ttemple he built
Rchambers all around, against the walls of the
temple, all around the sanctuary and the
*inner sanctuary. Thus he made side cham-
bers all around it.   Lit. house · Ezek. 41:6
6 The lowest chamber was five cubits
wide, the middle was six cubits wide, and the
third was seven cubits wide; for he made
narrow ledges around the outside of the
temple, so that the support beams would not
be fastened into the walls of the temple.
7 And the temple, when it was being built,
was built with stone finished at the quarry, so
that no hammer or chisel or any iron tool was
heard in the temple while it was being built.
8 The doorway for the *middle story was
on the right side of the temple. They went up
by stairs to the middle story, and from the
middle to the third.
9 RSo he built the Ttemple and finished it,
and he paneled the temple with beams and
boards of cedar.   1 Kin. 6:14, 38 · Lit. house
10 And he built side chambers against the
entire temple, each Tfive cubits high; they

5:16 So with MT, Tg., Vg.; LXX six hundred
5:17 Lit. house
6:1 So with MT, Tg., Vg.; LXX fortieth.
6:3 Heb. heykal; here the main room of the temple;
elsewhere called the Holy Place, Ex. 26:33; Ezek. 41:1 •
Lit. it
6:5 Heb. debir; here the inner room of the temple;
elsewhere called the Most Holy Place, v. 16
6:8 So with MT, Vg.; LXX upper story; Tg. ground story.

were attached to the temple with cedar beams.   7.5 ft.

11 Then the word of the LORD came to Solomon, saying:

12 "Concerning this ᵀtemple which you are building, if you walk in My statutes, execute My judgments, keep all My commandments, and walk in them, then I will perform My ᵀword with you, ᴿwhich I spoke to your father David.   Lit. *house* · *promise* · [2 Sam. 7:13]

13 "And ᴿI will dwell among the children of Israel, and will not ᴿforsake My people Israel."   Ex. 25:8 · [Deut. 31:6]

14 So Solomon built the temple and finished it.

15 And he built the inside walls of the temple with cedar boards; from the floor of the temple to the ceiling he paneled the inside with wood; and he covered the floor of the temple with planks of cypress.

16 Then he built the twenty-cubit room at the rear of the temple, from floor to ceiling, with cedar boards; he built *it* inside as the inner sanctuary, as the Most Holy *Place.*

17 And in front of it the temple sanctuary was ᵀforty cubits *long.*   60 ft.

18 The inside of the temple was cedar, carved with ornamental buds and open flowers. All *was* cedar; there was no stone *to be* seen.

19 And he prepared the ᵀinner sanctuary inside the temple, to set the ark of the covenant of the LORD there.   The Most Holy Place

20 The inner sanctuary *was* ᵀtwenty cubits long, twenty cubits wide, and twenty cubits high. He overlaid it with pure gold, and overlaid the altar of cedar.   30 ft.

21 So Solomon overlaid the inside of the temple with pure gold. He stretched gold chains across the front of the inner sanctuary, and overlaid it with gold.

22 The whole temple he overlaid with gold, until he had finished all the temple; also he overlaid with gold ᴿthe entire altar that *was* by the inner sanctuary.   Ex. 30:1, 3, 6

23 Inside the inner sanctuary he made two cherubim *of* olive wood, *each* ten cubits high.

24 One wing of the cherub *was* ᵀfive cubits, and the other wing of the cherub five cubits: ᵀten cubits from the tip of one wing to the tip of the other.   7.5 ft. · 15 ft.

25 And the other cherub *was* ten cubits; both cherubim *were* of the same size and shape.

26 The height of one cherub *was* ᵀten cubits, and so *was* the other cherub.   15 ft.

27 Then he set the cherubim inside the inner ᵀroom; and ᴿthey stretched out the wings of the cherubim so that the wing of the one touched *one* wall, and the wing of the other cherub touched the other wall. And their wings touched each other in the middle of the room.   Lit. *house* · 2 Chr. 5:8

28 Also he overlaid the cherubim with gold.

29 Then he carved all the walls of the temple all around, both the inner and outer *sanctuaries,* with carved ᴿfigures of cherubim, palm trees, and open flowers.   Ex. 36:8, 35

30 And the floor of the temple he overlaid with gold, both the inner and outer *sanctuaries.*

31 For the entrance of the inner sanctuary he made doors *of* olive wood; the lintel *and* doorposts *were* ᵀone-fifth *of the wall.*   5-sided

32 The two doors *were of* olive wood; and he carved on them figures of cherubim, palm trees, and open flowers, and overlaid *them* with gold; and he spread gold on the cherubim and on the palm trees.

33 So for the door of the ᵀsanctuary he also made doorposts *of* olive wood, ᵀone-fourth *of the wall.*   temple · Or 4-sided

34 And the two doors *were of* cypress wood; two panels *comprised* one folding door, and two panels *comprised* the other folding door.

35 Then he carved cherubim, palm trees, and open flowers *on them,* and overlaid *them* with gold applied evenly on the carved work.

36 And he built the ᴿinner court with three rows of hewn stone and a row of cedar beams.   1 Kin. 7:12

37 ᴿIn the fourth year the foundation of the house of the LORD was laid, in the month of ᵀZiv.   1 Kin. 6:1 · Or *Ayyar,* April or May

38 And in the eleventh year, in the month of ᵀBul, which is the eighth month, the house was finished in all its details and according to all its plans. So he was seven years in building it.   Or *Heshvan,* October or November

Solomon's Other Buildings

7 But Solomon took ᴿthirteen years to build his own house; so he finished all his house.   2 Chr. 8:1

2 He also built the House of the Forest of Lebanon; its length *was* ᵀone hundred cubits, its width ᵀfifty cubits, and its height thirty cubits, with four rows of cedar pillars, and cedar beams on the pillars.   150 ft. · 75 ft.

3 And *it was* paneled with cedar above the beams that *were* on forty-five pillars, fifteen *to* a row.

4 *There were* windows *with beveled frames* in three rows, and window *was* opposite window in three tiers.

5 And all the doorways and doorposts *had* rectangular frames; and window *was* opposite window in three tiers.

6 He also made the Hall of Pillars: its length *was* ᵀfifty cubits, and its width ᵀthirty cubits; and in front of them *was* a portico with pillars, and a canopy *was* in front of them.   75 ft. · 45 ft.

7 Then he made a hall for the throne, the Hall of Judgment, where he might judge; and

it was paneled with cedar from floor to
^Tceiling.   Lit. *floor*, of the upper level

8 And the house where he dwelt *had* another court inside the hall, of like workmanship. Solomon also made a house like this hall for Pharaoh's daughter, ^Rwhom he had taken as wife.   2 Chr. 8:11

9 All these *were of* costly stones cut to size, trimmed with saws, inside and out, from the foundation to the eaves, and also on the outside to the great court.

10 The foundation *was of* costly stones, large stones, some ^Tten cubits and some ^Teight cubits.   15 ft. • 12 ft.

11 And above *were* costly stones, hewn to size, and cedar wood.

12 The great court *was* enclosed with three rows of hewn stones and a row of cedar beams. So were the inner court of the house of the LORD and the vestibule of the temple.

Hiram the Craftsman

13 Now King Solomon sent and brought ^THuram from Tyre.   Heb. *Hiram*, cf. 2 Chr. 2:13, 14

14 He *was* the son of a widow from the tribe of Naphtali, and his father *was* a man of Tyre, a bronze worker; he was filled with wisdom and understanding and skill in working with all kinds of bronze work. So he came to King Solomon and did all his work.

The Bronze Pillars for the Temple

15 And he cast two pillars of bronze, each one eighteen cubits high, and a line of twelve cubits measured the circumference of each.

16 Then he made two capitals of cast bronze, to set on the tops of the pillars. The height of one capital *was* five cubits, and the height of the other capital *was* five cubits.

17 *He made* a lattice network, with wreaths of chainwork, for the capitals which *were* on top of the pillars: seven chains for one capital and seven for the other capital.

18 So he made the pillars, and two rows of pomegranates above the network all around to cover the capitals that *were* on top; and thus he did for the other capital.

19 The capitals which *were* on top of the pillars in the hall *were* in the shape of lilies, ^Tfour cubits.   6 ft.

20 The capitals on the two pillars also *had* pomegranates above, by the convex surface which *was* next to the network; and there *were* two hundred such pomegranates in rows on each of the capitals all around.

21 Then he set up the pillars by the vestibule of the temple; he set up the pillar on the right and called its name ^TJachin, and he set up the pillar on the left and called its name ^TBoaz.   Lit. *He Shall Establish* • Lit. *In It Is Strength*

22 The tops of the pillars were in the shape of lilies. So the work of the pillars was finished.

The Sea and the Oxen

23 And he made ^Rthe Sea of cast bronze, ^Tten cubits from one brim to the other; *it was* completely round. Its height *was* ^Tfive cubits, and a line of ^Tthirty cubits measured its circumference.   2 Chr. 4:2 • 15 ft. • 7.5 ft. • 45 ft.

24 Below its brim *were* ornamental buds encircling it all around, ten to a cubit, all the way around the Sea. The ornamental buds *were* cast in two rows when it was cast.

25 It stood on ^Rtwelve oxen: three looking toward the north, three looking toward the west, three looking toward the south, and three looking toward the east; the Sea *was* set upon them, and all their back parts pointed inward.   Jer. 52:20

26 It *was* a handbreadth thick; and its brim was shaped like the brim of a cup, *like* a lily blossom. It contained *two thousand baths.

The Carts and the Lavers

27 He also made ten ^Tcarts of bronze; four cubits *was* the length of each cart, four cubits its width, and three cubits its height. Or *stands*

28 And this *was* the design of the carts: They had panels, and the panels *were* between frames;

29 on the panels that *were* between the frames *were* lions, oxen, and cherubim. And on the frames *was* a pedestal on top. Below the lions and oxen *were* wreaths of plaited work.

30 Every cart had four bronze wheels and axles of bronze, and its four feet had supports. Under the laver *were* supports of cast *bronze* beside each wreath.

31 Its opening inside the crown at the top *was* ^Tone cubit in diameter; and the opening *was* round, shaped *like* a pedestal, ^Tone and a half cubits in outside diameter; and also on the opening *were* engravings, but the panels were square, not round.   18 in. • 27 in.

32 Under the panels *were* the four wheels, and the axles of the wheels *were joined* to the cart. The height of a wheel *was* ^Tone and a half cubits.   27 in.

33 The workmanship of the wheels *was* like the workmanship of a chariot wheel; their axle pins, their rims, their spokes, and their hubs *were* all of cast *bronze*.

34 And *there were* four supports at the four corners of each cart; its supports *were* part of the cart itself.

35 On the top of the cart, at the height of ^Thalf a cubit, *it was* perfectly round. And on the top of the cart, its flanges and its panels *were* of the same casting.   9 in.

36 On the plates of its flanges and on its panels he engraved cherubim, lions, and palm trees, wherever there was a clear space on each, with wreaths all around.

7:26 About 12,000 gallons; *three thousand*, 2 Chr. 4:5

37 Thus he made the ten carts. All of them were of ^Tthe same mold, one measure, *and* one shape.   *one*

38 Then ^Rhe made ten lavers of bronze; each laver contained ^Tforty baths, *and* each laver *was* ^Tfour cubits. On each of the ten carts *was* a laver.   2 Chr. 4:6 • 240 gal. • 6 ft.

39 And he put five carts on the right side of the house, and five on the left side of the house. He set the Sea on the right side of the house, toward the southeast.

Furnishings of the Temple

40 *Huram made the lavers and the shovels and the bowls. So Huram finished doing all the work that he was to do for King Solomon *for* the house of the LORD:

41 the two pillars, the *two* bowl-shaped capitals that *were* on top of the two pillars; the two ^Rnetworks covering the two bowl-shaped capitals which *were* on top of the pillars;   1 Kin. 7:17, 18

42 four hundred pomegranates for the two networks (two rows of pomegranates for each network, to cover the two bowl-shaped capitals that *were* on top of the pillars);

43 the ten carts, and ten lavers on the carts;

44 one Sea, and twelve oxen under the Sea;

45 ^Rthe pots, the shovels, and the bowls. All these articles which *Huram made for King Solomon *for* the house of the LORD *were of* burnished bronze.   Ex. 27:3

46 ^RIn the plain of Jordan the king had them cast in clay molds, between ^RSuccoth and ^RZaretan.   2 Chr. 4:17 • Gen. 33:17 • Josh. 3:16

47 And Solomon did not weigh all the articles, because *there were* so many; the weight of the bronze was not determined.

48 Thus Solomon had all the furnishings made for the house of the LORD: ^Rthe altar of gold, and ^Rthe table of gold on which *was* ^Rthe showbread;   Ex. 37:25, 26 • Ex. 37:10, 11 • Lev. 24:5–8

49 the lampstands of pure gold, five on the right *side* and five on the left in front of the inner sanctuary, with the flowers and the lamps and the wick-trimmers of gold;

50 the basins, the trimmers, the bowls, the ladles, and the ^Tcensers of pure gold; and the hinges of gold, *both* for the doors of the inner room (the Most Holy *Place*) *and* for the doors of the main hall of the temple.   *fire pans*

51 So all the work that King Solomon had done for the house of the LORD was finished; and Solomon brought in the things which his father David had dedicated: the silver and the gold and the furnishings. He put them in the treasuries of the house of the LORD.

The Ark Brought into the Temple

8 Now Solomon assembled the elders of Israel and all the heads of the tribes, the

7:40 Heb. *Hiram;* cf. 2 Chr. 2:13, 14
7:45 Heb. *Hiram;* cf. 2 Chr. 2:13, 14

chief fathers of the children of Israel, to King Solomon in Jerusalem, that they might bring up the ark of the covenant of the LORD from the City of David, which is Zion.

2 Therefore all the men of Israel assembled with King Solomon at the feast in the month of Ethanim, which *is* the seventh month.

3 So all the elders of Israel came, ^Rand the priests took up the ark.   Num. 4:15; 7:9

4 Then they brought up the ark of the LORD, the tabernacle of meeting, and all the holy furnishings that *were* in the tabernacle. The priests and the Levites brought them up.

5 Also King Solomon, and all the congregation of Israel who were assembled with him, *were* with him before the ark, ^Rsacrificing sheep and oxen that could not be counted or numbered for multitude.   2 Sam. 6:13

6 Then the priests ^Rbrought in the ark of the covenant of the LORD to ^Rits place, into the inner sanctuary of the temple, to the Most Holy *Place*, ^Runder the wings of the cherubim.   2 Sam. 6:17 • 1 Kin. 6:19 • 1 Kin. 6:27

7 For the cherubim spread *their* two wings over the place of the ark, and the cherubim overshadowed the ark and its poles.

8 The poles ^Rextended so that the ^Tends of the poles could be seen from the holy *place*, in front of the inner sanctuary; but they could not be seen from outside. And they are there to this day.   Ex. 25:13–15; 37:4, 5 • *heads*

9 Nothing *was* in the ark except the two tablets of stone which Moses put there at Horeb, when the LORD made *a covenant* with the children of Israel, when they came out of the land of Egypt.

10 And it came to pass, when the priests came out of the holy *place*, that the cloud ^Rfilled the house of the LORD,   Ex. 40:34, 35

11 so that the priests could not continue ministering because of the cloud; for the ^Rglory of the LORD filled the house of the LORD.   2 Chr. 7:1, 2

12 ^RThen Solomon spoke: 2 Chr. 6:1

"The LORD said
     He would dwell in the dark cloud.
13 ^RI have surely built You an exalted
     house,   2 Sam. 7:13
     ^RAnd a place for You to dwell in
     forever."   Ps. 132:14

Solomon's Speech at Completion of the Work

14 Then the king turned around and blessed the whole assembly of Israel, while all the assembly of Israel was standing.

15 And he said: ^R"Blessed *be* the LORD God of Israel, who ^Rspoke with His mouth to my father David, and with His hand has fulfilled *it*, saying,   Luke 1:68 • 2 Sam. 7:2, 12, 13, 25

16 'Since the day that I brought My people

Israel out of Egypt, I have chosen no city from any tribe of Israel *in which* to build a house, that My name might be there; but I chose David to be over My people Israel.'

17 "Now ᴿit was in the heart of my father David to build a *temple for the name of the LORD God of Israel.   2 Sam. 7:2, 3

18 ᴿ"But the LORD said to my father David, 'Whereas it was in your heart to temple a house for My name, you did well that it was in your heart.   2 Chr. 6:8, 9

19 'Nevertheless ᴿyou shall not build the temple, but your son who will come from your body, he shall build the temple for My name.'   2 Sam. 7:5, 12, 13

20 "So the LORD has fulfilled His word which He spoke; and I have ᵀfilled the position of my father David, and sit on the throne of Israel, ᴿas the LORD promised; and I have built a temple for the name of the LORD God of Israel.   *risen in the place of* · 1 Chr. 28:5, 6

21 "And there I have made a place for the ark, in which *is* the covenant of the LORD which He made with our fathers, when He brought them out of the land of Egypt."

Solomon's Prayer of Dedication

22 Then Solomon stood before ᴿthe altar of the LORD in the presence of all the assembly of Israel, and ᴿspread out his hands toward heaven;   2 Chr. 6:12 · Ezra 9:5

23 and he said: "LORD God of Israel, *there is* no God in heaven above or on earth below like You, ᴿwho keep *Your* covenant and mercy with Your servants who ᴿwalk before You with all their hearts.   [Neh. 1:5] · [Gen. 17:1]

24 "You have kept what You promised Your servant David my father; You have both spoken with Your mouth and fulfilled *it* with Your hand, as *it is* this day.

25 "Therefore, LORD God of Israel, now keep what You promised Your servant David my father, saying, ᴿ'You shall not fail to have a man sit before Me on the throne of Israel, only if your sons take heed to their way, that they walk before Me as you have walked before Me.'   1 Kin. 2:4; 9:5

26 "And now I pray, O God of Israel, let Your word come true, which You have spoken to Your servant David my father.

27 "But ᴮwill God indeed dwell on the earth? Behold, heaven and the heaven of heavens cannot contain You. How much less this temple which I have built! [Acts 7:49; 17:24]

28 "Yet regard the prayer of Your servant and his supplication, O LORD my God, and listen to the cry and the prayer which Your servant is praying before You today:

29 "that Your eyes may be open toward this ᵀtemple night and day, toward the place of which You said, 'My name shall be there,'

8:17 Lit. *house,* and so in vv. 18–20

that You may hear the prayer which Your servant makes toward this place. Lit. *house*

30 ᴿ"And may You hear the supplication of Your servant and of Your people Israel, when they pray toward this place. Hear in heaven Your dwelling place; and when You hear, forgive.   Neh. 1:6

31 "When anyone sins against his neighbor, and is forced to take ᴿan oath, and comes *and* takes an oath before Your altar in this temple,   Ex. 22:8–11

32 "then hear in heaven, and act, and judge Your servants, ᴿcondemning the wicked, bringing his way on his head, and justifying the righteous by giving him according to his righteousness.   Deut. 25:1

33 "When Your people Israel are defeated before an enemy because they have sinned against You, and when they turn back to You and confess Your name, and pray and make supplication to You in this temple,

34 "then hear in heaven, and forgive the sin of Your people Israel, and bring them back to the land which You gave to their fathers.

35 ᴿ"When the heavens are shut up and there is no rain because they have sinned against You, when they pray toward this place and confess Your name, and turn from their sin because You afflict them, Deut. 28:23

36 "then hear in heaven, and forgive the sin of Your servants, Your people Israel, that You may teach them ᴿthe good way in which they should walk; and send rain on Your land which You have given to Your people as an inheritance.   1 Sam. 12:23

37 "When there is famine in the land, pestilence *or* blight *or* mildew, locusts *or* grasshoppers; when their enemy besieges them in the land of their ᵀcities; whatever plague or whatever sickness *there is*;   Lit. *gates*

38 "whatever prayer, whatever supplication is made by anyone, *or* by all Your people Israel, when each one knows the plague of his own heart, and spreads out his hands toward this temple:

39 "then hear in heaven Your dwelling place, and forgive, and act, and give to everyone according to all his ways, whose heart You know (for You alone, ᴿknow the hearts of all the sons of men),   [1 Sam. 16:7]

40 ᴿ"that they may fear You all the days that they live in the land which You gave to our fathers.   [Ps. 130:4]

41 "Moreover, concerning a foreigner, who *is* not of Your people Israel, but has come from a far country for Your name's sake

42 "(for they will hear of Your great name and Your ᴿstrong hand and Your outstretched arm), when he comes and prays toward this temple,   Deut. 3:24

43 "hear in heaven Your dwelling place, and do according to all for which the foreigner calls to You, ᴿthat all peoples of the

earth may know Your name and ᴿfear You, as *do* Your people Israel, and that they may know that this temple which I have built is called by Your name. [1 Sam. 17:46] • Ps. 102:15

44 "When Your people go out to battle against their enemy, wherever You send them, and when they pray to the Lᴏʀᴅ toward the city which You have chosen and the temple which I have built for Your name,

45 "then hear in heaven their prayer and their supplication, and maintain their cause.

46 "When they sin against You (for *there is* no one who does not sin), and You become angry with them and deliver them to the enemy, and they take them captive ᴿto the land of the enemy, far or near; Lev. 26:34, 44

47 ᴿ"*yet* when they come to themselves in the land where they were carried captive, and repent, and make supplication to You in the land of those who took them captive, ᴿsaying, 'We have sinned and done wrong, we have committed wickedness'; [Lev. 26:40-42] • Dan. 9:5

48 "and *when* they ᴿreturn to You with all their heart and with all their soul in the land of their enemies who led them away captive, and ᴿpray to You toward their land which You gave to their fathers, the city which You have chosen and the temple which I have built for Your name: Jer. 29:12-14 • Dan. 6:10

49 "then hear in heaven Your dwelling place their prayer and their supplication, and maintain their ᵀcause,   *justice*

50 "and forgive Your people who have sinned against You, and all their transgressions which they have transgressed against You; and ᴿgrant them compassion before those who took them captive, that they may have compassion on them Ps. 106:46

51 "(for ᴿthey *are* Your people and Your inheritance, whom You brought out of Egypt, ᴿout of the iron furnace),   Deut. 9:26-29 • Jer. 11:4

52 ᴿ"that Your eyes may be open to the supplication of Your servant and the supplication of Your people Israel, to listen to them whenever they call to You.   1 Kin. 8:29

53 "For You separated them from among all the peoples of the earth *to be* Your inheritance, ᴿas You spoke by Your servant Moses, when You brought our fathers out of Egypt, O Lord Gᴏᴅ."   Ex. 19:5, 6

Solomon Blesses the Assembly

54 ᴿAnd so it was, when Solomon had finished praying all this prayer and supplication to the Lᴏʀᴅ, that he arose from before the altar of the Lᴏʀᴅ, from kneeling on his knees with his hands spread up to heaven. 2 Chr. 7:1

55 Then he stood and blessed all the assembly of Israel with a loud voice, saying:

56 "Blessed *be* the Lᴏʀᴅ, who has given ᵀrest to His people Israel, according to all that He promised. There has not failed one word of all His good promise, which He promised through His servant Moses.   *peace*

57 "May the Lᴏʀᴅ our God be with us, as He was with our fathers. ᴿMay He not leave us nor forsake us,   Deut. 31:6

58 "that He may ᴿincline our hearts to Himself, to walk in all His ways, and to keep His commandments and His statutes and His judgments, which He commanded our fathers.   Ps. 119:36

59 "And may these words of mine, with which I have made supplication before the Lᴏʀᴅ, be near the Lᴏʀᴅ our God day and night, that He may maintain the cause of His servant and the cause of His people Israel, as each day may require,

60 ᴿ"that all the peoples of the earth may know that ᴿthe Lᴏʀᴅ *is* God; *there is* no other.   1 Sam. 17:46 • Deut. 4:35, 39

61 "Let your heart therefore be loyal to the Lᴏʀᴅ our God, to walk in His statutes and keep His commandments, as at this day."

Solomon Dedicates the Temple

62 Then ᴿthe king and all Israel with him offered sacrifices before the Lᴏʀᴅ.   2 Chr. 7:4-10

63 And Solomon offered a sacrifice of peace offerings, which he offered to the Lᴏʀᴅ, twenty-two thousand bulls and one hundred and twenty thousand sheep. So the king and all the children of Israel dedicated the house of the Lᴏʀᴅ.

64 On the same day the king consecrated the middle of the court that *was* in front of the house of the Lᴏʀᴅ; for there he offered burnt offerings, grain offerings, and the fat of the peace offerings, because the bronze altar that *was* before the Lᴏʀᴅ *was* too small to receive the burnt offerings, the grain offerings, and the fat of the peace offerings.

65 At that time Solomon held a feast, and all Israel with him, a great assembly from the entrance of Hamath to the Brook of Egypt, before the Lᴏʀᴅ our God, seven days and seven *more* days—fourteen days.

66 On the eighth day he sent the people away; and they blessed the king, and went to their tents joyful and glad of heart for all the good that the Lᴏʀᴅ had done for His servant David, and for Israel His people.

God's Second Appearance to Solomon

9 And it came to pass, when Solomon had finished building the house of the Lᴏʀᴅ and the king's house, and ᴿall Solomon's desire which he wanted to do,   2 Chr. 8:6

2 that the Lᴏʀᴅ appeared to Solomon the second time, ᴿas He had appeared to him at Gibeon.   1 Kin. 3:5; 11:9

3 And the Lᴏʀᴅ said to him: "I have heard your prayer and your supplication that you have made before Me; I have consecrated this house which you have built ᴿto put My name there forever, and My eyes and My heart will be there perpetually.   1 Kin. 8:29

4 "Now if you walk before Me as your father David walked, in integrity of heart and in uprightness, to do according to all that I have commanded you, *and* if you ^Rkeep My statutes and My judgments,   1 Kin. 8:61

5 "then I will establish the throne of your kingdom over Israel forever, as I promised David your father, saying, 'You shall not fail to have a man on the throne of Israel.'

6 ^R"But if you or your sons at all ^Tturn from following Me, and do not keep My commandments *and* My statutes which I have set before you, but go and serve other gods and worship them,   2 Sam. 7:14-16 · turn back

7 "then I will ^Tcut off Israel from the land which I have given them; and this house which I have consecrated for My name I will cast out of My sight. Israel will be a proverb and a byword among all peoples.   destroy

8 "And *as for* this house, *which* is exalted, everyone who passes by it will be astonished and will hiss, and say, 'Why has the LORD done thus to this land and to this house?'

9 "Then they will answer, 'Because they forsook the LORD their God, who brought their fathers out of the land of Egypt, and have embraced other gods, and worshiped them and served them; therefore the LORD has brought all this calamity on them.' "

Solomon and Hiram Exchange Gifts

10 Now ^Rit happened at the end of twenty years, when Solomon had built the two houses, the house of the LORD and the king's house   2 Chr. 8:1

11 ^R(Hiram the king of Tyre had supplied Solomon with cedar and cypress and gold, as much as he desired), *that* King Solomon then gave Hiram twenty cities in the land of Galilee.   1 Kin. 5:1

12 Then Hiram went from Tyre to see the cities which Solomon had given him, but they did not please him.

13 So he said, "What *kind of* cities *are* these which you have given me, my brother?" And he called them the land of ^TCabul, as they are to this day.   Lit. *Good for Nothing*

14 Then Hiram sent the king ^Tone hundred and twenty talents of gold. $691,200,000

Solomon's Additional Achievements

15 And this *is* the reason for the labor force which King Solomon raised: to build the house of the LORD, his own house, *the ^RMillo, the wall of Jerusalem, ^RHazor, Megiddo, and Gezer.   2 Sam. 5:9 · Josh. 11:1; 19:36

16 (Pharaoh king of Egypt had gone up and taken Gezer and burned it with fire, ^Rhad killed the Canaanites who dwelt in the city, and had given it *as* a dowry to his daughter, Solomon's wife.)   Josh. 16:10

17 And Solomon built Gezer, Lower ^RBeth Horon,   2 Chr. 8:5

18 ^RBaalath, and Tadmor in the wilderness, in the land *of Judah*,   Josh. 19:44

19 all the storage cities that Solomon had, cities for his chariots and cities for his ^Rcavalry, and whatever Solomon ^Rdesired to build in Jerusalem, in Lebanon, and in all the land of his dominion.   1 Kin. 4:26 · 1 Kin. 9:1

20 ^RAll the people *who were* left of the Amorites, Hittites, Perizzites, Hivites, and Jebusites, who *were* not of the children of Israel—   2 Chr. 8:7

21 that is, their descendants who were left in the land after them, whom the children of Israel had not been able to destroy completely—from these Solomon raised ^Rforced labor, as it is to this day.   Ezra 2:55, 58

22 But of the children of Israel Solomon ^Rmade no forced laborers, because they *were* men of war and his servants: his officers, his captains, commanders of his chariots, and his cavalry.   [Lev. 25:39]

23 Others *were* chiefs of the officials who *were* over Solomon's work: ^Rfive hundred and fifty, who ruled over the people who did the work.   2 Chr. 8:10

24 But Pharaoh's daughter came up from the City of David to ^Rher house which ^TSolomon had built for her. ^RThen he built the Millo.   1 Kin. 7:8 · Lit. *he*, cf. 2 Chr. 8:11 · 2 Sam. 5:9

25 ^RNow three times a year Solomon offered burnt offerings and peace offerings on the altar which he had built for the LORD, and he burned incense with them *on the altar* that *was* before the LORD. So he finished the temple.   Ex. 23:14-17

26 King Solomon also built a fleet of ships at Ezion Geber, which *is* near *Elath on the shore of the Red Sea, in the land of Edom.

27 ^RThen Hiram sent his servants with the fleet, seamen who knew the sea, to work with the servants of Solomon.   1 Kin. 5:6, 9; 10:11

28 And they went to Ophir, and acquired four hundred and twenty talents of gold from there, and brought *it* to King Solomon.

The Queen of Sheba's Praise of Solomon

10 Now when the ^Rqueen of Sheba heard of the fame of Solomon concerning the name of the LORD, she came ^Rto test him with hard questions.   Matt. 12:42 · Judg. 14:12

2 She came to Jerusalem with a very great ^Tretinue, with camels that bore spices, very much gold, and precious stones; and when she came to Solomon, she spoke with him about all that was in her heart.   company

3 So Solomon answered all her questions; there was nothing ^Tso difficult for the king that he could not explain *it* to her.   too

4 And when the queen of Sheba had seen

all the wisdom of Solomon, the house that he had built,

5 the food on his table, the seating of his servants, the service of his waiters and their apparel, his cupbearers, ᴿand his entryway by which he went up to the house of the Lᴏʀᴅ, there was no more spirit in her.   1 Chr. 26:16

6 Then she said to the king: "It was a true report which I heard in my own land about your words and your wisdom.

7 "However I did not believe the words until I came and saw with my own eyes; and indeed the half was not told me. Your wisdom and prosperity exceed the fame of which I heard.

8 ᴿ"Happy *are* your men and happy *are* these your servants, who stand continually before you *and* hear your wisdom!   Prov. 8:34

9 ᴿ"Blessed be the Lᴏʀᴅ your God, who delighted in you, setting you on the throne of Israel! Because the Lᴏʀᴅ has loved Israel forever, therefore He made you king, ᴿto do justice and righteousness."   1 Kin. 5:7 • Ps. 72:2

10 Then she gave the king one hundred and twenty talents of gold, spices in great quantity, and precious stones. There never again came such abundance of spices as the queen of Sheba gave to King Solomon.

11 Also, the ships of Hiram, which brought gold from Ophir, brought great *quantities* of *almug wood and precious stones from Ophir.

12 ᴿAnd the king made ᵀsteps of the almug wood for the house of the Lᴏʀᴅ and for the king's house, also harps and stringed instruments for singers. There never again came such ᴿalmug wood, nor has the like been seen to this day.   2 Chr. 9:11 • Or *supports* • 2 Chr. 9:10

13 Now King Solomon gave the queen of Sheba all she desired, whatever she asked, besides what Solomon had given her according to the royal generosity. So she turned and went to her own country, she and her servants.

Solomon's Great Wealth

14 The weight of gold that came to Solomon yearly was ᵀsix hundred and sixty-six talents of gold, $3.83 billion

15 besides *that* from the ᴿtraveling merchants, from the income of traders, ᴿfrom all the kings of Arabia, and from the governors of the country.   2 Chr. 1:16 • Ps. 72:10

16 And King Solomon made two hundred large shields *of* hammered gold; six hundred *shekels* of gold went into each shield.

17 He also *made* three hundred shields *of* hammered gold; three minas of gold went into each shield. The king put them in the House of the Forest of Lebanon.

18 Moreover the king made a great throne of ivory, and overlaid it with pure gold.

19 The throne had six steps, and the top of the throne *was* round at the back; *there were* armrests on either side of the place of the seat, and two lions stood beside the armrests.

20 Twelve lions stood there, one on each side of the six steps; nothing like *this* had been made for any *other* kingdom.

21 ᴿAll King Solomon's drinking vessels *were* gold, and all the vessels of the House of the Forest of Lebanon *were* pure gold. Not one *was* silver, for this was accounted as nothing in the days of Solomon.   2 Chr. 9:20

22 For the king had *merchant ships at sea with the fleet of Hiram. Once every three years the merchant ships came bringing gold, silver, ivory, apes, and *monkeys.

23 So King Solomon surpassed all the kings of the earth in riches and wisdom.

24 Now all the earth sought the presence of Solomon to hear his wisdom, which God had put in his heart.

25 Each man brought his present: articles of silver and gold, garments, armor, spices, horses, and mules, at a set rate year by year.

26 And Solomon ᴿgathered chariots and horsemen; he had one thousand four hundred chariots and twelve thousand horsemen, whom he *stationed in the chariot cities and with the king at Jerusalem.   1 Kin. 9:19

27 ᴿThe king made silver as *common* in Jerusalem as stones, and he made cedar trees as abundant as the sycamores which *are* in the lowland.   2 Chr. 1:15–17

28 Also Solomon had horses imported from Egypt and Keveh; the king's merchants bought them in Keveh at the *current* price.

29 Now a chariot that was imported from Egypt cost six hundred *shekels* of silver, and a horse one hundred and fifty; ᴿand ᵀthus, through their agents, they exported *them* to all the kings of the Hittites and the kings of Syria.   2 Kin. 7:6, 7 • Lit. *by their hands*

Solomon's Heart Turns from the Lᴏʀᴅ

11 But King Solomon loved many foreign women, as well as the daughter of Pharaoh: women of the Moabites, Ammonites, Edomites, Sidonians, *and* Hittites—

2 from the nations of whom the Lᴏʀᴅ had said to the children of Israel, ᴿ"You shall not intermarry with them, nor they with you. Surely they will turn away your hearts after their gods." Solomon clung to these in love.   [Deut. 7:3, 4]

3 And he had seven hundred wives, princesses, and three hundred concubines; and his wives turned away his heart.

4 For it was so, when Solomon was old, ᴿthat his wives turned his heart after other

10:11 *algum*, 2 Chr. 9:10–11

10:22 Lit. *ships of Tarshish*, deep-sea vessels • Or *peacocks*

10:26 So with LXX, Syr., Tg., Vg. (cf. 2 Chr. 9:25); MT *led*

gods; and his heart was not [T]loyal to the LORD his God, [R]as *was* the heart of his father David.   [Deut. 17:17] • Lit. *at peace with* • 1 Kin. 9:4

5 For Solomon went after Ashtoreth the goddess of the Sidonians, and after Milcom the abomination of the Ammonites.

6 Solomon did evil in the sight of the LORD, and did not fully follow the LORD, as *did* his father David.

7 Then Solomon built a high place for Chemosh the abomination of Moab, on the hill that *is* east of Jerusalem, and for Molech the abomination of the people of Ammon.

8 And he did likewise for all his foreign wives, who burned incense and sacrificed to their gods.

9 So the LORD became angry with Solomon, because his heart had turned from the LORD God of Israel, [R]who had appeared to him twice,   1 Kin. 3:5; 9:2

10 and [R]had commanded him concerning this thing, that he should not go after other gods; but he did not keep what the LORD had commanded.   1 Kin. 6:12; 9:6, 7

11 Therefore the LORD said to Solomon, "Because you have done this, and have not kept My covenant and My statutes, which I have commanded you, [R]I will surely tear the kingdom away from you and give it to your [R]servant.   1 Kin. 11:31; 12:15, 16 • 1 Kin. 11:31, 37

12 "Nevertheless I will not do it in your days, for the sake of your father David; I will tear it out of the hand of your son.

13 "However I will not tear away the whole kingdom; I will give one tribe to your son for the sake of my servant David, and for the sake of Jerusalem which I have chosen."

Adversaries of Solomon

14 Now the LORD [R]raised up an adversary against Solomon, Hadad the Edomite; he *was* a descendant of the king in Edom.   1 Chr. 5:26

15 For it happened, when David was in Edom, and Joab the commander of the army had gone up to bury the slain, [R]after he had killed every male in Edom   Num. 24:18, 19

16 (because for six months Joab remained there with all Israel, until he had cut down every male in Edom),

17 that Hadad fled to go to Egypt, he and certain Edomites of his father's servants with him. Hadad *was* still a little child.

18 Then they arose from Midian and came to Paran; and they took men with them from Paran and came to Egypt, to Pharaoh king of Egypt, who gave him a house, apportioned food for him, and gave him land.

19 And Hadad found great favor in the sight of Pharaoh, so that he gave him as wife the sister of his own wife, that is, the sister of Queen Tahpenes.

20 Then the sister of Tahpenes bore him Genubath his son, whom Tahpenes weaned in Pharaoh's house. And Genubath was in Pharaoh's household among the sons of Pharaoh.

21 So when Hadad heard in Egypt that David rested with his fathers, and that Joab the commander of the army was dead, Hadad said to Pharaoh, [T]"Let me depart, that I may go to my own country."   Lit. *Send me away*

22 Then Pharaoh said to him, "But what have you lacked with me, that suddenly you seek to go to your own country?" So he answered, "Nothing, but do let me go anyway."

23 And God raised up *another* adversary against him, Rezon the son of Eliadah, who had fled from his lord, [R]Hadadezer king of Zobah.   2 Sam. 8:3; 10:16

24 So he gathered men to him and became captain over a band *of raiders,* [R]when David killed those *of Zobah.* And they went to Damascus and dwelt there, and reigned in Damascus.   2 Sam. 8:3; 10:8, 18

25 He was an adversary of Israel all the days of Solomon (besides the trouble that Hadad *caused*); and he abhorred Israel, and reigned over Syria.

Jeroboam's Rebellion

26 Then Solomon's servant, Jeroboam the son of Nebat, an Ephraimite from Zereda, whose mother's name *was* Zeruah, a widow, also [R]rebelled against the king.   2 Sam. 20:21

27 And this *is* what caused him to rebel against the king: Solomon had built the Millo *and* [T]repaired the damages to the City of David his father.   Lit. *closed up the breaches*

28 The man Jeroboam *was* a mighty man of valor; and Solomon, seeing that the young man was [R]industrious, made him the officer over all the labor force of the house of Joseph.   [Prov. 22:29]

29 Now it happened at that time, when Jeroboam went out of Jerusalem, that the prophet Ahijah the Shilonite met him on the way; and he had clothed himself with a new garment, and the two *were* alone in the field.

30 Then Ahijah took hold of the new garment that *was* on him, and [R]tore it *into* twelve pieces.   1 Sam. 15:27, 28; 24:5

31 And he said to Jeroboam, "Take for yourself ten pieces, for [R]thus says the LORD, the God of Israel: 'Behold, I will tear the kingdom out of the hand of Solomon and will give ten tribes to you   1 Kin. 11:11, 13

32 '(but he shall have one tribe for the sake of My servant David, and for the sake of Jerusalem, the city which I have chosen out of all the tribes of Israel),

33 'because *they have forsaken Me, and worshiped Ashtoreth the goddess of the Sidonians, Chemosh the god of the Moabites, and

11:33 So with MT, Tg., LXX, Syr., Vg. *he has*

Milcom the god of the people of Ammon, and have not walked in My ways to do *what is* right in My eyes and *keep* My statutes and My judgments, as *did* his father David.

34 'However I will not take the whole kingdom out of his hand, because I have made him ruler all the days of his life for the sake of My servant David, whom I chose because he kept My commandments and My statutes.

35 'But I will take the kingdom out of his son's hand and give it to you—ten tribes.

36 'And to his son I will give one tribe, that My servant David may always have a lamp before Me in Jerusalem, the city which I have chosen for Myself, to put My name there.

37 'So I will take you, and you shall reign over all your heart desires, and you shall be king over Israel.

38 'Then it shall be, if you heed all that I command you, walk in My ways, and do *what is* right in My sight, to keep My statutes and My commandments, as My servant David did, then I will be with you and ᴿbuild for you an enduring house, as I built for David, and will give Israel to you.   2 Sam. 7:11, 27

39 'And I will afflict the descendants of David because of this, but not forever.' "

40 Solomon therefore sought to kill Jeroboam. But Jeroboam arose and fled to Egypt, to ᴿShishak king of Egypt, and was in Egypt until the death of Solomon.   2 Chr. 12:2-9

Death of Solomon

41 Now the rest of the acts of Solomon, all that he did, and his wisdom, *are* they not written in the book of the acts of Solomon?

42 And the period that Solomon reigned in Jerusalem over all Israel *was* forty years.

43 Then Solomon ᵀrested with his fathers, and was buried in the City of David his father. And Rehoboam his son reigned in his ᴿplace.   Died and joined his ancestors • 2 Chr. 10:1

The Revolt Against Rehoboam

12 And ᴿRehoboam went to ᴿShechem, for all Israel had gone to Shechem to make him king.   2 Chr. 10:1 • Judg. 9:6

2 So it happened, when Jeroboam the son of Nebat heard *it* (he was still in Egypt, for he had fled from the presence of King Solomon and had been dwelling in Egypt),

3 that they sent and called him. Then Jeroboam and the whole assembly of Israel came and spoke to Rehoboam, saying,

4 "Your father made our yoke ᵀheavy; now therefore, lighten the burdensome service of your father, and his heavy yoke which he put on us, and we will serve you."   hard

5 So he said to them, "Depart *for* three days, then come back to me." And the people departed.

6 Then King Rehoboam consulted the elders who stood before his father Solomon

while he still lived, and he said, "How do you advise *me* to answer these people?"

7 And they spoke to him, saying, ᴿ"If you will be a servant to these people today, and serve them, and answer them, and speak good words to them, then they will be your servants forever."   2 Chr. 10:7

8 But he rejected the advice which the elders had given him, and consulted the young men who had grown up with him, who stood before him.

9 And he said to them, "What advice do you give? How should we answer this people who have spoken to me, saying, 'Lighten the yoke which your father put on us'?"

10 Then the young men who had grown up with him spoke to him, saying, "Thus you should speak to this people who have spoken to you, saying, 'Your father made our yoke heavy, but you make *it* lighter on us'—thus you shall say to them: 'My little *finger* shall be thicker than my father's waist!

11 'And now, whereas my father put a heavy yoke on you, I will add to your yoke; my father chastised you with whips, but I will chastise you with *scourges!' "

12 So Jeroboam and all the people came to Rehoboam the third day, as the king had directed, saying, "Come back to me the third day."

13 Then the king answered the people ᵀroughly, and rejected the advice which the elders had given him;   harshly

14 and he spoke to them according to the advice of the young men, saying, "My father made your yoke heavy, but I will add to your yoke; my father chastised you with whips, but I will chastise you with *scourges!"

15 So the king did not listen to the people; for the turn of *events* was from the LORD, that He might fulfill His word, which the LORD had ᴿspoken by Ahijah the Shilonite to Jeroboam the son of Nebat.   1 Kin. 11:11, 29, 31

16 Now when all Israel saw that the king did not listen to them, the people answered the king, saying:

ᴿ"What share have we in David?
We have no inheritance in the son of
    Jesus.   2 Sam. 20:1
To your tents, O Israel!
Now, see to your own house, O David!"

So Israel departed to their tents.

17 But Rehoboam reigned over ᴿthe children of Israel who dwelt in the cities of Judah.   1 Kin. 11:13, 36

18 Then King Rehoboam sent Adoram, who *was* in charge of the revenue; but all Israel stoned him with stones, and he died. Therefore King Rehoboam mounted his chariot in haste to flee to Jerusalem.

12:11 Scourges with points or barbs, lit. *scorpions*
12:14 Lit. *scorpions*

19 So ᴿIsrael has been in rebellion against the house of David to this day.   2 Kin. 17:21

20 Now it came to pass when all Israel heard that Jeroboam had come back, they sent for him and called him to the congregation, and made him king over all Israel. There was none who followed the house of David, but the tribe of Judah only.

21 And when ᴿRehoboam came to Jerusalem, he assembled all the house of Judah with the tribe of ᴿBenjamin, one hundred and eighty thousand chosen *men* who were warriors, to fight against the house of Israel, that he might restore the kingdom to Rehoboam the son of Solomon.   2 Chr. 11:1-4 • 2 Sam. 19:17

22 But ᴿthe word of God came to Shemaiah the man of God, saying,   2 Chr. 11:2; 12:5-7

23 "Speak to Rehoboam the son of Solomon, king of Judah, to all the house of Judah and Benjamin, and to the rest of the people, saying,

24 'Thus says the Lᴏʀᴅ: "You shall not go up nor fight against your brethren the children of Israel. Let every man return to his house, ᴿfor this thing is from Me." ' " Therefore they obeyed the word of the Lᴏʀᴅ, and turned back, according to the word of the Lᴏʀᴅ.   1 Kin. 12:15

Jeroboam's Gold Calves

25 Then Jeroboam built Shechem in the mountains of Ephraim, and dwelt there. Also he went out from there and built Penuel.

26 And Jeroboam said in his heart, "Now the kingdom may return to the house of David:

27 "If these people ᴿgo up to offer sacrifices in the house of the Lᴏʀᴅ at Jerusalem, then the heart of this people will turn back to their lord, Rehoboam king of Judah, and they will kill me and go back to Rehoboam king of Judah."   [Deut. 12:5-7, 14]

28 Therefore the king asked advice, made two calves of gold, and said to the people, "It is too much for you to go up to Jerusalem. ᴿHere are your gods, O Israel, which brought you up from the land of Egypt!"   Ex. 32:4, 8

29 And he set up one in ᴿBethel, and the other he put in ᴿDan.   Gen. 28:19 • Judg. 18:26-31

30 Now this thing became ᴿa sin, for the people went *to worship* before the one as far as Dan.   1 Kin. 13:34

31 He made ᵀshrines on the high places, and made priests from every class of people, who were not of the sons of Levi.   Lit. *houses*

32 Jeroboam ᵀordained a feast on the fifteenth day of the eighth month, like the feast that *was* in Judah, and offered sacrifices on the altar. So he did at Bethel, sacrificing to the calves that he had made. And at Bethel he installed the priests of the high places which he had made.   *instituted*

33 So he made offerings on the altar which he had made at Bethel on the fifteenth day of the eighth month, in the month which he had devised in his own heart. And he ordained a feast for the children of Israel, and offered sacrifices on the altar and burned incense.

The Message of the Man of God

13 And behold, ᴿa man of God went from Judah to Bethel ᵀby the word of the Lᴏʀᴅ, and Jeroboam stood by the altar to burn incense.   2 Kin. 23:17 • *at the Lᴏʀᴅ's command*

2 Then he cried out against the altar ᵀby the word of the Lᴏʀᴅ, and said, "O altar, altar! Thus says the Lᴏʀᴅ: 'Behold, a child, Josiah by name, shall be born to the house of David; and on you he shall sacrifice the priests of the high places who burn incense on you, and men's bones shall be ᴿburned on you.' "   *at the Lᴏʀᴅ's command* • [Lev. 26:30]

3 And he gave a sign the same day, saying, "This is the sign which the Lᴏʀᴅ has spoken: Surely the altar shall split apart, and the ashes on it shall be poured out."

4 So it came to pass when King Jeroboam heard the saying of the man of God, who cried out against the altar in Bethel, that he stretched out his hand from the altar, saying, "Arrest him!" Then his hand, which he stretched out toward him, withered, so that he could not pull it back to himself.

5 The altar also was split apart, and the ashes poured out from the altar, according to the sign which the man of God had given by the word of the Lᴏʀᴅ.

6 Then the king answered and said to the man of God, "Please entreat the favor of the Lᴏʀᴅ your God, and pray for me, that my hand may be restored to me." So the man of God entreated the Lᴏʀᴅ, and the king's hand was restored to him, and became as before.

7 Then the king said to the man of God, "Come home with me and refresh yourself, and ᴿI will give you a reward."   1 Sam. 9:7

8 But the man of God said to the king, ᴿ"If you were to give me half your house, I would not go in with you; nor would I eat bread nor drink water in this place.   Num. 22:18; 24:13

9 "For so it was commanded me by the word of the Lᴏʀᴅ, saying, ᴿ"You shall not eat bread, nor drink water, nor return by the same way you came.' "   [1 Cor. 5:11]

10 So he went another way and did not return by the way he came to Bethel.

Death of the Man of God

11 Now an old prophet dwelt in Bethel, and his ᵀsons came and told him all the works that the man of God had done that day in Bethel; they also told their father the words which he had spoken to the king.   Lit. *son*

12 And their father said to them, "Which

way did he go?" For his sons *had seen which way the man of God went who came from Judah.

13 Then he said to his sons, "Saddle the donkey for me." So they saddled the donkey for him; and he rode on it,

14 and went after the man of God, and found him sitting under an oak. Then he said to him, "Are you the man of God who came from Judah?" And he said, "I am."

15 Then he said to him, "Come home with me and eat bread."

16 And he said, "I cannot return with you nor go in with you; neither can I eat bread nor drink water with you in this place.

17 "For ᵀI have been told ᴿby the word of the LORD, 'You shall not eat bread nor drink water there, nor return by going the way you came.' "   Lit. *a command came to me by* • 1 Kin. 20:35

18 He said to him, "I too *am* a prophet as you *are*, and an angel spoke to me by the word of the LORD, saying, 'Bring him back with you to your house, that he may eat bread and drink water.' " (He was lying to him.)

19 So he went back with him, and ate bread in his house, and drank water.

20 Now it happened, as they sat at the table, that the word of the LORD came to the prophet who had brought him back;

21 and he cried out to the man of God who came from Judah, saying, "Thus says the LORD: 'Because you have disobeyed the word of the LORD, and have not kept the commandment which the LORD your God commanded you,

22 'but you came back, ate bread, and drank water in the ᴿplace of which *the LORD* said to you, "Eat no bread and drink no water," your corpse shall not come to the tomb of your fathers.' "   1 Kin. 13:9

23 So it was, after he had eaten bread and after he had drunk, that he saddled the donkey for him, the prophet whom he had brought back.

24 When he was gone, ᴿa lion met him on the road and killed him. And his corpse was thrown on the road, and the donkey stood by it. The lion also stood by the corpse. 1 Kin. 20:36

25 And there, men passed by and saw the corpse thrown on the road, and the lion standing by the corpse. Then they went and told *it* in the city where the old prophet dwelt.

26 Now when the prophet who had brought him back from the way heard *it*, he said, "It *is* the man of God who was disobedient to the word of the LORD. Therefore the LORD has delivered him to the lion, which has torn him and killed him, according to the word of the LORD which He spoke to him."

27 And he spoke to his sons, saying, "Saddle the donkey for me." So they saddled *it*.

28 Then he went and found his corpse thrown on the road, and the donkey and the lion standing by the corpse. The lion had not eaten the corpse nor torn the donkey.

29 And the prophet took up the corpse of the man of God, laid it on the donkey, and brought it back. So the old prophet came to the city to mourn, and to bury him.

30 Then he laid the corpse in his own tomb; and they mourned over him, *saying,* ᴿ"Alas, my brother!"   Jer. 22:18

31 So it was, after he had buried him, that he spoke to his sons, saying, "When I am dead, then bury me in the tomb where the man of God *is* buried; ᴿlay my bones beside his bones.   2 Kin. 23:17, 18

32 "For the saying which he cried out by the word of the LORD against the altar in Bethel, and against all the ᵀshrines on the high places which *are* in the cities of Samaria, will surely come to pass."   Lit. *houses*

33 After this event Jeroboam did not turn from his evil way, but again he made priests from every class of people for the high places; whoever wished, he consecrated him, and he became one of the priests of the high places.

34 ᴿAnd this thing was the sin of the house of Jeroboam, so as to exterminate and destroy *it* from the face of the earth.   1 Kin. 12:30

Judgment on the House of Jeroboam

14 At that time Abijah the son of Jeroboam became sick.

2 And Jeroboam said to his wife, "Please arise, and disguise yourself, that they may not recognize you as the wife of Jeroboam, and go to Shiloh. Indeed, Ahijah the prophet is there, who told me that ᴿI *would be* king over this people.   1 Kin. 11:29-31

3 "Also take with you ten loaves, *some* cakes, and a jar of honey, and go to him; he will tell you what will become of the child."

4 And Jeroboam's wife did so; she arose and went to Shiloh, and came to the house of Ahijah. But Ahijah could not see, for his eyes were ᵀglazed by reason of his age.   *set*

5 Now the LORD had said to Ahijah, "Here *is* the wife of Jeroboam, coming to ask you something about her son, for he *is* sick. Thus and thus you shall say to her; for it will be, when she comes in, that she will pretend *to be* another *woman.*"

6 And so it was, when Ahijah heard the sound of her footsteps as she came through the door, he said, "Come in, wife of Jeroboam. Why do you pretend *to be* another *person?* For I *have been* sent to you *with* bad *news.*

7 "Go, tell Jeroboam, 'Thus says the LORD God of Israel: ᴿ"Because I exalted you from among the people, and made you ruler over My people Israel,   1 Kin. 16:2

8 "and tore the kingdom away from the house of David, and gave it to you; and yet you have not been as My servant David, ᴿwho kept My commandments and who followed Me with all his heart, to do only what was right in My eyes;   1 Kin. 11:33, 38; 15:5

9 "but you have done more evil than all who were before you, ᴿfor you have gone and made for yourself other gods and molded images to provoke Me to anger, and ᴿhave cast Me behind your back—   1 Kin. 12:28 • Ps. 50:17

10 "therefore behold! I will bring disaster on the house of Jeroboam, and will cut off from Jeroboam every male in Israel, ᴿbond and free; I will take away the remnant of the house of Jeroboam, as one takes away refuse until it is all gone.   Deut. 32:36

11 "The dogs shall eat ᴿwhoever belongs to Jeroboam and dies in the city, and the birds of the air shall eat whoever dies in the field; for the LORD has spoken!" '   1 Kin. 16:4; 21:24

12 "Arise therefore, go to your own house. ᴿWhen your feet enter the city, the child shall die.   1 Kin. 14:17

13 "And all Israel shall mourn for him and bury him, for he is the only one of Jeroboam who shall come to the grave, because in him there is found something good toward the LORD God of Israel in the house of Jeroboam.

14 "Moreover the LORD will raise up for Himself a king over Israel who shall cut off the house of Jeroboam; ᵀthis is the day. What? Even now!   Or this day and from now on

15 "For the LORD will strike Israel, as a reed is shaken in the water. He will uproot Israel from this good land which He gave to their fathers, and will scatter them beyond ᵀthe River, ᴿbecause they have made their *wooden images, provoking the LORD to anger.   The Euphrates • [Ex. 34:13, 14]

16 "And He will give Israel up because of the sins of Jeroboam, ᴿwho sinned and who made Israel sin."   1 Kin. 12:30; 13:34; 15:30, 34; 16:2

17 Then Jeroboam's wife arose and departed, and came to ᴿTirzah. ᴿWhen she came to the threshold of the house, the child died.   Song 6:4 • 1 Kin. 14:12

18 And they buried him; and all Israel mourned for him, ᴿaccording to the word of the LORD which He spoke through His servant Ahijah the prophet.   1 Kin. 14:13

Death of Jeroboam

19 Now the rest of the acts of Jeroboam, how he ᴿmade war and how he reigned, indeed they are written in the book of the chronicles of the kings of Israel.   2 Chr. 13:2-20

20 The period that Jeroboam reigned was twenty-two years. So he rested with his fathers. Then ᴿNadab his son reigned in his place.   1 Kin. 15:25

Rehoboam Reigns in Judah

21 And Rehoboam the son of Solomon reigned in Judah. Rehoboam was forty-one years old when he became king. He reigned seventeen years in Jerusalem, the city which the LORD had chosen out of all the tribes of Israel, to put His name there. His mother's name was Naamah, an Ammonitess.

22 Now Judah did evil in the sight of the LORD, and they provoked Him to jealousy with their sins which they committed, more than all that their fathers had done.

23 For they also built for themselves ᵀhigh places, ᴿsacred pillars, and wooden images on every high hill and under every green tree.   Places for pagan worship • [Deut. 16:22]

24 And there were also *perverted persons in the land. They did according to all the abominations of the nations which the LORD had cast out before the children of Israel.

25 ᴿIt happened in the fifth year of King Rehoboam that Shishak king of Egypt came up against Jerusalem.   1 Kin. 11:40

26 ᴿAnd he took away the treasures of the house of the LORD and the treasures of the king's house; he took away everything. He also took away all the gold shields ᴿwhich Solomon had made.   2 Chr. 12:9-11 • 1 Kin. 10:17

27 Then King Rehoboam made bronze shields in their place, and ᵀcommitted them to the hands of the captains of the ᵀguard, who guarded the doorway of the king's house.   entrusted • Lit. runners

28 And whenever the king entered the house of the LORD, the guards carried them, then brought them back into the guardroom.

29 Now the rest of the acts of Rehoboam, and all that he did, are they not written in the book of the chronicles of the kings of Judah?

30 And there was ᴿwar between Rehoboam and Jeroboam all their days.   1 Kin. 12:21-24; 15:6

31 So Rehoboam rested with his fathers, and was buried with his fathers in the City of David. His mother's name was Naamah, an Ammonitess. Then ᵀAbijam his son reigned in his place.   Abijah, 2 Chr. 12:16 ff.

Abijam Reigns in Judah

15 Inᴿ in the eighteenth year of King Jeroboam the son of Nebat, Abijam became king over Judah.   2 Chr. 13:1

2 He reigned three years in Jerusalem. His mother's name was Maachah the granddaughter of ᴿAbishalom.   2 Chr. 11:21

3 And he walked in all the sins of his father, which he had done before him; ᴿhis heart was not loyal to the LORD his God, as was the heart of his father David.   Ps. 119:80

4 Nevertheless ᴿfor David's sake the LORD his God gave him a lamp in Jerusalem, by

14:15 Or Asherim, Canaanite deities

14:24 Heb. qedeshim, those practicing sodomy and prostitution in religious rituals

setting up his son after him and by establishing Jerusalem;   2 Sam. 21:17

5 because David did *what was* right in the eyes of the Lord, and had not turned aside from anything that He commanded him all the days of his life, [R]except in the matter of Uriah the Hittite.   2 Sam. 11:3, 15–17; 12:9, 10

6 And there was war between *Rehoboam and Jeroboam all the days of his life.

7 [R]Now the rest of the acts of Abijam, and all that he did, *are* they not written in the book of the chronicles of the kings of Judah? And there was war between Abijam and Jeroboam.   2 Chr. 13:2–22

8 [R]So Abijam rested with his fathers, and they buried him in the City of David. Then Asa his son reigned in his place.   2 Chr. 14:1

Asa Reigns in Judah

9 In the twentieth year of Jeroboam king of Israel, Asa became king over Judah.

10 And he reigned forty-one years in Jerusalem. His grandmother's name *was* Maachah the granddaughter of Abishalom.

11 [R]Asa did *what was* right in the eyes of the Lord, as *did* his father David.   2 Chr. 14:2

12 [R]And he banished the *perverted persons from the land, and removed all the idols that his fathers had made.   1 Kin. 14:24; 22:46

13 Also he removed Maachah his grandmother from *being* queen mother, because she had made an obscene image of *Asherah. And Asa cut down her obscene image and [R]burned *it* by the Brook Kidron.   Ex. 32:20

14 But the [T]high places were not removed. Nevertheless Asa's heart was loyal to the Lord all his days.   Places for pagan worship

15 He also brought into the house of the Lord the things which his father had dedicated, and the things which he himself had dedicated: silver and gold and utensils.

16 Now there was war between Asa and Baasha king of Israel all their days.

17 And [R]Baasha king of Israel came up against Judah, and built [R]Ramah, [R]that he might let none go out or come in to Asa king of Judah.   2 Chr. 16:1–6 · Josh. 18:25 · 1 Kin. 12:26–29

18 Then Asa took all the silver and gold *that was* left in the treasuries of the house of the Lord and the treasuries of the king's house, and delivered them into the hand of his servants. And King Asa sent them to [R]Ben-Hadad the son of Tabrimmon, the son of Hezion, king of Syria, who dwelt in [R]Damascus, saying,   2 Chr. 16:2 · 1 Kin. 11:23, 24

19 "Let there be a treaty between you and me, as there was between my father and your father. See, I have sent you a present of silver

15:6 So with MT, LXX, Tg., Vg.; some Heb. mss., Syr. *Abijam*
15:12 Heb. *qedeshim,* those practicing sodomy and prostitution in religious rituals
15:13 A Canaanite goddess

and gold. Come and break your treaty with Baasha king of Israel, so that he will withdraw from me."

20 So Ben-Hadad heeded King Asa, and sent the captains of his armies against the cities of Israel. He attacked Ijon, Dan, [R]Abel Beth Maachah, and all Chinneroth, with all the land of Naphtali.   2 Sam. 20:14, 15

21 Now it happened, when Baasha heard *it,* that he stopped building Ramah, and remained in [R]Tirzah.   1 Kin. 14:17; 16:15–18

22 Then King Asa made a proclamation throughout all Judah; none *was* exempted. And they took away the stones and timber of Ramah, which Baasha had used for building; and with them King Asa built [R]Geba of Benjamin, and [R]Mizpah.   Josh. 21:17 · Josh. 18:26

23 The rest of all the acts of Asa, all his might, all that he did, and the cities which he built, *are* they not written in the book of the chronicles of the kings of Judah? But in the time of his old age he was diseased in his feet.

24 So Asa rested with his fathers, and was buried with his fathers in the City of David his father. [R]Then [R]Jehoshaphat his son reigned in his place.   2 Chr. 17:1 · Matt. 1:8

Nadab Reigns in Israel

25 Now [R]Nadab the son of Jeroboam became king over Israel in the second year of Asa king of Judah, and he reigned over Israel two years.   1 Kin. 14:20

26 And he did evil in the sight of the Lord, and walked in the way of his father, and in his sin by which he had made Israel sin.

27 [R]Then Baasha the son of Ahijah, of the house of Issachar, conspired against him. And Baasha killed him at Gibbethon, which *belonged* to the Philistines, while Nadab and all Israel laid siege to Gibbethon.   1 Kin. 14:14

28 Baasha killed him in the third year of Asa king of Judah, and reigned in his place.

29 And it was so, when he became king, *that* he killed all the house of Jeroboam. He did not leave to Jeroboam anyone that breathed, until he had destroyed him, according to the word of the Lord which He had spoken by His servant Ahijah the Shilonite,

30 [R]because of the sins of Jeroboam, which he had sinned and by which he had made Israel sin, because of his provocation with which he had provoked the Lord God of Israel to anger.   1 Kin. 14:9, 16

31 Now the rest of the acts of Nadab, and all that he did, *are* they not written in the book of the chronicles of the kings of Israel?

32 [R]And there was war between Asa and Baasha king of Israel all their days.   1 Kin. 15:16

Baasha Reigns in Israel

33 In the third year of Asa king of Judah, Baasha the son of Ahijah became king over

all Israel in Tirzah, and *reigned* twenty-four years.

34 He did evil in the sight of the LORD, and walked in the way of Jeroboam, and in his sin by which he had made Israel sin.

16 Then the word of the LORD came to ᴿJehu the son of ᴿHanani, against Baasha, saying: 2 Chr. 19:2; 20:34 • 2 Chr. 16:7-10

2 "Inasmuch as I lifted you out of the dust and made you ruler over My people Israel, and you have walked in the way of Jeroboam, and have made My people Israel sin, to provoke Me to anger with their sins,

3 "surely I will ᵀtake away the posterity of Baasha and the posterity of his house, and I will make your house like the house of Jeroboam the son of Nebat.   *consume*

4 "The dogs shall eat whoever belongs to Baasha and dies in the city, and the birds of the air shall eat whoever dies in the fields."

5 Now the rest of the acts of Baasha, what he did, and his might, ᴿ*are* they not written in the book of the chronicles of the kings of Israel?   2 Chr. 16:11

6 So Baasha ᵀrested with his fathers and was buried in Tirzah. Then Elah his son reigned in his place.   Died and joined his ancestors

7 And also the word of the LORD came by the prophet Jehu the son of Hanani against Baasha and his house, because of all the evil that he did in the sight of the LORD in provoking Him to anger with the work of his hands, in being like the house of Jeroboam, and because ᴿhe killed them.   1 Kin. 15:27, 29

Elah Reigns in Israel

8 In the twenty-sixth year of Asa king of Judah, Elah the son of Baasha became king over Israel, *and reigned* two years in Tirzah.

9 Now his servant Zimri, commander of half *his* chariots, conspired against him as he was in Tirzah drinking himself drunk in the house of Arza, ᴿstewardᵀ of *his* house in Tirzah.   1 Kin. 18:3 • Lit. *who was over the house*

10 And Zimri went in and struck him and killed him in the twenty-seventh year of Asa king of Judah, and reigned in his place.

11 Then it came to pass, when he began to reign, as soon as he was seated on his throne, *that* he killed all the household of Baasha; he ᴿdid not leave him one male, neither of his relatives nor of his friends.   1 Sam. 25:22

12 Thus Zimri destroyed all the household of Baasha, ᴿaccording to the word of the LORD, which He spoke against Baasha by Jehu the prophet,   1 Kin. 16:3

13 for all the sins of Baasha and the sins of Elah his son, by which they had sinned and by which they had made Israel sin, in provoking the LORD God of Israel to anger ᴿwith their ᵀidols.   Deut. 32:21 • Lit. *vanities*

14 Now the rest of the acts of Elah, and all that he did, *are* they not written in the book of the chronicles of the kings of Israel?

Zimri Reigns in Israel

15 In the twenty-seventh year of Asa king of Judah, Zimri had reigned in Tirzah seven days. And the people *were* encamped ᴿagainst Gibbethon, which *belonged* to the Philistines.   1 Kin. 15:27

16 Now the people *who were* encamped heard it said, "Zimri has conspired and also has killed the king." So all Israel made Omri, the commander of the army, king over Israel that day in the camp.

17 Then Omri and all Israel with him went up from Gibbethon, and they besieged Tirzah.

18 And it happened, when Zimri saw that the city was ᵀtaken, that he went into the citadel of the king's house and burned the king's house ᵀdown upon himself with fire, and died,   *captured* • Lit. *over him*

19 because of the sins which he had committed in doing evil in the sight of the LORD, ᴿin walking in the ᴿway of Jeroboam, and in his sin which he had committed to make Israel sin.   1 Kin. 15:26, 34 • 1 Kin. 12:25-33

20 Now the rest of the acts of Zimri, and the treason he committed, *are* they not written in the book of the chronicles of the kings of Israel?

Omri Reigns in Israel

21 Then the people of Israel were divided into two parts: half of the people followed Tibni the son of Ginath, to make him king, and half followed Omri.

22 But the people who followed Omri prevailed over the people who followed Tibni the son of Ginath. So Tibni died and Omri reigned.

23 In the thirty-first year of Asa king of Judah, Omri became king over Israel, *and reigned* twelve years. Six years he reigned in ᴿTirzah.   1 Kin. 15:21

24 And he bought the hill of Samaria from Shemer for two talents of silver; then he built on the hill, and called the name of the city which he built, ᵀSamaria, after the name of Shemer, owner of the hill.   Heb. *Shomron*

25 Omri did evil in the eyes of the LORD, and did worse than all who *were* before him.

26 For he walked in all the ways of Jeroboam the son of Nebat, and in his sin by which he had made Israel sin, provoking the LORD God of Israel to anger with their idols.

27 Now the rest of the acts of Omri which he did, and the might that he showed, *are* they not written in the book of the chronicles of the kings of Israel?

28 So Omri rested with his fathers and was buried in Samaria. Then Ahab his son reigned in his place.

Ahab Reigns in Israel

29 In the thirty-eighth year of Asa king of Judah, Ahab the son of Omri became king

over Israel; and Ahab the son of Omri reigned over Israel in Samaria twenty-two years.

30 Now Ahab the son of Omri did evil in the sight of the LORD, more than all who *were* before him.

31 And it came to pass, as though it had been a trivial thing for him to walk in the sins of Jeroboam the son of Nebat, that he took as wife Jezebel the daughter of Ethbaal, king of the Sidonians; ᴿand he went and served Baal and worshiped him.　　　　1 Kin. 21:25, 26

32 Then he set up an altar for Baal in ᴿthe temple of Baal, which he had built in Samaria.　　　　2 Kin. 10:21, 26, 27

33 ᴿAnd Ahab made a *wooden image. Ahab did more to provoke the LORD God of Israel to anger than all the kings of Israel who were before him.　　　　1 Kin. 13:6

34 In his days Hiel of Bethel built Jericho. He laid its foundation ᵀwith Abiram his firstborn, and with his youngest *son* Segub he set up its gates, ᴿaccording to the word of the LORD, which He had spoken through Joshua the son of Nun.　　At the cost of the life of • Josh. 6:26

Elijah Proclaims a Drought

17 And Elijah the Tishbite, of the inhabitants of Gilead, said to Ahab, "*As the LORD God of Israel lives, before whom I stand, ᴿthere shall not be dew nor rain ᴿthese years, except at my word."　　James 5:17 • Luke 4:25

2 Then the word of the LORD came to him, saying,

3 "Get away from here and turn eastward, and hide by the Brook Cherith, which flows into the Jordan.

4 "And it will be *that* you shall drink from the brook, and I have commanded the ᴿravens to feed you there."　　Job 38:41

5 So he went and did according to the word of the LORD, for he went and stayed by the Brook Cherith, which flows into the Jordan.

6 The ravens brought him bread and meat in the morning, and bread and meat in the evening; and he drank from the brook.

7 And it happened after a while that the brook dried up, because there had been no rain in the land.

Elijah and the Widow

8 Then the word of the LORD came to him, saying,

9 "Arise, go to Zarephath, which *belongs* to Sidon, and dwell there. See, I have commanded a widow there to provide for you."

10 So he arose and went to Zarephath. And when he came to the gate of the city, indeed a widow *was* there gathering sticks. And he called to her and said, "Please bring me a little water in a cup, that I may drink."

11 And as she was going to get *it*, he called to her and said, "Please bring me a morsel of bread in your hand."

12 So she said, "As the LORD your God lives, I do not have bread, only a handful of flour in a bin, and a little oil in a jar; and see, I *am* gathering a couple of sticks that I may go in and prepare it for myself and my son, that we may eat it, and ᴿdie."　　Deut. 28:23, 24

13 And Elijah said to her, "Do not fear; go *and* do as you have said, but make me a small cake from it first, and bring *it* to me; and afterward make *some* for yourself and your son.

14 "For thus says the LORD God of Israel: 'The bin of flour shall not be used up, nor shall the jar of oil run dry, until the day the LORD sends rain on the earth.'"

15 So she went away and did according to the word of Elijah; and she and he and her household ate for *many* days.

16 The bin of flour was not used up, nor did the jar of oil run dry, according to the word of the LORD which He spoke by Elijah.

Elijah Revives the Widow's Son

17 Now it happened after these things *that* the son of the woman who owned the house became sick. And his sickness was so serious that there was no breath left in him.

18 So she said to Elijah, ᴿ"What have I to do with you, O man of God? Have you come to me to bring my sin to remembrance, and to kill my son?"　　Luke 5:8

19 And he said to her, "Give me your son." So he took him out of her arms and carried him to the upper room where he was staying, and laid him on his own bed.

20 Then he cried out to the LORD and said, "O LORD my God, have You also brought tragedy on the widow with whom I lodge, by killing her son?"

21 ᴿAnd he stretched himself out on the child three times, and cried out to the LORD and said, "O LORD my God, I pray, let this child's soul come back to him."　　2 Kin. 4:34, 35

22 Then the LORD heard the voice of Elijah; and the soul of the child came back to him, and he ᴿrevived.　　Heb. 11:35

23 And Elijah took the child and brought him down from the upper room into the house, and gave him to his mother. And Elijah said, "See, your son lives!"

24 Then the woman said to Elijah, "Now by this ᴿI know that you *are* a man of God, *and* that the word of the LORD in your mouth *is* the truth."　　John 2:11; 3:2; 16:30

Elijah's Message to Ahab

18 And it came to pass *after* ᴿmany days that the word of the LORD came to Elijah, in the third year, saying, "Go, present yourself to Ahab, and ᴿI will send rain on the earth."　　Luke 4:25 • Deut. 28:12

16:33 Or *Asherah,* a Canaanite goddess

2 So Elijah went to present himself to Ahab; and *there was* a severe famine in Samaria.

3 And Ahab had called Obadiah, who *was* ^Tin charge of *his* house. (Now Obadiah feared the LORD greatly.   Lit. *over the house*

4 For so it was, while Jezebel ^Tmassacred the prophets of the LORD, that Obadiah had taken one hundred prophets and hidden them, fifty to a cave, and had fed them with bread and water.)   Lit. *cut off*

5 And Ahab had said to Obadiah, "Go into the land to all the springs of water and to all the brooks; perhaps we may find grass to keep the horses and mules alive, so that we will not have to kill any livestock."

6 So they divided the land between them to explore it; Ahab went one way by himself, and Obadiah went another way by himself.

7 Now as Obadiah was on his way, suddenly Elijah met him; and he ^Rrecognized him, and fell on his face, and said, "*Is* that you, my lord Elijah?"   2 Kin. 1:6–8

8 And he answered him, "*It is* I. Go, tell your master, 'Elijah *is here.*' "

9 So he said, "How have I sinned, that you are delivering your servant into the hand of Ahab, to kill me?

10 "As the LORD your God lives, there is no nation or kingdom where my master has not sent someone to hunt for you; and when they said, '*He is* not *here,*' he took an oath from the kingdom or nation that they could not find you.

11 "And now you say, 'Go, tell your master, "Elijah *is here*"'!

12 "And it shall come to pass, *as soon as* I am gone from you, that ^Rthe Spirit of the LORD will carry you to a place I do not know; so when I go and tell Ahab, and he cannot find you, he will kill me. But I your servant have feared the LORD from my youth.   Acts 8:39

13 "Was it not reported to my lord what I did when Jezebel killed the prophets of the LORD, how I hid one hundred men of the LORD's prophets, fifty to a cave, and fed them with bread and water?

14 "And now you say, 'Go, tell your master, "Elijah *is here,*" ' He will kill me!"

15 Then Elijah said, "As the LORD of hosts lives, before whom I stand, I will surely present myself to him today."

16 So Obadiah went to meet Ahab, and told him; and Ahab went to meet Elijah.

17 Then it happened, when Ahab saw Elijah, that Ahab said to him, ^R"*Is that* you, O ^Rtroubler of Israel?"   1 Kin. 21:20 • Josh. 7:25

18 And he answered, "I have not troubled Israel, but you and your father's house *have,* ^Rin that you have forsaken the commandments of the LORD and have followed the Baals.   [2 Chr. 15:2]

19 "Now therefore, send *and* gather all Israel to me on Mount ^RCarmel, the four hundred and fifty prophets of Baal, and the four hundred prophets of ^TAsherah, who eat at Jezebel's table."   Josh. 19:26 • A Canaanite goddess

Elijah's Mount Carmel Victory

20 So Ahab sent for all the children of Israel, and ^Rgathered the prophets together on Mount Carmel.   1 Kin. 22:6

21 And Elijah came to all the people, and said, ^R"How long will you falter between two opinions? If the LORD *is* God, follow Him; but if Baal, ^Rfollow him." But the people answered him not a word.   [Matt. 6:24] • Josh. 24:15

22 Then Elijah said to the people, "I alone am left a prophet of the LORD; but Baal's prophets *are* four hundred and fifty men.

23 "Therefore let them give us two bulls; and let them choose one bull for themselves, cut it in pieces, and lay *it* on the wood, but put no fire *under it*; and I will prepare the other bull, and lay *it* on the wood, but put no fire *under it.*

24 "Then you call on the name of your gods, and I will call on the name of the LORD; and the God who ^Ranswers by fire, He is God." So all the people answered and said, ^T"It is well spoken." 1 Chr. 21:26 • Lit. *The word is good*

25 Now Elijah said to the prophets of Baal, "Choose one bull for yourselves and prepare *it* first, for you *are* many; and call on the name of your god, but put no fire *under it.*"

26 So they took the bull which was given them, and they prepared *it,* and called on the name of Baal from morning even till noon, saying, "O Baal, hear us!" But *there was* no voice; no one answered. Then they leaped about the altar which they had made.

27 And so it was, at noon, that Elijah mocked them and said, "Cry ^Taloud, for he *is* a god; either he is meditating, or he is busy, or he is on a journey, *or* perhaps he is sleeping and must be awakened."   with a loud voice

28 So they cried aloud, and cut themselves, as was their custom, with ^Tknives and lances, until the blood gushed out on them.   swords

29 And when midday was past, ^Rthey prophesied until the *time* of the offering of the *evening* sacrifice. But *there was* ^Rno voice; no one answered, no one paid attention.   Ex. 29:39, 41 • 1 Kin. 18:26

30 Then Elijah said to all the people, "Come near to me." So all the people came near to him. ^RAnd he repaired the altar of the LORD *that was* broken down.   2 Chr. 33:16

31 And Elijah took twelve stones, according to the number of the tribes of the sons of Jacob, to whom the word of the LORD had come, saying, *"Israel shall be your name."

32 Then with the stones he built an altar ^Rin the name of the LORD; and he made a trench

18:31 Gen. 32:28; 35:10; 2 Kin. 17:34

around the altar large enough to hold ᵀtwo seahs of seed.   [Col. 3:17] • 4.349 bu.

33 And he ᴿput the wood in order, cut the bull in pieces, and laid *it* on the wood, and said, "Fill four waterpots with water, and ᴿpour *it* on the burnt sacrifice and on the wood."   Lev. 1:6–8 • Judg. 6:20

34 Then he said, "Do *it* a second time," and they did *it* a second time; and he said, "Do *it* a third time," and they did *it* a third time.

35 So the water ran all around the altar; and he also filled the trench with water.

▼ 32–F. The Prayer of a Prophet at the Crossroads

36 And it came to pass, at *the time of* the offering of the *evening* sacrifice, that Elijah the prophet came near and said, "LORD God of Abraham, Isaac, and Israel, let it be known this day that You *are* God in Israel and I *am* Your servant, and *that* I have done all these things at Your word.

37 "Hear me, O LORD, hear me, that this people may know that You *are* the LORD God, and *that* You have turned their hearts
▲ back *to* You again."

38 Then ᴿthe fire of the LORD fell and consumed the burnt sacrifice, and the wood and the stones and the dust, and it licked up the water that *was* in the trench.   1 Chr. 21:26

39 Now when all the people saw *it*, they fell on their faces; and they said, ᴿ"The LORD, He *is* God! The LORD, He *is* God!"   1 Kin. 18:21, 24

40 And Elijah said to them, "Seize the prophets of Baal! Do not let one of them escape!" So they seized them; and Elijah brought them down to the Brook Kishon and ᴿexecuted them there.   [Deut. 13:5; 18:20]

The Drought Ends

41 Then Elijah said to Ahab, "Go up, eat and drink; for *there is* the sound of abundance of rain."

42 So Ahab went up to eat and drink. And Elijah went up to the top of Carmel; ᴿthen he bowed down on the ground, and put his face between his knees,   James 5:17, 18

43 and said to his servant, "Go up now, look toward the sea." So he went up and looked, and said, "*There is* nothing." And seven times he said, "Go again."

44 Then it came to pass the seventh *time,* that he said, "There is a cloud, as small as a man's hand, rising out of the sea!" So he said, "Go up, say to Ahab, ᵀ'Prepare *your chariot,* and go down before the rain stops you.' "   Lit. Bind or Harness

45 Now it happened in the meantime that the sky became black with clouds and wind, and there was a heavy rain. So Ahab rode away and went to Jezreel.

46 Then the hand of the LORD came upon Elijah; and he girded up his loins and ran ahead of Ahab to the entrance of Jezreel.

Elijah Escapes from Jezebel

19 And Ahab told Jezebel all that Elijah had done, also how he had ᴿexecuted all the prophets with the sword.   1 Kin. 18:40

2 Then Jezebel sent a messenger to Elijah, saying, "So let the gods do *to* me, and more also, if I do not make your life as the life of one of them by tomorrow about this time."

3 And when he saw *that,* he arose and ran for his life, and went to Beersheba, which *belongs* to Judah, and left his servant there.

4 But he himself went a day's journey into the wilderness, and came and sat down under a broom tree. And he prayed that he might

---

32–F. The Prayer of a Prophet at the Crossroads (1 Kings 18:36, 37)—The eyes of an entire nation were fastened upon Elijah (vv. 17–40). Baal's 450 prophets had failed to call down fire upon their altar, although they had prayed earnestly all day long. Elijah faced them defiantly. His very name, Elijah, meant "My God is Jehovah." It had been according to Elijah's word that no rain had fallen in the land for three years (1 Kin. 17:1, page 346). Now he had spoken again, openly challenging the men of Baal to this contest of power. Baal had failed. It was his turn. Would Jehovah send fire from heaven?

Elijah now ordered four containers of water to be poured over the altar and into its trenches. As Elijah approached the water-soaked altar, the nation held its breath; even as he was at the crossroads of his ministry, so Israel too was at a crossroads which would determine its destiny. Who was God—Baal or Jehovah? Would fire fall in answer to Elijah's prayer?

Let us look back at this moment on Mount Carmel and consider Elijah's prayer:

(1) He looked to the God of Abraham, Isaac, and Jacob (Israel), who answered the prayers of these patriarchs in their crises (v. 36).

(2) He prayed that the knowledge of the true God might fill his nation (v. 36).

(3) He asked for the vindication of his own words and deeds, that all might know that these were done at Jehovah's bidding—the cessation of rain, his rebuke of the evil rulers Ahab and Jezebel, and all of the resulting national consternation (v. 36; cf. 1 Kin. 17:1, 17, 18, page 346).

(4) He sought to bring back to the Lord the rebellious hearts of his nation (v. 37).

"Then the fire of the LORD fell" (v. 38). God answered the prayer of His servant at the crossroads. God will also answer you at your crossroads.

See Habakkuk 3:1–19, page 901, for **Point 32–G: A Prayer for Revival.**

die, and said, "It is enough! Now, LORD, take my life, for I *am* no better than my fathers!"

5 Then as he lay and slept under a broom tree, suddenly an ᵀangel touched him, and said to him, "Arise *and* eat."   Or *Angel*

6 Then he looked, and there by his head *was* a cake baked on ᵀcoals, and a jar of water. So he ate and drank, and lay down again.   *hot stones*

7 And the ᵀangel of the LORD came back the second time, and touched him, and said, "Arise *and* eat, because the journey *is* too great for you."   Or *Angel*

8 So he arose, and ate and drank; and he went in the strength of that food forty days and ᴿforty nights as far as ᴿHoreb, the mountain of God.   Matt. 4:2 · Ex. 3:1; 4:27

9 And there he went into a cave, and spent the night in that place; and behold, the word of the LORD *came* to him, and He said to him, "What are you doing here, Elijah?"

10 So he said, "I have been very zealous for the LORD God of hosts; for the children of Israel have forsaken Your covenant, torn down Your altars, and ᴿkilled Your prophets with the sword. ᴿI alone am left; and they seek to take my life."   1 Kin. 18:4 · 1 Kin. 18:22

God's Revelation to Elijah

11 Then He said, "Go out, and stand on the mountain before the LORD." And behold, the LORD ᴿpassed by, and ᴿa great and strong wind tore into the mountains and broke the rocks in pieces before the LORD, *but* the LORD *was* not in the wind; and after the wind an earthquake, *but* the LORD *was* not in the earthquake;   Ex. 33:21, 22 · Ezek. 1:4; 37:7

12 and after the earthquake a fire, *but* the LORD *was* not in the fire; and after the fire ᵀa still small voice.   *a delicate, whispering voice*

13 So it was, when Elijah heard *it*, that ᴿhe wrapped his face in his mantle and went out and stood in the entrance of the cave. Suddenly a voice *came* to him, and said, "What are you doing here, Elijah?"   Ex. 3:6

14 ᴿAnd he said, "I have been very zealous for the LORD God of hosts; because the children of Israel have forsaken Your covenant, torn down Your altars, and killed Your prophets with the sword. I alone am left; and they seek to take my life."   1 Kin. 19:10

15 Then the LORD said to him: "Go, return on your way to the Wilderness of Damascus; ᴿand when you arrive, anoint Hazael *as* king over Syria.   2 Kin. 8:8-15

16 "Also you shall anoint Jehu the son of Nimshi *as* king over Israel. And ᴿElisha the son of Shaphat of Abel Meholah you shall anoint *as* prophet in your place.   2 Kin. 2:9-15

17 "It shall be *that* whoever escapes the sword of Hazael, Jehu will kill; and whoever escapes the sword of Jehu, Elisha will kill.

18 ᴿ"Yet I have reserved seven thousand in Israel, all whose knees have not bowed to Baal, ᴿand every mouth that has not kissed him."   Rom. 11:4 · Hos. 13:2

Elisha Follows Elijah

19 So he departed from there, and found Elisha the son of Shaphat, who *was* plowing *with* twelve yoke *of oxen* before him, and he was with the twelfth. Then Elijah passed by him and threw his mantle on him.

20 And he left the oxen and ran after Elijah, and said, ᴿ"Please let me kiss my father and my mother, and *then* I will follow you." And he said to him, "Go back again, for what have I done to you?"   [Matt. 8:21, 22]

21 So *Elisha* turned back from him, and took a yoke of oxen and slaughtered them and ᴿboiled their flesh, using the oxen's equipment, and gave it to the people, and they ate. Then he arose and followed Elijah, and became his servant.   2 Sam. 24:22

Ahab Defeats the Syrians

20 Now Ben-Hadad the king of Syria gathered all his forces together; thirty-two kings were with him, with horses and chariots. And he went up and besieged Samaria, and made war against it.

2 Then he sent messengers into the city to Ahab king of Israel, and said to him, "Thus says Ben-Hadad:

3 'Your silver and your gold *are* mine; your loveliest wives and children are mine.' "

4 And the king of Israel answered and said, "My lord, O king, just as you say, I and all that I have *are* yours."

5 Then the messengers came back and said, "Thus speaks Ben-Hadad, saying, 'Indeed I have sent to you, saying, "You shall deliver to me your silver and your gold, your wives and your children";

6 'but I will send my servants to you tomorrow about this time, and they shall search your house and the houses of your servants. And it shall be, *that* whatever is ᵀpleasant in your eyes, they will put *it* in their hands and take *it*.' "   *pleasing*

7 So the king of Israel called all the elders of the land, and said, "Notice, please, and see how this *man* seeks trouble, for he sent to me for my wives, my children, my silver, and my gold; and I did not deny him."

8 And all the elders and all the people said to him, "Do not listen or consent."

9 Therefore he said to the messengers of Ben-Hadad, "Tell my lord the king, 'All that you sent for to your servant the first time I will do, but this thing I cannot do.' " And the messengers departed and brought back word to him.

10 Then Ben-Hadad sent to him and said, "The gods do so to me, and more also, if enough dust is left of Samaria for a handful for each of the people who follow me."

11 So the king of Israel answered and said, "Tell *him*, 'Let not the one who puts on *his* armor boast like the one who takes *it off*.' "

12 And it happened when *Ben-Hadad* heard this message, as he and the kings *were* drinking at the ᵀcommand post, that he said to his servants, "Get ready." And they got ready to attack the city.   Lit. *booths* or *shelters*

13 Suddenly a prophet approached Ahab king of Israel, saying, "Thus says the LORD: 'Have you seen all this great multitude? Behold, I will deliver it into your hand today, and you shall know that I *am* the LORD.' "

14 So Ahab said, "By whom?" And he said, "Thus says the LORD: 'By the young leaders of the provinces.' " Then he said, "Who will set the battle in order?" And he answered, "You."

15 Then he mustered the young leaders of the provinces, and there were two hundred and thirty-two; and after them he mustered all the people, all the children of Israel—seven thousand.

16 So they went out at noon. Meanwhile Ben-Hadad and the thirty-two kings helping him were ᴿgetting drunk at the command post.   1 Kin. 16:9; 20:12

17 The young leaders of the provinces went out first. And Ben-Hadad sent out *a patrol*, and they told him, saying, "Men are coming out of Samaria!"

18 So he said, "If they have come out for peace, take them alive; and if they have come out for war, take them alive."

19 Then these young leaders of the provinces went out of the city with the army which followed them.

20 And each one killed his man; so the Syrians fled, and Israel pursued them; and Ben-Hadad the king of Syria escaped on a horse with the cavalry.

21 Then the king of Israel went out and attacked the horses and chariots, and killed the Syrians with a great slaughter.

22 And the prophet came to the king of Israel and said to him, "Go, strengthen yourself; take note, and see what you should do, ᴿfor in the spring of the year the king of Syria will come up against you."   2 Sam. 11:1

The Syrians Again Defeated

23 Then the servants of the king of Syria said to him, "Their gods *are* gods of the hills. Therefore they were stronger than we; but if we fight against them in the plain, surely we will be stronger than they.

24 "So do this thing: Dismiss the kings, each from his position, and put captains in their ᵀplaces;   *positions*

25 "and you shall muster an army like the army ᵀthat you have lost, horse for horse and chariot for chariot. Then we will fight against them in the plain; surely we will be stronger

than they." And he listened to their voice and did so.   Lit. *that fell from you*

26 So it was, in the spring of the year, that Ben-Hadad mustered the Syrians and went up to ᴿAphek to fight against Israel.   Josh. 13:4

27 And the children of Israel were mustered and given provisions, and they went against them. Now the children of Israel encamped before them like two little flocks of goats, while the Syrians filled the countryside.

28 Then a man of God came and spoke to the king of Israel, and said, "Thus says the LORD: 'Because the Syrians have said, "The LORD *is* God of the hills, but He *is* not God of the valleys," therefore ᴿI will deliver all this great multitude into your hand, and you shall know that I *am* the LORD.' "   1 Kin. 20:13

29 And they encamped opposite each other for seven days. So it was that on the seventh day the battle was joined; and the children of Israel killed one hundred thousand foot soldiers *of* the Syrians in one day.

30 But the rest fled to Aphek, into the city; then a wall fell on twenty-seven thousand of the men *who were* left. And Ben-Hadad fled and went into the city, into an inner chamber.

Ahab's Treaty with Ben-Hadad

31 Then his servants said to him, "Look now, we have heard that the kings of the house of Israel *are* merciful kings. Please, let us put sackcloth around our waists and ropes around our heads, and go out to the king of Israel; perhaps he will spare your life."

32 So they wore sackcloth around their waists and *put* ropes around their heads, and came to the king of Israel and said, "Your servant Ben-Hadad says, 'Please let me live.' " And he said, "*Is* he still alive? He *is* my brother."

33 Now the men were watching closely to see whether *any sign of mercy would come* from him; and they quickly grasped *at this word* and said, "Your brother Ben-Hadad." So he said, "Go, bring him." Then Ben-Hadad came out to him; and he had him come up into the chariot.

34 So *Ben-Hadad* said to him, ᴿ"The cities which my father took from your father I will restore; and you may set up marketplaces for yourself in Damascus, as my father did in Samaria." Then *Ahab said*, "I will send you away with this treaty." So he made a treaty with him and sent him away.   1 Kin. 15:20

Ahab Condemned

35 Now a certain man of the sons of the prophets said to his neighbor ᴿby the word of the LORD, "Strike me, please." And the man refused to strike him.   1 Kin. 13:17, 18

36 Then he said to him, "Because you have not obeyed the voice of the LORD, surely, as

soon as you depart from me, a lion shall kill you." And as soon as he left him, ᴿa lion found him and killed him.   1 Kin. 13:24

37 And he found another man, and said, "Strike me, please." So the man struck him, inflicting a wound.

38 Then the prophet departed and waited for the king by the road, and disguised himself with a bandage over his eyes.

39 Now as the king passed by, he cried out to the king and said, "Your servant went out into the midst of the battle; and there, a man came over and brought a man to me, and said, 'Guard this man; if by any means he is missing, your life shall be for his life, or else you shall ᵀpay a talent of silver.'   Lit. *weigh*

40 "While your servant was busy here and there, he was gone." Then the king of Israel said to him, "So *shall* your judgment *be*; you yourself have decided *it*."

41 And he hastened to take the bandage away from his eyes; and the king of Israel recognized him as one of the prophets.

42 Then he said to him, "Thus says the LORD: 'Because you have let slip out of *your* hand a man whom I appointed to utter destruction, therefore your life shall go for his life, and your people for his people.'"

43 So the king of Israel went to his house sullen and displeased, and came to Samaria.

Naboth Is Murdered for His Vineyard

21 And it came to pass after these things *that* Naboth the Jezreelite had a vineyard which *was* in ᴿJezreel, next to the palace of Ahab king of Samaria.   1 Kin. 18:45, 46

2 So Ahab spoke to Naboth, saying, "Give me your vineyard, that I may have it for a vegetable garden, because it *is* near, next to my house; and for it I will give you a vineyard better than it. *Or*, if it seems good to you, I will give you its worth in money."

3 But Naboth said to Ahab, "The LORD forbid ᴿthat I should give the inheritance of my fathers to you!"   [Num. 36:7]

4 So Ahab went into his house sullen and displeased because of the word which Naboth the Jezreelite had spoken to him; for he had said, "I will not give you the inheritance of my fathers." And he lay down on his bed, and turned away his face, and would eat no food.

5 But ᴿJezebel his wife came to him, and said to him, "Why is your spirit so sullen that you eat no food?"   1 Kin. 19:1, 2

6 He said to her, "Because I spoke to Naboth the Jezreelite, and said to him, 'Give me your vineyard for money; or else, if it pleases you, I will give you *another* vineyard for it.' And he answered, 'I will not give you my vineyard.'"

7 Then Jezebel his wife said to him, "You now exercise authority over Israel! Arise, eat food, and let your heart be cheerful; I will give you the vineyard of Naboth the Jezreelite."

8 And she wrote letters in Ahab's name, sealed *them* with his seal, and sent the letters to the elders and the nobles who *were* dwelling in the city with Naboth.

9 She wrote in the letters, saying, "Proclaim a fast, and seat Naboth ᵀwith high honor among the people;   Lit. *at the head*

10 "and seat two men, scoundrels, before him to bear witness against him, saying, 'You have ᴿblasphemed God and the king.' Then take him out, and ᴿstone him, that he may die."   [Ex. 22:28] • [Lev. 24:14]

11 So the men of his city, the elders and nobles who were inhabitants of his city, did as Jezebel had sent to them, as it *was* written in the letters which she had sent to them.

12 They proclaimed a fast, and seated Naboth with high honor among the people.

13 And two men, scoundrels, came in and sat before him; and the scoundrels ᴿwitnessed against him, against Naboth, in the presence of the people, saying, "Naboth has blasphemed God and the king!" Then they took him outside the city and stoned him with stones, so that he died.   [Ex. 20:16; 23:1, 7]

14 Then they sent to Jezebel, saying, "Naboth has been stoned and is dead."

15 And it came to pass, when Jezebel heard that Naboth had been stoned and was dead, that Jezebel said to Ahab, "Arise, take possession of the vineyard of Naboth the Jezreelite, which he refused to give you for money; for Naboth is not alive, but dead."

16 So it was, when Ahab heard that Naboth was dead, that Ahab got up and went down to take possession of the vineyard of Naboth the Jezreelite.

The LORD Condemns Ahab

17 ᴿThen the word of the LORD came to ᴿElijah the Tishbite, saying,   [Ps. 9:12] • 1 Kin. 19:1

18 "Arise, go down to meet Ahab king of Israel, ᴿwho *lives* in Samaria. There *he is*, in the vineyard of Naboth, where he has gone down to take possession of it.   2 Chr. 22:9

19 "You shall speak to him, saying, 'Thus says the LORD: "Have you murdered and also taken possession?"' And you shall speak to him, saying, 'Thus says the LORD: "In the place where dogs licked the blood of Naboth, dogs shall lick your blood, even yours."'"

20 So Ahab said to Elijah, "Have you found me, O my enemy?" And he answered, "I have found *you*, because you have sold yourself to do evil in the sight of the LORD:

21 'Behold, I will bring calamity on you. I will take away your posterity, and will cut off from Ahab ᴿevery male in Israel, both ᴿbond and free.   1 Sam. 25:22 • 1 Kin. 14:10

22 'I will make your house like the house of Jeroboam the son of Nebat, and like the house of Baasha the son of Ahijah, because of

the provocation with which you have provoked *Me* to anger, and made Israel sin.'

23 "And ᴿconcerning Jezebel the Lᴏʀᴅ also
spoke, saying, 'The dogs shall eat Jezebel by
the *wall of Jezreel.'   2 Kin. 9:10, 30-37

24 "The dogs shall eat whoever belongs to
Ahab and dies in the city, and the birds of the
air shall eat whoever dies in the field."

25 But ᴿthere was no one like Ahab who
sold himself to do wickedness in the sight of
the Lᴏʀᴅ, ᴿbecause Jezebel his wife ᵀstirred
him up.   1 Kin. 16:30-33; 21:20 • 1 Kin. 16:31 • *incited him*

26 And he behaved very abominably in
following idols, according to all ᴿ*that* the
Amorites had done, whom the Lᴏʀᴅ had cast
out before the children of Israel.   2 Kin. 21:11

27 So it was, when Ahab heard those words,
that he tore his clothes and ᴿput sackcloth on
his body, and fasted and lay in sackcloth, and
went about mourning.   Gen. 37:34

28 And the word of the Lᴏʀᴅ came to Elijah
the Tishbite, saying,

29 "See how Ahab has humbled himself
before Me? Because he ᴿhas humbled himself
before Me, I will not bring the calamity in his
days. In the days of his son I will bring the
calamity on his house."   [2 Kin. 22:19]

Micaiah Warns Ahab

22 Now three years passed without war
between Syria and Israel.

2 Then it came to pass, in the third year,
that ᴿJehoshaphat the king of Judah went
down to *visit* the king of Israel.   2 Chr. 18:2

3 And the king of Israel said to his servants, "Do you know that ᴿRamoth in Gilead
is ours, but we hesitate to take it out of the
hand of the king of Syria?"   Deut. 4:43

4 So he said to Jehoshaphat, "Will you go
with me to fight at Ramoth Gilead?" Jehoshaphat said to the king of Israel, ᴿ"I *am* as you
are, my people as your people, my horses as
your horses."   2 Kin. 3:7

5 Also Jehoshaphat said to the king of
Israel, ᴿ"Please inquire for the word of the
Lᴏʀᴅ today."   2 Kin. 3:11

6 Then the king of Israel gathered ᵀthe
prophets together, about four hundred men,
and said to them, "Shall I go against Ramoth
Gilead to fight, or shall I refrain?" So they
said, "Go up, for the Lord will deliver *it* into
the hand of the king."   The false prophets

7 And ᴿJehoshaphat said, "*Is there* not still
a prophet of the Lᴏʀᴅ here, that we may
inquire of ᵀHim?"   2 Kin. 3:11 • Or *him*

8 So the king of Israel said to Jehoshaphat, "*There is* still one man, Micaiah the son
of Imlah, by whom we may inquire of the
Lᴏʀᴅ; but I hate him, because he does not
prophesy good concerning me, but evil." And

21:23 So with MT, LXX; some Heb. mss., Syr., Tg., Vg.
plot of ground instead of *wall* (cf. 2 Kin. 9:36)

Jehoshaphat said, "Let not the king say such
things!"

9 Then the king of Israel called an officer
and said, "Bring Micaiah the son of Imlah
quickly!"

10 The king of Israel and Jehoshaphat the
king of Judah, having put on *their* robes, sat
each on his throne, at a threshing floor at the
entrance of the gate of Samaria; and all the
prophets prophesied before them.

11 Now Zedekiah the son of Chenaanah
had made ᴿhorns of iron for himself; and he
said, "Thus says the Lᴏʀᴅ: 'With these you
shall ᴿgore the Syrians until they are destroyed.' "   Zech. 1:18-21 • Deut. 33:17

12 And all the prophets prophesied so, saying, "Go up to Ramoth Gilead and prosper,
for the Lᴏʀᴅ will deliver *it* into the king's
hand."

13 Then the messenger who had gone to
call Micaiah spoke to him, saying, "Now
listen, the words of the prophets with one
accord encourage the king. Please, let your
word be like the word of one of them, and
speak encouragement."

14 And Micaiah said, "*As* the Lᴏʀᴅ lives,
ᴿwhatever the Lᴏʀᴅ says to me, that I will
speak."   Num. 22:38; 24:13

15 Then he came to the king; and the king
said to him, "Micaiah, shall we go to war
against Ramoth Gilead, or shall we refrain?"
And he answered him, "Go and prosper, for
the Lᴏʀᴅ will deliver *it* into the hand of the
king!"

16 So the king said to him, "How many
times shall I make you swear that you tell me
nothing but the truth in the name of the
Lᴏʀᴅ?"

17 Then he said, "I saw all Israel ᴿscattered
on the mountains, as sheep that have no
shepherd. And the Lᴏʀᴅ said, 'These have no
master. Let each return to his house in
peace.' "   Matt. 9:36

18 And the king of Israel said to Jehoshaphat, "Did I not tell you he would not prophesy good concerning me, but evil?"

19 Then *Micaiah* said, "Therefore hear the
word of the Lᴏʀᴅ: I saw the Lᴏʀᴅ sitting on
His throne, and all the host of heaven standing by, on His right hand and on His left.

20 "And the Lᴏʀᴅ said, 'Who will persuade
Ahab to go up, that he may fall at Ramoth
Gilead?' So one spoke in this manner, and
another spoke in that manner.

21 "Then a spirit came forward and stood
before the Lᴏʀᴅ, and said, 'I will persuade
him.'

22 "The Lᴏʀᴅ said to him, 'In what way?'
So he said, 'I will go out and be a lying spirit
in the mouth of all his prophets.' And *the
Lᴏʀᴅ* said, ᴿ'You shall persuade *him*, and also
prevail. Go out and do so.'   Judg. 9:23

23 ᴿ"Therefore look! The Lᴏʀᴅ has put a

lying spirit in the mouth of all these prophets of yours, and the LORD has declared disaster against you." [Ezek. 14:9]

24 Now Zedekiah the son of Chenaanah went near and struck Micaiah on the cheek, and said, "Which way did the spirit from the LORD go from me to speak to you?"

25 And Micaiah said, "Indeed, you shall see on that day when you go into an ᴿinner chamber to hide!" 1 Kin. 20:30

26 So the king of Israel said, "Take Micaiah, and return him to Amon the governor of the city and to Joash the king's son;

27 "and say, 'Thus says the king: "Put this *fellow* in ᴿprison, and feed him with bread of affliction and water of affliction, until I come in peace." ' " 2 Chr. 16:10; 18:25-27

28 But Micaiah said, "If you ever return in peace, the LORD has not spoken by me." And he said, "Take heed, all you people!"

Ahab Dies in Battle

29 So the king of Israel and Jehoshaphat the king of Judah went up to Ramoth Gilead.

30 And the king of Israel said to Jehoshaphat, "I will disguise myself and go into battle; but you put on your robes." So the king of Israel ᴿdisguised himself and went into battle. 2 Chr. 35:22

31 Now the king of Syria had commanded the thirty-two ᴿcaptains of his chariots, saying, "Fight with no one small or great, but only with the king of Israel." 1 Kin. 20:24

32 So it was, when the captains of the chariots saw Jehoshaphat, that they said, "Surely it *is* the king of Israel!" Therefore they turned aside to fight against him, and Jehoshaphat ᴿcried out. 2 Chr. 18:31

33 And it happened, when the captains of the chariots saw that it *was* not the king of Israel, that they turned back from pursuing him.

34 Now a *certain* man drew a bow at random, and struck the king of Israel between the joints of his armor. So he said to the driver of his chariot, "Turn around and take me out of the battle, for I am wounded."

35 The battle increased that day; and the king was propped up in his chariot, facing the Syrians, and died at evening. The blood ran out from the wound onto the floor of the chariot.

36 Then, as the sun was going down, a shout went throughout the army, saying, "Every man to his city, and every man to his own country!"

37 So the king died, and was brought to Samaria. And they buried the king in Samaria.

38 Then *someone* washed the chariot at a pool in Samaria, and the dogs licked up his blood while *the harlots bathed, according to

the word of the LORD which He had spoken.

39 Now the rest of the acts of Ahab, and all that he did, ᴿthe ivory house which he built and all the cities that he built, *are* they not written in the book of the chronicles of the kings of Israel? Amos 3:15

40 So Ahab rested with his fathers. Then Ahaziah his son reigned in his place.

Jehoshaphat Reigns in Judah

41 ᴿJehoshaphat the son of Asa had become king over Judah in the fourth year of Ahab king of Israel. 2 Chr. 20:31

42 Jehoshaphat *was* thirty-five years old when he became king, and he reigned twenty-five years in Jerusalem. His mother's name *was* Azubah the daughter of Shilhi.

43 And he walked in all the ways of his father Asa. He did not turn aside from them, doing *what was* right in the eyes of the LORD. Nevertheless ᴿthe high places were not taken away, *for* the people offered sacrifices and burned incense on the high places. 2 Kin. 12:3

44 Also ᴿJehoshaphat made ᴿpeace with the king of Israel. 2 Chr. 19:2 • 2 Chr. 18:1

45 Now the rest of the acts of Jehoshaphat, the might that he showed, and how he made war, *are* they not written ᴿin the book of the chronicles of the kings of Judah? 2 Chr. 20:34

46 ᴿAnd the rest of the *perverted persons, who remained in the days of his father Asa, he banished from the land. 1 Kin. 14:24; 15:12

47 ᴿ*There was* then no king in Edom, only a deputy of the king. 2 Sam. 8:14

48 Jehoshaphat made *merchant ships to go to Ophir for gold; but they never sailed, for the ships were wrecked at Ezion Geber.

49 Then Ahaziah the son of Ahab said to Jehoshaphat, "Let my servants go with your servants in the ships." But Jehoshaphat would not.

50 And ᴿJehoshaphat rested with his fathers, and was buried with his fathers in the City of David his father. Then Jehoram his son reigned in his place. 2 Chr. 21:1

Ahaziah Reigns in Israel

51 ᴿAhaziah the son of Ahab became king over Israel in Samaria in the seventeenth year of Jehoshaphat king of Judah, and reigned two years over Israel. 1 Kin. 22:40

52 He did evil in the sight of the LORD, and ᴿwalked in the way of his father and in the way of his mother and in the way of Jeroboam the son of Nebat, who had made Israel sin; 1 Kin. 15:26; 21:25

53 for ᴿhe served Baal and worshiped him, and provoked the LORD God of Israel to anger, ᴿaccordingᵀ to all that his father had done. Judg. 2:11 • 1 Kin. 16:30-32 • In the same way that

22:46 Heb. *qadesh,* those practicing sodomy and prostitution in religious rituals
22:48 Lit. *ships of Tarshish*

22:38 Tg., Syr. *they washed his armor*

THE SECOND BOOK OF THE
Kings

AUTHORSHIP. To be sure, 2 Kings is adventuresome reading. But who wrote this fast-moving historical account of the two kingdoms? We do not know for certain who the human author is. There is no internal evidence; the author does not identify himself. The traditional view from the Jewish Talmud ascribes the book to the prophet Jeremiah. This seems most acceptable. Jeremiah is a logical candidate for several reasons: (1) He was the last prophet of Israel's independence. (2) He would be moved to preserve the record of Israel's history. (3) He demonstrated devotion to history in his own prophecy, the book that bears his name. (4) There are similarities between 2 Kings and the book of Jeremiah, not only in historical details but also in the style of writing as well. These reasons are not conclusive, but they do give us grounds for holding to Jeremiah as the author of 2 Kings.

CONTEXT. 1 and 2 Kings recount four centuries of Israelite kings, from the death of David to the liberation of Jehoiachin from prison (971–560 B.C.). If you are looking for exciting reading—here it is! 2 Kings reports to the world a most complete record of two tragedies in the national life of Israel: (1) the fall of Israel, the northern kingdom, in 722 B.C.; (2) the fall of the southern kingdom, Judah, and the burning of Jerusalem, in 586 B.C.

HOW 2 KINGS FITS INTO THE BIBLE. Actually, the history contained in 1 and 2 Kings forms a single volume in the original Hebrew canon. The division into two books goes back to the Greek translation, called the Septuagint, and a Latin version called the Vulgate.

The Septuagint is designated by the Roman numerals, LXX, after the seventy translators who worked on the translation. All this goes back to between 285–247 B.C. The Vulgate was a much later translation. A Christian scholar by the name of Jerome was commissioned by the bishop of Rome, in A.D. 383, to undertake a Latin translation of the Bible. In A.D. 392 Samuel and Kings were issued, and the entire Bible was complete in A.D. 405.

In both the Septuagint and the Vulgate Samuel and Kings were divided quite arbitrarily, not even at any marked epoch in the historical narrative. It was more than likely for convenience of use and reference that the division was made.

On a more inspiring note, we see in 2 Kings the miracle ministry of the great prophet Elisha. His ministry was quite long, extending through the reigns of at least five kings of Israel (93–95 years). He was very useful to these kings as he was able to furnish insight and counsel that related to the affairs of Israel. His advice, however, was not always appreciated. He spoke to man from God and boldly confronted the evil, even of kings. But in all his miracle-working ministry, Elisha attested Jehovah to be the living God over Israel.

SUMMARY STATEMENT. The writer is saying to all generations that there are significant spiritual lessons to be learned from the way God acts and interacts in the lives and history of His people. The central theme to keep in mind is the fall of the kingdom.

HOW 2 KINGS FITS TOGETHER. What do we have in this book? Is it simply a synchronized list of the kings of Israel and Judah, or is there a more fundamental purpose of its writing? The prophetic sayings throughout the book relate the events of that time to God and His government over His people. The sins of the people are brought forth, their repentance is recorded, God's punishment is pronounced and His forgiveness is conveyed.

There are two major divisions in the book: (1) The Corruption of the Divided Kingdom (1—16); (2) The Retribution upon the Divided Kingdom (17—25).

The book of 2 Kings is truly the Word and Works of God. You will read not so much what He had to say, but what He did, in and through man—be he evil or good.

It seems that God does not deal immediate retribution to evil men today; but the teaching of 2 Kings is still true: Man will reap what he sows.

—G.C.S.

God Judges Ahaziah

MOAB [R]rebelled against Israel [R]after
the death of Ahab.   2 Sam. 8:2 • 2 Kin. 3:5
2 Now Ahaziah fell through the lattice of his upper room in Samaria, and was
injured; so he sent messengers and said to
them, "Go, inquire of Baal-Zebub, the god of
Ekron, whether I shall recover from this
injury."

3 But the [T]angel of the LORD said to Elijah
the Tishbite, "Arise, go up to meet the messengers of the king of Samaria, and say to
them, 'Is it because there is no God in Israel
that you are going to inquire of Baal-Zebub,
the god of Ekron?'   Or Angel
4 "Now therefore, thus says the LORD:
'You shall not come down from the bed to
which you have gone up, but you shall surely
die.' " So Elijah departed.
5 And when the messengers returned to
[T]him, he said to them, "Why have you come
back?"   Ahaziah
6 So they said to him, "A man came up to
meet us, and said to us, 'Go, return to the
king who sent you, and say to him, "Thus
says the LORD: 'Is it because there is no God
in Israel that you are sending to inquire of
Baal-Zebub, the god of Ekron? Therefore you
shall not come down from the bed to which
you have gone up, but you shall surely
die.' " ' "
7 Then he said to them, "What kind of
man was it who came up to meet you and
told you these words?"
8 So they answered him, "A hairy man
wearing a leather belt around his waist." And
he said, [R]"It is Elijah the Tishbite."   1 Kin. 18:7
9 Then the king sent to him a captain of
fifty with his fifty men. So he went up to him;
and there he was, sitting on the top of a hill.
And he spoke to him: "Man of God, the king
has said, 'Come down!' "
10 So Elijah answered and said to the captain of fifty, "If I am a man of God, then let
fire come down from heaven and consume
you and your fifty men." And fire came down
from heaven and consumed him and his fifty.
11 Then he sent to him another captain of
fifty with his fifty men. And he answered and
said to him: "Man of God, thus has the king
said, 'Come down quickly!' "
12 So Elijah answered and said to them, "If
I am a man of God, let fire come down from
heaven and consume you and your fifty
men." And the fire of God came down from
heaven and consumed him and his fifty.
13 Again, he sent a third captain of fifty
with his fifty men. And the third captain of
fifty went up, and came and [T]fell on his knees
before Elijah, and pleaded with him, and said
to him: "Man of God, please let my life and
the life of these fifty servants of yours be
precious in your sight.   Lit. bowed down

14 "Look, fire has come down from heaven
and burned up the first two captains of fifties
with their fifties. But let my life now be
precious in your sight."
15 And the [T]angel of the LORD said to Elijah, "Go down with him; do not be afraid of
him." So he arose and went down with him to
the king.   Or Angel
16 Then he said to him, "Thus says the
LORD: 'Because you have sent messengers to
inquire of Baal-Zebub, the god of Ekron, is it
because there is no God in Israel to inquire of
His word? Therefore you shall not come
down from the bed to which you have gone
up, but you shall surely die.' "
17 So Ahaziah died according to the word
of the LORD which Elijah had spoken. Because he had no son, *Jehoram became king
in his place, in the second year of Jehoram
the son of Jehoshaphat, king of Judah.
18 Now the rest of the acts of Ahaziah
which he did, are they not written in the
book of the chronicles of the kings of Israel?

Elijah Ascends to Heaven

2 And it came to pass, when the LORD was
about to [R]take up Elijah into heaven by a
whirlwind, that Elijah went with [R]Elisha from
Gilgal.   Gen. 5:24 • 1 Kin. 19:16–21
2 Then Elijah said to Elisha, "Stay here,
please, for the LORD has sent me on to
Bethel." But Elisha said, "As the LORD lives,
and [R]as your soul lives, I will not leave you!"
So they went down to Bethel.   1 Sam. 1:26
3 Now the sons of the prophets who were
at Bethel came out to Elisha, and said to him,
"Do you know that the LORD will take away
your master from [T]over you today?" And he
said, "Yes, I know; keep silent!"   Lit. your head
4 Then Elijah said to him, "Elisha, stay
here, please, for the LORD has sent me on to
Jericho." But he said, "As the LORD lives, and
as your soul lives, I will not leave you!" So
they came to Jericho.
5 Now the sons of the prophets who were
at Jericho came to Elisha and said to him,
"Do you know that the LORD will take away
your master from over you today?" So he
answered, "Yes, I know; keep silent!"
6 Then Elijah said to him, "Stay here,
please, for the LORD has sent me on to the
Jordan." But he said, "As the LORD lives, and
as your soul lives, I will not leave you!" So
the two of them went on.
7 And fifty men of the sons of the prophets
went and stood facing them at a distance,
while the two of them stood by the Jordan.
8 Now Elijah took his mantle, rolled it up,
and struck the water; and [R]it was divided this
way and that, so that the two of them crossed
over on dry [R]ground.   Ex. 14:21, 22 • Josh. 3:17

1:17 The son of Ahab king of Israel, 2 Kin. 3:1

9 And so it was, when they had crossed over, that Elijah said to Elisha, "Ask! What may I do for you, before I am taken away from you?" Elisha said, "Please let a double portion of your spirit be upon me."

10 So he said, "You have asked a hard thing. *Nevertheless,* if you see me *when I am* taken from you, it shall be so for you; but if not, it shall not be *so.*"

11 Then it happened, as they continued on and talked, that suddenly ᴿa chariot of fire *appeared* with horses of fire, and separated the two of them; and Elijah ᴿwent up by a whirlwind into heaven.   2 Kin. 6:17 • Heb. 11:5

12 And Elisha saw *it,* and he cried out, ᴿ"My father, my father, the chariot of Israel and its horsemen!" So he saw him no more. And he took hold of his own clothes and tore them into two pieces.   2 Kin. 13:14

13 He also took up the mantle of Elijah that had fallen from him, and went back and stood by the bank of the Jordan.

14 Then he took the mantle of Elijah that had fallen from him, and struck the water, and said, "Where *is* the LORD God of Elijah?" And when he also had struck the water, ᴿit was divided this way and that; and Elisha crossed over.   2 Kin. 2:8

15 Now when the sons of the prophets who *were* ᴿfromᵀ Jericho saw him, they said, "The spirit of Elijah rests on Elisha." And they came to meet him, and bowed to the ground before him.   2 Kin. 2:7 • Or *at Jericho opposite him saw*

16 Then they said to him, "Look now, there are fifty strong men with your servants. Please let them go and search for your master, ᴿlest perhaps the Spirit of the LORD has taken him up and cast him upon some mountain or into some valley." And he said, "You shall not send anyone."   1 Kin. 18:12

17 But when they urged him till he was ᴿashamed, he said, "Send *them!*" Therefore they sent fifty men, and they searched for three days but did not find him.   2 Kin. 8:11

18 And when they came back to him, for he had stayed in Jericho, he said to them, "Did I not say to you, 'Do not go'?"

Elisha Performs Miracles

19 Then the men of the city said to Elisha, "Please notice, the situation of this city *is* pleasant, as my lord sees; but the water *is* bad, and the ground barren."

20 And he said, "Bring me a new bowl, and put salt in it." So they brought *it* to him.

21 Then he went out to the source of the water, and ᴿcast in the salt there, and said, "Thus says the LORD: 'I have ᵀhealed this water; from it there shall be no more death or barrenness.'"   Ex. 15:25, 26 • *purified*

22 So the water remains ᴿhealed to this day, according to the word of Elisha which he spoke.   Ezek. 47:8, 9

23 Then he went up from there to Bethel; and as he was going up the road, some youths came from the city and mocked him, and said to him, "Go up, you baldhead! Go up, you baldhead!"

24 So he turned around and looked at them, and ᴿpronounced a curse on them in the name of the LORD. And two female bears came out of the woods and mauled forty-two of the youths.   Deut. 27:13–26

25 Then he went from there to ᴿMount Carmel, and from there he returned to Samaria.   2 Kin. 4:25

Moab Rebels Against Israel

3 Now ᴿJehoram the son of Ahab became king over Israel at Samaria in the eighteenth year of Jehoshaphat king of Judah, and reigned twelve years.   2 Kin. 1:17

2 And he did evil in the sight of the LORD, but not like his father and mother; for he put away the *sacred* pillar of Baal ᴿthat his father had made.   1 Kin. 16:31, 32

3 Nevertheless he persisted in the sins of Jeroboam the son of Nebat, who had made Israel sin; he did not depart from them.

4 Now Mesha king of Moab was a sheep-breeder, and he regularly paid the king of Israel one hundred thousand lambs and the wool of one hundred thousand rams.

5 But it happened, when ᴿAhab died, that the king of Moab rebelled against the king of Israel.   2 Kin. 1:1

6 So King Jehoram went out of Samaria at that time and mustered all Israel.

7 Then he went and sent to Jehoshaphat king of Judah, saying, "The king of Moab has rebelled against me. Will you go with me to fight against Moab?" And he said, "I will go up; ᴿI *am* as you *are,* my people as your people, my horses as your horses."   1 Kin. 22:4

8 Then he said, "Which way shall we go up?" And he answered, "By way of the Wilderness of Edom."

9 So the king of Israel went with the king of Judah and the king of Edom, and they marched on that roundabout route seven days; and there was no water for the army, nor for the animals that followed them.

10 And the king of Israel said, "Alas! For the LORD has called these three kings together to deliver them into the hand of Moab."

11 But Jehoshaphat said, "*Is there* no prophet of the LORD here, that we may inquire of the LORD by him?" So one of the servants of the king of Israel answered and said, "Elisha the son of Shaphat *is* here, who poured water on the hands of Elijah."

12 And Jehoshaphat said, "The word of the LORD is with him." So the king of Israel and Jehoshaphat and the king of Edom ᴿwent down to him.   2 Kin. 2:25

13 Then Elisha said to the king of Israel, R"What have I to do with you? RGo to Rthe prophets of your father and the prophets of your mother." But the king of Israel said to him, "No, for the LORD has called these three kings *together* to deliver them into the hand of Moab."   [Ezek. 14:3] • Judg. 10:14 • 1 Kin. 22:6-11

14 And Elisha said, R"As the LORD of hosts lives, before whom I stand, surely were it not that I regard the presence of Jehoshaphat king of Judah, I would not look at you, nor see you.   1 Kin. 17:1

15 "But now bring me a musician." Then it happened, when the musician played, that the hand of the LORD came upon him.

16 And he said, "Thus says the LORD: 'Make this valley full of Tditches.'   canals

17 "For thus says the LORD: 'You shall not see wind, nor shall you see rain; yet that valley shall be filled with water, so that you, your cattle, and your animals may drink.'

18 "And this is a simple matter in the sight of the LORD; He will also deliver the Moabites into your hand.

19 "Also you shall attack every fortified city and every choice city, and shall cut down every good tree, and stop up every spring of water, and ruin every good piece of land with stones."

20 Now it happened in the morning, when Rthe grain offering was offered, that suddenly water came by way of Edom, and the land was filled with water.   Ex. 29:39, 40

21 And when all the Moabites heard that the kings had come up to fight against them, all who were able to bear arms and older were gathered; and they stood at the border.

22 Then they rose up early in the morning, and the sun was shining on the water; and the Moabites saw the water on the other side *as* red as blood.

23 And they said, "This is blood; the kings have surely struck swords and have killed one another; now therefore, Moab, to the spoil!"

24 So when they came to the camp of Israel, Israel rose up and attacked the Moabites, so that they fled before them; and they entered *their* land, killing the Moabites.

25 Then they destroyed the cities, and each man threw a stone on every good piece of land and filled it; and they stopped up all the springs of water and cut down all the good trees. But they left the stones of RKir Haraseth *intact.* However the slingers surrounded and attacked it.   Is. 16:7, 11

26 And when the king of Moab saw that the battle was too fierce for him, he took with him seven hundred men who drew swords, to break through to the king of Edom, but they could not.

27 Then Rhe took his eldest son who would have reigned in his place, and offered him *as*

a burnt offering upon the wall; and there was great Tindignation against Israel. RSo they departed from him and returned to *their* own land.   [Amos 2:1] • *wrath* • 2 Kin. 8:20

Elisha and the Widow's Oil

4 A certain woman of the wives of the sons of the prophets cried out to Elisha, saying, "Your servant my husband is dead, and you know that your servant feared the LORD. And the creditor is coming Rto take my two sons to be his slaves."   [Lev. 25:39-41, 48]

2 So Elisha said to her, "What shall I do for you? Tell me, what do you have in the house?" And she said, "Your maidservant has nothing in the house but a jar of oil."

3 Then he said, "Go, borrow vessels from everywhere, from all your neighbors—empty vessels; Rdo not gather just a few.   2 Kin. 3:16

4 "And when you have come in, you shall shut the door behind you and your sons; then pour it into all those vessels, and set aside the full ones."

5 So she went from him and shut the door behind her and her sons, who brought *the vessels* to her; and she poured *it* out.

6 Now it came to pass, when the vessels were full, that she said to her son, "Bring me another vessel." And he said to her, "There is not another vessel." So the oil ceased.

7 Then she came and told the man of God. And he said, "Go, sell the oil and pay your debt; and you *and* your sons live on the rest."

Elisha Raises the Shunammite's Son

8 Now it happened one day that Elisha went to Shunem, where there *was* a notable woman, and she persuaded him to eat some food. So it was, as often as he passed by, he would turn in there to eat some food.

9 And she said to her husband, "Look now, I know that this *is* a holy man of God, who passes by us regularly.

10 "Please, let us make a small upper room on the wall; and let us put a bed for him there, and a table and a chair and a lampstand; so it will be, whenever he comes to us, he can turn in there."

11 And it happened one day that he came there, and he turned in to the upper room and lay down there.

12 Then he said to Gehazi his servant, "Call this Shunammite woman." When he had called her, she stood before him.

13 And he said to him, "Say now to her, 'Look, you have been concerned for us with all this care. What *can I* do for you? Do you want me to speak on your behalf to the king or to the commander of the army?'" She answered, "I dwell among my own people."

14 So he said, "What then *is* to be done for her?" And Gehazi answered, "Actually, she has no son, and her husband is old."

15 So he said, "Call her." When he had called her, she stood in the doorway.

16 Then he said, ᵀ"About this time next year you shall embrace a son." And she said, "No, my lord. Man of God, do not lie to your maidservant!"   Lit. *About this season, as the time of life*

17 But the woman conceived, and bore a son when the appointed time had come, of which Elisha had told her.

18 And the child grew. Now it happened one day that he went out to his father, to the reapers.

19 And he said to his father, "My head, my head!" So he said to a servant, "Carry him to his mother."

20 When he had taken him and brought him to his mother, he sat on her knees till noon, and *then* died.

21 And she went up and laid him on the bed of the man of God, shut *the door* upon him, and went out.

22 Then she called to her husband, and said, "Please send me one of the young men and one of the donkeys, that I may run to the man of God and come back."

23 So he said, "Why are you going to him today? *It is* neither the New Moon nor the Sabbath." And she said, "*It is* well."

24 Then she saddled a donkey, and said to her servant, "Drive, and go forward; do not slacken the pace for me unless I tell you."

25 And so she departed, and went to the man of God ᴿat Mount Carmel.   2 Kin. 2:25

So it was, when the man of God saw her afar off, that he said to his servant Gehazi, "Look, the Shunammite woman!

26 "Please run now to meet her, and say to her, 'Is it well with you? Is it well with your husband? Is it well with the child?' " And she answered, "*It is* well."

27 Now when she came to the man of God at the hill, she caught him by the feet, but Gehazi came near to push her away. But the man of God said, "Let her alone; for her soul is in deep distress, and the LORD has hidden *it* from me, and has not told me."

28 So she said, "Did I ask a son of my lord? Did I not say, 'Do not deceive me'?"

29 Then he said to Gehazi, ᵀ"Get yourself ready, and take my staff in your hand, and be on your way. If you meet anyone, do not greet him; and if anyone greets you, do not answer him; but ᴿlay my staff on the face of the child."   Lit. *Gird up your loins* • Ex. 7:19; 14:16

30 And the mother of the child said, ᴿ"As the LORD lives, and as your soul lives, I will not ᴿleave you." So he arose and followed her.   2 Kin. 2:2 • 2 Kin. 2:4

31 Now Gehazi went on ahead of them, and laid the staff on the face of the child; but *there was* neither voice nor hearing. Therefore he went back to meet him, and told him, saying, "The child has not awakened."

32 When Elisha came into the house, there was the child, lying dead on his bed.

33 He ᴿwent in therefore, shut the door behind the two of them, ᴿand prayed to the LORD.   [Matt. 6:6] • 1 Kin. 17:20

34 And he went up and lay on the child, and put his mouth on his mouth, his eyes on his eyes, and his hands on his hands; and ᴿhe stretched himself out on the child, and the flesh of the child became warm.   1 Kin. 17:21–23

35 He returned and walked back and forth in the house, and again went up ᴿand stretched himself out on him; then ᴿthe child sneezed seven times, and the child opened his eyes.   1 Kin. 17:21 • 2 Kin. 8:1, 5

36 And he called Gehazi and said, "Call this Shunammite woman." So he called her. And when she came in to him, he said, "Pick up your son."

37 So she went in, fell at his feet, and bowed to the ground; then she ᴿpicked up her son and went out.   [Heb. 11:35]

Elisha Purifies the Pot of Stew

38 And Elisha returned to Gilgal, and *there was* a famine in the land. Now the sons of the prophets *were* sitting before him; and he said to his servant, "Put on the large pot, and boil stew for the sons of the prophets."

39 So one went out into the field to gather herbs, and found a wild vine, and gathered from it a lapful of wild gourds, and came and sliced *them* into the pot of stew, though they did not know *what they were*.

40 Then they served it to the men to eat. Now it happened, as they were eating the stew, that they cried out and said, "Man of God, *there is* ᴿdeath in the pot!" And they could not eat *it*.   Ex. 10:17

41 So he said, "Then bring some flour." And ᴿhe put *it* into the pot, and said, "Serve *it* to the people, that they may eat." And there was nothing harmful in the pot.   Ex. 15:25

Elisha Feeds One Hundred Men

42 Then a man came from ᴿBaal Shalisha, ᴿand brought the man of God bread of the firstfruits, twenty loaves of barley bread, and newly ripened grain in his knapsack. And he said, "Give *it* to the people, that they may eat."   1 Sam. 9:4 • [1 Cor. 9:11]

43 But his servant said, ᴿ"What? Shall I set this before one hundred men?" He said again, "Give it to the people, that they may eat; for thus says the LORD: ᴿ'They shall eat and have *some* left over.' "   John 6:9 • Luke 9:17

44 So he set *it* before them; and they ate ᴿand had *some* left over, according to the word of the LORD.   John 6:13

Naaman's Leprosy Healed

5 Now ᴿNaaman, commander of the army of the king of Syria, was ᴿa great and

honorable man in the eyes of his master, because by him the LORD had given victory to Syria. He was also a mighty man of valor, *but* a leper. Luke 4:27 · Ex. 11:3

2 And the Syrians had gone out ᵀon raids, and had brought back captive a young girl from the land of Israel. She ᵀwaited on Naaman's wife. Or *in bands* · Served, lit. *was before*

3 Then she said to her mistress, "If only my master *were* with the prophet who *is* in Samaria! For he would heal him of his leprosy."

4 And *Naaman* went in and told his master, saying, "Thus and thus said the girl who *is* from the land of Israel."

5 Then the king of Syria said, "Go now, and I will send a letter to the king of Israel." So he departed and ᴿtook with him ten talents of silver, six thousand *shekels* of gold, and ten changes of clothing. 1 Sam. 9:8

6 Then he brought the letter to the king of Israel, which said,

Now be advised, when this letter comes to you, that I have sent Naaman my servant to you, that you may heal him of his leprosy.

7 And it happened, when the king of Israel read the letter, that he tore his clothes and said, "*Am* I ᴿGod, to kill and make alive, that this man sends a man to me to heal him of his leprosy? Therefore please consider, and see how he seeks a quarrel with me." [Gen. 30:2]

8 So it was, when Elisha the man of God heard that the king of Israel had torn his clothes, that he sent to the king, saying, "Why have you torn your clothes? Please let him come to me, and he shall know that there is a prophet in Israel."

9 Then Naaman went with his horses and chariot, and he stood at the door of Elisha's house.

10 And Elisha sent a messenger to him, saying, "Go and ᴿwash in the Jordan seven times, and your flesh shall be restored to you, and *you shall* be clean." John 9:7

11 But Naaman became furious, and went away and said, "Indeed, I said to myself, 'He will surely come out *to me*, and stand and call on the name of the LORD his God, and wave his hand over the place, and heal the leprosy.'

12 "*Are* not the *Abanah and the Pharpar, the rivers of Damascus, better than all the waters of Israel? Could I not wash in them and be clean?" So he turned and went away in a rage.

13 And his servants came near and spoke to him, and said, "My father, *if* the prophet had told you *to do* something great, would you not have done *it*? How much more then, when he says to you, 'Wash, and be clean'?"

5:12 So with Kt., LXX, Vg.; Qr., Syr., Tg. *Amanah*

14 So he went down and dipped seven times in the Jordan, according to the saying of the man of God; and his flesh was restored like the flesh of a little child, and he was clean.

15 And he returned to the man of God, he and all his aides, and came and stood before him; and he said, "Indeed, now I know that *there is* ᴿno God in all the earth, except in Israel; now therefore, please take ᴿa gift from your servant." Dan. 2:47; 3:29; 6:26, 27 · Gen. 33:11

16 But he said, "*As* the LORD lives, before whom I stand, I will receive nothing." And he urged him to take *it*, but he refused.

17 So Naaman said, "Then, if not, please let your servant be given two mule-loads of earth; for your servant will no longer offer either burnt offering or sacrifice to other gods, but to the LORD.

18 "Yet in this thing may the LORD pardon your servant: when my master goes into the temple of Rimmon to worship there, and ᴿhe leans on my hand, and I bow down in the temple of Rimmon—when I bow down in the temple of Rimmon, may the LORD please pardon your servant in this thing." 2 Kin. 7:2, 17

19 Then he said to him, "Go in peace." So he departed from him a ᵀshort distance. 5 mi.

Gehazi's Greed

20 But ᴿGehazi, the servant of Elisha the man of God, said, "Look, my master has spared Naaman this Syrian, while not receiving from his hands what he brought; but *as* the LORD lives, I will run after him and take something from him." 2 Kin. 4:12; 8:4, 5

21 So Gehazi pursued Naaman. When Naaman saw *him* running after him, he got down from the chariot to meet him, and said, "*Is* all well?"

22 And he said, "All *is* ᴿwell. My master has sent me, saying, 'Indeed, just now two young men of the sons of the prophets have come to me from the mountains of Ephraim. Please give them a ᵀtalent of silver and two changes of garments.' " 2 Kin. 4:26 · $384,000

23 So Naaman said, "Please, take two talents." And he urged him, and bound two talents of silver in two bags, with two changes of garments, and handed *them* to two of his servants; and they carried *them* on ahead of him.

24 When he came to ᵀthe citadel, he took *them* from their hand, and stored *them* away in the house; then he let the men go, and they departed. Lit. *the hill*

25 Now he went in and stood before his master. Elisha said to him, "Where *did you* go, Gehazi?" And he said, "Your servant did not go anywhere."

26 Then he said to him, "Did not my heart go *with you* when the man turned back from his chariot to meet you? *Is it* ᴿtime to receive money and to receive clothing, olive groves

and vineyards, sheep and oxen, male and female servants? [Eccl. 3:1, 6]

27 "Therefore the leprosy of Naaman ᴿshall cling to you and your descendants forever." And he went out from his presence ᴿleprous, *as white* as snow. [1 Tim. 6:10] · Ex. 4:6

The Floating Ax Head

6 And ᴿthe sons of the prophets said to Elisha, "See now, the place where we dwell with you is too small for us. 2 Kin. 4:38

2 "Please, let us go to the Jordan, and let every man take a beam from there, and let us make there a place where we may dwell." So he answered, "Go."

3 Then one said, ᴿ"Please consent to go with your servants." And he answered, "I will go." 2 Kin. 5:23

4 So he went with them. And when they came to the Jordan, they cut down trees.

5 But as one was cutting down a tree, the iron *ax* head fell into the water; and he cried out and said, "Alas, master! For it was ᴿborrowed." [Ex. 22:14]

6 So the man of God said, "Where did it fall?" And he showed him the place. So ᴿhe cut off a stick, and threw *it* in there; and he made the iron float. 2 Kin. 2:21; 4:41

7 Therefore he said, "Pick *it* up for yourself." So he reached out his hand and took it.

The Blinded Syrians Captured

8 Now the ᴿking of Syria was making war against Israel; and he consulted with his servants, saying, "My camp *will be* in such and such a place." 2 Kin. 8:28, 29

9 And the man of God sent to the king of Israel, saying, "Beware that you do not pass this place, for the Syrians are coming down there."

10 Then the king of Israel sent *someone* to the place of which the man of God had told him. Thus he warned him, and he was watchful there, not just once or twice.

11 Therefore the heart of the king of Syria was greatly troubled by this thing; and he called his servants and said to them, "Will you not show me which of us *is* for the king of Israel?"

12 And one of his servants said, "None, my lord, O king; but Elisha, the prophet who *is* in Israel, tells the king of Israel the words that you speak in your bedroom."

13 So he said, "Go and see where he *is*, that I may send and get him." And it was told him, saying, "Surely *he is* in Dothan."

14 Therefore he sent horses and chariots and a great army there, and they came by night and surrounded the city.

15 And when the servant of the man of God arose early and went out, there was an army, surrounding the city with horses and chariots. And his servant said to him, "Alas, my master! What shall we do?"

27-D. Fear Not: God Is Your Power ▼

16 So he answered, ᴿ"Do not fear, for ᴿthose who *are* with us *are* more than those who *are* with them." Ex. 14:13 · [Rom. 8:31] ▲

17 And Elisha prayed, and said, "LORD, I pray, open his eyes that he may see." Then

---

27-D. Fear Not: God Is Your Power (2 Kings 6:16)—"Do not fear, for those who are with us are more than those who are with them" (v. 16). Elisha was a prophet with great faith. By that faith he knew that the Lord's army was encamped around Dothan, not to save the city but to deliver Elisha from the hands of Ben-Hadad, king of Syria. The king had sent his army to capture Elisha because the Lord had revealed to the prophet all of Ben-Hadad's military plans. Elisha, in turn, revealed those plans to Ben-Hadad's enemy, Jehoram, king of Israel, thus guaranteeing Ben-Hadad's defeat. So Ben-Hadad sent spies to locate Elisha. When Elisha was found, the king sent horses, chariots, and a great army, just to capture one unarmed prophet! But they were not enough (v. 14). They reached Dothan in darkness and surrounded the city. When Elisha's servant went about his morning duties, he saw the Syrian army and rushed in to Elisha, overcome by fear and crying, "Alas, my master! What shall we do?" (v. 15).

(1) Elisha taught the young man faith and the fear of the Lord. Elisha prayed that the Lord would open the young man's eyes so that he might see the unseen (v. 17; cf. 2 Cor. 4:18, page 1168). Only by faith can we see the invisible host of heaven and "not fear." The Lord opened the young man's spiritual eyes, and he saw God's army ready to protect His servant.

(2) Every servant of God has the edge over the enemies of righteousness. The psalmist said, "The LORD is on my side; I will not fear. What can man do to me?" (Ps. 118:6, page 579). The believer has these armaments in his fight against fear:

(a) *God's Word.* "For He Himself has said, 'I will never leave you nor forsake you.' So we may boldly say: 'The LORD is my helper; I will not fear. What can man do to me?' " (Heb. 13:5, 6, page 1252; cf. Deut. 31:12, 13, page 209).

(b) *God's power.* "This poor man cried out, and the LORD heard him, and saved him out of all his troubles. The angel of the LORD encamps all around those who fear Him, and delivers them" (Ps. 34:6, 7, page 530).

(c) *God's Holy Spirit.* "My Spirit remains among you; do not fear fear!" (Hag. 2:5, page 908). "I will

(Point 27-D continued on next page)

the LORD [R]opened the eyes of the young man, and he saw. And behold, the mountain *was* full of [R]horses and chariots of fire all around Elisha.   Num. 22:31 • 2 Kin. 2:11

18 So when *the Syrians* came down to him, Elisha prayed to the LORD, and said, "Strike this people, I pray, with blindness." And [R]He struck them with blindness according to the word of Elisha.   Gen. 19:11

19 Now Elisha said to them, "This *is* not the way, nor *is* this the city. Follow me, and I will bring you to the man whom you seek." But he led them to Samaria.

20 So it was, when they had come to Samaria, that Elisha said, "LORD, open the eyes of these *men*, that they may see." And the LORD opened their eyes, and they saw; and there *they were*, inside Samaria!

21 Now when the king of Israel saw them, he said to Elisha, "My [R]father, shall I kill *them*? Shall I kill *them*?"   2 Kin. 2:12; 5:13; 8:9

22 But he answered, "You shall not kill *them*. Would you kill those whom you have taken captive with your sword and your bow? [R]Set food and water before them, that they may eat and drink and go to their master."   [Rom. 12:20]

23 Then he prepared a great feast for them; and after they ate and drank, he sent them away and they went to their master. So [R]the bands of Syrian *raiders* came no more into the land of Israel.   2 Kin. 5:2; 6:8, 9

Syria Besieges Samaria in Famine

24 And it happened after this that [R]Ben-Hadad king of Syria gathered all his army, and went up and besieged Samaria.   1 Kin. 20:1

25 And there was a great famine in Samaria; and indeed they besieged it until a donkey's head was sold for eighty *shekels* of silver, and one-fourth of a [T]kab of dove droppings for five *shekels* of silver.   1 pt.

26 Then, as the king of Israel was passing by on the wall, a woman cried out to him, saying, "Help, my lord, O king!"

27 And he said, "If the LORD does not help you, where can I find help for you? From the threshing floor or from the winepress?"

(Point 27-D continued from previous page)
pray the Father, and He will give you another Helper [the Holy Spirit], that He may abide with you forever" (John 14:16, page 1075).

(d) *God's protection.* Isaiah said, "Be strong, do not fear! Behold, your God will come with vengeance, with the recompense of God; He will come and save you" (Is. 35:4, page 675). Isaiah 35 is a promise and a prophecy. "Be strong, do not fear! Behold, your God will come with vengeance." The promise is that the Messiah will come to establish God's kingdom on earth (Rev. 19:11–16, page 1312). The prophecy is that He will come with vengeance—at Armageddon (Rev. 19:17–21, page 1313).

(3) While we wait for His second coming we are to "be strong in the Lord and in the power of His might." How? "Put on the whole armor of God, that you may be able to stand against the wiles of the devil" (Eph. 6:10, 11, page 1192). Without God's armor, we fight a losing battle. God's armor consists of the following:

(a) *The belt of truth.* "Having girded your waist with truth" (Eph. 6:14, page 1192). This belt of truth is embodied in Christ. Jesus said, "And you shall know the truth, and the truth shall make you free" (John 8:31, 32, page 1063). Again He said, "I am . . . the truth" (John 14:6, page 1074). Every believer must bear witness to the truth (John 5:33, page 1057).

(b) *The breastplate of righteousness.* "Having put on the breastplate of righteousness" (Eph. 6:14, page 1192). This breastplate is the righteousness of the Lord Jesus Christ (Rom. 10:1–4, 10, page 1140). It must be reflected in our daily lives.

(c) *The gospel shoes.* "Having shod your feet with the preparation of the gospel [good news] of peace" (Eph. 6:15, page 1192). Christ is our peace, and without His gospel the sinner can never be at peace with God (Rom. 5:1, page 1133). It is our duty to go with the gospel—to tell those who do not know it.

(d) *The shield of faith.* "Above all, taking the shield of faith" (Eph. 6:16, page 1192). Christ is our shield of faith. God said to Abram, "Do not be afraid, Abram. I am your shield" (Gen. 15:1, page 20). "The just shall live by faith" (Heb. 10:38, page 1247). The shield of faith will quench all the fiery darts of the satanic kingdom.

(e) *The helmet of salvation.* "Take the helmet of salvation" (Eph. 6:17, page 1192). Christ is our deliverance (Luke 4:16–18, page 1016).

(f) *The sword of the Spirit.* "The sword of the Spirit [Holy Spirit], which is the word of God" (Eph. 6:17, page 1192). Christ also is the sword, the living Word (John 1:1, 14, page 1049). Let us exalt this Word in all that we do or say, and let us use it, our only *offensive* weapon.

(g) *Prayer.* "Praying always with all prayer and supplication in the Spirit" (Eph. 6:18, page 1192). The armor is God's, and as good soldiers of the cross we need to keep it polished with prayer. It is our "secret defense"!

"Be strong, do not fear! Behold, your God will come with vengeance" (Is. 35:4, page 675). Until then, put on the whole armor of God and do not fear, because "we are more than conquerors through Him who loved us" (Rom. 8:37, page 1138).

See Psalm 34:4, page 530, for **Point 27-E: Fear: Its Objects.**

28 Then the king said to her, "What is troubling you?" And she answered, "This woman said to me, 'Give your son, that we may eat him today, and we will eat my son tomorrow.'

29 "So ᴿwe boiled my son, and ate him. And I said to her on the next day, 'Give your son, that we may eat him'; but she has hidden her son."   Lev. 26:27-29

30 Now it happened, when the king heard the words of the woman, that he ᴿtore his clothes; and as he passed by on the wall, the people looked, and there underneath *he had* sackcloth on his body.   1 Kin. 21:27

31 Then he said, ᴿ"God do so to me and more also, if the head of Elisha the son of Shaphat remains on him today!"   Ruth 1:17

32 But Elisha was sitting in his house, and the elders were sitting with him. And *the king* sent a man ahead of him, but before the messenger came to him, he said to the elders, "Do you see how this son of a murderer has sent someone to take away my head? Look, when the messenger comes, shut the door, and hold him fast at the door. *Is* not the sound of his master's feet behind him?"

33 And while ᵀhe was still talking with them, there was the messenger, coming down to him; and then *the king* said, "Surely this calamity *is* from the LORD; ᴿwhy should I wait for the LORD any longer?"   Jehoram • Job 2:9

7 Then Elisha said, "Hear the word of the LORD. Thus says the LORD: 'Tomorrow about this time a ᵀseah of fine flour *shall be sold* for a shekel, and two seahs of barley for a shekel, at the gate of Samaria.'"   8 gal.

2 So an officer on whose hand the king leaned answered the man of God and said, "Look, ᴿif the LORD would make windows in heaven, could this thing be?" And he said, "In fact, you shall see *it* with your eyes, but you shall not eat of it."   Mal. 3:10

The Syrians Flee

3 Now there were four leprous men ᴿat the entrance of the gate; and they said to one another, "Why are we sitting here until we die?   [Num. 5:2-4; 12:10-14]

4 "If we say, 'We will enter the city,' the famine *is* in the city, and we shall die there. And if we sit here, we die also. Now therefore, come, let us surrender to the army of the Syrians. If they keep us alive, we shall live; and if they kill us, we shall only die."

5 And they rose at twilight to go to the camp of the Syrians; and when they had come to ᵀthe outskirts of the Syrian camp, to their surprise no one *was* there.

6 For the LORD had caused the army of the Syrians ᴿto hear the noise of chariots and the noise of horses—the noise of a great army; so they said to one another, "Look, the king of Israel has hired against us ᴿthe kings of the Hittites and the kings of the Egyptians to attack us!"   2 Sam. 5:24 • 1 Kin. 10:29

7 Therefore they ᴿarose and fled at twilight, and left the camp intact—their tents, their horses, and their donkeys—and they fled for their lives.   Ps. 48:4-6

8 And when these lepers came to the outskirts of the camp, they went into one tent and ate and drank, and carried from it silver and gold and clothing, and went and hid *them*; then they came back and entered another tent, and carried *some* from there *also*, and went and hid *it*.

9 Then they said to one another, "We are not doing right. This day *is* a day of good news, and we remain silent. If we wait until morning light, some ᵀpunishment will come upon us. Now therefore, come, let us go and tell the king's household."   Calamity

10 So they went and called to the gatekeepers of the city, and told them, saying, "We went to the Syrian camp, and surprisingly no one *was* there, not a human sound—only horses and donkeys tied, and the tents intact."

11 And the gatekeepers called out, and they told *it* to the king's household inside.

12 So the king arose in the night and said to his servants, "Let me now tell you what the Syrians have done to us. They know that we *are* ᴿhungry; therefore they have gone out of the camp to ᵀhide themselves in the field, saying, 'When they come out of the city, we shall catch them alive, and get into the city.'"   2 Kin. 6:24-29 • Hide themselves in ambush

13 And one of his servants answered and said, "Please, let several *men* take five of the remaining horses which are left in the city. Look, they *may either become* like all the multitude of Israel that are left in it; or indeed, *I say,* they *may become* like all the multitude of Israel left from those who are consumed; so let us send them and see."

14 Therefore they took two chariots with horses; and the king sent them in the direction of the Syrian army, saying, "Go and see."

15 And they went after them to the Jordan; and indeed all the road *was* full of garments and weapons which the Syrians had thrown away in their haste. So the messengers returned and told the king.

16 Then the people went out and plundered the tents of the Syrians. So a seah of fine flour was *sold* for a ᵀshekel, and two seahs of barley for a shekel, ᴿaccording to the word of the LORD. $128 • 2 Kin. 7:1

17 Now the king had appointed the officer on whose hand he leaned to have charge of the gate. But the people trampled him in the gate, and he died, just ᴿas the man of God had said, who spoke when the king came down to him.   2 Kin. 6:32; 7:2

18 So it happened just as the man of God had spoken to the king, saying, ᴿ"Two seahs

of barley for a shekel, and a seah of fine flour for a shekel, shall be *sold* tomorrow about this time in the gate of Samaria." 2 Kin. 7:1

19 Then that officer had answered the man of God, and said, "Now look, *if* the LORD would make windows in heaven, could such a thing be?" And he had said, "In fact, you shall see *it* with your eyes, but you shall not eat of it."

20 And so it happened to him, for the people trampled him in the gate, and he died.

The King Restores the Shunammite's Land

8 Then Elisha spoke to the woman whose son he had restored to life, saying, "Arise and go, you and your household, and stay wherever you can; for the LORD has called for a ᴿfamine, and furthermore, it will come upon the land for seven years." 2 Sam. 21:1

2 So the woman arose and did according to the saying of the man of God, and she went with her household and dwelt in the land of the Philistines seven years.

3 It came to pass, at the end of seven years, that the woman returned from the land of the Philistines; and she went to make an appeal to the king for her house and for her land.

4 Then the king talked with Gehazi, the servant of the man of God, saying, "Tell me, please, all the great things Elisha has done."

5 Now it happened, as he was telling the king how he had restored the dead to life, that there was the woman whose son he had restored to life, appealing to the king for her house and for her land. And Gehazi said, "My lord, O king, this *is* the woman, and this *is* her son whom Elisha restored to life."

6 And when the king asked the woman, she told him. So the king appointed a certain officer for her, saying, "Restore all that *was* hers, and all the proceeds of the field from the day that she left the land until now."

Death of Ben-Hadad

7 Then Elisha went to Damascus, and ᴿBen-Hadad king of Syria was sick; and it was told him, saying, "The man of God has come here." 2 Kin. 6:24

8 And the king said to Hazael, "Take a present in your hand, and go to meet the man of God, and inquire of the LORD by him, saying, 'Shall I recover from this disease?' "

9 So Hazael went to meet him and took a present with him, of every good thing of Damascus, forty camel-loads; and he came and stood before him, and said, "Your son Ben-Hadad king of Syria has sent me to you, saying, 'Shall I recover from this disease?' "

10 And Elisha said to him, "Go, say to him, 'You shall certainly recover.' However the LORD has shown me that he will really die."

11 Then he ᵀset his countenance in a stare

until he was ashamed; and the man of God ᴿwept. *fixed his gaze* • Luke 19:41

12 And Hazael said, "Why is my lord weeping?" And he answered, "Because I know the evil that you will do to the children of Israel: Their strongholds you will set on fire, and their young men you will kill with the sword; and you ᴿwill dash their children, and rip open their women with child." Hos. 13:16

13 So Hazael said, "But what ᴿis your servant—a dog, that he should do this gross thing?" And Elisha answered, ᴿ"The LORD has shown me that you *will* become king over Syria." 1 Sam. 17:43 • 1 Kin. 19:15

14 Then he departed from Elisha, and came to his master, who said to him, "What did Elisha say to you?" And he answered, "He told me you would surely recover."

15 But it happened on the next day that he took a thick cloth and dipped *it* in water, and spread *it* over his face so that he died; and Hazael reigned in his place.

Jehoram Reigns in Judah

16 Now ᴿin the fifth year of Joram the son of Ahab, king of Israel, Jehoshaphat *having been* king of Judah, ᴿJehoram the son of Jehoshaphat began to reign as ᵀking of Judah. 2 Kin. 1:17; 3:1 • 2 Chr. 21:3 • Co-regent with his father

17 He was ᴿthirty-two years old when he became king, and he reigned eight years in Jerusalem. 2 Chr. 21:5-10

18 And he walked in the way of the kings of Israel, just as the house of Ahab had done, for the daughter of Ahab was his wife; and he did evil in the sight of the LORD.

19 Yet the LORD would not destroy Judah, for the sake of his servant David, ᴿas He promised him to give a lamp to him *and* his sons forever. 2 Sam. 7:13

20 In his days ᴿEdom revolted against Judah's authority, ᴿand made a king over themselves. Gen. 27:40 • 1 Kin. 22:47

21 So Joram went to Zair, and all his chariots with him. Then he rose by night and attacked the Edomites who had surrounded him and the captains of the chariots; and the troops fled to their tents.

22 Thus Edom has been in revolt against Judah's authority to this day. ᴿAnd Libnah revolted at that time. Josh. 21:13

23 Now the rest of the acts of *Joram, and all that he did, *are* they not written in the book of the chronicles of the kings of Judah?

24 So Joram rested with his fathers, and was buried with his fathers in the City of David. Then ᴿAhaziahᵀ his son reigned in his place. 2 Chr. 22:1, 7 • Or *Azariah* or *Jehoahaz*

Ahaziah Reigns in Judah

25 In the twelfth year of Joram the son of Ahab, king of Israel, Ahaziah the son of Jehoram, king of Judah, began to reign.

26 Ahaziah *was* ᴿtwenty-two years old

8:23 *Jehoram*, v. 16

when he became king, and he reigned one year in Jerusalem. His mother's name *was* Athaliah the granddaughter of Omri, king of Israel.   2 Chr. 22:2

27 And he walked in the way of the house of Ahab, and did evil in the sight of the LORD, like the house of Ahab, for he *was* the son-in-law of the house of Ahab.

28 Now he went ᴿwith Joram the son of Ahab to war against Hazael king of Syria at ᴿRamoth Gilead; and the Syrians wounded Joram.   2 Chr. 22:5 • 1 Kin. 22:3, 29

29 Then King Joram went back to Jezreel to recover from the wounds which the Syrians had inflicted on him at ᵀRamah, when he fought against Hazael king of Syria. And Ahaziah the son of Jehoram, king of Judah, went down to see Joram the son of Ahab in Jezreel, because he was sick.   *Ramoth, v. 28*

Jehu Anointed King of Israel

9 And Elisha the prophet called one of the sons of the prophets, and said to him, "Get yourself ready, take this flask of oil in your hand, and go to Ramoth Gilead.

2 "Now when you arrive at that place, look there for Jehu the son of Jehoshaphat, the son of Nimshi, and go in and make him rise up from among ᴿhis associates, and take him to an inner room.   2 Kin. 9:5, 11

3 "Then take the flask of oil, and pour *it* on his head, and say, 'Thus says the LORD: "I have anointed you king over Israel." ' Then open the door and flee, and do not delay."

4 So the young man, the servant of the prophet, went to Ramoth Gilead.

5 And when he arrived, there *were* the captains of the army sitting; and he said, "I have a message for you, commander." Jehu said, "For which *one* of us?" And he said, "For you, commander."

6 Then he arose and went into the house. And he poured the oil on his head, and said to him, ᴿ"Thus says the LORD God of Israel: 'I have anointed you king over the people of the LORD, over Israel.   2 Chr. 22:7

7 'You shall strike down the house of Ahab your master, that I may ᴿavenge the blood of My servants the prophets, and the blood of all the servants of the LORD, ᴿat the hand of Jezebel.   [Deut. 32:35, 41] • 1 Kin. 18:4; 21:15

8 'For the whole house of Ahab shall perish; and I will cut off from Ahab all the males in Israel, both bond and free.

9 'So I will make the house of Ahab like the house of Jeroboam the son of Nebat, and like the house of Baasha the son of Ahijah.

10 'The dogs shall eat Jezebel on the plot of ground at Jezreel, and *there shall be* none to bury *her.*' " And he opened the door and fled.

11 Then Jehu came out to the servants of his master, and *one* said to him, "Is all well? Why did ᴿthis madman come to you?" And he

said to them, "You know the man and his babble."   Jer. 29:26

12 And they said, "A lie! Tell us now." So he said, "Thus and thus he spoke to me, saying, 'Thus says the LORD: "I have anointed you king over Israel." ' "

13 Then each man hastened ᴿto take his garment and put *it* ᵀunder him on the top of the steps; and they blew trumpets, saying, "Jehu is king!"   Matt. 21:7, 8 • Lit. *under his feet*

Joram of Israel Killed

14 So Jehu the son of Jehoshaphat, the son of Nimshi, conspired against Joram. (Now Joram had been defending Ramoth Gilead, he and all Israel, against Hazael king of Syria.

15 But King Joram had returned to Jezreel to recover from the wounds which the Syrians had inflicted on him when he fought with Hazael king of Syria.) And Jehu said, "If you are so minded, let no one leave or escape from the city to go and tell *it* in Jezreel."

16 So Jehu rode in a chariot and went to Jezreel, for Joram was laid up there; ᴿand Ahaziah king of Judah had come down to see Joram.   2 Kin. 8:29

17 Now a watchman stood on the tower in Jezreel, and he saw the company of Jehu as he came, and said, "I see a company of men." And Joram said, "Get a horseman and send him to meet them, and let him say, ᵀ'Is it peace?' "   *Are you peaceful?*

18 So the horseman went to meet him, and said, "Thus says the king: '*Is it* peace?' " And Jehu said, "What have you to do with peace? Turn around and follow me." So the watchman reported, saying, "The messenger went to them, but is not coming back."

19 Then he sent out a second horseman who came to them, and said, "Thus says the king: '*Is it* peace?' " And Jehu answered, "What have you to do with peace? Turn around and follow me."

20 So the watchman reported, saying, "He went up to them and is not coming back; and the driving *is* like the driving of Jehu the son of Nimshi, for he drives furiously!"

21 Then Joram said, ᵀ"Make ready." And his chariot was made ready. Then Joram king of Israel and Ahaziah king of Judah went out, each in his chariot; and they went out to meet Jehu, and ᵀmet him on the property of Naboth the Jezreelite.   *Harness up •* Lit. *found*

22 Now it happened, when Joram saw Jehu, that he said, "*Is it* peace, Jehu?" So he answered, "What peace, as long as the harlotries of your mother Jezebel and her witchcraft *are so* many?"

23 So Joram turned around and fled, and said to Ahaziah, "Treachery, Ahaziah!"

24 Now Jehu ᵀdrew his bow with full strength and shot Jehoram between his arms; and the arrow came out at his heart, and he sank down in his chariot.   Lit. *filled his hand*

25 Then *Jehu* said to Bidkar his captain, "Pick *him* up, *and* throw him into the tract of the field of Naboth the Jezreelite; for remember, when you and I were riding together behind Ahab his father, that ᴿthe LORD laid this ᴿburden upon him: 1 Kin. 21:19, 24–29 • Is. 13:1

26 'Surely I saw yesterday the blood of Naboth and the blood of his sons,' says the LORD, ᴿ'and I will repay you ᵀin this plot,' says the LORD. Now therefore, take *and* throw him on the plot *of* ground, according to the word of the LORD."   1 Kin. 21:13, 19 • *on this property*

Ahaziah of Judah Killed

27 But when Ahaziah king of Judah saw *this*, he fled by the road to Beth Haggan. So Jehu pursued him, and said, "Shoot him also in the chariot." And they shot him at the Ascent of Gur, which is by Ibleam. Then he fled to Megiddo, and died there.

28 And his servants carried him in the chariot to Jerusalem, and buried him in his tomb with his fathers in the City of David.

29 In the eleventh year of Joram the son of Ahab, Ahaziah had become king over Judah.

Jezebel's Violent Death

30 Now when Jehu had come to Jezreel, Jezebel heard *of it*; ᴿand she put paint on her eyes and adorned her head, and looked through a window.   Ezek. 23:40

31 Then, as Jehu entered at the gate, she said, ᴿ"*Is it* peace, Zimri, murderer of your master?"   1 Kin. 16:9–20

32 And he looked up at the window, and said, "Who *is* on my side? Who?" So two *or* three eunuchs looked out at him.

33 Then he said, "Throw her down." So they threw her down, and *some* of her blood spattered on the wall and on the horses; and he trampled her underfoot.

34 And when he had gone in, he ate and drank. Then he said, "Go now, see to this accursed *woman*, and bury her, for ᴿshe was a king's daughter."   1 Kin. 16:31

35 So they went to bury her, but they found no more of her than the skull and the feet and the palms of *her* hands.

36 Therefore they came back and told him. And he said, "This *is* the word of the LORD, which He spoke by His servant Elijah the Tishbite, saying, *'On the plot *of* ground at Jezreel dogs shall eat the flesh of Jezebel;

37 'and the corpse of Jezebel shall be ᴿas refuse on the surface of the field, in the plot at Jezreel, so that they shall not say, "Here lies Jezebel." ' "   Ps. 83:10

Ahab's Seventy Sons Killed

10 Now Ahab had seventy sons in Samaria. And Jehu wrote and sent letters

9:36 1 Kin. 21:23
10:1 So with MT, Syr., Tg.; LXX *Samaria*; Vg. *city*

to Samaria, to the rulers of *Jezreel, to the elders, and to ᵀthose who reared Ahab's *sons*, saying: *the guardians of*

2 Now as soon as this letter comes to you, since your master's sons *are* with you, and you have chariots and horses, a fortified city also, and weapons,

3 choose the ᵀbest qualified of your master's sons, set *him* on his father's throne, and fight for your master's house.   *most upright*

4 But they were exceedingly afraid, and said, "Look, two kings could not ᵀstand up to him; how then can we stand?"   Lit. *stand before*

5 And he who *was* in charge of the house, and he who *was* in charge of the city, the elders also, and those who reared *the sons*, sent to Jehu, saying, "We *are* your servants, we will do all you tell us; but we will not make anyone king. Do *what is* good in your sight."

6 Then he wrote a second letter to them, saying:

If you *are* for me and will obey my voice, take the heads of the men, your master's sons, and come to me at Jezreel by this time tomorrow.

Now the king's sons, seventy persons, *were* with the great men of the city, who were rearing them.

7 So it was, when the letter came to them, that they took the king's sons and slaughtered seventy persons, put their heads in baskets and sent *them* to him at Jezreel.

8 Then a messenger came and told him, saying, "They have brought the heads of the king's sons." And he said, "Lay them in two heaps at the entrance of the gate until morning."

9 So it was, in the morning, that he went out and stood, and said to all the people, "You *are* righteous. Indeed ᴿI conspired against my master and killed him; but who killed all these?   2 Kin. 9:14–24

10 "Know now that nothing shall ᴿfall to the earth of the word of the LORD which the LORD spoke concerning the house of Ahab; for the LORD has done what He spoke ᴿby His servant Elijah."   1 Sam. 3:19 • 1 Kin. 21:17–24, 29

11 So Jehu killed all who remained of the house of Ahab in Jezreel, and all his great men and his close acquaintances and his priests, until he left him none remaining.

Ahaziah's Forty-two Brothers Killed

12 And he arose and departed and went to Samaria. On the way, at *Beth Eked of the Shepherds,

13 ᴿJehu met with the brothers of Ahaziah king of Judah, and said, "Who *are* you?" So

10:12 Lit. *The Shearing House*

they answered, "We *are* the brothers of Ahaziah; we have come down to greet the sons of the king and the sons of the queen mother." 2 Chr. 22:8

14 And he said, "Take them alive!" So they took them alive, and ᴿkilled them at the well of ᵀBeth Eked, forty-two men; and he left none of them. 2 Chr. 22:8 · Lit. *The Shearing House*

The Rest of Ahab's Family Killed

15 Now when he departed from there, he ᵀmet Jehonadab the son of Rechab, *coming* to meet him; and he greeted him and said to him, "Is your heart right, as my heart *is* toward your heart?" And Jehonadab answered, "It is." *Jehu said,* "If it is, give *me* your hand." So he gave *him* his hand, and he took him up to him into the chariot. *found*

16 Then he said, "Come with me, and see my ᴿzeal for the Lᴏʀᴅ." So they had him ride in his chariot. 1 Kin. 19:10

17 And when he came to Samaria, ᴿhe killed all who remained to Ahab in Samaria, till he had destroyed them, according to the word of the Lᴏʀᴅ which He spoke to Elijah. 2 Kin. 9:8

Worshipers of Baal Killed

18 Then Jehu gathered all the people together, and said to them, "Ahab served Baal a little, Jehu will serve him much.

19 "Now therefore, call to me all the ᴿprophets of Baal, all his servants, and all his priests. Let no one be missing, for I have a great sacrifice for Baal. Whoever is missing shall not live." But Jehu acted deceptively, with the intent of destroying the worshipers of Baal. 1 Kin. 18:19; 22:6

20 And Jehu said, "Proclaim a solemn assembly for Baal." So they proclaimed *it.*

21 Then Jehu sent throughout all Israel; and all the worshipers of Baal came, so that there was not a man left who did not come. So they came into the *temple of Baal, and the ᴿtemple of Baal was full from one end to the other. 1 Kin. 16:32

22 And he said to the one in charge of the wardrobe, "Bring out vestments for all the worshipers of Baal." So he brought out vestments for them.

23 Then Jehu and Jehonadab the son of Rechab went into the temple of Baal, and said to the worshipers of Baal, "Search and see that no servants of the Lᴏʀᴅ are here with you, but only the worshipers of Baal."

24 So they went in to offer sacrifices and burnt offerings. Now Jehu had appointed for himself eighty men on the outside, and had said, "*If* any of the men whom I have brought into your hands escapes, *whoever lets him escape, it shall be ᴿhis life for the life of the other." 1 Kin. 20:39

25 Now it happened, as soon as he had

made an end of offering the burnt offering, that Jehu said to the guard and to the captains, "Go in *and* kill them; let no one come out!" And they killed them with the edge of the sword; then the guards and the officers threw *them* out, and went into the ᵀinner room of the temple of Baal. Lit. *city*

26 And they brought the *sacred* pillars out of the temple of Baal and burned them.

27 Then they broke down the *sacred* pillar of Baal, and tore down the temple of Baal and made it a refuse dump to this day.

28 Thus Jehu destroyed Baal from Israel.

29 However Jehu did not turn away from the sins of Jeroboam the son of Nebat, who had made Israel sin, *that is,* from the golden calves that *were* at Bethel and Dan.

30 And the Lᴏʀᴅ said to Jehu, "Because you have done well in doing *what is* right in My sight, *and* have done to the house of Ahab all that *was* in My heart, ᴿyour sons shall sit on the throne of Israel to the fourth generation." 2 Kin. 13:1, 10; 14:23; 15:8, 12

31 But Jehu took no heed to walk in the law of the Lᴏʀᴅ God of Israel with all his heart; for he did not depart from the sins of Jeroboam, who had made Israel sin.

Death of Jehu

32 In those days the Lᴏʀᴅ began to cut off *parts* of Israel; and ᴿHazael conquered them in all the territory of Israel 2 Kin. 8:12; 13:22

33 from the Jordan eastward: all the land of Gilead—Gad, Reuben, and Manasseh—from ᴿAroer, which *is* by the River Arnon, including ᴿGilead and Bashan. Deut. 2:36 · Amos 1:3-5

34 Now the rest of the acts of Jehu, all that he did, and all his might, *are* they not written in the book of the chronicles of the kings of Israel?

35 So Jehu rested with his fathers, and they buried him in Samaria. Then ᴿJehoahaz his son reigned in his place. 2 Kin. 13:1

36 And the period that Jehu reigned over Israel in Samaria *was* twenty-eight years.

Athaliah Reigns in Judah

11 When Athaliah the mother of Ahaziah saw that her son was ᴿdead, she arose and destroyed all the royal heirs. 2 Kin. 9:27

2 But ᵀJehosheba, the daughter of King Joram, sister of Ahaziah, took ᵀJoash the son of Ahaziah, and stole him away from among the king's sons *who were* being murdered; and they hid him and his nurse in the bedroom, from Athaliah, so that he was not killed. *Jehoshabeath,* 2 Chr. 22:11 · Or *Jehoash*

3 So he was hidden with her in the house of the Lᴏʀᴅ for six years, while Athaliah reigned over the land.

Joash Crowned King of Judah

4 In ᴿthe seventh year Jehoiada sent and brought the captains of hundreds—of the

bodyguards and the ᵀescorts—and brought them into the house of the LORD to him. And he made a covenant with them and took an oath from them in the house of the LORD, and showed them the king's son.   2 Chr. 23:1 · *guards*

5 Then he commanded them, saying, "This *is* what you shall do: One-third of you who come on duty on the Sabbath shall be keeping watch over the king's house,

6 "one-third *shall be* at the gate of Sur, and one-third at the gate behind the escorts. You shall keep the watch of the house, lest it be broken down.

7 "The two ᵀcontingents of you who go off duty on the Sabbath shall keep the watch of the house of the LORD for the king.   *companies*

8 "But you shall surround the king on all sides, every man with his weapons in his hand; and whoever comes within range, let him be put to death. You are to be with the king as he goes out and as he comes in."

9 So the captains of the hundreds did according to all that Jehoiada the priest commanded. Each of them took his men who were to be on duty on the Sabbath, with those who were going off duty on the Sabbath, and came to Jehoiada the priest.

10 And the priest gave the captains of hundreds the spears and shields which *had belonged* to King David, ᴿthat were in the temple of the LORD.   2 Sam. 8:7

11 Then the escorts stood, every man with his weapons in his hand, all around the king, from the right side of the temple to the left side of the temple, by the altar and the house.

12 And he brought out the king's son, put the crown on him, and *gave him* the ᵀTestimony; they made him king and anointed him, and they clapped their hands and said, "Long live the king!"   The Law, Ex. 25:16, 21; Deut. 31:9

Death of Athaliah

13 ᴿNow when Athaliah heard the noise of the escorts *and* the people, she came to the people *in* the temple of the LORD.   2 Chr. 23:12

14 When she looked, there was the king standing by ᴿa pillar according to custom; and the leaders and the trumpeters were by the king. All the people of the land were rejoicing and blowing trumpets. So Athaliah tore her clothes and cried out, "Treason! Treason!"   2 Chr. 34:31

15 And Jehoiada the priest commanded the captains of the hundreds, the officers of the army, and said to them, "Take her outside ᵀunder guard, and slay with the sword whoever follows her." For the priest had said, "Do not let her be killed in the house of the LORD."   Lit. *between ranks*

16 So they seized her; and she went by way of the horses' entrance *into* the king's house, and there she was killed.

17 Then Jehoiada made a covenant between the LORD, the king, and the people, that they should be the LORD's people, and *also* between the king and the people.

18 And all the people of the land went to the temple of Baal, and tore it down. They thoroughly broke in pieces its altars and ᵀimages, and killed Mattan the priest of Baal before the altars. And the priest appointed officers over the house of the LORD.   Idols

19 Then he took the captains of hundreds, the bodyguards, the escorts, and all the people of the land; and they brought the king down from the house of the LORD, and went by way of the gate of the escorts to the king's house. Then he sat on the throne of the kings.

20 So all the people of the land rejoiced; and the city was quiet, for they had slain Athaliah with the sword *in* the king's house.

21 Jehoash *was* ᴿseven years old when he became king.   2 Chr. 24:1–14

Jehoash Repairs the Temple

12 In the seventh year of Jehu, ᴿJehoashᵀ became king, and he reigned forty years in Jerusalem. His mother's name *was* Zibiah of Beersheba.   2 Chr. 24:1 · *Joash*, 2 Kin. 11:2ff.

2 Jehoash did *what was* right in the sight of the LORD all the days in which ᴿJehoiada the priest instructed him.   2 Kin. 11:4

3 But the ᵀhigh places were not taken away; the people still sacrificed and burned incense on the high places.   For pagan worship

4 And Jehoash said to the priests, "All the money of the dedicated gifts that are brought into the house of the LORD—each man's census money, each man's ᴿassessment money—*and* all the money that a man purposes in his heart to bring into the house of the LORD,   Lev. 27:2ff.

5 "let the priests take *it* themselves, each from his constituency; and let them repair the ᵀdamages of the temple, wherever any dilapidation is found."   Lit. *breaches*

6 Now it was so, by the twenty-third year of King Jehoash, ᴿthat the priests had not repaired the damages of the temple.   2 Chr. 24:5

7 So King Jehoash called Jehoiada the priest and the *other* priests, and said to them, "Why have you not repaired the damages of the temple? Now therefore, do not take *more* money from your constituency, but deliver it for repairing the damages of the temple."

8 And the priests agreed that they would neither receive *more* money from the people, nor repair the damages of the temple.

9 Then Jehoiada the priest took a chest, bored a hole in its lid, and set it beside the altar, on the right side as one comes into the house of the LORD; and the priests who kept the door put ᴿthere all the money brought into the house of the LORD.   Mark 12:41

10 So it was, whenever they saw that *there*

was much money in the chest, that the king's ^Tscribe and the high priest came up and put it in bags, and counted the money that was found in the house of the LORD.   *secretary*

11 Then they gave the money, which had been apportioned, into the hands of those who did the work, who had the oversight of the house of the LORD; and they ^Tpaid it out to the carpenters and builders who worked on the house of the LORD,   Lit. *weighed*

12 and to masons and stonecutters, and for buying timber and hewn stone, to repair the damage of the house of the LORD, and for all that was paid out to repair the temple.

13 However there were not made for the house of the LORD basins of silver, trimmers, sprinkling-bowls, trumpets, any articles of gold or articles of silver, from the money brought into the house of the LORD.

14 But they gave that to the workmen, and they repaired the house of the LORD with it.

15 Moreover ^Rthey did not require an account from the men into whose hand they delivered the money to be paid to workmen, for they dealt faithfully.   2 Kin. 22:7

16 ^RThe money from the trespass offerings and the money from the sin offerings was not brought into the house of the LORD. ^RIt belonged to the priests.   [Lev. 5:15, 18] • [Num. 18:9]

Hazael Threatens Jerusalem

17 Hazael king of Syria went up and fought against Gath, and took it; then Hazael set his face to go up to Jerusalem.

18 And Jehoash king of Judah ^Rtook all the sacred things that his fathers, Jehoshaphat and Jehoram and Ahaziah, kings of Judah, had dedicated, and his own sacred things, and all the gold found in the treasuries of the house of the LORD and in the king's house, and sent *them* to Hazael king of Syria. Then he went away from Jerusalem.   1 Kin. 15:18

Death of Joash

19 Now the rest of the acts of *Joash, and all that he did, *are* they not written in the book of the chronicles of the kings of Judah?

20 And ^Rhis servants arose and formed a conspiracy, and killed Joash in the house of *the Millo, which goes down to Silla.   2 Kin. 14:5

21 For *Jozachar the son of Shimeath and Jehozabad the son of *Shomer, his servants, struck him. So he died, and they buried him with his fathers in the City of David. Then Amaziah his son reigned in his place.

Jehoahaz Reigns in Israel

13 In the twenty-third year of *Joash the son of Ahaziah, king of Judah, Jehoa-

haz the son of Jehu became king over Israel in Samaria, *and reigned* seventeen years.

2 And he did evil in the sight of the LORD, and followed the ^Rsins of Jeroboam the son of Nebat, who had made Israel sin. He did not ^Tdepart from them.   1 Kin. 12:26-33 • Lit. *turn*

3 Then ^Rthe anger of the LORD was aroused against Israel, and He delivered them into the hand of ^RHazael king of Syria, and into the hand of ^RBen-Hadad the son of Hazael, all *their* days.   Judg. 2:14 • 2 Kin. 8:12 • Amos 1:4

4 So Jehoahaz ^Rpleaded with the LORD, and the LORD listened to him; for ^RHe saw the oppression of Israel, because the king of Syria oppressed them.   [Ps. 78:34] • [Ex. 3:7, 9]

5 ^RThen the LORD gave Israel a deliverer, so that they escaped from under the hand of the Syrians; and the children of Israel dwelt in their tents as before.   2 Kin. 13:25; 14:25, 27

6 Nevertheless they did not depart from the sins of the house of Jeroboam, who had made Israel sin, *but* walked in them; and the *wooden image also remained in Samaria.

7 For He left of the army of Jehoahaz only fifty horsemen, ten chariots, and ten thousand foot soldiers; for the king of Syria had destroyed them ^Rand made them ^Rlike the dust at threshing.   2 Kin. 10:32 • [Amos 1:3]

8 Now the rest of the acts of Jehoahaz, all that he did, and his might, *are* they not written in the book of the chronicles of the kings of Israel?

9 So Jehoahaz rested with his fathers, and they buried him in Samaria. Then ^TJoash his son reigned in his place.   Or *Jehoash*

Jehoash Reigns in Israel

10 In the thirty-seventh year of Joash king of Judah, ^TJehoash the son of Jehoahaz became king over Israel in Samaria, *and reigned* sixteen years.   *Joash,* v. 9

11 And he did evil in the sight of the LORD. He did not depart from all the sins of Jeroboam the son of Nebat, who made Israel sin, *but* walked in them.

12 Now the rest of the acts of Joash, all that he did, and ^Rhis might with which he fought against Amaziah king of Judah, *are* they not written in the book of the chronicles of the kings of Israel?   2 Kin. 14:9

13 So Joash rested with his fathers. Then Jeroboam sat on his throne. And Joash was buried in Samaria with the kings of Israel.

Death of Elisha

14 Elisha had become sick with the illness of which he would die. Then Joash the king of Israel came down to him, and wept over his face, and said, "O my father, my father, the chariots of Israel and their horsemen!"

15 And Elisha said to him, "Take a bow and

12:19 *Jehoash,* vv. 1-18
12:20 Lit. *The Landfill*
12:21 *Zabad,* 2 Chr. 24:26 • *Shimrith,* 2 Chr. 24:26
13:1 *Jehoash,* 2 Kin. 12:1-18

13:6 Or *Asherah,* a Canaanite goddess

some arrows." So he took himself a bow and some arrows.

16 Then he said to the king of Israel, "Put your hand on the bow." So he put his hand on it, and Elisha put his hands on the king's hands.

17 And he said, "Open the east window"; and he opened it. Then Elisha said, "Shoot"; and he shot. And he said, "The arrow of the LORD's deliverance and the arrow of deliverance from Syria; for you must strike the Syrians at ᴿAphek till you have destroyed them."   1 Kin. 20:26

18 Then he said, "Take the arrows"; so he took them. And he said to the king of Israel, "Strike the ground"; so he struck three times, and stopped.

19 And the man of God was angry with him, and said, "You should have struck five or six times; then you would have struck Syria till you had destroyed it! ᴿBut now you will strike Syria only three times."   2 Kin. 13:25

20 Then Elisha died, and they buried him. And the ᴿraiding bands from Moab invaded the land in the spring of the year.   2 Kin. 3:5

21 So it was, as they were burying a man, that suddenly they spied a band of raiders; and they put the man in the tomb of Elisha; and when the man was let down and touched the bones of Elisha, he revived and stood on his feet.

Israel Recaptures Cities from Syria

22 And ᴿHazael king of Syria oppressed Israel all the days of Jehoahaz.   2 Kin. 8:12, 13

23 But the LORD was gracious to them, had compassion on them, and regarded them, because of His covenant with Abraham, Isaac, and Jacob, and would not yet destroy them or cast them from His presence.

24 Now Hazael king of Syria died. Then Ben-Hadad his son reigned in his place.

25 And ᵀJehoash the son of Jehoahaz recaptured from the hand of Ben-Hadad, the son of Hazael, the cities which he had taken out of the hand of Jehoahaz his father by war. Three times Joash defeated him and recaptured the cities of Israel.   Joash, vv. 12–14

Amaziah Reigns in Judah

14 In the second year of Joash the son of Jehoahaz, king of Israel, Amaziah the son of Joash, king of Judah, became king.

2 He was twenty-five years old when he became king, and he reigned twenty-nine years in Jerusalem. His mother's name was Jehoaddan of Jerusalem.

3 And he did what was right in the sight of the LORD, yet not like his father David; he did everything as his father Joash had done.

4 However the high places were not taken away, and the people still sacrificed and burned incense on the high places.

5 Now it happened, as soon as the kingdom was established in his hand, that he executed his servants ᴿwho had murdered his father the king.   2 Kin. 12:20

6 But the children of the murderers he did not execute, according to what is written in the Book of the Law of Moses, in which the LORD commanded, saying, ᴿ"Fathers shall not be put to death for their children, nor shall their children be put to death for their fathers; but a person shall be put to death for his own sin."   Deut. 24:16; [Ezek. 18:4, 20]

7 He killed ten thousand Edomites in the Valley of Salt, and took ᵀSela by war, and called its name Joktheel to this day.   Petra

8 Then Amaziah sent messengers to *Jehoash the son of Jehoahaz, the son of Jehu, king of Israel, saying, "Come, let us face one another in battle."

9 And Jehoash king of Israel sent to Amaziah king of Judah, saying, "The thistle that was in Lebanon sent to the cedar that was in Lebanon, saying, 'Give your daughter to my son as wife'; and a wild beast that was in Lebanon passed by and trampled the thistle.

10 "You have indeed defeated Edom, and your heart has ᵀlifted you up. Glory in that, and stay at home; for why should you meddle with trouble so that you fall—you and Judah with you?"   Made you proud

11 But Amaziah would not heed. Therefore Jehoash king of Israel went out; so he and Amaziah king of Judah faced one another at Beth Shemesh, which belongs to Judah.

12 And Judah was defeated by Israel, and every man fled to his tent.

13 Then Jehoash king of Israel captured Amaziah king of Judah, the son of Jehoash, the son of Ahaziah, at Beth Shemesh; and he went to Jerusalem, and broke down the wall of Jerusalem from the Gate of Ephraim to the Corner Gate—four hundred cubits.

14 And he took all ᴿthe gold and silver, all the articles that were found in the house of the LORD and in the treasuries of the king's house, and hostages, and returned to Samaria.   1 Kin. 7:51

15 ᴿNow the rest of the acts of Jehoash which he did—his might, and how he fought with Amaziah king of Judah—are they not written in the book of the chronicles of the kings of Israel?   2 Kin. 13:12, 13

16 So Jehoash ᵀrested with his fathers, and was buried in Samaria with the kings of Israel. Then Jeroboam his son reigned in his place.   Died and joined his ancestors

17 Amaziah the son of Joash, king of Judah, lived fifteen years after the death of Jehoash the son of Jehoahaz, king of Israel.

18 Now the rest of the acts of Amaziah, are they not written in the book of the chronicles of the kings of Judah?

14:8 Joash, 2 Kin. 13:9, 12–14, 25; 2 Chr. 25:17ff.

19 And [R]they formed a conspiracy against him in Jerusalem, and he fled to [R]Lachish; but they sent after him to Lachish and killed him there.   2 Chr. 25:27 • Josh. 10:31

20 Then they brought him on horses, and he was buried at Jerusalem with his fathers in the City of David.

21 And all the people of Judah took *Azariah, who was sixteen years old, and made him king instead of his father Amaziah.

22 He built Elath and restored it to Judah, after the king rested with his fathers.

Jeroboam II Reigns in Israel

23 In the fifteenth year of Amaziah the son of Joash, king of Judah, Jeroboam the son of Joash, king of Israel, became king in Samaria, and reigned forty-one years.

24 And he did evil in the sight of the LORD; he did not depart from all the sins of Jeroboam the son of Nebat, who had made Israel sin.

25 He restored the territory of Israel from the entrance of Hamath to the Sea of the Arabah, according to the word of the LORD God of Israel, which He had spoken through His servant Jonah the son of Amittai, the prophet who was from Gath Hepher.

26 For the LORD saw that the affliction of Israel was very bitter; and whether bond or free, there was no helper for Israel.

27 [R]And the LORD did not say that He would blot out the name of Israel from under heaven; but He saved them by the hand of Jeroboam the son of Joash.   [2 Kin. 13:5, 23]

28 Now the rest of the acts of Jeroboam, and all that he did—his might, how he made war, and how he recaptured for Israel, from Damascus and Hamath, what had belonged to Judah—are they not written in the book of the chronicles of the kings of Israel?

29 So Jeroboam [T]rested with his fathers, the kings of Israel. Then Zechariah his son reigned in his place.   Died and joined his ancestors

Azariah Reigns in Judah

15 In the twenty-seventh year of Jeroboam king of Israel, Azariah the son of Amaziah, king of Judah, became king.

2 He was sixteen years old when he became king, and he reigned fifty-two years in Jerusalem. His mother's name was Jecholiah of Jerusalem.

3 And he did what was right in the sight of the LORD, according to all that his father Amaziah had done,

4 [R]except that the high places were not removed; the people still sacrificed and burned incense on the high places.   2 Kin. 12:3

5 Then the LORD struck the king, so that he was a leper until the day of his death; so

he [R]dwelt in an isolated house. And Jotham the king's son was over the royal house, judging the people of the land.   [Lev. 13:46]

6 Now the rest of the acts of Azariah, and all that he did, are they not written in the book of the chronicles of the kings of Judah?

7 So Azariah [T]rested with his fathers, and [R]they buried him with his fathers in the City of David. Then Jotham his son reigned in his place.   Died and joined his ancestors • 2 Chr. 26:23

Zechariah Reigns in Israel

8 In the thirty-eighth year of Azariah king of Judah, Zechariah the son of Jeroboam reigned over Israel in Samaria six months.

9 And he did evil in the sight of the LORD, [R]as his fathers had done; he did not depart from the sins of Jeroboam the son of Nebat, who had made Israel sin.   2 Kin. 14:24

10 Then Shallum the son of Jabesh conspired against him, and [R]struck and killed him in front of the people; and he reigned in his place.   Amos 7:9

11 Now the rest of the acts of Zechariah, indeed they are written in the book of the chronicles of the kings of Israel.

12 This was the word of the LORD which He spoke to Jehu, saying, [R]"Your sons shall sit on the throne of Israel to the fourth generation." And so it was.   2 Kin. 10:30

Shallum Reigns in Israel

13 Shallum the son of Jabesh became king in the thirty-ninth year of [T]Uzziah king of Judah; and he reigned a full month in Samaria.   Azariah, 2 Kin. 14:21ff.; 15:1ff.

14 For Menahem the son of Gadi went up from Tirzah, came to Samaria, and struck Shallum the son of Jabesh in Samaria and killed him; and he reigned in his place.

15 Now the rest of the acts of Shallum, and the conspiracy which he [T]led, indeed they are written in the book of the chronicles of the kings of Israel.   Lit. conspired

16 Then from Tirzah, Menahem attacked Tiphsah, all who were there, and its territory. Because they did not surrender, therefore he attacked it. All the women there who were with child he ripped open.

Menahem Reigns in Israel

17 In the thirty-ninth year of Azariah king of Judah, Menahem the son of Gadi became king over Israel, and reigned ten years in Samaria.

18 And he did evil in the sight of the LORD; he did not depart all his days from the sins of Jeroboam the son of Nebat, who had made Israel sin.

19 *Pul king of Assyria came against the land; and Menahem gave Pul a thousand

talents of silver, that his hand might be with him to strengthen the kingdom under his control.

20 And Menahem ᴿexactedᵀ the money from Israel, from all the very wealthy, from each man ᵀfifty shekels of silver, to give to the king of Assyria. So the king of Assyria turned back, and did not stay there in the land.   2 Kin. 23:35 · took · $6,400

21 Now the rest of the acts of Menahem, and all that he did, *are* they not written in the book of the chronicles of the kings of Israel?

22 So Menahem rested with his fathers. Then Pekahiah his son reigned in his place.

Pekahiah Reigns in Israel

23 In the fiftieth year of Azariah king of Judah, Pekahiah the son of Menahem became king over Israel in Samaria, *and* reigned two years.

24 And he did evil in the sight of the LORD; he did not depart from the sins of Jeroboam the son of Nebat, who had made Israel sin.

25 Then Pekah the son of Remaliah, an officer of his, conspired against him and ᵀkilled him in Samaria, in the citadel of the king's house, along with Argob and Arieh; and with him were fifty men of Gilead. He killed him and reigned in his place.   struck

26 Now the rest of the acts of Pekahiah, and all that he did, indeed they *are* written in the book of the chronicles of the kings of Israel.

Pekah Reigns in Israel

27 In the fifty-second year of Azariah king of Judah, ᴿPekah the son of Remaliah became king over Israel in Samaria, *and* reigned twenty years.   Is. 7:1

28 And he did evil in the sight of the LORD; he did not depart from the sins of Jeroboam the son of Nebat, who had made Israel sin.

29 In the days of Pekah king of Israel, ᵀTiglath-Pileser king of Assyria came and took Ijon, Abel Beth Maachah, Janoah, Kedesh, Hazor, Gilead, and Galilee, all the land of Naphtali; and he ᴿcarried them captive to Assyria.   A later name of *Pul*, v. 19 · 2 Kin. 17:6

30 Then Hoshea the son of Elah led a conspiracy against Pekah the son of Remaliah, and struck and killed him; so he ᴿreigned in his place in the twentieth year of Jotham the son of Uzziah.   [Hos. 10:3, 7, 15]

31 Now the rest of the acts of Pekah, and all that he did, indeed they *are* written in the book of the chronicles of the kings of Israel.

Jotham Reigns in Judah

32 In the second year of Pekah the son of Remaliah, king of Israel, Jotham the son of Uzziah, king of Judah, began to reign.

33 He was twenty-five years old when he became king, and he reigned sixteen years in Jerusalem. His mother's name *was* ᵀJerusha the daughter of Zadok.   *Jerushah*, 2 Chr. 27:1

34 And he did *what was* right in the sight of the LORD; he did ᴿaccording to all that his father Uzziah had done.   2 Kin. 15:3, 4

35 However the high places were not removed; the people still sacrificed and burned incense on the high places. He built the Upper Gate of the house of the LORD.

36 Now the rest of the acts of Jotham, and all that he did, *are* they not written in the book of the chronicles of the kings of Judah?

37 In those days the LORD began to send Rezin king of Syria and ᴿPekah the son of Remaliah against Judah.   2 Kin. 15:26, 27

38 So Jotham ᵀrested with his fathers, and was buried with his fathers in the City of David his father. Then Ahaz his son reigned in his place.   Died and joined his ancestors

Ahaz Reigns in Judah

16 In the seventeenth year of Pekah the son of Remaliah, Ahaz the son of Jotham, king of Judah, began to reign.

2 Ahaz *was* twenty years old when he became king, and he reigned sixteen years in Jerusalem; and he did not do *what was* right in the sight of the LORD his God, as his father David *had* done.

3 But he walked in the way of the kings of Israel; indeed he made his son pass through the fire, according to the ᴿabominations of the nations whom the LORD had cast out from before the children of Israel.   [Lev. 18:21]

4 And he sacrificed and burned incense on the ᴿhigh places, ᴿon the hills, and under every green tree.   2 Kin. 15:34, 35 · [Deut. 12:2]

5 ᴿThen Rezin king of Syria and Pekah the son of Remaliah, king of Israel, came up to Jerusalem to *make* war; and they besieged Ahaz but could not overcome *him.*   Is. 7:1, 4

6 At that time Rezin king of Syria captured Elath for Syria, and drove the men of Judah from Elath. Then the *Edomites went to Elath, and dwell there to this day.

7 So Ahaz sent messengers to ᵀTiglath-Pileser king of Assyria, saying, "I *am* your servant and your son. Come up and save me from the hand of the king of Syria and from the hand of the king of Israel, who rise up against me."   A later name of *Pul*, 2 Kin. 15:19

8 And Ahaz took the silver and gold that was found in the house of the LORD, and in the treasuries of the king's house, and sent *it* as a present to the king of Assyria.

9 So the king of Assyria heeded him; for the king of Assyria went up against Damascus and ᴿtook it, carried *its people* captive to ᴿKir, and killed Rezin.   Amos 1:5 · Amos 9:7

10 Now King Ahaz went to Damascus to meet Tiglath-Pileser king of Assyria, and saw an altar that *was* at Damascus; and King

16:6 A few ancient mss. *Syrians*

Ahaz sent to Urijah the priest the design of the altar and its pattern, according to all its workmanship.

11 Then Urijah the priest built an altar according to all that King Ahaz had sent from Damascus. So Urijah the priest made *it* before King Ahaz came back from Damascus.

12 And when the king came back from Damascus, the king saw the altar; and ᴿthe king approached the altar and made offerings on it.   2 Chr. 26:16, 19

13 So he burned his burnt offering and his grain offering; and he poured his drink offering and sprinkled the blood of his peace offerings on the altar.

14 He also brought ᴿthe bronze altar which *was* before the LORD, from the front of the ᵀtemple—from between the *new* altar and the house of the LORD—and put it on the north side of the *new* altar.   2 Chr. 4:1 • Lit. *house*

15 Then King Ahaz commanded Urijah the priest, saying, "On the great *new* altar burn ᴿthe morning burnt offering, the evening grain offering, the king's burnt sacrifice, and his grain offering, with the burnt offering of all the people of the land, their grain offering, and their drink offerings; and sprinkle on it all the blood of the burnt offering and all the blood of the sacrifice. And the bronze altar shall be for me to inquire *by.*"   Ex. 29:39-41

16 Thus did Urijah the priest, according to all that King Ahaz commanded.

17 And King Ahaz cut off ᴿthe panels of the carts, and removed the lavers from them; and he took down ᴿthe Sea from the bronze oxen that *were* under it, and put it on a pavement of stones.   1 Kin. 7:27-29 • 1 Kin. 7:23-25

18 Also he removed the Sabbath pavilion which they had built in the temple, and he removed the king's outer entrance from the house of the LORD, on account of the king of Assyria.

19 Now the rest of the acts of Ahaz which he did, *are* they not written in the book of the chronicles of the kings of Judah?

20 So Ahaz rested with his fathers, and ᴿwas buried with his fathers in the City of David. Then Hezekiah his son reigned in his place.   2 Chr. 28:27

Hoshea Reigns in Israel

17 In the twelfth year of Ahaz king of Judah, Hoshea the son of Elah became king of Israel in Samaria, *and he reigned* nine years.

2 And he did evil in the sight of the LORD, but not as the kings of Israel who were before him.

3 Shalmaneser king of Assyria came up against him; and Hoshea ᴿbecame his vassal, and paid him tribute money.   2 Kin. 24:1

4 And the king of Assyria uncovered a conspiracy by Hoshea; for he had sent mes-sengers to So, king of Egypt, and brought no tribute to the king of Assyria, as *he had done* year by year. Therefore the king of Assyria shut him up, and bound him in prison.

Israel Carried Captive to Assyria

5 Now ᴿthe king of Assyria went through-out all the land, and went up to Samaria and besieged it for three years.   Hos. 13:16

6 In the ninth year of Hoshea, the king of Assyria took Samaria and ᴿcarried Israel away to Assyria, and placed them in Halah and by the Habor, the River of Gozan, and in the cities of the Medes.   [Deut. 28:36, 64; 29:27, 28]

7 For so it was that the children of Israel had sinned against the LORD their God, who had brought them up out of the land of Egypt, from under the hand of Pharaoh king of Egypt; and they had feared other gods,

8 and ᴿhad walked in the statutes of the nations whom the LORD had cast out from before the children of Israel, and of the kings of Israel, which they had made.   [Lev. 18:3]

9 Also the children of Israel secretly did against the LORD their God things that *were* not right, and they built for themselves ᵀhigh places in all their cities, ᴿfrom watchtower to fortified city.   Places for pagan worship • 2 Kin. 18:8

10 They set up for themselves *sacred* pillars and *wooden images on every high hill and under every green tree.

11 There they burned incense on all the high places, like the nations whom the LORD had carried away before them; and they did wicked things to provoke the LORD to anger,

12 for they served idols, ᴿof which the LORD had said to them, ᴿ"You shall not do this thing."   [Ex. 20:3-5] • [Deut. 4:19]

13 Yet the LORD testified against Israel and against Judah, by all of His prophets, ᴿevery seer, saying, "Turn from your evil ways, and keep My commandments *and* My statutes, according to all the law which I commanded your fathers, and which I sent to you by My servants the prophets."   1 Sam. 9:9

14 Nevertheless they would not hear, but ᴿstiffened their necks, like the necks of their fathers, who ᴿdid not believe in the LORD their God.   [Acts 7:51] • Deut. 9:23

15 And they rejected His statutes and His covenant that He had made with their fa-thers, and His testimonies which He had testified against them; they followed idols, ᴿbecame idolaters, and *went* after the nations who *were* all around them, *concerning* whom the LORD had charged them that they should ᴿnot do like them.   [Rom. 1:21-23] • [Deut. 12:30, 31]

16 So they left all the commandments of the LORD their God, made for themselves a molded image *and* two calves, made a wooden image and worshiped all the ᴿhost of heaven, and served Baal.   [Deut. 4:19]

17:10 Or *Asherim*, Canaanite deities

17 And they caused their sons and daughters to pass through the fire, ᴿpracticed witchcraft and soothsaying, and sold themselves to do evil in the sight of the Lᴏʀᴅ, to provoke Him to anger.   [Deut. 18:10-12]

18 Therefore the Lᴏʀᴅ was very angry with Israel, and removed them from His sight; there was none left ᴿbut the tribe of Judah alone.   1 Kin. 11:13, 32

19 Also ᴿJudah did not keep the commandments of the Lᴏʀᴅ their God, but walked in the statutes of Israel which they made. Jer. 3:8

20 And the Lᴏʀᴅ rejected all the descendants of Israel, afflicted them, and delivered them into the hand of plunderers, until He had cast them from His ᴿsight.   2 Kin. 24:20

21 For ᴿHe tore Israel from the house of David, and ᴿthey made Jeroboam the son of Nebat king. Then Jeroboam drove Israel from following the Lᴏʀᴅ, and made them commit a great sin.   1 Kin. 11:11, 31 • 1 Kin. 12:20, 28

22 For the children of Israel walked in all the sins of Jeroboam which he did; they did not depart from them,

23 until the Lᴏʀᴅ removed Israel out of His sight, as He had said by all His servants the prophets. So Israel was carried away from their own land to Assyria, *as it is* to this day.

Assyria Resettles Samaria

24 ᴿThen the king of Assyria brought *people* from Babylon, Cuthah, ᴿAva, Hamath, and from Sepharvaim, and placed *them* in the cities of Samaria instead of the children of Israel; and they took possession of Samaria and dwelt in its cities.   Ezra 4:2, 10 • 2 Kin. 18:34

25 And it was so, at the beginning of their dwelling there, *that* they did not fear the Lᴏʀᴅ; therefore the Lᴏʀᴅ sent lions among them, which killed *some* of them.

26 So they spoke to the king of Assyria, saying, "The nations whom you have removed and placed in the cities of Samaria do not know the rituals of the God of the land; therefore He has sent lions among them, and indeed, they are killing them because they do not know the rituals of the God of the land."

27 Then the king of Assyria commanded, saying, "Send there one of the priests whom you brought from there; let him go and dwell there, and let him teach them the rituals of the God of the land."

28 Then one of the priests whom they had carried away from Samaria came and dwelt in Bethel, and taught them how they should fear the Lᴏʀᴅ.

29 However every nation continued to make gods of its own, and put *them* ᴿin the shrines on the high places which the Samaritans had made, *every* nation in the cities where they dwelt.   1 Kin. 12:31; 13:32

30 The men of ᴿBabylon made Succoth Benoth, the men of Cuth made Nergal, the men of Hamath made Ashima,   2 Kin. 17:24

31 and the Avites made Nibhaz and Tartak; and the Sepharvites ᴿburned their children in fire to Adrammelech and Anammelech, the gods of Sepharvaim.   [Deut. 12:31]

32 So they feared the Lᴏʀᴅ, and from every class they appointed for themselves priests of the high places, who sacrificed for them in the shrines of the high places.

33 ᴿThey feared the Lᴏʀᴅ, yet served their own gods—according to the rituals of the nations from among whom they were carried away.   Zeph. 1:5

34 To this day they continue practicing the former rituals; they do not fear the Lᴏʀᴅ, nor do they follow their statutes or their ordinances, or the law and commandment which the Lᴏʀᴅ had commanded the children of Jacob, ᴿwhom He named Israel, Gen. 32:28; 35:10

35 with whom the Lᴏʀᴅ had made a covenant and charged them, saying: "You shall not fear other gods, nor bow down to them nor serve them nor sacrifice to them;

36 "but the Lᴏʀᴅ, who brought you up from the land of Egypt with great power and ᴿan outstretched arm, ᴿHim you shall fear, Him you shall worship, and to Him you shall offer sacrifice.   Ex. 6:6; 9:15 • [Deut. 10:20]

37 "And the statutes, the ordinances, the law, and the commandment which He wrote for you, you shall be careful to observe forever; you shall not fear other gods.

38 "And the covenant that I have made with you, ᴿyou shall not forget, nor shall you fear other gods.   Deut. 4:23; 6:12

39 "But the Lᴏʀᴅ your God you shall fear; and He will deliver you from the hand of all your enemies."

40 However they did not obey, but they followed their former rituals.

41 ᴿSo these nations feared the Lᴏʀᴅ, yet served their carved images; also their children and their children's children have continued doing as their fathers did, even to this day.   2 Kin. 17:32, 33

Hezekiah Reigns in Judah

18 Now it came to pass in the third year of Hoshea the son of Elah, king of Israel, *that* ᴿHezekiah the son of Ahaz, king of Judah, began to reign.   2 Chr. 28:27; 29:1

2 He was twenty-five years old when he became king, and he reigned twenty-nine years in Jerusalem. His mother's name *was* *Abi the daughter of Zechariah.

3 And he did *what was* right in the sight of the Lᴏʀᴅ, according to all that his father David had done.

4 He removed the high places and broke the *sacred* pillars, cut down the *wooden

18:2 *Abijah,* 2 Chr. 29:1ff.
18:4 Or *Asherah,* a Canaanite goddess

image and broke in pieces the bronze serpent that Moses had made; for until those days the children of Israel burned incense to it, and called it ᵀNehushtan.   Lit. *Bronze Thing*

5 He ᴿtrusted in the LORD God of Israel, ᴿso that after him was none like him among all the kings of Judah, nor who were before him.   2 Kin. 19:10 • 2 Kin. 23:25

6 For he ᴿheld fast to the LORD; he did not depart from following Him, but kept His commandments, which the LORD had commanded Moses.   Deut. 10:20

7 The LORD was with him; he prospered wherever he went. And he rebelled against the king of Assyria and did not serve him.

8 ᴿHe ᵀsubdued the Philistines, as far as Gaza and its territory, ᴿfrom watchtower to fortified city.   Is. 14:29 • Lit. *struck* • 2 Kin. 17:9

9 Now ᴿit came to pass in the fourth year of King Hezekiah, which *was* the seventh year of Hoshea the son of Elah, king of Israel, *that* Shalmaneser king of Assyria came up against Samaria and besieged it.   2 Kin. 17:3

10 And at the end of three years they took it. In the sixth year of Hezekiah, that *is*, ᴿthe ninth year of Hoshea king of Israel, Samaria was taken.   2 Kin. 17:6

11 Then the king of Assyria carried Israel away captive to Assyria, and put them ᴿin Halah and by the Habor, the River of Gozan, and in the cities of the Medes,   1 Chr. 5:26

12 because they ᴿdid not obey the voice of the LORD their God, but transgressed His covenant *and* all that Moses the servant of the LORD had commanded; and they would neither hear nor do *them*.   2 Kin. 17:7-18

13 And ᴿin the fourteenth year of King Hezekiah, Sennacherib king of Assyria came up against all the fortified cities of Judah and took them.   2 Chr. 32:1

14 Then Hezekiah king of Judah sent to the king of Assyria at Lachish, saying, "I have done wrong; turn away from me; whatever you impose on me I will pay." And the king of Assyria assessed Hezekiah king of Judah ᵀthree hundred talents of silver and ᵀthirty talents of gold. $115,200,000 • $172,800,000

15 So Hezekiah gave *him* all the silver that was found in the house of the LORD and in the treasuries of the king's house.

16 At that time Hezekiah stripped *the gold from* the doors of the temple of the LORD, and *from* the pillars which Hezekiah king of Judah had overlaid, and gave ᵀit to the king of Assyria.   Lit. *them*

Sennacherib Boasts Against the LORD

17 Then the king of Assyria sent *the* *Tartan, *the* *Rabsaris, and *the* *Rabshakeh from Lachish, with a great army against Jerusa-

lem, to King Hezekiah. And they went up and came to Jerusalem. When they had come up, they went and stood by the ᴿaqueduct from the upper pool, which *was* on the highway to the Fuller's Field.   2 Kin. 20:20

18 And when they had called to the king, ᴿEliakim the son of Hilkiah, who *was* over the household, Shebna the ᵀscribe, and Joah the son of Asaph, the recorder, came out to them.   Is. 22:20 • *secretary*

19 Then *the* Rabshakeh said to them, "Say now to Hezekiah, 'Thus says the great king, the king of Assyria: ᴿ"What confidence is this in which you trust?   2 Chr. 32:10

20 "You speak of *having* plans and power for war; but *they are* ᵀmere words. And in whom do you trust, that you rebel against me?   Lit. *a word of the lips*

21 ᴿ"Now look! You are trusting in the staff of this broken reed, Egypt, on which if a man leans, it will go into his hand and pierce it. So *is* Pharaoh king of Egypt to all who trust in him.   Ezek. 29:6, 7

22 "But if you say to me, 'We trust in the LORD our God,' *is* it not He ᴿwhose ᵀhigh places and whose altars Hezekiah has taken away, and said to Judah and Jerusalem, 'You shall worship before this altar in Jerusalem'?" '   2 Kin. 18:4 • Places for pagan worship

23 "Now therefore, I urge you, give a pledge to my master the king of Assyria, and I will give you two thousand horses—if you are able on your part to put riders on them!

24 "How then will you repel one captain of the least of my master's servants, and put your trust in Egypt for chariots and horsemen?

25 "Have I now come up without the LORD against this place to destroy it? The LORD said to me, 'Go up against this land, and destroy it.' "

26 Then Eliakim the son of Hilkiah, Shebna, and Joah said to *the* Rabshakeh, "Please speak to your servants in Aramaic, for we understand *it*; and do not speak to us in ᵀHebrew in the hearing of the people who *are* on the wall."   Lit. *Judean*

27 But *the* Rabshakeh said to them, "Has my master sent me to your master and to you to speak these words, and not to the men who sit on the wall, who will eat and drink their own waste with you?"

28 Then *the* Rabshakeh stood and called out with a loud voice in ᵀHebrew, and spoke, saying, "Hear the word of the great king, the king of Assyria!   Lit. *Judean*

29 "Thus says the king: ᴿDo not let Hezekiah deceive you, for he shall not be able to deliver you from his hand;   2 Chr. 32:15

30 'nor let Hezekiah make you trust in the LORD, saying, "The LORD will surely deliver us; this city shall not be given into the hand of the king of Assyria."

18:17 A title, probably *Commander in Chief* • A title, probably *Chief Officer* • A title, probably *Chief of Staff* or *Governor*

31 "Do not listen to Hezekiah; for thus says the king of Assyria: 'Make *peace* with me by a ᵀpresent and come out to me; and every one of you eat from his own vine and every one from his own fig tree, and every one of you drink the waters of his own cistern;   Tribute

32 'until I come and take you away to a land like your own land, ᴿa land of grain and new wine, a land of bread and vineyards, a land of olive groves and honey, that you may live and not die. But do not listen to Hezekiah, lest he persuade you, saying, "The LORD will deliver us."   Deut. 8:7–9; 11:12

33 ᴿ'Has any of the gods of the nations at all delivered its land from the hand of the king of Assyria?   2 Kin. 19:12

34 'Where *are* the gods of Hamath and Arpad? Where *are* the gods of Sepharvaim and Hena and ᴿIvah? Indeed, have they delivered Samaria from my hand?   2 Kin. 17:24

35 'Who among all the gods of the lands have delivered their countries from my hand, ᴿthat the LORD should deliver Jerusalem from my hand?'"   Dan. 3:15

36 But the people held their peace and answered him not a word; for the king's commandment was, "Do not answer him."

37 Then Eliakim the son of Hilkiah, who *was* over the household, Shebna the scribe, and Joah the son of Asaph, the recorder, came to Hezekiah with *their* clothes torn, and told him the words of *the* Rabshakeh.

Isaiah Assures Deliverance

19 And ᴿso it was, when King Hezekiah heard *it*, that he tore his clothes, covered himself with ᴿsackcloth, and went into the house of the LORD.   Is. 37:1 • Ps. 69:11

2 Then he sent Eliakim, who *was* over the household, Shebna the scribe, and the elders of the priests, covered with sackcloth, to Isaiah the prophet, the son of Amoz.

3 And they said to him, "Thus says Hezekiah: 'This day *is* a day of trouble, and rebuke, and blasphemy; for the children have come to birth, but *there is* no strength to ᵀbring them forth.   give birth

4 'It may be that the LORD your God will hear all the words of *the* Rabshakeh, whom his master the king of Assyria has sent to ᴿreproach the living God, and will ᴿrebuke the words which the LORD your God has heard. Therefore lift up *your* prayer for the remnant that is left.'"   2 Kin. 18:35 • Ps. 50:21

5 So the servants of King Hezekiah came to Isaiah.

6 And Isaiah said to them, "Thus you shall say to your master, 'Thus says the LORD: "Do not be afraid of the words which you have heard, with which the servants of the king of Assyria have blasphemed Me.

7 "Surely I will send ᴿa spirit upon him, and he shall hear a rumor and return to his own land; and I will cause him to fall by the sword in his own land."'"   2 Kin. 19:35–37

Sennacherib's Threat and Hezekiah's Prayer

8 Then *the* Rabshakeh returned and found the king of Assyria warring against Libnah, for he heard that he had departed ᴿfrom Lachish.   2 Kin. 18:14, 17

9 And ᴿthe king heard concerning Tirhakah king of Ethiopia, "Look, he has come out to make war with you." So he again sent messengers to Hezekiah, saying,   1 Sam. 23:27

10 "Thus you shall speak to Hezekiah king of Judah, saying: 'Do not let your God ᴿin whom you trust deceive you, saying, "Jerusalem shall not be given into the hand of the king of Assyria."   2 Kin. 18:5

11 'Look! You have heard what the kings of Assyria have done to all lands by utterly destroying them; and shall you be delivered?

12 'Have the gods of the nations delivered those whom my fathers have destroyed, Gozan and Haran and Rezeph, and the people of ᴿEden who *were* in Telassar?   Ezek. 27:23

13 ᴿ'Where *is* the king of Hamath, the king of Arpad, and the king of the city of Sepharvaim, Hena, and Ivah?'"   2 Kin. 18:34

14 ᴿAnd Hezekiah received the letter from the hand of the messengers, and read it; and Hezekiah went up to the house of the LORD, and spread it before the LORD.   Is. 37:14

15 Then Hezekiah prayed before the LORD, and said: "O LORD God of Israel, *the One* who dwells *between* the cherubim, You are God, You alone, of all the kingdoms of the earth. You have made heaven and earth.

16 ᴿ"Incline Your ear, O LORD, and hear; open Your eyes, O LORD, and see; and hear the words of Sennacherib, ᴿwhich he has sent to reproach the living God.   Ps. 31:2 • 2 Kin. 19:4

17 "Truly, LORD, the kings of Assyria have laid waste the nations and their lands,

18 "and have cast their gods into the fire; for they *were* not gods, but ᴿthe work of men's hands—wood and stone. Therefore they destroyed them.   [Acts 17:29]

19 "Now therefore, O LORD our God, I pray, save us from his hand, ᴿthat all the kingdoms of the earth may ᴿknow that You *are* the LORD God, You alone."   Ps. 83:18 • 1 Kin. 8:42, 43

The Word of the LORD Concerning Sennacherib

20 Then Isaiah the son of Amoz sent to Hezekiah, saying, "Thus says the LORD God of Israel: ᴿ'Because you have prayed to Me against Sennacherib king of Assyria, ᴿI have heard.'   Is. 37:21 • 2 Kin. 20:5

21 "This *is* the word which the LORD has spoken concerning him:

'The virgin, ᴿthe daughter of Zion,

Has despised you, laughed you to scorn;
The daughter of Jerusalem   Lam. 2:13
Has shaken *her* head behind your back!

22 'Whom have you reproached and
blasphemed?
Against whom have you raised *your*
voice,
And lifted up your eyes on high?
Against the Holy *One* of Israel.
23 ᴿBy your messengers you have
reproached the Lord,   2 Kin. 18:17
And said: ᴿ"By the multitude of my
chariots   Ps. 20:7
I have come up to the height of the
mountains,
To the limits of Lebanon;
I will cut down its tall cedars
And its choice cypress trees;
I will enter the extremity of its borders,
To its fruitful forest.
24 I have dug and drunk strange water,
And with the soles of my feet I have
ᴿdried up   Is. 19:6
All the brooks of defense."

25 'Did you not hear long ago
How ᴿI made it,   [Is. 45:7]
From ancient times that I formed it?
Now I have brought it to pass,
That ᴿyou should be   Is. 10:5, 6
For crushing fortified cities *into* heaps
of ruins.
26 Therefore their inhabitants had little
power;
They were dismayed and confounded;
They were *as* the grass of the field
And the green herb,
As the grass on the housetops
And *grain* blighted before it is grown.

27 'But ᴿI know your dwelling place,
Your going out and your coming in,
And your rage against Me.   Ps. 139:1-3
28 Because your rage against Me and your
tumult
Have come up to My ears,
Therefore ᴿI will put My hook in your
nose   Ezek. 29:4; 38:4
And My bridle in your lips,
And I will turn you back
By the way which you came.

29 'This *shall be* a ᴿsign to you:

You shall eat this year such as grows
ᵀof itself,   2 Kin. 20:8, 9 • Without cultivation
And in the second year what springs
from the same;
Also in the third year sow and reap,
Plant vineyards
and eat the fruit of them.
30 ᴿAnd the remnant who have escaped of
the house of Judah
Shall again take root downward,
And bear fruit upward.   2 Chr. 32:22, 23

31 For out of Jerusalem shall go a
remnant,
And those who escape from Mount
Zion.
ᴿThe zeal of the Lᴏʀᴅ *of hosts will do
this.'   Is. 9:7

32 "Therefore thus says the Lᴏʀᴅ concerning the king of Assyria:

'He shall ᴿnot come into this city,
Nor shoot an arrow there,   Is. 8:7-10
Nor come before it with shield,
Nor build a siege mound against it.
33 By the way that he came,
By the same shall he return;
And he shall not come into this city,'
Says the Lᴏʀᴅ.
34 'For I will ᴿdefend this city, to save it
For My own sake and ᴿfor My servant
David's sake.' "   Is. 31:5 • 1 Kin. 11:12, 13

Sennacherib's Defeat and Death

35 And it came to pass on a certain night
that the ᵀangel of the Lᴏʀᴅ went out, and
killed in the camp of the Assyrians one
hundred and eighty-five thousand; and when
people arose early in the morning, there were
the corpses—all dead.   Or *Angel*
36 So Sennacherib king of Assyria departed
and went away, returned *home*, and remained at ᴿNineveh.   Gen. 10:11
37 Now it came to pass, as he was worshiping in the temple of Nisroch his god, that his
sons Adrammelech and Sharezer struck him
down with the sword; and they escaped into
the land of Ararat. Then ᴿEsarhaddon his son
reigned in his place.   Ezra 4:2

Hezekiah's Life Extended

20 In those days Hezekiah was sick and
near death. And Isaiah the prophet,
the son of Amoz, went to him and said to
him, "Thus says the Lᴏʀᴅ: 'Set your house in
order, for you shall die, and not live.' "
2 Then he turned his face toward the wall,
and prayed to the Lᴏʀᴅ, saying,
3 "Remember now, O Lᴏʀᴅ, I pray, how I
have walked before You in truth and with a
loyal heart, and have done *what was* good in
Your sight." And Hezekiah wept bitterly.
4 And it happened, before Isaiah had gone
out into the middle court, that the word of
the Lᴏʀᴅ came to him, saying,
5 "Return and tell Hezekiah the leader of
My people, 'Thus says the Lᴏʀᴅ, the God of
David your father: ᴿ"I have heard your
prayer, I have seen ᴿyour tears; surely I will
heal you. On the third day you shall go up to
the house of the Lᴏʀᴅ.   Ps. 65:2 • Ps. 39:12; 56:8

19:31 So with many Heb. mss. and ancient vss. (cf. Is.
37:32); MT omits *of hosts*.

6 "And I will add to your days fifteen years. I will deliver you and this city from the hand of the king of Assyria; and ᴿI will defend this city for My own sake, and for the sake of My servant David." ' "   2 Kin. 19:34

7 Then ᴿIsaiah said, "Take a lump of figs." So they took and laid it on the boil, and he recovered.   Is. 38:21

8 And Hezekiah said to Isaiah, ᴿ"What is the sign that the Lord will heal me, and that I shall go up to the house of the Lord the third day?"   Judg. 6:17, 37, 39

9 Then Isaiah said, ᴿ"This is the sign to you from the Lord, that the Lord will do the thing which He has spoken: shall the shadow go forward ten degrees or go backward ten degrees?"   Is. 38:7, 8

10 And Hezekiah answered, "It is an easy thing for the shadow to go down ten ᵀdegrees; no, but let the shadow go backward ten degrees."   Lit. steps

11 So Isaiah the prophet cried out to the Lord, and ᴿHe brought the shadow ten ᵀdegrees backward, by which it had gone down on the sundial of Ahaz.   Is. 38:8 • Lit. steps

The Babylonian Envoys

12 ᴿAt that time *Berodach-Baladan the son of Baladan, king of Babylon, sent letters and a present to Hezekiah, for he heard that Hezekiah had been sick.   Is. 39:1–8

13 And Hezekiah was attentive to them, and showed them all the house of his treasures—the silver and gold, the spices and precious ointment, and *all his armory—all that was found among his treasures. There was nothing in his house or in all his dominion that Hezekiah did not show them.

14 Then Isaiah the prophet went to King Hezekiah, and said to him, "What did these men say, and from where did they come to you?" So Hezekiah said, "They came from a far country, from Babylon."

15 And he said, "What have they seen in your house?" So Hezekiah answered, ᴿ"They have seen all that is in my house; there is nothing among my treasures that I have not shown them."   2 Kin. 20:13

16 Then Isaiah said to Hezekiah, "Hear the word of the Lord:

17 'Behold, the days are coming when all that is in your house, and what your fathers have accumulated until this day, ᴿshall be carried to Babylon; nothing shall be left,' says the Lord.   Jer. 27:21, 22; 52:17

18 'And they shall take away some of your sons who will ᵀdescend from you, whom you will beget; and they shall be eunuchs in the palace of the king of Babylon.' "   be born from

19 So Hezekiah said to Isaiah, ᴿ"The word

of the Lord which you have spoken is good!" For he said, "Will there not be peace and truth at least in my days?"   1 Sam. 3:18

Death of Hezekiah

20 Now the rest of the acts of Hezekiah—all his might, and how he made a pool and a ᵀtunnel and ᴿbrought water into the city—are they not written in the book of the chronicles of the kings of Judah?   aqueduct • 2 Chr. 32:3, 30

21 So Hezekiah rested with his fathers. Then Manasseh his son reigned in his place.

Manasseh Reigns in Judah

21 Manasseh ᴿwas twelve years old when he became king, and he reigned fifty-five years in Jerusalem. His mother's name was Hephzibah.   2 Chr. 33:1–9

2 And he did evil in the sight of the Lord, ᴿaccording to the abominations of the nations whom the Lord had cast out before the children of Israel.   2 Kin. 16:3

3 For he rebuilt the high places which Hezekiah his father had destroyed; he raised up altars for Baal, and made a *wooden image, as Ahab king of Israel had done; and he worshiped all ᵀthe host of heaven and served them.   The gods of the Assyrians

4 He also built altars in the house of the Lord, of which the Lord had said, ᴿ"In Jerusalem I will put My name."   1 Kin. 11:13

5 And he built altars for all the host of heaven in the ᴿtwo courts of the house of the Lord.   1 Kin. 6:36; 7:12

6 ᴿAlso he made his son pass through the fire, practiced ᴿsoothsaying, used witchcraft, and consulted spiritists and mediums. He did much evil in the sight of the Lord, to provoke Him to anger.   [Lev. 18:21; 20:2] • [Deut. 18:10–14]

7 He even set a carved image of *Asherah that he had made, in the ᵀhouse of which the Lord had said to David and to Solomon his son, ᴿ"In this house and in Jerusalem, which I have chosen out of all the tribes of Israel, I will put My name forever;   Temple • 1 Kin. 9:3

8 ᴿ"and I will not make the feet of Israel wander anymore from the land which I gave their fathers—only if they are careful to do according to all that I have commanded them, and according to all the law that My servant Moses commanded them."   2 Sam. 7:10

9 But they paid no attention, and Manasseh ᴿseduced them to do more evil than the nations whom the Lord had destroyed before the children of Israel.   [Prov. 29:12]

10 And the Lord spoke ᴿby His servants the prophets, saying,   2 Kin. 17:13

11 "Because Manasseh king of Judah has done these abominations (ᴿhe has acted more wickedly than all the ᴿAmorites who were

---

20:12 Merodach-Baladan, Is. 39:1
20:13 So with many Heb. mss., Syr., Tg.; MT omits all

21:3 Or Asherah, a Canaanite goddess
21:7 A Canaanite goddess

before him, and ᴿhas also made Judah sin with his idols),   1 Kin. 21:26 • Gen. 15:16 • 2 Kin. 21:9

12 "therefore thus says the LORD God of Israel: 'Behold, *I* am bringing *such* calamity upon Jerusalem and Judah, that whoever hears of it, both ᴿhis ears will tingle.   Jer. 19:3

13 'And I will stretch over Jerusalem ᴿthe measuring line of Samaria and the plummet of the house of Ahab; ᴿI will wipe Jerusalem as *one* wipes a dish, wiping *it* and turning *it* upside down.   Amos 7:7, 8 • 2 Kin. 22:16-19; 25:4-11

14 'So I will forsake the ᴿremnant of My inheritance and deliver them into the hand of their enemies; and they shall become victims of plunder to all their enemies,   Jer. 6:9

15 'because they have done evil in My sight, and have provoked Me to anger since the day their fathers came out of Egypt, even to this day.' "

16 ᴿMoreover Manasseh shed very much innocent blood, till he had filled Jerusalem from one end to another, besides his sin by which he made Judah sin, in doing evil in the sight of the LORD.   2 Kin. 24:4

17 Now the rest of the acts of Manasseh—all that he did, and the sin that he committed—*are* they not written in the book of the chronicles of the kings of Judah?

18 So ᴿManasseh rested with his fathers, and was buried in the garden of his own house, in the garden of Uzza. Then his son Amon reigned in his place.   2 Chr. 33:20

Amon's Reign and Death

19 Amon *was* twenty-two years old when he became king, and he reigned two years in Jerusalem. His mother's name *was* Meshullemeth the daughter of Haruz of Jotbah.

20 And he did evil in the sight of the LORD, as his father Manasseh had done.

21 So he walked in all the ways that his father had walked; and he served the idols that his father had served, and worshiped them.

22 He forsook the LORD God of his fathers, and did not walk in the way of the LORD.

23 ᴿThen the servants of Amon ᴿconspired against him, and killed the king in his own house.   2 Chr. 33:24, 25 • 2 Kin. 12:20; 14:19

24 But the people of the land ᴿexecuted all those who had conspired against King Amon. Then the people of the land made his son Josiah king in his place.   2 Kin. 14:5

25 Now the rest of the acts of Amon which he did, *are* they not written in the book of the chronicles of the kings of Judah?

26 And he was buried in his tomb in the garden of Uzza. Then Josiah his son reigned in his place.

Josiah Reigns in Judah

22 Josiah *was* eight years old when he became king, and he reigned thirty-

one years in Jerusalem. His mother's name *was* Jedidah the daughter of Adaiah of Bozkath.

2 And he did *what was* right in the sight of the LORD, and walked in all the ways of his father David; he ᴿdid not turn aside to the right hand or to the left.   Deut. 5:32

Hilkiah Finds the Book of the Law

3 Now it came to pass, in the eighteenth year of King Josiah, *that* the king sent Shaphan the scribe, the son of Azaliah, the son of Meshullam, to the house of the LORD, saying:

4 "Go up to Hilkiah the high priest, that he may count the money which has been ᴿbrought into the house of the LORD, which ᴿthe doorkeepers have gathered from the people.   2 Kin. 12:4 • 2 Kin. 12:9, 10

5 "And let them ᴿdeliver it into the hand of those doing the work, who are the overseers in the house of the LORD; let them give it to those who *are* in the house of the LORD doing the work, to repair the damages of the house—   2 Kin. 12:11-14

6 "to carpenters and builders and masons—and to buy timber and hewn stone to repair the house.

7 "However there need be no accounting made with them of the money delivered into their hand, because they deal faithfully."

8 Then Hilkiah the high priest said to Shaphan the scribe, ᴿ"I have found the Book of the Law in the house of the LORD." And Hilkiah gave the book to Shaphan, and he read it.   Deut. 31:24-26

9 So Shaphan the scribe went to the king, bringing the king word, saying, "Your servants have ᵀgathered the money that was found in the house, and have delivered it into the hand of those who do the work, who oversee the house of the LORD."   Lit. *poured out*

10 Then Shaphan the scribe showed the king, saying, "Hilkiah the priest has given me a book." And Shaphan read it before the king.

11 Now it happened, when the king heard the words of the Book of the Law, that he tore his clothes.

12 Then the king commanded Hilkiah the priest, ᴿAhikam the son of Shaphan, *Achbor the son of Michaiah, Shaphan the scribe, and Asaiah a servant of the king, saying,   Jer. 26:24

13 "Go, inquire of the LORD for me, for the people and for all Judah, concerning the words of this book that has been found; for great *is* ᴿthe wrath of the LORD that is aroused against us, because our fathers have not obeyed the words of this book, to do according to all that is written concerning us."   [Deut. 29:23-28; 31:17, 18]

22:12 *Abdon the son of Micah,* 2 Chr. 34:20

14 So Hilkiah the priest, Ahikam, Achbor, Shaphan, and Asaiah went to Huldah the prophetess, the wife of Shallum the son of Tikvah, the son of Harhas, keeper of the wardrobe. (She dwelt in Jerusalem in the Second Quarter.) And they spoke with her.

15 Then she said to them, "Thus says the LORD God of Israel, 'Tell the man who sent you to Me,

16 "Thus says the LORD: 'Behold, ᴿI will bring calamity on this place and on its inhabitants—all the words of the book which the king of Judah has read—   Deut. 29:27

17 ᴿ"because they have forsaken Me and burned incense to other gods, that they might provoke Me to anger with all the works of their hands. Therefore My wrath shall be aroused against this place and shall not be quenched.' " '   Deut. 29:25-27

18 "But as for ᴿthe king of Judah, who sent you to inquire of the LORD, in this manner you shall speak to him, 'Thus says the LORD God of Israel: "Concerning the words which you have heard—   2 Chr. 34:26

19 "because your heart was tender, and you humbled yourself before the LORD when you heard what I spoke against this place and against its inhabitants, that they would become a desolation and ᴿa curse, and you tore your clothes and wept before Me, I also have heard you," says the LORD.   Jer. 26:6; 44:22

20 "Surely, therefore, I will gather you to your fathers, and you shall be gathered to your grave in peace; and your eyes shall not see all the calamity which I will bring on this place." ' " So they brought back word to the king.

Josiah Restores True Worship

23 Now the king sent them to gather all the elders of Judah and Jerusalem to him.

2 The king went up to the house of the LORD with all the men of Judah, and with him all the inhabitants of Jerusalem—the priests and the prophets and all the people, both small and great. And he ᴿread in their hearing all the words of the Book of the Covenant ᴿwhich had been found in the house of the LORD.   Deut. 31:10-13 • 2 Kin. 22:8

3 Then the king ᴿstood by a pillar and made a ᴿcovenant before the LORD, to follow the LORD and to keep His commandments and His testimonies and His statutes, with all his heart and all his soul, to perform the words of this covenant that were written in this book. And all the people took a stand for the covenant.   2 Kin. 11:14 • 2 Kin. 11:17

4 And the king commanded Hilkiah the high priest, the priests of the second order, and the doorkeepers, to bring out of the temple of the LORD all the articles that were made for Baal, for *Asherah, and for all ᵀthe host of heaven; and he burned them outside Jerusalem in the fields of Kidron, and carried their ashes to Bethel.   The gods of the Assyrians

5 Then he removed the idolatrous priests whom the kings of Judah had ordained to burn incense on the high places in the cities of Judah, and in the places all around Jerusalem, and those who burned incense to Baal, to the sun, to the moon, to the ᵀconstellations, and to all the host of heaven.   Zodiac

6 And he brought out the ᵀwooden image from the house of the LORD, to the Brook Kidron outside Jerusalem, burned it at the Brook Kidron and ground it to ashes, and threw its ashes on ᴿthe graves of the common people.   Or Asherah, a Canaanite goddess • 2 Chr. 34:4

7 Then he tore down the ritual ᵀbooths of the *perverted persons that were in the house of the LORD, where the ᴿwomen wove hangings for the wooden image.   Lit. houses • Ex. 38:8

8 And he brought all the priests from the cities of Judah, and defiled the high places where the priests had burned incense, from ᴿGeba to Beersheba; also he broke down the high places at the gates which were at the entrance of the Gate of Joshua the governor of the city, which were to the left of the city gate.   Josh. 21:17

9 ᴿNevertheless the priests of the high places did not come up to the altar of the LORD in Jerusalem, but they ate unleavened bread among their brethren.   [Ezek. 44:10-14]

10 And he defiled ᴿTopheth, which is in the Valley of the ᵀSon of Hinnom, that no man might make his son or his daughter pass through the fire to Molech.   Is. 30:33 • Kt. sons

11 Then he removed the horses that the kings of Judah had ᵀdedicated to the sun, at the entrance to the house of the LORD, by the chamber of Nathan-Melech, the officer who was in the court; and he burned the chariots of the sun with fire.   given

12 The altars that were ᴿon the roof, the upper chamber of Ahaz, which the kings of Judah had made, and the altars which ᴿManasseh had made in the two courts of the house of the LORD, the king broke down and pulverized there, and threw their dust into the Brook Kidron.   Jer. 19:13 • 2 Kin. 21:5

13 Then the king defiled the high places that were east of Jerusalem, which were on the ᵀsouth of the ᵀMount of Corruption, which Solomon king of Israel had built for Ashtoreth the abomination of the Sidonians, for Chemosh the abomination of the Moabites, and for Milcom the abomination of the people of Ammon.   Lit. right of • Mount of Olives

14 And he broke in pieces the sacred pillars

23:4 A Canaanite goddess
23:7 Heb. qedeshim, those practicing sodomy and prostitution in religious rituals

and cut down the wooden images, and filled their places with the bones of men.

15 Moreover the altar that *was* at Bethel, *and* the ᵀhigh place ᴿwhich Jeroboam the son of Nebat, who made Israel sin, had made, both that altar and the high place he broke down; and he burned the high place *and* crushed *it* to powder, and burned the wooden image. A place for pagan worship • 1 Kin. 12:28-33

16 As Josiah turned, he saw the tombs that *were* there on the mountain. And he sent and took the bones out of the tombs and burned *them* on the altar, and defiled it according to the word of the LORD which the man of God proclaimed, who proclaimed these words.

17 Then he said, "What gravestone *is* this that I see?" So the men of the city told him, "*It is* ᴿthe tomb of the man of God who came from Judah and proclaimed these things which you have done against the altar of Bethel." 1 Kin. 13:1, 30, 31

18 And he said, "Let him alone; let no one move his bones." So they let his bones alone, with the bones of ᴿthe prophet who came from Samaria. 1 Kin. 13:11, 31

19 Now Josiah also took away all the ᵀshrines of the high places that *were* ᴿin the cities of Samaria, which the kings of Israel had made to provoke *the LORD to anger; and he did to them according to all the deeds he had done in Bethel. Lit. houses • 2 Chr. 34:6, 7

20 He executed all the priests of the ᵀhigh places who *were* there, on the altars, and burned men's bones on them; and he returned to Jerusalem. Places for pagan worship

21 Then the king commanded all the people, saying, ᴿ"Keep the Passover to the LORD your God, ᴿas *it is* written in this Book of the Covenant." 2 Chr. 35:1 • Deut. 16:2-8

22 ᴿSuch a Passover surely had never been held since the days of the judges who judged Israel, nor in all the days of the kings of Israel and the kings of Judah. 2 Chr. 35:18, 19

23 But in the eighteenth year of King Josiah this Passover was held before the LORD in Jerusalem.

24 Moreover Josiah put away those who consulted mediums and spiritists, the household gods and idols, all the abominations that were seen in the land of Judah and in Jerusalem, that he might perform the words of ᴿthe law which were written in the book ᴿthat Hilkiah the priest found in the house of the LORD. [Lev. 19:31; 20:27] • 2 Kin. 22:8

25 ᴿNow before him there was no king like him, who turned to the LORD with all his heart, with all his soul, and with all his might, according to all the Law of Moses; nor after him did *any* arise like him. 2 Kin. 18:5

23:19 So with LXX, Syr., Vg.; MT, Tg. omit *the LORD*

Impending Judgment on Judah

26 Nevertheless the LORD did not turn from the fierceness of His great wrath, with which His anger was aroused against Judah, ᴿbecause of all the provocations with which Manasseh had provoked Him. Jer. 15:4

27 And the LORD said, "I will also remove Judah from My sight, as I have removed Israel, and will cast off this city Jerusalem which I have chosen, and the house of which I said, ᴿ'My name shall be there.'" 1 Kin. 8:29

Josiah Dies in Battle

28 Now the rest of the acts of Josiah, and all that he did, *are* they not written in the book of the chronicles of the kings of Judah?

29 In his days Pharaoh Necho king of Egypt went to the aid of the king of Assyria, to the River Euphrates; and King Josiah went against him. And *Pharaoh Necho* killed him at Megiddo when he confronted him.

30 ᴿThen his servants moved his body in a chariot from Megiddo, brought him to Jerusalem, and buried him in his own tomb. And ᴿthe people of the land took Jehoahaz the son of Josiah, anointed him, and made him king in his father's place. 2 Chr. 35:24 • 2 Chr. 36:1-4

The Reign and Captivity of Jehoahaz

31 ᴿJehoahaz *was* twenty-three years old when he became king, and he reigned three months in Jerusalem. His mother's name *was* ᴿHamutal the daughter of Jeremiah of Libnah. Jer. 22:11 • 2 Kin. 24:18

32 And he did evil in the sight of the LORD, according to all that his fathers had done.

33 Now Pharaoh Necho put him in prison ᴿat Riblah in the land of Hamath, that he might not reign in Jerusalem; and he imposed on the land a tribute of one hundred talents of silver and a talent of gold. 2 Kin. 25:6

34 Then Pharaoh Necho made Eliakim the son of Josiah king in place of his father Josiah, and changed his name to Jehoiakim. And *Pharaoh* took Jehoahaz and went to Egypt, and ᵀhe died there. Jehoahaz

Jehoiakim Reigns in Judah

35 So Jehoiakim gave ᴿthe silver and gold to Pharaoh; but he taxed the land to give money according to the command of Pharaoh; he exacted the silver and gold from the people of the land, from every one according to his assessment, to give *it* to Pharaoh Necho. 2 Kin. 23:33

36 Jehoiakim *was* twenty-five years old when he became king, and he reigned eleven years in Jerusalem. His mother's name *was* Zebudah the daughter of Pedaiah of Rumah.

37 And he did evil in the sight of the LORD, according to all that his fathers had done.

Judah Overrun by Enemies

24 In ᴿhis days Nebuchadnezzar king of Babylon came up, and Jehoiakim became his vassal *for* three years. Then he turned and rebelled against him.   Dan. 1:1

2 And the LORD sent against him *raiding* ᵀbands of Chaldeans, bands of Syrians, bands of Moabites, and bands of the people of Ammon; He sent them against Judah to destroy it, ᴿaccording to the word of the LORD which He had spoken by His servants the prophets.   *troops* · 2 Kin. 20:17; 21:12–14; 23:27

3 Surely at the commandment of the LORD *this* came upon Judah, to remove *them* from His sight because of the sins of Manasseh, according to all that he had done,

4 ᴿand also because of the innocent blood that he had shed; for he had filled Jerusalem with innocent blood, which the LORD would not pardon.   2 Kin. 21:16

5 Now the rest of the acts of Jehoiakim, and all that he did, *are* they not written in the book of the chronicles of the kings of Judah?

6 So Jehoiakim rested with his fathers. Then Jehoiachin his son reigned in his place.

7 And ᴿthe king of Egypt did not come out of his land anymore, for ᴿthe king of Babylon had taken all that belonged to the king of Egypt from the Brook of Egypt to the River Euphrates.   Jer. 37:57 · Jer. 46:2

The Reign and Captivity of Jehoiachin

8 ᵀJehoiachin *was* eighteen years old when he became king, and he reigned in Jerusalem three months. His mother's name *was* Nehushta the daughter of Elnathan of Jerusalem.   *Jeconiah,* Jer. 24:1; or *Coniah,* Jer. 22:24, 28

9 And he did evil in the sight of the LORD, according to all that his father had done.

10 ᴿAt that time the servants of Nebuchadnezzar king of Babylon came up against Jerusalem, and the city was besieged.   Dan. 1:1

11 And Nebuchadnezzar king of Babylon came against the city, as his servants were besieging it.

12 Then Jehoiachin king of Judah, his mother, his servants, his princes, and his officers went out to the king of Babylon; and the king of Babylon, ᴿin the eighth year of his reign, took him prisoner.   2 Chr. 36:10

The Captivity of Jerusalem

13 And he carried out from there all the treasures of the house of the LORD and the treasures of the king's house, and he cut in pieces all the articles of gold which Solomon king of Israel had made in the temple of the LORD, ᴿas the LORD had said.   Jer. 20:5

14 Also he carried into captivity all Jerusalem: all the captains and all the mighty men of valor, ten thousand captives, and all the craftsmen and smiths. None remained except ᴿthe poorest people of the land.   2 Kin. 25:12

15 And ᴿhe carried Jehoiachin captive to Babylon. The king's mother, the king's wives, his officers, and the mighty of the land he carried into captivity from Jerusalem to Babylon.   Jer. 22:24–28

16 All the valiant men, seven thousand, and craftsmen and smiths, one thousand, all *who were* strong *and* fit for war, these the king of Babylon brought captive to Babylon.

Zedekiah Reigns in Judah

17 Then the king of Babylon made Mattaniah, ᵀ*Jehoiachin's* uncle, king in his place, and changed his name to Zedekiah.   Lit. *his*

18 ᴿZedekiah *was* twenty-one years old when he became king, and he reigned eleven years in Jerusalem. His mother's name *was* ᴿHamutal the daughter of Jeremiah of Libnah.   Jer. 52:1 · 2 Kin. 23:31

19 He also did evil in the sight of the LORD, according to all that Jehoiakim had done.

20 For because of the anger of the LORD *this* happened in Jerusalem and Judah, that He finally cast them out from His presence. ᴿThen Zedekiah rebelled against the king of Babylon.   Ezek. 17:15

The Fall and Captivity of Judah

25 Now it came to pass ᴿin the ninth year of his reign, in the tenth month, on the tenth *day* of the month, *that* Nebuchadnezzar king of Babylon and all his army came against Jerusalem and encamped against it; and they built a siege wall against it all around.   Jer. 6:6; 34:2

2 So the city was besieged until the eleventh year of King Zedekiah.

3 By the ninth *day* of the ᴿ*fourth* month the famine had become so severe in the city that there was no food for the people of the land.   Lam. 4:9, 10

4 Then the city wall was broken through, and all the men of war *fled* at night by way of the gate between two walls, which was by the king's garden, even though the Chaldeans *were* still encamped all around against the city. And ᴿ*the king*ᵀ went by way of the ᵀplain.   Ezek. 12:12 · Lit. *he* · Or *Arabah,* The Jordan Valley

5 But the army of the Chaldeans pursued the king, and they overtook him in the plains of Jericho. All his army was scattered from him.

6 So they took the king and brought him up to the king of Babylon ᴿat Riblah, and they pronounced judgment on him.   Jer. 52:9

7 Then they killed the sons of Zedekiah before his eyes, ᴿputᵀ out the eyes of Zedekiah, bound him with bronze fetters, and took him to Babylon.   Jer. 39:7 · *blinded*

8 And in the fifth month, ᴿon the seventh *day* of the month (which *was* ᴿthe nineteenth year of King Nebuchadnezzar king of Babylon), ᴿNebuzaradan the captain of the

guard, a servant of the king of Babylon, came to Jerusalem.   Jer. 52:12 • 2 Kin. 24:12 • Jer. 39:9

9 [R]He burned the house of the LORD [R]and the king's house; all the houses of Jerusalem, that is, all the houses of the great, [R]he burned with fire.   2 Chr. 36:19 • Jer. 39:8 • Jer. 17:27

10 And all the army of the Chaldeans who *were with* the captain of the guard broke down the walls of Jerusalem all around.

11 Then Nebuzaradan the captain of the guard carried away captive the rest of the people *who* remained in the city and the defectors who had deserted to the king of Babylon, with the rest of the multitude.

12 But the captain of the guard [R]left *some* of the poor of the land as vinedressers and farmers.   Jer. 39:10; 40:7; 52:16

13 The bronze pillars that *were* in the house of the LORD, and the carts and [R]the bronze Sea that *were* in the house of the LORD, the Chaldeans broke in pieces, and carried their bronze to Babylon.   1 Kin. 7:23

14 They also took away [R]the pots, the shovels, the trimmers, the spoons, and all the bronze utensils with which the priests ministered.   Ex. 27:3

15 The firepans and the basins, the things of solid gold and solid silver, the captain of the guard took away.

16 The two pillars, one Sea, and the carts, which Solomon had made for the house of the LORD, [R]the bronze of all these articles was beyond measure.   1 Kin. 7:47

17 The height of one pillar *was* eighteen cubits, and the capital on it *was* of bronze. The height of the capital was three cubits, and the network and pomegranates all around the capital were all of bronze. The second pillar was the same, with a network.

18 And the captain of the guard took Seraiah the chief priest, Zephaniah the second priest, and the three doorkeepers.

19 He also took out of the city an officer who had charge of the men of war, [R]five men of the king's close associates who were found in the city, the chief recruiting officer of the army, who mustered the people of the land, and sixty men of the people of the land *who* were found in the city.   Jer. 52:25

20 So Nebuzaradan, captain of the guard, took these and brought them to the king of Babylon at Riblah.

21 Then the king of Babylon struck them

and put them to death at Riblah in the land of Hamath. [R]Thus Judah was carried away captive from its own land.   Deut. 28:36, 64

Gedaliah Made Governor of Judah

22 Then he made Gedaliah the son of [R]Ahikam, the son of Shaphan, governor over [R]the people who remained in the land of Judah, whom Nebuchadnezzar king of Babylon had left.   2 Kin. 22:12 • Is. 1:9; Jer. 40:5

23 Now when all the [R]captains of the armies, they and *their* men, heard that the king of Babylon had made Gedaliah governor, they came to Gedaliah at Mizpah—Ishmael the son of Nethaniah, Johanan the son of Careah, Seraiah the son of Tanhumeth the Netophathite, and *Jaazaniah the son of a Maachathite, they and their men.   Jer. 40:7-9

24 And Gedaliah took an oath before them and their men, and said to them, "Do not be afraid of the servants of the Chaldeans. Dwell in the land and serve the king of Babylon, and it shall be well with you."

25 But [R]it happened in the seventh month that Ishmael the son of Nethaniah, the son of Elishama, of the royal family, came with ten men and struck and killed Gedaliah, the Jews, as well as the Chaldeans who were with him at Mizpah.   Jer. 41:1-3

26 And all the people, small and great, and the captains of the armies, arose and went to Egypt; for they were afraid of the Chaldeans.

Jehoiachin Released from Prison

27 Now it came to pass in the thirty-seventh year of the captivity of Jehoiachin king of Judah, in the twelfth month, on the twenty-seventh *day* of the month, *that* [T]Evil-Merodach king of Babylon, in the year that he began to reign, released Jehoiachin king of Judah from prison.   Lit. *Man of Marduk*

28 He spoke kindly to him, and gave him a more prominent seat than those of the kings who *were* with him in Babylon.

29 So Jehoiachin changed from his prison garments, and he [R]ate [T]bread regularly before the king all the days of his life.   2 Sam. 9:7 • Food

30 And as for his provisions, *there was* a regular ration given him by the king, a portion for each day, all the days of his life.

25:23 *Jezaniah*, Jer. 40:8

THE FIRST BOOK OF THE
Chronicles

AUTHORSHIP. No author for this book is mentioned in 1 or 2 Chronicles or elsewhere in the Scriptures.

The Jewish rabbis who produced the Talmud believed that Ezra was the author but provided no evidence for the claim. Traditionally, Christian scholars have accepted the Jewish belief. In more recent years, some scholars have rejected Ezra as the author and have preferred to speak of "the Chronicler," or of many unknown editors.

As a priest and skilled scribe who knew the law of Moses thoroughly, Ezra was well qualified to write 1 Chronicles. He had been empowered by King Artaxerxes to go from Persia to Jerusalem with funds to beautify the temple and also to be the religious leader of the Jewish people (ch. 7). While in Jerusalem he led the reading of the law of Moses before the people gathered in the temple courtyard. He also supervised a reform of religious life and practice in the land (Neh. 8).

Since 1 Chronicles (like 1 Samuel and 1 Kings) was originally the first part of one book, it is necessary to go to the end of 2 Chronicles to observe that the concluding verses are like the opening verses of the book of Ezra. Cyrus, the first emperor of the Persian Empire (550–529 B.C.), is mentioned. This ruler took over the Babylonian Empire by force in 539 B.C. Chronicles would not have been written before that date. Many scholars propose 450–425 B.C. as the time Chronicles was written, thus tying this event with Ezra. Others propose a time span of 390–350 B.C. because they believe Ezra is to be dated during that time. Even those who reject Ezra as the author suggest the fourth century B.C. as the time the book was compiled. The earlier date is more likely correct.

HOW 1 CHRONICLES FITS INTO THE BIBLE. As mentioned above, 1 Chronicles is one of a pair, the other being 2 Chronicles. In early manuscripts of the Hebrew Old Testament, both books were on one scroll and called by a Hebrew phrase meaning "accounts of the days." The Greek translation, the Septuagint, has the title *Paralipomena,* meaning "things omitted" or "supplements," for the combined books. Jerome, who produced the Latin translation called the Vulgate, seems to have been the first to suggest the present title, "Chronicles."

Until A.D. 1448 the two books were preserved by Jewish scribes on one scroll. However, copies of the Greek translation had two books of Chronicles by the fourth century A.D. and English translations do the same.

The Hebrew Old Testament places the Chronicles at the very end of the canon. In the Greek and Latin translations they are placed immediately after 2 Kings, and so they are in English Bibles, where they are also followed by Ezra. This is the more natural placement since 1 and 2 Chronicles cover much the same period as 2 Samuel and 1 and 2 Kings. Also, the last two verses of 2 Chronicles are repeated in Ezra 1:1–3, thus linking it with that book.

From chapter 10 on, 1 Chronicles parallels and supplements materials found in 1 Samuel 31, all of 2 Samuel and 1 Kings 1–2:12. 2 Chronicles then continues the historical correlation with 1 and 2 Kings and prepares the reader to see Ezra and Nehemiah as a historical sequel. 1 Chronicles is thus a link in a historical chain.

1 Chronicles, like 2 Chronicles, has a different interest than do the other historical books. This interest centers in the sovereignty of the Lord, who revealed Himself in a special way to the early founders of the kingdom, especially to King David. David was loyal to the Lord, and so should the people be who had returned from exile. David's concern about collecting funds and materials for a temple and organizing the priests and Levites so that temple worship would glorify God is prominent in this book. Nothing of David's private life is provided.

HOW 1 CHRONICLES FITS TOGETHER. The organization of 1 Chronicles is twofold. The first part (chs. 1–9) is genealogical, with one section given to the period from Adam to Jacob (1:1–2:2) and another given to the descendants of Jacob (2:3–9:44) extending well into the fifth century B.C. The second part (chs. 10–29) concentrates on David's reign, and has several subsections: Death of Saul (ch. 10); Jerusalem and David's Heroes (11–12); Glories of David's Reign (13–22:1); Organization for Proper Worship (22:2–26:32); Organization for Proper Government (ch. 27); Solomon Made King (28–29:25); David's Death (29:26-30).

KEY VERSE: 29:11—"Yours, O LORD, is the greatness, the power and the glory, the victory and

the majesty; for all that is in heaven and in earth is Yours; Yours is the kingdom, O LORD, and You are exalted as head over all."

SUMMARY SENTENCE. God is the Lord of all history beginning with Adam; but, because of His covenant with the patriarchs, He is especially the Lord of Jacob's descendents; one of them, King David, became the Lord's servant in forming Israel into a united and worshiping nation.

The writer of 1 Chronicles firmly believed that God was intimately involved in all that happened to His covenant people. He is a mighty God worthy of undivided loyalty, for Israel would be nothing apart from divine mercies. The people who had returned from the exile could look to the past and receive instruction; they could look to the future and hope.

—G.H.L.

The Family of Adam—Seth to Abraham

ADAM, [R]Seth, Enosh,   Gen. 4:25, 26; 5:3–9
2 [T]Cainan, Mahalalel, Jared, Heb. Qenan
3 Enoch, Methuselah, Lamech,
4 *Noah, Shem, Ham, and Japheth.

5 [R]The sons of Japheth were Gomer, Magog, Madai, Javan, Tubal, Meshech, and Tiras.   Gen. 10:2–4
6 The sons of Gomer were Ashkenaz, [T]Diphath, and Togarmah.   Riphath, Gen. 10:3
7 The sons of Javan were Elishah, *Tarshishah, Kittim, and *Rodanim.
8 [R]The sons of Ham were Cush, Mizraim, Put, and Canaan.   Gen. 10:6
9 The sons of Cush were Seba, Havilah, *Sabta, *Raama, and Sabtecha. The sons of Raama were Sheba and Dedan.
10 Cush [R]begot Nimrod; he began to be a mighty one on the earth.   Gen. 10:8–10, 13
11 Mizraim begot Ludim, Anamim, Lehabim, Naphtuhim,
12 Pathrusim, Casluhim (from whom came the Philistines and the [R]Caphtorim. Deut. 2:23
13 [R]Canaan begot Sidon, his firstborn, and Heth;   Gen. 9:18, 25–27; 10:15
14 the Jebusite, the Amorite, and the Girgashite;
15 the Hivite, the Arkite, and the Sinite;
16 the Arvadite, the Zemarite, and the Hamathite.
17 The sons of Shem were Elam, Asshur, [R]Arphaxad, Lud, Aram, Uz, Hul, Gether, and [T]Meshech.   Luke 3:36 • Mash, Gen. 10:23
18 Arphaxad begot Shelah, and Shelah begot Eber.
19 To Eber were born two sons: the name of one was *Peleg, for in his days the earth was divided; and his brother's name was Joktan.
20 [R]Joktan begot Almodad, Sheleph, Hazarmaveth, Jerah,   Gen. 10:26
21 Hadoram, Uzal, Diklah,
22 [T]Ebal, Abimael, Sheba,   Obal, Gen. 10:28
23 Ophir, Havilah, and Jobab. All these were the sons of Joktan.
24 [R]Shem, Arphaxad, Shelah,   Luke 3:34–36

25 [R]Eber, Peleg, Reu,   Gen. 11:15
26 Serug, Nahor, Terah,
27 and [R]Abram, who is Abraham.   Gen. 17:5
28 [R]The sons of Abraham were [R]Isaac and [R]Ishmael.   Gen. 21:2, 3 • Gen. 21:2 • Gen. 16:11, 15

The Family of Ishmael

29 These are their genealogies: The [R]firstborn of Ishmael was Nebajoth; then Kedar, Adbeel, Mibsam,   Gen. 25:13–16
30 Mishma, Dumah, Massa, *Hadad, Tema,
31 Jetur, Naphish, and Kedemah. These were the sons of Ishmael.

The Family of Keturah

32 Now [R]the sons born to Keturah, Abraham's concubine, were Zimran, Jokshan, Medan, Midian, Ishbak, and Shuah. The sons of Jokshan were Sheba and Dedan. Gen. 25:1–4
33 The sons of Midian were Ephah, Epher, Hanoch, Abida, and Eldaah. All these were the children of Keturah.

The Family of Isaac

34 And [R]Abraham begot Isaac. The sons of Isaac were Esau and Israel.   Gen. 21:2
35 The sons of [R]Esau were Eliphaz, Reuel, Jeush, Jaalam, and Korah.   Gen. 36:10–19
36 And the sons of Eliphaz were Teman, Omar, [T]Zephi, Gatam, and Kenaz; and by [R]Timna, Amalek.   Zepho, Gen. 36:11 • Gen. 36:12
37 The sons of Reuel were Nahath, Zerah, Shammah, and Mizzah.

The Family of Seir

38 The sons of Seir were Lotan, Shobal, Zibeon, Anah, Dishon, Ezer, and Dishan.
39 And the sons of Lotan were Hori and Homam; Lotan's sister was Timna.
40 The sons of Shobal were [T]Alian, Manahath, Ebal, *Shephi, and Onam. The sons of Zibeon were Ajah and Anah.   Alvan, Gen. 36:23
41 The son of Anah was [R]Dishon. The sons of Dishon were [T]Hamran, Eshban, Ithran, and Cheran.   Gen. 36:25 • Hemdan, Gen. 36:26
42 The sons of Ezer were Bilhan, Zaavan,

1:4 So with MT, Vg.; LXX adds the sons of Noah.
1:7 Tarshish, Gen. 10:4 • Dodanim, Gen. 10:4
1:9 Sabtah, Gen. 10:7 • Raamah, Gen. 10:7
1:19 Lit. Division, Gen. 10:25

1:30 Hadar, Gen. 25:15
1:40 Shepho, Gen. 36:23

and ᵀJaakan. The sons of Dishan were Uz and Aran.   *Akan, Gen. 36:27*

The Kings of Edom

43 Now these were the kings who reigned in the land of Edom before a king reigned over the children of Israel: Bela the son of Beor, and the name of his city was Dinhabah.

44 And when Bela died, Jobab the son of Zerah of Bozrah reigned in his place.

45 When Jobab died, Husham of the land of the Temanites reigned in his place.

46 And when Husham died, Hadad the son of Bedad, who ᵀattacked Midian in the field of Moab, reigned in his place. The name of his city was Avith.   *Lit. struck*

47 When Hadad died, Samlah of Masrekah reigned in his place.

48 And when Samlah died, Saul of Rehoboth-by-the-River reigned in his place.

49 When Saul died, Baal-Hanan the son of Achbor reigned in his place.

50 And when Baal-Hanan died, ᵀHadad reigned in his place; and the name of his city was ᵀPai. His wife's name was Mehetabel the daughter of Matred, the daughter of Mezahab.   *Hadar, Gen. 36:39 · Pau, Gen. 36:39*

51 Hadad died also. And the chiefs of Edom were Chief Timnah, Chief ᵀAliah, Chief Jetheth,   *Alvah, Gen. 36:40*

52 Chief Aholibamah, Chief Elah, Chief Pinon,

53 Chief Kenaz, Chief Teman, Chief Mibzar,

54 Chief Magdiel, and Chief Iram. These were the chiefs of Edom.

The Family of Israel

2 These were the sons of Israel: Reuben, Simeon, Levi, Judah, Issachar, Zebulun,
2 Dan, Joseph, Benjamin, Naphtali, Gad, and Asher.

From Judah to David

3 The sons of Judah were Er, Onan, and Shelah. These three were born to him by the daughter of Shua, the Canaanitess. ᴿEr, the firstborn of Judah, was wicked in the sight of the LORD; so He killed him.   *Gen. 38:7*

4 And ᴿTamar, his daughter-in-law, ᴿbore him Perez and Zerah. All the sons of Judah were five.   *Gen. 38:6 · Matt. 1:3*

5 The sons of ᴿPerez were Hezron and Hamul.   *Ruth 4:18*

6 The sons of Zerah were ᵀZimri, ᴿEthan, Heman, Calcol, and ᵀDara—five of them in all.   *Zabdi, Josh. 7:1 · 1 Kin. 4:31 · Darda, 1 Kin. 4:31*

7 The son of Carmi was *Achar, the troubler of Israel, who transgressed in the ᵀaccursed thing.   *banned or devoted*

8 The son of Ethan was Azariah.

2:7 Achan, Josh. 7:1

9 Also the sons of Hezron who were born to him were Jerahmeel, Ram, and *Chelubai.

10 Ram ᴿbegot Amminadab, and Amminadab begot Nahshon, ᴿleader of the children of Judah;   *Matt. 1:4 · Num. 1:7; 2:3*

11 Nahshon begot ᵀSalma, and Salma begot Boaz;   *Salmon, Ruth 4:21; Luke 3:32*

12 Boaz begot Obed, and Obed begot Jesse;

13 ᴿJesse begot Eliab his firstborn, Abinadab the second, *Shimea the third,   *1 Sam. 16:6*

14 Nethanel the fourth, Raddai the fifth,

15 Ozem the sixth, and David the seventh.

16 Now their sisters were Zeruiah and Abigail. ᴿAnd the sons of Zeruiah were Abishai, Joab, and Asahel—three.   *2 Sam. 2:18*

17 Abigail bore Amasa; and the father of Amasa was ᴿJether the Ishmaelite.   *2 Sam. 17:25*

The Family of Hezron

18 Caleb the son of Hezron had children by Azubah, his wife, and by Jerioth. Now these were her sons: Jesher, Shobab, and Ardon.

19 When Azubah died, Caleb took *Ephrath as his wife, who bore him Hur.

20 And Hur begot Uri, and Uri begot ᴿBezalel.   *Ex. 31:2; 38:22*

21 Now afterward Hezron went in to the daughter of ᴿMachir the father of Gilead, whom he married when he was sixty years old; and she bore him Segub.   *Num. 27:1*

22 Segub begot ᴿJair, who had twenty-three cities in the land of Gilead.   *Judg. 10:3*

23 ᴿ(Geshur and Syria took from them the towns of Jair, with Kenath and its towns—sixty towns.) All these belonged to the sons of Machir the father of Gilead.   *Deut. 3:14*

24 After Hezron died in Caleb Ephrathah, Hezron's wife Abijah bore him ᴿAshhur the father of Tekoa.   *1 Chr. 4:5*

The Family of Jerahmeel

25 The sons of Jerahmeel, the firstborn of Hezron, were Ram, the firstborn, and Bunah, Oren, Ozem, and Ahijah.

26 Jerahmeel had another wife, whose name was Atarah; she was the mother of Onam.

27 The sons of Ram, the firstborn of Jerahmeel, were Maaz, Jamin, and Eker.

28 The sons of Onam were Shammai and Jada. The sons of Shammai were Nadab and Abishur.

29 And the name of the wife of Abishur was Abihail, and she bore him Ahban and Molid.

30 And the sons of Nadab were Seled and Appaim; Seled died without children.

31 The son of Appaim was Ishi, the son of Ishi was Sheshan, and ᴿSheshan's son was Ahlai.   *1 Chr. 2:34, 35*

2:9 *Caleb*, vv. 18, 42
2:13 *Shammah*, 1 Sam. 16:9
2:19 Or *Ephrathah*

32 The sons of Jada, the brother of Shammai, *were* Jether and Jonathan; Jether died without children.

33 The sons of Jonathan *were* Peleth and Zaza. These were the sons of Jerahmeel.

34 Now Sheshan had no sons, only daughters. And Sheshan had an Egyptian servant whose name *was* Jarha.

35 Sheshan gave his daughter to Jarha his servant as wife, and she bore him Attai.

36 Attai begot Nathan, and Nathan begot ᴿZabad;   1 Chr. 11:41

37 Zabad begot Ephlal, and Ephlal begot ᴿObed;   2 Chr. 23:1

38 Obed begot Jehu, and Jehu begot Azariah;

39 Azariah begot Helez, and Helez begot Eleasah;

40 Eleasah begot Sismai, and Sismai begot Shallum;

41 Shallum begot Jekamiah, and Jekamiah begot Elishama.

The Family of Caleb

42 The descendants of Caleb the brother of Jerahmeel *were* Mesha, his firstborn, who was the father of Ziph, and the sons of Mareshah the father of Hebron.

43 The sons of Hebron *were* Korah, Tappuah, Rekem, and Shema.

44 Shema begot Raham the father of Jorkoam, and Rekem begot Shammai.

45 And the son of Shammai *was* Maon, and Maon *was* the father of Beth Zur.

46 Ephah, Caleb's concubine, bore Haran, Moza, and Gazez; and Haran begot Gazez.

47 And the sons of Jahdai *were* Regem, Jotham, Geshan, Pelet, Ephah, and Shaaph.

48 Maachah, Caleb's concubine, bore Sheber and Tirhanah.

49 She also bore Shaaph the father of Madmannah, Sheva the father of Machbenah and the father of Gibea. And the daughter of Caleb *was* ᴿAchsah.ᵀ   Josh. 15:17 · Or *Achsa*

50 These were the descendants of Caleb: The sons of Hur, the firstborn of Ephrathah, *were* Shobal the father of Kirjath Jearim,

51 Salma the father of Bethlehem, *and* Hareph the father of Beth Gader.

52 And Shobal the father of Kirjath Jearim had descendants: Haroeh, *and* half of the ᵀfamilies of Manuhoth.   Same as *Manahethites*, v. 54

53 The families of Kirjath Jearim *were* the Ithrites, the Puthites, the Shumathites, and the Mishraites. From these came the Zorathites and the Eshtaolites.

54 The sons of Salma *were* Bethlehem, the Netophathites, Atroth Beth Joab, half of the Manahethites, and the Zorites.

55 And the families of the scribes who dwelt at Jabez *were* the Tirathites, the Shimeathites, *and* the Suchathites. These *were* the ᴿKenites who came from Hammath, the father of the house of ᴿRechab.   Judg. 1:16 · Jer. 35:2

The Family of David

3 Now these were the sons of David who were born to him in Hebron: The firstborn *was* Amnon, by Ahinoam the Jezreelitess; the second, ᵀDaniel, by ᴿAbigail the Carmelitess;   *Chileab*, 2 Sam. 3:3 · 1 Sam. 25:39–42

2 the third, Absalom the son of Maacah, the daughter of Talmai, king of Geshur; the fourth, Adonijah the son of Haggith;

3 the fifth, Shephatiah, by Abital; the sixth, Ithream, by his wife ᴿEglah.   2 Sam. 3:5

4 *These* six were born to him in Hebron. ᴿThere he reigned seven years and six months, and ᴿin Jerusalem he reigned thirty-three years.   2 Sam. 2:11 · 2 Sam. 5:5

5 And these were born to him in Jerusalem: *Shimea, Shobab, Nathan, and Solomon—four by ᵀBathshua the daughter of ᵀAmmiel.   *Bathsheba*, 2 Sam. 11:3 · *Eliam*, 2 Sam. 11:3

6 Also *there* were Ibhar, ᵀElishama, ᵀEliphelet,   *Elishua*, 1 Chr. 14:5; 2 Sam. 5:15 · *Elpelet*, 1 Chr. 14:5

7 Nogah, Nepheg, Japhia,

8 Elishama, ᵀEliada, and Eliphelet—ᴿnine in *all*.   *Beeliada*, 1 Chr. 14:7 · 2 Sam. 5:14–16

9 *These were* all the sons of David, besides the sons of the concubines, and ᴿTamar their sister.   2 Sam. 13:1

The Family of Solomon

10 Solomon's son *was* ᴿRehoboam; ᵀAbijah *was* his son, Asa his son, Jehoshaphat his son,   1 Kin. 11:43 · *Abijam*, 1 Kin. 15:1

11 ᵀJoram his son, Ahaziah his son, ᵀJoash his son,   *Jehoram*, 2 Kin. 1:17; 8:16 · *Jehoash*, 2 Kin. 12:1

12 Amaziah his son, ᵀAzariah his son, Jotham his son,   *Uzziah*, Is. 6:1

13 Ahaz his son, Hezekiah his son, Manasseh his son,

14 Amon his son, *and* Josiah his son.

15 The sons of Josiah *were* Johanan the firstborn, the second Jehoiakim, the third Zedekiah, and the fourth *Shallum.

16 The sons of Jehoiakim *were* Jeconiah his son *and* ᵀZedekiah his son.   *Mattaniah*, 2 Kin. 24:17

The Family of Jeconiah

17 And the sons of *Jeconiah ᵀwere* Assir, Shealtiel his son,   Or *the captive were*

18 *and* Malchiram, Pedaiah, Shenazzar, Jecamiah, Hoshama, and Nedabiah.

19 The sons of Pedaiah *were* Zerubbabel and Shimei. The sons of Zerubbabel *were* Meshullam, Hananiah, Shelomith their sister,

20 and Hashubah, Ohel, Berechiah, Hasadiah, and Jushab-Hesed—five in *all*.

3:5 *Shammua*, 1 Chr. 14:4; 2 Sam. 5:14
3:15 *Jehoahaz*, 2 Kin. 23:31
3:17 *Jehoiachin*, 2 Kin. 24:8, or *Coniah*, Jer. 22:24

21 The sons of Hananiah *were* Pelatiah and Jeshaiah, the sons of Rephaiah, the sons of Arnan, the sons of Obadiah, and the sons of Shechaniah.

22 The son of Shechaniah was Shemaiah. The sons of Shemaiah *were* Hattush, Igal, Bariah, Neariah, and Shaphat—six *in all.*

23 The sons of Neariah *were* Elioenai, Hezekiah, and Azrikam—three *in all.*

24 The sons of Elioenai *were* Hodaviah, Eliashib, Pelaiah, Akkub, Johanan, Delaiah, and Anani—seven *in all.*

The Family of Judah

4 The sons of Judah *were* ᴿPerez, Hezron, Carmi, Hur, and Shobal.   Gen. 38:29; 46:12

2 And Reaiah the son of Shobal begot Jahath, and Jahath begot Ahumai and Lahad. These *were* the families of the Zorathites.

3 These *were* the sons *of the father* of Etam: Jezreel, Ishma, and Idbash; and the name of their sister *was* Hazelelponi;

4 and Penuel *was* the father of Gedor, and Ezer *was* the father of Hushah. These *were* the sons of ᴿHur, the firstborn of Ephrathah the father of Bethlehem.   1 Chr. 2:50

5 And ᴿAshhur the father of Tekoa had two wives, Helah and Naarah.   1 Chr. 2:24

6 Naarah bore him Ahuzzam, Hepher, Temeni, and Haahashtari. These *were* the sons of Naarah.

7 The sons of Helah *were* Zereth, Zohar, and Ethnan;

8 and Koz begot Anub, Zobebah, and the families of Aharhel the son of Harum.

9 Now Jabez was more honorable than his brothers, and his mother called his name *Jabez, saying, "Because I bore *him* in pain."

10 And Jabez called on the God of Israel saying, "Oh, that You would bless me indeed, and enlarge my ᵀterritory, that Your hand would be with me, and that You would keep *me* from evil, that I may not cause pain!" So God granted him what he requested.   *border*

11 Chelub the brother of Shuhah begot Mehir, who *was* the father of Eshton.

12 And Eshton begot Beth-Rapha, Paseah, and Tehinnah the father of ᵀIr-Nahash. These *were* the men of Rechah.   Lit. *City of Nahash*

13 The sons of Kenaz *were* Othniel and Seraiah. The sons of Othniel *were* *Hathath,

14 and Meonothai *who* begot Ophrah. Seraiah begot Joab the father of ᵀGe Harashim, for they were craftsmen.   Lit. *Valley of Craftsmen*

15 The sons of ᴿCaleb the son of Jephunneh *were* Iru, Elah, and Naam. The son of Elah *was* ᵀKenaz.   1 Chr. 6:56 • Or *Uknaz*

16 The sons of Jehallelel *were* Ziph, Ziphah, Tiria, and Asarel.

17 The sons of Ezrah *were* Jether, Mered, Epher, and Jalon. And ᵀMered's *wife* bore Miriam, Shammai, and Ishbah the father of Eshtemoa.   Lit. *she*

18 (ᵀHis wife Jehudijah bore Jered the father of Gedor, Heber the father of Sochoh, and Jekuthiel the father of Zanoah.) And these were the sons of Bithiah the daughter of Pharaoh, whom Mered took.   Or *His Judean wife*

19 The sons of Hodiah's wife, the sister of Naham, *were* the fathers of Keilah the Garmite and of Eshtemoa the Maachathite.

20 And the sons of Shimon *were* Amnon, Rinnah, Ben-Hanan, and Tilon. And the sons of Ishi *were* Zoheth and Ben-Zoheth.

21 The sons of ᴿShelah ᴿthe son of Judah *were* Er the father of Lecah, Laadah the father of Mareshah, and the families of the house of the linen workers of the house of Ashbea;   Gen. 38:11, 14 • Gen. 38:1-5; 46:12

22 also Jokim, the men of Chozeba, and Joash; Saraph, who ruled in Moab, and Jashubi-Lehem. Now the records are ancient.

23 These *were* the potters and those who dwell at ᵀNetaim and *Gederah; there they dwelt with the king for his work.   Lit. *Plants*

The Family of Simeon

24 The ᴿsons of Simeon *were* Nemuel, Jamin, *Jarib, *Zerah, *and* Shaul,   Num. 26:12-14

25 Shallum his son, Mibsam his son, and Mishma his son.

26 And the sons of Mishma *were* Hamuel his son, Zacchur his son, and Shimei his son.

27 Shimei had sixteen sons and six daughters; but his brothers did not have many children, ᴿnor did any of their families multiply as much as the children of Judah.   Num. 2:9

28 They dwelt at Beersheba, Moladah, Hazar Shual,

29 ᵀBilhah, Ezem, Tolad,   *Balah,* Josh. 19:3

30 Bethuel, Hormah, Ziklag,

31 Beth Marcaboth, ᵀHazar Susim, Beth Biri, and at Shaaraim. These *were* their cities until the reign of David.   *Hazar Susah,* Josh. 19:5

32 And their villages *were* Etam, Ain, Rimmon, Tochen, and Ashan—five cities—

33 and all the villages that *were* around these cities as far as ᵀBaal. These *were* their dwelling places, and they maintained their genealogy: Or *Baalath Beer,* Josh. 19:8

34 Meshobab, Jamlech, and Joshah the son of Amaziah;

35 Joel, and Jehu the son of Joshibiah, the son of Seraiah, the son of Asiel;

36 Elioenai, Jaakobah, Jeshohaiah, Asaiah, Adiel, Jesimiel, and Benaiah;

4:9 Lit. *He Will Cause Pain*
4:13 LXX, Vg. add *and Meonothai.*

4:23 Lit. *Hedges*
4:24 *Jachin,* Gen. 46:10; Num. 26:12 • *Zohar,* Gen. 46:10; Ex. 6:15

37 Ziza the son of Shiphi, the son of Allon, the son of Jedaiah, the son of Shimri, the son of Shemaiah—

38 these mentioned by name were leaders in their families, and their father's house increased greatly.

39 So they went to the entrance of Gedor, as far as the east side of the valley, to seek pasture for their flocks.

40 And they found rich, good pasture, and the land was broad, quiet, and peaceful; for some Hamites formerly lived there.

41 These recorded by name came in the days of Hezekiah king of Judah; and they ᵀattacked their tents and the Meunites who were found there, and ᴿutterly destroyed them, as it is to this day. So they dwelt in their place, because there was pasture for their flocks there.   Lit. *struck* • 2 Kin. 19:11

42 Now some of them, five hundred men of the sons of Simeon, went to Mount Seir, having as their captains Pelatiah, Neariah, Rephaiah, and Uzziel, the sons of Ishi.

43 And they ᵀdefeated ᴿthe rest of the Amalekites who had escaped. They have dwelt there to this day.   Lit. *struck* • 1 Sam. 15:8; 30:17

The Family of Reuben

5 Now the sons of Reuben the firstborn of Israel—he was indeed the firstborn, but because he ᴿdefiled his father's bed, his birthright was given to the sons of Joseph, the son of Israel, so that the genealogy is not listed according to the birthright;   Gen. 35:22

2 yet Judah prevailed over his brothers, and from him came a ruler, although ᵀthe birthright was Joseph's—   the right of the firstborn

3 the sons of ᴿReuben the firstborn of Israel were Hanoch, Pallu, Hezron, and Carmi.   Ex. 6:14

4 The sons of Joel were Shemaiah his son, Gog his son, Shimei his son,

5 Micah his son, Reaiah his son, Baal his son,

6 and Beerah his son, whom *Tiglath-Pileser king of Assyria ᴿcarried into captivity. He was leader of the Reubenites.   2 Kin. 18:11

7 And his brethren by their families, ᴿwhen the genealogy of their generations was registered: the chief, Jeiel, and Zechariah,   1 Chr. 5:17

8 and Bela the son of Azaz, the son of Shema, the son of Joel, who dwelt in ᴿAroer, as far as Nebo and Baal Meon.   Josh. 12:2

9 Eastward they settled as far as the ᵀentrance of the wilderness this side of the River Euphrates, because their cattle had ᵀmultiplied in the land of Gilead.   beginning • increased

10 Now in the days of Saul they made war ᴿwith the Hagrites, who fell by their hand;

5:6 Heb. *Tilgath-Pilneser*

and they dwelt in their tents throughout the entire area east of Gilead.   Gen. 25:12

The Family of Gad

11 And the children of Gad dwelt next to them in the land of Bashan as far as Salcah:

12 Joel was the chief, Shapham the next, then Jaanai and Shaphat in Bashan,

13 and their brethren of their father's house: Michael, Meshullam, Sheba, Jorai, Jachan, Zia, and Heber—seven in all.

14 These were the children of Abihail the son of Huri, the son of Jaroah, the son of Gilead, the son of Michael, the son of Jeshishai, the son of Jahdo, the son of Buz;

15 Ahi the son of Abdiel, the son of Guni, was chief of their father's house.

16 And the Gadites dwelt in Gilead, in Bashan and in its villages, and in all the ᵀcommon-lands of ᴿSharon within their borders.   open lands • 1 Chr. 27:29

17 All these were registered by genealogies in the days of Jotham king of Judah, and in the days of Jeroboam king of Israel.

18 The sons of Reuben, the Gadites, and half the tribe of Manasseh had forty-four thousand seven hundred and sixty valiant men, men able to bear shield and sword, to shoot with the bow, and skillful in war, who went to war.

19 They made war with the Hagrites, ᴿJetur, Naphish, and Nodab.   Gen. 25:15

20 And they were helped against them, and the Hagrites were delivered into their hand, and all who were with them, for they cried out to God in the battle. He heeded their prayer, because they put their trust in Him.

21 Then they took away their livestock—fifty thousand of their camels, two hundred and fifty thousand of their sheep, and two thousand of their donkeys—also one hundred thousand of their men;

22 for many fell dead, because the war ᴿwas God's. And they dwelt in their place until ᴿthe captivity.   [Josh. 23:10] • 2 Kin. 15:29; 17:6

The Family of Manasseh (East)

23 So the children of the half-tribe of Manasseh dwelt in the land. Their numbers increased from Bashan to Baal Hermon, that is, to ᴿSenir, or Mount Hermon.   Deut. 3:9

24 These were the heads of their fathers' houses: Epher, Ishi, Eliel, Azriel, Jeremiah, Hodaviah, and Jahdiel. They were mighty men of valor, famous men, and heads of their fathers' houses.

25 And they were unfaithful to the God of their fathers, and ᴿplayed the harlot after the gods of the peoples of the land, whom God had destroyed before them.   2 Kin. 17:7

26 So the God of Israel stirred up the spirit

of Pul king of Assyria, that is, *Tiglath-Pileser king of Assyria. He carried the Reubenites, the Gadites, and the half-tribe of Manasseh into captivity. He took them to Halah, Habor, Hara, and the river of Gozan to this day.

The Family of Levi

6 The sons of Levi were ᴿGershon,ᵀ Kohath, and Merari.   Ex. 6:16 · Or *Gershom*, v. 16
2 The sons of Kohath were Amram, ᴿIzhar, Hebron, and Uzziel.   1 Chr. 6:18, 22
3 The children of Amram were Aaron, Moses, and Miriam. And the sons of Aaron were Nadab, Abihu, Eleazar, and Ithamar.
4 Eleazar begot Phinehas, and Phinehas begot Abishua;
5 Abishua begot Bukki, and Bukki begot Uzzi;
6 Uzzi begot Zerahiah, and Zerahiah begot Meraioth;
7 Meraioth begot Amariah, and Amariah begot Ahitub;
8 ᴿAhitub begot ᴿZadok, and Zadok begot Ahimaaz;   2 Sam. 8:17 · 2 Sam. 15:27
9 Ahimaaz begot Azariah, and Azariah begot Johanan;
10 Johanan begot Azariah (it was he who ministered as priest in the ᵀtemple that Solomon built in Jerusalem);   Lit. *house*
11 ᴿAzariah begot ᴿAmariah, and Amariah begot Ahitub;   Ezra 7:3 · 2 Chr. 19:11
12 Ahitub begot Zadok, and Zadok begot ᵀShallum;   *Meshullam*, 1 Chr. 9:11
13 Shallum begot Hilkiah, and Hilkiah begot Azariah;
14 Azariah begot ᴿSeraiah, and Seraiah begot Jehozadak.   Neh. 11:11
15 Jehozadak went *into captivity* when the LORD carried Judah and Jerusalem into captivity by the hand of Nebuchadnezzar.
16 The sons of Levi were ᴿGershon,* Kohath, and Merari.   Ex. 6:16
17 These are the names of the sons of Gershon: Libni and Shimei.
18 The sons of Kohath were Amram, Izhar, Hebron, and Uzziel.
19 The sons of Merari were Mahli and Mushi. Now these are the families of the Levites according to their fathers:
20 Of Gershon were Libni his son, Jahath his son, ᴿZimmah his son,   1 Chr. 6:42
21 Joah his son, Iddo his son, Zerah his son, and Jeatherai his son.
22 The sons of Kohath were Amminadab his son, Korah his son, Assir his son,
23 Elkanah his son, Ebiasaph his son, Assir his son,
24 Tahath his son, Uriel his son, Uzziah his son, and Shaul his son.

25 The sons of Elkanah were ᴿAmasai and Ahimoth.   1 Chr. 6:35, 36
26 *As for* Elkanah, the sons of Elkanah were *Zophai his son, *Nahath his son,
27 ᵀEliab his son, Jeroham his son, *and* Elkanah his son.   *Eliel*, v. 34
28 The sons of Samuel *were* *Joel the firstborn, and Abijah ᵀthe second.   Heb. *Vasheni*
29 The sons of Merari were Mahli, Libni his son, Shimei his son, Uzzah his son,
30 Shimea his son, Haggiah his son, *and* Asaiah his son.

Musicians in the House of the LORD

31 Now these are ᴿthe men whom David appointed over the service of song in the house of the LORD, after the ᴿark came to rest.   1 Chr. 15:16–22, 27; 16:4–6 · 1 Chr. 15:25—16:1
32 They were ministering with music before the dwelling place of the tabernacle of meeting, until Solomon had built the house of the LORD in Jerusalem, and they served in their office according to their order.
33 And these *are* the ones who ᵀministered with their sons: Of the sons of the ᴿKohathites *were* Heman the singer, the son of Joel, the son of Samuel,   Lit. *stood with* · Num. 26:57
34 the son of Elkanah, the son of Jeroham, the son of *Eliel, the son of *Toah,
35 the son of Zuph, the son of Elkanah, the son of Mahath, the son of Amasai,
36 the son of Elkanah, the son of Joel, the son of Azariah, the son of Zephaniah,
37 the son of Tahath, the son of Assir, the son of ᴿEbiasaph, the son of Korah,   Ex. 6:24
38 the son of Izhar, the son of Kohath, the son of Levi, the son of Israel.
39 And his brother ᴿAsaph, who stood at his right hand, *was* Asaph the son of Berachiah, the son of Shimea,   2 Chr. 5:12
40 the son of Michael, the son of Baaseiah, the son of Malchijah,
41 the son of ᴿEthni, the son of Zerah, the son of Adaiah,   1 Chr. 6:21
42 the son of Ethan, the son of Zimmah, the son of Shimei,
43 the son of Jahath, the son of Gershon, the son of Levi.
44 Their brethren, the sons of Merari, on the left hand, *were* Ethan the son of Kishi, the son of Abdi, the son of Malluch,
45 the son of Hashabiah, the son of Amaziah, the son of Hilkiah,
46 the son of Amzi, the son of Bani, the son of Shamer,
47 the son of Mahli, the son of Mushi, the son of Merari, the son of Levi.
48 And their brethren, the Levites, *were* appointed to every ᴿkind of service of the tabernacle of the house of God.   1 Chr. 9:14–34

5:26 Heb. *Tilgath-Pilneser*
6:16 Heb. *Gershom*, an alternate spelling for *Gershon*, vv. 17, 20, 43, 62, 71

6:26 *Zuph*, v. 35; 1 Sam. 1:1 • *Toah*, v. 34
6:28 So with LXX, Syr., Arab.; cf. v. 33 and 1 Sam. 8:2
6:34 *Elihu*, 1 Sam. 1:1 • *Tohu*, 1 Sam. 1:1

The Family of Aaron

49 ᴿBut Aaron and his sons offered sacrifices on the altar of burnt offering and on the altar of incense, for all the work of the Most Holy *Place,* and to make atonement for Israel, according to all that Moses the servant of God had commanded. [Num. 18:1-8]
50 Now these *are* the ᴿsons of Aaron: Eleazar his son, Phinehas his son, Abishua his son, 1 Chr. 6:4-8
51 Bukki his son, Uzzi his son, Zerahiah his son,
52 Meraioth his son, Amariah his son, Ahitub his son,
53 Zadok his son, *and* Ahimaaz his son.

Dwelling Places of the Levites

54 Now these *are* their dwelling places throughout their settlements in their territory, for they were *given* by lot to the sons of Aaron, of the family of the Kohathites:
55 They gave them Hebron in the land of Judah, with its surrounding common-lands.
56 But the fields of the city and its villages they gave to Caleb the son of Jephunneh.
57 And ᴿto the sons of Aaron they gave *one of* the cities of refuge, Hebron; also Libnah with its common-lands, Jattir, Eshtemoa with its common-lands, Josh. 21:13, 19
58 ᵀHilen with its common-lands, Debir with its common-lands, Holon, Josh. 21:15
59 ᵀAshan with its common-lands, and Beth Shemesh with its common-lands. Ain, Josh. 21:16
60 And from the tribe of Benjamin: Geba with its common-lands, ᵀAlemeth with its common-lands, and Anathoth with its common-lands. All their cities among their families *were* thirteen. Almon, Josh. 21:18
61 To the rest of the family of the tribe of the Kohathites *they gave* ᴿby lot ten cities from half the tribe of Manasseh. Josh. 21:5
62 And to the sons of Gershon, throughout their families, *they gave* thirteen cities from the tribe of Issachar, from the tribe of Asher, from the tribe of Naphtali, and from the tribe of Manasseh in Bashan.
63 To the sons of Merari, throughout their families, *they gave* ᴿtwelve cities from the tribe of Reuben, from the tribe of Gad, and from the tribe of Zebulun. Josh. 21:7, 34-40
64 So the children of Israel gave *these* cities with their common-lands to the Levites.
65 And they gave by lot from the tribe of the children of Judah, from the tribe of the children of Simeon, and from the tribe of the children of Benjamin these cities which are called by *their* names.
66 Now ᴿsome of the families of the sons of Kohath *were given* cities as their territory from the tribe of Ephraim. 1 Chr. 6:61
67 ᴿAnd they gave them *one of* the cities of refuge, Shechem with its common-lands, in

the mountains of Ephraim, also Gezer with its common-lands, Josh. 21:21
68 ᴿJokmeam with its common-lands, Beth Horon with its common-lands, Josh. 21:22
69 Aijalon with its common-lands, and Gath Rimmon with its common-lands.
70 And from the half-tribe of Manasseh: Aner with its common-lands and Bileam with its common-lands, for the rest of the family of the sons of Kohath.
71 From the family of the half-tribe of Manasseh the sons of Gershon *were given* Golan in Bashan with its common-lands and ᴿAshtaroth with its common-lands. Josh. 21:27
72 And from the tribe of Issachar: ᵀKedesh with its common-lands, Daberath with its common-lands, Kishon, Josh. 21:28
73 Ramoth with its common-lands, and Anem with its common-lands.
74 And from the tribe of Asher: Mashal with its common-lands, Abdon with its common-lands,
75 Hukok with its common-lands, and Rehob with its common-lands.
76 And from the tribe of Naphtali: Kedesh in Galilee with its common-lands, Hammon with its common-lands, and Kirjathaim with its common-lands.
77 From the tribe of Zebulun the rest of the children of Merari *were given* *Rimmon with its common-lands and Tabor with its common-lands.
78 And on the other side of the Jordan, across from Jericho, on the east side of the Jordan, *they were given* from the tribe of Reuben: Bezer in the wilderness with its common-lands, Jahzah with its common-lands,
79 Kedemoth with its common-lands, and Mephaath with its common-lands.
80 And from the tribe of Gad: Ramoth in Gilead with its common-lands, Mahanaim with its common-lands,
81 Heshbon with its common-lands, and Jazer with its common-lands.

The Family of Issachar

7 The sons of Issachar *were* Tola, *Puah, Jashub, and Shimron—four *in all.*
2 The sons of Tola *were* Uzzi, Rephaiah, Jeriel, Jahmai, Jibsam, and Shemuel, heads of their father's house. *The sons* of Tola *were* mighty men of valor in their generations; their number *was* in the days of David *was* twenty-two thousand six hundred.
3 The son of Uzzi *was* Izrahiah, and the sons of Izrahiah *were* Michael, Obadiah, Joel, and Ishiah. All five of them *were* chief men.

6:77 Heb. *Rimmono,* an alternate spelling of Rimmon, 1 Chr. 4:32
7:1 *Puvah,* Gen. 46:13

4 And with them, by their generations, according to their fathers' houses, were thirty-six thousand troops ready for war; for they had many wives and sons.

5 Now their brethren among all the families of Issachar were mighty men of valor, listed by their genealogies, eighty-seven thousand in all.

The Family of Benjamin

6 The sons of ᴿBenjamin were Bela, Becher, and Jediael—three in all.   Gen. 46:21

7 The sons of Bela were Ezbon, Uzzi, Uzziel, Jerimoth, and Iri—five in all. They were heads of their fathers' houses, and they were listed by their genealogies, twenty-two thousand and thirty-four mighty men of valor.

8 The sons of Becher were Zemirah, Joash, Eliezer, Elioenai, Omri, Jerimoth, Abijah, Anathoth, and Alemeth. All these are the sons of Becher.

9 And they were recorded by genealogy according to their generations, heads of their fathers' houses, twenty thousand two hundred mighty men of valor.

10 The son of Jediael was Bilhan, and the sons of Bilhan were Jeush, Benjamin, Ehud, Chenaanah, Zethan, Tharshish, and Ahishahar.

11 All these sons of Jediael were heads of their fathers' houses; there were seventeen thousand two hundred mighty men of valor fit to go out for war and battle.

12 Shuppim and *Huppim were the sons of Ir, and Hushim was the son of Aher.

The Family of Naphtali

13 The sons of Naphtali were *Jahziel, Guni, Jezer, and *Shallum, the sons of Bilhah.

The Family of Manasseh (West)

14 The ᴿdescendants of Manasseh: his Syrian concubine bore him Machir the father of Gilead, the father of *Asriel.   Num. 26:29-34

15 Machir took as his wife the sister of ᴿHuppim and Shuppim, whose name was Maachah. The name of Gilead's ᵀgrandson was ᴿZelophehad, but Zelophehad begot only daughters.   1 Chr. 7:12 • Lit. the second • Num. 26:30-33

16 (Maachah the wife of Machir bore a son, and she called his name Peresh. The name of his brother was Sheresh, and his sons were Ulam and Rakem.

17 The son of Ulam was ᴿBedan.) These were the descendants of Gilead the son of Machir, the son of Manasseh.   1 Sam. 12:11

18 His sister Hammoleketh bore Ishhod, ᵀAbiezer, and Mahlah.   Jeezer, Num. 26:30

19 And the sons of Shemida were Ahian, Shechem, Likhi, and Aniam.

The Family of Ephraim

20 ᴿThe sons of Ephraim were Shuthelah, Bered his son, Tahath his son, Eladah his son, Tahath his son,   Num. 26:35-37

21 Zabad his son, Shuthelah his son, and Ezer and Elead. The men of Gath who were born in that land killed them because they came down to take away their cattle.

22 Then Ephraim their father mourned many days, and his brethren came to comfort him.

23 And when he went in to his wife, she conceived and bore a son; and he called his name ᵀBeriah, because tragedy had come upon his house.   Lit. In Tragedy

24 Now his daughter was Sheerah, who built Lower and Upper ᴿBeth Horon and Uzzen Sheerah;   Josh. 16:3, 5

25 and Rephah was his son, as well as Resheph, and Telah his son, Tahan his son,

26 Laadan his son, Ammihud his son, ᴿElishama his son,   Num. 10:22

27 *Nun his son, and Joshua his son.

28 Now their ᴿpossessions and dwelling places were Bethel and its towns: to the east ᵀNaaran, to the west Gezer and its towns, and Shechem and its towns, as far as *Ayyah and its towns;   Josh. 16:1-10 • Naarath, Josh. 16:7

29 and by the borders of the children of Manasseh were Beth Shean and its towns, Taanach and its towns, Megiddo and its towns, Dor and its towns. In these dwelt the children of Joseph, the son of Israel.

The Family of Asher

30 The sons of Asher were Imnah, Ishvah, Ishvi, Beriah, and their sister Serah.

31 The sons of Beriah were Heber and Malchiel, who was the father of *Birzaith.

32 And Heber begot Japhlet, ᵀShomer, *Hotham, and their sister Shua.   Shemer, v. 34

33 The sons of Japhlet were Pasach, Bimhal, and Ashvath. These were the children of Japhlet.

34 The sons of ᴿShemer were Ahi, Rohgah, Jehubbah, and Aram.   1 Chr. 7:32

35 And the sons of his brother Helem were Zophah, Imna, Shelesh, and Amal.

36 The sons of Zophah were Suah, Harnepher, Shual, Beri, Imrah,

37 Bezer, Hod, Shamma, Shilshah, ᵀJithran, and Beera.   Jether, v. 38

38 The sons of Jether were Jephunneh, Pispah, and Ara.

39 The sons of Ulla were Arah, Haniel, and Rizia.

7:27 Heb. Non
7:28 Or Azzah or Gazza
7:31 Or Birzavith or Birzoth
7:32 Helem, 1 Chr. 7:35

7:12 Hupham, Num. 26:39
7:13 Jahzeel, Gen. 46:24 • Shillem, Gen. 46:24
7:14 The son of Gilead (compare Num. 26:30, 31)

40 All these *were* the children of Asher, heads of *their* fathers' houses, choice men, mighty men of valor, chief leaders. And they were recorded by genealogies among the army fit for battle; their number *was* twenty-six thousand.

The Family Tree of King Saul of Benjamin

8 Now Benjamin begot Bela his firstborn, Ashbel the second, *Aharah the third,

2 Nohah the fourth, and Rapha the fifth.

3 The sons of Bela were ᵀAddar, Gera, Abihud,   *Ard*, Num. 26:40

4 Abishua, Naaman, Ahoah,

5 Gera, Shephuphan, and Huram.

6 These *are* the sons of Ehud, who were the heads of the fathers' *houses* of the inhabitants of ᴿGeba, and who forced them to move to ᴿManahath: 1 Chr. 6:60 · 1 Chr. 2:52

7 Naaman, Ahijah, and Gera who forced them to move. He begot Uzza and Ahihud.

8 Also Shaharaim had children in the country of Moab, after he had sent away Hushim and Baara his wives.

9 By Hodesh his wife he begot Jobab, Zibia, Mesha, Malcam,

10 Jeuz, Sachiah, and Mirmah. These *were* his sons, heads of their fathers' *houses*.

11 And by Hushim he begot Abitub and Elpaal.

12 The sons of Elpaal were Eber, Misham, and Shemed, who built Ono and Lod with its towns;

13 and Beriah and ᴿShema, who *were* heads of their fathers' *houses* of the inhabitants of Aijalon, who drove out the inhabitants of Gath.   1 Chr. 8:21

14 Ahio, Shashak, Jeremoth,

15 Zebadiah, Arad, Eder,

16 Michael, Ispah, and Joha *were* the sons of Beriah.

17 Zebadiah, Meshullam, Hizki, Heber,

18 Ishmerai, Jizliah, and Jobab *were* the sons of Elpaal.

19 Jakim, Zichri, Zabdi,

20 Elienai, Zillethai, Eliel,

21 Adaiah, Beraiah, and Shimrath *were* the sons of ᵀShimei.   *Shema*, 1 Chr. 7:13

22 Ishpan, Eber, Eliel,

23 Abdon, Zichri, Hanan,

24 Hananiah, Elam, Antothijah,

25 Iphdeiah, and Penuel *were* the sons of Shashak.

26 Shamsherai, Shehariah, Athaliah,

27 Jaareshiah, Elijah, and Zichri *were* the sons of Jeroham.

28 These *were* heads of the fathers' *houses* by their generations, chief men. These dwelt in Jerusalem.

29 Now the father of Gibeon, whose wife's name *was* Maacah, dwelt at Gibeon.

8:1 *Ahiram*, Num. 26:38

30 And his firstborn son *was* Abdon, then Zur, Kish, Baal, Nadab,

31 Gedor, Ahio, ᵀZecher,   *Zechariah*, 1 Chr. 9:37

32 and Mikloth, *who* begot *Shimeah. They also dwelt ᵀalongside their ᵀrelatives in Jerusalem, with their brethren. *Lit. opposite · brethren*

33 ᴿNer* begot Kish, Kish begot Saul, and Saul begot Jonathan, Malchishua, ᵀAbinadab, and *Esh-Baal.   1 Sam. 14:51 · *Jishui*, 1 Sam. 14:49

34 The son of Jonathan *was* *Merib-Baal, and Merib-Baal begot ᴿMicah.   2 Sam. 9:12

35 The sons of Micah *were* Pithon, Melech, ᵀTarea, and Ahaz.   *Tahrea*, 1 Chr. 9:41

36 And Ahaz begot ᵀJehoaddah; Jehoaddah begot Alemeth, Azmaveth, and Zimri; and Zimri begot Moza.   *Jarah*, 1 Chr. 9:42

37 Moza begot Binea, *Raphah his son, Eleasah his son, *and* Azel his son.

38 Azel had six sons whose names *were* these: Azrikam, Bocheru, Ishmael, Sheariah, Obadiah, and Hanan. All these *were* the sons of Azel.

39 And the sons of Eshek his brother *were* Ulam his firstborn, Jeush the second, and Eliphelet the third.

40 The sons of Ulam *were* mighty men of valor—archers. *They* had many sons and grandsons, one hundred and fifty *in all*. These *were* all sons of Benjamin.

9 So ᴿall Israel *was* ᵀrecorded by genealogies, and indeed, they *were* inscribed in the book of the kings of Israel. But Judah was carried away captive to Babylon because of their unfaithfulness.   Ezra 2:59 · *enrolled*

2 And the first inhabitants who *dwelt* in their possessions in their cities *were* Israelites, priests, Levites, and the Nethinim.

Dwellers in Jerusalem

3 Now in ᴿJerusalem the children of Judah dwelt, and some of the children of Benjamin, and of the children of Ephraim and Manasseh: Neh. 11:1, 2

4 Uthai the son of Ammihud, the son of Omri, the son of Imri, the son of Bani, of the descendants of Perez, the son of Judah.

5 Of the Shilonites: Asaiah the firstborn and his sons.

6 Of the sons of Zerah: Jeuel, and their brethren—six hundred and ninety.

7 Of the sons of Benjamin: Sallu the son of Meshullam, the son of Hodaviah, the son of Hassenuah;

8 Ibneiah the son of Jeroham; Elah the son

8:32 Or *Shimeam*, 1 Chr. 9:38

8:33 Also the son of Gibeon, 1 Chr. 9:36, 39 •

Ishbosheth, 2 Sam. 2:8

8:34 *Mephibosheth*, 2 Sam. 4:4

8:37 *Raphaiah*, 1 Chr. 9:43

of Uzzi, the son of Michri; Meshullam the son of Shephatiah, the son of Reuel, the son of Ibnijah;

9 and their brethren, according to their generations—nine hundred and fifty-six. All these men *were* heads of a father's *house* in their fathers' houses.

The Priests at Jerusalem

10 ᴿOf the priests: Jedaiah, Jehoiarib, and Jachin;   Neh. 11:10-14

11 ᵀAzariah the son of Hilkiah, the son of Meshullam, the son of Zadok, the son of Meraioth, the son of Ahitub, the ᴿofficer over the house of God;   Seraiah, Neh. 11:11 · Jer. 20:1

12 Adaiah the son of Jeroham, the son of Pashur, the son of Malchijah; Maasai the son of Adiel, the son of Jahzerah, the son of Meshullam, the son of Meshillemith, the son of Immer;

13 and their brethren, heads of their fathers' *houses*—one thousand seven hundred and sixty. They *were* very able men for the work of the service of the house of God.

The Levites at Jerusalem

14 Of the Levites: Shemaiah the son of Hasshub, the son of Azrikam, the son of Hashabiah, of the sons of Merari;

15 Bakbakkar, Heresh, Galal, and Mattaniah the son of Micah, the son of ᴿZichri, the son of Asaph;   Neh. 11:17

16 Obadiah the son of Shemaiah, the son of Galal, the son of Jeduthun; and Berechiah the son of Asa, the son of Elkanah, who lived in the villages of the Netophathites.

The Levite Gatekeepers

17 And the gatekeepers *were* Shallum, Akkub, Talmon, Ahiman, and their brethren. Shallum *was* the chief.

18 Until then *they had been* gatekeepers for the camps of the children of Levi at the King's Gate on the east.

19 Shallum the son of Kore, the son of Ebiasaph, the son of Korah, and his brethren, from his father's house, the Korahites, *were* in charge of the work of the service, ᵀgatekeepers of the tabernacle. Their fathers had been keepers of the entrance to the camp of the LORD.   Lit. *thresholds*

20 And ᴿPhinehas the son of Eleazar had been the officer over them in time past; the LORD *was* with him.   Num. 25:6-13; 31:6

21 ᴿZechariah the son of Meshelemiah *was* ᵀkeeper of the door of the tabernacle of meeting.   1 Chr. 26:2, 14 · *gatekeeper*

22 All those chosen as gatekeepers *were* two hundred and twelve. They were recorded by their genealogy, in their villages. David and Samuel ᴿthe seer had appointed them to their trusted office.   1 Sam. 9:9

23 So they and their children *were* in charge of the gates of the house of the LORD, the house of the tabernacle, by assignment.

24 The gatekeepers were assigned to the four directions: the east, west, north, and south.

25 And their brethren in their villages *had* to come with them from time to time ᴿfor seven days.   2 Kin. 11:4-7

26 For in this trusted office *were* four chief gatekeepers; they were Levites. And they had charge over the chambers and treasuries of the house of God.

27 And they lodged *all* around the house of God because ᵀthey *had* the responsibility, and they *were* in charge of opening *it* every morning.   *the watch was committed to them*

Other Levite Responsibilities

28 Now *some* of them were in charge of the serving vessels, for they brought them in and took them out by count.

29 *Some* of them *were* appointed over the furnishings and over all the implements of the sanctuary, and over the ᴿfine flour and the wine and the oil and the incense and the spices.   1 Chr. 23:29

30 And *some* of the sons of the priests made ᴿthe ointment of the spices.   Ex. 30:22-25

31 Mattithiah of the Levites, the firstborn of Shallum the Korahite, had the trusted office over the things that were baked in the pans.

32 And some of their brethren of the sons of the Kohathites ᴿ*were* in charge of preparing the showbread for every Sabbath.   Lev. 24:5-8

33 These are ᴿthe singers, heads of the fathers' *houses* of the Levites, *who lodged* in the chambers, *and were* free *from other duties;* for they were employed in *that* work day and night.   1 Chr. 6:31; 25:1

34 These heads of the fathers' *houses* of the Levites *were* heads throughout their generations. They dwelt at Jerusalem.

The Family of King Saul

35 Jeiel the father of Gibeon, whose wife's name *was* Maacah, dwelt at Gibeon.

36 His firstborn son *was* Abdon, then Zur, Kish, Baal, Ner, Nadab,

37 Gedor, Ahio, *Zechariah, and Mikloth.

38 And Mikloth begot ᵀShimeam. They also dwelt alongside their relatives in Jerusalem, with their brethren.   *Shimeah,* 1 Chr. 8:32

39 ᴿNer begot Kish, Kish begot Saul, and Saul begot Jonathan, Malchishua, Abinadab, and Esh-Baal.   1 Chr. 8:33-38

40 The son of Jonathan *was* Merib-Baal, and Merib-Baal begot Micah.

41 The sons of Micah *were* Pithon, Melech, ᵀTahrea, *and Ahaz.   *Tarea,* 1 Chr. 8:35

9:37 *Zecher,* 1 Chr. 8:31
9:41 So with Arab., Syr., Tg., Vg. (cf. 8:35); MT, LXX omit *and Ahaz.*

42 And Ahaz begot ᵀJarah; Jarah begot Alemeth, Azmaveth, and Zimri; and Zimri begot Moza; *Jehoaddah, 1 Chr. 8:36*

43 Moza begot Binea, *Rephaiah his son, Eleasah his son, and Azel his son.

44 And Azel had six sons whose names *were* these: Azrikam, Bocheru, Ishmael, Sheariah, Obadiah, and Hanan; these *were* the sons of Azel.

Tragic End of Saul and His Sons

10 Now ᴿthe Philistines fought against Israel; and the men of Israel fled from before the Philistines, and fell slain on Mount Gilboa.   *1 Sam. 31:1, 2*

2 Then the Philistines followed hard after Saul and his sons. And the Philistines killed Jonathan, ᵀAbinadab, and Malchishua, Saul's sons.   *Jishui, 1 Sam. 14:49*

3 The battle became fierce against Saul. The archers hit him, and he was wounded by the archers.

4 Then Saul said to his armorbearer, "Draw your sword, and thrust me through with it, lest these uncircumcised men come and abuse me." But his armorbearer would not, for he was greatly afraid. Therefore Saul took a sword and fell on it.

5 And when his armorbearer saw that Saul was dead, he also fell on his sword and died.

6 So Saul and his three sons died, and all his house died together.

7 And when all the men of Israel who *were* in the valley saw that they had fled and that Saul and his sons were dead, they forsook their cities and fled; then the Philistines came and dwelt in them.

8 So it happened the next day, when the Philistines came to ᵀstrip the slain, that they found Saul and his sons fallen on Mount Gilboa.   *plunder*

9 And they stripped him and took his head and his armor, and sent word *throughout* the land of the Philistines to proclaim the news *in the temple* of their idols and among the people.

10 ᴿThen they put his armor in the ᵀtemple of their gods, and fastened his head in the temple of Dagon.   *1 Sam. 31:10 • Lit. house*

11 And when all Jabesh Gilead heard all that the Philistines had done to Saul,

12 all the valiant men arose and took the body of Saul and the bodies of his sons; and they brought them to ᴿJabesh, and buried their bones under the tamarisk tree at Jabesh, and fasted seven days.   *2 Sam. 21:12*

13 So Saul died for his unfaithfulness which he had ᵀcommitted against the LORD, because he did not keep the word of the LORD, and also because ᴿhe consulted a medium for guidance.   *Lit. transgressed • 1 Sam. 28:7*

14 But *he* did not inquire of the LORD; therefore He killed him, and turned the kingdom over to David the son of Jesse.

David Made King over All Israel

11 Then ᴿall Israel came together to David at Hebron, saying, "Indeed we *are* your bone and your flesh.   *2 Sam. 5:1*

2 "Also, in time past, even when Saul was king, you *were* the one who led Israel out and brought them in; and the LORD your God said to you, 'You shall shepherd My people Israel, and be ruler over My people Israel.'"

3 Therefore all the elders of Israel came to the king at Hebron, and David made a covenant with them at Hebron before the LORD. And they anointed David king over Israel, according to the word of the LORD ᵀby ᴿSamuel.   *Lit. by the hand of Samuel • 1 Sam. 16:1, 4, 12, 13*

The City of David

4 And David and all Israel ᴿwent to Jerusalem, which is Jebus, where the Jebusites *were,* the inhabitants of the land.   *2 Sam. 5:6*

5 But the inhabitants of Jebus said to David, "You shall not come in here!" Nevertheless David took the stronghold of Zion (that is, the City of David).

6 Now David said, "Whoever attacks the Jebusites first shall be ᵀchief and captain." And Joab the son of Zeruiah went up first, and became chief.   *Lit. head*

7 Then David dwelt in the stronghold; therefore they called it the City of David.

8 And he built the city around it, from *the Millo to the surrounding area. Joab ᵀrepaired the rest of the city.   *Lit. revived*

9 So David went on and became great, and the LORD of hosts *was* with him.

The Mighty Men of David

10 Now these *were* the heads of the mighty men whom David had, who strengthened themselves with him in his kingdom, with all Israel, to make him king, according to the word of the LORD concerning Israel.

11 And this *is* the number of the mighty men whom David had: ᴿJashobeam the son of a Hachmonite, ᴿchief of *the captains; he had lifted up his spear against three hundred, killed *by him* at one time.   *1 Chr. 27:2 • 1 Chr. 12:18*

12 After him *was* Eleazar the son of ᴿDodo, the Ahohite, who *was* one of the three mighty men.   *1 Chr. 27:4*

13 He was with David at Pasdammim. Now there the Philistines were gathered for battle, and there was a piece of ground full of barley. So the people fled from the Philistines.

14 But they ᵀstationed themselves in the

11:8 Lit. *The Landfill*

11:11 So with Qr.; Kt., LXX, Vg. *the thirty* (cf. 2 Sam. 23:8)

middle of *that* field, defended it, and killed the Philistines. So the LORD brought about a great victory.   Lit. *took their stand*

15 Now three of the thirty chief men went down to the rock to David, into the cave of Adullam; and the army of the Philistines encamped in the Valley of ᵀRephaim.   *Giants*

16 David *was* then in the stronghold, and the garrison of the Philistines *was* then in Bethlehem.

17 And David said with longing, "Oh, that someone would give me a drink of water from the well of Bethlehem, which is by the gate!"

18 So the three broke through the camp of the Philistines, drew water from the well of Bethlehem that *was* by the gate, and took *it* and brought *it* to David. Nevertheless David would not drink it, but poured it out to the LORD.

19 And he said, "Far be it from me, O my God, that I should do this! Shall I drink the blood of these men *who have put* their lives *in jeopardy?* For at the risk of their lives they brought it." Therefore he would not drink it. These things were done by the three mighty men.

20 Abishai the brother of Joab was chief of *another* *three. He had lifted up his spear against three hundred *men,* killed *them,* and won a name among *these* three.

21 ᴿOf the three he was more honored than the other two men. Therefore he became their captain. However he did not attain to the *first* three.   2 Sam. 23:19

22 Benaiah was the son of Jehoiada, the son of a valiant man from Kabzeel, who ᵀhad done many deeds. ᴿHe had killed two lion-like heroes of Moab. He also had gone down and killed a lion in the midst of a pit on a snowy day.   *was great in deeds* · 2 Sam. 23:20

23 And he killed an Egyptian, a man of *great* height, ᵀfive cubits tall. In the Egyptian's hand *there was* a spear like a weaver's beam; and he went down to him with a staff, wrested the spear out of the Egyptian's hand, and killed him with his own spear.   7.5 ft.

24 These *things* Benaiah the son of Jehoiada did, and won a name among three mighty men.

25 Indeed he was more honored than the thirty, but he did not attain to the *first* three. And David appointed him over his guard.

26 Also the mighty warriors *were* ᴿAsahel the brother of Joab, Elhanan the son of Dodo of Bethlehem,   2 Sam. 23:24

27 ᵀShammoth the Harorite, Helez the *Pelonite,   *Shammah the Harodite,* 2 Sam. 23:25

28 ᴿIra the son of Ikkesh the Tekoite, ᴿAbiezer the Anathothite,   1 Chr. 27:9 · 1 Chr. 27:12

29 ᵀSibbechai the Hushathite, ᵀIlai the Ahohite,   *Mebunnai,* 2 Sam. 23:27 · *Zalmon,* 2 Sam. 23:28

30 ᴿMaharai the Netophathite, *Heled the son of Baanah the Netophathite,   1 Chr. 27:13

31 Ithai the son of Ribai of Gibeah, of the sons of Benjamin, Benaiah the Pirathonite,

32 ᵀHurai of the brooks of Gaash, ᵀAbiel the Arbathite,   *Hiddai,* 2 Sam. 23:30 · *Abi-Albon,* 2 Sam. 23:31

33 Azmaveth the ᵀBaharumite, Eliahba the Shaalbonite,   *Barhumite,* 2 Sam. 23:31

34 the sons of Hashem the Gizonite, Jonathan the son of Shageh the Hararite,

35 Ahiam the son of Sacar the Hararite, ᴿEliphal the son of Ur,   *Eliphelet,* 2 Sam. 23:34

36 Hepher the Mecherathite, Ahijah the Pelonite,

37 ᵀHezro the Carmelite, ᵀNaarai the son of Ezbai,   *Hezrai,* 2 Sam. 23:35 · *Paarai the Arbite,* 2 Sam. 23:35

38 Joel the brother of Nathan, Mibhar the son of Hagri,

39 Zelek the Ammonite, Naharai the ᵀBerothite (the armorbearer of Joab the son of Zeruiah),   *Beerothite,* 2 Sam. 23:37

40 Ira the Ithrite, Gareb the Ithrite,

41 Uriah the Hittite, ᵀZabad the son of Ahlai,   The last sixteen are not in 2 Sam. 23.

42 Adina the son of Shiza the Reubenite (a chief of the Reubenites) and thirty with him,

43 Hanan the son of Maachah, Joshaphat the Mithnite,

44 Uzzia the Ashterathite, Shama and Jeiel the sons of Hotham the Aroerite,

45 Jediael the son of Shimri, and Joha his brother, the Tizite,

46 Eliel the Mahavite, Jeribai and Joshaviah the sons of Elnaam, Ithmah the Moabite,

47 Eliel, Obed, and Jaasiel the Mezobaite.

The Growth of David's Army

12 Now ᴿthese *were* the men who came to David at ᴿZiklag while he was still a fugitive from Saul the son of Kish; and they *were* among the mighty men, helpers in the war,   1 Sam. 27:2 · 1 Sam. 27:6

2 armed with bows, using both the right hand and ᴿthe left in *hurling* stones and *shooting* arrows with the bow. They *were* of Benjamin, Saul's brethren.   Judg. 3:15; 20:16

3 The chief *was* Ahiezer, then Joash, the sons of ᵀShemaah the Gibeathite; Jeziel and Pelet the sons of Azmaveth; Berachah, and Jehu the Anathothite;   Or *Hasmaah*

4 Ishmaiah the Gibeonite, a mighty man among the thirty, and over the thirty; Jeremiah, Jahaziel, Johanan, and Jozabad the Gederathite;

5 Eluzai, Jerimoth, Bealiah, Shemariah, and Shephatiah the Haruphite;

6 Elkanah, Jisshiah, Azarel, Joezer, and Jashobeam, the Korahites;

7 and Joelah and Zebadiah the sons of Jeroham of Gedor.

8 *Some* Gadites joined David at the stronghold in the wilderness, mighty men of valor, men trained for battle, who could handle shield and spear, whose faces *were like* the faces of lions, and *were* ᴿas swift as gazelles on the mountains: 2 Sam. 2:18

9 Ezer the first, Obadiah the second, Eliab the third,

10 Mishmannah the fourth, Jeremiah the fifth,

11 Attai the sixth, Eliel the seventh,

12 Johanan the eighth, Elzabad the ninth,

13 Jeremiah the tenth, and Machbanai the eleventh,

14 These *were* from the sons of Gad, captains of the army; the least was over a hundred, and the greatest was over a thousand.

15 These *are* the ones who crossed the Jordan in the first month, when it had overflowed all its ᴿbanks; and they put to flight all *those* in the valleys, to the east and to the west.   Josh. 3:15; 4:18, 19

16 Then some of the sons of Benjamin and Judah came to David at the stronghold.

17 And David went out ᵀto meet them, and answered and said to them, "If you have come peaceably to me to help me, my heart will be united with you; but if to betray me to my enemies, since *there is* no ᵀwrong in my hands, may the God of our fathers look and bring judgment."   Lit. *before them* · Lit. *violence*

18 Then the Spirit ᵀcame upon ᴿAmasai, chief of the captains, *and he said:*

"*We are* yours, O David;
We *are* on your side, O son of Jesse!
Peace, peace to you,
And peace to your helpers!
For your God helps you."

So David received them, and made them captains of the troop.   Lit. *clothed* · 2 Sam. 17:25

19 And *some* from Manasseh defected to David ᴿwhen he was going with the Philistines to battle against Saul; but they did not help him, for the lords of the Philistines sent him away by agreement, saying, ᴿ"He may defect to his master Saul *and endanger* our heads."   1 Sam. 29:2 · 1 Sam. 29:4

20 When he went to Ziklag, those of Manasseh who defected to him were Adnah, Jozabad, Jediael, Michael, Jozabad, Elihu, and Zillethai, captains of the thousands who *were* from Manasseh.

21 And they helped David against ᴿthe bands *of raiders,* for they *were* all mighty men of valor, and they were captains in the army.   1 Sam. 30:1, 9, 10

22 For at *that* time they came to David day by day to help him, until *it was* a great army, ᴿlike the army of God.   Josh. 5:13-15

David's Army at Hebron

23 Now these *were* the numbers of the ᵀdivisions *that were* equipped for *the* war, *and* came to David at Hebron to turn over *the* kingdom of Saul to him, ᴿaccording to the word of the LORD: Lit. *heads of those* · 1 Sam. 16:1-4

24 of the sons of Judah bearing shield and spear, six thousand eight hundred ᵀarmed for war;   *equipped*

25 of the sons of Simeon, mighty men of valor fit for war, seven thousand one hundred;

26 of the sons of Levi four thousand six hundred;

27 Jehoiada, the leader of the Aaronites, and with him three thousand seven hundred;

28 ᴿZadok, a young man, a valiant warrior, and from his father's house twenty-two captains;   2 Sam. 8:17

29 of the sons of Benjamin, relatives of Saul, three thousand (until then ᴿthe greatest part of them had remained loyal to the house of Saul);   2 Sam. 2:8, 9

30 of the sons of Ephraim twenty thousand eight hundred, mighty men of valor, famous men throughout their father's house;

31 of the half-tribe of Manasseh eighteen thousand, who were designated by name to come and make David king;

32 of the sons of Issachar who had understanding of the times, to know what Israel ought to do, their chiefs were two hundred; and all their brethren were at their command;

33 of Zebulun there were fifty thousand who went out to battle, expert in war with all weapons of war, ᴿstouthearted men who could keep ranks;   Ps. 12:2

34 of Naphtali one thousand captains, and with them thirty-seven thousand with shield and spear;

35 of the Danites who could keep battle formation, twenty-eight thousand six hundred;

36 of Asher, those who could go out to war, able to keep battle formation, forty thousand;

37 of the Reubenites and the Gadites and the half-tribe of Manasseh, from the other side of the Jordan, one hundred and twenty thousand armed for battle with every *kind* of weapon of war.

38 All these men of war, who could keep ranks, came to Hebron with a loyal heart, to make David king over all Israel; and all the rest of Israel *were* of ᴿone mind to make David king.   2 Chr. 30:12

39 And they were there with David three days, eating and drinking, for their brethren had prepared for them.

40 Moreover those who were near to them, from as far away as Issachar and Zebulun and Naphtali, were bringing food on donkeys and camels, on mules and oxen—provisions of flour and cakes of figs and cakes of raisins,

wine and oil and oxen and sheep abundantly, for *there was* joy in Israel.

The Ark Brought from Kirjath Jearim

13 Then David consulted with the ᴿcaptains of thousands and hundreds, *and* with every leader.   1 Chr. 11:15; 12:34

2 And David said to all the assembly of Israel, "If *it seems* good to you, and if it is of the LORD our God, let us send out to our brethren everywhere *who are* ᴿleft in all the land of Israel, and with them to the priests and Levites *who are* in their cities *and* their common-lands, that they may gather together to us;   Is. 37:4

3 "and let us bring the ark of our God back to us, ᴿfor we have not inquired at it since the days of Saul."   1 Sam. 7:1, 2

4 Then all the assembly said that they would do so, for the thing was right in the eyes of all the people.

5 So ᴿDavid gathered all Israel together, from ᴿShihor in Egypt to as far as the entrance of Hamath, to bring the ark of God from Kirjath Jearim.   1 Sam. 7:5 • Josh. 13:3

6 And David and all Israel went up to *Baalah, to Kirjath Jearim, which belonged to Judah, to bring up from there the ark of God the LORD, who dwells *between* the cherubim, where *His* name is proclaimed.

7 So they carried the ark of God on a new cart ᴿfrom the house of Abinadab, and Uzza and Ahio drove the cart.   1 Sam. 7:1

8 Then David and all Israel played *music* before God with all *their* might, with singing, on harps, on stringed instruments, on tambourines, on cymbals, and with trumpets.

9 And when they came to ᵀChidon's threshing floor, Uzza put out his hand to hold the ark, for the oxen stumbled.   *Nachon,* 2 Sam. 6:6

10 Then the anger of the LORD was aroused against Uzza, and He struck him ᴿbecause he put his hand to the ark; and he ᴿdied there before God.   [Num. 4:15] • Lev. 10:2

11 And David became angry because of the LORD's outbreak against Uzza; therefore that place is called *Perez Uzza to this day.

12 David was afraid of God that day, saying, "How can I bring the ark of God to me?"

13 So David would not move the ark with him into the City of David, but took it aside into the house of Obed-Edom the Gittite.

14 The ark of God remained with the family of Obed-Edom in his house three months. And the LORD blessed ᴿthe house of Obed-Edom and all that he had.   1 Chr. 26:4–8

David Established at Jerusalem

14 Now Hiram king of Tyre sent messengers to David, and cedar trees, with masons and carpenters, to build him a house.

2 So David knew that the LORD had established him as king over Israel, for his kingdom was ᴿhighly exalted for the sake of His people Israel.   Num. 24:7

3 Then David took more wives in Jerusalem, and David begot more sons and daughters.

4 And these are the names of his children whom he had in Jerusalem: ᵀShammua, Shobab, Nathan, Solomon,   *Shimea,* 1 Chr. 3:5

5 Ibhar, ᵀElishua, *Elpelet,   *Elishama,* 1 Chr. 3:6

6 Nogah, Nepheg, Japhia,

7 Elishama, *Beeliada, and Eliphelet.

The Philistines Defeated

8 Now when the Philistines heard that ᴿDavid had been anointed king over all Israel, all the Philistines went up to search for David. And David heard *of it* and went out against them.   2 Sam. 5:17–21

9 Then the Philistines went and made a raid on the Valley of ᵀRephaim.   *Lit. Giants*

10 And David ᴿinquired of God, saying, "Shall I go up against the Philistines? Will You deliver them into my hand?" The LORD said to him, "Go up, for I will deliver them into your hand."   1 Sam. 23:2, 4; 30:8

11 So they went up to Baal Perazim, and David defeated them there. Then David said, "God has broken through my enemies by my hand like a breakthrough of water." Therefore they called the name of that place ᵀBaal Perazim.   *Lit. Master of Breakthroughs*

12 And when they left their gods there, David gave a commandment, and they were burned with fire.

13 ᴿThen the Philistines once again made a raid on the valley.   2 Sam. 5:22–25

14 Therefore David inquired again of God, and God said to him, "You shall not go up after them; circle around them, and come upon them in front of the mulberry trees.

15 "And it shall be, when you hear a sound of marching in the tops of the mulberry trees, then you shall go out to battle, for God has gone out before you to strike the camp of the Philistines."

16 So David did as God commanded him, and they drove back the army of the Philistines from Gibeon as far as Gezer.

17 Then ᴿthe fame of David went out into all lands, and the LORD ᴿbrought the fear of him upon all nations.   Josh. 6:27 • [Deut. 2:25; 11:25]

The Ark Brought to Jerusalem

15 David built houses for himself in the City of David; and he prepared a place for the ark of God, and pitched a tent for it.

2 Then David said, "No one may carry the ᴿark of God but the Levites, for the LORD has

chosen them to carry the ark of God and to minister before Him forever."   [Num. 4:15]

3 And David gathered all Israel together at Jerusalem, to bring up the ark of the Lord to its place, which he had prepared for it.

4 Then David assembled the children of Aaron and the Levites:

5 of the sons of Kohath, Uriel the chief, and one hundred and twenty of his brethren;

6 of the sons of Merari, Asaiah the chief, and two hundred and twenty of his brethren;

7 of the sons of Gershom, Joel the chief, and one hundred and thirty of his brethren;

8 of the sons of Elizaphan, Shemaiah the chief, and two hundred of his brethren;

9 of the sons of ᴿHebron, Eliel the chief, and eighty of his brethren;   Ex. 6:18

10 of the sons of Uzziel, Amminadab the chief, and one hundred and twelve of his brethren.

11 And David called for ᴿZadok and ᴿAbiathar the priests, and for the Levites: for Uriel, Asaiah, Joel, Shemaiah, Eliel, and Amminadab.   1 Chr. 12:28 • 1 Kin. 2:22, 26, 27

12 He said to them, "You are the heads of the fathers' houses of the Levites; sanctify yourselves, you and your brethren, that you may bring up the ark of the Lord God of Israel to the place I have prepared for it.

13 "For because you did not do it the first time, the Lord our God broke out against us, because we did not consult Him ᵀabout the proper order."   regarding the ordinance

14 So the priests and the Levites ᵀsanctified themselves to bring up the ark of the Lord God of Israel.   consecrated

15 And the children of the Levites bore the ark of God on their shoulders, by its poles, as ᴿMoses had commanded according to the word of the Lord.   Ex. 25:14

16 Then David spoke to the leaders of the Levites to appoint their brethren to be the singers accompanied by instruments of music, stringed instruments, harps, and cymbals, by raising the voice with resounding joy.

17 So the Levites appointed Heman the son of Joel; and of his brethren, Asaph the son of Berechiah; and of their brethren, the sons of Merari, Ethan the son of Kushaiah;

18 and with them their brethren of the second rank: Zechariah, *Ben, Jaaziel, Shemiramoth, Jehiel, Unni, Eliab, Benaiah, Maaseiah, Mattithiah, Elipheleh, Mikneiah, Obed-Edom, and Jeiel, the gatekeepers;

19 the singers, Heman, Asaph, and Ethan, were to sound the cymbals of bronze;

20 Zechariah, ᵀAziel, Shemiramoth, Jehiel, Unni, Eliab, Maaseiah, and Benaiah, with strings according to Alamoth;   Jaaziel, v. 18

21 Mattithiah, Elipheleh, Mikneiah, Obed-

15:18 So with MT, Vg.; LXX omits *Ben*

Edom, Jeiel, and Azaziah, to direct with harps on the ᴿSheminith;   Ps. 6:title

22 Chenaniah, leader of the Levites, was instructor in charge of the music, because he was skillful;

23 Berechiah and Elkanah were doorkeepers for the ark;

24 Shebaniah, Joshaphat, Nethanel, Amasai, Zechariah, Benaiah, and Eliezer, the priests, ᴿwere to blow the trumpets before the ark of God; and Obed-Edom and Jehiah, doorkeepers for the ark.   [Num. 10:8]

25 So ᴿDavid, the elders of Israel, and the captains over thousands went to bring up the ark of the covenant of the Lord from the house of Obed-Edom with joy.   1 Kin. 8:1

26 And so it was, when God helped the Levites who bore the ark of the covenant of the Lord, that they offered seven bulls and seven rams.

27 David was clothed with a robe of fine ᴿlinen, as were all the Levites who bore the ark, the singers, and Chenaniah the music master with the singers. David also wore a linen ephod.   1 Sam. 2:18, 28

28 ᴿThus all Israel brought up the ark of the covenant of the Lord with shouting and with the sound of the horn, with trumpets and with cymbals, making music with stringed instruments and harps.   1 Chr. 13:8

29 And it happened, ᴿas the ark of the covenant of the Lord came to the City of David, that Michal, Saul's daughter, looked through a window and saw King David whirling and playing music; and she despised him in her heart.   2 Sam. 3:13, 14; 6:16, 20-23

The Ark Placed in the Tabernacle

16 So they brought the ark of God, and set it in the midst of the tabernacle that David had erected for it. Then they offered burnt offerings and peace offerings before God.

2 And when David had finished offering the burnt offerings and the peace offerings, ᴿhe blessed the people in the name of the Lord.   1 Kin. 8:14

3 Then he distributed to everyone of Israel, both man and woman, to everyone a loaf of bread, a piece of meat, and a cake of raisins.

4 And he appointed some of the Levites to minister before the ark of the Lord, to ᴿcommemorate, to thank, and to praise the Lord God of Israel: Ps. 38:title; 70:title

5 Asaph the chief, and next to him Zechariah, then ᴿJeiel, Shemiramoth, Jehiel, Mattithiah, Eliab, Benaiah, and Obed-Edom: Jeiel with stringed instruments and harps, but Asaph made music with cymbals;   1 Chr. 15:18

6 Benaiah and Jahaziel the priests regularly blew the trumpets before the ark of the covenant of God.

David's Song of Thanksgiving

7 On that day David ᴿfirst delivered *this psalm* into the hand of Asaph and his brethren, to thank the LORD: Ps. 105:1-15

8 ᴿOh, give thanks to the LORD!
  Call upon His name;   Ps. 105:1-15
  Make known His deeds among the peoples!
9 Sing to Him, sing psalms to Him;
  Talk of all His wondrous works!
10 Glory in His holy name;
  Let the hearts of those rejoice who seek the LORD!
11 Seek the LORD and His strength;
  Seek His face evermore!
12 Remember His marvelous works which He has done,
  His wonders, and the judgments of His mouth,
13 O seed of Israel His servant,
  You children of Jacob, His chosen ones!

14 He *is* the LORD our God;
  His judgments *are* in all the earth.
15 Remember His covenant forever,
  The word which He commanded, for a thousand generations,
16 The ᴿcovenant which He made with Abraham,   Gen. 17:2; 26:3; 28:13; 35:11
  And His oath to Isaac,
17 And ᴿconfirmed it to ᴿJacob for a statute,   Gen. 35:11, 12 • Gen. 28:10-15
  To Israel *for* an everlasting covenant,
18 Saying, "To you I will give the land of Canaan
  As the allotment of your inheritance,"
19 When you were few in number,
  Indeed very few, and strangers in it.

20 When they went from one nation to another,
  And from *one* kingdom to another people,
21 He permitted no man to do them wrong;
  Yes, He rebuked kings for their sakes,
22 *Saying*, ᴿ"Do not touch My anointed ones,   Ps. 105:1-15
  And do My prophets no harm."

23 ᴿSing to the LORD, all the earth;   Ps. 96:1-13
  Proclaim the good news of His salvation from day to day.
24 Declare His glory among the nations,
  His wonders among all peoples.
25 For the LORD *is* great and greatly to be praised;
  He *is* also to be feared above all gods.
26 For all the gods ᴿof the peoples *are* ᵀidols,   Lev. 19:4 • *worthless things*
  But the LORD made the heavens.
27 Honor and majesty *are* before Him;
  Strength and gladness *are* in His place.

28 Give to the LORD, O families of the peoples,
  Give to the LORD glory and strength.
29 Give to the LORD the glory *due* His name;
  Bring an offering, and come before Him.
  Oh, worship the LORD in the beauty of holiness!
30 Tremble before Him, all the earth.
  The world also is firmly established,
  It shall not be moved.

31 Let the heavens rejoice, and let the earth be glad;
  And let them say among the nations,
  "The LORD reigns."
32 Let the sea roar, and all its fullness;
  Let the field rejoice, and all that *is* in it.
33 Then the ᴿtrees of the woods shall rejoice before the LORD,   Is. 55:12, 13
  For He is coming to judge the earth.

34 ᴿOh, give thanks to the LORD, for *He is* good!   Ps. 106:1; 107:1; 118:1; 136:1
  For His mercy *endures* forever.
35 ᴿAnd say, "Save us, O God of our salvation;   Ps. 106:47, 48
  Gather us together, and deliver us from the Gentiles,
  To give thanks to Your holy name,
  To triumph in Your praise."

36 ᴿBlessed *be* the LORD God of Israel
  From everlasting to everlasting!

And all ᴿthe people said, "Amen!" and praised the LORD.   1 Kin. 8:15, 56 • Deut. 27:15

Regular Worship Maintained

37 So he left ᴿAsaph and his brothers there before the ark of the covenant of the LORD to minister before the ark regularly, as every day's work ᴿrequired;   1 Chr. 16:4, 5 • Ezra 3:4
38 and Obed-Edom with his sixty-eight brethren, including Obed-Edom the son of Jeduthun, and Hosah, *to be* gatekeepers;
39 and Zadok the priest and his brethren the priests, before the tabernacle of the LORD at the high place that *was* at Gibeon,
40 to offer burnt offerings to the LORD on the altar of burnt offering regularly ᴿmorning and evening, and *to do* according to all that is written in the Law of the LORD which He commanded Israel;   [Ex. 29:38-42]
41 and with them Heman and Jeduthun and the rest who were chosen, who were designated by name, to give thanks to the LORD, because His mercy *endures* forever;
42 and with them Heman and Jeduthun, to sound aloud with trumpets and cymbals and the musical instruments of God. Now the sons of Jeduthun *were* gatekeepers.
43 ᴿThen all the people departed, every man to his house; and David returned to bless his house.   2 Sam. 6:18-20

God's Covenant with David

17 Now ᴿit came to pass, when David was dwelling in his house, that David said to Nathan the prophet, "See now, I dwell in a house of cedar, but the ark of the covenant of the LORD *is* under tent curtains."   2 Sam. 7:1

2 Then Nathan said to David, "Do all that *is* in your heart, for God *is* with you."

3 But it happened that night that the word of God came to Nathan, saying,

4 "Go and tell My servant David, 'Thus says the LORD: "You shall ᴿnot build Me a house to dwell in.   [1 Chr. 28:2, 3]

5 "For I have not dwelt in a house since the time that I brought up Israel, even to this day, but have gone from tent to tent, and from *one* tabernacle *to another.*

6 "Wherever I have moved about with all Israel, have I ever spoken a word to any of the judges of Israel, whom I commanded to shepherd My people, saying, 'Why have you not built Me a house of cedar?' " '

7 "Now therefore, thus shall you say to My servant David, 'Thus says the LORD of hosts: "I took you ᴿfrom the sheepfold, from following the sheep, to be ᵀruler over My people Israel.   1 Sam. 16:11-13 · *leader*

8 "And I have been with you wherever you have gone, and have cut off all your enemies from before you, and have ᵀmade you a name like the name of the great men who *are* on the earth.   *given you prestige*

9 "Moreover I will appoint a place for My people Israel, and will plant them, that they may dwell in a place of their own and move no more; nor shall the sons of wickedness oppress them anymore, as previously,

10 "since the time that I commanded judges *to be* over My people Israel. Also I will subdue all your enemies. Furthermore I tell you that the LORD will build you a *house.

11 "And it shall be, when your days are ᴿfulfilled, when you must go *to be* with your fathers, that I will ᴿset up your seed after you, who will be of your sons; and I will establish his kingdom.   1 Kin. 2:10 · Matt. 1:6

12 "He shall build Me a house, and I will establish his throne ᴿforever.   [Luke 1:33]

13 ᴿ"I will be his Father, and he shall be My son; and I will not take My mercy away from him, ᴿas I took *it* from *him* who was before you.   Heb. 1:5 · 1 Chr. 10:14

14 "And I will establish him in My house and in My kingdom forever; and his ᴿthrone shall be established forever." ' "   Acts 2:30

15 According to all these words and according to all this vision, so Nathan spoke to David.

16 ᴿThen King David went in and sat before the LORD; and he said: "Who *am* I, O LORD God? And what *is* my house, that You have brought me this far?   2 Sam. 7:18

17 "And *yet* this was a small thing in Your sight, O God; and You have *also* spoken of Your servant's house for a great while to come, and have regarded me according to the rank of a man of high degree, O LORD God.

18 "What more can David *say* to You for the honor of Your servant? For You know Your servant.

19 "O LORD, for Your servant's sake, and according to Your own heart, You have done all this greatness, in making known all these great things.

20 "O LORD, *there is* none like You, nor *is there any* God besides You, according to all that we have heard with our ears.

21 ᴿ"And who *is* like Your people Israel, the one nation on the earth whom God went to redeem for Himself *as* a people—to make for Yourself a name by great and awesome deeds, by driving out nations from before Your people whom You redeemed from Egypt?   Ps. 147:20

22 "For You have made Your people Israel Your very own people forever; and You, LORD, have become their God.

23 "And now, O LORD, the word which You have spoken concerning Your servant and concerning his house, *let it* be established forever, and do as You have said.

24 "So let it be established, that Your name may be magnified forever, saying, 'The LORD of hosts, the God of Israel, *is* Israel's God.' And let the house of Your servant David be established before You.

25 "For You, O my God, have ᵀrevealed to Your servant that You will build him a house. Therefore Your servant has found it *in his heart* to pray before You.   Lit. *uncovered the ear of*

26 "And now, LORD, You are God, and have promised this goodness to Your servant.

27 "Now You have been pleased to bless the house of Your servant, that it may continue before You forever; for You have blessed it, O LORD, and *it shall be* blessed forever."

David's Further Conquests

18 After this ᴿit came to pass that David ᵀattacked the Philistines, subdued them, and took Gath and its towns from the hand of the Philistines.   2 Sam. 8:1-18 · Lit. *struck*

2 Then he ᵀdefeated ᴿMoab, and the Moabites became David's ᴮservants, *and* brought tribute.   Lit. *struck* · 2 Sam. 8:2 · Ps. 60:8

3 And David defeated *Hadadezer king of Zobah *as far as* Hamath, as he went to establish his power by the River Euphrates.

4 David took from him one thousand

chariots, ᵀseven thousand horsemen, and twenty thousand foot soldiers. Also David ᵀhamstrung all the chariot *horses*, except that he spared enough of them for one hundred chariots.   Or *seven hundred,* 2 Sam. 8:4 · *crippled*

5 When the Syrians of Damascus came to help Hadadezer king of Zobah, David killed twenty-two thousand of the Syrians.

6 Then David put *garrisons* in Syria of Damascus; and the Syrians became David's servants, *and* brought tribute. So the LORD preserved David wherever he went.

7 And David took the shields of gold that were on the servants of Hadadezer, and brought them to Jerusalem.

8 Also from ᵀTibhath and from Chun, cities of Hadadezer, David brought a large amount of bronze, with which Solomon made the bronze ᵀSea, the pillars, and the articles of bronze.   *Betah,* 2 Sam. 8:8 · *Great basin*

9 Now when ᵀTou king of Hamath heard that David had defeated all the army of Hadadezer king of Zobah,   *Toi,* 2 Sam. 8:9, 10

10 he sent Hadoram his son to King David, to greet him and bless him, because he had fought against Hadadezer and ᵀdefeated him (for Hadadezer had been at war with Tou); and *Hadoram brought with him* all kinds of articles of gold, silver, and bronze.   Lit. *struck*

11 King David also dedicated these to the LORD, along with the silver and gold that he had brought from all *these* nations—from Edom, from Moab, from the ᴿpeople of Ammon, from the ᴿPhilistines, and from ᴿAmalek.   2 Sam. 10:12 · 2 Sam. 5:17–25 · 2 Sam. 1:1

12 Moreover Abishai the son of Zeruiah killed ᴿeighteen thousand ᵀEdomites in the Valley of Salt.   2 Sam. 8:13 · Or *Syrians,* 2 Sam. 8:13

13 He also put garrisons in Edom, and all the Edomites became David's servants. And the LORD preserved David wherever he went.

David's Administration

14 So David reigned over all Israel, and administered judgment and justice to all his people.

15 Joab the son of Zeruiah *was* over the army; Jehoshaphat the son of Ahilud *was* recorder;

16 Zadok the son of Ahitub and Abimelech the son of Abiathar *were* the priests; ᵀShavsha *was* the scribe;   *Seraiah,* 2 Sam. 8:17

17 ᴿBenaiah the son of Jehoiada *was* over the Cherethites and the Pelethites; and David's sons *were* ᵀchief ministers at the king's side.   2 Sam. 8:18 · Lit. *at the hand of the king*

The Ammonites and Syrians Defeated

19 Itᴿ happened after this that Nahash the king of the people of Ammon died, and his son reigned in his place.   2 Sam. 10:1–19

2 Then David said, "I will show kindness to Hanun the son of Nahash, because his father showed kindness to me." So David sent messengers to comfort him concerning his father. And David's servants came to Hanun in the land of the people of Ammon to comfort him.

3 And the princes of the people of Ammon said to Hanun, ᵀ"Do you think that David really honors your father because he has sent comforters to you? Did his servants not come to you to search and to overthrow and to spy out the land?"   Lit. *In your eyes does David honor*

4 Therefore Hanun took David's servants, shaved them, and cut off their garments ᵀin the middle, at their ᴿbuttocks, and sent them away.   *in half* · Is. 20:4

5 Then *some* went and told David about the men; and he sent to meet them, because the men were greatly ashamed. And the king said, "Wait at Jericho until your beards have grown, and *then* return."

6 When the people of Ammon saw that they had made themselves repulsive to David, Hanun and the people of Ammon sent a thousand talents of silver to hire for themselves chariots and horsemen from ᵀMesopotamia, from Syrian Maacah, and from ᵀZobah.   Heb. *Aram Naharaim* · *Zoba,* 2 Sam. 10:6

7 So they hired for themselves thirty-two thousand chariots, with the king of Maacah and his people, who came and encamped before Medeba. Also the people of Ammon gathered together from their cities, and came to battle.

8 Now when David heard *of it,* he sent Joab and all the army of the mighty men.

9 Then the people of Ammon came out and put themselves in battle array before the gate of the city, and the kings who had come *were* by themselves in the field.

10 When Joab saw that the battle line was against him before and behind, he chose some of Israel's best and put *them* in battle array against the Syrians.

11 And the rest of the people he put under the command of Abishai his brother, and they set *themselves* in battle array against the people of Ammon.

12 Then he said, "If the Syrians are too strong for me, then you shall help me; but if the people of Ammon are too strong for you, then I will help you.

13 "Be of good courage, and let us be strong for our people and for the cities of our God. And may the LORD do *what is* good in His sight."

14 So Joab and the people who *were* with him drew near for the battle against the Syrians, and they fled before him.

15 When the people of Ammon saw that the Syrians were fleeing, they also fled before Abishai his brother, and entered the city. So Joab went to Jerusalem.

16 Now when the Syrians saw that they had been defeated by Israel, they sent messengers and brought the Syrians who were beyond *the River, and *Shophach the commander of Hadadezer's army went before them.

17 When it was told David, he gathered all Israel, crossed over the Jordan and came upon them, and set up in battle array against them. So when David had set up in *battle* array against the Syrians, they fought with him.

18 Then the Syrians fled before Israel; and David killed ᵀseven thousand charioteers and forty thousand *foot soldiers of the Syrians, and killed Shophach the commander of the army.   *Or seven hundred,* 2 Sam. 10:18

19 And when the servants of Hadadezer saw that they were defeated by Israel, they made peace with David and became his servants. So the Syrians were not willing to help the people of Ammon anymore.

Rabbah Is Conquered

20 It happened ᵀin the spring of the year, at the time kings go out *to battle,* that Joab led out the armed forces and ravaged the country of the people of Ammon, and came and besieged Rabbah. But David stayed at Jerusalem. And Joab defeated Rabbah and overthrew it.   Lit. *at the return*

2 Then David ᴿtook their king's crown from his head, and found it to weigh a ᵀtalent of gold, and *there were* precious stones in it. And it was set on David's head. Also he brought out the ᵀspoil of the city in great abundance.   2 Sam. 12:30, 31 • $5,760,000 • *plunder*

3 And he brought out the people who *were* in it, and *put *them* to work with saws, with iron picks, and with axes. So David did to all the cities of the people of Ammon. Then David and all the people returned *to* Jerusalem.

Philistine Giants Destroyed

4 Now it happened afterward that war broke out at Gezer with the Philistines, at which time Sibbechai the Hushathite killed *Sippai, *who was one* of the sons of ᵀthe giant. And they were subdued.   Or *Raphah*

5 Again there was war with the Philistines, and Elhanan the son of *Jair killed Lahmi the brother of Goliath the Gittite, the shaft of whose spear *was* like a weaver's beam.

6 Yet again ᴿthere was war at Gath, where there was a man of *great* stature, with twenty-four fingers and toes, six *on each* hand and six *on each foot;* and he also was born to ᵀthe giant.   2 Sam. 21:20 • Or *Raphah*

7 So when he defied Israel, Jonathan the son of *Shimea, David's brother, killed him.

8 These were born to the giant in Gath, and they fell by the hand of David and by the hand of his servants.

The Census of Israel and Judah

21 Now Satan stood up against Israel, and moved David to number Israel.

2 So David said to Joab and to the leaders of the people, "Go, number Israel from Beersheba to Dan, ᴿand bring the number of them to me that I may know *it.*"   1 Chr. 27:23, 24

3 And Joab answered, "May the LORD make His people a hundred times more than they are. But, my lord the king, *are* they not all my lord's servants? Why then does my lord require this thing? Why should he be a cause of guilt in Israel?"

4 Nevertheless the king's word prevailed against Joab. Therefore Joab departed and went throughout all Israel and came to Jerusalem.

5 Then Joab gave the sum of the number of the people to David. All Israel *had* one million one hundred thousand men who drew the sword, and Judah *had* four hundred and seventy thousand men who drew the sword.

6 ᴿBut he did not count Levi and Benjamin among them, for the king's ᵀword was abominable to Joab.   1 Chr. 27:24 • *command*

7 And God was displeased with this thing; therefore He struck Israel.

8 So David said to God, "I have sinned greatly, because I have done this thing; but now, I pray, take away the iniquity of Your servant, for I have done very foolishly."

9 Then the LORD spoke to Gad, David's ᴿseer, saying,   1 Sam. 9:9

10 "Go and tell David, ᴿsaying, 'Thus says the LORD: "I offer you three *things;* choose one of them for yourself, that I may do *it* to you." ' "   2 Sam. 24:12-14

11 So Gad came to David and said to him, "Thus says the LORD: 'Choose for yourself,

12 'either *three years of famine, or three months to be defeated by your foes with the sword of your enemies overtaking *you,* or else for three days the sword of the LORD— the plague in the land, with the *angel of the LORD destroying throughout all the territory of Israel.' Now consider what answer I should take back to Him who sent me."

13 And David said to Gad, "I am in great distress. Please let me fall into the hand of the

---

19:16 The Euphrates • *Zoba,* 2 Sam. 10:6, or *Shobach,* 2 Sam. 10:16

19:18 *horsemen,* 2 Sam. 10:18

20:3 LXX *cut them with*

20:4 Saph, 2 Sam. 21:18

20:5 *Jaare-Oregim,* 2 Sam. 21:19

20:7 Shammah, 1 Sam. 16:9 or *Shimeah,* 2 Sam. 21:21

21:12 *seven,* 2 Sam. 24:13 • Or *Angel,* and so throughout the chapter

LORD, for His mercies *are* very great; but do not let me fall into the hand of man."

14 So the LORD sent a plague upon Israel, and seventy thousand men of Israel fell.

15 And God sent ᵀan angel to Jerusalem to destroy it. As *he was destroying, the LORD looked and relented of the disaster, and said to the angel who was destroying, "It is enough; now restrain *your hand." And the angel of the LORD stood by the threshing floor of *Ornan the Jebusite.   Or *the Angel*

16 Then David lifted his eyes and ᴿsaw the angel of the LORD standing between earth and heaven, having in his hand a drawn sword stretched out over Jerusalem. So David and the elders, clothed in sackcloth, fell on their faces.   2 Chr. 3:1

17 And David said to God, "Was it not I who commanded the people to be numbered? I am the one who has sinned and done evil indeed; but these ᴿsheep, what have they done? Let Your hand, I pray, O LORD my God, be against me and my father's house, but not against Your people that they should be plagued."   2 Sam. 7:8

18 Therefore, the ᴿangel of the LORD commanded Gad to say to David that David should go and erect an altar to the LORD on the threshing floor of Ornan the Jebusite.   2 Chr. 3:1

19 So David went up at the word of Gad, which he had spoken in the name of the LORD.

20 Now Ornan turned and saw the angel; and his four sons *who were* with him hid themselves, but Ornan continued threshing wheat.

21 So David came to Ornan, and Ornan looked and saw David. And he went out from the threshing floor, and bowed before David with *his* face to the ground.

22 Then David said to Ornan, ᵀ"Grant me the place of *this* threshing floor, that I may build an altar on it to the LORD. You shall grant it to me at the full price, that the plague may be withdrawn from the people."   Lit. *Give*

23 But Ornan said to David, "Take *it* to yourself, and let my lord the king do *what is* good in his eyes. Look, I *also* give *you* the oxen for burnt offerings, the threshing implements for wood, and the wheat for the grain offering; I give *it* all."

24 Then King David said to Ornan, "No, but I will surely buy *it* for the full price, for I will not take what is yours for the LORD, nor offer burnt offerings with *that which* costs *me* nothing."

25 So ᴿDavid gave Ornan six hundred shekels of gold by weight for the place.   2 Sam. 24:24

26 And David built there an altar to the LORD, and offered burnt offerings and peace

21:15 Or *He* • Or *Your* • Araunah, 2 Sam. 24:16, 18–24

offerings, and called on the LORD; and ᴿHe answered him from heaven by fire on the altar of burnt offering.   Lev. 9:24

27 So the LORD commanded the angel, and he returned his sword to its sheath.

28 At that time, when David saw that the LORD had answered him on the threshing floor of Ornan the Jebusite, he sacrificed there.

29 ᴿFor the tabernacle of the LORD and the altar of the burnt offering, which Moses had made in the wilderness, *were* at that time at the high place in ᴿGibeon.   1 Kin. 3:4 • 1 Chr. 16:39

30 But David could not go before it to inquire of God, for he was afraid of the sword of the angel of the LORD.

David Prepares to Build the Temple

22 Then David said, ᴿ"This *is* the house of the LORD God, and this *is* the altar of burnt offering for Israel."   Deut. 12:5

2 So David commanded to gather the aliens who *were* in the land of Israel; and he appointed masons to ᴿcut hewn stones to build the house of God.   1 Kin. 5:17, 18

3 And David prepared iron in abundance for the nails of the doors of the gates and for the joints, and bronze in abundance ᴿbeyond measure,   1 Kin. 7:47

4 and cedar trees in abundance; for the ᴿSidonians and those from Tyre brought much cedar wood to David.   1 Kin. 5:6–10

5 Now David said, ᴿ"Solomon my son *is* young and inexperienced, and the house to be built for the LORD *must be* exceedingly magnificent, famous and glorious throughout all countries. I will now make preparation for it." So David made abundant preparations before his death.   1 Chr. 29:1, 2

6 Then he called for his son Solomon, and ᵀcharged him to build a house for the LORD God of Israel.   *commanded*

7 And David said to Solomon: "My son, as for me, it was in my mind to build a house to the name of the LORD my God;

8 "but the word of the LORD came to me, saying, 'You have shed much blood and have made great wars; you shall not build a house for My name, because you have shed much blood on the earth in My sight.

9 'Behold, a son shall be born to you, who shall be a man of rest; and I will give him rest from all his enemies all around. His name shall be ᵀSolomon, for I will give peace and quietness to Israel in his days.   Lit. *Peaceful*

10 'He shall build a house for My name, and ᴿhe shall be My son, and I *will be* his Father; and I will establish the throne of his kingdom over Israel forever.'   Matt. 1:6

11 "Now, my son, may ᴿthe LORD be with you; and may you prosper, and build the house of the LORD your God, as He has said to you.   1 Chr. 22:16

12 "Only may the LORD ᴿgive you wisdom

and understanding, and give you charge concerning Israel, that you may keep the law of the LORD your God.   1 Kin. 3:9-12

13 "Then you will prosper, if you take care to fulfill the statutes and judgments with which the LORD ᵀcharged Moses concerning Israel. Be strong and of good courage; do not fear nor be dismayed.   commanded

14 "Indeed I have taken much trouble to prepare for the house of the LORD ᵀone hundred thousand talents of gold and ᵀone million talents of silver, and bronze and iron ᴿbeyond measure, for it is so abundant. I have prepared timber and stone also, and you may add to them. $576 billion • $384 billion • 1 Chr. 22:3

15 "Moreover there are workmen with you in abundance: woodsmen and stonecutters, and all types of skillful men for every kind of work.

16 "Of gold and silver and bronze and iron there is no limit. Arise and begin working, and ᴿthe LORD be with you."   1 Chr. 22:11

17 David also commanded all the leaders of Israel to help Solomon his son, saying,

18 "Is not the LORD your God with you? ᴿAnd has He not given you rest on every side? For He has given the inhabitants of the land into my hand, and the land is subdued before the LORD and before His people.   Josh. 22:4

19 "Now set your heart and your soul to seek the LORD your God. Therefore arise and build the sanctuary of the LORD God, to bring the ark of the covenant of the LORD and the holy articles of God into the house that is to be built for the name of the LORD."

The Divisions of the Levites

23 So when David was old and full of days, he made his son Solomon king over Israel.

2 And he gathered together all the leaders of Israel, with the priests and the Levites.

3 Now the Levites were numbered from the age of ᴿthirty years and above; and the number of individual males was thirty-eight thousand.   Num. 4:1-3

4 Of these, twenty-four thousand were to look after the work of the house of the LORD, six thousand were officers and judges,

5 four thousand were gatekeepers, and four thousand ᴿpraised the LORD with musical instruments, ᴿ"which I made," said David, "for giving praise."   1 Chr. 15:16 • 2 Chr. 29:25-27

6 Also ᴿDavid separated them into ᵀdivisions among the sons of Levi: Gershon, Kohath, and Merari.   Ex. 6:16 • groups

7 Of the ᴿGershonites: ᵀLaadan and Shimei.   1 Chr. 26:21 • Libni, Ex. 6:17

8 The sons of Laadan: the first Jehiel, then Zetham and Joel—three in all.

9 The sons of Shimei: Shelomith, Haziel, and Haran—three in all. These were the heads of the fathers' houses of Laadan.

10 And the sons of Shimei: Jahath, *Zina, Jeush, and Beriah. These were the four sons of Shimei.

11 Jahath was the first and Zizah the second. But Jeush and Beriah did not have many sons; therefore they were assigned as one father's house.

12 ᴿThe sons of Kohath: Amram, Izhar, Hebron, and Uzziel—four in all.   Ex. 6:18

13 The sons of Amram: Aaron and Moses; and Aaron was set apart, he and his sons forever, that he should ᵀsanctify the most holy things, to burn incense before the LORD, ᴿto minister to Him, and to give the blessing in His name forever.   consecrate • [Deut. 21:5]

14 Now the sons of Moses the man of God were reckoned to the tribe of Levi.

15 ᴿThe sons of Moses were ᵀGershon and Eliezer.   Ex. 18:3, 4 • Heb. Gershom, 1 Chr. 6:16

16 Of the sons of Gershon, ᴿShebuelᵀ was the first.   1 Chr. 26:24 • Shubael, 1 Chr. 24:20

17 Of the descendants of Eliezer, Rehabiah was the first. And Eliezer had no other sons, but the sons of Rehabiah were very many.

18 Of the sons of Izhar, ᴿShelomith was the first.   1 Chr. 24:22

19 ᴿOf the sons of Hebron, Jeriah was the first, Amariah the second, Jahaziel the third, and Jekameam the fourth.   1 Chr. 24:23

20 Of the sons of Uzziel, Michah was the first and Jesshiah the second.

21 ᴿThe sons of Merari were Mahli and Mushi. The sons of Mahli were Eleazar and ᴿKish.   1 Chr. 24:26 • 1 Chr. 24:29

22 And Eleazar died, and had no sons, but only daughters; and their ᵀbrethren, the sons of Kish, took them as wives.   kinsmen

23 ᴿThe sons of Mushi were Mahli, Eder, and Jeremoth—three in all.   1 Chr. 24:30

24 These were the sons of Levi by their fathers' houses—the heads of the fathers' houses as they were counted individually by the number of their names, who did the work for the service of the house of the LORD, from the age of ᴿtwenty years and above.   Ezra 3:8

25 For David said, "The LORD God of Israel ᴿhas given rest to His people, that they may dwell in Jerusalem forever";   1 Chr. 22:18

26 and also to the Levites, "They shall no longer ᴿcarry the tabernacle, or any of the articles for its service."   Num. 4:5, 15; 7:9

27 For by the ᴿlast words of David the Levites were numbered from twenty years old and above;   2 Sam. 23:1

28 because their duty was to help the sons of Aaron in the service of the house of the LORD, in the courts and in the chambers, in the purifying of all holy things and the work of the service of the house of God,

29 both with the showbread and the fine flour for the grain offering, with the unleav-

ened cakes and ᴿwhat is baked in the pan, with what is mixed and with all kinds of ᴿmeasures and sizes;   Lev. 2:5, 7 • Lev. 19:35

30 to stand every morning to thank and praise the LORD, and likewise at evening;

31 and at every presentation of a burnt offering to the LORD on the Sabbaths and on the New Moons and on the set feasts, by number according to the ordinance governing them, regularly before the LORD;

32 and that they should attend to the ᴿneeds of the tabernacle of meeting, the needs of the holy place, and the needs of the sons of Aaron their brethren in the work of the house of the LORD.   [Num. 1:53]

The Divisions of the Priests

24 Now these are the divisions of the sons of Aaron. The sons of Aaron were Nadab, Abihu, Eleazar, and Ithamar.

2 And Nadab and Abihu died before their father, and had no children; therefore Eleazar and Ithamar ministered as priests.

3 Then David with Zadok of the sons of Eleazar, and ᴿAhimelech of the sons of Ithamar, divided them according to the schedule of their service.   1 Chr. 18:16

4 There were more leaders found of the sons of Eleazar than of the sons of Ithamar, and thus they were divided. Among the sons of Eleazar were sixteen heads of their fathers' houses, and eight heads of their fathers' houses among the sons of Ithamar.

5 Thus they were divided by lot, one group as another, for there were officials of the sanctuary and officials of the house of God, from the sons of Eleazar and from the sons of Ithamar.

6 And the scribe, Shemaiah the son of Nethanel, one of the Levites, wrote them down before the king, the leaders, Zadok the priest, Ahimelech the son of Abiathar, and the heads of the fathers' houses of the priests and Levites, one father's house taken for Eleazar and one for Ithamar.

7 Now the first lot fell to Jehoiarib, the second to Jedaiah,

8 the third to Harim, the fourth to Seorim,

9 the fifth to Malchijah, the sixth to Mijamin,

10 the seventh to Hakkoz, the eighth to ᴿAbijah,   Luke 1:5

11 the ninth to Jeshua, the tenth to Shecaniah,

12 the eleventh to Eliashib, the twelfth to Jakim,

13 the thirteenth to Huppah, the fourteenth to Jeshebeab,

14 the fifteenth to Bilgah, the sixteenth to Immer,

15 the seventeenth to Hezir, the eighteenth to *Happizzez,

16 the nineteenth to Pethahiah, the twentieth to *Jehezekel,

17 the twenty-first to Jachin, the twenty-second to Gamul,

18 the twenty-third to Delaiah, the twenty-fourth to Maaziah.

19 This was the schedule of their service ᴿfor coming into the house of the LORD according to their ordinance by the hand of Aaron their father, as the LORD God of Israel had commanded him.   1 Chr. 9:25

Other Levites

20 And the rest of the sons of Levi: of the sons of Amram, ᵀShubael; of the sons of Shubael, Jehdeiah.   Shebuel, 1 Chr. 23:16

21 Concerning ᴿRehabiah, of the sons of Rehabiah, the first was Isshiah.   1 Chr. 23:17

22 Of the Izharites, ᵀShelomoth; of the sons of Shelomoth, Jahath.   Shelomith, 1 Chr. 23:18

23 Of the sons *of ᴿHebron, Jeriah *was the first, Amariah the second, Jahaziel the third, and Jekameam the fourth.   1 Chr. 23:19; 26:31

24 Of the sons of Uzziel, Michah; of the sons of Michah, Shamir.

25 The brother of Michah, Isshiah; of the sons of Isshiah, Zechariah.

26 ᴿThe sons of Merari were Mahli and Mushi; the son of Jaaziah, Beno.   Ex. 6:19

27 The sons of Merari by Jaaziah were Beno, Shoham, Zaccur, and Ibri.

28 Of Mahli: Eleazar, who had no sons.

29 Of Kish: the son of Kish, Jerahmeel.

30 Also the sons of Mushi were Mahli, Eder, and Jerimoth. These were the sons of the Levites according to their fathers' houses.

31 These also cast lots just as their brothers the sons of Aaron did, in the presence of King David, Zadok, Ahimelech, and the heads of the fathers' houses of the priests and Levites. The chief fathers did just as their younger brethren.

The Musicians

25 Moreover David and the captains of the army separated for the service some of the sons of ᴿAsaph, of Heman, and of Jeduthun, who should prophesy with harps, stringed instruments, and cymbals. And the number of the skilled men performing their service was: 1 Chr. 6:30, 33, 39, 44

2 Of the sons of Asaph: Zaccur, Joseph, Nethaniah, and ᵀAsharelah; the sons of Asaph were ᵀunder the direction of Asaph, who prophesied according to the order of the king.   Jesharelah, v. 14 • Lit. at the hands of

24:15 LXX, Vg. Aphses
24:16 MT Jehezkel
24:23 Supplied from 23:19 (following some Heb. mss. and LXX mss.) • See previous note

3 Of Jeduthun, the sons of Jeduthun: Gedaliah, Zeri, Jeshaiah, Shimei, Hashabiah, and Mattithiah, *six, under the direction of their father Jeduthun, who prophesied with a harp to give thanks and to praise the LORD.

4 Of Heman, the sons of Heman: Bukkiah, Mattaniah, ᵀUzziel, ᵀShebuel, *Jerimoth, Hananiah, Hanani, Eliathah, Giddalti, Romamti-Ezer, Joshbekashah, Mallothi, Hothir, *and* Mahazioth.   *Azarel, v. 18 · Shubael, v. 20*

5 All these *were* the sons of Heman the king's seer in the words of God, to ᵀexalt his horn. For God gave Heman fourteen sons and three daughters.   Increase his power or influence

6 All these *were* under the direction of their father for the music *in* the house of the LORD, with cymbals, stringed instruments, and ᴿharps, for the service of the house of God. Asaph, Jeduthun, and Heman *were* under the authority of the king.   *1 Chr. 15:16*

7 So the ᴿnumber of them, with their brethren who *were* instructed in the songs of the LORD, all who were skillful, *was* two hundred and eighty-eight.   *1 Chr. 23:5*

8 And they cast lots for their duty, the small as well as the great, ᴿthe teacher with the student.   *2 Chr. 23:13*

9 Now the first lot for Asaph came out for Joseph; the second for Gedaliah, him with his brethren and sons, twelve;

10 the third for Zaccur, his sons and his brethren, twelve;

11 the fourth for ᵀJizri, his sons and his brethren, twelve;   *Zeri, v. 3*

12 the fifth for Nethaniah, his sons and his brethren, twelve;

13 the sixth for Bukkiah, his sons and his brethren, twelve;

14 the seventh for ᵀJesharelah, his sons and his brethren, twelve;   *Asharelah, v. 2*

15 the eighth for Jeshaiah, his sons and his brethren, twelve;

16 the ninth for Mattaniah, his sons and his brethren, twelve;

17 the tenth for Shimei, his sons and his brethren, twelve;

18 the eleventh for ᵀAzarel, his sons and his brethren, twelve;   *Uzziel, v. 4*

19 the twelfth for Hashabiah, his sons and his brethren, twelve;

20 the thirteenth for ᵀShubael, his sons and his brethren, twelve;   *Shebuel, v. 4*

21 the fourteenth for Mattithiah, his sons and his brethren, twelve;

22 the fifteenth for ᵀJeremoth, his sons and his brethren, twelve;   *Jerimoth, v. 4*

23 the sixteenth for Hananiah, his sons and his brethren, twelve;

24 the seventeenth for Joshbekashah, his sons and his brethren, twelve;

25 the eighteenth for Hanani, his sons and his brethren, twelve;

26 the nineteenth for Mallothi, his sons and his brethren, twelve;

27 the twentieth for Eliathah, his sons and his brethren, twelve;

28 the twenty-first for Hothir, his sons and his brethren, twelve;

29 the twenty-second for Giddalti, his sons and his brethren, twelve;

30 the twenty-third for Mahazioth, his sons and his brethren, twelve;

31 the twenty-fourth for Romamti-Ezer, his sons and his brethren, twelve.

The Gatekeepers

26 Concerning the divisions of the gatekeepers: of the Korahites, Meshelemiah the son of Kore, of the sons of Asaph.

2 And the sons of Meshelemiah *were* Zechariah the firstborn, Jediael the second, Zebadiah the third, Jathniel the fourth,

3 Elam the fifth, Jehohanan the sixth, Elioenai the seventh.

4 Moreover the sons of ᴿObed-Edom *were* Shemaiah the firstborn, Jehozabad the second, Joah the third, Sacar the fourth, Nethanel the fifth,   *1 Chr. 15:18, 21*

5 Ammiel the sixth, Issachar the seventh, Peulthai the eighth; for God blessed him.

6 Also to Shemaiah his son were sons born who governed their fathers' houses, because they *were* men of great ability.

7 The sons of Shemaiah *were* Othni, Rephael, Obed, and Elzabad, whose brothers Elihu and Semachiah *were* able men.

8 All these *were* of the sons of Obed-Edom, they and their sons and their brethren, ᴿable men with strength for the work: sixty-two of Obed-Edom.   *1 Chr. 9:13*

9 And Meshelemiah had sons and brethren, eighteen able men.

10 Also Hosah, of the children of Merari, had sons: Shimri the first (for *though* he was not the firstborn, his father made him the first),

11 Hilkiah the second, Tebaliah the third, Zechariah the fourth; all the sons and brethren of Hosah *were* thirteen.

12 Among these *were* the divisions of the gatekeepers, among the chief men, *having* duties just like their brethren, to serve in the house of the LORD.

13 And they ᴿcast lots for each gate, the small as well as the great, according to their father's house.   *1 Chr. 24:5, 31; 25:8*

14 The lot for the East *Gate* fell to ᵀShelemiah. Then they cast lots *for* his son Zechariah, a wise counselor, and his lot came out for the North Gate;   *Meshelemiah, v. 1*

15 to Obed-Edom the South Gate, and to his sons the ᵀstorehouse.   Heb. *asuppim*

16 To Shuppim and Hosah *the lot came out* for the West Gate, with the Shallecheth Gate on the ᴿascending highway—watchman opposite watchman.   1 Kin. 10:5

17 On the east were *six* Levites, on the north four each day, on the south four each day, and for the *storehouse two by two.

18 As for the *Parbar on the west, *there were* four on the highway *and* two at the Parbar.

19 These were the divisions of the gatekeepers among the sons of Korah and among the sons of Merari.

The Treasuries and Other Duties

20 Of the Levites, Ahijah *was* over the treasuries of the house of God and over the treasuries of the ᵀdedicated things.   *holy*

21 The sons of ᵀLaadan, the descendants of the Gershonites of Laadan, heads of their fathers' *houses*, of Laadan the Gershonite: ᵀJehieli.   *Libni,* 1 Chr. 6:17 • *Jehiel,* 1 Chr. 23:8; 29:8

22 The sons of Jehieli, Zetham and Joel his brother, *were* over the treasuries of the house of the LORD.

23 Of the ᴿAmramites, the Izharites, the Hebronites, and the Uzzielites: Ex. 6:18

24 Shebuel the son of Gershom, the son of Moses, *was* overseer of the treasuries.

25 And his brethren by Eliezer *were* Rehabiah his son, Jeshaiah his son, Joram his son, Zichri his son, and Shelomith his son.

26 This Shelomith and his brethren *were* over all the treasuries of the dedicated things ᴿwhich King David and the heads of fathers' *houses*, the captains over thousands and hundreds, and the captains of the army, had dedicated.   2 Sam. 8:11

27 Some of the spoils won in battles they dedicated to maintain the house of the LORD.

28 And all that Samuel ᴿthe seer, Saul the son of Kish, Abner the son of Ner, and Joab the son of Zeruiah had dedicated, every dedicated *thing*, was under the hand of Shelomith and his brethren.   1 Sam. 9:9

29 Of the Izharites, Chenaniah and his sons *performed* duties as ᴿofficials and judges over Israel outside Jerusalem.   1 Chr. 23:4

30 Of the Hebronites, Hashabiah and his brethren, one thousand seven hundred able men, had the oversight of Israel on the west side of the Jordan for all the business of the LORD, and in the service of the king.

31 Among the Hebronites, ᴿJerijah *was* head of the Hebronites according to his genealogy of the fathers. In the fortieth year of the reign of David they were sought, and

there were found among them capable men ᴿat Jazer of Gilead.   1 Chr. 23:19 • Josh. 21:39

32 And his brethren *were* two thousand seven hundred able men, heads of fathers' *houses*, whom King David made officials over the Reubenites, the Gadites, and the half-tribe of Manasseh, for every matter pertaining to God and the affairs of the king.

The Military Divisions

27 And the children of Israel, according to their number, the heads of fathers' *houses*, the captains of thousands and hundreds and their officers, served the king in every matter of the *military* divisions. These *divisions* came in and went out month by month throughout all the months of the year, each division *having* twenty-four thousand.

2 Over the first division for the first month *was* Jashobeam the son of Zabdiel, and in his division *were* twenty-four thousand;

3 *he was* of the children of Perez, and the chief of all the captains of the army for the first month.

4 Over the division of the second month *was* *Dodai an Ahohite, and of his division Mikloth also *was* the leader; in his division *were* twenty-four thousand.

5 The third captain of the army for the third month *was* Benaiah, the son of Jehoiada the priest, who was chief; in his division *were* twenty-four thousand.

6 This was the Benaiah *who was* mighty among the thirty, and was over the thirty; in his division *was* Ammizabad his son.

7 The fourth *captain* for the fourth month *was* ᴿAsahel the brother of Joab, and Zebadiah his son after him; in his division *were* twenty-four thousand.   1 Chr. 11:26

8 The fifth *captain* for the fifth month *was* *Shamhuth the Izrahite; in his division *were* twenty-four thousand.

9 The sixth *captain* for the sixth month *was* Ira the son of Ikkesh the Tekoite; in his division *were* twenty-four thousand.

10 The seventh *captain* for the seventh month *was* ᴿHelez the Pelonite, of the children of Ephraim; in his division *were* twenty-four thousand.   1 Chr. 11:27

11 The eighth *captain* for the eighth month *was* ᴿSibbechai the Hushathite, of the Zarhites; in his division *were* twenty-four thousand.   2 Sam. 21:18

12 The ninth *captain* for the ninth month *was* ᴿAbiezer the Anathothite, of the Benjamites; in his division *were* twenty-four thousand.   1 Chr. 11:28

13 The tenth *captain* for the tenth month *was* ᴿMaharai the Netophathite, of the Zar-

26:17 Heb. *asuppim*
26:18 Probably a court or colonnade extending west of the temple

27:4 Heb. *Dodai,* usually spelled *Dodo,* 2 Sam. 23:9
27:8 *Shammah,* 2 Sam. 23:11, or *Shammoth,* 1 Chr. 11:27

hites; in his division *were* twenty-four thousand.   1 Chr. 11:30

14 The eleventh *captain* for the eleventh month *was* ᴿBenaiah the Pirathonite, of the children of Ephraim; in his division *were* twenty-four thousand.   1 Chr. 11:31

15 The twelfth *captain* for the twelfth month *was* ᵀHeldai the Netophathite, of Othniel; in his division *were* twenty-four thousand.   *Heleb,* 2 Sam. 23:29; *Heled,* 1 Chr. 11:30

Leaders of Tribes

16 Furthermore, over the tribes of Israel: the officer over the Reubenites *was* Eliezer the son of Zichri; over the Simeonites, Shephatiah the son of Maachah;

17 *over* the Levites, ᴿHashabiah the son of Kemuel; over the Aaronites, Zadok; 1 Chr. 26:30

18 *over* Judah, Elihu, *one* of David's brothers; *over* Issachar, Omri the son of Michael;

19 *over* Zebulun, Ishmaiah the son of Obadiah; *over* Naphtali, Jerimoth the son of Azriel;

20 *over* the children of Ephraim, Hoshea the son of Azaziah; *over* the half-tribe of Manasseh, Joel the son of Pedaiah;

21 *over* the half-*tribe* of Manasseh in Gilead, Iddo the son of Zechariah; *over* Benjamin, Jaasiel the son of Abner;

22 *over* Dan, Azarel the son of Jeroham. These *were* the leaders of the tribes of Israel.

23 But David did not take the number of those twenty years old and under, because ᴿthe Lᴏʀᴅ had said He would multiply Israel like the stars of the heavens.   [Deut. 6:3]

24 Joab the son of Zeruiah began a census, but he did not finish, for ᴿwrath came upon Israel because of this census; nor was the number recorded in the account of the chronicles of King David.   1 Chr. 21:1-7

Other State Officials

25 And Azmaveth the son of Adiel *was* over the king's treasuries; and Jehonathan the son of Uzziah *was* over the storehouses in the field, in the cities, in the villages, and in the fortresses.

26 Ezri the son of Chelub *was* over those who did the work of the field for tilling the ground.

27 And Shimei the Ramathite *was* over the vineyards, and Zabdi the Shiphmite *was* over the produce of the vineyards for the supply of wine.

28 Baal-Hanan the Gederite *was* over the olive trees and the sycamore trees that *were* in the lowlands, and Joash *was* over the store of oil.

29 And Shitrai the Sharonite *was* over the herds that fed in Sharon, and Shaphat the son of Adlai *was* over the herds *that were* in the valleys.

30 Obil the Ishmaelite *was* over the camels,

Jehdeiah the Meronothite *was* over the donkeys,

31 and Jaziz the ᴿHagrite *was* over the flocks. All these *were* the officials over King David's property.   1 Chr. 5:10

32 Also Jehonathan, David's uncle, *was* a counselor, a wise man, and a ᵀscribe; and Jehiel the ᵀson of Hachmoni *was* with the king's sons.   *secretary* • Or *Hachmonite*

33 ᴿAhithophel *was* the king's counselor, and ᴿHushai the Archite *was* the king's companion.   2 Sam. 15:12 • 2 Sam. 15:32-37

34 After Ahithophel *was* Jehoiada the son of Benaiah, then Abiathar. And the general of the king's army *was* ᴿJoab.   1 Chr. 11:6

Solomon Instructed to Build the Temple

28 Now David assembled at Jerusalem all the leaders of Israel: the officers of the tribes and the captains of the divisions who served the king, the captains over thousands and captains over hundreds, and ᴿthe stewards over all the substance and ᵀpossessions of the king and of his sons, with the officials, the valiant men, and all ᴿthe mighty men of valor.   1 Chr. 27:25 • Or *livestock* • 1 Chr. 11:10-47

2 Then King David rose to his feet and said, "Hear me, my brethren and my people: ᴿI *had* it in my heart to build a house of rest for the ark of the covenant of the Lᴏʀᴅ, and for ᴿthe footstool of our God, and had made preparations to build it.   2 Sam. 7:2 • Ps. 99:5; 132:7

3 "But God said to me, 'You shall not build a house for My name, because you *have been* a man of war and have shed blood.'

4 "However the Lᴏʀᴅ God of Israel chose me above all the house of my father to be king over Israel forever, for He has chosen Judah *to be* the ruler. And of the house of Judah, ᴿthe house of my father, and among the sons of my father, He was pleased with me to make *me* king over all Israel. 1 Sam. 16:1

5 "And of all my sons (for the Lᴏʀᴅ has given me many sons) ᴿHe has chosen my son Solomon to sit on the throne of the kingdom of the Lᴏʀᴅ over Israel.   1 Chr. 22:9; 29:1

6 "Now He said to me, 'It is ᴿyour son Solomon *who* shall build My house and My courts; for I have chosen him *to be* My son, and I will be his Father.   2 Sam. 7:13, 14

7 'Moreover ᴿI will establish his kingdom forever, ᴮif he is steadfast to observe My commandments and My judgments, as it is this day.'   Matt. 1:6 • 1 Chr. 22:13

8 "Now therefore, in the sight of all Israel, the assembly of the Lᴏʀᴅ, and in the hearing of our God, be careful to seek out all the commandments of the Lᴏʀᴅ your God, that you may possess this good land, and leave *it* as an inheritance for your children after you forever.

9 "As for you, my son Solomon, ᴿknow the God of your father, and serve Him with a

loyal heart and with a willing mind; for the LORD searches all hearts and understands all the intent of the thoughts. If you seek Him, He will be found by you; but if you forsake Him, He will cast you off forever. [John 17:3]

10 "Consider now, ^Rfor the LORD has chosen you to build a house for the sanctuary; be strong, and do it."   1 Chr. 22:13; 28:6

11 Then David gave his son Solomon ^Rthe plans for the vestibule, its houses, its treasuries, its upper chambers, its inner chambers, and the place of the mercy seat;   1 Chr. 28:19

12 and the plans for all that he had by the Spirit, of the courts of the house of the LORD, of all the chambers all around, ^Rof the treasuries of the house of God, and of the treasuries for the dedicated things;   1 Chr. 26:20, 28

13 also for the division of the priests and the ^RLevites, for all the work of the service of the house of the LORD, and for all the articles of service in the house of the LORD.   1 Chr. 23:6

14 He gave gold by weight for things of gold, for all articles used in every kind of service; also silver for all articles of silver by weight, for all articles used in every kind of service;

15 the weight for the ^Rlampstands of gold, and their lamps of gold, by weight for each lampstand and its lamps; for the lampstands of silver by weight, for the lampstand and its lamps, according to the use of each lampstand.   Ex. 25:31-39

16 And by weight he gave gold for the tables of the showbread, for each ^Rtable, and silver for the tables of silver;   1 Kin. 7:48

17 also pure gold for the forks, the basins, the pitchers of pure gold, and the golden bowls—he gave gold by weight for every bowl; and for the silver bowls, silver by weight for every bowl;

18 and refined gold by weight for the altar of incense, and for the construction of the chariot, that is, the gold ^Rcherubim that spread their wings and overshadowed the ark of the covenant of the LORD.   Ex. 25:18-22

19 "All this," said David, "the LORD made me understand in writing, by His hand upon me, all the ^Tworks of these plans."   details

20 And David said to his son Solomon, ^R"Be strong and of good courage, and do it; do not fear nor be dismayed, for the LORD God—my God—will be with you. ^RHe will not leave you nor forsake you, until you have finished all the work for the service of the house of the LORD.   1 Chr. 22:13 • Josh. 1:5

21 "Here are ^Rthe divisions of the priests and the Levites for all the service of the house of God; and ^Revery willing craftsman will be with you for all manner of workmanship, for every kind of service; also the leaders and all the people will be completely at your command."   1 Chr. 24—26 • Ex. 35:25-35; 36:1, 2

Offerings for Building the Temple

29 Furthermore King David said to all the assembly: "My son Solomon, whom alone God has chosen, is young and inexperienced; and the work is great, because the temple is not for man but for the LORD God.

2 "Now for the house of my God I have prepared with all my might: gold for things to be made of gold, silver for things of silver, bronze for things of bronze, iron for things of iron, wood for things of wood, ^Ronyx stones, stones to be set, glistening stones of various colors, all kinds of precious stones, and marble slabs in abundance.   Is. 54:11, 12

3 "Moreover, because I have set my affection on the house of my God, I have given to the house of my God, over and above all that I have prepared for the holy house, my own special treasure of gold and silver:

4 ^T"three thousand talents of gold, of the gold of ^ROphir, and ^Tseven thousand talents of refined silver, to overlay the walls of the houses; $17.280 billion • 1 Kin. 9:28 • $2.68 billion

5 "the gold for things of gold and the silver for things of silver, and for all kinds of work to be done by the hands of craftsmen. Who then is ^Rwilling to ^Tconsecrate himself this day to the LORD?"   [2 Cor. 8:5, 12] • Lit. fill his hand

6 Then the leaders of the fathers' houses, leaders of the tribes of Israel, the captains of thousands and of hundreds, with the officers over the king's work, offered willingly.

7 They gave for the work of the house of God five thousand talents and ten thousand darics of gold, ten thousand talents of silver, eighteen thousand talents of bronze, and one hundred thousand talents of iron.

8 And whoever had precious stones gave them to the treasury of the house of the LORD, into the hand of ^RJehiel^T the Gershonite.   1 Chr. 23:8 • Possibly the same as Jehieli, 1 Chr. 26:21, 22

9 Then the people rejoiced, for they had offered willingly, because with a loyal heart they had ^Roffered willingly to the LORD; and King David also rejoiced greatly.   2 Cor. 9:7

David's Praise to God

10 Therefore David blessed the LORD before all the assembly; and David said:

"Blessed are You, LORD God of Israel,
    our Father, forever and ever.
11 ^RYours, O LORD, is the greatness,
    The power and the glory,   1 Tim. 1:17
    The victory and the majesty;
    For all that is in heaven and in earth is
      Yours;
    Yours is the kingdom, O LORD,
    And You are exalted as head over all.
12 ^RBoth riches and honor come from You,
    And You reign over all.   Rom. 11:36
    In Your hand is power and might;

In Your hand *it is* to make great
And to give strength to all.

13 "Now therefore, our God,
  We thank You
  And praise Your glorious name.
14 But who *am* I, and who *are* my people,
  That we should be able to offer so
    willingly as this?
  For all things *come* from You,
  And of Your own we have given You.
15 For ᴿwe *are* ᵀaliens and ᵀpilgrims before
    You,   Heb. 11:13, 14 • *sojourners • transients*
  As *were* all our fathers;
  ᴿOur days on earth *are* as a shadow,
  And without hope.   Job 14:2

16 "O Lᴏʀᴅ our God, all this abundance
that we have prepared to build You a house
for Your holy name is from Your hand, and *is*
all Your own.
17 "I know also, my God, that You test the
heart and have pleasure in uprightness. As
for me, in the uprightness of my heart I have
willingly offered all these *things*; and now
with joy I have seen Your people, who are
present here to offer willingly to You.
18 "O Lᴏʀᴅ God of Abraham, Isaac, and
Israel, our fathers, keep this forever in the
intent of the thoughts of the heart of Your
people, and fix their heart toward You.
19 "And ᴿgive my son Solomon a loyal
heart to keep Your commandments and Your
testimonies and Your statutes, to do all *these*
things, and to build the ᵀtemple for which I
have made provision."   [1 Chr. 28:9] • Lit. *palace*
20 Then David said to all the assembly,
"Now bless the Lᴏʀᴅ your God." So all the
assembly blessed the Lᴏʀᴅ God of their fathers, and bowed their heads and prostrated
themselves before the Lᴏʀᴅ and the king.

Solomon Anointed King

21 And they made sacrifices to the Lᴏʀᴅ
and offered burnt offerings to the Lᴏʀᴅ on
the next day: a thousand bulls, a thousand
rams, a thousand lambs, with their drink
offerings, and ᴿsacrifices in abundance for all
Israel.   1 Kin. 8:62, 63
22 So they ate and drank before the Lᴏʀᴅ
with great gladness on that day. And they
made Solomon the son of David king the
second time, and anointed *him* before the
Lᴏʀᴅ *to be* the leader, and Zadok *to be* priest.
23 Then Solomon sat on the throne of the
Lᴏʀᴅ as king instead of David his father, and
prospered; and all Israel obeyed him.
24 All the leaders and the mighty men, and
also all the sons of King David, ᵀsubmitted
themselves to King Solomon.   Lit. *gave the hand*
25 So the Lᴏʀᴅ exalted Solomon exceedingly in the sight of all Israel, and ᴿbestowed
on him *such* royal majesty as had not been
on any king before him in Israel.   1 Kin. 3:13

The Close of David's Reign

26 Thus David the son of Jesse reigned over
all Israel.
27 ᴿAnd the period that he reigned over
Israel *was* forty years; ᴿseven years he
reigned in Hebron, and thirty-three *years* he
reigned in Jerusalem.   1 Kin. 2:11 • 2 Sam. 5:5
28 So he ᴿdied in a good old age, ᴿfull of
days and riches and honor; and Solomon his
son reigned in his place.   Gen. 25:8 • 1 Chr. 23:1
29 Now the acts of King David, first and
last, indeed they *are* written in the book of
Samuel the seer, in the book of Nathan the
prophet, and in the book of Gad the seer,
30 with all his reign and his might, ᴿand the
events that happened to him, to Israel, and to
all the kingdoms of the lands.   Dan. 2:21; 4:23, 25

THE SECOND BOOK OF THE
Chronicles

AUTHORSHIP. Jewish tradition has always assigned the authorship of 1 and 2 Chronicles to Ezra. This external evidence is strongly confirmed by two points of internal evidence: (1) The style of the books of Ezra and Chronicles are so similar that critics agree they must have been written by the same person. (2) The last two verses of 2 Chronicles are repeated in the beginning of Ezra. (See the introduction to 1 Chronicles for further details.)

CONTEXT. At the time when this book was written the people of Israel had reached a new crisis in their national history. When Ezra returned to Judea in 458 B.C. the monarchy had been in abeyance for 130 years. Nearly eighty years had passed since the first of those who returned from the captivity had begun to reestablish the nation in Jerusalem, but they and their descendants had accepted their position as subjects of the Persian government, and their civil government was on the same footing as that of a conquered people. It was for such an altered condition of the Hebrew people that Ezra rewrote the later history of their race.

HOW 2 CHRONICLES FITS INTO THE BIBLE. The author records events of the same period as that covered by the books of Samuel and Kings, and sometimes uses the same language; and so his work is properly placed where it is in the English Bible. However, he writes from a different standpoint and his work has a distinct character of its own.

SUMMARY STATEMENT. In 2 Chronicles God places before the Jews such an aspect of their past history as would strengthen the religious element of their nationality and teach them that their highest glory is the special sovereignty of God over them.

HOW 2 CHRONICLES FITS TOGETHER. 2 Chronicles divides into two parts, recording the history of Solomon in chapters 1—9 and the history of the Judahite kings in chapters 10—36. It closes with the edict of Cyrus.

The most effective teaching is by repetition. God is trying, again and again to remind the nation of Israel of their heritage, where they had been and where they could be. A strong appeal for national return to God is given in 7:14— "If My people who are called by My name will humble themselves, and pray and seek My face, and turn from their wicked ways, then I will hear from heaven, and will forgive their sin and heal their land."

—H.F.C.

Solomon Requests Wisdom

NOW ᴿSolomon the son of David was strengthened in his kingdom, and the LORD his God *was* with him and ᴿexalted him exceedingly.   1 Kin. 2:46 • 1 Chr. 29:25

2 And Solomon spoke to all Israel, to ᴿthe captains of thousands and of hundreds, to the judges, and to every leader in all Israel, the heads of the fathers' *houses*.   1 Chr. 27:1-34

3 Then Solomon, and all the assembly with him, went to the high place that *was* at Gibeon; for the tabernacle of meeting with God was there, which Moses the servant of the LORD had made in the wilderness.

4 ᴿBut David had brought up the ark of God from Kirjath Jearim to *the place* David had prepared for it, for he had pitched a tent for it at Jerusalem.   2 Sam. 6:2-17

5 Now the bronze altar that Bezalel the son of Uri, the son of Hur, had made, *he put before the tabernacle of the LORD; Solomon and the assembly sought Him *there*.

6 And Solomon went up there to the bronze altar before the LORD, which *was* at the tabernacle of meeting, and ᴿoffered a thousand burnt offerings on it.   1 Kin. 3:4

7 ᴿOn that night God appeared to Solomon, and said to him, "Ask! What shall I give you?"   1 Kin. 3:5-14; 9:2

8 And Solomon said to God: "You have shown great mercy to David my father, and have made me ᴿking in his place.   1 Chr. 28:5

9 "Now, O LORD God, let Your promise to David my father be established, for You have made me king over a people like the ᴿdust of the earth in multitude.   Gen. 13:16

10 ᴿ"Now give me wisdom and knowledge, that I may ᴿgo out and come in before this people; for who can judge this great people of Yours?"   1 Kin. 3:9 • Deut. 31:2

11 ᴿThen God said to Solomon: "Because this was in your heart, and you have not asked riches or wealth or honor or the life of your enemies, nor have you asked long life— but have asked wisdom and knowledge for yourself, that you may judge My people over whom I have made you king—   1 Kin. 3:11-13

1:5 Some authorities *it was there*

12 "wisdom and knowledge *are* granted to you; and I will give you riches and wealth and honor, such as ᴿnone of the kings have had who *were* before you, nor shall any after you have the like."   2 Chr. 9:22

Solomon's Military and Economic Power

13 So Solomon came to Jerusalem from ᵀthe high place that *was* at Gibeon, from before the tabernacle of meeting, and reigned over Israel.   Place for worship

14 ᴿAnd Solomon gathered chariots and horsemen; he had one thousand four hundred chariots and twelve thousand horsemen, whom he stationed in the chariot cities and with the king in Jerusalem.   1 Kin. 10:26

15 ᴿAlso the king made silver and gold as common in Jerusalem as stones, and he made cedars as abundant as the sycamores which *are* in the lowland.   2 Chr. 9:27

16 And Solomon had horses imported from Egypt and Keveh; the king's merchants bought them in Keveh at the *current* price.

17 They also acquired and imported from Egypt a chariot for six hundred *shekels* of silver, and a horse for one hundred and fifty; thus, ᵀthrough their agents, they exported them to all the kings of the Hittites and the kings of Syria.   Lit. *by their hands*

Solomon Prepares to Build the Temple

2 Then Solomon ᴿdetermined to build a temple for the name of the Lᴏʀᴅ, and a royal house for himself.   1 Kin. 5:5

2 Solomon selected seventy thousand men to bear burdens, eighty thousand to quarry *stone* in the mountains, and three thousand six hundred to oversee them.

3 Then Solomon sent to ᵀHiram king of Tyre, saying: Heb. *Huram*, 1 Kin. 5:1

ᴿAs you have dealt with David my father, and sent him cedars to build himself a house to dwell in, *so deal with me.*   1 Chr. 14:1

4 Behold, I am building a temple for the name of the Lᴏʀᴅ my God, to dedicate *it* to Him, to burn before Him ᵀsweet incense, for the continual showbread, for the burnt offerings morning and evening, on the Sabbaths, on the New Moons, and on the ᵀset feasts of the Lᴏʀᴅ our God. This *is an ordinance* forever to Israel.   *incense of spices · appointed*

5 And the temple which I build *will be* great, for ᴿour God is greater than all gods.   Ps. 135:5

6 But who is able to build Him a temple, since heaven and the heaven of heavens cannot contain Him? Who *am* I then, that I should build Him a temple, except to burn sacrifice before Him?

7 Therefore send me at once a man skillful to work in gold and silver, in bronze and iron, in purple and crimson and blue, who has skill to engrave with the skillful men who are with me in Judah and Jerusalem, ᴿwhom David my father provided.   1 Chr. 22:15

8 Also send me cedar and cypress and algum logs from Lebanon, for I know that your servants have skill to cut timber in Lebanon; and indeed my servants *will be* with your servants,

9 to prepare timber for me in abundance, for the ᵀtemple which I am about to build *shall be* great and wonderful.   *house*

10 ᴿAnd indeed I will give to your   1 Kin. 5:11 servants, the woodsmen who cut timber, twenty thousand kors of ground wheat, twenty thousand kors of barley, twenty thousand baths of wine, and twenty thousand baths of oil.

11 Then Hiram king of Tyre answered in writing, which he sent to Solomon:

ᴿBecause the Lᴏʀᴅ loves His people, He has made you king over them.   2 Chr. 9:8

12 ᵀHiram also said: Heb. *Huram*, 1 Kin. 5:1

ᴿBlessed *be* the Lᴏʀᴅ God of Israel, ᴿwho made heaven and earth, for He has given King David a wise son, endowed with prudence and understanding, who will build a temple for the Lᴏʀᴅ and a royal house for himself!   1 Kin. 5:7 · Rev. 10:6

13 And now I have sent a skillful man, endowed with understanding, *Huram my *master *craftsman*

14 ᴿ(the son of a woman of the daughters of Dan, and his father was a man of Tyre), skilled to work in gold and silver, bronze and iron, stone and wood, purple and blue, fine linen and crimson, and to make any engraving and to accomplish any plan which may be given to him, with your skillful men and with the skillful men of my lord David your father.   1 Kin. 7:13, 14

15 Now therefore, the wheat, the barley, the oil, and the wine which ᴿmy lord has spoken of, let him send to his servants.   2 Chr. 2:10

16 And we will cut wood from Lebanon, as much as you need; we will bring it to you in rafts by sea to ᵀJoppa, and you will carry it up to Jerusalem.   Heb. *Japho*

17 ᴿThen Solomon numbered all the aliens who *were* in the land of Israel, after the census in which ᴿDavid his father had numbered them; and there were found to be one

2:13 *Hiram*, 1 Kin. 7:13 • Lit. *father*, 1 Kin. 7:13, 14

hundred and fifty-three thousand six hundred. 1 Kin. 5:13 • 1 Chr. 22:2

18 And he made ᴿseventy thousand of them bearers of burdens, eighty thousand stonecutters in the mountain, and three thousand six hundred overseers to make the people work. 2 Chr. 2:2

Solomon Builds the Temple

3 Now Solomon began to build the house of the LORD at Jerusalem on Mount Moriah, where *the LORD had appeared to his father David, at the place that David had prepared on the threshing floor of ᴿOrnan* the Jebusite. 1 Chr. 21:18; 22:1

2 And he began to build on the second *day* of the second month in the fourth year of his reign.

3 This is the foundation which Solomon laid for building the house of God: The length *was* sixty cubits (by cubits according to the former measure) and the width twenty cubits.

4 And the vestibule that *was* in front of *the sanctuary* was twenty cubits long across the width of the house, and the height *was* *one hundred and twenty. He overlaid the inside with pure gold.

5 The larger room he paneled with cypress which he overlaid with fine gold, and he carved palm trees and chainwork on it.

6 And he decorated the house with precious stones for beauty, and the gold *was* gold from Parvaim.

7 He also overlaid the house—the beams and doorposts, its walls and doors—with gold; and he carved cherubim on the walls.

8 And he made the ᴿMost Holy Place. Its length was according to the width of the house, ᵀtwenty cubits, and its width twenty cubits. He overlaid it with ᵀsix hundred talents of fine gold. Ex. 26:33 • 30 ft. • $3.45 billion

9 The weight of the nails *was* ᵀfifty shekels of gold; and he overlaid the upper ᴿarea with gold. $96,000 • 1 Chr. 28:11

10 ᴿIn the Most Holy Place he made two cherubim, fashioned by carving, and overlaid them with gold. 1 Kin. 6:23-28

11 The wings of the cherubim *were* twenty cubits in *overall* length: one wing *of the one cherub was* five cubits, touching the wall of the room, and the other wing *was* five cubits, touching the wing of the other cherub;

12 *one* wing of the other cherub *was* ᵀfive cubits, touching the wall of the room, and the other wing *also was* five cubits, touching the wing of the other cherub. 7.5 ft.

13 The wings of these cherubim spanned ᵀtwenty cubits overall. They stood on their feet, and they faced inward. 30 ft.

14 And he made the ᴿveil of blue, purple, crimson, and fine linen, and wove cherubim into it. Ex. 26:31

15 Also he made in front of the ᵀtemple ᴿtwo pillars *thirty-five cubits ᵀhigh, and the capital that *was* on the top of each of *them* was five cubits. Lit. *house* • 1 Kin. 7:15-20 • Lit. *long*

16 He made wreaths of chainwork, as in the inner sanctuary, and put *them* on top of the pillars; and he made ᴿone hundred pomegranates, and put *them* on the wreaths of chainwork. 1 Kin. 7:20

17 Then he ᴿset up the pillars before the temple, one on the right hand and the other on the left; he called the name of the one on the right hand Jachin, and the name of the one on the left Boaz. 1 Kin. 7:21

Furnishings of the Temple

4 Moreover he made a bronze altar: twenty cubits *was* its length, twenty cubits its width, and ten cubits its height.

2 ᴿThen he made the ᵀSea of cast *bronze*, ten cubits from one brim to the other; *it was* completely round. Its height *was* five cubits, and a line of thirty cubits measured its circumference. 1 Kin. 7:23-26 • Great laver or basin

3 ᴿAnd under it *was* the likeness of oxen encircling it all around, ten to a ᵀcubit, all the way around the Sea. The oxen *were* cast in two rows, when it was cast. 1 Kin. 7:24-26 • 18 in.

4 It stood on twelve ᴿoxen: three looking toward the north, three looking toward the west, three looking toward the south, and three looking toward the east; the Sea *was* set upon them, and all their back parts *pointed* inward. 1 Kin. 7:25

5 It *was* a handbreadth thick; and its brim was shaped like the brim of a cup, *like* a lily blossom. It contained *three thousand baths.

6 He also made ten lavers, and put five on the right side and five on the left, to wash in them; such things as they offered for the burnt offering they would wash in them, but the Sea *was* for the priests to wash in.

7 ᴿAnd he made ten lampstands of gold ᴿaccording to their design, and set *them* in the temple, five on the right side and five on the left. 1 Kin. 7:49 • Ex. 25:31

8 ᴿHe also made ten tables, and placed *them* in the temple, five on the right side and five on the left. And he made one hundred ᴿbowls of gold. 1 Kin. 7:48 • 1 Chr. 28:17

9 Furthermore ᴿhe made the court of the priests, and the ᴿgreat court and doors for the court; and he overlaid these doors with bronze. 1 Kin. 6:36 • 2 Kin. 21:5

3:1 Lit. *He,* following MT, Vg.; LXX *the LORD;* Tg. *the Angel of the Lord* • *Araunah,* 2 Sam. 24:16

3:4 *the holy place,* the main room of the temple, 1 Kin. 6:3 • So with MT, LXX, Vg.; Arab., some LXX mss., Syr. *twenty*

3:15 *eighteen,* 1 Kin. 7:15; 2 Kin. 25:17; Jer. 52:21

4:5 About 8,000 gallons; *two thousand,* 1 Kin. 7:26

10 ᴿHe set the Sea on the right side, toward the southeast.   1 Kin. 7:39

11 Then ᴿHuram made the pots and the shovels and the bowls. So Huram finished doing the work that he was to do for King Solomon for the house of God: 1 Kin. 7:40-51

12 the two pillars and ᴿthe bowl-shaped capitals *that were* on top of the two pillars; the two networks covering the two bowl-shaped capitals which *were* on top of the pillars;   1 Kin. 7:41

13 ᴿfour hundred pomegranates for the two networks (two rows of pomegranates for each network, to cover the two bowl-shaped capitals that *were* on the pillars);   1 Kin. 7:20

14 he also made ᴿcarts and the lavers on the carts;   1 Kin. 7:27, 43

15 one Sea and twelve oxen under it;

16 also the pots, the shovels, the forks—and all their articles Huram his ᵀmaster *craftsman* made of burnished bronze for King Solomon for the house of the Lᴏʀᴅ.   Lit. *father*

17 In the plain of Jordan the king had them cast in clay molds, between Succoth and ᵀZeredah.   *Zaretan,* 1 Kin. 7:46

18 And Solomon had all these articles made in such great abundance that the weight of the bronze was not determined.

19 Thus Solomon had all the furnishings made for the house of God: the altar of gold and the tables on which *was* the showbread;

20 the lampstands with their lamps of pure gold, to burn ᴿin the prescribed manner in front of the inner sanctuary,   Ex. 27:20, 21

21 with ᴿthe flowers and the lamps and the wick-trimmers of gold, of purest gold; Ex. 25:31

22 the trimmers, the bowls, the ladles, and the censers of pure gold. As for the entry of the ᵀsanctuary, its inner doors to the Most Holy *Place*, and the doors of the main hall of the temple, *were* gold.   Lit. *house*

5 So all the work that Solomon had done for the house of the Lᴏʀᴅ was finished; and Solomon brought in the things which his father David had dedicated: the silver and the gold and all the furnishings. And he put *them* in the treasuries of the house of God.

The Ark Brought into the Temple

2 ᴿNow Solomon assembled the elders of Israel and all the heads of the tribes, the chief fathers of the children of Israel, in Jerusalem, that they might bring the ark of the covenant of the Lᴏʀᴅ up ᴿfrom the City of David, which *is* Zion.   1 Kin. 8:1-9 · 2 Sam. 6:12

3 ᴿTherefore all the men of Israel assembled with the king at the feast, which *was* in the seventh month.   1 Kin. 8:2

4 So all the elders of Israel came, and the ᴿLevites took up the ark.   1 Chr. 15:2, 15

5 Then they brought up the ark, the tabernacle of meeting, and all the holy furnishings that *were* in the tabernacle. The priests and the Levites brought them up.

6 Also King Solomon, and all the congregation of Israel who were assembled with him before the ark, were sacrificing sheep and oxen that could not be counted or numbered for multitude.

7 Then the priests brought in the ark of the covenant of the Lᴏʀᴅ to its place, into the inner sanctuary of the *temple, to the Most Holy *Place*, under the wings of the cherubim.

8 For the cherubim spread *their* wings over the place of the ark, and the cherubim overshadowed the ark and its poles.

9 The poles extended so that the ends of the poles of the ark could be seen from *the holy place*, in front of the inner sanctuary; but they could not be seen from outside. And ᵀthey are there to this day.   Lit. *it is*

10 Nothing was in the ark except the two tablets which Moses ᴿput *there* at Horeb, ᵀwhen the Lᴏʀᴅ made *a covenant* with the children of Israel, when they had come out of Egypt.   Deut. 10:2, 5 · Or *where*

11 And it came to pass when the priests came out of the Most Holy *Place* (for all the priests who *were* present had ᵀsanctified themselves, without keeping to their ᴿdivisions),   *consecrated* · 1 Chr. 24:1-5

12 and the Levites *who were* the singers, all those of Asaph and Heman and Jeduthun, with their sons and their brethren, stood at the east end of the altar, clothed in white linen, having cymbals, stringed instruments and harps, and with them one hundred and twenty priests sounding with trumpets—

13 indeed it came to pass, when the trumpeters and singers *were* as one, to make one sound to be heard in praising and thanking the Lᴏʀᴅ, and when they lifted up their voice with the trumpets and cymbals and instruments of music, and praised the Lᴏʀᴅ, *saying*:

ᴿ"*For He is* good,
For His mercy *endures* forever,"   Ps. 106:1

that the house, the house of the Lᴏʀᴅ, was filled with a cloud,

14 so that the priests could not continue ministering because of the cloud; for the glory of the Lᴏʀᴅ filled the house of God.

6 Then Solomon spoke:
"The Lᴏʀᴅ said
He would dwell in the dark cloud.

2 I have surely built You an exalted house,
And ᴿa place for You to dwell in forever."   2 Chr. 7:12

Solomon's Speech upon Completion of the Work

3 Then the king turned around and blessed the whole assembly of Israel, while all the assembly of Israel was standing.

5:7 Lit. *house*

4 And he said: "Blessed *be* the LORD God of Israel, who has fulfilled with His hands *what* He spoke with His mouth to my father David, ^Rsaying,   1 Chr. 17:5

5 'Since the day that I brought My people out of the land of Egypt, I have chosen no city from any tribe of Israel *in which* to build a house, that My name might be there, nor did I choose any man to be a ruler over My people Israel.

6 'Yet I have chosen Jerusalem, that My name may be there, and I have chosen David to be over My people Israel.'

7 "Now ^Rit was in the heart of my father David to build a *temple for the name of the LORD God of Israel.   2 Sam. 7:2

8 "But the LORD said to my father David, 'Whereas it was in your heart to build a temple for My name, you did well in that it was in your heart.

9 'Nevertheless you shall not build the temple, but your son who will come from your body, he shall build the temple for My ^Rname.'   1 Chr. 28:3-6

10 "So the LORD has fulfilled His word which He spoke, and I have filled the position of my father David, and ^Rsit on the throne of Israel, as the LORD promised; and I have built the temple for the name of the LORD God of Israel.   1 Kin. 2:12; 10:9

11 "And there I have put the ark, ^Rin which *is* the covenant of the LORD which He made with the children of Israel."   2 Chr. 5:7-10

Solomon's Prayer of Dedication

12 Then *Solomon stood before the altar of the LORD in the presence of all the assembly of Israel, and spread out his hands

13 (for Solomon had made a bronze platform five cubits long, five cubits wide, and three cubits high, and had set it in the midst of the court; and he stood on it, knelt down on his knees before all the assembly of Israel, and spread out his hands toward heaven);

14 and he said: "LORD God of Israel, ^R*there is* no God in heaven or on earth like You, who keep Your ^Rcovenant and mercy with Your servants who walk before You with all their hearts.   [Ex. 15:11] • [Deut. 7:9]

15 ^R"You have kept what You promised Your servant David my father; You have both spoken with Your mouth and fulfilled *it* with Your hand, as *it is* this day.   1 Chr. 22:9, 10

16 "Therefore, LORD God of Israel, now keep what You promised Your servant David my father, saying, ^R'You shall not fail to have a man sit before Me on the throne of Israel, ^Ronly if your sons take heed to their way, that they walk in My law as you have walked before Me.'   2 Chr. 7:18 • Ps. 132:12

6:7 Lit. *house,* and so in vv. 8–10
6:12 Lit. *he*

17 "And now, O LORD God of Israel, let Your word come true, which You have spoken to Your servant David.

18 "But will God indeed dwell with men on the earth? Behold, heaven and the heaven of heavens cannot contain You. How much less this ^Ttemple which I have built!   Lit. *house*

19 "Yet regard the prayer of Your servant and his supplication, O LORD my God, and listen to the cry and the prayer which Your servant is praying before You:

20 "that Your eyes may be open toward this temple day and night, toward the place where *You* said *You would* put Your name, that You may hear the prayer which Your servant makes ^Rtoward this place.   Dan. 6:10

21 "And may You hear the supplications of Your servant and of Your people Israel, when they pray toward this place. Hear from heaven Your dwelling place, and when You hear, ^Rforgive.   [Mic. 7:18]

22 "If anyone sins against his neighbor, and is forced to take an ^Roath, and comes *and* takes an oath before Your altar in this temple,   Ex. 22:8-11

23 "then hear from heaven, and act, and judge Your servants, bringing retribution on the wicked by bringing his way on his own head, and justifying the righteous by giving him according to his ^Rrighteousness.   [Job 34:11]

24 "Or if Your people Israel are defeated before an ^Renemy because they have sinned against You, and return and confess Your name, and pray and make supplication before You in this temple,   2 Kin. 21:14, 15

25 "then hear from heaven and forgive the sin of Your people Israel, and bring them back to the land which You gave to them and their fathers.

26 "When the ^Rheavens are shut up and there is no rain because they have sinned against You, when they pray toward this place and confess Your name, and turn from their sin because You afflict them,   1 Kin. 17:1

27 "then hear *in* heaven, and forgive the sin of Your servants, Your people Israel, that You may teach them the good way in which they should walk; and send rain on Your land which You have given to Your people as an inheritance.

28 "When there is famine in the land, pestilence or blight or mildew, locusts or grasshoppers; when their enemies besiege them in the land of their cities; whatever plague or whatever sickness *there is;*

29 "whatever prayer, whatever supplication is *made* by anyone, or by all Your people Israel, when each one knows his own burden and his own grief, and spreads out his hands to this temple:

30 "then hear from heaven Your dwelling place, and forgive, and give to everyone according to all his ways, whose heart You

know (for You alone ᴿknow the ᴿhearts of the sons of men), [1 Chr. 28:9] • [1 Sam. 16:7]

31 "that they may fear You, to walk in Your ways as long as they live in the land which You gave to our fathers.

32 "Moreover, concerning a foreigner, ᴿwho is not of Your people Israel, but has come from a far country for the sake of Your great name and Your mighty hand and Your outstretched arm, when they come and pray in this temple; John 12:20

33 "then hear from heaven Your dwelling place, and do according to all for which the foreigner calls to You, that all peoples of the earth may know Your name and fear You, as *do* Your people Israel, and that they may know that this temple which I have built is called by Your name.

34 "When Your people go out to battle against their enemies, wherever You send them, and when they pray to You toward this city which You have chosen and the temple which I have built for Your name,

35 "then hear from heaven their prayer and their supplication, and maintain their cause.

36 "When they sin against You (for *there is* ᴿno one who does not sin), and You become angry with them and deliver them to the enemy, and they take them ᴿcaptive to a land far or near; [Rom. 3:9, 19; 5:12] • Deut. 28:63-68

37 "yet when they ᵀcome to themselves in the land where they were carried captive, and repent, and make supplication to You in the land of their captivity, saying, 'We have sinned, we have done wrong, and have committed wickedness'; Lit. *bring back to their hearts*

38 "and *when* they return to You with all their heart and with all their soul in the land of their captivity, where they have been carried captive, and pray toward their land which You gave to their fathers, the city which You have chosen, and toward the temple which I have built for Your name:

39 "then hear from heaven Your dwelling place their prayer and their supplications, and maintain their cause, and forgive Your people who have sinned against You.

40 "Now, my God, I pray, let Your eyes be ᴿopen and *let* Your ears *be* attentive to the prayer *made* in this place. 2 Chr. 6:20

41 "Now ᴿ therefore, Ps. 132:8-10, 16
Arise, O Lᴏʀᴅ God, to Your ᴿresting
place, 1 Chr. 28:2
You and the ark of Your strength.
Let Your priests, O Lᴏʀᴅ God, be
clothed with salvation,
And let Your saints ᴿrejoice in
goodness. Neh. 9:25

42 "O Lᴏʀᴅ God, do not turn away the face of Your Anointed;
ᴿRemember the mercies of Your servant David." Ps. 89:49; 132:1, 8-10

Solomon Dedicates the Temple

7 When Solomon had finished praying, fire came down from heaven and consumed the burnt offering and the sacrifices; and the glory of the Lᴏʀᴅ filled the temple.

2 ᴿAnd the priests could not enter the house of the Lᴏʀᴅ, because the glory of the Lᴏʀᴅ had filled the Lᴏʀᴅ's house. 2 Chr. 5:14

3 When all the children of Israel saw how the fire came down, and the glory of the Lᴏʀᴅ on the temple, they bowed their faces to the ground on the pavement, and worshiped and praised the Lᴏʀᴅ, *saying:*

ᴿ"For *He is* good, Ps. 106:1; 136:1
For His mercy *endures* forever."

4 ᴿThen the king and all the people offered sacrifices before the Lᴏʀᴅ. 1 Kin. 8:62, 63

5 King Solomon offered a sacrifice of twenty-two thousand bulls and one hundred and twenty thousand sheep. So the king and all the people dedicated the house of God.

6 ᴿAnd the priests attended to their services; the Levites also with instruments of the music of the Lᴏʀᴅ, which King David had made to praise the Lᴏʀᴅ, saying, ᴿ"For His mercy *endures* forever," whenever David offered praise by their ministry. ᴿThe priests sounded trumpets opposite them, while all Israel stood. 1 Chr. 15:16 • Ps. 106:1 • 2 Chr. 5:12

7 Furthermore Solomon consecrated the middle of the court that *was* in front of the house of the Lᴏʀᴅ; for there he offered burnt offerings and the fat of the peace offerings, because the bronze altar which Solomon had made was not able to receive the burnt offerings, the grain offerings, and the fat.

8 At that time Solomon kept the feast seven days, and all Israel with him, a very great assembly from the entrance of Hamath to *the Brook of Egypt.

9 And on the eighth day they held a ᴿsacred assembly, for they observed the dedication of the altar seven days, and the feast seven days. Lev. 23:36

10 ᴿOn the twenty-third day of the seventh month he sent the people away to their tents, joyful and glad of heart for the good that the Lᴏʀᴅ had done for David, for Solomon, and for His people Israel. 1 Kin. 8:66

11 Thus ᴿSolomon finished the house of the Lᴏʀᴅ and the king's house; and Solomon successfully accomplished all that came into his heart to make in the house of the Lᴏʀᴅ and in his own house. 1 Kin. 9:1

God's Second Appearance to Solomon

12 Then the Lᴏʀᴅ appeared to Solomon by night, and said to him: "I have heard your prayer, and have chosen this ᴿplace for Myself as a house of sacrifice. 2 Chr. 6:20

7:8 The *Shihor*, 1 Chr. 13:5

13 "When I shut up heaven and there is no rain, or command the locusts to devour the land, or send pestilence among My people,

14 "if My people who are ᴿcalled by My name will humble themselves, and pray and seek My face, and turn from their wicked ways, then I will hear from heaven, and will forgive their sin and heal their land.   [Is. 43:7]

15 "Now My eyes will be open and My ears attentive to prayer *made* in this place.

16 "For now I have chosen and ᵀsanctified this house, that My name may be there forever; and ᵀMy eyes and ᵀMy heart will be there perpetually.   *set apart • My attention • My concern*

17 ᴿ"As for you, if you walk before Me as your father David walked, and do according to all that I have commanded you, and if you keep My statutes and My judgments, 1 Kin. 9:4

18 "then I will establish the throne of your kingdom, as I covenanted with David your father, saying, ᴿ'You shall not fail *to have* a man as ruler in Israel.'   2 Chr. 6:16

19 ᴿ"But if you turn away and forsake My statutes and My commandments which I have set before you, and go and serve other gods, and worship them,   Lev. 26:14, 33

20 "then I will uproot them from My land which I have given them; and this house which I have sanctified for My name I will cast out of My sight, and will make it a proverb and a byword among all peoples.

21 "And *as for* this house, which is exalted, everyone who passes by it will be astonished and say, 'Why has the Lᴏʀᴅ done thus to this land and this house?'

22 "Then they will answer, 'Because they forsook the Lᴏʀᴅ God of their fathers, who brought them out of the land of Egypt, and embraced other gods, and worshiped them and served them; therefore He has brought all this calamity on them.' "

Solomon's Additional Achievements

8 It came to pass at the end of twenty years, when Solomon had built the house of the Lᴏʀᴅ and his own house,

2 that the cities which Hiram had given to Solomon, Solomon built them; and he settled the children of Israel there.

3 And Solomon went to Hamath Zobah and seized it.

4 ᴿHe also built Tadmor in the wilderness, and all the storage cities which he built in ᴿHamath.   1 Kin. 9:17, 18 • 1 Chr. 18:3, 9

5 He built Upper Beth Horon and ᴿLower Beth Horon, fortified cities *with* walls, gates, and bars,   1 Chr. 7:24

6 also Baalath and all the storage cities that Solomon had, and all the chariot cities and the cities of the cavalry, and all that Solomon desired to build in Jerusalem, in Lebanon, and in all the land of his dominion.

7 ᴿAll the people *who were* left of the Hittites, Amorites, Perizzites, Hivites, and Jebusites, who *were* not of Israel—   1 Kin. 9:20

8 that is, their descendants who were left in the land after them, whom the children of Israel did not destroy—from these Solomon raised forced labor, as it is to this day.

9 But Solomon did not make the children of Israel ᵀservants for his work. Some *were* men of war, captains of his officers, captains of his chariots, and his cavalry.   Or *slaves*

10 And others *were* chiefs of the officials of King Solomon: ᴿtwo hundred and fifty, who ruled over the people.   1 Kin. 9:23

11 Now Solomon brought the daughter of Pharaoh up from the City of David to the house he had built for her, for he said, "My wife shall not dwell in the house of David king of Israel, because the *places* to which the ark of the Lᴏʀᴅ has come are holy."

12 Then Solomon offered burnt offerings to the Lᴏʀᴅ on the altar of the Lᴏʀᴅ which he had built before the vestibule,

13 according to the daily rate, offering according to the commandment of Moses, for the Sabbaths, the New Moons, and the ᴿthree appointed yearly feasts—the Feast of Unleavened Bread, the Feast of Weeks, and the Feast of Tabernacles.   Ex. 23:14–17; 34:22, 23

14 And, according to the ᵀorder of David his father, he appointed the divisions of the priests for their service, ᴿthe Levites for their duties (to praise and serve before the priests) as the duty of each day required, and the ᴿgatekeepers by their divisions at each gate; for so David the man of God had commanded.   *ordinance* • 1 Chr. 25:1 • 1 Chr. 9:17; 26:1

15 They did not depart from the command of the king to the priests and Levites concerning any matter or concerning the ᴿtreasuries.   1 Chr. 26:20–28

16 Now all the work of Solomon was well-ordered *from the day of the foundation of the house of the Lᴏʀᴅ until it was finished. So the house of the Lᴏʀᴅ was completed.

17 Then Solomon went to Ezion Geber and *Elath on the seacoast, in the land of Edom.

18 ᴿAnd Hiram sent him ships by the hand of his servants, and servants who knew the sea. They went with the servants of Solomon to ᴿOphir, and acquired four hundred and fifty talents of gold from there, and brought it to King Solomon.   2 Chr. 9:10, 13 • 1 Chr. 29:4

The Queen of Sheba's Praise of Solomon

9 Now ᴿwhen the queen of Sheba heard of the fame of Solomon, she came to Jerusalem to test Solomon with hard questions, *having* a very great retinue, camels that bore spices, gold in abundance, and precious

8:16 So with LXX, Syr., Vg.; MT *as far as*
8:17 Heb. *Eloth*, 2 Kin. 14:22

stones; and when she came to Solomon, she spoke with him about all that was in her heart.   [Matt. 12:42]

2 So Solomon answered all her questions; there was nothing so difficult for Solomon that he could not explain it to her.

3 And when the queen of Sheba had seen the wisdom of Solomon, the house that he had built,

4 the food on his table, the seating of his servants, the service of his waiters and their apparel, his ᴿcupbearers and their apparel, and his entryway by which he went up to the house of the Lᴏʀᴅ, there was no more spirit in her.   Neh. 1:11

5 Then she said to the king: "It was a true report which I heard in my own land about your words and your wisdom.

6 "However I did not believe their words until I came and saw with my own eyes; and indeed the half of the greatness of your wisdom was not told me. You exceed the fame of which I heard.

7 "Happy are your men and happy are these your servants, who stand continually before you and hear your wisdom!

8 "Blessed be the Lᴏʀᴅ your God, who delighted in you, setting you on His throne to be king for the Lᴏʀᴅ your God! Because your God has loved Israel, to establish them forever, therefore He made you king over them, to do justice and righteousness."

9 And she gave the king ᵀone hundred and twenty talents of gold, spices in great abundance, and precious stones; there never were any spices such as those the queen of Sheba gave to King Solomon. $691,200,000

10 Also, the servants of Hiram and the servants of Solomon, ᴿwho brought gold from Ophir, brought ᵀalgum wood and precious stones.   2 Chr. 8:18 • Or almug, 1 Kin. 10:11, 12

11 And the king made walkways of the ᵀalgum wood for the house of the Lᴏʀᴅ and for the king's house, also harps and stringed instruments for singers; and there were none such as these seen before in the land of Judah.   Or almug, 1 Kin. 10:11, 12

12 Now King Solomon gave to the queen of Sheba all she desired, whatever she asked, much more than she had brought to the king. So she turned and went to her own country, she and her servants.

Solomon's Great Wealth

13 ᴿThe weight of gold that came to Solomon yearly was ᵀsix hundred and sixty-six talents of gold,   1 Kin. 10:14-29 • $3.83 billion

14 besides what the traveling merchants and traders brought. And all the kings of Arabia and governors of the country brought gold and silver to Solomon.

15 And King Solomon made two hundred large shields of hammered gold; six hundred shekels of hammered gold went into each shield.

16 He also made three hundred shields of hammered gold; *three hundred shekels of gold went into each shield. The king put them in the House of the Forest of Lebanon.

17 Moreover the king made a great throne of ivory, and overlaid it with pure gold.

18 The throne had six steps, with a footstool of gold, which were fastened to the throne; there were ᵀarmrests on either side of the place of the seat, and two lions stood beside the armrests.   Lit. hands

19 Twelve lions stood there, one on each side of the six steps; nothing like this had been made for any other kingdom.

20 All King Solomon's drinking vessels were gold, and all the vessels of the House of the Forest of Lebanon were pure gold. Not one was silver, for this was accounted as nothing in the days of Solomon.

21 For the king's ships went to Tarshish with the servants of *Hiram. Once every three years the *merchant ships came, bringing gold, silver, ivory, apes, and *monkeys.

22 So King Solomon surpassed all the kings of the earth in riches and wisdom.

23 And all the kings of the earth sought the presence of Solomon to hear his wisdom, which God had put in his heart.

24 Each man brought his present: articles of silver and gold, garments, armor, spices, horses, and mules, at a set rate year by year.

25 Solomon had four thousand stalls for horses and chariots, and twelve thousand horsemen whom he stationed in the chariot cities and with the king at Jerusalem.

26 So he reigned over all the kings from ᵀthe River to the land of the Philistines, as far as the border of Egypt.   The Euphrates

27 ᴿThe king made silver as common in Jerusalem as stones, and he made cedar trees ᴿas abundant as the sycamores which are in the lowland.   1 Kin. 10:27 • 2 Chr. 1:15-17

28 ᴿAnd they brought horses to Solomon from Egypt and from all lands.   2 Chr. 1:16

Death of Solomon

29 ᴿNow the rest of the acts of Solomon, first and last, are they not written in the book of Nathan the prophet, in the prophecy of ᴿAhijah the Shilonite, and in the visions of ᴿIddo the seer concerning Jeroboam the son of Nebat?   1 Kin. 11:41 • 1 Kin. 11:29 • 2 Chr. 12:15; 13:22

30 ᴿSolomon reigned in Jerusalem over all Israel forty years.   1 Kin. 4:21; 11:42, 43

31 Then Solomon ᵀrested with his fathers, and was buried in the City of David his

9:16 three minas, 1 Kin. 10:17
9:21 Heb. Huram • Lit. ships of Tarshish, deep-sea vessels • Or peacocks

father. And Rehoboam his son reigned in his place.   *Died and joined his ancestors*

The Revolt Against Rehoboam

10 And ᴿRehoboam went to Shechem, for all Israel had gone to Shechem to make him king.   1 Kin. 12:1-20

2 So it happened, when Jeroboam the son of Nebat heard *it* (he was in Egypt, where he had fled from the presence of King Solomon), that Jeroboam returned from Egypt.

3 Then they sent for him and called him. And Jeroboam and all Israel came and spoke to Rehoboam, saying,

4 "Your father made our yoke heavy; now therefore, lighten the burdensome service of your father and his heavy yoke which he put on us, and we will serve you."

5 So he said to them, "Come back to me after three days." And the people departed.

6 Then King Rehoboam consulted the elders who stood before his father Solomon while he still lived, saying, "How do you advise *me* to answer these people?"

7 And they spoke to him, saying, "If you are kind to these people, and please them, and speak good words to them, they will be your servants forever."

8 ᴿBut he rejected the advice which the elders had given him, and consulted the young men who had grown up with him, who stood before him.   1 Kin. 12:8-11

9 And he said to them, "What advice do you give? How should we answer this people who have spoken to me, saying, 'Lighten the yoke which your father put on us'?"

10 Then the young men who had grown up with him spoke to him, saying, "Thus you should speak to the people who have spoken to you, saying, 'Your father made our yoke heavy, but you make *it* lighter on us'—thus you shall say to them: 'My little *finger* shall be thicker than my father's waist!

11 'And now, whereas my father put a heavy yoke on you, I will add to your yoke; my father chastised you with whips, but I *will* chastise *you* with ᵀscourges!' "   Lit. *scorpions*

12 So ᴿJeroboam and all the people came to Rehoboam on the third day, as the king had directed, saying, "Come back to me the third day."   1 Kin. 12:12-14

13 Then the king answered them roughly. King Rehoboam rejected the advice of the elders,

14 and he spoke to them according to the advice of the young men, saying, *"My father made your yoke heavy, but I will add to it; my father chastised you with whips, but I *will* chastise *you* with ᵀscourges!"   Lit. *scorpions*

10:14 So with many Heb. mss., LXX, Syr., Vg. (cf. v. 10, 1 Kin. 12:14); MT *I.*

15 So the king did not listen to the people; for the turn *of events* was from God, that the LORD might fulfill His ᴿword, which He had spoken by the hand of Ahijah the Shilonite to Jeroboam the son of Nebat.   1 Kin. 11:29-39

16 Now when all Israel *saw* that the king did not listen to them, the people answered the king, saying:

"What share have we in David?
We *have* no inheritance in the son of Jesse.
Every man to your tents, O Israel!
Now see to your own house, O David!"

So all Israel departed to their tents.

17 But Rehoboam reigned over the children of Israel who dwelt in the cities of Judah.

18 Then King Rehoboam sent Hadoram, who *was* in charge of revenue; but the children of Israel stoned him with stones, and he died. Therefore King Rehoboam mounted *his* chariot in haste to flee to Jerusalem.

19 ᴿSo Israel has been in rebellion against the house of David to this day.   1 Kin. 12:19

11 Now ᴿwhen Rehoboam came to Jerusalem, he assembled from the house of Judah and Benjamin one hundred and eighty thousand chosen *men* who were warriors, to fight against Israel, that he might restore the kingdom to Rehoboam.   1 Kin. 12:21-24

2 But the word of the LORD came ᴿto Shemaiah the man of God, saying,   1 Chr. 12:5

3 "Speak to Rehoboam the son of Solomon, king of Judah, and to all Israel in Judah and Benjamin, saying,

4 'Thus says the LORD: "You shall not go up or fight against your brethren! Let every man return to his house, for this thing is from Me." ' " Therefore they obeyed the words of the LORD, and turned back from attacking Jeroboam.

Rehoboam Fortifies the Cities

5 So Rehoboam dwelt in Jerusalem, and built cities for defense in Judah.

6 And he built Bethlehem, Etam, Tekoa,

7 Beth Zur, Sochoh, Adullam,

8 Gath, Mareshah, Ziph,

9 Adoraim, Lachish, Azekah,

10 Zorah, Aijalon, and Hebron, which are in Judah and Benjamin, fortified cities.

11 And he fortified the strongholds, and put captains in them, and stores of food, oil, and wine.

12 Also in every city he put shields and spears, and made them very strong, having Judah and Benjamin on his side.

Priests and Levites Move to Judah

13 And from all their territories the priests and the Levites who *were* in all Israel took their stand with him.

14 For the Levites left ᴿtheir common-lands and their possessions and came to Judah and Jerusalem, for ᴿJeroboam and his sons had rejected them from serving as priests to the Lᴏʀᴅ.   Num. 35:2-5 • 2 Chr. 13:9

15 Then he appointed for himself priests for the ᵀhigh places, for the demons, and the calf idols which he had made.   Center of worship

16 And ᵀafter *the Levites left*, those from all the tribes of Israel, such as set their heart to seek the Lᴏʀᴅ God of Israel, ᴿcame to Jerusalem to sacrifice to the Lᴏʀᴅ God of their fathers.   Lit. *after them* • 2 Chr. 15:9, 10; 30:11, 18

17 So they ᴿstrengthened the kingdom of Judah, and made Rehoboam the son of Solomon strong for three years, because they walked in the way of David and Solomon for three years.   2 Chr. 12:1, 13

The Family of Rehoboam

18 Then Rehoboam took for himself as wife Mahalath the daughter of Jerimoth the son of David, *and of* Abihail the daughter of ᴿEliah the son of Jesse.   1 Sam. 16:6

19 And she bore him children: Jeush, Shamariah, and Zaham.

20 After her he took ᴿMaachah the *granddaughter of Absalom; and she bore him Abijah, Attai, Ziza, and Shelomith.   2 Chr. 13:2

21 Now Rehoboam loved Maachah the granddaughter of Absalom more than all his wives and his concubines; for he took eighteen wives and sixty concubines, and begot twenty-eight sons and sixty daughters.

22 And Rehoboam ᴿappointed ᴿAbijah the son of Maachah as chief, *to be* leader among his brothers; for he *intended* to make him king.   Deut. 21:15-17 • 2 Chr. 13:1

23 He dealt wisely, and dispersed some of his sons throughout all the territories of Judah and Benjamin, to every fortified city; and he gave them provisions in abundance. He also sought many wives *for them*.

Egypt Attacks Judah

12 Now ᴿit came to pass, when Rehoboam had established the kingdom and had strengthened himself, that ᴿhe forsook the law of the Lᴏʀᴅ, and all Israel along with him.   2 Chr. 11:17 • 1 Kin. 14:22-24

2 ᴿAnd it happened in the fifth year of King Rehoboam *that* Shishak king of Egypt came up against Jerusalem, because they had transgressed against the Lᴏʀᴅ,   1 Kin. 11:40; 14:25

3 with twelve hundred chariots, sixty thousand horsemen, and people without number who came with him out of Egypt—ᴿthe Lubim and the Sukkiim and the Ethiopians.   2 Chr. 16:8

4 And he took the fortified cities of Judah and came to Jerusalem.

5 Then Shemaiah the prophet came to Rehoboam and the leaders of Judah, who were gathered together in Jerusalem because of Shishak, and said to them, "Thus says the Lᴏʀᴅ: 'You have forsaken Me, and therefore I also have left you in the hand of Shishak.' "

6 So the leaders of Israel and the king ᴿhumbled themselves; and they said, ᴿ"The Lᴏʀᴅ *is* righteous."   [James 4:10] • Ex. 9:27

7 Now when the Lᴏʀᴅ saw that they humbled themselves, ᴿthe word of the Lᴏʀᴅ came to Shemaiah, saying, "They have humbled themselves; *therefore* I will not destroy them, but I will grant them some deliverance. My wrath shall not be poured out on Jerusalem by the hand of Shishak.   1 Kin. 21:28, 29

8 "Nevertheless they will be his servants, that they may distinguish My service from the service of the kingdoms of the nations."

9 So Shishak king of Egypt came up against Jerusalem, and took away the treasures of the house of the Lᴏʀᴅ and the treasures of the king's house; he took everything. He also carried away the gold shields which Solomon had ᴿmade.   2 Chr. 9:15, 16

10 Then King Rehoboam made bronze shields in their place, and committed *them* to the hands of the captains of the guard, who guarded the doorway of the king's house.

11 And whenever the king entered the house of the Lᴏʀᴅ, the guard would go and bring them out; then they would take them back into the guardroom.

12 When he humbled himself, the wrath of the Lᴏʀᴅ turned from him, so as not to destroy *him* completely; and things also went well in Judah.

The End of Rehoboam's Reign

13 Thus King Rehoboam strengthened himself in Jerusalem and reigned. Now Rehoboam *was* forty-one years old when he became king; and he reigned seventeen years in Jerusalem, the city which the Lᴏʀᴅ had chosen out of all the tribes of Israel, to put His name there. His mother's name *was* Naamah, an ᴿAmmonitess.   1 Kin. 11:1, 5

14 And he did evil, because he did not prepare his heart to seek the Lᴏʀᴅ.

15 The acts of Rehoboam, first and last, *are* they not written in the book of Shemaiah the prophet, and of Iddo the seer concerning genealogies? And *there were* wars between Rehoboam and Jeroboam all their days.

16 So Rehoboam rested with his fathers, and was buried in the City of David. Then *Abijah his son reigned in his place.

Abijah Reigns in Judah

13 In the eighteenth year of King Jeroboam, Abijah became king over Judah.

11:20 Lit. *daughter*, but in the broader sense of granddaughter

12:16 *Abijam*, 1 Kin. 14:31

2 He reigned three years in Jerusalem. His mother's name *was* *Michaiah the daughter of Uriel of Gibeah. And there was war between Abijah and Jeroboam.

3 Abijah set the battle in order with an army of valiant warriors, four hundred thousand choice men. Jeroboam also drew up in battle formation against him with eight hundred thousand choice men, mighty men of valor.

4 Then Abijah stood on Mount Zemaraim, which *is* in the mountains of Ephraim, and said, "Hear me, Jeroboam and all Israel:

5 "Should you not know that the LORD God of Israel ᴿgave the dominion over Israel to David forever, to him and his sons, ᴿby a covenant of salt?   2 Sam. 7:8-16 • Num. 18:19

6 "Yet Jeroboam the son of Nebat, the servant of Solomon the son of David, rose up and ᴿrebelled against his lord.   1 Kin. 11:28; 12:20

7 "Then ᴿworthless rogues gathered to him, and strengthened themselves against Rehoboam the son of Solomon, when Rehoboam was ᴿyoung and inexperienced and could not withstand them.   Judg. 9:4 • 2 Chr. 12:13

8 "And now you think to withstand the kingdom of the LORD, which is in the hand of the sons of David; and you *are* a great multitude, and with you are the gold calves which Jeroboam made for you as gods.

9 "Have you not cast out the priests of the LORD, the sons of Aaron, and the Levites, and made for yourselves priests, like the peoples of *other* lands, ᴿso that whoever comes to consecrate himself with a young bull and seven rams may be a priest of ᴿthings that are not gods?   Ex. 29:29-33 • Jer. 2:11; 5:7

10 "But as for us, the LORD *is* our God, and we have not forsaken Him; and the priests who minister to the LORD *are* the sons of Aaron, and the Levites *attend* to *their* duties.

11 ᴿ"And they burn to the LORD every morning and every evening burnt sacrifices and sweet incense; *they* also *set* the ᴿshowbread *in order on* the pure *gold* table, and the lampstand of gold with its lamps ᴿto burn every evening; for we keep the command of the LORD our God, but you have forsaken Him.   2 Chr. 2:4 • Lev. 24:5-9 • Ex. 27:20, 21

12 "Now look, God Himself is with us as *our* ᴿhead, ᴿand His priests with sounding trumpets to sound the alarm against you. O children of Israel, do not fight against the LORD God of your fathers, for you shall not prosper!"   [Heb. 2:10] • [Num. 10:8-10]

13 But Jeroboam caused an ambush to go around behind them; so they were in front of Judah, and the ambush *was* behind them.

14 And when Judah looked around, to their surprise the battle line *was* at both front and rear; and they ᴿcried out to the LORD, and the priests sounded the trumpets.   2 Chr. 6:34, 35

13:2 *Maachah,* 1 Kin. 15:2; 2 Chr. 11:20, 21

15 Then the men of Judah gave a shout; and as the men of Judah shouted, it happened that God ᴿstruck Jeroboam and all Israel before Abijah and Judah.   2 Chr. 14:12

16 And the children of Israel fled before Judah, and God delivered them into their hand.

17 Then Abijah and his people struck them with a great slaughter; so five hundred thousand choice men of Israel fell slain.

18 Thus the children of Israel were subdued at that time; and the children of Judah prevailed, ᴿbecause they relied on the LORD God of their fathers.   2 Chr. 14:11

19 And Abijah pursued Jeroboam and took cities from him: Bethel with its villages, Jeshanah with its villages, and ᴿEphrainᵀ with its villages.   Josh. 15:9 • Or *Ephron*

20 So Jeroboam did not recover strength again in the days of Abijah; and the LORD struck him, and ᴿhe died.   1 Kin. 14:20

21 But Abijah grew mighty, married fourteen wives, and begot twenty-two sons and sixteen daughters.

22 Now the rest of the acts of Abijah, his ways, and his sayings *are* written in the ᵀannals of the prophet Iddo.   Or *commentary*

14 So Abijah rested with his fathers, and they buried him in the City of David. Then Asa his son reigned in his place. In his days the land was quiet for ten years.

Asa Reigns in Judah

2 Asa did *what was* good and right in the eyes of the LORD his God,

3 for he removed the altars of the foreign *gods* and the ᵀhigh places, and ᴿbroke down the *sacred* pillars and cut down the wooden images.   Places for pagan worship • [Ex. 34:13]

4 He commanded Judah to ᴿseek the LORD God of their fathers, and to observe the law and the commandment.   [2 Chr. 7:14]

5 He also removed the high places and the incense altars from all the cities of Judah, and the kingdom was quiet under him.

6 And he built fortified cities in Judah, for the land had rest; he had no war in those years, because the LORD had given him rest.

7 Therefore he said to Judah, "Let us build these cities and make walls around *them,* and towers, gates, and bars, *while* the land *is* yet before us, because we have sought the LORD our God; we have sought *Him,* and He has given us rest on every side." So they built and prospered.

8 And Asa had an army of three hundred thousand from Judah who carried ᵀshields and spears, and from Benjamin two hundred and eighty thousand men who carried shields and drew bows; all these *were* mighty men of ᴿvalor.   large shields • 2 Chr. 13:3

9 ᴿThen Zerah the Ethiopian came out against them with an army of a million men

and three hundred chariots, and he came to ᴿMareshah.   2 Chr. 12:2, 3; 16:8 • Josh. 15:44

10 So Asa went out against him, and they set the troops in battle array in the Valley of Zephathah at Mareshah.

11 And Asa cried out to the Lᴏʀᴅ his God, and said, "Lᴏʀᴅ, it is nothing for You to help, whether with many or with those who have no power; help us, O Lᴏʀᴅ our God, for we rest on You, and in Your name we go against this multitude. O Lᴏʀᴅ, You are our God; do not let man prevail against You!"

12 So the Lᴏʀᴅ struck the Ethiopians before Asa and Judah, and the Ethiopians fled.

13 And Asa and the people who were with him pursued them to ᴿGerar. So the Ethiopians were overthrown, and they could not recover, for they were broken before the Lᴏʀᴅ and His army. And they carried away very much ᵀspoil.   Gen. 10:19; 20:1 • plunder

14 Then they defeated all the cities around Gerar, for the fear of the Lᴏʀᴅ came upon them; and they plundered all the cities, for there was exceedingly much spoil in them.

15 They also ᵀattacked the livestock enclosures, and carried off sheep and camels in abundance, and returned to Jerusalem. struck

The Reforms of Asa

15 Now ᴿthe Spirit of God came upon Azariah the son of Oded.   2 Chr. 20:14; 24:20

2 And he went out to meet Asa, and said to him: "Hear me, Asa, and all Judah and Benjamin. ᴿThe Lᴏʀᴅ is with you while you are with Him. ᴿIf you seek Him, He will be found by you; but if you forsake Him, He will forsake you.   [James 4:8] • [1 Chr. 28:9]

3 ᴿ"For a long time Israel has been without the true God, without a ᴿteaching priest, and without ᴿlaw;   Hos. 3:4 • 2 Kin. 12:2 • Lev. 10:11

4 "but ᴿwhen in their trouble they turned to the Lᴏʀᴅ God of Israel, and sought Him, He was found by them.   [Deut. 4:29]

5 "And in those times there was no peace to the one who went out, nor to the one who came in, but great turmoil was on all the inhabitants of the lands.

6 ᴿ"So nation was ᵀdestroyed by nation, and city by city, for God troubled them with every adversity.   Matt. 24:7 • Lit. beaten in pieces

7 "But you, be strong and do not let your hands be weak, for your work shall be rewarded!"

8 And when Asa heard these words and the prophecy of *Oded the prophet, he took courage, and removed the abominable idols from all the land of Judah and Benjamin and from the cities ᴿwhich he had taken in the mountains of Ephraim; and he restored the

15:8 So with MT, LXX; Syr., Vg. Azariah the son of Oded (cf. v. 1)

altar of the Lᴏʀᴅ that was before the vestibule of the Lᴏʀᴅ.   2 Chr. 13:19

9 Then he gathered all Judah and Benjamin, and ᴿthose who dwelt with them from Ephraim, Manasseh, and Simeon, for they came over to him in great numbers from Israel when they saw that the Lᴏʀᴅ his God was with him.   2 Chr. 11:16

10 So they gathered together at Jerusalem in the third month, in the fifteenth year of the reign of Asa.

11 And they offered to the Lᴏʀᴅ at that time seven hundred bulls and seven thousand sheep from the spoil they had brought.

12 Then they ᴿentered into a covenant to seek the Lᴏʀᴅ God of their fathers with all their heart and with all their soul;   2 Kin. 23:3

13 ᴿand whoever would not seek the Lᴏʀᴅ God of Israel ᴿwas to be put to death, whether small or great, whether man or woman.   Ex. 22:20 • Deut. 13:5-15

14 Then they took an oath before the Lᴏʀᴅ with a loud voice, with shouting and trumpets and rams' horns.

15 And all Judah rejoiced at the oath, for they had sworn with all their heart and ᴿsought Him with all their soul; and He was found by them, and the Lᴏʀᴅ gave them ᴿrest all around.   2 Chr. 15:2 • 2 Chr. 14:7

16 Also he removed Maachah, the ᵀmother of Asa the king, from being queen mother, because she had made an obscene image of ᵀAsherah; and Asa cut down her obscene image, then crushed and burned it by the Brook Kidron.   Or grandmother • A Canaanite goddess

17 But the ᵀhigh places were not removed from Israel. Nevertheless the heart of Asa was loyal all his days.   Places for pagan worship

18 He also brought into the house of God the things that his father had dedicated and that he himself had dedicated: silver and gold and utensils.

19 And there was no war until the thirty-fifth year of the reign of Asa.

Asa's Treaty with Syria

16 In the thirty-sixth year of the reign of Asa, Baasha king of Israel came up against Judah and built Ramah, that he might let none go out or come in to Asa king of Judah.

2 Then Asa brought silver and gold from the treasuries of the house of the Lᴏʀᴅ and of the king's house, and sent to Ben-Hadad king of Syria, who dwelt in Damascus, saying,

3 "Let there be a treaty between you and me, as there was between my father and your father. See, I have sent you silver and gold; come, break your treaty with Baasha king of Israel, so that he will withdraw from me."

4 So Ben-Hadad heeded King Asa, and sent the captains of his armies against the cities of Israel. They attacked Ijon, Dan, Abel Maim, and all the storage cities of Naphtali.

5 Now it happened, when Baasha heard *it*, that he stopped building Ramah and ceased his work.

6 Then King Asa took all Judah, and they carried away the stones and timber of Ramah, which Baasha had used for building; and with them he built Geba and Mizpah.

Hanani's Message to Asa

7 And at that time ᴿHanani the seer came to Asa king of Judah, and said to him: ᴿ"Because you have relied on the king of Syria, and have not relied on the LORD your God, therefore the army of the king of Syria has escaped from your hand.   2 Chr. 19:2 • [Jer. 17:5]

8 "Were the Ethiopians and the Lubim not a huge army with very many chariots and horsemen? Yet, because you relied on the LORD, He delivered them into your hand.

9 "For the eyes of the LORD run to and fro throughout the whole earth, to show Himself strong on behalf of *those* whose heart *is* loyal to Him. In this you have done foolishly; therefore from now on you shall have wars."

10 Then Asa was angry with the seer, and ᴿput him in prison, for *he was* enraged at him because of this. And Asa oppressed *some* of the people at that time.   Jer. 20:2

Illness and Death of Asa

11 ᴿNote that the acts of Asa, first and last, are indeed written in the book of the kings of Judah and Israel.   1 Kin. 15:23, 24

12 And in the thirty-ninth year of his reign, Asa became diseased in his feet, and his malady was severe; yet in his disease he did not seek the LORD, but the physicians.

13 ᴿSo Asa rested with his fathers; he died in the forty-first year of his reign.   1 Kin. 15:24

14 They buried him in his own tomb, which he had ᵀmade for himself in the City of David; and they laid him in the bed which was filled with spices and various ingredients prepared in a mixture of ointments. They made a very great burning for him.   Lit. *dug*

Jehoshaphat Reigns in Judah

17 Then ᴿJehoshaphat his son reigned in his place, and strengthened himself against Israel.   1 Kin. 15:24

2 And he placed troops in all the fortified cities of Judah, and set garrisons in the land of ᴿJudah and in the cities of Ephraim ᴿwhich Asa his father had taken.   2 Chr. 11:5 • 2 Chr. 15:8

3 Now the LORD was with Jehoshaphat, because he walked in the former ways of his father David; he did not seek the Baals,

4 but sought *the God of his father, and walked in His commandments and not according to ᴿthe acts of Israel.   1 Kin. 12:28

5 Therefore the LORD established the kingdom in his hand; and all Judah ᴿgave presents

17:4 LXX the LORD God

to Jehoshaphat, ᴿand he had riches and honor in abundance.   1 Kin. 10:25 • 2 Chr. 18:1

6 And his heart took delight in the ways of the LORD; moreover he removed the high places and wooden images from Judah.

7 Also in the third year of his reign he sent his leaders, Ben-Hail, Obadiah, Zechariah, Nethanel, and Michaiah, ᴿto teach in the cities of Judah.   2 Chr. 15:3; 35:3

8 And with them *he sent* Levites: Shemaiah, Nethaniah, Zebadiah, Asahel, Shemiramoth, Jehonathan, Adonijah, Tobijah, and Tobadonijah—the Levites; and with them Elishama and Jehoram, the priests.

9 ᴿSo they taught in Judah, and *had* the Book of the Law of the LORD with them; they went throughout all the cities of Judah and taught the people.   Neh. 8:3, 7

10 And ᴿthe fear of the LORD fell on all the kingdoms of the lands that *were* around Judah, so that they did not make war against Jehoshaphat.   2 Chr. 14:14

11 Also *some* of the Philistines brought Jehoshaphat presents and silver as tribute; and the Arabians brought him flocks, seven thousand seven hundred rams and seven thousand seven hundred male goats.

12 So Jehoshaphat became increasingly powerful, and he built fortresses and storage cities in Judah.

13 He had much property in the cities of Judah; and the men of war, mighty men of valor, *were* in Jerusalem.

14 These *are* their numbers, according to their fathers' houses. Of Judah, the captains of thousands: Adnah the captain, and with him three hundred thousand mighty men of valor;

15 and next to him *was* Jehohanan the captain, and with him two hundred and eighty thousand;

16 and next to him *was* Amasiah the son of Zichri, ᴿwho willingly offered himself to the LORD, and with him two hundred thousand mighty men of valor.   Judg. 5:2, 9

17 Of Benjamin: Eliada a mighty man of valor, and with him two hundred thousand men armed with bow and shield;

18 and next to him *was* Jehozabad, and with him one hundred and eighty thousand prepared for war.

19 These served the king, besides ᴿthose the king put in the fortified cities throughout all Judah.   2 Chr. 17:2

Micaiah Warns Ahab

18 Jehoshaphat had riches and honor in abundance; and by marriage he ᴿallied himself with ᴿAhab.   2 Chr. 8:18 • 1 Kin. 22:40

2 ᴿAfter some years he went down to *visit* Ahab in Samaria; and Ahab killed sheep and oxen in abundance for him and the people who were with him, and persuaded him to go up *with him* to Ramoth Gilead.   1 Kin. 22:2

3 So Ahab king of Israel said to Jehoshaphat king of Judah, "Will you go with me *against* Ramoth Gilead?" And he answered him, "I *am* as you *are*, and my people as your people; *we will be* with you in the war."

4 Also Jehoshaphat said to the king of Israel, ᴿ"Please inquire for the word of the LORD today."   2 Sam. 2:1

5 Then the king of Israel gathered the prophets together, four hundred men, and said to them, "Shall we go to war against Ramoth Gilead, or shall I refrain?" So they said, "Go up, for God will deliver it into the king's hand."

6 But Jehoshaphat said, "*Is there* not still a prophet of the LORD here, that we may inquire of ᴿHim?"ᵀ   2 Kin. 3:11 · Or *him*

7 So the king of Israel said to Jehoshaphat, "*There is* still one man by whom we may inquire of the LORD; but I hate him, because he never prophesies good concerning me, but always evil. He *is* Micaiah the son of Imla." And Jehoshaphat said, "Let not the king say such things!"

8 Then the king of Israel called one *of his* officers and said, "Bring Micaiah the son of Imla quickly!"

9 The king of Israel and Jehoshaphat king of Judah, clothed in *their* robes, sat each on his throne; and they sat at a threshing floor at the entrance of the gate of Samaria; and all the prophets prophesied before them.

10 Now Zedekiah the son of Chenaanah had made ᴿhorns of iron for himself; and he said, "Thus says the LORD: 'With these you shall gore the Syrians until they are destroyed.' "   Zech. 1:18-21

11 And all the prophets prophesied so, saying, "Go up to Ramoth Gilead and prosper, for the LORD will deliver *it* into the king's hand."

12 Then the messenger who had gone to call Micaiah spoke to him, saying, "Now listen, the words of the prophets with one accord encourage the king. Therefore please let your word be like *the word of* one of them, and speak encouragement."

13 And Micaiah said, "*As* the LORD lives, whatever my God says, that I will speak."

14 Then he came to the king; and the king said to him, "Micaiah, shall we go to war against Ramoth Gilead, or shall I refrain?" And he said, "Go and prosper, and they shall be delivered into your hand!"

15 So the king said to him, "How many times shall I make you swear that you tell me nothing but the truth in the name of the LORD?"

16 Then he said, "I saw all Israel ᴿscattered on the mountains, as sheep that have no ᴿshepherd. And the LORD said, 'These have no master. Let each return to his house in peace.' "   [Jer. 23:1-8; 31:10] · Matt. 9:36

17 And the king of Israel said to Jehoshaphat, "Did I not tell you he would not prophesy good concerning me, but evil?"

18 Then *Micaiah* said, "Therefore hear the word of the LORD: I saw the LORD sitting on His throne, and all the host of heaven standing on His right hand and His left.

19 "And the LORD said, 'Who will persuade Ahab king of Israel to go up, that he may fall at Ramoth Gilead?' So one spoke in this manner, and another spoke in that manner.

20 "Then a spirit came forward and stood before the LORD, and said, 'I will persuade him.' The LORD said to him, 'In what way?'

21 "So he said, 'I will go out and be a lying spirit in the mouth of all his prophets.' And ᴿthe LORD said, 'You shall persuade *him* and also prevail; go out and do so.'   1 Kin. 22:22

22 "Therefore look! ᴿThe LORD has put a lying spirit in the mouth of these prophets of yours, and the LORD has declared disaster against you."   Ezek. 14:9

23 Then Zedekiah the son of Chenaanah went near and ᴿstruck Micaiah on the cheek, and said, "Which way did the spirit from the LORD go from me to speak to you?"   Jer. 20:2

24 And Micaiah said, "Indeed you shall see on that day when you go into an inner chamber to hide!"

25 Then the king of Israel said, "Take Micaiah, and return him to Amon the governor of the city and to Joash the king's son;

26 "and say, 'Thus says the king: ᴿ"Put this *fellow* in prison, and feed him with bread of affliction and water of affliction, until I return in peace." ' "   2 Chr. 16:10

27 But Micaiah said, "If you ever return in peace, the LORD has not spoken by me." And he said, "Take heed, all you people!"

Ahab Dies in Battle

28 So the king of Israel and Jehoshaphat the king of Judah went up to Ramoth Gilead.

29 And the king of Israel said to Jehoshaphat, "I will ᴿdisguise myself and go into battle; but you put on your robes." So the king of Israel disguised himself, and they went into battle.   2 Chr. 35:22

30 Now the king of Syria had commanded the captains of the chariots who *were* with him, saying, "Fight with no one small or great, but only with the king of Israel."

31 So it was, when the captains of the chariots saw Jehoshaphat, that they said, "It *is* the king of Israel!" Therefore they surrounded him to attack; but Jehoshaphat cried out, and the LORD helped him, and God diverted them from him.

32 For so it was, when the captains of the chariots saw that it was not the king of Israel, that they turned back from pursuing him.

33 Now a certain man drew a bow at random, and struck the king of Israel between

the joints of his armor. So he said to the driver of his chariot, "Turn around and take me out of the battle, for I am wounded."

34 The battle increased that day, and the king of Israel propped *himself* up in *his* chariot facing the Syrians until evening; and about the time of sunset he died.

19 Then Jehoshaphat the king of Judah returned safely to his house in Jerusalem.

2 And Jehu the son of Hanani the seer went out to meet him, and said to King Jehoshaphat, "Should you help the wicked and love those who hate the LORD? Therefore the wrath of the LORD *is* upon you.

3 "Nevertheless good things are found in you, in that you have removed the ᵀwooden images from the land, and have prepared your heart to seek God."   Heb. *Asheroth*

The Reforms of Jehoshaphat

4 So Jehoshaphat dwelt at Jerusalem; and he went out again among the people from Beersheba to the mountains of Ephraim, and brought them back to the LORD God of their ᴿfathers.   2 Chr. 15:8–13

5 Then he set ᴿjudges in the land throughout all the fortified cities of Judah, city by city,   [Deut. 16:18–20]

6 and said to the judges, "Take heed to what you are doing, for you do not judge for man but for the LORD, who *is* with you ᵀin the judgment.   Lit. *in the matter of the judgment*

7 "Now therefore, let the fear of the LORD be upon you; take care and do *it*, for *there is* no iniquity with the LORD our God, no ᴿpartiality, nor taking of bribes."   [Deut. 10:17, 18]

8 Moreover in Jerusalem, for the judgment of the LORD and for controversies, Jehoshaphat appointed some of the Levites and priests, and some of the chief fathers of Israel, *when they returned to Jerusalem.

9 And he commanded them, saying, "Thus you shall act ᴿin the fear of the LORD, faithfully and with a loyal heart: [2 Sam. 23:3]

10 ᴿ"Whatever case comes to you from your brethren who dwell in their cities, whether of bloodshed or offenses against law or commandment, against statutes or ordinances, you shall warn them, lest they trespass against the LORD and ᴿwrath come upon ᴿyou and your brethren. Do this, and you will not be guilty.   Deut. 17:8 • Num. 16:46 • [Ezek. 3:18]

11 "And take notice: Amariah the chief priest *is* over you ᴿin all matters of the LORD; and Zebadiah the son of Ishmael, the ruler of the house of Judah, for all the king's matters; also the Levites *will be* officials before you. Behave courageously, and the LORD will be ᴿwith the good."   1 Chr. 26:30 • [2 Chr. 15:2; 20:17]

19:8 LXX, [Syr.], [Vg.] *for the inhabitants of Jerusalem.*

Ammon, Moab, and Mount Seir Defeated

20 It happened after this *that* the people of Moab with the people of Ammon, and *others* with them besides the *Ammonites, came to battle against Jehoshaphat.

2 Then some came and told Jehoshaphat, saying, "A great multitude is coming against you from beyond the sea, from *Syria; and they are ᴿin Hazazon Tamar" (which *is* ᴿEn Gedi).   Gen. 14:7 • Josh. 15:62

3 And Jehoshaphat feared, and set ᵀhimself to seek the LORD, and ᴿproclaimed a fast throughout all Judah.   Lit. *his face* • Ezra 8:21

4 So Judah gathered together to ask ᴿhelp from the LORD; and from all the cities of Judah they came to seek the LORD.   2 Chr. 14:11

5 Then Jehoshaphat stood in the assembly of Judah and Jerusalem, in the house of the LORD, before the new court,

6 and said: "O LORD God of our fathers, *are* You not God in heaven, and do You *not* rule over all the kingdoms of the nations, and in Your hand *is there not* power and might, so that no one is able to withstand You?

7 "*Are* You not our God, *who* drove out the inhabitants of this land before Your people Israel, and gave it to the descendants of Abraham ᴿYour friend forever?   Is. 41:8

8 "And they dwell in it, and have built You a sanctuary in it for Your name, saying,

9 ᴿ'If disaster comes upon us—sword, judgment, pestilence, or famine—we will stand before this temple and in Your presence (for Your ᴿname *is* in this temple), and cry out to You in our affliction, and You will hear and save.'   2 Chr. 6:28–30 • 2 Chr. 6:20

10 "And now, here are the people of Ammon, Moab, and Mount Seir—whom You would not let Israel invade when they came out of the land of Egypt, but they turned from them and did not destroy them—

11 "here they are, rewarding us ᴿby coming to throw us out of Your possession which You have given us to inherit.   Ps. 83:1–18

12 "O our God, will You not ᴿjudge them? For we have no power against this great multitude that is coming against us; nor do we know what to do, but ᴿour eyes *are* upon You."   Judg. 11:27 • Ps. 25:15; 121:1, 2; 123:1, 2; 141:8

13 Now all Judah, with their little ones, their wives, and their children, stood before the LORD.

14 Then ᴿthe Spirit of the LORD came upon Jahaziel the son of Zechariah, the son of Benaiah, the son of Jeiel, the son of Mattaniah, a Levite of the sons of Asaph, in the midst of the assembly.   2 Chr. 15:1; 24:20

15 And he said, "Listen, all you of Judah and you inhabitants of Jerusalem, and you,

20:1 So with MT, Vg.; LXX *Meunites,* 2 Chr. 26:7
20:2 So with MT, LXX, Vg.; Heb. mss., Old Lat. *Edom*

King Jehoshaphat! Thus says the LORD to you: ᴿ'Do not be afraid nor dismayed because of this great multitude, for the battle is not yours, but God's.   [Deut. 1:29, 30; 31:6, 8]

16 'Tomorrow go down against them. They will surely come up by the Ascent of Ziz, and you will find them at the end of the ᵀbrook before the Wilderness of Jeruel.   *ravine or wadi*

17 'You will not *need* to fight in this *battle*. Position yourselves, stand still and see the salvation of the LORD, who is with you, O Judah and Jerusalem!' Do not fear or be dismayed; tomorrow go out against them, ᴿfor the LORD is with you."   Num. 14:9

18 And Jehoshaphat ᴿbowed his head with *his* face to the ground, and all Judah and the inhabitants of Jerusalem bowed before the LORD, worshiping the LORD.   Ex. 4:31

19 Then the Levites of the children of the Kohathites and of the children of the Korahites stood up to praise the LORD God of Israel with voices loud and high.

20 So they rose early in the morning and went out into the Wilderness of Tekoa; and as they went out, Jehoshaphat stood and said, "Hear me, O Judah and you inhabitants of Jerusalem: ᴿBelieve in the LORD your God, and you shall be established; believe His prophets, and you shall prosper."   Is. 7:9

21 And when he had consulted with the people, he appointed those who should sing to the LORD, ᴿand who should praise the beauty of holiness, as they went out before the army and were saying: 1 Chr. 16:29

ᴿ"Praise the LORD,   Ps. 106:1; 136:1
For His mercy *endures* forever."

22 Now when they began to sing and to praise, ᴿthe LORD set ambushes against the people of Ammon, Moab, and Mount Seir, who had come against Judah; and they were defeated.   Judg. 7:22

23 For the people of Ammon and Moab stood up against the inhabitants of Mount Seir to utterly kill and destroy *them*. And when they ᵀhad made an end of the inhabitants of Seir, ᴿthey helped to destroy one another.   *had finished* • 1 Sam. 14:20

24 So when Judah came to a place overlooking the wilderness, they looked toward the multitude; and there *were* their dead bodies, fallen on the earth. No one had escaped.

25 When Jehoshaphat and his people came to take away their spoil, they found among them an abundance of valuables on the *dead bodies, and precious jewelry, which they stripped off for themselves, more than they could carry away; and they were three days gathering the spoil because there was so much.

20:25 A few mss., Lat., Vg. *garments;* LXX *armor*

26 And on the fourth day they assembled in the Valley of ᵀBerachah, for there they blessed the LORD; therefore the name of that place was called The Valley of Berachah until this day.   Lit. *Blessing*

27 Then they returned, every man of Judah and Jerusalem, with Jehoshaphat in front of them, to go back to Jerusalem with joy, for the LORD had ᴿmade them rejoice over their enemies.   Neh. 12:43

28 So they came to Jerusalem, with stringed instruments and harps and trumpets, to the house of the LORD.

29 And ᴿthe fear of God was on all the kingdoms of *those* countries when they heard that the LORD had fought against the enemies of Israel.   2 Chr. 14:14; 17:10

30 Then the realm of Jehoshaphat was quiet, for his God gave him rest all around.

The End of Jehoshaphat's Reign

31 ᴿSo Jehoshaphat was king over Judah. *He was* thirty-five years old when he became king, and he reigned twenty-five years in Jerusalem. His mother's name *was* Azubah the daughter of Shilhi.   [1 Kin. 22:41–43]

32 And he walked in the way of his father Asa, and did not turn aside from it, doing *what was* right in the sight of the LORD.

33 Nevertheless the ᵀhigh places were not taken away, for as yet the people had not ᴿdirected their hearts to the God of their fathers.   *Places for pagan worship* • 2 Chr. 12:14; 19:3

34 Now the rest of the acts of Jehoshaphat, first and last, indeed they *are* written in the book of Jehu the son of Hanani, which *is* mentioned in the book of the kings of Israel.

35 After this Jehoshaphat king of Judah allied himself with Ahaziah king of Israel, who acted very ᴿwickedly.   [2 Chr. 19:2]

36 And he allied himself with him ᴿto make ships to go to Tarshish, and they made the ships in Ezion Geber.   1 Kin. 9:26; 10:22

37 But Eliezer the son of Dodavah of Mareshah prophesied against Jehoshaphat, saying, "Because you have allied yourself with Ahaziah, the LORD has destroyed your works." Then the ships were wrecked, so that they were not able to go ᴿto Tarshish.   2 Chr. 9:21

Jehoram Reigns in Judah

21 And ᴿJehoshaphat rested with his fathers, and was buried with his fathers in the City of David. Then Jehoram his son reigned in his place.   1 Kin. 22:50

2 He had brothers, the sons of Jehoshaphat: Azariah, Jehiel, Zechariah, Azaryahu, Michael, and Shephatiah; all these *were* the sons of Jehoshaphat king of Israel.

3 Their father gave them great gifts of silver and gold and precious things, with fortified cities in Judah; but he gave the

kingdom to Jehoram, because he *was* the firstborn.

4 Now when Jehoram ᵀwas established over the kingdom of his father, he strengthened himself and killed all his brothers with the sword, and also *others* of the princes of Israel.   Lit. *arose*

5 ᴿJehoram *was* thirty-two years old when he became king, and he reigned eight years in Jerusalem.   2 Kin. 8:17–22

6 And he walked in the way of the kings of Israel, just as the house of Ahab had done, for he had the daughter of Ahab as a wife; and he did evil in the sight of the LORD.

7 Yet the LORD would not destroy the house of David, because of the ᴿcovenant that He had made with David, and since He had promised to give a lamp to him and to his ᴿsons forever.   2 Sam. 7:8–17 • 1 Kin. 11:36

8 ᴿIn his days Edom revolted against Judah's authority, and made a king over themselves.   2 Kin. 8:20; 14:7, 10

9 So Jehoram went out with his officers, and all his chariots with him. And he rose by night and attacked the Edomites who had surrounded him and the captains of the chariots.

10 Thus Edom has been in revolt against Judah's authority to this day. At that time Libnah revolted against his rule, because he had forsaken the LORD God of his fathers.

11 Moreover he made ᵀhigh places in the mountains of Judah, and caused the inhabitants of Jerusalem to ᴿcommit harlotry, and led Judah astray.   Places for pagan worship • [Lev. 20:5]

12 And a letter came to him from Elijah the prophet, saying,

Thus says the LORD God of your father David:
Because you have not walked in the ways of Jehoshaphat your father, or in the ways of Asa king of Judah,

13 but have walked in the way of the kings of Israel, and have made Judah and the inhabitants of Jerusalem to ᴿplay the harlot like the ᴿharlotry of the house of Ahab, and also have ᴿkilled your brothers, those of your father's household, *who were* better than yourself,   Deut. 31:16 • 2 Kin. 9:22 • 2 Chr. 21:4

14 behold, the LORD will strike your people with a serious affliction—your children, your wives, and all your possessions;

15 and you *will become* very sick with a ᴿdisease of your intestines, until your intestines come out by reason of the sickness, day by day.   2 Chr. 21:18, 19

16 Moreover the LORD stirred up against Jehoram the spirit of the Philistines and the Arabians who *were* near the Ethiopians.

17 And they came up into Judah and invaded it, and carried away all the possessions that were found in the king's house, and also his sons and his wives, so that there was not a son left to him except ᵀJehoahaz, the youngest of his sons.   *Ahaziah,* 2 Chr. 22:1

18 After all this the LORD struck him in his intestines with an incurable disease.

19 Then it happened in the course of time, after the end of two years, that his intestines came out because of his sickness; so he died in severe pain. And his people made no ᵀburning for him, like ᴿthe burning for his fathers.   Burning of spices • 2 Chr. 16:14

20 He was thirty-two years old when he became king. He reigned in Jerusalem eight years and, to no one's sorrow, departed. However they buried him in the City of David, but not in the tombs of the kings.

Ahaziah Reigns in Judah

22 Then the inhabitants of Jerusalem made Ahaziah his youngest son king in his place, for the raiders who came with the ᴿArabians into the camp had killed all the ᴿolder *sons.* So Ahaziah the son of Jehoram, king of Judah, reigned.   2 Chr. 21:16 • 2 Chr. 21:17

2 Ahaziah *was* *forty-two years old when he became king, and he reigned one year in Jerusalem. His mother's name *was* Athaliah the ᵀgranddaughter of Omri.   See note at 11:20

3 He also walked in the ways of the house of Ahab, for his mother advised him to do wickedly.

4 Therefore he did evil in the sight of the LORD, like the house of Ahab; for they were his counselors after the death of his father, to his destruction.

5 He also followed their advice, and went with ᵀJehoram the son of Ahab king of Israel to war against Hazael king of Syria at Ramoth Gilead; and the Syrians wounded Joram.   *Joram,* vv. 5, 7; 2 Kin. 8:28

6 Then he returned to Jezreel to recover from the wounds which he had received at Ramah, when he fought against Hazael king of Syria. And *Azariah the son of Jehoram, king of Judah, went down to see Jehoram the son of Ahab in Jezreel, because he was sick.

7 His going to Joram was God's occasion for Ahaziah's downfall; for when he arrived, he went out with ᵀJehoram against Jehu the son of Nimshi, whom the LORD had anointed to cut off the house of Ahab.   See note at v. 5

8 And it happened, when Jehu was ᴿexecuting judgment on the house of Ahab, and ᴿfound the princes of Judah and the sons of Ahaziah's brothers who served Ahaziah, that he killed them.   2 Kin. 9:22–24 • 2 Kin. 10:10–14

9 ᴿThen he searched for Ahaziah; and they caught him (he was hiding in Samaria), and brought him to Jehu. When they had killed

22:2 *twenty-two,* 2 Kin. 8:26
22:6 Heb. mss., LXX, Syr., Vg. *Ahaziah* and 2 Kin. 8:29

him, they buried him, "because," they said, "he is the son of ᴿJehoshaphat, who sought the Lord with all his heart." So the house of Ahaziah had no one to assume power over the kingdom.   [2 Kin. 9:27] • 1 Kin. 15:24

Athaliah Reigns in Judah

10 ᴿNow when Athaliah the mother of Ahaziah saw that her son was dead, she arose and destroyed all the royal heirs of the house of Judah.   2 Kin. 11:1-3
11 But ᵀJehoshabeath, the daughter of the king, took ᴿJoash the son of Ahaziah, and stole him away from among the king's sons who were being murdered, and put him and his nurse in a bedroom. So Jehoshabeath, the daughter of King Jehoram, the wife of Jehoiada the priest (for she was the sister of Ahaziah), hid him from Athaliah so that she did not kill him.   Jehosheba, 2 Kin. 11:2 • 2 Kin. 12:18
12 And he was hidden with them in the house of God for six years, while Athaliah reigned over the land.

Joash Crowned King of Judah

23 In ᴿthe seventh year ᴿJehoiada strengthened himself, and made a covenant with the captains of hundreds: Azariah the son of Jeroham, Ishmael the son of Jehohanan, Azariah the son of ᴿObed, Maaseiah the son of Adaiah, and Elishaphat the son of Zichri.   2 Kin. 11:4 • 2 Kin. 12:2 • 1 Chr. 2:37, 38
2 And they went throughout Judah and gathered the Levites from all the cities of Judah, and the ᴿchief fathers of Israel, and they came to Jerusalem.   Ezra 1:5
3 Then all the assembly made a covenant with the king in the house of God. And he said to them, "Behold, the king's son shall reign, as the Lord has ᴿsaid of the sons of David.   2 Sam. 7:12
4 "This is what you shall do: One-third of you ᴿentering on the Sabbath, of the priests and the Levites, shall be keeping watch over the doors;   1 Chr. 9:25
5 "one-third shall be at the king's house; and one-third at the Gate of the Foundation. All the people shall be in the courts of the house of the Lord.
6 "But let no one come into the house of the Lord except the priests and ᴿthose of the Levites who serve. They may go in, for they are holy; but all the people shall keep the watch of the Lord.   1 Chr. 23:28-32
7 "And the Levites shall surround the king on all sides, every man with his weapons in his hand; and whoever comes into the house, let him be put to death. You are to be with the king when he comes in and when he goes out."
8 So the Levites and all Judah did according to all that Jehoiada the priest commanded. And each man took his men who were to be on duty on the Sabbath, with

those who were going off duty on the Sabbath; for Jehoiada the priest had not dismissed ᴿthe divisions.   1 Chr. 24:1-31
9 And Jehoiada the priest gave to the captains of hundreds the spears and the large and small shields which had belonged to King David, that were in the temple of God.
10 Then he set all the people, every man with his weapon in his hand, from the right side of the temple to the left side of the temple, along by the altar and by the temple, all around the king.
11 And they brought out the king's son, put the crown on him, ᴿgave him the ᵀTestimony, and made him king. Then Jehoiada and his sons anointed him, and said, "Long live the king!"   Deut. 17:18 • The Law, Ex. 25:16, 21; Deut. 31:9

Death of Athaliah

12 Now when Athaliah heard the noise of the people running and praising the king, she came to the people in the temple of the Lord.
13 When she looked, there was the king standing by his pillar at the entrance; and the leaders and the trumpeters were by the king. All the people of the land were rejoicing and blowing trumpets, also the singers with musical instruments, and ᴿthose who led in praise. So Athaliah tore her clothes and said, ᴿ"Treason! Treason!"   1 Chr. 25:8 • 2 Kin. 9:23
14 And Jehoiada the priest brought out the captains of hundreds who were set over the army, and said to them, "Take her outside under guard, and slay with the sword whoever follows her." For the priest had said, "Do not kill her in the house of the Lord."
15 So they seized her; and she went by way of the entrance of the Horse Gate into the king's house, and they killed her there.
16 Then Jehoiada made a ᴿcovenant between himself, the people, and the king, that they should be the Lord's people.   Josh. 24:24, 25
17 And all the people went to the temple of Baal, and tore it down. They broke in pieces its altars and images, and killed Mattan the priest of Baal before the altars.
18 Also Jehoiada appointed the oversight of the house of the Lord to the hand of the priests, the Levites, whom David had assigned in the house of the Lord, to offer the burnt offerings of the Lord, as it is written in the Law of Moses, with rejoicing and with singing, as it was established by David.
19 And he set the gatekeepers at the gates of the house of the Lord, so that no one who was in any way unclean should enter.
20 ᴿThen he took the captains of hundreds, the nobles, the governors of the people, and all the people of the land, and brought the king down from the house of the Lord; and they went through the Upper Gate to the king's house, and set the king on the throne of the kingdom.   2 Kin. 11:19

21 So all the people of the land rejoiced; and the city was quiet, for they had slain Athaliah with the sword.

Joash Repairs the Temple

24 Joash ᴿwas seven years old when he became king, and he reigned forty years in Jerusalem. His mother's name was Zibiah of Beersheba.   2 Kin. 11:21; 12:1–15
2 Joash did what was right in the sight of the Lᴏʀᴅ all the days of Jehoiada the priest.
3 And Jehoiada took two wives for him, and he had sons and daughters.
4 Now it happened after this that Joash set his heart on repairing the house of the Lᴏʀᴅ.
5 Then he gathered the priests and the Levites, and said to them, "Go out to the cities of Judah, and gather from all Israel money to repair the house of your God from year to year, and see that you do it quickly." However the Levites did not do it quickly.
6 So the king called Jehoiada the chief priest, and said to him, "Why have you not required the Levites to bring in from Judah and from Jerusalem the collection, according to the commandment of Moses the servant of the Lᴏʀᴅ and of the assembly of Israel, for the ᴿtabernacle of witness?"   Num. 1:50
7 For the sons of Athaliah, that wicked woman, had broken into the house of God, and had also presented all the dedicated things of the house of the Lᴏʀᴅ to the Baals.
8 Then at the king's command ᴿthey made a chest, and set it outside at the gate of the house of the Lᴏʀᴅ.   2 Kin. 12:9
9 And they made a proclamation throughout Judah and Jerusalem to bring to the Lᴏʀᴅ the collection that Moses the servant of God had imposed on Israel in the wilderness.
10 Then all the leaders and all the people rejoiced, brought their contributions, and put them into the chest until all had given.
11 So it was, at that time, when the chest was brought to the king's official by the hand of the Levites, and ᴿwhen they saw that there was much money, that the king's scribe and the high priest's officer came and emptied the chest, and took it and returned it to its place. Thus they did day by day, and gathered money in abundance.   2 Kin. 12:10
12 The king and Jehoiada gave it to those who did the work of the service of the house of the Lᴏʀᴅ; and they hired masons and carpenters to repair the house of the Lᴏʀᴅ, and also those who worked in iron and bronze to restore the house of the Lᴏʀᴅ.
13 So the workmen labored, and the work was completed by them; they restored the house of God to its original condition and reinforced it.
14 When they had finished, they brought the rest of the money before the king and Jehoiada; ᴿthey made from it articles for the house of the Lᴏʀᴅ, articles for serving and offering, spoons and vessels of gold and silver. And they offered burnt offerings in the house of the Lᴏʀᴅ continually all the days of Jehoiada.   2 Kin. 12:13

Apostasy of Joash

15 But Jehoiada grew old and was full of days, and he died; he was one hundred and thirty years old when he died.
16 And they buried him in the City of David among the kings, because he had done good in Israel, both toward God and His house.
17 Now after the death of Jehoiada the leaders of Judah came and bowed down to the king. And the king listened to them.
18 Therefore they left the house of the Lᴏʀᴅ God of their fathers, and served ᴿwooden images and idols; and ᴿwrath came upon Judah and Jerusalem because of their trespass.   1 Kin. 14:23 • [Ex. 34:12–14]
19 Yet He sent prophets to them, to bring them back to the Lᴏʀᴅ; and they testified against them, but they would not listen.
20 Then the Spirit of God ᵀcame upon Zechariah the son of Jehoiada the priest, who stood above the people, and said to them, "Thus says God: ᴿ'Why do you transgress the commandments of the Lᴏʀᴅ, so that you cannot prosper? ᴿBecause you have forsaken the Lᴏʀᴅ, He also has forsaken you.'"   Lit. clothed • Num. 14:41 • [2 Chr. 15:2]
21 So they conspired against him, and at the command of the king they ᴿstoned him with stones in the court of the house of the Lᴏʀᴅ.   [Neh. 9:26]
22 Thus Joash the king did not remember the kindness which Jehoiada his ᵀfather had done to him, but killed his son; and as he died, he said, "The Lᴏʀᴅ look on it, and ᴿrepay!"   Foster father • [Gen. 9:5]

Death of Joash

23 So it happened in the spring of the year that ᴿthe army of Syria came up against him; and they came to Judah and Jerusalem, and destroyed all the leaders of the people from among the people, and sent all their ᵀspoil to the king of Damascus.   2 Kin. 12:17 • plunder
24 For the army of the Syrians ᴿcame with a small company of men; but the Lᴏʀᴅ ᴿdelivered a very great army into their hand, because they had forsaken the Lᴏʀᴅ God of their fathers. So they ᴿexecuted judgment against Joash.   Lev. 26:8 • Lev. 26:25 • 2 Chr. 22:8
25 And when they had withdrawn from him (for they left him severely wounded), ᴿhis own servants conspired against him because of the blood of the *sons of Jehoiada the priest, and killed him on his bed. So he died. And they buried him in the City of David, but

24:25 LXX, Vg. son and vv. 20–22

they did not bury him in the tombs of the kings. 2 Kin. 12:20, 21

26 These are the ones who conspired against him: ᵀZabad the son of Shimeath the Ammonitess, and Jehozabad the son of *Shimrith the Moabitess.   Or *Jozachar,* 2 Kin. 12:21

27 Now *concerning* his sons, and the many oracles about him, and the repairing of the house of God, indeed they *are* written in the annals of the book of the kings. Then Amaziah his son reigned in his place.

Amaziah Reigns in Judah

25 Amaziah *was* twenty-five years old when he became king, and he reigned twenty-nine years in Jerusalem. His mother's name *was* Jehoaddan of Jerusalem.

2 And he did *what was* right in the sight of the LORD, but not with a loyal heart.

3 Now it happened, as soon as the kingdom was established for him, that he executed his servants who had murdered his father the king.

4 However he did not execute their children, but *did* as *it is* written in the Law in the Book of Moses, where the LORD commanded, saying, ᴿ"The fathers shall not be put to death for their children, nor shall the children be put to death for their fathers; but a person shall die for his own sin."   Deut. 24:16

The War Against Edom

5 Moreover Amaziah gathered Judah together and set over them captains of thousands and captains of hundreds, according to *their* fathers' houses, throughout all Judah and Benjamin; and he numbered them ᴿfrom twenty years old and above, and found them to be three hundred thousand choice *men, able* to go to war, who could handle spear and shield.   Num. 1:3

6 He also hired one hundred thousand mighty men of valor from Israel for ᵀone hundred talents of silver. $38,400,000

7 But a ᴿman of God came to him, saying, "O king, do not let the army of Israel go with you, for the LORD *is* not with Israel—*not with* any of the children of Ephraim.   2 Chr. 11:2

8 "But if you go, be gone! Be strong in battle! *Even* so, God shall make you fall before the enemy; for God has ᴿpower to help and to overthrow."   2 Chr. 14:11; 20:6

9 Then Amaziah said to the man of God, "But what *shall* we do about the ᵀhundred talents which I have given to the troops of Israel?" And the man of God answered, ᴿ"The LORD is able to give you much more than this." $38,400,000 · [Deut. 8:18]

10 So Amaziah discharged the troops that had come to him from Ephraim, to go back home. Therefore their anger was greatly

aroused against Judah, and they returned home in great anger.

11 Then Amaziah strengthened himself, and leading his people, he went to ᴿthe Valley of Salt and killed ten thousand of the people of Seir.   2 Kin. 14:7

12 Also the children of Judah took captive ten thousand alive, brought them to the top of the rock, and cast them down from the top of the rock, so that they all were dashed in pieces.

13 But as for the soldiers of the army which Amaziah had discharged, so that they would not go with him to battle, they raided the cities of Judah from Samaria to Beth Horon, killed three thousand in them, and took much ᵀspoil.   *plunder*

14 Now it was so, after Amaziah came from the slaughter of the Edomites, that he brought the gods of the people of Seir, set them up *to be* his gods, and bowed down before them and burned incense to them.

15 Therefore the anger of the LORD was aroused against Amaziah, and He sent him a prophet who said to him, "Why have you sought ᴿthe gods of the people, which ᴿcould not rescue their own people from your hand?"   [Ps. 96:5] · 2 Chr. 25:11

16 So it was, as he talked with him, that *the king* said to him, "Have we made you the king's counselor? Cease! Why should you be killed?" Then the prophet ceased, and said, "I know that God has ᴿdetermined to destroy you, because you have done this and have not heeded my advice."   [1 Sam. 2:25]

Israel Defeats Judah

17 Now Amaziah king of Judah asked advice and sent to *Joash the son of Jehoahaz, the son of Jehu, king of Israel, saying, "Come, let us face one another *in battle."*

18 And Joash king of Israel sent to Amaziah king of Judah, saying, "The thistle that *was* in Lebanon sent to the cedar that was in Lebanon, saying, 'Give your daughter to my son as wife'; and a wild beast that *was* in Lebanon passed by and trampled the thistle.

19 "Indeed you say that you have defeated the Edomites, and your heart is lifted up to ᴿboast. Stay at home now; why should you meddle with trouble, that you should fall— you and Judah with you?"   2 Chr. 26:16; 32:25

20 But Amaziah would not heed, for it *came* from God, that He might give them into the hand *of their enemies,* because they ᴿsought the gods of Edom.   2 Chr. 25:14

21 So Joash king of Israel went out; and he and Amaziah king of Judah faced one another at ᴿBeth Shemesh, which *belongs* to Judah.   Josh. 19:38

22 And Judah was defeated by Israel, and every man fled to his tent.

23 Then Joash the king of Israel captured Amaziah king of Judah, the son of Joash, the son of RJehoahaz, at Beth Shemesh; and he brought him to Jerusalem, and broke down the wall of Jerusalem from the Gate of Ephraim to the Corner Gate—Tfour hundred cubits.   2 Chr. 21:17; 22:1, 6 • 600 ft.

24 And *he took* all the gold and silver, all the articles that were found in the house of God with RObed-Edom, the treasures of the king's house, and hostages, and returned to Samaria.   1 Chr. 26:15

Death of Amaziah

25 Amaziah the son of Joash, king of Judah, lived fifteen years after the death of Joash the son of Jehoahaz, king of Israel.

26 Now the rest of the acts of Amaziah, from first to last, indeed *are* they not written in the book of the kings of Judah and Israel?

27 After the time that Amaziah turned away from following the LORD, they made a conspiracy against him in Jerusalem, and he fled to Lachish; but they sent after him to Lachish and killed him there.

28 Then they brought him on horses and buried him with his fathers in Tthe City of Judah.   *The City of David*

Uzziah Reigns in Judah

26 Now all the people of Judah took *Uzziah, who *was* sixteen years old, and made him king instead of his father Amaziah.

2 He built *Elath and restored it to Judah, after the king rested with his fathers.

3 Uzziah *was* sixteen years old when he became king, and he reigned fifty-two years in Jerusalem. His mother's name was Jecholiah of Jerusalem.

4 And he did *what was* Rright in the sight of the LORD, according to all that his father Amaziah had done.   2 Chr. 24:2

5 He sought God in the days of Zechariah, who had understanding in the *visions of God; and as long as he sought the LORD, God made him Rprosper.   [2 Chr. 15:2; 20:20; 31:21]

6 Now he went out and Rmade war against the Philistines, and broke down the wall of Gath, the wall of Jabneh, and the wall of Ashdod; and he built cities *around* Ashdod and among the Philistines.   Is. 14:29

7 God helped him against Rthe Philistines, against the Arabians who lived in Gur Baal, and against the Meunites.   2 Chr. 21:16

8 Also the Ammonites Rbrought tribute to Uzziah. His fame spread as far as the en-trance of Egypt, for he became exceedingly strong.   2 Chr. 17:11

9 And Uzziah built towers in Jerusalem at the RCorner Gate, at the Valley Gate, and at the corner buttress of the wall; then he fortified them.   Neh. 3:13, 19, 32

10 Also he built towers in the desert. He dug many wells, for he had much livestock, both in the lowlands and in the plains; *he also had* farmers and vinedressers in the mountains and in Carmel, for he loved the soil.

11 Moreover Uzziah had an army of fighting men who went out to war by companies, according to the number on their roll as prepared by Jeiel the scribe and Maaseiah the officer, under the hand of Hananiah, *one* of the king's captains.

12 The total number of Tchief officers of the mighty men of valor *was* two thousand six hundred.   Lit. *chief fathers*

13 And under their authority *was* an army of three hundred and seven thousand five hundred, that made war with mighty power, to help the king against the enemy.

14 Then Uzziah prepared for them, for the entire army, shields, spears, helmets, body armor, bows, and slings *to cast* stones.

15 And he made devices in Jerusalem, invented by Rskillful men, to be on the towers and the corners, to shoot arrows and large stones. So his fame spread far and wide, for he was marvelously helped till he became strong.   Ex. 39:3, 8

The Penalty for Uzziah's Pride

16 But Rwhen he was strong his heart was Rlifted up, to *his* destruction, for he transgressed against the LORD his God by entering the temple of the LORD to burn incense on the altar of incense.   [Deut. 32:15] • 2 Chr. 25:19

17 So RAzariah the priest went in after him, and with him were eighty priests of the LORD—valiant men.   1 Chr. 6:10

18 And they withstood King Uzziah, and said to him, "It Ris not for you, Uzziah, to burn incense to the LORD, but for the priests, the sons of Aaron, who are consecrated to burn incense. Get out of the sanctuary, for you have trespassed! You *shall have* no honor from the LORD God."   [Num. 3:10]

19 Then Uzziah became furious; and he *had* a censer in his hand to burn incense. And while he was angry with the priests, Rleprosy broke out on his forehead, before the priests in the house of the LORD, beside the incense altar.   2 Kin. 5:25-27

20 And Azariah the chief priest and all the priests looked at him, and there, on his forehead, he *was* leprous; so they thrust him out of that place. Indeed he also hurried to get out, because the LORD had struck him.

21 RKing Uzziah was a leper until the day of his death. He dwelt in an Risolated house,

26:1 *Azariah,* 2 Kin. 14:21ff.
26:2 Heb. *Eloth*
26:5 Heb. mss., LXX, Syr., Tg., Arab. *fear*

because he was a leper; for he was cut off from the house of the LORD. Then Jotham his son *was* over the king's house, judging the people of the land.   2 Kin. 15:5 • [Lev. 13:46]

22 Now the rest of the acts of Uzziah, from first to last, the prophet ᴿIsaiah the son of Amoz wrote.   Is. 1:1

23 So Uzziah ᵀrested with his fathers, and they buried him with his fathers in the field of burial which *belonged* to the kings, for they said, "He is a leper." Then Jotham his son reigned in his place.   *Died and joined his ancestors*

Jotham Reigns in Judah

27 Jotham *was* twenty-five years old when he became king, and he reigned sixteen years in Jerusalem. His mother's name *was* *Jerushah the daughter of Zadok.

2 And he did *what was* right in the sight of the LORD, according to all that his father Uzziah had done (although he did not enter the temple of the LORD). But still ᴿthe people acted corruptly.   2 Kin. 15:35

3 He built the Upper Gate of the house of the LORD, and he built extensively on the wall of ᴿOphel.   2 Chr. 33:14

4 Moreover he built cities in the mountains of Judah, and in the forests he built fortresses and towers.

5 He also fought with the king of the ᴿAmmonites and defeated them. And the people of Ammon gave him in that year one hundred talents of silver, ten thousand kors of wheat, and ten thousand of barley. The people of Ammon paid this to him in the second and third years also.   2 Chr. 26:8

6 So Jotham became mighty, because he prepared his ways before the LORD his God.

7 Now the rest of the acts of Jotham, and all his wars and his ways, indeed they *are* written in the book of the kings of Israel and Judah.

8 He was twenty-five years old when he became king, and he reigned sixteen years in Jerusalem.

9 ᴿSo Jotham rested with his fathers, and they buried him in the City of David. Then Ahaz his son reigned in his place.   2 Kin. 15:38

Ahaz Reigns in Judah

28 Ahaz ᴿwas twenty years old when he became king, and he reigned sixteen years in Jerusalem; and he did not do *what was* right in the sight of the LORD, as his father David *had done*.   2 Kin. 16:2-4

2 For he walked in the ways of the kings of Israel, and made ᴿmolded images for ᴿthe Baals.   Ex. 34:17 • Judg. 2:11

3 He burned incense in the Valley of the Son of Hinnom, and burned his children in the fire, according to the abominations of the

27:1 *Jerusha,* 2 Kin. 15:33

nations whom the LORD had ᴿcast out before the children of Israel.   [Lev. 18:24-30]

4 And he sacrificed and burned incense on the ᵀhigh places, on the hills, and under every green tree.   *Places for pagan worship*

Syria and Israel Defeat Judah

5 Therefore ᴿthe LORD his God delivered him into the hand of the king of Syria. They defeated him, and carried away a great multitude of them as captives, and brought *them* to Damascus. Then he was also delivered into the hand of the king of Israel, who defeated him with a great slaughter.   [Is. 10:5]

6 For Pekah the son of Remaliah killed one hundred and twenty thousand in Judah in one day, all valiant men, because they had forsaken the LORD God of their fathers.

7 Zichri, a mighty man of Ephraim, killed Maaseiah the king's son, Azrikam the officer over the house, and Elkanah *who was* second to the king.

8 And the children of Israel carried away captive of their brethren two hundred thousand women, sons, and daughters; and they also took away much ᵀspoil from them, and brought the spoil to Samaria.   *plunder*

Israel Returns the Captives

9 But a ᴿprophet of the LORD was there, whose name *was* Oded; and he went out before the army that came to Samaria, and said to them: "Look, ᴿbecause the LORD God of your fathers was angry with Judah, He has delivered them into your hand; but you have killed them in a rage *that* ᴿreaches up to heaven.   2 Chr. 25:15 • [Is. 10:5; 47:6] • Rev. 18:5

10 "And now you propose to force the children of Judah and Jerusalem to be your male and female slaves; *but are* you not also guilty before the LORD your God?

11 "Now hear me, therefore, and return the captives, whom you have taken captive from your brethren, ᴿfor the fierce wrath of the LORD *is* upon you."   James 2:13

12 Then some of the heads of the children of Ephraim, Azariah the son of Johanan, Berechiah the son of Meshillemoth, Jehizkiah the son of Shallum, and Amasa the son of Hadlai, stood up against those who came from the war,

13 and said to them, "You shall not bring the captives here, for we *already* have offended the LORD. You intend to add to our sins and to our guilt; for our guilt is great, and *there is* fierce wrath against Israel."

14 So the armed men left the captives and the ᵀspoil before the leaders and all the assembly.   *plunder*

15 Then the men who were designated by name rose up and took the captives, and from the spoil they clothed all who were naked among them, dressed them and gave them

sandals, gave them food and drink, and anointed them; and they let all the feeble ones ride on donkeys. So they brought them to their brethren at Jericho, the city of palm trees. Then they returned to Samaria.

Assyria Refuses to Help Judah

16 ^RAt the same time King Ahaz sent to the *kings of Assyria to help him.   2 Kin. 16:7

17 For again the Edomites had come, attacked Judah, and carried away captives.

18 ^RThe Philistines also had invaded the cities of the lowland and of the South of Judah, and had taken Beth Shemesh, Aijalon, Gederoth, Sochoh with its villages, Timnah with its villages, and Gimzo with its villages; and they dwelt there.   Ezek. 16:27, 57

19 For the LORD brought Judah low because of Ahaz king of Israel, for he had encouraged moral decline in Judah and had been continually unfaithful to the LORD.

20 Also ^RTiglath-Pileser^T king of Assyria came to him and distressed him, and did not assist him.   1 Chr. 5:26 • Heb. Tilgath-Pilneser

21 For Ahaz took part of the treasures from the house of the LORD, from the house of the king, and from the leaders, and he gave it to the king of Assyria; but he did not help him.

Apostasy and Death of Ahaz

22 Now in the time of his distress King Ahaz became increasingly unfaithful to the LORD. This is that King Ahaz.

23 For ^Rhe sacrificed to the gods of Damascus which had defeated him, saying, "Because the gods of the kings of Syria help them, I will sacrifice to them ^Rthat they may help me." But they were the ruin of him and of all Israel.   2 Chr. 25:14 • Jer. 44:17, 18

24 So Ahaz gathered the articles of the house of God, cut in pieces the articles of the house of God, ^Rshut up the doors of the house of the LORD, and made for himself altars in every corner of Jerusalem.   2 Chr. 29:3, 7

25 And in every single city of Judah he made ^Thigh places to burn incense to other gods, and provoked to anger the LORD God of his fathers.   Places for pagan worship

26 Now the rest of his acts and all his ways, from first to last, indeed they are written in the book of the kings of Judah and Israel.

27 So Ahaz ^Trested with his fathers, and they buried him in the city, in Jerusalem; but they did not bring him into the tombs of the kings of Israel. Then Hezekiah his son reigned in his place.   Died and joined his ancestors

Hezekiah Reigns in Judah

29 Hezekiah ^Rbecame king when he was twenty-five years old, and he reigned twenty-nine years in Jerusalem. His mother's

28:16 LXX, [Syr.], Vg. king (cf. v. 20)

name was ^TAbijah the daughter ^Rof Zechariah.   2 Kin. 18:1 • Abi, 2 Kin. 18:2 • 2 Chr. 26:5

2 And he did what was right in the sight of the LORD, according to all that his father David had done.

Hezekiah Cleanses the Temple

3 In the first year of his reign, in the first month, he ^Ropened the doors of the house of the LORD and repaired them.   2 Chr. 28:24; 29:7

4 Then he brought in the priests and the Levites, and gathered them in the East Square,

5 and said to them: "Hear me, Levites! Now sanctify yourselves, sanctify the house of the LORD God of your fathers, and carry out the rubbish from the holy place.

6 "For our fathers have trespassed and done evil in the eyes of the LORD our God; they have forsaken Him, have turned their faces away from the ^Tdwelling place of the LORD, and turned their backs on Him.   Temple

7 ^R"They have also shut up the doors of the vestibule, put out the lamps, and have not burned incense or offered burnt offerings in the holy place to the God of Israel.   2 Chr. 28:24

8 "Therefore the wrath of the LORD fell upon Judah and Jerusalem, and He has given them up to trouble, to desolation, and to jeering, as you see with your eyes.

9 "For indeed, because of this our fathers have fallen by the sword; and our sons, our daughters, and our wives are in captivity.

10 "Now it is in my heart to make a covenant with the LORD God of Israel, that His fierce wrath may turn away from us.

11 "My sons, do not be negligent now, for the LORD has ^Rchosen you to stand before Him, to serve Him, and that you should minister to Him and burn incense."   Num. 3:6

12 Then these Levites arose: Mahath the son of Amasai and Joel the son of Azariah, of the sons of the Kohathites; of the sons of Merari, Kish the son of Abdi and Azariah the son of Jehallelel; of the Gershonites, Joah the son of Zimmah and Eden the son of Joah;

13 of the sons of Elizaphan, Shimri and Jeiel; of the sons of Asaph, Zechariah and Mattaniah;

14 of the sons of Heman, Jehiel and Shimei; and of the sons of Jeduthun, Shemaiah and Uzziel.

15 And they gathered their brethren, sanctified themselves, and went according to the commandment of the king, at the words of the LORD, to cleanse the house of the LORD.

16 Then the priests went into the inner part of the house of the LORD to cleanse it, and brought out all the debris that they found in the temple of the LORD to the court of the house of the LORD. And the Levites took it out and carried it to the Brook Kidron.

17 Now they began to ^Tsanctify on the first

day of the first month, and on the eighth day of the month they came to the vestibule of the LORD. So they sanctified the house of the LORD in eight days, and on the sixteenth day of the first month they finished.   *consecrate*

18 So they went in to King Hezekiah and said, "We have cleansed all the house of the LORD, the altar of burnt offerings with all its articles, and the table of the showbread with all its articles.

19 "Moreover all the articles which King Ahaz in his reign had ᴿcast aside in his transgression we have prepared and ᵀsanctified; and there they *are*, before the altar of the LORD."   2 Chr. 28:24 · *consecrated*

Hezekiah Restores Temple Worship

20 Then King Hezekiah rose early, gathered the rulers of the city, and went up to the house of the LORD.

21 And they brought seven bulls, seven rams, seven lambs, and seven male goats for a ᴿsin offering for the kingdom, for the sanctuary, and for Judah. Then he commanded the priests, the sons of Aaron, to offer *them* on the altar of the LORD.   Lev. 4:3–14

22 So they killed the bulls, and the priests received the blood and ᴿsprinkled *it* on the altar. Likewise they killed the rams and sprinkled the blood on the altar. They also killed the lambs and sprinkled the blood on the altar.   Lev. 8:14, 15, 19, 24

23 Then they brought out the male goats *for* the sin offering before the king and the assembly, and they laid their hands on them.

24 And the priests killed them; and they presented their blood on the altar as a sin offering to make an atonement for all Israel, for the king commanded *that* the burnt offering and the sin offering *be made* for all Israel.

25 And he stationed the Levites in the house of the LORD with cymbals, with stringed instruments, and with harps, according to the commandment of David, of Gad the king's seer, and of Nathan the prophet; ᴿfor thus *was* the commandment of the LORD by his prophets.   2 Chr. 30:12

26 The Levites stood with the instruments of David, and the priests with the trumpets.

27 Then Hezekiah commanded *them* to offer the burnt offering on the altar. And when the burnt offering began, the song of the LORD *also* began, with the trumpets and with the instruments of David king of Israel.

28 So all the assembly worshiped, the singers sang, and the trumpeters sounded; all *this* continued until the burnt offering was finished.

29 And when they had finished offering, ᴿthe king and all who were present with him bowed and worshiped.   2 Chr. 20:18

30 Moreover King Hezekiah and the leaders commanded the Levites to sing praise to the LORD with the words of David and of Asaph the seer. So they sang praises with gladness, and they bowed their heads and worshiped.

31 Then Hezekiah answered and said, "Now *that* you have consecrated yourselves to the LORD, come near, and bring sacrifices and thank offerings into the house of the LORD." So the assembly brought in sacrifices and thank offerings, and as many as were of a willing heart *brought* burnt offerings.

32 And the number of the burnt offerings which the assembly brought was seventy bulls, one hundred rams, *and* two hundred lambs; all these *were* for a burnt offering to the LORD.

33 The consecrated things *were* six hundred bulls and three thousand sheep.

34 But the priests were too few, so that they could not skin all the burnt offerings; therefore their brethren the Levites helped them until the work was ended and until the *other* priests had ᵀsanctified themselves, for the Levites were more diligent in sanctifying themselves than the priests.   *consecrated*

35 Also the burnt offerings *were* in abundance, with ᴿthe fat of the peace offerings and *with* ᴿthe drink offerings for *every* burnt offering. So the service of the house of the LORD was set in order.   Lev. 3:16 · Num. 15:5–10

36 Then Hezekiah and all the people rejoiced that God had prepared the people, since the events took place so suddenly.

Hezekiah Keeps the Passover

30 And Hezekiah sent to all Israel and Judah, and also wrote letters to Ephraim and Manasseh, that they should come to the house of the LORD at Jerusalem, to keep the Passover to the LORD God of Israel.

2 For the king and his leaders and all the assembly in Jerusalem had agreed to keep the Passover in the second month.

3 For they could not keep it at *the regular time, because a sufficient number of priests had not consecrated themselves, nor had the people gathered together at Jerusalem.

4 And the matter pleased the king and all the assembly.

5 So they ᵀresolved to make a proclamation throughout all Israel, from Beersheba to Dan, that they should come to keep the Passover to the LORD God of Israel at Jerusalem, since they had not done *it* for a long *time* in the *prescribed* manner.   *established a decree to*

6 Then the runners went throughout all Israel and Judah with the letters from the king and his leaders, and spoke according to the command of the king: "Children of Israel, ᴿreturn to the LORD God of Abraham, Isaac, and Israel; then He will return to the remnant

30:3 The first month, Lev. 23:5; lit. *that time*

of you who have escaped from the hand of the kings of Assyria.   [Jer. 4:1]

7 "And do not be like your fathers and your brethren, who trespassed against the Lord God of their fathers, so that He gave them up to desolation, as you see.

8 "Now do not be ᵀstiff-necked, as your fathers *were, but* yield yourselves to the Lord; and enter His sanctuary, which He has sanctified forever, and serve the Lord your God, ᴿthat the fierceness of His wrath may turn away from you.   Rebellious • 2 Chr. 29:10

9 "For if you return to the Lord, your brethren and your children *will be treated* with compassion by those who lead them captive, so that they may come back to this land; for the Lord your God *is* ᴿgracious and merciful, and will not turn His face from you if you ᴿreturn to Him."   [Ex. 34:6] • [Is. 55:7]

10 So the runners passed from city to city through the country of Ephraim and Manasseh, as far as Zebulun; but ᴿthey laughed at them and mocked them.   2 Chr. 36:16

11 Nevertheless ᴿsome from Asher, Manasseh, and Zebulun humbled themselves and came to Jerusalem.   2 Chr. 11:16; 30:18, 21

12 Also ᴿthe hand of God was on Judah to give them singleness of heart to obey the command of the king and the leaders, ᴿat the word of the Lord.   [Phil. 2:13] • 2 Chr. 29:25

13 Now many people, a very great assembly, gathered at Jerusalem to keep the Feast of Unleavened Bread in the second month.

14 They arose and took away the ᴿaltars that *were* in Jerusalem, and they took away all the incense altars and cast *them* into the Brook ᴿKidron.   2 Chr. 28:24 • 2 Chr. 29:16

15 Then they slaughtered the Passover *lambs* on the fourteenth *day* of the second month. The priests and the Levites ᵀwere ashamed, and ᵀsanctified themselves, and brought the burnt offerings to the house of the Lord.   *humbled themselves • set themselves apart*

16 They stood in their place according to their custom, according to the Law of Moses the man of God; the priests sprinkled the blood *received* from the hand of the Levites.

17 For *there were* many in the assembly who had not sanctified themselves; therefore the Levites had charge of the slaughter of the Passover *lambs* for everyone who *was* not clean, to sanctify *them* to the Lord.

18 For a multitude of the people, ᴿmany from Ephraim, Manasseh, Issachar, and Zebulun, had not cleansed themselves, ᴿyet they ate the Passover contrary to what was written. But Hezekiah prayed for them, saying, "May the good Lord provide atonement for everyone   2 Chr. 30:1, 11, 25 • [Num. 9:10]

19 "*who* ᴿprepares his heart to seek God, the Lord God of his fathers, though *he is* not *cleansed* according to the purification of the sanctuary."   2 Chr. 19:3

20 And the Lord listened to Hezekiah and healed the people.

21 So the children of Israel who were present at Jerusalem kept ᴿthe Feast of Unleavened Bread seven days with great gladness; and the Levites and the priests praised the Lord day by day, *singing* to the Lord, accompanied by loud instruments.   Ex. 12:15; 13:6

22 And Hezekiah gave encouragement to all the Levites ᴿwho taught the good knowledge of the Lord; and they ate throughout the feast seven days, offering peace offerings and ᴿmaking confession to the Lord God of their fathers.   2 Chr. 17:9; 35:3 • Ezra 10:11

23 Then the whole assembly agreed to keep *the feast* ᴿanother seven days, and they kept it *another* seven days with gladness.   1 Kin. 8:65

24 For Hezekiah king of Judah gave to the assembly a thousand bulls and seven thousand sheep, and the leaders gave to the assembly a thousand bulls and ten thousand sheep; and a great number of priests ᴿsanctifiedᵀ themselves.   2 Chr. 29:34 • *consecrated*

25 The whole assembly of Judah rejoiced, also the priests and Levites, all the assembly that came from Israel, the sojourners ᴿwho came from the land of Israel, and those who dwelt in Judah.   2 Chr. 30:11, 18

26 So there was great joy in Jerusalem, for since the time of ᴿSolomon the son of David, king of Israel, *there had* been nothing like this in Jerusalem.   2 Chr. 7:8-10

27 Then the priests, the Levites, arose and ᴿblessed the people, and their voice was heard; and their prayer came *up* to ᴿHis holy dwelling place, to heaven.   Num. 6:23 • Deut. 26:15

The Reforms of Hezekiah

31 Now when all this was finished, all Israel who were present went out to the cities of Judah and ᴿbroke the sacred pillars in pieces, cut down the wooden images, and threw down the high places and the altars—from all Judah, Benjamin, Ephraim, and Manasseh—until they had utterly destroyed them all. Then all the children of Israel returned to their own cities, every man to his possession.   2 Kin. 18:4

2 And Hezekiah appointed ᴿthe divisions of the priests and the Levites according to their divisions, each man according to his service, the priests and Levites for burnt offerings and peace offerings, to serve, to give thanks, and to praise in the gates of the ᵀcamp of the Lord.   1 Chr. 23:6; 24:1 • Temple

3 The king also *appointed* a ᵀportion of his ᵀpossessions for the burnt offerings: for the morning and evening burnt offerings, the burnt offerings for the Sabbaths and the New Moons and the set feasts, as *it is* written in the Law of the Lord.   *share • property*

4 Moreover he commanded the people who dwelt in Jerusalem to contribute ᴿsupportᵀ for the priests and the Levites, that they

might devote themselves to [R]the Law of the LORD.   Num. 18:8 · *the portion due* · Mal. 2:7

5 As soon as the commandment was circulated, the children of Israel brought in abundance [R]the firstfruits of grain and wine, oil and honey, and of all the produce of the field; and they brought in abundantly the [R]tithe of everything.   Ex. 22:29 · [Lev. 27:30]

6 And the children of Israel and Judah, who dwelt in the cities of Judah, brought the tithe of oxen and sheep; also the [R]tithe of holy things which were consecrated to the LORD their God they laid in heaps.   Deut. 14:28

7 In the third month they began laying them in heaps, and they finished in the seventh month.

8 And when Hezekiah and the leaders came and saw the heaps, they blessed the LORD and His people Israel.

9 Then Hezekiah questioned the priests and the Levites concerning the heaps.

10 And Azariah the chief priest, from the house of Zadok, answered him and said, [R]"Since *the people* began to bring the offerings into the house of the LORD, we have had enough to eat and have plenty left, for the LORD has blessed His people; and what is left *is* this great [R]abundance."   [Mal. 3:10] · Ex. 36:5

11 Now Hezekiah commanded *them* to prepare [R]rooms[T] in the house of the LORD, and they prepared them.   1 Kin. 6:5–8 · *storerooms*

12 Then they faithfully brought in the offerings, the tithes, and the dedicated things; Cononiah the Levite had charge of them, and Shimei his brother *was* the next.

13 Jehiel, Azaziah, Nahath, Asahel, Jerimoth, Jozabad, Eliel, Ismachiah, Mahath, and Benaiah *were* overseers under the hand of Cononiah and Shimei his brother, at the commandment of Hezekiah the king and Azariah the ruler of the house of God.

14 Kore the son of Imnah the Levite, the keeper of the East Gate, *was* over the freewill offerings to God, to distribute the offerings of the LORD and the most holy things.

15 And under him *were* [R]Eden, Miniamin, Jeshua, Shemaiah, Amariah, and Shecaniah, *his* faithful assistants in [R]the cities of the priests, to distribute [R]allotments to their brethren by divisions, to the great as well as the small.   2 Chr. 29:12 · Josh. 21:1–3, 9 · 1 Chr. 9:26

16 Besides those males from three years old and up who were written in the genealogy, they distributed to everyone who entered the house of the LORD his daily portion for the work of his service, by his division,

17 and to the priests who were written in the genealogy according to their father's house, and to the Levites [R]from twenty years old and up according to their work, by their divisions,   1 Chr. 23:24, 27

18 and to all who were written in the gene-

alogy—their little ones and their wives, their sons and daughters, the whole company of them—for in their faithfulness they [T]sanctified themselves in holiness.   *consecrated*

19 Also for the sons of Aaron the priests, *who were* in the fields of the common-lands of their cities, in every single city, *there were* men who were [R]designated by name to distribute portions to all the males among the priests and to all who were listed by genealogies among the Levites.   2 Chr. 31:12–15

20 Thus Hezekiah did throughout all Judah, and he [R]did what *was* good and right and true before the LORD his God.   2 Kin. 20:3; 22:2

21 And in every work that he began in the service of the house of God, in the law and in the commandment, to seek his God, he did *it* with all his heart. So he [R]prospered.   Ps. 1:3

Sennacherib Boasts Against the LORD

32 After [R]these deeds of faithfulness, Sennacherib king of Assyria came and entered Judah; he encamped against the fortified cities, thinking to win them over to himself.   2 Kin. 18:13—19:37

2 And when Hezekiah saw that Sennacherib had come, and that his purpose was to make war against Jerusalem,

3 he consulted with his leaders and [T]commanders to stop the water from the springs which *were* outside the city; and they helped him.   Lit. *mighty men*

4 Thus many people gathered together who stopped all the [R]springs and the brook that ran through the land, saying, "Why should the *kings of Assyria come and find much water?"   2 Kin. 20:20

5 And he strengthened himself, [R]built up all the wall that was broken, raised *it* up to the towers, and *built* another wall outside; also he repaired [T]the Millo *in* the City of David, and made [T]weapons and shields in abundance.   2 Chr. 25:23 · Lit. *the Landfill* · *javelins*

6 Then he set military captains over the people, gathered them together to him in the open square of the city gate, and [R]gave them encouragement, saying,   2 Chr. 30:22

7 [R]"Be strong and courageous; [R]do not be afraid nor dismayed before the king of Assyria, nor before all the multitude that *is* with him; for [R]there are more with us than with him.   [Deut. 31:6] · 2 Chr. 20:15 · 2 Kin. 6:16

8 "With him *is* an [R]arm of flesh; but [R]with us *is* the LORD our God, to help us and to fight our battles." And the people were strengthened by the words of Hezekiah king of Judah.   [Jer. 17:5] · [Rom. 8:31]

9 After this Sennacherib king of Assyria sent his servants to Jerusalem (but he and all the forces with him *laid siege* against Lachish), to Hezekiah king of Judah, and to all Judah who *were* in Jerusalem, saying,

32:4 So with MT, Vg.; Arab., LXX, Syr. *king*

10 ^R"Thus says Sennacherib king of Assyria: 'In what do you trust, that you remain under siege in Jerusalem?   2 Kin. 18:19

11 'Does not Hezekiah persuade you to give yourselves over to die by famine and by thirst, saying, ^R"The LORD our God will deliver us from the hand of the king of Assyria"?   2 Kin. 18:30

12 'Has not the same Hezekiah taken away His high places and His altars, and commanded Judah and Jerusalem, saying, "You shall worship before one altar and burn incense on ^Rit"?   2 Chr. 31:1, 2

13 'Do you not know what I and my fathers have done to all the peoples of *other* lands? ^RWere the gods of the nations of those lands in any way able to deliver their lands out of my hand?   2 Kin. 18:33-35

14 'Who *was there* among all the gods of those nations that my fathers utterly destroyed that could deliver his people from my hand, that your God should be able to deliver you from my ^Rhand?   [Is. 10:5-12]

15 'Now therefore, ^Rdo not let Hezekiah deceive you or persuade you like this, and do not believe him; for no god of any nation or kingdom was able to deliver his people from my hand or the hand of my fathers. How much less will your God deliver you from my hand?' "   2 Kin. 18:29

16 Furthermore, his servants spoke against the LORD God and against His servant Hezekiah.

17 He also wrote letters to revile the LORD God of Israel, and to speak against Him, saying, "As the gods of the nations of *other* lands have not delivered their people from my hand, so the God of Hezekiah will not deliver His people from my hand."

18 Then they called out with a loud voice in *Hebrew to the people of Jerusalem who *were* on the wall, to frighten them and trouble them, that they might take the city.

19 And they spoke against the God of Jerusalem, as against the gods of the people of the earth—^Rthe work of men's hands.   [Ps. 96:5]

Sennacherib's Defeat and Death

20 ^RNow because of this King Hezekiah and ^Rthe prophet Isaiah, the son of Amoz, prayed and cried out to heaven.   2 Kin. 19:15 · 2 Kin. 19:2

21 ^RThen the LORD sent an angel who cut down every mighty man of valor, leader, and captain in the camp of the king of Assyria. So he returned ^Rshamefaced to his own land. And when he had gone into the temple of his god, some of his own offspring struck him down with the sword there.   Zech. 14:3 · Ps. 44:7

22 Thus the LORD saved Hezekiah and the inhabitants of Jerusalem from the hand of Sennacherib the king of Assyria, and from

the hand of all *others,* and *guided them on every side.

23 And many brought gifts to the LORD at Jerusalem, and ^Tpresents to Hezekiah king of Judah, so that he was exalted in the sight of all nations thereafter.   Lit. *precious things*

Hezekiah Humbles Himself

24 ^RIn those days Hezekiah was sick and near death, and he prayed to the LORD; and He spoke to him and gave him a sign. Is. 38:1-8

25 But Hezekiah did not repay according to the favor *shown* him, for ^Rhis heart was lifted up; therefore wrath was looming over him and over Judah and Jerusalem.   [Hab. 2:4]

26 ^RThen Hezekiah humbled himself for the pride of his heart, he and the inhabitants of Jerusalem, so that the wrath of the LORD did not come upon them ^Rin the days of Hezekiah.   Jer. 26:18, 19 · 2 Kin. 20:19

Hezekiah's Wealth and Honor

27 Hezekiah had very great riches and honor. And he made himself treasuries for silver, for gold, for precious stones, for spices, for shields, and for all kinds of desirable items;

28 storehouses for the harvest of grain, wine, and oil; and stalls for all kinds of livestock, and *folds for flocks.

29 Moreover he provided cities for himself, and possessions of flocks and herds in abundance; for ^RGod had given him very much property.   1 Chr. 29:12

30 This same Hezekiah also stopped the water outlet of Upper Gihon, and ^Tbrought the water by tunnel to the west side of the City of David. Hezekiah prospered in all his works.   Lit. *brought it straight to,* 2 Kin. 20:20

31 However, *regarding* the ambassadors of the princes of Babylon, whom they ^Rsent to him to inquire about the wonder that was *done* in the land, God withdrew from him, in order to ^Rtest him, that He might know all *that was* in his heart.   Is. 39:1 · [Deut. 8:2, 16]

Death of Hezekiah

32 Now the rest of the acts of Hezekiah, and his goodness, indeed they *are* written in ^Rthe vision of Isaiah the prophet, the son of Amoz, *and* in the ^Rbook of the kings of Judah and Israel.   Is. 36-39 · 2 Kin. 18-20

33 So Hezekiah ^Trested with his fathers, and they buried him in the upper tombs of the sons of David; and all Judah and the inhabitants of Jerusalem ^Rhonored him at his death. Then Manasseh his son reigned in his place.   Died and joined his ancestors · Prov. 10:7

32:22 LXX *gave them rest;* Vg. *gave them treasures*
32:28 So with LXX, Vg.; Arab., Syr. omit *folds for flocks;* MT *flocks for sheepfolds*

32:18 Lit. *Judean*

Manasseh Reigns in Judah

33 Manasseh Rwas twelve years old when he became king, and he reigned fifty-five years in Jerusalem.   2 Kin. 21:1-9

2 But he did evil in the sight of the LORD, according to the Rabominations of the nations whom the LORD had cast out before the children of Israel.   2 Chr. 28:3

3 For he rebuilt the high places which Hezekiah his father had broken down; he raised up altars for the Baals, and made wooden images; and he worshiped all *the host of heaven and served them.

4 He also built altars in the house of the LORD, of which the LORD had said, "In Jerusalem shall My name be forever."

5 And he built altars for all the host of heaven Rin the two courts of the house of the LORD.   2 Chr. 4:9

6 RAlso he caused his sons to pass through the fire in the Valley of the Son of Hinnom; he practiced soothsaying, used witchcraft and sorcery, and consulted mediums and spiritists. He did much evil in the sight of the LORD, to provoke Him to anger.   [Lev. 18:21]

7 He even set a carved image, the idol which he had made, in the house of God, of which God had said to David and to Solomon his son, R"In this house and in Jerusalem, which I have chosen out of all the tribes of Israel, I will put My name forever;   1 Kin. 9:3

8 R"and I will not again remove the foot of Israel from the land which I have appointed for your fathers—only if they are careful to do all that I have commanded them, according to the whole law and the statutes and the ordinances by the hand of Moses."   2 Sam. 7:10

9 So Manasseh seduced Judah and the inhabitants of Jerusalem to do more evil than the nations whom the LORD had destroyed before the children of Israel.

Manasseh Restored After Repentance

10 And the LORD spoke to Manasseh and his people, but they would not Tlisten.   obey

11 Therefore the LORD brought upon them the captains of the army of the king of Assyria, who took Manasseh with Thooks, bound him with Tbronze *fetters*, and carried him off to Babylon.   Nose hooks, 2 Kin. 19:28 · chains

12 Now when he was in affliction, he implored the LORD his God, and humbled himself greatly before the God of his fathers,

13 and prayed to Him; and He Rreceived his entreaty, heard his supplication, and brought him back to Jerusalem into his kingdom. Then Manasseh Rknew that the LORD was God.   Ezra 8:23 · Dan. 4:25

14 After this he built a wall outside the City of David on the west side of Gihon, in the valley, as far as the entrance of the Fish Gate;

and *it* enclosed Ophel, and he raised it to a very great height. Then he put military captains in all the fortified cities of Judah.

15 He took away Rthe foreign gods and the idol from the house of the LORD, and all the altars that he had built in the mount of the house of the LORD and in Jerusalem; and he cast *them* out of the city.   2 Chr. 33:3, 5, 7

16 He also repaired the altar of the LORD, sacrificed peace offerings and Rthank offerings on it, and commanded Judah to serve the LORD God of Israel.   Lev. 7:12

17 RNevertheless the people still sacrificed on the Thigh places, *but* only to the LORD their God.   2 Chr. 32:12 · Places for pagan worship

Death of Manasseh

18 Now the rest of the acts of Manasseh, his prayer to his God, and the words of Rthe seers who spoke to him in the name of the LORD God of Israel, indeed they *are written* in the Tbook of the kings of Israel.   1 Sam. 9:9 · Lit. *words*

19 Also his prayer and how *God* received his entreaty, and all his sin and trespass, and the sites where he built high places and set up wooden images and carved images, before he was humbled, indeed they *are* written among the sayings of *Hozai.

20 RSo Manasseh rested with his fathers, and they buried him in his own house. Then his son Amon reigned in his place.   2 Kin. 21:18

Amon's Reign and Death

21 RAmon *was* twenty-two years old when he became king, and he reigned two years in Jerusalem.   2 Kin. 21:19-24

22 But he did evil in the sight of the LORD, as his father Manasseh had done; for Amon sacrificed to all the carved images which his father Manasseh had made, and served them.

23 And he did not humble himself before the LORD, as his father Manasseh had humbled himself; but Amon trespassed more and more.

24 Then his servants conspired against him, and killed him in his own house.

25 But the people of the land executed all those who had conspired against King Amon. Then the people of the land made his son Josiah king in his place.

Josiah Reigns in Judah

34 Josiah Rwas eight years old when he became king, and he reigned thirty-one years in Jerusalem.   2 Kin. 22:1, 2

2 And he did *what was* right in the sight of the LORD, and walked in the ways of his father David; *he* did *not* turn aside to the right hand or to the left.

3 For in the eighth year of his reign, while he was still young, he began to seek the God

of his father David; and in the twelfth year he began to purge Judah and Jerusalem of the high places, the wooden images, the carved images, and the molded images.

4 They broke down the altars of the Baals in his presence, and the incense altars which *were* above them he cut down; and the wooden images, the carved images, and the molded images he broke in pieces, and made dust of them and scattered *it* on the graves of those who had sacrificed to them.

5 He also ᴿburned the bones of the priests on their ᴿaltars, and cleansed Judah and Jerusalem. 1 Kin. 13:2 • 2 Kin. 23:20

6 And *so he did* in the cities of Manasseh, Ephraim, and Simeon, as far as Naphtali and all around, with ᵀaxes. Lit. *swords*

7 When he had broken down the altars and the wooden images, had ᴿbeaten the carved images into powder, and cut down all the incense altars throughout all the land of Israel, he returned to Jerusalem. Deut. 9:21

Hilkiah Finds the Book of the Law

8 In the eighteenth year of his reign, when he had purged the land and the ᵀtemple, he sent Shaphan the son of Azaliah, Maaseiah the governor of the city, and Joah the son of Joahaz the recorder, to repair the house of the LORD his God. Lit. *house*

9 When they came to Hilkiah the high priest, they delivered the money that was brought into the house of God, which the Levites who kept the doors had gathered from the hand of Manasseh and Ephraim, from all the ᴿremnant of Israel, from all Judah and Benjamin, and *which* they had brought back to Jerusalem. 2 Chr. 30:6

10 Then they put *it* in the hand of the foremen who had the oversight of the house of the LORD; and they gave it to the workmen who worked in the house of the LORD, to repair and restore the house.

11 They gave *it* to the craftsmen and builders to buy hewn stone and timber for beams, and to floor the houses which the kings of Judah had destroyed.

12 And the men did the work faithfully. Their overseers *were* Jahath and Obadiah the Levites, of the sons of Merari, and Zechariah and Meshullam, of the sons of the Kohathites, to supervise. *Others of* the Levites, all of whom were skillful with instruments of music;

13 *were* ᴿover the burden bearers and *were* overseers of all who did work in any kind of service. And *some* of the Levites *were* scribes, officers, and gatekeepers. 2 Chr. 8:10

14 Now when they brought out the money that was brought into the house of the LORD, Hilkiah the priest ᴿfound the Book of the Law of the LORD *given* by Moses. 2 Kin. 22:8

15 Then Hilkiah answered and said to Sha-

phan the scribe, "I have found the Book of the Law in the house of the LORD." And Hilkiah gave the book to Shaphan.

16 So Shaphan carried the book to the king, bringing the king word, saying, "All that was committed to your servants they are doing.

17 "And they have ᵀgathered the money that was found in the house of the LORD, and have delivered it into the hand of the overseers and the workmen." Lit. *poured out*

18 Then Shaphan the scribe told the king, saying, "Hilkiah the priest has given me a book." And Shaphan read it before the king.

19 Thus it happened, when the king heard the words of the Law, that he tore his clothes.

20 Then the king commanded Hilkiah, Ahikam the son of Shaphan, *Abdon the son of Micah, Shaphan the scribe, and Asaiah a servant of the king, saying,

21 "Go, inquire of the LORD for me, and for those who are left in Israel and Judah, concerning the words of the book that is found; for great *is* the wrath of the LORD that is poured out on us, because our fathers have not kept the word of the LORD, to do according to all that is written in this book."

22 So Hilkiah and those the king *had appointed* went to Huldah the prophetess, the wife of Shallum the son of *Tokhath, the son of *Hasrah, keeper of the wardrobe. (She dwelt in Jerusalem in the Second Quarter.) And they spoke to her to that *effect*.

23 Then she answered them, "Thus says the LORD God of Israel, 'Tell the man who sent you to Me,

24 "Thus says the LORD: 'Behold, I will ᴿbring calamity on this place and on its inhabitants, all the curses that are written in the ᴿbook which they have read before the king of Judah, 2 Chr. 36:14–20 • Deut. 28:15–68

25 'because they have forsaken Me and burned incense to other gods, that they might provoke Me to anger with all the works of their hands. Therefore My wrath will be poured out on this place, and not be quenched.' " '

26 "But as for the king of Judah, who sent you to inquire of the LORD, in this manner you shall speak to him, 'Thus says the LORD God of Israel: "*Concerning* the words which you have heard—

27 "because your heart was tender, and you humbled yourself before God when you heard His words against this place and against its inhabitants, and you humbled yourself before Me, and you tore your clothes and wept before Me, I also have heard *you*," says the ᴿLORD. 2 Chr. 12:7; 30:6; 33:12, 13

28 "Surely I will gather you to your fathers, and you shall be gathered to your grave in

34:20 *Achbor, the son of Michaiah*, 2 Kin. 22:12
34:22 *Tikvah*, 2 Kin. 22:14 • *Harhas*, 2 Kin. 22:14

peace; and your eyes shall not see all the calamity which I will bring on this place and its inhabitants." ' " So they brought back word to the king.

Josiah Restores True Worship

29 ᴿThen the king sent and gathered all the elders of Judah and Jerusalem.   2 Kin. 23:1-3

30 The king went up to the house of the LORD, with all the men of Judah and the inhabitants of Jerusalem—the priests and the Levites, and all the people, great and small. And he read in their hearing all the words of the Book of the Covenant which had been found in the house of the LORD.

31 Then the king stood in ᴿhis place and made a ᴿcovenant before the LORD, to follow the LORD, and to keep His commandments and His testimonies and His statutes with all his heart and all his soul, to perform the words of the covenant that were written in this book.   2 Kin. 11:14; 23:3 • 2 Chr. 23:16; 29:10

32 And he made all who were present in Jerusalem and Benjamin take a stand. So the inhabitants of Jerusalem did according to the covenant of God, the God of their fathers.

33 Thus Josiah removed all the abominations from all the country that belonged to the children of Israel, and made all who were present in Israel diligently serve the LORD their God. All his days they did not depart from following the LORD God of their fathers.

Josiah Keeps the Passover

35 Now ᴿJosiah kept a Passover to the LORD in Jerusalem, and they slaughtered the Passover lambs on the ᴿfourteenth day of the first month.   2 Kin. 23:21, 22 • Ex. 12:6

2 And he set the priests in their ᴿduties and ᴿencouraged them for the service of the house of the LORD.   2 Chr. 23:18 • 2 Chr. 29:5-15

3 Then he said to the Levites who taught all Israel, who were holy to the LORD: ᴿ"Put the holy ark ᴿin the house which Solomon the son of David, king of Israel, built. ᴿIt shall no longer be a burden on your shoulders. Now serve the LORD your God and His people Israel.   2 Chr. 34:14 • 2 Chr. 5:7 • 1 Chr. 23:26

4 "Prepare yourselves according to your fathers' ᵀhouses, according to your divisions, following the written instruction of David king of Israel and the ᴿwritten instruction of Solomon his son.   households • 2 Chr. 8:14

5 "And stand in the holy place according to the divisions of the fathers' houses of your brethren the lay people, and according to the division of the father's house of the Levites.

6 "So slaughter the Passover offerings, consecrate yourselves, and prepare them for your brethren, that they may do according to the word of the LORD by the hand of Moses."

7 Then Josiah ᴿgave the lay people lambs and young goats from the flock, all for Pass-

over offerings for all who were present, to the number of thirty thousand, as well as three thousand cattle; these were from the king's ᴿpossessions.   2 Chr. 30:24 • 2 Chr. 31:3

8 And his leaders gave willingly to the people, to the priests, and to the Levites. Hilkiah, Zechariah, and Jehiel, rulers of the house of God, gave to the priests for the Passover offerings two thousand six hundred from the flock, and three hundred cattle.

9 Also Conaniah, his brothers Shemaiah and Nethanel, and Hashabiah and Jeiel and Jozabad, chief of the Levites, gave to the Levites for Passover offerings five thousand from the flock and five hundred cattle.

10 So the service was prepared, and the priests stood in their places, and the ᴿLevites in their divisions, according to the king's command.   2 Chr. 5:12; 7:6; 8:14, 15; 13:10; 29:25-34

11 And they slaughtered the Passover offerings; and the priests ᴿsprinkled the blood with their hands, while the Levites ᴿskinned the animals.   2 Chr. 29:22 • 2 Chr. 29:34

12 Then they removed the burnt offerings that they might give them to the divisions of the fathers' houses of the lay people, to offer to the LORD, as it is written in the Book of Moses. And so they did with the cattle.

13 Also they ᴿroasted the Passover offerings with fire according to the ordinance; but the other holy offerings they boiled in pots, in caldrons, and in pans, and divided them quickly among all the lay people.   Ex. 12:8, 9

14 Then afterward they prepared portions for themselves and for the priests, because the priests, the sons of Aaron, were busy in offering burnt offerings and fat until night; therefore the Levites prepared portions for themselves and for the priests, the sons of Aaron.

15 And the singers, the sons of Asaph, were in their places, according to the command of David, Asaph, Heman, and Jeduthun the king's seer. Also the gatekeepers ᴿwere at each gate; they did not have to leave their position, because their brethren the Levites prepared portions for them.   1 Chr. 9:17, 18

16 So all the service of the LORD was prepared the same day, to keep the Passover and to offer burnt offerings on the altar of the LORD, according to the command of King Josiah.

17 And the children of Israel who were present kept the Passover at that time, and the Feast of ᴿUnleavened Bread for seven days.   Ex. 12:15; 13:6

18 ᴿThere had been no Passover kept in Israel like that since the days of Samuel the prophet; and none of the kings of Israel had kept such a Passover as Josiah kept, with the priests and the Levites, all Judah and Israel who were present, and the inhabitants of Jerusalem.   2 Kin. 23:22, 23

19 In the eighteenth year of the reign of Josiah this Passover was kept.

Josiah Dies in Battle

20 After all this, when Josiah had prepared the temple, Necho king of Egypt came up to fight against ᴿCarchemish by the Euphrates; and Josiah went out against him.   Jer. 46:2

21 But he sent messengers to him, saying, "What have I to do with you, king of Judah? *I have* not *come* against you this day, but against the house with which I have war; for God commanded me to make haste. Refrain *from meddling with* God, who *is* with me, lest He destroy you."

22 Nevertheless Josiah would not turn his face from him, but disguised himself so that he might fight with him, and did not heed the words of Necho from the mouth of God. So he came to fight in the Valley of Megiddo.

23 And the archers shot King Josiah; and the king said to his servants, "Take me away, for I am severely wounded."

24 His servants therefore took him out of that chariot and put him in the second chariot that he had, and they brought him to Jerusalem. So he died, and was buried in *one of* the tombs of his fathers. And all Judah and Jerusalem mourned for Josiah.

25 Jeremiah also lamented for Josiah. And to this day all the singing men and the singing women speak of Josiah in their lamentations. They made it a custom in Israel; and indeed they *are* written in the Laments.

26 Now the rest of the acts of Josiah and his goodness, according to *what was* written in the Law of the LORD,

27 and his deeds from first to last, indeed they *are* written in the book of the kings of Israel and Judah.

The Reign and Captivity of Jehoahaz

36 Then the people of the land took Jehoahaz the son of Josiah, and made him king in his father's place in Jerusalem.

2 *Jehoahaz *was* twenty-three years old when he became king, and he reigned three months in Jerusalem.

3 Now the king of Egypt deposed him at Jerusalem; and he imposed on the land a tribute of ᵀone hundred talents of silver and a ᵀtalent of gold. $38,400,000 • $5,760,000

4 Then the king of Egypt made ᵀJehoahaz's brother Eliakim king over Judah and Jerusalem, and changed his name to Jehoiakim. And Necho took *Jehoahaz his brother and carried him off to Egypt.   Lit. *his*

The Reign and Captivity of Jehoiakim

5 Jehoiakim *was* twenty-five years old when he became king, and he reigned eleven

years in Jerusalem. And he did ᴿevil in the sight of the LORD his God.   [Jer. 22:13–19]

6 Nebuchadnezzar king of Babylon came up against him, and bound him in ᵀbronze *fetters* to carry him off to Babylon.   *chains*

7 ᴿNebuchadnezzar also carried off *some* of the articles from the house of the LORD to Babylon, and put them in his temple at Babylon.   Dan. 1:1, 2

8 Now the rest of the acts of Jehoiakim, the abominations which he did, and what was found against him, indeed they *are* written in the book of the kings of Israel and Judah. Then Jehoiachin his son reigned in his place.

The Reign and Captivity of Jehoiachin

9 ᴿJehoiachin *was* *eight years old when he became king, and he reigned in Jerusalem three months and ten days. And he did evil in the sight of the LORD.   2 Kin. 24:8–17

10 At the turn of the year ᴿKing Nebuchadnezzar summoned *him* and took him to Babylon, ᴿwith the costly articles from the house of the LORD, and made ᴿZedekiah,ᵀ *Jehoiakim's* brother, king over Judah and Jerusalem.   2 Kin. 24:10–17 • Dan. 1:1, 2 • Jer. 37:1 • Or *Mattaniah*

Zedekiah Reigns in Judah

11 ᴿZedekiah *was* twenty-one years old when he became king, and he reigned eleven years in Jerusalem.   Jer. 52:1

12 He did evil in the sight of the LORD his God, *and* ᴿdid not humble himself before Jeremiah the prophet, *who spoke* from the mouth of the LORD.   Jer. 21:3–7; 44:10

13 And he also ᴿrebelled against King Nebuchadnezzar, who had made him swear *an oath* by God; but he ᴿstiffened his neck and hardened his heart against turning to the LORD God of Israel.   Ezek. 17:15 • 2 Kin. 17:14

14 Moreover all the leaders of the priests and the people transgressed more and more, *according* to all the abominations of the nations, and defiled the house of the LORD which He had consecrated in Jerusalem.

The Fall of Jerusalem

15 ᴿAnd the LORD God of their fathers sent *warnings* to them by His messengers, rising up early and sending *them,* because He had compassion on His people and on His dwelling place.   Jer. 7:13; 25:3, 4

16 But they mocked the messengers of God, despised His words, and scoffed at His prophets, until the wrath of the LORD arose against His people, till *there was* no remedy.

17 Therefore He brought against them the king of the Chaldeans, who killed their young men with the sword in the house of their sanctuary, and had no compassion on young

36:9 Heb. mss., LXX, Syr. *eighteen* and 2 Kin. 24:8
36:10 Lit. *his brother,* 2 Kin. 24:17

man or virgin, on the aged or the weak; He gave *them* all into his hand.

18 ᴿAnd all the articles from the house of God, great and small, the treasures of the house of the LORD, and the treasures of the king and of his leaders, all *these* he took to Babylon.   2 Kin. 25:13-15

19 ᴿThen they burned the house of God, broke down the wall of Jerusalem, burned all its palaces with fire, and destroyed all its precious possessions.   2 Kin. 25:9

▼ 1-C. The Prophets of the Old Testament Received the Scriptures as Inerrant

20 And those who escaped from the sword he carried away to Babylon, ᴿwhere they became servants to him and his sons until the rule of the kingdom of Persia,   Jer. 17:4; 27:7

21 to fulfill the word of the LORD by the mouth of Jeremiah, until the land ᴿhad en-

joyed her Sabbaths. As long as she lay deso- ▽ late ᴿshe kept Sabbath, to fulfill seventy years.   Lev. 26:34-43 • Lev. 25:4, 5 ▲

The Proclamation of Cyrus

22 ᴿNow in the first year of Cyrus king of Persia, that the word of the LORD by the mouth of ᴿJeremiah might be fulfilled, the LORD stirred up the spirit of ᴿCyrus king of Persia, so that he made a proclamation throughout all his kingdom, and also *put it* in writing, saying,   Ezra 1:1-3 • Jer. 29:10 • Is. 44:28; 45:1

23 ᴿThus says Cyrus king of Persia: All the kingdoms of the earth the LORD God of heaven has given me. And He has commanded me to build Him a ᵀhouse at Jerusalem which is in Judah. Who *is* among you of all His people? May the LORD his God *be* with him, and let him go up!   Ezra 1:2, 3 • Temple

1-C. The Prophets of the Old Testament Received the Scriptures as Inerrant (2 Chronicles 36:20, 21)—In Point 1-B (page 1068) it was seen that Christ clearly believed the Holy Scriptures to be God's written Word to mankind, absolutely authoritative and inerrant in every matter which they treated (John 10:35, page 1068). Here we see that Christ was not announcing this as a new doctrine, but was placing His own seal of truth and authentication upon a belief held by Daniel and other prophets for centuries (Dan. 9:2, page 849; cf. Jer. 29:10, page 742). Note that:

(1) Moses, the author of the first five Old Testament books, was commanded by God Himself to record events in Israel's history and transmit them to Joshua (Ex. 17:14, page 77). He kept written records of Israel's journeys (Num. 33:1, 2, page 176). His writings were to be read and studied by future kings of Israel (Deut. 17:18, 19, page 197). He wrote down a body of law which the priests of Israel preserved. This law was to be read publicly every seven years in order to preserve godly living (Deut. 31:9-12, page 209). Moses' law was to be received and studied by Joshua as the secret of his success—by direct command of God (Josh. 1:7, 8, page 215).

(2) Joshua's generation saw Moses' writings not as the words of man, but as having the authority of God (Josh. 8:31-35, page 223).

(3) David charged Solomon to obey God's written law, especially the law of Moses (1 Kin. 2:3, page 327).

(4) Isaiah claimed that the words he spoke and recorded were the actual words of God, which were to be received and obeyed (Is. 1:10, page 642). Isaiah equated correctness with adherence to God's written Word (Is. 8:20, page 650).

(5) Daniel studied the writings of Jeremiah the prophet, and took these to be accurate and inerrant records of God's message to man (Dan. 9:2, page 849; cf. Jer. 25:11, 12, page 738).

(6) Malachi ends the Old Testament era with an admonition to "remember the Law of Moses . . . the statutes and judgments" (Mal. 4:4, page 926).

The Scriptures were uniformly and universally received by the Old Testament prophets and writers themselves as the perfect and inerrant Word of God, the only standard of faith and practice.

See 2 Peter 1:21, page 1273, for **Point 1-D: Christ and the Apostles Authenticated the New Testament as Inerrant.**

THE BOOK OF

Ezra

Ezra is named after the man who exercised a significant influence on the history of Israel between the years 536—458 B.C. His book was the revelation of God at this time in Israel's experience.

The importance of the book of Ezra is inestimable. It provides us with the only information available regarding the historical period immediately following the exile. Ezra chronicles the day-by-day events of those epochal times.

AUTHORSHIP. The book does not give the name of the author but the last four chapters (7—10) were clearly written by Ezra. Here he speaks in the first person. This suggests the likelihood that he wrote the whole book.

The name Ezra means "Help" in Hebrew. He was the faithful scribe and priest, descended from Hilkiah the high priest in the reign of Josiah. The only biblical record concerning Ezra is found in the last chapters of this book and from Nehemiah 8 and 12. Here we learn that Ezra was a priest of great piety and learning who lived in Babylon during the reign of Artaxerxes.

HOW EZRA FITS INTO THE BIBLE. The book is strategic because it perpetuates the scarlet thread of redemption found in the Holy Scriptures, by continuing the genealogical record of the seed of the woman (Gen. 3:15). The book registers the names of the families of Israel who returned from exile in Babylon. Those whose genealogy could not be established were rejected. Thus the purity of the race was maintained.

The book records the return of God's people to Jerusalem under the protecting hand of the Almighty. It was by the will of God that they had been taken captive to Babylon, as shown in the books of Kings and Chronicles. God had not abandoned His people; indeed, as the books of Ezekiel and Daniel demonstrate, He was continually watching over them. And now, by His sovereign will, they were coming home. The reader will be inspired by this account to practice the presence of God and depend on Him alone for protection and provision of every need.

KEY VERSE: 6:14b—"And they built and finished it, according to the commandment of the God of Israel, and according to the command of Cyrus, Darius, and Artaxerxes king of Persia."

HOW EZRA FITS TOGETHER. The book falls naturally into three parts: (1) The Return of the Exiles under Zerubbabel (1—2), (2) The Restoration of the Worship of the LORD (3—6), and (3) The Return of the Exiles under Ezra (7—10).

Besides recounting the Israelites' return to their land, the book also records the religious reformation among those who had departed from observing the divine ordinances following the death of their leaders, Zerubbabel and Joshua. There was a clarion call to repentance and renunciation of foreign wives and their idolatrous practices. The sorrow the Israelites expressed for sin reveals hearts broken before God. The penitential prayer that followed is beautiful. It could be a model prayer for confession of sin. The book closes with a list of those who had married foreign wives.

In conclusion, the book magnifies respect for the Word of God. It brings into focus the law of the Lord as the rule of human conduct and relationships to God and man. Reestablishment of the Mosaic institutions, ordinances, and feasts reminded them of the great redemption of God's people and strengthened their faith. The purpose of the book is crystal clear: that Israel might be nourished in the words of faith and good doctrine. It is a book of repentance, revival, restoration, and renewal of faith and confidence of Israel in her great redemptive God.

—C.W.B.

End of the Babylonian Captivity

▼ 34-D. From the Babylonian Captivity to the Crucifixion

NOW in the first year of Cyrus king of Persia, that the word of the LORD by the mouth of Jeremiah might be fulfilled, the LORD stirred up the spirit of Cyrus king of Persia, so that he made a proclamation throughout all his kingdom, and also *put it* in writing, saying,

2 Thus says Cyrus king of Persia: All the kingdoms of the earth the LORD God of heaven has given me. And He has commanded me to build Him a ᵀhouse at Jerusalem which *is* in Judah. Temple
3 Who *is* among you of all His people? May his God be with him, and let him go up to Jerusalem which *is* in Judah, and build the house of the LORD God of Israel ᴿ(He *is* God), which *is* in Jerusalem. Dan. 6:26
4 And whoever is left in any place where he dwells, let the men of his place help him with silver and gold, with goods and livestock, besides the freewill offerings for the house of God which *is* in Jerusalem.

5 Then the heads of the fathers' *houses* of Judah and Benjamin, and the priests and the Levites, with all whose spirits God had moved, arose to go up and build the house of the LORD which *is* in Jerusalem.
6 And all those who *were* around them ᵀencouraged them with articles of silver and gold, with goods and livestock, and with precious things, besides all *that* was ᴿwillingly offered. Lit. *strengthened their hands* • Ezra 2:68
7 King Cyrus also brought out the articles of the house of the LORD, ᴿwhich Nebuchadnezzar had taken from Jerusalem and put in the ᵀtemple of his gods; 2 Kin. 24:13 • Lit. *house*
8 and Cyrus king of Persia brought them out by the hand of Mithredath the treasurer, and counted them out to ᴿSheshbazzar the prince of Judah. Ezra 5:14, 16

9 This *is* the number of them: thirty gold ▽ platters, one thousand silver platters, twenty-nine knives,
10 thirty gold basins, four hundred and ten silver basins of a similar *kind, and* one thousand other articles.
11 All the articles of gold and silver *were* five thousand four hundred. All *these* Sheshbazzar took with the captives who were brought from Babylon to Jerusalem. ▲

The Captives Who Returned to Jerusalem

2 Now ᴿthese *are* the people of the province who came back from the captivity, of those who had been carried away, ᴿwhom Nebuchadnezzar the king of Babylon had carried away to Babylon, and who returned to Jerusalem and Judah, everyone to his *own* city. Neh. 7:6-73 • 2 Kin. 24:14-16; 25:11
2 *Those* who came with Zerubbabel *were* Jeshua, Nehemiah, Seraiah, Reelaiah, Mordecai, Bilshan, ᵀMispar, Bigvai, ᵀRehum, *and* Baanah. The number of the men of the people of Israel: *Mispereth,* Neh. 7:7 • *Nehum,* Neh. 7:7
3 the people of Parosh, two thousand one hundred and seventy-two;
4 the people of Shephatiah, three hundred and seventy-two;
5 the people of Arah, ᴿseven hundred and seventy-five; Neh. 7:10
6 the people of ᴿPahath-Moab, of the people of Jeshua *and* Joab, two thousand eight hundred and twelve; Neh. 7:11
7 the people of Elam, one thousand two hundred and fifty-four;
8 the people of Zattu, nine hundred and forty-five;
9 the people of Zaccai, seven hundred and sixty;
10 the people of ᵀBani, six hundred and forty-two; *Binnui,* Neh. 7:15
11 the people of Bebai, six hundred and twenty-three;
12 the people of Azgad, one thousand two hundred and twenty-two;
13 the people of Adonikam, six hundred and sixty-six;

34-D. From the Babylonian Captivity to the Crucifixion (over 600 years) (Ezra 1:1-11)—The books that cover the seventy years of captivity and the restoration of Judah and Benjamin are Jeremiah, Ezekiel, Daniel, Ezra, Nehemiah, Esther, Haggai, Zechariah, and Malachi. There were approximately four hundred years between Malachi and the birth of Christ. These are often called the silent years, because no God-inspired prophet arose in Judah during that time. Zerubbabel led 42,360 from the tribes of Judah, Benjamin, and Levi back to Jerusalem (after seventy years in Babylon) to rebuild the temple (Ezra 1, 2, page 444).

The Jews had much opposition in building the temple. They stopped until the preaching of Haggai and Zechariah drove them back to the work (Hag. 1, page 908; Zech. 1, page 911). The temple was completed and dedicated to the Lord in 516 B.C., seventy years after its destruction (Jer. 29:10, page 742). During the period from the Babylonian captivity to the Crucifixion, Daniel's prophecy of the four Gentile kingdoms began to come to pass (Dan. 2, page 832; 7, page 844). The people of Judah, the descendants of Abraham, were taken captive by the Babylonian empire. They returned to Jerusalem, under the Persian empire, and rebuilt the city and the temple. Then came the Greeks, followed by the Romans. Rome was in power during the time of Christ.

See Luke 21:20-24, page 1041, for **Point 34-E: From the Crucifixion to the Fall of Jerusalem.**

14 the people of Bigvai, two thousand and fifty-six;

15 the people of Adin, four hundred and fifty-four;

16 the people of Ater of Hezekiah, ninety-eight;

17 the people of Bezai, three hundred and twenty-three;

18 the people of ᵀJorah, one hundred and twelve;   Hariph, Neh. 7:24

19 the people of Hashum, two hundred and twenty-three;

20 the people of *Gibbar, ninety-five;

21 the people of Bethlehem, one hundred and twenty-three;

22 the men of Netophah, fifty-six;

23 the men of Anathoth, one hundred and twenty-eight;

24 the people of *Azmaveth, forty-two;

25 the people of *Kirjath Arim, Chephirah, and Beeroth, seven hundred and forty-three;

26 the people of Ramah and Geba, six hundred and twenty-one;

27 the men of Michmas, one hundred and twenty-two;

28 the men of Bethel and Ai, two hundred and twenty-three;

29 the people of Nebo, fifty-two;

30 the people of Magbish, one hundred and fifty-six;

31 the people of the other ᴿElam, one thousand two hundred and fifty-four;   Ezra 2:7

32 the people of Harim, three hundred and twenty;

33 the people of Lod, Hadid, and Ono, seven hundred and twenty-five;

34 the people of Jericho, three hundred and forty-five;

35 the people of Senaah, three thousand six hundred and thirty.

36 The priests: the sons of ᴿJedaiah, of the house of Jeshua, nine hundred and seventy-three;   1 Chr. 24:7-18

37 the sons of ᴿImmer, one thousand and fifty-two;   1 Chr. 24:14

38 the sons of ᴿPashhur, one thousand two hundred and forty-seven;   1 Chr. 9:12

39 the sons of ᴿHarim, one thousand and seventeen.   1 Chr. 24:8

40 The Levites: the sons of Jeshua and Kadmiel, of the sons of ᵀHodaviah, seventy-four.   Judah, Ezra 3:9, or Hodevah, Neh. 7:43

41 The singers: the sons of Asaph, one hundred and twenty-eight.

42 The sons of the gatekeepers: the sons of Shallum, the sons of Ater, the sons of Talmon, the sons of Akkub, the sons of Hatita, and the sons of Shobai, one hundred and thirty-nine in all.

43 The Nethinim: the sons of Ziha, the sons of Hasupha, the sons of Tabbaoth,

44 the sons of Keros, the sons of ᵀSiaha, the sons of Padon,   Sia, Neh. 7:47

45 the sons of Lebanah, the sons of Hagabah, the sons of Akkub,

46 the sons of Hagab, the sons of Shalmai, the sons of Hanan,

47 the sons of Giddel, the sons of Gahar, the sons of Reaiah,

48 the sons of Rezin, the sons of Nekoda, the sons of Gazzam,

49 the sons of Uzza, the sons of Paseah, the sons of Besai,

50 the sons of Asnah, the sons of Meunim, the sons of ᵀNephusim,   Nephishesim, Neh. 7:52

51 the sons of Bakbuk, the sons of Hakupha, the sons of Harhur,

52 the sons of ᵀBazluth, the sons of Mehida, the sons of Harsha,   Bazlith, Neh. 7:54

53 the sons of Barkos, the sons of Sisera, the sons of Tamah,

54 the sons of Neziah, and the sons of Hatipha.

55 The sons of Solomon's servants: the sons of Sotai, the sons of ᴿSophereth, the sons of ᵀPeruda,   Neh. 7:57-60 • Perida, Neh. 7:57

56 the sons of Jaala, the sons of Darkon, the sons of Giddel,

57 the sons of Shephatiah, the sons of Hattil, the sons of Pochereth of Zebaim, and the sons of ᵀAmi.   Amon, Neh. 7:59

58 All the ᴿNethinim and the children of ᴿSolomon's servants were three hundred and ninety-two.   1 Chr. 9:2 • 1 Kin. 9:21

59 And these were the ones who came up from Tel Melah, Tel Harsha, Cherub, *Addan, and Immer; but they could not ᵀidentify their father's house or their ᵀgenealogy, whether they were of Israel: Lit. tell • Lit. seed

60 the sons of Delaiah, the sons of Tobiah, and the sons of Nekoda, six hundred and fifty-two;

61 and of the sons of the priests: the sons of ᴿHabaiah, the sons of ᵀKoz, and the sons of ᴿBarzillai, who took a wife of the daughters of Barzillai the Gileadite, and was called by their name.   Neh. 7:63 • Or Hakkoz • 2 Sam. 17:27

62 These sought their listing among those who were registered by genealogy, but they were not found; therefore they were excluded from the priesthood as defiled.

63 And the ᵀgovernor said to them that they should not eat of the most holy things till a priest could consult with the ᴿUrim and Thummim.   Or Tirshatha • Ex. 28:30

64 The whole assembly together was forty-two thousand three hundred and sixty,

65 besides their male and female servants, of whom there were seven thousand three

hundred and thirty-seven; and they had two hundred men and women singers.

66 Their horses *were* seven hundred and thirty-six, their mules two hundred and forty-five,

67 their camels four hundred and thirty-five, and *their* donkeys six thousand seven hundred and twenty.

68 *Some* of the heads of the fathers' *houses,* when they came to the house of the LORD which *is* in Jerusalem, offered freely for the house of God, to erect it in its place:

69 According to their ability, they gave to the treasury for the work sixty-one thousand gold drachmas, five thousand minas of silver, and one hundred priestly garments.

70 ^RSo the priests and the Levites, *some of* the people, the singers, the gatekeepers, and the Nethinim, dwelt in their cities, and all Israel in their cities.   Neh. 7:73

Worship Restored at Jerusalem

3 And when the ^Rseventh month had come, and the children of Israel *were* in the cities, the people gathered together as one man to Jerusalem.   Neh. 7:73; 8:1, 2

2 Then ^TJeshua the son of *Jozadak and his brethren the priests, and Zerubbabel the son of Shealtiel and his brethren, arose and built the altar of the God of Israel, to offer burnt offerings on it, as *it is* written in the Law of Moses the man of God.   Or *Joshua*

3 Though fear *had come* upon them because of the people of those countries, they set the altar on its bases; and they offered burnt offerings on it to the LORD, *both* the morning and evening burnt offerings.

4 They also kept the Feast of Tabernacles, ^Ras *it is* written, and ^Roffered the daily burnt offerings in the number required by ordinance for each day.   Ex. 23:16 • Num. 29:12, 13

5 Afterwards *they offered* the ^Rregular burnt offering, and *those* for New Moons and for all the appointed feasts of the LORD that were consecrated, and *those* of everyone who willingly offered a freewill offering to the LORD.   Ex. 29:38

6 From the first day of the seventh month they began to offer burnt offerings to the LORD, although the foundation of the temple of the LORD had not been laid.

7 They also gave money to the masons and the carpenters, and food, drink, and oil to the people of Sidon and Tyre to bring cedar logs from Lebanon to the sea, to Joppa, ^Raccording to the permission which they had from Cyrus king of Persia.   Ezra 1:2; 6:3

Restoration of the Temple Begins

8 Now in the second month of the second year of their coming to the house of God at Jerusalem, Zerubbabel the son of Shealtiel,

Jeshua the son of *Jozadak, and the rest of their brethren the priests and the Levites, and all those who had come out of the captivity to Jerusalem, began *work* and appointed the Levites from twenty years old and above to oversee the work of the house of the LORD.

9 Then ^RJeshua *with* his sons and brothers, Kadmiel *with* his sons, and the sons of ^TJudah, arose as one to oversee those working on the house of God: the sons of Henadad *with* their sons and their brethren the Levites.   Ezra 2:40 • Or *Hodaviah,* Ezra 2:40

10 When the builders laid the foundation of the temple of the LORD, *the priests stood in their apparel with trumpets, and the Levites, the sons of Asaph, with cymbals, to praise the LORD, according to the ^Rordinance^T of David king of Israel.   1 Chr. 6:31; 16:4; 25:1 • Lit. *hands*

11 ^RAnd they sang responsively, praising and giving thanks to the LORD: Neh. 12:24

^R"For *He is* good,   Ps. 136:1
    ^RFor His mercy *endures* forever toward
        Israel."   Jer. 33:11

Then all the people shouted with a great shout, when they praised the LORD, because the foundation of the house of the LORD was laid.

12 But many of the priests and Levites and ^Rheads of the fathers' *houses,* old men who had seen the first temple, wept with a loud voice when the foundation of this temple was laid before their eyes. Yet many shouted aloud for joy,   Ezra 2:68

13 so that the people could not discern the noise of the shout of joy from the noise of the weeping of the people, for the people shouted with a loud shout, and the sound was heard afar off.

Resistance to Rebuilding the Temple

4 Now when ^Rthe ^Tadversaries of Judah and Benjamin heard that the descendants of the captivity were building the temple of the LORD God of Israel,   Ezra 4:7-9 • *enemies*

2 they came to Zerubbabel and the heads of the fathers' *houses,* and said to them, "Let us build with you, for we seek your God as you *do*; and we have sacrificed to Him ^Rsince the days of Esarhaddon king of Assyria, who brought us here."   2 Kin. 17:24; 19:37

3 But Zerubbabel and Jeshua and the rest of the heads of the fathers' *houses* of Israel said to them, "You may do nothing with us to build a house for our God; but we alone will build to the LORD God of Israel, as King Cyrus the king of Persia has commanded us."

4 Then ^Rthe people of the land tried to discourage the people of Judah. They troubled them in building,   Ezra 3:3

3:2 *Jehozadak,* 1 Chr. 6:14

3:8 *Jehozadak,* 1 Chr. 6:14
3:10 So with LXX, Syr., Vg.; MT *they stationed the priests*

5 and hired counselors against them to frustrate their purpose all the days of Cyrus king of Persia, even until the reign of ᴿDarius king of Persia.   Ezra 5:5; 6:1

Rebuilding of Jerusalem Opposed

6 In the reign of Ahasuerus, in the beginning of his reign, they wrote an accusation against the inhabitants of Judah and Jerusalem.

7 In the days of ᴿArtaxerxes also, ᵀBishlam, Mithredath, Tabel, and the rest of their companions wrote to Artaxerxes king of Persia; and the letter was written in ᴿAramaic script, and translated into the Aramaic language.   Ezra 7:1, 7, 21 • Or in peace • 2 Kin. 18:26

8 *Rehum the commander and Shimshai the scribe wrote a letter against Jerusalem to King Artaxerxes in this fashion:

9 ᵀFrom Rehum the commander, Shimshai the scribe, and the rest of their companions—representatives of the Dinaites, the Apharsathchites, the Tarpelites, the people of Persia and Erech and Babylon and ᵀShushan, the Dehavites, the Elamites,   Lit. Then • Or Susa

10 and the rest of the nations whom the great and noble Osnapper took captive and settled in the cities of Samaria and the remainder beyond *the River—ᵀand so forth.   Lit. and now

11 This is a copy of the letter that they sent him—

To King Artaxerxes from your servants the men of the region beyond the River, ᵀand so forth: Lit. and now

12 Let it be known to the king that the Jews who came up from you have come to us at Jerusalem, and are building the ᴿrebellious and evil city, and are finishing its ᴿwalls and repairing the foundations.   2 Chr. 36:13 • Ezra 5:3, 9

13 Let it now be known to the king that, if this city is built and the walls completed, they will not pay ᴿtax, tribute, or custom, and the king's treasury will be diminished.   Ezra 4:20; 7:24

14 Now because we receive support from the palace, it was not proper for us to see the king's dishonor; therefore we have sent and informed the king,

15 that search may be made in the book of the records of your fathers. And you will find in the book of the records and know that this city is a rebellious city, harmful to kings and provinces, and that they have incited sedition within

the city in former times, for which cause this city was destroyed.

16 We inform the king that if this city is rebuilt and its walls are completed, the result will be that you will have no dominion beyond the River.

17 Then the king sent an answer:

To Rehum the commander, to Shimshai the scribe, to the rest of their companions who dwell in Samaria, and to the remainder beyond the River:
Peace, ᵀand so forth.   Lit. and now

18 The letter which you sent to us has been clearly read before me.

19 And I gave the command, and a search has been made, and it was found that this city in former times has revolted against kings, and rebellion and sedition have been fostered in it.

20 There have also been mighty kings over Jerusalem, who have ruled over all the region beyond the River; and tax, tribute, and custom were paid to them.

21 Now give the command to make these men cease, that this city may not be built until the command is given by me.

22 Take heed now that you do not fail to do this. Why should damage increase to the hurt of the kings?

23 Now when the copy of King Artaxerxes' letter was read before Rehum, Shimshai the scribe, and their companions, they went up in haste to Jerusalem against the Jews, and by force of arms made them cease.

24 Thus the work of the house of God which is at Jerusalem ceased, and it was discontinued until the second year of the reign of Darius king of Persia.

Restoration of the Temple Resumed

5 Then the prophet ᴿHaggai and ᴿZechariah the son of Iddo, prophets, prophesied to the Jews who were in Judah and Jerusalem, in the name of the God of Israel, who was over them.   Hag. 1:1 • Zech. 1:1

2 So Zerubbabel the son of Shealtiel and Jeshua the son of ᵀJozadak rose up and began to build the house of God which is in Jerusalem; and the prophets of God were with them, helping them.   Jehozadak, 1 Chr. 6:14

3 At the same time Tattenai the governor of the region beyond ᵀthe River and Shethar-Boznai and their companions came to them and spoke thus to them: ᴿ"Who has commanded you to build this ᵀtemple and finish this wall?"   The Euphrates • Ezra 1:3; 5:9 • Lit. house

4 ᴿThen, accordingly, we told them the names of the men who were constructing this building.   Ezra 5:10

5 But ᴿthe eye of their God was upon the elders of the Jews, so that they could not

4:8 The original language of Ezra 4:8 through 6:18 is Aramaic.

4:10 The Euphrates

make them cease till a report could go to Darius. Then a ᴿwritten answer was returned concerning this *matter*.   Ps. 33:18 · Ezra 6:6

6 This is a copy of the letter that Tattenai sent:

The governor of *the region* beyond the River, and Shethar-Boznai, ᴿand his companions, the Persians who *were in the region* beyond the River, to Darius the king.   Ezra 4:7–10

7 They sent a letter to him, in which was written thus—

To Darius the king:
All peace.

8 Let it be known to the king that we went into the province of Judea, to the temple of the great God, which is being built with ᵀheavy stones, and timber is being laid in the walls; and this work goes on diligently and prospers in their hands.   Lit. *stones of rolling*

9 Then we asked those elders, *and* spoke thus to them: ᴿ"Who commanded you to build this temple and to finish these walls?"   Ezra 5:3, 4

10 We also asked them their names to inform you, that we might write the names of the men who *were* chief among them.

11 And thus they returned us an answer, saying: "We are the servants of the God of heaven and earth, and we are rebuilding the ᵀtemple that was built many years ago, which a great king of Israel built and completed.   Lit. *house*

12 "But because our fathers provoked the God of heaven to wrath, He gave them into the hand of Nebuchadnezzar king of Babylon, the Chaldean, *who* destroyed this temple and ᴿcarried the people away to Babylon.   Jer. 13:19

13 "However, in the first year of Cyrus king of Babylon, King Cyrus issued a decree to build this house of God.

14 "Also, the gold and silver articles of the house of God, which Nebuchadnezzar had taken from the temple that *was* in Jerusalem and carried into the temple of Babylon—those King Cyrus took from the temple of Babylon, and they were given to one named Sheshbazzar, whom he had made governor.

15 "And he said to him, 'Take these articles; go, carry them to the temple *site* that *is* in Jerusalem, and let the house of God be rebuilt on its former site.'

16 "Then the same Sheshbazzar came *and* ᴿlaid the foundation of the house of God which *is* in Jerusalem; but from that time even until now it has been

under construction, and ᴿit is not finished."   Ezra 3:8-10 · Ezra 6:15

17 Now therefore, if *it seems* good to the king, ᴿlet a search be made in the king's treasure house, which *is* there in Babylon, whether it is *so* that a decree was issued by King Cyrus to build this house of God at Jerusalem, and let the king send us his pleasure concerning this *matter*.   Ezra 6:1, 2

The Decree of Darius

6 Then King Darius issued a decree, ᴿand a search was made in the *archives, where the treasures were stored in Babylon. Ezra 5:17

2 And at *Achmetha, in the palace that *is* in the province of ᴿMedia, a scroll was found, and in it a record *was* written thus: 2 Kin. 17:6

3 In the first year of King Cyrus, King Cyrus issued a ᴿdecree *concerning* the house of God at Jerusalem: "Let the house be rebuilt, the place where they offered sacrifices; and let the foundations of it be firmly laid, its height ᵀsixty cubits *and* its width sixty cubits,   Ezra 1:1; 5:13 · 90 ft.

4 ᴿ*with* three rows of heavy stones and one row of new timber. Let the ᴿexpenses be paid from the king's treasury.   1 Kin. 6:36 · Ezra 3:7

5 Also let ᴿthe gold and silver articles of the house of God, which Nebuchadnezzar took from the temple which *is* in Jerusalem and brought to Babylon, be restored and taken back to the temple which *is* in Jerusalem, *each* to its place; and deposit *them* in the house of God"—   Ezra 1:7, 8; 5:14

6 ᴿNow *therefore*, Tattenai, governor of *the region* beyond the River, and Shethar-Boznai, and your companions the Persians who *are* beyond the River, keep yourselves far from there. Ezra 5:3, 6

7 Let the work of this ᵀhouse of God alone; let the governor of the Jews and the elders of the Jews build this house of God on its site.   Temple

8 Moreover I issue a decree as *to* what you shall do for the elders of these Jews, for the building of this ᵀhouse of God: Let the cost be paid at the king's expense from taxes *on the region* beyond the River; this is to be given immediately to these men, so that they are not hindered.   Temple

9 And whatever they need—young bulls, rams, and lambs for the burnt offerings of the God of heaven, wheat, salt, wine, and oil, according to the request of the

6:1 Lit. *house of the books*
6:2 Probably *Ecbatana*, the ancient capital of Media

priests who *are* in Jerusalem—let it be given them day by day without fail,

10 that they may offer sacrifices of sweet aroma to the God of heaven, and pray for the life of the king and his sons.

11 Also I issue a decree that whoever alters this edict, let a timber be pulled from his house and erected, and let him be hanged on it; and let his house be made a refuse heap because of this.

12 And may the God who causes His name to dwell there destroy any king or people who put their hand to alter it, or to destroy this ᵀhouse of God which is in Jerusalem. I Darius issue a decree; let it be done diligently.   Temple

The Temple Completed and Dedicated

13 Then Tattenai, governor of *the region* beyond the River, Shethar-Boznai, and their companions diligently did according to what King Darius had sent.

14 So the elders of the Jews built, and they prospered through the prophesying of Haggai the prophet and Zechariah the son of Iddo. And they built and finished *it*, according to the commandment of the God of Israel, and according to the ᵀcommand of Cyrus, Darius, and Artaxerxes king of Persia.   decree

15 Now the temple was finished on the third day of the month of Adar, which was in the sixth year of the reign of King Darius.

16 Then the children of Israel, the priests and the Levites and the rest of the descendants of the captivity, celebrated the dedication of this ᵀhouse of God with joy.   Temple

17 And they ᴿoffered sacrifices at the dedication of this house of God, one hundred bulls, two hundred rams, four hundred lambs, and as a sin offering for all Israel twelve male goats, according to the number of the tribes of Israel.   Ezra 8:35

18 They assigned the priests to their divisions and the Levites to their divisions, over the service of God in Jerusalem, ᴿas it is written in the Book of Moses.   Num. 3:6; 8:9

The Passover Celebrated

19 *And the descendants of the captivity kept the Passover ᴿon the fourteenth *day* of the first month.   Ex. 12:6

20 For the priests and the Levites had ᴿpurified themselves; all of them *were ritually* clean. And they ᴿslaughtered the Passover *lambs* for all the descendants of the captivity, for their brethren the priests, and for themselves.   2 Chr. 29:34; 30:15 • 2 Chr. 35:11

21 Then the children of Israel who had returned from the captivity ate together with all who had separated themselves from the

ᵀfilth of the nations of the land in order to seek the LORD God of Israel.   uncleanness

22 And they kept the Feast of Unleavened Bread seven days with joy; for the LORD made them joyful, and ᴿturned the heart of the king of Assyria toward them, to strengthen their hands in the work of the house of God, the God of Israel.   [Prov. 21:1]

The Arrival of Ezra

7 Now after these things, in the reign of Artaxerxes king of Persia, Ezra the ᴿson of Seraiah, ᴿthe son of Azariah, the son of ᴿHilkiah,   1 Chr. 6:14 • Jer. 52:24 • 2 Chr. 35:8

2 the son of Shallum, the son of Zadok, the son of Ahitub,

3 the son of Amariah, the son of Azariah, the son of Meraioth,

4 the son of Zerahiah, the son of Uzzi, the son of Bukki,

5 the son of Abishua, the son of Phinehas, the son of Eleazar, the son of Aaron the chief priest—

6 this Ezra came up from Babylon; and he *was* a skilled scribe in the Law of Moses, which the LORD God of Israel had given. The king granted him all his request, according to the hand of the LORD his God upon him.

7 *Some* of the children of Israel, the priests, the Levites, the singers, the gatekeepers, and the Nethinim came up to Jerusalem in the seventh year of King Artaxerxes.

8 And Ezra came to Jerusalem in the fifth month, which *was* in the seventh year of the king.

9 On the first *day* of the first month he began *his* journey from Babylon, and on the first *day* of the fifth month he came to Jerusalem, ᴿaccording to the good hand of his God upon him.   Neh. 2:8, 18

10 For Ezra had prepared his heart to seek the Law of the LORD, and to do *it*, and to teach statutes and ordinances in Israel.

The Letter of Artaxerxes to Ezra

11 This *is* a copy of the letter that King Artaxerxes gave Ezra the priest, the scribe, expert in the words of the commandments of the LORD, and of His statutes to Israel:

12 *Artaxerxes, ᴿking of kings,   Dan. 2:37
To Ezra the priest, a scribe of the Law of the God of heaven:
Perfect *peace*, ᴿand* so forth.   Ezra 4:10

13 I issue a decree that all those of the people of Israel and the priests and Levites in my realm, who volunteer to go up to Jerusalem, may go with you.

14 And whereas you are being sent by the king and his seven counselors to inquire concerning Judah and

---

6:19 The Hebrew language resumes in Ezra 6:19 and continues through 7:11.

7:12 The original language of Ezra 7:12 through 7:26 is Aramaic. • Lit. *and now*

Jerusalem, with regard to the Law of your God which *is* in your hand;

15 and *whereas you are* to carry the silver and gold which the king and his counselors have freely offered to the God of Israel, ^Rwhose dwelling *is* in Jerusalem;   Ezra 6:12

16 and *whereas* all the silver and gold that you may find in all the province of Babylon, along with the freewill offering of the people and the priests, *are to be* ^Rfreely offered for the house of their God in Jerusalem—   1 Chr. 29:6, 9

17 now therefore, be careful to buy with this money bulls, rams, and lambs, with their grain offerings and their drink offerings, and offer them on the altar of the house of your God in Jerusalem.

18 And whatever seems good to you and your brethren to do with the rest of the silver and the gold, do it according to the will of your God.

19 Also the articles that are given to you for the service of the house of your God, deliver in full before the God of Jerusalem.

20 And whatever more may be needed for the house of your God, which you may have occasion to provide, pay *for it* from the king's treasury.

21 And I, *even* I, Artaxerxes the king, issue a decree to all the treasurers who *are in the region* beyond the River, that whatever Ezra the priest, the scribe of the Law of the God of heaven, may require of you, let it be done diligently,

22 up to one hundred talents of silver, one hundred kors of wheat, ^Tone hundred baths of wine, one hundred baths of oil, and salt without prescribed limit.   600 gal.

23 Whatever is commanded by the God of heaven, let it diligently be done for the ^Thouse of the God of heaven. For why should there be wrath against the realm of the king and his sons?   Temple

24 Also we inform you that it shall not be lawful to impose tax, tribute, or custom *on* any of the priests, Levites, singers, gatekeepers, Nethinim, or servants of this house of God.

25 And you, Ezra, according to your God-given wisdom, ^Rset magistrates and judges who may judge all the people who *are in the region* beyond the River, all such as know the laws of your God; and ^Rteach those who do not know *them.*   Ex. 18:21, 22 • [Mal. 2:7]

26 Whoever will not observe the law of your God and the law of the king, let judgment be executed speedily on him, whether *it be* death, or banishment, or confiscation of goods, or imprisonment.

27 ^RBlessed* *be* the Lord God of our fathers, ^Rwho has put *such a thing* as this in the king's heart, to beautify the house of the Lord which *is* in Jerusalem, 1 Chr. 29:10 • Ezra 6:22

28 and ^Rhas extended mercy to me before the king and his counselors, and before all the king's mighty princes.   Ezra 9:9

So I was encouraged, as the hand of the Lord my God *was* upon me; and I gathered leading men of Israel to go up with me.

Heads of Families Who Returned with Ezra

8 These *are* the heads of their fathers' houses, and *this is* the genealogy of those who went up with me from Babylon, in the reign of King Artaxerxes:

2 of the sons of Phinehas, Gershom; of the sons of Ithamar, Daniel; of the sons of David, ^RHattush;   1 Chr. 3:22

3 of the sons of Shecaniah, of the sons of ^RParosh, Zechariah; and registered with him *were* one hundred and fifty males;   Ezra 2:3

4 of the sons of ^RPahath-Moab, Eliehoenai the son of Zerahiah, and with him two hundred males;   Ezra 10:30

5 of *the sons of Shechaniah, Ben-Jahaziel, and with him three hundred males;

6 of the sons of Adin, Ebed the son of Jonathan, and with him fifty males;

7 of the sons of Elam, Jeshaiah the son of Athaliah, and with him seventy males;

8 of the sons of Shephatiah, Zebadiah the son of Michael, and with him eighty males;

9 of the sons of Joab, Obadiah the son of Jehiel, and with him two hundred and eighteen males;

10 of *the sons of Shelomith, Ben-Josiphiah, and with him one hundred and sixty males;

11 of the sons of Bebai, Zechariah the son of Bebai, and with him twenty-eight males;

12 of the sons of Azgad, Johanan ^Tthe son of Hakkatan, and with him one hundred and ten males;   Or *the youngest son*

13 of the last sons of Adonikam, whose names *are* these—Eliphelet, Jeiel, and Shemaiah—and with them sixty males;

14 also of the sons of Bigvai, Uthai and Zabbud, and with them seventy males.

Servants for the Temple

15 Now I gathered them by the river that flows to Ahava, and we camped there three days. And I looked among the people and the priests, and found none of the ^Rsons of Levi there.   Ezra 7:7; 8:2

16 Then I sent for Eliezer, Ariel, Shemaiah, Elnathan, Jarib, Elnathan, Nathan, Zecha-

7:27 The Hebrew language resumes in Ezra 7:27.
8:5 So with MT, Vg.; LXX *the sons of Zatho,* Shechaniah
8:10 So with MT, Vg.; LXX *the sons of Banni,* Shalomith

riah, and ᴿMeshullam, leaders; also for Joiarib and Elnathan, men of understanding. Ezra 10:15

17 And I gave them a command for Iddo the chief man at the place Casiphia, and I told them what they should say *to Iddo *and his brethren the Nethinim at the place Casiphia—that they should bring us servants for the house of our God.

18 Then, by the good hand of our God upon us, they ᴿbrought us a man of understanding, of the sons of Mahli the son of Levi, the son of Israel, namely Sherebiah, with his sons and brothers, eighteen men;   Neh. 8:7

19 and ᴿHashabiah, and with him Jeshaiah of the sons of Merari, his brothers and their sons, twenty men;   Neh. 12:24

20 also of the Nethinim, whom David and the leaders had appointed for the service of the Levites, two hundred and twenty Nethinim. All of them were designated by name.

Fasting and Prayer for Protection

21 Then I ᴿproclaimed a fast there at the river of Ahava, that we might ᴿhumble ourselves before our God, to seek from Him the ᴿright way for us and our little ones and all our possessions.   1 Sam. 7:6 · Is. 58:3, 5 · Ps. 5:8

22 For ᴿI was ashamed to request of the king an escort of soldiers and horsemen to help us against the enemy on the road, because we had spoken to the king, saying, "The hand of our God is upon all those for ᴿgood who seek Him, but His power and His wrath are ᴿagainst all those who ᴿforsake Him."   1 Cor. 9:15 · [Rom. 8:28] · [Ps. 34:16] · [2 Chr. 15:2]

23 So we fasted and entreated our God for this, and He ᴿanswered our prayer.   2 Chr. 33:13

Gifts for the Temple

24 And I separated twelve of the leaders of the priests—Sherebiah, Hashabiah, and ten of their brethren with them—

25 and weighed out to them ᴿthe silver, the gold, and the articles, the offering for the house of our God which the king and his counselors and his princes, and all Israel *who were* present, had offered.   Ezra 7:15, 16

26 I weighed into their hand ᵀsix hundred and fifty talents of silver, silver articles *weighing* one hundred talents, ᵀone hundred talents of gold, $249,000,000 · $576,000,000

27 twenty gold basins *worth* a ᵀthousand drachmas, and two vessels of fine polished bronze, precious as gold. $1,424,176

28 And I said to them, "You *are* ᵀholy to the LORD; the articles *are* holy also; and the silver and the gold *are* a freewill offering to the LORD God of your fathers.   consecrated

29 "Watch and keep *them* until you weigh *them* before the leaders of the priests and the Levites and ᴿheads of the fathers' *houses* of Israel in Jerusalem, *in* the chambers of the house of the LORD."   Ezra 4:3

30 So the priests and the Levites received the silver and the gold and the articles by weight, to bring *them* to Jerusalem to the house of our God.

The Return to Jerusalem

31 Then we departed from the river of Ahava on the twelfth *day* of the first month, to go to Jerusalem. And ᴿthe hand of our God was upon us, and He delivered us from the hand of the enemy and from ambush along the road.   Ezra 7:6, 9, 28

32 So we ᴿcame to Jerusalem, and stayed there three days.   Neh. 2:11

33 Now on the fourth day the silver and the gold and the articles were weighed in the house of our God by the hand of Meremoth the son of Uriah the priest, and with him *was* Eleazar the son of Phinehas; with them *were* the Levites, ᴿJozabad the son of Jeshua and Noadiah the son of Binnui,   Neh. 11:16

34 with the number *and* weight of everything. All the weight was written down at that time.

35 The children of those who had been carried away captive, who had come from the captivity, ᴿoffered burnt offerings to the God of Israel: twelve bulls for all Israel, ninety-six rams, seventy-seven lambs, and twelve male goats *as* a sin offering. All *this was* a burnt offering to the LORD.   Ezra 6:17

36 And they delivered the king's orders to the king's satraps and the governors *in the region* beyond the River. So they gave support to the people and the house of God.

Intermarriage with Pagans

9 When these things were done, the leaders came to me, saying, "The people of Israel and the priests and the Levites have not separated themselves from the peoples of the lands, with respect to the abominations of the Canaanites, the Hittites, the Perizzites, the Jebusites, the Ammonites, the Moabites, the Egyptians, and the Amorites.

2 "For they have taken some of their daughters *as wives* for themselves and their sons, so that the holy seed is mixed with the peoples of *those* lands. Indeed, the hand of the leaders and rulers has been foremost in this ᵀtrespass."   unfaithfulness

3 So when I heard this thing, ᴿI tore my garment and my robe, and plucked out some of the hair of my head and beard, and sat down ᴿastonished.   Job 1:20 · Ps. 143:4

4 Then everyone who trembled at the words of the God of Israel assembled to me, because of the transgression of those who had been carried away captive, and I sat astonished until the evening sacrifice.

8:17 So with Vg.; MT *to Iddo his brother;* LXX *to their brethren.*

5 At the evening sacrifice I arose from my fasting; and having torn my garment and my robe, I fell on my knees and ᴿspread out my hands to the Lᴏʀᴅ my God.   Ex. 9:29

6 And I said: "O my God, I am too ᴿashamed and humiliated to lift up my face to You, my God; for ᴿour iniquities have risen higher than our heads, and our guilt has grown up to the heavens.   Dan. 9:7, 8 • Ps. 38:4

7 "Since the days of our fathers to this day we *have been* very guilty, and for our iniquities we, our kings, *and* our priests have been delivered into the hand of the kings of the lands, to the sword, to captivity, to plunder, and to humiliation, as *it is* this day.

8 "And now for a little while grace has been *shown* from the Lᴏʀᴅ our God, to leave us a remnant to escape, and to give us a peg in His holy place, that our God may ᴿenlighten our eyes and give us a measure of revival in our bondage.   Ps. 34:5

9 "For we *were* slaves. Yet our God did not forsake us in our bondage; but ᴿHe extended mercy to us in the sight of the kings of Persia, to revive us, to repair the house of our God, to rebuild its ruins, and to give us ᴿa wall in Judah and Jerusalem.   Ezra 7:28 • Is. 5:2

10 "And now, O our God, what shall we say after this? For we have forsaken Your commandments,

11 "which You commanded by Your servants the prophets, saying, 'The land which you are entering to possess is an unclean land, with the ᴿuncleanness of the peoples of the lands, with their abominations which have filled it from one end to another with their impurity.   Ezra 6:21

12 'Now therefore, do not give your daughters as wives for their sons, nor take their daughters to your sons; and never seek their peace or prosperity, that you may be strong and eat the good of the land, and leave *it* as an inheritance to your children forever.'

13 "And after all that has come upon us for our evil deeds and for our great guilt, since You our God ᴿhave punished us less than our iniquities *deserve*, and have given us *such* deliverance as this,   [Ps. 103:10]

14 "should we ᴿagain break Your commandments, and join in marriage with the people committing these abominations? Would You not be ᴿangry with us until You had ᵀconsumed *us*, so that *there would be* no remnant or survivor?   [John 5:14] • Deut. 9:8 • *destroyed*

15 "O Lᴏʀᴅ God of Israel, ᴿYou *are* righteous, for we are left as a remnant, as *it is* this day. ᴿHere we *are* before You, ᴿin our guilt, though no one can stand before You because of this!"   Dan. 9:14 • [Rom. 3:19] • 1 Cor. 15:17

Confession of Improper Marriages

10 Now while Ezra was praying, and while he was confessing, weeping, and bowing down before the house of God, a very large assembly of men, women, and children gathered to him from Israel; for the people wept very ᴿbitterly.   Neh. 8:1–9

2 And Shechaniah the son of Jehiel, *one* of the sons of Elam, spoke up and said to Ezra, "We have ᴿtrespassedᵀ against our God, and have taken pagan wives from the peoples of the land; yet now there is hope in Israel in spite of this.   Neh. 13:23–27 • *been unfaithful to*

3 "Now therefore, let us make a covenant with our God to put away all these wives and those who have been born to them, according to the advice of my master and of those who tremble at the commandment of our God; and let it be done according to the law.

4 "Arise, for *this* matter *is* your *responsibility*. We also *are* with you. ᴿBe of good courage, and do *it*."   1 Chr. 28:10

5 Then Ezra arose, and made the leaders of the priests, the Levites, and all Israel ᴿswear an oath that they would do according to this word. So they swore an oath.   Neh. 5:12; 13:25

6 Then Ezra rose up from before the house of God, and went into the chamber of Jehohanan the son of Eliashib; and *when* he came there, he ᴿate no bread and drank no water, for he mourned because of the guilt of those from the captivity.   Deut. 9:18

7 And they issued a proclamation throughout Judah and Jerusalem to all the descendants of the captivity, that they must gather at Jerusalem,

8 and that whoever would not come within three days, according to the instructions of the leaders and elders, all his property would be confiscated, and he himself would be separated from the assembly of those from the captivity.

9 So all the men of Judah and Benjamin gathered at Jerusalem within three days. It *was* the ninth month, on the twentieth of the month; and ᴿall the people sat in the open square of the house of God, trembling because of *this* matter and because of heavy rain.   1 Sam. 12:18

10 Then Ezra the priest stood up and said to them, "You have ᵀtransgressed and have ᵀtaken pagan wives, adding to the guilt of Israel.   *acted unfaithfully* • Heb. *brought back*

11 "Now therefore, make confession to the Lᴏʀᴅ God of your fathers, and do His will; ᴿseparate yourselves from the peoples of the land, and from the pagan wives."   Ezra 10:3

12 Then all the assembly answered and said with a loud voice, "Yes! As you have said, so we must do.

13 "But *there are* many people; it *is* the season for heavy rain, and we are not able to stand outside. Nor *is this* the work of one or two days, for *there are* many of us who have transgressed in this matter.

14 "Please, let the leaders of our entire assembly stand; and let all those in our cities

who have taken pagan wives come at appointed times, together with the elders and judges of their cities, until ᴿthe fierce wrath of our God is turned away from us in this matter."   2 Chr. 28:11-13; 29:10; 30:8

15 Only Jonathan the son of Asahel and Jahaziah the son of Tikvah opposed this, and ᴿMeshullam and Shabbethai the Levite gave them support.   Neh. 3:4

16 Then the descendants of the captivity did so. And Ezra the priest, with certain heads of the fathers' households, were set apart by the fathers' households, each of them by name; and they sat down on the first day of the tenth month to examine the matter.

17 By the first day of the first month they finished questioning all the men who had taken pagan wives.

Pagan Wives Put Away

18 And among the sons of the priests who had taken pagan wives the following were found of the sons of ᴿJeshua the son of ᵀJozadak, and his brothers: Maaseiah, Eliezer, Jarib, and Gedaliah.   Ezra 5:2 · Jehozadak, 1 Chr. 6:14

19 And they gave their promise that they would put away their wives; and being ᴿguilty, they presented a ram of the flock as their ᴿtrespass offering.   Lev. 6:4, 6 · Lev. 5:6, 15

20 Also of the sons of Immer: Hanani and Zebadiah;

21 of the sons of Harim: Maaseiah, Elijah, Shemaiah, Jehiel, and Uzziah;

22 of the sons of Pashhur: Elioenai, Maaseiah, Ishmael, Nethanel, Jozabad, and Elasah.

23 Also of the Levites: Jozabad, Shimei, Kelaiah (the same is Kelita), Pethahiah, Judah, and Eliezer.

24 Also of the singers: Eliashib; and of the gatekeepers: Shallum, Telem, and Uri.

25 And others of Israel: of the ᴿsons of Parosh: Ramiah, Jeziah, Malchiah, Mijamin, Eleazar, Malchijah, and Benaiah;   Ezra 2:3; 8:3

26 of the sons of Elam: Mattaniah, Zechariah, Jehiel, Abdi, Jeremoth, and Eliah;

27 of the sons of Zattu: Elioenai, Eliashib, Mattaniah, Jeremoth, Zabad, and Aziza;

28 of the ᴿsons of Bebai: Jehohanan, Hananiah, Zabbai, and Athlai;   Ezra 8:11

29 of the sons of Bani: Meshullam, Malluch, Adaiah, Jashub, Sheal, and *Ramoth;

30 of the ᴿsons of Pahath-Moab: Adna, Chelal, Benaiah, Maaseiah, Mattaniah, Bezalel, Binnui, and Manasseh;   Ezra 8:4

31 of the sons of Harim: Eliezer, Ishijah, Malchijah, Shemaiah, Shimeon,

32 Benjamin, Malluch, and Shemariah;

33 of the sons of Hashum: Mattenai, Mattattah, Zabad, Eliphelet, Jeremai, Manasseh, and Shimei;

34 of the sons of Bani: Maadai, Amram, Uel,

35 Benaiah, Bedeiah, *Cheluh,

36 Vaniah, Meremoth, Eliashib,

37 Mattaniah, Mattenai, ᵀJaasai,   Or Jaasu

38 Bani, Binnui, Shimei,

39 Shelemiah, Nathan, Adaiah,

40 Machnadebai, Shashai, Sharai,

41 Azarel, Shelemiah, Shemariah,

42 Shallum, Amariah, and Joseph;

43 of the sons of Nebo: Jeiel, Mattithiah, Zabad, Zebina, *Jaddai, Joel, and Benaiah.

44 All these had taken pagan wives, and some of them had wives by whom they had children.

10:29 Or Jeremoth
10:35 Or Cheluhi or Cheluhu
10:43 Or Jaddu

THE BOOK OF
Nehemiah

HOW NEHEMIAH FITS INTO THE BIBLE. It is noteworthy that each book in the Bible has a unique spiritual character, a oneness with truth that perfectly blends in with all the other books, both of the Old and New Testaments. A survey of the entire book of Nehemiah reveals that the scriptural principles of faith, fidelity, and fervency prevail. These characteristics are woven into the entire fabric of the Scriptures. In this book they are highly visible in the life and ministry of God's man, Nehemiah.

AUTHORSHIP. Scholars differ as to the authorship of the book of Nehemiah. There are those who believe Ezra was the author; others believe Nehemiah himself was the author. One thing is for certain: the Holy Spirit inspired the one who wrote this book (2 Peter 1:21).

Nehemiah was a man of stability and integrity. As cupbearer to King Artaxerxes, he was an important officer in the royal court. In the spiritual realm, he was not a priest, king, or prophet. Instead, he had the important responsibility of administrator. He was a leader of men, courageous and steadfast in purpose. He was an alert, exemplary patriot, unflinchingly facing the realities of life. The keystone of his activity was perseverance.

Nehemiah was a man of vision and also of action. When he saw a need, he took the responsibility to do something about it. When he learned of the deplorable state of the wall around Jerusalem and the broken-down condition of the gates, he sought permission from King Artaxerxes to return to the city so he could organize the work, repair the damage, and restore order.

In the midst of severe testing for the people who stood with him in his vision of restoration for the city of his "fathers' tombs" (2:3) he displayed a deep sense of compassion, a sensitivity to their dangers and their welfare. His conduct revealed the meaning of his name *Nehemiah*, "Comfort of Jehovah."

A dominant feature of Nehemiah's life was prayer. Eleven times in the book it is recorded that he prayed. Fasting, confession of sin, repentance and praise (worship) were vital to the success of his mission. He led the way in these spiritual exercises and the people followed.

Nehemiah was a man of the Book, the Word of God. By his direction the law of Moses was not only read "distinctly" but it also was explained (8:8). On occasions it was read "from morning until midday" (8:3).

As the book is read prayerfully, Nehemiah the man of God emerges as one who does God's work in God's way, a master builder implicitly following the plan of the Master Builder, the Lord God of Israel.

CONTEXT. Nehemiah went to Jerusalem in 444 B.C. as a civil administrator, with authority from Artaxerxes, king of Persia. Under cover of night, Nehemiah went around the wall, noting the damage and observing the condition of each gate on his lonely tour. He looked further than the visible damage. He saw the finished product. He knew it could be done. He knew it *must* be done. He rallied the people of God to the task, "everyone to his work" (4:15)—a key that is still effective. United effort gets the job done.

Considerable detail is given to the account of events concerning repairing the gates and rebuilding the wall surrounding the city of Jerusalem. High priority was given to this work. The wall had been a great protection to the inhabitants of the city, but it had greatly deteriorated. All the gates were in disrepair. Because of this breakdown of protection, the enemy could enter or leave the city at will.

Walls speak not only of protection but also of separation—both *from* the enemy (the world, the flesh, and the devil) and *to* the Lord, the God of Israel. Desire for this kind of defense and dedication caused the people to meet Nehemiah's challenge with the passionate response, "'Let us rise up and build.' . . . The people had a mind to work" (2:18; 4:6). Nehemiah is a building book—an action book.

The book of Nehemiah is one of those books that stand out with clarity as a challenge and guide in carrying out the work of God in the face of orchestrated opposition. Nehemiah and his dedicated followers ran the gauntlet of sarcasm, ridicule, and hatred. His indomitable spirit did not capitulate. He inspired the people of God to press onward. He exuded confidence in God. He negated the hostilities of the enemy. He reversed reverses. The enemy's devious ways of attacking, blocking, and hindering always met with a sterling quality of leadership in Nehemiah.

In the face of intense opposition from enemies of long standing—the Moabites, Ammonites, Ashdodites, Arabians, and Samaritans—Nehemiah led the people forward to victory, rebuilding the wall and repairing the gates in fifty-two days.

This man of vision led the train of workmen through valleys of discouragement, buffetings of enemies, and the toil of hard labor by encouragement, prayer, Bible reading, exhortation, and preaching the Word, and by full dependence on God. The Feast of Tabernacles was restored and fasting and repentance were revived. The city of Jerusalem and its inhabitants returned to a great degree of normalcy. Order was established. Watchmen of the gates, singers, and Levites were appointed.

Later Nehemiah, the successful, conquering builder of the wall and repairer of the gates, returned to his responsibilities in the court of King Artaxerxes at Shushan, the capital of Persia. During his absence from Jerusalem, Tobiah, who previously had opposed Nehemiah, gained entrance and was being entertained "in the courts of the house of God" (13:7). The sensitive soul of Nehemiah was grieved when he returned, and he proceeded to cleanse the house of God with an uncompromising purge.

To sum up, Nehemiah is a book of working and watching, praying and praising, confession and cleansing, dedication and devotion—a book of power-packed instructions for the people of God of all times.

—W.B.Y.

Nehemiah Prays for His People

THE words of ᴿNehemiah the son of Hachaliah.   Neh. 10:1
It came to pass in the month of Chislev, *in* the twentieth year, as I was in ᴿShushanᵀ the ᵀcitadel,   Esth. 1:1, 2, 5 • Or *Susa* • Or *fortified palace*

2 that ᴿHanani one of my brethren came with men from Judah; and I asked them concerning the Jews who had escaped, who had survived the captivity, and concerning Jerusalem.   Neh. 7:2

3 And they said to me, "The survivors who are left from the captivity in the ᴿprovince *are* there in great distress and reproach. The wall of Jerusalem *is* also broken down, and its gates *are* burned with fire."   Neh. 7:6

4 So it was, when I heard these words, that I sat down and wept, and mourned *for many* days; I was fasting and praying before the God of heaven.

5 And I said: "I pray, Lᴏʀᴅ God of heaven, O great and awesome God, ᴿ*You* who keep *Your* covenant and mercy with those who love ᵀYou and observe ᵀYour commandments,   [Ex. 20:6; 34:6, 7] • Lit. *Him* • Lit. *His*

6 "please let Your ear be attentive and ᴿYour eyes open, that You may hear the prayer of Your servant which I pray before You now, day and night, for the children of Israel Your servants, and ᴿconfess the sins of the children of Israel which we have sinned against You. Both my father's house and I have sinned.   2 Chr. 6:40 • Dan. 9:20

7 "We have acted very corruptly against You, and have ᴿnot kept the commandments, the statutes, nor the ordinances which You commanded Your servant Moses.   Deut. 28:15

8 "Remember, I pray, the word that You commanded Your servant Moses, saying, ᴿ'*If*

you ᵀare unfaithful, I will scatter you among the nations;   Lev. 26:33 • *act treacherously*

9 *but if* you return to Me, and keep My commandments and do them, though some of you were cast out to the farthest part of the heavens, *yet* I will gather them from there, and bring them to the place which I have chosen as a dwelling for My name.'

10 "Now these *are* Your servants and Your people, whom You have redeemed by Your great power, and by Your strong hand.

11 "O Lord, I pray, please ᴿlet Your ear be attentive to the prayer of Your servant, and to the prayer of Your servants who ᴿdesire to fear Your name; and let Your servant prosper this day, I pray, and grant him mercy in the sight of this man." For I was the king's ᴿcupbearer.   Neh. 1:6 • Is. 26:8 • Neh. 2:1

Nehemiah Sent to Judah

2 And it came to pass in the month of Nisan, in the twentieth year of King Artaxerxes, *when* wine *was* before him, that I took the wine and gave it to the king. Now I had never been sad in his presence before.

2 Therefore the king said to me, "Why *is* your face sad, since you *are* not sick? This *is* nothing but ᴿsorrow of heart." So I became ᵀdreadfully afraid,   Prov. 15:13 • Lit. *very much*

3 and said to the king, "May the king live forever! Why should my face not be sad, when ᴿthe city, the place of my fathers' tombs, *lies* waste, and its gates are burned with ᴿfire?"   2 Chr. 36:19 • Neh. 1:3

4 Then the king said to me, "What do you request?" So I prayed to the God of heaven.

5 And I said to the king, "If it pleases the

1:9 Deut. 30:4

king, and if your servant has found favor in your sight, I ask that you send me to Judah, to the city of my fathers' tombs, that I may rebuild it."

6 Then the king said to me (the queen also sitting beside him), "How long will your journey be? And when will you return?" So it pleased the king to send me; and I set him ᴿa time. Neh. 5:14; 13:6

7 Furthermore I said to the king, "If it pleases the king, let letters be given to me for the governors of the region beyond *the River, that they must permit me to pass through till I come to Judah,

8 "and a letter to Asaph the keeper of the king's forest, that he must give me timber to make beams for the gates of the citadel which pertains to the *temple, for the city wall, and for the house that I will occupy." And the king granted them to me according to the good hand of my God upon me.

9 Then I went to the governors in the region beyond the River, and gave them the king's letters. Now the king had sent captains of the army and horsemen with me.

10 When ᴿSanballat the Horonite and Tobiah the Ammonite ᵀofficial heard of it, they were deeply disturbed that a man had come to seek the well-being of the children of Israel. Neh. 2:19; 4:1 · Lit. servant, and so elsewhere

Nehemiah Views the Wall of Jerusalem

11 So I ᴿcame to Jerusalem and was there three days. Ezra 8:32

12 Then I arose in the night, I and a few men with me; I told no one what my God had put in my heart to do at Jerusalem; nor was there any animal with me, except the one on which I rode.

13 And I went out by night through the Valley Gate to the Serpent Well and the ᵀRefuse Gate, and ᵀviewed the walls of Jerusalem which were broken down and its gates which were burned with fire. Dung · examined

14 Then I went on to the Fountain Gate and to the King's Pool, but there was no room for the animal under me to pass.

15 So I went up in the night by the valley, and viewed the wall; then I turned back and entered by the Valley Gate, and so returned.

16 And the officials did not know where I had gone or what I had done; I had not yet told the Jews, the priests, the nobles, the officials, or the others who did the work.

17 Then I said to them, "You see the distress that we are in, how Jerusalem lies waste, and its gates are burned with fire. Come and let us build the wall of Jerusalem, that we may no longer be a reproach."

18 And I told them of the hand of my God which had been good upon me, and also of

the king's words that he had spoken to me. So they said, "Let us rise up and build." Then they set their hands to this good work.

19 But when Sanballat the Horonite, Tobiah the Ammonite official, and Geshem the Arab heard of it, they laughed at us and despised us, and said, "What is this thing that you are doing? ᴿWill you rebel against the king?" Neh. 6:6

20 So I answered them, and said to them, "The God of heaven Himself will prosper us; therefore we His servants will arise and build, ᴿbut you have no heritage or right or memorial in Jerusalem." Ezra 4:3

Rebuilding the Wall

3 Then Eliashib the high priest rose up with his brethren the priests and built the Sheep Gate; they consecrated it and hung its doors. They built as far as the Tower of *the Hundred, and consecrated it, then as far as the Tower of Hananel.

2 ᵀNext to Eliashib ᴿthe men of Jericho built. And next to them Zaccur the son of Imri built. Lit. On his hand · Neh. 7:36

3 Also the sons of Hassenaah built the Fish Gate; they laid its beams and ᴿhung its doors with its bolts and bars. Neh. 6:1; 7:1

4 And next to them ᴿMeremoth the son of Urijah, the son of ᵀKoz, made repairs. Next to them ᴿMeshullam the son of Berechiah, the son of Meshezabel, made repairs. Next to them Zadok the son of Baana made repairs. Ezra 8:33 · Or Hakkoz · Ezra 10:15

5 Next to them the Tekoites made repairs; but their nobles did not put their ᴿnecks to ᴿthe work of their Lord. Lit. necks · [Judg. 5:23]

6 Moreover Jehoiada the son of Paseah and Meshullam the son of Besodeiah repaired ᴿthe Old Gate; they laid its beams and hung its doors, with its bolts and bars. Neh. 12:39

7 And next to them Melatiah the Gibeonite, Jadon the Meronothite, the men of Gibeon and Mizpah, repaired the ᴿresidenceᵀ of the governor of the region ᵀbeyond the River. Neh. 2:7-9 · Lit. throne · West of the Euphrates

8 Next to him Uzziel the son of Harhaiah, one of the goldsmiths, made repairs. Also next to him Hananiah, ᵀone of the perfumers, made repairs; and they ᵀfortified Jerusalem as far as the Broad Wall. Lit. the son · restored

9 And next to them Rephaiah the son of Hur, leader of half the district of Jerusalem, made repairs.

10 Next to them Jedaiah the son of Harumaph made repairs in front of his house. And next to him Hattush the son of Hashabniah made repairs.

11 Malchijah the son of Harim and Hashub the son of Pahath-Moab repaired another section, as well as the Tower of the Ovens.

12 And next to him was Shallum the son of

Hallohesh, leader of half the district of Jerusalem; he and his daughters made repairs.

13 Hanun and the inhabitants of Zanoah repaired ᴿthe Valley Gate. They built it, hung its doors with its bolts and bars, and *repaired* a ᵀthousand cubits of the wall as far as ᴿthe Refuse Gate.   Neh. 2:13, 15 • 1500 ft. • Neh. 2:13

14 Malchijah the son of Rechab, leader of the district of ᴿBeth Haccerem, repaired the Refuse Gate; he built it and hung its doors with its bolts and bars.   Jer. 6:1

15 Shallun the son of Col-Hozeh, leader of the district of Mizpah, repaired the Fountain Gate; he built it, covered it, hung its doors with its bolts and bars, and repaired the wall of the Pool of ᴿShelahᵀ by the ᴿKing's Garden, as far as the stairs that go down from the City of David.   Is. 8:6 • Or *Shiloah* • 2 Kin. 25:4

16 After him Nehemiah the son of Azbuk, leader of half the district of Beth Zur, made repairs as far as the front of the *tombs of David, to the ᴿman-made pool, and as far as the House of the Mighty.   2 Kin. 20:20

17 After him the Levites, *under* Rehum the son of Bani, made repairs. Next to him Hashabiah, leader of half the district of Keilah, made repairs for his district.

18 After him their brethren, *under* *Bavai the son of Henadad, leader of the *other* half of the district of Keilah, made repairs.

19 And next to him Ezer the son of Jeshua, the leader of Mizpah, repaired another section in front of the Ascent to the Armory at the ᴿbuttress.ᵀ   2 Chr. 26:9 • Lit. *turning*

20 After him Baruch the son of *Zabbai carefully repaired the other section, from the ᵀbuttress to the door of the house of Eliashib the high priest.   Lit. *turning*

21 After him Meremoth the son of Urijah, the son of ᵀKoz, repaired another section, from the door of the house of Eliashib to the end of the house of Eliashib.   Or *Hakkoz*

22 And after him the priests, the men of the plain, made repairs.

23 After him Benjamin and Hasshub made repairs opposite their house. After them Azariah the son of Maaseiah, the son of Ananiah, made repairs by his house.

24 After him ᴿBinnui the son of Henadad repaired another section, from the house of Azariah to ᴿthe ᵀbuttress, even as far as the corner.   Ezra 8:33 • Neh. 3:19 • Lit. *turning*

25 Palal the son of Uzai *made repairs* opposite the buttress, and on the tower which projects from the king's upper house that *was* by the court of the prison. After him Pedaiah the son of Parosh *made repairs.*

26 Moreover ᴿthe Nethinim who dwelt in ᴿOphel *made repairs* as far as *the place* in front of the Water Gate toward the east, and on the projecting tower.   Neh. 11:21 • 2 Chr. 27:3

27 After them the Tekoites repaired another section, next to the great projecting tower, and as far as the wall of Ophel.

28 Beyond the Horse Gate the priests made repairs, each in front of his *own* house.

29 After them Zadok the son of Immer made repairs in front of his *own* house. After him Shemaiah the son of Shechaniah, the keeper of the East Gate, made repairs.

30 After him Hananiah the son of Shelemiah, and Hanun, the sixth son of Zalaph, repaired another section. After him Meshullam the son of Berechiah made repairs in front of his ᵀdwelling.   Lit. *room*

31 After him Malchijah, one of the goldsmiths, made repairs as far as the house of the Nethinim and of the merchants, in front of the ᵀMiphkad Gate, and as far as the upper room at the corner.   Lit. *Inspection* or *Recruiting*

32 And between the upper room at the corner, as far as the Sheep Gate, the goldsmiths and the merchants made repairs.

The Wall Defended Against Enemies

4 But it so happened, ᴿwhen Sanballat heard that we were rebuilding the wall, that he was furious and very indignant, and mocked the Jews.   Neh. 2:10, 19

2 And he spoke before his brethren and the army of Samaria, and said, "What are these feeble Jews doing? Will they fortify themselves? Will they offer sacrifices? Will they complete it in a day? Will they revive the stones from the heaps of rubbish—*stones* that are burned?"

3 Now ᴿTobiah the Ammonite *was* beside him, and he said, "Whatever they build, if even a fox goes up *on it,* he will break down their stone wall."   Neh. 2:10, 19

4 Hear, O our God, for we are despised; turn their reproach on their own heads, and give them as plunder to a land of captivity!

5 ᴿDo not cover their iniquity, and do not let their sin be blotted out from before You; for they have provoked You to anger before the builders.   Jer. 18:23

6 So we built the wall, and the entire wall was joined together up to half its *height,* for the people had a mind to work.

7 Now it happened, ᴿwhen Sanballat, Tobiah, ᴿthe Arabs, the Ammonites, and the Ashdodites heard that the walls of Jerusalem were being restored and the ᵀgaps were beginning to be closed, that they became very angry,   Neh. 4:1 • Neh. 2:19 • Lit. *breaks*

8 and all of them ᴿconspired together to come *and* attack Jerusalem and create confusion.   Ps. 83:3–5

9 Nevertheless ᴿwe made our prayer to our God, and because of them we set a watch against them day and night.   [Ps. 50:15]

3:16 LXX, Syr., Vg. *tomb*

3:18 So with MT, Vg.; some Heb. mss., LXX, Syr. *Binnui* (cf. v. 24)

3:20 A few Heb. mss., Syr., Vg. *Zaccai*

10 Then Judah said, "The strength of the laborers is failing, and *there is* so much rubbish that we are not able to build the wall."

11 And our adversaries said, "They will neither know nor see anything, till we come into their midst and kill them and cause the work to cease."

12 So it was, when the Jews who dwelt near them came, that they told us ten times, "From whatever place you turn, *they will be* upon us."

13 Therefore I positioned *men* behind the lower parts of the wall, at the openings; and I set the people according to their families, with their swords, their spears, and their bows.

14 And I looked, and arose and said to the nobles, to the leaders, and to the rest of the people, "Do not be afraid of them. Remember the Lord, ᴿgreat and awesome, and fight for your brethren, your sons, your daughters, your wives, and your houses." [Deut. 10:17]

15 And it happened, when our enemies heard that it was known to us, and *that* God had brought their plot to nothing, that all of us returned to the wall, everyone to his work.

16 So it was, from that time on, *that* half of my servants worked at construction, while the other half held the spears, the shields, the bows, and *wore* armor; and the leaders ᵀ*were* behind all the house of Judah. Supported

17 Those who built on the wall, and those who carried burdens, loaded themselves so that with one hand they worked at construction, and with the other held a weapon.

18 Every one of the builders had his sword girded at his side as he built. And the one who sounded the trumpet *was* beside me.

19 Then I said to the nobles, the rulers, and the rest of the people, "The work *is* great and extensive, and we are separated far from one another on the wall.

20 "Wherever you hear the sound of the trumpet, rally to us there. ᴿOur God will fight for us." Ex. 14:14, 25

21 So we labored in the work, and half of ᵀ*the men* held the spears from daybreak until the stars appeared. Lit. *them*

22 At the same time I also said to the people, "Let each man and his servant stay at night in Jerusalem, that they may be our guard by night and a working party by day."

23 So neither I, my brethren, my servants, nor the men of the guard who followed me took off our clothes, *except* that everyone took them off for washing.

Nehemiah Deals with Oppression

5 And there was a great ᴿoutcry of the people and their wives against their ᴿJewish brethren. Neh. 5:7, 8 • Deut. 15:7

2 For there were those who said, "We, our sons, and our daughters *are* many; therefore let us get grain, that we may eat and live."

3 There were also *some* who said, "We have mortgaged our lands and vineyards and houses, that we might buy grain because of the famine."

4 There were also those who said, "We have borrowed money for the king's tax *on* our lands and vineyards.

5 "Yet now our flesh *is* as the flesh of our brethren, our children as their children; and indeed we are forcing our sons and our daughters to be slaves, and *some* of our daughters have been brought into slavery. *It is* not in our power *to redeem them,* for other men have our lands and vineyards."

6 And I became very angry when I heard their outcry and these words.

7 After serious thought, I rebuked the nobles and rulers, and said to them, "Each of you is exacting usury from his brother." So I called a great assembly against them.

8 And I said to them, "According to our ability we have ᴿredeemed our Jewish brethren who were sold to the nations. Now indeed, will you even sell your brethren? Or should they be sold to us?" Then they were silenced and found nothing to *say.* Lev. 25:48

9 Then I said, "What you are doing *is* not good. Should you not walk ᴿin the fear of our God ᴿbecause of the reproach of the nations, our enemies?" Lev. 25:36 • 2 Sam. 12:14

10 "I also, *with* my brethren and my servants, am lending them money and grain. Please, let us stop this ᵀusury! *interest*

11 "Restore now to them, even this day, their lands, their vineyards, their olive groves, and their houses, also a hundredth of the money and the grain, the new wine and the oil, that you have charged them."

12 So they said, "We will restore *it,* and will require nothing from them; we will do as you say." Then I called the priests, ᴿand required an oath from them that they would do according to this promise. Ezra 10:5

13 Then I shook out ᵀthe fold of my garment and said, "So may God shake out each man from his house, and from his property, who does not perform this promise. Even thus may he be shaken out and emptied." And all the assembly said, "Amen!" and praised the Lord. ᴿThen the people did according to this promise. Lit. *my lap* • 2 Kin. 23:3

The Generosity of Nehemiah

14 Moreover, from the time that I was appointed to be their governor in the land of Judah, from the twentieth year until the thirty-second year of King Artaxerxes, twelve years, neither I nor my brothers ᴿate the governor's provisions. [1 Cor. 9:4-15]

15 But the former governors who *were* before me laid burdens on the people, and took from them bread and wine, besides forty

shekels of silver. Yes, even their servants bore rule over the people, but I did not do so, because of the ᴿfear of God.   Neh. 5:9

16 Indeed, I also continued the work on this wall, and we did not buy any land. All my servants *were* gathered there for the work.

17 And ᴿat my table *were* one hundred and fifty Jews and rulers, besides those who came to us from the nations around us.   1 Kin. 18:19

18 Now *that* which was prepared daily *was* one ox *and* six choice sheep. Also fowl were prepared for me, and once every ten days an abundance of all kinds of wine. Yet in spite of this ᴿI did not demand the governor's provisions, because the bondage was heavy on this people.   Neh. 5:14, 15

19 Remember me, my God, for good, *according to* all that I have done for this people.

Conspiracy Against Nehemiah

6 Now it happened when Sanballat, Tobiah, ᵀGeshem the Arab, and the rest of our enemies heard that I had rebuilt the wall, and *that* there were no breaks left in it ᴿ(though at that time I had not hung the doors in the gates),   Or *Gashmu* • Neh. 3:1, 3

2 that Sanballat and Geshem sent to me, saying, "Come, let us meet together among ᵀthe villages in the plain of Ono." But they thought to do me harm.   Or *in Kephirim*

3 So I sent messengers to them, saying, "I *am* doing a great work, so that I cannot come down. Why should the work cease while I leave it and go down to you?"

4 But they sent me this message four times, and I answered them in the same manner.

5 Then Sanballat sent his servant to me as before, the fifth time, with an open letter in his hand.

6 In it *was* written:

It is reported among the nations, and *Geshem says, that you and the Jews plan to rebel; therefore, according to these rumors, you are rebuilding the wall, that you may be their king.

7 And you have also appointed prophets to proclaim concerning you at Jerusalem, saying, "*There is* a king in Judah!" Now these matters will be reported to the king. So come, therefore, and let us consult together.

8 Then I sent to him, saying, "No such things as you say are being done, but you invent them in your own heart."

9 For they all *were trying to* make us afraid, saying, "Their hands will be weakened in the work, and it will not be done."

Now therefore, O *God*, strengthen my hands.

10 Afterward I came to the house of

6:6 Heb. *Gashmu*

Shemaiah the son of Delaiah, the son of Mehetabel, who *was* a secret informer; and he said, "Let us meet together in the house of God, within the temple, and let us close the doors of the temple, for they are coming to kill you; indeed, at night they will come to kill you."

11 And I said, "Should such a man as I flee? And who *is there* such as I who would go into the temple to save his life? I will not go in!"

12 Then I perceived that God had not sent him at all, but that ᴿhe pronounced *this* prophecy against me because Tobiah and Sanballat had hired him.   Ezek. 13:22

13 For this reason he *was* hired, that I should be afraid and act that way and sin, so *that* they might have *cause* for an evil report, that they might reproach me.

14 My God, remember Tobiah and Sanballat, according to these their works, and the prophetess Noadiah and the rest of the prophets who would have made me afraid.

The Wall Completed

15 So the wall was finished on the twenty-fifth *day* of Elul, in fifty-two days.

16 And it happened, when all our enemies heard *of it*, and all the nations around us saw *these things*, that they were very disheartened in their own eyes; for they perceived that this work was done by our God.

17 Also in those days the nobles of Judah sent many letters to Tobiah, and *the letters of* Tobiah came to them.

18 For many in Judah were pledged to him, because he was the ᴿson-in-law of Shechaniah the son of Arah, and his son Jehohanan had married the daughter of ᴿMeshullam the son of Berechiah.   Neh. 13:4, 28 • Ezra 10:15

19 Also they reported his good deeds before me, and reported my ᵀwords to him. Tobiah sent letters to frighten me.   Or *affairs*

7 Then it was, when the wall was built and I had ᴿhung the doors, when the gatekeepers, the singers, and the Levites had been appointed,   Neh. 6:1, 15

2 that I gave the charge of Jerusalem to my brother Hanani, and Hananiah the leader of the ᵀcitadel, for he *was* a faithful man and ᴿfeared God more than many.   *palace* • Ex. 18:21

3 And I said to them, "Do not let the gates of Jerusalem be opened until the sun is hot; and while they stand *guard*, let them shut and bar the doors; and appoint guards from among the inhabitants of Jerusalem, one at his watch station and another in front of his own house."

The Captives Who Returned to Jerusalem

4 Now the city *was* large and spacious, but the people in it *were* ᴿfew, and the houses *were* not rebuilt.   Deut. 4:27

5 Then my God put it into my heart to

gather the nobles, the rulers, and the people, that they might be registered by genealogy. And I found a register of the genealogy of those who had come up in the first *return*, and found written in it:

6 ^RThese *are* the people of the province who came back from the captivity, of those who had been carried away, whom Nebuchadnezzar the king of Babylon had carried away, and who returned to Jerusalem and Judah, everyone to his city.   Ezra 2:1-70

7 Those who came with Zerubbabel *were* Jeshua, Nehemiah, ^TAzariah, Raamiah, Nahamani, Mordecai, Bilshan, ^TMispereth, Bigvai, Nehum, and Baanah.

The number of the men of the people of Israel: Seraiah, Ezra 2:2 · Mispar, Ezra 2:2

8 the sons of Parosh, two thousand one hundred and seventy-two;

9 the sons of Shephatiah, three hundred and seventy-two;

10 the sons of Arah, six hundred and fifty-two;

11 the sons of Pahath-Moab, of the sons of Jeshua and Joab, two thousand eight hundred and eighteen;

12 the sons of Elam, one thousand two hundred and fifty-four;

13 the sons of Zattu, eight hundred and forty-five;

14 the sons of Zaccai, seven hundred and sixty;

15 the sons of ^TBinnui, six hundred and forty-eight;   Bani, Ezra 2:10

16 the sons of Bebai, six hundred and twenty-eight;

17 the sons of Azgad, two thousand three hundred and twenty-two;

18 the sons of Adonikam, six hundred and sixty-seven;

19 the sons of Bigvai, two thousand and sixty-seven;

20 the sons of Adin, six hundred and fifty-five;

21 the sons of Ater of Hezekiah, ninety-eight;

22 the sons of Hashum, three hundred and twenty-eight;

23 the sons of Bezai, three hundred and twenty-four;

24 the sons of ^THariph, one hundred and twelve;   Jorah, Ezra 2:18

25 the sons of *Gibeon, ninety-five;

26 the men of Bethlehem and Netophah, one hundred and eighty-eight;

27 the men of Anathoth, one hundred and twenty-eight;

28 the men of *Beth Azmaveth, forty-two;

29 the men of ^TKirjath Jearim, Chephirah, and Beeroth, seven hundred and forty-three;   Kirjath Arim, Ezra 2:25

30 the men of Ramah and Geba, six hundred and twenty-one;

31 the men of Michmas, one hundred and twenty-two;

32 the men of Bethel and Ai, one hundred and twenty-three;

33 the men of the other Nebo, fifty-two;

34 the sons of the other Elam, one thousand two hundred and fifty-four;

35 the sons of Harim, three hundred and twenty;

36 the sons of Jericho, three hundred and forty-five;

37 the sons of Lod, Hadid, and Ono, seven hundred and twenty-one;

38 the sons of Senaah, three thousand nine hundred and thirty.

39 The priests: the sons of ^RJedaiah, of the house of Jeshua, nine hundred and seventy-three;   1 Chr. 24:7

40 the sons of ^RImmer, one thousand and fifty-two;   1 Chr. 9:12

41 the sons of Pashhur, one thousand two hundred and forty-seven;

42 the sons of ^RHarim, one thousand and seventeen.   1 Chr. 24:8

43 The Levites: the sons of Jeshua, of Kadmiel, *and* of the sons of ^THodevah, seventy-four.   Hodaviah, Ezra 2:40

44 The singers: the sons of Asaph, one hundred and forty-eight.

45 The gatekeepers: the sons of Shallum, the sons of Ater, the sons of Talmon, the sons of Akkub, the sons of Hatita, the sons of Shobai, one hundred and thirty-eight.

46 The Nethinim: the sons of Ziha, the sons of Hasupha, the sons of Tabbaoth,

47 the sons of Keros, the sons of ^TSia, the sons of Padon,   Siaha, Ezra 2:44

48 the sons of *Lebana, the sons of *Hagaba, the sons of *Salmai,

49 the sons of Hanan, the sons of Giddel, the sons of Gahar,

50 the sons of Reaiah, the sons of Rezin, the sons of Nekoda,

51 the sons of Gazzam, the sons of Uzza, the sons of Paseah,

52 the sons of Besai, the sons of Meunim, the sons of *Nephishesim,

53 the sons of Bakbuk, the sons of Hakupha, the sons of Harhur,

54 the sons of *Bazlith, the sons of Mehida, the sons of Harsha,

55 the sons of Barkos, the sons of Sisera, the sons of Tamah,

---

7:25 *Gibbar*, Ezra 2:20
7:28 *Azmaveth*, Ezra 2:24

7:48 MT *Lebanah* • MT *Hogabah* • *Shalmai*, Ezra 2:46; or *Shamlai*
7:52 *Nephusim*, Ezra 2:50
7:54 *Bazluth*, Ezra 2:52

56 the sons of Neziah, and the sons of Hatipha.

57 The sons of Solomon's servants: the sons of Sotai, the sons of Sophereth, the sons of *Perida,

58 the sons of Jaala, the sons of Darkon, the sons of Giddel,

59 the sons of Shephatiah, the sons of Hattil, the sons of Pochereth of Zebaim, and the sons of *Amon.

60 All the Nethinim, and the sons of Solomon's servants, were three hundred and ninety-two.

61 And these were the ones who came up from Tel Melah, Tel Harsha, Cherub, *Addon, and Immer, but they could not identify their father's house nor their lineage, whether they were of Israel:

62 the sons of Delaiah, the sons of Tobiah, the sons of Nekoda, six hundred and forty-two;

63 and of the priests: the sons of Habaiah, the sons of ᵀKoz, the sons of Barzillai, who took a wife of the daughters of Barzillai the Gileadite, and was called by their name.   Or Hakkoz

64 These sought their listing among those who were registered by genealogy, but it was not found; therefore they were excluded from the priesthood as defiled.

65 And the ᵀgovernor said to them that they should not eat of the most holy things till a priest could consult with the Urim and Thummim.   Or Tirshatha

66 Altogether the whole assembly was forty-two thousand three hundred and sixty,

67 besides their male and female servants, of whom there were seven thousand three hundred and thirty-seven; and they had two hundred and forty-five men and women singers.

68 Their horses were seven hundred and thirty-six, their mules two hundred and forty-five,

69 their camels four hundred and thirty-five, and donkeys six thousand seven hundred and twenty.

70 And some of the heads of the fathers' houses gave to the work. ᴿThe ᵀgovernor gave to the treasury ᵀone thousand gold drachmas, fifty basins, and five hundred and thirty priestly garments.   Neh. 8:9 · Or Tirshatha · $1,424,176

71 Some of the heads of the fathers' houses gave to the treasury of the work twenty thousand gold drachmas, and two thousand two hundred silver minas.

72 And that which the rest of the people gave was twenty thousand gold drachmas, two thousand silver minas, and sixty-seven priestly garments.

73 So the priests, the Levites, the gatekeepers, the singers, some of the people, the Nethinim, and all Israel dwelt in their cities.

Ezra Reads the Law

ᴿWhen the seventh month came, the children of Israel were in their cities.   Ezra 3:1

8 Now all ᴿthe people gathered together as one man in the open square that was ᴿin front of the Water Gate; and they told Ezra the ᴿscribe to bring the Book of the Law of Moses, which the LORD had commanded Israel.   Ezra 3:1 · Neh. 3:26 · Ezra 7:6

2 So Ezra the priest brought the Law before the assembly, of men and women and all who could hear with understanding, on the first day of the seventh month.

3 Then he ᴿread from it in the open square that was in front of the Water Gate ᵀfrom morning until midday, before the men and women and those who could understand; and the ears of all the people were attentive to the Book of the Law.   2 Kin. 23:2 · Lit. from the light

4 So Ezra the scribe stood on a platform of wood which they had made for the purpose; and beside him, at his right hand, stood Mattithiah, Shema, Anaiah, Urijah, Hilkiah, and Maaseiah; and at his left hand Pedaiah, Mishael, Malchijah, Hashum, Hashbadana, Zechariah, and Meshullam.

5 And Ezra opened the book in the sight of all the people, for he was standing above all the people; and when he opened it, all the people ᴿstood up.   Judg. 3:20

6 And Ezra blessed the LORD, the great God. Then all the people answered, "Amen, Amen!" while lifting up their hands. And they bowed their heads and worshiped the LORD with their faces to the ground.

7 Also Jeshua, Bani, Sherebiah, Jamin, Akkub, Shabbethai, Hodijah, Maaseiah, Kelita, Azariah, Jozabad, Hanan, Pelaiah, and the Levites, helped the people to understand the Law; and the people stood in their place.

8 So they read distinctly from the book, in the Law of God; and they gave the sense, and helped them to understand the reading.

9 And Nehemiah, who was the *governor, Ezra the priest and scribe, and the Levites who taught the people said to all the people, "This day is holy to the LORD your God; do not mourn nor weep." For all the people wept, when they heard the words of the Law.

10 Then he said to them, "Go your way, eat the fat, drink the sweet, and send portions to those for whom nothing is prepared; for this

7:57 Peruda, Ezra 2:55
7:59 Ami, Ezra 2:57
7:61 Addan, Ezra 2:59

8:9 Heb. tirshathah

day *is* holy to our LORD. Do not sorrow, for the joy of the LORD is your strength."

11 So the Levites quieted all the people, saying, "Be still, for the day *is* holy; do not be grieved."

12 And all the people went their way to eat and drink, to ᴿsend portions and rejoice greatly, because they ᴿunderstood the words that were declared to them. Neh. 8:10 • Neh. 8:7, 8

The Feast of Tabernacles

13 Now on the second day the heads of the fathers' *houses* of all the people, with the priests and Levites, were gathered to Ezra the scribe, in order to understand the words of the Law.

14 And they found written in the Law, which the LORD had commanded by Moses, that the children of Israel should dwell in ᴿboothsᵀ during the feast of the seventh month, Lev. 23:34, 40, 42 • Temporary shelters

15 and that they should announce and proclaim in all their cities and in Jerusalem, saying, "Go out to the mountain, and bring olive branches, branches of oil trees, myrtle branches, palm branches, and branches of leafy trees, to make booths, as *it is* written."

16 Then the people went out and brought *them* and made themselves booths, each one on the roof of his house, or in their courtyards or the courts of the house of God, and in the open square of the Water Gate and in the open square of the Gate of Ephraim.

17 So the whole assembly of those who had returned from the captivity made ᵀbooths and sat under the booths; for since the days of Joshua the son of Nun until that day the children of Israel had not done so. And there was very great gladness. Temporary shelters

18 Also ᴿday by day, from the first day until the last day, he read from the Book of the Law of God. And they kept the feast ᴿseven days; and on the ᴿeighth day *there was* a sacred assembly, according to the *prescribed* manner. Deut. 31:11 • Lev. 23:36 • Num. 29:35

The People Confess Their Sins

9 Now on the twenty-fourth day of ᴿthis month the children of Israel were assembled with fasting, in sackcloth, and with ᵀdust on their heads. Neh. 8:2 • Lit. *earth on them*

2 Then ᴿthose of Israelite lineage separated themselves from all foreigners; and they stood and ᴿconfessed their sins and the iniquities of their fathers. Neh. 13:3, 30 • Neh. 1:6

3 And they stood up in their place and ᴿread from the Book of the Law of the LORD their God *for one*-fourth of the day; and *for another* fourth they confessed and worshiped the LORD their God. Neh. 8:7, 8

4 Then Jeshua, Bani, Kadmiel, Shebaniah, Bunni, Sherebiah, Bani, *and* Chenani stood on the stairs of the Levites and cried out with a loud voice to the LORD their God.

5 And the Levites, Jeshua, Kadmiel, Bani, Hashabniah, Sherebiah, Hodijah, Shebaniah, *and* Pethahiah, said:

"Stand up *and* bless the LORD your God Forever and ever!

"Blessed be ᴿYour glorious name,
Which is exalted above all blessing and praise! 1 Chr. 29:13
6 ᴿYou alone *are* the LORD; 2 Kin. 19:15, 19
ᴿYou have made heaven, Rev. 14:7
ᴿThe heaven of heavens, with ᴿall their host, [Deut. 10:14] • Gen. 2:1
The earth and everything on it,
The seas and all that is in them,
And You ᴿpreserve them all. [Ps. 36:6]
The host of heaven worships You.

7 "You *are* the LORD God,
Who chose ᴿAbram, Gen. 11:31
And brought him out of Ur of the Chaldeans,
And gave him the name Abraham;
8 You found his heart ᴿfaithful before You, Gen. 15:6; 22:1-3
And made a covenant with him
To give the land of the Canaanites,
The Hittites, the Amorites,
The Perizzites, the Jebusites,
And the Girgashites—
To give *it* to his descendants.
You ᴿhave performed Your words,
For You *are* righteous. Josh. 23:14

9 "Youᴿ saw the affliction of our fathers in Egypt, Ex. 2:25; 3:7
And heard their cry by the Red Sea.
10 You ᴿshowed signs and wonders against Pharaoh, Ex. 7—14
Against all his servants,
And against all the people of his land.
For You knew that they acted ᵀproudly against them. *presumptuously* or *insolently*
So You ᴿmade a name for Yourself, as *it is* this day. Jer. 32:20
11 ᴿAnd You divided the sea before them,
So that they went through the midst of the sea on the dry land; Ex. 14:20-28
And their persecutors You threw into the deep,
As a stone into the mighty waters.
12 Moreover You ᴿled them by day with a cloudy pillar, Ex. 13:21, 22
And by night with a pillar of fire,
To give them light on the road
Which they should travel.

13 "Youᴿ came down also on Mount Sinai,
And spoke with them from heaven,
And gave them ᴿjust ordinances and true laws, Ex. 20:1-18 • [Rom. 7:12]
Good statutes and commandments.

14 You made known to them Your ᴿholy
      Sabbath,   Gen. 2:3
   And commanded them precepts,
      statutes and laws,
   By the hand of Moses Your servant.
15 You ᴿgave them bread from heaven for
      their hunger,   Ex. 16:14–17
   And ᴿbrought them water out of the
      rock for their thirst,   Ex. 17:6
   And told them to ᴿgo in to possess the
      land   Deut. 1:8
   Which You had sworn to give them.

16 "But they and our fathers acted
      ᵀproudly,   presumptuously
   ᵀHardened their necks,   Became stubborn
   And did not heed Your commandments.
17 They refused to obey,
   And ᴿthey were not mindful of Your
      wonders   Ps. 78:11, 42–45
   That You did among them.
   But they hardened their necks,
   And *in their rebellion
   They appointed ᴿa leader   Num. 14:4
   To return to their bondage.
   But You are God,
   Ready to pardon,
   ᴿGracious and merciful,   Joel 2:13
   Slow to anger,
   Abundant in kindness,
   And did not forsake them.
18 "Even ᴿwhen they made a molded calf
      for themselves,   Ex. 32:4–8, 31
   And said, 'This is your god
   That brought you up out of Egypt,'
   And worked great provocations,
19 Yet in Your ᴿmanifold mercies
   You did not forsake them in the
      wilderness.   Ps. 106:45
   The ᴿpillar of the cloud did not depart
      from them by day,   1 Cor. 10:1
   To lead them on the road;
   Nor the pillar of fire by night,
   To show them light,
   And the way they should go.
20 You also gave Your ᴿgood Spirit to
      instruct them,   Num. 11:17
   And did not withhold Your ᴿmanna
      from their mouth,   Ex. 16:14–16
   And gave them water for their thirst.
21 ᴿForty years You sustained them in the
      wilderness;   Deut. 2:7
   They lacked nothing;
   Their ᴿclothes did not wear out Deut. 29:5
   And their feet did not swell.
22 "Moreover You gave them kingdoms
      and nations,
   And divided them into ᵀdistricts.
   So they took possession of the land of
      ᴿSihon,   Lit. corners • Num. 21:21–35

*The land of the king of Heshbon,
   And the land of Og king of Bashan.
23 You also multiplied ᴿtheir children as
      the stars of heaven,   Gen. 15:5; 22:17
   And brought them into the land
   Which You had told their fathers
   To go in and possess.
24 So ᴿthe ᵀpeople went in   Josh. 1:2–4
   And possessed the land;   Lit. sons
   ᴿYou subdued before them the
      inhabitants of the land,   [Ps. 44:2, 3]
   The Canaanites,
   And gave them into their hands,
   With their kings
   And the people of the land,
   That they might do with them as they
      would.
25 And they took strong cities and a ᴿrich
      land,   Num. 13:27
   And possessed ᴿhouses full of all goods,
   Cisterns already dug, vineyards, olive
      groves,   Deut. 6:11
   And ᵀfruit trees in abundance.
   So they ate and were filled and ᴿgrew
      fat,   Lit. trees for eating • [Deut. 32:15]
   And delighted themselves in Your great
      ᴿgoodness.   Hos. 3:5

26 "Nevertheless they ᴿwere disobedient
   And rebelled against You,   Judg. 2:11
   Cast Your law behind their backs
   And killed Your prophets, who ᵀtestified
      against them   warned them
   To turn them to Yourself;
   And they worked great provocations.
27 ᴿTherefore You delivered them into the
      hand of their enemies,   Judg. 2:14
   Who oppressed them;
   And in the time of their trouble,
   When they cried to You,
   You ᴿheard from heaven;   Ps. 106:44
   And according to Your abundant
      mercies
   ᴿYou gave them deliverers who saved
      them   Judg. 2:18
   From the hand of their enemies.

28 "But after they had rest,
   ᴿThey again did evil before You.
   Therefore You left them in the hand of
      their enemies,   Judg. 3:12
   So that they had dominion over them;
   Yet when they returned and cried out
      to You,
   You heard from heaven;
   And ᴿmany times You delivered them
      according to Your mercies,   Ps. 106:43
29 And ᵀtestified against them,
   That You might bring them back to
      Your law.   admonished them
   Yet they acted ᵀproudly,   presumptuously

And did not heed Your commandments,
But sinned against Your judgments,
R'Which if a man does, he shall live by
    them.'   Lev. 18:5
And they shrugged their shoulders,
TStiffened their necks,   Became stubborn
And would not hear.

30 Yet for many years You had patience
    with them,
And testified against them by Your
    Spirit Rin Your prophets.   [Acts 7:51]
Yet they would not listen;
RTherefore You gave them into the hand
    of the peoples of the lands.   Is. 5:5

31 Nevertheless in Your great mercy
RYou did not utterly consume them nor
    forsake them;   Jer. 4:27
For You are God, gracious and
    merciful.

32 "Now therefore, our God,
The great, the Rmighty, and awesome
    God,   [Ex. 34:6, 7]
Who keeps covenant and mercy:
Do not let all the Ttrouble seem small
    before You   hardship
That has come upon us,
Our kings and our princes,
Our priests and our prophets,
Our fathers and on all Your people,
RFrom the days of the kings of Assyria
    until this day.   2 Kin. 15:19; 17:3-6

33 However RYou are just in all that has
    befallen us;   [Dan. 9:14]
For You have dealt faithfully,
But we have done wickedly.

34 Neither our kings nor our princes,
Our priests nor our fathers,
Have kept Your law,
Nor heeded Your commandments and
    Your testimonies,
With which You testified against them.

35 For they have Rnot served You in their
    kingdom,   Deut. 28:47
Or in the many good things that You
    gave them,
Or in the large and rich land which You
    set before them;
Nor did they turn from their wicked
    works.

36 "Here Rwe are, servants today!
And the land that You gave to our
    fathers,   Deut. 28:48
To eat its fruit and its bounty,
Here we are, servants in it!

37 And Rit yields much increase to the
    kings   Deut. 28:33, 51
You have set over us,
Because of our sins;
Also they have Rdominion over our
    bodies and our cattle   Deut. 28:48
At their pleasure;
And we are in great distress.

38 "And because of all this,
We Rmake a sure covenant and write it;
Our leaders, our Levites, and our priests
    Rseal it."   2 Kin. 23:3 • Neh. 10:1

The People Who Sealed the Covenant

10 Now those who placed their seal on
the document were:
Nehemiah the Tgovernor, Rthe son of
Hacaliah, and Zedekiah,   Or Tirshatha • Neh. 1:1
2 RSeraiah, Azariah, Jeremiah,   Neh. 12:1-21
3 Pashhur, Amariah, Malchijah,
4 Hattush, Shebaniah, Malluch,
5 Harim, Meremoth, Obadiah,
6 Daniel, Ginnethon, Baruch,
7 Meshullam, Abijah, Mijamin,
8 Maaziah, Bilgai, and Shemaiah. These
were the priests.
9 The Levites: Jeshua the son of Azaniah,
Binnui of the sons of Henadad, and Kadmiel.
10 Their brethren: Shebaniah, Hodijah, Kelita, Pelaiah, Hanan,
11 Micha, Rehob, Hashabiah,
12 Zaccur, Sherebiah, Shebaniah,
13 Hodijah, Bani, and Beninu.
14 The leaders of the people: RParosh,
Pahath-Moab, Elam, Zattu, Bani,   Ezra 2:3
15 Bunni, Azgad, Bebai,
16 Adonijah, Bigvai, Adin,
17 Ater, Hezekiah, Azzur,
18 Hodijah, Hashum, Bezai,
19 Hariph, Anathoth, Nebai,
20 Magpiash, Meshullam, Hezir,
21 Meshezabel, Zadok, Jaddua,
22 Pelatiah, Hanan, Anaiah,
23 Hoshea, Hananiah, Hasshub,
24 Hallohesh, Pilha, Shobek,
25 Rehum, Hashabnah, Maaseiah,
26 Ahijah, Hanan, Anan,
27 Malluch, Harim, and Baanah.

The Covenant That Was Sealed

28 RNow the rest of the people—the priests,
the Levites, the gatekeepers, the singers, the
Nethinim, Rand all those who had separated
themselves from the peoples of the lands to
the Law of God, their wives, their sons, and
their daughters, everyone who had knowledge and understanding—   Ezra 2:36-43 • Neh. 13:3
29 these joined with their brethren, their
nobles, and entered into a curse and an oath
to walk in God's Law, which was given by
Moses the servant of God, and to observe and
do all the commandments of the LORD our
Lord, and His ordinances and His statutes:
30 We would not give Rour daughters as
wives to the peoples of the land, nor take
their daughters for our sons;   Ex. 34:16
31 if the peoples of the land brought Twares
or any grain to sell on the Sabbath day, we
would not buy it from them on the Sabbath,
or on a holy day; and we would forego the
seventh year's produce and the Texacting of
every debt.   merchandise • collection

32 Also we made ordinances for ourselves, to exact from ourselves yearly ᴿone-thirdᵀ of a shekel for the service of the house of our God: Matt. 17:24 • $45

33 for ᴿthe showbread, for the regular grain offering, for the ᴿregular burnt offering of the Sabbaths, the New Moons, and the set feasts; for the holy things, for the sin offerings to make atonement for Israel, and all the work of the house of our God.   Lev. 24:5 • Num. 28; 29

34 We cast lots among the priests, the Levites, and the people, for *bringing* the wood offering into the house of our God, according to our fathers' houses, at the appointed times year by year, to burn on the altar of the Lᴏʀᴅ our God as *it is* written in the Law.

35 And *we made ordinances* ᴿto bring the firstfruits of our ground and the firstfruits of all fruit of all trees, year by year, to the house of the Lᴏʀᴅ;   Ex. 23:19; 34:26

36 to bring the ᴿfirstborn of our sons and our cattle, as *it is* written in the Law, and the firstborn of our herds and our flocks, to the house of our God, to the priests who minister in the house of our God;   Ex. 13:2, 12, 13

37 to bring the firstfruits of our dough, our offerings, the fruit from all kinds of trees, *the* new wine and oil, to the priests, to the storerooms of the ᵀhouse of our God; and to bring ᴿthe tithes of our land to the Levites, for the Levites should receive the tithes in all our farming communities.   Temple • Lev. 27:30

38 And the priest, the descendant of Aaron, shall be with the Levites when the Levites receive tithes; and the Levites shall bring up a tenth of the tithes to the house of our God, to ᴿthe rooms of the storehouse.   1 Chr. 9:26

39 For the children of Israel and the children of Levi shall bring the offering of the grain, of the new wine and the oil, to the storerooms where the articles of the sanctuary *are, where* the priests who minister and the gatekeepers and the singers *are*; and we will not neglect the house of our God.

The People Dwelling in Jerusalem

11 Now the leaders of the people dwelt at Jerusalem; the rest of the people cast lots to bring one out of ten to dwell in Jerusalem, ᴿthe holy city, and nine-tenths *were* to dwell in *other* cities.   Matt. 4:5; 5:35; 27:53

2 And the people blessed all the men who ᴿwillingly offered themselves to dwell at Jerusalem.   Judg. 5:9

3 ᴿThese *are* the heads of the province who dwelt in Jerusalem. (But in the cities of Judah everyone dwelt in his own possession in their cities—Israelites, priests, Levites, ᴿNethinim, and ᴿdescendants of Solomon's servants.)   1 Chr. 9:2, 3 • Ezra 2:43 • Ezra 2:55

4 Also ᴿin Jerusalem dwelt *some* of the children of Judah and of the children of Benjamin.   1 Chr. 9:3

The children of Judah: Athaiah the son of Uzziah, the son of Zechariah, the son of Amariah, the son of Shephatiah, the son of Mahalalel, of the children of Perez;

5 and Maaseiah the son of Baruch, the son of Col-Hozeh, the son of Hazaiah, the son of Adaiah, the son of Joiarib, the son of Zechariah, the son of Shiloni.

6 All the sons of Perez who dwelt at Jerusalem *were* four hundred and sixty-eight valiant men.

7 And these are the sons of Benjamin: Sallu the son of Meshullam, the son of Joed, the son of Pedaiah, the son of Kolaiah, the son of Maaseiah, the son of Ithiel, the son of Jeshaiah;

8 and after him Gabbai *and* Sallai, nine hundred and twenty-eight.

9 Joel the son of Zichri *was* their overseer, and Judah the son of ᵀSenuah *was* second over the city.   Or Hassenuah

10 ᴿOf the priests: Jedaiah the son of Joiarib, and Jachin;   1 Chr. 9:10

11 Seraiah the son of Hilkiah, the son of Meshullam, the son of Zadok, the son of Meraioth, the son of Ahitub, *was* the leader of the house of God.

12 Their brethren who did the work of the house *were* eight hundred and twenty-two; and Adaiah the son of Jeroham, the son of Pelaliah, the son of Amzi, the son of Zechariah, the son of Pashhur, the son of Malchijah,

13 and his brethren, heads of the fathers' *houses, were* two hundred and forty-two; and Amashai the son of Azarel, the son of Ahzai, the son of Meshillemoth, the son of Immer,

14 and their brethren, mighty men of valor, *were* one hundred and twenty-eight. Their overseer *was* Zabdiel ᵀthe son of *one of* the great men.   Or the son of Haggedolim

15 Also of the Levites: Shemaiah the son of Hasshub, the son of Azrikam, the son of Hashabiah, the son of Bunni;

16 Shabbethai and Jozabad, of the heads of the Levites, *had* the oversight of the business outside of the house of God;

17 Mattaniah the son of ᵀMicha, the son of Zabdi, the son of Asaph, the leader *who* began the thanksgiving with prayer; Bakbukiah, the second among his brethren; and Abda the son of Shammua, the son of Galal, the son of Jeduthun.   Or Michah

18 All the Levites in ᴿthe holy city *were* two hundred and eighty-four.   Neh. 11:1

19 Moreover the gatekeepers, Akkub, Talmon, and their brethren who kept the gates, *were* one hundred and seventy-two.

20 And the rest of Israel, of the priests *and* Levites, *were* in all the cities of Judah, everyone in his inheritance.

21 But the Nethinim dwelt in Ophel. And Ziha and Gishpa *were* over the Nethinim.

22 Also the overseer of the Levites at Jerusalem *was* Uzzi the son of Bani, the son of Hashabiah, the son of Mattaniah, the son of Micha, of the sons of Asaph, the singers in charge of the service of the house of God.

23 For *it was* the king's command concerning them that a ᵀcertain portion should be for the singers, a quota day by day.   *fixed share*

24 Pethahiah the son of Meshezabel, of the children of Zerah the son of Judah, *was* ᴿtheᵀ king's deputy in all matters concerning the people.   1 Chr. 18:17 • Lit. *at the king's hand*

The People Dwelling Outside Jerusalem

25 And as for the villages with their fields, *some* of the children of Judah dwelt in ᴿKirjath Arba and its villages, Dibon and its villages, Jekabzeel and its villages;   Josh. 14:15

26 in Jeshua, Moladah, Beth Pelet,

27 Hazar Shual, and Beersheba and its villages;

28 in Ziklag and Meconah and its villages;

29 in En Rimmon, Zorah, Jarmuth,

30 Zanoah, Adullam, and their villages; in Lachish and its fields; in Azekah and its villages. They dwelt from Beersheba to the Valley of Hinnom.

31 Also the children of Benjamin from Geba *dwelt* in Michmash, Aija, and Bethel, and their villages;

32 in Anathoth, Nob, Ananiah;

33 in Hazor, Ramah, Gittaim;

34 in Hadid, Zeboim, Neballat;

35 in Lod, Ono, *and* ᴿthe Valley of Craftsmen.   1 Chr. 4:14

36 Some of the Judean divisions of Levites *were* in Benjamin.

The Priests and Levites

12 Now these *are* the ᴿpriests and the Levites who came up with ᴿZerubbabel the son of Shealtiel, and Jeshua: ᴿSeraiah, Jeremiah, Ezra,   Ezra 2:1, 2; 7:7 • Neh. 7:7 • Neh. 10:2–8

2 Amariah, ᵀMalluch, Hattush,   *Melichu*, v. 14

3 Shechaniah, Rehum, Meremoth,

4 Iddo, ᵀGinnethoi, Abijah,   Or *Ginnethon*, v. 16

5 Mijamin, ᵀMaadiah, Bilgah,   *Moadiah*, v. 17

6 Shemaiah, Joiarib, Jedaiah,

7 Sallu, Amok, Hilkiah, *and* Jedaiah.

These *were* the heads of the priests and their brethren in the days of ᴿJeshua. Zech. 3:1

8 Moreover the Levites *were* Jeshua, Binnui, Kadmiel, Sherebiah, Judah, *and* Mattaniah ᴿ*who* led the thanksgiving *psalms*, he and his brethren.   Neh. 11:17

9 Also Bakbukiah and Unni, their brethren, *stood* across from them in *their* duties.

10 Jeshua begot Joiakim, Joiakim begot Eliashib, Eliashib begot Joiada,

11 Joiada begot Jonathan, and Jonathan begot Jaddua.

12 Now in the days of Joiakim, the priests, the heads of the fathers' *houses were*: of Seraiah, Meraiah; of Jeremiah, Hananiah;

13 of Ezra, Meshullam; of Amariah, Jehohanan;

14 of ᵀMelichu, Jonathan; of ᵀShebaniah, Joseph;   Or *Malluch*, v. 2 • Or *Shechaniah*, v. 3

15 of *Harim, Adna; of *Meraioth, Helkai;

16 of Iddo, Zechariah; of Ginnethon, Meshullam;

17 of Abijah, Zichri; *the son of* ᵀMinjamin; of ᵀMoadiah, Piltai;   Or *Mijamin*, v. 5 • Or *Maadiah*, v. 5

18 of Bilgah, Shammua; of Shemaiah, Jehonathan;

19 of Joiarib, Mattenai; of Jedaiah, Uzzi;

20 of *Sallai, Kallai; of Amok, Eber;

21 of Hilkiah, Hashabiah; *and* of Jedaiah, Nethanel.

22 During the reign of Darius the Persian, a record *was also* kept of the Levites and priests *who had been* ᴿheads of their fathers' *houses* in the days of Eliashib, Joiada, Johanan, and Jaddua.   1 Chr. 24:6

23 The sons of Levi, the heads of the fathers' *houses* until the days of Johanan the son of Eliashib, *were* written in the book of the ᴿchronicles.   1 Chr. 9:14–22

24 And the heads of the Levites *were* Hashabiah, Sherebiah, and Jeshua the son of Kadmiel, with their brothers across from them, to praise *and* give thanks, group alternating with group, according to the command of David the man of God.

25 Mattaniah, Bakbukiah, Obadiah, Meshullam, Talmon, and Akkub *were* gatekeepers keeping the watch at the storerooms of the gates.

26 These *lived* in the days of Joiakim the son of Jeshua, the son of ᵀJozadak, and in the days of Nehemiah the governor, and of Ezra the priest, the scribe.   *Jehozadak*, 1 Chr. 6:14

Nehemiah Dedicates the Wall

27 Now at the dedication of the wall of Jerusalem they sought out the Levites in all their places, to bring them to Jerusalem to celebrate the dedication with gladness, both with thanksgivings and singing, *with* cymbals and stringed instruments and harps.

28 And the sons of the singers gathered together from the countryside around Jerusalem, from the villages of the Netophathites,

29 from the house of Gilgal, and from the fields of Geba and Azmaveth; for the singers had built themselves villages all around Jerusalem.

30 Then the priests and Levites ᴿpurified themselves, and purified the people, the gates, and the wall.   Neh. 13:22, 30

31 So I brought the leaders of Judah up on the wall, and appointed two large thanksgiving choirs. *One* went to the right hand on the wall toward the Refuse Gate.

12:15 *Rehum*, v. 3 • *Meremoth*, v. 3
12:20 *Sallu*, v. 7

32 After them went Hoshaiah and half of the leaders of Judah,

33 and Azariah, Ezra, Meshullam,

34 Judah, Benjamin, Shemaiah, Jeremiah,

35 and some of the priests' sons ᴿwith trumpets—Zechariah the son of Jonathan, the son of Shemaiah, the son of Mattaniah, the son of Michaiah, the son of Zaccur, the son of Asaph,   Num. 10:2, 8

36 and his brethren, Shemaiah, Azarel, Milalai, Gilalai, Maai, Nethanel, Judah, and Hanani, with ᴿthe musical ᴿinstruments of David the man of God. And Ezra the scribe went before them.   1 Chr. 23:5 • 2 Chr. 29:26, 27

37 By the Fountain Gate, in front of them, they went up the stairs of the City of David, on the stairway of the wall, beyond the house of David, as far as the Water Gate eastward.

38 ᴿThe other thanksgiving choir went the opposite way, and I was behind them with half of the people on the wall, going past the ᴿTower of the Ovens as far as ᴿthe Broad Wall,   Neh. 12:31 • Neh. 3:11 • Neh. 3:8

39 and above the Gate of Ephraim, above the Old Gate, above ᴿthe Fish Gate, the Tower of Hananel, the Tower of the Hundred, as far as the Sheep Gate; and they stopped by the Gate of the Prison.   Neh. 3:3

40 So the two thanksgiving choirs stood in the house of God, likewise I and the half of the rulers with me;

41 and the priests, Eliakim, Maaseiah, ᵀMinjamin, Michaiah, Elioenai, Zechariah, and Hananiah, with trumpets;   Or Mijamin, v. 5

42 also Maaseiah, Shemaiah, Eleazar, Uzzi, Jehohanan, Malchijah, Elam, and Ezer. The singers ᵀsang loudly with Jezrahiah the director.   Lit. made their voice to be heard

43 Also that day they offered great sacrifices, and rejoiced, for God had made them rejoice with great joy; the women also and the children also rejoiced, so that the joy of Jerusalem was heard ᴿafar off.   Ezra 3:13

Temple Responsibilities

44 And at the same time some were appointed over the rooms of the storehouse for the offerings, the firstfruits, and the tithes, to gather into them from the fields of the cities the portions specified by the Law for the priests and Levites; for Judah rejoiced over the priests and Levites who ministered.

45 Both the singers and the gatekeepers kept the charge of their God and the charge of the purification, according to the command of David and Solomon his son.

46 For in the days of David and Asaph of old there were chiefs of the singers, and songs of praise and thanksgiving to God.

47 In the days of Zerubbabel and in the days of Nehemiah all Israel gave the portions for the singers and the gatekeepers, a portion for each day. They also consecrated holy things for the Levites, and the Levites consecrated them for the children of Aaron.

Principles of Separation

13 On that day ᴿthey read from the Book of Moses in the hearing of the people, and in it was found written ᴿthat no Ammonite or Moabite should ever come into the assembly of God,   Neh. 8:3, 8; 9:3 • Deut. 23:3, 4

2 because they had not met the children of Israel with bread and water, but hired Balaam against them to curse them. However, our God turned the curse into a blessing.

3 So it was, when they had heard the Law, ᴿthat they separated all the mixed multitude from Israel.   Neh. 9:2; 10:28

The Reforms of Nehemiah

4 Now before this, Eliashib the priest, having authority over the storerooms of the house of our God, was allied with Tobiah.

5 And he had prepared for him a large room, ᴿwhere previously they had stored the grain offerings, the frankincense, the articles, the tithes of grain, the new wine and oil, ᴿwhich were commanded to be given to the Levites and singers and gatekeepers, and the offerings for the priests.   Neh. 12:44 • Num. 18:21, 24

6 But during all this I was not in Jerusalem, ᴿfor in the thirty-second year of Artaxerxes king of Babylon I had returned to the king. Then after certain days I obtained leave from the king,   Neh. 5:14–16

7 and I came to Jerusalem and discovered the evil that Eliashib had done for Tobiah, in ᴿpreparing a room for him in the courts of the ᵀhouse of God.   Neh. 13:1, 5 • Temple

8 And it grieved me bitterly; therefore I threw all the household goods of Tobiah out of the room.

9 Then I commanded them to ᴿcleanse the rooms; and I brought back into them the articles of the house of God, with the grain offering and the frankincense.   2 Chr. 29:5, 15, 16

10 I also realized that the portions for the Levites had ᴿnot been given them; for each of the Levites and the singers who did the work had gone back to ᴿhis field.   Neh. 10:37 • Num. 35:2

11 So ᴿI contended with the rulers, and said, ᴿ"Why is the house of God forsaken?" And I gathered them together and set them in their place.   Neh. 13:17, 25 • Neh. 10:39

12 ᴿThen all Judah brought the tithe of the grain and the new wine and the oil to the storehouse.   Neh. 10:38; 12:44

13 ᴿAnd I appointed as treasurers over the storehouse Shelemiah the priest and Zadok the scribe, and of the Levites, Pedaiah; and next to them was Hanan the son of Zaccur, the son of Mattaniah; for they were considered ᴿfaithful, and their task was to distribute to their brethren.   2 Chr. 31:12 • 1 Cor. 4:2

14 ^RRemember me, O my God, concerning this, and do not wipe out my good deeds that I have done for the house of my God, and for its services!   Neh. 5:19; 13:22, 31

15 In those days I saw in Judah *some people* treading wine presses ^Ron the Sabbath, and bringing in sheaves, and loading donkeys with wine, grapes, figs, and all *kinds of* burdens, ^Rwhich they brought into Jerusalem on the Sabbath day. And I warned *them* about the day on which they were selling provisions.   [Ex. 20:10] • [Jer. 17:21]

16 Men of Tyre dwelt there also, who brought in fish and all kinds of goods, and sold *them* on the Sabbath to the children of Judah, and in Jerusalem.

17 Then I contended with the nobles of Judah, and said to them, "What evil thing *is* this that you do, by which you profane the Sabbath day?

18 ^R"Did not your fathers do thus, and did not our God bring all this disaster on us and on this city? Yet you bring added wrath on Israel by profaning the Sabbath."   [Jer. 17:21]

19 So it was, at the gates of Jerusalem, as it began to be dark before the Sabbath, that I commanded the gates to be shut, and charged that they must not be opened till after the Sabbath. Then I posted *some* of my servants at the gates, *so that* no burdens would be brought in on the Sabbath day.

20 Now the merchants and sellers of all kinds of ^Twares ^Tlodged outside Jerusalem once or twice.   *merchandise* • *spent the night*

21 Then I warned them, and said to them, "Why do you spend the night ^Taround the wall? If you do *so* again, I will lay hands on you!" From that time on they came no *more* on the Sabbath.   Lit. *before*

22 And I commanded the Levites that ^Rthey should cleanse themselves, and that they should go and guard the gates, to sanctify the Sabbath day.

Remember me, O my God, *concerning* this also, and spare me according to the greatness of Your mercy!   Neh. 12:30

23 In those days I also saw Jews who ^Rhad married women of ^RAshdod, Ammon, *and* Moab.   Ezra 9:2 • Neh. 4:7

24 And half of their children spoke the language of Ashdod, and could not speak the language of Judah, but spoke according to the language of one or the other people.

25 So I ^Rcontended with them and cursed them, struck some of them and pulled out their hair, and made them swear by God, *saying,* "You shall not give your daughters as wives to their sons, nor take their daughters for your sons or yourselves.   Prov. 28:4

26 ^R"Did not Solomon king of Israel sin by these things? Yet among many nations there was no king like him, who was beloved of his God; and God made him king over all Israel. ^RNevertheless pagan women caused even him to sin.   1 Kin. 11:1, 2 • 1 Kin. 11:4–8

27 "Should we then hear of your doing all this great evil, ^Rtransgressing against our God by marrying pagan women?"   [Ezra 10:2]

28 And *one* of the sons ^Rof Joiada, the son of Eliashib the high priest, *was* a son-in-law of ^RSanballat the Horonite; therefore I drove him from me.   Neh. 12:10, 12 • Neh. 4:1, 7; 6:1, 2

29 Remember them, O my God, because they have defiled the priesthood and the covenant of the priesthood and the Levites.

30 Thus I cleansed them of everything pagan. I also assigned duties to the priests and the Levites, each to his service,

31 and to bringing ^Rthe wood offering and the firstfruits at appointed times.   Neh. 10:34

Remember me, O my God, for good!

THE BOOK OF
Esther

Esther is one of the most exciting books in the Old Testament, recounting how a Jewish orphan girl, by her beauty and courage, saved her people from extermination. It stands alone among all of the books of the Bible in being the only one which does not use the name of God (although Hebrew scholars have found His name in hidden form at crucial turning points in the narrative). It is fitting that God's name *not* be apparent in Esther because the book's theme is God's providential working *behind* the scenes of history. Also, the Jews in Esther were those who had been satisfied to stay in Persia after they could have gone back to the Holy Land.

AUTHORSHIP. The book of Esther gives no indication as to the identity of its author. Some have assumed from 9:20 that Mordecai wrote the entire book, but this verse simply states that Mordecai wrote letters regarding the observance of the feast of Purim. The book has also been ascribed to Ezra, Nehemiah, Joiakim the son of Jeshua the high priest (Neh. 12:10, 26), and the men of the Great Synagogue. These various theories of authorship are merely guesses.

The date of the book is as difficult to determine as the identity of the author. The book is not mentioned in either the Old or New Testament and is the only book in the Old Testament of which no trace has yet been found in the Dead Sea Scrolls. No mention is made either of Esther or Mordecai in Ben Sirach's roll of the heroes of Israel (Ecclesiasticus 44—49) about 180 B.C. However, we do know that the book was written in the pre-Christian era. It is found in the earliest manuscripts of the Septuagint. There is a reference to the feast of Purim in 2 Maccabees 15:36 (written about 50 B.C.). Josephus (who died in 95 A.D.) was well acquainted with Esther and considered it to be ancient.

CONTEXT. Because of centuries of disobedience to God, especially in religious compromise with the Gentiles, the Jews were scattered throughout Mesopotamia. Their sins of rebellion against God eventually resulted in divine judgment through captivity in foreign lands. However, most of the exiled Jews retained their own identity, culture and religion.

After seventy years of exile, God raised up a Gentile king who overthrew Babylon. King Cyrus encouraged the Jews to return to the land of their fathers and rebuild the temple. In 536 B.C., fifty thousand Jews returned to Jerusalem under the leadership of Zerubbabel the governor and Jeshua the high priest. Ezra and Nehemiah, the two Old Testament books preceding the book of Esther, tell of these Jews who returned to their homeland. The majority of Jews in Persia and Babylon, however, preferred to continue their easy and lucrative life under the Persians. There is no indication that Mordecai and Esther wished to be a part of the returning remnant to Jerusalem, a city reduced to thorns and briers.

KEY WORD AND KEY VERSE. The key word in Esther is *providence.* The book teaches the providence of God. Providence simply means that God will provide. It is the way that God leads the one who will not easily be led, just as Mordecai said to Esther in 4:14: "For if you remain completely silent at this time, relief and deliverance will arise for the Jews from another place, but you and your father's house will perish. Yet who knows whether you have come to the kingdom for such a time as this?"

HOW ESTHER FITS TOGETHER. The book may be outlined according to its twelve major events:

(1) Ahasuerus deposes Queen Vashti for refusing to appear at his banquet (ch. 1).
(2) Esther, cousin of Mordecai the Jew, is chosen queen (2:1-18).
(3) Mordecai tells Esther about a plot to kill the king (2:19-23).
(4) Mordecai refuses to bow to Haman, the king's favorite, who then plans to massacre the Jews on a fixed date (ch. 3).
(5) Mordecai persuades Esther to intercede for the Jews with the king (ch. 4).
(6) Esther invites the king and Haman to her banquet (ch. 5).
(7) The king orders Haman to honor Mordecai publicly as a reward for revealing the plot against him (ch. 6).
(8) At a second banquet Esther reveals Haman's plot to massacre the Jews, and Haman is hanged on a gallows that he made for Mordecai (ch. 7).
(9) Since the edict for the massacre cannot be revoked, the king orders a second edict allowing the Jews to defend themselves (ch. 8).
(10) The Jews destroy their enemies (9:1-19).

(11) The Jews' deliverance is commemorated at the feast of Purim (9:20-32).

(12) Mordecai is promoted to a position of authority (ch. 10).

Esther needs to be read because it supplies us with our only account of the origin of the feast of Purim. From it we also learn of the error of absolutism and dogmatism in the case of Ahasuerus; and in the case of Haman, the danger of pride and jealousy against God's providential design to fulfill His purpose in history.

—C.G.H.

The King Dethrones Queen Vashti

NOW it came to pass in the days of *Ahasuerus (this *was* the Ahasuerus who reigned over one hundred and twenty-seven provinces, from India to Ethiopia),

2 in those days when King Ahasuerus sat on the throne of his kingdom, which *was* in *Shushan the ᵀcitadel,   *Or fortified palace*

3 *that* in the third year of his reign he ᴿmade a feast for all his officials and servants—the powers of Persia and Media, the nobles, and the princes of the provinces *being* before him—   Gen. 40:20

4 when he showed the riches of his glorious kingdom and the splendor of his excellent majesty for many days, one hundred and eighty days *in all.*

5 And when these days were completed, the king made a feast lasting seven days for all the people who were present in Shushan the ᵀcitadel, from great to small, in the court of the garden of the king's palace.   *palace*

6 *There were* white and blue linen *curtains* fastened with cords of fine linen and purple on silver rods and marble pillars; *and the* ᴿcouches *were* of gold and silver on a *mosaic* pavement of alabaster, turquoise, and white and black marble.   Amos 2:8; 6:4

7 And they served drinks in golden vessels, each vessel being different from the other, with royal wine in abundance, ᴿaccording to the ᵀgenerosity of the king.   Esth. 2:18 • Lit. *hand*

8 In accordance with the law, the drinking was not compulsory; for so the king had ordered all the officers of his household, that they should do according to each man's pleasure.

9 Queen Vashti also made a feast for the women *in* the royal palace which *belonged* to King Ahasuerus.

10 On the seventh day, when the heart of the king was merry with wine, he commanded Mehuman, Biztha, ᴿHarbona, Bigtha, Abagtha, Zethar, and Carcas, seven eunuchs who served in the presence of King Ahasuerus,   Esth. 7:9

11 to bring Queen Vashti before the king, *wearing* her royal crown, in order to show her beauty to the people and the officials, for she *was* beautiful to behold.

12 But Queen Vashti refused to come at the king's command *brought* by *his* eunuchs; therefore the king was furious, and his anger burned within him.

13 Then the king said to the ᴿwise men ᴿwho understood the times (for this *was* the king's manner toward all who knew law and justice,   Dan. 2:12 • 1 Chr. 12:32

14 those closest to him *being* Carshena, Shethar, Admatha, Tarshish, Meres, Marsena, and Memucan, the ᴿseven princes of Persia and Media, ᴿwho had access to the king's presence, *and* who ᵀranked highest in the kingdom):   Ezra 7:14 • 2 Kin. 25:19 • Lit. *sat in first place*

15 "What *shall we* do to Queen Vashti, according to law, because she did not obey the command of King Ahasuerus *brought to her* by the eunuchs?"

16 And Memucan answered before the king and the princes: "Queen Vashti has not only wronged the king, but also all the princes, and all the people who *are* in all the provinces of King Ahasuerus.

17 "For the queen's behavior will become known to all women, so that they will ᴿdespise their husbands in their eyes, when they report, 'King Ahasuerus commanded Queen Vashti to be brought in before him, but she did not come.'   [Eph. 5:33]

18 "This very day the *noble* ladies of Persia and Media will say to all the king's officials that they have heard of the behavior of the queen. Thus *there will be* excessive contempt and wrath.

19 "If it pleases the king, let a royal ᵀdecree go out from him, and let it be recorded in the laws of the Persians and the Medes, so that it will ᴿnot ᵀbe altered, that Vashti shall come no more before King Ahasuerus; and let the king give her royal position to another who is better than she.   Lit. *word* • Esth. 8:8 • *pass away*

20 "When the king's decree which he will make is proclaimed throughout all his empire (for it is great), all wives will ᴿhonor their husbands, both great and small."   [Col. 3:18]

21 And the reply pleased the king and the princes, and the king did according to the word of Memucan.

22 Then he sent letters to all the king's provinces, ᴿto each province in its own script,

and to every people in their own language, that each man should ᴿbe master in his own house, and speak in the language of his own people.   Esth. 3:12; 8:9 • [Eph. 5:22–24]

Esther Becomes Queen

2 After these things, when the wrath of King Ahasuerus subsided, he remembered Vashti, ᴿwhat she had done, and what had been decreed against her.   Esth. 1:19, 20

2 Then the king's servants who attended him said: "Let beautiful young virgins be sought for the king;

3 "and let the king appoint officers in all the provinces of his kingdom, that they may gather all the beautiful young virgins to Shushan the citadel, into the women's quarters, under the custody of ᵀHegai the king's eunuch, custodian of the women. And let beauty preparations be given *them*.   Heb. Hege

4 "Then let the young woman who pleases the king be queen instead of Vashti." This thing pleased the king, and he did so.

5 In ᵀShushan the ᵀcitadel there was a certain Jew whose name *was* Mordecai the son of Jair, the son of Shimei, the son of ᴿKish, a Benjamite.   Or Susa • palace • 1 Sam. 9:1

6 ᵀKish had been carried away from Jerusalem with the captives who had been captured with ᵀJeconiah king of Judah, whom Nebuchadnezzar the king of Babylon had carried away.   Lit. Who • Jehoiachin, 2 Kin. 24:6

7 And *Mordecai* had brought up Hadassah, that *is*, Esther, ᴿhis uncle's daughter, for she had neither father nor mother. The young woman *was* lovely and beautiful. When her father and mother died, Mordecai took her as his own daughter.   Esth. 2:15

8 So it was, when the king's command and decree were heard, and when many young women were gathered at Shushan the citadel, *under* the custody of Hegai, that Esther also was taken to the king's palace, into the care of Hegai the custodian of the women.

9 Now the young woman pleased him, and she obtained his favor; so he readily gave beauty preparations to her, besides her allowance. Then seven choice maidservants were provided for her from the king's palace, and he moved her and her maidservants to the best *place* in the house of the women.

10 ᴿEsther had not ᵀrevealed her people or family, for Mordecai had charged her not to reveal *it*.   Esth. 2:20 • Revealed the identity of

11 And every day Mordecai paced in front of the court of the women's quarters, to learn of Esther's welfare and what was happening to her.

12 Each young woman's turn came to go in to King Ahasuerus after she had completed twelve months' preparation, according to the regulations for the women, for thus were the days of their preparation apportioned: six

months with oil of myrrh, and six months with perfumes and preparations for beautifying women.

13 Thus *prepared, each* young woman went to the king, and she was given whatever she desired to take with her from the women's quarters to the king's palace.

14 In the evening she went, and in the morning she returned to the second house of the women, to the custody of Shaashgaz, the king's eunuch who kept the concubines. She would not go in to the king again unless the king delighted in her and called for her by name.

15 Now when the turn came for Esther the daughter of Abihail the uncle of Mordecai, who had taken her as his daughter, to go in to the king, she requested nothing but what Hegai the king's eunuch, the custodian of the women, advised. And Esther ᴿobtained favor in the sight of all who saw her.   Esth. 5:2, 8

16 So Esther was taken to King Ahasuerus, into his royal palace, in the tenth month, which *is* the month of Tebeth, in the seventh year of his reign.

17 The king loved Esther more than all the *other* women, and she obtained grace and favor in his sight more than all the virgins; so he set the royal ᴿcrown upon her head and made her queen instead of Vashti.   Esth. 1:11

18 Then the king ᴿmade a great feast, the Feast of Esther, for all his officials and servants; and he proclaimed a holiday in the provinces and gave gifts according to the ᵀgenerosity of a king.   Esth. 1:3 • Lit. hand

Mordecai Discovers a Plot

19 When virgins were gathered together a second time, Mordecai sat within the king's gate.

20 *Now* Esther had not revealed her family and her people, just as Mordecai had charged her, for Esther obeyed the command of Mordecai as when she was brought up by him.

21 In those days, while Mordecai sat within the king's gate, two of the king's eunuchs, ᵀBigthan and Teresh, doorkeepers, became furious and sought to lay hands on King Ahasuerus.   Bigthana, Esth. 6:2

22 So the matter became known to Mordecai, who told Queen Esther, and Esther informed the king in Mordecai's name.

23 And when an inquiry was made into the matter, it was confirmed, and both were hanged on a gallows; and it was written in ᴿthe book of the chronicles in the presence of the king.   Esth. 6:1

Haman's Conspiracy Against the Jews

3 After these things King Ahasuerus promoted Haman, the son of Hammedatha the Agagite, and advanced him and set his seat above all the princes who *were* with him.

2 And all the king's servants who *were* within the king's gate bowed and paid homage to Haman, for so the king had commanded concerning him. But Mordecai ᴿwould not bow or pay homage. Ps. 15:4

3 Then the king's servants who *were* within the king's gate said to Mordecai, "Why do you transgress the ᴿking's command?" Esth. 3:2

4 Now it happened, when they spoke to him daily and he would not listen to them, that they told *it* to Haman, to see whether Mordecai's words would stand; for *Mordecai* had told them that he *was* a Jew.

5 When Haman saw that Mordecai ᴿdid not bow or pay him homage, Haman was ᴿfilled with wrath. Esth. 3:2; 5:9 · Dan. 3:19

6 But he disdained to lay hands on Mordecai alone, for they had told him of the people of Mordecai. Instead, Haman ᴿsought to destroy all the Jews who *were* throughout the whole kingdom of Ahasuerus—the people of Mordecai. Ps. 83:4

7 In the first month, which is the month of Nisan, in the twelfth year of King Ahasuerus, they cast Pur (that *is*, the lot), before Haman ᵀto determine the day and the *month, *until it fell on the twelfth *month*, which *is* the month of Adar. Lit. from day to day and month to month

8 Then Haman said to King Ahasuerus, "There is a certain people scattered and dispersed among the people in all the provinces of your kingdom; their laws *are* different from all *other* people's, and they do not keep the king's laws. Therefore it *is* not fitting for the king to let them remain.

9 "If it pleases the king, let *a decree* be written that they be destroyed, and I will pay ᵀten thousand talents of silver into the hands of those who do the work, to bring *it* into the king's treasuries." $3.84 billion

10 So the king ᴿtook ᴿhis signet ring from his hand and gave it to Haman, the son of Hammedatha the Agagite, the ᴿenemy of the Jews. Gen. 41:42 · Esth. 8:2, 8 · Esth. 7:6

11 And the king said to Haman, "The money and the people *are* given to you, to do with them as seems good to you."

12 ᴿThen the king's scribes were called on the thirteenth day of the first month, and *a decree* was written according to all that Haman commanded—to the king's satraps, to the governors who *were* over each province, to the officials of all people, to every province ᴿaccording to its script, and to every people in their language. ᴿIn the name of King Ahasuerus it was written, and sealed with the king's signet ring. Esth. 8:9 · Esth. 1:22 · Esth. 8:8–10

3:7 LXX adds *to destroy the people of Mordecai in one day;* Vg. adds *the nation of the Jews should be destroyed* • So with MT, Vg.; LXX *and the lot fell on the fourteenth of the month*

13 And the letters were sent by couriers into all the king's provinces, to destroy, to kill, and to annihilate all the Jews, both young and old, little children and women, in one day, on the thirteenth *day* of the twelfth *month*, which *is* the month of Adar, and ᴿto plunder their *possessions. Esth. 8:11; 9:10

14 ᴿA copy of the document was to be issued as law in every province, being published for all people, that they should be ready for that day. Esth. 8:13, 14

15 The couriers went out, hastened by the king's command; and the decree was proclaimed in Shushan the ᵀcitadel. So the king and Haman sat down to drink, but the city of Shushan was ᵀperplexed. *palace · in confusion*

Esther Agrees to Help the Jews

4 When Mordecai learned all that had happened, ᵀhe tore his clothes and put on sackcloth and ashes, and went out into the midst of the city. He ᴿcried out with a loud and bitter cry. Lit. *Mordecai* · Gen. 27:34

2 He went as far as the front of the king's gate, for no one *might* enter the king's gate clothed with sackcloth.

3 And in every province where the king's command and decree arrived, *there was* great mourning among the Jews, with fasting, weeping, and wailing; and many lay in sackcloth and ashes.

4 So Esther's maids and eunuchs came and told her, and the queen was deeply distressed. Then she sent garments to clothe Mordecai and take his sackcloth away from him, but he would not accept *them.*

5 Then Esther called Hathach, *one* of the king's eunuchs whom he had appointed to attend her, and she gave him a command concerning Mordecai, to learn what and why this *was.*

6 So Hathach went out to Mordecai in the city square that *was* in front of the king's gate.

7 And Mordecai told him all that had happened to him, and ᴿthe sum of money that Haman had promised to pay into the king's treasuries to destroy the Jews. Esth. 3:9

8 He also gave him ᴿa copy of the written decree for their destruction, which was given at ᵀShushan, that he might show it to Esther and explain it to her, and that he might command her to go in to the king to make supplication to him and plead before him for her people. Esth. 3:14, 15 · Or *Susa*

9 So Hathach returned and told Esther the words of Mordecai.

10 Then Esther spoke to Hathach, and gave him a command for Mordecai:

11 "All the king's servants and the people of the king's provinces know that any man or

3:13 LXX adds the text of the letter here.

woman who goes into the inner court to the king, who has not been called, *he has* but one law: put *all* to death, except the one to whom the king holds out the golden scepter, that he may live. Yet I myself have not been called to go in to the king these thirty days."

12 So they told Mordecai Esther's words.

13 And Mordecai told *them* to answer Esther: "Do not think in your heart that you will escape in the king's palace any more than all the other Jews.

14 "For if you remain completely silent at this time, relief and deliverance will arise for the Jews from another place, but you and your father's house will perish. Yet who knows whether you have come to the kingdom for *such* a time as this?"

15 Then Esther told *them* to reply to Mordecai:

16 "Go, gather all the Jews who are present in ᵀShushan, and fast for me; neither eat nor drink for ᴿthree days, night or day. My maids and I will fast likewise. And so I will go to the king, which *is* against the law; ᴿand if I perish, I perish!"   Or *Susa* • Esth. 5:1 • Gen. 43:14

17 So Mordecai went his way and did according to all that Esther commanded *him.

Esther's Banquet

5 Now it happened ᴿon the third day that Esther put on *her* royal *robes* and stood in ᴿthe inner court of the king's palace, across from the king's house, while the king sat on his royal throne in the royal house, facing the entrance of the *house.   Esth. 4:16 • Esth. 4:11; 6:4

2 So it was, when the king saw Queen Esther standing in the court, *that* ᴿshe found favor in his sight, and ᴿthe king held out to Esther the golden scepter that *was* in his hand. Then Esther went near and touched the top of the scepter.   [Prov. 21:1] • Esth. 4:11; 8:4

3 And the king said to her, "What do you wish, Queen Esther? What *is* your request? ᴿIt shall be given to you—up to half the kingdom!"   Mark 6:23

4 So Esther answered, "If it pleases the king, let the king and Haman come today to the banquet that I have prepared for him."

5 Then the king said, "Bring Haman quickly, that he may do as Esther has said." So the king and Haman went to the banquet that Esther had prepared.

6 At the banquet of wine the king said to Esther, ᴿ"What *is* your petition? It shall be granted you. What *is* your request, up to half the kingdom? It shall be done!"   Esth. 9:12

7 Then Esther answered and said, "My petition and request *is this*:

8 "If I have found favor in the sight of the king, and if it pleases the king to grant my

4:17 LXX adds a prayer of Mordecai here.
5:1 LXX adds many extra details in vv. 1, 2.

petition and ᵀfulfill my request, then let the king and Haman come to the ᴿbanquet which I will prepare for them, and tomorrow I will do as the king has said."   Lit. *to do* • Esth. 6:14

Haman's Plot Against Mordecai

9 So Haman went out that day ᴿjoyful and with a glad heart; but when Haman saw Mordecai in the king's gate, and that he did not stand or tremble before him, he was filled with indignation against Mordecai.   [Job 20:5]

10 Nevertheless Haman ᴿrestrained himself and went home, and he sent and called for his friends and his wife Zeresh.   2 Sam. 13:22

11 Then Haman told them of his great riches, the multitude of his children, everything in which the king had promoted him, and how he had ᴿadvanced him above the officials and servants of the king.   Esth. 3:1

12 Moreover Haman said, "Besides, Queen Esther invited no one but me to come in with the king to the banquet that she prepared; and tomorrow I am again invited by her, along with the king.

13 "Yet all this avails me nothing, so long as I see Mordecai the Jew sitting at the king's gate."

14 Then his wife Zeresh and all his friends said to him, "Let a gallowsᵀ be made, fifty cubits high, and in the morning ᴿsuggest to the king that Mordecai be hanged on it; then go merrily with the king to the banquet." And the thing pleased Haman; so he had ᴿthe gallows made.   Lit. *tree* or *wood* • Esth. 6:4 • Esth. 7:10

The King Honors Mordecai

6 That night ᵀthe king could not sleep. So one was commanded to bring the book of the records of the chronicles; and they were read before the king.   *the king's sleep fled*

2 And it was found written that Mordecai had told of Bigthana and Teresh, two of the king's eunuchs, the doorkeepers who had sought to lay hands on King Ahasuerus.

3 Then the king said, "What honor or dignity has been bestowed on Mordecai for this?" And the king's servants who attended him said, "Nothing has been done for him."

4 So the king said, "Who *is* in the court?" Now Haman had *just* entered ᴿthe outer court of the king's palace ᴿto suggest that the king hang Mordecai on the gallows that he had prepared for him.   Esth. 5:1 • Esth. 5:14

5 The king's servants said to him, "Haman is there, standing in the court." And the king said, "Let him come in."

6 So Haman came in, and the king asked him, "What shall be done for the man whom the king delights to honor?" Now Haman thought in his heart, "Whom would the king delight to honor more than ᴿme?"   [Prov. 16:18]

7 And Haman answered the king, "*For* the man whom the king delights to honor,

8 "let a royal robe be brought which the king has worn, and ᴿa horse on which the king has ridden, which has a royal ᵀcrest placed on its head.   1 Kin. 1:33 · *crown*

9 "Then let this robe and horse be delivered to the hand of one of the king's most noble princes, that he may array the man whom the king delights to honor. Then ᵀparade him on horseback through the city square, ᴿand proclaim before him: 'Thus shall it be done to the man whom the king delights to honor!' "   Lit. *cause him to ride* · Gen. 41:43

10 Then the king said to Haman, "Hurry, take the robe and the horse, as you have suggested, and do so for Mordecai the Jew who sits within the king's gate! Leave nothing undone of all that you have spoken."

11 So Haman took the robe and the horse, arrayed Mordecai and led him on horseback through the city square, and proclaimed before him, "Thus shall it be done to the man whom the king delights to honor!"

12 Afterward Mordecai went back to the king's gate. But Haman hurried to his house, mourning and with his head covered.

13 When Haman told his wife Zeresh and all his friends everything that had happened to him, his wise men and his wife Zeresh said to him, "If Mordecai, before whom you have begun to fall, is of Jewish descent, you will not prevail against ᴿhim but will surely fall before him."   Zech. 2:8

14 While they *were* still talking with him, the king's eunuchs came, and hastened to bring Haman to ᴿthe banquet which Esther had prepared.   Esth. 5:8

Haman Hanged Instead of Mordecai

7 So the king and Haman went to dine with Queen Esther.

2 And on the second day, ᴿat the banquet of wine, the king again said to Esther, "What *is* your petition, Queen Esther? It shall be granted you. And what *is* your request, up to half the kingdom? It shall be done!"   Esth. 5:6

3 Then Queen Esther answered and said, "If I have found favor in your sight, O king, and if it pleases the king, let my life be given me at my petition, and my people at my request.

4 "For we have been ᴿsold, my people and I, to be destroyed, to be killed, and to be annihilated. Had we been sold as ᴿmale and female slaves, I would have held my tongue, although the enemy could never compensate for the king's loss."   Esth. 3:9; 4:7 · Deut. 28:68

5 So King Ahasuerus answered and said to Queen Esther, "Who is he, and where is he, who would dare presume in his heart to do such a thing?"

6 And Esther said, "The adversary and enemy *is* this wicked Haman!" So Haman was terrified before the king and queen.

7 Then the king arose in his wrath from the banquet of wine *and went* into the palace garden; but Haman stood before Queen Esther, pleading for his life, for he saw that evil was determined against him by the king.

8 When the king returned from the palace garden to the place of the banquet of wine, Haman had fallen across ᴿthe couch where Esther *was*. Then the king said, "Will he also assault the queen while I *am* in the house?" As the word left the king's mouth, they ᴿcovered Haman's face.   Esth. 1:6 · Job 9:24

9 Now Harbonah, one of the eunuchs, said to the king, "Look! The ᵀgallows, fifty cubits high, which Haman made for Mordecai, who spoke good on the king's behalf, is standing at the house of Haman." Then the king said, "Hang him on it!"   Lit. *tree* or *wood*

10 So ᴿthey ᴿhanged Haman on the gallows that he had prepared for Mordecai. Then the king's wrath subsided.   [Ps. 7:16; 94:23] · Dan. 6:24

Esther Saves the Jews

8 On that day King Ahasuerus gave Queen Esther the house of Haman, the ᴿenemy of the Jews. And Mordecai came before the king, for Esther had told ᴿhow he *was related* to her.   Esth. 7:6 · Esth. 2:7, 15

2 So the king took off ᴿhis signet ring, which he had taken from Haman, and gave it to Mordecai; and Esther appointed Mordecai over the house of Haman.   Esth. 3:10

3 Now Esther spoke again to the king, fell down at his feet, and implored him with tears to counteract the evil of Haman the Agagite, and the scheme which he had devised against the Jews.

4 And ᴿthe king held out the golden scepter toward Esther. So Esther arose and stood before the king,   Esth. 4:11; 5:2

5 and said, "If it pleases the king, and if I have found favor in his sight, and the thing *seems* right to the king and I am pleasing in his eyes, let it be written to revoke the ᴿletters devised by Haman, the son of Hammedatha the Agagite, which he wrote to annihilate the Jews who *are* in all the king's provinces.   Esth. 3:13

6 "For how can I endure to see the evil that will come to my people? Or how can I endure to see the destruction of my countrymen?"

7 Then King Ahasuerus said to Queen Esther and Mordecai the Jew, "Indeed, I have given Esther the house of Haman, and they have hanged him on the gallows because he *tried to* lay his hand on the Jews.

8 "You yourselves write *a decree* concerning the Jews, ᵀas you please, in the king's name, and seal *it* with the king's signet ring; for whatever is written in the king's name and sealed with the king's signet ring ᴿno one can revoke."   Lit. *as is good in your eyes* · Dan. 6:8, 12, 15

9 ᴿSo the king's scribes were called at that time, in the third month, which is the month of Sivan, on the twenty-third day; and it was written, according to all that Mordecai commanded, to the Jews, the satraps, the governors, and the princes of the provinces ᴿfrom India to Ethiopia, one hundred and twenty-seven provinces in all, to every province ᴿin its own script, to every people in their own language, and to the Jews in their own script and language.   Esth. 3:12 • Esth. 1:1 • Esth. 1:22; 3:12

10 ᴿAnd he wrote in the name of King Ahasuerus, sealed it with the king's signet ring, and sent letters by couriers on horseback, riding on royal horses ᵀbred from swift steeds.   1 Kin. 21:8 • Lit. sons of the swift horses

11 By these letters the king permitted the Jews who were in every city to ᴿgather together and protect their lives—to ᴿdestroy, kill, and annihilate all the forces of any people or province that would assault them, both little children and women, and to plunder their possessions,   Esth. 9:2 • Esth. 9:10, 15, 16

12 on one day in all the provinces of King Ahasuerus, on the thirteenth day of the twelfth month, which is the month of *Adar.

13 ᴿA copy of the document was to be issued as a decree in every province and published for all people, so that the Jews would be ready on that day to avenge themselves on their enemies.   Esth. 3:14, 15

14 The couriers who rode on royal horses went out, hastened and pressed on by the king's command. And the decree was issued in ᵀShushan the ᵀcitadel.   Or Susa • palace

15 So Mordecai went out from the presence of the king in royal apparel of blue and white, with a great crown of gold and a garment of fine linen and purple; and the city of Shushan rejoiced and was glad.

16 The Jews had ᴿlight and gladness, joy and honor.   Ps. 97:11; 112:4

17 And in every province and city, wherever the king's command and decree came, the Jews had joy and gladness, a feast ᴿand a holiday. Then many of the people of the land ᴿbecame Jews, because ᴿfear of the Jews fell upon them.   Esth. 9:19 • Ps. 18:43 • Gen. 35:5

The Jews Destroy Their Tormentors

9 Now ᴿin the twelfth month, that is, the month of Adar, on the thirteenth day, ᴿthe time came for the king's command and his decree to be executed. On the day that the enemies of the Jews had hoped to overpower them, the opposite occurred, in that the Jews themselves ᴿoverpowered those who hated them.   Esth. 8:12 • Esth. 3:13 • 2 Sam. 22:41

2 The Jews ᴿgathered together in their cities throughout all the provinces of King Ahasuerus to lay hands on those who ᴿsought

8:12 LXX adds the text of the letter here.

their harm. And no one could withstand them, ᴿbecause fear of them fell upon all people.   Esth. 8:11; 9:15-18 • Ps. 71:13, 14 • Esth. 8:17

3 And all the officials of the provinces, the satraps, the governors, and all those doing the king's work, helped the Jews, because the fear of Mordecai fell upon them.

4 For Mordecai was great in the king's palace, and his fame spread throughout all the provinces; for this man Mordecai ᴿbecame increasingly prominent.   2 Sam. 3:1

5 Thus the Jews defeated all their enemies with the stroke of the sword, with slaughter and destruction, and did what they pleased with those who hated them.

6 And in Shushan the citadel the Jews killed and destroyed five hundred men.

7 Also Parshandatha, Dalphon, Aspatha,

8 Poratha, Adalia, Aridatha,

9 Parmashta, Arisai, Aridai, and Vajezatha—

10 the ten sons of Haman the son of Hammedatha, the enemy of the Jews—they killed; but they did not lay a hand on the plunder.

11 On that day the number of those who were killed in ᵀShushan the ᵀcitadel ᵀwas brought to the king.   Or Susa • palace • Lit. came

12 And the king said to Queen Esther, "The Jews have killed and destroyed five hundred men in Shushan the citadel, and the ten sons of Haman. What have they done in the rest of the king's provinces? Now what is your petition? It shall be granted to you. Or what is your further request? It shall be done."

13 Then Esther said, "If it pleases the king, let it be granted to the Jews who are in Shushan to do again tomorrow according to today's decree, and let Haman's ten sons ᴿbe hanged on the gallows."   2 Sam. 21:6, 9

14 So the king commanded this to be done; the decree was issued in Shushan, and they hanged Haman's ten sons.

15 And the Jews who were in ᵀShushan gathered together again on the fourteenth day of the month of Adar and killed three hundred men at Shushan; ᴿbut they did not lay a hand on the plunder.   Or Susa • Esth. 9:10

16 The remainder of the Jews in the king's provinces gathered together and protected their lives, had rest from their enemies, and killed seventy-five thousand of their enemies; but they did not lay a hand on the plunder.

17 This was on the thirteenth day of the month of Adar. And on the fourteenth of ᵀthe month they rested and made it a day of feasting and gladness.   Lit. it

The Feast of Purim

18 But the Jews who were at Shushan assembled together on the thirteenth day, as well as on the fourteenth; and on the fifteenth of ᵀthe month they rested, and made it a day of feasting and gladness.   Lit. it

19 Therefore the Jews of the villages who dwelt in the unwalled towns celebrated the fourteenth day of the month of Adar *with* gladness and feasting, as a holiday, and for sending presents to one another.

20 And Mordecai wrote these things and sent letters to all the Jews, near and far, who *were* in all the provinces of King Ahasuerus,

21 to establish among them that they should celebrate yearly the fourteenth and fifteenth days of the month of Adar,

22 as the days on which the Jews had rest from their enemies, as the month which was turned from sorrow to joy for them, and from mourning to a holiday; that they should make them days of feasting and joy, of ᴿsending presents to one another and gifts to the ᴿpoor.   Neh. 8:10 · [Deut. 15:7–11]

23 So the Jews accepted the custom which they had begun, as Mordecai had written to them,

24 because Haman, the son of Hammedatha the Agagite, the enemy of all the Jews, ᴿhad plotted against the Jews to annihilate them, and had cast Pur (that *is*, the lot), to consume them and destroy them;   Esth. 3:6, 7; 9:26

25 but when ᵀEsther came before the king, he commanded by letter that ᵀthis wicked plot which *Haman* had devised against the Jews should ᴿreturn on his own head, and that he and his sons should be hanged on the gallows.   Lit. *she* or *it* · Lit. *his* · Esth. 7:10

26 So they called these days Purim, after the name ᵀPur. Therefore, because of all the words of ᴿthis letter, what they had seen concerning this matter, and what had happened to them,   Lit. *Lot* · Esth. 9:20

27 the Jews established and imposed it upon themselves and their descendants and all who would ᴿjoin them, that without fail they should celebrate these two days every year, according to the written *instructions* and according to the *prescribed* time,   Esth. 8:17

28 *that* these days *should be* remembered and kept throughout every generation, every family, every province, and every city, that these days of Purim should not fail *to be observed* among the Jews, and *that* the memory of them should not perish among their descendants.

29 Then Queen Esther, ᴿthe daughter of Abihail, with Mordecai the Jew, wrote with full authority to confirm this ᴿsecond letter about Purim.   Esth. 2:15 · Esth. 8:10; 9:20, 21

30 And *Mordecai* sent letters to all the Jews, to ᴿthe one hundred and twenty-seven provinces of the kingdom of Ahasuerus, *with* words of peace and truth,   Esth. 1:1

31 to confirm these days of Purim at their *appointed* time, as Mordecai the Jew and Queen Esther had prescribed for them, and as they had decreed for themselves and their descendants concerning matters of their ᴿfasting and lamenting.   Esth. 4:3, 16

32 So the decree of Esther confirmed these matters of Purim, and it was written in the book.

Mordecai's Advancement

10 And King Ahasuerus imposed tribute on the land and *on* the islands of the sea.

2 Now all the acts of his power and his might, and the account of the greatness of Mordecai, to which the king advanced him, *are* they not written in the book of the chronicles of the kings of Media and Persia?

3 For Mordecai the Jew *was* second to King Ahasuerus, and was great among the Jews and well received by the multitude of his brethren, seeking the good of his people and speaking peace to all his *countrymen.

10:3 Lit. *seed* • LXX, Vg. add a dream of Mordecai here; Vg. adds six more chapters.

THE BOOK OF
Job

AUTHORSHIP. Although the Book of Job has inspired a great deal of study over the centuries, in many ways it remains a puzzle. There is still no agreement on who wrote it or when it was written.

Traditionally its authorship was assigned to Moses, or someone earlier. Modern scholarship places it much later, as late as the third century B.C. While there is insufficient evidence for a pre-Mosaic date, there is likewise no compelling support for a late date. Given the universal nature of suffering, the fact that the latter portion of Isaiah also deals with suffering is not a convincing argument for a later date for Job. Besides, Job's suffering is not vicarious, whereas that of Isaiah's suffering Servant is.

Perhaps the most plausible view is that Job is an anonymous work composed about the time of Solomon. Support for this comes from a comparison of the material in Job with other literature of the same type (e.g., comparing 15:8 and ch. 28 with Prov. 8). That period of time marked the beginning of Israel's wisdom writing and so would be a natural literary setting for this book. These ideas do not, however, rule out its being written a little earlier or later.

CONTEXT. The book of Job is named after the central figure in the drama. But the work makes no reference to any parallel historical event. All that we know of Job is that he lived in Uz, near Teman, the home of Eliphaz, south or east of Israel. This harmonizes with the fact that the cultural setting of the material does not appear to be Hebrew. In fact, the holy name Yahweh (Jehovah) is scarely used in the dialogues. The book just does not provide much information.

Many have suggested that the setting of this drama is in the patriarchal period. The name Job has indeed been found as early as the nineteenth century B.C., as well as in the Amarna letters. In addition the emphasis on the family unit with the father making sacrifices (1:5) fits that period. Moreover, the type of money mentioned in the book, the qesita' (translated "piece of silver," 42:11), occurs elsewhere only in Genesis 33:19 and Joshua 24:32, both texts referring to the earlier periods. These arguments should not be given too much weight, however, because ancient customs can survive for centuries in Arabian cultures.

In spite of the uncertainties about the work, there is no reason to doubt that Job and his friends existed, and that Job's misfortunes provided the occasion for their dialogues about human suffering and God's justice. Ezekiel refers to Job along with Noah and Daniel as righteous (Ezek. 14:14, 20), and James refers to Job's perseverance (James 5:11) with the assumption that he existed.

Except for the prologue and the epilogue, the book is written in poetry (poetry which preserves many rare words and difficult forms). Since it is unlikely that the speakers conversed in poetic meter, it is reasonable to suggest that the present composition of the book is a poetic dramatization of the dialogues between Job and his friends. Under the inspiration of the Holy Spirit the composition accurately represents the ideas expressed about Job's suffering.

HOW JOB FITS INTO THE BIBLE. The book of Job was placed in the third section of the Hebrew canon, the Writings, due to its anonymity and its poetic style. Most English Bibles follow the arrangement of the Latin Vulgate with Job placed before Psalms and Proverbs.

But Job's place within the literary genre of wisdom literature is more helpful for understanding its message. Throughout the ancient world wisdom literature was concerned with the established order in the world that rewards virtue and industry while bringing justice to evil and laziness. Any study of this type of literature in the Bible would have to include Proverbs, Ecclesiastes, and Psalms 1, 32, 37, and 49.

Wisdom literature usually stresses the fear of the LORD and the knowledge of His ways, the contrasting lifestyles of the righteous and the wicked, and the inevitability of reward and retribution. The problem of suffering forms a significant part of this material, because people would like to think that life is fair, that the righteous prosper and the wicked suffer. But God's rule over life is not so predictable. And it is on this point that Job challenges conventional human wisdom, and in so doing provides vitality to the faith by its unique message that the righteous suffer.

SUMMARY SENTENCE. Suffering reminds the righteous of their mortality and forces them to examine their spiritual condition, but ultimately it enables them to come to a deeper faith in the incomprehensible wisdom of God.

KEY VERSES. Several verses combine to give a synopsis of the message of the book. The words of Satan in Job 1:9 provide the quest of the suffering: "Does Job fear God for nothing?" Job's confidence in the LORD remains despite his perplexity: "Though He slay me, yet will I trust Him" (13:15); and his certainty of ultimate vindiction remains: "I know that my Redeemer lives, and He shall stand at last on the earth . . . in my flesh I shall see God" (19:25, 26). And finally, in response to all their dialogue about how He should rule the world, God says: "Where were you when I laid the foundations of the earth? Tell Me, if you have understanding" (38:4).

How Job Fits Together. The prologue to the book provides the reason for the suffering, Satan's challenge that Job's faith is related to his prosperity (chs. 1—2). But when the blow falls, Job retains his faith in an exemplary fashion (3).

Three friends then come to comfort Job, but when he laments his lot in life they give their opinions. In the first round of speeches Eliphaz advises Job to repent because suffering comes from guilt (4—5), to which Job responds by challenging them to prove he deserved such intense suffering (6—7); Bildad agrees that suffering is God's punishment (8), to which Job responds that God was unjust for creating him for this (9—10); and Zophar warns that because God's wisdom is inscrutable Job should repent (11), to which Job responds by questioning God's justice, noting that the good are not rewarded and the evil are unpunished (12—14).

The second cycle becomes more intense. Eliphaz accuses Job of presumption because ancient wisom is on the side of the three friends (15); but Job retorts that their being at ease leads them to their simplistic view (16—17). Bildad then lists the kinds of woes that afflict the wicked (18); but Job answers that he is innocent and will ultimately be vindicated (19). Zophar further explains how the wicked are punished (20); but Job undermines their argument by observing that the wicked prosper and death comes to everyone (21).

In the last round of speeches the friends have less to say. Eliphaz contends that suffering is a part of God's justice (22). Job remains convinced that he will be vindicated when God reveals his integrity (23—24). Bildad asks if a man can be justified with God (25). But Job remains resolute; he is aware of God's immense power, and his own punishable sins, and so he challenges God to reply (26—31).

In the dialogues with the three friends Job's argument that the wicked actually prosper is the undoing of their arguments. They give up on their traditional wisdom, because it is inadequate to explain the ways of God.

Elihu comes on the scene with a fresh approach. He explains that God uses suffering to teach people His ways (32—33); thus, His justice is vindicated (34). Because of this there are advantages to living piously (35). Ultimately Job must learn that God is far greater than he (36—37).

The final speeches of the book belong to God. He passes over all their theological questions and makes Job aware of His sovereign majesty. He shows that His creation displays His omniscience (38:1—40:5), and that His power overwhelms human frailty (40:6—42:6). This display of God's infinitely superior wisdom overshadows human wisdom.

The epilogue (42:7-17) reports how the humbled sufferer is restored to the fullness of life.

Everyone who experiences sufferings in life wonders what he has done to deserve them. Life seems so unfair at times that God's wisdom in ruling over the affairs of the world is easily questioned. The book of Job presents just such a case. As far as we know Job never received an answer to his questions. The suffering human might demand answers from God at these times, but when he learns more about God he is faced with totally different questions. What happens is that through the suffering comes a maturity that is characterized by a deepening faith in God's sovereign wisdom.

—A.P.R.

Job and His Family in Uz

THERE was a man in the land of Uz, whose name was Job; and that man was blameless and upright, and one who feared God and shunned evil.

2 And seven sons and three daughters were born to him.

3 Also, his possessions were seven thousand sheep, three thousand camels, five hundred yoke of oxen, five hundred female donkeys, and a very large household, so that this man was the greatest of all the ᵀpeople of the East.   Lit. sons

4 And his sons would go and feast in their houses, each on his appointed day, and would send and invite their three sisters to eat and drink with them.

5 So it was, when the days of feasting had

run their course, that Job would send and ᵀsanctify them, and he would rise early in the morning and offer burnt offerings *according to* the number of them all. For Job said, "It may be that my sons have sinned and *cursed God in their hearts." Thus Job did regularly.   consecrate

Satan Attacks Job's Character

▼ **12-G. Satan: His Present and Eternal Abodes**

6 Now there was a day when the sons of God came to present themselves before the LORD, and *Satan also came among them.

7 And the LORD said to Satan, "From where do you come?" So Satan answered the LORD and said, "From ᴿgoing to and fro on the earth, and from walking back and forth on it."   [1 Pet. 5:8]

8 Then the LORD said to Satan, "Have you ᵀconsidered My servant Job, that *there is* none like him on the earth, a blameless and upright man, one who fears God and ᵀshuns evil?"   Lit. *set your heart on* · Lit. *turns away from*

9 So Satan answered the LORD and said, "Does Job fear God for nothing?

10 "Have You not ᵀmade a hedge around him, around his household, and around all that he has on every side? You have blessed the work of his hands, and his possessions have increased in the land.   Protected him

11 ᴿ"But now, stretch out Your hand and touch all that he has, and he will surely ▽ ᴿcurse You to Your face!"   Job 2:5; 19:21 · Is. 8:21

12 And the LORD said to Satan, "Behold, all that he has *is* in your ᵀpower; only do not lay a hand on his *person.*" So Satan went out from the presence of the LORD.   Lit. *hand* ▲

Job Loses His Property and Children

13 Now there was a day ᴿwhen his sons and daughters *were* eating and drinking wine in their oldest brother's house;   [Eccl. 9:12]

14 and a messenger came to Job and said, "The oxen were plowing and the donkeys feeding beside them,

15 "when the *Sabeans ᵀraided *them* and took them away—indeed they have killed the servants with the edge of the sword; and I alone have escaped to tell you!"   Lit. *fell upon*

16 While he *was* still speaking, another also came and said, "The fire of God fell from heaven and burned up the sheep and the servants, and ᵀconsumed them; and I alone have escaped to tell you!"   destroyed

17 While he *was* still speaking, another also came and said, "The Chaldeans formed three bands, raided the camels and took them away, yes, and killed the servants with the edge of the sword; and I alone have escaped to tell you!"

18 While he *was* still speaking, another also came and said, ᴿ"Your sons and daughters *were* eating and drinking wine in their oldest brother's house,   Job 1:4, 13

19 "and suddenly a great wind came from

1:5 Lit. *blessed,* but in an evil sense, Job 1:11; 2:5, 9
1:6 Lit. *the Adversary*

1:15 Lit. *Sheba,* Job 6:19

12-G. Satan: His Present and Eternal Abodes (Job 1:6–12)—The Scriptures clearly teach that Satan, in his original creation, was "the anointed cherub" (Ezek. 28:14, page 806), a perfect angel; but he sinned, and God said, "I cast you as a profane thing out of the mountain of God" (Ezek. 28:16, page 806). Again, God spoke to Satan, saying, "How you are fallen from heaven, O Lucifer, son of the morning! How you are cut down to the ground" (Is. 14:12, page 657). Jesus said, "I saw Satan fall like lightning from heaven" (Luke 10:18, page 1026). These three Scriptures speak of Satan's spiritual fall. However, God, in His sovereign will, still allows this fallen angel some type of access, in person, into the very presence of God.

(1) His present abode is in the heavenly realm or on this earth (vv. 6–12). Satan seems to have the privilege and power to be on earth or in the heavens at will. He is not omnipresent, however—he cannot be in two places at the same time.

(2) He will reach his future, eternal abode in three stages:

(a) In the Great Tribulation, Satan and his angels (disembodied evil spirits) will be cast out of heaven and grounded upon the earth until the end of the Tribulation (Rev. 12:7–12, page 1305).

(b) At the end of the Great Tribulation and the beginning of the millennial reign of Jesus Christ, the King of kings and Lord of lords, Satan will be bound and cast into "the bottomless pit" for a thousand years (Rev. 20:1–3, page 1313).

(c) At the end of the thousand years, Satan will be released from the pit. He will go out to the nations and deceive those who have lived under the reign of Jesus and are not saved. The deceived will be as the sand of the sea and they will follow Satan to the "beloved city" (Rev. 20:9, page 1313). This is Satan's last great effort to conquer the holy city, and seat himself upon the kingdom throne as King of kings and Lord of lords. The fire of God will come down from heaven and consume his army, and he himself will be "cast into the lake of fire and brimstone where the beast and the false prophet are. And they [the beast, the false prophet, and Satan] will be tormented day and night forever and ever"—time without end. This is hell (Rev. 20:7–10, page 1313).

See John 12:31, page 1072, for **Point 12-H: Satan and the Death of Christ.**

*across the wilderness and struck the four corners of the house, and it fell on the young people, and they are dead; and I alone have escaped to tell you!"

20 Then Job arose, ᴿtore his robe, and shaved his head; and he ᴿfell to the ground and worshiped.   Gen. 37:29, 34 • [1 Pet. 5:6]

21 And he said:

"Naked I came from my mother's womb,
And naked shall I return there.
The LORD ᴿgave, and the LORD has
ᴿtaken away;   [James 1:17] • Gen. 31:16
Blessed be the name of the LORD."

22 ᴿIn all this Job did not sin nor charge God with wrong.   Job 2:10

Satan Attacks Job's Health

2 Again ᴿthere was a day when the sons of God came to present themselves before the LORD, and Satan came also among them to present himself before the LORD.   Job 1:6–8

2 And the LORD said to Satan, "From where do you come?" So ᴿSatan answered the LORD and said, "From going to and fro on the earth, and from walking back and forth on it."   Job 1:7

3 Then the LORD said to Satan, "Have you considered My servant Job, that there is none like him on the earth, a blameless and upright man, one who fears God and shuns evil? And still he holds fast to his integrity, although you incited Me against him, ᴿto ᵀdestroy him without cause."   Job 9:17 • Lit. consume

4 So Satan answered the LORD and said, "Skin for skin! Yes, all that a man has he will give for his life.

5 "But stretch out Your hand now, and touch his ᴿbone and his flesh, and he will surely curse You to Your face!"   Job 19:20

6 ᴿAnd the LORD said to Satan, "Behold, he is in your hand, but spare his life."   Job 1:12

7 So Satan went out from the presence of the LORD, and struck Job with painful boils ᴿfrom the sole of his foot to the crown of his head.   Is. 1:6

8 And he took for himself a potsherd with which to scrape himself ᴿwhile he sat in the midst of the ashes.   Ezek. 27:30

9 Then his wife said to him, "Do you still hold fast to your integrity? Curse God and die!"

10 But he said to her, "You speak as one of the foolish women speaks. ᴿShall we indeed accept good from God, and shall we not accept adversity?" ᴿIn all this Job did not ᴿsin with his lips.   Job 1:21, 22 • Job 1:22 • Ps. 39:1

Job's Three Friends

11 Now when Job's three friends heard of all this adversity that had come upon him,

each one came from his own place—Eliphaz the Temanite, Bildad the Shuhite, and Zophar the Naamathite. For they had made an appointment together to come ᴿand mourn with him, and to comfort him.   Rom. 12:15

12 And when they raised their eyes from afar, and did not recognize him, they lifted their voices and wept; and each one tore his robe and ᴿsprinkled dust on his head toward heaven.   Neh. 9:1

13 So they sat down with him on the ground ᴿseven days and seven nights, and no one spoke a word to him, for they saw that his grief was very great.   Gen. 50:10

Job Deplores His Birth

3 After this Job opened his mouth and cursed the day of his birth.

2 And Job ᵀspoke, and said: Lit. answered

3 "May ᴿthe day perish on which I was
born,   Jer. 20:14–18
And the night in which it was said,
'A male child is conceived.'

4 May that day be darkness;
May God above not seek it,
Nor the light shine upon it.

5 May darkness and ᴿthe shadow of death
claim it;   Jer. 13:16
May a cloud settle on it;
May the blackness of the day terrify it.

6 As for that night, may darkness seize it;
May it not *rejoice among the days of
the year,
May it not come into the number of the
months.

7 Oh, may that night be barren!
May no joyful shout come into it!

8 May those curse it who curse the day,
Those ᴿwho are ready to arouse
Leviathan.   Jer. 9:17

9 May the stars of its morning be dark;
May it look for light, but have none,
And not see the dawning of the day;

10 Because it did not shut up the doors of
my mother's womb,
Nor hide sorrow from my eyes.

11 "Why ᴿdid I not die at birth?
Why did I not ᵀperish when I came
from the womb?   Job 10:18, 19 • expire

12 ᴿWhy did the knees receive me?   Gen. 30:3
Or why the breasts, that I should
nurse?

13 For now I would have lain still and
been quiet,
I would have been asleep;
Then I would have been at rest

14 With kings and counselors of the earth,
Who ᴿbuilt ruins for themselves,   Job 15:28

15 Or with princes who had gold,
Who filled their houses with silver;

1:19 LXX omits across   3:6 LXX, Syr., Tg., Vg. be joined

16 Or *why* was I not hidden ᴿlike a
    stillborn child,   Ps. 58:8
    Like infants who never saw light?
17 There the wicked cease *from* troubling,
    And there the weary are at rest.
18 *There* the prisoners ᵀrest together;
    ᴿThey do not hear the voice of the
    oppressor.   *are at ease* • Job 39:7
19 The small and great are there,
    And the servant *is* free from his master.

20 "Whyᴿ is light given to him who is in
    misery,   Jer. 20:18
    And life to the ᴿbitter of soul,   2 Kin. 4:27
21 Who ᴿlongᵀ for death, but it does not
    come,
    And search for it more than ᴿhidden
    treasures;   Rev. 9:6 • Lit. *wait* • Prov. 2:4
22 Who rejoice exceedingly,
    And are glad when they can find the
    ᴿgrave?   Job 7:15, 16
23 *Why is light given* to a man whose way
    is hidden,
    ᴿAnd whom God has hedged in?   Job 19:8
24 For my sighing comes before *I eat,
    And my groanings pour out like water.
25 For the thing I greatly ᴿfeared has
    come upon me,
    And what I dreaded has happened to
    me.   [Job 9:28; 30:15]
26 I am not at ease, nor am I quiet;
    I have no rest, for trouble comes."

Eliphaz: Job Has Sinned

4 Then Eliphaz the Temanite answered and
    said:

2 "If one attempts a word with you, will
    you become weary?
    But who can withhold himself from
    speaking?
3 Surely you have instructed many,
    And you ᴿhave strengthened weak
    hands.   Is. 35:3
4 Your words have upheld him who was
    stumbling,
    And you ᴿhave strengthened the ᵀfeeble
    knees;   Is. 35:3 • Lit. *bending*
5 But now it comes upon you, and you
    are weary;
    It touches you, and you are troubled.
6 *Is* not ᴿyour reverence ᴿyour
    confidence?
    And the integrity of your ways your
    hope?   Job 1:1 • Prov. 3:26

7 "Remember now, ᴿwho *ever* perished
    being innocent?   [Ps. 37:25]
    Or where were the upright *ever* cut off?
8 Even as I have seen,
    ᴿThose who plow iniquity   [Prov. 22:8]
    And sow trouble reap the same.

3:24 Lit. *my bread*

9 By the blast of God they perish,
    And by the breath of His anger they are
    consumed.
10 The roaring of the lion,
    The voice of the fierce lion,
    And ᴿthe teeth of the young lions are
    broken.   Ps. 58:6
11 ᴿThe old lion perishes for lack of prey,
    And the cubs of the lioness are
    scattered.   Ps. 34:10

12 "Now a word was secretly brought to
    me,
    And my ear received a whisper of it.
13 ᴿIn disquieting thoughts from the visions
    of the night,   Job 33:15
    When deep sleep falls on men,
14 Fear came upon me, and trembling,
    Which made all my bones shake.
15 Then a spirit passed before my face;
    The hair on my body stood up.
16 It stood still,
    But I could not discern its appearance.
    A form *was* before my eyes;
    There was silence;
    Then I heard a voice *saying:*
17 'Can a mortal be more righteous than
    God?
    Can a man be more pure than his
    Maker?
18 If He puts no trust in His servants,
    If He charges His angels with error,
19 How much more those who dwell in
    houses of clay,
    Whose foundation is in the dust,
    Who are crushed before a moth?
20 ᴿThey are broken in pieces from
    morning till evening;
    They perish forever, with no one
    regarding.   Ps. 90:5, 6
21 Does not their own excellence go
    away?
    They die, even without wisdom.'

Job Is Chastened by God

5 "Call out now;
    Is there anyone who will answer you?
    And to which of the holy ones will you
    turn?
2 For wrath kills a foolish man,
    And envy slays a simple one.
3 I have seen the foolish taking root,
    But suddenly I cursed his dwelling
    place.
4 His sons are ᴿfar from safety,   Ps. 119:155
    They are crushed in the gate,
    And ᴿthere is no deliverer.   Ps. 109:12
5 Because the hungry eat up his harvest,
    *Taking it even from the thorns,
    *And a snare snatches their substance.

5:5 LXX *They shall not be taken from evil men;* Vg. *And
the armed men shall take him by violence* • LXX *The
might shall draw them off;* Vg. *And the thirsty shall drink
up their riches.*

6 For affliction does not come from the
dust,
Nor does trouble spring from the
ground;
7 Yet man is ^Rborn to ^Ttrouble,
As the sparks fly upward.   Job 14:1 · *labor*
8 "But as for me, I would seek God,
And to God I would commit my
cause—
9 Who does great things, and
unsearchable,
Marvelous things without number.
10 He gives rain on the earth,
And sends waters on the fields.
11 ^RHe sets on high those who are lowly,
And those who mourn are lifted to
safety.   Ps. 113:7
12 ^RHe frustrates the devices of the crafty,
So that their hands cannot carry out
their plans.   Neh. 4:15
13 He catches the ^Rwise in their own
craftiness,
And the counsel of the cunning comes
quickly upon them.   [1 Cor. 3:19]
14 They meet with darkness in the
daytime,
And grope at noontime as in the night.
15 But ^RHe saves the needy from the
sword,
From the mouth of the mighty,
And from their hand.   Ps. 35:10
16 ^RSo the poor have hope,   1 Sam. 2:8
And injustice shuts her mouth.

17 "Behold,^R happy is the man whom God
corrects;   Ps. 94:12
Therefore do not despise the chastening
of the Almighty.
18 For He bruises, but He binds up;
He wounds, but His hands make whole.
19 He shall deliver you in six troubles,
Yes, in seven no evil shall touch you.
20 ^RIn famine He shall redeem you from
death,   Ps. 33:19, 20; 37:19
And in war from the ^Tpower of the
sword.   Lit. *hand*
21 ^RYou shall be hidden from the scourge
of the tongue,
And you shall not be afraid of
destruction when it comes.   Ps. 31:20
22 You shall laugh at destruction and
famine,
And ^Ryou shall not be afraid of the
^Rbeasts of the earth.   Ezek. 34:25 · Hos. 2:18
23 ^RFor you shall have a covenant with the
stones of the field,
And the beasts of the field shall be at
peace with you.   Ps. 91:12
24 You shall know that your tent is in
peace;
You shall visit your dwelling and find
nothing amiss.

25 You shall also know that ^Ryour
descendants shall be many,
And your offspring ^Rlike the grass of
the earth.   Ps. 112:2 · Ps. 72:16
26 ^RYou shall come to the grave at a full
age,   [Prov. 9:11; 10:27]
As a sheaf of grain ripens in its season.
27 Behold, this we have ^Rsearched out;
It is true.
Hear it, and know for yourself."   Ps. 111:2

Job: My Complaint Is Just

6 Then Job answered and said:

2 "Oh, that my grief were fully weighed,
And my calamity laid with it on the
scales!
3 For then it would be heavier than the
sand of the sea—
therefore my words have been rash.
4 ^RFor the arrows of the Almighty are
within me;
My spirit drinks in their poison;
^RThe terrors of God are arrayed ^Ragainst
me.   Ps. 38:2 · Ps. 88:15, 16 · Job 30:15
5 Does the ^Rwild donkey bray when it has
grass,   Job 39:5-8
Or does the ox low over its fodder?
6 Can flavorless food be eaten without
salt?
Or is there any taste in the white of an
egg?
7 My soul refuses to touch them;
They are as loathsome food to me.

8 "Oh, that I might have my request,
That God would grant me the thing
that I long for!
9 That it would please God to crush me,
That He would loose His hand and ^Rcut
me off!   Job 7:16; 9:21; 10:1
10 Then I would still have comfort;
Though in anguish I would exult,
He will not spare;
For ^RI have not concealed the words of
^Rthe Holy One.   Acts 20:20 · [Is. 57:15]

11 "What strength do I have, that I should
hope?
And what is my end, that I should
prolong my life?
12 Is my strength the strength of stones?
Or is my flesh bronze?
13 Is my help not within me?
And is success driven from me?

14 "To^R him who is ^Tafflicted, kindness
should be shown by his friend,
Even though he forsakes the fear of the
Almighty.   [Prov. 17:17] · Or despairing
15 ^RMy brothers have dealt deceitfully like
a brook,
^RLike the streams of the brooks that
pass away,   Ps. 38:11 · Jer. 15:18

16 Which are dark because of the ice,
   And into which the snow vanishes.
17 When it is warm, they cease to flow;
   When it is hot, they vanish from their
   place.
18 The paths of their way turn aside,
   They go nowhere and perish.
19 The caravans of ᴿTema look,   Gen. 25:15
   The travelers of Sheba hope for them.
20 They are ᴿdisappointedᵀ because they
   were confident;   Jer. 14:3 · Lit. *ashamed*
   They come there and are confused.
21 For now ᴿyou are nothing,   Job 13:4
   You see terror and ᴿare afraid.   Ps. 38:11
22 Did I ever say, 'Bring *something* to me'?
   Or, 'Offer a bribe for me from your
   wealth'?
23 Or, 'Deliver me from the enemy's
   hand'?
   Or, 'Redeem me from the hand of
   oppressors'?
24 "Teach me, and I will hold my tongue;
   Cause me to understand wherein I have
   erred.
25 How forceful are right words!
   But what does your arguing prove?
26 Do you intend to rebuke *my* words,
   And the speeches of a desperate one,
   which are as wind?
27 Yes, you overwhelm the fatherless,
   And you ᴿundermine your friend.   Ps. 57:6
28 Now therefore, be pleased to look at
   me;
   For I would never lie to your face.
29 ᴿYield now, let there be no injustice!
   Yes, concede, my ᴿrighteousness ᵀstill
   stands!   Job 17:10 · Job 27:5, 6; 34:5 · Lit. *is in it*
30 Is there injustice on my tongue?
   Cannot my taste discern the unsavory?

Job: My Suffering Is Comfortless

7 "Is there not ᴿa time of hard service for
   man on earth?
   Are not his days also like the days of a
   hired man?   [Job 14:5, 13, 14]
2 Like a servant who ᵀearnestly desires
   the shade,
   And like a hired man who eagerly looks
   for his wages,   Lit. *pants for*
3 So I have been allotted ᴿmonths of
   futility,
   And wearisome nights have been
   appointed to me.   [Job 15:31]
4 ᴿWhen I lie down, I say, 'When shall I
   arise,
   And the night be ended?'
   For I have had my fill of tossing till
   dawn.   Deut. 28:67
5 My flesh is ᴿcaked with worms and
   dust,
   My skin is cracked and breaks out
   afresh.   Is. 14:11

6 "Myᴿ days are swifter than a weaver's
   shuttle,   Job 9:25; 16:22; 17:11
   And are spent without hope.
7 Oh, remember that my life *is* a breath!
   My eye will never again see good.
8 ᴿThe eye of him who sees me will see
   me no *more*;
   While your *eyes* are upon me, I shall no
   longer *be*.   Job 8:18; 20:9
9 *As* the cloud disappears and vanishes
   away,
   So ᴿhe who goes down to the grave
   does not come up.   2 Sam. 12:23
10 He shall never return to his house,
   Nor shall his place know him anymore.

11 "Therefore I will ᴿnot restrain my
   mouth;
   I will speak in the anguish of my spirit;
   I will ᴿcomplain in the bitterness of my
   soul.   Ps. 39:1, 9 · 1 Sam. 1:10
12 *Am* I a sea, or a sea serpent,
   That You set a guard over me?
13 When I say, 'My bed will comfort me,
   My couch will ease my complaint,'
14 Then You scare me with dreams
   And terrify me with visions,
15 So that my soul chooses strangling
   And death rather than *my body.
16 ᴿI loathe *my life*;   Job 10:1
   I would not live forever.
   ᴿLet me alone,   Job 14:6
   For my days *are but* a breath.

17 "Whatᴿ *is* man, that You should exalt
   him,   Ps. 8:4; 144:3
   That You should set Your heart on
   him,
18 That You should ᵀvisit him every
   morning,
   And test him every moment?   *attend to*
19 How long?
   Will You not look away from me,
   And let me alone till I swallow my
   saliva?
20 Have I sinned?
   What have I done to You, ᴿO watcher
   of men?   Ps. 36:6
   Why have You set me as Your target,
   So that I am a burden *to myself?
21 Why then do You not pardon my
   transgression,
   And take away my iniquity?
   For now I will lie down in the dust,
   And You will seek me diligently,
   But I *will* no longer *be*."

Bildad: Job Should Repent

8 Then Bildad the Shuhite answered and
   said:

7:15 Lit. *my bones*
7:20 So with MT, Tg., Vg.; LXX, Jewish tradition reads
to You

2 "How long will you speak these *things*,
And the words of your mouth *be like* a
strong wind?
3 ᴿDoes God subvert judgment?   [Deut. 32:4]
Or does the Almighty pervert justice?
4 If your sons have sinned against Him,
He has cast them away ᵀfor their
transgression.   Lit. *into the hand of*
5 ᴿIf you would earnestly seek God
And make your supplication to the
Almighty,   [Job 5:17–27; 11:13]
6 If you *were* pure and upright,
Surely now He would awake for you,
And prosper your rightful dwelling
place.
7 Though your beginning was small,
Yet your latter end would ᴿincrease
abundantly.   Job 42:12

8 "For ᴿ inquire, please, of the former age,
And consider the things discovered by
their fathers;   Deut. 4:32; 32:7
9 For ᴿwe *were born* yesterday, and know
ᵀnothing,
Because our days on earth *are* a
shadow.   Gen. 47:9 · Lit. *not*
10 Will they not teach you and tell you,
And utter words from their heart?

11 "Can the papyrus grow up without a
marsh?
Can the reeds flourish without water?
12 While it *is* yet green *and* not cut down,
It withers before any *other* plant.
13 So *are* the paths of all who ᴿforget God;
And the hope of the ᴿhypocrite shall
perish,   Ps. 9:17 · Job 11:20; 18:14; 27:8
14 Whose confidence shall be cut off,
And whose trust *is* a spider's ᵀweb.   *house*
15 ᴿHe leans on his house, but it does not
stand.   Job 8:22; 27:18
He holds it fast, but it does not endure.
16 He grows green in the sun,
And his branches spread out in his
garden.
17 His roots wrap around the rock heap,
And look for a place in the stones.
18 ᴿIf he is destroyed from his place,
Then *it* will deny him, *saying*, 'I have
not seen you.'   Job 7:10

19 "Behold, this is the joy of His way,
And out of the earth others will grow.
20 Behold, ᴿGod will not ᵀcast away the
blameless,   Job 4:7 · *reject*
Nor will He uphold the evildoers.
21 He will yet fill your mouth with
laughing,
And your lips with ᵀrejoicing.   *shouts of joy*
22 Those who hate you will be ᴿclothed
with shame,   Ps. 35:26; 109:29
And the dwelling place of the wicked
ᵀwill come to nothing."   Lit. *will not be*

Job: There Is No Mediator

9 Then Job answered and said:

2 "Truly I know *it is* so,
But how can a ᴿman be ᴿrighteous
before God?   [Job 4:17; 15:14–16] · [Hab. 2:4]
3 If one wished to ᵀcontend with Him,
He could not answer Him one time out
of a thousand.   *argue*
4 ᴿGod is wise in heart and mighty in
strength.
Who has hardened *himself* against Him
and prospered?   Job 36:5
5 He removes the mountains, and they do
not know
When He overturns them in His anger;
6 He shakes the earth out of its place,
And its ᴿpillars tremble;   Job 26:11
7 He commands the sun, and it does not
rise;
He seals off the stars;
8 He alone spreads out the heavens,
And treads on the waves of the sea;
9 ᴿHe made ᵀthe Bear, Orion, and the
Pleiades,   Amos 5:8 · Heb. *Ash, Kesil,* and *Kimah*
And the chambers of the south;
10 ᴿHe does great things past finding out,
Yes, wonders without number.   Job 5:9
11 ᴿIf He goes by me, I do not see *Him*;
If He moves past, I do not perceive
Him;   [Job 23:8, 9; 35:14]
12 ᴿIf He takes away, ᵀwho can hinder
Him?
Who can say to Him, 'What are You
doing?'   [Is. 45:9] · Lit. *who can turn him back?*
13 God will not withdraw His anger,
ᴿThe allies of ᵀthe proud lie prostrate
beneath Him.   Job 26:12 · Heb. *rahab*

14 "How then can I answer Him,
And choose my words *to reason* with
Him?
15 ᴿFor though I were righteous, I could
not answer Him;   Job 10:15; 23:1–7
I would beg mercy of my Judge.
16 If I called and He answered me,
I would not believe that He was
listening to my voice.
17 For He crushes me with a tempest,
And multiplies my wounds ᴿwithout
cause.   Job 2:3
18 He will not allow me to catch my
breath,
But fills me with bitterness.
19 If *it is a matter* of strength, indeed *He
is* strong;
And if of justice, who will appoint my
day *in court?*
20 Though I were righteous, my own
mouth would condemn me;
Though I *were* blameless, it would
prove me perverse.

21 "I am blameless, yet I do not know
   myself;
   I despise my life.
22 It *is* all one *thing*;
   Therefore I say, ᴿ'He destroys the
   blameless and the wicked.'   Ezek. 21:3
23 If the scourge slays suddenly,
   He laughs at the plight of the innocent.
24 The earth is given into the hand of the
   wicked.
   He covers the faces of its judges.
   If it is not *He*, who else could it be?

25 "Now ᴿmy days are swifter than a
   runner;   Job 7:6, 7
   They flee away, they see no good.
26 They pass by like swift ships,
   Like an eagle swooping on its prey.
27 ᴿIf I say, 'I will forget my complaint,
   I will put off my sad face and wear a
   smile,'   Job 7:13
28 ᴿI am afraid of all my sufferings;
   I know that You ᴿwill not hold me
   innocent.   Ps. 119:120 · Ex. 20:7
29 *If* I am condemned,
   Why then do I labor in vain?
30 If I wash myself with snow water,
   And cleanse my hands with ᵀsoap,   *lye*
31 Yet You will plunge me into the pit,
   And my own clothes will abhor me.

32 "For ᴿ*He is* not a man, as I *am*,
   That I may answer Him,
   And that we should go to court
   together.   [Is. 45:9]
33 Nor is there any mediator between us,
   Who may lay his hand on us both.
34 Let Him take His rod away from me,
   And do not let dread of Him terrify me.
35 *Then* I would speak and not fear Him,
   But it is not so with me.

Job: I Would Plead with God

10 "My ᴿsoul loathes my life;
   I will give free course to my
   complaint,   Job 7:16
   I will speak in the bitterness of my
   soul.
2 I will say to God, 'Do not condemn me;
   Show me why You contend with me.
3 *Does it* seem good to You that You
   should oppress,
   That You should despise the work of
   Your hands,
   And ᵀsmile on the counsel of the
   wicked?   *Look favorably*
4 Do You have eyes of flesh?
   Or ᴿdo You see as man sees?   [1 Sam. 16:7]
5 *Are* Your days like the days of a mortal
   man?
   Are Your years like the days of a
   mighty man,
6 That You should seek for my iniquity
   And search out my sin,

7 Although You know that I am not
   wicked,
   And *there is* no one who can deliver
   from Your hand?
8 'Yourᴿ hands have made me and
   fashioned me,   Ps. 119:73
   An intricate unity;
   Yet You would ᴿdestroy me.   [Job 9:22]
9 Remember, I pray, ᴿthat You have
   made me like clay.   Gen. 2:7
   And will You turn me into dust again?
10 ᴿDid You not pour me out like milk,
   And curdle me like cheese,   [Ps. 139:14-16]
11 Clothe me with skin and flesh,
   And knit me together with bones and
   sinews?
12 You have granted me life and favor,
   And Your care has preserved my spirit.

13 'And these *things* You have hidden in
   Your heart;
   I know that this *was* with You:
14 If I sin, then ᴿYou mark me,   Ps. 139:1
   And will not acquit me of my iniquity.
15 If I am wicked, ᴿwoe to me;   Is. 3:11
   ᴿEven *if* I am righteous, I ᵀcannot lift up
   my head.   [Job 9:12, 15] · Lit. *will not*
   I *am* full of disgrace;
   ᴿSee my misery!   Ps. 25:18
16 If *my head* is exalted,
   ᴿYou hunt me like a fierce lion,
   And again You show Yourself awesome
   against me.   Is. 38:13
17 You renew Your witnesses against me,
   And increase Your indignation toward
   me;
   Changes and war are *ever* with me.

18 'Whyᴿ then have You brought me out of
   the womb?
   Oh, that I had perished and no eye had
   seen me!   Job 3:11-13
19 I would have been as though I had not
   been.
   I would have been carried from the
   womb to the grave.
20 ᴿAre not my days few?   Ps. 39:5
   Cease! ᴿLeave me alone, that I may
   take a little comfort,   Job 7:16, 19
21 Before I go *to the place from which* I
   shall not return,
   ᴿTo the land of darkness ᴿand the
   shadow of death,   Ps. 88:12 · Ps. 23:4
22 A land as dark as darkness *itself*,
   As the shadow of death, without any
   order,
   Where even the light *is* like darkness.' "

Zophar Urges Job to Repent

11 Then Zophar the Naamathite answered and said:

2 "Should not the multitude of words be
   answered?

And should [T]a man full of talk be
vindicated?   Lit. *a man of lips*
3 Should your empty talk make men
[T]hold their peace?
And when you mock, should no one
rebuke you?   *be silent*
4 For you have said,
[R]'My doctrine *is* pure,
And I am clean in your eyes.'   Job 6:30
5 But oh, that God would speak,
And open His lips against you,
6 That He would show you the secrets of
wisdom!
For *they would* double *your* prudence.
Know therefore that God [T]exacts from
you   Lit. *forgets some of your iniquity for you*
Less than your iniquity *deserves.*

7 "Can[R] you search out the deep things of
God?
Can you find out the limits of the
Almighty?   [Eccl. 3:11]
8 *They are* higher than heaven—what
can you do?
Deeper than [T]Sheol—what can you
know?   *The abode of the dead*
9 Their measure *is* longer than the earth
And broader than the sea.

10 "If [R] He passes by, imprisons, and
gathers *to* judgment,   [Rev. 3:7]
Then who can [T]hinder Him?   *restrain*
11 For [R]He knows deceitful men;
He sees wickedness also.
Will He not then consider *it?*   [Ps. 10:14]
12 For an [R]empty-headed man will be wise,
When a wild donkey's colt is born a
man.   Rom. 1:22

13 "If you would [R]prepare your heart,
And [R]stretch out your hands toward
Him;   [1 Sam. 7:3] • Ps. 88:9
14 If iniquity *were* in your hand, *and you*
put it far away,
And [R]would not let wickedness dwell in
your tents;   Ps. 101:3
15 [R]Then surely you could lift up your face
without spot;
Yes, you could be steadfast, and not
fear;   Ps. 119:6
16 Because you would [R]forget *your* misery,
And remember *it* as waters *that have*
passed away,   Is. 65:16
17 And *your* life [R]would be brighter than
noonday.
Though you were dark, you would be
like the morning.   Is. 58:8, 10
18 And you would be secure, because
there is hope;
Yes, you would dig *around you, and*
[R]take your rest in safety.   Lev. 26:5, 6
19 You would also lie down, and no one
would make *you* afraid;
Yes, many would court your favor.

20 But [R]the eyes of the wicked will fail,
And they shall not escape,   Deut. 28:65
And [R]their hope—loss of life!"   [Prov. 11:7]

Job Answers His Critics

12 Then Job answered and said:

2 "No doubt you *are* the people,
And wisdom will die with you!
3 But I have [T]understanding as well as
you;
I *am* not [R]inferior to you.
Indeed, who does not *know* such things
as these?   Lit. *a heart* • Job 13:2

4 "I[R] am one mocked by his friends,
Who [R]called on God, and He answered
him,   Job 21:3 • Ps. 91:15
The just and blameless *who is* ridiculed.
5 A [T]lamp is despised in the thought of
one who is at ease;
It is made ready for [R]those whose feet
slip.   Or *disaster* • Prov. 14:2
6 [R]The tents of robbers prosper,
And those who provoke God are
secure—   [Job 9:24; 21:6-16]
In what God provides by His hand.

7 "But now ask the beasts, and they will
teach you;
And the birds of the air, and they will
tell you;
8 Or speak to the earth, and it will teach
you;
And the fish of the sea will explain to
you.
9 Who among all these does not know
That the hand of the LORD has done
this,
10 [R]In whose hand *is* the [T]life of every
living thing,   [Acts 17:28] • *soul*
And the breath of all mankind?
11 Does not the ear test words
And the [T]mouth taste its food?   *palate*
12 Wisdom *is* with aged men,
And with [T]length of days,
understanding.   *Long life*

13 "With Him *are* wisdom and strength,
He has counsel and understanding.
14 If [R]He breaks a *thing* down, it cannot
be rebuilt;
If He imprisons a man, there can be no
release.   Job 11:10
15 If He [R]withholds the waters, they dry
up;
If He [R]sends them out, they overwhelm
the earth.   [1 Kin. 8:35, 36] • Gen. 7:11-24
16 With Him *are* strength and prudence.
The deceived and the deceiver *are* His.
17 He leads counselors away plundered,
And makes fools of the judges.
18 He loosens the bonds of kings,
And binds their waist with a belt.

19 He leads *princes away plundered,
   And overthrows the mighty.
20 ᴿHe deprives the trusted ones of speech,
   And takes away the discernment of the
   elders.   Job 32:9
21 ᴿHe pours contempt on princes,   Ps. 107:40
   And ᵀdisarms the mighty.   loosens the belt of
22 He ᴿuncovers deep things out of
   darkness,
   And brings the shadow of death to
   light.   [1 Cor. 4:5]
23 ᴿHe makes nations great, and destroys
   them;   Is. 9:3; 26:15
   He enlarges nations, and guides them.
24 He takes away the ᵀunderstanding of
   the chiefs of the people of the earth,
   And ᴿmakes them wander in a pathless
   wilderness.   Lit. heart · Ps. 107:4
25 They grope in the dark without light,
   And He makes them ᴿstagger like a
   drunken man.   Ps. 107:27

13 "Behold, my eye has seen all *this*,
       My ear has heard and understood it.
2 ᴿWhat you know, I also know;
   I *am* not inferior to you.   Job 12:3
3 But I would speak to the Almighty,
   And I desire to reason with God.
4 But you forgers of lies,
   ᴿYou *are* all worthless physicians. Job 6:21
5 Oh, that you would be silent,
   And it would be your wisdom!
6 Now hear my reasoning,
   And heed the pleadings of my lips.
7 Will you speak ᵀwickedly for God,
   And talk deceitfully for Him?   unrighteously
8 Will you show partiality for Him?
   Will you contend for God?
9 Will it be well when He searches you
   out?
   Or can you mock Him as one mocks a
   man?
10 He will surely rebuke you
   If you secretly show partiality.
11 Will not His ᵀexcellence make you
   afraid,   Lit. exaltation
   And the dread of Him fall upon you?
12 Your platitudes *are* proverbs of ashes,
   Your defenses are defenses of clay.
13 "Holdᵀ your peace with me, and let me
   speak,
   Then let come on me what *may!*   Be silent
14 Why ᴿdo I take my flesh in my teeth,
   And put my life in my hands?   Job 18:4
15 ᴿThough He slay me, yet will I trust
   Him.
   ᴿEven so, I will defend my own ways
   before Him.   Ps. 23:4 · Job 27:5
16 He also *shall* be my salvation,
   For a ᴿhypocrite could not come before
   Him.   Job 8:13

17 Listen carefully to my speech,
   And to my declaration with your ears.
18 See now, I have prepared *my* case,
   I know that I shall be vindicated.
19 Who *is* he *who* will contend with me?
   If now I hold my tongue, I perish.

Job's Despondent Prayer

20 "Only two *things* do not do to me,
   Then I will not hide myself from You:
21 ᴿWithdraw Your hand far from me,
   And let not the dread of You make me
   afraid.   Ps. 39:10
22 Then call, and I will ᴿanswer;
   Or let me speak, then You respond to
   me.   Job 9:16; 14:15
23 How many *are* my iniquities and sins?
   Make me know my transgression and
   my sin.
24 ᴿWhy do You hide Your face,   [Deut. 32:30]
   And ᴿregard me as Your enemy?   Lam. 2:5
25 ᴿWill You frighten a leaf driven to and
   fro?
   And will You pursue dry stubble?   Is. 42:3
26 For You write bitter things against me,
   And ᴿmake me inherit the iniquities of
   my youth.   Job 20:11
27 You put my feet in the stocks,
   And watch closely all my paths.
   You ᵀset a limit for the ᵀsoles of my
   feet.   Lit. inscribe a print · roots
28 "Manᵀ decays like a rotten thing,   Lit. He
   Like a garment that is moth-eaten.

14 "Man *who is* born of woman
       Is of few days and full of trouble.
2 ᴿHe comes forth like a flower and fades
   away;
   He flees like a shadow and does not
   continue.   Job 8:9
3 And ᴿdo You open Your eyes on such a
   one,
   And ᴿbring *me to judgment with
   Yourself?   Ps. 8:4; 144:3 · [Ps. 143:2]
4 Who ᴿcan bring a clean *thing* out of an
   unclean?
   No one!   [Ps. 51:2, 5, 10]
5 ᴿSince his days *are* determined,
   The number of his months *is* with You;
   You have appointed his limits, so that
   he cannot pass.   Job 7:1; 21:21
6 ᴿLook away from him that he may ᵀrest,
   Till ᴿlike a hired man he finishes his
   day.   Ps. 39:13 · Lit. cease · Job 7:1

7 "For there is hope for a tree,
   If it is cut down, that it will sprout
   again,
   And that its tender shoots will not
   cease.

12:19 Lit. *priests,* but not in a technical sense

14:3 LXX, Syr., Vg. *him*

8 Though its root may grow old in the earth,
And its stump may die in the ground,
9 Yet at the scent of water it will bud
And bring forth branches like a plant.
10 But man dies and ᵀis laid away;
Indeed he ᵀbreathes his last
And where *is* he?   *lies prostrate • expires*
11 *As* water disappears from the sea,
And a river becomes parched and dries up,
12 So man lies down and does not rise.
ᴿTill the heavens *are* no more,
They will not awake   [Is. 51:6; 65:17; 66:22]
Nor be roused from their sleep.

13 "Oh, that You would hide me in the grave,
That You would conceal me until Your wrath is past,
That You would appoint me a set time, and remember me!
14 If a man dies, shall he live *again*?
All the days of my hard service ᴿI will wait,
Till my change comes.   Job 13:15
15 ᴿYou shall call, and I will answer You;
You shall desire the work of Your hands.   Job 13:22
16 For now ᴿYou number my steps,
But do not watch over my sin.   Prov. 5:21
17 My transgression *is* sealed up in a bag,
And You *cover my iniquity.

18 "But *as* a mountain falls *and* crumbles away,
And *as* a rock is moved from its place;
19 *As* water wears away stones,
And as torrents wash away the soil of the earth;
So You destroy the hope of man.
20 You prevail forever against him, and he passes on;
You change his countenance and send him away.
21 His sons come to honor, and ᴿhe does not know *it*;
They are brought low, and he does not perceive *it*.   Eccl. 9:5
22 But his flesh will be in pain over it,
And his soul will mourn over it."

Eliphaz Accuses Job of Folly

15 Then ᴿEliphaz the Temanite answered and said: Job 4:1

2 "Should a wise man answer with empty knowledge,
And fill himself with the east wind?
3 Should he reason with unprofitable talk,
Or by speeches with which he can do no good?

4 Yes, you cast off fear,
And restrain prayer before God.
5 For your iniquity teaches your mouth,
And you choose the tongue of the crafty.
6 ᴿYour own mouth condemns you, and not I;   [Luke 19:22]
Yes, your own lips testify against you.

7 "*Are* you the first man *who* was born?
Or were you made before the hills?
8 Have you heard the counsel of God?
Do you limit wisdom to yourself?
9 ᴿWhat do you know that we do not know?
What do you understand that *is* not in us?   Job 12:3; 13:2
10 ᴿBoth the gray-haired and the aged *are* among us,   Job 8:8–10; 12:12; 32:6, 7
Much older than your father.
11 *Are* the consolations of God too small for you,
And the word *spoken* *gently with you?
12 Why does your heart carry you away,
And what do your eyes wink at,
13 That you turn your spirit against God,
And let *such* words go out of your mouth?
14 "What ᴿ *is* man, that he could be pure?
And *he who is* born of a woman, that he could be righteous?   Prov. 20:9
15 ᴿIf *God* puts no trust in His saints,
And the heavens are not pure in His sight,   Job 4:18; 25:5
16 ᴿHow much less man, *who is* abominable and filthy,   Ps. 14:3; 53:3
ᴿWho drinks iniquity like water!   Prov. 19:28

17 "I will tell you, hear me;
What I have seen I will declare,
18 What wise men have told,
Not hiding *anything received* ᴿfrom their fathers,   Job 8:8; 20:4
19 To whom alone the ᵀland was given,
And no alien passed among them: *earth*
20 The wicked man writhes with pain all *his* days,
ᴿAnd the number of years is hidden from the oppressor.   Ps. 90:12
21 ᵀDreadful sounds *are* in his ears;
ᴿIn prosperity the destroyer comes upon him.   *Terrifying* • 1 Thess. 5:3
22 He does not believe that he will ᴿreturn from darkness,   Job 14:10–12
For a sword is waiting for him.
23 He ᴿwanders about for bread, *saying*,
'Where *is* it?'   Ps. 59:15; 109:10
He knows ᴿthat a day of darkness is ready at his hand.   Job 18:12
24 Trouble and anguish make him afraid;
They overpower him, like a king ready for ᵀbattle.   *attack*

14:17 Lit. *plaster over*

15:11 Or *a secret thing*

25 For he stretches out his hand against
   God,
   And acts defiantly against the
   Almighty,
26 Running stubbornly against Him
   With his strong, embossed shield.
27 "Though[R] he has covered his face with
   his fatness,   Ps. 17:10; 73:7; 119:70
   And made *his* waist heavy with fat,
28 He dwells in desolate cities,
   In houses which no one inhabits,
   Which are destined to become ruins.
29 He will not be rich,
   Nor will his wealth [R]continue,
   Nor will his possessions overspread the
   earth.   Job 20:28; 27:16, 17
30 He will not depart from darkness;
   The flame will dry out his branches,
   And [R]by the breath of His mouth he
   will go away.   Job 4:9
31 Let him not [R]trust in futile *things*,
   deceiving himself,
   For futility will be his reward.   Is. 59:4
32 It will be accomplished before his time,
   And his branch will not be green.
33 He will shake off his unripe grape like a
   vine,
   And cast off his blossom like an olive
   tree.
34 For the company of hypocrites *will be*
   barren,
   And fire will consume the tents of
   bribery.
35 [R]They conceive trouble and bring forth
   futility;
   Their womb prepares deceit."   Is. 59:4

Job Reproaches His Pitiless Friends

16 Then Job answered and said:

2 "I have heard many such things;
   Miserable comforters *are* you all!
3 Shall words of wind have an end?
   Or what provokes you that you
   answer?
4 I also could speak as you *do*,
   If your soul were in my soul's place.
   I could heap up words against you,
   And shake my head at you;
5 *But* I would strengthen you with my
   mouth,
   And the comfort of my lips would
   relieve *your* grief.

6 "Though I speak, my grief is not
   relieved;
   And *if* I remain silent, how am I eased?
7 But now He has [R]worn me out;
   You [R]have made desolate all my
   company.   Job 7:3 · Job 16:20; 19:13–15
8 You have shriveled me up,
   And it is a [R]witness *against* me;

My leanness rises up against me
   And bears witness to my face.   Job 10:17
9 He tears *me* in His wrath, and hates
   me;
   He gnashes at me with His teeth;
   My adversary sharpens His gaze on me.
10 They [R]gape at me with their mouth,
   They [R]strike me reproachfully on the
   cheek,   Ps. 22:13; 35:21 · Lam. 3:30
   They gather together against me.
11 God [R]has delivered me to the ungodly,
   And turned me over to the hands of the
   wicked.   Job 1:15, 17
12 I was at ease, but He has [R]shattered
   me;
   He also has taken *me* by my neck, and
   shaken me to pieces;   Job 9:17
   He has set me up for His target,
13 His archers surround me.
   He pierces my *heart and does not pity;
   He pours out my gall on the ground.
14 He breaks me with wound upon wound;
   He runs at me like a *warrior.
15 "I have sewn sackcloth over my skin,
   And laid my [T]head in the dust.   Lit. *horn*
16 My face is [T]flushed from weeping,
   And on my eyelids *is* the shadow of
   death;   Lit. *red*
17 Although no violence *is* in my hands,
   And my prayer *is* pure.

18 "O earth, do not cover my blood,
   And let my cry have no *resting* place!
19 Surely even now [R]my witness *is* in
   heaven,
   And my evidence *is* on high.   Rom. 1:9
20 My friends scorn me;
   My eyes pour out *tears* to God.
21 [R]Oh, that one might plead for a man
   with God,   Job 31:35
   As a man *pleads* for his [T]neighbor!   *friend*
22 For when a few years are finished,
   I shall go the way of no return.

Job Prays for Relief

17 "My spirit is broken,
   My days are extinguished,
   [R]The grave *is* ready for me.   Ps. 88:3, 4
2 *Are* not mockers with me?
   And does not my eye [T]dwell on their
   provocation?   Lit. *lodge*
3 "Now put down a pledge for me with
   Yourself.
   Who *is* he *who* [R]will shake hands with
   me?   Prov. 6:1; 17:18; 22:26
4 For You have hidden their heart from
   [R]understanding;   Job 12:20; 32:9
   Therefore You will not exalt them.
5 He who speaks flattery to *his* friends,
   Even the eyes of his children will fail.

16:13 Lit. *kidneys*
16:14 Vg. *giant*

6 "But He has made me ^{R}a byword of the people, Job 30:9
And I have become one in whose face men spit.

7 ^{R}My eye has also grown dim because of sorrow, Ps. 6:7; 31:9
And all my members *are* like shadows.

8 Upright *men* are astonished at this,
And the innocent stirs himself up against the hypocrite.

9 Yet the righteous will hold to his ^{R}way,
And he who has ^{R}clean hands will be stronger and stronger. Prov. 4:18 · Ps. 24:4

10 "But please, ^{R}come back again, *all of you, Job 6:29
For I shall not find *one* wise *man* among you.

11 ^{R}My days are past, Job 7:6
My purposes are broken off,
Even the ^{T}thoughts of my heart. *desires*

12 They change the night into day;
'The light *is* near,' *they say*, in the face of darkness.

13 If I wait *for* the grave *as* my house,
If I make my bed in the darkness,

14 If I say to corruption, 'You *are* my father,'
And to the worm, 'You *are* my mother and my sister,'

15 Where then *is* my ^{R}hope? Job 7:6; 13:15
As for my hope, who can see it?

16 *Will* they go down ^{R}to the gates of ^{T}Sheol? Jon. 2:6 · *The abode of the dead*
Shall *we have* ^{R}rest together in the dust?" Job 3:17–19; 21:33

Bildad: The Wicked Are Punished

18 Then ^{R}Bildad the Shuhite answered and said: Job 8:1

2 "How long *till* you put an end to words?
Gain understanding, and afterward we will speak.

3 Why are we counted ^{R}as beasts, Ps. 73:22
And regarded as stupid in your sight?

4 ^{R}You^T who tear yourself in anger,
Shall the earth be forsaken for you?
Or shall the rock be removed from its place? Job 13:14 · Lit. *one who tears his soul*

5 "The^R light of the wicked indeed goes out, Prov. 13:9; 20:20; 24:20
And the flame of his fire does not shine.

6 The light is dark in his tent,
And his lamp beside him is put out.

7 The steps of his strength are shortened,
And his own counsel casts him down.

8 For ^{R}he is cast into a net by his own feet,
And he walks into a snare. Job 22:10

9 The net takes *him* by the heel,
And ^{R}a snare lays hold of him. Job 5:5

10 A noose *is* hidden for him on the ground,
And a trap for him in the road.

11 ^{R}Terrors frighten him on every side,
And drive him to his feet. Jer. 6:25

12 His strength is starved,
And destruction *is* ready at his side.

13 It devours patches of his skin;
The firstborn of death devours his ^{T}limbs. *parts*

14 He is uprooted from ^{R}the shelter of his tent,
And they parade him before the king of terrors. Job 11:20

15 They dwell in his tent *who are* none of his;
Brimstone is scattered on his dwelling.

16 ^{R}His roots are dried out below,
And his branch withers above. Job 29:19

17 ^{R}The memory of him perishes from the earth, [Ps. 34:16]
And he has no name *among the renowned.

18 He is driven from light into darkness,
And chased out of the world.

19 ^{R}He has neither son nor posterity among his people, Is. 14:22
Nor any remaining in his dwellings.

20 Those ^{T}in the west are astonished ^{R}at his day, Lit. *who came after* · Ps. 37:13
As those in the east are frightened.

21 Surely such *are* the dwellings of the wicked,
And this *is* the place *of him who* ^{R}does not know God." Jer. 9:3

Job Trusts in His Redeemer

19 Then Job answered and said:

2 "How long will you torment my soul,
And break me in pieces with words?

3 These ten times you have ^{T}reproached me; *shamed* or *disgraced*
You are not ashamed *that* you *have wronged me.

4 And if indeed I have erred,
My error remains with me.

5 If indeed you ^{R}exalt *yourselves* against me, Ps. 35:26; 38:16; 55:12, 13
And plead my disgrace against me,

6 Know then that God has wronged me,
And has surrounded me with His net.

7 "If I cry out concerning ^{T}wrong, I am not heard. *violence*
If I cry aloud, *there is* no justice.

8 ^{R}He has ^{T}fenced up my way, so that I cannot pass; Job 3:23 · *walled off my way*
And He has set darkness in my paths.

18:17 Lit. *before the outside*, i.e., the distinguished or famous

19:3 A Jewish tradition reads *make yourselves strange to me*

9 ᴿHe has stripped me of my glory,   Ps. 89:44
And taken the crown *from* my head.
10 He breaks me down on every side,
And I am gone;
My hope He has uprooted like a tree.
11 He has also kindled His wrath against
me,
And ᴿHe counts me as *one of* His
enemies.   Job 13:24; 33:10
12 His troops come together
And build up their road against me;
They encamp all around my tent.

13 "Heᴿ has removed my brothers far from
me,   Ps. 31:11; 38:11; 69:8; 88:8, 18
And my acquaintances are completely
estranged from me.
14 My relatives have failed,
And my close friends have forgotten
me.
15 Those who dwell in my house, and my
maidservants,
Count me as a stranger;
I am an alien in their sight.
16 I call my servant, but he gives no
answer;
I beg him with my mouth.
17 My breath is offensive to my wife,
And I am ᵀrepulsive to the children of
my own body.   Lit. *strange*
18 Even young children despise me;
I arise, and they speak against me.
19 ᴿAll my close friends abhor me,
And those whom I love have turned
against me.   Ps. 38:11; 55:12, 13
20 ᴿMy bone clings to my skin and to my
flesh,   Ps. 102:5
And I have escaped by the skin of my
teeth.

21 "Have pity on me, have pity on me, O
you my friends,
For the hand of God has struck me!
22 Why do you persecute me as God *does*,
And are not satisfied with my flesh?

23 "Oh, that my words were written!
Oh, that they were inscribed in a book!
24 That they were engraved on a rock
With an iron pen and lead, forever!
25 For I know *that* my Redeemer lives,
And He shall stand at last on the earth;
26 And after my skin is ᵀdestroyed, this *I
know*,   Lit. *struck off*
That in my flesh I shall see God,
27 Whom I shall see for myself,
And my eyes shall behold, and not
another.
How my ᵀheart yearns within me! *kidneys*
28 If you should say, 'How shall we
persecute him?'—
Since the root of the matter is found in
me,
29 Be afraid of the sword for yourselves;

For wrath *brings* the punishment of the
sword,
That you may know *there is a*
judgment."

Zophar's Sermon on the Wicked Man

20 Then ᴿZophar the Naamathite answered and said: Job 11:1

2 "Therefore my anxious thoughts make
me answer,
Because of the turmoil within me.
3 I have heard the rebuke ᵀthat
reproaches me,   Lit. *of my insulting correction*
And the spirit of my understanding
causes me to answer.

4 "Do you *not* know this of old,
Since man was placed on earth,
5 ᴿThat the triumphing of the wicked is
short,   Ps. 37:35, 36
And the joy of the hypocrite is *but* for
a ᴿmoment?   [Job 8:13; 13:16; 15:34; 27:8]
6 ᴿThough his haughtiness mounts up to
the heavens,   Is. 14:13, 14
And his head reaches to the clouds,
7 *Yet* he will perish forever like his own
refuse;
Those who have seen him will say,
'Where is he?'
8 He will fly away ᴿlike a dream, and not
be found;   Ps. 73:20; 90:5
Yes, he ᴿwill be chased away like a
vision of the night.   Job 18:18; 27:21-23
9 The eye *that* saw him will *see him* no
more,
Nor will his place behold him anymore.
10 His children will seek the favor of the
poor,
And his hands will restore his wealth.
11 His bones are full of ᴿhis youthful vigor,
ᴿBut it will lie down with him in the
dust.   Job 13:26 · Job 21:26

12 "Though evil is sweet in his mouth,
And he hides it under his tongue,
13 *Though* he spares it and does not
forsake it,
But still keeps it in his ᵀmouth,   Lit. *palate*
14 *Yet* his food in his stomach turns sour;
It becomes cobra venom within him.
15 He swallows down riches
And vomits them up again;
God casts them out of his belly.
16 He will suck the poison of cobras;
The viper's tongue will slay him.
17 He will not see ᴿthe streams,
The rivers flowing with honey and
cream.   Jer. 17:8
18 He will restore that for which he
labored,
And will not swallow *it* down;
From the proceeds of business
He will get no enjoyment.

19 For he has ᵀoppressed *and* forsaken the
poor,
He has violently seized a house which
he did not build.   *crushed*

20 "Becauseᴿ he knows no quietness in his
ᵀheart,   Eccl. 5:13-15 · Lit. *belly*
He will not save anything he desires.

21 Nothing is left for him to eat;
Therefore his well-being will not last.

22 In his self-sufficiency he will be in
distress;
Every hand of ᵀmisery will come
against him.   Or *the wretched* or *sufferer*

23 *When* he is about to fill his stomach,
God will cast on him the fury of His
wrath,
And will rain *it* on him while he is
eating.

24 He will flee from the iron weapon;
A bronze bow will pierce him through.

25 It is drawn, and comes out of the body;
Yes, ᴿthe glittering *point comes* out of
his ᵀgall.   Job 16:13 · Gall bladder
ᴿTerrors *come* upon him;   Job 18:11, 14

26 Total darkness *is* reserved for his
treasures.
ᴿAn unfanned fire will consume him;
It shall go ill with him who is left in his
tent.   Ps. 21:9

27 The heavens will reveal his iniquity,
And the earth will rise up against him.

28 The increase of his house will depart,
And his goods will flow away in the day
of His ᴿwrath.   Job 20:15; 21:30

29 ᴿThis *is* the portion from God for a
wicked man,   Job 27:13; 31:2, 3
The heritage appointed to him by God."

Job's Discourse on the Wicked

21 Then Job answered and said:

2 "Listen carefully to my speech,
And let this be your ᵀconsolation.   *comfort*

3 Bear with me that I may speak,
And after I have spoken, keep
ᴿmocking.   Job 16:10

4 "As for me, *is* my complaint against
man?
And if *it were*, why should I not be
impatient?

5 Look at me and be astonished;
Put *your* hand over *your* mouth.

6 Even when I remember I am terrified,
And trembling takes hold of my flesh.

7 ᴿWhy do the wicked live *and* become
old,
Yes, become mighty in power?   [Jer. 12:1]

8 Their descendants are established with
them in their sight,
And their offspring before their eyes.

9 Their houses *are* safe from fear,
Neither *is* the rod of God upon them.

10 Their bull breeds without failure;
Their cow calves without miscarriage.

11 They send forth their little ones like a
flock,
And their children dance.

12 They sing to the tambourine and harp,
And rejoice to the sound of the flute.

13 They spend their days in wealth,
And ᵀin a moment go down to the
ᵀgrave.   *Without lingering* · Or *Sheol*

14 ᴿYet they say to God, 'Depart from us,
For we do not desire the knowledge of
Your ways.   Job 22:17

15 ᴿWho *is* the Almighty, that we should
serve Him?
And ᴿwhat profit do we have if we pray
to Him?'   Ex. 5:2 · Mal. 3:14

16 Indeed ᵀtheir prosperity *is* not in their
hand;   Lit. *their goal*
ᴿThe counsel of the wicked is far from
me.   Prov. 1:10

17 "How often is the lamp of the wicked
put out?
How often does their destruction come
upon them,
The sorrows God ᴿdistributes in His
anger?   [Luke 12:46]

18 ᴿThey are like straw before the wind,
And like chaff that a storm ᵀcarries
away.   Ps. 1:4; 35:5 · *steals away*

19 *They say*, 'God ᵀlays up ᵀone's iniquity
ᴿfor his children';
Let Him recompense him, that he may
know *it*.   *stores up* · Lit. *his* · [Ex. 20:5]

20 Let his eyes see his destruction,
And ᴿlet him drink of the wrath of the
Almighty.   Is. 51:17

21 For what does he care about his
household after him,
When the number of his months is cut
in half?

22 "Can *anyone* teach God knowledge,
Since He judges those on high?

23 One dies in his full strength,
Being wholly at ease and secure;

24 His *pails are full of milk,
And the marrow of his bones is moist.

25 Another man dies in the bitterness of
his soul,
Never having eaten with pleasure.

26 They ᴿlie down alike in the dust,
And worms cover them.   Eccl. 9:2

27 "Look, I know your thoughts,
And the schemes *with which* you
would wrong me.

28 For you say,
'Where *is* the house of the prince?
And where *is* *the tent,
The dwelling place of the wicked?'

21:24 LXX, Vg. *bowels*; Syr. *sides*; Tg. *breasts*
21:28 Vg. omits *the tent*

29 Have you not asked those who travel
the road?
And do you not know their signs?
30 ᴿFor the wicked are reserved for the day
of doom;
They shall be brought out on the day of
wrath.   [Prov. 16:4]
31 Who condemns his way to his face?
And who repays him *for what* he has
done?
32 Yet he shall be brought to the grave,
And a vigil kept over the tomb.
33 The clods of the valley shall be sweet to
him;
ᴿEveryone shall follow him,   Heb. 9:27
As countless *have gone* before him.
34 How then can you comfort me with
empty words,
Since ᵀfalsehood remains in your
answers?"   *faithlessness*

Eliphaz Accuses Job of Wickedness

22 Then ᴿEliphaz the Temanite answered
and said: Job 4:1; 15:1; 42:9

2 "Canᴿ a man be profitable to God,
Though he who is wise may be
profitable to himself?   [Luke 17:10]
3 *Is it* any pleasure to the Almighty that
you are righteous?
Or *is it* gain *to Him* that you make your
ways blameless?

4 "Is it because of your fear of Him that
He corrects you,
And enters into judgment with you?
5 *Is* not your wickedness great,
And your iniquity without end?
6 For you have ᴿtaken pledges from your
brother for no reason,
And stripped the naked of their
clothing.   [Ex. 22:26, 27]
7 You have not given the weary water to
drink,
And you ᴿhave withheld bread from the
hungry.   Deut. 15:7
8 But the ᵀmighty man possessed the
land,   Lit. *man of arm*
And the honorable man dwelt in it.
9 You have sent widows away empty,
And the ᵀstrength of the fatherless was
crushed.   Lit. *arms*
10 Therefore snares *are* all around you,
And sudden fear troubles you,
11 Or darkness *so that* you cannot see;
And an abundance of ᴿwater covers
you.   Ps. 69:1, 2; 124:5

12 "Is not God in the height of heaven?
And see the highest stars, how lofty
they are!
13 And you say, ᴿ'What does God know?
Can He judge through the deep
darkness?   Ps. 73:11

14 ᴿThick clouds cover Him, so that He
cannot see,
And He walks above the circle of
heaven.'   Ps. 139:11, 12
15 Will you keep to the old way
Which wicked men have trod,
16 Who ᴿwere cut down before their time,
Whose foundations were swept away
by a flood?   Job 14:19; 15:32
17 They said to God, 'Depart from us!
What can the Almighty do to *them?'
18 Yet He filled their houses with good
things;
But the counsel of the wicked is far
from me.

19 "The righteous see *it* and are glad,
And the innocent laugh at them:
20 'Surely our *adversaries are cut down,
And the fire consumes their remnant.'

21 "Now acquaint yourself with Him, and
ᴿbe at peace;   Is. 27:5
Thereby good will come to you.
22 Receive, please, ᴿinstruction from His
mouth,   Prov. 2:6
And lay up His words in your heart.
23 If you return to the Almighty, you will
be built up;
You will remove iniquity far from your
tents.
24 Then you will ᴿlay your gold in the
dust,
And the *gold* of Ophir among the stones
of the brooks.   2 Chr. 1:15
25 Yes, the Almighty will be your *gold
And your precious silver;
26 For then you will have your ᴿdelight in
the Almighty,
And lift up your face to God.   Job 27:10
27 ᴿYou will make your prayer to Him,
He will hear you,
And you will pay your vows.   [Is. 58:9-11]
28 You will also declare a thing,
And it will be established for you;
So light will shine on your ways.
29 When they cast *you* down, and you say,
'Exaltation *will come!'*
Then He will save the humble *person.*
30 He will *even* deliver one who is not
innocent;
Yes, he will be delivered by the purity
of your hands."

Job Proclaims God's Righteous Judgments

23 Then Job answered and said:

2 "Even today my ᴿcomplaint is bitter;

22:17 LXX, Syr. *us*
22:20 LXX *substance is*
22:25 Ancient vss. suggest *defense;* MT *gold,* and v. 24

*My hand is listless because of my
   groaning.   Job 7:11
3 ᴿOh, that I knew where I might find
   Him,   Job 13:3, 18; 16:21; 31:35
   That I might come to His seat!
4 I would present *my* case before Him,
   And fill my mouth with arguments.
5 I would know the words *which* He
   would answer me,
   And understand what He would say to
   me.
6 ᴿWould He contend with me in His great
   power?   Is. 57:16
   No! But He would take *note* of me.
7 There the upright could reason with
   Him,
   And I would be delivered forever from
   my Judge.
8 "Look,ᴿ I go forward, but He is not
   there,
   And backward, but I cannot perceive
   Him;   Job 9:11; 35:14
9 When He works on the left hand, I
   cannot behold *Him*;
   When He turns to the right hand, I
   cannot see *Him*.
10 But ᴿHe knows the way that I take;
   When ᴿHe has tested me, I shall come
   forth as gold.   [Ps. 1:6; 139:1–3] • [James 1:12]
11 ᴿMy foot has held fast to His steps;
   I have kept His way and not turned
   aside.   Ps. 17:5
12 I have not departed from the
   ᴿcommandment of His lips;
   ᴿI have treasured the words of His
   mouth   Job 6:10; 22:22 • Ps. 44:18
   More than my necessary *food*.

13 "But He *is* unique, and who can make
   Him change?
   And whatever ᴿHis soul desires, *that* He
   does.   [Ps. 115:3]
14 For He performs *what is* ᴿappointed for
   me,   [1 Thess. 3:2–4]
   And many such *things are* with Him.
15 Therefore I am terrified at His presence;
   When I consider *this*, I am afraid of
   Him.
16 For God ᴿmade my heart weak,
   And the Almighty terrifies me;   Ps. 22:14
17 Because I was not ᴿcut off ᵀfrom the
   presence of darkness,
   And He did *not* hide deep darkness
   from my face.   Job 10:18, 19 • Or *by* or *before*

Job Complaints of Violence on the Earth

24 "Since ᴿtimes are not hidden from the
   Almighty,
   Why do those who know Him see not
   His ᴿdays?   [Acts 1:7] • [Is. 2:12]

2 "*Some* remove ᴿlandmarks;
   They seize flocks violently and feed *on*
   them;   [Deut. 19:14; 27:17]
3 They drive away the donkey of the
   fatherless;
   They take the widow's ox as a pledge.
4 They push the needy off the road;
   All the ᴿpoor of the land are forced to
   hide.   Prov. 28:28
5 Indeed, *like* wild donkeys in the desert,
   They go out to their work, searching
   for food.
   The wilderness *yields* food for them *and*
   for *their* children.
6 They gather their fodder in the field
   And glean in the vineyard of the
   wicked.
7 They ᴿspend the night naked, without
   clothing,   Ex. 22:26, 27
   And have no covering in the cold.
8 They are wet with the showers of the
   mountains,
   And ᴿhuddle around the rock for want
   of shelter.   Lam. 4:5

9 "*Some* snatch the fatherless from the
   breast,
   And take a pledge from the poor.
10 They cause *the poor* to go naked,
   without ᴿclothing;
   And they take away the sheaves from
   the hungry.   Job 31:19
11 They press out oil within their walls,
   And tread winepresses, yet suffer thirst.
12 The dying groan in the city,
   And the souls of the wounded cry out;
   Yet God does not charge *them* with
   wrong.

13 "There are those who rebel against the
   light;
   They do not know its ways
   Nor abide in its paths.
14 The murderer rises with the light;
   He kills the poor and needy;
   And in the night he is like a thief.
15 ᴿThe eye of the adulterer waits for the
   twilight,   Prov. 7:7–10
   ᴿSaying, 'No eye will see me';   Ps. 10:11
   And he disguises *his* face.
16 In the dark they break into houses
   Which they marked for themselves in
   the daytime;
   ᴿThey do not know the light.   [John 3:20]
17 For the morning is the same to them as
   the shadow of death;
   If *someone* recognizes *them*,
   They are in the terrors of the shadow
   of death.

18 "They *should be* swift on the face of the
   waters,
   Their portion *should be* cursed in the
   earth,

So that no *one would* turn into the way
　of their vineyards.
19 As drought and heat ᵀconsume the
　snow waters,
　So the ᵀgrave *consumes those who*
　have sinned. 　　　　Lit. *seize* • Or *Sheol*
20 The womb *should* forget him,
　The worm *should* feed sweetly on him;
　ᴿHe *should* be remembered no more,
　And wickedness *should* be broken like a
　tree. 　　　　　　　　　　Prov. 10:7
21 For he ᵀpreys on the barren *who* do not
　bear, 　　　　　　　　　Lit. *feeds on*
　And does no good for the widow.

22 "But *God* draws the mighty away with
　His power;
　He rises up, but no *man* is sure of life.
23 He gives them security, and they rely
　on *it*;
　Yet His eyes *are* on their ways.
24 They are exalted for a little while,
　Then they are gone.
　They are brought low;
　They are taken out of the way like all
　others;
　They dry out like the heads of grain.

25 "Now if *it is* not *so*, who will prove me a
　liar,
　And make my speech worth nothing?"

Bildad: How Can Man Be Righteous?

25 Then ᴿBildad the Shuhite answered
　　and said: 　　　　　　　Job 8:1; 18:1

2 "Dominion and fear *belong* to Him;
　He makes peace in His high places.
3 Is there any number to His armies?
　Upon whom does His light not rise?
4 ᴿHow then can man be righteous before
　God? 　　　　　　　　　Job 4:17; 15:14
　Or how can he be ᴿpure *who is* born of
　a woman? 　　　　　　　　[Job 14:4]
5 If even the moon does not shine,
　And the stars are not pure in His sight,
6 How much less man, *who is* a maggot,
　And a son of man, *who is* a worm?"

Job: Man's Frailty and God's Majesty

26 But Job answered and said:

2 "How have you helped *him who is*
　without power?
　How have you saved the arm *that has*
　no strength?
3 How have you counseled *one who has*
　no wisdom?
　And *how* have you declared sound
　advice to many?
4 To whom have you uttered words?
　And whose spirit came from you?
5 "The dead tremble,
　Those under the waters and those
　inhabiting them.

6 Sheol *is* naked before Him,
　And Destruction has no covering.
7 ᴿHe stretches out the north over empty
　space; 　　　　　　　　　　Job 9:8
　He hangs the earth on nothing.
8 ᴿHe binds up the water in His thick
　clouds, 　　　　　　　　　Prov. 30:4
　Yet the clouds are not broken under it.
9 He covers the face of *His* throne,
　And spreads His cloud over it.
10 ᴿHe drew a circular horizon on the face
　of the waters, 　　　　　　Prov. 8:29
　At the boundary of light and darkness.
11 The pillars of heaven tremble,
　And are astonished at His rebuke.
12 ᴿHe stirs up the sea with His power,
　And by His understanding He breaks up
　ᵀthe storm. 　　　　　Is. 51:15 • Lit. *rahab*
13 By His Spirit He adorned the heavens;
　His hand pierced the fleeing serpent.
14 Indeed these *are* the mere edges of His
　ways,
　And how small a whisper we hear of
　Him!
　But the thunder of His power who can
　understand?"

Job Maintains His Integrity

27 Moreover Job continued his discourse,
　　and said:

2 "As God lives, ᴿ*who* has taken away my
　justice, 　　　　　　　　　Job 34:5
　And the Almighty, *who* has made my
　soul bitter;
3 As long as my breath *is* in me,
　And the breath of God in my nostrils,
4 My lips will not speak wickedness,
　Nor my tongue utter deceit.
5 Far be it from me
　That I should say you are right;
　Till I die ᴿI will not put away my
　integrity from me. 　　　Job 2:9; 13:15
6 My righteousness I ᴿhold fast, and will
　not let it go; 　　　　　　Job 2:3; 33:9
　ᴿMy heart shall not ᵀreproach *me* as
　long as I live. 　　　　Acts 24:16 • *reprove*

7 "May my enemy be like the wicked,
　And he who rises up against me like
　the unrighteous.
8 ᴿFor what is the hope of the hypocrite,
　Though he may gain *much*, 　Matt. 16:26
　If God takes away his life?
9 ᴿWill God hear his cry 　　　Jer. 14:12
　When trouble comes upon him?
10 ᴿWill he delight himself in the Almighty?
　Will he always call on God? 　Job 22:26, 27

11 "I will teach you ᵀabout the hand of
　God; 　　　　　　　　　　　　*by*
　What *is* with the Almighty I will not
　conceal.

12 Surely all of you have seen *it*;
Why then do you behave with complete
nonsense?

13 "This^R is the portion of a wicked man
with God,　　　　　Job 20:29
And the heritage of oppressors, received
from the Almighty:

14 ^RIf his children are multiplied, *it is* for
the sword;　　　　　Deut. 28:41
And his offspring shall not be satisfied
with bread.

15 Those who survive him shall be buried
in death,
And ^Ttheir widows shall not weep,　Lit. *his*

16 Though he heaps up silver like dust,
And piles up clothing like clay—

17 He may pile *it* up, but ^Rthe just will
wear *it*,　　　　　Prov. 28:8
And the innocent will divide the silver.

18 He builds his house like a *moth,
^RLike a ^Tbooth *which* a watchman
makes.　　　　Is. 1:8 • Temporary shelter

19 The rich man will lie down,
*But not be gathered *up*;
He opens his eyes,
And he *is* ^Rno more.　　Job 7:8, 21; 20:7

20 Terrors overtake him like a flood;
A tempest steals him away in the night.

21 The east wind carries him away, and he
is gone;
It sweeps him out of his place.

22 It hurls against him and does not
^Rspare;　　　　　Jer. 13:14
He flees desperately from its power.

23 *Men* shall clap their hands at him,
And shall hiss him out of his place.

Job's Discourse on Wisdom

28 "Surely there is a mine for silver,
And a place *where* gold is refined.

2 Iron is taken from the ^Tearth,
And copper *is* smelted *from* ore.　Lit. *dust*

3 *Man* puts an end to darkness,
And searches every recess
For ore in the darkness and the shadow
of death.

4 He breaks open a shaft away from
people;
In places forgotten by feet
They hang far away from men;
They swing to and fro.

5 *As for* the earth, from it comes bread,
But underneath it is turned up as by
fire;

6 Its stones *are* the source of sapphires,
And it contains gold dust.

7 *That* path no bird knows,
Nor has the falcon's eye seen it.

27:18 So with MT, Vg.; LXX, Syr. *spider* (cf. 8:14); Tg.
decay

27:19 So with MT, Tg.; LXX, Syr. *But shall not add* (i.e.,
do it again); Vg. *But take away nothing.*

8 The *proud lions have not trodden it,
Nor has the fierce lion passed over it.

9 He puts his hand on the flint;
He overturns the mountains ^Tat the
roots.　　　　　At the base

10 He cuts out channels in the rocks,
And his eye sees every precious thing.

11 He dams up the streams from trickling;
What is hidden he brings forth to light.

12 "But^R where can wisdom be found?
And where *is* the place of
understanding?　　　　Eccl. 7:24

13 Man does not know its ^Rvalue,　Prov. 3:15
Nor is it found in the land of the living.

14 ^RThe deep says, '*It is* not in me';　Job 28:22
And the sea says, '*It is* not with me.'

15 It cannot be purchased for gold,
Nor can silver be weighed *for* its price.

16 It cannot be valued in the gold of
Ophir,
In precious onyx or sapphire.

17 Neither ^Rgold nor crystal can equal it,
Nor can it be exchanged for ^Tjewelry of
fine gold.　　　Prov. 8:10; 16:16 • *vessels*

18 No mention shall be made of ^Tcoral or
quartz,
For the price of wisdom *is* above
^Rrubies.　　Heb. *ramoth* • Prov. 3:15; 8:11

19 The topaz of Ethiopia cannot equal it,
Nor can it be valued in pure gold.

20 "From^R where then does wisdom come?
And where *is* the place of
understanding?　　　　Job 28:12

21 It is hidden from the eyes of all living,
And concealed from the birds of the
^Tair.　　　　　heaven

22 ^RDestruction^T and Death say,
'We have heard a report about it with
our ears.'　Job 28:14 • Heb. *Abaddon*

23 God understands its way,
And He knows its place.

24 For He looks to the ends of the earth,
And sees under the whole heavens,

25 To establish a weight for the wind,
And apportion the waters by measure.

26 When He made a law for the rain,
And a path for the thunderbolt,

27 Then He saw ^Twisdom and declared it;
He prepared it, indeed, He searched it
out.　　　　　Lit. *it*

28 And to man He said,
'Behold, ^Rthe fear of the Lord, that *is*
wisdom,
And to depart from evil *is*
understanding.' "　　[Prov. 1:7; 9:10]

Job's Summary Defense

29 Job further continued his discourse,
and said:

28:8 Lit. *sons of pride*, figurative of the great lions

2 "Oh, that I were as *in* months ᴿpast,
As *in* the days *when* God ᴿwatched
over me;   Job 1:1–5 · Job 1:10

3 ᴿWhen His lamp shone upon my head,
And when by His light I walked
through darkness;   Job 18:6

4 Just as I was in the days of my prime,
When ᴿthe friendly counsel of God *was*
over my tent;   [Ps. 25:14]

5 When the Almighty *was* yet with me,
When my children *were* around me;

6 When ᴿmy steps were bathed with
*cream,
And ᴿthe rock poured out rivers of oil
for me!   Deut. 32:14 · Ps. 81:16

7 "When I went out to the gate by the
city,
When I took my seat in the open
square,

8 The young men saw me and hid,
And the aged arose *and* stood;

9 The princes refrained from talking,
And put *their* hand on their mouth;

10 The voice of nobles was hushed,
And their ᴿtongue stuck to the roof of
their mouth.   Ps. 137:6

11 When the ear heard, then it blessed me,
And when the eye saw, then it
approved me;

12 Because ᴿI delivered the poor who cried
out,
The fatherless and *the one who* had no
helper.   [Ps. 72:12]

13 The blessing of a perishing *man* came
upon me,
And I caused the widow's heart to sing
for joy.

14 ᴿI put on righteousness, and it clothed
me;
My justice *was* like a robe and a
turban.   [Is. 59:17; 61:10]

15 I *was* ᴿeyes to the blind,
And I *was* feet to the lame.   Num. 10:31

16 I *was* a father to the poor,
And ᴿI searched out the case *that* I did
not know.   Prov. 29:7

17 I broke the fangs of the wicked,
And plucked the victim from his teeth.

18 "Then I said, 'I shall die in my nest,
And multiply *my* days as the sand.

19 ᴿMy root *is* spread out ᴿto the waters,
And the dew lies all night on my
branch.   Job 18:16 · Ps. 1:3

20 My glory *is* fresh within me,
And my bow is renewed in my hand.'

21 "*Men* listened to me and waited,
And kept silence for my counsel.

22 After my words they did not speak
again,
And my speech settled on them *as dew*.

23 They waited for me *as* for the rain,
And they opened their mouth wide *as*
for ᴿthe spring rain.   [Zech. 10:1]

24 *If* I mocked at them, they did not
believe *it*,
And the light of my countenance they
did not cast down.

25 I chose the way for them, and sat as
chief;
So I dwelt as a king in the army,
As one *who* comforts mourners.

30 "But now they mock at me, *men*
ᵀyounger than I,
Whose fathers I disdained to put with
the dogs of my flock.   Lit. *of fewer days*

2 Indeed, what *profit is* the strength of
their hands to me?
Their vigor has perished.

3 *They are* gaunt from want and famine,
Fleeing late to the wilderness, desolate
and waste,

4 Who pluck mallow by the bushes,
And broom tree roots *for* their food.

5 They were driven out from among *men*,
They shouted at them as *at* a thief.

6 *They had* to live in the clefts of the
ᵀvalleys,   *wadis*
In caves of the earth and the rocks.

7 Among the bushes they brayed,
Under the nettles they nestled.

8 *They were* sons of fools,
Yes, sons of vile men;
They were scourged from the land.

9 "Andᴿ now I am their taunting song;
Yes, I am their byword.   Job 17:6

10 They abhor me, they keep far from me;
They do not hesitate to spit in my face.

11 Because ᴿHe has loosed *my bowstring
and afflicted me,   Job 12:18
They have cast off restraint before me.

12 At *my* right *hand* the rabble arises;
They push away my feet,
And ᴿthey raise against me their ways
of destruction.   Job 19:12

13 They break up my path,
They promote my calamity;
They have no helper.

14 They come as broad breakers;
Under the ruinous storm they roll
along.

15 Terrors are turned upon me;
They pursue my honor as the wind,
And my prosperity has passed like a
cloud.

16 "Andᴿ now my soul is ᴿpoured out
because of my *plight*;   Ps. 42:4 · Ps. 22:14
The days of affliction take hold of me.

17 My bones are pierced in me at night,
And my gnawing pains take no rest.

29:6 MT *wrath;* ancient vss. and a few Heb. mss. *cream*
and Job 20:17

30:11 So with MT, Syr., Tg.; LXX, Vg. *His*

18 By great force my garment is
    disfigured;
    It binds me about as the collar of my
    coat.
19 He has cast me into the mire,
    And I have become like dust and ashes.
20 "I ᴿcry out to You, but You do not
    answer me;
    I stand up, and You regard me.   Job 19:7
21 *But* You have become cruel to me;
    With the strength of Your hand You
    ᴿoppose me.   Job 10:3; 16:9, 14; 19:6, 22
22 You lift me up to the wind and cause
    me to ride *on it*;
    You spoil my success.
23 For I know *that* You will bring me *to*
    death,
    And *to* the house ᴿappointed for all
    living.   [Heb. 9:27]
24 "Surely He would not stretch out *His*
    hand against a heap of ruins,
    If they cry out when He destroys *it*.
25 ᴿHave I not wept for him who was in
    trouble?   Ps. 35:13, 14
    Has *not* my soul grieved for the poor?
26 ᴿBut when I looked for good, evil came
    to me;
    And when I waited for light, then came
    darkness.   Jer. 8:15
27 My heart is in turmoil and cannot rest;
    Days of affliction confront me.
28 ᴿI go about mourning, but not in the
    sun;
    I stand up in the assembly *and* cry out
    for help.   Ps. 38:6; 42:9; 43:2
29 ᴿI am a brother of jackals,
    And a companion of ostriches.   Mic. 1:8
30 My skin grows black and falls from me;
    ᴿMy bones burn with fever.   Ps. 102:3
31 My harp is *turned* to mourning,
    And my flute to the voice of those who
    weep.

31 "I have made a covenant with my
    eyes;
    Why then should I ᵀlook upon a
    young woman?   *look intently* or *gaze*
2 For what *is* the ᴿallotment of God from
    above,
    And the inheritance of the Almighty
    from on high?   Job 20:29
3 *Is* it not destruction for the wicked,
    And disaster for the workers of
    iniquity?
4 ᴿDoes He not see my ways,
    And count all my steps?   [2 Chr. 16:9]
5 "If I have walked with falsehood,
    Or if my foot has hastened to deceit,
6 Let me be weighed on honest scales,
    That God may know my integrity.
7 If my step has turned from the way,

Or my heart walked after my eyes,
    Or if any spot adheres to my hands,
8 *Then* let me sow, and another eat;
    Yes, let my harvest be rooted out.
9 "If my heart has been enticed by a
    woman,
    Or *if* I have lurked at my neighbor's
    door,
10 *Then* let my wife grind for another,
    And let others bow down over her.
11 For that *would be* wickedness;
    Yes, ᴿit *would be* iniquity *deserving of*
    judgment.   Gen. 38:24
12 For that *would be* a fire *that* consumes
    to destruction,
    And would root out all my increase.
13 "If I have despised the cause of my male
    or female servant
    When they complained against me,
14 What then shall I do when ᴿGod rises
    up?
    When He punishes, how shall I answer
    Him?   [Ps. 44:21]
15 ᴿDid not He who made me in the womb
    make them?
    Did not the same One fashion us in the
    womb?   Job 34:19
16 "If I have kept the poor from *their*
    desire,
    Or caused the eyes of the widow to
    ᴿfail,   Job 29:12
17 Or eaten my morsel by myself,
    So that the fatherless could not eat of it
18 (But from my youth I reared him as a
    father,
    And from my mother's womb I guided
    the widow);
19 If I have seen anyone perish for lack of
    clothing,
    Or any poor *man* without covering;
20 If his ᵀheart has not ᴿblessed me,
    And *if* he was *not* warmed with the
    fleece of my sheep;   Lit. *loins* • [Deut. 24:13]
21 If I have raised my hand ᴿagainst the
    fatherless,   Job 22:9
    When I saw I had help in the gate;
22 *Then* let my arm fall from my shoulder,
    Let my arm be torn from the socket.
23 For ᴿdestruction *from* God *is* a terror to
    me,
    And because of His magnificence I
    cannot endure.   Is. 13:6
24 "If ᴿ I have made gold my hope,
    Or said to fine gold, '*You are* my
    confidence';   [Mark 10:23-25]
25 ᴿIf I have rejoiced because my wealth
    was great,
    And because my hand had gained
    much;   Ps. 62:10
26 ᴿIf I have observed the ᵀsun when it
    shines,   Ezek. 8:16 • Lit. *light*
    Or the moon moving *in* brightness,

27 So that my heart has been secretly
    enticed,
    And my mouth has kissed my hand;
28 This also *would be* an iniquity
    deserving of judgment,
    For I would have denied God *who is*
    above.

29 "If^R I have rejoiced at the destruction of
    him who hated me,   [Prov. 17:5; 24:17]
    Or lifted myself up when evil found him
30 ^R(Indeed I have not allowed my mouth
    to sin   [Matt. 5:44]
    By asking for a curse on his soul);
31 If the men of my tent have not said,
    'Who is there that has not been satisfied
    with his meat?'
32 ^R(*But* no sojourner had to lodge in the
    street,
    For I have opened my doors to the
    *traveler);   Gen. 19:2, 3
33 If I have covered my transgressions
    ^Ras^T Adam,   [Prov. 28:13] · Or *as men do*
    By hiding my iniquity in my bosom,
34 Because I feared the great ^Rmultitude,
    And dreaded the contempt of families,
    So that I kept silence
    And did not go out of the door— Ex. 23:2
35 ^ROh, that I had one to hear me!
    Here is my mark.   Job 19:7; 30:20, 24, 28
    Oh, ^R*that* the Almighty would answer
    me,   Job 13:22, 24; 33:10
    That my ^TProsecutor had written a
    book!   Lit. *Accuser*
36 Surely I would carry it on my shoulder,
    And bind it on me *like* a crown;
37 I would declare to Him the number of
    my steps;
    Like a prince I would approach Him.

38 "If my land cries out against me,
    And its furrows weep together;
39 If ^RI have eaten its ^Tfruit without
    money,   Job 24:6, 10–12 · Lit. *strength*
    Or caused its owners to lose their lives;
40 *Then* let ^Rthistles grow instead of
    wheat,
    And weeds instead of barley."   Gen. 3:18

The words of Job are ended.

Elihu Contradicts Job's Friends

32 So these three men ceased answering
    Job, because he *was* ^Rrighteous in his
own eyes.   Job 6:29; 31:6; 33:9
2 Then the wrath of Elihu, the son of
Barachel the ^RBuzite, of the family of Ram,
was aroused against Job; his wrath was
aroused because he ^Rjustified himself rather
than God.   Gen. 22:21 · Job 27:5, 6
3 Also against his three friends his wrath
was aroused, because they had found no
answer, and *yet* had condemned Job.

4 Now because they *were* years older than
he, Elihu had waited *to speak to Job.
5 When Elihu saw that *there was* no answer in the mouth of these three men, his
wrath was aroused.
6 So Elihu, the son of Barachel the Buzite,
answered and said:

"I *am* ^Ryoung in years, and you *are* very
    old;
    Therefore I was afraid,
    And dared not declare my opinion to
    you.   Lev. 19:32
7 I said, ^T'Age should speak,
    And multitude of years should teach
    wisdom.'   Lit. *Days,* meaning *years*
8 But *there is* a spirit in man,
    And ^Rthe breath of the Almighty gives
    him understanding.   [Prov. 2:6]
9 ^RGreat^T men are not *always* wise,
    Nor do the aged *always* understand
    justice.   [1 Cor. 1:26] · Or *Men of many years*
10 "Therefore I say, 'Listen to me,
    I also will declare my opinion.'
11 Indeed I waited for your words,
    I listened to your reasonings, while you
    searched out what to say.
12 I paid close attention to you;
    And surely not one of you convinced
    Job,
    Or answered his words—
13 ^RLest you say,   [Jer. 9:23]
    'We have found wisdom';
    God will vanquish him, not man.
14 Now he has not ^Tdirected *his* words
    against me;
    So I will not answer him with your
    words.   *ordered*

15 "They are dismayed and answer no
    more;
    Words escape them.
16 And I have waited, because they did
    not speak,
    Because they stood still *and* answered
    no more.
17 I also will answer my part,
    I too will declare my opinion.
18 For I am full of words;
    The spirit within me compels me.
19 Indeed my ^Tbelly *is* like wine *that* has
    no ^Tvent;   *bosom* · *opening*
    It is ready to burst like new wineskins.
20 I will speak, that I may find relief;
    I must open my lips and answer.
21 Let me not, I pray, show partiality to
    anyone;
    Nor let me flatter any man.
22 For I do not know how to flatter,
    Else my Maker would soon take me
    ^Raway.   Job 27:8

31:32 So with LXX, Syr., Tg., Vg.; MT *road*   32:4 Vg. *till Job had spoken*

Elihu Contradicts Job

33 "But please, Job, hear my speech,
And listen to all my words.
2 Now, I open my mouth;
My tongue speaks in my mouth.
3 My words *come* from my upright heart;
My lips utter pure knowledge.
4 ᴿThe Spirit of God has made me,
And the breath of the Almighty gives
me life.   [Gen. 2:7]
5 If you can answer me,
Set *your words* in order before me;
Take your stand.
6 ᴿTruly I *am* ᵀas your spokesman before
God;   Job 4:19 · Lit. *as your mouth*
I also have been formed out of clay.
7 Surely no fear of me will terrify you,
Nor will my hand be heavy on you.

8 "Surely you have spoken in myᵀ hearing,
And I have heard the sound of *your*
words, *saying,*   Lit. *ears*
9 'Iᴿ *am* pure, without transgression;
I *am* innocent, and *there is* no iniquity
in me.   Job 10:7
10 Yet He finds occasions against me,
ᴿHe counts me as His enemy;   Job 13:24; 16:9
11 ᴿHe puts my feet in the stocks,
He watches all my paths.'   Job 13:27; 19:8

12 "Look, *in* this you are not righteous.
I will answer you,
For God is greater than man.
13 Why do you ᴿcontend with Him?
For He does not give an accounting of
any of His words.   [Is. 45:9]
14 ᴿFor God may speak in one way, or in
another,
Yet man does not perceive it.   Ps. 62:11
15 In a dream, in a vision of the night,
When deep sleep falls upon men,
While slumbering on their beds,
16 ᴿThen He opens the ears of men,
And seals their instruction.   [Job 36:10, 15]
17 In order to turn man *from his* deed,
And conceal pride from man,
18 He keeps back his soul from the Pit,
And his life from ᵀperishing by the
sword.   Lit. *passing*

19 "*Man* is also chastened with pain on his
ᴿbed,   Job 30:17
And with strong *pain* in many of his
bones,
20 ᴿSo that his life abhors bread,   Ps. 107:18
And his soul ᵀsucculent food.   *desirable*
21 His flesh wastes away from sight,
And his bones stick out *which once*
were not seen.
22 Yes, his soul draws near the Pit,
And his life to the executioners.

23 "If there is a messenger for him,

A mediator, one among a thousand,
To show man His uprightness,
24 Then He is gracious to him, and says,
'Deliver him from going down to the
Pit;
I have found ᵀa ransom';   *an atonement*
25 His flesh shall be young like a child's,
He shall return to the days of his youth.
26 He shall pray to God, and He will
delight in him,
He shall see His face with joy,
For He restores to man His
righteousness.
27 Then he looks at men and ᴿsays,
'I have sinned, and perverted *what was*
right,   [Luke 15:21]
And it ᴿdid not profit me.'   [Rom. 6:21]
28 He will ᴿredeem his soul from going
down to the Pit,   Is. 38:17
And *his life shall see the light.

29 "Behold, God works all these *things,*
Twice, *in fact,* three *times* with a man,
30 ᴿTo bring back his soul from the Pit,
That he may be enlightened with the
light of life.   Ps. 56:13

31 "Give ear, Job, listen to me;
Hold your peace, and I will speak.
32 If you have anything to say, answer
me;
Speak, for I desire to justify you.
33 If not, ᴿlisten to me;
ᵀHold your peace, and I will teach you
wisdom."   Ps. 34:11 · *Keep silent*

Elihu Proclaims God's Justice

34 Elihu further answered and said:

2 "Hear my words, you wise *men;*
Give ear to me, you who have
knowledge.
3 ᴿFor the ear tests words
As the palate tastes food.   Job 6:30; 12:11
4 Let us choose justice for ourselves;
Let us know among ourselves what *is*
good.

5 "For Job has said, 'I am righteous,
But God has taken away my justice;
6 Should I lie concerning my right?
My ᵀwound *is* incurable, *though I am*
without transgression.'   Lit. *arrow*
7 What man *is* like Job,
Who drinks ᵀscorn like water,   *derision*
8 Who goes in company with the workers
of iniquity,
And walks with wicked men?
9 For ᴿhe has said, 'It profits a man
nothing   Mal. 3:14
That he should delight in God.'

33:28 Kt. *my*

10 "Therefore listen to me, you men of
    ^Tunderstanding: Lit. *heart*
    ^RFar be it from God *to do* wickedness,
    And *from* the Almighty to *commit*
    iniquity.   Job 8:3; 36:23
11 ^RFor He repays man *according to* his
    work,
    And makes man to find a reward
    according to *his* way.   Ps. 62:12
12 Surely God will never do wickedly,
    Nor will the Almighty pervert justice.
13 Who gave Him charge over the earth?
    Or who appointed *Him over* the whole
    world?
14 If He should set His heart on it,
    If He should ^Rgather to Himself His
    Spirit and His breath,   Ps. 104:29
15 All flesh would perish together,
    And man would return to dust.
16 "If *you* have understanding, hear this;
    Listen to the sound of my words:
17 ^RShould one who hates justice govern?
    Will you ^Rcondemn *Him who is* most
    just?   2 Sam. 23:3 • Job 40:8
18 ^R*Is it fitting* to say to a king, '*You are*
    worthless,'   Ex. 22:28
    And to nobles, '*You are* wicked'?
19 Yet He ^Ris not partial to princes,
    Nor does He regard the rich more than
    the poor;   [Deut. 10:17]
    For they *are* all the work of His hands.
20 In a moment they die, ^Rin the middle of
    the night;
    The people are shaken and pass away;
    The mighty are taken away without a
    hand.   Ex. 12:29
21 "For^R His eyes *are* on the ways of man,
    And He sees all his steps.   Job 31:4
22 ^RThere is no darkness nor shadow of
    death
    Where the workers of iniquity may hide
    themselves.   [Amos 9:2, 3]
23 For He need not further consider a
    man,
    That he should go before God in
    judgment.
24 ^RHe breaks in pieces mighty men
    without inquiry,
    And sets others in their place.   [Dan. 2:21]
25 Therefore He knows their works;
    He overthrows *them* in the night,
    And they are crushed.
26 He strikes them as wicked *men*
    In the open sight of others,
27 Because they ^Rturned back from Him,
    And ^Rwould not consider any of His
    ways,   1 Sam. 15:11 • Is. 5:12
28 So that they ^Rcaused the cry of the
    poor to come to Him;   Job 35:9
    For He hears the cry of the afflicted.
29 When He gives quietness, who then can
    make trouble?

And when He hides *His* face, who then
    can see Him,
    Whether *it is* against a nation or a man
    alone?—
30 That the hypocrite should not reign,
    Lest the people be ensnared.

31 "For has *anyone* said to God,
    'I have borne *chastening*;
    I will offend no more;
32 Teach me *what* I do not see;
    If I have done iniquity, I will do no
    more'?
33 Should He repay *it* according to your
    terms,
    Just because you disavow it?
    You must choose, and not I;
    Therefore speak what you know.

34 "Men of understanding say to me,
    Wise men who listen to me:
35 'Job speaks without knowledge,
    His words *are* without wisdom.'
36 Oh, that Job were tried to the utmost,
    Because *his* answers *are like* those of
    wicked men!
37 For he adds rebellion to his sin;
    He claps *his hands* among us,
    And multiplies his words against God."

Elihu Condemns Self-Righteousness

35 Moreover Elihu answered and said:

2 "Do you think this is right?
    Do you say,
    'My righteousness is more than God's'?
3 For ^Ryou say,   Job 21:15; 34:9
    'What advantage will it be to You?
    What profit shall I have, more than *if* I
    had sinned?'

4 "I will answer you,
    And your companions with you.
5 ^RLook to the heavens and see;
    And behold the clouds—
    They are higher than you.   [Job 22:12]
6 If you sin, what do you accomplish
    ^Ragainst Him?   [Jer. 7:19]
    Or, *if* your transgressions are
    multiplied, what do you do to Him?
7 ^RIf you are righteous, what do you give
    Him?
    Or what does He receive from your
    hand?   Prov. 9:12
8 Your wickedness affects a man such as
    you,
    And your righteousness a son of man.

9 "Because^R of the multitude of
    oppressions they cry out;
    They cry out for help because of the
    arm of the mighty.   Job 34:28
10 But no one says, ^R'Where *is* God my
    Maker,   Is. 51:13
    ^RWho gives songs in the night,   Acts 16:25

11 Who ᴿteaches us more than the beasts
of the earth,
And makes us wiser than the birds of
heaven?'   Ps. 94:12
12 ᴿThere they cry out, but He does not
answer,   Prov. 1:28
Because of the pride of evil men.
13 ᴿSurely God will not listen to empty
talk,
Nor will the Almighty regard it.   [Is. 1:15]
14 ᴿAlthough you say you do not see Him,
Yet justice is before Him, and ᴿyou
must wait for Him.   Job 9:11 · [Ps. 37:5, 6]
15 And now, because He has not
ᴿpunished in His anger,
Nor taken much notice of folly,   Ps. 89:32
16 ᴿTherefore Job opens his mouth in vain;
He multiplies words without
knowledge."   Job 34:35; 38:2

Elihu Proclaims God's Goodness

36 Elihu also proceeded and said:

2 "Bear with me a little, and I will show
you
That there are yet words to speak on
God's behalf.
3 I will fetch my knowledge from afar;
I will ascribe righteousness to my
Maker.
4 For truly my words are not false;
One who is perfect in knowledge is
with you.

5 "Behold, God is mighty, but despises no
one;
ᴿHe is mighty in strength ᵀof
understanding.   Job 12:13, 16; 37:23 · of heart
6 He does not preserve the life of the
wicked,
But gives justice to the oppressed.
7 ᴿHe does not withdraw His eyes from
the righteous;   [Ps. 33:18; 34:15]
But ᴿthey are on the throne with kings,
For He has seated them forever,
And they are exalted.   Ps. 113:8
8 And if they are bound in ᵀfetters,
Held in the cords of affliction,   chains
9 Then He tells them their work and their
transgressions—
That they have acted ᵀdefiantly.   proudly
10 ᴿHe also opens their ear to ᵀinstruction,
And commands that they turn from
iniquity.   Job 33:16; 36:15 · discipline
11 If they obey and serve Him,
They shall ᴿspend their days in
prosperity,
And their years in pleasures.   [Is. 1:19, 20]
12 But if they do not obey,
They shall perish by the sword,
And they shall die *without knowledge.

36:12 MT as one without knowledge.

13 "But the hypocrites in heart ᴿstore up
wrath;   [Rom. 2:5]
They do not cry for help when He binds
them.
14 ᵀThey die in youth,   Lit. Their soul dies
And their life ends among the
*perverted persons.
15 He delivers the poor in their affliction,
And opens their ears in oppression.

16 "Indeed He would have brought you out
of dire distress,
ᴿInto a broad place where there is no
restraint;   Ps. 18:19; 31:8; 118:5
And ᴿwhat is set on your table would
be full of ᴿrichness.   Ps. 23:5 · Ps. 36:8
17 But you are filled with the judgment
due the ᴿwicked;   Job 22:5, 10, 11
Judgment and justice take hold of you.
18 Because there is wrath, beware lest He
take you away with one blow;
For ᴿa large ransom would not help you
avoid it.   Ps. 49:7
19 ᴿWill your riches,
Or all the mighty forces,
Keep you from distress?   [Prov. 11:4]
20 Do not desire the night,
When people are cut off in their place.
21 Take heed, ᴿdo not turn to iniquity,
For ᴿyou have chosen this rather than
affliction.   [Ps. 31:6; 66:18] · [Heb. 11:25]

22 "Behold, God is exalted by His power;
Who teaches like Him?
23 ᴿWho has assigned Him His way,
Or who has said, 'You have done
ᴿwrong'?   Job 34:13 · Job 8:3

Elihu Proclaims God's Majesty

24 "Remember to ᴿmagnify His work,
Of which men have sung.   [Rev. 15:3]
25 Everyone has seen it;
Man looks on it from afar.

26 "Behold, God is great, and we ᴿdo not
know Him;
ᴿNor can the number of His years be
discovered.   [1 Cor. 13:12] · Heb. 1:12
27 For He draws up drops of water,
Which distill as rain from the mist,
28 ᴿWhich the clouds drop down
And pour abundantly on man.   [Prov. 3:20]
29 Indeed, can anyone understand the
spreading of clouds,
The thunder from His canopy?
30 Look, He ᴿscatters His light upon it,
And covers the depths of the sea.   Job 37:3
31 For ᴿby these He judges the peoples;
He gives food in abundance.   [Acts 14:17]
32 He covers His hands with lightning,
And commands it to ᵀstrike.   strike the mark

36:14 Heb. qedeshim, those practicing sodomy or
prostitution in religious rituals

33 ᴿHis thunder declares it,
The cattle also, concerning ᵀthe rising
storm. 1 Kin. 18:41 • Lit. *what is rising*

37 "At this also my heart trembles,
And leaps from its place.
2 Hear attentively the thunder of His
voice,
And the rumbling *that* comes from His
mouth.
3 He sends it forth under the whole
heaven,
His lightning to the ends of the earth.
4 After it ᴿa voice roars;
He thunders with His majestic voice,
And He does not restrain them when
His voice is heard. Ps. 29:3
5 God thunders marvelously with His
voice;
ᴿHe does great things which we cannot
comprehend. Job 5:9; 9:10; 36:26
6 For ᴿHe says to the snow, 'Fall on the
earth'; Ps. 147:16, 17
Likewise to the ᵀgentle rain and the
heavy rain of His strength. *shower of rain*
7 He seals the hand of every man,
That all men may know His work.
8 The beasts ᴿgo into dens,
And remain in their lairs. Ps. 104:21, 22
9 From the chamber *of the south* comes
the whirlwind,
And cold from the scattering winds *of
the north.*
10 By the breath of God ice is given,
And the broad waters are frozen.
11 Also with moisture He saturates the
thick clouds;
He scatters His bright clouds.
12 And they swirl about, being turned by
His guidance,
That they may ᴿdo whatever He
commands them Job 36:32
On the face of *the whole earth.
13 ᴿHe causes it to come, Ex. 9:18, 23
Whether for ᵀcorrection, Lit. *a rod*
Or ᴿfor His land, Job 38:26, 27
Or ᴿfor mercy. 1 Kin. 18:41-46
14 "Listen to this, O Job;
Stand still and ᴿconsider the wondrous
works of God. Ps. 111:2
15 Do you know when God ᵀdispatches
them,
And causes the light of His cloud to
shine? *places them*
16 ᴿDo you know how the clouds are
balanced,
Those wondrous works of ᴿHim who is
perfect in knowledge? Job 36:29 • Job 36:4
17 Why *are* your garments hot,
When He quiets the earth by the south
wind?

37:12 Lit. *the world of the earth*

18 With Him, have you ᴿspread out the
ᴿskies, [Is. 44:24] • Ps. 104:2
Strong as a cast metal mirror?
19 "Teach us what we should say to Him,
For we can prepare nothing because of
the darkness.
20 Should He be told that I *wish to* speak?
If a man were to speak, surely he
would be swallowed up.
21 Even now *men* cannot look at the light
when it is bright in the skies,
When the wind has passed and cleared
them.
22 He comes from the north *as* golden
splendor;
With God *is* awesome majesty.
23 *As for* the Almighty, ᴿwe cannot find
Him; [1 Tim. 6:16]
ᴿHe is excellent in power,
In judgment and abundant justice;
He does not oppress. [Job 9:4; 36:5]
24 Therefore men ᴿfear Him;
He shows no partiality to any *who are*
ᴿwise of heart." [Matt. 10:28] • [Matt. 11:25]

The Lᴏʀᴅ Reveals His Omnipotence to Job

38 Then the Lᴏʀᴅ answered Job ᴿout of
the whirlwind, and said: Ex. 19:16

2 "Who *is* this who darkens counsel
By ᴿwords without knowledge? 1 Tim. 1:7
3 ᴿNow ᵀprepare yourself like a man;
I will question you, and you shall
answer Me. Job 40:7 • *gird up your loins*
4 "Where ᴿwere you when I laid the
foundations of the earth? Ps. 104:5
Tell *Me,* if you have understanding.
5 Who determined its measurements?
Surely you know!
Or who stretched the line upon it?
6 To what were its foundations fastened?
Or who laid its cornerstone,
7 When the morning stars sang together,
And all ᴿthe sons of God shouted for
joy? Job 1:6
8 "Or ᴿ*who* shut in the sea with doors,
When it burst forth *and* issued from the
womb; Gen. 1:9
9 When I made the clouds its garment,
And thick darkness its swaddling band;
10 When ᴿI fixed My limit for it,
And set bars and doors; Job 26:10
11 When I said,
'This far you may come, but no farther,
And here your proud waves must stop!'
12 "Have you ᴿcommanded the morning
since your days *began,* [Ps. 74: 6; 148:5]
And caused the dawn to know its place,
13 That it might take hold of the ends of
the earth,
And the wicked be shaken out of it?

14 It takes on form like clay *under* a seal,
And stands out like a garment.
15 From the wicked their ᴿlight is
withheld,   Job 18:5
And the ᵀupraised arm is broken.   *high*
16 "Have you ᴿentered the springs of the
sea?
Or have you walked in search of the
depths?   [Ps. 77:19]
17 Have ᴿthe gates of death been ᵀrevealed
to you?
Or have you seen the doors of the
shadow of death?   Ps. 9:13 · Lit. *opened*
18 Have you comprehended the breadth of
the earth?
Tell *Me*, if you know all this.
19 "Where *is* the way *to* the dwelling of
light?
And darkness, where *is* its place,
20 That you may take it to its territory,
That you may know the paths *to* its
home?
21 Do you know *it*, because you were born
then,
Or *because* the number of your days *is*
great?
22 "Have you entered ᴿthe treasury of
snow,   Ps. 135:7
Or have you seen the treasury of hail,
23 ᴿWhich I have reserved for the time of
trouble,
For the day of battle and war?   Is. 30:30
24 By what way is light ᵀdiffused,
Or the east wind scattered over the
earth?   Lit. *divided*
25 "Who ᴿhas divided a channel for the
overflowing *water*,
Or a path for the thunderbolt,   Job 28:26
26 To cause it to rain on a land *where*
there is no one,
A wilderness in which *there is* no man;
27 ᴿTo satisfy the desolate waste,
And cause to spring forth the growth of
tender grass?   Ps. 104:13, 14; 107:35
28 ᴿHas the rain a father?   Job 36:27, 28
Or who has begotten the drops of dew?
29 From whose womb comes the ice?
And the ᴿfrost of heaven, who gives it
birth?   Ps. 147:16, 17
30 The waters harden like stone,
And the surface of the deep is frozen.
31 "Can you bind the cluster of the
ᴿPleiades,ᵀ   Amos 5:8 · *the Seven Stars*
Or loose the belt of Orion?
32 Can you bring out ᵀMazzaroth in its
season?
Or can you guide ᵀthe Great Bear with
its cubs?   Lit. *Constellations* · Or *Arcturus*
33 Do you know ᴿthe ordinances of the
heavens?

Can you set their dominion over the
earth?   Jer. 31:35, 36
34 "Can you lift up your voice to the
clouds,
That an abundance of water may cover
you?
35 Can you send out lightnings, that they
may go,
And say to you, 'Here we *are!*'?
36 ᴿWho has put wisdom in ᵀthe mind?
Or who has given understanding to the
heart?   [Ps. 51:6] · Lit. *the inward parts*
37 Who can number the clouds by
wisdom?
Or who can pour out the bottles of
heaven,
38 When the dust hardens in clumps,
And the clods cling together?
39 "Canᴿ you hunt the prey for the lion,
Or satisfy the appetite of the young
lions,   Ps. 104:21
40 When they crouch in *their* dens,
Or lurk in their lairs to lie in wait?
41 Who provides food for the raven,
When its young ones cry to God,
And wander about for lack of food?

39 "Do you know the time when the wild
ᴿmountain goats bear young?
Or can you mark when ᴿthe deer gives
birth?   Ps. 104:18 · Ps. 29:9
2 Can you number the months *that* they
fulfill?
Or do you know the time when they
bear young?
3 They bow down,
They bring forth their young,
They deliver their *offspring.
4 Their young ones are healthy,
They grow strong with grain;
They depart and do not return to them.
5 "Who set the wild donkey free?
Who loosed the bonds of the onager,
6 ᴿWhose home I have made the
wilderness,   Jer. 2:24
And the barren land his dwelling?
7 He scorns the tumult of the city;
He does not heed the shouts of the
driver.
8 The range of the mountains *is* his
pasture,
And he searches after ᴿevery green
thing.   Gen. 1:29
9 "Will the ᴿwild ox be willing to serve
you?
Will he bed by your manger?   Num. 23:22
10 Can you bind the wild ox in the furrow
with ropes?
Or will he plow the valleys behind you?

39:3 Lit. *pangs*

11 Will you trust him because his strength
   is great?
   Or will you leave your labor to him?
12 Will you trust him to bring home your
   ᵀgrain,   Lit. *seed*
   And gather it to your threshing floor?

13 "The wings of the ostrich wave proudly,
   But are her wings and pinions *like the*
   kindly stork's?
14 For she leaves her eggs on the ground,
   And warms them in the dust;
15 She forgets that a foot may crush them,
   Or that a wild beast may break them.
16 She treats her young harshly, as though
   they were not hers;
   Her labor is in vain, without concern,
17 Because God deprived her of wisdom,
   And did not ᴿendow her with
   understanding.   Job 35:11
18 When she lifts herself on high,
   She scorns the horse and its rider.

19 "Have you given the horse strength?
   Have you clothed his neck with
   ᵀthunder?   Or *a mane*
20 Can you frighten him like a locust?
   His majestic snorting strikes terror.
21 He paws in the valley, and rejoices in
   his strength;
   ᴿHe gallops into the clash of arms.   Jer. 8:6
22 He mocks at fear, and is not frightened;
   Nor does he turn back from the sword.
23 The quiver rattles against him,
   The glittering spear and javelin.
24 He devours the distance with fierceness
   and rage;
   Nor does he come to a halt because the
   trumpet *has* sounded.
25 At *the blast of* the trumpet he says,
   'Aha!'
   He smells the battle from afar,
   The thunder of captains and shouting.

26 "Does the hawk fly by your wisdom,
   And spread its wings toward the south?
27 Does the ᴿeagle mount up at your
   command,   Prov. 30:18, 19
   And ᴿmake its nest on high?   Jer. 49:16
28 On the rock it dwells and resides,
   On the crag of the rock and the
   stronghold.
29 From there it spies out the prey;
   Its eyes observe from afar.
30 Its young ones suck up blood;
   And where the slain *are*, there it *is*."

40 Moreover the LORD ᴿanswered Job,
     and said: Job 38:1

2 "Shall ᴿthe one who contends with the
  Almighty correct *Him*?   Job 9:3; 10:2
  He who rebukes God, let him answer
  it."

Job's Response to God

3 Then Job answered the LORD and said:

4 "Behold,ᴿ I am vile;   Ezra 9:6
  What shall I answer You?
  ᴿI lay my hand over my mouth.   Job 29:9
5 Once I have spoken, but I will not
  answer;
  Yes, twice, but I will proceed no
  further."

God's Challenge to Job

6 ᴿThen the LORD answered Job out of the
whirlwind, and said: Job 38:1

7 "Now ᵀprepare yourself like a man;
  ᴿI will question you, and you shall
  answer Me: Lit. *gird up your loins* · Job 42:4

8 "Wouldᴿ you indeed ᵀannul My
  judgment?
  Would you condemn Me that you may
  be justified?   [Rom. 3:4] · *nullify*
9 Have you an arm like God?
  Or can you thunder with ᴿa voice like
  His?   [Ps. 29:3, 4]
10 ᴿThen adorn yourself *with* majesty and
   splendor,
   And array yourself with glory and
   beauty.   Ps. 93:1; 104:1
11 Disperse the rage of your wrath;
   Look on everyone *who is* proud, and
   humble him.
12 Look on everyone *who is* ᴿproud, *and*
   bring him low;   Dan. 4:37
   Tread down the wicked in their place.
13 Hide them in the dust together,
   Bind their faces in hidden *darkness*.
14 Then I will also confess to you
   That your own right hand can save
   you.

15 "Look now at the *behemoth, which I
   made *along* with you;
   He eats grass like an ox.
16 See now, his strength *is* in his hips,
   And his power *is* in his stomach
   muscles.
17 He moves his tail like a cedar;
   The sinews of his thighs are tightly
   knit.
18 His bones *are like* beams of bronze,
   His ribs like bars of iron.
19 He *is* the first of the ᴿways of God;
   Only He who made him can bring near
   His sword.   Job 26:14
20 Surely the mountains ᴿyield food for
   him,
   And all the beasts of the field play
   there.   Ps. 104:14
21 He lies under the lotus trees,
   In a covert of reeds and marsh.

40:15 A large animal, exact identity unknown

22 The lotus trees cover him *with their
    shade;
   The willows by the brook surround
    him.
23 Indeed the river may rage,
   Yet he is not disturbed;
   He is confident, though the Jordan
    gushes into his mouth.
24 *Though* he takes it in his eyes,
   Or one pierces *his* nose with a snare.

41 "Can you draw out *Leviathan with a
       hook,
   Or *snare* his tongue with a line *which*
    you lower?
2 Can you put a reed through his nose,
   Or pierce his jaw with a ᵀhook?   thorn
3 Will he make many supplications to
    you?
   Will he speak softly to you?
4 Will he make a covenant with you?
   Will you take him as a servant forever?
5 Will you play with him as *with* a bird,
   Or will you leash him for your maidens?
6 Will *your* companions ᵀmake a banquet
    of him?
   Will they apportion him among the
    merchants?   Or bargain over him
7 Can you fill his skin with harpoons,
   Or his head with fishing spears?
8 Lay your hand on him;
   Remember the battle—
   Never do it again!
9 Indeed, *any* hope of *overcoming* him is
    false;
   Shall *one not* be overwhelmed at the
    sight of him?
10 No one *is* so fierce that he would dare
    stir him up.
   Who then is able to stand against Me?
11 ᴿWho has preceded Me, that I should
    pay *him*?   [Rom. 11:35]
   Everything under heaven is Mine.

12 "I will not ᵀconceal his limbs,
   His mighty power, or his graceful
    proportions.   Lit. keep silent about
13 Who can ᵀremove his outer coat?
   Who can approach *him* with a double
    bridle?   Lit. take off the face of his garment
14 Who can open the doors of his face,
   With his terrible teeth all around?
15 *His* rows of ᵀscales are *his* pride,
   Shut up tightly *as with* a seal;   Lit. shields
16 One is so near another
   That no air can come between them;
17 They are joined one to another,
   They stick together and cannot be
    parted.
18 His sneezings flash forth light,
   And his eyes *are* like the eyelids of the
    morning.

19 Out of his mouth go burning lights;
   Sparks of fire shoot out.
20 Smoke goes out of his nostrils,
   As *from* a boiling pot and burning
    rushes.
21 His breath kindles coals,
   And a flame goes out of his mouth.
22 Strength dwells in his neck,
   And ᵀsorrow dances before him.   despair
23 The folds of his flesh are joined
    together;
   They are firm on him and cannot be
    moved.
24 His heart is as hard as stone,
   Even as hard as the lower *millstone.*
25 When he raises himself up, the mighty
    are afraid;
   Because of his crashings they ᵀare
    beside themselves.   Or purify themselves
26 *Though* the sword reaches him, it
    cannot avail;
   Nor does spear, dart, or javelin.
27 He regards iron as straw,
   And bronze as rotten wood.
28 The arrow cannot make him flee;
   Slingstones become like stubble to him.
29 Darts are regarded as straw;
   He laughs at the threat of javelins.
30 His undersides *are* like sharp potsherds;
   He spreads pointed *marks* in the mire.
31 He makes the deep boil like a pot;
   He makes the sea like a pot of
    ointment.
32 He leaves a shining wake behind him;
   One would think the deep had white
    hair.
33 On earth there is nothing like him,
   Which is made without fear.
34 He beholds every high *thing;*
   He *is* king over all the children of
    pride."

Job's Repentance and Restoration

42 Then Job answered the LORD and said:

2 "I know that You ᴿcan do everything,
   And that no purpose *of* Yours can be
    withheld from You.   [Matt. 19:26]
3 *You asked,* ᴿ'Who *is* this who hides
    counsel without knowledge?'   Job 38:2
   Therefore I have uttered what I did not
    understand,
   ᴿThings too wonderful for me, which I
    did not know.   Ps. 40:5; 131:1; 139:6
4 Listen, please, and let me speak;
   You said, ᴿ'I will question you, and you
    shall answer Me.'   Job 38:3; 40:7

5 "I have ᴿheard of You by the hearing of
    the ear,
   But now my eye sees You.   Job 26:14
6 Therefore I ᴿabhor *myself,*
   And repent in dust and ashes."   Ezra 9:6

7 And so it was, after the LORD had spoken

41:1 A large sea creature, exact identity unknown

these words to Job, that the LORD said to Eliphaz the Temanite, "My wrath is aroused against you and your two friends, for you have not spoken of Me *what is* right, as My servant Job *has.*

8 "Now therefore, take for yourselves seven bulls and seven rams, go to My servant Job, and offer up for yourselves a burnt offering; and My servant Job shall pray for you. For I will accept ^Thim, lest I deal with you *according to your* folly; because you have not spoken of Me *what is* right, as My servant Job *has.*"   Lit. *his face*

9 So Eliphaz the Temanite and Bildad the Shuhite *and* Zophar the Naamathite went and did as the LORD commanded them; for the LORD had ^Taccepted Job.   Lit. *Job's face*

10 And the LORD restored *Job's losses when he prayed for his friends. Indeed the LORD gave Job ^Rtwice as much as he had before.   Is. 40:2

11 Then all his brothers, all his sisters, and

42:10 Lit. *turned the captivity of Job,* what was captured from Job

all those who had been his acquaintances before, came to him and ate food with him in his house; and they consoled him and comforted him for all the adversity that the LORD had brought upon him. Each one gave him a piece of silver and each a ring of gold.

12 Now the LORD blessed ^Rthe latter *days* of Job more than his beginning; for he had ^Rfourteen thousand sheep, six thousand camels, one thousand yoke of oxen, and one thousand female donkeys.   James 5:11 • Job 1:3

13 ^RHe also had seven sons and three daughters.   Job 1:2

14 And he called the name of the first Jemimah, the name of the second Keziah, and the name of the third Keren-Happuch.

15 In all the land were found no women *so* beautiful as the daughters of Job; and their father gave them an inheritance among their brothers.

16 After this Job ^Rlived one hundred and forty years, and saw his children and grandchildren *for* four generations.   Job 5:26

17 So Job died, old and full of days.

THE BOOK OF
Psalms

How Psalms Fits into the Bible. Psalms is the first of the books in the Old Testament known as the Writings, which section completes the canon in the Hebrew order of books. Each section of the Old Testament—whether law, history, or prophecy—feeds history, biography, and instructions into the Psalms, while drawing from them a spiritual interpretation of that material.

This devotional commentary on the Old Testament also contains a vast treasury of prophetic teachings, providing an inspired bridge to the New Testament. The book of Psalms provides a background for the Gospels and the ministry of Christ, where it appears to have been His favorite Old Testament book (judging from His use of it). The Psalms are also widely quoted in the rest of the New Testament. They provide an important companion to that portion of the Bible, which helps explain the popularity of editions of the New Testament containing the Psalms.

Context. In Hebrew the title literally means "Praises." The Psalms were used as a guide for public and private worship in ancient Israel. Careful reading reveals some of these keys given for the worship leaders as well as for the congregation.

Following the return from exile in Babylon, the Psalms were used as the hymnbook and prayer book for worship in the rebuilt temple under the leadership of the restored priestly system. Formal guides such as "To the Chief Musician" (Psalm 12) and "On stringed instruments" (Psalm 67) were for the worship leaders and ministers in the temple. The "Selahs," such as those in Psalm 66 were for both congregation and leaders. This notation may have had a similar significance to the "Amens" in contemporary worship, as a formal response with the meaning and impact of "Forever!"

The Psalms also call for congregational participation, like contemporary responsive readings. An excellent example of this is found in Psalm 136 where the leader gives specific reasons for giving thanks to God and the congregation responds by repeating, "For His mercy endures forever"—a response that occurs in each of the psalm's twenty-six verses.

Other illustrations of style may be found in the pictorial language of the Psalms as well as the arrangement of ideas and verses. Some were arranged to help the student memorize them. For example, Psalm 119 is divided into twenty-two sections of eight verses each, corresponding to the twenty-two letters of the Hebrew alphabet. Other psalms use traditional Hebrew poetic devices such as repetition of ideas, repetition of sounds and phrases, and contrast between ideas to emphasize the main teachings of the Scriptures.

The Message. Given by God to minister to the whole person (mentally, physically, emotionally, and spiritually), the Psalms provide rich intellectual teachings, practical guidelines for living, sound psychology, and heart-centered means of reaching the person who longs for an intimate relationship with God. The wealth of the Bible is buried in the Psalms, waiting for the patient disciple to mine them systematically through a lifetime of study. Sacred history, doctrine, prophecy, psychology, and much more contribute to the devotional value of this inspired book.

Historically, the Psalms recall many major events in sacred history from creation (8:3, 4; 19; 24:1, 2; 102:25–27; 148) to consummation (2; 96:13; 98:9). The psalmist's interpretation of history teaches us that God is in control of the destinies of men and nations.

Doctrinally, the major beliefs of Scripture are woven into the fabric of the Psalms. These doctrinal threads include teachings about the Bible (19:7–11; 119), God's nature and perfections (2:1–5; 139), the tri-personal revelation of God as Father, Son, and Holy Spirit (2; 51:11), God's grace (51:1–12), the nature and destiny of man (8:4–8; 36:1–4; 58:3; 60:11, 12; 108:12; 146:3, 4), eternal rewards and retribution (9:17; 11:16; 23:6), and the existence of the supernatural realm (91:11, 12, et al.). Faithful study here will affirm most major convictions of the Christian faith.

Prophetically, Psalms gives an overview of the person and work of the Messiah as our Prophet, High Priest, and King. Descended from David (89:4; 132:11, 12, 17), He would have two natures—divine and human (110:1, studied in conjunction with Christ's self-understanding in Matthew 22:41–45, where He makes His point that the Messiah would be David's son, humanly speaking, and preexistent and alive in David's day as God's eternal Son). He would fulfill priestly and kingly functions (110:4), be rejected (118:22), persecuted and betrayed (69:21; 26; 41:9; 54:12–14), and crucified (22), and His last words prerecorded (31:5). But all these events would not end the Messiah's life and ministry. He would rise from the dead (2:7; 16:10) and come again some day to take His rightful place as King of Israel (2:6–9). The Psalms witness to events which would take place almost a millennium later!

Psychologically, the Psalms demonstrate the need in the human heart for a spiritual

foundation for mental health and a personal relationship with God (9:1; 19:14; 44:2; 139:23, 24). Anyone seeking this sure foundation for living will appreciate the perfect plan for an abundant life given in the Psalms: *trust* in the Lord, *delight* in the Lord, *commit* your way to the Lord, and *rest* in the Lord (37:1-7). This marvelous book is a sure guide for psychological well-being and assurance in an age of moral and spiritual confusion.

Devotionally, there is a lifetime of reading, meditation, and application in the Psalms. Many disciples read the Psalms daily. Some read five chapters per day and complete the Psalms monthly; others read one per day like "spiritual apples" to ward off self-destructive thoughts and actions. Anyone seeking a closer walk with God cannot neglect this book.

AUTHORSHIP AND HOW THE PSALMS FIT TOGETHER. The Psalms are presently arranged in five books, which many Bible students believe correspond to the order of the Torah, the first five books of the Bible (Genesis through Deuteronomy). One reason for this may be the close correlation between the teachings of the two sections and the need for both praise and obedience in a believer's life. The five books of the Psalms are as follows:

Book I —Psalms 1—41, mostly by David, are characterized by the use of the special name for God, Yahweh (Jehovah), identified in the text by LORD, and expressing the unchanging nature of God ("I AM WHO I AM," Ex. 3:14).

Book II —Psalms 42—72, including psalms of David (51—65; 68—70) and of the sons of Korah (42—49). The sons of Korah were descendants of the priestly line who were appointed to the music ministry in Israel (1 Chr. 6:22 ff.), and their psalms reflect this calling.

Book III—Psalms 73—89, by the sons of Korah (84—88) and by Asaph (73—83), a collector and arranger of hymns and poetry who directed the orchestra and choirs for both David and Solomon (1 Chr. 15:16-19; 16:4-7; 2 Chr. 5:1, 11-14).

Book IV—Psalms 90—106, beginning with a prayer of Moses (Psalm 90) and including two psalms by David (101; 103), with the rest anonymous. The dominant theme of these psalms is the work of the LORD on behalf of His people.

Book V —Psalms 107—150, including several by David and one by Solomon (127), with the rest anonymous. These are psalms of praise, thanksgiving, and ascent (believed to have been sung by pilgrims going up to Jerusalem during the major feast days of Israel). Of these, 113—118 were sung during Passover and are the hymns mentioned in the Gospels in connection with the Last Supper (Matt. 26:30; Mark 14:26).

—J.E.

BOOK ONE
Psalms 1—41

Psalm 1

The Way of the Righteous and the End of the Ungodly

BLESSED ᴿ*is* the man
  Who walks not in the counsel of the
  ᵀungodly,   Prov. 4:14 · wicked
  Nor stands in the path of sinners,
  Nor sits in the seat of the scornful;
2 But ᴿhis delight *is* in the law of the
  LORD,   Ps. 119:14, 16, 35
  And in His law he ᵀmeditates day and
  night.   *ponders* by talking to himself
3 He shall be like a tree
  ᴿPlanted by the ᵀrivers of water,
  That brings forth its fruit in its
  season,   Jer. 17:8 · *channels*

Whose leaf also shall not wither;
  And whatever he does shall prosper.

4 The ungodly *are* not so,
  But *are* ᴿlike the chaff which the wind
  drives away.   Job 21:18
5 Therefore the ungodly shall not stand
  in the judgment,
  Nor sinners in the congregation of the
  righteous.
6 For ᴿthe LORD knows the way of the
  righteous,   Ps. 37:18
  But the way of the ungodly shall perish.

Psalm 2

The Messiah's Triumph and Kingdom

9-G. The Messiah as King of Kings   ▼

WHY ᴿdo the nations rage,   [Acts 4:25-28]
  And the people plot a vain thing?

9-G. The Messiah as King of Kings (Psalm 2:1-12)—In this messianic psalm, Jehovah comes to the end of His patience with mankind. In the end time, ungodly philosophies will penetrate and permeate the hearts of kings, rulers, and most of the world's population. The psalm takes us through the Great Tribulation, up to the millennial throne of the Messiah, King of kings (Matt. 25:31-46, page 976).

(Point 9-G continued on next page)

▽ 2 The kings of the earth set themselves,
     And the rulers take counsel together,
     ᴿAgainst the Lᴏʀᴅ and against His
       ᵀAnointed, *saying,*   [John 1:41] • Christ
   3 "Let us break Their bonds in pieces
     And cast away Their cords from us."

   4 He who sits in the heavens shall laugh;
     The Lᴏʀᴅ shall hold them in derision.
   5 Then He shall speak to them in His
       wrath,
     And distress them in His deep
       displeasure:
   6 "Yet I have ᵀset My King   Lit. *installed*
     On My holy hill of Zion."

   7 "I will declare the decree:
     The Lᴏʀᴅ has said to Me,
       ᴿ'You *are* My Son,   [Luke 1:35]
     Today I have begotten You.
   8 Ask of Me, and I will give You
     The nations *for* Your inheritance,
     And the ends of the earth *for* Your
       possession.
   9 ᴿYou shall *break them with a rod of
       iron;
     You shall dash them to pieces like a
       potter's vessel.' "   Ps. 89:23; 110:5, 6

  10 Now therefore, be wise, O kings;
     Be instructed, you judges of the earth.
  11 Serve the Lᴏʀᴅ with fear,

   2:9 So with MT, Tg.; LXX, Syr., Vg. *rule* (cf. Rev. 2:27)

     And rejoice with trembling.   ▽
  12 ᵀKiss* the Son, lest *He be angry,
     And you perish *in* the way,
     When His wrath is kindled but a little.
     Blessed *are* all those who put their trust
     in Him.   An act of homage and submission ▲

Psalm 3

The Lᴏʀᴅ Helps His Troubled People
A Psalm of David when he fled
from Absalom his son.

Lᴏʀᴅ, how they have increased who
     trouble me!
   Many *are* they who rise up against me.
 2 Many *are* they who say of me,
   "*There is* no help for him in God."
     Selah

 3 But You, O Lᴏʀᴅ, *are* ᴿa shield ᵀfor me,
   My glory and ᴿthe One who lifts up my
     head.   Ps. 5:12; 28:7 • Lit. *around* • Ps. 9:13; 27:6
 4 I cried to the Lᴏʀᴅ with my voice,
   And ᴿHe heard me from His ᴿholy hill.
     Selah   Ps. 4:3; 34:4 • Ps. 2:6; 15:1; 43:3

 5 ᴿI lay down and slept;   Lev. 26:6
   I awoke, for the Lᴏʀᴅ sustained me.
 6 ᴿI will not be afraid of ten thousands of
     people
   Who have set *themselves* against me all
     around.   Ps. 23:4; 27:3

   2:12 LXX, Vg. *Embrace discipline;* Tg. *receive instruction*
   • LXX *the Lᴏʀᴅ*

(Point 9-G continued from previous page)
    The first two verses of this prophetic psalm were fulfilled at the crucifixion of Christ (Acts 4:23-29, page 1092). The fulfillment of the remaining verses began at Calvary when the leaders of nations and religions continued to cry, "Let us break Their bonds in pieces and cast away Their cords from us" (v. 3). This call to rebellion will continue until the Son sits upon the throne of David: "Yet I have set My King on My holy hill of Zion" (v. 6; cf. Is. 9:6, 7, page 651). When Jesus comes He will crush the ungodly nations: "You shall break them with a rod of iron; you shall dash them to pieces like a potter's vessel" (v. 9; cf. Rev. 19:11-16, page 1312). Christ is not yet upon the holy hill of Zion. He is seated at the right hand of the Father. He promised, "To him who overcomes I will grant to sit with Me on My throne, as I also overcame and sat down with My Father on His throne" (Rev. 3:21, page 1297).
    The psalmist asked a twofold question:

    (1) "Why do the nations rage?" (v. 1). Why do the nations act in an insane manner, in uncontrolled anger, against God and His Anointed (Messiah, Christ)?
    (2) "And the people plot a vain thing?" (v. 1). They will be convinced that they no longer need God. Today, much of the world has already reached this stage of delusion. The rulers, with their humanistic or atheistic convictions, will lead the people to believe that they will solve all the world's problems, that there will be no more hunger and that they will control the population growth. The people will not have the hope of eternal life in Christ. They will be persuaded that, sometime in the future, science will be able to extend life indefinitely. The great leaders of the world will convene a council to plot their strategy against Jehovah and against His Messiah. They will say, "Let us break Their bonds in pieces and cast away Their cords from us" (v. 3). They will refuse to recognize any of God's holy laws, and will revert to the corruption and violence that existed in the days of Noah. They will become totally corrupt (Matt. 24:36-39, page 974; cf. Gen. 6:1-7, page 11). According to Isaiah, God pronounces certain woes upon the wicked—the secular humanists—and their philosophies: "Woe to those who draw iniquity with cords of vanity" (Is. 5:18, page 647). They will break the cords of God that bind the sacrifice to the altar (Ps. 118:27, page 580), braiding cords of vanity, with which they will attempt to lift themselves above God.

    This is God's response (vv. 4-9):

    (1) He laughs: it is the laughter of ridicule and derision. "He who sits in the heavens shall laugh" (v. 4).
                                                                (Point 9-G continued on next page)

7 Arise, O Lord;
   Save me, O my God!
   ^RFor You have struck all my enemies on
     the cheekbone;
   You have broken the teeth of the
     ungodly.   Job 16:10
8 ^RSalvation *belongs* to the Lord.
   Your blessing *is* upon Your people.
   Selah   [Is. 43:11]

Psalm 4

The Safety of the Faithful

To the Chief Musician. With stringed instruments.
A Psalm of David.

HEAR me when I call, O God of my
    righteousness!
   You have relieved me in my distress;
   Have mercy on me, and hear my
     prayer.

2 How long, O you sons of men,
   Will you turn my glory to shame?
   How long will you love worthlessness
   And seek falsehood?   Selah
3 But know that the Lord has *set apart
     for Himself him who is godly;
   The Lord will hear when I call to Him.

4:3 Many Heb. mss., LXX, Tg., Vg. *made wonderful*

4 ^RBe angry, and do not sin.   [Eph. 4:26]
   ^RMeditate within your heart on your
     bed, and be still.   Selah   Ps. 77:6
5 Offer the sacrifices of righteousness,
   And put your trust in the Lord.

6 *There are* many who say,
   "Who will show us *any* good?"
   ^RLord, lift up the light of Your
     countenance upon us.   Num. 6:26
7 You have put ^Rgladness in my heart,
   More than in the season that their
     grain and wine increased.   Is. 9:3
8 ^RI will both lie down in peace, and sleep;
   ^RFor You alone, O Lord, make me dwell
     in safety.   Ps. 3:5 • [Lev. 25:18]

Psalm 5

A Prayer for Guidance

To the Chief Musician. With *flutes.
A Psalm of David.

GIVE ^Rear to my words, O Lord,   Ps. 4:1
    Consider my ^Tmeditation.   Lit. *groaning*
2 Give heed to the voice of my cry,
   My King and my God,
   For to You I will pray.

5:title, Heb. *nehiloth*

(Point 9–G continued from previous page)
   (2) He speaks: "Then He shall speak to them in His wrath" (v. 5). It is in derision that He laughs at them,
but it is in wrath that He speaks. God is a God of love, but His holiness demands the punishment of sin.
   (3) He agitates them: "Then He shall speak to them in His wrath, and distress [agitate] them in His deep
displeasure" (v. 5). Some may be shocked to imagine God laughing at them in derision, speaking to them in
His anger, and agitating them in His displeasure. Yet this happened when Pharaoh's army pursued Israel.
When they came to the Red Sea, God parted the waters and Israel marched through on dry land. Pharaoh
sent his army after them. When the army reached the middle of the sea, with walls of water on either side,
the Scriptures record that God "took off their chariot wheels." He distressed them, He confused them, He
made them realize that they were fighting against Almighty God. Then He brought the walls of water down
to destroy them (Ex. 14:24, 25, page 74).
   (4) He places the Messiah on the throne of David: "Yet I have set My King on My holy hill of Zion" (v.
6; cf. Is. 9:6, 7, page 651).
   (5) He decrees: "I will declare the decree" (v. 7; cf. Dan. 4:24, page 839).

   (a) "You are My Son" (v. 7). God's Son is the Messiah-King (Acts 13:33, page 1107).
   (b) "Today I have begotten You" (v. 7; cf. Heb. 1:5, page 1236). Jesus the Messiah, as God's only
begotten Son, is officially recognized as such (John 1:14, page 1049).
   (c) "Ask of Me, and I will give You the nations for Your inheritance, and the ends of the earth for
Your possession" (v. 8). The Messiah, the King of kings, will rule and reign forever over this world kingdom.
The thousand-year reign will be the beginning (Rev. 20:4, page 1313). After the thousand years, Christ will
continue to rule with His bride forever in the new heaven and new earth (Rev. 21:1–8, page 1314).
   (d) He will rule the nations with a scepter of righteousness (Heb. 1:8, page 1236), breaking the
ungodly with His rod of iron (Rev. 19:15, 16, page 1312).

   Now we come to the conclusion of this great messianic psalm (vv. 10–12). God in His mercy and love
makes one great final appeal to the wise and the rulers of this world—that they repent and accept the Lord
Jesus Christ as their Lord of lords and King of kings. "Be wise, O kings; be instructed, you judges of the
earth" (v. 10). This is God's call of grace. He called upon them to "serve the Lord with fear [reverence], and
rejoice with trembling. Kiss the Son," in love and worship, "lest He be angry" (vv. 11, 12). It is impossible to
worship God without loving "the Lord your God with all your heart, with all your soul, and with all your
mind" (Matt. 22:37, page 971; cf. Deut. 6:5, page 187).
   This psalm closes with these words: "Blessed are all those who put their trust in Him" (v. 12). This free
offer of salvation is still extended to the unsaved.
   See Index, page 17, for your next study.

3 My voice You shall hear in the
    morning, O LORD;
  RIn the morning I will direct *it* to You,
    And I will look up.   Ps. 55:17; 88:13

4 For You *are* not a God who takes
    pleasure in wickedness,
    Nor shall evil Tdwell with You.   Lit. *sojourn*

5 The Rboastful shall not Rstand in Your
    sight;   [Hab. 1:13] • Ps. 1:5
    You hate all workers of iniquity.

6 You shall destroy those who speak
    falsehood;
    The LORD abhors the Rbloodthirsty and
    deceitful man.   Ps. 55:23

▼ **28-B. Worship in the Old Testament**

7 But as for me, I will come into Your
    house in the multitude of Your
    mercy;
    In fear of You I will worship toward
▲   Your holy temple.

8 RLead me, O LORD, in Your
    righteousness because of my enemies;
    Make Your way straight before my
    face.   Ps. 25:4, 5; 27:11; 31:3

9 For *there is* no Tfaithfulness in their
    mouth;   *uprightness*
    Their inward part *is* destruction;
  RTheir throat *is* an open tomb;   Rom. 3:13
    They flatter with their tongue.

10 Pronounce them guilty, O God!
    Let them fall by their own counsels;
    Cast them out in the multitude of their
    transgressions,
    For they have rebelled against You.

11 But let all those rejoice who put their
    trust in You;
    Let them ever shout for joy, because
    You Tdefend them;
    Let those also who love Your name
    Be joyful in You.   *protect*, lit. *cover*

12 For You, O LORD, will bless the
    righteous;
    With favor You will surround him as
    with a shield.

Psalm 6

A Prayer of Faith in Time of Distress

To the Chief Musician. With stringed instruments.
On an *eight-stringed harp. A Psalm of David.

O LORD, Rdo not rebuke me in Your
    anger,   Ps. 38:1; 118:18
    Nor chasten me in Your hot
    displeasure.

2 Have mercy on me, O LORD, for I *am*
    weak;
    O LORD, Rheal me, for my bones are
    troubled.   [Hos. 6:1]

3 My soul also is greatly Rtroubled;
    But You, O LORD—how long?   Ps. 88:3

4 Return, O LORD, deliver me!
    Oh, save me for Your mercies' sake!

5 RFor in death *there is* no remembrance
    of You;   [Eccl. 9:10]
    In the grave who will give You thanks?

6 I am weary with my groaning;

6:title, Heb. *sheminith*

28-B. Worship in the Old Testament (Psalm 5:7)—

  (1) *Worship before the giving of the law.* Before God gave the law, with its elaborate instructions on how to worship Him properly, the unit of worship was the family. The father of each family acted as priest. From the time of Adam and Eve, animal sacrifices were made to atone for sin, as well as to worship God.
  The first use of the word *worship* in the Bible is in the beloved story of Abraham and Isaac (Gen. 22:1–18, page 26). When God spoke to Abraham and told him to offer Isaac as a sacrifice, His instructions were specific:
  (a) "Take now your son, your only son Isaac." He was to be the sacrifice.
  (b) "And go to the land of Moriah, and offer him there as a burnt offering on one of the mountains of which I shall tell you" (Gen. 22:2, page 26). God chose the site for Abraham to build an altar, and would later provide a sacrifice to take the place of Isaac.
  "And Abraham said to his young men, 'Stay here with the donkey; the lad and I will go yonder and worship, and we will come back to you'" (Gen. 22:5, page 27; see Point 20-C, "The Offering of Isaac," page 26).
  Not just any person may worship God, but only those who have accepted His provision. The system of animal sacrifice in the Old Testament prefigured the sacrifice of Christ in the New Testament. Not just any method of worship is allowed, but only such as God has prescribed. Even before the giving of the Law it was necessary to present a blood sacrifice; because Cain did not do so, his worship was refused. Old Testament worship was taken up with forms and ceremonies; New Testament worship is concerned with worshiping in spirit and truth (John 4:24, 25, page 1054). But in both Testaments the basis of worship is the shedding of blood, without which the unforgiven sin separates the would-be worshiper from a holy God.

  (2) *Worship in the tabernacle.* The book of Exodus gives elaborate and intricate instructions on the building of the tabernacle, and the book of Leviticus is equally detailed concerning the sacrifices that were to be offered. While these books can be read as history, their spiritual lesson is missed if they are read in this way only. 1 Corinthians 10:11 (page 1155) tells us that all these things happened for our instruction. Both the
(Point 28-B continued on next page)

Or *Every*
T All night I make my bed swim;
I drench my couch with my tears.
7 My eye wastes away because of grief;
It grows old because of all my enemies.

8 R Depart from me, all you workers of
iniquity;
For the Lord has R heard the voice of
my weeping.   [Matt. 25:41] • Ps. 3:4; 28:6
9 The Lord has heard my supplication;
The Lord will receive my prayer.
10 Let all my enemies be ashamed and
greatly troubled;
Let them turn back *and* be ashamed
suddenly.

Psalm 7

Prayer and Praise for Deliverance from Enemies

A *Meditation of David, which he sang
to the Lord concerning the words of Cush,
a Benjamite.

O LORD my God, in You I put my trust;
Save me from all those who persecute
me;
And R deliver me,   Ps. 31:15
2 R Lest they tear me like a lion,
R Rending *me* in pieces, while *there is*
none to deliver.   Is. 38:13 • Ps. 50:22

3 O Lord my God, if I have done this:
If there is iniquity in my hands,
4 If I have repaid evil to him who was at
peace with me,

7:title, Heb. *Shiggaion*

Or R have plundered my enemy without
cause,   1 Sam. 24:7; 26:9
5 Let the enemy pursue me and overtake
me;
Yes, let him trample my life to the
earth,
And lay my honor in the dust.   Selah

6 Arise, O Lord, in Your anger;
R Lift Yourself up because of the rage of
my enemies;   Ps. 94:2
R Rise up *for me to* the judgment You
have commanded!   Ps. 35:23; 44:23
7 So the congregation of the peoples shall
surround You;
For their sakes, therefore, return on
high.
8 The Lord shall judge the peoples;
R Judge me, O Lord, R according to my
righteousness,
And according to my integrity within
me.   Ps. 26:1; 35:24; 43:1 • Ps. 18:20; 35:24

9 Oh, let the wickedness of the wicked
come to an end,
But establish the just;
For the righteous God tests the hearts
and T minds.   Lit. *kidneys,* secret part of man
10 T My defense *is* of God,   Lit. *My shield is God*
Who saves the upright in heart.

11 God *is* a just judge,
And God is angry *with the wicked*
every day.

7:6 So with MT, Tg., Vg.; LXX *O Lord my God*

(Point 28-B continued from previous page)
tabernacle and the sacrifices are clear *types,* or illustrations, of Christ. Christ is the means by which the worshiper comes to God; without Him there can be no true worship. The colors, the materials, the metals, the arrangement, every detail of Old Testament worship prefigures some attribute of our Lord Jesus. All the sacrifices of Leviticus together picture the great sacrifice of the Lamb of God who takes away the sin of the world.

The worshiper in ancient Israel brought his animal to the door of the tabernacle and identified himself with it, but only the priest could officiate at its sacrifice; even the high priest could go through the veil into the Most Holy Place only once a year. In Christianity, however, the veil has been torn apart (Mark 15:38, page 1007), and any believer-priest may enter the Most Holy Place (1 Pet. 2:9, page 1265) spiritually, in prayer, through the one Mediator between God and man, the God-Man Christ Jesus (1 Tim. 2:5, page 1219).

(3) *Worship in the temple.* Solomon's temple continued the sacrificial system of the tabernacle. But there were differences:

(a) A building is more permanent than a tent, no matter how beautiful and elaborate that tent may be.

(b) The additional beauties of the temple choir's antiphonal hymns, which we learn about in Chronicles and the book of Psalms, surpassed the simpler tabernacle worship.

The typology of the temple apparently is less specific than that of the tabernacle, but the same sacrificial system was carried on as outlined for the tabernacle, and Christ was portrayed in the temple sacrifices. Our Lord Himself spoke of the temple as His "Father's house" (John 2:16, page 1051) when He threw out the money changers and those who would use religion as a means of monetary gain (1 Tim. 6:5, page 1222). He also pointed out that His own body was a temple that would be destroyed through death and yet in three days would rise again (John 2:19–21, page 1051). The believer-priest of the New Testament era is told that his or her body is also a temple of the Holy Spirit (1 Cor. 3:16, page 1149). The world is much impressed with Grecian temples and Gothic cathedrals with their high ceilings and beautifully colored windows, but God is more impressed with the humble heart of the believer in whom the Holy Spirit dwells.

See John 4:23, 24, page 1054, for **Point 28-C: Worship in the New Testament.**

12 If he does not turn back,
He will ᴿsharpen His sword;   Deut. 32:41
He bends His bow and makes it ready.
13 He also prepares for Himself
instruments of death;
He makes His arrows into fiery shafts.

14 ᴿBehold, *the wicked* brings forth
iniquity;
Yes, he conceives trouble and brings
forth falsehood.   Is. 59:4
15 He made a pit and dug it out,
ᴿAnd has fallen into the ditch *which* he
made.   [Job 4:8]
16 ᴿHis trouble shall return upon his own
head,   Esth. 9:25
And his violent dealing shall come
down on ᵀhis own crown.   *of his own head*

17 I will praise the LORD according to His
righteousness,
And will sing praise to the name of the
LORD Most High.

Psalm 8

The Glory of the LORD in Creation

To the Chief Musician. *On the instrument
of Gath. A Psalm of David.

▼ **9-A. The Messiah Exalted**

O LORD, our Lord,
How ᴿexcellent *is* Your name in all the
earth,
Who have ᴿset Your glory above the
heavens!   Ps. 148:13 • Ps. 113:4

2 ᴿOut of the mouth of babes and nursing
infants
You have ordained strength,
Because of Your enemies,   Matt. 21:15, 16

8:title, Heb. *Al Gittith*

That You may silence ᴿthe enemy and   ▽
the avenger.   Ps. 44:16

3 When I ᴿconsider Your heavens, the
work of Your fingers,
The moon and the stars, which You
have ordained,   Ps. 111:2
4 ᴿWhat is man that You are mindful of
him,   Job 7:17, 18
And the son of man that You ᴿvisitᵀ
him?   [Job 10:12] • *give attention to* or *care for*
5 For You have made him a little lower
than *the angels,
And You have crowned him with glory
and honor.

6 You have made him to have dominion
over the works of Your hands;
You have put all *things* under his feet,
7 All sheep and oxen—
Even the beasts of the field,
8 The birds of the air,
And the fish of the sea
That pass through the paths of the
seas.

9 ᴿO LORD, our Lord,
How excellent *is* Your name in all the
earth!   Ps. 8:1 ▲

Psalm 9

Prayer and Thanksgiving for the LORD's Righteous Judgments

To the Chief Musician. To the *tune of* *"Death of
the Son." A Psalm of David.

I WILL praise You, O LORD, with my
whole heart;
I will tell of all Your marvelous works.

8:5 Heb. *Elohim, God;* LXX, Syr., Tg., Jewish tradition
reads *angels*
9:title, Heb. *Muth Labben*

9-A. The Messiah Exalted (Psalm 8:1–9)—This messianic psalm exalts the name of Jesus. You can sense David's excitement as you read the first verse, "O LORD, our Lord, how excellent is Your name in all the earth, who have set Your glory above the heavens!" (v. 1). The name of Jesus is excellent in all the earth and His glory fills the universe. His name is above every name—every name in heaven, every name on earth, and every name throughout the vast universe (Phil. 2:9–11, page 1197). The day will come when every tongue will confess that glorious, excellent name of Jesus Christ as Lord. For those who are in hell it will be too late, but they *will* confess it nevertheless (Rev. 20:11–15, page 1313). But those of us who will be in the presence of our Savior will continue to confess and exalt that name throughout eternity (Rev. 21:6, 7, page 1315).

Christ is the center and principal subject of this messianic psalm, and it is so interpreted by the Lord Jesus Himself. Matthew tells us that, on one occasion, He entered the temple and drove out the religious commercializers. Jesus said to them, "It is written, 'My house shall be called a house of prayer,' but you have made it a 'den of thieves'" (Matt. 21:13, page 968). After cleansing the temple of the merchants, He brought in the lame and the blind, healed them and blessed them. Now when the children saw the miracles, their voices rang out in the temple, "Hosanna to the Son of David!" (Matt. 21:15, page 968). Hosanna means "Save now" (cf. Ps. 118:25, page 580). In other words, the children in the temple were calling upon the Messiah to deliver them now. The chief priests and scribes looked on in religious silence and contempt, ignorant of the fact that this was the fulfillment of verse 2. They said to Jesus, "Do You hear what these are saying?" (Matt. 21:16, page 968). They were shocked because the children proclaimed Him to be the promised Messiah. Then Jesus quoted verse 2: "Yes. Have you never read, 'Out of the mouth of babes and nursing infants You have perfected praise'?" (Matt. 21:12–16, page 968). God used the children in the temple to exalt the Messiah and fulfill this messianic prophecy.

See Psalm 118:22–29, page 580, for **Point 9-B: The Messiah Rejected.**

2 I will be glad and ^Rrejoice in You;
  I will sing praise to Your name, ^RO
  Most High.   Ps. 5:11; 104:34 • [Ps. 83:18; 92:1]

3 When my enemies turn back,
  They shall fall and perish at Your
  presence.

4 For You have maintained my right and
  my cause;
  You sat on the throne judging in
  righteousness.

5 You have rebuked the ^Tnations,
  You have destroyed the wicked;
  You have ^Rblotted out their name
  forever and ever.   Gentiles • Prov. 10:7

6 O enemy, destructions are finished
  forever!
  And you have destroyed cities;
  Even their memory has perished.

7 ^RBut the LORD shall endure forever;
  He has prepared His throne for
  judgment.   Heb. 1:11

8 ^RHe shall judge the world in
  righteousness,   [Ps. 96:13; 98:9]
  And He shall administer judgment for
  the peoples in uprightness.

9 The LORD also will be a ^Rrefuge^T for the
  oppressed,   Ps. 32:7; 46:1 • Lit. secure height
  A refuge in times of trouble.

10 And those who ^Rknow Your name will
   put their trust in You;
   For You, LORD, have not forsaken those
   who seek You.   Ps. 91:14

11 Sing praises to the LORD, who dwells in
   Zion!
   Declare His deeds among the people.

12 ^RWhen He avenges blood, He remembers
   them;
   He does not forget the cry of the
   ^Thumble.   [Ps. 72:14] • afflicted

13 Have mercy on me, O LORD!
   Consider my trouble from those who
   hate me,
   You who lift me up from the gates of
   death,

14 That I may tell of all Your praise
   In the gates of the daughter of ^TZion.
   I will rejoice in Your salvation.   Jerusalem

15 ^RThe ^Tnations have sunk down in the pit
   which they made;
   In the net which they hid, their own
   foot is caught.   Ps. 7:15, 16 • Gentiles

16 The LORD is ^Rknown by the judgment
   He executes;   Ex. 7:5
   The wicked is snared in the work of his
   own hands.

                *Meditation.   Selah

17–D. Hell Is a Place   ▼

17 The wicked shall be turned into hell,
   And all the nations that forget God.   ▲

18 ^RFor the needy shall not always be
   forgotten;
   ^RThe expectation of the poor shall not
   perish forever.   Ps. 9:12; 12:5 • Prov. 23:18

19 Arise, O LORD,
   Do not let man prevail;
   Let the nations be judged in Your sight.

20 Put them in fear, O LORD,

   9:16 Heb. Higgaion

17–D. Hell Is a Place (Psalm 9:17)—When we say that the Bible teaches that hell is an actual place, we are not using a figure of speech, a religious simile, or a metaphor; we are speaking of hell as a reality, in a real place, for real people who reject the only true God and Savior, the Lord Jesus Christ (John 3:36, page 1053).

  Let us look at some of the biblical concepts that speak of the ultimate fate of the wicked dead in the place called hell:

  (1) *Sheol*—the Old Testament Hebrew word for hell. "The wicked shall be turned into hell" (v. 17). In some Scriptures, Sheol means the grave. For example, Jacob said, "For I shall go down into the grave [Sheol] to my son in mourning" (Gen. 37:35, page 44). It is obvious in this text that Sheol refers to the grave, and it is just as clear in other texts that Sheol refers to the place for the spirits of wicked mankind, e. g., "The wicked shall be turned into hell [Sheol]" (v. 17). This Sheol is the temporary abode of the wicked dead.

  (2) *Hades*—the New Testament Greek word for hell. "And being in torments in Hades, he lifted up his eyes" (Luke 16:23, page 1035). Hades in the New Testament is the same as Sheol in the Old Testament. Sheol, or Hades, is the place where the spirits of the wicked dead are tormented until the last resurrection (Rev. 20:13, page 1314). The sea and the graves will give up the dead bodies of the wicked, Sheol-Hades will give up the spirits, and every body, soul, and spirit of the wicked dead will stand before Jesus Christ at the Great White Throne to be judged (Rev. 20:11–15, page 1313; John 5:22, page 1057).

  (3) *Gehenna*—Greek for the ever-burning fires in the Valley of Hinnom, a deep narrow valley just south of Jerusalem where the people of Judah sacrificed their children to the god Moloch (Jer. 32:35, page 747; cf. 19:2–6, page 732). The Valley of Hinnom later became a dumping place for trash and putrefying matter which was offensive to sight and smell. In the Valley of Hinnom the fires burned day and night. It became a prototype of eternal hell fire. Jesus, in His teachings, often warned the sinner of the results of sin, illustrating hell as an eternal place of fire and brimstone—a perpetual burning (Matt. 5:22, page 939). Jesus said, "I will show you whom you should fear: Fear Him [God, not Satan], who, after He has killed, has power to cast into hell [Gehenna]; yes, I say to you, fear Him!" (Luke 12:5, page 1029).

  See Acts 1:25, page 1087, for **Point 17-E: Hell Is the Sinner's Place.**

That the ᵀnations may know   *Gentiles*
themselves *to be but* men.   Selah

Psalm 10

A Song of Confidence in God's Triumph over Evil

WHY do You stand afar off, O Lᴏʀᴅ?
Why do You hide in times of trouble?
2 The wicked in *his* pride ᵀpersecutes the
  poor;   *hotly pursues*
  ᴿLet them be caught in the plots which
  they have devised.   Ps. 7:16; 9:16

3 For the wicked ᴿboasts of his heart's
  desire;
  He ᴿblesses the greedy *and* renounces
  the Lᴏʀᴅ.   Ps. 49:6; 94:3, 4 · Prov. 28:4
4 The wicked in his proud countenance
  does not seek *God;*
  God *is* in none of his ᴿthoughts.   Ps. 36:1

5 His ways ᵀare always prospering;
  Your judgments *are* far above, out of
  his sight;
  As *for* all his enemies, he sneers at
  them.   Lit. *are strong*
6 ᴿHe has said in his heart,   [Eccl. 8:11]
  "I shall not be moved;
  ᴿI shall never be in adversity."   Rev. 18:7
7 ᴿHis mouth is full of cursing and ᴿdeceit
  and oppression;
  Under his tongue *is* trouble and
  iniquity.   [Rom. 3:14] · Ps. 55:10, 11

8 He sits in the lurking places of the
  villages;
  In the secret places he murders the
  innocent;
  His eyes are secretly fixed on the
  helpless.
9 He lies in wait secretly, as a lion in his
  den;
  He lies in wait to catch the poor;
  He catches the poor when he draws
  him into his net.
10 So he ᵀcrouches, he lies low,
  That the helpless may fall by his
  ᵀstrength.   Or *is crushed* · Or *mighty ones*
11 He has said in his heart,
  "God has forgotten;
  He hides His face;
  He will never see."

12 Arise, O Lᴏʀᴅ!
  O God, ᴿlift up Your hand!   Mic. 5:9
  Do not forget the ᴿhumble.   Ps. 9:12
13 Why do the wicked renounce God?
  He has said in his heart,
  "You will not require *an account.*"

14 But You have ᴿseen, for You observe
  trouble and grief,   [Ps. 11:4]
  To repay *it* by Your hand.
  The helpless commits himself to You;
  You are the helper of the fatherless.

15 Break the arm of the wicked and the
  evil *man;*
  Seek out his wickedness *until* You find
  none.
16 ᴿThe Lᴏʀᴅ *is* King forever and ever;
  The nations have perished out of His
  land.   Ps. 29:10
17 Lᴏʀᴅ, You have heard the desire of the
  humble;
  You will prepare their heart;
  You will cause Your ear to hear,
18 To ᵀdo justice to the fatherless and the
  oppressed,
  That the man of the earth may ᵀoppress
  no more.   *vindicate* · *terrify*

Psalm 11

Faith in the Lᴏʀᴅ's Righteousness
To the Chief Musician. A Psalm of David.

IN ᴿthe Lᴏʀᴅ I put my trust;   Ps. 56:11
  How can you say to my soul,
  "Flee *as* a bird to your mountain"?
2 For look! ᴿThe wicked bend *their* bow,
  They make ready their arrow on the
  string,
  That they may shoot ᵀsecretly at the
  upright in heart.   Ps. 64:3, 4 · Lit. *in darkness*
3 ᴿIf the foundations are destroyed,
  What can the righteous do?   Ps. 82:5

4 The Lᴏʀᴅ *is* in His holy temple,
  The Lᴏʀᴅ's ᴿthrone *is* in heaven;
  ᴿHis eyes behold,   [Is. 66:1] · [Ps. 33:18]
  His eyelids test the sons of men.
5 The Lᴏʀᴅ ᴿtests the righteous,
  But the wicked and the one who loves
  violence His soul hates.   Gen. 22:1
6 Upon the wicked He will rain coals;
  Fire and brimstone and a burning wind
  Shall be the portion of their cup.

7 For the Lᴏʀᴅ *is* righteous,
  He ᴿloves righteousness;   Ps. 33:5; 45:7
  *His countenance beholds the upright.

Psalm 12

Man's Treachery and God's Constancy
To the Chief Musician. On an *eight-stringed
harp. A Psalm of David.

HELP,ᵀ Lᴏʀᴅ, for the godly man ᴿceases!
  For the faithful disappear from among
  the sons of men.   *Save* · [Is. 57:1]
2 ᴿThey speak idly everyone with his
  neighbor;   Ps. 10:7; 41:6
  With flattering lips *and* ᵀa double heart
  they speak.   *An inconsistent mind*

3 May the Lᴏʀᴅ ᵀcut off all flattering lips,
  And the tongue that speaks ᵀproud
  things,   *destroy* · *great*

11:7 Or *The upright beholds His countenance*
12:title, Heb. *sheminith*

4 Who have said,
   "With our tongue we will prevail;
   Our lips *are* our own;
   Who *is* lord over us?"

5 "For the oppression of the poor, for the
   sighing of the needy,
   Now I will arise," says the LORD;
   "I will set *him* in the safety for which he
   yearns."

6 The words of the LORD *are* ᴿpure words,
   Like silver tried in a furnace of earth,
   Purified seven times.   2 Sam. 22:31

7 You shall keep them, O LORD,
   You shall preserve them from this
   generation forever.

8 The wicked prowl on every side,
   When vileness is exalted among the
   sons of men.

Psalm 13

Trust in the Salvation of the LORD
To the Chief Musician. A Psalm of David.

HOW long, O LORD? Will You forget me
   forever?
   ᴿHow long will You hide Your face from
   me?   Job 13:24
2 How long shall I take counsel in my
   soul,
   Having sorrow in my heart daily?
   How long will my enemy be exalted
   over me?

3 Consider *and* hear me, O LORD my God;
   ᴿEnlighten my eyes,   Ezra 9:8
   ᴿLest I sleep the *sleep of* death;   Jer. 51:39
4 Lest my enemy say,
   "I have prevailed against him";
   Lest those who trouble me rejoice
   when I am moved.

5 But I have trusted in Your mercy;
   My heart shall rejoice in Your
   salvation.
6 I will sing to the LORD,
   Because He has dealt bountifully with
   me.

Psalm 14

*Folly of the Godless, and God's Final
Triumph*
To the Chief Musician. A Psalm of David.

THE ᴿfool has said in his heart,
   "*There is* no God."   Ps. 10:4; 53:1
   They are corrupt,
   They have done abominable works,
   There is none who does good.

2 ᴿThe LORD looks down from heaven
   upon the children of men,

To see if there are any who understand,
   who seek God.   Ps. 33:13, 14; 102:19
3 ᴿThey have all turned aside,
   They have together become corrupt;
   There is none who does good,
   No, not one.   Rom. 3:12

4 Have all the workers of iniquity no
   knowledge,
   Who eat up my people *as* they eat
   bread,
   And ᴿdo not call on the LORD?   Is. 64:7
5 There they are in great fear,
   For God *is* with the generation of the
   righteous.
6 You shame the counsel of the poor,
   But the LORD *is* his ᴿrefuge.   Ps. 9:9; 40:17

7 ᴿOh, that the salvation of Israel *would
   come* out of Zion!   Ps. 53:6
   ᴿWhen the LORD brings back the
   captivity of His people,   Job 42:10
   Let Jacob rejoice *and* Israel be glad.

Psalm 15

*The Character of Those Who May Dwell
with the LORD*
A Psalm of David.

LORD, ᴿwho may ᵀabide in Your
   tabernacle?   Ps. 24:3-5 • *sojourn*
   Who may dwell in Your holy hill?

2 He who walks uprightly,
   And works righteousness,
   And speaks the truth in his heart;
3 He *who* ᴿdoes not backbite with his
   tongue,   [Lev. 19:16-18]
   Nor does evil to his neighbor,
   ᴿNor does he ᵀtake up a reproach
   against his friend;   Ex. 23:1 • *receive*
4 ᴿIn whose eyes a vile person is despised,
   But he honors those who fear the
   LORD;
   He *who* ᴿswears to his own hurt and
   does not change;   Esth. 3:2 • Lev. 5:4
5 He *who* does not put out his money at
   usury,
   Nor does he take a bribe against the
   innocent.
   He who does these *things* ᴿshall never
   be moved.   2 Pet. 1:10

Psalm 16

*The Hope of the Faithful, and the
Messiah's Victory*
A Michtam of David.

9-E. The Messiah Resurrected   ▼

PRESERVE me, O God, for in You I put
   my trust.

9-E. The Messiah Resurrected (Psalm 16:1-11)—On the day of Pentecost, Simon Peter, under the anointing
of the Holy Spirit, preached the crucifixion and resurrection of the Messiah (Acts 2:14-39, page 1089).
(Point 9-E continued on next page)

▽ 2 *O my soul,* you have said to the LORD,
"You *are* my Lord,
    ᴿMy goodness is nothing apart from
    You.   Job 35:7
3 As for the saints who *are* on the earth,
"They are the excellent ones, in ᴿwhom
    is all my delight."   Ps. 119:63
4 Their sorrows shall be multiplied who
    hasten *after* another *god;*
Their drink offerings of ᴿblood I will not
    offer,   Ps. 106:37, 38
Nor take up their names on my lips.
5 O LORD, *You are* the portion of my
    inheritance and my cup;
You ᵀmaintain my lot.   Lit. *uphold*
6 The lines have fallen to me in pleasant
    places;
Yes, I have a good inheritance.

7 I will bless the LORD who has given me
    counsel;
My ᵀheart also instructs me in the night
    seasons.   Mind, lit. *kidneys*
8 ᴿI have set the LORD always before me;
Because *He is* at my right hand I shall
    not be moved.   [Acts 2:25–28]
9 Therefore my heart is glad, and my
    glory rejoices;
My flesh also will rest in hope.
10 ᴿFor You will not leave my soul in
    Sheol,
Nor will You allow Your Holy One to
    see corruption.   [Ps. 49:15; Acts 2:31, 32]
11 You will show me the ᴿpath of life;
In Your presence *is* fullness of joy;
At Your right hand *are* pleasures
    forevermore.   [Matt. 7:14]

Psalm 17
Prayer with Confidence in Final Salvation
A Prayer of David.

HEAR a just cause, O LORD,
    Attend to my cry;

Give ear to my prayer *which is* not
    from deceitful lips.
2 Let my vindication come from Your
    presence;
Let Your eyes look on the things that
    are upright.

3 You have tested my heart;
You have visited *me* in the night;
    ᴿYou have ᵀtried me and have found
    ᵀnothing;   Job. 23:10 · examined · Nothing evil
I have purposed that my mouth shall
    not ᴿtransgress.   Ps. 39:1
4 Concerning the works of men,
By the word of Your lips,
I have kept away from the paths of the
    destroyer.
5 ᴿUphold my steps in Your paths,   Ps. 44:18
That my footsteps may not slip.

6 ᴿI have called upon You, for You will
    hear me, O God;
Incline Your ear to me, *and* hear my
    speech.   Ps. 86:7; 116:2
7 Show Your marvelous lovingkindness
    by Your right hand,
O You who save those who trust *in*
    You
From those who rise up *against them.*
8 Keep me as the ᵀapple of Your eye;
Hide me under the shadow of Your
    wings,   *pupil*
9 From the wicked who oppress me,
From my deadly enemies who surround
    me.

10 They have closed up their fat *hearts;*
With their mouths they speak proudly.
11 They have now surrounded us in our
    steps;
They have set their eyes, crouching
    down to the earth,
12 As a lion is eager to tear his prey,
And like a young lion lurking in secret
    places.

(Point 9-E continued from previous page)
Quoting from this messianic psalm, Peter reminded his listeners that David was a prophet: "Therefore, being a prophet, and knowing that God had sworn with an oath to him that of the fruit of his body, according to the flesh, He would raise up the Christ to sit on his throne" (Acts 2:30, page 1089).
   This psalm reveals the Messiah's hope, born of His perfect knowledge. The Messiah said, "My flesh also will rest in hope" (v. 9; cf. Acts 2:26, page 1089). His death, burial, and resurrection were not without hope. He expressed His hope in glad expectation. His hope was at the joyful side of Calvary, where He would be seated with the Father (Heb. 12:2, page 1250).
   His hope was anchored in the knowledge that God the Father would not leave His soul in hell (Hades—the place of departed souls). "Nor will You allow Your Holy One to see corruption" (v. 10; cf. Acts 2:27, page 1089): He also knew that His body of flesh, which would remain three days and three nights in the tomb, would not decay or undergo corruption, because it was a perfect, sinless, holy body. He knew that the prophecy would be fulfilled when His soul returned to His body, and the Father would raise Him and seat Him at His right hand. There He would remain until He returned to earth, to sit on the throne of David.
   Simon Peter concluded his interpretation of this great psalm by pointing his hearers (Acts 2:34–36, page 1089) to the fact that David could not have been speaking of his *own* death and burial because his body still lay, decaying, in the tomb. Instead, he spoke of Jesus Christ, who rose from the dead on the third day and is alive forever. Jesus Christ is the resurrected Messiah of Psalm 16.
   See Psalm 110:1–7, page 576, for **Point 9-F: The Messiah as High Priest.**

13 Arise, O LORD,
　Confront him, cast him down;
　Deliver my life from the wicked with
　　Your sword,
14 With Your hand from men, O LORD,
　From men of the world *who have* their
　　portion in *this* life,
　And whose belly You fill with Your
　　hidden treasure.
　They are satisfied with children,
　And leave the rest of their *possession*
　　for their babes.

15 As for me, ᴿI will see Your face in
　　righteousness;   [1 John 3:2]
　ᴿI shall be satisfied when I ᴿawake in
　　Your likeness.   Ps. 4:6, 7; 16:11 • [Is. 26:19]

Psalm 18

God the Sovereign Savior

To the Chief Musician. A Psalm of David the
servant of the LORD, who spoke to the LORD the
words of this song on the day that the LORD
delivered him from the hand of all his enemies
and from the hand of Saul.
And he said:

I WILL love You, O LORD, my strength.
　2 The LORD is my rock and my fortress
　　and my deliverer;
　My God, ᵀmy strength, ᴿin whom I will
　　trust;   Lit. *rock* • Heb. 2:13
　My shield and the ᵀhorn of my
　　salvation, my stronghold.   Strength
3 I will call upon the LORD, ᴿ*who is*
　worthy to be praised;   Rev. 5:12
　So shall I be saved from my enemies.

4 ᴿThe pangs of death surrounded me,
　And the floods of ᵀungodliness made me
　　afraid.   Ps. 116:3 • Lit. *Belial*
5 The sorrows of Sheol surrounded me;
　The snares of death confronted me.
6 In my distress I called upon the LORD,
　And cried out to my God;
　He heard my voice from His temple,
　And my cry came before Him, *even* to
　　His ears.

7 ᴿThen the earth shook and trembled;
　The foundations of the hills also quaked
　　and were shaken,
　Because He was angry.   Acts 4:31
8 Smoke went up from His nostrils,
　And devouring fire from His mouth;
　Coals were kindled by it.
9 ᴿHe bowed the heavens also, and came
　　down
　With darkness under His feet.   Ps. 144:5
10 And He rode upon a cherub, and flew;
　He flew upon the wings of the wind.
11 He made darkness His secret place;
　ᴿHis canopy around Him *was* dark
　　waters
　And thick clouds of the skies.   Ps. 97:2

12 ᴿFrom the brightness before Him,
　His thick clouds passed with hailstones
　　and coals of fire.   Ps. 97:3; 140:10
13 The LORD thundered from heaven,
　And the Most High uttered His voice,
　*Hailstones and coals of fire.
14 ᴿHe sent out His arrows and scattered
　　the foe,
　Lightnings in abundance, and He
　　vanquished them.   Ps. 144:6
15 Then the channels of the sea were seen,
　The foundations of the world were
　　uncovered
　At Your rebuke, O LORD,
　At the blast of the breath of Your
　　nostrils.

16 He sent from above, He took me;
　He drew me out of many waters.
17 He delivered me from my strong
　　enemy,
　From those who hated me,
　For they were too strong for me.
18 They confronted me in the day of my
　　calamity,
　But the LORD was my support.
19 ᴿHe also brought me out into a broad
　　place;
　He delivered me because He delighted
　　in me.   Ps. 4:1; 31:8; 118:5

20 ᴿThe LORD rewarded me according to
　　my righteousness;
　According to the cleanness of my hands
　He has recompensed me.   1 Sam. 24:19
21 For I have kept the ways of the LORD,
　And have not wickedly departed from
　　my God.
22 For all His judgments *were* before me,
　And I did not put away His statutes
　　from me.
23 I was also blameless ᵀbefore Him,   *with*
　And I kept myself from my iniquity.
24 ᴿTherefore the LORD has recompensed
　　me according to my righteousness,
　According to the cleanness of my hands
　　in His sight.   1 Sam. 26:23

25 ᴿWith the merciful You will show
　　Yourself merciful;
　With a blameless man You will show
　　Yourself blameless;   [1 Kin. 8:32]
26 With the pure
　　You will show Yourself pure;
　And ᴿwith the devious You will show
　　Yourself shrewd.   [Lev. 26:23-28]
27 For You will save the humble people,
　But will bring down haughty looks.

28 ᴿFor You will light my lamp;
　The LORD my God will enlighten my
　　darkness.   Job 18:6

18:13 So with MT, Tg., Vg.; a few Heb. mss., LXX omit
Hailstones and coals of fire

29 For by You I can run against a troop,
   By my God I can leap over a wall.
30 *As for* God, His way *is* perfect;
   The word of the LORD is proven;
   He *is* a shield to all who trust in Him.
31 For who *is* God, except the LORD?
   And who *is* a rock, except our God?
32 *It is* God who ᴿarms me with strength,
   And makes my way perfect.   [Ps. 91:2]
33 He makes my feet like the *feet of* deer,
   And sets me on my high places.
34 ᴿHe teaches my hands to make war,
   So that my arms can bend a bow of
   bronze.   Ps. 144:1
35 You have also given me the shield of
   Your salvation;
   Your right hand has held me up,
   Your gentleness has made me great.
36 You enlarged my path under me,
   ᴿSo my feet did not slip.   Prov. 4:12

37 I have pursued my enemies and
   overtaken them;
   Neither did I turn back again till they
   were destroyed.
38 I have wounded them,
   So that they could not rise;
   They have fallen under my feet.
39 For You have armed me with strength
   for the battle;
   You have subdued under me those who
   rose up against me.
40 You have also given me
   the necks of my enemies,
   So that I destroyed those who hated
   me.
41 They cried out, but *there was* none to
   save;
   ᴿ*Even* to the LORD, but He did not
   answer them.   Job 27:9
42 Then I beat them as fine as the dust
   before the wind;
   I cast them out like dirt in the streets.

43 You have delivered me from the
   strivings of the people;
   ᴿYou have made me the head of the
   ᵀnations;
   ᴿA people I have not known shall serve
   me.   2 Sam. 8 · *Gentiles* · Is. 52:15
44 As soon as they hear of me they obey
   me;
   The foreigners submit to me.
45 ᴿThe foreigners fade away,
   And come frightened from their
   hideouts.   Mic. 7:17

46 The LORD lives!
   Blessed *be* my Rock!
   Let the God of my salvation be exalted.
47 *It is* God who avenges me,
   And subdues the peoples under me;
48 He delivers me from my enemies.
   ᴿYou also lift me up above those who
   rise against me;
   You have delivered me from the violent
   man.   Ps. 27:6; 59:1
49 Therefore I will give thanks to You,
   O LORD, among the ᵀGentiles,   *nations*
   And sing praises to Your name.
50 ᴿGreat deliverance He gives to His king,
   And shows mercy to His anointed,
   To David and his ᵀdescendants
   forevermore.   Ps. 21:1; 144:10 · Lit. *seed*

Psalm 19

The Perfect Revelation of the LORD
To the Chief Musician. A Psalm of David.

THE ᵀheavens declare the glory of God;
   And the ᵀfirmament shows His
   handiwork.   *expanse* · *the work of His hands*
2 Day unto day utters speech,
   And night unto night reveals
   knowledge.
3 *There is* no speech nor language
   Where their voice is not heard.
4 ᴿTheir ᵀline* has gone out through all
   the earth,   Rom. 10:18 · *measuring line*
   And their words to the end of the
   world.

   In them He has set a ᵀtabernacle for
   the sun,   *tent*
5 Which *is* like a bridegroom coming out
   of his chamber,
   ᴿ*And* rejoices like a strong man to run
   its race.   Eccl. 1:5
6 Its rising *is* from one end of heaven,
   And its circuit to the other end;
   And there is nothing hidden from its
   heat.

2-A. Know What the Bible Says About   ▼
   Itself

7 ᴿThe law of the LORD *is* perfect,
   ᵀconverting the soul;   Ps. 111:7 · *restoring*
   The testimony of the LORD *is* sure,
   making ᴿwise the simple;   Ps. 119:130 ▲
8 The statutes of the LORD *are* right,
   rejoicing the heart;
   The commandment of the LORD *is* pure,
   enlightening the eyes;

19:4 LXX, [Syr.], Vg. *sound;* Tg. *business*

2-A. Know What the Bible Says About Itself (Psalm 19:7)—"The law [Word] of the LORD is perfect,
converting the soul; the testimony of the LORD is sure, making wise the simple" (v. 7; cf. 2 Tim. 3:16, page
1227). Before reading further, you should review Point 1-A, "The Bible Declares Itself to Be the Word of
God" (page 1227), which accurately defines the Scriptures. To further help you in studying the Bible it will
be of value to know that:

(Point 2-A continued on next page)

9 The fear of the LORD *is* clean, enduring
    forever;
    The judgments of the LORD *are* true
    and righteous altogether.
10 More to be desired *are they* than ᴿgold,
     Yea, than much fine gold;   Ps. 119:72, 127
     Sweeter also than honey and the
     ᵀhoneycomb.   *honey in the combs*
11 Moreover by them Your servant is
     warned,
     And in keeping them *there is* great
     reward.

12 Who can understand *his* errors?
     ᴿCleanse me from secret *faults.*   [Ps. 51:1, 2]
13 Keep back Your servant also from
     ᴿpresumptuous *sins;*   Num. 15:30
     Let them not have ᴿdominion over me.
     Then I shall be blameless,
     And I shall be innocent of ᵀgreat
     transgression.   Ps. 119:133 · Or *much*

14 ᴿLet the words of my mouth and the
     meditation of my heart
     Be acceptable in Your sight,
     O LORD, my ᵀstrength and my
     ᴿRedeemer.   Ps. 51:15 · Lit. *rock* · Is. 47:4

Psalm 20

The Assurance of God's Saving Work
To the Chief Musician. A Psalm of David.

MAY the LORD answer you in the day of
    trouble;
    May the name of the God of Jacob
    ᵀdefend you;   Lit. *set you on high*
2 May He send you help from the
   sanctuary,
   And strengthen you out of Zion;

3 May He remember all your offerings,
   And accept your burnt sacrifice.   Selah
4 May He grant you according to your
   heart's *desire,*
   And fulfill all your ᵀpurpose.   *counsel*
5 We will rejoice in your salvation,
   And in the name of our God we will set
   up *our* banners!
   May the LORD fulfill all your petitions.

6 Now I know that the LORD saves His
   ᵀanointed;
   He will answer him from His holy
   heaven
   With the saving strength of His right
   hand.   Commissioned one, Heb. *messiah*
7 Some *trust* in chariots, and some in
   ᴿhorses;
   But we will remember the name of the
   LORD our God.   Ps. 33:16, 17
8 They have bowed down and fallen;
   But we have risen and stand upright.

9 Save, LORD!
   May the King answer us when we call.

Psalm 21

Joy in the Salvation of the LORD
To the Chief Musician. A Psalm of David.

THE king shall have joy in Your strength,
    O LORD;
    And in Your salvation how greatly shall
    he rejoice!
2 You have given him his heart's desire,
   And have not withheld the ᴿrequest of
   his lips.   Selah   2 Sam. 7:26-29
3 For You meet him with the blessings of
   goodness;

(Point 2-A continued from previous page)

(1) "Forever, O LORD, Your word is settled in heaven" (Ps. 119:89, page 583). The contents of Holy Scripture, in every detail, were in the mind of God from all eternity. Only God has existed from everlasting (Ps. 90:2, page 564). The words we read in Scripture are the record of what God has thought from eternity! Should not our hands tremble as we take up this Book, realizing that it is our greatest earthly treasure? As we turn its pages and peruse its phrases, reading the very utterances and wisdom of God Himself, our study becomes an exciting, lively experience, and our appetite for such words as these becomes insatiable! This promise is a good place to begin as we think about the value of Bible study: "Heaven and earth will pass away, but My words will by no means pass away" (Mark 13:31, page 1003).

(2) "The Scripture cannot be broken" (John 10:35, page 1068). As we study the Bible, these words of Jesus ought to be engraved on our minds. He means that the Scripture, given by the Holy Spirit to holy men who recorded it exactly as it was given, cannot be altered in the slightest detail. All students of the Bible, throughout history, have made and will make mistakes in their *interpretation,* but this does not devalue the objective Word of God as He originally gave it and as it has been faithfully handed down under the superintending care of the Holy Spirit.

This fact calls for our most careful attention to the Scriptures. "Let God be true but every man a liar" (Rom. 3:4, page 1130). His Word is true, but no one understands it perfectly. Let us have no confidence in the flesh. We all make errors, but the pure truth of God lies before us in His Word. In a sense, we should approach each line of Scripture as if for the first time, depending on the Holy Spirit, because we cannot have fully grasped, in previous reading, all that God intended for us. We can never assume that we have absorbed the full intent of what God has for us in His Word. That full message of God is permanent, unbreakable, and unchanging.

See Genesis 1:1, page 2, for **Point 2-B: Know What God Intended the Bible to Do for You.**

You set a crown of pure gold upon his
head.
4 ᴿHe asked life from You, *and* You gave
it to him—   Ps. 61:5, 6; 133:3
Length of days forever and ever.
5 His glory *is* great in Your salvation;
Honor and majesty You have placed
upon him.
6 For You have made him most blessed
forever;
You have made him exceedingly glad
with Your presence.
7 For the king trusts in the Lᴏʀᴅ,
And through the mercy of the Most
High he shall not be ᵀmoved.   *shaken*
8 Your hand will find all Your enemies;
Your right hand will find those who
hate You.
9 You shall make them as a fiery oven in
the time of Your anger;
The Lᴏʀᴅ shall swallow them up in His
wrath,
And the fire shall devour them.
10 Their offspring You shall destroy from
the earth,
And their ᵀdescendants from among the
sons of men.   Lit. *seed*
11 For they intended evil against You;
They devised a plot *which* they are not
able *to* ᴿperform.   Ps. 2:1–4
12 Therefore You will make them turn
their back;
You will make ready *Your arrows* on
Your string toward their faces.

13 Be exalted, O Lᴏʀᴅ, in Your own
strength!
We will sing and praise Your power.

Psalm 22

*The Suffering, Praise, and Posterity of the
Messiah*

To the Chief Musician. Set to *"The Deer
of the Dawn." A Psalm of David.

▼ 9-D. The Messiah Crucified

Mʏ ᴿGod, My God, why have You
forsaken Me?   [Mark 15:34]
Why are You so far from helping Me,
And from the words of My groaning?
2 O My God, I cry in the daytime, but
You do not hear;
And in the night season, and am not
silent.

22:title, Heb. *Aijeleth Hashahar*

3 But You *are* holy,   ▽
Enthroned in the praises of Israel.
4 Our fathers trusted in You;
They trusted, and You delivered them.
5 They cried to You, and were delivered;
ᴿThey trusted in You, and were not
ashamed.   Is. 49:23
6 But I ᴿ*am* a worm, and no man;
ᴿA reproach of men, and despised by the
people.   Is. 41:14 • [Is. 53:3]
7 All those who see Me ridicule Me;
ᵀThey shoot out the lip, they shake the
head, *saying,* Show contempt with their mouth
8 "Heᵀ *trusted in the Lᴏʀᴅ, let Him
rescue Him; Lit. *He rolled himself on the Lᴏʀᴅ
ᴿLet Him deliver Him, since He delights
in Him!"   Ps. 91:14; Matt. 27:43
9 ᴿBut You *are* He who took Me out of
the womb;
You made Me trust *while* on My
mother's breasts.   [Ps. 71:5, 6]
10 I was cast upon You from birth.
From My mother's womb
ᴿYou *have been* My God.   [Is. 46:3; 49:1]
11 Be not far from Me,
For trouble *is* near;
For *there is* none to help.
12 ᴿMany bulls have surrounded Me;
Strong *bulls* of ᴿBashan have encircled
Me.   Ps. 22:21; 68:30 • Deut. 32:14
13 ᴿThey gape at Me *with* their mouths,
Like a raging and roaring lion.   Job 16:10
14 I am poured out like water,
ᴿAnd all My bones are out of joint;
My heart is like wax;
It has melted within Me.   Dan. 5:6
15 ᴿMy strength is dried up like a potsherd,
And ᴿMy tongue clings to My jaws;
You have brought Me to the dust of
death.   Prov. 17:22 • John 19:28
16 For dogs have surrounded Me;
The congregation of the wicked has
enclosed Me.
*They pierced My hands and My feet;
17 I can count all My bones.
ᴿThey look *and* stare at Me.   John 19:37
18 They divide My garments among them,
And for My clothing they cast lots.
19 But You, O Lᴏʀᴅ, do not be far from
Me;
O My Strength, hasten to help Me!
20 Deliver Me from the sword,

22:8 LXX, [Syr.], Vg. hoped; Tg. *praised*
22:16 So with some Heb. mss., LXX, Syr., Vg.; MT *Like a
lion* instead of *They pierced*

9-D. The Messiah Crucified (Psalm 22:1–31)—This is the psalm of the Messiah's crucifixion. It stands alone,
and is the very heart of the messianic psalms. This vivid prophecy of the Crucifixion was written a thousand
years before the Romans adopted (from the Phoenicians) this inhuman method of executing their criminals.
Compare the prophecies of this psalm with the accounts of the Crucifixion in the four Gospels—Matthew 27
(Point 9-D continued on next page)

▽   [R]My[T] precious *life* from the power of the
     dog.   Ps. 35:17 • Lit. *My only one*
21 [R]Save Me from the lion's mouth
     And from the horns of the wild oxen!
     [R]You have answered Me.   2 Tim. 4:17 • Is. 34:7

22 [R]I will declare Your name to My
     brethren;
     In the midst of the assembly I will
     praise You.   Mark 1:21, 39; Heb. 2:12
23 [R]You who fear the LORD, praise Him!
     All you [T]descendants of Jacob, glorify
     Him,
     And fear Him, all you offspring of
     Israel!   Ps. 135:19, 20 • Lit. *seed*
24 For He has not despised nor abhorred
     the affliction of the afflicted;
     Nor has He hidden His face from Him;
     But when He cried to Him, He heard.
25 [R]My praise *shall be* of You in the great
     assembly;
     [R]I will pay My vows before those who
     fear Him.   Ps. 35:18; 40:9, 10 • Eccl. 5:4

26 The poor shall eat and be satisfied;   ▽
     Those who seek Him will praise the
     LORD.
     Let your heart live forever!

27 All the ends of the world
     Shall remember and turn to the LORD,
     And all the families of the [T]nations
     Shall worship before *You.   Gentiles
28 [R]For the kingdom *is* the LORD's,
     And He rules over the nations.   Matt. 6:13

29 [R]All the prosperous of the earth
     Shall eat and worship;   Ps. 17:10; 45:12
     [R]All those who go down to [T]the dust
     Shall bow before Him,   [Is. 26:19] • Death
     Even he who cannot keep himself alive.

30 A posterity shall serve Him.
     It will be recounted of the Lord to the
     next generation,
31 They will come and declare His

22:27 So with MT, LXX, Tg.; Arab., Syr., Vg. *Him*

(Point 9-D continued from previous page)
(page 979); Mark 15 (page 1005); Luke 23 (page 1044); John 19 (page 1080)—and stand amazed at the accuracy of this prophetic picture of the crucifixion of the Messiah.

In verse 1 the Messiah cries, "My God, My God, why have You forsaken Me?" When Jesus repeated these words from the cross (Matt. 27:46, page 980), it was His hour, the hour that He would be "made . . . to be sin for us, that we might become the righteousness of God in Him" (2 Cor. 5:21, page 1169). His cry came from the agony of His holy soul. He abhors sin, but loves the sinner so much that, in order that we might be made righteous, He was willing to be made that which He abhors. It is impossible for mere human beings to grasp the full significance of these exceedingly bitter words from the cross. He was brutally disfigured, "more than any man" (Is. 52:14, page 693). Yet His *physical* suffering cannot be compared with His *spiritual* agony, when He took on our sin and thus became separated from His Father. We cannot understand how God the Father could forsake His Son, the God-Man. All we know is that it happened—when God the Son suffered the total penalty of the sins of mankind, crying out, "My God, My God, why have You forsaken Me?"

In verse 6 the Messiah says, "I am a worm, and no man." The people hated Him so much that they esteemed Him to be little more than a worm, and they treated Him as such. As He hung on the cross, in total agony, that vulgar mob expressed their contempt for Him physically in three kinds of mockery (v. 7):

(1) "All those who see Me ridicule Me."
(2) "They shoot out the lip."
(3) "They shake the head" (cf. Matt. 27:39, page 980).

In verse 8 the people say of Him, "He trusted in the LORD, let Him rescue Him; let Him deliver Him, since He delights in Him!" They mocked Him on the cross, saying, "If You are the Son of God, come down from the cross." The chief priests, scribes, and elders joined the people, saying, "He saved others; Himself He cannot save" (Matt. 27:40-43, page 980). The Messiah suffered the insults and contempt of the people in the hour of His crucifixion. No mere human could endure such suffering.

"All My bones are out of joint" (v. 14). The cross was His rack, an instrument of torture. The soldiers stretched Him upon the cross until His bones were out of their sockets. This is greater pain than the average human being can endure; yet Jesus endured it, refusing to take the wine mixed with gall to lessen this excruciating pain. Think of His agony when the cross was raised, then allowed to plunge into the hole in the ground with a sudden jolt. The pain was so intense that the Messiah says in verse 14, "My heart is like wax; it has melted within Me." His physical strength dried up like a potsherd (a piece of dried, broken earthenware).

Again He says in verse 16, "For dogs have surrounded Me." The wicked people milled around the cross, howling for His blood, for His death. He continues: "They pierced My hands and My feet." After His resurrection, Jesus would say to unbelieving Thomas, "Reach your finger here, and look at My hands" (John 20:24-29, page 1083). Thomas and the other disciples with him would see our Lord's nail-pierced hands, and believe in Him as Messiah.

In verse 18 the Messiah says, "They divide My garments among them, and for My clothing they cast lots." This prophecy was fulfilled by the Roman soldiers who nailed Him to the cross and gambled for His seamless tunic (John 19:23, 24, page 1081).

See Psalm 16:1-11, page 517, for **Point 9-E: The Messiah Resurrected.**

▽   righteousness to a people who will be
     born,
▲   That He has done *this.*

Psalm 23

The LORD the Shepherd of His People

A Psalm of David.

▼ **4-F. Jehovah-Rohi: The LORD My
Shepherd**

▲ THE LORD is ᴿmy shepherd;
     ᴿI shall not ᵀwant.   [Is. 40:11] • [Phil. 4:19] • *lack*
2 He makes me to lie down in ᵀgreen
     pastures;   Lit. *pastures of tender grass*
   He leads me beside the still waters.
3 He restores my soul;
   ᴿHe leads me in the paths of
     righteousness
   For His name's sake.   Ps. 5:8; 31:3

4 Yea, though I walk through the valley
     of the shadow of death,
   ᴿI will fear no evil;
   ᴿFor You *are* with me;
   Your rod and Your staff, they comfort
     me.   [Ps. 3:6; 27:1] • [Is. 43:2]

5 You ᴿprepare a table before me in the
     presence of my enemies;
   You ᴿanoint my head with oil;
   My cup runs over.   Ps. 104:15 • Ps. 92:10
6 Surely goodness and mercy shall follow
     me
   All the days of my life;
   And I will *dwell in the house of the
     LORD
   ᵀForever.   Lit. *For length of days*

   23:6 So with LXX, [Syr.], Tg., Vg.; MT *return*

Psalm 24

The King of Glory and His Kingdom

A Psalm of David.

THE ᴿearth *is* the LORD's, and all its
     fullness,   1 Cor. 10:26, 28
   The world and those who dwell therein.
2 For He has founded it upon the seas,
   And established it upon the waters.

3 ᴿWho may ascend into the hill of the
     LORD?   Ps. 15:1-5
   Or who may stand in His holy place?
4 He who has ᴿclean hands and ᴿa pure
     heart,   [Job 17:9] • [Matt. 5:8]
   Who has not lifted up his soul to an
     idol,
   Nor ᴿsworn deceitfully.   Ps. 15:4
5 He shall receive blessing from the LORD,
   And righteousness from the God of his
     salvation.
6 This *is* Jacob, the generation of those
     who ᴿseek Him,
   Who seek Your face.   Selah   Ps. 27:4, 8

7 Lift up your heads, O you gates!
   And be lifted up, you everlasting doors!
   And the King of glory shall come in.
8 Who *is* this King of glory?
   The LORD strong and mighty,
   The LORD mighty in ᴿbattle.   Rev. 19:13-16
9 Lift up your heads, O you gates!
   Lift up, you everlasting doors!
   And the King of glory shall come in.
10 Who is this King of glory?
   The LORD of hosts,
   He *is* the King of glory.   Selah

4-F: Jehovah-Rohi: The LORD My Shepherd (Psalm 23:1)—The name *Jehovah-Rohi* is the Hebrew beginning of Psalm 23. It is both a name of God and an affirmation of faith. David, out on the hills of Bethlehem in the cool nights, watched the sheep, knowing that bears, wolves, lions, and thieves menaced his flock and himself. He was the shepherd who watched for the sheep's welfare. But David affirms that Jehovah-Rohi watched over the shepherd's own needs and safety. "The LORD My Shepherd" was present to protect, lead, and provide pasture for David.

This marvelous truth leads us to the following conclusions:

(1) Just as David's Shepherd was Jehovah, so today every parent, as well as every spiritual, business, and political leader should realize that Jehovah is their Shepherd.

(2) We belong to God's flock by faith in Christ. Jesus made it clear that those who rejected Him took the devil to be their father and were not part of His flock (John 8:42, 44, page 1063).

(3) Christ declared, "I am the good shepherd." As proof, He spoke of His coming death: "The good shepherd gives His life for the sheep" (John 10:11, page 1067).

(4) Christ specifically denied that all other religious leaders who became founders of religions were also shepherds of humanity. He calls them "thieves and robbers" (John 10:8, page 1067).

(5) Christ spoke of having "other sheep" who would "also" come and "be one flock." Here He prophesied of the worldwide call of the Gentile believers to join with the Jewish believers in "one flock"— His true church (John 10:16, page 1067).

(6) All of the wonderful and happy benefits described in Psalm 23 belong to the believer, by virtue of his belonging to Christ—his wonderful, strong, thoughtful, and caring Shepherd.

When we need guidance, food, protection, or comfort, let us, like David of old, look beyond the hills to Jehovah-Rohi, "The LORD My Shepherd."

See Index, page 17, for your next study.

Psalm 25

A Plea for Deliverance and Forgiveness
A Psalm of David.

TO You, O LORD, I lift up my soul.
2 O my God, I ᴿtrust in You;   Ps. 34:8
    Let me not be ashamed;
    Let not my enemies triumph over me.

3 Indeed, let no one ᵀwho waits on You
        be ashamed;   Waits for You in faith
    Let those be ashamed who deal
        treacherously without cause.

4 ᴿShow me Your ways, O LORD;
    Teach me Your paths.   Ex. 33:13
5 Lead me in Your truth and teach me,
    For You are the God of my salvation;
    On You I wait all the day.

6 Remember, O LORD, Your tender
        mercies and Your lovingkindnesses,
    For they are from of old.
7 Do not remember the sins of my youth,
        nor my transgressions;
    According to Your mercy remember
        me,
    For Your goodness' sake, O LORD.

8 Good and upright is the LORD;
    Therefore He teaches sinners in the
        way.
9 The humble He guides in justice,
    And the humble He teaches His way.
10 All the paths of the LORD are mercy
        and truth,
    To such as keep His covenant and His
        testimonies.
11 ᴿFor Your name's sake, O LORD,   Ps. 79:9
    Pardon my iniquity, for it is great.

12 Who is the man that fears the LORD?
    ᴿHim shall ᵀHe teach in the way ᵀHe
        chooses.   [Ps. 25:8; 37:23] · Or he
13 ᴿHe himself shall dwell in ᵀprosperity,
    And ᴿhis descendants shall inherit the
        earth.   [Prov. 19:23] · Lit. goodness · Matt. 5:5
14 ᴿThe secret of the LORD is with those
        who fear Him,   [John 7:17]
    And He will show them His covenant.
15 ᴿMy eyes are ever toward the LORD,
    For He shall ᵀpluck my feet out of the
        net.   [Ps. 123:2; 141:8] · Lit. bring out

16 ᴿTurn Yourself to me, and have mercy
        on me,   Ps. 69:16
    For I am ᵀdesolate and afflicted.   lonely
17 The troubles of my heart have enlarged;
    Bring me out of my distresses!
18 ᴿLook on my affliction and my pain,
    And forgive all my sins.   2 Sam. 16:12
19 Consider my enemies, for they are
        many;
    And they hate me with cruel hatred.
20 Keep my soul, and deliver me;

Let me not be ashamed, for I put my
        trust in You.
21 Let integrity and uprightness preserve
        me,
    For I wait for You.

22 ᴿRedeem Israel, O God,
    Out of all their troubles!   [Ps. 130:8]

Psalm 26

A Prayer for Divine Scrutiny and Redemption
A Psalm of David.

VINDICATE ᴿme, O LORD,   Ps. 7:8
    For I have ᴿwalked in my integrity.
    ᴿI have also trusted in the LORD;
    I shall not slip.   2 Kin. 20:3 · [Ps. 13:5; 28:7]
2 Examine me, O LORD, and ᵀprove me;
    Try my mind and my heart.   test me
3 For Your lovingkindness is before my
        eyes,
    And I have walked in Your truth.
4 I have not ᴿsat with idolatrous mortals,
    Nor will I go in with hypocrites.   Ps. 1:1
5 I have ᴿhated the assembly of evildoers,
    And will not sit with the wicked.   Ps. 31:6

6 I will wash my hands in innocence;
    So I will go about Your altar, O LORD,
7 That I may proclaim with the voice of
        thanksgiving,
    And tell of all Your wondrous works.
8 LORD, ᴿI have loved the habitation of
        Your house,   Ps. 27:4; 84:1-4, 10
    And the place where Your glory dwells.

9 Do not gather my soul with sinners,
    Nor my life with bloodthirsty men,
10 In whose hands is a sinister scheme,
    And whose right hand is full of bribes.

11 But as for me, I will walk in my
        integrity;
    Redeem me and be merciful to me.
12 ᴿMy foot stands in an even place;
    In the congregations I will bless the
        LORD.   Ps. 40:2

Psalm 27

An Exuberant Declaration of Faith
A Psalm of David.

THE LORD is my ᴿlight and my salvation;
    Whom shall I fear?   [Mic. 7:8]
    The ᴿLORD is the strength of my life;
    Of whom shall I be afraid?   Ps. 62:7; 118:14
2 When the wicked came against me
    To ᴿeatᵀ up my flesh,   Ps. 14:4 · devour
    My enemies and foes,
    They ᴿstumbled and fell.   John 18:6
3 ᴿThough an army may encamp against
        me,
    My heart shall not fear;

Though war may rise against me,
In this I *will be* confident.   Ps. 3:6

4 ᴿOne *thing* I have desired of the LORD,
That will I seek: Ps. 26:8; 65:4
That I may ᴿdwell in the house of the
LORD
All the days of my life,   Luke 2:37
To behold the ᵀbeauty of the LORD,
And to inquire in His temple.   *delightfulness*

5 For ᴿin the time of trouble
He shall hide me in His pavilion;
In the secret place of His tabernacle
He shall hide me;   Ps. 31:20; 91:1
He shall set me high upon a rock.

6 And now ᴿmy head shall be ᵀlifted up
above my enemies all around me;
Therefore I will offer sacrifices of ᵀjoy
in His tabernacle;
I will sing, yes, I will sing praises to the
LORD.   Ps. 3:3 · Lifted up in honor · *joyous shouts*

7 Hear, O LORD, *when* I cry with my
voice!
Have mercy also upon me, and answer
me.

8 *When You said,* "Seek My face,"
My heart said to You, "Your face,
LORD, I will seek."

9 ᴿDo not hide Your face from me;
Do not turn Your servant away in
anger;
You have been my help;
Do not leave me nor forsake me,
O God of my salvation.   Ps. 69:17; 143:7

10 ᴿWhen my father and my mother
forsake me,   Is. 49:15
Then the LORD will take care of me.

11 ᴿTeach me Your way, O LORD,
And lead me in a smooth path, because
of my enemies.   Ps. 25:4; 86:11; 119:33

12 Do not deliver me to the will of my
adversaries;
For ᴿfalse witnesses have risen against
me,   Ps. 35:11; Matt. 26:60, 61
And such as breathe out violence.

13 *I would have lost heart,* unless I had
believed
That I would see the goodness of the
LORD
ᴿIn the land of the living.   Ezek. 26:20

14 ᴿWaitᵀ on the LORD;   Is. 25:9 · Wait in faith
Be of good courage,
And He shall strengthen your heart;
Wait, I say, on the LORD!

Psalm 28
Rejoicing in Answered Prayer
A Psalm of David.

TO You I will cry, O LORD my Rock:
ᴿDo not be silent to me,
ᴿLest, if You *are* silent to me,
I become like those who go down to
the pit.   Ps. 35:22; 39:12; 83:1 · Ps. 88:4; 143:7

2 Hear the voice of my supplications
When I cry to You,
ᴿWhen I lift up my hands ᴿtoward Your
holy sanctuary.   Ps. 5:7 · Ps. 138:2

3 Do not ᵀtake me away with the wicked
And with the workers of iniquity,
ᴿWho speak peace to their neighbors,
But evil *is* in their hearts.   *drag* · Ps. 12:2

4 ᴿGive them according to their deeds,
And according to the wickedness of
their endeavors;   [Rev. 18:6; 22:12]
Give them according to the work of
their hands;
Render to them what they deserve.

5 Because ᴿthey do not regard the works
of the LORD,
Nor the operation of His hands,
He shall destroy them
And not build them up.   Is. 5:12

6 Blessed *be* the LORD,
Because He has heard the voice of my
supplications!

7 The LORD *is* ᴿmy strength and my
shield;   Ps. 18:2; 59:17
My heart ᴿtrusted in Him, and I am
helped;   Ps. 13:5; 112:7
Therefore my heart greatly rejoices,
And with my song I will praise Him.

8 The LORD *is* *their strength,
And He *is* the saving refuge of His
ᵀanointed.   Commissioned one, Heb. *messiah*

9 Save Your people,
And bless ᴿYour inheritance;
Shepherd them also,   [Deut. 9:29; 32:9]
ᴿAnd bear them up forever.   Deut. 1:31

Psalm 29
Praise to God in His Holiness and
Majesty
A Psalm of David.

GIVEᵀ ᴿunto the LORD, O you mighty
ones,   Ascribe · 1 Chr. 16:28, 29
Give unto the LORD glory and strength.

28-A. Worship: Some Fundamentals   ▼

2 ᵀGive unto the LORD the glory due to
His name;   Lit. *of His name*

28:8 So with MT, Tg.; LXX, Syr., Vg. *the strength of His
people*

28-A. Worship: Some Fundamentals (Psalm 29:2)—

(1) *The Definition of Worship.* The dictionary definition of worship is "the reverence or veneration
tendered a divine being or supernatural power; respect, admiration, or devotion for an object of esteem."

(Point 28-A continued on next page)

▽
▲ Worship the LORD in ᴿthe ᵀbeauty of
holiness.   2 Chr. 20:21 • *majesty*

3 The voice of the LORD *is* over the
waters;
ᴿThe God of glory thunders;   [Job 37:4, 5]
The LORD *is* over many waters.

4 The voice of the LORD *is* powerful;
The voice of the LORD *is* full of majesty.

5 The voice of the LORD breaks ᴿthe
cedars,
Yes, the LORD splinters the cedars of
Lebanon.   Is. 2:13; 14:8

6 ᴿHe makes them also skip like a calf,
Lebanon and ᴿSirion like a young
wild ox.   Ps. 114:4 • Deut. 3:9

7 The voice of the LORD ᵀdivides the
flames of fire.   *stirs up,* lit. *hews out*

8 The voice of the LORD shakes the
wilderness;
The LORD shakes the Wilderness of
ᴿKadesh.   Num. 13:26

9 The voice of the LORD makes the ᴿdeer
give birth,
And strips the forests bare;
And in His temple everyone says,
"Glory!"   Job 39:1

10 The LORD sat *enthroned* at the Flood,
And the LORD sits as King forever.

11 ᴿThe LORD will give strength to His
people;
The LORD will bless His people with
peace.   Ps. 28:8; 68:35

Psalm 30
The Blessedness of Answered Prayer
A Psalm. A Song at the dedication
of the house of David.

I WILL extol You, O LORD, for You have
ᴿlifted me up,
And have not let my foes ᴿrejoice over
me.   Ps. 28:9 • Ps. 25:2

2 O LORD my God, I cried out to You,
And You ᴿhealed me.   Ps. 6:2; 103:3

3 O LORD, ᴿYou brought my soul up from
the grave;
You have kept me alive, *that I should
not go down to the pit.   Ps. 86:13

4 ᴿSing praise to the LORD, you saints of
His,
And give thanks at the remembrance of
ᵀHis holy name.   Ps. 97:12 • Or *His holiness*

5 For ᴿHis anger *is but for* a moment,
ᴿHis favor *is for* life;   Ps. 103:9 • Ps. 63:3
Weeping may endure for a night,
But joy *comes* in the morning.

6 Now in my prosperity I said,
"I shall never be ᵀmoved."   *shaken*

7 LORD, by Your favor You have made
my mountain stand strong;
You hid Your face, *and* I was troubled.

8 I cried out to You, O LORD;
And to the LORD I made supplication:

9 "What profit *is there* in my blood,
When I go down to the pit?

30:3 So with Qr., Tg.; Kt., LXX, Syr., Vg. *from those who
descend to the pit*

(Point 28-A continued from previous page)
A simpler understanding of worship is in the very root of the English word, which is "worth-ship." In other words, it is the state of gladly recognizing the supreme worth of God. It is not coming to God to get something, as in prayer; it is not evangelizing people to bring them to God; it is not learning the Scriptures; rather it is heartfelt love, appreciation, an adoration of God for who He is and what He has done (Deut. 6:4, 5, page 187). One of the best illustrations of pure worship is a loyal dog, who will lie at its master's feet, gazing in adoration and seeking nothing but the privilege of being in his presence. Worship is difficult to define in cold print, because it is an exercise of the heart. As the Scottish lady put it, "It's better felt than telt." The Bible is full of worship. It is a book of worship from cover to cover. The most popular book in the Old Testament, the Psalms, is largely a worship book in poetic form.

(2) *The Object of Worship.* "For it is written, 'You shall worship the LORD your God, and Him only you shall serve' " (Matt. 4:10, page 934). In this quotation from Deuteronomy 6:13 (page 187), our Lord rebukes Satan for suggesting that Christ should worship him. The only true object of worship is God. That Jesus Himself received worship and is accorded worship in the book of the Revelation and elsewhere, is further evidence that He is the Son of God and God the Son. The Father, the Son, and the Holy Spirit are co-equal and co-eternal, and deserve equal honor in our worship. Anyone less than God, no matter how beloved or revered, should not be worshiped. The worship of angels (a heresy that apparently existed in Colosse), the adoration of the Virgin Mary or other "saints," the virtual deification of high-ranking church officials, are all completely forbidden by the Word of God. Only one is worthy of worship: our Creator and Redeemer, the one true God, eternally existent as Father, Son, and Holy Spirit.

In Acts 10:26 (page 1103) Peter refused to let Cornelius kneel before him, uttering a strong rebuke: "Stand up; I myself am also a man." Likewise, in the very last chapter of Revelation, the apostle John was so overwhelmed by what he had seen in the visions revealed to him by the angel, that he fell down to worship him. The angel answered, "See that you do not do that. For I am your fellow servant, and of your brethren the prophets, and of those who keep the words of this book. Worship God" (Rev. 22:9, page 1316). From start to finish the Bible makes it clear that there is only one true Object of worship as concisely summarized by the angel in Revelation 22:9: "Worship God."

See Psalm 5:7, page 512, for **Point 28-B: Worship in the Old Testament.**

^RWill the dust praise You?
Will it declare Your truth?   [Ps. 6:5]

10 Hear, O LORD, and have mercy on me;
LORD, be my helper!"

11 ^RYou have turned for me my mourning
into dancing;   Jer. 31:4
You have put off my sackcloth and
clothed me with gladness,

12 To the end that *my* ^Tglory may sing
praise to You and not be silent.
O LORD my God, I will give thanks to
You forever.   Soul

Psalm 31

The LORD a Fortress in Adversity

To the Chief Musician. A Psalm of David.

I N You, O LORD, ^TI put my trust;
Let me never be ashamed;   *have taken refuge*
Deliver me in Your righteousness.

2 Bow down Your ear to me,
Deliver me speedily;
Be my rock of ^Trefuge,   *strength*
A fortress of defense to save me.

3 ^RFor You *are* my rock and my fortress;
Therefore, for Your name's sake,
Lead me and guide me.   [Ps. 18:2]

4 Pull me out of the net which they have
secretly laid for me,
For You *are* my strength.

5 ^RInto Your hand I commit my spirit;
You have redeemed me, O LORD God of
^Rtruth.   Luke 23:46 • [Deut. 32:4]

6 I have hated those ^Rwho regard useless
idols;
But I trust in the LORD.   Jon. 2:8

7 I will be glad and rejoice in Your
mercy,
For You have considered my trouble;
You have ^Rknown my soul in
^Tadversities,   [John 10:27] • *troubles*

8 And have not ^Tshut me up into the
hand of the enemy;   *given me over*
You have set my feet in a wide place.

9 Have mercy on me, O LORD, for I am in
trouble;
^RMy eye wastes away with grief,   Ps. 6:7
Yes, my soul and my ^Tbody!   Lit. *belly*

10 For my life is spent with grief,
And my years with sighing;
My strength fails because of my
iniquity,
And my bones waste away.

11 I am a reproach among all my enemies,
But especially among my neighbors,
And *am* repulsive to my acquaintances;
Those who see me outside flee from me.

12 ^RI am forgotten like a dead man, out of
mind;   Ps. 88:4, 5
I am like ^Ta broken vessel.   Lit. *perishing*

13 ^RFor I hear the slander of many;
^RFear *is* on every side;

While they ^Rtake counsel together
against me,   Jer. 20:10 • Lam. 2:22 • Matt. 27:1
They scheme to take away my life.

14 But as for me, I trust in You, O LORD;
I say, "You *are* my God."

15 My times *are* in Your ^Rhand;
Deliver me from the hand of my
enemies,   [Job 14:5; 24:1]
And from those who persecute me.

16 ^RMake Your face shine upon Your
servant;   Ps. 4:6; 80:3
Save me for Your mercies' sake.

17 ^RDo not let me be ashamed, O LORD, for
I have called upon You;   Ps. 25:2, 20
Let the wicked be ashamed;
Let them be silent in the grave.

18 ^RLet the lying lips be put to silence,
Which ^Rspeak insolent things proudly
and contemptuously against the
righteous.   Ps. 109:2; 120:2 • Ps. 94:4

19 ^ROh, how great *is* Your goodness,
Which You have laid up for those who
fear You,   [Rom. 2:4; 11:22]
Which You have prepared for those
who trust in You
In the presence of the sons of men!

20 ^RYou shall hide them in the secret place
of Your presence   [Ps. 27:5; 32:7]
From the plots of man;
^RYou shall keep them secretly in ^Ta
pavilion   Job 5:21 • *shelter*
From the strife of tongues.

21 Blessed *be* the LORD,
For He has shown me His marvelous
kindness in a ^Tstrong city!   *fortified*

22 For I said in my haste,
"I am cut off from before Your eyes";
Nevertheless You heard the voice of my
supplications
When I cried out to You.

23 Oh, love the LORD, all you His saints!
For the LORD preserves the faithful,
And fully repays the proud person.

24 ^RBe of good courage,
And He shall strengthen your heart,
All you who hope in the LORD.   [Ps. 27:14]

Psalm 32

The Joy of Forgiveness

A Psalm of David. A *Contemplation.

B LESSED *is* he whose ^Rtransgression *is*
forgiven,
Whose sin *is* covered.   [Ps. 85:2; 103:3]

2 Blessed *is* the man to whom the LORD
does not ^Timpute iniquity,   *charge*
And in whose spirit *there is* no deceit.

3 When I kept silent, my bones grew old
Through my groaning all the day long.

32:title, Heb. *Maschil*

4 For day and night Your ᴿhand was
   heavy upon me;
My vitality was turned into the drought
   of summer. Selah   1 Sam. 5:6
5 I acknowledged my sin to You,
And my iniquity I have not hidden.
ᴿI said, "I will confess my transgressions
   to the Lᴏʀᴅ,"
And You forgave the iniquity of my sin.
   Selah   [Prov. 28:13]

6 ᴿFor this cause everyone who is godly
   shall ᴿpray to You   [1 Tim. 1:16] • Is. 55:6
In a time when You may be found;
Surely in a flood of great waters
They shall not come near him.
7 ᴿYou *are* my hiding place;
You shall preserve me from trouble;
You shall surround me with ᴿsongs of
   deliverance. Selah   Ps. 9:9 • Ex. 15:1

8 I will instruct you and teach you in the
   way you should go;
I will guide you with My eye.
9 Do not be like the ᴿhorse *or* like the
   mule,   Prov. 26:3
Which have no understanding,
Which must be harnessed with bit and
   bridle,
Else they will not come near you.

10 ᴿMany sorrows *shall be* to the wicked;
But ᴿhe who trusts in the Lᴏʀᴅ, mercy
   shall surround him.   [Rom. 2:9] • Prov. 16:20
11 ᴿBe glad in the Lᴏʀᴅ and rejoice, you
   righteous;

33:7 LXX, Tg., Vg. *in a vessel*

And shout for joy, all *you* upright in
   heart!   Ps. 64:10; 68:3; 97:12

Psalm 33

The Sovereignty of the Lᴏʀᴅ in Creation and History

R EJOICE in the Lᴏʀᴅ, O you righteous!
   For praise from the upright is beautiful.
2 Praise the Lᴏʀᴅ with the harp;
ᵀMake melody to Him with an
   instrument of ten strings. Lit. *Sing to Him*
3 Sing to Him a new song;
Play skillfully with a shout of joy.

4 For the word of the Lᴏʀᴅ *is* right,
And all His work *is done* in truth.
5 He loves righteousness and justice;
The earth is full of the goodness of the
   Lᴏʀᴅ.

6 ᴿBy the word of the Lᴏʀᴅ the heavens
   were made,   [Heb. 11:3]
And all the ᴿhost of them ᴿby the
   breath of His mouth.   Gen. 2:1 • [Job 26:13]
7 ᴿHe gathers the waters of the sea
   together *as a heap;   Job 26:10; 38:8
He lays up the deep in storehouses.

27-B. Fear, Godly

8 Let all the earth fear the Lᴏʀᴅ;
Let all the inhabitants of the world
   stand in awe of Him.
9 For ᴿHe spoke, and it was *done;*
He commanded, and it stood fast. Gen. 1:3

10 ᴿThe Lᴏʀᴅ brings the counsel of the
   nations to nothing;

27-B. Fear, Godly (Psalm 33:8)—"Let all the earth fear the Lᴏʀᴅ" (v. 8). All the earth will fear the Lord in His coming kingdom. Till then we thank God for those who fear Him in this sin-sick world (Rom. 3:18, page 1131). Let us remember:

(1) The fear of the Lord is the beginning of knowledge and wisdom (Prov. 1:7, page 598; 15:33, page 610).
(2) The fear of the Lord is godly fear (Heb. 12:28, page 1251).
(3) The fear of the Lord is righteous fear, "He loves righteousness" (Ps. 33:5, page 529).
(4) The fear of the Lord is holy fear (2 Cor. 7:1, page 1169).
(5) The fear of the Lord is reverential fear (Heb. 12:28, page 1251).
(6) The fear of the Lord is to stand in awe of Him. "Let all the inhabitants of the world stand in awe of Him" (Ps. 33:8, page 529).
(7) To fear the Lord is to worship Him in spirit and truth (John 4:24, page 1054).
(8) To fear the Lord is to "serve God acceptably with reverence and godly fear" (Heb. 12:28, page 1251).

Godly fear brings joy. The psalmist said, "Rejoice in the Lᴏʀᴅ, O you righteous! . . . Praise the Lᴏʀᴅ with the harp. . . . Sing to Him a new song" (Ps. 33:1–3, page 529). Speaking of joy, the apostle John said, "These things we write to you that your joy may be full. This is the message . . . that God is light" (1 John 1:4, 5, page 1278).

Is there godly fear in your heart? To be sure that you have godly fear, examine the following verses in 1 John 1:6–10 (page 1278).

(1) "If we [who say we are believers] say that we have fellowship with Him [the Lord Jesus Christ], and walk in darkness [live in known, unconfessed sin], we lie and do not practice the truth" (1 John 1:6, page 1278; cf. Acts 5:1–4, page 1093).
(2) "But if we walk in the light as He is in the light, we have fellowship with one another [we have fellowship with God because we are in His light—His righteousness], and the blood of Jesus Christ His Son

(Point 27-B continued on next page)

He makes the plans of the peoples of no
effect.   Is. 8:10; 19:3

11 ᴿThe counsel of the LORD stands forever,
The plans of His heart to all
generations.   [Job 23:13]

12 Blessed *is* the nation whose God *is* the
LORD,
The people He has ᴿchosen as His own
inheritance.   [Ex. 19:5]

13 ᴿThe LORD looks from heaven;
He sees all the sons of men.   Job 28:24

14 From the place of His dwelling He looks
On all the inhabitants of the earth;

15 He fashions their hearts individually;
He ᵀconsiders all their works.   *understands*

16 ᴿNo king *is* saved by the multitude of an
army;
A mighty man is not delivered by great
strength.   Ps. 44:6; 60:11

17 ᴿA horse *is* a ᵀvain hope for safety;
Neither shall it deliver *any* by its great
strength.   [Prov. 21:31] · *false*

18 ᴿBehold, the eye of the LORD *is* on those
who fear Him,   [Job 36:7]
On those who hope in His mercy,

19 To deliver their soul from death,
And to keep them alive in famine.

20 Our soul waits for the LORD;
He *is* our help and our shield.

21 For our heart shall rejoice in Him,
Because we have trusted in His holy
name.

22 Let Your mercy, O LORD, be upon us,
Just as we hope in You.

Psalm 34

The Happiness of Those Who Trust in God

A Psalm of David when he pretended madness
before Abimelech, who drove him away,
and he departed.

I WILL ᴿbless the LORD at all times;
His praise *shall* continually *be* in my
mouth.   [Eph. 5:20]

2 My soul shall make its boast in the
LORD;
The humble shall hear *of it* and be glad.

3 Oh, magnify the LORD with me,
And let us exalt His name together.

27-E. Fear: Its Objects   ▼

4 I sought the LORD, and He heard me,
And delivered me from all my fears.   ▲

5 They looked to Him and were radiant,
And their faces were not ashamed.

6 This poor man cried out, and the LORD
heard *him*,
And saved him out of all his troubles.

7 The ᵀangel of the LORD ᴿencamps all
around those who fear Him,
And delivers them.   Or *Angel* · 2 Kin. 6:17

8 Oh, ᴿtaste and see that the LORD *is*
good;   1 Pet. 2:3
Blessed *is* the man *who* trusts in Him!

9 Oh, fear the LORD, you His saints!
There is no ᵀwant to those who fear
Him.   *lack*

10 The young lions lack and suffer hunger;
ᴿBut those who seek the LORD shall not
lack any good *thing*.   [Ps. 84:11]

(Point 27-B continued from previous page)
cleanses us from all sin" (1 John 1:7, page 1278; cf. Rev. 1:5, page 1293). Godly fear can be known only by those who have been cleansed by the precious blood of Jesus (1 Pet. 1:18, 19, page 1263).

(3) "If we say that we have no sin, we deceive ourselves, and the truth is not in us" (1 John 1:8, page 1278; cf. Gal. 6:7, 8, page 1184).

(4) "If we confess our sins, He is faithful and just to forgive us our sins and to cleanse us from all unrighteousness" (1 John 1:9, page 1278). To be cleansed by the blood brings the lost or unsaved into a relationship with God the Father. To be cleansed from sins which you commit after you are born into the family of God, you must confess them to our Lord, calling each known sin by name. Godly fear will cause you to search your heart every time you go to God in prayer; and if you find any unconfessed sin in your heart, however small, judge it, confess it, and forsake it. Practice 1 John 1:9 every day, and thus stay in fellowship with the Lord.

(5) "If we say that we have not sinned, we make Him a liar, and His Word is not in us" (1 John 1:10, page 1278). Godly fear will not let you say, "I have no sin," or "I cannot sin in the flesh," or "I have not sinned since the Lord saved me." Yet godly fear can also help you to resist temptation (1 Cor. 10:13, page 1155).

"My little children, these things I write to you, so that you may not sin. And if anyone sins, we have an Advocate with the Father, Jesus Christ the righteous" (1 John 2:1, page 1278).

See Genesis 15:1, page 20, for **Point 27-C: Fear Not: God Is Your Protector.**

27-E. Fear: Its Objects (Psalm 34:4)—The following are some of the objects of fear:

(1) *Manifestations of Deity.* When John was exiled to the island of Patmos, he was visited by the risen, glorified Christ (Rev. 1:12-17, page 1293). John records that "I fell at His feet as dead," but Jesus reassured him, saying, "Do not be afraid." See Daniel 8:15-17 (page 848) for a similar visitation of the Lord.

(2) *Manifestations of angels.*

(Point 27-E continued on next page)

11 Come, you children, listen to me;
    I will teach you the fear of the LORD.
12 ᴿWho is the man who desires life,
    And loves many days, that he may see
    good?   [1 Pet. 3:10-12]
13 Keep your tongue from evil,
    And your lips from speaking deceit.
14 ᴿDepart from evil and do good;   Ps. 37:27
    ᴿSeek peace and pursue it.   [Rom. 14:19]

15 ᴿThe eyes of the LORD are on the
    righteous,   Job 36:7

And His ears are open to their cry.
16 ᴿThe face of the LORD is against those
    who do evil,   Lev. 17:10
    ᴿTo ᵀcut off the remembrance of them
    from the earth.   [Prov. 10:7] • destroy

17 The righteous cry out, and ᴿthe LORD
    hears,
    And delivers them out of all their
    troubles.   Ps. 34:6; 145:19
18 ᴿThe LORD is near ᴿto those who have a
    broken heart,   [Ps. 145:18] • [Is. 57:15]

(Point 27-E continued from previous page)
    (a) The aged priest Zacharias and his wife Elizabeth had no children (Elizabeth was barren), but longed and prayed for a child. One day, as Zacharias was burning incense in the temple, an angel of the Lord appeared to him. When he saw the angel, Zacharias was gripped by fear (Luke 1:5-25, page 1009).
    (b) When Jesus was born in Bethlehem, the shepherds were keeping watch over their flocks: "And behold, an angel of the Lord stood before them, and the glory of the Lord shone around them, and they were greatly afraid" (Luke 2:9, page 1012).
    (c) As the Roman soldiers guarded the tomb of Jesus, "an angel of the Lord descended from heaven, and came and rolled back the stone from the door, and sat on it. . . . And the guards shook for fear of him, and became like dead men" (Matt. 28:1-4, page 981). They were momentarily petrified with fear.

    (3) Fear of meeting God in our sins. The first mention of fear in the Bible is in Genesis 3 (page 5), when Adam and Eve sinned in the Garden of Eden. The Word says, "The eyes of both of them were opened, and they knew that they were naked" (Gen. 3:7, page 6). As we commonly do when we sin, they tried to deceive God. They made coverings for their nakedness out of fig leaves, and when they heard the voice of God they tried to hide. When God called out, "Where are you?" Adam finally appeared and made a fourfold confession (Gen. 3:9, 10, page 6):

    (a) "I heard Your voice."
    (b) "I was afraid." Adam and Eve had never known fear before. Now that they had sinned, they experienced guilt and fear.
    (c) "I was naked." Before they sinned, they had been clothed in innocence, free from guilt and the fear of judgment; but now as sinners they feared their Creator, who made them, loved them, and provided for them.
    (d) "I hid myself." God knew where they were, but Adam thought that they were well concealed. He soon learned that you cannot hide from our omnipotent, omniscient, omnipresent God!

    At the first mention of fear, God was gracious and merciful. He provided a covering of animal skins for Adam and Eve before He removed them from the Garden of Eden (Gen. 3:21, page 7). He gave them the promise of a Redeemer, who would come and shed His blood and cover their sins.
    The last mention of fear in the Bible is in Revelation 21:8 (page 1315). There we come to the end of all the dispensations of mankind, from Adam to the new heaven and the new earth. And the Lord says, "But the cowardly, unbelieving, abominable, murderers, sexually immoral, sorcerers, idolaters, and all liars shall have their part in the lake which burns with fire and brimstone, which is the second death" (Rev. 21:8, page 1315).
    (4) Fear of serving God in fleshly wisdom. The apostle Paul journeyed to Corinth and preached the gospel of the Lord Jesus Christ. Later he wrote back to the church at Corinth, "I was with you in weakness, in fear, and in much trembling." Paul was saying, in effect, "When I preached the gospel to you in Corinth, I feared lest I should do it in fleshly wisdom"; therefore, "my speech and my preaching were not with persuasive words of human wisdom, but in demonstration of the Spirit and of power" (1 Cor. 2:1-5, page 1148). Fear of serving God in the energy of the flesh is a good fear. We should strive to "do all in the name of the Lord Jesus, giving thanks to God the Father through Him" (Col. 3:17, page 1207).
    (5) Fear of the end times. At the end of the dispensation of the church age, and at the beginning of the Great Tribulation, "they will fall by the edge of the sword, and be led away captive into all nations. And Jerusalem will be trampled by Gentiles until the times of the Gentiles are fulfilled" (Luke 21:24, page 1041). The "times of the Gentiles" will end with the Tribulation.
    (6) Fear of death. The Lord Jesus Christ came to earth to die on Calvary, where He conquered death. To the believer, there need be no fear of death. Death has been conquered; death has been defeated. Through death Jesus destroyed "him who had the power of death, that is, the devil." He defeated Satan and death, delivering "those who through fear of death were all their lifetime subject to bondage" (Heb. 2:14, 15, page 1237). It is sad to see many who profess to believe in the Lord Jesus Christ, yet live in the dread of physical death. When Jesus returns to this earth, He will raise the bodies of all the saints who have experienced physical death. The Word of God tells us, "There shall be no more death" (Rev. 21:4, page 1315). This will be the end of death and fear for all eternity.

    See Index, page 17, for your next study.

And saves such as ᵀhave a contrite
spirit.   *are crushed in spirit*

19 ᴿMany *are* the afflictions of the
righteous,
ᴿBut the LORD delivers him out of them
all.   Prov. 24:16 · Ps. 34:4, 6, 17
20 He guards all his bones;
ᴿNot one of them is broken.   John 19:33, 36
21 ᴿEvil shall slay the wicked,
And those who hate the righteous shall
be ᵀcondemned.   Ps. 94:23; 140:11 · *held guilty*
22 The LORD ᴿredeems the soul of His
servants,
And none of those who trust in Him
shall be condemned.   1 Kin. 1:29

Psalm 35

The LORD the Avenger of His People

A Psalm of David.

PLEADᵀ *my cause,* O LORD, with those
who strive with me;
Fight against those who fight against
me.   *Contend for me*
2 Take hold of shield and ᵀbuckler,
And stand up for my help.   A small shield
3 Also draw out the spear,
And stop those who pursue me.
Say to my soul,
"I *am* your salvation."

4 ᴿLet those be put to shame and brought
to dishonor   Ps. 40:14, 15; 70:2, 3
Who seek after my life;
Let those be ᴿturned back and brought
to confusion
Who plot my hurt.   Ps. 129:5
5 ᴿLet them be like chaff before the wind,
And let the ᵀangel of the LORD chase
them.   Job 21:18 · Or *Angel*
6 Let their way be ᴿdark and slippery,
And let the angel of the LORD pursue
them.   Ps. 73:18
7 For without cause they have ᴿhidden
their net for me *in* a pit,
Which they have dug without cause for
my life.   Ps. 9:15
8 Let ᴿdestruction come upon him
unexpectedly,   [1 Thess. 5:3]
And let his net that he has hidden
catch himself;
Into that very destruction let him fall.

9 And my soul shall be joyful in the
LORD;
It shall rejoice in His salvation.
10 ᴿAll my bones shall say,
"LORD, ᴿwho *is* like You,
Delivering the poor from him who is
too strong for him,
Yes, the poor and the needy from him
who plunders him?"   Ps. 51:8 · [Ex. 15:11]

11 ᴿFierce witnesses rise up;   Mark 14:57, 58
They ask me *things* that I do not know.

12 ᴿThey reward me evil for good,
To the sorrow of my soul.   John 10:32
13 But as for me, ᴿwhen they were sick,
My clothing *was* sackcloth;
I humbled myself with fasting;
And my prayer would return to my
own ᵀheart.   Job 30:25 · Lit. *bosom*
14 I paced about as though *he were* my
friend *or* brother;
I bowed down ᵀheavily, as one who
mourns *for his* mother.   *in mourning*
15 But in my ᵀadversity they rejoiced
And gathered together;   *limping, stumbling*
Attackers gathered against me,
And I did not know *it;*
They tore *at me* and did not cease;
16 With ungodly mockers at feasts
They gnashed at me with their teeth.

17 Lord, how long will You ᴿlook on?
Rescue me from their destructions,
My precious *life* from the lions. [Hab. 1:13]
18 I will give You thanks in the great
assembly;
I will praise You among many people.

19 ᴿLet them not rejoice over me who are
wrongfully my enemies;   Ps. 69:4; 109:3
Nor let them wink with the eye who
ᴿhate me without a cause.   John 15:24, 25
20 For they do not speak peace,
But they devise deceitful matters
Against *the* quiet ones in the land.
21 They also opened their mouth wide
against me,
And said, "Aha, aha!
Our eyes have seen *it.*"

22 *This* You have seen, O LORD;
Do not keep silence.
O Lord, do not be far from me.
23 Stir up Yourself, and awake to my
vindication,
To my cause, my God and my Lord.
24 Vindicate me, O LORD my God,
according to Your righteousness;
And let them not rejoice over me.
25 Let them not say in their hearts, "Ah,
so we would have it!"
Let them not say, "We have swallowed
him up."

26 Let them be ashamed and brought to
mutual confusion
Who rejoice at my hurt;
Let them be ᴿclothed with shame and
dishonor   Ps. 109:29
Who exalt themselves against me.

27 ᴿLet them shout for joy and be glad,
Who favor my righteous cause;
And let them say continually,
"Let the LORD be magnified,
Who has pleasure in the prosperity of
His servant."   Rom. 12:15

28 And my tongue shall speak of Your
    righteousness
    And of Your praise all the day long.

Psalm 36

Man's Wickedness and God's Perfections

To the Chief Musician. A Psalm of David
the servant of the LORD.

AN oracle within my heart concerning the
    transgression of the wicked:
    There is no fear of God before his eyes.
2 For he flatters himself in his own eyes,
    When he finds out his iniquity *and*
        when he hates.
3 The words of his mouth *are* wickedness
        and deceit;
    ᴿHe has ceased to be wise *and* to do
        good.   Jer. 4:22
4 ᴿHe devises wickedness on his bed;
    He sets himself ᴿin a way *that is* not
        good;   Prov. 4:16 • Is. 65:2
    He does not ᵀabhor evil.   *reject, loathe*
5 Your mercy, O LORD, *is* in the heavens;
    Your faithfulness *reaches* to the clouds.
6 Your righteousness *is* like the ᵀgreat
        mountains;   Lit. *mountains of God*
    Your judgments *are* a great deep;
    O LORD, You preserve man and beast.
7 How precious *is* Your lovingkindness, O
        God!
    Therefore the children of men ᴿput
        their trust under the shadow of Your
        wings.   Ps. 17:8; 57:1; 91:4
8 ᴿThey are abundantly satisfied with the
        fullness of Your house,   Ps. 63:5; 65:4
    And You give them drink from ᴿthe
        river of Your pleasures.   Rev. 22:1
9 For with You *is* the fountain of life;
    ᴿIn Your light we see light.   [1 Pet. 2:9]
10 Oh, continue Your lovingkindness to
        those who know You,
    And Your righteousness to the upright
        in heart.
11 Let not the foot of pride come against
        me,
    And let not the hand of the wicked
        drive me away.
12 There the workers of iniquity have
        fallen;
    They have been cast down and are not
        able to rise.

Psalm 37

The Heritage of the Righteous and the Calamity of the Wicked

A Psalm of David.

DOᴿ not fret because of evildoers,
    Nor be envious of the workers of
        iniquity.   Ps. 73:3
2 For they shall soon be cut down ᴿlike
        the grass,   Ps. 90:5, 6; 92:7
    And wither as the green herb.

3 Trust in the LORD, and do good;
    Dwell in the land, and feed on His
        faithfulness.
4 ᴿDelight yourself also in the LORD,
    And He shall give you the desires of
        your ᴿheart.   Is. 58:14 • Ps. 21:2; 145:19
5 ᴿCommit ᵀyour way to the LORD,
    Trust also in Him,   [Ps. 55:22] • Lit. *Roll off onto*
    And He shall bring *it* to pass.
6 ᴿHe shall bring forth your righteousness
        as the light,   Job 11:17
    And your justice as the noonday.

7 Rest in the LORD, ᴿand wait patiently
        for Him;
    Do not fret because of him who
        ᴿprospers in his way,
    Because of the man who brings wicked
        schemes to pass.   [Lam. 3:26] • [Ps. 73:3–12]
8 Cease from anger, and forsake wrath;
    Do not fret—*it* only *causes* harm.

9 For evildoers shall be ᵀcut off;
    But those who wait on the LORD,
    They shall inherit the earth.   *destroyed*
10 For ᴿyet a little while and the wicked
        shall be no *more;*   [Heb. 10:36]
    Indeed, ᴿyou will look carefully for his
        place,
    But it *shall be* no *more.*   Job 7:10
11 ᴿBut the meek shall inherit the earth,
    And shall delight themselves in the
        abundance of peace.   [Matt. 5:5]

12 The wicked plots against the just,
    And gnashes at him with his teeth.
13 ᴿThe Lord laughs at him,   Ps. 2:4; 59:8
    For He sees that his day is coming.
14 The wicked have drawn the sword
    And have bent their bow,
    To cast down the poor and needy,
    To slay those who are of upright
        conduct.
15 Their sword shall enter their own heart,
    And their bows shall be broken.

16 ᴿA little that a righteous man has
    Is better than the riches of many
        wicked.   Prov. 15:16; 16:8
17 For the arms of the wicked shall be
        broken,
    But the LORD upholds the righteous.

18 The LORD knows the days of the
        upright,
    And their inheritance shall be forever.
19 They shall not be ashamed in the evil
        time,
    And in the days of famine they shall be
        satisfied.
20 But the wicked shall perish;
    And the enemies of the LORD,
    Like the splendor of the meadows, shall
        vanish.
    Into smoke they shall vanish away.

21 The wicked borrows and does not
        repay,

But ᴿthe righteous shows mercy and
gives.   Ps. 112:5, 9
22 ᴿFor *those* blessed by Him shall inherit
the earth,
But *those* cursed by Him shall be ᵀcut
off.   [Prov. 3:33] · *destroyed*

23 ᴿThe steps of a *good* man are ᵀordered
by the LORD,   [1 Sam. 2:9] · *established*
And He delights in his way.
24 ᴿThough he fall, he shall not be utterly
cast down;
For the LORD upholds *him with* His
hand.   Prov. 24:16

25 I have been young, and *now* am old;
Yet I have not seen the righteous
forsaken,
Nor his descendants begging bread.
26 *He is* ᵀever merciful, and lends;   *all the day*
And his descendants *are* blessed.

27 Depart from evil, and do good;
And dwell forevermore.
28 For the LORD loves justice,
And does not forsake His saints;
They are preserved forever,
But the descendants of the wicked shall
be cut off.
29 ᴿThe righteous shall inherit the land,
And dwell in it forever.   Prov. 2:21

30 ᴿThe mouth of the righteous speaks
wisdom,   [Matt. 12:35]
And his tongue talks of justice.
31 The law of his God *is* in his heart;
None of his steps shall ᵀslide.   *slip*
32 The wicked ᴿwatches the righteous,
And seeks to slay him.   Ps. 10:8; 17:11
33 The LORD ᴿwill not leave him in his
hand,   [2 Pet. 2:9]
Nor condemn him when he is judged.

34 ᴿWait on the LORD,
And keep His way,
And He shall exalt you to inherit the
land;
When the wicked are cut off, you shall
see *it.*   Ps. 27:14; 37:9
35 I have seen the wicked in great power,
And spreading himself like a native
green tree.
36 Yet *he passed away, and behold, he
was no *more;*
Indeed I sought him, but he could not
be found.
37 Mark the blameless *man,* and observe
the upright;
For the future of *that* man *is* peace.
38 ᴿBut the transgressors shall be destroyed
together;
The future of the wicked shall be cut
off.   [Ps. 1:4–6; 37:20, 28]
39 But the salvation of the righteous *is*
from the LORD;

37:36 So with MT, LXX, Tg.; Syr., Vg. *I passed by*

He *is* their strength ᴿin the time of
trouble.   Ps. 9:9; 37:19
40 And ᴿthe LORD shall help them and
deliver them;   Is. 31:5
He shall deliver them from the wicked,
And save them,
ᴿBecause they trust in Him.   1 Chr. 5:20

Psalm 38

Prayer in Time of Chastening

A Psalm of David. To bring to remembrance.

O LORD, do not ᴿrebuke me in Your
wrath,
Nor chasten me in Your hot
displeasure!   Ps. 6:1
2 For Your arrows pierce me deeply,
And Your hand presses me down.

3 *There is* no soundness in my flesh
Because of Your anger,
Nor *any* health in my bones
Because of my sin.
4 For my iniquities have gone over my
head;
Like a heavy burden they are too heavy
for me.
5 My wounds are foul *and* festering
Because of my foolishness.

6 I am ᵀtroubled, I am bowed down
greatly;   Lit. *bent down*
I go mourning all the day long.
7 For my loins are full of inflammation,
And *there is* no soundness in my flesh.
8 I am feeble and severely broken;
I groan because of the turmoil of my
heart.

9 Lord, all my desire *is* before You;
And my sighing is not hidden from
You.
10 My heart pants, my strength fails me;
As for the light of my eyes, it also has
gone from me.

11 My loved ones and my friends stand
aloof from my plague,
And ᵀmy relatives stand afar off.   *neighbors*
12 Those also who seek my life lay snares
for me;
Those who seek my hurt speak of
destruction,
And plan deception all the day long.

13 But I, like a deaf *man,* do not hear;
And *I am* like a ᴿmute *who* does not
open his mouth.   Matt. 27:12–14
14 Thus I am like a man who does not
hear,
And in whose mouth *is* no response.

15 For in You, O LORD, ᴿI hope;   [Ps. 39:7]
You will ᵀhear, O Lord my God.   *answer*
16 For I said, "*Hear me,* lest they rejoice
over me,
Lest, when my foot slips, they exalt
themselves against me."

17 ᴿFor I *am* ready to fall,
　　And my sorrow *is* continually before
　　me.　　　　　　　　　　Ps. 51:3
18 For I will ᴿdeclare my iniquity;　　Ps. 32:5
　　I will be in anguish over my sin.
19 But my enemies *are* vigorous, *and* they
　　are strong;
　　And those who hate me wrongfully
　　have multiplied.
20 Those also ᴿwho render evil for good,
　　They are my adversaries, because I
　　follow *what is* good.　　　Ps. 35:12

21 Do not forsake me, O Lᴏʀᴅ;
　　O my God, be not far from me!
22 Make haste to help me,
　　O Lord, my salvation!

Psalm 39

Prayer for Wisdom and Forgiveness

To the Chief Musician. To Jeduthun. A Psalm of
David.

I SAID, "I will guard my ways,
　　Lest I sin with my ᴿtongue;　　[James 3:5–12]
　　I will restrain my mouth with a muzzle,
　　While the wicked are before me."
2 ᴿI was mute with silence,
　　I held my peace *even* from good;
　　And my sorrow was stirred up.　　Ps. 38:13
3 My heart was hot within me;
　　While I was ᵀmusing, the fire burned.
　　Then I spoke with my tongue:　　*meditating*

4 "Lᴏʀᴅ, make me to know my end,
　　And what *is* the measure of my days,
　　That I may know how frail I *am*.
5 Indeed, You have made my days *as*
　　handbreadths,
　　And my age *is* as nothing before You;
　　Certainly every man at his best state *is*
　　but ᴿvapor. Selah　　　　　　Ps. 62:9
6 Surely every man walks about like a
　　shadow;
　　Surely they ᵀbusy themselves in vain;
　　He heaps up *riches*,
　　And does not know who will gather
　　them.　　　*make an uproar for nothing*

7 "And now, Lord, what do I wait for?
　　My ᴿhope *is* in You.　　　　　Ps. 38:15
8 Deliver me from all my transgressions;
　　Do not make me ᴿthe reproach of the
　　foolish.　　Ps. 44:13; 79:4; 119:22
9 I was mute, I did not open my mouth,
　　Because it was ᴿYou who did *it*.　　Job 2:10
10 ᴿRemove Your plague from me;
　　I am consumed by the blow of Your
　　hand.　　　　　　Job 9:34; 13:21
11 When with rebukes You correct man
　　for iniquity,
　　You make his beauty ᴿmelt away like a
　　moth;　　　　　　　　　Job 13:28
　　Surely every man *is* vapor. Selah

12 "Hear my prayer, O Lᴏʀᴅ,
　　And give ear to my cry;
　　Do not be silent at my tears;
　　For I *am* a stranger with You,
　　A sojourner, as all my fathers *were*.
13 ᴿRemove Your gaze from me, that I may
　　regain strength,　　Job 7:19; 10:20, 21; 14:6
　　Before I go away and am no more."

Psalm 40

Faith Persevering in Trial

To the Chief Musician. A Psalm of David.

I ᴿWAITED patiently for the Lᴏʀᴅ;
　　And He inclined to me,
　　And heard my cry.　　　Ps. 25:5; 27:14; 37:7
2 He also brought me up out of a horrible
　　pit,
　　Out of ᴿthe miry clay,　　　Ps. 69:2, 14
　　And ᴿset my feet upon a rock,　　Ps. 27:5
　　And established my steps.
3 ᴿHe has put a new song in my mouth—
　　Praise to our God;
　　Many will see *it* and fear,
　　And will trust in the Lᴏʀᴅ.　　Ps. 32:7; 33:3

4 ᴿBlessed *is* that man who makes the
　　Lᴏʀᴅ his trust,
　　And does not respect the proud, nor
　　such as turn aside to lies.　　Ps. 34:8; 84:12
5 ᴿMany, O Lᴏʀᴅ my God, *are* Your
　　wonderful works　　　　　　Job 9:10
　　Which You have done;
　　ᴿAnd Your thoughts toward us　　[Is. 55:8]
　　Cannot be recounted to You in order;
　　If I would declare and speak *of them*,
　　They are more than can be numbered.

6 ᴿSacrifice and offering You did not
　　desire;
　　My ears You have opened.
　　Burnt offering and sin offering You did
　　not require.　　　　　　[Heb. 10:5–9]
7 Then I said, "Behold, I come;
　　In the scroll of the book *it is* written of
　　me.
8 I delight to do Your will, O my God,
　　And Your law *is* within my heart."

9 ᴿI have proclaimed the good news of
　　righteousness　　　　　Ps. 22:22, 25
　　In the great assembly;
　　Indeed, ᴿI do not restrain my lips,
　　O Lᴏʀᴅ, You Yourself know.　　Ps. 119:13
10 ᴿI have not hidden Your righteousness
　　within my heart;　　　　Acts 20:20, 27
　　I have declared Your faithfulness and
　　Your salvation;
　　I have not concealed Your
　　lovingkindness and Your truth
　　From the great assembly.

11 Do not withhold Your tender mercies
　　from me, O Lᴏʀᴅ;
　　ᴿLet Your lovingkindness and Your
　　truth continually preserve me.　　Ps. 61:7

12 For innumerable evils have surrounded
   me;
   ᴿMy iniquities have overtaken me, so
     that I am not able to look up;
   They are more than the hairs of my
     head;
   Therefore my heart fails me.   Ps. 38:4; 65:3

13 ᴿBe pleased, O Lᴏʀᴅ, to deliver me;
   O Lᴏʀᴅ, make haste to help me!   Ps. 70:1
14 ᴿLet them be ashamed and brought to
     mutual confusion   Ps. 35:4, 26; 70:2
   Who seek to destroy my ᵀlife;   Or soul
   Let them be driven backward and
     brought to dishonor
   Who wish me evil.
15 Let them be ᴿconfounded because of
     their shame,
   Who say to me, "Aha, aha!"   Ps. 73:19

16 ᴿLet all those who seek You rejoice and
     be glad in You;
   Let such as love Your salvation ᴿsay
     continually,
   "The Lᴏʀᴅ be magnified!"   Ps. 70:4 • Ps. 35:27
17 ᴿBut I am poor and needy;   Ps. 70:5; 86:1
   Yet the Lᴏʀᴅ thinks upon me.
   You are my help and my deliverer;
   ᴿDo not delay, O my God.   1 Pet. 5:7

Psalm 41

The Blessing and Suffering of the Godly
To the Chief Musician. A Psalm of David.

Bᴸᴱˢˢᴱᴰ is he who considers the ᵀpoor;
   The Lᴏʀᴅ will deliver him in time of
     trouble.   helpless or powerless
2 The Lᴏʀᴅ will preserve him and keep
     him alive,
   And he will be blessed on the earth;
   ᴿYou will not deliver him to the will of
     his enemies.   Ps. 27:12
3 The Lᴏʀᴅ will strengthen him on his
     bed of illness;
   You will sustain him on his sickbed.

4 I said, "Lᴏʀᴅ, be merciful to me;
   ᴿHeal my soul, for I have sinned against
     You."   Ps. 6:2; 103:3; 147:3
5 My enemies speak evil of me:
   "When will he die, and his name perish?"
6 And if he comes to see me, he speaks
     ᵀlies;   empty words
   His heart gathers iniquity to itself;
   When he goes out, he tells it.

7 All who hate me whisper together
     against me;
   Against me they ᵀdevise my hurt.   plot
8 "Anᵀ evil disease," they say, "clings to
     him.
   And now that he lies down, he will rise
     up no more."   Lit. A thing of Belial
9 ᴿEven my own familiar friend in whom I
     trusted,   2 Sam. 15:12

ᴿWho ate my bread,   John 13:18, 21-30
   Has lifted up his heel against me.

10 But You, O Lᴏʀᴅ, be merciful to me,
     and raise me up,
   That I may repay them.
11 By this I know that You are well
     pleased with me,
   Because my enemy does not triumph
     over me.
12 As for me, You uphold me in my
     integrity,
   And set me before Your face forever.

13 ᴿBlessed be the Lᴏʀᴅ God of Israel
   From everlasting to everlasting!
   Amen and Amen.   Ps. 72:18, 19; 89:52; 106:48

BOOK TWO
Psalms 42–72

Psalm 42

*Yearning for God in the Midst of
Distresses*
To the Chief Musician. A *Contemplation
of the sons of Korah.

Aˢ the deer pants for the water brooks,
   So pants my soul for You, O God.
2 ᴿMy soul thirsts for God, for the ᴿliving
     God.
   When shall I come and *appear before
     God?   Ps. 63:1; 84:2; 143:6 • 1 Thess. 1:9
3 ᴿMy tears have been my food day and
     night,   Ps. 80:5; 102:9
   While they continually say to me,
   ᴿ"Where is your God?"   Ps. 79:10; 115:2

4 When I remember these things,
   ᴿI pour out my soul within me.
   For I used to go with the multitude;
   ᴿI went with them to the house of God,
   With the voice of joy and praise,
   With a multitude that kept a pilgrim
     feast.   Job 30:16 • Is. 30:29

5 Why are you cast down, O my soul?
   And why are you disquieted within me?
   Hope in God, for I shall yet praise Him
   *For the help of His countenance.

6 *O my God, my soul is cast down within
     me;
   Therefore I will remember You from
     the land of the Jordan,
   And from the heights of Hermon,
   From ᵀthe Hill Mizar.   Or Mount

42:title, Heb. Maschil
42:2 So with MT, Vg.; some Heb. mss., LXX, Syr., Tg. I
see the face of God
42:5 So with MT, Tg.; a few Heb. mss., LXX, Syr., [Vg.]
The help of my countenance, my God
42:6 So with MT, Tg.; a few Heb. mss., LXX, Syr., [Vg.]
put my God at the end of v. 5

7 Deep calls unto deep at the noise of
  Your waterfalls;
  ᴿAll Your waves and billows have gone
  over me.   Ps. 69:1, 2; 88:7
8 The LORD will ᴿcommand His
  lovingkindness in the daytime,
  And ᴿin the night His song *shall be*
  with me—   Deut. 28:8 · Job 35:10
  A prayer to the God of my life.

9 I will say to God my Rock,
  ᴿ"Why have You forgotten me?
  Why do I go mourning because of the
  oppression of the enemy?"   Ps. 38:6
10 *As* with a ᵀbreaking of my bones,
   My enemies ᵀreproach me,
   While they say to me all day long,
   "Where *is* your God?"   Lit. *shattering · revile*

11 ᴿWhy are you cast down, O my soul?
   And why are you disquieted within me?
   Hope in God;
   For I shall yet praise Him,
   The ᵀhelp of my countenance and my
   God.   Ps. 43:5 · Lit. *salvation*

Psalm 43

Prayer to God in Time of Trouble

VINDICATE ᴿme, O God,
  And ᴿplead my cause against an
  ungodly nation;
  Oh, deliver me from the deceitful and
  unjust man!   [Ps. 26:1; 35:24] · Ps. 35:1
2 For You *are* the God of my strength;
  Why do You cast me off?
  ᴿWhy do I go mourning because of the
  oppression of the enemy?   Ps. 42:9
3 ᴿOh, send out Your light and Your truth!
  Let them lead me;
  Let them bring me to ᴿYour holy hill
  And to Your tabernacle.   [Ps. 40:11] · Ps. 3:4
4 Then I will go to the altar of God,
  To God my exceeding joy;
  And on the harp I will praise You,
  O God, my God.
5 ᴿWhy are you cast down, O my soul?
  And why are you disquieted within me?
  Hope in God;
  For I shall yet praise Him,
  The ᵀhelp of my countenance and my
  God.   Ps. 42:5, 11 · Lit. *salvation*

Psalm 44

*Redemption Remembered in Present
Dishonor*

To the Chief Musician. A *Contemplation
of the sons of Korah.

WE have heard with our ears, O God,
  ᴿOur fathers have told us,
  The deeds You did in their days,
  In days of old: [Ex. 12:26, 27]

44:title, Heb. *Maschil*

2 ᴿYou drove out the ᵀnations with Your
  hand,
  But them You planted;
  You afflicted the peoples, and cast them
  out.   Ex. 15:17 · *Gentiles, heathen*
3 For ᴿthey did not gain possession of the
  land by their own sword,   [Deut. 8:17, 18]
  Nor did their own arm save them;
  But it was Your right hand, Your arm,
  and the light of Your countenance,
  Because You favored them.
4 ᴿYou are my King, *O God;
  *Command victories for Jacob.   [Ps. 74:12]
5 Through You ᴿwe will push down our
  enemies;
  Through Your name we will trample
  those who rise up against us.   [Dan. 8:4]
6 For ᴿI will not trust in my bow,
  Nor shall my sword save me.   Ps. 33:16
7 But You have saved us from our
  enemies,
  And have put to shame those who
  hated us.
8 ᴿIn God we boast all day long,   Ps. 34:2
  And praise Your name forever.   Selah

9 But ᴿYou have cast *us* off and put us to
  shame,   Ps. 60:1
  And You do not go out with our
  armies.
10 You make us ᴿturn back from the
   enemy,
   And those who hate us have taken
   ᵀspoil for themselves.   Lev. 26:17 · *plunder*
11 ᴿYou have given us up like sheep
   intended for food,
   And have ᴿscattered us among the
   nations.   Rom. 8:36 · Deut. 4:27; 28:64
12 You sell Your people for *next to*
   nothing,
   And are not enriched by selling them.

13 ᴿYou make us a reproach to our
   neighbors,
   A scorn and a derision to those all
   around us.   Deut. 28:37
14 ᴿYou make us a byword among the
   nations,
   ᴿA shaking of the head among the
   peoples.   Jer. 24:9 · Job 16:4
15 My dishonor *is* continually before me,
   And the shame of my face has covered
   me,
16 Because of the voice of him who
   reproaches and reviles,
   Because of the enemy and the avenger.
17 ᴿAll this has come upon us;
   But we have not forgotten You,
   Nor have we dealt falsely with Your
   covenant.   Dan. 9:13

44:4 So with MT, Tg.; LXX, Vg. *and my God* • So with
MT, Tg.; LXX, Syr., Vg. *who commands*

18 Our heart has not turned back,
    ^RNor have our steps departed from Your
       way;   Job 23:11
19 But You have severely broken us in
    ^Rthe place of jackals,
    And covered us ^Rwith the shadow of
       death.   Is. 34:13 • [Ps. 23:4]
20 If we had forgotten the name of our
       God,
    Or ^Rstretched^T out our hands to a
       foreign god,   [Deut. 6:14] • Worshiped
21 Would not God search this out?
    For He knows the secrets of the heart.
22 ^RYet for Your sake we are killed all day
       long;
    We are accounted as sheep for the
       slaughter.   Rom. 8:36
23 ^RAwake! Why do You sleep, O Lord?
    Arise! Do not cast us off forever.   Ps. 7:6
24 ^RWhy do You hide Your face,
    And forget our affliction and our
       oppression?   Job 13:24
25 For ^Rour soul is bowed down ^Tto the
       dust;   Ps. 119:25 • Ground, in humiliation
    Our body clings to the ground.
26 Arise for our help,
    And redeem us for Your mercies' sake.

Psalm 45

The Glories of the Messiah and His Bride

To the Chief Musician. Set to *"The Lilies."
A *Contemplation of the sons of Korah.
A Song of Love.

M Y heart is overflowing with a good
      theme;
    I recite my composition concerning the
       King;
    My tongue is the pen of a ready writer.

2   You are fairer than the sons of men;
    Grace is poured upon Your lips;
    Therefore God has blessed You forever.

45:title, Heb. Shoshannim • Heb. Maschil

3   ^TGird Your ^Rsword upon Your thigh,
    ^RO Mighty One,   Belt on • [Heb. 4:12] • [Is. 9:6]
    With Your glory and Your majesty.
4   ^RAnd in Your majesty ride prosperously
       because of truth, humility, and
       righteousness;
    And Your right hand shall teach You
       awesome things.   Rev. 6:2
5   Your arrows are sharp in the heart of
       the King's enemies;
    The peoples fall under You.

7-E. Jesus Is God, According to God the ▼
        Father

6   ^RYour throne, O God, is forever and
       ever;   Heb. 1:8
    A ^Rscepter of righteousness is the
       scepter of Your kingdom.   [Num. 24:17]
7   You love righteousness and hate
       wickedness;
    Therefore God, Your God, has
    ^Ranointed You
    With the oil of ^Rgladness more than
       Your companions.   Ps. 2:2 • Ps. 21:6 ▲
8   All Your garments are ^Rscented with
       myrrh and aloes and cassia,
    Out of the ivory palaces, by which they
       have made You glad.   Song 1:12, 13
9   ^RKings' daughters are among Your
       honorable women;
    ^RAt Your right hand stands the queen in
       gold from Ophir.   Song 6:8 • 1 Kin. 2:19

10 Listen, O daughter,
    Consider and incline your ear;
    ^RForget your own people also, and your
       father's house;   Deut. 21:13
11 So the King will greatly desire your
       beauty;
    Because He is your Lord, worship Him.
12 And the daughter of Tyre will come
       with a gift;
    ^RThe rich among the people will seek
       your favor.   Is. 49:23

7-E. Jesus Is God, According to God the Father (Psalm 45:6, 7)—"Your throne, O God" (v. 6). In the New Testament we learn that this is a messianic psalm, that Jesus is God the Messiah. "But to the Son He [God the Father] says: 'Your throne, O God, is forever and ever' " (Heb. 1:8, 9, page 1236). Only the spiritually blind (2 Cor. 4:3, 4, page 1167) can read God's Word and fail to see that Jesus is God (Col. 2:9, 10, page 1204).

"Your throne, O God, is forever and ever" (v. 6). The throne of the Lord Jesus Christ is forever and ever; it will never terminate. Jesus is no usurper; the kingdom throne is His according to God the Father. The Son and the Father are inseparable in essence, in attributes, in eternity, and in authority (John 10:30, page 1068).

"Your throne, O God, is forever and ever; a scepter of righteousness is the scepter of Your kingdom" (v. 6; cf. Heb. 1:8, page 1236). A scepter is a rod or a staff used by a sovereign to symbolize his royal authority. According to God, the scepter of King Jesus is a righteous scepter. Do not think that righteousness is weakness. It never is. When Jesus returns to this earth He will come as King of kings and Lord of lords, to war against the wicked, and His righteous scepter will be as strong as iron (Rev. 19:11-16, page 1312).

When the King of righteousness comes, He will continue to love righteousness and hate wickedness. His righteous kingdom is one of everlasting joy—joy unspeakable and full of glory (1 Pet. 1:7, 8, page 1263).

See John 1:14, page 1049, for **Point 7-F: Jesus Is the God-Man.**

13 The royal daughter *is* all glorious
    within *the palace;*
    Her clothing *is* woven with gold.
14 ᴿShe shall be brought to the King in
    robes of many colors;
    The virgins, her companions who follow
    her, shall be brought to You.   Song 1:4
15 With gladness and rejoicing they shall
    be brought;
    They shall enter the King's palace.

16 Instead of Your fathers shall be Your
    sons,
    ᴿWhom You shall make princes in all
    the earth.   [1 Pet. 2:9]
17 ᴿI will make Your name to be
    remembered in all generations;
    Therefore the people shall praise You
    forever and ever.   Mal. 1:11

Psalm 46

God the Refuge of His People and Conqueror of the Nations

To the Chief Musician. A Psalm of the sons
of Korah. A Song for Alamoth.

GOD *is* our ᴿrefuge and strength,   Ps. 62:7, 8
    A very present help in trouble.
2 Therefore we will not fear,
    Even though the earth be removed,
    And though the mountains be carried
    into the ᵀmidst of the sea;   Lit. *heart*
3 ᴿ*Though* its waters roar *and* be troubled,
    Though the mountains shake with its
    swelling. Selah   [Ps. 93:3, 4]

4 *There is* a ᴿriver whose streams shall
    make glad the city of God,
    The holy *place* of the ᵀtabernacle of the
    Most High.   [Ezek. 47:1–12] · *dwelling places*
5 God *is* ᴿin the midst of her, she shall
    not be ᵀmoved;   [Zeph. 3:15] · *shaken*
    God shall help her, just ᵀat the break of
    dawn.   Lit. *at the turning of the morning*
6 ᴿThe nations raged, the kingdoms were
    moved;   Ps. 2:1, 2
    He uttered His voice, the earth melted.

7 The ᴿLORD of hosts *is* with us;   Num. 14:9
    The God of Jacob *is* our refuge.   Selah

8 Come, behold the works of the LORD,
    Who has made desolations in the earth.
9 ᴿHe makes wars cease to the end of the
    earth;   Is. 2:4
    ᴿHe breaks the bow and cuts the spear
    in two;   Ps. 76:3
    ᴿHe burns the chariot in the fire. Ezek. 39:9

10 Be still, and know that I *am* God;
    ᴿI will be exalted among the nations,
    I will be exalted in the earth!   [Is. 2:11, 17]

11 The LORD of hosts *is* with us;
    The God of Jacob *is* our refuge.   Selah

Psalm 47

Praise to God, the Ruler of the Earth

To the Chief Musician.
A Psalm of the sons of Korah.

OH, clap your hands, all you peoples!
    Shout to God with the voice of
    triumph!
2 For the LORD Most High *is* awesome;
    He is a great King over all the earth.
3 ᴿHe will subdue the peoples under us,
    And the nations under our feet.   Ps. 18:47
4 He will choose our ᴿinheritance for us,
    The excellence of Jacob whom He
    loves. Selah   [1 Pet. 1:4]

5 God has gone up with a shout,
    The LORD with the sound of a trumpet.
6 Sing praises to God, sing praises!
    Sing praises to our King, sing praises!
7 For God *is* the King of all the earth;
    Sing praises with understanding.

8 ᴿGod reigns over the nations;   1 Chr. 16:31
    God sits on His ᴿholy throne.   Ps. 48:1
9 The princes of the people have gathered
    together,
    ᴿThe people of the God of Abraham.
    ᴿFor the shields of the earth *belong* to
    God;   [Rom. 4:11, 12] · [Ps. 89:18]
    He is greatly exalted.

Psalm 48

The Glory of God in Zion

A Song. A Psalm of the sons of Korah.

GREAT *is* the LORD, and greatly to be
    praised
    In the ᴿcity of our God,
    In His holy mountain.   Ps. 46:4; 87:3
2 ᴿBeautiful in ᵀelevation,
    The joy of the whole earth,
    Is Mount Zion *on* the sides of the
    north,
    The city of the great King.   Ps. 50:2 · *height*
3 God *is* in her palaces;
    He is known as her refuge.

4 For behold, ᴿthe kings assembled,
    They passed by together.   2 Sam. 10:6, 14
5 They saw *it, and* so they marveled;
    They were troubled, they hastened
    away.
6 Fear ᴿtook hold of them there,   Ex. 15:15
    And pain, as of a woman in birth pangs,
7 As *when* You break the ᴿships of
    Tarshish
    With an east wind.   Ezek. 27:25

8 As we have heard,
    So we have seen
    In the city of the LORD of hosts,
    In the city of our God:
    God will establish it forever. Selah

9 We have thought, O God, on ᴿYour
　lovingkindness,
　In the midst of Your temple.　Ps. 26:3
10 According to ᴿYour name, O God,
　So *is* Your praise to the ends of the
　earth;　Mal. 1:11
　Your right hand is full of righteousness.
11 Let Mount Zion rejoice,
　Let the daughters of Judah be glad,
　Because of Your judgments.

12 Walk about Zion,
　And go all around her.
　Count her towers;
13 Mark well her bulwarks;
　Consider her palaces;
　That you may ᴿtell *it* to the generation
　following.　[Ps. 78:5-7]
14 For this *is* God,
　Our God forever and ever;
　ᴿHe will be our guide
　Even to death.　Is. 58:11

Psalm 49

The Confidence of the Foolish

To the Chief Musician.
A Psalm of the sons of Korah.

H EAR this, all peoples;
　Give ear, all inhabitants of the world,
2 Both low and high,
　Rich and poor together.
3 My mouth shall speak wisdom,
　And the meditation of my heart *shall*
　give understanding.
4 I will incline my ear to a proverb;
　I will disclose my ᵀdark saying on the
　harp.　riddle

5 Why should I fear in the days of evil,
　When the iniquity at my heels
　surrounds me?
6 Those who ᴿtrust in their wealth
　And boast in the multitude of their
　riches,　[Mark 10:24]
7 None *of them* can by any means
　redeem *his* brother,
　Nor give to God a ransom for him—
8 For ᴿthe redemption of their souls *is*
　costly,
　And it shall cease forever—　[Matt. 16:26]
9 That he should continue to live
　eternally,
　And not ᵀsee the Pit.　experience corruption

10 For he sees wise men die;
　Likewise the fool and the senseless
　person perish,
　And leave their wealth to others.
11 *Their inner thought is that their houses
　will last* forever,

Their dwelling places to all generations;
　They ᴿcall *their* lands after their own
　names.　Gen. 4:17
12 Nevertheless man, *though* in honor,
　does not *remain;
　He is like the beasts *that* perish.

13 This is the way of those who *are*
　ᴿfoolish,
　And of their posterity who approve
　their sayings.　Selah　[Luke 12:20]
14 Like sheep they are laid in the grave;
　Death shall feed on them;
　ᴿThe upright shall have dominion over
　them in the morning;　[Dan. 7:18]
　And their beauty shall be consumed in
　the grave, far from their dwelling.
15 But God ᴿwill redeem my soul from the
　power of the grave,　Acts 2:31, 32
　For He shall receive me.　Selah

16 Do not be afraid when one becomes
　rich,
　When the glory of his house is
　increased;
17 For when he dies he shall carry nothing
　away;
　His glory shall not descend after him.
18 Though while he lives ᴿhe blesses
　himself
　(For *men* will praise you when you do
　well for yourself),　Deut. 29:19
19 He shall go to the generation of his
　fathers;
　They shall never see ᵀlight.　The light of life
20 A man *who is* in honor, yet does not
　understand,
　ᴿIs like the beasts *that* perish.　Eccl. 3:19

Psalm 50

God the Righteous Judge

A Psalm of Asaph.

T HE ᴿMighty One, God the Lᴏʀᴅ,
　Has spoken and called the earth
　From the rising of the sun to its going
　down.　Is. 9:6
2 Out of Zion, the perfection of beauty,
　ᴿGod will shine forth.　Ps. 80:1
3 Our God shall come, and shall not keep
　silent;
　ᴿA fire shall devour before Him,
　And it shall be very tempestuous all
　around Him.　[Ps. 97:3]
4 ᴿHe shall call to the heavens from above,
　And to the earth, that He may judge
　His people:　Is. 1:2
5 "Gather My saints together to Me,

48:14 So with MT, Syr.; LXX, Vg. *Forever*
49:11 LXX, Syr., Tg., Vg. *Their graves shall be their
houses forever*

49:12 So with MT, Tg.; LXX, [Syr.], Vg. *understand* (cf. v.
20)

ᴿThose who have ᵀmade a covenant with
Me by sacrifice."   Ex. 24:7 • Lit. cut
6 Let the ᴿheavens declare His
righteousness,   [Ps. 97:6]
For God Himself is Judge. Selah

7 "Hear, O My people, and I will speak,
O Israel, and I will testify against you;
ᴿI am God, your God!   Ex. 20:2
8 ᴿI will not rebuke you ᴿfor your
sacrifices   Jer. 7:22 • [Hos. 6:6]
Or your burnt offerings,
Which are continually before Me.
9 ᴿI will not take a bull from your house,
Nor goats out of your folds.   Ps. 69:31
10 For every beast of the forest is Mine,
And the cattle on a thousand hills.
11 I know all the birds of the mountains,
And the wild beasts of the field are
Mine.
12 "If I were hungry, I would not tell you;
ᴿFor the world is Mine, and all its
fullness.   Ex. 19:5
13 ᴿWill I eat the flesh of bulls,
Or drink the blood of goats? [Ps. 51:15-17]
14 ᴿOffer to God thanksgiving,   Heb. 13:15
And pay your vows to the Most High.
15 ᴿCall upon Me in the day of trouble;
I will deliver you, and you shall glorify
Me."   [Zech. 13:9]

16 But to the wicked God says:
"What right have you to declare My
statutes,
Or take My covenant in your mouth,
17 ᴿSeeing you hate instruction   Rom. 2:21
And cast My words behind you?
18 When you saw a thief, you ᴿconsented*
with him,
And have been a ᴿpartaker with
adulterers.   [Rom. 1:32] • 1 Tim. 5:22
19 You give your mouth to evil,
And ᴿyour tongue frames deceit.   Ps. 52:2
20 You sit and speak against your brother;
You slander your own mother's son.
21 These things you have done, and I kept
silent;
ᴿYou thought that I was altogether like
you;
But I will rebuke you,
And ᴿset them in order before your
eyes.   [Rom. 2:4] • [Ps. 90:8]

22 "Now consider this, you who ᴿforget
God,
Lest I tear you in pieces,
And there be none to deliver.   [Job 8:13]
23 Whoever offers praise glorifies Me;
And ᴿto him who orders his conduct
aright   Gal. 6:16
I will show the salvation of God."

50:18 LXX, [Syr.], [Tg.], Vg. run

Psalm 51

A Prayer of Repentance

To the Chief Musician. A Psalm of David when
Nathan the prophet went to him, after he had
gone in to Bathsheba.

Hᴬⱽᴱ mercy upon me, O God,
According to Your lovingkindness;
According to the multitude of Your
tender mercies,
ᴿBlot out my transgressions. [Is. 43:25; 44:22]
2 ᴿWash me thoroughly from my iniquity,
And cleanse me from my sin.   [Heb. 9:14]

3 For I acknowledge my transgressions,
And my sin is always before me.
4 ᴿAgainst You, You only, have I sinned,
And done this evil ᴿin Your sight—
ᴿThat You may be found just *when
You speak,   2 Sam. 12:13 • [Luke 5:21] • Rom. 3:4
And blameless when You judge.

5 Behold, I was brought forth in iniquity,
And in sin my mother conceived me.
6 Behold, You desire truth in the inward
parts,
And in the hidden part You will make
me to know wisdom.

7 ᴿPurge me with hyssop, and I shall be
clean;
Wash me, and I shall be ᴿwhiter than
snow.   Heb. 9:19 • [Is. 1:18]
8 Make me hear joy and gladness,
That the bones You have broken ᴿmay
rejoice.   [Matt. 5:4]
9 Hide Your face from my sins,
And blot out all my iniquities.

10 Create in me a clean heart, O God,
And renew a steadfast spirit within me.
11 Do not cast me away from Your
presence,
And do not take Your ᴿHoly Spirit from
me.   [Luke 11:13]
12 Restore to me the joy of Your
salvation,
And uphold me by Your ᴿgenerous
Spirit.   [2 Cor. 3:17]
13 Then I will teach transgressors Your
ways,
And sinners shall be converted to You.

14 Deliver me from the guilt of bloodshed,
O God,
The God of my salvation,
And my tongue shall sing aloud of Your
righteousness.
15 O Lord, open my lips,
And my mouth shall show forth Your
praise.

51:4 LXX, Tg., Vg. in Your words

16 For ^RYou do not desire sacrifice, or else
    I would give *it;*   [1 Sam. 15:22]
    You do not delight in burnt offering.
17 ^RThe sacrifices of God *are* a broken
    spirit,   Ps. 34:18
    A broken and a contrite heart—
    These, O God, You will not despise.
18 Do good in Your good pleasure to Zion;
    Build the walls of Jerusalem.
19 Then You shall be pleased with ^Rthe
    sacrifices of righteousness,
    With burnt offering and whole burnt
    offering;
    Then they shall offer bulls on Your
    altar.   Ps. 4:5

Psalm 52

The End of the Wicked and the Peace of the Godly

To the Chief Musician. A *Contemplation of David when Doeg the Edomite went and told Saul, and said to him, "David has gone to the house of Ahimelech."

W HY do you boast in evil, O mighty
    man?
    The goodness of God *endures*
    continually.
2 Your tongue devises destruction,
    Like a sharp razor, working deceitfully.
3 You love evil more than good,
    Lying rather than speaking
    righteousness.   Selah
4 You love all devouring words,
    You deceitful tongue.

5 God shall likewise destroy you forever;
    He shall take you away, and pluck you
    out of *your* dwelling place,
    And uproot you from the land of the
    living.   Selah
6 The righteous also shall see and fear,
    And shall laugh at him, *saying,*
7 "Here is the man *who* did not make God
    his strength,
    But trusted in the abundance of his
    riches,
    And strengthened himself in his
    ^Twickedness."   Lit. *desire,* in evil sense

8 But I *am* ^Rlike a green olive tree in the
    house of God;
    I trust in the mercy of God forever and
    ever.   Jer. 11:16
9 I will praise You forever,
    Because You have done *it;*
    And in the presence of Your saints
    I will wait on Your name, for *it is* good.

52:title, Heb. *Maschil*

Psalm 53

Folly of the Godless, and the Restoration of Israel

To the Chief Musician. Set to "Mahalath." A *Contemplation of David.

T HE ^Rfool has said in his heart,
    ^R"There is no God."   Ps. 10:4 • Rom. 3:10-12
    They are corrupt,
    and have done abominable iniquity;
    There is none who does good.

2 God looks down from heaven upon the
    children of men,
    To see if there are *any* who understand,
    who ^Rseek God.   [2 Chr. 15:2]
3 Every one of them has turned aside;
    They have together become corrupt;
    There is none who does good,
    No, not one.

4 Have the workers of iniquity ^Rno
    knowledge,
    Who eat up my people *as* they eat
    bread,
    And do not call upon God?   Jer. 4:22
5 ^RThere they are in great fear   Prov. 28:1
    Where no fear was,
    For God has scattered the bones of him
    who encamps against you;
    You have put *them* to shame,
    Because God has despised them.

6 ^ROh, that the salvation of Israel would
    come out of Zion!   Ps. 14:7
    When God brings back ^Tthe captivity of
    His people,   Or *His captive people*
    Let Jacob rejoice *and* Israel be glad.

Psalm 54

Answered Prayer for Deliverance from Adversaries

To the Chief Musician. With *stringed instruments. A *Contemplation of David when the Ziphites went and said to Saul, "Is David not hiding with us?"

S AVE me, O God, by Your name,
    And vindicate me by Your strength.
2 Hear my prayer, O God;
    Give ear to the words of my mouth.
3 For strangers have risen up against me,
    And oppressors have sought after my
    life;
    They have not set God before them.
    Selah

4 Behold, God *is* my helper;
    The Lord *is* with those who ^Tuphold my
    life.   *sustain my soul*
5 He will repay my enemies for their evil.
    Cut them off in Your ^Ttruth.   Or *faithfulness*

53:title, Heb. *Maschil*
54:title, Heb. *neginoth* • Heb. *Maschil*

6 I will freely sacrifice to You;
I will praise Your name, O LORD, for *it
is* good.
7 For He has delivered me out of all
trouble;
ᴿAnd my eye has seen *its desire* upon
my enemies.   Ps. 59:10

Psalm 55

*Trust in God Concerning the Treachery
of Friends*

To the Chief Musician. With *stringed
instruments. A *Contemplation of David.

GIVE ear to my prayer, O God,
And do not hide Yourself from my
supplication.
2 Attend to me, and hear me;
I ᴿamᵀ restless in my complaint, and
moan noisily,   Is. 38:14; 59:11 · *wander*
3 Because of the voice of the enemy,
Because of the oppression of the
wicked;
ᴿFor they bring down trouble upon me,
And in wrath they hate me.   2 Sam. 16:7, 8
4 ᴿMy heart is severely pained within me,
And the terrors of death have fallen
upon me.   Ps. 116:3
5 Fearfulness and trembling have come
upon me,
And horror has overwhelmed me.
6 So I said, "Oh, that I had wings like a
dove!
I would fly away and be at rest.
7 Indeed, I would wander far off,
And remain in the wilderness. Selah
8 I would hasten my escape
From the windy storm *and* tempest."

9 Destroy, O Lord, *and* divide their
ᵀtongues,
For I have seen ᴿviolence and strife in
the city.   *speech,* counsel · Jer. 6:7
10 Day and night they go around it on its
walls;
ᴿIniquity and trouble *are* also in the
midst of it.   Ps. 10:7
11 Destruction *is* in its midst;
ᴿOppression and deceit do not depart
from its streets.   Ps. 10:7

12 ᴿFor *it is* not an enemy *who* reproaches
me;   Ps. 41:9
Then I could bear *it.*
Nor *is it* one *who* hates me who has
exalted *himself* against me;
Then I could hide from him.
13 But *it was* you, a man my equal,
My companion and my acquaintance.
14 We took sweet counsel together,
And ᴿwalked to the house of God in the
throng.   Ps. 42:4

15 Let death seize them;
Let them ᴿgo down alive into ᵀhell,
For wickedness *is* in their dwellings *and*
among them.   Num. 16:30, 33 · Or *Sheol*
16 As for me, I will call upon God,
And the LORD shall save me.
17 ᴿEvening and morning and at noon
I will pray, and cry aloud,
And He shall hear my voice.   Dan. 6:10
18 He has redeemed my soul in peace
from the battle *that was* against me,
For there were many against me.
19 God will hear, and afflict them,
ᴿEven He who abides from of old.
Selah
Because they do not change,   [Deut. 33:27]
Therefore they do not fear God.

20 He has put forth his hands against
those who ᴿwere at peace with him;
He has broken his ᵀcovenant.   Ps. 7:4 · *treaty*
21 ᴿ*The words* of his mouth were smoother
than butter,   Ps. 28:3; 57:4
But war *was* in his heart;
His words were softer than oil,
Yet they *were* drawn swords.

22 ᴿCast your burden on the LORD,
And ᴿHe shall sustain you;
He shall never permit the righteous to
be ᵀmoved.   [Ps. 37:5] · Ps. 37:24 · *shaken*

23 But You, O God, shall bring them down
to the pit of destruction;
ᴿBloodthirsty and deceitful men ᴿshall
not live out half their days;
But I will trust in You.   Ps. 5:6 · Prov. 10:27

Psalm 56

Prayer for Relief from Tormentors

To the Chief Musician. Set to *"The Silent Dove
in Distant Lands." A Michtam of David when the
Philistines captured him in Gath.

BE ᴿmerciful to me, O God, for man
would swallow me up;   Ps. 57:1
Fighting all day he oppresses me.
2 My enemies would ᴿhound *me* all day,
For *there are* many who fight against
me, O Most High.   Ps. 57:3

3 Whenever I am afraid,
I will trust in You.
4 In God (I will praise His word),
In God I have put my trust;
ᴿI will not fear.
What can flesh do to me?   Ps. 118:6

5 All day they twist my words;
All their thoughts *are* against me for
evil.
6 They gather together,
They hide, they mark my steps,
When they lie in wait for my life.

55:title, Heb. *neginoth* • Heb. *Maschil*   56:title, Heb. *Jonath Elem Rechokim*

7 Shall they escape by iniquity?
  In anger cast down the peoples, O God!

8 You number my wanderings;
  Put my tears into Your bottle;
  R*Are they* not in Your book?   [Mal. 3:16]

9 When I cry out *to* You,
  Then my enemies will turn back;
  This I know, because God *is* for me.

10 In God (I will praise *His* word),
   In the LORD (I will praise *His* word),

11 In God I have put my trust;
   I will not be afraid.
   What can man do to me?

12 Vows *made* to You *are binding* upon
   me, O God;
   I will render praises to You,

13 RFor You have delivered my soul from
   death.   Ps. 116:8, 9
   Have You not *kept* my feet from falling,
   That I may walk before God
   In the Rlight of the living?   Job 33:30

Psalm 57

Prayer for Safety from Enemies

To the Chief Musician. Set to *"Do Not Destroy."
A Michtam of David when he fled from Saul into
the cave.

B E merciful to me, O God, be merciful to
  me!
  For my soul trusts in You;
  RAnd in the shadow of Your wings I will
  make my refuge,   Ps. 17:8; 63:7
  Until *these* calamities have passed by.

2 I will cry out to God Most High,
  To God Rwho performs *all things* for
  me.   [Ps. 138:8]

3 He shall send from heaven and save
  me;
  He reproaches the one who would
  Tswallow me up. Selah
  God shall send forth His mercy and His
  truth.   *snaps at or hounds me, or crushes me*

4 My soul *is* among lions;
  I lie *among* the sons of men
  Who are set on fire,
  Whose teeth *are* spears and arrows,
  And their tongue a sharp sword.

5 Be exalted, O God, above the heavens;
  Let Your glory *be* above all the earth.

6 RThey have prepared a net for my steps;
  My soul is bowed down;
  They have dug a pit before me;
  Into the midst of it they *themselves*
  have fallen. Selah   Ps. 9:15

7 RMy heart is steadfast, O God, my heart
  is steadfast;
  I will sing and give praise.   Ps. 108:1-5

8 Awake, Rmy glory!
  Awake, lute and harp!
  I will awaken the dawn.   Ps. 16:9

9 RI will praise You, O Lord, among the
  peoples;   Ps. 108:3
  I will sing to You among the nations.

10 RFor Your mercy reaches unto the
   heavens,   Ps. 103:11
   And Your truth unto the clouds.

11 Be exalted, O God, above the heavens;
   Let Your glory *be* above all the earth.

Psalm 58

The Just Judgment of the Wicked

To the Chief Musician. Set to *"Do Not Destroy."
A Michtam of David.

D O you indeed speak righteousness, you
  silent ones?
  Do you judge uprightly, you sons of
  men?

2 No, in heart you work wickedness;
  You weigh out the violence of your
  hands in the earth.

3 RThe wicked are estranged from the
  womb;
  They go astray as soon as they are
  born, speaking lies.   [Is. 48:8]

4 RTheir poison *is* like the poison of a
  serpent;
  They are like the deaf cobra *that* stops
  its ear,   Eccl. 10:11

5 Which will not Rheed the voice of
  charmers,
  Charming ever so skillfully.   Jer. 8:17

6 RBreak their teeth in their mouth, O
  God!
  TBreak out the fangs of the young lions,
  O LORD!   Job 4:10 · *Break away*

7 RLet them flow away as waters *which*
  run continually;   Josh. 2:11; 7:5
  When he bends *his* bow,
  Let his arrows be as if cut in pieces.

8 *Let them be* like a snail which melts
  away as it goes,
  RLike a stillborn child of a woman, that
  they may not see the sun.   Job 3:16

9 Before your Rpots can feel *the burning*
  thorns,
  He shall take them away Ras with a
  whirlwind,   Eccl. 7:6 · Prov. 10:25
  As in His living and burning wrath.

10 The righteous shall rejoice when he
   sees the Rvengeance;
   RHe shall wash his feet in the blood of
   the wicked,   Jer. 11:20 · Ps. 68:23

11 RSo that men will say,

"Surely *there is* a reward for the
righteous;
Surely He is God who ᴿjudges in the
earth."   Ps. 92:15 • Ps. 50:6; 75:7

Psalm 59

The Assured Judgment of the Wicked

To the Chief Musician. Set to *"Do Not Destroy."
A Michtam of David when Saul
sent men, and they watched the house
in order to kill him.

ELIVER me from my enemies, O my
God;
ᵀDefend me from those who rise up
against me.   Lit. *Set me on high*
2 Deliver me from the workers of
iniquity,
And save me from bloodthirsty men.

3 For look, they lie in wait for my life;
ᴿThe mighty gather against me,
Not *for* my transgression nor *for* my
sin, O Lᴏʀᴅ.   Ps. 56:6
4 They run and prepare themselves
through no fault *of* mine.

ᴿAwake to help me, and behold!   Ps. 35:23
5 You therefore, O Lᴏʀᴅ God of hosts,
the God of Israel,
Awake to punish all the ᵀnations;
Do not be merciful to any wicked
transgressors. Selah   *Gentiles*

6 ᴿAt evening they return,
They growl like a dog,
And go all around the city.   Ps. 59:14
7 Indeed, they belch with their mouth;
ᴿSwords *are* in their lips;   Prov. 12:18
For *they say,* ᴿ"Who hears?"   Ps. 10:11

8 But ᴿYou, O Lᴏʀᴅ, shall laugh at them;
You shall have all the ᵀnations in
derision.   Prov. 1:26 • *Gentiles*
9 I will wait for You,
O You *his Strength;
For God *is* my ᵀdefense.   Lit. *fortress*
10 *My God of mercy shall ᴿcome to meet
me;
God shall let ᴿme see *my desire* on my
enemies.   Ps. 21:3 • Ps. 54:7

11 Do not slay them, lest my people forget;
Scatter them by Your power,
And bring them down,
O Lord our shield.
12 ᴿFor the sin of their mouth *and* the
words of their lips,
Let them even be taken in their pride,

59:title, Heb. *Al Tashcheth*
59:9 So with MT, [Syr.]; some Heb. mss., LXX, Tg., Vg.
my Strength
59:10 So with Qr.; some Heb. mss., LXX, Vg. *My God,
His mercy;* Kt., some Heb. mss., Tg. *O God, my mercy;*
Syr. *O God, Your mercy*

And for the cursing and lying *which*
they speak.   Prov. 12:13
13 ᴿConsume *them* in wrath, consume
them,
That they *may* not *be;*
And ᴿlet them know that God rules in
Jacob   Ps. 104:35 • Ps. 83:18
To the ends of the earth. Selah

14 And ᴿat evening they return,
They growl like a dog,
And go all around the city.   Ps. 59:6
15 They wander up and down for food,
And *howl if they are not satisfied.

16 But I will sing of Your power;
Yes, I will sing aloud of Your mercy in
the morning;
For You have been my defense
And refuge in the day of my trouble.
17 To You, ᴿO my Strength, I will sing
praises;
For God *is* my defense,
My God of mercy.   Ps. 18:1

Psalm 60

Urgent Prayer for the Restored Favor of
God

To the Chief Musician. Set to *"Lily
of the Testimony." A Michtam of David.
For teaching. When he fought against
Mesopotamia and Syria of Zobah, and Joab
returned and killed twelve thousand Edomites in
the Valley of Salt.

GOD, ᴿYou have cast us off;
You have broken us down;
You have been displeased;
Oh, restore us again!   Ps. 44:9
2 You have made the earth tremble;
You have broken it;
Heal its breaches, for it is shaking.
3 ᴿYou have shown Your people hard
things;
ᴿYou have made us drink the wine of
ᵀconfusion.   Ps. 71:20 • Jer. 25:15 • *staggering*

4 ᴿYou have given a banner to those who
fear You,
That it may be displayed because of the
truth. Selah   Ps. 20:5
5 ᴿThat Your beloved may be delivered,
Save *with* Your right hand, and hear
me.   Ps. 108:6-13

6 God has ᴿspoken in His holiness:
"I will rejoice;   Ps. 89:35
I will ᴿdivide ᴿShechem
And measure out ᴿthe Valley of
Succoth.   Josh. 1:6 • Gen. 12:6 • Josh. 13:27
7 Gilead *is* Mine, and Manasseh *is* Mine;

59:15 So with LXX, Vg.; MT, Syr., Tg. *spend the night*
60:title, Heb. *Shushan Eduth*

Ephraim also *is* the ᵀhelmet for My
head;
Judah *is* My lawgiver.   Lit. *protection*
8 ᴿMoab *is* My washpot;
ᴿOver Edom I will cast My shoe;
ᴿPhilistia, shout in triumph because of
Me."   2 Sam. 8:2 • 2 Sam. 8:14 • 2 Sam. 8:1

9 Who will bring me *to* the strong city?
Who will lead me to Edom?
10 *Is it* not You, O God, ᴿwho cast us off?
And You, O God, *who* did ᴿnot go out
with our armies?   Ps. 108:11 • Josh. 7:12
11 Give us help from trouble,
ᴿFor the help of man *is* useless.   Ps. 146:3
12 Through God ᴿwe will do valiantly,
For *it is* He *who* shall tread down our
enemies.   Num. 24:18

Psalm 61

Assurance of God's Eternal Protection

To the Chief Musician. On *a stringed instrument.
A Psalm of David.

HEAR my cry, O God;
Attend to my prayer.
2 From the end of the earth I will cry to
You,
When my heart is overwhelmed;
Lead me to the rock that is higher
than I.

3 For You have been a shelter for me,
A strong tower from the enemy.
4 I will abide in Your ᵀtabernacle forever;
ᴿI will trust in the shelter of Your wings.
Selah   *tent* • Ps. 91:4

5 For You, O God, have heard my vows;
You have given *me* the heritage of
those who fear Your name.
6 You will prolong the king's life,
His years as many generations.
7 He shall abide before God forever.
Oh, prepare mercy and truth, *which*
may ᵀpreserve him!   Lit. *guard* or *keep*

8 So I will sing praise to Your name
forever,
That I may daily perform my vows.

Psalm 62

A Calm Resolve to Wait for the Salvation of God

To the Chief Musician. To Jeduthun.
A Psalm of David.

TRULY ᴿmy soul silently *waits* for God;
From Him *comes* my salvation.   Ps. 33:20
2 He alone *is* my rock and my salvation;
He *is* my ᵀdefense;   *strong tower*
I shall not be greatly ᵀmoved.   *shaken*

3 How long will you attack a man?
You shall be slain, all of you,

61:title, Heb. *neginah*

ᴿLike a leaning wall and a tottering
fence.   Is. 30:13
4 They only consult to cast *him* down
from his high position;
They ᴿdelight in lies;
They bless with their mouth,
But they curse inwardly.   Selah   Ps. 28:3

5 My soul, wait silently for God alone,
For my ᵀexpectation *is* from Him.   *hope*
6 He only *is* my rock and my salvation;
He is my defense;
I shall not be ᵀmoved.   *shaken*
7 ᴿIn God *is* my salvation and my glory;
The rock of my strength,
And my refuge, *is* in God.   [Jer. 3:23]

8 Trust in Him at all times, you people;
ᴿPour out your heart before Him;
God *is* a refuge for us.   Selah   1 Sam. 1:15

9 Surely men of low degree *are* ᵀa vapor,
Men of high degree *are* a lie;   *vanity*
If they are weighed on the scales,
They *are* altogether *lighter* than vapor.
10 Do not trust in oppression,
Nor vainly hope in robbery;
ᴿIf riches increase,   [Luke 12:15]
Do not set *your* heart *on them.*

11 God has spoken once,
Twice I have heard this:
That power *belongs* to God.
12 Also to You, O Lord, *belongs* mercy;
For ᴿYou ᵀrender to each one according
to his work.   [Matt. 16:27] • *reward*

Psalm 63

Joy in the Fellowship of God

A Psalm of David when he was
in the wilderness of Judah.

O GOD, You *are* my God;
Early will I seek You;
ᴿMy soul thirsts for You;
My flesh longs for You
In a dry and thirsty land
Where there is no water.   Ps. 42:2
2 So I have looked for You in the
sanctuary,
To see Your power and Your glory.

3 ᴿBecause Your lovingkindness *is* better
than life,
My lips shall praise You.   Ps. 138:2
4 Thus I will bless You while I live;
I will lift up my hands in Your name.
5 My soul shall be satisfied as with
ᵀmarrow and ᵀfatness,
And my mouth shall praise You with
joyful lips.   Lit. *fat* • Abundance

6 When I remember You on my bed,
I meditate on You in the *night* watches.

7 Because You have been my help,
Therefore in the shadow of Your wings
I will rejoice.
8 My soul follows close behind You;
Your right hand upholds me.

9 But those *who* seek my life, to destroy
it,
Shall go into the lower parts of the
earth.
10 They shall fall by the sword;
They shall be ᵀa portion for jackals. Prey

11 But the king shall rejoice in God;
ᴿEveryone who swears by Him shall
glory;
But the mouth of those who speak lies
shall be stopped. Deut. 6:13

Psalm 64

Oppressed by the Wicked but Rejoicing in the LORD

To the Chief Musician. A Psalm of David.

HEAR my voice, O God, in my
ᵀmeditation;
Preserve my life from fear of the
enemy. *complaint*
2 Hide me from the secret plots of the
wicked,
From the rebellion of the workers of
iniquity,
3 Who sharpen their tongue like a sword,
ᴿAnd bend *their bows to shoot* their
arrows—bitter words, Ps. 58:7
4 That they may shoot in secret at the
blameless;
Suddenly they shoot at him and do not
fear.

5 They encourage themselves *in* an evil
matter;
They talk of laying snares secretly;
They say, "Who will see them?"
6 They devise iniquities:
"We have perfected a shrewd scheme."
Both the inward thought and the heart
of man are deep.

7 But God shall shoot at them *with* an
arrow;
Suddenly they shall be wounded.
8 So He will make them stumble over
their own tongue;
ᴿAll who see them shall flee away. Ps. 31:11
9 All men shall fear,
And shall declare the work of God;
For they shall wisely consider His
doing.

10 ᴿThe righteous shall be glad in the LORD,
and trust in Him. Ps. 32:11
And all the upright in heart shall glory.

Psalm 65

Praise to God for His Salvation and Providence

To the Chief Musician. A Psalm of David. A Song.

PRAISE is awaiting You, O God, in Zion;
And to You the ᵀvow shall be
performed. Promised deed
2 O You who hear prayer,
ᴿTo You all flesh will come. [Is. 66:23]
3 Iniquities prevail against me;
As for our transgressions,
You will provide atonement for them.

4 ᴿBlessed *is the man* You ᴿchoose,
And cause to approach *You*,
That he may dwell in Your courts.
ᴿWe shall be satisfied with the goodness
of Your house, Ps. 33:12 • Ps. 4:3 • Ps. 36:8
Of Your holy temple.

5 *By* awesome deeds in righteousness
You will answer us,
O God of our salvation,
You who are the confidence of all the
ends of the earth,
And of the far-off seas;
6 Who established the mountains by His
strength,
ᴿ*Being* clothed with power; Ps. 93:1
7 ᴿYou who still the noise of the seas,
The noise of their waves, Matt. 8:26
ᴿAnd the tumult of the peoples. Is. 17:12, 13
8 They also who dwell in the farthest
parts are afraid of Your signs;
You make the outgoings of the
morning and evening rejoice.

9 You ᵀvisit the earth and water it,
You greatly enrich it; *give attention to*
ᴿThe river of God is full of water;
You provide their grain, Ps. 46:4; 104:13
For so You have prepared it.
10 You water its ridges abundantly,
You settle its furrows;
You make it soft with showers,
You bless its growth.

11 You crown the year with Your
goodness,
And Your paths drip *with* abundance.
12 They drop *on* the pastures of the
wilderness,
And the little hills rejoice on every side.
13 The pastures are clothed with flocks;
The valleys also are covered with grain;
They shout for joy, they also sing.

Psalm 66

Praise to God for His Awesome Works

To the Chief Musician. A Song. A Psalm.

MAKE ᴿa joyful shout to God, all the
earth! Ps. 100:1

2 Sing out the honor of His name;
　Make His praise glorious.
3 Say to God,
　"How ᴿawesome are Your works!
　ᴿThrough the greatness of Your power
　Your enemies shall submit themselves
　　to You.   Ps. 65:5 · Ps. 18:44
4 ᴿAll the earth shall worship You
　And sing praises to You;
　They shall sing praises *to* Your name."
　Selah   Ps. 117:1

5 Come and see the works of God;
　He is awesome *in His* doing toward the
　　sons of men.
6 ᴿHe turned the sea into dry *land;*
　They went through the river on foot.
　There we will rejoice in Him.   Ex. 14:21
7 He rules by His power forever;
　His eyes observe the nations;
　Do not let the rebellious exalt
　　themselves. Selah

8 Oh, bless our God, you peoples!
　And make the voice of His praise to be
　　heard,
9 Who keeps our soul among the living,
　And does not allow our feet to ᵀbe
　　moved.   *slip*
10 For You, O God, have tested us;
　You have refined us as silver is refined.
11 ᴿYou brought us into the net;
　You laid affliction on our backs. Lam. 1:13
12 ᴿYou have caused men to ride over our
　　heads;
　ᴿWe went through fire and through
　　water;
　But You brought us out to ᵀrich
　　fulfillment.   Is. 51:23 · Is. 43:2 · *abundance*

13 ᴿI will go into Your house with burnt
　　offerings;   Ps. 100:4; 116:14, 17–19
　I will pay You my ᵀvows,   Promises
14 Which my lips have uttered
　And my mouth has spoken when I was
　　in trouble.
15 I will offer You burnt sacrifices of fat
　　animals,
　With the sweet aroma of rams;
　I will offer bulls with goats. Selah

16 Come *and* hear, all you who fear God,
　And I will declare what He has done for
　　my soul.
17 I cried to Him with my mouth,
　And He was extolled with my tongue.
18 ᴿIf I regard iniquity in my heart,
　The Lord will not hear.   Is. 1:15
19 *But* certainly God ᴿhas heard *me;*
　He has attended to the voice of my
　　prayer.   Ps. 116:1, 2

20 Blessed *be* God,
　Who has not turned away my prayer,
　Nor His mercy from me!

Psalm 67

An Invocation and a Doxology

To the Chief Musician. On *stringed instruments.
A Psalm. A Song.

GOD be merciful to us and bless us,
　And ᴿcause His face to shine upon us,
　Selah   Num. 6:25
2 That ᴿYour way may be known on
　　earth,   Acts 18:25
　Your salvation among all nations.

3 Let the peoples praise You, O God;
　Let all the peoples praise You.
4 Oh, let the nations be glad and sing for
　　joy!
　For ᴿYou shall judge the people
　　righteously,
　And govern the nations on earth.
　Selah   [Ps. 96:10, 13; 98:9]

5 Let the peoples praise You, O God;
　Let all the peoples praise You.
6 *Then* the earth shall yield her increase;
　God, our own God, shall bless us.
7 God shall bless us,
　And all the ends of the earth shall fear
　　Him.

Psalm 68

The Glory of God in His Goodness to Israel

To the Chief Musician. A Psalm of David. A Song.

LET ᴿGod arise,
　Let His enemies be scattered;
　Let those also who hate Him flee before
　　Him.   Num. 10:35
2 ᴿAs smoke is driven away,
　So drive *them* away;
　ᴿAs wax melts before the fire,
　So let the wicked perish at the presence
　　of God.   [Is. 9:18] · Mic. 1:4
3 But ᴿlet the righteous be glad;
　Let them rejoice before God;   Ps. 32:11
　Yes, let them rejoice exceedingly.

4 Sing to God, sing praises to His name;
　ᵀExtol Him who rides on the *clouds,
　ᴿBy His name YAH,   *Praise* · [Ex. 6:3]
　And rejoice before Him.

5 ᴿA father of the fatherless, a defender of
　　widows,   [Ps. 10:14, 18; 146:9]
　Is God in His holy habitation.
6 ᴿGod sets the solitary in families;
　ᴿHe brings out those who are bound into
　　prosperity;   Ps. 107:4-7 · Acts 12:6
　But the rebellious dwell in a dry *land.*

7 O God, ᴿwhen You went out before
　　Your people,

67:title, Heb. *neginoth*
68:4 MT *deserts;* Tg. *heavens,* cf. v. 34 and Is. 19:1

When You marched through the
wilderness,   Selah   Ex. 13:21
8 The earth shook;
The heavens also dropped rain at the
presence of God;
Sinai itself was moved at the presence
of God, the God of Israel.
9 RYou, O God, sent a plentiful rain,
Whereby You confirmed Your
inheritance,
When it was weary.   Deut. 11:11
10 Your congregation dwelt in it;
RYou, O God, provided from Your
goodness for the poor.   Deut. 26:5
11 The Lord gave the word;
Great was the Tcompany of those who
proclaimed it: host
12 "KingsR of armies flee, they flee,
And she who remains at home divides
the Tspoil.   Josh. 10:16 · plunder
13 RThough you lie down among the
Tsheepfolds,   Ps. 81:6 · Or saddlebags
RYou will be like the wings of a dove
covered with silver,   Ps. 105:37
And her feathers with yellow gold."
14 RWhen the Almighty scattered kings in
it,   Josh. 10:10
It was white as snow in Zalmon.

15 A mountain of God is the mountain of
Bashan;
A mountain of many peaks is the
mountain of Bashan.
16 Why do you Tfume with envy, you
mountains of many peaks?   Lit. stare
RThis is the mountain which God desires
to dwell in;   [Deut. 12:5]
Yes, the LORD will dwell in it forever.

17 RThe chariots of God are twenty
thousand,
Even thousands of thousands;
The Lord is among them as in Sinai, in
the Holy Place.   Deut. 33:2
18 RYou have ascended on high,   Eph. 4:8
RYou have led captivity captive;   Judg. 5:12
You have received gifts among men,
Even from Rthe rebellious,   1 Tim. 1:13
That the LORD God might dwell there.

19 Blessed be the Lord,
Who daily loads us with benefits,
The God of our salvation!   Selah
20 Our God is the God of salvation;
And Rto GOD the Lord belong escapes
from death.   [Deut. 32:39]

21 But RGod will wound the head of His
enemies,   Hab. 3:13
RThe hairy scalp of the one who still
goes on in his trespasses.   Ps. 55:23

22 The Lord said, "I will bring Rback from
Bashan,
I will bring them back Rfrom the depths
of the sea,   Num. 21:33 · Ex. 14:22
23 RThat *your foot may crush them in
blood,   Ps. 58:10
And the tongues of your dogs may
have their portion from your
enemies."

24 They have seen Your Tprocession, O
God,
The procession of my God, my King,
into the sanctuary.   Lit. goings
25 RThe singers went before, the players on
instruments followed after;
Among them were the maidens playing
timbrels.   1 Chr. 13:8
26 Bless God in the congregations,
The Lord, from the fountain of Israel.
27 RThere is little Benjamin, their leader,
The princes of Judah and their
Tcompany,
The princes of Zebulun and the princes
of Naphtali.   1 Sam. 9:21 · throng
28 *Your God has Rcommanded your
strength;
Strengthen, O God, what You have
done for us.   Is. 26:12
29 Because of Your temple at Jerusalem,
Kings will bring presents to You.
30 Rebuke the beasts of the reeds,
RThe herd of bulls with the calves of the
peoples,   Ps. 22:12
Till everyone Rsubmits himself with
pieces of silver.   2 Sam. 8:2
Scatter the peoples who delight in war.
31 Envoys will come out of Egypt;
REthiopia will quickly Rstretch out her
hands to God.   Is. 45:14 · Ps. 44:20

32 Sing to God, you Rkingdoms of the
earth;   [Ps. 67:3, 4]
Oh, sing praises to the Lord,   Selah
33 To Him Rwho rides on the heaven of
heavens, which were of old!
Indeed, He sends out His voice, a
Rmighty voice.   Ps. 18:10 · Ps. 46:6
34 RAscribe strength to God;
His excellence is over Israel,   Ps. 29:1
And His strength is in the clouds.
35 O God, RYou are more awesome than
Your holy places.   Ps. 76:12
The God of Israel is He who gives
strength and power to His people.

Blessed be God!

68:23 LXX, [Syr.], Tg., Vg. you may dip your foot
68:28 LXX, [Syr.], Tg., Vg. Command, O God

Psalm 69

An Urgent Plea for Help in Trouble

To the Chief Musician.
Set to *"The Lilies." A Psalm of David.

▼ 9–C. The Messiah Forsaken

S AVE me, O God!
   For ᴿthe waters have come up to *my*
   ᵀneck.   Jon. 2:5 • Lit. *soul*

2 ᴿI sink in deep mire,

69:title, Heb. *Shoshannim*

Where *there is* no standing;   ▽
I have come into deep waters,
Where the floods overflow me.   Ps. 40:2
3 ᴿI am weary with my crying;
My throat is dry;   Ps. 6:6
My eyes fail while I wait for my God.

4 Those who ᴿhate me without a cause
Are more than the hairs of my head;
They are mighty who would destroy
me,
Being my enemies wrongfully;
Though I have stolen nothing,
I *still* must restore *it.*   John 15:25

9-C. The Messiah Forsaken (Psalm 69:1–21)—Psalms 22 and 69 are quoted by the writers of the New Testament more than any other segment of Scripture. Psalm 69 is one of the great messianic psalms.

In verse 4 the Messiah says, "Those who hate me without a cause are more than the hairs of my head; they are mighty who would destroy me, being my enemies wrongfully." Christ was hated from His birth without cause, first by King Herod the Great (Matt. 2:1–15, page 931), and also by Satan, demons, religious leaders, and virtually the entire Gentile and Jewish nations. The leaders, especially the religious leaders, attempted to kill Him many times. But no man could touch Him until His hour had come (John 17:1, page 1078).

In verse 8 the Messiah says, "I have become a stranger to my brothers, and an alien to my mother's children." He was ostracized by His own, even though He came healing the sick, cleansing the lepers, and opening the eyes of the blind. He raised the dead and fed the multitudes. "He came to His own [His own creation, His own things], and His own [people] did not receive Him" (John 1:11, page 1049). He was an alien to His mother's children. Notice, He did not say, "My father's children," because God was and is His only Father. John wrote that before His resurrection His half-brothers did not believe in Him (John 7:5, page 1060). (After His resurrection, however, they were converted. They believed in Him as the Lord Christ, the Messiah, God's only begotten Son. Two of them, James and Jude, wrote two New Testament epistles bearing their names.)

In verse 9 the Messiah says, "Because zeal for Your house has eaten me up." When Jesus went up to Jerusalem, at the time of the Passover, He found the temple desecrated by moneychangers and by those who sold oxen, sheep, and doves. These commercializers had not only turned temple worship into a business, they made it a dishonest business as well, cheating those who sincerely wanted to worship God. Jesus made a whip and drove them out of the temple, saying, " 'My house shall be called a house of prayer,' but you have made it a 'den of thieves' " (Matt. 21:13, page 968). When the disciples saw what Jesus did, and heard what He said, they remembered verse 9.

In verse 19 the Messiah says, "You know my reproach, my shame, and my dishonor; my adversaries are all before You." Four words in this verse express the contempt poured out on Him:

(1) "Reproach." In verse 20 He continues, "Reproach has broken my heart." Jesus died on the cross with a broken heart. During His crucifixion, a Roman soldier pierced His side with a spear, and blood and water flowed out. Water was evidence both of physical suffering (it builds up around the pericardium during intense agony) and of a broken heart (John 19:34, page 1081). Men chided Him: "If You are the Son of God, come down from the cross." The chief priests, with the scribes and elders, mocked Him: "He saved others; Himself He cannot save" (Matt. 27:35–44, page 980).

(2) "Shame." The shame of Calvary was the shame of the world. It is your shame and my shame. He so loved the world that He hung upon the cross and bore the shame of the world, loving us so much that He bore the shame for us. But now He is on the joyful side of Calvary, where there is no shame (Heb. 12:2, page 1250).

(3) "Dishonor." Here again, along with our shame, He also bore dishonor in our place, upon the cross.

(4) "Adversaries." His adversaries are our adversaries—Satan, the demons, and all those who crucified Jesus. Essentially, the Lord was saying to His disciples, "They will hate you; they will try to do the same to you if you are My disciples." Yet Jesus loved and prayed for those enemies who crucified Him. He prayed, "Father, forgive them, for they do not know what they do" (Luke 23:34, page 1045).

In verse 21 the Messiah says, "They also gave me gall for my food, and for my thirst they gave me vinegar to drink." On the cross "they gave Him sour wine mingled with gall to drink. But when He had tasted it, He would not drink" (Matt. 27:34, page 980). He refused the vinegar and gall because He knew they were given to Him to help deaden the pain. The Lord Jesus came into the world to suffer, to pay the price in full for our sins, that we might be redeemed and transformed into children of God. As the God-Man He would suffer physically, spiritually, and mentally, to the fullest extent, so that you and I might be saved (Col. 1:13, 14, page 1201).

See Psalm 22:1–31, page 522, for **Point 9-D: The Messiah Crucified.**

▽ 5 O God, You know my foolishness;
And my sins are not hidden from You.

6 Let not those who ᵀwait for You,
O Lord GOD of hosts, be ᵀashamed
because of me;
Let not those who seek You be
confounded because of me, O God of
Israel.   Wait in faith · *dishonored*

7 Because ᴿfor Your sake I have borne
reproach;   Rom. 15:3
Shame has covered my face.

8 ᴿI have become a stranger to my
brothers,   Is. 53:3; Mark 3:21
And an alien to my mother's children;

9 ᴿBecause zeal for Your house has eaten
me up,   John 2:17
And the reproaches of those who
reproach You have fallen on me.

10 When I wept *and chastened* my soul
with fasting,
That became my reproach.

11 I also made ᵀsackcloth my garment;
I became a byword to them.   Symbol of grief

12 Those who ᵀsit in the gate speak
against me,   Sit as judges
And I *am* the song of the drunkards.

13 But as for me, my prayer *is* to You,
O LORD, *in* the acceptable time;
O God, in the multitude of Your mercy,
Hear me in the truth of Your salvation.

14 Deliver me out of the mire,
And let me not sink;
Let me be delivered from those who
hate me,
And out of the deep waters.

15 Let not the floodwater overflow me,
Nor let the deep swallow me up;
And let not the pit shut its mouth on
me.

16 Hear me, O LORD, for Your
lovingkindness *is* good;
Turn to me according to the multitude
of Your tender mercies.

17 And do not hide Your face from Your
servant,
For I am in trouble;
Hear me speedily.

18 Draw near to my soul, *and* redeem it;
Deliver me because of my enemies.

19 You know ᴿmy reproach, my shame,
and my dishonor;   Ps. 22:6, 7
My adversaries *are* all before You.

20 ᴿReproach has broken my heart,
And I am full of heaviness;   Rom. 15:3
ᴿI looked *for someone* to take pity, but
there was none;   Is. 63:5
And for comforters, but I found none.

21 They also gave me gall for my food,
ᴿAnd for my thirst they gave me vinegar
to drink.   Matt. 27:34, 48

22 ᴿLet their table become a snare before
them,
And their well-being a trap.   Rom. 11:9, 10

23 ᴿLet their eyes be darkened, so that they
do not see;   Is. 6:9, 10
And make their loins shake continually.

24 ᴿPour out Your indignation upon them,
And let Your wrathful anger take hold
of them.   [1 Thess. 2:16]

25 ᴿLet their dwelling place be desolate;
Let no one live in their tents.   Matt. 23:38

26 For they persecute ᴿthe *ones* You have
struck,
And talk of the grief of those You have
wounded.   [Is. 53:4]

27 ᴿAdd iniquity to their iniquity,
ᴿAnd let them not come into Your
righteousness.   [Rom. 1:28] · [Is. 26:10]

28 Let them ᴿbe blotted out of the book of
the living,   [Ex. 32:32]
And not be written with the righteous.

29 But I *am* poor and sorrowful;
Let Your salvation, O God, set me up
on high.

30 ᴿI will praise the name of God with a
song,
And will magnify Him with
thanksgiving.   [Ps. 28:7]

31 ᴿThis also shall please the LORD better
than an ox *or* bull,   Ps. 50:13, 14, 23; 51:16
Which has horns and hooves.

32 ᴿThe humble shall see *this and* be glad;
And you who seek God, ᴿyour hearts
shall live.   Ps. 34:2 · Ps. 22:26

33 For the LORD hears the poor,
And does not despise His prisoners.

34 ᴿLet heaven and earth praise Him,
The seas ᴿand everything that moves in
them.   Ps. 96:11 · Is. 55:12

35 ᴿFor God will save Zion
And build the cities of Judah,
That they may dwell there and possess
it.   Is. 44:26

36 Also, ᴿthe ᵀdescendants of His servants
shall inherit it,
And those who love His name shall
dwell in it.   Ps. 102:28 · Lit. *seed*

Psalm 70

Prayer for Relief from Adversaries

To the Chief Musician. *A Psalm* of David.
To bring to remembrance.

MAKE *haste*, O God, to deliver me!
Make haste to help me, O LORD!

2 ᴿLet them be ashamed and confounded
Who seek my life;
Let them be turned back and confused
Who desire my hurt.   Ps. 35:4, 26

3 ᴿLet them be *turned back because of
their shame,   Ps. 40:15
Who say, ᵀ"Aha, aha!"   An expression of scorn

70:3 So with MT, LXX, Tg., Vg.; some Heb. mss., Syr.
appalled (cf. 40:15)

4 Let all those who seek You rejoice and
   be glad in You;
   And let those who love Your salvation
   say continually,
   "Let God be magnified!"

5 ᴿBut I *am* poor and needy;   Ps. 72:12, 13
   ᴿMake haste to me, O God!   Ps. 141:1
   You *are* my help and my deliverer;
   O Lᴏʀᴅ, do not delay.

Psalm 71

God the Rock of Salvation

IN ᴿYou, O Lᴏʀᴅ, I put my trust;
   Let me never be put to shame.   Ps. 25:2, 3
2 ᴿDeliver me in Your righteousness, and
   cause me to escape;   Ps. 31:1
   Incline Your ear to me, and save me.
3 Be my ᵀstrong refuge,
   To which I may resort continually;
   You have given the commandment to
   save me,   Lit. *rock of refuge* or *habitation*
   For You *are* my rock and my fortress.

4 ᴿDeliver me, O my God, out of the hand
   of the wicked,
   Out of the hand of the unrighteous and
   cruel man.   Ps. 140:1, 3
5 For You are my hope, O Lord Gᴏᴅ;
   You are my trust from my youth.
6 By You I have been ᵀupheld from birth;
   You are He who took me out of my
   mother's womb.   *sustained from the womb*
   My praise *shall be* continually of You.

7 ᴿI have become a wonder to many,
   But You *are* my strong refuge.   Is. 8:18
8 Let ᴿmy mouth be filled *with* Your
   praise   Ps. 35:28
   And with Your glory all the day.

9 Do not cast me off in the time of old
   age;
   Do not forsake me when my strength
   fails.
10 For my enemies speak against me;
   And those who lie in wait for my life
   ᴿtake counsel together,   2 Sam. 17:1
11 Saying, "God has forsaken him;
   Pursue and take him, for *there is* none
   to deliver *him*."

12 ᴿO God, do not be far from me;   Ps. 35:22
   O my God, make haste to help me!
13 Let them be ᵀconfounded *and*
   consumed
   Who are adversaries of my life;
   Let them be covered *with* reproach and
   dishonor
   Who seek my hurt.   *ashamed*

14 But I will hope continually,
   And will praise You yet more and more.

15 My mouth shall tell of Your
   righteousness
   And Your salvation all the day,
   For I do not know *their* limits.
16 I will go in the strength of the Lord
   Gᴏᴅ;
   I will make mention of Your
   righteousness, of Yours only.
17 O God, You have taught me from my
   ᴿyouth;
   And to this *day* I declare Your
   wondrous works.   Deut. 4:5; 6:7
18 Now also ᴿwhen *I am* old and
   grayheaded,
   O God, do not forsake me,
   Until I declare Your strength to *this*
   generation,
   Your power to everyone *who* is to
   come.   [Is. 46:4]
19 Also Your righteousness, O God, *is* very
   ᵀhigh,   *great, lit. to the height of heaven*
   You who have done great things;
   O God, who *is* like You?
20 ᴿYou, who have shown me great and
   severe troubles,
   ᴿShall revive me again,
   And bring me up again from the depths
   of the earth.   Ps. 60:3 • Hos. 6:1, 2
21 You shall increase my greatness,
   And comfort me on every side.

22 Also ᴿwith the lute I will praise You—
   And Your faithfulness, O my God!
   To You I will sing with the harp,
   O ᴿHoly One of Israel.   Ps. 92:1-3 • 2 Kin. 19:22
23 My lips shall greatly rejoice when I sing
   to You,
   And ᴿmy soul, which You have
   redeemed.   Ps. 103:4
24 My tongue also shall talk of Your
   righteousness all the day long;
   For they are confounded,
   For they are brought to shame
   Who seek my hurt.

Psalm 72

Glory and Universality of the Messiah's Reign

A Psalm of Solomon.

GIVE the king Your judgments, O God,
   And Your righteousness to the king's
   Son.
2 ᴿHe will judge Your people with
   righteousness,   [Is. 9:7; 11:2-5; 32:1]
   And Your poor with justice.
3 ᴿThe mountains will bring peace to the
   people,   Ps. 85:10
   And the little hills, by righteousness.
4 ᴿHe will bring justice to the poor of the
   people;   Is. 11:4

He will save the children of the needy,
And will break in pieces the oppressor.

5 *They shall fear You
  ᴿAs long as the sun and moon endure,
  Throughout all generations.   [Ps. 89:36]
6 ᴿHe shall come down like rain upon the
    grass before mowing,   Hos. 6:3
  Like showers *that* water the earth.
7 In His days the righteous shall flourish,
  ᴿAnd abundance of peace,
  Until the moon is no more.   Is. 2:4

8 ᴿHe shall have dominion also from sea to
    sea,
  And from the River to the ends of the
    earth.   Ex. 23:31
9 Those who dwell in the wilderness will
    ᴿbow before Him,   Is. 49:23
  And His enemies will lick the dust.
10 ᴿThe kings of Tarshish and of the isles
   Will bring presents;
   The kings of Sheba and Seba
   Will offer gifts.   2 Chr. 9:21
11 ᴿYes, all kings shall fall down before
     Him;
   All nations shall serve Him.   Is. 49:23

12 For He ᴿwill deliver the needy when he
     cries,   Job. 29:12
   The ᴿpoor also, and *him* who has no
     helper.   [Ps. 72:4]
13 He will spare the poor and needy,
   And will save the souls of the needy.
14 He will redeem their life from
     oppression and violence;
   And ᴿprecious shall be their blood in
     His sight.   [Ps. 116:15]

15 And He shall live;
   And the gold of ᴿSheba will be given to
     Him;
   Prayer also will be made for Him
     continually,
   And daily He shall be praised.   Is. 60:6

16 There will be an abundance of grain in
     the earth,
   On the top of the mountains;
   Its fruit shall wave like Lebanon;
   ᴿAnd *those* of the city shall flourish like
     grass of the earth.   1 Kin. 4:20

17 ᴿHis name shall endure forever;
   His name shall continue as long as the
     sun.   [Ps. 89:36]
   And *men* shall be blessed in Him;
   All nations shall call Him blessed.

18 ᴿBlessed *be* the LORD God, the God of
     Israel,   1 Chr. 29:10
   Who only does wondrous things!
19 And ᴿblessed *be* His glorious name
     forever!

   ᴿAnd let the whole earth be filled *with*
     His glory.   [Neh. 9:5] • Num. 14:21
   Amen and Amen.

20 The prayers of David the son of Jesse
     are ended.

BOOK THREE
Psalms 73–89

Psalm 73

The Tragedy of the Wicked, and the
Blessedness of Trust in God

A Psalm of Asaph.

TRULY God *is* good to Israel,
  To such as are pure in heart.
2 But as for me, my feet had almost
    stumbled;
  My steps had nearly ᴿslipped.   Job 12:5
3 ᴿFor I *was* envious of the boastful,
  When I saw the prosperity of the
    ᴿwicked.   Ps. 37:1, 7 • Job 21:5–16

4 For *there are* no ᵀpangs in their death,
  But their strength *is* firm.   *pains*
5 They *are* not in trouble as *other* men,
  Nor are they plagued like *other* men.
6 Therefore pride serves as their
    necklace;
  Violence covers them *like* a garment.
7 Their *eyes bulge with abundance;
  They have more than heart could wish.
8 ᴿThey scoff and speak wickedly   Ps. 53:1
    concerning oppression;
  They ᴿspeak ᵀloftily.   2 Pet. 2:18 • *Proudly*
9 They set their mouth ᴿagainst the
    heavens,
  And their tongue walks through the
    earth.   Rev. 13:6

10 Therefore his people return here,
   ᴿAnd waters of a full *cup* are drained by
     them.   [Ps. 75:8]
11 And they say, ᴿ"How does God know?
   And is there knowledge in the Most
     High?"   Job 22:13
12 Behold, these *are* the ungodly,
   Who are always at ease;
   They increase *in* riches.
13 Surely I have ᵀcleansed my heart ᴿin
     vain,   *kept my heart pure in vain* • Job 21:15; 35:3
   And washed my hands in innocence.
14 For all day long I have been plagued,
   And chastened every morning.

15 If I had said, "I will speak thus,"
   Behold, I would have been untrue to
     the generation of Your children.

72:5 So with MT, Tg.; LXX, Vg. *They shall continue*   73:7 Tg. *face bulges;* LXX, Syr., Vg. *iniquity bulges*

16 When I thought *how* to understand
   this,
   It *was* too ᵀpainful for me—   *troublesome*
17 Until I went into the sanctuary of God;
   Then I understood their ᴿend.   [Ps. 37:38]

18 Surely You set them in slippery places;
   You cast them down to destruction.
19 Oh, how they are *brought* to desolation,
   as in a moment!
   They are utterly consumed with terrors.
20 As a dream when *one* awakes,
   So, Lord, when You awake,
   You shall despise their image.

21 Thus my heart was grieved,
   And I was vexed in my mind.
22 ᴿI *was* so foolish and ignorant;
   I was *like* a beast before You.   Ps. 92:6
23 Nevertheless I *am* continually with
   You;
   You hold *me* by my right hand.
24 You will guide me with Your counsel,
   And afterward receive me *to* glory.

25 ᴿWhom have I in heaven *but You?*
   And *there is* none upon earth *that* I
   desire besides You.   [Phil. 3:8]
26 ᴿMy flesh and my heart fail;   Ps. 84:2
   But God *is* the ᵀstrength of my heart
   and my ᴿportion forever. Lit. *rock* · Ps. 16:5

27 For indeed, ᴿthose who are far from
   You shall perish;   [Ps. 119:155]
   You have destroyed all those who
   desert You for harlotry.
28 But *it is* good for me to ᴿdraw near to
   God;   [Heb. 10:22]
   I have put my trust in the Lord Goᴅ,
   That I may declare all Your works.

Psalm 74

A Plea for Relief from Oppressors

A *Contemplation of Asaph.

O GOD, why have You cast *us* off
   forever?
   Why does Your anger smoke against
   the sheep of Your pasture?
2 Remember Your congregation, *which*
   You have purchased of old,
   The tribe of Your inheritance, *which*
   You have redeemed—
   This Mount Zion where You have
   dwelt.
3 Lift up Your feet to the perpetual
   desolations.
   The enemy has damaged everything in
   the sanctuary.
4 ᴿYour enemies roar in the midst of Your
   meeting place;   Lam. 2:7
   They set up their banners *for* signs.

5 They seem like men who lift up
   Axes among the thick trees.
6 And now they break down its carved
   work, all at once,
   With axes and hammers.
7 They have set fire to Your sanctuary;
   They have defiled the dwelling place of
   Your name to the ground.
8 ᴿThey said in their hearts,
   "Let us ᵀdestroy them altogether."
   They have burned up all the meeting
   places of God in the land. Ps. 83:4 · *oppress*

9 We do not see our signs;
   ᴿ*There is* no longer any prophet;
   Nor *is there* any among us who knows
   how long.   Amos 8:11
10 O God, how long will the adversary
   ᵀreproach?
   Will the enemy blaspheme Your name
   forever?   *revile*
11 ᴿWhy do You withdraw Your hand, even
   Your right hand?
   Take it out of Your bosom and destroy
   them.   Lam. 2:3
12 For ᴿGod *is* my King from of old,
   Working salvation in the midst of the
   earth.   Ps. 44:4
13 You divided the sea by Your strength;
   You broke the heads of the ᵀsea
   serpents in the waters.   *sea monsters*
14 You broke the heads of ᵀLeviathan in
   pieces,   A large sea creature of unknown identity
   And gave him *as* food to the people
   inhabiting the wilderness.
15 ᴿYou broke open the fountain and the
   flood;   Ex. 17:5, 6
   ᴿYou dried up mighty rivers.   Josh. 2:10; 3:13
16 The day *is* Yours, the night also *is*
   ᴿYours;
   ᴿYou have prepared the light and the
   sun.   Job 38:12 · Gen. 1:14–18
17 You have ᴿset all the borders of the
   earth;   Acts 17:26
   You have made summer and winter.

18 Remember this, *that* the enemy has
   reproached, O Loʀᴅ,
   And *that* a foolish people has
   blasphemed Your name.
19 Oh, do not deliver the life of Your
   turtledove to the wild beast!
   Do not forget the life of Your poor
   forever.
20 Have respect to the covenant;
   For the dark places of the earth are full
   of the haunts of cruelty.
21 Oh, do not let the oppressed return
   ashamed!
   Let the poor and needy praise Your
   name.
22 Arise, O God, plead Your own cause;
   Remember how the foolish man
   ᵀreproaches You daily.   *reviles* or *taunts*

74:title, Heb. *Maschil*

23 Do not forget the voice of Your
    enemies;
  The tumult of those who rise up against
  You increases continually.

Psalm 75

*Thanksgiving for God's Righteous
Judgment*

To the Chief Musician. Set to *"Do Not Destroy."
A Psalm of Asaph. A Song.

WE give thanks to You, O God, we give
    thanks!
  For Your wondrous works declare *that*
  Your name is near.

2 "When I choose the ᵀproper time,
    I will judge uprightly.   appointed
3 The earth and all its inhabitants are
    dissolved;
  I set up its pillars firmly.   Selah

4 "I said to the boastful, 'Do not deal
    boastfully,'
  And to the wicked, 'Do not ᵀlift up the
  horn.   Raise the head proudly like a horned animal
5 Do not lift up your horn on high;
  Do *not* speak with ᵀa stiff neck.' "   Pride

6 For exaltation *comes* neither from the
    east
  Nor from the west nor from the south.
7 But ᴿGod *is* the Judge:
  ᴿHe puts down one,
  And exalts another.   Ps. 50:6 • 1 Sam. 2:7
8 For ᴿin the hand of the LORD *there is* a
    cup,
  And the wine is red;
  It is fully mixed, and He pours it out;
  Surely its dregs shall all the wicked of
    the earth
  Drain *and* drink down.   Jer. 25:15

9 But I will declare forever,
  I will sing praises to the God of Jacob.

10 "Allᴿ the ᵀhorns of the wicked I will also
    cut off,   Jer. 48:25 • Strength
  But ᴿthe horns of the righteous shall be
  ᴿexalted."   Ps. 89:17; 148:14 • 1 Sam. 2:1

Psalm 76

The Majesty of God in Judgment

To the Chief Musician. On *stringed instruments.
A Psalm of Asaph. A Song.

IN ᴿJudah God *is* known;
   His name *is* great in Israel.   Ps. 48:1, 3
2 In ᵀSalem also is His tabernacle,
  And His dwelling place in Zion.   Jerusalem
3 There He broke the arrows of the bow,
  The shield and sword of battle.   Selah

75:title, Heb. *Al Tashcheth*
76:title, Heb. *neginoth*

4 You *are* more glorious and excellent
  ᴿThan the mountains of prey.   Ezek. 38:12
5 The stouthearted were plundered;
  ᴿThey have sunk into their sleep;
  And none of the mighty men have
  found the use of their hands.   Ps. 13:3
6 ᴿAt Your rebuke, O God of Jacob,
  Both the chariot and horse were cast
  into a dead sleep.   Ex. 15:1–21

7 You, Yourself, *are* to be feared;
  And ᴿwho may stand in Your presence
  When once You are angry?   [Nah. 1:6]
8 ᴿYou caused judgment to be heard from
    heaven;   Ex. 19:9
  ᴿThe earth feared and was still, 2 Chr. 20:29
9 When God ᴿarose to judgment,
  To deliver all the oppressed of the
  earth.   Selah   [Ps. 9:7–9]
10 ᴿSurely the wrath of man shall praise
    You;
  With the remainder of wrath You shall
  gird Yourself.   Rom. 9:17

11 ᴿMake vows to the LORD your God, and
    pay *them;*
  ᴿLet all who are around Him bring
  presents to Him who ought to be
  feared.   [Eccl. 5:4–6] • 2 Chr. 32:22, 23
12 He shall cut off the spirit of princes;
  ᴿHe is awesome to the kings of the
  earth.   Ps. 68:35

Psalm 77

*The Consoling Memory of God's
Redemptive Works*

To the Chief Musician. To Jeduthun.
A Psalm of Asaph.

I CRIED out to God with my voice—
   To God with my voice;
   And He gave ear to me.
2 In the day of my trouble I sought the
    Lord;
  My hand was stretched out in the night
  without ceasing;
  My soul refused to be comforted.
3 I remembered God, and was troubled;
  I complained, and my spirit was
  overwhelmed.   Selah

4 You hold my eyelids *open;*
  I am so troubled that I cannot speak.
5 I have considered the days of old,
  The years of ancient times.
6 I call to remembrance my song in the
    night;
  I meditate within my heart,
  And my spirit makes diligent search.

7 Will the Lord cast off forever?
  And will He be favorable no more?
8 Has His mercy ceased forever?
  Has *His* promise failed forevermore?

9 Has God forgotten to be gracious?
   Has He in anger shut up His tender
      mercies? Selah

10 And I said, "This *is* my ᵀanguish;
   But I will remember the years of the
      right hand of the Most High."   *infirmity*

11 I will remember the works of the LORD;
   Surely I will remember Your wonders
      of old.

12 I will also meditate on all Your work,
   And talk of Your deeds.

13 Your way, O God, *is* in the sanctuary;
   Who *is* so great a God as *our* God?

14 You *are* the God who does wonders;
   You have declared Your strength
      among the peoples.

15 You have with *Your* arm redeemed
      Your people,
   The sons of Jacob and Joseph.   Selah

16 The waters saw You, O God;
   The waters saw You, they were ᴿafraid;
   The depths also trembled.   Ex. 14:21

17 The clouds poured out water;
   The skies sent out a sound;
   Your arrows also flashed about.

18 The voice of Your thunder *was* in the
      whirlwind;
   The lightnings lit up the world;
   The earth trembled and shook.

19 Your way *was* in the sea,
   Your path in the great waters,
   And Your footsteps were not known.

20 You led Your people like a flock
   By the hand of Moses and Aaron.

Psalm 78

God's Kindness to Rebellious Israel

A *Contemplation of Asaph.

G IVE ear, O my people, *to* my law;
   Incline your ears to the words of my
      mouth.

2 I will open my mouth in a parable;
   I will utter ᵀdark sayings of old,   *riddles*

3 Which we have heard and known,
   And our fathers have told us.

4 ᴿWe will not hide *them* from their
      children,   Deut. 4:9; 6:7
   ᴿTelling to the generation to come the
      praises of the LORD,   Ex. 13:8, 14
   And His strength and His wonderful
      works that He has done.

5 For ᴿHe established a testimony in
      Jacob,
   And appointed a law in Israel,
   Which He commanded our fathers,
   That ᵀthey should make them known to
      their children;   Ps. 147:19 · Deut. 4:9; 11:19

6 ᴿThat the generation to come might
      know *them*,

78:title, Heb. *Maschil*

The children *who* would be born,
   That they may arise and declare *them*
      to their children,   Ps. 102:18

7 That they may set their hope in God,
   And not forget the works of God,
   But keep His commandments;

8 And may not be like their fathers,
   A stubborn and rebellious generation,
   A generation ᴿ*that* did not ᵀset its heart
      aright,   Ps. 78:37 · Lit. *prepare its heart*
   And whose spirit was not faithful to
      God.

9 The children of Ephraim, *being* armed
      and ᵀcarrying bows,   Lit. *bow shooters*
   Turned back in the day of battle.

10 They did not keep the covenant of God;
   They refused to walk in His law,

11 And ᴿforgot His works
   And His wonders that He had shown
      them.   Ps. 106:13

12 ᴿMarvelous things He did in the sight of
      their fathers,
   In the land of Egypt, ᴿ*in* the field of
      Zoan.   Ex. 7—12 · Num. 13:22

13 ᴿHe divided the sea and caused them to
      pass through;
   And ᴿHe made the waters stand up like
      a heap.   Ex. 14:21 · Ex. 15:8

14 ᴿIn the daytime also He led them with
      the cloud,   Ex. 13:21
   And all the night with a light of fire.

15 ᴿHe split the rocks in the wilderness,
   And gave *them* drink in abundance like
      the depths.   Num. 20:11

16 He also brought ᴿstreams out of the
      rock,
   And caused waters to run down like
      rivers.   Num. 20:8, 10, 11

17 But they sinned even more against Him
   By ᴿrebelling against the Most High in
      the wilderness.   Heb. 3:16

18 And they tested God in their heart
   By asking for the food of their fancy.

19 ᴿYes, they spoke against God:
   They said, "Can God prepare a table in
      the wilderness?   Num. 11:4; 20:3; 21:5

20 ᴿBehold, He struck the rock,
   So that the waters gushed out,
   And the streams overflowed.
   Can He give bread also?   Num. 20:11
   Can He provide meat for His people?"

21 Therefore the LORD heard *this* and ᴿwas
      furious;   Num. 11:1
   So a fire was kindled against Jacob,
   And anger also came up against Israel,

22 Because they did not believe in God,
   And did not trust in His salvation.

23 Yet He had commanded the clouds
      above,
   And opened the doors of heaven,

24 ^RHad rained down manna on them to
      eat,
   And given them of the ^Tbread of
      ^Rheaven.   Ex. 16:4 • Lit. *grain* • John 6:31
25 Men ate angels' food;
   He sent them food to the ^Tfull.   *satiation*
26 ^RHe caused an east wind to blow in the
      heavens;
   And by His power He brought in the
      south wind.   Num. 11:31
27 He also rained meat on them like the
      dust,
   Feathered fowl like the sand of the
      seas;
28 And He let *them* fall in the midst of
      their camp,
   All around their dwellings.
29 So they ate and were well filled,
   For He gave them their own desire.
30 They were not ^Tdeprived of their
      craving;   Lit. *separated from*
   But ^Rwhile their food *was* still in their
      mouths,   Num. 11:33
31 The wrath of God came against them,
   And slew the stoutest of them,
   And struck down the choice *men* of
      Israel.
32 In spite of this ^Rthey still sinned,
   And ^Rdid not believe in His wondrous
      works.   Num. 14:16, 17 • Num. 14:11
33 ^RTherefore their days He consumed in
      futility,
   And their years in fear.   Num. 14:29, 35
34 ^RWhen He slew them, then they sought
      Him;
   And they returned and sought earnestly
      for God.   [Hos. 5:15]
35 Then they remembered that ^RGod *was*
      their rock,   [Deut. 32:4, 15]
   And the Most High God ^Rtheir
      Redeemer.   Is. 41:14; 44:6; 63:9
36 Nevertheless they ^Rflattered Him with
      their mouth,   Ezek. 33:31
   And they lied to Him with their tongue;
37 For their heart was not steadfast with
      Him,
   Nor were they faithful in His covenant.
38 ^RBut He, *being* full of compassion,
      forgave *their* iniquity,   [Num. 14:18–20]
   And did not destroy *them*.
   Yes, many a time ^RHe turned His anger
      away,   [Is. 48:9]
   And did not stir up all His wrath;
39 For ^RHe remembered ^Rthat they *were*
      but flesh,
   ^RA breath that passes away and does not
      come again.   Job 10:9 • John 3:6 • [Job 7:7, 16]
40 How often they ^Rprovoked^T Him in the
      wilderness,   Heb. 3:16 • *rebelled against Him*
   And grieved Him in the desert!

41 Yes, ^Ragain and again they tempted
      God,   Num. 14:22
   And limited the Holy One of Israel.
42 They did not remember His ^Tpower:
   The day when He redeemed them from
      the enemy,   Lit. *hand*
43 When He worked His signs in Egypt,
   And His wonders in the field of Zoan;
44 ^RTurned their rivers into blood,
   And their streams, that they could not
      drink.   Ex. 7:20
45 ^RHe sent swarms of flies among them,
      which devoured them,   Ex. 8:24
   And frogs, which destroyed them.
46 He also gave their crops to the
      caterpillar,
   And their labor to the ^Rlocust.   Ex. 10:14
47 He destroyed their vines with hail,
   And their sycamore trees with frost.
48 He also gave up their cattle to the hail,
   And their flocks to fiery lightning.
49 He cast on them the fierceness of His
      anger,
   Wrath, indignation, and trouble,
   By sending angels of destruction *among*
      them.
50 He made a path for His anger;
   He did not spare their soul from death,
   But gave their life over to the plague,
51 And destroyed all the ^Rfirstborn in
      Egypt,
   The first of *their* strength in the tents
      of Ham.   Ex. 12:29, 30
52 But He ^Rmade His own people go forth
      like sheep,
   And guided them in the wilderness like
      a flock;   Ps. 77:20
53 And He ^Rled them on safely, so that
      they did not fear;
   But the sea ^Roverwhelmed their
      enemies.   Ex. 14:19, 20 • Ex. 14:27, 28
54 And He brought them to His ^Rholy
      border,
   This mountain ^R*which* His right hand
      had acquired.   Ex. 15:17 • Ps. 44:3
55 ^RHe also drove out the nations before
      them,   Ps. 44:2
   ^RAllotted them an inheritance by
      ^Tsurvey,
   And made the tribes of Israel dwell in
      their tents.   Josh. 13:7 • Lit. *measuring cord*
56 ^RYet they tested and provoked the Most
      High God,   Judg. 2:11–13
   And did not keep His testimonies,
57 But ^Rturned back and acted unfaithfully
      like their fathers;
   They were turned aside ^Rlike a deceitful
      bow.   Ezek. 20:27, 28 • Hos. 7:16
58 ^RFor they provoked Him to anger with
      their ^Rhigh places,
   And moved Him to jealousy with their
      carved images.   Judg. 2:12 • Deut. 12:2

59 When God heard *this*, He was furious,
   And greatly abhorred Israel,
60 ^RSo that He forsook the tabernacle of
      Shiloh,   1 Sam. 4:11
   The tent He had placed among men,
61 ^RAnd delivered His strength into
      captivity,   Judg. 18:30
   And His glory into the enemy's hand.
62 ^RHe also gave His people over to the
      sword,   1 Sam. 4:10
   And was furious with His inheritance.
63 The fire consumed their young men,
   And ^Rtheir maidens were not given in
      marriage.   Jer. 7:34; 16:9; 25:10
64 ^RTheir priests fell by the sword,
   And ^Rtheir widows made no
      lamentation.   1 Sam. 4:17; 22:18 · Job 27:15

65 Then the Lord awoke as from sleep,
   ^RLike a mighty man who shouts because
      of wine.   Is. 42:13
66 And ^RHe beat back His enemies; 1 Sam. 5:6
   He put them to a perpetual reproach.

67 Moreover He rejected the tent of
      Joseph,
   And did not choose the tribe of
      Ephraim,
68 But chose the tribe of Judah,
   Mount Zion ^Rwhich He loved.   [Ps. 87:2]
69 And He built His ^Rsanctuary like the
      heights,
   Like the earth which He has established
      forever.   1 Kin. 6:1–38
70 He also chose David His servant,
   And took him from the sheepfolds;
71 From following ^Rthe ewes that had
      young He brought him,   [Is. 40:11]
   ^RTo shepherd Jacob His people,
   And Israel His inheritance.   2 Sam. 5:2
72 So he shepherded them according to
      the ^Rintegrity of his heart,
   And guided them by the skillfulness of
      his hands.   1 Kin. 9:4

Psalm 79

*A Dirge and a Prayer for Israel,
Destroyed by Enemies*

A Psalm of Asaph.

O GOD, the nations have come into
      ^RYour inheritance;   Ps. 74:2
   Your holy temple they have defiled;
   They have laid Jerusalem in ^Theaps. *ruins*
2 ^RThe dead bodies of Your servants
   They have given *as* food for the birds of
      the heavens,
   The flesh of Your saints to the beasts of
      the earth.   Jer. 7:33; 19:7; 34:20
3 Their blood they have shed like water
   all around Jerusalem,
   And *there was* no one to bury *them*.
4 We have become a reproach to our
      ^Rneighbors,

A scorn and derision to those who are
   around us.   Ps. 44:13

5 ^RHow long, LORD?   Ps. 74:1, 9
   Will You be angry forever?
   Will Your jealousy burn like fire?
6 ^RPour out Your wrath on the nations
      that do not know You,   Jer. 10:25
   And on the kingdoms that ^Rdo not call
      on Your name.   Ps. 53:4
7 For they have devoured Jacob,
   And laid waste his dwelling place.

8 Oh, do not remember ^Tformer iniquities
      against us!   Or *iniquities of those before us*
   Let Your tender mercies come speedily
      to meet us,
   For we have been brought very low.
9 Help us, O God of our salvation,
   For the glory of Your name;
   And deliver us, and provide atonement
      for our sins,
   ^RFor Your name's sake!   Jer. 14:7, 21
10 ^RWhy should the nations say,   Ps. 42:10
   "Where *is* their God?"
   Let there be known among the ^Tnations
      in our sight   *Gentiles*
   The avenging of the blood of Your
      servants *which has been* shed.

11 Let ^Rthe groaning of the prisoner come
      before You;
   According to the greatness of Your
      ^Tpower
   Preserve those who are appointed to
      die;   Ps. 102:20 · Lit. *arm*
12 And return to our neighbors ^Rsevenfold
      into their bosom   Gen. 4:15
   ^RTheir reproach with which they have
      reproached You, O Lord.   Ps. 74:10, 18, 22

13 So ^Rwe, Your people and sheep of Your
      pasture,
   Will give You thanks forever;
   ^RWe will show forth Your praise to all
      generations.   Ps. 74:1; 95:7 · Is. 43:21

Psalm 80

Prayer for Israel's Restoration

**To the Chief Musician. Set to *"The Lilies."
A *Testimony of Asaph. A Psalm.**

G IVE ear, O Shepherd of Israel,
   ^RYou who lead Joseph like a flock;
   You who dwell *between* the cherubim,
   ^Rshine forth!   [Ex. 25:20–22] · Deut. 33:2
2 Before ^REphraim, Benjamin, and
      Manasseh,
   Stir up Your strength,
   And come *and* save us!   Ps. 78:9, 67

80:title, Heb. *Shoshannim* • Heb. *Eduth*

3 ᴿRestore us, O God;
  ᴿCause Your face to shine,
  And we shall be saved!   Lam. 5:21 · Num. 6:25

4 O Lᴏʀᴅ God of hosts,
  ᴿHow long will You be angry   Ps. 79:5
  Against the prayer of Your people?
5 ᴿYou have fed them with the bread of
  tears,
  And given them tears to drink in great
  measure.   Is. 30:20
6 You have made us a strife to our
  neighbors,
  And our enemies laugh among
  themselves.

7 Restore us, O God of hosts;
  Cause Your face to shine,
  And we shall be saved!

8 You have brought ᴿa vine out of Egypt;
  ᴿYou have cast out the ᵀnations, and
  planted it.   [Is. 5:1, 7] · Ps. 44:2 · *Gentiles*
9 You prepared *room* for it,
  And caused it to take deep root,
  And it filled the land.
10 The hills were covered with its shadow,
  And the ᵀmighty cedars with its
  ᴿboughs.   Lit. *cedars of God* · Lev. 23:40
11 She sent out her boughs to *the Sea,
  And her branches to *the River.
12 Why have You ᴿbroken down her
  ᵀhedges,
  So that all who pass by the way pluck
  her *fruit*?   Is. 5:5 · *walls* or *fences*
13 The boar out of the woods uproots it,
  And the wild beast of the field devours
  it.

14 Return, we beseech You, O God of
  hosts;
  ᴿLook down from heaven and see,
  And visit this vine   Is. 63:15
15 And the vineyard which Your right
  hand has planted,
  And the branch *that* You made strong
  ᴿfor Yourself.   [Is. 49:5]
16 *It is* burned with fire, *it is* cut down;
  ᴿThey perish at the rebuke of Your
  countenance.   [Ps. 39:11]
17 ᴿLet Your hand be upon the man of
  Your right hand,
  Upon the son of man *whom* You made
  strong for Yourself.   Ps. 89:21
18 Then we will not turn back from You;
  Revive us, and we will call upon Your
  name.
19 Restore us, O Lᴏʀᴅ God of hosts;
  Cause Your face to shine,
  And we shall be saved!

Psalm 81

An Appeal for Israel's Repentance

To the Chief Musician. *On an instrument
of Gath. A Psalm of Asaph.

SING aloud to God our strength;
  Make a joyful shout to the God of
  Jacob.
2 Raise a song and strike the timbrel,
  The pleasant harp with the lute.

3 Blow the trumpet at the time of the
  New Moon,
  At the full moon, on our solemn feast
  day.
4 For ᴿthis *is* a statute for Israel,
  A law of the God of Jacob.   Num. 10:10
5 This He established in Joseph *as* a
  testimony,
  When He went throughout the land of
  Egypt,
  ᴿWhere I heard a language I did not
  understand.   Ps. 114:1

6 "I removed his shoulder from the
  burden;
  His hands were freed from the baskets.
7 ᴿYou called in trouble, and I delivered
  you;   Ex. 2:23; 14:10
  ᴿI answered you in the secret place of
  thunder;   Ex. 19:19; 20:18
  I ᴿtested you at the waters of Meribah.
  Selah   Ex. 17:6, 7

8 "Hear,ᴿ O My people, and I will
  admonish you!   [Ps. 50:7]
  O Israel, if you will listen to Me!
9 There shall be no ᴿforeign god among
  you;   [Is. 43:12]
  Nor shall you worship any foreign god.
10 ᴿI *am* the Lᴏʀᴅ your God,   Ex. 20:2
  Who brought you out of the land of
  Egypt;
  Open your mouth wide, and I will fill it.

11 "But My people would not heed My
  voice,
  And Israel would *have* none of Me.
12 ᴿSo I gave them over to their own
  stubborn heart,
  To walk in their own counsels.   [Acts 7:42]

13 "Oh, that My people would listen to Me,
  That Israel would walk in My ways!
14 I would soon subdue their enemies,
  And turn My hand against their
  adversaries.
15 ᴿThe haters of the Lᴏʀᴅ would pretend
  submission to Him,   Rom. 1:30
  But their fate would endure forever.
16 He would have fed them also with ᵀthe
  finest of wheat;   Lit. *fat of wheat*
  And with honey ᴿfrom the rock I would
  have satisfied you."   Job 29:6

Psalm 82

A Plea for Justice

A Psalm of Asaph.

Gᴏᴅ ᴿstands in the congregation of the ᵀmighty;   [2 Chr. 19:6] • Heb. *El*, lit. *God*
He judges among the *gods.

2 How long will you judge unjustly,
   And ᴿshow partiality to the wicked?
   Selah   [Deut. 1:17]
3 ᵀDefend the poor and fatherless;   *Vindicate*
   Do justice to the afflicted and needy.
4 Deliver the poor and needy;
   Free *them* from the hand of the wicked.

5 They do not know, nor do they
   understand;
   They walk about in darkness;
   All the ᴿfoundations of the earth are
   ᵀunstable.   Ps. 11:3 • *moved*

6 I said, "You *are* ᵀgods,   See note at v. 1
   And all of you *are* children of the Most
   High.
7 But you shall die like men,
   And fall like one of the princes."

8 Arise, O God, judge the earth;
   For You shall inherit all nations.

Psalm 83

Prayer to Frustrate Conspiracy Against Israel

A Song. A Psalm of Asaph.

Dᴼ not keep silent, O God!
   Do not hold Your peace,
   And do not be still, O God!   Ps. 28:1
2 For behold, ᴿYour enemies make a
   ᵀtumult;   Ps. 81:15 • *uproar*
   And those who hate You have ᵀlifted
   up their head.   Exalted themselves
3 They have taken crafty counsel against
   Your people,
   And consulted together ᴿagainst Your
   sheltered ones.   [Ps. 27:5]
4 They have said, "Come, and ᴿlet us cut
   them off from *being* a nation,
   That the name of Israel may be
   remembered no more."   Jer. 11:19; 31:36

5 For they have consulted together with
   one ᵀconsent;   Lit. *heart*
   They form a confederacy against You:
6 ᴿThe tents of Edom and the Ishmaelites;
   Moab and the Hagrites;   2 Chr. 20:1, 10, 11
7 Gebal, Ammon, and Amalek;
   Philistia with the inhabitants of Tyre;
8 Assyria also has joined with them;
   They have helped the children of Lot.
   Selah

9 Deal with them as *with* Midian,

As *with* ᴿSisera,   Judg. 4:15–24; 5:20, 21
As *with* Jabin at the Brook Kishon,
10 Who perished at En Dor,
    Who became *as* refuse on the earth.
11 Make their nobles like Oreb and like
    ᴿZeeb,   Judg. 7:25
    Yes, all their princes like ᴿZebah and
    Zalmunna,   Judg. 8:12–21
12 Who said, "Let us take for ourselves
    The pastures of God for a possession."

13 ᴿO my God, make them like the whirling
    dust,   Is. 17:13
    ᴿLike the chaff before the wind!   Ps. 35:5
14 As the fire burns the woods,
    And as the flame ᴿsets the mountains
    on fire,   Deut. 32:22
15 So pursue them with Your tempest,
    And frighten them with Your storm.
16 Fill their faces with shame,
    That they may seek Your name, O
    Lᴏʀᴅ.
17 Let them be ᵀconfounded and dismayed
    forever;
    Yes, let them be put to shame and
    perish,   *ashamed*
18 ᴿThat they may know that You, whose
    name alone *is* the Lᴏʀᴅ,   Ps. 59:13
    Are the Most High over all the earth.

Psalm 84

The Blessedness of Dwelling in the House of God

To the Chief Musician. *On an instrument of Gath. A Psalm of the sons of Korah.

Hᴼᵂ lovely ᵀis Your tabernacle,
    O Lᴏʀᴅ of hosts!   *are your dwellings*
2 ᴿMy soul longs, yes, even faints
   For the courts of the Lᴏʀᴅ;
   My heart and my flesh cry out for the
   living God.   Ps. 42:1, 2

3 Even the sparrow has found a home,
   And the swallow a nest for herself,
   Where she may lay her young—
   Even Your altars, O Lᴏʀᴅ of hosts,
   My King and my God.
4 Blessed *are* those who dwell in Your
   ᴿhouse;   [Ps. 65:4]
   They will still be praising You.   Selah

5 Blessed *is* the man whose strength *is* in
   You,
   Whose heart *is* set on pilgrimage.
6 *As they* pass through the Valley ᴿof
   ᵀBaca,   2 Sam. 5:22–25 • Lit. *Weeping*
   They make it a spring;
   The rain also covers it with pools.
7 They go from strength to strength;
   Each one appears before God in Zion.

84:title, Heb. *Al Gittith*
84:7 LXX, Syr., Vg. *The God of Gods shall be seen*

82:1 *Judges;* Heb. *elohim,* lit. *mighty ones* or *gods*

8 O Lord God of hosts, hear my prayer;
   Give ear, O God of Jacob! Selah
9 ᴿO God, behold our shield,   Gen. 15:1
   And look upon the face of Your
   ᵀanointed.   Commissioned one, Heb. *messiah*

10 For a day in Your courts *is* better than
    a thousand.
    I would rather ᵀbe a doorkeeper in the
    house of my God   *stand at the threshold*
    Than dwell in the tents of wickedness.
11 For the Lord God *is* a sun and shield;
    The Lord will give grace and glory;
    No good *thing* will He withhold
    From those who walk uprightly.

12 O Lord of hosts,
    Blessed *is* the man who trusts in You!

Psalm 85

Prayer that the Lord Will Restore Favor
to the Land

To the Chief Musician.
A Psalm of the sons of Korah.

LORD, You have been favorable to Your
land;
   You have ᴿbrought back the captivity
   of Jacob.   Joel 3:1
2 You have forgiven the iniquity of Your
   people;
   You have covered all their sin. Selah
3 You have taken away all Your wrath;
   You have turned from the fierceness of
   Your anger.

4 ᴿRestore us, O God of our salvation,
   And cause Your anger toward us to
   cease.   Ps. 80:3, 7
5 ᴿWill You be angry with us forever?
   Will You prolong Your anger to all
   generations?   Ps. 79:5
6 Will You not ᴿrevive us again,   Hab. 3:2
   That Your people may rejoice in You?
7 Show us Your mercy, Lord,
   And grant us Your salvation.

8 I will hear what God the Lord will
   speak,
   For He will speak peace
   To His people and to His saints;
   But let them not turn back to folly.
9 Surely ᴿHis salvation *is* near to those
   who fear Him,   Is. 46:13
   That glory may dwell in our land.

10 Mercy and truth have met together;
    Righteousness and peace have kissed.
11 Truth shall spring out of the earth,
    And righteousness shall look down
    from heaven.
12 Yes, the Lord will give *what is* good;
    And our land will yield its increase.
13 Righteousness will go before Him,
    And shall make His footsteps *our*
    pathway.

Psalm 86

Prayer for Mercy, with Meditation on the
Excellencies of the Lord

A Prayer of David.

BOW down Your ear, O Lord, hear me;
For I *am* poor and needy.
2 Preserve my ᵀlife, for I *am* holy;
   You are my God;   Lit. *soul*
   Save Your servant who trusts in You!
3 Be merciful to me, O Lord,
   For I cry to You all day long.
4 Rejoice the soul of Your servant,
   For to You, O Lord, I lift up my soul.
5 For ᴿYou, Lord, *are* good, and ready to
   forgive,
   And abundant in mercy to all those
   who call upon You.   [Joel 2:13]

6 Give ear, O Lord, to my prayer;
   And attend to the voice of my
   supplications.
7 In the day of my trouble I will call
   upon You,
   For You will answer me.

8 ᴿAmong the gods *there is* none like You,
   O Lord;
   Nor *are there any* works like Your
   works.   [Ex. 15:11]
9 All nations whom You have made
   Shall come and worship before You,
   O Lord,
   And shall glorify Your name.
10 For You *are* great, and ᴿdo wondrous
    things;
    ᴿYou alone *are* God.   [Ex. 15:11] · Deut. 6:4

11 ᴿTeach me Your way, O Lord;
   I will walk in Your truth;   Ps. 27:11; 143:8
   Unite my heart to fear Your name.
12 I will praise You, O Lord my God, with
    all my heart,
    And I will glorify Your name
    forevermore.
13 For great *is* Your mercy toward me,
    And You have delivered my soul from
    the ᵀdepths of Sheol. The abode of the dead

14 O God, the proud have risen against
    me,
    And a mob of violent *men* have sought
    my life,
    And have not set You before them.
15 But ᴿYou, O Lord, *are* a God full of
    compassion, and gracious,
    Longsuffering and abundant in mercy
    and truth.   Ex. 34:6

16 Oh, turn to me, and have mercy on me!
    Give Your strength to Your servant,
    And save the son of Your maidservant.
17 Show me a sign for good,
    That those who hate me may see *it* and
    be ashamed,

Because You, Lord, have helped me
and comforted me.

Psalm 87

The Glories of the City of God

A Psalm of the sons of Korah. A Song.

HIS foundation is in the holy mountains.
2 The Lord loves the gates of Zion
More than all the dwellings of Jacob.
3 RGlorious things are spoken of you,
O city of God! Selah　　　　　Is. 60:1

4 "I will make mention of TRahab and
Babylon to those who know Me;
Behold, O Philistia and Tyre, with
Ethiopia:
'This one was born there.' "　　　Egypt

5 And of Zion it will be said,
"This one and that one were born in her;
And the Most High Himself shall
establish her."
6 The Lord will record,
When He Rregisters the peoples:
"This one was born there." Selah　Is. 4:3

7 Both the singers and the players on
instruments say,
"All my springs are in you."

Psalm 88

A Prayer for Help in Despondency

A Song. A Psalm of the sons of Korah. To the
Chief Musician. Set to "Mahalath Leannoth." A
*Contemplation of Heman the Ezrahite.

O LORD, RGod of my salvation,
I have cried out day and night before
You.　　　　　Ps. 27:9
2 Let my prayer come before You;
TIncline Your ear to my cry.　　Listen to

3 For my soul is full of troubles,
And my life draws near to the grave.
4 I am counted with those who Rgo T
down to the pit;　[Ps. 28:1] • Die
I am like a man who has no strength,
5 TAdrift among the dead,　　Lit. Free
Like the slain who lie in the grave,
Whom You remember no more,
And who are cut off from Your hand.

6 You have laid me in the lowest pit,
In darkness, in the depths.
7 Your wrath lies heavy upon me,
And You have afflicted me with all
RYour waves. Selah　　　Ps. 42:7
8 RYou have Tput away my acquaintances
far from me;
You have made me an abomination to
them;　Job 19:13, 19 • taken away my friends
I am shut up, and I cannot get out;

9 My eye wastes away because of
affliction.

Lord, I have called daily upon You;
I have stretched out my hands to You.
10 Will You work wonders for the dead?
Shall Tthe dead arise and praise You?
Selah　　　　　shades, ghosts
11 Shall Your lovingkindness be declared
in the grave?
Or Your faithfulness in the place of
destruction?
12 Shall Your wonders be known in the
dark?
And Your righteousness in the land of
forgetfulness?

13 But to You I have cried out, O Lord,
And in the morning my prayer comes
before You.
14 Lord, why do You cast off my soul?
Why do You hide Your face from me?
15 I have been afflicted and ready to die
from my youth;
I suffer Your terrors;
I am distraught.
16 Your fierce wrath has gone over me;
Your terrors have cut me off.
17 They came around me all day long like
water;
They engulfed me altogether.
18 RLoved one and friend You have put far
from me,　　　　Ps. 31:11; 38:11
And my acquaintances into darkness.

Psalm 89

Remembering the Covenant with David, and Sorrow for Lost Blessings

A *Contemplation of Ethan the Ezrahite.

I WILL sing of the mercies of the Lord
forever;
With my mouth will I make known
Your faithfulness to all generations.
2 For I have said, "Mercy shall be built
up forever;
RYour faithfulness You shall establish in
the very heavens."　　[Ps. 119:89, 90]

3 "IR have made a covenant with My
chosen,　　　　　1 Kin. 8:16
I have sworn to My servant David:
4 'Your seed I will establish forever,
And build up your throne Rto all
generations.' " Selah　　[Luke 1:33]

5 And Rthe heavens will praise Your
wonders, O Lord;
Your faithfulness also in the assembly
of the saints.　　　　[Ps. 19:1]
6 RFor who in the heavens can be
compared to the Lord?

88:title, Heb. Maschil　　　　89:title, Heb. Maschil

Who among the sons of the mighty can
be likened to the LORD?   Ps. 86:8; 113:5

7 ^RGod is greatly to be feared in the
assembly of the saints,
And to be held in reverence by all *those*
around Him.   Ps. 76:7, 11

8 O LORD God of hosts,
Who *is* mighty like You, O LORD?
Your faithfulness also surrounds You.

9 You rule the raging of the sea;
When its waves rise, You still them.

10 ^RYou have broken ^TRahab in pieces, as
one who is slain;
You have scattered Your enemies with
Your mighty arm.   Ps. 87:4 · Egypt

11 ^RThe heavens *are* Yours, the earth also
is Yours;
The world and all its fullness, You have
founded them.   [Gen. 1:1]

12 The north and the south, You have
created them;
^RTabor and ^RHermon rejoice in Your
name.   Josh. 19:22 · Josh. 11:17; 12:1

13 You have a mighty arm;
Strong is Your hand, *and* high is Your
right hand.

14 Righteousness and justice *are* the
foundation of Your throne;
Mercy and truth go before Your face.

15 Blessed *are* the people who know the
^Rjoyful sound!
They walk, O LORD, in the light of Your
countenance.   Ps. 98:6

16 In Your name they rejoice all day long,
And in Your righteousness they are
exalted.

17 For You *are* the glory of their strength,
And in Your favor our horn is exalted.

18 For our shield *belongs* to the LORD,
And our king to the Holy One of Israel.

19 Then You spoke in a vision to Your
*holy one,
And said: "I have given help to *one
who is* mighty;
I have exalted one ^Rchosen from the
people.   1 Kin. 11:34

20 I have found My servant David;
With My holy oil I have anointed him,

21 ^RWith whom My hand shall be
established;   Ps. 80:17
Also My arm shall strengthen him.

22 The enemy shall not outwit him,
Nor the son of wickedness afflict him.

23 I will beat down his foes before his
face,
And plague those who hate him.

24 "But My faithfulness and My mercy
shall be with him,

And in My name his horn shall be
exalted.

25 Also I will set his hand over the sea,
And his right hand over the rivers.

26 He shall cry to Me, 'You *are* my Father,
My God, and the rock of my salvation.'

27 Also I will make him My firstborn,
The highest of the kings of the earth.

28 ^RMy mercy I will keep for him forever,
And My covenant shall stand firm with
him.   Is. 55:3

29 His seed also I will make *to endure*
forever,
And his throne as the days of heaven.

30 "If ^R his sons forsake My law   [2 Sam. 7:14]
And do not walk in My judgments,

31 If they ^Tbreak My statutes   *profane*
And do not keep My commandments,

32 Then I will ^Tpunish their transgression
with the rod,
And their iniquity with stripes.   *attend to*

33 Nevertheless My lovingkindness I will
not ^Tutterly take from him,   Lit. *break off*
Nor allow My faithfulness to fail.

34 My covenant I will not break,
Nor ^Ralter the word that has gone out
of My lips.   Jer. 33:20–22

35 Once I have sworn ^Rby My holiness;
I will not lie to David: Amos 4:2

36 ^RHis seed shall endure forever,   [Luke 1:33]
And his throne as the sun before Me;

37 It shall be established forever like the
moon,
Even *like* the faithful witness in the
sky." Selah

38 But You have cast off and ^Tabhorred,
You have been furious with Your
^Tanointed.   *rejected* · Commissioned one

39 You have renounced the covenant of
Your servant;
^RYou have ^Tprofaned his crown *by
casting it* to the ground.   Lam. 5:16 · *defiled*

40 You have broken down all his hedges;
You have brought his ^Tstrongholds to
ruin.   *fortresses*

41 All who pass by the way plunder him;
He is a reproach to his neighbors.

42 You have exalted the right hand of his
adversaries;
You have made all his enemies rejoice.

43 You have also turned back the edge of
his sword,
And have not sustained him in the
battle.

44 You have made his ^Tglory cease,
And cast his throne down to the
ground.   *splendor* or *brightness*

45 The days of his youth You have
shortened;
You have covered him with shame.
Selah

89:19 So with many Heb. mss.; MT, LXX, Tg., Vg. *holy
ones*

46 How long, LORD?
   Will You hide Yourself forever?
   Will Your wrath burn like fire?
47 Remember how short my time ᴿis;
   For what ᴿfutility have You created all
      the children of men?   Ps. 90:9 · Ps. 62:9
48 What man can live and not ᵀsee death?
   Can he deliver his life from the power
      of ᵀthe grave? Selah experience · Or Sheol

49 Lord, where are Your former
      lovingkindnesses,
   Which You ᴿswore to David ᴿin Your
      truth?   [2 Sam. 7:15] · Ps. 54:5
50 Remember, Lord, the reproach of Your
      servants—
   ᴿHow I bear in my bosom the reproach
      of all the many peoples,   Ps. 69:9, 19
51 ᴿWith which Your enemies have
      reproached, O LORD,   Ps. 74:10, 18, 22
   With which they have reproached the
      footsteps of Your ᵀanointed. Heb. messiah

52 ᴿBlessed be the LORD forevermore!
   Amen and Amen.   Ps. 41:13

BOOK FOUR
Psalms 90–106

Psalm 90

The Eternity of God, and Man's Frailty
A Prayer of Moses the man of God.

LORD, ᴿYou have been our *dwelling place
   in all generations.   [Ezek. 11:16]
2 ᴿBefore the mountains were brought
      forth,   [Prov. 8:25, 26]
   Or ever You ᵀhad formed the earth and
      the world,   Lit. gave birth to
   Even from everlasting to everlasting,
      You are God.

3 You turn man to destruction,
   And say, "Return, O children of men."
4 ᴿFor a thousand years in Your sight
   Are like yesterday when it is past,
   And like a watch in the night.   2 Pet. 3:8
5 You carry them away like a flood;
   ᴿThey are like a sleep.
   In the morning ᴿthey are like grass
      which grows up: Ps. 73:20 · Is. 40:6
6 In the morning it flourishes and grows
      up;
   In the evening it is cut down and
      withers.

7 For we have been consumed by Your
      anger,
   And by Your wrath we are terrified.
8 ᴿYou have set our iniquities before You,
   Our ᴿsecret sins in the light of Your
      countenance.   Ps. 50:21 · Ps. 19:12

90:1 LXX, [Tg.], Vg. refuge

9 For all our days have passed away in
      Your wrath;
   We finish our years like a sigh.
10 The days of our lives are seventy years;
   And if by reason of strength they are
      eighty years,
   Yet their boast is only labor and
      sorrow;
   For it is soon cut off, and we fly away.
11 Who knows the power of Your anger?
   For as the fear of You, so is Your
      wrath.
12 So teach us to number our days,
   That we may gain a heart of wisdom.

13 Return, O LORD!
   How long?
   And ᴿhave compassion on Your
      servants.   Deut. 32:36
14 Oh, satisfy us early with Your mercy,
   ᴿThat we may rejoice and be glad all our
      days!   Ps. 85:6
15 Make us glad according to the days in
      which You have afflicted us,
   The years in which we have seen evil.
16 Let ᴿYour work appear to Your
      servants,
   And Your glory to their children. Hab. 3:2
17 ᴿAnd let the beauty of the LORD our God
      be upon us,
   And ᴿestablish the work of our hands
      for us;   Ps. 27:4 · Is. 26:12
   Yes, establish the work of our hands.

Psalm 91

Safety of Abiding in the Presence of God

HE ᴿwho dwells in the secret place of the
   Most High
   Shall abide ᴿunder the shadow of the
      Almighty.   Ps. 27:5; 31:20; 32:7 · Ps. 17:8
2 ᴿI will say of the LORD, "He is my refuge
      and my fortress;
   My God, in Him I will trust."   Ps. 142:5

3 Surely He shall deliver you from the
   ᴿsnare of the *fowler   Ps. 124:7
   And from the perilous pestilence.
4 ᴿHe shall cover you with His feathers,
   And under His wings you shall take
      refuge;
   His truth shall be your shield and
      ᵀbuckler.   Ps. 17:8 · A small shield
5 ᴿYou shall not be afraid of the terror by
      night,   [Job 5:19]
   Nor of the arrow that flies by day,
6 Nor of the pestilence that walks in
      darkness,
   Nor of the destruction that lays waste
      at noonday.

7 A thousand may fall at your side,

91:3 One who catches birds in a trap or snare

And ten thousand at your right hand;
But it shall not come near you.
8 Only with your eyes shall you look,
And see the reward of the wicked.

9 Because you have made the LORD, *who*
    is ᴿmy refuge,   Ps. 91:2
Even the Most High, your dwelling
    place,
10 ᴿNo evil shall befall you,
Nor shall any plague come near your
    dwelling;   [Prov. 12:21]
11 ᴿFor He shall give His angels charge
    over you,
To keep you in all your ways.   [Heb. 1:14]
12 In *their* hands they shall bear you up,
Lest you dash your foot against a stone.
13 You shall tread upon the lion and the
    cobra,
The young lion and the serpent you
    shall trample underfoot.

14 "Because he has set his love upon Me,
    therefore I will deliver him;
I will ᵀset him on high, because he has
    ᴿknown My name.   exalt him · [Ps. 9:10]
15 He shall ᴿcall upon Me, and I will
    answer him;   Ps. 50:15
I *will be* with him in trouble;
I will deliver him and honor him.
16 With ᵀlong life I will satisfy him,
And show him My salvation." *length of days*

Psalm 92

Praise to the LORD for His Love and Faithfulness

A Psalm. A Song for the Sabbath day.

*I*T is ᴿgood to give thanks to the LORD,
    And to sing praises to Your name, O
    Most High;   Ps. 147:1
2 To ᴿdeclare Your lovingkindness in the
    morning,   Ps. 89:1
And Your faithfulness every night,
3 ᴿOn an instrument of ten strings,
On the lute,   1 Chr. 23:5
And on the harp,
With ᵀharmonious sound.   *melodic*
4 For You, LORD, have made me glad
    through Your work;
I will triumph in the works of Your
    hands.

5 O LORD, how great are Your works!
    ᴿYour thoughts are very deep.   [Is. 28:29]
6 ᴿA senseless man does not know,
Nor does a fool understand this.   Ps. 73:22
7 When ᴿthe wicked ᵀspring up like grass,
And when all the workers of iniquity
    flourish,   Job 12:6 · *sprout*
It is that they may be destroyed
    forever.

8 ᴿBut You, LORD, *are* on high
    forevermore.   [Ps. 83:18]
9 For behold, Your enemies, O LORD,
For behold, Your enemies shall perish;
All the workers of iniquity shall ᴿbe
    scattered.   Ps. 68:1
10 But ᴿmy ᵀhorn You have exalted like a
    wild ox;   Ps. 89:17 · Strength
I have been anointed with fresh oil.
11 ᴿMy eye also has seen *my desire* on my
    enemies;
My ears hear *my desire* on the wicked
Who rise up against me.   Ps. 54:7
12 ᴿThe righteous shall flourish like a palm
    tree,   Ps. 52:8
He shall grow like a cedar in Lebanon.
13 Those who are planted in the house of
    the LORD
Shall flourish in the courts of our God.
14 They shall still bear fruit in old age;
They shall be fresh and flourishing,
15 To declare that the LORD is upright;
He is my rock, and ᴿ*there is* no
    unrighteousness in Him.   [Rom. 9:14]

Psalm 93

The Eternal Reign of the LORD

*T*HE ᴿLORD reigns, He is clothed with
    majesty;   Ps. 96:10
The LORD is clothed,
    ᴿHe has girded Himself with strength.
Surely the world is established, so that
    it cannot be ᵀmoved.   Ps. 65:6 · shaken
2 ᴿYour throne *is* established from of old;
You *are* from everlasting.   Ps. 45:6

3 The floods have ᵀlifted up, O LORD,
The floods have lifted up their voice;
The floods lift up their waves.   *raised up*
4 ᴿThe LORD on high *is* mightier   Ps. 65:7
Than the noise of many waters,
Than the mighty waves of the sea.

5 Your testimonies are very sure;
Holiness adorns Your house,
O LORD, ᵀforever.   Lit. *for length of days*

Psalm 94

God the Refuge of the Righteous

O LORD God, ᴿto whom vengeance
    belongs—
O God, to whom vengeance belongs,
    shine forth!   [Nah. 1:2]
2 Rise up, O ᴿJudge of the earth; [Gen. 18:25]
Render punishment to the proud.
3 LORD, how long will the wicked,
How long will the wicked triumph?
4 They ᴿutter speech, *and* speak insolent
    things;

All the workers of iniquity boast in
   themselves.   Ps. 31:18
5 They break in pieces Your people, O
   LORD,
   And afflict Your heritage.
6 They slay the widow and the stranger,
   And murder the fatherless.
7 RYet they say, "The LORD does not see,
   Nor does the God of Jacob
   Tunderstand."   Ps. 10:11 · pay attention

8 Understand, you senseless among the
   people;
   And you fools, when will you be wise?
9 RHe who planted the ear, shall He not
   hear?
   He who formed the eye, shall He not
   see?   [Ex. 4:11]
10 He who Tinstructs the Tnations, shall He
   not correct,   disciplines · Gentiles
   He who teaches man knowledge?
11 The LORD Rknows the thoughts of man,
   That they are futile.   1 Cor. 3:20
12 Blessed is the man whom You Rinstruct,
   O LORD,
   And teach out of Your law,   [Heb. 12:5, 6]
13 That You may give him Trest from the
   days of adversity,
   Until the pit is dug for the wicked.   relief
14 For the LORD will not Tcast off His
   people,   abandon
   Nor will He forsake His inheritance.
15 But judgment will return to
   righteousness,
   And all the upright in heart will follow
   it.

16 Who will rise up for me against the
   evildoers?
   Who will stand up for me against the
   workers of iniquity?
17 Unless the LORD had been my help,
   My soul would soon have settled in
   silence.
18 If I say, "My foot slips,"
   Your mercy, O LORD, will hold me up.
19 In the multitude of my anxieties within
   me,
   Your comforts delight my soul.

20 Shall Rthe throne of iniquity, which
   devises evil by law,
   Have fellowship with You?   Amos 6:3
21 They gather together against the life of
   the righteous,
   And condemn Rinnocent blood.   [Ex. 23:7]
22 But the LORD has been my defense,
   And my God the rock of my refuge.
23 He has brought on them their own
   iniquity,
   And shall cut them off in their own
   wickedness;
   The LORD our God shall cut them off.

Psalm 95

A Call to Worship and Obedience

OH come, let us sing to the LORD!
   Let us shout joyfully to the Rock of
   our salvation.
2 Let us come before His presence with
   thanksgiving;
   Let us shout joyfully to Him with
   Rpsalms.   James 5:13
3 For Rthe LORD is the great God,   [Ps. 96:4]
   And the great King above all gods.
4 TIn His hand are the deep places of the
   earth;   In His possession
   The heights of the hills are His also.
5 RThe sea is His, for He made it; Gen. 1:9, 10
   And His hands formed the dry land.

6 Oh come, let us worship and bow down;
   Let Rus kneel before the LORD our
   Maker.   [Phil. 2:10]
7 For He is our God,
   And we are the people of His pasture,
   And the sheep Tof His hand. Under His care

   Today, if you will hear His voice:
8 "Do not harden your hearts, as in the
   Trebellion,   Or Meribah, lit. Strife
   As in the day of trial in the wilderness,
9 When Ryour fathers tested Me;
   They tried Me, though they Rsaw My
   work.   Ps. 78:18 · Num. 14:22
10 For Rforty years I was Tgrieved with
   that generation,   Heb. 3:10, 17 · disgusted
   And said, 'It is a people who go astray
   in their hearts,
   And they do not know My ways.'
11 So RI swore in My wrath,
   'They shall not enter My rest.' " Heb. 4:3, 5

Psalm 96

A Song of Praise to God Coming in
Judgment

OH, sing to the LORD a new song!
   Sing to the LORD, all the earth.
2 Sing to the LORD, bless His name;
   Proclaim the good news of His
   salvation from day to day.
3 Declare His glory among the Tnations,
   His wonders among all peoples.   Gentiles

4 For Rthe LORD is great and Rgreatly to
   be praised;   Ps. 145:3 · Ps. 18:3
   RHe is to be feared above all gods. Ps. 95:3
5 For Rall the gods of the peoples are
   idols,   [Jer. 10:11]
   RBut the LORD made the heavens. Is. 42:5
6 Honor and majesty are before Him;
   Strength and Rbeauty are in His
   sanctuary.   Ps. 29:2

7 RGiveT to the LORD, O families of the
   peoples,   Ps. 29:1, 2 · Ascribe
   Give to the LORD glory and strength.

8 ᵀGive to the LORD the glory *due* His
   name;
   Bring an offering, and come into His
   courts.   *Ascribe*
9 Oh, worship the LORD ᴿin the beauty of
   holiness!
   Tremble before Him, all the earth. Ps. 29:2

10 Say among the ᵀnations, ᴿ"The LORD
   reigns;   *Gentiles · Ps. 93:1; 97:1*
   The world also is firmly established,
   It shall not be ᵀmoved;   *shaken*
   He shall judge the peoples righteously."

11 ᴿLet the heavens rejoice, and let the
   earth be glad;   Ps. 69:34
   Let the sea roar, and all its fullness;
12 Let the field be joyful, and all that *is* in
   it.
   Then all the trees of the woods will
   rejoice before the LORD.
13 For He is coming, for He is coming to
   judge the earth.
   ᴿHe shall judge the world with
   righteousness,   [Rev. 19:11]
   And the peoples with His truth.

Psalm 97

A Song of Praise to the Sovereign LORD

THE LORD ᴿreigns;   [Ps. 96:10]
   Let the earth rejoice;
   Let the multitude of isles be glad!

2 Clouds and darkness surround Him;
   ᴿRighteousness and justice *are* the
   foundation of His throne.   [Ps. 89:14]
3 ᴿA fire goes before Him,   Ps. 18:8
   And burns up His enemies round about.
4 ᴿHis lightnings light the world;
   The earth sees and trembles.   Ex. 19:18
5 ᴿThe mountains melt like wax at the
   presence of the LORD,
   At the presence of the Lord of the
   whole earth.   Mic. 1:4
6 ᴿThe heavens declare His righteousness,
   And all the peoples see His glory.   Ps. 19:1

7 ᴿLet all be put to shame who serve
   carved images,   [Ex. 20:4]
   Who boast of idols.
   ᴿWorship Him, all *you* gods.   [Heb. 1:6]
8 Zion hears and is glad,
   And the daughters of Judah rejoice
   Because of Your judgments, O LORD.
9 For You, LORD, ᴿ*are* most high above
   all the earth;   Ps. 83:18
   You are exalted far above all gods.

10 You who love the LORD, ᴿhate evil!
   ᴿHe preserves the souls of His saints;
   ᴿHe delivers them out of the hand of the
   wicked.   [Ps. 34:14] · Prov. 2:8 · Ps. 37:40
11 ᴿLight is sown for the righteous,   Job 22:28
   And gladness for the upright in heart.

12 Rejoice in the LORD, you righteous,
   ᴿAnd give thanks at the remembrance of
   ᵀHis holy name.   Ps. 30:4 · Or *His holiness*

Psalm 98

A Song of Praise to the LORD for His Salvation and Judgment

A Psalm.

OH, ᴿsing to the LORD a new song!
   For He has ᴿdone marvelous things;
   His right hand and His holy arm have
   gained Him the victory.   Is. 42:10 · Ex. 15:11
2 ᴿThe LORD has made known His
   salvation;   Is. 52:10
   His righteousness He has revealed in
   the sight of the ᵀnations.   *Gentiles*
3 He has remembered His mercy and His
   faithfulness to the house of Israel;
   ᴿAll the ends of the earth have seen the
   salvation of our God.   Luke 3:6

4 Shout joyfully to the LORD, all the
   earth;
   Break forth in song, rejoice, and sing
   praises.
5 Sing to the LORD with the harp,
   With the harp and the sound of a
   psalm,
6 With trumpets and the sound of a horn;
   Shout joyfully before the LORD, the
   King.

7 Let the sea roar, and all its fullness,
   The world and those who dwell in it;
8 Let the rivers clap *their* hands;
   Let the hills be joyful together before
   the LORD,
9 For He is coming to ᴿjudge the earth.
   With righteousness He shall judge the
   world,   [Ps. 96:10, 13]
   And the peoples with ᵀequity.   *uprightness*

Psalm 99

Praise to the LORD for His Holiness

THE LORD reigns;
   Let the peoples tremble!
   ᴿHe dwells *between* the cherubim;
   Let the earth be ᵀmoved!   Ex. 25:22 · *shaken*
2 The LORD *is* great in Zion,
   And He *is* high above all the peoples.
3 Let them praise Your great and
   awesome name—
   ᵀHe *is* holy.   Or *It*

4 The King's strength also loves justice;
   You have established equity;
   You have executed justice and
   righteousness in Jacob.
5 Exalt the LORD our God,
   And worship at His footstool—
   He *is* holy.

6 Moses and Aaron were among His
priests,
And Samuel was among those who
   ^Rcalled upon His name;
They called upon the LORD, and He
answered them.   1 Sam. 7:9; 12:18
7 He spoke to them in the cloudy pillar;
They kept His testimonies and the
   ^Tordinance He gave them.   statute

8 You answered them, O LORD our God;
You were to them God-Who-Forgives,
Though You took vengeance on their
deeds.
9 Exalt the LORD our God,
And worship at His holy hill;
For the LORD our God *is* holy.

Psalm 100

A Song of Praise for the LORD's Faithfulness to His People

A Psalm of Thanksgiving.

MAKE ^Ra joyful shout to the LORD, ^Tall
you lands!   Ps. 95:1 · Lit. *all the earth*
2 Serve the LORD with gladness;
Come before His presence with singing.
3 Know that the LORD, He *is* God;
   ^R*It is* He *who* has made us, and *not we
ourselves;
   ^R*We are* His people and the sheep of His
pasture.   [Eph. 2:10] · Ezek. 34:30, 31

4 Enter into His gates with thanksgiving,
And into His courts with praise.
Be thankful to Him, *and* bless His
name.
5 For the LORD *is* good;
   ^RHis mercy *is* everlasting,
And His truth *endures* to all
generations.   Ps. 136:1

Psalm 101

Promised Faithfulness to the LORD

A Psalm of David.

I WILL sing of mercy and justice;
To You, O LORD, I will sing praises.

2 I will behave wisely in a ^Tperfect way.
Oh, when will You come to me?
I will ^Rwalk within my house with a
perfect heart.   *blameless* · 1 Kin. 11:4

3 I will set nothing ^Twicked before my
eyes;   *worthless*
   ^RI hate the work of those ^Rwho fall
away;   Ps. 97:10 · Josh. 23:6
It shall not cling to me.
4 A perverse heart shall depart from me;
I will not ^Rknow wickedness.   [Ps. 119:115]

100:3 So with Kt., LXX, Vg.; Qr., many Heb. mss., Tg. *we
are His*

5 Whoever secretly slanders his neighbor,
Him I will destroy;
   ^RThe one who has a haughty look and a
proud heart,
Him I will not endure.   Prov. 6:17

6 My eyes *shall be* on the faithful of the
land,
That they may dwell with me;
He who walks in a ^Tperfect way,
He shall serve me.   *blameless*
7 He who works deceit shall not dwell
within my house;
He who tells lies ^Tshall not continue in
my presence.   Lit. *be established*
8 ^REarly I will destroy all the wicked of
the land,   Jer. 21:12
That I may cut off all the evildoers
   ^Rfrom the city of the LORD.   Ps. 48:2, 8

Psalm 102

The LORD's Eternal Love

A Prayer of the afflicted, when he is overwhelmed
and pours out his complaint before the LORD.

HEAR my prayer, O LORD,
And let my cry come to You.
2 ^RDo not hide Your face from me
in the day of my trouble;
Incline Your ear to me;
In the day that I call, answer me
speedily.   Ps. 27:9; 69:17

3 For my days ^Tare ^Rconsumed like
smoke,   Lit. *end in* · James 4:14
And my bones are burned like a hearth.
4 My heart is stricken and withered like
grass,
So that I forget to eat my bread.
5 Because of the sound of my groaning
My bones cling to my ^Tskin.   *flesh*
6 I am like a pelican of the wilderness;
I am like an owl of the desert.
7 I lie awake,
And am like a sparrow alone on the
housetop.

8 My enemies reproach me all day long;
Those who deride me swear an oath
against me.
9 For I have eaten ashes like bread,
And mingled my drink with weeping,
10 Because of Your indignation and Your
wrath;
For You have lifted me up and cast me
away.
11 My days *are* like a shadow that
lengthens,
And I wither away like grass.

12 But You, O LORD, shall endure forever,
And the remembrance of Your name to
all generations.

13 You will arise *and* have mercy on Zion;
   For the time to favor her,
   Yes, the set time, has come.
14 For Your servants take pleasure in her
   stones,
   And show favor to her dust.
15 So the ᵀnations shall ᴿfear the name of
   the LORD,
   And all the kings of the earth Your
   glory.   *Gentiles* · 1 Kin. 8:43
16 For the LORD shall build up Zion;
   ᴿHe shall appear in His glory.   [Is. 60:1, 2]
17 ᴿHe shall regard the prayer of the
   destitute,   Neh. 1:6
   And shall not despise their prayer.

18 This will be ᴿwritten for the generation
   to come,
   That ᴿa people yet to be created may
   praise the LORD.   [Rom. 15:4] · Ps. 22:31
19 For He ᴿlooked down from the height
   of His sanctuary;
   From heaven the LORD viewed the
   earth,   Deut. 26:15
20 To hear the groaning of the prisoner,
   To release those appointed to death,
21 To ᴿdeclare the name of the LORD in
   Zion,
   And His praise in Jerusalem,   Ps. 22:22
22 ᴿWhen the peoples are gathered
   together,   [Is. 2:2, 3; 49:22, 23; 60:3]
   And the kingdoms, to serve the LORD.

23 He weakened my strength in the way;
   He ᴿshortened my days.   Job 21:21

▼ 3-E. God Is Eternal
24 ᴿI said, "O my God,
   Do not take me away in the midst of
   my days;
   ᴿYour years *are* throughout all
   generations.   Is. 38:10 · [Ps. 90:2]

25 ᴿOf old You laid the foundation of the   ▽
   earth,
   And the heavens *are* the work of Your
   hands.   [Heb. 1:10-12]
26 ᴿThey will perish, but You will ᵀendure;
   Yes, they will all grow old like a
   garment;   Is. 34:4; 51:6 · *continue*
   Like a cloak You will change them,
   And they will be changed.
27 But ᴿYou *are* the same,   [Mal. 3:6]
   And Your years will have no end.   ▲
28 ᴿThe children of Your servants will
   continue,
   And their descendants will be
   established before You."   Ps. 69:36

Psalm 103

Praise for the LORD's Mercies

A *Psalm* of David.

B LESS ᴿthe LORD, O my soul;
   And all that is within me, *bless* His
   holy name!   Ps. 104:1, 35
2 Bless the LORD, O my soul,
   And forget not all His benefits:
3 Who forgives all your iniquities,
   Who ᴿheals all your diseases,   [Ex. 15:26]
4 Who redeems your life from
   destruction,
   ᴿWho crowns you with lovingkindness
   and tender mercies,   [Ps. 5:12]
5 Who satisfies your mouth with good
   things,
   So that ᴿyour youth is renewed like the
   eagle's.   [Is. 40:31]

6 The LORD executes righteousness
   And justice for all who are oppressed.
7 He made known His ways to Moses,
   His acts to the children of Israel.

3-E. God Is Eternal (Psalm 102:24-27)—God had no beginning, but "in the beginning God created the heavens and the earth" (Gen. 1:1, page 2). He has no ending. He is eternal. Our God exists totally from Himself.

(1) "Abraham . . . called on the name of the LORD [Jehovah], the Everlasting God" (Gen. 21:33, page 26).

(2) Habakkuk asked, "Are You not from everlasting, O LORD [Jehovah] my God, my Holy One?" (Hab. 1:12, page 899).

(3) Moses prayed to God saying, "From everlasting to everlasting, You are God" (Ps. 90:2, page 564).

God's dimension is beyond geometric space, eternal, without bounds, without past or future. He is one eternal "Now." He is not a being of time as we are. He is eternal, self-existent life, and therefore free from all succession of time. The clock never ticks for God. He was not created, so there is none greater. He was not born, so He will never die. The one and only true and living God is eternal; all other gods are false. The first commandment is, "You shall have no other gods before Me" (Ex. 20:3, page 79).

"Your years are throughout all generations" (v. 24). Our true and living God is ageless. But His creation will grow old like a garment, and He will re-create the heavens and the earth, making them new, without the curse of sin (Is. 34:4, page 674). After Satan and all of his followers are judged and cast into the lake of eternal fire, there will come "a new heaven and a new earth, for the first heaven and the first earth had passed away" (Rev. 20:10—21:1, page 1313).

"But You are the same [God is immutable], and Your years will have no end [God is eternal]" (vv. 25-27).

See Index, page 17, for your next study.

8 The Lord *is* merciful and gracious,
  Slow to anger, and abounding in mercy.
9 He will not always strive *with us,*
  Nor will He keep *His anger* forever.
10 ᴿHe has not dealt with us according to
   our sins,
   Nor punished us according to our
   iniquities.   [Ezra 9:13]
11 For as the heavens are high above the
   earth,
   So great is His mercy toward those who
   fear Him;
12 As far as the east is from the west,
   So far has He ᴿremoved our
   transgressions from us.   [Is. 38:17; 43:25]
13 ᴿAs a father pities *his* children,   Mal. 3:17
   So the Lord pities those who fear Him.
14 For He ᵀknows our frame;   Understands
   He remembers that we *are* dust.
15 *As for* man, his days *are* like grass;
   As a flower of the field, so he flourishes.
16 ᴿFor the wind passes over it, and it is
   ᵀgone,   [Is. 40:7] • *not*
   *And its place remembers it no more.
17 But the mercy of the Lord *is* from
   everlasting to everlasting
   On those who fear Him,
   And His righteousness to children's
   children,

103:16 Job 7:10

18 ᴿTo such as keep His covenant,
   And to those who remember His
   commandments to do them.   [Deut. 7:9]

11–C. Angels: Their Nature   ▼

19 The Lord has established His throne in
   heaven,
   And His kingdom rules over all.

20 ᴿBless the Lord, you His angels,
   Who excel in strength, who ᴿdo His
   word,   Ps. 148:2 • [Matt. 6:10]
   Heeding the voice of His word.
21 Bless the Lord, all *you* His hosts,
   ᴿYou ᵀministers of His, who do His
   pleasure.   [Heb. 1:14] • *servants* ▲
22 Bless the Lord, all His works,
   In all places of His dominion.

   Bless the Lord, O my soul!

Psalm 104

*Praise to the Sovereign Lord for His
Creation and Providence*

BLESS ᴿthe Lord, O my soul!

  O Lord my God, You are very great:
  You are clothed with honor and
  majesty,   Ps. 103:1
2 Who cover *Yourself* with light as *with* a
  garment,

11–C. Angels: Their Nature (Psalm 103:19–21)—Angels are created, spiritual beings. They never die; they do not reproduce (Matt. 22:30, page 970). It is their nature:

(1) To "bless the Lord" and serve Him. They "excel in strength, who do His word" (v. 20). They obey His every command.

(2) To worship and praise the Lord. "Praise Him, all His angels; praise Him, all His hosts. . . . Let them praise the name of the Lord, for He commanded and they were created" (Ps. 148:1-6, page 595).

(3) To be intellectually superior to fallen man. "My lord [King David] is wise, according to the wisdom of the angel of God, to know everything that is in the earth" (2 Sam. 14:20, page 311). Angels know all that is in the earth, although they are not omniscient. By comparison, man knows very little.

(4) To dispense the judgment of God on:

(a) Armies. One angel, with supernatural power, destroyed the Assyrian army of 185,000 in one night. When the inhabitants of Jerusalem awoke the next morning, they saw the prophecy of Isaiah fulfilled (Is. 37:33-36, page 677).

(b) Cities. Two angels helped destroy Sodom and Gomorrah because these cities were filled with gross immorality. When people of Sodom heard that two men (the angels) were in Lot's house, they went there demanding to have them, that they might have homosexual relations with them. The angels struck the homosexuals with blindness, so that they could not find the door. The next morning, after Lot and his daughters departed from the city, God destroyed Sodom and Gomorrah and all the people (Gen. 19:1-24, page 23).

(c) Individuals. King Herod delivered an address, and while he was speaking the people cried out, " 'The voice of a god and not of a man!' Then immediately an angel of the Lord struck him, because he did not give glory to God. And he was eaten by worms and died" (Acts 12:22, 23, page 1105).

(5) To guard and guide the nation Israel. God sent an angel to guide Israel through forty years of wandering in the wilderness (Ex. 23:20-23, page 82). God did not reveal his identity, but he had authority over Israel. Exodus 23:21 suggests that this angel may be either:

(a) The Lord Jesus Christ, who often appears in the Scriptures as "the Angel of the Lord" (Gen. 22:11, 12, page 27);

(b) Michael, the archangel, "the great prince who stands watch over the sons of your [Daniel's] people" (Dan. 12:1, page 856).

See Revelation 5:11-14, page 1298, for **Point 11-D: Angels: Their Ministry in Heaven and on Earth.**

Who stretch out the heavens like a
curtain.

3 ᴿHe lays the beams of His upper
chambers in the waters,   [Amos 9:6]
Who makes the clouds His chariot,
Who walks on the wings of the wind,
4 Who makes His angels spirits,
His ᵀministers a flame of fire.   *servants*

5 You *who* ᵀlaid the foundations of the
earth,   Lit. *founded the earth upon her bases*
So *that* it should not be moved forever,
6 You ᴿcovered it with the deep as *with* a
garment;   Gen. 1:6
The waters stood above the mountains.
7 At Your rebuke they fled;
At the voice of Your thunder they
hastened away.
8 ᵀThey went up over the mountains;
They went down into the valleys,
To the place which You founded for
them.   Or *The mountains rose; The valleys sank*
9 You have ᴿset a boundary that they
may not pass over,
ᴿThat they may not return to cover the
earth.   [Jer. 5:22] • Gen. 9:11–15

10 He sends the springs into the valleys;
They flow among the hills.
11 They give drink to every beast of the
field;
The wild donkeys quench their thirst.
12 By them the birds of the heavens have
their home;
They sing among the branches.
13 ᴿHe waters the hills from His upper
chambers;
The earth is satisfied with ᴿthe fruit of
Your works.   Ps. 147:8 • Jer. 10:13

14 ᴿHe causes the grass to grow for the
cattle,
And vegetation for the service of man,
That he may bring forth ᴿfood from the
earth,   Gen. 1:29 • Job 28:5
15 And ᴿwine *that* makes glad the heart of
man,
Oil to make *his* face shine,
And bread *which* strengthens man's
heart.   Judg. 9:13
16 The trees of the Lᴏʀᴅ are full *of sap,*
The cedars of Lebanon which He
planted,
17 Where the birds make their nests;
The stork has her home in the fir trees.
18 The high hills *are* for the wild goats;
The cliffs are a refuge for the ᵀrock
badgers.   Or *rock hyraxes;* Lev. 11:5

19 He appointed the moon for seasons;
The ᴿsun knows its going down.   Ps. 19:6
20 ᴿYou make darkness, and it is night,
In which all the beasts of the forest
creep about.   [Is. 45:7]

21 ᴿThe young lions roar after their prey,
And seek their food from God.   Job 38:39
22 *When* the sun rises, they gather
together
And lie down in their dens.
23 Man goes out to ᴿhis work   Gen. 3:19
And to his labor until the evening.

24 O Lᴏʀᴅ, how manifold are Your works!
In wisdom You have made them all.
The earth is full of Your possessions—
25 This great and wide sea,
In which *are* innumerable teeming
things,
Living things both small and great.
26 There the ships sail about;
There is that ᴿLeviathan   Job 41:1
Which You have made to play there.

27 ᴿThese all wait for You,
That You may give *them* their food in
due season.   Ps. 136:25
28 *What* You give them they gather in;
You open Your hand, they are filled
with good.
29 You hide Your face, they are troubled;
ᴿYou take away their breath, they die
and return to their dust.   Job 34:15
30 ᴿYou send forth Your Spirit, they are
created;   Is. 32:15
And You renew the face of the earth.

31 May the glory of the Lᴏʀᴅ endure
forever;
May the Lᴏʀᴅ rejoice in His works.
32 He looks on the earth, and it trembles;
He touches the hills, and they smoke.

33 ᴿI will sing to the Lᴏʀᴅ as long as I live;
I will sing praise to my God while I
have my being.   Ps. 63:4
34 May my ᴿmeditation be sweet to Him;
I will be glad in the Lᴏʀᴅ.   Ps. 19:14
35 May ᴿsinners be consumed from the
earth,
And the wicked be no more.

Bless the Lᴏʀᴅ, O my soul!
ᵀPraise the Lᴏʀᴅ!   Ps. 37:38 • Heb. *Hallelujah*

Psalm 105

The Eternal Faithfulness of the Lᴏʀᴅ

OH, ᴿgive thanks to the Lᴏʀᴅ!
Call upon His name;
ᴿMake known His deeds among the
peoples!   Is. 12:4 • Ps. 145:12
2 Sing to Him, sing psalms to Him;
ᴿTalk of all His wondrous works!   Ps. 119:27
3 Glory in His holy name;
Let the hearts of those rejoice who
seek the Lᴏʀᴅ!
4 Seek the Lᴏʀᴅ and His strength;
ᴿSeek His face evermore!   Ps. 27:8
5 ᴿRemember His marvelous works which
He has done,

His wonders, and the judgments of His
    mouth,　　　　Ps. 77:11
6　O seed of Abraham His servant,
    You children of Jacob, His chosen ones!

7　He *is* the LORD our God;
    His judgments *are* in all the earth.
8　He ᴿremembers His covenant forever,
    The word *which* He commanded, for a
    thousand generations,　　　　Luke 1:72
9 ᴿ*The covenant* which He made with
    Abraham,
    And His oath to Isaac,　　　　Gen. 17:2
10　And confirmed it to Jacob for a statute,
    To Israel *as* an everlasting covenant,
11　Saying, ᴿ"To you I will give the land of
    Canaan　　　　Gen. 13:15; 15:18
    As the allotment of your inheritance,"
12　When they were few in number,
    Indeed very few, and strangers in it.

13　When they went from one nation to
    another,
    From *one* kingdom to another people,
14　He permitted no one to do them wrong;
    Yes, He rebuked kings for their sakes,
15　*Saying,* "Do not touch My anointed
    ones,
    And do My prophets no harm."

16　Moreover ᴿHe called for a famine in the
    land;　　　　Gen. 41:54
    He destroyed all the provision of bread.
17 ᴿHe sent a man before them—　　[Gen. 45:5]
    Joseph—*who* was sold as a slave.
18 ᴿThey hurt his feet with fetters,　Gen. 40:15
    ᵀHe was laid in irons.　　*His soul came into iron*
19　Until the time that his word came to
    pass,
    The word of the LORD tested him.
20　The king sent and released him,
    The ruler of the people let him go free.
21　He made him lord of his house,
    And ruler of all his possessions,
22　To ᵀbind his princes at his pleasure,
    And teach his elders wisdom.　　As prisoners

23 ᴿIsrael also came into Egypt,　　Gen. 46:6
    And Jacob dwelt in the land of Ham.
24 ᴿHe increased His people greatly,
    And made them stronger than their
    enemies.　　　　Ex. 1:7, 9
25 ᴿHe turned their heart to hate His
    people,
    To deal craftily with His servants.　Ex. 1:8–10; 4:21
26 ᴿHe sent Moses His servant,　Ex. 3:10; 4:12–15
    And Aaron whom He had chosen.
27　They ᴿperformed His signs among them,
    And wonders in the land of Ham.　Ps. 78:43
28　He sent darkness, and made *it* dark;
    And they did not rebel against His
    word.
29 ᴿHe turned their waters into blood,
    And killed their fish.　　　Ex. 7:20, 21

30 ᴿTheir land abounded with frogs,　Ex. 8:6
    Even in the chambers of their kings.
31 ᴿHe spoke, and there came swarms of
    flies,
    And lice in all their territory.　Ex. 8:16, 17
32 ᴿHe gave them hail for rain,
    And flaming fire in their land.　Ex. 9:23–25
33 ᴿHe struck their vines also, and their fig
    trees,
    And splintered the trees of their
    territory.　　　　Ps. 78:47
34 ᴿHe spoke, and locusts came,
    Young locusts without number,　Ex. 10:4
35　And ate up all the vegetation in their
    land,
    And devoured the fruit of their ground.
36 ᴿHe also ᵀdestroyed all the firstborn in
    their land,　Ex. 12:29; 13:15 • Lit. *struck down*
    ᴿThe first of all their strength.　Gen. 49:3

37 ᴿHe also brought them out with silver
    and gold,
    And *there was* none feeble among His
    tribes.　　　　Ex. 12:35, 36
38 ᴿEgypt was glad when they departed,
    For the fear of them had fallen upon
    them.　　　　Ex. 12:33
39　He spread a cloud for a covering,
    And fire to give light in the night.
40 ᴿ*The people* asked, and He brought
    quail,
    And ᴿsatisfied them with the bread of
    heaven.　　Ex. 16:12 • Ps. 78:24
41 ᴿHe opened the rock, and water gushed
    out;　　　　Ex. 17:6
    It ran in the dry places *like* a river.

42　For He remembered ᴿHis holy promise,
    And Abraham His servant.　Gen. 15:13, 14
43　He brought out His people with joy,
    His chosen ones with ᵀgladness.　*glad shout*
44 ᴿHe gave them the lands of the
    ᵀGentiles,
    And they inherited the labor of the
    nations,　Josh. 11:16–23; 13:7 • *nations*
45 ᴿThat they might observe His statutes
    And keep His laws.

ᵀPraise the LORD!　[Deut. 4:1, 40] • Heb. *Hallelujah*

Psalm 106

Joy in Forgiveness of Israel's Sins

PRAISEᵀ the LORD!
    Oh, ᴿgive thanks to the LORD, for *He is*
    good!　　Heb. *Hallelujah* • 1 Chr. 16:34, 41
    For His mercy *endures* forever.
2　Who can ᵀutter the mighty acts of the
    LORD?
    Who can declare all His praise?　*express*
3　Blessed *are* those who keep justice,
    And *he who ᴿdoes righteousness at ᴿall
    times!　　Ps. 15:2 • [Gal. 6:9]

106:3 LXX, [Syr.], Tg., Vg. *those who do*

4 Remember me, O Lord, with the favor
  You have toward Your people.
  Oh, visit me with Your salvation,
5 That I may see the benefit of Your
  chosen ones,
  That I may rejoice in the gladness of
  Your nation,
  That I may glory with ᵀYour
  inheritance.   The people of Your inheritance

6 ᴿWe have sinned with our fathers,
  We have committed iniquity,
  We have done wickedly.   [Dan. 9:5]
7 Our fathers in Egypt did not understand
  Your wonders;
  They did not remember the multitude
  of Your mercies,
  But rebelled by the sea—the Red Sea.

8 Nevertheless He saved them for His
  name's sake,
  ᴿThat He might make His mighty power
  known.   Ex. 9:16
9 ᴿHe rebuked the Red Sea also, and it
  dried up;   Ex. 14:21
  So ᴿHe led them through the depths,
  As through the wilderness.   Is. 63:11-13
10 He ᴿsaved them from the hand of him
   who hated *them,*
   And redeemed them from the hand of
   the enemy.   Ex. 14:30
11 The waters covered their enemies;
   There was not one of them left.
12 ᴿThen they believed His words;
   They sang His praise.   Ex. 15:1-21
13 ᴿThey soon forgot His works;   Ex. 17:1-7
   They did not wait for His counsel,
14 ᴿBut lusted exceedingly in the
   wilderness,
   And tested God in the desert.   1 Cor. 10:6
15 And He gave them their request,
   But sent leanness into their soul.

16 When they envied Moses in the camp,
   And Aaron the saint of the Lord,
17 ᴿThe earth opened up and swallowed
   Dathan,   Deut. 11:6
   And covered the faction of Abiram.
18 A fire was kindled in their company;
   The flame burned up the wicked.

19 ᴿThey made a calf in Horeb,   Ex. 32:1-4
   And worshiped the molded image.
20 Thus ᴿthey changed their glory   Rom. 1:23
   Into the image of an ox that eats grass.
21 They forgot God their Savior,
   Who had done great things in Egypt,
22 Wondrous works in the land of Ham,
   Awesome things by the Red Sea.
23 ᴿTherefore He said that He would
   destroy them,
   Had not Moses His chosen one ᴿstood
   before Him in the breach,
   To turn away His wrath, lest He
   destroy *them.*   Ex. 32:10 • Ezek. 22:30

24 Then they despised ᴿthe pleasant land;
   They did not believe His word,   Deut. 8:7
25 ᴿBut complained in their tents,   Num. 14:2, 27
   And did not heed the voice of the Lord.
26 ᴿTherefore He raised His hand *in an*
   oath against them,   Ezek. 20:15, 16
   To overthrow them in the wilderness,
27 To ᵀoverthrow their descendants among
   the nations,   *make their descendants fall also*
   And to scatter them in the lands.

28 ᴿThey joined themselves also to Baal of
   Peor,   Hos. 9:10
   And ate sacrifices made to the dead.
29 Thus they provoked *Him* to anger with
   their deeds,
   And the plague broke out among them.
30 Then Phinehas stood up and
   intervened,
   And the plague was stopped.
31 And that was accounted to him ᴿfor
   righteousness   Num. 25:11-13
   To all generations forevermore.

32 ᴿThey angered *Him* also at the waters of
   ᵀstrife,   Num. 20:3-13 • Heb. *Meribah*
   ᴿSo that it went ill with Moses on
   account of them;   Deut. 1:37; 3:26
33 Because they rebelled against His Spirit,
   So that he spoke rashly with his lips.

34 ᴿThey did not destroy the peoples,
   ᴿConcerning whom the Lord had
   commanded them,   Judg. 1:21 • [Deut. 7:2, 16]
35 ᴿBut they mingled with the Gentiles
   And learned their works;   Judg. 3:5, 6
36 ᴿThey served their idols,   Judg. 2:12
   ᴿWhich became a snare to them.   Deut. 7:16
37 They even sacrificed their sons
   And their daughters to demons,
38 And shed innocent blood,
   The blood of their sons and daughters,
   Whom they sacrificed to the idols of
   Canaan;
   And the land was polluted with blood.
39 Thus they ᵀwere ᴿdefiled by their own
   works,   *became unclean* • Ezek. 20:18
   And ᴿplayed the ᵀharlot by their own
   deeds.   [Lev. 17:7] • Were unfaithful

40 Therefore ᴿthe wrath of the Lord was
   kindled against His people,
   So that He abhorred ᴿHis own
   inheritance.   Judg. 2:14 • [Deut. 9:29; 32:9]
41 And ᴿHe gave them into the hand of
   the Gentiles,
   And those who hated them ruled over
   them.   Judg. 2:14
42 Their enemies also oppressed them,
   And they were brought into subjection
   under their hand.
43 ᴿMany times He delivered them;   Judg. 2:16
   But they rebelled in their counsel,
   And were brought low for their
   iniquity.

44 Nevertheless He regarded their
affliction,
When ᴿHe heard their cry; Judg. 3:9
45 ᴿAnd for their sake He remembered His
covenant, [Lev. 26:41, 42]
And relented ᴿaccording to the
multitude of His mercies. Ps. 69:16
46 ᴿHe also made them to be pitied
By all those who carried them away
captive. Ezra 9:9

47 ᴿSave us, O Lᴏʀᴅ our God, 1 Chr. 16:35, 36
And gather us from among the
Gentiles,
To give thanks to Your holy name,
To triumph in Your praise.

48 ᴿBlessed be the Lᴏʀᴅ God of Israel
From everlasting to everlasting!
And let all the people say, "Amen!"

ᵀPraise the Lᴏʀᴅ! Ps. 41:13 • Heb. Hallelujah

BOOK FIVE
Psalms 107–150

Psalm 107

*Thanksgiving to the Lᴏʀᴅ for His Great
Works of Deliverance*

OH, ᴿgive thanks to the Lᴏʀᴅ, for *He is*
good! Ps. 106:1
For His mercy *endures* forever.
2 Let the redeemed of the Lᴏʀᴅ say *so,*
Whom He has redeemed from the hand
of the enemy,
3 And ᴿgathered out of the lands, Is. 43:5, 6
From the east and from the west,
From the north and from the south.

4 They wandered in ᴿthe wilderness in a
desolate way; [Deut. 2:7; 32:10]
They found no city to dwell in.
5 Hungry and thirsty,
Their soul fainted in them.
6 ᴿThen they cried out to the Lᴏʀᴅ in
their trouble,
And He delivered them out of their
distresses. Ps. 50:15
7 And He led them forth by the ᴿright
way,
That they might go to a city for a
dwelling place. Ezra 8:21
8 ᴿOh, that *men* would give thanks to the
Lᴏʀᴅ *for* His goodness,
And *for* His wonderful works to the
children of men! Ps. 107:15, 21
9 For He satisfies the longing soul,
And fills the hungry soul with
goodness.

10 Those who ᴿsat in darkness and in the
shadow of death, [Luke 1:79]
ᵀBound in affliction and irons— Prisoners

11 Because they ᴿrebelled against the
words of God,
And ᵀdespised ᴿthe counsel of the Most
High, Lam. 3:42 • *scorned* • [Ps. 73:24]
12 Therefore He brought down their heart
with labor;
They fell down, and *there was* ᴿnone to
help. Ps. 22:11
13 Then they cried out to the Lᴏʀᴅ in
their trouble,
And He saved them out of their
distresses.
14 ᴿHe brought them out of darkness and
the shadow of death,
And broke their chains in pieces. Ps. 68:6
15 Oh, that *men* would give thanks to the
Lᴏʀᴅ *for* His goodness,
And *for* His wonderful works to the
children of men!
16 For He has ᴿbroken the gates of bronze,
And cut the bars of iron in two. Is. 45:1, 2

17 Fools, ᴿbecause of their transgression,
And because of their iniquities, were
afflicted. Lam. 3:39
18 ᴿTheir soul abhorred all manner of food,
And they ᴿdrew near to the gates of
death. Job 33:20 • Job 33:22
19 Then they cried out to the Lᴏʀᴅ in
their trouble,
And He saved them out of their
distresses.
20 ᴿHe sent His word and ᴿhealed them,
And ᴿdelivered *them* from their
destructions. Matt. 8:8 • Ps. 30:2 • Job 33:28, 30
21 Oh, that *men* would give thanks to the
Lᴏʀᴅ *for* His goodness,
And *for* His wonderful works to the
children of men!
22 ᴿLet them sacrifice the sacrifices of
thanksgiving, Lev. 7:12
And declare His works with rejoicing.

23 Those who go down to the sea in ships,
Who do business on great waters,
24 They see the works of the Lᴏʀᴅ,
And His wonders in the deep.
25 For He commands and ᴿraises the
stormy wind, Jon. 1:4
Which lifts up the waves of the sea.
26 They mount up to the heavens,
They go down again to the depths;
Their soul melts because of trouble.
27 They reel to and fro, and stagger like a
drunken man,
And are at their wits' end.
28 Then they cry out to the Lᴏʀᴅ in their
trouble,
And He brings them out of their
distresses.
29 ᴿHe calms the storm,
So that its waves are still. Ps. 89:9
30 Then they are glad because they are
quiet;

So He guides them to their desired
haven.
31 ᴿOh, that *men* would give thanks to the
Lᴏʀᴅ *for* His goodness,
And *for* His wonderful works to the
children of men!   Ps. 107:8, 15, 21
32 Let them exalt Him also ᴿin the
assembly of the people,
And praise Him in the company of the
elders.   Ps. 22:22, 25

33 He turns rivers into a wilderness,
And the watersprings into dry ground;
34 A ᴿfruitful land into ᵀbarrenness,
For the wickedness of those who dwell
in it.   Gen. 13:10 · Lit. *a salty waste*
35 ᴿHe turns a wilderness into pools of
water,
And dry land into watersprings. Ps. 114:8
36 There He makes the hungry dwell,
That they may establish a city for a
dwelling place,
37 And sow fields and plant vineyards,
That they may yield a fruitful harvest.
38 ᴿHe also blesses them, and they multiply
greatly;
And He does not let their cattle
ᴿdecrease.   Gen. 12:2; 17:16, 20 · [Deut. 7:14]

39 When they are ᴿdiminished and brought
low
Through oppression, affliction and
sorrow,   2 Kin. 10:32
40 He pours contempt on princes,
And causes them to wander in the
wilderness *where there is* no way;
41 ᴿYet He sets the poor on high, far from
affliction,   1 Sam. 2:8
And makes *their* families like a flock.
42 The righteous see *it* and rejoice,
And all iniquity stops its mouth.

43 ᴿWhoever *is* wise will observe these
things,
And they will understand the
lovingkindness of the Lᴏʀᴅ.   Jer. 9:12

Psalm 108

Assurance of God's Victory over Enemies
A Song. A Psalm of David.

Oᴿ GOD, my heart is steadfast;
I will sing and give praise, even with
my glory.   Ps. 57:7-11
2 ᴿAwake, lute and harp!
I will awaken the dawn.   Ps. 57:8-11
3 I will praise You, O Lᴏʀᴅ, among the
peoples,
And I will sing praises to You among
the nations.
4 For Your mercy *is* great above the
ᵀheavens,   skies
And Your truth *reaches* to the clouds.

5 Be exalted, O God, above the heavens,
And Your glory above all the earth;
6 ᴿThat Your beloved may be delivered,
Save *with* Your right hand, and ᵀhear
me.   Ps. 60:5-12 · Lit. *answer*

7 God has spoken in His holiness:
"I will rejoice;
I will divide Shechem
And measure out the Valley of Succoth.
8 Gilead *is* Mine; Manasseh *is* Mine;
Ephraim also *is* the ᵀhelmet for My
head;
Judah *is* My lawgiver.   Lit. *protection*
9 Moab *is* My washpot;
Over Edom I will cast My shoe;
Over Philistia I will triumph."

10 ᴿWho will bring me *into* the strong city?
Who will lead me to Edom?   Ps. 60:9
11 *Is it* not You, O God, *who* cast us off?
And You, O God, *who* did not go out
with our armies?
12 Give us help from trouble,
For the help of man is useless.
13 ᴿThrough God we will do valiantly,
For *it is* He *who* shall tread down our
enemies.   Ps. 60:12

Psalm 109

Plea for Judgment of False Accusers
To the Chief Musician. A Psalm of David.

Dᴼ not keep silent,
O God of my praise!   Ps. 83:1
2 For the mouth of the wicked and the
mouth of the deceitful
Have opened against me;
They have spoken against me with a
ᴿlying tongue.   Ps. 27:12
3 They have also surrounded me with
words of hatred,
And fought against me ᴿwithout a
cause.   John 15:23-25
4 In return for my love they are my
accusers,
But I *give myself to* prayer.
5 Thus ᴿthey have rewarded me evil for
good,
And hatred for my love. Ps. 35:7, 12; 38:20

6 Set a wicked man over him,
And let ᴿan ᵀaccuser stand at his right
hand.   Zech. 3:1 · Heb. *satan*
7 When he is judged, let him be found
guilty,
And ᴿlet his prayer become sin. [Prov. 28:9]
8 Let his days be ᴿfew,   [Ps. 55:23]
And ᴿlet another take his office. Acts 1:20
9 ᴿLet his children be fatherless,
And his wife a widow.   Ex. 22:24
10 Let his children ᵀcontinually be
vagabonds, and beg;

Let them *seek *their bread* also from
their desolate places.   *wander continuously*

11 Let the creditor seize all that he has,
And let strangers plunder his labor.

12 Let there be none to extend mercy to
him,
Nor let there be any to favor his
fatherless children.

13 Let his posterity be ᵀcut off,   *destroyed*
And in the generation following let
their ᴿname be blotted out.   Prov. 10:7

14 ᴿLet the iniquity of his fathers be
remembered before the Lᴏʀᴅ,
And let not the sin of his mother ᴿbe
blotted out.   [Ex. 20:5] • Neh. 4:5

15 Let them be continually before the
Lᴏʀᴅ,
That He may ᴿcut off the memory of
them from the earth;   Job 18:17

16 Because he did not remember to show
mercy,
But persecuted the poor and needy
man,
That he might even slay the ᴿbroken in
heart.   [Ps. 34:18]

17 ᴿAs he loved cursing, so let it come to
him;
As he did not delight in blessing, so let
it be far from him.   Prov. 14:14

18 As he clothed himself with cursing as
with his garment,
So let it ᴿenter his body like water,
And like oil into his bones.   Num. 5:22

19 Let it be to him like the garment which
covers him,
And for a belt with which he girds
himself continually.

20 *Let* this *be* the Lᴏʀᴅ's reward to my
accusers,
And to those who speak evil against my
person.

21 But You, O Gᴏᴅ the Lord,
Deal with me for Your name's sake;
Because Your mercy *is* good, deliver
me.

109:10 So with MT, Tg.; LXX, Vg. *be cast out*

22 For I *am* poor and needy,
And my heart is wounded within me.

23 I am gone ᴿlike a shadow when it
lengthens;
I am shaken off like a locust.   Ps. 102:11

24 My ᴿknees are weak through fasting,
And my flesh is feeble from lack of
fatness.   Heb. 12:12

25 I also have become ᴿa reproach to
them;
When they look at me, ᴿthey shake
their heads.   Ps. 22:7 • Matt. 27:39

26 Help me, O Lᴏʀᴅ my God!
Oh, save me according to Your mercy,

27 ᴿThat they may know that this *is* Your
hand—
That You, Lᴏʀᴅ, have done it!   Job 37:7

28 Let them curse, but You bless;
When they arise, let them be ashamed,
But let ᴿYour servant rejoice.   Is. 65:14

29 Let my accusers be clothed with shame,
And let them cover themselves with
their own disgrace as with a mantle.

30 I will greatly praise the Lᴏʀᴅ with my
mouth;
Yes, ᴿI will praise Him among the
multitude.   Ps. 35:18; 111:1

31 For ᴿHe shall stand at the right hand of
the poor,
To save *him* from those ᵀwho condemn
him.   [Ps. 16:8] • Lit. *judging his soul*

Psalm 110

Announcement of the Messiah's Reign
A Psalm of David.

9-F. The Messiah as High Priest   ▼

THE ᴿLᴏʀᴅ said to my Lord,
"Sit at My right hand,
Till I make Your enemies Your
ᴿfootstool."   Matt. 22:44 • [1 Cor. 15:25]

2 The Lᴏʀᴅ shall send the rod of Your
strength ᴿout of Zion.   [Rom. 11:26, 27]
Rule in the midst of Your enemies!

3 ᴿYour people *shall be* volunteers
In the day of Your power;

9-F. The Messiah as High Priest (Psalm 110:1–7)—In this messianic psalm, the prophet David affirms two
great doctrines:

(1) *The deity of the Messiah.* David prophesied that after the death, burial, and resurrection of the
Messiah, He would sit at the right hand of the Father. "The Lᴏʀᴅ [Jehovah] said to my Lord [Adonai], 'Sit at
My right hand, till I make Your enemies Your footstool' " (v. 1). This is one of the strongest declarations of
Christ's deity in the Bible. God the Father said to God the Son, "Sit at My right hand." The "Lᴏʀᴅ" of this
verse is *Jehovah* God; the "Lord" is *Adonai* God; both are Hebrew names for God. "Lᴏʀᴅ" (all capitals)
always stands for the personal name of God or Jehovah *(Yahweh).* "Lord" (in upper and lower case) stands
for *Adonai* ("master"). (Without the initial capital letter, "lord" refers merely to a human—or sometimes
angelic—leader or aristocrat.) After His resurrection, our High Priest, Adonai, sat down with Jehovah on His
throne, where He will remain until Jehovah makes His enemies His footstool. Then He will sit upon the
throne of David, His father by natural descent, and Jehovah God will say to Him, "Your throne, O God, is
forever and ever; a scepter of righteousness is the scepter of Your kingdom" (Heb. 1:8, page 1236).

(Point 9-F continued on next page)

▽ ᴿIn the beauties of holiness, from the
     womb of the morning,   Judg. 5:2 · Ps. 96:9
   You have the dew of Your youth.
4 The Lᴏʀᴅ has sworn
   And ᴿwill not relent,   [Num. 23:19]
   "You *are* a ᴿpriest forever   [Zech. 6:13]
   According to the order of
   ᴿMelchizedek."   [Heb. 5:6, 10; 6:20]

5 The Lord *is* ᴿat Your right hand;
   He shall ᵀexecute kings in the day of
      His wrath.   [Ps. 16:8] · Lit. *break kings in pieces*
6 He shall judge among the nations,
   He shall fill *the places* with dead bodies,
   ᴿHe shall ᵀexecute the heads of many
      countries.   Ps. 68:21 · Lit. *break in pieces*
7 He shall drink of the brook by the
      wayside;
▲   Therefore He shall lift up the head.

Psalm 111

*Praise to God for His Faithfulness and
Justice*

Pʀᴀɪsᴇᵀ the Lᴏʀᴅ!

   I will ᴿpraise the Lᴏʀᴅ with *my* whole
      heart,
   In the assembly of the upright and *in*
      the congregation.   Heb. *Hallelujah* · Ps. 35:18

2 ᴿThe works of the Lᴏʀᴅ *are* great,

ᴿStudied by all who have pleasure in
   them.   Ps. 92:5 · Ps. 143:5
3 His work *is* honorable and glorious,
   And His righteousness endures forever.
4 He has made His wonderful works to be
      remembered;
   ᴿThe Lᴏʀᴅ *is* gracious and full of
      compassion.   [Ps. 86:5]
5 He has given food to those who fear
      Him;
   He will ever be mindful of His
      covenant.
6 He has declared to His people the
      power of His works,
   In giving them the ᵀheritage of the
      nations.   *inheritance*
7 The works of His hands *are* ᴿverityᵀ and
      justice;
   All His precepts *are* sure.   [Rev. 15:3] · *truth*
8 They stand fast forever and ever,
   And are done in truth and uprightness.
9 ᴿHe has sent redemption to His people;
   He has commanded His covenant
      forever: Luke 1:68
   ᴿHoly and awesome *is* His name.   Luke 1:49
10 ᴿThe fear of the Lᴏʀᴅ *is* the beginning of
      wisdom;
   A good understanding have all those
      who do *His commandments.*
   His praise endures forever.   Eccl. 12:13

(Point 9-F continued from previous page)

   The first verse of this messianic psalm is quoted or alluded to often in the New Testament, always confirming the deity of the Messiah, seated at the right hand of the Father:

   At the Father's right hand,

       (a) He is David's Son by natural descent (Rom. 1:3, page 1128), but David's God because of His eternal and divine origin (Matt. 22:41–46, page 971).
       (b) He is both God and Messiah (Acts 2:34–36, page 1089).
       (c) He stood to welcome home Stephen, the first Christian martyr (Acts 7:55, page 1097).
       (d) He intercedes for all believers as Messiah-Priest (Rom. 8:34, page 1138; Heb. 9:24–26, page 1244).
       (e) He is exalted above all authority (Eph. 1:19–23, page 1187).
       (f) He is greater than angels (Heb. 1:4–13, page 1236).
       (g) He made atonement for all the sins of all believers as our High Priest (Heb. 10:11–14, page 1246). After He offered one sacrifice for sin—Himself—He ascended into heaven to sprinkle His blood upon the mercy seat.
       (h) He found eternal joy after Calvary (Heb. 12:2, page 1250). All believers can have joy now (1 John 1:4, page 1278). But when we see Him in our glorified bodies, we too will share His perfect, eternal joy (1 John 3:2, page 1279).
       (i) The whole host of heaven is subject to Him (1 Pet. 3:22, page 1267).

   (2) *The priesthood of the Messiah.* "The Lᴏʀᴅ has sworn and will not relent, 'You are a priest forever according to the order of Melchizedek' " (v. 4). Christ is the Messiah-Priest, ordained not by man, but by the oath of Jehovah God, who consecrated Him, saying, "You are a priest forever according to the order of Melchizedek." And Jehovah is not a man that He should repent, i.e., change His mind (Num. 23:19, page 164). He is immutable, that is, He does not change (Heb. 13:8, page 1252). The Messiah-Priest of this messianic psalm has no successor; His priesthood is eternally unique.

   Melchizedek is mentioned only twice in the Old Testament, here and in Genesis 14. He was a mysterious priest and king who went out to meet Abraham when the latter returned from battle after rescuing Lot (Gen. 14:17–20, page 19).

   As a king-priest, Melchizedek is a type of Christ who is our eternal King-Priest (Heb. 7:17, page 1242). As priest, he brought bread and wine to Abraham and then received tithes from him. In the New Testament our High Priest, who is "a priest forever according to the order of Melchizedek," served bread and wine to His disciples, instituting the Lord's Supper (Matt. 26:26–30, page 978).

   See Psalm 2:1–12, page 509, for **Point 9-G: The Messiah as King of Kings.**

Psalm 112

The Blessed State of the Righteous

PRAISE[T] the LORD!

Blessed *is* the man *who* fears the LORD,
Who [R]delights greatly in His
  commandments.   Heb. *Hallelujah* · Ps. 128:1

2 [R]His descendants will be mighty on
   earth;
   The generation of the upright will be
     blessed.   [Ps. 102:28]
3 Wealth and riches *will be* in his house,
   And his righteousness endures forever.
4 [R]Unto the upright there arises light in
   the darkness;
   He is gracious, and full of compassion,
   and righteous.   Job 11:17
5 [R]A good man deals graciously and lends;
   He will guide his affairs [R]with
   discretion.   [Luke 6:35] · [Eph. 5:15]
6 Surely he will never be shaken;
   [R]The righteous will be in everlasting
   remembrance.   Prov. 10:7
7 [R]He will not be afraid of evil tidings;
   His heart is steadfast, trusting in the
   LORD.   [Prov. 1:33]
8 His [R]heart *is* established;
   [R]He will not be afraid,
   Until he [R]sees *his desire* upon his
   enemies.   Heb. 13:9 · Prov. 1:33; 3:24 · Ps. 59:10

9 He has dispersed abroad,
   He has given to the poor;
   His righteousness endures forever;
   His horn will be exalted with honor.
10 The wicked will see *it* and be grieved;
   He will gnash his teeth and melt away;
   The desire of the wicked shall perish.

Psalm 113

The Majesty and Condescension of God

PRAISE[T] the LORD!   Heb. *Hallelujah*

Praise, O servants of the LORD,
Praise the name of the LORD!
2 Blessed be the name of the LORD
   From this time forth and forevermore!
3 [R]From the rising of the sun to its going
   down   Is. 59:19
   The LORD's name *is* to be praised.

4 The LORD *is* high above all nations,
   His glory above the heavens.
5 [R]Who *is* like the LORD our God,
   Who dwells on high,   [Is. 57:15]
6 [R]Who humbles Himself to behold
   The things that are in the heavens and
   in the earth?   [Ps. 11:4]

7 [R]He raises the poor out of the dust,
   And lifts the [R]needy out of the ash
   heap,   1 Sam. 2:8 · Ps. 72:12

8 That He may [R]seat *him* with princes—
   With the princes of His people.   [Job 36:7]
9 [R]He grants the [T]barren woman *a* home,
   Like a joyful mother of children.

Praise the LORD!   1 Sam. 2:5 · *childless*

Psalm 114

The Power of God in His Deliverance of Israel

WHEN Israel went out of Egypt,
The house of Jacob from a people [T]of
   strange language,   *who spoke unintelligibly*
2 [R]Judah became His sanctuary,
   And Israel His dominion.   Ex. 6:7; 19:6

3 [R]The sea saw *it* and fled;
   [R]Jordan turned back.   Ex. 14:21 · Josh. 3:13–16
4 [R]The mountains skipped like rams,
   The little hills like lambs.   Ps. 29:6
5 [R]What ails you, O sea, that you fled?
   O Jordan, *that* you turned back?   Hab. 3:8
6 O mountains, *that* you skipped like
   rams?
   O little hills, like lambs?

7 Tremble, O earth, at the presence of the
   Lord,
   At the presence of the God of Jacob,
8 [R]Who turned the rock *into* a pool of
   water,   Ex. 17:6
   The flint into a fountain of waters.

Psalm 115

The Futility of Idols and the Trustworthiness of God

NOT [R]unto us, O LORD, not unto us,
   But to Your name give glory,
   Because of Your mercy,
   Because of Your truth.   [Is. 48:11]
2 Why should the [T]Gentiles say,   *nations*
   [R]"So where *is* their God?"   Ps. 42:3, 10

3 [R]But our God *is* in heaven;   [1 Chr. 16:26]
   He does whatever He pleases.
4 [R]Their idols *are* silver and gold,
   The work of men's hands.   Jer. 10:3
5 They have mouths, but they do not
   speak;
   Eyes they have, but they do not see;
6 They have ears, but they do not hear;
   Noses they have, but they do not smell;
7 They have hands, but they do not
   handle;
   Feet they have, but they do not walk;
   Nor do they mutter through their
   throat.
8 Those who make them are like them;
   So is everyone who trusts in them.

9 [R]O Israel, trust in the LORD;   Ps. 118:2, 3
   [R]He *is* their help and their shield. Ps. 33:20

10 O house of Aaron, trust in the LORD;
   He *is* their help and their shield.
11 You who fear the LORD, trust in the
   LORD;
   He *is* their help and their shield.

12 The LORD ᵀhas been mindful of *us;*   *has remembered us*
   He will bless us;
   He will bless the house of Israel;
   He will bless the house of Aaron.
13 ᴿHe will bless those who fear the LORD,
   Both small and great.   Ps. 128:1, 4

14 May the LORD give you increase more
   and more,
   You and your children.
15 *May* you *be* blessed by the LORD,
   ᴿWho made heaven and earth.   Gen. 1:1

16 The heaven, *even* the heavens, *are* the
   LORD'S;
   But the earth He has given to the
   children of men.
17 The dead do not praise the LORD,
   Nor any who go down into silence.
18 ᴿBut we will bless the LORD
   From this time forth and forevermore.

   Praise the LORD!   Dan. 2:20

Psalm 116

Thanksgiving for Deliverance from Death

I ᴿLOVE the LORD, because He has heard
   My voice *and* my supplications.   Ps. 18:1
2 Because He has inclined His ear to me,
   Therefore I will call *upon Him* as long
   as I live.

3 The ᵀpains of death surrounded me,
   And the ᵀpangs of Sheol ᵀlaid hold of
   me;   Lit. *cords* · *distresses* · Lit. *found me*
   I found trouble and sorrow.
4 Then I called upon the name of the
   LORD:
   "O LORD, I implore You, deliver my
   soul!"

5 Gracious *is* the LORD, and ᴿrighteous;
   Yes, our God *is* merciful.   [Ezra 9:15]
6 The LORD preserves the simple;
   I was brought low, and He saved me.
7 Return to your ᴿrest, O my soul,
   For ᴿthe LORD has dealt bountifully
   with you.   [Jer. 6:16] · Ps. 13:6

8 ᴿFor You have delivered my soul from
   death,
   My eyes from tears,
   And my feet from falling.   Ps. 56:13
9 I will walk before the LORD
   ᴿIn the land of the living.   Ps. 27:13
10 ᴿI believed, therefore I spoke,
   "I am greatly afflicted."   2 Cor. 4:13
11 ᴿI said in my haste,
   ᴿ"All men *are* liars."   Ps. 31:22 · Rom. 3:4

12 What shall I render to the LORD
   For all His benefits toward me?
13 I will take up the cup of salvation,
   And call upon the name of the LORD.
14 ᴿI will pay my vows to the LORD   Ps. 116:18
   Now in the presence of all His people.

15 ᴿPrecious in the sight of the LORD
   Is the death of His saints.   Ps. 72:14

16 O LORD, truly ᴿI *am* Your servant;
   I *am* Your servant, ᴿthe son of Your
   maidservant;   Ps. 119:125; 143:12 · Ps. 86:16
   You have loosed my bonds.
17 I will offer to You ᴿthe sacrifice of
   thanksgiving,
   And will call upon the name of the
   LORD.   Lev. 7:12

18 I will pay my vows to the LORD
   Now in the presence of all His people,
19 In the ᴿcourts of the LORD's house,
   In the midst of you, O Jerusalem.

   ᵀPraise the LORD!   Ps. 96:8 · Heb. *Hallelujah*

Psalm 117

Let All Peoples Praise the LORD

P RAISE the LORD, all you Gentiles!
   ᵀLaud Him, all you peoples!   *Praise*
2 For His merciful kindness is great
   toward us,
   And ᴿthe truth of the LORD *endures*
   forever.

   Praise the LORD!   [Ps. 100:5]

Psalm 118

Praise to God for His Everlasting Mercy

O H, ᴿgive thanks to the LORD, for *He is*
   good!   1 Chr. 16:8, 34
   For His mercy *endures* forever.

2 ᴿLet Israel now say,
   "His mercy *endures* forever."   [Ps. 115:9]
3 Let the house of Aaron now say,
   "His mercy *endures* forever."
4 Let those who fear the LORD now say,
   "His mercy *endures* forever."

5 ᴿI called on the LORD in distress;
   The LORD answered me *and* ᴿset me in
   a broad place.   Ps. 120:1 · Ps. 18:19
6 ᴿThe LORD *is* on my side;
   I will not fear.
   What can man do to me?   Ps. 27:1; 56:9
7 ᴿThe LORD is for me among those who
   help me;
   Therefore ᴿI shall see *my desire* on
   those who hate me.   Ps. 54:4 · Ps. 59:10
8 ᴿ*It is* better to trust in the LORD
   Than to put confidence in man.   Ps. 40:4
9 ᴿ*It is* better to trust in the LORD   Ps. 146:3
   Than to put confidence in princes.

10 All nations surrounded me,
  But in the name of the LORD I will
    destroy them.
11 They ᴿsurrounded me,
  Yes, they surrounded me;
  But in the name of the LORD I will
    destroy them.   Ps. 88:17
12 They surrounded me ᴿlike bees;
  They were quenched ᴿlike a fire of
    thorns;   Deut. 1:44 • Nah. 1:10
  For in the name of the LORD I will
    ᵀdestroy them.   *cut them off*
13 You pushed me violently, that I might
    fall,
  But the LORD helped me.
14 ᴿThe LORD *is* my strength and song,
  And He has become my salvation. Ex. 15:2

15 The voice of rejoicing and salvation
  Is in the tents of the righteous;
  The right hand of the LORD does
    valiantly.
16 ᴿThe right hand of the LORD is exalted;
  The right hand of the LORD does
    valiantly.   Ex. 15:6
17 ᴿI shall not die, but live,   Hab. 1:12
  And declare the works of the LORD.
18 The LORD has chastened me severely,
  But He has not given me over to death.

19 ᴿOpen to me the gates of righteousness;
  I will go through them,
  And I will praise the LORD.   Is. 26:2
20 ᴿThis is the gate of the LORD,
  ᴿThrough which the righteous shall
    enter.   Ps. 24:7 • Is. 35:8

21 I will praise You,
  For You have ᴿanswered me,
  And have become my salvation.   Ps. 116:1

▼ **9–B. The Messiah Rejected**

22 The stone *which* the builders rejected
  Has become the chief cornerstone.

23 This ᵀwas the LORD's doing;   ▽
  It *is* marvelous in our eyes. *is from the LORD*
24 This is the day the LORD has made;
  We will rejoice and be glad in it.
25 Save now, I pray, O LORD;
  O LORD, I pray, send now prosperity.
26 ᴿBlessed *is* he who comes in the name of
    the LORD!
  We have blessed you from the house of
    the LORD.   Mark 11:9; Luke 19:38
27 God *is* the LORD,
  And He has given us ᴿlight;
  Bind the sacrifice with cords to the
    horns of the altar.   [1 Pet. 2:9]
28 You *are* my God, and I will praise You;
  ᴿYou *are* my God, I will exalt You. Is. 25:1
29 Oh, give thanks to the LORD, for *He is*
    good!
  For His mercy *endures* forever.   ▲

Psalm 119

*Meditations on the Excellencies of the
Word of God*

א ALEPH

B LESSED *are* the undefiled in the way,
    Who walk in the law of the LORD!
2 Blessed *are* those who keep His
    testimonies,
  Who seek Him with the whole heart!
3 ᴿThey also do no iniquity;
  They walk in His ways.   [1 John 3:9; 5:18]
4 You have commanded *us*
  To keep Your precepts diligently.
5 Oh, that my ways were directed
  To keep Your statutes!
6 ᴿThen I would not be ashamed,
  When I look into all Your
    commandments.   Job 22:26
7 I will praise You with uprightness of
    heart,

9-B. The Messiah Rejected (Psalm 118:22-29)—"The stone which the builders rejected has become the chief cornerstone" (v. 22). The builders who rejected their Messiah, the cornerstone of the promised kingdom, were the spiritual leaders of the Hebrew nation. John tells us that "He [the cornerstone] came to His own [Judaism, Israel], and His own [people] did not receive Him" (John 1:11, page 1049). When they rejected their Messiah, they rejected their King and His kingdom. Jesus said to them, "The kingdom of God will be taken from you [Israel] and given to a nation [Gentiles] bearing the fruits of it" (Matt. 21:43, page 969).

When Christ came the first time, national Israel rejected Him. They stumbled on the rock and became a broken, scattered nation. The kingdom of God was taken from them and given to the Gentiles. Largely from among the Gentile nations and the Jews the Messiah called His bride, the church (Matt. 21:43-46, page 969), though the earliest believers were *Jewish* Christians. To the true New Testament church, Christ is the chief cornerstone. The New Testament church is a "holy temple in the Lord" (Eph. 2:18-22, page 1188).

When the Messiah comes the second time, national Israel (Rom. 9:6, 7, page 1139) will be saved. "For I do not desire, brethren, that you should be ignorant of this mystery, lest you should be wise in your own opinion, that blindness in part has happened to Israel until the fullness of the Gentiles has come in. And so all Israel will be saved, as it is written: 'The Deliverer will come out of Zion, and He will turn away ungodliness from Jacob; for this is My covenant with them, when I take away their sins'" (Rom. 11:25-27, page 1141). Israel will enter the kingdom, and Christ (the Messiah) will be its cornerstone. But to the ungodly nations Christ will be a crushing stone. He will grind those corrupt nations to powder (Dan. 2:31-35, 44, 45, page 835). Christ is the cornerstone of the kingdom and the church.

See Psalm 69:1-21, page 550, for **Point 9-C: The Messiah Forsaken.**

When I learn Your righteous
   judgments.
8 I will keep Your statutes;
   Oh, do not forsake me utterly!

ב BETH

9 How can a young man cleanse his way?
   By taking heed according to Your
      word.
10 With my whole heart I have ᴿsought
      You;
   Oh, let me not wander from Your
      commandments!   2 Chr. 15:15
11 Your word I have hidden in my heart,
   That I might not sin against You.
12 Blessed *are* You, O LORD!
   Teach me Your statutes.
13 With my lips I have ᴿdeclared   Ps. 34:11
   All the judgments of Your mouth.
14 I have rejoiced in the way of Your
      testimonies,
   As *much as* in all riches.
15 I will meditate on Your precepts,
   And ᵀcontemplate Your ways.   *look into*
16 I will ᴿdelight myself in Your statutes;
   I will not forget Your word.   Ps. 1:2

ג GIMEL

17 Deal bountifully with Your servant,
   That I may live and keep Your word.
18 Open my eyes, that I may see
   Wondrous things from Your law.
19 ᴿI *am* a stranger in the earth;
   Do not hide Your commandments from
      me.   Heb. 11:13
20 My soul ᵀbreaks with longing   *is crushed*
   For Your judgments at all times.
21 You rebuke the proud—the cursed,
   Who stray from Your commandments.
22 ᴿRemove from me reproach and
      contempt,
   For I have kept Your testimonies. Ps. 39:8
23 Princes also sit *and* speak against me,
   But Your servant meditates on Your
      statutes.
24 Your testimonies also *are* my delight
   And my counselors.

ד DALETH

25 ᴿMy soul clings to the dust;   Ps. 44:25
   Revive me according to Your word.
26 I have declared my ways, and You
      answered me;
   ᴿTeach me Your statutes.   Ps. 25:4; 27:11
27 Make me understand the way of Your
      precepts;
   So ᴿshall I meditate on Your wonderful
      works.   Ps. 145:5, 6
28 My soul ᵀmelts from heaviness;   Lit. *drops*
   Strengthen me according to Your word.
29 Remove from me the way of lying,
   And grant me Your law graciously.

30 I have chosen the way of truth;
   Your judgments I have laid *before me.*
31 I cling to Your testimonies;
   O LORD, do not put me to shame!
32 I will run the course of Your
      commandments,
   For You shall ᴿenlarge my heart.   Is. 60:5

ה HE

33 ᴿTeach me, O LORD, the way of Your
      statutes,
   And I shall keep it *to* the end.   [Rev. 2:26]
34 ᴿGive me understanding, and I shall
      keep Your law;
   Indeed, I shall observe it with *my*
      whole heart.   [Prov. 2:6]
35 Make me walk in the path of Your
      commandments,
   For I delight in it.
36 Incline my heart to Your testimonies,
   And not to covetousness.
37 ᴿTurn away my eyes from ᴿlooking at
      worthless things,   Is. 33:15 • Prov. 23:5
   And revive me in *Your way.
38 ᴿEstablish Your word to Your servant,
   Who *is devoted* to fearing You.   2 Sam. 7:25
39 Turn away my reproach which I dread,
   For Your judgments *are* good.
40 Behold, I long for Your precepts;
   Revive me in Your righteousness.

ו WAW

41 Let Your mercies come also to me,
      O LORD—
   Your salvation according to Your word.
42 So shall I have an answer for him who
      ᵀreproaches me,
   For I trust in Your word.   *taunts*
43 And take not the word of truth utterly
      out of my mouth,
   For I have hoped in Your ordinances.
44 So shall I keep Your law continually,
   Forever and ever.
45 And I will walk ᵀat liberty,
   For I seek Your precepts.   *in a wide place*
46 ᴿI will speak of Your testimonies also
      before kings,
   And will not be ashamed.   Matt. 10:18
47 And I will delight myself in Your
      commandments,
   Which I love.
48 My hands also I will lift up to Your
      commandments,
   Which I love,
   And I will meditate on Your statutes.

ז ZAYIN

49 Remember the word to Your servant,
   Upon which You have caused me to
      hope.

119:37 So with MT, LXX, Vg.; [DSS], Tg. *Your words*

50 This *is* my comfort in my affliction,
   For Your word has given me life.
51 The proud have me in great derision,
   Yet I do not turn aside from Your law.
52 I remembered Your judgments of old,
   O Lord,
   And have comforted myself.
53 ^RIndignation has taken hold of me
   Because of the wicked, who forsake
   Your law.   Ezra 9:3
54 Your statutes have been my songs
   In the house of my pilgrimage.
55 ^RI remember Your name in the night,
   O Lord,
   And I keep Your law.   Ps. 63:6
56 This has become mine,
   Because I kept Your precepts.

ח HETH

57 ^R*You are* my portion, O Lord;
   I have said that I would keep Your
   words.   Jer. 10:16
58 I entreated Your favor with *my* whole
   heart;
   Be merciful to me according to Your
   word.
59 I ^Rthought about my ways,
   And turned my feet to Your
   testimonies.   Luke 15:17
60 I made haste, and did not delay
   To keep Your commandments.
61 The cords of the wicked have bound
   me,
   But I have not forgotten Your law.
62 ^RAt midnight I will rise to give thanks to
   You,   Acts 16:25
   Because of Your righteous judgments.
63 I *am* a companion of all who fear You,
   And of those who keep Your precepts.
64 ^RThe earth, O Lord, is full of Your
   mercy;
   Teach me Your statutes.   Ps. 33:5

ט TETH

65 You have dealt well with Your servant,
   O Lord, according to Your word.
66 Teach me good judgment and
   ^Rknowledge,   Phil. 1:9
   For I believe Your commandments.
67 Before I was ^Rafflicted I went astray,
   But now I keep Your word. [Heb. 12:5-11]
68 You *are* ^Rgood, and do good;
   Teach me Your statutes.   [Matt. 19:17]
69 The proud have ^Rforged^T a lie against
   me,   Job 13:4 • Lit. *smeared me with a lie*
   But I will keep Your precepts with *my*
   whole heart.
70 Their heart is ^Tas fat as grease,
   But I delight in Your law.   Insensible

71 *It is* good for me that I have been
   afflicted,
   That I may learn Your statutes.
72 ^RThe law of Your mouth *is* better to me
   Than thousands of *coins of* gold and
   silver.   Ps. 19:10

י YOD

73 ^RYour hands have made me and
   fashioned me;   Job 10:8; 31:15
   Give me understanding, that I may
   learn Your commandments.
74 ^RThose who fear You will be glad when
   they see me,   Ps. 34:2
   Because I have hoped in Your word.
75 I know, O Lord, ^Rthat Your judgments
   are ^Tright,
   And in faithfulness You have
   afflicted me.   [Heb. 12:10] • Lit. *righteous*
76 Let, I pray, Your merciful kindness be
   for my comfort,
   According to Your word to Your
   servant.
77 Let Your tender mercies come to me,
   that I may live;
   For Your law *is* my delight.
78 Let the proud ^Rbe ashamed,   Ps. 25:3
   For they treated me wrongfully with
   falsehood;
   But I will meditate on Your precepts.
79 Let those who fear You turn to me,
   Those who know Your testimonies.
80 Let my heart be blameless regarding
   Your statutes,
   That I may not be ashamed.

כ KAPH

81 ^RMy soul faints for Your salvation,
   But I hope in Your word. Ps. 73:26; 84:2
82 My eyes fail *from searching* Your word,
   Saying, "When will You comfort me?"
83 For ^RI have become like a wineskin in
   smoke,   Job 30:30
   Yet I do not forget Your statutes.
84 ^RHow many *are* the days of Your
   servant?   Ps. 39:4
   ^RWhen will You execute judgment on
   those who persecute me?   Rev. 6:10
85 ^RThe proud have dug pits for me, Ps. 35:7
   Which *is* not according to Your law.
86 All Your commandments *are* faithful;
   They persecute me ^Rwrongfully;
   Help me!   Ps. 35:19
87 They almost made an end of me on
   earth,
   But I did not forsake Your precepts.
88 Revive me according to Your
   lovingkindness,
   So that I may keep the testimony of
   Your mouth.

LAMED

▼ **1–G. Fulfilled Prophecy Shows the Inerrancy of the Bible**

89 ᴿForever, O Lord,   Matt. 24:35
▲   Your word is settled in heaven.
90 Your faithfulness *endures* to all
    generations;
    You established the earth, and it
    ᵀabides.   Lit. *stands*
91 They continue this day according to
    ᴿYour ordinances,
    For all *are* Your servants.   Jer. 33:25
92 Unless Your law *had been* my delight,
    I would then have perished in my
    affliction.
93 I will never forget Your precepts,
    For by them You have given me life.
94 I *am* Yours, save me;
    For I have sought Your precepts.
95 The wicked wait for me to destroy me,
    But I will consider Your testimonies.
96 ᴿI have seen the consummation of all
    perfection,
    But Your commandment *is* exceedingly
    broad.   Matt. 5:18

מ MEM

97 Oh, how I love Your law!
    ᴿIt *is* my meditation all the day.   Ps. 1:2

98 You, through Your commandments,
    make me ᴿwiser than my enemies;
    For they *are* ever with me.   Deut. 4:6
99 I have more understanding than all my
    teachers,
    ᴿFor Your testimonies *are* my
    meditation.   [2 Tim. 3:15]
100 I understand more than the ᵀancients,
    Because I keep Your precepts.   *aged*
101 I have restrained my feet from every
    evil way,
    That I may keep Your word.
102 I have not departed from Your
    judgments,
    For You Yourself have taught me.
103 How sweet are Your words to my taste,
    Sweeter than honey to my mouth!
104 Through Your precepts I get
    understanding;
    Therefore I hate every false way.

נ NUN

105 ᴿYour word *is* a lamp to my feet
    And a light to my path.   Prov. 6:23
106 ᴿI have sworn and confirmed   Neh. 10:29
    That I will keep Your righteous
    judgments.
107 I am afflicted very much;
    Revive me, O Lord, according to Your
    word.

1–G. Fulfilled Prophecy Shows the Inerrancy of the Bible (Psalm 119:89)—Jesus said, "Heaven and earth will pass away, but My words will by no means pass away" (Matt. 24:35, page 974). He was speaking in a context of prophetic predictions. He insisted that every predictive word would find its fulfillment because it comes from God, who knows and controls the future. Other prophets have spoken throughout world history; it is apparent that none of them really knew the future, especially the distant future. Only the prophecies of the Bible have been and will be fulfilled in every detail. These prophecies come to us in the exact words of Scripture. Their past fulfillment is a proof that the Bible is God's book—true, as it claims for itself, and inerrant even in its prophetic words. For example:

(1) Prophecies of past history have come true. Amos, in 760 B.C., prophesied judgment on various nations (Amos 1:1—2:16, page 874). All of these dire words have come to pass in history, one by one.

(2) Prophecies of the moral nature of man have come true. Christ said that wars would continue (Matt. 24:5–12, page 973) and poverty would continue (Matt. 26:11, page 977); Paul prophesied the future moral corruption of the world (1 Tim. 4:1–3, page 1220). Sadly, these words have stood the test of time.

(3) Prophecies concerning Israel's survival and restoration have come true. The Bible has predicted in many verses the survival of the Hebrew people and their eventual return to the land as survivors from many nations (Jer. 30:1–11, page 743; 31:1–11, page 744; Rom. 11:25, 27, page 1141). The ancient Moabites, Ammonites, Canaanites, and countless others have passed away, but the lasting endurance of Israel stands as a mark of prophetic fulfillment and truth.

(4) Prophecies concerning the coming, the life, and the death of Christ have come true in hundreds of details. Micah 5:2 (page 890), Isaiah 52:13—53:12 (page 693), Psalm 22 (page 522), Zechariah 12:10 (page 918), and other passages describe in minute detail Christ's birth in Bethlehem and His death by crucifixion. The accurate fulfillment of so many predictions, centuries in advance, demonstrates the divine origin of the Scriptures (Luke 24:27, 44, page 1047).

(5) Prophecies came true even when they ran counter to historical trends. Christ said that not one stone of the temple would remain standing upon another (Matt. 24:1, 2, page 972), and today not one does. By contrast, ancient temples still remain today in Persia, Babylon, Athens, Corinth, Ephesus, Egypt, and Rome; their stones, walls, and columns stand nobly after 2000 years.

(6) Prophecies of the end of the age are today coming into focus in the world. In our century several nations, including Russia, Iran, Ethiopia, and Libya, have opposed the new nation of Israel (Ezek. 38:2, 5, page 816).

(7) The prophecies of Christ's second coming will yet come to pass. Armies will come to Armageddon (Rev. 16:16, page 1310; 19:19, page 1313) and Christ will return to rescue Israel and put the world in order (Rev. 19:11–16, page 1312). The Word of God is, and shall be, true and inerrant in its every word.

See Index, page 17, for your next study.

108 Accept, I pray, ^Rthe freewill offerings of
      my mouth, O LORD,
      And teach me Your judgments.   Hos. 14:2
109 My life *is* continually ^Tin my hand,
      Yet I do not forget Your law.   In danger
110 ^RThe wicked have laid a snare for me,
      Yet I have not strayed from Your
      precepts.   Ps. 140:5
111 ^RYour testimonies I have taken as a
      ^Theritage forever,   Deut. 33:4 · *inheritance*
      For they *are* the rejoicing of my heart.
112 I have inclined my heart to perform
      Your statutes
      Forever, to the very end.

ℸ SAMEK

113 I hate the double-minded,
      But I love Your law.
114 ^RYou *are* my hiding place and my shield;
      I hope in Your word.   [Ps. 32:7]
115 ^RDepart from me, you evildoers,   Matt. 7:23
      For I will keep the commandments of
      my God!
116 Uphold me according to Your word,
      that I may live;
      And do not let me ^Rbe ashamed of my
      hope.   [Rom. 5:5; 9:33; 10:11]
117 ^THold me up, and I shall be safe,
      And I shall observe Your statutes
      continually.   Uphold me
118 You reject all those who stray from
      Your statutes,
      For their deceit *is* falsehood.
119 You put away all the wicked of the
      earth ^R*like* dross;   Ezek. 22:18, 19
      Therefore I love Your testimonies.
120 My flesh trembles for fear of You,
      And I am afraid of Your judgments.

ע AYIN

121 I have done justice and righteousness;
      Do not leave me to my oppressors.
122 Be surety for Your servant for good;
      Do not let the proud oppress me.
123 My eyes fail *from seeking* Your
      salvation
      And Your righteous word.
124 Deal with Your servant according to
      Your mercy,
      And teach me Your statutes.
125 ^RI *am* Your servant;   Ps. 116:16
      Give me understanding,
      That I may know Your testimonies.
126 *It is* time for *You* to act, O LORD,
      For they have ^Tregarded Your law as
      void.   broken Your law
127 Therefore I love Your commandments
      More than gold, yes, than fine gold!
128 Therefore all *Your* precepts *concerning*
      all *things*
      I consider *to be* right;
      I hate every false way.

פ PE

129 Your testimonies are wonderful;
      Therefore my soul keeps them.
130 The entrance of Your words gives light;
      It gives understanding to the simple.
131 I opened my mouth and ^Rpanted,   Ps. 42:1
      For I longed for Your commandments.
132 ^RLook upon me and be merciful to me,
      ^RAs Your custom *is* toward those who
      love Your name.   Ps. 106:4 · [2 Thess. 1:6]
133 ^RDirect my steps by Your word,
      And ^Rlet no iniquity have dominion
      over me.   Ps. 17:5 · [Rom. 6:12]
134 ^RRedeem me from the oppression of
      man,   Luke 1:74
      That I may keep Your precepts.
135 ^RMake Your face shine upon Your
      servant,   Ps. 4:6
      And teach me Your statutes.
136 ^RRivers of water run down from my
      eyes,   Jer. 9:1, 18; 14:17
      Because *men* do not keep Your law.

צ TSADDE

137 ^RRighteous *are* You, O LORD,   Neh. 9:33
      And upright *are* Your judgments.
138 ^RYour testimonies, *which* You have
      commanded,   [Ps. 19:7-9]
      Are righteous and very faithful.
139 ^RMy zeal has ^Tconsumed me,
      Because my enemies have forgotten
      Your words.   John 2:17 · *put an end to*
140 Your word is very ^Tpure;   Lit. *refined* or *tried*
      Therefore Your servant loves it.
141 I *am* small and despised,
      Yet I do not forget Your precepts.
142 Your righteousness *is* an everlasting
      righteousness,
      And Your law *is* ^Rtruth.   [John 17:17]
143 Trouble and anguish have ^Tovertaken
      me,   Lit. *found*
      Yet Your commandments *are* my
      delights.
144 The righteousness of Your testimonies
      is everlasting;
      Give me understanding, and I shall live.

ק QOPH

145 I cry out with *my* whole heart;
      Hear me, O LORD!
      I will keep Your statutes.
146 I cry out to You;
      Save me, and I will keep Your
      testimonies.
147 ^RI rise before the dawning of the
      morning,   Ps. 5:3
      And cry for help;
      I hope in Your word.
148 ^RMy eyes are awake through the *night*
      watches,   Ps. 63:1, 6
      That I may meditate on Your word.

149 Hear my voice according to Your
      lovingkindness;
    O Lord, revive me according to Your
      justice.
150 They draw near who follow after
      wickedness;
    They are far from Your law.
151 You *are* ᴿnear, O Lord,   [Ps. 145:18]
    And all Your commandments *are* truth.
152 Concerning Your testimonies,
    I have known of old that You have
      founded them ᴿforever.   Luke 21:33

ר RESH

153 ᴿConsider my affliction and deliver me,
    For I do not forget Your law.   Lam. 5:1
154 Plead my cause and redeem me;
    Revive me according to Your word.
155 Salvation *is* far from the wicked,
    For they do not seek Your statutes.
156 ᵀGreat *are* Your tender mercies, O Lord;
    Revive me according to Your
      judgments.   Or *Many*
157 Many *are* my persecutors and my
      enemies,
    Yet I do not ᴿturn from Your
      testimonies.   Ps. 44:18
158 I see the treacherous, and ᴿam
      disgusted,   Ezek. 9:4
    Because they do not keep Your word.
159 Consider how I love Your precepts;
    Revive me, O Lord, according to Your
      lovingkindness.
160 The entirety of Your word *is* truth,
    And every one of Your righteous
      judgments *endures* forever.

ש SHIN

161 ᴿPrinces persecute me without a cause,
    But my heart stands in awe of Your
      word.   1 Sam. 24:11; 26:18
162 I rejoice at Your word
    As one who finds great treasure.
163 I hate and abhor lying,
    But I love Your law.
164 Seven times a day I praise You,
    Because of Your righteous judgments.
165 ᴿGreat peace have those who love Your
      law,   [Is. 26:3; 32:17]
    And nothing causes them to stumble.
166 ᴿLord, I hope for Your salvation,
    And I do Your commandments.   Gen. 49:18
167 My soul keeps Your testimonies,
    And I love them exceedingly.
168 I keep Your precepts and Your
      testimonies,
    ᴿFor all my ways *are* before You.   Prov. 5:21

ת TAU

169 Let my cry come before You, O Lord;
    ᴿGive me understanding according to
      Your word.   Ps. 119:27, 144

170 Let my supplication come before You;
    Deliver me according to Your word.
171 ᴿMy lips shall utter praise,   Ps. 119:7
    For You teach me Your statutes.
172 My tongue shall speak of Your word,
    For all Your commandments *are*
      righteousness.
173 Let Your hand become my help,
    For I have chosen Your precepts.
174 ᴿI long for Your salvation, O Lord,
    And Your law *is* my delight.   Ps. 119:166
175 Let my soul live, and it shall praise
      You;
    And let Your judgments help me.
176 ᴿI have gone astray like a lost sheep;
    Seek Your servant,   [Is. 53:6]
    For I do not forget Your
      commandments.

Psalm 120

Plea for Relief from Bitter Foes
A Song of Ascents.

IN ᴿmy distress I cried to the Lord,
    And He heard me.   Jon. 2:2
2 Deliver my soul, O Lord, from lying lips
    And from a deceitful tongue.

3 What shall be given to you,
    Or what shall be done to you,
    You false tongue?
4 Sharp arrows of the ᵀwarrior,
    With coals of the broom tree!   *mighty one*

5 Woe is me, that I dwell in Meshech,
    That I dwell among the tents of Kedar!
6 My soul has dwelt too long
    With one who hates peace.
7 I *am for* peace;
    But when I speak, they *are* for war.

Psalm 121

God the Help of Those Who Seek Him
A Song of Ascents.

I ᴿWILL lift up my eyes to the hills—
    From whence comes my help?   [Jer. 3:23]
2 ᴿMy help *comes* from the Lord,
    Who made heaven and earth.   [Ps. 124:8]

3 ᴿHe will not allow your foot to ᵀbe
      moved;
                            1 Sam. 2:9 · *slip*
    He who keeps you will not slumber.
4 Behold, He who keeps Israel
    Shall neither slumber nor sleep.

5 The Lord *is* your ᵀkeeper;
    The Lord *is* ᴿyour shade ᴿat your right
      hand.   *protector* · Is. 25:4 · Ps. 16:8
6 ᴿThe sun shall not strike you by day,
    Nor the moon by night.   Is. 49:10

7 The Lord shall ᵀpreserve you from all
      evil;
    He shall ᴿpreserve your soul. *keep* · Ps. 41:2

8 The LORD shall ᴿpreserveᵀ your going
out and your coming in
From this time forth, and even
forevermore. Deut. 28:6 · keep

Psalm 122

The Joy of Going to the House of the LORD
A Song of Ascents. Of David.

I WAS glad when they said to me,
"Let us go into the house of the LORD."
2 Our feet have been standing
Within your gates, O Jerusalem!

3 Jerusalem is built
As a city that is compact together,
4 ᴿWhere the tribes go up,
The tribes of the LORD,
ᵀTo the Testimony of Israel,
To give thanks to the name of the
LORD. Deut. 16:16 · Or As a testimony to
5 For thrones are set there for judgment,
The thrones of the house of David.

6 ᴿPray for the peace of Jerusalem:
"May they prosper who love you. Ps. 51:18
7 Peace be within your walls,
Prosperity within your palaces."
8 For the sake of my brethren and
companions,
I will now say, "Peace be within you."
9 Because of the house of the LORD our
God
I will ᴿseek your good. Neh. 2:10

Psalm 123

Prayer for Relief from Contempt
A Song of Ascents.

UNTO You ᴿI lift up my eyes, Ps. 121:1
O You who dwell in the heavens.
2 Behold, as the eyes of servants look to
the hand of their masters,
As the eyes of a maid to the hand of
her mistress,
ᴿSo our eyes look to the LORD our God,
Until He has mercy on us. Ps. 25:15

3 Have mercy on us, O LORD, have mercy
on us!
For we are exceedingly filled with
contempt.
4 Our soul is exceedingly filled
With the scorn of those who are at
ease,
With the contempt of the proud.

Psalm 124

The LORD the Defense of His People
A Song of Ascents. Of David.

"IF it had not been the LORD who was
on our ᴿside,"
ᴿLet Israel now say— [Rom. 8:31] · Ps. 129:1

2 "If it had not been the LORD who was on
our side,
When men rose up against us,
3 Then they would have ᴿswallowed us
alive,
When their wrath was kindled against
us; Prov. 1:12
4 Then the waters would have
overwhelmed us,
The stream would have ᵀgone over our
soul; swept over
5 Then the swollen waters
Would have gone over our soul."

6 Blessed be the LORD,
Who has not given us as prey to their
teeth.
7 ᴿOur soul has escaped ᴿas a bird from
the snare of the *fowlers;
The snare is broken, and we have
escaped. Ps. 91:3 · Prov. 6:5
8 ᴿOur help is in the name of the LORD,
Who made heaven and earth. [Ps. 121:2]

Psalm 125

The LORD the Strength of His People
A Song of Ascents.

THOSE who trust in the LORD
Are like Mount Zion,
Which cannot be moved, but abides
forever.
2 As the mountains surround Jerusalem,
So the LORD surrounds His people
From this time forth and forever.

3 For ᴿthe scepter of wickedness shall not
rest
On the land allotted to the righteous,
Lest the righteous reach out their
hands to iniquity. Prov. 22:8

4 Do good, O LORD, to those who are
good,
And to those who are upright in their
hearts.

5 As for such as turn aside to their
ᴿcrooked ways,
The LORD shall lead them away
With the workers of iniquity.

ᴿPeace be upon Israel! Prov. 2:15 · [Gal. 6:16]

Psalm 126

A Joyful Return to Zion
A Song of Ascents.

WHEN the LORD brought back ᵀthe
captivity of Zion, Those of the captivity
ᴿWe were like those who dream. Acts 12:9
2 Then ᴿour mouth was filled with
laughter,

124:7 Persons who catch birds in a trap or snare

And our tongue with singing.
Then they said among the ^Tnations,
"The LORD has done great things for
them."   Job 8:21 · Gentiles
3 The LORD has done great things for us,
And we are glad.

4 Bring back our captivity, O LORD,
As the streams in the South.

5 ^RThose who sow in tears
Shall reap in joy.   Jer. 31:9
6 He who continually goes forth weeping,
Bearing ^Tseed for sowing,   Lit. a bag of seed
Shall doubtless come again ^Twith
^Rrejoicing,   with shouts of joy · Is. 61:3
Bringing his sheaves with him.

Psalm 127

Laboring and Prospering with the LORD
A Song of Ascents. Of Solomon.

UNLESS the LORD builds the house,
They labor in vain who build it;
Unless the LORD guards the city,
The watchman stays awake in vain.
2 It is vain for you to rise up early,
To sit up late,
To eat the bread of sorrows;
For so He gives His beloved sleep.

3 Behold, ^Rchildren are a heritage from
the LORD,   [Josh. 24:3, 4]
The fruit of the womb is a reward.
4 Like arrows in the hand of a warrior,
So are the children of one's youth.
5 ^RHappy is the man who has his quiver
full of them;
^RThey shall not be ashamed,
But shall speak with their enemies in
the gate.   Ps. 128:2, 3 · Prov. 27:11

Psalm 128

Blessings of Those Who Fear the LORD
A Song of Ascents.

BLESSED ^Ris every one who fears the
LORD,
Who walks in His ways.   Ps. 119:1

2 ^RWhen you eat the labor of your hands,
You shall be happy, and it shall be
^Rwell with you.   Is. 3:10 · Deut. 4:40
3 Your wife shall be ^Rlike a fruitful vine
In the very heart of your house,
Your ^Rchildren like olive plants
All around your table.   Ezek. 19:10 · Ps. 127:3-5
4 Behold, thus shall the man be blessed
Who fears the LORD.

5 ^RThe LORD bless you out of Zion,
And may you see the good of Jerusalem
All the days of your life.   Ps. 134:3
6 Yes, may you ^Rsee your children's
children.

^RPeace be upon Israel!   Job 42:16 · Ps. 125:5

Psalm 129

Song of Victory over Zion's Enemies
A Song of Ascents.

"MANY a time they have ^Tafflicted me
from my youth,"   persecuted
^RLet Israel now say—   Ps. 124:1
2 "Many a time they have afflicted me
from my youth;
Yet they have not prevailed against me.
3 The plowers plowed on my back;
They made their furrows long."
4 The LORD is righteous;
He has cut in pieces the cords of the
wicked.

5 Let all those who hate Zion
Be put to shame and turned back.
6 Let them be as the ^Rgrass on the
housetops,   Ps. 37:2
Which withers before it grows up,
7 With which the reaper does not fill his
hand,
Nor he who binds sheaves, his arms.
8 Neither let those who pass by them say,
"The blessing of the LORD be upon you;
We bless you in the name of the LORD!"

Psalm 130

Waiting for the Redemption of the LORD
A Song of Ascents.

OUT ^Rof the depths I have cried to You,
O LORD;   Lam. 3:55
2 Lord, hear my voice!
Let Your ears be attentive
To the voice of my supplications.

3 If You, LORD, should ^Tmark iniquities,
O Lord, who could stand?   take note of
4 But there is forgiveness with You,
That ^RYou may be feared.   [1 Kin. 8:39, 40]

5 ^RI wait for the LORD, my soul waits,
And in His word I do hope.   [Ps. 27:14]
6 ^RMy soul waits for the Lord
More than those who watch for the
morning—
Yes, more than those who watch for
the morning.   Ps. 119:147

7 ^RO Israel, hope in the LORD;   Ps. 131:3
For with the LORD there is mercy,
And with Him is abundant redemption.
8 And ^RHe shall redeem Israel
From all his iniquities.   [Ps. 103:3, 4]

Psalm 131

Simple Trust in the LORD
A Song of Ascents. Of David.

LORD, my heart is not ^Thaughty,   Proud
Nor my eyes ^Tlofty.   Arrogant
^RNeither do I ^Tconcern myself with great
matters,   [Rom. 12:16] · Lit. walk
Nor with things too profound for me.

2 Surely I have calmed and quieted my
     soul,
   RLike a weaned child with his mother;
   Like a weaned child *is* my soul within
     me.   [Matt. 18:3]

3 RO Israel, hope in the LORD   [Ps. 130:7]
   From this time forth and forever.

Psalm 132

The Eternal Dwelling of God in Zion
A Song of Ascents.

LORD, remember David
     And all his afflictions;
2 How he swore to the LORD,
   R*And* vowed to Rthe Mighty One of
     Jacob: Ps. 65:1 • Gen. 49:24
3 "Surely I will not go into the chamber of
     my house,
   Or go up to the comfort of my bed;
4 I will Rnot give sleep to my eyes
   Or slumber to my eyelids.   Prov. 6:4
5 Until I Rfind a place for the LORD,
   A dwelling place for the Mighty One of
     Jacob."   Acts 7:46

6 Behold, we heard of it in Ephrathah;
   We found it in the fields of *the woods.
7 Let us go into His tabernacle;
   RLet us worship at His footstool.   Ps. 99:5
8 Arise, O LORD, to Your resting place,
   You and the ark of Your strength.
9 Let Your priests Rbe clothed with
     righteousness,   Job 29:14
   And let Your saints shout for joy.

10 For Your servant David's sake,
   Do not turn away the face of Your
     TAnointed.   *Commissioned One, Heb. Messiah*

11 RThe LORD has sworn *in* truth to David;
   He will not turn from it: [Ps. 89:3, 4, 33]
   "I will set upon your throne Rthe Tfruit
     of your body.   2 Sam. 7:12 • *offspring*
12 If your sons will keep My covenant
   And My testimony which I shall teach
     them,
   Their sons also shall sit upon your
     throne forevermore."

13 RFor the LORD has chosen Zion;   [Ps. 48:1, 2]
   He has desired *it* for His dwelling place:
14 "This *is* My resting place forever;
   Here I will dwell, for I have desired it.
15 I will abundantly bless her Tprovision;
   I will satisfy her poor with bread.   *food*
16 I will also Rclothe her priests with
     salvation,   2 Chr. 6:41
   And her saints shall shout aloud for
     joy.
17 RThere I will make the horn of David
     grow;   Ezek. 29:21
   I will prepare a lamp for My Anointed.

132:6 Or *Jaar,* lit. *Woods*

18 His enemies I will Rclothe with shame,
   But upon Himself His crown shall
     flourish."   Ps. 35:26

Psalm 133

Blessed Unity of the People of God
A Song of Ascents. Of David.

BEHOLD, how good and how pleasant *it*
     is
   For Rbrethren to dwell together in
     unity!   Gen. 13:8
2 *It is* like the precious oil upon the head,
   Running down on the beard,
   The beard of Aaron,
   Running down on the edge of his
     garments.
3 *It is* like the dew of RHermon,
   Descending upon the mountains of
     Zion;
   For Rthere the LORD commanded the
     blessing—
   Life forevermore.   Deut. 4:48 • Lev. 25:21

Psalm 134

Praising the LORD in His House at Night
A Song of Ascents.

BEHOLD, bless the LORD,
     All *you* servants of the LORD,
   Who by night stand in the house of the
     LORD!
2 RLift up your hands *in* the sanctuary,
   And bless the LORD.   [1 Tim. 2:8]
3 The LORD who made heaven and earth
   Bless you from Zion!

Psalm 135

Praise to God in Creation and
Redemption

PRAISE the LORD!
   Praise the name of the LORD;
   Praise *Him,* O you servants of the
     LORD!
2 RYou who stand in the house of the
     LORD,   Luke 2:37
   In the courts of the house of our God,
3 Praise the LORD, for Rthe LORD *is* good;
   Sing praises to His name, Rfor *it is*
     pleasant.   [Ps. 119:68] • Ps. 147:1
4 For Rthe LORD has chosen Jacob for
     Himself,
   Israel for His special treasure.   [Ex. 19:5]

5 For I know that Rthe LORD *is* great,
   And our Lord *is* above all gods.   Ps. 95:3
6 RWhatever the LORD pleases He does,
   In heaven and in earth,   Ps. 115:3
   In the seas and in all deep places.
7 He causes the Tvapors to ascend from
   the ends of the earth;   *Water vapor*

ᴿHe makes lightning for the rain;
He brings the wind out of His
   ᴿtreasures.   Job 28:25, 26; 38:24-28 · Jer. 51:16

8 He destroyed the firstborn of Egypt,
   ᵀBoth of man and beast.   From man to beast
9 ᴿHe sent signs and wonders into the
   midst of you, O Egypt,   Ex. 7:10
   Upon Pharaoh and all his servants.
10 ᴿHe defeated many nations
   And slew mighty kings—   Num. 21:24
11 Sihon king of the Amorites,
   Og king of Bashan,
   And all the kingdoms of Canaan—
12 And gave their land as a ᵀheritage,
   A heritage to Israel His people.   inheritance

13 ᴿYour name, O Lᴏʀᴅ, endures forever,
   Your fame, O Lᴏʀᴅ, throughout all
   generations.   [Ex. 3:15]
14 ᴿFor the Lᴏʀᴅ will judge His people,
   And He will have compassion on His
   servants.   Deut. 32:36

15 ᴿThe idols of the nations are silver and
   gold,
   The work of men's hands.   [Ps. 115:4-8]
16 They have mouths, but they do not
   speak;
   Eyes they have, but they do not see;
17 They have ears, but they do not hear;
   Nor is there any breath in their mouths.
18 Those who make them are like them;
   So is everyone who trusts in them.

19 Bless the Lᴏʀᴅ, O house of Israel!
   Bless the Lᴏʀᴅ, O house of Aaron!
20 Bless the Lᴏʀᴅ, O house of Levi!
   You who fear the Lᴏʀᴅ, bless the Lᴏʀᴅ!
21 Blessed be the Lᴏʀᴅ ᴿout of Zion,
   Who dwells in Jerusalem!

       Praise the Lᴏʀᴅ!   Ps. 134:3

Psalm 136

*Thanksgiving to God for His Enduring
Mercy*

OH, ᴿgive thanks to the Lᴏʀᴅ, for He is
   good!   Ps. 106:1
   For His mercy endures forever.
2 Oh, give thanks to the God of gods!
   For His mercy endures forever.
3 Oh, give thanks to the Lord of lords!
   For His mercy endures forever:

4 To Him ᴿwho alone does great wonders,
   For His mercy endures forever; Ps. 72:18
5 ᴿTo Him who by wisdom made the
   heavens,   Jer. 51:5
   For His mercy endures forever;
6 ᴿTo Him who laid out the earth above
   the waters,   Jer. 10:12
   For His mercy endures forever;
7 To Him who made great lights,
   For His mercy endures forever—

8 ᴿThe sun to rule by day,   Gen. 1:16
   For His mercy endures forever;
9 The moon and stars to rule by night,
   For His mercy endures forever.

10 ᴿTo Him who struck Egypt in their
   firstborn,   Ex. 12:29
   For His mercy endures forever;
11 ᴿAnd brought out Israel from among
   them,   Ex. 12:51; 13:3, 16
   For His mercy endures forever;
12 ᴿWith a strong hand, and with ᵀan
   outstretched arm,   Ex. 6:6 · Mighty power
   For His mercy endures forever;
13 ᴿTo Him who divided the Red Sea in
   two,   Ex. 14:21
   For His mercy endures forever;
14 And made Israel pass through the midst
   of it,
   For His mercy endures forever;
15 ᴿBut overthrew Pharaoh and his army in
   the Red Sea,   Ex. 14:27
   For His mercy endures forever;
16 ᴿTo Him who led His people through the
   wilderness,   Ex. 13:18; 15:22
   For His mercy endures forever;
17 To Him who struck down great kings,
   For His mercy endures forever;
18 ᴿAnd slew famous kings,   Deut. 29:7
   For His mercy endures forever—
19 ᴿSihon king of the Amorites,   Num. 21:21
   For His mercy endures forever;
20 ᴿAnd Og king of Bashan,   Num. 21:33
   For His mercy endures forever—
21 And gave their land as a heritage,
   For His mercy endures forever;
22 A heritage to Israel His servant,
   For His mercy endures forever.

23 Who ᴿremembered us in our lowly
   state,
   For His mercy endures forever; Gen. 8:1
24 And ᴿrescued us from our enemies,
   For His mercy endures forever; Ps. 44:7
25 ᴿWho gives food to all flesh,   Ps. 104:27
   For His mercy endures forever.

26 Oh, give thanks to the God of heaven!
   For His mercy endures forever.

Psalm 137

Longing for Zion in a Foreign Land

BY the rivers of Babylon,
   There we sat down, yea, we wept
   When we remembered Zion.
2 We hung our harps
   Upon the willows in the midst of it.
3 For there those who carried us away
   captive asked of us a song,
   And those who ᴿplundered us requested
   mirth,
   Saying, "Sing us one of the songs of
   Zion!"   Ps. 79:1

4 How shall we sing the Lord's song
    In a foreign land?
5 If I forget you, O Jerusalem,
    Let my right hand forget *its skill!*
6 If I do not remember you,
    Let my ^Rtongue cling to the roof of my
        mouth—
    If I do not exalt Jerusalem
    Above my chief joy.   Ezek. 3:26

7 Remember, O Lord, against ^Rthe sons
        of Edom   Jer. 49:7–22
    The day of Jerusalem,
    Who said, ^T"Raze *it,* raze *it,*
    To its very foundation!"   Lit. *Make it bare*

8 O daughter of Babylon, ^Rwho are to be
        destroyed,   Is. 13:1–6; 47:1
    Happy the one ^Rwho repays you as you
        have served us!   Jer. 50:15
9 Happy the one who takes and ^Rdashes
    Your little ones against the rock!   Is. 13:16

Psalm 138

The Lord's Goodness to the Faithful

A *Psalm* of David.

I WILL praise You with my whole heart;
    ^RBefore the gods I will sing praises to
        You.   Ps. 119:46
2 ^RI will worship ^Rtoward Your holy
        temple,   Ps. 28:2 · 1 Kin. 8:29
    And praise Your name
    For Your lovingkindness and Your
        truth;
    For You have ^Rmagnified Your word
        above all Your name.   Is. 42:21
3 In the day when I cried out, You
        answered me,
    And made me bold *with* strength in my
        soul.

4 ^RAll the kings of the earth shall praise
        You, O Lord,
    When they hear the words of Your
        mouth.   Ps. 102:15
5 Yes, they shall sing of the ways of the
        Lord,
    For great *is* the glory of the Lord.
6 ^RThough the Lord *is* on high,   [Ps. 113:4–7]
    Yet ^RHe regards the lowly;   [James 4:6]
    But the proud He knows from afar.

7 ^RThough I walk in the midst of trouble,
        You will revive me;   [Ps. 23:3, 4]
    You will stretch out Your hand
    Against the wrath of my enemies,
    And Your right hand will save me.
8 ^RThe Lord will ^Tperfect *that which*
        concerns me;   Ps. 57:2 · *complete*
    Your mercy, O Lord, *endures* forever;
    ^RDo not forsake the works of Your
        hands.   Job 10:3, 8

Psalm 139

God's Perfect Knowledge of Man

For the Chief Musician. A Psalm of David.

O LORD, ^RYou have searched me and
    known *me.*   Ps. 17:3
2 ^RYou know my sitting down and my
        rising up;   2 Kin. 19:27
    You understand my thought afar off.
3 ^RYou ^Tcomprehend my path and my
        lying down,   Job 14:16; 31:4 · Lit. *winnow*
    And are acquainted with all my ways.
4 For *there is* not a word on my tongue,
    But behold, O Lord, ^RYou know it
        altogether.   [Heb. 4:13]
5 You have ^Thedged me behind and
        before,
    And laid Your hand upon me.   *enclosed*
6 ^RSuch knowledge *is* too wonderful for
        me;
    It is high, I cannot *attain* it.   Job 42:3

7 ^RWhere can I go from Your Spirit?
    Or where can I flee from Your
        presence?   [Jer. 23:24]
8 ^RIf I ascend into heaven, You *are* there;
    ^RIf I make my bed in ^Thell, behold, You
        are there.   [Amos 9:2–4] · [Job 26:6] · Or *Sheol*
9 *If* I take the wings of the morning,
    And dwell in the uttermost parts of the
        sea,
10 Even there Your hand shall lead me,
    And Your right hand shall hold me.
11 If I say, "Surely the darkness shall *fall
        on me,"
    Even the night shall be light about me;
12 Indeed, ^Rthe darkness ^Tshall not hide
        from You,
    But the night shines as the day;
    The darkness and the light *are* both
        alike *to* You.   Job 26:6; 34:22 · Lit. *is not dark*

13 For You formed my inward parts;
    You covered me in my mother's womb.
14 I will praise You, for *I am fearfully
    and wonderfully made;
    Marvelous are Your works,
    And *that* my soul knows very well.
15 ^RMy ^Tframe was not hidden from You,
    When I was made in secret,   Job 10:8, 9
    And skillfully wrought in the lowest
        parts of the earth.   Lit. *bones were*
16 Your eyes saw my substance, being yet
        unformed.
    And in Your book they all were
        written,
    The days fashioned for me,
    When *as yet there were* none of them.

139:11 Vg., Symmachus cover
139:14 So with MT, Tg.; LXX, Syr., Vg. *You are fearfully
    wonderful*

17 ^RHow precious also are Your thoughts to
   me, O God!
   How great is the sum of them!   [Ps. 40:5]
18 *If* I should count them, they would be
   more in number than the sand;
   When I awake, I am still with You.

19 Oh, that You would ^Rslay the wicked,
   O God!   [Is. 11:4]
   Depart from me, therefore, you
   ^Tbloodthirsty men.   Lit. *men of bloodshed*
20 For they speak against You wickedly;
   *Your enemies take *Your name* in vain.
21 ^RDo I not hate them, O Lord, who hate
   You?
   And do I not loathe those who rise up
   against You?   2 Chr. 19:2
22 I hate them with ^Tperfect hatred;
   I count them my enemies.   *complete*

23 ^RSearch me, O God, and know my heart;
   Try me, and know my anxieties;   Job 31:6
24 And see if *there is any* wicked way in
   me,
   And lead me in the way everlasting.

Psalm 140

Prayer for Deliverance from Evil Men

To the Chief Musician. A Psalm of David.

DELIVER me, O Lord, from evil men;
   Preserve me from violent men,
2 Who plan evil things in *their* hearts;
   ^RThey continually gather together *for*
   war.   Ps. 56:6
3 They sharpen their tongues like a
   serpent;
   The ^Rpoison of asps *is* under their lips.
   Selah   Ps. 58:4

4 ^RKeep me, O Lord, from the hands of
   the wicked;
   Preserve me from violent men,
   Who have purposed to make my steps
   stumble.   Ps. 71:4
5 The proud have hidden a ^Rsnare for me,
   and cords;   Jer. 18:22
   They have spread a net by the wayside;
   They have set traps for me.   Selah

6 I said to the Lord: "You *are* my God;
   Hear the voice of my supplications,
   O Lord.
7 O God the Lord, the strength of my
   salvation,
   You have ^Tcovered my head in the day
   of battle.   *sheltered*
8 Do not grant, O Lord, the desires of the
   wicked;
   Do not further his *wicked* scheme,
   ^R*Lest* they be exalted. Selah   Deut. 32:27

139:20 LXX, Vg. *they take your cities in vain*

9 *"As for* the head of those who surround
   me,
   Let the evil of their lips cover them;
10 ^RLet burning coals fall upon them;
   Let them be cast into the fire,
   Into deep pits, that they rise not up
   again.   Ps. 11:6
11 Let not a slanderer be established in the
   earth;
   Let evil hunt the violent man to
   overthrow *him*."

12 I know that the Lord will ^Rmaintain
   The cause of the afflicted,
   And justice for the poor.   1 Kin. 8:45
13 Surely the righteous shall give thanks
   to Your name;
   The upright shall dwell in Your
   presence.

Psalm 141

Prayer for Safekeeping from Wickedness

A Psalm of David.

LORD, I cry out to You;
   Make haste to me!
   Give ear to my voice when I cry out to
   You.
2 Let my prayer be set before You ^Ras
   incense,   [Rev. 5:8; 8:3, 4]
   ^RThe lifting up of my hands *as* ^Rthe
   evening sacrifice.   [1 Tim. 2:8] • Ex. 29:39, 41

3 Set a guard, O Lord, over my mouth;
   Keep watch over the door of my lips.
4 Do not incline my heart to any evil
   thing,
   To practice wicked works
   With men who work iniquity;
   ^RAnd do not let me eat of their
   delicacies.   Prov. 23:6

5 ^RLet the righteous strike me;
   It shall be a kindness.
   And let him rebuke me;
   It shall be as excellent oil;
   Let my head not refuse it.

   For still my prayer *is* against the deeds
   of the wicked.   [Prov. 9:8]
6 Their judges are overthrown by the
   sides of the ^Tcliff,
   And they hear my words, for they are
   sweet.   *rock*
7 Our bones are scattered at the mouth
   of the grave,
   As when one plows and breaks up the
   earth.

8 But ^Rmy eyes *are* upon You, O God the
   Lord;
   In You I take refuge;
   Do not leave my soul destitute. Ps. 25:15
9 Keep me from ^Rthe snares they have
   laid for me,

And from the traps of the workers of
iniquity.   Ps. 119:110
10 ^RLet the wicked fall into their own nets,
While I escape safely.   Ps. 35:8

Psalm 142

A Plea for Relief from Persecutors

A *Contemplation of David.
A Prayer when he was in the cave.

I CRY out to the LORD with my voice;
With my voice to the LORD I make my
supplication.
2 I pour out my complaint before Him;
I declare before Him my trouble.
3 When my spirit ^Twas ^Roverwhelmed
within me,   Lit. *fainted* · Ps. 77:3
Then You knew my path.
In the way in which I walk
They have secretly set a snare for me.
4 Look on *my* right hand and see,
For *there is* no one who acknowledges
me;
Refuge has failed me;
No one cares for my soul.
5 I cried out to You, O LORD:
I said, "You *are* my refuge,
My portion in the land of the living.
6 ^TAttend to my cry,
For I am brought very low;
Deliver me from my persecutors,
For they are stronger than I.   *Give heed*
7 Bring my soul out of prison,
That I may ^Rpraise Your name; Ps. 34:1, 2
The righteous shall surround me,
For You shall deal bountifully with
me."

Psalm 143

An Earnest Appeal for Guidance and Deliverance

A Psalm of David.

H EAR my prayer, O LORD,
Give ear to my supplications!
In Your faithfulness answer me,
And in Your righteousness.
2 Do not enter into judgment with Your
servant,
^RFor in Your sight no one living is
righteous.   [Gal. 2:16]
3 For the enemy has persecuted my soul;
He has crushed my life to the ground;
He has made me dwell in darkness,
Like those who have long been dead.
4 ^RTherefore my spirit is overwhelmed
within me;

142:title, Heb. *Maschil*

My heart within me is distressed. Ps. 77:3
5 ^RI remember the days of old; Ps. 77:5, 10, 11
I meditate on all Your works;
I muse on the work of Your hands.
6 I spread out my hands to You;
^RMy soul *longs* for You like a thirsty
land. Selah   Ps. 63:1
7 Answer me speedily, O LORD;
My spirit fails!
Do not hide Your face from me,
^RLest I ^Tbe like those who ^Tgo down into
the pit.   Ps. 28:1 · *become* · Die
8 Cause me to hear Your lovingkindness
^Rin the morning,   Ps. 46:5
For in You do I trust;
^RCause me to know the way in which I
should walk,   Ps. 5:8
For ^RI lift up my soul to You.   Ps. 25:1
9 Deliver me, O LORD, from my enemies;
*In You I take shelter.
10 ^RTeach me to do Your will,   Ps. 25:4, 5
For You *are* my God;
^RYour Spirit *is* good.   Neh. 9:20
Lead me in the land of uprightness.
11 ^RRevive me, O LORD, for Your name's
sake!
For Your righteousness' sake bring my
soul out of trouble.   Ps. 119:25
12 In Your mercy ^Rcut^T off my enemies,
And destroy all those who afflict my
soul;   Ps. 54:5 · *put an end to*
For I *am* Your servant.

Psalm 144

A Song to the LORD Who Preserves and Prospers His People

A Psalm of David.

B LESSED *be* the LORD my Rock,
^RWho trains my hands for war,
And my fingers for battle—   2 Sam. 22:35
2 My lovingkindness and my fortress,
My high tower and my deliverer,
My shield and *the One* in whom I take
refuge,
Who subdues *my people under me.

14-A. How Did Mankind Appear on ▼ This Planet?

3 ^RLORD, what *is* man, that You take
knowledge of him?

143:9 LXX, Vg. *To You I flee*
144:2 So with MT, LXX, Vg.; Syr., Tg. *the peoples* (cf.
18:47)

14-A. How Did Mankind Appear on This Planet? (Psalm 144:3)—Our human logic requires a cause for
everything, and we are ultimately forced to recognize the first cause—God. He is eternal and self-existent.
His being and operation are beyond human scientific knowledge and reasoning. The origin of mankind lies
(Point 14-A continued on next page)

▽ *Or* the son of man, that You are
▲ mindful of him?   Heb. 2:6
4 RMan is like a breath;   Ps. 39:11
   His days *are* like a passing shadow.

5 RBow down Your heavens, O LORD, and
   come down;
   RTouch the mountains, and they shall
   smoke.   Ps. 18:9 • Ps. 104:32

6 RFlash forth lightning and scatter them;
   Shoot out Your arrows and destroy
   them.   Ps. 18:13, 14

7 Stretch out Your hand from above;
   Rescue me and deliver me out of great
   waters,
   From the hand of foreigners,

8 Whose mouth Rspeaks Tlying words,
   And whose right hand *is* a right hand
   of falsehood.   Ps. 12:2 • *empty* or *worthless*

9 I will Rsing a new song to You, O God;
   On a harp of ten strings I will sing
   praises to You,   Ps. 33:2, 3; 40:3

10 *The One* who gives Tsalvation to kings,
   RWho delivers David His servant
   From the deadly sword.   *deliverance* • Ps. 18:50

11 Rescue me and deliver me from the
   hand of foreigners,
   Whose mouth speaks lying words,
   And whose right hand *is* a right hand
   of falsehood—

12 That our sons *may be* Ras plants grown
   up in their youth;   Ps. 128:3
   That our daughters *may be* as Tpillars,
   Sculptured in palace style;   *corner pillars*

13 *That* our barns *may be* full,
   Supplying all kinds of produce;

That our sheep may bring forth
thousands
And ten thousands in our fields;

14 *That* our oxen *may be* well-laden;
   That there be no Tbreaking in or going
   out;   Lit. *breach*
   That there be no outcry in our streets.

15 RHappy *are* the people who are in such a
   state;
   Happy *are* the people whose God *is* the
   LORD!   [Ps. 33:12]

Psalm 145

A Song of God's Majesty and Love
A Praise of David.

I WILL Textol You, my God, O King;
  And I will bless Your name forever and
  ever.   *praise*

2 Every day I will bless You,
  And I will praise Your name forever
  and ever.

3 RGreat *is* the LORD, and greatly to be
  praised;   [Ps. 147:5]
  And His greatness *is* unsearchable.

4 ROne generation shall praise Your works
  to another,   Is. 38:19
  And shall declare Your mighty acts.

5 *I will meditate on the glorious splendor
  of Your majesty,
  And *on Your wondrous works.

6 *Men* shall speak of the might of Your
  awesome acts,
  And I will declare Your greatness.

145:5 So with MT, Tg.; DSS, LXX, Syr., Vg. *they* • Lit. *on
the words of Your wondrous works*

(Point 14-A continued from previous page)
with God as the Creator; the ultimate purpose of human existence cannot be discovered or determined by
humanity—it must be declared by God Himself.
   With respect to such questions, certain biblical truths come forward:
   (1) Mankind was created by God on the sixth day of creation, in the "image" and "likeness" of God
(Gen. 1:26–28, page 4). Christ Himself endorsed the truth of this creation account (Matt. 19:4–6, page 965).
   (2) Mankind was fashioned by a creative act of God. Man did not evolve (Gen. 2:7, page 4). Not only do
we have the Genesis testimony of Moses and the word of Christ about this, but paleontology (the study of
prehistoric life by means of fossils) and anthropology (the study of man) have failed to develop a satisfactory
scheme by which man could have evolved. The gaps in the fossil record are many and confusing, and there
is no tidy scientific theory to explain them. So-called "evolution" would require many billions of accidental
developments, both simple and complex, involving both man and the earth, without a biological engineer's
guidance. It makes more sense to accept God's Word—that He is in control of biological forces far beyond
our grasp, and that He made mankind in the beginning (Ps. 139:14, page 590).
   (3) God placed man on a planet that was biologically prepared to sustain him. Prior to the space
journeys of the Voyager and Mariner camera probes, some scientists assured us that primal forms of life
would be found on Mars, Jupiter, or Saturn. Years before, basic life forms on the moon had been predicted.
All such notions are now abandoned in the face of the bleak, dry, or frozen planetary surfaces. God alone
prepared the free oxygen in the air, the running water on the surface, the self-sustaining plant life for food,
the animal life, the workable minerals of the ground, the freedom from atmospheric poisons, and the
acceptable temperature range for ideal human life (Gen. 1:29–31, page 4).
   (4) Man was given a body fitted for dominion over the planet, as well as for an ideal social and moral life
(Gen. 1:27, 28, page 4). Such was no evolutionary accident, but the design of an all-wise Creator who
planned the partner-family system for the mutual happiness of men, women, and children (Gen. 2:24, page
5; Matt. 19:4–6, page 965).
   See Romans 3:23, page 1131, for **Point 14-B: How Did Mankind Fall, and What Were the Effects?**

7 They shall ᵀutter the memory of Your
     great goodness,   *eagerly utter,* lit. *bubble forth*
   And shall sing of Your righteousness.

8 ᴿThe LORD *is* gracious and full of
     compassion,   [Num. 14:18]
   Slow to anger and great in mercy.

9 ᴿThe LORD *is* good to all,
   And His tender mercies *are* over all His
     works.   Nah. 1:7

10 ᴿAll Your works shall praise You, O
     LORD,
   And Your saints shall bless You.   Ps. 19:1

11 They shall speak of the glory of Your
     kingdom,
   And talk of Your power,

12 To make known to the sons of men His
     mighty acts,
   And the glorious majesty of His
     kingdom.

13 ᴿYour kingdom *is* an everlasting
     kingdom,
   And Your dominion *endures*
     throughout all *generations.   [1 Tim. 1:17]

14 The LORD upholds all who fall,
   And ᴿraises up all *who are* bowed
     down.   Ps. 146:8

15 ᴿThe eyes of all look expectantly to You,
   And ᴿYou give them their food in due
     season.   Ps. 104:27 · Ps. 136:25

16 You open Your hand
   ᴿAnd satisfy the desire of every living
     thing.   Ps. 104:21, 28

17 The LORD *is* righteous in all His ways,
   Gracious in all His works.

18 ᴿThe LORD *is* near to all who call upon
     Him,   [Deut. 4:7]
   To all who call upon Him in truth.

19 He will fulfill the desire of those who
     fear Him;
   He also will hear their cry and save
     them.

20 The LORD preserves all who love Him,
   But all the wicked He will destroy.

21 My mouth shall speak the praise of the
     LORD,
   And all flesh shall bless His holy name
   Forever and ever.

Psalm 146

The Happiness of Those Whose Help Is
the LORD

PRAISEᵀ the LORD!   Heb. *Hallelujah*
   Praise the LORD, O my soul!
2 ᴿWhile I live I will praise the LORD;
   I will sing praises to my God while I
     have my being.   Ps. 104:33

145:13 So with MT, Tg; DSS, LXX, Syr., Vg. add *The LORD*
is faithful in all His words, and holy in all His works

3 ᴿDo not put your trust in princes,
   Nor in ᵀa son of man, in whom *there is*
     no ᵀhelp.   [Is. 2:22] · A human being · *salvation*
4 ᴿHis spirit departs, he returns to his
     earth;   [Eccl. 12:7]
   In that very day his plans perish.

5 ᴿHappy *is* he who *has* the God of Jacob
     for his help,   Jer. 17:7
   Whose hope *is* in the LORD his God,
6 ᴿWho made heaven and earth,
   The sea, and all that *is* in them;
   Who keeps truth forever,   Rev. 14:7
7 ᴿWho executes justice for the oppressed,
   ᴿWho gives food to the hungry.
   ᴿThe LORD gives freedom to the
     prisoners.   Ps. 103:6 · Ps. 107:9 · Ps. 107:10

8 ᴿThe LORD opens *the eyes of* the blind;
   ᴿThe LORD raises those who are bowed
     down;   Matt. 9:30 · Luke 13:13
   The LORD loves the righteous.
9 The LORD watches over the strangers;
   He relieves the fatherless and widow;
   ᴿBut the way of the wicked He ᵀturns
     upside down.   Ps. 147:6 · Lit. *makes crooked*

10 ᴿThe LORD shall reign forever—
   Your God, O Zion, to all generations.

   Praise the LORD!   Ex. 15:18

Psalm 147

Praise to God for His Word and
Providence

PRAISEᵀ the LORD!   Heb. *Hallelujah*
   For ᴿ*it* is good to sing praises to our
     God;   Ps. 92:1
   ᴿFor *it* is pleasant, *and* ᴿpraise is
     beautiful.   Ps. 135:3 · Ps. 33:1

2 The LORD ᴿbuilds up Jerusalem;
   ᴿHe gathers together the outcasts of
     Israel.   Ps. 102:16 · Deut. 30:3
3 ᴿHe heals the brokenhearted   [Ps. 51:17]
   And binds up their ᵀwounds.   Lit. *sorrows*
4 ᴿHe counts the number of the stars;
   He calls them all by name.   Is. 40:26
5 ᴿGreat *is* our Lord, and ᴿmighty in
     power;   Ps. 48:1 · Nah. 1:3
   ᴿHis understanding *is* infinite.   Is. 40:28
6 ᴿThe LORD lifts up the humble;
   He casts the wicked down to the
     ground.   Ps. 146:8, 9

7 Sing to the LORD with thanksgiving;
   Sing praises on the harp to our God,
8 ᴿWho covers the heavens with clouds,
   Who prepares rain for the earth,
   Who makes grass to grow on the
     mountains.   Job 38:26
9 ᴿHe gives to the beast its food,   Job 38:41
   And to the young ravens that cry.

10 ᴿHe does not delight in the strength of
     the horse;

He takes no pleasure in the legs of a
   man.   Ps. 33:16, 17
11 The LORD takes pleasure in those who
   fear Him,
   In those who hope in His mercy.

12 Praise the LORD, O Jerusalem!
   Praise your God, O Zion!
13 For He has strengthened the bars of
   your gates;
   He has blessed your children within
   you.
14 He makes peace in your borders,
   And fills you with the finest wheat.

15 ᴿHe sends out His command to the
   earth;
   His word runs very swiftly.   [Ps. 107:20]
16 ᴿHe gives snow like wool;
   He scatters the frost like ashes;   Job 37:6
17 He casts out His hail like ᵀmorsels;
   Who can stand before His cold?   crumbs
18 ᴿHe sends out His word and melts them;
   He causes His wind to blow, and the
   waters flow.   Job 37:10
19 ᴿHe declares His word to Jacob,
   ᴿHis statutes and His judgments to
   Israel.   Deut. 33:4 · Mal. 4:4
20 ᴿHe has not dealt thus with any nation;
   And as for His judgments, they have
   not known them.

   ᵀPraise the LORD!   [Rom. 3:1, 2] · Heb. Hallelujah

Psalm 148

Praise to the LORD from Creation

Praise the LORD from the heavens;
   Praise Him in the heights!   Heb. Hallelujah
2 Praise Him, all His angels;
   Praise Him, all His hosts!
3 Praise Him, sun and moon;
   Praise Him, all you stars of light!
4 Praise Him, you heavens of heavens,
   And you waters above the heavens!

5 Let them praise the name of the LORD,
   For ᴿHe commanded and they were
   created.   Gen. 1:1, 6
6 ᴿHe also established them forever and
   ever;
   He made a decree which shall not pass
   away.   Ps. 89:37

7 Praise the LORD from the earth,
   ᴿYou great sea creatures and all the
   depths;   Is. 43:20
8 Fire and hail, snow and clouds;
   Stormy wind, fulfilling His word;
9 ᴿMountains and all hills;
   Fruitful trees and all cedars;   Is. 44:23; 49:13
10 Beasts and all cattle;
   Creeping things and flying fowl;

11 Kings of the earth and all peoples;
   Princes and all judges of the earth;
12 Both young men and maidens;
   Old men and children.

13 Let them praise the name of the LORD,
   For His ᴿname alone is exalted;   Ps. 8:1
   His glory is above the earth and
   heaven.
14 And He ᴿhas exalted the ᵀhorn of His
   people,   Ps. 75:10 · Strength or dominion
   The praise of ᴿall His saints—
   Of the children of Israel,
   ᴿA people near to Him.   Ps. 149:9 · Eph. 2:17

   ᵀPraise the LORD!   Heb. Hallelujah

Psalm 149

Praise to God for His Salvation and Judgment

Praise the LORD!   Heb. Hallelujah

   ᴿSing to the LORD a new song,
   And His praise in the assembly of
   saints.   Ps. 33:3

2 Let Israel rejoice in their Maker;
   Let the children of Zion be joyful in
   their ᴿKing.   Zech. 9:9
3 ᴿLet them praise His name with the
   dance;
   Let them sing praises to Him with the
   timbrel and harp.   Ps. 81:2
4 For ᴿthe LORD takes pleasure in His
   people;
   ᴿHe will beautify the ᵀhumble with
   salvation.   Ps. 35:27 · Ps. 132:16 · meek

5 Let the saints be joyful in glory;
   Let them sing aloud on their beds.
6 Let the high praises of God be in their
   mouth,
   And a two-edged sword in their hand,
7 To execute vengeance on the nations,
   And punishments on the peoples;
8 To bind their kings with chains,
   And their nobles with fetters of iron;
9 ᴿTo execute on them the written
   judgment—   Deut. 7:1, 2
   ᴿThis honor have all His saints.

   ᵀPraise the LORD!   1 Cor. 6:2 · Heb. Hallelujah

Psalm 150

Let All Things Praise the LORD

Praise the LORD!   Ps. 145:5, 6

   Praise God in His sanctuary;
   Praise Him in His mighty firmament!

2 Praise Him for His mighty acts;
   Praise Him according to His excellent
   ᴿgreatness!   Deut. 3:24

3 Praise Him with the sound of the
   ᵀtrumpet;
   Praise Him with the lute and harp! *cornet*
4 Praise Him with the timbrel and dance;
   Praise Him with stringed instruments
   and flutes!

5 Praise Him with loud cymbals;
   Praise Him with clashing
   cymbals!
6 Let everything that has breath praise
   the LORD.

   ᵀPraise the LORD!   Heb. *Hallelujah*

THE BOOK OF
Proverbs

The past three decades have seen a tragic emptiness and lack of direction in the Western world. Almost persistently the old foundations have been eroded; and we are left with the dilemma that befell Israel during the time of the judges: "everyone did what was right in his own eyes" (Judg. 17:6).

Alongside this aimlessness is a marvelous sign of hope. In the latter part of the twentieth century a new, worldwide sense of urgency for evangelism is setting the stage for the coming of the Lord Jesus. Accompanying this fervor for souls is an intense desire to know the Word of God.

One book that is being rediscovered in the Word of God is the book of Proverbs. It has often been neglected, yet in this library of God-given practical wisdom are the formulas for living a life of purpose and direction.

The supreme purpose of this book is to teach us that to know God personally is more important than everything else (1:7). The goal of Proverbs, then, is to equip man for every good work (2 Tim. 3:15-17). Here godly, practical principles are set forth so that from them we may learn how to walk in righteousness, equity, and love.

KEY VERSE. The key to Proverbs hangs right inside the door in the first sentence (1:1-6), and the book's teaching is well stated in 1:7—"The fear of the LORD is the beginning of knowledge, but fools despise wisdom and instruction."

Proverbs is not a mere book of good manners. In its pages is the key to genuine living. To the youth preparing to leave home, to the family member seeking to maintain godly order in the home, or to the leader concerned about social ills, the book gives one essential standard for making decisions: "Is this wisdom or folly? Does God lead in this path?"

The word *proverb* derives from the Latin words *pro*, meaning "for," and *verb*, meaning "word"; thus a proverb takes the place of a many-worded discourse. Proverbs are short, catchy truisms which are true because they come from God, and are not to be discounted because of their brevity. They are to be weighed by their fullness, their superior value, and their applicability to the situations of life. To be conversant in other important books, but ignorant of the depth of this book, is infinite folly, for here is practical religion.

AUTHORSHIP. Solomon wrote the bulk of the Proverbs. This wisdom literature was begun by Solomon, passed around orally and in segmented writings, and probably finalized in its composition during Hezekiah's reign (25:1).

Proverbs in a general statement is the practical expression of our day-to-day living. Its purpose is to direct our daily, relational life just as the Psalms express our heart's worship of God. The Proverbs demonstrate how mankind is to live successfully, accomplish worthy goals by making right decisions, and please God in relationships with other people.

KEY WORD. The key word is *wisdom*. This wisdom derives from God as a gift (chs. 2 and 8), but expresses itself in our dealings not only with God but with all others as well.

HOW PROVERBS FITS TOGETHER. There are three main divisions of the book, each beginning with a reminder that these are "the proverbs of Solomon." If we follow the compiler's lead, the divisions are: (1) A Father's Praise of Wisdom (chs. 1—9); (2) A General Collection Concerning Prudence (10—24, written mostly by Solomon); and (3) A Collection from Hezekiah (25—31, written by Solomon, Agur, and others).

The ultimate desire of Proverbs is that we may be led to the One in whom "all the fullness" dwells (Col. 1:19), to claim Him as the source of all wisdom and knowledge, and to see the working out of "Christ in you, the hope of glory" (Col. 1:27). To that end may God bless you as you dig into this spiritual gold mine where God's wisdom is stored.

—J.R.W.

The Beginning of Knowledge

THE ᴿproverbs of Solomon the son of David, king of Israel: 1 Kin. 4:32

2 To know wisdom and instruction,
To ᵀperceive the words of
understanding,   understand or discern
3 To receive the instruction of wisdom,
Justice, judgment, and equity;
4 To give prudence to the ᴿsimple,
To the young man knowledge and
discretion—   Prov. 9:4
5 ᴿA wise *man* will hear and increase
learning,
And a man of understanding will
ᵀattain wise counsel,   Prov. 9:9 · acquire
6 To understand a proverb and an
enigma,
The words of the wise and their
ᴿriddles.   Ps. 78:2

7 ᴿThe fear of the Lᴏʀᴅ *is* the beginning of
knowledge,
But fools despise wisdom and
instruction.   Job 28:28

Shun Evil Counsel

8 ᴿMy son, hear the instruction of your
father,
And do not forsake the law of your
mother;   Prov. 4:1
9 For they *will be* a ᴿgraceful ornament
on your head,
And chains about your neck.   Prov. 3:22

10 My son, if sinners entice you,
ᴿDo not consent.   Gen. 39:7-10
11 If they say, "Come with us,
Let us ᴿlie in wait to *shed* blood;
Let us lurk secretly for the innocent
without cause;   Jer. 5:26
12 Let us swallow them alive like ᵀSheol,
And whole, ᴿlike those who go down to
the Pit;   Or *the grave* · Ps. 28:1
13 We shall find all *kinds* of precious
ᵀpossessions,   Lit. *wealth*
We shall fill our houses with spoil;
14 Cast in your lot among us,
Let us all have one purse"—
15 My son, ᴿdo not walk in the way with
them,   Ps. 1:1
Keep your foot from their path;
16 ᴿFor their feet run to evil,   [Is. 59:7]
And they make haste to shed blood.
17 Surely, in ᵀvain the net is spread   futility
In the sight of any ᵀbird;   Lit. *lord of the wing*
18 But they lie in wait for their *own* blood,
They lurk secretly for their *own* lives.
19 ᴿSo *are* the ways of everyone who is
greedy for gain;   [1 Tim. 6:10]
It takes away the life of its owners.

The Call of Wisdom

20 ᴿWisdom calls aloud ᵀoutside;
She raises her voice in the open
squares.   [John 7:37] · *in the street*
21 She cries out in the *chief concourses,
At the openings of the gates in the city
She speaks her words:
22 "How long, you ᵀsimple ones, will you
love ᵀsimplicity?
For scorners delight in their scorning,
And fools hate knowledge.   naive · naivete
23 Turn at my rebuke;
Surely I will pour out my spirit on you;
I will make my words known to you.
24 ᴿBecause I have called and you refused,
I have stretched out my hand and no
one regarded,   Jer. 7:13
25 Because you disdained all my counsel,
And would have none of my rebuke,
26 I also will laugh at your calamity;
I will mock when your terror comes,
27 When ᴿyour terror comes like a storm,
And your destruction comes like a
whirlwind,
When distress and anguish come upon
you.   [Prov. 10:24, 25]
28 "Thenᴿ they will call on me, but I will
not answer;
They will seek me diligently, but they
will not find me.   Is. 1:15
29 Because they ᴿhated knowledge
And did not ᴿchoose the fear of the
Lᴏʀᴅ,   Job 21:14 · Ps. 119:173
30 ᴿThey would have none of my counsel
And despised my every rebuke.   Ps. 81:11
31 Therefore ᴿthey shall eat the fruit of
their own way,
And be filled to the full with their own
fancies.   Job 4:8
32 For the ᵀturning away of the simple will
slay them,
And the complacency of fools will
destroy them;   waywardness
33 But whoever listens to me will dwell
ᴿsafely,
And ᴿwill be ᵀsecure, without fear of
evil."   Prov. 3:24-26 · Ps. 112:7 · *at ease*

The Value of Wisdom

2 My son, if you receive my words,
And ᴿtreasure my commands within
you,   [Prov. 4:21]
2 So that you incline your ear to wisdom,
And apply your heart to understanding;
3 Yes, if you cry out for discernment,
And lift up your voice for
understanding,
4 ᴿIf you seek her as silver,
And search for her as *for* hidden
treasures;   [Prov. 3:14]

1:21 LXX, [Syr.], [Tg.] *top of the walls;* Vg. *the head of
the multitudes*

5 ᴿThen you will understand the fear of
  the LORD,   [James 1:5, 6]
  And find the knowledge of God.
6 ᴿFor the LORD gives wisdom;
  From His mouth *come* knowledge and
  understanding;   1 Kin. 3:9, 12
7 He stores up sound wisdom for the
  upright;
  ᴿ*He is* a shield to those who walk
  uprightly;   [Ps. 84:11]
8 He guards the paths of justice,
  And preserves the way of His saints.
9 Then you will understand righteousness
  and justice,
  Equity *and* every good path.

10 When wisdom enters your heart,
   And knowledge is pleasant to your soul,
11 Discretion will preserve you;
   Understanding will keep you,
12 To deliver you from the way of evil,
   From the man who speaks perverse
   things,
13 From those who leave the paths of
   uprightness
   To walk in the ways of darkness;
14 ᴿWho rejoice in doing evil,
   And delight in the perversity of the
   wicked;   [Rom. 1:32]
15 ᴿWhose ways *are* crooked,   Ps. 125:5
   And *who are* devious in their paths;
16 To deliver you from ᴿthe immoral
   woman,
   ᴿFrom the seductress *who* flatters with
   her words,   Prov. 5:20; 6:24; 7:5 · Prov. 5:3
17 Who forsakes the companion of her
   youth,
   And forgets the covenant of her God.
18 For ᴿher house ᵀleads down to death,
   And her paths to the dead;   Prov. 7:27 · *sinks*
19 None who go to her return,
   Nor do they regain the paths of life—
20 So you may walk in the way of
   goodness,
   And keep *to* the paths of righteousness.
21 For the upright will dwell in the land,
   And the blameless will remain in it;
22 But the wicked will be ᵀcut off from the
   ᵀearth,
   And the unfaithful will be uprooted
   from it.   *destroyed · land*

Guidance for the Young

3 My son, do not forget my law,
    But let your heart keep my commands;
2 For length of days and long life
  And peace they will add to you.

3 Let not ᵀmercy and truth forsake you;
  Bind them around your neck, *lovingkindness*
  Write them on the tablet of your heart,
4 ᴿ*And* so find favor and high esteem
  In the sight of God and man.   Rom. 14:18

5 ᴿTrust in the LORD with all your heart,
  ᴿAnd lean not on your own
  understanding;   [Ps. 37:3, 5] · [Jer. 9:23, 24]
6 In all your ways acknowledge Him,
  And He shall *direct your paths.
7 Do not be wise in your own eyes;
  Fear the LORD and depart from evil.
8 It will be health to your *flesh,
  And *strength to your bones.

9 ᴿHonor the LORD with your possessions,
  And with the firstfruits of all your
  increase;   Ex. 22:29
10 ᴿSo your barns will be filled with plenty,
   And your vats will overflow with new
   wine.   Deut. 28:8

11 ᴿMy son, do not despise the chastening
   of the LORD,
   Nor detest His correction;   Job 5:17
12 For whom the LORD loves He corrects,
   ᴿJust as a father the son *in whom* he
   delights.   Deut. 8:5

13 Happy *is* the man *who* finds wisdom,
   And the man *who* gains understanding;
14 ᴿFor her proceeds *are* better than the
   profits of silver,
   And her gain than fine gold.   Job 28:13
15 She *is* more precious than rubies,
   And ᴿall the things you may desire
   cannot compare with her.   Matt. 13:44
16 Length of days *is* in her right hand,
   In her left hand riches and honor.
17 ᴿHer ways *are* ways of pleasantness,
   And all her paths *are* peace.   [Matt. 11:29]
18 She *is* ᴿa tree of life to those who take
   hold of her,   Gen. 2:9
   And happy *are* all who retain her.

19 ᴿThe LORD by wisdom founded the
   earth;
   By understanding He established the
   heavens;   Ps. 104:24
20 By His knowledge the depths were
   ᴿbroken up,   Gen. 7:11
   And clouds drop down the dew.

21 My son, let them not depart from your
   eyes—
   Keep sound wisdom and discretion;
22 So they will be life to your soul
   And grace to your neck.
23 ᴿThen you will walk safely in your way,
   And your foot will not stumble.   Prov. 10:9
24 When you lie down, you will not be
   afraid;
   Yes, you will lie down and your sleep
   will be sweet.
25 ᴿDo not be afraid of sudden terror,
   Nor of trouble from the wicked when it
   comes;   Ps. 91:5

3:6 Or *make smooth* or *straight*
3:8 Body, lit. *navel* • Lit. *drink*

26 For the LORD will be your confidence,
And will keep your foot from being
caught.

27 ᴿDo not withhold good from ᵀthose to
whom it is due,
When it is in the power of your hand to
do *so*.   Rom. 13:7 · Lit. *its owners*
28 ᴿDo not say to your neighbor,
"Go, and come back,
And tomorrow I will give *it*,"
When *you* have it with you.   Lev. 19:13
29 Do not devise evil against your
neighbor,
For he dwells by you for safety's sake.
30 ᴿDo not strive with a man without
cause,
If he has done you no harm.   [Rom. 12:18]

31 ᴿDo not envy the oppressor,
And choose none of his ways;   Ps. 37:1
32 For the perverse *person is* an
abomination to the LORD,
ᴿBut His secret *counsel is* with the
upright.   Ps. 25:14
33 ᴿThe curse of the LORD *is* on the house
of the wicked,   Zech. 5:3, 4
But He blesses the home of the just.
34 ᴿSurely He scorns the scornful,
But gives grace to the humble.   James 4:6
35 The wise shall inherit glory,
But shame shall be the legacy of fools.

Security in Wisdom

4 Hear, ᴿmy children, the instruction of a
father,
And give attention to know
understanding;   Ps. 34:11
2 For I give you good doctrine:
Do not forsake my law.
3 When I was my father's son,
ᴿTender and the only one in the sight of
my mother,   1 Chr. 29:1
4 He also taught me, and said to me:
"Let your heart retain my words;
ᴿKeep my commands, and live.   Prov. 7:2
5 ᴿGet wisdom! Get understanding!
Do not forget, nor turn away from the
words of my mouth.   Prov. 2:2, 3
6 Do not forsake her, and she will
preserve you;
Love her, and she will keep you.
7 ᴿWisdom *is* the principal thing;
Therefore get wisdom.
And in all your getting, get
understanding.   Matt. 13:44
8 ᴿExalt her, and she will promote you;
She will bring you honor, when you
embrace her.   1 Sam. 2:30
9 She will place on your head ᴿan
ornament of grace;   Prov. 3:22
A crown of glory she will deliver to
you."

10 Hear, my son, and receive my sayings,
And the years of your life will be many.
11 I have ᴿtaught you in the way of
wisdom;
I have led you in right paths.   1 Sam. 12:23
12 When you walk, ᴿyour steps will not be
hindered,
ᴿAnd when you run, you will not
stumble.   Ps. 18:36 · [Ps. 91:11]
13 Take firm hold of instruction, do not let
go;
Keep her, for she *is* your life.

14 Do not enter the path of the wicked,
And do not walk in the way of evil.
15 Avoid it, do not travel on it;
Turn away from it and pass on.
16 ᴿFor they do not sleep unless they have
done evil;   Ps. 36:4
And their sleep is ᵀtaken away unless
they make *someone* fall.   Lit. *robbed*
17 For they eat the bread of wickedness,
And drink the wine of violence.
18 But the path of the just ᴿis like the
shining ᵀsun,
That shines ever brighter unto the
perfect day.   2 Sam. 23:4 · Lit. *light*
19 ᴿThe way of the wicked *is* like darkness;
They do not know what makes them
stumble.   [Is. 59:9, 10]

20 My son, give attention to my words;
Incline your ear to my sayings.
21 Do not let them depart from your eyes;
Keep them in the midst of your heart;
22 For they *are* life to those who find
them,
And health to all their flesh.
23 Keep your heart with all diligence,
For out of it *spring* the issues of life.
24 Put away from you a deceitful mouth,
And put perverse lips far from you.
25 Let your eyes look straight ahead,
And your eyelids look right before you.
26 Ponder the path of your ᴿfeet,   Heb. 12:13
And let all your ways be established.
27 Do not turn to the right or the left;
Remove your foot from evil.

The Peril of Adultery

5 My son, pay attention to my wisdom;
Lend your ear to my understanding,
2 That you may preserve discretion,
And your lips may keep knowledge.
3 ᴿFor the lips of ᵀan immoral woman drip
honey,   Prov. 2:16 · Lit. *a strange*
And her mouth *is* smoother than oil;
4 But in the end she is bitter as
wormwood,
Sharp as a two-edged sword.
5 Her feet go down to death,
Her steps lay hold of ᵀhell.   Or *Sheol*

6 Lest you ponder *her* path of life—
  Her ways are unstable;
  You do not know *them*.

7 Therefore hear me now, *my* children,
  And do not depart from the words of
  my mouth.

8 Remove your way far from her,
  And do not go near the door of her
  house,

9 Lest you give your ^Thonor to others,
  And your years to the cruel *one*;   vigor

10 Lest aliens be filled with your ^Twealth,
   And your labors go to the house of a
   foreigner;   Lit. *strength*

11 And you mourn at last,
   When your flesh and your body are
   consumed,

12 And say:
   "How I have hated instruction,
   And my heart despised correction!

13 I have not obeyed the voice of my
   teachers,
   Nor inclined my ear to those who
   instructed me!

14 I was on the verge of total ruin,
   In the midst of the assembly and
   congregation."

15 Drink water from your own cistern,
   And running water from your own well.

16 Should your fountains be dispersed
   abroad,
   ^TStreams of water in the streets?   Channels

17 Let them be only your own,
   And not for strangers with you.

18 Let your fountain be blessed,
   And rejoice with ^Rthe wife of your
   youth.   Mal. 2:14

19 ^RAs a loving deer and a graceful doe,
   Let her breasts satisfy you at all times;
   And always be ^Tenraptured with her
   love.   Song 2:9 · Lit. *intoxicated*

20 For why should you, my son, be
   enraptured by ^Ran immoral woman,
   And be embraced in the arms of a
   seductress?   Prov. 2:16

21 ^RFor the ways of man *are* before the
   eyes of the LORD,   Hos. 7:2
   And He ^Tponders all his paths.   Lit. *weighs*

22 ^RHis own iniquities entrap the wicked
   man,   Num. 32:23
   And he is caught in the cords of his sin.

23 ^RHe shall die for lack of instruction,
   And in the greatness of his folly he
   shall go astray.   Job 4:21

Dangerous Promises

6 My son, ^Rif you become ^Tsurety for your
friend,   Prov. 11:15 · *guaranty* or *collateral*
   If you have ^Tshaken hands in pledge for
   a stranger,   Lit. *struck*

2 You are snared by the words of your
  mouth;

You are taken by the words of your
mouth.

3 So do this, my son, and deliver yourself;
  For you have come into the hand of
  your friend:
  Go and humble yourself;
  Plead with your friend.

4 ^RGive no sleep to your eyes,
  Nor slumber to your eyelids.   Ps. 132:4

5 Deliver yourself like a gazelle from the
  hand *of the hunter*,
  And like a bird from the hand of the
  *fowler.

The Folly of Indolence

6 ^RGo to the ant, you sluggard!
  Consider her ways and be wise,   Job 12:7

7 Which, having no ^Tcaptain,
  Overseer or ruler,   Lit. *leader*

8 Provides her supplies in the summer,
  And gathers her food in the harvest.

9 ^RHow long will you ^Tslumber, O
  sluggard?   Prov. 24:33, 34 · Lit. *lie down*
  When will you rise from your sleep?

10 A little sleep, a little slumber,
   A little folding of the hands to sleep—

11 ^RSo shall your poverty come on you like
   a prowler,   Prov. 10:4
   And your need like an armed man.

The Wicked Man

12 A worthless person, a wicked man,
   Walks with a perverse mouth;

13 ^RHe ^Twinks with his
   eyes,   Job 15:12 · *gives signals*
   He ^Tshuffles his feet,   Lit. *scrapes*
   He points with his fingers;

14 Perversity *is* in his heart,
   ^RHe devises evil continually,
   ^RHe sows discord.   Mic. 2:1 · Prov. 6:19

15 Therefore his calamity shall come
   ^Rsuddenly;
   Suddenly he shall ^Rbe broken ^Rwithout
   remedy.   Is. 30:13 · Jer. 19:11 · 2 Chr. 36:16

16 These six *things* the LORD hates,
   Yes, seven *are* an abomination to Him:

17 ^RA^T proud look,   Ps. 101:5 · *Haughty eyes*
   ^RA lying tongue,   Ps. 120:2
   ^RHands that shed innocent blood,   Is. 1:15

18 A heart that devises wicked plans,
   Feet that are swift in running to evil,

19 ^RA false witness *who* speaks lies,
   And one who ^Rsows discord among
   brethren.   Ps. 27:12 · Prov. 6:14

Beware of Adultery

20 ^RMy son, keep your father's command,
   And do not forsake the law of your
   mother.   Eph. 6:1

21 ^RBind them continually upon your heart;
   Tie them around your neck.   Prov. 3:3

6:5 One who catches birds in a trap or snare

22 ᴿWhen you roam, ᵀthey will lead you;
   When you sleep, ᴿthey will keep you;
   And *when* you awake, they will speak
   with you.   [Prov. 3:23] • Lit. *it* • Prov. 2:11

23 ᴿFor the commandment *is* a lamp,
   And the law a light;
   Reproofs of instruction *are* the way of
   life,   Ps. 19:8

24 ᴿTo keep you from the evil woman,
   From the flattering tongue of a
   seductress.   Prov. 2:16

25 ᴿDo not lust after her beauty in your
   heart,   Matt. 5:28
   Nor let her allure you with her eyelids.

26 For ᴿby means of a harlot   Prov. 29:3
   A man is reduced to a crust of bread;
   And ᵀan adulteress will prey upon his
   precious life.   Wife of another, lit. *a man's wife*

27 Can a man take fire to his bosom,
   And his clothes not be burned?

28 Can one walk on hot coals,
   And his feet not be seared?

29 So *is* he who goes in to his neighbor's
   wife;
   Whoever touches her shall not be
   innocent.

30 *People* do not despise a thief
   If he steals to satisfy himself when he is
   starving.

31 Yet *when* he is found, ᴿhe must restore
   sevenfold;
   He may have to give up all the
   substance of his house.   Ex. 22:1-4

32 Whoever commits adultery with a
   woman ᴿlacks understanding;   Prov. 7:7
   He *who* does so destroys his own soul.

33 Wounds and dishonor he will get,
   And his reproach will not be wiped
   away.

34 For ᴿjealousy *is* a husband's fury;
   Therefore he will not spare in the day
   of vengeance.   Song 8:6

35 He will ᵀaccept no recompense,
   Nor will he be appeased though you
   give many gifts.   Lit. *lift up the face of any*

7 My son, keep my words,
   And ᴿtreasure my commands within
   you.   Prov. 2:1

2 ᴿKeep my commands and live,   Lev. 18:5
   And my law as the apple of your eye.

3 ᴿBind them on your fingers;   Deut. 6:8
   Write them on the tablet of your heart.

4 Say to wisdom, "You *are* my sister,"
   And call understanding *your* nearest
   kin,

5 ᴿThat they may keep you from the
   immoral woman,
   From the seductress *who* flatters with
   her words.   Prov. 2:16; 5:3

The Crafty Harlot

6 For at the window of my house
   I looked through my lattice,

7 And saw among the simple,
   I perceived among the ᵀyouths,   Lit. *sons*
   A young man ᴿdevoidᵀ of
   understanding,   [Prov. 6:32; 9:4, 16] • *lacking*

8 Passing along the street near her
   corner;
   And he took the path to her house

9 ᴿIn the twilight, in the evening,
   In the black and dark night.   Job 24:15

10 And there a woman met him,
   With the attire of a harlot, and a crafty
   heart.

11 ᴿShe *was* loud and rebellious,   Prov. 9:13
   Her feet would not stay at home.

12 At times *she was* outside, at times in
   the open square,
   Lurking at every corner.

13 So she caught him and kissed him;
   With an impudent face she said to him:

14 "*I have* peace offerings with me;
   Today I have paid my vows.

15 So I came out to meet you,
   Diligently to seek your face,
   And I have found you.

16 I have spread my bed with tapestry,
   Colored coverings of Egyptian linen.

17 I have perfumed my bed
   With myrrh, aloes, and cinnamon.

18 Come, let us take our fill of love until
   morning;
   Let us delight ourselves with love.

19 For my husband *is* not at home;
   He has gone on a long journey;

20 He has taken a bag of money ᵀwith
   him,
   And will come home ᵀon the appointed
   day."   Lit. *in his hand* • *at the full moon*

21 With ᵀher enticing speech she caused
   him to yield,   *By the greatness of her words*
   ᴿWith her flattering lips she ᵀseduced
   him.   Ps. 12:2 • *compelled*

22 Immediately he went after her, as an ox
   goes to the slaughter,
   Or *as a fool to the correction of the
   ᵀstocks,   *shackles*

23 Till an arrow struck his liver.
   ᴿAs a bird hastens to the snare,   Eccl. 9:12
   He did not know it *would* cost his life.

24 Now therefore, listen to me, *my*
   children;
   Pay attention to the words of my
   mouth:

25 Do not let your heart turn aside to her
   ways,
   Do not stray into her paths;

7:22 LXX, Syr., Tg. *as a dog to bonds;* Vg. *as a
lamb . . . to bonds*

26 For she has cast down many wounded,
   And ᴿall who were slain by her were
   strong men.   Neh. 13:26
27 Her house is the way to ᵀhell,   Or Sheol
   Descending to the chambers of death.

The Excellence of Wisdom

8 Does not ᴿwisdom cry out,   Prov. 1:20, 21
   And understanding lift up her voice?
2 She takes her stand on the top of the
   ᵀhigh hill,   Lit. heights
   Beside the way, where the paths meet.
3 She cries out by the gates, at the entry
   of the city,
   At the entrance of the doors:
4 "To you, O men, I call,
   And my voice is to the sons of men.
5 O you ᵀsimple ones, understand
   prudence,
   And you fools, be of an understanding
   heart.   naive
6 Listen, for I will speak of ᴿexcellent
   things,
   And from the opening of my lips will
   come right things;   Prov. 22:20
7 For my mouth will speak truth;
   Wickedness is an abomination to my
   lips.
8 All the words of my mouth are with
   righteousness;
   Nothing crooked or perverse is in them.
9 They are all plain to him who
   understands,
   And right to those who find knowledge.
10 Receive my instruction, and not silver,
   And knowledge rather than choice
   gold;
11 ᴿFor wisdom is better than rubies,
   And all the things one may desire
   cannot be compared with her. Job 28:15

12 "I, wisdom, dwell with prudence,
   And find out knowledge and discretion.
13 The fear of the Lᴏʀᴅ is to hate evil;
   Pride and arrogance and the evil way
   And the perverse mouth I hate.
14 Counsel is mine, and sound wisdom;
   I am understanding, I have strength.
15 ᴿBy me kings reign,
   And rulers decree justice.   Rom. 13:1
16 By me princes rule, and nobles,
   All the judges of *the earth.
17 ᴿI love those who love me,
   And ᴿthose who seek me diligently will
   find me.   [John 14:21] • James 1:5
18 ᴿRiches and honor are with me,   Prov. 3:16
   Enduring riches and righteousness.
19 My fruit is better than gold, yes, than
   fine gold,
   And my revenue than choice silver.

20 I traverse the way of righteousness,
   In the midst of the paths of justice,
21 That I may cause those who love me to
   inherit wealth,
   That I may fill their treasuries.

22 "Theᴿ Lᴏʀᴅ possessed me at the
   beginning of His way,
   Before His works of old.   Prov. 3:19
23 ᴿI have been established from
   everlasting,
   From the beginning, before there was
   ever an earth.   [Ps. 2:6]
24 When there were no depths I was
   brought forth,
   When there were no fountains
   abounding with water.
25 Before the mountains were settled,
   Before the hills, I was brought forth;
26 While as yet He had not made the earth
   or the ᵀfields,   outer places
   Or the primal dust of the world.
27 When He prepared the heavens, I was
   there,
   When He drew a circle on the face of
   the deep,
28 When He established the clouds above,
   When He strengthened the fountains of
   the deep,
29 ᴿWhen He assigned to the sea its limit,
   So that the waters would not transgress
   His command,
   When ᴿHe marked out the foundations
   of the earth,   Gen. 1:9, 10 • Job 28:4, 6
30 Then I was beside Him as *a master
   craftsman;
   ᴿAnd I was daily His delight,   [Matt. 3:17]
   Rejoicing always before Him,
31 Rejoicing in His inhabited world,
   And ᴿmy delight was with the sons of
   men.   Ps. 16:3

32 "Now therefore, listen to me, my
   children,
   For ᴿblessed are those who keep my
   ways.   Luke 11:28
33 Hear instruction and be wise,
   And do not disdain it.
34 ᴿBlessed is the man who listens to me,
   Watching daily at my gates,   Prov. 3:13, 18
   Waiting at the posts of my doors.
35 For whoever finds me finds life,
   And obtains favor from the Lᴏʀᴅ;
36 But he who sins against me ᴿwrongs his
   own soul;   Prov. 20:2
   All those who hate me love death."

The Way of Wisdom

9 Wisdom has ᴿbuilt her house,   [Matt. 16:18]
   She has hewn out her seven pillars;
2 ᴿShe has slaughtered her meat,
   She has mixed her wine,   Matt. 22:4
   She has also ᵀfurnished her table.   arranged

8:16 MT, Syr., Tg., Vg. righteousness; LXX, Bg., some
mss. and editions earth

8:30 A Jewish tradition one brought up

3 She has sent out her maidens,
    She cries out from the highest places of
    the city,
4 "Whoever[R] *is* simple, let him turn in
    here!"
    As for him who lacks understanding,
      she says to him,   Ps. 19:7
5 "Come,[R] eat of my bread   Is. 55:1
    And drink of the wine I have mixed.
6 Forsake foolishness and live,
    And go in the way of understanding.

7 "He who corrects a scoffer gets shame
    for himself,
    And he who rebukes a wicked *man*
      only harms himself.
8 [R]Do not correct a scoffer, lest he hate
    you;
    [R]Rebuke a wise *man*, and he will love
      you.   Matt. 7:6 · Ps. 141:5
9 Give *instruction* to a wise *man*, and he
    will be still wiser;
    Teach a just *man*, [R]and he will increase
      in learning.   [Matt. 13:12]
10 "The[R] fear of the LORD *is* the beginning
    of wisdom,
    And the knowledge of the Holy One *is*
      understanding.   Job 28:28
11 For by me your days will be multiplied,
    And years of life will be added to you.
12 [R]If you are wise, you are wise for
    yourself,   Job 35:6, 7
    And *if* you scoff, you will bear *it* alone."

The Way of Folly

13 A foolish woman is [T]clamorous; *boisterous*
    She is simple, and knows nothing.
14 For she sits at the door of her house,
    On a seat [R]*by* the highest places of the
    city,   Prov. 9:3
15 To call to those who pass by,
    Who go straight on their way:
16 "Whoever[R] *is* [T]simple, let him turn in
    here";   Prov. 7:7, 8 · *naive*
    And *as for* him who lacks
      understanding, she says to him,
17 "Stolen[R] water is sweet,   Prov. 20:17
    And bread *eaten* in secret is pleasant."
18 But he does not know that [R]the dead
    are there,
    That her guests *are* in the depths of
    [T]hell.   Prov. 2:18; 7:27 · *Or Sheol*

Wise Sayings of Solomon

10

The proverbs of [R]Solomon: Prov. 1:1; 25:1

    [R]A wise son makes a glad father,
    But a foolish son *is* the grief of his
      mother.   Prov. 15:20; 17:21, 25; 19:13; 29:3, 15

2 Treasures of wickedness profit nothing,
    But righteousness delivers from death.

3 [R]The LORD will not allow the righteous
    soul to famish,
    But He casts away the desire of the
      wicked.   Ps. 34:9, 10; 37:25
4 [R]He who has a slack hand becomes poor,
    But [R]the hand of the diligent makes
      rich.   Prov. 19:15 · Prov. 12:24; 13:4; 21:5
5 He who gathers in [R]summer *is* a wise
    son;
    He who sleeps in harvest *is* [R]a son who
      causes shame.   Prov. 6:8 · Prov. 19:26

6 Blessings *are* on the head of the
    righteous,
    But violence covers the mouth of the
      wicked.
7 The memory of the righteous *is* blessed,
    But the name of the wicked will rot.

8 The wise in heart will receive
    commands,
    But a prating fool will [T]fall.   *be thrust down*
9 [R]He who walks with integrity walks
    securely,
    But he who perverts his ways will
      become known.   [Ps. 23:4]

10 He who winks with the eye causes
    trouble,
    But a prating fool will fall.

11 The mouth of the righteous *is* a well of
    life,
    But violence covers the mouth of the
      wicked.

12 Hatred stirs up strife,
    But [R]love covers all sins.   [1 Cor. 13:4–7]

13 Wisdom is found on the lips of him who
    has understanding,
    But a rod *is* for the back of him who [T]is
      devoid of understanding.   *lacks heart*

14 Wise *people* store up knowledge,
    But [R]the mouth of the foolish *is* near
      destruction.   Prov. 18:7

15 The [R]rich man's wealth *is* his strong
    city;
    The destruction of the poor *is* their
      poverty.   Job 31:24

16 The labor of the righteous *leads* to life,
    The wages of the wicked to sin.

17 He who keeps instruction *is in* the way
    of life,
    But he who refuses correction [T]goes
      astray.   *leads*

18 Whoever hides hatred *has* lying lips,
    And whoever spreads slander *is* a fool.

19 [R]In the multitude of words sin is not
    lacking,   Eccl. 5:3
    But he who restrains his lips *is* wise.

20 The tongue of the righteous *is* choice
   silver;
   The heart of the wicked *is worth* little.
21 The lips of the righteous feed many,
   But fools die for lack of *wisdom.

22 ᴿThe blessing of the Lᴏʀᴅ makes one
   rich,   Gen. 24:35; 26:12
   And He adds no sorrow with it.

23 ᴿTo do evil *is* like sport to a fool,
   But a man of understanding has
   wisdom.   Prov. 2:14; 15:21
24 ᴿThe fear of the wicked will come upon
   him,
   And ᴿthe desire of the righteous will be
   granted.   Job 15:21 • Ps. 145:19
25 When the whirlwind passes by, ᴿthe
   wicked *is* no *more*,
   But ᴿthe righteous *has* an everlasting
   foundation.   Ps. 37:9, 10 • Ps. 15:5
26 As vinegar to the teeth and smoke to
   the eyes,
   So *is* the lazy *man* to those who send
   him.
27 ᴿThe fear of the Lᴏʀᴅ prolongs days,
   But ᴿthe years of the wicked will be
   shortened.   Prov. 9:11 • Job 15:32
28 The hope of the righteous *will be*
   gladness,
   But the ᴿexpectation of the wicked will
   perish.   Job 8:13
29 The way of the Lᴏʀᴅ *is* strength for the
   upright,
   But ᴿdestruction *will come* to the
   workers of iniquity.   Ps. 1:6
30 ᴿThe righteous will never be removed,
   But the wicked will not inhabit the
   ᵀearth.   Ps. 37:22 • *land*
31 ᴿThe mouth of the righteous brings forth
   wisdom,   Ps. 37:30
   But the perverse tongue will be cut out.
32 The lips of the righteous know what is
   acceptable,
   But the mouth of the wicked *what is*
   perverse.

11 Dishonestᴿ scales *are* an abomination
     to the Lᴏʀᴅ,   Lev. 19:35, 36
     But a just weight *is* His delight.

2 When pride comes, then comes shame;
  But with the humble *is* wisdom.
3 The integrity of the upright will guide
  ᴿthem,
  But the perversity of the unfaithful will
  destroy them.   Prov. 13:6
4 Riches do not profit in the day of
  wrath,
  But righteousness delivers from death.

5 The righteousness of the blameless will
  ᵀdirect his way aright,
  But the wicked will fall by his own
  wickedness.   Or *make smooth* or *straight*
6 The righteousness of the upright will
  deliver them,
  But the unfaithful will be caught by
  their lust.

7 When a wicked man dies, *his*
  expectation will ᴿperish,   Prov. 10:28
  And the hope of the unjust perishes.
8 The righteous is delivered from trouble,
  And it comes to the wicked instead.
9 The hypocrite with *his* mouth destroys
  his neighbor,
  But through knowledge the righteous
  will be delivered.
10 ᴿWhen it goes well with the righteous,
   the city rejoices;
   And when the wicked perish, *there is*
   jubilation.   Prov. 28:12
11 By the blessing of the upright the city
   is ᴿexalted,
   But it is overthrown by the mouth of
   the wicked.   Prov. 14:34
12 He who ᵀis devoid of wisdom despises
   his neighbor,
   But a man of understanding holds his
   peace.   Lit. *lacks heart*
13 ᴿA talebearer reveals secrets,
   But he who is of a faithful spirit
   ᴿconceals a matter.   Lev. 19:16 • Prov. 19:11
14 ᴿWhere *there is* no counsel, the people
   fall;
   But in the multitude of counselors *there*
   is safety.   1 Kin. 12:1
15 He who is ᴿsuretyᵀ for a stranger will
   suffer,   Prov. 6:1, 2 • *guaranty*
   But one who hates ᵀbeing surety is
   secure.   Lit. *those who strike hands*

16 A gracious woman retains honor,
   But ruthless *men* retain riches.
17 ᴿThe merciful man does good for his
   own soul,
   But *he who is* cruel troubles his own
   flesh.   [Matt. 5:7; 25:34–36]
18 The wicked *man* does deceptive work,
   But ᴿhe who sows righteousness *will*
   have a sure reward.   Hos. 10:12
19 As righteousness *leads* to ᴿlife,
   So he who pursues evil *pursues it* to his
   own ᴿdeath.   Prov. 10:16; 12:28 • [Rom. 6:23]
20 Those who are of a perverse heart *are*
   an abomination to the Lᴏʀᴅ,
   But the blameless in their ways *are* His
   delight.
21 *Though they join* ᵀforces, the wicked
   will not go unpunished;
   But ᴿthe posterity of the righteous will
   be delivered.   Lit. *hand in hand* • Ps. 112:2

10:21 Lit. *heart*

22 *As* a ring of gold in a swine's snout,
So *is* a lovely woman who lacks
ᵀdiscretion.　　　　　*taste*

23 The desire of the righteous *is* only
good,
But the expectation of the wicked ᴿ*is*
wrath.　　　　　Rom. 2:8, 9

24 There is *one* who ᴿscatters, yet
increases more;
And there is *one* who withholds more
than is right,
But it *leads* to poverty.　　　Ps. 112:9

25 ᴿThe generous soul will be made rich,
ᴿAnd he who waters will also be watered
himself.　　　[2 Cor. 9:6, 7] · [Matt. 5:7]

26 The people will curse ᴿhim who
withholds grain,
But ᴿblessing *will be* on the head of him
who sells *it*.　　　Amos 8:5, 6 · Job 29:13

27 He who earnestly seeks good ᵀfinds
favor,
ᴿBut trouble will come to him who seeks
evil.　　　Lit. *seeks* · Esth. 7:10

28 ᴿHe who trusts in his riches will fall,
But ᴿthe righteous will flourish like
foliage.　　　Job 31:24 · Ps. 1:3

29 He who troubles his own house ᴿwill
inherit the wind,
And the fool *will be* ᴿservant to the
wise of heart.　　　Eccl. 5:16 · Prov. 14:19

30 The fruit of the righteous *is a* tree of
life,
And he who wins souls *is* wise.

31 ᴿIf the righteous will be ᵀrecompensed
on the earth,
How much more the ungodly and the
sinner.　　　Jer. 25:29 · *rewarded*

12 Whoever loves instruction loves
knowledge,
But he who hates correction *is* stupid.

2 A good *man* obtains favor from the
LORD,
But a man of wicked intentions He will
condemn.

3 A man is not established by
wickedness,
But the ᴿroot of the righteous cannot
be moved.　　　[Prov. 10:25]

4 ᴿAnᵀ excellent wife *is* the crown of her
husband,　　　1 Cor. 11:7 · Lit. *A wife of valor*
But she who causes shame *is* ᴿlike
rottenness in his bones.　　　Prov. 14:30

5 The thoughts of the righteous *are* right,
But the counsels of the wicked *are*
deceitful.

6 ᴿThe words of the wicked *are*, "Lie in
wait for blood,"　　　Prov. 1:11, 18

ᴿBut the mouth of the upright will
deliver them.　　　Prov. 14:3

7 ᴿThe wicked are overthrown and *are* no
more,　　　Matt. 7:24–27
But the house of the righteous will
stand.

8 A man will be commended according to
his wisdom,
ᴿBut he who is of a perverse heart will
be despised.　　　1 Sam. 25:17

9 ᴿBetter *is the* one who is ᵀslighted but
has a servant,
Than he who honors himself but lacks
bread.　　　Prov. 13:7 · *lightly esteemed*

10 ᴿA righteous *man* regards the life of his
animal,　　　Deut. 25:4
But the tender mercies of the wicked
are cruel.

11 ᴿHe who ᵀtills his land will be satisfied
with bread,　　　Gen. 3:19 · *works* or *cultivates*
But he who follows ᵀfrivolity *is* devoid
of *understanding.　　　Lit. *vain things*

12 The wicked covet the catch of evil *men*,
But the root of the righteous yields
fruit.

13 ᴿThe wicked is ensnared by the
transgression of *his* lips,
ᴿBut the righteous will come through
trouble.　　　Prov. 18:7 · [2 Pet. 2:9]

14 ᴿA man will be satisfied with good by
the fruit of *his* mouth,　　　Prov. 13:2; 15:23
ᴿAnd the recompense of a man's hands
will be rendered to him.　　　[Is. 3:10, 11]

15 ᴿThe way of a fool *is* right in his own
eyes,　　　Luke 18:11
But he who heeds counsel *is* wise.

16 A fool's wrath is known at once,
But a prudent *man* covers shame.

17 ᴿHe *who* speaks truth declares
righteousness,　　　Prov. 14:5
But a false witness, deceit.

18 ᴿThere is one who speaks like the
piercings of a sword,　　　Ps. 57:4
But the tongue of the wise *promotes*
health.

19 The truthful lip shall be established
forever,
But a lying tongue *is* but for a moment.

20 Deceit is in the heart of those who
devise evil,
But counselors of peace have joy.

21 ᴿNo grave ᵀtrouble will overtake the
righteous,　　　1 Pet. 3:13 · *harm*
But the wicked shall be filled with evil.

22 ᴿLying lips *are* an abomination to the
LORD,　　　Rev. 22:15
But those who deal truthfully *are* His
delight.

12:11 Lit. *heart*

23 [R]A prudent man conceals knowledge,
But the heart of fools proclaims
foolishness.   Prov. 13:16

24 [R]The hand of the diligent will rule,
But the lazy *man* will be put to forced
labor.   Prov. 10:4

25 [R]Anxiety in the heart of man causes
depression,   Prov. 15:13
But a good word makes it glad.

26 The righteous should choose his friends
carefully,
For the way of the wicked leads them
astray.

27 The lazy *man* does not roast what he
took in hunting,
But diligence *is* man's precious
possession.

28 In the way of righteousness *is* life,
And in *its* pathway *there is* no death.

13 A wise son *heeds* his father's
instruction,
But a scoffer does not listen to rebuke.

2 [R]A man shall eat well by the fruit of *his*
mouth,
But the soul of the unfaithful feeds on
violence.   Prov. 12:14

3 [R]He who guards his mouth preserves his
life,
But he who opens wide his lips shall
have destruction.   Prov. 21:23

4 [R]The soul of a lazy *man* desires, and *has*
nothing;
But the soul of the diligent shall be
made rich.   Prov. 10:4

5 A righteous *man* hates lying,
But a wicked *man* is loathsome and
comes to shame.

6 [R]Righteousness guards *him whose* way is
blameless,   Prov. 11:3, 5, 6
But wickedness overthrows the sinner.

7 [R]There is one who makes himself rich,
yet *has* nothing;
And one who makes himself poor, yet
has great riches.   [Prov. 11:24; 12:9]

8 The ransom of a man's life *is* his riches,
But the poor does not hear rebuke.

9 The light of the righteous rejoices,
[R]But the lamp of the wicked will be put
out.   Prov. 24:20

10 By pride comes nothing but strife,
But with the well-advised *is* wisdom.

11 [R]Wealth *gained by* dishonesty will be
diminished,
But he who gathers by labor will
increase.   Prov. 10:2; 20:21

12 Hope deferred makes the heart sick,
But [R]*when* the desire comes, *it is* a tree
of life.   Prov. 13:19

13 He who [R]despises the word will be
destroyed,
But he who fears the commandment
will be rewarded.   Num. 15:31

14 [R]The law of the wise *is* a fountain of life,
To turn *one* away from [R]the snares of
death.   Prov. 6:22; 10:11; 14:27 • 2 Sam. 22:6

15 Good understanding [T]gains favor,   *gives*
But the way of the unfaithful *is* hard.

16 [R]Every prudent *man* acts with
knowledge,
But a fool lays open *his* folly.   Prov. 12:23

17 A wicked messenger falls into trouble,
But [R]a faithful ambassador *brings*
health.   Prov. 25:13

18 Poverty and shame *will come* to him
who [T]disdains correction,
But [R]he who regards a rebuke will be
honored.   Lit. *ignores* • Prov. 15:5, 31, 32

19 A desire accomplished is sweet to the
soul,
But *it is* an abomination to fools to
depart from evil.

20 He who walks with wise *men* will be
wise,
But the companion of fools will be
destroyed.

21 [R]Evil pursues sinners,
But to the righteous, good shall be
repaid.   Prov. 32:10

22 A good *man* leaves an inheritance to
his children's children,
But [R]the wealth of the sinner is stored
up for the righteous.   [Eccl. 2:26]

23 [R]Much food *is in* the [T]fallow *ground* of
the poor,   Prov. 12:11 • *uncultivated*
And for lack of justice there is *waste.

24 [R]He who spares his rod hates his son,
But he who loves him disciplines him
[T]promptly.   Prov. 19:18 • *early*

25 [R]The righteous eats to the satisfying of
his soul,
But the stomach of the wicked shall be
in want.   Ps. 34:10

14 The wise woman builds her house,
But the foolish pulls it down with her
hands.

2 He who walks in his uprightness fears
the LORD,
[R]But *he who is* perverse in his ways
despises Him.   [Rom. 2:4]

13:23 Lit. *what is swept away*

3 In the mouth of a fool *is* a rod of pride,
   ᴿBut the lips of the wise will preserve
   them.   Prov. 12:6

4 Where no oxen *are*, the ᵀtrough *is*
   clean;
   But much increase *comes* by the
   strength of an ox.   *manger* or *feed trough*

5 A faithful witness does not lie,
   But a false witness will utter lies.

6 A scoffer seeks wisdom and does not
   find it,
   But ᴿknowledge *is* easy to him who
   understands.   Prov. 8:9; 17:24

7 Go from the presence of a foolish man,
   When you do not perceive *in him* the
   lips of ᴿknowledge.   Prov. 23:9

8 The wisdom of the prudent *is* to
   understand his way,
   But the folly of fools *is* deceit.

9 ᴿFools mock at ᵀsin,   Prov. 10:23 · Lit. *guilt*
   But among the upright *there is* favor.

10 The heart knows its own bitterness,
   And a stranger does not share its joy.

▼ **14-F. What Is the Final Destiny of Man?**

11 ᴿThe house of the wicked will be
   overthrown,   Job 8:15
   But the tent of the upright will flourish.

12 ᴿThere is a way *that seems* right to a
   man,   Prov. 16:25
▲   But its end *is* the way of death.

13 Even in laughter the heart may sorrow,
   And the end of mirth *may be* grief.

14 The backslider in heart will be ᴿfilled
   with his own ways,   Prov. 1:31; 12:15
   But a good man *will be satisfied* ᵀfrom
   ᴿabove. Lit. *from above himself* · Prov. 13:2; 18:20

15 The simple believes every word,
   But the prudent considers well his
   steps.

16 A wise *man* fears and departs from evil,
   But a fool rages and is self-confident.

17 A quick-tempered *man* acts foolishly,
   And a man of wicked intentions is
   hated.

18 The simple inherit folly,
   But the prudent are crowned with
   knowledge.

19 The evil will bow before the good,
   And the wicked at the gates of the
   righteous.

20 ᴿThe poor *man* is hated even by his own
   neighbor,   Prov. 19:7
   But the rich *has* many ᴿfriends.   Prov. 19:4

21 He who despises his neighbor sins;
   ᴿBut he who has mercy on the poor,
   happy *is* he.   Ps. 112:9

22 Do they not go astray who devise evil?
   But mercy and truth *belong* to those
   who devise good.

23 In all labor there is profit,
   But *idle chatter *leads* only to poverty.

24 The crown of the wise is their riches,
   But the foolishness of fools *is* folly.

25 A true witness ᵀdelivers souls,   *saves lives*
   But a deceitful *witness* speaks lies.

26 In the fear of the LORD *there is* strong
   confidence,
   And His children will have a place of
   refuge.

27 ᴿThe fear of the LORD *is* a fountain of
   life,   Prov. 13:14

14:23 Lit. *talk of the lips*

14-F. What Is the Final Destiny of Man? (Proverbs 14:11, 12)—Man's final destiny is death if he chooses the way that seems right to him. As Isaiah said, "All we like sheep have gone astray; we have turned, every one, to his own way" (Is. 53:6, page 693). Man's way is the broad way, the way of least resistance, a road that narrows down to destruction—eternal separation from God (Matt. 7:13, page 945).

Man's final destiny is life if he chooses God's way, which is through His Son, the Lord Jesus Christ. Jesus said, "Narrow is the gate and difficult is the way which leads to life" (Matt. 7:14, page 945). Then He said, "I am the way, the truth, and the life. No one comes to the Father except through Me" (John 14:6, page 1074). He is God's only way to eternal life (Acts 4:12, page 1091).

(1) Christ will come soon to establish righteousness on earth, to judge the wicked, and to inaugurate His millennial (thousand-year) kingdom (Matt. 25:31–46, page 976; Rev. 20:1–10, page 1313).

(2) The lost of all the ages will be cast into the lake of fire, which was prepared for the Devil and his angels (Rev. 20:11–15, page 1313).

(3) The earth, where man dwells, shall burn with such intense fire that the elements themselves will melt. A new world shall be established, clean and ready for its redeemed population (2 Pet. 3:10–13, page 1276).

(4) The saved of all the ages will live forever

(a) on the new earth and in the New Jerusalem, in a world of total righteousness, in which there is no death (Rev. 21:1—22:5, page 1314; cf. Ps. 23:6, page 524);

(b) in a world of sinless happiness and bliss (Rev. 21:4, page 1315; Rev. 22:1–5, page 1315);

(c) in the presence of God and the Lamb, who is Christ (Rev. 21:22–24, page 1315; 22:3–5, page 1316).

See Index, page 17, for your next study.

To turn *one* away from the snares of death.

28 In a multitude of people *is* a king's honor,
But in the lack of people *is* the downfall of a prince.

29 [R]He who *is* slow to wrath has great understanding,   James 1:19
But *he who is* *impulsive exalts folly.

30 A sound heart *is* life to the body,
But envy *is* rottenness to the bones.

31 [R]He who oppresses the poor reproaches [R]his Maker,
But he who honors Him has mercy on the needy.   Matt. 25:40 • [Prov. 22:2]

32 The wicked is banished in his wickedness,
But [R]the righteous has a refuge in his death.   Job 13:15

33 Wisdom rests in the heart of him who has understanding,
But [R]*what is* in the heart of fools is made known.   Prov. 12:16

34 Righteousness exalts a [R]nation,   Prov. 11:11
But sin *is* a reproach to *any* people.

35 [R]The king's favor *is* toward a wise servant,   Matt. 24:45-47
But his wrath *is* against him who causes shame

15

A soft answer turns away wrath,
But a harsh word stirs up anger.

2 The tongue of the wise uses knowledge rightly,
[R]But the mouth of fools pours forth foolishness.   Prov. 12:23

3 [R]The eyes of the LORD *are* in every place,
Keeping watch on the evil and the good.   Job 34:21

4 A wholesome tongue *is* a tree of life,
But perverseness in it breaks the spirit.

5 A fool despises his father's instruction,
But he who receives correction is prudent.

6 *In* the house of the righteous *there is* much treasure,
But in the revenue of the wicked is trouble.

7 The lips of the wise [T]disperse knowledge,   spread
But the heart of the fool *does* not *do* so.

8 [R]The sacrifice of the wicked *is* an abomination to the LORD,

But the prayer of the upright *is* His delight.   Is. 1:11

9 The way of the wicked *is* an abomination to the LORD,
But He loves him who [R]follows righteousness.   Prov. 21:21

10 [R]Harsh discipline *is* for him who forsakes the way,   1 Kin. 22:8
And he who hates correction will die.

11 [R]Hell[T] and [T]Destruction *are* before the LORD;   Job 26:6 • Or *Sheol* • Heb. *Abaddon*
So how much more [R]the hearts of the sons of men.   2 Chr. 6:30

12 [R]A scoffer does not love one who corrects him,   Amos 5:10
Nor will he go to the wise.

13 [R]A merry heart makes a cheerful [T]countenance,   Prov. 12:25 • *face*
But [R]by sorrow of the heart the spirit is broken.   Prov. 17:22

14 The heart of him who has understanding seeks knowledge,
But the mouth of fools feeds on foolishness.

15 All the days of the afflicted *are* evil,
[R]But he who is of a merry heart *has* a continual feast.   Prov. 17:22

16 [R]Better *is* a little with the fear of the LORD,   Ps. 37:16
Than great treasure with trouble.

17 [R]Better *is* a dinner of [T]herbs where love is,   Prov. 17:1 • Or *vegetables*
Than a fatted calf with hatred.

18 [R]A wrathful man stirs up strife,
But *he who is* slow to anger allays contention.   Prov. 26:21

19 [R]The way of the lazy *man is* like a hedge of thorns,   Prov. 22:5
But the way of the upright *is* a highway.

20 A wise son makes a father glad,
But a foolish man despises his mother.

21 [R]Folly *is* joy to him *who is* destitute of [T]discernment,   Prov. 10:23 • *heart*
[R]But a man of understanding walks uprightly.   Eph. 5:15

22 [R]Without counsel, plans go awry,
But in the multitude of counselors they are established.   Prov. 11:14

23 A man has joy by the answer of his mouth,
And a word *spoken* [T]in due season, how good *it is!*   Lit. *in its time*

24 [R]The way of life *winds* upward for the wise,   Phil. 3:20
That he may [R]turn away from [T]hell below.   Prov. 14:16 • Or *Sheol*

14:29 Lit. *short of spirit*

25 ^RThe LORD will destroy the house of the proud,   Prov. 12:7
But ^RHe will establish the boundary of the widow.   Ps. 68:5, 6

26 ^RThe thoughts of the wicked *are* an abomination to the LORD,   Prov. 6:16, 18
But *the words* of the pure *are* pleasant.

27 ^RHe who is greedy for gain troubles his own house,   Is. 5:8
But he who hates bribes will live.

28 The heart of the righteous ^Rstudies how to answer,   1 Pet. 3:15
But the mouth of the wicked pours forth evil.

29 ^RThe LORD *is* far from the wicked,
But ^RHe hears the prayer of the righteous.   Ps. 10:1; 34:16 • Ps. 145:18

30 The light of the eyes rejoices the heart,
And a good report makes the bones ^Thealthy.   Lit. *fat*

31 The ear that hears the rebukes of life Will abide among the wise.

32 He who disdains instruction despises his own soul,
But he who heeds rebuke gets understanding.

33 ^RThe fear of the LORD *is* the instruction of wisdom,   Prov. 1:7
And ^Rbefore honor *is* humility.   Prov. 18:12

16 The ^Rpreparations^T of the heart *belong* to man,   Jer. 10:23 • *plans*
^RBut the answer of the tongue *is* from the LORD.   Matt. 10:19

2 All the ways of a man *are* pure in his own ^Reyes,   Prov. 21:2
But the LORD weighs the spirits.

3 ^RCommit your works to the LORD,   Ps. 37:5
And your thoughts will be established.

4 The LORD has made all for Himself,
^RYes, even the wicked for the day of ^Tdoom.   [Rom. 9:22] • Lit. *evil*

5 ^REveryone proud in heart is an abomination to the LORD;   Prov. 6:17; 8:13
Though they join ^Tforces, none will go unpunished.   Lit. *hand in hand*

6 ^RIn mercy and truth   Dan. 4:27
Atonement is provided for iniquity;
And ^Rby the fear of the LORD *one* departs from evil.   Prov. 8:13; 14:16

7 When a man's ways please the LORD,
He makes even his enemies to be at peace with him.

8 Better *is* a little with righteousness,
Than vast revenues without justice.

9 ^RA man's heart plans his way,   Prov. 19:21
^RBut the LORD directs his steps.   Jer. 10:23

10 Divination *is* on the lips of the king;
His mouth must not transgress in judgment.

11 ^RHonest weights and scales *are* the LORD'S;   Lev. 19:36
All the weights in the bag *are* His ^Twork.   *concern*

12 *It is* an abomination for kings to commit wickedness,
For ^Ra throne is established by righteousness.   Prov. 25:5

13 ^RRighteous lips *are* the delight of kings,
And they love him who speaks *what is* right.   Prov. 14:35

14 As messengers of death *is* the king's wrath,
But a wise man will appease it.

15 In the light of the king's face *is* life,
And his favor *is* like a ^Rcloud of the latter rain.   Zech. 10:1

16 ^RHow much better to get wisdom than gold!   Prov. 8:10, 11, 19
And to get understanding is to be chosen rather than silver.

17 The highway of the upright *is* to depart from evil;
He who keeps his way preserves his soul.

18 Pride *goes* before destruction,
And a haughty spirit before a fall.

19 Better *to be* of a humble spirit with the lowly,
Than to divide the ^Tspoil with the proud.   *plunder*

20 He who heeds the word wisely will find good,
And whoever ^Rtrusts in the LORD, happy *is* he.   Ps. 34:8

21 The wise in heart will be called prudent,
And sweetness of the lips increases learning.

22 Understanding *is* a wellspring of life to him who has it.
But the correction of fools *is* folly.

23 The heart of the wise teaches his mouth,
And adds learning to his lips.

24 Pleasant words *are like* a honeycomb,
Sweetness to the soul and health to the bones.

25 There is a way *that seems* right to a man,
But its end *is* the way of death.

26 The person who labors, labors for himself,
For his *hungry* mouth drives him *on.*

27 An ungodly man digs up evil,
And *it is* on his lips like a burning fire.
28 A perverse man sows strife,
And ᴿa whisperer separates the best of
friends.   Prov. 17:9
29 A violent man entices his neighbor,
And leads him in a way *that is* not
good.
30 He winks his eye to devise perverse
things;
He ᵀpurses his lips *and* brings about
evil.   Lit. *compresses*

31 ᴿThe silver-haired head *is* a crown of
glory,   Prov. 20:29
If it is found in the way of
righteousness.

32 ᴿ*He who is* slow to anger *is* better than
the mighty,   Prov. 14:29; 19:11
And he who rules his spirit than he
who takes a city.

33 The lot is cast into the lap,
But its every decision *is* from the Lᴏʀᴅ.

17 Better *is* ᴿa dry morsel with
quietness,
Than a house full of ᵀfeasting *with*
strife.   Prov. 15:17 • Or *sacrificial meals*

2 A wise servant will rule over ᴿa son
who causes shame,
And will share an inheritance among
the brothers.   Prov. 10:5

3 The refining pot *is* for silver and the
furnace for gold,
ᴿBut the Lᴏʀᴅ tests the hearts.   Jer. 17:10

4 An evildoer gives heed to false lips;
A liar listens eagerly to a ᵀspiteful
tongue.   Lit. *destructive*

5 ᴿHe who mocks the poor reproaches his
Maker;
ᴿHe who is glad at calamity will not go
unpunished.   Prov. 14:31 • Job 31:29

6 ᴿChildren's children *are* the crown of old
men,   [Ps. 127:3; 128:3]
And the glory of children *is* their father.

7 Excellent speech is not becoming to a
fool,
Much less lying lips to a prince.

8 A present *is* a precious stone in the
eyes of its possessor;
Wherever he turns, he prospers.

9 ᴿHe who covers a transgression seeks
love,   [Prov. 10:12]
But ᴿhe who repeats a matter separates
friends.   Prov. 16:28

10 ᴿRebuke is more effective for a wise
man   [Mic. 7:9]
Than a hundred blows on a fool.

11 An evil *man* seeks only rebellion;
Therefore a cruel messenger will be
sent against him.

12 Let a man meet ᴿa bear robbed of her
cubs,
Rather than a fool in his folly.   Hos. 13:8

13 Whoever rewards evil for good,
Evil will not depart from his house.

14 The beginning of strife *is like* releasing
water;
Therefore ᴿstop contention before a
quarrel starts.   [Prov. 20:3]

15 ᴿHe who justifies the wicked, and he
who condemns the just,
Both of them alike *are* an abomination
to the Lᴏʀᴅ.   Ex. 23:7

16 Why *is there* in the hand of a fool the
purchase price of wisdom,
Since *he has* no heart *for it?*

17 ᴿA friend loves at all times,   Ruth 1:16
And a brother is born for adversity.

18 A man devoid of ᵀunderstanding shakes
hands in a pledge,   Lit. *heart*
And becomes surety for his friend.

19 He who loves transgression loves strife,
And ᴿhe who exalts his gate seeks
destruction.   Prov. 16:18

20 He who has a ᵀdeceitful heart finds no
good,
And he who has ᴿa perverse tongue
falls into evil.   *crooked* • James 3:8

21 He who begets a scoffer *does so* to his
sorrow,
And the father of a fool has no joy.

22 A merry heart ᵀdoes good, *like*
medicine,   Or *makes medicine even better*
But a broken spirit dries the bones.

23 A wicked *man* accepts a bribe ᵀbehind
the back   Under cover, lit. *from the bosom*
To pervert the ways of justice.

24 ᴿWisdom *is* in the sight of him who has
understanding,
But the eyes of a fool *are* on the ends
of the earth.   Eccl. 2:14

25 A foolish son *is* a grief to his father,
And bitterness to her who bore him.

26 Also, to punish the righteous *is* not
good,
Nor to strike princes for *their*
uprightness.

27 ᴿHe who has knowledge spares his
words,
And a man of understanding is of a
calm spirit.   James 1:19

28 ᴿEven a fool is counted wise when he
  holds his peace;   Job 13:5
  When he shuts his lips, *he is considered*
  perceptive.

18 A man who isolates himself seeks his
  own desire;
  He rages against all wise judgment.

2 A fool has no delight in understanding,
  But in expressing his own heart.

3 When the wicked comes, contempt
  comes also;
  And with dishonor *comes* reproach.

4 ᴿThe words of a man's mouth *are* deep
  waters;   Prov. 10:11
  ᴿThe wellspring of wisdom *is* a flowing
  brook.   [James 3:17]

5 *It is* not good to show partiality to the
  wicked,
  Or to overthrow the righteous in
  ᴿjudgment.   Prov. 17:15

6 A fool's lips enter into contention,
  And his mouth calls for blows.

7 A fool's mouth *is* his destruction,
  And his lips *are* the snare of his soul.

8 ᴿThe words of a ᵀtalebearer *are* like
  *tasty trifles,   Prov. 12:18 · *gossip* or *slander*
  And they go down into the ᵀinmost
  body.   Lit. *rooms of the belly*

9 He who is slothful in his work
  Is a brother to him who is a great
  destroyer.

10 The name of the Lᴏʀᴅ *is* a strong
   ᴿtower;   2 Sam. 22:2, 3, 33
   The righteous run to it and are safe.

11 The rich man's wealth *is* his strong city,
   And like a high wall in his own esteem.

12 ᴿBefore destruction the heart of a man is
   haughty,   Prov. 15:33; 16:18
   And before honor *is* humility.

13 He who answers a matter before he
   hears *it,*
   It *is* folly and shame to him.

14 The spirit of a man will sustain him in
   sickness,
   But who can bear a broken spirit?

15 The heart of the prudent acquires
   knowledge,
   And the ear of the wise seeks
   knowledge.

16 A man's gift makes room for him,
   And brings him before great men.

17 The first *one* to plead his cause *seems*
   right,
   Until his neighbor comes and examines
   him.

18 Casting ᴿlots causes contentions to
   cease,   [Prov. 16:33]
   And keeps the mighty apart.

19 A brother offended *is harder to win*
   than a strong city,
   And contentions *are* like the bars of a
   castle.

20 ᴿA man's stomach shall be satisfied from
   the fruit of his mouth;   Prov. 12:14; 14:14
   From the produce of his lips he shall be
   filled.

21 ᴿDeath and life *are* in the power of the
   tongue,   Matt. 12:37
   And those who love it will eat its fruit.

22 *He who* finds a wife finds a good *thing,*
   And obtains favor from the Lᴏʀᴅ.

23 The poor *man* uses entreaties,
   But the rich answers roughly.

24 A man *who has* friends *must himself
   be friendly,
   ᴿBut there is a friend *who* sticks closer
   than a brother.   Prov. 17:17

19 Better ᴿ*is* the poor who walks in his
  integrity
  Than *one who is* perverse in his lips,
  and is a fool.   Prov. 28:6

2 Also it is not good *for* a soul *to be*
  without knowledge,
  And he sins who hastens with *his* feet.

3 The foolishness of a man twists his
  way,
  And his heart frets against the Lᴏʀᴅ.

4 ᴿWealth makes many friends,
  But the poor is separated from his
  friend.   Prov. 14:20

5 A false witness will not go unpunished,
  And *he who* speaks lies will not escape.

6 Many entreat the favor of the nobility,
  And every man *is* a friend to one who
  gives gifts.

7 ᴿAll the brothers of the poor hate him;
  How much more do his friends go ᴿfar
  from him!   Prov. 14:20 · Ps. 38:11
  He may pursue *them with* words, *yet*
  they ᵀabandon *him.*   Lit. *are not*

8 He who gets ᵀwisdom loves his own
  soul;
  He who keeps understanding ᴿwill find
  good.   Lit. *heart* · Prov. 16:20

9 A false witness will not go unpunished,
  And *he who* speaks lies shall perish.

10 Luxury is not fitting for a fool,
   Much less ᴿfor a servant to rule over
   princes.   Prov. 30:21, 22

18:8 A Jewish tradition reads *wounds*   18:24 Or *may come to ruin*

11 ^RThe discretion of a man makes him
slow to anger,
^RAnd his glory is to overlook a
transgression.   James 1:19 · Eph. 4:32

12 ^RThe king's wrath is like the roaring of a
lion,   Prov. 16:14
But his favor is like dew on the grass.

13 A foolish son is the ruin of his father,
^RAnd the contentions of a wife are a
continual ^Tdripping.   Prov. 21:9, 19 · Irritation

14 ^RHouses and riches are an inheritance
from fathers,   2 Cor. 12:14
But a prudent wife is from the LORD.

15 Laziness casts one into a deep sleep,
And an idle person will suffer hunger.

16 ^RHe who keeps the commandment keeps
his soul,
But he who *is careless of his ways will
die.   Luke 10:28; 11:28

17 ^RHe who has pity on the poor lends to
the LORD,
And He will pay back what he has
given.   [2 Cor. 9:6–8]

18 ^RChasten your son while there is hope,
And do not set your heart *on his
destruction.   Prov. 13:24

19 A man of great wrath will suffer
punishment;
For if you rescue him, you will have to
do it again.

20 Listen to counsel and receive
instruction,
That you may be wise ^Rin your latter
days.   Ps. 37:37

21 There are many plans in a man's heart,
^RNevertheless the LORD's counsel—that
will stand.   Heb. 6:17

22 What is desired in a man is kindness,
And a poor man is better than a liar.

23 ^RThe fear of the LORD leads to life,
And he who has it will abide in
satisfaction;   [1 Tim. 4:8]
He will not be visited with evil.

24 ^RA lazy man buries his hand in the
*bowl,
And will not so much as bring it to his
mouth again.   Prov. 15:19

25 Strike a scoffer, and the simple ^Rwill
become wary;   Deut. 13:11
^RRebuke one who has understanding,
and he will discern knowledge. Prov. 9:8

26 He who mistreats his father and chases
away his mother
Is ^Ra son who causes shame and brings
reproach.   Prov. 17:2

27 Cease listening to instruction, my son,
And you will stray from the words of
knowledge.

28 A ^Tdisreputable witness scorns justice,
And the mouth of the wicked devours
iniquity.   Lit. witness of Belial, worthless witness

29 Judgments are prepared for scoffers,
And beatings for the backs of fools.

20 Wine ^Ris a mocker,   Gen. 9:21
Strong drink is a brawler,
And whoever is led astray by it is not
wise.

2 The *wrath of a king is like the roaring
of a lion;
Whoever provokes him to anger sins
against his own life.

3 ^RIt is honorable for a man to stop
striving,   Prov. 17:14
Since any fool can start a quarrel.

4 ^RThe lazy man will not plow because of
winter;   Prov. 10:4
^RHe will beg during harvest and have
nothing.   Prov. 19:15

5 Counsel in the heart of man is like deep
water,
But a man of understanding will draw it
out.

6 Most men will proclaim each his own
^Tgoodness,   Lit. mercy
But who can find a faithful man?

7 ^RThe righteous man walks in his
integrity;   2 Cor. 1:12
His children are blessed after him.

8 A king who sits on the throne of
judgment
Scatters all evil with his eyes.

9 ^RWho can say, "I have made my heart
clean,   [1 Kin. 8:46]
I am pure from my sin"?

10 ^RDiverse weights and diverse measures,
They are both alike, an abomination to
the LORD.   Deut. 25:13

11 Even a child is ^Rknown by his deeds,
Whether what he does is pure and
right.   Matt. 7:16

12 The hearing ear and the seeing eye,
The LORD has made them both.

13 ^RDo not love sleep, lest you come to
poverty;   Rom. 12:11

19:16 Is reckless, lit. despises
19:18 Lit. to put him to death, a Jewish tradition reads
on his crying
19:24 LXX, Syr. bosom; Tg., Vg. armpit

20:2 Lit. fear or terror, produced by the king's wrath

Open your eyes, *and* you will be satisfied with bread.

14 "*It is* ᵀgood for nothing," cries the buyer;
But when he has gone his way, then he boasts. Lit. *evil, evil*

15 There is gold and a multitude of rubies,
But ᴿthe lips of knowledge *are* a precious jewel. [Prov. 3:13–15]

16 ᴿTake the garment of one who is surety *for* a stranger, Prov. 22:26
And hold it as a pledge *when it* is for a seductress.

17 ᴿBread gained by deceit *is* sweet to a man, Prov. 9:17
But afterward his mouth will be filled with gravel.

18 ᴿPlans are established by counsel; Prov. 24:6
ᴿBy wise counsel wage war. Luke 14:31

19 ᴿHe who goes about *as* a talebearer reveals secrets; Prov. 11:13
Therefore do not associate with one ᴿwho flatters with his lips. Rom. 16:18

20 ᴿWhoever curses his father or his mother, Matt. 15:4
ᴿHis lamp will be put out in deep darkness. Job 18:5, 6

21 ᴿAn inheritance gained hastily at the beginning Prov. 28:20
Will not be blessed at the end.

22 ᴿDo not say, "I will ᵀrecompense evil";
ᴿWait for the LORD, and He will save you. [Rom. 12:17–19] · *repay* · 2 Sam. 16:12

23 Diverse weights *are* an abomination to the LORD,
And dishonest scales *are* not good.

24 A man's steps *are* of the LORD;
How then can a man understand his own way?

25 *It is* a snare for a man to devote rashly *something as* holy,
And afterward to reconsider *his* vows.

26 ᴿA wise king sifts out the wicked,
And brings the threshing wheel over them. Ps. 101:8

27 ᴿThe spirit of a man *is* the lamp of the LORD, 1 Cor. 2:11
Searching all the ᵀinner depths of his heart. Lit. *rooms of the belly*

28 ᴿMercy and truth preserve the king,
And by ᵀlovingkindness he upholds his throne. Prov. 21:21 · *mercy*

29 The glory of young men *is* their strength,

And ᴿthe splendor of old men *is* their gray head. Prov. 16:31

30 Blows that hurt cleanse away evil,
As *do* stripes the ᵀinner depths of the heart. Lit. *rooms of the belly*

21 The king's heart *is* in the hand of the LORD,
Like the ᵀrivers of water; channels
He turns it wherever He wishes.

2 ᴿEvery way of a man *is* right in his own eyes, Prov. 16:2
ᴿBut the LORD weighs the hearts. Prov. 24:12

3 ᴿTo do righteousness and justice
Is more acceptable to the LORD than sacrifice. 1 Sam. 15:22

4 ᴿA haughty look, a proud heart, Prov. 6:17
And the *plowing of the wicked *are* sin.

5 ᴿThe plans of the diligent *lead* surely to plenty, Prov. 10:4
But *those of* everyone *who is* hasty, surely to poverty.

6 ᴿGetting treasures by a lying tongue
*Is the fleeting fantasy of those who seek death. 2 Pet. 2:3

7 The violence of the wicked will ᵀdestroy them, Lit. *drag them away*
Because they refuse to do justice.

8 *The way of a guilty man *is* perverse;
But *as for* the pure, his work *is* right.

9 Better to dwell in a corner of a housetop,
Than in a house shared with ᴿa contentious woman. Prov. 19:13

10 The soul of the wicked desires evil;
His neighbor finds no favor in his eyes.

11 When the scoffer is punished, the simple is made wise;
But when the ᴿwise is instructed, he receives knowledge. Prov. 19:25

12 The righteous God wisely considers the house of the wicked,
Overthrowing the wicked for *their* wickedness.

13 ᴿWhoever shuts his ears to the cry of the poor [Matt. 7:2; 18:30–34]
Will also cry himself and not be heard.

21:4 Or *lamp*
21:6 LXX *Pursue vanity on the snares of death;* Vg. *Is vain and foolish, and shall stumble on the snares of death;* Tg. *They shall be destroyed, and they shall fall who seek death*
21:8 Or *The way of a man is perverse and strange*

14 A gift in secret pacifies anger,
And a bribe [T]behind the back, strong
wrath.   Under cover, lit. *in the bosom*

15 *It is* a joy for the just to do justice,
But destruction *will come* to the
workers of iniquity.

16 A man who wanders from the way of
understanding
Will rest in the assembly of the dead.

17 He who loves pleasure *will be* a poor
man;
He who loves wine and oil will not be
rich.

18 The wicked *shall be* a ransom for the
righteous,
And the unfaithful for the upright.

19 Better to dwell [T]in the wilderness,
Than with a contentious and angry
woman.   Lit. *in the land of the desert*

20 [R]*There is* desirable treasure,   Ps. 112:3
And oil in the dwelling of the wise,
But a foolish man squanders it.

21 [R]He who follows righteousness and
mercy   Matt. 5:6
Finds life, righteousness and honor.

22 A [R]wise *man* [T]scales the city of the
mighty,   Prov. 24:5 · Climbs over the walls of
And brings down the trusted
stronghold.

23 [R]Whoever guards his mouth and tongue
Keeps his soul from troubles.   [James 3:2]

24 A proud *and* haughty *man*—
"Scoffer" *is* his name;
He acts with arrogant pride.

25 The [R]desire of the lazy *man* kills him,
For his hands refuse to labor.   Prov. 13:4
26 He covets greedily all day long,
But the righteous [R]gives and does not
spare.   [Prov. 22:9]

27 [R]The sacrifice of the wicked *is* an
abomination;   Jer. 6:20
How much more *when* he brings it with
wicked intent!

28 A false witness shall perish,
But the man who hears *him* will speak
endlessly.

29 A wicked man hardens his face,
But *as for* the upright, he *establishes
his way.

30 [R]*There is* no wisdom or understanding
Or counsel against the LORD.   [Jer. 9:23, 24]

21:29 Qr., LXX *understands*

31 The horse *is* prepared for the day of
battle,
But [R]deliverance *is* of the LORD.   Ps. 3:8

22 A [R]good name is to be chosen rather
than great riches,   Eccl. 7:1
Loving favor rather than silver and
gold.

2 The [R]rich and the poor have this in
common,   Prov. 29:13
The LORD *is* the maker of them all.

3 A prudent *man* foresees evil and hides
himself,
But the simple pass on and are
[R]punished.   Prov. 27:12

4 By humility *and* the fear of the LORD
Are riches and honor and life.

5 Thorns *and* snares *are* in the way of
the perverse;
He who guards his soul will be far from
them.

6 [R]Train up a child in the way he should
go,   Eph. 6:4
[T]And when he is old he will not depart
from it.   *Even*

7 The [R]rich rules over the poor,
And the borrower *is* servant to the
lender.   James 2:6

8 He who sows iniquity will reap
[R]sorrow,[T]   Job 4:8 · *trouble*
And the rod of his anger will fail.

9 [R]He who has a [T]generous eye will be
[R]blessed,   2 Cor. 9:6 · Lit. *good* · [Prov. 19:17]
For he gives of his bread to the poor.

10 [R]Cast out the scoffer, and contention
will leave;   Ps. 101:5
Yes, strife and reproach will cease.

11 [R]He who loves purity of heart   Ps. 101:6
And has grace on his lips,
The king *will be* his friend.

12 The eyes of the LORD preserve
knowledge,
But He overthrows the words of the
faithless.

13 [R]The lazy *man* says, "There *is* a lion
outside!   Prov. 26:13
I shall be slain in the streets!"

14 [R]The mouth of an immoral woman *is* a
deep pit;   Prov. 2:16; 5:3; 7:5
[R]He who is abhorred by the LORD will
fall there.   Eccl. 7:26

15 Foolishness *is* bound up in the heart of
a child;
[R]The rod of correction will drive it far
from him.   Prov. 13:24; 23:13, 14

16 He who oppresses the poor to increase
   his *riches*,
   And he who gives to the rich, *will*
   surely *come* to poverty.

Sayings of the Wise

17 Incline your ear and hear the words of
   the wise,
   And apply your heart to my knowledge;
18 For *it is* a pleasant thing if you keep
   them within you;
   Let them all be fixed upon your lips,
19 So that your trust may be in the LORD;
   I have instructed you today, even you.
20 Have I not written to you excellent
   things
   Of counsels and knowledge,
21 That I may make you know the
   certainty of the words of truth,
   That you may answer words of truth
   To those who ᵀsend to you?   Or *send you*

22 Do not rob the ᴿpoor because he *is*
   poor,   Ex. 23:6
   Nor oppress the afflicted at the gate;
23 ᴿFor the LORD will plead their cause,
   And plunder the soul of those who
   plunder them.   1 Sam. 24:12

24 Make no friendship with an angry man,
   And with a furious man do not go,
25 Lest you learn his ways
   And set a snare for your soul.

26 ᴿDo not be one of those who ᵀshakes
   hands in a pledge,   Prov. 11:15 · Lit. *strikes*
   One of those who is surety for debts;
27 If you have nothing *with which* to pay,
   Why should he take away your bed
   from under you?

28 Do not remove the ancient ᵀlandmark
   Which your fathers have set.   *boundary*

29 Do you see a man *who* ᵀexcels in his
   work?   *is prompt in his business*
   He will stand before kings;
   He will not stand before ᵀunknown
   men.   *obscure*

23

When you sit down to eat with a
   ruler,
   Consider carefully what *is* before you;
2 And put a knife to your throat
   If you *are* a man given to appetite.
3 Do not desire his delicacies,
   For they *are* deceptive food.

4 ᴿDo not overwork to be rich;
   ᴿBecause of your own understanding,
   cease!   1 Tim. 6:9, 10 · Rom. 12:16
5 Will you set your eyes on that which is
   not?
   For *riches* certainly make themselves
   wings;
   They fly away like an eagle *toward*
   heaven.

6 Do not eat the bread of ᴿa* miser,
   Nor desire his delicacies;   Deut. 15:9

26-A. Think like a Dynamic Servant of ▼
God

7 For as he thinks in his heart, so *is* he.
   "Eat and drink!" ᴿhe says to you,
   But his heart is not with you.   Prov. 12:2 ▲
8 The morsel you have eaten, you will
   vomit up,
   And waste your pleasant words.

9 ᴿDo not speak in the hearing of a fool,
   For he will despise the wisdom of your
   words.   Matt. 7:6
10 Do not remove the ancient landmark,
   Nor enter the fields of the fatherless;
11 ᴿFor their Redeemer *is* mighty; Prov. 22:23
   He will plead their cause against you.

12 Apply your heart to instruction,
   And your ears to words of knowledge.
13 ᴿDo not withhold correction from a
   child,   Prov. 13:24
   For *if* you beat him with a rod, he will
   not die.
14 You shall beat him with a rod,
   And deliver his soul from ᵀhell.   Or *Sheol*

15 My son, if your heart is wise,
   My heart will rejoice—indeed, I myself;
16 Yes, my inmost being will rejoice
   When your lips speak right things.

17 ᴿDo not let your heart envy sinners,
   But ᴿ*be zealous* for the fear of the LORD
   all the day;   Ps. 37:1 · Prov. 28:14
18 For surely there is a ᵀhereafter,   Future
   And your hope will not be cut off.

19 Hear, my son, and be wise;
   And guide your heart in the way.
20 ᴿDo not mix with winebibbers,   Is. 5:22
   Or with gluttonous eaters of meat;
21 For the drunkard and the glutton will
   come to poverty,

23:6 Lit. *one who has an evil eye*

26-A. Think like a Dynamic Servant of God (Proverbs 23:7)—A dynamic servant of God thinks by faith, not
by fear. Fear says, "God can't," but faith says, "God can." Fear doubts God's Word, but faith believes every
word of God. Fear leads to certain defeat, but faith leads to sure victory. Faith believes God's promise: "I will
never leave you nor forsake you," so that we may boldly say, "The LORD is my helper; I will not fear. What
can man do to me?" (Heb. 13:5, 6, page 1252; Deut. 31:1–8, page 209). Believers do not think as unbelievers
think. Believers are justified by faith; therefore they live and walk by faith, because, as dynamic servants of
(Point 26-A continued on next page)

And drowsiness will clothe *a man* with
rags.

22 [R]Listen to your father who begot you,
And do not despise your mother when
she is old.   Prov. 1:8

23 [R]Buy the truth, and do not sell *it*,
Also wisdom and instruction and
understanding.   Matt. 13:44

24 [R]The father of the righteous will greatly
rejoice,   Prov. 10:1
And he who begets a wise *child* will
delight in him.

25 Let your father and your mother be
glad,
And let her who bore you rejoice.

26 My son, give me your heart,
And let your eyes observe my ways.

27 [R]For a harlot *is* a deep pit,   Prov. 22:14
And a seductress *is* a narrow well.

28 [R]She also lies in wait as *for* a victim,
And increases the unfaithful among
men.   Prov. 7:12

29 [R]Who has woe?   Is. 5:11, 22
Who has sorrow?
Who has contentions?
Who has complaints?
Who has wounds without cause?
Who [R]has redness of eyes?   Gen. 49:12

30 Those who linger long at the wine,
Those who go in search of mixed wine.

31 Do not look on the wine when it is red,
When it sparkles in the cup,
When it swirls around smoothly;

32 At the last it bites like a serpent,
And stings like a viper.

33 Your eyes will see strange things,
And your heart will utter perverse
things.

34 Yes, you will be like one who lies down
in the [T]midst of the sea,   Lit. *heart*
Or like one who lies at the top of the
mast, *saying*:

35 "They[R] have struck me, *but* I was not
hurt;   Jer. 5:3
They have beaten me, but I did not feel
it.
When shall [R]I awake, that I may seek
another *drink*?"   Eph. 4:19

24 Do not be [R]envious of evil men,
Nor desire to be with them;   Ps. 1:1; 37:1

2 For their heart devises violence,
And their lips talk of troublemaking.

3 Through wisdom a house is built,
And by understanding it is established;

4 By knowledge the rooms are filled
With all precious and pleasant riches.

5 [R]A wise man *is* strong,   Prov. 21:22
Yes, a man of knowledge increases
strength;

6 [R]For by wise counsel you will wage your
own war,   Luke 14:31
And in a multitude of counselors *there*
is safety.

7 [R]Wisdom *is* too lofty for a fool;   Ps. 10:5
He does not open his mouth in the
gate.

8 He who [R]plots to do evil   Rom. 1:30
Will be called a schemer.

9 The devising of foolishness *is* sin,
And the scoffer *is* an abomination to
men.

10 *If* you [R]faint in the day of adversity,
Your strength *is* small.   Heb. 12:3

11 [R]Deliver *those who* are drawn toward
death,   Ps. 82:4
And hold back *those* stumbling to the
slaughter.

12 If you say, "Surely we did not know
this,"
Does not [R]He who weighs the hearts
consider *it*?   Prov. 21:2
He who keeps your soul, does He *not*
know *it*?

(Point 26-A continued from previous page)
God, they think by faith. They know that if they draw back from this life of faith, the Lord will be displeased
(Heb. 10:38, 39, page 1247). For "without faith it is impossible to please Him" (Heb. 11:6, page 1247).

(1) A dynamic servant of God thinks by faith and is thus victorious over this world system (1 John 5:5,
page 1282), because he is not in love with the things of this world (1 John 2:15–17, page 1279).

(2) A dynamic servant of God thinks by faith and can sing with David, "The LORD is my light and my
salvation; whom shall I fear? The LORD is the strength of my life; of whom shall I be afraid?" (Ps. 27:1–5, page
525).

(3) A dynamic servant of God thinks by faith and boldly evangelizes without fear of man (Phil. 1:12–14,
page 1195).

(4) A dynamic servant of God thinks in terms of God's power, and not of his own weakness (Acts 1:8,
page 1086).

(5) A dynamic servant of God thinks thoughts of forgiveness, not of guilt (Eph. 1:7, page 1186).

(6) A dynamic servant of God thinks thoughts of love, not of hate (1 John 4:7–11, page 1280).

(7) A dynamic servant of God thinks, "I can," not "I can't." He thinks like the apostle Paul, who said, "I
can do all things through Christ who strengthens me" (Phil. 4:13, page 1198).

(8) A dynamic servant of God is unafraid of natural weakness, because God says, "My strength is made
perfect in weakness" (2 Cor. 12:9, page 1175).

See Romans 12:3, page 1142, for **Point 26-B: You Are What You Think.**

And will He *not* render to *each* man
Raccording to his deeds?   Ps. 62:12

13 My son, Reat honey because *it is* good,
And the honeycomb *which is* sweet to
your taste;   Song 5:1
14 RSo *shall* the knowledge of wisdom *be* to
your soul;   Ps. 19:10; 58:11
If you have found *it*, there is a
Tprospect,   Lit. *latter end*
And your hope will not be cut off.

15 Do not lie in wait, O wicked *man*,
against the dwelling of the righteous;
Do not plunder his resting place;
16 RFor a righteous *man* may fall seven
times   [Mic. 7:8]
And rise again,
But the wicked shall fall by calamity.

17 RDo not rejoice when your enemy falls,
And do not let your heart be glad when
he stumbles;   Obad. 12
18 Lest the LORD see *it*, and Tit displease
Him,   Lit. *it is evil in His eyes*
And He turn away His wrath from him.

19 RDo not fret because of evildoers,
Nor be envious of the wicked;   Ps. 37:1
20 For there will be no prospect for the
evil *man*;
The lamp of the wicked will be put out.

21 My son, Rfear the LORD and the king;
Do not associate with those given to
change;   [1 Pet. 2:17]
22 For their calamity will rise suddenly,
And who knows the ruin those two can
bring?

Further Sayings of the Wise

23 These *things* also *belong* to the wise:

It is not good to Tshow partiality in
judgment.   Lit. *recognize faces*
24 RHe who says to the wicked, "You *are*
righteous,"   Is. 5:23
Him the people will curse;
Nations will abhor him.
25 But those who rebuke *the wicked* will
have Rdelight,   Prov. 28:23
And a good blessing will come upon
them.

26 He who gives a right answer kisses the
lips.

27 RPrepare your outside work,   Prov. 27:23-27
Make it fit for yourself in the field;
And afterward build your house.

28 RDo not be a witness against your
neighbor without cause,   Eph. 4:25
*For would you deceive with your lips?

24:28 LXX, Vg. *Do not deceive*

29 RDo not say, "I will do to him just as he
has done to me;   [Prov. 20:22]
I will render to the man according to
his work."

30 I went by the field of the lazy *man*,
And by the vineyard of the man devoid
of understanding;
31 And there it was, Rall overgrown with
thorns;   Gen. 3:18
Its surface was covered with nettles;
Its stone wall was broken down.
32 When I saw *it*, I considered *it* well;
I looked on *it and* received instruction:
33 RA little sleep, a little slumber,   Prov. 6:9, 10
A little folding of the hands to rest;
34 So shall your poverty come *like* Ta
prowler,   Lit. *one who walks about*
And your need like an armed man.

Further Wise Sayings of Solomon

25 TheseR also *are* proverbs of Solomon
which the men of Hezekiah king of
Judah copied: 1 Kin. 4:32

2 RIt is the glory of God to conceal a
matter,
But the glory of kings *is* to search out a
matter.   Deut. 29:29

3 As the heavens for height and the earth
for depth,
So the heart of kings *is* unsearchable.

4 RTake away the dross from silver,
And it will go to the silversmith *for*
jewelry.   2 Tim. 2:21
5 Take away the wicked from before the
king,
And his throne will be established in
Rrighteousness.   Prov. 16:12; 20:8

6 Do not exalt yourself in the presence of
the king,
And do not stand in the place of the
great;
7 RFor *it is* better that he say to you,
"Come up here,"
Than that you should be put lower in
the presence of the prince,
Whom your eyes have seen.   Luke 14:7-11

8 Do not go hastily to Tcourt;
For what will you do in the end,
When your neighbor has put you to
shame?   Lit. *contend* or *bring a lawsuit*
9 RDebate your case with your neighbor,
And do not disclose the secret to
another;   [Matt. 18:15]
10 Lest he who hears *it* expose your
shame,
And your reputation be ruined.

11 A word fitly Rspoken *is like* apples of
gold
In settings of silver.   Prov. 15:23

12 *Like* an earring of gold and an
    ornament of fine gold
    Is a wise rebuker to an obedient ear.

13 ᴿLike the cold of snow in time of harvest
    Is a faithful messenger to those who
    send him,   Prov. 13:17
    For he refreshes the soul of his masters.

14 ᴿWhoever falsely boasts of giving Prov. 20:6
    Is like clouds and wind without rain.

15 ᴿBy long forbearance a ruler is
    persuaded,   Prov. 15:1
    And a gentle tongue breaks a bone.

16 Have you found honey?
    Eat only as much as you need,
    Lest you be filled with it and vomit.

17 Seldom set foot in your neighbor's
    house,
    Lest he become weary of you and hate
    you.

18 ᴿA man who bears false witness against
    his neighbor
    Is like a club, a sword, and a sharp
    arrow.   Ps. 57:4

19 Confidence in an unfaithful *man* in
    time of trouble
    Is like a bad tooth and a foot out of
    joint.

20 *Like* one who takes away a garment in
    cold weather,
    And like vinegar on soda,
    Is one who ᴿsings songs to a heavy
    heart.   Dan. 6:18

21 ᴿIf your enemy is hungry, give him
    bread to eat;
    And if he is thirsty, give him water to
    drink;   Rom. 12:20
22 For *so* you will heap coals of fire on his
    head,
    And the Lᴏʀᴅ will reward you.

23 The north wind brings forth rain,
    And ᴿa backbiting tongue an angry
    countenance.   Ps. 101:5

24 ᴿ*It is* better to dwell in a corner of a
    housetop,
    Than in a house shared with a
    contentious woman.   Prov. 19:13

25 *As* cold water to a weary soul,
    So *is* good news from a far country.

26 A righteous *man* who falters before the
    wicked
    Is like a murky spring and a ᵀpolluted
    well.   ruined

27 *It is* not good to eat much honey;
    So to seek one's own glory *is not* glory.

28 ᴿWhoever *has* no rule over his own
    spirit

Is like a city broken down, without
    walls.   Prov. 16:32

26 As snow in summer and rain in
    harvest,
    So honor is not fitting for a fool.

2 Like a flitting sparrow, like a flying
    swallow,
    So ᴿa curse without cause shall not
    alight.   Deut. 23:5

3 ᴿA whip for the horse,   Ps. 32:9
    A bridle for the donkey,
    And a rod for the fool's back.

4 Do not answer a fool according to his
    folly,
    Lest you also be like him.

5 Answer a fool according to his folly,
    Lest he be wise in his own eyes.

6 He who sends a message by the hand of
    a fool
    Cuts off *his own* feet *and* drinks
    violence.

7 *Like* the legs of the lame that hang
    limp
    Is a proverb in the mouth of fools.

8 Like one who binds a stone in a sling
    Is he who gives honor to a fool.

9 *Like* a thorn *that* goes into the hand of
    a drunkard
    Is a proverb in the mouth of fools.

10 *The great *God* who formed everything
    Gives the fool *his* hire and the
    transgressor *his* wages.

11 As a dog returns to his own vomit,
    ᴿSo a fool repeats his folly.   Ex. 8:15
12 ᴿDo you see a man wise in his own eyes?
    There is more hope for a fool than for
    him.   [Rev. 3:17]

13 The lazy *man* says, "*There is* a lion in
    the road!
    A fierce lion *is* in the ᵀstreets!"   square
14 As a door turns on its hinges,
    So *does* the lazy *man* on his bed.
15 The ᴿlazy *man* buries his hand in the
    *bowl;   Prov. 19:24
    It wearies him to bring it back to his
    mouth.
16 The lazy *man is* wiser in his own eyes
    Than seven men who can answer
    sensibly.

17 He who passes by *and* meddles in a
    quarrel not his own
    Is like one who takes a dog by the ears.

18 Like a madman who throws firebrands,
    arrows, and death,
19 *Is* the man *who* deceives his neighbor,
    And says, ᴿ"I was only joking!"   Eph. 5:4

26:10 Heb. difficult in v. 10; ancient and modern
translators differ greatly
26:15 LXX, Syr. *bosom;* Tg., Vg. *armpit*

20 Where *there is* no wood, the fire goes out;
And where *there is* no ^Ttalebearer, strife ceases.   *gossip, lit. whisperer*
21 ^RAs charcoal *is* to burning coals, and wood to fire,   Prov. 15:18
So *is* a contentious man to kindle strife.
22 The words of a ^Ttalebearer *are* like tasty *trifles,   gossip, lit. whisperer*
And they go down into the inmost body.

23 Fervent lips with a wicked heart
Are like earthenware covered with silver dross.

24 He who hates, disguises *it* with his lips,
And lays up deceit within himself;
25 ^RWhen ^The speaks kindly, do not believe him,   Ps. 28:3 • *Lit. his voice is gracious*
For *there are* seven abominations in his heart;
26 *Though his* hatred is covered by deceit,
His wickedness will be revealed before the assembly.

27 ^RWhoever digs a pit will fall into it,
And he who rolls a stone will have it roll back on him.   Ps. 7:15

28 A lying tongue hates *those who are* crushed by it,
And a flattering mouth works ruin.

27 Do^R not boast about tomorrow,
For you do not know what a day may bring forth.   James 14:13–16

2 ^RLet another man praise you, and not your own mouth;   Prov. 25:27
A stranger, and not your own lips.

3 A stone *is* heavy and sand *is* weighty,
But a fool's wrath *is* heavier than both of them.

4 Wrath *is* cruel and anger a torrent,
But ^Rwho *is* able to stand before jealousy?   1 John 3:12

5 ^ROpen rebuke *is* better   [Prov. 28:23]
Than love carefully concealed.

6 Faithful *are* the wounds of a friend,
But the kisses of an enemy *are* ^Rdeceitful.   Matt. 26:49

7 A satisfied soul ^Tloathes the honeycomb,
But to a hungry soul every bitter thing *is* sweet.   *Lit. tramples on*

8 Like a bird that wanders from its nest
Is a man who wanders from his place.

9 Ointment and perfume delight the heart,

And the sweetness of a man's friend *gives delight* by hearty counsel.

10 Do not forsake your own friend or your father's friend,
Nor go to your brother's house in the day of your calamity;
^RBetter *is* a neighbor nearby than a brother far away.   Prov. 17:17; 18:24

11 My son, be wise, and make my heart glad,
^RThat I may answer him who reproaches me.   Prov. 10:1; 23:15–26

12 A prudent *man* foresees evil *and* hides himself;
The simple pass on *and* are punished.

13 Take the garment of him who is surety for a stranger,
And hold it in pledge *when* he is surety for a seductress.

14 He who blesses his friend with a loud voice, rising early in the morning,
It will be counted a curse to him.

15 A ^Rcontinual dripping on a very rainy day   Prov. 19:13
And a contentious woman are alike;
16 Whoever ^Trestrains her restrains the wind,   *hides*
And grasps oil with his right hand.

17 *As* iron sharpens iron,
So a man sharpens the countenance of his friend.

18 ^RWhoever ^Tkeeps the fig tree will eat its fruit;   [1 Cor. 3:8; 9:7–13] • *protects or tends*
So he who waits on his master will be honored.

19 As in water face *reflects* face,
So a man's heart *reveals* the man.

20 *Hell and *Destruction are never full;
So the eyes of man are never satisfied.

21 ^RThe refining pot *is* for silver and the furnace for gold,   Prov. 17:3
And a man *is valued* by what others say of him.

22 ^RThough you grind a fool in a mortar with a pestle along with crushed grain,   Jer. 5:3
Yet his foolishness will not depart from him.

23 Be diligent to know the state of your ^Rflocks,   Prov. 24:27
And attend to your herds;
24 For riches *are* not forever,
Nor does a crown *endure* to all generations.

26:22 A Jewish tradition reads *wounds*

27:20 Or *Sheol* • Heb. *Abaddon*

25 RWhen the hay is removed, and the
    tender grass shows itself,
  And the herbs of the mountains are
    gathered in,   Ps. 104:14
26 The lambs *will provide* your clothing,
  And the goats the price of a field;
27 *You shall have* enough goats' milk for
    your food,
  For the food of your household,
  And the nourishment of your
    maidservants.

28 The wicked flee when no one
      pursues,
  But the righteous are bold as a lion.

2 Because of the transgression of a land,
    many *are* its princes;
  But by a man of understanding *and*
    knowledge
  Right will be prolonged.

3 RA poor man who oppresses the poor
  Is like a driving rain Twhich leaves no
    food.   Matt. 18:28 · Lit. *and there is no bread*

4 RThose who forsake the law praise the
    wicked,
  RBut such as keep the law contend with
    them.   Ps. 49:18 · 1 Kin. 18:18

5 REvil men do not understand justice,
  But Rthose who seek the LORD
    understand all.   Ps. 92:6 · John 17:17

6 Better *is* the poor who walks in his
    integrity
  Than one perverse *in his* ways, though
    he *be* rich.

7 Whoever keeps the law *is* a discerning
    son,
  But a companion of gluttons shames his
    father.

8 One who increases his possessions by
    usury and extortion
  Gathers it for him who will pity the
    poor.

9 One who turns away his ear from
    hearing the law,
  Even his prayer *is* an abomination.

10 RWhoever causes the upright to go
    astray in an evil way,   Prov. 26:27
  He himself will fall into his own pit;
  But the blameless will inherit good.

11 The rich man *is* wise in his own eyes,
  But the poor who has understanding
    searches him out.

12 When the righteous rejoice, *there is*
    great Rglory;   Prov. 11:10; 29:2
  But when the wicked arise, men Thide
    themselves.   Lit. *will be searched for*

13 RHe who covers his sins will not prosper,
  But whoever confesses and forsakes
    them will have mercy.   Ps. 32:3-5

14 Happy *is* the man who is always
    reverent,
  But he who hardens his heart will fall
    into calamity.

15 *Like* a roaring lion and a charging bear
  Is a wicked ruler over poor people.

16 A ruler who lacks understanding *is* a
    great Roppressor,
  But he who hates covetousness will
    prolong *his* days.   Eccl. 10:16

17 RA man burdened with bloodshed will
    flee into a pit;
  Let no one help him.   Gen. 9:6

18 Whoever walks blamelessly will be
    Tsaved,
  But *he who is* perverse *in his* ways will
    suddenly fall.   *delivered*

19 RHe who tills his land will have plenty of
    bread,
  But he who follows frivolity will have
    poverty enough!   Prov. 12:11; 20:13

20 A faithful man will abound with
    blessings,
  RBut he who hastens to be rich will not
    go unpunished.   1 Tim. 6:9

21 To Tshow partiality *is* not good,
  RBecause for a piece of bread a man will
    transgress.   Lit. *recognize faces* · Ezek. 13:19

22 A man with an evil eye hastens after
    riches,
  And does not consider that Rpoverty
    will come upon him.   Prov. 21:5

23 RHe who rebukes a man will find more
    favor afterward   Prov. 27:5, 6
  Than he who flatters with the tongue.

24 Whoever robs his father or his mother,
  And says, "*It is* no transgression,"
  The same *is* companion to a destroyer.

25 RHe who is of a proud heart stirs up
    strife,
  RBut he who trusts in the LORD will be
    prospered.   Prov. 13:10 · 1 Tim. 6:6

26 He who Rtrusts in his own heart is a
    fool,
  But whoever walks wisely will be
    delivered.   Prov. 3:5

27 RHe who gives to the poor will not lack,
  But he who hides his eyes will have
    many curses.   Deut. 15:7

28 When the wicked arise, Rmen hide
    themselves;
  But when they perish, the righteous
    increase.   Job 24:4

29 HeR who is often rebuked, *and*
      hardens *his* neck,
  Will suddenly be destroyed, and that
    without remedy.   2 Chr. 36:16

2 When the righteous ᵀare in authority,
   the people rejoice;   *become great*
   But when a wicked *man* rules, ᴿthe
   people groan.   Esth. 4:3

3 Whoever loves wisdom makes his
   father rejoice,
   But a companion of harlots wastes *his*
   wealth.

4 The king establishes the land by justice,
   But he who receives bribes overthrows
   it.

5 A man who ᴿflatters his neighbor
   Spreads a net for his feet.   Prov. 26:28

6 By transgression an evil man is snared,
   But the righteous sings and rejoices.

7 The righteous ᴿconsiders the cause of
   the poor,
   But the wicked does not understand
   such knowledge.   Job 29:16

8 Scoffers ᴿset a city aflame,   Prov. 11:11
   But wise *men* turn away wrath.

9 *If* a wise man contends with a foolish
   man,
   ᴿWhether *the fool* rages or laughs, *there*
   is no peace.   Matt. 11:17

10 The bloodthirsty hate the blameless,
    But the upright seek his well-being.

11 A fool vents all his ᵀfeelings,   Lit. *spirit*
    But a wise *man* holds them back.

12 If a ruler pays attention to lies,
    All his servants *become* wicked.

13 The poor *man* and the oppressor have
    this in common:
    ᴿThe Lᴏʀᴅ gives light to the eyes of
    both.   [Matt. 5:45]

14 The king who judges the ᴿpoor with
    truth,   Is. 11:4
    His throne will be established forever.

15 The rod and rebuke give ᴿwisdom,
    But a child left *to himself* brings shame
    to his mother.   Prov. 22:15

16 When the wicked are multiplied,
    transgression increases;
    But the righteous will see their fall.

17 Correct your son, and he will give you
    rest;
    Yes, he will give delight to your soul.

45-B. Noah: A Man of Vision   ▼

18 Where *there is* no ᵀrevelation, the
    people cast off restraint;   *prophetic vision*
    But happy *is* he who keeps the law.   ▲

19 A servant will not be corrected by mere
    words;
    For though he understands, he will not
    respond.

20 Do you see a man hasty in his words?
    ᴿ*There is* more hope for a fool than for
    him.   Prov. 26:12

21 He who pampers his servant from
    childhood
    Will have him as a son in the end.

22 ᴿAn angry man stirs up strife,
    And a furious man abounds in
    transgression.   Prov. 26:21

23 ᴿA man's pride will bring him low,
    But the humble in spirit will retain
    honor.   Is. 66:2

24 Whoever is a partner with a thief hates
    his own life;
    He ᵀswears to tell the truth, but reveals
    nothing.   Lit. *hears the adjuration* or *oath*

25 ᴿThe fear of man brings a snare,
    But whoever trusts in the Lᴏʀᴅ shall be
    ᵀsafe.   Gen. 12:12; 20:2 • *secure*, lit. *set on high*

26 ᴿMany seek the ruler's ᵀfavor,

45-B. Noah: A Man of Vision (Proverbs 29:18)—"Where there is no revelation, the people cast off restraint" (v. 18). As a consequence, people fall apart; they lose all consciousness of righteousness. They go to pieces spiritually and morally. The last verse in the book of Judges illustrates: "In those days there was no king in Israel; everyone did what was right in his own eyes" (Judg. 21:25, page 263). The Lord is saying, as it were, "Where there is no vision (revelation) of God in all His love, power, and glory, the people perish, fall apart, and turn to spiritual anarchy." Jesus said, "But as the days of Noah were, so also will the coming of the Son of Man be" (Matt. 24:36–39, page 974).

At the second coming of Christ, history will repeat itself. Noah's family is a type of the body of Christ—those who have found grace in the eyes of the Lord. Those who drowned in the Flood were comparable in that day to those who will have heard and rejected the gospel of salvation in the day to come. Without a vision of God in His coming glory, they will perish.

Noah was a man of vision. The word "vision" is not found in the Bible until Genesis 15:1 (page 20); yet it is found over a hundred times in the remaining Scriptures. It suggests a supernatural experience; it is something or someone seen other than by natural sight (Acts 16:8–10, page 1110). Noah had a vision of the grace of God; he found grace and knew it. How did he know? By faith. Noah had a vision of God's plans for the ark. For 120 years he was true to that vision. He worked on the ark and walked with God. He had a supernatural vision of the unseen that was more real than anything seen with his natural vision (2 Cor. 4:18, page 1168).

See 2 Peter 2:5, page 1274, for **Point 45-C: Noah: A Preacher of Righteousness.**

But justice for man *comes* from the
LORD.   Ps. 20:9 • Lit. *face*

27 An unjust man *is* an abomination to
the righteous,
And *he who is* upright in the way *is* an
abomination to the wicked.

The Wisdom of Agur

30 The words of Agur the son of Jakeh,
his utterance. This man declared to
Ithiel—to Ithiel and Ucal:

2 ᴿSurely I *am* more stupid than *any* man,
And do not have the understanding of a
man.   Ps. 73:22
3 I neither learned wisdom
Nor have knowledge of the Holy One.

4 ᴿWho has ascended into heaven, or
descended?   [John 3:13]
ᴿWho has gathered the wind in His fists?
Who has bound the waters in a
garment?   Job 38:4
Who has established all the ends of the
earth?
What *is* His name, and what *is* His
Son's name,
If you know?

5 ᴿEvery word of God *is* ᵀpure;
He *is* a shield to those who put their
trust in Him.   Ps. 12:6 • *tested, refined*
6 ᴿDo not add to His words,
Lest He rebuke you, and you be found
a liar.   Deut. 4:2; 12:32

7 Two *things* I request of You
(Deprive me not before I die):
8 Remove falsehood and lies far from me;
Give me neither poverty nor riches—
Feed me with the food alloted to me;
9 ᴿLest I be full and deny *You,*
And say, "Who *is* the LORD?"   Deut. 8:12-14
Or lest I be poor and steal,
And profane the name of my God.

10 Do not malign a servant to his master,
Lest he curse you, and you be found
guilty.

11 *There is* a generation *that* curses its
ᴿfather,
And does not bless its mother.   Ex. 21:17
12 *There is* a generation ᴿ*that* is pure in its
own eyes,   Luke 18:11
Yet is not washed from its filthiness.
13 *There is* a generation—oh, how ᴿlofty
are their eyes!   Prov. 6:17
And their eyelids are lifted up.
14 ᴿ*There is* a generation whose teeth *are*
like swords,   Job 29:17
And whose fangs *are like* knives,
ᴿTo devour the poor from off the earth,
And the needy from *among* men.   Amos 8:4

15 The leech has two daughters—
Give *and* Give!

There are three *things that* are never
satisfied,
Four never say, "Enough!":
16 ᴿTheᵀ grave,   Prov. 27:20 • Or *Sheol*
The barren womb,
The earth *that* is not satisfied with
water—
And the fire never says, "Enough!"

17 ᴿThe eye *that* mocks *his* father,   Gen. 9:22
And scorns obedience to *his* mother,
The ravens of the valley will pick it out,
And the young eagles will eat it.

18 There are three *things which* are too
wonderful for me,
Yes, four *which* I do not understand:
19 The way of an eagle in the air,
The way of a serpent on a rock,
The way of a ship in the ᵀmidst of the
sea,   Lit. *heart*
And the way of a man with a virgin.

20 This *is* the way of an adulterous
woman:
She eats and wipes her mouth,
And says, "I have done no wickedness."

21 For three *things* the earth is perturbed,
Yes, for four it cannot bear up:
22 ᴿFor a servant when he reigns,   Prov. 19:10
A fool when he is filled with food,
23 A ᵀhateful *woman* when she is married,
And a maidservant who succeeds her
mistress.   Or *hated*

24 There are four *things which* are little
on the earth,
But they *are* exceedingly wise:
25 ᴿThe ants *are* a people not strong,
Yet they prepare their food in the
summer;   Prov. 6:6
26 The *rock badgers are a feeble folk,
Yet they make their homes in the
crags;
27 The locusts have no king,
Yet they all advance in ranks;
28 The ᵀspider skillfully grasps with its
hands,
And it is in kings' palaces.   Or *lizard*

29 There are three *things which* are
majestic in pace,
Yes, four *which* are stately in walk:
30 A lion, *which is* mighty among beasts
And does not turn away from any;
31 A ᵀgreyhound,   Exact identity unknown
A male goat also,
And *a king *whose* troops *are* with
him.

32 If you have been foolish in exalting
yourself,

30:26 *rock hyraxes*
30:31 A Jewish tradition reads *a king against whom there
is no uprising*

Or if you have devised evil, ^R*put your*
hand on *your* mouth.   Mic. 7:16
33 For *as* the churning of milk produces
butter,
And wringing the nose produces blood,
So the forcing of wrath produces strife.

The Words of King Lemuel's Mother

31 The words of King Lemuel, the utterance which his mother taught him:

2 What, my son?
And what, son of my womb?
And what, ^Rson of my vows?   Is. 49:15
3 ^RDo not give your strength to women,
Nor your ways ^Rto that which destroys
kings.   Prov. 5:9 • Deut. 17:17

4 ^R*It is* not for kings, O Lemuel,   Eccl. 10:17
It is not for kings to drink wine,
Nor for princes intoxicating drink;
5 ^RLest they drink and forget the law,
And pervert the justice of all ^Tthe
afflicted.   Hos. 4:11 • Lit. *sons of affliction*
6 ^RGive strong drink to him who is
perishing,
And wine to those who are bitter of
heart.   Ps. 104:15
7 Let him drink and forget his poverty,
And remember his misery no more.

8 ^ROpen your mouth for the speechless,
In the cause of all *who are* ^Tappointed
to die.   Job 29:15, 16 • Lit. *sons of passing away*
9 Open your mouth, ^Rjudge righteously,
And ^Rplead the cause of the poor and
needy.   Lev. 19:15 • Jer. 22:16

The Virtuous Wife

10 ^RWho* can find *a virtuous wife? Prov. 12:4
For her worth *is* far above rubies.
11 The heart of her husband safely trusts
her;
So he will have no lack of gain.
12 She does him good and not evil
All the days of her life.
13 She seeks wool and flax,
And willingly works with her hands.

31:10 Vv. 10–31 are an alphabetic acrostic in Hebrew cf.
Ps. 119 • Lit. *a wife of valor,* in the sense of all forms of
excellence

14 She is like the merchant ships,
She brings her food from afar.
15 She also rises while it is yet night,
And provides food for her household,
And a portion for her maidservants.
16 She considers a field and buys it;
From her profits she plants a vineyard.
17 She girds herself with strength,
And strengthens her arms.
18 She perceives that her merchandise *is*
good,
And her lamp does not go out by night.
19 She stretches out her hands to the
distaff,
And her hand holds the spindle.
20 ^RShe extends her hand to the poor,
Yes, she reaches out her hands to the
needy.   Eph. 4:28
21 She is not afraid of snow for her
household,
For all her household *is* clothed with
scarlet.
22 She makes tapestry for herself;
Her clothing *is* fine linen and purple.
23 ^RHer husband is known in the gates,
When he sits among the elders of the
land.   Prov. 12:4
24 She makes linen garments and sells
them,
And supplies sashes for the merchants.
25 Strength and honor *are* her clothing;
She shall rejoice in time to come.
26 She opens her mouth with wisdom,
And on her tongue *is* the law of
kindness.
27 She watches over the ways of her
household,
And does not eat the bread of idleness.
28 Her children rise up and call her
blessed;
Her husband *also,* and he praises her:
29 "Many daughters have done well,
But you excel them all."
30 Charm *is* deceitful and beauty *is*
passing,
But a woman *who* fears the Lord, she
shall be praised.
31 Give her of the fruit of her hands,
And let her own works praise her in the
gates.

THE BOOK OF
Ecclesiastes

AUTHORSHIP AND CONTEXT. Although the author's name is not given in the book, sufficient evidence is found in the text to indicate clearly that King Solomon wrote the book of Ecclesiastes. In the first verse the writer refers to himself as "the son of David, king in Jerusalem," and in 1:12 he says that he "was king over Israel in Jerusalem."

After the death of King David, his father, Solomon became king in Israel and reigned forty years (1 Kin. 11:42; 2 Chr. 9:30) until his death, around 970 B.C. He implies in the book that at the time of writing he had ceased the behavior that had characterized the latter part of his reign, so the book is dated sometime just before 970 B.C.

Solomon, a young man hardly twenty years of age when he ascended the throne in Jerusalem, rose to great heights of prominence and popularity. In answer to prayer God gave him remarkable wisdom that made him a great counselor not only to the common man but even to kings. Outstanding among the many notable achievements of this wise man were the building of the temple and an enormous personal palace, and the writing of three thousand proverbs and more than one thousand songs (1 Kin. 4:32).

As much as we would like to remember Solomon for his virtues, we must be aware of his vices. Lust and the love of luxury caused him to turn away from the Lord to "many foreign women" (1 Kin. 11:1) and to idolatry (1 Kin. 11:4, 5). His rejection of the Lord's counsel brought God's chastening judgment upon his kingdom. Soon after his death, chaos, rebellion, and the division of the kingdom resulted.

HOW ECCLESIASTES FITS INTO THE BIBLE. The Bible is a progressive unfolding of the truth, and Ecclesiastes is a vital link in the chain of truth. Under divine inspiration the writer takes a position of human reasoning and shows the "vanity" (emptiness, futility, folly) of such a position. The entire book is a confession of the vanity of man's life when God is left out. Solomon, the Preacher (1:1), delivers the message that life is not worth living when it is lived without God.

SUMMARY STATEMENT. A self-centered and worldly life is "vanity;" nothing "under the sun" (man's natural life apart from God) can bring satisfaction to the human heart.

KEY WORD, PHRASE, AND VERSE. The key word in the book is *vanity*. The key phrase is "under the sun." The key verse is 1:3— "What profit has a man from all his labor in which he toils under the sun?"

HOW ECCLESIASTES FITS TOGETHER. Ecclesiastes may be divided into three parts: (1) The subject stated—the vanity of life without God (1:1-3); (2) the subject substantiated—evidence supporting his claim of the vanity of life without God (1:4—10:20); and (3) the subject summarized (11:1—12:14). In this third and final part of the book the writer gives an encouragement to faith (11:1-6), an entreaty to remember that the end of life is coming and to rejoice in the opportunities and blessings of life (11:7—12:7), and an exhortation to obedience, by fearing God and keeping His commandments (12:8-14).

All truth is not given in a single book of the Bible. The apostle Paul tells us that the Holy Spirit teaches us by "comparing spiritual things with spiritual" (1 Cor. 2:13). In our quest for wisdom and understanding, therefore, we are to compare Scripture with Scripture.

Ecclesiastes should be interpreted in the light of the New Testament. One should not linger in the twilight, but move on to the greater light of revelation in the New Testament where the message of Solomon is expounded in a clearer and broader way. However, there is a time in many people's lives when Ecclesiastes is the only book that seems to make sense.

According to Solomon the wise thing to do in this empty and unsatisfying world—where disappointment, trouble, and death are unavoidable—is to yield to the providence of God and enjoy the blessings of life now. The Lord Jesus said, "One's life does not consist in the abundance of the things he possesses" (Luke 12:15). He admonishes us, "Seek first the kingdom of God and His righteousness" instead (Matt. 6:33), and promises us a full and satisfying life: "I have come that they may have life, and that they may have it more abundantly" (John 10:10).

Solomon tells us that everything "under the sun" (i.e., apart from God) is vain. In contrast, Paul tells us that our labor "is not in vain in the Lord" (1 Cor. 15:58). The reason why our labor is not in vain in the Lord is that we have the wonderful promise, the blessed hope, of Christ's

coming—and the assurance of His eternal presence. "Therefore comfort one another with these words," says Paul (1 Thess. 4:18).

Without God life is indeed vain; but in Christ life is a satisfying victory.

—S.W.

The Vanity of Life

THE words of the Preacher, the son of David, ^Rking in Jerusalem.   Prov. 1:1

2 "Vanity* of vanities," says the Preacher;
   "Vanity of vanities, all is vanity."

3 What profit has a man from all his
    labor
   In which he ^Ttoils under the sun?   labors
4 One generation passes away, and
    another generation comes;
   ^RBut the earth abides forever.   Ps. 104:5
5 ^RThe sun also rises, and the sun goes
    down,
   And ^Thastens to the place where it
    arose.   Ps. 19:4-6 • Is eager for, lit. panting
6 ^RThe wind goes toward the south,
   And turns around to the north;
   The wind whirls about continually,
   And comes again on its circuit.   John 3:8
7 ^RAll the rivers run into the sea,
   Yet the sea is not full;
   To the place from which the rivers
    come,
   There they return again.   [Jer. 5:22]
8 All things are ^Tfull of labor;   wearisome
   Man cannot express it.
   ^RThe eye is not satisfied with seeing,
   Nor the ear filled with hearing.   Prov. 27:20
9 ^RThat which has been is what will be,
   That which is done is what will be
    done,
   And there is nothing new under the
    sun.   Eccl. 3:15
10 Is there anything of which it may be
    said,
   "See, this is new"?
   It has already been in ancient times
    before us.
11 There is ^Rno remembrance of former
    things,
   Nor will there be any remembrance of
    things that are to come
   By those who will come after.   Eccl. 2:16

The Grief of Wisdom

12 I, the Preacher, was king over Israel in Jerusalem.
13 And I set my heart to seek and ^Rsearch out by wisdom concerning all that is done under heaven; this burdensome task God has

given to the sons of man, by which they may be ^Texercised.   [Eccl. 7:25; 8:16, 17] • Or afflicted
14 I have seen all the works that are done under the sun; and indeed, all is vanity and grasping for the wind.

15 ^RWhat is crooked cannot be made
    straight,
   And what is lacking cannot be
    numbered.   Eccl. 7:13

16 I communed with my heart, saying, "Look, I have attained greatness, and have gained more wisdom than all who were before me in Jerusalem. My heart has understood great wisdom and knowledge."
17 And I set my heart to know wisdom and to know madness and folly. I perceived that this also is grasping for the wind.

18 For ^Rin much wisdom is much grief,
   And he who increases knowledge
    increases sorrow.   Eccl. 12:12

The Vanity of Pleasure

2 I said in my heart, "Come now, I will test you with mirth; therefore enjoy pleasure"; but surely, this also was vanity.
2 I said of laughter—"Madness!"; and of mirth, "What does it accomplish?"
3 I searched in my heart how ^Tto gratify my flesh with wine, while guiding my heart with wisdom, and how to lay hold on folly, till I might see what was ^Rgood for the sons of men to do under heaven all the days of their lives.   Lit. to draw my flesh • [Eccl. 3:12, 13; 5:18; 6:12]
4 I made my works great, I built myself houses, and planted myself vineyards.
5 I made myself gardens and orchards, and I planted all kinds of fruit trees in them.
6 I made myself water pools from which to ^Twater the growing trees of the grove.   irrigate
7 I acquired male and female servants, and had servants born in my house. Yes, I had greater possessions of herds and flocks than all who were in Jerusalem before me.
8 ^RI also gathered for myself silver and gold and the special treasures of kings and of the provinces. I acquired male and female singers, the delights of the sons of men, and *musical instruments of all kinds.   1 Kin. 9:28
9 So I became great and excelled more than all who were before me in Jerusalem. Also my wisdom remained with me.
10 Whatever my eyes desired I did not
    keep from them.

1:2 Or Absurdity, Frustration, Futility, Nonsense; and so throughout the book

2:8 Exact meaning unknown

I did not withhold my heart from any
  pleasure,
For my heart rejoiced in all my labor;
And ^Rthis was my ^Treward from all my
  labor.   Eccl. 3:22; 5:18; 9:9 · Lit. *portion*
11 Then I looked on all the works that my
  hands had done
And on the labor in which I had toiled;
And indeed all *was* ^Rvanity and
  grasping for the wind.   Eccl. 1:3, 14
There was no profit under the sun.

The End of the Wise and the Fool

12 Then I turned myself to consider
  wisdom ^Rand madness and folly;
For what *can* the man *do* who succeeds
  the king?—   Eccl. 1:17; 7:25
Only what he has already ^Rdone.   Eccl. 1:9
13 Then I saw that wisdom ^Rexcels folly
As light excels darkness.   Eccl. 7:11, 14, 19
14 ^RThe wise man's eyes *are* in his head,
But the fool walks in darkness.
Yet I myself perceived
That ^Rthe same event happens to them
  all.   Prov. 17:24 · Ps. 49:10
15 So I said in my heart,
"As it happens to the fool,
It also happens to me,
And why was I then more wise?"
Then I said in my heart,
"This also *is* vanity."
16 For *there is* ^Rno more remembrance of
  the wise than of the fool forever,
Since all that now *is* will be forgotten
  in the days to come.
And how does a wise *man* die?
As the fool!   Eccl. 1:11; 4:16

17 Therefore I hated life because the work
that was done under the sun *was* distressing
to me, for all *is* vanity and grasping for the
wind.
18 Then I hated all my labor in which I had
toiled under the sun, because ^RI must leave it
to the man who will come after me.   Ps. 49:10
19 And who knows whether he will be wise
or a fool? Yet he will rule over all my labor in
which I toiled and in which I have shown
myself wise under the sun. This also *is* vanity.
20 Therefore I turned my heart and despaired of all the labor in which I had toiled
under the sun.
21 For there is a man whose labor *is* with
wisdom, knowledge, and skill; yet he must
leave his ^Theritage to a man who has not
labored for it. This also *is* vanity and a great
evil.   Lit. *portion*
22 ^RFor what has man for all his labor, and
for the striving of his heart with which he has
toiled under the sun?   Eccl. 1:3; 3:9
23 For all his days *are* ^Rsorrowful, and his
work burdensome; even in the night his heart
takes no rest. This also *is* vanity.   Job 5:7; 14:1

24 Nothing *is* better for a man *than* that he
should eat and drink, and *that* his soul should
enjoy good in his labor. This also, I saw, was
from the hand of God.
25 For who can eat, or who can have enjoyment, *more than I?
26 For *God* gives ^Rwisdom and knowledge
and joy to a man who *is* good in His sight; but
to the sinner He gives the work of gathering
and collecting, that ^Rhe may give to *him who*
is good before God. This also *is* vanity and
grasping for the wind.   Prov. 2:6 · Prov. 28:8

Everything Has Its Time

3 To everything *there is* a season,
  A ^Rtime for every purpose under
  heaven: Eccl. 3:17; 8:6
2 A time ^Tto be born,   Lit. *to bear*
And ^Ra time to die;   Heb. 9:27
A time to plant,
And a time to pluck *what is* planted;
3 A time to kill,
And a time to heal;
A time to break down,
And a time to build up;
4 A time to ^Rweep,
And a time to laugh;
A time to mourn,
And a time to dance;   Rom. 12:15
5 A time to cast away stones,
And a time to gather stones;
^RA time to embrace,
And a time to refrain from
  embracing;   Joel 2:16
6 A time to gain,
And a time to lose;
A time to keep,
And a time to throw away;
7 A time to tear,
And a time to sew;
^RA time to keep silence,   Amos 5:13
And a time to ^Rspeak;   Prov. 25:11
8 A time to love,
And a time to ^Rhate;
A time of war,
And a time of peace.   Luke 14:26

The God-Given Task

9 ^RWhat profit has the worker from that in
which he labors?   Eccl. 1:3
10 I have seen the God-given task with
which the sons of men are to be occupied.
11 He has made everything beautiful in its
time. Also He has put eternity in their hearts,
except that no one can find out the work that
God does from beginning to end.
12 I know that nothing *is* better for them
than to rejoice, and to do good in their lives,
13 and also that ^Revery man should eat and
drink and enjoy the good of all his labor—it *is*
the gift of God.   Eccl. 2:24

2:25 So with MT, Tg., Vg.; some Heb. mss., LXX, Syr.
without Him

14 I know that whatever God does,
It shall be forever.
^RNothing can be added to it,
And nothing taken from it.
God does *it*, that men should fear
before Him.   James 1:17
15 ^RThat which is has already been,
And what is to be has already been;
And God ^Trequires an account of ^Twhat
is past.   Eccl. 1:9 · Lit. *seeks · what is pursued*

Injustice Seems to Prevail

16 Moreover ^RI saw under the sun: Eccl. 5:8

In the place of ^Tjudgment,   *justice*
Wickedness *was* there;
And *in* the place of righteousness,
^TIniquity *was* there.   *Wickedness*

17 I said in my heart,

^R"God shall judge the righteous and the
wicked,   [Rom. 2:6–10]
For *there is* a time there for every
^Tpurpose and for every work."   *desire*

18 I said in my heart, "Concerning the
condition of the sons of men, God tests them,
that they may see that they themselves are
like animals."
19 ^RFor what happens to the sons of men
also happens to animals; one thing befalls
them: as one dies, so dies the other. Surely,
they all have one breath; man has no advan-
tage over animals, for all is vanity.   [Eccl. 2:16]
20 All go to one place: ^Rall are from the
dust, and all return to dust.   Gen. 3:19
21 *Who knows the spirit of the sons of
men, which goes upward, and the spirit of the
animal, which goes down to the earth?
22 So I perceived that nothing *is* better
than that a man should rejoice in his own
works, for that *is* his heritage. For who can
bring him to see what will happen after him?

4 Then I returned and considered all the
^Roppression that is done under the sun:

And look! The tears of the oppressed,
But they have no comforter—
^TOn the side of their oppressors *there is*
power,   Eccl. 3:16; 5:8 · Lit. *At the hand*
But they have no comforter.
2 ^RTherefore I praised the dead who were
already dead,   Job 3:17, 18
More than the living who are still alive.
3 ^RYet, better than both *is* he who has
never existed,
Who has not seen the evil work that is
done under the sun.   Job 3:11–22

The Vanity of Selfish Toil

4 Again, I saw that for all toil and every
skillful work a man is envied by his neighbor.

3:21 LXX, Syr., Tg., Vg. *Who knows whether the spirit
. . . goes upward, and whether . . . goes downward to
the earth?*

This also *is* vanity and grasping for the wind.

5 ^RThe fool folds his hands   Prov. 6:10; 24:33
And consumes his own flesh.
6 Better a handful *with* quietness
Than both hands full, *together with* toil
and grasping for the wind.

7 Then I returned, and I saw vanity under
the sun:

8 There is one alone, without companion:
He has neither son nor brother.
Yet *there is* no end to all his labors,
Nor is his ^Reye satisfied with riches.
But ^Rhe never asks,   [1 John 2:16] · Ps. 39:6
"For whom do I toil and deprive myself
of ^Rgood?"   Eccl. 2:18–21
This also *is* vanity and a ^Tgrave
misfortune.   Lit. *evil task*

The Value of a Friend

9 Two *are* better than one,
Because they have a good reward for
their labor.
10 For if they fall, one will lift up his
companion.
But woe to him *who is* alone when he
falls,
For *he has* no one to help him up.
11 Again, if two lie down together, they
will keep warm;
But how can one be warm *alone?*
12 Though one may be overpowered by
another, two can withstand him.
And a threefold cord is not quickly
broken.

Popularity Passes Away

13 Better a poor and wise youth
Than an old and foolish king who will
be admonished no more.
14 For he comes out of prison to be king,
Although ^The was born poor in his
kingdom.   *The youth*
15 I saw all the living who walk under the
sun;
They were with the second youth who
stands in his place.
16 *There was* no end of all the people over
whom he was made king;
Yet those who come afterward will not
rejoice in him.
Surely this also *is* vanity and grasping
for the wind.

Fear God, Keep Your Vows

5 Walk ^Rprudently when you go to the
house of God; and draw near to hear
rather than to give the sacrifice of fools, for
they do not know that they do evil.   Ex. 3:5

2 Do not be ^Rrash with your mouth,
And let not your heart utter anything
hastily before God.   Prov. 20:25
For God *is* in heaven, and you on earth;
Therefore let your words be few.

3 For a dream comes through much
　　activity,
　　And ᴿa fool's voice *is known by his*
　　many words.　　　　　　Prov. 10:19

4 ᴿWhen you make a vow to God, do not
　　delay to ᴿpay it;　　Num. 30:2 • Ps. 66:13, 14
　　For *He* has no pleasure in fools.
　　Pay what you have vowed—
5 ᴿBetter not to vow than to vow and not
　　pay.　　　　　　　　　　　　　Acts 5:4

6 Do not let your ᴿmouth cause your flesh
to sin, ᴿnor say before the messenger *of God*
that it *was* an error. Why should God be
angry at your ᵀexcuse and destroy the work
of your hands?　　　Prov. 6:2 • 1 Cor. 11:10 • Lit. *voice*
7 For in the multitude of dreams and many
words *there is* also vanity. But fear God.

The Vanity of Gain and Honor

8 If you ᴿsee the oppression of the poor,
and the violent ᵀperversion of justice and
righteousness in a province, do not marvel at
the matter; for ᴿhigh official watches over
high official, and higher officials are over
them.　　　　Eccl. 3:16 • *wresting* • [Ps. 12:5; 58:11; 82:1]
9 Moreover the profit of the land is for all;
even the king is served from the field.

10 He who loves silver will not be satisfied
　　with silver;
　　Nor he who loves abundance, with
　　　increase.
　　This also *is* vanity.

11 When goods increase,
　　They increase who eat them;
　　So what profit have the owners
　　Except to see *them* with their eyes?

12 The sleep of a laboring man *is* sweet,
　　Whether he eats little or much;
　　But the abundance of the rich will not
　　　permit him to sleep.

13 ᴿThere is a severe evil *which* I have seen
　　under the sun:　　　　　　　Eccl. 6:1, 2
　　Riches kept for their owner to his hurt.
14 But those riches perish through
　　ᵀmisfortune;
　　When he begets a son, *there is* nothing
　　　in his hand.　　　　　　Lit. *bad business*
15 ᴿAs he came from his mother's womb,
　　naked shall he return,　　　　1 Tim. 6:7
　　To go as he came;
　　And he shall take nothing from his
　　　labor
　　Which he may carry away in his hand.

16 And this also *is* a severe evil—
　　Just exactly as he came, so shall he go.
　　And what profit has he ᴿwho has
　　　labored for the wind?　　　Prov. 11:29
17 All his days ᴿhe also eats in darkness,
　　And *he has* much sorrow and sickness
　　and anger.　　　　　　　　Ps. 127:2

18 Here is what I have seen: *It is* good and
fitting *for one* to eat and drink, and to enjoy
the good of all his labor in which he toils
under the sun all the days of his life which
God gives him; for it *is* his heritage.
19 As for every man to whom God has
given riches and wealth, and given him
power to eat of it, to receive his heritage and
rejoice in his labor—this *is* the gift of God.
20 For he will not dwell unduly on the days
of his life, because God keeps *him* busy with
the joy of his heart.

6 There is an evil which I have seen under
the sun, and it *is* common among men:
2 A man to whom God has given riches
and wealth and honor, ᴿso that he lacks
nothing for himself of all he desires; ᴿyet God
does not give him power to eat of it, but a
foreigner consumes it. This *is* vanity, and it *is*
an evil ᵀaffliction.　　Job 21:10 • Luke 12:20 • *disease*
3 If a man begets a hundred *children* and
lives many years, so that the days of his years
are many, but his soul is not satisfied with
goodness, or indeed he has no burial, I say
that a stillborn child *is* better than he—
4 for it comes in vanity and departs in
darkness, and its name is covered with darkness.
5 Though it has not seen the sun or known
anything, this has more rest than that man,
6 even if he lives a thousand years twice—
but has not seen goodness. Do not all go to
one ᴿplace?　　　　　　　　Eccl. 2:14, 15

7 All the labor of man *is* for his mouth,
　　And yet the soul is not satisfied.
8 For what more has the wise *man* than
　　the fool?
　　What does the poor man have,
　　Who knows *how* to walk before the
　　　living?
9 Better *is* ᵀthe ᴿsight of the eyes than
　　the wandering of ᵀdesire.
　　This also *is* vanity and grasping for the
　　wind.　　　　What the eyes see • Eccl. 11:9 • Lit. *soul*

10 Whatever one is, he has been named
　　ᴿalready,　　　　　　　Eccl. 1:9; 3:15
　　For it is known that he *is* man;
　　ᴿAnd he cannot contend with Him who
　　　is mightier than he.　　　　Job 9:32
11 Since there are many things that
　　increase vanity,
　　How *is* man the better?

12 For who knows what *is* good for man in
life, all the days of his vain life which he
passes like a shadow? Who can tell a man
what will happen after him under the sun?

The Value of Practical Wisdom

7 A good ᴿname *is* better than precious
ointment,
And the day of death than the day of
one's ᴿbirth;　　　Prov. 15:30; 22:1 • Eccl. 4:2

2 Better to go to the house of mourning
Than to go to the house of feasting,
For that is the end of all men;
And the living will take it to heart.
3 ᵀSorrow is better than laughter,
ᴿFor by a sad countenance the heart is
made better.   Vexation or Grief · [2 Cor. 7:10]
4 The heart of the wise is in the house of
mourning,
But the heart of fools is in the house of
mirth.

5 ᴿIt is better to ᵀhear the rebuke of the
wise
Than for a man to hear the song of
fools.   Ps. 141:5 · listen to
6 ᴿFor like the ᵀcrackling of thorns under
a pot,
So is the laughter of the fool.
This also is vanity.   Eccl. 2:2 · Lit. sound
7 Surely oppression destroys a wise man's
reason,
And a bribe ᵀdebases the heart.   destroys

8 The end of a thing is better than its
beginning;
ᴿThe patient in spirit is better than the
proud in spirit.   Prov. 14:29
9 ᴿDo not hasten in your spirit to be
angry,   James 1:19
For anger rests in the bosom of fools.
10 Do not say,
"Why were the former days better than
these?"
For you do not inquire wisely
concerning this.

11 Wisdom is good with an inheritance,
And profitable ᴿto those who see the
sun.   Eccl. 11:7
12 For wisdom is ᵀa defense as money is a
defense,   A protective shade, lit. shadow
But the ᵀexcellence of knowledge is
that wisdom gives ᴿlife to those who
have it.   advantage or profit · Prov. 3:18

13 Consider the work of God;
For ᴿwho can make straight what He
has made crooked?   Job 12:14
14 ᴿIn the day of prosperity be joyful,
But in the day of adversity consider:
Surely God has appointed the one ᵀas
well as the other,
So that man can find out nothing that
will come after him.   Deut. 28:47 · alongside

15 I have seen everything in my days of
vanity:
ᴿThere is a just man who perishes in his
righteousness,   Eccl. 8:12-14

And there is a wicked man who
prolongs life in his wickedness.

16 ᴿDo not be overly righteous,
ᴿNor be overly wise: Prov. 25:16 · Rom. 12:3
Why should you destroy yourself?
17 Do not be overly wicked,
Nor be foolish:
Why should you die before your time?
18 It is good that you grasp this,
And also not remove your hand from
the other;
For he who fears God will ᵀescape them
all.   Lit. come forth from all of them

19 ᴿWisdom strengthens the wise   Prov. 21:22
More than ten rulers of the city.
20 ᴿFor there is not a just man on earth
who does good
And does not sin.   1 John 1:8

21 Also do not take to heart everything
people say,
Lest you hear your servant cursing you.
22 For many times, also, your own heart
has known
That even you have cursed others.

23 All this I have ᵀproved by wisdom.
ᴿI said, "I will be wise";
But it was far from me.   tested · Rom. 1:22
24 ᴿAs for that which is far off and
ᴿexceedingly deep,
Who can find it out?   1 Tim. 6:16 · Rom. 11:33
25 ᴿI applied my heart to know,   Eccl. 1:17
To search and seek out wisdom and the
reason of things,
To know the wickedness of folly,
Even of foolishness and madness.
26 ᴿAnd I find more bitter than death
The woman whose heart is snares and
nets,   Prov. 5:3, 4
Whose hands are fetters.
ᵀHe who pleases God shall escape from
her,   Lit. He who is good before God
But the sinner shall be trapped by her.

27 "Here is what I have found," says ᴿthe
Preacher,
"Adding one thing to the other to find
out the reason,   Eccl. 1:1, 2
28 Which my soul still seeks but I cannot
find:
ᴿOne man among a thousand I have
found,
But a woman among all these I have
not found.   Job 33:23

14-E. What Are the Various States of Man with God?   ▼

29 Truly, this only I have found:
ᴿThat God made man upright,

14-E. What Are the Various States of Man with God? (Ecclesiastes 7:29)—"Truly, this only I have found: that
God made man upright, but they [men and women] have sought out many schemes [for evil intent]" (v. 29).
(Point 14-E continued on next page)

But ᴿthey have sought out many
schemes." Gen. 1:27 • Gen. 3:6, 7

8 Who *is* like a wise *man?*
And who knows the interpretation of a
thing?
ᴿA man's wisdom makes his face shine,
And ᴿthe ᵀsternness of his face is
changed. Acts 6:15 • Deut. 28:50 • Lit. *strength*

Obey Authorities for God's Sake

2 I *say,* "Keep the king's commandment
for the sake of your oath to God.
3 "Do not be hasty to go from his presence. Do not take your stand for an evil
thing, for he does whatever pleases him."

4 Where the word of a king *is, there is*
power;
And ᴿwho may say to him, "What are
you doing?" Job 34:18
5 He who keeps his command will
experience nothing harmful;
And a wise man's heart ᵀdiscerns both
time and judgment, Lit. *knows*
6 Because ᴿfor every matter there is a
time and judgment,
Though the misery of man ᵀincreases
greatly. Eccl. 3:1, 17 • *is great upon him*
7 ᴿFor he does not know what will
happen; Eccl. 6:12
So who can tell him when it will occur?
8 ᴿNo one has power over the spirit to
retain the spirit, Ps. 49:6, 7
And no one has power in the day of
death.
There is ᴿno release from that war,
And wickedness will not deliver those
who are given to it. Deut. 20:5-8

9 All this I have seen, and applied my
heart to every work that is done under the
sun: *There is* a time in which one man rules
over another to his own hurt.

Death Comes to All

10 Then I saw the wicked buried, who had
come and gone from the place of holiness,
and they were *forgotten in the city where
they had so done. This also *is* vanity.
11 ᴿBecause the sentence against an evil
work is not executed speedily, therefore the
heart of the sons of men is fully set in them to
do evil. Is. 26:10
12 Though a sinner does evil a hundred
times, and his *days* are prolonged, yet I
surely know that ᴿit will be well with those
who fear God, who fear before Him. [Is. 3:10]
13 But it will not be well with the wicked;
nor will he prolong *his* days, *which are* as a
shadow, because he does not fear before God.
14 There is a vanity which occurs on earth,
that there are just *men* to whom it ᴿhappens
according to the work of the wicked; again,
there are wicked *men* to whom it happens
according to the work of the righteous. I said
that this also *is* vanity. Ps. 73:14
15 ᴿSo I commended enjoyment, because a
man has nothing better under the sun than to
eat, drink, and be merry; for this will remain
with him in his labor *all* the days of his life
which God gives him under the sun. Eccl. 2:24
16 When I applied my heart to know wisdom and to see the business that is done on
earth, even though one sees no sleep day or
night,
17 then I saw all the work of God, that ᴿa
man cannot find out the work that is done
under the sun. For though a man labors to
discover *it,* yet he will not find *it;* moreover,
though a wise *man* attempts to know *it,* he
will not be able to find *it.* Rom. 11:33

9 For I ᵀconsidered all this in my heart, so
that I could declare it all: that the righteous and the wise and their works *are* in the
hand of God. People know neither love nor
hatred *by* anything *they see* before them. *put*

8:10 Some Heb. mss., LXX, Vg. *praised*

(Point 14-E continued from previous page)
This verse describes the condition of man, before and after Adam fell through disobedience to God. Man's
condition has clearly changed since Creation, particularly in his relationship with God:

(1) *Adam before the Fall.* Theologians have agreed that Adam was not neutral, but was in an original
(though untested and unconfirmed) state of righteousness. In his state of innocence he was disposed to do
good, with no desire to do evil. He was created perfect, but not a robot.
(2) *Man after the Fall.* When Adam fell, and death entered into the world (Rom. 5:12, page 1133), Adam
acquired a sinful nature which was inherited by all generations (Rom. 3:9–19, page 1130). "For all have
sinned and fall short of the glory of God" (Rom. 3:23, page 1131).
(3) *Redeemed man.* Saved man, at the new birth, is now judged legally righteous by God on the basis of
Christ's substitutionary death (John 3:5–18, page 1052). Through the Holy Spirit, who now dwells in the
believer (Rom. 8:9, page 1137), he can resist sin. However, the rudiments of the sinful "old nature" still
indwell the personality, and so even saved people can sin. A struggle exists between the two natures (Rom.
7:14–25, page 1136). When Christians allow the old nature to dominate their lives, they become part of the
group Paul termed as "carnal" (1 Cor. 3:3, page 1149).
(4) *Glorified man.* In heaven, and then in the New Jerusalem, the saints, in their eternal state (like Christ),
will be unable to sin by virtue of their glorified (perfect) state of holiness (1 John 3:1, 2, page 1279).

See Proverbs 14:11, 12, page 608, for **Point 14-F: What Is the Final Destiny of Man?**

2 ᴿAll things *come* alike to all: Mal. 3:15

One event *happens* to the righteous
and the wicked;
To the *good, the clean, and the
unclean;
To him who sacrifices and him who
does not sacrifice.
As is the good, so *is* the sinner;
He who takes an oath as *he* who fears
an oath.

3 This *is* an evil in all that is done under
the sun: that one thing *happens* to all. Truly
the hearts of the sons of men are full of evil;
madness *is* in their hearts while they live, and
after that *they* go to the dead.

4 But for him who is joined to all the living
there is hope, for a living dog is better than a
dead lion.

5 For the living know that they will die;
But ᴿthe dead know nothing,   Is. 63:16
And they have no more reward,
For the memory of them is forgotten.

6 Also their love, their hatred, and their
envy have now perished;
Nevermore will they have a share
In anything done under the sun.

7 Go, ᴿeat your bread with joy,
And drink your wine with a merry
heart;
For God has already accepted your
works.   Eccl. 8:15

8 Let your garments always be white,
And let your head lack no oil.

9 Live joyfully with the wife whom you
love all the days of your vain life which He
has given you under the sun, all your days of
vanity; for that *is* your portion in life, and in
the labor which you perform under the sun.

10 ᴿWhatever your hand finds to do, do *it*
with your ᴿmight; for *there is* no work or
device or knowledge or wisdom in the grave
where you are going.   [Col. 3:17] • Rom. 12:11

11 I returned ᴿand saw under the sun
that—

The race *is* not to the swift,
Nor the battle to the strong,
Nor bread to the wise,
Nor riches to men of understanding,
Nor favor to men of skill;
But time and ᴿchance happen to them
all.   Amos 2:14, 15 • 1 Sam. 6:9

12 For ᴿman also does not know his time:
Like fish taken in a cruel net,   Eccl. 8:7
Like birds caught in a snare,
So the sons of men *are* ᴿsnared in an
evil time,   Prov. 29:6
When it falls suddenly upon them.

9:2 LXX, Syr., Vg. *good and bad*

Wisdom Superior to Folly

13 This wisdom I have also seen under the
sun, and it *seemed* great to me:
14 *There was* a little city with few men in it;
and a great king came against it, besieged it,
and built great *snares around it.
15 Now there was found in it a poor wise
man, and he by his wisdom delivered the city.
Yet no one remembered that same poor man.
16 Then I said:

"Wisdom *is* better than ᴿstrength.
Nevertheless ᴿthe poor man's wisdom *is*
despised,   Eccl. 7:12, 19 • Mark 6:2, 3
And his words are not heard.

17 Words of the wise, *spoken* quietly,
should be heard
Rather than the shout of a ruler of
fools.

18 Wisdom *is* better than weapons of war;
But one sinner destroys much good."

10 Dead flies *putrefy the perfumer's
ointment,
And cause it to give off a foul odor;
So does a little folly to one respected
for wisdom *and* honor.

2 A wise man's heart *is* at his right hand,
But a fool's heart at his left.

3 Even when a fool walks along the way,
He lacks wisdom,
ᴿAnd he shows everyone *that* he *is* a
fool.   Prov. 13:16; 18:2

4 If the spirit of the ruler rises against
you,
ᴿDo not leave your post;   Eccl. 8:3
For conciliation pacifies great offenses.

5 There is an evil I have seen under the
sun,
As an error proceeding from the ruler:
6 ᴿFolly is set in great dignity,   Esth. 3:1
While the rich sit in a lowly place.

7 I have seen servants ᴿon horses,
While princes walk on the ground like
servants.   Prov. 19:10; 30:22

8 ᴿHe who digs a pit will fall into it,
And whoever breaks through a wall
will be bitten by a serpent.   Prov. 26:27

9 He who quarries stones may be hurt by
them,
And he who splits wood may be
endangered by it.

10 If the ax is dull,
And one does not sharpen the edge,
Then he must use more strength;
But wisdom brings success.

11 A serpent may bite when *it is* not
charmed;
The babbler is no different.

9:14 LXX, Syr., Vg. *bulwarks*
10:1 Tg., Vg. omit *putrefy*

12 RThe words of a wise man's mouth *are* gracious,   Prov. 10:32
But Rthe lips of a fool shall swallow him up;   Prov. 10:14

13 The words of his mouth begin with foolishness,
And the end of his talk *is* raving madness.

14 RA fool also multiplies words.   [Prov. 15:2]
No man knows what is to be;
Who can tell him Rwhat will be after him?   Eccl. 3:22; 8:7

15 The labor of fools wearies them,
For they do not even know how to go to the city!

16 RWoe to you, O land, when your king *is* a child,   Is. 3:4, 5; 5:11
And your princes feast in the morning!

17 Blessed *are* you, O land, when your king *is* the son of nobles,
And your Rprinces feast at the proper time—   Prov. 31:4
For strength and not for drunkenness!

18 Because of laziness the Tbuilding decays,   Lit. *rafters sink*
And Rthrough idleness of hands the house leaks.   Prov. 24:30-34

19 A feast is made for laughter,
And Rwine makes merry;   Ps. 104:15
But money answers everything.

20 RDo not curse the king, even in your thought;   Acts 23:5
Do not curse the rich, even in your bedroom;
For a bird of the air may carry your voice,
And a bird in flight may tell the matter.

The Value of Diligence

11 Cast your bread upon the waters,
For you will find it after many days.

2 RGive a serving Rto seven, and also to eight,   [1 Tim. 6:18, 19] • Mic. 5:5
RFor you do not know what evil will be on the earth.   Eph. 5:16

3 If the clouds are full of rain,
They empty *themselves* upon the earth;
And if a tree falls to the south or the north,
In the place where the tree falls, there it shall lie.

4 He who observes the wind will not sow,
And he who regards the clouds will not reap.

5 As Ryou do not know what *is* the way of the Twind,   John 3:8 • Or *spirit*
ROr how the bones *grow* in the womb of her who is with child,   Ps. 139:14
So you do not know the works of God who makes everything.

6 In the morning sow your seed,
And in the evening do not withhold your hand;
For you do not know which will prosper,
Either this or that,
Or whether both alike *will be* good.

7 Truly the light is sweet,
And *it is* pleasant for the eyes Rto behold the sun;   Eccl. 7:11

8 But if a man lives many years
And Rrejoices in them all,
Yet let him Rremember the days of darkness,   Eccl. 9:7 • Eccl. 12:1
For they will be many.
All that is coming *is* vanity.

Seek God in Early Life

9 Rejoice, O young man, in your youth,
And let your heart cheer you in the days of your youth;
Walk in the ways of your heart,
And Tin the sight of your eyes;   As you see best
But know that for all these
God will bring you into judgment.

10 Therefore remove Tsorrow from your heart,   *vexation*
And put away evil from your flesh,
For childhood and youth *are* vanity.

12 RememberR now your Creator in the days of your youth,   Lam. 3:27
Before the Tdifficult days come,   *evil*
And the years draw near Rwhen you say,   2 Sam. 19:35
"I have no pleasure in them":

2 While the sun and the light,
The moon and the stars,
Are not darkened,
And the clouds do not return after the rain;

3 In the day when the keepers of the house tremble,
And the strong men bow down;
When the grinders cease because they are few,
And those that look through the windows grow dim;

4 When the doors are shut in the streets,
And the sound of grinding is low;
When one rises up at the sound of a bird,
And all Rthe daughters of music are brought low.   2 Sam. 19:35

5 Also they are afraid of height,
And of terrors in the way;
When the almond tree blossoms,
The grasshopper is a burden,
And desire fails.
For man goes to his eternal home,
And the mourners go about the streets.

6 *Remember your Creator* before the
   silver cord is *loosed,
   Or the golden bowl is broken,
   Or the pitcher shattered at the
      fountain,
   Or the wheel broken at the well.
7 ᴿThen the dust will return to the earth
   as it was,   Gen. 3:19
   ᴿAnd the spirit will return to God ᴿwho
   gave it.   Eccl. 3:21 • Job 34:14

8 "Vanityᴿ of vanities," says the Preacher,
   "All *is* vanity."   Ps. 62:9

The Whole Duty of Man

9 And moreover, because the Preacher
was wise, he still taught the people knowledge; yes, he pondered and sought out *and*
ᴿsetᵀ in order many proverbs. 1 Kin. 4:32 • *arranged*

12:6 So with Qr., Tg.; Kt. *removed;* LXX, Vg. *broken*

10 The Preacher sought to find ᵀacceptable
words; and *what was* written *was* upright—
words of truth.   *delightful*
11 The words of the wise are like goads, and
the words of *scholars are like well-driven
nails, given by one Shepherd.
12 And further, my son, be admonished by
these. Of making many books *there is* no
end, and ᴿmuch study *is* wearisome to the
flesh.   Eccl. 1:18
13 Let us hear the conclusion of the whole
matter:

   Fear God and keep His commandments,
   For this is man's all.
14 For ᴿGod will bring every work into
      judgment,   Matt. 12:36
   Including every secret thing,
   Whether good or evil.

12:11 Lit. *masters of assemblies*

THE
Song of Solomon

AUTHORSHIP. Solomon wrote 1,005 songs, according to 1 Kings 4:32, but the Song of Solomon is the only one that has survived. We know it is the finest because the expression "Song of Songs" (the book's Hebrew title, taken from 1:1 is the Hebrew way of making a superlative; it means, therefore, "the most exquisite, or best, song." It is, in fact, one of the loveliest poems in all literature, if not *the* loveliest. Tradition says that Solomon wrote the Song when he was young, in his first experience of true love, before the multiple political marriages and the concubinage that later so damaged his spiritual life and testimony (1 Kin. 11:8–10).

CONTEXT. The book dates from about 965 B.C., and tells the true story of King Solomon's love for a lovely country maiden, the Shulamite. An alternate theory posits a love triangle—Solomon the king trying to steal the maiden from her beloved rustic shepherd. Such a situation is most unlikely, however, since it would make the king of Israel the villain of a book named after himself!

HOW THE SONG OF SOLOMON FITS INTO THE BIBLE. Love is the greatest of personal qualities (1 Cor. 13:13), and surely the mutual love of a man and wife is one of the most important of God-ordained loves. Today there is a popular theory that the Song of Solomon is a "marriage manual" for young couples. Aside from the fact that the poem is too subtle to be a "manual" for anything not already understood, neither the Jewish temple nor the Christian church has ever regarded the book in this light. The Jews, in fact, forbade the reading of the Song until a man was thirty years of age! Ancient Jews saw the book as a portrayal of Israel's relationship to the Lord as the wife of Jehovah (cf. Is. 54:5; Jer. 2:2; Ezek. 16:8–14; Hos. 2:16–20).

The Christian church extended this view to refer specifically to the Lord Jesus, the person of the Godhead who, for the love of God, came to earth to seek and to save the lost. Luke 24:27 says that Christ expounded to the Emmaus travelers "in *all* the Scriptures the things concerning Himself" (emphasis added). Since the chapter and verse divisions are man-made and late, there is no need to say that Christ is specifically predicted or typified in each individual verse of Holy Writ, but it certainly is inconceivable that an entire book of the Bible could have nothing of Christ in it. Luther, as is well known, saw Christ as the key to all Bible books, and in this he was no doubt correct. Also, 2 Corinthians 11:2, Ephesians 5:24, and Revelation 19:7–9 and 21:9 all picture the Church as a bride and Christ as the husband, which fits in with the general flow of the Song of Solomon.

SUMMARY STATEMENT. The Song of Songs poetically relates the growing love, the separation, and the final consummation of love between King Solomon and the Shulamite maiden, giving *literally* poetic praise of married love and *spiritually* a picture of the love of God for Israel and of Christ for His Bride, the Church.

KEY WORDS AND KEY VERSE. The key words in the Song of Songs are *love* and *beloved*. Several verses would make good theme verses, such as 2:4 and 7:10, but perhaps the best verse to express the theme of the book is 8:7—"Many waters cannot quench love, nor can the floods drown it. If a man would give for love all the wealth of his house, it would be utterly despised."

HOW THE SONG OF SOLOMON FITS TOGETHER. As a poem, the Song is difficult to outline, and no two interpreters agree on the *exact* flow of action. It *is* a unified poem, however, as is shown by unity of character and by the repetition of such refrains as "I charge you, O daughters of Jerusalem. . ." The book may be broadly divided as follows: Love Beginning (1:1—3:5); Love Uniting (3:6—5:1); Love Struggling (5:2—7:10); Love Progressing (7:11—8:14).

Among the varied books in the Word of God, the Song of Songs is unique. This unified dramatic poem is full of observations and comparisons involving plants and animals. In its eight short chapters, Solomon mentions fifteen animals, twenty-one plants, and fifteen geographical sites from Lebanon in the north to Egypt in the south.

The Song has been an inspiration to centuries of poets and musicians. Hymns such as "Emmanuel's Land" and many others draw heavily on its wording. The titles "Rose of Sharon" and "Lily of the Valley" are often applied by poets to the Lord Jesus, but *in context* they are feminine comparisons by the Shulamite of herself with common field flowers (2:1). The titles from this book that are most suitable for our Lord are "Altogether Lovely" (5:16) and "Chief Among Ten Thousand" (5:10).

—A.L.F.

THE song of songs, which *is* Solomon's.

The Banquet

THE *SHULAMITE

2 Let him kiss me with the kisses of his
    mouth—
  For *your love *is* better than wine.
3 Because of the fragrance of your good
    ointments,
  Your name *is* ointment poured forth;
  Therefore the virgins love you.
4 RDraw me away!   Hos. 11:4

THE DAUGHTERS OF JERUSALEM

  RWe will run after *you.   Phil. 3:12-14

THE SHULAMITE

  The king Rhas brought me into his
    chambers.   Ps. 45:14, 15

THE DAUGHTERS OF JERUSALEM

  We will be glad and rejoice in *you.

  We will remember *your love more
    than wine.

THE SHULAMITE

  Rightly do they love you.

5 I *am* dark, but lovely,
  O daughters of Jerusalem,
  Like the tents of Kedar,
  Like the curtains of Solomon.
6 Do not look upon me, because I *am*
    dark,
  Because the sun has tanned me.
  My mother's sons were angry with me;
  They made me the keeper of the
    vineyards,
  But my own vineyard I have not kept.

(TO HER BELOVED)

7 Tell me, O you whom I love,
  Where you feed *your flock*,
  Where you make *it* rest at noon.
  For why should I be as one who *veils
    herself
  By the flocks of your companions?

THE BELOVED

8 If you do not know, RO fairest among
    women,   Song 5:9
  TFollow in the footsteps of the flock,
  And feed your little goats
  Beside the shepherds' tents.   Lit. Go out

1:1 A Palestinian young woman, Song 6:13. The speaker
and audience are identified according to the number,
gender, and person of the Hebrew words. Occasionally
the identity is not certain.
1:2 The Beloved
1:4 The Beloved • The Shulamite • The Beloved
1:7 LXX, Syr., Vg. *wanders*

9 I have compared you, my love,
  To my filly among Pharaoh's chariots.
10 RYour cheeks are lovely with ornaments,
   Your neck with chains *of* gold. Ezek. 16:11

THE DAUGHTERS OF JERUSALEM

11 We will make *you ornaments of gold
   With studs of silver.

THE SHULAMITE

12 While the king *is* at his table,
   My spikenard sends forth its fragrance.
13 A bundle of myrrh *is* my beloved to me,
   That lies all night between my breasts.
14 My beloved *is* to me a cluster of henna
     blooms
   In the vineyards of En Gedi.

THE BELOVED

15 Behold, you *are* fair, my Tlove!
   Behold, you *are* fair!
   You *have* dove's eyes.   companion, friend

THE SHULAMITE

16 Behold, you *are* Rhandsome, my
     beloved!   Song 5:10-16
   Yes, pleasant!
   Also our Tbed *is* green.   couch
17 The beams of our houses *are* cedar,
   And our rafters of fir.

2 I *am* the rose of Sharon,
  And the lily of the valleys.

THE BELOVED

2 Like a lily among thorns,
  So *is* my love among the daughters.

THE SHULAMITE

3 Like an apple tree among the trees of
    the woods,
  So *is* my beloved among the sons.
  I sat down in his shade with great
    delight,
  And his fruit *was* sweet to my taste.

THE SHULAMITE TO THE DAUGHTERS
OF JERUSALEM

4 He brought me to the Tbanqueting
    house,   Lit. *house of wine*
  And his banner over me *was* love.
5 Sustain me with cakes of raisins,
  Refresh me with apples,
  For I *am* lovesick.
6 RHis left hand *is* under my head, Song 8:3
  And his right hand embraces me.
7 RI Tcharge you, O daughters of
    Jerusalem,
  By the gazelles or by the does of the
    field,

1:11 The Shulamite

Do not stir up nor awaken love
Until it pleases.   Song 3:5; 8:4 · *adjure*

The Beloved's Request

THE SHULAMITE

8 The voice of my beloved!
Behold, he comes
Leaping upon the mountains,
Skipping upon the hills.
9 ᴿMy beloved is like a gazelle or a young
   stag.
Behold, he stands behind our wall;
He is looking through the windows,
Gazing through the lattice.   Song 2:17

10 My beloved spoke, and said to me:
"Rise up, my love, my fair one,
And come away.
11 For lo, the winter is past,
The rain is over *and* gone.
12 The flowers appear on the earth;
The time of singing has come,
And the voice of the turtledove
Is heard in our land.
13 The fig tree puts forth her green figs,
And the vines *with* the tender grapes
Give a good smell.
Rise up, my love, my fair one,
And come away!
14 "O my dove, in the clefts of the rock,
In the secret *places* of the cliff,
Let me see your ᵀface,
Let me hear your voice;   Lit. *appearance*
For your voice *is* sweet,
And your face *is* lovely."

HER BROTHERS

15 Catch us ᴿthe foxes,   Ezek. 13:4
The little foxes that spoil the vines,
For our vines *have* tender grapes.

THE SHULAMITE

16 My beloved *is* mine, and I *am* his.
He feeds *his flock* among the lilies.

(TO HER BELOVED)

17 ᴿUntil the day breaks   Song 4:6
And the shadows flee away,
Turn, my beloved,
And be ᴿlike a gazelle   Song 8:14
Or a young stag
Upon the mountains of *Bether.

A Troubled Night

THE SHULAMITE

3 By ᴿnight on my bed I sought the one I
      .love;   Is. 26:9
I sought him, but I did not find him.

2:17 Lit. *Separation*

2 "I will rise now," *I said,*
"And go about the city;
In the streets and in the squares
I will seek the one I love."
I sought him, but I did not find him.
3 ᴿThe watchmen who go about the city
   found me;
I said,
"Have you seen the one I love?"   Song 5:7

4 Scarcely had I passed by them,
When I found the one I love.
I held him and would not let him go,
Until I had brought him to the ᴿhouse
   of my mother,
And into the ᵀchamber of her who
   conceived me.   Song 8:2 · *room*

5 ᴿI ᵀcharge you, O daughters of
   Jerusalem,
By the gazelles or by the does of the
   field,
Do not stir up nor awaken love
Until it pleases.   Song 2:7; 8:4 · *adjure*

The Coming of Solomon

THE SHULAMITE

6 ᴿWho *is* this coming out of the
   wilderness
Like pillars of smoke,
Perfumed with myrrh and frankincense,
With all the merchant's fragrant
   powders?   Song 8:5
7 Behold, it *is* Solomon's couch,
With sixty valiant men around it,
Of the valiant of Israel.
8 They all hold swords,
Being expert in war.
Every man *has* his sword on his thigh
Because of fear in the night.
9 Of the wood of Lebanon
Solomon the King
Made himself a ᵀpalanquin: A portable chair
10 He made its pillars *of* silver,
Its support *of* gold,
Its seat *of* purple,
Its interior paved *with* love
By the daughters of Jerusalem.
11 Go forth, O daughters of Zion,
And see King Solomon with the crown
With which his mother crowned him
On the day of his wedding,
The day of the gladness of his heart.

THE BELOVED

4 Behold, ᴿyou *are* fair, my love!
Behold, you *are* fair!   Song 1:15; 5:12
You *have* dove's eyes behind your veil.
Your hair *is* like a ᴿflock of goats,
Going down from Mount Gilead.   Song 6:5
2 ᴿYour teeth *are* like a flock of shorn
   sheep   Song 6:6

Which have come up from the washing,
Every one of which bears twins,
And none *is* barren among them.
3 Your lips *are* like a strand of scarlet,
And your mouth is lovely.
    ^RYour temples behind your veil
    Are like a piece of pomegranate.   Song 6:7
4 ^RYour neck *is* like the tower of David,
    Built ^Rfor an armory,   Song 7:4 • Neh. 3:19
    On which hang a thousand ^Tbucklers,
    All shields of mighty men.   Small shields
5 ^RYour two breasts *are* like two fawns,
    Twins of a gazelle,   Song 7:3
    Which feed among the lilies.

6 ^RUntil the day breaks   Song 2:17
    And the shadows flee away,
    I will go my way to the mountain of
       myrrh
    And to the hill of frankincense.

7 ^RYou *are* all fair, my love,
    And *there is* no spot in you.   Eph. 5:27
8 Come with me from Lebanon, *my*
       spouse,
    With me from Lebanon.
    Look from the top of Amana,
    From the top of Senir ^Rand Hermon,
    From the lions' dens,   Deut. 3:9
    From the mountains of the leopards.

9 You have ravished my heart,
    My sister, *my* spouse;
    You have ravished my heart
    With one *look* of your eyes,
    With one link of your necklace.
10 How fair is your love,
    My sister, *my* spouse!
    ^RHow much better than wine is your
       love,
    And the ^Tscent of your perfumes
    Than all spices!   Song 1:2, 4 • *fragrance*
11 Your lips, O *my* spouse,
    Drip as the honeycomb;
    Honey and milk *are* under your tongue;
    And the fragrance of your garments
    Is like the fragrance of Lebanon.

12 A garden ^Tenclosed
    Is my sister, *my* spouse,
    A spring shut up,
    A fountain sealed.   *locked* or *barred*
13 Your plants *are* an orchard of
       pomegranates
    With pleasant fruits,
    Fragrant henna with spikenard,
14 Spikenard and saffron,
    Calamus and cinnamon,
    With all trees of frankincense,
    Myrrh and aloes,
    With all the chief spices—
15 A fountain of gardens,
    A well of ^Rliving waters,   Zech. 14:8
    And streams from Lebanon.

THE SHULAMITE

16 Awake, O north *wind,*
    And come, O south!
    Blow upon my garden,
    That its spices may flow out.
    ^RLet my beloved come to his garden
    And eat its pleasant fruits.   Song 5:1

THE BELOVED

5 I ^Rhave come to my garden, my ^Rsister,
    my spouse;   Song 4:16 • Song 4:9
    I have gathered my myrrh with my
       spice;
    ^RI have eaten my honeycomb with my
       honey;   Song 4:11
    I have drunk my wine with my milk.

(To His Friends)

    Eat, O ^Rfriends!   Luke 15:7, 10
    Drink, yes, drink deeply,
    O beloved ones!

The Shulamite's Troubled Evening

THE SHULAMITE

2 I sleep, but my heart is awake;
    It is the voice of my beloved!
    ^RHe knocks, *saying,*   Rev. 3:20
    "Open for me, my sister, my love,
    My dove, my perfect one;
    For my head is covered with dew,
    My locks with the drops of the night."
3 I have taken off my robe;
    How can I put it on *again?*
    I have washed my feet;
    How can I ^Tdefile them?   *dirty*
4 My beloved put his hand
    By the ^Tlatch *of the door,*
    And my heart yearned for him.   *opening*
5 I arose to open for my beloved,
    And my hands dripped *with* myrrh,
    My fingers with liquid myrrh,
    On the handles of the lock.

6 I opened for my beloved,
    But my beloved had turned away *and*
       was gone.
    My heart leaped up when he spoke.
    I sought him, but I could not find him;
    I called him, but he gave me no answer.
7 ^RThe watchmen who went about the city
       found me.
    They struck me, they wounded me;
    The keepers of the walls
    Took my veil away from me.   Song 3:3
8 I charge you, O daughters of Jerusalem,
    If you find my beloved,
    That you tell him I *am* lovesick!

THE DAUGHTERS OF JERUSALEM

9 What *is* your beloved
    More than *another* beloved,
    ^RO fairest among women?   Song 1:8; 6:1

What *is* your beloved
More than *another* beloved,
That you so ᵀcharge us?   *adjure*

THE SHULAMITE

10 My beloved *is* white and ruddy,
   ᵀChief among ten thousand.   *Distinguished*
11 His head *is like* the finest gold;
   His locks *are* wavy,
   And black as a raven.
12 ᴿHis eyes *are* like doves   Song 1:15; 4:1
   By the rivers of waters,
   Washed with milk,
   And ᵀfitly set.   *sitting in a setting*
13 His cheeks *are* like a bed of spices,
   Banks of scented herbs.
   His lips *are* lilies,
   Dripping liquid myrrh.

14 His hands *are* rods of gold
   Set with beryl.
   His body *is* carved ivory
   Inlaid *with* sapphires.
15 His legs *are* pillars of marble
   Set on bases of fine gold.
   His countenance *is* like Lebanon,
   Excellent as the cedars.
16 His mouth *is* most sweet,
   Yes, he *is* altogether lovely.
   This *is* my beloved,
   And this *is* my friend,
   O daughters of Jerusalem!

THE DAUGHTERS OF JERUSALEM

6 Where has your beloved gone,
   ᴿO fairest among women?   Song 1:8; 5:9
   Where has your beloved turned aside,
   That we may seek him with you?

THE SHULAMITE

2 My beloved has gone to his ᴿgarden,
   To the beds of spices,   Song 4:16; 5:1
   To feed *his* flock in the gardens,
   And to gather lilies.
3 ᴿI *am* my beloved's,   Song 2:16; 7:10
   And my beloved *is* mine.
   He feeds *his* flock among the lilies.

Praise of the Shulamite's Beauty

THE BELOVED

4 O my love, you *are as* beautiful as
   Tirzah,
   Lovely as Jerusalem,
   Awesome as *an army* with banners!
5 Turn your eyes away from me,
   For they have ᵀovercome me.   *overwhelmed*
   Your hair *is* ᴿlike a flock of goats
   Going down from Gilead.   Song 4:1
6 ᴿYour teeth *are* like a flock of sheep
   Which have come up from the washing;
   Every one bears twins,   Song 4:2
   And none *is* ᵀbarren among them. *bereaved*

7 ᴿLike a piece of pomegranate   Song 4:3
   Are your temples behind your veil.

8 There are sixty queens
   And eighty concubines,
   And ᴿvirgins without number.   Song 1:3
9 My dove, my ᴿperfect one,
   Is the only one,
   The only one of her mother,
   The favorite of the one who bore her.
   The daughters saw her
   And called her blessed,
   The queens and the concubines,
   And they praised her.   Song 2:14; 5:2

10 Who is she who looks forth as the
   morning,
   Fair as the moon,
   Clear as the sun,
   Awesome as *an army* with banners?

THE SHULAMITE

11 I went down to the garden of nuts
   To see the verdure of the valley,
   To see whether the vine had budded
   And the pomegranates had bloomed.
12 Before I was even aware,
   My soul had made me
   As the chariots of *my noble people.

THE BELOVED AND HIS FRIENDS

13 Return, return, O Shulamite;
   Return, return, that we may look upon
   you!

THE SHULAMITE

   What would you see in the Shulamite—
   As it were, the dance of the two camps?

Expressions of Praise

THE BELOVED

7 How beautiful are your feet in sandals,
   ᴿO prince's daughter!
   The curves of your thighs *are* like
   jewels,
   The work of the hands of a skillful
   workman.   Ps. 45:13
2 Your navel *is* a rounded goblet;
   It lacks no ᵀblended beverage.
   Your waist *is* a heap of wheat
   Set about with lilies.   Lit. *mixed* or *spiced drink*
3 ᴿYour two breasts *are* like two fawns,
   Twins of a gazelle.   Song 4:5
4 ᴿYour neck *is* like an ivory tower,
   Your eyes *like* the pools in Heshbon
   By the gate of Bath Rabbim.
   Your nose *is* like the tower of Lebanon
   Which looks toward Damascus.   Song 4:4
5 Your head *crowns* you like *Mount*
   Carmel,
   And the hair of your head *is* like
   purple;
   A king *is* held captive by *your* tresses.

6:12 Or *Ammi Nadib*

6 How fair and how pleasant you are,
O love, with your delights!

7 This stature of yours is like a palm tree,
And your breasts *like* its clusters.

8 I said, "I will go up to the palm tree,
I will take hold of its branches."
Let now your breasts be like clusters of
the vine,
The fragrance of your ᵀbreath like
apples,   Lit. *nose*

9 And the roof of your mouth like the
best wine.

THE SHULAMITE

The wine goes *down* smoothly for my
beloved,
Moving gently the *lips of sleepers.

10 ᴿI *am* my beloved's,   Song 2:16; 6:3
And ᴿhis desire *is* toward me.   Ps. 45:11

11 Come, my beloved,
Let us go forth to the field;
Let us lodge in the villages.

12 Let us get up early to the vineyards;
Let us ᴿsee if the vine has budded,
Whether the grape blossoms are open,
And the pomegranates are in bloom.
There I will give you my love.   Song 6:11

13 The ᴿmandrakes give off a fragrance,
And at our gates ᴿ*are* pleasant *fruits,*
All manner, new and old,
Which I have laid up for you, my
beloved.   Gen. 30:14 · Matt. 13:52

8 Oh, that you were like my brother,
Who nursed at my mother's breasts!
If I should find you outside,
I would kiss you;
I would not be despised.

2 I would lead you *and* bring you
Into the ᴿhouse of my mother,
She *who* used to instruct me.
I would cause you to drink of ᴿspiced
wine,   Song 3:4 · Prov. 9:2
Of the juice of my pomegranate.

(TO THE DAUGHTERS OF JERUSALEM)

3 His left hand *is* under my head,
And his right hand embraces me.

4 ᴿI charge you, O daughters of Jerusalem,
Do not stir up nor awaken love
Until it pleases.   Song 2:7; 3:5

Love Renewed in Lebanon

A RELATIVE

5 ᴿWho *is* this coming up from the
wilderness,   Song 3:6
Leaning upon her beloved?

7:9 LXX, Syr., Vg. *lips and teeth.*

I awakened you under the apple tree.
There your mother brought you forth;
There she *who* bore you brought *you*
forth.

THE SHULAMITE TO HER BELOVED

6 ᴿSet me as a seal upon your heart,
As a seal upon your arm;   Jer. 22:24
For love *is as* strong as death,
Jealousy *as* ᵀcruel as ᵀthe grave;
Its flames *are* flames of fire,
*A most vehement flame.   severe · Or *Sheol*

7 Many waters cannot quench love,
Nor can the floods drown it.
ᴿIf a man would give for love
All the wealth of his house,   Prov. 6:35
It would be utterly despised.

THE SHULAMITE'S BROTHERS

8 ᴿWe have a little sister,   Ezek. 23:33
And she has no breasts.
What shall we do for our sister
In the day when she is spoken for?

9 If she *is* a wall,
We will build upon her
A battlement of silver;
And if she *is* a door,
We will enclose her
With boards of cedar.

THE SHULAMITE

10 I *am* a wall,
And my breasts like towers;
Then I became in his eyes
As one who found peace.

11 Solomon had a vineyard at Baal
Hamon;
He leased the vineyard to keepers;
Everyone was to bring for its fruit
A thousand silver coins.

(TO SOLOMON)

12 My own vineyard *is* before me.
You, O Solomon, *may have* a thousand,
And those who tend its fruit two
hundred.

THE BELOVED

13 You who dwell in the gardens,
The companions listen for your voice—
ᴿLet me hear it!   Song 2:14

THE SHULAMITE

14 ᵀMake haste, my beloved,   Hurry, lit. *Flee*
And ᴿbe like a gazelle   Song 2:7, 9, 17
Or a young stag
On the mountains of spices.

8:6 Lit. *A flame of YAH,* poetic form of *YHWH, the*
LORD

THE BOOK OF

Isaiah

The last forty years of the eighth century B.C. produced some outstanding men. One who stood head and shoulders above the rest was the prophet Isaiah. Isaiah's character and genius have been summarized under the fourfold characterization of statesman, reformer, theologian, and poet. The prominent part Isaiah played in his country's affairs made him a national figure. He had great concern for social justice and national righteousness. He was a poetic genius. His brilliance of expression and freshness of style are unsurpassed.

How Isaiah Fits into the Bible. Isaiah was the first prophet of the southern kingdom of Judah and one of the four major prophets. Of the many prophets God called to minister to his people Israel sixteen were chosen to add their writings to the Old Testament canon; twelve of these prophets are considered "minor" (largely because of the brevity of the books) and four of them—Isaiah, Jeremiah, Ezekiel, and Daniel—are considered major. Isaiah is a major prophet not only because of the length of the book that bears his name but also because of the depth and importance of his message. Indeed, Isaiah has been called the "Prince of Prophets."

Isaiah was a native of Jerusalem in the southern kingdom of Judah. Tradition says he was a cousin of Uzziah, king of Judah. His ministry lasted from youth to old age—according to tradition about sixty years of service. His ministry occurred during the reigns of Uzziah, Jotham, Ahaz, and Hezekiah, kings of Judah (1:1).

In the year of King Uzziah's death, 740 B.C., Isaiah received his special commission to a prophetic ministry while in the temple in Jerusalem (6:1-13). This vision of the thrice-holy God (v. 3) was the greatest spiritual influence in his life. Although it came to him after some years of experience in preaching, this special encounter with God was definitely used to deepen his insights about God's character and the nature of his prophetic calling.

Isaiah's call was a dramatic experience—a vision of the holiness and purity of God. He saw his own unworthiness, confessed his sins, received cleansing from the Lord, and made himself available to God. God gave him a commission to go to a sinful, needy people with a message of warning and judgment, but also with the good news of forgiveness and deliverance.

When Isaiah preached that God was about to abandon Judah, no doubt many thought it was a harsh and cruel message. The chastening of the Lord, however, was meant to lead His people to repentance and righteousness. The Lord is far more concerned about the purity of His people than with their general prosperity.

Context. About a quarter of a century after Isaiah's birth, the northern kingdom met its downfall at the hands of Assyria. Isaiah's mighty message from God to Judah is what saved the southern kingdom during those trying times. The security of the southern kingdom, however, was fragile. Because of the spiritual and moral decadence of Judah, in the realm of religion, politics, and society, the southern kingdom continued to be threatened with defeat and bondage.

Isaiah spoke boldly to the conditions of his time. He was both a *forthteller* and a *foreteller*. As a *forthteller,* he said that judgment must fall on Judah because of the rotten political, social, and religious conditions which were preventing her from fulfilling her mission in the world. He warned her of the danger posed by the strong and aggressive nations surrounding her. He called on his people to repent and turn back to God.

As a *foreteller,* Isaiah told how God's ultimate plan would finally triumph through His preserving a remnant of His people and through the suffering and death of His appointed Servant, the Lord Jesus Christ (52:13—53:12). The Messiah of whom he prophesied would be a descendant of King David who would ultimately establish peace and justice on earth and propagate the knowledge of God. Isaiah foretold the Messiah's birth, family, anointing, character, simplicity of life, gentleness, death, resurrection, and glorious reign.

How Isaiah Fits Together. With its sixty-six chapters, the book of Isaiah may be compared to a miniature Bible (the Bible having sixty-six books). As with the Bible, the book of Isaiah has two great divisions, with thirty-nine chapters in the first (like the thirty-nine books of the Old Testament) and twenty-seven chapters in the second (like the twenty-seven books of the New Testament).

The Old Testament opens with God's case against man because of his sin (Gen. 3) and closes with the prophet's prediction of the coming kingdom (Mal. 4). In the same way, the first section

of Isaiah (1—39) opens with a description of the wickedness of Judah (ch. 1) and closes with the prophecy of the coming King of Righteousness and the redemption of all Israel.

The New Testament opens with the announcement of John the Baptist, the forerunner of Jesus Christ (Matt. 3) and closes with John's vision of a new heaven and a new earth (Rev. 21—22). Likewise, the second part of Isaiah (40—66) opens with "the voice of one crying in the wilderness" (40:3) and includes prophetic messages about the person and work of Jesus Christ. It closes with the vision of new heavens and a new earth in which righteousness dwells.

AUTHORSHIP. Since the book of Isaiah is written with these two distinct styles and emphases, some scholars believe that there was more than one author. In fact, some have said there must have been at least three writers, and call the three parts of the book by the names *Proto-, Deutero-,* and *Trito-Isaiah.*

Conservative Bible scholars reject the concept of multiple authorship of the book, believing instead that it was written by one man with two major messages. They contend that tradition has always held that the book was written by the prophet. The inspired writers of the New Testament quoted from both sections of the book and ascribed them to Isaiah; see for example John 12:38–41, in which the apostle specifically quotes Isaiah 53:1 and Isaiah 6:10 as spoken by the prophet himself. Furthermore, the discovery of the Dead Sea Scrolls from the Qumran community is more recent evidence of the unity of the book, since there is no indication of any break in the Isaiah scroll. Therefore, Isaiah's authorship of the whole book of Isaiah is very defensible.

A Jewish tradition recorded in the Talmud tells us that Isaiah resisted King Manasseh's idolatrous decrees. Because of this he suffered the death of a martyr by being "sawn in two." Many believe this is the event referred to in Hebrews 11:37.

—M.W.

THE vision of Isaiah the son of Amoz, which he saw concerning Judah and Jerusalem in the days of Uzziah, Jotham, Ahaz, *and* Hezekiah, kings of Judah.

The Wickedness of Judah

2 ᴿHear, O heavens, and give ear, O earth!
  For the LORD has spoken: Jer. 2:12
  "I have nourished and brought up
    children,
  And they have rebelled against Me;
3 ᴿThe ox knows its owner   Jer. 8:7
  And the donkey its master's crib;
  But Israel ᴿdoes not know,   Jer. 9:3, 6
  My people do not ᵀconsider."   *understand*

4 Alas, sinful nation,
  A people ᵀladen with iniquity,   *heavy*
  A ᵀbrood of evildoers,   *offspring, seed*
  Children who are corrupters!
  They have forsaken the LORD,
  They have provoked to anger
  The Holy One of Israel,
  They have turned away backward.

5 ᴿWhy should you be stricken again?
  You will revolt more and more.
  The whole head is sick,
  And the whole heart faints.   Jer. 5:3
6 From the sole of the foot even to the
    head,
  There is no soundness in it,
  But wounds and bruises and putrefying
    sores;
  They have not been closed or bound up,
  Or soothed with ointment.

7 ᴿYour country *is* desolate,
  Your cities *are* burned with fire;
  Strangers devour your land in your
    presence;
  And *it is* desolate, as overthrown by
    strangers.   Deut. 28:51, 52
8 So the daughter of Zion is left ᴿas a
    ᵀbooth in a vineyard,
  As a hut in a garden of cucumbers,
  ᴿAs a besieged city.   Job 27:18 · *shelter* · Jer. 4:17
9 ᴿUnless the LORD of hosts
  Had left to us a very small remnant,
  We would have become like ᴿSodom,
  We would have been made like
    Gomorrah.   Lam. 3:22 · Gen. 19:24

10 Hear the word of the LORD,
   You rulers ᴿof Sodom;
   Give ear to the law of our God,
   You people of Gomorrah: Deut. 32:32
11 "To what purpose *is* the multitude of
     your ᴿsacrifices to Me?"
   Says the LORD.
   "I have had enough of burnt offerings of
     rams
   And the fat of fed cattle.
   I do not delight in the blood of bulls,
   Or of lambs or goats.   [1 Sam. 15:22]

12 "When you come ᴿto appear before Me,
   Who has required this from your hand,
   To trample My courts?   Ex. 23:17
13 Bring no more ᴿfutileᵀ sacrifices;
   Incense is an abomination to Me.

The New Moons, the Sabbaths, and
  ᴿthe calling of assemblies—
I cannot endure iniquity and the sacred
  meeting.   Matt. 15:9 · worthless · Joel 1:14
14 Your ᴿNew Moons and your ᴿappointed
    feasts
  My soul hates;   Num. 28:11 · Lam. 2:6
  They are a trouble to Me,
  I am weary of bearing *them.*
15 When you ᵀspread out your hands, Pray
  I will hide My eyes from you;
  ᴿEven though you make many prayers,
  I will not hear.   Mic. 3:4
  Your hands are full of ᵀblood. bloodshed

▼ 33-C. The Plan of Salvation: "For the Jew First"

16 "Washᴿ yourselves, make yourselves
    clean;
  Put away the evil of your doings from
    before My eyes.
  ᴿCease to do evil,   Jer. 4:14 · Rom. 12:9
17 Learn to do good;
  Seek justice,
  Rebuke *the oppressor;

1:17 Some ancient vss. *the oppressed*

ᵀDefend the fatherless,
Plead for the widow.   Vindicate
18 "Come now, and let us ᴿreason
    together,"
  Says the Lᴏʀᴅ,
  "Though your sins are like scarlet,
  ᴿThey shall be as white as snow;
  Though they are red like crimson,
  They shall be as wool.   Is. 43:26 · Ps. 51:7
19 If you are willing and obedient,
  You shall eat the good of the land;
20 But if you refuse and rebel,
  You shall be devoured by the sword";
  For the mouth of the Lᴏʀᴅ has spoken.

The Degenerate City

21 ᴿHow the faithful city has become a
    ᵀharlot!   Jer. 2:20 · Unfaithful
  It was full of justice;
  Righteousness lodged in it,
  But now ᴿmurderers.   Mic. 3:1-3
22 ᴿYour silver has become dross,
  Your wine mixed with water.   Jer. 6:28
23 ᴿYour princes *are* rebellious,   Hos. 9:15
  And ᴿcompanions of thieves;   Prov. 29:24
  ᴿEveryone loves bribes,   Jer. 22:17

33-C. The Plan of Salvation: "For the Jew First" (Isaiah 1:16-19)—A significant number of Jewish people in recent years have become believers in Christ. The Christian invitation of salvation to the Jews (God's ancient people—Israel) is in harmony with the promises of both the Old and New Testaments.

    (1) In the Old Testament Israel was invited to salvation:

        (a) God declared that the Hebrews too were sinners (despite having been chosen in Abraham), as is all mankind (Is. 1:3-14, page 642).
        (b) As a result of their sins, God said He would not hear their prayers (v. 15; Is. 59:1-3, page 698).
        (c) God exhorted them to repent of their sins and be cleansed (v. 16).
        (d) God exhorted them to live so as to outwardly reflect their inward cleansing (v. 17).
        (e) God promised them total cleansing and forgiveness (v. 18).
        (f) God pledged that if they repented, their blessings at His hand would continue (v. 19).

    (2) In the Old Testament, Israel was promised a Messiah-Savior who would suffer as God's lamb for the sins of those who would turn to God (Is. 53:4-7, page 693).

    (3) In the New Testament, Israel is still invited to salvation, which is "for the Jew first and also for the Greek" (Rom. 1:16, page 1128).

        (a) The gospel, the Good News, is God's power to save people. The Holy Spirit uses this message to touch the hearts of unbelievers, that they might believe and be saved (1 Cor. 15:1-4, page 1161).
        (b) The gospel is able to save everyone who believes—Jew or Gentile.
        (c) Salvation in the New Testament was specifically offered to "the Jew first" (Rom. 1:16, page 1128), out of historical necessity or courtesy, just as the Messiah-Savior was promised to the Jewish people by the Old Testament prophets.
        (d) Salvation was offered to "the Jew first" (Rom. 1:16, page 1128; John 1:11, page 1049), according to the apostle Paul's inspired words. It thus requires that we who know Christ should continue to share the gospel with the Jewish people (Rom. 11:1-5, 11, 12, page 1141).

    (4) The apostle Paul

        (a) Showed an earnest desire for Israelites to be saved (Rom. 9:1-4, page 1139). He prayed for Israel's salvation (Rom. 10:1, page 1140).
        (b) Declared that any Jew or Gentile will be saved if he or she calls upon God through Christ (Rom. 10:11, 12, page 1140).
        (c) Stated that God had not "cast away" Israel (Rom. 11:1, page 1141).
        (d) Affirmed that Israel, as a nation, would at some future time turn in faith to Christ (Rom. 11:26-28, page 1141; Zech. 12:10, page 918).

    See Isaiah 53:10, page 693, for **Point 33-D: The Parties to the Crucifixion of Christ.**

And follows after rewards.
They ^Rdo not defend the fatherless,
Nor does the cause of the widow come
before them.   Jer. 5:28

24 Therefore the Lord says,
The LORD of hosts, the Mighty One of
Israel,
"Ah, ^RI will ^Trid Myself of My
adversaries,   Deut. 28:63 · *be relieved of*
And take vengeance on My enemies.
25 I will turn My hand against you,
And ^Rthoroughly^T purge away your
dross,   Mal. 3:3 · *refine with lye*
And take away all your alloy.
26 I will restore your judges ^Ras at the
first,   Jer. 33:7–11
And your counselors as at the
beginning.
Afterward you shall be called the city
of righteousness, the faithful city."
27 Zion shall be redeemed with justice,
And her penitents with righteousness.
28 The ^Rdestruction of transgressors and of
sinners *shall be* together,
And those who forsake the LORD shall
be consumed.   [2 Thess. 1:8, 9]
29 For *they shall be ashamed of the
^Tterebinth trees   Sites of pagan worship
Which you have desired;
And you shall be embarrassed because
of the gardens
Which you have chosen.
30 For you shall be as a terebinth whose
leaf fades,
And as a garden that has no water.
31 ^RThe strong shall be as tinder,   Ezek. 32:21
And the work of it as a spark;
Both will burn together,
And no one shall ^Rquench *them.*   Mark 9:43

The Future House of God

2 The word that Isaiah the son of Amoz
saw concerning Judah and Jerusalem.

2 Now ^Rit shall come to pass ^Rin the latter
days   Mic. 4:1–3 · Gen. 49:1
^R*That* the mountain of the LORD's house
Shall be established on the top of the
mountains,   Ps. 68:15
And shall be exalted above the hills;
And all nations shall flow to it.
3 Many people shall come and say,
^R"Come, and let us go up to the mountain
of the LORD,
To the house of the God of Jacob;
He will teach us His ways,
And we shall walk in His paths."
^RFor out of Zion shall go forth the law,
And the word of the LORD from
Jerusalem.   Jer. 50:5 · Is. 51:4, 5

1:29 So with MT, LXX, Vg.; some Heb. mss., Tg. *you*

4 He shall judge between the nations,
And rebuke many people;
^RThey shall beat their swords into
plowshares,   Is. 32:17, 18
And their spears into pruning ^Thooks;
Nation shall not lift up sword against
nation,   *knives*
Neither shall they learn war anymore.

The Day of the LORD

5 O house of Jacob, come and let us
^Rwalk
In the light of the LORD.   Eph. 5:8

6 For You have forsaken Your people,
the house of Jacob,
Because they are filled ^Rwith eastern
ways;   Num. 23:7
They *are* ^Rsoothsayers like the
Philistines,   Deut. 18:14
^RAnd they are pleased with the children
of foreigners.   Ps. 106:35
7 ^RTheir land is also full of silver and gold,
And there is no end to their treasures;
Their land is also full of horses,   Deut. 17:16
And there is no end to their chariots.
8 ^RTheir land is also full of idols;
They worship the work of their own
hands,
That which their own fingers have
made.   Jer. 2:28
9 People bow down,
And each man humbles himself;
Therefore do not forgive them.

10 ^REnter into the rock, and hide in the
dust,   Rev. 6:15, 16
From the terror of the LORD
And the glory of His majesty.
11 The ^Tlofty looks of man shall be
^Rhumbled,
The haughtiness of men shall be bowed
down,
And the LORD alone shall be exalted ^Rin
that day.   *proud* · Prov. 16:5 · Hos. 2:16
12 For the day of the LORD of hosts
Shall come upon everything proud and
lofty,
Upon everything lifted up—
And it shall be brought low—
13 Upon all ^Rthe cedars of Lebanon *that
are* high and lifted up,   Zech. 11:1, 2
And upon all the oaks of Bashan;
14 ^RUpon all the high mountains,   Is. 30:25
And upon all the hills *that are* lifted up;
15 Upon every high tower,
And upon every fortified wall;
16 ^RUpon all the ships of Tarshish,   1 Kin. 10:22
And upon all the beautiful sloops.
17 The ^Tloftiness of man shall be bowed
down,
And the haughtiness of men shall be
brought low;

The LORD alone will be exalted in that
day,   *pride*
18 But the idols He shall utterly abolish.

19 They shall go into the ᴿholes of the
rocks,   Hos. 10:8
And into the caves of the ᵀearth,
ᴿFrom the terror of the LORD
And the glory of His majesty,
When He arises ᴿto shake the earth
mightily.   Lit. *dust* • [2 Thess. 1:9] • Hag. 2:6, 7

20 In that day a man will cast away his
idols of silver
And his idols of gold,
Which they made, *each* for himself to
worship,
To the moles and bats,
21 To go into the clefts of the rocks,
And into the crags of the rugged rocks,
From the terror of the LORD
And the glory of His majesty,
When He arises to shake the earth
mightily.
22 Sever yourselves from such a man,
Whose ᴿbreath *is* in his nostrils;
For of what account is he?   Job 27:3

Judgment on Judah and Jerusalem

3 For behold, the Lord, the LORD of hosts,
ᴿTakes away from Jerusalem and from
Judah   Jer. 37:21
ᵀThe stock and the store,   Every support
The whole supply of bread and the
whole supply of water;
2 ᴿThe mighty man and the man of war,
The judge and the prophet,   2 Kin. 24:14
And the diviner and the elder;
3 The captain of fifty and the ᵀhonorable
man,   Eminent looking men
The counselor and the skillful artisan,
And the expert enchanter.

4 "I will give ᵀchildren *to be* their princes,
And babes shall rule over them.   *boys*
5 The people will be oppressed,
Every one by another and every one by
his neighbor;
The child will be insolent toward the
ᵀelder,   *aged*
And the base toward the honorable."

6 When a man takes hold of his brother
In the house of his father, *saying*,
"You have clothing;
You be our ruler,
And *let* these ruins *be* under your
ᵀpower,"   Lit. *hand*
7 In that day he will protest, saying,
"I cannot cure *your* ills,
For in my house *is* neither food nor
clothing;
Do not make me a ruler of the people."

8 For ᴿJerusalem stumbled,   Mic. 3:12
And Judah is fallen,

Because their tongue and their doings
Are against the LORD,
To provoke the eyes of His glory.
9 The look on their countenance
witnesses against them,
And they declare their sin as ᴿSodom;
They do not hide *it.*
Woe to their soul!
For they have brought evil upon
themselves.   Gen. 13:13
10 "Say to the righteous ᴿthat *it shall be*
well *with them,*
ᴿFor they shall eat the fruit of their
doings.   [Eccl. 8:12] • Ps. 128:2
11 Woe to the wicked! ᴿ*It shall be* ill *with
him,*
For the reward of his hands shall be
ᵀgiven him.   [Ps. 11:6] • *done to him*
12 *As for* My people, children *are* their
oppressors,
And women rule over them.
O My people! ᴿThose who lead you
ᵀcause *you* to err,   Is. 9:16 • *lead you astray*
And destroy the way of your paths."

Oppression and Luxury Condemned

13 The LORD stands up to ᵀplead,   *contend*
And stands to judge the people.
14 The LORD will enter into judgment
With the elders of His people
And His princes:
"For you have ᵀeaten up ᴿthe vineyard;
The plunder of the poor *is* in your
houses.   *burned* • Matt. 21:33
15 What do you mean by ᴿcrushing My
people
And grinding the faces of the poor?"
Says the Lord GOD of hosts.   Mic. 3:2, 3

16 Moreover the LORD says:

"Because the daughters of Zion are
haughty,
And walk with outstretched necks
And ᵀwanton eyes,   *seductive, ogling*
Walking and mincing *as* they go,
Making a jingling with their feet,
17 Therefore the Lord will strike with ᴿa
scab
The crown of the head of the daughters
of Zion,
And the LORD will ᴿuncover their secret
parts."   Deut. 28:27 • Jer. 13:22

18 In that day the Lord will take away the
finery:
The jingling anklets, the ᵀscarves, and
the ᴿcrescents;   *headbands* • Judg. 8:21, 26
19 The pendants, the bracelets, and the
veils;
20 The headdresses, the leg ornaments,
and the headbands;
The perfume boxes, the charms,

21   and the rings;
      The nose jewels,
22   the festal apparel, and the mantles;
      The outer garments, the purses,
23   and the mirrors;
      The fine linen, the turbans, and the
      robes.

24 And so it shall be:

      Instead of a sweet smell there will be a
         stench;
      Instead of a sash, a rope;
      Instead of well-set hair, ᴿbaldness;
      Instead of a rich robe, a girding of
         sackcloth;   Is. 22:12
      And branding instead of beauty.
25   Your men shall fall by the sword,
      And your ᵀmighty in the war.   Lit. *strength*

26 ᴿHer gates shall lament and mourn,
      And she *being* desolate ᴿshall sit on the
         ground.   Jer. 14:2 • Lam. 2:10

4 And ᴿin that day seven women shall
      take hold of one man, saying,   Is. 2:11, 17
"We will ᴿeat our own food and wear
      our own apparel;   2 Thess. 3:12
Only let us be called by your name,
To take away ᴿour reproach."   Luke 1:25

The Renewal of Zion

2 In that day ᴿthe Branch of the LORD
      shall be beautiful and glorious;
      And the fruit of the earth *shall be*
         excellent and appealing   [Jer. 23:5]
      For those of Israel who have escaped.

3 And it shall come to pass that *he who is*
left in Zion and remains in Jerusalem ᴿwill be
called holy—everyone who is recorded
among the living in Jerusalem.   Is. 60:21
4 When ᴿthe Lord has washed away the
filth of the daughters of Zion, and purged
the ᵀblood of Jerusalem from her midst, by
the spirit of judgment and by the spirit of
burning,   Mal. 3:2, 3 • *bloodshed*
5 then the LORD will create above every
dwelling place of Mount Zion, and above her
assemblies, a cloud and smoke by day and the
shining of a flaming fire by night. For over all
the glory there *will be* a covering.
6 And there will be a tabernacle for shade
in the daytime from the heat, for a place of
refuge, and for a shelter from storm and rain.

God's Disappointing Vineyard

5 Now let me sing to my Well-beloved
      A song of my Beloved ᴿregarding His
      vineyard: Matt. 21:33

      My Well-beloved has a vineyard
      On a very fruitful hill.
2 He dug it up and cleared out its stones,
      And planted it with the choicest vine.

He built a tower in its midst,
      And also made a winepress in it;
      ᴿSo He expected *it* to bring forth *good*
         grapes,   Deut. 32:6
      But it brought forth wild grapes.

3 "And now, O inhabitants of Jerusalem
      and men of Judah,
      ᴿJudge, please, between Me and My
         vineyard.   [Rom. 3:4]
4 What more could have been done to
      My vineyard
      That I have not done in ᴿit?
      Why then, when I expected *it* to bring
         forth *good* grapes,   2 Chr. 36:15, 16
      Did it bring forth wild grapes?
5 And now, please let Me tell you what I
      will do to My vineyard:
      ᴿI will take away its hedge, and it shall
         be burned;
      And break down its wall, and it shall be
         trampled down.   Ps. 80:12; 89:40, 41
6 I will lay it ᴿwaste;   2 Chr. 36:19–21
      It shall not be pruned or ᵀdug,   *hoed*
      But there shall come up briers and
         ᴿthorns.   Is. 7:19–25
      I will also command the clouds
      That they rain no rain on it."

7 For the vineyard of the LORD of hosts *is*
      the house of Israel,
      And the men of Judah are His pleasant
         plant.
      He looked for justice, but behold,
         oppression;
      For righteousness, but behold, a cry *for*
         help.

Impending Judgment on Excesses

8 Woe to those who ᵀjoin ᴿhouse to
      house;   Accumulate houses • Mic. 2:2
      They add field to field,
      Till *there is* no place
      Where they may dwell alone in the
         midst of the land!
9 ᴿIn my hearing the LORD of hosts *said*,
      "Truly, many houses shall be desolate,
      Great and beautiful ones, without
         inhabitant.   Is. 22:14
10 For ᵀten acres of vineyard shall yield
      one ᴿbath,ᵀ   6.81 acres • Ezek. 45:11 • 6 gal.
      And a ᵀhomer of seed shall yield one
      ᵀephah."   6.524 bu. • .65 bu.

11 ᴿWoe to those who rise early in the
      morning,
      That they may ᵀfollow intoxicating
      drink;
      Who continue until night, *till* wine
         inflames them!   Prov. 23:29, 30 • *pursue*
12 ᴿThe harp and the strings,
      The tambourine and flute,
      And wine are in their feasts;

But ᴿthey do not regard the work of the
  LORD,
Nor consider the operation of His
  hands.   Amos 6:5 · Job 34:27

13 ᴿTherefore my people have gone into
     captivity,
   Because *they have* no ᴿknowledge;
   Their honorable men *are* famished,
   And their multitude dried up with
     thirst.   2 Kin. 24:14–16 · Hos. 4:6
14 Therefore Sheol has enlarged itself
   And opened its mouth beyond measure;
   Their glory and their multitude and
     their pomp,
   And he who is jubilant, shall descend
     into it.
15 People shall be brought down,
   ᴿEach man shall be humbled,
   And the eyes of the lofty shall be
     humbled.   Is. 2:9, 11
16 But the LORD of hosts shall be ᴿexalted
     in judgment,
   And God who is holy shall be hallowed
     in righteousness.   Is. 2:11
17 Then the lambs shall feed in their
     pasture,
   And in the waste places of the ᵀfat ones
     strangers shall eat.   *fatlings,* rich ones

18 Woe to those who ᵀdraw iniquity with
     cords of ᵀvanity,   *drag · emptiness* or *falsehood*
   And sin as if with a cart rope;
19 ᴿThat say, "Let Him make speed *and*
     hasten His work,
   That we may see *it*;
   And let the counsel of the Holy One of
     Israel draw near and come,
   That we may know *it.*"   Jer. 17:15

20 Woe to those who call evil good, and
     good evil;
   Who put darkness for light, and light
     for darkness;
   Who put bitter for sweet, and sweet for
     bitter!

21 Woe to *those who are* ᴿwise in their
     own eyes,   Rom. 1:22; 12:16
   And prudent in their own sight!

22 Woe to men mighty at drinking wine,
   Woe to men valiant for mixing
     intoxicating drink,
23 Who ᴿjustify the wicked for a bribe,
   And take away justice from the
     righteous man!   Prov. 17:15

24 Therefore, ᴿas the ᵀfire devours the
     stubble,   Ex. 15:7 · Lit. *tongue of fire*
   And the flame consumes the chaff,
   So ᴿtheir root will be as rottenness,
   And their blossom will ascend like dust;

Because they have rejected the law of
  the LORD of hosts,   Job 18:16
And despised the word of the Holy One
  of Israel.
25 ᴿTherefore the anger of the LORD is
     aroused against His people;
   He has stretched out His hand against
     them   2 Kin. 22:13, 17
   And stricken them,
   And ᴿthe hills trembled.   Jer. 4:24
   Their carcasses *were* as refuse in the
     midst of the streets.
   ᴿFor all this His anger is not turned
     away,   Is. 9:12, 17
   But His hand *is* stretched out still.

26 ᴿHe will lift up a banner to the nations
     from afar,   Is. 11:10, 12
   And will ᴿwhistle to them from ᴿthe end
     of the earth;   Is. 7:18 · Mal. 1:11
   Surely ᴿthey shall come with speed,
     swiftly.   Joel 2:7
27 No one will be weary or stumble among
     them,
   No one will slumber or sleep;
   Nor ᴿwill the belt on their loins be
     loosed,
   Nor the strap of their sandals be
     broken;   Dan. 5:6
28 ᴿWhose arrows *are* sharp,
   And all their bows bent;
   Their horses' hooves will ᵀseem like
     flint,   Jer. 5:16 · Lit. *be regarded as*
   And their wheels like a whirlwind.
29 Their roaring *will be* like a lion,
   They will roar like young lions;
   Yes, they will roar
   And lay hold of the prey;
   They will carry *it* away safely,
   And no one will deliver.
30 In that day they will roar against them
   Like the roaring of the sea.
   And if one ᴿlooks to the land,   Is. 8:22
   Behold, darkness *and* ᵀsorrow;   *distress*
   And the light is darkened by the clouds.

Isaiah Called to Be a Prophet

6 In the year that ᴿKing Uzziah died, I ᴿsaw
   the Lord sitting on a throne, high and
lifted up, and the train of His robe filled the
temple.   2 Kin. 15:7 · John 12:41
  2 Above it stood seraphim; each one had
six wings: with two he covered his face, with
two he covered his feet, and with two he flew.
  3 And one cried to another and said:

  "Holy, holy, holy *is* the LORD of hosts;
   The whole earth *is* full of His glory!"

  4 And the posts of the door were shaken
by the voice of him who cried out, and the
house was filled with smoke.

▼ **32-A. The Prayer of the Penitent Prophet**

5 So I said:

"Woe *is* me, for I am ᵀundone!
Because I *am* a man of ᴿunclean lips,
And I dwell in the midst of a people of
    unclean lips;   *destroyed, cut off* · Ex. 6:12, 30
For my eyes have seen the King,
▲   The LORD of hosts."

6 Then one of the seraphim flew to me,
having in his hand a live coal *which* he had
taken with the tongs from ᴿthe altar.   Rev. 8:3
7 And he ᴿtouched my mouth *with it*, and
said:

"Behold, this has touched your lips;
Your iniquity is taken away,
And your sin ᵀpurged."   Jer. 1:9 · *atoned for*

8 Also I heard the voice of the Lord, saying:

"Whom shall I send,
And who will go for ᴿUs?"   Gen. 1:26

Then I said, "Here *am* I! Send me."

9 And He said, "Go, and tell this people:

ᴿ'Keep on hearing, but do not
    understand;   Matt. 13:14, 15
Keep on seeing, but do not perceive.'

10 "Make ᴿthe heart of this people dull,
And their ears heavy,   Mark 6:1-6
And shut their eyes;
ᴿLest they see with their eyes,   Jer. 5:21
And hear with their ears,
And understand with their heart,
And return and be healed."

11 Then I said, "Lord, how long?" And He
answered:

ᴿ"Until the cities are laid waste and
    without inhabitant,
The houses are without a man,
The land is utterly desolate,   Mic. 3:12
12 ᴿThe LORD has removed men far away,
And the forsaken places *are* many in
    the midst of the land.   2 Kin. 25:21
13 But yet a tenth *will be* in it,
And will return and be for consuming,
As a terebinth tree or as an oak,
Whose stump *remains* when it is cut
    down.
So the holy seed *shall be* its stump."

Isaiah Sent to King Ahaz

7 Now it came to pass in the days of Ahaz
the son of Jotham, the son of Uzziah,
king of Judah, *that* Rezin king of Syria and
Pekah the son of Remaliah, king of Israel,
went up to Jerusalem to *make* war against it,
but could not prevail against it.

32-A. The Prayer of the Penitent Prophet (Isaiah 6:5)—This prayer marks Isaiah's personal plea for God's cleansing and also his entry into God's service. The significance of the verse that begins this passage should be noted: "In the year that King Uzziah died, I saw the Lord" (v. 1, page 647). King Uzziah, otherwise a good king of Judah, willfully attempted to take over the priest's office and burn incense in the temple. For this sin God plagued him with leprosy, which remained with him until he died (2 Chr. 26:16-21, page 431). Uzziah's leprosy was a vivid reminder to Isaiah of the absolute, holy standards of God, which not even a king could violate with impunity. Against this background we see

(1) *Isaiah's vision.* Isaiah saw a glimmer of heaven as he entered the temple. In this glimpse of the heavenly throne, Isaiah heard and beheld

(a) the majesty of God, above all kings (v. 1);
(b) the court of God, surrounded by winged seraphim (v. 2);
(c) the acclamation of God's holiness, given threefold, as in Revelation 4:8 (page 1297), implying God's tri-unity, or the Trinity (v. 3).

(2) *Isaiah's reaction.* Isaiah's response to this vision of God's holiness is voiced in the prayer of the penitent prophet (v. 5). Here he exclaims

(a) his realization that he is a sinner—"Woe is me, for I am undone!";
(b) his confession that he is unclean before God—"I am a man of unclean lips";
(c) his acknowledgment that his entire nation is a sinful people—"a people of unclean lips."

(3) *Isaiah's call.* As a result of Isaiah's confession came God's cleansing and invitation to service. Note that since Isaiah confessed

(a) his sinfulness, God cleansed him (vv. 6, 7);
(b) his sinful lips, God consecrated his lips to be used in the future to prophesy for Him (vv. 7-9);
(c) the sinfulness of his nation, God called him to go to the people with the message of God's salvation, which the majority of that generation would not receive (vv. 9-13).

Isaiah's prayer of confession was also Peter's prayer at seeing Christ's holiness and majesty (Luke 5:8, page 1018). It was Paul's prayer, too (Acts 9:4-6, page 1100). Someday, in the future, it will be Israel's prayer (Zech. 12:10, page 918). May we follow the prophets and apostles ourselves, in praying the prayer of the penitent prophet when we are confronted with God's holiness. May we heed His call for servants to deliver His message of life.

See Isaiah 25:1-9, page 665, for **Point 32-B: Kingdom Prayer and Praise.**

2 And it was told to the house of David, saying, "Syria's forces are ᵀdeployed in Ephraim." So his heart and the heart of his people were moved as the trees of the woods are moved with the wind.   Lit. *settled upon*

3 Then the LORD said to Isaiah, "Go out now to meet Ahaz, you and ᵀShear-Jashub your son, at the end of the aqueduct from the upper pool, on the highway to the Fuller's Field,   Lit. *A Remnant Shall Return*

4 "and say to him: ᵀ'Take heed, and ᵀbe ᴿquiet; do not fear or be fainthearted for these two stubs of smoking firebrands, for the fierce anger of Rezin and Syria, and the son of Remaliah.   *Be careful · be calm ·* Is. 30:15

5 'Because Syria, Ephraim, and the son of Remaliah have plotted evil against you, saying,

6 "Let us go up against Judah and ᵀtrouble it, and let us make a gap in its wall for ourselves, and set a king over them, the son of Tabel"—   *cause a sickening dread*

7 'thus says the Lord GOD:

ᴿ"It shall not stand,
Nor shall it come to pass.   Is. 8:10
8 ᴿFor the head of Syria *is* Damascus,
And the head of Damascus *is* Rezin.
Within sixty-five years Ephraim will be
ᵀbroken,   2 Sam. 8:6 · Lit. *shattered*
So that it *will* not *be* a people.
9 The head of Ephraim *is* Samaria,
And the head of Samaria *is* Remaliah's son.
ᴿIf you will not believe,   2 Chr. 20:20
Surely you shall not be established." ' "

The Immanuel Prophecy

10 Moreover the LORD spoke again to Ahaz, saying,

11 "Ask a sign for yourself from the LORD your God; ᵀask it either in the depth or in the height above."   Lit. *make the request deep or high above*

12 But Ahaz said, "I will not ask, nor will I test the LORD!"

13 Then he said, "Hear now, O house of David! *Is it* a small thing for you to weary men, but will you weary my God also?

7-C. Jesus Is Immanuel   ▼

14 "Therefore the Lord Himself will give you a sign: ᴿBehold, the virgin shall conceive and bear a ᴿSon, and shall call His name *Immanuel.   Matt. 1:23; Luke 1:31, 34, 35 · [Is. 9:6]

15 "Curds and honey He shall eat, that He may know to refuse the evil and choose the good.

16 ᴿFor before the Child shall know to refuse the evil and choose the good, the land that you dread will be forsaken by ᴿboth her kings.   Is. 8:4 · 2 Kin. 15:30 ▲

17 "The LORD will bring the king of Assyria upon you and your people and your father's house—days that have not come since the day that Ephraim departed from Judah."

18 And it shall come to pass in that day
That the LORD ᴿwill whistle for the fly
That *is* in the farthest part of the rivers of Egypt,
And for the bee that *is* in the land of Assyria.   Is. 5:26
19 They will come, and all of them will rest
In the desolate valleys and in ᴿthe clefts of the rocks,   Jer. 16:16
And on all thorns and in all pastures.
20 In the same day the Lord will shave with a ᴿhired razor,   Is. 10:5, 15

7:14 Lit. *God with Us*

7-C. Jesus Is Immanuel (Isaiah 7:14–16)—As we study the prophecies of the Old Testament, we discover that some have a dual fulfillment. The first event is often close at hand, and its greatest value is in its *typology*, that is, in its typifying a greater, future event or truth. The second event might be hundreds—even thousands—of years in the future.

God spoke to the house of David saying, "Before the Child shall know to refuse the evil and choose the good, the land that you dread [Syria and Israel] will be forsaken by both her kings" (v. 16; cf. Is. 7:1–7). So the child in verse 16 is not the virgin-born Immanuel. He is a type of Immanuel. He is the son that was to be born to Isaiah and to the unnamed virgin he would marry (his second wife). This virgin is a type of the Virgin Mary who would give birth to Immanuel.

At the time God gave this prophecy to the house of David, Isaiah's betrothed was a virgin (Is. 8:3, 4, page 650). When Isaiah's son became old enough to refuse evil and choose good, the Lord said, "The land that you dread [Syria and Israel] will be forsaken by both her kings" (v. 16). Soon after, Syria and Israel were indeed defeated by Assyria. The defeat was the fulfillment of an impending event; but the definitive fulfillment of this wonderful prophecy would not occur for seven hundred years.

Read how Immanuel was born of the Virgin Mary, and fulfilled the prophecy of Isaiah. "So all this was done that it might be fulfilled which was spoken by the Lord through the prophet [Isaiah], saying: 'Behold, the virgin shall be with child, and bear a Son, and they shall call His name Immanuel,' which is translated, 'God with us.' Then Joseph, being aroused from sleep, did as the angel of the Lord commanded him and took to him his wife, and did not know her till she had brought forth her firstborn Son. And he called His name JESUS" (Matt. 1:18–25, page 930). The virgin-born Jesus, our Lord and Savior, is Immanuel, GOD WITH US.

See Isaiah 9:6, 7, page 651, for **Point 7-D: Jesus Is the Father's Gift to Us.**

With those from beyond ᵀthe River,
with the king of Assyria, The Euphrates
The head and the hair of the legs,
And will also remove the beard.

21 It shall be in that day,
That a man will keep alive a young cow
and two sheep;
22 So it shall be, from the abundance of
milk they give,
That he will eat curds;
For curds and honey everyone will eat
who is left in the land.

23 It shall happen in that day,
That wherever there could be a
thousand vines
Worth a thousand *shekels* of silver,
ᴿIt will be for briers and thorns.   Is. 5:6
24 With arrows and bows men will come
there,
Because all the land will become briers
and thorns.

25 And to any hill which could be dug
with the hoe,
You will not go there for fear of briers
and thorns;
But it will become a range for oxen
And a place for sheep to roam.

Assyria Will Invade the Land

8 Moreover the LORD said to me, "Take a
large scroll, and write on it with a man's
pen concerning Maher-Shalal-Hash-Baz.
2 "And I will take for Myself faithful witnesses to record, ᴿUriah the priest and Zechariah the son of Jeberechiah."   2 Kin. 16:10
3 Then I went to the prophetess, and she
conceived and bore a son. Then the LORD said
to me, "Call his name Maher-Shalal-Hash-
Baz;
4 ᴿ"for before the child ᵀshall have knowledge to cry 'My father' and 'My mother,' ᴿthe
riches of Damascus and the ᵀspoil of Samaria
will be taken away before the king of As-
syria."   2 Kin. 17:6 • *knows how* • 2 Kin. 15:29 • *plunder*
5 The LORD also spoke to me again, say-
ing:

6"Inasmuch as these people refused
The waters of ᴿShiloah that flow softly,
And rejoice ᴿin Rezin and in Remaliah's
son;   John 9:7 • Is. 7:1, 2
7 Now therefore, behold, the Lord brings
up over them
The waters of ᵀthe River, strong and
mighty—   The Euphrates
The king of Assyria and all his glory;
He will ᵀgo up over all his channels
And go over all his banks.   Overflow
8 He will pass through Judah,
He will overflow and pass over,
ᴿHe will reach up to the neck;   Is. 30:28

And the stretching out of his wings
Will ᵀfill the breadth of Your land, O
ᴿImmanuel.*   Lit. *be fullness of* • Is. 7:14

9"Beᴿ shattered, O you peoples, and be
broken in pieces!
Give ear, all you from far countries.
Gird yourselves, but be broken in
pieces;
Gird yourselves, but be broken in
pieces.   Joel 3:9
10 ᴿTake counsel together, but it will come
to nothing;   Is. 7:7
Speak the word, but it will not stand,
For ᵀGod *is* with us."   Heb. *Immanuel*

Fear God, Heed His Word

11 For the LORD spoke thus to me with a
strong hand, and instructed me that I should
not walk in the way of this people, saying:

12"Do not say, 'A conspiracy,'
Concerning all that this people call a
conspiracy,
Nor be afraid of their ᵀthreats, nor be
ᵀtroubled.   Lit. *fear* or *terror* • Lit. *in dread*
13 The LORD of hosts, Him you shall
hallow;
Let Him *be* your fear,
And *let* Him *be* your dread.
14 He will be as a ᵀsanctuary,   *holy abode*
But a ᴿstone of stumbling and a rock of
ᵀoffense   Luke 2:34; 20:17 • *stumbling over*
To both the houses of Israel,
As a trap and a snare to the inhabitants
of Jerusalem.
15 And many among them shall ᴿstumble;
They shall fall and be broken,
Be snared and ᵀtaken."   Matt. 21:44 • *captured*

16 Bind up the testimony,
Seal the law among my disciples.
17 And I will wait on the LORD,
Who ᴿhides His face from the house of
Jacob;
And I ᴿwill hope in Him.   Is. 54:8 • Hab. 2:3
18 ᴿHere am I and the children whom the
LORD has given me!   Heb. 2:13
We ᴿ*are* for signs and wonders in Israel
From the LORD of hosts,   Ps. 71:7
Who dwells in Mount Zion.

19 And when they say to you, ᴿ"Seek those
who are mediums and wizards, ᴿwho whisper
and mutter," should not a people seek their
God? *Should they* ᴿ*seek* the dead on behalf of
the living?   1 Sam. 28:8 • Is. 29:4 • Ps. 106:28
20 To the law and to the testimony! If they
do not speak according to this word, *it is*
because ᴿthere *is* no light in them.   Mic. 3:6
21 They will pass through it hard pressed
and hungry; and it shall happen, when they
are hungry, that they will be enraged and

8:8 Lit. *God With Us*

curse ᵀtheir king and their God, and look
upward.   *Or by their king and by their God*
22 Then they will look to the earth, and see
trouble and darkness, gloom of anguish; and
they will be driven into darkness.

The Government of the Promised Son

9 Nevertheless ᴿthe gloom *will not be*
upon her who *is* distressed,   Is. 8:22
As when at first He lightly esteemed
ᴿThe land of Zebulun and the land of
Naphtali,   Matt. 4:13-16
And afterward more heavily oppressed
her,
By the way of the sea, beyond the
Jordan,
In Galilee of the Gentiles.
2 The ᴿpeople who walked in darkness
Have seen a great light;   Luke 1:79
Those who dwelt in the land of the
shadow of death,
Upon them a light has shined.

3 You have multiplied the nation
And *increased its joy;
They rejoice before You
According to the joy of harvest,
As *men* rejoice ᴿwhen they divide the
spoil.   Judg. 5:30
4 For You have broken the yoke of his
burden
And the staff of his shoulder,
The rod of his oppressor,
As in the day of ᴿMidian.   Judg. 7:22
5 For every warrior's ᵀsandal from the
noisy battle,
And garments rolled in blood,

9:3 So with Qr., Tg.; Kt., Vg. *not increased joy;* LXX *most
of the people You brought down in Your joy*

ᴿWill be used for burning *and* fuel ᵀof
fire.   *boot • Is. 66:15 • for the fire*

7-D. Jesus Is the Father's Gift to Us ▼

6 ᴿFor unto us a Child is born,
Unto us a Son is given;   [Is. 7:14; Luke 2:11]
And ᴿthe government will be upon His
shoulder.   [Matt. 28:18]
And His name will be called
Wonderful, Counselor, Mighty God,
Everlasting Father, Prince of Peace.
7 Of the increase of *His* government and
peace
ᴿ*There will be* no end,
Upon the throne of David and over His
kingdom,   Dan. 2:44; Luke 1:32, 33
To order it and establish it with
judgment and justice
From that time forward, even forever.
The ᴿzeal of the LORD of hosts will
perform this.   Is. 37:32 ▲

The Punishment of Samaria

8 The LORD sent a word against ᴿJacob,
And it has fallen on Israel.   Gen. 32:28
9 All the people will know—
Ephraim and the inhabitant of
Samaria—
Who say in pride and arrogance of
heart:
10 "The bricks have fallen down,
But we will rebuild with hewn stones;
The sycamores are cut down,
But we will replace *them* with cedars."
11 Therefore the LORD shall set up
The adversaries of Rezin against him,
And spur his enemies on,
12 The Syrians before and the Philistines
behind;

7-D. Jesus Is the Father's Gift to Us (Isaiah 9:6, 7)—"For unto us a Child is born" (v. 6). The "us" is the Hebrew nation and all believers of all nations. John tells us, "He came to His own, and His own did not receive Him. But as many as received Him [individuals, Jews or Gentiles], to them He gave the right to become children of God, to those who believe in His name" (John 1:11, 12, page 1049).

"Unto us a Son is given" (v. 6). "For God so loved the world that He gave His only begotten Son" (John 3:16, page 1052). Jesus, "who Himself bore our sins in His own body on the tree" (1 Pet. 2:24, page 1266) is God the Father's gift to us. This portion of the prophecy was fulfilled when the Virgin Mary "brought forth her firstborn Son, and wrapped Him in swaddling cloths, and laid Him in a manger" (Luke 2:1-7, page 1012).

The rest of the prophecy (vv. 6, 7) will not come to pass until Jesus the Messiah returns to earth (Acts 1:9-11, page 1087; cf. Matt. 24:44, page 975).

(1) When He comes again, "the government will be upon His shoulder" (v. 6). What a great day that will be, when He carries the government upon His all-powerful shoulders! Only then will the world know righteous government (Heb. 1:8, page 1236).

(2) When He comes again, His kingdom name (not *names*) will be "Wonderful, Counselor, Mighty God, Everlasting Father, Prince of Peace" (v. 6).

(a) *"Wonderful."* Before the days of His flesh, when Christ manifested Himself as "the Angel of the LORD" announcing the birth of Samson to Manoah and his wife, Manoah asked, "What is Your name?" Christ answered, "Why do you ask My name, seeing it is wonderful?" (Judg. 13:17, 18, page 255).

(b) *"Counselor."* Jesus is the perfect counselor. Therefore, He never sought or needed counseling from any man (Rom. 11:33, 34, page 1142).

(c) *"Mighty God."* In the kingdom, Jesus is "the great God, mighty and awesome" (Deut. 10:17, page 191). When Jesus, the "Mighty God," sits on the throne of His glory in His kingdom, all nations will come

(Point 7-D continued on next page)

And they shall devour Israel with an open mouth.

For all this His anger is not turned away,
But His hand *is* stretched out still.

13 For the people do not turn to Him who strikes them,
Nor do they seek the LORD of hosts.

14 Therefore the LORD will cut off head and tail from Israel,
Palm branch and bulrush in one day.

15 The elder and honorable, he *is* the head;
The prophet who teaches lies, he *is* the tail.

16 For ᴿthe leaders of this people cause *them* to err,
And *those who are* led by them are destroyed.   Is. 3:12

17 Therefore the LORD ᴿwill have no joy in their young men,   Ps. 147:10
Nor have mercy on their fatherless and widows;
For everyone *is* a hypocrite and an evildoer,
And every mouth speaks folly.

ᴿFor all this His anger is not turned away,   Is. 5:25
But His hand *is* stretched out still.

18 For wickedness burns as the fire;
It shall devour the briers and thorns,
And kindle in the thickets of the forest;
They shall mount up *like* rising smoke.

19 Through the wrath of the LORD of hosts
ᴿThe land is burned up,   Is. 8:22
And the people shall be as fuel for the fire;
ᴿNo man shall spare his brother.   Mic. 7:2, 6

20 And he shall ᵀsnatch on the right hand
And be hungry;
He shall devour on the left hand
ᴿAnd not be satisfied;
ᴿEvery man shall eat the flesh of his own arm.   *slice off* or *tear* · Lev. 26:26 · Jer. 19:9

21 Manasseh *shall devour* Ephraim, and Ephraim Manasseh,
Together they *shall be* against Judah.

ᴿFor all this His anger is not turned away,   Is. 9:12, 17
But His hand *is* stretched out still.

10 "Woe to those who ᴿdecree   Ps. 58:2
unrighteous decrees,
Who write misfortune,
Which they have prescribed

2 To rob the needy of justice,
And to take what is right from the poor of My people,
That widows may be their prey,
And *that* they may rob the fatherless.

3 ᴿWhat will you do in ᴿthe day of punishment,   Job 31:14 · Hos. 9:7
And in the desolation *which* will come from ᴿafar?   Is. 5:26
To whom will you flee for help?
And where will you leave your glory?

4 Without Me they shall bow down among the ᴿprisoners,   Is. 24:22
And they shall fall among the slain."

ᴿFor all this His anger is not turned away,   Is. 5:25
But His hand *is* stretched out still.

Arrogant Assyria Also Judged

5 "Woe to Assyria, ᴿthe rod of My anger
And the staff in whose hand is My indignation.   Jer. 51:20

(Point 7-D continued from previous page)
before Him to be judged. He will separate the righteous from the unrighteous. The unrighteous will learn what it means to stand in judgment before God (Matt. 25:31–46, page 976).

(d) *"Everlasting Father."* Jesus is the Father Eternal who watches over His own. He said, "I and My Father are one" (John 10:30, page 1068). Jesus did not say that the Son and the Father are one person; they are two persons in one substance. When Jesus was baptized in the Jordan River, God His Father spoke from heaven, saying, "This is My beloved Son, in whom I am well pleased" (Matt. 3:17, page 934). Philip said to Jesus, "Lord, show us the Father." Jesus answered Philip, "He who has seen Me has seen the Father. . . . Do you not believe that I am in the Father, and the Father in Me?" (John 14:7–11, page 1074). The Father, the Son and the Holy Spirit are one God in three persons.

(e) *"Prince of Peace."* Until the everlasting kingdom is established, there will be no lasting world peace (Matt. 24:4–8, page 973; cf. 1 Thess. 5:1–3, page 1212). But Paul tells us that, in the midst of a world in which there is no peace, we can have "peace with God through our Lord Jesus Christ" (Rom. 5:1, page 1133).

(3) When He comes again, there will be no end to the increase of His government or of peace (v. 7). His government will not become stagnant; there will be no end to its growth, and we will continue to grow in grace and knowledge with it (2 Pet. 3:18, page 1276).

(4) When He comes again, He will sit on the throne of David. David's throne will be an actual throne. He is not on David's throne now, but when He comes He will rule the world in righteousness. He is now seated with His Father on His Father's throne (Rev. 3:21, page 1297), and He will remain on the Father's throne until His bride, the church, is ready (2 Cor. 11:2, page 1174).

Verses 6 and 7 cover both the first and second coming of Jesus. It is one of the clearest and most revealing messianic prophecies in the Old Testament.
See Psalm 45:6, 7, page 538, for **Point 7-E: Jesus Is God, According to God the Father.**

6 I will send him against ᴿan ungodly
    nation,   Is. 9:17
  And against the people of My wrath
  I will ᴿgive him charge,   Jer. 34:22
  To seize the spoil, to take the prey,
  And to tread them down like the mire
    of the streets.
7 ᴿYet he does not mean so,   Gen. 50:20
  Nor does his heart think so;
  But *it is* in his heart to destroy,
  And cut off not a few nations.
8 ᴿFor he says,   2 Kin. 19:10
  '*Are* not my princes altogether kings?
9 *Is* not ᴿCalno like Carchemish?
  Is not Hamath like Arpad?   Amos 6:2
  Is not Samaria ᴿlike Damascus?   2 Kin. 16:9
10 As my hand has found the kingdoms of
    the idols,
  Whose carved images excelled those of
    Jerusalem and Samaria,
11 As I have done to Samaria and her
    idols,
  Shall I not do also to Jerusalem and her
    idols?' "

12 Therefore it shall come to pass, when the
Lᴏʀᴅ has ᵀperformed all His work ᴿon Mount
Zion and on Jerusalem, *that He will say,* ᴿ"I
will punish the fruit of the arrogant heart of
the king of Assyria, and the glory of his
haughty looks."   *completed* · 2 Kin. 19:31 · Jer. 50:18
13 ᴿFor he says: Is. 37:24-27

  "By the strength of my hand I have
    done *it,*
  And by my wisdom, for I am prudent;
  Also I have removed the boundaries of
    the people,
  And have robbed their treasuries;
  So I have put down the inhabitants like
    a ᵀvaliant *man.*   *mighty*
14 ᴿMy hand has found like a nest the
    riches of the people,   Job 31:25
  And as one gathers eggs *that are* left,
  I have gathered all the earth;
  And there was no one who moved *his*
    wing,
  Nor opened *his* mouth with even a
    peep."

15 Shall ᴿthe ax boast itself against him
    who chops with it?   Jer. 51:20
  Or shall the saw exalt itself against him
    who saws with it?
  As if a rod could wield *itself* against
    those who lift it up,
  Or as if a staff could lift up, *as if it
    were* not wood!
16 Therefore the Lord, the *Lord of hosts,
  Will send leanness among his fat ones;
  And under his glory
  He will kindle a burning
  Like the burning of a fire.

17 So the Light of Israel will be for a fire,
  And his Holy One for a flame;
  ᴿIt will burn and devour   Is. 9:18
  His thorns and his briers in one day.
18 And it will consume the glory of his
    forest and of ᴿhis fruitful field,
  Both soul and body;   2 Kin. 19:23
  And they will be as when a sick man
    wastes away.
19 Then the rest of the trees of his forest
  Will be so few in number
  That a child may write them.

The Returning Remnant of Israel

20 And it shall come to pass in that day
  That the remnant of Israel,
  And such as have escaped of the house
    of Jacob,
  ᴿWill never again depend on him who
    ᵀdefeated them,   2 Kin. 16:7 · *struck*
  But will depend on the Lᴏʀᴅ, the Holy
    One of Israel, in truth.
21 The remnant will return, the remnant
    of Jacob,
  To the ᴿMighty God.   [Is. 9:6]
22 ᴿFor though your people, O Israel, be as
    the sand of the sea,   Rom. 9:27, 28
  ᴿA remnant of them will return;
  The destruction decreed shall overflow
    with righteousness.   Is. 6:13
23 ᴿFor the Lord Gᴏᴅ of hosts   Dan. 9:27
  Will make a determined end
  In the midst of all the land.

24 Therefore thus says the Lord Gᴏᴅ of
hosts: "O My people, who dwell in Zion, ᴿdo
not be afraid of the Assyrian. He shall strike
you with a rod and lift up his staff against
you, in the manner of Egypt.   Is. 7:4; 12:2
25 "For yet a very little while ᴿand the
indignation will cease, as will My anger in
their destruction."   Dan. 11:36
26 And the Lᴏʀᴅ of hosts will ᵀstir up ᴿa
scourge for him like the slaughter of ᴿMidian
at the rock of Oreb; ᴿ*as* His rod *was* on the
sea, so will He lift it up in the manner of
Egypt.   *arouse* · 2 Kin. 19:35 · Is. 9:4 · Ex. 14:26, 27

27 It shall come to pass in that day
  That his burden will be taken away
    from your shoulder,
  And his yoke from your neck,
  And the yoke will be destroyed because
    of ᴿthe anointing oil.   Ps. 105:15
28 He has come to Aiath,
  He has passed Migron;
  At Michmash he has attended to his
    equipment.
29 They have gone ᵀalong ᴿthe ridge,
  They have taken up lodging at Geba.
  Ramah is afraid,   Or *over the pass* · 1 Sam. 13:23
  ᴿGibeah of Saul has fled.   1 Sam. 11:4
30 ᵀLift up your voice,   *Or Cry shrilly*
  O daughter ᴿof Gallim!   1 Sam. 25:44

10:16 So with Bg.; MT, DSS *YHWH, the* Lᴏʀᴅ

Cause it to be heard as far as ᴿLaish—
*O poor Anathoth!   Judg. 18:7
31 ᴿMadmenah has fled,   Josh. 15:31
The inhabitants of Gebim seek refuge.
32 As yet he will remain at Nob that day;
He will ᴿshake his fist at the mount of
ᴿthe daughter of Zion,
The hill of Jerusalem.   Is. 13:2 • Is. 37:22
33 Behold, the Lord,
The Lᴏʀᴅ of hosts,
Will lop off the bough with terror;
ᴿThose of high stature *will be* hewn
down,   Amos 2:9
And the haughty will be humbled.
34 He will cut down the thickets of the
forest with iron,
And Lebanon will fall by the Mighty
One.

The Reign of Jesse's Offspring

11 There ᴿshall come forth a Rod from
the stem of Jesse,   [Zech. 6:12]
And ᴿa Branch shall ᵀgrow out of his
roots.   Is. 4:2 • *be fruitful*
2 ᴿThe Spirit of the Lᴏʀᴅ shall rest upon
Him,
The Spirit of wisdom and
understanding,
The Spirit of counsel and might,
The Spirit of knowledge and of the fear
of the Lᴏʀᴅ.   [John 1:32]
3 His delight *is* in the fear of the Lᴏʀᴅ,
ᴿAnd He shall not judge by the sight of
His eyes,   John 2:25
Nor decide by the hearing of His ears;
4 But ᴿwith righteousness He shall judge
the poor,
And decide with equity for the meek of
the earth;
He shall ᴿstrike the earth with the rod
of His mouth,
And with the breath of His lips He shall
slay the wicked.   Rev. 19:11 • Job 4:9
5 Righteousness shall be the belt of His
loins,
And faithfulness the belt of His waist.

▼ 33-F. The Peace That Someday Will Be Israel's

6 "Theᴿ wolf also shall dwell with the
lamb,   Hos. 2:18
The leopard shall lie down with the
young goat,
The calf and the young lion and the
fatling together;

10:30 So with MT, Tg., Vg.; LXX, Syr. *Listen to her, O
Anathoth*

And a little child shall lead them.   ▽
7 The cow and the bear shall graze;
Their young ones shall lie down
together;
And the lion shall eat straw like the ox.
8 The nursing child shall play by the
cobra's hole,
And the weaned child shall put his
hand in the viper's den.
9 ᴿThey shall not hurt nor destroy in all
My holy mountain,   Job 5:23
For ᴿthe earth shall be full of the
knowledge of the Lᴏʀᴅ   Hab. 2:14
As the waters cover the sea.

10 "Andᴿ in that day ᴿthere shall be a ᴿRoot
of Jesse,   Is. 2:11 • Rom. 15:12 • Is. 11:1
Who shall stand as a ᴿbanner to the
people;   Is. 27:12, 13
For the Gentiles shall seek Him,
And His resting place shall be glorious."

11 It shall come to pass in that day
That the Lᴏʀᴅ shall set His hand again
the second time
To recover the remnant of His people
who are left,
ᴿFrom Assyria and Egypt,
From Pathros and Cush,
From Elam and Shinar,
From Hamath and the ᵀislands of the
sea.   Zech. 10:10 • Or *coastlands*

12 He will set up a banner for the nations,
And will ᵀassemble the outcasts of
Israel,   *gather*
And gather together ᴿthe dispersed of
Judah   John 7:35
From the four corners of the earth.   ▲
13 Also ᴿthe envy of Ephraim shall depart,
And the adversaries of Judah shall be
cut off;   Jer. 3:18
Ephraim shall not envy Judah,
And Judah shall not harass Ephraim.
14 But they shall fly down upon the
shoulder of the Philistines toward the
west;
Together they shall plunder the ᵀpeople
of the East;
ᴿThey shall lay their hand on Edom and
Moab;
And the people of Ammon shall obey
them.   Lit. *sons* • Dan. 11:41
15 The Lᴏʀᴅ will utterly *destroy the
tongue of the Sea of Egypt;
With His mighty wind He will shake
His fist over ᵀthe River,   The Euphrates

11:15 So with MT, Vg.; LXX, [Syr.]; Tg. *dry up*

33-F. The Peace That Someday Will Be Israel's (Isaiah 11:6–12)—Today, most Jewish people are scattered
over the world, some have returned to Israel, and some are still looking for the Messiah. The nation of Israel
itself lives in an atmosphere of tension concerning the future. Someday, according to the Bible, after the
struggle and tribulation of this age, the Jewish people will at last find their long-awaited rest. All peoples,
(Point 33-F continued on next page)

And strike it in the seven streams,
And make *men* cross over dryshod.
16 ^RThere will be a highway for the
  remnant of His people
Who will be left from Assyria,
  ^RAs it was for Israel
In the day that he came up from the
  land of Egypt.   Is. 19:23 · Ex. 14:29

A Hymn of Praise

12 And ^Rin that day you will say:

"O LORD, I will praise You;
  Though You were angry with me,
  Your anger is turned away, and You
  comfort me.   Is. 2:11
2 Behold, God *is* my salvation,
  I will trust and not be afraid;
  ^R'For ^RYAH, the LORD, *is* my strength and
  song;   Ex. 15:2 · Ps. 83:18
  He also has become my salvation.' "

3 Therefore with joy you will draw
  ^Rwater
From the wells of salvation.   [John 4:10, 14]

4 And in that day you will say:

  ^R"Praise the LORD, call upon His name;
  ^RDeclare His deeds among the peoples,

Make mention that His ^Rname is
  exalted.   1 Chr. 16:8 · Ps. 145:4–6 · Ps. 34:3
5 ^RSing to the LORD,
  For He has done excellent things;
  This *is* known in all the earth.   Ex. 15:1
6 ^RCry out and shout, O inhabitant of
  Zion,
  For great *is* ^Rthe Holy One of Israel in
  your midst!"   Zeph. 3:14, 15 · Ps. 89:18

Proclamation Against Babylon

13 The burden against Babylon which
  Isaiah the son of Amoz saw.

2 "Lift^R up a banner ^Ron the high
  mountain,   Is. 18:3 · Jer. 51:25
  Raise your voice to them;
  ^RWave your hand, that they may enter
  the gates of the nobles.   Is. 10:32
3 I have commanded My ^Tsanctified ones;
  I have also called ^RMy mighty ones for
  My anger—   *consecrated* or *set apart* · Joel 3:11
  Those who rejoice in My exaltation."

4 The ^Rnoise of a multitude in the
  mountains,
  Like that of many people!
  A tumultuous noise of the kingdoms of
  nations gathered together!
  The LORD of hosts musters
  The army for battle.   Is. 17:12

(Point 33-F continued from previous page)
including Jews and Arabs, will at last live side by side in the unity of peace (Zech. 14:16–21, page 919). God desires, invites, and demands fellowship with Egyptians and all Arab peoples, in Jerusalem, in the millennial age of peace.

(1) The nation Israel was founded during a search for a refuge.
      (a) The British Balfour Declaration (1917) committed England to work toward the establishment of a Jewish homeland in Palestine. This was the beginning of the return of a remnant.
      (b) In World War I, General Allenby conquered the Turks (allies of the Axis powers) who were then occupying the west side of the Jordan. At the same time, independent Arab armies (spurred by Lawrence of Arabia) conquered the lands east of the Jordan from the Turks.
      (c) The Jews in Russia were especially persecuted. In 1917 when the Czar of Russia was removed by the communist revolution, some Jews thought that communism (where all workers are equal) would bring in a new state of equality where all men would be brothers. This ideal was soon betrayed, and ultimately Jews were again persecuted by the atheistic communist state, even as they had been under the Czar.
      (d) Hitler's Nazi machine, as a tool of Satan, in 1939–1945, placed the Jews of Poland, Germany, Austria, France, and Holland into concentration camps; six million Jews were exterminated in this holocaust.
      (e) The British governed Palestine from 1917–1948 under a mandate from the League of Nations.
      (f) When the British left Palestine in 1948, war broke out; on May 14, 1948, Israel declared itself an independent nation. A welcome was announced for all Jewish people who wished to return to their historic homeland—a land which had been theirs in the days of Joshua, the judges, and the kings, and from where the Romans had driven them in A.D. 70.
      (g) In 1956 Israel fought Egypt, which was armed by Russia, in the Sinai campaign.
      (h) In 1967 the Six-Day War was fought. Israel regained the entire land west of the Jordan, including Jerusalem and the central west bank of the Jordan River, which the nation Jordan had held.
      (i) In 1973, Israel was suddenly attacked in the Yom Kippur War by Egypt and Syria.
(2) Christ, at His second coming, will rescue Israel from its tribulation and will "destroy all the nations that come against Jerusalem" (Zech. 12:9, page 918; cf. 14:3, 4, page 919).
(3) The Jewish people will then find spiritual peace as "they will look on Me whom they pierced" (Zech. 12:10, page 918; cf. 13:1, 2, page 918).
(4) Christ will bring His peace to the entire millennial world and will regather the Jewish people (vv. 4–12). "New Jerusalem" (Rev. 21:2, page 1315) will be the capital city of the eternal state which will someday come, and which will remain at peace forever and ever. "Even so, come, Lord Jesus!" (Rev. 22:20, page 1317).

See Index, page 17, for your next study.

5 They come from a far country,
From the end of heaven—
The ᴿLORD and His ᵀweapons of
indignation,   Is. 42:13 · Or *instruments*
To destroy the whole land.

6 Wail, ᴿfor the day of the LORD *is* at
hand!   Zeph. 1:7
ᴿIt will come as destruction from the
Almighty.   Joel 1:15
7 Therefore all hands will be limp,
Every man's heart will melt,
8 And they will be afraid.
ᴿPangsᵀ and sorrows will take hold of
them;   Ps. 48:6 · *Sharp pains*
They will be in pain as a woman in
childbirth;
They will be amazed at one another;
Their faces *will be like* flames.

9 Behold, ᴿthe day of the LORD comes,
Cruel, with both wrath and fierce
anger,
To lay the land desolate;   Mal. 4:1
And He will destroy its sinners from it.
10 For the stars of heaven and their
constellations
Will not give their light;
The sun will be ᴿdarkened in its going
forth,
And the moon will not cause its light to
shine.   Joel 2:31
11 "I will ᴿpunish the world for *its* evil,
And the wicked for their iniquity;
ᴿI will halt the arrogance of the proud,
And will lay low the haughtiness of the
ᵀterrible.   Is. 26:21 · [Is. 2:17] · Or *tyrants*
12 I will make a mortal more rare than
fine gold,
A man more than the golden wedge of
Ophir.
13 ᴿTherefore I will shake the heavens,
And the earth will move out of her
place,   Hag. 2:6
In the wrath of the LORD of hosts
And in the day of His fierce anger.
14 It shall be as the hunted gazelle,
And as a sheep that no man takes up;
Every man will turn to his own people,
And everyone will flee to his own land.
15 Everyone who is found will be thrust
through,
And everyone who is captured will fall
by the sword.
16 Their children also will be ᴿdashed to
pieces before their eyes;   Nah. 3:10
Their houses will be plundered
And their wives ᴿravished.   Zech. 14:2

17 "Behold,ᴿ I will stir up the Medes against
them,
Who will not ᵀregard silver;
And *as for* gold, they will not delight in
it.   Dan. 5:28, 31 · *esteem*

18 Also *their* bows will dash the young
men to pieces,
And they will have no pity on the fruit
of the womb;
Their eye will not spare children.
19 ᴿAnd Babylon, the glory of kingdoms,
The beauty of the Chaldeans' pride,
Will be as when God overthrew ᴿSodom
and Gomorrah.   Is. 14:4 · Gen. 19:24
20 ᴿIt will never be inhabited,
Nor will it be settled from generation to
generation;
Nor will the Arabian pitch tents there,
Nor will the shepherds make their
sheepfolds there.   Jer. 50:3
21 ᴿBut wild beasts of the desert will lie
there,   Is. 34:11–15
And their houses will be full of owls;
Ostriches will dwell there,
And wild goats will caper there.
22 The hyenas will howl in their citadels,
And jackals in their pleasant palaces.
ᴿHer time *is* near to come,   Jer. 51:33
And her days will not be prolonged."

Mercy on Jacob

14 For the LORD ᴿwill have mercy on
Jacob, and will still choose Israel, and
settle them in their own land. ᴿThe strangers
will be joined with them, and they will cling
to the house of Jacob.   Ps. 102:13 · Is. 60:4, 5, 10
2 Then people will take them ᴿand bring
them to their place, and the house of Israel
will possess them for servants and maids in
the land of the LORD; they will take them
captive whose captives they were, ᴿand rule
over their oppressors.   Is. 49:22; 60:9; 66:20 · Is. 60:14

Fall of the King of Babylon

3 It shall come to pass in the day the LORD
gives you rest from your sorrow, and from
your fear and the hard bondage in which you
were made to serve,
4 that you ᴿwill take up this proverb
against the king of Babylon, and say: Hab. 2:6

"How the oppressor has ceased,
The ᵀgolden city ceased!   Or *insolent*
5 The LORD has broken ᴿthe staff of the
wicked,
The scepter of the rulers;   Ps. 125:3
6 He who struck the people in wrath with
a continual stroke,
He who ruled the nations in anger,
Is persecuted *and* no one hinders.
7 The whole earth is at rest *and* quiet;
They break forth into singing.
8 ᴿIndeed the cypress trees rejoice over
you,   Ezek. 31:16
And the cedars of Lebanon,
Saying, 'Since you were cut down,
No woodsman has come up against us.'
9 "Hellᴿ from beneath is excited about
you,   Ezek. 32:21

To meet you at your coming;
It stirs up the dead for you,
All the chief ones of the earth;
It has raised up from their thrones
All the kings of the nations.
10 They all shall ᴿspeak and say to you:
'Have you also become as weak as we?
Have you become like us?   Ezek. 32:21
11 Your pomp is brought down to Sheol,
And the sound of your stringed
   instruments;
The maggot is spread under you,
And worms cover you.'

▼ 12-B. Satan: His Fall

The Fall of Lucifer

12 "How you are fallen from heaven,
O *Lucifer, son of the morning!
How you are cut down to the ground,
You who weakened the nations!
13 For you have said in your heart:
   ᴿᵗI will ascend into heaven,   Ezek. 28:2
   ᴿI will exalt my throne above the stars
      of God;   Dan. 8:10
   I will also sit on the ᴿmount of the
      congregation   Ezek. 28:14
   ᴿOn the farthest sides of the north; Ps. 48:2
14 I will ascend above the heights of the
      clouds,
   ᴿI will be like the Most High.'   2 Thess. 2:4

14:12 Lit. Day Star

15 Yet you ᴿshall be brought down to
      Sheol,   Matt. 11:23   ▽
   To the ᵀlowest depths of the Pit. recesses ▲
16 "Those who see you will gaze at you,
   And consider you, saying:
   'Is this the man who made the earth
      tremble,
   Who shook kingdoms,
17 Who made the world as a wilderness
   And destroyed its cities,
   Who ᵀdid not open the house of his
      prisoners?'   Would not release
18 "All the kings of the nations,
   All of them, sleep in glory,
   Everyone in his own house;
19 But you are cast out of your grave
   Like an ᵀabominable branch,
   Like the garment of those who are
      slain,   despised
   ᵀThrust through with a sword,   Pierced
   Who go down to the stones of the pit,
   Like a corpse trodden underfoot.
20 You will not be joined with them in
      burial,
   Because you have destroyed your land
   And slain your people.
   ᴿThe brood of evildoers shall never be
      named.   Ps. 21:10; 109:13
21 Prepare slaughter for his children
   ᴿBecause of the iniquity of their fathers,
   Lest they rise up and possess the land,

12-B. Satan: His Fall (Isaiah 14:12–15)—If we are to understand this portion of Scripture, it must be interpreted in the same manner as the messianic psalms (Ezek. 28:11–19, page 805; also Point 12-A, "Satan: His Origin," page 805). When the king of Babylon had been snared and taken captive "by him [Satan] to do his will" (2 Tim. 2:26, page 1227), Isaiah prophesied that the enslaved would take up a taunting chant against the king (vv. 3–11). This Babylonian monarch, filled with satanic splendor, power, and pride, was a visible symbol of the invisible "prince of the power of the air," who controlled and perhaps dwelled in him (Eph. 2:2, page 1187).

"How you are fallen from heaven, O Lucifer, son of the morning!" (v. 12). Jesus said, "I saw Satan [the morning star] fall like lightning from heaven" (Luke 10:18, page 1026). Verses 12–14 mark the fall of Satan, "the anointed cherub" (Ezek. 28:14, page 806). This could have been the original sin; however, we cannot be certain.

Satan fell from his original exalted office when he desired to put his self-will above God's perfect will. Five times he said, "I will."

(1) "I will ascend into heaven" (v. 13). It is possible that Satan was God's exalted ruler of this planet before his fall. The planet earth could have been the first Eden (Gen. 1:1, page 2). In this verse we see the original creation of the earth: "[God] did not create it in vain" (Is. 45:18, page 686). In Genesis 1:1 (page 2) the earth may have been "without form, and void" as it clearly was in verse 2. There may have been a gap between Genesis 1:1 and Genesis 1:2. The events in verses 1 and 2 may have happened eons apart.

(2) "I will exalt my throne above the stars of God" (v. 13). Satan was not satisfied to rule only the angels under his delegated authority; he tried to will himself into authority over all of God's creatures.

(3) "I will also sit on the mount of the congregation on the farthest sides of the north" (v. 13). Satan desired to sit on the mountain of God where the host of heaven assembled to worship God. He tried to will that he would receive worship along with God.

(4) "I will ascend above the heights of the clouds" (v. 14). His throne was beneath the clouds. Thus it could have been a spiritual world, or it could have been this planet earth in its original, created state.

(5) "I will be like the Most High" (v. 14). Satan did not will to overthrow God and rule the universe; he wanted equality with God.

See 2 Corinthians 4:3, 4, page 1167, for **Point 12-C: Satan: The God of This World.**

And fill the face of the world with
cities."   Ex. 20:5

Babylon Destroyed

22 "For I will rise up against them," says
the LORD of hosts,
"And cut off from Babylon ^Rthe name
and ^Rremnant,
^RAnd offspring and posterity," says the
LORD.   Prov. 10:7 • 1 Kin. 14:10 • Job 18:19
23 "I will also make it a possession for the
^Rporcupine,   Zeph. 2:14
And marshes of muddy water;
I will sweep it with the broom of
destruction," says the LORD of hosts.

Assyria Destroyed

24 The LORD of hosts has sworn, saying,
"Surely, as I have thought, so it shall
come to pass,
And as I have purposed, so it shall
^Rstand: Is. 43:13
25 That I will break the ^RAssyrian in My
land,
And on My mountains tread him under
foot.
Then ^Rhis yoke shall be removed from
them,
And his burden removed from their
shoulders.   Mic. 5:5, 6 • Is. 10:27
26 This is the ^Rpurpose that is purposed
against the whole earth,
And this is the hand that is stretched
out over all the nations.   Is. 23:9
27 For the LORD of hosts has ^Rpurposed,
And who will annul it?
His hand is stretched out,
And who will turn it back?"   Dan. 4:31, 35

Philistia Destroyed

28 This is the ^Tburden which came in the
year that King Ahaz died.   oracle, prophecy

29 "Do not rejoice, all you of Philistia,
^RBecause the rod that struck you is
broken;
For out of the serpent's roots will come
forth a viper,
^RAnd its offspring will be a fiery flying
serpent.   2 Chr. 26:6 • 2 Kin. 18:8
30 The firstborn of the poor will feed,
And the needy will lie down in safety;
I will kill your roots with famine,
And it will slay your remnant.
31 Wail, O gate! Cry, O city!
All you of Philistia are dissolved;
For smoke will come from the north,
And no one will be alone in his
^Tappointed times."   Or ranks

32 What will they answer the messengers
of the nation?
That ^Rthe LORD has founded Zion,

And ^Rthe poor of His people shall take
refuge in it.   Ps. 87:1, 5 • Zech. 11:11

Proclamation Against Moab

15 The burden against Moab.

Because in the night ^RAr of ^RMoab is
laid waste
And destroyed,   Deut. 2:9 • Amos 2:1-3
Because in the night Kir of Moab is laid
waste
And destroyed,
2 He has gone up to the ^Ttemple and
Dibon,   Heb. bayith, lit. house
To the high places to weep.
Moab will wail over Nebo and over
Medeba;
^ROn all their heads will be baldness,
And every beard cut off.   Lev. 21:5
3 In their streets they will clothe
themselves with sackcloth;
On the tops of their houses
And in their streets
Everyone will wail, weeping bitterly.
4 Heshbon and Elealeh will cry out,
Their voice shall be heard as far as
^RJahaz;   Jer. 48:34
Therefore the *armed soldiers of Moab
will cry out;
His life will be burdensome to him.

5 "My^R heart will cry out for Moab;   Jer. 48:31
His fugitives shall flee to Zoar,
Like *a three-year-old heifer.
For ^Rby the Ascent of Luhith   Jer. 48:5
They will go up with weeping;
For in the way of Horonaim
They will raise up a cry of destruction,
6 For the waters ^Rof Nimrim will be
desolate,   Num. 32:36
For the green grass has withered away;
The grass fails, there is nothing green.
7 Therefore the abundance they have
gained,
And what they have laid up,
They will carry away to the Brook of
the Willows.
8 For the cry has gone all around the
borders of Moab,
Its wailing to Eglaim
And its wailing to Beer Elim.
9 For the waters of *Dimon will be full of
blood;
Because I will bring more upon
*Dimon,
^RLions upon him who escapes from
Moab,   2 Kin. 17:25
And on the remnant of the land."

15:4 So with MT, Tg., Vg.; LXX, Syr. loins
15:5 Or The Third Eglath, an unknown city, Jer. 48:34
15:9 So with MT, Tg.; DSS, Vg. Dibon; LXX Rimon • See
preceding note

Moab Destroyed

16 Send the lamb to the ruler of the land,
From [T]Sela to the wilderness,   Lit. Rock
To the mount of the daughter of Zion.
2 For it shall be as a [R]wandering bird
  thrown out of the nest;   Prov. 27:8
  So shall be the daughters of Moab at
  the fords of the [R]Arnon.   Num. 21:13

3 "Take counsel, execute judgment;
  Make your shadow like the night in the
  middle of the day;
  Hide the outcasts,
  Do not betray him who escapes.
4 Let My outcasts dwell with you, O
  Moab;
  Be a shelter to them from the face of
  the [T]spoiler.
  For the extortioner is at an end,
  Devastation ceases,
  The oppressors are consumed out of the
  land.   devastator
5 In mercy [R]the throne will be
  established;   Dan. 7:14
  And One will sit on it in truth, in the
  tabernacle of David,
  Judging and seeking justice and
  hastening [R]righteousness."   Is. 9:7
6 We have heard of the [R]pride of Moab—
  He is very proud—   Jer. 48:29
  Of his haughtiness and his pride and his
  wrath;
  But his [T]lies shall not be so.   Lit. vain talk
7 Therefore Moab shall [R]wail for Moab;
  Everyone shall wail.   Jer. 48:20
  For the foundations [R]of Kir Hareseth
  you shall mourn;
  Surely they are stricken.   2 Kin. 3:25
8 For [R]the fields of Heshbon languish,
  And [R]the vine of Sibmah;
  The lords of the nations have broken
  down its choice plants,   Is. 24:7 · Is. 16:9
  Which have reached to Jazer
  And wandered through the wilderness.
  Her branches are stretched out,
  They are gone over the [R]sea.   Jer. 48:32
9 Therefore I will bewail the vine of
  Sibmah,
  With the weeping of Jazer;
  I will drench you with my tears,
  [R]O Heshbon and Elealeh;
  For [T]battle cries have fallen
  Over your summer fruits and your
  harvest.   Is. 15:4 · Or shouting has
10 [R]Gladness is taken away,   Is. 24:8
  And joy from the plentiful field;
  In the vineyards there will be no
  singing,
  Nor will there be shouting;
  No treaders will tread out wine in the
  presses;
  I have made their shouting cease.

11 Therefore [R]my [T]heart shall resound like
  a harp for Moab,   Jer. 48:36 · Lit. belly
  And my inner being for Kir Heres.
12 And it shall come to pass,
  When it is seen that Moab is weary on
  [R]the high place,
  That he will come to his sanctuary to
  pray;
  But he will not prevail.   Is. 15:2

13 This is the word which the LORD has
spoken concerning Moab since that time.
14 But now the LORD has spoken, saying,
"Within three years, [R]as the years of a hired
man, the glory of Moab will be despised with
all that great multitude, and the remnant will
be very small and feeble."   Is. 21:16

Proclamation Against Syria and Israel

17 The [R]burden[T] against Damascus.

"Behold, Damascus will cease from being
a city,   Zech. 9:1 · oracle, prophecy
And it will be a ruinous heap.
2 *The cities of [R]Aroer are forsaken;
  They will be for flocks
  Which lie down, and [R]no one will make
  them afraid.   Num. 32:34 · Jer. 7:33
3 [R]The fortress also will cease from
  Ephraim,   Is. 7:16; 8:4
  The kingdom from Damascus,
  And the remnant of Syria;
  They will be as the glory of the children
  of Israel,"
  Says the LORD of hosts.

4 "In that day it shall come to pass
  That the glory of Jacob will wane,
  And the fatness of his flesh grow lean.
5 [R]It shall be as when the harvester
  gathers the grain,
  And reaps the heads with his arm;
  It shall be as he who gathers heads of
  grain
  In the Valley of Rephaim.   Jer. 51:33
6 [R]Yet gleaning grapes will be left in it,
  Like the shaking of an olive tree,
  Two or three olives at the top of the
  uppermost bough,   Is. 24:13
  Four or five in its most fruitful
  branches,"
  Says the LORD God of Israel.

7 In that day a man will [R]look to his
  Maker,   Mic. 7:7
  And his eyes will have respect for the
  Holy One of Israel.
8 He will not look to the altars,
  The work of his hands;
  He will not respect what his [R]fingers
  have made,   Is. 2:8; 31:7

17:2 So with MT, Vg.; LXX It shall be forsaken forever;
Tg. Its cities shall be forsaken and desolate

Nor the ᵀwooden images nor the incense altars. Or *Asherah,* a Canaanite goddess

9 In that day his strong cities will be as a forsaken *bough
And *an uppermost branch,
Which they left because of the children of Israel;
And there will be desolation.

10 Because you have forgotten ᴿthe God of your salvation,   Ps. 68:19
And have not been mindful of the Rock of your ᵀstronghold,   *refuge*
Therefore you will plant pleasant plants
And set out foreign seedlings;
11 In the day you will make your plant to grow,
And in the morning you will make your seed to flourish;
But the harvest *will be* a heap of ruins
In the day of grief and desperate sorrow.

12 Woe to the multitude of many people
Who make a noise ᴿlike the roar of the seas,
And to the rushing of nations
That make a rushing like the rushing of mighty waters!   Jer. 6:23
13 The nations will rush like the rushing of many waters;
But *God* will ᴿrebuke them and they will flee far away,
And ᴿbe chased like the chaff of the mountains before the wind,
Like a rolling thing before the whirlwind.   Ps. 9:5 · Hos. 13:3
14 Then behold, at eventide, trouble!
And before the morning, he *is* no more.
This *is* the portion of those who plunder us,
And the lot of those who rob us.

Proclamation Against Ethiopia

18 Woe ᴿto the land shadowed with buzzing wings,   Zeph. 2:12; 3:10
Which *is* beyond the rivers of Ethiopia,
2 Which sends ambassadors by sea,
Even in vessels of reed on the waters, *saying,*
"Go, swift messengers, to a nation tall and smooth *of skin,*
To a people terrible from their beginning onward,
A nation powerful and treading down,
Whose land the rivers divide."

3 All inhabitants of the world and dwellers on the earth;
ᴿWhen he lifts up a banner on the mountains, you see *it;*

And when he blows a trumpet, you hear *it.*   Is. 5:26
4 For so the Lᴏʀᴅ said to me,
"I will take My rest,
And I will ᵀlook from My dwelling place
Like clear heat in sunshine,
Like a cloud of dew in the heat of harvest."   *watch*
5 For before the harvest, when the bud is perfect
And the sour grape is ripening in the flower,
He will both cut off the sprigs with pruning hooks
And take away *and* cut down the branches.
6 They will be left together for the mountain birds of prey
And for the beasts of the earth;
The birds of prey will summer on them,
And all the beasts of the earth will winter on them.

7 In that time ᴿa present will be brought to the Lᴏʀᴅ of hosts
*From a people tall and smooth *of skin,*
And from a people terrible from their beginning onward,
A nation powerful and treading down,
Whose land the rivers divide—
To the place of the name of the Lᴏʀᴅ of hosts,
To Mount Zion.   Zeph. 3:10

Proclamation Against Egypt

19 The ᵀburden against Egypt.   *oracle*

Behold, the Lᴏʀᴅ ᴿrides on a swift cloud,   Ps. 18:10; 104:3
And will come into Egypt;
ᴿThe idols of Egypt will ᵀtotter at His presence,   Jer. 43:12 · Lit. *shake*
And the heart of Egypt will melt in its midst.

2 "I will ᴿset Egyptians against Egyptians;
Everyone will fight against his brother,
And everyone against his neighbor,
City against city, kingdom against kingdom.   Judg. 7:22
3 The spirit of Egypt will fail in its midst;
I will destroy their counsel,
And they will ᴿconsult the idols and the charmers,   Is. 8:19; 47:12
The mediums and the sorcerers.
4 And the Egyptians I will give
Into the hand of a cruel master,
And a fierce king will rule over them,"
Says the Lord, the Lᴏʀᴅ of hosts.

5 ᴿThe waters will fail from the sea,
And the river will be wasted and dried up.   Jer. 51:36

17:9 LXX *Hivites;* Tg. *laid waste;* Vg. *as the plows* •
LXX *Amorites;* Tg. *in ruins;* Vg. *corn*

18:7 So with DSS, LXX, Vg.; MT omits *From;* Tg. *To*

6 The rivers will turn foul;
The brooks ^Rof defense will be emptied
and dried up;   2 Kin. 19:24
The reeds and rushes will wither.
7 The papyrus reeds by ^Tthe River, by the
mouth of the River,
And everything sown by the River,
Will wither, be driven away, and be no
more.   The Nile
8 The fishermen also will mourn;
All those will lament who cast hooks
into the River,
And they will languish who spread nets
on the waters.
9 Moreover those who work in ^Rfine flax
And those who weave fine fabric will be
ashamed;   Prov. 7:16
10 And its foundations will be broken.
All who make wages *will be* troubled of
soul.

11 Surely the princes of ^RZoan *are* fools;
Pharaoh's wise counselors give foolish
counsel.   Num. 13:22
^RHow do you say to Pharaoh, "I *am* the
son of the wise,   1 Kin. 4:29, 30
The son of ancient kings?"
12 ^RWhere *are* they?   1 Cor. 1:20
Where are your wise men?
Let them tell you now,
And let them know what the LORD of
hosts has purposed against Egypt.
13 The princes of Zoan have become fools;
^RThe princes of ^TNoph are deceived;
They have also deluded Egypt,
Those who are the ^Tmainstay of its
tribes.   Jer. 2:16 • Ancient Memphis • *cornerstone*
14 The LORD has mingled ^Ra perverse spirit
in her midst;
And they have caused Egypt to err in
all her work,
As a drunken man staggers in his
vomit.   Is. 29:10
15 Neither will there be *any* work for
Egypt,
Which ^Rthe head or tail,   Is. 9:14–16
Palm branch or bulrush, may do.

16 In that day Egypt will ^Rbe like women,
and will be afraid and fear because of the
waving of the hand of the LORD of hosts,
^Rwhich He waves over it.   Nah. 3:13 • Is. 11:15
17 And the land of Judah will be a terror to
Egypt; everyone who makes mention of it
will be afraid in himself, because of the
counsel of the LORD of hosts which He has
^Rdetermined against it.   Dan. 4:35

Egypt, Assyria, and Israel Blessed

18 In that day five cities in the land of
Egypt will speak the language of Canaan and
^Rswear by the LORD of hosts; one will be
called the City of *Destruction.   Is. 45:23
19 In that day there will be an altar to the
LORD in the midst of the land of Egypt, and a
pillar to the ^RLORD at its border.   Ps. 68:31
20 And ^Rit will be for a sign and for a
witness to the LORD of hosts in the land of
Egypt; for they will cry to the LORD because
of the oppressors, and He will send them a
^RSavior and a Mighty One, and He will deliver
them.   Josh. 4:20; 22:27 • Is. 43:11
21 Then the LORD will be known to Egypt,
and the Egyptians will ^Rknow the LORD in
that day, and ^Rwill make sacrifice and offering; yes, they will make a vow to the LORD
and perform *it*.   [Is. 2:3, 4; 11:9] • Mal. 1:11
22 And the LORD will strike Egypt, He will
strike and ^Rheal *it*; they will return to the
LORD, and He will be entreated by them and
heal them.   Deut. 32:39
23 In that day there will be a highway from
Egypt to Assyria, and the Assyrian will come
into Egypt and the Egyptian into Assyria, and
the Egyptians will serve with the Assyrians.
24 In that day Israel will be one of three
with Egypt and Assyria—a blessing in the
midst of the land,
25 whom the LORD of hosts shall bless,
saying, "Blessed *is* Egypt My people, and
Assyria ^Rthe work of My hands, and Israel
My inheritance."   Is. 29:23

The Sign Against Egypt and Ethiopia

20 In the year that ^RTartan^T came to
Ashdod, when Sargon the king of As-
syria sent him, and he fought against Ashdod
and took it,   2 Kin. 18:17 • Or *the Commander in Chief*
2 at the same time the LORD spoke by
Isaiah the son of Amoz, saying, "Go, and
remove the sackcloth from your ^Tbody, and
take your sandals off your feet." And he did
so, walking naked and barefoot.   Lit. *loins*
3 Then the LORD said, "Just as My servant
Isaiah has walked naked and barefoot three
years ^R*for* a sign and a wonder against Egypt
and Ethiopia,   Is. 8:18
4 "so shall the ^Rking of Assyria lead away
the Egyptians as prisoners and the Ethiopians
as captives, young and old, naked and barefoot, ^Rwith their buttocks uncovered, to the
shame of Egypt.   Is. 19:4 • Jer. 13:22
5 ^R"Then they shall be afraid and ashamed
of Ethiopia their expectation and Egypt their
glory.   2 Kin. 18:21
6 "And the inhabitant of this territory will
say in that day, 'Surely such *is* our expectation, wherever we flee for ^Rhelp to be delivered from the king of Assyria; and how shall
we escape?' "   Is. 30:5, 7

19:18 Some Heb. mss., Arab., DSS, Tg., Vg. *Sun;* LXX
Asedek, lit. *Righteousness*

The Fall of Babylon Proclaimed

21 The ᵀburden against the Wilderness of the Sea.

As ᴿwhirlwinds in the South pass
  through,
So it comes from the desert, from a
  terrible land.   *oracle, prophecy* · Zech. 9:14

2 A distressing vision is declared to me;
ᴿThe treacherous dealer deals
    treacherously,
And the plunderer plunders.
ᴿGo up, O Elam!
Besiege, O Media!   Is. 33:1 · Jer. 49:34
All its sighing I have made to cease.

3 Therefore my loins are filled with pain;
ᴿPangs have taken hold of me, like the
    pangs of a woman in labor.   Is. 13:8
I was ᵀdistressed when I heard *it*;
I was dismayed when *I* saw *it.*   Lit. *bowed*

4 My heart wavered, fearfulness
    frightened me;
ᴿThe night for which I longed He turned
    into fear for me.   Deut. 28:67

5 ᴿPrepare the table,
Set a watchman in the tower,
Eat and drink.
Arise, you princes,
Anoint the shield!   Dan. 5:5

6 For thus has the Lord said to me:
"Go, set a watchman,
Let him declare what he sees."

7 And he saw a chariot *with* a pair of
    horsemen,
A chariot of donkeys, *and* a chariot of
    camels,
And he listened earnestly with great
    care.

8 *Then he cried, "A lion, my Lord!
I stand continually on the ᴿwatchtower
    in the daytime;   Hab. 2:1
I have sat at my post every night.

9 And look, here comes a chariot of men
    with a pair of horsemen!"
Then he answered and said,
ᴿ"Babylon is fallen, is fallen!   Jer. 51:8
And ᴿall the carved images of her gods
He has broken to the ground."   Is. 46:1

10 ᴿOh, my threshing and the grain of my
    floor!
That which I have heard from the Lord
    of hosts,
The God of Israel,
I have declared to you.   Jer. 51:33

Proclamation Against Edom

11 The burden against Dumah.

He calls to me out of ᴿSeir,   Gen. 32:3
"Watchman, what of the night?
Watchman, what of the night?"

21:8 DSS *Then the observer cried, "My Lord!*

12 The watchman said,
"The morning comes, and also the night.
If you will inquire, inquire;
Return! Come back!"

Proclamation Against Arabia

13 The ᵀburden against Arabia.

In the forest in Arabia you will lodge,
O you traveling companies ᴿof
    Dedanites.   *oracle, prophecy* · 1 Chr. 1:9, 32

14 O inhabitants of the land of Tema,
Bring water to him who is thirsty;
With their bread they met him who
    fled.

15 For they fled from the swords, from the
    drawn sword,
From the bent bow, and from the
    distress of war.

16 For thus the Lord has said to me:
"Within a year, according to the year of a
hired man, all the glory of Kedar will fail;
17 "and the remainder of the number of
archers, the mighty men of the people of
Kedar, will be diminished; for the Lord God
of Israel has spoken *it.*"

Proclamation Against Jerusalem

22 The ᵀburden against the Valley of
    Vision.   *oracle, prophecy*

What ails you now, that you have all
    gone up to the housetops,
2 You who are full of noise,
A ᵀtumultuous city, ᴿa joyous city?
Your slain *men are* not slain with the
    sword,
Nor dead in battle.   *boisterous* · Is. 32:13

3 All your rulers have fled together;
They are captured by the archers.
All who are found in you are bound
    together;
They have fled from afar.

4 Therefore I said, "Look away from me,
ᴿI will weep bitterly;
Do not labor to comfort me
Because of the plundering of the
    daughter of my people."   Jer. 4:19

5 ᴿFor *it is* a day of trouble and treading
    down and perplexity   Is. 37:3
ᴿBy the Lord God of hosts   Lam. 1:5; 2:2
In the Valley of Vision—
Breaking down the walls
And of crying to the mountain.

6 ᴿElam bore the quiver   Jer. 49:35
With chariots of men *and* horsemen,
And ᴿKir uncovered the shield.   Is. 15:1

7 It shall come to pass *that* your choicest
    valleys
Shall be full of chariots,
And the horsemen shall set themselves
    in array at the gate.

8 He removed the ᵀprotection of Judah.
   You looked in that day to the armor of
   the House of the Forest;   Lit. *covering*
9 ᴿYou also saw the ᵀdamage to the city of
   David,   2 Kin. 20:20 · Lit. *breaches* in the city walls
   That it was great;
   And you gathered together the waters
   of the lower pool.
10 You numbered the houses of Jerusalem,
   And the houses you broke down
   To fortify the wall.
11 ᴿYou also made a reservoir between the
   two walls   Neh. 3:16
   For the water of the old ᴿpool.
   But you did not look to its Maker,
   Nor did you have respect for Him who
   fashioned it long ago.   2 Chr. 32:3, 4

12 And in that day the Lord Gᴏᴅ of hosts
   ᴿCalled for weeping and for mourning,
   ᴿFor baldness and for girding with
   sackcloth.   Joel 1:13; 2:17 · Mic. 1:16
13 But instead, joy and gladness,
   Slaying oxen and killing sheep,
   Eating meat and ᴿdrinking wine:
   ᴿ"Let us eat and drink, for tomorrow we
   die!"   Luke 17:26–29 · 1 Cor. 15:32
14 ᴿThen it was revealed in my hearing by
   the Lᴏʀᴅ of hosts,
   "Surely for this iniquity there ᴿwill be no
   atonement for you,
   Even to your death," says the Lord Gᴏᴅ
   of hosts.   Is. 5:9 · Ezek. 24:13

The Judgment on Shebna

15 Thus says the Lord Gᴏᴅ of hosts:

   "Go, proceed to this steward,
   To ᴿShebna, who *is* over the house, *and*
   say: Is. 36:3
16 'What have you here, and whom have
   you here,
   That you have hewn a sepulcher here,
   As he ᴿwho hews himself a sepulcher
   on high,
   Who carves a tomb for himself in a
   rock?   Matt. 27:60
17 Indeed, the Lᴏʀᴅ will throw you away
   violently,
   O mighty man,
   ᴿAnd will surely seize you.   Esth. 7:8
18 He will surely turn violently and toss
   you like a ball
   Into a large country;
   There you shall die, and there ᴿyour
   glorious chariots
   Shall be the shame of your master's
   house.   Is. 2:7
19 So I will drive you out of your office,
   And from your position *he will pull
   you down.

20 'Then it shall be in that day,
   That I will call My servant ᴿEliakim the
   son of Hilkiah;   2 Kin. 18:18
21 I will clothe him with your robe
   And strengthen him with your belt;
   I will commit your responsibility into
   his hand.
   He shall be a father to the inhabitants
   of Jerusalem
   And to the house of Judah.
22 The key of the house of David
   I will lay on his ᴿshoulder;
   So he shall ᴿopen, and no one shall
   shut;
   And he shall shut, and no one shall
   open.   Is. 9:6 · Rev. 3:7
23 I will fasten him *as* ᴿa peg in a secure
   place,
   And he will become a glorious throne
   to his father's house.   Ezra 9:8

24 'They will hang on him all the glory of
his father's house, the offspring and the
posterity, all vessels of small quantity, from
the cups to all the pitchers.
25 'In that day,' says the Lᴏʀᴅ of hosts, 'the
peg that is fastened in the secure place will
be removed and be cut down and fall, and the
burden that *was* on it will be cut off; for the
Lᴏʀᴅ has spoken.' "

Proclamation Against Tyre

23 The ᴿburden against Tyre.

   Wail, you ships of Tarshish!
   For it is laid waste,
   So that there is no house, no harbor;
   From the land of *Cyprus it is revealed
   to them.   Zech. 9:2, 4

2 Be still, you inhabitants of the
   coastland,
   You merchants of Sidon,
   *Whom those who cross the sea have
   filled.
3 And on great waters the grain of
   Shihor,
   The harvest of ᵀthe River, *is* her
   revenue;
   And ᴿshe is a marketplace for the
   nations.   The Nile · Ezek. 27:3–23

4 Be ashamed, O Sidon;
   For the sea has spoken,
   The strength of the sea, saying,
   "I do not labor, nor bring forth children;
   Neither do I rear young men,
   *Nor bring up virgins."
5 ᴿWhen the report *reaches* Egypt,
   They also will be in agony at the report
   of Tyre.   Is. 19:16

22:19 LXX omits *he will pull you down;* Syr., Tg., Vg. *I
will pull you down*

23:1 Heb. *Kittim,* western lands, especially Cyprus
23:2 So with MT, Vg.; LXX, Tg. *passing over the water;*
DSS *your messengers passing over the sea*

6 Cross over to Tarshish;
Wail, you inhabitants of the coastland!
7 *Is* this your ^Rjoyous *city,*   Is. 22:2; 32:13
Whose antiquity *is* from ancient days,
Whose feet carried her far off to dwell?
8 Who has taken this counsel against
Tyre, ^Rthe crowning *city,*
Whose merchants *are* princes,
Whose traders *are* the honorable of the
earth?   Ezek. 28:2, 12
9 The LORD of hosts has purposed it,
To ^Tbring to dishonor the ^Rpride of all
glory,
To bring into contempt all the
honorable of the earth.   *pollute* · Dan. 4:37
10 Overflow through your land like ^Tthe
River,   The Nile
O daughter of Tarshish;
There is no more ^Tstrength.   *restraint*
11 He stretched out His hand over the sea,
He shook the kingdoms;
The LORD has given a commandment
^Ragainst Canaan
To destroy its strongholds.   Zech. 9:2-4
12 And He said, "You will rejoice no more,
O you oppressed virgin daughter of
Sidon.
Arise, ^Rcross over to Cyprus;   Rev. 18:22
There also you will have no rest."
13 Behold, the land of the ^RChaldeans,
This people *which* was not;
Assyria founded it for ^Rwild beasts of
the desert.
They set up its towers,
They raised up its palaces,
And brought it to ruin.   Is. 47:1 · Ps. 72:9
14 ^RWail, you ships of Tarshish!   Ezek. 27:25-30
For your strength is laid waste.

15 Now it shall come to pass in that day
that Tyre will be forgotten seventy years,
according to the days of one king. At the end
of seventy years it will happen to Tyre as *in*
the song of the harlot:

16 "Take a harp, go about the city,
You forgotten harlot;
Make sweet melody, sing many songs,
That you may be remembered."

17 And it shall be, at the end of seventy
years, that the LORD will deal with Tyre. She
will return to her hire, and ^Rcommit fornication with all the kingdoms of the world on
the face of the earth.   Rev. 17:2
18 Her gain and her pay ^Rwill be set apart
for the LORD; it will not be treasured nor laid
up, for her gain will be for those who dwell
before the LORD, to eat sufficiently, and for
^Tfine clothing.   Zech. 14:20, 21 · *choice*

Impending Judgment on the Earth

24 Behold, the LORD makes the earth
empty and makes it waste,

Distorts its surface
And scatters abroad its inhabitants.
2 And it shall be:
As with the people, so with the ^Rpriest;
As with the servant, so with his master;
As with the maid, so with her mistress;
^RAs with the buyer, so with the seller;
As with the lender, so with the
borrower;   Hos. 4:9 · Ezek. 7:12, 13
As with the creditor, so with the
debtor.
3 The land shall be entirely emptied and
utterly plundered,
For the LORD has spoken this word.

4 The earth mourns *and* fades away,
The world languishes *and* fades away;
The ^Rhaughty^T people of the earth
languish.   Is. 25:11 · *proud*
5 ^RThe earth is also defiled under its
inhabitants,
Because they have ^Rtransgressed the
laws,   Num. 35:33 · Is. 59:12
Changed the ordinance,
Broken the everlasting covenant.
6 Therefore ^Rthe curse has devoured the
earth,   Mal. 4:6
And those who dwell in it are ^Tdesolate.
Therefore the inhabitants of the earth
are ^Rburned,   Or *held guilty* · Is. 9:19
And few men *are* left.

7 ^RThe new wine fails, the vine languishes,
All the merry-hearted sigh.   Joel 1:10, 12
8 The mirth ^Rof the tambourine ceases,
The noise of the jubilant ends,
The joy of the harp ceases.   Ezek. 26:13
9 They shall not drink wine with a song;
Strong drink is bitter to those who
drink it.
10 The city of confusion is broken down;
Every house is shut up, so that none
may go in.
11 *There is* a cry for wine in the streets,
All joy is darkened,
The mirth of the land is gone.
12 In the city desolation is left,
And the gate is stricken with
destruction.
13 When it shall be thus in the midst of
the land among the people,
^R*It shall be* like the shaking of an olive
tree,
Like the gleaning of grapes when the
vintage is done.   [Is. 17:5, 6; 27:12]

14 They shall lift up their voice, they shall
sing;
For the majesty of the LORD
They shall cry aloud from the sea.
15 Therefore ^Rglorify the LORD in the
dawning light,   Is. 25:3
^RThe name of the LORD God of Israel in
the coastlands of the sea.   Mal. 1:11

16 From the ends of the earth we have
    heard songs:
"Glory to the righteous!"
But I said, [T]"I am ruined, ruined!
Woe to me!   Lit. *Leanness to me, leanness to me*
[R]The treacherous dealers have dealt
    treacherously,   Jer. 3:20; 5:11
Indeed, the treacherous dealers have
    dealt very treacherously."

17 [R]Fear and the pit and the snare
    Are upon you, O inhabitant of the
    earth.   Jer. 48:43
18 And it shall be
    That he who flees from the noise of the
        fear
    Shall fall into the pit,
    And he who comes up from the midst
        of the pit
    Shall be [T]caught in the snare;
    For [R]the windows from on high are
        open,
    And [R]the foundations of the earth are
        shaken.   Lit. *taken* • Gen. 7:11 • Ps. 18:7; 46:2

19 [R]The earth is violently broken,
    The earth is split open,
    The earth is shaken exceedingly.   Jer. 4:23
20 The earth shall [R]reel[T] to and fro like a
        drunkard,   Is. 19:14; 24:1; 28:7 • *stagger*
    And shall totter like a hut;
    Its transgression shall be heavy upon it,
    And it will fall, and not rise again.

21 It shall come to pass in that day
    That the LORD will punish on high the
        host of exalted ones,
    And on the earth [R]the kings of the
        earth.   Ps. 76:12
22 They will be gathered together,

As prisoners are gathered in the pit,
And will be shut up in the prison;
After many days they will be punished.
23 Then the [R]moon will be disgraced
    And the sun ashamed;   Is. 13:10; 60:19
    For the LORD of hosts will reign
    On Mount Zion and in Jerusalem
    And before His elders, gloriously.

Praise to God

32-B. Kingdom Prayer and Praise   ▼

25 O LORD, You *are* my God.
    [R]I will exalt You,
    I will praise Your name,
    [R]For You have done wonderful *things*;
    [R]*Your* counsels of old *are* faithfulness
        and truth.   Ex. 15:2 • Ps. 98:1 • Num. 23:19
2 For You have made [R]a city a ruin,
    A fortified city a ruin,
    A palace of foreigners to be a city no
        more;
    It will never be rebuilt.   Jer. 51:37
3 Therefore the strong people will [R]glorify
        You;
    The city of the [T]terrible nations will
        fear You.   Is. 24:15 • *terrifying*
4 For You have been a strength to the
        poor,
    A strength to the needy in his distress,
    [R]A refuge from the storm,
    A shade from the heat;
    For the blast of the terrible ones *is* as a
        storm *against* the wall.   Is. 4:6
5 You will reduce the noise of aliens,
    As heat in a dry place;
    As heat in the shadow of a cloud,
    The song of the terrible ones will be
        [T]diminished.   *humbled*

32-B. Kingdom Prayer and Praise (Isaiah 25:1-9)—Isaiah had just announced the Lord's coming judgment on the nations—Assyria (Is. 10:12, page 653), Babylon (Is. 13:1, 17–19, page 655), Moab (Is. 15:1, page 658), Syria (Is. 17:1, page 659), Ethiopia (Is. 18:1, 5, page 660), Egypt (Is. 19:1, 2, page 660), and Tyre (Is. 23:1, page 663). Once these great messages of judgment had been uttered, the prophet delivered two great themes of heartfelt prayer and praise: awe at the sovereign power of God, who will judge wicked nations by His holiness; and praise to God, who will in the future establish His millennial kingdom on earth. Every child of God who is appalled at today's calamities on our planet, and who contemplates the great prophecies of the future, must share Isaiah's two reactions. This wonderful prayer expresses

(1) awe at God's bringing to pass those events which He prophesied long ago (v. 1);
(2) awe at God's judgment of the cities of wicked nations (vv. 2, 3);
(3) praise for God's defense of the helpless who placed their trust in His strength (vv. 4, 5);
(4) praise for the coming millennial kingdom on earth, including

(a) praise for God's coming banquet, a time of unbounded spiritual rejoicing centering at (or near to) Jerusalem (v. 6; cf. Zech. 14:16–21, page 919);
(b) praise for God's coming elimination of death, tears, and suffering, which still grip the nations of the world (vv. 7, 8; cf. Rev. 21:4, page 1315);
(c) praise for God's future silencing of all reproaches from His earthly followers (v. 8; cf. Rev. 19:7–9, page 1312);
(d) praise for God's certain fulfillment of His promised future kingdom of salvation, peace, and joy (v. 9; cf. Matt. 26:29, page 978).

Surely, we who know Christ join Isaiah in this kingdom prayer—"Your kingdom come" (Matt. 6:10, page 943); "come, Lord Jesus!" (Rev. 22:20, page 1317).

See Jeremiah 1:6, page 710, for **Point 32-C: The Prayer of an Inadequate Man.**

▽ **6** And in ᴿthis mountain   [Is. 2:2-4; 56:7]
ᴿThe Lᴏʀᴅ of hosts will make for ᴿall
people   Prov. 9:2 • [Dan. 7:14]
A feast of ᵀchoice pieces,   Lit. *fat things*
A feast of wines on the lees,
Of fat things full of marrow,
Of well-refined wines on the lees.
7 And He will destroy on this mountain
The surface of the covering cast over
all people,
And ᴿthe veil that is spread over all
nations.   [Eph. 4:18]
8 He will swallow up death forever,
And the Lord Gᴏᴅ will ᴿwipe away
tears from all faces;   Rev. 7:17; 21:4
The rebuke of His people
He will take away from all the earth;
For the Lᴏʀᴅ has spoken.

9 And it will be said in that day:
"Behold, this *is* our God;
ᴿWe have waited for Him, and He will
save us.
This *is* the Lᴏʀᴅ;
We have waited for Him;
ᴿWe will be glad and rejoice in His
▲ salvation."   Gen. 49:18 • Ps. 20:5

10 For on this mountain the hand of the
Lᴏʀᴅ will rest,
And ᴿMoab shall be trampled down
under Him,
As straw is trampled down for the
refuse heap.   Amos 2:1-3
11 And He will spread out His hands in
their midst
As a swimmer reaches out to swim,
And He will bring down their ᴿpride
Together with the trickery of their
hands.   Is. 24:4; 26:5
12 The ᴿfortress of the high fort of your
walls
He will bring down, lay low,
And bring to the ground, down to the
dust.   Is. 26:5

A Song of Salvation

26 In ᴿthat day this song will be sung in
the land of Judah:

"We have a strong city;
ᴿGod will appoint salvation *for* walls and
bulwarks.   Is. 2:11; 12:1 • Is. 60:18
2 ᴿOpen the gates,   Ps. 118:19, 20
That the righteous nation which ᵀkeeps
the truth may enter in.   Or *remains faithful*
3 You will keep *him* in perfect ᴿpeace,
Whose mind *is* stayed *on* You,
Because he trusts in You.   Is. 57:19
4 Trust in the Lᴏʀᴅ forever,
ᴿFor in Yᴀʜ, the Lᴏʀᴅ, *is* ᵀeverlasting
strength.   Is. 12:2; 45:17 • Or *Rock of Ages*
5 For He brings ᵀdown those who dwell
on high,   *low*
ᴿThe lofty city;   Is. 25:11, 12

He lays it low,
He lays it low to the ground,
He brings it down to the dust.
6 The foot shall ᵀtread it down—
The feet of the poor
And the steps of the needy."   *trample*

7 The way of the just *is* uprightness;
ᴿO Most Upright,   Ps. 37:23
You weigh the path of the just.
8 Yes, ᴿin the way of Your judgments,
O Lᴏʀᴅ, we have waited for You;
The desire of *our* soul *is* for Your name
And for the remembrance of You.   Is. 64:5
9 ᴿWith my soul I have desired You in the
night,
Yes, by my spirit within me I will seek
You early;
For when Your judgments *are* in the
earth,
The inhabitants of the world will learn
righteousness.   Ps. 63:6
10 ᴿLet grace be shown to the wicked,
Yet he will not learn righteousness;
In ᴿthe land of uprightness he will deal
unjustly,
And will not behold the majesty of the
Lᴏʀᴅ.   [Rom. 2:4] • Ps. 143:10
11 Lᴏʀᴅ, *when* Your hand is lifted up,
ᴿthey will not see.   Is. 5:12
But they will see and be ashamed
For ᵀtheir envy of people;
Yes, the fire of Your enemies shall
devour them.   Or *Your zeal for the people*

12 Lᴏʀᴅ, You will establish peace for us,
For You have also done all our works
ᵀin us.   Or *for us*
13 O Lᴏʀᴅ our God, ᴿmasters besides You
Have had dominion over us;
But by You only we make mention of
Your name.   2 Chr. 12:8
14 They *are* dead, they will not live;
They are deceased, they will not rise.
Therefore You have punished and
destroyed them,
And made all their memory to perish.
15 You have increased the nation, O Lᴏʀᴅ,
You have ᴿincreased the nation;
You are glorified;
You have expanded all the ᵀborders of
the land.   Is. 9:3 • Or *ends*
16 Lᴏʀᴅ, ᴿin trouble they have visited You,
They poured out a prayer *when* Your
chastening *was* upon them.   Hos. 5:15
17 As ᴿa woman with child
Is in pain and cries out in her ᵀpangs,
When she draws near the time of her
delivery,   [John 16:21] • *sharp pains*
So have we been in Your sight, O Lᴏʀᴅ.
18 We have been with child, we have been
in pain;

We have, as it were, [T]brought forth
wind;
We have not accomplished any
deliverance in the earth,
Nor have [R]the inhabitants of the world
fallen.   *given birth to* · Ps. 17:14

19 [R]Your dead shall live;   [Ezek. 37:1–14]
Together with *my dead body they shall
arise.
Awake and sing, you who dwell in dust;
For your dew *is like* the dew of herbs,
And the earth shall cast out the dead.

Take Refuge from the Coming Judgment

20 Come, my people, [R]enter your
chambers,
And shut your doors behind you;
Hide yourself, as it were, [R]for a little
moment,   Ex. 12:22, 23 · [Ps. 30:5]
Until the indignation is past.

21 For behold, the LORD [R]comes out of His
place   Mic. 1:3
To punish the inhabitants of the earth
for their iniquity;
The earth will also disclose her blood,
And will no more cover her slain.

27 In that day the LORD with His severe
sword, great and strong,
Will punish Leviathan the fleeing
serpent,
[R]Leviathan that twisted serpent;
And He will slay [R]the reptile that *is* in
the sea.   Ps. 74:13, 14 · Is. 51:9

The Restoration of Israel

2 In that day [R]sing to her,   Is. 5:1
[R]"A vineyard of *red wine!   Is. 5:7

3 [R]I, the LORD, keep it,   Is. 31:5
I water it every moment;
Lest any hurt it,
I keep it night and day.

4 Fury *is* not in Me.
Who would set [R]briers *and* thorns
Against Me in battle?   2 Sam. 23:6
I would go through them,
I would burn them together.

5 Or let him take hold of My strength,
That he may make peace with Me;
And he shall make peace with Me."

6 Those who come He shall cause [R]to
take root in Jacob;   Is. 37:31
Israel shall blossom and bud,
And fill the face of the world with fruit.

7 [R]Has He struck [T]Israel as He struck
those who struck him?

26:19 So with MT, Vg.; Syr., Tg. *their dead bodies;* LXX
those in the tombs

27:2 So with MT (Kittel's *Biblia Hebraica*), Bg., Vg.; MT
(*Biblia Hebraica Stuttgartensia*), some Heb. mss., LXX
delight; Tg. *choice vineyard*

Or has He been slain according to the
slaughter of those who were slain by
Him?   Is. 10:12, 17; 30:30–33 · Lit. *him*

8 [R]In measure, by sending it away,
You contended with it.   Job 23:6
[R]He removes *it* by His rough wind
In the day of the east wind.   [Ps. 78:38]

9 Therefore by this the iniquity of Jacob
will be covered;
And this *is* all the fruit of taking away
his sin:
When he makes all the stones of the
altar
Like chalkstones that are beaten to
dust,
*Wooden images and incense altars shall
not stand.

10 Yet the fortified city *will be* [R]desolate,
The habitation forsaken and left like a
wilderness;   Is. 5:6, 17; 32:14
There the calf will feed, and there it
will lie down
And consume its branches.

11 When its boughs are withered, they will
be broken off;
The women come *and* set them on fire.
For [R]it *is* a people of no understanding;
Therefore He who made them will [R]not
have mercy on them,   Deut. 32:28 · Is. 9:17
And [R]He who formed them will show
them no favor.   Deut. 32:18

12 And it shall come to pass in that day
That the LORD will thresh,
From the channel of [T]the River to the
Brook of Egypt;   The Euphrates
And you will be [R]gathered one by one,
O you children of Israel.   [Is. 11:11; 56:8]

13 [R]So it shall be in that day: Is. 2:11
[R]The great trumpet will be blown;
They will come, who are about to
perish in the land of Assyria,   Rev. 11:15
And they who are outcasts in the land
of [R]Egypt,   Is. 19:21, 22
And shall [R]worship the LORD in the holy
mount at Jerusalem.   Zech. 14:16

Woe to Ephraim and Jerusalem

28 Woe to the crown of pride, to the
drunkards of Ephraim,
Whose glorious beauty *is* a fading
flower
Which *is* at the head of the [T]verdant
valleys,   Lit. *valleys of fatness*
To those who are overcome with wine!

2 Behold, the Lord has a mighty and
strong one,
[R]Like a tempest of hail and a destroying
storm,
Like a flood of mighty waters
overflowing,

27:9 Or *Asherim, Canaanite deities*

Who will bring *them* down to the earth
with *His* hand.   Ezek. 13:11

3 The crown of pride, the drunkards of
Ephraim,
Will be trampled underfoot;

4 And the glorious beauty is a fading
flower
Which *is* at the head of the ᵀverdant
valley,   Lit. *valley of fatness*
Like the first fruit before the summer,
Which an observer sees;
He eats it up while it is still in his hand.

5 In that day the LORD of hosts will be
For a crown of glory and a diadem of
beauty
To the remnant of His people,

6 For a spirit of justice to him who sits in
judgment,
And for strength to those who turn
back the battle at the gate.

7 But they also ᴿhave erred through wine,
And through intoxicating drink are out
of the way;   Hos. 4:11
ᴿThe priest and the prophet have erred
through intoxicating drink,   Is. 56:10, 12
They are swallowed up by wine,
They are out of the way through
intoxicating drink;
They err in vision, they stumble *in*
judgment.

8 For all tables are full of vomit *and* filth;
No place *is* clean.

9 "Whomᴿ will he teach knowledge?
And whom will he make to understand
the message?   Jer. 6:10
Those *just* weaned from milk?
Those *just* drawn from the breasts?

10 ᴿFor precept *must be* upon precept,
precept upon precept,
Line upon line, line upon line,
Here a little, there a little."   [2 Chr. 36:15]

11 For with ᴿstammering lips and another
tongue
He will speak to this people,   1 Cor. 14:21

12 To whom He said, "This *is* the ᴿrest
with which
You may cause the weary to rest,"
And, "This *is* the refreshing";
Yet they would not hear.   Is. 30:15

13 But the word of the LORD was to them,
"Precept upon precept, precept upon
precept,
Line upon line, line upon line,
Here a little, there a little,"
That they might go and fall backward,
and be broken
And snared and caught.

14 Therefore hear the word of the LORD,
you scornful men,
Who rule this people who *are* in
Jerusalem,

15 Because you have said, "We have made
a covenant with death,
And with Sheol we are in agreement.
When the overflowing scourge passes
through,
It will not come to us,
ᴿFor we have made lies our refuge,
And under falsehood we have hidden
ourselves."   Is. 9:15

A Cornerstone in Zion

16 Therefore thus says the Lord GOD:

"Behold, I lay in Zion ᴿa stone for a
foundation,   Matt. 21:42; 1 Pet. 2:6–8
A tried stone, a precious cornerstone, a
sure foundation;
Whoever believes will not act hastily.

17 Also I will make justice the measuring
line,
And righteousness the plummet;
The hail will sweep away the refuge of
lies,
And the waters will overflow the hiding
place.

18 Your covenant with death will be
annulled,
And your agreement with Sheol will
not stand;
When the overflowing scourge passes
through,
Then you will be trampled down by it.

19 As often as it goes out it will take you;
For morning by morning it will pass
over,
And by day and by night;
It will be a terror just to understand
the report."

20 For the bed is too short to stretch out
on,
And the covering so narrow that one
cannot wrap himself *in it.*

21 For the LORD will rise up as *at* Mount
ᴿPerazim,   2 Sam. 5:20
He will be angry as in the Valley of
ᴿGibeon—
That He may do His work, ᴿHis
awesome work,
And bring to pass His act, His ᵀunusual
act.   Josh. 10:10, 12 • [Lam. 3:33] • Lit. *foreign*

22 Now therefore, do not be mockers,
Lest your bonds be made strong;
For I have heard from the Lord GOD of
hosts,
ᴿA ᵀdestruction determined even upon
the whole earth.   Is. 10:22 • Lit. *complete end*

Listen to the Teaching of God

23 Give ear and hear my voice,
Listen and hear my speech.

24 Does the plowman keep plowing all day
to sow?
Does he keep turning his soil and
breaking the clods?

25 When he has leveled its surface,
    Does he not sow the black cummin
    And scatter the cummin,
    Plant the wheat in rows,
    The barley in the appointed place,
    And the ᵀspelt in its place?   *rye*
26 For He instructs him in right judgment,
    His God teaches him.
27 For the black cummin is not threshed
        with a threshing sledge,
    Nor is a cartwheel rolled over the
        cummin;
    But the black cummin is beaten out
        with a stick,
    And the cummin with a rod.
28 Bread *flour* must be ground;
    Therefore he does not thresh it forever,
    Break *it with* his cartwheel,
    Or crush *it with* his horsemen.
29 This also comes from the LORD of hosts,
    ᴿ*Who* is wonderful in counsel *and*   Ps. 92:5
        excellent in ᵀguidance.   *sound wisdom*

Woe to Jerusalem

29 "Woe to ᵀAriel, to Ariel, the city
        where David dwelt!
    Add year to year;   *Jerusalem, lit. Lion of God*
    Let feasts come around.
2 Yet I will distress Ariel;
    There shall be heaviness and sorrow,
    And it shall be to Me as Ariel.
3 I will encamp against you all around,
    I will lay siege against you with a
        mound,
    And I will raise siegeworks against you.
4 You shall be brought down,
    You shall speak out of the ground;
    Your speech shall be low, out of the
        dust;
    Your voice shall be like a medium's,
    ᴿout of the ground;   Is. 8:19
    And your speech shall whisper out of
        the dust.

5 "Moreover the multitude of your ᴿfoes
    Shall be like fine dust,   Is. 25:5
    And the multitude of the terrible ones
    Like chaff that passes away;
    Yes, it shall be in an instant, suddenly.
6 ᴿYou will be punished by the LORD of
        hosts   Is. 28:2; 30:30
    With thunder and ᴿearthquake and
        great noise,   Rev. 16:18, 19
    With storm and tempest
    And the flame of devouring fire.
7 ᴿThe multitude of all the nations who
        fight against ᵀAriel,
    Even all who fight against her and her
        fortress,   Mic. 4:11, 12 • Jerusalem
    And distress her,
    Shall be as a dream of a night vision.
8 ᴿIt shall even be as when a hungry man
        dreams,

    And look—he eats;
    But he awakes, and his soul is still
        empty;
    Or as when a thirsty man dreams,
    And look—he drinks;
    But he awakes, and indeed *he is* faint,
    And his soul still craves:
    So the multitude of all the nations shall
        be,
    Who fight against Mount Zion."   Ps. 73:20

The Blindness of Disobedience

9 Pause and wonder!
    Blind yourselves and be blind!
    ᴿThey are drunk, ᴿbut not with wine;
    They stagger, but not with intoxicating
        drink.   Is. 28:7, 8 • Is. 51:21
10 For ᴿthe LORD has poured out on you
    The spirit of deep sleep,   Rom. 11:8
    And has ᴿclosed your eyes, namely, the
        prophets;   Ps. 69:23
    And He has covered your heads,
    namely, ᴿthe seers.   Is. 44:18

11 The whole vision has become to you like
the words of a ᵀbook ᴿthat is sealed, which
men deliver to one who is literate, saying,
"Read this, please." ᴿAnd he says, "I cannot,
for it *is* sealed."   *scroll* • Is. 8:16 • Dan. 12:4, 9
12 Then the book is delivered to one who ᵀis
illiterate, saying, "Read this, please." And he
says, "I am not literate."   Lit. *does not know books*
13 Therefore the Lord said:

    ᴿ"Inasmuch as these people draw near
        with their mouths   Ezek. 33:31
    And honor Me ᴿwith their lips,   Col. 2:22
    But have removed their hearts far from
        Me,
    And their fear toward Me is taught by
        the commandment of men,
14 ᴿTherefore, behold, I will again do a
        marvelous work
    Among this people,
    A marvelous work and a wonder;
    ᴿFor the wisdom of their wise *men* shall
        perish,
    And the understanding of their prudent
        men shall be hidden."   Hab. 1:5 • Jer. 49:7

15 ᴿWoe to those who seek deep to hide
        their counsel far from the LORD,
    And their works are in the dark;
    ᴿThey say, "Who sees us?" and, "Who
        knows us?"   Is. 30:1 • Ps. 10:11; 94:7
16 Surely you have things turned around!
    Shall the potter be esteemed as the
        clay;
    For shall the ᴿthing made say of him
        who made it,
    "He did not make me"?
    Or shall the thing formed say of him
        who formed it,
    "He has no understanding"?   Is. 45:9

Future Recovery of Wisdom

17 Is it not yet a very little while
 Till ᴿLebanon shall be turned into a
  fruitful field,
 And the fruitful field be esteemed as a
  forest? Is. 32:15
18 ᴿIn that day the deaf shall hear the
  words of the book, Is. 35:5
 And the eyes of the blind shall see out
  of obscurity and out of darkness.
19 ᴿThe humble also shall increase their joy
  in the Lᴏʀᴅ, [Is. 11:4; 61:1]
 And ᴿthe poor among men shall rejoice
  In the Holy One of Israel. [James 2:5]
20 For the ᵀterrible one is brought to
  nothing,
 ᴿThe scornful one is consumed,
 And all who ᴿwatch for iniquity are cut
  off— terrifying • Is. 28:14 • Mic. 2:1
21 Who make a man an offender by a
  word,
 And ᴿlay a snare for him who reproves
  in the gate,
 And turn aside the just ᴿby empty
  words. Amos 5:10, 12 • Prov. 28:21

22 Therefore thus says the Lᴏʀᴅ, ᴿwho
redeemed Abraham, concerning the house of
Jacob: Josh. 24:3

 "Jacob shall not now be ᴿashamed,
 Nor shall his face now grow pale; Is. 45:17
23 But when he sees his children,
 ᴿThe work of My hands, in his midst,
 They will hallow My name,
 And hallow the Holy One of Jacob,
 And fear the God of Israel. [Is. 45:11]
24 These also ᴿwho erred in spirit will
  come to understanding,
 And those who complained will learn
  doctrine." Is. 28:7

Futile Confidence in Egypt

30 "Woe to the rebellious children," says
  the Lᴏʀᴅ,
 ᴿ"Who take counsel, but not of Me,
 And who ᵀdevise plans, but not of My
  Spirit, Is. 29:15 • Lit. weave a web
 ᴿThat they may add sin to sin; Deut. 29:19
2 ᴿWho walk to go down to Egypt,
 And ᴿhave not asked My advice,
 To strengthen themselves in the
  strength of Pharaoh, Is. 31:1 • Josh. 9:14
 And to trust in the shadow of Egypt!
3 ᴿTherefore the strength of Pharaoh
 Shall be your shame,
 And trust in the shadow of Egypt
 Shall be your humiliation. Is. 20:5
4 For his princes were at ᴿZoan, Is. 19:11
 And his ambassadors came to Hanes.
5 ᴿThey were all ashamed of a people who
  could not benefit them,
 Or be help or benefit, Jer. 2:36
 But a shame and also a reproach."

6 ᴿThe ᵀburden against the beasts of the
South. Is. 57:9 • oracle, prophecy

 Through a land of trouble and anguish,
 From which came the lioness and lion,
 ᴿThe viper and fiery flying serpent,
 They will carry their riches on the
  backs of young donkeys, Deut. 8:15
 And their treasures on the humps of
  camels,
 To a people who shall not profit;
7 ᴿFor the Egyptians shall help in vain and
  to no purpose. Jer. 37:7
 Therefore I have called her
 ᵀRahab-Hem-Shebeth. Lit. Rahab Sits Idle

A Rebellious People

8 Now go, ᴿwrite it before them on a
  tablet,
 And note it on a scroll,
 That it may be for time to come,
 Forever and ever: Hab. 2:2
9 That ᴿthis is a rebellious people,
 Lying children,
 Children who will not hear the law of
  the Lᴏʀᴅ; Is. 1:2, 4; 65:2
10 ᴿWho say to the seers, "Do not see,"
 And to the prophets, "Do not prophesy
  to us right things;
 ᴿSpeak to us smooth things, prophesy
  deceits. Jer. 11:21 • 1 Kin. 22:8, 13
11 Get out of the way,
 Turn aside from the path,
 Cause the Holy One of Israel
 To cease from before us."

12 Therefore thus says the Holy One of
Israel:

 "Because you ᴿdespise this word,
 And trust in oppression and perversity,
 And rely on them, Is. 5:24
13 Therefore this iniquity shall be to you
 ᴿLike a breach ready to fall,
 A bulge in a high wall,
 Whose breaking ᴿcomes suddenly, in an
  instant. Ps. 62:3, 4 • Is. 29:5
14 And ᴿHe shall break it like the breaking
  of the potter's vessel, Jer. 19:11
 Which is broken in pieces;
 He shall not spare.
 So there shall not be found among its
  fragments
 A shard to take fire from the hearth,
 Or to take water from the cistern."

15 For thus says the Lord Gᴏᴅ, the Holy
One of Israel:

 ᴿ"In returning and rest you shall be
  saved;
 In quietness and confidence shall be
  your strength."
 ᴿBut you would not, Is. 7:4; 28:12 • Matt. 23:37

16 And you said, "No, for we will flee on
   horses"—
   Therefore you shall flee!
   And, "We will ride on swift *horses*"—
   Therefore those who pursue you shall
   be swift!
17 [R]One thousand *shall flee* at the threat of
   one,   Josh. 23:10
   At the threat of five you shall flee,
   Till you are left as a [T]pole on top of a
   mountain   A tree stripped of branches
   And as a banner on a hill.

God Will Be Gracious

18 Therefore the LORD will wait, that He
   may be [R]gracious to you;   Is. 33:2
   And therefore He will be exalted, that
   He may have mercy on you.
   For the LORD *is* a God of justice;
   Blessed *are* all those who wait for Him.
19 For the people [R]shall dwell in Zion at
   Jerusalem;   Is. 65:9
   You shall [R]weep no more.   Is. 25:8
   He will be very gracious to you at the
   sound of your cry;
   When He hears it, He will answer you.
20 And *though* the Lord gives you
   [R]The bread of adversity and the water of
   [T]affliction,   1 Kin. 22:27 • *oppression*
   Yet [R]your teachers will not be moved
   into a corner anymore,   Amos 8:11
   But your eyes shall see your teachers.
21 Your ears shall hear a word behind you,
   saying,
   "This *is* the way, walk in it,"
   Whenever you [R]turn to the right hand
   Or whenever you turn to the left. Josh. 1:7
22 [R]You will also defile the covering of your
   images of silver,   Is. 2:20; 31:7
   And the ornament of your molded
   images of gold.
   You will throw them away as an
   unclean thing;
   You will say to them, "Get away!"
23 [R]Then He will give the rain for your seed
   With which you sow the ground,
   And bread of the increase of the earth;
   It will be [T]fat and plentiful.
   In that day your cattle will feed
   In large pastures.   [Matt. 6:33] • *rich*
24 Likewise the oxen and the young
   donkeys that work the ground
   Will eat cured fodder,
   Which has been winnowed with the
   shovel and fan.
25 There will be [R]on every high mountain
   And on every high hill   Is. 2:14, 15
   Rivers *and* streams of waters,
   In the day of the [R]great slaughter,
   When the towers fall.   Is. 2:10–21; 34:2

26 Moreover [R]the light of the moon will be
   as the light of the sun,   [Is. 60:19, 20]
   And the light of the sun will be
   sevenfold,
   As the light of seven days,
   In the day that the LORD binds up the
   bruise of His people
   And heals the stroke of their wound.

Judgment on Assyria

27 Behold, the name of the LORD comes
   from afar,
   Burning *with* His anger,
   And *His* burden *is* heavy;
   His lips are full of indignation,
   And His tongue like a devouring fire.
28 [R]His breath is like an overflowing
   stream,   Is. 11:4
   [R]Which reaches up to the neck,
   To sift the nations with the sieve of
   futility;   Is. 8:8
   And *there shall be* [R]a bridle in the jaws
   of the people,   Is. 37:29
   Causing *them* to err.
29 You shall have a song
   As in the night *when* a holy festival is
   kept,
   And gladness of heart as when one
   goes with a flute,
   To come into [R]the mountain of the
   LORD,   [Is. 2:3]
   To [T]the Mighty One of Israel. Lit. *the Rock*
30 [R]The LORD will cause His glorious voice
   to be heard,
   And show the descent of His arm,
   With the indignation of *His* anger
   And the flame of a devouring fire,
   With scattering, tempest, [R]and
   hailstones.   Is. 29:6 • Is. 28:2
31 For through the voice of the LORD
   Assyria will be [T]beaten down, Lit. *shattered*
   As He strikes with the [R]rod.   Is. 10:5, 24
32 And *in* every place where the staff of
   punishment passes,
   Which the LORD lays on him,
   It will be with tambourines and harps;
   And in battles of [R]brandishing He will
   fight with it.   Is. 11:15
33 [R]For Tophet *was* established of old,
   Yes, for the king it is prepared.
   He has made *it* deep and large;
   Its pyre *is* fire with much wood;
   The breath of the LORD, like a stream
   of brimstone,
   Kindles it.   Jer. 7:31

The Folly of Not Trusting God

31 Woe to those [R]who go down to Egypt
     for help,   Is. 30:1, 2
   And [R]rely on horses,   Ps. 20:7
   Who trust in chariots because *they are*
   many,

And in horsemen because they are very
   strong,
But who do not look to the Holy One of
   Israel,
^RNor seek the LORD!   Dan. 9:13

2 Yet He also *is* wise and will bring
   disaster,
And ^Rwill not ^Tcall back His words,
But will arise against the house of
   evildoers,
And against the help of those who
   work iniquity.   Num. 23:19 · Retract

3 Now the Egyptians *are* men, and not
   God;
And their horses are flesh, and not
   spirit.
When the LORD stretches out His hand,
Both he who helps will fall,
And he who is helped will fall down;
They all will perish ^Rtogether.   Is. 20:6

God Will Deliver Jerusalem

4 For thus the LORD has spoken to me:

^R"As a lion roars,   Hos. 11:10
   And a young lion over his prey
   (When a multitude of shepherds is
     summoned against him,
   He will not be afraid of their voice
   Nor be disturbed by their noise),
   So the LORD of hosts will come down
   To fight for Mount Zion and for its hill.
5 ^RLike birds flying about,   Deut. 32:11
   So will the LORD of hosts defend
    Jerusalem.
   Defending, He will also deliver *it*;
   Passing over, He will preserve *it*."

6 Return *to* Him against whom the chil-
dren of Israel have ^Rdeeply revolted.   Hos. 9:9

7 For in that day every man shall ^Rthrow
away his idols of silver and his idols of gold—
^Rsin, which your own hands have made for
yourselves.   Is. 2:20; 30:22 · 1 Kin. 12:30

8 "Then Assyria shall ^Rfall by a sword not
   of man,
   And a sword not of mankind shall
    ^Rdevour him.
   But he shall flee from the sword,
   And his young men shall become forced
    labor.   2 Kin. 19:35, 36 · Is. 37:36
9 ^RHe shall cross over to his stronghold for
   fear,   Is. 37:37
   And his princes shall be afraid of the
    banner,"
   Says the LORD,
   Whose fire *is* in Zion
   And whose furnace *is* in Jerusalem.

A Reign of Righteousness

32 Behold, ^Ra king will reign in
     righteousness,   Ps. 45:1
   And princes will rule with justice.

2 A man will be as a hiding place from
   the wind,
And ^Ra ^Tcover from the tempest,
As rivers of water in a dry place,
As the shadow of a great rock in a
   weary land.   Is. 4:6 · *shelter*
3 ^RThe eyes of those who see will not be
   dim,
And the ears of those who hear will
   listen.   Is. 29:18; 35:5
4 Also the heart of the ^Trash will
   ^Runderstand knowledge,
And the tongue of the stammerers will
   be ready to speak plainly.   *hasty* · Is. 29:24

5 The foolish person will no longer be
   called ^Tgenerous,
Nor the miser said *to be* bountiful;   *noble*
6 For the foolish person will speak
   foolishness,
And his heart will work ^Riniquity:
To practice ungodliness,
To utter error against the LORD,
To keep the hungry unsatisfied,
And he will cause the drink of the
   thirsty to fail.   Prov. 24:7–9
7 Also the schemes of the schemer *are*
   evil;
He devises wicked plans
To destroy the poor with lying words,
Even when the needy speaks justice.
8 But a ^Tgenerous man devises generous
   things,
And by generosity he shall stand.   *noble*

Consequences of Complacency

9 Rise up, you women ^Rwho are at ease,
   Hear my voice;
   You complacent daughters,
   Give ear to my speech.   Amos 6:1
10 In a year and *some* days
   You will be troubled, you complacent
    women;
   For the vintage will fail,
   The gathering will not come.
11 Tremble, you *women* who are at ease;
   Be troubled, you complacent ones;
   Strip yourselves, make yourselves bare,
   And gird *sackcloth* on *your* waists.

12 People shall mourn upon their breasts
   For the pleasant fields, for the fruitful
    vine.
13 ^ROn the land of my people will come up
   thorns *and* briers,
   Yes, on all the happy homes *in* ^Rthe
    joyous city;   Hos. 9:6 · Is. 22:2
14 ^RBecause the palaces will be forsaken,
   The bustling city will be deserted.
   The forts and towers will become lairs
    forever,
   A joy of wild donkeys, a pasture of
    flocks—   Is. 27:10
15 Until ^Rthe Spirit is poured upon us from
   on high,

And ᴿthe wilderness becomes a fruitful
field,
And the fruitful field is counted as a
forest.   [Joel 2:28] · Is. 29:17

The Peace of God's Reign

16 Then justice will dwell in the
wilderness,
And righteousness remain in the
fruitful field.
17 ᴿThe work of righteousness will be
peace,   James 3:18
And the effect of righteousness,
quietness and assurance forever.
18 My people will dwell in a peaceful
habitation,
In secure dwellings, and in quiet
ᴿresting places,   [Zech. 2:5; 3:10]
19 ᴿThough hail comes down ᴿon the forest,
And the city is brought low in
humiliation.   Is. 30:30 · Zech. 11:2
20 Blessed are you who sow beside all
waters,
Who send out freely the feet of ᴿthe ox
and the donkey.   Is. 30:23, 24

A Prayer in Deep Distress

33 Woe to you who plunder, though you
have not been plundered;
And you who deal treacherously,
though they have not dealt
treacherously with you!
ᴿWhen you cease plundering,   Rev. 13:10
You will be ᴿplundered;   Is. 10:12; 14:25; 31:8
When you make an end of dealing
treacherously,
They will deal treacherously with you.

2 O Lᴏʀᴅ, be gracious to us;
ᴿWe have waited for You.   Is. 25:9; 26:8
Be *their arm every morning,
Our salvation also in the time of
trouble.
3 At the noise of the tumult the people
ᴿshall flee;
When You lift Yourself up, the nations
shall be scattered;   Is. 17:13
4 And Your plunder shall be gathered
Like the gathering of the caterpillar;
As the running to and fro of locusts,
He shall run upon them.

5 ᴿThe Lᴏʀᴅ is exalted, for He dwells on
high;
He has filled Zion with justice and
righteousness.   Ps. 97:9
6 Wisdom and knowledge will be the
stability of your times,
And the strength of salvation;
The fear of the Lᴏʀᴅ is His treasure.

7 Surely their valiant ones shall cry
outside,
ᴿThe ambassadors of peace shall weep
bitterly.   2 Kin. 18:18, 37
8 ᴿThe highways lie waste,
The traveling man ceases.
ᴿHe has broken the covenant,
*He has despised the *cities,
He regards no man.   Judg. 5:6 · 2 Kin. 18:13-17
9 ᴿThe earth mourns and languishes,
Lebanon is shamed and shriveled;
Sharon is like a wilderness,
And Bashan and Carmel shake off their
fruits.   Is. 24:4

Impending Judgment on Zion

10 "Nowᴿ I will rise," says the Lᴏʀᴅ;
"Now I will be exalted,
Now I will lift Myself up.   Ps. 12:5
11 ᴿYou shall conceive chaff,   [Ps. 7:14]
You shall bring forth stubble;
Your breath, as fire, shall devour you.
12 And the people shall be like the
burnings of lime;
ᴿLike thorns cut up they shall be burned
in the fire.   Is. 9:18
13 Hear, ᴿyou who are afar off, what I
have done;
And you who are near, acknowledge
My might."   Is. 49:1
14 The sinners in Zion are afraid;
Fearfulness has seized the hypocrites:
"Who among us shall dwell with the
devouring ᴿfire?
Who among us shall dwell with
everlasting burnings?"   Heb. 12:29
15 He who ᴿwalks righteously and speaks
uprightly,   Ps. 15:2; 24:3, 4
He who despises the gain of
oppressions,
Who gestures with his hands, refusing
bribes,
Who stops his ears from hearing of
bloodshed,
And shuts his eyes from seeing evil:
16 He will dwell on ᵀhigh;
His place of defense will be the fortress
of rocks;
Bread will be given him,
His water will be sure.   Lit. heights

The Land of the Majestic King

17 Your eyes will see the King in His
ᴿbeauty;
They will see the land that is very far
off.   Ps. 27:4
18 Your heart will meditate on terror:
ᴿ"Where is the scribe?   1 Cor. 1:20
Where is he who weighs?
Where is he who counts the towers?"

33:2 LXX omits their; Syr., Tg., Vg. our

33:8 Tg. They have been removed from their cities • So
with MT, Vg.; DSS witnesses; LXX omits cities

19 ᴿYou will not see a fierce people,
  ᴿA people of obscure speech, beyond
    perception,   2 Kin. 19:32 · Jer. 5:15
  Of a ᵀstammering tongue *that you*
    cannot understand.   Unintelligible speech

20 ᴿLook upon Zion, the city of our
    appointed feasts;   Ps. 48:12
  Your eyes will see ᴿJerusalem, a quiet
    home,   Ps. 46:5; 125:1
  A tabernacle *that* will not be taken
    down;
  ᴿNot one of ᴿits stakes will ever be
    removed,   Is. 37:33 · Is. 54:2
  Nor will any of its cords be broken.
21 But there the majestic LORD *will be* for
    us
  A place of broad rivers *and* streams,
  In which no ᵀgalley with oars will sail,
  Nor majestic ships pass by   *ship*
22 (For the LORD *is* our ᴿJudge,   [Acts 10:42]
  The LORD *is* our ᴿLawgiver,   James 4:12
  ᴿThe LORD *is* our King;   Ps. 89:18
  He will save us);
23 Your tackle is loosed,
  They could not strengthen their mast,
  They could not spread the sail.

  Then the prey of great plunder is
    divided;
  The lame take the prey.
24 And the inhabitant will not say, "I am
    sick";
  ᴿThe people who dwell in it *will be*
    forgiven *their* iniquity.   Is. 40:2

Judgment on the Nations

34 Come ᴿnear, you nations, to hear;
  And heed, you people!
  ᴿLet the earth hear, and all that is in it,
  The world and all things that come
    forth from it.   Ps. 49:1 · Deut. 32:1
2 For the indignation of the LORD *is*
    against all nations,
  And *His* fury against all their armies;
  He has utterly destroyed them,
  He has given them over to the
    ᴿslaughter.   Is. 13:5
3 Also their slain shall be thrown out;
  ᴿTheir stench shall rise from their
    corpses,
  And the mountains shall be melted with
    their blood.   Joel 2:20
4 ᴿAll the host of heaven shall be
    dissolved,   Is. 13:13
  And the heavens shall be rolled up like
    a scroll;
  ᴿAll their host shall fall down   Is. 14:12
  As the leaf falls from the vine,
  And as *fruit* falling from a fig tree.

5 "For ᴿMy sword shall be bathed in
    heaven;
  Indeed it ᴿshall come down on Edom,

  And on the people of My curse, for
    judgment.   Jer. 46:10 · Mal. 1:4
6 The ᴿsword of the LORD is filled with
    blood,
  It is made ᵀoverflowing with fatness,
  With the blood of lambs and goats,
  With the fat of the kidneys of rams.
  For ᴿthe LORD has a sacrifice in Bozrah,
  And a great slaughter in the land of
    Edom.   Is. 66:16 · Lit. *fat* · Zeph. 1:7
7 The wild oxen shall come down with
    them,
  And the young bulls with the mighty
    bulls;
  Their land shall be soaked with blood,
  And their dust saturated with fatness."

8 For *it is* the day of the LORD's
    ᴿvengeance,   Is. 63:4
  The year of recompense for the cause
    of Zion.
9 ᴿIts streams shall be turned into pitch,
  And its dust into brimstone;   Deut. 29:23
  Its land shall become burning pitch.
10 It shall not be quenched night or day;
  ᴿIts smoke shall ascend forever.
  ᴿFrom generation to generation it shall
    lie waste;
  No one shall pass through it forever
    and ever.   Rev. 14:11; 18:18; 19:3 · Mal. 1:3, 4
11 But the ᵀpelican and the ᵀporcupine
    shall possess it,   Or *owl* · Or *hedgehog*
  Also the owl and the raven shall dwell
    in it.
  And ᴿHe shall stretch out over it   Lam. 2:8
  The line of confusion and the stones of
    emptiness.
12 They shall call its nobles to the
    kingdom,
  But none *shall be* there, and all its
    princes shall be nothing.

13 And ᴿthorns shall come up in its
    palaces,   Is. 32:13
  Nettles and brambles in its fortresses;
  ᴿIt shall be a habitation of jackals,
  A courtyard for ostriches.   Is. 13:21
14 The wild beasts of the desert shall also
    meet with the ᵀjackals,
  And the wild goat shall bleat to its
    companion;   Lit. *howling creatures*
  Also the night creature shall rest there,
  And find for herself a place of rest.
15 There the arrow snake shall make her
    nest and lay *eggs*
  And hatch, and gather *them* under her
    shadow;
  There also shall the hawks be gathered,
  Every one with her mate.

16 "Search from ᴿthe book of the LORD, and
    read: [Mal. 3:16]
  Not one of these shall fail;
  Not one shall lack her mate.

For My mouth has commanded it, and
His Spirit has gathered them.
17 He has cast the lot for them,
And His hand has divided it among
them with a measuring line.
They shall possess it forever;
From generation to generation they
shall dwell in it."

The Future Glory of Zion

35 The wilderness and the wasteland
shall be glad for them,   Is. 32:15; 55:12
And the ᴿdesertᵀ shall rejoice and
blossom as the rose;   Is. 41:19 • Heb. Arabah
2 ᴿIt shall blossom abundantly and rejoice,
Even with joy and singing.   Is. 32:15
The glory of Lebanon shall be given to
it,
The excellence of Carmel and Sharon.
They shall see the ᴿglory of the LORD,
The excellency of our God.   Is. 40:5

3 Strengthen the ᵀweak hands,   Lit. sinking
And make firm the feeble knees.
4 Say to those who are fearful-hearted,
"Be strong, do not fear!
Behold, your God will come with
ᴿvengeance,   Is. 34:8
With the recompense of God;
He will come and ᴿsave you."   Is. 33:22

5 Then the ᴿeyes of the blind shall be
opened,
And ᴿthe ears of the deaf shall be
unstopped.   Is. 29:18; John 9:6, 7 • [Matt. 11:5]
6 Then the ᴿlame shall leap like a deer,
And the ᴿtongue of the dumb sing.
For ᴿwaters shall burst forth in the
wilderness,   Matt. 15:30 • Is. 32:4 • [John 7:38]
And streams in the desert.
7 The parched ground shall become a
pool,
And the thirsty land springs of water;
In ᴿthe habitation of jackals, where
each lay,   Is. 34:13
There shall be grass with reeds and
rushes.

8 A ᴿhighway shall be there, and a road,
And it shall be called the Highway of
Holiness.   Is. 19:23
ᴿThe unclean shall not pass over it,
But it shall be for others.   Joel 3:17
Whoever walks the road, although a
fool,
Shall not go astray.
9 ᴿNo lion shall be there,   Lev. 26:6
Nor shall any ravenous beast go up on
it;
It shall not be found there.
But the redeemed shall walk there,
10 And the ᴿransomed of the LORD shall
return,
And come to Zion with singing,

With everlasting joy on their heads.
They shall obtain joy and gladness,
And ᴿsorrow and sighing shall flee
away.   Is. 51:11 • [Rev. 7:17; 21:4]

Sennacherib Boasts Against the LORD

36 Now it came to pass in the fourteenth
year of King Hezekiah that Sennacherib king of Assyria came up against all the
fortified cities of Judah and took them.
2 Then the king of Assyria sent the *Rabshakeh with a great army from Lachish to
King Hezekiah at Jerusalem. And he stood by
the aqueduct from the upper pool, on the
highway to the Fuller's Field.
3 And ᴿEliakim the son of Hilkiah, who
was over the household, ᴿShebna the scribe,
and Joah the son of Asaph, the recorder,
came out to him.   Is. 22:20 • Is. 22:15
4 ᴿThen the Rabshakeh said to them, "Say
now to Hezekiah, 'Thus says the great king,
the king of Assyria: "What confidence is this
in which you trust?   2 Kin. 18:19
5 "I say you speak of having plans and
power for war; but they are ᵀmere words.
Now in whom do you trust, that you rebel
against me?   Lit. a word of the lips
6 "Look! You are trusting in the ᴿstaff of
this broken reed, Egypt, on which if a man
leans, it will go into his hand and pierce it. So
is Pharaoh king of Egypt to all who ᴿtrust in
him.   Ezek. 29:6 • Ps. 146:3
7 "But if you say to me, 'We trust in the
LORD our God,' is it not He whose high places
and whose altars Hezekiah has taken away,
and said to Judah and Jerusalem, 'You shall
worship before this altar'?" '
8 "Now therefore, I urge you, give a
pledge to my master the king of Assyria, and
I will give you two thousand horses—if you
are able on your part to put riders on them!
9 "How then will you repel one captain of
the least of my master's servants, and put
your trust in Egypt for chariots and horsemen?
10 "Have I now come up without the LORD
against this land to destroy it? The LORD said
to me, 'Go up against this land, and destroy
it.' "
11 Then Eliakim, Shebna, and Joah said to
the Rabshakeh, "Please speak to your servants in Aramaic, for we understand it; and
do not speak to us in ᵀHebrew in the hearing
of the people who are on the wall."   Lit. Judean
12 But the Rabshakeh said, "Has my master
sent me to your master and to you to speak
these words, and not to the men who sit on
the wall, who will eat and drink their own
waste with you?"
13 Then the Rabshakeh stood and called
out with a loud voice in Hebrew, and said,

36:2 A title, probably Chief of Staff or Governor

"Hear the words of the great king, the king of Assyria!

14 "Thus says the king: 'Do not let Hezekiah deceive you, for he will not be able to deliver you;

15 'nor let Hezekiah make you trust in the LORD, saying, "The LORD will surely deliver us; this city will not be given into the hand of the king of Assyria." '

16 "Do not listen to Hezekiah; for thus says the king of Assyria: 'Make *peace* with me *by a* present and come out to me; ᴿand every one of you eat from his own vine and every one from his own fig tree, and every one of you drink the waters of his own cistern;   Zech. 3:10

17 'until I come and take you away to a land like your own land, a land of grain and new wine, a land of bread and vineyards.

18 '*Beware* lest Hezekiah persuade you, saying, "The LORD will deliver us." Has any one of the gods of the nations delivered its land from the hand of the king of Assyria?

19 'Where *are* the gods of Hamath and Arpad? Where *are* the gods of Sepharvaim? Indeed, have they delivered ᴿSamaria from my hand?   2 Kin. 17:6

20 'Who among all the gods of these lands have delivered their countries from my hand, that the LORD should deliver Jerusalem from my hand?' "

21 But they ᵀheld their peace and answered him not a word; for the king's commandment was, "Do not answer him."   were silent

22 Then Eliakim the son of Hilkiah, who *was* over the household, Shebna the scribe, and Joah the son of Asaph, the recorder, came to Hezekiah with *their* clothes torn, and told him the words of *the* Rabshakeh.

Isaiah Assures Deliverance

37 And ᴿso it was, when King Hezekiah heard *it,* that he tore his clothes, covered himself with sackcloth, and went into the house of the LORD.   2 Kin. 19:1-37

2 Then he sent Eliakim, who *was* over the household, Shebna the scribe, and the elders of the priests, covered with sackcloth, to Isaiah the prophet, the son of Amoz.

3 And they said to him, "Thus says Hezekiah: 'This day *is* a day of ᴿtrouble and rebuke and ᵀblasphemy; for the children have come to birth, but *there is* no strength to bring them forth.   Is. 22:5; 26:16; 33:2 • *contempt*

4 'It may be that the LORD your God will hear the words of *the* Rabshakeh, whom his master the king of Assyria has sent to ᴿreproach the living God, and will rebuke the words which the LORD your God has heard. Therefore lift up *your* prayer for the remnant that is left.' "   Is. 36:15, 18, 20

5 So the servants of King Hezekiah came to Isaiah.

6 And Isaiah said to them, "Thus you shall say to your master, 'Thus says the LORD: "Do not be afraid of the words which you have heard, with which the servants of the king of Assyria have blasphemed Me.

7 "Surely I will send a spirit upon him, and he shall hear a rumor and return to his own land; and I will cause him to fall by the sword in his own land." ' "

Sennacherib's Threat and Hezekiah's Prayer

8 Then *the* Rabshakeh returned, and found the king of Assyria warring against Libnah, for he heard that he had departed from Lachish.

9 And the king heard concerning Tirhakah king of Ethiopia, "He has come out to make war with you." So when he heard *it,* he sent messengers to Hezekiah, saying,

10 "Thus you shall speak to Hezekiah king of Judah, saying: 'Do not let your God in whom you trust deceive you, saying, "Jerusalem shall not be given into the hand of the king of Assyria."

11 'Look! You have heard what the kings of Assyria have done to all lands by utterly destroying them; and shall you be delivered?

12 'Have the ᴿgods of the nations delivered those whom my fathers have destroyed, Gozan and Haran and Rezeph, and the people of Eden who *were* in Telassar?   Is. 36:18, 19

13 'Where *is* the king of ᴿHamath, the king of Arpad, and the king of the city of Sepharvaim, Hena, and Ivah?' "   Is. 49:23

14 And Hezekiah received the letter from the hand of the messengers, and read it; and Hezekiah went up to the house of the LORD, and spread it before the LORD.

15 Then Hezekiah prayed to the LORD, saying:

16 "O LORD of hosts, God of Israel, *the* One who dwells *between* the cherubim, You *are* God, You alone, of all the kingdoms of the earth. You have made heaven and earth.

17 ᴿ"Incline Your ear, O LORD, and hear; open Your eyes, O LORD, and see; and hear all the words of Sennacherib, which he has sent to reproach the living God.   Dan. 9:18

18 "Truly, LORD, the kings of Assyria have laid waste all the nations and their lands,

19 "and have cast their gods into the fire; for they *were* ᴿnot gods, but the work of men's hands—wood and stone. Therefore they destroyed them.   Is. 40:19, 20

20 "Now therefore, O LORD our God, ᴿsave us from his hand, that all the kingdoms of the earth may ᴿknow that You *are* the LORD, You alone."   Is. 33:22 • Ps. 83:18

The Word of the LORD Concerning Sennacherib

21 Then Isaiah the son of Amoz sent to Hezekiah, saying, "Thus says the LORD God

of Israel, 'Because you have prayed to Me
against Sennacherib king of Assyria,
22 'this *is* the word which the LORD has
spoken concerning him:

"The virgin, the daughter of Zion,
Has despised you, laughed you to scorn;
The daughter of Jerusalem Has shaken
her head behind your back!

23 "Whom have you reproached and
blasphemed?
Against whom have you raised *your*
voice,
And lifted up your eyes on high?
Against the Holy One of Israel.
24 By your servants you have reproached
the Lord,
And said, 'By the multitude of my
chariots
I have come up to the height of the
mountains,
To the limits of Lebanon;
I will cut down its tall cedars
And its choice cypress trees;
I will enter its farthest height,
To its fruitful forest.
25 I have dug and drunk water,
And with the soles of my feet I have
dried up
All the brooks of ᵀdefense.'   Or perhaps *Egypt*
26 "Did you not hear ᴿlong ago
How I made it,
From ancient times that I formed it?
Now I have brought it to pass,
That you should be
For crushing fortified cities *into* heaps
of ruins.   Is. 25:1; 40:21; 45:21
27 Therefore their inhabitants *had* little
power;
They were dismayed and confounded;
They were *as* the grass of the field
And the green herb,
As the grass on the housetops
And *grain* blighted before it is grown.

28 "But I know your dwelling place,
Your going out and your coming in,
And your rage against Me.
29 Because your rage against Me and your
tumult
Have come up to My ears,
Therefore ᴿI will put My hook in your
nose   Is. 30:28
And My bridle in your lips,
And I will ᴿturn you back   Ezek. 38:4; 39:2
By the way which you came." '

30 "This *shall be* a sign to you:

You shall eat this year such as grows of
itself,
And the second year what springs from
the same;
Also in the third year sow and reap,

Plant vineyards and eat the fruit of
them.
31 And the remnant who have escaped of
the house of Judah
Shall again take root downward,
And bear fruit upward.
32 For out of Jerusalem shall go a
remnant,
And those who escape from Mount
Zion.
The ᴿzeal of the LORD of hosts will do
this.   2 Kin. 19:31

33 "Therefore thus says the LORD
concerning the king of Assyria:

'He shall not come into this city,
Nor shoot an arrow there,
Nor come before it with shield,
Nor build a siege mound against it.
34 By the way that he came,
By the same shall he return;
And he shall not come into this city,'
Says the LORD.
35 'For I will ᴿdefend this city, to save it
For My own sake and for My servant
ᴿDavid's sake.' "   Is. 31:5; 38:6 • 1 Kin. 11:13

Sennacherib's Defeat and Death

36 Then the ᵀangel of the LORD went out,
and killed in the camp of the Assyrians one
hundred and eighty-five thousand; and when
people arose early in the morning, there were
the corpses—all dead.   Or *Angel*
37 So Sennacherib king of Assyria departed
and went away, returned *home,* and remained at Nineveh.
38 Now it came to pass, as he was worshiping in the house of Nisroch his god, that
Adrammelech and Sharezer his sons struck
him down with the sword; and they escaped
into the land of Ararat. Then ᴿEsarhaddon his
son reigned in his place.   Ezra 4:2

Hezekiah's Life Extended

38 In those days Hezekiah was sick and
near death. And Isaiah the prophet,
the son of Amoz, went to him and said to
him, "Thus says the LORD: 'Set your house in
order, for you shall die and not live.' "
2 Then Hezekiah turned his face toward
the wall, and prayed to the LORD,
3 and said, ᴿ"Remember now, O LORD, I
pray, how I have walked before You in truth
and with a ᵀloyal heart, and have done *what
is* good in Your ᴿsight." And Hezekiah wept
bitterly.   Neh. 13:14 • *whole* or *peaceful* • 2 Kin. 18:5, 6
4 And the word of the LORD came to Isa-
iah, saying,
5 "Go and tell Hezekiah, 'Thus says the
LORD, the God of David your father: "I have
heard your prayer, I have seen your tears;
surely I will add to your days fifteen years.

6 "I will deliver you and this city from the hand of the king of Assyria, and ᴿI will defend this city." '   Is. 31:5; 37:35

7 "And this *is* ᴿthe sign to you from the LORD, that the LORD will do this thing which He has spoken: Is. 7:11

8 "Behold, I will bring the shadow on the sundial, which has gone down with the sun on the sundial of Ahaz, ten degrees backward." So the sun returned ten degrees on the dial by which it had gone down.

9 This is the writing of Hezekiah king of Judah, when he had been sick and had recovered from his sickness:

10 I said,
"In the prime of my life
    I shall go to the gates of Sheol;
    I am deprived of the remainder of my
       years."
11 I said,
"I shall not see ᵀYAH,   Heb. YAH, YAH
    The LORD in the land of the living;
    I shall observe man no more *among
       the inhabitants of *the world.
12 ᴿMy life span is gone,
    Taken from me like a shepherd's tent;
    I have cut off my life like a weaver.
    He cuts me off from the loom;
    From day until night You make an end
       of me.   Job 7:6
13 I have considered until morning—
    Like a lion,
    So He breaks all my bones;
    From day until night You make an end
       of me.
14 Like a crane *or* a swallow, so I
       chattered;
    ᴿI mourned like a dove;
    My eyes fail *from looking* upward.
    O *LORD, I am oppressed;
    ᵀUndertake for me!   Is. 59:11 · *Be my surety*

15 "What shall I say?
    *He has both spoken to me,
    And He Himself has done *it*.
    I shall walk carefully all my years
    ᴿIn the bitterness of my soul.   Job 7:11; 10:1
16 O LORD, by these *things men* live;
    And in all these *things is* the life of my
       spirit;
    So You will restore me and make me
       live.
17 Indeed *it was* for *my own* peace
    That I had great bitterness;
    But You have lovingly *delivered* my
       soul from the pit of corruption,

38:11 LXX omits *among the inhabitants of the world* • So with some Heb. mss.; MT, Vg. *rest;* Tg. *land*
38:14 So with Bg.; MT, DSS *Lord*
38:15 So with MT, Vg.; DSS, Tg. *And shall I say to Him;* LXX omits first half of this verse

For You have cast all my sins behind
    Your back.
18 For ᴿSheol cannot thank You,
    Death cannot praise You;
    Those who go down to the pit cannot
       hope for Your truth.   Ps. 6:5; 30:9; 88:11
19 The living, the living man, he shall
       praise You,
    As I *do* this day;
    ᴿThe father shall make known Your
       truth to the children.   Deut. 4:9; 6:7
20 "The LORD *was ready* to save me;
    Therefore we will sing my songs with
       stringed instruments
    All the days of our life, in the house of
       the LORD."

21 Now ᴿIsaiah had said, "Let them take a lump of figs, and apply *it* as a poultice on the boil, and he shall recover."   2 Kin. 20:7
22 And ᴿHezekiah had said, "What *is* the sign that I shall go up to the house of the LORD?"   2 Kin. 20:8

The Babylonian Envoys

39 At that time *Merodach-Baladan the son of Baladan, king of Babylon, sent letters and a present to Hezekiah, for he heard that he had been sick and had recovered.

2 And Hezekiah was pleased with them, and showed them the house of his treasures—the silver and gold, the spices and precious ointment, and all his armory—all that was found among his treasures. There was nothing in his house or in all his dominion that Hezekiah did not show them.

3 Then Isaiah the prophet went to King Hezekiah, and said to him, "What did these men say, and from where did they come to you?" So Hezekiah said, "They came to me from a ᴿfar country, from Babylon."   Deut. 28:49

4 And he said, "What have they seen in your house?" So Hezekiah answered, "They have seen all that *is* in my house; there is nothing among my treasures that I have not shown them."

5 Then Isaiah said to Hezekiah, "Hear the word of the LORD of hosts:

6 'Behold, the days are coming ᴿwhen all that *is* in your house, and what your fathers have accumulated until this day, shall be carried to Babylon; nothing shall be left,' says the LORD.   Jer. 20:5

7 'And they shall take away *some* of your ᴿsons who will descend from you, whom you will beget; and they shall be eunuchs in the palace of the king of Babylon.' "   Dan. 1:1-7

8 So Hezekiah said to Isaiah, ᴿ"The word of the LORD which you have spoken *is* good!" For he said, "At least there will be peace and truth in my days."   1 Sam. 3:18

39:1 *Berodach-Baladan,* 2 Kin. 20:12

God's People Are Comforted

40 "Comfort, yes, comfort My people!"
Says your God.

2 "Speak ^Tcomfort to Jerusalem, and cry
out to her,   Lit. *to the heart of*
That her warfare is ended,
That her iniquity is pardoned;
^RFor she has received from the LORD's
hand   Is. 61:7
Double for all her sins."

3 ^RThe voice of one crying in the
wilderness: Matt. 3:3
"Prepare the way of the LORD;
^RMake straight *in the desert   Ps. 68:4
A highway for our God.
4 Every valley shall be exalted
And every mountain and hill brought
low;
^RThe crooked places shall be made
^Tstraight   Is. 45:2 · Or *a plain*
And the rough places smooth;
5 The ^Rglory of the LORD shall be
revealed,   Is. 35:2
And all flesh shall see *it* together;
For the mouth of the LORD has
spoken."

6 The voice said, "Cry out!"
And *he said, "What shall I cry?"

^R"All flesh *is* grass,   Job 14:2
And all its loveliness *is* like the flower
of the field.
7 The grass withers, the flower fades,
Because the breath of the LORD blows
upon it;
Surely the people *are* grass.
8 The grass withers, the flower fades,
But ^Rthe word of our God stands
forever."   [John 12:34]

9 O Zion,
You who bring good tidings,
Get up into the high mountain;
O Jerusalem,
You who bring good tidings,
Lift up your voice with strength,
Lift *it* up, be not afraid;
Say to the cities of Judah, "Behold your
God!"

10 Behold, the Lord GOD shall come ^Rwith^T
a strong *hand*,   Is. 9:6, 7 · *in strength*
And His arm shall rule for Him;
Behold, His reward *is* with Him,
And His ^Twork before Him.   *recompense*
11 He will ^Rfeed His flock like a shepherd;
He will gather the lambs with His arm,
And carry *them* in His bosom,
And gently lead those who are with
young.   Mic. 5:4; [John 10:11, 14–16]

12 ^RWho has measured the *waters in the
hollow of his hand,   Prov. 30:4
Measured heaven with a span
And calculated the dust of the earth in
a measure?
Weighed the mountains in scales
And the hills in a balance?
13 ^RWho has directed the Spirit of the
LORD,   [1 Cor. 2:16]
Or *as* His counselor has taught Him?
14 With whom did He take counsel, and
who instructed Him,
And ^Rtaught Him in the path of justice?
Who taught Him knowledge,
And showed Him the way of
understanding?   Job 36:22, 23
15 Behold, the nations *are* as a drop in a
bucket,
And are counted as the small dust on
the scales;
Look, He lifts up the isles as a very
little thing.
16 And Lebanon *is* not sufficient to burn,
Nor its beasts sufficient for a burnt
offering.
17 All nations before Him *are* as nothing,
And ^Rthey are counted by Him less than
nothing and worthless.   Ps. 62:9

18 To whom then will you ^Rliken God?
Or what likeness will you compare to
Him?   Is. 46:5
19 The workman molds an image,
The goldsmith overspreads it with gold,
And the silversmith casts silver chains.
20 Whoever *is* too impoverished for *such*
^Ta contribution
Chooses a tree *that* will not rot;
He seeks for himself a skillful workman
^RTo prepare a carved image *that* will not
totter.   *an offering* · Is. 41:7; 46:7

21 ^RHave you not known?
Have you not heard?
Has it not been told you from the
beginning?
Have you not understood from the
foundations of the earth?   Rom. 1:19
22 *It is* He who sits above the circle of the
earth,
And its inhabitants *are* like
grasshoppers,
Who ^Rstretches out the heavens like a
curtain,
And spreads them out like a ^Rtent to
dwell in.   Jer. 10:12 · Ps. 19:4
23 He ^Tbrings the ^Rprinces to nothing;
He makes the judges of the earth
useless.   *reduces* · Ps. 107:40

24 Scarcely shall they be planted,
Scarcely shall they be sown,

Scarcely shall their stock take root in
the earth,
When He will also blow on them,
And they will wither,
And the whirlwind will take them away
like stubble.

25 "To^R whom then will you liken Me,
Or *to whom* shall I be equal?" says the
Holy One.   Is. 40:18

26 Lift up your eyes on high,
And see who has created these *things,*
Who brings out their host by number;
^RHe calls them all by name,
By the greatness of His might
And the strength of *His* power;
Not one is missing.   Ps. 147:4

27 ^RWhy do you say, O Jacob,
And speak, O Israel:
"My way is hidden from the LORD,
And my just claim is passed over by my
God"?   Is. 54:7, 8

28 Have you not known?
Have you not heard?
The everlasting God, the LORD,
The Creator of the ends of the earth,
Neither faints nor is weary.
His understanding is unsearchable.

29 He gives power to the weak,
And to *those who have* no might He
increases strength.

30 Even the youths shall faint and be
weary,
And the young men shall utterly fall,

31 But those who ^Rwait on the LORD
^RShall renew *their* strength;
They shall mount up with wings like
eagles,   Is. 30:15; 49:23 · Ps. 103:5
They shall run and not be weary,
They shall walk and not faint.

Israel Assured of God's Help

41 "Keep ^Rsilence before Me, O
coastlands,
And let the people renew *their* strength!
Let them come near, then let them
speak;
Let us ^Rcome near together for
judgment.   Zech. 2:13 · Is. 1:18

2 "Who raised up one ^Rfrom the east?
Who in righteousness called him to His
feet?   Is. 46:11
Who ^Rgave the nations before him,
And made *him* rule over kings?
Who gave *them* as the dust *to* his
sword,   Is. 45:1, 13
As driven stubble to his bow?

3 Who pursued them, *and* passed ^Tsafely
By the way *that* he had not gone with
his feet?   Lit. *in peace*

4 ^RWho has performed and done *it,*
Calling the generations from the
beginning?   Is. 41:26

'I, the LORD, am ^Rthe first;   Rev. 1:8, 17; 22:13
And with the last I *am* ^RHe.' "   Is. 43:10

5 The coastlands saw *it* and feared,
The ends of the earth were afraid;
They drew near and came.

6 ^REveryone helped his neighbor,
And said to his brother,
^TBe of good courage!"   Is. 40:19 · Lit. *Be strong*

7 ^RSo the craftsman encouraged the
^Rgoldsmith;^T   Is. 44:13 · Is. 40:19 · *refined*
He who smooths *with* the hammer
inspired him who strikes the anvil,
Saying, "It *is* ready for the soldering";
Then he fastened it with pegs,
^RThat it might not totter.   Is. 40:20

8 "But you, Israel, *are* My servant,
Jacob whom I have ^Rchosen,
The descendants of Abraham My
^Rfriend.   Deut. 7:6; 10:15 · James 2:23

9 *You* whom I have taken from the ends
of the earth,
And called from its farthest regions,
And said to you,
'You *are* My servant,
I have chosen you and have not cast
you away:

10 ^RFear not, ^Rfor I *am* with you;
Be not dismayed, for I *am* your God.
I will strengthen you,
Yes, I will help you,
I will uphold you with My righteous
right hand.'   Is. 41:13, 14; 43:5 · [Deut. 31:6]

11 "Behold, all those who were incensed
against you
Shall be ^Rashamed and disgraced;
They shall be as nothing,
And those who strive with you shall
perish.   Zech. 12:3

12 You shall seek them and not find
them—
^TThose who contended with you.
Those who war against you
Shall be as nothing,   Lit. *Men of your strife*
As a nonexistent thing.

13 For I, the LORD your God, will hold
your right hand,
Saying to you, 'Fear not, I will help
you.'

14 "Fear not, you ^Rworm Jacob,
You men of Israel!
I will help you," says the LORD
And your Redeemer, the Holy One of
Israel.   Job 25:6

15 "Behold, ^RI will make you into a new
threshing sledge with sharp teeth;
You shall thresh the mountains and
beat *them* small,
And make the hills like chaff.   Mic. 4:13

16 You shall ^Rwinnow them, the wind shall
carry them away,   Jer. 51:2
And the whirlwind shall scatter them;

You shall ᴿrejoice in the LORD,   Is. 25:9
And glory in the Holy One of Israel.

17 "The poor and needy seek water, but
    there is none,
Their tongues fail for thirst.
I, the LORD, will hear them;
I, the God of Israel, will not ᴿforsake
    them.   Rom. 11:2
18 I will open ᴿrivers in desolate heights,
And fountains in the midst of the
    valleys;
I will make the ᴿwilderness a pool of
    water,   Is. 35:6, 7; 43:19; 44:3 • Ps. 107:35
And the dry land springs of water.
19 I will plant in the wilderness the cedar
    and the acacia tree,
The myrtle and the oil tree;
I will set in the ᴿdesert the cypress tree
    and the pine
And the box tree together,   Is. 35:1
20 ᴿThat they may see and know,
And consider and understand together,
That the hand of the LORD has done
    this,
And the Holy One of Israel has created
    it.   Job 12:9

The Futility of Idols

21 "Present your case," says the LORD.
    "Bring forth your strong *reasons,*" says
    the ᴿKing of Jacob.   Is. 43:15
22 "Letᴿ them bring forth and show us
    what will happen;   Is. 45:21
Let them show the ᴿformer things,
    what they *were,*   Is. 43:9
That we may consider them,
And know the latter end of them;
Or declare to us things to come.
23 ᴿShow the things that are to come
    hereafter,
That we may know that you *are* gods;
Yes, ᴿdo good or do evil,
That we may be dismayed and see *it*
    together.   [John 13:19] • Jer. 10:5
24 Indeed ᴿyou *are* nothing,   [1 Cor. 8:4]
And your work *is* nothing;
He who chooses you *is* an abomination.

25 "I have raised up one from the north,
And he shall come;
From the ᵀrising of the sun ᴿhe shall
    call on My name;
And he shall come against princes as
    though mortar,
As the potter treads clay.   East • Ezra 1:2
26 ᴿWho has declared from the beginning,
    that we may know?
And former times, that we may say, 'He
    is righteous'?
Surely *there is* no one who shows,
Surely *there is* no one who declares,
Surely *there is* no one who hears your
    words.   Is. 43:9

27 ᴿThe first time ᴿI *said* to Zion,
    'Look, there they are!'
And I will give to Jerusalem one who
    brings good tidings.   Is. 41:4 • Is. 40:9
28 ᴿFor I looked, and *there was* no man;
I looked among them, but *there was* no
    counselor,
Who, when I asked of them, could
    answer a word.   Is. 63:5
29 ᴿIndeed they *are* all *worthless;
Their works *are* nothing;
Their molded images *are* wind and
    confusion.   Is. 41:24

The Servant of the LORD

42 "Behold! ᴿMy Servant whom I
    uphold,   Luke 3:22
My ᵀElect One *in whom* My soul
    ᴿdelights!   Chosen • Matt. 3:17; 17:5
ᴿI have put My Spirit upon Him;
He will bring forth justice to the
    Gentiles.   [Is. 11:2]
2 He will not cry out, nor raise *His* voice,
Nor cause His voice to be heard in the
    street.
3 A bruised reed He will not break,
And smoking flax He will not quench;
He will bring forth justice for truth.
4 He will not fail nor be discouraged,
Till He has established justice in the
    earth;
ᴿAnd the coastlands shall wait for His
    law."   [Gen. 49:10]

5 Thus says God the LORD,
ᴿWho created the heavens and stretched
    them out,   Zech. 12:1
Who spread forth the earth and that
    which comes from it,
Who gives breath to the people on it,
And spirit to those who walk on it:
6 "I,ᴿ the LORD, have called You in
    ᴿrighteousness,   Is. 43:1 • Jer. 23:5, 6
And will hold Your hand;
I will keep You ᴿand give You as a
    covenant to the people,   Is. 49:8
As ᴿa light to the Gentiles,   Luke 2:32
7 ᴿTo open blind eyes,
To ᴿbring out prisoners from the prison,
Those who sit in ᴿdarkness from the
    prison house.   Is. 35:5 • Luke 4:18 • Is. 9:2
8 I *am* the LORD, that *is* My name;
And My ᴿglory I will not give to
    another,
Nor My praise to carved images. Is. 48:11
9 Behold, the former things have come to
    pass,
And new things I declare;
Before they spring forth I tell you of
    them."

41:29 So with MT, Vg.; DSS, Syr., Tg. *nothing;* LXX omits
first line

Praise to the LORD

10 ᴿSing to the LORD a new song,
  And His praise from the ends of the
    earth,   Ps. 33:3; 40:3; 98:1
  ᴿYou who go down to the sea, and ᵀall
    that is in it,
  You coastlands and you inhabitants of
    them!   Ps. 107:23 · Lit. *its fullness*
11 Let the wilderness and its cities lift up
    their voice,
  The villages *that* Kedar inhabits.
  Let the inhabitants of Sela sing,
  Let them shout from the top of the
    mountains.
12 Let them give glory to the LORD,
  And declare His praise in the
    coastlands.
13 The LORD shall go forth like a mighty
    man;
  He shall stir up *His* zeal like a man of
    war.
  He shall cry out, yes, shout aloud;
  He shall prevail against His enemies.

Promise of the LORD's Help

14 "I have held My peace a long time,
  I have been still and restrained Myself.
  Now I will cry like a woman in ᵀlabor,
  I will pant and gasp at once.   *childbirth*
15 I will lay waste the mountains and hills,
  And dry up all their vegetation;
  I will make the rivers coastlands,
  And I will dry up the pools.
16 I will bring the blind by a way they did
    not know;
  I will lead them in paths they have not
    known.
  I will make darkness light before them,
  And crooked places straight.
  These things I will do for them,
  And not forsake them.
17 They shall be ᴿturned back,
  They shall be greatly ashamed,
  Who trust in carved images,
  Who say to the molded images,
  'You *are* our gods.'   Ps. 97:7

18 "Hear, you deaf;
  And look, you blind, that you may see.
19 ᴿWho *is* blind but My servant,   [John 9:39, 41]
  Or deaf as My messenger *whom* I send?
  Who *is* blind as *he who is* perfect,
  And blind as the LORD's servant?
20 Seeing many things, ᴿbut you do not
    observe;
  Opening the ears, but he does not
    hear."   Rom. 2:21

Israel's Obstinate Disobedience

21 The LORD is well pleased for His
    righteousness' sake;
  He will exalt the law and make *it*
    honorable.

22 But this *is* a people robbed and
    plundered;
  All of them are ᵀsnared in holes,
  And they are hidden in prison houses;
  They are for prey, and no one delivers;
  For plunder, and no one says,
    "Restore!"   Or *trapped in caves*
23 Who among you will give ear to this?
  Who will listen and hear for the time to
    come?
24 Who gave Jacob for plunder, and Israel
    to the robbers?
  Was it not the LORD,
  He against whom we have sinned?
  For they would not walk in His ways,
  Nor were they obedient to His law.
25 Therefore He has poured on him the
    fury of His anger
  And the strength of battle;
  ᴿIt has set him on fire all around,
  ᴿYet he did not know;   2 Kin. 25:9 · Hos. 7:9
  And it burned him,
  Yet he did not take *it* to ᴿheart.   Is. 29:13

The Redeemer of Israel

43 But now, thus says the LORD, who
      created you, O Jacob,
  And He who formed you, O Israel:
  "Fear not, ᴿfor I have redeemed you;
  ᴿI have called *you* by your name;
  You *are* Mine.   Is. 43:5; 44:6 · Is. 42:6; 45:4
2 ᴿWhen you pass through the waters, ᴿI
    will be with you;   [Ps. 66:12; 91:3] · [Deut. 31:6]
  And through the rivers, they shall not
    overflow you.
  When you ᴿwalk through the fire, you
    shall not be burned,   Dan. 3:25
  Nor shall the flame scorch you.
3 For I *am* the LORD your God,
  The Holy One of Israel, your Savior;
  ᴿI gave Egypt for your ransom,   [Prov. 21:18]
  Ethiopia and Seba in your place.
4 Since you were precious in My sight,
  You have been honored,
  And I have ᴿloved you;
  Therefore I will give men for you,
  And people for your life.   Is. 63:9
5 ᴿFear not, for I *am* with you;   Is. 41:10; 44:2
  I will bring your descendants from the
    east,
  And ᴿgather you from the west;   Is. 54:7
6 I will say to the ᴿnorth, 'Give them up!'
  And to the south, 'Do not keep them
    back!'
  Bring My sons from afar,
  And My daughters from the ends of the
    earth—   Is. 49:12
7 Everyone who is ᴿcalled by My name,
  Whom ᴿI have created for My glory;
  I have formed him, yes, I have made
    him."   James 2:7 · 2 Cor. 5:17

8 ᴿBring out the blind people who have
   eyes,   Ezek. 12:2
And the ᴿdeaf who have ears.   Is. 29:18
9 Let all the nations be gathered
   together,
And let the people be assembled.
   ᴿWho among them can declare this,
And show us former things?
Let them bring out their witnesses, that
   they may be justified;   Is. 41:21, 22, 26
Or let them hear and say, "*It is* truth."
10 "You *are* My witnesses," says the LORD,
   "And My servant whom I have chosen,
That you may know and ᴿbelieve Me,
And understand that I *am* He.
Before Me there was no God formed,
Nor shall there be after Me.   Is. 41:4; 44:6
11 I, *even* I, ᴿ*am* the LORD,   Hos. 13:4
And besides Me *there is* no savior.
12 I have declared and saved,
   I have proclaimed,
And *there was* no ᴿforeign *god* among
   you;   Deut. 32:16
ᴿTherefore you *are* My witnesses,"
Says the LORD, "that I *am* God.   Is. 44:8
13 ᴿIndeed before the day *was*, I *am* He;
And *there is* no one who can deliver
   out of My hand;   Ps. 90:2
I work, and who will ᴿreverse it?" Job 9:12

14 Thus says the LORD, your Redeemer,
   The Holy One of Israel:
"For your sake I will send to Babylon,
And bring them all down as fugitives—
The Chaldeans, who rejoice in their
   ships.
15 I *am* the LORD, your Holy One,
The Creator of Israel, your King."

16 Thus says the LORD, who ᴿmakes a way
   in the sea   Ex. 14:16, 21, 22
And a path through the mighty waters,
17 Who ᴿbrings forth the chariot and
   horse,
The army and the power
(They shall lie down together, they
   shall not rise;
They are extinguished, they are
   quenched like a wick):   Ex. 14:4–9, 25
18 "Doᴿ not remember the former things,
Nor consider the things of old.   Jer. 16:14
19 Behold, I will do a ᴿnew thing,
Now it shall spring forth;
Shall you not know it?
ᴿI will even make a road in the
   wilderness   [2 Cor. 5:17] · Ex. 17:6
And rivers in the desert.
20 The beast of the field will honor Me,
The jackals and the ostriches,
Because ᴿI give waters in the
   wilderness
And rivers in the desert.   Is. 48:21
To give drink to My people, My chosen.

21 This people I have formed for Myself;
They shall declare My ᴿpraise.   Jer. 13:11

Pleading with Unfaithful Israel

22 "But you have not called upon Me, O
   Jacob;
And you ᴿhave been weary of Me, O
   Israel.   Mal. 1:13; 3:14
23 ᴿYou have not brought Me the sheep for
   your burnt offerings,
Nor have you honored Me with your
   sacrifices.
I have not caused you to serve with
   grain offerings,
Nor wearied you with incense.   Amos 5:25
24 You have bought Me no sweet cane
   with money,
Nor have you satisfied Me with the fat
   of your sacrifices;
But you have burdened Me with your
   sins,
You have ᴿwearied Me with your
   iniquities.   Is. 1:14; 7:13

25 "I, *even* I, *am* He who blots out your
   transgressions for My own sake;
And I will not remember your sins.
26 Put Me in remembrance;
Let us contend together;
State your *case*, that you may be
   ᵀacquitted.   *justified*
27 Your first father sinned,
And your ᵀmediators have transgressed
   against Me.   *interpreters*
28 Therefore I will profane the princes of
   the sanctuary;
ᴿI will give Jacob to the curse,
And Israel to reproaches.   Dan. 9:11

God's Blessing on Israel

44 "Yet hear now, O Jacob My servant,
   And Israel whom I have chosen.
2 Thus says the LORD who made you
And formed you from the womb, *who*
   will help you:
'Fear not, O Jacob My servant;
And you, Jeshurun, whom I have
   chosen.
3 For I will pour water on him who is
   thirsty,
And floods on the dry ground;
I will pour My Spirit on your
   descendants,
And My blessing on your offspring;
4 They will spring up among the grass
Like willows by the watercourses.'
5 One will say, 'I *am* the LORD's';
Another will call *himself* by the name
   of Jacob;
Another will write *with* his hand, 'The
   LORD's,'
And name *himself* by the name of
   Israel.

There Is No Other God

6 "Thus says the LORD, the King of Israel,
And his Redeemer, the LORD of hosts:
^R'I *am* the First and I *am* the Last;
Besides Me *there is* no God.   Is. 41:4
7 And ^Rwho can proclaim as I do?
Then let him declare it and set it in
   order for Me,
Since I appointed the ancient people.
And the things that are coming and
   shall come,   Is. 41:4, 22, 26
Let them show these to them.
8 Do not fear, nor be afraid;
^RHave I not told you from that time, and
   declared *it?*   Is. 41:22
^RYou *are* My witnesses.   Is. 43:10, 12
Is there a God besides Me?
Indeed ^R*there is* no other Rock;   1 Sam. 2:2
I know not one.' "

Idolatry Is Foolishness

9 ^RThose who make an image, all of them
   are useless,
And their precious things shall not
   profit;
They *are* their own witnesses;
^RThey neither see nor know, that they
   may be ashamed.   Is. 41:24 • Ps. 115:4
10 Who would form a god or mold an
   image
^R*That* profits him nothing?   Hab. 2:18
11 Surely all his companions would be
   ^Rashamed;
And the workmen, they *are* mere men.
Let them all be gathered together,
Let them stand up;
Yet they shall fear,
They shall be ashamed together.   Ps. 97:7

12 ^RThe blacksmith with the tongs works
   one in the coals,   Jer. 10:3–5
Fashions it with hammers,
And works it with the strength of his
   arms.
Even so, he is hungry, and his strength
   fails;
He drinks no water and is faint.

13 The craftsman stretches out *his* rule,
He marks one out with chalk;
He fashions it with a plane,
He marks it out with the compass,
And makes it like the figure of a man,
According to the beauty of a man, that
   it may remain in the house.
14 He cuts down cedars for himself,
And takes the cypress and the oak;
He ^Tsecures *it* for himself among the
   trees of the forest.
He plants a pine, and the rain nourishes
   it.   Lit. *appropriates*

15 Then it shall be for a man to burn,
For he will take some of it and warm
   himself;
Yes, he kindles *it* and bakes bread;
Indeed he makes a god and worships *it;*
He makes it a carved image, and falls
   down to it.
16 He burns half of it in the fire;
With this half he eats meat; ,
He roasts a roast, and is satisfied.
He even warms *himself* and says,
"Ah! I am warm,
I have seen the fire."
17 And the rest of it he makes into a god,
His carved image.
He falls down before it and worships *it,*
Prays to it and says,
"Deliver me, for you *are* my god!"
18 ^RThey do not know nor understand;
For He has shut their eyes, so that they
   cannot see,   Is. 45:20
And their hearts, so that they cannot
   ^Runderstand.   Jer. 10:14
19 And no one ^Rconsiders in his heart,
Nor *is there* knowledge nor
   understanding to say,
"I have burned half of it in the fire,
Yes, I have also baked bread on its
   coals;
I have roasted meat and eaten *it;*
And shall I make the rest of it an
   abomination?
Shall I fall down before a block of
   wood?"   Is. 46:8
20 He feeds on ashes;
^RA deceived heart has turned him aside;
And he cannot deliver his soul,
Nor say, "*Is there* not a ^Rlie in my right
   hand?"   2 Thess. 2:11 • Rom. 1:25

Israel Is Not Forgotten

21 "Remember these, O Jacob,
And Israel, for you *are* My servant;
I have formed you, you *are* My servant;
O Israel, you will not be ^Rforgotten by
   Me!   Is. 49:15
22 ^RI have blotted out, like a thick cloud,
   your transgressions,
And like a cloud, your sins.
Return to Me, for ^RI have redeemed
   you."   Is. 43:25 • 1 Cor. 6:20
23 ^RSing, O heavens, for the LORD has done
   it!   Ps. 69:34
Shout, you lower parts of the earth;
Break forth into singing, you
   mountains,
O forest, and every tree in it!
For the LORD has redeemed Jacob,
And ^Rglorified Himself in Israel.   Is. 60:21

Judah Will Be Restored

24 Thus says the LORD, ^Ryour Redeemer,
And ^RHe who formed you from the
womb:
"I *am* the LORD, who makes all *things*,
^RWho stretches out the heavens ^Tall
alone,
Who spreads abroad the earth by
Myself;   Is. 43:14 · Is. 43:1 · Job 9:8 · By Himself
25 Who ^Rfrustrates the signs ^Rof the
babblers;   Is. 47:13 · Jer. 50:36
And drives diviners mad;
Who turns wise men backward,
And makes their knowledge foolishness;
26 ^RWho confirms the word of His servant,
And performs the counsel of His
messengers;   Zech. 1:6
Who says to Jerusalem, 'You shall be
inhabited,'
To the cities of Judah, 'You shall be
built,'
And I will raise up her waste places;
27 ^RWho says to the deep, 'Be dry!
And I will dry up your rivers';   Jer. 50:38
28 Who says of ^RCyrus, '*He is* My
shepherd,
And he shall perform all My pleasure,
Saying to Jerusalem, ^R"You shall be
built,"
And to the temple, "Your foundation
shall be laid." '   Ezra 1:1 · Ezra 6:7

Cyrus, God's Instrument

45 "Thus says the LORD to His anointed,
To ^RCyrus, whose right hand I have
^Theld—   Is. 44:28 · *strengthened* or *sustained*
^RTo subdue nations before him   Dan. 5:30
And ^Rloose the armor of kings,   Job 12:21
To open before him the double doors,
So that the gates will not be shut:
2 'I will go before you
^RAnd* make the *crooked places
straight;
^RI will break in pieces the gates of
bronze   Is. 40:4 · Ps. 107:16
And cut the bars of iron.
3 I will give you the treasures of
darkness
And hidden riches of secret places,
^RThat you may know that I, the LORD,
Who ^Rcall *you* by your name,
Am the God of Israel.   Is. 41:23 · Ex. 33:12
4 For ^RJacob My servant's sake,
And Israel My elect,
I have even called you by your name;
I have named you, though you have
not known Me.   Is. 44:1
5 I *am* the LORD, and ^R*there is* no other;
There is no God besides Me.   Is. 45:14, 18

45:2 Tg. *I will trample down the walls;* Vg. *I will humble
the great ones of the earth* • DSS, LXX *mountains*

^RI will gird you, though you have not
known Me,   Ps. 18:32
6 That they may ^Rknow from the rising of
the sun to its setting   [Is. 11:9; 52:10]
That *there is* none besides Me.
I *am* the LORD, and *there is* no other;
7 I form the light and create darkness,
I make peace and ^Rcreate calamity;
I, the LORD, do all these *things*.'   Amos 3:6

8 "Rain^R down, you heavens, from above,
And let the skies pour down
righteousness;   Ps. 85:11
Let the earth open, let them bring forth
salvation,
And let righteousness spring up
together.
I, the LORD, have created it.

9 "Woe to him who strives with ^Rhis
Maker!
Let the potsherd *strive* with the
potsherds of the earth!
^RShall the clay say to him who forms it,
'What are you making?'
Or shall your handiwork *say*, 'He has
no hands'?   Is. 64:8 · Jer. 18:6
10 Woe to him who says to *his* father,
'What are you begetting?'
Or to the woman, 'What have you
brought forth?' "

11 Thus says the LORD,
The Holy One of Israel and his Maker:
^R"Ask Me of things to come concerning
^RMy sons;   Is. 8:19 · Jer. 31:9
And concerning ^Rthe work of My
hands, you command Me.   Is. 29:23; 60:21
12 ^RI have made the earth,   Is. 42:5
And ^Rcreated man on it.   Gen. 1:26
I—My hands—stretched out the
heavens,
And all their host I have commanded.
13 ^RI have raised him up in righteousness,
And I will direct all his ways;   Is. 41:2
He shall ^Rbuild My city   2 Chr. 36:22
And let My exiles go free,
^RNot for price nor reward,"   [Rom. 3:24]
Says the LORD of hosts.

The LORD, the Only Savior

14 Thus says the LORD:

^R"The labor of Egypt and merchandise of
Cush   Zech. 8:22, 23
And of the Sabeans, men of stature,
Shall come over to you, and they shall
be yours;
They shall walk behind you,
They shall come over in chains;
And they shall bow down to you.
They will make supplication to you,
saying, ^R'Surely God *is* in you,
And *there is* no other;   1 Cor. 14:25
^R*There is* no other God.' "   Is. 45:5

15 Truly You *are* God, ᴿwho hide Yourself,
　O God of Israel, the Savior!　　Ps. 44:24
16 They shall be ᴿashamed
　And also disgraced, all of them;
　They shall go in confusion together,
　Who are makers of idols.　　Is. 44:11
17 ᴿ*But* Israel shall be saved by the Lᴏʀᴅ
　With an ᴿeverlasting salvation;
　You shall not be ashamed or ᴿdisgraced
　Forever and ever.　　Is. 26:4 • Is. 51:6 • Is. 29:22

18 For thus says the Lᴏʀᴅ,
　ᴿWho created the heavens,
　Who is God,　　Is. 42:5
　Who formed the earth and made it,
　Who has established it,
　Who did not create it ᵀin vain,　　Or *a waste*
　Who formed it to be ᴿinhabited:　　Ps. 115:16
　I *am* the Lᴏʀᴅ, and *there is* no other.
19 I have not spoken in ᴿsecret,　　Deut. 30:11
　In a dark place of the earth;
　I did not say to the seed of Jacob,
　'Seek Me ᵀin vain';　　Or *in a waste place*
　ᴿI, the Lᴏʀᴅ, speak righteousness,
　I declare things that are right.　　Ps. 19:8

20 "Assemble yourselves and come;
　Draw near together,
　You *who have* escaped from the
　　nations.
　ᴿThey have no knowledge,
　Who carry the wood of their carved
　　image,　　Is. 44:9; 46:7
　And pray to a god *that* cannot save.
21 Tell and bring forth *your case*;
　Yes, let them take counsel together.
　ᴿWho has declared this from ancient
　　time?　　Is. 41:22; 43:9
　Who has told it from that time?
　Have not I, the Lᴏʀᴅ?
　ᴿAnd *there is* no other God besides Me,
　A just God and a Savior;　　Is. 44:8
　There is none besides Me.

22 "Look to Me, and be saved,
　ᴿAll you ends of the earth!　　Ps. 22:27; 65:5
　For I *am* God, and *there is* no other.
23 ᴿI have sworn by Myself;　　[Heb. 6:13]
　The word has gone out of My mouth *in*
　　righteousness,
　And shall not return,
　That to Me every knee shall bow,
　Every tongue shall take an oath.
24 He shall say,
　'Surely in the Lᴏʀᴅ I have
　　ᴿrighteousness and strength.
　To Him *men* shall come,　　[1 Cor. 1:30]
　And ᴿall shall be ashamed　　Is. 41:11
　Who are incensed against Him.

25 ᴿIn the Lᴏʀᴅ all the descendants of
　　Israel　　Is. 45:17
　Shall be justified, and shall glory.' "

Dead Idols and the Living God

46 Bel ᴿbows down, Nebo stoops;
　Their idols were on the beasts and on
　　the cattle.　　Jer. 50:2
　Your carriages *were* heavily loaded,
　ᴿA burden to the weary *beast*.　　Jer. 10:5
2 They stoop, they bow down together;
　They could not deliver the burden,
　ᴿBut have themselves gone into
　　captivity.　　Jer. 48:7

3 "Listen to Me, O house of Jacob,
　And all the remnant of the house of
　　Israel,
　ᴿWho have been upheld *by Me* from
　　ᵀbirth,　　Ps. 71:6 • Lit. *the belly*
　Who have been carried from the womb:
4 Even to *your* old age, ᴿI *am* He,
　And *even* to gray hairs ᴿI will carry
　　you!　　Mal. 3:6 • Ps. 48:14
　I have made, and I will bear;
　Even I will carry, and will deliver *you*.

5 "Toᴿ whom will you liken Me, and make
　　Me equal　　Is. 40:18, 25
　And compare Me, that we should be
　　alike?
6 ᴿThey lavish gold out of the bag,
　And weigh silver on the scales;
　They hire a ᴿgoldsmith, and he makes it
　　a god;
　They prostrate themselves, yes, they
　　worship.　　Is. 40:19; 41:6 • Is. 44:12
7 ᴿThey bear it on the shoulder, they carry
　　it　　Jer. 10:5
　And set it in its place, and it stands;
　From its place it shall not move.
　Though ᴿone cries out to it, yet it
　　cannot answer　　Is. 45:20
　Nor save him out of his trouble.

8 "Remember this, and ᵀshow yourselves
　　men;　　*be men,* take courage
　Recall to mind, O you transgressors.

29-A. God's Will Is Sovereign　　▼

9 Remember the former things of old,
　For I *am* God, and *there is* no other;
　I am God, and *there is* none like Me,
10 ᴿDeclaring the end from the beginning,
　And from ancient times *things that are*
　　not *yet* done,　　Is. 45:21; 48:3
　Saying, ᴿ'My counsel shall stand,
　And I will do all My pleasure,'　　Ps. 33:11
11 Calling a bird of prey ᴿfrom the east,
　The man ᴿwho executes My counsel,
　from a far country.　　Is. 41:2, 25 • Is. 44:28

29-A. God's Will Is Sovereign (Isaiah 46:9-11)—"I am God, and there is none like Me, declaring the end from the beginning . . . My counsel shall stand, and I will do all My pleasure" (vv. 9, 10). These verses declare the fact that God's sovereign will is in control of all things in heaven and on earth and throughout His universe. No one can alter His purposes. He said, "I will do all My pleasure" (v. 10).

(Point 29-A continued on next page)

▽ Indeed ᴿI have spoken *it*;   Num. 23:19
I will also bring it to pass.
I have purposed *it*;
▲ I will also do it.

12 "Listen to Me, you ᴿstubborn-hearted,
   Who *are* far from righteousness: Ps. 76:5
13 ᴿI bring My righteousness near, it shall
   not be far off;   [Rom. 1:17]
   My salvation shall not ᵀlinger.   *delay*
   And I will place ᴿsalvation in Zion,
   For Israel My glory.   Is. 62:11

The Humiliation of Babylon

47 "Come ᴿdown and ᴿsit in the dust,
      O virgin daughter of Babylon;
   Sit on the ground without a throne,
   O daughter of the Chaldeans!   Jer. 48:18
   For you shall no more be called
   Tender and ᵀdelicate.   Is. 3:26 · *dainty*
2 ᴿTake the millstones and grind meal.
   Remove your veil,
   Take off the skirt,
   Uncover the thigh,
   Pass through the rivers.   Ex. 11:5
3 ᴿYour nakedness shall be uncovered,
   Yes, your shame will be seen;   Is. 3:17; 20:4
   ᴿI will take vengeance,   [Rom. 12:19]
   And I will not arbitrate with a man."

4 As for ᴿour Redeemer, the LORD of
   hosts *is* His name,   Jer. 50:34
   The Holy One of Israel.

5 "Sit in ᴿsilence, and go into darkness,
   O daughter of the Chaldeans;   1 Sam. 2:9
   ᴿFor you shall no longer be called
   The Lady of Kingdoms.   [Dan. 2:37]
6 ᴿI was angry with My people;   2 Sam. 24:14
   ᴿI have profaned My inheritance,

And given them into your hand.
You showed them no mercy;
ᴿOn the elderly you laid your yoke very
   heavily.   Is. 43:28 · Deut. 28:49, 50
7 And you said, 'I shall be ᴿa lady
   forever,'   Rev. 18:7
   So that you did not ᴿtake these *things*
   to heart,   Is. 42:25; 46:8
   Nor remember the latter end of them.

8 "Therefore hear this now, *you who are*
   given to pleasures,
   Who dwell securely,
   Who say in your heart,
   'I *am*, and *there is* no one else besides
      me;
   I shall not sit *as* a widow,
   Nor shall I know the loss of children';
9 But these two *things* shall come to you
   ᴿIn a moment, in one day:
   The loss of children, and widowhood.
   They shall come upon you in their
      fullness
   Because of the multitude of your
      sorceries,
   For the great abundance of your
      enchantments.   1 Thess. 5:3

10 "For you have trusted in your
      wickedness;
   You have said, 'No one ᴿsees me';
   Your wisdom and your knowledge have
   ᵀwarped you;
   And you have said in your heart,
   'I *am*, and *there is* no one else besides
      me.'   Is. 29:15 · *led you astray*
11 Therefore evil shall come upon you;
   You shall not know from where it
      arises.
   And trouble shall fall upon you;

(Point 29-A continued from previous page)
   His sovereign will is established in the fulfilling of prophecy. He has declared the end, even from the beginning. He continued, "Indeed I have spoken it; I will also bring it to pass. I have purposed it; I will also do it" (v. 11). In context, God is saying that He has prophesied Israel's future, and will bring the prophecy to pass. What He has proposed, He will do. God's sovereign will determines the end of everything; His purpose cannot be circumvented (Dan. 4:35, page 840).
   The part of God's sovereign will that is not revealed is often called His secret will. Though we cannot know all of God's sovereign will, by faith we can know that part revealed through the Scriptures (Deut. 29:29, page 208). Most of God's sovereign will is secret, and we cannot know His secret will until He is ready to reveal it (Acts 1:6, 7, page 1086; Amos 9:11-15, page 880).
   We can, however, know God's sovereign purpose in history for the Jew and the Gentile, for He has made it known to us in His Word. He said to Abraham, "I will make you a great nation. . . . and in you all the families [nations] of the earth shall be blessed" (Gen. 12:2, 3, page 17). His sovereign will for Israel is well established in the Old and New Testaments, beginning with His promise to make Abraham's seed (Israel) a great nation, and to bless all the nations of the earth through his seed, which is Christ (Gal. 3:6-9, page 1181). Ultimately, true Israel will be saved and enter the kingdom where Christ is King of kings (Rom. 11:26-29, page 1141; Matt. 25:31-46, page 976). We also know God's sovereign will for all who, by faith, will accept the Lord Jesus Christ as personal Savior (John 3:16, 17, page 1052). They are predestined for eternal life with God (John 14:1-6, page 1074); but those who reject Christ as personal Savior are predestined to the lake of fire (Rev. 20:15, page 1314).
   Calvary is a proof of God's sovereign will. About a thousand years before Christ died on the cross, David prophesied that the Messiah would be crucified (Ps. 22:14-18, page 522). About seven hundred years before Calvary, Isaiah prophesied the ignominious death of Jesus Christ, who suffered for our sins (Is. 52:13—53:12, page 693). God's will is sovereign.
   See Malachi 3:6, page 924, for **Point 29-B: God's Will Is Immutable.**

You will not be able ᵀto put it off.
And desolation shall come upon you
   suddenly,   Lit. *to cover it* or *atone for it*
Which you shall not know.

12 "Stand now with your enchantments
   And the multitude of your sorceries,
   In which you have labored from your
      youth—
   Perhaps you will be able to profit,
   Perhaps you will prevail.
13 ᴿYou are wearied in the multitude of
      your counsels;   Is. 57:10
   Let now ᴿthe astrologers, the
      stargazers,   Dan. 2:2, 10
   And the monthly prognosticators
   Stand up and save you
   From what shall come upon you.
14 Behold, they shall be ᴿas stubble,
   The fire shall ᴿburn them;
   They shall ᴿnot deliver themselves
   From the power of the flame;
   It shall not *be* a coal to be warmed by,
   Nor a fire to sit before!   Nah. 1:10 · Jer. 51:58
15 Thus shall they be to you
   With whom you have labored,
   ᴿYour merchants from your youth;
   They shall wander each one to his
      ᵀquarter.   Rev. 18:11 · *own side* or *way*
   No one shall save you.

Israel Refined for God's Glory

48 "Hear this, O house of Jacob,
   Who are called by the name of Israel,
   And have come forth from the
      wellsprings of Judah;
   Who swear by the name of the LORD,
   And make mention of the God of Israel,
   But not in truth or in righteousness;
2 For they call themselves ᴿafter the holy
      city,   Is. 52:1; 64:10
   And ᴿlean on the God of Israel;   Mic. 3:11
   The LORD of hosts *is* His name:

3 "I have ᴿdeclared the former things from
      the beginning;   Is. 44:7, 8; 46:10
   They went forth from My mouth, and I
      caused them to hear it.
   Suddenly I did *them,* ᴿand they came to
      pass.   Josh. 21:45
4 Because I knew that you *were*
      ᵀobstinate,   Heb. *hard*
   And ᴿyour neck *was* an iron sinew,
   And your brow bronze,   Deut. 31:27
5 Even from the beginning I have
      declared *it* to you;
   Before it came to pass I proclaimed *it*
      to you,
   Lest you should say, 'My idol has done
      them,
   And my carved image and my molded
      image
   Have commanded them.'

6 "You have heard;
   See all this.
   And will you not declare *it?*
   I have made you to hear new things from
      this time,
   Even hidden things, and you did not
      know them.
7 They are created now and not from the
      beginning;
   And before this day you have not heard
      them,
   Lest you should say, 'Of course I knew
      them.'
8 Surely you did not hear,
   Surely you did not know;
   Surely from long ago your ear was not
      opened.
   For I knew that you would deal very
      treacherously,
   And were called ᴿa transgressor from
      the womb.   Ps. 58:3
9 "Forᴿ My name's sake ᴿI will ᵀdefer My
      anger,   Ezek. 20:9, 14, 22, 44 · Ps. 78:38 · *delay*
   And *for* My praise I will restrain it from
      you,
   So that I do not cut you off.
10 Behold, ᴿI have refined you, but not as
      silver;
   I have tested you in the ᴿfurnace of
      affliction.   Ps. 66:10 · Deut. 4:20
11 For My own sake, for My own sake, I
      will do *it;*
   For ᴿhow should *My name* be profaned?
   And ᴿI will not give My glory to
      another.   Ezek. 20:9 · Is. 42:8

God's Ancient Plan to Redeem Israel

12 "Listen to Me, O Jacob,
   And Israel, My called:
   I *am* He, ᴿI *am* the ᴿFirst,
   I *am* also the Last.   Deut. 32:39 · [Rev. 22:13]
13 Indeed ᴿMy hand has laid the
      foundation of the earth,
   And My right hand has stretched out
      the heavens;
   When ᴿI call to them,   Ps. 102:25 · Is. 40:26
   They stand up together.

14 "All of you, assemble yourselves, and
      hear!
   Who among them has declared these
      things?
   ᴿThe LORD loves him;
   ᴿHe shall do His pleasure on Babylon,
   And His arm *shall be against* the
      Chaldeans.   Is. 45:1 · Is. 44:28; 47:1-15
15 I, *even* I, have spoken;
   Yes, ᴿI have called him,
   I have brought him, and his way will
      prosper.   Is. 45:1, 2
16 "Come near to Me, hear this:
   ᴿI have not spoken in secret from the
      beginning;   Is. 45:19

From the time that it was, I *was* there.
And now the Lord God and His Spirit
ᵀHave sent Me."   Heb. verb is singular

17 Thus says ᴿthe LORD, your Redeemer,
The Holy One of Israel:
"I *am* the LORD your God,
Who teaches you to profit,
ᴿWho leads you by the way you should
go.   Is. 43:14 · Ps. 32:8
18 ᴿOh, that you had heeded My
commandments!
ᴿThen your peace would have been like
a river,
And your righteousness like the waves
of the sea.   Ps. 81:13 · Ps. 119:165
19 ᴿYour descendants also would have been
like the sand,   Gen. 22:17
And the offspring of your body like the
grains of sand;
His name would not have been cut off
Nor destroyed from before Me."

20 ᴿGo forth from Babylon!
Flee from the Chaldeans!
With a voice of singing,
Declare, proclaim this,
Utter it to the end of the earth;
Say, "The LORD has ᴿredeemed
His servant Jacob!"   Zech. 2:6, 7 · [Ex. 19:4–6]
21 And they ᴿdid not thirst
When He led them through the deserts;
He ᴿcaused the waters to flow from the
rock for them;
He also split the rock, and the waters
gushed out.   [Is. 41:17, 18] · Ex. 17:6

22 "ThereᴿR is no peace," says the LORD, "for
the wicked."   [Is. 57:21]

The Servant, the Light to the Gentiles

49 "Listen, ᴿO coastlands, to Me,
And take heed, you peoples from
afar!   Is. 41:1
ᴿThe LORD has called Me from the
womb;   Jer. 1:5
From the ᵀmatrix of My mother He has
made mention of My name.   *inward parts*
2 And He has made ᴿMy mouth like a
sharp sword;   Rev. 1:16; 2:12
ᴿIn the shadow of His hand He has
hidden Me,   Is. 51:16
And made Me ᴿa polished shaft;   Ps. 45:5
In His quiver He has hidden Me."

3 "And He said to me,
ᴿ'You *are* My servant, O Israel,   [Zech. 3:8]
ᴿIn whom I will be glorified.'   Is. 44:23
4 ᴿThen I said, 'I have labored in vain,
I have spent my strength for nothing
and in vain;   [Ezek. 3:19]
Yet surely my ᵀjust reward *is* with the
LORD,   *justice*
And my work with my God.' "

5 "And now the LORD says,
Who formed Me from the womb *to be*
His Servant,
To bring Jacob back to Him,
So that Israel ᴿis *gathered to Him
(For I shall be glorious in the eyes of
the LORD,   Matt. 23:37
And My God shall be My strength),
6 Indeed He says,
'It is too small a thing that You should
be My Servant
To raise up the tribes of Jacob,
And to restore the preserved ones of
Israel;
I will also give You as a ᴿlight to the
Gentiles,   [Luke 2:32]
That You should be My salvation to the
ends of the earth.' "

7 Thus says the LORD,
The Redeemer of Israel, ᵀtheir Holy
One,   Lit. *his* or *its*
ᴿTo Him whom man despises,
To Him whom the nation abhors,
To the Servant of rulers: [Ps. 22:6–8]
ᴿ"Kings shall see and arise,   [Is. 52:15]
Princes also shall worship,
Because of the LORD who is faithful,
The Holy One of Israel;
And He has chosen You."

8 Thus says the LORD:

"In an ᴿacceptableᵀ time I have heard
You,   2 Cor. 6:2 · *favorable*
And in the day of salvation I have helped
You;
I will ᵀpreserve You ᴿand give You
As a covenant to the people,
To restore the earth,   *keep* · Is. 42:6
To cause them to inherit the desolate
ᵀheritages;   *inheritances*
9 That You may say ᴿto the prisoners,
'Go forth,'   Is. 61:1; Luke 4:18
To those who *are* in darkness, 'Show
yourselves.'

"They shall feed along the roads,
And their pastures *shall be* on all
desolate heights.
10 They shall neither ᴿhunger nor thirst,
ᴿNeither heat nor sun shall strike them;
For He who has mercy on them ᴿwill
lead them,
Even by the springs of water He will
guide them.   Rev. 7:16 · Ps. 121:6 · Ps. 23:2
11 ᴿI will make each of My mountains a
road,   Is. 40:4
And My highways shall be elevated.
12 Surely ᴿthese shall come from afar;
Look! Those from the north and the
west,   Is. 43:5, 6
And these from the land of Sinim."

49:5 Qr., DSS, LXX *gathered to Him;* Kt. *not gathered*

13 ᴿSing, O heavens!　　Is. 44:23
　　Be joyful, O earth!
　　And break out in singing, O mountains!
　　For the Lᴏʀᴅ has comforted His people,
　　And will have mercy on His afflicted.

God Will Remember Zion

14 ᴿBut Zion said, "The Lᴏʀᴅ has forsaken
　　me,
　　And my Lord has forgotten me."　　Is. 40:27

15 "Can a woman forget her nursing child,
　　ᵀAnd not have compassion on the son of
　　her womb?　　Lit. From having compassion
　　Surely they may forget,
　　ᴿYet I will not forget you.　　Rom. 11:29
16 See, ᴿI have inscribed you on the palms
　　of My hands;　　Song 8:6
　　Your walls are continually before Me.
17 Your *sons shall make haste;
　　Your destroyers and those who laid you
　　waste
　　Shall go away from you.
18 ᴿLift up your eyes, look around and see;
　　All these gather together and come to
　　you.　　Is. 60:4
　　As I live," says the Lᴏʀᴅ,
　　"You shall surely clothe yourselves with
　　them all ᴿas an ornament,　　Prov. 17:6
　　And bind them on you as a bride does.

19 "For your waste and desolate places,
　　And the land of your destruction,
　　ᴿWill even now be too small for the
　　inhabitants;
　　And those who swallowed you up will
　　be far away.　　Zech. 10:10
20 ᴿThe children you will have,　　Is. 60:4
　　ᴿAfter you have lost the others,
　　Will say again in your ears,　　[Rom. 11:11]
　　'The place is too small for me;
　　Give me a place where I may dwell.'
21 Then you will say in your heart,
　　'Who has begotten these for me,
　　Since I have lost my children and am
　　desolate,
　　A captive, and wandering to and fro?
　　And who has brought these up?
　　There I was, left alone;
　　But these, where were they?' "

22 ᴿThus says the Lord Gᴏᴅ:　　Is. 60:4

　　"Behold, I will lift My hand in an oath to
　　the nations,
　　And set up My ᵀstandard for the
　　peoples;　　banner
　　They shall bring your sons in their
　　ᵀarms,
　　And your daughters shall be carried on
　　their shoulders;　　Lit. bosom
23 ᴿKings shall be your foster fathers,
　　And their queens your nursing mothers;

They shall bow down to you with their
　　faces to the earth,
　　And ᴿlick up the dust of your feet.
　　Then you will know that I am the
　　Lᴏʀᴅ,
　　ᴿFor they shall not be ashamed who
　　wait for Me."　　Is. 52:15 • Ps. 72:9 • [Rom. 5:5]

24 ᴿShall the prey be taken from the
　　mighty,
　　Or the captives *of the righteous be
　　delivered?　　Luke 11:21, 22

25 But thus says the Lᴏʀᴅ:

　　"Even the captives of the mighty shall
　　be taken away,
　　And the prey of the terrible be
　　delivered;
　　For I will contend with him who
　　contends with you,
　　And I will save your children.
26 I will ᴿfeed those who oppress you with
　　their own flesh,
　　And they shall be drunk with their own
　　ᴿblood as with sweet wine.
　　All flesh ᴿshall know
　　That I, the Lᴏʀᴅ, am your Savior,
　　And your Redeemer, the Mighty One of
　　Jacob."　　Is. 9:20 • Rev. 14:20 • Ps. 9:16

The Servant, Israel's Hope

50 Thus says the Lᴏʀᴅ:

　　"Where is ᴿthe certificate of your
　　mother's divorce,　　Deut. 24:1
　　Whom I have put away?
　　Or which of My ᴿcreditors is it to whom
　　I have sold you?　　Deut. 32:30
　　For your iniquities ᴿyou have sold
　　yourselves,　　Is. 52:3
　　And for your transgressions your
　　mother has been put away.
2 Why, when I came, was there no man?
　　Why, when I called, was there none to
　　answer?
　　Is My hand shortened at all that it
　　cannot redeem?
　　Or have I no power to deliver?
　　Indeed with My ᴿrebuke I dry up the
　　sea,
　　I make the rivers a wilderness;
　　Their fish stink because there is no
　　water,
　　And die of thirst.　　Nah. 1:4
3 I clothe the heavens with blackness,
　　And I make sackcloth their covering."

4 "The ᴿ Lord Gᴏᴅ has given Me　　Ex. 4:11
　　The tongue of the learned,
　　That I should know how to speak
　　A word in season to him who is ᴿweary.

49:17 DSS, LXX, Tg., Vg. builders
49:24 So with MT, Tg.; DSS, Syr., Vg. of the mighty; LXX
unjustly

He awakens Me morning by morning,
He awakens My ear   Matt. 11:28
To hear as the learned.
5 The Lord GOD has opened My ear;
And I was not ᴿrebellious,
Nor did I turn away.   Matt. 26:39; John 14:31
6 ᴿI gave My back to those who struck
Me,   Matt. 27:26
And ᴿMy cheeks to those who plucked
out the beard;   Matt. 26:67; 27:30
I did not hide My face from shame and
ᴿspitting.   Lam. 3:30

7 "For the Lord GOD will help Me;
Therefore I will not be disgraced;
Therefore ᴿI have set My face like a
flint,   Luke 9:51
And I know that I will not be ashamed.
8 ᴿHe is near who justifies Me; [Rom. 8:32–34]
Who will contend with Me?
Let us stand together.
Who is My adversary?
Let him come near Me.
9 Surely the Lord GOD ᴿwill help Me;
Who is he who will condemn Me?
ᴿIndeed they will all grow old like a
garment;   Acts 2:24 • Job 13:28
ᴿThe moth will eat them up.   Is. 51:6, 8

10 "Who among you fears the LORD?
Who obeys the voice of His Servant?
Who ᴿwalks in darkness   Ps. 23:4
And has no light?
ᴿLet him trust in the name of the LORD
And rely upon his God.   2 Chr. 20:20
11 Look, all you who kindle a fire,
Who encircle yourselves with sparks:
Walk in the light of your fire and in the
sparks you have kindled—
This you shall have from My hand:
You shall lie down ᴿin torment.   Ps. 16:4

The LORD Comforts Zion

51 "Listen to Me, ᴿyou who ᵀfollow after
righteousness,
You who seek the LORD:
Look to the rock from which you were
hewn,
And to the hole of the pit from which
you were dug.   [Rom. 9:30–32] • pursue
2 ᴿLook to Abraham your father,   Heb. 11:11
And to Sarah who bore you;
ᴿFor I called him alone,   Gen. 12:1
And blessed him and increased him."

3 For the LORD will ᴿcomfort Zion,
He will comfort all her waste places;
He will make her wilderness like Eden,
And her desert ᴿlike the garden of the
LORD;   Is. 40:1; 52:9 • Gen. 13:10
Joy and gladness will be found in it,
Thanksgiving and the voice of melody.

4 "Listen to Me, My people;
And give ear to Me, O My nation:

ᴿFor law will proceed from Me,   Is. 2:3
And I will make My justice rest
ᴿAs a light of the peoples.   Is. 42:6
5 ᴿMy righteousness is near,   Is. 46:13
My salvation has gone forth,
And My arms will judge the peoples;
ᴿThe coastlands will wait upon Me,
And on My arm they will trust.   Is. 60:9
6 ᴿLift up your eyes to the heavens,
And look on the earth beneath.   Is. 40:26
For ᴿthe heavens will vanish away like
smoke,   Matt. 24:35
ᴿThe earth will grow old like a garment,
And those who dwell in it will die in
like manner;   Is. 24:19, 20; 50:9
But My salvation will be ᴿforever,
And My righteousness will not be
ᵀabolished.   Is. 45:17 • broken

7 "Listen to Me, you who know
righteousness,
You people ᴿin whose heart is My law:
Do not fear the reproach of men,
Nor be afraid of their insults.   Ps. 37:31
8 For ᴿthe moth will eat them up like a
garment,   Is. 50:9
And the worm will eat them like wool;
But My righteousness will be forever,
And My salvation from generation to
generation."

9 ᴿAwake, awake, ᴿput on strength,
O arm of the LORD!   Ps. 44:23 • Ps. 93:1
Awake ᴿas in the ancient days,
In the generations of old.   Ps. 44:1
ᴿAre You not the arm that cut ᴿRahab
apart,   Job 26:12 • Ps. 87:4
And wounded the ᴿserpent?   Ps. 74:13

10 Are You not the One who ᴿdried up the
sea,   Ex. 14:21
The waters of the great deep;
That made the depths of the sea a road
For the redeemed to cross over?
11 So ᴿthe ransomed of the LORD shall
return,   Is. 35:10
And come to Zion with singing,
With everlasting joy on their heads.
They shall obtain joy and gladness;
Sorrow and sighing shall flee away.

12 "I, even I, am He ᴿwho comforts you.
Who are you that you should be afraid
ᴿOf a man who will die,   2 Cor. 1:3 • Ps. 118:6
And of the son of a man who will be
made ᴿlike grass;   Is. 40:6, 7
13 And ᴿyou forget the LORD your Maker,
Who stretched out the heavens   Is. 17:10
And laid the foundations of the earth;
You have feared continually every day
Because of the fury of the oppressor,
When he has prepared to destroy.
And where is the fury of the oppressor?
14 The captive exile hastens, that he may
be loosed,

That he should not die in the pit,
And that his bread should not fail.
15 But I *am* the LORD your God,
   Who ^Rdivided the sea whose waves
      roared—
   The LORD of hosts *is* His name.　Job 26:12
16 And ^RI have put My words in your
      mouth;　Deut. 18:18
   ^RI have covered you with the shadow of
      My hand,　Is. 49:2
   That I may ^Tplant the heavens,　*establish*
   Lay the foundations of the earth,
   And say to Zion, 'You *are* My people.' "

God's Fury Removed

17 ^RAwake, awake!　Is. 52:1
   Stand up, O Jerusalem,
   You who ^Rhave drunk at the hand of
      the LORD　Job 21:20
   The cup of His fury;
   You have drunk the dregs of the cup of
      trembling,
   And drained *it* out.
18 *There is* no one to guide her
   Among all the sons she has brought
      forth;
   Nor *is there any* who takes her by the
      hand
   Among all the sons she has brought up.
19 ^RThese two *things* have come to you;
   Who will be sorry for you?—　Is. 47:9
   Desolation and destruction, famine and
      sword—
   ^RBy whom will I comfort you?　Amos 7:2
20 ^RYour sons have fainted,
   They lie at the head of all the streets,
   Like an antelope in a net;
   They are full of the fury of the LORD,
   The rebuke of your God.　Lam. 2:11

21 Therefore please hear this, you afflicted,
   And drunk ^Rbut not with wine.　Lam. 3:15
22 Thus says your Lord,
   The LORD and your God,
   Who ^Rpleads the cause of His people:
   "See, I have taken out of your hand
   The cup of trembling,
   The dregs of the cup of My fury;
   You shall no longer drink it.　Jer. 50:34
23 ^RBut I will put it into the hand of those
      who afflict you,
   Who have said to ^Tyou,
   'Lie down, that we may walk over you.'
   And you have laid your body like the
      ground,
   And as the street, for those who walk
      over."　Zech. 12:2 • Lit. *your soul*

God Redeems Jerusalem

52 Awake, awake!
   Put on your strength, O Zion;
   Put on your beautiful garments,
   O Jerusalem, the holy city!

For the uncircumcised ^Rand the unclean
   Shall no longer come to you.　[Rev. 21:2-27]
2 ^RShake yourself from the dust, arise;
   Sit down, O Jerusalem!　Is. 3:26
   ^RLoose yourself from the bonds of your
      neck,　Zech. 2:7
   O captive daughter of Zion!

3 For thus says the LORD:

   ^R"You have sold yourselves for nothing,
   And you shall be redeemed ^Rwithout
      money."　Ps. 44:12 • Is. 45:13

4 For thus says the Lord GOD:

   "My people went down at first
   Into ^REgypt to ^Tdwell there;
   Then the Assyrian oppressed them
      without cause.　Gen. 46:6 • As resident aliens
5 Now therefore, what have I here," says
      the LORD,
   "That My people are taken away for
      nothing?
   Those who rule over them
   Make them wail," says the LORD,
   "And My name *is* ^Rblasphemed
      continually every day.　Ezek. 36:20, 23
6 Therefore My people shall know My
      name;
   Therefore *they shall know* in that day
   That I *am* He who speaks:
   'Behold, *it is* I.' "

7 ^RHow beautiful upon the mountains
   Are the feet of him who brings good
      news,
   Who proclaims peace,
   Who brings glad tidings of good *things*,
   Who proclaims salvation,
   Who says to Zion,
   ^R"Your God reigns!"　Rom. 10:15 • Ps. 93:1
8 Your watchmen shall lift up *their*
      voices,
   With their voices they shall sing
      together;
   For they shall see eye to eye
   When the LORD brings back Zion.
9 Break forth into joy, sing together,
   You waste places of Jerusalem!
   For the LORD has comforted His people,
   He has redeemed Jerusalem.
10 The LORD has made bare His holy arm
   In the eyes of ^Rall the nations;　Luke 3:6
   And all the ends of the earth shall see
   The salvation of our God.

11 ^RDepart! Depart! Go out from there,
   Touch no unclean *thing*;
   Go out from the midst of her,
   ^RBe clean,　Is. 48:20 • Lev. 22:2
   You who bear the vessels of the LORD.

52:5 DSS *Mock*; LXX *Marvel and wail*; Tg. *Boast
themselves*; Vg. *Treat them unjustly*

12 For ᴿyou shall not go out with haste,
   Nor go by flight;
   ᴿFor the LORD will go before you,
   ᴿAnd the God of Israel *will be* your rear
   guard.   Ex. 12:11, 33 • Mic. 2:13 • Ex. 14:19, 20

The Sin-Bearing Servant

13 Behold, ᴿMy Servant shall ᵀdeal
   prudently;   Is. 42:1 • *prosper*
   ᴿHe shall be exalted and ᵀextolled and be
   very high.   Phil. 2:9 • Lit. *be lifted up*
14 Just as many were astonished at you,
   So His ᴿvisageᵀ was marred more than
   any man,
   And His form more than the sons of
   men;   Ps. 22:6, 7; Is. 53:2, 3 • *appearance*
15 ᴿSo shall He ᵀsprinkle many nations.
   Kings shall shut their mouths at Him;
   For ᴿwhat had not been told them they
   shall see,
   And what they had not heard they shall
   consider.   1 Pet. 1:2 • Or *startle* • Rom. 15:21

53 Who ᴿhas believed our report?
      And to whom has the arm of the
   LORD been revealed?   Rom. 10:16
2 For He shall grow up before Him as a
   tender plant,
   And as a root out of dry ground.
   He has no form or comeliness;
   And ᴿwhen we see Him,   Mark 15:32
   There is no ᵀbeauty that we should
   desire Him.   Lit. *appearance*
3 ᴿHe is despised and rejected by men,
   A Man of sorrows and acquainted with
   grief.   Ps. 22:6; [Is. 49:7]
   And we hid, as it were, *our* faces from
   Him;
   He was despised, and ᴿwe did not
   esteem Him.   [John 1:10, 11]

4 Surely ᴿHe has borne our griefs
   And carried our sorrows;   [Matt. 8:17]
   Yet we esteemed Him stricken,
   Smitten by God, and afflicted.
5 But He *was* ᴿwounded for our
   transgressions,   [Rom. 4:25; 1 Pet. 2:24, 25]
   He *was* ᵀbruised for our iniquities;
   The chastisement for our peace *was*
   upon Him,   *crushed*
   And by His stripes we are healed.
6 All we like sheep have gone astray;
   We have turned, every one, to his own
   way;
   And the LORD has ᴿlaid on Him the
   iniquity of us all.   Heb. 9:28

7 He was oppressed and He was afflicted,
   Yet ᴿHe opened not His mouth;
   ᴿHe was led as a lamb to the slaughter,
   And as a sheep before its shearers is
   silent,   Matt. 26:63; Mark 15:4, 5 • Acts 8:32
   So He opened not His mouth.
8 He was ᴿtaken from ᵀprison and from
   judgment,   Luke 23:1-25 • *confinement*
   And who will declare His generation?
   For ᴿHe was cut off from the land of
   the living;   [Dan. 9:26]
   ᴿFor the transgressions of My people He
   was stricken.   1 Cor. 15:3
9 ᴿAnd ᵀthey made His grave with the
   wicked—   Matt. 27:38, 57-60 • Lit. *he*
   But with the rich at His death,
   Because He had done no violence,
   Nor *was any* deceit in His mouth.

33-D. The Parties to the Crucifixion of ▼ Christ

10 Yet it pleased the LORD to ᵀbruise Him;
   He has put *Him* to grief.   *crush*

33-D. The Parties to the Crucifixion of Christ (Isaiah 53:10)—Over the centuries, efforts to evangelize the Jews have been obstructed by various persons who have unjustly blamed Christ's death on the Jewish people as a whole. Thus it is difficult to invite the Jewish person to accept the Christian faith if that person envisions himself joining a group which actively persecutes the Jewish people. The question then, of who really crucified Christ, is one of vital importance to a true understanding of Scripture and to Jewish evangelism. Those who crucified Christ were

(1) *God the Father*. "Yet it pleased the LORD to bruise Him" (v. 10). This passage, amidst the great prophecy of the suffering of the Christ for humanity's sins, clearly states that Christ's crucifixion was a part of God's plan of salvation. He was "slain from the foundation of the world" (Rev. 13:8, page 1306). At the Garden of Gethsemane, Christ, facing the cross amid the agony of knowing He was soon to bear the sins of the world, said, "Not as I will, but as You will," and "Your will be done" (Matt. 26:39, 42, page 978). Christ did not attempt to avoid the cross because He saw it as the will of the Father to be crucified, to pay for sin, and to give salvation to the believers of the ages (Eph. 2:8, 9, page 1187).

(2) *God the Son*. Christ told Peter to put away his sword when He was arrested in the garden, since Christ could (if He wished) call for "more than twelve legions of angels" (Matt. 26:52-54, page 978). It was His own will to fulfill the Scriptures and to die as a substitute for sinners. Christ said that He came as the Good Shepherd to give His life for His sheep; "No one takes it [His life] from Me" (John 10:17, 18, page 1067).

(3) *Satan*. That fallen unseen spirit, from the beginning, sought to
   (a) slay Christ at His birth (Rev. 12:4, page 1305);
   (b) tempt Him to sin or to be killed by leaping off the temple (Matt. 4:5, 6, page 934);
(Point 33-D continued on next page)

▽   When You make His soul ^Ran offering
for sin,   [John 1:29; 2 Cor. 5:21]
He shall see *His* seed, ^RHe shall prolong
His days,   Acts 2:24
And the pleasure of the LORD shall
▲   prosper in His hand.
11 *He shall see the labor of His soul, *and*
be satisfied.

   ^RBy His knowledge My righteous
Servant shall justify many,   Rom 5:18, 19
For He shall bear their iniquities.
12 ^RTherefore I will divide Him a portion
with the great,   Ps. 2:8
^RAnd He shall divide the ^Tspoil with the
strong,   Col. 2:15 • *plunder*
Because He ^Rpoured out His soul unto
death,   Is. 50:6
And He was ^Rnumbered with the
transgressors,   Matt. 27:38; Luke 22:37
And He bore the sin of many,
And ^Rmade intercession for the
transgressors.   Luke 23:34

A Perpetual Covenant of Peace

54 "Sing, O ^Rbarren,
You *who* have not borne!
Break forth into singing, and cry aloud,
You *who* have not labored with child!
For more *are* the children of the
desolate

53:11 So with MT, Tg., Vg.; DSS, LXX *From the labor of
His soul He shall see light*

Than the children of the married
woman," says the LORD.   Gal. 4:27
2 "Enlarge^R the place of your tent,
And let them stretch out the curtains of
your dwellings;
Do not spare;
Lengthen your cords,
And strengthen your stakes.   Is. 49:19, 20
3 For you shall expand to the right and
to the left,
And your descendants will ^Rinherit the
nations,   Is. 14:2; 49:22, 23; 60:9
And make the desolate cities inhabited.

4 "Do^R not fear, for you will not be
ashamed;   Is. 41:10
Neither be disgraced, for you will not
be put to shame;
For you will forget the shame of your
youth,
And will not remember the reproach of
your widowhood anymore.
5 ^RFor your Maker *is* your husband,
The LORD of hosts *is* His name;
And your Redeemer *is* the Holy One of
Israel;
He is called ^Rthe God of the whole
earth.   Jer. 3:14 • Zech. 14:9
6 For the LORD ^Rhas called you
Like a woman forsaken and grieved in
spirit,
Like a youthful wife when you were
refused,"
Says your God.   Is. 62:4

(Point 33-D continued from previous page)

     (c) have Christ slain (John 13:26, 27, page 1073). When Satan entered Judas, Judas betrayed Christ and was consequently responsible for His crucifixion.

     (4) *The Jewish leaders and the people.* The high priests and Sanhedrin court were angered by Christ's repeated healings on the Sabbath, violating the law (according to their traditional interpretation of the law). So they condemned Christ and handed Him over to the Romans for death (Matt. 27:15–25, page 980).

     (5) *Herod Antipas.* The Herodian family were Edomites from the deserts south of Jerusalem. Since Christ was a Galilean by residence, Pontius Pilate sent Christ to Herod—who had previously killed John the Baptist, mocked Christ and sent Him back to Pilate to His death (Luke 23:6–12, page 1044).

     (6) *The Romans.* Pilate sentenced Christ to death by crucifixion (Luke 23:24, page 1045). Pilate was guilty for having killed Christ even after admitting that He was an innocent man (Luke 23:22, page 1044). The Roman soldiers, representing several Gentile nations, carried out the actual crucifixion of Christ (Mark 15:16–25, page 1006).

     (7) *The original sinners—Adam and Eve.* By eating from the forbidden tree, they had plunged the race of mankind into sin. Their aprons of fig leaves (a non-blood offering) could not cover their sin; therefore, God killed animals to cover them. This foreshadowed Christ's need to shed His blood on the cross, and to provide the human race with an eternal, covering robe of righteousness. Thus, by their original sin, Adam and Eve were parties to the crucifixion of Christ (Gen. 3:6, 7, 21, page 5; cf. Rev. 19:8, page 1312).

     (8) *All mankind.* All mankind, having fallen and in need of a Savior to bear their sins that they might live, required Christ to die for them (John 3:16, page 1052).

     (9) *You.* Christ "bore our sins in His own body on the tree"—Your sins and my sins nailed Him to the cross (1 Pet. 2:24, page 1266). He died for *you.* Your sins, seen from the beginning by a loving and compassionate heavenly Father, put Christ on the cross in your place to save you. Thus God the Father, God the Son, Satan, the Jewish leaders and the people, the Edomites, the Gentile nations, Adam and Eve, as well as all of mankind, including you and me, each crucified God the Son. So no individual or nation should blame another individual or nation for the death of the Lord Jesus Christ.

     See Luke 23:34, page 1045, for **Point 33-E: The Barrier to Evangelism: Persecution of the Jewish People.**

7 "For[R] a mere moment I have forsaken
you,
But with great mercies [R]I will gather
you.   Is. 26:20; 60:10 · [Is. 43:5; 56:8]
8 With a little wrath I hid My face from
you for a moment;
[R]But with everlasting kindness I will
have mercy on you,"   Jer. 31:3
Says the LORD, your Redeemer.

9 "For this is like the waters of [R]Noah to
Me;   Gen. 8:21; 9:11
For as I have sworn
That the waters of Noah would no
longer cover the earth,
So have I sworn
That I would not be angry with [R]you,
nor rebuke you.   Ezek. 39:29
10 For [R]the mountains shall depart
And the hills be removed,   Is. 51:6
[R]But My kindness shall not depart from
you,   Ps. 89:33, 34
Nor shall My covenant of peace be
removed,"
Says the LORD, who has mercy on you.

11 "O you afflicted one,
Tossed with tempest, and not
comforted,
Behold, I will lay your stones with
[R]colorful gems,
And lay your foundations with
sapphires.   Rev. 21:18, 19
12 I will make your pinnacles of rubies,
Your gates of crystal,
And all your walls of precious stones.
13 All your children shall be [R]taught by
the LORD,
And [R]great shall be the peace of your
children.   [John 6:45] · Ps. 119:165
14 In righteousness you shall be
established;
You shall be far from oppression, for
you shall not fear;
And from terror, for it shall not come
near you.
15 Indeed they shall surely assemble, but
not because of Me.
Whoever assembles against you shall
[R]fall for your sake.   Is. 41:11-16

16 "Behold, I have created the blacksmith
Who blows the coals in the fire,

Who brings forth an [T]instrument for his
work;
And I have created the [T]spoiler to
destroy.   Or weapon · destroyer
17 No weapon formed against you shall
[R]prosper,   Is. 17:12-14; 29:8
And every tongue which rises against
you in judgment
You shall condemn.
This is the heritage of the servants of
the LORD,
[R]And their righteousness is from Me,"
Says the LORD.   Is. 45:24, 25; 54:14

An Invitation to Abundant Life

55 "Ho! [R]Everyone who thirsts,
Come to the waters;   [John 4:14; 7:37]
And you who have no money,
[R]Come, buy and eat.   [Rev. 3:18]
Yes, come, buy wine and milk
Without money and without price.
2 Why do you [T]spend money for what is
not bread,
And your wages for what does not
satisfy?
Listen carefully to Me, and eat what is
good,
And let your soul delight itself in
abundance.   Lit. weigh out silver
3 Incline your ear, and [R]come to Me.
Hear, and your soul shall live;   Matt. 11:28
[R]And I will make an everlasting
covenant with you—   Jer. 32:40
The [R]sure mercies of David.   2 Sam. 7:8
4 Indeed I have given him as [R]a witness
to the people,   [Rev. 1:5]
A leader and commander for the people.
5 [R]Surely you shall call a nation you do
not know,   Is. 52:15; Eph. 2:11, 12
[R]And nations who do not know you shall
run to you,   Is. 60:5
Because of the LORD your God,
And the Holy One of Israel;
[R]For He has glorified you."   Is. 60:9

6 [R]Seek the LORD while He may be found,
Call upon Him while He is near. [Heb. 3:13]

26-C. Thinking Makes the Person   ▼

7 Let the [T]wicked forsake his way,
And the unrighteous man his thoughts;
Let him return to the LORD,

26-C. Thinking Makes the Person (Isaiah 55:7-9)—"Let the wicked forsake his way, and the unrighteous man
his thoughts" (v. 7). There are only two ways to think: the righteous way or the unrighteous way. Tell me
what you think and I will tell you what you are, because you are what you think. You cannot live a righteous
life and think unrighteous thoughts. Jesus said, "A good tree cannot bear bad fruit, nor can a bad tree bear
good fruit" (Matt. 7:18-20, page 946). A person who thinks good thoughts cannot live a bad life. James said,
"Thus no spring yields both salt water and fresh" (James 3:11, 12, page 1258). No one can live a righteous
and unrighteous life at the same time. You can, however, forsake your unrighteous thoughts and return to
the Lord, and "He will abundantly pardon" (v. 7). A thief is a thief because he thinks like a thief. A liar is a
liar because he thinks like a liar. An adulterer is an adulterer because he thinks like an adulterer (Matt. 5:28,
page 940). "For as he thinks in his heart, so is he" (Prov. 23:7, page 616).

(Point 26-C continued on next page)

▽   ^RAnd He will have mercy on him;
And to our God,   Lit. *man of iniquity* · Jer. 3:12
For He will abundantly pardon.

8 "For^R My thoughts *are* not your
thoughts,
Nor *are* your ways My ways," says the
LORD.   2 Sam. 7:19
9 "For^R *as* the heavens are higher than the
earth,   Ps. 103:11

▲   So are My ways higher than your ways,
And My thoughts than your thoughts.

10 "For ^Ras the rain comes down, and the
snow from heaven,
And do not return there,
But water the earth,
And make it bring forth and bud,
That it may give seed to the sower
And bread to the eater,   Deut. 32:2
11 ^RSo shall My word be that goes forth
from My mouth;   Is. 45:23
It shall not return to Me ^Tvoid,
But it shall accomplish what I please,
And it shall ^Rprosper *in the thing* for
which I sent it.   *empty* · Is. 46:9–11

12 "For^R you shall go out with joy,
And be led out with peace;
The mountains and the hills
Shall ^Rbreak forth into singing before
you,
And ^Rall the trees of the field shall clap
their hands.   Is. 35:10 · Ps. 98:8 · 1 Chr. 16:33
13 ^RInstead of ^Rthe thorn shall come up the
cypress tree,
And instead of the brier shall come up
the myrtle tree;
And it shall be to the LORD ^Rfor a name,
For an everlasting sign *that* shall not be
cut off."   Is. 41:19 · Mic. 7:4 · Jer. 13:11

Salvation for the Gentiles

56 Thus says the LORD:

"Keep justice, and do righteousness,

For My salvation *is* about to come,
And My righteousness to be revealed.
2 Blessed *is* the man *who* does this,
And the son of man *who* lays hold on
it;
^RWho keeps from defiling the Sabbath,
And keeps his hand from doing any
evil."   Is. 58:13
3 Do not let ^Rthe son of the foreigner
Who has joined himself to the LORD
Speak, saying,   [Eph. 2:12–19]
"The LORD has utterly separated me
from His people";
Nor let the eunuch say,
"Here I am, a dry tree."
4 For thus says the LORD:
"To the eunuchs who keep My Sabbaths,
And choose what pleases Me,
And hold fast My covenant,
5 Even to them I will give in ^RMy house
And within My walls a place ^Rand a
name   1 Tim. 3:15 · [1 John 3:1, 2]
Better than that of sons and daughters;
I will give *them an everlasting name
That shall not be cut off.
6 "Also the sons of the foreigner
Who join themselves to the LORD, to
serve Him,
And to love the name of the LORD, to
be His servants—
Everyone who keeps from defiling the
Sabbath,
And holds fast My covenant—
7 Even them I will ^Rbring to My holy
mountain,   [Is. 2:2, 3; 60:11]
And make them joyful in My ^Rhouse of
prayer.   Mark 11:17
^RTheir burnt offerings and their
sacrifices
Will be accepted on My altar;   [Rom. 12:1]
For My house shall be called a house of
prayer ^Rfor all nations."   [Mal. 1:11]

56:5 Lit. *him*

(Point 26-C continued from previous page)

Someone once said, "You are what you eat," but this is not entirely so. You are also what you think. Man is "spirit, soul, and body" (1 Thess. 5:23, page 1213). Your body is affected by what you eat, but your body is not all of you. It is only the temporary house in which you live. "The things which are seen [such as your body] are temporary, but the things which are not seen [such as your spirit and soul] are eternal" (2 Cor. 4:18, page 1168).

At the resurrection, we will have bodies of flesh and bone, but without sin, like the glorified body of our risen Lord and Savior, Jesus Christ (Luke 24:39, page 1047; 1 John 3:2, page 1279). Until the Lord releases us from these houses of clay, we are to present our bodies as "a living sacrifice, holy, acceptable to God, which is [our] reasonable service." This cannot be accomplished apart from "the renewing of your mind" (Rom. 12:1, 2, page 1142). To renew your mind means to forsake unrighteous thoughts, and become righteous in all of your thinking. By applying our hearts and minds to the Scriptures with the guidance of the Holy Spirit, our hearts and minds become renewed, and begin to think God's thoughts, and to have the mind of Christ (Phil. 2:5, page 1197). If you have been saved by grace, through faith (Eph. 2:8, page 1187), the Holy Spirit indwells you (1 Cor. 6:19, 20, page 1152). Therefore, let the Word of God and the indwelling Holy Spirit motivate your every thought. Remember, thinking makes the person!

See Hebrews 3:7, page 1238, for **Point 26-D: Keep Your Thought Processes Active and Open to the Voice of God.**

8 The Lord God, ^Rwho gathers the
   outcasts of Israel, says,   Is. 11:12; 27:12
  ^R"Yet I will gather to him   [John 10:16]
   Others besides those who are gathered
   to him."

Israel's Irresponsible Leaders

9 ^RAll you beasts of the field, come to
   devour,
   All you beasts in the forest.   Jer. 12:9
10 His watchmen *are* ^Rblind,   Matt. 15:14
   They are all ignorant;
  ^RThey *are* all dumb dogs,   Phil. 3:2
   They cannot bark;
   Sleeping, lying down, loving to slumber.
11 Yes, *they are* ^Rgreedy dogs   [Mic. 3:5, 11]
   Which ^Rnever have enough.   Ezek. 34:2–10
   And they *are* shepherds
   Who cannot understand;
   They all look to their own way,
   Every one for his own gain,
   From his *own* territory.
12 "Come," *one* says, "I will bring wine,
   And we will fill ourselves with
   intoxicating ^Rdrink;   Is. 28:7
   Tomorrow will be ^Ras today,   2 Pet. 3:4
   And much more abundant."

Israel's Futile Idolatry

57 The righteous perishes,
   And no man takes *it* to heart;
  ^RMerciful men *are* taken away,
  ^RWhile no one considers
   That the righteous is taken away from
   ^Tevil.   Ps. 12:1 • 1 Kin. 14:13 • Lit. *the face of evil*
2 He shall enter into peace;
   They shall rest in ^Rtheir beds,   2 Chr. 16:14
   Each one walking *in* his uprightness.

3 "But come here,
  ^RYou sons of the sorceress,   Matt. 16:4
   You offspring of the adulterer and the
   harlot!
4 Whom do you ridicule?
   Against whom do you make a wide
   mouth
   And stick out the tongue?
   Are you not children of transgression,
   Offspring of falsehood,
5 Inflaming yourselves with gods ^Runder
   every green tree,   2 Kin. 16:4
  ^RSlaying the children in the valleys,
   Under the clefts of the rocks?   Jer. 7:31
6 Among the smooth ^Rstones of the
   stream   Jer. 3:9
   Is your portion;
   They, they, *are* your lot!
   Even to them you have poured a drink
   offering,
   You have offered a grain offering.
   Should I receive comfort in these?

7 "On^R a lofty and high mountain
   You have set ^Ryour bed;

   Even there you went up
   To offer sacrifice.   Ezek. 16:16 • Ezek. 23:41
8 Also behind the doors and their posts
   You have set up your remembrance;
   For you have uncovered yourself *to*
   those other than Me,
   And have gone up to them;
   You have enlarged your bed
   And ^Tmade *a covenant* with them;
   You have loved their bed,
   Where you saw *their* *nudity.   Lit. *cut*
9 ^RYou went to the king with ointment,
   And increased your perfumes;   Hos. 7:11
   You sent your messengers far off,
   And *even* descended to Sheol.
10 You are wearied in the length of your
   way;
   Yet you did not say, 'There is no hope.'
   You have found the life of your hand;
   Therefore you were not grieved.

11 "And ^Rof whom have you been afraid, or
   feared,   Is. 51:12, 13
   That you have lied
   And not remembered Me,
   Nor taken *it* to your heart?
   Is it not because ^RI have ^Theld My
   peace from of old   Ps. 50:21 • remained silent
   That you do not fear Me?
12 I will declare your righteousness
   And your works,
   For they will not profit you.
13 When you cry out,
   Let your collection *of idols* deliver you.
   But the wind will carry them all away,
   A breath will take *them*.
   But he who puts his trust in Me shall
   possess the land,
   And shall inherit My holy mountain."

Healing for the Backslider

14 And one shall say,
  ^R"Heap it up! Heap it up!
   Prepare the way,
   Take the stumbling block out of the
   way of My people."   Is. 40:3; 62:10
15 For thus says the High and Lofty One
   Who inhabits eternity, ^Rwhose name *is*
   Holy: Job 6:10
  ^R"I dwell in the high and holy *place*,
  ^RWith him *who* has a contrite and
   humble spirit,   Zech. 2:13 • Ps. 34:18; 51:17
  ^RTo revive the spirit of the humble,
   And to revive the heart of the contrite
   ones.   Is. 61:1–3
16 ^RFor I will not contend forever,   [Mic. 7:18]
   Nor will I always be angry;
   For the spirit would fail before Me,
   And the souls *which* I have made.
17 For the iniquity of ^Rhis covetousness
   I was angry and struck him;   Jer. 6:13

57:8 Lit. *hand*, a euphemism

^RI hid and was angry,   Is. 8:17; 45:15; 59:2
^RAnd he went on ^Tbacksliding in the way
of his heart.   Is. 9:13 • Or *turning back*
18 I have seen his ways, and ^Rwill heal
him;
I will also lead him,
And restore comforts to him
And to ^Rhis mourners.   Jer. 3:22 • Is. 61:2

19 "I create ^Rthe fruit of the lips:
Peace, peace ^Rto *him who is* far off and
to *him who is* near,"
Says the LORD,   Heb. 13:15 • Eph. 2:17
"And I will heal him."
20 ^RBut the wicked *are* like the troubled
sea,   Job 15:20
When it cannot rest,
Whose waters cast up mire and dirt.

21 "There ^R is no peace,"
Says my God, "for the wicked."   Is. 48:22

Fasting that Pleases God

58 "Cry aloud, ^Tspare not;   *do not hold back*
Lift up your voice like a trumpet;
^RTell My people their
transgression,   Mic. 3:8
And the house of Jacob their sins.
2 Yet they seek Me daily,
And delight to know My ways,
As a nation that did righteousness,
And did not forsake the ordinance of
their God.
They ask of Me the ordinances of
justice;
They take delight in approaching God.
3 'Why^R have we fasted,' *they say,* 'and
You have not seen?   Mal. 3:13–18
Why have we ^Rafflicted our souls, and
You take no notice?'   Lev. 16:29; 23:27

"In fact, in the day of your fast you find
pleasure,
And ^Texploit all your laborers.   *drive hard*
4 ^RIndeed you fast for strife and debate,
And to strike with the fist of
wickedness.   1 Kin. 21:9
You will not fast as *you do* this day,
To make your voice heard on high.
5 Is ^Rit a fast that I have chosen,
^RA day for a man to afflict his soul?
Is it to bow down his head like a
bulrush,   Zech. 7:5 • Lev. 16:29
And ^Rto spread out sackcloth and
ashes?   Esth. 4:3
Would you call this a fast,
And an acceptable day to the LORD?

6 "*Is* this not the fast that I have chosen:
To loose the bonds of wickedness,
^RTo undo the heavy burdens,   Neh. 5:10–12
^RTo let the oppressed go free,   Jer. 34:9
And that you break every yoke?
7 *Is it* not ^Rto share your bread with the
hungry,   Ezek. 18:7

And that you bring to your house the
poor who are ^Tcast out;   *wandering*
^RWhen you see the naked, that you
cover him,
And not hide yourself from ^Ryour own
flesh?   Job 31:19–22 • Neh. 5:5
8 ^RThen your light shall break forth like
the morning,
Your healing shall spring forth speedily,
And your righteousness shall go before
you;
^RThe glory of the LORD shall be your
rear guard.   Job 11:17 • Ex. 14:19
9 Then you shall call, and the LORD will
answer;
You shall cry, and He will say, 'Here I
am.'

"If you take away the yoke from your
midst,
The ^Tpointing of the finger, and
speaking wickedness,   Lit. *sending out of*
10 *If* you extend your soul to the hungry
And satisfy the afflicted soul,
Then your light shall dawn in the
darkness,
And your ^Tdarkness shall *be* as the
noonday.   Or *gloom*
11 The LORD will guide you continually,
And satisfy your soul in drought,
And strengthen your bones;
You shall be like a watered garden,
And like a spring of water, whose
waters do not fail.
12 Those from among you
^RShall build the old waste places;
You shall raise up the foundations of
many generations;   Is. 61:4
And you shall be called the Repairer of
the Breach,
The Restorer of Streets to Dwell In.

13 "If ^Ryou turn away your foot from the
Sabbath,   Is. 56:2, 4, 6
From doing your pleasure on My holy
day,
And call the Sabbath a delight,
The holy *day* of the LORD honorable,
And shall honor Him, not doing your
own ways,
Nor finding your own pleasure,
Nor speaking *your own* words,
14 ^RThen you shall delight yourself in the
LORD;   Job 22:26
And I will cause you to ^Rride on the
high hills of the earth,   Deut. 32:13; 33:29
And feed you with the heritage of
Jacob your father.
The mouth of the LORD has spoken."

Separated from God

59 Behold, the LORD's hand is not
^Rshortened,
That it cannot save;

Nor His ear heavy,
That it cannot hear.   Num. 11:23
2 But your iniquities have separated you
   from your God;
   And your sins have hidden *His* face
   from you,
   So that He will ^Rnot hear.   Is. 1:15
3 For ^Ryour hands are defiled with ^Tblood,
   And your fingers with iniquity;   Ezek. 7:23
   Your lips have spoken lies,   *bloodshed*
   Your tongue has muttered perversity.

4 No one calls for justice,
   Nor does *any* plead for truth.
   They trust in ^Rempty words and speak
   lies;
   ^RThey conceive ^Tevil and bring forth
   iniquity.   Jer. 7:4 · Job 15:35 · *trouble*
5 They hatch vipers' eggs and weave the
   spider's web;
   He who eats of their eggs dies,
   And *from* that which is crushed a viper
   breaks out.

6 ^RTheir webs will not become garments,
   Nor will they cover themselves with
   their works;
   Their works *are* works of iniquity,
   And the act of violence *is* in their
   hands.   Job 8:14
7 ^RTheir feet run to evil,   Rom. 3:15
   And they make haste to shed ^Rinnocent
   blood;   Prov. 6:17
   ^RTheir thoughts *are* thoughts of iniquity;
   Wasting and ^Rdestruction *are* in their
   paths.   Is. 55:7 · Rom. 3:16, 17
8 The way of ^Rpeace they have not
   known,
   And *there is* no justice in their ways;
   ^RThey have made themselves crooked
   paths;
   Whoever takes that way shall not know
   peace.   Is. 57:20, 21 · Prov. 2:15

Sin Confessed

9 Therefore justice is far from us,
   Nor does righteousness overtake us;
   ^RWe look for light, but there is darkness!
   For brightness, *but* we walk in
   blackness!   Jer. 8:15
10 We grope for the wall like the blind,
   And we grope as if *we had* no eyes;
   We stumble at noonday as at twilight;
   We are as dead *men* in desolate places.
11 We all growl like bears,
   And ^Rmoan sadly like doves;   Ezek. 7:16
   We look for justice, but *there is* none;
   For salvation, *but* it is far from us.
12 For our ^Rtransgressions are multiplied
   before You,
   And our sins testify against us;
   For our transgressions *are* with us,
   And *as for* our iniquities, we know
   them: Is. 24:5; 58:1

13 In transgressing and lying against the
   LORD,
   And departing from our God,
   Speaking oppression and revolt,
   Conceiving and uttering ^Rfrom the
   heart words of falsehood.   Matt. 12:34
14 Justice is turned back,
   And righteousness stands afar off;
   For truth is fallen in the street,
   And equity cannot enter.
15 So truth fails,
   And he *who* departs from evil makes
   himself a ^Rprey.   Is. 5:23; 10:2; 29:21; 32:7

The Redeemer of Zion

Then the LORD saw *it*, and ^Tit displeased
Him   Lit. *it was evil in His eyes*
That *there was* no justice.
16 ^RHe saw that *there was* no man,
   And ^Rwondered that *there was* no
   intercessor;
   ^RTherefore His own arm brought
   salvation for Him;
   And His own righteousness, it sustained
   Him.   Ezek. 22:30 · Mark 6:6 · Ps. 98:1
17 ^RFor He put on righteousness as a
   breastplate,   Eph. 6:14, 17
   And a helmet of salvation on His head;
   He put on the garments of vengeance
   for clothing,
   And was clad with zeal as a cloak.
18 ^RAccording to *their* deeds, accordingly
   He will repay,   Is. 63:6
   Fury to His adversaries,
   Recompense to His enemies;
   The coastlands He will fully repay.
19 ^RSo shall they fear   Mal. 1:11
   The name of the LORD from the west,
   And His glory from the rising of the
   sun;
   When the enemy comes in ^Rlike a flood,
   The Spirit of the LORD will lift up a
   standard against him.   Rev. 12:15

20 "The^R Redeemer will come to Zion,
   And to those who turn from
   transgression in Jacob,"
   Says the LORD.   Rom. 11:26

21 "As^R for Me," says the LORD, "this *is* My
covenant with them: My Spirit who *is* upon
you, and My words which I have put in your
mouth, shall not depart from your mouth, nor
from the mouth of your descendants, nor
from the mouth of your descendants' descendants," says the LORD, "from this time
and forevermore."   [Heb. 8:10; 10:16]

The Gentiles Bless Zion

60 Arise, ^Rshine;
     For your light has come!
And ^Rthe glory of the LORD is risen
upon you.   Eph. 5:14 · Mal. 4:2

2 For behold, the darkness shall cover the
    earth,
    And deep darkness the people;
    But the LORD will arise over you,
    And His glory will be seen upon you.
3 The ᴿGentiles shall come to your light,
    And kings to the brightness of your
    rising.   Is. 49:6, 23; Rev. 21:24

4 "Lift ᴿ up your eyes all around, and see:
    They all gather together, ᴿthey come to
    you;   Is. 49:18 • Is. 49:20–22
    Your sons shall come from afar,
    And your daughters shall be nursed at
    your side.
5 Then you shall see and become radiant,
    And your heart shall swell with joy;
    Because ᴿthe abundance of the sea shall
    be turned to you,
    The wealth of the Gentiles shall come
    to you.   [Rom. 11:25–27]
6 The multitude of camels shall cover
    your land,
    The dromedaries of Midian and ᴿEphah;
    All those from ᴿSheba shall come;
    They shall bring ᴿgold and incense,
    And they shall proclaim the praises of
    the LORD.   Gen. 25:4 • Ps. 72:10 • Matt. 2:11
7 All the flocks of ᴿKedar shall be
    gathered together to you,
    The rams of Nebaioth shall minister to
    you;
    They shall ascend with ᴿacceptance on
    My altar,
    And ᴿI will glorify the house of My
    glory.   Gen. 25:13 • Is. 56:7 • Hag. 2:7, 9

8 "Who are these who fly like a cloud,
    And like doves to their roosts?
9 ᴿSurely the coastlands shall wait for Me;
    And the ships of Tarshish will come
    first,   Ps. 72:10
    ᴿTo bring your sons from afar,   [Gal. 4:26]
    ᴿTheir silver and their gold with them,
    To the name of the LORD your God,
    And to the Holy One of Israel,   Jer. 3:17
    ᴿBecause He has glorified you.   Is. 55:5

10 "The ᴿ sons of foreigners shall build up
    your walls,   Zech. 6:15
    And their kings shall minister to you;
    For ᴿin My wrath I struck you,   Is. 57:17
    ᴿBut in My favor I have had mercy on
    you.   Is. 54:7, 8
11 Therefore your gates ᴿshall be open
    continually;   Rev. 21:25, 26
    They shall not be shut day or night,
    That men may bring to you the wealth
    of the Gentiles,
    And their kings in procession.
12 ᴿFor the nation and kingdom which will
    not serve you shall perish,
    And those nations shall be utterly
    ruined.   Zech. 14:17

13 "The ᴿ glory of Lebanon shall come to
    you,
    The cypress, the pine, and the box tree
    together,
    To beautify the place of My sanctuary;
    And I will make ᴿthe place of My feet
    glorious.   Is. 35:2 • 1 Chr. 28:2
14 Also the sons of those who afflicted you
    Shall come ᴿbowing to you,   Is. 45:14
    And all those who despised you shall
    ᴿfall prostrate at the soles of your
    feet;   Rev. 3:9
    And they shall call you The City of the
    LORD,
    ᴿZion of the Holy One of Israel. [Heb. 12:22]

15 "Whereas you have been forsaken and
    hated,
    So that no one went through you,
    I will make you an eternal excellence,
    A joy of many generations.
16 You shall drink the milk of the
    Gentiles,
    ᴿAnd milk the breast of kings;
    You shall know that ᴿI, the LORD, am
    your Savior
    And your Redeemer, the Mighty One of
    Jacob.   Is. 49:23 • Is. 43:3

17 "Instead of bronze I will bring gold,
    Instead of iron I will bring silver,
    Instead of wood, bronze,
    And instead of stones, iron.
    I will also make your officers peace,
    And your magistrates righteousness.
18 Violence shall no longer be heard in
    your land,
    Neither ᵀwasting nor destruction within
    your borders;
    But you shall call ᴿyour walls Salvation,
    And your gates Praise.   devastation • Is. 26:1

God the Glory of His People

19 "The ᴿsun shall no longer be your light
    by day,   Rev. 21:23; 22:5
    Nor for brightness shall the moon give
    light to you;
    But the LORD will be to you an
    everlasting light,
    And ᴿyour God your glory.   Zech. 2:5
20 ᴿYour sun shall no longer go down,
    Nor shall your moon withdraw itself;
    For the LORD will be your everlasting
    light,
    And the days of your mourning shall be
    ended.   Amos 8:9
21 Also your people shall all be righteous;
    ᴿThey shall inherit the land forever,
    ᴿThe branch of My
    planting,   Ps. 37:11 • Is. 61:3
    ᴿThe work of My hands,   [Eph. 2:10]
    That I may be glorified.
22 A little one shall become a thousand,

And a small one a strong nation.
I, the LORD, will hasten it in its time."

The Good News of Salvation

61 "The ᴿSpirit of the Lord GOD *is* upon
Me,   Is. 11:2; Luke 4:18
Because the LORD has anointed Me
To preach good tidings to the poor;
He has sent Me ᴿto ᵀheal the
brokenhearted,   Ps. 147:3 · Lit. *bind up*
To proclaim ᴿliberty to the captives,
And the opening of the prison to *those
who are* bound;   Is. 42:7
2 ᴿTo proclaim the acceptable year of the
LORD,   Lev. 25:9
And the day of vengeance of our God;
ᴿTo comfort all who mourn,   Matt. 5:4
3 To ᵀconsole those who mourn in Zion,
ᴿTo give them beauty for ashes,
The oil of joy for mourning,
The garment of praise for the spirit of
heaviness;   Lit. *appoint* · Ps. 30:11
That they may be called trees of
righteousness,
ᴿThe planting of the LORD, ᴿthat He may
be glorified."   Is. 60:21 · [John 15:8]

4 And they shall ᴿrebuild the old ruins,
They shall raise up the former
desolations,   Ezek. 36:33
And they shall repair the ruined cities,
The desolations of many generations.
5 ᴿStrangers shall stand and feed your
flocks,
And the sons of the foreigner
Shall be your plowmen and your
vinedressers.   [Eph. 2:12]
6 ᴿBut you shall be named the priests of
the LORD,   Ex. 19:6
They shall call you the servants of our
God.
You shall eat the riches of the Gentiles,
And in their glory you shall boast.
7 ᴿInstead of your shame *you shall have*
double *honor*,
And *instead of* confusion they shall
rejoice in their portion.
Therefore in their land they shall
possess double;
Everlasting joy shall be theirs.   Zech. 9:12

8 "For ᴿI, the LORD, love justice;   Ps. 11:7
ᴿI hate robbery ᵀfor burnt offering;
I will direct their work in truth, Is. 1:11, 13
ᴿAnd will make with them an
everlasting covenant.   Or *in* · Is. 55:3
9 Their descendants shall be known
among the Gentiles,
And their offspring among the people.
All who see them shall acknowledge
them,
ᴿThat they *are* the posterity *whom* the
LORD has blessed."   Is. 65:23

10 ᴿI will greatly rejoice in the LORD,
My soul shall be joyful in my God;
For ᴿHe has clothed me with the
garments of salvation,
He has covered me with the robe of
righteousness,
ᴿAs a bridegroom decks *himself* with
ornaments,
And as a bride adorns *herself* with her
jewels.   Hab. 3:18 · Ps. 132:9, 16 · Is. 49:18
11 For as the earth brings forth its bud,
As the garden causes the things that
are sown in it to spring forth,
So the Lord GOD will cause
righteousness and praise to spring
forth before all the nations.

Assurance of Zion's Salvation

62 For Zion's sake I will not ᵀhold My
peace,   *keep silent*
And for Jerusalem's sake I will not rest,
Until her righteousness goes forth as
brightness,
And her salvation as a lamp *that* burns.
2 ᴿThe Gentiles shall see your
righteousness,   Is. 60:3
And all ᴿkings your glory.   Ps. 102:15, 16
ᴿYou shall be called by a new name,
Which the mouth of the LORD will
name.   Is. 62:4, 12; 65:15
3 You shall also be ᴿa crown of glory
In the hand of the LORD,
And a royal diadem
In the hand of your God.   Zech. 9:16
4 You shall no longer be termed
ᴿForsaken,ᵀ   Is. 49:14; 54:6, 7 · Heb. *Azubah*
Nor shall your land any more be termed
ᴿDesolate;ᵀ   Is. 54:1 · Heb. *Shemamah*
But you shall be called *Hephzibah, and
your land *Beulah;
For the LORD delights in you,
And your land shall be married.
5 For *as* a young man marries a virgin,
So shall your sons marry you;
And *as* the bridegroom rejoices over
the bride,
So shall your God rejoice over you.

6 ᴿI have set watchmen on your walls, O
Jerusalem;   Ezek. 3:17; 33:7
They shall ᵀnever hold their peace day
or night.   *not be silent*
You who ᵀmake mention of the LORD,
do not keep silent,   *remember*
7 And give Him no rest till He establishes
And till He makes Jerusalem ᴿa praise
in the earth.   Zeph. 3:19, 20

8 The LORD has sworn by His right hand
And by the arm of His strength:
"Surely I will no longer ᴿgive your grain
As food for your enemies;

62:4 Lit. *My Delight Is in Her* · Lit. *Married*

And the sons of the foreigner shall not
  drink your new wine,   Deut. 28:31, 33
For which you have labored.
9 But those who have gathered it shall
  eat it,
And praise the LORD;
Those who have brought it together
  shall drink it in My holy courts."

10 Go through,
  Go through the gates!
  RPrepare the way for the people;
  Build up,   Is. 40:3; 57:14
  Build up the highway!
  Take out the stones,
  RLift up a banner for the peoples!   Is. 11:12

11 Indeed the LORD has proclaimed
  To the end of the world:
  R"Say to the daughter of Zion,   Zech. 9:9
  'Surely your salvation is coming;
  Behold, His reward is with Him,
  And His Twork before Him.' "   recompense
12 And they shall call them The Holy
  People,
The Redeemed of the LORD;
And you shall be called Sought Out,
A City Not Forsaken.

The LORD in Judgment and Salvation

63 Who is this who comes from Edom,
  With dyed garments from Bozrah,
This One who is Tglorious in His
  apparel,   Or adorned
Traveling in the greatness of His
  strength?—

"I who speak in righteousness, mighty to
  save."

2 Why Ris Your apparel red,   [Rev. 19:13, 15]
And Your garments like one who treads
  in the winepress?

3 "I have Rtrodden the winepress alone,
And from the peoples no one was with
  Me.   Rev. 14:19, 20; 19:15
For I have trodden them in My anger,
And trampled them in My fury;
Their blood is sprinkled upon My
  garments,
And I have stained all My robes.
4 For the Rday of vengeance is in My
  heart,
And the year of My redeemed has
  come.   Is. 34:8; 35:4; 61:2
5 RI looked, but Rthere was no one to help,
And I wondered   Is. 41:28; 59:16 • [John 16:32]
That there was no one to uphold;
Therefore My own Rarm brought
  salvation for Me;   Ps. 98:1
And My own fury, it sustained Me.
6 I have trodden down the peoples in My
  anger,
Made them drunk in My fury,

And brought down their strength to the
  earth."

God's Mercy Remembered

7 I will mention the lovingkindnesses of
  the LORD
And the praises of the LORD,
According to all that the LORD has
  bestowed on us,
And the great goodness toward the
  house of Israel,
Which He has bestowed on them
  according to His mercies,
According to the multitude of His
  lovingkindnesses.
8 For He said, "Surely they are My
  people,
Children who will not lie."
So He became their RSavior.   Is. 60:16
9 RIn all their affliction He was *afflicted,
RAnd the Angel of His Presence saved
  them;   Judg. 10:16 • Ex. 14:19
RIn His love and in His pity He redeemed
  them;   Deut. 7:7
And RHe bore them and carried them
All the days of old.   Ex. 19:4
10 But they Rrebelled and Rgrieved His
  Holy Spirit;   Ex. 15:24 • Ps. 78:40
RSo He turned Himself against them as
  an enemy,   Ex. 23:21
And He fought against them.

11 Then he Rremembered the days of old,
Moses and his people, saying: Ps. 106:44, 45
"Where is He who Rbrought them up out
  of the sea   Ex. 14:30
With the *shepherd of His flock?
RWhere is He who put His Holy Spirit
  within them,   Num. 11:17, 25, 29
12 Who led them by the right hand of
  Moses,
RWith His glorious arm,
RDividing the water before them
To make for Himself an everlasting
  name,   Ex. 15:6 • Ex. 14:21, 22
13 RWho led them through the deep,
As a horse in the wilderness,
That they might not stumble?"   Ps. 106:9

14 As a beast goes down into the valley,
And the Spirit of the LORD causes him
  to rest,
So You lead Your people,
To make Yourself a glorious name.

A Prayer of Penitence

15 RLook down from heaven,   Deut. 26:15
And see Rfrom Your habitation, holy
  and glorious.   Ps. 33:14
Where are Your zeal and Your
  strength,

63:9 Kt., LXX, Syr. not afflicted
63:11 MT, Vg. shepherds

The yearning ᴿof Your heart and Your
mercies toward me?   Jer. 31:20
Are they restrained?

16 ᴿDoubtless You *are* our Father,
Though Abraham ᴿwas ignorant of us,
And Israel does not acknowledge us.
You, O LORD, *are* our Father;
Our Redeemer from Everlasting *is* Your
name.   Deut. 32:6 · Job 14:21

17 O LORD, why have You ᴿmade us stray
from Your ways,
And hardened our heart from Your
fear?
Return for Your servants' sake,
The tribes of Your inheritance.   John 12:40

18 ᴿYour holy people have possessed *it* but
a little while;
ᴿOur adversaries have trodden down
Your sanctuary.   Deut. 7:6 · Ps. 74:3-7

19 We have become *like* those of old, over
whom You never ruled,
Those who were never called by Your
name.

64 Oh, that You would ᵀrend the
heavens!
That You would come down!
That the mountains might shake at
Your ᴿpresence—   *tear open* · Mic. 1:3, 4

2 As fire burns brushwood,
As fire causes water to boil—
To make Your name known to Your
adversaries,
That the nations may tremble at Your
presence!

3 When ᴿYou did awesome things *for*
which we did not look,   Ex. 34:10
You came down,
The mountains shook at Your presence.

4 For since the beginning of the world
ᴿ*Men* have not heard nor perceived by
the ear,   Ps. 31:19
Nor has the eye seen any God besides
You,
Who acts for the one who waits for
Him.

5 You meet him who rejoices and does
righteousness,
Who remembers You in Your ways.
You are indeed angry, for we have
sinned—
ᴿIn these ways we continue;
And we need to be saved.   Mal. 3:6

6 But we are all like an unclean *thing*,
And all ᴿour righteousnesses *are* like
ᵀfilthy rags;   [Phil. 3:9] · Lit. *a filthy garment*
We all ᴿfade as a leaf,   Ps. 90:5, 6
And our iniquities, like the wind,
Have taken us away.

7 And *there is* no one who calls on Your
name,
Who stirs himself up to take hold of
You;

For You have hidden Your face from
us,
And have ᵀconsumed us because of our
iniquities.   Lit. *caused us to melt*

8 But now, O LORD,
You *are* our Father;
We *are* the clay, and You our potter;
And all we *are* the work of Your hand.

9 Do not be furious, O LORD,
Nor remember iniquity forever;
Indeed, please look—we all *are* Your
people!

10 Your holy cities are a wilderness,
Zion is a wilderness,
Jerusalem a desolation.

11 Our holy and beautiful ᵀtemple,
Where our fathers praised You,
Is burned up with fire;
And all ᴿour pleasant things are laid
waste.   Lit. *house* · Ezek. 24:21

12 ᴿWill You restrain Yourself because of
these *things*, O LORD?   Is. 42:14
ᴿWill You ᵀhold Your peace, and afflict
us very severely?   Ps. 83:1 · *keep silent*

The Righteousness of God's Judgment

65 "I was ᴿsought by *those who* did not
ask *for Me*;
I was found by *those who* did not seek
Me.
I said, 'Here I am, here I am,'
To a nation *that* ᴿwas not called by My
name.   Rom. 9:24; 10:20 · Is. 63:19

2 ᴿI have stretched out My hands all day
long to a rebellious people,   Rom. 10:21
Who ᴿwalk in a way *that* is not good,
According to their own thoughts; Is. 42:24

3 A people ᴿwho provoke Me to anger
continually to My face;   Deut. 32:21
ᴿWho sacrifice in gardens,
And burn incense on altars of brick; Is. 1:29

4 ᴿWho sit among the graves,   Deut. 18:11
And spend the night in the tombs;
ᴿWho eat swine's flesh,   Is. 66:17
And the broth of ᵀabominable things is
in their vessels;   Unclean meats, Lev. 7:18

5 ᴿWho say, 'Keep to yourself,   Matt. 9:11
Do not come near me,
For I am holier than you!'
These *are* smoke in My nostrils,
A fire that burns all the day.

6 "Behold, *it is* written before Me:
I will not keep silence, ᴿbut will repay—
Even repay into their bosom—   Ps. 79:12

7 Your iniquities and ᴿthe iniquities of
your fathers together,"   Ex. 20:5
Says the LORD,
ᴿ"Who have burned incense on the
mountains   Ezek. 18:6
ᴿAnd blasphemed Me on the hills;
Therefore I will measure their former
work into their bosom."   Ezek. 20:27, 28

8 Thus says the LORD:

"As the new wine is found in the cluster,
And one says, 'Do not destroy it,
For ^{R}a blessing is in it,'   Joel 2:14
So will I do for My servants' sake,
That I may not destroy them all.
9 I will bring forth descendants from
Jacob,
And from Judah an heir of My
mountains;
My ^{R}elect shall inherit it,   Matt. 24:22
And My servants shall dwell there.
10 ^{R}Sharon shall be a fold of flocks,   Is. 33:9
And ^{R}the Valley of Achor a place for
herds to lie down,   Josh. 7:24
For My people who have sought Me.
11 "But you are those who forsake the
LORD,
Who forget ^{R}My holy mountain,   Is. 56:7
Who prepare a table for *Gad,
And who furnish a drink offering for
*Meni.
12 Therefore I will number you for the
sword,
And you shall all bow down to the
slaughter;
^{R}Because, when I called, you did not
answer;
When I spoke, you did not hear,
But did evil before My eyes,
And chose that in which I do not
delight."   Prov. 1:24

65:11 Lit. Troop or Fortune; a pagan deity • Lit. Number
or Destiny; a pagan deity

13 Therefore thus says the Lord GOD:

"Behold, My servants shall eat,
But you shall be hungry;
Behold, My servants shall drink,
But you shall be thirsty;
Behold, My servants shall rejoice,
But you shall be ashamed;
14 Behold, My servants shall sing for joy
of heart,
But you shall cry for sorrow of heart,
And wail for ^{T}grief of spirit.   broken
15 You shall leave your name ^{R}as a curse
to ^{R}My chosen;   Jer. 29:22 • Is. 65:9, 22
For the Lord GOD will slay you,
And call His servants by another name;
16 ^{R}So that he who blesses himself in the
earth
Shall bless himself in the God of truth;
And ^{R}he who swears in the earth
Shall swear by the God of truth;
Because the former troubles are
forgotten,
And because they are hidden from My
eyes.   Jer. 4:2 • Zeph. 1:5

The Glorious New Creation

17-C. Heaven Is an Eternal Place ▼

17 "For behold, I create ^{R}new heavens and
a new earth;   Rev. 21:1
And the former shall not be
remembered or come to mind.   ▲
18 But be glad and rejoice forever in what
I create;
For behold, I create Jerusalem as a
rejoicing,
And her people a joy.

17-C. Heaven Is an Eternal Place (Isaiah 65:17)—Isaiah is the only Old Testament prophet who permits us a glimpse of the new heavens and the new earth that the Lord will create after the Millennium. God spoke to Isaiah saying, "For behold, I create new heavens and a new earth" (v. 17). In Isaiah 65:18-25 God allowed Isaiah to foresee some of the characteristics of the Millennium which would precede the "new heavens and a new earth." About 790 years after Isaiah's prophecy, the Lord revealed even more of this heavenly vision to the apostle John and enlarged the scope of this heavenly revelation (Rev. 21:1—22:9, page 1314). John wrote, "Now I saw a new heaven and a new earth, for the first heaven and the first earth had passed away. Also there was no more sea. Then I, John, saw the holy city, New Jerusalem, coming down out of heaven from God, prepared as a bride adorned for her husband" (Rev. 21:1, 2, page 1314).

The new heaven, the new earth, and the New Jerusalem are the beginning of God's eternal kingdom—including heaven on earth. It is not the Millennium viewed in retrospect. This future kingdom will come to an end after one thousand years (Rev. 20:7, page 1313). But the inhabitants of the new heaven, the new earth, and the New Jerusalem, along with the new things God will create, will never end, but "shall reign forever and ever" (Rev. 22:5, page 1316). Revelation chapters 21 and 22 (page 1314) are not a recapitulation of the millennial reign of Christ (Rev. 20:1-15, page 1313); they describe a new eternal order.

(1) The New Heaven. God will create a new, pure atmosphere for His new earth and New Jerusalem. No longer will Satan be the "prince of the power of the air" (Eph. 2:2, page 1187); the air will be clean and there will be no more storms. Satan and all his demons will be in the lake of fire (Rev. 20:10, page 1313).

(2) The New Earth. Under the curse of sin (Gen. 3:17-19, page 7) the old earth will be destroyed by fire (2 Pet. 3:10, page 1276). The Lord will create a new earth and there will be no more sea (Rev. 21:1, page 1314). With the curse lifted, every foot of the earth will become suitable for habitation. The new heaven and the new earth will then be ready for the Holy City.

(3) The New Jerusalem. The old Jerusalem, which was built by man, will be destroyed by fire with the rest of the earth. The New Jerusalem will be the work of the Lord Jesus Christ, our God and Savior. He said, "In My Father's house are many mansions; if it were not so, I would have told you. I go to prepare a place for you. And if I go and prepare a place for you, I will come again and receive you to Myself; that where I

(Point 17-C continued on next page)

19 ^RI will rejoice in Jerusalem,   Is. 62:4, 5
   And joy in My people;
   The ^Rvoice of weeping shall no longer
      be heard in her,   Rev. 7:17; 21:4
   Nor the voice of crying.

20 "No more shall an infant from there *live*
      but a few days,
   Nor an old man who has not fulfilled
      his days;
   For the child shall die one hundred
      years old,
   ^RBut the sinner *being* one hundred years
      old shall be accursed.   Eccl. 8:12, 13
21 ^RThey shall build houses and inhabit
      them;
   They shall plant vineyards and eat their
      fruit.   Amos 9:14
22 They shall not build and another
      inhabit;
   They shall not plant and another eat;
   For ^Ras the days of a tree, *so shall be*
      the days of My people,   Ps. 92:12

And ^RMy elect shall long enjoy the
   work of their hands.   Is. 65:9, 15
23 They shall not labor in vain,
   Nor bring forth children for trouble;
   For ^Rthey *shall be* the descendants of
      the blessed of the LORD,   Is. 61:9
   And their offspring with them.

24 "It shall come to pass
   That ^Rbefore they call, I will answer;
   And while they are still speaking, I will
      ^Rhear.   Is. 58:9 · Dan. 9:20-23
25 The ^Rwolf and the lamb shall feed
      together,
   The lion shall eat straw like the ox,
   ^RAnd dust *shall be* the serpent's food.
   They shall not hurt nor destroy in all
      My holy mountain,"
   Says the LORD.   Is. 11:6-9 · Gen. 3:14

True Worship and False

66 Thus says the LORD:

^R"Heaven *is* My throne,   1 Kin. 8:27

(Point 17-C continued from previous page)
am, there you may be also" (John 14:2, 3, page 1074). The New Jerusalem is the bride's eternal dwelling place, created for her by the Lord Jesus Christ. "One of the seven angels" spoke to John, saying, " 'Come, I will show you the bride, the Lamb's wife.' And he [the angel] carried me away in the Spirit to a great and high mountain, and showed me the great city, the holy Jerusalem, descending out of heaven from God" (Rev. 21:9, 10, page 1315). The bride, the Lamb's wife, will be in the New Jerusalem when it descends from heaven, to become the capital of heaven on earth. John describes the New Jerusalem magnificently (Rev. 21:9-27, page 1315).

(a) *The dimensions.* The exact specifications defy comprehension: 12,000 furlongs (or 1,500 miles) square. "Its length, breadth, and height are equal." Try to visualize a city of "pure gold, like clear [flawless] glass," 6,000 miles around and 1,500 miles high—in square miles covering more than half of the United States (Rev. 21:15-18, page 1315). Many believe the city will be in the shape of a pyramid, others, in the form of a cube.

(b) *The wall.* It "had a great and high wall" (216 feet tall) made of *jasper,* a pure stone believed to be diamond. Each of the four walls will have three gates with the names of the twelve tribes of Israel written thereon. Each of the twelve gates, which shall never be closed, will be made of pearl, with an angel at each gate (Rev. 21:12, 17, 21, 25, page 1315).

(c) *The foundations.* The wall will have twelve foundations, adorned with many assorted precious stones; on the foundations will be the names of the twelve apostles of the Lamb (Rev. 21:14, 19, 20, page 1315).

(d) *The street.* "The street of the city was pure gold, like transparent glass" (Rev. 21:21, page 1315).

(e) *The temple.* There will be no structural temple in the new heaven, new earth, or the New Jerusalem. John said, "I saw no temple in it, for the Lord God Almighty and the Lamb are its temple" (Rev. 21:22). Therefore, this new heaven and new earth are not a kingdom viewed in retrospect, for there will be a newly structured temple in the Great Tribulation (Matt. 24:15, page 973; Dan. 9:27, page 851), and in the Millennium (Rev. 15:8, page 1308).

(f) *The river of life.* "And he [the angel] showed me a pure river of water of life, clear as crystal, proceeding from the throne of God and of the Lamb" (Rev. 22:1, page 1315). This crystal river of life will flow out from the New Jerusalem to the nations of the new earth.

(g) *The tree of life.* "On either side of the river, was the tree of life, which bore twelve fruits, each tree yielding its fruit every month" (Rev. 22:1, 2, page 1315; Gen. 3:24, page 7). Yes, we will eat and drink in heaven.

(h) *The new eternal light.* This new heaven on earth will have a new light. It will be "like a jasper stone, clear as crystal" (Rev. 21:11, 23, 24, page 1315). The glory of God will light the city, and the nations. "There shall be no night there: They need no lamp nor light of the sun, for the Lord God gives them light. And they shall reign forever and ever" (Rev. 22:5, page 1316). The glory of God's essence will light the heaven, the earth, and the Holy City. The Lord Jesus Christ gave Peter, James, and John a glimpse of His glory on the mountain when He talked with Moses and Elijah, where He "was transfigured before them. His face shone like the sun, and His clothes became as white as the light" (Matt. 17:1-3, page 963). In God's new
(Point 17-C continued on next page)

And earth *is* My footstool.
Where *is* the house that you will build
    Me?
And where *is* the place of My rest?
2 For all those *things* My hand has made,
And all those *things* exist,"
    Says the LORD.
R"But on this *one* will I look:
  ROn *him who is* poor and of a contrite
    spirit,   [Is. 57:15; 61:1] • Ps. 34:18; 51:17
And who trembles at My word.

3 "HeR who kills a bull *is as if* he slays a
    man;   [Is. 1:10–17; 58:1–7]
He who sacrifices a lamb, *as if* he
  Rbreaks a dog's neck;   Deut. 23:18
He who offers a grain offering, *as if he
  offers* swine's blood;
He who burns incense, *as if* he blesses
    an idol.
Just as they have chosen their own
    ways,
And their soul delights in their
    abominations,

4 So will I choose their delusions,
And bring their fears on them;
  RBecause, when I called, no one
    answered,
When I spoke they did not hear;
But they did evil before My eyes,
And chose *that* in which I do not
    delight."   Is. 65:12

The LORD Vindicates Zion

5 Hear the word of the LORD,
You who tremble at His word:
"Your brethren who Rhated you,   Is. 60:15
Who cast you out for My name's sake,
    said,
R'Let the LORD be glorified,   Is. 5:19
That Rwe may see your joy.'   [Titus 2:13]
But they shall be ashamed."

6 The sound of noise from the city!
A voice from the temple!
The voice of the LORD,
Who fully repays His enemies!

(Point 17-C continued from previous page)
order, the bride and the nations of the world will bask in the effulgence of His glory, which will be the eternal light of the world. "This is the message which we have heard from Him and declare to you, that God is light and in Him is no darkness at all" (1 John 1:5, page 1278). "There shall be no night there" (Rev. 22:5, page 1316)—we will never need to sleep in heaven because God will be with His people forever and ever. That eternal light will radiate from the throne of God, in the New Jerusalem (Rev. 21:3, 23; 22:3, page 1315).

(4) The inhabitants of the new heaven, the new earth, and the New Jerusalem are to be

(a) God the Father, Son, and Holy Spirit (1 John 5:7, page 1282);
(b) The bride of Christ, the church, who will dwell in the New Jerusalem (Rev. 21:9, 10, page 1315);
(c) The Old Testament saints who will occupy the new earth (Is. 65:22, page 705; Heb. 11:10, 13–16, page 1248; Rev. 21:3, page 1315);
(d) The Tribulation and millennial saints who will also occupy the heaven on earth outside the New Jerusalem—the eternal home of the bride of Christ (Matt. 25:31–46, page 976). All the inhabitants of the new earth will have eternal access to the Holy City, where the twelve gates of pearl will never be closed (Rev. 21:24–26, page 1315);
(e) Angels who will worship and serve God (Heb. 12:22, 23, page 1251). They will also serve the bride and the nations.

The Lamb's wife and the nations will be busy worshiping and serving the Father, Son, and Holy Spirit. We will have perfect bodies, and therefore perfect brains. Throughout eternity we will be learning about all the wonders of our God. Paul said, "That in the ages to come [heaven] He might show the exceeding riches of His grace in His kindness toward us in Christ Jesus" (Eph. 2:7, page 1187). "But as it is written: 'Eye has not seen, nor ear heard, nor have entered into the heart of man the things which God has prepared for those who love Him'" (1 Cor. 2:9, page 1149; Is. 64:4, page 703). It will take ages upon ages for God to show us the greatness of His grace.

(5) In the new heaven "there shall be no more curse" on man, beast, or the earth (Rev. 22:3–5, page 1316; Gen. 3:14–19, page 7).

(a) There will be no tears or crying (Rev. 21:4, page 1315). There will never be a reason to cry.
(b) There will be no more death or separation (Rev. 21:4, page 1315; Rom. 8:38, 39, page 1138). Death is man's last enemy to be destroyed (1 Cor. 15:26, page 1162).
(c) There will be no sorrow, pain, or suffering, "for the former things have passed away" forever and ever (Rev. 21:4, page 1315).
(d) There will be no sin or sinners (Rev. 21:7, 8, page 1315; 22:14, 15, page 1316); only those who by faith have "washed their robes and made them white in the blood of the Lamb" (Rev. 7:9–17, page 1300; 1 Pet. 1:18, 19, page 1263), "who are written in the Lamb's Book of Life" (Rev. 21:27, page 1315).

When John saw and heard all this, he said, "Amen. Even so [he prayed], come, Lord Jesus!" (Rev. 22:20, page 1317). We shall see our God face to face, and reign with Him forever and ever (Rev. 22:4, 5, page 1316). See Psalm 9:17, page 515, for **Point 17-D: Hell Is a Place.**

7 "Before she was in labor, she gave birth;
  Before her pain came,
  She delivered a male child.
8 Who has heard such a thing?
  Who has seen such things?
  Shall the earth be made to give birth in
    one day?
  Or shall a nation be born at once?
  For as soon as Zion was in labor,
  She gave birth to her children.
9 Shall I bring to the time of birth, and
    not cause delivery?" says the LORD.
  "Shall I who cause delivery shut up *the
    womb?*" says your God.
10 "Rejoice with Jerusalem,
  And be glad with her, all you who love
    her;
  Rejoice for joy with her, all you who
    mourn for her;
11 That you may feed and be satisfied
  With the consolation of her bosom,
  That you may drink deeply and be
    delighted
  With the abundance of her glory."

12 For thus says the LORD:

  "Behold, ᴿI will extend peace to her like
    a river,   Is. 48:18; 60:5
  And the glory of the Gentiles like a
    flowing stream.
  Then you shall ᴿfeed;   Is. 60:16
  On *her* sides shall you be carried,
  And be dandled on *her* knees.
13 As one whom his mother comforts,
  So I will ᴿcomfort you;
  And you shall be comforted in
    Jerusalem."   Is. 51:3

The Reign and Indignation of God

14 When you see *this,* your heart shall
    rejoice,
  And ᴿyour bones shall flourish like
    grass;   Ezek. 37:1
  The hand of the LORD shall be known
    to His servants,
  And *His* indignation to His enemies.

15 ᴿFor behold, the LORD will come with
    fire
  And with His chariots, like a whirlwind,
  To render His anger with fury,   Is. 9:5
  And His rebuke with flames of fire.
16 For by fire and by ᴿHis sword
  The LORD will judge all flesh;
  And the slain of the LORD shall be
    ᴿmany.   Is. 27:1 • Is. 34:6

17 "Thoseᴿ who sanctify themselves and
  purify themselves,
  To go to the gardens
  ᵀAfter an *idol* in the midst,
  Eating swine's flesh and the
    abomination and the mouse,
  Shall ᵀbe consumed together," says the
    LORD.   Is. 65:3–8 • Lit. *After one* • *come to an end*

18 "For I *know* their works and their
ᴿthoughts. It shall be that I will ᴿgather all
nations and tongues; and they shall come and
see My glory.   Is. 59:7 • Jer. 3:17
19 "I will set a sign among them; and those
among them who escape I will send to the
nations: *to* Tarshish and *Pul and Lud, who
draw the bow, and Tubal and Javan, *to* the
coastlands afar off who have not heard My
fame nor seen My glory. And they shall
declare My glory among the Gentiles.
20 "Then they shall ᴿbring all your brethren
ᴿfor an offering to the LORD out of all nations,
on horses and in chariots and in litters, on
mules and on camels, to My holy mountain
Jerusalem," says the LORD, "as the children of
Israel bring an offering in a clean vessel into
the house of the LORD.   Is. 49:22 • [Rom. 15:16]
21 "And I will also take some of them for
ᴿpriests *and* Levites," says the LORD.   Ex. 19:6

34–G. From the Millennium to the New ▼
Heaven and the New Earth

22 "For as ᴿthe new heavens and the new
    earth
  Which I will make shall remain before
  Me," says the LORD,

66:19 So with MT, Tg., [Vg.]; LXX *Put* (cf. Jer. 46:9)

34-G. From the Millennium to the New Heaven and the New Earth (1000 years) (Isaiah 66:22, 23)—These
are some of the prophecies pertaining to Israel that will come to pass during the millennial reign of Christ:

(1) Satan, the accuser of the brethren (Israel) will be cast out of heaven in the middle of the seven-year
Tribulation (Rev. 12:7–12, page 1305), and at the beginning of the kingdom age will be imprisoned in the
bottomless pit for a thousand years (Rev. 20:1, 3, page 1313).

(2) The Tribulation saints who willingly become martyrs for Christ and the gospel of the kingdom will be
resurrected and will enter the kingdom with Christ (Rev. 20:4, 5, page 1313).

(3) The judgment of the nations (Matt. 25:31–46, page 976). These are people out of all the nations on
the earth who will have lived through the Tribulation. These are divided into three groups:

  (a) *Sheep.* They are the saved from all nations (Rev. 7:9–17, page 1300).
  (b) *Goats.* They are the lost of all nations (Matt. 25:41, page 976).
  (c) *Brethren.* They are the saved Israel (Rev. 7:1–8, page 1300).

(Point 34-G continued on next page)

▽   "So shall your descendants and your
        name remain.   Rev. 21:1
   23 And ᴿit shall come to pass   Zech. 14:16
        That from one New Moon to another,
        And from one Sabbath to another,
        ᴿAll flesh shall come to worship before
▲   Me," says the LORD.   Zech. 14:17-21

24 "And they shall go forth and look
    Upon the corpses of the men
    Who have transgressed against Me.
    For their ᴿworm does not die,
    And their fire is not quenched.
    They shall be an abhorrence to all
    flesh."   Mark 9:44, 46, 48

(Point 34-G continued from previous page)
    (4) Israel will become innumerable in the kingdom age (Gen. 22:17, page 28; Heb. 11:12, 13, page 1248).
    (5) Longevity will be restored during the Millennium (Is. 65:20, page 705).
    (6) At the end of the thousand years, Satan will be released from the bottomless pit, "and will go out to
deceive the nations" (Rev. 20:7, 8), and shall raise a huge army of unbelievers to fight against the saints and
the beloved city. During the thousand years, children will be born to those who enter the kingdom in their
physical bodies (Matt. 25:34, page 976). They will be born in sin and will need to be saved by faith in Christ.
Not all will believe, even under the perfect condition of the kingdom. Satan will deceive them, and God will
destroy them with fire from heaven (Rev. 20:7-9, page 1313).
    (7) Then will come the new heaven and the new earth (Rev. 21:1, page 1314; 2 Pet. 3:12, 13, page 1276;
Is. 65:17, page 704). God promised Abraham and his descendants the land forever (Gen. 13:14, 15, page 19).
God will keep His promise to Abraham and give the land to his "descendants forever." The history of Israel
is without parallel. It is the only ancient civilization to have been utterly destroyed and yet to have been
raised again to a place of prestige among the nations.

    See Index, page 17, for your next study.

THE BOOK OF
Jeremiah

AUTHORSHIP. These are the words of Jeremiah, the warning, weeping, and sometimes willing prophet of God. He was the son of Hilkiah, one of the priests of the city of Anathoth, in the territory of Benjamin (1:1). His hometown was about two-and-one-half miles northeast of Jerusalem, and he was born into a family of exiled priests (1 Kin. 2:26). Although Jeremiah is the confirmed author of this writing, his scribe, Baruch, collected the prophecies.

CONTEXT. The events described in this book took place between 626 B.C. and 587 B.C., and unlike Isaiah, Jeremiah is not chronological. Rather, it is an arrangement of Jeremiah's prophecies through this forty-year period of Judah's history. Jeremiah is seen to be a heartbroken prophet with a heartbreaking message. He labored almost half a century proclaiming a message of judgment and doom to the stiff-necked people of Judah. Although the prophecies themselves are difficult to arrange either chronologically or topically, their overall message comes through loud and clear: Surrender to God's will is the only way to escape judgment.

HOW JEREMIAH FITS INTO THE BIBLE. This writing is a part of the history of the kingdom of Judah. Following Solomon's death, his kingdom was divided into the northern kingdom (Israel) and the southern kingdom (Judah). Judah experienced four religious declines and three religious revivals. Josiah was the last good king, and Jeremiah began to prophesy in the thirteenth year of his reign, after the king had already begun a reformation. After the final revival, Judean history is marked by decline, not only in religious life but also in political and moral life. This decline eventually culminated in the Babylonian exile.

During this dark period of Judah's history—with the mighty army of Nebuchadnezzar, king of Babylon, preparing to march against Jerusalem—Jeremiah delivered his prophecies. He presented Jehovah, the God of Israel, as the sovereign Creator and Lord of all peoples and nations, the only true God, who hates idolatry and the immorality it produces.

SUMMARY STATEMENT. The book of Jeremiah is God's final, last-minute call to Judah, and its theme is the judgment and certain destruction of Jerusalem.

KEY VERSES: 7:23, 24; 8:11, 12. Chapter 31 is key also because of the promises found therein. Even though God's people have broken His covenant, He will make a new covenant whereby He will "put My law in their minds, and write it on their hearts; and I will be their God, and they shall be My people" (31:33).

HOW JEREMIAH FITS TOGETHER. Chapter 1 deals with the call of Jeremiah; chapters 2—45 are the prophecies to Judah; chapters 46—51 are a series of prophecies against nine Gentile nations; and chapter 52 deals with the fall of Jerusalem.

In the opening verses of the book, Jeremiah is spoken of as having been chosen to be a prophet before he was born (1:5). He received his call at quite an early age, and he was forbidden to take a wife, due to the certain misery and doom that was forthcoming. God spared His servant (and emphasized to His people) the many sorrows of being a husband and father during this time. Jeremiah was a prophet for many years; in fact, he prophesied for approximately half of a century. He is characterized as a reproving prophet, a weeping prophet, and a suffering prophet.

The style of Jeremiah's writing is plain enough to be understood by people in every walk of life. The time had come in Judah's history when plain talk was more needful than fancy words. He presented a clear, last-minute warning to Judah, which was on the brink of national ruin, due to moral and spiritual decay. Jeremiah condemned the soft, soothing words of the false prophets and corrupt priests who cried "Peace, peace!" when there was and would be no peace (6:14; 8:11).

Jeremiah's message of judgment and doom was unpopular, causing him to suffer ridicule and persecution, but it was the true message of his Lord. At a certain point in Jeremiah's ministry, he wanted to quit his unpopular task and escape the burden of his commitment: "Oh, that I had in the wilderness a lodging place for travelers; that I might leave my people, and go from them!" (9:2). To Jeremiah's credit, however, he did not leave his people, but stayed on the job, suffering their abuse, as he faithfully proclaimed the message of God.

Although the warning was clear, Judah failed to repent, which resulted in the Babylonian captivity. Jeremiah listed the moral and spiritual causes for their catastrophe, but he also brought

the good news of God's gracious promise of hope and restoration. There would always be a handful of survivors, a faithful remnant with whom God would establish a new covenant (31:31–34).

Jeremiah's prophecy of the new covenant was given its foundation in the ministry, crucifixion, and resurrection of the Lord Jesus Christ (Matt. 26:28; Mark 14:24; Luke 22:20; 1 Cor. 11:25; Heb. 7:22—9:20; 10:16, 29; 12:24; 13:20). The very term "The New Testament" means "The New Covenant."

Just as Jeremiah spoke plainly to Judah in the hour of her greatest need, today it is important also that God's message of salvation and judgment be clearly proclaimed to the world in this time of spiritual and moral crisis. The apostle Paul said that God has made us "ministers of the new covenant" (2 Cor. 3:6). Just as Jeremiah faithfully delivered God's message, so today men called to the ministry are to proclaim the Word of God with authority and power. Every believer in Jesus Christ is a minister of one sort or another, according to the gifts bestowed upon him by the Holy Spirit.

Following in the footsteps of Jesus—and also in the footsteps of Jeremiah—may bring ridicule and persecution, for the truth of God is still unpopular to the unbelieving world. But, as the Lord Jesus Christ said, "Blessed are those who are persecuted for righteousness' sake, for theirs is the kingdom of heaven. Blessed are you when they revile and persecute you, and say all kinds of evil against you falsely for My sake. Rejoice and be exceedingly glad, for great is your reward in heaven, for so they persecuted the prophets who were before you" (Matt. 5:10–12).

—F.W.O.

THE words of Jeremiah the son of Hilkiah, of the priests who were ᴿin Anathoth in the land of Benjamin, Josh. 21:18 2 to whom the word of the LORD came in the days of Josiah the son of Amon, king of Judah, in the thirteenth year of his reign.

3 It came also in the days of ᴿJehoiakim the son of Josiah, king of Judah, ᴿuntil the end of the eleventh year of Zedekiah the son of Josiah, king of Judah, ᴿuntil the carrying away of Jerusalem captive ᴿin the fifth month.   2 Kin. 23:34 • Jer. 39:2 • Jer. 52:12 • 2 Kin. 25:8

The Prophet Is Called

4 Then the word of the LORD came to me, saying:

5 "Before I ᴿformed you in the womb ᴿI knew you;   Is. 49:1, 5 • Ex. 33:12
Before you were born I ᴿsanctifiedᵀ you;
I ᵀordained you a prophet to the nations."   [Luke 1:15] • set you apart • appointed

▼ 32-C. The Prayer of an Inadequate Man

6 Then said I:
ᴿ"Ah, Lord GOD!
Behold, I cannot speak, for I am a youth."   Ex. 4:10; 6:12, 30

7 But the LORD said to me:
"Do not say, 'I am a youth,'
For you shall go to all to whom I send you,

And ᴿwhatever I command you, you shall speak.   Num. 22:20, 38
8 ᴿDo not be afraid of their faces,
For ᴿI am with you to deliver you," says the LORD.   Ezek. 2:6; 3:9 • Ex. 3:12

9 Then the LORD put forth His hand and ᴿtouched my mouth, and the LORD said to me:

"Behold, I have ᴿput My words in your mouth.   Is. 6:7 • Is. 51:16
10 See, I have this day set you over the nations and over the kingdoms,
To ᴿroot out and to pull down,
To destroy and to throw down,
To build and to plant."   [2 Cor. 10:4, 5]

11 Moreover the word of the LORD came to me, saying, "Jeremiah, what do you see?" And I said, "I see a ᵀbranch of an almond tree."   Lit. rod
12 Then the LORD said to me, "You have seen well, for I am ᵀready to perform My word."   Lit. watching
13 And the word of the LORD came to me the second time, saying, "What do you see?" And I said, "I see ᴿa boiling pot, and it is facing away from the north."   Ezek. 11:3; 24:3
14 Then the LORD said to me:

"Out of the ᴿnorth calamity shall break forth   Jer. 6:1
On all the inhabitants of the land.
15 For behold, I am ᴿcalling   Jer. 6:22; 25:9

32-C. The Prayer of an Inadequate Man (Jeremiah 1:6)—God announced to Jeremiah that he was His chosen prophet to address nations, kings, and peoples (vv. 4, 5). From the chronological data of verses 2 and 3 we learn that the years of his prophecy were from 627 B.C. to 586 B.C., forty-two years of proclaiming dreadful judgment on a hardened people. However,

(Point 32-C continued on next page)

All the families of the kingdoms of the
north," says the LORD;
"They shall come and ᴿeach one set his
throne   Jer. 39:3
At the entrance of the gates of
Jerusalem,
Against all its walls all around,
And against all the cities of Judah.
16 I will utter My judgments
Against them concerning all their
wickedness,
Because ᴿthey have forsaken Me,
Burned ᴿincense to other gods,
And worshiped the works of their own
ᴿhands.   Deut. 28:20 • Jer. 7:9 • Is. 37:19

17 "Therefore ᴿprepare yourself and arise,
And speak to them all that I command
you.   Job 38:3
ᴿDo not be dismayed before their faces,
Lest I dismay you before them.   Ezek. 2:6
18 For behold, I have made you this day
ᴿA fortified city and an iron pillar,
And bronze walls against the whole
land—   Is. 50:7
Against the kings of Judah,
Against its princes,
Against its priests,
And against the people of the land.
19 They will fight against you,
But they shall not prevail against you.
For I am with you," says the LORD, "to
deliver you."

God's Case Against Israel

2 Moreover the word of the LORD came to
me, saying,
2 "Go and cry in the hearing of Jerusalem,
saying, 'Thus says the LORD:

"I remember you,
The kindness of your ᴿyouth,   Ezek. 16:8
The love of your betrothal,
ᴿWhen you ᵀwent after Me in the
wilderness,   Deut. 2:7 • followed
In a land not sown.
3 ᴿIsrael was holiness to the LORD,
The firstfruits of His increase.
All that devour him will offend;
Disaster will ᴿcome upon them," says
the LORD.'"   [Ex. 19:5, 6] • Is. 41:11

4 Hear the word of the LORD, O house of
Jacob and all the families of the house of
Israel.
5 Thus says the LORD:

ᴿ"What injustice have your fathers found
in Me,   Is. 5:4
That they have gone far from Me,
Have followed ᵀidols,   vanities or futilities
And have become idolaters?
6 Neither did they say, 'Where is the
LORD,
Who ᴿbrought us up out of the land of
Egypt,   Is. 63:11
Who led us through ᴿthe wilderness,
Through a land of deserts and pits,
Through a land of drought and the
shadow of death,   Deut. 8:15; 32:10
Through a land that no one crossed
And where no one dwelt?'
7 I brought you into ᴿa bountiful country,
To eat its fruit and its goodness.
But when you entered, you ᴿdefiled My
land   Num. 13:27 • Num. 35:33
And made My heritage an abomination.
8 The priests did not say, 'Where is the
LORD?'

(Point 32-C continued from previous page)
(1) they would not listen to his call for repentance;
(2) they disbelieved his warning that God was going to permit pagan Babylon to pull down the temple
of Jehovah;
(3) they hated him for even uttering God's message of doom.

When he was called, Jeremiah perhaps already sensed the sinfulness of the age, and that his role would
be to warn and to rebuke. The rulers of the nation and its cities were called "elders" (Ezra 10:14, page 452).
He lived in an age when the elderly were respected and when young people kept silent in their presence. So
Jeremiah, who must have been a young man at the time, might well be overwhelmed at the prospect of such
a ministry. Plainly, Jeremiah sensed his own inadequacy as he faced the mission which God had called him
to perform. Many times the believer shares with Jeremiah this sense of personal insufficiency. So we join him
in voicing our own prayer of inadequacy.

In verse 6, Jeremiah's prayer disclaims both

(1) his ability, "I cannot speak";
(2) his person, "I am a youth."

God's reply contains several lessons for us (vv. 7-10).

(1) Don't make excuses (when I, God, call you).
(2) I shall go with you (I am wiser, stronger than they).
(3) You shall be speaking My words (I always speak truth).
(4) Do not fear them (I, God, can and will deliver you).
(5) Your authority comes from Me (I rule over nations and kingdoms).

Whenever we feel inadequate to do God's will, let us turn away from our doubts, and pray for God's
presence and strength to become our sufficiency.

See Jeremiah 12:1-4, page 724, for **Point 32-D: The Prayer of a Puzzled Prophet.**

And those who handle the ᴿlaw did not
know Me;   Rom. 2:20
The rulers also transgressed against Me;
ᴿThe prophets prophesied by Baal,
And walked after *things that* do not
profit.   Jer. 23:13

9 "Therefore ᴿI will yet ᵀbring charges
against you," says the Lᴏʀᴅ,
"And against your children's children I
will bring charges.   Mic. 6:2 • *contend with*
10 For pass beyond the coasts of *Cyprus
and see,
Send to *Kedar and consider diligently,
And see if there has been such *a* thing.
11 ᴿHas a nation changed *its* gods,
Which *are* ᴿnot gods?
ᴿBut My people have changed their
Glory   Mic. 4:5 • Is. 37:19 • Rom. 1:23
For *what* does not profit.
12 Be astonished, O heavens, at this,
And be horribly afraid;
Be very desolate," says the Lᴏʀᴅ.
13 "For My people have committed two
evils:
They have forsaken Me, the ᴿfountain
of living waters,   Ps. 36:9
And hewn themselves cisterns—broken
cisterns that can hold no water.

14 "*Is* Israel ᴿa servant?
Is he a homeborn *slave?*
Why is he plundered?   [Ex. 4:22]
15 ᴿThe young lions roared at him, *and*
growled;
They made his land waste;
His cities are burned, without
inhabitant.   Is. 1:7
16 Also the people of ᵀNoph and
Tahpanhes   Memphis in ancient Egypt
Have broken the crown of your head.
17 ᴿHave you not brought this on yourself,
In that you have forsaken the Lᴏʀᴅ
your God   Jer. 4:18
When ᴿHe led you in the way?   Deut. 32:10
18 And now why take the road to Egypt,
To drink the waters of ᴿSihor?   Josh. 13:3
Or why take the road to Assyria,
To drink the waters of *the River?
19 Your own wickedness will ᴿcorrect you,
And your backslidings will rebuke you.
Know therefore and see that *it is* an
evil and bitter *thing*   Jer. 4:18
That you have forsaken the Lᴏʀᴅ your
God,
And the ᵀfear of Me *is* not in you,"
Says the Lord Gᴏᴅ of hosts.   *dread*

20 "For of old I have ᴿbroken your yoke
and burst your bonds;   Lev. 26:13

2:10 Heb. *Kittim,* representative of western cultures • In
northern Arabian desert, representative of eastern
cultures
2:18 The Euphrates

And ᴿyou said, 'I will not *transgress,'
When ᴿon every high hill and under
every green tree   Judg. 10:16 • Deut. 12:2
You lay down, playing the harlot.
21 Yet I had ᴿplanted you a noble vine, a
seed of highest quality.
How then have you turned before Me
Into ᴿthe degenerate plant of an alien
vine?   Ex. 15:17 • Is. 5:4
22 For though you wash yourself with lye,
and use much soap,
Yet your iniquity is ᵀmarked before
Me," says the Lord Gᴏᴅ.   *stained*

23 "HowᴿR can you say, 'I am not ᵀpolluted,
I have not gone after the Baals'?
See your way in the valley;
Know what you have done:
You are a swift dromedary breaking
loose in her ways,   Prov. 30:12 • *defiled*
24 A wild donkey used to the wilderness,
That sniffs at the wind in her desire;
In her time of mating, who can turn
her away?
All those who seek her will not weary
themselves;
In her month they will find her.
25 Withhold your foot from being unshod,
and your throat from thirst.
But you said, ᴿ'There is no hope.
No! For I have loved ᴿaliens, and after
them I will go.'   Jer. 18:12 • Jer. 3:13

26 "As the thief is ashamed when he is
found out,
So is the house of Israel ashamed;
They and their kings and their princes,
and their priests and their prophets,
27 Saying to a tree, 'You *are* my father,'
And to a ᴿstone, 'You gave birth to me.'
For they have turned *their* back to Me,
and not *their* face.   Jer. 3:9
But in the time of their ᴿtrouble   Is. 26:16
They will say, 'Arise and save us.'
28 But ᴿwhere *are* your gods that you
have made for yourselves?   Judg. 10:14
Let them arise,
If they ᴿcan save you in the time of
your ᵀtrouble;   Is. 45:20 • Or *evil*
For ᴿaccording *to* the number of your
cities   Jer. 11:13
Are your gods, O Judah.

29 "Why will you plead with Me?
You all have transgressed against Me,"
says the Lᴏʀᴅ.
30 "In vain I have ᴿchastened your
children;
They received no correction.   Is. 9:13
Your sword has ᴿdevoured your
prophets
Like a destroying lion.   Neh. 9:26

2:20 Kt. *serve*

31 "O generation, see the word of the LORD!
   Have I been a wilderness to Israel,
   Or a land of darkness?
   Why do My people say, 'We are lords;
   ^RWe will come no more to You'? Deut. 32:15
32 Can a virgin forget her ornaments,
   Or a bride her attire?
   Yet My people ^Rhave forgotten Me days
   without number.   Ps. 106:21
33 "Why do you beautify your way to seek
   love?
   Therefore you have also taught
   The wicked women your ways.
34 Also on your skirts is found
   ^RThe blood of the lives of the poor
   innocents.   Ps. 106:38
   I have not found it by ^Tsecret search,
   But plainly on all these things.   digging
35 ^RYet you say, 'Because I am innocent,
   Surely His anger shall turn from me.'
   Behold, ^RI will plead My case against
   you,   Jer. 2:23, 29 · Jer. 2:9
   Because you say, 'I have not sinned.'
36 ^RWhy do you gad about so much to
   change your way?   Hos. 5:13; 12:1
   Also ^Ryou shall be ashamed of Egypt as
   you were ashamed of Assyria.   Is. 30:3
37 Indeed you will go forth from him
   With your hands on ^Ryour head;
   For the LORD has rejected your trusted
   allies,   2 Sam. 13:19
   And you will not prosper by them.

Israel Is Shameless

3 "They say, 'If a man divorces his wife,
   And she goes from him
   And becomes another man's,
   ^RMay he return to her again?'
   Would not that ^Rland be greatly
   polluted?   Deut. 24:1-4 · Jer. 2:7
   But you have ^Rplayed the harlot with
   many lovers;   Ezek. 16:26
   Yet return to Me," says the LORD.

2 "Lift up your eyes to ^Rthe desolate
   heights and see: Deut. 12:2
   Where have you not *lain *with men*?
   ^RBy the road you have sat for them
   Like an Arabian in the wilderness;
   ^RAnd you have polluted the land
   With your harlotries and your
   wickedness.   Prov. 23:28 · Jer. 2:7
3 Therefore the ^Rshowers have been
   withheld,   Lev. 26:19
   And there has been no latter rain.
   You have had a ^Rharlot's forehead;
   You refuse to be ashamed.   Zeph. 3:5
4 Will you not from this time cry to Me,
   'My Father, You *are* ^Rthe guide of ^Rmy
   youth?   Prov. 2:17 · Jer. 2:2
5 ^RWill He remain angry forever?
   Will He keep it to the end?'

3:2 Kt. *been violated*

Behold, you have spoken and done evil
   things,
As you were able."   [Is. 57:16]

A Call to Repentance

6 The LORD said also to me in the days of
Josiah the king: "Have you seen what backsliding Israel has done? She has ^Rgone up on
every high mountain and under every green
tree, and there played the harlot.   Jer. 2:20
7 "And I said, after she had done all these
things, 'Return to Me.' But she did not return.
And her treacherous sister Judah saw it.
8 "Then I saw that ^Rfor all the causes for
which backsliding Israel had committed adultery, I had ^Rput her away and given her a
certificate of divorce; ^Ryet her treacherous
sister Judah did not fear, but went and played
the harlot also.   Ezek. 23:9 · 2 Kin. 17:6 · Ezek. 23:11
9 "So it came to pass, through her casual
harlotry, that she defiled the land and committed adultery with stones and trees.
10 "And yet for all this her treacherous
sister Judah has not turned to Me with her
whole heart, but in pretense," says the LORD.
11 Then the LORD said to me, ^R"Backsliding
Israel has shown herself more righteous than
treacherous Judah.   Ezek. 16:51, 52
12 "Go and proclaim these words toward
^Rthe north, and say: 2 Kin. 17:6

   'Return, backsliding Israel,' says the
     LORD;
   'I will not cause My anger to fall on
     you.
   For I *am* merciful,' says the LORD;
   'I will not remain angry forever.
13 ^ROnly acknowledge your iniquity,
   That you have transgressed against the
     LORD your God,   Deut. 30:1, 2
   And have ^Rscattered your ^Tcharms
   To ^Ralien deities under every green
     tree,   Ezek. 16:15 · Lit. *ways* · Jer. 2:25
   And you have not obeyed My voice,'
     says the LORD.

14 "Return, O backsliding children," says
the LORD; "for I am married to you. I will
take you, one from a city and two from a
family, and I will bring you to Zion.
15 "And I will give you shepherds according to My heart, who will ^Rfeed you with
knowledge and understanding.   Acts 20:28
16 "Then it shall come to pass, when you
are multiplied and ^Rincreased in the land in
those days," says the LORD, "that they will
say no more, 'The ark of the covenant of the
LORD.' ^RIt shall not come to mind, nor shall
they remember it, nor shall they visit *it*, nor
shall it be made anymore. Is. 49:19 · Is. 65:17
17 "At that time Jerusalem shall be called
The Throne of the LORD, and all the nations
shall be gathered to it, to the name of the
LORD, to Jerusalem. No more shall they follow the dictates of their evil hearts.

18 "In those days ᴿthe house of Judah shall walk with the house of Israel, and they shall come together out of the land of ᴿthe north to ᴿthe land that I have given as an inheritance to your fathers.   Is. 11:13 · Jer. 31:8 · Amos 9:15

19 "But I said:

'How can I put you among the children
And give you ᴿa pleasant land,
A beautiful heritage of the hosts of
    nations?'   Ps. 106:24

"And I said:

'You shall call Me, ᴿ"My Father,"
And not turn away from Me.'   Is. 63:16

20 Surely, *as* a wife treacherously departs
    from her ᵀhusband,   Lit. *companion*
So ᴿhave you dealt treacherously with
    Me,   Is. 48:8
O house of Israel," says the Lᴏʀᴅ.

21 A voice was heard on ᴿthe desolate
    heights,
Weeping *and* supplications of the
    children of Israel.
For they have perverted their way;
They have forgotten the Lᴏʀᴅ their
    God.   Is. 15:2

22 "Return, you backsliding children,
    And I will ᴿheal your backslidings."

"Indeed we do come to You,   Hos. 6:1; 14:4
For You are the Lᴏʀᴅ our God.
23 ᴿTruly, in vain *is salvation hoped for*
    from the hills,   Ps. 121:1, 2
And from the multitude of mountains;
ᴿTruly, in the Lᴏʀᴅ our God   Ps. 3:8
Is the salvation of Israel.
24 ᴿFor shame has devoured
The labor of our fathers from our
    youth—
Their flocks and their herds,
Their sons and their daughters.   Hos. 9:10
25 We lie down in our shame,
And our ᵀreproach covers us.   *disgrace*
ᴿFor we have sinned against the Lᴏʀᴅ
    our God,   Ezra 9:6, 7
We and our fathers,
From our youth even to this day,
And ᴿhave not obeyed the voice of the
    Lᴏʀᴅ our God."   Jer. 22:21

4 "If you will return, O Israel," says the
    Lᴏʀᴅ,
ᴿ"Return to Me;   Joel 2:12
And if you will put away your
    abominations out of My sight,
Then you shall not be moved.
2 ᴿAnd you shall swear, 'The Lᴏʀᴅ lives,'
ᴿIn truth, in ᵀjudgment, and in
    righteousness;   Deut. 10:20 · Zech. 8:8 · *justice*
ᴿThe nations shall bless themselves in
    Him,   [Gen. 22:18]
And in Him they shall ᴿglory."   1 Cor. 1:31

3 For thus says the Lᴏʀᴅ to the men of Judah and Jerusalem:

ᴿ"Break up your fallow ground,   Hos. 10:12
And ᴿdo not sow among thorns.   Matt. 13:7
4 Circumcise yourselves to the Lᴏʀᴅ,
And take away the foreskins of your
    hearts,   Deut. 10:16; 30:6
You men of Judah and inhabitants of
    Jerusalem,
Lest My fury come forth like fire,
And burn so that no one can quench *it*,
Because of the evil of your doings."

An Imminent Invasion

5 Declare in Judah and proclaim in Jerusalem, and say:

ᴿ"Blow the trumpet in the land;
Cry, 'Gather together,'   Hos. 8:1
And say, ᴿ'Assemble yourselves,   Jer. 8:14
And let us go into the fortified cities.'
6 Set up the ᵀstandard toward Zion.
Take refuge! Do not delay!
For I will bring disaster from the
    ᴿnorth,   *banner* · Jer. 1:13–15; 6:1, 22; 50:17
And great destruction."

7 ᴿThe lion has come up from his thicket,
And ᴿthe destroyer of nations is on his
    way.   Dan. 7:4 · Jer. 25:9
He has gone forth from his place
ᴿTo make your land desolate.   Is. 1:7; 6:11
Your cities will be laid waste,
Without inhabitant.
8 For this, ᴿclothe yourself with
    sackcloth,   Is. 22:12
Lament and wail.
For the fierce anger of the Lᴏʀᴅ
Has not turned back from us.

9 "And it shall come to pass in that day,"
    says the Lᴏʀᴅ,
"*That* the heart of the king shall perish,
And the heart of the princes;
The priests shall be astonished,
And the prophets shall wonder."

10 Then I said, "Ah, Lord Gᴏᴅ!
ᴿSurely You have greatly deceived this
    people and Jerusalem,   Ezek. 14:9
ᴿSaying, 'You shall have peace,'
Whereas the sword reaches to the
    ᵀheart."   Jer. 5:12; 14:13 · *soul*

11 At that time it will be said
To this people and to Jerusalem,
ᴿ"A dry wind of the desolate heights
    blows in the wilderness   Hos. 13:15
Toward the daughter of My people—
Not to fan or to cleanse—
12 A wind too strong for these will come
    for Me;
Now ᴿI will also speak judgment
    against them."   Jer. 1:16

13 "Behold, he shall come up like clouds,
   And his chariots like a whirlwind.
   His horses are swifter than eagles.
   Woe to us, for we are plundered!"

14 O Jerusalem, ^Rwash your heart from
   wickedness,   James 4:8
   That you may be saved.
   How long shall your evil thoughts lodge
   within you?

15 For a voice declares ^Rfrom Dan
   And proclaims ^Taffliction from Mount
   Ephraim: Jer. 8:16; 50:17 · Or wickedness

16 "Make mention to the nations,
   Yes, proclaim against Jerusalem,
   That watchers come from a ^Rfar
   country   Is. 39:3
   And raise their voice against the cities
   of Judah.

17 ^RLike keepers of a field they are against
   her all around,   2 Kin. 25:1, 4
   Because she has been rebellious against
   Me," says the LORD.

18 "Your^R ways and your doings   Is. 50:1
   Have procured these things for you.
   This is your wickedness,
   Because it is bitter,
   Because it reaches to your heart."

Sorrow for the Doomed Nation

19 O my ^Rsoul, my soul!
   I am pained in my very heart!
   My heart makes a noise in me;
   I cannot hold my peace,
   Because you have heard, O my soul,
   The sound of the trumpet,
   The alarm of war.   Is. 15:5; 16:11; 21:3; 22:4

20 Destruction upon destruction is cried,
   For the whole land is plundered.
   Suddenly ^Rmy tents are plundered,
   And my curtains in a moment.   Jer. 10:20

21 How long will I see the standard,
   And hear the sound of the trumpet?

22 "For My people are foolish,
   They have not known Me.
   They are ^Tsilly children,   foolish
   And they have no understanding.
   ^RThey are wise to do evil,   Rom. 16:19
   But to do good they have no
   knowledge."

23 ^RI beheld the earth, and indeed it was
   without form, and void;   Is. 24:19
   And the heavens, they had no light.

24 ^RI beheld the mountains, and indeed
   they trembled,   Ezek. 38:20
   And all the hills moved back and forth.

25 I beheld, and indeed there was no man,
   And ^Rall the birds of the heavens had
   fled.   Zeph. 1:3

26 I beheld, and indeed the fruitful land
   was a ^Rwilderness,   Jer. 9:10
   And all its cities were broken down

At the presence of the LORD,
By His fierce anger.

27 For thus says the LORD:

   "The whole land shall be desolate;
   Yet I will not make a full end.

28 For this ^Rshall the earth mourn,
   And ^Rthe heavens above be black,
   Because I have spoken.   Hos. 4:3 · Is. 50:3
   I have ^Rpurposed and will not relent,
   Nor will I turn back from it.   [Dan. 4:35]

29 The whole city shall flee from the noise
   of the horsemen and bowmen.
   They shall go into thickets and climb
   up on the rocks.
   Every city shall be forsaken,
   And not a man shall dwell in it.

30 "And when you are plundered,
   What will you do?
   Though you clothe yourself with
   crimson,
   Though you adorn yourself with
   ornaments of gold,
   ^RThough you enlarge your eyes with
   paint,   2 Kin. 9:30
   In vain you will make yourself fair;
   ^RYour lovers will despise you;
   They will seek your life.   Jer. 22:20, 22

31 "For I have heard a voice as of a woman
   in ^Tlabor,   childbirth
   The anguish as of her who brings forth
   her first child,
   The voice of the daughter of Zion
   bewailing herself;
   She ^Rspreads her hands, saying,
   'Woe is me now, for my soul is ^Tweary
   Because of murderers!'   Lam. 1:17 · faint

The Justice of God's Judgment

5 "Run to and fro through the streets of
   Jerusalem;
   See now and know;
   And seek in her open places
   ^RIf you can find a man,   Ezek. 22:30
   ^RIf there is anyone who executes
   ^Tjudgment,   Gen. 18:23-32 · justice
   Who seeks the truth,
   ^RAnd I will pardon her.   Gen. 18:26

2 Though they say, 'As ^Rthe LORD lives,'
   Surely they ^Rswear falsely."   Jer. 4:2 · Jer. 7:9

3 O LORD, are not ^RYour eyes on the
   truth?   [2 Chr. 16:9]
   You have ^Rstricken them,
   But they have not grieved;
   You have consumed them,
   But ^Rthey have refused to receive
   correction.   Is. 1:5; 9:13 · Zeph. 3:2
   They have made their faces harder than
   rock;
   They have refused to return.

4 Therefore I said, "Surely these *are* poor.
   They are foolish;
   For ᴿthey do not know the way of the
   LORD,   Jer. 8:7
   The judgment of their God.
5 I will go to the great men and speak to
   them,
   For ᴿthey have known the way of the
   LORD,   Mic. 3:1
   The judgment of their God."

   But these have altogether ᴿbroken the
   yoke   Ps. 2:3
   And burst the bonds.
6 Therefore ᴿa lion from the forest shall
   slay them,   Jer. 4:7
   ᴿA wolf of the deserts shall destroy
   them;   Zeph. 3:3
   ᴿA leopard will watch over their cities.
   Everyone who goes out from there shall
   be torn in pieces,   Hos. 13:7
   Because their transgressions are many;
   Their backslidings have increased.

7 "How shall I pardon you for this?
   Your children have forsaken Me
   And ᴿsworn by *those* ᴿ*that are* not
   gods.
   When I had fed them to the full,
   Then they committed adultery
   And assembled themselves by troops in
   the harlots' houses.   Zeph. 1:5 • Deut. 32:21
8 ᴿThey were *like* well-fed lusty stallions;
   Every one neighed after his neighbor's
   wife.   Ezek. 22:11
9 Shall I not punish *them* for these
   things?" says the LORD.
   "And shall I not ᴿavenge Myself on such
   a nation as this?   Jer. 9:9
10 "Go up on her walls and destroy,
   But do not make a ᴿcomplete end.
   Take away her branches,   Jer. 4:27
   For they *are* not the LORD's.
11 For ᴿthe house of Israel and the house
   of Judah   Jer. 3:6, 7, 20
   Have dealt very treacherously with
   Me," says the LORD.

12 They have lied about the LORD,
   And said, ᴿ"*It is* not He.   Jer. 23:17
   Neither will evil come upon us,
   Nor shall we see sword or famine.
13 And the prophets become wind,
   For the word *is* not in them.
   Thus shall it be done to them."

14 Therefore thus says the LORD God of
hosts:

   "Because you speak this word,
   ᴿBehold, I will make My words in your
   mouth fire,   Jer. 1:9; 23:29
   And this people wood,
   And it shall devour them.
15 Behold, I will bring a ᴿnation against
   you ᴿfrom afar,   Deut. 28:49 • Jer. 4:16

O house of Israel," says the LORD.
"It *is* a mighty nation,
   It *is* an ancient nation,
   A nation whose language you do not
   know,
   Nor can you understand what they say.
16 Their quiver *is* like an open tomb;
   They *are* all mighty men.
17 And they shall eat up your ᴿharvest and
   your bread,   Lev. 26:16
   Which your sons and daughters should
   eat.
   They shall eat up your flocks and your
   herds;
   They shall eat up your vines and your
   fig trees;
   They shall destroy your fortified cities,
   In which you trust, with the sword.

18 "Nevertheless in those days," says the
LORD, "I ᴿwill not ᵀmake a complete end of
you.   Jer. 30:11 • *completely destroy*
19 "And it will be when you say, ᴿ'Why
does the LORD our God do all these *things* to
us?' then you shall answer them, 'Just as you
have ᴿforsaken Me and served foreign gods in
your land, so you shall serve aliens in a land
that is not yours.'   Deut. 29:24–29 • Jer. 1:16; 2:13

20 "Declare this in the house of Jacob
   And proclaim it in Judah, saying,
21 'Hear this now, O foolish people,
   Without ᵀunderstanding,   *heart*
   Who have eyes and see not,
   And who have ears and hear not:
22 ᴿDo you not fear Me?' says the LORD.
   'Will you not tremble at My presence,
   Who have placed the sand as the
   ᴿbound of the sea,
   By a perpetual decree, that it cannot
   pass beyond it?
   And though its waves toss to and fro,
   Yet they cannot prevail;
   Though they roar, yet they cannot pass
   over it.   [Rev. 15:4] • Job 26:10
23 But this people has a defiant and
   rebellious heart;
   They have revolted and departed.
24 They do not say in their heart,
   "Let us now fear the LORD our God,
   ᴿWho gives rain, both the former and
   the latter, in its season.   Acts 14:17
   ᴿHe reserves for us the appointed weeks
   of the harvest."   [Gen. 8:22]
25 ᴿYour iniquities have turned these *things*
   away,   Jer. 3:3
   And your sins have withheld good from
   you.
26 'For among My people are found wicked
   men;
   They ᴿlie in wait as one who sets
   snares;   Hab. 1:15
   They set a trap;
   They catch men.

27 As a cage is full of birds,
So their houses *are* full of deceit.
Therefore they have become great and
grown rich.
28 They have grown ᴿfat, they are sleek;
Yes, they ᵀsurpass the deeds of the
wicked;   Deut. 32:15 · *pass over* or *overlook*
They do not plead ᴿthe cause,
The cause of the fatherless;
ᴿYet they prosper,
And the right of the needy they do not
defend.   Zech. 7:10 · Job 12:6
29 ᴿShall I not punish *them* for these
things?' says the Lᴏʀᴅ.   Mal. 3:5
'Shall I not avenge Myself on such a
nation as this?'

30 "An astonishing and horrible thing
Has been committed in the land:
31 The prophets prophesy ᴿfalsely,
And the priests rule by their *own*
power;   Ezek. 13:6
And My people love *to have it* so.
But what will you do in the end?

Impending Destruction from the North

6 "O you children of Benjamin,
Gather yourselves to flee from the
midst of Jerusalem!
Blow the trumpet in Tekoa,
And set up a signal-fire in ᴿBeth
Haccerem;   Neh. 3:14
ᴿFor disaster appears out of the north,
And great destruction.   Jer. 4:6
2 I have likened the daughter of Zion
To a lovely and delicate woman.
3 The ᴿshepherds with their flocks shall
come to her.   2 Kin. 25:1-4
They shall pitch *their* tents against her
all around.
Each one shall pasture in his own
place."

4 "Prepareᴿ war against her;
Arise, and let us go up ᴿat noon.
Woe to us, for the day goes away,
For the shadows of the evening are
lengthening.   Joel 3:9 · Jer. 15:8
5 Arise, and let us go by night,
And let us destroy her palaces."

6 For thus has the Lᴏʀᴅ of hosts said:

"Cut down trees,
And build a mound against Jerusalem.
This *is* the city to be punished.
She *is* full of oppression in her midst.
7 ᴿAs a fountain ᵀwells up with water,
So she wells up with her wickedness.
ᴿViolence and plundering are heard in
her.   Is. 57:20 · *gushes* · Ps. 55:9
Before Me continually *are* ᵀgrief and
wounds.   *sickness*
8 Be instructed, O Jerusalem,
Lest ᴿMy soul depart from you;

Lest I make you desolate,
A land not inhabited."   Hos. 9:12

9 Thus says the Lᴏʀᴅ of hosts:

"They shall thoroughly glean as a vine
the remnant of Israel;
As a grape-gatherer, put your hand
back into the branches."

10 To whom shall I speak and give
warning,
That they may hear?
Indeed their ᴿear *is* uncircumcised,
And they cannot give heed.   [Acts 7:51]
Behold, ᴿthe word of the Lᴏʀᴅ is a
reproach to them;   Jer. 8:9; 20:8
They have no delight in it.
11 Therefore I am full of the fury of the
Lᴏʀᴅ.
ᴿI am weary of holding *it* in.
"I will pour it out ᴿon the children
outside,   Jer. 20:9 · Jer. 9:21
And on the assembly of young men
together;
For even the husband shall be taken
with the wife,
The aged with *him who is* full of days.
12 And ᴿtheir houses shall be turned over
to others,   Deut. 28:30
Fields and wives together;
For I will stretch out My hand
Against the inhabitants of the land,"
says the Lᴏʀᴅ.
13 "Because from the least of them even to
the greatest of them,
Everyone *is* given to ᴿcovetousness;
And from the prophet even to the
ᴿpriest,   Is. 56:11 · Jer. 5:31; 23:11
Everyone deals falsely.
14 They have also healed the ᵀhurt of My
people ᵀslightly,   Lit. *crushing* · Superficially
ᴿSaying, 'Peace, peace!'   Jer. 4:10; 23:17
When *there is* no peace.
15 Were they ᴿashamed when they had
committed abomination?
No! They were not at all ashamed;
Nor did they know how to blush.
Therefore they shall fall among those
who fall;   Jer. 3:3; 8:12
At the time I punish them,
They shall be cast down," says the
Lᴏʀᴅ.

16 Thus says the Lᴏʀᴅ:

"Stand in the ways and see,
And ask for the ᴿold paths, where the
good way *is*,   Jer. 18:15
And walk in it;
Then you will find rest for your souls.
But they said, 'We will not walk *in it.*'
17 Also, I set watchmen over you, *saying,*
'Listen to the sound of the trumpet!'
But they said, 'We will not listen.'

18 Therefore hear, you nations,
And know, O congregation, what *is*
among them.
19 ᴿHear, O earth!   Is. 1:2
Behold, I will certainly bring ᴿcalamity
on this people—   Jer. 19:3, 15
ᴿThe fruit of their thoughts,
Because they have not heeded My
words   Prov. 1:31
Nor My law, but rejected it.
20 ᴿFor what purpose to Me   Mic. 6:6, 7
Comes frankincense ᴿfrom Sheba,
And sweet cane from a far country?
Your burnt offerings *are* not acceptable,
Nor your sacrifices sweet to Me."   Is. 60:6

21 Therefore thus says the Lᴏʀᴅ:

"Behold, I will lay stumbling blocks
before this people,
And the fathers and the sons together
shall fall on them.
The neighbor and his friend shall
perish."

22 Thus says the Lᴏʀᴅ:

"Behold, a people comes from the ᴿnorth
country,   Jer. 1:15; 10:22; 50:41-43
And a great nation will be raised from
the farthest parts of the earth.
23 They will lay hold on bow and spear;
They *are* cruel and have no mercy;
Their voice ᴿroars like the sea;
And they ride on horses,   Is. 5:30
As men of war set in array against you,
O daughter of Zion."

24 We have heard the report of it;
Our hands grow feeble.
ᴿAnguish has taken hold of us,   Jer. 4:31
Pain as of a woman in ᵀlabor.   *childbirth*
25 Do not go out into the field,
Nor walk by the way.
Because of the sword of the enemy,
Fear *is* on every side.
26 O daughter of my people,
ᴿDress in sackcloth
ᴿAnd roll about in ashes!
ᴿMake mourning *as for* an only son,
most bitter lamentation;
For the plunderer will suddenly come
upon us.   Jer. 4:8 · Mic. 1:10 · [Zech. 12:10]
27 "I have set you *as* an assayer *and* ᴿa
fortress among My people,   Jer. 1:18
That you may know and test their way.
28 ᴿThey *are* all stubborn rebels, ᴿwalking
as slanderers.   Jer. 5:23 · Jer. 9:4
They *are* ᴿbronze and iron,   Ezek. 22:18
They *are* all corrupters;
29 The bellows blow fiercely,
The lead is consumed by the fire;
The smelter refines in vain,
For the wicked are not drawn off.

30 *People* will call them rejected silver,
Because the Lᴏʀᴅ has rejected them."

Trusting in Lying Words

7 The word that came to Jeremiah from the
Lᴏʀᴅ, saying,
2 "Stand in the gate of the Lᴏʀᴅ's house,
and proclaim there this word, and say, 'Hear
the word of the Lᴏʀᴅ, all *you of* Judah who
enter in at these gates to worship the Lᴏʀᴅ!' "
3 Thus says the Lᴏʀᴅ of hosts, the God of
Israel: "Amend your ways and your doings,
and I will cause you to dwell in this place.
4 ᴿ"Do not trust in these lying words,
saying, 'The temple of the Lᴏʀᴅ, the temple
of the Lᴏʀᴅ, the temple of the Lᴏʀᴅ *are*
these.'   Mic. 3:11
5 "For if you thoroughly amend your ways
and your doings, if you thoroughly execute
judgment between a man and his neighbor,
6 "*if* you do not oppress the stranger, the
fatherless, and the widow, and do not shed
innocent blood in this place, ᴿor walk after
other gods to your hurt,   Deut. 6:14, 15
7 ᴿ"then I will cause you to dwell in this
place, in ᴿthe land that I gave to your fathers
forever and ever.   Deut. 4:40 · Jer. 3:18
8 "Behold, you trust in ᴿlying words that
cannot profit.   Jer. 5:31; 14:13, 14
9 ᴿ"Will you steal, murder, commit adultery, swear falsely, burn incense to Baal, and
ᴿwalk after other gods whom you do not
know,   1 Kin. 18:21 · Ex. 20:3
10 ᴿ"and *then* come and stand before Me in
this house ᴿwhich is called by My name, and
say, 'We are delivered to do all these abominations'?   Ezek. 23:39 · Jer. 7:11, 14; 32:34; 34:15
11 "Has ᴿthis house, which is called by My
name, become a ᴿden of thieves in your eyes?
Behold, I, even I, have seen *it*," says the
Lᴏʀᴅ.   Is. 56:7 · Matt. 21:13
12 "But go now to ᴿMy place which *was* in
Shiloh, ᴿwhere I set My name at the first, and
see what I did to it because of the wickedness
of My people Israel.   Josh. 18:1 · Deut. 12:11
13 "And now, because you have done all
these works," says the Lᴏʀᴅ, "and I spoke to
you, ᴿrising up early and speaking, but you
did not hear, and I ᴿcalled you, but you did
not answer,   2 Chr. 36:15 · Prov. 1:24
14 "therefore I will do to the house which is
called by My name, in which you trust, and to
this place which I gave to you and your
fathers, as I have done to ᴿShiloh. 1 Sam. 4:10, 11
15 "And I will cast you out of My sight, ᴿas
I have cast out all your brethren—ᴿthe whole
posterity of Ephraim.   2 Kin. 17:23 · Ps. 78:67
16 "Therefore do not pray for this people,
nor lift up a cry or prayer for them, nor make
intercession to Me; for I will not hear you.
17 "Do you not see what they do in the
cities of Judah and in the streets of Jerusalem?

18 "The children gather wood, the fathers kindle the fire, and the women knead dough, to make cakes for the queen of heaven; and *they* pour out drink offerings to other gods, that they may provoke Me to anger.

19 R"Do they provoke Me to anger?" says the LORD. "*Do they* not *provoke* themselves, to the shame of their own faces?" Deut. 32:16, 21

20 Therefore thus says the Lord GOD: "Behold, My anger and My fury will be poured out on this place—on man and on beast, on the trees of the field and on the fruit of the ground. And it will burn and not be quenched."

21 Thus says the LORD of hosts, the God of Israel: R"Add your burnt offerings to your sacrifices and eat meat.   Jer. 6:20

22 R"For I did not speak to your fathers, or command them in the day that I brought them out of the land of Egypt, concerning burnt offerings or sacrifices.   [Hos. 6:6]

23 "But this is what I commanded them, saying, 'Obey My voice, and RI will be your God, and you shall be My people. And walk in all the ways that I have commanded you, that it may be well with you.'   [Ex. 19:5, 6]

24 R"Yet they did not obey or incline their ear, but *followed the counsels *and the *dictates of their evil hearts, and Twent backward and not forward.   Ps. 81:11 • *they were*

25 "Since the day that your fathers came out of the land of Egypt until this day, I have even sent to you all My servants the prophets, daily rising up early and sending *them*.

26 R"Yet they did not obey Me or incline their ear, but Rstiffened their neck. They did worse than their fathers.   Jer. 11:8 • Neh. 9:17

27 "Therefore Ryou shall speak all these words to them, but they will not obey you. You shall also call to them, but they will not answer you.   Ezek. 2:7

Judgment on Obscene Religion

28 "So you shall say to them, 'This *is* a nation that does not obey the voice of the LORD their God Rnor receive correction. RTruth has perished and has been cut off from their mouth.   Jer. 5:3 • Jer. 9:3

29 R"Cut off your hair and cast *it* away, and take up a lamentation on the desolate heights; for the LORD has rejected and forsaken the generation of His wrath.'   Mic. 1:16

30 "For the children of Judah have done evil in My sight," says the LORD. "They have set their abominations in the house which is called by My name, to Tpollute it.   *defile*

31 "And they have built the Rhigh places of Tophet, which *is* in the Valley of the Son of Hinnom, to burn their sons and their daughters in the fire, which I did not command, nor did it come into My heart.   2 Kin. 23:10

32 "Therefore behold, Rthe days are coming," says the LORD, "when it will no more be called Tophet, or the Valley of the Son of Hinnom, but the Valley of Slaughter; Rfor they will bury in Tophet until there is no room.   Jer. 19:6 • 2 Kin. 23:10

33 "The Rcorpses of this people will be food for the birds of the heaven and for the beasts of the earth. And no one will frighten *them away*.   Jer. 9:22; 19:11

34 "Then I will cause to Rcease from the cities of Judah and from the streets of Jerusalem the voice of mirth and the voice of gladness, the voice of the bridegroom and the voice of the bride. For Rthe land shall be desolate.   Is. 24:7, 8 • Lev. 26:33

8 "At that time," says the LORD, "they shall bring out the bones of the kings of Judah, and the bones of its princes, and the bones of the priests, and the bones of the prophets, and the bones of the inhabitants of Jerusalem, out of their graves.

2 "They shall spread them before the sun and the moon and all the host of heaven, which they have loved and which they have served and after which they have walked, which they have sought and Rwhich they have worshiped. They shall not be gathered Rnor buried; they shall be like refuse on the face of the earth.   2 Kin. 23:5 • Jer. 22:19

3 "Then Rdeath shall be chosen rather than life by all the Tresidue of those who remain of this evil family, who remain in all the places where I have driven them," says the LORD of hosts.   Rev. 9:6 • *remnant*

The Peril of False Teaching

4 "Moreover you shall say to them, 'Thus says the LORD:

"Will they fall and not rise?
Will one turn away and not return?
5 Why has this people slidden back,
Jerusalem, in a perpetual backsliding?
RThey hold fast to deceit,
RThey refuse to return.   Jer. 9:6 • Jer. 5:3
6 RI listened and heard,   Ps. 14:2
But they do not speak aright.
RNo man repented of his wickedness,
Saying, 'What have I done?'   Mic. 7:2
Everyone turned to his own course,
As the horse rushes into the battle.

7 "Even Rthe stork in the heavens
Knows her appointed times;
And the turtledove, the swift, and the
swallow   Song 2:12
Observe the time of their coming.
But RMy people do not know the
judgment of the LORD.   Jer. 5:4; 9:3

8 "How can you say, 'We *are* wise,
RAnd the law of the LORD *is* with us'?
Look, the false pen of the scribe
certainly works falsehood.   Rom. 2:17

7:24 *walked in* • *stubbornness, or imagination*

9 ᴿThe wise men are ashamed,   Jer. 6:15
   They are dismayed and taken.
   Behold, they have rejected the word of
      the Lᴏʀᴅ;
   So ᴿwhat wisdom do they have?   Jer. 4:22
10 Therefore ᴿI will give their wives to
      others,   Deut. 28:30
   And their fields to those who will
      inherit *them*;
   Because from the least even to the
      greatest
   Everyone is given to ᴿcovetousness;
   From the prophet even to the priest
   Everyone deals falsely.   Is. 56:11; 57:17
11 For they have healed the hurt of the
      daughter of My people ᵀslightly,
   Saying, 'Peace, peace!'
   When *there is* no peace.   Superficially
12 Were they ᴿashamed when they had
      committed abomination?
   No! They were not at all ashamed,
   Nor did they know how to blush.
   Therefore they shall fall among those
      who fall;
   In the time of their punishment
   They shall be cast down," says the
      Lᴏʀᴅ.   Jer. 3:3; 6:15
13 "I will surely ᵀconsume them," says the
      Lᴏʀᴅ.   Or *take them away*
   "No grapes *shall be* on the vine,
   Nor figs on the ᴿfig tree,   Matt. 21:19
   And the leaf shall fade;
   And *the things* I have given them shall
      pass away from them." ' "
14 "Why do we sit still?
   ᴿAssemble yourselves,   Jer. 4:5
   And let us enter the fortified cities,
   And let us be silent there.
   For the Lᴏʀᴅ our God has put us to
      silence
   And given us ᴿwaterᵀ of gall to drink,
   Because we have sinned against the
      Lᴏʀᴅ.   Jer. 9:15 • Bitter or poisonous water
15 "*We* ᴿlooked for peace, but no good
      came;
   And for a time of health, and there was
      trouble!   Jer. 14:19
16 The snorting of His horses was heard
      from ᴿDan.   Jer. 4:15
   The whole land trembled at the sound
      of the neighing of His ᴿstrong ones;
   For they have come and devoured the
      land and all that is in it,   Jer. 47:3
   The city and those who dwell in it."
17 "For behold, I will send serpents among
      you,
   Vipers which cannot be charmed,
   And they shall bite you," says the
      Lᴏʀᴅ.

The Prophet Mourns for the People

18 I would comfort myself in sorrow;
   My heart *is* faint in me.

19 Listen! The voice,
   The cry of the daughter of my people
   From ᴿa far country:
   "*Is* not the Lᴏʀᴅ in Zion?
   Is not her King in her?"   Is. 39:3

   "Why have they provoked Me to anger
   With their carved images—
   With foreign idols?"

20 "The harvest is past,
   The summer is ended,
   And we are not saved!"

21 ᴿFor the hurt of the daughter of my
      people I am hurt.
   I am ᴿmourning;   Jer. 9:1 • Joel 2:6
   Astonishment has taken hold of me.
22 *Is there* no ᴿbalm in Gilead,
   Is there no physician there?
   Why then is there no recovery
   For the health of the daughter of my
      people?   Jer. 46:11

9 Oh, ᴿthat my head were waters,
   And my eyes a fountain of tears,
   That I might weep day and night
   For the slain of the daughter of my
      people!   Is. 22:4
2 Oh, that I had in the wilderness
   A lodging place for travelers;
   That I might leave my people,
   And go from them!
   For ᴿthey *are* all adulterers,   Jer. 5:7, 8
   An assembly of treacherous men.

3 "And *like* their bow ᴿthey have bent
      their tongues *for* lies.   Ps. 64:3
   They are not valiant for the truth on
      the earth.
   For they proceed from ᴿevil to evil,
   And they ᴿdo not know Me," says the
      Lᴏʀᴅ.   Jer. 4:22; 13:23 • 1 Sam. 2:12
4 "Everyoneᴿ take heed to his ᵀneighbor,
   And do not trust any brother;
   For every brother will utterly supplant,
   And every neighbor will walk with
      slanderers.   Mic. 7:5, 6 • *friend*
5 Everyone will ᴿdeceive his neighbor,
   And will not speak the truth;   Is. 59:4
   They have taught their tongue to speak
      lies;
   Weary themselves to commit iniquity.
6 Your dwelling place *is* in the midst of
      deceit;
   Through deceit they refuse to know
      Me," says the Lᴏʀᴅ.

7 Therefore thus says the Lᴏʀᴅ of hosts:

   "Behold, ᴿI will refine them and ᵀtry
      them;   Is. 1:25 • *test*
   ᴿFor how shall I deal with the daughter
      of My people?   Hos. 11:8
8 Their tongue *is* an arrow shot out;
   It speaks ᴿdeceit;   Ps. 12:2

One speaks ᴿpeaceably to his neighbor
  with his mouth,
But in his heart he lies in wait.   Ps. 55:21
9 ᴿShall I not punish them for these
  things?" says the LORD.
"Shall I not avenge Myself on such a
  nation as this?"   Jer. 5:9, 29

10 I will take up a weeping and wailing for
  the mountains,
And ᴿfor the ᵀdwelling places of the
  wilderness a lamentation,
Because they are burned up,
So that no one can pass through;
Nor can *men* hear the voice of the
  cattle.   Hos. 4:3 · *pastures*
ᴿBoth the birds of the heavens and the
  beasts have fled;
They are gone.   Jer. 4:25

11 "I will make Jerusalem ᴿa heap of ruins,
ᴿa den of jackals.
I will make the cities of Judah desolate,
  without an inhabitant."   Is. 25:2 · Is. 13:22

12 ᴿWho *is* the wise man who may understand this? And *who is he* to whom the
mouth of the LORD has spoken, that he may
declare it? Why does the land perish *and* burn
up like a wilderness, so that no one can pass
through?   Hos. 14:9
13 And the LORD said, "Because they have
forsaken My law which I set before them,
and have ᴿnot obeyed My voice, nor walked
according to it,   Jer. 3:25; 7:24
14 "but they have walked according to the
*dictates of their own hearts and after the
Baals, which their fathers taught them,"
15 therefore thus says the LORD of hosts,
the God of Israel: "Behold, I will feed them,
this people, with wormwood, and give them
ᵀwater of gall to drink.   Bitter or poisonous water
16 "I will scatter them also among the
Gentiles, whom neither they nor their fathers
have known. ᴿAnd I will send a sword after
them until I have consumed them."   Ezek. 5:2

The People Mourn in Judgment

17 Thus says the LORD of hosts:

"Consider and call for ᴿthe mourning
  women,   2 Chr. 35:25
That they may come;
And send for skillful wailing women,
That they may come.
18 Let them make haste
And take up a wailing for us,
That our eyes may run with tears,
And our eyelids gush with water.
19 For a voice of wailing is heard from
  Zion:
'How we are plundered!

9:14 Lit. *stubbornness;* LXX, Tg. *imagination*

We are greatly ashamed,
Because we have forsaken the land,
Because we have been cast out of ᴿour
  dwellings.' "   Lev. 18:28
20 Yet hear the word of the LORD, O
  women,
And let your ear receive the word of
  His mouth;
Teach your daughters wailing,
And everyone her neighbor a
  lamentation.
21 For death has come through our
  windows,
Has entered our palaces,
To kill off the children—ᵀ*no longer to
  be* outside!   Lit. *from outside*
And the young men—ᵀ*no longer* on the
  streets!   Lit. *from the square*
22 Speak, "Thus says the LORD:

'Even the carcasses of men shall fall ᴿas
  refuse on the open field,   Jer. 8:1, 2
Like cuttings after the harvester,
And no one shall gather *them*.' "

23 Thus says the LORD:

ᴿ"Let not the wise *man* glory in his
  wisdom,   [Eccl. 9:11]
Let not the mighty *man* glory in his
  ᴿmight,   Ps. 33:16–18
Nor let the rich *man* glory in his riches;
24 But ᴿlet him who glories glory in this,
That he understands and knows Me,
That I *am* the LORD, exercising
  lovingkindness, judgment, and
  righteousness in the earth.   1 Cor. 1:31
For in these I delight," says the LORD.

25 "Behold, the days are coming," says the
LORD, "that I will punish all *who are* circumcised with the uncircumcised—
26 "Egypt, Judah, Edom, the people of Ammon, Moab, and all *who are* in the ᴿfarthest
corners, who dwell in the wilderness. For all
these nations *are* uncircumcised, and all the
house of Israel *are* ᴿuncircumcised in the
heart."   Jer. 25:23 · [Rom. 2:28]

Idols and the True God

10 Hear the word which the LORD speaks
       to you, O house of Israel.
2 Thus says the LORD:

ᴿ"Do not learn the way of the Gentiles;
Do not be dismayed at the signs of
  heaven,   [Lev. 18:3; 20:23]
For the Gentiles are dismayed at them.
3 For the customs of the peoples *are*
  ᵀfutile;
For ᴿone cuts a tree from the forest,
The work of the hands of the workman,
  with the ax.   Lit. *vanity* · Is. 40:19; 45:20
4 They decorate it with silver and gold;
They ᴿfasten it with nails and hammers
So that it will not topple.   Is. 41:7

5 They *are* upright, like a palm tree,
   And ᴿthey cannot speak;   Ps. 115:5
   They must be ᴿcarried,   Ps. 115:7
   Because they cannot go *by themselves.*
   Do not be afraid of them,
   For ᴿthey cannot do evil,   Is. 41:23, 24
   Nor can they do any good."

6 Inasmuch as *there is* none ᴿlike You, O
   Lᴏʀᴅ
   (You *are* great, and Your name *is* great
   in might),   Ex. 15:11
7 ᴿWho would not fear You, O King of the
   nations?
   For this is Your rightful due,
   For ᴿamong all the wise *men* of the
   nations,
   And in all their kingdoms,
   There is none like You.   Rev. 15:4 • Ps. 89:6
8 But they are altogether ᴿdull-hearted
   and foolish;   Hab. 2:18
   A wooden idol *is* a worthless doctrine.
9 Silver is beaten into plates;
   It is brought from Tarshish,
   And ᴿgold from Uphaz,   Dan. 10:5
   The work of the craftsman
   And of the hands of the metalsmith;

Blue and purple *are* their clothing;
They *are* all the work of skillful *men.*

3–A. God Is a Personal Being   ▼

10 But the Lᴏʀᴅ *is* the true God;
   He *is* ᴿthe living God and the
      ᴿeverlasting King.   1 Tim. 6:17 • Ps. 10:16
   At His wrath the earth will tremble,
   And the nations will not be able to
   endure His indignation.

11 Thus you shall say to them: ᴿ"The gods
   that have not made the heavens and the
   earth ᴿshall perish from the earth and from
   under these heavens."   Ps. 96:5 • Zeph. 2:11

12 He ᴿhas made the earth by His power,
   He has ᴿestablished the world by His
   wisdom,
   And ᴿhas stretched out the heavens at
   His discretion.   Jer. 51:15 • Ps. 93:1 • Job 9:8
13 ᴿWhen He utters His voice,
   There is a ᵀmultitude of waters in the
   heavens:
   ᴿ"And He causes the vapors to ascend
      from the ends of the earth.
   He makes lightning for the rain,

3–A. God Is a Personal Being (Jeremiah 10:10–16)—"The Lᴏʀᴅ [Jehovah] is the true God; He is the living God and the everlasting King" (v. 10). He is not dead. He is the eternal, living God, King of kings and Lord of lords (Rev. 19:16, page 1313; cf. Dan. 2:47, page 835). He created the heavens and the earth and every living thing in His universe (Gen. 1:1, page 2; cf. Is. 45:18, page 686). "And: 'You, Lᴏʀᴅ, in the beginning [the same beginning as in Gen. 1:1, page 2] laid the foundation of the earth, and the heavens are the work of Your hands. They will perish, but You remain; and they will all grow old like a garment; like a cloak You will fold them up, and they will be changed. But You are the same, and Your years will not fail' " (Heb. 1:10–12, page 1237; cf. Ps. 102:24–28, page 569). This messianic psalm, as quoted in Hebrews, attributes the act of creating all things to Christ, and is evidence that God is a living person (Col. 1:15–19, page 1202). In the light of the Scriptures, who can deny that Jesus Christ, the God-Man, is a living person seated at the right hand of God the Father (Heb. 1:3, page 1236)?

Scripture reveals the fact that God is a person, possessing self-consciousness and self-determination. He is the true and living God. The personality of God was seen when He revealed Himself to Moses in the burning bush. He said, "I am the God of your father—the God of Abraham, the God of Isaac, and the God of Jacob" (Ex. 3:6, page 60). To these words Jesus added, "God is not the God of the dead, but of the living" (Matt. 22:32, page 970). To be the God of the living, He must be a living person, infinitely greater than His subjects. "Then Moses said to God, 'Indeed, when I come to the children of Israel and say to them, "The God of your fathers has sent me to you," and they say to me, "What is His name?" what shall I say to them?' And God said to Moses, 'I AM WHO I AM.' And He said, 'Thus you shall say to the children of Israel, "I AM has sent me to you." ' Moreover God said to Moses, 'Thus you shall say to the children of Israel: "The Lᴏʀᴅ God of your fathers, the God of Abraham, the God of Isaac, and the God of Jacob, has sent me to you. This is My name forever, and this is My memorial to all generations" ' " (Ex. 3:13–15, page 60). God said, "I AM WHO I AM"—the only uncaused, self-existing God (Ex. 20:1–6, page 79).

Personality consists of intellect, emotion, and will. The personality of God is seen in certain characteristics ascribed to Him in the Scriptures.

(1) God grieves. "He was grieved in His heart" (Gen. 6:6, page 12).
(2) God becomes angry. "The Lᴏʀᴅ became angry with Solomon" (1 Kin. 11:9, page 339).
(3) God is jealous. "For I, the Lᴏʀᴅ your God, am a jealous God" (Ex. 20:5, page 79).
(4) God laughs. "He who sits in the heavens shall laugh" (Ps. 2:4, page 510).
(5) God hates. "These six things the Lᴏʀᴅ [Jehovah] hates, yes, seven are an abomination to Him" (Prov. 6:16–19, page 601).
(6) God cares. "Casting all your care upon Him, for He cares for you" (1 Pet. 5:7, page 1268).
(7) God hears. "He who planted the ear, shall He not hear?" (Ps. 94:9, page 566).
(8) God sees. "He who formed the eye, shall He not see?" (Ps. 94:9, page 566; Ps. 11:4, page 516).

Our God is an eternal, living, personal being.
See Luke 3:21, 22, page 1014, for **Point 3-B: God Is a Trinity.**

▽ He brings the wind out of His
 treasuries." Job 38:34 • Or *noise* • Ps. 135:7

14 ᴿEveryone is ᴿdull-hearted, without
 knowledge; Jer. 51:17 • Prov. 30:2
 ᴿEvery metalsmith is put to shame by an
 image; Is. 42:17; 44:11
 ᴿFor his molded image *is* falsehood,
 And *there is* no breath in them. Hab. 2:18
15 They *are* futile, a work of errors;
 In the time of their punishment they
 shall perish.
16 ᴿThe Portion of Jacob *is* not like them,
 For He *is* the Maker of all *things,*
 And ᴿIsrael *is* the tribe of His
 inheritance; Lam. 3:24 • Deut. 32:9
▲ ᴿThe Lᴏʀᴅ of hosts *is* His name. Is. 47:4

The Coming Captivity of Judah

17 ᴿGather up your wares from the land,
 O inhabitant of the fortress! Jer. 6:1

18 For thus says the Lᴏʀᴅ:

"Behold, I will ᴿthrow out at this time
 The inhabitants of the land,
 And will distress them, 1 Sam. 25:29
 ᴿThat they may find *it* so." Ezek. 6:10

19 ᴿWoe is me for my hurt! Jer. 8:21
 My wound is severe.
 But I say, ᴿ"Truly this *is* an infirmity,
 And ᴿI must bear it." Ps. 77:10 • Mic. 7:9
20 ᴿMy tent is plundered,
 And all my cords are broken;
 My children have gone from me,
 And they *are* ᴿno more.
 There is no one to pitch my tent
 anymore,
 Or set up my curtains. Jer. 4:20 • Jer. 31:15

21 For the shepherds have become dull-
 hearted,
 And have not sought the Lᴏʀᴅ;
 Therefore they shall not prosper,
 And all their flocks shall be scattered.
22 Behold, the noise of the report has
 come,
 And a great commotion out of the
 ᴿnorth country,
 To make the cities of Judah desolate, a
 ᴿden of jackals. Jer. 5:15 • Jer. 9:11

23 O Lᴏʀᴅ, I know the ᴿway of man *is* not
 in himself;
 It is not in man who walks to direct his
 own steps. Prov. 16:1; 20:24
24 O Lᴏʀᴅ, ᴿcorrect me, but with justice;
 Not in Your anger, lest You bring me
 to nothing. Jer. 30:11
25 ᴿPour out Your fury on the Gentiles,
 ᴿwho do not know You,
 And on the families who do not call on
 Your name; Ps. 79:6, 7 • Job 18:21
 For they have eaten up Jacob,

Devoured him and consumed him,
And made his dwelling place desolate.

The Broken Covenant

11 The word that came to Jeremiah from
 the Lᴏʀᴅ, saying,
2 "Hear the words of this covenant, and
speak to the men of Judah and to the inhabitants of Jerusalem;
3 "and say to them, 'Thus says the Lᴏʀᴅ
God of Israel: ᴿ"Cursed *is* the man who does
not obey the words of this covenant Deut. 27:26
4 "which I commanded your fathers in the
day I brought them out of the land of Egypt,
ᴿfrom the iron furnace, saying, ᴿ'Obey My
voice, and do according to all that I command you; so shall you be My people, and I
will be your God,' Deut. 4:20 • Lev. 26:3
5 "that I may establish the ᴿoath which I
have sworn to your fathers, to give them ᴿ'a
land flowing with milk and honey,' as *it is*
this day.'" And I answered and said, ᵀ"So
be it, Lᴏʀᴅ." Ps. 105:9 • Ex. 3:8 • Heb. *Amen*
6 Then the Lᴏʀᴅ said to me, "Proclaim all
these words in the cities of Judah and in the
streets of Jerusalem, saying: 'Hear the words
of this covenant ᴿand do them. [Rom. 2:13]
7 'For I earnestly exhorted your fathers in
the day I brought them up out of the land of
Egypt, until this day, ᴿrising early and exhorting, saying, "Obey My voice." Jer. 35:15
8 'Yet they did not obey or incline their
ear, but everyone followed the dictates of his
evil heart; therefore I will bring upon them all
the words of this covenant, which I commanded *them* to do, but *which* they have not
done.' "
9 And the Lᴏʀᴅ said to me, "A conspiracy
has been found among the men of Judah and
among the inhabitants of Jerusalem.
10 "They have turned back to ᴿthe iniquities of their forefathers who refused to hear
My words, and they have gone after other
gods to serve them; the house of Israel and
the house of Judah have broken My covenant
which I made with their fathers." Ezek. 20:18
11 Therefore thus says the Lᴏʀᴅ: "Behold, I
will surely bring calamity on them which
they will not be able to escape; and though
they cry out to Me, I will not listen to them.
12 "Then the cities of Judah and the
inhabitants of Jerusalem will go and ᴿcry out
to the gods to whom they offer incense, but
they will not save them at all in the time of
their trouble. Deut. 32:37
13 "For *according to* the number of your
ᴿcities were your gods, O Judah; and *according to* the number of the streets of Jerusalem
you have set up altars to *that* shameful thing,
altars to burn incense to Baal. Jer. 2:28
14 "So ᴿdo not pray for this people, or lift up
a cry or prayer for them; for I will not hear
them in the time that they cry out to Me
because of their trouble. Ex. 32:10

15 "What^R has My beloved to do in My
  house,   Ps. 50:16
Having ^Rdone lewd deeds with many?
And ^Rthe holy flesh has passed from
  you.   Ezek. 16:25 • [Titus 1:15]
When you do evil, then you rejoice.
16 The LORD called your name,
  ^RGreen Olive Tree, Lovely *and* of Good
  Fruit.
With the noise of a great tumult
He has kindled fire on it,
And its branches are broken.   Ps. 52:8

17 "For the LORD of hosts, ^Rwho planted
you, has pronounced doom against you for
the evil of the house of Israel and of the
house of Judah, which they have done
against themselves to provoke Me to anger in
offering incense to Baal."   Is. 5:2

Jeremiah's Life Threatened

18 Now the LORD gave me knowledge *of it,*
and I know *it;* for You showed me their
doings.
19 But I *was* like a docile lamb brought to
the slaughter; and I did not know that they
had devised schemes against me, *saying,* "Let

us destroy the tree with its fruit, and let us
cut him off from the land of the living, that
his name may be remembered no more."

20 But, O LORD of hosts,
  You who judge righteously,
Testing the ^Tmind and the heart,   *kidneys*
Let me see Your vengeance on them,
For to You I have revealed my cause.

21 "Therefore thus says the LORD concerning the men of Anathoth who seek your life,
saying, ^R'Do not prophesy in the name of the
LORD, lest you die by our hand'—   Mic. 2:6
22 "therefore thus says the LORD of hosts:
'Behold, I will punish them. The young men
shall die by the sword, their sons and their
daughters shall ^Rdie by famine;   Jer. 9:21
23 'and there shall be no remnant of them,
for I will bring catastrophe on the men of
Anathoth, *even* ^Rthe year of their punishment.' "   Jer. 23:12

Jeremiah's Question

32-D. The Prayer of a Puzzled Prophet ▼

12 Righteous ^R*are* You, O LORD, when I
      plead with You;

32-D. The Prayer of a Puzzled Prophet (Jeremiah 12:1–4)—While Jeremiah was preaching in his home village
of Anathoth (which lay a few miles north of Jerusalem), he was informed by certain men that if he continued
to preach to them, rebuking them for their sin and warning them to repent lest God should bring the
Babylonians down upon them, they would kill him (Jer. 11:21–23, page 724). Because of the blatant evil of
this group, and their open defiance of God, Jeremiah, in frustration and anger, prayed to God and asked,
"Why?" That is, "Why do You allow this bunch to get away with their sins and arrogance, although You are
a righteous God and cannot remain silent in the face of wickedness?" In every generation God's people
have joined with Jeremiah in this prayer of puzzlement at the seeming immunity from judgment of
evildoers, who flaunt their prosperity and taunt God's poorer servants. This prayer and God's answer help us
to understand what has perplexed many throughout time.

  (1) Jeremiah's prayer teaches us that

      (a) the most devout servants of God still have questions (v. 1);
      (b) we must begin all such questions with the acknowledgment that God is just (v. 1);
      (c) even the prophets have observed that the wicked prosper (vv. 1, 2);
      (d) godly people may well feel frustrated over such apparent injustice (vv. 1, 2);
      (e) godly people do long for righteousness to triumph, and for evil men to be brought to judgment
by a righteous God (v. 3);
      (f) unchecked evildoers cause everyone around them to suffer (v. 4).

  (2) God's answer teaches us that

      (a) We should be prepared to see even more frustrating circumstances in this world of sin (v. 5);
      (b) Sometimes our own friends or families do not share our revulsion at the open sinfulness of
evildoers (v. 6);
      (c) Eventually God's forbearance will come to an end, and He will bring the wicked to justice,
whoever they may be. The sword of the Lord will arrive at God's appointed hour (Jer. 12:12, page 725);
      (d) Yet, for those who repent and are punished there is forgiveness, mercy, and restoration by God's
own hand (Jer. 12:14–16, page 725).

  An old, popular saying sums it up well: "God's wheel of justice may grind slowly, but it grinds
exceedingly fine." When frustrated by the momentary success of the wicked, remember this prayer of a
puzzled prophet and God's reply—then take heart. Also see Peter's answer to this same question in 2 Peter
3:3, 4, 8–10 (page 1275).
  The wicked enjoy the long-suffering of God (2 Pet. 3:9, page 1275). Unless they repent and believe on
the Lord Jesus Christ, they will come to the end of God's long-suffering and will be judged at the Great
White Throne judgment (Rev. 20:11–15, page 1313).
  See Jonah 2:1–9, page 885, for **Point 32-E: The Prayer of a Backslidden Prophet.**

▽ Yet let me talk with You about *Your*
  judgments.
  ᴿWhy does the way of the wicked
  prosper?
  Why are those happy who deal so
  treacherously?   Ps. 51:14 • Mal. 3:15
2 You have planted them, yes, they have
  taken root;
  They grow, yes, they bear fruit.
  ᴿYou *are* near in their mouth   Matt. 15:8
  But far from their ᵀmind.   Lit. *kidneys*

3 But You, O Lᴏʀᴅ, ᴿknow me;
  You have seen me,
  And You have ᴿtested my heart toward
  You.
  Pull them out like sheep for the
  slaughter,
  And prepare them for ᴿthe day of
  slaughter.   Ps. 17:3 • Jer. 11:20 • James 5:5
4 How long will ᴿthe land mourn,
  And the herbs of every field wither?
  ᴿThe beasts and birds are consumed,
  ᴿFor the wickedness of those who dwell
  there,
  Because they said, "He will not see our
▲ final end."   Hos. 4:3 • Jer. 9:10 • Ps. 107:34

The Lᴏʀᴅ Answers Jeremiah

5 "If you have run with the footmen, and
  they have wearied you,
  Then how can you contend with
  horses?
  And *if* in the land of peace,
  In which you trusted, *they wearied you*,
  Then how will you do in ᴿthe ᵀflood
  plain of the Jordan?   Josh. 3:15 • Or *thicket*
6 For even ᴿyour brothers, the house of
  your father,   Jer. 9:4, 5
  Even they have dealt treacherously
  with you;
  Yes, they have called ᵀa multitude after
  you.   Or *abundantly*
  ᴿDo not believe them,   Prov. 26:25
  Even though they speak ᵀsmooth words
  to you.   Lit. *good*

7 "I have forsaken My house, I have left
  My heritage;
  I have given the dearly beloved of My
  soul into the hand of her enemies.
8 My heritage is to Me like a lion in the
  forest;
  It cries out against Me;
  Therefore I have ᴿhated it.   Hos. 9:15
9 My ᵀheritage *is* to Me *like* a speckled
  vulture;   *inheritance*
  The vultures all around *are* against her.
  Come, assemble all the beasts of the
  field,
  ᴿBring them to devour!   Lev. 26:22

10 "Many ᵀrulers have destroyed ᴿMy
   vineyard,   Lit. *shepherds* or *pastors* • Is. 5:1-7

They have ᴿtrodden My portion
  underfoot;   Is. 63:18
They have made My ᵀpleasant portion a
  desolate wilderness.   *desired portion* of land
11 They have made it ᴿdesolate;
Desolate, it mourns to Me;   Jer. 10:22; 22:6
The whole land is made desolate,
Because no one takes *it* to heart.
12 The plunderers have come
On all the desolate heights in the
  wilderness,
For the sword of the Lᴏʀᴅ shall devour
From *one* end of the land to the *other*
  end of the land;
No flesh shall have peace.
13 ᴿThey have sown wheat but reaped
  thorns;
They have ᵀput themselves to pain *but*
  do not profit.
But be ashamed of your harvest
Because of the fierce anger of the
  Lᴏʀᴅ."   Hag. 1:6 • Or *strained*

14 Thus says the Lᴏʀᴅ: "Against all My evil
neighbors who ᴿtouch the inheritance which
I have caused My people Israel to inherit—
behold, I will ᴿpluck them out of their land
and pluck out the house of Judah from
among them.   Zech. 2:8 • Deut. 30:3
15 "Then it shall be, after I have plucked
them out, that I will return and have compassion on them and bring them back, everyone
to his heritage and everyone to his land.
16 "And it shall be, if they will learn carefully the ways of My people, to swear by My
name, 'As the Lᴏʀᴅ lives,' as they taught My
people to swear by Baal, then they shall be
established in the midst of My people.
17 "But if they do not ᴿobey, I will utterly
pluck up and destroy that nation," says the
Lᴏʀᴅ.   Is. 60:12

Symbol of the Linen Sash

13 Thus the Lᴏʀᴅ said to me: "Go and get
yourself a linen sash, and put it around
your waist, but do not put it in water."
2 So I got a sash according to the word of
the Lᴏʀᴅ, and put *it* around my waist.
3 And the word of the Lᴏʀᴅ came to me
the second time, saying,
4 "Take the ᵀsash that you acquired,
which is ᵀaround your waist, and arise, go to
the ᵀEuphrates, and hide it there in a hole in
the rock."   *waistband* • Lit. *upon your loins* • Heb. *Perath*
5 So I went and hid it by the Euphrates, as
the Lᴏʀᴅ commanded me.
6 Now it came to pass after many days
that the Lᴏʀᴅ said to me, "Arise, go to the
Euphrates, and take from there the sash
which I commanded you to hide there."
7 Then I went to the Euphrates and dug,
and I took the ᵀsash from the place where I
had hidden it; and there was the sash, ruined.
It was profitable for nothing.   *waistband*

8 Then the word of the LORD came to me, saying,

9 "Thus says the LORD: 'In this manner ᴿI will ruin the pride of Judah and the great ᴿpride of Jerusalem.   Lev. 26:19 • Zeph. 3:11

10 'This evil people, who ᴿrefuse to hear My words, who follow the dictates of their hearts, and walk after other gods to serve them and worship them, shall be just like this sash which is profitable for nothing.   Jer. 16:12

11 'For as the sash clings to the waist of a man, so I have caused the whole house of Israel and the whole house of Judah to cling to Me,' says the LORD, 'that they may become My people, for renown, for praise, and for glory; but they would not hear.'

Symbol of the Wine Bottles

12 "Therefore you shall speak to them this word: 'Thus says the LORD God of Israel: "Every bottle shall be filled with wine." ' And they will say to you, 'Do we not certainly know that every bottle will be filled with wine?'

13 "Then you shall say to them, 'Thus says the LORD: "Behold, I will fill all the inhabitants of this land—even the kings who sit on David's throne, the priests, the prophets, and all the inhabitants of Jerusalem—ᴿwith drunkenness!   Is. 51:17; 63:6

14 "And ᴿI will dash them ᵀone against another, even the fathers and the sons together," says the LORD. "I will not pity nor spare nor have mercy, but will destroy them." ' "   Jer. 19:9-11 • Lit. a man against his brother

Pride Precedes Captivity

15 Hear and give ear:
Do not be proud,
For the LORD has spoken.

16 ᴿGive glory to the LORD your God
Before He causes ᴿdarkness,
And before your feet stumble
On the dark mountains,   Josh. 7:19 • Amos 8:9
And while you are looking for light,
He turns it into ᴿthe shadow of death
And makes it dense darkness.   Ps. 44:19

17 But if you will not hear it,
My soul will ᴿweep in secret for your pride;
My eyes will weep bitterly
And run down with tears,
Because the LORD's flock has been taken captive.   Jer. 9:1; 14:17

18 Say to ᴿthe king and to the queen mother,
"Humble yourselves;
Sit down,
For your rule shall collapse, the crown of your glory."   Jer. 22:26

19 The cities of the South shall be shut up,
And no one shall open them;

Judah shall be carried away captive, all of it;
It shall be wholly carried away captive.

20 Lift up your eyes and see
Those who come from the ᴿnorth.
Where is the flock that was given to you,
Your beautiful sheep?   Jer. 10:22; 46:20

21 What will you say when He punishes you?
For you have taught them
To be chieftains, to be head over you.
Will not ᴿpangs seize you,
Like a woman in ᵀlabor?   Jer. 6:24 • childbirth

22 And if you say in your heart,
"Why have these things come upon me?"
For the greatness of your iniquity
Your skirts have been uncovered,
Your heels ᵀmade bare.   Lit. suffer violence

23 Can the Ethiopian change his skin or the leopard its spots?
Then may you also do good who are accustomed to do evil.

24 "Therefore I will ᴿscatter them ᴿlike stubble
That passes away by the wind of the wilderness.   Jer. 9:16 • Hos. 13:3

25 ᴿThis is your lot,   Job 20:29
The portion of your measures from Me," says the LORD,
"Because you have forgotten Me
And trusted in ᴿfalsehood.   Jer. 10:14

26 Therefore ᴿI will uncover your skirts over your face,
That your shame may appear.   Lam. 1:8

27 I have seen your adulteries
And your lustful ᴿneighings,
The lewdness of your harlotry,
Your abominations ᴿon the hills in the fields.   Jer. 5:7, 8 • Is. 65:7
Woe to you, O Jerusalem!
Will you still not be made clean?"

Sword, Famine, and Pestilence

14 The word of the LORD that came to Jeremiah concerning the droughts.

2 "Judah mourns,
And ᴿher gates languish;   Is. 3:26
They ᴿmourn for the land,   Jer. 8:21
And the cry of Jerusalem has gone up.

3 Their nobles have sent their lads for water;
They went to the cisterns and found no water.
They returned with their vessels empty;
They were ashamed and confounded
ᴿAnd covered their heads.   2 Sam. 15:30

4 Because the ground is parched,
For there was ᴿno rain in the land,
The plowmen were ashamed;
They covered their heads.   Jer. 3:3

5 Yes, the deer also gave birth in the
    field,
  But left because there was no grass.
6 And ᴿthe wild donkeys stood in the
    desolate heights;   Jer. 2:24
  They sniffed at the wind like jackals;
  Their eyes failed because *there was* no
    grass."

7 O Lᴏʀᴅ, though our iniquities testify
    against us,
  Do it ᴿfor Your name's sake;   Ps. 25:11
  For our backslidings are many,
  We have sinned against You.
8 ᴿO the Hope of Israel, his Savior in time
    of trouble,
  Why should You be like a stranger in
    the land,
  And like a traveler *who* turns aside to
    tarry for a night?   Jer. 17:13
9 Why should You be like a man
    astonished,
  Like a mighty one ᴿ*who* cannot save?
  Yet You, O Lᴏʀᴅ, ᴿ*are* in our midst,
  And we are called by Your name;
  Do not leave us!   Is. 59:11 • Ex. 29:45

10 Thus says the Lᴏʀᴅ to this people:

  ᴿ"Thus they have loved to wander;
  They have not restrained their feet.
  Therefore the Lᴏʀᴅ does not accept
    them;   Jer. 2:23-25
  ᴿHe will remember their iniquity now,
  And punish their sins."   Hos. 8:13

11 Then the Lᴏʀᴅ said to me, ᴿ"Do not pray
for this people, for *their* good.   Ex. 32:10
12 "When they fast, I will not hear their
cry; and when they offer burnt offering and
grain offering, I will not accept them. But ᴿI
will consume them by the sword, by the
famine, and by the pestilence.   Jer. 9:16
13 Then I said, "Ah, Lord Gᴏᴅ! Behold, the
prophets say to them, 'You shall not see the
sword, nor shall you have famine, but I will
give you assured peace in this place.' "
14 And the Lᴏʀᴅ said to me, "The prophets
prophesy lies in My name. I have not sent
them, commanded them, nor spoken to them;
they prophesy to you a false vision, ᵀdivina-
tion, a worthless thing, and the deceit of their
heart.   Telling the future by signs and omens
15 "Therefore thus says the Lᴏʀᴅ concerning the prophets who prophesy in My name,
whom I did not send, ᴿand who say, 'Sword
and famine shall not be in this land'—'By
sword and famine those prophets shall be
consumed!   Ezek. 14:10
16 'And the people to whom they prophesy
shall be cast out in the streets of Jerusalem
because of the famine and the sword; they
will have no one to bury them—them nor
their wives, their sons nor their daughters—
for I will pour their wickedness on them.'

17 "Therefore you shall say this word to
them:

  ᴿ"Let my eyes flow with tears night and
    day,   Jer. 9:1; 13:17
  And let them not cease;
  ᴿFor the virgin daughter of my people
  Has been broken with a mighty stroke,
    with a very severe blow.   Jer. 8:21
18 If I go out to ᴿthe field,
  Then behold, those slain with the
    sword!   Ezek. 7:15
  And if I enter the city,
  Then behold, those sick from famine!
  Yes, both prophet and ᴿpriest go about
    in a land they do not know.' "   Jer. 23:11

The People Plead for Mercy

19 ᴿHave You utterly rejected Judah?
  Has Your soul loathed Zion?
  Why have You stricken us so that
  ᴿ*there is* no healing for us?
  ᴿWe looked for peace, but *there was* no
    good;
  And for the time of healing, and there
    was trouble.   Lam. 5:22 • Jer. 15:18 • Jer. 8:15
20 We acknowledge, O Lᴏʀᴅ, our
    wickedness
  And the iniquity of our fathers,
  For we have sinned against You.
21 Do not abhor *us*, for Your name's sake;
  Do not disgrace the throne of Your
    glory.
  ᴿRemember, do not break Your
    covenant with us.   Ps. 106:45
22 Are there any among the idols of the
    nations that can cause ᴿrain?   Jer. 5:24
  Or can the heavens give showers?
  ᴿ*Are* You not He, O Lᴏʀᴅ our God?
  Therefore we will wait for You,
  Since You have made all these.   Ps. 135:7

The Lᴏʀᴅ Will Not Relent

15 Then the Lᴏʀᴅ said to me, "*Even* if
Moses and ᴿSamuel stood before Me,
My ᵀmind *would* not *be* favorable toward this
people. Cast *them* out of My sight, and let
them go forth.   1 Sam. 7:9 • Lit. *soul was not toward*
2 "And it shall be, if they say to you,
'Where should we go?' then you shall tell
them, 'Thus says the Lᴏʀᴅ:

  ᴿ"Such as *are* for death, to death;
  And such as *are* for the sword, to the
    sword;
  And such as *are* for the famine, to the
    famine;
  And such as *are* for the ᴿcaptivity, to
    the captivity." '   Zech. 11:9 • Jer. 9:16; 16:13

3 "And I will ᴿappoint over them four
forms *of destruction*," says the Lᴏʀᴅ: "the
sword to slay, the dogs to drag, ᴿthe birds of
the heavens and the beasts of the earth to
devour and destroy.   Ezek. 14:21 • Jer. 7:33

4 "I will hand them over to ᴿtrouble, to all kingdoms of the earth, because of ᴿManasseh the son of Hezekiah, king of Judah, for what he did in Jerusalem.   Deut. 28:25 • 2 Kin. 24:3, 4

5 "For who will have pity on you, O
    Jerusalem?
Or who will bemoan you?
Or who will turn aside to ask how you
    are doing?

6 ᴿYou have forsaken Me," says the Lᴏʀᴅ,
"You have gone backward.
Therefore I will stretch out My hand
    against you and destroy you;
I am ᵀweary of relenting!   Jer. 2:13 • tired

7 And I will winnow them with a
    winnowing fan in the gates of the
    land;
I will ᴿbereave them of children;
I will destroy My people,
Since they ᴿdo not return from their
    ways.   Jer. 18:21 • Is. 9:13

8 Their widows will be increased to Me
    more than the sand of the seas;
I will bring against them,
Against the mother of the young men,
A plunderer at noonday;
I will cause anguish and terror to fall
    on them ᴿsuddenly.   Is. 29:5

9 "Sheᴿ languishes who has borne seven;
She has breathed her last;
ᴿHer sun has gone down
While it was yet day;
She has been ashamed and confounded.
And the remnant of them I will deliver
    to the sword   1 Sam. 2:5 • Amos 8:9
Before their enemies," says the Lᴏʀᴅ.

Jeremiah's Dejection

10 ᴿWoe is me, my mother,   Job 3:1
That you have borne me,
A man of strife and a man of
    contention to the whole ᵀearth!
I have neither lent for interest,
Nor have men lent to me for interest.
Every one of them curses me.   Or land

11 The Lᴏʀᴅ said:

"Surely it will be well with your
    remnant;
Surely I will cause ᴿthe enemy to
    intercede with you
In the time of adversity and in the time
    of affliction.   Jer. 40:4, 5

12 Can anyone break iron,
The northern iron and the bronze?

13 Your wealth and your treasures
I will give as ᴿplunder without price,
Because of all your sins,
Throughout all your territories.   Ps. 44:12

14 And I will *make you cross over with
    your enemies

15:14 So with MT, Vg.; LXX, Syr., Tg. cause you to serve (cf. 17:4)

Into a land which you do not know;
For a ᴿfire is kindled in My anger,
Which shall burn upon you."   Deut. 32:22

15 O Lᴏʀᴅ, ᴿYou know;   Jer. 12:3
Remember me and ᵀvisit me,   attend to
And ᴿtake vengeance for me on my
    persecutors.   Jer. 20:12
In Your enduring patience, do not take
    me away.
Know that ᴿfor Your sake I have
    suffered rebuke.   Ps. 69:7-9

16 Your words were found, and I ᴿate
    them,   Ezek. 3:1, 3
And ᴿYour word was to me the joy and
    rejoicing of my heart;   [Job 23:12]
For I am called by Your name,
O Lᴏʀᴅ God of hosts.

17 ᴿI did not sit in the assembly of the
    mockers,
Nor did I rejoice;
I sat alone because of Your hand,
For You have filled me with
    indignation.   Ps. 26:4, 5

18 Why is my ᴿpain perpetual   Jer. 10:19; 30:15
And my wound incurable,
Which refuses to be healed?
Will You surely be to me ᴿlike an
    unreliable stream,   Job 6:15
As waters that ᵀfail?   Or cannot be trusted

The Lᴏʀᴅ Reassures Jeremiah

19 Therefore thus says the Lᴏʀᴅ:

ᴿ"If you return,
Then I will bring you back;
You shall ᴿstand before Me;
If you ᴿtake out the precious from the
    vile,   Zech. 3:7 • Jer. 15:1 • Ezek. 22:26; 44:23
You shall be as My mouth.
Let them return to you,
But you must not return to them.

20 And I will make you to this people a
    fortified bronze ᴿwall;   Ezek. 3:9
And they will fight against you,
But ᴿthey shall not prevail against you;
For I am with you to save you
And deliver you," says the
    Lᴏʀᴅ.   Jer. 1:8, 19

21 "I will deliver you from the hand of the
    wicked,
And I will redeem you from the grip of
    the terrible."

Jeremiah's Life-Style and Message

16 The word of the Lᴏʀᴅ also came to me, saying,

2 "You shall not take a wife, nor shall you have sons or daughters in this place."

3 For thus says the Lᴏʀᴅ concerning the sons and daughters who are born in this place, and concerning their mothers who bore them and their fathers who begot them in this land:

4 "They shall die gruesome deaths; they shall not be lamented nor shall they be buried, *but* they shall be ᴿlike refuse on the face of the earth. They shall be consumed by the sword and by famine, and their ᴿcorpses shall be meat for the birds of heaven and for the beasts of the earth." Ps. 83:10 · Ps. 79:2

5 For thus says the Lᴏʀᴅ: ᴿ"Do not enter the house of mourning, nor go to lament or bemoan them; for I have taken away My peace from this people," says the Lᴏʀᴅ, "lovingkindness and mercies. Ezek. 24:17, 22, 23

6 "Both the great and the small shall die in this land. They shall not be buried; neither shall men lament for them, cut themselves, nor make themselves bald for them.

7 "Nor shall *men* break *bread* in mourning for them, to comfort them for the dead; nor shall *men* give them the cup of consolation to drink for their father or their mother.

8 "Also you shall not go into the house of feasting to sit with them, to eat and drink."

9 For thus says the Lᴏʀᴅ of hosts, the God of Israel: "Behold, ᴿI will cause to cease from this place, before your eyes and in your days, the voice of ᵀmirth and the voice of gladness, the voice of the bridegroom and the voice of the bride. Rev. 18:23 · *rejoicing*

10 "And it shall be, when you show this people all these words, and they say to you, ᴿ'Why has the Lᴏʀᴅ pronounced all this great disaster against us? Or what *is* our iniquity? Or what *is* our sin that we have committed against the Lᴏʀᴅ our God?' Deut. 29:24

11 "then you shall say to them, 'Because your fathers have forsaken Me,' says the Lᴏʀᴅ; 'they have walked after other gods and have served them and worshiped them, and have forsaken Me and not kept My law.

12 'And you have done worse than your fathers, for behold, each one follows the dictates of his own evil heart, so that no one listens to Me.

13 'Therefore I will cast you out of this land ᴿinto a land that you do not know, neither you nor your fathers; and there you shall serve other gods day and night, where I will not show you favor.' Jer. 15:14

God Will Restore Israel

14 "Therefore behold, the days are coming," says the Lᴏʀᴅ, "that it shall no more be said, 'The Lᴏʀᴅ lives who brought up the children of Israel from the land of Egypt,'

15 "but, 'The Lᴏʀᴅ lives who brought up the children of Israel from the land of the north and from all the lands where He had driven them.' For I will bring them back into their land which I gave to their fathers.

16 "Behold, I will send for many ᴿfishermen," says the Lᴏʀᴅ, "and they shall fish them; and afterward I will send for many hunters, and they shall hunt them from every

mountain and every hill, and out of the holes of the rocks. Amos 4:2

17 "For My ᴿeyes *are* on all their ways; they are not hidden from My face, nor is their iniquity hidden from My eyes. Heb. 4:13

18 "And first I will repay ᴿdouble for their iniquity and their sin, because ᴿthey have defiled My land; they have filled My inheritance with the carcasses of their detestable and abominable idols." Jer. 17:18 · [Ezek. 43:7]

19 O Lᴏʀᴅ, ᴿmy strength and my fortress,
ᴿMy refuge in the day of affliction,
The Gentiles shall come to You
From the ends of the earth and say,
"Surely our fathers have inherited lies,
Worthlessness and ᴿunprofitable
    things." Ps. 18:1, 2 · Jer. 17:17 · Is. 44:10
20 Will a man make gods for himself,
ᴿWhich *are* not gods? Gal. 4:8

21 "Therefore behold, I will this once cause
    them to know,
I will cause them to know
My hand and My might;
And they shall know that ᴿMy name *is*
    the Lᴏʀᴅ. Amos 5:8

Judah's Sin and Punishment

17 "The sin of Judah *is* ᴿwritten with a
    ᴿpen of iron; Jer. 2:22 · Job 19:24
With the point of a diamond *it is*
    ᴿengraved 2 Cor. 3:3
On the tablet of their heart,
And on the horns of your altars,
2 While their children remember
Their altars and their *wooden images
By the green trees on the high hills.
3 O My mountain in the field,
I will give as plunder your wealth, all
    your treasures,
And your high places of sin within all
    your borders.
4 And you, even yourself,
Shall let go of your heritage which I
    gave you;
And I will cause you to serve your
    enemies
In the land which you do not know;
For you have kindled a fire in My anger
    which shall burn forever."

5 Thus says the Lᴏʀᴅ:

"Cursed *is* the man who trusts in man
And makes flesh his ᵀstrength, Lit. *arm*
Whose heart departs from the Lᴏʀᴅ.
6 For he shall be ᴿlike a shrub in the
    desert, Jer. 48:6
And ᴿshall not see when good comes,
But shall inhabit the parched places in
    the wilderness, Job 20:17
In a salt land *which is* not inhabited.

17:2 Or *Asherim,* Canaanite deities

7 "Blessed[R] *is* the man who trusts in the
  LORD,
  And whose hope is the LORD.   [Is. 30:18]
8 For he shall be [R]like a tree planted by
  the waters,   [Ps. 1:3]
  Which spreads out its roots by the
  river,
  And will not *fear when heat comes;
  But its leaf will be green,
  And will not be anxious in the year of
  drought,
  Nor will cease from yielding fruit.

9 "The heart *is* deceitful above all *things,*
  And [T]desperately wicked;   *incurably sick*
  Who can know it?
10 I, the LORD, [R]search the heart,   Rev. 2:23
  I test the [T]mind,   Most secret parts, lit. *kidneys*
  [R]Even to give every man according to
  his ways,   Rom. 2:6
  According to the fruit of his doings.
11 "*As* a partridge that [T]broods but does
  not hatch,   Sits on eggs
  So is he who gets riches, but not by
  right;
  It [R]will leave him in the midst of his
  days,   Ps. 55:23
  And at his end he will be a fool."

12 A glorious high throne from the
  beginning
  Is the place of our sanctuary.
13 O LORD, [R]the hope of Israel,   Jer. 14:8
  [R]All who forsake You shall be ashamed.

  "Those who depart from Me   [Is. 1:28]
  Shall be [R]written in the earth,   Luke 10:20
  Because they have forsaken the LORD,
  The [R]fountain of living waters."   Jer. 2:13

Jeremiah Prays for Deliverance

14 Heal me, O LORD, and I shall be healed;
  Save me, and I shall be saved,
  For [R]You *are* my praise.   Deut. 10:21
15 Indeed they say to me,
  [R]"Where *is* the word of the LORD?
  Let it come now!"   Is. 5:19
16 As for me, [R]I have not hurried away
  from *being* a shepherd *who* follows
  You,
  Nor have I desired the woeful day;
  You know what came out of my lips;
  It was right there before You.   Jer. 1:4-12
17 Do not be a terror to me;
  You *are* my hope in the day of doom.
18 [R]Let them be ashamed who persecute
  me,   Ps. 35:4; 70:2
  But [R]do not let me be put to shame.

  17:8 Qr., Tg. *see*

Let them be dismayed,
But do not let me be dismayed.
Bring on them the day of doom,
And [R]destroy[T] them with double
destruction!   Ps. 25:2 · Jer. 11:20 · Lit. *crush*

Hallow the Sabbath Day

19 Thus the LORD said to me: "Go and stand
in the gate of the children of the people, by
which the kings of Judah come in and by
which they go out, and in all the gates of
Jerusalem;
20 "and say to them, [R]'Hear the word of the
LORD, you kings of Judah, and all Judah, and
all the inhabitants of Jerusalem, who enter by
these gates.   Jer. 19:3, 4
21 'Thus says the LORD: [R]"Take heed to
yourselves, and bear no burden on the Sabbath day, nor bring *it* in by the gates of
Jerusalem;   Neh. 13:19
22 "nor carry a burden out of your houses
on the Sabbath day, nor do any work, but
hallow the Sabbath day, as I [R]commanded
your fathers.   Ex. 20:8; 31:13
23 "But they did not obey nor incline their
ear, but made their neck stiff, that they might
not hear nor receive instruction.
24 "And it shall be, [R]if you heed Me carefully," says the LORD, "to bring no burden
through the gates of this city on the [R]Sabbath
day, but hallow the Sabbath day, to do no
work in it,   Jer. 11:4; 26:3 · Ex. 16:23-30; 20:8-10
25 [R]"then shall enter the gates of this city
kings and princes sitting on the throne of
David, riding in chariots and on horses, they
and their princes, accompanied by the men of
Judah and the inhabitants of Jerusalem; and
this city shall remain forever.   Jer. 22:4
26 "And they shall come from the cities of
Judah and from the places around Jerusalem,
from the land of Benjamin and from the
lowland, from the mountains and from the
South, bringing burnt offerings and sacrifices,
grain offerings and incense, bringing sacrifices of praise to the house of the LORD.
27 "But if you will not heed Me to hallow
the Sabbath day, such as not carrying a
burden when entering the gates of Jerusalem
on the Sabbath day, then I will kindle a fire in
its gates, and it shall devour the palaces of
Jerusalem, and it shall not be quenched." ' "

The Potter and the Clay

5-C. The Sovereignty of God Illustrated   ▼

18 The word which came to Jeremiah
   from the LORD, saying:
2 "Arise and go down to the potter's
house, and there I will cause you to hear My
words."

5-C. The Sovereignty of God Illustrated (Jeremiah 18:1-12)—In the darkest hour of Jeremiah's ministry, God
gave him a vision of His sovereign throne. It is called "a glorious high throne from the beginning . . . the
place of our sanctuary" (Jer. 17:12, page 730). His throne is the place of worship and refuge. Without this

(Point 5-C continued on next page)

▽ 3 Then I went down to the potter's house, and there he was, making something at the ᵀwheel.   Potter's wheel

4 And the vessel that he ᵀmade of clay was ᵀmarred in the hand of the potter; so he made it again into another vessel, as it seemed good to the potter to make.   was making · ruined

5 Then the word of the LORD came to me, saying:

6 "O house of Israel, can I not do with you as this potter?" says the LORD. "Look, ᴿas the clay is in the potter's hand, so are you in My hand, O house of Israel!   Is. 64:8

7 "The instant I speak concerning a nation and concerning a kingdom, to ᴿpluck up, to pull down, and to destroy it,   Jer. 1:10

8 "if that nation against whom I have spoken turns from its evil, I will relent of the disaster that I thought to bring upon it.

9 "And the instant I speak concerning a nation and concerning a kingdom, to build and to plant it,

10 "if it does evil in My sight so that it does not obey My voice, then I will relent concerning the good with which I said I would benefit it.

11 "Now therefore, speak to the men of Judah and to the inhabitants of Jerusalem, saying, 'Thus says the LORD: "Behold, I am fashioning a disaster and devising a plan against you. ᴿReturn now every one from his evil way, and make your ways and your doings ᴿgood." ' "   2 Kin. 17:13 · Jer. 7:3-7

God's Warning Rejected

12 And they said, ᴿ"That is hopeless! So we will walk according to our own plans, and we will every one ᵀobey the dictates of his evil
▲ heart."   Jer. 2:25 · Lit. do

13 Therefore thus says the LORD:

ᴿ"Ask now among the Gentiles,
Who has heard such things?
The virgin of Israel has done ᴿa very
   horrible thing.   Jer. 2:10, 11 · Jer. 5:30

14 Will a man ᵀleave the snow water of
   Lebanon,
Which comes from the rock of the
   field?
Will the cold flowing waters be
   forsaken for strange waters?   forsake

15 "Because My people have forgotten ᴿMe,
They have burned incense to worthless
   idols.
And they have caused themselves to
   stumble in their ways,
From the ᴿancient paths,
To walk in pathways and not on a
   highway,   Jer. 2:13, 32 · Jer. 6:16

16 To make their land ᴿdesolate and a
   perpetual ᴿhissing;
Everyone who passes by it will be
   astonished
And shake his head.   Jer. 19:8 · 1 Kin. 9:8

17 ᴿI will scatter them ᴿas with an east
   wind before the enemy;
ᴿI will *show them the back and not the
   face   Jer. 13:24 · Ps. 48:7 · Jer. 2:27
In the day of their calamity."

Jeremiah Persecuted

18 Then they said, "Come and let us devise plans against Jeremiah; for the law shall not perish from the priest, nor counsel from the wise, nor the word from the prophet. Come and let us attack him with the tongue, and let us not give heed to any of his words."

19 Give heed to me, O LORD,
   And listen to the voice of those who
   contend with me!

18:17 So with LXX, Syr., Tg., Vg.; MT look them in

(Point 5-C continued from previous page)
great and comforting truth, the doctrine of the sovereignty of God would be a dreaded and frightening fact. We would live in constant fear. But now we know that His throne "is the place of our [the believers'] sanctuary"—a refuge to flee to. And someday we, who are believers, can come bodily to the place where Jesus is seated with the Father, on the Father's throne (Rev. 3:21, page 1297). It is also called "the throne of grace" (Heb. 4:16, page 1239), where we can find refuge from the powers of Satan, demons, temptations, and sins of the flesh. It is truly a "glorious high throne."

In chapter 18, on the background of the vision of the sovereign throne in chapter 17, Jeremiah can better understand sovereignty as it is illustrated and interpreted at the potter's house. The first thing Jeremiah learned from the potter was that God is sovereign, that He has unlimited authority over all things, and that He always creates and molds everything perfectly. Now we come to the purpose of sovereignty. The potter was molding a clay vessel on the potter's wheel; he was a skilled craftsman; he had a purpose for his work; and he knew what he was making. But his purpose was thwarted when the clay "was marred in [emphasis added] the hand of the potter [not by the hand of the potter]; so he made it again into another vessel, as it seemed good to the potter to make" (v. 4). Now the lesson shines forth in sovereign grace: " 'O house of Israel, can I not do with you as this potter?' says the Lord. 'Look, as the clay is in the potter's hand, so are you in My hand, O house of Israel!' " (v. 6). God, in sovereign grace, would make Judah and Jerusalem into another vessel; but they refused. So God sent them into captivity for seventy years. By doing so, He remolded them as He desired.

God is sovereign over all nations and individuals. He either dispenses sovereign judgment or bestows sovereign grace, according to His just nature. But He never punishes or shows grace arbitrarily; He always has a purpose that befits His holy character.

See Romans 8:29, 30, page 1137, for **Point 5-D: The Sovereignty of God and Salvation.**

20 Shall evil be repaid for good?
   For they have dug a pit for my life.
   Remember that I ᴿstood before You
   To speak good for them,   Jer. 14:7—15:1
   To turn away Your wrath from them.
21 Therefore ᴿdeliver up their children to
      the famine,   Ps. 109:9-20
   And pour out their *blood*
   By the force of the sword;
   Let their wives *become* widows
   And ᴿbereaved of their children.
   Let their men be put to death,
   Their young men *be* slain
   By the sword in battle.   Jer. 15:7, 8
22 Let a cry be heard from their houses,
   When You bring a troop suddenly upon
      them;
   For they have dug a pit to take me,
   And hidden snares for my feet.
23 Yet, Lᴏʀᴅ, You know all their counsel
   Which is against me, to slay *me*.
   ᴿProvide no atonement for their iniquity,
   Nor blot out their sin from Your sight;
   But let them be overthrown before You.
   Deal *thus* with them   Ps. 35:14; 109:14
   In the time of Your ᴿanger.   Jer. 7:20

The Sign of the Broken Flask

19 Thus says the Lᴏʀᴅ: "Go and get a
   potter's earthen flask, and *take* some
of the elders of the people and some of the
elders of the priests.
2 "And go out to ᴿthe Valley of the Son of
Hinnom, which *is* by the entry of the Potsherd Gate; and proclaim there the words
that I will tell you,   Josh. 15:8
3 ᴿ"and say, 'Hear the word of the Lᴏʀᴅ, O
kings of Judah and inhabitants of Jerusalem.
Thus says the Lᴏʀᴅ of hosts, the God of
Israel: "Behold, I will bring such a catastrophe on this place, that whoever hears of it,
his ears will ᴿtingle.   Jer. 17:20 · 1 Sam. 3:11
4 "Because they ᴿhave forsaken Me and
made this an alien place, because they have
burned incense in it to other gods whom
neither they, their fathers, nor the kings of
Judah have known, and have filled this place
with the blood of the innocents   Is. 65:11
5 "(they have also built the high places of
Baal, to burn their sons with fire *for* burnt
offerings to Baal, which I did not command
or speak, nor did it come into My mind),
6 "therefore behold, the days are coming,"
says the Lᴏʀᴅ, "that this place shall no more
be called Tophet or ᴿthe Valley of the Son of
Hinnom, but the Valley of Slaughter. Josh. 15:8
7 "And I will make void the counsel of
Judah and Jerusalem in this place, ᴿand I will
cause them to fall by the sword before their
enemies and by the hands of those who seek
their lives; their ᴿcorpses I will give as meat
for the birds of the heaven and for the beasts
of the earth.   Lev. 26:17 · Ps. 79:2

8 "I will make this city desolate and a
hissing; everyone who passes by it will be
astonished and hiss because of all its plagues.
9 "And I will cause them to eat the ᴿflesh
of their sons and the flesh of their daughters,
and everyone shall eat the flesh of his friend
in the siege and in the desperation with
which their enemies and those who seek their
lives shall drive them to despair." ' Lev. 26:29
10 ᴿ"Then you shall break the flask in the
sight of the men who go with you,   Jer. 51:63, 64
11 "and say to them, 'Thus says the Lᴏʀᴅ of
hosts: ᴿ"Even so I will break this people and
this city, as *one* breaks a potter's vessel,
which cannot be ᵀmade whole again; and
they shall ᴿbury *them* in Tophet till *there is*
no place to bury.   Is. 30:14 · *restored* · Jer. 7:32
12 "Thus I will do to this place," says the
Lᴏʀᴅ, "and to its inhabitants, and make this
city like Tophet.
13 "And the houses of Jerusalem and the
houses of the kings of Judah shall be defiled
like the place of Tophet, because of all the
houses on whose roofs they have burned
incense to all the host of heaven, and poured
out drink offerings to other gods." ' "
14 Then Jeremiah came from Tophet,
where the Lᴏʀᴅ had sent him to prophesy;
and he stood in ᴿthe court of the Lord's house
and said to all the people,   2 Chr. 20:5
15 "Thus says the Lᴏʀᴅ of hosts, the God of
Israel: 'Behold, I will bring on this city and on
all her towns all the doom that I have pronounced against it, because ᴿthey have stiffened their necks that they might not hear
My words.' "   Neh. 9:17, 29

The Word of God to Pashhur

20 Now ᴿPashhur the son of ᴿImmer, the
   priest who *was* also chief governor in
the house of the Lᴏʀᴅ, heard that Jeremiah
prophesied these things. Ezra 2:37, 38 · 1 Chr. 24:14
2 Then Pashhur struck Jeremiah the
prophet, and put him in the stocks that *were*
in the high ᴿgate of Benjamin, which *was* by
the house of the Lᴏʀᴅ.   Jer. 37:13
3 And it happened on the next day that
Pashhur brought Jeremiah out of the stocks.
Then Jeremiah said to him, "The Lᴏʀᴅ has
not called your name Pashhur, but ᵀMagor-
Missabib.   Lit. *Fear on Every Side*
4 "For thus says the Lᴏʀᴅ: 'Behold, I will
make you a terror to yourself and to all your
friends; and they shall fall by the sword of
their enemies, and your eyes shall see *it*. I will
give all Judah into the hand of the king of
Babylon, and he shall carry them captive to
Babylon and slay them with the sword.
5 'Moreover I ᴿwill deliver all the wealth of
this city, all its produce, and all its precious
things; all the treasures of the kings of Judah
I will give into the hand of their enemies,

who will plunder them, seize them, and
[R]carry them to Babylon.   2 Kin. 20:17 • Is. 39:6
6 'And you, Pashhur, and all who dwell in
your house, shall go into captivity. You shall
go to Babylon, and there you shall die, and be
buried there, you and all your friends, to
whom you have [R]prophesied lies.' "   Jer. 14:13-15

Jeremiah's Unpopular Ministry

7 O LORD, You [T]induced me, and I was
    persuaded;   enticed or persuaded
    [R]You are stronger than I, and have
    prevailed.   Jer. 1:6, 7
    I am [T]in derision daily;
    Everyone mocks me.   Lit. a laughingstock
8 For when I spoke, I cried out;
    [R]I shouted, "Violence and plunder!"
    Because the word of the LORD was
        made to me
    A reproach and a derision daily.   Jer. 6:7
9 Then I said, "I will not make mention
        of Him,
    Nor speak anymore in His name."
    But His word was in my heart like a
        [R]burning fire
    Shut up in my bones;
    I was weary of holding it back,
    And [R]I could not.   Ps. 39:3 • Job 32:18
10 [R]For I heard many [T]mocking:
    "Fear on every side!"   Ps. 31:13 • slandering
    "Report," they say, "and we will report
        it!"
    [R]All my acquaintances watched for my
        stumbling, saying,   Ps. 41:9; 55:13, 14
    "Perhaps he can be induced;
    Then we will prevail against him,
    And we will take our revenge on him."
11 But the LORD is [R]with me as a mighty,
    awesome One.   Jer. 1:18, 19
    Therefore my persecutors will stumble,
    and will not [R]prevail.   Jer. 15:20; 17:18
    They will be greatly ashamed, for they
        will not prosper.
    Their [R]everlasting confusion will never
        be forgotten.   Jer. 23:40
12 But, O LORD of hosts,
    You who [R]test the
        righteous,   [Jer. 11:20; 17:10]
    And see the [T]mind and heart,
    Let me see Your vengeance on them;
    For I have pleaded my cause before
        You.   Most secret parts, lit. kidneys
13 Sing to the LORD! Praise the LORD!
    For [R]He has delivered the life of the
        poor   Ps. 35:9, 10; 109:30, 31
    From the hand of evildoers.
14 [R]Cursed be the day in which I was born!
    Let the day not be blessed in which my
        mother bore me!   Job 3:3
15 Let the man be cursed
    Who brought news to my father,
        saying,

"A male child has been born to you!"
    Making him very glad.
16 And let that man be like the cities
    Which the LORD [R]overthrew, and did
        not relent;   Gen. 19:25
    Let him [R]hear the cry in the morning
    And the shouting at noon,   Jer. 18:22
17 [R]Because he did not kill me from the
        womb,
    That my mother might have been my
        grave,
    And her womb always enlarged with
        me.   Job 3:10, 11
18 [R]Why did I come forth from the womb
        to [R]see [T]labor and sorrow,
    That my days should be consumed with
        shame?   Job 3:20 • Lam. 3:1 • toil

Jerusalem's Doom Is Sealed

21 The word which came to Jeremiah
    from the LORD when [R]King Zedekiah
sent to him [R]Pashhur the son of Melchiah,
and [R]Zephaniah the son of Maaseiah, the
priest, saying,   2 Kin. 24:17, 18 • Jer. 38:1 • 2 Kin. 25:18
2 [R]"Please inquire of the LORD for us, for
*Nebuchadnezzar king of Babylon makes
war against us. Perhaps the LORD will deal
with us according to all His wonderful works,
that the king may go away from us."   Jer. 37:3, 7
3 Then Jeremiah said to them, "Thus you
shall say to Zedekiah,
4 'Thus says the LORD God of Israel: "Behold, I will turn back the weapons of war that
are in your hands, with which you fight
against the king of Babylon and the *Chaldeans who besiege you outside the walls; and I
will assemble them in the midst of this city.
5 "I Myself will fight against you with an
outstretched hand and with a strong arm,
even in anger and fury and great wrath.
6 "I will strike the inhabitants of this city,
both man and beast; they shall die of a great
pestilence.
7 "And afterward," says the LORD, "I will
deliver Zedekiah king of Judah, his servants
and the people, and such as are left in this
city from the pestilence and the sword and
the famine, into the hand of Nebuchadnezzar
king of Babylon, into the hand of their enemies, and into the hand of those who seek
their life; and he shall strike them with the
edge of the sword. [R]He shall not spare them,
or have pity or mercy." '   2 Chr. 36:17
8 "Now you shall say to this people, 'Thus
says the LORD: "Behold, [R]I set before you the
way of life and the way of death.   Deut. 30:15, 19
9 "He who remains in this city shall die by
the sword, by famine, and by pestilence; but
he who goes out and [T]defects to the Chalde-

21:2 Heb. Nebuchadrezzar, and so elsewhere in the
book
21:4 Or Babylonians, and so elsewhere in the book

ans who besiege you, he shall live, and his life shall be as a prize to him. Lit. *falls away*

10 "For I have ᴿset My face against this city for adversity and not for good," says the LORD. ᴿ"It shall be given into the hand of the king of Babylon, and he shall ᴿburn it with fire." ' Amos 9:4 · Jer. 38:3 · Jer. 34:2, 22; 37:10

Message to the House of David

11 "And concerning the house of the king of Judah, *say,* 'Hear the word of the LORD,
12 'O house of David! Thus says the LORD:

"Execute judgment in the morning;
And deliver *him who is* plundered
Out of the hand of the oppressor,
Lest My fury go forth like fire
And burn so that no one can quench *it,*
Because of the evil of your doings.

13 "Behold, ᴿI *am* against you, O
ᵀinhabitant of the valley,
And rock of the plain," says the LORD,
"Who say, ᴿ'Who shall come down
against us? [Ezek. 13:8] · *dweller* · Jer. 49:4
Or who shall enter our dwellings?'
14 But I will punish you according to the
ᴿfruit of your ᵀdoings," says the
LORD;
"I will kindle a fire in its forest,
And ᴿit shall devour all things around
it." ' " Is. 3:10, 11 · *deeds* · 2 Chr. 36:19

22 Thus says the LORD: "Go down to the house of the king of Judah, and there speak this word,
2 "and say, ᴿ'Hear the word of the LORD, O king of Judah, you who sit on the throne of David, you and your servants and your people who enter these gates! Jer. 17:20
3 'Thus says the LORD: "Execute judgment and righteousness, and deliver the plundered out of the hand of the oppressor. Do no wrong and do no violence to the stranger, the ᴿfatherless, or the widow, nor shed innocent blood in this place. Jer. 7:6
4 "For if you indeed do this thing, ᴿthen shall enter the gates of this house, riding on horses and in chariots, accompanied by servants and people, kings who sit on the throne of David. Jer. 17:25
5 "But if you will not ᵀhear these words, I swear by Myself," says the LORD, "that this house shall become a desolation." ' " Obey
6 For thus says the LORD to the house of the king of Judah:

"You *are* ᴿGilead to Me, Song 4:1
The head of Lebanon;
Yet I surely will make you a wilderness,
Cities *which* are not inhabited.
7 I will prepare destroyers against you,
Everyone with his weapons;
They shall cut down ᴿyour choice
cedars Is. 37:24
ᴿAnd cast *them* into the fire. Jer. 21:14

8 "And many nations will pass by this city; and everyone will say to his neighbor, 'Why has the LORD done so to this great city?'
9 "Then they will answer, ᴿ'Because they have forsaken the covenant of the LORD their God, and worshiped other gods and served them.' " 2 Chr. 34:25

10 Weep not for ᴿthe dead, nor bemoan
him; 2 Kin. 22:20
Weep bitterly for him who goes away,
For he shall return no more,
Nor see his native country.

Message to the Sons of Josiah

11 For thus says the LORD concerning ᵀShallum the son of Josiah, king of Judah, who reigned instead of Josiah his father, ᴿwho went from this place: "He shall not return here anymore, Or *Jehoahaz* · 2 Kin. 23:34
12 "but he shall die in the place where they have led him captive, and shall see this land no more.

13 "Woeᴿ to him who builds his house by
unrighteousness 2 Kin. 23:35
And his chambers by injustice,
ᴿ*Who* uses his neighbor's service
without wages James 5:4
And gives him nothing for his work,
14 Who says, 'I will build myself a wide
house with spacious chambers,
And cut out windows for it,
Paneling *it* with cedar
And painting *it* with vermilion.'
15 "Shall you reign because you enclose
yourself in cedar?
Did not your father eat and drink,
And do justice and righteousness?
Then ᴿ*it was* well with him. Ps. 128:2
16 He ᵀjudged the cause of the poor and
needy;
Then *it was* well.
Was not this knowing Me?" says the
LORD. Defended
17 "Yetᴿ your eyes and your heart *are* for
nothing but your covetousness,
For shedding innocent blood,
And practicing oppression and
violence." Ezek. 19:6

18 Therefore thus says the LORD concerning Jehoiakim the son of Josiah, king of Judah:

ᴿ"They shall not lament for him,
Saying, ᴿ'Alas, my brother!' or 'Alas, my
sister!'
They shall not lament for him,
Saying, 'Alas, master!' or 'Alas, his
glory!' Jer. 16:4, 6 · 1 Kin. 13:30
19 ᴿHe shall be buried with the burial of a
donkey,
Dragged and cast out beyond the gates
of Jerusalem. Jer. 36:30

20 "Go up to Lebanon, and cry out,
   And lift up your voice in Bashan;
   Cry from Abarim,
   For all your lovers are destroyed.
21 I spoke to you in your prosperity,
   But you said, 'I will not hear.'
   R This *has been* your manner from your
   youth,   Jer. 3:24, 25; 32:30
   That you did not obey My voice.
22 The wind shall eat up all R your T rulers,
   And your lovers shall go into captivity;
   Surely then you will be ashamed and
   humiliated   Jer. 23:1 • Lit. *shepherds*
   For all your wickedness.
23 O inhabitant of Lebanon,
   Making your nest in the cedars,
   How gracious will you be when pangs
   come upon you,
   Like the pain of a woman in labor?

Message to Coniah

24 "*As* I live," says the LORD, "though
   T Coniah the son of Jehoiakim, king of Judah,
   were the signet on My right hand, yet I
   would pluck you off;   Or *Jeconiah* or *Jehoiachin*
25 R "and I will give you into the hand of
   those who seek your life, and into the hand
   of those whose face you fear—the hand of
   Nebuchadnezzar king of Babylon and the
   hand of the T Chaldeans.   Jer. 34:20 • Or *Babylonians*
26 "So I will cast you out, and your mother
   who bore you, into another country where
   you were not born; and there you shall die.
27 "But to the land to which they desire to
   return, there they shall not return.

28 "Is this man T Coniah a despised, broken
   idol—
   R A vessel in which *is* no pleasure?
   Why are they cast out, he and his
   descendants,
   And cast into a land which they do not
   know?   Jehoiachin, v. 24 • Hos. 8:8
29 R O earth, earth, earth,
   Hear the word of the LORD!   Deut. 32:1
30 Thus says the LORD:

'Write this man down as R childless,
   A man *who* shall not prosper in his
   days;   Matt. 1:12
   For R none of his descendants shall
   prosper,   Jer. 36:30
   Sitting on the throne of David,
   And ruling anymore in Judah.' "

The Branch of Righteousness

23 "Woe R to the shepherds who destroy
   and scatter the sheep of My pasture!"
says the LORD.   Jer. 10:21
2 Therefore thus says the LORD God of
Israel against the shepherds who feed My
people: "You have scattered My flock, driven
them away, and not attended to them. R Behold, I will attend to you for the evil of your
doings," says the LORD.   Ex. 32:34
3 "But R I will gather the remnant of My
flock out of all countries where I have driven
them, and bring them back to their folds; and
they shall be fruitful and increase. Jer. 32:37
4 "I will set up R shepherds over them who
will feed them; and they shall fear no more,
nor be dismayed, nor shall they be lacking,"
says the LORD.   Jer. 3:15

5 "Behold, R *the* days are coming," says the
   LORD,   Jer. 33:14
   "That I R will raise to David a Branch of
   righteousness;   Matt. 1:1, 6
   A King shall reign and prosper,
   And execute T judgment and
   righteousness in the T earth.   *justice • land*

4-E. Jehovah-Tsidkenu: The LORD Our   ▼
Righteousness

6 In His days Judah will be saved,
   And Israel R will dwell safely;
   Now R this *is* His name by which He will
   be called: Jer. 32:37 • [1 Cor. 1:30]

*THE LORD OUR RIGHTEOUSNESS.   ▲

7 "Therefore, behold, R *the* days are coming," says the LORD, "that they shall no

23:6 Heb. *YHWH Tsidkenu*

4-E. Jehovah-Tsidkenu: The LORD Our Righteousness (Jeremiah 23:6)—Jeremiah prophesied until the time
of the Babylonian exile. He warned Israel that because of her sins, God was going to allow the Babylonians
to invade, destroy Solomon's temple, and lead them away into a seventy-year captivity—one from which
many would never return, not even their children. Babylon's first invasion came in 606 B.C., the second in 597
B.C., and the third in 586 B.C. Then Jerusalem and the temple were destroyed, and the people were deported.

   God blamed the idolatrous and faithless kings and the false religious teachers for leading Israel into sin,
causing Him to send the people into captivity. To them He exclaims, "You have scattered My flock" (Jer.
23:2, page 735). He then looked far into the future, to the end-times and the millennial kingdom, when Israel
shall praise the Lord for returning them from their captivity among the nations (v. 8). Here Jeremiah
proclaims that the final return of the children of Israel will coincide with God's raising up the Messiah—"I
will raise to David a Branch of righteousness" (v. 5). Next he adds that "Israel will dwell safely" (v. 6)—
signifying that in the messianic age the existence of Israel in the Middle East is guaranteed by God; no longer
will nations threaten to destroy her. The Messiah's name is *Jehovah-Tsidkenu*, "THE LORD OUR
RIGHTEOUSNESS" (v. 6). There is much to be gleaned from this.

   (1) Paul, writing the letter to the Romans 650 years later, echoed Jeremiah, and declared that unbelieving
(Point 4-E continued on next page)

longer say, 'As the LORD lives who brought up the children of Israel from the land of Egypt,'   Jer. 16:14

8 but, 'As the LORD lives who brought up and led the descendants of the house of Israel from the north country and from all the countries where I had driven them.' And they shall dwell in their own land."

False Prophets and Empty Oracles

9 My heart within me is broken
    Because of the prophets;
    ^RAll my bones shake.
    I am like a drunken man,
    And like a man whom wine has
      overcome,
    Because of the LORD,
    And because of His holy words.   Hab. 3:16
10 For ^Rthe land is full of adulterers;
    For ^Rbecause of a curse the land
      mourns.   Jer. 9:2 • Hos. 4:2
    ^RThe pleasant places of the wilderness
      are dried up.   Jer. 9:10
    Their course of life is evil,
    And their might *is* not right.

11 "For ^Rboth prophet and priest are
    profane;   Zeph. 3:4
    Yes, ^Rin My house I have found their
      wickedness," says the LORD.   Jer. 7:30
12 "Therefore^R their way shall be to them
    Like slippery *ways*;
    In the darkness they shall be driven on
    And fall in them;
    For I ^Rwill bring disaster on them,
    The year of their punishment," says the
    LORD.   [Prov. 4:19] • Jer. 11:23
13 "And I have seen ^Tfolly in the prophets
    of Samaria: Lit. *distastefulness*
    ^RThey prophesied by Baal   Jer. 2:8
    And caused My people Israel to err.
14 Also I have seen a horrible thing in the
    prophets of Jerusalem:
    ^RThey commit adultery and walk in lies;
    They also ^Rstrengthen the hands of
      evildoers,   Jer. 29:23 • Ezek. 13:22, 23

So that no one turns back from his
    wickedness.
All of them are like Sodom to Me,
And her inhabitants like Gomorrah.
15 "Therefore thus says the LORD of hosts
    concerning the prophets:
    'Behold, I will feed them with
      ^Rwormwood,
    And make them drink the water of gall;
    For from the prophets of Jerusalem
    ^TProfaneness has gone out into all the
      land.' "   Jer. 9:15 • Or *Pollution*

16 Thus says the LORD of hosts:

    "Do not listen to the words of the
      prophets who prophesy to you.
    They make you worthless;
    They speak a vision of their own heart,
    Not from the mouth of the LORD.
17 They continually say to those who
      despise Me,
    'The LORD has said, ^R"You shall have
      peace" ';   Ezek. 13:10
    And to everyone who walks according
      to the dictates of his own heart,
    ^R'No evil shall come upon you.' "   Mic. 3:11

18 For ^Rwho has stood in the counsel of
      the LORD,
    And has perceived and heard His word?
    Who has marked His word and heard
      it?   [1 Cor. 2:16]
19 Behold, a ^Rwhirlwind of the LORD has
      gone forth in fury—
    A violent whirlwind!
    It will fall violently on the head of the
      wicked.   Amos 1:14
20 The ^Ranger of the LORD will not turn
      back
    Until He has executed and performed
      the thoughts of His heart.
    ^RIn the latter days you will understand it
      perfectly.   Jer. 30:24 • Gen. 49:1

21 "I^R have not sent these prophets, yet
    they ran.

(Point 4-E continued from previous page)
Israel is still hunting for her righteousness, while Jehovah-Jesus is "righteousness to everyone who believes" (Rom. 10:1–4, page 1140).

     (2) Israel will yet know Jesus who is her righteousness in the millennial age to come (Rom. 10:1–4, page 1140; 11:25–27, page 1141; cf. Matt. 25:31–34, page 976).

     (3) Our own efforts at being righteous—trying to be upright and free from sin—are called "filthy rags" (Is. 64:6, page 703).

     (4) The psalmist says that God's search for a righteous person ended in His declaration that "there is none who does good, no, not one" (Ps. 14:2, 3, page 517).

     (5) The parable of the wedding feast, told by Christ, shows that no one will be allowed into heaven wearing his own good deeds for righteousness. God (the King) orders the dismissal of the one who refused the pure garment of righteousness (Christ), which He had provided for all guests to wear (Matt. 22:11–13, page 970).

     That perfect moral uprightness, demanded by God's holy standards, is provided only by God Himself, through faith in Christ; for it is He who is Jehovah-Tsidkenu, "THE LORD OUR RIGHTEOUSNESS" (cf. 2 Cor. 5:21, page 1169).

     See Psalm 23:1, page 524, for **Point 4-F: Jehovah-Rohi: The LORD My Shepherd.**

I have not spoken to them, yet they prophesied.   Jer. 14:14; 23:32; 27:15

22 But if they had stood in My counsel,
And had caused My people to hear My
   words,
Then they would have ^Rturned them
   from their evil way
And from the evil of their doings. Jer. 25:5

23 "*Am* I a God near at hand," says the
   Lord,
   "And not a God afar off?
24 Can anyone ^Rhide himself in secret
   places,
   So I shall not see him?" says the Lord;
   ^R"Do I not fill heaven and earth?" says
   the Lord.   [Ps. 139:7] · [1 Kin. 8:27]

25 "I have heard what the prophets have
said who prophesy lies in My name, saying, 'I
have dreamed, I have dreamed!'
26 "How long will *this* be in the heart of the
prophets who prophesy lies? Indeed *they are*
prophets of the deceit of their own heart,
27 "who try to make My people forget My
name by their dreams which everyone tells
his neighbor, ^Ras their fathers forgot My
name for Baal.   Judg. 3:7

28 "The prophet who has a dream, let him
   tell a dream;
   And he who has My word, let him
      speak My word faithfully.
   What *is* the chaff to the wheat?" says
      the Lord.
29 "*Is* not My word like a ^Rfire?" says the
   Lord,
   "And like a hammer *that* breaks the
      rock in pieces?   Jer. 5:14

30 "Therefore behold, ^RI *am* against the
prophets," says the Lord, "who steal My
words every one from his neighbor. Deut. 18:20
31 "Behold, I *am* ^Ragainst the prophets,"
says the Lord, "who use their tongues and
say, 'He says.'   Ezek. 13:9
32 "Behold, I *am* against those who prophesy false dreams," says the Lord, "and tell
them, and cause My people to err by their
^Rlies and by ^Rtheir recklessness. Yet I did not
send them or command them; therefore they
shall not ^Rprofit this people at all," says the
Lord.   Lam. 2:14; 3:37 · Zeph. 3:4 · Jer. 7:8
33 "So when these people or the prophet or
the priest ask you, saying, 'What is ^Rthe
^Toracle of the Lord?' you shall then say to
them, *'What oracle?' I will even forsake
you," says the Lord.   Mal. 1:1 · *burden, prophecy*
34 "And *as for* the prophet and the priest
and the people who say, 'The ^Toracle of the
Lord!' I will even punish that man and his
house.   *burden, prophecy*
35 "Thus every one of you shall say to his

23:33 LXX, Tg., Vg. *'You are the burden'*

neighbor, and every one to his brother, 'What
has the Lord answered?' and, 'What has the
Lord spoken?'
36 "And the ^Toracle of the Lord you shall
mention no more. For every man's word will
be his oracle, for you have ^Rperverted the
words of the living God, the Lord of hosts,
our God.   *burden, prophecy* · Deut. 4:2
37 "Thus you shall say to the prophet,
'What has the Lord answered you?' and,
'What has the Lord spoken?'
38 "But since you say, 'The ^Toracle of the
Lord!' therefore thus says the Lord: 'Because
you say this word, "The oracle of the Lord!"
and I have sent to you, saying, "Do not say,
'The oracle of the Lord!' "   *burden, prophecy*
39 'therefore behold, I, even I, ^Rwill utterly
forget you and forsake you, and the city that
I gave you and your fathers, and *will cast you
out of My presence.   Hos. 4:6
40 'And I will bring an everlasting reproach
upon you, and a perpetual ^Rshame, which
shall not be forgotten.' "   Mic. 3:5-7

The Sign of Two Baskets of Figs

24 The ^RLord showed me, and there were
two baskets of figs set before the tem-
ple of the Lord, after Nebuchadnezzar ^Rking
of Babylon had carried away captive Jeconiah the son of Jehoiakim, king of Judah, and
the princes of Judah with the craftsmen and
smiths, from Jerusalem, and had brought
them to Babylon.   Amos 7:1, 4; 8:1 · 2 Kin. 24:12-16
2 One basket *had* very good figs, like the
figs *that are* first ripe; and the other basket
had very bad figs which could not be eaten,
they were so ^Rbad.   Jer. 29:17
3 Then the Lord said to me, "What do you
see, Jeremiah?" And I said, "Figs, the good
figs, very good; and the bad, very bad, which
cannot be eaten, they are so bad."
4 Again the word of the Lord came to me,
saying,
5 "Thus says the Lord, the God of Israel:
'Like these good figs, so will I ^Tacknowledge
those who are carried away captive from
Judah, whom I have sent out of this place for
their own good, into the land of the Chaldeans.   *regard*
6 'For I will set My eyes on them for good,
and I will bring them back to this land; I will
build them and not pull *them* down, and I will
plant them and not pluck *them* up.
7 'Then I will give them a heart to know
Me, that I *am* the Lord; and they shall be My
people, and I will be their God, for they shall
return to Me with their whole heart.
8 'And as the bad figs which cannot be
eaten, they are so bad'—surely thus says the
Lord—'so will I give up Zedekiah the king of
Judah, his princes, the residue of Jerusalem
who remain in this land, and ^Rthose who
dwell in the land of Egypt.   Jer. 44:1, 26-30

9 'I will deliver them to trouble into all the kingdoms of the earth, for *their* harm, *to be* a reproach and a byword, a taunt and a curse, in all places where I shall drive them.

10 'And I will send the sword, the famine, and the pestilence among them, till they are ^Tconsumed from the land that I gave to them and their fathers.' " *destroyed*

Seventy Years of Desolation

25 The word that came to Jeremiah concerning all the people of Judah, ^Rin the fourth year of Jehoiakim the son of Josiah, king of Judah (which *was* the first year of Nebuchadnezzar king of Babylon), Jer. 36:1

2 which Jeremiah the prophet spoke to all the people of Judah and to all the inhabitants of Jerusalem, saying:

3 ^R"From the thirteenth year of Josiah the son of Amon, king of Judah, even to this day, this *is* the twenty-third year in which the word of the LORD has come to me; and I have spoken to you, rising early and speaking, ^Rbut you have not listened. Jer. 1:2 • Jer. 7:13; 11:7, 8, 10

4 "And the LORD has sent to you all His servants the prophets, ^Rrising early and sending *them*, but you have not listened nor inclined your ear to hear. Jer. 7:13, 25

5 "They said, ^R'Repent now everyone of his evil way and his evil doings, and dwell in the land that the LORD has given to you and your fathers forever and ever. Jer. 18:11

6 'Do not go after other gods to serve them and worship them, and do not provoke Me to anger with the works of your hands; and I will not harm you.'

7 "Yet you have not listened to Me," says the LORD, "that you might ^Rprovoke Me to anger with the works of your hands to your own hurt. Deut. 32:21

8 "Therefore thus says the LORD of hosts: 'Because you have not heard My words,

9 'behold, I will send and take all the families of the north,' says the LORD, 'and Nebuchadnezzar the king of Babylon, My servant, and will bring them against this land, against its inhabitants, and against these nations all around, and will utterly destroy them, and ^Rmake them an astonishment, a hissing, and perpetual desolations. Jer. 18:16

10 'Moreover I will ^Ttake from them the voice of mirth and the voice of gladness, the voice of the bridegroom and the voice of the bride, the sound of the millstones and the light of the lamp. Lit. *cause to perish from them*

11 'And this whole land shall be a desolation *and* an astonishment, and these nations shall serve the king of Babylon seventy years.

12 'Then it will come to pass, ^Rwhen seventy years are completed, *that* I will punish the king of Babylon and that nation, the land of the Chaldeans, for their iniquity,' says the

LORD; ^Rand I will make it a perpetual desolation. Ezra 1:1 • Is. 13:20

13 'So I will bring on that land all My words which I have pronounced against it, all that is written in this book, which Jeremiah has prophesied concerning all the nations.

14 '(For many nations and great kings shall ^Rbe served by them also; and I will repay them according to their deeds and according to the works of their own hands.)' " Jer. 27:7

Judgment on the Nations

15 For thus says the LORD God of Israel to me: "Take this ^Rwine cup of ^Tfury from My hand, and cause all the nations, to whom I send you, to drink it. Rev. 14:10 • *wrath*

16 "And ^Rthey will drink and stagger and go mad because of the sword that I will send among them." Nah. 3:11

17 Then I took the cup from the LORD's hand, and made all the nations drink, to whom the LORD had sent me:

18 Jerusalem and the cities of Judah, its kings and its princes, to make them ^Ra desolation, an astonishment, a hissing, and ^Ra curse, as *it is* this day; Jer. 25:9, 11 • Jer. 24:9

19 Pharaoh king of Egypt, his servants, his princes, and all his people;

20 all the mixed multitude, all the kings of the land of Uz, all the kings of the land of the Philistines (namely, Ashkelon, Gaza, Ekron, and the remnant of Ashdod);

21 Edom, Moab, and the people of Ammon;

22 all the kings of ^RTyre, all the kings of Sidon, and the kings of the coastlands which *are* across the ^Rsea; Jer. 47:4 • Jer. 49:23

23 ^RDedan, Tema, Buz, and all *who are* in the farthest corners; Jer. 49:7, 8

24 all the kings of Arabia and all the kings of the ^Rmixed multitude who dwell in the desert; Ezek. 30:5

25 all the kings of Zimri, all the kings of Elam, and all the kings of the Medes;

26 ^Rall the kings of the north, far and near, one with another; and all the kingdoms of the world which *are* on the face of the earth. Also the king of ^TSheshach shall drink after them. Jer. 50:9 • A code word for *Babylon*, Jer. 51:41

27 "Therefore you shall say to them, 'Thus says the LORD of hosts, the God of Israel: ^R"Drink, ^Rbe drunk, and vomit! Fall and rise no more, because of the sword which I will send among you." ' Hab. 2:16 • Is. 63:6

28 "And it shall be, if they refuse to take the cup from your hand to drink, then you shall say to them, 'Thus says the LORD of hosts: "You shall certainly drink!

29 "For behold, ^RI begin to bring calamity on the city ^Rwhich is called by My name, and should you be utterly unpunished? You shall not be unpunished, for ^RI will call for a sword on all the inhabitants of the earth," says the LORD of hosts.' Ezek. 9:6 • Dan. 9:18 • Ezek. 38:21

30 "Therefore prophesy against them all these words, and say to them:

'The LORD will ᴿroar from on high,
And utter His voice from ᴿHis holy
　habitation;　　　　　Amos 1:2 · Ps. 11:4
He will roar mightily against ᴿHis fold.
He will give ᴿa shout, as those who
　tread *the grapes,*　　1 Kin. 9:3 · Is. 16:9
Against all the inhabitants of the earth.
31 A noise will come to the ends of the
　earth—
For the LORD has ᴿa controversy with
　the nations;　　　　　　　　Mic. 6:2
ᴿHe will plead His case with all flesh.
He will give those *who are* wicked to
　the sword,' says the LORD."　　Is. 66:16

32 Thus says the LORD of hosts:

"Behold, disaster shall go forth
From nation to nation,
And ᴿa great whirlwind shall be raised
　up　　　　　　　　　Jer. 23:19; 30:23
From the farthest parts of the earth.

33 "And at that day the slain of the LORD shall be from *one* end of the earth even to the *other* end of the earth. They shall not be lamented, ᴿor gathered, or buried; they shall become refuse on the ground.　　Ps. 79:3

34 "Wail,ᴿ shepherds, and cry!　Jer. 4:8; 6:26
Roll about *in the ashes,*
You leaders of the flock!
For the days of your slaughter and your
　dispersions are fulfilled;
You shall fall like a precious vessel.
35 And the shepherds will have no ᵀway to
　flee,　　　　　　　　Or *refuge*
Nor the leaders of the flock to escape.
36 A voice of the cry of the shepherds,
And a wailing of the leaders to the
　flock *will be heard.*
For the LORD has plundered their
　pasture,
37 And the peaceful dwellings are cut
　down
Because of the fierce anger of the LORD.
38 He has left His lair like the lion;
For their land is desolate
Because of the fierceness of the
　Oppressor,
And because of His fierce anger."

Jeremiah Saved from Death

26 In the beginning of the reign of Jehoiakim the son of Josiah, king of Judah, this word came from the LORD, saying,

2 "Thus says the LORD: 'Stand in ᴿthe court of the LORD's house, and speak to all the cities of Judah, which come to worship *in* the LORD's house, ᴿall the words that I command you to speak to them. ᴿDo not diminish a word.　　Jer. 19:14 · Matt. 28:20 · Acts 20:27

3 'Perhaps everyone will listen and turn from his evil way, that I may relent concerning the calamity which I purpose to bring on them because of the evil of their doings.'

4 "And you shall say to them, 'Thus says the LORD: "If you will not listen to Me, to walk in My law which I have set before you,

5 "to heed the words of My servants the prophets ᴿwhom I sent to you, both rising up early and sending *them* (but you have not heeded),　　　　　　　Jer. 25:4; 29:19

6 "then I will make this house like ᴿShiloh, and will make this city ᴿa curse to all the nations of the earth." ' "　　1 Sam. 4:10, 11 · Is. 65:15

7 So the priests and the prophets and all the people heard Jeremiah speaking these words in the house of the LORD.

8 Now it happened, when Jeremiah had made an end of speaking all that the LORD had commanded *him* to speak to all the people, that the priests and the prophets and all the people seized him, saying, "You will surely die!

9 "Why have you prophesied in the name of the LORD, saying, 'This house shall be like Shiloh, and this city shall be ᴿdesolate, without an inhabitant'?" And all the people were gathered against Jeremiah in the house of the LORD.　　　　　　　　　　Jer. 9:11

10 When the princes of Judah heard these things, they came up from the king's house to the house of the LORD and sat down in the entry of the New Gate of the LORD's *house.*

11 And the priests and the prophets spoke to the princes and all the people, saying, "This man deserves to ᴿdie! For he has prophesied against this city, as you have heard with your ears."　　　　　　　Jer. 38:4

12 Then Jeremiah spoke to all the princes and all the people, saying: "The LORD sent me to prophesy against this house and against this city with all the words that you have heard.

13 "Now therefore, ᴿamend your ways and your doings, and obey the voice of the LORD your God; then the LORD will relent concerning the doom that He has pronounced against you.　　　　　　　　　　Jer. 7:3

14 "As for me, here I am, in your hand; do with me as seems good and proper to you.

15 "But know for certain that if you put me to death, you will surely bring innocent blood on yourselves, on this city, and on its inhabitants; for truly the LORD has sent me to you to speak all these words in your hearing."

16 So the princes and all the people said to the priests and the prophets, "This man does not deserve to die. For he has spoken to us in the name of the LORD our God."

17 ᴿThen certain of the elders of the land rose up and spoke to all the assembly of the people, saying:　　　　　　Acts 5:34

18 ᴿ"Micah of Moresheth prophesied in the days of Hezekiah king of Judah, and spoke to all the people of Judah, saying, 'Thus says the LORD of hosts: Mic. 1:1

ᴿ"Zion shall be plowed *like* a field, Mic. 3:12
Jerusalem shall become heaps of ruins,
And the mountain of the *temple
Like the bare hills of the forest."'

19 "Did Hezekiah king of Judah and all Judah ever put him to death? Did he not fear the LORD and seek the LORD's favor? And the LORD relented concerning the doom which He had pronounced against them. But we are doing great evil against ourselves."

20 Now there was also a man who prophesied in the name of the LORD, Urijah the son of Shemaiah of Kirjath Jearim, who prophesied against this city and against this land according to all the words of Jeremiah.

21 And when Jehoiakim the king, with all his mighty men and all the princes, heard his words, the king sought to put him to death; but when Urijah heard *it*, he was afraid and fled, and went to Egypt.

22 Then Jehoiakim the king sent men to Egypt: Elnathan the son of Achbor, and *other* men *who went* with him to Egypt.

23 And they brought Urijah from Egypt and brought him to Jehoiakim the king, who killed him with the sword and cast his dead body into the graves of the common people.

24 Nevertheless ᴿthe hand of Ahikam the son of Shaphan was with Jeremiah, so that they should not give him into the hand of the people to put him to death.   2 Kin. 22:12-14

Symbol of the Bonds and Yokes

27 In* the beginning of the reign of *Jehoiakim the son of Josiah, king of Judah, this word came to Jeremiah from the LORD, saying,

2 "Thus says the LORD to me: 'Make for yourselves bonds and yokes, ᴿand put them on your neck,   Jer. 28:10, 12

3 'and send them to the king of Edom, the king of Moab, the king of the Ammonites, the king of Tyre, and the king of Sidon, by the hand of the messengers who come to Jerusalem to Zedekiah king of Judah.

4 'And command them to say to their masters, "Thus says the LORD of hosts, the God of Israel—thus you shall say to your masters:

5 ᴿ'I have made the earth, the man and the beast that *are* on the ground, by My great power and by My outstretched arm, and ᴿhave given it to whom it seemed proper to Me.   Is. 45:12 • Dan. 4:17, 25, 32

26:18 Lit. *house*
27:1 LXX omits v. 1 • So with MT, Tg., Vg.; some Heb. mss., Arab., Syr. *Zedekiah* (cf. 27:3, 12; 28:1)

6 'And now I have given all these lands into the hand of Nebuchadnezzar the king of Babylon, My servant; and the beasts of the field I have also given him to serve him.

7 'So all nations shall serve him and his son and his son's son, until the time of his land comes; and then many nations and great kings shall make him serve them.

8 'And it shall be, *that* the nation and kingdom which will not serve Nebuchadnezzar the king of Babylon, and which will not put its neck under the yoke of the king of Babylon, that nation I will punish,' says the LORD, 'with the sword, the famine, and the pestilence, until I have consumed them by his hand.

9 'Therefore do not listen to your prophets, your diviners, your ᵀdreamers, your soothsayers, or your sorcerers, who speak to you, saying, "You shall not serve the king of Babylon."   Lit. *dreams*

10 'For they prophesy a ᴿlie to you, to remove you far from your land; and I will drive you out, and you will perish.   Jer. 23:16

11 'But the nations that bring their necks under the yoke of the king of Babylon and serve him, I will let them remain in their own land,' says the LORD, 'and they shall till it and dwell in it.'"'"

12 I also spoke to ᴿZedekiah king of Judah according to all these words, saying, "Bring your necks under the yoke of the king of Babylon, and serve him and his people, and live!   Jer. 28:1; 38:17

13 ᴿ"Why will you die, you and your people, by the sword, by the famine, and by the pestilence, as the LORD has spoken against the nation that will not serve the king of Babylon?   [Ezek. 18:31]

14 "Therefore ᴿdo not listen to the words of the prophets who speak to you, saying, 'You shall not serve the king of Babylon,' for they prophesy a lie to you;   Jer. 23:16

15 "for I have ᴿnot sent them," says the LORD, "yet they prophesy a lie in My name, that I may drive you out, and that you may perish, you and the prophets who prophesy to you."   Jer. 23:21; 29:9

16 Also I spoke to the priests and to all this people, saying, "Thus says the LORD: 'Do not listen to the words of your prophets who prophesy to you, saying, "Behold, ᴿthe vessels of the LORD's house will now shortly be brought back from Babylon"; for they prophesy a lie to you.   Dan. 1:2

17 'Do not listen to them; serve the king of Babylon, and live! Why should this city be laid waste?

18 'But if they *are* prophets, and if the word of the LORD is with them, let them now make intercession to the LORD of hosts, that the vessels which are left in the house of the

LORD, *in* the house of the king of Judah, and at Jerusalem, do not go to Babylon.'

19 "For thus says the LORD of hosts ᴿconcerning the pillars, concerning the Sea, concerning the carts, and concerning the remainder of the vessels that remain in this city,   2 Kin. 25:13-17

20 "which Nebuchadnezzar king of Babylon did not take, when he carried away ᴿcaptive Jeconiah the son of Jehoiakim, king of Judah, from Jerusalem to Babylon, and all the nobles of Judah and Jerusalem—   Jer. 24:1

21 "yes, thus says the LORD of hosts, the God of Israel, concerning the vessels that remain in the house of the LORD, and in the house of the king of Judah and of Jerusalem:

22 'They shall be carried to Babylon, and there they shall be until the day that I visit them,' says the LORD. 'Then I will bring them up and restore them to this place.' "

Hananiah's Falsehood and Doom

28 And it happened in the same year, at the beginning of the reign of Zedekiah king of Judah, in the fourth year *and* in the fifth month, *that* Hananiah the son of Azur the prophet, who *was* from Gibeon, spoke to me in the house of the LORD in the presence of the priests and of all the people, saying,

2 "Thus speaks the LORD of hosts, the God of Israel, saying: 'I have broken ᴿthe yoke of the king of Babylon.   Jer. 27:12

3 ᴿWithin two full years I will bring back to this place all the vessels of the LORD's house, that Nebuchadnezzar king of Babylon ᴿtook away from this place and carried to Babylon.   Jer. 27:16 • Dan. 1:2

4 'And I will bring back to this place Jeconiah the son of Jehoiakim, king of Judah, with all the captives of Judah who went to Babylon,' says the LORD, 'for I will break the yoke of the king of Babylon.' "

5 Then the prophet Jeremiah spoke to the prophet Hananiah in the presence of the priests and in the presence of all the people who stood in the house of the LORD,

6 and the prophet Jeremiah said, ᴿ"Amen! The LORD do so; the LORD perform your words which you have prophesied, to bring back the vessels of the LORD's house and all who were carried away captive, from Babylon to this place.   1 Kin. 1:36

7 "Nevertheless hear now this word that I speak in your hearing and in the hearing of all the people:

8 "The prophets who have been before me and before you of old prophesied against many countries and great kingdoms—of war and disaster and pestilence.

9 "As for the prophet who prophesies of ᴿpeace, when the word of the prophet comes to pass, the prophet will be known *as* one whom the LORD has truly sent."   Jer. 23:17

10 Then Hananiah the prophet took the ᴿyoke off the prophet Jeremiah's neck and broke it.   Jer. 27:2

11 And Hananiah spoke in the presence of all the people, saying, "Thus says the LORD: 'Even so I will break the yoke of Nebuchadnezzar king of Babylon from the neck of all nations within the space of two full years.' " And the prophet Jeremiah went his way.

12 Now the word of the LORD came to Jeremiah, after Hananiah the prophet had broken the yoke from the neck of the prophet Jeremiah, saying,

13 "Go and tell Hananiah, saying, 'Thus says the LORD: "You have broken the yokes of wood, but you have made in their place yokes of iron."

14 'For thus says the LORD of hosts, the God of Israel: ᴿ"I have put a yoke of iron on the neck of all these nations, that they may serve Nebuchadnezzar king of Babylon; and they shall serve him. ᴿI have given him the beasts of the field also." ' "   Deut. 28:48 • Jer. 27:6

15 Then the prophet Jeremiah said to Hananiah the prophet, "Hear now, Hananiah, the LORD has not sent you, but ᴿyou make this people trust in a ᴿlie.   Ezek. 13:22 • Jer. 27:10; 29:9

16 "Therefore thus says the LORD: 'Behold, I will cast you from the face of the earth. This year you shall die, because you have taught ᴿrebellion against the LORD.' "   Deut. 13:5

17 So Hananiah the prophet died the same year in the seventh month.

Jeremiah's Letter to the Captives

29 Now these *are* the words of the letter that Jeremiah the prophet sent from Jerusalem to the remainder of the elders who were ᴿcarried away captive—to the priests, the prophets, and all the people whom Nebuchadnezzar had carried away captive from Jerusalem to Babylon.   Jer. 27:20

2 (This happened after Jeconiah the king, the queen mother, the eunuchs, the princes of Judah and Jerusalem, the craftsmen, and the smiths had departed from Jerusalem.)

3 *The letter was sent* by the hand of Elasah the son of ᴿShaphan, and Gemariah the son of Hilkiah, whom Zedekiah king of Judah sent to Babylon, to Nebuchadnezzar king of Babylon, saying,   2 Chr. 34:8

4 Thus says the LORD of hosts, the God of Israel, to all who were carried away captive, whom I have caused to be carried away from Jerusalem to Babylon:

5 Build houses and dwell in *them*; plant gardens and eat their fruit.

6 Take wives and beget sons and daughters; and take wives for your sons and give your daughters to husbands, so that they may bear sons and

daughters—that you may be increased there, and not diminished.

7 And seek the peace of the city where I have caused you to be carried away captive, and pray to the LORD for it; for in its peace you will have peace.

8 For thus says the LORD of hosts, the God of Israel: Do not let your prophets and your diviners who are in your midst deceive you, nor listen to your dreams which you cause to be dreamed.

9 For they prophesy ^Rfalsely to you in My name; I have not sent them, says the LORD.   Jer. 28:15; 37:19

10 For thus says the LORD: After ^Rseventy years are completed at Babylon, I will visit you and perform My good word toward you, and cause you to ^Rreturn to this place.   Dan. 9:2 • [Jer. 24:6, 7]

11 For I know the thoughts that I think toward you, says the LORD, thoughts of peace and not of evil, to give you a future and a hope.

12 Then you will call upon Me and go and pray to Me, and I will listen to you.

13 And ^Ryou will seek Me and find Me, when you search for Me ^Rwith all your heart.   Deut. 30:1-3 • Jer. 24:7

14 I will be found by you, says the LORD, and I will bring you back from your captivity; I will gather you from all the nations and from all the places where I have driven you, says the LORD, and I will bring you to the place from which I cause you to be carried away captive.

15 Because you have said, "The LORD has raised up prophets for us in Babylon"—

16 therefore thus says the LORD concerning the king who sits on the throne of David, concerning all the people who dwell in this city, and concerning your brethren who have not gone out with you into captivity—

17 thus says the LORD of hosts: Behold, I will send on them the sword, the famine, and the pestilence, and will make them like ^Rrotten figs that cannot be eaten, they are so bad.   Jer. 24:3, 8-10

18 And I will pursue them with the sword, with famine, and with pestilence; and I ^Rwill deliver them to trouble among all the kingdoms of the earth—to be ^Ra curse, an astonishment, a hissing, and a reproach among all the nations where I have driven them,   Deut. 28:25 • Jer. 26:6; 42:18

19 because they have not heeded My words, says the LORD, which I sent to them by My servants the prophets, rising up early and sending them; neither would you hear, says the LORD.

20 Therefore hear the word of the LORD, all you of the captivity, whom I have sent from Jerusalem to Babylon.

21 Thus says the LORD of hosts, the God of Israel, concerning Ahab the son of Kolaiah, and Zedekiah the son of Maaseiah, who prophesy a ^Rlie to you in My name: Behold, I will deliver them into the hand of Nebuchadnezzar king of Babylon, and he shall slay them before your eyes.   Lam. 2:14

22 ^RAnd because of them a curse shall be taken up by all the captivity of Judah who are in Babylon, saying, "The LORD make you like Zedekiah and Ahab, ^Rwhom the king of Babylon roasted in the fire";   Is. 65:15 • Dan. 3:6, 21

23 because they have done disgraceful things in Israel, have committed adultery with their neighbors' wives, and have spoken lying words in My name, which I have not commanded them. Indeed I ^Rknow, and am a witness, says the LORD.   [Prov. 5:21]

24 You shall also speak to Shemaiah the Nehelamite, saying,

25 Thus speaks the LORD of hosts, the God of Israel, saying: You have sent letters in your name to all the people who are at Jerusalem, ^Rto Zephaniah the son of Maaseiah the priest, and to all the priests, saying,   Jer. 21:1

26 "The LORD has made you priest instead of Jehoiada the priest, so that there should be ^Rofficers in the house of the LORD over every man who is ^Rdemented and considers himself a prophet, that you should ^Rput him in prison and in the stocks.   Jer. 20:1 • John 10:20 • Jer. 20:1, 2

27 Now therefore, why have you not rebuked Jeremiah of Anathoth who makes himself a prophet to you?

28 For he has sent to us in Babylon, saying, 'This captivity is long; build houses and dwell in them, and plant gardens and eat their fruit.' "

29 Now Zephaniah the priest read this letter in the hearing of Jeremiah the prophet.

30 Then the word of the LORD came to Jeremiah, saying:

31 Send to all those in captivity, saying, Thus says the LORD concerning Shemaiah the Nehelamite: Because Shemaiah has prophesied to you, and I have not sent him, and he has caused you to trust in a lie—

32 therefore thus says the LORD: Behold, I will punish Shemaiah the Nehelamite and his family: he shall not have anyone to dwell among this people, nor shall he see the good that I will do for My people, says the LORD, because he has taught rebellion against the LORD.

Restoration of Israel and Judah

30 The word that came to Jeremiah from the LORD, saying,

2 "Thus speaks the LORD God of Israel, saying: 'Write in a book for yourself all the words that I have spoken to you.

3 'For behold, the days are coming,' says the LORD, 'that ᴿI will bring back from captivity My people Israel and Judah,' says the LORD. ᴿ'And I will cause them to return to the land that I gave to their fathers, and they shall possess it.'" Ezek. 39:25 • Jer. 16:15

4 Now these *are* the words that the LORD spoke concerning Israel and Judah.

5 "For thus says the LORD:

'We have heard a voice of trembling,
Of ᵀfear, and not of peace.   *dread*
6 Ask now, and see,
Whether a ᵀman is ever in labor with
child?   Lit. *a male can give birth*
So why do I see every man *with* his
hands on his loins
ᴿLike a woman in labor,
And all faces turned pale?   Jer. 4:31; 6:24
7 ᴿAlas! For that day *is* great,   Amos 5:18
ᴿSo that none *is* like it;   Dan. 9:23; 12:1
And it *is* the time of Jacob's trouble,
But he shall be saved out of it.

8 'For it shall come to pass in that day,'
Says the LORD of hosts,
'*That* I will break his yoke from your
neck,
And will burst your bonds;
Foreigners shall no more enslave them.
9 But they shall serve the LORD their
God,
And ᴿDavid their king,   [Luke 1:69]
Whom I will raise up for them.

10 'Therefore ᴿdo not fear, O My servant
Jacob,' says the LORD,
'Nor be dismayed, O Israel;
For behold, I will save you from afar,
And your seed ᴿfrom the land of their
captivity.   Is. 41:13; 43:5; 44:2 • Jer. 3:18
Jacob shall return, have rest and be
quiet,
And no one shall make *him* afraid.
11 For I *am* with ᴿyou,' says the LORD, 'to
save you;   [Is. 43:2-5]
ᴿThough I make a full end of all nations
where I have scattered you,   Amos 9:8
ᴿYet I will not make a complete end of
you.   Jer. 4:27; 46:27, 28
But I will correct you ᴿin justice,
And will not let you go altogether
unpunished.'   Ps. 6:1

12 "For thus says the LORD:

ᴿYour affliction *is* incurable,
Your wound *is* severe.   Jer. 15:18

13 *There is* no one to plead your cause,
That you may be bound up;
ᴿYou have no healing medicines.   Jer. 8:22
14 ᴿAll your lovers have forgotten you;   Lam. 1:2
They do not seek you;
For I have wounded you with the
wound ᴿof an enemy, Job 13:24; 16:9; 19:11
With the chastisement of a cruel one,
For the multitude of your iniquities,
ᴿBecause your sins have increased.   Jer. 5:6
15 Why ᴿdo you cry about your affliction?
Your sorrow *is* incurable.   Jer. 15:18
Because of the multitude of your
iniquities,
Because your sins have increased,
I have done these things to you.

16 'Therefore all those who devour you
ᴿshall be devoured;   Jer. 10:25
And all your adversaries, every one of
them, shall go into ᴿcaptivity;   Is. 14:2
Those who plunder you shall become
ᴿplunder,   Ezek. 39:10
And all who prey upon you I will make
a ᴿprey.   Jer. 2:3
17 ᴿFor I will restore health to you
And heal you of your wounds,' says the
LORD,
'Because they called you an outcast
saying:
"This *is* Zion;
No one seeks her." '   Jer. 33:6

18 "Thus says the LORD:

'Behold, I will bring back the captivity
of Jacob's tents,
And ᴿhave mercy on his dwelling
places;
The city shall be built upon its own
ᵀmound,
And the palace shall remain according
to its own plan.   Ps. 102:13 • *ruins*
19 Then ᴿout of them shall proceed
thanksgiving
And the voice of those who make
merry;
ᴿI will multiply them, and they shall not
diminish;
I will also glorify them, and they shall
not be small.   Is. 51:11 • Zech. 10:8
20 Their children also shall be ᴿas before,
And their congregation shall be
established before Me;   Is. 1:26
And I will punish all who oppress them.
21 Their nobles shall be from among them,
ᴿAnd their governor shall come from
their midst;   Gen. 49:10
Then I will ᴿcause him to draw near,
And he shall approach Me;   Num. 16:5
For who *is* this who pledged his heart
to approach Me?' says the LORD.
22 'You shall be ᴿMy people,
And I will be your God.' "   Ezek. 36:28

23 Behold, the ᴿwhirlwind of the Lᴏʀᴅ
    Goes forth with fury,
    A ᵀcontinuing whirlwind;
    It will fall violently on the head of the
    wicked.   Jer. 23:19, 20; 25:32 · Or *sweeping*
24 The fierce anger of the Lᴏʀᴅ will not
    return until He has done it,
    And until He has performed the intents
    of His heart.

In the latter days you will consider it.

The Remnant of Israel Saved

▼ **33–A. The Permanence of God's Love to Israel**

31 "At the same time," says the Lᴏʀᴅ, "I will be the God of all the families of Israel, and they shall be My people."

2 Thus says the Lᴏʀᴅ:

"The people who survived the sword
    Found grace in the wilderness—
Israel, when I went to give him rest."

3 The Lᴏʀᴅ has appeared ᵀof old to me,
    saying: Lit. *from afar*
"Yes, ᴿI have loved you with ᴿan
    everlasting love;   Mal. 1:2 · Rom. 11:28
Therefore with lovingkindness I have
    ᴿdrawn you.   Hos. 11:4
4 Again ᴿI will build you, and you shall
    be rebuilt,
    O virgin of Israel!
    You shall again be adorned with your
    ᴿtambourines,

And shall go forth in the dances of   ▽
    those who rejoice.   Jer. 33:7 · Judg. 11:34
5 ᴿYou shall yet plant vines on the
    mountains of Samaria;   Amos 9:14
    The planters shall plant and ᵀeat *them*
    as ordinary food.   Lit. *treat them as common*
6 For there shall be a day
    When the watchmen will cry on Mount
    Ephraim,
    ᴿ'Arise, and let us go up *to* Zion,
    To the Lᴏʀᴅ our God.' "   [Mic. 4:2]

7 For thus says the Lᴏʀᴅ:

    ᴿ"Sing with gladness for Jacob,
    And shout among the chief of the
    nations;
    Proclaim, give praise, and say,
    'O Lᴏʀᴅ, save Your people,
    The remnant of Israel!'   Is. 12:5, 6
8 Behold, I will bring them ᴿfrom the
    north country,   Jer. 3:12, 18; 23:8
    And ᴿgather them from the ends of the
    earth,   Ezek. 20:34, 41; 34:13
    Among them the blind and the lame,
    The woman with child
    And the one who labors with child,
    together;
    A great throng shall return there.
9 ᴿThey shall come with weeping,   [Jer. 50:4]
    And with supplications I will lead them.
    I will cause them to walk ᴿby the rivers
    of waters,   Is. 35:8; 43:19; 49:10, 11
    In a straight way in which they shall
    not stumble;

33-A. The Permanence of God's Love to Israel (Jeremiah 31:1-40)—In light of today's world situation, it is vital that all believers understand God's everlasting love for Israel, especially when sharing one's faith with Jewish people. God's love for Israel is revealed in many ways.

(1) *An everlasting love.* God Himself declared that His love for the nation Israel is everlasting (v. 3), despite the fact that He has judged that nation (v. 2).

(2) *Her weeping shall cease.* God comforted weeping Rachel—herself a symbol of Israel—assuring her that in the end-time her children would return to her (vv. 15-17).

(3) *They shall return.* Jews shall return both to Ephraim, Israel's northern kingdom scattered in 721 B.C. by Assyria, and to Judah, Israel's southern kingdom (vv. 20, 23), which was scattered by the Babylonians in 606, 597, and 586 B.C. In A.D. 70 the Romans destroyed Jerusalem and dispersed the Jewish people. They began to return before World War I, and after World War II (1948) became a modern nation (Jer. 30:1-11, page 743).

(4) *A new covenant.* God promised that He would make a new covenant with the house of Israel. At its consummation, the members of this nation will experience a loving, personal relationship with God. They will be forgiven of all past national sins (vv. 31-34; Zech. 12:10, page 918; 1 Cor. 11:25, page 1156).

(5) *Never abandoned.* God, in forceful language within Jeremiah's prophecy of judgment on the nation, pledged that Israel would never be totally destroyed, nor would He ever abandon them (vv. 35-37). Thus, despite New Testament events, God never has and never will "cast off" Israel (vv. 36, 37). The New Testament directly confirms this, when the apostle Paul answered his own rhetorical question, "Has God cast away His people? Certainly not . . . God has not cast away His people whom He foreknew" (Rom. 11:1, 2, page 1141).

(6) *God's ancient people.* The term "the seed of Israel" promises the nation of Israel (today's Jewish people) an eventual, peaceful restoration to their land (vv. 36, 37). Other blessings are promised to the church in manifold quantities, but in these verses the offspring of ancient Israel is the topic.

(7) *Full restoration.* God's will, in the future, is to reestablish the nation of Israel. Jerusalem will be rebuilt; it will be holy and dedicated to the Lord (vv. 38-40; cf. Zech. 14:16-21, page 919). God says it shall yet come to pass; that makes it certain.

See Micah 5:2, page 890, for **Point 33-B: The Prophecies of Israel's Messiah.**

▽ For I am a Father to Israel,
And Ephraim *is* My ᴿfirstborn.   Ex. 4:22

10 "Hear the word of the Lᴏʀᴅ, O nations,
And declare *it* in the ᵀisles afar off, and
say,
'He who scattered Israel ᴿwill gather
him,
And keep him as a shepherd *does* his
flock.'   Or *coastlands* · Is. 40:11
11 For the Lᴏʀᴅ has redeemed Jacob,
And ransomed him ᴿfrom the hand of
one stronger than he.   Is. 49:24
12 Therefore they shall come and sing in
ᴿthe height of Zion,   Ezek. 17:23
Streaming to ᴿthe goodness of the
Lᴏʀᴅ—   Hos. 3:5
For wheat and new wine and oil,
For the young of the flock and the
herd;
Their souls shall be like a ᴿwell-watered
garden,   Is. 58:11
And they shall sorrow no more at all.

13 "Then shall the virgin rejoice in the
dance,
And the young men and the old,
together;
For I will turn their mourning to joy,
Will comfort them,
And make them rejoice rather than
sorrow.
14 I will ᵀsatiate the soul of the priests
with abundance,   Fill to the full
And My people shall be satisfied with
My goodness, says the Lᴏʀᴅ."

Mercy on Ephraim

15 Thus says the Lᴏʀᴅ:

"A voice was heard in Ramah,
Lamentation *and* bitter weeping,
Rachel weeping for her children,
Refusing to be comforted for her
ᴿchildren,   Gen. 42:13; Matt. 2:17
Because ᴿthey *are* no more."   Jer. 10:20

16 Thus says the Lᴏʀᴅ:

"Refrain your voice from ᴿweeping,
And your eyes from tears;
For your work shall be rewarded, says
the Lᴏʀᴅ,
And they shall come back from the
land of the enemy.   [Is. 25:8; 30:19]
17 There is ᴿhope in your future, says the
Lᴏʀᴅ,
That *your* children shall come back to
their own border.   Jer. 29:11
18 "I have surely heard Ephraim bemoaning
himself:
'You have ᴿchastised me, and I was
chastised,   Ps. 94:12
Like an untrained bull;

ᴿRestore me, and I will return,   Lam. 5:21 ▽
For You *are* the Lᴏʀᴅ my God.
19 Surely, ᴿafter my turning, I repented;
And after I was instructed, I struck
myself on the thigh;
I was ᴿashamed, yes, even humiliated,
Because I bore the reproach of my
youth.'   Deut. 30:2 · Ezek. 36:31
20 *Is* Ephraim My dear son?
Is he a pleasant child?
For though I spoke against him,
I earnestly remember him still;
Therefore My ᵀheart yearns for him;
ᴿI will surely have mercy on him, says
the Lᴏʀᴅ.   Lit. *inward parts* · [Hos. 14:4]

21 "Set up signposts,
Make landmarks;
ᴿSet your heart toward the highway,
The way in *which* you went.   Jer. 50:5
ᵀTurn back, O virgin of Israel,   Or *Return*
Turn back to these your cities.
22 How long will you ᴿgad about,
O you ᴿbacksliding daughter?
For the Lᴏʀᴅ has created a new thing
in the earth—   Jer. 2:18, 23, 36 · Jer. 3:6, 8, 11
A woman shall encompass a man."

Future Prosperity of Judah

23 Thus says the Lᴏʀᴅ of hosts, the God of
Israel: "They shall again use this speech in
the land of Judah and in its cities, when I
bring back their captivity: ᴿ'The Lᴏʀᴅ bless
you, O home of justice, *and* ᴿmountain of
holiness!'   Is. 1:26 · [Zech. 8:3]
24 "And there shall dwell in Judah itself,
and ᴿin all its cities together, farmers and
those going out with flocks.   Jer. 33:12
25 "For I have satiated the weary soul, and
I have replenished every sorrowful soul."
26 After this I awoke and looked around,
and my sleep was ᴿsweet to me.   Prov. 3:24
27 "Behold, the days are coming, says the
Lᴏʀᴅ, that ᴿI will sow the house of Israel and
the house of Judah with the seed of man and
the seed of beast.   Ezek. 36:9-11
28 "And it shall come to pass, *that* as I have
watched over them ᴿto pluck up, to break
down, to throw down, to destroy, and to
afflict, so I will watch over them ᴿto build and
to plant, says the Lᴏʀᴅ.   Jer. 1:10 · Jer. 24:6
29 ᴿ"In those days they shall say no more:

'The fathers have eaten sour grapes,
And the children's teeth are set on
edge.'   Ezek. 18:2, 3

30 ᴿ"But every one shall die for his own
iniquity; every man who eats the sour grapes,
his teeth shall be set on edge.   [Gal. 6:5, 7]

A New Covenant

31 "Behold, the ᴿdays are coming, says the
Lᴏʀᴅ, when I will make a ᴿnew covenant

▽ with the house of Israel and with the house of Judah—   Heb. 8:8–12; 10:16, 17 • [Luke 22:20]

32 "not according to the covenant that I made with their fathers in the day *that* ᴿI took them by the hand to lead them out of the land of Egypt, My covenant which they broke, *though I was a husband to them, says the LORD.   Deut. 1:31

33 "But this *is* the covenant that I will make with the house of Israel after those days, says the LORD: ᴿI will put My law in their minds, and write it on their ᵀhearts; ᴿand I will be their God, and they shall be My people.   Ps. 40:8 • Lit. *inward parts* • Heb. 10:15–17

34 "No more shall every man teach his neighbor, and every man his brother, saying, 'Know the LORD,' for ᴿthey all shall know Me, from the least of them to the greatest of them, says the LORD. For ᴿI will forgive their iniquity, and their sin I will remember no more."   [John 6:45] • Is. 11:9

35 Thus says the LORD,
ᴿWho gives the sun for a light by day,
The ordinances of the moon and the
          stars for a light by night,
Who disturbs ᴿthe sea,   Gen. 1:14–18 • Is. 51:15
And its waves roar
(The LORD of hosts *is* His name):

36 "If ᴿthose ordinances depart
From before Me, says the LORD,
Then the seed of Israel shall also cease
From being a nation before Me
          forever."   Ps. 148:6

37 Thus says the LORD:

ᴿ"If heaven above can be measured,
And the foundations of the earth
          searched out beneath,
I will also ᴿcast off all the seed of Israel
For all that they have done, says the
          LORD.   Jer. 33:22 • [Rom. 11:2–5, 26, 27]

38 "Behold, the days are coming, says the LORD, that the city shall be built for the LORD ᴿfrom the Tower of Hananel to the Corner Gate.   Zech. 14:10

39 ᴿ"The surveyor's line shall again extend straight forward over the hill Gareb; then it shall turn toward Goath.   Zech. 2:1, 2

40 "And the whole valley of the dead bodies and of the ashes, and all the fields as far as the Brook Kidron, ᴿto the corner of the Horse Gate toward the east, ᴿ*shall be* holy to the LORD. It shall not be plucked up or thrown
▲ down anymore forever."   Neh. 3:28 • [Joel 3:17]

Jeremiah Buys a Field

32 The word that came to Jeremiah from the LORD ᴿin the tenth year of Zede-kiah king of Judah, which was the eighteenth year of Nebuchadnezzar.   Jer. 39:1, 2

2 For then the king of Babylon's army besieged Jerusalem, and Jeremiah the prophet was shut up ᴿin the court of the prison, which *was in* the king of Judah's house.   Jer. 33:1; 37:21; 39:14

3 For Zedekiah king of Judah had shut him up, saying, "Why do you ᴿprophesy and say, 'Thus says the LORD: ᴿ"Behold, I will give this city into the hand of the king of Babylon, and he shall take it;   Jer. 26:8, 9 • Jer. 21:3–7; 34:2

4 "and Zedekiah king of Judah shall not escape from the hand of the Chaldeans, but shall surely be delivered into the hand of the king of Babylon, and shall speak with him *face to face, and see him eye to eye;

5 "then he shall lead Zedekiah to Babylon, and there he shall be until I visit him," says the LORD; "though you fight with the Chalde-ans, you shall not succeed" '?"

6 And Jeremiah said, "The word of the LORD came to me, saying,

7 'Behold, Hanamel the son of Shallum your uncle will come to you, saying, "Buy my field which *is* in Anathoth, for the ᴿright of redemption *is* yours to buy *it*." '   Ruth 4:4

8 "Then Hanamel my uncle's son came to me in the court of the prison according to the word of the LORD, and said to me, 'Please buy my field that *is* in Anathoth, which *is* in the country of Benjamin; for the right of inheri-tance *is* yours, and the redemption yours; buy *it* for yourself.' Then I knew that this was the word of the LORD.

9 "So I bought the field from Hanamel, the son of my uncle who *was* in Anathoth, and ᴿweighed *out to* him the money—ᵀseventeen shekels of silver.   Zech. 11:12 • $2176

10 "And I signed the ᵀdeed and sealed *it*, took witnesses, and weighed the money on the scales.   Lit. *book*

11 "So I took the purchase deed, *both* that which was sealed *according* to the law and custom, and that which was open;

12 "and I gave the purchase deed to Baruch the son of Neriah, son of Mahseiah, in the presence of Hanamel my uncle's *son*, and in the presence of the ᴿwitnesses who signed the purchase deed, before all the Jews who sat in the court of the prison.   Is. 8:2

13 "Then I charged ᴿBaruch before them, saying,   Jer. 36:4

14 'Thus says the LORD of hosts, the God of Israel: "Take these deeds, both this purchase deed which is sealed and this deed which is open, and put them in an earthen vessel, that they may last many days."

15 'For thus says the LORD of hosts, the God of Israel: "Houses and fields and vineyards shall be possessed again in this land." '

31:32 So with MT, Tg., Vg.; LXX, Syr. *and I turned away from them*

32:4 Lit. *mouth to mouth*

Jeremiah Prays for Understanding

16 "Now when I had delivered the purchase deed to Baruch the son of Neriah, I prayed to the LORD, saying:

17 'Ah, Lord GOD! Behold, You have made the heavens and the earth by Your great power and outstretched arm. ᴿThere is nothing too ᵀhard for You.   Luke 18:27 · *difficult*

18 '*You* show ᴿlovingkindness to thousands, and repay the iniquity of the fathers into the bosom of their children after them—the Great, ᴿthe Mighty God, whose name *is* ᴿthe LORD of hosts.   Deut. 5:9, 10 · [Is. 9:6] · Jer. 10:16

19 '*You are* ᴿgreat in counsel and mighty in ᵀwork, for your ᴿeyes *are* open to all the ways of the sons of men, ᴿto give everyone according to his ways and according to the fruit of his doings.   Is. 28:29 · *deed* · Prov. 5:21 · Jer. 17:10

20 'You have set signs and wonders in the land of Egypt, to this day, and in Israel and among *other* men; and You have made Yourself ᴿa name, as it is this day.   Is. 63:12

21 'You ᴿhave brought Your people Israel out of the land of Egypt with signs and wonders, with a strong hand and an outstretched arm, and with great terror;   Ex. 6:6

22 'You have given them this land, of which You swore to their fathers to give them—ᴿ"a land flowing with milk and honey."   Ex. 3:8, 17

23 'And they came in and took possession of it, but ᴿthey have not obeyed Your voice or walked in Your law. They have done nothing of all that You commanded them to do; therefore You have caused all this calamity to come upon them.   [Neh. 9:26]

24 'Look, the siege mounds! They have come to the city to take it; and the city has been given into the hand of the Chaldeans who fight against it, because of the sword and famine and pestilence. What You have spoken has happened; there You see *it*!

25 'And You have said to me, O Lord GOD, "Buy the field for money, and take witnesses"!—yet the city has been given into the hand of the Chaldeans.' "

God's Assurance of the People's Return

26 Then the word of the LORD came to Jeremiah, saying,

27 "Behold, I *am* the LORD, the God of all flesh. Is there anything too hard for Me?

28 "Therefore thus says the LORD: 'Behold, I will give this city into the hand of the Chaldeans, into the hand of Nebuchadnezzar king of Babylon, and he shall take it.

29 'And the Chaldeans who fight against this city shall come and ᴿset fire to this city and burn it, with the houses ᴿon whose roofs they have offered incense to Baal and poured out drink offerings to other gods, to provoke Me to anger;   2 Chr. 36:19 · Jer. 19:13

30 'because the children of Israel and the children of Judah have done only evil before Me from their youth. For the children of Israel have provoked Me only to anger with the work of their hands,' says the LORD.

31 'For this city has been to Me *a provocation of* My anger and My fury from the day that they built it, even to this day; ᴿso I will remove it from before My face   2 Kin. 23:27; 24:3

32 'because of all the evil of the children of Israel and the children of Judah, which they have done to provoke Me to anger—ᴿthey, their kings, their princes, their priests, ᴿtheir prophets, the men of Judah, and the inhabitants of Jerusalem.   Dan. 9:8 · Jer. 23:14

33 'And they have turned to Me the back, and not the face; though I taught them, rising up early and teaching *them*, yet they have not listened to receive instruction.

34 'But they set their abominations in the house which is called by My name, to defile it.

35 'And they built the high places of Baal which *are* in the Valley of the Son of Hinnom, to cause their sons and their daughters to pass through *the fire* to Molech, ᴿwhich I did not command them, nor did it come into My mind that they should do this abomination, to cause Judah to sin.'   Jer. 7:31

36 "Now therefore, thus says the LORD, the God of Israel, concerning this city of which you say, 'It shall be delivered into the hand of the king of Babylon by the sword, by the famine, and by the pestilence':

37 'Behold, I will ᴿgather them out of all countries where I have driven them in My anger, in My fury, and in great wrath; I will bring them back to this place, and I will cause them ᴿto dwell safely.   Deut. 30:3 · Jer. 33:16

38 'They shall be ᴿMy people, and I will be their God;   [Jer. 24:7; 30:22; 31:33]

39 'then I will give them one heart and one way, that they may fear Me forever, for the good of them and their children after them.

40 'And ᴿI will make an everlasting covenant with them, that I will not turn away from doing them good; but ᴿI will put My fear in their hearts so that they will not depart from Me.   Is. 55:3 · [Jer. 31:33]

41 'Yes, I will rejoice over them to do them good, and I will assuredly plant them in this land, with all My heart and with all My soul.'

42 "For thus says the LORD: ᴿ'Just as I have brought all this great calamity on this people, so I will bring on them all the good that I have promised them.   Jer. 31:28

43 'And fields will be bought in this land ᴿof which you say, "*It is* desolate, without man or beast; it has been given into the hand of the Chaldeans."   Jer. 33:10

44 'Men will buy fields for money, sign deeds and seal *them*, and take witnesses, in ᴿthe land of Benjamin, in the places around Jerusalem, in the cities of Judah, in the cities of the mountains, in the cities of the ᵀlow-

land, and in the cities of the ᵀSouth; for I will cause their captives to return,' says the LORD." Jer. 17:26 • Heb. *Shephelah* • Heb. *Negev*

Excellence of the Restored Nation

33 Moreover the word of the LORD came to Jeremiah a second time, while he was still ᴿshut up in the court of the prison, saying, Jer. 32:2, 3

2 "Thus says the LORD ᴿwho made it, the LORD who formed it to establish it ᴿ(the ᵀLORD *is* His name): Is. 37:26 • Ex. 15:3 • Heb. *YHWH*

3 ᴿ'Call to Me, and I will answer you, and show you great and ᵀmighty things, which you do not know.' Jer. 29:12 • *inaccessible*

4 "For thus says the LORD, the God of Israel, concerning the houses of this city and the houses of the kings of Judah, which have been pulled down ᴿ*to fortify* against the siege mounds and the sword: Is. 22:10

5 'They come to fight with the Chaldeans, but *only* ᴿto fill their places with the dead bodies of men whom I will slay in My anger and My fury, all for whose wickedness I have hidden My face from this city. 2 Kin. 23:14

6 'Behold, ᴿI will bring it health and healing; I will heal them and reveal to them the abundance of peace and truth. Jer. 30:17

7 'And I will cause the captives of Judah and the captives of Israel to return, and will rebuild those places ᴿas at the first. Is. 1:26

8 'I will ᴿcleanse them from all their iniquity by which they have sinned against Me, and I will pardon all their iniquities by which they have sinned and by which they have transgressed against Me. Zech. 13:1

9 ᴿ'Then it shall be to Me a name of joy, a praise, and an honor before all nations of the earth, who shall hear all the good that I do to them; they shall ᴿfear and tremble for all the goodness and all the prosperity that I provide for it.' Is. 62:7 • Is. 60:5

10 "Thus says the LORD: 'Again there shall be heard in this place—of which you say, "It *is* desolate, without man and without beast" —in the cities of Judah, in the streets of Jerusalem that are desolate, without man and without inhabitant and without beast,

11 'the ᴿvoice of joy and the voice of gladness, the voice of the bridegroom and the voice of the bride, the voice of those who will say: Rev. 18:23

ᴿ"Praise the LORD of hosts, Is. 12:4
  For the LORD *is* good,
  For His mercy *endures* forever"—

and of those *who will* bring ᴿthe sacrifice of praise into the house of the LORD. For I will cause the captives of the land to return as at the first,' says the LORD. Lev. 7:12

12 "Thus says the LORD of hosts: ᴿ'In this place which is desolate, without man and without beast, and in all its cities, there shall

again be a dwelling place of shepherds causing *their* flocks to lie down. Is. 65:10

13 'In the cities of the mountains, in the cities of the lowland, in the cities of the South, in the land of Benjamin, in the places around Jerusalem, and in the cities of Judah, the flocks shall again pass under the hands of him who counts *them*,' says the LORD.

14 'Behold, the days are coming,' says the LORD, 'that ᴿI will perform that good thing which I have promised to the house of Israel and to the house of Judah: Jer. 29:10; 32:42

15 'In those days and at that time
  I will cause to grow up to David
  A ᴿBranch of righteousness; Zech. 6:12, 13
  He shall execute judgment and
    righteousness in the earth.
16 In those days ᴿJudah will be saved,
  And Jerusalem will dwell safely.
  And this *is the name* by which she will
    be called: Is. 45:17, 22

*THE LORD OUR RIGHTEOUSNESS.'

17 "For thus says the LORD: 'David shall never ᴿlack a man to sit on the throne of the house of Israel; 2 Sam. 7:16

18 'nor shall the ᴿpriests, the Levites, lack a man to ᴿoffer burnt offerings before Me, to ᵀkindle grain offerings, and to sacrifice continually.' " Ezek. 44:15 • [1 Pet. 2:5, 9] • *burn*

The Permanence of God's Covenant

19 And the word of the LORD came to Jeremiah, saying,

20 "Thus says the LORD: 'If you can break My covenant with the day and My covenant with the night, so that there will not be day and night in their season,

21 'then My covenant may also be broken with David My servant, so that he shall not have a son to reign on his throne, and with the Levites, the priests, My ministers.

22 'As ᴿthe host of heaven cannot be numbered, nor the sand of the sea measured, so will I ᴿmultiply the descendants of David My servant and the ᴿLevites who minister to Me.' " Gen. 15:5; 22:17 • Jer. 30:19 • Is. 66:21

23 Moreover the word of the LORD came to Jeremiah, saying,

24 "Have you not considered what these people have spoken, saying, 'The two families which the LORD has chosen, He has also cast them off'? Thus they have ᴿdespised My people, as if they should no more be a nation before them. Esth. 3:6–8

25 "Thus says the LORD: 'If ᴿMy covenant *is* not with day and night, *and if* I have not ᴿappointed the ordinances of heaven and earth, Gen. 8:22 • Ps. 74:16; 104:19

26 'then I will cast away the descendants of Jacob and David My servant, *so* that I will

33:16 Heb. *YHWH Tsidkenu*; cf. Jer. 23:5, 6

not take *any* of his descendants *to be* rulers over the descendants of Abraham, Isaac, and Jacob. For I will cause their captives to return, and will have mercy on them.' "

Zedekiah Warned by God

34 The word which came to Jeremiah from the LORD, Rwhen Nebuchadnezzar king of Babylon and all his army, Rall the kingdoms of the earth under his dominion, and all the people, fought against Jerusalem and all its cities, saying,   2 Kin. 25:1 • Jer. 1:15; 25:9

2 "Thus says the LORD, the God of Israel: 'Go and speak to Zedekiah king of Judah and tell him, "Thus says the LORD: 'Behold, I will give this city into the hand of the king of Babylon, and he shall burn it with fire.

3 'And you shall not escape from his hand, but shall surely be taken and delivered into his hand; your eyes shall see the eyes of the king of Babylon, he shall speak with you RfaceT to face, and you shall go to Babylon.' "   Jer. 32:4; 39:5, 6 • Lit. *mouth to mouth*

4 "Yet hear the word of the LORD, O Zedekiah king of Judah! Thus says the LORD concerning you: 'You shall not die by the sword.

5 'You shall die in peace; as in the ceremonies of your fathers, the former kings who were before you, Rso they shall burn incense for you and Rlament for you, *saying*, "Alas, lord!" For I have pronounced the word, says the LORD.' "   Dan. 2:46 • Jer. 22:18

6 Then Jeremiah the prophet spoke all these words to Zedekiah king of Judah in Jerusalem,

7 when the king of Babylon's army fought against Jerusalem and all the cities of Judah that were left, against Lachish and Azekah; for *only* Rthese fortified cities remained of the cities of Judah.   2 Kin. 18:13; 19:8

Treacherous Treatment of Slaves

8 *This is* the word that came to Jeremiah from the LORD, after King Zedekiah had made a covenant with all the people who *were* at Jerusalem to proclaim Rliberty to them: Ex. 21:2

9 Rthat every man should set free his male and female slave—a Hebrew man or woman—Rthat no one should keep a Jewish brother in bondage.   Neh. 5:11 • Lev. 25:39-46

10 Now when all the princes and all the people, who had entered into the covenant, heard that everyone should set free his male and female slaves, that no one should keep them in bondage anymore, they obeyed and let *them* go.

11 But afterward they changed their minds and made the male and female slaves return, whom they had set free, and brought them into subjection as male and female slaves.

12 Therefore the word of the LORD came to Jeremiah from the LORD, saying,

13 "Thus says the LORD, the God of Israel: 'I made a covenant with your fathers in the day that I brought them out of the land of Egypt, out of the house of bondage, saying,

14 "At the end of Rseven years let every man set free his Hebrew brother, who Thas been sold to him; and when he has served you six years, you shall let him go free from you." But your fathers did not obey Me nor incline their ear.   Deut. 15:12 • Or *sold himself*

15 'Then you Trecently turned and did what was right in My sight—every man proclaiming liberty to his neighbor; and you Rmade a covenant before Me Rin the house which is called by My name.   Lit. *today* • Neh. 10:29 • Jer. 7:10

16 'Then you turned around and Rprofaned My name, and every one of you brought back his male and female slaves, whom he had set at liberty, at their pleasure, and brought them back into subjection, to be your male and female slaves.'   Ex. 20:7

17 "Therefore thus says the LORD: 'You have not obeyed Me in proclaiming liberty, every one to his brother and every one to his neighbor. Behold, I proclaim liberty to you,' says the LORD—'to the sword, to pestilence, and to famine! And I will deliver you to trouble among all the kingdoms of the earth.

18 'And I will give the men who have transgressed My covenant, who have not performed the words of the covenant which they made before Me, when they cut the calf in two and passed between the parts of it—

19 'the princes of Judah, the princes of Jerusalem, the Teunuchs, the priests, and all the people of the land who passed between the parts of the calf—   Or *officers*

20 'I will Rgive them into the hand of their enemies and into the hand of those who seek their life. Their Rdead bodies shall be for meat for the birds of the heaven and the beasts of the earth.   Jer. 22:25 • Jer. 7:33; 16:4; 19:7

21 'And I will give Zedekiah king of Judah and his princes into the hand of their enemies, into the hand of those who seek their life, and into the hand of the king of Babylon's army which has gone back from you.

22 'Behold, I will command,' says the LORD, 'and cause them to return to this city. They will fight against it and take it and burn it with fire; and I will make the cities of Judah a desolation without inhabitant.' "

The Obedient Rechabites

35 The word which came to Jeremiah from the LORD in the days of Jehoiakim the son of Josiah, king of Judah, saying,

2 "Go to the house of the RRechabites, speak to them, and bring them into the house of the LORD, into one of Rthe chambers, and give them wine to drink."   1 Chr. 2:55 • 1 Kin. 6:5, 8

3 Then I took Jaazaniah the son of Jeremiah, the son of Habazziniah, his brothers

and all his sons, and the whole house of the Rechabites,

4 and I brought them into the house of the LORD, into the chamber of the sons of Hanan the son of Igdaliah, a man of God, which *was* by the chamber of the princes, above the chamber of Maaseiah the son of Shallum, the keeper of the ᵀdoor.   Lit. *threshold*

5 Then I set before the sons of the house of the Rechabites bowls full of wine, and cups; and I said to them, "Drink wine."

6 But they said, "We will drink no wine, for Jonadab the son of Rechab, our father, commanded us, saying, 'You shall drink ᴿno wine, you nor your sons, forever.   Luke 1:15

7 'You shall not build a house, sow seed, plant a vineyard, nor have *any of these*; but all your days you shall dwell in tents, ᴿthat you may live many days in the land where you are sojourners.'   Ex. 20:12

8 "Thus we have ᴿobeyed the voice of Jonadab the son of Rechab, our father, in all that he charged us, to drink no wine all our days, we, our wives, our sons, or our daughters,   [Col. 3:20]

9 "nor to build ourselves houses to dwell in; nor do we have vineyard, field, or seed.

10 "But we have dwelt in tents, and have obeyed and done according to all that Jonadab our father commanded us.

11 "But it came to pass, when Nebuchadnezzar king of Babylon came up into the land, that we said, 'Come, let us ᴿgo to Jerusalem for fear of the army of the Chaldeans and for fear of the army of the Syrians.' So we dwell at Jerusalem."   Jer. 4:5-7; 8:14

12 Then came the word of the LORD to Jeremiah, saying,

13 "Thus says the LORD of hosts, the God of Israel: 'Go and tell the men of Judah and the inhabitants of Jerusalem, "Will you not ᴿreceive instruction to ᵀobey My words?" says the LORD.   Jer. 6:10; 17:23; 32:33 • *listen to*

14 "The words of Jonadab the son of Rechab, which he commanded his sons, not to drink wine, are performed; for to this day they drink none, and obey their father's commandment. ᴿBut although I have spoken to you, ᴿrising early and speaking, you did not ᵀobey Me.   2 Chr. 36:15 • Jer. 7:13; 25:3 • *listen to*

15 "I have also sent to you all My servants the prophets, rising up early and sending *them*, saying, ᴿ'Turn now everyone from his evil way, amend your doings, and do not go after other gods to serve them; then you will ᴿdwell in the land which I have given you and your fathers.' But you have not inclined your ear, nor obeyed Me.   Jer. 18:11 • Jer. 7:7; 25:5, 6

16 "Surely the sons of Jonadab the son of Rechab have performed the commandment of their father, which he commanded them, but this people has not obeyed Me." '

17 "Therefore thus says the LORD God of hosts, the God of Israel: 'Behold, I will bring on Judah and on all the inhabitants of Jerusalem all the doom that I have pronounced against them; because I have spoken to them but they have not heard, and I have called to them but they have not answered.' "

18 And Jeremiah said to the house of the Rechabites, "Thus says the LORD of hosts, the God of Israel: 'Because you have obeyed the commandment of Jonadab your father, and kept all his precepts and done according to all that he commanded you,

19 'therefore thus says the LORD of hosts, the God of Israel: "Jonadab the son of Rechab shall not lack a man to ᴿstand before Me forever." ' "   Jer. 15:19

The Scroll Read in the Temple

36 Now it came to pass in the ᴿfourth year of Jehoiakim the son of Josiah, king of Judah, *that* this word came to Jeremiah from the LORD, saying: Jer. 25:1, 3; 45:1

2 "Take a scroll of a book and write on it all the words that I have spoken to you against Israel, against Judah, and against all the nations, from the day I spoke to you, from the days of Josiah even to this day.

3 "It ᴿmay be that the house of Judah will hear all the adversities which I purpose to bring upon them, that everyone may ᴿturn from his evil way, that I may forgive their iniquity and their sin."   Jer. 26:3 • Jon. 3:8

4 Then Jeremiah ᴿcalled Baruch the son of Neriah; and ᴿBaruch wrote on a scroll of a book, ᵀat the instruction of Jeremiah, all the words of the LORD which He had spoken to him.   Jer. 32:12 • Jer. 45:1 • Lit. *from Jeremiah's mouth*

5 And Jeremiah commanded Baruch, saying, "I *am* confined, I cannot go into the house of the LORD.

6 "You go, therefore, and read from the scroll which you have written ᵀat my instruction, the words of the LORD, in the hearing of the people in the LORD's house on ᴿthe day of fasting. And you shall also read them in the hearing of all Judah who come from their cities.   Lit. *from my mouth* • Acts 27:9

7 "It may be that they will present their supplication before the LORD, and everyone will turn from his evil way. For great *is* the anger and the fury that the LORD has pronounced against this people."

8 And Baruch the son of Neriah did according to all that Jeremiah the prophet commanded him, reading from the book the words of the LORD in the LORD's house.

9 Now it came to pass in the fifth year of Jehoiakim the son of Josiah, king of Judah, in the ninth month, *that* they proclaimed a fast before the LORD to all the people in Jerusalem, and to all the people who came from the cities of Judah to Jerusalem.

10 Then Baruch read from the book the words of Jeremiah in the house of the LORD, in the chamber of Gemariah the son of Shaphan the scribe, in the upper court at the entry of the New Gate of the LORD's house, in the ᵀhearing of all the people.   Lit. *ears*

The Scroll Read in the Palace

11 When Michaiah the son of Gemariah, the son of Shaphan, heard all the words of the LORD from the book,

12 he then went down to the king's house, into the scribe's chamber; and there all the princes were sitting—ᴿElishama the scribe, Delaiah the son of Shemaiah, ᴿElnathan the son of Achbor, Gemariah the son of Shaphan, Zedekiah the son of Hananiah, and all the princes.   Jer. 41:1 • Jer. 26:22

13 Then Michaiah declared to them all the words that he had heard when Baruch read the book in the hearing of the people.

14 Therefore all the princes sent Jehudi the son of Nethaniah, the son of Shelemiah, the son of Cushi, to Baruch, saying, "Take in your hand the scroll from which you have read in the hearing of the people, and come." So Baruch the son of Neriah took the scroll in his hand and came to them.

15 And they said to him, "Sit down now, and read it in our hearing." So Baruch read *it* in their hearing.

16 Now it happened, when they had heard all the words, that they looked in fear from one to another, and said to Baruch, "We will surely tell the king of all these words."

17 And they asked Baruch, saying, "Tell us now, how did you write all these words—ᵀat his instruction?"   Lit. *with his mouth*

18 So Baruch answered them, "He proclaimed with his mouth all these words to me, and I wrote *them* with ink in the book."

19 Then the princes said to Baruch, "Go and hide, you and Jeremiah; and let no one know where you are."

The King Destroys Jeremiah's Scroll

20 And they went to the king, into the court; but they stored the scroll in the chamber of Elishama the scribe, and told all the words in the hearing of the king.

21 So the king sent Jehudi to bring the scroll, and he took it from Elishama the scribe's chamber. And Jehudi read it in the hearing of the king and in the hearing of all the princes who stood beside the king.

22 Now the king was sitting in ᴿthe winter house in the ninth month, with *a fire* burning on the hearth before him.   Amos 3:15

23 And it happened, when Jehudi had read three or four columns, *that the king* cut it with the scribe's knife and cast *it* into the fire that *was* on the hearth, until all the scroll was consumed in the fire that *was* on the hearth.

24 Yet they were ᴿnot afraid, nor did they tear their garments, the king nor any of his servants who heard all these words.   [Ps. 36:1]

25 Nevertheless Elnathan, Delaiah, and Gemariah implored the king not to burn the scroll; but he would not listen to them.

26 And the king commanded Jerahmeel ᵀthe king's son, Seraiah the son of Azriel, and Shelemiah the son of Abdeel, to seize Baruch the scribe and Jeremiah the prophet, but the LORD hid them.   Or *son of Hammelech*

Jeremiah Rewrites the Scroll

27 Now after the king had burned the scroll with the words which Baruch had written *at the instruction of Jeremiah, the word of the LORD came to Jeremiah, saying:

28 "Take yet another scroll, and write on it all the former words that were in the first scroll which Jehoiakim the king of Judah has burned.

29 "And you shall say to Jehoiakim king of Judah, 'Thus says the LORD: "You have burned this scroll, saying, 'Why have you written in it that the king of Babylon will certainly come and destroy this land, and cause man and beast to cease from here?' "

30 'Therefore thus says the LORD concerning Jehoiakim king of Judah: "He shall have no one to sit on the throne of David, and his dead body shall be ᴿcast out to the heat of the day and the frost of the night.   Jer. 22:19

31 "I will punish him, his ᵀfamily, and his servants for their iniquity; and I will bring on them, on the inhabitants of Jerusalem, and on the men of Judah all the doom that I have pronounced against them; but they did not heed." ' "   Lit. *seed*

32 Then Jeremiah took another scroll and gave it to Baruch the scribe, the son of Neriah, who wrote on it ᵀat the instruction of Jeremiah all the words of the book which Jehoiakim king of Judah had burned in the fire. And besides, there were added to them many similar words.   Lit. *from Jeremiah's mouth*

Zedekiah's Vain Hope

37 Now King Zedekiah the son of Josiah reigned instead of Coniah the son of Jehoiakim, whom Nebuchadnezzar king of Babylon made king in the land of Judah.

2 ᴿBut neither he nor his servants nor the people of the land gave heed to the words of the LORD which He spoke by the prophet Jeremiah.   2 Chr. 36:12–16

3 And Zedekiah the king sent Jehucal the son of Shelemiah, and ᴿZephaniah the son of Maaseiah, the priest, to the prophet Jeremiah, saying, ᴿ"Pray now to the LORD our God for us."   Jer. 21:1, 2; 29:25; 52:24 • Jer. 42:2

4 Now Jeremiah was coming and going

36:27 Lit. *from Jeremiah's mouth*

among the people, for they had not *yet* put him in prison.

5 Then ^RPharaoh's army came up from Egypt; and when the Chaldeans who were besieging Jerusalem heard news of them, they departed from Jerusalem.   Ezek. 17:15

6 Then the word of the LORD came to the prophet Jeremiah, saying,

7 "Thus says the LORD, the God of Israel, 'Thus you shall say to the king of Judah, ^Rwho sent you to Me to inquire of Me: "Behold, Pharaoh's army which has come up to help you will return to Egypt, to their own land.   Jer. 21:2

8 ^R"And the Chaldeans shall come back and fight against this city, and take it and burn it with fire." '   Jer. 34:22

9 "Thus says the LORD: 'Do not deceive yourselves, saying, "The Chaldeans will surely depart from us," for they will not depart.

10 'For though you had defeated the whole army of the Chaldeans who fight against you, and there remained *only* wounded men among them, they would rise up, every man in his tent, and burn the city with fire.' "

Jeremiah Imprisoned

11 And it happened, when the army of the Chaldeans left *the siege* of Jerusalem for fear of Pharaoh's army,

12 that Jeremiah went out of Jerusalem to go into the land of Benjamin to claim his property there among the people.

13 And when he was in the Gate of Benjamin, a captain of the guard *was* there whose name *was* Irijah the son of Shelemiah, the son of Hananiah; and he seized Jeremiah the prophet, saying, "You are defecting to the Chaldeans!"

14 Then Jeremiah said, ^T"False! I am not defecting to the Chaldeans." But he did not listen to him. So Irijah seized Jeremiah and brought him to the princes.   *a lie*

15 Therefore the princes were angry with Jeremiah, and they struck him ^Rand put him in prison in the house of Jonathan the scribe. For they had made that the prison.   Jer. 20:2

16 When Jeremiah entered ^Rthe dungeon and the cells, and Jeremiah had remained there many days,   Jer. 38:6

17 then Zedekiah the king sent and took him *out*. The king asked him secretly in his house, and said, "Is there *any* word from the LORD?" And Jeremiah said, "There is." Then he said, "You shall be ^Rdelivered into the hand of the king of Babylon!"   Jer. 21:7

18 Moreover Jeremiah said to King Zedekiah, "What offense have I committed against you, against your servants, or against this people, that you have put me in prison?

19 "Where now *are* your prophets who prophesied to you, saying, 'The king of Bab-

ylon will not come against you or against this land?'

20 "Therefore please hear now, O my lord the king. Please, let my petition be accepted before you, and do not make me return to the house of Jonathan the scribe, lest I die there."

21 Then Zedekiah the king commanded that they should commit Jeremiah ^Rto the court of the prison, and that they should give him daily a piece of bread from the bakers' street, ^Runtil all the bread in the city was gone. Thus Jeremiah remained in the court of the prison.   Jer. 32:2; 38:13, 28 · Jer. 38:9; 52:6

Jeremiah in the Dungeon

38 Now Shephatiah the son of Mattan, Gedaliah the son of Pashhur, *Jucal the son of Shelemiah, and Pashhur the son of Malchiah heard the words that Jeremiah had spoken to all the people, saying,

2 "Thus says the LORD: ^R'He who remains in this city shall die by the sword, by famine, and by pestilence; but he who goes over to the Chaldeans shall live; his life shall be as a prize to him, and he shall live.'   Jer. 21:9

3 "Thus says the LORD: 'This city shall surely be given into the hand of the king of Babylon's army, which shall take it.' "

4 Therefore the princes said to the king, "Please, ^Rlet this man be put to death, for thus he weakens the hands of the men of war who remain in this city, and the hands of all the people, by speaking such words to them. For this man does not seek the welfare of this people, but their harm."   Jer. 26:11

5 Then Zedekiah the king said, "Look, he *is* in your hand. For the king can *do* nothing against you."

6 ^RSo they took Jeremiah and cast him into the dungeon of Malchiah *the king's son, which *was* in the court of the prison, and they let Jeremiah down with ropes. And in the dungeon *there was* no water, but mire. So Jeremiah sank in the mire.   Jer. 37:21

7 ^RNow Ebed-Melech the Ethiopian, one of the ^Teunuchs, who was in the king's house, heard that they had put Jeremiah in the dungeon. When the king was sitting at the Gate of Benjamin,   Jer. 39:16 · Or *officers*

8 Ebed-Melech went out of the king's house and spoke to the king, saying:

9 "My lord the king, these men have done evil in all that they have done to Jeremiah the prophet, whom they have cast into the dungeon, and he is likely to die from hunger in the place where he is. For *there is* ^Rno more bread in the city."   Jer. 37:21

10 Then the king commanded Ebed-Melech the Ethiopian, saying, "Take from here thirty

38:1 *Jehucal*, Jer. 37:3
38:6 Or *son of Hammelech*

men with you, and lift Jeremiah the prophet out of the dungeon before he dies."

11 So Ebed-Melech took the men with him and went into the house of the king under the treasury, and took from there old clothes and old rags, and let them down by ropes into the dungeon to Jeremiah.

12 Then Ebed-Melech the Ethiopian said to Jeremiah, "Please put these old clothes and rags under your armpits, under the ropes." And Jeremiah did so.

13 So they pulled Jeremiah up with ropes and lifted him out of the dungeon. And Jeremiah remained ᴿin the court of the prison.   Jer. 37:21

Zedekiah's Fears and Jeremiah's Advice

14 Then Zedekiah the king sent and had Jeremiah the prophet brought to him at the third entrance of the house of the LORD. And the king said to Jeremiah, "I will ask you something. Hide nothing from me."

15 Jeremiah said to Zedekiah, "If I declare it to you, will you not surely put me to death? And if I give you advice, you will not listen to me."

16 So Zedekiah the king swore secretly to Jeremiah, saying, "As the LORD lives, ᴿwho made our very souls, I will not put you to death, nor will I give you into the hand of these men who seek your life."   Is. 57:16

17 Then Jeremiah said to Zedekiah, "Thus says the LORD, the God of hosts, the God of Israel: 'If you surely ᵀsurrender to the king of Babylon's princes, then your soul shall live; this city shall not be burned with fire, and you and your house shall live.   Lit. go out

18 'But if you do not ᵀsurrender to the king of Babylon's princes, then this city shall be given into the hand of the Chaldeans; they shall burn it with fire, and you shall not escape from their hand.' "   Lit. go out

19 And Zedekiah the king said to Jeremiah, "I am afraid of the Jews who have defected to the Chaldeans, lest they deliver me into their hand, and they ᴿabuse me."   1 Sam. 31:4

20 But Jeremiah said, "They shall not deliver you. Please, obey the voice of the LORD which I speak to you. So it shall be ᴿwell with you, and your soul shall live.   Jer. 40:9

21 "But if you refuse to surrender, this is the word that the LORD has shown me:

22 'Now behold, all the ᴿwomen who are left in the king of Judah's house shall be surrendered to the king of Babylon's princes, and those women shall say: Jer. 8:10

"Your close friends have ᵀset upon you
And prevailed against you;   Or misled
Your feet have sunk in the mire,
And they have turned away again."

23 'So they shall surrender all your wives and ᴿchildren to the Chaldeans. ᴿYou shall not escape from their hand, but shall be taken by the hand of the king of Babylon. And you shall cause this city to be burned with fire.' "   Jer. 39:6; 41:10 · Jer. 39:5

24 Then Zedekiah said to Jeremiah, "Let no one know of these words, and you shall not die.

25 "But if the princes hear that I have talked with you, and they come to you and say to you, 'Declare to us now what you have said to the king, and also what the king said to you; do not hide it from us, and we will not put you to death,'

26 "then you shall say to them, ᴿ'I presented my request before the king, that he would not make me return ᴿto Jonathan's house to die there.' "   Jer. 37:20 · Jer. 37:15

27 Then all the princes came to Jeremiah and asked him. And he told them according to all these words that the king had commanded. So they stopped speaking with him, for the conversation had not been heard.

28 Now ᴿJeremiah remained in the court of the prison until the day that Jerusalem was taken. And he was there when Jerusalem was taken.   Jer. 37:21; 39:14

The Fall of Jerusalem

39 In the ninth year of Zedekiah king of Judah, in the tenth month, Nebuchadnezzar king of Babylon and all his army came against Jerusalem, and besieged it.

2 In the eleventh year of Zedekiah, in the fourth month, on the ninth day of the month, the ᵀcity was penetrated.   city wall was breached

3 Then all the princes of the king of Babylon came in and sat in the Middle Gate: Nergal-Sharezer, Samgar-Nebo, Sarsechim, *Rabsaris, Nergal-Sarezer, *Rabmag, with the rest of the princes of the king of Babylon.

4 So it was, when Zedekiah the king of Judah and all the men of war saw them, that they fled and went out of the city by night, by way of the king's garden, by the gate between the two walls. And he went out by way of the ᵀplain.   Or Arabah, the Jordan Valley

5 But the Chaldean army pursued them and overtook Zedekiah in the plains of Jericho. And when they had captured him, they brought him up to Nebuchadnezzar king of Babylon, to Riblah in the land of Hamath, where he pronounced judgment on him.

6 Then the king of Babylon killed the sons of Zedekiah before his ᴿeyes in Riblah; the king of Babylon also killed all the ᴿnobles of Judah.   Deut. 28:34 · Jer. 34:19–21

7 Moreover ᴿhe put out Zedekiah's eyes, and bound him with bronze ᵀfetters to carry him off to Babylon.   Ezek. 12:13 · chains

8 And the Chaldeans burned the king's

39:3 A title, probably Chief Officer; also v. 13 • A title, probably Troop Commander; also v. 13

house and the houses of the people with fire, and broke down the walls of Jerusalem.

9 Then Nebuzaradan the captain of the guard carried away captive to Babylon the remnant of the people who remained in the city and those who defected to him, with the rest of the people who remained.

10 But Nebuzaradan the captain of the guard left in the land of Judah the poor people, who had nothing, and gave them vineyards and fields at the same time.

Jeremiah Goes Free

11 Now Nebuchadnezzar king of Babylon gave charge concerning Jeremiah to Nebuzaradan the captain of the guard, saying,

12 "Take him and look after him, and do him no ᴿharm; but do to him just as he says to you."   Jer. 1:18, 19; 15:20, 21

13 So Nebuzaradan the captain of the guard sent Nebushasban, Rabsaris, Nergal-Sharezer, Rabmag, and all the king of Babylon's chief officers;

14 then they sent someone to take Jeremiah from the court of the prison, and committed him to Gedaliah the son of Ahikam, the son of Shaphan, that he should take him home. So he dwelt among the people.

15 Meanwhile the word of the LORD had come to Jeremiah while he was shut up in the court of the prison, saying,

16 "Go and speak to ᴿEbed-Melech the Ethiopian, saying, 'Thus says the LORD of hosts, the God of Israel: "Behold, ᴿI will bring My words upon this city for adversity and not for good, and they shall be performed in that day before you.   Jer. 38:7, 12 • [Dan. 9:12]

17 "But I will deliver you in that day," says the LORD, "and you shall not be given into the hand of the men of whom you are afraid.

18 "For I will surely deliver you, and you shall not fall by the sword; but your life shall be as a prize to you, ᴿbecause you have put your trust in Me," says the LORD.' "   Ps. 37:40

Jeremiah with Gedaliah the Governor

40 The word that came to Jeremiah from the LORD ᴿafter Nebuzaradan the captain of the guard had let him go from Ramah, when he had taken him bound in chains among all who were carried away captive from Jerusalem and Judah, who were carried away captive to Babylon.   Jer. 39:9, 11

2 And the captain of the guard took Jeremiah and said to him: "The LORD your God has pronounced this doom on this place.

3 "Now the LORD has brought it, and has done just as He said. ᴿBecause you people have sinned against the LORD, and not obeyed His voice, therefore this thing has come upon you.   Dan. 9:11

4 "And now look, I free you this day from the chains that ᵀwere on your hand. If it

seems good to you to come with me to Babylon, come, and I will look after you. But if it seems wrong for you to come with me to Babylon, remain here. See, all the land is before you; wherever it seems good and convenient for you to go, go there."   Or are

5 Now while Jeremiah had not yet gone back, Nebuzaradan said, "Go back to ᴿGedaliah the son of Ahikam, the son of Shaphan, ᴿwhom the king of Babylon has made governor over the cities of Judah, and dwell with him among the people. Or go wherever it seems convenient for you to go." So the captain of the guard gave him rations and a gift and let him go.   Jer. 39:14 • Jer. 41:10

6 ᴿThen Jeremiah went to Gedaliah the son of Ahikam, to ᴿMizpah, and dwelt with him among the people who were left in the land.   Jer. 39:14 • Judg. 20:1

7 ᴿAnd when all the captains of the armies who were in the fields, they and their men, heard that the king of Babylon had made Gedaliah the son of Ahikam governor in the land, and had committed to him men, women, children, and ᴿthe poorest of the land who had not been carried away captive to Babylon,   2 Kin. 25:23, 24 • Jer. 39:10

8 then they came to Gedaliah at Mizpah—Ishmael the son of Nethaniah, Johanan and Jonathan the sons of Kareah, Seraiah the son of Tanhumeth, the sons of Ephai the Netophathite, and ᵀJezaniah the son of a Maachathite, they and their men.   Jaazaniah, 2 Kin. 25:23

9 And Gedaliah the son of Ahikam, the son of Shaphan, took an oath before them and their men, saying, "Do not be afraid to serve the Chaldeans. Dwell in the land and serve the king of Babylon, and it shall be ᴿwell with you.   Jer. 27:11; 38:17-20

10 "As for me, I will indeed dwell at Mizpah and serve the Chaldeans who come to us. But you, gather wine and summer fruit and oil, put them in your vessels, and dwell in your cities that you have taken."

11 Likewise, when all the Jews who were in Moab, among the Ammonites, in Edom, and who were in all the countries, heard that the king of Babylon had left a remnant of Judah, and that he had set over them Gedaliah the son of Ahikam, the son of Shaphan,

12 then all the Jews ᴿreturned out of all places where they had been driven, and came to the land of Judah, to Gedaliah at Mizpah, and gathered wine and summer fruit in abundance.   Jer. 43:5

13 Moreover Johanan the son of Kareah and all the captains of the forces that were in the fields came to Gedaliah at Mizpah,

14 and said to him, "Do you certainly know that Baalis the king of the Ammonites has sent Ishmael the son of Nethaniah to murder you?" But Gedaliah the son of Ahikam did not believe them.

15 Then Johanan the son of Kareah spoke secretly to Gedaliah in Mizpah, saying, "Let me go, please, and I will kill Ishmael the son of Nethaniah, and no one will know *it*. Why should he murder you, so that all the Jews who are gathered to you would be scattered, and the ᴿremnant in Judah perish?"   Jer. 42:2

16 But Gedaliah the son of Ahikam said to Johanan the son of Kareah, "You shall not do this thing, for you speak falsely concerning Ishmael."

Insurrection Against Gedaliah

41 Now it came to pass in the seventh month *that* Ishmael the son of Nethaniah, the son of Elishama, of the royal family and of the officers of the king, came with ten men to Gedaliah the son of Ahikam, at Mizpah. And there they ate bread together in Mizpah.

2 Then Ishmael the son of Nethaniah, and the ten men who were with him, arose and ᴿstruck Gedaliah the son of ᴿAhikam, the son of Shaphan, with the sword, and killed him whom the king of Babylon had made ᴿgovernor over the land.   2 Kin. 25:25 • Jer. 26:24 • Jer. 40:5

3 Ishmael also struck down all the Jews who were with him, *that is,* with Gedaliah at Mizpah, and the Chaldeans who were found there, the men of war.

4 And it happened, on the second day after he had killed Gedaliah, when as yet no one knew *it,*

5 that certain men came from Shechem, from Shiloh, and from Samaria, eighty men ᴿwith their beards shaved and their clothes torn, having cut themselves, with offerings and incense in their hand, to bring *them* to ᴿthe house of the Lᴏʀᴅ.   Deut. 14:1 • 1 Sam. 1:7

6 Now Ishmael the son of Nethaniah went out from Mizpah to meet them, weeping as he went along; and it happened as he met them that he said to them, "Come to Gedaliah the son of Ahikam!"

7 So it was, when they came into the midst of the city, that Ishmael the son of Nethaniah killed them *and cast them* into the midst of a pit, he and the men who were with him.

8 But ten men were found among them who said to Ishmael, "Do not kill us, for we have treasures of wheat, barley, oil, and honey in the field." So he desisted and did not kill them among their brethren.

9 Now the ᵀpit into which Ishmael had cast all the dead bodies of the men whom he had slain, because of Gedaliah, *was* ᴿthe same one Asa the king had made for fear of Baasha king of Israel. Ishmael the son of Nethaniah filled it with *the* slain.   Or *cistern* • 1 Kin. 15:22

10 Then Ishmael carried away captive all the rest of the people who *were* in Mizpah, the king's daughters and all the people who remained in Mizpah, whom Nebuzaradan the captain of the guard had committed to Gedaliah the son of Ahikam. And Ishmael the son of Nethaniah carried them away captive and departed to go over to the Ammonites.

11 But when ᴿJohanan the son of Kareah and all the captains of the forces that *were* with him heard of all the evil that Ishmael the son of Nethaniah had done,   Jer. 40:7, 8, 13–16

12 they took all the men and went to fight with Ishmael the son of Nethaniah; and they found him by ᴿthe great pool that *is* in Gibeon.   2 Sam. 2:13

13 So it was, when all the people who *were* with Ishmael saw Johanan the son of Kareah, and all the captains of the forces who *were* with him, that they were glad.

14 Then all the people whom Ishmael had carried away captive from Mizpah turned around and came back, and went to Johanan the son of Kareah.

15 But Ishmael the son of Nethaniah escaped from Johanan with eight men and went to the Ammonites.

16 Then Johanan the son of Kareah, and all the captains of the forces that were with him, took from Mizpah all the ᴿrest of the people whom he had recovered from Ishmael the son of Nethaniah after he had murdered Gedaliah the son of Ahikam—the mighty men of war and the women and the children and the eunuchs, whom he had brought back from Gibeon.   Jer. 40:11, 12; 43:4–7

17 And they departed and dwelt in the habitation of Chimham, which is near Bethlehem, as they went on their way to Egypt,

18 because of the Chaldeans; for they were afraid of them, because Ishmael the son of Nethaniah had murdered Gedaliah the son of Ahikam, ᴿwhom the king of Babylon had made governor in the land.   Jer. 40:5

The Flight to Egypt Forbidden

42 Now all the captains of the forces, Johanan the son of Kareah, Jezaniah the son of Hoshaiah, and all the people, from the least to the greatest, came near

2 and said to Jeremiah the prophet, "Please, let our petition be acceptable to you, and pray for us to the Lᴏʀᴅ your God, for all this remnant (since we are left *but* ᴿa few of many, as you can see),   Lev. 26:22

3 "that the Lᴏʀᴅ your God may show us ᴿthe way in which we should walk and the thing we should do."   Ezra 8:21

4 Then Jeremiah the prophet said to them, "I have heard. Indeed, I will pray to the Lᴏʀᴅ your God according to your words, and it shall be, *that* whatever the Lᴏʀᴅ answers you, I will declare *it* to you. I will ᴿkeep nothing back from you."   1 Sam. 3:17, 18

5 So they said to Jeremiah, "Let the Lᴏʀᴅ be a true and faithful witness between us, if

we do not do according to everything which the LORD your God sends us by you.

6 "Whether *it is* ^Tpleasing or ^Tdispleasing, we will ^Robey the voice of the LORD our God to whom we send you, ^Rthat it may be well with us when we obey the voice of the LORD our God." Lit. *good* · Lit. *evil* · Ex. 24:7 · Jer. 7:23

7 And it happened after ten days that the word of the LORD came to Jeremiah.

8 Then he called Johanan the son of Kareah, all the captains of the forces which *were* with him, and all the people from the least even to the greatest,

9 and said to them, "Thus says the LORD, the God of Israel, to whom you sent me to present your petition before Him:

10 'If you will still remain in this land, then ^RI will build you and not pull *you* down, and I will plant you and not pluck *you* up. For I ^Rrelent concerning the disaster that I have brought upon you. Jer. 24:6; 31:28; 33:7 · [Jer. 18:8]

11 'Do not be afraid of the king of Babylon, of whom you are afraid; do not be afraid of him,' says the LORD, 'for I *am* with you, to save you and deliver you from his hand.

12 'And ^RI will show you mercy, that he may have mercy on you and cause you to return to your own land.' Ps. 106:46

13 "But if ^Ryou say, 'We will not dwell in this land,' disobeying the voice of the LORD your God, Jer. 44:16

14 "saying, 'No, but we will go to the land of ^REgypt where we shall see no war, nor hear the sound of the trumpet, nor be hungry for bread, and there we will dwell'— Jer. 41:17; 43:7

15 "Then hear now the word of the LORD, O remnant of Judah! Thus says the LORD of hosts, the God of Israel: 'If you ^Rwholly^T set ^Ryour faces to enter Egypt, and go to dwell there, Deut. 17:16 · Or *surely* · Luke 9:51

16 'then it shall be *that* the ^Rsword which you feared shall overtake you there in the land of Egypt; the famine of which you were afraid shall follow close after you there *in* Egypt; and there you shall die. Ezek. 11:8

17 'So shall it be with all the men who set their faces to go to Egypt to dwell there. They shall die by the sword, by famine, and by pestilence. And ^Rnone of them shall remain or escape from the disaster that I will bring upon them.' Jer. 44:14, 28

18 "For thus says the LORD of hosts, the God of Israel: 'As My anger and My fury have been poured out on the inhabitants of Jerusalem, so will My fury be poured out on you when you enter Egypt. And you shall be an oath, an astonishment, a curse, and a reproach; and you shall see this place no more.'

19 "The LORD has said concerning you, O remnant of Judah, ^R'Do not go to Egypt!' Know certainly that I have ^Tadmonished you this day. Deut. 17:16 · *warned*

20 "For you were hypocrites in your hearts when you sent me to the LORD your God, saying, 'Pray for us to the LORD our God, and according to all that the LORD your God says, so declare to us and we will do *it.*'

21 "And I have this day declared *it* to you, but you have ^Rnot obeyed the voice of the LORD your God, or anything which He has sent you by me. Is. 30:1-7

22 "Now therefore, know certainly that you ^Rshall die by the sword, by famine, and by pestilence in the place where you desire to go to dwell." Ezek. 6:11

Jeremiah Taken to Egypt

43 Now it happened, when Jeremiah had stopped speaking to all the people all the ^Rwords of the LORD their God, for which the LORD their God had sent him to them, all these words, Jer. 42:9-18

2 that Azariah the son of Hoshaiah, Johanan the son of Kareah, and all the proud men spoke, saying to Jeremiah, "You speak falsely! The LORD our God has not sent you to say, 'Do not go to Egypt to dwell there.'

3 "But Baruch the son of Neriah has set you against us, to deliver us into the hand of the Chaldeans, that they may put us to death or carry us away captive to Babylon."

4 So Johanan the son of Kareah, all the captains of the forces, and all the people would ^Rnot obey the voice of the LORD, to remain in the land of Judah. 2 Kin. 25:26

5 But Johanan the son of Kareah and all the captains of the forces took ^Rall the remnant of Judah who had returned to dwell in the land of Judah, from all nations where they had been driven— Jer. 40:11, 12

6 men, women, children, the king's daughters, ^Rand every person whom Nebuzaradan the captain of the guard had left with Gedaliah the son of Ahikam, the son of Shaphan, and Jeremiah the prophet and Baruch the son of Neriah. Jer. 39:10; 40:7

7 ^RSo they went to the land of Egypt, for they did not obey the voice of the LORD. And they went as far as Tahpanhes. Jer. 42:19

8 Then the ^Rword of the LORD came to Jeremiah in Tahpanhes, saying, Jer. 44:1-30

9 "Take large stones in your hand, and hide them in the sight of the men of Judah, in the ^Tclay in the brick courtyard which *is* at the entrance to Pharaoh's house in Tahpanhes; Or *mortar*

10 "and say to them, 'Thus says the LORD of hosts, the God of Israel: "Behold, I will send and bring Nebuchadnezzar the king of Babylon, My servant, and will set his throne above these stones that I have hidden. And he will spread his royal pavilion over them.

11 "When he comes, he shall strike the land of Egypt *and deliver* to death ^Rthose *appointed* for death, and to captivity *those*

appointed for captivity, and to the sword *those appointed* for the sword.   Jer. 15:2

12 *"I will kindle a fire in the houses of ᴿthe gods of Egypt, and he shall burn them and carry them away captive. And he shall array himself with the land of Egypt, as a shepherd puts on his garment, and he shall go out from there in peace.   Jer. 46:25

13 "He shall also break the sacred pillars of *Beth Shemesh that *are* in the land of Egypt; and the houses of the gods of the Egyptians he shall burn with fire." ' "

Israelites Will Be Punished in Egypt

44 The word that came to Jeremiah concerning all the Jews who dwell in the land of Egypt, who dwell at Migdol, at Tahpanhes, at ᴿNoph,ᵀ and in the country of Pathros, saying,   Is. 19:13 · Ancient Memphis

2 "Thus says the LORD of hosts, the God of Israel: 'You have seen all the calamity that I have brought on Jerusalem and on all the cities of Judah; and behold, this day they *are* a desolation, and no one dwells in them,

3 'because of their wickedness which they have committed to provoke Me to anger, in that they went to burn incense *and* to ᴿserve other gods whom they did not know, they nor you nor your fathers.   Deut. 13:6; 32:17

4 "However ᴿI have sent to you all My servants the prophets, rising early and sending *them,* saying, "Oh, do not do this abominable thing that I hate!"   Jer. 7:25; 25:4; 26:5; 29:19

5 'But they did not listen or incline their ear to turn from their wickedness, to burn no incense to other gods.

6 'So My fury and My anger were poured out and kindled in the cities of Judah and in the streets of Jerusalem; and they are wasted *and* desolate, as it is this day.'

7 "Now therefore, thus says the LORD, the God of hosts, the God of Israel: 'Why do you commit *this* great evil against yourselves, to cut off from you man and woman, child and infant, out of Judah, leaving none to remain,

8 'in that you provoke Me to wrath with the works of your hands, burning incense to other gods in the land of Egypt where you have gone to dwell, that you may cut yourselves off and be a curse and a reproach among all the nations of the earth?

9 'Have you forgotten the wickedness of your fathers, the wickedness of the kings of Judah, the wickedness of their wives, your own wickedness, and the wickedness of your wives, which they committed in the land of Judah and in the streets of Jerusalem?

10 'They have not been ᵀhumbled, to this day, nor have they feared; they have not

43:12 So with MT, Tg.; LXX, Syr., Vg. *He*
43:13 Lit. *House of the Sun,* ancient On, later called Heliopolis

walked in My law or in My statutes that I set before you and your fathers.'   Lit. *crushed*

11 "Therefore thus says the LORD of hosts, the God of Israel: 'Behold, ᴿI will set My face against you for catastrophe and for ᵀcutting off all Judah.   Amos 9:4 · Destroying

12 'And I will take the remnant of Judah who have set their faces to go into the land of Egypt to dwell there, and they shall all be consumed and fall in the land of Egypt. They shall be consumed by the sword *and* by famine. They shall die, from the least to the greatest, by the sword and by famine; and ᴿthey shall be an oath, an astonishment, a curse and a reproach!   Is. 65:15

13 'For I will punish those who dwell in the land of Egypt, as I have punished Jerusalem, by the sword, by famine, and by pestilence,

14 'so that none of the remnant of Judah who have gone into the land of Egypt to dwell there shall escape or survive, lest they return to the land of Judah, to which they desire to return and dwell. For none shall return except those who escape.' "

15 Then all the men who knew that their wives had burned incense to other gods, with all the women who stood by, a great multitude, and all the people who dwelt in the land of Egypt, in Pathros, answered Jeremiah, saying:

16 "*As for* the word that you have spoken to us in the name of the LORD, ᴿwe will not listen to you!   Jer. 6:16

17 "But we will certainly do whatever has gone out of our own mouth, to burn incense to the queen of heaven and pour out drink offerings to her, as we have done, we and our fathers, our kings and our princes, in the cities of Judah and in the streets of Jerusalem. For *then* we had plenty of ᵀfood, were well-off, and saw no trouble.   Lit. *bread*

18 "But since we stopped burning incense to the queen of heaven and pouring out drink offerings to her, we have lacked everything and have been consumed by the sword and by famine."

19 *The women also said,* ᴿ"And when we burned incense to the queen of heaven and poured out drink offerings to her, did we make cakes for her, to worship her, and pour out drink offerings to her without our husbands' *permission?*"   Jer. 7:18

20 Then Jeremiah spoke to all the people— the men, the women, and all the people who had given him *that* answer—saying:

21 "The incense that you burned in the cities of Judah and in the streets of Jerusalem, you and your fathers, your kings and your princes, and the people of the land, did not the LORD remember them, and did it *not* come into His mind?

22 "So the LORD could no longer bear *it,* because of the evil of your doings *and* be-

cause of the abominations which you committed. Therefore your land is a desolation, an astonishment, a curse, and without an inhabitant, ᴿas *it is* this day.   Jer. 25:11, 18, 38

23 "Because you have burned incense and because you have sinned against the Lᴏʀᴅ, and have not obeyed the voice of the Lᴏʀᴅ or walked in His law, in His statutes or in His testimonies, ᴿtherefore this calamity has happened to you, as *at* this day."   Dan. 9:11, 12

24 Moreover Jeremiah said to all the people and to all the women, "Hear the word of the Lᴏʀᴅ, all Judah who *are* in the land of Egypt! 25 "Thus says the Lᴏʀᴅ of hosts, the God of Israel, saying: 'You and your wives have spoken with your mouths and fulfilled with your hands, saying, "We will surely keep our vows that we have made, to burn incense to the queen of heaven and pour out drink offerings to her." You will surely keep your vows and perform your vows!'

26 "Therefore hear the word of the Lᴏʀᴅ, all Judah who dwell in the land of Egypt: 'Behold, ᴿI have sworn by My ᴿgreat name,' says the Lᴏʀᴅ, 'that ᴿMy name shall no more be named in the mouth of any man of Judah in all the land of Egypt, saying, "The Lord Gᴏᴅ lives."   Heb. 6:13 · Jer. 10:6 · Ezek. 20:39

27 'Behold, I will watch over them for adversity and not for good. And all the men of Judah who *are* in the land of Egypt ᴿshall be consumed by the sword and by famine, until there is an end to them.   Ezek. 7:6

28 'Yet ᴿa small number who escape the sword shall return from the land of Egypt to the land of Judah; and all the remnant of Judah, who have gone to the land of Egypt to dwell there, shall know whose words will stand, Mine or theirs.   Is. 10:19; 27:12, 13

29 'And this *shall be* a sign to you,' says the Lᴏʀᴅ, 'that I will punish you in this place, that you may know that My words will surely ᴿstand against you for adversity.'   [Ps. 33:11]

30 "Thus says the Lᴏʀᴅ: 'Behold, I will give Pharaoh Hophra king of Egypt into the hand of his enemies and into the hand of those who seek his life, as I gave Zedekiah king of Judah into the hand of Nebuchadnezzar king of Babylon, his enemy who sought his life.' "

Assurance to Baruch

45 The word that Jeremiah the prophet spoke to Baruch the son of Neriah, when he had written these words in a book at the instruction of Jeremiah, in the ᴿfourth year of Jehoiakim the son of Josiah, king of Judah, saying,   Jer. 25:1; 36:1; 46:2

2 "Thus says the Lᴏʀᴅ, the God of Israel, to you, O Baruch:

3 'You said, "Woe is me now! For the Lᴏʀᴅ has added grief to my sorrow. I fainted in my sighing, and I find no rest." '

4 "Thus you shall say to him, 'Thus says the Lᴏʀᴅ: "Behold, ᴿwhat I have built I will break down, and what I have planted I will pluck up, that is, this whole land.   Is. 5:5

5 "And do you seek great things for yourself? Do not seek *them*; for behold, ᴿI will bring adversity on all flesh," says the Lᴏʀᴅ. "But I will give your life to you as a prize in all places, wherever you go." ' "   Jer. 25:26

Judgment on Egypt

46 The word of the Lᴏʀᴅ which came to Jeremiah the prophet against ᴿthe nations.   Jer. 25:15

2 Against Egypt.

Concerning the army of Pharaoh Necho, king of Egypt, which was by the River Euphrates in Carchemish, and which Nebuchadnezzar king of Babylon ᴿdefeated in the ᴿfourth year of Jehoiakim the son of Josiah, king of Judah: 2 Chr. 35:20 · Jer. 45:1

3 "Order the ᵀbuckler and shield,
 And draw near to battle!   A small shield
4 Harness the horses,
 And mount up, you horsemen!
 Stand forth with *your* helmets,
 Polish the spears,
 ᴿPut on the armor!   Jer. 51:11, 12
5 Why have I seen them dismayed *and*
 turned back?
 Their mighty ones are beaten down;
 They have speedily fled,
 And did not look back,
 For ᴿfear *was* all around," says the
 Lᴏʀᴅ.   Jer. 49:29
6 "Do not let the swift flee away,
 Nor the mighty man escape;
 They will ᴿstumble and fall
 Toward the north, by the River
 Euphrates.   Dan. 11:19
7 "Who *is* this coming up like a flood,
 Whose waters move like the rivers?
8 Egypt rises up like a flood,
 And *its* waters move like the rivers;
 And he says, 'I will go up *and* cover the
 earth,
 I will destroy the city and its
 inhabitants.'
9 Come up, O horses, and rage, O
 chariots!
 And let the mighty men come forth:
 ᵀThe Ethiopians and ᵀthe Libyans who
 handle the shield,
 And the Lydians ᴮwho handle *and* bend
 the bow.   Heb. Cush · Heb. Put · Is. 66:19
10 For this *is* ᴿthe day of the Lord Gᴏᴅ of
 hosts,   Joel 1:15
 A day of vengeance,
 That He may avenge Himself on His
 adversaries.
 ᴿThe sword shall devour;   Deut. 32:42

It shall be ᵀsatiated and made drunk
with their blood;   Filled to the full
For the Lord GOD of hosts ᴿhas a
sacrifice   Is. 34:6
In the north country by the River
Euphrates.

11 "Go up to Gilead and take balm,
ᴿO virgin, the daughter of Egypt;
In vain you will use many medicines;
ᴿYou shall not be cured.   Is. 47:1 • Ezek. 30:21
12 The nations have heard of your ᴿshame,
And your cry has filled the land;
For the mighty man has stumbled
against the mighty;
They both have fallen together."   Jer. 2:36

Babylonia Will Strike Egypt

13 The word that the LORD spoke to Jeremiah the prophet, how Nebuchadnezzar king
of Babylon would come and ᴿstrike the land
of Egypt.   Is. 19:1

14 "Declare in Egypt, and proclaim in
ᴿMigdol;   Jer. 44:1
Proclaim in *Noph and in Tahpanhes;
Say, 'Stand fast and prepare yourselves,
For the sword devours all around you.'
15 Why are your valiant men swept away?
They did not stand
Because the LORD drove them away.
16 He made many fall;
Yes, ᴿone fell upon another.   Lev. 26:36, 37
And they said, 'Arise!
ᴿLet us go back to our own people
And to the land of our nativity   Jer. 51:9
From the oppressing sword.'
17 They cried there,
'Pharaoh, king of Egypt, is but a noise.
He has passed by the appointed time!'
18 "As I live," says the King,
ᴿWhose name is the LORD of hosts,
"Surely as Tabor is among the
mountains
And as Carmel by the sea, so he shall
come.   Jer. 48:15
19 O you daughter dwelling in Egypt,
Prepare yourself ᴿto go into captivity!
For *Noph shall be waste and desolate,
without inhabitant.   Is. 20:4

20 "Egypt is a very pretty ᴿheifer,
But destruction comes, it comes ᴿfrom
the north.   Hos. 10:11 • Jer. 1:14
21 Also her mercenaries are in her midst
like ᵀfat bulls,   Lit. calves of the stall
For they also are turned back,
They have fled away together.
They did not stand,

For ᴿthe day of their calamity had come
upon them,   [Ps. 37:13]
The time of their punishment.
22 ᴿHer noise shall go like a serpent,
For they shall march with an army
And come against her with axes,
Like those who chop wood.   [Is. 29:4]

23 "They shall ᴿcut down her forest," says
the LORD,
"Though it cannot be searched,
Because they are innumerable,
And more numerous than
ᴿgrasshoppers.   Is. 10:34 • Judg. 6:5; 7:12
24 The daughter of Egypt shall be
ashamed;
She shall be delivered into the hand
Of ᴿthe people of the north."   Jer. 1:15

25 The LORD of hosts, the God of Israel,
says: "Behold, I will bring punishment on
ᵀAmon of *No, and Pharaoh and Egypt, with
their gods and their kings—Pharaoh and
those who ᴿtrust in him.   A sun god • Is. 30:1-5
26 ᴿ"And I will deliver them into the hand
of those who seek their lives, into the hand of
Nebuchadnezzar king of Babylon and the
hand of his servants. ᴿAfterward it shall be
inhabited as in the days of old," says the
LORD.   Ezek. 32:11 • Ezek. 29:8-14

God Will Preserve Israel

27 "Butᴿ do not fear, O My servant Jacob,
And do not be dismayed, O Israel!
For behold, I will ᴿsave you from afar,
And your offspring from the land of
their captivity;
Jacob shall return, have rest and be at
ease;   Is. 41:13, 14; 43:5; 44:2 • Is. 11:11
No one shall make him afraid.
28 Do not fear, O Jacob My servant," says
the LORD,
"For I am with you;
For I will make a complete end of all
the nations
To which I have driven you,
But I will not make ᴿa complete end of
you.
I will rightly ᴿcorrect you,
For I will not leave you wholly
unpunished."   Amos 9:8, 9 • Jer. 30:11

Judgment on Philistia

47 The word of the LORD that came to
Jeremiah the prophet against the Philistines, before Pharaoh attacked Gaza.
2 Thus says the LORD:

"Behold, ᴿwaters rise ᴿout of the north,
And shall be an overflowing flood;
They shall overflow the land and all
that is in it,

46:14 Ancient Memphis
46:19 Ancient Memphis   46:25 Ancient Thebes

The city and those who dwell within;
Then the men shall cry,
And all the inhabitants of the land shall
wail. Is. 8:7, 8 • Jer. 1:14

3 At the ᴿnoise of the stamping hooves of
his strong horses, Jer. 8:16
At the rushing of his chariots,
At the rumbling of his wheels,
The fathers will not look back for *their*
children,
ᵀLacking courage, Lit. *From sinking hands*
4 Because of the day that comes to
plunder all the ᴿPhilistines, Is. 14:29–31
To cut off from ᴿTyre and Sidon every
helper who remains; Jer. 25:22
For the LORD shall plunder the
Philistines,
The remnant of the country of
ᵀCaphtor. Cappadocia in Asia Minor
5 ᴿBaldness has come upon Gaza, Mic. 1:16
ᴿAshkelon is cut off Jer. 25:20
With the remnant of their valley.
How long will you cut yourself?

6 "O you ᴿsword of the LORD,
How long until you are quiet?
Put yourself up into your scabbard,
Rest and be still! Ezek. 21:3–5
7 How can ᵀit be quiet, Lit. *you*
Seeing the LORD has ᴿgiven it a charge
Against Ashkelon and against the
seashore? Ezek. 14:17
There He has ᴿappointed it." Mic. 6:9

Judgment on Moab

48 Against ᴿMoab. Is. 15:1—16:14; 25:10
Thus says the LORD of hosts, the God
of Israel:

"Woe to ᴿNebo! Is. 15:2
For it is plundered,
ᴿKirjathaim is shamed *and* taken;
ᵀThe high stronghold is shamed and
dismayed— Num. 32:37 • Or *Misgab*
2 ᴿNo more praise of Moab. Is. 16:14
In ᴿHeshbon they have devised evil
against her: Jer. 49:3
'Come, and let us cut her off as a
nation.'
You also shall be cut down, O
ᴿMadmen!ᵀ Is. 10:31 • A city of Moab
The sword shall pursue you;
3 A voice of crying *shall be* from
ᴿHoronaim: Is. 15:5
'Plundering and great destruction!'

4 "Moab is destroyed;
*Her little ones have caused a cry to be
heard;
5 ᴿFor in the Ascent of Luhith they ascend
with continual weeping;

48:4 So with MT, Tg., Vg.; LXX *Proclaim it in Zoar*

For in the descent of Horonaim the
enemies have heard a cry of
destruction. Is. 15:5

6 "Flee, save your lives!
And be like ᵀthe ᴿjuniper in the
wilderness. Or *Aroer, a city of Moab* • Jer. 17:6
7 For because you have trusted in your
works and your ᴿtreasures,
You also shall be taken.
And ᴿChemosh shall go forth into
captivity, Jer. 9:23 • Jer. 48:7
His priests and his princes together.
8 And ᴿthe plunderer shall come against
every city;
No one shall escape.
The valley also shall perish,
And the plain shall be destroyed,
As the LORD has spoken. Jer. 6:26

9 "Giveᴿ wings to Moab,
That she may flee and get away;
For her cities shall be desolate,
Without any to dwell in them. Ps. 55:6
10 ᴿCursed *is* he who does the work of the
LORD deceitfully,
And cursed *is* he who keeps back his
sword from blood. 1 Sam. 15:3

11 "Moab has been at ease from *his youth;
He ᴿhas settled on his dregs,
And has not been emptied from vessel
to vessel, Zeph. 1:12
Nor has he gone into captivity.
Therefore his taste remained in him,
And his scent has not changed.

12 "Therefore behold, the days are coming,"
says the LORD,
"That I shall send him ᵀwine-workers
Who will tip him over
And empty his vessels
And break the bottles. *tippers* of wine bottles
13 Moab shall be ashamed of Chemosh,
As the house of Israel ᴿwas ashamed of
Bethel, their confidence. Hos. 10:6

14 "How can you say, ᴿ'We *are* mighty
And strong men for the war'? Is. 16:6
15 Moab is plundered and gone up *from*
her cities;
Her chosen young men have ᴿgone
down to the slaughter," says ᴿthe
King, Jer. 50:27 • Jer. 46:18; 51:57
Whose name *is* the LORD of hosts.

16 "The calamity of Moab *is* near at hand,
And his affliction comes quickly.
17 Bemoan him, all you who are around
him;
And all you who know his name,
Say, ᴿ'How the strong staff is broken,
The beautiful rod!' Is. 9:4; 14:4, 5

48:11 Heb. uses masc. and fem. pronouns
interchangeably in this chapter.

18 "O ᴿdaughter inhabiting ᴿDibon,
　　Come down from *your* glory,
　　And sit in thirst;　　　　Is. 47:1 • Is. 15:2
　　For the plunderer of Moab has come
　　　against you,
　　He has destroyed your strongholds.
19 O inhabitant of ᴿAroer,　　Deut. 2:36
　　ᴿStand by the way and watch;
　　Ask him who flees　　1 Sam. 4:13, 14, 16
　　And her who escapes;
　　Say, 'What has happened?'
20 Moab is shamed, for he is broken down.
　　ᴿWail and cry!
　　Tell it in ᴿArnon, that Moab is
　　　plundered.　　　　Is. 16:7 • Num. 21:13
21 "And judgment has come on the plain
　　　country:
　　On Holon and Jahzah and Mephaath,
22 On Dibon and Nebo and Beth
　　　Diblathaim,
23 On Kirjathaim and Beth Gamul and
　　　Beth Meon,
24 On ᴿKerioth and Bozrah,
　　On all the cities of the land of Moab,
　　Far or near.　　　　Amos 2:2
25 ᴿThe horn of Moab is cut off,　　Ps. 75:10
　　And his arm is broken," says the Lᴏʀᴅ.

26 "Make ᴿhim drunk,　　　　Jer. 25:15
　　Because he exalted *himself* against the
　　　Lᴏʀᴅ.
　　Moab shall wallow in his vomit,
　　And he shall also be in derision.
27 For was not Israel a derision to you?
　　ᴿWas he found among thieves?　　Jer. 2:26
　　For whenever you speak of him,
　　You shake *your* head *in* ᴿscorn.　　Lam. 2:15
28 You who dwell in Moab,
　　Leave the cities and ᴿdwell in the rock,
　　And be like ᴿthe dove *which* makes her
　　　nest　　　　Ps. 55:6, 7 • Song 2:14
　　In the sides of the cave's mouth.

29 "We have heard the ᴿpride of Moab
　　(He *is* exceedingly proud),
　　Of his loftiness and arrogance and
　　　ᴿpride,　　　　Is. 16:6 • Jer. 49:16
　　And of the haughtiness of his heart."
30 "I know his wrath," says the Lᴏʀᴅ,
　　"But it *is* not right;
　　His lies have made nothing right.
31 Therefore I will wail for Moab,
　　And I will cry out for all Moab;
　　*I will mourn for the men of Kir Heres.
32 ᴿO vine of Sibmah! I will weep for you
　　　with the weeping of Jazer.　　Is. 16:8, 9
　　Your plants have gone over the sea,
　　They reach to the sea of Jazer.
　　The plunderer has fallen on your
　　　summer fruit and your vintage.

33 ᴿJoy and gladness are taken
　　From the plentiful field
　　And from the land of Moab;
　　I have caused wine to ᵀfail from the
　　　winepresses;
　　No one will tread with joyous
　　　shouting—
　　Not joyous shouting!　　Joel 1:12 • *cease*

34 "Fromᴿ the cry of Heshbon to ᴿElealeh
　　　and to Jahaz　　Is. 15:4–6 • Num. 32:3, 37
　　They have uttered their voice,
　　ᴿFrom Zoar to Horonaim,　　Is. 15:5, 6
　　Like *a three-year-old heifer;
　　For the waters of Nimrim also shall be
　　　desolate.

35 "Moreover," says the Lᴏʀᴅ,
　　"I will cause to cease in Moab
　　The one who offers *sacrifices* in the
　　　ᵀhigh places　　Places for pagan worship
　　And burns incense to his gods.
36 Therefore ᴿMy heart shall wail like
　　　flutes for Moab,　　Is. 15:5; 16:11
　　And like flutes My heart shall wail
　　For the men of Kir Heres.
　　Therefore ᴿthe riches they have
　　　acquired have perished.　　Is. 15:7
37 "For ᴿevery head *shall be* bald, and
　　　every beard clipped;　　Is. 15:2, 3
　　On all the hands *shall be* cuts, and ᴿon
　　　the loins sackcloth—　　Gen. 37:34
38 A general lamentation
　　On all the ᴿhousetops of Moab,
　　And in its streets;
　　For I have ᴿbroken Moab like a vessel
　　　in which *is* no pleasure," says the
　　　Lᴏʀᴅ.　　　　Is. 15:3 • Jer. 22:28
39 "They shall wail:
　　'How she is broken down!
　　How Moab has turned her back with
　　　shame!'
　　So Moab shall be a derision
　　And a dismay to all those about her."

40 For thus says the Lᴏʀᴅ:

　　"Behold, one shall fly like an eagle,
　　And ᴿspread his wings over Moab.　　Is. 8:8
41 Kerioth is taken,
　　And the strongholds are surprised;
　　ᴿThe mighty men's hearts in Moab on
　　　that day shall be
　　Like the heart of a woman in birth
　　　pangs.　　　　Is. 13:8; 21:3
42 And Moab shall be destroyed ᴿas a
　　　people,
　　Because he exalted *himself* against the
　　　Lᴏʀᴅ.　　　　Ps. 83:4
43 ᴿFear and the pit and the snare *shall be*
　　　upon you,　　Is. 24:17, 18
　　O inhabitant of Moab," says the Lᴏʀᴅ.

48:31 So with DSS, LXX, Vg.; MT *He*

48:34 Or *The Third Eglath*, an unknown city, Is. 15:5

44 "He who flees from the fear shall fall
 into the pit,
And he who gets out of the pit shall be
 caught in the ᴿsnare.
For upon Moab, upon it ᴿI will bring
The year of their punishment," says the
 LORD.   Is. 24:18 • Jer. 11:23

45 "Those who fled stood under the shadow
 of Heshbon
Because of exhaustion.
But a fire shall come out of Heshbon,
A flame from the midst of ᴿSihon,
And ᴿshall devour the brow of Moab,
The crown of the head of the sons of
 tumult.   Ps. 135:11 • Num. 24:17
46 ᴿWoe to you, O Moab!
The people of Chemosh perish;
For your sons have been taken captive,
And your daughters captive. Num. 21:29

47 "Yet I will bring back the captives of
 Moab
In the latter days," says the LORD.

Thus far is the judgment of Moab.

Judgment on Ammon

49 Against the Ammonites.
Thus says the LORD:

"Has Israel no sons?
Has he no heir?
Why then does *Milcom inherit Gad,
And his people dwell in its cities?
2 ᴿTherefore behold, the days are coming,"
 says the LORD,   Amos 1:13-15
"That I will cause to be heard an alarm
 of war
In ᴿRabbah of the Ammonites;
It shall be a desolate mound,
And her ᵀvillages shall be burned with
 fire.   Ezek. 25:5 • Lit. daughters
Then Israel shall take possession of his
 inheritance," says the LORD.

3 "Wail, O Heshbon, for Ai is plundered!
Cry, you daughters of Rabbah,
Gird yourselves with sackcloth!
Lament and run to and fro by the walls;
For ᵀMilcom shall go into captivity
With his priests and his princes
 together. An Ammonite god, Molech
4 Why ᴿdo you boast in the valleys,
ᵀYour flowing valley, O backsliding
 daughter? Jer. 9:23 • Lit. Your valley is flowing
Who trusted in her treasures, ᴿsaying,
'Who will come against me?' Jer. 21:13
5 Behold, I will bring fear upon you,"
Says the Lord GOD of hosts,
"From all those who are around you;
You shall be driven out, everyone
 headlong,

49:1 Heb. Malcam, lit. their king; an Ammonite god,
1 Kin. 11:5; Molech, Lev. 18:21

And no one will gather those who
 wander off.
6 But ᴿafterward I will bring back
The captives of the people of Ammon,"
 says the LORD.   Jer. 48:47

Judgment on Edom

7 ᴿAgainst Edom. Ezek. 25:12-14; 35:1-15
Thus says the LORD of hosts:

"Is wisdom no more in Teman?
ᴿHas counsel perished from the prudent?
Has their wisdom vanished? Is. 19:11
8 Flee, turn back, dwell in the depths, O
 inhabitants of ᴿDedan! Jer. 25:23
For I will bring the calamity of Esau
 upon him,
The time that I will punish him.
9 ᴿIf grape-gatherers came to you,
Would they not leave some gleaning
 grapes?
If thieves by night,
Would they not destroy until they have
 enough?   Obad. 5, 6
10 ᴿBut I have made Esau bare;
I have uncovered his secret places,
And he shall not be able to hide
 himself. Obad. 5, 6; Mal. 1:3
His descendants are plundered,
His brethren and his neighbors,
And ᴿhe is no more. Is. 17:14
11 Leave your fatherless children,
I will preserve them alive;
And let your widows trust in Me."

12 For thus says the LORD: "Behold, ᴿthose
whose judgment was not to drink of the cup
have assuredly drunk. And are you the one
who will altogether go unpunished? You shall
not go unpunished, but you shall surely drink
of it.   Jer. 25:29
13 "For I have sworn by Myself," says the
LORD, "that Bozrah shall become a desolation, a reproach, a waste, and a curse. And all
its cities shall be perpetual wastes."

14 ᴿI have heard a message from the LORD,
And an ambassador has been sent to
 the nations:
"Gather together, come against her,
And rise up to battle! Obad. 1-4

15 "For indeed, I will make you small
 among nations,
Despised among men.
16 ᴿYour fierceness has deceived you,
The ᴿpride of your heart,
O you who dwell in the clefts of the
 rock, Obad. 3, 4 • Jer. 48:29
Who hold the height of the hill!
Though you make your ᴿnest as high as
 the eagle, Job 39:27
ᴿI will bring you down from there," says
 the LORD. Amos 9:2

17 "Edom also shall be an astonishment;
   REveryone who goes by it will be
      astonished   Jer. 18:16; 49:13; 50:13
   And will hiss at all its plagues.
18 RAs in the overthrow of Sodom and
      Gomorrah   Deut. 29:23
   And their neighbors," says the LORD,
   "No one shall remain there,
   Nor shall a son of man dwell in it.

19 "Behold,R he shall come up like a lion
      from Rthe Tflood plain of the Jordan
   Against the dwelling place of the
      strong;
   But I will suddenly make him run away
      from her.   Jer. 50:44 · Jer. 12:5 · Or thicket
   And who is a chosen man that I may
      appoint over her?
   For Rwho is like Me?   Ex. 15:11
   Who will arraign Me?
   And Rwho is that shepherd   Job 41:10
   Who will withstand Me?"

20 RTherefore hear the counsel of the LORD
      that He has taken against Edom,
   And His purposes that He has proposed
      against the inhabitants of Teman:
   Surely the least of the flock shall Tdraw
      them out;   Jer. 50:45 · Or drag them away
   Surely He shall make their dwelling
      places desolate with them.
21 RThe earth shakes at the noise of their
      fall;
   At the cry its noise is heard at the Red
      Sea.   Jer. 50:46
22 Behold, RHe shall come up and fly like
      the eagle,
   And spread His wings over Bozrah;
   The heart of the mighty men of Edom
      in that day shall be
   Like the heart of a woman in birth
      pangs.   Jer. 48:40, 41

Judgment on Damascus

23 RAgainst Damascus.   Amos 1:3, 5
   R"Hamath and Arpad are shamed,
      For they have heard bad news.
   They are fainthearted;   Jer. 39:5
   RThere is Ttrouble on the sea;
      It cannot be quiet.   [Is. 57:20] · anxiety
24 Damascus has grown feeble;
   She turns to flee,
   And fear has seized her.
   RAnguish and sorrows have taken her
      like a woman in Tlabor.   Is. 13:8 · childbirth
25 Why is Rthe city of praise not deserted,
      the city of My joy?   Jer. 33:9
26 RTherefore her young men shall fall in
      her streets,   Jer. 50:30
   And all the men of war shall be cut off
      in that day," says the LORD of hosts.
27 "IR will kindle a fire in the wall of
      Damascus,

And it shall consume the palaces of
   Ben-Hadad."   Amos 1:4

Judgment on Kedar and Hazor

28 RAgainst Kedar and against the kingdoms of Hazor, which Nebuchadnezzar king
of Babylon shall strike.   Ezek. 27:21
Thus says the LORD:

"Arise, go up to Kedar,
   And devastate the men of the East!
29 Their Rtents and their flocks they shall
      take away.
   They shall take for themselves their
      curtains,
   All their vessels and their camels;
   And they shall cry out to them,
   R'Fear is on every side!'   Ps. 120:5 · Jer. 46:5

30 "Flee, get far away! Dwell in the depths,
   O inhabitants of Hazor!" says the LORD.
   "For Nebuchadnezzar king of Babylon
      has taken counsel against you,
   And has conceived a plan against you.

31 "Arise, go up to Rthe wealthy nation that
      dwells securely," says the LORD,
   "Which has neither gates nor bars,
   RDwelling alone.   Ezek. 38:11 · Num. 23:9
32 Their camels shall be for booty,
   And the multitude of their cattle for
      plunder.
   I will Rscatter to all winds those in the
      farthest corners,   Ezek. 5:10
   And I will bring their calamity from all
      its sides," says the LORD.
33 "Hazor Rshall be a dwelling for jackals, a
      desolation forever;
   No one shall reside there,
   Nor son of man dwell in it."   Mal. 1:3

Judgment on Elam

34 The word of the LORD that came to
Jeremiah the prophet against RElam, in the
Rbeginning of the reign of Zedekiah king of
Judah, saying,   Jer. 25:25 · 2 Kin. 24:17, 18
35 "Thus says the LORD of hosts:

'Behold, I will break the Tbow of Elam,
   The foremost of their might.   Power
36 Against Elam I will bring the four
      winds
   From the four quarters of heaven,
   And scatter them toward all those
      winds;
   There shall be no nations where the
      outcasts of Elam will not go.
37 For I will cause Elam to be dismayed
      before their enemies
   And before those who seek their life.
   RI will bring disaster upon them,
   My fierce anger,' says the LORD;
   'And I will send the sword after them
   Until I have consumed them.   Jer. 9:16

38 I will ᴿset My throne in Elam,   Jer. 43:10
And will destroy from there the king
and the princes,' says the LORD.

39 'But it shall come to pass ᴿin the latter
days:
I will bring back the captives of Elam,'
says the LORD."   Jer. 48:47

Judgment on Babylon and Babylonia

50 The word that the LORD spoke
against Babylon *and* against the land
of the Chaldeans by Jeremiah the prophet.

2 "Declare among the nations,
Proclaim, and ᵀset up a standard;   *lift*
Proclaim—do not conceal *it*—
Say, 'Babylon is taken, Bel is shamed.
*Merodach is broken in pieces;
ᴿHer idols are humiliated,   Jer. 43:12, 13
Her images are broken in pieces.'
3 ᴿFor out of the north ᴿa nation comes up
against her,   Jer. 51:48 • Is. 13:17, 18, 20
Which shall make her land desolate,
And no one shall dwell therein.
They shall ᵀmove, they shall depart,
Both man and beast.   Or *wander*

4 "In those days and in that time," says
the LORD,
"The children of Israel shall come,
ᴿThey and the children of Judah
together;   Hos. 1:11
ᴿWith continual weeping they shall
come,   Ezra 3:12, 13
ᴿAnd seek the LORD their God.   Hos. 3:5
5 They shall ask the way to Zion,
With their faces toward it, *saying,*
'Come and let us join ourselves to the
LORD
In ᴿa perpetual covenant   Jer. 31:31
That will not be forgotten.'

6 "My people have been ᴿlost sheep.
Their shepherds have led them astray;
They have turned them away *on* ᴿthe
mountains.   Is. 53:6 • [Jer. 2:20; 3:6, 23]
They have gone from mountain to hill;
They have forgotten their resting place.
7 All who found them have ᴿdevoured
them;   Ps. 79:7
And ᴿtheir adversaries said, ᴿ'We have
not offended,   Zech. 11:5 • Jer. 2:3
Because they have sinned against the
LORD, the habitation of justice,
The LORD, the hope of their fathers.'

8 "Move from the midst of Babylon,
Go out of the land of the Chaldeans;
And be like the rams before the flocks.
9 ᴿFor behold, I will raise and cause to
come up against Babylon
An assembly of great nations from the
north country,   Jer. 15:14; 51:27

And they shall array themselves against
her;
From there she shall be captured.
Their arrows *shall be* like *those* of *an
expert warrior;
ᴿNone shall return in vain.   2 Sam. 1:22
10 And Chaldea shall become plunder;
ᴿAll who plunder her shall be satisfied,"
says the LORD.   [Rev. 17:16]

11 "Becauseᴿ you were glad, because you
rejoiced,   Is. 47:6
You destroyers of My heritage,
Because you have grown fat ᴿlike a
heifer threshing grain,   Hos. 10:11
And you bellow like bulls,
12 Your mother shall be deeply ashamed;
She who bore you shall be ashamed.
Behold, the least of the nations *shall be*
a ᴿwilderness,
A dry land and a desert.   Jer. 51:43
13 Because of the wrath of the LORD
She shall not be inhabited,
ᴿBut she shall be wholly desolate.
ᴿEveryone who goes by Babylon shall be
horrified   Jer. 25:12 • Jer. 49:17
And hiss at all her plagues.

14 "Putᴿ yourselves in array against
Babylon all around,   Jer. 51:2
All you who bend the bow;
Shoot at her, spare no arrows,
For she has sinned against the LORD.
15 Shout against her all around;
She has ᴿgiven her hand,   Lam. 5:6
Her foundations have fallen,
ᴿHer walls are thrown down;   Jer. 51:58
For ᴿit *is* the vengeance of the LORD.
Take vengeance on her.   Jer. 51:6, 11
As she has done, so do to her.
16 Cut off the sower from Babylon,
And him who handles the sickle at
harvest time.
For fear of the oppressing sword
Everyone shall turn to his own people,
And everyone shall flee to his own land.

17 "Israel *is* like scattered sheep;
The lions have driven *him* away.
First the king of Assyria devoured him;
Now at last this Nebuchadnezzar king
of Babylon has broken his bones."

18 Therefore thus says the LORD of hosts,
the God of Israel:

"Behold, I will punish the king of
Babylon and his land,
As I have punished the king of Assyria.
19 ᴿBut I will bring back Israel to his home,
And he shall feed on Carmel and
Bashan;

50:9 So with some Heb. mss., LXX, Syr.; MT, Tg., Vg. *a
warrior who makes childless*

50:2 Or *Marduk;* a Babylonian god

His soul shall be satisfied on Mount
    Ephraim and Gilead.   Is. 65:10
20 In those days and in that time," says
    the LORD,
  R"The iniquity of Israel shall be sought,
    but *there shall be* none;
  And the sins of Judah, but they shall
    not be found;
  For I will pardon those Rwhom I
    preserve.   [Jer. 31:34] · Is. 1:9

21 "Go up against the land of Merathaim,
    against it,
  And against the inhabitants of Pekod.
  TWaste and utterly destroy them," says
    the LORD,   Or *Attack* with the sword
  "And do Raccording to all that I have
    commanded you.   2 Sam. 16:11
22 RA sound of battle *is* in the land,
  And of great destruction.   Jer. 51:54
23 How Rthe hammer of the whole earth
    has been cut apart and broken!
  How Babylon has become a desolation
    among the nations!
  I have laid a snare for you;   Jer. 51:20–24
24 You have indeed been Rtrapped, O
    Babylon,
  And you were not aware;
  You have been found and also caught,
  Because you have Rcontended against
    the Lord.   Dan. 5:30 · [Is. 45:9]
25 The LORD has opened His armory,
  And has brought out Rthe weapons of
    His indignation;
  For this *is* the work of the Lord GOD of
    hosts
  In the land of the Chaldeans.   Is. 13:5
26 Come against her from the farthest
    border;
  Open her storehouses;
  Cast her up as heaps of ruins,
  And destroy her utterly;
  Let nothing of her be left.
27 Slay all her Rbulls,
  Let them go down to the slaughter.
  Woe to them!
  For their day has come, the time of
    Rtheir punishment.   Is. 34:7 · Jer. 48:44
28 The voice of those who flee and escape
    from the land of Babylon
  RDeclares in Zion the vengeance of the
    LORD our God,
  The vengeance of His temple.   Jer. 51:10

29 "Call together the archers against
    Babylon.
  All you who bend the bow, encamp
    against it all around;
  Let none of them *escape.
  RRepay her according to her work;
  According to all she has done, do to
    her;   Jer. 51:56

50:29 Qr., some Heb. mss., LXX, Tg. add *to her*

RFor she has been proud against the
    LORD,   [Is. 47:10]
  Against the Holy One of Israel.
30 RTherefore her young men shall fall in
    the streets,   Jer. 49:26; 51:4
  And all her men of war shall be cut off
    in that day," says the LORD.
31 "Behold, I *am* against you,
  O most haughty one!" says the Lord
    GOD of hosts;
  "For your day has come,
  *The time *that* I will punish you.
32 The most Rproud shall stumble and fall,
  And no one will raise him up;   Mal. 4:1
  RI will kindle a fire in his cities,   Jer. 21:14
  And it will devour all around him."

33 Thus says the LORD of hosts:

  "The children of Israel *were* oppressed,
  Along with the children of Judah;
  All who took them captive have held
    them fast;
  They have refused to let them go.
34 RTheir Redeemer *is* strong;   Rev. 18:8
  RThe LORD of hosts *is* His name.   Is. 47:4
  He will thoroughly plead their case,
  That He may give rest to the land,
  And disquiet the inhabitants of
    Babylon.

35 "A sword *is* against the Chaldeans," says
    the LORD,
  "Against the inhabitants of Babylon,
  And Ragainst her princes and Rher wise
    men.   Dan. 5:30 · Is. 47:13
36 A sword *is* Ragainst the soothsayers,
    and they will be fools.
  A sword *is* against her mighty men, and
    they will be dismayed.   Is. 44:25
37 A sword *is* against their horses,
  Against their chariots,
  And against all Rthe mixed peoples who
    are in her midst;
  And Rthey will become like women.
  A sword *is* against her treasures, and
    they will be robbed. Jer. 25:20 · Jer. 51:30
38 RA *drought *is* against her waters, and
    they will be dried up.   Rev. 16:12
  For it *is* the land of carved images,
  And they are insane with *their* idols.

39 "ThereforeR the wild desert beasts shall
    dwell *there* with the jackals,
  And the ostriches shall dwell in it.
  RIt shall be inhabited no more forever,
  Nor shall it be dwelt in from generation
    to generation.   Rev. 18:2 · Is. 13:20
40 RAs God overthrew Sodom and
    Gomorrah   Is. 13:19

50:31 So with MT, [Tg.]; LXX, Vg. *The time of your
punishment*
50:38 So with MT, Tg., Vg; Syr. *sword;* LXX omits *A
drought is*

And their neighbors," says the LORD,
"So no one shall reside there,
Nor son of man [R]dwell in it.   Is. 13:20

41 "Behold,[R] a people shall come from the
    north,
    And a great nation and many kings
    Shall be raised up from the ends of the
    earth.   Jer. 6:22; 25:14; 51:27
42 [R]They shall hold the bow and the lance;
    [R]They *are* cruel and shall not show
    mercy.   Jer. 6:23 · Is. 13:18
    [R]Their voice shall roar like the sea;
    They shall ride on horses,   Is. 5:30
    Set in array, like a man for the battle,
    Against you, O daughter of Babylon.

43 "The king of Babylon has [R]heard the
    report about them,   Jer. 51:31
    And his hands grow feeble;
    Anguish has taken hold of him,
    Pangs as of a woman in childbirth.

44 "Behold,[R] he shall come up like a lion
    from the [T]flood plain of the Jordan
    Against the dwelling place of the
    strong;
    But I will make them suddenly run
    away from her.   Jer. 49:19–21 · Or *thicket*
    And who *is* a chosen *man that* I may
    appoint over her?
    For who *is* like Me?
    Who will arraign Me?
    And [R]who *is* that shepherd   Job 41:10
    Who will withstand Me?"

45 Therefore hear the counsel of the LORD
    that He has taken against Babylon,
    And His [R]purposes that He has
    proposed against the land of the
    Chaldeans:
    [R]Surely the least of the flock shall draw
    them out;   Jer. 51:29 · Jer. 49:19, 20
    Surely He will make their dwelling
    place desolate with them.
46 [R]At the noise of the taking of Babylon
    The earth trembles,   Rev. 18:9
    And the cry is heard among the
    nations.

The Utter Destruction of Babylon

51 Thus says the LORD:

"Behold, I will raise up against Babylon,
Against those who dwell in *Leb
    Kamai,
A destroying wind.
2 And I will send [R]winnowers to Babylon,
    Who shall winnow her and empty her
    land.   Jer. 15:7
    [R]For in the day of doom   Jer. 50:14
    They shall be against her all around.

51:1 Lit. *The Midst of Those Who Rise Up Against Me;* a
code word for Chaldea, Babylonia

3 Against *her* [R]let the archer bend his
    bow,   Jer. 50:14, 29
    And lift himself up against *her* in his
    armor.
    Do not spare her young men;
    [R]Utterly destroy all her army.   Jer. 50:21
4 Thus the slain shall fall in the land of
    the Chaldeans,
    And *those* thrust through in her streets.
5 For Israel is not forsaken, nor Judah,
    By his God, the LORD of hosts,
    Though their land was filled with sin
    against the Holy One of Israel."

6 [R]Flee from the midst of Babylon,
    And every one save his life!
    Do not be cut off in her iniquity,
    For [R]this *is* the time of the LORD's
    vengeance;   Rev. 18:4 · Jer. 50:15
    [R]He shall recompense her.   Jer. 25:14
7 [R]Babylon *was* a golden cup in the LORD's
    hand,   Rev. 17:4
    That made all the earth drunk.
    [R]The nations drank her wine;   Rev. 14:8
    Therefore the nations are deranged.
8 Babylon has suddenly [R]fallen and been
    destroyed.   Is. 21:9
    [R]Wail for her!   Rev. 18:9, 11, 19
    [R]Take balm for her pain;   Jer. 46:11
    Perhaps she may be healed.

9 We would have healed Babylon,
    But she is not healed.
    Forsake her, and [R]let us go everyone to
    his own country;   Is. 13:14
    [R]For her judgment reaches to heaven
    and is lifted up to the skies.   Rev. 18:5
10 The LORD has [R]revealed our
    righteousness.   Ps. 37:6
    Come and let us [R]declare in Zion the
    work of the LORD our God.   Jer. 50:28

11 [T]Make the arrows bright!
    Gather the shields!   *Polish the arrows*
    [R]The LORD has raised up the spirit of the
    kings of the Medes.   Is. 13:17
    [R]For His plan *is* against Babylon to
    destroy it,   Jer. 50:45
    Because it *is* [R]the vengeance of the
    LORD,   Jer. 50:28
    The vengeance for His temple.
12 [R]Set up the standard on the walls of
    Babylon;
    Make the guard strong,
    Set up the watchmen,
    Prepare the ambushes.
    For the LORD has both devised and
    done
    What He spoke against the inhabitants
    of Babylon.   Nah. 2:1; 3:14
13 [R]O you who dwell by many waters,
    Abundant in treasures,   Rev. 17:1, 15
    Your end has come,
    The measure of your covetousness.

14 ᴿThe LORD of hosts has sworn by
  Himself:
  "Surely I will fill you with men, ᴿas with
    locusts,
  And they shall lift ᴿup a shout against
    you."   Jer. 49:13 • Nah. 3:15 • Jer. 50:15

15 ᴿHe has made the earth by His power;
  He has established the world by His
    wisdom,
  And ᴿstretched out the heaven by His
    understanding.   Gen. 1:1, 6 • Job 9:8
16 When He utters *His* voice—
  There is a multitude of waters in the
    heavens:
  ᴿ"He causes the vapors to ascend from
    the ends of the earth;
  He makes lightnings for the rain;
  He brings the wind out of His
    treasuries."   Ps. 135:7
17 ᴿEveryone is dull-hearted, without
    knowledge;   Jer. 10:14
  Every metalsmith is put to shame by
    the carved image;
  ᴿFor his molded image *is* falsehood,
  And *there is* no breath in them.   Jer. 50:2
18 They *are* futile, a work of errors;
  In the time of their punishment they
    shall perish.
19 The Portion of Jacob *is* not like them,
  For He *is* the Maker of all things;
  And *Israel is* the tribe of His
    inheritance.
  The LORD of hosts *is* His name.

20 "Youᴿ *are* My battle-ax *and* weapons of
    war: Is. 10:5, 15
  For with you I will break the nation in
    pieces;
  With you I will destroy kingdoms;
21 With you I will break in pieces the
    horse and its rider;
  With you I will break in pieces the
    chariot and its rider;
22 With you also I will break in pieces
    man and woman;
  With you I will break in pieces ᴿold and
    young;
  With you I will break in pieces the
    young man and the maiden;   2 Chr. 36:17
23 With you also I will break in pieces the
    shepherd and his flock;
  With you I will break in pieces the
    farmer and his yoke of oxen;
  And with you I will break in pieces
    governors and rulers.

24 "Andᴿ I will repay Babylon   Jer. 50:15, 29
  And all the inhabitants of Chaldea
  For all the evil they have done
  In Zion in your sight," says the LORD.

25 "Behold, I *am* against you, ᴿO destroying
    mountain,   Zech. 4:7

Who destroys all the earth," says the
  LORD.
"And I will stretch out My hand against
    you,
  Roll you down from the rocks,
  And make you a burnt mountain.
26 They shall not take from you a stone
    for a corner
  Nor a stone for a foundation,
  ᴿBut you shall be desolate forever," says
    the LORD.   Jer. 50:26, 40

27 ᴿSet up a banner in the land,   Is. 13:2
  Blow the trumpet among the nations!
  ᴿPrepare the nations against her,
  Call ᴿthe kingdoms together against
    her: Jer. 25:14 • Jer. 50:41, 42
  Ararat, Minni, and Ashkenaz.
  Appoint a general against her;
  Cause the horses to come up like the
    bristling locusts.
28 Prepare against her the nations,
  With the kings of the Medes,
  Its governors and all its rulers,
  All the land of his dominion.
29 And the land will tremble and sorrow;
  For every ᴿpurpose of the LORD shall be
    performed against Babylon,   Jer. 50:45
  ᴿTo make the land of Babylon a
    desolation without inhabitant.   Jer. 50:13
30 The mighty men of Babylon have
    ceased fighting,
  They have remained in their
    strongholds;
  Their might has failed,
  ᴿThey became *like* women;   Is. 19:16
  They have burned her dwelling places,
  ᴿThe bars of her *gate* are broken. Lam. 2:9
31 ᴿOne runner will run to meet another,
  And one messenger to meet another,
  To show the king of Babylon that his
    city is taken on *all* sides;   Jer. 50:24
32 ᴿThe passages are blocked,   Jer. 50:38
  The reeds they have burned with fire,
  And the men of war are terrified.

33 For thus says the LORD of hosts, the God
  of Israel:

  "The daughter of Babylon *is* ᴿlike a
    threshing floor   Is. 21:10
  When ᴿ*it is* time to thresh her;
  Yet a little while   Hab. 3:12
  And the time of her harvest will come."

34 "Nebuchadnezzar the king of Babylon
  Has ᴿdevoured me, he has crushed me;
  He has made me an ᴿempty vessel,
  He has swallowed me up like a
    monster;
  He has filled his stomach with my
    delicacies,
  He has spit me out.   Jer. 50:17 • Is. 24:1-3
35 Let the violence *done* to me and my
    flesh *be* upon Babylon,"

The inhabitant of Zion will say;
"And my blood be upon the inhabitants
of Chaldea!"
Jerusalem will say.

36 Therefore thus says the LORD:

"Behold, ᴿI will plead your case and take
vengeance for you.
ᴿI will dry up her sea and make her
springs dry.   Jer. 50:34 · Jer. 50:38
37 ᴿBabylon shall become a heap,   Is. 13:22
A dwelling place for jackals,
ᴿAn astonishment and a hissing,
Without an inhabitant.   Jer. 25:9, 11
38 They shall roar together like lions,
They shall growl like lions' whelps.
39 In their excitement I will prepare their
feasts;
ᴿI will make them drunk,   Jer. 51:57
That they may rejoice,
And sleep a perpetual sleep
And not awake," says the LORD.
40 "I will bring them down
Like lambs to the slaughter,
Like rams with male goats.

41 "Oh, how ᵀSheshach is taken!
Oh, how the praise of the whole earth
is seized!   A code word for *Babylon,* Jer. 25:26
How Babylon has become desolate
among the nations!
42 ᴿThe sea has come up over Babylon;
She is covered with the multitude of its
waves.   Is. 8:7, 8
43 ᴿHer cities are a desolation,   Jer. 50:39, 40
A dry land and a wilderness,
A land where ᴿno one dwells,   Is. 13:20
Through which no son of man passes.
44 I will punish ᵀBel in Babylon,
And I will bring out of his mouth what
he has swallowed;   A Babylonian god
And the nations shall not stream to him
anymore.
Yes, the wall of Babylon shall fall.

45 "My people, go out of the midst of her!
And let everyone deliver ᵀhimself from
the fierce anger of the LORD.   Lit. *his soul*
46 And lest your heart faint,
And you fear ᴿfor the rumor that *will
be* heard in the land
(A rumor will come *one* year,
And after that, in *another* year
A rumor *will come,*
And violence in the land,
Ruler against ruler),   2 Kin. 19:7
47 Therefore behold, the days are coming
That I will bring judgment on the
carved images of Babylon;
Her whole land shall be ashamed,
And all her slain shall fall in her midst.
48 Then ᴿthe heavens and the earth and
all that *is* in them   Is. 44:23; 48:20; 49:13

Shall sing joyously over Babylon;
For the plunderers shall come to her
from the north," says the LORD.

49 As Babylon *has caused* the slain of
Israel to fall,
So at Babylon the slain of all the earth
shall fall.
50 ᴿYou who have escaped the sword,
Get away! Do not stand still!   Jer. 44:28
Remember the LORD afar off,
And let Jerusalem come to your mind.

51 ᴿWe are ashamed because we have
heard reproach.   Ps. 44:15; 79:4
Shame has covered our faces,
For strangers have come into the
sanctuaries of the LORD's house.

52 "Therefore behold, the days are coming,"
says the LORD,
"That I will bring judgment on her
carved images,
And throughout all her land the
wounded shall groan.
53 ᴿThough Babylon were to ᵀmount up to
heaven,
And though she were to fortify the
height of her strength,
Yet from Me plunderers would come to
her," says the LORD.   Amos 9:2 · *ascend*
54 ᴿThe sound of a cry *comes* from
Babylon,
And great destruction from the land of
the Chaldeans,   Jer. 50:22
55 Because the LORD is plundering
Babylon
And silencing her loud voice,
Though her waves roar like great
waters,
And the noise of their voice is uttered,
56 Because the plunderer comes against
her, against Babylon,
And her mighty men are taken.
Every one of their bows is broken;
ᴿFor the LORD *is* the God of recompense,
He will surely repay.   Jer. 50:29

57 "And I will make drunk
Her princes and ᴿwise men,
Her governors, her deputies, and her
mighty men.   Jer. 50:35
And they shall sleep a perpetual sleep
And not awake," says the King,
Whose name *is* the LORD of hosts.

58 Thus says the LORD of hosts:

"The broad walls of Babylon shall be
utterly ᵀbroken,   Lit. *laid utterly bare*
And her high gates shall be burned
with fire;
ᴿThe people will labor in vain,   Hab. 2:13
And the nations, because of the fire;
And they shall be weary."

Jeremiah's Command to Seraiah

59 The word which Jeremiah the prophet commanded Seraiah the son of ᴿNeriah, the son of Mahseiah, when he went with Zedekiah the king of Judah to Babylon in the fourth year of his reign. And Seraiah *was* the quartermaster.   Jer. 32:12

60 So Jeremiah wrote in a book all the evil that would come upon Babylon, all these words that are written against Babylon.

61 And Jeremiah said to Seraiah, "When you arrive in Babylon and see it, and read all these words,

62 "then you shall say, 'O LORD, You have spoken against this place to cut it off, so that none shall remain in it, neither man nor beast, but it shall be desolate forever.'

63 "Now it shall be, when you have finished reading this book, *that* you shall tie a stone to it and throw it out into the Euphrates.

64 "Then you shall say, 'Thus Babylon shall sink and not rise from the catastrophe that I will bring upon her. And they shall be weary.' " Thus far *are* the words of Jeremiah.

The Fall of Jerusalem Reviewed

52 Zedekiah *was* ᴿtwenty-one years old when he became king, and he reigned eleven years in Jerusalem. His mother's name *was* Hamutal the daughter of Jeremiah of ᴿLibnah.   2 Kin. 24:18 • Josh. 10:29

2 He also did evil in the sight of the LORD, according to all that Jehoiakim had done.

3 For because of the anger of the LORD *this* happened in Jerusalem and Judah, till He finally cast them out from His presence. Then Zedekiah ᴿrebelled against the king of Babylon.   2 Chr. 36:13

4 Now it came to pass in the ᴿninth year of his reign, in the tenth month, on the tenth *day* of the month, *that* Nebuchadnezzar king of Babylon and all his army came against Jerusalem and encamped against it; and *they* built a siege wall against it all around. Jer. 39:1

5 So the city was besieged until the eleventh year of King Zedekiah.

6 By the fourth month, on the ninth day of the month, the famine had become so severe in the city that there was no food for the people of the land.

7 Then the city wall was broken through, and all the men of war fled and went out of the city at night by way of the gate between the two walls, which *was* by the king's garden, even though the Chaldeans *were* near the city all around. And they went by way of the ᵀplain.   Or *arabah*, the Jordan Valley

8 But the army of the Chaldeans pursued the king, and they overtook Zedekiah in the plains of Jericho. All his army was scattered from him.

9 ᴿSo they took the king and brought him up to the king of Babylon at Riblah in the land of Hamath, and he pronounced judgment on him.   Jer. 32:4; 39:5

10 Then the king of Babylon killed the sons of Zedekiah before his eyes. And he killed all the princes of Judah in Riblah.

11 He also put out the eyes of Zedekiah; and the king of Babylon bound him in bronze fetters, took him to Babylon, and put him in prison till the day of his death.

The Temple and City Plundered and Burned

12 ᴿNow in the fifth month, on the tenth *day* of the month (ᴿwhich *was* the nineteenth year of King Nebuchadnezzar king of Babylon), ᴿNebuzaradan, the captain of the guard, *who* served the king of Babylon, came to Jerusalem.   2 Kin. 25:8–21 • Jer. 52:29 • Jer. 39:9

13 He burned the house of the LORD and the king's house; all the houses of Jerusalem, that is, all the houses of the great, he burned with fire.

14 And all the army of the Chaldeans who *were* with the captain of the guard broke down all the walls of Jerusalem all around.

15 ᴿThen Nebuzaradan the captain of the guard carried away captive *some* of the poor people, the rest of the people who remained in the city, the defectors who had deserted to the king of Babylon, and the rest of the craftsmen.   Jer. 39:9

16 But Nebuzaradan the captain of the guard left *some* of the poor of the land as vinedressers and farmers.

17 ᴿThe bronze pillars that *were* in the house of the LORD, and the carts and the bronze Sea that *were* in the house of the LORD, the Chaldeans broke in pieces, and carried all their bronze to Babylon. Jer. 27:19

18 They also took away ᴿthe pots, the shovels, the trimmers, the ᵀbowls, the spoons, and all the bronze utensils with which the priests ministered.   Ex. 27:3 • *basins*

19 The basins, the firepans, the bowls, the pots, the lampstands, the spoons, and the cups, whatever *was* solid gold and whatever *was* solid silver, the captain of the guard took away.

20 The two pillars, one Sea, the twelve bronze bulls which *were* under *it*, *and* the carts, which King Solomon had made for the house of the LORD—ᴿthe bronze of all these articles was beyond measure.   1 Kin. 7:47

21 Now concerning the ᴿpillars: the height of one pillar *was* ᵀeighteen cubits, a measuring line of twelve cubits could measure its circumference, and its thickness *was* ᵀfour fingers; *it was* hollow.   2 Kin. 25:17 • 27 ft. • 3 in.

22 A capital of bronze *was* on it; and the height of one capital *was* ᵀfive cubits, with a network and pomegranates all around the capital, all of bronze. The second pillar, with pomegranates was the same.   7.5 ft.

23 There were ninety-six pomegranates on the sides; ^Rall the pomegranates, all around on the network, *were* one hundred.   1 Kin. 7:20

The People Taken Captive to Babylonia

24 The captain of the guard took Seraiah the chief priest, ^RZephaniah the second priest, and the three doorkeepers.   Jer. 21:1; 29:25

25 He also took out of the city an ^Tofficer who had charge of the men of war, seven men of the king's close associates who were found in the city, the principal scribe of the army who mustered the people of the land, and sixty men of the people of the land who were found in the midst of the city.   Lit. *eunuch*

26 And Nebuzaradan the captain of the guard took these and brought them to the king of Babylon at Riblah.

27 Then the king of Babylon struck them and put them to death at Riblah in the land of Hamath. Thus Judah was carried away captive from its own land.

28 These *are* the people whom Nebuchadnezzar carried away captive: in the seventh year, three thousand and twenty-three Jews;

29 ^Rin the eighteenth year of Nebuchadnezzar he carried away captive from Jerusalem eight hundred and thirty-two persons;   Jer. 39:9

30 in the twenty-third year of Nebuchadnezzar, Nebuzaradan the captain of the guard carried away captive of the Jews seven hundred and forty-five persons. All the persons *were* four thousand six hundred.

Jehoiachin Released from Prison

31 Now it came to pass in the thirty-seventh year of the captivity of Jehoiachin king of Judah, in the twelfth month, on the twenty-fifth *day* of the month, *that* Evil-Merodach king of Babylon, in the first *year* of his reign, lifted up the head of Jehoiachin king of Judah and brought him out of prison.

32 And he spoke kindly to him and gave him a more prominent seat than those of the kings who *were* with him in Babylon.

33 So ^TJehoiachin changed from his prison garments, and he ate bread regularly before the king all the days of his life.   Lit. *he*

34 And as for his provisions, there was a regular ration given him by the king of Babylon, a portion for each day until the day of his death, all the days of his life.

THE BOOK OF
Lamentations

CONTEXT. The composition of Lamentations was most assuredly prompted by the destruction of Jerusalem and the accompanying exile of the people of Judah under the conquering Babylonians in 586 B.C. Lamentations is a collection of five songs, or poems, of mourning written as if for a national funeral; they reflect the author's observations as he viewed the devastation of Jerusalem. The ancient custom of composing and singing lamentations over deceased friends was extended by the prophets to cities, nations, and countries.

The title of this book in Hebrew is the first word of chapters 1, 2, and 4, which literally means "Alas!" or "How . . . !" This designation is similar to the name "Lamentations" since it is the usual word used for funeral laments in the Old Testament. Either title projects the mood of the entire book, namely, that of weeping over the downfall of Jerusalem.

AUTHORSHIP. Although no one is named as the author in the book itself, from ancient times Lamentations has been attributed to the prophet Jeremiah. The Septuagint (the Greek translation of the Old Testament) places the following preface before the text of Lamentations: "And it came to pass after the captivity of Israel and the desolation of Jerusalem that Jeremiah sat weeping, and he lamented this lament over Jerusalem." Various scholars indicate that there are enough similarities between Lamentations and the poetical sections of Jeremiah to substantiate the possibility of a common author. Additionally, the Scripture implies in 2 Chronicles 35:25 that Jeremiah is the author of a lament type of literature. Careful study of authorship proves that the tradition that Jeremiah was the writer is as well founded as any other possibility.

THE TIME AND PLACE OF WRITING. It is clear that the date of Lamentations is after the destruction of Jerusalem by the Babylonians in 586 B.C. but sometime before the release of the Jews from Babylonian captivity in 538 B.C. The fact that there is nothing in the book indicating any expectation of immediate relief or restoration suggests a time close to 586 B.C.

Because there are so many explicit descriptions of the desolate city of Jerusalem, it seems that the author was reporting what he saw with his own eyes. Tradition says that there is a cave just outside the north wall of Jerusalem where the author wept bitter tears and composed Lamentations.

HOW LAMENTATIONS FITS TOGETHER. The book is a collection of five separate songs, or poems, each comprising a chapter. Four of the five songs of mourning are acrostic, that is, each verse begins with a letter of the Hebrew alphabet in alphabetic sequence. This was a favorite form of Hebrew poetry, adopted to help in memorizing. The fifth song is more a prayer than a dirge and gives place to free and natural feeling rather than the careful consideration necessary for alphabetic arrangement.

Lamentations expresses both individual and community sorrow. The city of Jerusalem, once grand and beautiful, is now reduced to rubble. Stunned, dazed, and broken with grief, the prophet walks the streets reporting what he hears, sees, and feels.

The first lamentation (ch. 1) begins by portraying Jerusalem's miserable condition after the Babylonian destruction. Her greatness has departed and now she stands humiliated. She has made wrong choices as a result of preoccupation with temporal things. Beginning with 1:12, the city is personified and answers the author as she observes her emptiness and destruction. She cries for understanding and sympathy because of the magnitude of her sorrow, yet states that this punishment from God is just.

The second lamentation (ch. 2) records the fierce anger of God. Little is spared in the description of God's displeasure over Judah's failure. The people and their leaders had been warned repeatedly, but they continued to disobey. The prophet deliberately stresses the fact that God has caused the suffering in Jerusalem in order to teach a much-needed lesson.

The third lamentation (ch. 3) is a reminder of the mercy and compassion of God despite so much affliction. As the prophet looks over the ruins of Jerusalem, he personally feels the pain and anguish of God's judgment. In the midst of this experience he remembers that the Lord's mercy never ceases, His compassion never fails, and His faithfulness never diminishes (3:22, 23).

The fourth lamentation (ch. 4) vividly describes the harsh realities of God's judgment. Things which were once considered priceless became valueless and those previously deemed insignificant became precious. The prophet pictures the situation as being overwhelmingly hopeless and the people as being beyond comfort.

The final song in Lamentations (ch. 5) is not a funeral dirge like the first four, but a prayer for restoration. The prophet reflects the thoughts of the captives as they walked away from Jerusalem to captivity. Some had lived to tell the story of the terrible consequences of their sin. The prophet concludes by recording the people's request to God. Their plea is simple and direct: "Turn us back to You, O LORD . . . renew our days as of old" (5:21).

In the book of Lamentations the author presents to the community, in their deep sorrow, words to direct the grieving heart to the only Source of true comfort. He seeks to give expression to the people's grief that he may weep with them. At the same time he seeks to motivate his fellow countrymen to acknowledge God's justice in this devastating experience. His desire is to keep them from despair under the burden of unutterable woe and to teach them how to submit to the judgment which has come. His purpose is to lead them back to God.

The Jewish synagogue, recognizing the importance of Lamentations as a reminder of God's judgment on Judah, requires that the book be read throughout the world on the ninth day of the fourth month (Jer. 52:6).

—N.B.C.

Jerusalem in Affliction

HOW lonely sits the city
    That was full of people!
    ^R*How* like a widow is she,   Is. 47:7-9
Who *was* great among the nations!
The princess among the provinces
Has become a ^Tslave!   Lit. *forced laborer*

2 She ^Rweeps bitterly in the ^Rnight,
    Her tears *are* on her cheeks;
Among all her lovers
She has none to comfort *her*.
All her friends have dealt treacherously
    with her;   Jer. 13:17 • Job 7:3
They have become her enemies.

3 ^RJudah has gone into captivity,   Jer. 52:27
    Under affliction and hard servitude;
^RShe dwells among the ^Tnations,
She finds no ^Rrest;
All her persecutors overtake her in dire
    straits.   Lam. 2:9 • *Gentiles* • Deut. 28:65

4 The roads to Zion mourn
    Because no one comes to the ^Tset
      feasts.
All her gates are ^Rdesolate;
Her priests sigh,
Her virgins are afflicted,
And she *is* in bitterness.   appointed • Is. 27:10

5 Her adversaries ^Rhave become ^Tthe
    master,   Deut. 28:43 • Lit. *her head*
Her enemies prosper;
For the LORD has afflicted her
^RBecause of the multitude of her
    transgressions.   Dan. 9:7, 16
Her ^Rchildren have gone into captivity
    before the enemy.   Jer. 52:28

6 And from the daughter of Zion
    All her splendor has departed.
Her princes have become like deer
That find no pasture,
That ^Tflee without strength
Before the pursuer.   Lit. *are gone*

7 In the days of her affliction and
    roaming,
Jerusalem ^Rremembers all her pleasant
    things   Ps. 137:1
That she had in the days of old.
When her people fell into the hand of
    the enemy,
With no one to help her,
The adversaries saw her
And mocked at her *downfall.

8 ^RJerusalem has sinned gravely,
    Therefore she has become *vile.
All who honored her despise her
Because they have seen her nakedness;
Yes, she sighs and turns away.   [1 Kin. 8:46]

9 Her uncleanness *is* in her skirts;
    She ^Rdid not consider her destiny;
Therefore her collapse was awesome;
She had no comforter.   Is. 47:7
"O LORD, behold my affliction,
For *the* enemy is exalted!"

10 The adversary has spread his hand
    Over all her ^Tpleasant things;   desirable
For she has seen ^Rthe nations enter her
    ^Tsanctuary,   Jer. 51:51 • *holy place,* the temple
Those whom You commanded
^RNot to enter Your assembly.   Deut. 23:3

11 All her people sigh,
    ^RThey ^Tseek bread;   Jer. 38:9; 52:6 • *hunt food*
They have given their ^Tvaluables for
    food to restore life.   desirable things
"See, O LORD, and consider,
For I am scorned."

12 "*Is it* nothing to you, all you who pass
    by?
Behold and see
^RIf there is any sorrow like my sorrow,
Which has been brought on me,

1:7 Vg. *Sabbaths*
1:8 LXX, Vg. *moved* or *removed*

What

Which

Which the Lord has inflicted
In the day of His fierce anger.　Dan. 9:12

13 "From above He has sent fire into my
bones,
And it overpowered them;
He has [R]spread a net for my feet
And turned me back;
He has made me desolate
And faint all the day.　Ezek. 12:13; 17:20

14 "The[R] yoke of my transgressions was
*bound;
They were woven together by His
hands,
And thrust upon my neck.
He made my strength fail;
The Lord delivered me into the hands
of those whom I am not able to
withstand.　Deut. 28:48

15 "The Lord has trampled underfoot all my
mighty men in my midst;
He has called an assembly against me
To crush my young men;
[R]The Lord trampled as in a winepress
The virgin daughter of Judah.　[Rev. 14:19]

16 "For these things I weep;
My eye, [R]my eye overflows with water;
Because the comforter, who should
restore my life,
Is far from me.
My children are desolate
Because the enemy prevailed."　Eccl. 4:1

17 [R]Zion [T]spreads out her hands,
But no one comforts her;
The Lord has commanded concerning
Jacob
That those [R]around him become his
adversaries;
Jerusalem has become an unclean thing
among them.　Jer. 4:31 • Prays • 2 Kin. 24:2–4

18 "The Lord is [R]righteous,　Dan. 9:7, 14
For I rebelled against His
[T]commandment.　Lit. mouth
Hear now, all peoples,
And behold my sorrow;
My virgins and my young men
Have gone into captivity.

19 "I called for my lovers,
But they deceived me;
My priests and my elders
Breathed their last in the city,
While they sought food
To restore their life.

20 "See, O Lord, that I am in distress;
My [T]soul is troubled;　Lit. inward parts
My heart is overturned within me,
For I have been very rebellious.

[R]Outside the sword bereaves,　Ezek. 7:15
At home it is like death.

21 "They have heard that I sigh,
But no one comforts me.
All my enemies have heard of my
trouble;
They are [R]glad that You have done it.
Bring on [R]the day You have
[T]announced,　Ps. 35:15 • [Jer. 46] • proclaimed
That they may become like me.

22 "Let[R] all their wickedness come before
You,
And do to them as You have done to
me
For all my transgressions;
For my sighs are many,
And my heart is faint."　Ps. 109:15; 137:7, 8

God's Anger with Jerusalem

2 How the Lord has covered the daughter
of Zion
With a [R]cloud in His anger!　[Lam. 3:44]
[R]He cast down from heaven to the earth
[R]The beauty of Israel,　Matt. 11:23 • 2 Sam. 1:19
And did not remember [R]His footstool
In the day of His anger.　Ps. 99:5

2 The Lord has swallowed up and has
[R]not pitied
All the dwelling places of Jacob.
He has thrown down in His wrath
The strongholds of the daughter of
Judah;
He has brought them down to the
ground;
[R]He has profaned the kingdom and its
princes.　Lam. 3:43 • Ps. 89:39, 40

3 He has cut off in fierce anger
Every [T]horn of Israel;　Strength
[R]He has drawn back His right hand
From before the enemy.　Ps. 89:46
[R]He has blazed against Jacob like a
flaming fire
Devouring all around.　Ps. 74:11

4 [R]Standing like an enemy, He has bent
His bow;　Is. 63:10
With His right hand, like an adversary,
He has slain [R]all who were pleasing to
His eye;　Ezek. 24:25
On the tent of the daughter of Zion,
He has poured out His fury like fire.

5 [R]The Lord was like an enemy.
He has swallowed up Israel,
He has swallowed up all her palaces;
[R]He has destroyed her strongholds,
And has increased mourning and
lamentation　Jer. 30:14 • Jer. 52:13
In the daughter of Judah.

6 He has done violence [R]to His
[T]tabernacle,　Ps. 80:12; 89:40 • Lit. booth
[R]As if it were a garden;　Is. 1:8

He has destroyed His place of assembly;
The Lord has caused
The appointed feasts and Sabbaths to
be forgotten in Zion.
In His burning indignation He has
spurned the king and the priest.

7 The Lord has spurned His altar,
He has ^Rabandoned His sanctuary;
He has ^Tgiven up the walls of her
palaces   Ezek. 24:21 • delivered
Into the hand of the enemy.
^RThey have made a noise in the house of
the Lord   Ps. 74:3–8
As on the day of a set feast.

8 The Lord has ^Tpurposed to destroy
The ^Rwall of the daughter of Zion.
^RHe has stretched out a line;
He has not withdrawn His hand from
destroying;   determined • Jer. 52:14 • [Is. 34:11]
Therefore He has caused the rampart
and wall to lament;
They languished together.

9 Her gates have sunk into the ground;
He has destroyed and ^Rbroken her bars.
^RHer king and her princes are among the
^Tnations;   Jer. 51:30 • Deut. 28:36 • Gentiles
^RThe Law is no more,   2 Chr. 15:3
And her ^Rprophets find no ^Tvision from
the Lord.   Ps. 74:9 • Prophetic revelation

10 The elders of the daughter of Zion
Sit on the ground and keep silence;
^TThey throw dust on their heads
And gird themselves with sackcloth.
The virgins of Jerusalem   A sign of mourning
Bow their heads to the ground.

11 ^RMy eyes fail with tears,   Lam. 3:48
My ^Theart is troubled;   Lit. inward parts
^RMy ^Tbile is poured on the ground
Because of the destruction of the
daughter of my people,   Job 16:13 • Lit. liver
Because ^Rthe children and the infants
Faint in the streets of the city.   Lam. 4:4

12 They say to their mothers,
"Where is grain and wine?"
As they swoon like the wounded
In the streets of the city,
As their life is poured out
In their mothers' bosom.

13 How shall I ^Tconsole you?
To what shall I liken you,
O daughter of Jerusalem?
What shall I compare with you, that I
may comfort you,
O virgin daughter of Zion?
For your ruin is spread wide as the sea;
Who can heal you?   Or bear witness to

14 Your ^Rprophets have seen for you
False and deceptive visions;

They have not ^Runcovered your
iniquity,   Jer. 2:8; 23:25–29 • Is. 58:1
To bring back your captives,
But have envisioned for you false
^Rprophecies and delusions.   Jer. 23:33–36

15 All who ^Tpass by ^Rclap their hands at
you;   Lit. pass by this way • Ezek. 25:6
They hiss ^Rand shake their heads
At the daughter of Jerusalem: Ps. 44:14
"Is this the city that is called
^R'The perfection of beauty,   [Ps. 48:2; 50:2]
The joy of the whole earth'?"

16 ^RAll your enemies have opened their
mouth against you;   Job 16:9, 10
They hiss and gnash their teeth.
They say, ^R"We have swallowed her up!
Surely this is the ^Rday we have waited
for;   Ps. 56:2; 124:3 • Lam 1:21
We have found it, we have seen it!"

17 The Lord has done what He ^Rpurposed;
He has fulfilled His word
Which He commanded in days of old.
He has thrown down and has not
pitied,
And He has caused an enemy to
^Rrejoice over you;
He has exalted the ^Thorn of your
adversaries.   Lev. 26:16 • Ps. 38:16 • Strength

18 Their heart cried out to the Lord,
"O wall of the daughter of Zion,
^RLet tears run down like a river day and
night;   Jer. 14:17
Give yourself no relief;
Give your eyes no rest.

19 "Arise, ^Rcry out in the night,   Ps. 119:147
At the beginning of the watches;
^RPour out your heart like water before
the face of the Lord.   Ps. 42:4; 62:8
Lift your hands toward Him
For the life of your young children,
Who faint from hunger ^Rat the head of
every street."   Is. 51:20

20 "See, O Lord, and consider!
To whom have You done this?
^RShould the women eat their offspring,
The children *they have cuddled?
Should the priest and prophet be slain
In the sanctuary of the Lord?   Lev. 26:29

21 "Young^R and old lie
On the ground in the streets;
My virgins and my young men
Have fallen by the ^Rsword;
You have slain them in the day of Your
anger,   2 Chr. 36:17 • Jer. 18:21
You have slaughtered and not pitied.

22 "You have invited as to a feast day
^RThe terrors that surround me.

2:20 Vg. a span long

In the day of the LORD's anger
There was no refugee or survivor.
RThose whom I have borne and brought
  up   Ps. 31:13 • Hos. 9:12
My enemies have destroyed."

The Prophet's Anguish and Hope

3 I *am* the man *who* has seen affliction
    by the rod of His wrath.
2 He has led me and made *me* walk
  In darkness and not *in* light.
3 Surely He has turned His hand against
  me
  Time and time again throughout the
  day.
4 He has aged Rmy flesh and my skin,
  And Rbroken my bones.   Job 16:8 • Ps. 51:8
5 He has besieged me
  And surrounded *me* with bitterness and
  Twoe.   hardship or weariness
6 RHe has set me in dark places
  Like the dead of long ago. [Ps. 88:5, 6; 143:3]
7 RHe has hedged me in so that I cannot
  get out;
  He has made my chain heavy.   Hos. 2:6
8 Even Rwhen I cry and shout,
  He shuts out my prayer.   Job 30:20
9 He has blocked my ways with hewn
  stone;
  He has made my paths crooked.
10 He *has been* to me a bear lying in wait,
   Like a lion in Tambush.   Lit. *secret places*
11 He has turned aside my ways and Rtorn
   me in pieces;
   He has made me desolate.   Hos. 6:1
12 He has bent His bow
   And Rset me up as a target for the
   arrow.   Job 7:20; 16:12
13 He has caused Rthe Tarrows of His
   quiver   Job 6:4 • Lit. *sons of*
   To pierce my Tloins.   Lit. *kidneys*
14 I have become the Rridicule of all my
   people—   Jer. 20:7
   Their taunting song all the day.
15 RHe has filled me with bitterness, Jer. 9:15
   He has made me drink wormwood.
16 He has also broken my teeth Rwith
   gravel,   [Prov. 20:17]
   And covered me with ashes.
17 You have moved my soul far from
   peace;
   I have forgotten Tprosperity.   Lit. *good*
18 RAnd I said, "My strength and my hope
   Have perished from the LORD."   Ps. 31:22
19 Remember my affliction and roaming,
   The wormwood and the Tgall.   bitterness
20 My soul still remembers
   And Tsinks within me.   Lit. *bowed down*

21 This I recall to my mind,
   Therefore I have Rhope.   Ps. 130:7
22 RThrough the LORD's mercies we are not
   consumed,   [Mal. 3:6]
   Because His compassions fail not.
23 They *are* new Revery morning;
   Great *is* Your faithfulness.   Is. 33:2
24 "The LORD *is* my portion," says my soul,
   "Therefore I Rhope in Him!"   Mic. 7:7
25 The LORD *is* good to those who Rwait
   for Him,
   To the soul *who* seeks Him.   Is. 30:18
26 *It is* good that *one* should Rhope Rand
   wait quietly   [Rom. 4:16–18] • Ps. 37:7
   For the salvation of the LORD.
27 RIt *is* good for a man to bear
   The yoke in his youth.   Ps. 94:12

28 Let him sit alone and keep silent,
   Because *God* has laid *it* on him;
29 RLet him put his mouth in the dust—
   There may yet be hope.   Job 42:6
30 RLet him give *his* cheek to the one who
   strikes him,
   And be full of reproach.   Is. 50:6

31 For the Lord will not cast off forever.
32 Though He causes grief,
   Yet He will show compassion
   According to the multitude of His
   mercies.
33 For He does not afflict willingly,
   Nor grieve the children of men.

34 To crush under one's feet
   All the prisoners of the earth,
35 To turn aside the justice *due* a man
   Before the face of the Most High,
36 Or subvert a man in his cause—
   RThe Lord does not approve.   [Hab. 1:13]

37 Who *is* he Rwho speaks and it comes to
   pass,   [Ps. 33:9–11]
   When the Lord has not commanded *it*?
38 *Is it* not from the mouth of the Most
   High
   That woe and well-being proceed?
39 Why should a living man complain,
   A man for the punishment of his sins?

40 Let us search out and examine our
   ways,
   And turn back to the LORD;
41 RLet us lift our hearts and hands
   To God in heaven.   Ps. 86:4
42 RWe have transgressed and rebelled;
   You have not pardoned.   Dan. 9:5

43 You have covered *Yourself* with anger
   And pursued us;
   You have slain *and* not pitied.
44 You have covered Yourself with a
   cloud,
   That prayer should not pass through.

45 You have made us an ᴿoffscouring and
refuse
In the midst of the peoples.   1 Cor. 4:13

46 ᴿAll our enemies   Lam. 2:16
Have opened their mouths against us.

47 Fear and a snare have come upon us,
ᴿDesolation and destruction.   Is. 51:19

48 ᴿMy eyes overflow with rivers of water
For the destruction of the daughter of
my people.   Jer. 4:19; 14:17

49 ᴿMy eyes flow and do not cease,
Without interruption,   Jer. 14:17

50 Till the LORD from heaven
ᴿLooks down and sees.   Is. 63:15

51 My eyes bring suffering to my soul
Because of all the daughters of my city.

52 My enemies ᴿwithout cause
Hunted me down like a bird.   Ps. 35:7, 19

53 They *silenced my life in the pit
And threw ᵀstones at me.   Lit. a stone on

54 ᴿThe waters flowed over my head;
ᴿI said, "I am cut off!"   Ps. 69:2 • Is. 38:10

55 ᴿI called on Your name, O LORD,
From the lowest ᴿpit.   Ps. 130:1 • Jer. 38:6–13

56 ᴿYou have heard my voice:
"Do not hide Your ear
From my sighing, from my cry for
help."   Ps. 3:4

57 You ᴿdrew near on the day I called on
You,   James 4:8
And said, ᴿ"Do not fear!"   Is. 41:10, 14

58 O Lord, You have ᴿpleaded the case for
my soul;   Jer. 51:36
ᴿYou have redeemed my life.   Ps. 71:23

59 O LORD, You have seen ᵀhow I am
wronged;
ᴿJudge my case.   Lit. my wrong • Ps. 9:4

60 You have seen all their vengeance,
All their ᴿschemes against me.   Jer. 11:19

61 You have heard their reproach, O LORD,
All their schemes against me,

62 The lips of my enemies
And their whispering against me all the
day.

63 Look at their ᴿsitting down and their
rising up;
I am their taunting song.   Ps. 139:2

64 ᴿRepay them, O LORD,   Ps. 28:4
According to the work of their hands.

65 Give them *a veiled heart;
Your curse be upon them!

66 In Your anger,
Pursue and destroy them
From under the heavens of the LORD.

The Degradation of Zion

4 How the gold has become dim!
How changed the fine gold!

3:53 LXX put to death
3:65 A Jewish tradition reads sorrow of

The stones of the sanctuary are
ᵀscattered   Lit. poured out
At the head of every street.

2 The precious sons of Zion,
ᵀValuable as fine gold,   Lit. Weighed against
How they are regarded as clay pots,
The work of the hands of the potter!

3 Even the jackals present their breasts
To nurse their young;
But the daughter of my people is cruel,
Like ostriches in the wilderness.

4 The tongue of the infant clings
To the roof of its mouth for thirst;
ᴿThe young children ask for bread,
But no one breaks it for them.   Ps. 22:15

5 Those who ate delicacies
Are desolate in the streets;
Those who were brought up in scarlet
ᴿEmbrace ash heaps.   Job 24:8

6 The punishment of the iniquity of the
daughter of my people
Is greater than the punishment of the
ᴿsin of Sodom,   Ezek. 16:48
Which was ᴿoverthrown in a moment,
With no hand to help her!   Gen. 19:25

7 Her ᵀNazirites were ᵀbrighter than snow
And whiter than milk;   Or nobles • Or purer
They were more ruddy in body than
rubies,
Like sapphire in their appearance.

8 Now their appearance is blacker than
soot;
They go unrecognized in the streets;
ᴿTheir skin clings to their bones,   Ps. 102:5
It has become as dry as wood.

9 Those slain by the sword are better off
Than those who die of hunger;
For these ᴿpine away,   Lev. 26:39
Stricken for lack of the fruits of the
ᴿfield.   Jer. 16:4

10 The hands of the ᴿcompassionate
women   Lam. 2:20
Have ᵀcooked their ᴿown children;
They became ᴿfood for them
In the destruction of the daughter of
my people.   boiled • Is. 49:15 • Deut. 28:57

11 The LORD has fulfilled His fury,
He has poured out His fierce anger.
ᴿHe kindled a fire in Zion,   Deut. 32:22
And it has devoured its foundations.

12 The kings of the earth,
And all inhabitants of the world,
Would not have believed
That the adversary and the enemy
Could enter the gates of Jerusalem—

13 ᴿBecause of the sins of her prophets
And the iniquities of her priests,

ᴿWho shed in her midst
The blood of the just.　Jer. 5:31 • Matt. 23:31

14 They wandered blind in the streets;
ᴿThey have defiled themselves with
blood,　Jer. 2:34
ᴿSo that no one would touch their
garments.　Num. 19:16

15 They cried out to them,
"Go away, ᴿunclean!　Lev. 13:45, 46
Go away, go away,
Do not touch us!"
When they fled and wandered,
Those among the nations said,
"They shall no longer dwell *here*."

16 The *face of the Lᴏʀᴅ scattered them;
He no longer regards them.
ᴿ*The people* do not respect the priests
Nor show favor to the elders.　Lam. 5:12

17 Still ᴿour eyes failed us,　2 Kin. 24:7
Watching vainly for our help;
In our watching we watched
For a nation *that* could not save *us*.

18 ᴿThey ᵀtracked our steps
So that we could not walk in our
streets.　2 Kin. 25:4 • Lit. *hunted*
ᴿOur end was near,　Ezek. 7:2, 3, 6
Our days were over,
For our end had come.

19 Our pursuers were ᴿswifter　Deut. 28:49
Than the eagles of the heavens.
They pursued us on the mountains
And lay in wait for us in the wilderness.

20 The ᴿbreath of our nostrils, the
anointed of the Lᴏʀᴅ,　Gen. 2:7
ᴿWas caught in their pits,　Jer. 52:9
Of whom we said, "Under his shadow
We shall live among the nations."

21 Rejoice and be glad, O daughter of
ᴿEdom,　Ps. 83:3-6
You who dwell in the land of Uz!
ᴿThe cup shall also pass over to you
And you shall become drunk and make
yourself naked.　Jer. 25:15

22 ᴿ*The punishment of* your iniquity ᵀis
accomplished,　[Is. 40:2] • *has been completed*
O daughter of Zion;
He will no longer send you into
captivity.
ᴿHe will punish your iniquity,　Ps. 137:7
O daughter of Edom;
He will uncover your sins!

4:16 Tg. *anger*

A Prayer for Restoration

5 Remember, ᴿO Lᴏʀᴅ, what has come
upon us;　Ps. 89:50
Look, and behold our reproach!

2 ᴿOur inheritance has been turned over
to aliens,
And our houses to foreigners.　Ps. 79:1

3 We have become orphans and waifs,
Our mothers *are* like ᴿwidows.　Jer. 15:8

4 We pay for the water we drink,
And our wood comes at a price.

5 *They* pursue at our ᵀheels;　Lit. *necks*
We labor *and* have no rest.

6 ᴿWe have given our hand ᴿto the
Egyptians
And the ᴿAssyrians, to be satisfied with
bread.　Gen. 24:2 • Hos. 9:3; 12:1 • Hos. 5:13

7 ᴿOur fathers sinned *and are* no more,
But we bear their iniquities.　Jer. 31:29

8 Servants rule over us;
There is none to deliver *us* from their
hand.

9 We get our bread *at the risk* of our
lives,
Because of the sword in the wilderness.

10 Our skin is hot as an oven,
Because of the fever of famine.

11 They ravished the women in Zion,
The maidens in the cities of Judah.

12 Princes were hung up by their hands,
And elders were not respected.

13 Young men ground at the millstones;
Boys staggered under *loads of* wood.

14 The elders have ceased *gathering at the*
gate,
And the young men from their music.

15 The joy of our heart has ceased;
Our dance has turned into mourning.

16 ᴿThe crown has fallen *from* our head.
Woe to us, for we have sinned!　Ps. 89:39

17 Because of this our heart is faint;
ᴿBecause of these *things* our eyes grow
dim;　Ps. 6:7

18 Because of Mount Zion which is
ᴿdesolate,
With foxes walking about on it.　Is. 27:10

19 You, O Lᴏʀᴅ, ᴿremain forever;
ᴿYour throne from generation to
generation.　Ps. 9:7 • Ps. 45:6

20 ᴿWhy do You forget us forever,　Ps. 13:1
And forsake us for so long a time?

21 ᴿTurn us back to You, O Lᴏʀᴅ, and we
will be ᵀrestored;　Jer. 31:18 • *returned*
Renew our days as of old,

22 Unless You have utterly rejected us,
And are very angry with us!

THE BOOK OF
Ezekiel

AUTHORSHIP AND CONTEXT. Ezekiel, a priest in Jerusalem, was taken captive to Babylon with King Jehoiachin in 597 B.C. In about 592 B.C. (1:2) he was directed by the Lord to speak the Lord's words to the rebellious Israelites in captivity (2:7). The book of Ezekiel is this priest's record of God's words to Israel through his faithful servant, over a twenty-two-year period (29:17; 40:1).

Through the centuries scholars have traditionally held Ezekiel the priest, the son of Buzi (1:3), to be the author of the book of Ezekiel. In recent years, however, some few have contended that it was impossible for one who was a captive in Babylon to have such intimate knowledge of events then occurring in distant Jerusalem. They insist, therefore, that much of the book must have been written by one who lived in a later time. This struggle to explain an imagined difficulty stems from the refusal to acknowledge that these revelations were given by the omniscient, omnipresent God to his faithful servant, Ezekiel, the mystical visionary dwelling in his house beside the River Chebar in Babylon (1:1, 3; 3:15, 23; 10:15, 20, 22; 43:3).

HOW EZEKIEL FITS INTO THE BIBLE. The book of Ezekiel is generally regarded—along with Isaiah, Jeremiah, and Daniel—as one of the "major" books of prophecy. Isaiah was an eighth-century prophet, a contemporary of Hosea, Micah, and Amos; all four of these prophets deal primarily with the fall of the northern kingdom of Israel to Assyria.

Jeremiah also was a contemporary of Ezekiel. He lived in Jerusalem during the first twenty-five years of Ezekiel's life, before the latter was carried into exile in Babylon. Still, Jeremiah belongs to the group of prophets of the seventh century, along with Habakkuk, Nahum, and Zephaniah, whose writings are concerned with the impending destruction of Judah because of its iniquity and idolatry.

Ezekiel, Daniel, and Obadiah were contemporary prophets of the Babylonian exile in the early part of the sixth century B.C.

As Ezekiel had prophesied of the return of the remnant of the chosen people, the restoration to the Holy Land began about 538 B.C., and continued under the leadership of Zerubbabel, Ezra, and Nehemiah, and the prophets Haggai, Zechariah, and Malachi.

Although the book of Ezekiel is not specifically mentioned in the New Testament, the marvelous imagery of the book in proclaiming and manifesting the glory of God is strikingly reflected in the book of Revelation (written by the apostle John, a more modern mystic). The authenticity of Ezekiel is substantiated by the fulfillment of its prophecies concerning the restoration of Israel to her own land, beginning about 538 B.C. Corroboration of the book's canonicity is to be found in the prophetic writings of both Old and New Testaments, and more especially by the prophecies of Jesus Christ, concerning the glory of the chosen people in the end times.

SUMMARY STATEMENT AND KEY PHRASE. The consistent theme of the book of Ezekiel is the inevitable judgment of a holy God upon a rebellious, wicked, and unrepentant people, Israel, and upon all others who, by their iniquity, heap to themselves judgment from the one true God. According to the book of Ezekiel, however, when the exiles from Judah at last acknowledge their sins and the justness of God's judgment upon them, and repent of their sins (36:31), God promises to cleanse them and to restore them to their homeland and to fellowship with Himself.

In summary: God's purpose in dealing with His people in judgment is that they might come to know Him in His holiness, righteousness, and justice.

The key phrase, which repeatedly resounds as a clarion call throughout the book, first occurs in 6:7, 10—the witness to judgment "shall know that I am the LORD."

HOW EZEKIEL FITS TOGETHER. The book of Ezekiel falls into the following divisions: (1) the Lord's calling and preparation of Ezekiel as His spokesman (chs. 1—3); (2) prophecies of Jerusalem's destruction (4—24); (3) prophecies against pagan nations (25—32); (4) prophecies of Israel's restoration and blessing (33—39); and (5) prophecies of Israel's sharing in the millennial glory of God (40—48).

In one sense, the revelation of God is greater in the book of Ezekiel than in any other book of the Bible. No other book consists of the direct speech of God as does Ezekiel; virtually all of its contents is God's own language, rather than that of the human author. Thus we here discover in a unique revelation the heart and mind of God Himself. In the pages of Ezekiel, God unburdens His grief and deep hurt resulting from the grievous rejection of His love by His

beloved. How very personal and vulnerable do we come to know our great God to be as He pours out His anguish—an anguish which is caused by the idolatry of His own chosen people! Even as God reveals His mighty anger, wrath, and indignation against the abominable wickedness of Israel—the nation which He had raised up from the utter degradation of slavery—we seem to hear His great heart of love breaking. As God, in the person of Jesus Christ His Son, died from a broken heart upon the cruel cross of redemption, so the God of Israel suffers heartbreak because the forefathers of Jesus' crucifiers rejected and scoffed at their own Creator and Savior.

God exercised extreme care to insure that rebellious Israel understood fully the reasons for the judgments which were to befall her. He not only instructed His prophet to convey His spoken messages, but He also directed Ezekiel to enact dramatically the reasons for, and the nature of, God's imminent judgments.

Perhaps in no other portion of Scripture is the God of Glory so awesomely presented. In Ezekiel's graphic and unfathomable visions the overwhelming glory and majesty of the LORD God is portrayed. The prophet magnifies the sovereignty of God in Israel, among the nations, and throughout the entire universe.

Ezekiel the priest manifests his consuming interest in worship of the glorious and sovereign God. This is seen, in part, in his emphasis upon worship in the magnificent temple during the Golden Age of the returned, reigning Messiah.

Striking parallels may be seen between the writings of Ezekiel and the book of Revelation. Ezekiel the prophet and John the apostle were both remarkable mystics. Even as John in his spirit was caught away into heaven to receive the visions of the future, so Ezekiel was carried in his spirit from Babylon to Jerusalem to see and record the future fate of Jerusalem. John heard the command of the Lord, "Come up here" (Rev. 4:1)—into the very presence of God. As Ezekiel was lifted by the Spirit of God and borne away in his spirit to be shown future events, it is as though he was being commanded to "come up here."

In turn Ezekiel became a pioneer of thought in the formation of Judaism, and thereby lifted higher the worship of those of his people who followed him. He clearly stated the doctrine of individual responsibility before God (18:1-4). He prophesied eschatologically so profoundly as virtually to establish the pathway between prophecy and the apocalyptic.

Of course, Ezekiel knew nothing of the church. He was concerned only for the nation of Israel. His inspired prophecy of God's dealings with Israel in a time of tribulation, as well as in the future age of restoration and glorification, bears great similarity to the prophetic utterances of John's revelation of God's treatment of His chosen nation in the last days.

Both of these great mystical prophets, Ezekiel and John, describe the unmitigated terror of the wrath of God against the wickedness of rebellious, sinful mankind. Ezekiel records the messages of the Lord as He pronounces in great detail and in graphic language the judgment He is bringing those whom He has loved and nurtured. The justice of God is shown as demanding such condemnation and destruction. This terrible time of tribulation which God imposes upon rebellious Israel is shown to have a threefold purpose: punishment for sin, purification of a remnant to be saved out of the fires of judgment, and glory for the Almighty God of Holiness.

The love of God for all men is discernible in His messages to the nations. The redemptive, forgiving spirit of God is evinced as He literally cries out to a wicked people to turn from their sin and receive His freely offered salvation. Even though God pronounces judgment upon the sins of the nations, He discloses His love and concern for those who will turn from their idolatry to worship the true God.

Ezekiel is a book of revelation in that therein God reveals much concerning the future destiny of the nation Israel, and concerning the glorious reign of the Messiah upon earth in the Golden Age to come. The nation Israel, restored and glorified, living in their promised land in the day of true peace and pure worship of their great Messiah during His reign upon earth in the millennial age, is disclosed by God through His faithful servant Ezekiel.

While Ezekiel's central theme is the glory of God, the sweet, golden tones of the love of the great Redeemer rings and throbs throughout all this wonderful book.

—E.D.

Ezekiel's Vision of God

NOW it came to pass in the thirtieth year, in the fourth *month*, on the fifth *day* of the month, as I *was* among the captives by the River Chebar, *that* the heavens were opened and I saw visions* of God.

2 On the fifth *day* of the month, which *was* in the fifth year of King Jehoiachin's captivity,

3 the word of the LORD came expressly to Ezekiel the priest, the son of Buzi, in the land of the *Chaldeans by the River Chebar; and the hand of the LORD was upon him there.

4 Then I looked, and behold, ᴿa whirlwind was coming ᴿout of the north, a great cloud with raging fire engulfing itself; and brightness *was* all around it and radiating out of its midst like the color of amber, out of the midst of the fire.   Jer. 23:19; 25:32 • Jer. 1:14

5 Also from within it *came* the likeness of four living creatures. And this *was* their appearance: they had the likeness of a man.

6 Each one had four faces, and each one had four wings.

7 Their ᵀlegs *were* straight, and the soles of their feet *were* like the soles of calves' feet. They sparkled ᴿlike the color of burnished bronze.   Lit. *feet* • Dan. 10:6

8 ᴿThe hands of a man *were* under their wings on their four sides; and each of the four had faces and wings.   Ezek. 10:8, 21

9 Their wings touched one another. *The creatures* did not turn when they went, but each one went straight ᴿforward.   Ezek. 1:12

10 As for the likeness of their faces, *each* had the face of a man; each of the four had the face of a lion on the right side, each of the four had the face of an ox on the left side, and each of the four had the face of an eagle.

11 Thus *were* their faces. Their wings stretched upward; two *wings* of each one touched one another, and ᴿtwo covered their bodies.   Is. 6:2

12 And each one went straight forward; they went wherever the spirit wanted to go, and they did not turn when they went.

13 As for the likeness of the living creatures, their appearance *was* like burning coals of fire, like the appearance of torches going back and forth among the living creatures. The fire was bright, and out of the fire went lightning.

14 And the living creatures ran back and forth, in appearance like a flash of lightning.

15 Now as I looked at the living creatures, behold, a wheel *was* on the earth beside each living creature with its four faces.

16 ᴿThe appearance of the wheels and their workings *was* ᴿlike the color of beryl, and all four had the same likeness. The appearance

of their workings *was*, as it were, a wheel in the middle of a wheel.   Ezek. 10:9, 10 • Dan. 10:6

17 When they moved, they went toward any one of four directions; they did not turn aside when they went.

18 As for their rims, they were so high they were awesome; and their rims *were* ᴿfull of eyes, all around the four of them.   Ezek. 10:12

19 ᴿWhen the living creatures went, the wheels went beside them; and when the living creatures were lifted up from the earth, the wheels were lifted up.   Ezek. 10:16, 17

20 Wherever the spirit wanted to go, they went, *because* there the spirit went; and the wheels were lifted together with them, ᴿfor the spirit of the living creatures *was* in the wheels.   Ezek. 10:17

21 When those went, *these* went; when those stood, *these* stood; and when those were lifted up from the earth, the wheels were lifted up together with them, for the spirit of the *living creatures *was* in the wheels.

22 The likeness of the ᵀfirmament above the heads of the *living creatures *was* like the color of an awesome ᴿcrystal, stretched out ᴿover their heads.   Or *expanse* • Rev. 4:6 • Ezek. 10:1

23 And under the firmament their wings spread out straight, one toward another. Each one had two which covered one side, and each one had two which covered the other side of the body.

24 When they went, I heard the noise of their wings, like the noise of many waters, like ᴿthe voice of the Almighty, a tumult like the noise of an army; and when they stood still, they let down their wings.   Job 37:4, 5

25 A voice came from above the firmament that *was* over their heads; whenever they stood, they let down their wings.

26 And above the firmament over their heads *was* the likeness of a throne, in appearance like a sapphire stone; on the likeness of the throne *was* a likeness with the appearance of a man high above it.

27 Also from the appearance of His waist and upward I saw, as it were, the color of amber with the appearance of fire all around within it; and from the appearance of His waist and downward I saw, as it were, the appearance of fire with brightness all around.

28 ᴿLike the appearance of a rainbow in a cloud on a rainy day, so *was* the appearance of the brightness all around it. ᴿThis *was* the appearance of the likeness of the glory of the LORD.   Rev. 4:3; 10:1 • Ezek. 3:23; 8:4

Ezekiel Sent to Rebellious Israel

So when I saw *it*, ᴿI fell on my face, and I heard a voice of One speaking.   Dan. 8:17

1:1 So with MT, LXX, Vg.; Syr., Tg. *a vision*
1:3 Or *Babylonians*, and so elsewhere in the book
1:21 Lit. *living creature;* LXX, Vg. *spirit of life;* Tg. *creatures*
1:22 So with LXX, Tg., Vg.; MT reads *living creature*

2 And He said to me, "Son of man, stand on your feet, and I will speak to you."

2 Then ᴿthe Spirit entered me when He spoke to me, and set me on my feet; and I heard Him who spoke to me. Ezek. 3:24

3 And He said to me: "Son of man, I am sending you to the children of Israel, to a rebellious nation that has rebelled against Me; ᴿthey and their fathers have transgressed against Me to this very day. Jer. 3:25

4 "For *they are* impudent and stubborn children. I am sending you to them, and you shall say to them, 'Thus says the Lord God.'

5 "As for them, whether they hear or whether they refuse—for they *are* a rebellious house—yet they ᴿwill know that a prophet has been among them. Ezek. 33:33

6 "And you, son of man, do not be afraid of them nor be afraid of their words, though briers and thorns *are* with you and you dwell among scorpions; do not be afraid of their words or dismayed by their looks, ᴿthough they *are* a rebellious house. Ezek. 3:9, 26, 27

7 ᴿ"You shall speak My words to them, whether they hear or whether they refuse, for they *are* rebellious. Jer. 1:7, 17

8 "But you, son of man, hear what I say to you. Do not be rebellious like that rebellious house; open your mouth and ᴿeat what I give you." Rev. 10:9

9 Now when I looked, there was ᴿa hand stretched out to me; and behold, ᴿa scroll of a book *was* in it. [Ezek. 8:3] · Ezek. 3:1

10 Then He spread it before me; and *there was* writing on the inside and on the outside, and written on it *were* lamentations and mourning and woe.

3 Moreover He said to me, "Son of man, eat what you find; ᴿeat this scroll, and go, speak to the house of Israel." Ezek. 2:8, 9

2 So I opened my mouth, and He caused me to eat that scroll.

3 And He said to me, "Son of man, feed your belly, and fill your stomach with this scroll that I give you." So I ate, and it was in my mouth like honey in sweetness.

4 Then He said to me: "Son of man, go to the house of Israel and speak with My words to them.

5 "For you *are* not sent to a people of unfamiliar speech and of hard language, *but* to the house of Israel,

6 "not to many people of unfamiliar speech and of hard language, whose words you cannot understand. Surely, had I sent you to them, they would have listened to you.

7 "But the house of Israel will not listen to you, because they will not listen to Me; ᴿfor all the house of Israel *are* ᵀimpudent and hard-hearted. Ezek. 2:4 · Lit. *strong of forehead*

8 "Behold, I have made your face strong against their faces, and your forehead strong against their foreheads.

9 ᴿ"Like adamant stone, harder than flint, I have made your forehead; do not be afraid of them, nor be dismayed at their looks, though they *are* a rebellious house." Mic. 3:8

10 Moreover He said to me: "Son of man, receive into your heart all My words that I speak to you, and hear with your ears.

11 "And go, get to the captives, to the children of your people, and speak to them and tell them, 'Thus says the Lord God,' whether they hear, or whether they refuse."

12 Then the Spirit lifted me up, and I heard behind me a great thunderous voice: "Blessed *is* the glory of the Lord from His place!"

13 *I* also *heard* the noise of the wings of the living creatures that touched one another, and the noise of the wheels beside them, and a great thunderous noise.

14 So the Spirit lifted me up and took me away, and I went in bitterness, in the ᵀheat of my spirit; but ᴿthe hand of the Lord was strong upon me. Or *anger* · 2 Kin. 3:15

15 Then I came to the captives at Tel Abib, who dwelt by the River Chebar; and ᴿI sat where they sat, and remained there astonished among them seven days. Job 2:13

Ezekiel Is a Watchman

16 Now it ᴿcame to pass at the end of seven days that the word of the Lord came to me, saying, Jer. 42:7

17 ᴿ"Son of man, I have made you ᴿa watchman for the house of Israel; therefore hear a word from My mouth, and give them ᴿwarning from Me: Ezek. 33:7-9 · Jer. 6:17 · [Lev. 19:17]

18 "When I say to the wicked, 'You shall surely die,' and you give him no warning, nor speak to warn the wicked from his wicked way, to save his life, that same wicked *man* ᴿshall die in his iniquity; but his blood I will require at your hand. [John 8:21, 24]

19 "Yet, if you warn the wicked, and he does not turn from his wickedness, nor from his wicked way, he shall die in his iniquity; but you have delivered your soul.

20 "Again, when a ᴿrighteous *man* turns from his righteousness and commits iniquity, and I lay a stumbling block before him, he shall die; because you did not give him warning, he shall die in his sin, and his righteousness which he has done shall not be remembered; but his blood I will require at your hand. Ezek. 18:24; 33:18

21 "Nevertheless if you warn the righteous *man* that the righteous should not sin, and he does not sin, he shall surely live because he took warning; also you will have delivered your soul."

22 ᴿThen the hand of the Lord was upon me there, and He said to me, "Arise, go out ᴿinto the plain, and there I shall talk with you." Ezek. 1:3 · Ezek. 8:4

23 So I arose and went out into the plain, and behold, the glory of the LORD stood there, like the glory which I saw by the River Chebar; and I fell on my face.

24 Then the Spirit entered me and set me on my feet, and spoke with me and said to me: "Go, shut yourself inside your house.

25 "And you, O son of man, surely they will put ropes on you and bind you with them, so that you cannot go out among them.

26 "I will make your tongue cling to the roof of your mouth, so that you shall be mute and ^Rnot be one to rebuke them, ^Rfor they *are* a rebellious house.   Hos. 4:17 · Ezek. 2:5–7

27 "But when I speak with you, I will open your mouth, and you shall say to them, ^R'Thus says the Lord GOD.' He who hears, let him hear; and he who refuses, let him refuse; for they *are* a rebellious house.   Ezek. 3:11

The Siege of Jerusalem Portrayed

4 "You also, son of man, take a clay tablet and lay it before you, and portray on it a city, Jerusalem.

2 ^R"Lay siege against it, build a siege wall against it, and heap up a ^Rmound against it; set camps against it also, and place battering rams against it all around.   Jer. 6:6 · 2 Kin. 25:1

3 "Moreover take for yourself an iron plate, and set it *as* an iron wall between you and the city. Set your face against it, and it shall be ^Rbesieged, and you shall lay siege against it. ^RThis *will be* a sign to the house of Israel.   Jer. 39:1, 2 · Ezek. 12:6, 11; 24:24, 27

4 "Lie also on your left side, and lay the iniquity of the house of Israel upon it. *According* to the number of the days that you lie on it, you shall bear their iniquity.

5 "For I have laid on you the years of their iniquity, according to the number of the days, three hundred and ninety days; so you shall bear the iniquity of the house of Israel.

6 "And when you have completed them, lie again on your right side; then you shall bear the iniquity of the house of Judah forty days. I have laid on you a day for each year.

7 "Therefore you shall set your face toward the siege of Jerusalem; your arm *shall be* uncovered, and you shall prophesy against it.

8 "And surely I will restrain you so that you cannot turn from one side to another till you have ended the days of your siege.

9 "Also take for yourself wheat, barley, beans, lentils, millet, and spelt; put them into one vessel, and make bread of them for yourself. *During* the number of days that you lie on your side, three hundred and ninety days, you shall eat it.

10 "And your food which you eat *shall be* by weight, ^Ttwenty shekels a day; from time to time you shall eat it. $2,560

11 "You shall also drink water by measure, ^Tone-sixth of a hin; from time to time you shall drink.   21.3 oz.

12 "And you shall eat it *as* barley cakes; and bake it using fuel of human waste in their sight."

13 Then the LORD said, "So ^Rshall the children of Israel eat their defiled bread among the Gentiles, where I will drive them." Hos. 9:3

14 So I said, "Ah, Lord GOD! Indeed I have never defiled myself from my youth till now; I have never eaten what died of itself or was torn by beasts, nor has ^Tabominable flesh ever come into my mouth."   Ritually unclean

15 Then He said to me, "See, I am giving you cow dung instead of human waste, and you shall prepare your bread over it."

16 Moreover He said to me, "Son of man, surely I will cut off the ^Rsupply of bread in Jerusalem; they shall eat bread by weight and with anxiety, and shall ^Rdrink water by measure and with dread,   Is. 3:1 · Ezek. 4:11

17 "that they may lack bread and water, and be dismayed with one another, and waste away because of their iniquity.

A Sword Against Jerusalem

5 "And you, son of man, take a sharp sword, take it as a barber's razor, and pass *it* over your head and your beard; then take scales to weigh and divide the hair.

2 "You shall burn with fire one-third in the midst of the city, when the days of the siege are finished; then you shall take one-third and strike around *it* with the sword, and one-third you shall scatter in the wind: I will draw out a sword after ^Rthem.   Lev. 26:25

3 ^R"You shall also take a small number of them and bind them in the edge of your *garment.*   Jer. 40:6; 52:16

4 "Then take some of them again and throw them into the midst of the fire, and burn them in the fire. From there a fire will go out into all the house of Israel.

5 "Thus says the Lord GOD: 'This *is* Jerusalem; I have set her in the midst of the nations and the countries all around her.

6 'She has rebelled against My judgments by doing wickedness more than the nations, and against My statutes more than the countries that *are* all around her; for they have refused My judgments, and they have not walked in My statutes.'

7 "Therefore thus says the Lord GOD: 'Because you have ^Tmultiplied *disobedience* more than the nations that *are* all around you, have not walked in My statutes ^Rnor kept My judgments, *nor even done according to the judgments of the nations that *are* all around you'—   Or *raged* · Jer. 2:10, 11

5:7 So with MT, LXX, Tg., Vg.; many Heb. mss., Syr. *but have done* (cf. 11:12)

8 "therefore thus says the Lord GOD: 'Indeed I, even I, *am* against you and will execute judgments in your midst in the sight of the nations.

9 'And I will do among you what I have never done, and the like of which I will never do again, because of all your abominations.

10 'Therefore fathers ᴿshall eat *their* sons in your midst, and sons shall eat their fathers; and I will execute judgments among you, and all of you who remain I will ᴿscatter to all the winds.   Jer. 19:9 · Zech. 2:6; 7:14

11 'Therefore, *as* I live,' says the Lord GOD, 'surely, because you have ᴿdefiled My sanctuary with all your ᴿdetestable things and with all your abominations, therefore I will also diminish *you*; My eye will not spare, nor will I have any pity.   [Jer. 7:9-11] · Ezek. 11:21

12 ᴿ'One-third of you shall die of the pestilence, and be consumed with famine in your midst; and one-third shall fall by the sword all around you; and ᴿI will scatter another third to all the winds, and I will draw out a sword after ᴿthem.   Ezek. 6:12 · Jer. 9:16 · Jer. 43:10, 11; 44:27

13 'Thus shall My anger be spent, and I will cause My fury to rest upon them, and I will be avenged; ᴿand they shall know that I, the LORD, have spoken *it* in My zeal, when I have spent My fury upon them.   Ezek. 36:6; 38:19

14 'Moreover I will make you a waste and a reproach among the nations that *are* all around you, in the sight of all who pass by.

15 'So *it shall be a ᴿreproach, a taunt, a ᴿlesson, and an astonishment to the nations that *are* all around you, when I execute judgments among you in anger and in fury and in ᴿfurious rebukes. I, the LORD, have spoken.   Jer. 24:9 · [Is. 26:9] · Ezek. 5:8; 25:17

16 'When I send against them the terrible arrows of famine which shall be for destruction, which I will send to destroy you, I will increase the famine upon you and cut off your ᴿsupply of bread.   Lev. 26:26

17 'So I will send against you famine and ᴿwild beasts, and they will bereave you. ᴿPestilence and blood shall pass through you, and I will bring the sword against you. I, the LORD, have spoken.' "   Lev. 26:22 · Ezek. 38:22

Judgment on Idolatrous Israel

6 Now the word of the LORD came to me, saying:

2 "Son of man, ᴿset your face toward the ᴿmountains of Israel, and prophesy against them,   Ezek. 20:46; 21:2; 25:2 · Ezek. 36:1

3 "and say, 'O mountains of Israel, hear the word of the Lord GOD! Thus says the Lord GOD to the mountains, to the hills, to the ravines, and to the valleys: "Indeed I, *even* I,

will bring a sword against you, and ᴿI will destroy your high places.   Lev. 26:30

4 "Then your altars shall be desolate, your incense altars shall be broken, and I will cast down your slain *men* before your idols.

5 "And I will lay the corpses of the children of Israel before their idols, and I will scatter your bones all around your altars.

6 "In all your dwelling places the cities shall be laid waste, and the ᵀhigh places shall be desolate, so that your altars may be laid waste and made desolate, your idols may be broken and made to cease, your incense altars may be cut down, and your works may be abolished.   Places for pagan worship

7 "The slain shall fall in your midst, and you shall know that I *am* the LORD.

8 ᴿ"Yet I will leave a remnant, so that you may have *some* who escape the sword among the nations, when you are ᴿscattered through the countries.   Jer. 44:28 · Ezek. 5:12

9 "Then those of you who escape will remember Me among the nations where they are carried captive, because ᴿI was crushed by their adulterous heart which has departed from Me, and by their eyes which play the harlot after their idols; they will loathe themselves for the evils which they committed in all their abominations.   Ps. 78:40

10 "And they shall know that I *am* the LORD; I have not said in vain that I would bring this calamity upon them."

11 'Thus says the Lord GOD: ᵀ"Pound your fists and stamp your feet, and say, 'Alas, for all the evil abominations of the house of Israel! For they shall fall by the sword, by famine, and by pestilence.   Lit. *Strike your hands*

12 'He who is far off shall die by the pestilence, he who is near shall fall by the sword, and he who remains and is besieged shall die by the famine. ᴿThus will I spend My fury upon them.   Ezek. 5:13

13 'Then you shall know that I *am* the LORD, when their slain are among their idols all around their altars, on every high hill, on all the mountaintops, under every green tree, and under every thick oak, wherever they offered sweet incense to all their idols.

14 'So I will ᴿstretch out My hand against them and make the land desolate, yes, more desolate than the wilderness toward Diblah, in all their dwelling places. Then they shall know that I *am* the LORD.' " ' "   Is. 5:25

Judgment on Israel Is Near

7 Moreover the word of the LORD came to me, saying,

2 "And you, son of man, thus says the Lord GOD to the land of Israel:

ᴿ'An end! The end has come upon the
    four corners of the land.   Amos 8:2, 10
3 Now the end *has come* upon you,
    And I will send My anger against you;

I will judge you ᴿaccording to your
ways,
And I will repay you for all your
abominations.   [Rom. 2:6]
4 ᴿMy eye will not spare you,
Nor will I have pity;
But I will repay your ways,
And your abominations will be in your
midst;
ᴿThen you shall know that I *am* the
Lᴏʀᴅ!'   Ezek. 5:11 · Ezek. 12:20

5 "Thus says the Lord Gᴏᴅ:

'A disaster, a singular ᴿdisaster;
Behold, it has come!   2 Kin. 21:12, 13
6 An end has come,
The end has come;
It has dawned for you;
Behold, it has come!
7 ᴿDoom has come to you, you who dwell
in the land;   Ezek. 7:10
ᴿThe time has come,   Zeph. 1:14, 15
A day of trouble *is* near,
And not of rejoicing in the mountains.
8 Now upon you I will soon ᴿpour out My
fury,
And spend My anger upon you;
I will judge you according to your
ways,
And I will repay you for all your
abominations.   Ezek. 20:8, 21

9 'My eye will not spare,
Nor will I have pity;
I will ᵀrepay you according to your
ways,
And your abominations will be in your
midst.
Then you shall know that I *am* the
Lᴏʀᴅ who strikes.   Lit. *give*

10 'Behold, the day!
Behold, it has come!
ᴿDoom has gone out;
The rod has blossomed,
Pride has budded.   Ezek. 7:7
11 ᴿViolence has risen up into a rod of
wickedness;   Jer. 6:7
None of them *shall remain,*
None of their multitude,
None of ᵀthem;   Or *their wealth*
Nor *shall there be* wailing for them.
12 The time has come,
The day draws near.

'Let not the buyer ᴿrejoice,   Prov. 20:14
Nor the seller ᴿmourn,   Is. 24:2
For wrath *is* on their whole multitude.
13 For the seller shall not return to what
has been sold,
Though he may still be alive;
For the vision concerns the whole
multitude,
And it shall not turn back;

No one will strengthen himself
Who lives in iniquity.

14 'They have blown the trumpet and
made everyone ready,
But no one goes to battle;
For My wrath *is* on all their multitude.
15 ᴿThe sword *is* outside,   Jer. 14:18
And the pestilence and famine within.
Whoever *is* in the field
Will die by the sword;
And whoever *is* in the city,
Famine and pestilence will devour him.

16 'Those who ᴿsurvive will escape and be
on the mountains
Like doves of the valleys,
All of them mourning,
Each for his iniquity.   Ezek. 6:8; 14:22
17 Every ᴿhand will be feeble,
And every knee will be *as* weak *as*
water.   Is. 13:7
18 They will also ᴿbe girded with
sackcloth;
Horror will cover them;
Shame *will be* on every face,
Baldness on all their heads.   Amos 8:10
19 'They will throw their silver into the
streets,
And their gold will be like refuse;
Their ᴿsilver and their gold will not be
able to deliver them
In the day of the wrath of the Lᴏʀᴅ;
They will not satisfy their souls,
Nor fill their stomachs,
Because it became their stumbling
block of iniquity.   Zeph. 1:18

20 'As for the beauty of his ornaments,
He set it in majesty;
ᴿBut they made from it
The images of their abominations—
Their detestable things;
Therefore I have made it
Like refuse to them.   Jer. 7:30
21 I will give it as ᴿplunder
Into the hands of strangers,
And to the wicked of the earth as spoil;
And they shall defile it.   2 Kin. 24:13
22 I will turn My face from them,
And they will defile My secret place;
For robbers shall enter it and defile it.

23 'Make a chain,
For ᴿthe land is filled with crimes of
blood,   2 Kin. 21:16
And the city is full of violence.
24 Therefore I will bring the ᴿworst of the
Gentiles,   Ezek. 21:31; 28:7
And they will possess their houses;
I will cause the pomp of the strong to
cease,
And their holy places shall be defiled.

25 Destruction comes;
They will seek peace, but *there shall be none.*
26 ᴿDisaster will come upon disaster,
And rumor will be upon rumor.
ᴿThen they will seek a vision from a prophet;   Jer. 4:20 • Ps. 74:9
But the law will perish from the priest,
And counsel from the elders.

27 'The king will mourn,
The prince will be clothed with desolation,
And the hands of the common people will tremble.
I will do to them according to their way,
And according to what they deserve I will judge them;
Then they shall know that I *am* the LORD!' "

Abominations in the Temple

8 And it came to pass in the sixth year, in the sixth *month,* on the fifth *day* of the month, as I sat in my house with the elders of Judah sitting before me, that ᴿthe hand of the Lord GOD fell upon me there.   Ezek. 1:3
2 Then I looked, and there was a likeness, like the appearance of fire—from the appearance of His waist and downward, fire; and from His waist and upward, like the appearance of brightness, like the color of amber.
3 He stretched out the form of a hand, and took me by a lock of my hair; and the Spirit lifted me up between earth and heaven, and brought me in visions of God to Jerusalem, to the door of the north gate of the inner *court,* where the seat of the image of jealousy *was,* which provokes to jealousy.
4 And behold, the ᴿglory of the God of Israel *was* there, like the vision that I ᴿsaw in the plain.   Ezek. 3:12; 9:3 • Ezek. 1:28; 3:22, 23
5 Then He said to me, "Son of man, lift your eyes now toward the north." So I lifted my eyes toward the north, and there, north of the altar gate, was this image of jealousy in the entrance.
6 Furthermore He said to me, "Son of man, do you see what they are doing, the great ᴿabominations that the house of Israel commits here, to make Me go far away from My sanctuary? Now turn again, you will see greater abominations."   2 Kin. 23:4, 5
7 So He brought me to the door of the court; and when I looked, there was a hole in the wall.
8 Then He said to me, "Son of man, dig into the wall"; and when I dug into the wall, there was a door.
9 And He said to me, "Go in, and see the wicked abominations which they are doing there."
10 So I went in and saw, and there—every

sort of creeping thing, abominable beasts, and all the idols of the house of Israel, ᵀportrayed all around on the walls.   Or *carved*
11 And there stood before them seventy men of the elders of the house of Israel, and in their midst stood Jaazaniah the son of Shaphan. Each man had a censer in his hand, and a thick cloud of incense went up.
12 Then He said to me, "Son of man, have you seen what the elders of the house of Israel do in the dark, every man in the room of his idols? For they say, 'The LORD does not see us; the LORD has forsaken the land.' "
13 And He said to me, "Turn again, *and* you will see greater abominations that they are doing."
14 So He brought me to the door of the north gate of the LORD's house; and to my dismay, women were sitting there weeping for ᵀTammuz.   A Sumerian god similar to Gr. god Adonis
15 Then He said to me, "Have you seen *this,* O son of man? Turn again, you will see greater abominations than these."
16 So He brought me into the inner court of the LORD's house; and there, at the door of the temple of the LORD, ᴿbetween the porch and the altar, ᴿ*were* about twenty-five men ᴿwith their backs toward the temple of the LORD and their faces toward the east, and they were worshiping ᴿthe sun toward the east.   Joel 2:17 • Ezek. 11:1 • Jer. 2:27; 32:33 • Deut. 4:19
17 And He said to me, "Have you seen *this,* O son of man? Is it a trivial thing to the house of Judah to commit the abominations which they commit here? For they have ᴿfilled the land with violence; then they have returned to provoke Me to anger. Indeed they put the branch to their nose.   Ezek. 9:9
18 "Therefore I also will act in fury. My eye will not spare nor will I have pity; and though they ᴿcry in My ears with a loud voice, I will not hear them."   Mic. 3:4

The Wicked Are Slain

9 Then He called out in my hearing with a loud voice, saying, "Let those who have charge over the city draw near, each *with* a ᵀdeadly weapon in his hand."   Or *destroying*
2 And suddenly six men came from the direction of the upper gate, which faces north, each with his ᵀbattle-ax in his hand. ᴿOne man among them *was* clothed with linen and had a writer's inkhorn ᵀat his side. They went in and stood beside the bronze altar.   Lit. *shattering weapon* • Lev. 16:4 • Lit. *upon his loins*
3 Now the glory of the God of Israel had gone up from the cherub, where it had been, to the threshold of the ᵀtemple. And He called to the man clothed with linen, who *had* the writer's inkhorn at his side;   Lit. *house*
4 and the LORD said to him, "Go through the midst of the city, through the midst of Jerusalem, and put a mark on the foreheads

of the men who sigh and cry over all the abominations that are done within it."

5 To the others He said in my hearing, "Go after him through the city and kill; do not let your eye spare, nor have any pity.

6 "Utterly slay old *and* young men, maidens and little children and women; but do not come near anyone on whom *is* the mark; and begin at My sanctuary." So they began with the elders who *were* before the temple.

7 Then He said to them, "Defile the ᵀtemple, and fill the courts with the slain. Go out!" And they went out and killed in the city.   Lit. *house*

8 So it was, that while they were killing them, I was left *alone*; and I fell on my face and cried out, and said, "Ah, Lord GOD! Will You destroy all the remnant of Israel in pouring out Your fury on Jerusalem?"

9 Then He said to me, "The iniquity of the house of Israel and Judah *is* exceedingly great, and ᴿthe land is full of bloodshed, and the city full of perversity; for they say, ᴿ'The LORD has forsaken the land, and ᴿthe LORD does not see!'   2 Kin. 21:16 · Ezek. 8:12 · Is. 29:15

10 "And as for Me also, My eye will neither spare, nor will I have pity, *but* I will recompense their deeds on their own head."

11 Just then, the man clothed with linen, who *had* the inkhorn at his side, reported back and said, "I have done as You commanded me."

The Glory Departs from the Temple

10 And I looked, and there in the ᴿfirmamentᵀ that was above the head of the cherubim, there appeared something like a sapphire stone, having the appearance of the likeness of a throne.   Ezek. 1:22, 26 · *expanse*

2 ᴿThen He spoke to the man clothed with linen, and said, "Go in among the wheels, under the cherub, fill your hands with ᴿcoals of fire from among the cherubim, and ᴿscatter *them* over the city." And he went in as I watched.   Dan. 10:5 · Ezek. 1:13 · Rev. 8:5

3 Now the cherubim were standing on the south side of the *temple when the man went in, and the cloud filled the inner court.

4 Then the glory of the LORD went up from the cherub, *and* paused over the threshold of the ᵀtemple; and the house was filled with the cloud, and the court was full of the brightness of the LORD's glory.   Lit. *house*

5 And the ᴿsound of the wings of the cherubim was heard *even* in the outer court, like ᴿthe voice of Almighty God when He speaks.   Ezek. 1:24 · [Ps. 29:3]

6 Then it happened, when He commanded the man clothed in linen, saying, "Take fire from among the wheels, from among the cherubim," that he went in and stood beside the wheels.

7 And the cherub stretched out his hand from among the cherubim to the fire that *was* among the cherubim, and took *some of it* and put *it* into the hands of the *man* clothed with linen, who took *it* and went out.

8 The cherubim appeared to have the form of a man's hand under their wings.

9 ᴿAnd when I looked, there were four wheels by the cherubim, one wheel by one cherub and another wheel by each other cherub; the wheels appeared *to have* the color of a ᴿberyl stone.   Ezek. 1:15 · Ezek. 1:16

10 *As for* their appearance, all four looked alike—as it were, a wheel in the middle of a wheel.

11 ᴿWhen they went, they went toward *any* of their four directions; they did not turn aside when they went, but followed in the direction the head was facing. They did not turn aside when they went.   Ezek. 1:17

12 And their whole body, with their back, their hands, their wings, and the wheels that the four had, *were* full of eyes all around.

13 As for the wheels, they were called in my ᵀhearing, "Wheel."   Lit. *ears*

14 ᴿEach one had four faces: the first face *was* the face of a cherub, the second face the face of a man, the third the face of a lion, and the fourth the face of an eagle.   Ezek. 1:6, 10, 11

15 And the cherubim were lifted up. This *was* ᴿthe living creature I saw by the River Chebar.   Ezek. 1:3, 5

16 ᴿWhen the cherubim went, the wheels went beside them; and when the cherubim lifted their wings to mount up from the earth, the same wheels also did not turn from beside them.   Ezek. 1:19

17 When *the cherubim stood still, *the wheels stood still, and when *one was lifted up, *the other lifted itself up, for the spirit of the living creature *was* in them.

18 Then ᴿthe glory of the LORD ᴿdeparted from the threshold of the ᵀtemple and stood over the cherubim.   Ezek. 10:4 · Hos. 9:12 · Lit. *house*

19 And the cherubim lifted their wings and mounted up from the earth in my sight. When they went out, the wheels *were* beside them; and they stood at the door of the ᴿeast gate of the LORD's house, and the glory of the God of Israel *was* above them.   Ezek. 11:1

20 ᴿThis *is* the living creature I saw under the God of Israel ᴿby the River Chebar, and I knew they *were* cherubim.   Ezek. 1:22 · Ezek. 1:1

21 ᴿEach one had four faces and each one four wings, and the likeness of the hands of a man *was* under their wings.   Ezek. 1:6, 8; 10:14

22 And the likeness of their faces *was* the same *as* the faces which I had seen by the River Chebar, their appearance and their persons. They each went straight forward.

Judgment on Wicked Counselors

11 Then Rthe Spirit lifted me up and brought me to the East Gate of the LORD's house, which faces eastward; and there at the door of the gate were twenty-five men, among whom I saw Jaazaniah the son of Azzur, and Pelatiah the son of Benaiah, princes of the people.   Ezek. 3:12, 14

2 And He said to me: "Son of man, these *are* the men who devise iniquity and give wicked Tcounsel in this city,   Advice

3 "who say, '*The time is* not Rnear to build houses; Rthis *city is* the Tcaldron, and we *are* the meat.'   2 Pet. 3:4 • Jer. 1:13 • Pot

4 "Therefore prophesy against them, prophesy, O son of man!"

5 Then Rthe Spirit of the LORD fell upon me, and said to me, "Speak! 'Thus says the LORD: "Thus you have said, O house of Israel; for RI know the things that come into your mind.   Ezek. 2:2; 3:24 • [Jer. 16:17; 17:10]

6 R"You have multiplied your slain in this city, and you have filled its streets with the slain."   Ezek. 7:23; 22:2-6, 9, 12, 27

7 'Therefore thus says the Lord GOD: R"Your slain whom you have laid in its midst, they *are* the meat, and this *city is* the caldron; Rbut I shall bring you out of the midst of it.   Mic. 3:2, 3 • Ezek. 11:9

8 "You have feared the sword; and I will bring a sword upon you," says the Lord GOD.

9 "And I will bring you out of its midst, and deliver you into the hands of strangers, and Rexecute judgments on you.   Ezek. 5:8

10 "You shall fall by the sword. I will judge you at the border of Israel. RThen you shall know that I *am* the LORD.   Ps. 9:16

11 "This *city* shall not be your Tcaldron, nor shall you be the meat in its midst. I will judge you at the border of Israel.   Pot

12 "And you shall know that I *am* the LORD; for you have not walked in My statutes nor executed My judgments, but Rhave done according to the customs of the Gentiles which *are* all around you." '   Deut. 12:30, 31

13 Now it happened, while I was prophesying, that RPelatiah the son of Benaiah died. Then RI fell on my face and cried with a loud voice, and said, "Ah, Lord GOD! Will You make a complete end of the remnant of Israel?"   Acts 5:5 • Ezek. 9:8

God Will Restore Israel

14 Again the word of the LORD came to me, saying,

15 "Son of man, your brethren, your relatives, your countrymen, and all the house of Israel in its entirety, *are* those about whom the inhabitants of Jerusalem have said, 'Get far away from the LORD; this land has been given to us as a possession.'

16 "Therefore say, 'Thus says the Lord GOD: "Although I have cast them far off among the

Gentiles, and although I have scattered them among the countries, Ryet I shall be a little Tsanctuary for them in the countries where they have gone." '   Is. 8:14 • *holy place*

17 "Therefore say, 'Thus says the Lord GOD: R"I will gather you from the peoples, assemble you from the countries where you have been scattered, and I will give you the land of Israel." '   Jer. 3:12, 18; 24:5

18 "And they will go there, and they will take away all its Rdetestable things and all its abominations from there.   Ezek. 37:23

19 "Then I will give them one heart, and I will put a new spirit within Tthem, and take Rthe stony heart out of their flesh, and give them a heart of flesh,   Lit. *you* (pl.) • Zech. 7:12

20 "that they may walk in My statutes and keep My judgments and do them; and they shall be My people, and I will be their God.

21 "But *as for those* whose hearts follow the desire for their detestable things and their abominations, I will recompense their deeds on their own heads," says the Lord GOD.

22 So the cherubim lifted up their wings, with the wheels beside them, and the glory of the God of Israel *was* high above them.

23 And Rthe glory of the LORD went up from the midst of the city and stood Ron the mountain, Rwhich *is* on the east side of the city.   Ezek. 8:4; 9:3 • Zech. 14:4 • Ezek. 43:2

24 Then the Spirit took me up and brought me in a vision by the Spirit of God into *Chaldea, to those in captivity. And the vision that I had seen went up from me.

25 So I spoke to those in captivity of all the things the LORD had shown me.

Judah's Captivity Portrayed

12 Now the word of the LORD came to me, saying:

2 "Son of man, you dwell in the midst of a rebellious house, which has eyes to see but does not see, and ears to hear but does not hear; for they *are* a rebellious house.

3 "Therefore, son of man, prepare your belongings for captivity, and go into captivity by day in their sight. You shall go from your place into captivity to another place in their sight. It may be that they will consider, though they *are* a rebellious house.

4 "By day you shall bring out your belongings in their sight, as though going into captivity; and at evening you shall go in their sight, like those who go into captivity.

5 "Dig through the wall in their sight, and carry your belongings out through it.

6 "In their sight you shall bear *them* on *your* shoulders *and* carry *them* out at twilight; you shall cover your face, so that you

11:24 Or *Babylon,* and so elsewhere in the book

cannot see the ground, ^Rfor I have made you a sign to the house of Israel." Ezek. 4:3; 24:24

7 So I did as I was commanded. I brought out my belongings by day, as though going into captivity, and at evening I dug through the wall with my hand. I brought *them* out at twilight, *and* I bore *them* on *my* shoulder in their sight.

8 And in the morning the word of the Lord came to me, saying,

9 "Son of man, has not the house of Israel, ^Rthe rebellious house, said to you, ^R'What are you doing?' Ezek. 2:5 • Ezek. 17:12; 24:19

10 "Say to them, 'Thus says the Lord God: "This ^Rburden^T *concerns* the prince in Jerusalem and all the house of Israel who are among them." ' Mal. 1:1 • *oracle, prophecy*

11 "Say, ^R'I *am* a sign to you. As I have done, so shall it be done to them; they shall be carried away into captivity.' Ezek. 12:6

12 "And ^Rthe prince who *is* among them shall bear *his* belongings on *his* shoulder at twilight and go out. They shall dig through the wall to carry *them* out through it. He shall cover his face, so that he cannot see the ground with *his* eyes. Jer. 39:4; 52:7

13 "I will also spread My ^Rnet over him, and he shall be caught in My snare. ^RI will bring him to Babylon, *to* the land of the Chaldeans; yet he shall not see it, though he shall die there. Jer. 52:9 • Jer. 52:11

14 "I will scatter to every wind all who *are* around him to help him, and all his troops; and I will draw out the sword after them.

15 ^R"Then they shall know that I *am* the Lord, when I scatter them among the nations and disperse them throughout the countries. Ezek. 6:7, 14; 12:16, 20

16 "But I will spare a few of their men from the sword, from famine, and from pestilence, that they may declare all their abominations among the Gentiles wherever they go. Then they shall know that I *am* the Lord."

Judgment Not Postponed

17 Moreover the word of the Lord came to me, saying,

18 "Son of man, ^Reat your bread with ^Tquaking, and drink your water with trembling and anxiety. Ezek. 4:16 • *shaking*

19 "And say to the people of the land, 'Thus says the Lord God to the inhabitants of Jerusalem *and* to the land of Israel: "They shall eat their bread with anxiety, and drink their water with dread, so that her land may be emptied of all who are in it, because of the violence of all those who dwell in it.

20 "Then the cities that are inhabited shall be laid waste, and the land shall become desolate; and you shall know that I *am* the Lord." ' "

21 And the word of the Lord came to me, saying,

22 "Son of man, what *is* this proverb *that* you *people* have about the land of Israel, which says, ^R'The days are prolonged, and every vision fails'? Ezek. 11:3; 12:27

23 "Tell them therefore, 'Thus says the Lord God: "I will lay this proverb to rest, and they shall no more use it as a proverb in Israel." ' But say to them, "The days are at hand, and the fulfillment of every vision.

24 "For ^Rno more shall there be any ^Rfalse^T vision or flattering divination within the house of Israel. Ezek. 13:6 • Lam. 2:14 • Lit. *vain*

25 "For I *am* the Lord. I speak, and the word which I speak will come to pass; it will no more be postponed; for in your days, O rebellious house, I will say the word and ^Rperform it," says the Lord God.' " [Is. 14:24]

26 Again the word of the Lord came to me, saying,

27 ^R"Son of man, look, the house of Israel is saying, 'The vision that he sees *is* ^Rfor many days *from now*, and he prophesies of times far off.' Ezek. 12:22 • Dan. 10:14

28 "Therefore say to them, 'Thus says the Lord God: "None of My words will be postponed any more, but the word which I speak ^Rwill be done," says the Lord God.' " Jer. 4:7

Woe to Foolish Prophets

13 And the word of the Lord came to me, saying,

2 "Son of man, prophesy against the prophets of Israel who prophesy, and say to those who prophesy out of their own heart, 'Hear the word of the Lord!' "

3 Thus says the Lord God: "Woe to the foolish prophets, who follow their own spirit and have seen ^Tnothing! No vision

4 "O Israel, your prophets are ^Rlike foxes in the deserts. Song 2:15

5 "You ^Rhave not gone up into the ^Tgaps to build a wall for the house of Israel to stand in battle on the day of the Lord. Ps. 106:23 • *breaches*

6 "They have envisioned futility and false divination, saying, 'Thus says the Lord!' But the Lord has not sent them; yet they hope that the word may ^Tbe confirmed. Come true

7 "Have you not seen a futile vision, and have you not spoken false divination? You say, 'The Lord says,' but I have not spoken."

8 Therefore thus says the Lord God: "Because you have spoken nonsense and envisioned lies, therefore I *am* indeed against you," says the Lord God.

9 "My hand will be against the prophets who envision futility and who divine lies; they shall not be in the assembly of My people, nor be written in the record of the house of Israel, ^Rnor shall they enter into the land of Israel. ^RThen you shall know that I *am* the Lord God. Jer. 20:3–6 • Ezek. 11:10, 12

10 "Because, indeed, because they have seduced My people, saying, ^R'Peace!' when

there is no peace—and one builds a wall, and they ᴿplasterᵀ it with untempered *mortar—*   Jer. 6:14; 8:11 • Ezek. 22:28 • Or *whitewash*

11 "say to those who plaster *it* with untempered *mortar*, that it will fall. ᴿThere will be flooding rain, and you, O great hailstones, shall fall; and a stormy wind shall tear *it* down.   Ezek. 38:22

12 "Surely, when the wall has fallen, will it not be said to you, 'Where *is* the mortar with which you plastered *it?* "

13 Therefore thus says the Lord Gᴏᴅ: "I will cause a stormy wind to break forth in My fury; and there shall be a flooding rain in My anger, and great hailstones in fury to consume *it.*

14 "So I will break down the wall you have plastered with untempered *mortar*, and bring it down to the ground, so that its foundation will be uncovered; it will fall, and you shall be consumed in the midst of it. ᴿThen you shall know that I *am* the Lᴏʀᴅ.   Ezek. 13:9, 21, 23; 14:8

15 "Thus will I accomplish My wrath on the wall and on those who have plastered it with untempered *mortar*; and I will say to you, 'The wall *is no more*, nor those who plastered it,

16 '*that is*, the prophets of Israel who prophesy concerning Jerusalem, and who ᴿsee visions of peace for her when *there is* no peace,' " says the Lord Gᴏᴅ.   Jer. 6:14; 8:11; 28:9

17 "Likewise, son of man, ᴿset your face against the daughters of your people, ᴿwho prophesy out of their own ᵀheart; prophesy against them,   Ezek. 20:46; 21:2 • Ezek. 13:2 • Inspiration

18 "and say, 'Thus says the Lord Gᴏᴅ: "Woe to the *women* who sew *magic* charms *on their sleeves and make veils for the heads of people of every height to hunt souls! Will you hunt the souls of My people, and keep yourselves alive?

19 "And will you profane Me among My people ᴿfor handfuls of barley and for pieces of bread, killing people who should not die, and keeping people alive who should not live, by your lying to My people who listen to lies?"   Mic. 3:5

20 'Therefore thus says the Lord Gᴏᴅ: "Behold, I *am* against your *magic* charms by which you hunt souls there like ᵀbirds. I will tear them from your arms, and let the souls go, the souls you hunt like birds.   Lit. *flying ones*

21 "I will also tear off your veils and deliver My people out of your hand, and they shall no longer be as prey in your hand. ᴿThen you shall know that I *am* the Lᴏʀᴅ.   Ezek. 13:9

22 "Because with lies you have made the heart of the righteous sad, whom I have not made sad; and you have strengthened the

hands of the wicked, so that he does not turn from his wicked way to save his life.

23 "Therefore ᴿyou shall no longer envision futility nor practice divination; for I will deliver My people out of your hand, and you shall know that I *am* the Lᴏʀᴅ." ' "   Mic. 3:5, 6

Idolatry Will Be Punished

14 Now some of the elders of Israel came to me and sat before me.

2 And the word of the Lᴏʀᴅ came to me, saying,

3 "Son of man, these men have set up their idols in their hearts, and put before them ᴿthat which causes them to stumble into iniquity. ᴿShould I let Myself be inquired of at all by them?   Ezek. 7:19 • Ezek. 20:3, 31

4 "Therefore speak to them, and say to them, 'Thus says the Lord Gᴏᴅ: "Everyone of the house of Israel who sets up his idols in his heart, and puts before him what causes him to stumble into iniquity, and then comes to the prophet, I the Lᴏʀᴅ will answer him who comes, according to the multitude of his idols,

5 "that I may seize the house of Israel by their heart, because they are all estranged from Me by their idols." '

6 "Therefore say to the house of Israel, 'Thus says the Lord Gᴏᴅ: "Repent, turn away from your idols, and ᴿturn your faces away from all your abominations.   Is. 2:20; 30:22; 55:6, 7

7 "For anyone of the house of Israel, or of the strangers who dwell in Israel, who separates himself from Me and sets up his idols in his heart and puts before him what causes him to stumble into iniquity, then comes to a prophet to inquire of him concerning Me, I the Lᴏʀᴅ will answer him by Myself.

8 "I will set My face against that man and make him a sign and a proverb, and I will cut him off from the midst of My people. Then you shall know that I *am* the Lᴏʀᴅ.

9 "And if the prophet is induced to speak anything, I the Lᴏʀᴅ ᴿhave induced that prophet, and I will stretch out My hand against him and destroy him from among My people Israel.   2 Thess. 2:11

10 "And they shall bear their iniquity; the punishment of the prophet shall be the same as the punishment of the one who inquired,

11 "that the house of Israel may ᴿno longer stray from Me, nor be profaned anymore with all their transgressions, ᴿbut that they may be My people and I may be their God," says the Lord Gᴏᴅ.' "   2 Pet. 2:15 • Ezek. 11:20; 37:27

Judgment on Persistent Unfaithfulness

12 The word of the Lᴏʀᴅ came again to me, saying:

13 "Son of man, when a land sins against Me by persistent unfaithfulness, I will stretch out My hand against it; I will cut off its

---

13:18 Lit. *over all the joints of My hands;* Vg. *under every elbow;* LXX, Tg. *on all elbows of the hands*

ᴿsupply of bread, send famine on it, and cut off man and beast from it.   Is. 3:1

14 ᴿ"Even if these three men, Noah, Daniel, and Job, were in it, they would deliver only themselves ᴿby their righteousness," says the Lord GOD.   Jer. 15:1 • [Prov. 11:4]

15 "If I cause wild beasts to pass through the land, and they ᵀempty it, and make it so desolate that no man may pass through because of the beasts,   Lit. bereave it of children

16 "even though these three men were ᵀin it, as I live," says the Lord GOD, "they would deliver neither sons nor daughters; only they would be delivered, and the land would be ᴿdesolate.   Lit. in the midst of it • Ezek. 15:8; 33:28, 29

17 "Or if ᴿI bring a sword on that land, and say, 'Sword, go through the land,' and I ᴿcut off man and beast from it,   Lev. 26:25 • Zeph. 1:3

18 "even ᴿthough these three men were in it, as I live," says the Lord GOD, "they would deliver neither sons nor daughters, but only they themselves would be delivered.   Ezek. 14:14

19 "Or if I send ᴿa pestilence into that land and ᴿpour out My fury on it in blood, and cut off from it man and beast,   2 Sam. 24:15 • Ezek. 7:8

20 "even ᴿthough Noah, Daniel, and Job were in it, as I live," says the Lord GOD, "they would deliver neither son nor daughter; they would deliver only themselves by their righteousness."   Ezek. 14:14

21 For thus says the Lord GOD: "How much more it shall be when I send My four ᵀsevere judgments on Jerusalem—the sword and famine and wild beasts and pestilence—to cut off man and beast from it?   Lit. evil

22 "Yet behold, there shall be left in it a remnant who will be brought out, both sons and daughters; surely they will come out to you, and you will see their ways and their doings. Then you will be comforted concerning the disaster that I have brought upon Jerusalem, all that I have brought upon it.

23 "And they will comfort you, when you see their ways and their doings; and you shall know that I have done nothing ᴿwithout cause that I have done in it," says the Lord GOD.   Jer. 22:8, 9

The Outcast Vine

15 Then the word of the LORD came to me, saying:

2 "Son of man, how is the wood of the vine better than any other wood, the vine branch which is among the trees of the forest?

3 "Is wood taken from it to make any object? Or can men make a peg from it to hang any vessel on?

4 "Instead, it is thrown into the fire for fuel; the fire devours both ends of it, and its middle is burned. Is it useful for any work?

5 "Indeed, when it was whole, no object could be made from it. How much less will it be useful for any work when the fire has devoured it, and it is burned?

6 "Therefore thus says the Lord GOD: 'Like the wood of the vine among the trees of the forest, which I have given to the fire for fuel, so I will give up the inhabitants of Jerusalem;

7 'and ᴿI will set My face against them. ᴿThey will go out from one fire, but another fire shall devour them. ᴿThen you shall know that I am the LORD, when I set My face against them.   Ezek. 14:8 • Is. 24:18 • Ezek. 7:4

8 'Thus I will make the land desolate, because they have persisted in unfaithfulness,' says the Lord GOD."

God's Love for Jerusalem

16 Again the word of the LORD came to me, saying,

2 "Son of man, ᴿcause Jerusalem to know her abominations,   Ezek. 20:4; 22:2

3 "and say, 'Thus says the Lord GOD to Jerusalem: "Your birth and your nativity are from the land of Canaan; your father was an Amorite and your mother a Hittite.

4 "As for your nativity, ᴿon the day you were born your navel cord was not cut, nor were you washed in water to cleanse you; you were not rubbed with salt nor wrapped in swaddling cloths.   Hos. 2:3

5 "No eye pitied you, to do any of these things for you, to have compassion on you; but you were thrown out into the open field, when you yourself were ᵀloathed on the day you were born.   abhorred

6 "And when I passed by you and saw you struggling in your own blood, I said to you in your blood, 'Live!' Yes, I said to you in your blood, 'Live!'

7 "I made you thrive like a plant in the field; and you grew, matured, and became very beautiful. Your breasts were formed, your hair grew, but you were naked and bare.

8 "When I passed by you again and looked upon you, indeed your time was the time of love; so I spread ᵀMy wing over you and covered your nakedness. Yes, I swore an oath to you and entered into a covenant with you, and ᴿyou became Mine," says the Lord GOD.   Or the corner of My garment • [Ex. 19:5]

9 "Then I washed you in water; yes, I thoroughly washed off your blood, and I anointed you with oil.

10 "I clothed you in embroidered cloth and gave you sandals of badger skin; I clothed you with fine linen and covered you with silk.

11 "I adorned you with ornaments, ᴿput bracelets on your wrists, ᴿand a chain on your neck.   Gen. 24:22, 47 • Prov. 1:9

12 "And I put a ᵀjewel in your nose, earrings in your ears, and a beautiful crown on your head.   Lit. ring

13 "Thus you were adorned with gold and silver, and your clothing was of fine linen,

silk, and embroidered cloth. You ate *pastry of fine flour*, honey, and oil. You were exceedingly beautiful, and succeeded to royalty.

14 "Your fame went out among the nations because of your beauty, for it *was* perfect through My splendor which I had bestowed on you," says the Lord GOD.

Jerusalem's Harlotry

15 R"But you trusted in your own beauty, Rplayed the harlot because of your fame, and poured out your harlotry on everyone passing by who *would have* it.   Mic. 3:11 · Is. 1:21; 57:8

16 R"You took some of your garments and adorned multicolored high places for yourself, and played the harlot on them. *Such* things should not happen, nor be.   Ezek. 7:20

17 "You have also taken your beautiful jewelry from My gold and My silver, which I had given you, and made for yourself male images and played the harlot with them.

18 "You took your embroidered garments and covered them, and you set My oil and My incense before them.

19 "Also My food which I gave you—the pastry of fine flour, oil, and honey *which* I fed you—you set it before them as sweet incense; and so it was," says the Lord GOD.

20 R"Moreover you took your sons and your daughters, whom you bore to Me, and these you sacrificed to them to be devoured. *Were* your *acts* of harlotry a small matter,   Jer. 7:31

21 "that you have slain My children and offered them up to them by causing them to pass through the Rfire?   Jer. 19:5

22 "And in all your abominations and acts of harlotry you did not remember the days of your youth, Rwhen you were naked and bare, struggling in your blood.   Ezek. 16:4-6

23 "Then it was so, after all your wickedness—'Woe, woe to you!' says the Lord GOD—

24 "*that* you also built for yourself a shrine, and Rmade a Thigh place for yourself in every street.   Jer. 2:20; 3:2 · Place for pagan worship

25 "You built your high places Rat the head of every road, and made your beauty to be abhorred. You offered yourself to everyone who passed by, and multiplied your acts of harlotry.   Prov. 9:14

26 "You also committed harlotry with Rthe Egyptians, your very fleshly neighbors, and increased your acts of harlotry to Rprovoke Me to anger.   Ezek. 16:26; 20:7, 8 · Deut. 31:20

27 "Behold, therefore, I stretched out My hand against you, diminished your Tallotment, and gave you up to the will of those who hate you, Rthe daughters of the Philistines, who were ashamed of your lewd behavior.   Allowance of food · Ezek. 16:57

28 "You also played the harlot with the RAssyrians, because you were insatiable;

indeed you played the harlot with them and still were not satisfied.   Jer. 2:18, 36

29 "Moreover you multiplied your acts of harlotry as far as the land of the trader, RChaldea; and even then you were not satisfied.   Ezek. 23:14-17

30 "How degenerate is your heart!" says the Lord GOD, "seeing you do all these *things*, the deeds of a brazen harlot.

Jerusalem's Adultery

31 "You erected your shrine at the head of every road, and built your high place in every street. Yet you were not like a harlot, because you scorned Rpayment.   Is. 52:3

32 "*You are* an adulterous wife, *who* takes strangers instead of her husband.

33 "Men make payment to all harlots, but Ryou made your payments to all your lovers, and Thired them to come to you from all around for your harlotry.   Hos. 8:9, 10 · Or *bribed*

34 "You are the opposite of *other* women in your harlotry, because no one solicited you to be a harlot. In that you gave payment but no payment was given you, therefore you are the opposite."

Jerusalem's Lovers Will Abuse Her

35 'Now then, O harlot, hear the word of the LORD!

36 'Thus says the Lord GOD: "Because your filthiness was poured out and your nakedness uncovered in your harlotry with your lovers, and with all your abominable idols, and because of Rthe blood of your children which you gave to them,   Jer. 2:34

37 "surely, therefore, RI will gather all your lovers with whom you took pleasure, all those you loved, *and* all those you hated; I will gather them from all around against you and will uncover your nakedness to them, that they may see all your nakedness.   Lam. 1:8

38 "And I will judge you as Rwomen who break wedlock or Rshed blood are judged; I will bring blood upon you in fury and jealousy.   Lev. 20:10 · Gen. 9:6

39 "I will also give you into their hand, and they shall throw down your shrines and break down Ryour Thigh places. RThey shall also strip you of your clothes, take your beautiful jewelry, and leave you naked and bare.   Ezek. 16:24, 31 · Places for pagan worship · Hos. 2:3

40 R"They shall also bring up an assembly against you, Rand they shall stone you with stones and thrust you through with their swords.   Ezek. 23:45-47 · John 8:5, 7

41 "They shall burn your houses with fire, and Rexecute judgments on you in the sight of many women; and I will make you Rcease playing the harlot, and you shall no longer hire lovers.   Ezek. 5:8; 23:10, 48 · Ezek. 23:27

42 "So I will lay to rest My fury toward you, and My jealousy shall depart from you. I will be quiet, and be angry no more.

43 "Because you did not remember the days of your youth, but *agitated Me with all these *things,* surely I will also recompense your deeds on *your own* head," says the Lord GOD. "And you shall not commit lewdness in addition to all your abominations.

More Wicked than Samaria and Sodom

44 "Indeed everyone who quotes proverbs will use *this* proverb against you: 'Like mother, like daughter!'

45 "You *are* your mother's daughter, ᵀloathing husband and children; and you *are* the sister of your sisters, who loathed their husbands and children; your mother *was* a Hittite and your father an Amorite.   *despising*

46 "Your elder sister *is* Samaria, who dwells with her daughters to the north of you; and ᴿyour younger sister, who dwells to the south of you, *is* Sodom and her daughters.   Is. 1:10

47 "You did not walk in their ways nor act according to their abominations; but, as *if that were* too little, ᴿyou became more corrupt than they in all your ways.   Ezek. 5:6, 7

48 "*As* I live," says the Lord GOD, "neither your sister Sodom nor her daughters have done as you and your daughters have done.

49 "Look, this was the iniquity of your sister Sodom: She and her daughter had pride, ᴿfullness of food, and abundance of idleness; neither did she strengthen the hand of the poor and needy.   Gen. 13:10

50 "And they were haughty and committed abomination before Me; therefore ᴿI took them away as *I saw fit.   Gen. 19:24

51 "Samaria did not commit ᴿhalf of your sins; but you have multiplied your abominations more than they, and ᴿhave justified your sisters by all the abominations which you have done.   Ezek. 23:11 • Jer. 3:8–11

52 "You who judged your sisters, bear your own shame also, because the sins which you committed were more abominable than theirs; they are more righteous than you. Yes, be disgraced also, and bear your own shame, because you justified your sisters.

53 ᴿ"When I bring back their captives, the captives of Sodom and her daughters, and the captives of Samaria and her daughters, then *I will also bring back* ᴿthe captives of your captivity among them,   Is. 1:9 • Jer. 20:16

54 "that you may bear your own shame and be disgraced by all that you did when ᴿyou comforted them.   Ezek. 14:22

55 "When your sisters, Sodom and her daughters, return to their former state, and Samaria and her daughters return to their former state, then you and your daughters will return to your former state.

56 "For your sister Sodom was not a byword in your mouth in the days of your pride,

57 "before your wickedness was uncovered. It was like the time of the reproach of the daughters of *Syria and all *those* around her, and of ᴿthe daughters of the Philistines, who despise you everywhere.   Ezek. 16:27

58 ᴿ"You have paid for your lewdness and your abominations," says the LORD.   Ezek. 23:49

59 'For thus says the Lord GOD: "I will deal with you as you have done, who despised the oath by breaking the covenant.

An Everlasting Covenant

60 "Nevertheless I will ᴿremember My covenant with you in the days of your youth, and I will establish ᴿan everlasting covenant with you.   Ps. 106:45 • Is. 55:3

61 "Then you will remember your ways and be ashamed, when you receive your older and your younger sisters; for I will give them to you for ᴿdaughters, ᴿbut not because of My covenant with you.   [Gal. 4:26] • Jer. 31:31

62 ᴿ"And I will establish My covenant with you. Then you shall know that I *am* the LORD,   Hos. 2:19, 20

63 "that you may ᴿremember and be ashamed, ᴿand never open your mouth anymore because of your shame, when I provide you an atonement for all you have done," says the Lord GOD.' "   Ezek. 36:31, 32 • [Rom. 3:19]

The Eagles and the Vine

17 And the word of the LORD came to me, saying,

2 "Son of man, pose a riddle, and speak a ᴿparable to the house of Israel,   Ezek. 20:49; 24:3

3 "and say, 'Thus says the Lord GOD:

ᴿ"A great eagle with large wings and long
   pinions,
Full of feathers of various colors,
Came to Lebanon
And ᴿtook from the cedar the highest
   branch.   Ezek. 17:12 • 2 Kin. 24:12

4 He cropped off its topmost young twig
And carried it to a land of trade;
He set it in a city of merchants.

5 Then he took some of the seed of the
   land
And planted it in a fertile field;
He placed *it* by abundant waters
And set it ᴿlike a willow tree.   Is. 44:4

6 And it grew and became a spreading
   vine ᴿof low stature;   Ezek. 17:14
Its branches turned toward him,
But its roots were under it.
So it became a vine,
Brought forth branches,
And put forth shoots.

7 "But there was *another great eagle
  with large wings and many feathers;
And behold, ᴿthis vine bent its roots
  toward him,   Ezek. 17:15
And stretched its branches toward him,
From the garden terrace where it had
  been planted,
That he might water it.
8 It was planted in ᵀgood soil by many
  waters,   Lit. *a good field*
To bring forth branches, bear fruit,
And become a majestic vine." '

9 "Say, 'Thus says the Lord GOD:

"Will it thrive?
ᴿWill he not pull up its roots,
  Cut off its fruit,
  And leave it to wither?
All of its spring leaves will wither,
And no great power or many people
Will be needed to pluck it up by its
  roots.   2 Kin. 25:7
10 Behold, *it is* planted,
  Will it thrive?
ᴿWill it not utterly wither when the east
  wind touches it?
It will wither in the garden terrace
  where it grew." ' "   Hos. 13:15

11 Moreover the word of the LORD came to
me, saying,
12 "Say now to the rebellious house: 'Do
you not know what these *things mean*?' Tell
them, 'Indeed ᴿthe king of Babylon went to
Jerusalem and took its king and princes, and
led them with him to Babylon.   2 Kin. 24:11-16
13 ᴿ'And he took the king's offspring, made
a covenant with him, ᴿand put him under
oath. He also took away the mighty of the
land,   2 Kin. 24:17 · 2 Chr. 36:13
14 'that the kingdom might be ᴿbrought low
and not lift itself up, *but* that by keeping his
covenant it might stand.   Ezek. 29:14
15 'But ᴿhe rebelled against him by sending
his ambassadors to Egypt, ᴿthat they might
give him horses and many people. ᴿWill he
prosper? Will he who does such *things* escape? Can he break a covenant and still be
delivered?   2 Kin. 24:20 · Deut. 17:16 · Ezek. 17:9
16 '*As* I live,' says the Lord GOD, 'surely ᴿin
the place *where* the king *dwells* who made
him king, whose oath he despised and whose
covenant he broke—with him in the midst of
Babylon he shall die.   Ezek. 12:13
17 'Nor will Pharaoh with *his* mighty army
and great company do anything in the war,
when they heap up a siege mound and build a
ᵀwall to cut off many persons.   Or *siege wall*
18 'Since he despised the oath by breaking
the covenant, and in fact gave his hand and
still did all these *things*, he shall not escape.' "

17:7 So with LXX, Syr., Vg; MT, Tg. *one*

19 Therefore thus says the Lord GOD: "*As* I
live, surely My oath which he despised, and
My covenant which he broke, I will recompense on his own head.
20 "I will spread My net over him, and he
shall be taken in My snare. I will bring him to
Babylon and try him there for the treason
which he committed against Me.
21 "All his *fugitives with all his troops
shall fall by the sword, and those who remain
shall be scattered to every wind; and you
shall know that I, the LORD, have spoken."

Israel Exalted at Last

22 Thus says the Lord GOD: "I will take also
one of the highest ᴿbranches of the high
cedar and set *it* out. I will crop off from the
topmost of its young twigs ᴿa tender one, and
will ᴿplant *it* on a high and prominent mountain.   [Zech. 3:8] · Is. 53:2 · [Ps. 2:6]
23 ᴿ"On the mountain height of Israel I will
plant it; and it will bring forth boughs, and
bear fruit, and be a majestic cedar. Under it
will dwell birds of every sort; in the shadow
of its branches they will dwell.   [Is. 2:2, 3]
24 "And all the trees of the field shall know
that I, the LORD, have brought down the high
tree and exalted the low tree, dried up the
green tree and made the dry tree flourish; I,
the LORD, have spoken and have done *it*."

A False Proverb Refuted

18 The word of the LORD came to me
again, saying,
2 "What do you mean when you use this
proverb concerning the land of Israel, saying:

'The ᴿfathers have eaten sour grapes,
And the children's teeth are set on
  edge'?   Lam. 5:7

3 "*As* I live," says the Lord GOD, "you
shall no longer use this proverb in Israel.

4 "Behold, all souls are ᴿMine;
The soul of the father   Num. 16:22; 27:16
As well as the soul of the son is Mine;
ᴿThe soul who sins shall die.   [Rom. 6:23]
5 But if a man is just
And does what is lawful and right;
6 If he has not eaten ᵀon the mountains,
Nor lifted up his eyes to the idols of the
  house of Israel,   At the mountain shrines
Nor ᴿdefiled his neighbor's wife,
Nor approached ᴿa woman during her
  impurity;   Lev. 18:20; 20:10 · Lev. 18:19; 20:18
7 If he has not ᴿoppressed anyone,   Ex. 22:21
But has restored to the debtor his
  ᴿpledge,   Deut. 24:12
Has robbed no one by violence,

17:21 So with MT, Vg.; many Heb. mss., Syr. *choice
men*; Tg. *mighty men*; LXX omits *All his fugitives*

But has given his bread to the hungry
And covered the naked with clothing;
8 If he has not ᵀexacted ᴿusury
Nor taken any increase,
But has withdrawn his hand from
iniquity   Lent money at interest · Ex. 22:25
And ᴿexecuted true ᵀjudgment between
man and man;   Zech. 8:16 · *justice*
9 *If* he has walked in My statutes
And kept My judgments faithfully—
He *is* just;
He shall surely ᴿlive!"
Says the Lord Gᴏᴅ.   Amos 5:4

10 "If he begets a son *who is* a robber
Or ᴿa shedder of blood,
Who does any of these *things*   Num. 35:31
11 And does none of those *duties*,
But has eaten on the mountains
Or defiled his neighbor's wife;
12 If he has oppressed the poor and needy,
Robbed by violence,
Not restored the pledge,
Lifted his eyes to the idols,
Or ᴿcommitted abomination;   Ezek. 8:6, 17
13 If he has exacted usury
Or taken increase—
Shall he then live?
He shall not live!
If he has done any of these
abominations,
He shall surely die;
His blood shall be upon him.

14 "If, however, he begets a son
Who sees all the sins which his father
has done,
And considers but does not do likewise;
15 *Who* has not eaten ᵀon the mountains,
Nor lifted his eyes to the idols of the
house of Israel,   At the mountain shrines
Nor defiled his neighbor's wife;
16 Has not oppressed anyone,
Nor withheld a pledge,
Nor robbed by violence,
But has given his bread to the hungry
And covered the naked with clothing;
17 *Who* has withdrawn his hand from *the
poor
And not received usury or increase,
But has executed My judgments
And walked in My statutes—
He shall not die for the iniquity of his
father;
He shall surely live!

18 "As for his father,
Because he cruelly oppressed,
Robbed his brother by violence,
And did what is not good among his
people,
Behold, he shall die for his iniquity.

18:17 So with MT, Tg., Vg.; LXX *iniquity* (cf. v. 8)

Turn and Live

19 "Yet you say, 'Why ᴿshould the son not
bear the guilt of the father?' Because the son
has done what is lawful and right, and has
kept all My statutes and observed them, he
shall surely live.   Ex. 20:5
20 "The soul who sins shall die. The son
shall not bear the guilt of the father, nor the
father bear the guilt of the son. ᴿThe righteousness of the righteous shall be upon
himself, ᴿand the wickedness of the wicked
shall be upon himself.   Is. 3:10, 11 · Rom. 2:6-9
21 "But ᴿif a wicked man turns from all his
sins which he has committed, keeps all My
statutes, and does what is lawful and right, he
shall surely live; he shall not die.   Ezek. 18:27
22 "None of the transgressions which he
has committed shall be remembered against
him; because of the righteousness which he
has done, he shall ᴿlive.   [Ps. 18:20-24]
23 ᴿ"Do I have any pleasure at all that the
wicked should die?" says the Lord Gᴏᴅ, "and
not that he should turn from his ways and
live?   [Ezek. 18:32; 33:11]
24 "But ᴿwhen a righteous man turns away
from his righteousness and commits iniquity,
and does according to all the abominations
that the wicked *man* does, shall he live? ᴿAll
the righteousness which he has done shall
not be remembered; because of the unfaithfulness of which he is guilty and the sin
which he has committed, because of them he
shall die.   Ezek. 3:20; 18:26; 33:18 · [2 Pet. 2:20]
25 "Yet you say, ᴿ'The way of the Lord is
not fair.' Hear now, O house of Israel, is it not
My way which is fair, and your ways which
are not fair?   Ezek. 18:29; 33:17, 20
26 ᴿ"When a righteous *man* turns away
from his righteousness, commits iniquity, and
dies in it, it is because of the iniquity which
he has done that he dies.   Ezek. 18:24
27 "Again, ᴿwhen a wicked *man* turns away
from the wickedness which he committed,
and does what is lawful and right, he preserves himself alive.   Ezek. 18:21
28 "Because he considers and turns away
from all the transgressions which he committed, he shall surely live; he shall not die.
29 ᴿ"Yet the house of Israel says, 'The way
of the Lord is not fair.' O house of Israel, is it
not My ways which are fair, and your ways
which are not fair?   Ezek. 18:25
30 ᴿ"Therefore I will judge you, O house of
Israel, every one according to his ways," says
the Lord Gᴏᴅ. ᴿ"Repent, and turn from all
your transgressions, so that iniquity will not
be your ruin.   Ezek. 7:3; 33:20 · Matt. 3:2
31 "Cast away from you all the transgressions which you have committed, and get
yourselves a new heart and a new spirit. For
why should you die, O house of Israel?
32 "For ᴿI have no pleasure in the death of

one who dies," says the Lord God. "Therefore turn and ᴿlive!"   Lam. 3:33 • [Prov. 4:2, 5, 6]

Israel Degraded

19 "Moreover ᴿtake up a lamentation for the princes of Israel,   Ezek. 26:17
2 "and say:

'What *is* your mother? A lioness:
She lay down among the lions;
Among the young lions she nourished her cubs.

3 She brought up one of her cubs,
And ᴿhe became a young lion;
He learned to catch prey,
And he devoured men.   2 Kin. 23:31, 32

4 The nations also heard of him;
He was trapped in their pit,
And they brought him with chains to the land of ᴿEgypt.   2 Kin. 23:33, 34

5 'When she saw that she waited, *that* her hope was lost,
She took ᴿanother of her cubs *and* made him a young lion.   2 Kin. 23:34

6 ᴿHe roved among the lions,
And ᴿbecame a young lion;
He learned to catch prey;
He devoured men.   Jer. 22:13-17 • Ezek. 19:3

7 *He knew their desolate places,
And laid waste their cities;
The land with its fullness was desolated
By the noise of his roaring.

8 Then the nations set against him from the provinces on every side,
And spread their net over him;
ᴿHe was trapped in their pit.   Ezek. 19:4

9 ᴿThey put him in a cage with ᵀchains,
And brought him to the king of Babylon;   2 Chr. 36:6 • Or *hooks*
They brought him in nets,
That his voice should no longer be heard on the mountains of Israel.

10 'Your mother *was* ᴿlike a vine in your *bloodline,   Ezek. 17:6
Planted by the waters,
ᴿFruitful and full of branches   Deut. 8:7-9
Because of many waters.

11 She had strong branches for scepters of rulers.
ᴿShe towered in stature above the thick branches,
And was seen in her height amid the ᵀdense foliage.   Dan. 4:11 • Or *many branches*

12 But she was ᴿplucked up in fury,
She was cast down to the ground,
And the ᴿeast wind dried her fruit.
Her strong branches were broken and withered;   Jer. 31:27, 28 • Hos. 13:5
The fire consumed them.

19:7 LXX *He stood in insolence;* Tg. *He destroyed its palaces;* Vg. *He learned to make widows*
19:10 Lit. *blood.* So with MT, Syr., Vg.; LXX *like a flower on a pomegranate tree;* Tg. *in your likeness*

13 And now she *is* planted in the wilderness,
In a dry and thirsty land.

14 ᴿFire has come out from a rod of her branches
And devoured her fruit,
So that she has no strong branch—a scepter for ruling.' "

ᴿThis *is* a lamentation, and has become a lamentation.   Judg. 9:15 • Lam. 2:5

The Rebellions of Israel

20 It came to pass in the seventh year, in the fifth *month*, on the tenth *day* of the month, *that* ᴿcertain of the elders of Israel came to inquire of the LORD, and sat before me.   Ezek. 8:1, 11, 12; 14:1

2 Then the word of the LORD came to me, saying,

3 "Son of man, speak to the elders of Israel, and say to them, 'Thus says the Lord God: "Have you come to inquire of Me? *As* I live," says the Lord God, ᴿ"I will not be inquired of by you." '   Ezek. 7:26; 14:3

4 "Will you judge them, son of man, will you judge *them?* Then make known to them the abominations of their fathers.

5 "Say to them, 'Thus says the Lord God: "On the day when ᴿI chose Israel and raised My hand in an oath to the descendants of the house of Jacob, and made Myself ᴿknown to them in the land of Egypt, I raised My hand in an oath to them, saying, ᴿ'I *am* the LORD your God.'   Ex. 6:6-8 • Deut. 4:34 • Ex. 20:2

6 "On that day I raised My hand in an oath to them, to bring them out of the land of Egypt into a land that I had searched out for them, ᴿ'flowing with milk and honey,' ᴿthe glory of all lands.   Ex. 3:8 • Jer. 11:5; 32:22

7 "Then I said to them, 'Each of you, ᴿthrow away ᴿthe abominations which are before his eyes, and do not defile yourselves with ᴿthe idols of Egypt. I *am* the LORD your God.'   Ezek. 18:31 • 2 Chr. 15:8 • Lev. 18:3

8 "But they rebelled against Me and would not ᵀobey Me. They did not all cast away the abominations which were before their eyes, nor did they forsake the idols of Egypt. Then I said, 'I will ᴿpour out My fury on them and fulfill My anger against them in the midst of the land of Egypt.'   Lit. *listen to* • Ezek. 7:8

9 "But I acted for My name's sake, that it should not be profaned before the Gentiles among whom they *were,* in whose sight I had made Myself ᴿknown to them, to bring them out of the land of Egypt.   Josh. 2:10; 9:9, 10

10 "Therefore I ᴿmade them go out of the land of Egypt and brought them into the wilderness.   Ex. 13:18

11 "And I gave them My statutes and showed them My judgments, ᴿ'which, *if* a man does, he shall live by them.'   Lev. 18:5

12 "Moreover I also gave them My ᴿSabbaths, to be a sign between them and Me, that they might know that I *am* the LORD who sanctifies them.　Deut. 5:12

13 "Yet the house of Israel rebelled against Me in the wilderness; they did not walk in My statutes; they despised My judgments, 'which, *if* a man does, he shall live by them;' and they greatly ᴿdefiled My Sabbaths. Then I said I would pour out My fury on them in the wilderness, to consume them.　Ex. 16:27

14 "But I acted for My name's sake, that it should not be profaned before the Gentiles, in whose sight I had brought them out.

15 "So ᴿI also raised My hand in an oath to them in the wilderness, that I would not bring them into the land which I had given *them*, ᴿ'flowing with milk and honey,' ᴿthe glory of all lands,　Ex. 3:8 • Num. 14:28 • Ezek. 20:6

16 ᴿ"because they despised My judgments and did not walk in My statutes, but profaned My Sabbaths; for ᴿtheir heart went after their idols.　Ezek. 20:13, 24 • Amos 5:25

17 ᴿ"Nevertheless My eye spared them from destruction. I did not make an end of them in the wilderness.　[Ps. 78:38]

18 "But I said to their children in the wilderness, 'Do not walk in the statutes of your fathers, nor observe their judgments, nor defile yourselves with their idols.

19 'I *am* the LORD your God: Walk in My statutes, keep My judgments, and do them;

20 ᴿ'hallow My Sabbaths, and they will be a sign between Me and you, that you may know that I *am* the LORD your God.'　Jer. 17:22

21 "Notwithstanding, ᴿthe children rebelled against Me; they did not walk in My statutes, and were not careful to observe My judgments, ᴿ'which, *if* a man does, he shall live by them'; but they profaned My Sabbaths. Then I said I would pour out My fury on them and fulfill My anger against them in the wilderness.　Num. 25:1 • Lev. 18:5

22 "Nevertheless I withdrew My hand and acted for My name's sake, that it should not be profaned in the sight of the Gentiles, in whose sight I had brought them out.

23 "Also I raised My hand in an oath to those in the wilderness, that ᴿI would scatter them among the Gentiles and disperse them throughout the countries,　Lev. 26:33

24 "because they had not executed My judgments, but had despised My statutes, profaned My Sabbaths, and ᴿtheir eyes were fixed on their fathers' idols.　Ezek. 6:9

25 "Therefore ᴿI also gave them up to statutes *that were* not good, and judgments by which they could not live;　Rom. 1:24

26 "and I pronounced them unclean because of their ritual gifts, in that they caused all their firstborn to pass through *the fire*, that I might make them desolate and that they might know that I *am* the LORD." '

27 "Therefore, son of man, speak to the house of Israel, and say to them, 'Thus says the Lord GOD: "In this too your fathers have blasphemed Me, by being unfaithful to Me.

28 "When I brought them into the land *concerning* which I had raised My hand in an oath to give them, and ᴿthey saw all the high hills and all the thick trees, there they offered their sacrifices and provoked Me with their offerings. There they also sent up their ᴿsweet aroma and poured out their drink offerings.　Ezek. 6:13 • Ezek. 16:19

29 "Then I said to them, 'What *is* this high place to which you go?' So its name is called ᵀBamah to this day." '　Lit. *High Place*

30 "Therefore say to the house of Israel, 'Thus says the Lord GOD: "Are you defiling yourselves in the manner of your ᴿfathers, and committing harlotry according to their ᴿabominations?　Judg. 2:19 • Jer. 7:26; 16:12

31 "For when you offer your gifts and make your sons pass through the fire, you defile yourselves with all your idols, even to this day. So shall I be inquired of by you, O house of Israel? *As* I live," says the Lord GOD, "I will not be inquired of by you.

32 ᴿ"What you have in your mind shall never be, when you say, 'We will be like the Gentiles, like the families in other countries, serving wood and stone.'　Ezek. 11:5

God Will Restore Israel

33 "As I live," says the Lord GOD, "surely with a mighty hand, ᴿwith an outstretched arm, and with fury poured out, I will rule over you.　Jer. 21:5

34 "I will bring you out from the peoples and gather you out of the countries where you are scattered, with a mighty hand, with an outstretched arm, and with fury poured out.

35 "And I will bring you into the wilderness of the peoples, and there ᴿI will plead My case with you face to face.　Jer. 2:9, 35

36 ᴿ"Just as I pleaded My case with your fathers in the wilderness of the land of Egypt, so I will plead My case with you," says the Lord GOD.　Num. 14:21–23, 28

37 "I will make you ᴿpass under the rod, and I will bring you into the bond of the ᴿcovenant;　Lev. 27:32 • Ps. 89:30–34

38 ᴿ"I will purge the rebels from among you, and those who transgress against Me; I will bring them out of the country where they dwell, but ᴿthey shall not enter the land of Israel. Then you will know that I *am* the LORD.　Ezek. 34:17 • Jer. 44:14

39 "As for you, O house of Israel," thus says the Lord GOD: ᴿ"Go, serve every one of you his idols—and hereafter—if you will not obey Me; ᴿbut profane My holy name no more with your gifts and your idols.　Amos 4:4 • Is. 1:13–15

40 "For on My holy mountain, on the mountain height of Israel," says the Lord GOD, "there all the house of Israel, all of them in the land, shall serve Me; there I will accept them, and there I will require your offerings and the firstfruits of your ᵀsacrifices, together with all your holy things.   *offerings*

41 "I will accept you as a ᴿsweet aroma when I bring you out from the peoples and gather you out of the countries where you have been scattered; and I will be hallowed in you before the Gentiles.   Phil. 4:18

42 "Then you shall know that I *am* the LORD, when I bring you into the land of Israel, into the country *for* which I raised My hand in an oath to give to your fathers.

43 "And there you shall remember your ways and all your doings with which you were defiled; and you shall ᵀloathe yourselves in your own sight because of all the evils that you have committed.   Or *despise*

44 "Then you shall know that I *am* the LORD, when I have dealt with you for My name's sake, not according to your wicked ways nor according to your corrupt doings, O house of Israel," says the Lord GOD.' "

Fire in the Forest

45 Furthermore the word of the LORD came to me, saying,

46 "Son of man, set your face toward the south; preach against the south and prophesy against the forest land, the ᵀSouth,   Heb. *Negev*

47 "and say to the forest of the South, 'Hear the word of the LORD! Thus says the Lord GOD: "Behold, I will kindle a fire in you, and it shall devour every green tree and every dry tree in you; the blazing flame shall not be quenched, and all faces ᴿfrom the south to the north shall be scorched by it.   Ezek. 21:4

48 "All flesh shall see that I, the LORD, have kindled it; it shall not be quenched." ' "

49 Then I said, "Ah, Lord GOD! They say of me, 'Does he not speak parables?' "

Babylon, the Sword of God

21 And the word of the LORD came to me, saying,

2 "Son of man, set your face toward Jerusalem, ᴿpreach against the holy places, and prophesy against the land of Israel;   Amos 7:16

3 "and say to the land of Israel, 'Thus says the LORD: "Behold, I *am* against you, and I will draw My sword out of its sheath and cut off both righteous and wicked from you.

4 "Because I will cut off both righteous and wicked from you, therefore My sword shall go out of its sheath against all flesh ᴿfrom south *to* north,   Ezek. 20:47

5 "that all flesh may know that I, the LORD, have drawn My sword out of its sheath; it shall not return anymore." '

6 "Sigh therefore, son of man, with ᵀa breaking heart, and sigh with bitterness before their eyes.   Lit. *the breaking of your loins*

7 "And it shall be when they say to you, 'Why are you sighing?' that you shall answer, 'Because of the news; when it comes, every heart will melt, all hands will be feeble, every spirit will faint, and all knees will be weak *as* water. Behold, it is coming and shall be brought to pass,' says the Lord GOD."

8 Again the word of the LORD came to me, saying,

9 "Son of man, prophesy and say, 'Thus says the LORD!' Say:

ᴿ'A sword, a sword is sharpened
    And also polished!   Deut. 32:41
10 Sharpened to make a dreadful
        slaughter,
    Polished to flash like lightning!
    Should we then make mirth?
    It despises the scepter of My son,
    As it does all wood.
11 And He has given it to be polished,
        That it may be handled;
    This sword is sharpened, and it is
        polished
    To be given into the hand of ᴿthe
        slayer.'   Ezek. 21:19
12 "Cry and wail, son of man;
    For it will be against My people,
    Against all the princes of Israel.
    Terrors including the sword will be
        against My people;
    Therefore ᴿstrike *your* thigh.   Jer. 31:19
13 "Because *it is* ᴿa testing,   Job 9:23
    And what if *the sword* despises even
        the scepter?
    ᴿ*The scepter* shall be no *more*,"   Ezek. 21:27

says the Lord GOD.

14 "You therefore, son of man, prophesy,
    And ᴿstrike *your* hands together.
    The third time let the sword do double
        damage.   Num. 24:10
    It *is* the sword *that* slays,
    The sword that slays the great *men*,
    That enters their private chambers.
15 I have set the point of the sword
        against all their gates,
    That the heart may melt and many may
        stumble.
    Ah! ᴿ*It is* made bright;
    It is grasped for slaughter: Ezek. 21:10, 28
16 "Swordsᴿ at the ready!   Ezek. 14:17
    Thrust right!
    Set your blade!
    Thrust left—
    Wherever your ᵀedge is ordered!   Lit. *face*

17 "I also will ᴿbeat My fists together,
And I will cause My fury to rest;
I, the LORD, have spoken."　　　Ezek. 22:13

18 The word of the LORD came to me again, saying:
19 "And son of man, appoint for yourself two ways for the sword of the king of Babylon to go; both of them shall go from the same land. Make a sign; put *it* at the head of the road to the city.
20 "Appoint a road for the sword to go to ᴿRabbah of the Ammonites, and to Judah, into fortified Jerusalem.　　　Jer. 49:2
21 "For the king of Babylon stands at the parting of the road, at the fork of the two roads, to use divination: he shakes the arrows, he consults the ᵀimages, he looks at the liver.　　　Heb. *teraphim*
22 "In his right hand is the divination for Jerusalem: to set up battering rams, to call for a slaughter, to lift the voice with shouting, to set battering rams against the gates, to heap up a *siege* mound, and to build a wall.
23 "And it will be to them like a false divination in the eyes of those who ᴿhave sworn oaths with them; but he will bring their iniquity to remembrance, that they may be taken.　　　Ezek. 17:16, 18
24 "Therefore thus says the Lord GOD: 'Because you have made your iniquity to be remembered, in that your transgressions are uncovered, so that in all your doings your sins appear—because you have come to remembrance, you shall be taken in hand.
25 'Now to you, O ᴿprofane, wicked prince of Israel, ᴿwhose day has come, whose iniquity *shall* end,　　　Jer. 52:2 · Ezek. 21:29
26 'thus says the Lord GOD:

"Remove the turban, and take off the crown;
Nothing *shall remain* the same.
Exalt the humble, and humble the exalted.
27 ᵀOverthrown, overthrown,　　　Or *Ruin*
I will make it overthrown!
ᴿIt shall be no *longer,*　　　[Luke 1:32, 33]
Until He comes whose right it is,
And I will give it to ᴿHim." '　　　[Jer. 23:5, 6]

A Sword Against the Ammonites

28 "And you, son of man, prophesy and say, 'Thus says the Lord GOD ᴿconcerning the Ammonites and concerning their reproach,' and say:

'A sword, a sword *is* drawn,
Polished for slaughter,
For consuming, for flashing—　　　Ezek. 25:1-7
29 While they ᴿsee false visions for you,
While they divine a lie to you,

To bring you on the necks of the wicked, the slain　　　Ezek. 12:24; 13:6-9; 22:28
ᴿWhose day has come,　　　Job 18:20
Whose iniquity *shall* end.
30 'Returnᴿ *it* to its sheath.　　　Jer. 47:6, 7
ᴿI will judge you　　　Gen. 15:14
In the place where you were created,
In the land of your ᵀnativity.　　　Or *origin*
31 I will ᴿpour out My indignation on you;
I will ᴿblow against you with the fire of My wrath,　　　Ezek. 7:8 · Ezek. 22:20, 21
And deliver you into the hands of brutal men *who are* skillful to destroy.
32 You shall be fuel for the fire;
Your blood shall be in the midst of the land.
ᴿYou shall not be remembered,
For I the LORD have spoken.' "　　　Ezek. 25:10

Sins of Jerusalem

22 Moreover the word of the LORD came to me, saying,
2 "Now, son of man, ᴿwill you judge, will you judge ᴿthe bloody city? Yes, show her all her abominations!　　　Ezek. 20:4 · Nah. 3:1
3 "Then say, 'Thus says the Lord GOD: "The city sheds ᴿblood in her own midst, that her time may come; and she makes idols within herself to defile herself.　　　Ezek. 24:6, 7
4 "You have become guilty by the blood which you have shed, and have defiled yourself with the idols which you have made. You have caused your days to draw near, and have come to *the end of* your years; therefore I have made you a reproach to the nations, and a mockery to all countries.
5 "*Those* near and *those* far from you will mock you as infamous *and* full of tumult.
6 "Look, the princes of Israel: each one has used his power to shed blood in you.
7 "In you they have made light of father and mother; in your midst they have oppressed the stranger; in you they have mistreated the fatherless and the widow.
8 "You have despised My holy things and ᴿprofaned My Sabbaths.　　　Lev. 19:30
9 "In you are ᴿmen who slander to cause bloodshed; ᴿin you are those who eat on the mountains; in your midst they commit lewdness.　　　Lev. 19:16 · Ezek. 18:6, 11
10 "In you men uncover their fathers' nakedness; in you they violate women who are set apart during their impurity.
11 "One commits abomination with his neighbor's wife; another lewdly defiles his daughter-in-law; and another in you violates his sister, his father's ᴿdaughter.　　　Lev. 18:9
12 "In you they take bribes to shed blood; you take usury and increase; you have made profit from your neighbors by extortion, and have forgotten Me," says the Lord GOD.

13 "Behold, therefore, I beat My fists at the dishonest profit which you have made, and at the bloodshed which has been in your midst.

14 ᴿ"Can your heart endure, or can your hands remain strong, in the days when I shall deal with you? ᴿI, the LORD, have spoken, and will do *it*.   Ezek. 21:7 · Ezek. 17:24

15 "I will scatter you among the nations, disperse you throughout the countries, and remove your filthiness completely from you.

16 "You shall defile yourself in the sight of the nations; then ᴿyou shall know that I *am* the LORD." ' "   Ps. 9:16

Israel in the Furnace

17 The word of the LORD came to me, saying,

18 "Son of man, the house of Israel has become dross to Me; they *are* all bronze, tin, iron, and lead, in the midst of a ᴿfurnace; they have become dross from silver.   Prov. 17:3

19 "Therefore thus says the Lord GOD: 'Because you have all become dross, therefore behold, I will gather you into the midst of Jerusalem.

20 *As men* gather silver, bronze, iron, lead, and tin into the midst of a furnace, to blow fire on it, to ᴿmelt *it*; so I will gather *you* in My anger and in My fury, and I will leave *you there* and melt you.   Is. 1:25

21 'Yes, I will gather you and blow on you with the fire of My wrath, and you shall be melted in its midst.

22 'As silver is melted in the midst of a furnace, so shall you be melted in its midst; then you shall know that I, the LORD, have ᴿpoured out My fury on you.' "   Ezek. 20:8, 33

Israel's Wicked Leaders

23 And the word of the LORD came to me, saying,

24 "Son of man, say to her: 'You *are* a land that is ᴿnot *cleansed or rained on in the day of indignation.'   Ezek. 24:13

25 "The conspiracy of her *prophets in her midst is like a roaring lion tearing the prey; they have devoured ᵀpeople; they have taken treasure and precious things; they have made many widows in her midst.   Lit. *souls*

26 "Her priests have violated My law and profaned My holy things; they have not ᴿdistinguished between the holy and unholy, nor have they made known *the difference* between the unclean and the clean; and they have hidden their eyes from My Sabbaths, so that I am profaned among them.   Lev. 10:10

27 "Her princes in her midst *are* like wolves tearing the prey, to shed blood, to destroy people, and to get dishonest gain.

28 "Her prophets plastered them with untempered *mortar*, seeing false visions, and divining lies for them, saying, 'Thus says the Lord GOD,' when the LORD had not spoken.

29 "The people of the land have used oppressions, committed robbery, and mistreated the poor and needy; and they wrongfully ᴿoppress the stranger.   Ex. 23:9

30 "So I sought for a man among them who would make a wall, and stand in the gap before Me on behalf of the land, that I should not destroy it; but I found no one.

31 "Therefore I have ᴿpoured out My indignation on them; I have consumed them with the fire of My wrath; and I have recompensed ᴿtheir deeds on their own heads," says the Lord GOD.   Ezek. 22:22 · Ezek. 9:10

Two Harlot Sisters

23 The word of the LORD came again to me, saying:

2 "Son of man, there were two women,
The daughters of one mother.
3 ᴿThey committed harlotry in Egypt,
They committed harlotry in ᴿtheir
    youth;   Lev. 17:7 · Ezek. 16:22
Their breasts were there embraced,
Their virgin bosom was there pressed.
4 Their names: *Oholah the elder and
    *Oholibah her sister;
ᴿThey were Mine,   Ezek. 16:8, 20
And they bore sons and daughters.
As for their names,
Samaria *is* Oholah, and Jerusalem *is*
    Oholibah.

The Older Sister, Samaria

5 "Oholah played the harlot even though
    she was Mine;
And she lusted for her lovers, the
    neighboring ᴿAssyrians,   Hos. 5:13; 8:9, 10
6 *Who were* clothed in purple,
Captains and rulers,
All of them desirable young men,
Horsemen riding on horses.
7 Thus she committed her harlotry with
    them,
All of them choice men of Assyria;
And with all for whom she lusted,
With all their idols, she defiled herself.
8 She has never given up her harlotry
    brought ᴿfrom Egypt,
For in her youth they had lain with her,
Pressed her virgin bosom,
And poured out their immorality upon
    her.   Ezek. 23:3, 19

9 "Therefore I have delivered her
Into the hand of her lovers,

22:24 So with MT, Syr., Vg.; LXX *showered upon*
22:25 So with MT, Vg.; LXX *princes*; Tg. *scribes*

23:4 Lit. *Her Own Tabernacle* • Lit. *My Tabernacle Is in Her*

Into the hand of the ᴿAssyrians,
For whom she lusted.   2 Kin. 17:3

10 They uncovered her nakedness,
Took away her sons and daughters,
And slew her with the sword;
She became a byword among women,
For they had executed judgment on
her.

The Younger Sister, Jerusalem

11 "Now although her sister Oholibah saw
this, ᴿshe became more corrupt in her lust
than she, and in her harlotry more corrupt
than her sister's harlotry.   Jer. 3:8–11

12 "She lusted for the neighboring
ᴿAssyrians,   2 Kin. 16:27, 28
ᴿCaptains and rulers,   Ezek. 23:6, 23
Clothed most gorgeously,
Horsemen riding on horses,
All of them desirable young men.

13 Then I saw that she was defiled;
Both *took* the same way.

14 But she increased her harlotry;
She looked at men portrayed on the
wall,
Images of ᴿChaldeans portrayed in
vermilion,   Ezek. 8:10; 16:29

15 Girded with belts around their waists,
Flowing turbans on their heads,
All of them looking like captains,
In the manner of the Babylonians of
Chaldea,
The land of their nativity.

16 ᴿAs soon as her eyes saw them,
She lusted for them
And sent ᴿmessengers to them in
Chaldea.   2 Kin. 24:1 · Is. 57:9

17 "Then the ᵀBabylonians came to her,
into the bed of love,   Lit. *sons of Babel*
And they defiled her with their
immorality;
So she was defiled by them, and
alienated herself from them.

18 She revealed her harlotry and
uncovered her nakedness.
Then ᴿI ᴿalienated Myself from her,
As I had alienated Myself from her
sister.   Jer. 6:8 · Jer. 12:8

19 "Yet she multiplied her harlotry
In calling to remembrance the days of
her youth,
ᴿWhen she had played the harlot in the
land of Egypt.   Ezek. 23:2

20 For she lusted for her ᵀparamours,
Whose flesh *is like* the flesh of donkeys,
And whose issue *is like* the issue of
horses.   Illicit lovers

21 Thus you called to remembrance the
lewdness of your youth,
When the ᴿEgyptians pressed your
bosom   Ezek. 16:26
Because of your youthful breasts.

Judgment on Jerusalem

22 "Therefore, Oholibah, thus says the Lord
Gᴏᴅ:

ᴿBehold, I will stir up your lovers against
you,
From whom you have alienated
yourself,
And I will bring them against you from
every side: Ezek. 16:37–41; 23:28

23 The Babylonians,
All the Chaldeans,
ᴿPekod, Shoa, Koa,   Jer. 50:21
ᴿAll the Assyrians with them,
All of them desirable young men,
Governors and rulers,   Ezek. 23:12
Captains and men of renown,
All of them riding on horses.

24 And they shall come against you
With chariots, wagons, and war-horses,
With a horde of people.
They shall array against you
Buckler, shield, and helmet all around.

'I will delegate judgment to them,
And they shall judge you according to
their judgments.

25 I will set My ᴿjealousy against you,
And they shall deal furiously with you;
They shall remove your nose and your
ears,
And your remnant shall fall by the
sword;
They shall take your sons and your
daughters,
And your remnant shall be devoured by
fire.   Ex. 34:14

26 They shall also strip you of your clothes
And take away your beautiful jewelry.

27 'Thus ᴿI will make you cease your
lewdness and your ᴿharlotry
Brought from the land of Egypt,
So that you will not lift your eyes to
them,   Ezek. 16:41; 22:15 · Ezek. 23:3, 19
Nor remember Egypt anymore.'

28 "For thus says the Lord Gᴏᴅ: 'Surely I
will deliver you into the hand of ᴿthose you
hate, into the hand *of those* ᴿfrom whom you
alienated yourself.   Ezek. 16:37–41 · Ezek. 23:17

29 ᴿThey will deal hatefully with you, take
away all you have worked for, and ᴿleave you
naked and bare. The nakedness of your harlotry shall be uncovered, both your lewdness
and your harlotry.   Deut. 28:48 · Ezek. 16:39

30 'I will do these *things* to you because
you have ᴿgone as a harlot after the Gentiles,
because you have become defiled by their
idols.   Ezek. 6:9

31 'You have walked in the way of your
sister; therefore I will put her ᴿcup in your
hand.'   Jer. 7:14, 15; 25:15

32 "Thus says the Lord GOD:

'You shall drink of your sister's cup,
The deep and wide one;
^RYou shall be laughed to scorn
And held in derision;
It contains much.   Ezek. 22:4, 5
33 You will be filled with drunkenness and
    sorrow,
The cup of horror and desolation,
The cup of your sister Samaria.
34 You shall ^Rdrink and drain it,   Is. 51:17
You shall break its ^Tshards,
And tear at your own breasts;
For I have spoken,'
Says the Lord GOD.   Earthenware fragments

35 "Therefore thus says the Lord GOD:

'Because you ^Rhave forgotten Me and
    cast Me behind your back,   Jer. 3:21
Therefore you shall bear the *penalty*
Of your lewdness and your harlotry.' "

Both Sisters Judged

36 The LORD also said to me: "Son of man,
will you judge Oholah and Oholibah? Then
^Rdeclare to them their abominations.   Is. 58:1
37 "For they have committed adultery, and
^Rblood *is* on their hands. They have com-
mitted adultery with their idols, and even
sacrificed their sons ^Rwhom they bore to Me,
passing them through *the fire*, to devour
them.   Ezek. 16:38 · Ezek. 16:20, 21, 36, 45; 20:26, 31
38 "Moreover they have done this to Me:
They have defiled My sanctuary on the same
day and ^Rprofaned My Sabbaths.   Ezek. 22:8
39 "For after they had slain their children
for their idols, on the same day they came
into My sanctuary to profane it; and indeed
^Rthus they have done in the midst of My
house.   2 Kin. 21:2–8
40 "Furthermore you sent for men to come
from afar, to whom a messenger *was* sent;
and there they came. And you washed yourself for them, ^Rpainted your eyes, and
adorned yourself with ornaments.   Jer. 4:30
41 "You sat on a stately ^Rcouch, with a
table prepared before it, ^Ron which you had
set My incense and My oil.   Is. 57:7 · Prov. 7:17
42 "The sound of a carefree multitude *was*
with her, and ^TSabeans *were* brought from
the wilderness with men of the common sort,
who put bracelets on their ^Twrists and beautiful crowns on their heads.   Or *drunkards* · Lit. *hands*
43 "Then I said concerning *her who had
grown* old in adulteries, 'Will they commit
harlotry with her now, and she *with them*?'
44 "Yet they went in to her, as men go in to
a woman who plays the harlot; thus they
went in to Oholah and Oholibah, the lewd
women.
45 "But righteous men will ^Rjudge them
after the manner of adulteresses, and after

the manner of women who shed blood, be-
cause they *are* adulteresses, and ^Rblood *is* on
their hands.   Ezek. 16:38 · Ezek. 23:37
46 "For thus says the Lord GOD: ^R'Bring up
an assembly against them, give them up to
trouble and plunder.   Ezek. 16:40
47 'The assembly shall stone them with
stones and execute them with their swords;
they shall slay their sons and their daughters,
and burn their houses with fire.
48 'Thus I will cause lewdness to cease from
the land, ^Rthat all women may be taught not
to practice your lewdness.   Deut. 13:11
49 'They shall repay you for your lewdness,
and you shall ^Rpay for your idolatrous sins.
^RThen you shall know that I *am* the Lord
GOD.' "   Ezek. 23:35 · Ezek. 20:38, 42, 44; 25:5

Symbol of the Cooking Pot

24 Again, in the ninth year, in the tenth
month, on the tenth *day* of the month,
the word of the LORD came to me, saying,
2 "Son of man, write down the name of
the day, this very day—the king of Babylon
started his siege against Jerusalem ^Rthis very
day.   2 Kin. 25:1
3 ^R"And utter a parable to the rebellious
house, and say to them, 'Thus says the Lord
GOD: Ezek. 17:12

^R"Put on a pot, set *it* on,   Jer. 1:13
And also pour water into it.
4 Gather pieces *of meat* in it,
Every good piece,
The thigh and the shoulder.
Fill *it* with choice ^Tcuts;   Lit. *bones*
5 Take the choice of the flock.
Also pile *fuel* bones under it,
Make it boil well,
And let the cuts simmer in it."

6 'Therefore thus says the Lord GOD:

"Woe to ^Rthe bloody city,   Ezek. 22:2, 3, 27
To the pot whose scum *is* in it,
And whose scum is not gone from it!
Bring it out piece by piece,
On which no ^Rlot has fallen.   Nah. 3:10
7 For her blood is in her midst;
She set it on top of a rock;
^RShe did not pour it on the ground,
To cover it with dust.   Lev. 17:13
8 That it may raise up fury and take
    vengeance,
^RI have set her blood on top of a rock,
That it may not be covered."   [Matt. 7:2]

9 'Therefore thus says the Lord GOD:

^R"Woe to the bloody city!
I too will make the pyre great.   Hab. 2:12
10 Heap on the wood,
Kindle the fire;
Cook the meat well,
Mix in the spices,
And let the ^Tcuts be burned up.   Lit. *bones*

11 "Then set the pot empty on the coals,
    That it may become hot and its bronze
      may burn,
    That its filthiness may be melted in it,
    That its scum may be consumed.
12 She has ᵀgrown weary with ᵀlies,
    And her great scum has not gone from
      her.   Or *wearied Me* • Or *toil*
    Let her scum be in the fire!
13 In your ᴿfilthiness *is* lewdness.
    Because I have cleansed you, and you
      were not cleansed,   Ezek. 23:36–48
    You will ᴿnot be cleansed of your
      filthiness anymore,   Jer. 6:28–30
    ᴿTill I have caused My fury to rest upon
      you.   Ezek. 5:13; 8:18; 16:42
14 ᴿI, the LORD, have spoken *it*;   [1 Sam. 15:29]
    ᴿIt shall come to pass, and I will do *it*;
    I will not hold back,   Is. 55:11
    ᴿNor will I spare,   Ezek. 5:11
    Nor will I relent;
    According to your ways
    And according to your deeds
    *They will judge you,"
    Says the Lord GOD.' "

The Prophet's Wife Dies

15 Also the word of the LORD came to me,
saying,
16 "Son of man, behold, I take away from
you the desire of your eyes with one stroke;
yet you shall ᴿneither mourn nor weep, nor
shall your tears run down.   Jer. 16:5
17 "Sigh in silence, make no mourning for
the dead; bind your turban on your head, and
ᴿput your sandals on your feet; ᴿdo not cover
your ᵀlips, and do not eat man's bread *of*
sorrow."   2 Sam. 15:30 • Mic. 3:7 • Lit. *moustache*
18 So I spoke to the people in the morning,
and at evening my wife died; and the next
morning I did as I was commanded.
19 And the people said to me, ᴿ"Will you
not tell us what these *things signify* to us,
that you behave so?"   Ezek. 12:9; 37:18
20 Then I answered them, "The word of the
LORD came to me, saying,
21 'Speak to the house of Israel, "Thus says
the Lord GOD: 'Behold, I will profane My
sanctuary, ᵀyour arrogant boast, the desire of
your eyes, the delight of your soul; and your
sons and daughters whom you left behind
shall fall by the sword.   the pride of your strength
22 'And you shall do as I have done; ᴿyou
shall not cover *your* ᵀlips nor eat man's bread
of sorrow.   Jer. 16:6, 7 • Lit. *moustache*
23 'Your turbans shall be on your heads and
your sandals on your feet; you shall neither
mourn nor weep, but you shall pine away in
your iniquities and mourn with one another.
24 'Thus ᴿEzekiel is a sign to you; according
to all that he has done you shall do; ᴿand

when this comes, ᴿyou shall know that I *am*
the Lord GOD.' "   Is. 20:3 • Jer. 17:15 • Ezek. 6:7; 25:5
25 'And you, son of man—*will it* not *be* in
the day when I take from them their stronghold, their joy and their glory, the desire of
their eyes, and that on which they set their
minds, their sons and their daughters:
26 'on that day one who escapes will come
to you to let *you* hear *it* with *your* ears;
27 ᴿ'on that day your mouth will be opened
to him who has escaped; you shall speak and
no longer be mute. Thus you will be a sign to
them, and they shall know that I *am* the
LORD.' "   Ezek. 3:26; 33:22

Proclamation Against Ammon

25 The word of the LORD came to me,
saying,
2 "Son of man, set your face against the
Ammonites, and prophesy against them.
3 "Say to the Ammonites, 'Hear the word
of the Lord GOD! Thus says the Lord GOD:
ᴿ"Because you said, 'Aha!' against My sanctuary when it was profaned, and against the
land of Israel when it was desolate, and
against the house of Judah when they went
into captivity,   Ezek. 26:2
4 "indeed, therefore, I will deliver you as a
possession to the men of the East, and they
shall set their encampments among you and
make their dwellings among you; they shall
eat your fruit, and they shall drink your milk.
5 "And I will make Rabbah a stable for
camels and Ammon a resting place for flocks.
Then you shall know that I *am* the LORD."
6 'For thus says the Lord GOD: "Because
you ᴿclapped *your* hands, stamped your feet,
and ᴿrejoiced in heart with all your disdain
for the land of Israel,   Job 27:23 • Ezek. 36:5
7 "indeed, therefore, I will ᴿstretch out My
hand against you, and give you as plunder to
the nations; I will cut you off from the
peoples, and I will cause you to perish from
the countries; I will destroy you, and you
shall know that I *am* the LORD."   Ezek. 35:3

Proclamation Against Moab

8 'Thus says the Lord GOD: "Because
Moab and ᴿSeir say, 'Look! The house of
Judah *is* like all the nations,'   Ezek. 35:2, 5
9 "therefore, behold, I will clear the territory of Moab of cities, of the cities on its
frontier, the glory of the country, Beth Jeshimoth, Baal Meon, and ᴿKirjathaim.   Jer. 48:23
10 ᴿ"To the men of the East I will give it as
a possession, together with the Ammonites,
that the Ammonites ᴿmay not be remem-
bered among the nations.   Ezek. 25:4 • Ezek. 21:32
11 "And I will execute judgments upon
Moab, and they shall know that I *am* the
LORD."

Proclamation Against Edom

12 'Thus says the Lord GOD: R"Because of what Edom did against the house of Judah by taking vengeance, and has greatly offended by avenging itself on them," Obad. 10-14
13 'therefore thus says the Lord GOD: "I will also stretch out My hand against Edom, cut off man and beast from it, and make it desolate from Teman; TDedan shall fall by the sword. Or *even to Dedan they shall fall*
14 R"I will lay My vengeance on Edom by the hand of My people Israel, that they may do in Edom according to My anger and according to My fury; and they shall know My vengeance," says the Lord GOD. Is. 11:14

Proclamation Against Philistia

15 'Thus says the Lord GOD: "Because the Philistines dealt vengefully and took vengeance with Ta spiteful heart, to destroy because of the old hatred," Lit. *spite in soul*
16 'therefore thus says the Lord GOD: "I will stretch out My hand against the Philistines, and I will cut off the Cherethites and destroy the remnant of the seacoast.
17 "I will Rexecute great vengeance on them with furious rebukes; Rand they shall know that I *am* the LORD, when I lay My vengeance upon them." ' " Ezek. 5:15 · Ps. 9:16

Proclamation Against Tyre

26 And it came to pass in the eleventh year, on the first *day* of the month, *that* the word of the LORD came to me, saying,
2 "Son of man, Rbecause Tyre has said against Jerusalem, R'Aha! She is broken who *was* the gateway of the peoples; now she is turned over to me; I shall be filled; she is laid waste.' Jer. 25:22 · Ezek. 25:3
3 'Therefore thus says the Lord GOD: 'Behold, I *am* against you, O Tyre, and will cause many nations to come up against you, as the sea causes its waves to come up.
4 'And they shall destroy the walls of Tyre and break down her towers; I will also scrape her dust from her, and Rmake her like the top of a rock. Ezek. 26:14
5 'It shall be *a place for* spreading nets Rin the midst of the sea, for I have spoken,' says the Lord GOD; 'it shall become plunder for the nations. Ezek. 27:32
6 'Also her daughter *villages* which *are* in the fields shall be slain by the sword. RThen they shall know that I am the LORD.' Ezek. 25:5
7 "For thus says the Lord GOD: 'Behold, I will bring against Tyre from the north *Nebuchadnezzar king of Babylon, king of kings, with horses, with chariots, and with horsemen, and an army with many people.

8 'He will slay with the sword your daughter *villages* in the fields; he will heap up a siege mound against you, build a wall against you, and raise a Tdefense against you. shield
9 'He will direct his battering rams against your walls, and with his axes he will break down your towers.
10 'Because of the abundance of his horses, their dust will cover you; your walls will shake at the noise of the horsemen, the wagons, and the chariots, when he enters your gates, as men enter a city that has been breached.
11 'With the hooves of his Rhorses he will trample all your streets; he will slay your people by the sword, and your strong pillars will fall to the ground. Hab. 1:8
12 'They will plunder your riches and pillage your merchandise; they will break down your walls and destroy your pleasant houses; they will lay your stones, your timber, and your soil in the midst of the water.
13 R'I will put an end to the sound of Ryour songs, and the sound of your harps shall be heard no more. Is. 14:11; 24:8 · Rev. 18:22
14 R'I will make you like the top of a rock; you shall be *a place for* spreading nets, and you shall never be rebuilt, for I the LORD have spoken,' says the Lord GOD. Ezek. 26:4, 5
15 "Thus says the Lord GOD to Tyre: 'Will the coastlands not shake at the sound of your fall, when the wounded cry, when slaughter is made in the midst of you?
16 'Then all the princes of the sea will come down from their thrones, lay aside their robes, and take off their embroidered garments; they will clothe themselves with trembling; they will sit on the ground, tremble *every* moment, and be astonished at you.
17 'And they will take up a Rlamentation for you, and say to you:

"How you have perished,
   O one inhabited by seafaring men,
   O renowned city,
   Who was Rstrong at sea,
   She and her inhabitants,
   Who caused their terror *to be* on all her
      inhabitants! Ezek. 27:2-36 · Is. 23:4
18 Now Rthe coastlands tremble on the day
      of your fall; Ezek. 26:15
   Yes, the coastlands by the sea are
      troubled at your departure." '

19 "For thus says the Lord GOD: 'When I make you a desolate city, like cities that are not inhabited, when I bring the deep upon you, and great waters cover you,
20 'then I will bring you down with those who descend into the Pit, to the people of old, and I will make you dwell in the lowest part of the earth, in places desolate from antiquity, with those who go down to the Pit, so

26:7 Heb. *Nebuchadrezzar,* and so elsewhere in the book

that you may never be inhabited; and I shall establish glory in the land of the living.

21 ᴿI will make you a terror, and you *shall be* no *more*; ᴿthough you are sought for, you will never be found again,' says the Lord GOD." Ezek. 27:36; 28:19 · Ps. 37:10, 36

Lamentation for Tyre

27 The word of the LORD came again to me, saying,

2 "Now, son of man, ᴿtake up a lamentation for Tyre, Ezek. 26:17

3 "and say to Tyre, ᴿYou who ᵀare situated at the entrance of the sea, ᴿmerchant of the peoples on many coastlands, thus says the Lord GOD: Ezek. 26:17; 28:2 · Lit. *sit* or *dwell* · Is. 23:3

"O Tyre, you have said,
ᴿ'I *am* perfect in beauty.' Ezek. 28:12

4 Your borders *are* in the midst of the
    seas.
Your builders have perfected your
    beauty.

5 They ᵀmade all *your* planks of fir trees
    from ᴿSenir;
They took a cedar from Lebanon to
    make you a mast. built · Deut. 3:9

6 *Of* oaks from Bashan they made your
    oars;
The company of Ashurites have inlaid
    your planks
With ivory from the coasts of *Cyprus.

7 Fine embroidered linen from Egypt was
    what you spread for your sail;
Blue and purple from the coasts of
    Elishah was what covered you.

8 "Inhabitants of Sidon and Arvad were
    your oarsmen;
Your wise men, O Tyre, were in you;
They became your pilots.

9 Elders of ᴿGebal and its wise men
Were in you to caulk your seams;
All the ships of the sea
And their oarsmen were in you
To market your merchandise. 1 Kin. 5:18

10 "Those from Persia, ᵀLydia, and *Libya
Were in your army as men of war;
They hung shield and helmet in you;
They gave splendor to you. Heb. *Lud*

11 Men of Arvad with your army *were* on
    your walls *all* around,
And the men of Gammad were in your
    towers;
They hung their shields on your walls
    all around;
They made your beauty perfect.

12 "Tarshish *was* your merchant because of your many luxury goods. They gave you silver, iron, tin, and lead for your goods.

13 "Javan, Tubal, and Meshech *were* your traders. They bartered human lives and vessels of bronze for your merchandise.

14 "Those from the house of ᴿTogarmah traded for your wares with horses, steeds, and mules. Gen. 10:3

15 "The men of ᴿDedan *were* your traders; many isles *were* the market of your hand. They brought you ivory tusks and ebony as payment. Gen. 10:7

16 "Syria *was* your merchant because of the abundance of goods you made. They gave you for your wares emeralds, purple, embroidery, fine linen, corals, and rubies.

17 "Judah and the land of Israel *were* your traders. They traded for your merchandise wheat of ᴿMinnith, millet, honey, oil, and ᴿbalm. Judg. 11:33 · Jer. 8:22

18 "Damascus *was* your merchant because of the abundance of goods you made, because of your many luxury items, with the wine of Helbon and with white wool.

19 "Dan and Javan paid for your wares, *traversing back and forth. Wrought iron, cassia, and cane were among your merchandise.

20 ᴿ"Dedan *was* your merchant in saddlecloths for riding. Gen. 25:3

21 "Arabia and all the princes of ᴿKedar *were* your regular merchants. They traded with you in lambs, rams, and goats. Is. 60:7

22 "The merchants of ᴿSheba and Raamah *were* your merchants. They traded for your wares the choicest spices, all kinds of precious stones, and gold. Gen. 10:7

23 ᴿ"Haran, Canneh, Eden, the merchants of ᴿSheba, Assyria, *and* Chilmad *were* your merchants. 2 Kin. 19:12 · Gen. 25:3

24 "These *were* your merchants in choice items—in purple clothes, in embroidered garments, in chests of multicolored apparel, in sturdy woven cords, which were in your marketplace.

25 "The ᴿships of Tarshish were carriers of
    your merchandise.
You were filled and very glorious ᴿin
    the midst of the seas. Is. 2:16 · Ezek. 27:4

26 Your oarsmen brought you into many
    waters,
But ᴿthe east wind broke you in the
    midst of the seas. Ps. 48:7

27 "Your ᴿriches, wares, and merchandise,
Your mariners and pilots,
Your caulkers and merchandisers,
All your men of war who *are* in you,
And the entire company which *is* in
    your midst,
Will fall into the midst of the seas on
    the day of your ruin. [Prov. 11:4]

27:6 Heb. *Kittim*, western lands, especially Cyprus
27:10 Heb. *Put*

27:19 LXX, Syr. *from Uzal*

28 The common-land will shake at the
   sound of the cry of your pilots.

29 "All ᴿwho handle the oar,
   The mariners,
   All the pilots of the sea
   Will come down from their ships *and*
   stand on the ᵀshore.   Rev. 18:17 · Lit. *land*
30 They will make their voice heard
   because of you;
   They will cry bitterly and ᴿcast dust on
   their heads;   Rev. 18:19
   They ᴿwill roll about in ashes; Jer. 6:26
31 They will ᴿshave themselves completely
   bald because of you,
   Gird themselves with sackcloth,
   And weep for you
   With bitterness of heart *and* bitter
   wailing.   Ezek. 29:18
32 In their wailing for you
   They will ᴿtake up a lamentation,
   And lament for you: Ezek. 26:17
   ᴿ'What *city is* like Tyre, Rev. 18:18
   Destroyed in the midst of the sea?
33 'Whenᴿ your wares went out by sea,
   You satisfied many people;
   You enriched the kings of the earth
   With your many luxury goods and your
   merchandise.   Rev. 18:19
34 But ᴿyou are broken by the seas in the
   depths of the waters;   Ezek. 26:19
   Your merchandise and the entire
   company will fall in your midst.
35 ᴿAll the inhabitants of the isles will be
   astonished at you;   Ezek. 26:15, 16
   Their kings will be greatly afraid,
   And *their* countenance will be troubled.
36 The merchants among the peoples ᴿwill
   hiss at you;   Jer. 18:16
   ᴿYou will become a horror, and *be* no
   ᴿmore forever.' " ' "   Ezek. 26:2 · Ps. 37:10, 36

Proclamation Against the King of Tyre

28 The word of the Lord came to me
      again, saying,
2 "Son of man, say to the prince of Tyre,
'Thus says the Lord God:

"Because your heart *is* ᴿliftedᵀ up,
   And you say, 'I *am* a god,
   I sit *in* the seat of gods,   Jer. 49:16 · Proud
   ᴿIn the midst of the seas,'   Ezek. 27:3, 4
   ᴿYet you *are* a man, and not a god,

Though you set your heart as the heart
   of a god.   Is. 31:3
3 (Behold, ᴿyou *are* wiser than Daniel!
   There is no secret that can be hidden
   from you!   Dan. 1:20; 2:20–23, 28; 5:11, 12
4 With your wisdom and your
   understanding
   You have gained ᴿriches for yourself,
   And gathered gold and silver into your
   treasuries;   Zech. 9:1–3
5 ᴿBy your great wisdom in trade you
   have increased your riches,
   And your heart is lifted up because of
   your riches),"   Ps. 62:10

6 'Therefore thus says the Lord God:

"Because you have set your heart as the
   heart of a god,
7 Behold, therefore, I will bring ᴿstrangers
   against you,   Ezek. 26:7
   ᴿThe most terrible of the nations;
   And they shall draw their swords
   against the beauty of your wisdom,
   And defile your splendor. Ezek. 7:24; 30:11
8 They shall throw you down into the
   ᴿPit,
   And you shall die the death of the slain
   In the midst of the seas. Is. 14:15

9 "Will you still ᴿsay before him who slays
   you,   Ezek. 28:2
   'I *am* a god'?
   But you *shall be* a man, and not a god,
   In the hand of him who slays you.
10 You shall die the death of ᴿthe
   uncircumcised
   By the hand of aliens;
   For I have spoken," says the Lord
   God.' "   Ezek. 31:18; 32:19, 21, 25, 27

Lamentation for the King of Tyre

12-A. Satan: His Origin   ▼

11 Moreover the word of the Lord came to
me, saying,
12 "Son of man, ᴿtake up a lamentation for
the king of Tyre, and say to him, 'Thus says
the Lord God: Ezek. 27:2

"You *were* the seal of perfection,
   Full of wisdom and perfect in beauty.
13 You were in ᴿEden, the garden of God;
   Every precious stone *was* your
   covering: Ezek. 31:8, 9; 36:35

12-A. Satan: His Origin (Ezekiel 28:11–19)—"You were perfect in your ways from the day you were created"
(v. 15). Like everything God creates, Satan was perfect until iniquity was discovered in him. Verses 11–19
give us a glimpse of Satan's past (what he was), his present state (what he is), and his future (what he will
be). In this portion of Scripture, Ezekiel addresses the king of Tyre, who was a self-proclaimed god. By no
stretch of the imagination does the king of Tyre fit the description of this created supernatural person.
   Thus, if we are to understand verses 11–19, it must be interpreted in the same manner as some of the
messianic psalms. Following this method of interpretation, there is only one created supernatural person
who fits this Scripture in Ezekiel 28—that person is Satan.

(Point 12-A continued on next page)

▽

The sardius, topaz, and diamond,
Beryl, onyx, and jasper,
Sapphire, turquoise, and emerald with
   gold.
The workmanship of ^Ryour timbrels and
   pipes   Ezek. 26:13
Was prepared for you on the day you
   were created.

14 "You *were* the anointed ^Rcherub who
   covers;
   I established you;
   You were on ^Rthe holy mountain of
   God;
   You walked back and forth in the midst
   of fiery stones.   Ex. 25:20 • Ezek. 20:40
15 You *were* perfect in your ways from
   the day you were created,
   Till ^Riniquity was found in you.   [Is. 14:12]

16 "By the abundance of your trading
   You became filled with violence within,
   And you sinned;
   Therefore I cast you as a profane thing
   Out of the mountain of God;
   And I destroyed you, ^RO covering
   cherub,   Ezek. 28:14
   From the midst of the fiery stones.

17 "Your ^Rheart was ^Tlifted up because of
   your beauty;   Ezek. 28:2, 5 • Proud

You corrupted your wisdom for the
   sake of your splendor;
I cast you to the ground,
I laid you before kings,
That they might gaze at you.

18 "You defiled your sanctuaries
   By the multitude of your iniquities,
   By the iniquity of your trading;
   Therefore I brought fire from your
   midst;
   It devoured you,
   And I turned you to ashes upon the
   earth
   In the sight of all who saw you.
19 All who knew you among the peoples
   are astonished at you;
   ^RYou have become a horror,   Ezek. 26:21
   And *shall be* no more forever.' "

▲

Proclamation Against Sidon

20 Then the word of the LORD came to me,
saying,
21 "Son of man, ^Rset your face toward
Sidon, and prophesy against her,   Ezek. 6:2
22 "and say, 'Thus says the Lord GOD:

   ^R"Behold, I *am* against you, O Sidon;
   I will be glorified in your midst;
   And ^Rthey shall know that I *am* the
   LORD,   Ex. 14:4, 17 • Ps. 9:16

(Point 12-A continued from previous page)
   (1) He was God's masterpiece. There are three things said about Satan in his origin. He was

   (a) "The seal of perfection" (v. 12). He was the sum of God's creation, one-of-a-kind, without peer
in the angelic realm.
   (b) "Full of wisdom" (v. 12). The Scriptures indicate that God endowed Satan with supernatural
wisdom, but not complete wisdom. His wisdom is seen in the fall of Adam and Eve. Satan chose to tempt
Eve, perhaps sensing that Adam would not be tricked. Paul suggests that "Adam was not deceived" (1 Tim.
2:14, page 1219). Satan knew that Eve could be deceived and that Adam would fall because of his great love
for her. So Satan, full of cunning, used the serpent to tempt Eve, and Eve to tempt Adam—who would eat
the forbidden fruit in disobedience to God, rather than be eternally separated from the one he loved (Gen.
3:1–24, page 5).
   (c) "Perfect in beauty" (v. 12). Satan was the most beautiful creature that God had ever created. His
beauty filled him with pride (v. 17). Beauty can be a blessing or a curse. Satan had physical beauty,
supernatural wisdom, and the seal of perfection, but he wanted more. He fell when God found him full of
iniquity (v. 15).

   (2) He was God's "anointed cherub who covers" (v. 14). A cherub is an angel. One of his duties was to
cover the throne of God (Ex. 25:20, page 85). Satan was not just a cherub, he was "the anointed cherub who
covers" (v. 14). God anoints for three offices: prophet, priest, and king. Satan could have been anointed for
one or all three offices. He is the only known angel the Lord anointed for any office.
   (3) He was in "Eden, the garden of God" (v. 13). A careful reading tells us that this Eden was not the
same Garden of Eden in Genesis 3. When Satan was in the Eden of Genesis 3, he was already a fallen angel.
But, in this Eden, he was the sum of perfection, full of wisdom, and perfect in beauty. And "every precious
stone was your covering" (v. 13). This covering is similar to the breastplate of the high priest (vv. 15–20, page
87). So perhaps Satan had indeed been anointed as high priest of Eden. The Scriptures also tell us that this
covering was prepared for him "on the day you were created" (v. 13). This means that Satan had access to
the very presence of God. In the Old Testament we find that only the high priest had this privilege (Lev.
16:2–4, 17, page 123). So in the first Eden, Satan was without sin—he was perfect. He fell when iniquity was
found in him. God said, "I cast you as a profane thing out of the mountain of God." However, he still has
access to the throne of God (Job 1:6, page 479). "And I destroyed you" (v. 16). God's future judgments are
so certain that they are often written in past tense (Rev. 20:10, page 1313).

   See Isaiah 14:12–15, page 657, for **Point 12-B: Satan: His Fall.**

When I execute judgments in her and
am ᴿhallowed in her.   Ezek. 28:25

23 ᴿFor I will send pestilence upon her,
And blood in her streets;
The wounded shall be judged in her
midst
By the sword against her on every side;
Then they shall know that I *am* the
Lᴏʀᴅ.   Ezek. 38:22

24 "And there shall no longer be a pricking
brier or a painful thorn for the house of Israel
from among all *who are* around them, who
ᴿdespise them. Then they shall know that I
am the Lord Gᴏᴅ."   Ezek. 16:57; 25:6, 7

Israel's Future Blessing

25 'Thus says the Lord Gᴏᴅ: "When I have
gathered the house of Israel from the peoples
among whom they are scattered, and am
ᴿhallowed in them in the sight of the Gentiles,
then they will dwell in their own land which I
gave to My servant Jacob.   Ezek. 28:22

26 "And they will ᴿdwell ᵀsafely there, build
houses, and ᴿplant vineyards; yes, they will
dwell securely, when I execute judgments on
all those around them who despise them.
Then they shall know that I *am* the Lᴏʀᴅ
their God." ' "   Jer. 23:6 • *securely* • Jer. 31:5

Proclamation Against Egypt

29 In the tenth year, in the tenth *month*,
on the twelfth *day* of the month, the
word of the Lᴏʀᴅ came to me, saying,

2 "Son of man, ᴿset your face against
Pharaoh king of Egypt, and prophesy against
him, and ᴿagainst all Egypt.   Ezek. 28:21 • Is. 19:1

3 "Speak, and say, 'Thus says the Lord
Gᴏᴅ:

ᴿ"Behold, I *am* against you,   Jer. 44:30
O Pharaoh king of Egypt,
O great ᴿmonster who lies in the midst
of his rivers,   Ps. 74:13, 14
Who has said, 'My ᵀRiver *is* my own;
I have made *it* for myself.'   The Nile

4 But ᴿI will put hooks in your jaws,
And cause the fish of your rivers to
stick to your scales;
I will bring you up out of the midst of
your rivers,
And all the fish in your rivers will stick
to your scales.   Ezek. 38:4

5 I will leave you in the wilderness,
You and all the fish of your rivers;
You shall fall on the open field;
ᴿYou shall not be picked up or
*gathered.
I have given you as food   Jer. 8:2; 16:4; 25:33
To the beasts of the field
And to the birds of the heavens.

29:5 So with MT, LXX, Vg.; some Heb. mss., Tg. *buried*
29:7 So with MT, Vg.; LXX, [Syr.] *hand*

6 "Then all the inhabitants of Egypt
Shall know that I *am* the Lᴏʀᴅ,
Because they have been a ᴿstaff of reed
to the house of Israel.   Is. 36:6

7 ᴿWhen they took hold of you with the
hand,
You broke and tore all their *shoulders;
When they leaned on you,
You broke and made all their backs
quiver."   Ezek. 17:17

8 'Therefore thus says the Lord Gᴏᴅ:
"Surely I will bring ᴿa sword upon you and
cut off from you man and beast.   Ezek. 14:17

9 "And the land of Egypt shall become
ᴿdesolate and waste; then they will know that
I *am* the Lᴏʀᴅ, because he said, 'The River *is*
mine, and I have made *it*.'   Ezek. 30:7, 8

10 "Indeed, therefore, I *am* against you and
against your rivers, ᴿand I will make the land
of Egypt utterly waste and desolate, ᴿfrom
ᵀMigdol *to* Syene, as far as the border of
Ethiopia.   Ezek. 30:12 • Ezek. 30:6 • Or *the tower*

11 ᴿ"Neither foot of man shall pass through
it nor foot of beast pass through it, and it
shall be uninhabited forty years.   Ezek. 32:13

12 "I will make the land of Egypt desolate
in the midst of the countries *that are* desolate; and among the cities *that are* laid waste,
her cities shall be desolate forty years; and I
will scatter the Egyptians among the nations
and disperse them throughout the countries."

13 'Yet, thus says the Lord Gᴏᴅ: "At the
ᴿend of forty years I will gather the Egyptians
from the peoples among whom they were
scattered.   Jer. 46:26

14 "I will bring back the captives of Egypt
and cause them to return to the land of
Pathros, to the land of their origin, and there
they shall be a ᴿlowly kingdom.   Ezek. 17:6, 14

15 "It shall be the lowliest of kingdoms; it
shall never again exalt itself above the nations, for I will diminish them so that they
will not rule over the nations anymore.

16 "No longer shall it be ᴿthe confidence of
the house of Israel, but will remind them of
their iniquity when they turned to follow
them. Then they shall know that I *am* the
Lord Gᴏᴅ." ' "   Is. 30:2, 3; 36:4, 6

Babylonia Will Plunder Egypt

17 And it came to pass in the twenty-
seventh year, in the first *month*, on the first
day of the month, that the word of the Lᴏʀᴅ
came to me, saying,

18 "Son of man, Nebuchadnezzar king of
Babylon caused his army to labor strenuously
against Tyre; every head *was* made bald, and
every shoulder rubbed raw; yet neither he
nor his army received wages from Tyre, for
the labor which they expended on it.

19 "Therefore thus says the Lord Gᴏᴅ:
'Surely I will give the land of Egypt to ᴿNebuchadnezzar king of Babylon; he shall take

away her wealth, carry off her spoil, and remove her pillage; and that will be the wages for his army.   Jer. 43:10-13

20 'I have given him the land of Egypt for his labor, because they ᴿworked for Me,' says the Lord GOD.   Jer. 25:9

21 'In that day I will cause the horn of the house of Israel to spring forth, and I will open your mouth to speak in their midst. Then they shall know that I am the LORD.' "

Egypt and Her Allies Will Fall

30 The word of the LORD came to me again, saying,

2 "Son of man, prophesy and say, 'Thus says the Lord GOD:

ᴿ"Wail, 'Woe to the day!'   Is. 13:6; 15:2
3 For ᴿthe day is near,
Even the day of the LORD is near;
It will be a day of clouds, the time of the Gentiles.   Joel 2:1
4 The sword shall come upon Egypt,
And great anguish shall be in ᵀEthiopia,
When the slain fall in Egypt,   Heb. Cush
And they take away her wealth,
And her foundations are broken down.

5 "Ethiopia, ᵀLibya, ᵀLydia, ᴿall the mingled people, Chub, and the men of the lands who are allied, shall fall with them by the sword."   Heb. Put · Heb. Lud · Jer. 25:20, 24
6 'Thus says the LORD:

"Those who uphold Egypt shall fall,
And the pride of her power shall come down.
ᴿFrom ᵀMigdol to Syene
Those within her shall fall by the sword,"
Says the Lord GOD.   Ezek. 29:10 · Or the tower

7 "Theyᴿ shall be desolate in the midst of the desolate countries,   Ezek. 29:12
And her cities shall be in the midst of the cities that are laid waste.
8 Then they will know that I am the LORD,
When I have set a fire in Egypt
And all her helpers are destroyed.
9 On that day ᴿmessengers shall go forth from Me in ships   Is. 18:1, 2
To make the ᵀcareless Ethiopians afraid,
And great anguish shall come upon them,   Or secure
As on the day of Egypt;
For indeed it is coming!"

10 'Thus says the Lord GOD:

ᴿ"I will also make a multitude of Egypt to cease
By the hand of Nebuchadnezzar king of Babylon.   Ezek. 29:19
11 He and his people with him, ᴿthe most terrible of the nations,   Ezek. 28:7; 31:12

Shall be brought to destroy the land;
They shall draw their swords against Egypt,
And fill the land with the slain.
12 ᴿI will make the rivers dry,   Is. 19:5, 6
And ᴿsell the land into the hand of the wicked;   Is. 19:4
I will make the land waste, and all that is in it,
By the hand of aliens.
I, the LORD, have spoken."

13 'Thus says the Lord GOD:

"I will also ᴿdestroy the idols,   Is. 19:1
And cause the images to cease from ᵀNoph;   Ancient Memphis
ᴿThere shall no longer be princes from the land of Egypt;   Zech. 10:11
I will put fear in the land of Egypt.
14 I will make ᴿPathros desolate,   Ezek. 29:14
Set fire to ᴿZoan,   Ps. 78:12, 43
And execute judgments in *No.
15 I will pour My fury on ᵀSin, the strength of Egypt;   Ancient Pelusium
ᴿI will cut off the multitude of No,   Jer. 46:25
16 And ᴿset a fire in Egypt;   Ezek. 30:8
Sin shall have great pain,
No shall be split open,
And Noph shall be in distress daily.
17 The young men of *Aven and Pi Beseth shall fall by the sword,
And these cities shall go into captivity.
18 ᴿAt ᵀTehaphnehes the day shall also be *darkened,
When I break the yokes of Egypt there.
And her arrogant strength shall cease in her;
As for her, a cloud shall cover her,
And her daughters shall go into captivity.   Jer. 2:16 · Tahpanhes, Jer. 43:7
19 Thus I will ᴿexecute judgments on Egypt,
Then they shall know that I am the LORD." '   [Ps. 9:16]

Proclamation Against Pharaoh

20 And it came to pass in the eleventh year, in the first month, on the seventh day of the month, that the word of the LORD came to me, saying,
21 "Son of man, I have ᴿbroken the arm of Pharaoh king of Egypt; and see, ᴿit has not been bandaged for healing, nor a ᵀsplint put on to bind it, to make it strong enough to hold a sword.   Jer. 48:25 · Jer. 46:11 · Lit. bandage
22 "Therefore thus says the Lord GOD: 'Surely I am against Pharaoh king of Egypt,

30:14 Ancient Thebes
30:17 Ancient On, Heliopolis
30:18 So with many Heb. mss., Bg., LXX, [Syr.], Tg., Vg.; MT refrained

and will ᴿbreak his arms, both the strong one and the one that was broken; and I will make the sword fall out of his hand.   Ps. 37:17

23 ᴿ'I will scatter the Egyptians among the nations, and disperse them throughout the countries.   Ezek. 29:12; 30:17, 18, 26

24 'I will strengthen the arms of the king of Babylon and put My sword in his hand; but I will break Pharaoh's arms, and he will groan before him with the groanings of a mortally wounded *man.*

25 'Thus I will strengthen the arms of the king of Babylon, but the arms of Pharaoh shall fall down; ᴿthey shall know that I *am* the Lᴏʀᴅ, when I put My sword into the hand of the king of Babylon and he stretches it out against the land of Egypt.   Ps. 9:16

26 ᴿ'I will scatter the Egyptians among the nations and disperse them throughout the countries. Then they shall know that I *am* the Lᴏʀᴅ.' "   Ezek. 29:12

Egypt Cut Down Like a Great Tree

31 Now it came to pass in the ᴿeleventh year, in the third *month,* on the first *day* of the month, *that* the word of the Lᴏʀᴅ came to me, saying,   Ezek. 30:20; 32:1

2 "Son of man, say to Pharaoh king of Egypt and to his multitude:

'Whom are you like in your greatness?
3 ᴿIndeed Assyria *was* a cedar in Lebanon,
With fine branches that shaded the forest,
And of high stature;
And its top was among the thick boughs.   Dan. 4:10, 20-23
4 ᴿThe waters made it grow;
Underground waters gave it height,
With their rivers running around the place where it was planted,
And sent out ᵀrivulets to all the trees of the field.   Jer. 51:36 • Or *channels*
5 'Therefore ᴿits height was exalted above all the trees of the field;
Its boughs were multiplied,
And its branches became long because of the abundance of water,
As it sent them out.   Dan. 4:11
6 All the ᴿbirds of the heavens made their nests in its boughs;   Dan. 4:12, 21
Under its branches all the beasts of the field brought forth their young;
And in its shadow all great nations ᵀmade their home.   Lit. *dwelt*
7 'Thus it was beautiful in greatness and in the length of its branches,
Because its roots reached to abundant waters.
8 The cedars in the ᴿgarden of God could not hide it;   Gen. 2:8, 9; 13:10
The fir trees were not like its boughs,

And the ᵀchestnut trees were not like its branches;   Or *plane,* Heb. *armon*
No tree in the garden of God was like it in beauty,
9 I made it beautiful with a multitude of branches,
So that all the trees of Eden envied it,
That *were* in the garden of God.'

10 "Therefore thus says the Lord Gᴏᴅ: 'Because you have increased in height, and it set its top among the thick boughs, and ᴿits heart was lifted up in its height,   Dan. 5:20

11 'therefore I will deliver it into the hand of the ᴿmighty one of the nations, and he shall surely deal with it; I have driven it out for its wickedness.   Ezek. 30:10

12 'And aliens, the most terrible of the nations, have cut it down and left it; its branches have fallen ᴿon the mountains and in all the valleys; its boughs lie ᴿbroken by all the rivers of the land; and all the peoples of the earth have gone from under its shadow and left it.   Ezek. 32:5; 35:8 • Ezek. 30:24, 25

13 'On ᴿits ruin will remain all the birds of the heavens,
And all the beasts of the field will come to its branches—   Is. 18:6

14 'So that no trees by the waters may ever again exalt themselves for their height, nor set their tops among the thick boughs, that no tree which drinks water may ever be high enough to reach up to them.

'For ᴿthey have all been delivered to death,
ᴿTo the depths of the earth,
Among the children of men who go down to the Pit.'   Ps. 82:7 • Ezek. 32:18

15 "Thus says the Lord Gᴏᴅ: 'In the day when it went down to ᵀhell, I caused mourning. I covered the deep because of it. I restrained its rivers, and the great waters were held back. I caused Lebanon to ᵀmourn for it, and all the trees of the field wilted because of it.   Or *Sheol* • Lit. *be darkened*

16 'I made the nations shake at the sound of its fall, when I cast it down to ᵀhell together with those who descend into the Pit; and all the trees of Eden, the choice and best of Lebanon, all that drink water, were comforted in the depths of the earth.   Or *Sheol*

17 'They also went down to hell with it, with those *slain* by the sword; and *those who were* its *strong* arm ᴿdwelt in its shadows among the nations.   Lam. 4:20

18 'To which of the trees in Eden will you then be likened in glory and greatness? Yet you shall be brought down with the trees of Eden to the depths of the earth; you shall lie in the midst of the uncircumcised, with *those* slain by the sword. This *is* Pharaoh and all his multitude,' says the Lord Gᴏᴅ."

Lamentation for Pharaoh and Egypt

32 And it came to pass in the twelfth year, in the ᴿtwelfth *month*, on the first *day* of the month, *that* the word of the LORD came to me, saying,   Ezek. 31:1; 33:21

2 "Son of man, ᴿtake up a lamentation for Pharaoh king of Egypt, and say to him:

ᴿ'You are like a young lion among the
   nations,   Ezek. 27:2 · Ezek. 19:2-6
And you *are* like a monster in the seas,
ᴿBursting forth in your rivers,   Jer. 46:7, 8
Troubling the waters with your feet,
And ᴿfouling their rivers.'   Ezek. 34:18

3 "Thus says the Lord GOD:

'I will therefore spread My net over you
   with a company of many people,
And they will draw you up in My net.
4 Then I will leave you on the land;
I will cast you out on the open fields,
ᴿAnd cause to ᵀsettle on you all the birds
   of the heavens,   Is. 18:6 · Lit. *sit* or *dwell*
And with you I will fill the beasts of the
   whole earth.
5 I will lay your flesh on the mountains,
And fill the valleys with your carcass.

6 'I will also water the land with the flow
   of your blood,
Even to the mountains;
And the riverbeds will be full of you.
7 When *I* put out your light,
ᴿI will cover the heavens, and make its
   stars dark;   Rev. 6:12, 13; 8:12
I will cover the sun with a cloud,
And the moon shall not give her light.
8 All the ᵀbright lights of the heavens I
   will make dark over you,
And bring darkness upon your land,'
Says the Lord GOD.   Or *shining*

9 'I will also trouble the hearts of many peoples, when I bring your destruction among the nations, into the countries which you have not known. 10 'Yes, I will make many peoples astonished at you, and their kings shall be horribly afraid of you when I brandish My sword before them; and ᴿthey shall tremble *every* moment, every man for his own life, in the day of your fall.'   Ezek. 26:16
11 ᴿ"For thus says the Lord GOD: 'The sword of the king of Babylon shall come upon you.   Jer. 46:26
12 'By the swords of the mighty warriors, all of them the most terrible of the nations, I will cause your multitude to fall.

'They shall plunder the pomp of Egypt,
And all its multitude shall be destroyed.
13 Also I will destroy all its animals
From beside its great waters;
ᴿThe foot of man shall muddy them no
   more,

Nor shall the hooves of animals muddy
   them.   Ezek. 29:11
14 Then I will make their waters ᵀclear,
And make their rivers run like oil,'
Says the Lord GOD.   Lit. *sink*; settle, grow clear

15 'When I make the land of Egypt
   desolate,
And the country is destitute of all that
   once filled it,
When I strike all who dwell in it,
ᴿThen they shall know that I *am* the
   LORD.   Ps. 9:16

16 'This *is* the ᴿlamentation
With which they shall lament her;
The daughters of the nations shall
   lament her;
They shall lament for her, for Egypt,
And for all her multitude,'
Says the Lord GOD."   Ezek. 26:17

Egypt and Others Consigned to the Pit

17 It came to pass also in the twelfth year, on the fifteenth *day* of the month, that the word of the LORD came to me, saying:

18 "Son of man, wail over the multitude of
   Egypt,
And ᴿcast them down to the depths of
   the earth,   Ezek. 26:20; 31:14
Her and the daughters of the famous
   nations,
With those who go down to the Pit:
19 'Whom ᴿdo you surpass in beauty?
ᴿGo down, be placed with the
   uncircumcised.'   Ezek. 31:2, 18 · Ezek. 28:10

20 "They shall fall in the midst of *those*
   slain by the sword;
She is delivered to the sword,
Drawing her and all her multitudes.
21 ᴿThe strong among the mighty
Shall speak to him out of the midst of
   hell   Is. 1:31; 14:9, 10
With those who help him:
'They have ᴿgone down,   Ezek. 32:19, 25
They lie with the uncircumcised, slain
   by the sword.'

22 "Assyria *is* there, and all her company,
With their graves all around her,
All of them slain, fallen by the sword.
23 ᴿHer graves are set in the recesses of the
   Pit,
And her company is all around her
   grave,
All of them slain, fallen by the sword,
Who ᴿcaused terror in the land of the
   living.   Is. 14:15 · Ezek. 32:24-27, 32

24 "There *is* ᴿElam and all her multitude,
All around her grave,   Jer. 25:25; 49:34-39
All of them slain, fallen by the sword,
Who have gone down uncircumcised to
   the lower parts of the earth,

[R]Who caused their terror in the land of
   the living;   Ezek. 32:23
Now they bear their shame with those
   who go down to the Pit.
25 They have set her [R]bed in the midst of
   the slain,   Ps. 139:8
With all her multitude,
With her graves all around it,
All of them uncircumcised, slain by the
   sword;
Though their terror was caused
In the land of the living,
Yet they bear their shame
With those who go down to the Pit;
It was put in the midst of the slain.

26 "There are [R]Meshech and Tubal and all
   their multitudes,
With all their graves around it,
All of them [R]uncircumcised, slain by the
   sword,
Though they caused their terror in the
   land of the living.   Gen. 10:2 · Ezek. 32:19
27 [R]They do not lie with the mighty
Who are fallen of the uncircumcised,
Who have gone down to hell with their
   weapons of war;
They have laid their swords under their
   heads,
But their iniquities will be on their
   bones,
Because of the terror of the mighty in
   the land of the living.   Is. 14:18, 19
28 Yes, you shall be broken in the midst of
   the uncircumcised,
And lie with those slain by the sword.

29 "There is [R]Edom,   Ezek. 25:12-14
Her kings and all her princes,
Who despite their might
Are laid beside those slain by the
   sword;
They shall lie with the uncircumcised,
And with those who go down to the
   Pit.
30 [R]There are the princes of the north,
All of them, and all the [R]Sidonians,
Who have gone down with the slain
In shame at the terror which they
   caused by their might;
They lie uncircumcised with those slain
   by the sword,   Jer. 1:15; 25:26 · Ezek. 28:21-23
And bear their shame with those who
   go down to the Pit.

31 "Pharaoh will see them
And be [R]comforted over all his
   multitude,
Pharaoh and all his army,
Slain by the sword,"
Says the Lord GOD.   Ezek. 14:22; 31:16

32 "For I have caused My terror in the land
   of the living;

And he shall be placed in the midst of
   the uncircumcised
With those slain by the sword,
Pharaoh and all his multitude,"
Says the Lord GOD.

The Watchman and His Message

33 Again the word of the LORD came to
me, saying,
2 "Son of man, speak to the children of
your people, and say to them: 'When I bring
the sword upon a land, and the people of the
land take a man from their territory and
make him their [R]watchman,   2 Sam. 18:24, 25
3 'when he sees the sword coming upon
the land, if he blows the trumpet and warns
the people,
4 'then whoever hears the sound of the
trumpet and does [R]not take warning, if the
sword comes and takes him away, [R]his blood
shall be on his own head.   Zech. 1:4 · [Acts 18:6]
5 'He heard the sound of the trumpet, but
did not take warning; his blood shall be upon
himself. But he who takes warning will [T]save
his life.   Or deliver his soul
6 'But if the watchman sees the sword
coming and does not blow the trumpet, and
the people are not warned, and the sword
comes and takes any person from among
them, [R]he is taken away in his iniquity; but
his blood I will require at the watchman's
hand.'   Ezek. 33:8
7 [R]"So you, son of man: I have made you a
watchman for the house of Israel; therefore
you shall hear a word from My mouth and
warn them for Me.   Is. 62:6
8 "When I say to the wicked, 'O wicked
man, you shall surely die!' and you do not
speak to warn the wicked from his way, that
wicked man shall die in his iniquity; but his
blood I will require at your hand.
9 "Nevertheless if you warn the wicked to
turn from his way, and he does not turn from
his way, he shall die in his iniquity; but you
have [T]delivered your soul.   Or saved your life
10 "Therefore you, O son of man, say to the
house of Israel: 'Thus you say, "If our transgressions and our sins lie upon us, and we
[R]pine[T] away in them, [R]how can we then
live?" '   Ezek. 24:23 · Or waste away · Is. 49:14
11 "Say to them: 'As I live,' says the Lord
GOD, 'I have no pleasure in the death of the
wicked, but that the wicked turn from his
way and live. Turn, turn from your evil ways!
For why should you die, O house of Israel?'

The Fairness of God's Judgment

12 "Therefore you, O son of man, say to the
children of your people: 'The [R]righteousness
of the righteous man shall not deliver him in
the day of his transgression; as for the wickedness of the wicked, [R]he shall not fall because of it in the day that he turns from his

wickedness; nor shall the righteous be able to live because of *his righteousness* in the day that he sins.' Ezek. 3:20; 18:24, 26 • [2 Chr. 7:14]

13 "When I say to the righteous *that* he shall surely live, ᴿbut he trusts in his own righteousness and commits iniquity, none of his righteous works shall be remembered; but because of the iniquity that he has committed, he shall die. Ezek. 3:20; 18:24

14 "Again, when I say to the wicked, 'You shall surely die,' if he turns from his sin and does ᵀwhat is lawful and right, *justice*

15 "*if* the wicked restores the pledge, gives back what he has stolen, and walks in the statutes of life without committing iniquity, he shall surely live; he shall not die.

16 ᴿ"None of his sins which he has committed shall be remembered against him; he has done what is lawful and right; he shall surely live. [Is. 1:18; 43:25]

17 "Yet the children of your people say, 'The way of the Lᴏʀᴅ is not ᵀfair.' But it is their way which is not fair! *Or equitable*

18 ᴿ"When the righteous turns from his righteousness and commits iniquity, he shall die because of it. Ezek. 18:26

19 "But when the wicked turns from his wickedness and does what is lawful and right, he shall live because of it.

20 "Yet you say, 'The way of the Lᴏʀᴅ is not fair.' O house of Israel, I will judge every one of you according to his own ways."

The Fall of Jerusalem

21 And it came to pass in the twelfth year of our captivity, in the tenth *month*, on the fifth *day* of the month, *that* one who had escaped from Jerusalem came to me and said, "The city has been ᵀcaptured!" *struck down*

22 Now ᴿthe hand of the Lᴏʀᴅ had been upon me the evening before the man came who had escaped. And He had ᴿopened my mouth; so when he came to me in the morning, my mouth was opened, and I was no longer mute. Ezek. 1:3; 8:1; 37:1 • Ezek. 24:27

The Cause of Judah's Ruin

23 Then the word of the Lᴏʀᴅ came to me, saying:

24 "Son of man, they who inhabit those ruins in the land of Israel are saying, 'Abraham was only one, and he inherited the land. ᴿBut we *are* many; the land has been given to us as a ᴿpossession.' [Matt. 3:9] • Ezek. 11:15

25 "Therefore say to them, 'Thus says the Lord Gᴏᴅ: "You eat *meat* with blood, you ᴿlift up your eyes toward your idols, and ᴿshed blood. Should you then possess the ᴿland? Ezek. 18:6 • Ezek. 22:6, 9 • Deut. 29:28

26 "You rely on your sword, you commit abominations, and you defile one another's wives. Should you then possess the land?"'

27 "Say thus to them, 'Thus says the Lord Gᴏᴅ: "*As* I live, surely ᴿthose who *are* in the ruins shall fall by the sword, and the one who *is* in the open field ᴿI will give to the beasts to be devoured, and those who *are* in the strongholds and ᴿcaves shall die of the pestilence. Ezek. 33:24 • Ezek. 39:4 • 1 Sam. 13:6

28 ᴿ"For I will make the land most desolate, her arrogant strength shall cease, and the mountains of Israel shall be so desolate that no one will pass through. Jer. 44:2, 6, 22

29 "Then they shall know that I *am* the Lᴏʀᴅ, when I have made the land most desolate because of all their abominations which they have committed."'

Hearing and Not Doing

30 "As for you, son of man, the children of your people are talking about you beside the walls and in the doors of the houses; and they ᴿspeak to one another, everyone saying to his brother, 'Please come and hear what the word is that comes from the Lᴏʀᴅ.' Is. 29:13

31 "So they come to you as people do, they sit before you *as* My people, and they ᴿhear your words, but they do not do them; for with their mouth they show much love, *but* their hearts pursue their *own* gain. Is. 58:2

32 "Indeed you *are* to them as a very lovely song of one who has a pleasant voice and can play well on an instrument; for they hear your words, but they do not do them.

33 "And when this comes to pass—surely it will come—then ᴿthey will know that a prophet has been among them." Ezek. 2:5

Irresponsible Shepherds

34 And the word of the Lᴏʀᴅ came to me, saying,

2 "Son of man, prophesy against the shepherds of Israel, prophesy and say to them, 'Thus says the Lord Gᴏᴅ to the shepherds: ᴿ"Woe to the shepherds of Israel who feed themselves! Should not the shepherds feed the flocks? Zech. 11:17

3 "You eat the fat and clothe yourselves with the wool; you ᴿslaughter the fatlings, *but* you do not feed the flock. Ezek. 33:25, 26

4 "The weak you have not strengthened, nor have you healed those who were sick, nor bound up the broken, nor brought back what was driven away, nor ᴿsought what was lost; but with ᴿforce and ᵀcruelty you have ruled them. Luke 15:4 • [1 Pet. 5:3] • *harshness or rigor*

5 ᴿ"So they were ᴿscattered because *there was* no shepherd; ᴿand they became food for all the beasts of the field when they were scattered. Ezek. 33:21 • Matt. 9:36 • Is. 56:9

6 "My sheep ᴿwandered through all the mountains, and on every high hill; yes, My flock was scattered over the whole face of the earth, and no one was seeking or searching *for them*." 1 Pet. 2:25

7 'Therefore, you shepherds, hear the word of the LORD:

8 "*as* I live," says the Lord GOD, "surely because My flock became a prey, and My flock ᴿbecame food for every beast of the field, because *there was* no shepherd, nor did My shepherds search for My flock, ᴿbut the shepherds fed themselves and did not feed My flock"—   Ezek. 34:5, 6 · Ezek. 34:2, 10

9 'therefore, O shepherds, hear the word of the LORD!

10 'Thus says the Lord GOD: "Behold, I *am* against the shepherds, and I will require My flock at their hand; I will cause them to cease feeding the sheep, and the shepherds shall feed themselves no more; for I will ᴿdeliver My flock from their mouths, that they may no longer be food for them."   Ezek. 13:23

God, the True Shepherd

11 'For thus says the Lord GOD: "Indeed I Myself will search for My sheep and seek them out.

12 "As a ᴿshepherd seeks out his flock on the day he is among his scattered sheep, so will I seek out My sheep and deliver them from all the places where they were scattered on ᴿa cloudy and dark day.   Jer. 31:10 · Ezek. 30:3

13 "And ᴿI will bring them out from the peoples and gather them from the countries, and will bring them to their own land; I will feed them on the mountains of Israel, ᵀin the valleys and in all the inhabited places of the country.   Jer. 23:3 · Or *by the streams*

14 ᴿ"I will feed them in good pasture, and their fold shall be on the high mountains of Israel. ᴿThere they shall lie down in a good fold and feed in rich pasture on the mountains of Israel.   [John 10:9] · Jer. 33:12

15 "I will feed My flock, and I will make them lie down," says the Lord GOD.

16 ᴿ"I will seek what was lost and bring back what was driven away, bind up the broken and strengthen what was sick; but I will destroy ᴿthe fat and the strong, and feed them ᴿin judgment."   Mic. 4:6 · Is. 10:16 · Jer. 10:24

17 'And *as for* you, O My flock, thus says the Lord GOD: ᴿ"Behold, I shall judge between sheep and sheep, between rams and goats.   [Matt. 25:32]

18 "*Is it* too little for you to have eaten up the good pasture, that you must tread down with your feet the residue of your pasture— and to have drunk of the clear waters, that you must foul the residue with your feet?

19 "And *as for* My flock, they eat what you have trampled with your feet, and they drink what you have fouled with your feet."

20 'Therefore thus says the Lord GOD to them: ᴿ"Behold, I Myself will judge between the fat and the lean sheep.   Ezek. 34:17

21 "Because you have pushed with side and

shoulder, butted all the weak ones with your horns, and scattered them abroad,

22 "therefore I will save My flock, and they shall no longer be a prey; and I will judge between sheep and sheep.

23 "I will establish one ᴿshepherd over them, and he shall feed them—ᴿMy servant David. He shall feed them and be their shepherd.   [Is. 40:11] · Jer. 30:9

24 "And ᴿI, the LORD, will be their God, and My servant David ᴿa prince among them; I, the LORD, have spoken.   Ex. 29:45 · Ezek. 37:24, 25

25 "I will make a covenant of peace with them, and cause wild beasts to cease from the land; and they ᴿwill dwell safely in the wilderness and sleep in the woods.   Jer. 23:6

26 "I will make them and the places all around ᴿMy hill a blessing; and I will cause showers to come down in their season; there shall be ᴿshowers of blessing.   Is. 56:7 · Ps. 68:9

27 "Then ᴿthe trees of the field shall yield their fruit, and the earth shall yield her increase. They shall be safe in their land; and they shall know that I *am* the LORD, when I have ᴿbroken the bands of their yoke and delivered them from the hand of those who ᴿenslaved them.   Is. 4:2 · Jer. 2:20 · Jer. 25:14

28 "And they shall no longer be a prey for the nations, nor shall beasts of the land devour them; but ᴿthey shall dwell safely, and no one shall make *them* afraid.   Jer. 30:10

29 "I will raise up for them a ᴿgarden of renown, and they shall no longer be consumed with hunger in the land, nor bear the shame of the Gentiles anymore.   [Is. 11:1]

30 "Thus they shall know that ᴿI, the LORD their God, *am* with them, and they, the house of Israel, *are* ᴿMy people," says the Lord GOD.' "   Ezek. 34:24 · Ezek. 14:11; 36:28

31 "You are My ᴿflock, the flock of My pasture; you *are* men, *and* I *am* your God," says the Lord GOD.   Ps. 100:3

Judgment on Mount Seir

35 Moreover the word of the LORD came to me, saying,

2 "Son of man, set your face against Mount Seir and prophesy against it,

3 "and say to it, 'Thus says the Lord GOD:

"Behold, O Mount Seir, I *am* against
    you;
ᴿI will stretch out My hand against you,
    And make you most desolate;   Ezek. 6:14
4 I shall lay your cities waste,
    And you shall be desolate.
Then you shall know that I *am* the
    LORD.

5 "Because you have had an ᵀancient hatred, and have shed *the blood of* the children of Israel by the power of the sword at the time of their calamity, ᴿ*when their iniquity came to an* end,   Or *everlasting* · Ps. 137:7

6 "therefore, *as* I live," says the Lord GOD, "I will prepare you for blood, and blood shall pursue you; since you have not hated ^Tblood, therefore blood shall pursue you.   Or *bloodshed*

7 "Thus I will make Mount Seir most desolate, and cut off from it the ^Rone who leaves and the one who returns.   Judg. 5:6

8 "And I will fill its mountains with the slain; on your hills and in your valleys and in all your ravines those who are slain by the sword shall fall.

9 "I will make you perpetually desolate, and your cities shall be uninhabited; then you shall know that I *am* the LORD.

10 "Because you have said, 'These two nations and these two countries shall be mine, and we will ^Rpossess them,' although the LORD was there,   Ps. 83:4–12

11 "therefore, *as* I live," says the Lord GOD, "I will do ^Raccording to your anger and according to the envy which you showed in your hatred against them; and I will make Myself known among them when I judge you.   [James 2:13]

12 "Then you shall know that I *am* the LORD. I have heard all your ^Rblasphemies which you have spoken against the mountains of Israel, saying, 'They are desolate; they are given to us to consume.'   Is. 52:5

13 "Thus with your mouth you have boasted against Me and multiplied your words against Me; I have heard *them*."

14 'Thus says the Lord GOD: "The whole earth will rejoice when I make you desolate.

15 "As you rejoiced because the inheritance of the house of Israel was desolate, so I will do to you; you shall be desolate, O Mount Seir, as well as all of Edom—all of it! Then they shall know that I *am* the LORD."'

Blessing on Israel

36 "And you, son of man, prophesy to the ^Rmountains of Israel, and say, 'O mountains of Israel, hear the word of the LORD!   Ezek. 6:2, 3

2 'Thus says the Lord GOD: "Because the enemy has said of you, 'Aha! The ancient heights have become our possession,'"'

3 "therefore prophesy, and say, 'Thus says the Lord GOD: "Because they made *you* desolate and swallowed you up on every side, so that you became the possession of the rest of the nations, and you are taken up by the lips of talkers and slandered by the people"—

4 'therefore, O mountains of Israel, hear the word of the Lord GOD! Thus says the Lord GOD to the mountains, the hills, the ^Trivers, the valleys, the desolate wastes, and the cities that have been forsaken, which became plunder and ^Rmockery to the rest of the nations all around—   Or *ravines* · Ps. 79:4

5 'therefore thus says the Lord GOD: ^R"Surely I have spoken in My burning jeal-

ousy against the rest of the nations and against all Edom, who gave My land to themselves as a possession, with whole-hearted joy *and* spiteful minds, in order to plunder its open country." '   Deut. 4:24

6 "Therefore prophesy concerning the land of Israel, and say to the mountains, the hills, the rivers, and the valleys, 'Thus says the Lord GOD: "Behold, I have spoken in My jealousy and My fury, because you have ^Rborne the shame of the nations."   Ps. 74:10

7 'Therefore thus says the Lord GOD: "I have ^Rraised My hand in an oath that surely the nations that *are* around you shall ^Rbear their own shame.   Ezek. 20:5 · Jer. 25:9, 15, 29

8 "But you, O mountains of Israel, you shall shoot forth your branches and yield your fruit to My people Israel, for they are about to come.

9 "For indeed I *am* for you, and I will turn to you, and you shall be tilled and sown.

10 "I will multiply men upon you, all the house of Israel, all of it; and the cities shall be inhabited and ^Rthe ruins rebuilt.   Amos 9:14

11 "I will multiply upon you man and beast; and they shall increase and ^Tbear young; I will make you inhabited as in former times, and do ^Rbetter *for you* than at your beginnings. ^RThen you shall know that I *am* the LORD.   Lit. *be fruitful* · Is. 51:3 · Ezek. 35:9; 37:6, 13

12 "Yes, I will cause men to walk on you, My people Israel; they shall take possession of you, and you shall be their inheritance; no more shall you bereave them *of children*."

13 'Thus says the Lord GOD: "Because they say to you, ^R'You devour men and bereave your nation *of children*,'   Num. 13:32

14 "therefore you shall devour men no more, nor bereave your nation anymore," says the Lord GOD.

15 ^R"Nor will I let you hear the taunts of the nations anymore, nor bear the reproach of the peoples anymore, nor shall you cause your nation to stumble anymore," says the Lord GOD.' "   Ezek. 34:29

The Renewal of Israel

16 Moreover the word of the LORD came to me, saying:

17 "Son of man, when the house of Israel dwelt in their own land, ^Rthey defiled it by their own ways and deeds; to Me their way was like ^Rthe uncleanness of a woman in her customary impurity.   Jer. 2:7 · Lev. 15:19

18 "Therefore I poured out My fury on them ^Rfor the blood they had shed on the land, and for their idols *with which* they had defiled it.   Ezek. 16:36, 38; 23:37

19 "So I scattered them among the nations, and they were dispersed throughout the countries; I judged them ^Raccording to their ways and their deeds.   [Rom. 2:6]

20 "When they came to the nations, wherever they went, they ᴿprofaned My holy name—when they said of them, 'These *are* the people of the LORD, *and* yet they have gone out of His land.'   Rom. 2:24

21 "But I had concern for My holy name, which the house of Israel had profaned among the nations wherever they went.

22 "Therefore say to the house of Israel, 'Thus says the Lord GOD: "I do not do *this* for your sake, O house of Israel, but for My holy name's sake, which you have profaned among the nations wherever you went.

23 "And I will sanctify My great name, which has been profaned among the nations, which you have profaned in their midst; and the nations shall know that I *am* the LORD," says the Lord GOD, "when I am ᴿhallowed in you before their eyes.   Ezek. 20:41; 28:22

24 "For ᴿI will take you from among the nations, gather you out of all countries, and bring you into your own land.   Ezek. 34:13; 37:21

25 ᴿ"Then I will sprinkle clean water on you, and you shall be clean; I will cleanse you ᴿfrom all your filthiness and from all your idols.   Heb. 9:13, 19; 10:22 · Jer. 33:8

26 "I will give you a ᴿnew heart and put a new spirit within you; I will take the heart of stone out of your flesh and give you a heart of flesh.   Ezek. 11:19

27 "I will put My Spirit within you and cause you to walk in My statutes, and you will keep My judgments and do *them.*

28 "Then you shall dwell in the land that I gave to your fathers; ᴿyou shall be My people, and I will be your God.   Jer. 30:22

29 "I will deliver you from all your uncleannesses. I will call for the grain and multiply it, and bring no famine upon you.

30 ᴿ"And I will multiply the fruit of your trees and the increase of your fields, so that you need never again bear the reproach of famine among the nations.   Ezek. 34:27

31 "Then ᴿyou will remember your evil ways and your deeds that *were* not good; and you ᴿwill ᵀloathe yourselves in your own sight, for your iniquities and your abominations.   Ezek. 16:61, 63 · Ezek. 6:9; 20:43 · *despise*

32 ᴿ"Not for your sake do I do *this,*" says the Lord GOD, "let it be known to you. Be ashamed and confounded for your own ways, O house of Israel!"   Deut. 9:5

33 'Thus says the Lord GOD: "On the day that I cleanse you from all your iniquities, I will also enable *you* to dwell in the cities, ᴿand the ruins shall be rebuilt.   Ezek. 36:10

34 "The desolate land shall be tilled instead of lying desolate in the sight of all who pass by.

35 "So they will say, 'This land that was desolate has become like the garden of ᴿEden; and the wasted, desolate, and ruined cities *are now* fortified *and* inhabited.'   Joel 2:3

36 "Then the nations which are left all around you shall know that I, the LORD, have rebuilt the ruined places *and* planted what was desolate. ᴿI, the LORD, have spoken *it,* and I will do *it.*"   Ezek. 17:24; 22:14; 37:14

37 'Thus says the Lord GOD: ᴿ"I will also let the house of Israel inquire of Me to do this for them: I will ᴿincrease their men like a flock.   Ezek. 14:3; 20:3, 31 · Ezek. 36:10

38 "Like a ᵀflock *offered as* holy *sacrifices,* like the flock at Jerusalem on its ᵀfeast days, so shall the ruined cities be filled with flocks of men. Then they shall know that I *am* the LORD." ' "   Lit. *holy flock · appointed feasts*

The Dry Bones Live

37 The hand of the LORD came upon me and brought me out ᴿin the Spirit of the LORD, and set me down in the midst of the valley; and it *was* full of bones.   Ezek. 3:14

2 Then He caused me to pass by them all around, and behold, *there were* very many in the open valley; and indeed *they were* very dry.

3 And He said to me, "Son of man, can these bones live?" So I answered, "O Lord GOD, ᴿYou know."   [1 Sam. 2:6]

4 Again He said to me, "Prophesy to these bones, and say to them, 'O dry bones, hear the word of the LORD!

5 'Thus says the Lord GOD to these bones: "Surely I will ᴿcause breath to enter into you, and you shall live.   Ps. 104:29, 30

6 "I will put sinews on you and bring flesh upon you, cover you with skin and put breath in you; and you shall live. ᴿThen you shall know that I *am* the LORD." ' "   Joel 2:27; 3:17

7 So I prophesied as I was commanded; and as I prophesied, there was a noise, and suddenly a rattling; and the bones came together, bone to bone.

8 Indeed, as I looked, the sinews and the flesh came upon them, and the skin covered them over; but *there was* no breath in them.

9 Also He said to me, "Prophesy to the breath, prophesy, son of man, and say to the breath, 'Thus says the Lord GOD: "Come from the four winds, O breath, and breathe on these slain, that they may live." ' "

10 So I prophesied as He commanded me, ᴿand ᵀbreath came into them, and they lived, and stood upon their feet, an exceedingly great army.   Rev. 11:11 · Breath of life

11 Then He said to me, "Son of man, these bones are the whole house of Israel. They indeed say, ᴿ'Our bones are dry, our hope is lost, and we ourselves are cut off!'   Ps. 141:7

12 "Therefore prophesy and say to them, 'Thus says the Lord GOD: "Behold, ᴿO My people, I will open your graves and cause you to come up from your graves, and ᴿbring you into the land of Israel.   Is. 26:19; 66:14 · Ezek. 36:24

13 "Then you shall know that I *am* the LORD, when I have opened your graves, O My people, and brought you up from your graves.
14 "I ᴿwill put My Spirit in you, and you shall live, and I will place you in your own land. Then you shall know that I, the LORD, have spoken *it* and performed *it*," says the LORD.' "   Ezek. 36:27

One Kingdom, One King

15 Again the word of the LORD came to me, saying,
16 "As for you, son of man, ᴿtake a stick for yourself and write on it: 'For Judah and for the children of Israel, his companions.' Then take another stick and write on it, 'For Joseph, the stick of Ephraim, and *for* all the house of Israel, his companions.'   Num. 17:2, 3
17 "Then ᴿjoin them one to another for yourself into one stick, and they will become one in your hand.   Hos. 1:11
18 "And when the children of your people speak to you, saying, ᴿ'Will you not show us what you *mean* by these?'—   Ezek. 12:9; 24:19
19 ᴿ"say to them, 'Thus says the Lord GOD: "Surely I will take ᴿthe stick of Joseph, which *is* in the hand of Ephraim, and the tribes of Israel, his companions; and I will join them with it, with the stick of Judah, and make them one stick, and they will be one in My hand." '   Zech. 10:6 · Ezek. 37:16, 17
20 "And the sticks on which you write will be in your hand ᴿbefore their eyes.   Ezek. 12:3
21 "Then say to them, 'Thus says the Lord GOD: "Surely ᴿI will take the children of Israel from among the nations, wherever they have gone, and will gather them from every side and bring them into their own land;   Ezek. 36:24
22 "and I will make them one nation in the land, on the mountains of Israel; and ᴿone king shall be king over them all; they shall no longer be two nations, nor shall they ever be divided into two kingdoms again.   Ezek. 34:23
23 "They shall not defile themselves anymore with their idols, nor with their detestable things, nor with any of their transgressions; but I will deliver them from all their dwelling places in which they have sinned, and will cleanse them. Then they shall be My people, and I will be their God.
24 ᴿ"David My servant *shall* be king over them, and they shall all have one shepherd; they shall also walk in My judgments and observe My statutes, and do them.   Is. 11:1
25 "Then they shall dwell in the land that I have given to Jacob My servant, where your fathers dwelt; and they shall dwell there, they, their children, and their children's children, forever; and ᴿMy servant David *shall be* their prince forever.   John 12:34
26 "Moreover I will ᵀmake a covenant of peace with them, and it shall be an ever-

lasting covenant with them; I will establish them and multiply them, and I will set My sanctuary in their midst forevermore.   *cut*
27 ᴿ"My tabernacle also shall be with them; indeed I will be ᴿtheir God, and they shall be My people.   [John 1:14] · Ezek. 11:20
28 "The nations also will know that I, the LORD, ᴿsanctify Israel, when My sanctuary is in their midst forevermore." ' "   Ezek. 20:12

Gog and Allies Attack Israel

38 Now the word of the LORD came to me, saying,
2 "Son of man, set your face against ᴿGog, of the land of ᴿMagog, *the prince of Rosh, ᴿMeshech, and Tubal, and prophesy against him,   Rev. 20:8 · Gen. 10:2 · Ezek. 32:26
3 "and say, 'Thus says the Lord GOD: "Behold, I *am* against you, O Gog, the prince of Rosh, Meshech, and Tubal.
4 "I will turn you around, put hooks into your jaws, and lead you out, with all your army, horses, and horsemen, all splendidly clothed, a great company *with* bucklers and shields, all of them handling swords.
5 "Persia, *Ethiopia, and *Libya are with them, all of them *with* shield and helmet;
6 ᴿ"Gomer and all its troops; the house of Togarmah *from* the far north and all its troops—many people *are* with you.   Gen. 10:2
7 ᴿ"Prepare yourself and be ready, you and all your companies that are gathered about you; and be a guard for them.   Is. 8:9, 10
8 "After many days you will be visited. In the latter years you will come into the land of those brought back from the sword *and* gathered from many people on ᴿthe mountains of Israel, which had long been desolate; they were brought out of the nations, and now all of them dwell safely.   Ezek. 36:1, 4
9 "You will ascend, coming like a storm, covering the land like a cloud, you and all your troops and many peoples with you."
10 'Thus says the Lord GOD: "On that day it shall come to pass *that* thoughts will arise in your mind, and you will make an evil plan:
11 "You will say, 'I will go up against a land of ᴿunwalled villages; I will ᴿgo to a peaceful people, ᴿwho dwell ᵀsafely, all of them dwelling without walls, and having neither bars nor gates'—   Zech. 2:4 · Jer. 49:31 · Ezek. 38:8 · *securely*
12 "to take plunder and to take booty, to stretch out your hand against the waste places *that are again* inhabited, ᴿand against a people gathered from the nations, who have acquired livestock and goods, who dwell in the midst of the land.   Ezek. 38:8
13 "Sheba, ᴿDedan, the merchants ᴿof Tarshish, and all ᴿtheir young lions will say to

---

38:2 Tg., Vg., Aquila *the chief prince of Meshech,* also v. 3
38:5 Heb. *Cush* • Heb. *Put*

you, 'Have you come to take plunder? Have you gathered your army to take booty, to carry away silver and gold, to take away livestock and goods, to take great plunder?' " ' Ezek. 27:15, 20 • Ezek. 27:12 • Ezek. 19:3, 5

14 "Therefore, son of man, prophesy and say to Gog, 'Thus says the Lord GOD: ᴿ"On that day when My people Israel ᴿdwell safely, will you not know *it*? Is. 4:1 • Ezek. 38:8, 11

15 ᴿ"Then you will come from your place out of the far north, you and many peoples with you, all of them riding on horses, a great company and a mighty army. Ezek. 39:2

16 "You will come up against My people Israel like a cloud, to cover the land. It will be in the latter days that I will bring you against My land, so that the nations may ᴿknow Me, when I am ᴿhallowed in you, O Gog, before their eyes." Ezek. 35:11 • Ezek. 28:22

17 Thus says the Lord GOD: "Are *you* he of whom I have spoken in former days by My servants the prophets of Israel, who prophesied for years in those days that I would bring you against them?

Judgment on Gog

18 "And it will come to pass at the same time, when Gog comes against the land of Israel," says the Lord GOD, "*that* My fury will show in My face.

19 "For in My jealousy ᴿ*and* in the fire of My wrath I have spoken: ᴿ'Surely in that day there shall be a great ᵀearthquake in the land of Israel, Ps. 89:46 • Rev. 16:8 • Lit. *shaking*

20 'so that the fish of the sea, the birds of the heavens, the beasts of the field, all creeping things that creep on the earth, and all men who *are* on the face of the earth shall shake at My presence. The mountains shall be thrown down, the steep places shall fall, and every wall shall fall to the ground.'

21 "I will ᴿcall for ᴿa sword against Gog throughout all My mountains," says the Lord GOD. ᴿ"Every man's sword will be against his brother. Ps. 105:16 • Ezek. 14:17 • 1 Sam. 14:20

22 "And I will bring him to judgment with pestilence and bloodshed; I will rain down on him, on his troops, and on the many peoples who *are* with him, flooding rain, great hailstones, fire, and brimstone.

23 "Thus I will magnify Myself and ᴿsanctify Myself, ᴿand I will be known in the eyes of many nations. Then they shall know that I *am* the LORD." ' Ezek. 36:23 • Ezek. 37:28; 38:16

Gog's Armies Destroyed

39 "And you, son of man, prophesy against Gog, and say, 'Thus says the Lord GOD: "Behold, I *am* against you, O Gog, *the chief prince of Rosh, Meshech, and Tubal;

39:1 Tg., Vg., Aquila *the chief prince of Meshech*

2 "and I will ᴿturn you around and lead you on, ᴿbringing you up from the far north, and bring you against the mountains of Israel. Ezek. 38:8 • Ezek. 38:15

3 "Then I will knock the bow out of your left hand, and cause the arrows to fall out of your right hand.

4 "You shall ᵀfall upon the mountains of Israel, you and all your troops and the peoples who *are* with you; ᴿI will give you to birds of prey of every sort and *to* the beasts of the field to be devoured. Be slain • Ezek. 33:27

5 "You shall ᵀfall on the open field; for I have spoken," says the Lord GOD. Be slain

6 "And I will send fire on Magog and on those who live in security in the coastlands. Then they shall know that I *am* the LORD.

7 "So I will make My holy name known in the midst of My people Israel, and I will not let *them* profane My holy name anymore. ᴿThen the nations shall know that I *am* the LORD, the Holy One in Israel. Ezek. 38:16

8 "Surely it is coming, and it shall be done," says the Lord GOD. "This *is* the day ᴿof which I have spoken. Ezek. 38:17

9 "Then those who dwell in the cities of Israel will go out and set on fire and burn the weapons, both the shields and bucklers, the bows and arrows, the ᵀjavelins and spears; and they will make fires with them for seven years. Lit. *hand staffs*

10 "They will not take wood from the field nor cut down *any* from the forests, because they will make fires with the weapons; ᴿand they will plunder those who plundered them, and pillage those who pillaged them," says the Lord GOD. Is. 14:2; 33:1

The Burial of Gog

11 "It will come to pass in that day *that* I will give Gog a burial place there in Israel, the valley of those who pass by east of the sea; and it will obstruct travelers, because there they will bury Gog and all his multitude. Therefore they will call *it* the Valley of ᵀHamon Gog. Lit. *The Multitude of Gog*

12 "For seven months the house of Israel will be burying them, ᴿin order to cleanse the land. Deut. 21:23

13 "Indeed all the people of the land will be burying, and they will gain ᴿrenown for it on the day that ᴿI am glorified," says the Lord GOD. Zeph. 3:19, 20 • Ezek. 28:22

14 "They will set apart men regularly employed, with the help of ᵀa search party, to pass through the land and bury those bodies remaining on the ground, in order ᴿto cleanse it. At the end of seven months they will make a search. Lit. *those who pass through* • Ezek. 39:12

15 "The search party will pass through the land; and when anyone sees a man's bone, he shall set up a marker by it, till the buriers have buried it in the Valley of Hamon Gog.

16 "The name of the city will also be
ᵀHamonah. Thus they shall ᴿcleanse the
land." ʾ   Lit. *Multitude* • Ezek. 39:12

A Triumphant Festival

17 "And as for you, son of man, thus says
the Lord Goᴅ, ᴿ'Speak to every sort of bird
and to every beast of the field: Rev. 19:17, 18

ᴿ"Assemble yourselves and come;   Is. 18:6
Gather together from all sides to My
      ᴿsacrificial meal   Zeph. 1:7
Which I am sacrificing for you,
A great sacrificial meal ᴿon the
      mountains of Israel,   Ezek. 39:4
That you may eat flesh and drink blood.
18 ᴿYou shall eat the flesh of the mighty,
Drink the blood of the princes of the
      earth,   Rev. 19:18
Of rams and lambs,
Of goats and bulls,
All of them fatlings of Bashan.
19 You shall eat fat till you are full,
And drink blood till you are drunk,
At My sacrificial meal
Which I am sacrificing for you.
20 ᴿYou shall be filled at My table
With horses and riders,
ᴿWith mighty men
And with all the men of war," says the
Lord Goᴅ.   Ps. 76:5, 6 • Rev. 19:18

Israel Restored to the Land

21 ᴿ"I will set My glory among the nations;
all the nations shall see My judgment which I
have executed, and ᴿMy hand which I have
laid on them.   Ezek. 36:23; 38:23 • Ex. 7:4
22 ᴿ"So the house of Israel shall know that
I am the Loʀᴅ their God from that day
forward.   Ex. 39:7, 28
23 "The Gentiles shall know that the house
of Israel went into captivity for their iniquity;
because they were unfaithful to Me, therefore ᴿI hid My face from them. I ᴿgave them
into the hand of their enemies, and they all
fell by the sword.   Is. 1:15; 59:2 • Lev. 26:25
24 "According to their uncleanness and
according to their transgressions I have dealt
with them, and hidden My face from them." ʾ
25 "Therefore thus says the Lord Goᴅ:
ᴿ'Now I will bring back the captives of Jacob,
and have mercy on the ᴿwhole house of
Israel; and I will be jealous for My holy
name—   Ezek. 34:13; 36:24 • Hos. 1:11
26 ᴿ'after they have borne their shame, and
all their unfaithfulness in which they were
unfaithful to Me, when they ᴿdwelt safely
in their own land and no one made them
afraid.   Dan. 9:16 • Lev. 26:5, 6
27 'When I have brought them back from
the peoples and gathered them out of their
enemies' lands, and I ᴿam hallowed in them in
the sight of many nations,   Ezek. 36:23, 24; 38:16

28 ᴿ'then they shall know that I am the
Loʀᴅ their God, who sent them into captivity
among the nations, but also brought them
back to their land, and left none of them
ᵀcaptive any longer.   Ezek. 34:30 • Lit. *there*
29 ᴿ'And I will not hide My face from them
anymore; for I shall have ᴿpoured out My
Spirit on the house of Israel,' says the Lord
Goᴅ."   Is. 54:8, 9 • [Joel 2:28]

A New City, a New Temple

40 In the twenty-fifth year of our captivity, at the beginning of the year, on
the tenth day of the month, in the fourteenth
year after the city was ᵀcaptured, on the very
same day the hand of the Loʀᴅ was upon me;
and He took me there.   Lit. *struck*
2 In the visions of God He took me into
the land of Israel and ᴿset me on a very high
mountain; on it toward the south was something like the structure of a city.   Rev. 21:10
3 He took me there, and behold, there was
a man whose appearance was like the appearance of bronze. ᴿHe had a line of flax
ᴿand a measuring rod in his hand, and he
stood in the gateway.   Ezek. 47:3 • Rev. 11:1
4 And the man said to me, "Son of man,
look with your eyes and hear with your ears,
and ᵀfix your mind on everything I show you;
for you were brought here so that I might
show them to you. Declare to the house of
Israel everything you see."   Lit. *set your heart*
5 Now there was ᴿa wall all around the
outside of the *temple. In the man's hand
was a measuring rod six cubits long, each
being a cubit and a handbreadth; and he
measured the width of the wall structure, one
rod; and the height, one rod.   Ezek. 42:20

The Eastern Gateway of the Temple

6 Then he went to the gateway which
faced ᴿeast; and he went up its stairs and
measured the threshold of the gateway,
which was ᵀone rod wide, and the other
threshold was one rod wide.   Ezek. 43:1 • 10.5 ft.
7 Each gate chamber was one rod long
and one rod wide; between the gate chambers
was a space of ᵀfive cubits; and the threshold
of the gateway by the vestibule of the inside
gate was ᵀone rod.   8.75 ft. • 10.5 ft.
8 He also measured the vestibule of the
inside gate, one rod.
9 Then he measured the vestibule of the
gateway, ᵀeight cubits; and the gateposts,
ᵀtwo cubits. The vestibule of the gate was on
the inside.   14 ft. • 42 in.
10 In the eastern gateway were three gate
chambers on one side and three on the other;
the three were all the same size; also the
gateposts were of the same size on this side
and that side.

40:5 Lit. *house*

11 He measured the width of the entrance to the gateway, ^Tten cubits; *and* the length of the gate, ^Tthirteen cubits.   17.5 ft. · 22.75 ft.

12 *There was* a ^Tspace in front of the gate chambers, ^Tone cubit *on this side* and one cubit on that side; the gate chambers *were* ^Tsix cubits on this side and six cubits on that side.   Lit. *border* · 21 in. · 10.5 ft.

13 Then he measured the gateway from the roof of *one* gate chamber to the roof of the other; the width *was* ^Ttwenty-five cubits, as door faces door.   43.75 ft.

14 He measured the gateposts, ^Tsixty cubits high, and the court all around the gateway *extended* to the gatepost.   105 ft.

15 *From* the front of the entrance gate to the front of the vestibule of the inner gate *was* ^Tfifty cubits.   87.5 ft.

16 *There were* ^Rbeveled window *frames* in the gate chambers and in their intervening archways on the inside of the gateway all around, and likewise in the vestibules. *There were* windows all around on the inside. And on each gatepost *were* palm trees.   1 Kin. 6:4

The Outer Court

17 Then he brought me into the outer court; and *there were* chambers and a pavement made all around the court; ^Rthirty chambers faced the pavement.   Ezek. 45:5

18 The pavement was by the side of the gateways, corresponding to the length of the gateways; *this was* the lower pavement.

19 Then he measured the width from the front of the lower gateway to the front of the inner court exterior, ^Tone hundred cubits toward the east and the north.   175 ft.

The Northern Gateway

20 On the outer court was also a gateway facing north, and he measured its length and its width.

21 Its gate chambers, three on this side and three on that side, its gateposts and its archways, had the same measurements as the first gate; its length *was* ^Tfifty cubits and its width ^Ttwenty-five cubits.   87.5 ft. · 43.75 ft.

22 Its windows and those of its archways, and also its palm trees, *had* the same measurements as the gateway facing east; it was ascended by seven steps, and its archway *was* in front of it.

23 A gate of the inner court was opposite the northern gateway, just as the eastern *gateway*; and he measured from gateway to gateway, ^Tone hundred cubits.   175 ft.

The Southern Gateway

24 After that he brought me toward the south, and there a gateway was facing south; and he measured its gateposts and archways according to these same measurements.

25 *There were* windows in it and in its archways all around like those windows; its length *was* ^Tfifty cubits and its width ^Ttwenty-five cubits.   87.5 ft. · 43.75 ft.

26 Seven steps led up to it, and its archway *was* in front of them; and it had palm trees on its gateposts, one on this side and one on that side.

27 *There was* also a gateway on the inner court, facing south; and he measured from gateway to gateway toward the south, ^Tone hundred cubits.   175 ft.

Gateways of the Inner Court

28 Then he brought me to the inner court through the southern gateway; he measured the southern gateway according to these same measurements.

29 Also its gate chambers, its gateposts, and its archways *were* according to these same measurements; *there were* windows in it and in its archways all around; it *was* ^Tfifty cubits long and twenty-five cubits wide.   87.5 ft.

30 *There were* archways all around, twenty-five cubits long and five cubits wide.

31 Its archways faced the outer court, palm trees *were* on its gateposts, and going up to it *were* eight steps.

32 And he brought me into the inner court facing east; he measured the gateway according to these same measurements.

33 Also its gate chambers, its gateposts, and its archways *were* according to these same measurements; and *there were* windows in it and in its archways all around; it *was* fifty cubits long and twenty-five cubits wide.

34 Its archways faced the outer court, and palm trees *were* on its gateposts on this side and on that side; and going up to it *were* eight steps.

35 Then he brought me to the north gateway and measured *it* according to these same measurements—

36 also its gate chambers, its gateposts, and its archways. It had windows all around; its length *was* fifty cubits and its width twenty-five cubits.

37 Its gateposts faced the outer court, palm trees *were* on its gateposts on this side and on that side, and going up to it *were* eight steps.

Where Sacrifices Were Prepared

38 *There was* a chamber and its entrance by the gateposts of the gateway, where they ^Rwashed the burnt offering.   2 Chr. 4:6

39 In the vestibule of the gateway *were* two tables on this side and two tables on that side, on which to slay the burnt offering, ^Rthe sin offering, and the trespass offering.   Lev. 4:2, 3

40 At the outer side of the vestibule, as one goes up to the entrance of the northern gateway, *were* two tables; and on the other

side of the vestibule of the gateway were two tables.

41 Four tables were on this side and four tables on that side, by the side of the gateway, eight tables on which they slaughtered the sacrifices.

42 There were also four tables of hewn stone for the burnt offering, ᵀone cubit and a half long, one cubit and a half wide, and ᵀone cubit high; on these they laid the instruments with which they slaughtered the burnt offering and the sacrifice. 31.5 in. • 21 in.

43 Inside were hooks, a handbreadth wide, fastened all around; and the flesh of the sacrifices was on the tables.

Chambers for Singers and Priests

44 Outside the inner gate were the chambers for ᴿthe singers in the inner court, one facing south at the side of the northern gateway, and the other facing north at the side of the southern gateway. 1 Chr. 6:31, 32

45 Then he said to me, "This chamber which faces south is for ᴿthe priests who have charge of the temple. Lev. 8:35

46 "The chamber which faces north is for the priests ᴿwho have charge of the altar; these are the sons of ᴿZadok, from the sons of Levi, who come near the LORD to minister to Him." Num. 18:5 • 1 Kin. 2:35

Dimensions of the Inner Court and Vestibule

47 And he measured the court, ᵀone hundred cubits long and one hundred cubits wide, foursquare. The altar was in front of the temple. 175 ft.

48 Then he brought me to the ᴿvestibule of the temple and measured the doorposts of the vestibule, ᵀfive cubits on this side and five cubits on that side; and the width of the gateway was ᵀthree cubits on this side and three cubits on that side. 1 Kin. 6:3 • 8.75 ft. • 5.25 ft.

49 ᴿThe length of the vestibule was ᵀtwenty cubits, and the width eleven cubits; and by the steps which led up to it there were ᴿpillars by the doorposts, one on this side and another on that side. 1 Kin. 6:3 • 35 ft. • 1 Kin. 7:15-22

Dimensions of the Sanctuary

41 Then he brought me into the *sanctuary and measured the doorposts, six cubits wide on one side and six cubits wide on the other side—the width of the tabernacle.

2 The width of the entryway was ᵀten cubits, and the side walls of the entrance were five cubits on this side and five cubits on the other side; and he measured its length, forty cubits, and its width, twenty cubits. 17.5 ft.

41:1 Heb. heykal; the main room in the temple, the holy place, Ex. 26:33

3 Also he went inside and measured the doorposts, ᵀtwo cubits; and the entrance, ᵀsix cubits high; and the width of the entrance, ᵀseven cubits. 3.5 ft. • 10.5 ft. • 12.25 ft.

4 ᴿHe measured the length, ᵀtwenty cubits; and the width, twenty cubits, beyond the sanctuary; and he said to me, "This is the Most Holy Place." 1 Kin. 6:20 • 35 ft.

The Side Chambers on the Wall

5 Next, he measured the wall of the ᵀtemple, ᵀsix cubits. The width of each side chamber all around the temple was ᵀfour cubits on every side. Lit. house • 10.5 ft. • 7 ft.

6 ᴿThe side chambers were in three stories, one above the other, thirty chambers in each story; they rested on ᵀledges which were for the side chambers all around, that they might be supported, but ᴿnot fastened to the wall of the temple. 1 Kin. 6:5-10 • Lit. the wall • 1 Kin. 6:6, 10

7 As one went up from story to story, the side chambers ᴿbecame wider all around, because their supporting ledges in the wall of the temple ascended like steps; therefore the width of the structure increased as one went up from the lowest story to the highest by way of the middle one. 1 Kin. 6:8

8 I also saw an elevation all around the temple; it was the foundation of the side chambers, a full rod, that is, six cubits high.

9 The thickness of the outer wall of the side chambers was ᵀfive cubits, and so also the remaining terrace by the place of the side chambers of the ᵀtemple. 8.75 ft. • Lit. house

10 And between it and the wall chambers was a width of ᵀtwenty cubits all around the temple on every side. 35 ft.

11 The doors of the side chambers opened on the terrace, one door toward the north and another toward the south; and the width of the terrace was five cubits all around.

The Building at the Western End

12 The building that faced the separating courtyard at its western end was ᵀseventy cubits wide; the wall of the building was ᵀfive cubits thick all around, and its length ᵀninety cubits. 122.5 ft. • 8.75 ft. • 157.5 ft.

Dimensions and Design of the Temple Area

13 So he measured the temple, ᵀone ᴿhundred cubits long; and the separating courtyard with the building and its walls was one hundred cubits long; 175 ft. • Ezek. 40:47

14 also the width of the eastern face of the temple, including the separating courtyard, was one hundred cubits.

15 He measured the length of the building behind it, facing the separating courtyard, with its galleries on the one side and on the other side, one hundred cubits, as well as the inner temple and the porches of the court,

16 their doorposts and the beveled window frames. And the galleries all around their three stories opposite the threshold were paneled with wood from the ground to the windows—the windows were covered—

17 from the space above the door, even to the inner ᵀroom, as well as outside, and on every wall all around, inside and outside, by measure.   Lit. *house*, here the Most Holy Place

18 And *it was* made with cherubim and palm trees, a palm tree between cherub and cherub. *Each* cherub had two faces,

19 ᴿso that the face of a man *was* toward a palm tree on one side, and the face of a young lion toward a palm tree on the other side; thus *it was* made throughout the temple all around.   Ezek. 1:10; 10:14

20 From the floor to the space above the door, and on the wall of the sanctuary, cherubim and palm trees *were* carved.

21 The ᴿdoorposts of the temple *were* square, *as was* the front of the sanctuary; their appearance was similar.   1 Kin. 6:33

22 ᴿThe altar *was* of wood, three cubits high, and its length ᵀtwo cubits. Its corners, its length, and its sides *were* of wood; and he said to me, "This *is* ᴿthe table that *is* ᴿbefore the LORD."   Ex. 30:1-3 • 3.5 ft. • Ex. 25:23, 30 • Ex. 30:8

23 ᴿThe temple and the sanctuary had two doors.   1 Kin. 6:31-35

24 The doors had two ᴿpanels *apiece*, two folding panels: two *panels* for one door and two panels for the other *door*.   1 Kin. 6:34

25 Cherubim and palm trees *were* carved on the doors of the temple just as they *were* carved on the walls. A wooden canopy *was* on the front of the vestibule outside.

26 *There were* beveled window *frames* and palm trees on one side and on the other, on the sides of the vestibule—also on the side chambers of the temple and on the canopies.

The Chambers for the Priests

42 Then he brought me out into the outer court, by the way toward the north; and he brought me into the chamber which *was* opposite the separating courtyard, and which *was* opposite the building toward the north.

2 Facing the length, *which was* ᵀone hundred cubits (the width *was* ᵀfifty cubits), *was* the north door.   175 ft. • 87.5 ft.

3 Opposite the inner court of ᵀtwenty *cubits*, and opposite the ᴿpavement of the outer court, *was* ᴿgallery against gallery in three *stories*.   35 ft. • Ezek. 40:17 • Ezek. 41:15, 16; 42:5

4 In front of the chambers, toward the inside, *was* a walk ᵀten cubits wide, at a distance of ᵀone cubit; and their doors faced north.   17.5 ft. • 21 in.

5 Now the upper chambers *were* shorter, because the galleries took away *space* from them more than from the lower and middle stories of the building.

6 For they *were* in three *stories* and did not have pillars like the pillars of the courts; therefore *the upper level* was ᵀshortened more than the lower and middle levels from the ground up.   Or *narrowed*

7 And a wall which *was* outside ran parallel to the chambers, at the front of the chambers, toward the outer court; its length *was* ᵀfifty cubits.   87.5 ft.

8 The length of the chambers toward the outer court *was* fifty cubits, whereas that facing the temple *was* one hundred cubits.

9 At the lower chambers *was* the entrance on the east side, as one goes into them from the outer court.

10 Also *there were* chambers in the thickness of the wall of the court toward the east, opposite the separating courtyard and opposite the building.

11 *There was* a walk in front of them also, and their appearance *was* like the chambers which *were* toward the north; they *were* as long and as wide as the others, and all their exits and entrances *were* according to plan.

12 And corresponding to the doors of the chambers that *were* facing south, as one enters them, *there was* a door in front of the walk, the way directly in front of the wall toward the east.

13 Then he said to me, "The north chambers *and* the south chambers, which *are* opposite the separating courtyard, *are* the holy chambers where the priests who approach the LORD ᴿshall eat the most holy offerings. There they shall lay the most holy offerings—ᴿthe grain offering, the sin offering, and the trespass offering—for the place *is* holy.   Lev. 6:16, 26; 24:9 • Lev. 2:3, 10; 6:14, 17, 25

14 ᴿ"When the priests enter them, they shall not go out of the holy *chamber* into the outer court; but there they shall leave their garments in which they minister, for they *are* holy. They shall put on other garments; then they may approach *that* which *is* for the people."   Ezek. 44:19

Outer Dimensions of the Temple

15 Now when he had finished measuring the inner ᵀtemple, he brought me out through the gateway that faces toward the ᴿeast, and measured it all around.   Lit. *house* • Ezek. 40:6; 43:1

16 He measured the east side with the measuring rod, ᵀfive hundred rods by the ᴿmeasuring rod all around.   1 mi. • Ezek. 40:5

17 He measured the north side, ᵀfive hundred rods by the measuring rod all around.   1 mi.

18 He measured the south side, ᵀfive hundred rods by the measuring rod.   1 mi.

19 He came around to the west side *and*

measured ᵀfive hundred rods by the measuring rod.   1 mi.

20 He measured it on the four sides; it had a wall all around, ᴿfive hundred *cubits* long and five hundred wide, to separate the holy areas from the ᵀcommon.   Ezek. 45:2 · Or *profane*

The Temple, the LORD's Dwelling Place

43 Afterward he brought me to the gate, the gate that faces toward the east.

2 And behold, the glory of the God of Israel came from the way of the east. His voice *was* like the sound of many waters; and the earth shone with His glory.

3 *It was* like the appearance of the vision which I saw—like the vision which I saw when *I came to destroy the city. The visions *were* like the vision which I saw by the River Chebar; and I fell on my face.

4 ᴿAnd the glory of the LORD came into the ᵀtemple by way of the gate which faces toward the east.   Ezek. 10:19; 11:23 · Lit. *house*

5 The Spirit lifted me up and brought me into the inner court; and behold, the glory of the LORD filled the ᵀtemple.   Lit. *house*

6 Then I heard *Him* speaking to me from the temple, while a man stood beside me.

7 And He said to me, "Son of man, *this is* the place of My throne and the place of the soles of My feet, ᴿwhere I will dwell in the midst of the children of Israel forever. ᴿNo more shall the house of Israel defile My holy name, they nor their kings, by their harlotry or with ᴿthe carcasses of their kings on their high places.   Joel 3:17 · Ezek. 39:7 · Lev. 26:30

8 ᴿ"When they set their threshold by My threshold, and their doorpost by My doorpost, with a wall between them and Me, they defiled My holy name by the abominations which they committed; therefore I have consumed them in My anger.   Ezek. 8:3

9 "Now let them put their harlotry and the carcasses of their kings far away from Me, and I will dwell in their midst forever.

10 "Son of man, ᴿdescribe the ᵀtemple to the house of Israel, that they may be ashamed of their iniquities; and let them measure the pattern.   Ezek. 40:4 · Lit. *house*

11 "And if they are ashamed of all that they have done, make known to them the design of the ᵀtemple and its arrangement, its exits and its entrances, its entire design and all its ordinances, all its forms and all its laws. Write *it* down in their sight, so that they may keep its whole design and all its ordinances, and ᴿperform them.   Lit. *house* · Ezek. 11:20

12 "This *is* the law of the ᵀtemple: The whole area surrounding ᴿthe mountaintop *is* most holy. Behold, this *is* the law of the temple.   Lit. *house* · Ezek. 40:2

Dimensions of the Altar

13 "These are the measurements of the altar in cubits (the *cubit is* one cubit and a handbreadth): the base one cubit high and one cubit wide, with a rim all around its edge of one span. This *is* the height of the altar:

14 "from the base on the ground to the lower ledge, ᵀtwo cubits; the width of the ledge, ᵀone cubit; from the smaller ledge to the larger ledge, ᵀfour cubits; and the width of the ledge, *one* cubit.   3.5 ft. · 21 in. · 7 ft.

15 "The altar hearth *is* four cubits high, with four ᴿhorns extending upward from the ᵀhearth.   Ex. 27:2 · Heb. *ariel*

16 "The altar hearth *is* twelve cubits long, twelve wide, square at its four corners;

17 "the ledge, fourteen *cubits* long and fourteen wide on its four sides, with a rim of half a cubit around it; its base, one cubit all around; and its steps face toward the east."

Consecrating the Altar

18 And He said to me, "Son of man, thus says the Lord GOD: 'These *are* the ordinances for the altar on the day when it is made, for sacrificing ᴿburnt offerings on it, and for ᴿsprinkling blood on it.   Ex. 40:29 · Lev. 1:5, 11

19 'You shall give a young bull for a sin offering to the priests, the Levites, who are of the seed of Zadok, who approach Me to minister to Me,' says the Lord GOD.

20 'You shall take some of its blood and put *it* on the four horns of the altar, on the four corners of the ledge, and on the rim around it; thus you shall cleanse it and make atonement for it.

21 'Then you shall also take the bull of the sin offering, and burn it in the appointed place of the temple, outside the sanctuary.

22 'On the second day you shall offer a kid of the goats without blemish for a sin offering; and they shall cleanse the altar, as they cleansed *it* with the bull.

23 'When you have finished cleansing *it*, you shall offer a young bull without blemish, and a ram from the flock without blemish.

24 'When you offer them before the LORD, ᴿthe priests shall throw salt on them, and they will offer them up *as* a burnt offering to the LORD.   Lev. 2:13

25 'Every day for ᴿseven days you shall prepare a goat *for* a sin offering; they shall also prepare a young bull and a ram from the flock, both without blemish.   Ex. 29:35

26 'Seven days they shall make atonement for the altar and purify it, and so ᵀconsecrate *it*.   Lit. *fill its hands*

27 'When these days are over it shall be, on the eighth day and thereafter, that the priests shall offer your burnt offerings and your

---

43:3 Some mss., Vg. *He*   43:26 LXX, Syr. *themselves*

peace offerings on the altar; and I will ᴿaccept you,' says the Lord GOD." Ezek. 20:40, 41

The East Gate and the Prince

44 Then He brought me back to the outer gate of the sanctuary ᴿwhich faces toward the east, but it was shut. Ezek. 43:1

2 And the LORD said to me, "This gate shall be shut; it shall not be opened, and no man shall enter by it, ᴿbecause the LORD God of Israel has entered by it; therefore it shall be shut. Ezek. 43:2-4

3 "As for the ᴿprince, because he is the prince, he may sit in it to ᴿeat bread before the LORD; he shall enter by way of the vestibule of the gateway, and go out the same way." Gen. 31:54 · Ezek. 46:2, 8

Those Admitted to the Temple

4 Also He brought me by way of the north gate to the front of the temple; so I looked, and behold, the glory of the LORD filled the house of the LORD; and I fell on my face.

5 And the LORD said to me, "Son of man, mark well, see with your eyes and hear with your ears, all that I say to you concerning all the ordinances of the house of the LORD and all its laws. Mark well who may enter the house and all who go out from the sanctuary.

6 "Now say to the ᴿrebellious, to the house of Israel, 'Thus says the Lord GOD: "O house of Israel, ᴿlet Us have no more of all your abominations. Ezek. 2:5 · 1 Pet. 4:3

7 "When you brought in foreigners, uncircumcised in heart and uncircumcised in flesh, to be in My sanctuary to defile it—My house—and when you offered My food, the fat and the blood, then they broke My covenant because of all your abominations.

8 "And you have not ᴿkept charge of My holy things, but you have set others to keep charge of My sanctuary for you." Lev. 22:2

9 'Thus says the Lord GOD: "No foreigner, uncircumcised in heart or uncircumcised in flesh, shall enter My sanctuary, including any foreigner who is among the children of Israel.

Laws Governing Priests

10 ᴿ"And the Levites who went far from Me, when Israel went astray, who strayed away from Me after their idols, they shall bear their iniquity. 2 Kin. 23:8

11 "Yet they shall be ministers in My sanctuary, as gatekeepers of the house and ministers of the house; ᴿthey shall slay the burnt offering and the sacrifice for the people, and ᴿthey shall stand before them to minister to them. 2 Chr. 29:34; 30:17 · Num. 16:9

12 "Because they ministered to them before their idols and caused the house of Israel to fall into iniquity, therefore I have raised My hand in an oath against them," says the Lord GOD, "that they shall bear their iniquity.

13 ᴿ"And they shall not come near Me to minister to Me as priest, nor come near any of My holy things, nor into the Most Holy Place; but they shall ᴿbear their shame and their abominations which they have committed. 2 Kin. 23:9 · Ezek. 32:30

14 "Nevertheless I will make them ᴿkeep charge of the temple, for all its work, and for all that has to be done in it. Num. 18:4

15 "But the priests, the Levites, ᴿthe sons of Zadok, who kept charge of My sanctuary ᴿwhen the children of Israel went astray from Me, they shall come near Me to minister to Me; and they ᴿshall stand before Me to offer to Me the ᴿfat and the blood," says the Lord GOD. [1 Sam. 2:35] · Ezek. 44:10 · Deut. 10:8 · Ezek. 44:7

16 "They shall enter My sanctuary, and they shall come near My table to minister to Me, and they shall keep My charge.

17 "And it shall be, whenever they enter the gates of the inner court, that they shall put on linen garments; no wool shall come upon them while they minister within the gates of the inner court or within the house.

18 ᴿ"They shall have linen turbans on their heads and linen trousers on their bodies; they shall not clothe themselves with anything that causes sweat. Ex. 28:40; 39:28

19 "When they go out to the outer court, to the outer court to the people, they shall take off their garments in which they have ministered, leave them in the holy chambers, and put on other garments; and in their holy garments they shall not sanctify the people.

20 ᴿ"They shall neither shave their heads, nor let their hair grow ᴿlong; but they shall keep their hair well trimmed. Lev. 21:5 · Num. 6:5

21 ᴿ"No priest shall drink wine when he enters the inner court. Lev. 10:9

22 "They shall not take as wife a ᴿwidow or a divorced woman, but take virgins of the descendants of the house of Israel, or widows of priests. Lev. 21:7, 13, 14

23 "And ᴿthey shall teach My people the difference between the holy and the unholy, and cause them to ᴿdiscern between the unclean and the clean. Mal. 2:6-8 · Lev. 20:25

24 "In controversy they shall stand as judges, and judge it according to My judgments. They shall keep My laws and My statutes in all My appointed meetings, ᴿand they shall hallow My Sabbaths. Ezek. 22:26

25 "They shall not defile themselves by coming near a dead person. Only for father or mother, for son or daughter, for brother or unmarried sister may they defile themselves.

26 ᴿ"After he is cleansed, they shall count seven days for him. Num. 6:10; 19:11, 13-19

27 "And on the day that he goes to the sanctuary to minister in the sanctuary, ᴿhe must offer his sin offering ᴿin the inner court," says the Lord GOD. Lev. 5:3, 6 · Ezek. 44:17

28 "It shall be, in regard to their inheritance, *that* I ᴿ*am* their inheritance. You shall give them no ᴿpossession in Israel, for I *am* their possession.   Num. 18:20 • Ezek. 45:4

29 "They shall eat the grain offering, the sin offering, and the trespass offering; every dedicated thing in Israel shall be theirs.

30 "The ᵀbest of all firstfruits of any kind, and every sacrifice of any kind from all your sacrifices, shall be the priest's; also you ᴿshall give to the priest the first of your ground meal, ᴿto cause a blessing to rest on your house.   Lit. *first* • Neh. 10:37 • [Mal. 3:10]

31 "The priests shall not eat anything, bird or beast, that ᴿdied naturally or was torn *by wild beasts.*   Lev. 22:8

The Holy District

45 "Moreover, when you ᴿdivide the land by lot into inheritance, you shall ᴿset apart a district for the Lᴏʀᴅ, a holy section of the land; its length *shall be* twenty-five thousand *cubits,* and the width ten thousand. It *shall be* holy throughout its territory all around.   Ezek. 47:22 • Ezek. 48:8, 9

2 "Of this there shall be a square plot for the sanctuary, ᴿfive hundred by five hundred *rods,* with fifty cubits around it for an open space.   Ezek. 42:20

3 "So this is the district you shall measure: ᵀtwenty-five thousand *cubits* long and ᵀten thousand wide; ᴿin it shall be the sanctuary, the Most Holy *Place.*   8.3 mi. • 3.3 mi. • Ezek. 48:10

4 "It shall be ᴿa holy *section* of the land, belonging to the priests, the ministers of the sanctuary, who come near to minister to the Lᴏʀᴅ; it shall be a place for their houses and a holy place for the sanctuary.   Ezek. 48:10, 11

5 "*An area* twenty-five thousand *cubits* long and ten thousand wide shall belong to the Levites, the ministers of the temple; they shall have *twenty chambers as a possession.

Properties of the City and the Prince

6 ᴿ"You shall appoint as the property of the city *an area* ᵀfive thousand *cubits* wide and twenty-five thousand long, adjacent to the district of the holy *section;* it shall belong to the whole house of Israel.   Ezek. 48:15 • 1.6 mi.

7 ᴿ"The prince shall have *a section* on one side and the other of the holy district and the city's property; and bordering on the holy district and the city's property, extending westward on the west side and eastward on the east side, the length *shall be* side by side with one of the *tribal* portions, from the west border to the east border.   Ezek. 48:21

8 "The land shall be his possession in Israel; and ᴿMy princes shall no more oppress My people, but they shall give *the rest of* the

land to the house of Israel, according to their tribes."   Ezek. 22:27

Laws Governing the Prince

9 'Thus says the Lord Gᴏᴅ: ᴿ"Enough, O princes of Israel! ᴿRemove violence and plundering, execute justice and righteousness, and stop dispossessing My people," says the Lord Gᴏᴅ.   Ezek. 44:6 • Jer. 22:3

10 "You shall have honest ᴿscales, an honest ephah, and an honest bath.   Lev. 19:36

11 "The ephah and the bath shall be of the same measure, so that the bath contains one-tenth of a homer, and the ephah one-tenth of a homer; their measure shall be according to the ᵀhomer.   6.524 bu. or 60 gal.

12 "The ᴿshekel *shall be* twenty gerahs; twenty shekels, twenty-five shekels, *and* fifteen shekels shall be your mina.   Ex. 30:13

13 "This *is* the offering which you shall offer: you shall give ᵀone-sixth of an ephah from a homer of wheat, and one-sixth of an ephah from a homer of barley.   1.087 bu.

14 "The ordinance concerning oil, the bath of oil, *is* one-tenth of a bath from a kor. A kor *is* a homer or ten baths, for ten baths *are* a homer.

15 "And one lamb shall be given from a flock of two hundred, from the rich pastures of Israel. These shall be for grain offerings, burnt offerings, and peace offerings, to make atonement for them," says the Lord Gᴏᴅ.

16 "All the people of the land shall give this offering for the prince in Israel.

17 "Then it shall be the prince's part *to give* burnt offerings, grain offerings, and drink offerings, at the feasts, the New Moons, the Sabbaths, and at all the appointed seasons of the house of Israel. He shall prepare the sin offering, the grain offering, the burnt offering, and the peace offerings to make atonement for the house of Israel."

Keeping the Feasts

18 'Thus says the Lord Gᴏᴅ: "In the first *month,* on the first *day* of the month, you shall take a young bull without blemish and ᴿcleanse the sanctuary.   Lev. 16:16, 33

19 ᴿ"The priest shall take some of the blood of the sin offering and put *it* on the doorposts of the ᵀtemple, on the four corners of the ledge of the altar, and on the gateposts of the gate of the inner court.   Ezek. 43:20 • Lit. *house*

20 "And so you shall do on the seventh *day* of the month ᴿfor everyone who has sinned unintentionally or in ignorance. Thus you shall make atonement for the temple.   Lev. 4:27

21 ᴿ"In the first *month,* on the fourteenth day of the month, you shall observe the Passover, a feast of seven days; unleavened bread shall be eaten.   Ex. 12:18

22 "And on that day the prince shall pre-

45:5 So with MT, Tg., Vg.; LXX *a possession, cities of dwelling*

pare for himself and for all the people of the land ^{R}a bull *for* a sin offering.   Lev. 4:14

23 "On the ^{R}seven days of the feast he shall prepare a burnt offering to the LORD, seven bulls and seven rams without blemish, daily for seven days, and a kid of the goats daily *for* a sin offering.   Lev. 23:8

24 ^{R}"And he shall prepare a grain offering of ^{T}one ephah for each bull and one ephah for each ram, together with a ^{T}hin of oil for each ephah.   Ezek. 46:5, 7 • .65 bu. • 1 gal.

25 "In the seventh *month*, on the fifteenth day of the month, at the ^{R}feast, he shall do likewise for seven days, according to the sin offering, the burnt offering, the grain offering, and the oil."   Num. 29:12

The Manner of Worship

46 ¹Thus says the Lord GOD: "The gateway of the inner court that faces toward the east shall be shut the six working days; but on the Sabbath it shall be opened, and on the day of the New Moon it shall be opened.

2 ^{R}"The prince shall enter by way of the vestibule of the gateway from the outside, and stand by the gatepost. The priests shall prepare his burnt offering and his peace offerings. He shall worship at the threshold of the gate. Then he shall go out, but the gate shall not be shut until evening.   Ezek. 44:3

3 "Likewise the people of the land shall worship at the entrance to this gateway before the LORD on the Sabbaths and the New Moons.

4 "The burnt offering that ^{R}the prince offers to the LORD on the ^{R}Sabbath day *shall be* six lambs without blemish, and a ram without blemish;   Ezek. 45:17 • Num. 28:9, 10

5 "and the grain offering *shall be one* ephah for a ram, and the grain offering for the lambs, as much as he wants to give, as well as a hin of oil with every ephah.

6 "On the day of the New Moon *it shall be* a young bull without blemish, six lambs, and a ram; they shall be without blemish.

7 "He shall prepare a grain offering of an ^{T}ephah for a bull, an ephah for a ram, as much as he wants to give for the lambs, and a ^{T}hin of oil with every ephah.   .65 bu. • 1 gal.

8 ^{R}"When the prince enters, he shall go in by way of the vestibule of the gateway, and go out the same way.   Ezek. 44:3; 46:2

9 "But when the people of the land come before the LORD on the appointed feast days, whoever enters by way of the north ^{R}gate to worship shall go out by way of the south gate; and whoever enters by way of the south gate shall go out by way of the north gate. He shall not return by way of the gate through which he came, but shall go out through the opposite gate.   Ezek. 48:31, 33

10 "The prince shall then be in their midst.

When they go in, he shall go in; and when they go out, he shall go out.

11 "At the festivals and the appointed feast days ^{R}the grain offering shall be an ^{T}ephah for a bull, an ephah for a ram, as much as he wants to give for the lambs, and a ^{T}hin of oil with every ephah.   Ezek. 46:5, 7 • .65 bu. • 1 gal.

12 "Now when the prince makes a voluntary burnt offering or voluntary peace offering to the LORD, the gate that faces toward the east ^{R}shall then be opened for him; and he shall prepare his burnt offering and his peace offerings as he did on the Sabbath day. Then he shall go out, and after he goes out the gate shall be shut.   Ezek. 44:3; 46:1, 2, 8

13 ^{R}"You shall daily make a burnt offering to the LORD *of* a lamb of the first year without blemish; you shall prepare it ^{T}every morning.   Num. 28:3-5 • Lit. *morning by morning*

14 "And you shall prepare a grain offering with it every morning, a sixth of an ephah, and a third of a hin of oil to moisten the fine flour. This grain offering is a perpetual ordinance, to be made regularly to the LORD.

15 "Thus they shall prepare the lamb, the grain offering, and the oil, *as* a ^{R}regular burnt offering every morning."   Ex. 29:42

The Prince and Inheritance Laws

16 'Thus says the Lord GOD: "If the prince gives a gift *of some* of his inheritance to any of his sons, it shall belong to his sons; it is their possession by inheritance.

17 "But if he gives a gift of some of his inheritance to one of his servants, it shall be his until ^{R}the year of liberty, after which it shall return to the prince. But his inheritance shall belong to his sons; it shall become theirs.   Lev. 25:10

18 "Moreover ^{R}the prince shall not take any of the people's inheritance by evicting them from their property; he shall provide an inheritance for his sons from his own property, so that none of My people may be scattered from his property."'"   Ezek. 45:8

How the Offerings Were Prepared

19 Now he brought me through the entrance, which *was* at the side of the gate, into the holy chambers of the priests which face toward the north; and there a place *was* situated at their extreme western end.

20 And he said to me, "This *is* the place where the priests shall boil the trespass offering and the sin offering, *and* where they shall ^{R}bake the grain offering, so that they do not bring *them* out into the outer court ^{R}to sanctify the people."   Lev. 2:4, 5, 7 • Ezek. 44:19

21 Then he brought me out into the outer court and caused me to pass by the four corners of the court; and in fact, in every corner of the court *there was another* court.

22 In the four corners of the court *were* enclosed courts, forty *cubits* long and thirty wide; all four corners *were* the same size.

23 *There was* a row *of building stones* all around in them, all around the four of them; and ᵀcooking hearths were made under the rows of stones all around.   Lit. *boiling places*

24 And he said to me, "These *are* the kitchens where the ministers of the ᵀtemple shall boil the sacrifices of the people."   Lit. *house*

The Healing Waters and Trees

47 Then he brought me back to the door of the ᵀtemple; and there was ᴿwater, flowing from under the threshold of the temple toward the east, for the front of the temple faced east; the water was flowing from under the right side of the temple, south of the altar.   Lit. *house* • Joel 3:18

2 He brought me out by way of the north gate, and led me around on the outside to the outer gateway that faces east; and there was water, running out on the right side.

3 And when the man went out to the east with the line in his hand, he measured one thousand cubits, and he brought me through the waters; the water *came up to my* ankles.

4 Again he measured ᵀone thousand and brought me through the waters; the water *came up to my* knees. Again he measured one thousand and brought me through; the water *came up to my* waist.   1750 ft.

5 Again he measured one thousand, *and it was* a river that I could not cross; for the water was too deep, water in which one must swim, a river that could not be crossed.

6 He said to me, "Son of man, have you seen *this*?" Then he brought me and returned me to the bank of the river.

7 When I returned, there, along the bank of the river, *were* very many ᴿtrees on one side and the other.   [Rev. 22:2]

8 Then he said to me: "This water flows toward the eastern region, goes down into the valley, and enters the sea. *When it* reaches the sea, *its* waters are healed.

9 "And it shall be *that* every living thing that moves, wherever ᵀthe rivers go, will live. There will be a very great multitude of fish, because these waters go there; for they will be healed, and everything will live wherever the river goes.   Lit. *two rivers*

10 "It shall be *that* fishermen will stand by it from En Gedi to En Eglaim; they will be *places* for spreading their nets. Their fish will be of the same kinds as the fish ᴿof the Great Sea, exceedingly many.   Num. 34:3

11 "But its swamps and marshes will not be healed; they will be given over to salt.

12 "Along the bank of the river, on this side and that, will grow all *kinds of* trees used for food; their leaves will not wither, and their fruit will not fail. They will bear fruit every month, because their water flows from the sanctuary. Their fruit will be for food, and their leaves for ᴿmedicine."   [Rev. 22:2]

Borders of the Land

13 Thus says the Lord GOD: "These *are* the borders by which you shall divide the land as an inheritance among the twelve tribes of Israel. Joseph *shall have two* portions.

14 "You shall inherit it equally with one another; for I raised My hand in an oath to give it to your fathers, and this land shall ᴿfall to you as your inheritance.   Ezek. 48:29

15 "This *shall be* the border of the land on the north: from the Great Sea, *by* the road to Hethlon, as one goes to ᴿZedad,   Num. 34:7, 8

16 "Hamath, ᴿBerothah, Sibraim (which *is* between the border of Damascus and the border of Hamath), to Hazar Hatticon (which *is* on the border of Hauran).   2 Sam. 8:8

17 "Thus the boundary shall be from the Sea to Hazar Enan, the border of Damascus; and as for the north, northward, it is the border of Hamath. *This is* the north side.

18 "On the east side you shall mark out the border from between Hauran and Damascus, and between Gilead and the land of Israel, along the Jordan, and along the eastern side of the sea. *This is* the east side.

19 "The south side, toward the *South, shall be* from Tamar to the waters of Meribah by Kadesh, along the brook to the Great Sea. *This is* the south side, toward the South.

20 "The west side *shall be* the Great Sea, from the *southern* boundary until one comes to a point opposite Hamath. This *is* the west side.

21 "Thus you shall divide this land among yourselves according to the tribes of Israel.

22 "It shall be that you will divide it by lot as an inheritance for yourselves, and for the strangers who dwell among you and who bear children among you. ᴿThey shall be to you as native-born among the children of Israel; they shall have an inheritance with you among the tribes of Israel.   [Col. 3:11]

23 "And it shall be *that* in whatever tribe the stranger dwells, there you shall give *him* his inheritance," says the Lord GOD.

Division of the Land

48 "Now these *are* the names of the tribes: ᴿFrom the northern border along the road to Hethlon at the entrance of Hamath, to Hazar Enan, the border of Damascus northward, in the direction of Hamath, *there shall be* one *section* for Dan from its east to its west side;   Ezek. 47:15

2 "by the border of Dan, from the east side to the west, one *section* for Asher;

47:19 Heb. *Negev*

3 "by the border of Asher, from the east side to the west, one *section for* Naphtali;

4 "by the border of Naphtali, from the east side to the west, one *section for* Manasseh;

5 "by the border of Manasseh, from the east side to the west, one *section for* ᴿEphraim;   Josh. 16:5–10; 17:8–10, 14–18

6 "by the border of Ephraim, from the east side to the west, one *section for* Reuben;

7 "by the border of Reuben, from the east side to the west, one *section for* Judah;

8 "by the border of Judah, from the east side to the west, shall be the district which you shall set apart, twenty-five thousand *cubits* in width, and *in* length the same as one of the *other* portions, from the east side to the west, with the sanctuary in the center.

9 "The district that you shall set apart for the Lᴏʀᴅ *shall be* twenty-five thousand *cubits* in length and ten thousand in width.

10 "To these—to the priests—the holy district shall belong: on the north twenty-five thousand *cubits in length*, on the west ten thousand in width, on the east ten thousand in width, and on the south twenty-five thousand in length. The sanctuary of the Lᴏʀᴅ shall be in the center.

11 ᴿ"*It shall be* for the priests of the sons of Zadok, who are sanctified, who have kept My charge, who did not go astray when the children of Israel went astray, ᴿas the Levites went astray.   Ezek. 40:46; 44:15 • Ezek. 44:10, 12

12 "And *this* district of land that is set apart shall be to them a thing most ᴿholy by the border of the Levites.   Ezek. 45:4

13 "Opposite the border of the priests, the Levites *shall have an area* twenty-five thousand *cubits* in length and ten thousand in width; its entire length *shall be* twenty-five thousand and its width ten thousand.

14 "And they shall not sell or exchange any of it; they may not alienate this best *part* of the land, for *it is* holy to the Lᴏʀᴅ.

15 ᴿ"The five thousand *cubits* in width that remain, along the edge of the twenty-five thousand, shall be ᴿfor general use by the city, for dwellings and common-land; and the city shall be in the center.   Ezek. 45:6 • Ezek. 42:20

16 "These *shall be* its measurements: the north side four thousand five hundred *cubits*, the south side four thousand five hundred, the east side four thousand five hundred, and the west side four thousand five hundred.

17 "The common-land of the city shall be: to the north ᵀtwo hundred and fifty *cubits*, to the south two hundred and fifty, to the east two hundred and fifty, and to the west two hundred and fifty.   437.5 ft.

18 "The rest of the length, alongside the district of the holy *section*, *shall be* ten thousand *cubits* to the east and ten thousand to the west. It shall be adjacent to the district

of the holy *section*, and its produce shall be food for the workers of the city.

19 ᴿ"The workers of the city, from all the tribes of Israel, shall cultivate it.   Ezek. 45:6

20 "The entire district *shall be* twenty-five thousand *cubits* by twenty-five thousand *cubits*, foursquare. You shall set apart the holy district with the property of the city.

21 "The rest *shall belong* to the prince, on one side and on the other of the holy district and of the city's property, next to the twenty-five thousand *cubits* of the *holy* district as far as the eastern border, and westward next to the twenty-five thousand as far as the western border, adjacent to the *tribal* portions; *it shall belong* to the prince. It shall be the holy district, ᴿand the sanctuary of the ᵀtemple *shall be* in the center.   Ezek. 48:8, 10 • Lit. *house*

22 "Moreover, apart from the possession of the Levites and the possession of the city *which are* in the midst of what *belongs* to the prince, *the area* between the border of Judah and the border of ᴿBenjamin shall belong to the prince.   Josh. 18:21–28

23 "As for the rest of the tribes, from the east side to the west, Benjamin *shall have* one *section*;

24 "by the border of Benjamin, from the east side to the west, ᴿSimeon *shall have* one *section*;   Josh. 19:1–9

25 "by the border of Simeon, from the east side to the west, ᴿIssachar *shall have* one *section*;   Josh. 19:17–23

26 "by the border of Issachar, from the east side to the west, ᴿZebulun *shall have* one *section*;   Josh. 19:10–16

27 "by the border of Zebulun, from the east side to the west, Gad *shall have* one *section*;

28 "by the border of Gad, on the south side, toward the ᵀSouth, the border shall be from Tamar *to* the waters of Meribah *by* Kadesh, along the brook to the Great Sea.   Heb. *Negev*

29 ᴿ"This *is* the land which you shall divide by lot as an inheritance among the tribes of Israel, and these *are* their portions," says the Lord Gᴏᴅ.   Ezek. 47:14, 21, 22

The Gates of the City and Its Name

30 "These *are* the exits of the city. On the north side, measuring ᵀfour thousand five hundred *cubits*   1.5 mi.

31 ᴿ"(the gates of the city *shall be* named after the tribes of Israel), the three gates northward: one gate for Reuben, one gate for Judah, and one gate for Levi;   [Rev. 21:10–14]

32 "on the east side, ᵀfour thousand five hundred *cubits*, three gates: one gate for Joseph, one gate for Benjamin, and one gate for Dan;   1.5 mi.

33 "on the south side, measuring ᵀfour thousand five hundred *cubits*, three gates: one gate for Simeon, one gate for Issachar, and one gate for Zebulun;   1.5 mi.

34 "on the west side, ᵀfour thousand five hundred *cubits* with their three gates: one gate for Gad, one gate for Asher, and one gate for Naphtali.   1.5 mi.

35 "All the way around *shall be* eighteen thousand cubits; ᴿand the name of the city from *that* day *shall be:* ᵀTHE LORD *IS* THERE."   Joel 3:21 • Heb. *YHWH Shammah*

THE BOOK OF
Daniel

The book of Daniel is the most astounding of all the Old Testament prophets. The personal life of Daniel is hard to rival with its extremes of danger and advancement, and the prophecies of Daniel are the best summaries to be found in the Bible of God's plan for human history. Although twenty-six centuries separate Daniel from us today, we are bombarded with the cruelty and turmoil of wars, threatened wars, political transitions, and ruthless despots. All of this is illustrated during Daniel's life and foretold in his prophetic writings. As a teen-age exile from Jerusalem in 605 B.C., Daniel must have experienced a ruptured family, personal suffering, humiliation, and despair. Yet his faith, prayer life, national leadership, and prophetic insight are honored and no incident of sin or weakness is recorded.

Many Christians pay minimal attention to Gentile nations, focusing their attention instead on God's covenant people Israel. However, the Scriptures include reference to the historical tides of Gentiles which periodically overflowed into Israel, whether for temporary association, alliance, or total conquest. In the book of Daniel these nations are noted historically and then become the pattern for future instances of wickedness, covetousness, and blasphemy toward the God of Israel.

AUTHORSHIP. The book of Daniel is the last of the four Major Prophets of the Old Testament (the other three being Isaiah, Jeremiah, and Ezekiel). In the Hebrew Bible, however, Daniel is not found in the second section of the biblical canon (the Prophets) but in the third section (the Writings). The canon of the Prophets was closed about 200 B.C., and some modern scholars argue that this indicates Daniel was written later, during the Maccabean period. These scholars relate the visions of "Daniel" to the persecution of the Jews under Antiochus IV Epiphanes, a Seleucid (Greek) ruler who reigned from about 175 B.C. to about 163 B.C.

According to this view, the book of Daniel was penned by an anonymous writer (or writers) who used the respected figure of Daniel (Ezek. 14:14, 20; 28:3) to lend authority, credence, and persuasive power to their composition. Their purpose was to support the faith of the Jews during the terrible persecutions then raging under Antiochus Epiphanes, and to encourage them to remain courageous and steadfast even in the face of martyrdom. Because the book does not mention the cleansing of the temple, which took place under Judas Maccabeus in December, 165 B.C., these scholars suggest that the book was written sometime between 168 and 165 B.C. This theory has found widespread support.

As plausible and convincing as the theory may appear, however, it has one fatal flaw. The basic reason why some scholars deny the genuineness of Daniel's authorship is that they have rejected the possibility of predictive prophecy. Denying that an omniscient God could have revealed *future* events to Daniel or any other prophet, they claim that all "prophecy" is actually written *after* the historical events have occurred.

Conservative scholars reject such rationalistic skepticism about the biblical text and believe that the author of the book of Daniel was indeed the prophet Daniel who lived during the time of Nebuchadnezzar, Belshazzar, Cyrus, and Darius. By the revelation of God Daniel was able to see events that were to transpire hundreds of years in the future, to envision the fall of empires that had not yet arisen on the world scene. It would indeed have been impossible for Daniel to pen such a chronicle of future events on his own; but, as our Lord Jesus Christ said, "The things which are impossible with men are possible with God" (Luke 18:27).

KEY VERSES: 2:20-22, 44—"Daniel answered and said: 'Blessed be the name of God forever and ever, for wisdom and might are His. And He changes the times and the seasons; He removes kings and raises up kings; He gives wisdom to the wise and knowledge to those who have understanding. He reveals deep and secret things; He knows what is in the darkness, and light dwells with Him.' . . . 'And in the days of these kings the God of heaven will set up a kingdom which shall never be destroyed; and the kingdom shall not be left to other people; it shall break in pieces and consume all these kingdoms, and it shall stand forever.' "

The principal idea of the book of Daniel is the ultimate triumph of the kingdom of God. The book contains prophecies of the nations of the world and of Israel's future in relation to them in the sovereign plan of God. Throughout world history a succession of empires rise, have their day of glory and power, and then fall. When their allotted time span is fulfilled, they are overthrown. The wicked rulers and nations that shake their fist at the Almighty wind up on the ash heap of history; those who abide in righteousness and faithfulness to the Lord, even though they are

presently persecuted and even martyred, will receive their ultimate reward: "And many of those who sleep in the dust of the earth shall awake, some to everlasting life, some to shame and everlasting contempt" (12:2). Nowhere in the Old Testament is the Christian doctrine of resurrection more clearly enunciated than in this verse.

HOW DANIEL FITS TOGETHER. After a lengthy historical introduction describing the education of Daniel and his friends Shadrach, Meshach, and Abed-Nego (ch. 1), the book of Daniel falls into two clearly distinct parts: (1) events and prophecies concerning the nations of earth—their character, relations, succession, and destiny (chs. 2—6) and (2) a collection of visions describing the Hebrew nation, its relation to gentile dominion, and its future in the plan of God (7—12).

The first part of the book contains five sections: (a) Nebuchadnezzar's dream of a great image: a prophecy of "the times of the Gentiles" (Luke 21:24), when Israel will be ruled by gentile powers (2:1-49); (b) Nebuchadnezzar's trial of the confessors' faith—the image of gold and the deliverance from the fiery furnace: a lesson in steadfast faith (3:1-30); (c) Nebuchadnez-zar's vision of a tree whose height reached to the heavens, and his affliction and humiliation: a lesson in humility (4:1-37); (d) Belshazzar's drunken feast and Daniel's interpretation of the handwriting on the wall: a lesson in sin and its punishment (5:1-31); and (e) Darius the Mede in the role of unwilling religious persecutor, and the plot against Daniel and his deliverance in the lions' den: a lesson in faith, prayer, and courage in the face of persecution (6:1-28).

The second part of the book, a collection of visions seen by Daniel, contains four visions: (a) a vision of four beasts, the Ancient of Days, and the Son of Man: the conflict of Christ with Antichrist (7:1-28); (b) a vision of a ram, a goat, and a little horn: Israel in conflict with Antiochus Epiphanes, the Old Testament foreshadowing of the future Antichrist (8:1-27); (c) a vision of the seventy weeks and Daniel's prayer for his people: Israel's future in the plan of God (9:1-27); and (d) a final vision of Israel through the centuries, and the consummation in the hands of enemies and in the hands of God: a prophecy of the end time (10:1—12:13).

Daniel's prophecies are first panoramic (e.g., chs. 2 and 7), and then more specific. Chapter 9 contains probably the most definitive Old Testament prophecy of the time of our Lord's first advent, the period between the sixty-ninth and seventieth "week" which allows for the present church age, the duration of the Great Tribulation, and the menace of the Antichrist. Chapters 11-12 give us further insight into the culmination of human rebellion against God, and the blessed promise of resurrection for those who are loyal to Christ in the midst of world apostasy and the conflagration called Armageddon.

The book of Daniel will not be clear to everyone. The casual reader will simply skim the surface and benefit little. The spiritually indifferent reader will conclude with frightening details and problem passages which precipitate arguments. The key to understanding is to begin with Daniel's prayer of 9:1-19. It may be the most overlooked prayer of penitence in the Bible. It creates the proper view of the relations between God and His backslidden people. Daniel identifies with Israel's wickedness, confesses it, and pleads with God for His response in forgiveness for His own glory. God answered Daniel's prayer by giving him revelation and insight.

Let the spirit of this prayer enable the reader to claim the help of the Holy Spirit in understanding this astounding revelation of the future.

—J.R.D.

Daniel and His Friends Obey God
▼ 50-A. History, Prophecy, and Biography

I N the third year of the reign of Jehoiakim king of Judah, Nebuchadnezzar king of Babylon came to Jerusalem and besieged it.

2 And the Lord gave Jehoiakim king of Judah into his hand, with some of the articles of ᵀthe house of God, which he carried into the land of Shinar to the house of his god;

and he brought the articles into the treasure ▽ house of his god.   The temple

3 Then the king instructed Ashpenaz, the master of his eunuchs, to bring ᴿsome of the children of Israel and some of the king's descendants and some of the nobles,   Is. 39:7

4 young men in whom *there was* no blemish, but good-looking, gifted in all wisdom, possessing knowledge and quick to understand, who *had* ability to serve in the king's

---

50-A. History, Prophecy, and Biography (Daniel 1:1-21)—"In the third year of the reign of Jehoiakim king of Judah [606 B.C.], Nebuchadnezzar king of Babylon came to Jerusalem and besieged it" (v. 1). Nebuchadnezzar had defeated the Egyptian army and was moving to besiege Jerusalem, an event that
(Point 50-A continued on next page)

▽ palace, and whom they might teach the language and literature of the Chaldeans.

5 And the king appointed for them a daily provision of the king's delicacies and of the wine which he drank, and three years of training for them, so that at the end of *that time* they might serve before the king.

6 Now from among those of the sons of Judah were Daniel, Hananiah, Mishael, and Azariah.

7 ᴿTo them the chief of the eunuchs gave names: he gave Daniel *the name* Belteshazzar; to Hananiah, Shadrach; to Mishael, Meshach; and to Azariah, Abed-Nego.   2 Kin. 24:17

8 But Daniel purposed in his heart that he would not defile himself ᴿwith the portion of the king's delicacies, nor with the wine which he drank; therefore he requested of the chief of the eunuchs that he might not defile himself.   Hos. 9:3

9 Now ᴿGod had brought Daniel into the favor and ᵀgoodwill of the chief of the eunuchs.   Gen. 39:21 · *kindness*

10 And the chief of the eunuchs said to Daniel, "I fear my lord the king, who has appointed your food and drink. For why should he see your faces looking worse than the young men who *are* your age? Then you would endanger my head before the king."

11 So Daniel said to ᵀthe steward whom the chief of the eunuchs had set over Daniel, Hananiah, Mishael, and Azariah,   Or *Melzar*

12 "Please test your servants for ten days, ▽ and let them give us vegetables to eat and water to drink.

13 "Then let our appearance be examined before you, and the appearance of the young men who eat the portion of the king's delicacies; and as you see fit, *so* deal with your servants."

14 So he consented with them in this matter, and tested them ten days.

15 And at the end of ten days their features appeared better and fatter in flesh than all the young men who ate the portion of the king's delicacies.

16 Thus ᵀthe steward took away their portion of delicacies and the wine that they were to drink, and gave them vegetables.   Or *Melzar*

17 As for these four young men, ᴿGod gave them ᴿknowledge and skill in all literature and wisdom; and Daniel had understanding in all visions and dreams.   [James 1:5–7] · Acts 7:22

18 Now at the end of the days, when the king had said that they should be brought in, the chief of the eunuchs brought them in before Nebuchadnezzar.

19 Then the king ᵀinterviewed them, and among them all none was found like Daniel, Hananiah, Mishael, and Azariah; therefore they served before the king.   Lit. *talked with them*

20 ᴿAnd in all matters of wisdom *and* understanding about which the king examined them, he found them ten times better than all

---

(Point 50-A continued from previous page)
marked the beginning of the fall of Jerusalem and the seventy years of Babylonian captivity (vv. 1, 2). It was also the beginning of "the times of the Gentiles" (Luke 21:24, page 1041), which is to continue through the seven years of the Great Tribulation, called "the time of Jacob's trouble" (Jer. 30:7, page 743). The final assault on the city of Jerusalem came during the reign of Zedekiah, Judah's last king. Jeremiah, the prophet, prophesied the end of Judah and Jerusalem (Jer. 21:1–10, page 733). The prophecy was fulfilled, and then recorded by Jeremiah (Jer. 52:1–34, page 769).

(1) Three figurehead kings: The last three monarchs of Judah were puppet kings. Jehoiakim, who reigned for eleven years (2 Kin. 23:36—24:5, page 380; 2 Chr. 36:5-8, page 441); Jehoiachin, his son, who reigned for three months (2 Kin. 24:8, 9, page 381); and Zedekiah, who ruled for eleven years (2 Kin. 24:17—25:7, page 381; 2 Chr. 36:10-13, page 441). All three kings were evil in the sight of God, who accordingly brought judgment upon them, sending Nebuchadnezzar to take the people into captivity in Babylon and to burn the city of Jerusalem. Jehoiakim was so evil Jeremiah prophesied that upon his death the king would be given the burial of a donkey (Jer. 22:18, 19, page 734). Jehoiachin, after serving thirty-seven years as a prisoner, was given his freedom and finally exalted by Evil-Merodach, king of Babylon, in his first year as king. Jehoiachin was then lifted above all the kings that had been captured by the Babylonians (Jer. 52:31-34, page 770). Zedekiah did not fare so well. The king of Babylon brutally killed Zedekiah's sons before his very eyes, and then blinded him. The last thing this wicked king saw was the brutal execution of his sons. He must have carried that picture in his mind until the day he died in a Babylonian prison (Jer. 52:10, 11, page 769).

(2) Four courageous young Hebrews, Daniel, Hananiah, Mishael, and Azariah, of royal blood, descendants of godly Hezekiah (vv. 3–7), were chosen by God to know His will for their lives (Acts 22:13, 14, page 1118). About a hundred years before Judah was taken captive to Babylon, Isaiah had prophesied that Hezekiah's descendants would be made eunuchs in the palace of the king of Babylon (Is. 39:5-7, page 678). Daniel and his companions were of the spiritual nobility of the Hebrew captives. They were selected by Ashpenaz (master of Nebuchadnezzar's eunuchs) to become eunuchs. But unlike others who compromised and conformed to the Babylonian system, these four young believers were sustained by the power of God. They took their stand for Him, and God stood with them and gave them victory (v. 8; cf. 1 John 5:4, page 1282). They dared to do the will of God in a pagan land filled with false gods.

(3) In Babylon they were tested by Satan's world system (1 John 2:15, 16, page 1279).

(Point 50-A continued on next page)

▽ the magicians *and* astrologers who *were* in all his realm.   1 Kin. 10:1

21 ᴿThus Daniel continued until the first
▲ year of King Cyrus.   Dan. 6:28; 10:1

Nebuchadnezzar's Dream

▼ **50-B. The Times of the Gentiles**

2 Now in the second year of Nebuchadnezzar's reign, Nebuchadnezzar had dreams;
ᴿand his spirit was *so* troubled that ᴿhis sleep
left him.   Gen. 40:5–8; 41:1, 8 · Esth. 6:1

2 Then the king gave the command to call
the magicians, the astrologers, the sorcerers,
and the Chaldeans to tell the king his dreams.
So they came and stood before the king.

3 And the king said to them, "I have had a
dream, and my spirit is anxious to ᵀknow the
dream."   Or *understand*

4 Then the Chaldeans spoke to the king in
Aramaic, ᴿ"O* king, live forever! Tell your
servants the dream, and we will give the
interpretation."   Dan. 3:9; 5:10; 6:6, 21

5 The king answered and said to the Chal-

2:4 The original language of Daniel 2:4b through 7:28 is
Aramaic.

deans, "My decision is firm: if you do not ▽
make known the dream to me, and its interpretation, you shall be cut in pieces, and your
houses shall be made an ash heap.

6 "However, if you tell the dream and its
interpretation, you shall receive from me
gifts, rewards, and great honor. Therefore tell
me the dream and its interpretation."

7 They answered again and said, "Let the
king tell his servants the dream, and we will
give its interpretation."

8 The king answered and said, "I know for
certain that you would gain time, because
you see that my decision is firm:

9 "if you do not make known the dream to
me, *there is only* one decree for you! For you
have agreed to speak lying and corrupt words
before me till the ᵀtime has changed. Therefore tell me the dream, and I shall know that
you can give me its interpretation."   Situation

10 The Chaldeans answered the king, and
said, "There is not a man on earth who can
tell the king's matter; therefore no king, lord,
or ruler has *ever* asked such things of any
magician, astrologer, or Chaldean.

11 "*It is a* ᵀdifficult thing that the king

(Point 50-A continued from previous page)

(a) *The lust of the flesh.* The king changed their food, but not their faith. They were appointed a daily provision of the king's meat, and of the wine which he drank (v. 5). This was food and drink that was contrary to Hebrew dietary laws (Lev. 11:1–8, page 116). "But Daniel purposed in his heart that he would not defile himself with the portion of the king's delicacies, nor with the wine" (v. 8). Daniel's three Hebrew friends agreed: if God's children would dare to take their stand for Christ, and practice righteousness, God would bless their obedience and bend His enemies to His will (vv. 9–16). After three years of vegetables and water, God gave the young men superior knowledge and skill in all learning and wisdom. The king found them ten times better than all the wise men of the palace (vv. 17–20).

(b) *The lust of the eyes.* The Babylonians had changed the country of residence, but not the character of the young men (vv. 3, 4). The four young Hebrews were in a strange land filled with pagan gods, steeped in immorality and idolatry (Ex. 20:1–6, page 79). Babylon was very beautiful and magnificent, especially in its architecture. Its hanging gardens were considered among the seven wonders of the world. It is easy to understand how the eyes of most men (1 John 2:15, 16, page 1279) would be filled with lust. Satan made Babylon pleasant to behold. But Daniel, Hananiah, Mishael, and Azariah did not conform to the Babylonian way of life. Transformed by the power of God, they would "prove what is that good and acceptable and perfect will of God" (Rom. 12:1, 2, page 1142).

(c) *The pride of life.* The Babylonians had changed the names of the young men, but not their nature (vv. 6, 7). It is evident that they were partakers of the divine nature of God (2 Pet. 1:4, page 1272), and were new creatures in the Messiah (2 Cor. 5:17, page 1169). They were devoted students of the Old Testament books already written by the time of their captivity, not of the learning of Babylon. After reading Isaiah, they looked for the promised Messiah, who would be crucified, wounded for man's transgressions, bruised for his iniquities, and brought as a lamb to the slaughter (Is. 53:1–12, page 693). When John the Baptist saw Jesus, he said, "Behold! The Lamb of God who takes away the sin of the world!" (John 1:29, page 1050). John had learned this great truth from the Old Testament, and it was there for Daniel and his friends to learn. They were saved and given a new nature, because of what Christ would do at Calvary, just as in this day, we are saved by looking back to Calvary. They were given names that honored false gods, but they did not honor their new names. We learn, then, that it does not matter what you are called; it is what you are in Christ that counts. The Babylonians changed the young men's food, their country, and their names; but Daniel and his friends remained the same in faith, character, and nature. Babylon could not change them, but they made many changes in Babylon—they even converted Nebuchadnezzar (Dan. 4, page 837).

See Daniel 2:1–49, above, for **Point 50-B: The Times of the Gentiles.**

50-B. The Times of the Gentiles (Daniel 2:1–49)—Nebuchadnezzar had a dream that troubled his spirit so much that he could not sleep (vv. 1–11). "Then the king gave the command to call the magicians, the astrologers, the sorcerers, and the Chaldeans to tell the king his dreams. So they came and stood before the
(Point 50-B continued on next page)

▽ requests, and there is no other who can tell it to the king ᴿexcept the gods, whose dwelling is not with flesh." Or *rare* • Dan. 5:11

12 For this reason the king was angry and very furious, and gave the command to destroy all the wise *men* of Babylon.

13 So the decree went out, and they began killing the wise *men*; and they sought ᴿDaniel and his companions, to kill *them*. Dan. 1:19, 20

God Reveals Nebuchadnezzar's Dream

14 Then with counsel and wisdom Daniel answered Arioch, the captain of the king's guard, who had gone out to kill the wise *men* of Babylon;

15 he answered and said to Arioch the king's captain, "Why *is* the decree from the king so ᵀurgent?" Then Arioch made the decision known to Daniel. Or *harsh*

16 So Daniel went in and asked the king to give him time, that he might tell the king the interpretation.

17 Then Daniel went to his house, and ▽ made the decision known to Hananiah, Mishael, and Azariah, his companions,

18 that they might seek mercies from the God of heaven concerning this secret, so that Daniel and his companions might not perish with the rest of the wise *men* of Babylon.

19 Then the secret was revealed to Daniel ᴿin a night vision. So Daniel blessed the God of heaven. Job 33:15

20 Daniel answered and said:

ᴿ"Blessed be the name of God forever and
  ever, Ps. 113:2
ᴿFor wisdom and might are His. [Jer. 32:19]
21 And He changes ᴿthe times and the
  seasons; Esth. 1:13
ᴿHe removes kings and raises up kings;
ᴿHe gives wisdom to the wise
And knowledge to those who have
  understanding. [Ps. 75:6, 7] • [James 1:5]
22 He reveals deep and secret things;

(Point 50-A continued from previous page)
king" (v. 2). All claimed to have magical powers beyond the ordinary man. Astrologers claimed to know the future by divining the heavens. Those Chaldeans claiming to have astrological powers were considered to be the priests of the Chaldean people. Isaiah warned Babylon of God's coming judgment, because they trusted in the astrologers. Isaiah said, "Let now the astrologers, the stargazers . . . save you from what [God's judgments] shall come upon you" (Is. 47:12–14, page 688). This stargazing cult has continued to grow throughout the world to this very day; and God still condemns it. The spiritualists claim power to communicate with the dead; they are known as mediums. This, too, is condemned by the Lord (1 Sam. 28:7–19, page 294).

(1) The dream disturbed the king and exposed the fraudulent wise men of Babylon (vv. 3–12). Nebuchadnezzar told them, "I have had a dream, and my spirit is anxious to know the dream" (v. 3). The crafty Chaldeans said, "O king, live forever! Tell your servants the dream, and we will give the interpretation" (v. 4). King Nebuchadnezzar replied, "If you do not make the dream known to me, and its interpretation, you shall be cut in pieces" (v. 5), going on to say, "Therefore tell me the dream, and I shall know that you can give me its interpretation" (v. 9). The king's reasoning made sense—surely anyone who could foretell the future could also explain the dream. But the wise men failed, and the king decreed they should all be put to death, including Daniel and his friends, who were not with the wise men when they appeared before Nebuchadnezzar.

(2) Daniel came to the rescue of the wise men, his three friends, and himself (vv. 13–25). Hearing the bad news, Daniel responded like a man of action in seven important ways:

(a) He went to Arioch, the king's appointed executioner, asking, "Why is the decree from the king so urgent?" (v. 15), and requested to be taken before the king.

(b) He went before the king and requested time so that he could learn the dream, and master its interpretation. This was an act of great faith.

(c) He went to his three friends who had faith in the God of heaven, and the courage of their convictions.

(d) He and his three friends addressed God in prayer.

(e) When God revealed the dream and the interpretation to him in the night vision, Daniel blessed, praised, and exalted the God of heaven (vv. 19–23). Read these beautiful words of exaltation and praise to God for answered prayer. We should always thank God for every answer to prayer. In fact, if we really believe that God is going to answer our prayers, we should thank Him before we get the answer.

(f) He then went back to Arioch, who was under orders from the king to destroy all wise men in Babylon, and requested that he be brought again before the king.

(g) Drawing power from God in heaven, he went before the king, ready to reveal the dream and the interpretation which God had made known to him "in a night vision" (v. 19).

(3) Daniel made known to the king his dream and the interpretation (vv. 26–45). The king asked Daniel, "Are you able to make known to me the dream which I have seen, and its interpretation?" (v. 26). Daniel seized the opportunity to witness for the God of heaven, but first he reminded the king that his wise men could not explain the meaning of his dream. Then Daniel said, "There is a God in heaven who reveals secrets, and He has made known to King Nebuchadnezzar what will be in the latter days" (v. 28). Daniel
(Point 50-B continued on next page)

▽ ᴿHe knows what *is* in the darkness,
And light dwells with Him.   [Heb. 4:13]

23 "I thank You and praise You,
O God of my fathers;
You have given me wisdom and might,
And have now made known to me
    what we ᴿasked of You,   Dan. 2:18, 29, 30
For You have made known to us the
    king's ᵀdemand."   Lit. *word*

Daniel Explains the Dream

24 Therefore Daniel went to Arioch, whom the king had appointed to destroy the wise *men* of Babylon. He went and said thus to him: "Do not destroy the wise *men* of Babylon; take me before the king, and I will tell the king the interpretation."

25 Then Arioch quickly brought Daniel before the king, and said thus to him, "I have found a man of the ᵀcaptives of Judah, who

will make known to the king the interpreta- ▽
tion."   Lit. *sons of the captivity*

26 The king answered and said to Daniel, whose name *was* Belteshazzar, "Are you able to make known to me the dream which I have seen, and its interpretation?"

27 Daniel answered in the presence of the king, and said, "The secret which the king has demanded, the wise *men*, the astrologers, the magicians, and the soothsayers cannot declare to the king.

28 "But there is a God in heaven who reveals secrets, and He has made known to King Nebuchadnezzar what will be in the latter days. Your dream, and the visions of your head upon your bed, were these:

29 "As for you, O king, thoughts came *to* your *mind while* on your bed, *about* what would come to pass after this; ᴿand He who reveals secrets has made known to you what will be.   [Dan. 2:22, 28]

(Point 50-A continued from previous page)
gave God all the glory, saying, "But as for me, this secret has not been revealed to me because I have more wisdom than anyone living" (v. 30). This was true humility.

(4) Now we come to the dream (vv. 31–35). In these five short verses, God gave to the world a prophetic picture of the Times of the Gentiles (Luke 21:24, page 1041), starting with the seventy years of Hebrew captivity in Babylon beginning in 606 B.C., and continuing to the end of the Great Tribulation, when Christ (whom Nebuchadnezzar saw in his dream as the stone "cut out without hands") will crush the Gentile world powers and establish His kingdom on this earth (Matt. 25:31–46, page 976). The stone "cut out without hands" does not portray the first coming of the Lord Jesus Christ, who emerged initially as "the Lamb of God who takes away the sin of the world!" (John 1:29, page 1050). But when Jesus comes the second time, it will be in power as great as that of the stone cut out without hands, and will grind the Gentile kingdoms to powder; He will rule and reign on the throne of His father David as "KING OF KINGS AND LORD OF LORDS" (Rev. 19:11–16, page 1312).

(5) Daniel interpreted the dream (vv. 36–45). He said, "This is the dream. Now we will tell the interpretation of it before the king. . . . you are this head of gold" (vv. 36–38). God had given this pagan king power over the earth, man, and beast, making Nebuchadnezzar the greatest of all the world rulers. Fulfilling God's sovereign purpose, Nebuchadnezzar was summoned to punish Israel because they had forsaken their God in favor of false gods. The Lord said, "And now I have given all these lands into the hand of Nebuchadnezzar the king of Babylon, My servant" (Jer. 27:6, page 740).

God called Nebuchadnezzar, this heathen king, His servant. Why? Because Nebuchadnezzar, without knowing it, was doing the will of God. Nebuchadnezzar was fulfilling God's purpose. For God in His foreknowledge had predestined the salvation of this mighty king (see Point 5-D, "The Sovereignty of God and Salvation," page 1137). God had ordained that Nebuchadnezzar would come to the place where he would place his faith in the Most High God, and humbly commit himself to the Lord. At that time in history, Babylon was the first of the four Gentile world powers.

After Daniel said of the great image, "You are this head of gold" (v. 38) he added, "After you shall arise another kingdom inferior to yours"—on the part of the image that was silver (v. 39). The latter kingdom was the Medo-Persian Empire that overthrew the Babylonians. The third kingdom (of brass) was the Greek Empire. The fourth and last of the great Gentile world powers was the Roman Empire (of iron). The ten toes of the image represent the ten kings that will be in power in the Great Tribulation, when Christ, the crushing stone, finally will fall on the feet and grind the entire Gentile world system into powder.

Following the four Gentile world empires, there will come a fifth—the kingdom of God on earth. The stone that is hewn without hands, the Lord Jesus Christ, will rule and reign on the throne of His father David for a thousand years. But at the end of that time, the kingdom of God will continue. Only then will there be a new heaven and a new earth (Rev. 21:1, page 1314).

(6) When King Nebuchadnezzar heard the dream, and its analysis, he grew excited. "The king answered Daniel, and said, 'Truly your God is the God of gods, the Lord of kings, and a revealer of secrets, since you could reveal this secret' " (v. 47). And what did Daniel do after Nebuchadnezzar honored him as a great man? He requested of the king that his three Hebrew friends be exalted with him, and the king complied.

When we give God the glory for our successes in life, then the kingdom of God has been spiritually set up in our hearts. Until Jesus comes, the Lord reigns in our lives. God is given His proper place, and we are given ours, which is under His rule. We need more Daniels serving God.

See Daniel 3:1–30, page 835, for **Point 50-C: The Image of Gold.**

▽ 30 ᴿ"But as for me, this secret has not been revealed to me because I have more wisdom than anyone living, but for *our* sakes who make known the interpretation to the king, ᴿand that you may ᵀknow the thoughts of your heart. Acts 3:12 • Dan. 2:47 • Understand

31 "You, O king, were watching; and behold, a great image! This great image, whose splendor *was* excellent, stood before you; and its form *was* awesome.

32 ᴿ"This image's head *was* of fine gold, its chest and arms of silver, its belly and ᵀthighs of bronze, Dan. 2:38, 45 • Or *sides*

33 "its legs of iron, its feet partly of iron and partly of ᵀclay. Or *baked clay,* and so in vv. 34, 35, 42

34 "You watched while a stone was cut out ᴿwithout hands, which struck the image on its feet of iron and clay, and broke them in pieces. [Zech. 4:6]

35 "Then the iron, the clay, the bronze, the silver, and the gold were crushed together, and became like chaff from the summer threshing floors; the wind carried them away so that no trace of them was found. And the stone that struck the image became a great mountain and filled the whole earth.

36 "This *is* the dream. Now we will tell the interpretation of it before the king.

37 ᴿ"You, O king, *are* a king of kings. ᴿFor the God of heaven has given you a kingdom, power, strength, and glory; Jer. 27:6, 7 • Ezra 1:2

38 ᴿ"and wherever the children of men dwell, or the beasts of the field and the birds of the heaven, He has given *them* into your hand, and has made you ruler over them all— ᴿyou *are* this head of gold. Dan. 4:21, 22 • Dan. 2:32

39 "But after you shall arise ᴿanother kingdom ᴿinferior to yours; then another, a third kingdom of bronze, which shall rule over all the earth. Dan. 5:28, 31 • Dan. 2:32

40 "And ᴿthe fourth kingdom shall be as strong as iron, inasmuch as iron breaks in pieces and shatters everything; and like iron that crushes, *that kingdom* will break in pieces and crush all the others. Dan. 7:7, 23

41 "Whereas you saw the feet and toes, partly of potter's clay and partly of iron, the kingdom shall be divided; yet the strength of the iron shall be in it, just as you saw the iron mixed with ceramic clay.

42 "And *as* the toes of the feet *were* partly of iron and partly of clay, *so* the kingdom shall be partly strong and partly fragile.

43 "As you saw iron mixed with ceramic clay, they will mingle with the seed of men; but they will not adhere to one another, just as iron does not mix with clay.

44 "And in the days of these kings the God of heaven will ᴿset up a kingdom which shall never be destroyed; and the kingdom shall not be left to other people; it shall break in pieces and ᵀconsume all these kingdoms, and it shall stand forever. Is. 9:7 • Lit. *put an end to* ▽

45 "Inasmuch as you saw that the stone was cut out of the mountain without hands, and that it broke in pieces the iron, the bronze, the clay, the silver, and the gold—the great God has made known to the king what will come to pass after this. The dream is certain, and its interpretation is sure."

Daniel and His Friends Promoted

46 ᴿThen King Nebuchadnezzar fell on his face, prostrate before Daniel, and commanded that they should present an offering ᴿand incense to him. Acts 10:25; 14:13 • Ezra 6:10

47 The king answered Daniel, and said, "Truly your God *is* the God of ᴿgods, the Lord of kings, and a revealer of secrets, since you could reveal this secret." [Deut. 10:17]

48 ᴿThen the king promoted Daniel ᴿand gave him many great gifts; and he made him ruler over the whole province of Babylon, and ᴿchief administrator over all the wise *men* of Babylon. [Prov. 14:35; 21:1] • Dan. 2:6 • Dan. 4:9; 5:11

49 Also Daniel petitioned the king, and he set Shadrach, Meshach, and Abed-Nego over the affairs of the province of Babylon; but Daniel *sat* in the ᵀgate of the king. Court ▲

The Image of Gold

50–C. The Image of Gold ▼

3 Nebuchadnezzar the king made an image of gold, whose height *was* sixty cubits *and* its width six cubits. He set it up in the plain of Dura, in the province of Babylon.

2 And King Nebuchadnezzar sent *word* to gather together the satraps, the administrators, the governors, the counselors, the treasurers, the judges, the magistrates, and all the officials of the provinces, to come to the dedication of the image which King Nebuchadnezzar had set up.

3 So the satraps, the administrators, the governors, the counselors, the treasurers, the judges, the magistrates, and all the officials of the provinces gathered together for the dedication of the image that King Nebuchadnezzar had set up; and they stood before the image that Nebuchadnezzar had set up.

4 Then a herald cried ᵀaloud: "To you it is commanded, ᴿO peoples, nations, and languages, Lit. *with strength* • Dan. 4:1; 6:25

50-C. The Image of Gold (Daniel 3:1–30)—Chapter 3 introduces us to Nebuchadnezzar's image made of gold. He must have been influenced by Daniel's interpretation of his dream in chapter 2: "You are this head of gold" (Dan. 2:38, page 835). So Nebuchadnezzar built a great image of gold, a precious metal that does not deteriorate or tarnish, to immortalize himself.

(Point 50-C continued on next page)

▽ 5 "*that* at the time you hear the sound of the horn, flute, harp, lyre, *and* psaltery, in symphony with all kinds of music, you shall fall down and worship the gold image that King Nebuchadnezzar has set up;

6 "and whoever does not fall down and worship shall ᴿbe cast immediately into the midst of a burning fiery furnace."   Jer. 29:22

7 So at that time, when all the people heard the sound of the horn, flute, harp, *and* lyre, in symphony with all kinds of music, all the people, nations, and languages fell down *and* worshiped the gold image which King Nebuchadnezzar had set up.

Daniel's Friends Disobey the King

8 Therefore at that time certain Chaldeans came forward and accused the Jews.

9 They spoke and said to King Nebuchadnezzar, ᴿ"O king, live forever!   Dan. 2:4; 5:10

10 "You, O king, have made a decree that everyone who hears the sound of the horn, flute, harp, lyre, *and* psaltery, in symphony with all kinds of music, shall fall down and worship the gold image;

11 "and whoever does not fall down and worship shall be cast into the midst of a burning fiery furnace.

12 ᴿ"There are certain Jews whom you have set over the affairs of the province of Babylon: Shadrach, Meshach, and Abed-Nego; these men, O king, have ᴿnot paid due regard to you. They do not serve your gods or worship the gold image which you have set up."   Dan. 2:49 · Dan. 1:8; 6:12, 13

13 Then Nebuchadnezzar, in ᴿrage and fury, gave the command to bring Shadrach, Meshach, and Abed-Nego. So they brought these men before the king.   Dan. 2:12; 3:19

14 Nebuchadnezzar spoke, saying to them, "*Is it* true, Shadrach, Meshach, and Abed-Nego, *that* you do not serve my gods or worship the gold image which I have set up?

(Point 50-C continued from previous page)

(1) Nebuchadnezzar's golden image was ninety feet high and nine feet wide (v. 1). If this seems out of proportion, remember that this image could have been much shorter if the pedestal were part of its measurement. Perhaps Nebuchadnezzar's image was dedicated to one of his favorite gods, or it may have been declared a new god. Either way, in the sight of God it was the folly of a self-centered king (recalling the Pharaohs of Egypt, who built great pyramids to ensure their immortality). When the image of gold was completed, Nebuchadnezzar summoned all the dignitaries of his kingdom to the dedication. The image was erected outside Babylon, in the plain of Dura, where there would be nothing to distract from it (such as the magnificent hanging gardens and other architectural marvels). When all the guests were gathered before the image, Nebuchadnezzar directed his herald to declare the king's decree: at the sound of the music, they all were to fall down and worship the image—or be thrown into a fiery furnace (vv. 4-7).

(2) This was a real test of faith for the Hebrew nonconformists (vv. 8–22). They refused to bow down and worship the image. Knowing that they would not worship any god but Jehovah, the Chaldeans were watching them carefully. When they failed to bow down, the Chaldeans came to Nebuchadnezzar and accused the Jews. So the king summoned Shadrach, Meshach, and Abed-Nego. Because they were very prominent in his kingdom, he gave them a second chance. He said, in effect, "We will play the music again, and this time you will fall down and worship the image, or be thrown into a fiery furnace." This was quite a test of faith! The three Hebrews replied, "We have no need to answer you in this matter. If that is the case, our God whom we serve is able to deliver us from the burning fiery furnace, and He will deliver us from your hand, O king. But if not, let it be known to you, O king, that we do not serve your gods, nor will we worship the gold image which you have set up" (vv. 16–18). Their faith was not presumptuous. While they believed that God had the power to deliver them from the fiery furnace, they knew they could not demand it of God. They left it to His sovereign will. They did not have to talk it over; all three knew in their hearts they could not deny their God. Such was their great faith.

(3) Shadrach, Meshach, and Abed-Nego remind us of the remnant of the people of God who will endure all the fiery furnaces of this godless world, until their Messiah (the Lord Jesus Christ) comes back to this earth to usher them into the kingdom (Matt. 25:31–34, page 976). God speaks often of the remnant of Judah and Israel. The Scriptures record that

(a) God saved a remnant of Judah after they were besieged by the Assyrians for three years (Is. 37:1–4, 30–38, page 676; 2 Kin. 19:32–35, page 376);

(b) God has promised to save a remnant of the twelve tribes out of the Great Tribulation (Rev. 7:1–14, page 1300);

(c) God will bless the remnant of His people in the kingdom, and they will multiply and become innumerable (Zech. 8:12–17, page 915; cf. Matt. 25:31–34, page 976; Gen. 22:17, 18, page 28; Heb. 11:12, 13, page 1248).

Now we all know how God delivered these three courageous Hebrew young people from the fiery furnace. More than just deliver them, He joined them in the fire and they fellowshiped together. The faith of Shadrach, Meshach, and Abed-Nego shone brighter and more lasting than Nebuchadnezzar's image of gold. For over two thousand years there has been no trace of this golden statue; but the faith of Shadrach, Meshach, and Abed-Nego shines as bright as the sun on a cloudless day.

See Daniel 4:1–37, page 837, for **Point 50-D: Delegated Sovereignty.**

▽ 15 "Now if you are ready at the time you hear the sound of the horn, flute, harp, lyre, *and* psaltery, in symphony with all kinds of music, and you fall down and worship the image which I have made, ᴿ*good!* But if you do not worship, you shall be cast immediately into the midst of a burning fiery furnace. ᴿAnd who *is* the god who will deliver you from my hands?"   Luke 13:9 • Ex. 5:2

16 Shadrach, Meshach, and Abed-Nego answered and said to the king, "O Nebuchadnezzar, ᴿwe have no need to answer you in this matter.   [Matt. 10:19]

17 "If *that is the case,* our ᴿGod whom we serve is able to ᴿdeliver us from the burning fiery furnace, and He will deliver *us* from your hand, O king.   [Is. 26:3, 4] • 1 Sam. 17:37

18 "But if not, let it be known to you, O king, that we do not serve your gods, nor will we ᴿworship the gold image which you have set up."   Job 13:15

Saved in Fiery Trial

19 Then Nebuchadnezzar was full of fury, and the expression on his face changed toward Shadrach, Meshach, and Abed-Nego. He spoke and commanded that they heat the furnace seven times more than it was usually heated.

20 And he commanded certain mighty men of valor who *were* in his army to bind Shadrach, Meshach, and Abed-Nego, *and* cast *them* into the burning fiery furnace.

21 Then these men were bound in their coats, their trousers, their turbans, and their *other* garments, and were cast into the midst of the burning fiery furnace.

22 Therefore, because the king's command was ᵀurgent, and the furnace exceedingly hot, the flame of the fire killed those men who took up Shadrach, Meshach, and Abed-Nego.   Or *harsh*

23 And these three men, Shadrach, Meshach, and Abed-Nego, fell down bound into the midst of the burning fiery furnace.

24 Then King Nebuchadnezzar was astonished; and he rose in haste *and* spoke, saying to his ᵀcounselors, "Did we not cast three men bound into the midst of the fire?" They answered and said to the king, "True, O king."   High officials

25 "Look!" he answered, "I see four men loose, walking in the midst of the fire; and they are not hurt, and the form of the fourth is like ᵀthe Son of God." Or *a son of the gods* ▽

Nebuchadnezzar Praises God

26 Then Nebuchadnezzar went near the ᵀmouth of the burning fiery furnace and spoke, saying, "Shadrach, Meshach, and Abed-Nego, servants of the ᴿMost High God, come out, and come *here.*" Then Shadrach, Meshach, and Abed-Nego came from the midst of the fire.   Lit. *door* • [Dan. 4:2, 3, 17, 34, 35]

27 And the satraps, administrators, governors, and the king's counselors gathered together, and they saw these men ᴿon whose bodies the fire had no power; the hair of their head was not singed nor were their garments affected, and the smell of fire was not on them.   Heb. 11:34

28 Nebuchadnezzar spoke, saying, "Blessed be the God of Shadrach, Meshach, and Abed-Nego, who sent His ᴿAngelᵀ and delivered His servants who trusted in Him, and they have frustrated the king's word, and yielded their bodies, that they should not serve nor worship any god except their own God!   [Ps. 34:7, 8] • Or *angel*

29 ᴿ"Therefore I make a decree that any people, nation, or language which speaks anything amiss against the God of Shadrach, Meshach, and Abed-Nego shall be ᴿcut in pieces, and their houses shall be made an ash heap; ᴿbecause there is no other God who can deliver like this."   Dan. 6:26 • Dan. 2:5 • Dan. 6:27

30 Then the king ᵀpromoted Shadrach, Meshach, and Abed-Nego in the province of Babylon.   Lit. *caused to prosper* ▲

Nebuchadnezzar's Second Dream

50–D. Delegated Sovereignty   ▼

4 Nebuchadnezzar the king,
ᴿTo all peoples, nations, and languages that dwell in all the earth:
Peace be multiplied to you.   Dan. 3:4; 6:25

2 I thought it good to declare the signs and wonders ᴿthat the Most High God has worked for me.   Dan. 3:26

3 ᴿHow great *are* His signs,   2 Sam. 7:16
And how mighty His wonders!
His kingdom *is* ᴿan everlasting kingdom,   [Dan. 2:44; 4:34; 6:26]
And His dominion *is* from generation to generation.

50–D. Delegated Sovereignty (Daniel 4:1–37)—No king ever had a more prosperous or powerful kingdom than Nebuchadnezzar. His was the first and greatest of the four Gentile world empires (Dan. 2:31–45, page 835). Why? Because God, in His sovereign will, chose Nebuchadnezzar and exalted him to delegated autocracy. Then, in His sovereign grace, God humbled Nebuchadnezzar and brought him to repentance and faith in "the Most High [GᴏD]" (v. 34). In the study of this fourth chapter, God, in His sovereign power, having stripped this mighty king of his delegated power, reestablishes Nebuchadnezzar's authority with more greatness than before.

(Point 50-D continued on next page)

▽ 4 I, Nebuchadnezzar, was at rest in my house, and flourishing in my palace.

5 I saw a dream which made me afraid, and the thoughts on my bed and the visions of my head ᴿtroubled me. Dan. 2:1

6 Therefore I issued a decree to bring in all the wise *men* of Babylon before me, that they might make known to me the interpretation of the dream.

7 ᴿThen the magicians, the astrologers, the Chaldeans, and the soothsayers came in, and I told them the dream; but they did not make known to me its interpretation. Dan. 2:2

8 But at last Daniel came before me (his name *is* Belteshazzar, according to the ▽ name of my god; ᴿin him *is* the Spirit of the Holy God), and I told the dream before him, *saying:* Dan. 2:11; 4:18; 5:11, 14

9 "Belteshazzar, ᴿchief of the magicians, because I know that the Spirit of the Holy God *is* in you, and no secret troubles you, explain to me the visions of my dream that I have seen, and its interpretation. Dan. 2:48; 5:11

10 "These *were* the visions of my head *while* on my bed:
I was looking, and behold,
ᴿA tree in the midst of the earth,
And its height was great. Ezek. 31:3

(Point 50-D continued from previous page)

(1) *Nebuchadnezzar's confession of faith* (vv. 1–3). This chapter was written by Nebuchadnezzar after he came to know the Most High God as his personal Savior. He said, "I thought it good to declare the signs and wonders that the Most High God has worked for me" (v. 2). He was ready to witness to the saving power of his sovereign Savior. The psalmist said, "Let the redeemed of the LORD say so" (Ps. 107:2, page 574).

The Most High God used Daniel, his Hebrew friends and their works as "signs and wonders" (v. 2) to bring this mighty king to repentance. At conversion, Nebuchadnezzar immediately recognized the sovereignty of God, saying, "His kingdom is an everlasting kingdom, and His dominion is from generation to generation" (v. 3). After living with the beasts of the fields for seven years, and eating grass like cattle, he knew that no earthly monarch could be truly sovereign or everlasting. Now God did all of this to Nebuchadnezzar "that the living may know that the Most High [Sovereign] rules in the kingdom of men, and gives it [delegated rulership] to whomever He will, and sets over it the lowest of men" (v. 17).

(2) *Nebuchadnezzar's dream* (vv. 4–18). In his dream he saw a large tree reaching to the sky. It was a tree of comfort, supplying fruit for the nations. This tree is a symbol of Nebuchadnezzar's delegated power. As he gazed, he saw an angelic "watcher, a holy one, coming down from heaven" (v. 13), who commanded the great tree be chopped down.

(3) *Nebuchadnezzar's dream interpreted* (vv. 19–27). Daniel answered the king and said, "The tree that you saw . . . it is you, O king" (vv. 20, 22). The angelic watcher came down and said, "Chop down the tree and destroy it, but leave its stump and roots in the earth, bound with a band of iron and bronze" (v. 23). God would protect the stump of the great tree and restore it to power. Now Daniel pleaded with the king to "break off your sins" (v. 27). But the king continued in his sins until God divested him of his delegated authority.

(4) *Nebuchadnezzar stripped of his delegated power* (vv. 28–33). One year later, while walking proudly in his palace (Prov. 16:18, page 610), he declared, "Is not this great Babylon, that I have built for a royal dwelling by my mighty power and for the honor of my majesty?" (v. 30). So saying, Nebuchadnezzar brought to an end the long-suffering of God (2 Pet. 3:9, page 1275).

Then the Most High God said from heaven, "King Nebuchadnezzar, to you it is spoken: the kingdom has departed from you!" (v. 31). Here is a great lesson. Our sovereign God gives, and He takes away. He exalts, and He humbles. The great difference between the power of man and the sovereignty of God is that man has no power to strip God of His sovereignty. "The LORD has established His throne in heaven, and His kingdom rules over all" (Ps. 103:19, page 570).

(5) *Nebuchadnezzar's authority restored* (vv. 34–36). When God restored Nebuchadnezzar to his kingship, the latter said, "I, Nebuchadnezzar, lifted my eyes to heaven . . . and I blessed the Most High and praised and honored Him who lives forever: For His dominion is an everlasting dominion, and His kingdom is from generation to generation" (v. 34). He recognized the sovereignty of God, and for the first time he understood the difference between absolute and delegated power.

(6) *Nebuchadnezzar recognized the Sovereign God as his God.* In essence he declared (v. 37) that he, Nebuchadnezzar, would

(a) praise the King of heaven;
(b) extol the King of heaven;
(c) honor the King of heaven;
(d) declare that His works are truth;
(e) declare that His ways are just;
(f) know from experience that He is able to humble those who walk in pride, and strip them of all power, pride, and worldly pretense.

Nebuchadnezzar declared that the Lord is Sovereign Ruler, the Most High God.

See Daniel 5:1–31, page 840, for **Point 50-E: The Fall of Babylon.**

▽ 11 The tree grew and became strong;
Its height reached to the heavens,
And it could be seen to the ends of all
the earth.

12 Its leaves *were* lovely,
Its fruit abundant,
And in it *was* food for all.
    ᴿThe beasts of the field found shade
under it,
The birds of the heavens dwelt in its
branches,
And all flesh was fed from it.   Lam. 4:20

13 "I saw in the visions of my head *while*
on my bed, and there was a watcher, a
holy one, coming down from heaven.

14 He cried aloud and said thus:

    ᴿ'Chop down the tree and cut off its
branches,   Ezek. 31:10–14
Strip off its leaves and scatter its fruit.
Let the beasts get out from under it,
And the birds from its branches.

15 Nevertheless leave the stump and roots
in the earth,
Bound with a band of iron and bronze,
In the tender grass of the field.
Let it be wet with the dew of heaven,
And *let* him graze with the beasts
On the grass of the earth.

16 Let his heart be changed from *that of* a
man,
Let him be given the heart of a beast,
And let *seven times pass over him.

17 'This decision *is* by the decree of the
watchers,
And the sentence by the word of the
holy ones,
In order ᴿthat the living may know
That the Most High rules in the
kingdom of men,   Ps. 9:16; 83:18
ᴿGives it to whomever He will,   Jer. 27:5-7
And sets over it the lowest of men.'

18 "This dream I, King Nebuchadnezzar,
have seen. Now you, Belteshazzar,
declare its interpretation, ᴿsince all the
wise *men* of my kingdom are not able
to make known to me the interpretation; but you *are* able, for the Spirit of
the Holy God *is* in you."   Gen. 41:8, 15

Daniel Explains the Second Dream

19 Then Daniel, whose name was
Belteshazzar, was astonished for a time,
and his thoughts troubled him. *So* the
king spoke, and said, "Belteshazzar, do
not let the dream or its interpretation
trouble you." Belteshazzar answered
and said, "My lord, *may* the dream
concern those who hate you, and its
interpretation concern your enemies!

20 ᴿThe tree that you saw, which grew
and became strong, whose height
reached to the heavens and which

4:16 Possibly *years*

could be seen by all the earth, Dan. 4:10-12 ▽

21 whose leaves *were* lovely and its fruit
abundant, in which *was* food for all,
under which the beasts of the field
dwelt, and in whose branches the birds
of the heaven had their home—

22 it *is* you, O king, who have grown and
become strong; for your greatness has
grown and reaches to the heavens, and
your dominion to the end of the earth.

23 ᴿAnd inasmuch as the king saw a
watcher, a holy one, coming down from
heaven and saying, 'Chop down the
tree and destroy it, but leave its stump
and roots in the earth, *bound* with a
band of iron and bronze in the tender
grass of the field; let it be wet with the
dew of heaven, ᴿand let him graze with
the beasts of the field, till seven times
pass over him';   Dan. 4:13-15 · Dan. 5:21

24 this is the interpretation, O king, and
this is the decree of the Most High,
which has come upon my lord the king:

25 They shall drive you from men, your
dwelling shall be with the beasts of the
field, and they shall make you eat grass
like oxen. They shall wet you with the
dew of heaven, and seven ᵀtimes shall
pass over you, till you know that the
Most High rules in the kingdom
of men, and gives it to whomever He
chooses.   Possibly *years*

26 And inasmuch as they gave the
command to leave the stump *and* roots
of the tree, your kingdom shall be
assured to you, after you come to know
that ᴿHeavenᵀ rules.   Matt. 21:25 · God

27 Therefore, O king, let my advice be
acceptable to you; break off your sins
by *being* righteous, and your iniquities
by showing mercy to *the* poor.
Perhaps there may be ᴿa ᵀlengthening
of your prosperity."   1 Kin. 21:29 · *prolonging*

Nebuchadnezzar's Humiliation

28 All *this* came upon King
Nebuchadnezzar.

29 At the end of the twelve months he
was walking ᵀabout the royal palace of
Babylon.   Or *upon*

30 The king ᴿspoke, saying, "Is not this
great Babylon, that I have built for a
royal dwelling by my mighty power and
for the honor of my majesty?"   Prov. 16:18

31 While the word *was* still in the king's
mouth, a voice fell from heaven: "King
Nebuchadnezzar, to you it is spoken:
the kingdom has departed from you!

32 And they shall drive you from men,
and your dwelling *shall be* with the
beasts of the field. They shall make you
eat grass like oxen; and seven ᵀtimes
shall pass over you, until you know
that the Most High rules in the

▽ kingdom of men, and gives it to whomever He chooses." *Possibly years*

33 That very hour the word was fulfilled concerning Nebuchadnezzar; he was driven from men and ate grass like oxen; his body was wet with the dew of heaven till his hair had grown like eagles' *feathers* and his nails like birds' *claws.*

Nebuchadnezzar Praises God

34 And ᴿat the end of the ᵀtime I, Nebuchadnezzar, lifted my eyes to heaven, and my understanding returned to me; and I blessed the Most High and praised and honored Him ᴿwho lives forever: *Dan. 4:26 · Lit. days · [Rev. 4:10]*

For His dominion *is* ᴿan everlasting dominion, *[Luke 1:33]*
And His kingdom *is* from generation to generation.

35 ᴿAll the inhabitants of the earth *are* reputed as nothing; *Is. 40:15, 17*
ᴿHe does according to His will in the army of heaven *Ps. 115:3; 135:6*
And *among* the inhabitants of the earth.
ᴿNo one can restrain His hand *Job 34:29*
Or say to Him, ᴿ"What have You done?" *Rom. 9:20*

36 At the same time my reason returned to me, and for the glory of my kingdom, my honor and splendor returned to me. My counselors and nobles resorted to me, I was restored to my kingdom, and excellent majesty was added to me.

37 Now I, Nebuchadnezzar, praise and extol and honor the King of heaven, all of whose works *are* truth, and His ways justice. And those who walk in ▲ pride He is able to ᵀput down. *humble*

Belshazzar's Feast

▼ 50-E. The Fall of Babylon

5 Belshazzar the king made a great feast for a thousand of his lords, and drank wine in the presence of the thousand.

2 While he tasted the wine, Belshazzar gave the command to bring the gold and silver vessels ᴿwhich his ᵀfather Nebuchadnezzar had taken from the temple which *had been* in Jerusalem, that the king and his lords, his wives, and his concubines might drink from them. *Dan. 1:2 · Or ancestor*

3 Then they brought the gold ᴿvessels that had been taken from the temple of the house ▽ of God which *had been* in Jerusalem; and the king and his lords, his wives, and his concubines drank from them. *2 Chr. 36:10*

4 They drank wine, ᴿand praised the gods of gold and silver, bronze and iron, wood and stone. *Rev. 9:20*

5 ᴿIn the same hour the fingers of a man's hand appeared and wrote opposite the lampstand on the plaster of the wall of the king's palace; and the king saw the part of the hand that wrote. *Dan. 4:31*

6 Then the king's countenance changed, and his thoughts troubled him, so that the joints of his hips were loosened and his ᴿknees knocked against each other. *Dan. 4:6*

7 The king cried ᵀaloud to bring in the astrologers, the Chaldeans, and the soothsayers. The king spoke, saying to the wise *men* of Babylon, "Whoever reads this writing, and tells me its interpretation, shall be clothed with purple and *have* a chain of gold around his neck; ᴿand he shall be the third ruler in the kingdom." *Lit. with · Dan. 6:2, 3*

8 Now all the king's wise *men* came, ᴿbut they could not read the writing, or make known to the king its interpretation. *Dan. 2:27*

9 Then King Belshazzar was greatly ᴿtroubled, his countenance was changed, and his lords were ᵀastonished. *Dan. 2:1; 5:6 · perplexed*

10 The queen, because of the words of the king and his lords, came to the banquet hall. The queen spoke, saying, "O king, live forever! Do not let your thoughts trouble you, nor let your countenance change.

11 "There is a man in your kingdom in whom *is* the Spirit of the Holy God. And in the days of your father, light and understanding and wisdom, like the wisdom of the gods, were found in him; and King Nebuchadnezzar your father—your father the king—made him chief of the magicians, astrologers, Chaldeans, *and* soothsayers.

12 "Inasmuch as an excellent spirit, knowledge, understanding, interpreting dreams, solving riddles, and ᵀexplaining enigmas were found in this Daniel, whom the king named Belteshazzar, now let Daniel be called, and he will give the interpretation." *Lit. untying knots*

The Writing on the Wall Explained

13 Then Daniel was brought in before the king. The king spoke, and said to Daniel, "Are you that Daniel *who is one of the captives from Judah, whom my ᵀfather the king brought from Judah? *Or ancestor*

5:13 Lit. *who is of the sons of the captivity*

50-E. The Fall of Babylon (Daniel 5:1–31)—Babylon was one of the most remarkable cities of the ancient world, famed for its architecture and, above all, for its hanging gardens.

(1) *Babylon, the city.* Babylon was built in a square, fifteen miles on each side, or a sixty-mile perimeter.

(Point 50-E continued on next page)

▽ 14 "I have heard of you, that the Spirit of God *is* in you, and *that* light and understanding and excellent wisdom are found in you.

15 Now ᴿthe wise *men*, the astrologers, have been brought in before me, that they should read this writing and make known to me its interpretation, but they could not give the interpretation of the thing.   Dan. 5:7, 8

16 "And I have heard of you, that you can give interpretations and ᵀexplain enigmas. ᴿNow if you can read the writing and make known to me its interpretation, you shall be clothed with purple and *have* a chain of gold around your neck, and shall be the third ruler in the kingdom."   Lit. *untie knots* • Dan. 5:7, 29

17 Then Daniel answered, and said before the king, "Let your gifts be for yourself, and give your rewards to another; yet I will read the writing to the king, and make known to him the interpretation.

18 "O king, ᴿthe Most High God gave Nebuchadnezzar your ᵀfather a kingdom and majesty, glory and honor.   Dan. 4:17 • Or *ancestor* ▽

19 "And because of the majesty that He gave him, ᴿall peoples, nations, and languages trembled and feared before him. Whomever he wished, he ᴿexecuted; whomever he wished, he kept alive; whomever he wished, he set up; and whomever he wished, he put down.   Jer. 27:7 • Dan. 2:12, 13; 3:6

20 ᴿ"But when his heart was lifted up, and his spirit was hardened in pride, he was deposed from his kingly throne, and they took his glory from him.   Dan. 4:30, 37

21 "Then he was driven from the sons of men, his heart was made like the beasts, and his dwelling *was* with the wild donkeys. They fed him with grass like oxen, and his body was wet with the dew of heaven, ᴿtill he ᵀknew that the Most High God rules in the kingdom of men, and appoints over it whom-

(Point 50-E continued from previous page)
Its wall was 350 feet high, 87 feet thick, with over two hundred lookout towers. The great Euphrates River flowed from north to south through the city, dividing Babylon into two sections. The banks of the river were walled with great bronze or brass gates at each of the avenues. There was a bridge at the central gate and ferry boats for all the other gates. The palace stood in the center of the city, with one section on each side of the river. It was connected by a subterranean passageway under the river, where large banquet rooms were located.

(2) *Belshazzar's last feast.* Even though besieged by the Medes and the Persians (Cyrus and his great army had besieged the city for many months), Belshazzar entertained the city of Babylon with festivity and drinking. He invited a thousand of his lords and princes, his wives and concubines, to a great feast (v. 1), perhaps in one of the subterranean banquet rooms. Despite the siege by the Medes and Persians, the Babylonians believed that their city was impregnable. Little did they know that Cyrus had been working for months, changing the course of the great river so that it would bypass the city. On the night when they were feasting, drinking, and blaspheming the God of heaven, the river dried up, and Cyrus' army advanced down the riverbed (perhaps on both sides of the city). Careless in their drinking and partying, the Babylonians left the gates open and the Medes and Persians took the city. It was prophesied a hundred years before Cyrus was born that he would take Babylon (Is. 44:28—45:5, page 685).

(3) *Belshazzar's great sin.* During the drunken orgy, Belshazzar "gave the command to bring the gold and silver vessels which his father Nebuchadnezzar had taken from the temple which had been in Jerusalem" (v. 2). So far as we know, these sacred vessels had probably never been used until that night. When they were brought in, Belshazzar stood before the great banquet crowd and filled one of the vessels (perhaps a golden one) and "drank wine, and praised the gods of gold and silver, bronze and iron, wood and stone" (v. 4). This was blasphemy—for these vessels had been sprinkled with blood and set apart for the worship of Jehovah God (Heb. 9:21, 22, page 1244).

(4) *The handwriting on the wall.* While they were drinking and blaspheming God, they saw that the "fingers of a man's hand appeared and wrote opposite the lampstand on the plaster of the wall of the king's palace" (v. 5). The king was petrified with fear. His "countenance changed, and his thoughts troubled him, so that the joints of his hips were loosened and his knees knocked against each other" (v. 6). This wicked, ungodly king immediately sent for his wise men: "the astrologers, the Chaldeans, and the soothsayers" (v. 7). But none of them could read the writing on the wall. Then the queen came in and said, "There is a man in your kingdom in whom is the Spirit of the Holy God. And in the days of your father, light and understanding and wisdom, like the wisdom of the gods, were found in him" (v. 11). King Belshazzar summoned Daniel, saying, "Now if you can read the writing and make known to me its interpretation, you shall be clothed with purple and have a chain of gold around your neck, and shall be the third ruler in the kingdom" (v. 16). Daniel said to the king, "Let your gifts be for yourself" (v. 17), for he knew that the king would be dead before dawn. He was saying in effect, "The rewards I don't want, give them to somebody else." Then Daniel preached a great sermon to this wicked king (vv. 18–24): "This is the inscription that was written: MENE, MENE, TEKEL, UPHARSIN. This is the interpretation of each word. MENE: God has numbered your kingdom, and finished it; TEKEL: You have been weighed in the balances, and found wanting; PERES [the plural form of UPHARSIN]: Your kingdom has been divided, and given to the Medes and Persians" (vv. 25–28). This, then, was a day of reckoning. Even though Daniel told this ungodly king that he did not want the rewards, the king proceeded to do what he had promised for Daniel (v. 29). Then before the sun rose over the city of Babylon, the Medes and the Persians had conquered it, slaying Belshazzar "and Darius the Mede received the kingdom" (vv. 30, 31).

See Daniel 6:1–28, page 842, **for Point 50-F: Daniel: A Picture of the Tribulation Remnant.**

▽ ever He chooses.   Ezek. 17:24 · Recognized

22 "But you his son, Belshazzar, ᴿhave not humbled your heart, although you knew all this.   2 Chr. 33:23; 36:12

23 "And you have lifted yourself up against the Lord of heaven. They have brought the vessels of His house before you, and you and your lords, your wives and your concubines, have drunk wine from them. And you have praised the gods of silver and gold, bronze and iron, wood and stone, which do not see or hear or know; and the God who *holds* your breath in His hand and owns all your ways, you have not glorified.

24 "Then the *fingers of the hand were sent from Him, and this writing was written.

25 "And this is the inscription that was written:

*MENE, MENE, *TEKEL, *UPHARSIN.

26 "This *is* the interpretation of *each* word. Mᴇɴᴇ: God has numbered your kingdom, and finished it;

27 "Tᴇᴋᴇʟ: You have been weighed in the balances, and found wanting;

5:24 Lit. *palm*
5:25 Lit. *a mina* (50 shekels) from the verb "to number"
• Lit. *a shekel* from the verb "to weigh" • Lit. *and half-shekels* from the verb "to divide"; pl. of *Peres*, v. 28

---

28 "Pᴇʀᴇs: Your kingdom has been divided, ▽ and given to the Medes and *Persians."

29 Then Belshazzar gave the command, and they clothed Daniel with purple and *put a* chain of gold around his neck, and made a proclamation concerning him ᴿthat he should be the third ruler in the kingdom.   Dan. 5:7, 16

Belshazzar's Fall

30 ᴿThat very night Belshazzar, king of the Chaldeans, was slain.   Jer. 51:31, 39, 57

31 And Darius the Mede received the kingdom, *being* about sixty-two years old.   ▲

The Plot Against Daniel

50-F. Daniel: A Picture of the   ▼ Tribulation Remnant

6 It pleased Darius to set over the kingdom one hundred and twenty satraps, to be over the whole kingdom;

2 and over these, three governors, of whom Daniel *was* one, that the satraps might give account to them, so that the king would suffer no loss.

3 Then this Daniel distinguished himself above the governors and satraps, because an excellent spirit *was* in him; and the king gave thought to setting him over the whole realm.

5:28 Aram. *Para,* consonant with *Peres*

50-F. Daniel: A Picture of the Tribulation Remnant (Daniel 6:1-28)—The Tribulation remnant consists of 144,000 members of the twelve tribes of Israel, pledged by "the seal of the living God" to serve God during the Great Tribulation (Rev. 7:1-8, page 1300). They will evangelize the nations and turn a countless multitude to Christ the Messiah. Jeremiah, the prophet, prophesied that in the end of the Times of the Gentiles, God would bring Israel and Judah out of all the nations of the world, back to their original homeland. God said, " 'For I am with you,' says the Lᴏʀᴅ, 'to save you; though I make a full end of all nations where I have scattered you, yet I will not make a complete end of you. But I will correct you in justice, and will not let you go altogether unpunished' " (Jer. 30:1-11, page 743). Even though Israel has been persecuted and scattered throughout the world, and without a homeland until 1948, God has never forsaken his chosen nation. For almost two thousand years they were a nation without a home; yet they have retained their national identity. When you see a Hebrew, you are looking upon a miracle. God did not make an end of all nations after the seventy years of captivity in Babylon; therefore, this prophecy is to be fulfilled in the future (Matt. 25:31-46, page 976). At this time of judgment of the nations, God will make an end of all the ungodly nations. The Jews' punishment will not be completed until the end of the seven years of Great Tribulation which are called "the time of Jacob's trouble" (Jer. 30:7, page 743). Israel's God will save 144,000 of the twelve tribes and seal on their foreheads the mark of ownership (Rev. 7:3, page 1300). The 144,000 will not comprise the church: those of the church are not sealed on their foreheads; they are sealed with the Holy Spirit of promise (Eph. 1:13, page 1186; 4:30, page 1191) after having received the Lord Jesus Christ into their hearts as personal Savior (Rom. 10:9, 10, page 1140).

(1) *Daniel's political prominence* (vv. 1-3). This chapter ushers in the second Gentile world empire. After sixty-seven years the "head of gold" is replaced by the silver, an inferior kingdom (Dan. 5:30, 31, above). Daniel prophesied that the Medes and Persians would come and overthrow the Babylonian kingdom, and rule the known Gentile world.

(2) *Daniel's jealous colleagues* (vv. 4-9). Because King Darius favored Daniel over the other two presidents and all the princes, there was much jealousy; so they swore they would destroy Daniel, saying, "We shall not find any charge against this Daniel unless we find it against him concerning the law of his God" (v. 5). Now the presidents and princes had a voice in making laws for the Medes and Persians. When the laws were ratified by the king, no man could alter them. The difference between Nebuchadnezzar's kingdom and that of the Medes and Persians is simply that Nebuchadnezzar had total power. He was above all the laws of Babylon. But the Medo-Persian kings had to obey every statute. The law was the most powerful thing, more powerful than the king. Hence we have the phrase, "the law of the Medes and Persians, which does not alter" (v. 8). After drafting a law that would destroy Daniel, these two presidents and princes met the king, flattering him and lying to him (vv. 6, 7).

(Point 50-F continued on next page)

▽ 4 ᴿSo the governors and satraps sought to
find *some* charge against Daniel concerning
the kingdom; but they could find no charge
or fault, because he *was* faithful; nor was
there any error or fault found in him. Eccl. 4:4
5 Then these men said, "We shall not find
any charge against this Daniel unless we find
it against him concerning the law of his
God."
6 So these governors and satraps thronged
before the king, and said thus to him: ᴿ"King
Darius, live forever!   Neh. 2:3
7 "All the governors of the kingdom, the
administrators and satraps, the counselors
and advisors, have ᴿconsulted together to
establish a royal statute and to make a firm
decree, that whoever petitions any god or
man for thirty days, except you, O king, shall
be cast into the den of lions. Ps. 59:3; 62:4; 64:2-6
8 "Now, O king, establish the decree and
sign the writing, so that it cannot be
changed, according to the law of the Medes
and Persians, which does not alter."
9 Therefore King Darius signed the written decree.

Daniel in the Lions' Den

10 Now when Daniel knew that the writing
was signed, he went home. And in his upper
room, with his windows open toward Jerusalem, he knelt down on his knees three times
that day, and prayed and gave thanks before
his God, as was his custom since early days.

11 Then these men assembled and found ▽
Daniel praying and making supplication before his God.
12 And they went before the king, and
spoke concerning the king's decree: "Have
you not signed a decree that every man who
petitions any god or man within thirty days,
except you, O king, shall be cast into the den
of lions?" The king answered and said, "The
thing *is* true, according to the law of the
Medes and Persians, which does not alter."
13 So they answered and said before the
king, "That Daniel, who is ᵀone of the captives from Judah, does not show due regard
for you, O king, or for the decree that you
have signed, but makes his petition three
times a day."   Lit. *of the sons of the captivity*
14 And the king, when he heard *these*
words, ᴿwas greatly displeased with himself,
and set *his* heart on Daniel to deliver him;
and he ᵀlabored till the going down of the sun
to deliver him.   Mark 6:26 • *strove*
15 Then these men ᵀapproached the king,
and said to the king, "Know, O king, that *it is*
ᴿthe law of the Medes and Persians that no
decree or statute which the king establishes
may be changed." Lit. *thronged before* • Dan. 6:8, 12
16 So the king gave the command, and they
brought Daniel and cast *him* into the den of
lions. *But* the king spoke, saying to Daniel,
"Your God, whom you serve continually, He
will deliver you."
17 Then a stone was brought and laid on

(Point 50-F continued from previous page)

   (3) *Daniel's prayer life* (vv. 10, 11). The two presidents and princes knew that Daniel prayed to his God
three times a day, at an open window facing Jerusalem. When Daniel heard the news, "he went home. And
in his upper room, with his windows open toward Jerusalem," he prayed (v. 10), knowing that he would be
cast into the den of lions, because "the law of the Medes and Persians . . . does not alter." For Daniel valued
prayer and his faith in God more than he valued his physical life. God has always preserved a remnant of
Israel who value their faith in God more than they value their lives (Rom. 11:1–5, page 1141).
   (4) *Daniel's powerless king* (vv. 12–18). When Daniel's enemies came before the king, citing evidence
that Daniel had broken the law of the Medes and Persians, King Darius tried to save Daniel but ultimately
had to obey the law. So he had Daniel thrown into the den of lions. "Now the king went to his palace and
spent the night fasting; and no musicians were brought before him. Also his sleep went from him" (vv. 16,
18).
   (5) *Daniel's all-powerful God* (vv. 19–23). What the king could not do, Daniel's God could do. He
delivered Daniel from the lion's den, so that "no injury whatever was found on him, because he believed in
his God" (v. 23).
   (6) *Daniel's enemies destroyed* (v. 24). The king commanded that these men who "framed" Daniel and
who tried to destroy this great man of God, be cast "into the den of lions—them, their children, and their
wives" (v. 24). These wicked men, who would have destroyed Daniel, themselves suffered the fate which
they had planned for God's prophet. So it will be, at the end of the Great Tribulation, when the nations of
the world will be judged by God and destroyed, never to persecute God's people again (Rev. 19:11–21, page
1312). The book of Esther dramatized this, when Haman conspired to hang Mordecai the Jew, whom he
hated. Haman built a great gallows on which to hang Mordecai, but never got to use it. Actions taken against
God, and against His perfect will for His people, are always frustrated at last. Instead of Mordecai hanging
on the gallows, the king hanged Haman on Haman's own gallows (Esth. 7:10, page 474). This recalls the old
axiom: "the chickens come home to roost." So they will, when all the ungodly nations that have persecuted
the remnant of God's people for the past twenty-five hundred years are judged by God.
   (7) *Daniel's honor and prosperity* (vv. 25–28). Now King Darius decreed "that in every dominion of my
kingdom men must tremble and fear before the God of Daniel" (v. 26). They were not to fear Daniel nor to
tremble in his presence, but they were to respect and revere Daniel's God. Daniel was honored by the king,
and he prospered in his kingdom because he was an upright, righteous, honest, God-fearing man. What a
marvelous glorification of the Tribulation remnant, who "did not love their lives to the death" (Rev. 12:11,
page 1305).
   See Master Outline 51: "Daniel, the Prophet: His Visions," page 58, for your next study.

▽ the mouth of the den, ᴿand the king sealed it with his own signet ring and with the signets of his lords, that the purpose concerning Daniel might not be changed.   Matt. 27:66

Daniel Saved from the Lions

18 Now the king went to his palace and spent the night fasting; and no *musicians were brought before him. ᴿAlso his sleep ᵀwent from him.   Dan. 2:1 · Or *fled*

19 Then the ᴿking arose very early in the morning and went in haste to the den of lions.   Dan. 3:24

20 And when he came to the den, he cried out with a ᵀlamenting voice to Daniel. The king spoke, saying to Daniel, "Daniel, servant of the living God, ᴿhas your God, whom you serve continually, been able to deliver you from the lions?"   Or *grieved* · Dan. 3:17

21 Then Daniel said to the king, ᴿ"O king, live forever!   Dan. 2:4; 6:6

22 ᴿ"My God sent His angel and ᴿshut the lions' mouths, so that they have not hurt me, because I was found innocent before Him; and also, O king, I have done no wrong before you."   Dan. 3:28 · Heb. 11:33

23 Now the king was exceedingly glad for him, and commanded that they should take Daniel up out of the den. So Daniel was taken up out of the den, and no injury whatever was found on him, ᴿbecause he believed in his God.   Heb. 11:33

Darius Honors God

24 And the king gave the command, and they brought those men who had accused Daniel, and they cast *them* into the den of lions—them, ᴿtheir children, and their wives; and the lions overpowered them, and broke all their bones in pieces before they ever came to the bottom of the den.   Deut. 24:16

25 ᴿThen King Darius wrote:

To all peoples, nations, and languages that dwell in all the earth:

Peace be multiplied to you.   Dan. 4:1

26 ᴿI make a decree that in every   Dan. 3:29 dominion of my kingdom *men must* ᴿtremble and fear before the God of Daniel.   Ps. 99:1

ᴿFor He is the living God,   Dan. 4:34; 6:20 And steadfast forever; His kingdom *is* the one which shall not be ᴿdestroyed,   Dan. 2:44; 4:3; 7:14, 27 And His dominion *shall endure* to the end.

27 He delivers and rescues,

6:18 Exact meaning unknown

ᴿAnd He works signs and wonders   ▽ In heaven and on earth, Who has delivered Daniel from the ᵀpower of the lions.   Dan. 4:2, 3 · Lit. *hand*

28 So this Daniel prospered in the reign of Darius ᴿand in the reign of ᴿCyrus the Persian.   Dan. 1:21 · Ezra 1:1, 2 ▲

Vision of the Four Beasts

51-A. The Vision of the Four Beasts   ▼

7 In the first year of Belshazzar king of Babylon, ᴿDaniel ᵀhad a dream and ᴿvisions of his head *while* on his bed. Then he wrote down the dream, telling *the main facts.   [Amos 3:7] · Lit. *saw* · [Dan. 2:28]

2 Daniel spoke, saying, "I saw in my vision by night, and behold, the four winds of heaven were stirring up the Great Sea.

3 "And four great beasts came up from the sea, each different from the other.

4 "The first *was* like a lion, and had eagle's wings. I watched till its wings were plucked off; and it was lifted up from the earth and made to stand on two feet like a man, and a man's heart was given to it.

5 ᴿ"And suddenly another beast, a second, like a bear. It was raised up on one side, and *had* three ribs in its mouth between its teeth. And they said thus to it: 'Arise, devour much flesh!'   Dan. 2:39

6 "After this I looked, and there was another, like a leopard, which had on its back four wings of a bird. The beast also had four heads, and dominion was given to it.

7 "After this I saw in the night visions, and behold, ᴿa fourth beast, dreadful and terrible, exceedingly strong. It had huge iron teeth; it was devouring, breaking in pieces, and trampling the residue with its feet. It *was* different from all the beasts that *were* before it, ᴿand it had ten horns.   Dan. 2:40 · Rev. 12:3; 13:1

8 "I was considering the horns, and ᴿthere was another horn, a little one, coming up among them, before whom three of the first horns were plucked out by the roots. And there, in this horn, *were* eyes like the eyes ᴿof a man, ᴿand a mouth speaking ᵀpompous words.   Dan. 8:9 · Rev. 9:7 · Rev. 13:5, 6 · Lit. *great things*

Vision of the Ancient of Days

9 "Iᴿ watched till thrones were ᵀput in place,   [Rev. 20:4] · Or *set up* And ᴿthe Ancient of Days was seated; ᴿHis garment *was* white as snow, And the hair of His head *was* like pure wool.   Ps. 90:2 · Rev. 1:14

7:1 Lit. *the head* or *chief of the words*

51-A. The Vision of the Four Beasts (Daniel 7:1-28)—The empires in Daniel's vision (chapter 7) are identical to the empires of Nebuchadnezzar's dream in chapter 2. The difference is that Nebuchadnezzar saw the four Gentile empires from man's standpoint: he saw only their human glory. Daniel saw them from God's viewpoint: corrupt and ruthless.

(1) Daniel's vision occurred in the first year of Belshazzar's reign over Babylon (about 553 B.C.). So

(Point 51-A continued from previous page)

His throne *was* a fiery flame,
^RIts wheels a burning fire;   Ezek. 1:15
10 ^RA fiery stream issued
And came forth from before Him.
^RA thousand thousands ministered to
Him;   Is. 30:33; 66:15 • Rev. 5:11
Ten thousand times ten thousand stood
before Him.
^RThe ^Tcourt was seated,   [Rev. 20:11–15]
And the books were opened.   Or *judgment*

11 "I watched then because of the sound of
the ^Tpompous words which the horn was
speaking; ^RI watched till the beast was slain,
and its body destroyed and given to the
burning flame.   Lit. *great* • [Rev. 19:20; 20:10]
12 "As for the rest of the beasts, they had
their dominion taken away, yet their lives
were prolonged for a season and a time.

13 "I was watching in the night visions,
And behold, *One* like the Son of Man,
Coming with the clouds of heaven!
He came to the Ancient of Days,
And they brought Him near before
Him.

14 ^RThen to Him was given dominion and
glory and a kingdom,   [John 3:35, 36]
That all ^Rpeoples, nations, and
languages should serve Him.   Dan. 3:4
His dominion *is* ^Ran everlasting
dominion,   Mic. 4:7; [Luke 1:33]
Which shall not pass away,
And His kingdom *the one*
Which shall not be destroyed.

Daniel's Visions Interpreted

15 "I, Daniel, was grieved in my spirit
^Twithin *my* body, and the visions of my head
troubled me.   Lit. *in the midst of its sheath*
16 "I came near to one of those who stood
by, and asked him the truth of all this. So he
told me and made known to me the interpretation of these things:
17 'Those great beasts, which are four, *are*
four *kings *which* arise out of the earth.
18 'But the saints of the Most High shall
receive the kingdom, and possess the kingdom forever, even forever and ever.'

7:17 Representing their kingdoms, v. 23

(Point 51-A continued from previous page)
chronologically, Daniel's vision in chapter 7 came before chapter 5, but the Holy Spirit inspired Daniel to
insert it in the second half of the book of Daniel. The first half of Daniel (1—6, page 830) is historical and
biographical and includes some generalized prophecy, and typology as well.
  Chapters 7—12 (page 844) prophesy *details* covering the Times of the Gentiles from the Babylonian
captivity to the seven years of the Great Tribulation in the future, which is called "the time of Jacob's
trouble" (Jer. 30:7, page 743; cf. Rev. 7:14, page 1301).
  (2) Chapter 7 spans the Times of the Gentiles, from Nebuchadnezzar (606 B.C.) to the Antichrist (the little
horn), who will come to power during the Great Tribulation.
  Now let us compare Daniel's vision of the four great beasts with Nebuchadnezzar's dream of the image.
    (a) *"The first was like a lion"* (v. 4). This is the same as Nebuchadnezzar's head of gold (Dan. 2:37, 38,
page 835)—the Babylonian Empire. Nebuchadnezzar was the one outstanding king of this first Gentile world
empire.
    (b) *"A second, like a bear"* (v. 5). This is the same as the breast and arms of silver (Dan. 2:32, 39, page
835)—the Medo-Persian Empire. Cyrus was the outstanding king of this second Gentile world empire. Cyrus,
a Gentile who did not know Jehovah God, was selected by the Lord over a hundred years before he was
born. God anointed Cyrus to do His will, and to deliver Israel from the Babylonians and help rebuild their
temple (Is. 44:28—45:4, page 685; cf. Ezra 1:1–4, page 444).
    (c) *"There was another, like a leopard"* (v. 6). This is the same as the belly and thighs of brass (Dan.
2:32-39, page 835)—the Greek Empire. Alexander the Great was the outstanding king of this third Gentile
world empire.
    (d) *"I saw . . . a fourth beast"* (v. 7). The fourth beast in Daniel's vision was unlike any other—he was
dreadful and exceedingly strong, with teeth of iron (vv. 7, 8). He represents the same world power as the
legs of iron and the feet of iron and clay (Dan. 2:40-43, page 835). The outstanding ruler (the Antichrist) of
this empire is yet to appear. The ten horns in the head of the beast are the same as the ten toes of
Nebuchadnezzar's image (Dan. 2:41-44, page 835). These ten horns or ten toes represent the ten kings who
will lead the revived Roman Empire during the Tribulation (Rev. 13:1, page 1305). The first phase of the
Roman Empire lasted over 650 years, longer than the other three empires combined. The second phase of
the revived Roman Empire will last throughout the Great Tribulation. During this time, the little horn
(Antichrist) will be in power. In the first half of the Tribulation he will befriend the Jews and confirm a
covenant for seven years (Dan. 9:27, page 851). During the last half of the Tribulation he will be empowered
by Satan (v. 25; cf. Rev. 13:2, page 1305). He will dethrone three of the kings (v. 8). The other seven will
become puppets (v. 20). The book of Revelation details the satanic powers he will exert during the three-
and-one-half-year reign (Rev. 13:1-8, page 1305). He will possess all the characteristics of Satan (Rev. 13:2,
page 1305). In the days of the ten kings with the little horn (the Antichrist), Christ will come and establish the
kingdom of God upon earth (vv. 13, 22, above; cf. Dan. 2:34, 35, 44, 45, page 835; Luke 1:31-33, page 1010;
Rev. 11:15, page 1305). When Christ comes, He will sit upon the throne of His human ancestor, King David
(Is. 9:6, 7, page 651), and will rule in eternal righteousness (Heb. 1:8, 9, page 1236).

  See Daniel 8:1-27, page 846, for **Point 51-B: The Vision of the Ram and Goat.**

19 "Then I wished to know the truth about the fourth beast, which was different from all the others, exceedingly dreadful, *with* its teeth of iron and its nails of bronze, *which* devoured, broke in pieces, and trampled the residue with its feet;

20 "and the ten horns that *were* on its head, and the other *horn* which came up, before which three fell, namely, that horn which had eyes and a mouth which spoke [T]pompous words, whose appearance *was* greater than his fellows.   Lit. *great things*

21 "I was watching; [R]and the same horn was making war against the saints, and prevailing against them,   Rev. 11:7; 13:7; 17:14

22 "until the Ancient of Days came, [R]and a judgment was made *in favor* of the saints of the Most High, and the time came for the saints to possess the kingdom.   [Rev. 1:6]

23 "Thus he said:

'The fourth beast shall be
[R]A fourth kingdom on earth,   Dan. 2:40
    Which shall be different from all *other*
        kingdoms,
And shall devour the whole earth,
    Trample it and break it in pieces.

24 [R]The ten horns *are* ten kings   Rev. 13:1
    Who shall arise from this kingdom.
And another shall rise after them;
He shall be different from the first *ones*,
And shall subdue three kings.

25 [R]He shall speak *pompous* words against
    the Most High,   Rev. 13:1–6
Shall [R]persecute[T] the saints of the Most
    High,   Rev. 17:6 · Lit. *wear out*
And shall [R]intend to change times and
    law.   Dan. 2:21
Then [R]*the saints* shall be given into his
    hand   Rev. 13:7; 18:24
For a time and times and half a time.

26 'But[R] the court shall be seated,
And they shall [R]take away his
    dominion,   [Dan. 2:35; 7:10, 22] · Rev. 19:20
To consume and destroy *it* forever.

27 Then the [R]kingdom and dominion,
    And the greatness of the kingdoms
        under the whole heaven,   Dan. 7:14, 18, 22
Shall be given to the people, the saints
    of the Most High.
[R]His kingdom *is* an everlasting kingdom,
[R]And all dominions shall serve and obey
    Him.'   [Luke 1:33, 34] · Is. 60:12

28 "This *is* the end of the [T]account. As for me, Daniel, my thoughts greatly troubled me, and my countenance changed; but I kept the matter in my heart."   Lit. *word* ▲

Vision of a Ram and a Goat

51-B. The Vision of the Ram and Goat   ▼

8 In* the third year of the reign of King Belshazzar a vision appeared *to* me—to

8:1 The Hebrew language resumes in Dan. 8:1.

51-B. The Vision of the Ram and Goat (Daniel 8:1-27)—About two years after his first vision (Dan. 7:1, page 844), Daniel experienced his second vision (v. 1) during Belshazzar's third year as king of Babylon. His first vision had covered the four Gentile empires. His second vision covered the second and third empires (Medo-Persian and Greek). During the reign of these two empires, about 339 years, some of the most amazing prophecies in the Bible were fulfilled. Chronologically, chapters 7 and 8 occurred *before* Belshazzar's feast in chapter 5.

Daniel 1:1—2:3, because it was written in Hebrew, gave spiritual guidance and inspiration to the Hebrew captives. Daniel 2:4—7:28 was written in Aramaic, the popular language of the day, perhaps so that some of the Gentiles might read it and come to know the God of heaven as Nebuchadnezzar did (in chapter 4). Daniel wrote a portion of his book in Hebrew (8:1—12:13), so the Hebrew people could know God's plan for their nation from the seventy years of captivity prophesied by Jeremiah (Jer. 25:11, 12, page 738), to the return of their Messiah, the Lord Jesus Christ, at the end of the Great Tribulation.

Daniel was in Babylon when he had this second vision but was transported in the vision to Shushan (or Susa), in the province of Elam, north of the head of the Persian Gulf (v. 2). In a matter of moments, the God of heaven revealed to Daniel the future of Israel under the rule of the Medo-Persian and Greek empires for 339 years.

(1) In his vision he saw by the river of Ulai a ram with one horn higher than the other (vv. 3, 4). As he was pondering the vision, there appeared before him what looked like a man, even as a voice between the banks of the river was saying, "Gabriel, make this man understand the vision" (vv. 15, 16). Gabriel said to Daniel, "The ram which you saw, having the two horns—they are the kings of Media and Persia" (vv. 19, 20). Darius was then the king of the Medes, and Cyrus (the stronger of the two) was the king of the Persians. In his first year's reign, Cyrus had sent a written proclamation throughout his kingdom: "All the kingdoms of the earth the LORD God of heaven has given me. And He has commanded me to build Him a house at Jerusalem which is in Judah" (Ezra 1:2, page 444; cf. 6:1–3, page 448). Cyrus must have read Isaiah's prophecy where Jehovah God called him by name, saying, "He is My shepherd, and he shall perform all My pleasure, saying to Jerusalem, 'You shall be built,' and to the temple, 'Your foundation shall be laid' " (Is. 44:28, page 685).

Cyrus was called God's anointed for God had said, "I will go before you and make the crooked places straight; I will break in pieces the gates of bronze and cut the bars of iron" (Is. 45:1-7, page 685). God did

(Point 51-B continued on next page)

▽ me, Daniel—after the one that appeared to me ᴿthe first time. *Dan. 7:1*

2 I saw in the vision, and it so happened while I was looking, that I *was* in ᴿShushan,ᵀ the ᵀcitadel, which *is* in the province of Elam; and I saw in the vision that I was by the River Ulai. *Esth. 1:2; 2:8 · Or Susa · Or fortified palace*

3 Then I lifted my eyes and saw, and there, standing beside the river, was a ram which had two horns, and the two horns *were* high; but one *was* ᴿhigher than the other, and the higher *one* came up last. *Dan. 7:5*

4 I saw the ram pushing westward, northward, and southward, so that no animal could ᵀwithstand him; nor *was there any* that could deliver from his hand, but he did according to his will and became great. *Lit. stand before*

5 And as I was considering, suddenly a male goat came from the west, across the surface of the whole earth, without touching the ground; and the goat *had* a notable ᴿhorn between his eyes. *Dan. 8:8, 21; 11:3*

6 Then he came to the ram that had two horns, which I had seen standing beside the river, and ran at him with furious power.

7 And I saw him confronting the ram; he was moved with rage against him, ᵀattacked the ram, and broke his two horns. There was

no power in the ram to withstand him, but he ▽ cast him down to the ground and trampled him; and there was no one that could deliver the ram from his hand. *Lit. struck*

8 Therefore the male goat grew very great; but when he became strong, the large horn was broken, and in place of it ᴿfour notable ones came up toward the four winds of heaven. *Dan. 7:6; 8:22; 11:4*

9 ᴿAnd out of one of them came a little horn which grew exceedingly great toward the south, ᴿtoward the east, and toward the ᴿGlorious *Land*. *Dan. 11:21 · Dan. 11:25 · Ps. 48:2*

10 ᴿAnd it grew up to ᴿthe host of heaven; and ᴿit cast down *some* of the host and *some* of the stars to the ground, and trampled them. *Dan. 11:28 · Is. 14:13 · Rev. 12:4*

11 He even exalted *himself* as high as the Prince of the host; and by him the daily *sacrifices* were taken away, and the place of ᵀHis sanctuary was cast down. *The temple*

12 Because of transgression, an army was given over *to the horn* to oppose the daily *sacrifices*; and he cast truth down to the ground. He did *all this* and prospered.

13 Then I heard ᴿa holy one speaking; and *another* holy one said to that certain *one* who was speaking, "How long *will* the vision *be*,

---

(Point 51-B continued from previous page)
all of this for the Jews who were captives in Babylon. Cyrus was chosen by God to bring about the Jews' return to Judea, and the rebuilding of the city of Jerusalem and the temple. Those who first returned (approximately 50,000) came under Zerubbabel and Jeshua (Ezra 2:64, page 445). Upon arriving in Jerusalem, they immediately built the altar for their morning and evening burnt offerings to God (Ezra 3:1–7, page 446). The Jews gradually rebuilt the city of Jerusalem, the walls, and the temple under Zerubbabel, Jeshua, Ezra, Nehemiah, and Zechariah.

(2) The male goat from the west was Greece (vv. 5–8, 21). The words "without touching the ground" refer to the swiftness of the attack and conquest by the "notable horn," Alexander the Great (v. 5). With foot soldiers and cavalry, Alexander conquered the Medo-Persian Empire in an unparalleled campaign (336–323 B.C.) of military conquest. The words "furious" (v. 6) and "rage" (v. 7) are the only adequate words to describe Alexander's implacable hatred of the Persians, who for two centuries had humiliated and trampled on the beauty of the cities of Greece. His conquest of Persia, Palestine, Babylon, Egypt, and western India helped spread Greek culture and language everywhere, which is why the "good news" of the New Testament was later to be penned in Greek, the world language of the day.

(3) The Greek Empire split into four parts (v. 8). Alexander the Great died suddenly at Babylon in 323 B.C., at the age of thirty-three. Upon his death, Alexander's four generals (and then their heirs) became rulers of the conquered empire. These newly created Greek dynasties fought battle after battle to redivide the conquered land. The four horns represent these kings, and correspond to the four wings and four heads on the Greek leopard in the vision in Daniel 7:6 (page 844). Palestine became a football to be fought over by the Greek kings of Syria and the Hellenistic kings of Egypt.

(4) Out of the Syrian-Greek horn was to come a persecutor of Judah (vv. 9–12). From the dynasty of the Hellenistic kings of Syria would arise Antiochus Epiphanes who persecuted Israel from 168–165 B.C. He was the little horn of the Greek Empire as well as a type of the little horn of the revived Roman Empire . . . the Antichrist. He sought to erase the worship of the one true and living God from the earth:

   (a) He ordered the Sabbath day to be violated.
   (b) He sprinkled God's temple in Jerusalem with swine's blood.
   (c) He set up an idol of Jupiter in the temple.

Over the next decade God used a pious, priestly family, the Maccabees (or "Hammers"), whose family name was Hasmon, to lead Israel to defeat four Syrian armies. The temple was recovered, cleansed, and rededicated (165 B.C.). The security and freedom brought about by God through the Maccabees was maintained even when the Romans came in 63 B.C. God always destroys the persecutors of Israel and brings their works to nothing.

See Daniel 9:1–27, page 848, for **Point 51-C: The Vision of the Seventy Weeks.**

▽ concerning the daily *sacrifices* and the transgression ᵀof desolation, the giving of both the sanctuary and the host to be trampled underfoot?"   Dan. 4:13, 23 · Or *making desolate*

14 And he said to me, "For two thousand three hundred ᵀdays; then the sanctuary shall be cleansed."   Lit. *evening-mornings*

Gabriel Interprets the Vision

15 Then it happened, when I, Daniel, had seen the vision and was seeking the meaning, that suddenly there stood before me ᴿone having the appearance of a man.   Ezek. 1:26

16 And I heard a man's voice ᴿbetween *the banks of* the Ulai, who called, and said, ᴿ"Gabriel, make this *man* understand the vision."   Dan. 12:6, 7 · Luke 1:19, 26

17 So he came near where I stood, and when he came I was afraid and ᴿfell on my face; but he said to me, "Understand, son of man, that the vision *refers* to the time of the end."   Rev. 1:17

18 Now, as he was speaking with me, I was in a deep sleep with my face to the ground; but he touched me, and stood me upright.

19 And he said, "Look, I am making known to you what shall happen in the latter time of the indignation; ᴿfor at the appointed time the end *shall be*.   Hab. 2:3

20 "The ram which you saw, having the two horns—*they are* the kings of Media and Persia.

21 "And the male goat *is* the *kingdom of Greece. The large horn that *is* between its eyes ᴿis the first king.   Dan. 11:3

22 ᴿ"As for the broken *horn* and the four that stood up in its place, four kingdoms shall arise out of that nation, but not with its power.   Dan. 11:4

8:21 Lit. *king*, representing his kingdom, Dan. 7:17, 23

23 "And in the latter time of their kingdom, ▽ When the transgressors have reached their fullness,
A king shall arise,
Having fierce ᵀfeatures,   Lit. *countenance*
Who understands sinister schemes.

24 His power shall be mighty, ᴿbut not by his own power;   Rev. 17:13
He shall destroy ᵀfearfully,   *extraordinarily*
ᴿAnd shall prosper and thrive;   Dan. 11:36
ᴿHe shall destroy the mighty, and *also* the holy people.   Dan. 7:25

25 "Throughᴿ his cunning   Dan. 11:21
He shall cause deceit to prosper under his ᵀrule;   Lit. *hand*
And he shall exalt *himself* in his heart.
He shall destroy many in *their* prosperity.
ᴿHe shall even rise against the Prince of princes;   Rev. 19:19
But he shall be ᴿbroken without *human* ᵀmeans.   Job 34:20 · Lit. *hand*

26 "And the vision of the evenings and mornings
Which was told is true;
ᴿTherefore seal up the vision,
For *it refers* to many days in the future."   Ezek. 12:27

27 ᴿAnd I, Daniel, fainted and was sick for days; afterward I arose and went about the king's business. I was astonished by the vision, but no one understood it.   Dan. 7:28 ▲

Daniel's Prayer for the People

51-C. The Vision of the Seventy Weeks   ▼

9 In the first year ᴿof Darius the son of Ahasuerus, of the lineage of the Medes,

---

51-C. The Vision of the Seventy Weeks (Daniel 9:1–27)—This complex chapter is crucial to biblical prophecy. If we correctly interpret the seventy weeks (literally, seventy "heptads" or "sevens") that "are determined for your people and for your holy city" (v. 24), we will better understand the things that will come to pass in the last days before the rapture of the church and the Great Tribulation. Most scholars translate "sevens" as periods of seven years, so seventy sevens would be 490 years. This would take us up to the coming of Christ; and the last week goes beyond, to the Tribulation.

It was through studying Daniel's Seventieth Week that Leopold Cohn, a Russian rabbi, realized that the time for the coming of the Messiah had *already* passed, and he concluded that the Messiah must have come by A.D. 70! Cohn sought advice from an older rabbi who told him that you could find anything in New York, and to go to New York to find the Messiah. Cohn took the older rabbi quite literally, sold nearly all that he had to finance the journey to New York and there started his search for the Messiah. One day, as he was walking by a building, he heard singing. Entering the hall, he heard the gospel being preached and later that day accepted Jesus as his Messiah. He then bought a stable, cleaned it out, procured folding chairs, and started holding gospel meetings of his own. Thus, from a literal understanding of this passage in Daniel was born the American Board of Missions to the Jews!

We must remember that all prophecy concerning Israel and the Messiah is linked to the period of "seventy sevens." Also, we must allow Scripture to interpret Scripture (2 Pet. 1:20, 21, page 1273).

(1) In the first year of Darius' reign as king of the Chaldeans, Daniel began to understand Jeremiah's prophecy about the seventy years of captivity (Jer. 25:11, 12, page 738). He noted the fact that for 490 years Israel had failed to keep even one sabbatical year for the land (Lev. 25:1–7, page 132), so that now their God was collecting the entire seventy years they owed (vv. 1, 2).

(Point 51-C continued on next page)

▽ who was made king over the realm of the Chaldeans—

Dan. 1:21

2 in the first year of his reign I, Daniel, understood by the books the number of the years *specified* by the word of the LORD through ᴿJeremiah the prophet, that He would accomplish seventy years in the desolations of Jerusalem.

2 Chr. 36:21

3 ᴿThen I set my face toward the Lord God to make request by prayer and supplications, with fasting, sackcloth, and ashes.

Neh. 1:4

4 And I prayed to the LORD my God, and made confession, and said, "O Lord, great and awesome God, who keeps His covenant and mercy with those who love Him, and with ▽ those who keep His commandments,

5 ᴿ"we have sinned and committed iniquity, we have done wickedly and rebelled, even by departing from Your precepts and Your judgments.

1 Kin. 8:47, 48

6 ᴿ"Neither have we heeded Your servants the prophets, who spoke in Your name to our kings and our princes, to our fathers and all the people of the land.

2 Chr. 36:15

7 "O Lord, righteousness *belongs* to You, but to us shame of face, as *it is* this day—to the men of Judah, to the inhabitants of Jerusalem and all Israel, those near and those

---

(Point 51-C continued from previous page)

(2) Daniel felt deeply burdened by his concern for the future of his people and the city of Jerusalem. In prayer he sought the mercy of God for Israel:

   (a) His prayer was bold—"I set my face toward the Lord God" (v. 3).
   (b) His attitude was humble—"to make request by prayer and supplications, with fasting, sackcloth, and ashes" (v. 3).
   (c) He confessed the greatness of God—"O Lord, great and awesome God, who keeps His covenant and mercy with those who love Him, and with those who keep His commandments" (v. 4).
   (d) He confessed the sins of the nation Israel—"We have sinned" (vv. 4-16).
   (e) His plea—"Now therefore, our God, hear the prayer of Your servant" (vv. 17-19).

(3) The angel Gabriel interrupted Daniel's prayer and revealed to him Israel's future. Daniel wrote, "Yes, while I was speaking in prayer, the man Gabriel, whom I had seen in the vision at the beginning, being caused to fly swiftly, reached me about the time of the evening offering. And he informed me . . .

   (a) 'I have now come forth to give you skill to understand';
   (b) 'And I have come to tell you . . . consider the matter, and understand the vision' " (vv. 21-23).

God wanted Daniel to know and understand the seventy sevens of years that he had determined for Israel and Jerusalem. Israel had lived through sixty-nine sevens of years, or 483 years, with but seven years remaining judged upon them and their city.

(4) "Seventy weeks are determined for your people and for your holy city" (v. 24). The Hebrew word for week is *shavua*, which literally means "seven." But is this seven days or seven years? There is a clue in another chapter where Daniel said, "In those days I, Daniel, was mourning three full weeks"—or shavua, in the original (Dan. 10:2, 3, page 852). Here it means weeks of days, literally "three sevens of days."

If the seventy weeks were weeks of days, this would mean that the holy city and the walls would be rebuilt and destroyed again, and the Messiah would be "cut off," crucified (Matt. 27:35, page 980), and the six prophecies of Daniel (v. 24) would all come to pass in 490 *days*—obviously impossible.

The Hebrew people had sevens of years as well as sevens of days. For example, when Jacob had served Laban seven years for his daughter Rachel, he was given Leah, the first born, and Laban said unto him, "Fulfill her week, and we will give you this one also for the service which you will serve with me still another seven years" (Gen. 29:21-28, page 35). Here, one "week" is a seven of years.

(5) The three periods of the seventy sevens of years:

   (a) The first period of seven sevens of years, or forty-nine years, began "in the month of Nisan [April], in the twentieth year of King Artaxerxes"—445 B.C. (Neh. 2:1-8, page 455). Artaxerxes commissioned Nehemiah to rebuild Jerusalem and the walls (v. 25). See Ezra (page 444), Nehemiah (page 455), and Zechariah (page 911).

   (b) The second period of sixty-two sevens of years, or 434 years plus forty-nine years, totals 483 years with the Messiah (Christ) being cut off (crucified) in the month of Nisan (April) in A.D. 32. Allowing for Hebrew prophetic "years" of 360 days, this comes out to be exactly 483 years from the time Nehemiah was commissioned by King Artaxerxes to build the walled city. Actually, that Hebrew calculation dates back to the Flood. According to the book of Genesis, the Flood began in the six hundredth year of Noah's life, on the seventeenth day of the second month (Gen. 7:11, page 13); and the Flood came to an end on the seventeenth day of the seventh month (Gen. 8:4, page 14). This was a period of five months of thirty days each, exactly 150 days (Gen. 7:4, page 13). This indicates that as far back as the Flood, a year was reckoned to be 360 days, not 365 days as we calculate (v. 26).

   (c) The third period, the seventieth seven of years, or seven years plus 483 years, brings Israel down to the close of 490 years that Jehovah determined for the city and the people Israel. This is the Time of Jacob's Trouble (Jer. 30:7, page 743)—the seven years of Great Tribulation (Matt. 24:21, 22, page 973; Rev. 7:13, 14, page 1301).

(Point 51-C continued on next page)

▽ far off in all the countries to which You have driven them, because of the unfaithfulness which they have committed against You.

8 "O Lord, to us *belongs* shame of face, to our kings, our princes, and our fathers, because we have sinned against You.

9 ᴿ"To the Lord our God *belong* mercy and forgiveness, though we have rebelled against Him.   [Ps. 130:4, 7]

10 "We have not obeyed the voice of the LORD our God, to walk in His laws, which He set before us by His servants the prophets.

11 "Yes, ᴿall Israel has transgressed Your ▽ law, and has departed so as not to obey Your voice; therefore the curse and the oath written in the ᴿLaw of Moses the servant of God have been poured out on us, because we have sinned against Him.   Is. 1:3-6 • Lev. 26:14

12 "And He has ᴿconfirmed His words, which He spoke against us and against our judges who judged us, by bringing upon us a great disaster; ᴿfor under the whole heaven such has never been done as what has been done to Jerusalem.   Zech. 1:6 • Lam. 1:12; 2:13

(Point 51-C continued from previous page)

In the synagogue at Nazareth our Lord read from Isaiah 61:1 and 2, ending with "the acceptable year of the LORD," detailing the blessings of His First Advent in grace to Israel. He told them, "Today this Scripture is fulfilled in your hearing" (Luke 4:16–21, page 1016). The next line in Isaiah reads (but is not quoting Christ), "And the day of vengeance of our God." This is still in the future. Our Lord acknowledged the gap between His first and second comings, a gap surveyed in several Old Testament prophecies with comment.

Now there is a similar gap between verses 26 and 27. The 69 sevens of years, or 483 years were fulfilled by the crucifixion of Christ. However, the seventieth seven, or the last seven years, are still in the future because there are six prophecies that must be fulfilled during the seventy sevens of years before the 490 years determined for Israel come completely to pass. Gabriel said to Daniel (v. 24), "Seventy weeks are determined for your people and for your holy city

(a) "to finish the transgression"—the end of backsliding for the Hebrew nation, who will never again be apostate; this is yet future;

(b) "to make an end of sins"—as a nation they will no longer make a practice of sinning; this is yet future;

(c) "to make reconciliation for iniquity"—they will be reconciled to God by faith in the death, burial, and resurrection of Christ, their Messiah (Zech. 12:9–11, page 918; Rom. 11:25–27, page 1141)—as a nation they will repent; this is yet future;

(d) "to bring in everlasting righteousness"—this is God's righteous kingdom that Christ will establish on earth when He comes again (Heb. 1:8, 9, page 1236; cf. Is. 9:6, 7, page 651; Rev. 19:11–16, page 1312); this is yet future;

(e) "to seal up the vision and prophecy"—there will be no more need for visions and prophecies for Israel, for all will have come to pass; this is yet future;

(f) "to anoint the Most Holy"—or the Most Holy Place, the kingdom temple; this is yet future.

The Messiah was "cut off" on Calvary over 1900 years ago. This means that the first 483 years of the seventy sevens are past; they were literally fulfilled in every detail. Doesn't it stand to reason that the seventieth seven will also have a literal fulfillment? The Great Tribulation is yet to be.

We know from history that between verses 26 and 27 the church age occurred. This was a mystery to the prophets; none of the writers of the Old Testament books possessed any foreknowledge of the New Testament church (Eph. 3:9, page 1189; Col. 1:26, 27, page 1203).

(6) The seventieth week—"Then he [the prince] shall confirm a covenant with many for one week"—or seven years (v. 27). There are two princes mentioned in this chapter:

(a) "Messiah the Prince" (v. 25).

(b) The prince that shall come—"the people of the prince who is to come shall destroy the city and the sanctuary" (v. 26).

Christ the Messiah will not return to this earth until the end of the Tribulation (Rev. 19:11–21, page 1312). The Roman army under Titus destroyed Jerusalem in A.D. 70. Therefore, this prince (v. 26) who ratifies the covenant with the Jews for seven years will be a Roman—the little horn of Daniel (Dan. 7:8, page 844). He is also "the man of sin" (2 Thess. 2:3, 4, page 1215) and "a beast . . . out of the sea"—the sea being the ten kingdoms of the revived Roman Empire (Rev. 13:1–10, page 1305). "In the middle of the week [seven years] he shall bring an end to sacrifice and offering. And on the wing of abominations shall be one who makes desolate" (v. 27; cf. Matt. 24:15–22, page 973). He will stop the sacrificial offerings and worship, and desecrate the Holy Place, the temple. However, before the seventieth week can come to pass

(a) a remnant of Israel and Judah will return and possess the land of Israel in troublesome times (Jer. 30:1–24, page 743). In 1948 Israel became a nation; this *could* be the beginning of the end of the Times of the Gentiles (Luke 21:24, page 1041).

(b) the temple will be rebuilt either before or during the first three-and-one-half years of the Tribulation. Unless the temple be rebuilt, the prophecy of the "abomination of desolation" (Matt. 24:15, page 973) spoken of by Daniel the prophet could not come to pass.

See Daniel 10:1–21, page 851, for **Point 51-D: The Vision of the Angel in Linen.**

▽ 13 "As *it is* written in the Law of Moses, all this disaster has come upon us; ᴿyet we have not made our prayer before the Lᴏʀᴅ our God, that we might turn from our iniquities and understand Your truth.   Is. 9:13

14 "Therefore the Lᴏʀᴅ has ᴿkept the disaster in mind, and brought it upon us; for ᴿthe Lᴏʀᴅ our God *is* righteous in all the works which He does, though we have not obeyed His voice.   Jer. 31:28; 44:27 • Neh. 9:33

15 "And now, O Lord our God, ᴿwho brought Your people out of the land of Egypt with a mighty hand, and made Yourself ᴿa name, as *it is* this day—we have sinned, we have done wickedly!   Neh. 1:10 • Neh. 9:10

16 "O Lord, according to all Your righteousness, I pray, let Your anger and Your fury be turned away from Your city Jerusalem, Your holy mountain; because for our sins, and for the iniquities of our fathers, Jerusalem and Your people ᴿ*are* a reproach to all *those* around us.   Ps. 79:4

17 "Now therefore, our God, hear the prayer of Your servant, and his supplications, and for the Lord's sake cause Your face to shine on Your sanctuary, which is desolate.

18 "O my God, incline Your ear and hear; open Your eyes and see our desolations, and the city ᴿwhich is called by Your name; for we do not present our supplications before You because of our righteous deeds, but because of Your great mercies.   Jer. 25:29

19 "O Lord, hear! O Lord, forgive! O Lord, listen and act! Do not delay for Your own sake, my God, for Your city and Your people are called by Your name."

The Seventy-Weeks Prophecy

20 Now while I *was* speaking, praying, and confessing my sin and the sin of my people Israel, and presenting my supplication before the Lᴏʀᴅ my God for the holy mountain of my God,

21 yes, while I *was* speaking in prayer, the man ᴿGabriel, whom I had seen in the vision at the beginning, being caused to fly swiftly, reached me about the time of the evening offering.   Dan. 8:16

22 And he informed me, and talked with me, and said, "O Daniel, I have now come forth to give you skill to understand.

23 "At the beginning of your supplications the ᵀcommand went out, and I have come to tell you, for you *are* greatly ᴿbeloved; there-

fore ᴿconsider the matter, and understand the ▽ vision: Lit. *word* • Dan. 10:11, 19 • Matt. 24:15

24 "Seventy *weeks are determined
For your people and for your holy city,
To finish the transgression,
*To make an end of sins,
ᴿTo make reconciliation for iniquity,
To bring in everlasting righteousness,
To seal up vision and prophecy,   [Is. 53:10]
ᴿAnd to anoint the Most Holy.   Ps. 45:7

25 "Know therefore and understand,
That from the going forth of the
     command
To restore and build Jerusalem
Until ᴿMessiah ᴿthe Prince,
There shall be seven weeks and sixty-
     two weeks;   John 1:41; 4:25 • Is. 55:4
The ᵀstreet shall be built again, and the
ᵀwall,   Or *open square* • Or *moat*
Even in troublesome times.

26 "And after the sixty-two weeks
ᴿMessiah shall be cut off, ᴿbut not for
     Himself;   [Is. 53:8]; Matt. 27:50 • [1 Pet. 2:21]
And ᴿthe people of the prince who is to
     come   Matt. 22:7
ᴿShall destroy the city and the
     sanctuary.   Luke 19:43, 44
The end of it *shall be* with a flood,
And till the end of the war desolations
     are determined.

27 Then he shall confirm a ᵀcovenant with
ᴿmany for one week;   *treaty* • [Matt. 26:28]
But in the middle of the week
He shall bring an end to sacrifice and
     offering.
And on the wing of abominations shall
     be one who makes desolate,
ᴿEven until the consummation, which is
     determined,   Dan. 11:36
Is poured out on the desolate."   ▲

Vision of the Glorious Man

51-D. The Vision of the Angel in Linen ▼

10 In the third year of Cyrus king of Persia a message was revealed to Daniel, whose name was called Belteshazzar. The message *was* true, *but the appointed time *was* long; and he understood the message, and had understanding of the vision.

9:24 Lit. *sevens,* and so throughout the chapter • So with Qr., LXX, Syr., Vg.; Kt., Theodotion *To seal up*
10:1 Or *and of great conflict*

51-D. The Vision of the Angel in Linen (Daniel 10:1–21)—Daniel, chapters 10—12, is one complete vision in three parts. (Daniel's pagan name, in the courts of Babylon and Persia, was Belteshazzar; meaning "the god Bel is strong." However, from his daily walk everyone realized that his real name was Daniel, "God is my judge.") This vision came to Daniel in the third year of Cyrus, 536 B.C. It was a true vision of coming events. "The appointed time was long" (v. 1). Chapters 11 and 12 cover the Times of the Gentiles from the Medes and Persians to the coming kingdom of God.

(Point 51-D continued on next page)

▽ 2 In those days I, Daniel, was mourning three full weeks.

3 I ate no pleasant food, no meat or wine came into my mouth, nor did I anoint myself at all, till three whole weeks were fulfilled.

4 Now on the twenty-fourth day of the first month, as I was by the side of the great river, that is, the ᵀTigris,   Heb. *Hiddekel*

5 I lifted my eyes and looked, and behold, a certain man clothed in linen, whose waist was ᴿgirded with gold of Uphaz!   Rev. 1:13

6 His body was like beryl, his face like the appearance of lightning, his eyes like torches of fire, his arms and feet like burnished bronze in color, ᴿand the sound of his words like the voice of a multitude.   [Rev. 1:15]

7 And I, Daniel, alone saw the vision, for the men who were with me did not see the vision; but a great terror fell upon them, so that they fled to hide themselves.

8 Therefore I was left alone when I saw this great vision, and no strength remained in me; for my ᵀvigor was turned to frailty in me, and I retained no strength.   Lit. *splendor*

9 Yet I heard the sound of his words; and while I heard the sound of his words I was in a deep sleep on my face, with my face to the ground.

Prophecies Concerning Persia and Greece

10 ᴿSuddenly, a hand touched me, which made me tremble on my knees and on the palms of my hands.   Dan. 9:21

11 And he said to me, "O Daniel, man greatly beloved, understand the words that I ▽ speak to you, and stand upright, for I have now been sent to you." While he was speaking this word to me, I stood trembling.

12 Then he said to me, "Do not fear, Daniel, for from the first day that you set your heart to understand, and to humble yourself before your God, your words were heard; and I have come because of your words.

13 ᴿ"But the prince of the kingdom of Persia withstood me twenty-one days; and behold, ᴿMichael, one of the chief princes, came to help me, for I had been left alone there with the kings of Persia. Dan. 10:20 • Dan. 10:21; 12:1

14 "Now I have come to make you understand what will happen to your people ᴿin the latter days, ᴿfor the vision refers to many days yet to come."   Dan. 2:28 • Dan. 8:26; 10:1

15 When he had spoken such words to me, ᴿI ᵀturned my face toward the ground and became speechless.   Dan. 8:18; 10:9 • Lit. *set*

16 And suddenly, one having the likeness of *the sons of men touched my lips; then I opened my mouth and spoke, saying to him who stood before me, "My lord, because of the vision my sorrows have overwhelmed me, and I have retained no strength.

17 "For how can this servant of my lord talk with you, my lord? As for me, no strength remains in me now, nor is any breath left in me."

18 Then again, the one having the likeness of a man touched me and strengthened me.

10:16 Theodotion, Vg. *the son;* LXX *a hand*

(Point 51-D continued from previous page)

(1) In Daniel's vision he saw himself "by the side of the great river, that is, the Tigris," where he saw "a certain man clothed in linen" (vv. 4–9), quite possibly our Lord Jesus Christ. The vision was an Old Testament *Christophany,* or appearance of Christ. Scripture should interpret Scripture. In Daniel we have an Old Testament Christophany, and in the book of Revelation (1:9–18, page 1293) we have a New Testament Christophany which embraces Christ's death, burial, and resurrection.

(2) "Then, suddenly, a hand touched me" (v. 10). The pre-incarnate Christ was not alone in this vision. It was the manifestation of an angel, perhaps Gabriel. The angel was sent by the Lord to answer Daniel's prayer on the first day that he prayed. Gabriel was hindered by "the prince of the kingdom of Persia" (v. 13) who delayed him for twenty-one days until Michael (God's warring angel) could come and help him defeat the evil prince—Satan, or one of his fallen angels from the kingdom of darkness (Eph. 6:12, page 1192). Christ, the Man in linen, did not need Michael to fight His battle and defeat Satan. When He was tested in the wilderness, He met Satan in his own kingdom of darkness and was victorious (Matt. 4:1–11, page 934)— for prayer can produce actions behind the scenes (vv. 12, 13). Yet there occurred a struggle for twenty-one days (v. 13), and from this we can each learn patience through the power of prayer. God hears and He works according to His will. He is accomplishing many things in the lives of men and nations. He may require us to wait many days, but prayer *is* answered.

(3) Angels are assigned to watch over God's people. The words, "Michael your prince" (v. 21) show that there exists an assigned bond between certain people and/or nations and God's angels (Heb. 1:14, page 1237).

(4) It is God's will that both His Old Testament people, Israel, and His New Testament people, the church, should "understand what will happen to" them "in the latter days" (vv. 14, 21). Prophecy should not be ignored, for it can give us stability during difficult days (Matt. 24:6, page 973). We should know that whatever happens to us personally or as a nation, God triumphs, as do we as His ransomed children, in the near future (Rev. 3:11, page 1296; 22:12, 17, page 1316).

See Daniel 11:1–45, page 853, for **Point 51-E: The Vision of the Struggling Kings.**

▽ 19 And he said, "O man greatly beloved, ᴿfear not! Peace *be* to you; be strong, yes, be strong!" So when he spoke to me I was strengthened, and said, "Let my lord speak, for you have strengthened me."   Judg. 6:23

20 Then he said, "Do you know why I have come to you? And now I must return to fight ᴿwith the prince of Persia; and when I have gone forth, indeed the prince of Greece will come.   Dan. 10:13

21 "But I will tell you what is noted in the Scripture of Truth. (No one upholds me

▲ against these, except Michael your prince.

▼ **51-E. The Vision of the Struggling Kings**

11 "Also ᴿin the first year of ᴿDarius the Mede, I, *even* I, stood up to confirm and strengthen him.)   Dan. 9:1 · Dan. 5:31

2 "And now I will tell you the truth: Behold, three more kings will arise in Persia, and the fourth shall be far richer than *them* all; by his strength, through his riches, he shall stir up all against the realm of Greece.

3 "Then ᴿa mighty king shall arise, who shall rule with great dominion, and ᴿdo according to his will.   Dan. 7:6; 8:5 · Dan. 8:4; 10:16, 36

4 "And when he has arisen, his kingdom ▽ shall be broken up and divided toward the four winds of heaven, but not among his posterity nor according to his dominion with which he ruled; for his kingdom shall be uprooted, even for others besides these.

Warring Kings of North and South

5 "Also the king of the South shall become strong, as well as *one* of his princes; and he shall gain power over him and have dominion. His dominion *shall be* a great dominion.

6 "And at the end of *some* years they shall join forces, for the daughter of the king of the South shall go to the king of the North to make an agreement; but she shall not retain the power of her ᵀauthority, and neither he nor his authority shall stand; but she shall be given up, with those who brought her, and with him who begot her, and with him who strengthened her in *those* times.   Lit. *arm*

7 "But from a branch of her roots *one* shall arise in his place, who shall come with an army, enter the fortress of the king of the North, and deal with them and prevail.

8 "And he shall also carry their gods cap-

51-E. The Vision of the Struggling Kings (Daniel 11:1–45)—This chapter is as detailed and complex as any in the entire Bible. Once we admit that Almighty God does indeed reveal the future, we begin to appreciate and accept the wondrous detail and specific prophecies in this chapter as an outflowing of His omnipotence and omniscience. Knowing the future, He assures its certainty. Christ testified that the book of Daniel is inspired, genuine, and true (Matt. 24:15, page 973) because it is from God. Let us review this chapter's content and direction:

(1) *Verse 2.* The four great and powerful rulers of Persia were Cyrus, Ahasuerus (Cambyses), Darius Hystaspes, and Xerxes. Malachi, the last Old Testament author, ended the Old Testament canon in 420 B.C. During this intertestamental period (420–4 B.C.) the Jews were living in the far-flung Persian world.

(2) *Verses 3, 4.* Alexander the Great of Greece, at twenty years of age, inherited the Macedonian armies of his assassinated father, Philip II, and united the Greek city-states to the south by threat of annihilation. In thirteen years (336–323 B.C.) he conquered the western world. At his early death in Babylon, his conquered world split into four warring quarters which pitted Hellenistic general-kings against one another for the next 150 years (Dan. 7:6, page 844; cf. 8:21, 22, page 848).

(3) *Verses 5–12.* Two of these kingdoms, Syria and Egypt, continually fought over Israel (323–200 B.C.), which lay as the prize between them. Syria was "the king of the North" and Egypt "the king of the South." The king's daughter (v. 6) was Bernice, daughter of Ptolemy II, the Greek ruler of Egypt, who had married Antiochus Theous of Syria. Bernice was poisoned by him. Verses 7–9 speak of her brother, Ptolemy Energetes of Egypt. Verse 11 tells of Ptolemy Philopater of Egypt, victorious over and possessor of Palestine; verse 12 bemoans his later licentious life.

(4) *Verses 13–20.* Antiochus III (reigning 200–187 B.C.), greatest of Greek-Syrian kings, is mentioned in verses 13–19. While attempting to conquer Egypt, he recaptured Palestine for Syria at the Battle of Panias (198 B.C.). Verse 17 describes his futile attempt at marrying into Egypt through his daughter, Cleopatra (not the famous Cleopatra, queen of Egypt 150 years later). Verses 18 and 19 predict Antiochus' battle with the Romans as well as his death. Verse 20 foreshadows his short-lived follower, Seleucus Philopater (reigning 187–176 B.C.), who imposed taxes.

(5) *Verses 21–30.* Antiochus IV, the Greek ruler of Syria, was also called Epiphanes, meaning "illustrious," but because of his evil ways, he was notorious as Epimanes, or "maniac." Verses 21 and 23 call him vile and his reign deceitful. Verses 25–29 recount how the Romans, fearing Syria would become a rival to their fast-rising empire, in 168 B.C., forbade him to enlarge his kingdom (v. 30).

(6) *Verses 30–35.* When the Romans checked Antiochus' plan to attack Egypt, in rage he unleashed his army upon Jerusalem, which he hated because of the Jews' rejection of the Greek Jupiter cult. Verse 31 describes how he polluted the holy temple by sprinkling it with the blood of a pig (ceremonially unclean animal), and erecting within it a statue of Jupiter. The non-canonical, intertestamental (apocryphal) book of 1 Maccabees describes the revolt of the pious Jews, 168–165 B.C., under the courageous and consecrated

(Point 51-E continued on next page)

▽ tive to Egypt, with their ᵀprinces *and* their precious articles of silver and gold; and he shall continue *more* years than the king of the North.   Or *molded images*

9 "Also *the king of the North* shall come to the kingdom of the king of the South, but shall return to his own land.

10 "However his sons shall stir up strife, and assemble a multitude of great forces; and *one* shall certainly come ᴿand overwhelm and pass through; then he shall return ᴿto his fortress and stir up strife.   Is. 8:8 · Dan. 11:7

11 "And the king of the South shall be moved with rage, and go out and fight with him, with the king of the North, who shall muster a great multitude; but the multitude shall be given into the hand of his *enemy.*

12 "When he has taken away the multitude, his heart will be ᵀlifted up; and he will cast down tens of thousands, but he will not prevail.   Proud

13 "For the king of the North will return and muster a multitude greater than the former, and shall certainly come at the end of some years with a great army and much equipment.

14 "Now in those times many shall rise up ▽ against the king of the South. Also, *violent men of your people shall exalt themselves in fulfillment of the vision, but they shall fall.

15 "So the king of the North shall come and ᴿbuild a siege mound, and take a fortified city; and the ᵀforces of the South shall not withstand *him.* Even his choice troops *shall have* no strength to resist.   Ezek. 4:2 · Lit. *arms*

16 "But he who comes against him shall do according to his own will, and no one shall stand against him. He shall stand in the Glorious Land with destruction in his *power.

17 "He shall also ᴿset his face to enter with the strength of his whole kingdom, and *upright ones with him; thus shall he do. And he shall give him the daughter of women to destroy it; but she shall not stand *with him,* ᴿor be for him.   2 Chr. 20:3 · Dan. 9:26

18 "After this he shall turn his face to the coastlands, and shall take many. But a ruler shall bring the reproach against them to an

11:14 Or *robbers*, lit. *sons of breakage*
11:16 Lit. *hand*
11:17 Or *bring equitable terms*

(Point 51-E continued from previous page)
leadership of Judas the Maccabee ("Hammer"). Relying on God's strength and name, Judas "turned to flight the armies of the aliens" (Heb. 11:34, page 1249). The Hebrew feast of Hanukkah celebrates the recapture and rededication of the temple in Jerusalem in the month of Kislev (December), 165 B.C., and the consequent burning of the olive oil lamps for eight days (John 10:22, 23, page 1068).

Note: Verse 31 and Daniel 9:27 (page 851) place this abomination of desolation in the future. Christ, two hundred years later in A.D. 32, spoke of this "abomination of desolation" (Matt. 24:15, page 973). Thus He showed that the abomination by Antiochus was to be taken as a foreshadowing of the public blasphemy yet to be committed by Antichrist in the middle of the seven years of Tribulation (Dan. 9:27, page 851). This would identify the Antichrist to those on earth at the time, and would launch the beginning of the final half of the seven years of "the Great Tribulation," stopped at last by Christ's return, in glory, at Armageddon (Matt. 24:15, 21, 31, page 973). Paul also confirmed this event (2 Thess. 2:3, 4, page 1215). The theory that the Roman general Titus committed this abomination in A.D. 70 does not fit the history of those events. Titus did not *desecrate* the temple (his soldiers burned it against his orders); he never blasphemed God in it as Paul describes in 2 Thessalonians 2:3, 4. There was no opportunity for flight after the temple was captured, as would be necessary to reflect Matthew 24:15–18 (page 973). The "tribulation" of the Jews in A.D. 70 chiefly took place before, not after, the seizure of the temple, as would have been required by Matthew 24:15, 21 (page 973). Furthermore, Christ did not come again "immediately after the tribulation of those days" (Matt. 24:29, page 974). The abomination of desolation lies ahead, and Middle East events point to its imminence. When it occurs it will again be like that of Antiochus IV who is the prototype of the Antichrist—the little horn of Daniel 7:7, 8 (page 844) and the Beast "out of the sea" in Revelation 13:1–10 (page 1305).

(7) *Verses 36–45.* Scenes in Scripture sometimes shift from one location immediately in view to one in a distant vista. For example, Isaiah 14:4–17 (page 656), addresses the king of Babylon, then shifts to Satan who stands behind him. In Ezekiel 28:2 (page 805) the king of Tyre is the subject, but in verses 12–19 the shift is to Satan behind the king. So it is here: verse 36 shifts us to the satanic Antichrist, who is so much like Antiochus Epiphanes, and more. The Antichrist is here described in terms similar to the "little horn" of Daniel 7:8, 24, 25 (page 844), the "man of sin" of 2 Thessalonians 2:3, 4 (page 1215), and the "beast" of Revelation 13 (page 1305) who will reign supreme over all nations. "He was given authority to continue for forty-two months" (Rev. 13:5, page 1306). Today it is frequently speculated that he will be the ruler of the west (Rome revived—a confederated Europe); that the "king of the South" (v. 40) will rule the now-confederated Arab nations; that the "king of the North" (vv. 40, 44) is the head of the Union of Soviet Socialist Republics; and that "the east" (v. 44) is a confederation led by China. The events will happen in God's own time (Matt. 24:36, page 974; Acts 1:7, page 1086), and he, the Antichrist, will at last be destroyed (v. 45) at Armageddon (Rev. 16:16, page 1310; cf. 19:11–21, page 1312).

See Daniel 12:1–13, page 856, for **Point 51-F: The Vision of the Angel's Oath.**

▽ end; and with the reproach removed, he shall turn back on him.

19 "Then he shall turn his face toward the fortress of his own land; but he shall ᴿstumble and fall, ᴿand not be found.   Jer. 46:6 · Ps. 37:36

20 "There shall arise in his place one who imposes taxes on the glorious kingdom; but within a few days he shall be destroyed, but not in anger or in battle.

21 "And in his place ᴿshall arise a vile person, to whom they will not give the honor of royalty; but he shall come in peaceably, and seize the kingdom by intrigue.   Dan. 7:8

22 "With the ᵀforce of a flood they shall be swept away from before him and be broken, and also the prince of the covenant.   Lit. *arms*

23 "And after the league *is made* with him ᴿhe shall act deceitfully, for he shall come up and become strong with a small *number of* people.   Dan. 8:25

24 "He shall enter peaceably, even into the richest places of the province; and he shall do *what* his fathers have not done, nor his forefathers: he shall disperse among them the plunder, ᵀspoil, and riches; and he shall devise his plans against the strongholds, but *only* for a time.   *booty*

25 "He shall stir up his power and his courage against the king of the South with a great army. And the king of the South shall be stirred up to battle with a very great and mighty army; but he shall not stand, for they shall devise plans against him.

26 "Yes, those who eat of the portion of his delicacies shall destroy him; his army shall ᵀbe swept away, and many shall fall down slain.   Or *overflow*

27 "Both these kings' hearts *shall be* bent on evil, and they shall speak lies at the same table; but it shall not prosper, for the end *will* still *be* at the ᴿappointed time.   Hab. 2:3

28 "While returning to his land with great riches, his heart shall be *moved* against the holy covenant; so he shall do *damage* and return to his own land.

The Northern King's Blasphemies

29 "At the appointed time he shall return and go toward the south; but it shall not be like the former or the latter.

30 "For ships from ᵀCyprus shall come against him; therefore he shall be grieved, and return in rage against the holy covenant, and do *damage*. So he shall return and show regard for those who forsake the holy covenant.   Heb. *Kittim*, western lands, especially Cyprus

31 "And ᵀforces shall be mustered by him, ᴿand they shall defile the sanctuary fortress; then they shall take away the daily *sacrifices*, and place *there* the abomination of desolation.   Lit. *arms* · Dan. 8:11–13; 12:11

32 "Those who do wickedly against the ▽ covenant he shall ᵀcorrupt with flattery; but the people who know their God shall be strong, and carry out *great exploits*.   *pollute*

33 "And those of the people who understand shall instruct many; yet *for many* days they shall fall by sword and flame, by captivity and plundering.

34 "Now when they fall, they shall be aided with a little help; but many shall join with them by ᵀintrigue.   Or *slipperiness, flattery*

35 "And *some* of those of understanding shall fall, to refine them, purify *them*, and make *them* white, *until* the time of the end; because *it is* still for the appointed time.

36 "Then the king shall do according to his own will: he shall ᴿexalt and magnify himself above every god, shall speak blasphemies against the God of gods, and shall prosper till the wrath has been accomplished; for what has been determined shall be done.   Dan. 7:8, 25

37 "He shall regard neither the God of his fathers nor the desire of women, ᴿnor regard any ᵀgod; for he shall exalt himself above *them* all.   Is. 14:13 · Or *gods*

38 "But in their place he shall honor a god of fortresses; and a god which his fathers did not know he shall honor with gold and silver, with precious stones and pleasant things.

39 "Thus he shall act against the strongest fortresses with a foreign god, which he shall acknowledge, *and* advance *its* glory; and he shall cause them to rule over many, and divide the land for ᵀgain.   *profit*

The Northern King's Conquests

40 "At the time of the end the king of the South shall attack him; and the king of the North shall come against him ᴿlike a whirlwind, with chariots, horsemen, and with many ships; and he shall enter the countries, overwhelm *them*, and pass through.   Is. 21:1

41 "He shall also enter the Glorious Land, and many *countries* shall be overthrown; but these shall escape from his hand: Edom, Moab, and the prominent people of Ammon.

42 "He shall stretch out his hand against the countries, and the land of ᴿEgypt shall not escape.   Joel 3:19

43 "He shall have power over the treasures of gold and silver, and over all the precious things of Egypt; also the Libyans and Ethiopians *shall follow* ᴿat his heels.   Ex. 11:8

44 "But news from the east and the north shall trouble him; therefore he shall go out with great fury to destroy and annihilate many.

45 "And he shall plant the tents of his palace between the seas and ᴿthe glorious holy mountain; ᴿyet he shall come to his end, and no one will help him.   Ps. 48:2 · Rev. 19:20 ▲

Prophecy of the End Time

▼ **51–F. The Vision of the Angel's Oath**

12 "At that time Michael shall stand up,
The great prince who stands *watch*
over the sons of your people;
ᴿAnd there shall be a time of trouble,
Such as never was since there was a
nation,
Even to that time.
And at that time your people ᴿshall be
delivered,

Every one who is found ᴿwritten in the ▽
book.   Jer. 30:7 • Rom. 11:26 • Ex. 32:32

2 And many of those who sleep in the
dust of the earth shall awake,
ᴿSome to everlasting life,   [John 5:28, 29]
Some to shame ᴿ*and* everlasting
ᵀcontempt.   [Is. 66:24] • Lit. *abhorrence*
3 Those who are wise shall ᴿshine
Like the brightness of the firmament,
ᴿAnd those who turn many to
righteousness   Matt. 13:43 • [James 5:19, 20]
Like the stars forever and ever.

51–F. The Vision of the Angel's Oath (Daniel 12:1–13)—This wonderful book of prophecy closes with another *Christophany* (a pre-incarnate appearance of the glorious Christ). "I heard the man clothed in linen" who "swore by Him who lives forever" (v. 7; Heb. 6:13, page 1241). A great lesson from this book is that God, His Word, and His Christ live on forever, while evil and its satanic forces will one day be removed for eternity. Praise God for His grace that brought Jesus to bear our sins, that we too might one day abide by His side always.

(1) The main events of the end (vv. 1–3):

(a) "Michael" shall "stand up . . . [for] the sons of your people" (v. 1). This refers to the future. Revelation 12:7–10 (page 1305) describes Michael warring with Satan and casting him out of heaven, as Satan makes his final attempt to destroy Israel and the Tribulation saints—those who believe on Christ during the final seven years (Rev. 12:13, page 1305).

(b) It shall be "a time of trouble, such as never was since there was a nation" (v. 1). Christ said there "will be great tribulation" (Matt. 24:21, 22, page 973; cf. Rev. 7:13, 14, page 1301).

(c) "Your people shall be delivered" (v. 1). So states Revelation 12:11, 14–16, (page 1305) as well as Zechariah 12:9; 13:9; and 14:3, 4, (page 918).

(d) The dead will be resurrected (v. 2). This is the clearest Old Testament testimony to the Resurrection. It was pronounced in its absolute fullness only after Christ Himself conquered the grave and death for us forever (Rev. 1:18, page 1294; cf. 1 Cor. 15:35–44, page 1162).

(e) There will be rewards for 144,000 from the twelve tribes of the children of Israel, as well as for a great host of Gentiles who will evangelize the nations during the Tribulation, having turned many to righteousness—in heaven they will shine "like the stars forever and ever" (v. 3; cf. Rev. 7:1–17, page 1300). Saved souls of all denominations will receive a special reward in heaven (1 Thess. 2:19, 20, page 1210).

(2) A sealed book until the end (v. 4):

(a) "The words are closed up and sealed" (v. 9). Until Christ came and the New Testament church was formed, the understanding of prophetic details was veiled. In Revelation 6:1 (page 1299) Christ is shown unsealing a book and revealing the events during the seven years of Tribulation.

(b) "Many shall run to and fro" (v. 4). The end time would be characterized by excessive activity.

(c) "Knowledge shall increase" (v. 4). The end time will be characterized by an explosion of worldly knowledge and information.

(3) An angelic oath for the end (vv. 5–10). When asked, "How long?" the angel swears that it will be "time, times, and half a time," or that already familiar three-and-one-half-year period of the final "great tribulation" (Matt. 24:21, page 973; cf. Dan. 9:27, page 851; Rev. 13:5, page 1306). This is paralleled in Revelation when there is a similar angel, there too lifting up his hand to heaven, similarly standing astride water and land, swearing there should be "delay no longer" (Rev. 10:6, page 1303). The angel announces that the Tribulation events have at last arrived (Rev. 11—13, page 1303). During this time Satan, through Antichrist, persecutes Israel and all those left on earth who will not wear the mark of the beast, which is 666 (Rev. 13:16–18, page 1306). God commences to judge, destroy, and remove Satan's kingdom from the earth (Rev. 16:1, 2, 10, page 1308).

(4) Days beyond the end (vv. 11, 12). Verse 11 speaks of thirty days beyond the 1,260 of the Great Tribulation (Rev. 12:6, page 1305). Verse 12 attaches a blessing to the time of seventy-five days after the 1,260. Possibly these refer to the calendar of God's final judgments and rewards as Christ establishes His millennial reign on earth (Matt. 25:31–46, page 976). It may be that by seventy-five days after Armageddon and Christ's glorious coming, the millennial reign will at last be established in all of its prophesied perfections. Hence he that waits for this time is blessed.

(5) Abiding until the end (v. 13). This is what Christ commanded Peter in John 21:22 (page 1084): "You follow Me." Everyone is called to serve God faithfully during all the days He has given, and find rest and peace in His service. Then, because Jesus died on the cross in their stead, all "will arise to your inheritance at the end of the days" (v. 13; cf. 1 Cor. 3:11–15, page 1149).

See Index, page 17, for your next study.

▽ 4 "But you, Daniel, ᴿshut up the words, and seal the book until the time of the end; many shall ᴿrun to and fro, and knowledge shall increase."   Rev. 22:10 · Amos 8:12

5 Then I, Daniel, looked; and there stood two others, one on this riverbank and the other on that ᴿriverbank.   Dan. 10:4

6 And one said to the man clothed in ᴿlinen, who was above the waters of the river, ᴿ"How long shall the fulfillment of these wonders be?"   Ezek. 9:2 · Dan. 8:13; 12:8

7 Then I heard the man clothed in linen, who was above the waters of the river, when he held up his right hand and his left hand to heaven, and swore by Him who lives forever, that it shall be for a time, times, and half a time; and when the power of ᴿthe holy people has been completely shattered, all these things shall be finished.   Dan. 8:24

8 Although I heard, I did not understand. ▽ Then I said, "My lord, what shall be the end of these things?"

9 And he said, "Go your way, Daniel, for the words are closed up and sealed till the time of the end.

10 "Many shall be purified, made white, and refined, but the wicked shall do wickedly; and none of the wicked shall understand, but the wise shall understand.

11 "And from the time that the daily sacrifice is taken away, and the abomination of desolation is set up, there shall be one thousand two hundred and ninety days.

12 "Blessed is he who waits, and comes to the one thousand three hundred and thirty-five days.

13 "But you, go your way till the end; ᴿfor you shall rest, ᴿand will arise to your inheritance at the end of the days."   Rev. 14:13 · Ps. 1:5 ▲

THE BOOK OF
Hosea

Hosea is the first of the so-called Minor Prophets. They are so called because of the size of the books and not because of their content. The name *Hosea* means "salvation," and is closely related to the name *Joshua* (which in turn is identical with the name of our Savior, *Jesus*). Hosea's name fits his task well, for he was the last prophet to Israel before that kingdom fell in 722 B.C. He pleaded for his people to turn to God and be saved.

AUTHORSHIP. All that we know about the prophet is discovered from the autobiographical sections of the book itself. Hosea probably saw the ten tribes of his beloved Israel dragged away from the land which they had shamefully defiled by idolatry and immorality, into that exile and dispersion among the nations from which, even yet, they have not been regathered.

Hosea was a prophet to the northern kingdom, as the content of the book reveals. He was a contemporary with Amos, another prophet to Israel, and also with Micah and Isaiah, prophets to Judah. His ministry extended over half a century, and he lived to see the fulfillment of his prophecy in the captivity of Israel.

CONTEXT. Hosea may be called the prophet of the decline and fall of the northern kingdom. He sought to call the sinful and estranged nation back to God. Hosea was the prophet of Israel's zero hour. The prophet stood midway in time between Moses and Christ, and began to prophesy two hundred years after the division of the united kingdom. His ministry included the last years of the northern kingdom. Most of his prophetic ministry evidently took place from 750 to 725 B.C.

HOW HOSEA FITS TOGETHER. The book of Hosea may be divided into three major parts, as follows: (1) The Prophet's Married Life (chs. 1—3); (2) Israel's Unfaithfulness to Yahweh and Consequent Judgment (chs. 4—13); and (3) Israel's Conversion and Renewal: The Call to Repentance and the Promise of Forgiveness (ch. 14).

Hosea married a woman named Gomer, who bore him two sons and a daughter. Afterward she became a harlot and left home. Hosea's heart was broken beyond description. But God commanded Hosea to take this unfaithful harlot back into his home and to love her again. Out of this experience, Hosea grasped with rare insight the pain that is in the heart of God when His people forsake Him and sin against Him. Through the heartbreaking experience of his tragic marriage, the prophet had come to see Israel's sin against God in its deepest and most awful significance.

Beginning with chapter four, the private life of Hosea fades into the background and the emphasis is upon the Lord and Israel. The theme is the unfaithful nation and her faithful Lord. The book emphasizes the shame of sin, the fruit of backsliding, the love of the Lord for His wayward people, and the conditions of their restoration. The language of the book is plain and frank. Hosea's message is needed in our day when sin is glossed over and soft words are substituted for hard facts.

—T.J.C.

THE word of the LORD that came to Hosea the son of Beeri, in the days of Uzziah, Jotham, ᴿAhaz, *and* Hezekiah, kings of Judah, and in the days of Jeroboam the son of Joash, king of Israel. 2 Chr. 28

The Family of Hosea

2 When the LORD began to speak by Hosea, the LORD said to Hosea:

ᴿ"Go, take yourself a wife of harlotry
And children of harlotry, Hos. 3:1
For ᴿthe land has committed great
ᵀharlotry Jer. 2:13 · Spiritual adultery
By *departing* from the LORD."

3 So he went and took Gomer the daughter of Diblaim, and she conceived and bore him a son.

4 Then the LORD said to him:

"Call his name Jezreel,
For in a little *while*
ᴿI will avenge the bloodshed of Jezreel
on the house of Jehu, 2 Kin. 10:11
ᴿAnd bring an end to the kingdom of the
house of Israel. 2 Kin. 15:8–10; 17:6, 23
5 ᴿIt shall come to pass in that day
That I will break the bow of Israel in
the Valley of Jezreel." 2 Kin. 15:29

6 And she conceived again and bore a daughter. Then *God* said to him:

"Call her name ᵀLo-Ruhamah,

^RFor I will no longer have mercy on the
house of Israel,　　Lit. *No-Mercy* • 2 Kin. 17:6
*But I will utterly take them away.
7 ^RYet I will have mercy on the house of
Judah,　　　　　　2 Kin. 19:29-35
Will save them by the LORD their God,
And ^Rwill not save them by bow,
Nor by sword or battle,
By horses or horsemen."　　[Zech. 4:6]

8 Now when she had weaned Lo-Ruhamah, she conceived and bore a son.
9 Then *God* said:

"Call his name ^TLo-Ammi,　Lit. *Not-My-People*
For you *are* not My people,
And I will not be your *God*.

The Restoration of Israel

10 "Yet ^Rthe number of the children of
Israel　　　　　　Gen. 22:17; 32:12
Shall be as the sand of the sea,
Which cannot be measured or
numbered.
^RAnd it shall come to pass　　1 Pet. 2:10
In the place where it was said to them,
'You *are* ^Tnot My people,'　Heb. *Lo-Ammi*, v. 9
There it shall be said to them,
'*You are* sons of the living God.'
11 ^RThen the children of Judah and the
children of Israel　　Is. 11:11-13
Shall be gathered together,
And appoint for themselves one head;
And they shall come up out of the land,
For great *will be* the day of Jezreel!
2 Say to your brethren, *'My people,'
And to your sisters, *'Mercy *is shown*.'

God's Unfaithful People

2 "Bring^T charges against your mother,
^Tbring charges;　Or *Contend with* • Or *contend*
For ^Rshe *is* not My wife, nor *am* I her
Husband!　　　　　　Is. 50:1
Let her put away her ^Rharlotries from
her sight,　　　　　Ezek. 16:25
And her adulteries from between her
breasts;
3 Lest ^RI strip her naked　　Jer. 13:22, 26
And expose her, as in the day she was
^Rborn,　　　　　　Ezek. 16:4-7, 22
And make her like a wilderness,
And set her like a dry land,
And slay her with ^Rthirst.　　Amos 8:11-13

4 "I will not have mercy on her children,
For they *are* the children of harlotry.
5 For their mother has played the harlot;
She who conceived them has behaved
shamefully.
For she said, 'I will go after my lovers,
^RWho give *me* my bread and my water,

1:6 Or *That I may forgive them at all*
2:1 Heb. *Ammi,* Hos. 1:9, 10 • Heb. *Ruhamah,* Hos. 1:6

My wool and my linen,　　Hos. 2:8, 12
My oil and my drink.'
6 "Therefore, behold,
I will hedge up your way with thorns,
And ^Twall her in,　　Lit. *wall up her wall*
So that she cannot find her paths.
7 She will ^Tchase her lovers,　Or *pursue*
But not overtake them;
Yes, she will seek them, but not find
them.
Then she will say,
^RI will go and return to my ^Rfirst
husband,
For then *it was* better for me than
now.'　　Luke 15:17, 18 • Ezek. 16:8; 23:4
8 For she did not ^Rknow　　Is. 1:3
That I gave her grain, new wine, and
oil,
And multiplied her silver and gold—
Which they prepared for Baal.

9 "Therefore I will return and take away
My grain in its time
And My new wine in its season,
And will take back My wool and My
linen,
Given to cover her nakedness.
10 Now ^RI will uncover her lewdness in
the sight of her lovers,　　Ezek. 16:37
And no one shall deliver her from My
hand.
11 ^RI will also cause all her mirth to cease,
Her feast days,
Her New Moons,
Her Sabbaths—
All her appointed feasts.　　Amos 5:21; 8:10

12 "And I will destroy her vines and her fig
trees,
Of which she has said,
'These *are* my wages that my lovers
have given me.'
So I will make them a forest,
And the beasts of the field shall eat
them.
13 I will punish her
For the days of the Baals to which she
burned incense.
She decked herself with her earrings
and jewelry,
And went after her lovers;
But Me she forgot," says the LORD.

God's Mercy on His People

14 "Therefore, behold, I will allure her,
Will bring her into the wilderness,
And speak ^Tcomfort to her.　Lit. *to her heart*
15 I will give her her vineyards from there,
And ^Rthe Valley of Achor as a door of
hope;　　　　　　Josh. 7:26
She shall sing there,
As in ^Rthe days of her youth,
^RAs in the day when she came up from
the land of Egypt.　　Ezek. 16:8-14 • Ex. 15:1

16 "And it shall be, in that day,"
Says the LORD,
"*That* you will call Me *'My Husband,'
And no longer call Me *'My Master,'
17 For ᴿI will take from her mouth the
names of the Baals,
And they shall be remembered by their
name no more.   Ex. 23:13
18 In that day I will make a ᴿcovenant for
them   Job 5:23
With the beasts of the field,
With the birds of the air,
And *with* the creeping things of the
ground.
Bow and sword of battle ᴿI will shatter
from the earth,   Is. 2:4
To make them ᴿlie down safely.   Lev. 26:5

19 "I will betroth you to Me forever;
Yes, I will betroth you to Me
In righteousness and justice,
In lovingkindness and mercy;
20 I will betroth you to Me in faithfulness,
And you shall know the LORD.

21 "It shall come to pass in that day
That ᴿI will answer," says the LORD;
"I will answer the heavens,   Zech. 8:12
And they shall answer the earth.
22 The earth shall answer
With grain,
With new wine,
And with oil;
They shall answer ᵀJezreel. Lit. *God Will Sow*
23 Then ᴿI will sow her for Myself in the
earth,   Jer. 31:27
And I will have mercy on *her who had*
ᵀnot obtained mercy;   Heb. *Lo-Ruhamah*
Then ᴿI will say to *those who were* ᵀnot
My people,   Hos. 1:10 • Heb. *Lo-Ammi*
'You *are* ᵀMy people!'   Heb. *Ammi*
And they shall say, '*You are* my God!' "

Israel Will Return to God

3 Then the LORD said to me, "Go again,
love a woman *who is* loved by a ᴿloverᵀ
and is committing adultery, just like the love
of the LORD for the children of Israel, who
look to other gods and love *the* raisin cakes
of the pagans."   Jer. 3:20 • Lit. *friend* or *husband*
2 So I bought her for myself for ᵀfifteen
shekels of silver, and ᵀone and one-half ho-
mers of barley. $1920 • 9.786 bu.
3 And I said to her, "You shall ᴿstay with
me many days; you shall not play the harlot,
nor shall you have a man—so, too, *will* I *be*
toward you."   Deut. 21:13
4 For the children of Israel shall abide
many days ᴿwithout king or prince, without
sacrifice or sacred pillar, without ᴿephod or
ᴿteraphim.   Hos. 10:3 • Ex. 28:4–12 • Judg. 17:5; 18:14, 17
5 Afterward the children of Israel shall

return and seek the LORD their God and
David their king. They shall fear the LORD
and His goodness in the latter days.

God's Charge Against Israel

4 Hear the word of the LORD,
You children of Israel,
For the LORD *brings* a ᴿcharge against
the inhabitants of the land: Is. 1:18

"There is no truth or mercy
Or knowledge of God in the land.
2 By swearing and lying,
Killing and stealing and committing
adultery,
They break all restraint,
With bloodshed upon bloodshed.
3 Therefore ᴿthe land will mourn;
And ᴿeveryone who dwells there will
waste away
With the beasts of the field
And the birds of the air;
Even the fish of the sea will be taken
away.   Amos 5:16; 8:8 • Zeph. 1:3

4 "Now let no man contend, or rebuke
another;
For your people *are* like those ᴿwho
contend with the priest.   Deut. 17:12
5 Therefore you shall stumble ᴿin the day;
The prophet also shall stumble with
you in the night;
And I will destroy your mother.   Jer. 15:8
6 ᴿMy people are destroyed for lack of
knowledge.   Is. 5:13
Because you have rejected knowledge,
I also will reject you from being priest
for Me;
ᴿBecause you have forgotten the law of
your God,   Ezek. 22:26
I also will forget your children.

7 "The more they increased,
The more they sinned against Me;
*I will change *their glory into shame.
8 They eat up the sin of My people;
They set their heart on their iniquity.
9 And it shall be: like people, like priest.
So I will punish them for their ways,
And ᵀreward them for their deeds.   *repay*
10 For ᴿthey shall eat, but not have
enough;
They shall commit harlotry, but not
increase;
Because they have ceased obeying the
LORD.   Lev. 26:26

The Idolatry of Israel

11 "Harlotry, wine, and new wine ᴿenslave
the heart.   Is. 5:12; 28:7

4:7 So with MT, LXX, Vg.; scribal tradition, Syr., Tg. *They
will change* • So with MT, LXX, Syr., Tg., Vg.; scribal
tradition *My glory*

2:16 Heb. *Ishi* • Heb. *Baali*

12 My people ask counsel from their
  ᴿwooden *idols*,   Jer. 2:27
  And their ᵀstaff informs them.
  For ᴿthe spirit of harlotry has caused
    them to stray,
  And they have played the harlot
    against their God.   Diviner's rod • Is. 44:19, 20
13 ᴿThey offer sacrifices on the
    mountaintops,
  And burn incense on the hills,
  Under oaks, poplars, and terebinths,
  Because their shade *is* good.
  ᴿTherefore your daughters commit
    harlotry,   Is. 1:29; 57:5, 7 • Amos 7:17
  And your brides commit adultery.

14 "I will not punish your daughters when
    they commit harlotry,
  Nor your brides when they commit
    adultery;
  For *the men* themselves go apart with
    harlots,
  And offer sacrifices with a
    ᴿritual harlot.   Deut. 23:18
  Therefore people *who* do not
    understand will be trampled.

15 "Though you, Israel, play the harlot,
  Let not Judah offend.
  ᴿDo not come up to Gilgal,   Hos. 9:15; 12:11
  Nor go up to Beth Aven,
  Nor swear an oath, *saying*, 'As the
    Lᴏʀᴅ lives'—
16 "For Israel ᴿis stubborn
  Like a stubborn calf;
  Now the Lᴏʀᴅ will let them forage   Jer. 3:6; 7:24; 8:5
  Like a lamb in ᵀopen country.   *a large place*
17 "Ephraim *is* joined to idols,
  ᴿLet him alone.   Matt. 15:14
18 Their drink ᵀis rebellion,   Or *has turned aside*
  They commit harlotry continually.
  *Her ᵀrulers dearly love dishonor.   *shields*
19 ᴿThe wind has wrapped her up in its
    wings,
  And ᴿthey shall be ashamed because of
    their sacrifices.   Jer. 51:1 • Is. 1:29

Impending Judgment on Israel and Judah

5 "Hear this, O priests!
  Take heed, O house of Israel!
  Give ear, O house of the king!
  For ᵀyours *is* the judgment,
  Because ᴿyou have been a snare to
    Mizpah   Or *to you* • Hos. 6:9
  And a net spread on Tabor.
2 The revolters are ᴿdeeply involved in
    slaughter,
  Though I rebuke them all.   Is. 29:15
3 ᴿI know Ephraim,
  And Israel is not hidden from Me;

4:18 Heb. difficult; a Jewish tradition reads *shamefully
love, 'Give!'*

For now, O Ephraim, ᴿyou commit
    harlotry;
  Israel is defiled.   Amos 3:2; 5:12 • Hos. 4:17
4 "Theyᵀ do not direct their deeds
  Toward turning to their God,
  For the spirit of harlotry is in their
    midst,   Or *Their deeds will not allow them to turn*
  And they do not know the Lᴏʀᴅ.
5 The ᴿpride of Israel testifies to his face;
  Therefore Israel and Ephraim stumble
    in their iniquity;
  Judah also stumbles with them.   Hos. 7:10
6 "With their flocks and herds
  ᴿThey shall go to seek the Lᴏʀᴅ,
  But they will not find *Him*;   Prov. 1:28
  He has withdrawn Himself from them.
7 They have ᴿdealt treacherously with the
    Lᴏʀᴅ,   Jer. 3:20
  For they have begotten ᵀpagan
    children.
  Now a New Moon shall devour them
    and their heritage.   Lit. *strange*

8 "Blowᴿ the ram's horn in Gibeah,
  The trumpet in Ramah!   Joel 2:1
  ᴿCry aloud *at* Beth Aven,   Is. 10:30
  '*Look* behind you, O Benjamin!'
9 Ephraim shall be desolate in the day of
    rebuke;
  Among the tribes of Israel I make
    known what is sure.
10 "The princes of Judah are like those who
  ᴿremove a landmark;
  I will pour out my wrath on them like
    water.   Deut. 19:14; 27:17
11 Ephraim is ᴿoppressed *and* broken in
    judgment,
  Because he willingly walked by ᴿ*human*
    precept.   Deut. 28:33 • Mic. 6:16
12 Therefore I *will be* to Ephraim like a
    moth,
  And to the house of Judah ᴿlike
    rottenness.   Prov. 12:4
13 "When Ephraim saw his sickness,
  And Judah *saw* his ᴿwound,   Jer. 30:12-15
  Then Ephraim went ᴿto Assyria
  And sent to King Jareb;
  Yet he cannot cure you,
  Nor heal you of your wound.   2 Kin. 15:19
14 For ᴿI *will be* like a lion to Ephraim,
  And like a young lion to the house of
    Judah.
  ᴿI, *even* I, will tear *them* and go away;
  I will take *them* away, and no one shall
    rescue.   Lam. 3:10 • Ps. 50:22
15 I will return again to My place
  Till they ᵀacknowledge their offense.
  Then they will seek My face;
  In their affliction they will earnestly
    seek Me."   Lit. *become guilty*

A Call to Repentance

6 Come, and let us return to the LORD;
For He has torn, but He will heal us;
He has stricken, but He will bind us up.

2 ᴿAfter two days He will revive us;
On the third day He will raise us up,
That we may live in His sight.   [1 Cor. 15:4]

3 ᴿLet us know,
Let us pursue the knowledge of the
LORD.   Is. 54:13
His going forth is established ᴿas the
morning;   2 Sam. 23:4
ᴿHe will come to us ᴿlike the rain,
Like the latter *and* former rain to the
earth.   Ps. 72:6 • Job 29:23

Impenitence of Israel and Judah

4 "O Ephraim, what shall I do to you?
O Judah, what shall I do to you?
For your faithfulness is like a morning
cloud,
And like the early dew it goes away.

5 Therefore I have hewn *them* by the
prophets,
I have slain them by ᴿthe words of My
mouth;   [Jer. 23:29]
And ᵀyour judgments *are like* light *that*
goes forth.   Or *the judgments on you*

6 For I desire ᵀmercy and not sacrifice,
And the knowledge of God more than
burnt offerings.   Or *faithfulness* or *loyalty*

7 "But like ᵀmen they transgressed the
covenant;   Or *Adam*
There they dealt treacherously with Me.

8 ᴿGilead *is* a city of evildoers   Hos. 12:11
And ᵀdefiled with blood.   Lit. *foot-tracked*

9 As bands of robbers lie in wait for a
man,
So the company of ᴿpriests ᴿmurder on
the way to Shechem;   Hos. 5:1 • Jer. 7:9, 10
Surely they commit lewdness.

10 I have seen a horrible thing in the
house of Israel:
There *is* the ᵀharlotry of Ephraim;
Israel is defiled.   Spiritual adultery

11 Also, O Judah, a harvest is appointed
for you,
When I return the captives of My
people.

7 "When I would have healed Israel,
Then the iniquity of Ephraim was
uncovered,
And the wickedness of Samaria.
For ᴿthey have committed fraud;
A thief comes in;   Hos. 5:1
A band of robbers takes spoil outside.

2 They ᵀdo not consider in their hearts
That ᴿI remember all their wickedness;
Now their own deeds have surrounded
them;   Lit. *do not say to* • Jer. 14:10; 17:1
They are before My face.

3 They make a ᴿking glad with their
wickedness,   Hos. 1:1
And princes ᴿwith their lies.   [Rom. 1:32]

4 "Theyᴿ *are* all adulterers.   Jer. 9:2; 23:10
Like an oven heated by a baker—
He ceases stirring *the fire* after
kneading the dough,
Until it is leavened.

5 In the day of our king
Princes have made *him* sick, ᵀinflamed
with ᴿwine;   Lit. *with the heat of* • Is. 28:1, 7
He stretched out his hand with scoffers.

6 They prepare their heart like an oven,
While they lie in wait;
*Their baker sleeps all night;
In the morning it burns like a flaming
fire.

7 They are all hot, like an oven,
And have devoured their judges;
All their kings have fallen.
ᴿNone among them calls upon Me.   Is. 64:7

8 "Ephraim ᴿhas mixed himself among the
peoples;   Ps. 106:35
Ephraim is a cake unturned.

9 ᴿAliens have devoured his strength,
But he does not know *it;*
Yes, gray hairs are here and there on
him,
Yet he does not know *it.*   Hos. 8:7

10 And the ᴿpride of Israel testifies to his
face,
But ᴿthey do not return to the LORD
their God,
Nor seek Him for all this.   Hos. 5:5 • Is. 9:13

Futile Reliance on the Nations

11 "Ephraimᴿ also is like a silly dove,
without ᵀsense—   Hos. 11:11 • Lit. *heart*
ᴿThey call to Egypt,   Is. 30:3
They go to ᴿAssyria.   Hos. 5:13; 8:9

12 Wherever they go, I will ᴿspread My
net on them;
I will bring them down like birds of the
air;
I will chastise them
ᴿAccording to what their congregation
has heard.   Ezek. 12:13 • Lev. 26:14

13 "Woe to them, for they have fled from
Me!
Destruction to them,
Because they have transgressed against
Me!
Though ᴿI redeemed them,   Mic. 6:4
Yet they have spoken lies against Me.

14 ᴿThey did not cry out to Me with their
heart   Job 35:9, 10
When they wailed upon their beds.

7:6 So with MT, Vg., Syr., Tg. *Their anger;* LXX *Ephraim*

"They *assemble together for grain and
    new ᴿwine,
*They rebel against Me;   Amos 2:8
15 Though I disciplined *and* strengthened
    their arms,
Yet they devise evil against Me;
16 They return, *but* not to the Most High;
They are like a treacherous bow.
Their princes shall fall by the sword
For the ᴿcursings of their tongue.
This *shall be* their derision ᴿin the land
    of Egypt.   Ps. 73:9 • Hos. 8:13; 9:3

The Apostasy of Israel

8 "Set the ᵀtrumpet to your mouth!
    He shall come like an eagle against the
    house of the LORD,
Because they have transgressed My
    covenant   Heb. *shophar,* ram's horn
And rebelled against My law.
2 ᴿIsrael will cry to Me,   Ps. 78:34
'My God, ᴿwe know You!'   Titus 1:16
3 Israel has rejected the good;
The enemy will pursue him.

4 "Theyᴿ set up kings, but not by Me;
They made princes, but I did not
    acknowledge *them.*
From their silver and gold
They made idols for themselves—
That they might be cut off.   2 Kin. 15:23, 25
5 Your calf ᵀis rejected, O Samaria!
My anger is aroused against them—
ᴿHow long until they attain to
    innocence?   Or *has rejected you* • Jer. 13:27
6 For from Israel *is* even this:
A ᴿworkman made it, and it *is* not God;
But the calf of Samaria shall be broken
    to pieces.   Is. 40:19

7 "Theyᴿ sow the wind,   Prov. 22:8
And reap the whirlwind.
The stalk has no bud;
It shall never produce meal.
If it should produce,
ᴿAliens would swallow it up.   Hos. 7:9
8 ᴿIsrael is swallowed up;   2 Kin. 17:6
Now they are among the Gentiles
Like a vessel in which *is* no pleasure.
9 For they have gone up to Assyria,
Like a wild donkey alone by itself;
Ephraim ᴿhas hired lovers.   Ezek. 16:33, 34
10 Yes, though they have hired among the
    nations,
Now ᴿI will gather them;   Ezek. 16:37; 22:20
And they shall *sorrow a little,

7:14 So with MT, Tg.; Vg. *thought upon;* LXX *slashed
themselves for* (cf. 1 Kin. 18:28) • So with MT, [Syr.], Tg.;
LXX omits *They rebel against Me;* Vg. *They departed
from Me*
8:10 Or *begin to diminish*

Because of the ᵀburden of ᴿthe king of
    princes.   Or *oracle* or *proclamation* • Is. 10:8
11 "Because Ephraim has made many altars
    for sin,
They have become for him altars for
    sinning.
12 I have written for him ᴿthe great things
    of My law,
But they were considered a strange
    thing.   [Deut. 4:6-8]
13 *For* the sacrifices of My offerings ᴿthey
    sacrifice flesh and eat *it,*   Zech. 7:6
ᴿ*But* the LORD does not accept them.
ᴿNow He will remember their iniquity
    and punish their sins. Jer. 14:10 • Amos 8:7
They shall return to Egypt.

14 "For Israel has forgotten his Maker,
And has built ᵀtemples;   Or *palaces*
Judah also has multiplied ᴿfortified
    cities;   Jer. 17:27
But I will send fire upon his cities,
And it shall devour his ᵀpalaces."   citadels

Judgment of Israel's Sin

9 Doᴿ not rejoice, O Israel, with joy like
    other peoples,
For you have played the harlot against
    your God.
You have made love *for* ᴿhire on every
    threshing floor.   Is. 22:12, 13 • Jer. 44:17
2 The threshing floor and the winepress
Shall not feed them,
And the new wine shall fail in her.

3 They shall not dwell in ᴿthe LORD's
    land,   [Lev. 25:23]
ᴿBut Ephraim shall return to Egypt,
And ᴿshall eat unclean *things* in
    Assyria.   Hos. 7:16; 8:13 • Ezek. 4:13
4 They shall not offer wine *offerings* to
    the LORD,
Nor ᴿshall their ᴿsacrifices be pleasing
    to Him.
It shall be like bread of mourners to
    them;
All who eat it shall be defiled.
For their bread *shall be* for their *own*
    life;
It shall not come into the house of the
    LORD.   Jer. 6:20 • Hos. 8:13

5 What will you do in the appointed day,
And in the day of the feast of the
    LORD?
6 For indeed they are gone because of
    destruction.
Egypt shall gather them up;
Memphis shall bury them.
ᴿNettles shall possess their valuables of
    silver;   Is. 5:6; 7:23
Thorns *shall be* in their tents.

7 The days of punishment have come;
  The days of recompense have come.
  Israel ᴿknows!   Is. 10:3
  The prophet *is* a ᴿfool,   Lam. 2:14
  ᴿThe spiritual man *is* insane,   Mic. 2:11
  Because of the greatness of your
    iniquity and great enmity.
8 The ᴿwatchman of Ephraim *is* with my
    God;
  But the prophet *is* a *fowler's snare in
    all his ways—   Ezek. 3:17; 33:7
  Enmity in the house of his God.
9 ᴿThey are deeply corrupted,   Hos. 10:9
  As in the days of ᴿGibeah.   Judg. 19:22
  He will remember their iniquity;
  He will punish their sins.

10 "I found Israel
  Like grapes in the ᴿwilderness;
  I saw your fathers   Jer. 2:2
  As the ᴿfirstfruits on the fig tree in its
    first season.   Is. 28:4
  But they went to ᴿBaal Peor,   Num. 25:3
  And ᵀseparated themselves *to that*
    shame;   Or *dedicated*
  ᴿThey became an abomination like the
    thing they loved.   Ps. 81:12
11 *As for* Ephraim, their glory shall fly
    away like a bird—
  No birth, no pregnancy, and no
    conception!
12 Though they bring up their children,
  Yet I will bereave them to the last man.
  Yes, ᴿwoe to them when I depart from
    them!   Deut. 31:17
13 Just ᴿas I saw Ephraim like Tyre,
    planted in a pleasant place,
  So Ephraim will bring out his children
    to the murderer."   Ezek. 26—28

14 Give them, O Lᴏʀᴅ—
  What will You give?
  Give them ᴿa miscarrying womb
  And dry breasts!   Luke 23:29

15 "All their wickedness *is* in ᴿGilgal,
  For there I hated them.   Hos. 4:15; 12:11
  Because of the evil of their deeds
  I will drive them from My house;
  I will love them no more.
  ᴿAll their princes *are* rebellious.   Is. 1:23
16 Ephraim is ᴿstricken,
  Their root is dried up;
  They shall bear no fruit.
  Yes, were they to bear children,
  I would kill the darlings of their
    womb."   Hos. 5:11

17 My God will ᴿcast them away,
  Because they did not obey Him;
  And they shall be ᴿwanderers among
    the nations.   [Zech. 10:6] · Lev. 26:33

9:8 One who catches birds in a trap or snare

Israel's Sin and Captivity

10 Israel ᴿempties *his* vine;
  He brings forth fruit for himself.
  According to the multitude of his fruit
  ᴿHe has increased the altars;
  According to the bounty of his land
  They have embellished *his* sacred
    pillars.   Nah. 2:2 · Jer. 2:28
2 Their heart is ᵀdivided;   In loyalty
  Now they are held guilty.
  He will break down their altars;
  He will ruin their sacred pillars.

3 For now they say,
  "We have no king,
  Because we did not fear the Lᴏʀᴅ.
  And as for a king, what would he do
    for us?"
4 They have spoken words,
  Swearing falsely in making a covenant.
  Thus judgment springs up ᴿlike   Amos 5:7
  hemlock in the furrows of the field.

5 The inhabitants of Samaria fear
  Because of the ᴿcalf* of Beth Aven.
  For its people mourn for it,   Hos. 8:5, 6
  And its priests shriek for it—
  Because its glory has departed from it.
6 *The idol* also shall be carried to Assyria
  As a present for King ᴿJareb.
  Ephraim shall receive shame,
  And Israel shall be ashamed of his own
    counsel.   Hos. 5:13

7 *As for* Samaria, her king is cut off
  Like a twig on the water.
8 Also the ᴿhigh places of ᵀAven, ᴿthe sin
    of Israel,   Hos. 4:15 · Lit. *Idolatry* · 1 Kin. 13:34
  Shall be destroyed.
  The thorn and thistle shall grow on
    their altars;
  ᴿThey shall say to the mountains,
    "Cover us!"   Luke 23:30
  And to the hills, "Fall on us!"

9 "O Israel, you have sinned from the days
    of ᴿGibeah;   Hos. 9:9
  There they stood.
  The battle in Gibeah against the
    children of *iniquity
  Did not ᵀovertake them.   Or *overcome*
10 When *it is* My desire, I will chasten
    them.
  Peoples shall be gathered against them
  When I bind them ᵀfor their two
    transgressions.   Or *in their two habitations*
11 Ephraim *is* ᴿa trained heifer   [Mic. 4:13]
  That loves to thresh *grain;*
  But I harnessed her fair neck,
  I will make Ephraim ᵀpull *a* plow.   Lit. *to ride*
  Judah shall plow;
  Jacob shall break his clods."

10:5 Lit. *calves,* images
10:9 So with many Heb. mss., LXX, Vg., MT *unruliness*

12 Sow for yourselves righteousness;
   Reap in mercy;
   ^RBreak up your fallow ground,
   For *it is* time to seek the LORD,
   Till He ^Rcomes and rains righteousness
      on you.   Jer. 4:3 · Hos. 6:3

13 ^RYou have plowed wickedness;
   You have reaped iniquity.   [Prov. 22:8]
   You have eaten the fruit of lies,
   Because you trusted in your own way,
   In the multitude of your mighty men.
14 Therefore tumult shall arise among
      your people,
   And all your fortresses shall be
      plundered
   As Shalman plundered Beth Arbel in
      the day of battle—
   A mother dashed in pieces upon *her*
      children.
15 Thus it shall be done to you, O Bethel,
   Because of your great wickedness.
   At dawn the king of Israel
   Shall be cut off utterly.

God's Continuing Love for Israel

11 "When Israel *was* a ^Tchild, I loved
         him,   Or *youth*
      And out of Egypt I called My son.
   2 *As they called them,
      So they ^Rwent *from them;   2 Kin. 17:13-15
      They sacrificed to the Baals,
      And burned incense to carved images.
   3 "I^R taught Ephraim to walk,
      Taking them by *their arms;
      But they did not know that ^RI healed
         them.   Deut. 1:31; 32:10, 11 · Ex. 15:26
   4 I drew them with ^Tgentle cords,
      With bands of love,   Lit. *cords of a man*
      And I was to them as those who take
         the yoke from their ^Tneck.   Lit. *jaws*
      ^RI stooped *and* fed them.   Ps. 78:25

   5 "He shall not return to the land of
         Egypt;
      But the Assyrian shall be his king,
      Because they refused to repent.
   6 And the sword shall slash in his cities,
      Devour his districts,
      And consume *them,*
      Because of their own counsels.
   7 My people are bent on ^Rbacksliding
         from Me.   Jer. 3:6, 7; 8:5
      Though ^Tthey call *to the Most High,
      None at all exalt *Him.*   The prophets

   8 "How can I give you up, Ephraim?
      How can I hand you over, Israel?

How can I make you like Admah?
   How can I set you like Zeboiim?
   My heart ^Tchurns within Me;
   My sympathy is stirred.   Lit. *turns over*
9 I will not execute the fierceness of My
      anger;
   I will not again destroy Ephraim.
   ^RFor I *am* God, and not man,   Num. 23:19
   The Holy One in your midst;
   And I will not *come with terror.
10 "They shall walk after the LORD.
   ^RHe will roar like a lion.
   When He roars,
   Then *His* sons shall come trembling
      from the west;   [Joel 3:16]
11 They shall come trembling like a bird
      from Egypt,
   ^RLike a dove from the land of Assyria.
   ^RAnd I will let them dwell in their
      houses,"
   Says the LORD.   Is. 11:11; 60:8 · Ezek. 28:25, 26

12 "Ephraim has encircled Me with lies,
   And the house of Israel with deceit;
   But Judah still walks with God,
   Even with the ^THoly One *who is*
      faithful.   Or *holy ones*

12 "Ephraim feeds on the wind,
      And pursues the east wind;
   He daily increases lies and ^Tdesolation.
   ^RAlso they make a ^Tcovenant with the
      Assyrians,   *ruin* · 2 Kin. 17:4 · Or *treaty*
   And ^Roil is carried to Egypt.   Is. 30:6

God's Charge Against Judah and Jacob

2 "The^R LORD also *brings* a ^Tcharge against
      Judah,
   And will punish Jacob according to his
      ways;   Mic. 6:2 · A legal complaint
   According to his deeds He will
      recompense him.
3 He took his brother ^Rby the heel in the
      womb,
   And in his strength he ^Rstruggled with
      God.   Gen. 25:26 · Gen. 32:24-28
4 Yes, he struggled with the Angel and
      prevailed;
   He wept, and sought favor from Him.
   He found Him *in* ^RBethel,   [Gen. 28:12-19]
   And there He spoke to us—
5 That is, the LORD God of hosts.
   The LORD *is* His memorable name.
6 ^RSo you, by *the help of* your God,
      return;
   Observe mercy and justice,   Mic. 6:8
   And wait on your God continually.

7 "A cunning ^TCanaanite!   Or *merchant*
   ^RDeceitful scales *are* in his hand;
   He loves to oppress.   Amos 8:5

11:2 So with MT, Vg.; LXX *Just as I called them;* Tg.
interpreted as *I sent prophets to a thousand of them* •
So with MT, Tg., Vg.; LXX *from My face*
11:3 Some Heb. mss., LXX, Syr., Vg. *My arms*
11:7 Or *upward*

11:9 Or *enter a city*

8 And Ephraim said,
  'Surely[R] I have become rich,   Rev. 3:17
  I have found wealth for myself;
  In all my labors
  They shall find in me no iniquity that *is*
    sin.'

9 "But I *am* the LORD your God,
  Ever since the land of Egypt;
  I will again make you dwell in tents,
  As in the days of the appointed feast.

10 [R]I have also spoken by the prophets,
  And have multiplied visions;   2 Kin. 17:13
  I have given [T]symbols through the
    witness of the prophets."   *Or parables*

11 Though [R]Gilead *has* idols—   Hos. 6:8
  Surely they are [T]vanity—   *worthless*
  Though they sacrifice bulls in [R]Gilgal,
  Indeed their altars *shall be* heaps in the
    furrows of the field.   Hos. 9:15

12 Jacob fled to the country of Syria;
  [R]Israel served for a spouse,   Gen. 29:20, 28
  And for a wife he tended *sheep*.

13 [R]By a prophet the LORD brought Israel
    out of Egypt,   Ex. 12:50, 51; 13:3
  And by a prophet he was preserved.

14 Ephraim [R]provoked *Him* to anger most
    bitterly;   Ezek. 18:10-13
  Therefore his Lord will leave the guilt
    of his bloodshed upon him,
  And return his reproach upon him.

Relentless Judgment on Israel

13 When Ephraim spoke, trembling,
      He exalted *himself* in Israel;
  But when he offended through Baal
    worship, he died.

2 Now they sin more and more,
  And have made for themselves molded
    images,
  Idols of their silver, according to their
    skill;
  All of it *is* the work of craftsmen.
  They say of them,
  "Let [T]the men who sacrifice kiss the
    calves!"   Or *those who offer human sacrifice*

3 Therefore they shall be like the
    morning cloud
  And like the early dew that passes
    away,
  [R]Like chaff blown off from a threshing
    floor   Dan. 2:35
  And like smoke from a chimney.

4 "Yet [R]I *am* the LORD your God   Is. 43:11
  Ever since the land of Egypt,
  And you shall know no God but Me;
  For *there is* no savior besides Me.

5 I [T]knew you in the wilderness,
  In the land of great drought.   Cared for you

6 [R]When they had pasture, they were
    filled;   Deut. 8:12, 14; 32:13-15

They were filled and their heart was
    exalted;
  Therefore they forgot Me.

7 "So [R]I will be to them like a lion; Lam. 3:10
  Like a leopard by the road I will lurk;

8 I will meet them [R]like a bear deprived
    of *her cubs*;
  I will tear open their rib cage,
  And there I will devour them like a
    lion.
  The wild beast shall tear them.   2 Sam. 17:8

9 "O Israel, *you are destroyed,
  But [T]your help *is* from Me.   Lit. *in your help*

10 *I will be your King;
  [R]Where *is any other*,   Deut. 32:38
  That he may save you in all your cities?
  And your judges to whom [R]you said,
  'Give me a king and princes'?   1 Sam. 8:5, 6

11 I gave you a king in My anger,
  And took *him* away in My wrath.

12 "The[R] iniquity of Ephraim *is* bound up;
  His sin *is* stored up.   Deut. 32:34, 35

13 [R]The sorrows of a woman in childbirth
    shall come upon him.
  He *is* an unwise son,
  For he should not stay long where
    children are born.   Is. 13:8

14 "I will ransom them from the [T]power of
    [T]the grave;   Lit. *hand* · Or *Sheol*
  I will redeem them from death.
  O Death, *I will be your plagues!
  O [T]Grave, *I will be your destruction!
  Pity is hidden from My eyes."   Or *Sheol*

15 Though he is fruitful among *his*
    brethren,
  [R]An east wind shall come;
  The wind of the LORD shall come up
    from the wilderness.
  Then his spring shall become dry,
  And his fountain shall be dried up.
  He shall plunder the treasury of every
    desirable prize.   Jer. 4:11, 12

16 Samaria *is held guilty,
  For she has [R]rebelled against her God.
  They shall fall by the sword,
  Their infants shall be dashed in pieces,
  And their women with child [R]ripped
    open.   2 Kin. 8:12 · 2 Kin. 15:16

Israel Restored at Last

14 O Israel, [R]return to the LORD your
      God,
  For you have stumbled because of your
    iniquity;   [Joel 2:13]

13:9 Lit. *it or he destroyed you*
13:10 LXX, Syr., Tg., Vg. *Where is your king?*
13:14 LXX *where is your punishment?* • LXX *where is
your sting?*
13:16 LXX *shall be disfigured*

2 Take words with you,
And return to the LORD.
Say to Him,
"Take away all iniquity;
Receive *us* graciously,
For we will offer the ^Rsacrifices* of our
lips.   [Heb. 13:15]
3 Assyria shall ^Rnot save us,
We will not ride on horses,   Hos. 7:11; 10:13
Nor will we say anymore to the work of
our hands,
'*You are* our gods.'
For in You the fatherless finds mercy."

4 "I will heal their ^Rbacksliding,
I will ^Rlove them freely,
For My anger has turned away from
him.   Jer. 14:7 • [Eph. 1:6]
5 I will be like the ^Rdew to Israel;   Prov. 19:12
He shall ^Tgrow like the lily,   Lit. *bud* or *sprout*
And lengthen his roots like Lebanon.

14:2 Lit. *bull calves;* LXX *fruit*

6 His branches shall ^Tspread;   Lit. *go*
His beauty shall be like an olive tree,
And his fragrance like Lebanon.
7 ^RThose who dwell under his shadow
shall return;   Dan. 4:12
They shall be revived *like* grain,
And ^Tgrow like a vine.   Lit. *bud*
Their ^Tscent *shall be* like the wine of
Lebanon.   Lit. *remembrance*

8 "Ephraim *shall say,*
'What have I to do anymore with idols?'
I have heard and observed him.
I *am* like a green cypress tree;
^RYour fruit is found in Me."   [John 15:4]

9 Who *is* wise?
Let him understand these things.
Who is prudent?
Let him know them.
For ^Rthe ways of the LORD *are* right;
The righteous walk in them,   [Prov. 10:29]
But transgressors stumble in them.

THE BOOK OF

Joel

Like a burst of sunlight on a darkened world the apocalyptic book of Joel had its impact on his time and culture. It later helped to vitalize the apostle Peter's sermon at Pentecost about the living Messiah (Acts 2:16-21) and Paul's exposition of the unfathomable grace of God in the gospel (Rom. 10:13). It remains undimmed through the years in the darkness of our hedonistic society, and the darkness has not conquered it.

AUTHORSHIP. We know very little about Joel, the prophet who wrote this little book, either of his life or of the period of his prophecy. Perhaps this mystery is part of what makes Joel so constantly contemporary. The name *Joel* means "Jehovah is God," which may indicate the religious faith of his father Pethuel and his mother. There are thirteen other men named Joel in the Old Testament, but none of them can be identified with this prophet.

SUMMARY STATEMENT. Using a devastating plague of locusts as an illustration, Joel teaches that the day of the Lord—the time when He will reveal Himself in the destruction of His enemies and the exaltation of His friends—is surely coming.

HOW JOEL FITS INTO THE BIBLE. Joel is the second of the twelve so-called Minor Prophets, which in the Hebrew text constitute one book called "The Twelve." While Joel is a very short book, its prediction of the worldwide outpouring of the Holy Spirit is most important.

HOW JOEL FITS TOGETHER. The three chapters of Joel fall into two main parts: (1) The day of the Lord is heralded through the description of a plague of locusts (1:2—2:17); and (2) judgment is averted and blessings are bestowed (2:18—3:21).

KEY VERSE. The best single verse to characterize Joel from a positive viewpoint is 2:32a, which Paul quotes in Romans—"And it shall come to pass that whoever calls on the name of the LORD shall be saved." The most famous passage is 2:28-32, quoted by Peter in his Pentecost sermon.

—C.R.N. and J.C.N.

THE word of the LORD that came to ^RJoel the son of Pethuel.   Acts 2:16

The Land Laid Waste

2 Hear this, you elders,
  And give ear, all you inhabitants of the land!
  ^RHas *anything like* this happened in your days,   Joel 2:2
  Or even in the days of your fathers?
3 ^RTell your children about it,   Ps. 78:4
  Let your children *tell* their children,
  And their children another generation.

4 What the chewing *locust left, the ^Rswarming locust has eaten;   Is. 33:4
  What the swarming locust left, the crawling locust has eaten;
  And what the crawling locust left, the consuming locust has eaten.

5 Awake, you ^Rdrunkards, and weep;
  And wail, all you drinkers of wine,
  Because of the new wine,
  ^RFor it has been cut off from your mouth.   Is. 5:11; 28:1 • Is. 32:10
6 For ^Ra nation has come up against My land,   Joel 2:2, 11, 25

1:4 Exact identity of these locusts unknown

Strong, and without number;
  ^RHis teeth *are* the teeth of a lion,   Rev. 9:8
  And he has the fangs of a fierce lion.
7 He has ^Rlaid waste My vine,   Is. 5:6
  And ^Truined My fig tree;   Or *splintered*
  He has stripped it bare and thrown *it* away;
  Its branches are made white.

8 ^RLament like a virgin girded with sackcloth   Is. 22:12
  For ^Rthe husband of her youth.   Jer. 3:4
9 ^RThe grain offering and the drink offering
  Have been cut off from the house of the LORD;
  The priests ^Rmourn, who minister to the LORD.   Joel 1:13; 2:14 • Joel 2:17
10 The field is wasted,
  ^RThe land mourns;
  For the grain is ruined,
  ^RThe new wine is dried up,
  The oil fails.   Jer. 12:11 • Is. 24:7

11 ^RBe ashamed, you farmers,
  Wail, you vinedressers,
  For the wheat and the barley;
  Because the harvest of the field has perished.   Jer. 14:3, 4
12 ^RThe vine has dried up,
  And the fig tree has withered;

The pomegranate tree,
The palm tree also,
And the apple tree—
All the trees of the field are withered;
Surely ᴿjoy has withered away from the
  sons of men.   Joel 1:10 • Jer. 48:33

Mourning for the Land

13 ᴿGird yourselves and lament, you priests;
Wail, you who minister before the altar;
Come, lie all night in sackcloth,
You who minister to my God;
For the grain offering and the drink
  offering
Are withheld from the house of your
  God.   Jer. 4:8
14 ᴿConsecrate a fast,   Joel 2:15, 16
Call ᴿa sacred assembly;   Lev. 23:36
Gather the elders
And ᴿall the inhabitants of the land
Into the house of the Lord your God,
And cry out to the Lord.   2 Chr. 20:13

15 ᴿAlas for the day!
For ᴿthe day of the Lord is at hand;
It shall come as destruction from the
  Almighty.   [Jer. 30:7] • Is. 13:6
16 Is not the food ᴿcut off before our eyes,
ᴿJoy and gladness from the house of our
  God?   Is. 3:1 • Deut. 12:7
17 The seed shrivels under the clods,
Storehouses are in shambles;
Barns are broken down,
For the grain has withered.
18 How ᴿthe animals groan!   Hos. 4:3
The herds of cattle are restless,
Because they have no pasture;
Even the flocks of sheep *suffer
  punishment.

19 O Lord, ᴿto You I cry out;   [Ps. 50:15]
For fire has devoured the ᵀopen
  pastures,   Lit. pastures of the wilderness
And a flame has burned all the trees of
  the field.
20 The beasts of the field also ᴿcry out to
  You,   Ps. 104:21; 147:9
For ᴿthe water brooks are dried up,
And fire has devoured the open
  pastures.   1 Kin. 17:7; 18:5

The Day of the Lord

2 Blow ᴿthe ᵀtrumpet in Zion,
And ᴿsound an alarm in My holy
  mountain!   Jer. 4:5 • ram's horn • Num. 10:5
Let all the inhabitants of the land
  tremble;
For ᴿthe day of the Lord is coming,
For it is at hand: [Obad. 15]
2 ᴿA day of darkness and gloominess,
A day of clouds and thick darkness,

Like the morning *clouds* spread over
  the mountains.   Amos 5:18
ᴿA people *come*, great and strong,
ᴿThe like of whom has never been;
Nor will there ever be any *such* after
  them,   Joel 1:6; 2:11, 25 • Dan. 9:12; 12:1
Even for many successive generations.

3 A fire devours before them,
And behind them a flame burns;
The land *is* like ᴿthe Garden of Eden
  before them,   Is. 51:3
And behind them a desolate wilderness;
Surely nothing shall escape them.
4 ᴿTheir appearance is like the appearance
  of horses;
And like swift steeds, so they run.   Rev. 9:7
5 ᴿWith a noise like chariots   Rev. 9:9
Over mountaintops they leap,
Like the noise of a flaming fire that
  devours the stubble,
Like a strong people set in battle array.

6 Before them the people writhe in pain;
ᴿAll faces *are drained of color.   Nah. 2:10
7 They run like mighty men,
They climb the wall like men of war;
Every one marches in formation,
And they do not break ᴿranks.   Prov. 30:27
8 They do not push one another;
Every one marches in his own ᵀcolumn.
Though they lunge between the
  weapons,   Lit. highway
They are not ᵀcut down.   Halted by losses
9 They run to and fro in the city,
They run on the wall;
They climb into the houses,
They ᴿenter at the windows ᴿlike a
  thief.   Jer. 9:21 • John 10:1

10 ᴿThe earth quakes before them,   Ps. 18:7
The heavens tremble;
ᴿThe sun and moon grow dark,   Is. 13:10
And the stars diminish their brightness.
11 ᴿThe Lord gives voice before His army,
For His camp is very great;   Jer. 25:30
ᴿFor strong *is the* One who executes His
  word.   Rev. 18:8
For the ᴿday of the Lord is great and
  very terrible;   Amos 5:18
ᴿWho can endure it?   [Mal. 3:2]

A Call to Repentance

12 "Now, therefore," says the Lord,
ᴿ"Turn to Me with all your heart,
With fasting, with weeping, and with
  mourning."   Jer. 4:1
13 So ᴿrend your heart, and not ᴿyour
  garments;   [Ps. 34:18; 51:17] • Gen. 37:34
Return to the Lord your God,
For He *is* ᴿgracious and merciful,
Slow to anger, and of great kindness;
And He relents from doing harm.   [Ex. 34:6]

1:18 LXX, Vg. *are made desolate*   2:6 LXX, Tg., Vg. *gather blackness*

14 ᴿWho knows *if* He will turn and relent,
And leave ᴿa blessing behind Him—
A grain offering and a drink offering
For the Lᴏʀᴅ your God?   Jer. 26:3 • Hag. 2:19

15 Blow the ᵀtrumpet in Zion,   *ram's horn*
ᴿConsecrate a fast,   Joel 1:14
Call a sacred assembly;
16 Gather the people,
ᴿSanctify the congregation,
Assemble the elders,
Gather the children and nursing babes;
ᴿLet the bridegroom go out from his
chamber,   Ex. 19:10 • Ps. 19:5
And the bride from her dressing room.
17 Let the priests, who minister to the
Lᴏʀᴅ,
Weep ᴿbetween the porch and the altar;
Let them say, ᴿ"Spare Your people, O
Lᴏʀᴅ,   Matt. 23:35 • Ex. 32:11, 12
And do not give Your heritage to
reproach,
That the nations should ᵀrule over
them.   *Or speak a proverb against them*
ᴿWhy should they say among the
peoples,   Ps. 42:10
'Where *is* their God?' "

The Land Refreshed

18 Then the Lᴏʀᴅ will ᴿbe zealous for His
land,
And pity His people.   [Is. 60:10; 63:9, 15]
19 The Lᴏʀᴅ will answer and say to His
people,
"Behold, I will send you ᴿgrain and new
wine and oil,
And you will be satisfied by them;
I will no longer make you a reproach
among the nations.   [Mal. 3:10]

20 "But ᴿI will remove far from you ᴿthe
northern *army,*   Ex. 10:19 • Jer. 1:14, 15
And will drive him away into a barren
and desolate land,
With his face toward the eastern sea
And his back ᴿtoward the western sea;
His stench will come up,   Deut. 11:24
And his foul odor will rise,
Because he has done ᵀmonstrous
things."   Lit. *great*

21 Fear not, O land;
Be glad and rejoice,
For the Lᴏʀᴅ has done ᵀmarvelous
things!   Lit. *great*
22 Do not be afraid, you beasts of the
field;
For ᴿthe open pastures are springing
up,
And the tree bears its fruit;
The fig tree and the vine yield their
strength.   Joel 1:19

23 Be glad then, you children of Zion,
And ᴿrejoice in the Lᴏʀᴅ your God;
For He has given you *the former rain
faithfully,   Is. 41:16
And He ᴿwill cause the rain to come
down for you—
The former rain,
And the latter rain in the first *month.*
24 The threshing floors shall be full of
wheat,
And the vats shall overflow with new
wine and oil.
25 "So I will restore to you the years that
the swarming ᴿlocust has eaten,
The crawling locust,
The consuming locust,
And the chewing locust,   Joel 1:4
My great army which I sent among
you.
26 You shall ᴿeat in plenty and be
satisfied,
And praise the name of the Lᴏʀᴅ your
God,
Who has dealt wondrously with you;
And My people shall never be put to
ᴿshame.   Lev. 26:5 • Is. 45:17
27 Then you shall know that I *am* ᴿin the
midst of Israel: Lev. 26:11, 12
ᴿI *am* the Lᴏʀᴅ your God
And there is no other.   [Is. 45:5, 6]
My people shall never be put to shame.

God's Spirit Poured Out

28 "Andᴿ it shall come to pass afterward
That ᴿI will pour out My Spirit on all
flesh;   Ezek. 39:29 • Zech. 12:10
ᴿYour sons and your ᴿdaughters shall
prophesy,   Is. 54:13 • Acts 21:9
Your old men shall dream dreams,
Your young men shall see visions.
29 And also on *My* ᴿmenservants and on
My maidservants   [Gal. 3:28]
I will pour out My Spirit in those days.

30 "And ᴿI will show wonders in the
heavens and in the earth: Matt. 24:29
Blood and fire and pillars of smoke.
31 ᴿThe sun shall be turned into darkness,
And the moon into blood,   Is. 13:9, 10; 34:4
ᴿBefore the coming of the great and
awesome day of the Lᴏʀᴅ.   [Mal. 4:1, 5, 6]
32 And it shall come to pass
That ᴿwhoever calls on the name of the
Lᴏʀᴅ   Rom. 10:13
Shall be ᵀsaved.   Or *delivered*
For ᴿin Mount Zion and in Jerusalem
there shall be ᵀdeliverance,
As the Lᴏʀᴅ has said,   Is. 46:13 • Or *salvation*
Among ᴿthe remnant whom the Lᴏʀᴅ
calls.   [Mic. 4:7]

2:23 Or *teacher of righteousness*

God Judges the Nations

3 "For behold, ᴿin those days and at that
time,
When I bring back the captives of
Judah and Jerusalem,   Jer. 30:3
2 ᴿI will also gather all nations,   Zech. 14:2
And bring them down to the Valley of
Jehoshaphat;
And I ᴿwill enter into judgment with
them there   Is. 66:16
On account of My people, My heritage
Israel,
Whom they have scattered among the
nations;
They have also divided up My land.
3 They have ᴿcast lots for My people,
Have given a boy *as payment* for a
harlot,   Nah. 3:10
And sold a girl for wine, that they may
drink.

4 "Indeed, what have you to do with Me,
ᴿO Tyre and Sidon, and all the coasts of
Philistia?   Amos 1:6–8
Will you retaliate against Me?
But if you ᵀretaliate against Me, *repay Me*
Swiftly and speedily I will return your
retaliation upon your own head.
5 Because you have taken My silver and
My gold,
And have carried into your temples My
ᵀprized possessions. Lit. *precious good things*
6 Also the people of Judah and the people
of Jerusalem
You have sold to the Greeks,
That you may remove them far from
their borders.

7 "Behold, ᴿI will raise them
Out of the place to which you have sold
them,
And will return your ᵀretaliation upon
your own head.   Jer. 23:8 • Or *repayment*
8 I will sell your sons and your daughters
Into the hand of the people of Judah,
And they will sell them to the
ᴿSabeans,*   Ezek. 23:42
To a people ᴿfar off;   Jer. 6:20
For the LORD has spoken."

9 ᴿProclaim this among the nations:
"Prepare for war!
Wake up the mighty men,
Let all the men of war draw near,
Let them come up.   Ezek. 38:7
10 ᴿBeat your plowshares into swords [Is. 2:4]
And your pruning hooks into spears;
Let the weak say, 'I *am* strong.' "

49–D. The Establishment of the Millennial Kingdom

▼

11 Assemble and come, all you nations,
And gather together all around.
Cause ᴿYour mighty ones to go down
there, O LORD.   Is. 13:3

12 "Let the nations be wakened, and come
up to the Valley of Jehoshaphat;
For there I will sit to ᴿjudge all the
surrounding nations.   Is. 2:4
13 ᴿPut in the sickle, for ᴿthe harvest is
ripe.   Rev. 14:15 • Jer. 51:33
Come, go down;
For the ᴿwinepress is full,   [Is. 63:3]
The vats overflow—
For their wickedness *is* great."

14 Multitudes, multitudes in the valley of
decision!
For ᴿthe day of the LORD *is* near in the
valley of decision.   Joel 2:1

3:8 Lit. *Shebaites,* Is. 60:6; Ezek. 27:22

49–D. The Establishment of the Millennial Kingdom (Joel 3:11–17)—

(1) Verses 11–17 recount the Battle of Armageddon and the establishment of the millennial kingdom (Matt. 25:31–46, page 976). "Millennium" (Latin for "thousand years") refers to the thousand-year reign of Christ on earth (Rev. 20:1–7, page 1313).

(2) Satan will be *bound* (restrained) for a thousand years (Rev. 20:1–3, page 1313). Christ will come and cast the Beast (Antichrist) and the False Prophet "alive into the lake of fire burning with brimstone" (Rev. 19:20, page 1313).

(3) Christ will judge the nations (Matt. 25:31–46, page 976).

(a) This judgment for entrance into the millennial kingdom on earth should not be confused with the judgment seat of Christ meant for rewarding believers (2 Cor. 5:10, page 1168), nor with the Great White Throne judgment, the final judgment of all the lost (Rev. 20:11–15, page 1313).
(b) This judgment occurs "immediately after the tribulation" (Matt. 24:29–31, page 974).
(c) The judgment will separate "sheep" and "goat" individuals (Matt. 25:31, 32, page 976).
(d) The basis for the judgment is faith, the kind of saving faith demonstrated by those who help Christ's brethren flee from persecution during the Tribulation (Matt. 25:40–46, page 976). While the focus may be on those who helped His brethren during the Antichrist's persecution, the term "saving faith" may rightly be applied to the lives and works of every generation. Who are Christ's brethren? They are the Jews who will be persecuted, the 144,000 (Matt. 24:16–25, page 973; Rev. 12:10, 11, page 1305; 14:1, page 1306); as well as that great Gentile host from every nation, the Tribulation saints (Rev. 7:14, page 1301).

(4) The nations will not be deceived during the thousand years (Rev. 20:3, 7, 8, page 1313).

See Index, page 17, for your next study.

▽ 15 The sun and moon will grow dark,
And the stars will diminish their
brightness.
16 The LORD also will roar from Zion,
And utter His voice from Jerusalem;
The heavens and earth will shake;
ᴿBut the LORD will be a shelter for His
people,
And the strength of the children of
Israel.   [Is. 51:5, 6]

17 "So you shall know that I *am* the LORD
your God,
Dwelling in Zion My ᴿholy mountain.
Then Jerusalem shall be holy,
And no aliens shall ever pass through
▲   her again."   Zech. 8:3

God Blesses His People

18 And it will come to pass in that day

That the mountains shall drip with new
wine,
The hills shall flow with milk,
And all the brooks of Judah shall be
flooded with water;
A ᴿfountain shall flow from the house
of the LORD   Ezek. 47:1
And water the Valley of ᵀAcacias. *Shittim*

19 "Egypt shall be a desolation,
And Edom a desolate wilderness,
Because of violence *against* the people
of Judah,
For they have shed innocent blood in
their land.
20 But Judah shall abide forever,
And Jerusalem from generation to
generation.
21 "For I will ᴿacquit them of the guilt of
bloodshed, whom I had not acquitted;
For the LORD dwells in Zion."   Is. 4:4

THE BOOK OF
Amos

Amos is one of the most exciting and forward-looking books in the Bible. It is God's print-out for today's happenings to a people called Israel.

AUTHORSHIP. The author, whose name comes from a Hebrew verb meaning "to carry a burden," by his own confession was "no prophet, nor was I the son of a prophet" (7:14), but in his case God bypassed the professionals to enlist a sheepbreeder and a gatherer of fruit from the sycamore tree. His hometown was Tekoa in the desert twelve miles south of Jerusalem and six miles south of Bethlehem, overlooking the Dead Sea. Here he was occupied with managing sheep and pinching the fruit in such a way that it might grow and ripen properly as food for the poor.

CONTEXT. Often the people God uses are those who have a period of solitude in a desert place with Him. Think of God's theological college for Moses—the backside of the desert; Abraham—in the wilderness of Hebron; David—in the fields with his sheep, and later in the wilderness running from King Saul; Paul—three years in the Arabian desert; and here Amos, from the wild wilderness to Bethel, the capital of the northern kingdom of Israel, where Jeroboam I had erected one of his golden calves for idolatrous worship. It was during the reign of Jeroboam II in the eighth century B.C. that the prophet from Tekoa opened an exciting portion of God's eternal drama. The stage is set for us to see in this small book God's zeal for righteousness and the eternal hope that He gives.

SUMMARY STATEMENT. Amos, a Southerner from Judah, calls the idolatrous Northerners, Israel, to repent of their violence and social injustice and serve the Lord in righteousness.

HOW AMOS FITS TOGETHER AND KEY VERSE. The seed of God's eternal purpose for the Jewish nation and their land is germinated in this revealing and remarkable book of nine chapters, which shows how today's struggles become tomorrow's triumphs. The book may be divided into four main parts, all of which are highlighted by the key verse, 4:12—"Therefore thus will I do to you, O Israel; because I will do this to you, prepare to meet your God, O Israel!"

(1) Prior to this verse we see the patience of God in punishment. Chapters 1 and 2 proclaim God's judgment on the nations, and include indictments against Syria, Philistia, Phoenicia, Edom, Ammon, Moab, and Judah, finally focusing on Israel itself. The almighty and righteous God has not acted immediately by punishing the sinners, but finally His patience has been exhausted and to each nation He says, "I will send a fire" upon you!

(2) Chapters 3—6 are three sermons on the doom of Israel. The first announces coming judgment on Israel's present sins (ch. 3); the second denounces Israel's past depravity in failing to accept God's correction (4), and the third contains a lamentation for Israel's sin and doom, a call to repentance, and warnings concerning the coming day of the Lord (5—6).

(3) The curtain now rises on the final act in this drama of God with a fivefold vision of His judgment in chapters 7—9. God illustrates His will through the figures of locusts (7:1-3); a devouring fire (7:4-6); a plumb line (7:7-9); and a basket of summer fruit, ripe as Israel was ripe for judgment (8:1-14); and finally Amos sees the Lord Himself announcing the destruction of Israel (9:1-10). This section also contains a parenthetical account in which Amaziah the priest complains against Amos (7:10-17).

(4) After these messages of ruin and calamity, Amos ends his prophecy with the promise of Israel's restoration (9:11-15). God is almighty and thorough in His judgment, but He is also the same in His mercy. With this bright promise He brings to a conclusion His eternal and triumphant drama.

We do not depend on the flip of a coin, the editor of the morning newspaper, or the advice of a successful entrepreneur for a report on what will happen. No, the Lord who stands on the circle of the universe Himself gathers a people—a land—the history of the past—the glories of the future—and places them in the last chapter of Amos (and also in Acts 15:14-17) so that by looking to *Him* we recognize the fulfillment today of what He gave to Amos the prophet from Tekoa twenty-eight centuries ago.

—C.S.

THE words of Amos, who was among the *sheepbreeders of Tekoa, which he saw concerning Israel in the days of ᴿUzziah king of Judah, and in the days of Jeroboam the son of Joash, king of Israel, two years before the ᴿearthquake.   2 Chr. 26:1-23 • Zech. 14:5

2 And he said:

"The LORD ᴿroars from Zion,   Joel 3:16
And utters His voice from Jerusalem;
The pastures of the shepherds mourn,
And the top of Carmel withers."

Judgment on the Nations

3 Thus says the LORD:

"For three transgressions of ᴿDamascus,
    and for four,   Is. 8:4; 17:1-3
I will not turn away its *punishment*,
Because they have ᴿthreshed Gilead
    with implements of iron.   2 Kin. 10:32, 33
4 ᴿBut I will send a fire into the house of
    Hazael,
Which shall devour the palaces of ᴿBen-
    Hadad.   Jer. 49:27; 51:30 • 2 Kin. 6:24
5 I will also break the *gate* ᴿbar of
    Damascus,
And cut off the inhabitant from the
    Valley of Aven,
And the one who ᵀholds the scepter
    from ᵀBeth Eden.
The people of Syria shall go captive to
    Kir,"   Jer. 51:30 • Rules • Lit. *House of Eden*
Says the LORD.

6 Thus says the LORD:

"For three transgressions of ᴿGaza, and
    for four,
I will not turn away its *punishment*,
Because they took captive the whole
    captivity
To deliver *them* up to Edom.   Jer. 47:1, 5
7 ᴿBut I will send a fire upon the wall of
    Gaza,
Which shall devour its palaces.   Jer. 47:1
8 I will cut off the inhabitant ᴿfrom
    Ashdod,   Zeph. 2:4
And the one who holds the scepter
    from Ashkelon;
I will ᴿturn My hand against Ekron,
And ᴿthe remnant of the Philistines
    shall perish,"   Ps. 81:14 • Ezek. 25:16
Says the Lord GOD.

9 Thus says the LORD:

"For three transgressions of ᴿTyre, and
    for four,
I will not turn away its *punishment*,
Because they delivered up the whole
    captivity to Edom,
And did not remember the covenant of
    brotherhood.   Is. 23:1-18

10 But I will send a fire upon the wall of
    Tyre,
Which shall devour its palaces."

11 Thus says the LORD:

"For three transgressions of ᴿEdom, and
    for four,   Is. 21:11
I will not turn away its *punishment*,
Because he pursued his ᴿbrother with
    the sword,   Obad. 10-12
And cast off all pity;
His anger tore perpetually,
And he kept his wrath forever.
12 But ᴿI will send a fire upon Teman,
Which shall devour the palaces of
    Bozrah."   Obad. 9, 10

13 Thus says the LORD:

"For three transgressions of ᴿthe people
    of Ammon, and for four,   Ezek. 25:2
I will not turn away its *punishment*,
Because they ripped open the women
    with child in Gilead,
That they might enlarge their territory.
14 But I will kindle a fire in the wall of
    ᴿRabbah,
And it shall devour its palaces,
ᴿAmid shouting in the day of battle,
And a tempest in the day of the
    whirlwind.   Deut. 3:11 • Amos 2:2
15 ᴿTheir king shall go into captivity,
He and his princes together,"
Says the LORD.   Jer. 49:3

2 Thus says the LORD:

ᴿ"For three transgressions of Moab, and
    for four,   Zeph. 2:8-11
I will not turn away its *punishment*,
Because he ᴿburned the bones of the
    king of Edom to lime.   2 Kin. 3:26, 27
2 But I will send a fire upon Moab,
And it shall devour the palaces of
    ᴿKerioth;   Jer. 48:24, 41
Moab shall die with tumult,
With shouting *and* trumpet sound.
3 And I will cut off ᴿthe judge from its
    midst,   Num. 24:17
And slay all its princes with him,"
Says the LORD.

Judgment on Judah

4 Thus says the LORD:

"For three transgressions of ᴿJudah, and
    for four,   Hos. 12:2
I will not turn away its *punishment*,
ᴿBecause they have despised the law of
    the LORD,   Lev. 26:14
And have not kept His commandments.
ᴿTheir lies lead them astray,   Jer. 16:19
Lies which their fathers followed.
5 ᴿBut I will send a fire upon Judah,
And it shall devour the palaces of
    Jerusalem."   Hos. 8:14

1:1 2 Kin. 3:4

Judgment on Israel

6 Thus says the LORD:

"For three transgressions of ᴿIsrael, and
for four,   2 Kin. 17:7–18; 18:12
I will not turn away its *punishment,*
Because ᴿthey sell the righteous for
silver,   Is. 19:21
And the poor for a pair of sandals.
7 They ᵀpant after the dust of the earth
which is on the head of the poor,
And ᴿpervert the way of the humble.
ᴿA man and his father go in to the *same*
girl,   Or *trample on* · Amos 5:12 · Ezek. 22:11
ᴿTo defile My holy name.   Lev. 20:3
8 They lie down by every altar on clothes
ᴿtaken in pledge,   Ex. 22:26
And drink the wine of the condemned
in the house of their god.

9 "Yet *it was* I *who* destroyed the
ᴿAmorite before them,   Num. 21:25
Whose height *was* like the ᴿheight of
the cedars,   Ezek. 31:3
And he *was as* strong as the oaks;
Yet I ᴿdestroyed his fruit above
And his roots beneath.   [Mal. 4:1]
10 Also *it was* ᴿI *who* brought you up
from the land of Egypt,   Ex. 12:51
And ᴿled you forty years through the
wilderness,   Deut. 2:7
To possess the land of the Amorite.
11 I raised up some of your sons as
ᴿprophets,   Num. 12:6
And some of your young men as
ᴿNazirites.   Num. 6:2, 3
Is it not so, O you children of Israel?"
Says the LORD.
12 "But you gave the Nazirites wine to
drink,
And commanded the prophets ᴿsaying,
'Do not prophesy!'   Is. 30:10

13 "Behold, I am ᵀweighed down by you,
As a cart full of sheaves ᵀis weighed
down.   *tottering under · totters*

14 ᴿTherefore ᵀflight shall perish from the
swift,   Jer. 46:6 · Or *the place of refuge*
The strong shall not strengthen his
power,
Nor shall the mighty deliver himself;
15 He shall not stand who handles the
bow,
The swift of foot shall not ᵀescape,
Nor shall he who rides a horse deliver
himself.   Or *save*
16 The most courageous men of might
Shall flee naked in that day,"
Says the LORD.

Authority of the Prophet's Message

3 Hear this word that the LORD has spoken
against you, O children of Israel, against
the whole family which I brought up from
the land of Egypt, saying:

2 "Youᴿ only have I known of all the
families of the earth;
ᴿTherefore I will punish you for all your
iniquities."   [Deut. 7:6] · [Rom. 2:9]

**44-D. Enoch Walked in Agreement with ▼
God**

3 Can two walk together, unless they are
agreed?   ▲
4 Will a lion roar in the forest, when he
has no prey?
Will a young lion ᵀcry out of his den, if
he has caught nothing?   Lit. *give his voice*
5 Will a bird fall into a snare on the
earth, where there is no ᵀtrap for it?
Will a snare spring up from the earth, if
it has caught nothing at all?   Or *bait*
6 If a ᵀtrumpet is blown in a city, will not
the people be afraid?   *ram's horn*
ᴿIf there is calamity in a city, will not
the LORD have done *it?*   Is. 45:7

7 Surely the Lord GOD does nothing,
Unless ᴿHe reveals His secret to His
servants the prophets.   [John 15:15]

44-D. Enoch Walked in Agreement with God (Amos 3:3)—"Can two walk together, unless they are agreed?"
(v. 3). Enoch walked in agreement with God for three hundred years, continuously conforming his life to the
counsel of God. He must have learned that "the LORD brings the counsel of the nations to nothing . . . [but]
the counsel of the LORD stands forever" (Ps. 33:10, 11, page 529). Enoch chose to walk into eternity with the
infinite God; and as he traveled, he was guided by God's counsel day after day until he was translated into
His heavenly presence (Ps. 73:24, page 554). Enoch had a choice, to walk in agreement with God, or to walk
in the counsel of the ungodly (Ps. 1:1, page 509).
God gave Judah a choice before He sent them into seventy years of captivity: " 'Come now, and let us
reason together,' says the LORD, 'Though your sins are like scarlet, they shall be as white as snow; though
they are red like crimson, they shall be as wool' " (Is. 1:18, page 643). Judah was out of step with God, its
people walking in the counsel of the ungodly. When they refused to walk with Him, He sent them into
captivity. Every nation and individual has this choice: they can walk in agreement with God, as Enoch did, or
walk in the way that seems right to man, though the end of the walk that seems right to man is eternal
separation from God (Prov. 14:12, page 608).
Enoch began his walk with God in the year that Methuselah was born (Gen. 5:21, 22, page 9). For three
hundred years Enoch walked in faith, and in agreement with God.
See Genesis 5:24, page 10, for **Point 44-E: Enoch Walked All the Way to Heaven with God.**

8 A lion has roared!
  Who will not fear?
  The Lord God has spoken!
  ᴿWho can but prophesy?   Acts 4:20

Punishment of Israel's Sins

9 "Proclaim in the palaces at Ashdod,
  And in the palaces in the land of Egypt,
    and say:
  'Assemble on the mountains of Samaria;
  See great tumults in her midst,
  And the ᵀoppressed within her.   oppression
10 For they ᴿdo not know to do right,'
  Says the Lord,
  'Who store up violence and ᵀrobbery in
    their palaces.' "   Jer. 4:22 · Or devastation

11 Therefore thus says the Lord God:

  "An adversary shall be all around the
    land;
  He shall sap your strength from you,
  And your palaces shall be plundered."

12 Thus says the Lord:

  "As a shepherd ᵀtakes from the mouth of
    a lion   Or snatches
  Two legs or a piece of an ear,
  So shall the children of Israel be taken
    out
  Who dwell in Samaria—
  In the corner of a bed and ᵀon the edge
    of a couch!   Heb. is uncertain
13 Hear and testify against the house of
    Jacob,"
  Says the Lord God, the God of hosts,
14 "That in the day I punish Israel for their
    transgressions,
  I will also visit destruction on the altars
    of ᴿBethel;
  And the horns of the altar shall be cut
    off
  And fall to the ground.   Amos 4:4
15 I will ᵀdestroy the winter house along
    with ᴿthe summer house;
  The ᴿhouses of ivory shall perish,
  And the great houses shall have an
    end,"   Lit. strike · Judg. 3:20 · 1 Kin. 22:39
  Says the Lord.

4 Hear this word, you ᴿcows of Bashan,
    who are on the mountain of Samaria,
  Who oppress the ᴿpoor,   Ps. 22:12 · Amos 2:6
  Who crush the needy,
  Who say to ᵀyour husbands, "Bring
    wine, let us drink!"   Lit. their lords or masters
2 ᴿThe Lord God has sworn by His
    holiness: Ps. 89:35
  "Behold, the days shall come upon you
  When He will take you away ᴿwith
    fishhooks,   Jer. 16:16
  And your posterity with fishhooks.
3 ᴿYou will go out through broken walls,
  Each one straight ahead of her,

And you will ᵀbe cast into Harmon,"
  Says the Lord.   Ezek. 12:5 · Or cast them

4 "Come to Bethel and transgress,
  At Gilgal multiply transgression;
  Bring your sacrifices every morning,
  Your tithes every three *days.
5 ᴿOffer a sacrifice of thanksgiving with
    leaven,
  Proclaim and announce ᴿthe freewill
    offerings;
  For this you love,
  You children of Israel!"
  Says the Lord God.   Lev. 7:13 · Lev. 22:18

Israel Did Not Accept Correction

6 "Also I gave you ᵀcleanness of teeth in
    all your cities.
  And lack of bread in all your places;
  ᴿYet you have not returned to Me,"
  Says the Lord.   Hunger · Jer. 5:3

7 "I also withheld rain from you,
  When there were still three months to
    the harvest.
  I made it rain on one city,
  I withheld rain from another city.
  One part was rained upon,
  And where it did not rain the part
    withered.
8 So two or three cities wandered to
    another city to drink water,
  But they were not satisfied;
  Yet you have not returned to Me,"
  Says the Lord.

9 "Iᴿ blasted you with blight and mildew.
  When your gardens increased,
  Your vineyards,
  Your fig trees,
  And your olive trees,
  ᴿThe locust devoured them;
  Yet you have not returned to Me,"
  Says the Lord.   Hag. 2:17 · Joel 1:4, 7

10 "I sent among you a plague ᴿafter the
    manner of Egypt;
  Your young men I killed with a sword,
  Along with your captive horses;
  I made the stench of your camps come
    up into your nostrils;
  Yet you have not returned to Me,"
  Says the Lord.   Ps. 78:50

11 "I overthrew some of you,
  As God overthrew ᴿSodom and
    Gomorrah,
  And you were like a firebrand plucked
    from the burning;
  Yet you have not returned to Me,"
  Says the Lord.   Is. 13:19

12 "Therefore thus will I do to you, O
    Israel;

4:4 Or years, Deut. 14:28

Because I will do this to you,
Prepare to meet your God, O Israel!"

13 For behold,
He who forms mountains,
And creates the ᵀwind,   Or *spirit*
ᴿWho declares to man what ᵀhis thought
is,   Ps. 139:2 · Or *His*
And makes the morning darkness,
ᴿWho treads the high places of the
earth—   Mic. 1:3
The Lᴏʀᴅ God of hosts *is* His name.

A Lament for Israel

5 Hear this word which I take up against
you, a lamentation, O house of Israel:

2 The virgin of Israel has fallen;
She will rise no more.
She lies forsaken on her land;
There is no one to raise her up.

3 For thus says the Lord Gᴏᴅ:

"The city that goes out by a thousand
Shall have a hundred left,
And that which goes out by a hundred
Shall have ten left to the house of
Israel."

A Call to Repentance

4 For thus says the Lᴏʀᴅ to the house of
Israel:

ᴿ"Seek Me ᴿand live;   [Jer. 29:13] · [Is. 55:3]
5 But do not seek ᴿBethel,   Amos 4:4
Nor enter Gilgal,
Nor pass over to ᴿBeersheba;   Amos 8:14
For Gilgal shall surely go into captivity,
And Bethel shall come to nothing.
6 ᴿSeek the Lᴏʀᴅ and live,   [Is. 55:3, 6, 7]
Lest He break out like fire *in* the house
of Joseph,
And devour *it*,
With no one to quench *it* in Bethel—
7 You who ᴿturn justice to wormwood,
And lay righteousness to rest in the
earth!"   Amos 6:12

8 He made the ᴿPleiades and Orion;
He turns the shadow of death into
morning   Job 9:9; 38:31
ᴿAnd makes the day dark as night;
He ᴿcalls for the waters of the sea
And pours them out on the face of the
earth;   Ps. 104:20 · Job 38:34
ᴿThe Lᴏʀᴅ *is* His name.   [Amos 4:13]
9 He rains ruin upon the strong,
So that fury comes upon the fortress.

10 ᴿThey hate the one who rebukes in the
gate,
And they ᴿabhor the one who speaks
uprightly.   Is. 29:21; 66:5 · 1 Kin. 22:8
11 ᴿTherefore, because you ᵀtread down the
poor   Amos 2:6 · *trample*
And take grain ᵀtaxes from him, Or *tribute*

Though ᴿyou have built houses of hewn
stone,   Mic. 6:15
Yet you shall not dwell in them;
You have planted ᵀpleasant vineyards,
But you shall not drink wine from
them.   *desirable*
12 For I ᴿknow your manifold
transgressions
And your mighty sins:
ᴿAfflicting the just *and* taking bribes;
ᴿDiverting the poor *from justice* at the
gate.   Hos. 5:3 · Amos 2:6 · Is. 29:21
13 Therefore ᴿthe prudent keep silent at
that time,
For it *is* an evil time.   Amos 6:10

14 Seek good and not evil,
That you may live;
So the Lᴏʀᴅ God of hosts will be with
you,
ᴿAs you have spoken.   Mic. 3:11
15 ᴿHate evil, love good;
Establish justice in the gate.
ᴿIt may be that the Lᴏʀᴅ God of hosts
Will be gracious to the remnant of
Joseph.   Rom. 12:9 · Joel 2:14

The Day of the Lᴏʀᴅ

16 Therefore the Lᴏʀᴅ God of hosts, the
Lord, says this:

"There shall be wailing in all streets,
And they shall say in all the highways,
'Alas! Alas!'
They shall call the farmer to mourning,
ᴿAnd skillful lamenters to wailing.   Jer. 9:17
17 In all vineyards *there shall be* wailing,
For ᴿI will pass through you,"
Says the Lᴏʀᴅ.   Ex. 12:12

18 ᴿWoe to you who desire the day of the
Lᴏʀᴅ!   Is. 5:19
For what good *is* ᴿthe day of the Lᴏʀᴅ
to you?
It *will be* darkness, and not light.   Joel 2:2
19 It *will be* ᴿas though a man fled from a
lion,
And a bear met him!
Or *as though* he went into the house,
Leaned his hand on the wall,
And a serpent bit him!   Jer. 48:44
20 *Is* not the day of the Lᴏʀᴅ darkness,
and not light?
Is it not very dark, with no brightness
in it?

21 "Iᴿ hate, I despise your feast days,
And ᴿI do not savor your sacred
assemblies.   Is. 1:11–16 · Lev. 26:31
22 ᴿThough you offer Me burnt offerings
and your grain offerings,
I will not regard *them*,
Nor will I regard your fattened peace
offerings.   Mic. 6:6, 7
23 Take away from Me the noise of your
songs,

For I will not hear the melody of your
   stringed instruments.
24 But let justice run down like water,
   And righteousness like a mighty
     stream.

25 "Did^R you offer Me sacrifices and
   offerings
   In the wilderness forty years, O house
   of Israel?   Deut. 32:17
26 You also carried *Sikkuth your king
   And ^TChiun, your idols,   A pagan deity
   The star of your gods,
   Which you made for yourselves.
27 Therefore I will send you into captivity
   ^Rbeyond Damascus,"
   Says the LORD, ^Rwhose name is the God
   of hosts.   2 Kin. 17:6 • Amos 4:13

Warnings to Zion and Samaria

6 Woe ^Rto you who are at ease in Zion,
   And trust in Mount Samaria,   Luke 6:24
   Notable persons in the chief nation,
   To whom the house of Israel comes!
2 ^RGo over to ^RCalneh and see;
   And from there go to ^RHamath the
   great;   Jer. 2:10 • Is. 10:9 • 2 Kin. 18:34
   Then go down to Gath of the
   Philistines.
   ^RAre you better than these kingdoms?
   Or is their territory greater than your
   territory?   Nah. 3:8

3 Woe to you who ^Rput far off the day of
   ^Rdoom,   Is. 56:12 • Amos 5:18
   ^RWho cause ^Rthe seat of violence to
   come near;   Amos 5:12 • Ps. 94:20
4 Who lie on beds of ivory,
   Stretch out on your couches,
   Eat lambs from the flock
   And calves from the midst of the stall;
5 ^RWho sing idly to the sound of stringed
   instruments,   Is. 5:12
   And invent for yourselves musical
   instruments ^Rlike David;   1 Chr. 23:5
6 Who ^Rdrink wine from bowls,
   And anoint yourselves with the best
   ointments,
   ^RBut are not grieved for the affliction of
   Joseph.   Amos 2:8; 4:1 • Gen. 37:25
7 Therefore they shall now go ^Rcaptive as
   the first of the captives,   Amos 5:27
   And those who recline at banquets shall
   be removed.

8 ^RThe Lord GOD has sworn by Himself,
   The LORD God of hosts says: Jer. 51:14
   "I abhor ^Rthe pride of Jacob,   Amos 8:7
   And hate his palaces;
   Therefore I will deliver up the city
   And all that is in it."

9 Then it shall come to pass, that if ten
men remain in one house, they shall die.

5:26 LXX, Vg. tabernacle of Moloch • A pagan deity

10 And when ^Ta relative of the dead, with
one who will burn the bodies, picks up the
^Tbodies to take them out of the house, he will
say to one inside the house, "Are there any
more with you?" Then someone will say,
"None." And he will say, "Hold your tongue!
^RFor we dare not mention the name of the
LORD."   Lit. his loved one or uncle • Lit. bones • Amos 8:3

11 For behold, ^Rthe LORD gives a
   command: Is. 55:11
   ^RHe will break the great house into bits,
   And the little house into pieces.   Amos 3:15
12 Do horses run on rocks?
   Does one plow there with oxen?
   Yet ^Ryou have turned justice into gall,
   And the fruit of righteousness into
   wormwood,   Hos. 10:4
13 You who rejoice over *Lo Debar,
   Who say, "Have we not taken
   Karnaim for ourselves
   By our own strength?"

14 "But, behold, ^RI will raise up a nation
   against you,   Jer. 5:15
   O house of Israel,"
   Says the LORD God of hosts;
   "And they will afflict you from the
   ^Rentrance of Hamath   1 Kin. 8:65
   To the Valley of the Arabah."

Vision of the Locusts

7 Thus the Lord GOD showed me: Behold,
   He formed locust swarms at the beginning of the late crop; indeed it was the late
crop after the king's mowings.
2 And so it was, when they had finished
eating the grass of the land, that I said:

   "O Lord GOD, forgive, I pray!
   ^TOh, that Jacob may stand,
   For he is small!"   Or How shall Jacob stand
3 So ^Rthe LORD relented concerning this.
   "It shall not be," said the LORD.   Jon. 3:10

Vision of the Fire

4 Thus the Lord GOD showed me: Behold,
the Lord GOD called ^Tfor conflict by fire, and
it consumed the great deep and devoured the
^Tterritory.   to contend • Lit. portion
5 Then I said:

   "O Lord GOD, cease, I pray!
   ^ROh, that Jacob may stand,
   For he is small!"   Amos 7:2, 3
6 So the LORD relented concerning this.
   "This also shall not be," said the Lord
   GOD.

Vision of the Plumb Line

7 Thus He showed me: Behold, the Lord
stood on a wall made with a plumb line, with
a plumb line in His hand.
8 And the LORD said to me, "Amos, what

do you see?" And I said, "A plumb line." Then the Lord said:

"Behold, I am setting a plumb line
In the midst of My people Israel;
I will not pass by them anymore.
9 RThe Thigh places of Isaac shall be
desolate,   Gen. 46:1 • Places of pagan worship
And the Tsanctuaries of Israel shall be
laid waste.   Or *holy places*
RI will rise with the sword against the
house of Jeroboam."   2 Kin. 15:8-10

Amaziah's Complaint

10 Then Amaziah the priest of RBethel sent to RJeroboam king of Israel, saying, "Amos has conspired against you in the midst of the house of Israel. The land is not able to Tbear all his words.   Amos 4:4 • 2 Kin. 14:23 • Or *endure*

11 "For thus Amos has said:

'Jeroboam shall die by the sword,
And Israel shall surely be led away
Rcaptive
From their own land.' "   Amos 5:27; 6:7

12 Then Amaziah said to Amos:

"Go, you seer!
Flee to the land of Judah.
There eat bread,
And there prophesy.
13 But Rnever again prophesy at Bethel,
For it *is* the king's sanctuary,   Amos 2:12
And it *is* the royal Tresidence."   Lit. *house*

14 Then Amos answered, and said to Amaziah:

"I *was* no prophet,
Nor *was* I a son of a prophet,
But I *was* a Rsheepbreeder   2 Kin. 3:4
And a tender of sycamore fruit.
15 Then the Lord took me Tas I followed
the flock,   Lit. *from behind*
And the Lord said to me,
'Go, prophesy to My people Israel.'
16 Now therefore, hear the word of the
Lord:
You say, 'Do not prophesy against
Israel,
And Rdo not Tspout against the house of
Isaac.'   Ezek. 21:2 • Lit. *drip*

17 "ThereforeR thus says the Lord:

R'Your wife shall be a harlot in the city;
Your sons and daughters shall fall by
the sword;   Jer. 28:12; 29:21, 32 • Zech. 14:2
Your land shall be divided by *survey*
line;
You shall die in a Rdefiled land;
And Israel shall surely be led away
captive   Hos. 9:3
From his own land.' "

Vision of the Summer Fruit

8 Thus the Lord God showed me: Behold, a basket of summer fruit.

2 And He said, "Amos, what do you see?" So I said, "A basket of summer fruit." Then the Lord said to me:

R"The end has come upon My people
Israel;   Ezek. 7:2
RI will not pass by them anymore. Amos 7:8
3 And Rthe songs of the temple   Amos 5:23
Shall be wailing in that day,"
Says the Lord God—
"Many dead bodies everywhere,
They shall be thrown out in silence."

4 Hear this, you who Tswallow up the
needy,   Or *trample on,* Amos 2:7
And make the poor of the land fail,

5 Saying:

"When will the New Moon be past,
That we may sell grain?
And Rthe Sabbath,   Neh. 13:15
That we may Ttrade wheat?   Lit. *open*
RMaking the ephah small and the shekel
large,   Mic. 6:10, 11
Falsifying the scales by deceit,
6 That we may buy the poor for Rsilver,
And the needy for a pair of sandals—
Even sell the bad wheat?"   Amos 2:6

7 The Lord has sworn by Rthe pride of
Jacob: Amos 6:8
"Surely RI will never forget any of their
works.   Hos. 7:2; 8:13
8 RShall the land not tremble for this,
And everyone mourn who dwells in it?
All of it shall swell like *the River,
Heave and subside
RLike the River of Egypt.   Hos. 4:3 • Amos 9:5

9 "And it shall come to pass in that day,"
says the Lord God,
R"That I will make the sun go down at
noon,
And I will darken the earth in Tbroad
daylight;   Job 5:14 • Lit. *a day of light*
10 I will turn your feasts into Rmourning,
RAnd all your songs into lamentation;
RI will bring sackcloth on every waist,
And baldness on every head;
I will make it like mourning for an only
son,   Ezek. 7:18 • Ezek. 27:31 • [Zech. 12:10]
And its end like a bitter day.

11 "Behold, the days are coming," says the
Lord God,
"That I will send a famine on the land,
Not a famine of bread,
Nor a thirst for water,
But of hearing the words of the Lord.
12 They shall wander from sea to sea,
And from north to east;
They shall run to and fro, seeking the
word of the Lord,
But shall Rnot find *it.*   Hos. 5:6

8:8 The Nile; some Heb. mss., LXX, Tg., Syr., Vg. *River*
(cf. 9:5); MT *the light*

13 "In that day the fair virgins
And strong young men
Shall faint from thirst.
14 Those who ᴿswear by the ᵀsin of
Samaria,   Hos. 4:15 · Or *Ashima,* a Syrian goddess
Who say,
'As your god lives, O Dan!'
And, 'As the way of Beersheba lives!'
They shall fall and never rise again."

The Destruction of Israel

9 I saw the Lord standing by the altar, and
He said:

"Strike the ᵀdoorposts, that the
thresholds may shake,   Capital of the pillars
And ᴿbreak them on the heads of them
all.   Hab. 3:13
I will slay the last of them with the
sword.
ᴿHe who flees from them shall not get
away,   Amos 2:14
And he who escapes from them shall
not be delivered.

2 "Though they dig into ᵀhell,   Or *Sheol*
From there My hand shall take them;
ᴿThough they climb up to heaven,   Jer. 51:53
From there I will bring them down;
3 And though they ᴿhide themselves on
top of Carmel,
From there I will search and take them;
Though they hide from My sight at the
bottom of the sea,
From there I will command the serpent,
and it shall bite them;   Jer. 23:24
4 Though they go into captivity before
their enemies,
From there ᴿI will command the sword,
And it shall slay them.   Lev. 26:33
ᴿI will set My eyes on them for harm
and not for good."   Jer. 21:10; 39:16; 44:11

5 The Lord GOD of hosts,
He who touches the earth and it ᴿmelts,
And all who dwell there mourn;   Mic. 1:4
All of it shall swell like *the ᵀRiver,
And subside like the River of Egypt.
6 He who builds His ᴿlayersᵀ in the sky,
And has founded His strata in the
earth;
Who ᴿcalls for the waters of the sea,
And pours them out on the face of the
earth—   Ps. 104:3, 13 · Or *stairs* · Amos 5:8
ᴿThe LORD *is* His name.   Amos 4:13; 5:27

7 "*Are* you not like the ᵀpeople of Ethiopia
to Me,   Lit. *song of the Ethiopians*
O children of Israel?" says the LORD.

9:5 The Nile

"Did I not bring up Israel from the land
of Egypt,
The Philistines from ᵀCaphtor,   Crete
And the Syrians from ᴿKir?   Amos 1:5

8 "Behold, ᴿthe eyes of the Lord GOD *are*
on the sinful kingdom,   Amos 9:4
And I ᴿwill destroy it from the face of
the earth;   Jer. 5:10; 30:11
Yet I will not utterly destroy the house
of Jacob,"
Says the LORD.

9 "For surely I will command,
And will ᵀsift the house of Israel among
all nations,
As *grain* is sifted in a sieve;
ᴿYet not the smallest ᵀgrain shall fall to
the ground.   *shake* · [Is. 65:8–16] · Lit. *pebble*
10 All the sinners of My people shall die
by the sword,
ᴿWho say, 'The calamity shall not
overtake nor confront us.'   Amos 6:3

Israel Will Be Restored

11 "Onᴿ that day I will raise up   Acts 15:16–18
The *tabernacle of David, which has
fallen down,
And repair its damages;
I will raise up its ruins,
And rebuild it as in the days of old;
12 ᴿThat they may possess the remnant of
ᴿEdom,*   Obad. 19 · Num. 24:18
And all the Gentiles who are called by
My name,"
Says the LORD who does this thing.

13 "Behold, ᴿthe days are coming," says the
LORD,
"When the plowman shall overtake the
reaper,
And the treader of grapes him who
sows seed;
ᴿThe mountains shall drip with sweet
wine,   Lev. 26:5 · Joel 3:18
And all the hills shall flow *with it.*
14 ᴿI will bring back the captives of My
people Israel;
ᴿThey shall build the waste cities and
inhabit *them;*
They shall plant vineyards and drink
wine from them;
They shall also make gardens and eat
fruit from them.   Jer. 30:3, 18 · Is. 61:4
15 I will plant them in their land,
ᴿAnd no longer shall they be pulled up
From the land I have given them,"
Says the LORD your God.   Ezek. 34:28; 37:25

9:11 Lit. *booth;* a figure of a deposed dynasty
9:12 LXX *mankind*

THE BOOK OF
Obadiah

God's view of human pride and His response to it are just two of the important themes contained in Obadiah, the shortest prophecy in the Old Testament. The book is named after the prophet whose message it bears; the name *Obadiah* simply means "Servant of Jehovah."

Obadiah's prophecy is set against the background of the hatred which existed between Israel and Edom, a tension that had its origins in the marked differences between Jacob and Esau (Gen. 25:21-34).

The message of the book focuses on the nation of Edom, which had exploited its neighbors by extracting heavy taxes from the caravans forced to travel through its territory, had engaged in slave trade (2 Chr. 28:17; Amos 1:6, 9), and had acted treacherously toward Israel (vv. 10-14). Edom's absolute control of the rugged territory southeast of the Dead Sea had produced a false sense of security and an arrogant disposition (v. 3).

AUTHORSHIP. Although there are a number of individuals bearing the name *Obadiah* in the Old Testament, it is not possible to identify this prophet confidently with any of them. The straightforward and uncompromising nature of his prophecy, however, marks him as a man of courage.

CONTEXT. Obadiah did not identify any of the kings who reigned during his ministry. The date of this book, therefore, must be established by internal evidence alone. Obadiah's reference to the invasion of Jerusalem by "strangers" (v. 11) has led some to associate this event with the great destruction of Judah and Jerusalem by the Babylonians in 586 B.C. The prophet's description of Jerusalem's humiliation is so unlike that of all the other prophets in scope and nature, however, that it seems better to relate the events of verses 10-14 with the raids on Jerusalem by the Philistines and Arabians during the reign of Jehoram of Judah (2 Chr. 21:16, 17). This would place the date of the book and the events described therein in the middle of the ninth century B.C.

HOW OBADIAH FITS TOGETHER. The subject matter of Obadiah naturally divides into four parts, as follows: (1) The Certainty of Edom's Destruction (vv. 1-4); (2) The Character of Edom's Destruction (vv. 5-9); (3) The Cause of Edom's Destruction (vv. 10-14); and (4) The Climax of Edom's Destruction: The Day of the Lord (vv. 15-21).

The dominant theme of the book is God's judgment upon Edom because of her sinful attitudes and actions. Pride was at the heart of Edom's sinful attitudes and God declared that He would humble the inhabitants of Edom before all the surrounding nations (vv. 1-9).

The Old Testament is filled with warnings against personal and national pride. The book of Proverbs, for example, gives special attention to the matter (Prov. 6:17; 11:2; 15:25; 16:5; 21:4, 24; 26:12; 29:23); the writer declares, "Pride goes before destruction, and a haughty spirit before a fall" (Prov. 16:18). The book of Obadiah illustrates exactly how God deals with the matter of pride in terms of historical realities.

While the condemnation of Edom dominates most of Obadiah's message, there is also a message of hope to the suffering Hebrews. The conclusion to the whole matter would be Israel's final triumph—the ultimate blessing of Zion and the people of God (vv. 17-21).

Even the most casual reading of Obadiah should produce a sense of awe for the perfection with which God accomplishes His purpose and upholds His moral standards. Nations which have rebelled against the rule of the Almighty have fallen in the past; those who choose to lift their voices in arrogant defiance against God will also fall in the future (Ps. 2).

—J.J.D.

The Coming Judgment on Edom

THE vision of Obadiah.

Thus says the Lord GOD ᴿconcerning
Edom
    ᴿ(We have heard a report from the
    LORD,
    And a messenger has been sent among
    the nations, *saying*,
    "Arise, and let us rise up against her for
    battle"):   Is. 21:11 · Jer. 49:14–16

2 "Behold, I will make you small among
    the nations;
    You shall be greatly despised.
3 The ᴿpride of your heart has deceived
    you,
    You who dwell in the clefts of the rock,
    Whose habitation is high;
    ᴿ*You* who say in your heart,
    'Who will bring me down to the
    ground?'   Jer. 49:16 · Rev. 18:7
4 ᴿThough you ascend *as* high as the
    eagle,   Job 20:6
    And though you ᴿset your nest among
    the stars,   Hab. 2:9
    From there I will bring you down," says
    the LORD.

5 "If ᴿthieves had come to you,
    If robbers by night—   Jer. 49:9
    Oh, how you will be cut off!—
    Would they not have stolen till they
    had enough?
    If grape-gatherers had come to you,
    ᴿWould they not have left *some*
    gleanings?   Deut. 24:21
6 "Oh, how Esau shall be searched out!
    How his hidden treasures shall be
    sought after!
7 All the men in your confederacy
    Shall force you to the border;
    ᴿThe men at peace with you   Jer. 38:22
    Shall deceive you *and* prevail against
    you.
    Those who eat your bread shall lay a
    ᵀtrap for you.   Or *wound* or *plot*
    ᴿNo one is aware of it.   Is. 19:11

8 "WillR I not in that day," says the LORD,
    "Even destroy the wise *men* from Edom,
    And understanding from the mountains
    of Esau?   [Job 5:12–14]
9 Then your ᴿmighty men, O ᴿTeman,
    shall be dismayed,   Ps. 76:5 · Jer. 49:7
    To the end that everyone from the
    mountains of Esau
    May be cut off by slaughter.

Edom Mistreated His Brother

10 "For ᴿviolence against your brother
    Jacob,   Gen. 27:41
    Shame shall cover you,
    And you shall be cut off forever.

11 In the day that you ᴿstood on the other
    side—   Ps. 83:5–8
    In the day that strangers carried
    captive his forces,
    When foreigners entered his gates
    And ᴿcast lots for Jerusalem—
    Even you *were* as one of them.   Nah. 3:10
12 But you should not have ᴿgazed on the
    day of your brother   Mic. 4:11; 7:10
    *In the day of his captivity;
    Nor should you have ᴿrejoiced over the
    children of Judah   [Prov. 17:5]
    In the day of their destruction;
    Nor should you have spoken proudly
    In the day of distress.
13 You should not have entered the gate
    of My people
    In the day of their calamity.
    Indeed, you should not have ᵀgazed on
    their affliction
    In the day of their calamity,
    Nor laid *hands* on their substance
    In the day of their calamity.   Gloated over
14 You should not have stood at the
    crossroads
    To cut off those among them who
    escaped;
    Nor should you have ᵀdelivered up
    those among them who remained
    In the day of distress.   To the enemy

15 "ForR the day of the LORD upon all the
    nations *is* near;
    ᴿAs you have done, it shall be done to
    you;
    Your ᵀreprisal shall return upon your
    own head.   Ezek. 30:3 · Hab. 2:8 · Or *reward*
16 ᴿFor as you drank on my holy mountain,
    So shall all the nations drink
    continually;
    Yes, they shall drink, and swallow,
    And they shall be as though they had
    never been.   Joel 3:17

Israel's Final Triumph

17 "But on Mount Zion there ᴿshall be
    ᵀdeliverance,
    And there shall be holiness;
    The house of Jacob shall possess their
    possessions.   Amos 9:8 · Or *salvation*
18 The house of Jacob shall be a fire,
    And the house of Joseph ᴿa flame;
    But the house of Esau *shall be* stubble;
    They shall kindle them and devour
    them,
    And no survivor shall *remain* of the
    house of Esau,"
    For the LORD has spoken.   Zech. 12:6

19 The ᵀSouth ᴿshall possess the
    mountains of Esau,   Heb. *Negev* · Is. 11:14

12 Lit. *On the day he became a foreigner*

And the Lowland shall possess Philistia.
They shall possess the fields of Ephraim
And the fields of Samaria.
Benjamin *shall possess* Gilead.
20 And the captives of this host of the
children of Israel
Shall possess the land of the
Canaanites
As ᴿfar as Zarephath.   1 Kin. 17:9

The captives of Jerusalem who are in
Sepharad
Shall possess the cities of the *South.
21 Then ᴿsaviorsᵀ shall come to Mount
Zion   [James 5:20] • Or *deliverers*
To judge the mountains of Esau,
And the kingdom shall be the Lᴏʀᴅ's.

20 Heb. *Negev*

THE BOOK OF

Jonah

Jonah is unique, being the only book among the prophets that consists chiefly of narrative (except for the second chapter, which is in the form of a psalm). Jonah's stay in the belly of the great fish is used by our Lord in the New Testament to picture His burial and resurrection. Although it has been traditional to speak of "Jonah and the whale," the Hebrew word here and the Greek word in the New Testament do not mean "whale." There have been other historical incidents recorded of men (and even men on horseback!) swept overboard in the Mediterranean and swallowed whole by giant sharks. A few have lived to tell the story, as Jonah did, but this does not take away from the perfection of God's timing or from the other miracles in the book. Unbelief has stumbled over the miraculous in this book, and some have even said that it is a parable, rather than history. There is nothing to indicate a parable, however, and Christ speaks of Jonah as a historical prophet who actually experienced the things recorded in this little book.

AUTHORSHIP. Jonah has traditionally been credited with being the author of this book named for him. Because of the personal information contained in the book, logic makes him the best candidate as author, although there is no absolute proof of his authorship.

CONTEXT. Jonah was active during the reign of Jeroboam II (793–753 B.C.). The northern kingdom fell in 722 B.C. Based on these two historical facts and the logic that Jonah was the source of information, if not the author of the book, and that he would have written prior to the fall of the northern kingdom and after the beginning of Jeroboam II's reign, the best time frame for this book to have been written would be 790–722 B.C.

HOW JONAH FITS INTO THE BIBLE. The book of Jonah illustrates God's love and concern for Gentiles even during the time of the favorable relationship the children of Israel had with God. It becomes a prelude to God's reaching out to all the world through His Son Jesus Christ.

SUMMARY STATEMENT. God demonstrates His love for even His greatest enemies and for His angry and stubborn prophet.

KEY VERSE: 2:9d—"Salvation is of the LORD." God shows His love through His plan of salvation for Nineveh (and today through His plan of salvation in Christ Jesus).

HOW JONAH FITS TOGETHER. Initially we see Jonah rejecting God's call to reach a lost people (ch. 1). Even though Jonah attempts to run from God he fails, resulting in his repentance (ch. 2). Released from the belly of the fish, Jonah is recommissioned to his great evangelistic calling, which results in the repentance of the people of Nineveh and the demonstration of God's grace (ch. 3). Finally, we see Jonah showing his anger and lack of compassion in sharp contrast to God's mercy and love while remaining just (ch. 4).

In Jonah we can see how bitter and unforgiving we can become when we are out of God's will. It is God's desire that none should perish.

Today is a good time for each of us to consider where we are in relationship to God's will for our lives. What a tragedy it would be if we were unforgiving, angry, and bitter persons like Jonah.

—J.R.

Jonah's Disobedience

NOW the word of the LORD came to ᴿJonah the son of Amittai, saying, 2 Kin. 14:25

2 "Arise, go to ᴿNineveh, that great city, and cry out against it; for ᴿtheir wickedness has come up before Me." Is. 37:37 • Gen. 18:20

3 But Jonah arose to flee to Tarshish from the presence of the LORD. He went down to ᴿJoppa, and found a ship going to Tarshish; so he paid the fare, and went down into it, to go with them to ᴿTarshish ᴿfrom the presence of the LORD. Josh. 19:46 • Is. 23:1 • Gen. 4:16

The Storm at Sea

4 But ᴿthe LORD ᵀsent out a great wind on the sea, and there was a mighty tempest on the sea, so that the ship was about to be broken up. Ps. 107:25 • Lit. hurled

5 Then the mariners were afraid; and every man cried out to his god, and threw the cargo that was in the ship into the sea, to lighten the load. But Jonah had gone down ᴿinto the lowest parts of the ship, had lain down, and was fast asleep. 1 Sam. 24:3

6 So the captain came to him, and said to him, "What do you mean, sleeper? Arise, call

on your God; perhaps your God will consider us, so that we may not perish."

7 And they said to one another, "Come, let us cast lots, that we may know for whose cause this trouble *has come* upon us." So they cast lots, and the lot fell on Jonah.

8 Then they said to him, R"Please tell us! For whose cause *is* this trouble upon us? What is your occupation? And where do you come from? What is your country? And of what people are you?"   Josh. 7:19

9 So he said to them, "I *am* a Hebrew; and I fear the Lord, the God of heaven, who made the sea and the dry *land*."

Jonah Thrown into the Sea

10 Then the men were exceedingly afraid, and said to him, "Why have you done this?" For the men knew that he fled from the presence of the Lord, because he had told them.

11 Then they said to him, "What shall we do to you that the sea may be calm for us?"— for the sea was growing more tempestuous.

12 And he said to them, "Pick me up and Tthrow me into the sea; then the sea will become calm for you. For I know that this great tempest *is* because of me."   Lit. *hurl*

13 Nevertheless the men rowed hard to return to land, Rbut they could not, for the sea continued to grow more tempestuous against them.   [Prov. 21:30]

14 Therefore they cried out to the Lord and said, "We pray, O Lord, please do not let us perish for this man's life, and Rdo not charge us with innocent blood; for You, O Lord, have done as it pleased You."   Deut. 21:8

15 So they picked up Jonah and threw him into the sea, Rand the sea ceased from its raging.   [Ps. 89:9; 107:29]

16 Then the men Rfeared the Lord exceedingly, and offered a sacrifice to the Lord and took vows.   Acts 5:11

Jonah's Prayer and Deliverance

17 Now the Lord had prepared a great fish to swallow Jonah. And Jonah was in the belly of the fish three days and three nights.

32-E. The Prayer of a Backslidden Prophet   ▼

2 Then Jonah prayed to the Lord his God from the fish's belly.

2 And he said:

"I Rcried out to the Lord because of my affliction,   Ps. 120:1
RAnd He answered me.   Ps. 65:2

"Out of the belly of Sheol I cried,
And You heard my voice.
3 RFor You cast me into the deep,
Into the heart of the seas,
And the floods surrounded me;
RAll Your billows and Your waves
passed over me.   Ps. 88:6 · Ps. 42:7
4 RThen I said, 'I have been cast out of
Your sight;
Yet I will look again Rtoward Your holy
temple.'   Ps. 31:22 · 1 Kin. 8:38
5 The Rwaters surrounded me, *even* to my
soul;   Lam. 3:54
The deep closed around me;
Weeds were wrapped around my head.

32-E. The Prayer of a Backslidden Prophet (Jonah 2:1–9)—The "fish" of Jonah was probably a whale, which should disturb no one's faith. The original Hebrew (v. 1) *dag gadol* means "great fish," or huge, finned sea creature, including true fish (like the tiger shark), and mammals (whales).

Jonah fled from the Lord rather than going to preach in the Assyrian capital of Nineveh, as he was called to do. Then, by God's arrangement, he was swallowed by the "great fish." Some have speculated that Jonah died but that God revived him. Others, citing an actual case in which a man was coughed up alive after being swallowed by a whale, believe that Jonah could have remained alive naturally. Whatever the details, we are dealing with God's supernatural intervention on His prophet's behalf. The entire event is certified by Christ Himself and offered as a sign of His own death, burial, and resurrection (Matt. 12:39, 40, page 954).

In his humanly hopeless position, brought about by his own rebellion, Jonah finally prayed the prayer of a backslidden prophet. We can learn much from it:

(1) Often we do not cry to the Lord until we are in distress (vv. 1, 2).
(2) God can hear us in our hour of need, when we are in the very depths of despair (v. 2).
(3) It is right to acknowledge that our difficulty sometimes comes to us from God's hand (v. 3; cf. Matt. 10:29, page 950).
(4) When deliverance comes, we ought to give God the glory for our rescue (v. 6).
(5) We should thank Him for delivering us (v. 9).
(6) If we vow to correct our misdeeds, when delivered from the depths of our agony and need, we *must* keep our promise (v. 9).
(7) We are obligated to acknowledge that salvation comes from the Lord (v. 9).

However low we may have sunk let us not be discouraged. Rather let us take heart that God answers the prayer of the truly penitent person. Let us sink no longer, but rise in prayer, allowing God's power to buoy us up to renewed heights of fellowship with Him (Is. 40:29–31, page 680; cf. 1 John 1:9, page 1278; cf. 1 Kin. 21:27–29, page 352).

See 1 Kings 18:36, 37, page 348, for **Point 32-F: The Prayer of a Prophet at the Crossroads.**

▽ 6 I went down to the ᵀmoorings of the
mountains;   *foundations* or *bases*
The earth with its bars *closed* behind
me forever;
Yet You have brought up my ᴿlife from
the pit,   [Ps. 16:10]
O LORD, my God.

7 "When my soul fainted within me,
I remembered the LORD;
ᴿAnd my prayer went *up* to You,
Into Your holy temple.   Ps. 18:6

8 "Those who regard ᴿworthless idols Jer.10:8
Forsake their own ᵀMercy. Or *Lovingkindness*
9 But I will ᴿsacrifice to You   Hos. 14:2
With the voice of thanksgiving;
I will pay what I have ᴿvowed. [Eccl.5:4, 5]
▲   Salvation *is* of the ᴿLORD."   [Jer. 3:23]

10 So the LORD spoke to the fish, and it
vomited Jonah onto dry *land.*

Jonah Preaches at Nineveh

3 Now the word of the LORD came to Jonah
the second time, saying,
2 "Arise, go to Nineveh, that great city,
and preach to it the message that I tell you."
3 So Jonah arose and went to Nineveh,
according to the word of the LORD. Now
Nineveh was an exceedingly great city, *a
three-day journey *in extent.*
4 And Jonah began to enter the city on the
first ᵀday's walk. Then ᴿhe cried out and said,
"Yet forty days, and Nineveh shall be overthrown!"   20 mi. • [Deut. 18:22]

The People of Nineveh Believe

5 So the ᴿpeople of Nineveh believed God,
proclaimed a fast, and put on sackcloth, from
the greatest to the least of them.   [Matt. 12:41]
6 Then word came to the king of Nineveh;
and he arose from his throne and laid aside
his robe, covered *himself* with sackcloth ᴿand
sat in ashes.   Job 2:8
7 And he caused *it* to be proclaimed and
published throughout Nineveh by the decree
of the king and his nobles, saying,

Let neither man nor beast, herd nor
flock, taste anything; do not let them
eat, or drink water.
8 But let man and beast be covered with
sackcloth, and cry mightily to God; yes,
let every one turn from his evil way
and from ᴿthe violence that is in his
hands.   Is. 59:6

3:3 Exact meaning unknown

9 Who can tell *if* God will turn and
relent, and turn away from His fierce
anger, so that we may not perish?

10 ᴿThen God saw their works, that they
turned from their evil way; and God relented
from the disaster that He had said He would
bring upon them, and He did not do it. Jer. 18:8

Jonah's Anger and God's Kindness

4 But it displeased Jonah exceedingly, and
he became angry.
2 So he prayed to the LORD, and said, "Ah,
LORD, was not this what I said when I was
still in my country? Therefore I ᴿfled previously to Tarshish; for I know that You *are* a
ᴿgracious and merciful God, slow to anger
and abundant in lovingkindness, One who
relents from doing harm.   Jon. 1:3 • Joel 2:13
3 ᴿ"Therefore now, O LORD, please take
my life from me, for ᴿ*it is* better for me to die
than to live!"   1 Kin. 19:4 • Jon. 4:8
4 Then the LORD said, "Is it right for you
to be angry?"
5 So Jonah went out of the city and sat on
the east side of the city. There he made
himself a shelter and sat under it in the
shade, till he might see what would become
of the city.
6 And the LORD God prepared a ᵀplant and
made it come up over Jonah, that it might be
shade for his head to deliver him from his
misery. So Jonah was very grateful for the
plant.   Heb. *kikayon,* exact identity unknown
7 But as morning dawned the next day
God prepared a worm, and it *so* damaged the
plant that it withered.
8 And it happened, when the sun arose,
that God prepared a vehement east wind; and
the sun beat on Jonah's head, so that he grew
faint. Then he wished death for himself, and
said, "It *is* better for me to die than to live."
9 Then God said to Jonah, "Is *it* right for
you to be angry about the plant?" And he
said, "It *is* right for me to be angry, even to
death!"
10 But the LORD said, "You have had pity
on the plant for which you have not labored,
nor made it grow, which ᵀcame up in a night
and perished in a night.   Lit. *was a son of a night*
11 "And should I not pity Nineveh, that
great city, in which are more than one hundred and twenty thousand persons who cannot discern between their right hand and
their left—and much livestock?"

THE BOOK OF

Micah

The book of Micah was written by a country preacher who moved from the backwoods to the boulevards to preach to the cities. We know very little about him beyond the statement found in the first chapter: "The word of the LORD that came to Micah of Moresheth in the days of Jotham, Ahaz, and Hezekiah, kings of Judah" (1:1; see also Jer. 26:18; Mic. 1:14).

The name *Micah* means "Who is like Jehovah?"—a name which is an index to his character. Micah had an exalted conception of the holiness, righteousness, and compassion of God. The heart of his book is expressed in the closing chapter: "Who is a God like You . . . ?" (7:18). (The unspoken answer, of course, is an exultant "None!") His writings indicate that he was a man of strong convictions, yet tenderhearted and compassionate. He spoke with courage to the sins of his day and called for a return of the people to the principles of God.

Micah is a thrilling book to read because it is filled with poetic beauty. It contains remarkable prophecy concerning Jerusalem and the future glory of that city. As proof that it is the Word of God, the book of Micah names the birthplace of the Savior; this passage prophesying the coming Messiah (5:2-5a), a brief poem of eight lines in Hebrew, is one of the most spiritual and exquisite passages in the Old Testament.

KEY VERSE: 6:8—"He has shown you, O man, what is good; and what does the LORD require of you but to do justly, to love mercy, and to walk humbly with your God?"

HOW MICAH FITS TOGETHER. Some have advocated that the book consists of three sermons, each beginning with the word *Hear*. According to this interpretation, the sermons deal with the coming judgment, the coming Deliverer, and the call to repentance today. By reading the book, however, one sees that there are not three but at least six uses of the word *Hear* (1:2; 3:1, 9; 6:1, 2, 9).

The book of Micah basically divides itself into two main parts. The first part, chapters 1—3, is a denunciation. God is against the idolatry in high places as people worship things which they can manufacture such as clothes, houses, and money. He promises to destroy all these things. Covetousness is so rampant that people lie awake at night thinking on how they can get more things; then they awaken early in the morning to execute their greedy plans (2:1-2; cf. Amos 8:5-6).

The second main division, chapters 4—7, is consolatory. In the first part of chapter 4, there is a change of tone in Micah's preaching, as he seeks to console the people by turning from a message of judgment to a message of the future glories of Israel. She is to be gathered and delivered from Babylonian captivity. In chapter 5 Micah pleads for a return to spiritual worship and service. Sin and evil must be denounced and judged for people to receive the blessings of God. The last chapter of the book reveals Micah preaching and mourning for Israel's sins. Even the home has been invaded by deceit and hatred (7:5-6). The prophet then turns to God and confesses Israel's sins and counts on God's grace for the future (7:14-20). The only way for anyone—a nation or an individual—to receive the blessings of God is by repentance and confession of sin.

—B.W.

THE word of the LORD that came to Micah of Moresheth in the days of Jotham, Ahaz, *and* Hezekiah, kings of Judah, which he saw concerning Samaria and Jerusalem.

The Coming Judgment on Israel

2 Hear, all you peoples!
Listen, O earth, and all that is in it!
Let the Lord GOD be a witness against you,
The Lord from ᴿHis holy temple. [Ps. 11:4]

3 For behold, the LORD is coming out of His place;

He will come down
And tread on the high places of the earth.
4 ᴿThe mountains will melt under Him,
And the valleys will split   Amos 9:5
Like wax before the fire,
Like waters poured down a steep place.
5 All this is for the transgression of Jacob
And for the sins of the house of Israel.
What *is* the transgression of Jacob?
Is it not Samaria?
And what *are* the ᴿhigh places of Judah?
Are they not Jerusalem?   Deut. 32:13; 33:29

6 "Therefore I will make Samaria ᴿa heap
of ruins in the field,   2 Kin. 19:25
Places for planting a vineyard;
I will pour down her stones into the
valley,
And I will uncover her foundations.
7 All her carved images shall be beaten to
pieces,
And all her ᴿpay as a harlot shall be
burned with the fire;
All her idols I will lay desolate,
For she gathered *it* from the pay of a
harlot,
And they shall return to the ᴿpay of a
harlot."   Hos. 2:5 • Deut. 23:18

Mourning for Israel and Judah

8 Therefore I will wail and howl,
I will go stripped and naked;
I will make a wailing like the jackals
And a mourning like the ostriches,
9 For her wounds *are* incurable.
For ᴿit has come to Judah;
It has come to the gate of My people—
To Jerusalem.   2 Kin. 18:13
10 ᴿTell *it* not in Gath,
Weep not at all in ᵀBeth Aphrah,   2 Sam. 1:20
Roll yourself in the dust.   Lit. *House of Dust*
11 Pass by in naked shame, you inhabitant
of ᵀShaphir;
The inhabitant of ᵀZaanan does not go
out.
Beth Ezel mourns;
Its place to stand is taken away from
you.   Lit. *Beautiful* • Lit. *Going Out*
12 For the inhabitant of ᵀMaroth ᵀpined
for good,   Lit. *Bitterness* • Lit. *was sick*
But ᴿdisaster came down from the Lᴏʀᴅ
To the gate of Jerusalem.   Is. 59:9-11
13 O inhabitant of ᴿLachish,
Harness the chariot to the swift steeds
(She *was* the beginning of sin to the
daughter of Zion),
For the transgressions of Israel were
ᴿfound in you.   Is. 36:2 • Ezek. 23:11
14 Therefore you shall give presents to
ᵀMoresheth Gath;   Lit. *Possession of Gath*
The houses of ᴿAchzibᵀ *shall be* a lie to
the kings of Israel.   Josh. 15:44 • Lit. *Lie*
15 I will yet bring an heir to you, O
inhabitant of ᵀMareshah;
The glory of Israel shall come to
ᵀAdullam.   Lit. *Inheritance* • Lit. *Refuge*
16 Make yourself ᴿbald and cut off your
hair,
Because of your ᴿprecious children;
Enlarge your baldness like an eagle,
For they shall go from you into
ᴿcaptivity.   Job 1:20 • Lam. 4:5 • Amos 7:11, 17

Woe to Evildoers

2 Woe to those who devise iniquity,
And ᵀwork out evil on their beds!   Plan
At morning light they practice it,
Because it is in the power of their hand.
2 They ᴿcovet fields and take *them* by
violence,
Also houses, and seize *them*.
So they oppress a man and his house,
A man and his inheritance.   Is. 5:8

3 Therefore thus says the Lᴏʀᴅ:

"Behold, against this ᴿfamily I am
devising ᴿdisaster,
From which you cannot remove your
necks;
Nor shall you walk haughtily,
For this *is* an evil time.   Jer. 8:3 • Amos 5:13
4 In that day one shall take up a proverb
against you,
And ᴿlament with a bitter lamentation,
saying: 2 Sam. 1:17
'We are utterly destroyed!
He has changed the ᵀheritage of my
people;   Lit. *portion*
How He has removed *it* from me!
To ᵀa turncoat He has divided our
fields.' "   Lit. *one turning back*, an apostate
5 Therefore you will have no *one to
determine boundaries by lot
In the assembly of the Lᴏʀᴅ.

Lying Prophets

6 "Do not prattle," *you say to those who
ᵀprophesy.   Or *preach*, lit. *drip* words
So they shall not prophesy *to you;
They shall not return insult for insult.
7 *You who are* named the house of Jacob:
"Is the Spirit of the Lᴏʀᴅ restricted?
Are these His doings?
Do not My words do good
To him who walks uprightly?

8 "Lately My people have risen up as an
enemy—
You pull off the robe with the garment
From those who trust *you*, as they pass
by,
Like men returned from war.
9 The women of My people you cast out
From their pleasant houses;
From their children
You have taken away My glory forever.

10 "Arise and depart,
For this *is* not *your* ᴿrest;   Deut. 12:9
Because it is defiled, it shall destroy,
Yes, with utter destruction.
11 If a man should walk in a false spirit
And speak a lie, *saying*,

2:5 Lit. *one casting a surveyor's line*
2:6 Lit. *to these*

'I will ^Tprophesy to you ^Tof wine and drink,'   Or *preach*, lit. *drip* · *concerning*
Even he would be the ^Rprattler of this people.   Is. 30:10

Israel Restored

12 "I^R will surely assemble all of you, O Jacob,   [Mic. 4:6, 7]
I will surely gather the remnant of Israel;
I will put them together ^Rlike sheep of ^Tthe fold,   Jer. 31:10 · Or *Bozrah*
Like a flock in the midst of their pasture;
^RThey shall make a loud noise because of *so many* people.   Ezek. 33:22; 36:37
13 The one who breaks open will come up before them;
They will break out,
Pass through the gate,
And go out by it;
Their king will pass before them,
^RWith the LORD at their head."   Is. 52:12

Wicked Rulers and Prophets

3 And I said:

"Hear now, O heads of Jacob,
And you rulers of the house of Israel:
Is it not for you to know justice?
2 You who hate good and love evil;
Who strip the skin from ^TMy people,
And the flesh from their bones;   Lit. *them*
3 Who also ^Reat the flesh of My people,
Flay their skin from them,   Ps. 14:4; 27:2
Break their bones,
And chop *them* in pieces
Like *meat* for the pot,
^RLike flesh in the caldron."   Ezek. 11:3, 6, 7

4 Then ^Rthey will cry to the LORD,   Jer. 11:11
But He will not hear them;
He will even hide His face from them at that time,

Because they have been evil in their deeds.
5 Thus says the LORD ^Rconcerning the prophets   Ezek. 13:10, 19
Who make my people stray;
Who chant ^T"Peace"   All is well
While they chew with their teeth,
But who prepare war against him
Who puts nothing into their mouths:
6 "Therefore^R you shall have night without ^Tvision,   Is. 8:20–22; 29:10–12 · Prophetic revelation
And you shall have darkness without divination;
The sun shall go down on the prophets,
And the day shall be dark for them.
7 So the seers shall be ashamed,
And the diviners abashed;
Indeed they shall all cover their lips;
For *there is* no answer from God."

8 But truly I am full of power by the Spirit of the LORD,
And of justice and might,
^RTo declare to Jacob his transgression
And to Israel his sin.   Is. 58:1
9 Now hear this,
You heads of the house of Jacob
And rulers of the house of Israel,
Who abhor justice
And ^Tpervert all equity,   Lit. *twist*
10 Who build up Zion with ^Rbloodshed
And Jerusalem with iniquity: Hab. 2:12
11 ^RHer heads judge for a bribe,   Is. 1:23
^RHer priests teach for pay,   Jer. 6:13
And her prophets divine for ^Tmoney.
Yet they lean on the LORD, and say,
"Is not the LORD among us?   Lit. *silver*
No harm can come upon us."
12 Therefore because of you
Zion shall be plowed *like* a field,
Jerusalem shall become heaps of ruins,
And the mountain of the ^Ttemple
Like the bare hills of the forest.   Lit. *house*

The LORD's Reign in Zion

4 Now ^Rit shall come to pass in the latter days
That the mountain of the LORD's house
Shall be established on the top of the mountains,
And shall be exalted above the hills;
And peoples shall flow to it.   Is. 2:2–4
2 Many nations shall come and say,
"Come, and let us go up to the mountain of the LORD,
To the house of the God of Jacob;
He will teach us His ways,
And we shall walk in His paths."
For out of Zion the law shall go forth,
And the word of the LORD from Jerusalem.
3 He shall judge between many peoples,
And rebuke strong nations afar off;
They shall beat their swords into ^Rplowshares,   Is. 2:2–4
And their spears into ^Tpruning hooks;
Nation shall not lift up sword against nation,   *pruning knives*
Neither shall they learn war anymore.

4 ^RBut everyone shall sit under his vine and under his fig tree,
And no one shall make *them* afraid;
For the mouth of the LORD of hosts has spoken.   Zech. 3:10
5 For all people walk each in the name of his god,
But ^Rwe will walk in the name of the LORD our God
Forever and ever.   Zech. 10:12

Zion's Future Triumph

6 "In that day," says the LORD,
^R"I will assemble the lame,   Ezek. 34:16

R I will gather the outcast   Ps. 147:2
And those whom I have afflicted;
7 I will make the lame Ra remnant,
And the outcast a strong nation;
So the LORD Rwill reign over them in
Mount Zion   Mic. 2:12 • [Is. 9:6; 24:23]
From now on, even forever.
8 And you, O tower of the flock,
The stronghold of the daughter of Zion,
To you shall it come,
Even the former dominion shall come,
The kingdom of the daughter of
Jerusalem."

9 Now why do you cry aloud?
Is there no king in your midst?
Has your counselor perished?
For Rpangs have seized you like a
woman in Tlabor.   Is. 13:8 • childbirth
10 Be in pain, and labor to bring forth,
O daughter of Zion,
Like a woman in birth pangs.
For now you shall go forth from the
city,
You shall dwell in the field,
And to RBabylon you shall go.
There you shall be delivered;   Amos 5:27
There the RLORD will redeem you
From the hand of your enemies.   [Is. 45:13]

11 RNow also many nations have gathered
against you,   Lam. 2:16
Who say, "Let her be defiled,
And let our eye look upon Zion."
12 But they do not know Rthe thoughts of
the LORD,
Nor do they understand His counsel;
For He will gather them Rlike sheaves
to the threshing floor.   [Is. 55:8, 9] • Is. 21:10
13 "Arise and Rthresh, O daughter of Zion;
For I will make your horn iron,   Is. 41:15
And I will make your hooves bronze;
You shall Rbeat in pieces many peoples;
RI will consecrate their gain to the LORD,
And their substance to Rthe Lord of the
whole earth."   Dan. 2:44 • Is. 18:7 • Zech. 4:14

5 Now gather yourself in troops,
O daughter of troops;
He has laid siege against us;
They will Rstrike the judge of Israel
with a rod on the cheek.   Mark 15:19

The Coming Messiah

33-B. The Prophecies of Israel's Messiah ▼

2 "But you, RBethlehem Ephrathah,
Though you are little among the
thousands of Judah,   Luke 2:4-7

33-B. The Prophecies of Israel's Messiah (Micah 5:2)—The *Messiah* in Hebrew means "anointed," that is, "set apart by oil," and refers to a king, high priest, or prophet who has had the oil poured on his head (1 Sam. 16:13, page 283; Ex. 40:13, page 102). The oil is a *type* of the Spirit of God (Zech. 4:3, 6, page 913). Thus the Messiah was to be that messenger of the Lord of whom it was prophesied, "The Spirit of the LORD shall rest upon Him" (Is. 11:2, page 654). The Greek word for such an anointed is *Christos,* origin of "Christ."

Through the centuries the Old Testament prophets prophesied that a Messiah would come. Gradually, they put together the picture of what He would be like, what His mission would be, and how He could be recognized. Through the years many had analyzed and debated these prophecies, as they awaited the Messiah. Christians believe, and the New Testament demonstrates, that Jesus alone—among all religious or secular leaders that are or ever have been—matches perfectly these predictive descriptions. He was:

Messianic Prophecy	Old Testament Prophecy	New Testament Fulfillment
1. To be born in Bethlehem	1. Mic. 5:2 (page 890)	1. Matt. 2:1–6 (page 931)
2. To be of the tribe of Judah	2. Gen. 49:10 (page 55)	2. Matt. 1:1 (page 930)
3. To inherit the throne of David	3. 2 Sam. 7:12–17 (page 305); Is. 9:6, 7 (page 651)	3. Luke 1:32, 33 (page 1010)
4. To come 483 years after the restoration of Jerusalem and the temple, under Ezra and Nehemiah	4. Dan. 9:25 (page 851)	4. Matt. 2:1, 2 (page 931)
5. To be born of a virgin	5. Is. 7:14 (page 649)	5. Matt. 1:18–25 (page 930)
6. To be announced by a messenger from God	6. Mal. 3:1 (page 924)	6. Luke 7:24–27 (page 1021)
7. To appear in Galilee	7. Is. 9:1, 2 (page 651)	7. Matt. 4:13–16 (page 935)
8. To be a prophet like Moses	8. Deut. 18:15 (page 198)	8. Acts 3:21–24 (page 1091)
9. To enter Jerusalem on a donkey	9. Zech. 9:9 (page 916)	9. John 12:12–14 (page 1071)
10. To be rejected by His own people	10. Is. 53:3, 4 (page 693)	10. John 1:11 (page 1049)
11. To have His garments divided by His executioners	11. Ps. 22:18 (page 522)	11. Matt. 27:35 (page 980)
12. To be pierced	12. Zech. 12:10 (page 918); Ps. 22:16 (page 522)	12. Matt. 27:35 (page 980)
13. To suffer innocently, as a substitute for the guilty	13. Is. 53:4, 5 (page 693)	13. Luke 23:14–16 (page 1044)
14. To be resurrected	14. Ps. 16:10 (page 518); Is. 53:10, 12 (page 693)	14. Mark 16:6, 7 (page 1007)

See Isaiah 1:16–19, page 643, for **Point 33-C: The Plan of Salvation: "For the Jew First."**

▽   Yet out of you shall come forth to Me
The One to be ^RRuler in Israel,   Ex. 18:25
▲   Whose goings forth *are* from *of old,*
From ^Teverlasting."   Lit. *the days of eternity*

3 Therefore He shall give them up,
Until the time *that* ^Rshe who is in labor
has given birth;   Mic. 4:10
Then the remnant of His brethren
Shall return to the children of Israel.
4 And He shall stand and ^Rfeed^T *His flock*
In the strength of the LORD,
In the majesty of the name of the LORD
His God;   [Is. 40:11; 49:9] • *shepherd*
And they shall abide,
For now He ^Rshall be great   Ps. 72:8
To the ends of the earth;
5 And this *One* ^Rshall be peace.   [Is. 9:6]

Judgment on Israel's Enemies

When the Assyrian comes into our
land,
And when he treads in our palaces,
Then we will raise against him
Seven shepherds and eight princely
men.
6 They shall ^Twaste with the sword the
land of Assyria,   devastate
And the land of ^RNimrod at its
entrances;   Gen. 10:8–11
Thus He shall ^Rdeliver *us* from the
Assyrian,   Is. 14:25
When he comes into our land
And when he treads within our borders.

7 Then ^Rthe remnant of Jacob   Mic. 5:3
Shall be in the midst of many peoples,
^RLike dew from the LORD,   Deut. 32:2
Like showers on the grass,
That ^Ttarry for no man   wait
Nor ^Twait for the sons of men.   delay
8 And the remnant of Jacob
Shall be among the Gentiles,
In the midst of many peoples,
Like a ^Rlion among the beasts of the
forest,   Num. 24:9
Like a young lion among flocks of
sheep,
Who, if he passes through,
Both treads down and tears in pieces,
And none can deliver.
9 Your hand shall be lifted against your
adversaries,
And all your enemies shall be cut off.

10 "And it shall be in that day," says the
LORD,
"That I will ^Rcut^T off your ^Rhorses from
your midst   Zech. 9:10 • *destroy* • Deut. 17:16
And destroy your ^Rchariots.   Is. 2:7; 22:18
11 I will cut off the cities of your land
And throw down all your strongholds.

12 I will cut off sorceries from your hand,
And you shall have no soothsayers.
13 ^RYour carved images I will also cut off,
And your sacred pillars from your
midst;
You shall ^Rno more worship the work
of your hands;   Zech. 13:2 • Is. 2:8
14 I will pluck your ^Twooden images from
your midst;   Or *Asherim,* Canaanite deities
Thus I will destroy your cities.
15 And I will ^Rexecute vengeance in anger
and fury   [2 Thess. 1:8]
On the nations that have not *heard."

God Pleads with Israel

6 Hear now what the LORD says:

"Arise, plead your case before the
mountains,
And let the hills hear your voice.
2 ^RHear, O you mountains, ^Rthe LORD's
complaint,   Ps. 50:1, 4 • Hos. 12:2
And you strong foundations of the
earth;
For ^Rthe LORD has a complaint against
His people,   [Is. 1:18]
And He will contend with Israel.

3 "O My people, what ^Rhave I done to
you?
And how have I ^Rwearied you?
Testify against Me.   Jer. 2:5, 31 • Is. 43:22, 23
4 ^RFor I brought you up from the land of
Egypt,
I redeemed you from the house of
bondage;
And I sent before you Moses, Aaron,
and Miriam.   [Deut. 4:20]
5 O My people, remember now
What ^RBalak king of Moab counseled,
And what Balaam the son of Beor
answered him,   Num. 22:5, 6
From *Acacia Grove to Gilgal,
That you may know ^Rthe righteousness
of the LORD."   Judg. 5:11

6 With what shall I come before the
LORD,
And bow myself before the High God?
Shall I come before Him with burnt
offerings,
With calves a year old?
7 ^RWill the LORD be pleased with
thousands of rams,   Is. 1:11
Ten thousand ^Rrivers of oil?   Job 29:6
^RShall I give my firstborn *for* my
transgression,   2 Kin. 16:3
^TThe fruit of my body *for* the sin of my
soul?   My own child

5:15 *obeyed*
6:5 Heb. *Shittim,* Num. 25:1; Josh. 2:1; 3:1

▼ 44-C. Enoch Walked Humbly with God

8 He has ^Rshown you, O man, what *is*
   good;   [Deut. 10:12]
   And what does the LORD require of you
   But ^Rto do justly,   Gen. 18:19
   To love ^Tmercy,   Or *lovingkindness*
▲ And to walk humbly with your God?

Punishment of Israel's Injustice

9 The LORD's voice cries to the city—
   Wisdom shall see Your name:

   "Hear the rod!
   Who has appointed it?
10 Are there yet the treasures of
   wickedness
   In the house of the wicked,
   And the short measure *that is* an
   abomination?
11 Shall I count pure *those* with ^Rthe
   wicked scales,   Hos. 12:7
   And with the bag of deceitful weights?
12 For her rich men are full of ^Rviolence,
   Her inhabitants have spoken lies,
   And ^Rtheir tongue is deceitful in their
   mouth.   Mic. 2:1, 2 • Jer. 9:2–6, 8

13 "Therefore I will also ^Rmake you sick by
   striking you,
   By making you desolate because of
   your sins.   Lev. 26:16
14 You shall eat, but not be satisfied;
   ^THunger *shall be* in your midst.
   *You may carry *some* away, but shall
   not save *them;*   Or *Emptiness* or *Humiliation*
   And what you do rescue I will give
   over to the sword.

6:14 Tg., Vg. *You shall take hold*

15 "You shall ^Rsow, but not reap;
   You shall tread the olives, but not
   anoint yourselves with oil;
   And *make* sweet wine, but not drink
   wine.   Amos 5:11
16 For the statutes of Omri are ^Rkept;
   All the works of Ahab's house *are done;*
   And you walk in their counsels,   Hos. 5:11
   That I may make you a ^Tdesolation,
   And your inhabitants a hissing.
   Therefore you shall bear the ^Rreproach
   of *My people."   Or *object of horror* • Is. 25:8

Sorrow for Israel's Sins

7 Woe is me!
   For I am like those who gather summer
   fruits,
   Like those who ^Rglean vintage grapes;
   There is no cluster to eat
   Of the first-ripe fruit which ^Rmy soul
   desires.   Is. 17:6 • Is. 28:4
2 The ^Rfaithful^T *man* has perished from
   the earth,   Is. 57:1 • Or *loyal*
   And *there is* no one upright among
   men.
   They all lie in wait for blood;
   Every man hunts his brother with a
   net.

3 That they may successfully do evil with
   both hands—
   The prince asks *for gifts,*
   The judge *seeks* a ^Rbribe,
   And the great *man* utters his evil
   desire;
   So they scheme together.   Mic. 3:11

6:16 So with MT, Tg., Vg.; LXX *nations*

44-C. Enoch Walked Humbly with God (Micah 6:8)—All who walk with God are required to "walk humbly" (v. 8) with Him. We know that Enoch was a humble man, because he "walked with God three hundred years" (Gen. 5:22, page 9). To understand true humility we must know some of the characteristics of a humble person.

(1) He is gentle, but never weak. Jesus said of Himself, "I am gentle and lowly in heart" (Matt. 11:29, page 952). He was the most meek person this world will ever know—yet He once took a whip and drove the moneychangers from the temple (John 2:13–16, page 1051). This was not the act of a weak man.

(2) He is bold for the Lord, but never brazen. "Now when they [the Sanhedrin] saw the boldness of Peter and John, and perceived that they were uneducated and untrained men, they marveled. And they realized that they had been with Jesus" (Acts 4:1–22, page 1091). Peter and John were bold because they had accompanied Jesus for three years, and had witnessed His death, burial, and resurrection.

(3) He is aggressive for the Lord, but never contentious or hostile. The apostles never held back with the gospel of Jesus Christ, even though the Sanhedrin warned them, "Did we not strictly command you not to teach in this name? And look, you have filled Jerusalem with your doctrine, and intend to bring this Man's blood on us!" (Acts 5:22–32, page 1094).

(4) He is poor in spirit, but never spiritually poor (Matt. 5:3, page 936). The poor in spirit never think more highly of themselves than they ought (Rom. 12:3, page 1142). They believe themselves to be a new creation in Christ, knowing that "old things have passed away; behold, all things have become new" (2 Cor. 5:17, page 1169). The poor in spirit know that before honor can come their way, they must walk humbly with God (v. 8), who gives to the humble preference and honor among those in Christ. There is no room for arrogance, pride, or jealousy in the heart or mind of the person who walks humbly with God (Prov. 15:33, page 610).

See Amos 3:3, page 875, for **Point 44-D: Enoch Walked in Agreement with God.**

4 The best of them *is* ^Rlike a brier;
The most upright *is* sharper than a
  thorn hedge;
The day of your watchman and your
  punishment comes;
Now shall be their perplexity.   Ezek. 2:6

5 ^RDo not trust in a friend;
Do not put your confidence in a
  companion;   Jer. 9:4
Guard the doors of your mouth
From her who lies in your bosom.

6 For ^Rson dishonors father,
Daughter rises against her mother,
Daughter-in-law against her mother-in-
  law;
A man's enemies *are* the men of his
  own household.   Matt. 10:36

7 Therefore I will look to the LORD;
I will ^Rwait for the God of my salvation;
My God will hear me.   Is. 25:9

Israel's Confession and Comfort

8 Do not rejoice over me, my enemy;
^RWhen I fall, I will arise;   [Prov. 24:16]
When I sit in darkness,
The LORD *will be* a light to me.

9 I will bear the indignation of the LORD,
Because I have sinned against Him,
Until He pleads my ^Rcase   Jer. 50:34
And executes justice for me.
He will bring me forth to the light;
I will see His righteousness.

10 Then *she who is* my enemy will see,
And ^Rshame will cover her who said to
  me,
^R"Where is the LORD your God?"
My eyes will see her;
Now she will be trampled down
Like mud in the streets.   Ps. 35:26 · Ps. 42:3

11 *In* the day when your ^Rwalls are to be
  built,   [Amos 9:11]
In that day ^Tthe decree shall go far and
  wide.   Or *the boundary shall be extended*

12 *In* that day *they shall come to you
From Assyria and the *fortified cities,

7:12 Lit. *he,* collective of the captives • Heb. *arey mazor,*
possibly *cities of Egypt* • Heb. *mazor,* possibly *Egypt*

From the *fortress to ^Tthe River,
From sea to sea,   The Euphrates
And mountain *to* mountain.

13 Yet the land shall be desolate
Because of those who dwell in it,
And for the fruit of their deeds.

God Will Forgive Israel

14 Shepherd Your people with Your staff,
The flock of Your heritage,
Who dwell ^Tsolitarily in a ^Rwoodland,
In the midst of Carmel;
Let them feed *in* Bashan and Gilead,
As in days of old.   Alone · Is. 37:24

15 "As^R in the days when you came out of
  the land of Egypt,   Ps. 68:22; 78:12
I will show *them wonders."

16 The nations ^Rshall see and be ashamed
  of all their might;
^RThey shall put *their* hand over *their*
  mouth;
Their ears shall be deaf.   Is. 26:11 · Job 21:5

17 They shall lick the ^Rdust like a serpent;
They shall crawl from their holes like
  ^Tsnakes of the earth.   [Is.49:23] · Lit. *crawlers*
^RThey shall be afraid of the LORD our
  God,   Jer. 33:9
And shall fear because of You.

18 ^RWho *is* a God like You,   Ex. 15:11
^RPardoning iniquity   Ex. 34:6, 7, 9
And passing over the transgression of
^Rthe remnant of His heritage?   Mic. 4:7

He does not retain His anger forever,
Because He delights *in* mercy.

19 He will again have compassion on us,
And will subdue our iniquities.

You will cast all ^Tour sins
Into the depths of the sea.   Lit. *their*

20 ^RYou will give truth to Jacob
And ^Tmercy to Abraham,   Luke 1:72, 73
^RWhich You have sworn to our fathers
From days of old.   Or *lovingkindness* · Ps. 105:9

7:15 Lit. *him,* collective for the captives

THE BOOK OF
Nahum

God will not tolerate perennial rebellion. Our God is truly longsuffering (2 Pet. 3:9); but in His time His extended mercy is withdrawn and certain judgment comes like a whirlwind. No man can stand against the fierceness of God's wrath.

In the book of Nahum God's forecast for punishment against Nineveh brings chills to our bones and revives our awesome reverence for our holy God. Our God is shown here as a jealous God bent on divine justice. Never be mistaken: God is merciful but His wrath is sure and powerful.

AUTHORSHIP AND CONTEXT. The only reference in Scripture to "Nahum the Elkoshite" is in the first verse in this book. Elkosh was probably a village of Palestine, although some believe it may have been somewhere near Nineveh. Nahum prophesied sometime between the destruction of No Amon—ancient Thebes—in 663 B.C. (3:8–10) and Nineveh's fall in 612 B.C.

Nineveh was the capital of the cruel Assyrian Empire, which almost a century before had carried the northern kingdom away into captivity (722 B.C.). Nahum may not have preached there, but only spoken *about* the city *to* the people of Judah (1:15)—his name in Hebrew means "Comfort" or "Consolation," and the ruin of this violent people would indeed be comforting to the often-victimized Judah. If he actually went, however, it would not be the first time God had spoken to Nineveh, for the prophet Jonah had been sent there one-and-a-half centuries before. But it would be the last time. Now it was in the purpose of God to visit judgment upon Nineveh, the capital of the empire that had been the rod of God's anger upon the northern kingdom of Israel.

HOW NAHUM FITS TOGETHER. Chapter 1 proclaims God's power and majesty as it is shown by His wrath against the evil city. Chapter 2 vividly describes the siege and destruction of Nineveh, in one of the most exciting passages of Scripture. Finally, chapter 3 tells why Nineveh deserved God's judgment and how that judgment is inescapable.

KEY VERSES: 1:7, 8—"The LORD is good, a stronghold in the day of trouble; and He knows those who trust in Him. But with an overflowing flood He will make an utter end of its place, and darkness will pursue His enemies."

God's irrevocable indictments against Nineveh, that ruthless, bloodthirsty city, come like swift, hot arrows from the divine bow. Nineveh is an enemy of God. She has received evil counsel from the wicked. She is vile and despised, hated by all. She is a liar and a thief, full of false religion and the tyrannical abuse of power. Judgment against her is sure!

The prophet Jonah, fresh from the belly of a great fish, had preached repentance to Nineveh and she had indeed repented. But now, some 150 years later, the message of the prophet Nahum is not an offer to repent but a prophecy of impending judgment. God's wrath is pledged upon these sinners who had turned away from God. Their vileness, their hopeless pagan idolatry, their blatant self-reliance, their cocky ungodliness—all would be rewarded with destruction.

The book of Nahum provides a rare display of divine sarcasm. As the Neo-Babylonian Empire marches against Assyria, and a coalition of Medes and Chaldeans prepare to lay siege to the great city of Nineveh, God's prophet taunts the hated enemy: "Man the fort! Watch the road! Strengthen your flanks! Fortify your power mightily" (2:1). This challenge mocks a cruel tyrant who had long enslaved and oppressed the peoples of the ancient Near East. Now the destroyer will be destroyed! In the words of the Lord Jesus Christ: "All who take the sword will perish by the sword" (Matt. 26:52).

Nahum also gives us a forecast of the inevitable reaction of Nineveh to God's terrible judgment. It is a vivid portrait of pitiful people who foolishly fought against our holy God. These sinners in the hands of an angry God are seen retreating in fear and agony. They run naked, leaving all their riches behind, fleeing like cowards, with no place to hide. Their pomp and pride and haughtiness are gone. Their kings and noblemen are dead, their people are scattered, and their enemies clap their hands, rejoicing. Nineveh is punished and her voice is silenced forever.

"It is a fearful thing to fall into the hands of the living God" (Heb. 10:31).

—J.S.

THE burden against Nineveh. The book of the vision of Nahum the Elkoshite.

God's Wrath on His Enemies

2 God is ᴿjealous, and the LORD avenges;
The LORD avenges and is furious.
The LORD will take vengeance on His
adversaries,   Ex. 20:5
And He reserves wrath for His enemies;
3 The LORD is ᴿslow to anger and ᴿgreat
in power,   Ex. 34:6, 7 · [Job 9:4]
And will not at all acquit the wicked.

ᴿThe LORD has His way   Ps. 18:17
In the whirlwind and in the storm,
And the clouds are the dust of His feet.
4 ᴿHe rebukes the sea and makes it dry,
And dries up all the rivers.   Matt. 8:26
ᴿBashan and Carmel wither,   Is. 33:9
And the flower of Lebanon wilts.
5 The mountains quake before Him,
The hills melt,
And the earth *heaves at His presence,
Yes, the world and all who dwell in it.

6 Who can stand before His indignation?
And ᴿwho can endure the fierceness of
His anger?
His fury is poured out like fire,
And the rocks are thrown down by
Him.   [Mal. 3:2]

7 ᴿThe LORD is good,   [Jer. 33:11]
A stronghold in the day of trouble;
And He knows those who trust in Him.

8 But with an overflowing flood
He will make an utter end of its place,
And darkness will pursue His enemies.
9 ᴿWhat do you ᵀconspire against the
LORD?   Ps. 2:1 · Or devise
ᴿHe will make an utter end of it. 1 Sam. 3:12
Affliction will not rise up a second time.
10 For while tangled ᴿlike thorns,
ᴿAnd while drunken like drunkards,
ᴿThey shall be devoured like stubble
fully dried.   2 Sam. 23:6 · Nah. 3:11 · Mal. 4:1
11 From you comes forth one
Who plots evil against the LORD,
A ᵀwicked counselor.   Lit. counselor of Belial

12 Thus says the LORD:

"Though they are ᵀsafe, and likewise
many,   Or at peace or complete
Yet in this manner they will be ᴿcut
down   [Is. 10:16–19, 33, 34]
When he passes through.
Though I have afflicted you,
I will afflict you no more;
13 For now I will break off his yoke from
you,
And burst your bonds apart."

1:5 Tg. burns

14 The LORD has given a command
concerning you:
ᵀ"Your name shall be perpetuated no
longer. Lit. No more of your name shall be fruitful
Out of the house of your gods
I will cut off the carved image and the
molded image.
I will dig your ᴿgrave,   Ezek. 32:22, 23
For you are ᴿvile."ᵀ   Nah. 3:6 · Or contemptible
15 Behold, on the mountains
The ᴿfeet of him who brings good
tidings,   Rom. 10:15
Who proclaims peace!
O Judah, keep your appointed feasts,
Perform your vows.
For the ᵀwicked one shall no more pass
through you;   Lit. one of Belial
He is ᴿutterly cut off.   Is. 29:7, 8

The Destruction of Nineveh

2 He* who scatters has come up before
your face.
Man the fort!
Watch the road!
Strengthen your flanks!
Fortify your power mightily.

2 For the LORD will restore the excellence
of Jacob
Like the excellence of Israel,
For the emptiers have emptied them
out
And ruined their vine branches.

3 The shields of his mighty men are made
red,
The valiant men are in scarlet.
The chariots come with flaming torches
In the day of his preparation,
And *the spears are brandished.
4 The chariots rage in the streets,
They jostle one another in the broad
roads;
They seem like torches,
They run like lightning.

5 He remembers his nobles;
They stumble in their walk;
They make haste to her walls,
And the defense is prepared.
6 The gates of the rivers are opened,
And the palace is dissolved.
7 ᵀIt is decreed: Heb. Huzzab
She shall be led away captive,
She shall be brought up;
And her maidservants shall lead her as
with the voice of doves,
Beating their breasts.

8 Though Nineveh of old was like a pool
of water,
Now they flee away.

2:1 Vg. He who destroys
2:3 Lit. the cypresses are shaken; LXX, Syr. the horses
rush about; Vg. the drivers are stupefied

T"Halt! Halt!" *they* cry;   Lit. *Stand*
But no one turns back.

9 TTake spoil of silver!   *Plunder*
Take spoil of Rgold!   Zeph. 1:18
There is no end of treasure,
Or wealth of every desirable prize.

10 She is empty, desolate, and waste!
The heart melts, and the knees shake;
Much pain *is* in every side,
And all their faces *are drained of
color.

11 Where *is* the dwelling of the Rlions,
And the feeding place of the young
lions,
Where the lion walked, the lioness *and*
lion's cub,
And no one made *them* afraid?   Job 4:10,11

12 The lion tore in pieces enough for his
cubs,
TKilled for his lionesses,   Lit. *Strangled*
RFilled his caves with prey,   Jer. 51:34
And his dens with Tflesh.   *torn flesh*

13"Behold, RI *am* against you," says the
LORD of hosts, "I will burn Tyour chariots in
smoke, and the sword shall devour your
young lions; I will cut off your prey from the
earth, and the voice of your messengers shall
be heard no more."   Nah. 3:5 · Lit. *her*

The Woe of Nineveh

3 Woe to the Rbloody city!   Hab. 2:12
It *is* all full of lies *and* robbery.
Its Tvictim never departs.   Lit. *prey*

2 The noise of a whip
And the noise of rattling wheels,
Of galloping horses,
Of Tclattering chariots!   *bounding* or *jolting*

3 Horsemen charge with bright sword
and glittering spear.
There is a multitude of slain,
A great number of bodies,
Countless corpses—
They stumble over the corpses—

4 Because of the multitude of Tharlotries
of the seductive harlot,
RThe mistress of sorceries,
Who sells nations through her
harlotries,   Spiritual unfaithfulness · Is. 47:9–12
And families through her sorceries.

5"Behold, I *am* Ragainst you," says the
LORD of hosts;   Nah. 2:13
R"I will lift your skirts over your face,
I will show the nations your nakedness,
And the kingdoms your shame.   Is. 47:2, 3

6 I will cast abominable filth upon you,
Make you Rvile,T   Nah. 1:14 · *despicable*
And make you Ra spectacle.   Heb. 10:33

7 It shall come to pass *that* all who look
upon you
RWill flee from you, and say,   Rev. 18:10

R"Nineveh is laid waste!   Jon. 3:3; 4:11
RWho will bemoan her?'   Jer. 15:5
Where shall I seek comforters for you?"

8 Are you better than *No Amon
That was situated by the *River,
That had the waters around her,
Whose rampart *was* the sea,
Whose wall *was* the sea?

9 Ethiopia and Egypt *were* her strength,
And *it was* boundless;
Put and Lubim were *your helpers.

10 Yet she *was* carried away,
She went into captivity;
RHer young children also were dashed to
pieces
RAt the head of every street;
They Rcast lots for her honorable men,
And all her great men were bound in
chains.   Hos. 13:16 · Lam. 2:19 · Joel 3:3

11 You also will be Rdrunk;
You will be hidden;
You also will seek refuge from the
enemy.   Nah. 1:10

12 All your strongholds *are* Rfig trees with
ripened figs: Rev. 6:12, 13
If they are shaken,
They fall into the mouth of the eater.

13 Surely, Ryour people in your midst *are*
women!
The gates of your land are wide open
for your enemies;
Fire shall devour the Rbars of your
gates.   Is. 19:16 · Jer. 51:30

14 Draw your water for the siege!
RFortify your strongholds!
Go into the clay and tread the mortar!
Make strong the brick kiln!   Nah. 2:1

15 There the fire will devour you,
The sword will cut you off;
It will eat you up like a Rlocust.   Joel 1:4

Make yourself many—like the locust!
Make yourself many—like the
swarming locusts!

16 You have multiplied your merchants
more than the stars of heaven.
The locust plunders and flies away.

17 RYour commanders *are* like *swarming*
locusts,
And your generals like great
grasshoppers,
Which camp in the hedges on a cold
day;
When the sun rises they flee away,
And the place where they *are* is not
known.   Rev. 9:7

18 RYour shepherds slumber, O Rking of
Assyria;   Ps. 76:5, 6 · Jer. 50:18

2:10 LXX, Tg., Vg. *gather blackness;* Joel 2:6

3:8 Lit. *rivers,* the Nile and the surrounding canals
3:9 LXX *her*

Your nobles rest *in the dust.*
Your people are ^Rscattered on the
mountains,   1 Kin. 22:17
And no one gathers them.
19 Your injury *has* no healing,

^RYour wound is severe.   Mic. 1:9
^RAll who hear news of you   Lam. 2:15
Will clap *their* hands over you,
For upon whom has not your
wickedness passed continually?

THE BOOK OF
Habakkuk

Although the personal history of Habakkuk as a man is unknown, much is known about the times in which he lived and prophesied for the Lord God. His timeless words echo down the ages encouraging the followers of God to take comfort in God who takes the long view—the right view—the view of eternity.

AUTHORSHIP AND CONTEXT. Habakkuk's name comes from a Hebrew verb meaning "to embrace or clasp." Two nuances of this word are both reflected in his book: he loved his God fervently, and he willingly wrestled with hard questioning. He was a contemporary of the prophets Zephaniah and Jeremiah, prophesying sometime after the fall of the city of Nineveh (612 B.C.) and before the first Babylonian invasion of Judah (605 B.C.). He spoke during a time of great decadence following the death of the good king Josiah at Pharaoh Necho's hand, when Josiah's reforms were quickly forgotten. It was a time when moral and social evils were rampant in Israelite society. At that time the international balance of power shifted suddenly and dramatically with the abrupt rise of the Chaldeans (Babylonians). These conditions forced anguished questions from the prophet. From Habakkuk a new note sounded in prophecy: his words, instead of addressing Judah on behalf of God, addressed God on behalf of Judah. His prophecy was a dialogue between a man and God, in which he questioned God but did not speak against Him. He was a man of faith wondering what was happening.

Two questions confront each generation. One is, "Why do the wicked prosper?" The other is closely related: "Why doesn't God hurry up and do something about all the evil in the society?" Is God aware of it? Does He care? Doesn't He understand the injustice of the seeming prosperity of the wicked while the righteous suffer?

Habakkuk was a prophet whom God used to consider these problems, problems that all who follow the Lord have addressed at some time. We today can certainly identify with Habakkuk's dilemma. We too live in an age of abundant evil, when multitudes live in wickedness, working violence, destroying foundations, ignoring the laws of God, and perverting justice. Is the Lord asleep? Is He away on a journey? Absolutely not! He is working right now, within the framework of history. When all is done, He will bring justice—punishment and reward—to all peoples.

HOW HABAKKUK FITS TOGETHER AND KEY VERSE. The first round in Habakkuk's dialogue occurs in 1:1-11. Habakkuk had been grappling with the problem of God's silence and Judah's wickedness, and he presented this problem to his Lord. Just as the Lord God had told Moses that He would use the children of Israel to judge the pagan nations dwelling in Canaan (Lev. 18:24ff.), He told Habakkuk that He was raising up the Chaldeans to punish the children of Israel for their sinful rebellion. This puzzled the prophet. It was not what he expected!

When what the Lord does is different from what we would do, it puzzles us. We see such a small piece of the picture; God sees the whole. We see from our viewpoint alone, here and now. God sees from all viewpoints, timelessly.

The second round of dialogue begins in 1:12 and continues to the end of chapter 2. Habakkuk understood the need for Israel to be punished . . . but at the hands of the *Chaldeans?* Their sins were worse than Israel's! How could this possibly be just, or solve anything?

Instead of doing as so many people who, when they find themselves in baffling circumstances, leave the service of the Lord, Habakkuk provides the example of what should be done in the midst of a dilemma. He waited patiently, faithfully, in his place of service for the Lord to speak. Then the Lord revealed that in time He would deal with the Chaldeans also, and their multitude of sins would not go unpunished.

In 2:4 we find the book's key verse: "Behold the proud, his soul is not upright in him; but the just shall live by his faith." The follower of God, the justified man, must live by his faith. This faith is in the Lord God, the God of yesterday, today, and tomorrow—the God of eternity. And in this faith Habakkuk finds his answer.

To remind the people of God's faithfulness, chapter 3 contains a psalm of triumph sung in the temple worship, reminding Israel of the Lord's former dealings with her. He did not forsake her then; He would not forsake her now. He is the God of the long view. He is the God with a plan, working in the midst of His people. Regardless of present difficulties, regardless of tragic circumstance, regardless of seeming answerless prayers at this moment—as Habakkuk rejoiced,

so must we rejoice in the Lord, for He is the God of our salvation. He is our strength. In the long run, He will deliver us and allow us to walk on the high hills of final victory and peace.

—R.E.W.

▼ 5-B. The Sovereignty of God at Work

THE [T]burden which the prophet Habakkuk saw.   *oracle, prophecy*

The Prophet's Question

2 O LORD, how long shall I cry,
   [R]And You will not hear?   Lam. 3:8
   Even cry out to You, "Violence!"
   And You will [R]not save.   [Job 21:5–16]
3 Why do You show me iniquity,
   And cause *me* to see [T]trouble?   Or *toil*
   For plundering and violence *are* before me;
   There is strife, and contention arises.
4 Therefore the law is powerless,
   And justice never goes forth.
   For the wicked surround the righteous;
   Therefore perverse judgment proceeds.

The LORD's Reply

5 "Look[R] among the nations and watch—
   Be utterly astounded!
   For *I will* work a work in your days
   Which you would not believe, though it were told *you*.   Is. 29:14
6 For indeed I am [R]raising up the Chaldeans,
   A bitter and hasty [R]nation
   Which marches through the breadth of the earth,
   To possess dwelling places *that are* not theirs.   2 Kin. 24:2 · Ezek. 7:24; 21:31
7 They are terrible and dreadful;
   Their judgment and their dignity proceed from themselves.

8 Their horses also are [R]swifter than leopards,   Jer. 4:13
   And more fierce than evening wolves.
   Their [T]chargers [T]charge ahead;
   Their cavalry comes from afar;
   They fly as the [R]eagle *that* hastens to eat.   Lit. *horsemen* · Lit. *spring about* · Hos. 8:1
9 "They all come for violence;
   Their faces are set *like* the east wind.
   They gather captives like sand.
10 They scoff at kings,
   And princes are scorned by them.
   They deride every stronghold,
   For they heap up earthen *mounds* and seize it.
11 Then *his* [T]mind changes and he transgresses;   Lit. *spirit* or *wind*
   He commits offense,
   [R]*Ascribing* this power to his god."   Dan. 5:4 ▲

The Prophet's Second Question

12 Are You not [R]from everlasting,
   O LORD my God, my Holy One?
   We shall not die.   Ps. 90:2; 93:2
   O LORD, [R]You have appointed them for judgment;
   O Rock, You have marked them for [R]correction.   Is. 10:5–7 · Jer. 25:9
13 *You are* of purer eyes than to behold evil,
   And cannot look on wickedness.
   Why do You look on those who deal treacherously,
   And hold Your tongue when the wicked devours
   A *person* more righteous than he?

5-B. The Sovereignty of God at Work (Habakkuk 1:1–11)—Like so many of God's children, Habakkuk did not understand how his sovereign God worked. He was frustrated and baffled: why had not Almighty God corrected the corruption in Judah? He prayed, "O LORD, how long shall I cry, and You will not hear?" (v. 2). Then Habakkuk listed the evils of Judah—violence, iniquity, oppression, tyranny, strife, discord, lawlessness—and said, "The wicked surround the righteous; therefore perverse judgment proceeds" (v. 4).

God answered Habakkuk: "I will work a work in your days which you would not believe, though it were told you" (v. 5). God is the sovereign "I AM WHO I AM" (Ex. 3:13, 14, page 60). He is not obligated to reveal the what or why of His works, even when we think God is not working and we cry, "Why, O Lord?"

God did tell Habakkuk what He was doing (vv. 6–11)—using an ungodly nation (the Chaldeans) to punish Judah, "the apple of His eye" (Zech. 2:8, page 912). Judah was shocked and refused to believe what Habakkuk told them that God was doing. So, Habakkuk prayed, "O LORD, revive Your work in the midst of the years . . . in wrath remember mercy" (Hab. 3:2, page 901). His prayer was highly emotional, because he could not understand God's unusual actions. But who can fully understand the workings of our sovereign God? No one. For if we could, we would have knowledge that spans all eternity. Only our sovereign God is omniscient.

When we cry, "Why, O Lord?" the answer is: "Whatever the LORD pleases He does, in heaven and in earth" (Ps. 135:6, page 588; cf. Ps. 115:3, page 578). God's sovereignty is free from imperfection; it is absolute.

See Jeremiah 18:1–12, page 730, for **Point 5-C: The Sovereignty of God Illustrated.**

14 Why do You make men like fish of the
　　sea,
　　Like creeping things *that have* no ruler
　　over them?

15 They take up all of them with a hook,
　　They catch them in their net,
　　And gather them in their dragnet.
　　Therefore they rejoice and are glad.

16 Therefore ᴿthey sacrifice to their net,
　　And burn incense to their dragnet;
　　Because by them their share *is*
　　　　ᵀsumptuous　　　　Deut. 8:17 · Lit. *fat*
　　And their food plentiful.

17 Shall they therefore empty their net,
　　And continue to slay nations without
　　pity?

2 I will ᴿstand my watch
　　And set myself on the rampart,
　　And watch to see what He will say to
　　me,
　　And what I will answer when I am
　　corrected.　　　　Is. 21:8, 11

The Just Live by Faith

2 Then the Lᴏʀᴅ answered me and said:

ᴿ"Write the vision
　　And make *it* plain on tablets,
　　That he may run who reads it.　　Is. 8:1

3 For ᴿthe vision *is* yet for an appointed
　　time;　　　　Dan. 8:17, 19; 10:14
　　But at the end it will speak, and it will
　　ᴿnot lie.　　　　Ezek. 12:24, 25
　　ᴿThough it tarries, wait for it;
　　Because it will ᴿsurely come,
　　It will not tarry.　　[Heb. 10:37, 38] · [2 Pet. 3:9]

4 "Behold the proud,
　　His soul is not upright in him;
　　But the just shall live by his faith.

Woe to the Wicked

5 "Indeed, because he transgresses by
　　wine,
　　He is a proud man,
　　And he does not stay at home.
　　Because he ᴿenlarges his desire as ᵀhell,
　　And he *is* like death, and cannot be
　　satisfied,　　　　Is. 5:11–15 · Or *Sheol*
　　He gathers to himself all nations
　　And heaps up for himself all peoples.

6 "Will not all these ᴿtake up a proverb
　　against him,　　　　Mic. 2:4
　　And a taunting riddle against him, and
　　say,
　　'Woe to him who increases
　　What is not his—how long?
　　And to him who loads himself with
　　*many pledges'?

7 Will not ᵀyour creditors rise up
　　suddenly?　　　　Lit. *those who bite you*

2:6 Syr., Vg. *thick clay*

Will they not awaken who oppress you?
And you will become their booty.

8 ᴿBecause you have plundered many
　　nations,　　　　Is. 33:1
　　All the remnant of the people shall
　　plunder you,
　　Because of men's ᵀblood　　Or *bloodshed*
　　And the violence of the land *and* the
　　city,
　　And of all who dwell in it.

9 "Woe to him who covets evil gain for his
　　house,
　　That he may ᴿset his nest on high,
　　That he may be delivered from the
　　ᵀpower of disaster!　Obad. 4 · Lit. *hand of evil*

10 You give shameful counsel to your
　　house,
　　Cutting off many peoples,
　　And sin *against* your soul.

11 For the stone will cry out from the
　　wall,
　　And the beam from the timbers will
　　answer it.

12 "Woe to him who builds a town with
　　bloodshed,
　　Who establishes a city by iniquity!

13 Behold, *is it* not of the Lᴏʀᴅ of hosts
　　That the peoples labor *to feed the fire,
　　And nations weary themselves in vain?

14 For the earth will be filled
　　With the knowledge of the glory of the
　　Lᴏʀᴅ,
　　As the waters cover the sea.

15 "Woe to him who gives drink to his
　　neighbor,
　　*Pressing *him* to your ᴿbottle,　　Hos. 7:5
　　Even to make *him* drunk,
　　That you may look on his nakedness!

16 You are filled with shame instead of
　　glory.
　　You also—drink!
　　And *be exposed as uncircumcised!
　　The cup of the Lᴏʀᴅ's right hand *will
　　be* turned against you,
　　And utter shame will be on your glory.

17 For the violence *done to* Lebanon will
　　cover you,
　　And the plunder of beasts *which* made
　　them afraid,
　　Because of men's blood
　　And the violence of the land *and* the
　　city,
　　And of all who dwell in it.

18 "What profit is the image, that its maker
　　should carve it,
　　The molded image, a teacher of lies,

2:13 Lit. *for what satisfies fire,* for what is of no lasting
value
2:15 Lit. *Attaching* or *Joining*
2:16 DSS, LXX *reel;* [Syr.], Vg. *fall fast asleep*

That the maker of its mold should trust
  in it,
To make mute idols?
19 Woe to him who says to wood,
   'Awake!'
To silent stone, 'Arise! It shall teach!'
Behold, it is overlaid with gold and
   silver,
Yet in it there is no breath at all.

20 "But^R the LORD is in His holy temple.
   Let all the earth keep silence before
   Him."   Zeph. 1:7

The Prophet's Prayer

▼ **32-G. A Prayer for Revival**

3 A prayer of Habakkuk the prophet, on
  ^TShigionoth.   Exact meaning unknown

2 O LORD, I have heard your speech *and*
   was afraid;
O LORD, revive Your work in the midst
   of the years!
In the midst of the years make *it*
   known;
In wrath remember mercy.

3 God came from Teman,
  The Holy One from Mount Paran. Selah

His glory covered the heavens,   ▽
And the earth was full of His praise.
4 *His* brightness was like the light;
He had rays *flashing* from His hand,
And there His power *was* hidden.
5 Before Him went pestilence,
And fever followed at His feet.
6 He stood and measured the earth;
He looked and startled the nations.
^RAnd the everlasting mountains were
   scattered,   Nah. 1:5
The perpetual hills bowed.
His ways *are* everlasting.
7 I saw the tents of Cushan in affliction;
The curtains of the land of Midian
   trembled.
8 O LORD, were You displeased with the
   rivers,
Was Your anger against the rivers,
Was Your wrath against the sea,
That You rode on Your horses,
Your chariots of salvation?
9 Your bow was made quite ready;
Oaths were sworn over *Your*
   *arrows.   Selah
You divided the earth with rivers.

3:9 Lit. *tribes* or *rods,* cf. v. 14

32-G. A Prayer for Revival (Habakkuk 3:1–19)—Through the ages, God's people have joined Habakkuk in prayer, asking God for revival, praying that He would cause His work to live again. God's people—whether a congregation, church, mission, school, family, or even an individual—sometimes leave their "first love," as did the church of Ephesus (Rev. 2:4, page 1294). Difficulties arise, time passes, emphases change, key people move away, and—almost unnoticed—the life and zeal for the Lord have vanished.

Habakkuk's prayer for revival, containing at least eleven separate elements, is remarkable for its scope of thought and piety. We might well heed its example. It includes

(1) taking God's Word seriously (v. 2);
(2) the direct request for revival: "Revive your work in the midst of the years!" (v. 2);
(3) an appeal for mercy—not for what we think we deserve (v. 2);
(4) an acknowledgment of the great power God has over His entire creation (vv. 3–7);
(5) the acknowledgment that God, in righteous anger, punishes sinful men and nations (vv. 8–12);
(6) praise to God for saving His people (vv. 13–15);
(7) an acceptance of God's will for the future (v. 16);
(8) an affirmation of faith in God, whatever events should come our way (vv. 17, 18);
(9) an affirmation that God is our strength (v. 19);
(10) an affirmation that God is the source of our walk: "He will make my feet like deer's feet" (v. 19);
(11) an affirmation that God is the source of our blessings (v. 19).

Habakkuk, some six centuries before Christ, prayed for revival. He desired to see God's work live again. Revival today would reflect

(1) a renewed living faith;
(2) a new commitment to God to be faithful in worship and church attendance;
(3) a greater zeal and desire to study God's Word and to pray;
(4) a renewed effort to win souls and participate in missions;
(5) a putting away of sins, including criticism, grumbling, and gossip;
(6) a renewed joy in the Lord;
(7) a greater spirit of love and forbearance among God's people;
(8) a greater impact of witness in the community and nation;
(9) a rising love and praise to God for His abundant goodness;
(10) a loyalty to sound doctrine (Rev. 2:14–16, 20, page 1295).

Let us pray that we, too, may experience true revival and "walk on my high hills" again! (v. 19). It all must begin, however, with a prayer for revival.

See Index, page 17, for your next study.

▽ 10 The mountains saw You *and* trembled;
The overflowing of the water passed by.
The deep uttered its voice,
And ᴿlifted its hands on high.　Ex. 14:22

11 The ᴿsun and moon stood still in their
habitation;　Josh. 10:12-14
At the light of Your arrows they went,
At the shining of Your glittering spear.

12 You marched through the land in
indignation;
You trampled the nations in anger.

13 You went forth for the salvation of
Your people,
For salvation with Your Anointed.
You struck the head from the house of
the wicked,
By laying bare from foundation to
neck.　Selah

14 You thrust through with his own
arrows
The head of his villages.
They came out like a whirlwind to
scatter me;
Their rejoicing was like feasting on the
poor in secret.

15 ᴿYou walked through the sea with Your ▽
horses,　Ps. 77:19
Through the heap of great waters.

16 When I heard, ᴿmy body trembled;
My lips quivered at *the* voice;
Rottenness entered my bones;
And I trembled in myself,　Ps. 119:120
That I might rest in the day of trouble.
When he comes up to the people,
He will invade them with his troops.

A Hymn of Faith

17 Though the fig tree may not blossom,
Nor fruit be on the vines;
Though the labor of the olive may fail,
And the fields yield no food;
Though the flock may be cut off from
the fold,
And there be no herd in the stalls—

18 Yet I will ᴿrejoice in the LORD,　Is. 61:10
I will joy in the God of my salvation.

19 The LORD God is my strength;
He will make my feet like deer's *feet*,
And He will make me ᴿwalk on my
high hills.　Deut. 32:13; 33:29

To the Chief Musician. With my stringed
instruments.　▲

THE BOOK OF
Zephaniah

AUTHORSHIP AND CONTEXT. Zephaniah's name means "Jehovah Hides," i.e., shelters or protects. This great-great-grandson of the good King Hezekiah prophesied during the reign of King Josiah of Judah (640–608 B.C.), including Josiah's reformation which began in 621 B.C. He was also related to King Josiah, who was a great-grandson of Hezekiah. Zephaniah thereby probably had access to the king's court and would have been influential in helping to bring about the great reformation, which unfortunately was more superficial than real. He was also a contemporary of Jeremiah, Nahum, and Habakkuk.

KEY VERSE: 2:3, recalling the prophet's name—"Seek the LORD, all you meek of the earth, who have upheld His justice. Seek righteousness, seek humility. It may be that you will be hidden in the day of the LORD's anger."

HOW ZEPHANIAH FITS TOGETHER. Rampant lawlessness, profaned worship, deceitful prophets, and virtually extinct religious convictions among the people occasioned this prophet's message. Its theme is "the day of the LORD," a phrase repeated many times. Zephaniah was a flaming evangelist who preached effectively a message burning with rebuke to a people reluctant to respond. In the midst of severe denunciation, he called for repentance which alone could save the nation from impending doom. Finally, his thunder and sternness gave way to sweetness and love, joy and triumph, rest and salvation, as he foretold the bright future that would ultimately be Judah's.

His book may thus be divided according to its chapter breaks: chapter 1 proclaims God's coming *retribution* for the people's sins, chapter 2 seeks their *repentance,* and chapter 3 predicts their ultimate *restoration.* Terror turns to tenderness with a promise of redemption in the last twelve verses, and thus this prophet of doom reveals the heart of God, the goodness of the Lord, and the tenderness of His love. Affliction gives way to salvation and praise.

—R.J.W.

THE word of the LORD which came to Zephaniah the son of Cushi, the son of Gedaliah, the son of Amariah, the son of Hezekiah, in the days of ᴿJosiah the son of Amon, king of Judah.　　2 Kin. 22:1, 2

The Great Day of the LORD

2 "I will ᵀutterly consume everything
　　From the face of the land,"
　　Says the LORD;　　Lit. *make a complete end of*
3 "Iᴿ will consume man and beast;
　　I will consume the birds of the heavens,
　　The fish of the sea,　　Hos. 4:3
　　And the ᵀstumbling blocks along with
　　　　the wicked.　　Figurative of idols
　　I will cut off man from the face of the
　　　　ᵀland,"
　　Says the LORD.　　ground

4 "I will stretch out My hand against
　　Judah,
　　And against all the inhabitants of
　　　　Jerusalem.
　　ᵀI will cut off every trace of Baal from
　　　　this place,　　Fulfilled in 2 Kin. 23:4, 5
　　The names of the ᵀidolatrous priests
　　　　with the *pagan* priests—　　Heb. *chemarim*
5 Those ᴿwho worship the host of heaven
　　on the housetops;　　2 Kin. 23:12

Those who worship and swear *oaths* by
　　the LORD,
　　But who *also* swear by *Milcom;
6 ᴿThose who have turned back from
　　following the LORD,　　Is. 1:4
　　And ᴿhave not sought the LORD, nor
　　　　inquired of Him."　　Hos. 7:7

7 ᴿBe silent in the presence of the Lord
　　GOD;　　Zech. 2:13
　　For the day of the LORD *is* at hand,
　　For the LORD has prepared a sacrifice;
　　He has *invited His guests.

8 "And it shall be,
　　In the day of the LORD's sacrifice,
　　That I will punish ᴿthe princes and the
　　　　king's children,
　　And all such as are clothed with foreign
　　　　apparel.　　Jer. 39:6
9 In the same day I will punish
　　All those who ᴿleap over the threshold,
　　Who fill their masters' houses with
　　　　violence and deceit.　　1 Sam. 5:5

10 "And there shall be on that day," says
　　the LORD,
　　"The sound of a mournful cry from ᴿthe
　　　　Fish Gate,　　2 Chr. 33:14

1:5 Or *Malcam,* An Ammonite god, 1 Kin. 11:5; Jer. 49:1;
Molech, Lev. 18:21
1:7 Lit. *set apart, consecrated*

A wailing from the Second Quarter,
And a loud crashing from the hills.
11 Wail, you inhabitants of ᵀMaktesh!
For all the merchant people are cut
down;   A market district of Jerusalem, lit. *Mortar*
All those who handle money are cut off.

12 "And it shall come to pass at that time
That I will search Jerusalem with
lamps,
And punish the men
Who are ᴿsettled *in complacency,
ᴿWho say in their heart,   Jer. 48:11 · Ps. 94:7
'The LORD will not do good,
Nor will He do evil.'
13 Therefore their goods shall become
booty,
And their houses a desolation;
They shall build houses, but not inhabit
them;
They shall plant vineyards, but ᴿnot
drink their wine."   Deut. 28:39
14 ᴿThe great day of the LORD *is* near;
It is near and hastens quickly.
The noise of the day of the LORD is
bitter;   Joel 2:1, 11
There the mighty men shall cry out.
15 ᴿThat day *is* a day of wrath,   Is. 22:5
A day of trouble and distress,
A day of devastation and desolation,
A day of darkness and gloominess,
A day of clouds and thick darkness,
16 A day of ᴿtrumpet and alarm
Against the fortified cities
And against the high towers.   Jer. 4:19
17 "I will bring distress upon men,
And they shall ᴿwalk like blind men,
Because they have sinned against the
LORD;
Their blood shall be poured out like
dust,
And their flesh like refuse."   Deut. 28:29
18 ᴿNeither their silver nor their gold
Shall be able to deliver them   Ezek. 7:19
In the day of the LORD's wrath;
But the whole land shall be devoured
By the fire of His jealousy,
For He will make speedy riddance
Of all those who dwell in the land.

A Call to Repentance

2 Gatherᴿ yourselves together, yes, gather
together,   Joel 1:14; 2:16
O ᵀundesirable nation,   Or *shameless*
2 Before the decree is issued,
Or the day passes like chaff,
Before the LORD's fierce anger comes
upon you,
Before the day of the LORD's anger
comes upon you!

3 ᴿSeek the LORD, ᴿall you meek of the
earth,   Amos 5:6 · Ps. 76:9
Who have upheld His justice.
Seek righteousness, seek humility.
It may be that you will be hidden
In the day of the LORD's anger.

Judgment on Nations

4 For ᴿGaza shall be forsaken,
And Ashkelon desolate;
They shall drive out Ashdod ᴿat
noonday,   Zech. 9:5 · Jer. 6:4
And Ekron shall be uprooted.
5 Woe to the inhabitants of ᴿthe seacoast,
The nation of the Cherethites!
The word of the LORD *is* against you,
O ᴿCanaan, land of the Philistines:
"I will destroy you;   Ezek. 25:15–17 · Josh. 13:3
So there shall be no inhabitant."
6 The seacoast shall be pastures,
With *shelters for shepherds ᴿand folds
for flocks.   Is. 17:2
7 The coast shall be for ᴿthe remnant of
the house of Judah;   [Mic. 5:7, 8]
They shall feed *their* flocks there;
In the houses of Ashkelon they shall lie
down at evening.
For the LORD their God will ᴿinterveneᵀ
for them,   Luke 1:68 · Lit. *visit them*
And ᴿreturn their captives.   Jer. 29:14

8 "Iᴿ have heard the reproach of Moab,
And ᴿthe insults of the people of
Ammon,   Jer. 48:27 · Ezek. 25:3
With which they have reproached My
people,
And ᴿmade arrogant threats against
their borders.   Jer. 49:1
9 Therefore, *as* I live,"
Says the LORD of hosts, the God of
Israel,
"Surely ᴿMoab shall be like Sodom,
And ᴿthe people of Ammon like
Gomorrah—   Is. 15:1–9 · Amos 1:13
ᴿOverrun with weeds and saltpits,
And a perpetual desolation.
The residue of My people shall plunder
them,
And the remnant of My people shall
possess them."   Deut. 29:23
10 This they shall have ᴿfor their pride,
Because they have reproached and
made arrogant threats   Is. 16:6
Against the people of the LORD of hosts.
11 The LORD *will be* awesome to them,
For He will reduce to nothing all the
gods of the earth;
ᴿPeople shall worship Him,   Mal. 1:11
Each one from his place,
Indeed all the shores of the nations.

1:12 Lit. *on their lees;* like the dregs of wine   2:6 Underground huts or cisterns, lit. *excavations*

12 "You^R Ethiopians also,   Is. 18:1-7
    You shall be slain by My sword."

13 And He will stretch out His hand
       against the north,
    ^RDestroy Assyria,   Is. 10:5-27; 14:24-27
    And make Nineveh a desolation,
    As dry as the wilderness.

14 The herds shall lie down in her midst,
    ^REvery beast of the nation.   Is. 13:21
    Both the ^Rpelican and the bittern
    Shall lodge on the capitals *of her
       pillars;*   Is. 14:23; 34:11
    Their voice shall sing in the windows;
    Desolation *shall be* at the threshold;
    For He will lay bare the cedar work.

15 This is the rejoicing city
    ^RThat dwelt securely,   Is. 47:8
    ^RThat said in her heart,   Rev. 18:7
    "I *am it,* and *there is* none besides me."
    How has she become a desolation,
    A place for beasts to lie down!
    Everyone who passes by her
    Shall hiss and ^Rshake his fist.   Nah. 3:19

The Wickedness of Jerusalem

3 Woe to her who is rebellious and
       polluted,
    To the oppressing city!

2 She has not obeyed *His* voice,
    She has not received correction;
    She has not trusted in the LORD,
    She has not drawn near to her God.

3 ^RHer princes in her midst *are* roaring
       lions;   Ezek. 22:27
    Her judges *are* ^Revening wolves   Hab. 1:8
    That leave not a bone till morning.

4 Her ^Rprophets are insolent, treacherous
       people;   Hos. 9:7
    Her priests have ^Tpolluted the
       sanctuary,   Or *profaned*
    They have done violence to the law.

5 The LORD *is* righteous in her midst,
    He will do no unrighteousness.
    ^TEvery morning He brings His justice to
       light;   Lit. *Morning by morning*
    He never fails,
    But ^Rthe unjust knows no shame.   Jer. 3:3

6 "I have cut off nations,
    Their fortresses are devastated;
    I have made their streets desolate,
    With none passing by.
    Their cities are destroyed;
    There is no one, no inhabitant.

7 ^RI said, 'Surely you will fear Me,   Jer. 8:6
    You will receive instruction'—
    So that her dwelling would not be cut
       off,
    Despite everything for which I
       punished her.
    But ^Tthey rose early and ^Rcorrupted all
       their deeds.   They were eager · Gen. 6:12

A Faithful Remnant

8 "Therefore ^Rwait for Me," says the LORD,
    "Until the day I rise up *for plunder;
    My determination *is* to ^Rgather the
       nations   Hab. 2:3 · Joel 3:2
    To My assembly of kingdoms,
    To pour on them My indignation,
    All my fierce anger;
    All the earth ^Rshall be devoured
    With the fire of My jealousy.   Zeph. 1:18

9 "For then I will restore to the peoples ^Ra
       pure ^Tlanguage,   Is. 19:18; 57:19 · Lit. *lip*
    That they all may call on the name of
       the LORD,
    To serve Him with one accord.

10 ^RFrom beyond the rivers of Ethiopia
    My worshipers,
    The daughter of My dispersed ones,
    Shall bring My offering.   Ps. 68:31

11 In that day you shall not be shamed for
       any of your deeds
    In which you transgress against Me;
    For then I will take away from your
       midst
    Those who ^Rrejoice in your pride,
    And you shall no longer be haughty
    In My holy mountain.   Is. 2:12; 5:15

12 I will leave in your midst
    ^RA meek and humble people,
    And they shall trust in the name of the
       LORD.   Is. 14:32

13 ^RThe remnant of Israel ^Rshall do no
       unrighteousness   [Mic. 4:7] · Is. 60:21
    ^RAnd speak no lies,   Rev. 14:5
    Nor shall a deceitful tongue be found in
       their mouth;
    For ^Rthey shall feed *their* flocks and lie
       down,   Ezek. 34:13-15, 28
    And no one shall make *them* afraid."

Joy in God's Faithfulness

14 ^RSing, O daughter of Zion!
    Shout, O Israel!
    Be glad and rejoice with all *your* heart,
    O daughter of Jerusalem!   Is. 12:6

15 The LORD has taken away your
       judgments,
    He has cast out your enemy.
    ^RThe King of Israel, the LORD, ^R*is* in your
       midst;   [John 1:49] · Ezek. 48:35
    You shall *see disaster no more.

16 In that day ^Rit shall be said to
       Jerusalem: Is. 35:3, 4
    "Do not fear;
    Zion, let not your hands be weak.

17 The LORD your God ^Rin your midst,
    The Mighty One, will save;   Zeph. 3:5, 15

3:8 LXX, [Syr.] *for witness;* Tg. *for the day of My
revelation for judgment;* Vg. *for the day of My
resurrection that is to come*
3:15 So with Heb. mss., LXX, Bg.; MT, Vg. *fear*

ᴿHe will rejoice over you with gladness,
He will quiet *you* with His love,   Is. 62:5
He will rejoice over you with singing."

18 "I will gather those who ᴿsorrow over
    the appointed assembly,   Lam. 2:6
Who are among you,
To whom its reproach *is* a burden.
19 Behold, at that time
I will deal with all who afflict you;
I will save the ᴿlame,

And gather those who were driven out;
I will appoint them for praise and fame
In every land where they were put to
    shame.   [Mic. 4:6, 7]
20 At that time ᴿI will bring you back,
Even at the time I gather you;
For I will give you ᵀfame and praise
Among all the peoples of the earth,
When I return your captives before
    your eyes,"
Says the Lᴏʀᴅ.   Is. 11:12 • Lit. *a name*

THE BOOK OF
Haggai

AUTHORSHIP. Haggai, meaning "Festive," could have been the name given to the prophet in anticipation of the victorious return from exile. He was the first prophet who arose in the congregation of Judah upon its return from Babylon. Possibly he was a man up in years. Some infer from 2:3 that he had seen Solomon's temple, which was destroyed in 586 B.C.

His postexilic ministry continued only four months, and he left us only four messages in print. Nevertheless a four-month ministry under God excels forty years without His enduement. And four sermons in the power of the Spirit deliver greater blessing and benefit than four hundred preached in the energy of the flesh.

CONTEXT. Haggai's prophecy focuses on covenant renewal. Underlying his proclamations regarding the will and redemptive purposes of God can be found this emphasis. God had not abolished His covenant with Israel though He had suspended it.

Throughout the history of Israel God had always accompanied a covenant with a visible expression. The continuation of the ancient covenant, or the kingdom of God in Israel, was externalized and symbolized in the temple. Neglect of the temple demonstrated poverty of spirit and a breach of the covenant.

Upon the return of the captives of Judah and Benjamin, in just a matter of months, they restored God's altar of burnt offering and reestablished the sacrificial worship prescribed by law. In the second month of the second year after their return, they laid the foundation for the new temple (Ezra 3). Almost immediately adversaries obtained a decree that the building would cease. Fear doubtlessly did its nefarious work. The people pressed forward, trying to advance their own fortunes, building their own paneled houses while abandoning the temple construction (Hag. 1:4).

Their sin lay in their indifference to the building of God's house, while using any excuse to build their own houses. Haggai insisted God's work must have first priority in the lives of His people.

"The time has not come, the time that the LORD's house should be built," they said (1:2). Contemporary as this century, isn't it? Men don't treat business this way. They don't say, "Now is not the time to make money, to acquire property, build a great business, provide for a luxurious old age and the fortunes of our children." Their caution looks to one cause: God's. This curse has plagued the church in all ages.

If the covenant, breached with the desecration and destruction of the temple, was to be reestablished in its Old Testament form, rebuilding the temple demanded top priority. Pursuit of this with all possible zeal would testify to their burning desire to resume the covenant fellowship which for years had been interrupted. This task completed, they could know that God, restoring the former connection, would fulfill all His covenant promises.

God predicates every command and every promise upon the assumption of self-interest (not selfishness). So, His message through Haggai emphasizes divine chastisement upon selfish disobedience and divine blessings upon spiritual obedience.

HOW HAGGAI FITS TOGETHER. Haggai's first message (ch. 1) condemns the selfish neglect of the people towards the building of the temple. He identifies their crop failure and the curse under which they were suffering as divine punishment for that neglect. They respond by resuming the building after a fifteen-year hiatus.

Then, in his second message (2:1-9), Haggai comforts those who pine over the inferiority of the new temple to the old by assuring them that the Lord will keep His covenant promise made when the Hebrews fled from Egypt. He will shake the whole world and all the heathen, and He will give the new temple greater glory than irradiated Solomon's temple.

Haggai's third message (2:10-19) predicts the rescinding of the previous curse and the reactivation of the blessings of nature promised to those who remained faithful to the covenant.

Finally (2:20-23), Haggai assures the continuity of the throne of Israel, represented in the person and attitude of Zerubbabel, amidst the turbulence which will explode upon the kingdoms of this world. He will destroy the might and durability of the shaken kingdoms.

KEY VERSES: 2:7, 9—" 'I will shake all nations, and they shall come to the Desire of All Nations, and I will fill this temple with glory,' says the LORD of hosts. . . . 'The glory of this latter temple shall be greater than the former,' says the LORD of hosts. 'And in this place I will give peace,' says the LORD of hosts."

One final note: In this new temple there would be no ark of the covenant, no tablets of the law. They could not be restored inasmuch as Almighty God had written them. While the old covenant was not to be restored in its Sinaitic form, they had the promise of God through Jeremiah (31:31–34) that the Lord would make a new covenant with Israel and Judah: He would put His law into their hearts and write it in their minds.

—J.H.

The Command to Build God's House

IN the second year of King Darius, in the sixth month, on the first day of the month, the word of the LORD came by ᴿHaggai the prophet to Zerubbabel the son of Shealtiel, governor of Judah, and to ᴿJoshua the son of ᴿJehozadak, the high priest, saying,   Ezra 5:1; 6:14 · Ezra 5:2, 3 · 1 Chr. 6:15

2 "Thus speaks the LORD of hosts, saying: 'This people says, "The time has not come, the time that the LORD's house should be built."'"

3 Then the word of the LORD ᴿcame by Haggai the prophet, saying,   Ezra 5:1

4 "Is it ᴿtime for you yourselves to dwell in your paneled houses, and this ᵀtemple to lie in ruins?"   2 Sam. 7:2 · Lit. house, and so in v. 8

5 Now therefore, thus says the LORD of hosts: ᴿ"Consider your ways!   Lam. 3:40

6 "You have ᴿsown much, and bring in little;
You eat, but do not have enough;
You drink, but you are not filled with drink;
You clothe yourselves, but no one is warm;
And ᴿhe who earns wages,
Earns wages to put into a bag with holes."   Deut. 28:38–40 · Zech. 8:10

7 Thus says the LORD of hosts: "Consider your ways!

8 "Go up to the mountains and bring wood and build the temple, that I may take pleasure in it and be glorified," says the LORD.

9 "You looked for much, but indeed it came to little; and when you brought it home, I blew it away. Why?" says the LORD of hosts. "Because of My house that is in ruins, while every one of you runs to his own house.

10 "Therefore ᴿthe heavens above you withhold the dew, and the earth withholds its fruit.   Deut. 28:23

11 "For I called for a drought on the land and the mountains, on the grain and the new wine and the oil, on whatever the ground brings forth, on men and livestock, and on ᴿall the labor of your hands."   Hag. 2:17

The People's Obedience

12 ᴿThen Zerubbabel the son of Shealtiel, and Joshua the son of Jehozadak, the high priest, with all the remnant of the people, obeyed the voice of the LORD their God, and the words of Haggai the prophet, as the LORD their God had sent him; and the people feared the presence of the LORD.   Ezra 5:2

13 Then Haggai, the LORD's messenger, spoke the LORD's message to the people, saying, "I am with you, says the LORD."

14 So ᴿthe LORD stirred up the spirit of Zerubbabel the son of Shealtiel, ᴿgovernor of Judah, and the spirit of Joshua the son of Jehozadak, the high priest, and the spirit of all the remnant of the people; ᴿand they came and worked on the house of the LORD of hosts, their God,   Ezra 1:1 · Hag. 2:21 · Ezra 5:2, 8

15 on the twenty-fourth day of the sixth month, in the second year of King Darius.

The Coming Glory of God's House

2 In the seventh month, on the twenty-first of the month, the word of the LORD came by Haggai the prophet, saying:

2 "Speak now to Zerubbabel the son of Shealtiel, governor of Judah, and to Joshua the son of Jehozadak, the high priest, and to the remnant of the people, saying:

3 'Who is left among you who saw this *temple in its former glory? And how do you see it now? In comparison with it, ᴿis this not in your eyes as nothing?   Zech. 4:10

4 'Yet now ᴿbe strong, Zerubbabel,' says the LORD; 'and be strong, Joshua, son of Jehozadak, the high priest; and be strong, all you people of the land,' says the LORD, 'and work; for I am with you,' says the LORD of hosts.   Zech. 8:9

5 ᴿ'According to the word that I covenanted with you when you came out of Egypt, so ᴿMy Spirit remains among you; do not fear!'   Ex. 29:45, 46 · [Neh. 9:20]

6 "For thus says the LORD of hosts: 'Once more (it is a little while) ᴿI will shake heaven and earth, the sea and dry land;   [Joel 3:16]

7 'and I will shake all nations, and they shall come to the ᵀDesire of All Nations, and I will fill this ᵀtemple with glory,' says the LORD of hosts.   Or desire of all nations · Lit. house

8 'The silver is Mine, and the gold is Mine,' says the LORD of hosts.

9 'The ᴿ glory of this latter temple shall be greater than the former,' says the LORD of hosts. 'And in this place I will give ᴿpeace,' says the LORD of hosts."   [John 1:14] · Ps. 85:8, 9

2:3 Lit. house

The People Are Defiled

10 On the twenty-fourth *day* of the ninth *month*, in the second year of Darius, the word of the LORD came by Haggai the prophet, saying,

11 "Thus says the LORD of hosts: 'Now, ^Rask the priests *concerning the* law, saying,   Mal. 2:7

12 "If one carries holy meat in the fold of his garment, and with the edge he touches bread or stew, wine or oil, or any food, will it become holy?" ' " Then the priests answered and said, "No."

13 And Haggai said, "If *one who is* ^Runclean *because* of a dead body touches any of these, will it be unclean?" So the priests answered and said, "It shall be unclean."   Num. 19:11, 22

14 Then Haggai answered and said, " 'So is this people, and so is this nation before Me,' says the LORD, 'and so is every work of their hands; and what they offer there is unclean.

Promised Blessing

15 'And now, carefully consider from this day forward: from before stone was laid upon stone in the temple of the LORD—

16 'since those *days,* ^Rwhen *one* came to a heap of twenty ephahs, there were *but* ten; when *one* came to the wine vat to draw out fifty baths from the press, there were *but* twenty.   Zech. 8:10

17 'I struck you with blight and mildew and hail in all the labors of your hands; yet you did not *turn* to Me,' says the LORD.

18 'Consider now from this day forward, from the twenty-fourth day of the ninth month, from the day that the foundation of the LORD's temple was laid—consider it:

19 'Is the seed still in the barn? As yet the vine, the fig tree, the pomegranate, and the olive tree have not yielded *fruit. But* from this day I will bless *you.'* "

Zerubbabel Chosen as a Signet

20 And again the word of the LORD came to Haggai on the twenty-fourth day of the month, saying,

21 "Speak to Zerubbabel, ^Rgovernor of Judah, saying: Zech. 4:6-10

^R'I will shake heaven and earth.   Hag. 2:6, 7
22 ^RI will overthrow the throne of
    kingdoms;   [Dan. 2:44]
I will destroy the strength of the
    Gentile kingdoms.
^RI will overthrow the chariots   Mic. 5:10
And those who ride in them;
The horses and their riders shall come
    down,
Every one by the sword of his brother.

23 'In that day,' says the LORD of hosts, 'I will take you, Zerubbabel My servant, the son of Shealtiel,' says the LORD, 'and will make you like a signet *ring;* for I have chosen you,' says the LORD of hosts."

THE BOOK OF
Zechariah

The book of Zechariah is the eleventh of the twelve Old Testament books known as the Minor Prophets. The name *Zechariah* means "Jehovah Remembers." Like the prophet Haggai, Zechariah prophesied to the Jews who were in Judah and Jerusalem after the return from captivity in Babylon (Ezra 5:1; 6:14).

AUTHORSHIP AND DATE. The prophet Zechariah was "the son of Berechiah, the son of Iddo the prophet" (1:1, 7). Ezra calls Zechariah "the son of Iddo" (Ezra 5:1; 6:14), using the word "son" in the sense of "descendant." Like Haggai, Zechariah began his ministry in the second year of the reign of Darius I the Great, the king of Persia from 522 to 486 B.C. Therefore, his prophecy may be dated specifically in the year 520 B.C. (1:1, 7). According to the dates mentioned in chapters 1—8, Zechariah was active from 520 to 518 B.C.

Some scholars believe that Zechariah wrote only the first eight chapters of the book that bears his name. They believe that the remaining part of the book, chapters 9—14, which they see as describing the victories of Alexander the Great (9:1-8) and the victories of the Maccabees (9:11-17), must be credited to another writer who lived several centuries after Zechariah. Some go even further, crediting chapters 9—11 and 12—14 to a second and third writer. Conservative scholars, however, believe that Zechariah wrote chapters 9—14 at a later time to disclose the apocalyptic events connected with the coming of the Messiah and his earthly kingdom and that this accounts for the difference in style and subject matter. All internal evidence points to one author rather than several.

KEY VERSES. Selecting one key verse from Zechariah is quite difficult; therefore, several representative verses should be considered: 4:6—" 'Not by might nor by power, but by My Spirit,' says the LORD of hosts"; 7:9, 10; (see also 8:16, 17)—"Execute true justice, show mercy and compassion everyone to his brother. Do not oppress the widow or the fatherless, the alien or the poor. Let none of you plan evil in his heart against his brother"; and 9:9—"Rejoice greatly, O daughter of Zion! Shout, O daughter of Jerusalem! Behold, your King is coming to you; He is just and having salvation, lowly and riding on a donkey, a colt, the foal of a donkey."

HOW ZECHARIAH FITS TOGETHER AND CONTEXT. The book of Zechariah may be divided into four major parts: (1) a call to repentance (1:1-6); (2) the night visions of Zechariah (1:7—6:15); (3) a section dealing with fasting, disobedience, and Jerusalem, the holy city of the future (7:1—8:23); and (4) the future of the nations, Israel, and Messiah's kingdom (9:1—14:21).

The immediate purpose of Zechariah's prophesying was to encourage the rebuilding of the temple. The Jews lent their efforts first to the restoration of the temple and its ritual, and only later to rebuilding the city walls. The book of Ezra tells us that this rebuilding was begun almost immediately after the exiles reached Jerusalem after returning from the Babylonian captivity. Then work was interrupted by the opposition of people of the land, who were not permitted to cooperate in the work. Later Darius would issue a strongly worded decree that would cause the work to be taken up again with renewed vigor, and the temple would be finished four years afterward—but that decree was yet future. Now the work was at a standstill.

Zechariah came into this troubled scene. The introductory section of his book (1:1-6) is a call to repentance. Zechariah says that the people had not heeded the warnings of "the former prophets" (v. 4) and that their stubborn disobedience had issued in calamities.

This section is followed by eight night visions and their interpretations: (a) the four horsemen among the myrtle trees (1:7-17), in which God indicates His renewed interest in Jerusalem; (b) the four horns and the four craftsmen (1:18-21), which foretells the punishment of the nations who brought about the dispersion of Judah; (c) a man with a measuring line (2:1-13), which points to a new and larger Jerusalem with Yahweh both its glory and its protection; (d) a vision of Joshua the hight priest, whose filthy garments are cleansed (3:1-10), probably picturing the land cleansed of its iniquity; (e) the seven-branched golden lampstand flanked by the two olive trees, Joshua and Zerubbabel (4:1-14); (f) the flying scroll (5:1-4), a picture of Jehovah's curse carried out; (g) a woman in a basket (5:5-11), portraying the carrying away of the wickedness of the land to a home in Babylon; and (h) the four chariots (6:1-8), depicting the four winds bringing God's spirit of anger to bear on the north country. This section is concluded with the command to crown Joshua and the prophecy of the coming of the BRANCH, usually understood as a messianic prophecy (6:9-15).

The third major part of the book of Zechariah (7:1—8:23) contains the response of the Lord concerning the fasts held during the years of exile (7:1-7); then come ten oracles introduced by

the phrase "Thus says the LORD" (7:9; 8:2, 3, 4, 6, 7, 9, 14, 18, 20), contrasting the past with the promise of the future, when a season of joy and gladness will displace mourning and fasting.

The fourth major part of the book of Zechariah (9:1—14:21) contains two sections, both beginning with the words "The burden of the word of the LORD" (9:1; 12:1). These "burdens" depict the inauguration of Jehovah's rule, the reassembling of Judah and Joseph (that is, the regathering of the nation of Israel), and the overthrow of the world power. Portrayed further is the attack of the nations on Jerusalem, repelled by Jehovah in a terrible vengeance. The Lord establishes His kingdom and the nations come to Jerusalem to worship Him.

The prophet emphasizes the permanence and unchangeableness of Jehovah's words and statutes. The Lord is confronted with the fallibility and variability of those whom He has chosen as His own, but He cannot revoke His word. Indeed, He meets the challenge with mercy and forgiveness: " 'Return to me,' says the LORD of hosts, 'and I will return to you' " (1:3).

The New Jerusalem will be enlarged and will become a prosperous city, Jehovah bringing to it peace and salvation. Law and order will reign; the forcible seizure of another's property will cease (8:10); the land will be blessed from heaven (8:12). These blessings are to be enjoyed by a purified, sanctified remnant (8:12). "They shall be My people and I will be their God, in truth and righteousness" (8:8). Through it all runs the messianic figure who will be at their head to direct them.

The book of Zechariah breathes consolation and peace. Jehovah is to him a God who attracts, a stern but loving God. But the prophet goes on in chapter 12 to speak of Jerusalem as a burdensome stone for all people occupying its place when the nations that come against it are destroyed when there shall be universal mourning.

In chapter 14 we have Jerusalem taken and spoiled, a Jerusalem to which the remnant of the warring nations shall go up to worship under the threat of famine and plague. There is a ritualistic purification, a fountain is opened for sin and uncleanness. The prophet foretells the coming of a King in humble state to Jerusalem bringing salvation and peace.

—H.A.

A Call to Repentance

I N the eighth month ᴿof the second year of Darius, the word of the LORD came ᴿto Zechariah the son of Berechiah, the son of Iddo the prophet, saying, Zech. 7:1 • Matt. 23:35

2 "The LORD has been very angry with your fathers.

3 "Therefore say to them, 'Thus says the LORD of hosts: "Return ᴿto Me," says the LORD of hosts, "and I will return to you," says the LORD of hosts. [Mal. 3:7-10]

4 "Do not be like your fathers, ᴿto whom the former prophets preached, saying, 'Thus says the LORD of hosts: ᴿ"Turn now from your evil ways and your evil deeds." ' But they did not hear nor heed Me," says the LORD. 2 Chr. 36:15, 16 • Is. 31:6

5 "Your fathers, where are they?
And the prophets, do they live forever?

6 Yet surely ᴿMy words and My statutes,
Which I commanded My servants the
prophets— [Is. 55:11]
Did they not overtake your fathers?' "

So they returned and said:

ᴿ"Just as the LORD of hosts determined to
do to us, Lam. 1:18; 2:17
According to our ways and according to
our deeds,
So He has dealt with us."

Vision of the Horses

7 On the twenty-fourth day of the eleventh month, which is the month Shebat, in the second year of Darius, the word of the LORD came to Zechariah the son of Berechiah, the son of Iddo the prophet:

8 I saw by night, and behold, a man riding on a red horse, and it stood among the myrtle trees in the hollow; and behind him were ᴿhorses: red, sorrel, and white. [Zech. 6:2-7]

9 Then I said, "My lord, what are these?" So the angel who talked with me said to me, "I will show you what they are."

10 And the man who stood among the myrtle trees answered and said, ᴿ"These are the ones whom the LORD has sent to walk to and fro throughout the earth." [Heb. 1:14]

11 ᴿSo they answered the Angel of the LORD, who stood among the myrtle trees, and said, "We have walked to and fro throughout the earth, and behold, all the earth is ᵀresting quietly." [Ps. 103:20, 21] • Lit. sitting and quiet

The LORD Will Comfort Zion

12 Then the Angel of the LORD answered and said, "O LORD of hosts, ᴿhow long will You not have mercy on Jerusalem and on the cities of Judah, against which You were angry these seventy years?" Ps. 74:10

13 And the LORD answered the angel who talked to me, with ᴿgood and comforting words. Jer. 29:10

14 So the angel who spoke with me said to me, ^T"Proclaim, saying, 'Thus says the LORD of hosts: Lit. *Cry out*

"I am ^Rzealous for Jerusalem   Zech. 8:2
And for Zion with great ^Tzeal.   Or *jealousy*
15 I am exceedingly angry with the
    nations at ease;
For ^RI was a little angry,   Is. 47:6
And they helped—*but* with evil *intent*."

16 'Therefore thus says the LORD:

^R"I am returning to Jerusalem with
    mercy;   [Zech. 2:10; 8:3]
My ^Rhouse ^Rshall be built in it," says
    the LORD of hosts,   Ezra 6:14, 15 · Is. 44:28
"And a *surveyor's* line shall be stretched
    out over Jerusalem." '

17 "Again proclaim, saying, 'Thus says the LORD of hosts:

"My cities shall again ^Tspread out
    through prosperity;   Or *overflow with good*
The LORD will again comfort Zion,
And will again choose Jerusalem." ' "

Vision of the Horns

18 Then I raised my eyes and looked, and there *were* four ^Rhorns.   [Lam. 2:17]
19 And I said to the angel who talked with me, "What *are* these?" So he answered me, "These *are* the ^Thorns that have scattered Judah, Israel, and Jerusalem."   Kingdoms
20 Then the LORD showed me four craftsmen.
21 And I said, "What are these coming to do?" So he said, "These *are* the ^Rhorns that scattered Judah, so that no one could lift up his head; but ^T*the craftsmen* are coming to terrify them, to cast out the horns of the nations that lifted up *their* horn against the land of Judah to scatter it."   [Ps. 75:10] · Lit. *these*

Vision of the Measuring Line

2 Then I raised my eyes and looked, and behold, ^Ra man with a measuring line in his hand.   Jer. 31:39
2 So I said, "Where are you going?" And he said to me, "To measure Jerusalem, to see what *is* its width and what *is* its length."
3 And there *was* the angel who talked with me, going out; and another angel was coming out to meet him,
4 who said to him, "Run, speak to this young man, saying: 'Jerusalem shall be inhabited *as* towns without walls, because of the multitude of men and livestock in it.
5 'For I,' says the LORD, 'will be ^Ra wall of fire all around her, ^Rand I will be the glory in her midst.' "   [Is. 26:1] · [Is. 60:19]

Future Joy of Zion and Many Nations

6 "Up, up! Flee ^Rfrom the land of the north," says the LORD; "for I have ^Rspread

you abroad like the four winds of heaven," says the LORD.   Is. 48:20 · Deut. 28:64
7 "Up, Zion! ^REscape, you who dwell with the daughter of Babylon."   Is. 48:20
8 For thus says the LORD of hosts: "He sent Me after glory, to the nations which plunder you; for he who ^Rtouches you touches the apple of His eye.   Deut. 32:10
9 "For surely I will shake My hand against them, and they shall become ^Tspoil for their servants. Then you will know that the LORD of hosts has sent Me.   *booty*
10 ^R"Sing and rejoice, O daughter of Zion! For behold, I am coming and I ^Rwill dwell in your midst," says the LORD.   Is. 12:6 · [Lev. 26:12]
11 ^R"Many nations shall be joined to the LORD ^Rin that day, and they shall become ^RMy people. And I will dwell in your midst. Then you will know that the LORD of hosts has sent Me to you.   [Is. 2:2, 3] · Zech. 3:10 · Ex. 12:49
12 "And the LORD will ^Rtake possession of Judah as His inheritance in the Holy Land, and will again choose Jerusalem.   [Deut. 32:9]
13 "Be silent, all flesh, before the LORD, for He is aroused from His holy habitation!"

Vision of the High Priest

3 Then he showed me ^RJoshua the high priest standing before the Angel of the LORD, and ^RSatan^T standing at his right hand to oppose him.   Hag. 1:1 · Ps. 109:6 · Lit. *the Adversary*
2 And the LORD said to Satan, "The LORD rebuke you, Satan! The LORD who ^Rhas chosen Jerusalem rebuke you! *Is* this not a brand plucked from the fire?"   [Rom. 8:33]
3 Now Joshua was clothed with filthy garments, and was standing before the Angel.
4 Then He answered and spoke to those who stood before Him, saying, "Take away the filthy garments from him." And to him He said, "See, I have removed your iniquity from you, ^Rand I will clothe you with rich robes."   Is. 61:10
5 And I said, "Let them put a clean ^Rturban on his head." So they put a clean turban on his head, and they put the clothes on him. And the Angel of the LORD stood by.   Ex. 29:6

The Coming Branch

6 Then the Angel of the LORD admonished Joshua, saying,
7 "Thus says the LORD of hosts:

'If you will walk in My ways,
And if you will ^Rkeep My command,
Then you shall also judge My house,
And likewise have charge of My courts;
I will give you places to walk   Lev. 8:35
Among these who ^Rstand here.   Zech. 4:4

8 'Hear, O Joshua, the high priest,
You and your companions who sit
    before you,
For they are ^Ra wondrous sign;

For behold, I am bringing forth ᴿMy
Servant the BRANCH.   Ps. 71:7 • Is. 42:1
9 For behold, the stone
That I have laid before Joshua:
ᴿUpon the stone *are* seven eyes.
Behold, I will engrave its inscription,'
Says the Lᴏʀᴅ of hosts,   [Zech. 4:10]
'And ᴿI will remove the iniquity of that
land in one day.   Jer. 31:34; 50:20
10 In that day,' says the Lᴏʀᴅ of hosts,
'Everyone will invite his neighbor
Under his vine and under his fig tree.' "

Vision of the Lampstand and Olive Trees

4 Now ᴿthe angel who talked with me came
back and wakened me, ᴿas a man who is
wakened out of his sleep.   Zech. 1:9; 2:3 • Dan. 8:18
2 And he said to me, "What do you see?"
So I said, "I am looking, and there is ᴿa
lampstand of solid gold with a bowl on top of
it, ᴿand on the *stand* seven lamps with seven
pipes to the seven lamps.   Rev. 1:12 • [Rev. 4:5]
3 "Two olive trees *are* by it, one at the
right of the bowl and the other at its left."
4 So I answered and spoke to the angel
who talked with me, saying, "What *are* these,
my lord?"
5 Then the angel who talked with me
answered and said to me, "Do you not know
what these are?" And I said, "No, my lord."
6 So he answered and said to me:

"This *is* the word of the Lᴏʀᴅ to
ᴿZerubbabel:
ᴿ'Not by might nor by power, but by My
Spirit,'
Says the Lᴏʀᴅ of hosts.   Hag. 1:1 • Hos. 1:7
7 'Who *are* you, ᴿO great mountain?
Before Zerubbabel *you shall become* a
plain!   Jer. 51:25
And he shall bring forth the capstone
With shouts of "Grace, grace to it!" ' "

8 Moreover the word of the Lᴏʀᴅ came to
me, saying:

9 "The hands of Zerubbabel
ᴿHave laid the foundation of this
ᵀtemple;   Ezra 3:8–10; 5:16 • Lit. *house*
His hands ᴿshall also finish *it.*   Ezra 6:14, 15
Then ᴿyou will know   Zech. 2:9, 11; 6:15
That the ᴿLᴏʀᴅ of hosts has sent Me to
you.   [Is. 43:16]
10 For who has despised the day of ᴿsmall
things?   Hag. 2:3
For these seven rejoice to see
The ᵀplumb line in the hand of
Zerubbabel.   Lit. *plummet stone*
ᴿThey are the eyes of the Lᴏʀᴅ,
Which scan to and fro throughout the
whole earth."   2 Chr. 16:9

11 Then I answered and said to him, "What
are these two olive trees—at the right of the
lampstand and at its left?"

12 And I further answered and said to him,
"What *are these* two olive branches that *drip*
into the ᵀreceptacles of the two gold pipes
from which the golden *oil* drains?"   Lit. *hands*
13 Then he answered me and said, "Do you
not know what these *are*?" And I said, "No,
my lord."
14 So he said, "These *are* the two ᵀanointed
ones, ᴿwho stand beside the Lord of the
whole earth."   Lit. *sons of fresh oil* • Zech. 3:1–7

Vision of the Flying Scroll

5 Then I turned and raised my eyes, and
saw there a flying ᴿscroll.   Ezek. 2:9
2 And he said to me, "What do you see?"
So I answered, "I see a flying scroll. Its length
is ᵀtwenty cubits and its width ᵀten
cubits."   30 ft. • 15 ft.
3 Then he said to me, "This *is* the ᴿcurse
that goes out over the face of the whole
earth: 'Every thief shall be expelled,' according *to* this side of *the scroll*; and, 'Every
perjurer shall be expelled,' according *to* that
side of it."   Mal. 4:6

4 "I will send out *the curse*," says the
Lᴏʀᴅ of hosts;
"It shall enter the house of the ᴿthief
And the house of ᴿthe one who swears
falsely by My name.
It shall remain in the midst of his house
And consume ᴿit, with its timber and
stones."   Ex. 20:15 • Lev. 19:12 • Lev. 14:34, 35

Vision of the Woman in a Basket

5 Then the angel who talked with me
came out and said to me, "Lift your eyes now,
and see what this *is* that goes forth."
6 So I asked, "What *is* it?" And he said, "It
is a ᵀbasket that is going forth." He also said,
"This *is* their resemblance throughout the
earth: Heb. *ephah,* a measuring container, and so elsewhere
7 "Here *is* a lead disc lifted up, and this *is* a
woman sitting inside the basket";
8 then he said, "This *is* Wickedness!" And
he thrust her down into the basket, and
threw the lead *cover over its mouth.
9 Then I raised my eyes and looked, and
there *were* two women, coming with the
wind in their wings; for they had wings like
the wings of a ᴿstork, and they lifted up the
basket between earth and heaven.   Lev. 11:13, 19
10 So I said to the angel who talked with
me, "Where are they carrying the basket?"
11 And he said to me, "To build a house for
it in the land of ᵀShinar; when it is ready, *the
basket* will be set there on its base."   Babylon

Vision of the Four Chariots

6 Then I turned and raised my eyes and
looked, and behold, four chariots *were*

5:8 Lit. *stone*

coming from between two mountains, and the mountains *were* mountains of bronze.

2 With the first chariot *were* red horses, with the second chariot black horses,

3 with the third chariot white horses, and with the fourth chariot dappled horses— strong *steeds.*

4 Then I answered Rand said to the angel who talked with me, "What *are* these, my lord?"   Zech. 5:10

5 And the angel answered and said to me, R"These *are* four spirits of heaven, who go out from *their* Rstation before the Lord of all the earth.   [Heb. 1:7, 14] · Dan. 7:10

6 T"The one with the black horses is going to Rthe north country, the white are going after them, and the dappled are going toward the south country."   The chariot · Jer. 1:14

7 Then the strong *steeds* went out, eager to go, that they might walk to and fro throughout the earth. And He said, "Go, walk to and fro throughout the earth." So they walked to and fro throughout the earth.

8 And He called to me, and spoke to me, saying, "See, those who go toward the north country have given rest to My RSpirit in the north country."   Eccl. 10:4

The Command to Crown Joshua

9 Then the word of the Lord came to me, saying:

10 "Receive *the gift* from the captives— from Heldai, Tobijah, and Jedaiah, who have come from Babylon—and go the same day and enter the house of Josiah the son of Zephaniah.

11 "Take the silver and gold, make an elaborate crown, and set *it* on the head of Joshua the son of Jehozadak, the high priest.

12 "Then speak to him, saying, 'Thus says the Lord of hosts, saying:

"Behold, Rthe Man whose name *is* the
RBRANCH!   John 1:45 · Is. 11:1
From His place He shall Tbranch out,
RAnd He shall build the temple of the
  Lord;   Lit. *sprout up* · [Eph. 2:20]
13 Yes, He shall build the temple of the
  Lord.
He Rshall bear the glory,   Is. 22:24
And shall sit and rule on His throne;
So RHe shall be a priest on His throne,
And the counsel of peace shall be
  between them both.' "   [Ps. 110:4-7]

14 "Now the Telaborate crown shall be Rfor a memorial in the temple of the Lord *for Helem, Tobijah, Jedaiah, and Hen the son of Zephaniah.   Lit. *crowns* · Ex. 12:14

15 "Even Rthose from afar shall come and build the temple of the Lord. Then you shall know that the Lord of hosts has sent Me to

you. And *this* shall come to pass if you diligently obey the voice of the Lord your God."   Is. 57:19

Obedience Better than Fasting

7 Now in the fourth year of King Darius it came to pass *that* the word of the Lord came to Zechariah, on the fourth day of the ninth month, Chislev,

2 when *the people sent *Sherezer, with Regem-Melech and his men, *to Tthe house of God, to pray before the Lord,   Or *Bethel*

3 *and* to ask the priests who *were* in the house of the Lord of hosts, and the prophets, saying, "Should I weep in the fifth month and fast as I have done for so many years?"

4 Then the word of the Lord of hosts came to me, saying,

5 "Say to all the people of the land, and to the priests: 'When you Rfasted and mourned in the fifth and seventh *months* Rduring those seventy years, did you really fast Rfor Me— for Me?   [Is. 58:1-9] · Zech. 1:12 · [Rom. 14:6]

6 'When you eat and when you drink, do you not eat and drink *for yourselves?*

7 'Should *you* not have obeyed the words which the Lord proclaimed through the Rformer prophets when Jerusalem and the cities around it were inhabited and prosperous, and Rthe TSouth and the Lowland were inhabited?' "   Zech. 1:4 · Jer. 17:26 · Heb. *Negev*

Disobedience Resulted in Captivity

8 Then the word of the Lord came to Zechariah, saying,

9 "Thus says the Lord of hosts:

R'Execute true justice,   Jer. 7:28
Show Tmercy and compassion
Everyone to his brother.   Or *lovingkindness*
10 RDo not oppress the widow or the
  fatherless,
The alien or the poor.
RLet none of you plan evil in his heart
Against his brother.'   Ex. 22:22 · Mic. 2:1

11 "But they refused to heed, Rshrugged their shoulders, and Rstopped their ears so that they could not hear.   Neh. 9:29 · Jer. 17:23

12 "Yes, they made their hearts like flint, refusing to hear the law and the words which the Lord of hosts had sent by His Spirit through the former prophets. Thus great wrath came from the Lord of hosts.

13 "Therefore it happened, *that* just as He proclaimed and they would not hear, so Rthey called out and I would not listen," says the Lord of hosts.   Prov. 1:24-28

14 "But RI scattered them with a whirlwind among all the nations which they had not known. Thus the land became desolate after them, so that no one passed through or

6:14 So with MT, Tg., Vg.; Syr. *for Heldai* (cf. v. 10); LXX *for the patient ones*

7:2 Lit. *they*, cf. v. 5 · Or *Sar-Ezer*

returned; for they made the pleasant land desolate.'" Deut. 4:27; 28:64

Jerusalem, Holy City of the Future

8 Again the word of the LORD of hosts came, saying, 2 "Thus says the LORD of hosts:

'I am zealous for Zion with great zeal;
With great fervor I am zealous for her.'

3 "Thus says the LORD:

R'I will return to Zion,   Zech. 1:16
And Rdwell in the midst of Jerusalem.
Jerusalem Rshall be called the City of
    Truth,   Zech. 2:10, 11 • Is. 1:21
RThe Mountain of the LORD of hosts,
RThe Holy Mountain.'   [Is. 2:2, 3] • Jer. 31:23

4 "Thus says the LORD of hosts:

R'Old men and old women shall again sit
In the streets of Jerusalem,   Is. 65:20
Each one with his staff in his hand
Because of Tgreat age.   Lit. many days
5 The streets of the city
Shall be Rfull of boys and girls
Playing in its streets.'   Jer. 30:19, 20

6 "Thus says the LORD of hosts:

'If it is Tmarvelous in the eyes of the
    remnant of this people in these days,
Will it also be marvelous in My eyes?'
Says the LORD of hosts.   Or wonderful

7 "Thus says the LORD of hosts:

'Behold, RI will save My people from the
    land of the Teast   Is. 11:11 • Lit. rising sun
And from the land of the Twest; setting sun
8 I will Rbring them back,   Zeph. 3:20
And they shall dwell in the midst of
    Jerusalem.
RThey shall be My people   [Jer. 30:22; 31:1, 33]
And I will be their God,
RIn truth and righteousness.'   Jer. 4:2

9 "Thus says the LORD of hosts:

R'Let your hands be strong,   Hag. 2:4
You who have been hearing in these
    days
These words by the mouth of Rthe
    prophets,   Ezra 5:1, 2; 6:14
Who spoke in Rthe day the foundation
    was laid   Hag. 2:18
For the house of the LORD of hosts,
That the temple might be built.
10 For before these days
There were no Rwages for man nor any
    hire for beast;
There was no peace from the enemy for
    whoever went out or came in;
For I set all men, everyone, against his
    neighbor.   Hag. 1:6, 9

11 RBut now I will not treat the remnant of

this people as in the former days,' says the LORD of hosts.   Hag. 2:15-19

12 'For the Tseed shall be prosperous,
The vine shall give its fruit,   seed of peace
The ground shall give her increase,
And Rthe heavens shall give their dew—
I will cause the remnant of this people
To possess all these.   Hag. 1:10
13 And it shall come to pass
That just as you were Ra curse among
    the nations,   Jer. 42:18
O house of Judah and house of Israel,
So I will save you, and Ryou shall be a
    blessing.
Do not fear,
Let your hands be strong.'   Gen. 12:2

14 "For thus says the LORD of hosts:

R'Just as I determined to Tpunish you
When your fathers provoked Me to
    wrath,'   Jer. 31:28 • Lit. bring calamity to you
Says the LORD of hosts,
R'And I would not relent,   [2 Chr. 36:16]
15 So again in these days
I am determined to do good
To Jerusalem and to the house of
    Judah.
Do not fear.
16 These are the things you shall Rdo:
RSpeak each man the truth to his
    neighbor;   Zech. 7:9, 10 • [Eph. 4:25]
Give judgment in your gates for truth,
    justice, and peace;
17 RLet none of you think evil in Tyour
    heart against your neighbor;
And do not love a false oath.
For all these are things that I hate,'
Says the LORD."   Prov. 3:29 • Lit. his

18 Then the word of the LORD of hosts came to me, saying, 19 "Thus says the LORD of hosts:

RThe fast of the fourth month,   Jer. 52:6
RThe fast of the fifth,   Jer. 52:12
RThe fast of the seventh,   2 Kin. 25:25
RAnd the fast of the tenth,   Jer. 52:4
Shall be Rjoy and gladness and cheerful
    feasts   Esth. 8:17
For the house of Judah.
RTherefore love truth and peace.'   Zech. 8:16

20 "Thus says the LORD of hosts:

'Peoples shall yet come,
Inhabitants of many cities;
21 The inhabitants of one city shall go to
    another, saying,
R"Let us continue to go and pray before
    the LORD,
And seek the LORD of hosts.
I myself will go also."   [Is. 2:2, 3]
22 Yes, Rmany peoples and strong nations

Shall come to seek the LORD of hosts in
Jerusalem,   Is. 60:3; 66:23
And to pray before the LORD.'

23 "Thus says the LORD of hosts: 'In those
days ten men from every language of the
nations shall ^Rgrasp the sleeve of a Jewish
man, saying, "Let us go with you, for we have
heard *that* God *is* with you." ' "   [Is. 45:14]

Israel Defended Against Enemies

9 The ^Tburden of the word of the LORD
Against the land of Hadrach,   *oracle*
And ^RDamascus its resting place
(For ^Rthe eyes of men   Is. 17:1 • Amos 1:3–5
And all the tribes of Israel
Are on the LORD);

2 Also *against* ^RHamath, *which* borders
on it,   Jer. 49:23
And *against* ^RTyre and ^RSidon, though
they are very wise.   Is. 23 • 1 Kin. 17:9

3 For Tyre built herself a tower,
Heaped up silver like the dust,
And gold like the mire of the streets.

4 Behold, ^Rthe LORD will cast her out;
He will destroy her power in the sea,
And she will be devoured by fire.   Is. 23:1

5 Ashkelon shall see *it* and fear;
Gaza also shall be very sorrowful;
And ^REkron, for He dried up her
expectation.   Zeph. 2:4, 5
The king shall perish from Gaza,
And Ashkelon shall not be inhabited.

6 "A mixed race shall settle ^Rin Ashdod,
And I will cut off the pride of the
^RPhilistines.   Amos 1:8 • Ezek. 25:15–17

7 I will take away the blood from his
mouth,
And the abominations from between his
teeth.
But he who remains, even he *shall be*
for our God,
And shall be like a leader in Judah,
And Ekron like a Jebusite.

8 ^RI will camp around My house   [Ps. 34:7]
Because of the army,
Because of him who passes by and him
who returns.
No more shall an oppressor pass
through them,
For now I have seen with My eyes.

The Coming King

9 "Rejoice ^Rgreatly, O daughter of Zion!
Shout, O daughter of Jerusalem!
Behold, your King is coming to you;
He *is* just and having salvation,
Lowly and riding on a donkey,
A colt, the foal of a donkey.   Matt. 21:4, 5

10 I ^Rwill cut off the chariot from Ephraim
And the horse from Jerusalem;
The ^Rbattle bow shall be cut off.

He shall speak ^Rpeace to the nations;
His dominion *shall be* ^R'from sea to sea,
And from the River to the ends of the
earth.'   Hos. 1:7 • Hos. 2:18 • Mic. 4:2–4 • Ps. 72:8

God Will Save His People

11 "As for you also,
Because of the blood of your covenant,
I will set your ^Rprisoners free from the
waterless pit.   Is. 42:7

12 Return to the stronghold,
^RYou prisoners of hope.   Is. 49:9
Even today I declare
That I will restore ^Rdouble to you.   Is. 61:7

13 For I have bent Judah, My *bow*,
Fitted the bow with Ephraim,
And raised up your sons, O Zion,
Against your sons, O Greece,
And made you like the sword of a
mighty man."

14 Then the LORD will be seen over them,
And ^RHis arrow will go forth like
lightning.
The Lord GOD will blow the trumpet,
And go ^Rwith whirlwinds from the
south.   Ps. 18:14 • Is. 21:1

15 The LORD of hosts will ^Rdefend them;
They shall devour and subdue with
slingstones.   Zech. 12:8
They shall drink *and* roar as if with
wine;
They shall be filled *with blood* like
^Tbasins,   Sacrificial basins
Like the corners of the altar.

16 The LORD their God will ^Rsave them in
that day,   Jer. 31:10, 11
As the flock of His people.
For ^Rthey *shall be like* the ^Tjewels of a
crown,   Is. 62:3 • Lit. *stones*
Lifted like a banner over His land—

17 For how great is *its goodness
And how great *its ^Rbeauty!   Ps. 45:1–16
Grain shall make the young men thrive,
And new wine the young women.

Restoration of Judah and Israel

10 Ask the LORD for ^Rrain   [Deut. 11:13, 14]
In the time of the ^Tlatter rain. Spring rain
The LORD will make ^Tflashing clouds;
He will give them showers of rain,
Grass in the field for everyone. Or *lightning*

2 For the ^Tidols speak delusion; Heb. *teraphim*
The diviners envision ^Rlies,
And tell false dreams;   Jer. 27:9
They ^Rcomfort in vain.   Job 13:14
Therefore *the people* wend their way
like ^Rsheep;   Jer. 50:6, 7
They are ^Tin trouble ^Rbecause *there is*
no shepherd.   *afflicted* • Ezek. 34:5–8

9:17 Or *His*

3 "My anger is kindled against the
 ᴿshepherds,   Jer. 25:34–36
 ᴿAnd I will punish the ᵀgoatherds.
 For the LORD of hosts ᴿwill visit His
   flock,   Ezek. 34:17 • Leaders • Luke 1:68
 The house of Judah,
 And ᴿwill make them as His royal horse
   in the battle.   Song 1:9
4 From him comes ᴿthe cornerstone,
 From him ᴿthe tent peg,   Is. 28:16 • Is. 22:23
 From him the battle bow,
 From him every ᵀruler together. Or despot
5 They shall be like mighty men,
 Who ᴿtread down their enemies
 In the mire of the streets in the battle.
 They shall fight because the LORD is
   with them,
 And the riders on horses shall be put to
   shame.   Ps. 18:42
6 "I will strengthen the house of Judah,
 And I will save the house of Joseph.
 ᴿI will bring them back,   Jer. 3:18
 Because I ᴿhave mercy on them.   Hos. 1:7
 They shall be as though I had not cast
   them aside;
 For I am the LORD their God,
 And I ᴿwill hear them.   Zech. 13:9
7 Those of Ephraim shall be like a mighty
   man,
 And their ᴿheart shall rejoice as if with
   wine.   Ps. 104:15
 Yes, their children shall see it and be
   glad;
 Their heart shall rejoice in the LORD.
8 I will ᴿwhistle for them and gather
   them,
 For I will redeem them;
 ᴿAnd they shall increase as they once
   increased.   Is. 5:26 • Ezek. 36:37
9 "Iᴿ will ᵀsow them among the peoples,
 And they shall ᴿremember Me in far
   countries;   Hos. 2:23 • Or scatter • Deut. 30:1
 They shall live, together with their
   children,
 And they shall return.
10 ᴿI will also bring them back from the
   land of Egypt,   Is. 11:11
 And gather them from Assyria.
 I will bring them into the land of Gilead
   and Lebanon,
 Until no more room is found for them.
11 ᴿHe shall pass through the sea with
   affliction,   Is. 11:15
 And strike the waves of the sea:
 All the depths of ᵀthe River shall dry
   up.   The Nile
 Then ᴿthe pride of Assyria shall be
   brought down,   Zeph. 2:13
 And the scepter of Egypt shall depart.
12 "So I will strengthen them in the LORD,

And ᴿthey shall walk up and down in
   His name,"
 Says the LORD.   Mic. 4:5

Desolation of Israel

11 Open your doors, O Lebanon,
       That fire may devour your cedars.
2 Wail, O cypress, for the ᴿcedar has
   fallen,   Ezek. 31:3
 Because the mighty trees are ruined.
 Wail, O oaks of Bashan,
 For the thick forest has come down.
3 There is the sound of wailing
   ᴿshepherds!   Jer. 25:34–36
 For their glory is in ruins.
 There is the sound of roaring lions!
 For the *pride of the Jordan is in ruins.

Prophecy of the Shepherds

4 Thus says the LORD my God, "Feed the
flock for slaughter,
5 "whose owners slaughter them and ᴿfeel
no guilt; those who sell them ᴿsay, 'Blessed be
the LORD, for I am rich'; and their shepherds
do not pity them.   [Jer. 2:3] • 50:7 • Hos. 12:8
6 "For I will no longer pity the inhabitants
of the land," says the LORD. "But indeed I will
give everyone into his neighbor's hand and
into the hand of his king. They shall ᵀattack
the land, and I will not deliver them from
their hand."   Lit. strike
7 So I fed the flock for slaughter, *in
particular ᴿthe poor of the flock. I took for
myself two staffs: the one I called ᵀBeauty,
and the other I called ᵀBonds; and I fed the
flock.   Zeph. 3:12 • Or Grace • Or Unity
8 I ᵀdismissed the three shepherds ᴿin one
month. My soul loathed them, and their soul
also abhorred me.   Or destroyed, lit. cut off • Hos. 5:7
9 Then I said, "I will not feed you. ᴿLet
what is dying die, and what is perishing
perish. Let those that are left eat each other's
flesh."   Jer. 15:2
10 And I took my staff, Beauty, and cut it in
two, that I might break the covenant which I
had made with all the peoples.
11 So it was broken on that day. Thus *the
poor of the flock, who were watching me,
knew that it was the word of the LORD.
12 Then I said to them, "If it is agreeable to
you, give me my wages; and if not, refrain."
So they ᴿweighed out for my wages ᵀthirty
pieces of silver.   Matt. 27:9 • $3840
13 And the LORD said to me, "Throw it to
the ᴿpotter"—that princely price they set on
me. So I took the ᵀthirty pieces of silver and
threw them into the house of the LORD for
the potter.   Matt. 27:3–10 • $3840
14 Then I cut in two my other staff, ᵀBonds,

11:3 Or flood plain, thicket
11:7 So with MT, Tg., Vg; LXX for the Canaanites
11:11 So with MT, Tg., Vg; LXX the Canaanites

that I might break the brotherhood between Judah and Israel.   Or *Unity*

15 And the LORD said to me, R"Next, take for yourself the implements of a foolish shepherd.   Is. 56:11

16 "For indeed I will raise up a shepherd in the land *who* will not care for those who are cut off, nor seek the young, nor heal those that are broken, nor feed those that still stand. But he will eat the flesh of the fat and tear their hooves in Rpieces.   Ezek. 34:1–10

17 "WoeR to the worthless shepherd,
   Who leaves the flock!
A sword *shall be* against his arm
   And against his right eye;
His arm shall completely wither,
   And his right eye shall be totally
      blinded."   Jer. 23:1

The Coming Deliverance of Judah

12 The Tburden of the word of the LORD against Israel. Thus says the LORD, Rwho stretches out the heavens, lays the foundation of the earth, and forms the spirit of man within him: *oracle, prophecy* • Is. 42:5; 44:24

2 "Behold, I will make Jerusalem Ra cup of Tdrunkenness to all the surrounding peoples, when they lay siege against Judah and Jerusalem.   Is. 51:17 • Lit. *reeling*

3 "And it shall happen in that day that I will make Jerusalem Ra very heavy stone for all peoples; all who would heave it away will surely be cut in pieces, though all nations of the earth are gathered against it.   Matt. 21:44

4 "In that day," says the LORD, R"I will strike every horse with confusion, and its rider with madness; I will open My eyes on the house of Judah, and will strike every horse of the peoples with blindness.   Ezek. 38:4

5 "And the governors of Judah shall say in their heart, 'The inhabitants of Jerusalem *are* my strength in the LORD of hosts, their God.'

6 "In that day I will make the governors of Judah like a firepan in the woodpile, and like a fiery torch in the sheaves; they shall devour all the surrounding peoples on the right hand and on the left, but Jerusalem shall be inhabited again in her own place—Jerusalem.

7 "The LORD will save the tents of Judah first, so that the glory of the house of David and the glory of the inhabitants of Jerusalem shall not become greater than that of Judah.

8 "In that day the LORD will defend the inhabitants of Jerusalem; the one who is feeble among them in that day shall be like David, and the house of David *shall be* like God, like the Angel of the LORD before them.

9 "It shall be in that day that I will seek to Rdestroy all the nations that come against Jerusalem.   Hag. 2:22

Mourning for the Pierced One

10 R"And I will pour on the house of David and on the inhabitants of Jerusalem the Spirit of grace and supplication; then they will Rlook on Me whom they pierced. Yes, they will mourn for Him as one mourns for *his* only *son*, and grieve for Him as one grieves for a firstborn.   [Joel 2:28, 29] • John 19:34, 37; 20:27

11 "In that day there shall be a great mourning in Jerusalem, like the mourning at Hadad Rimmon in the plain of *Megiddo.

12 R"And the land shall mourn, every family by itself: the family of the house of David by itself, and their wives by themselves; the family of the house of RNathan by itself, and their wives by themselves;   [Matt. 24:30] • Luke 3:31

13 "the family of the house of Levi by itself, and their wives by themselves; the family of Shimei by itself, and their wives by themselves;

14 "all the families that remain, every family by itself, and their wives by themselves.

Idolatry Cut Off

13 "In that Rday Ra fountain shall be opened for the house of David and for the inhabitants of Jerusalem, for sin and for Runcleanness.   [Rev. 21:6, 7] • [Heb. 9:14] • Ezek. 36:25

2 "It shall be in that day," says the LORD of hosts, "*that* I will Rcut off the names of the idols from the land, and they shall no longer be remembered. I will also cause Rthe prophets and the unclean spirit to depart from the land.   Ex. 23:13 • Jer. 23:14, 15

3 "It shall come to pass *that* if anyone still prophesies, then his father and mother who begot him will say to him, 'You shall not live, because you have spoken lies in the name of the LORD.' And his father and mother who begot him Rshall thrust him through when he prophesies.   Deut. 13:6–11

4 "And it shall be in that day *that* Revery prophet will be ashamed of his vision when he prophesies; they will not wear Ra robe of coarse hair to deceive.   [Mic. 3:6, 7] • 2 Kin. 1:8

5 R"But he will say, 'I *am* no prophet, I *am* a farmer; for a man taught me to keep cattle from my youth.'   Amos 7:14

6 "And *one* will say to him, 'What are these wounds between your Tarms?' Then he will answer, 'Those with which I was wounded in the house of my friends.'   Or *hands*

The Shepherd Savior

7 "Awake, O sword, against RMy
      Shepherd,
   Against the Man Rwho is My
      Companion,"   Is. 40:11 • [John 10:30]
Says the LORD of hosts.
R"Strike the Shepherd,   Matt. 26:31, 56, 67
   And the sheep will be scattered;

12:11 Heb. *Megiddon*

Then I will turn My hand against ᴿthe
little ones.   Luke 12:32
8 And it shall come to pass in all the
land,"
Says the Lᴏʀᴅ,
"That ᴿtwo-thirds in it shall be cut off
and die,   Ezek. 5:2, 4, 12
ᴿBut one-third shall be left in it: [Rom. 11:5]
9 I will bring the one-third ᴿthrough the
fire,   Is. 48:10
Will ᴿrefine them as silver is refined,
And test them as gold is tested.   1 Pet. 1:6
ᴿThey will call on My name,   Ps. 50:15
And I will answer them.
ᴿI will say, 'This is My people';   Hos. 2:23
And each one will say, 'The Lᴏʀᴅ is my
God.' "

The Day of the Lᴏʀᴅ

14 Behold, ᴿthe day of the Lᴏʀᴅ is
coming,
And your ᵀspoil will be divided in your
midst.   [Is. 13:6, 9] • plunder or booty
2 For ᴿI will gather all the nations to
battle against Jerusalem;   Zech. 12:2, 3
The city shall be taken,
The houses ᵀrifled,   plundered
And the women ravished.
Half of the city shall go into captivity,
But the remnant of the people shall not
be cut off from the city.
3 Then the Lᴏʀᴅ will go forth
And fight against those nations,
As He fights in the day of battle.
4 And in that day His feet will stand ᴿon
the Mount of Olives,   Ezek. 11:23
Which faces Jerusalem on the east.
And the Mount of Olives shall be split
in two,
From east to west,
ᴿMaking a very large valley;   Joel 3:12
Half of the mountain shall move toward
the north
And half of it toward the south.
5 Then you shall flee through My
mountain valley,
For the mountain valley shall reach to
Azal.
Yes, you shall flee
As you fled from the ᴿearthquake Amos 1:1
In the days of Uzziah king of Judah.

Thus the Lᴏʀᴅ my God will come,
And ᴿall the saints with *You.   Joel 3:11
6 It shall come to pass in that day
That there will be no light;
The ᵀlights will diminish.   Lit. glorious ones
7 It shall be one day
ᴿWhich is known to the Lᴏʀᴅ—
Neither day nor night.   Matt. 24:36

14:5 Or you; LXX, Tg., Vg. Him

But at ᴿevening time it shall happen
That it will be light.   Is. 30:26
8 And in that day it shall be
That living ᴿwaters shall flow from
Jerusalem,   Ezek. 47:1–12
Half of them toward ᵀthe eastern sea
And half of them toward ᵀthe western
sea;   Dead Sea • Mediterranean Sea
In both summer and winter it shall
occur.
9 And the Lᴏʀᴅ shall be ᴿKing over all
the earth.
In that day it shall be—
ᴿ"The Lᴏʀᴅ is one,"
And His name one.   [Rev. 11:15] • Deut. 6:4

10 All the land shall be turned into a plain
from Geba to Rimmon south of Jerusalem.
ᵀJerusalem shall be raised up and ᴿinhabited
in her place from Benjamin's Gate to the
place of the First Gate and the Corner Gate,
ᴿand from the Tower of Hananel to the king's
winepresses.   Lit. She • Zech. 12:6 • Jer. 31:38
11 The people shall dwell in it;
And ᴿno longer shall there be utter
destruction,   Jer. 31:40
But Jerusalem shall be safely inhabited.

12 And this shall be the plague with which
the Lᴏʀᴅ will strike all the people who fought
against Jerusalem:

Their flesh shall ᵀdissolve while they
stand on their feet,
Their eyes shall dissolve in their
sockets,
And their tongues shall dissolve in their
mouths.   Lit. decay
13 It shall come to pass in that day
That ᴿa great panic from the Lᴏʀᴅ will
be among them.
Everyone will seize the hand of his
neighbor,
And raise ᴿhis hand against his
neighbor's hand; 1 Sam. 14:15, 20 • Judg. 7:22
14 Judah also will fight at Jerusalem.
ᴿAnd the wealth of all the surrounding
nations
Shall be gathered together:
Gold, silver, and apparel in great
abundance.   Ezek. 39:10, 17
15 ᴿSuch also shall be the plague
On the horse and the mule,
On the camel and the donkey,
And on all the cattle that will be in
those camps.
So shall this plague be.   Zech. 14:12

The Nations Worship the King

16 And it shall come to pass that everyone
who is left of all the nations which came
against Jerusalem shall go up from year to
year to worship the King, the Lᴏʀᴅ of hosts,
and to keep the Feast of Tabernacles.

17 ᴿAnd it shall be *that* whichever of the families of the earth do not come up to Jerusalem to worship the King, the Lᴏʀᴅ of hosts, on them there will be no rain.   Is. 60:12

18 If the family of Egypt will not come up and enter in, ᴿthey *shall have no rain*; they shall receive the plague with which the Lᴏʀᴅ strikes the nations who do not come up to keep the Feast of Tabernacles.   Deut. 11:10

19 This shall be the ᵀpunishment of Egypt and the punishment of all the nations that do not come up to keep the Feast of Tabernacles.   Lit. *sin*

20 In that day ᴿ"HOLINESS TO THE LORD" shall be *engraved* on the bells of the horses. The pots in the Lᴏʀᴅ's house shall be like the bowls before the altar.   Is. 23:18

21 Yes, *every pot in Jerusalem and Judah shall be holiness to the Lᴏʀᴅ of hosts. Everyone who sacrifices shall come and take them and cook in them. In that day there shall no longer be a Canaanite in the house of the Lᴏʀᴅ of hosts.

14:21 Or *on every pot . . . shall be engraved "HOLINESS TO THE LORD OF HOSTS"*

THE BOOK OF
Malachi

In reading books of the Old Testament and particularly the books of the prophets, we may wonder what they have to say to our day and to our problems since they lived so long ago. You will soon discover in reading Malachi that he is indeed the "messenger of God" and speaks clearly both to his generation and to ours. He speaks out of the mind of God and offers wise counsel and solutions. This is a small book of great significance. It is divinely inspired and as you read it you will discover it is fearfully up to date.

AUTHORSHIP. The book of Malachi is the last of the twelve Old Testament books that are called the Minor Prophets. The name *Malachi* means "My Messenger"; it may be an abbreviation of *Malachiah*, a Hebrew personal name meaning "The Messenger of Jehovah." Nothing is known of Malachi except what may be learned from the book that bears his name.

Some scholars believe that *Malachi* is not a proper name, but is the title—perhaps taken from "My messenger" in 3:1—of an unknown prophet or leader of the Jews after the Babylonian captivity. Some of those who suggest that this book is anonymous suggest Ezra as the possible author. But since each of the eleven other minor prophets identified himself by name, there is no problem in presuming Malachi has done the same thing.

CONTEXT. The content of the book presupposes that the temple has been rebuilt following the Babylonian captivity (the reconstructed temple was dedicated in 516 B.C.), that the people have been taught God's law (Ezra 7:10, 14, 25, 26), and that they have since departed from the Mosaic ordinances. Malachi therefore likely wrote during the third quarter of the fifth century B.C. (Other scholars believe, however, that while the book clearly presupposes the rebuilt temple, it does not reflect the reconstruction of the religious community that took place under Ezra and Nehemiah about 450 B.C., and so belongs to the first half of the fifth century.)

KEY VERSES: 2:17; 3:1—"You have wearied the LORD with your words; yet you say, 'In what way have we wearied Him?' In that you say, 'Everyone who does evil is good in the sight of the LORD, and He delights in them,' or, 'Where is the God of justice?' 'Behold, I send My messenger, and he will prepare the way before Me. And the Lord, whom you seek, will suddenly come to His temple, even the Messenger of the covenant, in whom you delight. Behold, He is coming,' says the LORD of hosts."

HOW MALACHI FITS TOGETHER. The book of Malachi has six distinct sections, each involving a question-and-answer dialogue. In this exchange God confronts His people's stubborn refusal of His love and His righteous standards:

(1) "In what way have You loved us?" God proves His love for Israel by contrasting their fate with that of Edom (1:2-5).

(2) "In what way have we despised Your name?" The Lord rebukes the ministry: corrupt priests offer polluted offerings (1:6—2:9).

(3) "For what reason" does He no longer accept the people's offerings? God exposes the treachery of infidelity: the degradation of marriage by divorce and remarriage to pagan women (2:10-16).

(4) "In what way have we wearied Him" with words? God rebukes them for denying His holiness and saying that He delights in evil. He tells them of the coming Messenger of the covenant, the Lord Himself, who will purify His people (2:17—3:5).

(5) "In what way shall we return" to God? He tells them to forsake their former ways, wherein they have robbed Him by withholding tithes and offerings (3:6-12).

(6) "What have we spoken against You?" The Lord condemns those who have turned their back on serving Him, and predicts the coming "great and dreadful day of the LORD," which will burn the wicked like stubble but will bring salvation to the righteous. In conclusion, both to this book and to the entire Old Testament, God exhorts His people to keep His law and promises the coming of Elijah (3:13—4:6).

With the exception of Joel this is the only document that illustrates the religious life of a period which is very dark as far as historical records are concerned. Malachi addresses three groups of people: the people in general, the priests as spiritual leaders, and the doubting saints. These addresses were delivered at various times, but there is a close connection between them. The teaching of Malachi is very practical for believers today.

The Jewish nation tended more and more to become a people of "the Book" and increasing stress was laid upon them to observe perfunctory rituals and correct observance of the

ordinances. As a result, they developed an ecclesiastical pattern that destroyed prophetic inspiration and the stagnant replaced the dynamic. Prophetic ideas had to be translated into life; Malachi lived his message in the Spirit, with a warm spirituality that could not be absorbed in ritual and ceremonial functions. He gave prophecy *with* the law, which is totally different from prophecy *under* the law.

The message of Malachi was sorely needed. There were many abuses in the land. The people were living in open sin, the priests were corrupt, temple worship was a disgrace, and a godless indifference had settled over the nation.

Blind and crippled animals were offered on the altar. Sacrifice and tithes were important to the prophet, but only because they were an outward index to a right inner spirit. Because there was a fundamental lack of reverence for God (1:12) and because His people refused the divine grace of God (3:7) things were going wrong in the community and a distressed condition prevailed. The men were divorcing their Jewish wives and marrying heathen women. They were even robbing God by withholding their tithes and offerings.

Malachi spoke to the priests, who were to be the spiritual leaders of the people. Many of the problems were due to their poor example: like priests, like people. Their poor concept of God and His requirements caused confusion of conduct in human relationships and produced a defective society needing many adjustments. Because of their low perception of God, the priests held governors and kings in higher esteem than they did God. Their worship became fraudulent and without sincerity. Lies entered into the soul and it was so because the priests did not know the real character of God whom they presumed to serve. Malachi sought to lift the priesthood to a higher level through a fuller concept of God and a new, stern responsibility in discharging their duties. Loyalty and conscience were sadly lacking and sorely needed.

Malachi reminded the people of God's love. God is gracious and abundant in mercy. God's purpose of election still stands. Israel must have lost sight of the divine purpose, but it could not be obscured forever. He not only talked about God's love but also told them that the divine love is a holy love—a truth that must never be forgotten by His people.

Malachi was a faithful preacher and understood the purpose of his ministry. He tried not only to help reach the unsaved but also to build up the saints. He found everything so out of perspective that even good people were beginning to wonder if being religious was worthwhile.

Malachi reminds them that marriage is something that must be entered into in the fear of the Lord. It is a divine ordinance and covenant that links a man to his wife. It is a covenant no less sacred and indissoluble than the covenant that binds a man to God. This is closely related to the teachings of the apostle Paul in Ephesians 5.

The prophet speaks to the doubters, in effect saying, "Return to the Lord; He still loves you." The rich promise of Malachi is: "In spite of your sins, God still loves you and is willing to forgive His sinful people." These words of comfort to a faltering faithful people are brightened with another beautiful promise: "A book of remembrance was written before Him for those who fear the LORD and who meditate on His name" (3:16). Then God says, "I will spare them as a man spares his own son who serves him" (3:17).

Malachi believed that God demands social righteousness and is willing to bestow rich gifts upon His people according to their response to His call to them. Obedient loyalty would bring rich blessings: "But to you who fear My name the Sun of Righteousness shall arise with healing in His wings" (4:2)—a messianic prophecy foretelling the coming of our Lord and Savior Jesus Christ. Truly, Malachi spoke out of the heart and mind of God.

—W.R.H.

T HE ᵀburden of the word of the LORD to Israel by Malachi.   *oracle, prophecy*

Israel Beloved of God

2 "Iᴿ have loved you," says the LORD.
  "Yet you say, 'In what way have You loved us?'   Deut. 4:37; 7:8; 23:5
  Was not Esau Jacob's brother?"
  Says the LORD.
  "Yet ᴿJacob I have loved;   Rom. 9:13
3 But Esau I have hated,

And ᴿlaid waste his mountains and his heritage   Jer. 49:18
For the jackals of the wilderness."

4 Even though Edom has said,
  "We have been impoverished,
  But we will return and build the desolate places,"

Thus says the LORD of hosts:

"They may build, but I will ᴿthrow down;

They shall be called the Territory of
  Wickedness,   Jer. 49:16-18
And the people against whom the LORD
  will have indignation forever.
5 Your eyes shall see,
  And you shall say,
  R'The LORD is magnified beyond the
    border of Israel.'   Ps. 35:27

Polluted Offerings

6 "A son Rhonors his father,   [Ex. 20:12]
  And a servant his master.
  RIf then I am the Father,   Luke 6:46
  Where is My honor?
  And if I am a Master,
  Where is My reverence?
  Says the LORD of hosts
  To you priests who despise My name.
  RYet you say, 'In what way have we
    despised Your name?'   Mal. 2:14
7 "You offer Rdefiled food on My altar,
  But say,   Deut. 15:2
  'In what way have we defiled You?'
  By saying,
  'The table of the LORD is contemptible.'
8 And Rwhen you offer the blind as a
  sacrifice,   Lev. 22:22
  Is it not evil?
  And when you offer the lame and sick,
  Is it not evil?
  Offer it then to your governor!
  Would he be pleased with you?
  Would he Taccept you favorably?"
  Says the LORD of hosts.   Lit. lift up your face

9 "But now entreat God's favor,
  That He may be gracious to us.
  RWhile this is being done by your hands,
  Will He accept you favorably?"
  Says the LORD of hosts.   Hos. 13:9
10 "Who is there even among you who
  would shut the doors,
  RSo that you would not kindle fire on
  My altar in vain?
  I have no pleasure in you,"
  Says the LORD of hosts,
  R"Nor will I accept an offering from your
  hands.   1 Cor. 9:13 • Is. 1:11
11 For Rfrom the rising of the sun, even to
  its going down,   Is. 59:19
  My name shall be great Ramong the
  Gentiles;   Is. 60:3, 5
  RIn every place Rincense shall be offered
  to My name,   1 Tim. 2:8 • Rev. 8:3
  And a pure offering;
  RFor My name shall be great among the
  nations,"   Is. 66:18, 19
  Says the LORD of hosts.
12 "But you profane it,
  In that you say,
  RThe table of the *LORD is defiled; Mal. 1:7
  And its fruit, its food, is contemptible.'

1:12 So with Bg.; MT Lord

13 You also say,
  'Oh, what a Rweariness!'
  And you sneer at it,"
  Says the LORD of hosts.
  "And you bring the stolen, the lame, and
    the sick;
  Thus you bring an offering!
  RShould I accept this from your hand?"
  Says the LORD.   Is. 43:22 • Lev. 22:20
14 "But cursed be Rthe deceiver
  Who has in his flock a male,
  And takes a vow,
  But sacrifices to the Lord Rwhat is
    blemished—
  For RI am a great King,"
  Says the LORD of hosts,
  "And My name is to be feared among
    the nations.   Mal. 1:8 • Lev. 22:18-20 • Ps. 47:2

Corrupt Priests

2 "And now, O Rpriests, this
  commandment is for you.   Mal. 1:6
2 RIf you will not hear,   [Deut. 28:15]
  And if you will not take it to heart,
  To give glory to My name,"
  Says the LORD of hosts,
  "I will send a curse upon you,
  And I will curse your blessings.
  Yes, I have cursed them Ralready, Mal. 3:9
  Because you do not take it to heart.
3 "Behold, I will rebuke your descendants
  And spread Rrefuse on your faces, Ex. 29:14
  The refuse of your solemn feasts;
  And one will take you away with it.
4 Then you shall know that I have sent
    this commandment to you,
  That My covenant with Levi may
    continue,"
  Says the LORD of hosts.
5 "MyR covenant was with him, one of life
    and peace,   Num. 25:12
  And I gave them to him Rthat he might
    fear Me;   Deut. 33:9
  So he feared Me
  And was reverent before My name.
6 TThe law of truth was in his mouth,
  And Tinjustice was not found on his
    lips.   Or true instruction • Or unrighteousness
  He walked with Me in peace and
    equity,
  And turned many away from iniquity.
7 "ForR the lips of a priest should keep
    knowledge,
  And people should seek the law from
    his mouth;
  RFor he is the messenger of the LORD of
    hosts.   Deut. 17:8-11 • [Gal. 4:14]
8 But you have departed from the way;
  You Rhave caused many to stumble at
    the law.   Jer. 18:15
  RYou have corrupted the covenant of
    Levi,"   Neh. 13:29
  Says the LORD of hosts.

9 "Therefore ᴿI also have made you
    contemptible and base   1 Sam. 2:30
  Before all the people,
  Because you have not kept My ways
  But have shown partiality in the law."

Treachery of Infidelity

10 ᴿHave we not all one Father?
  ᴿHas not one God created us?
  Why do we deal treacherously with one
    another
  By profaning the covenant of the
    fathers?   1 Cor. 8:6 · Job 31:15
11 Judah has dealt treacherously,
  And an abomination has been
    committed in Israel and in Jerusalem,
  For Judah has ᴿprofaned
  The Loʀᴅ's holy *institution* which He
    loves:
  He has married the daughter of a
    foreign god.   Ezra 9:1, 2
12 May the Loʀᴅ cut off from the tents of
    Jacob
  The man who does this, being *awake
    and aware,
  Yet ᴿwho brings an offering to the
    Loʀᴅ of hosts!   Neh. 13:29

13 And this is the second thing you do:
  You cover the altar of the Loʀᴅ with
    tears,
  With weeping and crying;
  So He does not regard the offering
    anymore,
  Nor receive *it* with goodwill from your
    hands.
14 Yet you say, "For what reason?"
  Because the Loʀᴅ has been witness
  Between you and ᴿthe wife of your
    youth,   Mal. 3:5
  With whom you have dealt
    treacherously;
  ᴿYet she is your companion   Prov. 2:17
  And your wife by covenant.
15 But ᴿdid He not make *them* one,
  Having a remnant of the Spirit?
  And why one?   Matt. 19:4, 5
  He seeks ᴿgodly offspring.   [1 Cor. 7:14]
  Therefore take heed to your spirit,
  And let none deal treacherously with
    the wife of his youth.

16 "For ᴿthe Loʀᴅ God of Israel says
  That He hates divorce,
  For it covers one's garment with
    violence,"   [Matt. 5:31; 19:6–8]

2:12 Talmud, Vg. *teacher and student*

Says the Loʀᴅ of hosts.
  "Therefore take heed to your spirit,
  That you do not deal treacherously."

17 ᴿYou have wearied the Loʀᴅ with your
    words;   Is. 43:22, 24
  Yet you say,
  "In what way have we wearied *Him?*"
  In that you say,
  ᴿ"Everyone who does evil   Is. 5:20
  Is good in the sight of the Loʀᴅ,
  And He delights in them,"
  Or, "Where *is* the God of justice?"

The Coming Messenger

3 "Behold, ᴿI send My messenger,   Luke 1:76
  And he will prepare the way before Me.
  And the Lord, whom you seek,
  Will suddenly come to His temple,
  ᴿEven the Messenger of the covenant,
  In whom you delight.   Is. 63:9
  Behold, ᴿHe is coming,"   Hab. 2:7
  Says the Loʀᴅ of hosts.

2 "But who can endure ᴿthe day of His
    coming?   [Mal. 4:1]
  And who can stand when He appears?
  For ᴿHe *is* like a refiner's fire   [Matt. 3:10–12]
  And like launderers' soap.
3 ᴿHe will sit as a refiner and a purifier of
    silver;   Is. 1:25
  He will purify the sons of Levi,
  And ᵀpurge them as gold and silver,
  That they may offer to the Loʀᴅ
  An offering in righteousness.   Or *refine*

4 "Then ᴿthe offering of Judah and
    Jerusalem
  Will be ᵀpleasant to the Loʀᴅ,
  As in the days of old,
  As in former years.   Mal. 1:11 · *pleasing*
5 And I will come near you for judgment;
  I will be a swift witness
  Against sorcerers,
  Against adulterers,
  ᴿAgainst perjurers,   Zech. 5:4
  Against those who exploit wage earners
    and widows and orphans,
  And against those who turn away an
    alien—
  Because they do not fear Me,"
  Says the Loʀᴅ of hosts.

29–B. God's Will Is Immutable   ▼

6 "For I *am* the Loʀᴅ, ᴿI do not change;
  ᴿTherefore you are not consumed, O
    sons of Jacob.   [Rom. 11:29] · [Lam. 3:22] ▲
7 Yet from the days of ᴿyour fathers

29–B. God's Will Is Immutable (Malachi 3:6)—"For I am the Loʀᴅ, I do not change" (v. 6). He does not change: "God is not a man, that He should lie, nor a son of man, that He should repent [change]. Has He said, and will He not do? Or has He spoken, and will He not make it good?" (Num. 23:19, page 164). God will keep His Word and perform His unchangeable will.

(Point 29-B continued on next page)

You have gone away from My
ordinances Acts 7:51
And have not kept *them*.
ᴿReturn to Me, and I will return to you,"
Says the LORD of hosts. Zech. 1:3
ᴿ"But you said, Mal. 1:6
'In what way shall we return?'

Do Not Rob God

8 "Will a man rob God?
Yet you have robbed Me!
But you say,
'In what way have we robbed You?'
ᴿIn tithes and offerings. Neh. 13:10–12
9 You are cursed with a curse,
For you have robbed Me,
Even this whole nation.
10 Bring all the tithes into the ᴿstorehouse,
That there may be food in My house,
And try Me now in this,"
Says the LORD of hosts, 1 Chr. 26:20
"If I will not open for you the ᴿwindows
of heaven Gen. 7:11
And ᴿpour out for you *such* blessing

That *there will* not *be room* enough *to*
receive it. 2 Chr. 31:10
11 "And I will rebuke ᴿthe devourer for
your sakes,
So that he will not destroy the fruit of
your ground,
Nor shall the vine fail to bear fruit for
you in the field,"
Says the LORD of hosts; Amos 4:9
12 "And all nations will call you blessed,
For you will be ᴿa delightful land,"
Says the LORD of hosts. Dan. 8:9

The People Complain Harshly

13 "Yourᴿ words have been ᵀharsh against
Me," Mal. 2:17 · Lit. *strong*
Says the LORD,
"Yet you say,
'What have we spoken against You?'
14 ᴿYou have said,
'It is useless to serve God;
What profit *is it* that we have kept His
ordinance,
And that we have walked as mourners
Before the LORD of hosts? Job 21:14

(Point 29-B continued from previous page)
Note that according to God's unchangeable will, "all Israel will be saved . . . 'The Deliverer will come out of Zion, and He will turn away ungodliness from Jacob; for this is My covenant with them, when I take away their sins' " (Rom. 11:26, 27, page 1141). This no more means that every Hebrew who ever lived will be saved than that every Gentile will be saved. But it does mean that all elect Jews (the remnant believers) will be saved. "The Redeemer will come to Zion" (Is. 59:20, 21, page 699), which refers to the second coming of Christ. Every good and perfect gift is a part of God's unchangeable will. "Of His own will He brought us forth by the word of truth" (James 1:17, 18, page 1256). It is God's purpose that this "word of truth" (the gospel)—the death, burial, and resurrection of Jesus Christ—be preached to Israel, so that "all Israel will be saved." God's will was immutable (or unchangeable) yesterday, today, and forever (Heb. 13:8, page 1252). God reveals His immutable will in His eternal Word.
God's will is immutable

(1) *in salvation*. We are saved by grace through faith, not through works (Eph. 2:8, 9, page 1187; cf. Acts 4:12, page 1091; Rom. 10:8–10, page 1140).
(2) *in judgment*. "For the Father judges no one, but has committed all judgment to the Son" (John 5:22, page 1057).

(a) Christ will judge the believer's works at "the judgment seat of Christ" (2 Cor. 5:10, page 1168), to take place at the rapture of the church (Rev. 22:12, page 1316). Believers will be rewarded for their good works, but for their bad works they will suffer the loss of rewards, not the loss of salvation (1 Cor. 3:11–15, page 1149). This is evidence that works alone cannot merit the salvation of God.
(b) Christ will judge all nations of the world at the beginning of His millennial reign (Matt. 25:31–46, page 976).
(c) Christ will judge the wicked at the end of His millennial reign (Rev. 20:11–15, page 1313).

(3) *in morals.*

(a) "You shall have no other gods before Me."
(b) "You shall not make for yourself a carved image."
(c) "You shall not take the name of the LORD your God in vain."
(d) "Honor your father and your mother."
(e) "You shall not murder."
(f) "You shall not commit adultery."
(g) "You shall not steal."
(h) "You shall not bear false witness against your neighbor."
(i) "You shall not covet" (Ex. 20:1–17, page 79).

To know God's immutable will, you must know His Word.
See Romans 12:1, 2, page 1142, for **Point 29-C: God's Will Is Good, Acceptable, and Perfect.**

15 So now ^Rwe call the proud blessed,
For those who do wickedness are
^Traised up;   Ps. 73:12 · Lit. *built*
They even tempt God and go free.' "

A Book of Remembrance

16 Then those ^Rwho feared the LORD
^Rspoke to one another,   Ps. 66:16 · Heb. 3:13
And the LORD listened and heard *them;*
So ^Ra book of remembrance was
written before Him   Ps. 56:8
For those who fear the LORD
And who meditate on His name.

17 "They^R shall be Mine," says the LORD of
hosts,   Ex. 19:5
"On the day that I make them My
^Rjewels.^T   Is. 62:3 · Lit. *special treasure*
And ^RI will spare them   Ps. 103:13
As a man spares his own son who
serves him."

18 ^RThen you shall again discern
Between the righteous and the wicked,
Between one who serves God   [Ps. 58:11]
And one who does not serve Him.

The Great Day of God

4 "For behold, ^Rthe day is coming,
Burning like an oven,   [2 Pet. 3:7]
And all the proud, yes, all who do
wickedly will be ^Rstubble.   Obad. 18

And the day which is coming shall burn
them up,"
Says the LORD of hosts,
"That will ^Rleave them neither root nor
branch.   Amos 2:9
2 But to you who ^Rfear My name   Mal. 3:16
The ^RSun of Righteousness shall arise
With healing in His wings;   Luke 1:78
And you shall go out
And grow fat like stall-fed calves.
3 ^RYou shall trample the wicked,
For they shall be ashes under the soles
of your feet
On the day that I do *this,*"
Says the LORD of hosts.   Mic. 7:10

4 "Remember the ^RLaw of Moses, My
servant,   Ex. 20:3
Which I commanded him in Horeb for
all Israel,
With the statutes and judgments.
5 Behold, I will send you ^RElijah the
prophet   [Matt. 11:14; 17:10-13]
^RBefore the coming of the great and
dreadful day of the LORD.   Joel 12:31
6 And he will turn
The hearts of the fathers to the
children,
And the hearts of the children to their
fathers,
Lest I come and ^Rstrike the earth with
^Ra curse."   Is. 11:4 · Zech. 5:3

The
New Testament
of
Our Lord and Savior
Jesus Christ

The New King James Version

THE GOSPEL ACCORDING TO
Matthew

The book of Matthew was written to convince Jews that Jesus is the Messiah and that He came to build a kingdom that was based on spiritual principles that would survive material empires. Thus, the word *kingdom* is used more than a hundred times in Matthew. One can never understand this great Gospel until he realizes that in Jesus' day there was a great hunger for a kingdom that would overthrow the Roman empire, which controlled Palestine. Many Jews were looking for a political Messiah who would defeat Rome and establish Israel as the reigning power. The people of that day, both rulers and common folk, saw in Jesus a possible Messiah of this type. Matthew was addressed to the Jews to show them that Jesus was indeed the Messiah, but that His kingdom was not of this world.

SUMMARY STATEMENT. Matthew presents Jesus Christ as the Messiah who fulfills the Old Testament prophecies, stressing His kingship, His kingdom and the principles of that kingdom.

HOW MATTHEW FITS INTO THE BIBLE. Matthew is the bridge between the Old and New Testaments. It is traditionally thought to be the oldest Gospel, but whether it is or not, it is definitely in the right position, since it ties the strong Jewish flavor of the Old Testament into the more universal outlook of the New. The genealogy in chapter one immediately throws the reader back to Abraham, David and the earthly people of God.

In his concern to convince the Jews that Jesus is the Messiah, the One promised by God, Matthew employs the Old Testament extensively. More than one hundred quotations from, and allusions to the Old Testament are used. Most Bible students agree that there are five major discourses in Matthew; it might have been that the author was trying to structure his presentation after the five books of Moses, a sort of New Testament Pentateuch.

HOW MATTHEW FITS TOGETHER. Matthew may be divided in the following seven sections: (1) The King's Pedigree and Birth (chs. 1, 2); (2) The King's Early Ministry (3, 4); (3) The King's Sermon on the Mount (5—7); (4) The King's Power, Program and Rejection (8—14); (5) The King's Ministry after Rejection (14—23); (6) The King's Olivet Discourse (24, 25); (7) The King's Death, Resurrection and Great Commission (26, 27).

The Gospel was probably written in A.D. 65, though some reputable Bible scholars contend that it could have been written ten or even twenty years earlier. Some liberal scholars place it after the destruction of Jerusalem, but they do this in order to convert prophecy into history, claiming that Matthew wrote *after* the events that he prophesied. This is sheer unbelief.

AUTHORSHIP. Matthew, the writer of this first Gospel, was one of the disciples of Jesus. His name appears in the four lists where His apostles are named (Matt. 10:3, Mark 3:18, Luke 6:15, Acts 1:13). His name means "gift of Jehovah" (he was also called Levi). A tax collector by profession, serving under Herod Antipas in the region of Capernaum, he was exercising his office when Jesus called him (9:9; 10:3). His function was to collect taxes on merchandise, the fishing industry, and other businesses in the area. Tradition contends that Matthew wrote this Gospel before Mark and Luke. Origen accepted this tradition and so did Papias and Augustine. This also harmonizes with the findings of Irenaeus, who listed Matthew's Gospel as the first; the Muratorian canon concurs. Many Bible students give importance to the statement of Eusebius, who quoted Papias (early second century) to the effect that Matthew wrote this Gospel.

Matthew's handling of historical events and the report of Jesus' discourses has no parallel in sacred or secular writings. He presents Jesus as human and divine, Son of God and the son of Abraham. The Savior is called by many names: King of the Jews, Immanuel, Son of God, Son of Man, Son of David, Servant of God, Lord, and Christ. Matthew concentrates on letting Jesus speak for Himself, so the book sparkles with the many discourses of the Lord. In these utterances Jesus reveals how He fulfills the law, how He redeems man from his sins, how He builds His church, how He gives the world a glimpse of the Father. In these many talks Jesus reveals the nature of demons, sickness and death, and how He is the victor over these difficult encounters that make life sad and lonely.

Of the twelve thousand days that Jesus lived on the earth, the Gospels record only fifty-one days, so the writers were selective with their material. Matthew reveals a beautiful blend of particularism and universalism; that is, he talks about Jesus and His Jewish heritage, but he also

includes the Gentile world. Jesus was a Jew, and came to His own, but this Gospel does not fail to recognize that when Jesus was born, it was Gentiles who came from the east to offer their gifts to the Jewish babe. And also, when the life of the baby was in danger from Herod, it was a Gentile land, Egypt, that offered Him asylum and protection. And though the Gospel of Matthew overflows with Jewish allusions and customs, it ends with the command that the Good News should be preached to all nations; we know it as the Great Commission.

The inspiration of the Holy Spirit alone could cause Matthew to remember and record the many incidents and discourses narrated in his Gospel, although he may have taken notes as well. So according to Matthew, the human Christ, who could suffer, grow weary, and be tempted is also the Christ who was virgin-born, performed miracles as only God could do, went to the cross and performed the miracle of the atonement, rose from the dead on the third day, and will return visibly and victoriously. This is the Christ that Matthew presents. He is the central theme of this wonderful book.

—A.M.

The Genealogy of Jesus Christ

THE book of the genealogy of Jesus Christ, ᴿthe Son of David, ᴿthe Son of Abraham: Ps. 132:11; Jer. 23:5 · Gen. 12:3; 22:18
2 Abraham begot Isaac, Isaac begot Jacob, and Jacob begot Judah and his brothers.
3 Judah begot Perez and Zerah by Tamar, Perez begot Hezron, and Hezron begot Ram.
4 Ram begot Amminadab, Amminadab begot Nahshon, and Nahshon begot Salmon.
5 Salmon begot Boaz by Rahab, Boaz begot Obed by Ruth, Obed begot Jesse,
6 and ᴿJesse begot David the king.

David the king begot Solomon by her *who had been the wife* of Uriah.   Is. 11:1, 10
7 Solomon begot Rehoboam, Rehoboam begot Abijah, and Abijah begot *Asa.
8 Asa begot Jehoshaphat, Jehoshaphat begot Joram, and Joram begot Uzziah.
9 Uzziah begot Jotham, Jotham begot ᴿAhaz, and Ahaz begot Hezekiah.   2 Kin. 15:38
10 Hezekiah begot Manasseh, Manasseh begot *Amon, and Amon begot Josiah.
11 Josiah begot ᵀJeconiah and his brothers about the time they were ᴿcarried away to Babylon.   Or Coniah or Jehoiachin · 2 Kin. 24:14-16
12 And after they were brought to Babylon, ᴿJeconiah begot Shealtiel, and Shealtiel begot ᴿZerubbabel.   1 Chr. 3:17 · Ezra 3:2
13 Zerubbabel begot Abiud, Abiud begot Eliakim, and Eliakim begot Azor.
14 Azor begot Zadok, Zadok begot Achim, and Achim begot Eliud.
15 Eliud begot Eleazar, Eleazar begot Matthan, and Matthan begot Jacob.
16 And Jacob begot Joseph the husband of ᴿMary, of whom was born Jesus who is called Christ.   Matt. 13:55

17 So all the generations from Abraham to David *are* fourteen generations, from David until the captivity in Babylon *are* fourteen generations, and from the captivity in Babylon until the Christ *are* fourteen generations.

Christ Born of Mary

18 Now the birth of Jesus Christ was as follows: After His mother Mary was betrothed to Joseph, ᴿbefore they came together, she was found with child of the Holy Spirit.   Is 7:14; 49:1, 5
19 Then Joseph her husband, being ᵀa just *man*, and not wanting ᴿto make her a public example, was minded to put her away secretly.   an upright · Deut. 24:1
20 But while he thought about these things, behold, an angel of the Lord appeared to him in a dream, saying, "Joseph, son of David, do not be afraid to take to you Mary your wife, ᴿfor that which is ᵀconceived in her is of the Holy Spirit.   Luke 1:35 · Lit. begotten
21 "And she will bring forth a Son, and you shall call His name JESUS, for He ᴿwill save His people from their sins."   Rom. 5:18, 19
22 So all this was done that it might be fulfilled which was spoken by the Lord through the prophet, saying:
23 ᴿ"Behold,* the virgin shall be with child, and bear a Son, and they shall call His name Immanuel," which is translated, "God with us."   Is. 7:14
24 Then Joseph, being aroused from sleep, did as the angel of the Lord commanded him and took to him his wife,
25 and did not know her till she had brought forth her firstborn *Son. And he ᴿcalled His name JESUS.   Luke 2:7, 21

1:6 Words in italic type have been added for clarity. They are not found in the original Greek.
1:7 NU Asaph
1:10 NU Amos

1:23 Words in oblique type in the New Testament are quoted from the Old Testament.
1:25 NU a Son

Wise Men from the East

▼ **37-A. The World into Which Christ Came**

2 Now after ᴿJesus was ᴿborn in Bethlehem of Judea in the days of Herod the king, behold, ᵀwise men from the East came to Jerusalem,   Luke 2:4–7 • Mic. 5:2 • Gr. *magoi*
2 saying, "Where is He who has been born King of the Jews? For we have seen His star in the East and have come to worship Him."
3 When Herod the king heard *this*, he was troubled, and all Jerusalem with him.

4 And when he had gathered all ᴿthe chief ▽ priests and ᴿscribes of the people together, ᴿhe inquired of them where the Christ was to be born.   2 Chr. 36:14 • 2 Chr. 34:13 • Mal. 2:7
5 So they said to him, "In Bethlehem of Judea, for thus it is written by the prophet:

6 '*But*ᴿ *you, Bethlehem, in the land of Judah,*   Mic. 5:2; John 7:42
Are not the least among the rulers of Judah;
For out of you shall come a Ruler Who will shepherd My people Israel.'"

37-A. The World into Which Christ Came (Matthew 2:1–12)—The coming of the promised Messiah into the world, to die for man's sin, was truly God's great gift to mankind. The circumstances of the waiting world at that time were ideal for the long-awaited arrival of the Christ. Scripture says, "When the fullness of the time had come, God sent forth His Son" (Gal. 4:4, page 1182).

(1) *His birth in Bethlehem prophesied.* Herod asked the religious leaders of Israel where Christ was to be born (vv. 3–6). They quoted Micah's prophecy (Mic. 5:2, page 890), given seven hundred years before, naming Bethlehem as the place from which the "Ruler in Israel" was to come. The virgin birth of the Savior was also prophesied (Is. 7:14, page 649). It should not seem strange to us that the conception of the unique Son of God should occur in a miraculous way.

(2) *Childhood of Christ.* In His infinite wisdom, God permitted the childhood of Jesus to pass us by quietly. These are "silent years." We are given only the account in Luke's Gospel concerning Jesus, the twelve-year-old boy, who already was

(a) amazing the rabbis with His questions and answers;
(b) completely conscious of His unique relationship to God the Father;
(c) fully aware of His unique mission (Luke 2:41–52, page 1013).

All non-biblical stories of the boy Jesus are fabricated and of late origin. Jesus did no miracles as a boy; John's Gospel makes that fact unmistakably clear (John 2:11, page 1051).

(3) *Greek language and culture.* The Roman chief captain asked Paul, "Can you speak Greek?" (Acts 21:37, page 1117). The language of the Western world in New Testament times was Greek (though some early church fathers claimed that Matthew originally wrote his Gospel in Hebrew or Aramaic). The reason was that from 336 to 323 B.C. Alexander the Great conquered Persia, Egypt, and the Middle Eastern world, spreading the Greek language and culture to all conquered areas. In the providence of God, this provided an almost universal language that would carry the message of God's salvation in Christ throughout the Mediterranean and Middle Eastern world. That the New Testament was written in Greek, the international language of the day (in contrast to the Old Testament which was written in Hebrew, a language of only one people), fit God's purpose to form the church out of believers of all kindreds, nations, and peoples (Acts 2:4–12, page 1088). At this same time, many Greek intellectuals had lost faith in the pagan gods and goddesses of Mt. Olympus, and at last were open and longing for a faith that would meet their real needs and answer their questions about life. Such a faith came with Christianity (Acts 17:15–34, page 1111).

(4) *The rule of Augustus Caesar.* During the reign of Augustus Caesar (31 B.C.—A.D. 14), the world saw a brief era of peace, unparalleled in history, called the *Pax Romana*. In the providence of God it allowed the first missionaries to travel safely throughout the Roman world. At the time of Christ's ministry, Pontius Pilate was governing Judea (including Jerusalem) from his headquarters, the Roman-dominated coastal city of Caesarea.

(5) *The rule of Herod.* Herod the Great ruled by intrigue and murder from 37 to 4 B.C. He was an Idumean, descended from the Edomites, a people south of the Dead Sea who had often treated the Jews cruelly (Amos 1:11, 12, page 874). Herod was the great builder of Palestine. He constructed the architectural and engineering marvel of the mountain fortress of Masada (on a cliff thirteen hundred feet high), as well as the Herodium, and the city of Caesarea with its amazing man-made harbor. He also built the three great battle towers by the Jaffa Gate in Jerusalem, the Praetorian Fortress (the "Antonia," named for Mark Antony), and the Jewish temple where Christ sometimes taught. He had the temple sanctuary dramatically refaced and then set about rebuilding all of the porticos, walls, courtyards, and outer buildings of the second temple.

But Herod is more commonly known for the series of murders he committed to protect his throne. He murdered Antipater, his eldest son and heir, his wife Mariam, and two more of their sons, and then hunted down the survivors of the previous royal family—the Hasmoneans (descendants of the Maccabees). Satan had a servant well prepared to kill the infants of Bethlehem as he sought to murder the newly born Christ child (Matt. 2:16, page 932; cf. Rev. 12:4, page 1305).

(Point 37-A continued on next page)

▽ 7 Then Herod, when he had secretly called the ᵀwise men, determined from them what time the ᴿstar appeared.   Gr. *magoi* · Num. 24:17

8 And he sent them to Bethlehem and said, "Go and search carefully for the young Child, and when you have found *Him*, bring back word to me, that I may come and worship Him also."

9 When they heard the king, they departed; and behold, the star which they had seen in the East went before them, till it came and stood over where the young Child was.

10 When they saw the star, they rejoiced with exceedingly great joy.

11 And when they had come into the house, they saw the young Child with Mary His mother, and fell down and worshiped Him. And when they had opened their treasures, ᴿthey presented gifts to Him: gold, frankincense, and myrrh.   Is. 60:6

12 Then, being divinely warned in a dream that they should not return to Herod, they ▲ departed for their own country another way.

The Flight into Egypt

13 Now when they had departed, behold, an angel of the Lord appeared to Joseph in a dream, saying, "Arise, take the young Child and His mother, flee to Egypt, and stay there until I bring you word; for ᴿHerod will seek the young Child to destroy Him."   Matt. 2:16

14 When he arose, he took the young Child and His mother by night and departed for Egypt,

15 and was there until the death of Herod, that it might be fulfilled which was spoken by the Lord through the prophet, saying, ᴿ"*Out of Egypt I called My Son.*"   Hos. 11:1

Massacre of the Innocents

16 Then Herod, when he saw that he was deceived by the wise men, was exceedingly angry; and he sent forth and put to death all the male children who were in Bethlehem and in all its districts, from two years old and under, according to the time which he had determined from the wise men.

17 Then was fulfilled what was spoken by ᴿJeremiah the prophet, saying: Jer. 31:15

18 "*Aᴿ voice was heard in Ramah,
Lamentation, weeping, and great
    mourning,
Rachel weeping for her children,
Refusing to be comforted,
Because they are no more.*"   Jer. 31:15

The Home in Nazareth

19 Now when Herod was dead, behold, an angel of the Lord appeared in a dream to Joseph in Egypt,

20 ᴿsaying, "Arise, take the young Child and His mother, and go to the land of Israel, for those who ᴿsought the young Child's life are dead."   Luke 2:39 · Matt. 2:16

21 Then he arose, took the young Child and His mother, and came into the land of Israel.

22 But when he heard that Archelaus was reigning over Judea instead of his father Herod, he was afraid to go there. And being warned by God in a ᴿdream, he turned aside into the region of Galilee.   Matt. 2:12, 13, 19

23 And he came and dwelt in a city called ᴿNazareth, that it might be fulfilled ᴿwhich was spoken by the prophets, "He shall be called a Nazarene."   John 1:45, 46 · Judg. 13:5

John the Baptist Prepares the Way

39–A. The Baptism of John the Baptist   ▼

3 In those days John the Baptist came preaching in the wilderness of Judea,

2 and saying, "Repent, for ᴿthe kingdom of heaven is at hand!"   Dan. 2:44; Mal. 4:5, 6

(Point 37-A continued from previous page)

(6) *Judaism.* The Jewish world of the day was divided into various parties and sects. Chief among these were:

(a) The Pharisees (meaning "separated ones")—scrupulously legalistic in their religion, and seeking righteousness through their works (Matt. 23:2, 3, page 971).

(b) The Sadducees—religious liberals of the day. They accepted the first five books of Moses, but denied the other writings, the possibility of resurrection, and the existence of angels (Matt. 22:23, 29, page 970; Acts 23:8, page 1119).

(c) The Herodians—members of the Jewish political party that backed the Herodian family reign. They favored home rule and compromised with Rome in order to keep the peace (Mark 3:6, page 987).

(d) The high priesthood—descended from the new Hasmonean family line which led the fight against the Syrians in 168–165 B.C. The high priest, as the religious ruler of Israel, was always from the tribe of Levi, and headed the Sanhedrin (the important council of seventy). He also had great legal and civil power. Annas and his son-in-law, Caiaphas, were high priests during Christ's ministry, Caiaphas serving at the time of the Crucifixion (John 18:13, 14, 19–23, page 1079).

See Mark 11:7–11, page 998, for Point 37-B: The Earthly Ministry of Jesus.

39-A. The Baptism of John the Baptist (Matthew 3:1–12)—The mother of John the Baptist, Elizabeth, was the cousin of Mary, the mother of Jesus, so, John the Baptist and Jesus were second cousins (Luke 1:36, page 1010). John the Baptist must not be confused with John the apostle. John the Baptist was beheaded in A.D.

(Point 39-A continued on next page)

▽ 3 For this is he who was spoken of by the prophet Isaiah, saying:

R "The voice of one crying in the
    wilderness: Is. 40:3
R 'Prepare the way of the LORD;
    Make His paths straight.' "   Luke 1:76

4 Now John himself was clothed in camel's hair, with a leather belt around his waist; and his food was locusts and wild honey.

5 Then Jerusalem, all Judea, and all the region around the Jordan went out to him

6 Rand were baptized by him in the Jordan, confessing their sins.   Acts 19:4, 18

7 But when he saw many of the Pharisees and Sadducees coming to his baptism, he said to them, "Brood of vipers! Who warned you to flee from the wrath to come?

8 "Therefore bear fruits worthy of repentance,

9 "and do not think to say to yourselves, ▽ R'We have Abraham as our father.' For I say to you that God is able to raise up children to Abraham from these stones.   John 8:33

10 "And even now the ax is laid to the root of the trees. RTherefore every tree which does not bear good fruit is cut down and thrown into the fire.   Matt. 7:19

11 R"I indeed baptize you with water unto repentance, but He who is coming after me is mightier than I, whose sandals I am not worthy to carry. He will baptize you with the Holy Spirit *and fire.   Acts 2:4, 33

12 R"His winnowing fan is in His hand, and He will thoroughly clean out His threshing floor, and gather His wheat into the barn; but He will Rburn up the chaff with unquenchable fire."   Mal. 3:3 • Matt. 13:30 ▲

3:11 M omits and fire

(Point 39-A continued from previous page)

28 by Herod Antipas, while John the apostle outlived all the other apostles (dying in A.D. 99) and was the writer of the Gospel of John, three epistles, and the book of Revelation. Let us consider these elements in the career of John the Baptist:

(1) John's birth announcement (Luke 1:13–17, page 1009). When Zacharias entered the temple alone to burn incense, an angel spoke to him, "Do not be afraid." This broke a silence of over four hundred years from God (and His angels and prophets) to the Jewish people. The angel announced to Zacharias that he would have a son, to be named John, who would "make ready a people prepared for the Lord"—the Christ who was to come (Luke 1:17, page 1009; cf. Mal. 3:1, page 924).

(2) John's mission (vv. 1–4, page 932). John was selected by God, from before his birth, to be the one to announce the coming of the Messiah (Luke 1:13–17, page 1009). Isaiah the prophet, in 700 B.C., prophesied of a "voice" that would come from the Judean wilderness and desert, announcing the arrival of the long-awaited messianic kingdom (Is. 40:3–5, page 679). Isaiah spoke of straightening the crooked places in preparation for the great King. Thus John the Baptist had the task of proclaiming that the Messiah's kingdom was imminent and that all should make their hearts ready by repenting of their sins (vv. 1, 2, page 932).

(3) John's identity (Mark 9:11–13, page 995). The Old Testament closes with the book of Malachi, which predicts the coming of the Messiah and His messenger (Mal. 3:1–3, page 924). Christ and the angel both affirm that John fitted the "Elijah" description as the announcer of the Christ, at His first advent, when John went before Christ "in the spirit and power of Elijah" (Luke 1:17, page 1009; cf. Mark 9:13, page 995).

(4) John's baptism (v. 6, page 933). John's baptism was an outward washing by water depicting an inward cleansing of the soul by repentance. John preached repentance in preparation for Christ's coming; he warned of the awful consequences of unforgiven sin (vv. 2, 10, 12). He preached in the power of the Holy Spirit (Luke 1:15, page 1009), and multitudes responded. They confessed their sins and came for baptism. The exact manner of John's baptism has been debated for many centuries. The Greek word baptizo means "dip" or "immerse," and symbolized that God forgave and washed away the sin of the one who repented and confessed to God. This baptism was not yet "into Christ" since the Savior had not yet died for man's sins (Acts 2:37, 38, page 1089).

(5) John's warnings.

(a) To the self-righteous Pharisees and Sadducees he spoke with special force, calling them a "brood of vipers" and warning them that they too were sinners (v. 7).

(b) To the casual listener he said that repentant people must "therefore bear fruits worthy of repentance" (v. 8).

(c) To those who relied on their Jewish birth he said that God could raise up other children of Abraham from stones (v. 9).

(d) To the crowds who procrastinated he spoke urgently, saying that the farmer, God, has the ax ready to chop the tree, Israel (v. 10).

See Matthew 3:13–17, page 934, for Point 39-B: The Baptism of Jesus.

John Baptizes Jesus

▼ 39-B. The Baptism of Jesus

13 Then Jesus came from Galilee to John at the Jordan to be baptized by him.

14 And John *tried to* prevent Him, saying, "I need to be baptized by You, and are You coming to me?"

15 But Jesus answered and said to him, "Permit it to be so now, for thus it is fitting for us to fulfill all righteousness." Then he allowed Him.

16 When He had been baptized, Jesus came up immediately from the water; and behold, the heavens were opened to Him, and He saw the ᴿSpirit of God descending like a dove and alighting upon Him.   Is. 11:2; 42:1

17 ᴿAnd suddenly a voice *came* from heaven, saying, ᴿ"This is My beloved Son, in

▲ whom I am well pleased."   John 12:28 · Ps. 2:7

Satan Tempts Jesus

▼ 12-E. Satan: The Tempter

4 Then Jesus was led up by the Spirit into the wilderness to be tempted by the devil.

2 And when He had fasted forty days and forty nights, afterward He was hungry.

3 Now when the tempter came to Him, he said, "If You are the Son of God, command that these stones become bread."

4 But He answered and said, "It is written, ▽ ᴿ'Man shall not live by bread alone, but by every word that proceeds from the mouth of God.'"   Deut. 8:3

5 Then the devil took Him up ᴿinto the holy city, set Him on the pinnacle of the temple,   Neh. 11:1, 18

6 and said to Him, "If You are the Son of God, throw Yourself down. For it is written:

ᴿ*He shall give His angels charge over you,'*   Ps. 91:11

and,

ᴿ*In their hands they shall bear you up, Lest you dash your foot against a stone.'"*   Ps. 91:12

7 Jesus said to him, "It is written again, *'You shall not tempt the LORD your God.'"*

8 Again, the devil took Him up on an exceedingly high mountain, and ᴿshowed Him all the kingdoms of the world and their glory.   [1 John 2:15–17]

9 And he said to Him, "All these things I will give You if You will fall down and worship me."

10 Then Jesus said to him, *"Away with you, Satan! For it is written, ᴿ*You shall*

4:7 Deut. 6:16

4:10 M *Get behind Me*

39-B. The Baptism of Jesus (Matthew 3:13–17)—John the Baptist's mother, Elizabeth, had surely told him at least part of the story concerning Jesus' birth and its angelic announcements (Luke 1:35–45, page 1010). He also must have known that Jesus had been born in Bethlehem, the prophesied birthplace of the Christ (Mic. 5:2, page 890). A heavenly voice instructed John that the Christ would be positively identified by a visible manifestation of the Holy Spirit, descending like a dove and remaining on Him (John 1:33, page 1050; Mark 1:10, 11, page 984; Is. 11:2, page 654). This final identifying sign appeared when Jesus came to John for baptism (vv. 16, 17).

(1) It was Jesus who came to John to be baptized (v. 13). Christ is an example to all believers. The rule of courtesy has always been that the lesser walks over to the greater; the one seeking mercy seeks out his master. Jesus did not wait for John to come to Him, but in humility He came to John to be baptized. As He said, "Thus it is fitting for us to fulfill all righteousness" (v. 15). Because He was not a sinner, Jesus did not need to repent. He came to be baptized because it was the right thing to do in order to identify Himself with the God-seekers in the land.

(2) Jesus actually was baptized by John (v. 15). If Christ submitted to baptism by John because it was the proper thing to do, how much more important it is that every convert to Christ "follow the Lord" in baptism when we, as sinners now cleansed, have been plainly directed to be baptized (Matt. 28:19, page 982). Baptism is a picture of the believer's faith in the death, burial, and resurrection of Jesus Christ (Rom. 6:4, 5, page 1134). Baptism is an outward symbol of an inward cleansing.

See Acts 2:41, 42, page 1090, for **Point 39-C: The Baptism of the Believer.**

12-E. Satan: The Tempter (Matthew 4:1–11)—The word *tempt* has a dual meaning: (1) to test, to search out, to try, to put to the proof; (2) to entice to commit evil. If God is the tempter, as He was when He tempted Abraham (Gen. 22:1, page 26), or if He Himself is tempted, as He was in the wilderness by the children of Israel (Ex. 17:2, page 77), then in such cases the word means to test, or to put to the proof. God never entices people or angels to commit evil, nor can He be enticed to sin, not by man or Satan or demons. "Let no one say when he is tempted [enticed to commit evil], 'I am tempted by God'; for God cannot be tempted by evil, nor does He Himself tempt anyone" to commit evil (James 1:12–15, page 1255). But Satan, demons, and fallen humanity can entice others to commit evil, because they are evil within. Before we examine the encounter between the God-Man and Satan, "the god of this age" (2 Cor. 4:4, page 1167), we must keep in mind certain biblical facts:

(Point 12-E continued on next page)

▽ *worship the LORD your God, and Him only you shall serve.'"*   Deut. 6:13; 10:20

▲ 11 Then the devil left Him, and behold, angels came and ministered to Him.

Jesus Begins His Galilean Ministry

12 Now when Jesus heard that John had been put in prison, He departed to Galilee. 13 And leaving Nazareth, He came and dwelt in Capernaum, which is by the sea, in the regions of Zebulun and Naphtali,

14 that it might be fulfilled which was spoken by Isaiah the prophet, saying:

15 *"The^R land of Zebulun and the land of Naphtali,*
By the way of the sea, beyond the Jordan,
Galilee of the Gentiles: Is. 9:1, 2
16 ^R*The people who sat in darkness have seen a great light,*

(Point 12-E continued from previous page)

(1) Jesus is God. God can be tested (Mal. 3:10, page 925), but He cannot be enticed to commit evil (James 1:13, page 1256).

(2) Jesus is more than mere man; He is not God and man separately, He is the God-Man (see Point 7-D, "Jesus Is the Father's Gift to Us," page 651; also Point 6-B, "He Was Unique in His Birth," page 1010). His God nature and His human nature were joined together, in the womb of the Virgin Mary, in such a way that the two natures were manifested in one person.

(3) "In Him there is no sin" (1 John 3:5, page 1280). Because He was not born of the seed of fallen Adam, His conception was a biological miracle (Luke 1:35, page 1010). Hence He is free of every sin.

(4) "Who committed no sin" (1 Pet. 2:22, page 1266). He never sinned in thought, word, or deed. "The lust of the flesh, the lust of the eyes, and the pride of life" (1 John 2:15-17, page 1279) were never a part of His humanity. He did only the will of His Father. God sent His only begotten Son "in the likeness of sinful flesh, on account of sin: He condemned sin in the flesh" (Rom. 8:3, page 1136).

(5) "Who knew no sin" (2 Cor. 5:21, page 1169). He never experienced sin; He never desired to sin. He "was in all points tempted as we are, yet without sin" (Heb. 4:15, page 1239).

(6) "Then Jesus was led up by the Spirit into the wilderness to be tempted of the devil" (v. 1). Satan did not plan this encounter with Jesus; it was according to the will of God and the work of the Holy Spirit (John 6:38, page 1059). Satan sought to corrupt the first Adam, tempting him through Eve. Adam fell. The last Adam, Jesus (1 Cor. 15:45, page 1162) sought Satan. In His humanity, in the wilderness, Jesus defeated the Devil. Satan is a defeated foe, and we know that "He [Jesus] who is in you [every believer] is greater than he [Satan] who is in the world" (1 John 4:4, page 1280).

(7) The purpose of His coming into the world was "that He might destroy the works of the devil" (1 John 3:8, page 1280). However, the judgment of Satan and his works will be final only at the end of the kingdom age (Rev. 20:7-10, page 1313). Then all of creation will be eternally free of Satan, his demons, and his evil works.

The three points on which Jesus was tempted were:

(1) "The lust of the flesh" (1 John 2:16, page 1279). Satan said to Jesus, "If You are the Son of God, command that these stones become bread" (v. 3). He tempted Jesus to act independently of God the Father and God the Holy Spirit, to satisfy a natural hunger in an unnatural way. Though Satan wanted Jesus to do the right thing in the wrong way, Jesus had no desire or inclination to obey the tempter and turn stones into bread.

Armed with the "sword of the Spirit, which is the word of God" (Eph. 6:17, page 1192), Jesus met Satan and defeated him. Let this great lesson edify you: when tempted by Satan, demons, or man, don't be afraid to use the "sword of the Spirit, which is the word of God," to resist the Devil (James 4:7, page 1259)! The Scripture that Jesus quoted in resisting the Devil is Deuteronomy 8:3 (page 189).

(2) "The pride of life" (1 John 2:16, page 1279). The Devil took Jesus up into Jerusalem, placing Him on the pinnacle of the temple and saying, "If You are the Son of God, throw Yourself down" (v. 6). Then Satan quoted from a prophetic psalm. In effect, he was saying:

(a) "Cast Yourself down and the people will know that You are the Messiah";

(b) "Prove to me that You trust the Father to deliver You. After all, 'in their hands they [the angels] shall bear you up, lest you dash your foot against a stone' " (cf. Ps. 91:11, 12, page 565).

Again, Jesus used the "sword of the Spirit" (Eph. 6:17, page 1192): "You shall not tempt the LORD your God" (Deut. 6:16, page 187).

(3) "The lust of the eyes" (1 John 2:16, page 1279)—the desire for what can be seen. The Devil took Jesus to a high mountain and showed Him "the kingdoms of the world and their glory" (v. 8). Satan was offering a shortcut to the kingdom apart from the Cross. Jesus would not have to wait; it would be His now, "if You will fall down and worship me" (v. 9). But Jesus said, "Away with you, Satan! For it is written, 'You shall worship the LORD your God, and Him only you shall serve' " (v. 10). The Scripture Jesus quoted to resist the Devil is Deuteronomy 6:13 (page 187). This sums up God's program for the believer: Come and worship God, then go and serve Him.

See 1 Peter 5:8, page 1269, for **Point 12-F: Satan: His Work.**

*And upon those who sat in the region
and shadow of death
Light has dawned."*   Luke 2:32

17 ᴿFrom that time Jesus began to preach
and to say, "Repent, for the kingdom of
heaven ᵀis at hand."   Mark 1:14, 15 • *has drawn near*

Four Fishermen Called as Disciples

18 And Jesus, walking by the Sea of Galilee,
saw two brothers, Simon ᴿcalled Peter, and
Andrew his brother, casting a net into the
sea; for they were fishermen.   John 1:40–42
19 Then He said to them, "Follow Me, and
ᴿI will make you fishers of men."   Luke 5:10
20 ᴿThey immediately left *their* nets and
followed Him.   Mark 10:28
21 Going on from there, He saw two other
brothers, James *the son* of Zebedee, and John
his brother, in the boat with Zebedee their
father, mending their nets. He called them,
22 and immediately they left the boat and
their father, and followed Him.

Jesus Heals a Great Multitude

23 And Jesus went about all Galilee, ᴿteaching in their synagogues, preaching ᴿthe gospel of the kingdom, ᴿand healing all kinds of
sickness and all kinds of disease among the
people.   Ps. 22:22 • [Matt. 24:14] • Mark 1:34

24 Then ᵀHis fame went throughout all
Syria; and they ᴿbrought to Him all sick
people who were afflicted with various diseases and torments, and those who were
demon-possessed, epileptics, and paralytics;
and He healed them.   Lit. *the report of Him* • Luke 4:40
25 Great multitudes followed Him—from
Galilee, and *from* ᵀDecapolis, Jerusalem, Judea, and beyond the Jordan.   Lit. *Ten Cities*

The Beatitudes

40-A. The Poor in Spirit   ▼

5 And seeing the multitudes, ᴿHe went up
on a mountain, and when He was seated
His disciples came to Him.   Mark 3:13
2 Then He opened His mouth and ᴿtaught
them, saying: [Matt. 7:29]

3 "Blessedᴿ *are* the poor in spirit,   Luke 6:20–23
   For theirs is the kingdom of heaven.   ▲

40-B. The Mourners   ▼

4 ᴿBlessed *are* those who mourn,
   For they shall be comforted.   Rev. 21:4   ▲

40-C. The Meek   ▼

5 ᴿBlessed *are* the meek,   Ps. 37:11
   For they shall inherit the earth.   ▲

40-A. The Poor in Spirit (Matthew 5:1–3)—"Blessed are the poor in spirit, for theirs is the kingdom of
heaven" (v. 3). The poor in spirit are empty of all spiritual pride; they know that spiritual pride is the spirit
of this age of which Satan is god (2 Cor. 4:4, page 1167).

To be poor in spirit is to have "a contrite and humble spirit" (Is. 57:15, page 697)—to be conscious of
your unworthiness. Peter demonstrated this quality when he fell at the knees of Jesus, saying, "Depart from
me, for I am a sinful man, O Lord!" (Luke 5:1–11, page 1018). The Pharisee of the parable boasted in his
religious pride, but the contrite and humble tax collector was truly "poor in spirit" (Luke 18:9–14, page 1037).

See Matthew 5:4, above, for **Point 40-B: The Mourners.**

40-B. The Mourners (Matthew 5:4)—"Blessed are those who mourn, for they shall be comforted" (v. 4). This
paradoxical Beatitude can be understood only by the believer. How can a bereaved person be blessed amid
grief? Because he knows that "weeping may endure for a night, but joy comes in the morning" (Ps. 30:5,
page 527), that God has promised to comfort the mourner in this life and in the life to come. Heaven's joys
will abundantly compensate for earth's sorrows.

We should also mourn for lost souls. Paul grieved for his "countrymen according to the flesh," and
longed desperately for their salvation (Rom. 9:1–5, page 1139). Some lost souls lament their life of sin when
they repent and believe on the Lord Jesus Christ as their personal Savior. The penitent publican "beat his
breast, saying, 'God be merciful to me a sinner!'" (Luke 18:13, page 1037). Mourning is a part of true
repentance. "Blessed are those who mourn, for they shall be comforted."

See Matthew 5:5, above, for **Point 40-C: The Meek.**

40-C. The Meek (Matthew 5:5)—"Blessed are the meek [gentle], for they shall inherit the earth" (v. 5; Ps.
37:11, page 533). The philosophy of the world is the exact opposite of this Beatitude. People of the world
consider the meek person to be weak and cowardly, a Caspar Milquetoast to be treated with contempt. The
most gentle, meek, humble person that ever lived on this earth was the Lord Jesus Christ, who said, "I am
gentle and lowly [humble] in heart, and you [that come to Me] will find rest for your souls" (Matt. 11:28–30,
page 952). This gentle Son of God entered the temple as the Jews were preparing for the Passover and the
Feast of Unleavened Bread (Ex. 12:1–51, page 69). He overturned the tables of the moneychangers, and with
a whip of cords He drove out those who sold oxen, sheep, and doves in the sanctity of the temple. He said,
"Do not make My Father's house a house of merchandise!" (John 2:13–16, page 1051). Was this the act of

(Point 40-C continued on next page)

▼ **40-D. The Hungry and Thirsty**   **40-E. The Merciful**   ▼

6 Blessed *are* those who ᴿhunger and
thirst for righteousness,   Luke 1:53   7 Blessed *are* the merciful,
▲   ᴿFor they shall be filled. [Is. 55:1; 65:13]   ᴿFor they shall obtain mercy.   Ps. 41:1 ▲

(Point 40-C continued from previous page)
a weak and cowardly man? Yet He is the Man who said, "Blessed are the meek, for they shall inherit the earth" (v. 5).

To know the characteristics of a truly meek (gentle) person, study this passage: "Therefore I ask that you do not lose heart at my tribulations for you, which is your glory. For this reason I bow my knees to the Father of our Lord Jesus Christ, from whom the whole family in heaven and earth is named, that He would grant you, according to the riches of His glory, to be strengthened with might through His Spirit in the inner man, that Christ may dwell in your hearts through faith; that you, being rooted and grounded in love, may be able to comprehend with all the saints what is the width and length and depth and height—to know the love of Christ which passes knowledge; that you may be filled with all the fullness of God" (Eph. 3:13-19, page 1189).

No, the meek are not weak; they are "strong in the Lord and in the power of His might" (Eph. 6:10, page 1192)!

See Matthew 5:6, above, for **Point 40-D: The Hungry and Thirsty.**

40-D. The Hungry and Thirsty (Matthew 5:6)—"Blessed are those who hunger and thirst for righteousness, for they shall be filled" (v. 6). We have often heard it said that the world is hungry for the gospel of the grace of God. But if this were so, the whole world would be saved in a very short time. The truth is that people of the world hunger and thirst, not for righteousness, but to satisfy the lust of the flesh, the lust of the eyes, and the pride of life (1 John 2:16, 17, page 1279). This yields no lasting happiness. By faith Moses chose to suffer affliction alongside God's people, rather than enjoy the passing happiness and fleeting pleasures of sin. The happiness of sin is short-lived, but the happiness of the godly life is eternal (Heb. 11:23-29, page 1249).

The Scriptures describe two kinds of righteousness:

(1) Legal or self-righteousness, which is man's vain effort to establish his own righteousness by his own works—works of the law (Rom. 10:1-3, page 1140). Such "law works" cannot save (Titus 3:5, page 1231; Eph. 2:8, 9, page 1187); they produce only self-righteousness, which in the sight of God is "filthy rags" (Is. 64:6, page 703).

(2) The righteousness of God in Christ. "For Christ is the end of the law for righteousness to everyone who believes" (Rom. 10:4, page 1140). Faith alone brings lasting happiness. "For with the heart one believes unto righteousness, and with the mouth confession is made unto salvation" (Rom. 10:10, page 1140). Believers live the righteous life, but they do so not in order to *be* saved, but because they know they *are* saved. Happiness is salvation's reward; in this life there is no greater joy. And there is even better to come: John said, "We know that when He is revealed [when Jesus comes again], we shall be like Him, for we shall see Him as He is" (1 John 3:2, page 1279). We shall see Him in all His glory. This will be heavenly happiness.

See Matthew 5:7, above, for **Point 40-E: The Merciful.**

40-E. The Merciful (Matthew 5:7)—"Blessed are the merciful, for they shall obtain mercy" (v. 7). This Beatitude does not mean that, if you show mercy to people, they in turn will show mercy to you. Some will, but not all; some may even persecute you in return. We cannot expect to receive mercy from those who do not know our merciful Savior. Jesus Christ showed mercy throughout His earthly ministry. He healed the sick, He cleansed the lepers, and He made the dumb speak, the deaf hear, the blind see, and the lame walk. He raised the dead and fed the multitudes. He never failed to show mercy, but did He obtain mercy from the people? No, the Roman army, the religious leaders, and many of their followers joined efforts to put Him to death. They showed only religious hatred for God the Son (Matt. 26 and 27, page 977; cf. Is. 53:1-12, page 693). "Blessed are the merciful, for they shall obtain mercy"—but not from sinful humanity!

We are to show mercy, knowing well that the recipient may never show mercy in return. We are to bestow it in the name of our merciful Christ, who Himself will reward us in this life and in heaven. An illustration is the parable of the Good Samaritan, spoken by Jesus in answer to a lawyer who asked, "And who is my neighbor?" (Luke 10:29, page 1027). Jesus told of a man traveling from Jerusalem to Jericho who was robbed, wounded, and left half dead by thieves. A priest came by and saw the man, but did not stop to help; he showed no mercy. A Levite also came along, stopped to look, then continued on his journey; he showed no mercy. But a Samaritan saw him, had compassion on him, and helped him without expecting anything in return. Jesus asked the lawyer, "So which of these three do you think was neighbor to him who fell among the thieves?" When the lawyer answered, "He who showed mercy on him," Jesus said, "Go and do likewise" (Luke 10:25-37, page 1026). "Blessed are the merciful, for they shall obtain mercy."

See Matthew 5:8, page 938, for **Point 40-F: The Pure in Heart.**

▼ **40-F. The Pure in Heart**

8 ᴿBlessed *are* the pure in heart,   Ps. 15:2; 24:4
▲   For ᴿthey shall see God.   1 Cor. 13:12

▼ **40-G. The Peacemakers**

9 Blessed *are* the peacemakers,
▲   For they shall be called sons of God.

▼ **40-H. The Persecuted**

10 ᴿBlessed *are* those who are persecuted
    for righteousness' sake,   1 Pet. 3:14
    For theirs is the kingdom of heaven.

11 "Blessed are you when they revile and ▽
persecute you, and say all kinds of ᴿevil
against you falsely for My sake.   1 Pet. 4:14
12 ᴿ"Rejoice and be exceedingly glad, for
great is your reward in heaven, for ᴿso they
persecuted the prophets who were before
you.   1 Pet. 4:13, 14 • Acts 7:52 ▲

Believers Are Salt and Light

41-A. Believers Are Salt and Light   ▼

13 "You are the salt of the earth; ᴿbut if the
salt loses its flavor, how shall it be seasoned?

40-F. The Pure in Heart (Matthew 5:8)—"Blessed are the pure in heart, for they shall see God" (v. 8). The unsaved man cannot have a pure heart as long as he rejects the Lord Jesus as Savior (Acts 4:12, page 1091); the things of God are foolishness to him (1 Cor. 2:14, page 1166). The natural (unregenerate) "heart is deceitful above all things, and desperately wicked" (Jer. 17:9, page 730).

Who are the pure in heart?

(1) They are void of hypocrisy (Ps. 24:3-5, page 524).
(2) They have room for only one master, Christ (Matt. 6:24, page 943).
(3) They thirst for God as a deer thirsts for the water brook (Ps. 42:1, page 536).
(4) They have a newly created heart (2 Cor. 5:17, page 1169). David prayed, "Create in me a clean heart, O God" (Ps. 51:10, page 541).
(5) They confess and forsake all known sin (Prov. 28:13, page 621).
(6) They never try to hide sin from God (Ps. 32:5, page 529).
(7) They are able to sin but cannot be happy in sin (Ps. 51:1-4, page 541). When they sin, they repent and seek forgiveness (1 John 1:9, page 1278).
(8) They are spiritually minded; they have the mind of Christ (1 Cor. 2:15, 16, page 1149).

Only they will see God.
See Matthew 5:9, above, for **Point 40-G: The Peacemakers.**

40-G. The Peacemakers (Matthew 5:9)—"Blessed are the peacemakers, for they shall be called sons of God" (v. 9). To become this kind of peacemaker, we must first be "justified freely by His grace through the redemption that is in Christ Jesus" (Rom. 3:24, page 1131). To be justified is to be declared just by Almighty God because of the imputed righteousness of the Lord Jesus Christ. For God to declare us just, we must believe that

(1) Christ was offered on the cross to bear our sins (Heb. 9:28, page 1245);
(2) He was buried and in the tomb three days and nights;
(3) He rose again the third day according to the Scriptures (1 Cor. 15:3, 4, page 1161).

"Therefore, having been justified by faith, we have peace with God through our Lord Jesus Christ" (Rom. 5:1, page 1133). Now that we have peace with God, we can also share our faith with those at enmity against God (Rom. 8:7, 8, page 1137). A peacemaker is one who shares the gospel with those who are lost, showing them how they can have peace with God, after being justified by grace through faith in the Lord Jesus Christ (Eph. 2:8, 9, page 1187).
See Matthew 5:10-12, above, for **Point 40-H: The Persecuted.**

40-H. The Persecuted (Matthew 5:10-12)—"Blessed are those who are persecuted for righteousness' sake, for theirs is the kingdom of heaven" (vv. 10-12). This is a beautiful and vivid description of mature Christians. They are reviled and persecuted because they love the Lord Jesus Christ, and have been given the righteousness of God. How do mature Christians respond to such persecution? They rejoice and are exceedingly glad, because they know the speeches against them are lies. They also know that a great reward awaits them in heaven.
Persecution harassed the church from the start. The apostles were arrested and tried before the Sanhedrin for preaching Christ and for doing many miracles in His name. Some wanted to put them to death, and even though Gamaliel persuaded the Sanhedrin to let them go, they were beaten before their release.
But this did not stop them from preaching the gospel. "They departed from the presence of the council, rejoicing that they were counted worthy to suffer shame for His name" (Acts 5:33-42, page 1094).
See Master Outline 41, "Manifesting Kingdom Principles," page 54, for your next study.

41-A. Believers Are Salt and Light (Matthew 5:13-16)—Believers are salt and light (vv. 13-16). The teachings of Jesus are rich in parabolic metaphors. In these verses He uses two familiar and important elements of everyday life: salt and light.

(Point 41-A continued on next page)

▽ It is then good for nothing but to be thrown out and trampled underfoot by men. Luke 14:34

14 ᴿ"You are the light of the world. A city that is set on a hill cannot be hidden. [John 8:12]

15 "Nor do they light a lamp and put it under a basket, but on a lampstand, and it gives light to all *who are* in the house.

16 "Let your light so shine before men, that they may see your good works and ᴿglorify
▲ your Father in heaven.   [John 15:8]

Christ Fulfills the Law

▼ **41-B. Christ, the Law, and the Prophets**

17 ᴿ"Do not think that I came to destroy the Law or the Prophets. I did not come to destroy but to fulfill.   Rom. 10:4

18 "For assuredly, I say to you, ᴿtill heaven and earth pass away, one jot or one ᵀtittle will by no means pass from the law till all is fulfilled.   Luke 16:17 • The smallest stroke in a Heb. letter

19 ᴿ"Whoever therefore breaks one of the least of these commandments, and teaches ▽ men so, shall be called least in the kingdom of heaven; but whoever does and teaches *them*, he shall be called great in the kingdom of heaven.   [James 2:10]

20 "For I say to you, that unless your righteousness exceeds ᴿ*the righteousness* of the scribes and Pharisees, you will by no means enter the kingdom of heaven. [Rom. 10:3] ▲

Murder Begins in the Heart

▼ **41-C. The King's Moral Requirements** ▼

21 "You have heard that it was said to those of old, *'You shall not murder,* and whoever murders will be in danger of the judgment.'

22 "But I say to you that whoever is angry with his brother *without a cause shall be in

5:21 Ex. 20:13; Deut. 5:17

5:22 NU omits *without a cause*

(Point 41-A continued from previous page)

(1) "You are the salt of the earth" (v. 13). Salt is aseptic; it does not cure corruption, but it can prevent decay from occurring. It also seasons food, making it more palatable to the taste. Similarly, your Christian influence in the world—measured by your conformity to the Beatitudes—is like salt that checks the spread of sin (corruption). However, "if the salt loses its flavor, how shall it be seasoned [made salty]? It is then good for nothing" (v. 13). Jesus is warning believers not to lose their Christian influence—their saltiness—in this corrupt world.

(2) "You are the light of the world" (v. 14). Light does not shine to be seen, but to enable others to see—and what they are to see is not the Christian, but Christ. "Let your light so shine before men, that they may see your good works [not you] and glorify your Father [not you] in heaven" (v. 16). He said, "A city that is set on a hill cannot be hidden" (v. 14), suggesting a city whose streetlamps and home lights shine through the darkest night. This is a beautiful metaphor of a congregation filled with that spiritual light that comes from Him who is light, in whom "is no darkness at all" (1 John 1:5–7, page 1278). He added, "Nor do they light a lamp and put it under a basket, but on a lampstand and it gives light to all who are in the house" (v. 15). In this part of the metaphor, believers are taught to let their light shine, in their homes and elsewhere, to light the way to Jesus for the family and others. When congregated together, believers become a city on a hill, a beacon lighting the way to Jesus for all who can see the light.

See Matthew 5:17–20, above, for **Point 41-B: Christ, the Law, and the Prophets.**

41-B. Christ, the Law, and the Prophets (Matthew 5:17-20)—Christ said, "Do not think that I came to destroy . . . but to fulfill" the Law and the Prophets (v. 17). With these words He placed His seal of authenticity on the Old Testament—the Law and the Prophets. He is the only Man who kept the whole law of God from the moment of birth, never breaking the least commandment, not "one jot or one tittle" (v. 18). "For whoever shall keep the whole law, and yet stumble in one point, he is guilty of all" (James 2:10, page 1256). Jesus walked this earth for some thirty-three years, and even after all those years He could challenge His enemies, saying, "Which of you convicts Me of sin?" (John 8:46, page 1063). Pilate said of Jesus, "I find no fault in Him at all" (John 18:38, page 1080). There is only one righteousness that is worthy of the kingdom of heaven, and that is the righteousness of Christ, who "is the end of the law for righteousness to everyone who believes. . . . For with the heart one believes unto righteousness" (Rom. 10:4, 9, 10, page 1140).

See Matthew 5:21–32, above, for **Point 41-C: The King's Moral Requirements.**

41-C. The King's Moral Requirements (Matthew 5:21-32)—In this portion of the Sermon on the Mount, our Lord contrasts the false teachings of the scribes and the Pharisees with His authoritative teaching on the moral commandments. "He taught them as one having authority, and not as the scribes" (Matt. 7:29, page 947). He appealed to no higher authority, because there is none higher: His authority is sovereign, because He is the God-Man. "And the Word [God] became flesh and dwelt among us" (John 1:14, page 1049). In this part of His manifesto, the King disputed the scribes' and the Pharisees' interpretation of the moral law. Six times He made this challenging statement: "You have heard that it was said . . . But I say to you . . ." (vv. 21, 22). It is no wonder that when He ended the Sermon, "the people were astonished [amazed, speechless, dumbfounded] at His teaching" (Matt. 7:28, page 947).

(Point 41-C continued on next page)

▽ danger of the judgment. And whoever says to his brother, 'Raca!' shall be in danger of the council. But whoever says, 'You fool!' shall be in danger of ᵀhell fire.   Gr. *Gehenna*

23 "Therefore ᴿif you bring your gift to the altar, and there remember that your brother has something against you,   Matt. 8:4

24 "leave your gift there before the altar, and go your way. First be reconciled to your brother, and then come and offer your gift.

25 ᴿ"Agree with your adversary quickly, ᴿwhile you are on the way with him, lest your adversary deliver you to the judge, the judge hand you over to the officer, and you be thrown into prison.   Luke 12:58, 59 · [Is. 55:6]

26 "Assuredly, I say to you, you will by no means get out of there till you have paid the last ᵀpenny.   ¹⁄₆₄ of a day's wage, or 50¢

Adultery in the Heart

27 "You have heard that it was said *to those of old, ᴿ*You shall not commit adultery.*'   Ex. 20:14; Deut. 5:18

5:27 NU, M omit *to those of old*

28 "But I say to you that whoever ᴿlooks at ▽ a woman to lust for her has already committed adultery with her in his heart. Prov. 6:25

29 "If your right eye causes you to ᵀsin, ᴿpluck it out and cast *it* from you; for it is more profitable for you that one of your members perish, than for your whole body to be cast into hell.   Lit. *stumble* or *offend* · [Col. 3:5]

30 "And if your right hand causes you to ᵀsin, cut it off and cast *it* from you; for it is more profitable for you that one of your members perish, than for your whole body to be cast into hell.   Lit. *stumble* or *offend*

Marriage Is Sacred and Binding

31 "Furthermore it has been said, ᴿ'Whoever divorces his wife, let him give her a certificate of divorce.'   Deut. 24:1

32 "But I say to you that ᴿwhoever divorces his wife for any reason except ᵀsexual immorality causes her to commit adultery; and whoever marries a woman who is divorced commits adultery.   [Luke 16:18] · Or *fornication* ▲

(Point 41-C continued from previous page)

(1) "You have heard that it was said to those of old, 'You shall not murder' " (vv. 21–26). "You shall not murder" is the sixth commandment (Ex. 20:13, page 80). There is a difference between killing in general and murder. It is not murder when you kill to protect your home, family, self, or country. To murder is to kill a person with malice (premeditated or not). The Pharisees taught that as long as you did not shed innocent blood, that is, unlawfully take a life, you were innocent of transgressing the sixth commandment. Jesus corrected this interpretation, saying to the people and to the Pharisees, "But I say to you that whoever is angry with his brother without a cause shall be in danger of the judgment" (v. 22). Malice becomes murder in the heart, and God will judge such "murder." If you commit murder in your heart, or call a brother a fool, and later, while worshiping, you remember this transgression, you must leave the place of worship and make amends to your brother. It is as if you owed someone who is about to take you to court: settle it out of court, for you cannot escape your obligation. Paul said, "Owe no one anything except to love one another" (Rom. 13:8–10, page 1144). There is one debt that can never be paid in full—the debt of love. Without love it is impossible to fulfill God's holy law.

(2) "You have heard that it was said to those of old, 'You shall not commit adultery' " (vv. 27–30). The Pharisees defined adultery as the act itself; they must have thought that God did not know the heart of man. Again Jesus said to the people and the Pharisees, "But I say to you that whoever looks at a woman to lust for her has already committed adultery with her in his heart" (v. 28); correspondingly, a woman has already committed adultery who lusts in *her* heart. You can easily commit adultery in your heart, aided today by books, magazines, movies, and television, until your eyes, in Peter's words, are "full of adultery" (2 Pet. 2:12–17, page 1274). Your mind can control what the eye sees or what the hand touches. Job said, "I have made a covenant with my eyes; why then should I look upon a young woman?" (Job 31:1, page 498).

(3) "It has been said, 'Whoever divorces his wife, let him give her a certificate of divorce' " (v. 31). Here again, Jesus corrects the teachings of the scribes and the Pharisees: "But I say to you that whoever divorces his wife for any reason except sexual immorality causes her to commit adultery" (v. 32).

Later, when the Pharisees came to Jesus to test Him, asking, "Is it lawful for a man to divorce his wife for just any reason?" (Matt. 19:3, page 965), they were trying to get Jesus to contradict the teachings of Moses on divorce (Deut. 24:1–4, page 202). In their narrow, legalistic interpretation of Moses' law, a man could simply write out a note saying that he was divorcing his wife for some trivial reason. His response, however, was to repeat His earlier teaching—basing it on the Creation account written by Moses (Matt. 19:1–9, page 965)! (The apostle Paul gives still another reason for divorce, one which did not exist until after the formation of the New Testament church—1 Cor. 7:10–15, page 1152).

Adultery is a sin, but no sin of immorality is unpardonable. Jesus forgave an adulterous woman, saying, "Go and sin no more" (John 8:1–12, page 1062). To the Samaritan woman, married five times and now living with a man who was not her husband, Jesus revealed that He was the Messiah, inviting her to drink the water of eternal life so that she might never thirst again (John 4:1–42, page 1053).

See Matthew 5:33–37, page 941, for **Point 41-D: Christ Speaks on Oaths.**

Jesus Forbids Oaths

▼ 41-D. Christ Speaks on Oaths

33 "Again you have heard that it was said to those of old, 'You shall not swear falsely, but shall perform your oaths to the Lord.'

34 "But I say to you, do not swear at all: neither by heaven, for it is God's throne;

35 "nor by the earth, for it is His footstool; nor by Jerusalem, for it is the city of ᴿthe great King.   Ps. 48:2

36 "Nor shall you swear by your head, because you cannot make one hair white or black.

37 ᴿ"But let ᵀyour 'Yes' be 'Yes,' and your 'No,' 'No.' For whatever is more than these is

▲ from the evil one.   [Col. 4:6] • Lit. *your word be yes yes*

Go the Second Mile

41-E. Turn the Other Cheek, Go the Second Mile, and Love Your Enemy   ▼

38 "You have heard that it was said, *'An eye for an eye and a tooth for a tooth.'*

39 "But I tell you not to resist an evil person. ᴿBut whoever slaps you on your right cheek, turn the other to him also.   Is. 50:6

40 "If anyone wants to sue you and take away your tunic, let him have *your* cloak also.

41 "And whoever ᴿcompels you to go one mile, go with him two.   Matt. 27:32

42 "Give to him who asks you, and ᴿfrom

5:38 Ex. 21:24; Lev. 24:20; Deut. 19:21

41-D. Christ Speaks on Oaths (Matthew 5:33–37)—"Again you have heard that it was said to those of old, 'You shall not swear falsely, but shall perform your oaths to the Lord.' But I say to you, do not swear at all" (vv. 33, 34). In other words, if we were living up to the Sermon on the Mount, we would never need to take an oath, in or out of court.

Is your word your bond? Or do you speak with a forked tongue, or from both sides of your mouth? When you make a business transaction, do you say one thing and mean another? Are you a double-talk artist? Jesus said, "Let your 'Yes' be 'Yes,' and your 'No,' 'No.' For whatever is more than these is from the evil one" (v. 37; cf. John 8:44, page 1063). To the honest person, yes is yes and no is no. There is no gray area—truth is truth and a lie is a lie; even though we may call it a "little white lie," it is still a lie, and we are liars (James 3:5–10, page 1258).

If the world could live up to the teaching of this kingdom manifesto, most of the world's problems could be solved. When the King of kings returns to this earth and establishes His kingdom, His manifesto will be obeyed and mankind will learn to tell the truth—God's truth.

See Matthew 5:38–48, above, for **Point 41-E: Turn the Other Cheek, Go the Second Mile, and Love Your Enemy.**

41-E. Turn the Other Cheek, Go the Second Mile, and Love Your Enemy (Matthew 5:38–48)—"You have heard that it was said, 'An eye for an eye and a tooth for a tooth.' But I tell you not to resist an evil person" (vv. 38, 39). If they slap you on the cheek, give them the other cheek to strike. If anyone sues you for your tunic, give him your cloak also. If he compels you to carry his burden for a mile (Roman soldiers could do this, under Roman law), offer to carry it a second mile (vv. 38–42). The believer has the ability to demonstrate his new life in Christ, "because the love of God has been poured out in our hearts by the Holy Spirit who was given to us" (Rom. 5:5, page 1133).

"You have heard . . . 'You shall love your neighbor and hate your enemy' " (v. 43). This was the teaching of the scribes and the Pharisees. But Jesus said, "Love your enemies, bless those who curse you, do good to those who hate you, and pray for those who spitefully use you and persecute you" (v. 44). Pray for them in love, from a heart filled with the love of God (1 Pet. 1:22, 23, page 1264).

Why? Because God loves them and shows them that love throughout their wicked lives. His sun shines on the evil and the good; His rain falls on the just (those who have been justified by faith—Rom. 5:1, page 1133), and on the unjust (the unsaved). But if we love only those who love us, we are no better than the ungodly, who do the same.

Even if we love our antagonist, and show it by turning the other cheek and by going the second mile for a taskmaster, we may suffer persecution, even as the apostles were beaten for daring to preach Christ. They responded by "rejoicing that they were counted worthy to suffer shame for His name" (Acts 5:40–42, page 1095). They practiced the kingdom principle by turning the other cheek and loving their enemies, because the love of God filled their hearts (Rom. 5:5, page 1133); they "will receive the crown of life [a reward] which the Lord has promised to those who love Him" (James 1:12, page 1255).

As subjects of God's kingdom, not only are we to do what is demanded of us by the laws of man, we are to go beyond the demands of the law, even though it may be an unjust law. If someone takes your shirt, give him your coat also. If you are compelled to go a mile for someone, go two miles in the spirit of the Lord. Do you love your family and friends? You should love those who love you; this is easy. But do you love your enemy? This is the true test of the kingdom principle.

See Master Outline 42, "Making Kingdom Choices," page 51 for your next study.

▽ him who wants to borrow from you do not turn away.   Luke 6:30-34

Love Your Enemies

43 "You have heard that it was said, ᴿ'*You shall love your neighbor* ᴿand hate your enemy.'   Lev. 19:18 • Deut. 23:3-6

44 *"But I say to you, love your enemies, bless those who curse you, ᴿdo good to those who hate you, and pray for those who spitefully use you and persecute you,   [Rom. 12:20]

45 "that you may be sons of your Father in heaven; for ᴿHe makes His sun rise on the evil and on the good, and sends rain on the just and on the unjust.   Job 25:3

46 ᴿ"For if you love those who love you, what reward have you? Do not even the tax collectors do the same?   Luke 6:32

47 "And if you greet your *brethren only, what do you do more *than* others? Do not even the *tax collectors do so?

48 "Therefore you shall be perfect, just ᴿas
▲ your Father in heaven is perfect.   Eph. 5:1

5:44 NU *But I say to you, love your enemies and pray for those who persecute you*

5:47 M *friends* • NU *Gentiles*

Do Good to Please God

42-A. A Threefold Hypocrite   ▼

6 Take heed that you do not do your charitable deeds before men, to be seen by them. Otherwise you have no reward from your Father in heaven.

2 "Therefore, ᴿwhen you do a charitable deed, do not sound a trumpet before you as the hypocrites do in the synagogues and in the streets, that they may have glory from men. Assuredly, I say to you, they have their reward.   Rom. 12:8

3 "But when you do a charitable deed, do not let your left hand know what your right hand is doing,

4 "that your charitable deed may be in secret; and your Father who sees in secret ᴿwill Himself reward you *openly.   Luke 14:12-14

The Model Prayer

5 "And when you pray, you shall not be like the ᵀhypocrites. For they love to pray standing in the synagogues and on the corners of the streets, that they may be seen by

6:4 NU *omits openly*

42-A. A Threefold Hypocrite (Matthew 6:1-18)—The Jew had three ways to practice righteousness and demonstrate the depth of his religious commitment: giving alms and doing charitable deeds, prayer, and fasting. Hypocrites did these right things in the wrong way, with wrong motives. Jesus exposed their religious hypocrisy:

(1) "Therefore, when you do a charitable deed, do not sound a trumpet" (v. 2), do not "blow your horn" as the hypocrites do. A hypocrite is a pretender, an actor; he pretends to be what he is not, or to have a faith that he does not have. He has a form of godliness, but it is empty inside (2 Tim. 3:5, page 1227). Some of the scribes, Pharisees, and other Jews gave alms as if for the glory of God, while at the same time making sure that people knew of their generosity. The main Christian motive for giving is the glory of God, "and your Father who sees in secret will Himself reward you openly" (v. 4). Jesus is our great example—He gave all of His riches, making Himself poor, that all believers might be rich (2 Cor. 8:9, page 1171).

(2) "When you pray, you shall not be like the hypocrites" (vv. 5-8). Here again He exposes the hypocrisy of the Pharisees, scribes, and rabbis. However, many of us are just as guilty before God, reading these verses without coming under conviction for sins committed during the very act of prayer. When we pray in public, is it to be heard or seen by other people? Or do we say the same prayer over and over in order to be heard? Or do we think we have to pray a lengthy prayer to reach God? If so, then we are hypocrites too. Jesus said, "Therefore do not be like them [the hypocrites]" (v. 8).

(3) "In this manner, therefore, pray" (vv. 9-13). This model prayer tells us to pray directly to our heavenly Father, recognizing that we are in the presence of eternal, holy deity. In this prayer we are to seek His kingdom and His perfect will for our lives, declare our physical needs, forgive all who have wronged us, and pray for strength to endure temptation (for we *will* be tempted). This prayer has often been called the "prayer perfect."

(4) "When you fast, do not be like the hypocrites" (vv. 16-18). In giving alms we make contact with people; in prayer we make contact with God; in fasting we make contact with self. Fasting is both physically and spiritually beneficial. When the disciples failed to heal a demon-possessed, epileptic boy, they brought him to Jesus and Jesus healed him. Then they asked, "Why could we not cast it [the demon] out?" Jesus answered, "Because of your unbelief" (Matt. 17:14-21, page 964). They failed first in prayer and fasting before they failed to heal the epileptic.

Fasting is a form of self-denial. It is time we talked less about giving, praying, and fasting, and practiced them more. When you fast, don't be like the Pharisees, who, when they fasted, appeared in public with sad faces, seeking the admiration of men. Twice a week they fasted, but their only reward was the empty praise of men. Jesus observed, "Assuredly, I say to you, they have their reward" (v. 16). There will be no reward for them at the judgment seat of Christ (2 Cor. 5:10, page 1168), where all our works will be judged (1 Cor. 3:12-15, page 1149). Therefore, we should not be concerned with what people say or think about our giving, praying, or fasting.

See Matthew 6:19-21, page 943, for **Point 42-B: Where Is Your Heart?**

▽ men. Assuredly, I say to you, they have their
reward.   *pretenders*

6 "But you, when you pray, ᴿgo into your
room, and when you have shut your door,
pray to your Father who *is* in the secret
place; and your Father who sees in secret will
reward you *openly.   2 Kin. 4:33

7 "And when you pray, ᴿdo not use vain
repetitions as the heathen *do*. ᴿFor they
think that they will be heard for their many
words.   Eccl. 5:2 • 1 Kin. 18:26

8 "Therefore do not be like them. For your
Father ᴿknows the things you have need of
before you ask Him.   [Rom. 8:26, 27]

9 "In this manner, therefore, pray:

ᴿOur Father in heaven,   [Matt. 5:9, 16]
Hallowed be Your ᴿname.   Mal. 1:11

10 Your kingdom come.
ᴿYour will be done   Matt. 26:42
On earth ᴿas *it is* in heaven.   Ps. 103:20

11 Give us this day our daily bread.

12 And ᴿforgive us our debts,
As we forgive our debtors.   [Matt. 18:21, 22]

13 And do not lead us into temptation,
But deliver us from the evil one.
*For Yours is the kingdom and the
power and the glory forever. Amen.

14 "For if you forgive men their trespasses,
your heavenly Father will also forgive you.

15 "But ᴿif you do not forgive men their
trespasses, neither will your Father forgive
your trespasses.   Matt. 18:35

Fasting to Be Seen Only by God

16 "Moreover, ᴿwhen you fast, do not be
like the hypocrites, with a sad countenance.

6:6 NU omits *openly*
6:13 NU omits the rest of v. 13.

For they disfigure their faces that they may ▽
appear to men to be fasting. Assuredly, I say
to you, they have their reward.   Is. 58:3-7

17 "But you, when you fast, ᴿanoint your
head and wash your face,   Ruth 3:3

18 "so that you do not appear to men to be
fasting, but to your Father who *is* in the
secret *place*; and your Father who sees in
secret will reward you *openly.

Lay Up Treasures in Heaven

42-B. Where Is Your Heart?   ▼

19 ᴿ"Do not lay up for yourselves treasures
on earth, where moth and rust destroy and
where thieves break in and steal;   Prov. 23:4

20 "but lay up for yourselves treasures in
heaven, where neither moth nor rust destroys
and where thieves do not break in and steal.

21 "For where your treasure is, there your
heart will be also.   ▲

The Lamp of the Body

42-C. Do You Have a Good or Evil Eye?   ▼

22 ᴿ"The lamp of the body is the eye. If
therefore your eye is ᵀgood, your whole body
will be full of light. Luke 11:34, 35 • Clear or healthy

23 "But if your eye is ᵀbad, your whole body
will be full of darkness. If therefore the light
that is in you is darkness, how great *is* that
darkness!   Evil or unhealthy ▲

You Cannot Serve God and Riches

42-D. Who Is Your Master?   ▼

24 ᴿ"No one can serve two masters; for
either he will hate the one and love the other,

6:18 NU, M omit *openly*

42-B. Where Is Your Heart? (Matthew 6:19–21)—"For where your treasure is, there your heart will be also" (v. 21). Here the King's subjects are asked to choose between earthly and eternal treasures. Someone once said, "What I hoard, I lose; but what I give, I keep." We cannot take our earthly treasures with us, but we can send them on ahead by sharing with others and supporting kingdom work. If your riches are here on earth, your heart will be bound to this world system. If your riches are in heaven, you will seek those things which are above and use the things of this world to the glory of God (Col. 3:1, 2, page 1205).
See Matthew 6:22, 23, above, for **Point 42-C: Do You Have a Good or Evil Eye?**

42-C. Do You Have a Good or Evil Eye? (Matthew 6:22, 23)—The good eye looks for the will of God, that the body may be filled with the presence of God, who is light; for "in Him is no darkness at all" (1 John 1:5, page 1278). The good eye places greatest value on things that cannot pass away, "for the things which are seen are temporary, but the things which are not seen are eternal" (2 Cor. 4:18, page 1168). For this reason the apostle Paul said, "Yet indeed I also count all things loss for the excellence of the knowledge of Christ Jesus my Lord, for whom I have suffered the loss of all things" (Phil. 3:3–9, page 1197).
The evil eye looks for the things of this age, this world system, where Satan is god (2 Cor. 4:4, page 1167). What are our real priorities? Are we Christians merely in name, who have "sold out," having an evil eye, seeing only the passing pleasures and possessions of this life, which soon fly away (1 John 2:15–17, page 1279)? Or have we truly seen the Master, who invites us to receive a heavenly possession "that does not fade away" (1 Pet. 1:4, page 1263)?
See Matthew 6:24, above, for **Point 42-D: Who Is Your Master?**

42-D. Who Is Your Master? (Matthew 6:24)—You can serve either a good or a bad master, but not both. "You cannot serve God and mammon," i.e., money, riches (v. 24). If God is your Master, you will deny
(Point 42-D continued on next page)

▽ or else he will be loyal to the one and despise the other. ᴿYou cannot serve God and ᵀmam-
▲ mon.   Luke 16:9, 11, 13 • [Gal. 1:10] • Lit., in Aram., *riches*

Do Not Worry

▼ **42-E. A Good or Bad Sphere**

25 "Therefore I say to you, ᴿdo not worry about your life, what you will eat or what you will drink; nor about your body, what you will put on. Is not life more than food and the body more than clothing?   Luke 12:22

26 ᴿ"Look at the birds of the air, for they neither sow nor reap nor gather into barns; yet your heavenly Father feeds them. Are you not of more value than they?   Luke 12:24

27 "Which of you by worrying can add one ᵀcubit to his ᵀstature?   18 in. • *height*

28 "So why do you worry about clothing? Consider the lilies of the field, how they grow: they neither toil nor spin;

29 "and yet I say to you that even Solomon in all his glory was not ᵀarrayed like one of these.   *dressed*

30 "Now if God so clothes the grass of the field, which today is, and tomorrow is thrown into the oven, *will He* not much more *clothe* you, O you of little faith?

31 "Therefore do not worry, saying, 'What shall we eat?' or 'What shall we drink?' or 'What shall we wear?'

32 "For after all these things the Gentiles seek. For your heavenly Father knows that you need all these things.

33 "But ᴿseek first the kingdom of God and His righteousness, and all these things shall be added to you.   [1 Tim. 4:8]

34 "Therefore do not worry about tomorrow, for tomorrow will worry about its own things. Sufficient for the day *is* its own trouble.   ▲

Do Not Judge

42-F. Judge Not   ▼

7 "Judge not, that you be not judged. **2** "For with what judgment you judge, you will be judged; and with the measure you use, it will be measured back to you.

3 "And why do you look at the speck in your brother's eye, but do not consider the plank in your own eye?

4 "Or how can you say to your brother, 'Let me remove the speck from your eye'; and look, a plank *is* in your own eye?

5 "Hypocrite! First remove the plank from your own eye, and then you will see clearly to remove the speck from your brother's eye.

(Point 42-D continued from previous page)
yourself and take up your cross and follow Him (Mark 8:34–38, page 994). If wealth is your master, it will fail you in this life and in eternal life to come (Luke 16:19–31, page 1035).
          See Matthew 6:25–34, above, for **Point 42-E: A Good or Bad Sphere.**

42-E. A Good or Bad Sphere (Matthew 6:25–34)—Faith is the good sphere, and worry is the bad. You must choose. You cannot live in both at the same time. To make the right choice, "seek first the kingdom of God and His righteousness," i.e., the righteousness of Christ (v. 33). When you become a part of His kingdom, by faith in Christ, and are robed in His righteousness, God will supply all your material needs according to His riches in glory by Christ Jesus (Phil. 4:19, page 1199).
          See Matthew 7:1–6, above, for **Point 42-F: Judge Not.**

42-F. Judge Not (Matthew 7:1–6)—In this last chapter of the manifesto of the King, He opens with a negative command: "Judge not," i.e., condemn not (v. 1). Keep in mind that God's negative commands always yield positive results.

          (1) If we judge (condemn) another believer, we will be condemning ourselves.
          (2) We cannot correctly judge another, because our knowledge of the facts is limited.
          (3) We are not spiritually qualified to judge another.
          (4) To sit in judgment on another believer is to usurp "the judgment seat of Christ" (2 Cor. 5:10, page 1168). Only He has the right to judge. Even "the Father judges no one, but has committed all judgment to the Son" (John 5:22, page 1057).

          To sit in judgment of a brother or sister in Christ demonstrates a spirit of bitterness and lack of love. But "judge not" does not mean that we are not to distinguish between good and evil. Neither are we to excuse or condone sin. To "judge not" means that we are not to assume the role of a judge and magnify the speck in the eye of another Christian. When we see sin in the life of another believer, then, how are we to cope with it?

          (1) Practice self-judgment—take a critical view of your own life-style for the purpose of improving yourself and understanding others (1 Cor. 11:31, 32, page 1157).
          (2) Practice the Golden Rule. "Therefore, whatever you want men to do to you, do also to them, for this is the Law and the Prophets" (Matt. 7:12, page 945).

          See Master Outline 43, "Entering the Kingdom," page 55 for your next study.

▽ 6 ᴿ"Do not give what is holy to the dogs;
nor cast your pearls before swine, lest they
trample them under their feet, and turn and
▲ tear you in pieces.   Prov. 9:7, 8

Keep Asking, Seeking, Knocking

▼ **43-A. Prayer Is Asking, Seeking, and
Knocking**

7 ᴿ"Ask, and it will be given to you; seek,
and you will find; knock, and it will be
opened to you.   [Mark 11:24]
8 "For ᴿeveryone who asks receives, and
he who seeks finds, and to him who knocks it
will be opened.   Prov. 8:17
9 ᴿ"Or what man is there among you who,
if his son asks for bread, will give him a
stone?   Luke 11:11
10 "Or if he asks for a fish, will he give him
a serpent?

11 "If you then, ᴿbeing evil, know how to ▽
give good gifts to your children, how much
more will your Father who is in heaven give
good things to those who ask Him!   Gen. 6:5 ▲

43-B. The Key to the Kingdom   ▼

12 "Therefore, ᴿwhatever you want men to
do to you, do also to them, for ᴿthis is the
Law and the Prophets.   Luke 6:31 • Gal. 5:14 ▲

The Narrow Way

43-C. Two Ways: The Broad and the   ▼
Narrow

13 ᴿ"Enter by the narrow gate; for wide *is*
the gate and broad *is* the way that leads to
destruction, and there are many who go in by
it.   Luke 13:24
14 *"Because narrow *is* the gate and ᵀdiffi-

7:14 NU, M *How narrow . . . !*

43-A. Prayer Is Asking, Seeking, and Knocking (Matthew 7:7–11)—"Ask, and it will be given to you; seek, and you will find; knock, and it will be opened to you" (v. 7). This is a precious, positive promise for all of God's children. It should motivate every believer to become bold in prayer, knowing that our heavenly Father has promised to give good things to all those who ask Him.

Before you ask the Father for anything, however, examine your motives. James said, "You ask and do not receive, because you ask amiss, that you may spend it on your pleasures" (James 4:3, page 1259). If your motives pass these tests, you will not be asking amiss:

(1) Are you obeying His command, "Seek first the kingdom of God and His righteousness" (Matt. 6:33, page 944)?

(2) Are you adhering to the principles of the Golden Rule, "Whatever you want men to do to you, do also to them, for this is the Law and the Prophets" (Matt. 7:12, above)?

(3) What are your Christian ethics in your relationships with your brothers and sisters in Christ? Do you treat them, in all matters, as you would have them treat you?

(4) Do the Beatitudes determine your daily Christian walk or practice?

Verses 7–11 are not a *carte blanche* promise for all who cry, "Lord, Lord" (Matt. 7:21, page 946). It is one thing to understand mentally the Sermon on the Mount, but quite another to practice it. If you are a hearer of the Word but not a doer, you are deceiving yourself (James 1:22–25, page 1256). Jesus gave us the Sermon on the Mount to help even the *weakest* Christian to know and walk in the will of God. When your life reflects the ethics of the Sermon on the Mount, you can ask and receive, you can seek and find, you can knock and God will open wide the door.

See Matthew 7:12, above, for **Point 43-B: The Key to the Kingdom.**

43-B. The Key to the Kingdom (Matthew 7:12)—The Golden Rule is the summation of the Sermon on the Mount. It established the Christian's ethical relationship with other believers, and revealed the purpose of the manifesto, which is to fulfill the Law and the Prophets (v. 12). Jesus said, "Do not think that I came to destroy the Law or the Prophets. I did not come to destroy but to fulfill" (Matt. 5:17, page 939). Jesus came to do for us what we could not do for ourselves, to make His righteousness available to all believers. "For Christ is the end of the law for righteousness to everyone who believes" (Rom. 10:4, page 1140). Now that we are "made righteous" (Rom. 5:19, page 1134) with the righteousness of Christ, we are to do to others every good thing to help them reach their highest spiritual goals, because this is what we would have other believers do for us.

The Golden Rule is the most concise, most inclusive ethical statement ever written or spoken. If it were obeyed by all of mankind, there would be no need for armies or law-enforcement officers; there would be heaven on earth. Make the Golden Rule *your* standard of ethics and you will make the world a better place in which to live.

See Matthew 7:13, 14, above, for **Point 43-C: Two Ways: The Broad and the Narrow.**

43-C. Two Ways: The Broad and the Narrow (Matthew 7:13, 14)—The Sermon on the Mount presents two paths—the way to heaven and the way to hell (vv. 13, 14). The choice is yours—and not to choose is itself a choice, the *wrong* choice (John 3:18, page 1053). You are already on one of these two ways:

(1) The broad way is the way of Satan, "the god of this age" (2 Cor. 4:4, page 1167). The broad way appeals to "the lust of the flesh, the lust of the eyes, and the pride of life" (1 John 2:15–17, page 1279).

(2) The narrow way is the way of Christ, "which leads to life" (v. 14; John 14:6, page 1074). You enter the

(Point 43-C continued on next page)

▽ cult is the way which leads to life, and there
▲ are few who find it.   *confined*

You Will Know Them by Their Fruits

▼ **43-D. Two Prophets: The False and the True**

15 ᴿ"Beware of false prophets, ᴿwho come to you in sheep's clothing, but inwardly they are ravenous wolves.   Jer. 23:16 • Mic. 3:5
16 ᴿ"You will know them by their fruits. ᴿDo men gather grapes from thornbushes or figs from thistles?   Matt. 7:20; 12:33 • Luke 6:43
17 "Even so, ᴿevery good tree bears good fruit, but a bad tree bears bad fruit.   Matt. 12:33
18 "A good tree cannot bear bad fruit, nor can a bad tree bear good fruit.
19 "Every tree that does not bear good fruit is cut down and thrown into the fire.
20 "Therefore by their fruits you will know
▲ them.

I Never Knew You

43-E. Religious but Lost   ▼

21 "Not everyone who says to Me, ᴿ'Lord, Lord,' shall enter the kingdom of heaven, but he who ᴿdoes the will of My Father in heaven.   Luke 6:46 • Rom. 2:13
22 "Many will say to Me in that day, 'Lord, Lord, have we ᴿnot prophesied in Your name, cast out demons in Your name, and done many wonders in Your name?'   Num. 24:4
23 "And ᴿthen I will declare to them, 'I never knew you; ᴿdepart from Me, you who practice lawlessness!'   [2 Tim. 2:19] • Ps. 5:5; 6:8 ▲

Build on the Rock

43-F. Two Builders: The Wise and the Foolish   ▼

24 "Therefore whoever hears these sayings of Mine, and does them, I will liken him to a wise man who built his house on the rock:

(Point 43-C continued from previous page)
"narrow gate" by faith in Christ (John 3:36, page 1053), and you walk this difficult way by following Christ (Mark 8:34–38, page 994).

You may travel on the broad way, but it will narrow down to death. "There is a way that seems right to a man," a broad and easy way with no restraints, appealing to the carnal nature; "but its end is the way of death," or eternal separation from God (Prov. 14:12, page 608).

If you have entered the narrow gate, by faith in Christ, you are on the narrow way. The way is difficult, but as you follow Christ, the way will widen out into abundant life (John 10:10, page 1067).

Thank God, you can leave the broad way to enter the narrow gate by faith in Christ, and follow Him. His promise is, "The one who comes to Me I will by no means cast out" (John 6:37, page 1059).

See Matthew 7:15-20, above, for **Point 43-D: Two Prophets: The False and the True.**

43-D. Two Prophets: The False and the True (Matthew 7:15-20)—Jesus said, "I am the good shepherd," the True Prophet (John 10:14, page 1067). In the present verses He warned the sheep, "Beware of false prophets, who come to you in sheep's clothing" (v. 15).

He added, "By their fruits you will know them" (v. 20; cf. James 3:16, 17, page 1259). By their teaching you will know the true from the false. Paul said, "I marvel that you are turning away so soon from Him who called you in the grace of Christ, to a different gospel" (Gal. 1:6–10, page 1178). The curse of God is on anyone who preaches any gospel other than the gospel of the grace of God (Eph. 2:8, 9, page 1187). Paul defined this gospel when he said, "Christ died for our sins according to the Scriptures, and that He was buried, and that He rose again the third day according to the Scriptures" (1 Cor. 15:1–4, page 1161). As we approach the end of the dispensation of grace, false prophets will multiply until the time when the church is raptured, the Antichrist is revealed (1 John 2:18, page 1279), and Christ the True Prophet comes to establish His kingdom (Matt. 25:31–46, page 976).

See Matthew 7:21-23, above, for **Point 43-E: Religious but Lost.**

43-E. Religious but Lost (Matthew 7:21-23)—Anyone who cries, "Lord, Lord," (v. 21) but does not believe that Jesus is the God-Man, the only Savior, has a false religion. At the Great White Throne judgment Jesus will say to them, "I never knew you; depart from Me, you who practice lawlessness!" (v. 23).

It is difficult to know the false from the true, because man has a finite and corrupt mind. How can he know the heart of another person, when he does not even understand his own heart (Jer. 17:9, 10, page 730)? Only the omniscient God has the capacity to understand the true relation of the human heart to His kingdom (1 Sam. 16:7, page 283). One may act the part of a Christian and cry, "Lord! Lord!" and even preach in His name, cast out demons in His name, perform miracles in His name, and do wonderful works in His name, deceiving many Christians—but such a person cannot fool the Lord, who knows the heart.

See Matthew 7:24-27, above, for **Point 43-F: Two Builders: The Wise and the Foolish.**

43-F. Two Builders: The Wise and the Foolish (Matthew 7:24-27)—There are two foundations, the false and the true (vv. 24–27). In these verses Jesus taught that there are two builders, the wise and the foolish. The foolish builder builds on sand, a false foundation. The materials may be good, but when the storm comes the house will fall because of its weak foundation. The wise builder erects his house on the Rock, and when the storm comes, it will stand because of its solid foundation. Christ is the true foundation of His church (Matt.

(Point 43-F continued on next page)

▽ 25 "and the rain descended, the floods came, and the winds blew and beat on that house; and it did not fall, for it was founded on the rock.

26 "But everyone who hears these sayings of Mine, and does not do them, will be like a foolish man who built his house on the sand:

27 "and the rain descended, the floods came, and the winds blew and beat on that
▲ house; and it fell. And great was its fall."

▼ 43-G. Two Authorities: Sovereign and Human

28 And so it was, when Jesus had ended these sayings, that ᴿthe people were astonished at His teaching,   Matt. 13:54
29 ᴿfor He taught them as one having au-
▲ thority, and not as the scribes.   [John 7:46]

Jesus Cleanses a Leper

8 When He had come down from the mountain, great multitudes followed Him.

2 ᴿAnd behold, a leper came and ᴿworshiped Him, saying, "Lord, if You are willing, You can make me clean."   Mark 1:40–45 • John 9:38

3 Then Jesus put out *His* hand and touched him, saying, "I am willing; be cleansed." Immediately his leprosy ᴿwas cleansed.   Luke 4:27

4 And Jesus said to him, "See that you tell no one; but go your way, show yourself to the priest, and offer the gift that Moses commanded, as a testimony to them."

Jesus Heals a Centurion's Servant

5 ᴿNow when Jesus had entered Capernaum, a ᴿcenturion came to Him, pleading with Him,   Luke 7:1–3 • Matt. 27:54

6 saying, "Lord, my servant is lying at home paralyzed, dreadfully tormented."

7 And Jesus said to him, "I will come and heal him."

8 The centurion answered and said, "Lord, I am not worthy that You should come under my roof. But only ᴿspeak a word, and my servant will be healed.   Ps. 107:20

9 "For I also am a man under authority, having soldiers under me. And I say to this *one*, 'Go,' and he goes; and to another, 'Come,' and he comes; and to my servant, 'Do this,' and he does *it*."

10 When Jesus heard *it*, He marveled, and said to those who followed, "Assuredly, I say to you, I have not found such great faith, not even in Israel!

11 "And I say to you that ᴿmany will come from east and west, and sit down with Abraham, Isaac, and Jacob in the kingdom of heaven.   Is. 49:12; 59:19; Mal. 1:11; Eph. 3:6

12 "But ᴿthe sons of the kingdom will be cast out into outer darkness. There will be weeping and gnashing of teeth."   [Matt. 21:43]

13 Then Jesus said to the centurion, "Go your way; and as you have believed, so let it be done for you." And his servant was healed that same hour.

Peter's Mother-in-Law Healed

14 ᴿNow when Jesus had come into Peter's house, He saw ᴿhis wife's mother lying sick with a fever.   Mark 1:29–31 • 1 Cor. 9:5

15 So He touched her hand, and the fever left her. And she arose and served *them.

Many Healed After Sabbath Sunset

16 ᴿWhen evening had come, they brought to Him many who were demon-possessed. And He cast out the spirits with a word, and healed all who were sick,   Luke 4:40, 41

17 that it might be fulfilled which was spoken by Isaiah the prophet, saying:

ᴿ*"He Himself took our infirmities
    And bore our sicknesses."*   Is. 53:4

The Cost of Discipleship

18 And when Jesus saw great multitudes about Him, He gave a command to depart to the other side.

8:15 NU, M *Him*

(Point 43-F continued from previous page)
16:18, page 962) and kingdom (1 Cor. 3:11, page 1149). The prophet Isaiah said, "Therefore thus says the Lord GOD: 'Behold, I lay in Zion a stone for a foundation, a tried stone, a precious cornerstone, a sure foundation; whoever believes will not act hastily' " (Is. 28:16, page 668). The church and kingdom stand upon Christ, the solid Rock. All other ground is sinking sand.
    See Matthew 7:28, 29, above, for **Point 43-G: Two Authorities: Sovereign and Human.**

43-G. Two Authorities: Sovereign and Human (Matthew 7:28, 29)—In this chapter we have briefly examined the two ways, the two prophets, the two religions, the two foundations, and now we consider the two authorities. This is the epilogue of the King's manifesto: "The people were astonished at His teaching" (v. 28). After almost two thousand years, people are still astonished at the supreme authority with which He taught.
    Unlike the scribes and Pharisees, whose authority was merely human, Jesus taught by His own divine authority. And so the people, not at all accustomed to this kind of teaching, were astonished. Jesus' authority is by virtue of the fact that He, the God-Man, has been given all authority in heaven and on earth (Matt. 28:18, page 982).
    His authority was, is, and always shall be, absolute.
    See Index, page 17, for your next study.

19 ᴿThen a certain scribe came and said to Him, "Teacher, I will follow You wherever You go."   Luke 9:57, 58

20 And Jesus said to him, "Foxes have holes and birds of the air *have* nests, but the Son of Man has nowhere to lay *His* head."

21 ᴿThen another of His disciples said to Him, "Lord, ᴿlet me first go and bury my father."   Luke 9:59, 60 • 1 Kin. 19:20

22 But Jesus said to him, "Follow Me, and let the dead bury their own dead."

Wind and Wave Obey Jesus

23 Now when He got into a boat, His disciples followed Him.

24 ᴿAnd suddenly a great tempest arose on the sea, so that the boat was covered with the waves. But He was asleep.   Mark 4:37

25 Then His disciples came to *Him* and awoke Him, saying, "Lord, save us! We are perishing!"

26 But He said to them, "Why are you fearful, O you of little faith?" Then ᴿHe arose and rebuked the winds and the sea, and there was a great calm.   Ps. 65:7; 89:9; 107:29

27 So the men marveled, saying, ᵀ"Who can this be, that even the winds and the sea obey Him?"   Lit. *What sort of man is this*

Two Demon-Possessed Men Healed

28 ᴿWhen He had come to the other side, to the country of the *Gergesenes, there met Him two demon-possessed *men*, coming out of the tombs, exceedingly fierce, so that no one could pass that way.   Mark 5:1-4

29 And suddenly they cried out, saying, "What have we to do with You, Jesus, You Son of God? Have You come here to torment us before the time?"

30 Now a good way off from them there was a herd of many swine feeding.

31 So the demons begged Him, saying, "If You cast us out, *permit us to go away into the herd of swine."

32 And He said to them, "Go." So when they had come out, they went into the herd of swine. And suddenly the whole herd of swine ran violently down the steep place into the sea, and perished in the water.

33 Then those who kept *them* fled; and they went away into the city and told everything, including what *had happened* to the demon-possessed *men*.

34 And behold, the whole city came out to meet Jesus. And when they saw Him, they begged *Him* to depart from their region.

Jesus Forgives and Heals a Paralytic

9 So He got into a boat, crossed over, ᴿand came to His own city.   Matt. 4:13; 11:23

2 Then behold, they brought to Him a paralytic lying on a bed. When Jesus saw their faith, He said to the paralytic, "Son, be of good cheer; your sins are forgiven you."

3 And at once some of the scribes said within themselves, "This Man blasphemes!"

4 But Jesus, knowing their thoughts, said, "Why do you think evil in your hearts?

5 "For which is easier, to say, '*Your* sins are forgiven you,' or to say, 'Arise and walk'?

6 "But that you may know that the Son of Man has power on earth to forgive sins"— then He said to the paralytic, "Arise, take up your bed, and go to your house."

7 And he arose and departed to his house.

8 Now when the multitudes saw *it*, they ᴿmarveled* and glorified God, who had given such power to men.   John 7:15

Matthew the Tax Collector

9 ᴿAs Jesus passed on from there, He saw a man named Matthew sitting at the tax office. And He said to him, "Follow Me." So he arose and followed Him.   Luke 5:27

10 ᴿNow it happened, as Jesus sat at the table in the house, *that* behold, many tax collectors and sinners came and sat down with Him and His disciples.   Mark 2:15

11 And when the Pharisees saw *it*, they said to His disciples, "Why does your Teacher eat with tax collectors and ᴿsinners?"   [Gal. 2:15]

12 When Jesus heard *that*, He said to them, "Those who are well have no need of a physician, but those who are sick.

13 "But go and learn what *this* means: ᴿ'*I desire mercy and not sacrifice.*' For I did not come to call the righteous, ᴿbut sinners, *to repentance."   Hos. 6:6 • 1 Tim. 1:15

Jesus Is Questioned About Fasting

14 Then the disciples of John came to Him, saying, "Why do we and the Pharisees fast *often, but Your disciples do not fast?"

15 And Jesus said to them, "Can the friends of the bridegroom mourn as long as the bridegroom is with them? But the days will come when the bridegroom will be taken away from them, and then they will fast.

16 "No one puts a piece of unshrunk cloth on an old garment; for ᵀthe patch pulls away from the garment, and the tear is made worse.   Lit. *that which is put on*

17 "Nor do they put new wine into old wineskins, or else the wineskins ᵀbreak, the wine is spilled, and the wineskins are ruined. But they put new wine into new wineskins, and both are preserved."   *burst*

8:28 NU *Gadarenes*
8:31 NU *send us into*

9:8 NU *were afraid*
9:13 NU omits *to repentance*
9:14 NU brackets *often* as disputed.

A Girl Restored to Life and a Woman Healed

18 While He spoke these things to them, behold, a ruler came and worshiped Him, saying, "My daughter has just died, but come and lay Your hand on her and she will live."

19 So Jesus arose and followed him, and so did His ᴿdisciples. Matt. 10:2–4

20 And suddenly, a woman who had a flow of blood for twelve years came from behind and touched the hem of His garment.

21 For she said to herself, "If only I may touch His garment, I shall be made well."

22 But Jesus turned around, and when He saw her He said, "Be of good cheer, daughter; your faith has made you well." And the woman was made well from that hour.

23 ᴿWhen Jesus came into the ruler's house, and saw ᴿthe flute players and the noisy crowd wailing, Mark 5:38 · 2 Chr. 35:25

24 He said to them, ᴿ"Make room, for the girl is not dead, but sleeping." And they ridiculed Him. Acts 20:10

25 But when the crowd was put outside, He went in and ᴿtook her by the hand, and the girl arose. Mark 1:31

26 And the ᴿreport of this went out into all that land. Matt. 4:24

Two Blind Men Healed

27 When Jesus departed from there, two blind men followed Him, crying out and saying, "Son of David, have mercy on us!"

28 And when He had come into the house, the blind men came to Him. And Jesus said to them, "Do you believe that I am able to do this?" They said to Him, "Yes, Lord."

29 Then He touched their eyes, saying, "According to your faith let it be to you."

30 And their eyes were opened. And Jesus sternly warned them, saying, ᴿ"See that no one knows it." Matt. 8:4

31 ᴿBut when they had departed, they ᵀspread the news about Him in all that ᵀcountry. Mark 7:36 · Lit. made Him known · Lit. land

A Mute Man Speaks

32 As they went out, behold, they brought to Him a man, mute and demon-possessed.

33 And when the demon was cast out, the mute spoke. And the multitudes marveled, saying, "It was never seen like this in Israel!"

34 But the Pharisees said, ᴿ"He casts out demons by the ruler of the demons." Luke 11:15

The Compassion of Jesus

35 Then Jesus went about all the cities and villages, ᴿteaching in their synagogues, preaching the gospel of the kingdom, and healing every sickness and every disease *among the people. Matt. 4:23

9:35 NU omits among the people

36 ᴿBut when He saw the multitudes, He was moved with compassion for them, because they were *weary and scattered, like sheep having no shepherd. Mark 6:34

37 Then He said to His disciples, ᴿ"The harvest truly is plentiful, but the laborers are few. Luke 10:2

38 "Therefore pray the Lord of the harvest to send out laborers into His harvest."

The Twelve Apostles

10 And when He had called His twelve disciples to Him, He gave them power over unclean spirits, to cast them out, and to heal all kinds of sickness and all kinds of disease.

2 Now the names of the twelve apostles are these: first, Simon, ᴿwho is called Peter, and Andrew his brother; James the son of Zebedee, and John his brother; John 1:42

3 Philip and Bartholomew; Thomas and Matthew the tax collector; James the son of Alphaeus, and *Lebbaeus, whose surname was Thaddaeus;

4 Simon the *Canaanite, and Judas ᴿIscariot, who also betrayed Him. John 13:2, 26

Sending Out the Twelve

5 These twelve Jesus sent out and commanded them, saying: ᴿ"Do not go into the way of the Gentiles, and do not enter a city of ᴿthe Samaritans. Matt. 4:15 · John 4:9

6 ᴿ"But go rather to the ᴿlost sheep of the house of Israel. Matt. 15:24 · Jer. 50:6

7 ᴿ"And as you go, preach, saying, 'The kingdom of heaven is at hand.' Luke 9:2

8 "Heal the sick, *cleanse the lepers, *raise the dead, cast out demons. ᴿFreely you have received, freely give. [Acts 8:18]

9 ᴿ"Provide neither gold nor silver nor ᴿcopper in your moneybelts, 1 Sam. 9:7 · Mark 6:8

10 "nor bag for your journey, nor two tunics, nor sandals, nor staffs; ᴿfor a worker is worthy of his food. 1 Tim. 5:18

11 ᴿ"Now whatever city or town you enter, inquire who in it is worthy, and stay there till you go out. Luke 10:8

12 "And when you go into a household, greet it.

13 ᴿ"If the household is worthy, let your peace come upon it. ᴿBut if it is not worthy, let your peace return to you. Luke 10:5 · Ps. 35:13

14 ᴿ"And whoever will not receive you nor hear your words, when you depart from that house or city, ᴿshake off the dust from your feet. Mark 6:11 · Acts 13:51

15 "Assuredly, I say to you, it will be more

9:36 NU, M harassed
10:3 NU omits Lebbaeus, whose surname was
10:4 NU Canaanaean
10:8 NU raise the dead, cleanse the lepers • M omits raise the dead

tolerable for the land of Sodom and Gomorrah in the day of judgment than for that city!

Persecutions Are Coming

16 "Behold, I send you out as sheep in the midst of wolves. Therefore be wise as serpents and ᴿharmless as doves.   [Phil. 2:14-16]

17 "But beware of men, for ᴿthey will deliver you up to councils and ᴿscourge you in their synagogues.   Mark 13:9 • Acts 5:40; 22:19; 26:11

18 ᴿ"You will be brought before governors and kings for My sake, as a testimony to them and to the Gentiles.   2 Tim. 4:16

19 ᴿ"But when they deliver you up, do not worry about how or what you should speak. For ᴿit will be given to you in that hour what you should speak;   Luke 12:11, 12; 21:14, 15 • Ex. 4:12

20 "for it is not you who speak, but the Spirit of your Father who speaks in you.

21 ᴿ"Now brother will deliver up brother to death, and a father *his* child; and children will rise up against parents and cause them to be put to death.   Mic. 7:6

22 "And ᴿyou will be hated by all for My name's sake. ᴿBut he who endures to the end will be saved.   Luke 21:17 • Mark 13:13

23 "When they persecute you in this city, flee to another. For assuredly, I say to you, you will not have gone through the cities of Israel before the Son of Man comes.

▼ 27-A. Fear, Constructive and Destructive

24 ᴿ"A disciple is not above *his* teacher, nor a servant above his master.   John 15:20

25 "It is enough for a disciple that he be like his teacher, and a servant like his master. If ᴿthey have called the master of the house

*Beelzebub, how much more *will they call* ▽ those of his household!   John 8:48, 52

26 "Therefore do not fear them. ᴿFor there is nothing covered that will not be revealed, and hidden that will not be known.   Mark 4:22

Jesus Teaches the Fear of God

27 "Whatever I tell you in the dark, ᴿspeak in the light; and what you hear in the ear, preach on the housetops.   Acts 5:20

28 ᴿ"And do not fear those who kill the body but cannot kill the soul. But rather ᴿfear Him who is able to destroy both soul and body in ᵀhell.   Luke 12:4 • Luke 12:5 • Gr. *Gehenna*

29 "Are not two sparrows sold for a ᵀcopper coin? And not one of them falls to the ground apart from your Father's will. $2

30 ᴿ"But the very hairs of your head are all numbered.   Luke 21:18

31 "Do not fear therefore; you are of more value than many sparrows.   ▲

Confess Christ Before Men

32 ᴿ"Therefore whoever confesses Me before men, ᴿhim I will also confess before My Father who is in heaven.   Luke 12:8 • [Rev. 3:5]

33 ᴿ"But whoever denies Me before men, him I will also deny before My Father who is in heaven.   2 Tim. 2:12

Christ Brings Division

34 ᴿ"Do not think that I came to bring peace on earth. I did not come to bring peace but a sword.   [Luke 12:49]

35 "For I have come to ᴿ'set ᵀ a man against his father, a daughter against her mother, and a daughter-in-law against her mother-in-law';   Mic. 7:6 • *alienate a man from*

10:25 NU, M *Beelzebul;* a Philistine deity, 2 Kin. 1:2, 3

27-A. Fear, Constructive and Destructive (Matthew 10:24-31)—Jesus said to His fearful disciples, "do not fear those who kill the body but cannot kill the soul" (v. 28). This is *destructive* fear. Jesus warned them that they would be persecuted for preaching the gospel, and would have no physical defense. He said, "Behold, I send you out as sheep in the midst of wolves" (vv. 16-23). The apostles suffered severe persecution; indeed, nearly all the apostles were put to death. They could have denied their faith and lived—but they refused.

Consider these five great biblical saints who trusted God and overcame fear, even in the face of death:

(1) Moses chose "rather to suffer affliction with the people of God than to enjoy the passing pleasures of sin . . . By faith he forsook Egypt, not fearing the wrath of the king" (Heb. 11:25-27, page 1249).

(2) The three Hebrew children, because of their faith, were unafraid of Nebuchadnezzar and his fiery furnace (Dan. 3:16-18, page 837).

(3) Daniel was not afraid of the decree of King Darius and the den of lions. By faith he defied the king's command, knowing that he would be cast into a den of hungry lions. Like his three Hebrew friends, he was courageous (Dan. 6:1-28, page 842).

(4) Stephen, one of the first deacons, "full of faith and power, did great wonders and signs among the people" (Acts 6:8, page 1095). He was the first Christian to suffer a martyr's death for exalting Christ. Stephen died on his knees, stoned by the enemies of Jesus. Unafraid, he prayed, "Lord, do not charge them with this sin" (Acts 7:54-60, page 1097).

(5) Paul wrote to young Timothy from Rome about his own coming death: "For I am already being poured out as a drink offering, and the time of my departure is at hand. I have fought the good fight, I have finished the race, I have kept the faith" (2 Tim. 4:6, 7, page 1228). In his letter to the church at Philippi, he said, "For to me, to live is Christ, and to die is gain" (Phil. 1:21, page 1196). By faith Paul was not afraid of death; to him it would be eternal gain.

(Point 27-A continued on next page)

36 "and *a man's* ᴿenemies will be those of his own household.'   Ps. 41:9; John 13:18

37 ᴿ"He who loves father or mother more than Me is not worthy of Me. And he who loves son or daughter more than Me is not worthy of Me.   Luke 14:26

38 "And he who does not take his cross and follow after Me is not worthy of Me.

39 "He who finds his life will lose it, and he who loses his life for My sake will find it.

A Cup of Cold Water

40 ᴿ"He who receives you receives Me, and he who receives Me receives Him who sent Me.   Luke 9:48

41 ᴿ"He who receives a prophet in the name of a prophet shall receive a prophet's reward. And he who receives a righteous man in the name of a righteous man shall receive a righteous man's reward.   1 Kin. 17:10

42 ᴿ"And whoever gives one of these little ones only a cup of cold *water* in the name of a disciple, assuredly, I say to you, he shall by no means lose his reward."   Mark 9:41

John the Baptist Sends Messengers to Jesus

11 Now it came to pass, when Jesus finished commanding His twelve disciples, that He departed from there to ᴿteach and to preach in their cities.   Luke 23:5

2 ᴿAnd when John had heard ᴿin prison about the works of Christ, he *sent two of his disciples   Luke 7:18–35 • Matt. 4:12; 14:3

11:2 NU *sent by his*

3 and said to Him, "Are You ᴿthe Coming One, or do we look for another?"   John 6:14

4 Jesus answered and said to them, "Go and tell John the ᴿthings which you hear and see: Is. 29:18, 19; 35:4–6

5 "*The* blind see and *the* lame walk; *the* lepers are cleansed and *the* deaf hear; *the* dead are raised up and *the* poor have the gospel preached to them.

6 "And blessed is he who is not ᴿoffended because of Me."   [Rom. 9:32]

7 ᴿAs they departed, Jesus began to say to the multitudes concerning John: "What did you go out into the wilderness to see? ᴿA reed shaken by the wind?   Luke 7:24 • [Eph. 4:14]

8 "But what did you go out to see? A man clothed in soft garments? Indeed, those who wear soft *clothing* are in kings' houses.

9 "But what did you go out to see? A prophet? Yes, I say to you, ᴿand more than a prophet.   Luke 1:76; 20:6

10 "For this is *he* of whom it is written:

ᴿ'*Behold, I send My messenger before Your face,*
Who will prepare Your way before You.'   Mal. 3:1

11 "Assuredly, I say to you, among those born of women there has not risen one greater than John the Baptist; but he who is least in the kingdom of heaven is greater than he.

12 "And from the days of John the Baptist until now the kingdom of heaven suffers violence, and the violent take it by force.

(Point 27-A continued from previous page)
There are two elements that will deliver you from destructive fear, whether fear of death or life, fear of failure or loss, fear of people or position, or fear of rank or power. These elements are:

(1) *Faith.* You cannot trust God and be fearful at the same time. The psalmist said, "Whenever I am afraid, I will trust in You. In God (I will praise His word), in God I have put my trust; I will not fear. What can flesh do to me?" (Ps. 56:3, 4, page 543). Sudden fear gripped the psalmist for a moment, then he cried, "Whenever I am afraid . . . " At the moment fear grips you, turn to God in faith. The psalmist went on to say, "I will trust in You." When faith came to him, he was able to say, "I will not fear. What can flesh do to me?" You cannot truly trust God and worry.

Paul tells us to take "the shield of faith with which you will be able to quench all the fiery darts of the wicked one" (Eph. 6:16, page 1192), and that ability is there the moment you lift up the shield. Fear is one of Satan's fiery darts. The shield of faith will extinguish it.

(2) *Love.* "There is no fear in love; but perfect love casts out fear" (1 John 4:18, page 1282). There is but one perfect love—the love of God. Let the Holy Spirit fill your heart with God's perfect love and there will be no room for destructive fear (Rom. 5:5, page 1133).

With your faith in God and your heart filled with His love, you are equipped with the two elements necessary to give you victory over all destructive fear.

Now let us examine *constructive,* or reverential fear. "But rather fear Him who is able to destroy both soul and body in hell" (v. 28). Some believe Jesus is telling us here to fear Satan, but Satan does *not* have this kind of power. Only God has the power and right to cast both soul and body into hell. Satan is a defeated foe. James urges us to "submit to God. Resist the devil and he will flee from you" (James 4:7, page 1259). When our lives are committed to God, we can resist Satan by faith, actually causing him to flee from us. We are to fear our holy God with a reverential fear—fear that bows in awe as we worship and praise Him. Remember, "There is no [destructive] fear in love" (1 John 4:18, page 1282). Perfect love produces reverential fear. We are to worship, praise, and exalt God in holy fear.

See Psalm 33:8, page 529, for **Point 27-B: Fear, Godly.**

13 ᴿ"For all the prophets and the law prophesied until John.   Mal. 4:4-6

14 "And if you are willing to receive *it*, he is ᴿElijah who is to come.   Luke 1:17

15 "He who has ears to hear, let him hear!

16 ᴿ"But to what shall I liken this generation? It is like children sitting in the marketplaces and calling to their companions,   Luke 7:31

17 "and saying:

'We played the flute for you,
And you did not dance;
We mourned to you,
And you did not ᵀlament.'   *beat your breast*

18 "For John came neither eating nor drinking, and they say, 'He has a demon.'

19 "The Son of Man came eating and drinking, and they say, 'Look, a glutton and a ᵀwinebibber, ᴿa friend of tax collectors and sinners!' ᴿBut wisdom is justified by her *children."   *wine drinker · Matt. 9:10 · Luke 7:35*

Woe to the Impenitent Cities

20 Then He began to ᵀrebuke the cities in which most of His mighty works had been done, because they did not repent: *reproach*

21 "Woe to you, Chorazin! Woe to you, Bethsaida! For if the mighty works which were done in you had been done in Tyre and Sidon, they would have repented long ago ᴿin sackcloth and ashes.   Jon. 3:6-8

22 "But I say to you, ᴿit will be more tolerable for Tyre and Sidon in the day of judgment than for you.   Matt. 10:15; 11:24

23 "And you, Capernaum, ᴿwho* are exalted to heaven, will be brought down to Hades; for if the mighty works which were done in you had been done in Sodom, it would have remained until this day.   Is. 14:13

24 "But I say to you ᴿthat it shall be more tolerable for the land of Sodom in the day of judgment than for you."   Matt. 10:15

Jesus Gives True Rest

25 ᴿAt that time Jesus answered and said, "I thank You, Father, Lord of heaven and earth, that ᴿYou have hidden these things from *the* wise and prudent and have revealed them to babes.   Luke 10:21, 22 · Ps. 8:2

26 "Even so, Father, for so it seemed good in Your sight.

27 ᴿ"All things have been delivered to Me by My Father, and no one knows the Son except the Father. Nor does anyone know the Father except the Son, and *the one* to whom the Son wills to reveal *Him*.   Matt. 28:18

28 "Come to Me, all *you* who labor and are heavy laden, and I will give you rest.

29 "Take My yoke upon you and learn from Me, for I am ᵀgentle and lowly in heart, and you will find rest for your souls.   *meek*

30 ᴿ"For My yoke *is* easy and My burden is light."   [1 John 5:3]

Jesus Is Lord of the Sabbath

12 At that time ᴿJesus went through the grainfields on the Sabbath. And His disciples were hungry, and began to ᴿpluck heads of grain and to eat.   Luke 6:1-5 · Deut. 23:25

2 And when the Pharisees saw *it*, they said to Him, "Look, Your disciples are doing what is not lawful to do on the Sabbath!"

3 But He said to them, "Have you not read ᴿwhat David did when he was hungry, he and those who were with him: 1 Sam. 21:6

4 "how he entered the house of God and ate ᴿthe showbread which was not lawful for him to eat, nor for those who were with him, ᴿbut only for the priests?   Lev. 24:5 · Ex. 29:32

5 "Or have you not read in the law that on the Sabbath the priests in the temple profane the Sabbath, and are blameless?

6 "Yet I say to you that in this place there is ᴿOne greater than the temple.   [Is. 66:1, 2]

7 "But if you had known what *this* means, ᴿ'I desire mercy and not sacrifice,' you would not have condemned the guiltless.   [Hos. 6:6]

8 "For the Son of Man is Lord *even of the Sabbath."

Healing on the Sabbath

9 ᴿNow when He had departed from there, He went into their synagogue.   Mark 3:1-6

10 And behold, there was a man who had a withered hand. And they asked Him, saying, ᴿ"Is it lawful to heal on the Sabbath?"—that they might accuse Him.   John 9:16

11 Then He said to them, "What man is there among you who has one sheep, and if it falls into a pit on the Sabbath, will not lay hold of it and lift *it* out?

12 "Of how much more value then is a man than a sheep? Therefore it is lawful to do good on the Sabbath."

13 Then He said to the man, "Stretch out your hand." And he stretched *it* out, and it was restored as whole as the other.

14 Then ᴿthe Pharisees went out and plotted against Him, how they might destroy Him.   Mark 3:6

Behold, My Servant

15 But when Jesus knew *it*, He withdrew from there. ᴿAnd great *multitudes followed Him, and He healed them all.   Matt. 19:2

16 Yet He ᴿwarned them not to make Him known,   Matt. 8:4; 9:30; 17:9

17 that it might be fulfilled which was spoken by Isaiah the prophet, saying:

11:19 NU *works*
11:23 NU *will you be exalted to heaven? No, you will be*

12:8 NU, M omit *even*
12:15 NU brackets *multitudes* as disputed.

18 *"Behold!* [R] *My Servant whom I have*
   chosen,
   My Beloved [R] *in whom My soul is well*
   pleased!
   I will put My Spirit upon Him,
   And He will declare justice to the
   Gentiles.   Is. 42:1-4 • Matt. 3:17; 17:5
19 *He will not quarrel nor cry out,*
   Nor will anyone hear His voice in the
   streets.
20 *A bruised reed He will not break,*
   And smoking flax He will not quench,
   Till He sends forth justice to victory;
21 *And in His name Gentiles will trust."*

A House Divided Cannot Stand

22 [R]Then one was brought to Him who was
demon-possessed, blind and mute; and He
healed him, so that the *blind and mute man
both spoke and saw.   Luke 11:14, 15
23 And all the multitudes were amazed and
said, "Could this be the Son of David?"

▼ **13-B. Demons: Servants of Satan**

24 [R]Now when the Pharisees heard *it* they
said, "This *fellow* does not cast out demons
except by *Beelzebub, the ruler of the de-
▲ mons."   Matt. 9:34

  12:22 NU omits *blind and*
  12:24 NU, M *Beelzebul*, a Philistine deity

25 But Jesus knew their thoughts, and said
to them: "Every kingdom divided against
itself is brought to desolation, and every city
or house divided against itself will not stand.
26 "If Satan casts out Satan, he is divided
against himself. How then will his kingdom
stand?
27 "And if I cast out demons by Beelzebub,
by whom do your sons cast *them* out? Therefore they shall be your judges.
28 "But if I cast out demons by the Spirit of
God, [R]surely the kingdom of God has come
upon you.   [Dan. 2:44; 7:14]
29 [R]"Or how can one enter a strong man's
house and plunder his goods, unless he first
binds the strong man? And then he will
plunder his house.   Is. 49:24
30 "He who is not with Me is against Me,
and he who does not gather with Me scatters
abroad.

The Unpardonable Sin

31 "Therefore I say to you, [R]every sin and
blasphemy will be forgiven men, [R]but the
blasphemy *against* the Spirit will not be
forgiven men.   Mark 3:28-30 • Acts 7:51
32 "Anyone who [R]speaks a word against
the Son of Man, [R]it will be forgiven him; but
whoever speaks against the Holy Spirit, it will
not be forgiven him, either in this age or in
the *age* to come.   John 7:12, 52 • 1 Tim. 1:13

13-B. Demons: Servants of Satan (Matthew 12:24)—Satan is "the ruler of the demons" (v. 24). He is their god
and they are his servants, to do his will. The Scriptures tell us that "the god of this age has blinded [the minds
of those] who do not believe" (2 Cor. 4:4, page 1167). How can Satan blind the minds of all unbelievers and
keep them in spiritual darkness, since he is not omnipresent? His servants (the demons) assist him in this evil
work. They can keep unbelievers in spiritual darkness until they are cast out by "the word of His power"
(Heb. 1:3, page 1236). Jesus said to a man with a demon, "Come out of the man, unclean spirit" (Mark 5:8,
page 990), and the demon came out of the man. The power of God's Word can help us resist Satan and his
demonic servants.

Satan and his servants are great counterfeiters. For example, as believers, we worship the Lord when we
partake of His Supper. Paul rebuked members of the Corinthian church for allowing the servants of Satan to
corrupt the Lord's Table. He had instructed the church in the proper observance of the Lord's Supper. This
instruction was itself a revelation from the risen Christ. Paul said, "I received from the Lord that which I also
delivered to you" (1 Cor. 11:17–34, page 1156). They, however, had allowed Satan and his demons to pollute
the Lord's Supper. Demons can influence believers and use them to destroy a whole congregation. Paul's
warning to the church was fourfold (1 Cor. 10:20, 21, page 1155):

  (1) Do not sacrifice to demons.
  (2) Have no fellowship with demons.
  (3) "You cannot drink the cup of the Lord and the cup of demons."
  (4) "You cannot partake of the Lord's table and of the table of demons." Satan and his demons are anti-
Christian and often make a show of "religion" (James 2:19, page 1257)!

The apostle Paul warned Timothy that in the latter days some will depart from the faith, giving heed to
deceiving spirits (demons); and will believe and teach "doctrines of demons." All of the doctrines of
demons are lies. In the last days, lying will become a way of life; it is almost that way today.

  (1) "Speaking lies in hypocrisy." Many people will live a lie, pretending to be what they are not.
  (2) "Having their own conscience seared with a hot iron" there will be no conviction of sin.
  (3) "Forbidding to marry." This may mean enforced celibacy, but also may mean that in the last days the
holy bonds of marriage will be widely abolished.
  (4) "Commanding to abstain from foods which God created" for mankind (1 Tim. 4:1–5, page 1220).

Satan, his demons, and all unbelievers who accept their doctrines, "shall have their part in the lake which
burns with fire and brimstone, which is the second death" (Rev. 21:8, page 1315).
See 2 Corinthians 12:7–10, page 1175, for **Point 13-C: Demons: Their Work.**

A Tree Known by Its Fruit

33 "Either make the tree good and its fruit good, or else make the tree bad and its fruit bad; for a tree is known by *its* fruit.

34 "Brood of vipers! How can you, being evil, speak good things? For out of the abundance of the heart the mouth speaks.

35 "A good man out of the good treasure *of his heart brings forth good things, and an evil man out of the evil treasure brings forth evil things.

36 "But I say to you that for every idle word men may speak, they will give account of it in the day of judgment.

37 "For by your words you will be justified, and by your words you will be condemned."

The Scribes and Pharisees Ask for a Sign

38 ᴿThen some of the scribes and Pharisees answered, saying, "Teacher, we want to see a sign from You."   Mark 8:11

39 But He answered and said to them, "An evil and ᴿadulterous generation seeks after a sign, and no sign will be given to it except the sign of the prophet Jonah.   Matt. 16:4

▼ **1–F. Christ and the Apostles Accepted the Books Most Attacked by Critics**

40 ᴿ"For as Jonah was three days and three nights in the belly of the great fish, so will the

12:35 NU, M omit *of his heart*

Son of Man be three days and three nights in ▽ the heart of the earth.   Jon. 1:17

41 ᴿ"The men of Nineveh will rise up in the judgment with this generation and ᴿcondemn it, ᴿbecause they repented at the preaching of Jonah; and indeed a greater than Jonah *is* here.   Luke 11:32 • Jer. 3:11 • Jon. 3:5 ▲

42 "The queen of the South will rise up in the judgment with this generation and condemn it, for she came from the ends of the earth to hear the wisdom of Solomon; and indeed a greater than Solomon *is* here.

An Unclean Spirit Returns

43 ᴿ"When an unclean spirit goes out of a man, ᴿhe goes through dry places, seeking rest, and finds none.   Luke 11:24–26 • [1 Pet. 5:8]

44 "Then he says, 'I will return to my house from which I came.' And when he comes, he finds *it* empty, swept, and put in order.

45 "Then he goes and takes with him seven other spirits more wicked than himself, and they enter and dwell there; and the last *state* of that man is worse than the first. So shall it also be with this wicked generation."

Jesus' Mother and Brothers Send for Him

46 While He was still talking to the multitudes, behold, His mother and brothers stood outside, seeking to speak with Him.

47 Then one said to Him, "Look, ᴿYour mother and Your brothers are standing outside, seeking to speak with You." Matt. 13:55, 56

48 But He answered and said to the one

1-F. Christ and the Apostles Accepted the Books Most Attacked by Critics (Matthew 12:40, 41)—The book of Jonah, claimed by some to be fiction, was personally authorized by the all-knowing Christ. Nor is this the only disputed book He attested:

(1) The Pentateuch (the first five Old Testament books) was written by Moses. (Moses' final death account [Deut. 34, page 213] was probably added by Joshua.) Note that in Matthew 4:4, 7, 10 (page 934), Christ defeats Satan by quoting from Deuteronomy 6:16 (page 187); 8:3 (page 189); and 10:20 (page 191).

Next to Genesis, Deuteronomy is the book most attacked by critics. Yet it was Christ's first choice in fighting Satan. Our conclusion: Deuteronomy was authenticated as inerrant Scripture, once and forever, by the all-knowing Christ.

(2) The book of Daniel was written by Daniel, about 600–550 B.C., although critics say that it was written four hundred years later at about 168 B.C. They allege this because Daniel's prophecies in chapters 2 (page 832), 7 (page 844), and 8 (page 846) seem to extend this far into history (although, indeed, they extend much farther). These critics do not believe it possible that God's prophets could miraculously predict the future. Jesus, however, quotes Daniel as a God-inspired foreteller of the future (Matt. 24:15, page 973; Mark 13:14, page 1002). To Christ, and therefore to us, the book of Daniel came from God, was written by Daniel, foretells the future, and is inerrant in all of its words.

(3) Some scholars divide Isaiah into three sections: "First Isaiah," chapters 1—39 (page 642); "Second Isaiah," chapters 40—55 (page 679); "Third Isaiah," chapters 56—66 (page 696). Because of the three divisions of subject matter, different emphases, and alleged variations in style, some maintain that different authors wrote each section. However, Isaiah is mentioned by name in the New Testament some twenty-one times. For example:

(a) Matthew 15:7–9 (page 960; cf. Is. 29:13, page 669)
(b) Matthew 3:3 (page 933; cf. Is. 40:3, page 679)
(c) Acts 8:28–33 (page 1099; cf. Is. 53:7, 8, page 693)

Along with these three quotations (one of which was spoken by the Lord Jesus Christ) from the three different sections of Isaiah, there are at least eighteen others from Matthew through Romans. All New Testament writers accept the unity of the book and that it is the work of one prophet.

See Psalm 119:89, page 583, for **Point 1-G: Fulfilled Prophecy Shows the Inerrancy of the Bible.**

who told Him, "Who is My mother and who are My brothers?"

49 And He stretched out His hand toward His disciples and said, "Here are My mother and My ᴿbrothers!   John 20:17

50 "For ᴿwhoever does the will of My Father in heaven is My brother and sister and mother."   John 15:14

The Parable of the Sower

13 On the same day Jesus went out of the house ᴿand sat by the sea.   Mark 4:1–12

2 ᴿAnd great multitudes were gathered together to Him, so that ᴿHe got into a boat and sat; and the whole multitude stood on the shore.   Luke 8:4 • Luke 5:3

▼ **47-A. The Sower**

3 Then He spoke many things to them in parables, saying: ᴿ"Behold, a sower went out to sow.   Luke 8:5

4 "And as he sowed, some *seed* fell by the wayside; and the birds came and devoured them.

5 "Some fell on stony places, where they did not have much earth; and they immediately sprang up because they had no depth of earth.

6 "But when the sun was up they were scorched, and because they had no root they withered away.

7 "And some fell among thorns, and the thorns sprang up and choked them.

8 "But others fell on good ground and ▽ yielded a crop: some ᴿa hundredfold, some sixty, some thirty.   Gen. 26:12

9 "He who has ears to hear, let him hear!" ▲

The Purpose of Parables

10 And the disciples came and said to Him, "Why do You speak to them in parables?"

11 He answered and said to them, "Because it has been given to you to know the ᵀmysteries of the kingdom of heaven, but to them it has not been given.   *secret or hidden truths*

12 ᴿ"For whoever has, to him more will be given, and he will have abundance; but whoever does not have, even what he has will be taken away from him.   Matt. 25:29

13 "Therefore I speak to them in parables, because seeing they do not see, and hearing they do not hear, nor do they understand.

14 "And in them the prophecy of Isaiah is fulfilled, which says:

ᴿ*'Hearing you will hear and shall not understand,*
And seeing you will see and not
ᴿ*perceive;*   Is. 6:9, 10 • [John 3:36]

15 *For the hearts of this people have grown dull.*
Their ears ᴿ*are hard of hearing,*   Heb. 5:11
And their eyes they have ᴿ*closed,*
Lest they should see with their eyes
and hear with their ears,   Luke 19:42

47-A. The Sower (Matthew 13:3–9, 18–23)—This parable is easy to understand, because the Lord Jesus interpreted it for His apostles (vv. 18–23):

(1) The sower is one who sows the Word of the kingdom in the world.
(2) The seed is the gospel of Jesus Christ (1 Cor. 15:1–4, page 1161; cf. John 3:17, 18, page 1053).
(3) The ground onto which the gospel seed is sown is the heart of man (Rom. 10:9, 10, page 1140).

There are four different responses to the gospel message—four different types of ground upon which the seed of the gospel falls. Christ did not teach that all the world would be converted during this age (Matt. 7:21–23, page 946). The various reactions are not caused by different qualities of *seed*—for example, more thrilling or compelling preaching. Christ placed the responsibility for faith or unbelief on the *soil*—the *hearer*.

(1) The first response comes from a *hard* heart (v. 4; cf. John 12:37–41, page 1072; Heb. 3:7–13, page 1238). Wayside soil is hard and unprepared for seed. The fowls that devour the seed that fell on the hard ground are Satan and his demons.

(2) The second response comes from a *shallow* heart (vv. 5, 6). Such a person has no spiritual depth, no commitment to God's Word. He holds to his religious decision for a while; but when tribulation or persecution come, "because of the word" of God, he is offended and falls away from his profession of faith (vv. 20, 21; cf. Matt. 7:21–23, page 946).

(3) The third response comes from a *worldly* heart (v. 7). A heart that loves this world system is a heart alienated from God (1 Cor. 3:1–4, page 1149). The love of money, success, and the pleasures of this world choke out the influence of the Word of God in the life of the professing believer so that he becomes unfruitful (v. 22). Many profess Christ but love the world and the things of the world more than they love God (1 John 2:15–17, page 1279).

(4) The fourth response comes from an *understanding* heart (vv. 8, 23). Note that only one man *understood* the Word of God, and brought forth fruit (Acts 8:26–39, page 1099).

The parable of the sower will apply to the ministry of the Lord Jesus Christ until the harvest at the end of the present age (John 4:35–39, page 1054). This parable should warn unconverted people that they need to receive the "good seed," the message of Christ's forgiveness, into their hearts. It also should encourage Christians to witness boldly, because the seed *does* produce fruit. However, the parable also puts to rest the unbiblical expectation that everyone who "hears" will enter the kingdom. Only those who hear, *understand*, and believe will make the true entrance.

See Matthew 13:24–30, 36–43, page 956, for **Point 47-B: The Tares.**

Lest they should understand with their hearts and turn,
So that I *should heal them.'

16 "But ᴿblessed *are* your eyes for they see, and your ears for they hear; Luke 10:23, 24

17 "for assuredly, I say to you ᴿthat many prophets and righteous *men* desired to see what you see, and did not see *it*, and to hear what you hear, and did not hear *it*. Heb. 11:13

The Parable of the Sower Explained

▼ 18 ᴿ"Therefore hear the parable of the sower: Mark 4:13-20

19 "When anyone hears the word ᴿof the kingdom, and does not understand *it*, then the wicked *one* comes and snatches away what was sown in his heart. This is he who received seed by the wayside. Matt. 4:23

20 "But he who received the seed on stony places, this is he who hears the word and immediately ᴿreceives it with joy; Is. 58:2

21 "yet he has no root in himself, but endures only for a while. For when ᴿtribulation or persecution arises because of the word, immediately ᴿhe stumbles. [Acts 14:22] • Matt. 11:6

22 "Now ᴿhe who received seed ᴿamong the thorns is he who hears the word, and the cares of this world and the deceitfulness of riches choke the word, and he becomes unfruitful. 1 Tim. 6:9 • Jer. 4:3

23 "But he who received seed on the good ground is he who hears the word and under-

13:15 NU, M *would*

stands *it*, who indeed bears ᴿfruit and produces: some a hundredfold, some sixty, some thirty." Col. 1:6 ▲

The Parable of the Wheat and the Tares

47-B. The Tares ▼

24 Another parable He put forth to them, saying: "The kingdom of heaven is like a man who sowed good seed in his field;

25 "but while men slept, his enemy came and sowed tares among the wheat and went his way.

26 "But when the grain had sprouted and produced a crop, then the tares also appeared.

27 "So the servants of the owner came and said to him, 'Sir, did you not sow good seed in your field? How then does it have tares?'

28 "He said to them, 'An enemy has done this.' The servants said to him, 'Do you want us then to go and gather them up?'

29 "But he said, 'No, lest while you gather up the tares you also uproot the wheat with them.

30 'Let both grow together until the harvest, and at the time of harvest I will say to the reapers, "First gather together the tares and bind them in bundles to burn them, but ᴿgather the wheat into my barn." ' " Matt. 3:12 ▲

The Parable of the Mustard Seed

47-C. The Mustard Seed ▼

31 Another parable He put forth to them, saying: ᴿ"The kingdom of heaven is like a

---

47-B. The Tares (Matthew 13:24-30, 36-43)—As He did with the parable of the sower, our Lord interpreted this parable for us:

(1) The sower of the good seed is the Son of Man, the Lord Jesus Christ (vv. 24, 37).

(2) The field is the world (vv. 24, 38). While here on earth He sowed the good seed in person; but before ascending into heaven, He commissioned His church to proclaim the gospel to every person in every nation (Matt. 28:19, 20, page 982).

(3) The good seed in this parable is not the gospel, but rather the children of the kingdom (vv. 24, 38). He began to sow (scatter) the good seed (the children of God) first in Jerusalem, then in Judea and Samaria; and He continues to scatter His children among all parts of the world. The good seed, as they are sown, are to share their faith with that part of the world in which they have been scattered (Acts 1:8, page 1086; cf. 8:1-4, page 1098).

(4) "The tares are the sons of the wicked one," Satan (vv. 25, 38). Jesus said to the unsaved religious leaders of His day, "You are of your father the devil" (John 8:44, page 1063). Where Jesus sends His children, Satan also sends his. You will find in most churches children of God and children of the Devil (Matt. 7:21-23, page 946).

(5) The enemy that sowed the tares is the Devil (vv. 28, 39).

(6) The harvest is the end of the age (vv. 30, 39). Christ's second coming will conclude this age. He will send His angels to reap the harvest and separate the wheat from the tares. He will rapture the "wheat," the children of the kingdom, and burn the "tares," the children of Satan. Note the contrast: The children of the Devil will be cast into "the furnace of fire" (hell), while the children of God "will shine forth as the sun in the kingdom of their Father" (vv. 30, 40-43; cf. Rev. 20:15, page 1314).

See Matthew 13:31, 32, above, for **Point 47-C: The Mustard Seed.**

47-C. The Mustard Seed (Matthew 13:31, 32)—"The kingdom of heaven is like a mustard seed, which a man took and sowed in his field" (v. 31). The mustard seed is one of the smallest of seeds.

(1) The mustard seed is the church in its numerically insignificant beginning—Christ and the twelve

(Point 47-C continued on next page)

▽ mustard seed, which a man took and sowed
in his field,   Luke 13:18, 19

32 "which indeed is the least of all the
seeds; but when it is grown it is greater than
the herbs and becomes a ᴿtree, so that the
birds of the air come and nest in its
▲ branches."   Ezek. 17:22–24; 31:3–9

The Parable of the Leaven

▼ **47-D. The Leaven**

33 Another parable He spoke to them: "The
kingdom of heaven is like leaven, which a
woman took and hid in three *measures of
▲ meal till it was all leavened."

Prophecy and the Parables

34 ᴿAll these things Jesus spoke to the
multitude in parables; and without a parable
He did not speak to them,   Mark 4:33, 34
35 that it might be fulfilled which was spoken by the prophet, saying:

> ᴿ"*I will open My mouth in parables;
> I will utter things kept secret from the
> foundation of the world.*"   Ps. 78:2

The Parable of the Tares Explained

▼ **36** Then Jesus sent the multitude away and
went into the house. And His disciples came

13:33 Gr. *saton,* same as a Heb. *seah;* approximately 2
pecks in all

to Him, saying, "Explain to us the parable of ▽
the tares of the field."

37 He answered and said to them: "He who
sows the good seed is the Son of Man.
38 ᴿ"The field is the world, the good seeds
are the sons of the kingdom, but the tares are
ᴿthe sons of the wicked *one.* Rom. 10:18 • John 8:44
39 "The enemy who sowed them is the
devil, the harvest is the end of the age, and
the reapers are the angels.   Rev. 14:15
40 "Therefore as the tares are gathered and
burned in the fire, so it will be at the end of
this age.
41 "The Son of Man will send out His angels, ᴿand they will gather out of His kingdom
all things that offend, and those who practice
lawlessness,   Matt. 18:7
42 ᴿ"and will cast them into the furnace of
fire. ᴿThere will be wailing and gnashing of
teeth.   Rev. 19:20; 20:10 • Matt. 8:12; 13:50
43 "Then the righteous will shine forth as
the sun in the kingdom of their Father. He
who has ears to hear, let him hear!   ▲

The Parable of the Hidden Treasure

▼ **47-E. The Hidden Treasure**

44 "Again, the kingdom of heaven is like
treasure hidden in a field, which a man found
and hid; and for joy over it he goes and sells
all that he has and ᴿbuys that field. [Is. 55:1] ▲

(Point 47-C continued from previous page)
apostles. On the Day of Pentecost, the small kingdom began its phenomenal expansion. Like the mustard
tree it continued to grow, branching out into other nations of the known world.
 (2) The man who sowed the seed is the God-Man, Christ Jesus.
 (3) His field is the world.
 (4) The fowls of the air that lodged in the branches are probably the same as in the parable of the
sower—Satan and his demons (Matt. 13:4, 19, page 955).

 This mustard tree (the church), in its early existence, was pure and powerful until Satan's followers found
a way to nest in its branches. Christendom will continue with the true children of God, as well as the
imposters who profess to be God's children. Just as the wheat and the tares will grow together until the
harvest, so the saved and the unsaved will nest in the mustard tree until Jesus comes to separate the wheat
from the tares, the sheep from the goats, the saved from the unsaved (Matt. 25:31–34, 41, 46, page 976).
 See Matthew 13:33, above, for **Point 47-D: The Leaven.**

47-D. The Leaven (Matthew 13:33)—
 (1) The woman is the harlot church (Rev. 17, page 1310).
 (2) The leaven represents the subtle working of evil, for which the same symbol is used elsewhere in
Scripture (e.g., Ex. 12:15, 19, page 70; Matt. 16:6–12, page 961). It is religious hypocrisy (Luke 12:1, page
1029). The leaven is the evil doctrine of the apostate church.
 (3) The three measures of meal represent Christendom from its inception through the Tribulation. After
the true church is raptured, Christendom will be totally corrupt (1 Cor. 5:6–9, page 1150). The "mystery of
lawlessness" (2 Thess. 2:7, page 1215) has been working as leaven in the church from its early days (Rev.
2:2–15, page 1294) and will continue to work until the whole of Christendom is evil.

 This parable teaches that as the years and centuries roll on, the pure Christianity of the early church will
become progressively corrupt until the entire lump (Christendom) is leavened.
 See Matthew 13:44, above, for **Point 47-E: The Hidden Treasure.**

47-E. The Hidden Treasure (Matthew 13:44)—This profound parable is one of the deepest and most
misinterpreted of all the parables. It involves both revelation and mystery (Rom. 16:25, 26, page 1146; cf.
Mark 4:11, 12, page 988).

(Point 47-E continued on next page)

The Parable of the Pearl of Great Price

▼ **47-F. The Pearl of Great Price**

45 "Again, the kingdom of heaven is like a merchant seeking beautiful pearls,

46 "who, when he had found ᴿone pearl of great price, went and sold all that he had and ▲ bought it.   Prov. 2:4; 3:14, 15; 8:10, 19

The Parable of the Dragnet

▼ **47-G. The Net**

47 "Again, the kingdom of heaven is like a dragnet that was cast into the sea and ᴿgathered some of every kind,   Matt. 22:9, 10

48 "which, when it was full, they drew to ▽ shore; and they sat down and gathered the good into vessels, but threw the bad away.

49 "So it will be at the end of the age. The angels will come forth, ᴿseparate the wicked from among the just,   Matt. 25:32

50 "and cast them into the furnace of fire. There will be wailing and gnashing of teeth." ▲

51 *Jesus said to them, "Have you understood all these things?" They said to Him, "Yes, *Lord."

52 Then He said to them, "Therefore every

13:51 NU omits *Jesus said to them* • NU omits *Lord*

(Point 47-E continued from previous page)

(1) The revelation is that the hidden treasure is the kingdom of God, not specifically the church, although the church is part of God's kingdom. This parable deals with the total kingdom, and not merely with a part.

(2) The mystery is that when the Lord Jesus found the treasure in the field, He hid it. The kingdom of God in its totality is still a mystery, hidden from man. However, Christ has revealed to us the King's manifesto, found in the Sermon on the Mount.

(3) The treasure is hidden in the field (the world). When Adam and Eve sinned and were driven from the Garden of Eden and God put a curse upon the world (Gen. 3:4–19, page 5), Satan, the god of this age, attempted to usurp a kingdom (2 Cor. 4:4, page 1167). Satan's kingdom, the kingdom of evil, is seen everywhere. The treasure, the kingdom of God that is hidden in the world, will be revealed in all power when the King returns and establishes His kingdom.

Jesus journeyed to Calvary with the promise of joy before Him (Heb. 12:2, page 1250). It was the joy of knowing that on the other side of the Cross was His purchased kingdom. After His resurrection He went back to heaven to await the Father's time, when He will return to this earth as King of kings and Lord of lords to claim the kingdom (Matt. 25:31–46, page 976; cf. Rev. 19:16, page 1313).

See Matthew 13:45, 46, above, for **Point 47-F: The Pearl of Great Price.**

47-F. The Pearl of Great Price (Matthew 13:45, 46)—The "pearl of great price" (v. 46) is perhaps the easiest to understand of all of Jesus' parables.

Again we have the merchant, representing the God-Man, Christ Jesus, who came into the world "to seek and to save that which was lost" (Luke 19:10, page 1038). The merchant came seeking beautiful pearls, and found one pearl of exquisite beauty. This speaks of the church, the body of Christ (Col. 1:18, page 1202). It is a beautiful picture of the growth, unity, and purity of the church.

The seeking Savior comes, and men, women, and children hear the gospel of how He was pierced, "wounded for our transgressions" (Is. 53:5, page 693). A pearl is formed in an oyster—a grain of sand lodged in the oyster's shell causes irritation, triggering a secretion that surrounds the sand . . . and in time a pearl is formed. Similarly, through the centuries the Lord has been adding to the church those who are being saved (Acts 2:47, page 1090). Thus, all born-again children of God together are valuable pearls in the eyes of the Father, Son, and Holy Spirit, because we were spiritually shaped by the blood that came from the Savior's pierced side.

This is a great mystery: that billions of individuals, living and dead, of differing backgrounds, cultures, customs, and languages, are one body. Tragically, sometimes differences in doctrine, opinion, and will are so pronounced between believers that it seems there will never be unity among them. Many refuse to "speak the same thing" and "be perfectly joined together in the same mind and in the same judgment" (1 Cor. 1:10, page 1148). Nonetheless they are all one in "the unity of the Spirit," in "one body" (Eph. 4:3, 4, page 1190). And just as the merchant sold all that he had and bought the one pearl of great price, so "Christ also loved the church and gave Himself for her" (Eph. 5:25, page 1192).

This pure, pearl-like unity of the church may never be visible on this earth, during this age. It will be realized, though, when the dead in Christ are raised and, with those who are alive, are caught up to meet Him in the air (1 Thess. 4:16–18, page 1212). Then we will be perfect in body and mind—"conformed to His glorious body" (Phil. 3:21, page 1198) and knowing "just as [we] also [are] known" (1 Cor. 13:12, page 1160). Then we shall be revealed as one body, one bride, or, as in the parable, "one pearl of great price"—paid for by His death, burial, and resurrection.

See Matthew 13:47-50, above, for **Point 47-G: The Net.**

47-G. The Net (Matthew 13:47–50)—This parable depicts the consummation of what the foregoing parables describe, as the kingdom moves from mystery to open, visible presence.

(1) The kingdom of heaven is a net filled with fish—a catch of all kinds.

(Point 47-G continued on next page)

scribe instructed ᵀconcerning the kingdom of heaven is like a householder who brings out of his treasure *things* new and old." Or *for*

Jesus Rejected at Nazareth

53 Now it came to pass, when Jesus had finished these parables, that He departed from there.

54 ᴿWhen He had come to His own country, He ᴿtaught them in their synagogue, so that they were astonished and said, "Where did this *Man* get this wisdom and *these* mighty works? Luke 4:16 · Ps. 22:22

55 "Is this not the carpenter's son? Is not His mother called Mary? And His brothers ᴿJames, *Joses, Simon, and Judas? Mark 15:40

56 "And His sisters, are they not all with us? Where then did this *Man* get all these things?"

57 So they ᴿwere offended at Him. But Jesus said to them, ᴿ"A prophet is not without honor except in his own country and in his own house." Matt. 11:6 · Luke 4:24

58 Now ᴿHe did not do many mighty works there because of their unbelief. Mark 6:5, 6

John the Baptist Beheaded

14 At that time ᴿHerod the tetrarch heard the report about Jesus Mark 6:14-29

2 and said to his servants, "This is John the Baptist; he is risen from the dead, and therefore these powers are at work in him."

3 For Herod had laid hold of John and bound him, and put *him* in prison for the sake of Herodias, his brother Philip's wife.

4 Because John had said to him, ᴿ"It is not lawful for you to have her." Lev. 18:16; 20:21

5 And although he wanted to put him to death, he feared the multitude, ᴿbecause they counted him as a prophet. Luke 20:6

6 But when Herod's birthday was celebrated, the daughter of Herodias danced before them and pleased Herod.

7 Therefore he promised with an oath to give her whatever she might ask.

8 So she, having been prompted by her mother, said, "Give me John the Baptist's head here on a platter."

9 And the king was sorry; nevertheless, because of the oaths and because of those

13:55 NU *Joseph*

who sat with him, he commanded *it* to be given to *her.*

10 So he sent and had John beheaded in prison.

11 And his head was brought on a platter and given to the girl, and she brought *it* to her mother.

12 Then his disciples came and took away the body and buried it, and went and told Jesus.

Feeding the Five Thousand

13 ᴿWhen Jesus heard *it,* He departed from there by boat to a deserted place by Himself. But when the multitudes heard it, they followed Him on foot from the cities. John 6:1, 2

14 And when Jesus went out He saw a great multitude; and He was moved with compassion for them, and healed their sick.

15 ᴿWhen it was evening, His disciples came to Him, saying, "This is a deserted place, and the hour is already late. Send the multitudes away, that they may go into the villages and buy themselves food." Luke 9:12

16 But Jesus said to them, "They do not need to go away. You give them something to eat."

17 And they said to Him, "We have here only five loaves and two fish."

18 He said, "Bring them here to Me."

19 Then He commanded the multitudes to sit down on the grass. And He took the five loaves and the two fish, and looking up to heaven, ᴿHe blessed and broke and gave the loaves to the disciples; and the disciples gave to the multitudes. Matt. 15:36; 26:26

20 So they all ate and were filled, and they took up twelve baskets full of the fragments that remained.

21 Now those who had eaten were about five thousand men, besides women and children.

Jesus Walks on the Sea

22 Immediately Jesus ᵀmade His disciples get into the boat and go before Him to the other side, while He sent the multitudes away. *strongly urged*

23 ᴿAnd when He had sent the multitudes away, He went up on a mountain by Himself to pray. ᴿNow when evening came, He was alone there. Mark 6:46 · John 6:16

(Point 47-G continued from previous page)

(2) The sea is the nations of the world who will come before the King to be judged.

(3) The catch is made up of good and bad. Just as the King allows the tares to grow amid the wheat until He comes to establish His kingdom, so the good and bad fish will co-exist until the Master Fisherman casts His net and draws them into His presence at the end of the age (v. 49). The angels will then separate the good from the bad (Matt. 25:31-46, page 976). The good (the saved, who did the will of God—John 6:40, page 1060) will be received into God's kingdom. The bad (the lost, who were disobedient) will be "cast . . . into the furnace of fire. There will be wailing and gnashing of teeth" (v. 50).

See Index, page 17, for your next study.

24 But the boat was now *in the middle of the sea, tossed by the waves, for the wind was contrary.

25 Now in the fourth watch of the night Jesus went to them, walking on the sea.

26 And when the disciples saw Him ᴿwalking on the sea, they were troubled, saying, "It is a ghost!" And they cried out for fear.   Job 9:8

27 But immediately Jesus spoke to them, saying, ᵀ"Be of good ᴿcheer! ᵀIt is I; do not be afraid."   Take courage • Acts 23:11; 27:22, 25, 36 • Lit. I am

28 And Peter answered Him and said, "Lord, if it is You, command me to come to You on the water."

29 So He said, "Come." And when Peter had come down out of the boat, he walked on the water to go to Jesus.

30 But when he saw *that the wind was boisterous, he was afraid; and beginning to sink he cried out, saying, "Lord, save me!"

31 And immediately Jesus stretched out His hand and caught him, and said to him, "O you of little faith, why did you doubt?"

32 And when they got into the boat, the wind ceased.

33 Then those who were in the boat *came and worshiped Him, saying, "Truly ᴿYou are the Son of God."   Ps. 2:7

Many Touch Him and Are Made Well

34 ᴿWhen they had crossed over, they came *to the land of Gennesaret.   Mark 6:53

35 And when the men of that place recognized Him, they sent out into all that surrounding region, brought to Him all who were sick,

36 and begged Him that they might only touch the hem of His garment. And as many as touched it were made perfectly well.

Defilement Comes from Within

15 Then the scribes and Pharisees who were from Jerusalem came to Jesus, saying,

2 ᴿ"Why do Your disciples transgress the tradition of the elders? For they do not wash their hands when they eat bread."   Mark 7:5

3 He answered and said to them, "Why do you also transgress the commandment of God because of your tradition?

4 "For God commanded, saying, ᴿ'Honor your father and your mother'; and, ᴿ'He who curses father or mother, let him be put to death.'   Ex. 20:12; Deut. 5:16 • Ex. 21:17

5 "But you say, 'Whoever says to his father or mother, "Whatever profit you might have received from me is a gift to God"—

6 'then he need not honor his father *or mother.' Thus you have made the *commandment of God of no effect by your tradition.

7 ᴿ"Hypocrites! Well did Isaiah prophesy about you, saying: Mark 7:6

8 'Theseᴿ people *draw near to Me with
       their mouth,   Is. 29:13
   And honor Me with their lips,
   But their heart is far from Me.
9 And in vain they worship Me,
   ᴿTeaching as doctrines the
       commandments of men.'"   [Col. 2:18–22]

10 ᴿWhen He had called the multitude to Himself, He said to them, "Hear and understand: Mark 7:14

11 ᴿ"Not what goes into the mouth defiles a man; but what comes out of the mouth, this defiles a man."   [Acts 10:15]

12 Then His disciples came and said to Him, "Do You know that the Pharisees were offended when they heard this saying?"

13 But He answered and said, ᴿ"Every plant which My heavenly Father has not planted will be uprooted.   [John 15:2]

14 "Let them alone. ᴿThey are blind leaders of the blind. And if the blind leads the blind, both will fall into a ditch."   Luke 6:39

15 ᴿThen Peter answered and said to Him, "Explain this parable to us."   Mark 7:17

16 So Jesus said, ᴿ"Are you also still without understanding?   Matt. 16:9

17 "Do you not yet understand that ᴿwhatever enters the mouth goes into the stomach and is eliminated?   [1 Cor. 6:13]

18 "But ᴿthose things which proceed out of the mouth come from the heart, and they defile a man.   [James 3:6]

19 ᴿ"For out of the heart proceed evil thoughts, murders, adulteries, fornications, thefts, false witness, blasphemies.   Prov. 6:14

20 "These are the things which defile a man, but to eat with unwashed hands does not defile a man."

A Gentile Shows Her Faith

21 Then Jesus went out from there and departed to the region of Tyre and Sidon.

22 And behold, a woman of Canaan came from that region and cried out to Him, saying, "Have mercy on me, O Lord, ᴿSon of David! My daughter is severely demon-possessed."   Matt. 1:1; 22:41, 42

23 But He answered her not a word. And His disciples came and urged Him, saying, "Send her away, for she cries out after us."

24 But He answered and said, ᴿ"I was not sent except to the lost sheep of the house of Israel."   Matt. 10:5, 6

14:24 NU many furlongs away from the land
14:30 NU brackets that and boisterous as disputed.
14:33 NU omits came and
14:34 NU to land at

15:6 NU omits or mother • NU word
15:8 NU omits draw near to Me with their mouth, And

25 Then she came and worshiped Him, saying, "Lord, help me!"

26 But He answered and said, "It is not good to take the children's bread and throw *it* to the little ᴿdogs." Matt. 7:6

27 And she said, "Yes, Lord, yet even the little dogs eat the crumbs which fall from their masters' table."

28 Then Jesus answered and said to her, "O woman, ᴿgreat *is* your faith! Let it be to you as you desire." And her daughter was healed from that very hour. Luke 7:9

Jesus Heals Great Multitudes

29 ᴿJesus departed from there, ᴿskirted the Sea of Galilee, and went up on the mountain and sat down there. Mark 7:31-37 • Matt. 4:18

30 ᴿThen great multitudes came to Him, having with them *the* lame, blind, mute, ᵀmaimed, and many others; and they laid them down at Jesus' ᴿfeet, and He healed them. Is. 35:5, 6 • *crippled* • Luke 7:38; 8:41; 10:39

31 So the multitude marveled when they saw *the* mute speaking, *the* maimed made whole, *the* lame walking, and *the* blind seeing; and they glorified the God of Israel.

Feeding the Four Thousand

32 ᴿNow Jesus called His disciples to *Himself* and said, "I have compassion on the multitude, because they have now continued with Me three days and have nothing to eat. And I do not want to send them away hungry, lest they faint on the way." Mark 8:1-10

33 ᴿThen His disciples said to Him, "Where could we get enough bread in the wilderness to fill such a great multitude?" 2 Kin. 4:43

34 Jesus said to them, "How many loaves do you have?" And they said, "Seven, and a few little fish."

35 So He commanded the multitude to sit down on the ground.

36 And ᴿHe took the seven loaves and the fish and ᴿgave thanks, broke *them* and gave *them* to His disciples; and the disciples *gave* to the multitude. Matt. 14:19; 26:27 • Luke 22:19

37 So they all ate and were filled, and they took up seven large baskets full of the fragments that were left.

38 Now those who ate were four thousand men, besides women and children.

39 ᴿAnd He sent away the multitude, got into the boat, and came to the region of *Magdala. Mark 8:10

15:39 NU *Magadan*

The Pharisees and Sadducees Seek a Sign

16 Then the ᴿPharisees and Sadducees came, and testing Him asked that He would show them a sign from heaven. Mark 8:11

2 He answered and said to them, "When it is evening you say, '*It will be* fair weather, for the sky is red';

3 "and in the morning, '*It will be* foul weather today, for the sky is red and threatening.' *Hypocrites! You know how to discern the face of the sky, but you cannot *discern* the signs of the times.

4 ᴿ"A wicked and adulterous generation seeks after a sign, and no sign shall be given to it except the sign of *the prophet Jonah." And He left them and departed. Matt. 12:39

The Leaven of the Pharisees and Sadducees

5 Now when His disciples had come to the other side, they had forgotten to take bread.

6 Then Jesus said to them, ᴿ"Take heed and beware of the ᵀleaven of the Pharisees and the Sadducees." Luke 12:1 • *yeast*

7 And they reasoned among themselves, saying, "It is because we have taken no bread."

8 But Jesus, being aware of *it*, said to them, "O you of little faith, why do you reason among yourselves because you *have brought no bread?

9 ᴿ"Do you not yet understand, or remember the five loaves of the five thousand and how many baskets you took up? Matt. 14:15-21

10 ᴿ"Nor the seven loaves of the four thousand and how many large baskets you took up? Matt. 15:32-38

11 "How is it you do not understand that I did not speak to you concerning bread?—but to beware of the ᵀleaven of the Pharisees and Sadducees." *yeast*

12 Then they understood that He did not tell *them* to beware of the leaven of bread, but of the ᵀdoctrine of the Pharisees and Sadducees. *teaching*

Peter Confesses Jesus as the Christ

38-E. The Church: Its Builder ▼

13 When Jesus came into the region of Caesarea Philippi, He asked His disciples,

16:3 NU omits *Hypocrites*
16:4 NU omits *the prophet*
16:8 NU *have no bread*

38-E. The Church: Its Builder (Matthew 16:13-20)—In this portion of Scripture, Jesus continued to reveal more of who He was and what He had come to do. First He asked His disciples two questions; then, adding to their answers, He gave them new revelation concerning Himself.

(1) "Who do men say that I, the Son of Man, am?" They all gave the same answer: "One of the prophets" (vv. 13, 14).

(Point 38-E continued on next page)

∇ saying, ᴿ"Who do men say that I, the Son of Man, am?"   Luke 9:18

14 So they said, ᴿ"Some *say* John the Baptist, some Elijah, and others Jeremiah or ᴿone of the prophets."   Matt. 14:2 • Matt. 21:11

15 He said to them, "But who do ᴿyou say that I am?"   John 6:67

16 Simon Peter answered and said, "You are the Christ, the Son of the living God."

17 Jesus answered and said to him, "Blessed are you, Simon Bar-Jonah, ᴿfor flesh and blood has not revealed *this* to you, but ᴿMy Father who is in heaven.   [Eph. 2:8] • Gal. 1:16

18 "And I also say to you that you are Peter, and ᴿon this rock I will ᴿbuild My church, and the gates of Hades shall not prevail against it.   [Eph. 2:20] • Acts 2:41, 47

19 ᴿ"And I will give you the keys of the kingdom of heaven, and whatever you bind on earth *will be bound in heaven, and whatever you loose on earth will be loosed in heaven."   Matt. 18:18

20 ᴿThen He commanded His disciples that they should tell no one that He was Jesus the ▲ Christ.   Luke 9:21

16:19 Or *will have been bound . . . will have been loosed*

Jesus Predicts His Death and Resurrection

21 From that time Jesus began to show to His disciples that He must go to Jerusalem, and suffer many things from the elders and chief priests and scribes, and be killed, and be ᴿraised the third day.   Acts 10:40; 1 Cor. 15:4

22 Then Peter took Him aside and began to rebuke Him, saying, "Far be it from You, Lord; this shall not happen to You!"

23 But He turned and said to Peter, "Get behind Me, Satan! You are ᵀan offense to Me, for you are not mindful of the things of God, but the things of men."   *a stumbling block*

Take Up the Cross and Follow Him

24 ᴿThen Jesus said to His disciples, "If anyone desires to come after Me, let him deny himself, and take up his cross, and ᴿfollow Me.   [2 Tim. 3:12] • [1 Pet. 2:21]

25 "For ᴿwhoever desires to save his life will lose it, but whoever loses his life for My sake will find it.   John 12:25

26 "For what ᴿprofit is it to a man if he gains the whole world, and loses his own soul? Or ᴿwhat will a man give in exchange for his soul?   Luke 12:20, 21 • Ps. 49:7, 8

(Point 38-E continued from previous page)

(2) "But who do you say that I am?" (v. 15). Peter answered, "You are the Christ [Messiah], the Son of the living God" (v. 16). Peter's answer to this question was itself a revelation from God the Father (v. 17). Note its profound implications:

(a) The incarnation of God's only begotten Son was the fullest revelation of God's plan of salvation. John said, "The Word [Christ, God's Son] became flesh"—the Incarnation (John 1:14, page 1049). God the Son was given a complete but sinless human nature, thus becoming the God-Man, having two natures in one person.

(b) The next step in God's revelation of eternal salvation was when God the Father's only begotten Son was made to "be sin" for us. In His incarnation He was made flesh. He was not part God and part man; He was fully God and fully man. In His vicarious death on Calvary, He was made "to be sin for us, that we might become the righteousness of God in Him" (2 Cor. 5:21, page 1169). To be saved, one must believe in His incarnation (that He was virgin-born, conceived by the Holy Spirit—Luke 1:26–38, page 1010), and that He died as our substitute on Calvary, was buried, resurrected, and ascended into heaven with the promise to come again and resurrect the dead in Christ—His church (1 Cor. 15:1–4, page 1161; cf. Acts 1:6–9, page 1086).

(3) Then Jesus told them, "On this rock I will build My church" (v. 18). Jesus—who has all authority in heaven and on earth (Matt. 28:18, page 982), who walked upon the waters of Galilee (Matt. 14:22–36, page 959), who rebuked the wind and the raging of the water, causing the storms to cease (Luke 8:22–25, page 1023), who spoke as no man ever spoke (John 7:46, page 1062)—said, "You are Peter [*petros*—a stone], and on this rock [*petra*—a rocky ledge] I will build My church" (v. 18). There is no question about it: Christ is the one foundation of His church.

Christ is not only the foundation of His church, He is its architect and builder. The church is a holy temple, a habitation of God, through the Holy Spirit who indwells every born-again child of God (1 Cor. 6:19, 20, page 1152). He is building His church "on the foundation [doctrine] of the apostles and prophets, Jesus Christ Himself being the chief cornerstone" (Eph. 2:19–22, page 1188). Israel drank from Christ, that "Rock" that followed them in the wilderness (1 Cor. 10:4, page 1154); now He is the foundation and chief cornerstone of His church (1 Cor. 3:11, page 1149; cf. Is. 28:16, page 668). He is building His church upon Himself using only "living stones"—sinners saved by His grace. At no time did Peter believe that *he* was the foundation of the church. He spoke of Christ as the "living stone . . . chosen by God . . . a chief cornerstone, elect, precious," but to unbelievers He is "a stone of stumbling and a rock of offense" (1 Pet. 2:4–8, page 1264).

See Index, page 17, for your next study.

▼ 6-G. He Will Be Unique in His Second Coming

27 "For ^Rthe Son of Man will come in the glory of His Father ^Rwith His angels, ^Rand then He will reward each according to his ▲ works.   Mark 8:38 • [Dan. 7:10] • Rom. 2:6

Jesus Transfigured on the Mount

28 "Assuredly, I say to you, ^Rthere are some standing here who shall not taste death till they see the Son of Man coming in His kingdom."   Luke 9:27

17 Now after six days Jesus took Peter, James, and John his brother, led them up on a high mountain by themselves;

2 and He was transfigured before them. His face shone like the sun, and His clothes became as white as the light.

3 And behold, Moses and Elijah appeared to them, talking with Him.

4 Then Peter answered and said to Jesus, "Lord, it is good for us to be here; if You wish, *let us make here three tabernacles: one for You, one for Moses, and one for Elijah."

5 While he was still speaking, behold, a bright cloud overshadowed them; and suddenly a voice came out of the cloud, saying, ^R"This is My beloved Son, in whom I am well pleased. Hear Him!"   Is. 42:1; 2 Pet. 1:17

6 And when the disciples heard it, they fell on their faces and were greatly afraid.

7 But Jesus came and ^Rtouched them and said, "Arise, and do not be afraid."   Dan. 8:18

8 When they had lifted up their eyes, they saw no one but Jesus only.

9 Now as they came down from the mountain, Jesus commanded them, saying, "Tell the vision to no one until the Son of Man is risen from the dead."

10 And His disciples asked Him, saying, ^R"Why then do the scribes say that Elijah must come first?"   Mal. 4:5

11 Jesus answered and said to them, "Indeed, Elijah is coming *first and will ^Rrestore all things.   [Mal. 4:6]

12 ^R"But I say to you that Elijah has come already, and they ^Rdid not know him but did to him whatever they wished. Likewise ^Rthe Son of Man is also about to suffer at their hands."   Mark 9:12, 13 • Matt. 14:3, 10 • Matt. 16:21

13 ^RThen the disciples understood that He spoke to them of John the Baptist.   Matt. 11:14

17:4 NU I will make   17:11 NU omits first

6-G. He Will Be Unique in His Second Coming (Matthew 16:27)—"For the Son of Man will come in the glory of His Father with His angels" (v. 27). When Jesus came the first time, angels heralded His birth (Luke 2:7-14, page 1012; Heb. 1:6, page 1236). When He comes the second time, to establish the kingdom and sit upon the throne of David (Is. 9:6, 7, page 651), His angels will accompany Him, "and they will gather together His elect from the four winds, from one end of heaven to the other" (Matt. 24:29-31, page 974).

Forty days after His resurrection, as He ascended, "two men stood by them [the apostles] in white apparel, who also said, 'Men of Galilee, why do you stand gazing up into heaven? This same Jesus, who was taken up from you into heaven, will so come in like manner as you saw Him go into heaven'" (Acts 1:10, 11, page 1087). Thus was the promise again given that Christ alone, of all religious leaders throughout history, would someday return to earth personally and bodily. Buddha, Confucius, and every world leader is gone forever—but the unique Christ is coming again!

Christ's second coming will:

(1) See Him return, not as the "Lamb as though it had been slain" (Rev. 5:6, page 1297), but in the power and the majesty of His deity, as "the Lion of the tribe of Judah" (Rev. 5:5, page 1297).

(2) Raise "the dead in Christ . . . Then we who are alive and remain shall be caught up together with them in the clouds to meet the Lord in the air. And thus we shall always be with the Lord" (1 Thess. 4:16, 17, page 1212). This is the rapture of the church.

(3) Be "as a thief in the night" (1 Thess. 5:2, page 1212). "That day and hour no one knows" (Matt. 24:36, 42-44, page 974).

(4) Inaugurate the promised millennial kingdom of peace on earth among men, who will be judged (Matt. 25:31, 32, page 976) and ruled (Ps. 2:6-12, page 510), and among animals, who will live in harmony with mankind and with each other (Is. 11:4-9, page 654).

(5) Put away or destroy the forces of evil who will be gathered against Him:

    (a) Antichrist (2 Thess. 2:8, page 1215)
    (b) the False Prophet (Rev. 13:1-18, page 1305)
    (c) the evil armies gathered at Armageddon (Rev. 19:17-21, page 1313)
    (d) all evildoers (2 Thess. 1:7-9, page 1215)
    (e) Satan himself, who will be imprisoned (Rev. 19:11—20:14, page 1312)

(6) Rescue the Tribulation saints (Matt. 24:22, 29-31, page 973) and bring about the national conversion of Israel (Zech. 12:9—13:1, page 918).

Christ's second coming may be soon. "Now when these things begin to happen, look up and lift up your heads, because your redemption draws near" (Luke 21:28, page 1042).

See Index, page 17, for your next study.

A Boy Is Healed

14 ᴿAnd when they had come to the multitude, a man came to Him, kneeling down to Him and saying,   Mark 9:14–28

15 "Lord, have mercy on my son, for he is *an epileptic and suffers severely; for he often falls into the fire and often into the water.

16 "So I brought him to Your disciples, but they could not cure him."

17 Then Jesus answered and said, "O ᵀfaithless and perverse generation, how long shall I be with you? How long shall I bear with you? Bring him here to Me."   *unbelieving*

18 And Jesus ᴿrebuked the demon, and it came out of him; and the child was cured from that very hour.   Luke 4:41

19 Then the disciples came to Jesus privately and said, "Why could we not cast it out?"

20 So Jesus said to them, "Because of your *unbelief; for assuredly, I say to you, ᴿif you have faith as a mustard seed, you will say to this mountain, 'Move from here to there,' and it will move; and nothing will be impossible for you.   Luke 17:6

21 *"However, this kind does not go out except by prayer and fasting."

Jesus Again Predicts His Death and Resurrection

22 Now while they were *staying in Galilee, Jesus said to them, "The Son of Man is about to be betrayed into the hands of men,

23 "and they will ᴿkill Him, and the third day He will be raised up." And they were exceedingly sorrowful.   Mark 15:37; Acts 10:40

Peter and His Master Pay Their Taxes

24 When they had come to *Capernaum, those who received the *temple* tax came to Peter and said, "Does your Teacher not pay the *temple* tax?"

25 He said, "Yes." And when he had come into the house, Jesus anticipated him, saying, "What do you think, Simon? From whom do the kings of the earth take customs or taxes, from their sons or from strangers?"

26 Peter said to Him, "From strangers." Jesus said to him, "Then the sons are free.

27 "Nevertheless, lest we offend them, go to the sea, cast in a hook, and take the fish that comes up first. And when you have opened its mouth, you will find a *piece of money; take that and give it to them for Me and you."

Who Is the Greatest?

18 At ᴿthat time the disciples came to Jesus, saying, "Who then is greatest in the kingdom of heaven?"   Luke 9:46–48; 22:24–27

2 Then Jesus called a little ᴿchild to Him, set him in the midst of them,   Matt. 19:14

3 and said, "Assuredly, I say to you, ᴿunless you are converted and become as little children, you will by no means enter the kingdom of heaven.   Luke 18:16

4 ᴿ"Therefore whoever humbles himself as this little child is the greatest in the kingdom of heaven.   [Matt. 20:27; 23:11]

5 ᴿ"Whoever receives one little child like this in My name receives Me.   [Matt. 10:42]

Jesus Warns of Offenses

6 ᴿ"But whoever causes one of these little ones who believe in Me to sin, it would be better for him if a millstone were hung around his neck, and he were drowned in the depth of the sea.   Mark 9:42

7 "Woe to the world because of ᵀoffenses! For offenses must come, but woe to that man by whom the offense comes!   *enticements*

8 ᴿ"If your hand or foot causes you to sin, cut it off and cast *it* from you. It is better for you to enter into life lame or maimed, rather than having two hands or two feet, to be cast into the everlasting fire.   Matt. 5:29, 30

9 "And if your eye causes you to sin, pluck it out and cast *it* from you. It is better for you to enter into life with one eye, rather than having two eyes, to be cast into ᵀhell fire.   Gr. *Gehenna*

The Parable of the Lost Sheep

10 "Take heed that you do not despise one of these little ones, for I say to you that in heaven ᴿtheir angels always see the face of My Father who is in heaven.   [Heb. 1:14]

11 ᴿ"For* the Son of Man has come to save that which was lost.   Luke 9:56

12 ᴿ"What do you think? If a man has a hundred sheep, and one of them goes astray, does he not leave the ninety-nine and go to the mountains to seek the one that is straying?   Luke 15:4–7

13 "And if he should find it, assuredly, I say to you, he rejoices more over that *sheep* than over the ninety-nine that did not go astray.

14 "Even so it is not the ᴿwill of your Father who is in heaven that one of these little ones should perish.   [1 Tim. 2:4]

Dealing with a Sinning Brother

15 "Moreover ᴿif your brother sins against you, go and tell him his fault between you and him alone. If he hears you, ᴿyou have gained your brother.   Lev. 19:17 • [James 5:20]

17:15 Lit. *moonstruck*
17:20 NU *little faith*
17:21 NU omits v. 21.
17:22 NU *gathering together*
17:24 NU *Capharnaum,* here and elsewhere
17:27 Gr. *stater,* the exact temple tax for two

18:11 NU omits v. 11.

16 "But if he will not hear, take with you one or two more, that R*by the mouth of two or three witnesses every word may be established.'   Deut. 17:6; 19:15

17 "And if he refuses to hear them, tell it to the church. But if he refuses even to hear the church, let him be to you like a Rheathen and a tax collector.   [2 Thess. 3:6, 14]

18 "Assuredly, I say to you, Rwhatever you bind on earth will be bound in heaven, and whatever you loose on earth will be loosed in heaven.   [John 20:22, 23]

19 R"Again* I say to you that if two of you agree on earth concerning anything that they ask, Rit will be done for them by My Father in heaven.   [1 Cor. 1:10] • [1 John 3:22; 5:14]

20 "For where two or three are gathered Rtogether in My name, I am there in the midst of them."   Acts 20:7

The Parable of the Unforgiving Servant

21 Then Peter came to Him and said, "Lord, how often shall my brother sin against me, and I forgive him? Up to seven times?"

22 Jesus said to him, "I do not say to you, Rup to seven times, but up to seventy times seven.   Col. 3:13

23 "Therefore the kingdom of heaven is like a certain king who wanted to settle accounts with his servants.

24 "And when he had begun to settle accounts, one was brought to him who owed him Tten thousand talents. $3,840,000,000

25 "But as he was not able to pay, his master commanded Rthat he be sold, with his wife and children and all that he had, and that payment be made.   2 Kin. 4:1

26 "The servant therefore fell down before him, saying, 'Master, have patience with me, and I will pay you all.'

27 "Then the master of that servant was moved with compassion, released him, and forgave him the debt.

28 "But that servant went out and found one of his fellow servants who owed him a Thundred denarii; and he laid hands on him and took him by the throat, saying, 'Pay me what you owe!'   100 days' wages or $3,200

18:19 NU, M *Again, assuredly, I say*

29 "So his fellow servant fell down *at his feet and begged him, saying, 'Have patience with me, and I will pay you *all.'

30 "And he would not, but went and threw him into prison till he should pay the debt.

31 "So when his fellow servants saw what had been done, they were very grieved, and came and told their master all that had been done.

32 "Then his master, after he had called him, said to him, 'You wicked servant! I forgave you Rall that debt because you begged me.   Luke 7:41-43

33 'Should you not also have had compassion on your fellow servant, just as I had pity on you?'

34 "And his master was angry, and delivered him to the torturers until he should pay all that was due to him.

35 R"So My heavenly Father also will do to you if each of you, from his heart, does not forgive his brother *his trespasses."   James 2:13

Marriage and Divorce

19 Now it came to pass, Rwhen Jesus had finished these sayings, that He departed from Galilee and came to the region of Judea beyond the Jordan.   Mark 10:1-12

2 RAnd great multitudes followed Him, and He healed them there.   Matt. 12:15

3 The Pharisees also came to Him, testing Him, and saying to Him, "Is it lawful for a man to divorce his wife for just any reason?"

1-E. Christ and the Apostles Accepted Genesis as a Factual Account   ▼

4 And He answered and said to them, "Have you not read that He who *made them at the beginning R'made them male and female,'   Gen. 1:27; 5:2 ▲

5 "and said, R'For this reason a man shall leave his father and mother and be joined to his wife, and Rthe two shall become one flesh'?   Gen. 2:24 • [1 Cor. 6:16; 7:2]

6 "So then, they are no longer two but one flesh. Therefore what God has joined together, let not man separate."

18:29 NU omits *at his feet* • NU, M omit *all*
18:35 NU omits *his trespasses*
19:4 NU *created*

1-E. Christ and the Apostles Accepted Genesis as a Factual Account (Matthew 19:4)—Some skeptics have dismissed the Genesis account of creation and miracles as impossible. But the Bible says that Christ was present with God "in the beginning" and "all things were made through Him" (John 1:1–3, page 1049). He alone, who came from heaven, was present at Creation. He witnessed all events in biblical history. He was in a position to know truth from error, fact from myth. What He accepted as true becomes our most certain guide to truth.

(1) Christ accepted the Creation account, as well as the Adam and Eve accounts, as true (vv. 4, 5). Here He quoted Genesis 1:27 (page 4) and 2:24 (page 5).

(2) Paul the apostle accepted the Adam and Eve account (1 Cor. 15:22, 45, page 1161; 1 Tim. 2:13, page 1219).

(Point 1-E continued on next page)

7 They said to Him, R"Why then did Moses command to give a certificate of divorce, and to put her away?"   Deut. 24:1-4

8 He said to them, "Moses, because of the Rhardness of your hearts, permitted you to divorce your Rwives, but from the beginning it was not so.   Heb. 3:15 • Mal. 2:16

9 R"And I say to you, whoever divorces his wife, except for Tsexual immorality, and marries another, commits adultery; and whoever marries her who is divorced commits adultery."   [Matt. 5:32] • Or fornication

10 His disciples said to Him, R"If such is the case of the man with his wife, it is better not to marry."   [Prov. 21:19]

Jesus Teaches on Celibacy

11 But He said to them, R"All cannot accept this saying, but only those to whom it has been given: [1 Cor. 7:2, 7, 9, 17]

12 "For there are Teunuchs who were born thus from their mother's womb, and Rthere are eunuchs who were made eunuchs by men, and there are eunuchs who have made themselves eunuchs for the kingdom of heaven's sake. He who is able to accept it, let him accept it."   Emasculated men • [1 Cor. 7:32]

Jesus Blesses Little Children

13 Then little children were brought to Him that He might put His hands on them and pray, but the disciples rebuked them.

14 But Jesus said, "Let the little children come to Me, and do not forbid them; for Rof such is the kingdom of heaven."   Matt. 18:3, 4

15 And He laid His hands on them and departed from there.

Jesus Counsels the Rich Young Ruler

16 Now behold, one came and said to Him, R"Good* Teacher, what good thing shall I do that I may have eternal life?"   Luke 10:25

19:16 NU omits Good

17 So He said to him, *"Why do you call Me good? *No one is Rgood but One, that is, God. But if you want to enter into life, Rkeep the commandments."   Nah. 1:7 • Lev. 18:5

18 He said to Him, "Which ones?" Jesus said, *"'You shall not murder,' 'You shall not commit adultery,' 'You shall not steal,' 'You shall not bear false witness,'

19 R'Honor your father and your mother,' and, R'You shall love your neighbor as yourself.'"   Ex. 20:12; Deut. 5:16 • Lev. 19:18

20 The young man said to Him, "All these things I have Rkept *from my youth. What do I still lack?"   [Phil. 3:6, 7]

21 Jesus said to him, "If you want to be perfect, Rgo, sell what you have and give to the poor, and you will have treasure in heaven; and come, follow Me."   Acts 2:45; 4:34, 35

22 But when the young man heard that saying, he went away sorrowful, for he had great possessions.

With God All Things Are Possible

23 Then Jesus said to His disciples, "Assuredly, I say to you that it is hard for a rich man to enter the kingdom of heaven.

24 "And again I say to you, it is easier for a camel to go through the eye of a needle than for a rich man to enter the kingdom of God."

25 When His disciples heard it, they were greatly astonished, saying, "Who then can be saved?"

26 But Jesus looked at them and said to them, "With men this is impossible, but Rwith God all things are possible."   Jer. 32:17

27 Then Peter answered and said to Him, "See, Rwe have left all and followed You. Therefore what shall we have?"   Deut. 33:9

19:17 NU Why do you ask Me about what is good? •
NU There is One who is good. But
19:18 Ex. 20:13–16; Deut. 5:17–20
19:20 NU omits from my youth

(Point 1-E continued from previous page)

(3) Christ accepted the reality of Satan and his part in the fall of man (Mark 3:23, page 987; Luke 10:18, page 1026; John 8:44, page 1063).

(4) John, in the book of Revelation, called Satan "that serpent of old," thus attesting Genesis 3 (page 5) and the Fall (Rev. 12:9, page 1305).

(5) Jude accepted the reality of Cain, who killed Abel, and Enoch, who "walked with God" (Jude 11, 14, page 1290; cf. Gen. 4:1–15, page 7; 5:18, 21–24, page 9).

(6) Christ and the writer of the New Testament book of Hebrews accepted the reality of Cain and Abel (Matt. 23:35, page 972; Heb. 11:4, page 1247; cf. Gen. 4:1–15, page 7).

(7) Christ affirmed His eternal existence prior to Abraham, and taught that Abraham knew of Christ's coming (John 8:56, 58, page 1064).

(8) Christ accepted the account of Lot's wife (Luke 17:32, page 1036; cf. Gen. 19:26, page 24).

(9) Christ accepted the reality of Noah and the Flood (Matt. 24:37–39, page 974; cf. Gen. 6—9, page 11).

The above are only examples of the many supporting references available. Clearly, Christ and the apostles accepted Genesis as part of the Bible; they regarded its accounts as true, and its words as true and inerrant.

See Matthew 12:40, 41, page 954, for **Point 1-F: Christ and the Apostles Accepted the Books Most Attacked by Critics.**

28 So Jesus said to them, "Assuredly I say to you, that in the regeneration, when the Son of Man sits on the throne of His glory, ᴿyou who have followed Me will also sit on twelve thrones, judging the twelve tribes of Israel.   Luke 22:28–30

29 ᴿ"And everyone who has left houses or brothers or sisters or father or mother *or wife or children or ᵀlands, for My name's sake, shall receive a hundredfold, and inherit eternal life.   Mark 10:29, 30 • Lit. *fields*

30 ᴿ"But many *who are* first will be last, and the last first.   Luke 13:30

The Parable of the Workers in the Vineyard

20 "For the kingdom of heaven is like a landowner who went out early in the morning to hire laborers for his vineyard.

2 "Now when he had agreed with the laborers for a ᵀdenarius a day, he sent them into his vineyard.   1 day's usual wage, about $32

3 "And he went out about the third hour and saw others standing idle in the market-place,

4 "and said to them, 'You also go into the vineyard, and whatever is right I will give you.' So they went.

5 "Again he went out about the sixth and the ninth hour, and did likewise.

6 "And about the eleventh hour he went out and found others standing *idle, and said to them, 'Why have you been standing here idle all day?'

7 "They said to him, 'Because no one hired us.' He said to them, 'You also go into the vineyard, *and whatever is right you will receive.'

8 "So when evening had come, the owner of the vineyard said to his steward, 'Call the laborers and give them *their* wages, beginning with the last to the first.'

9 "And when those came who *were hired* about the eleventh hour, they each received a denarius.

10 "But when the first came, they supposed that they would receive more; and they likewise received each a denarius.

11 "And when they had received *it*, they ᵀcomplained against the landowner,   *grumbled*

12 "saying, 'These last *men* have worked *only* one hour, and you made them equal to us who have borne the burden and the heat of the day.'

13 "But he answered one of them and said, 'Friend, I am doing you no wrong. Did you not agree with me for a denarius?

14 'Take *what is* yours and go your way. I wish to give to this last man *the same* as to you.

15 ᴿ'Is it not lawful for me to do what I wish with my own things? Or ᴿis your eye evil because I am good?'   [Rom. 9:20, 21] • Deut. 15:9

16 "So the last will be first, and the first last. *For many are called, but few chosen."

Jesus a Third Time Predicts His Death and Resurrection

17 ᴿNow Jesus, going up to Jerusalem, took the twelve disciples aside on the road and said to them,   Mark 10:32–34

18 "Behold, we are going up to Jerusalem, and the Son of Man will be ᴿbetrayed to the chief priests and to the scribes; and they will condemn Him to death,   Matt. 26:46, 66

19 ᴿ"and deliver Him to the Gentiles to mock and to scourge and to crucify. And the third day He will rise again."   Acts 2:23, 24

Greatness Is Serving

20 ᴿThen the mother of Zebedee's sons came to Him with her sons, kneeling down and asking something from Him.   Mark 10:35–45

21 And He said to her, "What do you wish?" She said to Him, "Grant that these two sons of mine may sit, one on Your right hand and the other on the left, in Your kingdom."

22 But Jesus answered and said, "You do not know what you ask. Are you able to drink ᴿthe cup that I am about to drink, *and be baptized with ᴿthe baptism that I am baptized with?" They said to Him, "We are able."   Luke 22:42 • Luke 12:50

23 So He said to them, ᴿ"You will indeed drink My cup, *and be baptized with the baptism that I am baptized with; but to sit on My right hand and on My left is not Mine to give, but *it is for those* for whom it is prepared by My Father."   [Acts 12:2]

24 And when the ten heard *it*, they were greatly displeased with the two brothers.

25 But Jesus called them to *Himself* and said, "You know that the rulers of the Gentiles lord it over them, and those who are great exercise authority over them.

26 "Yet ᴿit shall not be so among you; but whoever desires to become great among you, let him be your servant.   [1 Pet. 5:3]

27 ᴿ"And whoever desires to be first among you, let him be your slave—   [Matt. 18:4]

28 "just as the Son of Man did not come to be served, but to serve, and ᴿto give His life a ransom for many."   Is. 53:12

Two Blind Men Receive Their Sight

29 ᴿNow as they went out of Jericho, a great multitude followed Him.   Mark 10:46-52

30 And behold, two blind men sitting by the road, when they heard that Jesus was passing by, cried out, saying, "Have mercy on us, O Lord, ᴿSon of David!"   [Ezek. 37:21-25]

31 Then the multitude ᴿwarned them that they should be quiet; but they cried out all the more, saying, "Have mercy on us, O Lord, Son of David!"   Matt. 19:13

32 So Jesus stood still and called them, and said, "What do you want Me to do for you?"

33 They said to Him, "Lord, that our eyes may be opened."

34 So Jesus had compassion and touched their eyes. And immediately their eyes received sight, and they followed Him.

The Triumphal Entry

21 Now when they drew near Jerusalem, and came to *Bethphage, at the Mount of Olives, then Jesus sent two disciples,

2 saying to them, "Go into the village opposite you, and immediately you will find a donkey tied, and a colt with her. Loose them and bring them to Me.

3 "And if anyone says anything to you, you shall say, 'The Lord has need of them,' and immediately he will send them."

4 *All this was done that it might be fulfilled which was spoken by the prophet, saying:

5 "Tellᴿ the daughter of Zion,
   'Behold, your King is coming to you,
   Lowly, and sitting on a donkey,
   A colt, the foal of a donkey.'"   Zech. 9:9

6 ᴿSo the disciples went and did as Jesus commanded them.   Mark 11:4

7 They brought the donkey and the colt, ᴿlaid their clothes on them, *and set Him on them.   2 Kin. 9:13

8 And a very great multitude spread their clothes on the road; ᴿothers cut down branches from the trees and spread them on the road.   Lev. 23:40

9 Then the multitudes who went before and those who followed cried out, saying:

ᴿ"Hosanna to the Son of David!
   ᴿ'Blessed is He who comes in the name
      of the Lord!'   Matt. 23:39 • Ps. 118:26
   Hosanna in the highest!"

10 And when He had come into Jerusalem, all the city was moved, saying, "Who is this?"

11 So the multitudes said, "This is Jesus, the prophet from Nazareth of Galilee."

21:1 M *Bethphage*
21:4 NU omits *All*
21:7 NU *and He sat*

Jesus Cleanses the Temple

12 ᴿThen Jesus went into the temple *of God and drove out all those who bought and sold in the temple, and overturned the tables of the ᴿmoneychangers and the seats of those who sold doves.   Mal. 3:1 • Deut. 14:25

13 And He said to them, "It is written, * 'My house shall be called a house of prayer,' but you have made it a * 'den of thieves.'"

14 Then the blind and the lame came to Him in the temple, and He healed them.

15 But when the chief priests and scribes saw the wonderful things that He did, and the children crying out in the temple and saying, "Hosanna to the ᴿSon of David!" they were ᵀindignant   John 7:42 • angry

16 and said to Him, "Do You hear what these are saying?" And Jesus said to them, "Yes. Have you never read,

ᴿ'Out of the mouth of babes and nursing
      infants
   You have perfected praise'? "   Ps. 8:2

17 Then He left them and went out of the city to Bethany, and He lodged there.

The Fig Tree Withered

18 ᴿNow in the morning, as He returned to the city, He was hungry.   Mark 11:12-14, 20-24

19 ᴿAnd seeing a fig tree by the road, He came to it and found nothing on it but leaves, and said to it, "Let no fruit grow on you ever again." Immediately the fig tree withered away.   Mark 11:13

The Lesson of the Withered Fig Tree

20 ᴿAnd when the disciples saw it, they marveled, saying, "How did the fig tree wither away so soon?"   Mark 11:20

30-E. Pray Believing

21 So Jesus answered and said to them, "Assuredly, I say to you, if you have faith and do not doubt, you will not only do what was done to the fig tree, ᴿbut also if you say to this mountain, 'Be removed and be cast into the sea,' it will be done.   1 Cor. 13:2

22 "And ᴿwhatever things you ask in prayer, believing, you will receive." Matt. 7:7-11 ▲

Jesus' Authority Questioned

23 ᴿNow when He came into the temple, the chief priests and the elders of the people confronted Him as He was teaching, and ᴿsaid, "By what authority are You doing these things? And who gave You this authority?"   Luke 20:1-8 • Ex. 2:14

24 But Jesus answered and said to them, "I also will ask you one thing, which if you tell

21:12 NU omits *of God*
21:13 Is. 56:7 • Jer. 7:11

Me, I likewise will tell you by what authority I do these things:

25 "The ᴿbaptism of John—where was it from? From heaven or from men?" And they reasoned among themselves, saying, "If we say, 'From heaven,' He will say to us, 'Why then did you not believe him?'   [John 1:29-34]

26 "But if we say, 'From men,' we fear the multitude, for all count John as a prophet."

27 So they answered Jesus and said, "We do not know." And He said to them, "Neither will I tell you by what authority I do these things.

The Parable of the Two Sons

28 "But what do you think? A man had two sons, and he came to the first and said, 'Son, go, work today in my ᴿvineyard.'   Matt. 20:1

29 "He answered and said, 'I will not,' but afterward he regretted it and went.

30 "Then he came to the second and said likewise. And he answered and said, 'I go, sir,' but he did not go.

31 "Which of the two did the will of his father?" They said to Him, "The first." Jesus said to them, ᴿ'Assuredly, I say to you that tax collectors and harlots enter the kingdom of God before you.   Luke 7:29, 37-50

32 "For John came to you in the way of righteousness, and you did not believe him; ᴿbut tax collectors and harlots believed him; and when you saw it, you did not afterward ᵀrelent and believe him.   Luke 3:12, 13 • regret it

The Parable of the Wicked Vinedressers

33 "Hear another parable: There was a certain landowner who planted a vineyard and set a hedge around it, dug a winepress in it and built a tower. And he leased it to vinedressers and went into a far country.

34 "Now when vintage-time drew near, he sent his servants to the vinedressers, that they might receive its fruit.

35 "And the vinedressers took his servants, beat one, killed one, and stoned another.

36 "Again he sent other servants, more than the first, and they did likewise to them.

37 "Then last of all he sent his ᴿson to them, saying, 'They will respect my son.'   [John 3:16]

38 "But when the vinedressers saw the son, they said among themselves, ᴿ'This is the heir. ᴿCome, let us kill him and seize his inheritance.'   [Heb. 1:2] • John 11:53

39 ᴿ'So they took him and cast him out of the vineyard and killed him.   [Acts 2:23]

40 "Therefore, when the owner of the vineyard comes, what will he do to those vinedressers?"

41 They said to Him, "He will destroy those wicked men miserably, and lease his vineyard to other vinedressers who will ᵀrender to him the fruits in their seasons."   give

42 Jesus said to them, "Have you never read in the Scriptures:

ᴿ'The stone which the builders rejected
Has become the chief cornerstone.
This was the LORD's doing,   Ps. 118:22, 23
And it is marvelous in our eyes'?

43 "Therefore I say to you, ᴿthe kingdom of God will be taken from you and given to a nation bearing the fruits of it.   [Matt. 8:12]

44 "And ᴿwhoever falls on this stone will be

30-E. Pray Believing (Matthew 21:21, 22)—Faith is based on the knowledge that the Bible is God's inspired, infallible Word (2 Tim. 3:16, page 1227). We believe in God's almighty ability and desire to answer our prayers from the evidence and testimony of the Scriptures. We must pray with the understanding that all things were created, and therefore can be controlled, by the spoken Word of God (Heb. 11:1–3, page 1247).

It is possible to pray insincerely, too casually, irreverently, or even flippantly, just as a person can say words that he or she doesn't really mean (Matt. 6:5–8, page 942). Such a prayer is a false prayer, because it shows no interest in God's power or purpose.

By contrast, true prayer, according to Scripture, includes faith in God's power and will to accomplish what we ask. If we ask God for anything, but do not think it is His will, or do not believe He is able to perform it, in a sense we are not praying. We must be confident in what we know of God's will, and have faith in His almighty power, before we can ask and receive the answer. "For whatever is not from faith is sin" (Rom. 14:23, page 1145).

We must

(1) "Ask in prayer" (v. 22). God delights in our seeking His face. He cannot allow us to think that great spiritual victories happen by chance or by our own efforts. He wants to accomplish His great works *through* us—just as He fed the five thousand with the lad's lunch through the hands of the twelve apostles (John 6:1–14, page 1058).

(2) Ask "believing" (v. 22). "If you have faith and do not doubt . . . if you say to this mountain, 'Be removed . . . ' it will be done" (v. 21). Some spiritual problems are as stubborn as mountains. Attempting to solve them in our own strength is hopeless. We must, by faith, ask and expect great things from God.

The prayer of faith lifts us above all outward circumstances, filling our hearts with joy and peace (John 16:33, page 1078). Prayer not only helps us to find the mind of God and His peace, it helps us yield to His will. Beyond all this, however, Christ Himself has promised that our prayers will be answered (Matt. 7:7, 8, page 945).

See John 16:23, 24, page 1077, for **Point 30-F: Pray in His Name.**

broken; but on whomever it falls, ᴿit will grind him to powder."   Is. 8:14, 15 • [Dan. 2:44]

45 Now when the chief priests and Pharisees heard His parables, they ᵀperceived that He was speaking of them.   knew

46 But when they sought to lay hands on Him, they feared the multitudes, because ᴿthey took Him for a prophet.   Matt. 21:11

The Parable of the Wedding Feast

22 And Jesus answered and spoke to them again by parables and said:

2 "The kingdom of heaven is like a certain king who arranged a marriage for his son,

3 "and sent out his servants to call those who were invited to the wedding; and they were not willing to come.

4 "Again, he sent out other servants, saying, 'Tell those who are invited, "See, I have prepared my dinner; ᴿmy oxen and fatted cattle are killed, and all things are ready. Come to the wedding." '   Prov. 9:2

5 "But they made light of it and went their ways, one to his own farm, another to his business.

6 "And the rest seized his servants, treated them ᵀspitefully, and killed them.   insolently

7 "But when the king heard about it, he was furious. And he sent out ᴿhis armies, destroyed those murderers, and burned up their city.   [Dan. 9:26]

8 "Then he said to his servants, 'The wedding is ready, but those who were invited were not ᴿworthy.   Matt. 10:11

9 'Therefore go into the highways, and as many as you find, invite to the wedding.'

10 "So those servants went out into the highways and gathered together all whom they found, both bad and good. And the wedding hall was filled with guests.

11 "But when the king came in to see the guests, he saw a man there ᴿwho did not have on a wedding garment.   [Col. 3:10, 12]

12 "So he said to him, 'Friend, how did you come in here without a wedding garment?' And he was ᴿspeechless.   [Rom. 3:19]

13 "Then the king said to the servants, 'Bind him hand and foot, *take him away, and cast him into outer darkness; there will be weeping and gnashing of teeth.'

14 ᴿ"For many are called, but few are chosen."   Matt. 20:16

The Pharisees: Is It Lawful to Pay Taxes to Caesar?

15 Then the Pharisees went and plotted how they might entangle Him in His talk.

16 And they sent to Him their disciples with the Herodians, saying, "Teacher, we know that You are true, and teach the way of God

in truth; nor do You care about anyone, for You do not regard the person of men.

17 "Tell us, therefore, what do You think? Is it lawful to pay taxes to Caesar, or not?"

18 But Jesus ᵀperceived their wickedness, and said, "Why do you test Me, you hypocrites?   knew

19 "Show Me the tax money." So they brought Him a ᵀdenarius.   1 day's wage, about $32

20 And He said to them, "Whose image and inscription is this?"

21 They said to Him, "Caesar's." And He said to them, ᵀ"Render therefore to Caesar the things that are ᴿCaesar's, and to God the things that are God's."   Pay • [Rom. 13:1-7]

22 When they had heard these words, they marveled, and left Him and went their way.

The Sadducees: What About the Resurrection?

23 ᴿThe same day the Sadducees, ᴿwho say there is no resurrection, came to Him and asked Him,   Luke 20:27-40 • Acts 23:8

24 saying: "Teacher, ᴿMoses said that if a man dies, having no children, his brother shall marry his wife and raise up offspring for his brother.   Deut. 25:5

25 "Now there were with us seven brothers. The first died after he had married, and having no offspring, left his wife to his brother.

26 "Likewise the second also, and the third, even to the seventh.

27 "Last of all the woman died also.

28 "Therefore, in the resurrection, whose wife of the seven will she be? For they all had her."

29 Jesus answered and said to them, "You are ᵀmistaken, ᴿnot knowing the Scriptures nor the power of God.   deceived • John 20:9

30 "For in the resurrection they neither marry nor are given in marriage, but ᴿare like angels *of God in heaven.   [1 John 3:2]

31 "But concerning the resurrection of the dead, have you not read what was spoken to you by God, saying,

32 ᴿ'I am the God of Abraham, the God of Isaac, and the God of Jacob'? God is not the God of the dead, but of the living."   Ex. 3:6, 15

33 And when the multitudes heard this, they were astonished at His teaching.

The Scribes: Which Is the First Commandment of All?

34 ᴿBut when the Pharisees heard that He had silenced the Sadducees, they gathered together.   Mark 12:28-31

35 Then one of them, a lawyer, asked Him a question, testing Him, and saying,

36 "Teacher, which is the great commandment in the law?"

22:13 NU omits takes him away and   22:30 NU omits of God

37 Jesus said to him, R"*You shall love the* LORD *your God with all your heart, with all your soul, and with all your mind.'*   Deut. 6:5
38 "This is *the* first and great commandment.
39 "And *the* second *is* like it: R*'You shall love your neighbor as yourself.'*   Lev. 19:18
40 R"On these two commandments hang all the Law and the Prophets."   [Matt. 7:12]

Jesus: How Can David Call His Descendant Lord?

41 RWhile the Pharisees were gathered together, Jesus asked them,   Luke 20:41-44
42 saying, "What do you think about the Christ? Whose Son is He?" They said to Him, "*The* RSon of David."   Matt. 1:1; 21:9
43 He said to them, "How then does David in the Spirit call Him 'Lord,' saying:

44 'TheR LORD said to my Lord,
   "Sit at My right hand,
   Till I make Your enemies Your
       footstool" '?   Ps. 110:1

45 "If David then calls Him 'Lord,' how is He his Son?"
46 RAnd no one was able to answer Him a word, Rnor from that day on did anyone dare question Him anymore.   Luke 14:6 • Mark 12:34

Woe to the Scribes and Pharisees

23 Then Jesus spoke to the multitudes and to His disciples,
2 saying: R"The scribes and the Pharisees sit in Moses' seat.   Neh. 8:4, 8
3 "Therefore whatever they tell you *to observe, *that* observe and do, but do not do according to their works; for Rthey say, and do not do.   [Rom. 2:19]
4 R"For they bind heavy burdens, hard to bear, and lay *them* on men's shoulders; but they *themselves* will not move them with one of their fingers.   Luke 11:46
5 "But all their works they do to be seen by men. They make their phylacteries broad and enlarge the borders of their garments.
6 "They love the Tbest places at feasts, the best seats in the synagogues,   Or *place of honor*
7 "greetings in the marketplaces, and to be called by men, 'Rabbi, Rabbi.'
8 R"But you, do not be called 'Rabbi'; for One is your TTeacher, *the Christ, and you are all brethren.   [James 3:1] • *Leader*
9 "Do not call anyone on earth your father; Rfor One is your Father, He who is in heaven.   [Mal. 1:6]
10 "And do not be called teachers; for One is your Teacher, the Christ.
11 "But Rhe who is greatest among you shall be your servant.   Matt. 20:26, 27

12 R"And whoever exalts himself will be humbled, and he who humbles himself will be Texalted.   Luke 14:11; 18:14 • *lifted up*
13 "But Rwoe to you, scribes and Pharisees, hypocrites! For you shut up the kingdom of heaven against men; for you neither go in yourselves, nor do you allow those who are entering to go in.   Luke 11:52
14 *"Woe to you, scribes and Pharisees, hypocrites! For you devour widows' houses, and for a pretense make long prayers. Therefore you will receive greater condemnation.
15 "Woe to you, scribes and Pharisees, hypocrites! For you travel land and sea to win one proselyte, and when he is won, you make him twice as much a son of Thell as yourselves.   Gr. *Gehenna*
16 "Woe to you, blind guides, who say, 'Whoever swears by the temple, it is nothing; but whoever swears by the gold of the temple, he is obliged *to perform it.'*
17 "Fools and blind! For which is greater, the gold Ror the temple that *sanctifies the gold?   Ex. 30:29
18 "And, 'Whoever swears by the altar, it is nothing; but whoever swears by the gift that is on it, he is obliged *to perform it.'*
19 "Fools and blind! For which is greater, the gift or the altar that sanctifies the gift?
20 "Therefore he who Tswears by the altar, swears by it and by all things on it. Swears an oath
21 "He who swears by the temple, swears by it and by Him who *dwells in it.
22 "And he who swears by heaven, swears by Rthe throne of God and by Him who sits on it.   Matt. 5:34
23 "Woe to you, scribes and Pharisees, hypocrites! For you pay tithe of mint and anise and cummin, and have neglected the weightier *matters* of the law: justice and mercy and faith. These you ought to have done, without leaving the others undone.
24 "Blind guides, who strain out a gnat and swallow a camel!
25 "Woe to you, scribes and Pharisees, hypocrites! RFor you cleanse the outside of the cup and dish, but inside they are full of extortion and *self-indulgence.   Luke 11:39
26 "Blind Pharisee, first cleanse the inside of the cup and dish, that the outside of them may be clean also.
27 "Woe to you, scribes and Pharisees, hypocrites! RFor you are like whitewashed tombs which indeed appear beautiful outwardly, but inside are full of dead *men's* bones and all uncleanness.   Acts 23:3
28 "Even so you also outwardly appear

23:3 NU omits *to observe*
23:8 NU omits *the Christ*

23:14 NU omits v. 14.
23:17 NU *sanctified*
23:21 M *dwelt*
23:25 M *unrighteousness*

righteous to men, but inside you are full of hypocrisy and lawlessness.

29 ᴿ"Woe to you, scribes and Pharisees, hypocrites! Because you build the tombs of the prophets and ᵀadorn the monuments of the righteous,   Luke 11:47, 48 • decorate

30 "and say, 'If we had lived in the days of our fathers, we would not have been partakers with them in the blood of the prophets.'

31 "Therefore you are witnesses against yourselves that ᴿyou are sons of those who murdered the prophets.   [Acts 7:51, 52]

32 ᴿ"Fill up, then, the measure of your fathers' guilt.   [1 Thess. 2:16]

33 "Serpents, brood of vipers! How can you escape the condemnation of hell?

34 ᴿ"Therefore, indeed, I send you prophets, wise men, and scribes: *some* of them you will kill and crucify, and ᴿ*some* of them you will scourge in your synagogues and persecute from city to city,   Luke 11:49 • 2 Cor. 11:24, 25

35 "that on you may come all the righteous blood shed on the earth, ᴿfrom the blood of righteous Abel to the blood of Zechariah, son of Berechiah, whom you murdered between the temple and the altar.   Gen. 4:8

36 "Assuredly, I say to you, all these things will come upon this generation.

Jesus Laments over Jerusalem

34-F. From the Fall of Jerusalem to the Millennium   ▼

37 "O Jerusalem, Jerusalem, the one who kills the prophets and stones those who are sent to her! How often ᴿI wanted to gather your children together, as a hen gathers her chicks under *her* wings, but you ᴿwere not willing!   Deut. 32:11, 12 • Is. 49:5

38 "See! Your house is left to you desolate;

39 "for I say to you, you shall see Me no more till you say, ᴿ*'Blessed is He who comes in the name of the Lord!'"*   Ps. 118:26

Jesus Predicts the Destruction of the Temple

24 Then Jesus went out and departed from the temple, and His disciples came up to show Him the buildings of the temple.

2 And Jesus said to them, "Do you not see all these things? Assuredly, I say to you, ᴿnot one stone shall be left here upon another, that shall not be thrown down."   Luke 19:44 ▲

The Signs of the Times and the End of the Age

3 Now as He sat on the Mount of Olives, ᴿthe disciples came to Him privately, saying,

---

34-F. From the Fall of Jerusalem to the Millennium (to date, over 1,900 years) (Matthew 23:37—24:2)— Three things must come to pass before the millennial kingdom is restored to Israel:

(1) When the Hebrew people say, "Blessed is He [Christ] who comes in the name of the Lord!" (23:39). They must repent of their sins, return to the Lord, and accept Christ as their Messiah, as they certainly will do (Zech. 12:10, page 918; 13:6, page 918; Rom. 11:26, 27, page 1141). About twenty-seven hundred years ago, God gave an open invitation to the nation Israel. It is valid today, and will be valid until Israel accepts Christ as her Messiah and is saved. God said, " 'Come now, and let us reason together,' says the Lord, 'though your sins are like scarlet, they shall be as white as snow; though they are red like crimson, they shall be as wool' " (Is. 1:18, page 643).

(2) When "the times of the Gentiles" are fulfilled (Luke 21:24, page 1041; cf. Rom. 11:25, page 1141). "The times of the Gentiles" began with the captivity of Jerusalem in 586 B.C. by Nebuchadnezzar, king of Babylon (2 Chr. 36:11-21, page 441). It will end when Christ returns to earth and restores the kingdom to Israel. He will be the King and sit on the throne of His father David (Is. 9:6, 7, page 651).

(3) "Till all these things take place" (Matt. 24:32-35, page 974). All prophecies pertaining to the Hebrew people, until the kingdom, must come to pass before God will restore the kingdom to Israel. The fig tree, in the parable, is unsaved Israel regathered into the land. When you see prophecy being fulfilled pertaining to Israel, you can know that the second coming of Christ is near, and that "this generation will by no means pass away till all these things [prophecies] take place" (Matt. 24:34, page 974). The word "generation" may refer to the race in its sinful unbelief, or more simply to the literal generation alive at the time these things begin to happen and following. The last prophecy to be fulfilled before Christ returns to earth is the seven years of Great Tribulation. It is called "the time of Jacob's trouble" (Jer. 30:7, page 743). Many prophecies that will come to pass during the Great Tribulation are found in Matthew 24:9-51 (page 973) and in Revelation 4—19 (page 1297).

At the beginning of this period in the history of the Hebrew people, they were driven from their homeland and scattered among all the nations. Since A.D. 70 they have been without a country, without a temple, without a king, without a prophet, and without a Messiah. But they are not without God's promise that He will, in the last days, "bring back from captivity My people Israel and Judah . . . to the land" (Jer. 30:3, page 743). After World War I, the Jews began to return to Palestine in significant numbers; and in 1948, although small in number, they became a nation. In the last days the Lord will reestablish a remnant from all twelve tribes in the land of Israel (Hos. 3:4, 5, page 860).

See Isaiah 66:22, 23, page 707, for **Point 34-G: From the Millennium to the New Heaven and the New Earth.**

R"Tell us, when will these things be? And what *will be* the sign of Your coming, and of the end of the age?"   Mark 13:3 • [1 Thess. 5:1-3]

4 And Jesus answered and said to them: "Take heed that no one deceives you.

5 "For many will come in My name, saying, 'I am the Christ,' and will deceive many.

6 "And you will hear of Rwars and rumors of wars. See that you are not troubled; for *all *these things* must come to pass, but the end is not yet.   [Rev. 6:2-4]

7 "For Rnation will rise against nation, and kingdom against kingdom. And there will be Rfamines, *pestilences, and earthquakes in various places.   Hag. 2:22 • Rev. 6:5, 6

8 "All these *are* the beginning of sorrows.

▼ 49-B. The Tribulation on the Earth

9 R"Then they will deliver you up to tribulation and kill you, and you will be hated by all nations for My name's sake.   Matt. 10:17

10 "And then many will be offended, will betray one another, and will hate one another.

11 "Then Rmany false prophets will rise up and Rdeceive many.   2 Pet. 2:1 • [1 Tim. 4:1]

12 "And because lawlessness will abound, the love of many will grow Rcold.   [2 Thess. 2:3]

13 R"But he who endures to the end shall be saved.   Matt. 10:22

14 "And this gospel of the kingdom will be

preached in all the world as a witness to all ▽ the nations, and then the end will come.

The Great Tribulation

15 "Therefore when you see the *'abomination of desolation,' spoken of by Daniel the prophet, standing in the holy place" R(whoever reads, let him understand),   Dan. 9:23

16 "then let those who are in Judea flee to the mountains.

17 "Let him who is on the housetop not go down to take anything out of his house.

18 "And let him who is in the field not go back to get his clothes.

19 "But Rwoe to those who are pregnant and to those who are nursing babies in those days!   Luke 23:29

20 "And pray that your flight may not be in winter or on the Sabbath.

21 "For Rthen there will be great tribulation, such as has not been since the beginning of the world until this time, no, nor ever shall be.   Dan. 9:26

22 "And unless those days were shortened, no flesh would be saved; but for the elect's sake those days will be shortened.

23 "Then if anyone says to you, 'Look, here *is* the Christ!' or 'There!' do not believe *it.*

24 "For false christs and false prophets will rise and show great signs and wonders to deceive, if possible, even the elect.

25 "See, I have told you beforehand.

26 "Therefore if they say to you, 'Look, He

24:6 NU omits *all*
24:7 NU omits *pestilences*

24:15 Dan. 9:27; 11:31; 12:11

49-B. The Tribulation on the Earth (Matthew 24:9-30)—

(1) It will be a period of God's wrath. Christ describes a time of great tribulation (pressure, agony, suffering) on the earth (vv. 21, 22), during which Christ will let loose three successive series of judgments: the seven seals (Rev. 6:1-17, page 1299; 8:1, page 1301), the seven trumpets (Rev. 8:7—9:21, page 1302; 11:15-19, page 1305), and the seven bowls of God's wrath (Rev. 15, 16, page 1308). Since God will be pouring out His wrath on a wicked and rebellious earth (Rev. 6:17, page 1300), it is fitting that the true church will not be here then, since "God did not appoint us to wrath" (1 Thess. 5:9, page 1212).

(2) It will last seven years. Christ refers us to Daniel 9:27 (page 851) for the length of this period, which is set forth as seven years—one "week" of years (v. 15).

(3) It will begin with the signing of a covenant. "He [the Antichrist, who will come out of the revived Roman Empire] shall confirm a covenant with many" (Dan. 9:27, page 851).

(4) The Antichrist will set up the "abomination of desolation" in the middle of the seven years (v. 15; Dan. 9:27, page 851). This will be a dreadful, public sin perpetrated in Jerusalem at the rebuilt temple (2 Thess. 2:3, 4, page 1215). This prophesied abomination could not have been Titus' destruction of the temple in A.D. 70 because those actions do not fit either 2 Thessalonians 2:3, 4 (page 1215), nor the events described in Matthew 24:22, 29 (page 973). Clearly it is a future event.

(5) The abomination will start a fierce persecution. This final three-and-one-half-year period is the actual time of "great tribulation" (v. 21), although the entire seven years are commonly so labeled. Verse 21 describes the ferocity of this period. The book of Revelation shows that it will be a satanic attack against Israel and all those from the nations who turn to Christ (Rev. 7:9-14, page 1300; 12:13, 15, page 1305; cf. Zech. 12:2, 3, page 918; 14:2, page 919).

(6) The Antichrist will reign during this last three-and-one-half-years (Rev. 13:5, page 1306), leading his beast empire (the revived Roman Empire, in ten confederate states). During this period God and Satan will war with one another: God's anger (Rev. 6:17, page 1300) will be roused against Satan's persecution of "the woman [Israel] who gave birth to the male Child [Christ]" (Rev. 12:11-13, page 1305).

(7) The Tribulation will close at Armageddon (Rev. 16:16, 17, page 1310).

See Revelation 16:13-16, page 1309, for **Point 49-C: The Battle of Armageddon.**

▽ is in the desert!' do not go out; or 'Look, *He is* in the inner rooms!' do not believe *it.*

27 ᴿ"For as the lightning comes from the east and flashes to the west, so also will the coming of the Son of Man be.   Luke 17:24

28 ᴿ"For wherever the carcass is, there the eagles will be gathered together.   Luke 17:37

The Coming of the Son of Man

29 ᴿ"Immediately after the tribulation of those days ᴿthe sun will be darkened, and the moon will not give its light; the stars will fall from heaven, and the powers of the heavens will be shaken.   [Dan. 7:11] • Ezek. 32:7

30 "Then the sign of the Son of Man will appear in heaven, ᴿand then all the tribes of the earth will mourn, and they will see the Son of Man coming on the clouds of heaven

▲ with power and great glory.   Rev. 1:7

31 "And He will send His angels with a great sound of a trumpet, and they will gather together His elect from the four winds, from one end of heaven to the other.

The Parable of the Fig Tree

32 "Now learn ᴿthis parable from the fig tree: When its branch has already become tender and puts forth leaves, you know that summer *is* near.   Luke 21:29

33 "So you also, when you see all these things, know that it is near—at the doors!

34 "Assuredly, I say to you, ᴿthis generation will by no means pass away till all these things take place.   [Matt. 10:23; 16:28; 23:36]

35 "Heaven and earth will pass away, but My words will by no means pass away.

No One Knows the Day or Hour

36 ᴿ"But of that day and hour no one knows, not even the angels of *heaven, ᴿbut My Father only.   Acts 1:7 • Zech. 14:7

45–A. Noah: A Man Convicted   ▼

37 "But as the days of Noah *were,* so also will the coming of the Son of Man be.

24:36 NU adds *nor the Son*

45-A. Noah: A Man Convicted (Matthew 24:37–39)—"And the Lᴏʀᴅ said, 'My Spirit shall not strive with man forever' " (Gen. 6:3, page 11). The Holy Spirit began His ministry of convicting mankind of sin, of righteousness, and of judgment (John 16:7–11, page 1077) in the age before the Flood. He has continued to "strive with man" in every dispensation, and will continue as long as there are lost souls on earth. God began to strive with man in the Garden of Eden. When Adam and Eve fell, the Lᴏʀᴅ came and called to Adam saying, "Where are you?" (Gen. 3:1–10, page 5). Thus, God began His ministry of reaching out to lost humanity. From the first He was "longsuffering toward us, not willing that any should perish but that all should come to repentance" (2 Pet. 3:9, page 1275).

When the Holy Spirit convicted Noah of sin, of righteousness, and of judgment, he repented and "found grace in the eyes of the Lᴏʀᴅ" (Gen. 6:8, page 12). The question is often asked, how were the lost saved before the death of Christ on Calvary? The answer is, they were saved by grace through faith, looking forward to the death, burial, and resurrection of the Lord Jesus Christ. Today we are saved by grace through faith, looking *back* to the death, burial, and resurrection of the Lord Jesus Christ. The only way anyone can be saved is through the Lord Jesus Christ (Acts 4:10–12, page 1091; Rom. 3:25, page 1132).

Now, the people who lived before the Flood had the gospel preached through prophecy and through typology. Therefore, those who rejected the gospel, which was preached by Adam and his descendants, were without excuse (Rom. 1:20, page 1128).

(1) The pre-Flood people had the gospel preached through prophecy. When Adam and Eve sinned, the Lord cursed the serpent for allowing Satan to possess it and speak with Eve, tempting her to sin (2 Cor. 11:3, page 1174). Then the Lord said to the serpent, "I will put enmity between you and the woman, and between your seed and her Seed; He shall bruise your head, and you shall bruise His heel" (Gen. 3:15, page 7). This is the first promise of the virgin-born Redeemer. There is no seed of a woman. The woman produces the egg and the man the seed. This prophecy is a biological miracle. No woman can reproduce without the seed of the man. Yet the Virgin Mary gave birth to the Lord Jesus Christ while she was still a virgin (Luke 1:30–35, page 1010). Those who lived before the Flood had the promise of the Savior who would bruise the head of Satan.

(2) The pre-Flood people had the gospel preached through typology. God in His grace provided a covering for the nakedness of Adam and Eve: "Also for Adam and his wife the Lᴏʀᴅ God made tunics of skin, and clothed them" (Gen. 3:21, page 7). They did not need a theologian to tell them that the innocent had died to atone for the guilty. Before God drove Adam and Eve out of the Garden, He gave them the gospel in prophecy: the Seed of the woman would bruise the head of the serpent. And the Seed of the woman would shed His blood to atone for lost souls.

This gospel was handed down from Adam to Cain and Abel; Cain rejected the gospel, but Abel accepted (Gen. 4:1–16, page 7). Then Seth was born; Adam gave him the gospel, and Seth believed. "Then men began to call on the name of the Lᴏʀᴅ" (Gen. 4:25, 26, page 9). Adam gave the gospel to each of his descendants. He lived on for 243 years after Methuselah was born, and Methuselah lived 600 years after Noah was born. Adam had 243 years in which to give the gospel to Methuselah, and Methuselah had 600 years in which to pass it on to Noah.

See Proverbs 29:18, page 622, for **Point 45-B: Noah: A Man of Vision.**

▽ 38 ᴿ"For as in the days before the flood, they were eating and drinking, marrying and giving in marriage, until the day that Noah entered the ark,   [Gen. 6:3-5]

39 "and did not know until the flood came and took them all away, so also will the
▲ coming of the Son of Man be.

40 ᴿ"Then two *men* will be in the field: one will be taken and the other left.   Luke 17:34

41 "Two *women will be* grinding at the mill: one will be taken and the other left.

42 ᴿ"Watch therefore, for you do not know what *hour your Lord is coming.   Matt. 25:13

43 ᴿ"But know this, that if the master of the house had known what hour the thief would come, he would have watched and not allowed his house to be broken into.   Luke 12:39

44 ᴿ"Therefore you also be ready, for the Son of Man is coming at an hour you do not expect.   [1 Thess. 5:6]

The Faithful Servant and the Evil Servant

45 "Who then is a faithful and wise servant, whom his master made ruler over his household, to give them food in due season?

46 "Blessed *is* that servant whom his master, when he comes, will find so doing.

47 "Assuredly, I say to you that he will make him ruler over all his goods.

48 "But if that evil servant says in his heart, 'My master is delaying *his coming,'

49 "and begins to beat *his* fellow servants, and to eat and drink with the drunkards,

50 "the master of that servant will come on a day when he is not looking for *him* and at an hour that he is ᴿnot aware of,   Mark 13:32

51 "and will cut him in two and appoint *him* his portion with the hypocrites. There shall be weeping and gnashing of teeth.

The Parable of the Wise and Foolish Virgins

25 "Then the kingdom of heaven shall be likened to ten virgins who took their lamps and went out to meet the bridegroom.

2 ᴿ"Now five of them were wise, and five *were* foolish.   Matt. 13:47; 22:10

3 "Those who *were* foolish took their lamps and took no oil with them,

4 "but the wise took oil in their vessels with their lamps.

5 "But while the bridegroom was delayed, ᴿthey all slumbered and slept.   1 Thess. 5:6

6 "And at midnight ᴿa cry was *heard:* 'Behold, the bridegroom *is coming; go out to meet him!'   [1 Thess. 4:16]

7 "Then all those virgins arose and ᴿtrimmed their lamps.   Luke 12:35

8 "And the foolish said to the wise, 'Give us *some* of your oil, for our lamps are going out.'

9 "But the wise answered, saying, 'No, lest there should not be enough for us and you; but go rather to those who sell, and buy for yourselves.'

10 "And while they went to buy, the bridegroom came, and those who were ready went in with him to the wedding; and ᴿthe door was shut.   Luke 13:25

11 "Afterward the other virgins came also, saying, ᴿ'Lord, Lord, open to us!'   [Matt. 7:21-23]

12 "But he answered and said, 'Assuredly, I say to you, ᴿI do not know you.'   [Hab. 1:13]

13 ᴿ"Watch therefore, for you ᴿknow neither the day nor the hour *in which the Son of Man is coming.   Mark 13:35 · Matt. 24:36, 42

The Parable of the Talents

14 ᴿ"For *the kingdom of heaven is* ᴿlike a man traveling to a far country, *who* called his own servants and delivered his goods to them.   Luke 19:12-27 · Matt. 21:33

15 "And to one he gave five talents, to another two, and to another one, ᴿto each according to his own ability; and immediately he went on a journey.   [Rom. 12:6]

16 "Then he who had received the five talents went and traded with them, and made another five talents.

17 "And likewise he who *had received* two gained two more also.

18 "But he who had received one went and dug in the ground, and hid his lord's money.

19 "After a long time the lord of those servants came and settled accounts with them.

20 "So he who had received five talents came and brought five other talents, saying, 'Lord, you delivered to me five talents; look, I have gained five more talents besides them.'

21 "His lord said to him, 'Well *done,* good and faithful servant; you were faithful over a few things, I will make you ruler over many things. Enter into the joy of your lord.'

22 "He also who had received two talents came and said, 'Lord, you delivered to me two talents; look, I have gained two more talents besides them.'

23 "His lord said to him, 'Well *done,* good and faithful servant; you have been faithful over a few things, I will make you ruler over many things. Enter into the joy of your lord.'

24 "Then he who had received the one talent came and said, 'Lord, I knew you to be a hard man, reaping where you have not sown, and gathering where you have not scattered seed.

24:42 NU *day*
24:48 NU omits *his coming*
25:6 NU omits *is coming*

25:13 NU omits the rest of v. 13.

25 'And I was afraid, and went and hid your talent in the ground. Look, *there* you have *what is* yours.'

26 "But his lord answered and said to him, 'You wicked and lazy servant, you knew that I reap where I have not sown, and gather where I have not scattered seed.

27 'So you ought to have deposited my money with the bankers, and at my coming I would have received back my own with interest.

28 'Therefore take the talent from him, and give *it* to him who has ten talents.

29 ᴿ'For to everyone who has, more will be given, and he will have abundance; but from him who does not have, even what he has will be taken away.   Matt. 13:12

30 'And cast the unprofitable servant into the outer darkness. ᴿThere will be weeping and ᴿgnashing of teeth.'   Matt. 24:51 • Ps. 112:10

The Son of Man Will Judge the Nations

▼ **18–D. The Judgment of the Nations**

31 "When the Son of Man comes in His glory, and all the *holy angels with Him, then He will sit on the throne of His glory.

32 ᴿ"All the nations will be gathered before Him, and ᴿHe will separate them one from

25:31 NU omits *holy*

another, as a shepherd divides *his* sheep from ▽ the goats.   [2 Cor. 5:10] • Ezek. 20:38

33 "And He will set the ᴿsheep on His right hand, but the goats on the left. [John 10:11, 27, 28]

34 "Then the King will say to those on His right hand, 'Come, you blessed of My Father, ᴿinherit the kingdom prepared for you from the foundation of the world: [Rom. 8:17]

35 ᴿ'for I was hungry and you gave Me food; I was thirsty and you gave Me drink; I was a stranger and you took Me in;   Is. 58:7

36 'I *was* ᴿnaked and you clothed Me; I was sick and you visited Me; ᴿI was in prison and you came to Me.'   [James 2:15, 16] • 2 Tim. 1:16

37 "Then the righteous will answer Him, saying, 'Lord, when did we see You hungry and feed *You*, or thirsty and give *You* drink?

38 'When did we see You a stranger and take *You* in, or naked and clothe *You*?

39 'Or when did we see You sick, or in prison, and come to You?'

40 "And the King will answer and say to them, 'Assuredly, I say to you, ᴿinasmuch as you did *it* to one of the least of these My brethren, you did *it* to Me.'   Mark 9:41

17–F. Hell Is an Eternal Place ▼

41 "Then He will also say to those on the left hand, ᴿ'Depart from Me, you cursed, ᴿinto

---

18–D. The Judgment of the Nations (Matthew 25:31–46)—This judgment is not that of the Great White Throne (Rev. 20:11–15, page 1313). A careful comparison of the two judgments will establish the following facts:

(1) The judgment of the nations will take place "when the Son of Man comes in His glory . . . [and] then He will sit on the throne of His glory" (v. 31). The Great White Throne is never called "the throne of His glory."

(2) At this judgment, He will judge the living nations (Joel 3:11–16, page 871). At the Great White Throne, He will judge the wicked dead.

(3) At this judgment, there will be no resurrection of the dead. At the Great White Throne, all the wicked dead are raised: "the sea gave up the dead who were in it, and Death and Hades delivered up the dead who were in them" (Rev. 20:13, page 1314).

(4) At this judgment, the judge is specifically Christ "the King" (v. 34) judging the nations in His earthly kingdom. At the Great White Throne, the kingdom is no longer in view—indeed, the earth itself has "fled away" (Rev. 20:11, page 1313).

(5) At this judgment, no books will be opened. At the Great White Throne, there will be books opened (Rev. 20:12, page 1313).

(6) At this judgment, there are three classes judged:

(a) "Sheep"—the saved (v. 33; Rev. 7:9–17, page 1300).
(b) "Goats"—the unsaved (v. 33; 2 Thess. 1:7–10, page 1215).
(c) "Brethren"—the elect of Israel (v. 40; Rev. 7:1–8, page 1300; Rom. 11:25–28, page 1141). At the Great White Throne, there is only one class, "the dead" (Rev. 20:12, page 1313).

(7) At this judgment, the King will give the kingdom to those who have eternal life. At the Great White Throne, there will be no saved and no kingdom; all those judged will be "cast into the lake of fire" (Rev. 20:15, page 1314).

See Revelation 20:11–15, page 1313, for **Point 18–E: The Judgment of the Wicked.**

17–F. Hell Is an Eternal Place (Matthew 25:41)—This is the final hell. It was not prepared for mankind. God prepared it for Satan and his angels. They have no choice, but you must make a choice—either Satan's prepared hell or the believers' prepared heaven (John 14:1-6, page 1074). Christ the Judge will say to the living wicked at the judgment, "Depart from Me, you cursed, into the everlasting fire prepared for the devil

(Point 17-F continued on next page)

▽ the everlasting fire prepared for ᴿthe devil
▲ and his angels: Matt. 7:23 • Matt. 13:40, 42 • [2 Pet. 2:4]
42 'for I was hungry and you gave Me no
food; I was thirsty and you gave Me no drink;
43 'I was a stranger and you did not take
Me in, naked and you did not clothe Me, sick
and in prison and you did not visit Me.'
44 "Then they also will answer *Him, saying, 'Lord, when did we see You hungry or
thirsty or a stranger or naked or sick or in
prison, and did not minister to You?'
45 "Then He will answer them, saying,
'Assuredly, I say to you, ᴿinasmuch as you
did not do *it* to one of the least of these, you
did not do *it* to Me.'   Prov. 14:31
46 "And ᴿthese will go away into everlasting punishment, but the righteous into
▲ eternal life."   [Dan. 12:2]

The Plot to Kill Jesus

26 Now it came to pass, when Jesus had
finished all these sayings, *that* He said
to His disciples,
2 ᴿ"You know that after two days is the
Passover, and the Son of Man will be delivered up to be crucified."   Luke 22:1, 2
3 ᴿThen the chief priests, *the scribes, and
the elders of the people assembled at the
palace of the high priest, who was called
Caiaphas,   John 11:47
4 and ᴿplotted to take Jesus by ᵀtrickery
and kill *Him.*   Acts 4:25-28 • *deception*
5 But they said, "Not during the feast, lest
there be an uproar among the people."

25:44 NU, M omit *Him*
26:3 NU omits *the scribes*

The Anointing at Bethany

6 And when Jesus was in ᴿBethany at the
house of Simon the leper,   Mark 14:3-9
7 a woman came to Him having an alabaster flask of very costly fragrant oil, and she
poured *it* on His head as He sat *at the table.*
8 ᴿBut when His disciples saw *it,* they were
indignant, saying, "Why this waste?   John 12:4
9 "For this fragrant oil might have been
sold for much and given to *the poor.*"
10 But when Jesus was aware of *it,* He said
to them, "Why do you trouble the woman?
For she has done a good work for Me.
11 "For you have the poor with you always,
but Me you do not have always.
12 "For in pouring this fragrant oil on My
body, she did *it* for My ᴿburial.   John 19:38-42
13 "Assuredly, I say to you, wherever this
gospel is preached in the whole world, what
this woman has done will also be told as a
memorial to her."

Judas Agrees to Betray Jesus

14 Then one of the twelve, called ᴿJudas
Iscariot, went to the chief priests   Matt. 10:4
15 and said, "What are you willing to give
me if I deliver Him to you?" And they
counted out to him thirty pieces of silver.
16 So from that time he sought opportunity
to betray Him.

Jesus Celebrates Passover
with His Disciples

17 Now on the first *day* of the *Feast of* the
Unleavened Bread the disciples came to
Jesus, saying to Him, "Where do You want us
to prepare for You to eat the Passover?"

(Point 17-F continued from previous page)
and his angels" (v. 41). The wicked will know that they are in hell by choice; this will make their hell more
hellish.
   At the beginning of the thousand-year reign of Christ, the Antichrist and the False Prophet will be "cast
alive into the lake of fire burning with brimstone" (Rev. 19:20, page 1313). Satan will be bound by chains and
imprisoned during this Millennium in the bottomless pit. "Now when the thousand years have expired, Satan
will be released from his prison and will go out to deceive the nations" (Rev. 20:7-9, page 1313), and lead
them to fight against God. Just as God rained fire and brimstone on Sodom and Gomorrah (Gen. 19:24-29,
page 24), once again He will send fire from heaven on those wicked nations who think that, with the help of
Satan, they can overthrow God and His kingdom.
   Then Satan will be cast into hell, the lake of fire, where the Antichrist and the False Prophet will still be
alive after one thousand years. The evil triad will at last be together in their eternal abode, where "they will
be tormented day and night forever and ever" (Rev. 20:10, page 1313). This is proof that the eternal fires of
hell do not annihilate the body, soul, or spirit of man or angels. Hell is a place of *eternal* torment.
   At the Last Judgment, all of the wicked dead will be resurrected and will stand in body, soul, and spirit
before God at the Great White Throne. White represents holiness, righteousness, and purity. Christ will be
the Judge (John 5:22, page 1057). When the wicked see Him in His resurrected, glorified human body, they
will know that He has every right to judge them and cast them into the lake of fire along with their gods, the
evil triad.
   The lake of fire is called the second death. The first death began in the Garden of Eden, when Adam and
Eve ate the forbidden fruit and were separated from God by sin. Christ, the last Adam, was born of a virgin
and was given a complete human nature without sin, so that on Calvary He could be our substitute, and that
those who trust in Him may be made righteous with the righteousness of Christ, make heaven their home
(2 Cor. 5:21, page 1169) and escape the lake of fire, the second death (Rev. 20:11-15, page 1313).
   See Luke 16:19-31, page 1035, for **Point 17-G: You Must Choose: Heaven or Hell.**

18 And He said, "Go into the city to a certain man, and say to him, 'The Teacher says, "My time is at hand; I will keep the Passover at your house with My disciples." ' "

19 So the disciples did as Jesus had directed them; and they prepared the Passover.

20 ᴿWhen evening had come, He sat down with the twelve.   Mark 14:17-21

21 Now as they were eating, He said, "Assuredly, I say to you, one of you will ᴿbetray Me."   John 6:70, 71; 13:21

22 And they were exceedingly sorrowful, and each of them began to say to Him, "Lord, is it I?"

23 He answered and said, "He who dipped *his* hand with Me in the dish will betray Me.

24 "The Son of Man indeed goes just as it is written of Him, but woe to that man by whom the Son of Man is betrayed! It would have been good for that man if he had not been born."

25 Then Judas, who was betraying Him, answered and said, "Rabbi, is it I?" He said to him, "You have said it."

Jesus Institutes the Lord's Supper

26 ᴿAnd as they were eating, ᴿJesus took bread, *blessed and broke *it*, and gave *it* to the disciples and said, "Take, eat; ᴿthis is My body."   Mark 14:22-25 · 1 Cor. 11:23-25 · [1 Pet. 2:24]

27 Then He took the cup, and gave thanks, and gave *it* to them, saying, ᴿ"Drink from it, all of you.   Mark 14:23

28 "For ᴿthis is My blood ᴿof the *new covenant, which is shed for many for the ᵀremission of sins.   [Ex. 24:8] · Jer. 31:31 · *forgiveness*

29 "But ᴿI say to you, I will not drink of this fruit of the vine from now on ᴿuntil that day when I drink it new with you in My Father's kingdom."   Mark 14:25 · Acts 10:41

30 ᴿAnd when they had sung a hymn, they went out to the Mount of Olives.   Mark 14:26-31

Jesus Predicts Peter's Denial

31 Then Jesus said to them, ᴿ"All of you will ᴿbe made to stumble because of Me this night, for it is written: John 16:32 · [Matt. 11:6]

> ᴿ'I will strike the Shepherd,
> And the sheep of the flock will be
>   scattered.'   Zech. 13:7

32 "But after I have been raised, ᴿI will go before you to Galilee."   Matt. 28:7, 10, 16

33 Peter answered and said to Him, "Even if all are made to stumble because of You, I will never be made to stumble."

34 Jesus said to him, ᴿ"Assuredly, I say to you that this night, before the rooster crows, you will deny Me three times."   Matt. 26:74, 75

35 Peter said to Him, "Even if I have to die with You, I will not deny You!" And so said all the disciples.

The Prayer in the Garden

36 Then Jesus came with them to a place called Gethsemane, and said to the disciples, "Sit here while I go and pray over there."

37 And He took with Him Peter and ᴿthe two sons of Zebedee, and He began to be sorrowful and deeply distressed.   Matt. 4:21; 17:1

38 Then He said to them, ᴿ"My soul is exceedingly sorrowful, even to death. Stay here and watch with Me."   John 12:27

39 He went a little farther and fell on His face, and prayed, saying, "O My Father, if it is possible, let this cup pass from Me; nevertheless, not as I will, but as You *will.*"

40 Then He came to the disciples and found them sleeping, and said to Peter, "What? Could you not watch with Me one hour?

41 ᴿ"Watch and pray, lest you enter into temptation. ᴿThe spirit indeed *is* willing, but the flesh *is* weak."   Luke 22:40, 46 · [Gal. 5:17]

42 Again, a second time, He went away and prayed, saying, "O My Father, *if this cup cannot pass away from Me unless I drink it, ᴿYour will be done."   Is. 50:5

43 And He came and found them asleep again, for their eyes were heavy.

44 So He left them, went away again, and prayed the third time, saying the same words.

45 Then He came to His disciples and said to them, "Are *you* still sleeping and resting? Behold, the hour ᵀis at hand, and the Son of Man is being ᴿbetrayed into the hands of sinners.   *has drawn near* · Matt. 17:22, 23; 20:18, 19

46 "Rise, let us be going. See, My ᴿbetrayer is at hand."   Matt. 20:18; 26:21

Betrayal and Arrest in Gethsemane

47 And ᴿwhile He was still speaking, behold, Judas, one of the twelve, with a great multitude with swords and clubs, came from the chief priests and elders of the people.   Acts 1:16

48 Now His betrayer had given them a sign, saying, "Whomever I kiss, He is the One; seize Him."

49 Immediately he went up to Jesus and said, "Greetings, Rabbi!" and kissed Him.

50 But Jesus said to him, ᴿ"Friend, why have you come?" Then they came and laid hands on Jesus and took Him.   Ps. 41:9; 55:13

51 And suddenly, ᴿone of those *who were* with Jesus stretched out *his* hand and drew his sword, struck the servant of the high priest, and cut off his ear.   John 18:10

52 But Jesus said to him, "Put your sword in its place, ᴿfor all who take the sword will *perish by the sword.   Rev. 13:10

26:26 M *gave thanks for*
26:28 NU omits *new*
26:42 NU *if this may not pass away unless*
26:52 M *die*

53 "Or do you think that I cannot now pray to My Father, and He will provide Me with ᴿmore than twelve legions of angels? Dan. 7:10
54 "How then could the Scriptures be fulfilled, ᴿthat it must happen thus?" Is. 50:6
55 In that hour Jesus said to the multitudes, "Have you come out, as against a robber, with swords and clubs to take Me? I sat daily with you, teaching in the temple, and you did not seize Me.
56 "But all this was done that the Scriptures of the prophets might be fulfilled." Then all the disciples forsook Him and fled.

Jesus Faces the Sanhedrin

57 ᴿAnd those who had laid hold of Jesus led Him away to Caiaphas the high priest, where the scribes and the elders were assembled. John 18:12, 19–24
58 But Peter followed Him at a distance to the high priest's courtyard. And he went in and sat with the servants to see the end.
59 Now the chief priests, *the elders, and all the council sought ᴿfalse testimony against Jesus to put Him to death, Ps. 35:11
60 *but found none. Even though ᴿmany false witnesses came forward, they found none. But at last ᴿtwo *false witnesses came forward Ps. 27:12 · Deut. 19:15
61 and said, "This fellow said, ᴿ'I am able to destroy the temple of God and to build it in three days.' " John 2:19
62 ᴿAnd the high priest arose and said to Him, "Do You answer nothing? What is it these men testify against You?" Mark 14:60
63 But ᴿJesus kept silent. And the high priest answered and said to Him, ᴿ"I put You under oath by the living God: Tell us if You are the Christ, the Son of God!" Is. 53:7 · Lev. 5:1
64 Jesus said to him, "It is as you said. Nevertheless, I say to you, ᴿhereafter you will see the Son of Man ᴿsitting at the right hand of the Power, and coming on the clouds of heaven." Dan. 7:13 · [Acts 7:55]
65 Then the high priest tore his clothes, saying, "He has spoken blasphemy! What further need do we have of witnesses? Look, now you have heard His blasphemy!
66 "What do you think?" They answered and said, "He is deserving of death."
67 ᴿThen they spat in His face and beat Him; and ᴿothers struck Him with ᵀthe palms of their hands, Is. 50:6; 53:3 · Luke 22:63–65 · rods
68 saying, ᴿ"Prophesy to us, Christ! Who is the one who struck You?" Mark 14:65

Peter Denies Jesus, and Weeps Bitterly

69 ᴿNow Peter sat outside in the courtyard. And a servant girl came to him, saying, "You also were with Jesus of Galilee." John 18:17

26:59 NU omits the elders
26:60 NU but found none, even though many false witnesses came forward • NU omits false witnesses

70 But he denied it before them all, saying, "I do not know what you are saying."
71 And when he had gone out to the gateway, another girl saw him and said to those who were there, "This fellow also was with Jesus of Nazareth."
72 But again he denied with an oath, "I do not know the Man!"
73 And a little later those who stood by came up and said to Peter, "Surely you also are one of them, for your ᴿspeech betrays you." Luke 22:59
74 Then ᴿhe began to curse and swear, saying, "I do not know the Man!" Immediately a rooster crowed. Matt. 26:34
75 And Peter remembered the word of Jesus who had said to him, ᴿ"Before the rooster crows, you will deny Me three times." So he went out and wept bitterly. Matt. 26:34

Jesus Handed over to Pontius Pilate

27 When morning came, all the chief priests and elders of the people plotted against Jesus to put Him to death.
2 And when they had bound Him, they led Him away and ᴿdelivered Him to *Pontius Pilate the governor. Luke 18:32; Acts 3:13

Judas Hangs Himself

3 Then Judas, His betrayer, seeing that He had been condemned, was remorseful and brought back the ᵀthirty ᴿpieces of silver to the chief priests and elders, $3,840 · Matt. 26:15
4 saying, "I have sinned by betraying innocent blood." And they said, "What is that to us? You see to it!"
5 Then he threw down the pieces of silver in the temple and ᴿdeparted, and went and hanged himself. Matt. 18:7; 26:24
6 But the chief priests took the silver pieces and said, "It is not lawful to put them into the treasury, because they are the price of blood."
7 And they consulted together and bought with them the potter's field, to bury strangers in.
8 Therefore that field has been called ᴿthe Field of Blood to this day. Acts 1:19
9 Then was fulfilled what was spoken by Jeremiah the prophet, saying, ᴿ"And they took the thirty pieces of silver, the value of Him who was priced, whom they of the children of Israel priced, Zech. 11:12
10 "and ᴿgave them for the potter's field, as the Lᴏʀᴅ directed me." Jer. 32:6–9; Zech. 11:13

Jesus Faces Pilate

11 Now Jesus stood before the governor. ᴿAnd the governor asked Him, saying, "Are You the King of the Jews?" Jesus said to him, ᴿ"It is as you say." Mark 15:2–5 · John 18:37

27:2 NU omits Pontius

12 And while He was being accused by the chief priests and elders, ᴿHe answered nothing.   John 19:9

13 Then Pilate said to Him, ᴿ"Do You not hear how many things they testify against You?"   Matt. 26:62

14 But He answered him not one word, so that the governor marveled greatly.

Taking the Place of Barabbas

15 ᴿNow at the feast the governor was accustomed to releasing to the multitude one prisoner whom he wished.   Luke 23:17-25

16 And at that time they had a notorious prisoner called *Barabbas.

17 Therefore, when they had gathered together, Pilate said to them, "Whom do you want me to release to you? Barabbas, or Jesus who is called Christ?"

18 For he knew that they had handed Him over because of ᴿenvy.   Matt. 21:38

19 While he was sitting on the judgment seat, his wife sent to him, saying, "Have nothing to do with that just Man, for I have suffered many things today in a dream because of Him."

20 ᴿBut the chief priests and elders persuaded the multitudes that they should ask for Barabbas and destroy Jesus.   Acts 3:14

21 The governor answered and said to them, "Which of the two do you want me to release to you?" They said, "Barabbas!"

22 Pilate said to them, "What then shall I do with Jesus who is called Christ?" They all said to him, "Let Him be crucified!"

23 Then the governor said, ᴿ"Why, what evil has He done?" But they cried out all the more, saying, "Let Him be crucified!" Acts 3:13

24 When Pilate saw that he could not prevail at all, but rather that a ᵀtumult was rising, he ᴿtook water and washed his hands before the multitude, saying, "I am innocent of the blood of this *just Person. You see to it."   an uproar · Deut. 21:6-8

25 And all the people answered and said, "His blood be on us and on our children."

26 Then he released Barabbas to them; and when ᴿhe had scourged Jesus, he delivered Him to be crucified.   [Is. 50:6; 53:5]

The Soldiers Mock Jesus

27 Then the soldiers of the governor took Jesus into the Praetorium and gathered the whole ᵀgarrison around Him.   cohort

28 And they ᴿstripped Him and ᴿput a scarlet robe on Him.   John 19:2 · Luke 23:11

29 ᴿWhen they had ᵀtwisted a crown of thorns, they put it on His head, and a reed in His right hand. And they bowed the knee before Him and mocked Him, saying, "Hail, King of the Jews!"   Ps. 69:19; Is. 53:3 · Lit. woven

30 Then ᴿthey spat on Him, and took the reed and struck Him on the head.   Is. 50:6

31 And when they had mocked Him, they took the robe off Him, put His own clothes on Him, and led Him away to be crucified.

The King on a Cross

32 Now as they came out, ᴿthey found a man of Cyrene, Simon by name. Him they compelled to bear His cross.   Mark 15:21

33 ᴿAnd when they had come to a place called Golgotha, that is to say, Place of a Skull,   John 19:17

34 ᴿthey gave Him *sour wine mingled with gall to drink. But when He had tasted it, He would not drink.   Ps. 69:21

35 Then they crucified Him, and divided His garments, casting lots, *that it might be fulfilled which was spoken by the prophet:

> ᴿ"They divided My garments among
>   them,   Ps. 22:18
>   And for My clothing they cast lots."

36 ᴿSitting down, they kept watch over Him there.   Ps. 22:17; Matt. 27:54

37 And they ᴿput up over His head the accusation written against Him: John 19:19

THIS IS JESUS THE KING OF THE JEWS.

38 Then two robbers were crucified with Him, one on the right and another on the left.

39 ᴿthose who passed by blasphemed Him, wagging their heads   Ps. 22:7

40 and saying, ᴿ"You who destroy the temple and build it in three days, save Yourself! ᴿIf You are the Son of God, come down from the cross."   John 2:19 · Matt. 26:63

41 Likewise the chief priests also, ᴿmocking with the *scribes and elders, said,   Matt. 20:19

42 "He ᴿsaved others; Himself He cannot save. ᴿIf* He is the King of Israel, let Him now come down from the cross, and we will believe *Him.   [John 3:14, 15] · Ps. 22:6; 69:9

43 ᴿ"He trusted in God; let Him deliver Him now if He will have Him; for He said, 'I am the Son of God.'"   Ps. 22:8

44 Even the robbers who were crucified with Him reviled Him with the same thing.

Jesus Dies on the Cross

45 Now from the sixth hour until the ninth hour there was darkness over all the land.

46 And about the ninth hour ᴿJesus cried out with a loud voice, saying, "Eli, Eli, lama sabachthani?" that is, ᴿ"My God, My God, why have You forsaken Me?"   [Heb. 5:7] · Ps. 22:1

47 Some of those who stood there, when they heard that, said, "This Man is calling for Elijah!"

27:16 NU Jesus Barabbas
27:24 NU omits just
27:34 NU omits sour
27:35 NU, M omit the rest of v. 35.
27:41 M scribes, the Pharisees, and the elders
27:42 NU omits If • NU, M in Him

48 Immediately one of them ran and took a sponge, ᴿfilled it with sour wine and put it on a reed, and offered it to Him to drink. Ps. 69:21

49 The rest said, "Let Him alone; let us see if Elijah will come to save Him."

50 And Jesus cried out again with a loud voice, and yielded up His spirit.

51 Then, behold, ᴿthe veil of the temple was torn in two from top to bottom; and the earth quaked, and the rocks were split, Zech. 11:10, 11

52 and the graves were opened; and many bodies of the saints who had fallen asleep were raised;

53 and coming out of the graves after His resurrection, they went into the holy city and appeared to many.

54 ᴿSo when the centurion and those with him, who were guarding Jesus, saw the earthquake and the things that had happened, they feared greatly, saying, ᴿ"Truly this was the Son of God!" Mark 15:39 · Matt. 14:33

55 And many women ᴿwho followed Jesus from Galilee, ministering to Him, were there looking on from afar, Luke 8:2, 3

56 ᴿamong whom were Mary Magdalene, Mary the mother of James and *Joses, and the mother of Zebedee's sons. Mark 15:40, 47

Jesus Buried in Joseph's Tomb

57 Now ᴿwhen evening had come, there came a rich man from Arimathea, named Joseph, who himself had also become a disciple of Jesus. John 19:38-42

58 This man went to Pilate and asked for the body of Jesus. Then Pilate commanded the body to be given to him.

59 When Joseph had taken the body, he wrapped it in a clean linen cloth,

60 and ᴿlaid it in his new tomb which he had hewn out of the rock; and he rolled a large stone against the door of the tomb, and departed. Is. 53:9

61 And Mary Magdalene was there, and the other Mary, sitting opposite the tomb.

Pilate Sets a Guard

62 On the next day, which followed the Day of Preparation, the chief priests and Pharisees gathered together to Pilate,

63 saying, "Sir, we remember, while He was still alive, how that deceiver said, ᴿ'After three days I will rise.' Mark 8:31; 10:34

64 "Therefore command that the tomb be made secure until the third day, lest His disciples come *by night and steal Him away, and say to the people, 'He has risen from the dead.' So the last deception will be worse than the first."

65 Pilate said to them, "You have a guard; go your way, make it as secure as you know how."

66 So they went and made the tomb secure, sealing the stone and setting the guard.

He Is Risen

28 Now ᴿafter the Sabbath, as the first day of the week began to dawn, Mary Magdalene ᴿand the other Mary came to see the tomb. Luke 24:1-10 · Matt. 27:56, 61

2 And behold, there was a great earthquake; for an angel of the Lord descended from heaven, and came and rolled back the stone *from the door, and sat on it.

3 ᴿHis countenance was like lightning, and his clothing as white as snow. Dan. 7:9; 10:6

4 And the guards shook for fear of him, and became like ᴿdead men. Rev. 1:17

5 But the angel answered and said to the women, "Do not be afraid, for I know that you seek Jesus who was crucified.

6 "He is not here; ᴿfor He is risen, as He said. Come, see the place where the Lord lay. Matt. 12:40; 16:21

7 "And go quickly and tell His disciples that He is risen from the dead, and indeed He is going before you into Galilee; there you will see Him. Behold, I have told you."

8 So they went out quickly from the tomb with fear and great joy, and ran to bring His disciples word.

The Women Worship the Risen Lord

9 And *as they went to tell His disciples, behold, ᴿJesus met them, saying, "Rejoice!" So they came and held Him by the feet and worshiped Him. John 20:14

10 Then Jesus said to them, "Do not be afraid. Go and tell ᴿMy brethren to go to Galilee, and there they will see Me." John 20:17

The Soldiers Are Bribed

11 Now while they were going, behold, some of the guard came into the city and reported to the chief priests all the things that had happened.

12 When they had assembled with the elders and consulted together, they gave a large sum of money to the soldiers,

13 saying, "Tell them, 'His disciples came at night and stole Him away while we slept.'

14 "And if this comes to the governor's ears, we will appease him and make you secure."

15 So they took the money and did as they were instructed; and this saying is commonly reported among the Jews until this day.

27:56 NU Joseph
27:64 NU omits by night

28:2 NU omits from the door
28:9 NU omits as they went to tell His disciples

The Great Commission

▼ **38-C. The Church: Its Mission**

16 Then the eleven disciples went away into Galilee, to the mountain ᴿwhich Jesus had appointed for them.   Matt. 26:32; 28:7, 10
17 When they saw Him, they worshiped Him; but some ᴿdoubted.   John 20:24-29
18 And Jesus came and spoke to them, saying, ᴿ"All authority has been given to Me in heaven and on earth.   [Dan. 7:13, 14]

19 ᴿ"Go *therefore and ᴿmake disciples of ▽ all the nations, baptizing them in the name of the Father and of the Son and of the Holy Spirit,   Mark 16:15 · Luke 24:47
20 ᴿ"teaching them to observe all things that I have commanded you; and lo, I am ᴿwith you always, *even* to the end of the age." *Amen.   [Acts 2:42] · [Acts 4:31; 18:10; 23:11] ▲

28:19 M omits *therefore*
28:20 NU omits *Amen*

38-C. The Church: Its Mission (Matthew 28:16–20)—The key Scripture passage for the mandate of the church during this present age is the passage we often call the Great Commission (vv. 18–20):

(1) The church is commanded to *make* disciples of all nations (v. 19).

(a) "Go" implies that the church, as a company of believers, is to be active and aggressive in winning the lost "in Jerusalem, and in all Judea and Samaria, and to the end of the earth" (Acts 1:8, page 1086). This shows us that our disciple-making must begin at our own home and continue moving outward until eventually, as a church, we reach all the nations of the world. We are to be *active*—not passive, defensive, or reactionary.

(b) "Make disciples of all the nations, baptizing them in the name of the Father and of the Son and of the Holy Spirit, teaching them to observe all things that I have commanded you" (vv. 19, 20). This is evangelism. Every born-again believer is commissioned to go with the gospel and evangelize the world. We are to teach the lost their obligation to heed the Word of God, to believe in the Lord Jesus Christ.

(2) The church is commanded to *baptize* its disciples (v. 19). Surely this implies that they are admitted, recognized, loved, and accepted by His church. We are not to win them and then forget them; rather, we are to win them and establish them in the faith. Thus Paul did not merely preach the saving gospel; he also organized his converts into churches. He instructed them, cared for them, and visited and revisited them again and again. He admonished and encouraged them to obey the Lord in their service to Him and in their spiritual growth (Acts 15:36, page 1110).

(3) The church is commanded to *teach* its disciples "to observe all things that I have commanded you" (v. 20). Not only must we teach the lost so that they may believe and be baptized "in the name of the Father and of the Son and of the Holy Spirit" (v. 19), we must also teach those whom we have won to Christ to obey their Lord and Master Jesus Christ, and grow in grace and knowledge of Him.

See Ephesians 3:1–11, page 1188, for **Point 38-D: The Church: A Mystery.**

THE GOSPEL ACCORDING TO
Mark

AUTHORSHIP. John Mark, nephew of Barnabas, was led by the Holy Spirit to write the book bearing his name, perhaps in Rome. Mark was a native of Jerusalem, where his mother Mary had a house in which the early Christians met. It was Mark's privilege to accompany his uncle Barnabas and the apostle Paul on the first missionary journey, but for some reason Mark did not complete the journey, causing a separation between Paul and Barnabas over Mark's defection. Fortunately, Mark later proved himself a worthwhile servant of the Lord, and it is widely believed that his Gospel embodies the reminiscences of the apostle Peter. In fact, the outline of the book seems similar to Peter's presentation in Acts.

HOW MARK FITS INTO THE BIBLE. Mark is thought by most modern scholars to be the oldest Gospel, although the traditional view is that Matthew, who wrote especially for the Jews, was first. Mark was definitely written before the destruction of Jerusalem (A.D. 70), and may have been written as early as the middle of the first century. Because of Mark's appeal to Gentiles, his book forms a nice bridge between the Jewish-oriented Gospel of Matthew and the only books in the New Testament written by a Gentile, Luke and its companion volume, Acts.

KEY VERSE: 10:45—"For even the Son of Man did not come to be served, but to serve, and to give His life a ransom for many."

SUMMARY STATEMENT. Mark presents the Lord Jesus as the Servant of the Lord, and for this reason stresses action and deeds rather than words or family pedigree.

HOW MARK FITS TOGETHER. In light of the key verse, the Gospel of Mark may be divided into two parts, the first half stressing Christ's service (chs. 1—10) and the second His sacrificial death (chs. 11—16). Also, the book may be nicely divided according to the geography of Palestine: (1) Jesus' Preparation for Ministry (1:1-13); (2) Jesus' Preaching in Galilee (1:14—9:50); (3) Jesus' Preaching in Perea (ch. 10); (4) Jesus' Passion and Resurrection at Jerusalem (chs. 11—16).

CONTEXT. Because Gentile Romans were interested in power, action, and service, and not concerned with genealogy, as Jews would be, Mark omits the birth and childhood of Jesus. He immediately establishes Christ's deity by giving seventeen miracles showing His power over disease, nine miracles showing His power over nature, six miracles showing His power over demons, and three miracles proving His power over death. Christ is truly LORD over disease, demons, death and all nature.

Since the Roman mind was attuned to obedient, loyal servants, Mark uses the word *euthus* ("immediately") forty-two times, more than all the other New Testament writers combined. Christ indeed is our loyal Servant-Savior.

Let us study Mark and thank God that Christ, our Savior, loves us enough to minister to our every need.

—E.J.D.

John the Baptist Prepares the Way

▼ **22-B. Repentance Preached**

THE beginning of the gospel of Jesus Christ, ᴿthe Son of God.   Matt. 14:33
2 As it is written in *the Prophets:

ᴿ"Behold, I send My messenger before
    Your face,   Mal. 3:1

1:2 NU *Isaiah the prophet*

Who will prepare Your way before   ▽
    You."
3 "The ᴿ voice of one crying in the
    wilderness:
'Prepare the way of the LORD;
Make His paths straight.' "   Is. 40:3

4 ᴿJohn came baptizing in the wilderness and preaching a ᴿbaptism of repentance for the remission of sins.   Matt. 3:1 • Mal. 4:6 ▲
5 ᴿThen all the land of Judea, and those

22-B. Repentance Preached (Mark 1:1-4)—Repentance was preached in the Old Testament before the birth of Christ, during the life and ministry of Christ, on the Day of Pentecost, in the book of Acts after Pentecost, and in the Epistles and the book of Revelation. It is a doctrine to be preached and practiced in all dispensations and ages.

(Point 22-B continued on next page)

from Jerusalem, went out to him and were all baptized by him in the Jordan River, confessing their sins.   Matt. 3:5

6 Now John was [R]clothed with camel's hair and with a leather belt around his waist, and he ate locusts and wild honey.   Matt. 3:4

7 And he preached, saying, [R]"There comes One after me who is mightier than I, whose sandal strap I am not worthy to stoop down and loose.   John 1:27

8 "I indeed baptized you with water, but He will baptize you with the Holy Spirit."

John Baptizes Jesus

9 [R]It came to pass in those days that Jesus came from Nazareth of Galilee, and was baptized by John in the Jordan.   Matt. 3:13–17

10 And immediately, coming up *from the water, He saw the heavens parting and the Spirit descending upon Him like a dove.

11 Then a voice came from heaven, [R]"You are My beloved Son, in whom I am well pleased."   Is. 42:1

Satan Tempts Jesus

12 [R]Immediately the Spirit [T]drove Him into the wilderness.   Matt. 4:1–11 · sent Him out

13 And He was there in the wilderness forty days, tempted by Satan, and was with the wild beasts; [R]and the angels ministered to Him.   Matt. 4:10, 11

Jesus Begins His Galilean Ministry

14 [R]Now after John was put in prison, Jesus came to Galilee, [R]preaching the gospel *of the kingdom of God,   Matt. 4:12 · Matt. 4:23

15 and saying, [R]"The time is fulfilled, and the kingdom of God [T]is at hand. Repent, and believe in the gospel."   [Gal. 4:4] · has drawn near

Four Fishermen Called as Disciples

16 [R]And as He walked by the Sea of Galilee, He saw Simon and Andrew his brother casting a net into the sea; for they were fishermen.   Luke 5:2–11

17 Then Jesus said to them, "Follow Me, and I will make you become fishers of men."

18 [R]They immediately left their nets and followed Him.   [Luke 14:26]

19 When He had gone a little farther from there, He saw James the son of Zebedee, and John his brother, who also were in the boat mending their nets.

20 And immediately He called them, and they left their father Zebedee in the boat with the hired servants, and went after Him.

Jesus Casts Out an Unclean Spirit

6–C. He Was Unique in His Ministry   ▼

21 [R]Then they went into Capernaum, and immediately on the Sabbath He entered the [R]synagogue and taught.   Luke 4:31–37 · Matt. 4:23

1:10 NU out of   **1:14** NU omits of the kingdom

(Point 22-B continued from previous page)

(1) John the Baptist preached repentance:

(a) He preached the baptism of repentance (Luke 3:3, page 1014): "Repent, for the kingdom of heaven is at hand!" (Matt. 3:2, page 932).

(b) He was thus "The voice of one crying in the wilderness: 'Prepare the way of the LORD'" (Matt. 3:3, page 933).

John's preaching of repentance exalted Christ, denounced sin, and warned of judgment; it also cost him his head (Matt. 14:6–11, page 959).

(2) Jesus preached repentance:

(a) He preached, "Repent, and believe in the gospel" (vv. 14, 15). He went about doing mighty works, calling sinners to repent and have faith in the good news of God.

(b) His preaching was an ultimatum: repent or perish (Luke 13:1–5, page 1031). Salvation by grace is for the repentant soul, and judgment without mercy is for those who resist.

(3) Peter preached repentance:

(a) At Pentecost he commanded, "Repent, and let every one of you be baptized in the name of Jesus Christ for the remission of sins" (Acts 2:38, page 1089).

(b) In his second epistle he wrote that the Lord "is longsuffering toward us, not willing that any should perish but that all should come to repentance" (2 Pet. 3:9, page 1275). Every soul that goes to hell makes that choice contrary to the revealed will of God, who calls upon all to repent.

(4) Paul preached repentance. He declared that God "commands all men everywhere to repent" (Acts 17:30, page 1112). This message was given on Mars Hill to the intelligentsia of Athens. The results were threefold: some mocked, some procrastinated, but some believed (Acts 17:32–34, page 1112).

See Hebrews 6:1, page 1240, for **Point 22-C: Repentance from Dead Works.**

6-C. He Was Unique in His Ministry (Mark 1:21–28)—He preached with such absolute authority that He was recognized both by His followers and by the self-righteous Pharisees and scribes as being different from all

(Point 6-C continued on next page)

▽ 22 ᴿAnd they were astonished at His teaching, for He taught them as one having authority, and not as the scribes.   Matt. 7:28, 29
23 Now there was a man in their synagogue with an unclean spirit. And he cried out,
24 saying, "Let us alone! What have we to do with You, Jesus of Nazareth? Did You come to destroy us? I ᴿknow who You are— the ᴿHoly One of God!"   James 2:19 · Ps. 16:10
25 But Jesus rebuked him, saying, ᵀ"Be quiet, and come out of him!"   Lit. Be muzzled
26 And when the unclean spirit ᴿhad convulsed him and cried out with a loud voice, he came out of him.   Mark 9:20
27 Then they were all amazed, so that they questioned among themselves, saying, *"What is this? What new ᵀdoctrine is this? For with authority He commands even the unclean spirits, and they obey Him."   teaching
▲ 28 And immediately His fame spread throughout all the region around Galilee.

Peter's Mother-in-Law Healed

29 Now as soon as they had come out of the synagogue, they entered the house of Simon and Andrew, with James and John.
30 But Simon's wife's mother lay sick with a fever, and they told Him about her at once.

1:27 NU What is this? A new doctrine with authority. He

31 So He came and took her by the hand and lifted her up, and immediately the fever left her. And she served them.

Many Healed After Sabbath Sunset

32 ᴿAt evening, when the sun had set, they brought to Him all who were sick and those who were demon-possessed.   Matt. 8:16, 17
33 And the whole city was gathered together at the door.
34 Then He healed many who were sick with various diseases, and ᴿcast out many demons; and He did not allow the demons to speak, because they knew Him.   Luke 13:32

Preaching in Galilee

35 Now ᴿin the morning, having risen a long while before daylight, He went out and departed to a ᵀsolitary place; and there He ᴿprayed.   Luke 4:42, 43 · deserted · Luke 5:16; 6:12; 9:28, 29
36 And Simon and those who were with Him searched for Him.
37 When they found Him, they said to Him, "Everyone ᴿis looking for You."   [Heb. 11:6]
38 But He said to them, "Let us go into the next towns, that I may preach there also, because for this purpose I have come forth."
39 ᴿAnd He was preaching in their synagogues throughout all Galilee, and ᴿcasting out demons.   Matt. 4:23; 9:35 · Mark 5:8, 13; 7:29, 30

(Point 6-C continued from previous page)
the rabbis who had ever gone before. He was not, as some believed, just another rabbi. His ministry was unique in that

(1) He was the greatest teacher who ever lived. His Sermon on the Mount (Matt. 5—7, page 936), His "Lord's Prayer" (Matt. 6:9–13, page 943), His Olivet Discourse (Matt. 24—25, page 972), and His wonderful parables, such as that of the Good Samaritan (Luke 10:25–37, page 1026), are unmatched by any religious or secular teacher who ever lived.

(2) He performed the mightiest miracles (Mark 6:35–44, page 992). Christ fed the 5,000; He also fed another 4,000. He quieted storms more than once, caused miraculous drafts of fish to be pulled into nets, healed countless multitudes, walked on water, cast out demons, raised the dead, and turned water into wine. Some said He was Elijah (Luke 9:8, page 1024)—but He was far greater than even Elijah.

(3) Jesus was the greatest healer. He cured an adult who was blind from birth (John 9:30–33, page 1066). He made the deaf to hear, the crippled to walk, and cleansed the lepers (Matt. 11:5, page 951). He healed the palsied and cast out demons (Matt. 4:24, page 936), and on three occasions He even raised the dead (Luke 7:11–17, page 1021; 8:40–56, page 1023; John 11:39–44, page 1070).

(4) Jesus made messianic claims for Himself which were never made by any other prophet or rabbi (John 5:19–30, page 1056). Jesus said that like the Father, He Himself had power to give life and that He would be the final judge of men on Judgment Day. He said, "He who does not honor the Son does not honor the Father who sent Him" (John 5:23, page 1057). These are not the sayings of mere rabbis or prophets; they are messianic claims.

(5) Jesus was absolutely holy and sinless in His person, His actions, and His standards. He spoke of His own sinlessness: "Which of you convicts Me of sin?" (John 8:46; page 1063). Even the Roman governor Pontius Pilate confessed Christ's righteousness as he publicly washed his hands in water, saying, "I am innocent of the blood of this just Person" (Matt. 27:24, page 980).

(6) He was a friend of sinners, offering them salvation (Luke 7:44–50, page 1022). Christ was even called by His self-righteous foes "a friend of [the hated] tax collectors and sinners!" (Luke 7:34, page 1021).

(7) His ministry alone fulfilled the Old Testament messianic prophecies in Luke 4:16–22 (page 1016). Christ declared that by preaching the good news of God's forgiveness He was fulfilling Isaiah 61:1 (page 701). Of history's messianic claimants, only He fulfilled Zechariah 9:9 (page 916) which said that the Messiah was to enter Jerusalem triumphantly, riding upon a colt (Mark 11:7–11, page 998). Even when His own people rejected His ministry, they were fulfilling prophecy (Is. 53:3, page 693).

See John 19:16–30, page 1080, for Point 6-D: He Was Unique in His Death.

Jesus Cleanses a Leper

40 ^RNow a leper came to Him, imploring Him, kneeling down to Him and saying to Him, "If You are willing, You can make me clean."   Luke 5:12-14

41 Then Jesus, moved with compassion, stretched out *His* hand and touched him, and said to him, "I am willing; be cleansed."

42 As soon as He had spoken, immediately the leprosy left him, and he was cleansed.

43 And He strictly warned him and sent him away at once,

44 and said to him, "See that you say nothing to anyone; but go your way, show yourself to the priest, and offer for your cleansing those things ^Rwhich Moses commanded, as a testimony to them."   Lev. 14:1-32

45 However, he went out and began to proclaim *it* freely, and to spread the matter, so that Jesus could no longer openly enter the city, but was outside in deserted places; and they came to Him from every direction.

Jesus Forgives and Heals a Paralytic

2 And again ^RHe entered Capernaum after some days, and it was heard that He was in the house.   Matt. 9:1

2 *Immediately many gathered together, so that there was no longer room to receive *them*, not even near the door. And He preached the word to them.

3 Then they came to Him, bringing a paralytic who was carried by four *men*.

4 And when they could not come near Him because of the crowd, they uncovered the roof where He was. So when they had broken through, they let down the bed on which the paralytic was lying.

5 When Jesus saw their faith, He said to the paralytic, "Son, your sins are forgiven you."

6 And some of the scribes were sitting there and reasoning in their hearts,

7 "Why does this *Man* speak blasphemies like this? ^RWho can forgive sins but God alone?"   Is. 43:25

8 But immediately, when Jesus perceived in His spirit that they reasoned thus within themselves, He said to them, "Why do you reason about these things in your hearts?

9 ^R"Which is easier, to say to the paralytic, 'Your sins are forgiven you,' or to say, 'Arise, take up your bed and walk'?   Matt. 9:5

10 "But that you may know that the Son of Man has ^Tpower on earth to forgive sins"— He said to the paralytic,   authority

11 "I say to you, arise, take up your bed, and go to your house."

12 Immediately he arose, took up the bed, and went out in the presence of them all, so that all were amazed and glorified God, saying, "We never saw *anything* like this!"

Matthew the Tax Collector

13 ^RThen He went out again by the sea; and all the multitude came to Him, and He taught them.   Matt. 9:9

14 As He passed by, He saw Levi the *son* of Alphaeus sitting at the tax office. And He said to him, ^R"Follow Me." So he arose and ^Rfollowed Him.   John 1:43; 12:26; 21:22 • Luke 18:28

15 ^RNow it happened, as He was dining in *Levi's* house, that many tax collectors and sinners also sat together with Jesus and His disciples; for there were many, and they followed Him.   Matt. 9:10

16 And when the scribes *and Pharisees saw Him eating with the tax collectors and sinners, they said to His disciples, "How *is it* that He eats and drinks with tax collectors and sinners?"

17 When Jesus heard *it*, He said to them, ^R"Those who are well have no need of a physician, but those who are sick. I did not come to call *the* righteous, but sinners, *to repentance."   Matt. 9:12, 13; 18:11

Jesus Is Questioned About Fasting

18 ^RThe disciples of John and of the Pharisees were fasting. Then they came and said to Him, "Why do the disciples of John and of the Pharisees fast, but Your disciples do not fast?"   Luke 5:33-38

19 And Jesus said to them, "Can the friends of the bridegroom fast while the bridegroom is with them? As long as they have the bridegroom with them they cannot fast.

20 "But the days will come when the bridegroom will be ^Rtaken away from them, and then they will fast in those days.   Acts 1:9

21 "No one sews a piece of unshrunk cloth on an old garment; or else the new piece pulls away from the old, and the tear is made worse.

22 "And no one puts new wine into old wineskins; or else the new wine bursts the wineskins, the wine is spilled, and the wineskins are ruined. But new wine must be put into new wineskins."

Jesus Is Lord of the Sabbath

23 ^RNow it happened that He went through the grainfields on the Sabbath; and as they went His disciples began ^Rto pluck the heads of grain.   Luke 6:1-5 • Deut. 23:25

24 And the Pharisees said to Him, "Look, why do they do what is ^Rnot lawful on the Sabbath?"   Ex. 20:10; 31:15

25 But He said to them, "Have you never read what David did when he was in need and hungry, he and those with him:

2:16 NU *of the*
2:17 NU omits *to repentance*

2:2 NU omits *Immediately*

26 "how he went into the house of God *in the days* of Abiathar the high priest, and ate the showbread, ᴿwhich is not lawful to eat except for the priests, and also gave some to those who were with him?"   Lev. 24:5-9

27 And He said to them, "The Sabbath was made for man, and not man for the Sabbath.

28 "Therefore ᴿthe Son of Man is also Lord of the Sabbath."   Matt. 12:8

Healing on the Sabbath

3 And ᴿHe entered the synagogue again, and a man was there who had a withered hand.   Luke 6:6-11

2 So they ᴿwatched Him closely, whether He would heal him on the Sabbath, so that they might accuse Him.   Luke 14:1; 20:20

3 And He said to the man who had the withered hand, "Step forward."

4 Then He said to them, "Is it lawful on the Sabbath to do good or to do evil, to save life or to kill?" But they kept silent.

5 And when He had looked around at them with anger, being grieved by the hardness of their hearts, He said to the man, "Stretch out your hand." And he stretched *it* out, and his hand was restored *as whole as the other.

6 ᴿThen the Pharisees went out and immediately plotted with the Herodians against Him, how they might destroy Him.   Ps. 2:2

A Great Multitude Follows Jesus

7 But Jesus withdrew with His disciples to the sea. And a great multitude from Galilee followed Him, ᴿand from Judea   Luke 6:17

8 and Jerusalem and Idumea and beyond the Jordan; and those from Tyre and Sidon, a great multitude, when they heard how ᴿmany things He was doing, came to Him.   Mark 5:19

9 So He told His disciples that a small boat should be kept ready for Him because of the multitude, lest they should crush Him.

10 For He healed ᴿmany, so that as many as had afflictions pressed about Him to ᴿtouch Him.   Luke 7:21 • Matt. 9:21; 14:36

11 ᴿAnd the unclean spirits, whenever they saw Him, fell down before Him and cried out, saying, "You are the Son of God."   Luke 4:41

12 But ᴿHe sternly warned them that they should not make Him known.   Mark 1:25, 34

The Twelve Apostles

13 ᴿAnd He went up on the mountain and called to Him those He Himself wanted. And they came to Him.   Luke 9:1

14 Then He appointed twelve, *that they might be with Him and that He might send them out to preach,

15 and to have ᵀpower *to heal sicknesses and to cast out demons: *authority*

16 *Simon, ᴿto whom He gave the name Peter;   John 1:42

17 James the *son* of Zebedee and John the brother of James, to whom He gave the name Boanerges, that is, "Sons of Thunder";

18 Andrew, Philip, Bartholomew, Matthew, Thomas, James the *son* of Alphaeus, Thaddaeus, Simon the Canaanite;

19 and Judas Iscariot, who also betrayed Him. And they went into a house.

A House Divided Cannot Stand

20 Then the multitude came together again, so that they could not so much as eat bread.

21 But when His ᴿown people heard *about this*, they went out to lay hold of Him, for they said, "He is out of His mind."   Mark 6:3

22 And the scribes who came down from Jerusalem said, ᴿ"He has Beelzebub," and, "By the ᴿruler of the demons He casts out demons."   Matt. 9:34; 10:25 • [John 12:31; 14:30; 16:11]

23 ᴿSo He called them to *Himself* and said to them in parables: "How can Satan cast out Satan?   Matt. 12:25-29

24 "If a kingdom is divided against itself, that kingdom cannot stand.

25 "And if a house is divided against itself, that house cannot stand.

26 "And if Satan has risen up against himself, and is divided, he cannot stand, but has an end.

27 ᴿ"No one can enter a strong man's house and plunder his goods, unless he first binds the strong man. And then he will plunder his house.   [Is. 49:24, 25]

The Unpardonable Sin

28 ᴿ"Assuredly, I say to you, all sins will be forgiven the sons of men, and whatever blasphemies they may utter;   Luke 12:10

29 "but he who blasphemes against the Holy Spirit never has forgiveness, but is subject to eternal condemnation"—

30 because they ᴿsaid, "He has an unclean spirit."   Matt. 9:34

Jesus' Mother and Brothers Send for Him

31 ᴿThen His brothers and His mother came, and standing outside they sent to Him, calling Him.   Matt. 12:46-50

32 And a multitude was sitting around Him; and they said to Him, "Look, Your mother and Your brothers *are outside seeking You."

33 But He answered them, saying, "Who is My mother, or My brothers?"

34 And He looked around in a circle at

3:5 NU omits *as whole as the other*
3:14 NU adds *whom He also named apostles*
3:15 NU omits *to heal sicknesses and*
3:16 NU *and He appointed the twelve: Simon . . .*
3:32 NU, M add *and your sisters*

those who sat about Him, and said, "Here are My mother and My brothers!

35 "For whoever does the ᴿwill of God is My brother and My sister and mother."   Eph. 6:6

The Parable of the Sower

4 And ᴿagain He began to teach by the sea. And a great multitude was gathered to Him, so that He got into a boat and sat *in it* on the sea; and the whole multitude was on the land facing the sea.   Luke 8:4-10

2 Then He taught them many things by parables, and said to them in His teaching:

3 "Listen! Behold, a sower went out to sow.

4 "And it happened, as he sowed, *that* some *seed* fell by the wayside; and the birds *of the air came and devoured it.

5 "Some fell on stony ground, where it did not have much earth; and immediately it sprang up because it had no depth of earth.

6 "But when the sun was up it was scorched, and because it had no root it withered away.

7 "And some *seed* fell among thorns; and the thorns grew up and choked it, and it yielded no ᵀcrop.   Lit. *fruit*

8 "But other *seed* fell on good ground and yielded a crop that sprang up, increased and produced: some thirtyfold, some sixty, and some a hundred."

9 And He said *to them, "He who has ears to hear, let him hear!"

The Purpose of Parables

10 ᴿBut when He was alone, those around Him with the twelve asked Him about the parable.   Luke 8:9

11 And He said to them, "To you it has been given to ᴿknow the mystery of the kingdom of God; but to those who are outside, all things come in parables,   [1 Cor. 2:10-16]

12 "so that

> ᴿ'Seeing they may see and not perceive,
> And hearing they may hear and not
>   understand;
> Lest they should turn,
> And their sins be forgiven them.' "   Is. 6:9, 10; 43:8

The Parable of the Sower Explained

13 And He said to them, "Do you not understand this parable? How then will you understand all the parables?

14 ᴿ"The sower sows the word.   Matt. 13:18-23

15 "And these are the ones by the wayside where the word is sown. When they hear, Satan comes immediately and takes away the word that was sown in their hearts.

16 "These likewise are the ones sown on

4:4 NU, M omit *of the air*
4:9 NU, M omit *to them*

stony ground who, when they hear the word, immediately receive it with gladness;

17 "and they have no root in themselves, and so endure only for a time. Afterward, when tribulation or persecution arises for the word's sake, immediately they stumble.

18 "Now these are the ones sown among thorns; *they are* the ones who hear the word,

19 "and the ᴮcares of this world, ᴮthe deceitfulness of riches, and the desires for other things entering in choke the word, and it becomes unfruitful.   Luke 21:34 • 1 Tim. 6:9, 10, 17

20 "But these are the ones sown on good ground, those who hear the word, ᵀaccept *it*, and bear ᴿfruit: some thirtyfold, some sixty, and some a hundred."   *receive* • [Rom. 7:4]

Light Under a Basket

21 Also He said to them, "Is a lamp brought to be put under a basket or under a bed? Is it not to be set on a lampstand?

22 "For there is nothing hidden which will not be revealed, nor has anything been kept secret but that it should come to light.

23 ᴿ"If anyone has ears to hear, let him hear."   Matt. 11:15; 13:9, 43

24 Then He said to them, "Take heed what you hear. ᴿWith the same measure you use, it will be measured to you; and to you who hear, more will be given.   Matt. 7:2

25 "For whoever has, to him more will be given; but whoever does not have, even what he has will be taken away from him."

The Parable of the Growing Seed

26 And He said, "The kingdom of God is as if a man should scatter seed on the ground,

27 "and should sleep by night and rise by day, and the seed should sprout and ᴿgrow, he himself does not know how.   [2 Pet. 3:18]

28 "For the earth ᴮyields crops by itself: first the blade, then the head, after that the full grain in the head.   [John 12:24]

29 "But when the grain ripens, immediately ᴿhe puts in the sickle, because the harvest has come."   Rev. 14:15

The Parable of the Mustard Seed

30 Then He said, ᴿ"To what shall we liken the kingdom of God? Or with what parable shall we picture it?   Matt. 13:31, 32

31 "*It is* like a mustard seed which, when it is sown on the ground, is smaller than all the seeds on earth;

32 "but when it is sown, it grows up and becomes greater than all herbs, and shoots out large branches, so that the birds of the air may nest under its shade."

Jesus' Use of Parables

33 And with many such parables He spoke the word to them as they were able to hear *it*.

34 But without a parable He did not speak to them. And when they were alone, He explained all things to His disciples.

Wind and Wave Obey Jesus

35 ᴿOn the same day, when evening had come, He said to them, "Let us cross over to the other side."   Luke 8:22, 25

36 Now when they had left the multitude, they took Him along in the boat as He was. And other little boats were also with Him.

37 And a great windstorm arose, and the waves beat into the boat, so that it was already filling.

38 But He was in the stern, asleep on a pillow. And they awoke Him and said to Him, ᴿ"Teacher, ᴿdo You not care that we are perishing?"   [Matt. 23:8-10] • Ps. 44:23

39 Then He arose and rebuked the wind, and said to the sea, "Peace, be still!" And the wind ceased and there was a great calm.

40 But He said to them, "Why are you so fearful? *How is it that you have no faith?"

41 And they feared exceedingly, and said to

4:40 NU Have you still no faith?

one another, "Who can this be, that even the wind and the sea obey Him!"

A Demon-Possessed Man Healed

13-D. Demons: Their Power   ▼

5 Then they came to the other side of the sea, to the country of the *Gadarenes.

2 And when He had come out of the boat, immediately there met Him out of the tombs a man with an ᴿunclean spirit,   Mark 1:23; 7:25

3 who had his dwelling among the tombs; and no one could bind *him, not even with chains,

4 because he had often been bound with shackles and chains. And the chains had been pulled apart by him, and the shackles broken in pieces; neither could anyone tame him.

5 And always, night and day, he was in the mountains and in the tombs, crying out and cutting himself with stones.

6 When he saw Jesus from afar, he ran and worshiped Him.

5:1 NU Gerasenes
5:3 NU adds anymore

13-D. Demons: Their Power (Mark 5:1–20)—This demon-possessed man (v. 2) had the physical strength of many men. When Jesus asked the demon his name, he replied, "My name is Legion; for we are many" (v. 9). A Roman legion consisted of three thousand to six thousand troops, and this man had the strength of a legion of demons. Demons are not only strong, but they can also work miracles. John wrote, "And I saw three unclean spirits like frogs. . . . they are spirits of demons, performing signs" (Rev. 16:13, 14, page 1309). Yes, Satan and his demons can perform miracles and deceive those who are not rooted and grounded in God's Word. In the last days signs and wonders by occult groups may prepare the world for the coming of the Antichrist (2 Thess. 2:9, page 1215).

Satan and his demons often appear "religious." Do not be deceived by occult groups, false religions, or even merely professing Christians. They all have one thing in common: they deny the deity of Jesus Christ. The apostle John warns the believer, "Beloved, do not believe every spirit [some are evil spirits], but test the spirits, whether they are of God; because many false prophets have gone out into the world" (1 John 4:1–6, page 1280). How can we test the spirits? John said, "Every spirit that confesses that Jesus Christ [the Messiah] has come in the flesh [that Jesus is the God-Man] is of God." All other religions are satanically inspired and demonically controlled. Their adherents may even pray in the name of Jesus and call Him "Lord, Lord." Some of these false prophets will stand before Christ at the Great White Throne judgment and say, "Have we not prophesied in Your name, cast out demons in Your name, and done many wonders in Your name?" And Jesus will say, "I never knew you; depart from Me" (Matt. 7:21–23, page 946). You can know false teachers: all you need to do is ask them if they believe that Jesus is God (John 1:1, 14, page 1049). If they answer, "No," they are false prophets. They may be leaders of large congregations and even thought to be outstanding Christian leaders, but if they deny the deity of Jesus they are Satan's prophets.

God warned Israel, as they entered the Promised Land, to beware of spiritist mediums, saying, "You shall not learn to follow the abominations of those nations" (Deut. 18:9-14, page 198). They were not to worship Molech, who required human sacrifice of young children; the Lord called this demon religion an "abomination," and no wonder. Yet the Israelites briefly worshiped Molech and offered their sons and daughters to this demon god. Even Solomon in all his wisdom sinned in erecting an altar to Molech (1 Kin. 11:7, page 339). Don't underestimate the power of Satan and his demons (Ezek. 16:20-23, page 791).

Furthermore, do not let the Devil lead you into some so-called innocent cult. Our Lord calls all believers to "come out from among them and be separate, says the Lord. Do not touch what is unclean" (2 Cor. 6:14-18, page 1169). God says we are not to touch the following:

(1) Divination—those who claim to have secret knowledge of the future (fortune-tellers). This practice is demon-controlled (Ezek. 13:6-8, page 788).

(2) Witchcraft. Witches will be on the increase in the last days. During Saul's reign one even had the ability—and permission—to bring up the dead (1 Sam. 28:7-20, page 294).

(3) Mediums—those who claim to have familiar spirits (demons). "For all who do these things are an abomination to the LORD" (Deut. 18:12, page 198).

See 1 Corinthians 6:3, page 1151, for **Point 13-E: Demons: Their Judgment.**

▽ 7 And he cried out with a loud voice and said, "What have I to do with You, Jesus, Son of the Most High God? I ᵀimplore You by God that You do not torment me."   *adjure*

8 For He said to him, ᴿ"Come out of the man, unclean spirit!"   Mark 1:25; 9:25

9 Then He asked him, "What *is* your name?" And he answered, saying, "My name is Legion; for we are many."

10 Also he begged Him earnestly that He would not send them out of the country.

11 Now a large herd of ᴿswine was feeding there near the mountains.   Deut. 14:8

12 So all the demons begged Him, saying, "Send us to the swine, that we may enter them."

13 And *at once Jesus gave them permission. Then the unclean spirits went out and entered the swine (there were about two thousand); and the herd ran violently down the steep place into the sea, and drowned in the sea.

14 So those who fed the swine fled, and they told *it* in the city and in the country. And they went out to see what it was that had happened.

15 Then they came to Jesus, and saw the one *who had been* demon-possessed and had the legion, sitting and ᴿclothed and in his right mind. And they were afraid.   [Is. 61:10]

16 And those who saw it told them how it happened to him *who had been* demon-possessed, and about the swine.

17 Then ᴿthey began to plead with Him to depart from their region.   Acts 16:39

18 And when He got into the boat, ᴿhe who had been demon-possessed begged Him that he might be with Him.   Luke 8:38, 39

19 However, Jesus did not permit him, but said to him, "Go home to your friends, and tell them what great things the Lord has done for you, and how He has had compassion on you."

20 And he departed and began to proclaim in ᵀDecapolis all that Jesus had done for him; ▲ and all ᴿmarveled.   Lit. *Ten Cities* • Matt. 9:8, 33

A Girl Restored to Life and a Woman Healed

21 Now when Jesus had crossed over again by boat to the other side, a great multitude gathered to Him; and He was by the sea.

22 ᴿAnd behold, one of the rulers of the synagogue came, Jairus by name. And when he saw Him, he fell at His feet   Matt. 9:18–26

23 and begged Him earnestly, saying, "My little daughter lies at the point of death. Come and ᴿlay Your hands on her, that she may be healed, and she will live."   Acts 9:17; 28:8

24 So *Jesus* went with him, and a great multitude followed Him and thronged Him.

25 Now a certain woman ᴿhad a flow of blood for twelve years,   Lev. 15:19, 25

26 and had suffered many things from many physicians. She had spent all that she had and was no better, but rather grew worse.

27 When she heard about Jesus, she came behind *Him* in the crowd and ᴿtouched His garment.   Matt. 14:35, 36

28 For she said, "If only I may touch His clothes, I shall be made well."

29 Immediately the fountain of her blood was dried up, and she felt in *her* body that she was healed of the ᵀaffliction.   *suffering*

30 And Jesus, immediately knowing in Himself that ᴿpower had gone out of Him, turned around in the crowd and said, "Who touched My clothes?"   Luke 6:19; 8:46

31 But His disciples said to Him, "You see the multitude thronging You, and You say, 'Who touched Me?' "

32 And He looked around to see her who had done this thing.

33 But the woman, ᴿfearing and trembling, knowing what had happened to her, came and fell down before Him and told Him the whole truth.   [Ps. 89:7]

34 And He said to her, "Daughter, your faith has made you well. ᴿGo in peace, and be healed of your affliction."   Luke 7:50; 8:48

35 ᴿWhile He was still speaking, *some* came from the ruler of the synagogue's *house* who said, "Your daughter is dead. Why trouble the Teacher any further?"   Luke 8:49

36 As soon as Jesus heard the word that was spoken, He said to the ruler of the synagogue, "Do not be afraid; only believe."

37 And He permitted no one to follow Him except Peter, James, and John the brother of James.

38 Then He came to the house of the ruler of the synagogue, and saw ᵀa tumult and those who wept and wailed loudly.   *an uproar*

39 When He came in, He said to them, "Why make this commotion and weep? The child is not dead, but ᴿsleeping."   John 11:4, 11

40 And they ridiculed Him. ᴿBut when He had put them all outside, He took the father and the mother of the child, and those *who were* with Him, and entered where the child was lying.   Acts 9:40

41 Then He took the child by the hand, and said to her, "Talitha, cumi," which is translated, "Little girl, I say to you, arise."

42 Immediately the girl arose and walked, for she was twelve years *of age.* And they were overcome with great amazement.

43 But ᴿHe commanded them strictly that no one should know it, and said that *something* should be given her to eat.   Matt. 8:4

5:13 NU *He gave*

Jesus Rejected at Nazareth

6 Then ᴿHe went out from there and came to His own country, and His disciples followed Him.   Matt. 13:54

2 And when the Sabbath had come, He began to teach in the synagogue. And many hearing *Him* were ᴿastonished, saying, ᴿ"Where *did* this Man *get* these things? And what wisdom *is* this which is given to Him, that such mighty works are performed by His hands!   Matt. 7:28 • John 6:42

3 "Is this not the carpenter, the Son of Mary, and brother of James, Joses, Judas, and Simon? And are not His sisters here with us?" So they were offended at Him.

4 But Jesus said to them, ᴿ"A prophet is not without honor except in his own country, among his own relatives, and in his own house."   John 4:44

5 ᴿNow He could do no mighty work there, except that He laid His hands on a few sick people and healed *them*.   Gen. 19:22; 32:25

6 And ᴿHe marveled because of their unbelief. ᴿThen He went about the villages in a circuit, teaching.   Is. 59:16 • Matt. 9:35

Sending Out the Twelve

7 And He called the twelve to *Himself*, and began to send them out two *by* two, and gave them power over unclean spirits.

8 He commanded them to take nothing for the journey except a staff—no bag, no bread, no copper in *their* money belts—

9 but ᴿto wear sandals, and not to put on two tunics.   [Eph. 6:15]

10 ᴿAlso He said to them, "In whatever place you enter a house, stay there till you depart from that place.   Matt. 10:11

11 ᴿ"And *whoever will not receive you nor hear you, when you depart from there, ᴿshake off the dust under your feet as a testimony against them. *Assuredly, I say to you, it will be more tolerable for Sodom and Gomorrah in the day of judgment than for that city!"   Matt. 10:14 • Acts 13:51; 18:6

12 So they went out and preached that *people* should repent.

13 And they cast out many demons, ᴿand anointed with oil many who were sick, and healed *them*.   [James 5:14]

John the Baptist Beheaded

14 Now King Herod heard *of Him*, for His name had become well known. And he said, "John the Baptist is risen from the dead, and therefore these powers are at work in him."

15 ᴿOthers said, "It is Elijah." And others said, "It is the ᴿProphet, *or like one of the prophets."   Mark 8:28 • Matt. 21:11

16 ᴿBut when Herod heard, he said, "This is John, whom I beheaded; he has been raised from the dead!"   Luke 3:19

17 For Herod himself had sent and laid hold of John, and bound him in prison for the sake of Herodias, his brother Philip's wife; for he had married her.

18 Because John had said to Herod, "It is not lawful for you to have your brother's wife."

19 Therefore Herodias held it against him and wanted to kill him, but she could not;

20 for Herod ᴿfeared John, knowing that he *was* a just and holy man, and he protected him. And when he heard him, he did many things, and heard him gladly.   Matt. 14:5; 21:26

21 ᴿThen an opportune day came when Herod ᴿon his birthday gave a feast for his nobles, the high officers, and the chief *men* of Galilee.   Matt. 14:6 • Gen. 40:20

22 And when Herodias' daughter herself came in and danced, and pleased Herod and those who sat with him, the king said to the girl, "Ask me whatever you want, and I will give *it* to you."

23 He also swore to her, ᴿ"Whatever you ask me, I will give you, up to half my kingdom."   Esth. 5:3, 6; 7:2

24 So she went out and said to her mother, "What shall I ask?" And she said, "The head of John the Baptist!"

25 Immediately she came in with haste to the king and asked, saying, "I want you to give me at once the head of John the Baptist on a platter."

26 ᴿAnd the king was exceedingly sorry; *yet*, because of the oaths and because of those who sat with him, he did not want to refuse her.   Matt. 14:9

27 Immediately the king sent an executioner and commanded his head to be brought. And he went and beheaded him in prison,

28 brought his head on a platter, and gave it to the girl; and the girl gave it to her mother.

29 When his disciples heard *of it*, they came and ᴿtook away his corpse and laid it in a tomb.   1 Kin. 13:29, 30

Feeding the Five Thousand

30 ᴿThen the apostles gathered to Jesus and told Him all things, both what they had done and what they had taught.   Luke 9:10

31 And He said to them, "Come aside by yourselves to a deserted place and rest a while." For there were many coming and going, and they did not even have time to eat.

32 ᴿSo they departed to a deserted place in the boat by themselves.   Matt. 14:13–21

33 But *the multitudes saw them departing, and many ᴿknew Him and ran there on foot

---

6:11 NU *whatever place* • NU omits the rest of v. 11.
6:15 NU, M *a prophet, like one*

6:33 NU, M *they*

from all the cities. They arrived before them and came together to Him. [Col. 1:6]

34 And Jesus, when He came out, saw a great multitude and was moved with compassion for them, because they were like ᴿsheep not having a shepherd. So ᴿHe began to teach them many things. Num. 27:17 • Luke 9:11

35 When the day was now far spent, His disciples came to Him and said, "This is a deserted place, and already the hour is late.

36 "Send them away, that they may go into the surrounding country and villages and buy themselves *bread; for they have nothing to eat."

37 But He answered and said to them, "You give them something to eat." And they said to Him, ᴿ"Shall we go and buy two hundred denarii worth of bread and give them something to eat?" 2 Kin. 4:43

38 But He said to them, "How many loaves do you have? Go and see." And when they found out they said, "Five, and two fish."

39 Then He ᴿcommanded them to make them all sit down in groups on the green grass. Matt. 15:35

40 So they sat down in ranks, in hundreds and in fifties.

41 And when He had taken the five loaves and the two fish, He looked up to heaven, blessed and broke the loaves, and gave them to His disciples to set before them; and the two fish He divided among them all.

42 So they all ate and were filled.

43 And they took up twelve baskets full of fragments and of the fish.

44 Now those who had eaten the loaves were *about five thousand men.

Jesus Walks on the Sea

45 ᴿImmediately He ᵀmade His disciples get into the boat and go before Him to the other side, to Bethsaida, while He sent the multitude away. John 6:15-21 • strongly urged

46 And when He had sent them away, He ᴿdeparted to the mountain to pray. Luke 5:16

47 Now when evening came, the boat was in the middle of the sea; and He was alone on the land.

48 Then He saw them straining at rowing, for the wind was against them. Now about the fourth watch of the night He came to them, walking on the sea, and ᴿwould have passed them by. Luke 24:28

49 And when they saw Him walking on the sea, they supposed it was a ᴿghost, and cried out; Matt. 14:26

50 for they all saw Him and were troubled. But immediately He talked with them and said to them, ᴿ"Beᵀ of good cheer! It is I; do not be ᴿafraid." Matt. 9:2 • Take courage • Is. 41:10

51 Then He went up into the boat to them, and the wind ᴿceased. And they were greatly ᴿamazed in themselves beyond measure, and marveled. Ps. 107:29 • Mark 1:27; 2:12; 5:42; 7:37

52 For they had not understood about the loaves, because their heart was hardened.

Many Touch Him and Are Made Well

53 ᴿWhen they had crossed over, they came to the land of Gennesaret and anchored there. Matt. 14:34-36

54 And when they came out of the boat, immediately the people recognized Him,

55 ran through that whole surrounding region, and began to carry about on beds those who were sick to wherever they heard He was.

56 Wherever He entered, into villages, cities, or the country, they laid the sick in the marketplaces, and begged Him that ᴿthey might just touch the ᴿhem of His garment. And as many as touched Him were made well. Matt. 9:20 • Num. 15:38, 39

Defilement Comes from Within

7 Then ᴿthe Pharisees and some of the scribes came together to Him, having come from Jerusalem. Matt. 15:1-20

2 Now *when they saw some of His disciples eat bread with defiled, that is, with unwashed hands, *they found fault.

3 For the Pharisees and all the Jews do not eat unless they wash their hands in a special way, holding the tradition of the elders.

4 When they come from the marketplace, they do not eat unless they wash. And there are many other things which they have received and hold, like the washing of cups, pitchers, copper vessels, and couches.

5 ᴿThen the Pharisees and scribes asked Him, "Why do Your disciples not walk according to the tradition of the elders, but eat bread with unwashed hands?" Matt. 15:2

6 He answered and said to them, "Well did Isaiah prophesy of you ᴿhypocrites, as it is written: Matt. 23:13-29

ᴿ*This people honors Me with their lips,
 But their heart is far from Me.* Is. 29:13

7 *And in vain they worship Me,
 Teaching as doctrines the
 commandments of men.'*

8 "For laying aside the commandment of God, you hold the tradition of men—*the washing of pitchers and cups, and many other such things you do."

9 He said to them, "All too well ᴿyou ᵀreject the commandment of God, that you may keep your tradition. Prov. 1:25 • set aside

10 "For Moses said, *'Honor your father

6:36 NU *something to eat* and omits the rest of v. 36.
6:44 NU, M omit *about*

7:2 NU omits *when* • NU omits *they found fault*
7:8 NU omits the rest of v. 8.
7:10 Ex. 20:12; Deut. 5:16; Matt. 15:4

and your mother'; and, *'He who curses father or mother, let him be put to death.'*

11 "But you say, 'If a man says to his father or mother, ᴿ"Whatever profit you might have received from me is Corban'—' (that is, a gift to God); Matt. 15:5; 23:18

12 "and you no longer let him do anything for his father or his mother,

13 "making the word of God of no effect through your tradition which you have handed down. And many such things you do."

14 When He had called all the multitude to Himself, He said to them, "Hear Me, everyone, and ᴿunderstand: Matt. 16:9, 11, 12

15 "There is nothing that enters a man from outside which can defile him; but the things which come out of him, those are the things that ᴿdefile a man. Is. 59:3

16 ᴿ"If* anyone has ears to hear, let him hear!" Matt. 11:15

17 ᴿWhen He had entered a house away from the crowd, His disciples asked Him concerning the parable. Matt. 15:15

18 So He said to them, ᴿ"Are you thus without understanding also? Do you not perceive that whatever enters a man from outside cannot defile him, [Heb. 5:11-14]

19 "because it does not enter his heart but his stomach, and is eliminated, *thus* *purifying all foods?"

20 And He said, ᴿ"What comes out of a man, that defiles a man. Ps. 39:1

21 "For from within, out of the heart of men, ᴿproceed evil thoughts, ᴿadulteries, fornications, murders, [Gal. 5:19-21] · 2 Pet. 2:14

22 "thefts, covetousness, wickedness, deceit, ᴿlewdness, an evil eye, ᴿblasphemy, ᴿpride, foolishness. 1 Pet. 4:3 · Rev. 2:9 · 1 John 2:16

23 "All these evil things come from within and defile a man."

A Gentile Shows Her Faith

24 From there He arose and went to the region of Tyre *and Sidon. And He entered a house and wanted no one to know *it*, but He could not be ᴿhidden. Mark 2:1, 2

25 For a woman whose young daughter had an unclean spirit heard about Him, and she came and ᴿfell at His feet. John 11:32

26 The woman was a Greek, a Syro-Phoenician by birth, and she kept asking Him to cast the demon out of her daughter.

27 But Jesus said to her, "Let the children be filled first, for it is not good to take the children's bread and throw *it* to the little dogs."

28 And she answered and said to Him, "Yes, Lord, yet even the little dogs under the table eat from the children's crumbs."

29 Then He said to her, "For this saying go your way; the demon has gone out of your daughter."

30 And when she had come to her house, she found the demon gone out, and her daughter lying on the bed.

Jesus Heals a Deaf Mute

31 ᴿAgain, departing from the region of Tyre and Sidon, He came through the midst of the region of Decapolis to the Sea of Galilee. Matt. 15:29

32 Then they brought to Him one who was deaf and had an impediment in his speech, and they begged Him to put His hand on him.

33 And He took him aside from the multitude, and put His fingers in his ears, and ᴿHe spat and touched his tongue. Mark 8:23

34 Then, ᴿlooking up to heaven, ᴿHe sighed, and said to him, "Ephphatha," that is, "Be opened." Mark 6:41 · John 11:33, 38

35 ᴿImmediately his ears were opened, and the ᵀimpediment of his tongue was loosed, and he spoke plainly. Is. 35:5, 6 · Lit. *bond*

36 Then ᴿHe commanded them that they should tell no one; but the more He commanded them, the more widely they proclaimed *it*. Mark 5:43

37 And they were ᴿastonished beyond measure, saying, "He has done all things well. He ᴿmakes both the deaf to hear and the mute to speak." Mark 6:51; 10:26 · Matt. 12:22

Feeding the Four Thousand

8 In those days, the multitude being very great and having nothing to eat, Jesus called His disciples *to Him* and said to them,

2 "I have compassion on the multitude, because they have now continued with Me three days and have nothing to eat.

3 "And if I send them away hungry to their own houses, they will faint on the way; for some of them have come from afar."

4 Then His disciples answered Him, "How can one satisfy these people with bread here in the wilderness?"

5 ᴿHe asked them, "How many loaves do you have?" And they said, "Seven." Mark 6:38

6 So He commanded the multitude to sit down on the ground. And He took the seven loaves and gave thanks, broke *them* and gave *them* to His disciples to set before *them*; and they set *them* before the multitude.

7 They also had a few small fish; and ᴿhaving blessed them, He said to set them also before *them*. Matt. 14:19

8 So they ate and were filled, and they took up seven large baskets of leftover fragments.

9 Now those who had eaten were about four thousand. And He sent them away, 10 Rimmediately got into the boat with His disciples, and came to the region of Dalmanutha. Matt. 15:39

The Pharisees Seek a Sign

11 RThen the Pharisees came out and began to dispute with Him, seeking from Him a sign from heaven, testing Him. Matt. 12:38; 16:1
12 But He Rsighed deeply in His spirit, and said, "Why does this generation seek a sign? Assuredly, I say to you, Rno sign shall be given to this generation." Mark 7:34 • Matt. 12:39

Beware of the Leaven of the Pharisees and Herod

13 And He left them, and getting into the boat again, departed to the other side.
14 RNow *the disciples had forgotten to take bread, and they did not have more than one loaf with them in the boat. Matt. 16:5
15 RThen He charged them, saying, "Take heed, beware of the Tleaven of the Pharisees and the leaven of Herod." Luke 12:1 • yeast
16 And they reasoned among themselves, saying, "It is because we have no bread."
17 But Jesus, being aware of it, said to them, "Why do you reason because you have no bread? Do you not yet perceive nor understand? Is your heart *still hardened?
18 "Having eyes, do you not see? And having ears, do you not hear? And do you not remember?
19 R"When I broke the five loaves for the five thousand, how many baskets full of fragments did you take up?" They said to Him, "Twelve." Matt. 14:20
20 "Also, Rwhen I broke the seven for the four thousand, how many large baskets full of fragments did you take up?" And they said, "Seven." Matt. 15:37
21 So He said to them, "How is it Ryou do not understand?" [Mark 6:52]

A Blind Man Healed at Bethsaida

22 Then He came to Bethsaida; and they brought a Rblind man to Him, and begged Him to Rtouch him. John 9:1 • Luke 18:15
23 So He took the blind man by the hand and led him out of the town. And when He had spit on his eyes and put His hands on him, He asked him if he saw anything.
24 And he looked up and said, "I see men like trees, walking."
25 Then He put His hands on his eyes again and made him look up. And he was restored and saw everyone clearly.
26 Then He sent him away to his house,

saying, *"Neither go into the town, Rnor tell anyone in the town." Mark 5:43; 7:36

Peter Confesses Jesus as the Christ

27 RNow Jesus and His disciples went out to the towns of Caesarea Philippi; and on the road He asked His disciples, saying to them, "Who do men say that I am?" Luke 9:18-20
28 So they answered, R"John the Baptist; but some say, RElijah; and others, one of the prophets." Matt. 14:2 • Luke 9:7, 8
29 He said to them, "But who do you say that I am?" Peter answered and said to Him, R"You are the Christ." John 1:41; 4:42
30 RThen He strictly warned them that they should tell no one about Him. Matt. 8:4; 16:20

Jesus Predicts His Death and Resurrection

31 And He began to teach them that the Son of Man must suffer many things, and be Rrejected by the elders and chief priests and scribes, and be Rkilled, and after three days rise again. Mark 10:33 • Mark 9:31; 10:34; Luke 24:46
32 He spoke this word openly. Then Peter took Him aside and began to rebuke Him.
33 But when He had turned around and looked at His disciples, He Rrebuked Peter, saying, "Get behind Me, Satan! For you are not Tmindful of the things of God, but the things of men." [Rev. 3:19] • setting your mind on

Take Up the Cross and Follow Him

34 When He had called the people to Himself, with His disciples also, He said to them, R"Whoever desires to come after Me, let him deny himself, and take up his cross, and follow Me. Luke 14:27
35 "For Rwhoever desires to save his life will lose it, but whoever loses his life for My sake and the gospel's will save it. John 12:25
36 "For what will it profit a man if he gains the whole world, and loses his own soul?
37 "Or what will a man give in exchange for his soul?
38 R"For whoever is ashamed of Me and My words in this adulterous and sinful generation, of him the Son of Man also will be ashamed when He comes in the glory of His Father with the holy angels." Matt. 10:33

Jesus Transfigured on the Mount

9 And He said to them, "Assuredly, I say to you that there are some standing here who will not taste death till they see the kingdom of God present with power."
2 RNow after six days Jesus took Peter, James, and John, and led them up on a high mountain apart by themselves; and He was transfigured before them. Matt. 17:1-8

8:14 NU, M they
8:17 NU omits still

8:26 NU Do not even go into the town

3 His clothes became shining, exceedingly ᴿwhite, like snow, such as no launderer on earth can whiten them.   Dan. 7:9

4 And Elijah appeared to them with Moses, and they were talking with Jesus.

5 Then Peter answered and said to Jesus, "Rabbi, it is good for us to be here; and let us make three tabernacles: one for You, one for Moses, and one for Elijah"—

6 because he did not know what to say, for they were greatly afraid.

7 And a cloud came and overshadowed them; and a voice came out of the cloud, saying, "This is ᴿMy beloved Son. Hear Him!"   Ps. 2:7; Is. 42:1; Luke 1:35

8 Suddenly, when they had looked around, they saw no one anymore, but only Jesus with themselves.

9 Now as they came down from the mountain, He commanded them that they should tell no one the things they had seen, till the Son of Man had risen from the dead.

10 So they kept this word to themselves, questioning ᴿwhat the rising from the dead meant.   John 2:19–22

11 And they asked Him, saying, "Why do the scribes say that Elijah must come first?"

12 Then He answered and told them, "Indeed, Elijah is coming first and restores all things. And ᴿhow is it written concerning the Son of Man, that He must suffer many things and be treated with contempt?   Ps. 22:6; Is. 53:3

13 "But I say to you that ᴿElijah has also come, and they did to him whatever they wished, as it is written of him."   Luke 1:17

A Boy Is Healed

14 ᴿAnd when He came to the disciples, He saw a great multitude around them, and scribes disputing with them.   Matt. 17:14–19

15 Immediately, when they saw Him, all the people were greatly amazed, and running to Him, greeted Him.

16 And He asked the scribes, "What are you discussing with them?"

17 Then ᴿone of the crowd answered and said, "Teacher, I brought You my son, who has a mute spirit.   Luke 9:38

18 "And wherever it seizes him, it throws him down; he foams at the mouth, gnashes his teeth, and becomes rigid. So I spoke to Your disciples, that they should cast it out, but they could not."

19 He answered him and said, "O ᴿfaithlessᵀ generation, how long shall I be with you? How long shall I ᵀbear with you? Bring him to Me."   John 4:48 · unbelieving · put up with

20 Then they brought him to Him. And ᴿwhen he saw Him, immediately the spirit convulsed him, and he fell on the ground and wallowed, foaming at the mouth.   Mark 1:26

21 So He asked his father, "How long has this been happening to him?" And he said, "From childhood.

22 "And often he has thrown him both into the fire and into the water to destroy him. But if You can do anything, have compassion on us and help us."

23 Jesus said to him, *"If you can believe, all things are possible to him who believes."

24 Immediately the father of the child cried out and said with tears, "Lord, I believe; ᴿhelp my unbelief!"   Luke 17:5

25 When Jesus saw that the people came running together, He ᴿrebuked the unclean spirit, saying to it: "Deaf and dumb spirit, I command you, come out of him and enter him no more!"   Mark 1:25

26 Then the spirit cried out, convulsed him greatly, and came out of him. And he became as one dead, so that many said, "He is dead."

27 But Jesus took him by the hand and lifted him up, and he arose.

28 ᴿAnd when He had come into the house, His disciples asked Him privately, "Why could we not cast it out?"   Matt. 17:19

29 So He said to them, "This kind can come out by nothing but prayer *and fasting."

Jesus Again Predicts His Death and Resurrection

30 Then they departed from there and passed through Galilee, and He did not want anyone to know it.

31 For He taught His disciples and said to them, "The Son of Man is being betrayed into the hands of men, and they will kill Him. And after He is killed, He will rise the third day."

32 But they ᴿdid not understand this saying, and were afraid to ask Him.   Luke 2:50; 18:34

Who Is the Greatest?

33 ᴿThen He came to Capernaum. And when He was in the house He asked them, "What was it you ᵀdisputed among yourselves on the road?"   Matt. 18:1–5 · discussed

34 But they kept silent, for on the road they had ᴿdisputed among themselves who would be the ᴿgreatest.   [Prov. 13:10] · Luke 22:24; 23:46; 24:46

35 And He sat down, called the twelve, and said to them, "If anyone desires to be first, he shall be last of all and servant of all."

36 Then He took a little child and set him in the midst of them. And when He had taken him in His arms, He said to them,

37 "Whoever receives one of these little children in My name receives Me; and ᴿwhoever receives Me, receives not Me but Him who sent Me."   Matt. 10:40

Jesus Forbids Sectarianism

38 ᴿNow John answered Him, saying, "Teacher, we saw someone who does not

9:23 NU If you can! All things
9:29 NU omits and fasting

follow us casting out demons in Your name, and we forbade him because he does not follow us." Num. 11:27-29

39 But Jesus said, "Do not forbid him, ᴿfor no one who works a miracle in My name can soon afterward speak evil of Me. 1 Cor. 12:3

40 "For ᴿhe who is not *against us is on our side. [Matt. 12:30]

41 ᴿ"For whoever gives you a cup of water to drink in My name, because you belong to Christ, assuredly, I say to you, he will by no means lose his reward. Matt. 10:42

Jesus Warns of Offenses

42 ᴿ"But whoever causes one of these little ones who believe in Me ᵀto stumble, it would be better for him if a millstone were hung around his neck, and he were thrown into the sea. Luke 17:1, 2 · to fall into sin

43 ᴿ"If your hand causes you to sin, cut it off. It is better for you to enter into life ᵀmaimed, rather than having two hands, to go to ᵀhell, into the fire that shall never be quenched— Matt. 5:29, 30 · crippled · Gr. Gehenna

44 *"where

> ᴿ'Their worm does not die
> And the fire is not quenched.' Is. 66:24

45 "And if your foot causes you to sin, cut it off. It is better for you to enter life lame, rather than having two feet, to be cast into hell, *into the fire that shall never be quenched—

46 "where

> ᴿ'Their worm does not die
> And the fire is not quenched.' Is. 66:24

47 "And if your eye causes you to sin, pluck it out. It is better for you to enter the kingdom of God with one eye, rather than having two eyes, to be cast into ᵀhell fire— Gr. Gehenna

48 "where

> ᴿ'Their worm does not die Is. 66:24
> And the ᴿfire is not quenched.' Jer. 7:20

Tasteless Salt Is Worthless

49 "For everyone will be ᴿseasoned with fire, ᴿand* every sacrifice will be seasoned with salt. [Matt. 3:11] · Lev. 2:13

50 ᴿ"Salt is good, but if the salt loses its flavor, how will you season it? ᴿHave salt in yourselves, and ᴿhave peace with one another." Matt. 5:13 · Col. 4:6 · Rom. 12:18; 14:19

Marriage and Divorce

10 Then ᴿHe arose from there and came to the region of Judea by the other

side of the Jordan. And multitudes gathered to Him again, and as He was accustomed, He taught them again. Matt. 19:1-9

2 ᴿThe Pharisees came and asked Him, "Is it lawful for a man to divorce his wife?" testing Him. Matt. 19:3

3 And He answered and said to them, "What did Moses command you?"

4 They said, ᴿ"Moses permitted a man to write a certificate of divorce, and to dismiss her." Deut. 24:1-4

5 And Jesus answered and said to them, "Because of the hardness of your heart he wrote you this ᵀprecept. command

6 "But from the beginning of the creation, God * 'made them male and female.'

7 * 'For this reason a man shall leave his father and mother and be joined to his wife,

8 'and the two shall become one flesh'; so then they are no longer two, but one flesh.

9 "Therefore what God has joined together, let not man separate."

10 In the house His disciples also asked Him again about the same matter.

11 So He said to them, ᴿ"Whoever divorces his wife and marries another commits adultery against her. [Matt. 5:32; 19:9]

12 "And if a woman divorces her husband and marries another, she commits adultery."

Jesus Blesses Little Children

13 Then they brought little children to Him, that He might touch them; but the disciples rebuked those who brought them.

14 But when Jesus saw it, He was greatly displeased and said to them, "Let the little children come to Me, and do not forbid them; for ᴿof such is the kingdom of God. [1 Pet. 2:2]

15 "Assuredly, I say to you, whoever does not receive the kingdom of God as a little child will ᴿby no means enter it." Luke 13:28

16 And He took them up in His arms, laid His hands on them, and blessed them.

Jesus Counsels the Rich Young Ruler

17 Now as He was going out on the road, one came running, knelt before Him, and asked Him, "Good Teacher, what shall I ᴿdo that I may inherit eternal life?" John 6:28

18 So Jesus said to him, "Why do you call Me good? No one is good but One, that is, ᴿGod. 1 Sam. 2:2

19 "You know the commandments: ᴿ'Do not commit adultery,' 'Do not murder,' 'Do not steal,' 'Do not bear false witness,' 'Do not defraud,' 'Honor your father and your mother.'" Ex. 20:12-16; Deut. 5:16-20

20 And he answered and said to Him, "Teacher, all these things I have ᴿkept from my youth." Phil. 3:6

9:40 M you • M your
9:44 NU omits v. 44.
9:45 NU omits the rest of v. 45 and all of v. 46.
9:49 NU omits the rest of v. 49.

10:6 Gen. 1:27; 5:2
10:7 Gen. 2:24; [1 Cor. 6:16]; Eph. 5:31

21 Then Jesus, looking at him, loved him, and said to him, "One thing you lack: Go your way, ᴿsell whatever you have and give to the poor, and you will have treasure in heaven; and come, ᴿtake up the cross, and follow Me."   [Luke 12:33; 16:9] • [Mark 8:34]
22 But he was sad at this word, and went away sorrowful, for he had great possessions.

With God All Things Are Possible

23 Then Jesus looked around and said to His disciples, "How hard it is for those who have riches to enter the kingdom of God!"
24 And the disciples were astonished at His words. But Jesus answered again and said to them, "Children, how hard it is *for those ᴿwho trust in riches to enter the kingdom of God!   [1 Tim. 6:17]
25 "It is easier for a camel to go through the eye of a needle than for a ᴿrich man to enter the kingdom of God."   [Matt. 13:22; 19:24]
26 And they were greatly astonished, saying among themselves, "Who then can be saved?"
27 But Jesus looked at them and said, "With men *it is* impossible, but not with God; for with God all things are possible."
28 ᴿThen Peter began to say to Him, "See, we have left all and followed You."   Luke 18:28
29 So Jesus answered and said, "Assuredly, I say to you, there is no one who has left house or brothers or sisters or father or mother *or wife or children or ᵀlands, for My sake and the gospel's,   Lit. *fields*
30 ᴿ"who shall not receive a hundredfold now in this time—houses and brothers and sisters and mothers and children and lands, with ᴿpersecutions—and in the age to come, eternal life.   Luke 18:29, 30 • [1 Pet. 4:12, 13]
31 ᴿ"But many *who are* first will be last, and the last first."   Luke 13:30

Jesus a Third Time Predicts His Death and Resurrection

32 Now they were on the road, going up to Jerusalem, and Jesus was going before them; and they were amazed. And as they followed they were afraid. ᴿThen He took the twelve aside again and began to tell them the things that would happen to Him: Mark 8:31; 9:31

10:24 NU omits *for those who trust in riches*
10:29 NU omits *or wife*

33 "Behold, we are going up to Jerusalem, and the Son of Man will be ᴿbetrayed to the chief priests and to the scribes; and they will condemn Him to death and deliver Him to the Gentiles;   Mark 14:53, 64
34 "and ᴿthey will mock Him, and scourge Him, and spit on Him, and kill Him. And the third day He will rise again."   Luke 24:46

Greatness Is Serving

35 ᴿThen James and John, the sons of Zebedee, came to Him, saying, "Teacher, we want You to do for us whatever we ask."   [James 4:3]
36 And He said to them, "What do you want Me to do for you?"
37 They said to Him, "Grant us that we may sit, one on Your right hand and the other on Your left, in Your glory."
38 But Jesus said to them, "You do not know what you ask. Are you able to drink the cup that I drink, and be baptized with the ᴿbaptism that I am baptized with?"   Luke 12:50
39 They said to Him, "We are able." So Jesus said to them, ᴿ"You will indeed drink the cup that I drink, and with the baptism I am baptized with you will be baptized; Acts 12:2
40 "but to sit on My right hand and on My left is not Mine to give, but *it is for* those ᴿfor whom it is prepared."   [Heb. 11:16]
41 And when the ten heard *it*, they began to be greatly displeased with James and John.
42 But Jesus called them to *Himself* and said to them, ᴿ"You know that those who are considered rulers over the Gentiles lord it over them, and their great ones exercise authority over them.   Luke 22:25
43 ᴿ"Yet it shall not be so among you; but whoever desires to become among you shall be your servant.   Mark 9:35
44 "And whoever of you desires to be first shall be slave of all.

19-D. God's Remedy for Man's Ruin   ▼

45 "For even ᴿthe Son of Man did not come to be served, but to serve, and ᴿto give His life a ransom for many."   [Phil. 2:7, 8] • Is. 53:12 ▲

Jesus Heals Blind Bartimaeus

46 ᴿNow they came to Jericho. As He went out of Jericho with His disciples and a great multitude, blind Bartimaeus, the son of Timaeus, sat by the road begging.   Luke 18:35-43

19-D. God's Remedy for Man's Ruin (Mark 10:45)—God's unique remedy for man's ruin is "His only begotten Son" (John 3:16, page 1052), who came into this sin-cursed world through the womb of the Virgin Mary (Luke 1:26–38, page 1010), and lived a holy, sinless life because He was conceived by the Holy Spirit and not by a father bearing the sin of Adam. He had no human father (Matt. 1:18–25, page 930). In sinless human flesh He "was in all points tempted as we are, yet without sin" (Heb. 4:15, page 1239). Jesus was pure in thought, word, and deed; He never

(1) Entertained an evil thought: "Who knew no sin" (2 Cor. 5:21, page 1169);
(2) Spoke an evil word: "Who committed no sin, nor was deceit found in His mouth" (1 Pet. 2:22, page 1266);

(Point 19-D continued on next page)

47 And when he heard that it was Jesus of Nazareth, he began to cry out and say, "Jesus, Son of David, have mercy on me!"

48 Then many warned him to be quiet; but he cried out all the more, "Son of David, have mercy on me!"

49 So Jesus stood still and commanded him to be called. Then they called the blind man, saying to him, "Be of good cheer. Rise, He is calling you."

50 And throwing aside his garment, he rose and came to Jesus.

51 So Jesus answered and said to him, "What do you want Me to do for you?" The blind man said to Him, ᵀ"Rabboni, that I may receive my sight."   Lit. *My Great One*

52 Then Jesus said to him, "Go your way; ᴿyour faith has ᵀmade you well." And immediately he received his sight and followed Jesus on the road.   Matt. 9:22 · Lit. *saved you*

The Triumphal Entry

11 Now when they drew near Jerusalem, to *Bethphage and Bethany, at the Mount of Olives, He sent two of His disciples;

11:1 M *Bethsphage*

2 and He said to them, "Go into the village opposite you; and as soon as you have entered it you will find a colt tied, on which no one has sat. Loose it and bring *it*.

3 "And if anyone says to you, 'Why are you doing this?' say, 'The Lord has need of it,' and immediately he will send it here."

4 So they went their way, and found *the colt tied by the door outside on the street, and they loosed it.

5 But some of those who stood there said to them, "What are you doing, loosing the colt?"

6 And they spoke to them just as Jesus had commanded. So they let them go.

37-B. The Earthly Ministry of Jesus   ▼

7 Then they brought the colt to Jesus and threw their clothes on it, and He sat on it.

8 And many spread their clothes on the road, and others cut down leafy branches from the trees and spread *them* on the road.

9 Then those who went before and those who followed ᴿcried out, saying: Zech. 9:9

11:4 NU, M *a*

(Point 19-D continued from previous page)

(3) Committed an evil deed: "In Him there is no sin" (1 John 3:5, page 1280). He could stand before His enemies and challenge them to convict Him of sin (John 8:46, page 1063).

God the Father sent His Son into the world to do two things: "to serve, and to give His life a ransom for many" (Mark 10:45, page 997). From His baptism in Jordan to His death on Calvary, the Lord Jesus Christ

(1) Served the people. At Cana He turned water into wine (John 2:1-11, page 1050). Beside the Sea of Galilee He multiplied five loaves and two fishes into enough to feed five thousand (John 6:1-14, page 1058). The people reasoned that if He were king they would always have food to eat. However, Jesus came to serve, not to be served, and so He refused their kingdom (John 6:15, page 1059);

(2) Gave "His life a ransom for many" (v. 45). He came to pay the debt of sin with His life: "For the wages of sin is death, but the gift of God is eternal life in Christ Jesus our Lord" (Rom. 6:23, page 1134). God's remedy for man's ruin was completed when Jesus suffered the supreme penalty on Calvary. He paid the believer's debt of sin in full (John 1:12, 29, page 1049; cf. 1 John 2:2, page 1278).

In Adam all died, spiritually and physically, but in Christ all believers are made alive (Eph. 2:5, page 1187; cf. 1 Cor. 15:20-23, page 1161). In Adam all were created and then ruined through the Fall, but in Christ all (believers) are new creations (2 Cor. 5:17, page 1169). In Adam all are separated from God by sin (Is. 59:1, 2, page 698), but in Christ all believers are redeemed from the ruin (Gal. 3:13, page 1181).

See 1 Peter 1:18, 19, page 1263, for **Point 19-E: The Results of God's Remedy for Man's Ruin.**

37-B. The Earthly Ministry of Jesus (Mark 11:7-11)—When Jesus rode triumphantly into Jerusalem (vv. 7-11), He was aware that He was making a messianic entry, fulfilling the prophecy of Zechariah 9:9 (page 916) that the Messiah would someday come into Jerusalem on a donkey. He had sent for the donkey and approved of the messianic shouts of *Hosanna* ("Save now"—Ps. 118:25, 26, page 580). He had come to live and die as the Christ, to purchase human redemption (Mark 10:45, page 997). Claims that "He was just another Rabbi," or that "He never claimed to be the Messiah," appear wholly fallacious in light of His claims in the Gospels (e.g., John 8:56-59, page 1064; 11:23-26, page 1069).

Christ's ministry may be divided into the following eight chronological periods:

(1) *The birth and childhood years.* We have the scriptural account of Jesus' virgin birth (Luke 1:26-38, page 1010; 2:7, page 1012), the visit of the wise men, the flight into Egypt (Matt. 2:1-23, page 931), and His return to dwell in Nazareth. At the age of twelve He astounded the doctors of the Law in the temple (Luke 2:41-47, page 1013). The other years are not recounted until the beginning of His ministry at the age of thirty (John 2:11, page 1051).

(2) *The ministry of John the Baptist.* John was the forerunner of Christ, fulfilling Isaiah 40:2-5 (page 679). He preached repentance and baptized with water, outwardly signifying the inward cleansing. A fearless preacher, he was imprisoned and later beheaded by Herod (Matt. 14:1-12, page 959).

(Point 37-B continued on next page)

▽ "Hosanna!
R *Blessed is He who comes in the name
   of the LORD!'*   Ps. 118:26
10 Blessed is the kingdom of our father
   David
   That comes *in the name of the Lord!
   R Hosanna in the highest!"   Ps. 148:1

11 And Jesus went into Jerusalem and into
the temple. So when He had looked around at
all things, as the hour was already late, He
▲ went out to Bethany with the twelve.

The Fig Tree Withered

12 Now the next day, when they had come
out from Bethany, He was hungry.
13 R And seeing from afar a fig tree having
leaves, He went to see if perhaps He would
find something on it. When He came to it, He
found nothing but leaves, for it was not the
season for figs.   Matt. 21:19
14 In response Jesus said to it, "Let no one
eat fruit from you ever again." And His
disciples heard it.

Jesus Cleanses the Temple

15 So they came to Jerusalem. Then Jesus
went into the temple and began to drive out
those who bought and sold in the temple, and
overturned the tables of the moneychangers
and the seats of those who sold doves.
16 And He would not allow anyone to carry
wares through the temple.
17 Then He taught, saying to them, "Is it
not written, *'My R house shall be called a
house of prayer for all nations'*? R But you
have made it a *'den of thieves.'"* Is. 56:7 • Jer. 7:11

11:10 NU omits *in the name of the Lord*

18 And the scribes and chief priests heard it
and sought how they might destroy Him; for
they feared Him, because R all the people were
astonished at His teaching.   Matt. 7:28
19 When evening had come, He went out of
the city.

The Lesson of the Withered Fig Tree

20 Now in the morning, as they passed by,
they saw the fig tree dried up from the roots.
21 And Peter, remembering, said to Him,
"Rabbi, look! The fig tree which You cursed
has withered away."
22 So Jesus answered and said to them,
"Have faith in God.
23 "For assuredly, I say to you, whoever
says to this mountain, 'Be removed and be
cast into the sea,' and does not doubt in his
heart, but believes that those things he says
will be done, he will have whatever he says.
24 "Therefore I say to you, whatever things
you ask when you pray, believe that you
receive *them*, and you will have *them*.

Forgiveness and Prayer

25 "And whenever you stand praying, R if
you have anything against anyone, forgive
him, that your Father in heaven may also
forgive you your trespasses.   [Col. 3:13]
26 *"But R if you do not forgive, neither will
your Father in heaven forgive your trespasses."   Matt. 6:15; 18:35

Jesus' Authority Questioned

27 Then they came again to Jerusalem.
R And as He was walking in the temple, the
chief priests, the scribes, and the elders came
to Him.   Luke 20:1-8

11:26 NU omits v. 26.

(Point 37-B continued from previous page)
(3) *The year of introductions.* Jesus' baptism, temptation, and initial teaching ministries in Judea,
Jerusalem, Samaria, and Galilee took place during that time.
(4) *The year of popularity.* This was the year of His great Galilean ministry, when He chose the twelve
disciples, delivered the Sermon on the Mount, and worked many miracles around Capernaum. Huge crowds
eagerly followed Jesus in those days.
(5) *The year of antagonism.* After the feeding of the five thousand in Galilee, when He refused to
become a political King in opposition to Rome, the huge crowds for the most part deserted Him (John 6:66,
page 1060). He then began to minister in the Caesarea Philippi region to build the faith of His disciples
(Matt. 16:13-16, page 961). By this time the leaders at Jerusalem were set against Him, so He avoided
overexposure in Jerusalem (John 7:1, page 1060). He still taught, healed, and did many other good works.
(6) *The final months.* Toward the end of His earthly career, He ministered east of the Jordan River and
periodically visited Judea. During this time He raised Lazarus (the brother of Mary and Martha of Bethany)
from the dead, thus showing His glory (John 11:1-44, page 1069).
(7) *The last week.* This week was filled with drama for heaven and earth: His triumphal entry into
Jerusalem; His rebuking of the Pharisees and scribes (Matt. 23:1-36, page 971); His Olivet Discourse on
future events (Matt. 24:3-51, page 972); the Last Supper; His betrayal, arrest, and trials before the high priest,
the Sanhedrin, Pilate, Herod, and the mob; and His crucifixion for the sins of mankind on the hill of Calvary
(Matt. 26:47-68, page 978; 27:33-54, page 980).
(8) *The risen ministry.* After three days He arose from the dead and appeared frequently both in
Jerusalem and at the Sea of Galilee, to the twelve disciples and to others, "to whom He also presented
Himself alive after His suffering by many infallible proofs, being seen by them during forty days and
speaking of the things pertaining to the kingdom of God" (Acts 1:3, page 1086).

See Acts 8:1-8, page 1098, for **Point 37-C: The Church: Its Beginning and Development.**

28 And they said to Him, "By what authority are You doing these things? And who gave You this authority to do these things?"

29 But Jesus answered and said to them, "I also will ask you one question; then answer Me, and I will tell you by what authority I do these things:

30 "The baptism of John—was it from heaven or from men? Answer Me."

31 And they reasoned among themselves, saying, "If we say, 'From heaven,' He will say, 'Why then did you not believe him?'

32 "But if we say, 'From men' "—they feared the people, for [R]all counted John to have been a prophet indeed.   Matt. 3:5; 14:5

33 So they answered and said to Jesus, "We do not know." And Jesus answered and said to them, "Neither will I tell you by what authority I do these things."

The Parable of the Wicked Vinedressers

12 Then He began to speak to them in parables: "A man planted a vineyard and set a hedge around it, dug a place for the wine vat and built a tower. And he leased it to vinedressers and went into a far country.

2 "Now at vintage-time he sent a servant to the vinedressers, that he might receive some of the fruit of the vineyard from the vinedressers.

3 "And they took him and beat him and sent him away empty-handed.

4 "Again he sent them another servant, *and at him they threw stones, wounded him in the head, and sent him away shamefully treated.

5 "And again he sent another, and him they killed; and many others, [R]beating some and killing some.   2 Chr. 36:16

6 "Therefore still having one son, his beloved, he also sent him to them last, saying, 'They will respect my son.'

7 "But those vinedressers said among themselves, 'This is the heir. Come, let us kill him, and the inheritance will be ours.'

8 "So they took him and [R]killed him and cast him out of the vineyard.   [Acts 2:23]

9 "Therefore what will the owner of the vineyard do? He will come and destroy the vinedressers, and give the vineyard to others.

10 "Have you not even read this Scripture:

**The stone which the builders rejected
Has become the chief cornerstone.**

11 *This was the LORD's doing,
And it is marvelous in our eyes'?"*

12 [R]And they sought to lay hands on Him, but feared the multitude, for they knew He had spoken the parable against them. So they left Him and went away.   John 7:25, 30, 44

The Pharisees: Is It Lawful to Pay Taxes to Caesar?

13 [R]Then they sent to Him some of the Pharisees and the Herodians, to catch Him in His words.   Luke 20:20–26

14 When they had come, they said to Him, "Teacher, we know that You are true, and [T]care about no one; for You do not [T]regard the person of men, but teach the way of God in truth. Is it lawful to pay taxes to Caesar, or not?   Court no man's favor • Lit. look at the face of men

15 "Shall we pay, or shall we not pay?" But He, knowing their [R]hypocrisy, said to them, "Why do you test Me? Bring Me a [T]denarius that I may see it."   Luke 12:1 • 1 day's wage, $32

16 So they brought it. And He said to them, "Whose image and inscription is this?" They said to Him, "Caesar's."

17 And Jesus answered and said to them, [T]"Render to Caesar the things that are Caesar's, and to [R]God the things that are God's." And they marveled at Him.   Pay • [Eccl. 5:4, 5]

The Sadducees: What About the Resurrection?

18 [R]Then some Sadducees, [R]who say there is no resurrection, came to Him; and they asked Him, saying: Luke 20:27–38 • Acts 23:8

19 "Teacher, [R]Moses wrote to us that if a man's brother dies, and leaves his wife behind, and leaves no children, his brother should take his wife and raise up offspring for his brother.   Deut. 25:5

20 "Now there were seven brothers. The first took a wife; and dying, he left no offspring.

21 "And the second took her, and he died; nor did he leave any offspring. And the third likewise.

22 "So the seven had her and left no offspring. Last of all the woman died also.

23 "Therefore, in the resurrection, when they rise, whose wife will she be? For all seven had her as wife."

24 Jesus answered and said to them, "Are you not therefore [T]mistaken, because you do not know the Scriptures nor the power of God?   Or deceived

25 "For when they rise from the dead, they neither marry nor are given in marriage, but [R]are like angels in heaven.   [1 Cor. 15:42, 49, 52]

26 "But concerning the dead, that they rise, have you not read in the book of Moses, in the burning bush passage, how God spoke to him, saying, *'I am the God of Abraham, the God of Isaac, and the God of Jacob'?*

27 "He is not the God of the dead, but the God of the living. You are therefore greatly [T]mistaken."   Or deceived

12:4 NU omits and at him they threw stones
12:10 Ps. 118:22, 23

12:26 Ex. 3:6, 15

The Scribes: Which Is the First Commandment of All?

28 ᴿThen one of the scribes came, and having heard them reasoning together, *perceiving that He had answered them well, asked Him, "Which is the ᵀfirst commandment of all?"　　　　Matt. 22:34-40 · foremost

29 Jesus answered him, "The ᵀfirst of all the commandments is: ᴿ'Hear, O Israel, the Lᴏʀᴅ our God, the Lᴏʀᴅ is one.　　foremost · Deut. 6:4, 5

30 'And you shall ᴿlove the Lᴏʀᴅ your God with all your heart, with all your soul, with all your mind, and with all your strength.' *This is the first commandment.　　[Deut. 10:12; 30:6]

31 "And the second, like it, is this: ᴿ'You shall love your neighbor as yourself.' There is no other commandment greater than ᴿthese."　　　　Lev. 19:18 · [Rom. 13:9]

32 So the scribe said to Him, "Well said, Teacher. You have spoken the truth, for there is one God, ᴿand there is no other but He.　　　　Deut. 4:39

33 "And to love Him with all the heart, with all the understanding, *with all the soul, and with all the strength, and to love one's neighbor as oneself, ᴿis more than all the whole burnt offerings and sacrifices."　　[Hos. 6:6]

34 Now when Jesus saw that he answered wisely, He said to him, "You are not far from the kingdom of God." ᴿBut after that no one dared question Him.　　　　Matt. 22:46

Jesus: How Can David Call His Descendant Lord?

35 ᴿThen Jesus answered and said, while He taught in the temple, "How is it that the scribes say that the Christ is the Son of David?　　　　Luke 20:41-44

36 "For David himself said ᴿby the Holy Spirit:　　　　2 Sam. 23:2

ᴿ'The Lᴏʀᴅ said to my Lord,
"Sit at My right hand,
Till I make Your enemies Your
footstool."'　　　　Ps. 110:1

37 "Therefore David himself calls Him 'Lord'; how is He then his ᴿSon?" And the common people heard Him gladly. [Acts 2:29-31]

Beware of the Scribes

38 Then ᴿHe said to them in His teaching, ᴿ"Beware of the scribes, who desire to go around in long robes, ᴿlove greetings in the marketplaces,　　Mark 4:2 · Matt. 23:1-7 · Matt. 23:7

39 "the ᴿbest seats in the synagogues, and the best places at feasts,　　　　Luke 14:7

40 ᴿ"who devour widows' houses, and for a pretense make long prayers. These will receive greater condemnation."　　Matt. 23:14

The Widow's Two Mites

41 ᴿNow Jesus sat opposite the treasury and saw how the people put money ᴿinto the treasury. And many who were rich put in much.　　　　Luke 21:1-4 · 2 Kin. 12:9

42 Then one poor widow came and threw in two *mites, which make a ᵀquadrans.　　$1

43 So He called His disciples to Himself, and said to them, "Assuredly, I say to you that this poor widow has put in more than all those who have given to the treasury;

44 "for they all put in out of their abundance, but she out of her poverty put in all that she had, ᴿher whole livelihood." Deut. 24:6

Jesus Predicts the Destruction of the Temple

13 Then ᴿas He went out of the temple, one of His disciples said to Him, "Teacher, see what manner of stones and what buildings are here!"　　Luke 21:5-36

2 And Jesus answered and said to him, "Do you see these great buildings? ᴿNot one stone shall be left upon another, that shall not be thrown down."　　　　Luke 19:44

The Signs of the Times and the End of the Age

3 Now as He sat on the Mount of Olives opposite the temple, Peter, James, John, and ᴿAndrew asked Him privately,　John 1:40

4 ᴿ"Tell us, when will these things be? And what will be the sign when all these things will be fulfilled?"　　　　Matt. 24:3

5 And Jesus, answering them, began to say: "Take heed that no one deceives you.

6 "For many will come in My name, saying, 'I am He,' and will deceive many.

7 "But when you hear of wars and rumors of wars, do not be troubled; for such things must happen, but the end is not yet.

8 "For nation will rise against nation, and kingdom against kingdom. And there will be earthquakes in various places, and there will be famines *and troubles. ᴿThese are the beginnings of ᵀsorrows.　Matt. 24:8 · Lit. birth pangs

9 "But ᴿwatch out for yourselves, for they will deliver you up to councils, and you will be beaten in the synagogues. You will *be brought before rulers and kings for My sake, for a testimony to them.　　Matt. 10:17, 18

10 "And ᴿthe gospel must first be preached to all the nations.　　　　Matt. 24:14

11 "But when they arrest you and deliver you up, do not worry beforehand, *or premeditate what you will speak. But whatever is given you in that hour, speak that; for it is not you who speak, but the Holy Spirit.

12:42 Gr. lepta, very small copper coins
13:8 NU omits and troubles
13:9 NU, M stand
13:11 NU omits or premeditate

12:28 NU seeing
12:30 NU omits the rest of v. 30.
12:33 NU omits with all the soul

12 "Now ᴿbrother will betray brother to death, and a father *his* child; and children will rise up against parents and cause them to be put to death.   Mic. 7:6

13 ᴿ"And you will be hated by all for My name's sake. But he who ᵀendures to the end shall be saved.   Luke 21:17 • *bears patiently*

The Great Tribulation

14 "So when you see the * '*abomination of desolation,*' *spoken of by Daniel the prophet, standing where it ought not" (let the reader understand), "then ᴿlet those who are in Judea flee to the mountains.   Luke 21:21

15 "Let him who is on the housetop not go down into the house, nor enter to take anything out of his house.

16 "And let him who is in the field not go back to get his clothes.

17 "But woe to those who are pregnant and to those nursing babies in those days!

18 "And pray that your flight may not be in winter.

19 ᴿ"For *in* those days there will be tribulation, such as has not been since the beginning of the creation which God created until this time, nor ever shall be.   Dan. 9:26; 12:1

20 "And unless the Lord had shortened those days, no flesh would be saved; but for

13:14 Dan. 9:27; 11:31; 12:11 • NU omits *spoken of by Daniel the prophet*

the elect's sake, whom He chose, He shortened the days.

21 ᴿ"Then if anyone says to you, 'Look, here *is* the Christ!' or, 'Look, *He is* there!' do not believe it.   Luke 17:23; 21:8

22 "For false christs and false prophets will rise and show signs and wonders to deceive, if possible, even the ᵀelect.   *chosen ones*

23 "But ᴿtake heed; see, I have told you all things beforehand.   [2 Pet. 3:17]

The Coming of the Son of Man

24 ᴿ"But in those days, after that tribulation, the sun will be darkened, and the moon will not give its light;   Zeph. 1:15

25 "the stars of heaven will fall, and the powers in the heavens will be shaken.

11-E. Angels: Their Part in the Second   ▼
Coming of Christ

26 ᴿ"Then they will see the Son of Man coming in the clouds with great power and glory.   [Dan. 7:13, 14; Matt. 16:27]

27 "And then He will send His angels, and gather together His ᵀelect from the four winds, from the farthest part of earth to the farthest part of heaven.   *chosen ones* ▲

The Parable of the Fig Tree

28 ᴿ"Now learn this parable from the fig tree: When its branch has already become

11-E. Angels: Their Part in the Second Coming of Christ (Mark 13:26, 27)—Angels had a very important part in the life and ministry of the Lord Jesus Christ. They were created by Him and for Him (Col. 1:16, page 1202). They were created to worship Him (Heb. 1:6, page 1236), to minister to Him (Matt. 4:11, page 935), and to fight for Him (Rev. 12:7, page 1305). The angel Gabriel was sent to

(1) Zacharias the priest, to announce the birth of John the Baptist, who was to prepare the way for the Lord Jesus (John 3:28, page 1053; cf. Mal. 4:5, page 926; Matt. 17:11, 12, page 963);

(2) the Virgin Mary, to announce the birth of Jesus and John the Baptist (Luke 1:13, 26–38, page 1009).

An angel of the Lord rolled the stone from the tomb of Jesus and announced His resurrection (Matt. 28:1–8, page 981). When Jesus ascended to heaven after His resurrection and the apostles looked steadfastly toward heaven as He went up, "two men stood by them in white apparel" and announced that He would come again "in like manner as you saw Him go into heaven" (Acts 1:9–11, page 1087). The Scriptures do not tell us who the "two men" are. It is believed by some that they were angels.

It should not surprise us that angels will also have a great part in Christ's second coming, which will be in two stages.

(1) Jesus will come and rapture (take up) His bride, the church, out of the world to meet Him in the air, and His angels will assist Him. At the Rapture, Christ shall cry aloud and wake the dead (John 5:28, 29, page 1057); then the archangel (probably Michael) will shout and he, or some other angel, will blow God's trumpet (1 Thess. 4:13–18, page 1211). The resurrected saints and the living saints will be caught up together to meet the Lord Jesus in the air.

(2) Jesus will come back to this earth with His bride seven years later to put the world in order. "Then they [the people on earth] will see the Son of Man coming in the clouds with great power and glory. And then He will send His angels, and gather together His elect from the four winds, from the farthest part of earth to the farthest part of heaven" (vv. 26, 27).

Jesus' angels will assist at the rapture of His church before the seven-year Tribulation. His angels will then gather the elect from around the world and bring them to the judgment of the nations, after the Tribulation (Matt. 25:31–46, page 976). Jesus will come with an army of angels, all riding on white horses, to establish His kingdom and reign for a thousand years as "KING OF KINGS AND LORD OF LORDS" (Rev. 19:11–16, page 1312).

See Index, page 17, for your next study.

tender, and puts forth leaves, you know that summer is near.   Luke 21:29

29 "So you also, when you see these things happening, know that [T]it is near—at the doors!   Or *He*

30 "Assuredly, I say to you, this generation will by no means pass away till all these things take place.

31 "Heaven and earth will pass away, but My words will by no means pass away.

No One Knows the Day or Hour

32 "But of that day and hour [R]no one knows, not even the angels in heaven, nor the Son, but only the [R]Father.   Matt. 25:13 · Acts 1:7

33 [R]"Take heed, watch and pray; for you do not know when the time is.   1 Thess. 5:6

34 "*It is* like a man going to a far country, who left his house and gave authority to his servants, and to each his work, and commanded the doorkeeper to watch.

35 [R]"Watch therefore, for you do not know when the master of the house is coming—in the evening, at midnight, at the crowing of the rooster, or in the morning—   Matt. 24:42, 44

36 "lest, coming suddenly, he find you sleeping.

37 "And what I say to you, I say to all: Watch!"

The Plot to Kill Jesus

14 After [R]two days it was the Passover and [R]*the Feast* of Unleavened Bread. And the chief priests and the scribes sought how they might take Him by [T]trickery and put *Him* to death.   Luke 22:1, 2 · Ex. 12:1-27 · *deception*

2 But they said, "Not during the feast, lest there be an uproar of the people."

The Anointing at Bethany

3 [R]And being in Bethany at the house of Simon the leper, as He sat at the table, a woman came having an alabaster flask of very costly oil of spikenard. Then she broke the flask and poured *it* on His head.   Luke 7:37

4 But there were some who were indignant among themselves, and said, "Why was this fragrant oil wasted?

5 "For it might have been sold for more than three hundred denarii and given to the poor." And they criticized her sharply.

6 But Jesus said, "Let her alone. Why do you trouble her? She has done a good work for Me.

7 "For you have the poor with you always, and whenever you wish you may do them good; but Me you do not have always.

8 "She has done what she could. She has come beforehand to anoint My body for [R]burial.   John 19:40-42

9 "Assuredly, I say to you, wherever this gospel is [R]preached in the whole world, what this woman has done will also be told as a memorial to her."   Luke 24:47

Judas Agrees to Betray Jesus

10 [R]Then Judas Iscariot, one of the twelve, went to the chief priests to betray Him to them.   Matt. 10:2-4

11 And when they heard *it*, they were glad, and promised to give him money. So he sought how he might conveniently betray Him.

Jesus Celebrates the Passover with His Disciples

39-D. The Lord's Supper   ▼

12 [R]Now on the first day of Unleavened Bread, when they [T]killed the Passover *lamb*, His disciples said to Him, "Where do You want us to go and prepare, that You may eat the Passover?"   Matt. 26:17-19 · *sacrificed*

39-D. The Lord's Supper (Mark 14:12-26)—The Lord's Supper was Christ's adaptation of the Jewish Passover feast for His church (vv. 12-14). The Passover was primarily for Israel; it looked back to the deliverance from Egypt and forward to the dying of the Messiah—the Lamb of God, sacrificed for the sins of all (Jew and Gentile) who would believe.

(1) Partaking of the Lord's Supper allows us to look back to Christ's death to save sinners, and forward to His second coming (1 Cor. 11:26, page 1156).

(2) The broken bread represents Christ's body, broken on the cross for our sins (v. 22).

(3) The cup represents Christ's "blood of the new covenant, which is shed for many" (v. 24). Jeremiah 31:31-34 (page 745) describes this new covenant, in beautiful words, as someday being made with Israel and Judah; this will occur in the future (Rom. 11:26, 27, page 1141). Christ here extends it in the present to "many"—to all nations.

(4) When we partake of the Lord's Supper, we must examine ourselves. This does not mean that we are to try to remember all of our sins that we have committed since the last Lord's Supper, nor that we are to abstain from the Lord's Supper until we feel worthy. It means just the opposite. The Lord's Supper is a memorial to Him. He said, "Do this in remembrance of Me" (1 Cor. 11:24, page 1156)—not in remembrance of your sins. We do not come to the Lord's Table to dwell on our sins, we are to practice 1 John 1:9 (page 1278) before we come to the Lord's Table: "If we [Christians] confess our sins, He is faithful and just to forgive us our sins and to cleanse us from all unrighteousness." When we come to partake of the Lord's Supper, we are to focus our thoughts on Christ's broken body when He bore our sins and shed His blood that cleanses us from all sin. This memorial is to be repeated "till He comes" (1 Cor. 11:26, page 1156).

(Point 39-D continued on next page)

▽ 13 And He sent out two of His disciples and said to them, "Go into the city, and a man will meet you carrying a pitcher of water; follow him.

14 "Wherever he goes in, say to the master of the house, 'The Teacher says, "Where is the guest room in which I may eat the Passover with My disciples?"'

15 "Then he will show you a large upper room, furnished *and* prepared; there make ready for us."

16 So His disciples went out, and came into the city, and found it just as He had said to them; and they prepared the Passover.

17 ᴿIn the evening He came with the twelve.   Matt. 26:20-24

18 Now as they sat and ate, Jesus said, "Assuredly, I say to you, ᴿone of you who eats with Me will betray Me."   Ps. 41:9

19 And they began to be sorrowful, and to say to Him one by one, "*Is* it I?" *And another *said*, "*Is* it I?"

20 He answered and said to them, "*It is* one of the twelve, who dips with Me in the dish.

21 ᴿ"The Son of Man indeed goes just as it is written of Him, but woe to that man by whom the Son of Man is betrayed! It would have been good for that man if he had never been born."   Luke 22:22

Jesus Institutes the Lord's Supper

22 And as they were eating, Jesus took bread, blessed and broke *it*, and gave *it* to them and said, "Take, *eat; this is My body."

23 Then He took the cup, and when He had given thanks He gave *it* to them, and they all drank from it.

24 And He said to them, "This is My blood of the *new covenant, which is shed for many.

14:19 NU omits the rest of v. 19.
14:22 NU omits *eat*
14:24 NU omits *new*

25 "Assuredly, I say to you, I will no longer ▽ drink of the fruit of the vine until that day when I drink it new in the kingdom of God."

26 And when they had sung ᵀa hymn, they went out to the Mount of Olives.   Or *hymns* ▲

Jesus Predicts Peter's Denial

27 ᴿThen Jesus said to them, "All of you will be made to stumble *because of Me this night, for it is written: Matt. 26:31-35

ᴿ'*I will strike the Shepherd,*   Zech. 13:7
And the sheep will be scattered.'

28 "But ᴿafter I have been raised, I will go before you to Galilee."   Mark 16:7

29 Peter said to Him, "Even if all are made to stumble, yet I *will* not *be*."

30 Jesus said to him, "Assuredly, I say to you ᴿthat today, *even* this night, before the rooster crows twice, you will deny Me three times."   Mark 14:72; Luke 22:61

31 But he spoke more vehemently, "If I have to die with You, I will not deny You!" And they all said likewise.

The Prayer in the Garden

32 ᴿThen they came to a place which was named Gethsemane; and He said to His disciples, "Sit here while I pray."   Luke 22:40-46

33 And He ᴿtook Peter, James, and John with Him, and He began to be troubled and deeply distressed.   Mark 5:37; 9:2; 13:3

34 Then He said to them, ᴿ"My soul is exceedingly sorrowful, *even* to death. Stay here and watch."   John 12:27

35 He went a little farther, and fell on the ground, and prayed that if it were possible, the hour might pass from Him.

36 And He said, ᴿ"Abba, Father, ᴿall things *are* possible for You. Take this cup away from Me; ᴿnevertheless, not what I will, but what You *will*."   Gal. 4:6 • [Heb. 5:7] • Is. 50:5

14:27 NU omits *because of Me this night*

(Point 39-D continued from previous page)
"But let a man examine himself" (1 Cor. 11:28, page 1156). The partaker of the Lord's Supper must examine his own heart and be assured that he truly is "in Christ," that he truly repents of his sins, and that the blood of Christ has covered his guilt. The Lord's Supper should never be taken casually, in haste, or merely as a formal religious ceremony (1 Cor. 11:27-31, page 1156).

(5) The Lord's Supper is His, not ours. Jesus said, "This is My body . . . My blood" (vv. 22-24). The invitation comes directly from Jesus to the obedient believer.

(6) The Lord's Supper signifies the fulfillment of the Old Testament Passover (Mark 14:15, 16, page 1004). The Lord instructed Israel that each family was to take a lamb, as specified by the Lord, kill it in the evening, and roast it over the fire. Using hyssop, they were to apply the blood to the two sideposts and the crossbar (lintel) of the door to each house. This prefigured the time when God's Lamb would bleed and die on the cross for our sins.

Partaking of the Lord's Supper should promote a spirit of repentance and worship. The Lord's Supper is a time of the richest spiritual blessing, where we experience true communion in the fellowship of His love with other believers, for "in Your presence is fullness of joy; at Your right hand are pleasures forevermore" (Ps. 16:11, page 518).

See Index, page 17, for your next study.

37 Then He came and found them sleeping, and said to Peter, "Simon, are you sleeping? Could you not watch one hour?

38 ᴿ"Watch and pray, lest you enter into temptation. ᴿThe spirit indeed *is* willing, but the flesh *is* weak."   Luke 21:36 • [Rom. 7:18, 21-24]

39 Again He went away and prayed, and spoke the same words.

40 And when He returned, He found them asleep again, for their eyes were heavy; and they did not know what to answer Him.

41 Then He came the third time and said to them, "Are you still sleeping and resting? It is enough! ᴿThe hour has come; behold, the Son of Man is being betrayed into the hands of sinners.   John 13:1; 17:1

42 ᴿ"Rise, let us be going. See, My ᴿbetrayer is at hand."   John 13:21; 18:1, 2 • Matt. 20:18; 26:21

Betrayal and Arrest in Gethsemane

43 ᴿAnd immediately, while He was still speaking, Judas, one of the twelve, with a great multitude with swords and clubs, came from the chief priests and the scribes and the elders.   Luke 22:47-53

44 Now His betrayer had given them a signal, saying, "Whomever I kiss, He is the One; seize Him and lead *Him* away safely."

45 As soon as He had come, immediately he went up to Him and said to Him, "Rabbi, Rabbi!" and kissed Him.

46 Then they laid their hands on Him and took Him.

47 And one of those who stood by drew his sword and struck the servant of the high priest, and cut off his ear.

48 ᴿThen Jesus answered and said to them, "Have you come out, as against a robber, with swords and clubs to take Me?   Matt. 26:55

49 "I was daily with you in the temple ᴿteaching, and you did not seize Me. But ᴿthe Scriptures must be fulfilled."   Matt. 21:23 • Is. 53:7

50 Then they all forsook Him and fled.

A Young Man Flees Naked

51 Now a certain young man followed Him, having a linen cloth thrown around *his* naked *body*. And the young men laid hold of him,

52 and he left the linen cloth and fled from them naked.

Jesus Faces the Sanhedrin

53 And they led Jesus away to the high priest; and with him were assembled all the chief priests, the elders, and the scribes.

54 But ᴿPeter followed Him at a distance, right into the courtyard of the high priest. And he sat with the servants and warmed himself at the fire.   John 18:15

55 ᴿNow the chief priests and all the council sought testimony against Jesus to put Him to death, but found none.   Matt. 26:59

56 For many bore false witness against Him, but their testimonies did not agree.

57 Then ᴿsome rose up and bore false witness against Him, saying,   Ps. 27:12; 35:11

58 "We heard Him say, ᴿ'I will destroy this temple made with hands, and within three days I will build another made without hands.' "   John 2:19

59 But not even then did their testimony agree.

60 ᴿAnd the high priest stood up in the midst and asked Jesus, saying, "Do You answer nothing? What *is it* these men testify against You?"   Matt. 26:62

61 But ᴿHe kept silent and answered nothing. ᴿAgain the high priest asked Him, saying to Him, "Are You the Christ, the Son of the Blessed?"   Is. 53:7 • Luke 22:67-71

62 Jesus said, "I am. ᴿAnd you will see the Son of Man sitting at the right hand of the Power, and coming with the clouds of heaven."   Luke 22:69

63 Then the high priest tore his clothes and said, "What further need do we have of witnesses?

64 "You have heard the blasphemy! What do you think?" And they all ᴿcondemned Him to be deserving of death.   Matt. 20:18; Mark 10:33

65 Then some began to ᴿspit on Him, and to blindfold Him, and to beat Him, and to say to Him, "Prophesy!" And the officers *struck Him with the palms of their hands.   Is. 50:6

Peter Denies Jesus, and Weeps

66 ᴿNow as Peter was below in the courtyard, one of the servant girls of the high priest came.   John 18:16-18, 25-27

67 And when she saw Peter warming himself, she looked at him and said, "You also were with ᴿJesus of Nazareth."   John 1:45

68 But he denied it, saying, "I neither know nor understand what you are saying." And he went out on the porch, and a rooster crowed.

69 ᴿAnd the servant girl saw him again, and began to say to those who stood by, "This is one of them."   Matt. 26:71

70 But he denied it again. And a little later those who stood by said to Peter again, "Surely you are *one* of them; for you are a Galilean, *and your speech shows *it*."

71 Then he began to curse and swear, "I do not know this Man of whom you speak!"

72 A second time *the* rooster crowed. Then Peter called to mind the word that Jesus had said to him, "Before the rooster crows twice, you will deny Me three times." And when he thought about it, he wept.

Jesus Faces Pilate

15 Immediately, in the morning, the chief priests ᴿheld a consultation with the

14:65 NU *received Him with slaps*
14:70 NU omits the rest of v. 70.

elders and scribes and the whole council; and they bound Jesus, led *Him* away, and ᴿdelivered *Him* to Pilate.   Ps. 2:2 • Is. 53:7

2 ᴿThen Pilate asked Him, "Are You the King of the Jews?" He answered and said to him, "*It is as* you say."   Matt. 27:11-14

3 And the chief priests accused Him of many things, but He answered nothing.

4 ᴿThen Pilate asked Him again, saying, "Do You answer nothing? See how many things *they testify against You!"   Matt. 27:13

5 ᴿBut Jesus still answered nothing, so that Pilate marveled.   Ps. 38:13, 14; Is. 53:7; John 19:9

Taking the Place of Barabbas

6 Now ᴿat the feast he was accustomed to releasing one prisoner to them, whomever they requested.   Matt. 27:15-26

7 And there was one named Barabbas, *who was* chained with his fellow rebels; they had committed murder in the rebellion.

8 Then the multitude, *crying aloud, began to ask *him to do* just as he had always done for them.

9 But Pilate answered them, saying, "Do you want me to release to you the King of the Jews?"

10 For he knew that the chief priests had handed Him over because of envy.

11 But ᴿthe chief priests stirred up the crowd, so that he should rather release Barabbas to them.   Acts 3:14

12 Pilate answered and said to them again, "What then do you want me to do *with Him* whom you call the ᴿKing of the Jews?"   Mic. 5:2

13 So they cried out again, "Crucify Him!"

14 Then Pilate said to them, "Why, ᴿwhat evil has He done?" But they cried out all the more, "Crucify Him!"   1 Pet. 2:21-23

15 ᴿSo Pilate, wanting to gratify the crowd, released Barabbas to them; and he delivered Jesus, after he had scourged *Him*, to be ᴿcrucified.   Matt. 27:26 • [Is. 53:8]

The Soldiers Mock Jesus

16 Then the soldiers led Him away into the hall called ᵀPraetorium, and they called together the whole garrison.   Governor's headquarters

17 And they clothed Him with purple; and they twisted a crown of thorns, put it on His *head*,

18 and began to salute Him, "Hail, King of the Jews!"

19 Then they ᴿstruck Him on the head with a reed and spat on Him; and bowing the knee, they worshiped Him.   Is. 52:14; Mic. 5:1

20 And when they had mocked Him, they took the purple off Him, put His own clothes on Him, and led Him out to crucify Him.

The King on a Cross

21 Then they compelled a certain man, Simon a Cyrenian, the father of Alexander and Rufus, as he was coming out of the country and passing by, to bear His cross.

22 ᴿAnd they brought Him to the place Golgotha, which is translated, Place of a Skull.   John 19:17-24

23 Then they gave Him wine mingled with myrrh to drink, but He did not take *it*.

24 And when they crucified Him, they divided His garments, casting lots for them to determine what every man should take.

25 Now ᴿit was the third hour, and they crucified Him.   John 19:14

26 And ᴿthe inscription of His ᵀaccusation was written above: Matt. 27:37 • *crime*

THE KING OF THE JEWS.

27 ᴿWith Him they also crucified two robbers, one on His right and the other on His left.   Is. 53:9, 12

28 *So the Scripture was fulfilled which says, ᴿ *"And He was numbered with the transgressors."*   Is. 53:12; Luke 22:37

29 And ᴿthose who passed by blasphemed Him, ᴿwagging their heads and saying, "Aha! ᴿYou who destroy the temple and build *it* in three days,   Ps. 22:6, 7; 69:7 • Ps. 109:25 • John 2:19-21

30 ᴿ"save Yourself, and come down from the cross!"   Ps. 22:8

31 Likewise the chief priests also, mocking among themselves with the scribes, said, "He saved others; Himself He cannot save.

32 ᴿ"Let the Christ, the King of Israel, descend now from the cross, that we may see and *believe." Even ᴿthose who were crucified with Him reviled Him.   Ps. 22:8 • Matt. 27:44

Jesus Dies on the Cross

33 Now ᴿwhen the sixth hour had come, there was darkness over the whole land until the ninth hour.   Amos 8:9

34 And at the ninth hour Jesus cried out with a loud voice, saying, "Eloi, Eloi, lama sabachthani?" which is translated, ᴿ *"My God, My God, why have You forsaken Me?"*   Ps. 22:1

35 Some of those who stood by, when they heard *that*, said, "Look, He is calling for Elijah!"

36 Then ᴿsomeone ran and filled a sponge full of sour wine, put *it* on a reed, and ᴿoffered *it* to Him to drink, saying, "Let Him alone; let us see if Elijah will come to take Him down."   John 19:29 • Ps. 69:21

37 ᴿAnd Jesus cried out with a loud voice, and breathed His last.   Matt. 17:23

15:4 NU *of which they accuse You*
15:8 NU *going up*

15:28 NU omits v. 28.
15:32 M *believe Him*

38 Then ᴿthe veil of the temple was torn in two from top to bottom.   Zech. 11:10, 11

39 So ᴿwhen the centurion, who stood opposite Him, saw that *He cried out like this and breathed His last, he said, "Truly this Man was the Son of God!"   Luke 23:47

40 ᴿThere were also women looking on ᴿfrom afar, among whom were Mary Magdalene, Mary the mother of James the Less and of Joses, and Salome,   Matt. 27:55 · Ps. 38:11

41 who also ᴿfollowed Him and ministered to Him when He was in Galilee, and many other women who came up with Him to Jerusalem.   Luke 8:2, 3

Jesus Buried in Joseph's Tomb

42 ᴿNow when evening had come, because it was the Preparation Day, that is, the day before the Sabbath,   John 19:38-42

43 ᴿJoseph of Arimathea, a prominent council member, who ᴿwas himself waiting for the kingdom of God, coming and taking courage, went in to Pilate and asked for the body of Jesus.   Is. 53:9 · Luke 23:51

44 Pilate marveled that He was already dead; and summoning the centurion, he asked him if He had been dead for some time.

45 So when he found out from the centurion, he granted the body to Joseph.

46 Then he bought fine linen, took Him down, and wrapped Him in the linen. And he ᴿlaid Him in a tomb which had been hewn out of the rock, and rolled a stone against the door of the tomb.   Matt. 26:12; Mark 14:8

47 And Mary Magdalene and Mary the mother of Joses observed where He was laid.

He Is Risen

16 Now ᴿwhen the Sabbath was past, Mary Magdalene, Mary the mother of James, and Salome ᴿbought spices, that they might come and anoint Him. John 20:1-8 · Luke 23:56

2 ᴿVery early in the morning, on the first day of the week, they came to the tomb when the sun had risen.   Luke 24:1

3 And they said among themselves, "Who will roll away the stone from the door of the tomb for us?"

4 But when they looked up, they saw that the stone had been rolled away—for it was very large.

5 ᴿAnd entering the tomb, they saw a young man clothed in a long white robe sitting on the right side; and they were alarmed.   John 20:11, 12

6 But he said to them, "Do not be alarmed. You seek Jesus of Nazareth, who was crucified. He is ᴿrisen! He is not here. See the place where they laid Him.   Hos. 6:2

7 "But go, tell His disciples—and Peter—that He is going before you into Galilee; there you will see Him, as He said to you."

8 So they went out *quickly and fled from the tomb, for they trembled and were amazed. ᴿAnd they said nothing to anyone, for they were afraid.   Matt. 28:8

Mary Magdalene Sees the Risen Lord

9 Now when He rose early on the first day of the week, He appeared first to Mary Magdalene, ᴿout of whom He had cast seven demons.   Luke 8:2

10 She went and told those who had been with Him, as they mourned and wept.

11 ᴿAnd when they heard that He was alive and had been seen by her, they did not believe.   Luke 24:11, 41

Jesus Appears to Two Disciples

12 After that, He appeared in another form ᴿto two of them as they walked and went into the country.   Luke 24:13-35

13 And they went and told it to the rest, but they did not believe them either.

The Great Commission

14 ᴿLater He appeared to the eleven as they sat at the table; and He rebuked their unbelief and hardness of heart, because they did not believe those who had seen Him after He had risen.   1 Cor. 15:5

15 ᴿAnd He said to them, "Go into all the world ᴿand preach the gospel to every creature.   Matt. 28:19 · [Col. 1:23]

16 ᴿ"He who believes and is baptized will be saved; ᴿbut he who does not believe will be condemned.   [John 3:18, 36] · [John 12:48]

17 "And these signs will follow those who believe: In My name they will cast out demons; they will speak with new tongues;

18 ᴿ"they* will take up serpents; and if they drink anything deadly, it will by no means hurt them; ᴿthey will lay hands on the sick, and they will recover."   Acts 28:3-6 · James 5:14

Christ Ascends to God's Right Hand

19 So then, after the Lord had spoken to them, He was ᴿreceived up into heaven, and sat down at the right hand of God.   Is. 9:7

20 And they went out and preached everywhere, the Lord working with them ᴿand confirming the word through the accompanying signs. *Amen.   [Heb. 2:4]

16:8 NU, M omit quickly
16:18 NU and in their hands they will
16:20 Vv. 9–20 are bracketed in NU as not in the original text. They are lacking in Codex Sinaiticus and Codex Vaticanus, although nearly all other mss. of Mark contain them.

15:39 NU He thus breathed His last

THE GOSPEL ACCORDING TO
Luke

The Gospel of Luke has been referred to as "the most beautiful book in the world." Those who have made an in-depth study of this book would certainly agree. The reason for such a consensus is that this lovely book includes all of us. Regardless of your standing in this world, the Gospel of Luke was intended for you.

There is no other book in the Old or New Testament that contains an internal introduction as complete as does the Gospel of Luke (1:1-4). These verses contain definite suggestions for answers to questions that should be asked about any book. The questions are: Who is the author? To whom is the author writing? What is the purpose of the author in writing this book? The answers to these questions prepare us for the intriguing account of our Savior's life and work as they are traced from the time of the announcement of His birth until He was carried up into heaven.

AUTHORSHIP. From the first account of the appearance of this Gospel among Christians, it was concluded that Luke is the author. Luke was quite modest; although he was involved in important early Christian events, such as accompanying Paul on his second and third missionary journeys as recorded in Acts, he never mentioned his own name, preferring instead the pronoun *we*. The caption "According to Luke" was included in early Greek manuscripts of his Gospel. There is internal evidence that Luke is the author in the specific medical terms that suggest a doctor as writer. The connection of Luke 1:1-4 with Acts 1:1 leads us to believe Luke is the author of Acts also. There is no other information about Luke other than what we find in the New Testament. His name is given in Colossians 4:14, Philemon 1:24, and 2 Timothy 4:9-11. He is described by Paul as "the beloved physician." This statement suggests Luke was intelligent, possessor of a scientific mind and, because of his good Greek writing style, evidently quite cultured. Luke was a true friend to Paul and was one friend who remained faithful to him at the time of his approaching death. His vocation helps us understand the completeness of this narrative. He did not omit details. His training had taught him to be sympathetic and compassionate, especially to women and children.

CONTEXT. The opening paragraph gives us the name "Theophilus" ("Lover of God" or "Loved by God"). Nothing is known about this friend of Luke's. Although a name is given, it is evident from the content of the narrative that Luke was writing to the entire world. In observing the authors of the Gospels, it is apparent that all of them had access to the same material; but these men were chosen by the Holy Spirit to magnify different phases of the Savior's life. Luke reveals the beauty of our Lord as the ideal Man, the Savior of the world. Luke details the life of Jesus Christ so every person who reads his account can know that Jesus Christ was intended just for him or her.

Luke wanted the world, and particularly Theophilus, to have an accurate written account of the life of our Lord, since all that the world at large knew about Jesus until that time was by oral tradition. We are made aware of the theme of a book or chapter in the Bible by repetition of words or phrases. "Son of Man" is found twenty-six times in this Gospel. This tells us that Jesus Christ is the perfect God-Man who came into this world to provide a perfect Savior for all humanity. The Gospel of Luke presents Jesus as the perfect Man who provides salvation for imperfect people. Luke was thorough in his presentation, telling more about the birth of John the Baptist, the birth of Jesus, and His boyhood than the other Gospel writers. The Gospel of Luke appeals to women because more is said about womanhood than in any other Gospel. More than one-half of the material found in Luke is not found in the other Gospels. Luke includes history, poetry, and science, as well as spiritual teaching. It is a Gospel of prayer and praise.

HOW LUKE FITS INTO THE BIBLE. If Matthew was written especially for the Jews, and Mark for the Romans, Luke is especially aimed at the Greeks, who were seeking the perfect man. The Lord Jesus Christ is presented in Luke not merely as a perfect human, but as one who possessed the best attributes of mankind in general with none of its defects. Historically Luke was part of a two-volume work addressed to Theophilus, taking the Christian story from its beginning with John the Baptist through the Ascension in Luke, and from the Ascension to Paul's voyage to Rome in Acts. If Luke-Acts were omitted from the New Testament it would be a terrible loss, not only in content and beauty, but also because Luke actually wrote more material than the apostle Paul (the second contributor to the New Testament in volume).

HOW LUKE FITS TOGETHER. Luke follows the same general pattern as the other two synoptic Gospels, emphasizing Jesus as the Son of Man: (1) The Preparation of the Son of Man (1:1—4:13); (2) The Ministry of the Son of Man (4:14—9:50); (3) The Rejection and Death of the Son of Man (9:51—23:56); (4) The Resurrection and Ascension of the Son of Man (ch. 24).

SUMMARY STATEMENT. Luke presents Jesus Christ as the perfect Man, strong yet compassionate, the universal Savior of all who will accept Him.

Much more than a perfect human life and humanitarian work is found in this beautiful Gospel. Luke tells us not only about One who is the ultimate in manhood, but who is also the Savior of the world. The salvation Jesus provides is unlimited. It is intended for the Samaritans, the Gentiles, women, children, the lowest, the highest, the despised, the outcast, the hated and the thief. Luke clearly states that this salvation for all the world is dependent upon our personal faith in Jesus Christ. Like the other Gospel writers, Luke invites us to share this Good News with all the world.

—J.A.P.

Dedication to Theophilus

INASMUCH as many have taken in hand to set in order a narrative of those things which *have been fulfilled among us,

2 just as those who from the beginning were ᴿeyewitnesses and ministers of the word ᴿdelivered them to us,   Acts 1:2 • Heb. 2:3

3 it seemed good to me also, having ᵀhad perfect understanding of all things from the very first, to write to you an orderly account, most excellent Theophilus,   *accurately followed*

4 that you may know the certainty of those things in which you were instructed.

John's Birth Announced to Zacharias

5 There was ᴿin the days of Herod, the king of Judea, a certain priest named Zacharias, of the division of ᴿAbijah. His ᴿwife *was* of the daughters of Aaron, and her name *was* Elizabeth.   Matt. 2:1 • Neh. 12:4 • Lev. 21:13, 14

6 And they were both righteous before God, walking in all the commandments and ordinances of the Lord blameless.

7 But they had no child, because Elizabeth was barren, and they were both well advanced in years.

8 So it was, that while he was serving as priest before God in the order of his division,

9 according to the custom of the priesthood, his lot fell ᴿto burn incense when he went into the temple of the Lord.   Ex. 30:7, 8

10 And the whole multitude of the people was praying outside at the hour of incense.

11 Then an angel of the Lord appeared to him, standing on the right side of ᴿthe altar of incense.   Ex. 30:1

12 And when Zacharias saw *him*, ᴿhe was troubled, and fear fell upon him.   Luke 2:9

13 But the angel said to him, "Do not be afraid, Zacharias, for your prayer is heard; and your wife Elizabeth will bear you a son, and you shall call his name John.

14 "And you will have joy and gladness, and ᴿmany will rejoice at his birth.   Luke 1:58

15 "For he will be great in the sight of the Lord, and shall drink neither wine nor strong drink. He will also be filled with the Holy Spirit, even from his mother's womb.

16 "And he will turn many of the children of Israel to the Lord their God.

17 "He will also go before Him in the spirit and power of Elijah, ᴿ*'to turn the hearts of the fathers to the children,'* and the disobedient to the wisdom of the just, to make ready a people prepared for the Lord."   Mal. 4:5, 6

18 And Zacharias said to the angel, ᴿ"How shall I know this? For I am an old man, and my wife is well advanced in years."   Gen. 17:17

19 And the angel answered and said to him, "I am ᴿGabriel, who stands in the presence of God, and was sent to speak to you and bring you ᵀthese glad tidings.   Dan. 8:16 • *this good news*

20 "But behold, you will be mute and not able to speak until the day these things take place, because you did not believe my words which will be fulfilled in their own time."

21 And the people waited for Zacharias, and marveled that he lingered so long in the temple.

22 But when he came out, he could not speak to them; and they perceived that he had seen a vision in the temple, for he beckoned to them and remained speechless.

23 So it was, as soon as ᴿthe days of his service were completed, that he departed to his own house.   2 Kin. 11:5

24 Now after those days his wife Elizabeth conceived; and she hid herself five months, saying,

25 "Thus the Lord has dealt with me, in the days when He looked on *me*, to ᴿtake away my reproach among people."   Gen. 30:23

1:1 Or *are most surely believed*

Christ's Birth Announced to Mary

▼ **6-B. He Was Unique in His Birth**

26 Now in the sixth month the angel Gabriel was sent by God to a city of Galilee named Nazareth,

27 to a ᴿvirgin ᴿbetrothed to a man whose name was Joseph, of the house of David. The virgin's name *was* Mary.   Is. 7:14 · Matt. 1:18

28 And having come in, the angel said to her, "Rejoice, highly favored *one*, the Lord *is* with you; *blessed *are* you among women!"

29 But *when she saw *him*, ᴿshe was troubled at his saying, and considered what manner of greeting this was.   Luke 1:12

30 Then the angel said to her, "Do not be afraid, Mary, for you have found ᴿfavor with God.   Luke 2:52

31 ᴿ"And behold, you will conceive in your womb and bring forth a Son, and ᴿshall call His name Jesus.   Is. 7:14 · Matt. 1:21, 25; Luke 2:21

32 "He will be great, ᴿand will be called the Son of the Highest; and the Lord God will give Him the throne of His father David.   Mark 5:7

1:28 NU omits *blessed are you among women*
1:29 NU omits *when she saw him*

33 ᴿ"And He will reign over the house of Jacob ᴿforever, and of His kingdom there will be no end."   [Dan. 2:44] · Ps. 89:36, 37

34 Then Mary said to the angel, "How can this be, since I do not know a man?"

35 And the angel answered and said to her, *"The Holy Spirit will come upon you, and the power of the Highest will overshadow you; therefore, also, that Holy One who is to be born will be called the Son of God.   ▲

36 "Now indeed, Elizabeth your relative has also conceived a son in her old age; and this is now the sixth month for her who was called barren.

37 "For ᴿwith God nothing will be impossible."   Jer. 32:17

38 Then Mary said, "Behold the maidservant of the Lord! Let it be to me according to your word." And the angel departed from her.

Mary Visits Elizabeth

39 Now Mary arose in those days and went into the hill country with haste, ᴿto a city of Judah,   Josh. 21:9

40 and entered the house of Zacharias and greeted Elizabeth.

41 And it happened, when Elizabeth heard the greeting of Mary, that the babe leaped in

---

6-B. He Was Unique in His Birth (Luke 1:26–35)—Adam, the first man, was not born: he was made from the dust of the earth. Eve, the first woman, was not born: she was taken from the man. All other human beings were born of human parents, except the God-Man, who had no earthly father. Conceived apart from the seed of sinful man, He had a perfect, sinless human nature (John 1:14, page 1049; 1 Tim. 3:16, page 1220). Not only His conception, but also the circumstances surrounding His birth were unique, beyond even those that accompany the birth of earthly kings.

(1) He was born of a virgin, as prophesied by Isaiah seven hundred years before (Matt. 1:22, 23, page 930; cf. Is. 7:14, page 649). Note that the "of whom" of Matthew 1:16 (page 930) is feminine singular in the original Greek, indicating that Jesus was physically born of Mary, not of Joseph.

(2) He was the incarnate God (born in flesh). Isaiah called Him "Immanuel" ("God with Us"), meaning that He was the preexistent, eternal God, now in a human body (Is. 7:14, page 649).

(3) He was born in the city of Bethlehem, as prophesied by Micah seven hundred years before (Matt. 2:4–6, page 931; cf. Mic. 5:2, page 890).

(4) His birth was announced by angels (v. 26; Luke 2:9–11, page 1012).

(5) His birth occurred several weeks after the birth of John the Baptist, who had been announced by the angel Gabriel as the forerunner of the Messiah (vv. 11–19; John 1:6, 7, 23, page 1049).

(6) He was born as a Man, sharing the lot of men; He was poor, born in a stable and cared for in a feeding trough (Luke 2:7, page 1012). Yet this son of lowly Galileans was worshiped by kings (Matt. 2:2, 9–11, page 931).

(7) His birth was signaled by a once-in-history star which guided the wise men from the east to Him (Matt. 2:1, 2, 7, page 931).

(8) Hosts of angels gave forth praises at His birth, and shouted proclamations of coming "peace," while shepherds flocked to catch a glimpse of His face (Luke 2:8–16, page 1012).

(9) Satan prepared a murderer to slay the Christ child at birth: Herod the Great, a foreigner-king. Herod's sinful hands were already drenched with the blood of rivals and of the whole royal house of the Hasmoneans, the previous Hebrew ruling line. He was a hardened and ready agent for the murder of the Bethlehem children (Matt. 2:3–18, page 931).

(10) His birth was uniquely hailed by two aged holy persons, Simeon and Anna. Seeing the babe presented to the Lord in the temple, they identified Him through the Spirit of God as the Messiah who was to bring deliverance to His people (Luke 2:25–38, page 1013).

(11) Just prior to His birth an angel gave Him the name "Jesus" (the Greek form of the Hebrew *Jeshua*, "Jehovah Saves"), with the announcement, "For He will save His people from their sins," thus announcing the unique purpose for which He came (Matt. 1:21, page 930).

See Mark 1:21-28, page 984, for **Point 6-C: He Was Unique in His Ministry.**

her womb; and Elizabeth was ᴿfilled with the
Holy Spirit.   Acts 6:3

42 Then she spoke out with a loud voice
and said, "Blessed *are* you among women,
and blessed *is* the fruit of your womb!

43 "But why *is* this *granted* to me, that the
mother of my Lord should come to me?

44 "For indeed, as soon as the voice of your
greeting sounded in my ears, the babe leaped
in my womb for joy.

45 ᴿ"Blessed *is* she who believed, for there
will be a fulfillment of those things which
were told her from the Lord."   John 20:29

The Song of Mary

46 And Mary said:

ᴿ"My soul magnifies the Lord,   1 Sam. 2:1-10
47 And my spirit has ᴿrejoiced in ᴿGod my
      Savior.   Hab. 3:18 • 1 Tim. 1:1; 2:3
48 For ᴿHe has regarded the lowly state of
      His maidservant;
      For behold, henceforth ᴿall generations
      will call me blessed.   Ps. 138:6 • Luke 11:27
49 For He who is mighty ᴿhas done great
      things for me,   Ps. 71:19; 126:2, 3
      And ᴿholy *is* His name.   Ps. 111:9
50 And ᴿHis mercy *is* on those who fear
      Him
      From generation to generation. Ps. 103:17
51 He has shown strength with His arm;
      ᴿHe has scattered *the* proud in the
      imagination of their hearts.   [1 Pet. 5:5]
52 ᴿHe has put down the mighty from *their*
      thrones,
      And exalted *the* lowly.   1 Sam. 2:7, 8
53 He has ᴿfilled *the* hungry with good
      things,   [Matt. 5:6]
      And *the* rich He has sent away empty.
54 He has helped His servant Israel,
      ᴿIn remembrance of *His* mercy,   [Jer. 31:3]
55 As He spoke to our ᴿfathers,   [Rom. 11:28]
      To Abraham and to his seed forever."

56 And Mary remained with her about
three months, and returned to her house.

Birth of John the Baptist

57 Now Elizabeth's full time came for her to
be delivered, and she brought forth a son.

58 When her neighbors and relatives heard
how the Lord had shown great mercy to her,
they ᴿrejoiced with her.   [Rom. 12:15]

Circumcision of John the Baptist

59 So it was, ᴿon the eighth day, that they
came to circumcise the child; and they would
have called him by the name of his father,
Zacharias.   Gen. 17:12

60 His mother answered and said, ᴿ"No; he
shall be called John."   Luke 1:13, 63

61 But they said to her, "There is no one
among your relatives who is called by this
name."

62 So they made signs to his father—what
he would have him called.

63 And he asked for a writing tablet, and
wrote, saying, "His name is John." So they all
marveled.

64 Immediately his mouth was opened and
his tongue *loosed*, and he spoke, praising
God.

65 Then fear came on all who dwelt around
them; and all these sayings were discussed
throughout all the hill country of Judea.

66 And all those who heard *them* ᴿkept
them in their hearts, saying, "What kind of
child will this be?" And ᴿthe hand of the Lord
was with him.   Luke 2:19 • Acts 11:21

Zacharias' Prophecy

67 Now his father Zacharias was filled with
the Holy Spirit, and prophesied, saying:

68 "Blessedᴿ *is* the Lord God of Israel,
      For ᴿHe has visited and redeemed His
      people,   1 Kin. 1:48 • Ex. 3:16
69 ᴿAnd has raised up a horn of salvation
      for us   Ps. 132:17
      In the house of His servant David,
70 ᴿAs He spoke by the mouth of His holy
      prophets,   Rom. 1:2
      Who *have been* since the world began,
71 That we should be saved from our
      enemies
      And from the hand of all who hate us,
72 ᴿTo perform the mercy *promised* to our
      fathers   Lev. 26:42
      And to remember His holy covenant,
73 ᴿThe oath which He swore to our father
      Abraham: Gen. 12:3; 22:16-18
74 To grant us that we,
      Being delivered from the hand of our
      enemies,
      Might ᴿserve Him without fear,   [Heb. 9:14]
75 ᴿIn holiness and righteousness before
      Him all the days of our life.   [Eph. 4:24]

76 And you, child, will be called the
      ᴿprophet of the Highest;   Matt. 11:9, 10
      For ᴿyou will go before the face of the
      Lord to prepare His ways,   Is. 40:3
77 To give ᴿknowledge of salvation to His
      people
      By the remission of their sins,   [Mark 1:4]
78 Through the tender mercy of our God,
      With which the Dayspring from on
      high *has visited us;
79 ᴿTo give light to those who sit in
      darkness and the shadow of death,
      To ᴿguide our feet into the way of
      peace."   Is. 9:2 • John 14:27; 16:33

80 So ᴿthe child grew and became strong in
spirit, and ᴿwas in the deserts till the day of
his manifestation to Israel.   Luke 2:40 • Matt. 3:1

1:78 NU *shall visit*

Christ Born of Mary

2 And it came to pass in those days *that* a decree went out from Caesar Augustus that all the world should be registered.

2 ᴿThis census first took place while Quirinius was governing Syria.   Acts 5:37

3 So all went to be registered, everyone to his own city.

4 Joseph also went up from Galilee, out of the city of Nazareth, into Judea, to ᴿthe city of David, which is called ᴿBethlehem, ᴿbecause he was of the house and lineage of David,   1 Sam. 16:1 · Mic. 5:2 · Matt. 1:16

5 to be registered with Mary, his betrothed *wife, who was with child.

6 So it was, that while they were there, the days were completed for her to be delivered.

7 And ᴿshe brought forth her firstborn Son, and wrapped Him in swaddling cloths, and laid Him in a ᵀmanger, because there was no room for them in the inn.   Matt. 1:25 · *feed trough*

2:5 NU omits *wife*

Glory in the Highest

8 Now there were in the same country shepherds living out in the fields, keeping watch over their flock by night.

9 And *behold, an angel of the Lord stood before them, and the glory of the Lord shone around them, and they were greatly afraid.

10 Then the angel said to them, "Do not be afraid, for behold, I bring you good tidings of great joy which will be to all people.

11 ᴿ"For there is born to you this day in the city of David ᴿa Savior, ᴿwho is Christ the Lord.   Is. 9:6 · Matt. 1:21 · Acts 2:36

12 "And this *will be* the sign to you: You will find a Babe wrapped in swaddling cloths, lying in a ᵀmanger."   *feed trough*

28–D. Worship: Its Importance   ▼

13 ᴿAnd suddenly there was with the angel a multitude of the heavenly host praising God and saying: Dan. 7:10

2:9 NU omits *behold*

28–D. Worship: Its Importance (Luke 2:13, 14)—"Let all the angels of God worship Him" (Heb. 1:6, page 1236). Worship is the paramount activity in heaven among all the angels of God. They looked to Christ and worshiped Him, because the Father said to Him, "Your throne, O God, is forever and ever" (Heb. 1:8, page 1236; cf. Ps. 45:6, page 538). Jesus is worshiped because He is the only begotten Son of God, and God the Son (John 3:16, page 1052).

The truth of Jesus' deity is one of the most profound facts ever revealed by the heavenly Father. When Jesus was born in Bethlehem of Judea, God the Father sent "a multitude of the heavenly host praising God and saying: 'Glory to God in the highest, and on earth peace, good will toward men!' " (vv. 13, 14). Christ came to His own, but His own did not know Him; so they did not worship Him (John 1:10, page 1049). But God the Father sent the heavenly host to earth to worship the virgin-born Messiah.

(1) The seraphim know God's worth, and in great joy and ecstasy they cry one to another, "Holy, holy, holy is the LORD of hosts; the whole earth is full of His glory!" (Is. 6:1–3, page 647).

(2) The cherubim are always seen in connection with the throne of God. They worship the Lord and guard His throne. They cover the mercy seat in the Most Holy Place in heaven (Heb. 9:1–5, page 1243); accordingly, God told Moses to make golden cherubim and put them above the mercy seat in the Most Holy Place in the tabernacle (Ex. 25:17–19, page 85). They were not to be worshiped (Ex. 20:3–5, page 79), but to remind the high priest and the people that all the angels of God worship Him day and night (Rev. 4:8, page 1297). All the angels of God, as well as mankind, were created to bow down and worship the Creator.

(3) John said, "I heard the voice of many angels around the throne, the living creatures, and the elders; and the number of them was ten thousand times ten thousand, and thousands of thousands" (Rev. 5:8–14, page 1297). All were engaged in pure worship.

(a) The elders and the living creatures fell down before the Lamb.
(b) They brought the prayers of the saints as a gift to the Lamb.
(c) They sang a new song of praise.
(d) They worshiped the Lamb in word, and then the elders fell down to worship the One who lives forever and ever.

(4) The Tribulation saints will join all the host of heaven and worship the Lamb of God at the end of the Great Tribulation (Rev. 7:9–17, page 1300).

(5) Just as worship is paramount with the host of heaven, so it must have priority in all our thoughts and plans here on earth, because it is the most important thing we do as believers. Worship must take precedence over prayer, although prayer is vital to Christian growth and power. Worship must take precedence over reading God's Word, unless you are reading Scriptures to motivate worship. Worship must take precedence over music, unless the music is used to enhance worship.

Worship is an indispensable part of the Christian's life—now and in eternity. Evangelism and Bible teaching, like faith and hope, will cease. Worship, like love, will occupy our hearts forever (1 Cor. 13:8–10, page 1160).

See Index, page 17, for your next study.

▽ 14 "Glory^R to God in the highest,
    And on earth ^Rpeace, ^Rgoodwill* toward
▲   men!" Luke 19:38 • Is. 57:19 • [Eph. 2:4, 7]

15 So it was, when the angels had gone away from them into heaven, that the shepherds said to one another, "Let us now go to Bethlehem and see this thing that has come to pass, which the Lord has made known to us."

16 And they came with haste and found Mary and Joseph, and the Babe lying in a manger.

17 Now when they had seen *Him*, they made *widely known the saying which was told them concerning this Child.

18 And all those who heard *it* marveled at those things which were told them by the shepherds.

19 ^RBut Mary kept all these things and pondered *them* in her heart. Gen. 37:11

20 Then the shepherds returned, glorifying and praising God for all the things that they had heard and seen, as it was told them.

Circumcision of Jesus

21 And when eight days were completed *for the circumcision of the Child, His name was called JESUS, the name given by the angel before He was conceived in the womb.

Jesus Presented in the Temple

22 Now when ^Rthe days of her purification according to the law of Moses were completed, they brought Him to Jerusalem to present Him to the Lord Lev. 12:2-8

23 (as it is written in the law of the Lord, ^R "Every male who opens the womb shall be called holy to the LORD"), Ex. 13:2, 12, 15

24 and to offer a sacrifice according to what is said in the law of the Lord, ^R "A pair of turtledoves or two young pigeons." Lev. 12:2, 8

Simeon Sees God's Salvation

25 And behold, there was a man in Jerusalem whose name was Simeon, and this man was just and devout, ^Rwaiting for the Consolation of Israel, and the Holy Spirit was upon him. Mark 15:43

26 And it had been revealed to him by the Holy Spirit that he would not see death before he had seen the Lord's Christ.

27 So he came ^Rby the Spirit into the temple. And when the parents brought in the Child Jesus, to do for Him according to the custom of the law, Matt. 4:1

28 he took Him up in his arms and blessed God and said:

2:14 NU toward men of goodwill
2:17 NU omits widely
2:21 NU for His circumcision

29 "Lord, ^Rnow You are letting Your
    servant depart in peace,
    According to Your word; Gen. 46:30

30 For my eyes have seen Your salvation

31 Which You have prepared before the
    face of all peoples,

32 ^RA light to *bring* revelation to the
    Gentiles, Is. 9:2; 42:6
    And the glory of Your people Israel."

33 *And Joseph and His mother marveled at those things which were spoken of Him.

34 Then Simeon blessed them, and said to Mary His mother, "Behold, this *Child* is destined for the ^Rfall and rising of many in Israel, and for ^Ra sign which will be spoken against Is. 8:14; [1 Pet. 2:7, 8] • Acts 4:2; 17:32; 28:22

35 (yes, ^Ra sword will pierce through your own soul also), that the thoughts of many hearts may be revealed." Ps. 42:10

Anna Bears Witness to the Redeemer

36 Now there was one, Anna, a prophetess, the daughter of Phanuel, of the tribe of ^RAsher. She was of a great age, and had lived with a husband seven years from her virginity; Josh. 19:24

37 and this woman *was* a widow *of about eighty-four years, who did not depart from the temple, but served *God* with fastings and prayers ^Rnight and day. 1 Tim. 5:5

38 And coming in that instant she gave thanks to *the Lord, and spoke of Him to all those who ^Rlooked for redemption in Jerusalem. Mark 15:43

The Family Returns to Nazareth

39 So when they had performed all things according to the law of the Lord, they returned to Galilee, to their *own* city, Nazareth.

40 ^RAnd the Child grew and became strong *in spirit, filled with wisdom; and the grace of God was upon Him. Luke 1:80; 2:52

The Boy Jesus Amazes the Scholars

41 His parents went to ^RJerusalem every year at the Feast of the Passover. John 4:20

42 And when He was twelve years old, they went up to Jerusalem according to the ^Rcustom of the feast. Ex. 23:14, 15

43 When they had finished the ^Rdays, as they returned, the Boy Jesus lingered behind in Jerusalem. And *Joseph and His mother did not know *it;* Ex. 12:15

44 but supposing Him to have been in the company, they went a ^Tday's journey, and sought Him among *their* relatives and acquaintances. 20 mi.

2:33 NU And His father and mother
2:37 NU until she was eighty-four
2:38 NU God
2:40 NU omits in spirit
2:43 NU His parents

45 So when they did not find Him, they returned to Jerusalem, seeking Him.

46 Now so it was *that* after three days they found Him in the temple, sitting in the midst of the teachers, both listening to them and asking them questions.

47 And ᴿall who heard Him were astonished at His understanding and answers.   Matt. 7:28

48 So when they saw Him, they were amazed; and His mother said to Him, "Son, why have You done this to us? Look, Your father and I have sought You anxiously."

49 And He said to them, "Why did you seek Me? Did you not know that I must be about ᴿMy Father's business?"   [Luke 4:22, 32]

50 But ᴿthey did not understand the statement which He spoke to them.   John 7:15, 46

Jesus Advances in Wisdom and Favor

51 Then He went down with them and came to Nazareth, and was subject to them, but His mother kept all these things in her heart.

52 And Jesus increased in wisdom and stature, and in favor with God and men.

John the Baptist Prepares the Way

3 Now in the fifteenth year of the reign of Tiberius Caesar, ᴿPontius Pilate being governor of Judea, Herod being tetrarch of Galilee, his brother Philip tetrarch of Iturea and the region of Trachonitis, and Lysanias tetrarch of Abilene,   Matt. 27:2

2 while Annas* and Caiaphas were high priests, the word of God came to John the son of Zacharias in the wilderness.

3 And he went into all the region around the Jordan, preaching a baptism of repentance ᴿfor the remission of sins,   Luke 1:17, 77

4 as it is written in the book of the words of Isaiah the prophet, saying:

> ᴿ"The voice of one crying in the
>   wilderness:
> 'Prepare the way of the Lord;
>   Make His paths straight.   Is. 40:3–5
> 5 Every valley shall be filled
>   And every mountain and hill brought
>   low;
>   The crooked places shall be made
>   straight
>   And the rough ways smooth;
> 6 And all flesh shall see the salvation of
>   God.'"

John Preaches to the People

7 Then he said to the multitudes that came out to be baptized by him, ᴿ"Broodᵀ of vipers! Who warned you to flee from the wrath to come?   Matt. 3:7; 12:34; 23:33 • *Offspring*

8 "Therefore bear fruits ᴿworthy of repentance, and do not begin to say to yourselves, 'We have Abraham as *our* father.' For I say to you that God is able to raise up children to Abraham from these stones.   [2 Cor. 7:9–11]

9 "And even now the ax is laid to the root of the trees. Therefore ᴿevery tree which does not bear good fruit is cut down and thrown into the fire."   Matt. 7:19

10 So the people asked him, saying, ᴿ"What shall we do then?"   [Acts 2:37, 38; 16:30, 31]

11 He answered and said to them, ᴿ"He who has two tunics, let him give to him who has none; and he who has food, ᴿlet him do likewise."   2 Cor. 8:14 • Is. 58:7

12 Then ᴿtax collectors also came to be baptized, and said to him, "Teacher, what shall we do?"   Luke 7:29

13 And he said to them, ᴿ"Collect no more than what is appointed for you."   Luke 19:8

14 Likewise the soldiers asked him, saying, "And what shall we do?" So he said to them, "Do not intimidate anyone or accuse falsely, and be content with your wages."

15 Now as the people were in expectation, and all reasoned in their hearts about John, whether he was the Christ *or* not,

16 John answered, saying to all, "I indeed baptize you with water; but One mightier than I is coming, whose sandal strap I am not worthy to loose. He will baptize you with the Holy Spirit and fire.

17 "His winnowing fan *is* in His hand, and He will thoroughly clean out His threshing floor, and gather the wheat into His barn; but the chaff He will burn with unquenchable fire."

18 And with many other exhortations he preached to the people.

19 ᴿBut Herod the tetrarch, being rebuked by him concerning Herodias, his *brother Philip's wife, and for all the evils which Herod had done,   Mark 6:17

20 also added this, above all, that he shut John up in prison.

John Baptizes Jesus

3-B. God Is a Trinity   ▼

21 When all the people were baptized, it came to pass that Jesus also was baptized; and while He prayed, the heaven was opened.

22 And the Holy Spirit descended in bodily form like a dove upon Him, and a voice came

---

3:2 NU, M *in the high priesthood of Annas and Caiaphas*   3:19 NU *brother's wife*

3-B. God Is a Trinity (Luke 3:21, 22)—By the Trinity, we mean that God is three persons in one Being. The Trinity is His tri-personal existence in one Godhead, as Father, Son, and Holy Spirit (Matt. 3:16, 17, page 934). They are three distinct persons in one God. "Hear, O Israel: The Lord [Jehovah] our God, the Lord is one!"
(Point 3-B continued on next page)

▽ from heaven which said, "You are My be-
▲ loved Son; in You I am well pleased."

The Genealogy of Jesus Christ

23 Now Jesus Himself began *His* ministry at about thirty years of age, being (as was supposed) *the* son of Joseph, *the* son of Heli, **24** *the* son of Matthat, *the* son of Levi, *the* son of Melchi, *the* son of Janna, *the* son of Joseph, **25** *the* son of Mattathiah, *the* son of Amos, *the* son of Nahum, *the* son of Esli, *the* son of Naggai, **26** *the* son of Maath, *the* son of Mattathiah, *the* son of Semei, *the* son of Joseph, *the* son of Judah, **27** *the* son of Joannas, *the* son of Rhesa, *the* son of ᴿZerubbabel, *the* son of Shealtiel, *the* son of Neri,   Ezra 2:2; 3:8 **28** *the* son of Melchi, *the* son of Addi, *the* son of Cosam, *the* son of Elmodam, *the* son of Er, **29** *the* son of Jose, *the* son of Eliezer, *the* son of Jorim, *the* son of Matthat, *the* son of Levi,

30 *the* son of Simeon, *the* son of Judah, *the* son of Joseph, *the* son of Jonan, *the* son of Eliakim, **31** *the* son of Melea, *the* son of Menan, *the* son of Mattathah, *the* son of ᴿNathan, ᴿ*the* son of David,   Zech. 12:12 • Is. 9:7 **32** ᴿ*the* son of Jesse, *the* son of Obed, *the* son of Boaz, *the* son of Salmon, *the* son of Nahshon,   Is. 11:1, 10 **33** *the* son of Amminadab, *the* son of Ram, *the* son of Hezron, *the* son of Perez, ᴿ*the* son of Judah,   Gen. 49:10 **34** *the* son of Jacob, *the* son of Isaac, *the* son of Abraham, ᴿ*the* son of Terah, *the* son of Nahor,   Gen. 11:24, 26–30; 12:3 **35** *the* son of Serug, *the* son of Reu, *the* son of Peleg, *the* son of Eber, *the* son of Shelah, **36** ᴿ*the* son of Cainan, *the* son of ᴿArphaxad, *the* son of Shem, *the* son of Noah, *the* son of Lamech,   Gen. 11:12 • Gen. 10:22, 24; 11:10–13 **37** *the* son of Methuselah, *the* son of Enoch,

---

(Point 3-B continued from previous page)
(Deut. 6:4, page 187). The Father is Jehovah, the Son is Jehovah, and the Holy Spirit is Jehovah, and the three are a tri-unity, as the following passages demonstrate:

(1) Peter speaks of the "elect according to the foreknowledge of God the Father" (1 Pet. 1:2, page 1263). God the Father is the fullness of the Godhead, unseeable. "No one has seen God at any time" (John 1:18, page 1049).

(2) The Father says to God the Son, "Your throne, O God, is forever and ever; a scepter of righteousness is the scepter of Your Kingdom" (Heb. 1:8, page 1236). God the Son is the fullness of the Godhead bodily. "And the Word [Christ] became flesh and dwelt among us" (John 1:14, page 1049).

(3) "But Peter said, 'Ananias, why has Satan filled your heart to lie to the Holy Spirit? . . . You have not lied to men but to God' " (Acts 5:3, 4, page 1093). God the Holy Spirit is the fullness of the Godhead, convicting man of sin, of righteousness, and of judgment (John 16:7–11, page 1077).

The Trinity is also seen

(1) In the Creation:

(a) "In the beginning God [God the Father] created the heavens and the earth" (Gen. 1:1, page 2).

(b) "And the Spirit of God [God the Holy Spirit] was hovering over the face of the waters" (Gen. 1:2, page 2).

(c) "You, LORD [God the Son], in the beginning laid the foundation of the earth, and the heavens are the work of Your hands" (Heb. 1:10, page 1237). God the Son, Jesus Christ, "is the image of the invisible God, the firstborn over all creation. For by Him [Jesus Christ] all things were created that are in heaven and that are on earth, visible and invisible, whether thrones or dominions or principalities or powers. All things were created through Him and for Him. And He is before all things, and in Him all things consist" (Col. 1:15–17, page 1202).

In the above verses we see the Trinity creating and sustaining the heavens and the earth.

(2) In the baptism of the believer: "Go therefore and make disciples of all the nations, baptizing them in the name of the Father and of the Son and of the Holy Spirit" (Matt. 28:19, page 982). We are to baptize in the name (not names) of the Father, Son, and Holy Spirit, because the three are *one God*.

(3) In the baptism of Jesus:

(a) Jesus was baptized in the Jordan by John the Baptist.

(b) The Holy Spirit descended like a dove and alighted upon Him.

(c) God the Father spoke from heaven saying, "This is My beloved Son, in whom I am well pleased" (Matt. 3:13–17, page 934).

The Lord our God is one God in three persons. Paul closes 2 Corinthians with a trinitarian blessing: "The grace of the Lord Jesus Christ, and the love of God, and the communion of the Holy Spirit be with you all" (2 Cor. 13:14, page 1177).

See 1 John 1:5, page 1278, for **Point 3-C: God Is Light.**

the son of Jared, *the son* of Mahalalel, *the son* of Cainan,

38 *the son* of Enosh, *the son* of Seth, *the son* of Adam, ᴿ*the son* of God.   Gen. 5:1, 2

Satan Tempts Jesus

4 Then Jesus, being filled with the Holy Spirit, returned from the Jordan and was led by the Spirit *into the wilderness,

2 being ᵀtempted for forty days by the devil. And ᴿin those days He ate nothing, and afterward, when they had ended, He was hungry.   tested · Ex. 34:28

3 And the devil said to Him, "If You are ᴿthe Son of God, command this stone to become bread."   John 20:31

4 But Jesus answered him, saying, ᴿ"It is written, *'Man shall not live by bread alone, *but by every word of God.'"*   Deut. 8:3

5 *Then the devil, taking Him up on a high mountain, showed Him all the kingdoms of the world in a moment of time.

6 And the devil said to Him, "All this authority I will give You, and their glory; for ᴿ*this* has been delivered to me, and I give it to whomever I wish.   [Rev. 13:2, 7]

7 "Therefore, if You will worship before me, all will be Yours."

8 And Jesus answered and said to him, *"Get behind Me, Satan! *For it is written, ᴿ*'You shall worship the LORD your God, and Him only you shall serve.'"*   Deut. 6:13; 10:20

9 ᴿThen he brought Him to Jerusalem, set Him on the pinnacle of the temple, and said to Him, "If You are the Son of God, throw Yourself down from here.   Matt. 4:5-7

10 "For it is written:

ᴿ*'He shall give His angels charge over you,
To keep you,'*   Ps. 91:11

11 "and,

ᴿ*'In their hands they shall bear you up,
Lest you dash your foot against a stone.'"*   Ps. 91:12

12 And Jesus answered and said to him, "It has been said, ᴿ*'You shall not ᵀtempt the LORD your God.'"*   Deut. 6:16 · test

13 Now when the devil had ended every ᵀtemptation, he departed from Him ᴿuntil an opportune time.   testing · [Heb. 4:15]

Jesus Begins His Galilean Ministry

14 Then Jesus returned in the power of the Spirit to Galilee, and news of Him went out through all the surrounding region.

15 And He ᴿtaught in their synagogues, ᴿbeing glorified by all.   Matt. 4:23 · Is. 52:13

Jesus Rejected at Nazareth

16 So He came to Nazareth, where He had been brought up. And as His custom was, ᴿHe went into the synagogue on the Sabbath day, and stood up to read.   Ps. 22:22

17 And He was handed the book of the prophet Isaiah. And when He had opened the book, He found the place where it was written:

18 *"The*ᴿ *Spirit of the LORD is upon Me,
Because He has anointed Me to preach
the gospel to the poor;*   Is. 61:1, 2
*He has sent Me *to heal.the
brokenhearted,
To proclaim liberty to the captives
And recovery of sight to the blind,
To *ᴿset at liberty those who are
ᵀoppressed;*   [Dan. 9:24] · *downtrodden*
19 *To proclaim the acceptable year of the
LORD."*

20 Then He closed the book, and gave *it* back to the attendant and sat down. And the eyes of all who were in the synagogue were fixed on Him.

21 And He began to say to them, "Today this Scripture is fulfilled in your hearing."

22 So all bore witness to Him, and ᴿmarveled at the gracious words which proceeded out of His mouth. And they said, ᴿ"Is this not Joseph's son?"   [Ps. 45:2] · John 6:42

23 He said to them, "You will surely say this proverb to Me, 'Physician, heal yourself! Whatever we have heard done in *Capernaum, do also here in Your country.'"

24 Then He said, "Assuredly, I say to you, no prophet is accepted in his own country.

25 "But I tell you truly, ᴿmany widows were in Israel in the days of Elijah, when the heaven was shut up three years and six months, and there was a great famine throughout all the land;   1 Kin. 17:9

26 "but to none of them was Elijah sent except to ᵀZarephath, *in the region* of Sidon, to a woman *who was* a widow.   Gr. *Sarepta*

27 "And many lepers were in Israel in the time of Elisha the prophet, and none of them was cleansed except Naaman the Syrian."

28 So all those in the synagogue, when they heard these things, were filled with wrath,

29 ᴿand rose up and thrust Him out of the city; and they led Him to the brow of the hill on which their city was built, that they might throw Him down over the cliff.   John 8:37; 10:31

30 Then ᴿpassing through the midst of them, He went His way.   John 8:59; 10:39

4:1 NU *in*
4:4 NU omits *but by every word of God*
4:5 NU *And taking Him up, he showed Him*
4:8 NU omits *Get behind Me, Satan* • NU, M omit *For*

4:18 NU omits *to heal the brokenhearted*
4:23 NU *Capharnaum,* here and elsewhere

Jesus Casts Out an Unclean Spirit

▼ **7–G. Jesus Is Sovereign**

31 Then ᴿHe went down to Capernaum, a city of Galilee, and was teaching them on the Sabbaths.   Matt. 4:13

32 And they were astonished at His teaching, for His word was with authority.

33 ᴿNow in the synagogue there was a man who had a spirit of an unclean demon. And he cried out with a loud voice,   Mark 1:23

34 saying, "Let *us* alone! What have we to do with You, Jesus of Nazareth? Did You come to destroy us? ᴿI know who You are— ᴿthe Holy One of God!"   Luke 4:41 • Ps. 16:10

35 But Jesus rebuked him, saying, "Be quiet, and come out of him!" And when the demon had thrown him in *their* midst, it came out of him and did not hurt him.

36 Then they were all amazed and spoke among themselves, saying, "What a word this *is*! For with authority and power He commands the unclean spirits, and they come out."

37 And the report about Him went out into every place in the surrounding region.

Peter's Mother-in-Law Healed

38 Now He arose from the synagogue and entered Simon's house. But Simon's wife's

mother was sick with a high fever, and they made request of Him concerning her.

39 So He stood over her and ᴿrebuked the fever, and it left her. And immediately she arose and served them.   Luke 8:24

Many Healed After Sabbath Sunset

40 When the sun was setting, all those who had any that were sick with various diseases brought them to Him; and He laid His hands on every one of them and healed them.

41 And demons also came out of many, crying out and saying, "You are *the Christ, the Son of God!" And He, rebuking *them*, did not allow them to ᵀspeak, for they knew that He was the Christ.   Or *say that they knew*

Jesus Preaches in Galilee

42 ᴿNow when it was day, He departed and went into a deserted place. And the crowd sought Him and came to Him, and tried to keep Him from leaving them;   Mark 1:35-38

43 but He said to them, "I must preach the kingdom of God to the other cities also, because for this purpose I have been sent."

44 ᴿAnd He was preaching in the synagogues of *Galilee.   Matt. 4:23; 9:35

4:41 NU omits *the Christ*
4:44 NU *Judea*

7-G. Jesus Is Sovereign (Luke 4:31, 32)—When Jesus was rejected in Nazareth, "He went down to Capernaum, a city of Galilee, and was teaching them on the Sabbaths. And they were astonished at His teaching, for His word was with authority" (vv. 31, 32). Throughout His ministry, all that He did and taught was with total authority.

At the conclusion of the Sermon on the Mount, "the people were astonished at His teaching." Why were they so amazed? Because they heard the Messiah King deliver His kingdom manifesto. "He taught them as one having authority, and not as the scribes" (Matt. 7:28, 29, page 947). He did not derive His authority from the high priest, the Sanhedrin, the Pharisees, or the ancient rabbis, as the scribes did. His authority came from Himself, from His own divine nature.

On another occasion, while He was teaching in the temple, the chief priest and the Pharisees sent temple officers to arrest Him. But they returned without Jesus, explaining, "No man ever spoke like this Man!" (John 7:40-46, page 1061). Even the officers sent to arrest Jesus were captivated by His words, which were spoken with supreme authority.

His authority was based on truth. Jesus is the embodiment of truth (John 8:32, page 1063), declaring "I am the way, the truth, and the life" (John 14:6, page 1074). By contrast, Satan personifies all that is false and evil (John 8:44, page 1063). No wonder that during His earthly ministry He impressed people with the profound validity of His teaching. It rang simply, but deeply, *true*—because He is true.

In His resurrected body He appeared to His disciples on a mountain in Galilee, saying, "All authority has been given to Me in heaven and on earth" (Matt. 28:18, page 982). This means that He has all authority, is over all authority, and is over all the universe; Jesus is sovereign. He has this supreme authority because He is

(1) *Omniscient*. Peter said to Him, "Lord, You know all things; You know that I love You" (John 21:17, page 1084). Paul said of Jesus, "In whom are hidden all the treasures of wisdom and knowledge" (Col. 2:3, page 1203);

(2) *Omnipotent*. The book of Hebrews describes Him as "upholding all things by the word of His power" (Heb. 1:1-3, page 1236). This means that Jesus has ultimate power. He has all power in heaven and on earth. The word of His power sustains the universe (Col. 1:16, 17, page 1202);

(3) *Omnipresent*. In His deity He fills the universe. He promised to be with all believers always; He said, "Lo, I am with you always, even to the end of the age" (Matt. 28:20, page 982).

Only the almighty God is omniscient, omnipotent, and omnipresent. Both the Old Testament and the New Testament are filled with evidence for the deity of Christ.

See Master Outline 8, "The Deity of Christ: His Signs," page 24 for your next study.

Four Fishermen Called as Disciples

5 So it was, as the multitude pressed about Him to hear the word of God, that He stood by the Lake of Gennesaret,

2 and saw two boats standing by the lake; but the fishermen had gone from them and were washing *their* nets.

3 Then He got into one of the boats, which was Simon's, and asked him to put out a little from the land. And He ᴿsat down and taught the multitudes from the boat. John 8:2

4 When He had stopped speaking, He said to Simon, ᴿ"Launch out into the deep and let down your nets for a catch." John 21:6

5 But Simon answered and said to Him, "Master, we have toiled all night and caught ᴿnothing; nevertheless ᴿat Your word I will let down the net." John 21:3 • Ps. 33:9

6 And when they had done this, they caught a great number of fish, and their net was breaking.

7 So they signaled to *their* partners in the other boat to come and help them. And they came and filled both the boats, so that they began to sink.

8 When Simon Peter saw *it*, he fell down at Jesus' knees, saying, ᴿ"Depart from me, for I am a sinful man, O Lord!" 1 Kin. 17:18

9 For he and all who were with him were ᴿastonished at the catch of fish which they had taken; Mark 5:42; 10:24, 26

10 and so also *were* James and John, the sons of Zebedee, who were partners with Simon. And Jesus said to Simon, "Do not be afraid. From now on you will catch men."

11 So when they had brought their boats to land, they forsook all and followed Him.

Jesus Cleanses a Leper

12 And it happened when He was in a certain city, that behold, a man who was full of leprosy saw Jesus; and he fell on *his* face and ᵀimplored Him, saying, "Lord, if You are willing, You can make me clean." begged

13 Then He put out *His* hand and touched him, saying, "I am willing; be cleansed." ᴿImmediately the leprosy left him. John 5:9

14 And He charged him to tell no one, "But go and show yourself to the priest, and to be healed an offering for your cleansing, as a testimony to them, just as Moses commanded."

15 However, ᴿthe report went around concerning Him all the more; and ᴿgreat multitudes came together to hear, and to be healed by Him of their infirmities. Mark 1:45 • John 6:2

16 ᴿSo He Himself *often* withdrew into the wilderness and ᴿprayed. Luke 9:10 • Matt. 14:23

Jesus Forgives and Heals a Paralytic

17 Now it happened on a certain day, as He was teaching, that there were Pharisees and teachers of the law sitting by, who had come out of every town of Galilee, Judea, and Jerusalem. And the power of the Lord was *present* *to heal them.

18 Then behold, men brought on a bed a man who was paralyzed, whom they sought to bring in and lay before Him.

19 And when they could not find how they might bring him in, because of the crowd, they went up on the housetop and let him down with *his* bed through the tiling into the midst ᴿbefore Jesus. Matt. 15:30

20 When He saw their faith, He said to him, "Man, your sins are forgiven you."

21 ᴿAnd the scribes and the Pharisees began to reason, saying, "Who is this who speaks blasphemies? ᴿWho can forgive sins but God alone?" Mark 2:6, 7 • Is. 43:25

22 But when Jesus perceived their thoughts, He answered and said to them, "Why are you reasoning in your hearts?

23 "Which is easier, to say, 'Your sins are forgiven you,' or to say, 'Rise up and walk'?

24 "But that you may know that the Son of Man has power on earth to forgive sins"—He said to the man who was paralyzed, ᴿ"I say to you, arise, take up your bed, and go to your house." Luke 7:14

25 Immediately he rose up before them, took up what he had been lying on, and departed to his own house, glorifying God.

26 And they were all amazed, and they glorified God and were filled with fear, saying, "We have seen strange things today!"

Matthew the Tax Collector

27 After these things He went out and saw a tax collector named Levi, sitting at the tax office. And He said to him, "Follow Me."

28 So he left all, rose up, and followed Him.

29 ᴿThen Levi gave Him a great feast in his own house. And ᴿthere were a great number of tax collectors and others who sat down with them. Matt. 9:9, 10 • Luke 15:1

30 *And their scribes and the Pharisees ᵀcomplained against His disciples, saying, ᴿ"Why do You eat and drink with tax collectors and sinners?" grumbled • Luke 15:2

31 Jesus answered and said to them, "Those who are well have no need of a physician, but those who are sick.

32 ᴿ"I have not come to call *the* righteous, but sinners, to repentance." 1 Tim. 1:15

Jesus Is Questioned About Fasting

33 Then they said to Him, ᴿ"Why* do the disciples of John fast often and make prayers, and likewise those of the Pharisees, but Yours eat and drink?" Matt. 9:14

34 And He said to them, "Can you make the friends of the bridegroom fast while the ᴿbridegroom is with them? John 3:29

5:17 NU *with Him to heal*
5:30 NU *But the Pharisees and their scribes*
5:33 NU omits *Why do*, making the verse a statement

35 "But the days will come when the bridegroom will be taken away from them; then they will fast in those days."

36 ᴿThen He spoke a parable to them: "No one *puts a piece from a new garment on an old one; otherwise the new makes a tear, and also the piece that was *taken* out of the new does not match the old.   Mark 2:21, 22

37 "And no one puts new wine into old wineskins; or else the new wine will burst the wineskins and be spilled, and the wineskins will be ruined.

38 "But new wine must be put into new wineskins, *and both are preserved.

39 "And no one, having drunk old *wine*, *immediately desires new; for he says, 'The old is *better.' "

Jesus Is Lord of the Sabbath

6 Now ᴿit happened *on the second Sabbath after the first that He went through the grainfields. And His disciples plucked the heads of grain and ate *them*, rubbing *them* in their hands.   Matt. 12:1–8

2 And some of the Pharisees said to them, "Why are you doing ᴿwhat is not lawful to do on the Sabbath?"   Ex. 20:10

3 But Jesus answering them said, "Have you not even read this, ᴿwhat David did when he was hungry, he and those who were with him: 1 Sam. 21:6

4 "how he went into the house of God, took and ate the showbread, and also gave some to those with him, which is not lawful for any but the priests to eat?"

5 And He said to them, "The Son of Man is also Lord of the Sabbath."

Healing on the Sabbath

6 ᴿNow it happened on another Sabbath, also, that He entered the synagogue and taught. And a man was there whose right hand was withered.   Mark 3:1–6

7 So the scribes and Pharisees watched Him closely, whether He would ᴿheal on the Sabbath, that they might find an ᴿaccusation against Him.   Luke 13:14; 14:1–6 • Luke 20:20

8 But He knew their thoughts, and said to the man who had the withered hand, "Arise and stand here." And he arose and stood.

9 Then Jesus said to them, "I will ask you one thing: ᴿIs it lawful on the Sabbath to do good or to do evil, to save life or *to destroy?"   John 7:23

10 And when He had looked around at them all, He said to *the man, "Stretch out your hand." And he did so, and his hand was restored *as whole as the other.

11 But they were filled with rage, and discussed with one another what they might do to Jesus.

The Twelve Apostles

12 Now it came to pass in those days that He went out to the mountain to pray, and continued all night in ᴿprayer to God.   Mark 1:35

13 And when it was day, He called His disciples to *Himself*; and from them He chose twelve whom He also named apostles:

14 Simon, ᴿwhom He also named Peter, and Andrew his brother; James and John; Philip and Bartholomew;   John 1:42

15 Matthew and Thomas; James the *son* of Alphaeus, and Simon called the Zealot;

16 Judas ᴿthe *son* of James, and Judas Iscariot who also became a traitor.   Jude 1

Jesus Heals a Great Multitude

17 And He came down with them and stood on a level place with a crowd of His disciples ᴿand a great multitude of people from all Judea and Jerusalem, and from the seacoast of Tyre and Sidon, who came to hear Him and be healed of their diseases,   Mark 3:7, 8

18 as well as those who were tormented with unclean spirits. And they were healed.

19 And the whole multitude sought to ᴿtouch Him, for ᴿpower went out from Him and healed *them* all.   Mark 5:27, 28 • Luke 8:46

The Beatitudes

20 Then He lifted up His eyes toward His disciples, and said:

ᴿ"Blessed *are you* poor,   Matt. 5:3–12
    For yours is the kingdom of God.
21 Blessed *are you* who hunger now,
    For you shall ᵀfilled.   satisfied
ᴿBlessed *are you* who weep now,
    For you shall ᴿlaugh.   [Is. 61:3] • Ps. 126:5
22 Blessed are you when men hate you,
    And when they ᴿexclude you,
    And revile *you*, and cast out your
        name as evil,   [John 16:2]
    For the Son of Man's sake.
23 ᴿRejoice in that day and leap for joy!
    For indeed your reward *is* great in
        heaven,
    For ᴿin like manner their fathers did
        to the prophets.   James 1:2 • Acts 7:51

Jesus Pronounces Woes

24 "But woe to you ᴿwho are rich,
    For ᴿyou have received your
        consolation.   Luke 12:21 • Luke 16:25

5:36 NU *tears a piece from a new garment and puts it
    on an old one*
5:38 NU omits *and both are preserved*
5:39 NU omits *immediately* • NU *good*
6:1 NU *on a Sabbath that He went*
6:9 M *to kill*

6:10 NU, M *him*, • NU omits *as whole as the other*

25 ᴿWoe to you who are full,   [Is. 65:13]
    For you shall hunger.
    ᴿWoe to you who laugh now,   [Prov. 14:13]
    For you shall mourn and weep.
26 ᴿWoe *to you when *all men speak well
    of you,   [John 15:19]
    For so did their fathers to the false
    prophets.

Love Your Enemies

27 "But I say to you who hear: Love your enemies, do good to those who hate you,
28 "bless those who curse you, and ᴿpray for those who spitefully use you.   Acts 7:60
29 ᴿ"To him who strikes you on the one cheek, offer the other also. ᴿAnd from him who takes away your cloak, do not withhold your tunic either.   Matt. 5:39–42 • [1 Cor. 6:7]
30 ᴿ"Give to everyone who asks of you. And from him who takes away your goods do not ask them back.   Deut. 15:7, 8
31 ᴿ"And just as you want men to do to you, you also do to them likewise.   Matt. 7:12
32 ᴿ"But if you love those who love you, what credit is that to you? For even sinners love those who love them.   Matt. 5:45
33 "And if you do good to those who do good to you, what credit is that to you? For even sinners do the same.
34 ᴿ"And if you lend to those from whom you hope to receive back, what credit is that to you? For even sinners lend to sinners to receive as much back.   Matt. 5:42
35 "But ᴿlove your enemies, ᴿdo good, and ᴿlend, hoping for nothing in return; and your reward will be great, and you will be sons of the Most High. For He is kind to the unthankful and evil.   [Rom. 13:10] • Heb. 13:16 • Ps. 37:26
36 ᴿ"Therefore be merciful, just as your Father also is merciful.   Matt. 5:48

Do Not Judge

37 "Judge not, and you shall not be judged. Condemn not, and you shall not be condemned. Forgive, and you will be forgiven.
38 "Give, and it will be given to you: good measure, pressed down, shaken together, and running over will be put into your bosom. For ᴿwith the same measure that you use, it will be measured back to you."   James 2:13
39 And He spoke a parable to them: ᴿ"Can the blind lead the blind? Will they not both fall into the ditch?   Matt. 15:14; 23:16
40 ᴿ"A disciple is not above his teacher, but everyone who is perfectly trained will be like his teacher.   [John 13:16; 15:20]
41 ᴿ"And why do you look at the speck in your brother's eye, but do not perceive the plank in your own eye?   Matt. 7:3
42 "Or how can you say to your brother, 'Brother, let me remove the speck that is in

your eye,' when you yourself do not see the plank that is in your own eye? Hypocrite! First remove the plank from your own eye, and then you will see clearly to remove the speck that is in your brother's eye.

A Tree Is Known by Its Fruit

43 "For a good tree does not bear bad fruit, nor does a bad tree bear good fruit.
44 "For ᴿevery tree is known by its own fruit. For men do not gather figs from thorns, nor do they gather grapes from a bramble bush.   Matt. 12:33
45 ᴿ"A good man out of the good treasure of his heart brings forth good; and an evil man out of the evil *treasure of his heart brings forth evil. For out of the abundance of the heart his mouth speaks.   Matt. 12:34, 35

Build on the Rock

46 ᴿ"But why do you call Me 'Lord, Lord,' and not do the things which I say?   Mal. 1:6
47 ᴿ"Whoever comes to Me, and hears My sayings and does them, I will show you whom he is like: James 1:22–25
48 "He is like a man building a house, who dug deep and laid the foundation on the rock. And when the flood arose, the stream beat vehemently against that house, and could not shake it, for it was *founded on the rock.
49 "But he who heard and did nothing is like a man who built a house on the earth without a foundation, against which the stream beat vehemently; and immediately it *fell. And the ruin of that house was great."

Jesus Heals a Centurion's Servant

7 Now when He concluded all His sayings in the hearing of the people, He ᴿentered Capernaum.   Matt. 8:5–13
2 And a certain centurion's servant, who was dear to him, was sick and ready to die.
3 So when he heard about Jesus, he sent elders of the Jews to Him, pleading with Him to come and heal his servant.
4 And when they came to Jesus, they begged Him earnestly, saying that the one for whom He should do this was deserving,
5 "for he loves our nation, and has built us a synagogue."
6 Then Jesus went with them. And when He was already not far from the house, the centurion sent friends to Him, saying to Him, "Lord, do not trouble Yourself, for I am not worthy that You should enter under my roof.
7 "Therefore I did not even think myself worthy to come to You. But ᴿsay the word, and my servant will be healed.   Ps. 33:9; 107:20
8 "For I also am a man placed under ᴿauthority, having soldiers under me. And I

6:45 NU omits treasure of his heart
6:48 NU well built.
6:49 NU collapsed

6:26 NU, M omit to you • M omits all

say to one, 'Go,' and he goes; and to another, 'Come,' and he comes; and to my servant, 'Do this,' and he does *it*."   [Mark 13:34]

9 When Jesus heard these things, He marveled at him, and turned around and said to the crowd that followed Him, "I say to you, I have not found such great faith, not even in Israel!"

10 And those who were sent, returning to the house, found the servant well *who had been sick.

Jesus Raises the Son of the Widow of Nain

11 Now it happened, the day after, *that* He went into a city called Nain; and many of His disciples went with Him, and a large crowd.

12 And when He came near the gate of the city, behold, a dead man was being carried out, the only son of his mother; and she was a widow. And a large crowd from the city was with her.

13 When the Lord saw her, He had ᴿcompassion on her and said to her, ᴿ"Do not weep."   John 11:35 · Luke 8:52

14 Then He came and touched the open coffin, and those who carried *him* stood still. And He said, "Young man, I say to you, ᴿarise."   Acts 9:40

15 So he who was dead ᴿsat up and began to speak. And He ᴿpresented him to his mother.   John 11:44 · 2 Kin. 4:36

16 Then fear ᵀcame upon all, and they glorified God, saying, ᴿ"A great prophet has risen up among us"; and, ᴿ"God has visited His people."   seized them all · Luke 24:19 · Luke 1:68

17 And this report about Him went throughout all Judea and all the surrounding region.

John the Baptist Sends Messengers to Jesus

18 ᴿThen the disciples of John reported to him concerning all these things.   Matt. 11:2-19

19 And John, calling two of his disciples to *him*, sent *them* to *Jesus, saying, "Are You ᴿthe Coming One, or ᵀdo we look for another?"   [Zech. 9:9] · should we expect

20 When the men had come to Him, they said, "John the Baptist has sent us to You, saying, 'Are You the Coming One, or do we look for another?'"

21 And that very hour He cured many of ᵀinfirmities, afflictions, and evil spirits; and to many blind He gave sight.   illnesses

22 Jesus answered and said to them, "Go and tell John the things you have seen and heard: that ᴿthe blind see, *the* lame walk, *the* lepers are cleansed, *the* deaf hear, *the* dead are raised, *the* poor have the gospel preached to them.   Is. 35:5; 61:1

23 "And ᴿblessed is *he* who is not ᵀoffended because of Me."   Ps. 2:12 · caused to stumble

24 ᴿWhen the messengers of John had departed, He began to speak to the multitudes concerning John: "What did you go out into the wilderness to see? A reed shaken by the wind?   Matt. 11:7

25 "But what did you go out to see? A man clothed in soft garments? Indeed those who are gorgeously appareled and live in luxury are in kings' courts.

26 "But what did you go out to see? A prophet? Yes, I say to you, and more than a prophet.

27 "This is *he* of whom it is written:

> ᴿ'*Behold, I send My messenger before Your face,*
> *Who will prepare Your way before You.*'   Mal. 3:1

28 "For I say to you, among those born of women there is *not a greater prophet than John the Baptist; but he who is least in the kingdom of God is greater than he."

29 And when all the people heard *Him*, even the tax collectors justified God, having been baptized with the baptism of John.

30 But the Pharisees and lawyers rejected ᴿthe will of God for themselves, not having been baptized by him.   Acts 20:27

31 *And the Lord said, ᴿ"To what then shall I liken the men of this generation, and what are they like?   Matt. 11:16

32 "They are like children sitting in the marketplace and calling to one another, saying:

> 'We played the flute for you,
> And you did not dance;
> We mourned to you,
> And you did not weep.'

33 "For ᴿJohn the Baptist came ᴿneither eating bread nor drinking wine, and you say, 'He has a demon.'   Matt. 3:1 · Luke 1:15

34 "The Son of Man has come ᴿeating and drinking, and you say, 'Look, a glutton and a ᵀwinebibber, a friend of tax collectors and sinners!'   Luke 15:2 · An excessive drinker

35 ᴿ"But wisdom is justified by all her children."   Matt. 11:19

A Sinful Woman Forgiven

36 ᴿThen one of the Pharisees asked Him to eat with him. And He went to the Pharisee's house, and sat down to eat.   John 11:2

37 And behold, a woman in the city who was a sinner, when she knew that *Jesus* sat at the table in the Pharisee's house, brought an alabaster flask of fragrant oil,

---

7:10 NU omits *who had been sick*
7:19 NU *the Lord*

7:28 NU *none greater than John;*
7:31 NU, M omit *And the Lord said*

38 and stood at His feet behind *Him* weeping; and she began to wash His feet with her tears, and wiped *them* with the hair of her head; and she kissed His feet and anointed *them* with the fragrant oil.

39 Now when the Pharisee who had invited Him saw *this,* he spoke to himself, saying, "This man, if He were a prophet, would know who and what manner of woman *this is* who is touching Him, for she is a sinner."

40 And Jesus answered and said to him, "Simon, I have something to say to you." So he said, "Teacher, say it."

41 "There was a certain creditor who had two debtors. One owed ᵀfive hundred ᴿdenarii, and the other ᵀfifty. $16,000 · Matt. 18:28 · $1,600

42 "And when they had nothing with which to repay, he freely forgave them both. Tell Me, therefore, which of them will love him more?"

43 Simon answered and said, "I suppose the *one* whom he forgave more." And He said to him, "You have rightly judged."

44 Then He turned to the woman and said to Simon, "Do you see this woman? I entered your house; you gave Me no ᴿwater for My feet, but she has washed My feet with her tears, and wiped *them* with the hair of her head.   Gen. 18:4; 19:2; 43:24

45 "You gave Me no ᴿkiss, but this woman has not ceased to kiss My feet since the time I came in.   Rom. 16:16

46 ᴿ"You did not anoint My head with oil, but this woman has anointed My feet with fragrant oil.   Ps. 23:5

47 ᴿ"Therefore I say to you, her sins, *which are* many, are forgiven, for she loved much. But to whom little is forgiven, *the same* loves little."   [1 Tim. 1:14]

48 Then He said to her, ᴿ"Your sins are forgiven."   Matt. 9:2

49 And those who sat at the table with Him began to say to themselves, ᴿ"Who is this who even forgives sins?"   Luke 5:21

50 Then He said to the woman, ᴿ"Your faith has saved you. Go in peace."   Matt. 9:22

Many Women Minister to Jesus

8 Now it came to pass, afterward, that He went through every city and village, preaching and ᵀbringing the glad tidings of the kingdom of God. And the twelve *were* with Him,   *proclaiming the good news*

2 and ᴿcertain women who had been healed of evil spirits and ᵀinfirmities—Mary called Magdalene, ᴿout of whom had come seven demons,   Matt. 27:55 · *sicknesses* · Mark 16:9

3 and Joanna the wife of Chuza, Herod's steward, and Susanna, and many others who provided for *Him from their substance.

8:3 NU, M *them*

The Parable of the Sower

4 ᴿAnd when a great multitude had gathered, and they had come to Him from every city, He spoke by a parable: Mark 4:1-9

5 "A sower went out to sow his seed. And as he sowed, some fell by the wayside; and it was trampled down, and the birds of the air devoured it.

6 "Some fell on rock; and as soon as it sprang up, it withered away because it lacked moisture.

7 "And some fell among thorns, and the thorns sprang up with it and choked it.

8 "But others fell on good ground, sprang up, and yielded ᵀa crop a hundredfold." When He had said these things He cried, "He who has ears to hear, let him hear!"   *fruit*

The Purpose of Parables

9 ᴿThen His disciples asked Him, saying, "What does this parable mean?"   Matt. 13:10-23

10 And He said, "To you it has been given to know the mysteries of the kingdom of God, but to the rest *it is given* in parables, that

> ᴿ'Seeing they may not see,   Is. 6:9
> And hearing they may not understand.'

The Parable of the Sower Explained

11 ᴿ"Now the parable is this: The seed is the ᴿword of God.   [1 Pet. 1:23] · Luke 5:1; 11:28

12 "Those by the wayside are the ones who hear; then the devil comes and takes away the word out of their hearts, lest they should believe and be saved.

13 "But the ones on the rock *are those* who, when they hear, receive the word with joy; and these have no root, who believe for a while and in time of temptation fall away.

14 "Now the ones *that* fell among thorns are those who, when they have heard, go out and are choked with cares, riches, and pleasures of life, and bring no fruit to maturity.

15 "But the ones *that* fell on the good ground are those who, having heard the word with a noble and good heart, keep *it* and bear fruit with ᴿpatience.ᵀ   [Heb. 10:36-39] · *endurance*

The Parable of the Revealed Light

16 ᴿ"No one, when he has lit a lamp, covers it with a vessel or puts *it* under a bed, but sets *it* on a lampstand, that those who enter may see the ᴿlight.   Luke 11:33 · Matt. 5:14

17 "For nothing is secret that will not be ᴿrevealed, nor *anything* hidden that will not be known and come to light.   [2 Cor. 5:10]

18 "Therefore take heed how you hear. For whoever has, to him *more* will be given; and whoever does not have, even what he seems to have will be taken from him."

Jesus' Mother and Brothers Come to Him

19 ᴿThen His mother and brothers came to Him, and could not approach Him because of the crowd.   Mark 3:31-35

20 And it was told Him by some, who said, "Your mother and Your brothers are standing outside, desiring to see You."

21 But He answered and said to them, "My mother and My brothers are these who hear the word of God and do it."

Wind and Wave Obey Jesus

22 Now it happened, on a certain day, that He got into a boat with His disciples. And He said to them, "Let us cross over to the other side of the lake." And they launched out.

23 But as they sailed He fell asleep. And a windstorm came down on the lake, and they were filling with water, and were in ᵀjeopardy.   danger

24 And they came to Him and awoke Him, saying, "Master, Master, we are perishing!" Then He arose and rebuked the wind and the raging of the water. And they ceased, and there was a calm.

25 But He said to them, ᴿ"Where is your faith?" And they were afraid, and marveled, saying to one another, ᴿ"Who can this be? For He commands even the winds and water, and they obey Him!"   Luke 9:41 • Luke 4:36; 5:26

A Demon-Possessed Man Healed

26 Then they sailed to the country of the *Gadarenes, which is opposite Galilee.

27 And when He stepped out on the land, there met Him a certain man from the city who had demons *for a long time. And he wore no clothes, nor did he live in a house but in the tombs.

28 When he saw Jesus, he ᴿcried out, fell down before Him, and with a loud voice said, ᴿ"What have I to do with ᴿYou, Jesus, Son of the Most High God? I beg You, do not torment me!"   Mark 1:26; 9:26 • Mark 1:23, 24 • Luke 4:41

29 For He had commanded the unclean spirit to come out of the man. For it had often seized him, and he was kept under guard, bound with chains and shackles; and he broke the bonds and was driven by the demon into the wilderness.

30 Jesus asked him, saying, "What is your name?" And he said, "Legion," because many demons had entered him.

31 And they begged Him that He would not command them to go out into the abyss.

32 Now a herd of many ᴿswine was feeding there on the mountain. So they begged Him that He would permit them to enter them. And He permitted them.   Lev. 11:7

33 Then the demons went out of the man and entered the swine, and the herd ran violently down the steep place into the lake and drowned.

34 When those who fed them saw what had happened, they fled and told it in the city and in the country.

35 Then they went out to see what had happened, and came to Jesus, and found the man from whom the demons had departed, sitting at the feet of Jesus, clothed and in his right mind. And they were afraid.

36 They also who had seen it told them by what means he who had been demon-possessed was ᵀhealed.   delivered

37 Then the whole multitude of the surrounding region of the *Gadarenes ᴿasked Him to ᴿdepart from them, for they were seized with great ᴿfear. And He got into the boat and returned.   Luke 4:34 • Acts 16:39 • Luke 5:26

38 Now the man from whom the demons had departed begged Him that he might be with Him. But Jesus sent him away, saying,

39 "Return to your own house, and tell what great things God has done for you." And he went his way and proclaimed throughout the whole city what great things Jesus had done for him.

A Girl Restored to Life and a Woman Healed

40 So it was, when Jesus returned, that the multitude welcomed Him, for they were all waiting for Him.

41 ᴿAnd behold, there came a man named Jairus, and he was a ruler of the synagogue. And he fell down at Jesus' feet and begged Him to come to his house,   Mark 5:22-43

42 for he had an only daughter about twelve years of age, and she was dying. But as He went, the multitudes thronged Him.

43 ᴿNow a woman, having a ᴿflow of blood for twelve years, who had spent all her livelihood on physicians and could not be healed by any,   Matt. 9:20 • Luke 15:19-22

44 came from behind and ᴿtouched the border of His garment. And immediately her flow of blood stopped.   Mark 6:56

45 And Jesus said, "Who touched Me?" When all denied it, Peter *and those with him said, "Master, the multitudes throng and press You, *and You say, 'Who touched Me?' "

46 But Jesus said, "Somebody touched Me, for I perceived power going out from Me."

47 Now when the woman saw that she was not hidden, she came trembling; and falling down before Him, she declared to Him in the presence of all the people the reason she had

8:26 NU Gerasenes
8:27 NU and for a long time wore no clothes

8:37 NU Gerasenes
8:45 NU omits and those with him • NU omits the rest of v. 45.

touched Him and how she was healed immediately.

48 And He said to her, "Daughter, *be of good cheer; ᴿyour faith has made you well. ᴿGo in peace."   Luke 7:50 · John 8:11

49 ᴿWhile He was still speaking, someone came from the ruler of the synagogue's *house*, saying to him, "Your daughter is dead. Do not trouble the *Teacher."   Mark 5:35

50 But when Jesus heard *it*, He answered him, saying, "Do not be afraid; ᴿonly believe, and she will be made well."   [Mark 11:22-24]

51 When He came into the house, He permitted no one to go *in except Peter, *James, and John, and the father and mother of the girl.

52 Now all wept and mourned for her; but He said, ᴿ"Do not weep; she is not dead, ᴿbut sleeping."   Luke 7:13 · [John 11:11, 13]

53 And they ridiculed Him, knowing that she was dead.

54 But He *put them all outside, took her by the hand and called, saying, "Little girl, arise."

55 Then her spirit returned, and she arose immediately. And He commanded that she be given *something* to eat.

56 And her parents were astonished, but ᴿHe charged them to tell no one what had happened.   Matt. 8:4; 9:30

Sending Out the Twelve

9 Then He called His twelve disciples together and gave them power and authority over all demons, and to cure diseases.

2 ᴿHe sent them to preach the kingdom of God and to heal the sick.   Matt. 10:7, 8

3 ᴿAnd He said to them, "Take nothing for the journey, neither staffs nor bag nor bread nor money; and do not have two tunics apiece.   Luke 10:4-12; 22:35

4 ᴿ"Whatever house you enter, stay there, and from there depart.   Mark 6:10

5 ᴿ"And whoever will not receive you, when you go out of that city, ᴿshake off the very dust from your feet as a testimony against them."   Matt. 10:14 · Acts 13:51

6 ᴿSo they departed and went through the towns, preaching the gospel and healing everywhere.   Mark 6:12

Herod Seeks to See Jesus

7 ᴿNow Herod the tetrarch heard of all that was done by Him; and he was perplexed, because it was said by some that John had risen from the dead,   Matt. 14:1, 2

8 and by some that Elijah had appeared, and by others that one of the old prophets had risen again.

9 Herod said, "John I have beheaded, but who is this of whom I hear such things?" ᴿSo he sought to see Him.   Luke 23:8

Feeding the Five Thousand

10 ᴿAnd the apostles, when they had returned, told Him all that they had done. ᴿThen He took them and went aside privately into a deserted place belonging to the city called Bethsaida.   Mark 6:30 · Matt. 14:13

11 But when the multitudes knew *it*, they followed Him; and He received them and spoke to them about the kingdom of God, and healed those who had need of healing.

12 ᴿWhen the day began to wear away, the twelve came and said to Him, "Send the multitude away, that they may go into the surrounding towns and country, and lodge and get provisions; for we are in a deserted place here."   John 6:1, 5

13 But He said to them, "You give them something to eat." And they said, "We have no more than five loaves and two fish, unless we go and buy food for all these people."

14 For there were about five thousand men. Then He said to His disciples, "Make them sit down in groups of fifty."

15 And they did so, and made them all sit down.

16 Then He took the five loaves and the two fish, and looking up to heaven, He blessed and broke *them*, and gave *them* to the disciples to set before the multitude.

17 So they all ate and were ᵀfilled, and twelve baskets of the leftover fragments were taken up by them.   satisfied

Peter Confesses Jesus as the Christ

18 ᴿAnd it happened, as He was alone praying, *that* His disciples joined Him, and He asked them, saying, "Who do the crowds say that I am?"   Matt. 16:13-16

19 So they answered and said, "John the Baptist, but some *say* Elijah; and others *say* that one of the old prophets has risen again."

20 He said to them, "But who do you say that I am?" ᴿPeter answered and said, "The Christ of God."   John 6:68, 69

Jesus Predicts His Death and Resurrection

21 And He strictly warned and commanded them to tell this to no one,

22 saying, ᴿ"The Son of Man must suffer many things, and be rejected by the elders and chief priests and scribes, and be killed, and be raised the third day."   John 19:7

Take Up the Cross and Follow Him

23 ᴿThen He said to *them* all, "If anyone desires to come after Me, let him deny himself, and take up his cross *daily, and follow Me.   Matt. 10:38; 16:24

8:48 NU omits *be of good cheer*
8:49 NU adds *anymore*
8:51 NU adds *with Him* • NU, M *Peter, John, and James*
8:54 NU omits *put them all outside*

9:23 M omits *daily*

24 ᴿ"For whoever desires to save his life will lose it, but whoever loses his life for My sake will save it.   [John 12:25]

25 ᴿ"For what profit is it to a man if he gains the whole world, and is himself destroyed or lost?   Mark 8:36

26 "For whoever is ashamed of Me and My words, of him the Son of Man will be ashamed when He comes in His own glory, and in His Father's, and of the holy angels.

Jesus Transfigured on the Mount

27 ᴿ"But I tell you truly, there are some standing here who shall not taste death till they see the kingdom of God."   Acts 7:55, 56

28 ᴿNow it came to pass, about eight days after these sayings, that He took Peter, John, and James and went up on the mountain to pray.   Mark 9:2-8

29 As He prayed, the appearance of His face was altered, and His robe became white and glistening.

30 And behold, two men talked with Him, who were Moses and ᴿElijah,   2 Kin. 2:1-11

31 who appeared in glory and spoke of His ᵀdecease which He was about to accomplish at Jerusalem.   death, lit. departure

32 But Peter and those with him ᴿwere heavy with sleep; and when they were fully awake, they saw His glory and the two men who stood with Him.   Dan. 8:18; 10:9

33 Then it happened, as they were parting from Him, that Peter said to Jesus, "Master, it is good for us to be here; and let us make three ᵀtabernacles: one for You, one for Moses, and one for Elijah"—not knowing what he said.   tents

34 While he was saying this, a cloud came and overshadowed them; and they were fearful as they entered the ᴿcloud.   Ex. 13:21

35 And a voice came out of the cloud, saying, ᴿ"This is *My beloved Son. Hear Him!"   Ps. 2:7; Is. 42:1; Matt. 3:17

36 When the voice had ceased, Jesus was found alone. ᴿBut they kept quiet, and told no one in those days any of the things they had seen.   Matt. 17:9

A Boy Is Healed

37 ᴿNow it happened on the next day, when they had come down from the mountain, that a great multitude met Him.   Mark 9:14-27

38 Suddenly a man from the multitude cried out, saying, "Teacher, I implore You, look on my son, for he is my only child.

39 "And behold, a spirit seizes him, and he suddenly cries out; it convulses him so that he foams at the mouth; and it departs from him with great difficulty, bruising him.

40 "So I implored Your disciples to cast it out, but they could not."

41 Then Jesus answered and said, "O ᵀfaithless and perverse generation, how long shall I be with you and ᵀbear with you? Bring your son here."   unbelieving · put up with

42 And as he was still coming, the demon threw him down and convulsed him. Then Jesus rebuked the unclean spirit, healed the child, and gave him back to his father.

Jesus Again Predicts His Death

43 And they were all amazed at the majesty of God. But while everyone marveled at all the things which Jesus did, He said to His disciples,

44 "Let these words sink down into your ears, for the Son of Man is about to be ᴿbetrayed into the hands of men."   Luke 22:54

45 ᴿBut they did not understand this saying, and it was hidden from them so that they did not perceive it; and they were afraid to ask Him about this saying.   Mark 9:32

Who Is the Greatest?

46 ᴿThen a dispute arose among them as to which of them would be greatest.   Matt. 18:1-5

47 And Jesus, ᴿperceiving the thought of their heart, took a ᴿlittle child and set him by Him,   Matt. 9:4 · Luke 18:17

48 and said to them, "Whoever receives this little child in My name receives Me; and ᴿwhoever receives Me ᴿreceives Him who sent Me. ᴿFor he who is least among you all will be great."   John 12:44 · John 13:20 · Eph. 3:8

Jesus Forbids Sectarianism

49 ᴿNow John answered and said, "Master, we saw someone casting out demons in Your name, and we forbade him because he does not follow with us."   Mark 9:38-40

50 But Jesus said to him, "Do not forbid him, for he who is not against *us is on *our side."

A Samaritan Village Rejects the Savior

51 Now it came to pass, when the time had come for Him to be received up, that He steadfastly set His face to go to Jerusalem,

52 and sent messengers before His face. And as they went, they entered a village of the Samaritans, to prepare for Him.

53 But they did not receive Him, because His face was set for the journey to Jerusalem.

54 And when His disciples James and John saw this, they said, "Lord, do You want us to command fire to come down from heaven and consume them, *just as Elijah did?"

55 But He turned and rebuked them, *and said, "You do not know what manner of ᴿspirit you are of.   [2 Tim. 1:7]

9:50 NU against you is on your side • NU your
9:54 NU omits just as Elijah did
9:55 NU omits the rest of v. 55.

9:35 NU My Son, My Chosen One

56 *"For ᴿthe Son of Man did not come to destroy men's lives but to save *them.*" And they went to another village.   John 3:17; 12:47

The Cost of Discipleship

57 Now it happened as they journeyed on the road, *that* someone said to Him, "Lord, I will follow You wherever You go."
58 And Jesus said to him, "Foxes have holes and birds of the air *have* nests, but the Son of Man has nowhere to lay *His* head."
59 ᴿThen He said to another, "Follow Me." But he said, "Lord, let me first go and bury my father."   Matt. 8:21, 22
60 Jesus said to him, "Let the dead bury their own dead, but you go and preach the kingdom of God."
61 And another also said, "Lord, ᴿI will follow You, but let me first go *and* bid them farewell who are at my house."   1 Kin. 19:20
62 But Jesus said to him, "No one, having put his hand to the plow, and looking back, is ᴿfit for the kingdom of God."   2 Tim. 4:10

The Seventy Sent Out

10 After these things the Lord appointed *seventy others also, and sent them two by two before His face into every city and place where He Himself was about to go.
2 Then He said to them, ᴿ"The harvest truly *is* great, but the laborers *are* few; therefore ᴿpray the Lord of the harvest to send out laborers into His harvest.   John 4:35 • 2 Thess. 3:1
3 "Go your way; ᴿbehold, I send you out as lambs among wolves.   Matt. 10:16
4 "Carry neither money bag, knapsack, nor sandals; and greet no one along the road.
5 ᴿ"But whatever house you enter, first say, 'Peace to this house.'   Matt. 10:12
6 "And if a son of peace is there, your peace will rest on it; if not, it will return to you.
7 ᴿ"And remain in the same house, eating and drinking such things as they give, for ᴿthe laborer is worthy of his wages. Do not go from house to house.   Matt. 10:11 • 1 Tim. 5:18
8 "Whatever city you enter, and they receive you, eat such things as are set before you.
9 ᴿ"And heal the sick there, and say to them, ᴿ'The kingdom of God has come near to you.'   Mark 3:15 • Matt. 3:2; 10:7
10 "But whatever city you enter, and they do not receive you, go out into its streets and say,
11 ᴿ'The very dust of your city which clings to *us* we wipe off against you. Nevertheless know this, that the kingdom of God has come near you.'   Acts 13:51

12 *"But I say to you that ᴿit will be more tolerable in that Day for Sodom than for that city.   Matt. 10:15; 11:24

Woe to the Impenitent Cities

13 "Woe to you, Chorazin! Woe to you, Bethsaida! For if the mighty works which were done in you had been done in Tyre and Sidon, they would have repented long ago, sitting in sackcloth and ashes.
14 "But it will be more tolerable for Tyre and Sidon at the judgment than for you.
15 ᴿ"And you, Capernaum, *who are ᴿexalted to heaven, ᴿwill be brought down to Hades.   Matt. 11:23 • Is. 14:13-15 • Ezek. 26:20
16 "He who hears you hears Me, he who rejects you rejects Me, and ᴿhe who rejects Me rejects Him who sent Me."   John 5:23

The Seventy Return with Joy

17 Then ᴿthe *seventy returned with joy, saying, "Lord, even the demons are subject to us in Your name."   Luke 10:1
18 And He said to them, ᴿ"I saw Satan fall like lightning from heaven.   John 12:31
19 "Behold, ᴿI give you the authority to trample on serpents and scorpions, and over all the power of the enemy, and nothing shall by any means hurt you.   Mark 16:18
20 "Nevertheless do not rejoice in this, that the spirits are subject to you, but *rather rejoice because ᴿyour names are written in heaven."   Is. 4:3

Jesus Rejoices in the Spirit

21 ᴿIn that hour Jesus rejoiced in the Spirit and said, "I thank You, Father, Lord of heaven and earth, that You have hidden these things from *the* wise and prudent and revealed them to babes. Even so, Father, for so it seemed good in Your sight.   Matt. 11:25-27
22 *"All things have been delivered to Me by My Father, and ᴿno one knows who the Son is except the Father, and who the Father is except the Son, and *the one* to whom the Son wills to reveal *Him.*"   [John 1:18; 6:44, 46]
23 And He turned to *His* disciples and said privately, ᴿ"Blessed *are* the eyes which see the things you see;   Matt. 13:16, 17
24 "for I tell you ᴿthat many prophets and kings have desired to see what you see, and have not seen *it,* and to hear what you hear, and have not heard *it.*"   1 Pet. 1:10, 11

The Parable of the Good Samaritan

25 And behold, a certain ᵀlawyer stood up and tested Him, saying, "Teacher, what shall I do to inherit eternal life?"   *expert in the law*

9:56 NU omits *For the Son of Man did not come to destroy men's lives but to save them.*
10:1 NU *seventy-two others*
10:11 NU *our feet*

10:12 NU, M omit *But*
10:15 NU *will you be exalted to heaven? You will be thrust down to Hades!*
10:17 NU *seventy-two*
10:20 NU, M omit *rather*
10:22 M *And turning to the disciples He said, "All*

26 He said to him, "What is written in the law? What is your reading *of it?*"

27 So he answered and said, ^R"'*You shall love the LORD your God with all your heart, with all your soul, with all your strength, and with all your mind,'* and ^R'*your neighbor as yourself.'*"   Deut. 6:5 · Lev. 19:18

28 And He said to him, "You have answered rightly; do this and you will live."

29 But he, wanting to ^Rjustify himself, said to Jesus, "And who is my neighbor?"   Luke 16:15

30 Then Jesus answered and said: "A certain *man* went down from Jerusalem to Jericho, and fell among ^Tthieves, who stripped him of his clothing, wounded *him*, and departed, leaving *him* half dead.   robbers

31 "Now by chance a certain priest came down that road. And when he saw him, ^Rhe passed by on the other side.   Ps. 38:11

32 "Likewise a Levite, when he arrived at the place, came and looked, and passed by on the other side.

33 "But a certain Samaritan, as he journeyed, came where he was. And when he saw him, he had compassion.

34 "So he went to *him* and bandaged his wounds, pouring on oil and wine; and he set him on his own animal, brought him to an inn, and took care of him.

35 "On the next day, *when he departed, he took out ^Ttwo ^Rdenarii, gave *them* to the innkeeper, and said to him, 'Take care of him; and whatever more you spend, when I come again, I will repay you.'   2 days' wages · Matt. 20:2

36 "So which of these three do you think was neighbor to him who fell among the thieves?"

37 And he said, "He who showed mercy on him." Then Jesus said to him, ^R"Go and do likewise."   Prov. 14:21

Mary and Martha Worship and Serve

38 Now it happened as they went that He entered a certain village; and a certain

10:35 NU omits *when he departed*

woman named ^RMartha welcomed Him into her house.   John 11:1; 12:2, 3

39 And she had a sister called Mary, who also sat at *Jesus' feet and heard His word.

40 But Martha was distracted with much serving, and she approached Him and said, "Lord, do You not care that my sister has left me to serve alone? Therefore tell her to help me."

41 And *Jesus answered and said to her, "Martha, Martha, you are worried and troubled about many things.

42 "But ^Rone thing is needed, and Mary has chosen that good part, which will not be taken away from her."   [Ps. 27:4]

The Model Prayer

30-A. Pray As the Lord Prayed   ▼

11 Now it came to pass, as He was praying in a certain place, when He ceased, *that* one of His disciples said to Him, "Lord, teach us to pray, as John also taught his disciples."

2 So He said to them, "When you pray, say:

^ROur* Father *in heaven,   Matt. 6:9–13
Hallowed be Your name.
Your kingdom come.
*Your will be done
On earth as *it is* in heaven.

3 Give us day by day our daily bread.

4 And ^Rforgive us our sins,   [Eph. 4:32]
For we also forgive everyone who is
    indebted to us.
And do not lead us into temptation,
*But deliver us from the evil one."   ▲

10:39 NU *the Lord's*
10:41 NU *the Lord*
11:2 NU omits *Our* • NU omits *in heaven* • NU omits the rest of v. 2.
11:4 NU omits *But deliver us from the evil one*

30-A. Pray As the Lord Prayed (Luke 11:1–4)—Our Lord's disciples asked Him, "Lord, teach us to pray, as John also taught his disciples" (v. 1). In the ancient world of the Old Testament, everyone did not pray as freely as we do nowadays. In fact, the prevailing opinion was that only a great rabbi could compose the words of a new prayer. Thus, many of the common people would say aloud the great prayers of the rabbis. John the Baptist had taught his disciples to pray; our Lord's disciples asked Him to do the same. However, He did more than give them a beautiful prayer to recite. He provided them with a model to guide them in their daily prayers. This model prayer contains numerous lessons, including the following:

(1) "As He was praying" (v. 1). Christ is our example of a person of prayer. Not only did He show others how to pray, He first set the example. This, in itself, made others desire to follow His example.

(2) "Our Father in heaven" (v. 2). True prayer depends upon our belonging to God's family, through faith in Christ. For example, David began his "shepherd's prayer" with the words, "The LORD is my shepherd," with the word "my" showing the personal relationship that existed by faith between David and the Lord (Ps. 23:1, page 524).

(3) "Hallowed be Your name. Your kingdom come. Your will be done on earth as it is in heaven" (v. 2). Thus at the outset we honor the holiness of God and submit ourselves to His will. Indeed, we should desire

(Point 30-A continued on next page)

A Friend Comes at Midnight

5 And He said to them, "Which of you shall have a friend, and go to him at midnight and say to him, 'Friend, lend me three loaves;

6 'for a friend of mine has come to me on his journey, and I have nothing to set before him';

7 "and he will answer from within and say, 'Do not trouble me; the door is now shut, and my children are with me in bed; I cannot rise and give to you'?

8 "I say to you, ʳthough he will not rise and give to him because he is his friend, yet because of his persistence he will rise and give him as many as he needs. [Luke 18:1-5]

Keep Asking, Seeking, Knocking

9 ᴿ"So I say to you, ask, and it will be given to you; ᴿseek, and you will find; knock, and it will be opened to you. [John 15:7] · Is. 55:6

10 "For everyone who asks receives, and he who seeks finds, and to him who knocks it will be opened.

11 ᴿ"If a son asks for *bread from any father among you, will he give him a stone? Or if he asks for a fish, will he give him a serpent instead of a fish? Matt. 7:9

12 "Or if he asks for an egg, will he offer him a scorpion?

13 "If you then, being evil, know how to give ᴿgood gifts to your children, how much more will *your* heavenly Father give the Holy Spirit to those who ask Him!" James 1:17

A House Divided Cannot Stand

14 ᴿAnd He was casting out a demon, and it was mute. So it was, when the demon had gone out, that the mute spoke; and the multitudes marveled. Matt. 9:32-34; 12:22, 24

15 But some of them said, ᴿ"He casts out demons by *Beelzebub, the ruler of the demons." Matt. 9:34; 12:24

11:11 NU omits *bread from any father among you, will he give him a stone? Or if he asks for*
11:15 NU, M *Beelzebul.*

16 Others, testing *Him*, ᴿsought from Him a sign from heaven. Matt. 12:38; 16:1

17 But ᴿHe, knowing their thoughts, said to them: "Every kingdom divided against itself is brought to desolation, and a house *divided* against a house falls. John 2:25

18 "If Satan also is divided against himself, how will his kingdom stand? Because you say I cast out demons by Beelzebub.

19 "And if I cast out demons by Beelzebub, by whom do your sons cast *them* out? Therefore they will be your judges.

20 "But if I cast out demons ᴿwith the finger of God, surely the kingdom of God has come upon you. Ex. 8:19

21 "When a strong man, fully armed, guards his own palace, his goods are in peace.

22 "But ᴿwhen a stronger than he comes upon him and overcomes him, he takes from him all his armor in which he trusted, and divides his ᵀspoils. [Is. 53:12] · *plunder*

23 "He who is not with Me is against Me, and he who does not gather with Me scatters.

An Unclean Spirit Returns

24 ᴿ"When an unclean spirit goes out of a man, he goes through dry places, seeking rest; and finding none, he says, 'I will return to my house from which I came.' Matt. 12:43-45

25 "And when he comes, he finds *it* swept and put in order.

26 "Then he goes and takes with *him* seven other spirits more wicked than himself, and they enter and dwell there; and ᴿthe last *state* of that man is worse than the first." [2 Pet. 2:20]

Keeping the Word

27 And it happened, as He spoke these things, that a certain woman from the crowd raised her voice and said to Him, ᴿ"Blessed *is* the womb that bore You, and *the* breasts which nursed You!" Luke 1:28, 48

28 But He said, ᴿ"More than that, blessed *are* those who hear the word of God and keep it!" [Luke 8:21]

(Point 30-A continued from previous page)
not only our own perfect submission, but that of all on earth. Therefore we long also for His coming kingdom.

(4) "Give us day by day our daily bread" (v. 3). Christ sympathizes with our need for daily necessities, and it is perfectly proper to pray for these anew each day. As God made the earth to spin, He made our bodies and minds to function day by day, with day-by-day needs; we are to come afresh each morning to Him who supplies all things to His children (Mark 1:35, page 985).

(5) "Forgive us our sins, for we also forgive everyone who is indebted to us" (v. 4). Our own fellowship with God and daily spiritual cleansing require that we forgive others who have wronged us, because we ourselves have been redeemed through His blood (Matt. 6:14, 15, page 943). We have forgiveness of our sins because He is rich in grace (Eph. 1:7, page 1186). We are to forgive "up to seventy times seven" (Matt. 18:21, 22, page 965), because God has forgiven *us* for so much more.

(6) "Do not lead us into temptation, but deliver us from the evil one" (v. 4). We should not pray with pride in our ability to withstand any test which God might allow to come our way. Rather, we must constantly, humbly remember our weaknesses and each day ask Him to protect us against Satan's temptations.

See Jude 20, page 1290, for **Point 30-B: Pray in the Spirit.**

Seeking a Sign

29 And while the crowds were thickly gathered together, He began to say, "This is an evil generation. It seeks a sign, and no sign will be given to it except ᴿthe sign of Jonah *the prophet.   Luke 24:46; Acts 10:40

30 "For as ᴿJonah became a sign to the Ninevites, ᴿso also the Son of Man will be to this generation.   Jon. 1:17; 2:10; 3:3–10 · 1 Cor. 15:4

31 ᴿ"The queen of the South will rise up in the judgment with the men of this generation and condemn them, for she came from the ends of the earth to hear the wisdom of Solomon; and indeed a ᴿgreater than Solomon *is* here.   1 Kin. 10:1–9 · [Rom. 9:5]

32 "The men of Nineveh will rise up in the judgment with this generation and condemn it, for ᴿthey repented at the preaching of Jonah; and indeed a greater than Jonah *is* here.   Jon. 3:5

The Lamp of the Body

33 ᴿ"No one, when he has lit a lamp, puts *it* in a secret place or under a ᴿbasket, but on a lampstand, that those who come in may see the light.   Mark 4:21 · Matt. 5:15

34 "The lamp of the body is the eye. Therefore, when your eye is ᵀgood, your whole body also is full of light. But when *your eye* is ᵀbad, your body also is full of darkness.   Clear or healthy · Evil or unhealthy

35 "Therefore take heed that the light which is in you is not darkness.

36 "If then your whole body *is* full of light, having no part dark, *the* whole *body* will be full of light, as when the bright shining of a lamp gives you light."

Woe to the Pharisees and Lawyers

37 And as He spoke, a certain Pharisee asked Him to dine with him. So He went in and sat down to eat.

38 When the Pharisee saw *it*, he marveled that He had not first washed before dinner.

39 Then the Lord said to him, "Now you Pharisees make the outside of the cup and dish clean, but your inward part is full of ᵀgreed and wickedness.   *eager grasping* or *robbery*

40 "Foolish ones! Did not ᴿHe who made the outside make the inside also?   Gen. 1:26, 27

41 ᴿ"But rather give alms of ᵀsuch things as you have; then indeed all things are clean to you.   [Luke 12:33; 16:9] · Or *what is inside*

42 "But woe to you Pharisees! For you tithe mint and rue and all manner of herbs, and ᴿpass by justice and the ᴿlove of God. These you ought to have done, without leaving the others undone.   [Mic. 6:7, 8] · John 5:42

43 "Woe to you Pharisees! For you love the ᵀbest seats in the synagogues and greetings in the marketplaces.   Or *places of honor*

44 ᴿ"Woe to you, *scribes and Pharisees, hypocrites! For you are like graves which are not seen, and the men who walk over *them* are not aware *of them*."   Matt. 23:27

45 Then one of the lawyers answered and said to Him, "Teacher, by saying these things You reproach us also."

46 And He said, "Woe to you also, lawyers! For you load men with burdens hard to bear, and you yourselves do not touch the burdens with one of your fingers.

47 "Woe to you! For you build the tombs of the prophets, and your fathers killed them.

48 "In fact, you bear witness that you approve the deeds of your fathers; for they indeed killed them, and you build their tombs.

49 "Therefore the wisdom of God also said, 'I will send them prophets and apostles, and *some* of them they will kill and persecute,'

50 "that the blood of all the prophets which was shed from the foundation of the world may be required of this generation,

51 "from the blood of Abel to ᴿthe blood of Zechariah who perished between the altar and the temple. Yes, I say to you, it shall be required of this generation.   2 Chr. 24:20, 21

52 ᴿ"Woe to you lawyers! For you have taken away the key of knowledge. You did not enter in yourselves, and those who were entering in you hindered."   Matt. 23:13

53 *And as He said these things to them, the scribes and the Pharisees began to assail *Him* vehemently, and to cross-examine Him about many things,

54 lying in wait for Him, *and ᴿseeking to catch Him in something He might say, *that they might accuse Him.   Mark 12:13

Beware of Hypocrisy

12 In ᴿthe meantime, when an innumerable multitude of people had gathered together, so that they trampled one another, He began to say to His disciples first *of all*, ᴿ"Beware of the ᵀleaven of the Pharisees, which is hypocrisy.   Mark 8:15 · Matt. 16:12 · *yeast*

2 ᴿ"For there is nothing covered that will not be revealed, nor hidden that will not be known.   Matt. 10:26

3 "Therefore whatever you have spoken in the dark will be heard in the light, and what you have spoken in the ear in inner rooms will be proclaimed on the housetops.

Jesus Teaches the Fear of God

4 "And I say to you, My friends, do not be afraid of those who kill the body, and after that have no more that they can do.

5 "But I will show you whom you should

11:44 NU omits *scribes and Pharisees, hypocrites*
11:53 NU *And when He left there*
11:54 NU omits *and seeking* • NU omits *that they might accuse Him*

11:29 NU omits *the prophet*

fear: Fear Him who, after He has killed, has power to cast into hell; yes, I say to you, Rfear Him!   Ps. 119:120

6 "Are not five sparrows sold for Ttwo *copper coins? And Rnot one of them is forgotten before God.   1/8 day's wage, $4 • Matt. 6:26

7 "But the very hairs of your head are all numbered. Do not fear therefore; you are of more value than many sparrows.

Confess Christ Before Men

8 "Also I say to you, whoever confesses Me Rbefore men, him the Son of Man also will confess before the angels of God.   Ps. 119:46

9 "But he who Rdenies Me before men will be denied before the angels of God. Matt. 10:33

10 "And anyone who speaks a word against the Son of Man, it will be forgiven him; but to him who blasphemes against the Holy Spirit, it will not be forgiven.

11 R"Now when they bring you to the synagogues and magistrates and authorities, do not worry about how or what you should answer, or what you should say.   Mark 13:11

12 "For the Holy Spirit will teach you in that very hour what you ought to say."

The Parable of the Rich Fool

13 Then one from the crowd said to Him, "Teacher, tell my brother to divide the inheritance with me."

14 But He said to him, "Man, who made Me a judge or an arbitrator over you?"

15 And He said to them, R"Take heed and beware of *covetousness, for one's life does not consist in the abundance of the things he possesses."   [1 Tim. 6:6-10]

16 Then He spoke a parable to them, saying: "The ground of a certain rich man yielded plentifully.

17 "And he thought within himself, saying, 'What shall I do, since I have no room to store my crops?'

18 "So he said, 'I will do this: I will pull down my barns and build greater, and there I will store all my crops and my goods.

19 'And I will say to my soul, "Soul, you have many goods laid up for many years; take your ease; eat, drink, and be merry."'

20 "But God said to him, 'Fool! This night Ryour soul will be required of you; Rthen whose will those things be which you have provided?'   Ps. 52:7 • Ps. 39:6

21 "So is he who lays up treasure for himself, and is not rich toward God."

Do Not Worry

22 Then He said to His disciples, "Therefore I say to you, Rdo not worry about your life, what you will eat; nor about the body, what you will put on.   Matt. 6:25-33

23 "Life is more than food, and the body is more than clothing.

24 "Consider the ravens, for they neither sow nor reap, which have neither storehouse nor barn; and God feeds them. Of how much more value are you than the birds?

25 "And which of you by worrying can add one cubit to his stature?

26 "If you then are not able to do the least, why Tare you anxious for the rest?   do you worry

27 "Consider the lilies, how they grow: they neither toil nor spin; and yet I say to you, even RSolomon in all his glory was not Tarrayed like one of these.   1 Kin. 10:4-7 • clothed

28 "If then God so clothes the grass, which today is in the field and tomorrow is thrown into the oven, how much more will He clothe you, O you of Rlittle faith?   Matt. 6:30; 8:26

29 "And do not seek what you should eat or what you should drink, nor have an anxious mind.

30 "For all these things the nations of the world seek after, and your Father Rknows that you need these things.   Matt. 6:31, 32

31 R"But seek *the kingdom of God, and all these things shall be added to you.   Matt. 6:33

32 "Do not fear, little Rflock, for Rit is your Father's good pleasure to give you the kingdom.   Is. 40:11; Zech. 13:7 • [Matt. 11:25, 26]

33 R"Sell what you have and give Ralms; Rprovide yourselves money bags which do not grow old, a treasure in the heavens that does not fail, where no thief approaches nor moth destroys.   Matt. 19:21 • Luke 11:41 • Matt. 6:20

34 "For where your treasure is, there your heart will be also.

The Faithful Servant and the Evil Servant

35 R"Let your waist be girded and Ryour lamps burning;   [1 Pet. 1:13] • [Matt. 25:1-13]

36 "and you yourselves be like men who wait for their master, when he will return from the wedding, that when he comes and knocks they may open to him immediately.

37 R"Blessed are those servants whom the master, when he comes, will find watching. Assuredly, I say to you that he will gird himself and have them sit down to eat, and will come and serve them.   Matt. 24:46

38 "And if he should come in the second watch, or come in the third watch, and find them so, blessed are those servants.

39 R"But know this, that if the master of the house had known what hour the thief would come, he would *have watched and not allowed his house to be broken into.   Rev. 3:3

40 R"Therefore you also be ready, for the Son of Man is coming at an hour you do not expect."   Mark 13:33

12:6 Gr. assarion, a coin worth about 1/16 of a denarius
12:15 NU all covetousness

12:31 NU His kingdom, and these things
12:39 NU not have allowed

41 Then Peter said to Him, "Lord, do You speak this parable *only* to us, or to all *people?*"

42 And the Lord said, "Who then is that faithful and wise steward, whom *his* master will make ruler over his household, to give *them their* portion of food in due season?

43 "Blessed *is* that servant whom his master will find so doing when he comes.

44 ᴿ"Truly, I say to you that he will make him ruler over all that he has.   Matt. 24:47; 25:21

45 "But if that servant says in his heart, 'My master is delaying his coming,' and begins to beat the male and female servants, and to eat and drink, and be drunk,

46 "the master of that servant will come on a ᴿday when he is not looking for *him*, and at an hour when he is not aware, and will cut him in two and appoint *him* his portion with the unbelievers.   1 Thess. 5:3

47 "And ᴿthat servant who ᴿknew his master's will, and did not prepare *himself* or do according to his will, shall be beaten with many *stripes*.   Deut. 25:2 · [James 4:17]

48 "But he who did not know, yet committed things deserving of stripes, shall be beaten with few. For everyone to whom much is given, from him much will be required; and to whom much has been committed, of him they will ask the more.

Christ Brings Division

49 ᴿ"I came to send fire on the earth, and how I wish it were already kindled!   Luke 12:51

50 "But ᴿI have a baptism to be baptized with, and how distressed I am till it is ᴿaccomplished!   Mark 10:38 · John 12:27; 19:30

51 ᴿ"Do *you* suppose that I came to give peace on earth? I tell you, not at all, ᴿbut rather division.   Matt. 10:34-36 · John 7:43; 9:16; 10:19

52 ᴿ"For from now on five in one house will be divided: three against two, and two against three.   Mark 13:12

53 ᴿ"Father will be divided against son and son against father, mother against daughter and daughter against mother, mother-in-law against her daughter-in-law and daughter-in-law against her mother-in-law."   Matt. 10:21, 36

Discern the Time

54 Then He also said to the multitudes, ᴿ"Whenever you see a cloud rising out of the west, immediately you say, 'A shower is coming'; and so it is.   Matt. 16:2, 3

55 "And when you see the ᴿsouth wind blow, you say, 'There will be hot weather'; and there is.   Job 37:17

56 "Hypocrites! You can discern the face of the sky and of the earth, but how *is it* you do not discern ᴿthis time?   Luke 19:41-44

Make Peace with Your Adversary

57 "Yes, and why, even of yourselves, do you not judge what is right?

58 "When you go with your adversary to the magistrate, make every effort along the way to settle with him, lest he drag you to the judge, the judge deliver you to the officer, and the officer throw you into prison.

59 "I tell you, you shall not depart from there till you have paid the very last mite."

Repent or Perish

13 There were present at that season some who told Him about the Galileans whose blood Pilate had ᵀmingled with their sacrifices.   *mixed*

2 And Jesus answered and said to them, "Do you suppose that these Galileans were worse sinners than all *other* Galileans, because they suffered such things?

3 "I tell you, no; but unless you repent you will all likewise perish.

4 "Or those eighteen on whom the tower in Siloam fell and killed them, do you think that they were worse sinners than all *other* men who dwelt in Jerusalem?

5 "I tell you, no; but unless you repent you will all likewise perish."

The Parable of the Barren Fig Tree

6 He also spoke this parable: ᴿ"A certain *man* had a fig tree planted in his vineyard, and he came seeking fruit on it and found none.   Matt. 21:19

7 "Then he said to the keeper of his vineyard, 'Look, for three years I have come seeking fruit on this fig tree and find none. Cut it down; why does it use up the ground?'

8 "But he answered and said to him, 'Sir, let it alone this year also, until I dig around it and fertilize *it.*

9 *And if it bears fruit, *well.* But if not, after that you can ᴿcut it down.' "   [John 15:2]

A Spirit of Infirmity

10 Now He was teaching in one of the synagogues on the Sabbath.

11 And behold, there was a woman who had a spirit of infirmity eighteen years, and was bent over and could in no way ᵀraise *herself* up.   *straighten up*

12 But when Jesus saw her, He called *her* to *Him* and said to her, "Woman, you are loosed from your ᴿinfirmity."   Luke 7:21; 8:2

13 ᴿAnd He laid *His* hands on her, and immediately she was made straight, and glorified God.   Acts 9:17

14 But the ruler of the synagogue answered with indignation, because Jesus had healed on the Sabbath; and he said to the crowd, "There are six days on which men ought to work; therefore come and be healed on them, and ᴿnot on the Sabbath day."   Mark 3:2

13:9 NU *And if it bears fruit after that, well. But if not, you can*

15 The Lord then answered him and said, *"Hypocrite! Does not each one of you on the Sabbath loose his ox or donkey from the stall, and lead *it* away to water it?

16 "So ought not this woman, being a daughter of Abraham, whom Satan has bound—think of it—for eighteen years, be loosed from this bond on the Sabbath?"

17 And when He said these things, all His adversaries were put to shame; and all the multitude rejoiced for all the glorious things that were ᴿdone by Him.   Mark 5:19, 20

The Parable of the Mustard Seed

18 Then He said, "What is the kingdom of God like? And to what shall I compare it?

19 "It is like a mustard seed, which a man took and put in his garden; and it grew and became a *large tree, and the birds of the air nested in its branches."

The Parable of the Leaven

20 And again He said, "To what shall I liken the kingdom of God?

21 "It is like ᵀleaven, which a woman took and hid in three ᴿmeasures* of meal till it was all leavened."   *yeast* · Matt. 13:33

The Narrow Way

22 ᴿAnd He went through the cities and villages, teaching, and journeying toward Jerusalem.   Mark 6:6

23 Then one said to Him, "Lord, are there few who are saved?" And He said to them,

24 ᴿ"Strive to enter through the narrow gate, for many, I say to you, will seek to enter and will not be able.   [Matt. 7:13]

25 ᴿ"When once the Master of the house has risen up and shut the door, and you begin to stand outside and knock at the door, saying, 'Lord, Lord, open for us,' and He will answer and say to you, ᴿ'I do not know you, where you are from,'   Is. 55:6 · Matt. 7:23; 25:12

26 "then you will begin to say, 'We ate and drank in Your presence, and You taught in our streets.'

27 "But He will say, 'I tell you I do not know you, where you are from. ᴿDepart from Me, all you workers of iniquity.'   Ps. 6:8

28 "There will be weeping and gnashing of teeth, ᴿwhen you see Abraham and Isaac and Jacob and all the prophets in the kingdom of God, and yourselves thrust out.   Matt. 8:11

29 "They will come from the east and the west, from the north and the south, and sit down in the kingdom of God.

30 "And indeed there are last who will be first, and there are first who will be last."

31 *On that very day some Pharisees came, saying to Him, "Get out and depart from here, for Herod wants to kill You."

32 And He said to them, "Go, tell that fox, 'Behold, I cast out demons and perform cures today and tomorrow, and the ᴿthird *day* I shall be perfected.'   Luke 24:46; Acts 10:40

33 "Nevertheless I must journey today, tomorrow, and the *day* following; for it cannot be that a prophet should perish outside of Jerusalem.

Jesus Laments over Jerusalem

34 ᴿ"O Jerusalem, Jerusalem, the one who kills the prophets and stones those who are sent to her! How often I wanted to gather your children together, as a hen *gathers* her brood under *her* wings, but you were not willing!   Matt. 23:37-39

35 ᴿSee! ᴿYour house is left to you desolate; and *assuredly, I say to you, you shall not see Me until *the* time comes when you say, ᴿ'Blessed is He who comes in the name of the LORD!'"   Jer. 22:5 · Lev. 26:31, 32 · Ps. 118:26

A Man with Dropsy Healed on the Sabbath

14 Now it happened, as He went into the house of one of the rulers of the Pharisees to eat bread on the Sabbath, that they watched Him closely.

2 And behold, there was a certain man before Him who had dropsy.

3 And Jesus, answering, spoke to the lawyers and Pharisees, saying, ᴿ"Is it lawful to heal on the *Sabbath?"   Matt. 12:10

4 But they kept silent. And He took *him* and healed him, and let him go.

5 Then He answered them, saying, ᴿ"Which of you, having a *donkey or an ox that has fallen into a pit, will not immediately pull him out on the Sabbath day?"   [Ex. 23:5]

6 And they could not answer Him regarding these things.

Take the Lowly Place

7 So He told a parable to those who were invited, when He noted how they chose the best places, saying to them:

8 "When you are invited by anyone to a wedding feast, do not sit down in the best place, lest one more honorable than you be invited by him;

9 "and he who invited you and him come and say to you, 'Give place to this man,' and then you begin with shame to take the lowest place.

13:15 NU, M *Hypocrites*
13:19 NU omits *large*
13:21 Gr. *saton,* same as Heb. *seah;* Approximately 2 pecks in all

13:31 NU *In that very hour*
13:35 NU, M omit *assuredly*
14:3 NU adds *or not*
14:5 NU, M *son*

10 ^R"But when you are invited, go and sit down in the lowest place, so that when he who invited you comes he may say to you, 'Friend, go up higher.' Then you will have glory in the presence of those who sit at the table with you.   Prov. 25:6, 7
11 ^R"For whoever exalts himself will be ^Thumbled, and he who humbles himself will be exalted."   Matt. 23:12 · humbled
12 Then He also said to him who invited Him, "When you give a dinner or a supper, do not ask your friends, your brothers, your relatives, nor rich neighbors, lest they also invite you back, and you be repaid.
13 "But when you give a feast, invite the poor, the maimed, the lame, the blind.
14 "And you will be ^Rblessed, because they cannot repay you; for you shall be repaid at the resurrection of the just."   [Matt. 25:34–40]

The Parable of the Great Supper

15 Now when one of those who sat at the table with Him heard these things, he said to Him, ^R"Blessed is he who shall eat *bread in the kingdom of God!"   Rev. 19:9
16 Then He said to him, "A certain man gave a great supper and invited many,
17 "and ^Rsent his servant at supper time to say to those who were invited, 'Come, for all things are now ready.'   Prov. 9:2, 5
18 "But they all with one accord began to make excuses. The first said to him, 'I have bought a piece of ground, and I must go and see it. I ask you to have me excused.'
19 "And another said, 'I have bought five yoke of oxen, and I am going to test them. I ask you to have me excused.'
20 "Still another said, 'I have married a wife, and therefore I cannot come.'
21 "So that servant came and reported these things to his master. Then the master of the house, being angry, said to his servant, 'Go out quickly into the streets and lanes of the city, and bring in here the poor and the ^Tmaimed and the lame and the blind.'   crippled
22 "And the servant said, 'Master, it is done as you commanded, and still there is room.'
23 "Then the master said to the servant, 'Go out into the highways and hedges, and compel them to come in, that my house may be filled.
24 'For I say to you that none of those men who were invited shall taste my supper.' "

Leaving All to Follow Christ

25 Now great multitudes went with Him. And He turned and said to them,
26 "If anyone comes to Me and does not hate his father and mother, wife and children, brothers and sisters, ^Ryes, and his own life also, he cannot be My disciple.   Rev. 12:11

27 "And whoever does not bear his cross and come after Me cannot be My disciple.
28 "For which of you, intending to build a tower, does not sit down first and count the cost, whether he has enough to finish it—
29 "lest, after he has laid the foundation, and is not able to finish, all who see it begin to mock him,
30 "saying, 'This man began to build and was not able to finish.'
31 "Or what king, going to make war against another king, does not sit down first and consider whether he is able with ten thousand to meet him who comes against him with twenty thousand?
32 "Or else, while the other is still a great way off, he sends a delegation and asks conditions of peace.
33 "So likewise, whoever of you does not forsake all that he has cannot be My disciple.

Tasteless Salt Is Worthless

34 ^R"Salt is good; but if the salt has lost its flavor, how shall it be seasoned?   [Mark 9:50]
35 "It is neither fit for the land nor for the ^Tdunghill, but men throw it out. He who has ears to hear, let him hear!"   rubbish heap

The Parable of the Lost Sheep

15 Then all the tax collectors and the sinners drew near to Him to hear Him.
2 And the Pharisees and scribes complained, saying, "This Man ^Treceives sinners ^Rand eats with them."   welcomes · Gal. 2:12
3 So He spoke this parable to them, saying:
4 "What man of you, having a hundred sheep, if he loses one of them, does not leave the ninety-nine in the wilderness, and go after the one which is lost until he finds it?
5 "And when he has found it, he lays it on his shoulders, rejoicing.
6 "And when he comes home, he calls together his friends and neighbors, saying to them, 'Rejoice with me, for I have found my sheep ^Rwhich was lost!'   [1 Pet. 2:10, 25]
7 "I say to you that likewise there will be more joy in heaven over one sinner who repents than over ninety-nine ^Tjust persons who ^Rneed no repentance.   upright · [Mark 2:17]

The Parable of the Lost Coin

8 "Or what woman, having *ten silver coins, if she loses one coin, does not light a lamp, sweep the house, and search carefully until she finds it?
9 "And when she has found it, she calls her friends and neighbors together, saying, 'Rejoice with me, for I have found the piece which I lost!'

14:15 M the best

15:8 Gr. *drachma,* a valuable coin often worn in a ten-piece garland by married women

10 "Likewise, I say to you, there is joy in the presence of the angels of God over one sinner who repents."

The Parable of the Lost Son

11 Then He said: "A certain man had two sons.
12 "And the younger of them said to *his* father, 'Father, give me the portion of goods that falls *to me.*' So he divided to them ᴿ*his* livelihood.   Mark 12:44
13 "And not many days after, the younger son gathered all together, journeyed to a far country, and there wasted his possessions with ᵀprodigal living.   *wasteful*
14 "But when he had spent all, there arose a severe famine in that land, and he began to be in want.
15 "Then he went and joined himself to a citizen of that country, and he sent him into his fields to feed swine.
16 "And he would gladly have filled his stomach with the ᵀpods that the swine ate, and no one gave him *anything.*   *carob pods*
17 "But when he came to himself, he said, 'How many of my father's hired servants have bread enough and to spare, and I perish with hunger!
18 'I will arise and go to my father, and will say to him, "Father, ᴿI have sinned against heaven and before you,   2 Sam. 12:13; 24:10, 17
19 and I am no longer worthy to be called your son. Make me like one of your hired servants." '
20 "And he arose and came to his father. But when he was still a great way off, his father saw him and had compassion, and ran and fell on his neck and kissed him.
21 "And the son said to him, 'Father, I have sinned against heaven and in your sight, and am no longer worthy to be called your son.'
22 "But the father said to his servants, **'Bring out the best robe and put *it* on him, and put a ring on his hand and sandals on *his* feet.
23 'And bring the fatted calf here and kill *it,* and let us eat and be merry;
24 ᴿ'for this my son was dead and is alive again; he was lost and is found.' And they began to be merry.   Luke 9:60; 15:32
25 "Now his older son was in the field. And as he came and drew near to the house, he heard music and dancing.
26 "So he called one of the servants and asked what these things meant.
27 "And he said to him, 'Your brother has come, and because he has received him safe and sound, your father has killed the fatted calf.'
28 "But he was angry and would not go in.

15:22 NU *Quickly bring*

Therefore his father came out and pleaded with him.
29 "So he answered and said to *his* father, 'Lo, these many years I have been serving you; I never transgressed your commandment at any time; and yet you never gave me a young goat, that I might make merry with my friends.
30 'But as soon as this son of yours came, who has devoured your livelihood with harlots, you killed the fatted calf for him.'
31 "And he said to him, 'Son, you are always with me, and all that I have is yours.
32 'It was right that we should make merry and be glad, for your brother was dead and is alive again, and was lost and is found.' "

The Parable of the Unjust Steward

16 He also said to His disciples: "There was a certain rich man who had a steward, and an accusation was brought to him that this man was wasting his goods.
2 "So he called him and said to him, 'What is this I hear about you? Give an ᴿaccount of your stewardship, for you can no longer be steward.'   [Rom. 14:12]
3 "Then the steward said within himself, 'What shall I do? For my master is taking the stewardship away from me. I cannot dig; I am ashamed to beg.
4 'I have resolved what to do, that when I am put out of the stewardship, they may receive me into their houses.'
5 "So he called every one of his master's debtors to *him,* and said to the first, 'How much do you owe my master?'
6 "And he said, 'A ᵀhundred *measures of oil.' So he said to him, 'Take your bill, and sit down quickly and write fifty.'   600 gal.
7 "Then he said to another, 'And how much do you owe?' So he said, 'A hundred *measures of wheat.' And he said to him, 'Take your bill, and write eighty.'
8 "So the master commended the unjust steward because he had dealt shrewdly. For the sons of this world are more shrewd in their generation than the sons of light.
9 "And I say to you, make friends for yourselves by unrighteous ᵀmammon, that when *you fail, they may receive you into an everlasting home.   Lit., in Aram., *wealth*
10 ᴿ"He who *is* faithful in *what is* least is faithful also in much; and he who is unjust in *what is* least is unjust also in much.   Matt. 25:21
11 "Therefore if you have not been faithful in the unrighteous mammon, who will commit to your trust the true *riches?*
12 "And if you have not been faithful in what is another man's, who will give you what is your ᴿown?   [1 Pet. 1:3, 4]

16:6 Gr. *batos,* same as Heb. *bath;* 8 or 9 gallons each
16:7 Gr. *koros,* same as Heb. *kor;* 10 or 12 bushels each
16:9 NU *it fails*

13 ᴿ"No servant can serve two masters; for either he will hate the one and love the other, or else he will be loyal to the one and despise the other. You cannot serve God and mammon."   Matt. 6:24

The Law, the Prophets, and the Kingdom

14 Now the Pharisees, ᴿwho were lovers of money, also heard all these things, and they ᵀderided Him.   Matt. 23:14 • Lit. turned up their nose at

15 And He said to them, "You are those who justify yourselves ᴿbefore men, but ᴿGod knows your hearts. For what is highly esteemed among men is an abomination in the sight of God.   [Matt. 6:2, 5, 16] • Ps. 7:9

16 ᴿ"The law and the prophets were until John. Since that time the kingdom of God has been preached, and everyone is pressing into it.   Matt. 3:1–12; 4:17; 11:12, 13

17 ᴿ"And it is easier for heaven and earth to pass away than for one ᵀtittle of the law to fail.   Is. 40:8; 51:6 • The smallest stroke in a Heb. letter

18 ᴿ"Whoever divorces his wife and marries another commits adultery; and whoever marries her who is divorced from her husband commits adultery.   1 Cor. 7:10, 11

The Rich Man and Lazarus

▼ 17–G. You Must Choose: Heaven or Hell

19 "There was a certain rich man who was clothed in purple and fine linen and ᵀfared sumptuously every day.   lived in luxury

20 "But there was a certain beggar named Lazarus, full of sores, who was laid at his ▽ gate,

21 "desiring to be fed with *the crumbs which fell from the rich man's table. Moreover the dogs came and licked his sores.

22 "So it was that the beggar died, and was carried by the angels to Abraham's bosom. The rich man also died and was buried.

23 "And being in torments in Hades, he lifted up his eyes and saw Abraham afar off, and Lazarus in his bosom.

24 "Then he cried and said, 'Father Abraham, have mercy on me, and send Lazarus that he may dip the tip of his finger in water and ᴿcool my tongue; for I ᴿam tormented in this flame.'   Zech. 14:12 • [Mark 9:42–48]

25 "But Abraham said, 'Son, remember that in your lifetime you received your good things, and likewise Lazarus evil things; but now he is comforted and you are tormented.

26 'And besides all this, between us and you there is a great gulf fixed, so that those who want to pass from here to you cannot, nor can those from there pass to us.'

27 "Then he said, 'I beg you therefore, father, that you would send him to my father's house,

28 'for I have five brothers, that he may testify to them, lest they also come to this place of torment.'

29 "Abraham said to him, 'They have Moses and the prophets; let them hear them.'

16:21 NU what fell

17–G. You Must Choose: Heaven or Hell (Luke 16:19–31)—We have already seen that hell is a prepared place for the Devil (Satan) and his angels (Matt. 25:41, page 976), and is the destiny of all who do the will of their father, the Devil (John 8:44, page 1063). Satan is the spiritual father of all who reject the God-Man.

Just one day before His death, Jesus said to the eleven depressed disciples, "Let not your heart be troubled; you believe in God [the Father], believe also in Me [God the Son]" (John 14:1, page 1074). Earlier, in the temple at the Feast of Dedication, some of the Jews had come to Jesus and said to Him, "How long do You keep us in doubt? If You are the Christ, tell us plainly." Jesus had answered, "I and My Father are one." At this they prepared to stone Him (John 10:22–31, page 1068). Why? Because when He said, "I and My Father are one," He was claiming equality with God the Father. "I and My Father are one" in unity, essence, substance, authority, power, and eternity; but not one person. This is what He meant when He later said, "You believe in God, believe also in Me."

After thus reminding His disciples of who He was, He assured them, "I go to prepare a place for you" (John 14:2, page 1074). Heaven is a place, somewhere in God's universe, that is prepared for His believing people (2 Cor. 11:2, page 1174), the body of Christ (Rom. 12:4, 5, page 1143).

You have a choice: Either you must choose eternal life with Christ in the place that He is preparing for all who will by faith accept Him as their personal Savior, or you must choose eternal death with Satan in the hell prepared for him and his angels (John 3:16–18, page 1052). In its full biblical meaning, death is not annihilation; it is separation. Hell is called "the second death" (Rev. 21:8, page 1315); to experience this second death is to be eternally separated from the mercy, grace, and love of God forever and ever (Rev. 20:10, page 1313). The love of God does not extend beyond the gates of hell. In Satan's hell there is no love, no fellowship, no hope.

You have a choice of one of two ways (Matt. 7:13, 14, page 945):

(1) The broad way that leads to eternal hell. This way seems to be right to lost mankind, but the end of the broad way is eternal separation from God (Prov. 14:12, page 608).

(2) The narrow way that leads to eternal life in heaven. Jesus Christ is the narrow way. He is the only way (Acts 4:12, page 1091)—the only way to God the Father, the only way to heaven (John 14:6, page 1074).

YOU HAVE A CHOICE!
See Index, page 17, for your next study.

▽ 30 "And he said, 'No, father Abraham; but if one goes to them from the dead, they will repent.'

▲ 31 "But he said to him, 'If they do not hear Moses and the prophets, neither will they be persuaded though one rise from the dead.' "

Jesus Warns of Offenses

17 Then He said to the disciples, R"It is impossible that no Toffenses should come, but Rwoe to him through whom they do come!   [1 Cor. 11:19] · *stumbling blocks* · [2 Thess. 1:6]

2 "It would be better for him if a millstone were hung around his neck, and he were thrown into the sea, than that he should offend one of these little ones.

3 "Take heed to yourselves. If your brother sins *against you, Rrebuke him; and if he repents, forgive him.   [Prov. 17:10]

4 "And if he sins against you seven times in a day, and seven times in a day returns *to you, saying, 'I repent,' you shall forgive him."

Faith and Duty

5 And the apostles said to the Lord, "Increase our faith."

6 So the Lord said, "If you have faith as a mustard seed, you can say to this mulberry tree, 'Be pulled up by the roots and be planted in the sea,' and it would obey you.

7 "And which of you, having a servant plowing or tending sheep, will say to him when he has come in from the field, 'Come at once and sit down to eat'?

8 "But will he not rather say to him, 'Prepare something for my supper, and gird yourself and serve me till I have eaten and drunk, and afterward you will eat and drink'?

9 "Does he thank that servant because he did the things that were *commanded *him? I think not.

10 "So likewise you, when you have done all those things which you are commanded, say, 'We are Runprofitable servants. We have done what was our duty to do.' "   Rom. 3:12; 11:35

Ten Lepers Cleansed

11 Now it happened Ras He went to Jerusalem that He passed through the midst of Samaria and Galilee.   Luke 9:51, 52

12 Then as He entered a certain village, there met Him ten men who were lepers, Rwho stood afar off.   Lev. 13:46

13 And they lifted up *their* voices and said, "Jesus, Master, have mercy on us!"

14 So when He saw *them*, He said to them, R"Go, show yourselves to the priests." And so it was that as they went, they were cleansed.   Matt. 8:4

15 And one of them, when he saw that he was healed, returned, and with a loud voice Rglorified God,   Luke 5:25; 18:43

16 and fell down on *his* face at His feet, giving Him thanks. And he was a RSamaritan.   2 Kin. 17:24

17 So Jesus answered and said, "Were there not ten cleansed? But where *are* the nine?

18 "Were there not any found who returned to give glory to God except this foreigner?"

19 RAnd He said to him, "Arise, go your way. Your faith has made you well."   Matt. 9:22

The Coming of the Kingdom

20 Now when He was asked by the Pharisees when the kingdom of God would come, He answered them and said, "The kingdom of God does not come with observation;

21 R"nor will they say, *'See here!' or 'See there!' For indeed, Rthe kingdom of God is Twithin you."   Luke 17:23 · [Rom. 14:17] · *in your midst*

22 Then He said to the disciples, R"The days will come when you will desire to see one of the days of the Son of Man, and you will not see *it*.   Matt. 9:15

23 R"And they will say to you, *'Look here!' or 'Look there!' Do not go after *them* or follow *them*.   Matt. 24:23

24 R"For as the lightning that flashes out of one *part* under heaven shines to the other *part* under heaven, so also the Son of Man will be in His day.   Matt. 24:27

25 "But first He must suffer many things and be Rrejected by this generation.   Luke 9:22

26 "And as it was in the days of Noah, so it will be also in the days of the Son of Man:

27 "They ate, they drank, they married wives, they were given in marriage, until the day that Noah entered the ark, and the flood came and Rdestroyed them all.   Gen. 7:19-23

28 R"Likewise as it was also in the days of Lot: They ate, they drank, they bought, they sold, they planted, they built;   Gen. 19

29 "but on Rthe day that Lot went out of Sodom it rained fire and brimstone from heaven and destroyed *them* all.   Gen. 19:16, 24, 29

30 "Even so will it be in the day when the Son of Man Ris revealed.   [2 Thess. 1:7]

31 "In that day, he Rwho is on the housetop, and his Tgoods *are* in the house, let him not come down to take them away. And likewise the one who is in the field, let him not turn back.   Mark 13:15 · *possessions*

32 R"Remember Lot's wife.   Gen. 19:26

33 "Whoever seeks to save his life will lose it, and whoever loses his life will preserve it.

34 R"I tell you, in that night there will be two Tmen in one bed: the one will be taken and the other will be left.   [1 Thess. 4:17] · Or *people*

17:3 NU omits *against you*
17:4 M omits *to you*
17:9 NU omits the rest of v. 9; M omits *him*

17:21 NU reverses *here* and *there*
17:23 NU reverses *here* and *there*

35 "Two *women* will be grinding together: the one will be taken and the other left.

36 *"Two *men* will be in the field: the one will be taken and the other left."

37 And they answered and said to Him, R"Where, Lord?" So He said to them, "Wherever the body is, there the eagles will be gathered together."   Matt. 24:28

The Parable of the Persistent Widow

18 Then He spoke a parable to them, that men Ralways ought to pray and not lose heart,   Luke 11:5-10

2 saying: "There was in a certain city a judge who did not fear God nor regard man.

3 "Now there was a widow in that city; and she came to him, saying, T'Get justice for me from my adversary.'   Vindicate me against

4 "And he would not for a while; but afterward he said within himself, 'Though I do not fear God nor regard man,

5 R'yet because this widow troubles me I will Tavenge her, lest by her continual coming she weary me.' "   Luke 11:8 · vindicate

6 Then the Lord said, "Hear what the unjust judge said.

7 "And Rshall God not avenge His own elect who cry out day and night to Him, though He bears long with them?   Rev. 6:10

8 "I tell you that He will avenge them speedily. Nevertheless, when the Son of Man comes, will He really find faith on the earth?"

The Parable of the Pharisee and the Tax Collector

9 Also He spoke this parable to some Rwho trusted in themselves that they were righteous, and despised others: Luke 10:29; 16:15

10 "Two men went up to the temple to pray, one a Pharisee and the other a tax collector.

11 "The Pharisee stood and prayed thus with himself, 'God, I thank You that I am not like other men—extortioners, unjust, adulterers, or even as this tax collector.

12 'I fast twice a week; I give tithes of all that I possess.'

13 "And the tax collector, standing afar off, would not so much as raise *his* eyes to heaven, but beat his breast, saying, 'God be merciful to me a sinner!'

14 "I tell you, this man went down to his house justified *rather* than the other; for everyone who exalts himself will be humbled, and he who humbles himself will be exalted."

Jesus Blesses Little Children

15 Then they also brought infants to Him that He might touch them; but when the disciples saw *it*, they rebuked them.

16 But Jesus called them to *Him* and said, "Let the little children come to Me, and do not forbid them; for Rof such is the kingdom of God.   1 Pet. 2:2

17 R"Assuredly, I say to you, whoever does not receive the kingdom of God as a little child will by no means enter it."   Mark 10:15

Jesus Counsels the Rich Young Ruler

18 RNow a certain ruler asked Him, saying, "Good Teacher, what shall I do to inherit eternal life?"   Matt. 19:16-29

19 So Jesus said to him, "Why do you call Me good? No one *is* good but ROne, *that is,* God.   Ps. 86:5; 119:68

20 "You know the commandments: * 'Do not commit adultery,' 'Do not murder,' 'Do not steal,' 'Do not bear false witness,' R 'Honor your father and your mother.' "   Eph. 6:2

21 And he said, "All Rthese things I have kept from my youth."   Phil. 3:6

22 So when Jesus heard these things, He said to him, "You still lack one thing. RSell all that you have and distribute to the poor, and you will have treasure in heaven; and come, follow Me."   Matt. 6:19, 20; 19:21

23 But when he heard this, he became very sorrowful, for he was very rich.

With God All Things Are Possible

24 And when Jesus saw that he became very sorrowful, He said, R"How hard it is for those who have riches to enter the kingdom of God!   Mark 10:23

25 "For it is easier for a camel to go through the eye of a needle than for a rich man to enter the kingdom of God."

26 And those who heard it said, "Who then can be saved?"

27 But He said, "The things which are impossible with men are possible with God."

28 RThen Peter said, "See, we have left *all and followed You."   Matt. 19:27

29 So He said to them, "Assuredly, I say to you, Rthere is no one who has left house or parents or brothers or wife or children, for the sake of the kingdom of God,   Deut. 33:9

30 R"who shall not receive many times more in this present time, and in the age to come eternal life."   Job 42:10

Jesus a Third Time Predicts His Death and Resurrection

31 RThen He took the twelve aside and said to them, "Behold, we are going up to Jerusalem, and all things Rthat are written by the prophets concerning the Son of Man will be Taccomplished.   Matt. 16:21; 17:22 · Ps. 22 · fulfilled

32 "For RHe will be delivered to the Gentiles and will be mocked and insulted and spit upon.   Luke 23:1, 11, 36; Mark 15:19

18:20 Ex. 20:12-16; Deut. 5:16-20; Mark 10:19; Rom. 13:9
18:28 NU *our own*

17:36 NU, M omit this verse.

33 "They will scourge *Him* and kill Him. And the third day He will rise again."

34 ᴿBut they understood none of these things; this saying was hidden from them, and they did not know the things which were spoken.   Luke 2:50; 9:45

A Blind Man Receives His Sight

35 ᴿThen it happened, that as He was coming near Jericho, that a certain blind man sat by the road begging.   Matt. 20:29-34

36 And hearing a multitude passing by, he asked what it meant.

37 So they told him that Jesus of Nazareth was passing by.

38 And he cried out, saying, "Jesus, ᴿSon of David, have mercy on me!"   Matt. 9:27

39 Then those who went before warned him that he should be quiet; but he cried out all the more, "Son of David, have mercy on me!"

40 So Jesus stood still and commanded him to be brought to Him. And when he had come near, He asked him,

41 saying, "What do you want Me to do for you?" He said, "Lord, that I may receive my sight."

42 Then Jesus said to him, "Receive your sight; ᴿyour faith has made you well." Luke 17:19

43 And immediately he received his sight, and followed Him, ᴿglorifying God. And all the people, when they saw *it*, gave praise to God.   Luke 5:26

Jesus Comes to Zacchaeus' House

19 Then *Jesus* entered and passed through ᴿJericho.   Josh. 6:26

2 Now behold, *there was* a man named Zacchaeus who was a chief tax collector, and he was rich.

3 And he sought to ᴿsee who Jesus was, but could not because of the crowd, for he was of short stature.   John 12:21

4 So he ran ahead and climbed up into a sycamore tree to see Him, for He was going to pass that *way*.

5 And when Jesus came to the place, He looked up *and saw him, and said to him, "Zacchaeus, ᵀmake haste and come down, for today I must stay at your house."   *hurry*

6 So he ᵀmade haste and came down, and received Him joyfully.   *hurried*

7 But when they saw *it*, they all ᵀcomplained, saying, "He has gone to be a guest with a man who is a sinner."   *grumbled*

8 Then Zacchaeus stood and said to the Lord, "Look, Lord, I give half of my goods to the ᴿpoor; and if I have taken anything from anyone by ᴿfalse accusation, ᴿI restore fourfold."   [Ps. 41:1] • Luke 3:14 • Ex. 22:1

9 And Jesus said to him, "Today salvation has come to this house, because ᴿhe also is ᴿa son of Abraham;   [Gal. 3:7] • [Luke 13:16]

10 ᴿ"for the Son of Man has come to seek and to save that which was lost."   Matt. 18:11

The Parable of the Minas

11 Now as they heard these things, He spoke another parable, because He was near Jerusalem and because they thought the kingdom of God would appear immediately.

12 ᴿTherefore He said: "A certain nobleman went into a far country to receive for himself a kingdom and to return.   Matt. 25:14-30

13 "So he called ten of his servants, delivered to them ten *minas, and said to them, 'Do business till I come.'

14 ᴿBut his citizens hated him, and sent a delegation after him, saying, 'We will not have this *man* to reign over us.'   [John 1:11]

15 "And so it was that when he returned, having received the kingdom, he then commanded these servants, to whom he had given the money, to be called to him, that he might know how much every man had gained by trading.

16 "Then came the first, saying, 'Master, your mina has earned ᵀten minas.' $64,000

17 "And he said to him, 'Well *done*, good servant; because you were faithful in a very little, have authority over ten cities.'

18 "And the second came, saying, 'Master, your mina has earned ᵀfive minas.' $32,000

19 "Likewise he said to him, 'You also be over five cities.'

20 "Then another came, saying, 'Master, here is your mina, which I have kept put away in a handkerchief.

21 'For I feared you, because you are an austere man. You collect what you did not deposit, and reap what you did not sow.'

22 "And he said to him, ᴿ'Out of your own mouth I will judge you, you wicked servant. ᴿYou knew that I was an austere man, collecting what I did not deposit and reaping what I did not sow.   Job 15:6 • Matt. 25:26

23 'Why then did you not put my money in the bank, that at my coming I might have collected it with interest?'

24 "And he said to those who stood by, 'Take the mina from him, and give *it* to him who has ten minas.'

25 ("But they said to him, 'Master, he has ten minas.')

26 'For I say to you, ᴿthat to everyone who has will be given; and from him who does not have, even what he has will be taken away from him.   Luke 8:18

27 'But bring here those enemies of mine, who did not want me to reign over them, and slay *them* before me.' "

19:5 NU omits *and saw him*

19:13 Gr. *mna*, same as Heb. *minah*, each worth about three months' salary

The Triumphal Entry

28 When He had said this, ᴿHe went on ahead, going up to Jerusalem.   Mark 10:32

29 ᴿAnd it came to pass, when He drew near to *Bethphage and ᴿBethany, at the mountain called ᴿOlivet, *that* He sent two of His disciples,   Matt. 21:1 • John 12:1 • Acts 1:12

30 saying, "Go into the village opposite *you*, where as you enter you will find a colt tied, on which no one has ever sat. Loose it and bring *it here*.

31 "And if anyone asks you, 'Why are you loosing *it*?' thus you shall say to him, 'Because the Lord has need of it.' "

32 So those who were sent went their way and found *it* just as He had said to them.

33 But as they were loosing the colt, the owners of it said to them, "Why are you loosing the colt?"

34 And they said, "The Lord has need of him."

35 Then they brought him to Jesus. ᴿAnd they threw their own clothes on the colt, and they set Jesus on him.   2 Kin. 9:13

36 And as He went, *many* spread their clothes on the road.

37 Then, as He was now drawing near the descent of the Mount of Olives, the whole multitude of the disciples began to ᴿrejoice and praise God with a loud voice for all the mighty works they had seen,   Luke 13:17; 18:43

38 saying:

ᴿ" *'Blessed is the King who comes in the name of the Lᴏʀᴅ!'*
ᴿPeace in heaven and glory in the highest!"   Ps. 118:26 • [Eph. 2:14]

39 And some of the Pharisees called to Him from the crowd, "Teacher, rebuke Your disciples."

40 But He answered and said to them, "I tell you that if these should keep silent, ᴿthe stones would immediately cry out."   Hab. 2:1ᵢ

Jesus Weeps over Jerusalem

41 Now as He drew near, He saw the city and ᴿwept over it,   John 11:35

42 saying, "If you had known, even you, especially in this your day, the things *that* ᴿmake for your ᴿpeace! But now they are hidden from your eyes.   [Acts 10:36] • [Rom. 5:1]

43 "For days will come upon you when your enemies will ᴿbuild an embankment around you, surround you and close you in on every side,   Jer. 6:3, 6

44 "and level you, and your children within you, to the ground; and they will not leave in you one stone upon another, because you did not know the time of your visitation."

19:29 M *Bethsphage*

Jesus Cleanses the Temple

45 ᴿThen He went into the temple and began to drive out those who *bought and sold in it,   Mal. 3:1

46 saying to them, "It is written, ᴿ*'My house *is a house of prayer,'* but ᴿyou have made it a *'den of thieves.'* "   Is. 56:7 • Jer. 7:11

47 And He ᴿwas teaching daily in the temple. But ᴿthe chief priests, the scribes, and the leaders of the people sought to destroy Him,   Luke 21:37; 22:53 • John 7:19; 8:37

48 and were unable to do anything; for all the people were very attentive to hear Him.

Jesus' Authority Questioned

20 Now ᴿit happened on one of those days, as He taught the people in the temple and preached the gospel, *that* the chief priests and the scribes, together with the elders, confronted *Him*   Matt. 21:23-27

2 and spoke to Him, saying, "Tell us, by what authority are You doing these things? Or who is he who gave You this authority?"

3 But He answered and said to them, "I also will ask you one thing, and answer Me:

4 "The ᴿbaptism of John—was it from heaven or from men?"   John 1:26, 31

5 And they reasoned among themselves, saying, "If we say, 'From heaven,' He will say, 'Why *then did you not believe him?'

6 "But if we say, 'From men,' all the people will stone us, ᴿfor they are persuaded that John was a prophet."   Luke 7:24-30

7 So they answered that they did not know where *it was* from.

8 And Jesus said to them, "Neither will I tell you by what authority I do these things."

The Parable of the Wicked Vinedressers

9 Then He began to tell the people this parable: "A certain man planted a vineyard, leased it to ᵀvinedressers, and went into a far country for a long time.   tenant farmers

10 "Now at ᵀvintage-time he ᴿsent a servant to the vinedressers, that they might give him some of the fruit of the vineyard. But the vinedressers beat him and sent *him* away empty-handed.   Lit. *the season* • [1 Thess. 2:15]

11 "Again he sent another servant; and they beat him also, treated *him* shamefully, and sent *him* away empty-handed.

12 "And again he sent a third; and they wounded him also and cast *him* out.

13 "Then the owner of the vineyard said, 'What shall I do? I will send my beloved son. Probably they will respect *him* when they see him.'

14 "But when the vinedressers saw him, they reasoned among themselves, saying,

19:45 NU *were selling, saying*
19:46 NU *shall be*
20:5 NU, M omit *then*

'This is the heir. Come, let us kill him, that the inheritance may be ^Rours.'   John 11:47, 48

15 "So they cast him out of the vineyard and ^Rkilled *him*. Therefore what will the owner of the vineyard do to them?   Luke 23:33

16 "He will come and destroy those vinedressers and give the vineyard to ^Rothers." And when they heard *it* they said, "Certainly not!"   Rom. 11:1, 11

17 Then He looked at them and said, "What then is this that is written:

'The stone which the builders rejected
     Has become the chief cornerstone'?

18 "Whoever falls on that stone will be broken; but ^Ron whomever it falls, it will grind him to powder."   [Dan. 2:34, 35, 44, 45]

19 And the chief priests and the scribes that very hour sought to lay hands on Him, but they *feared the people—for they knew He had spoken this parable against them.

The Pharisees: Is It Lawful to Pay Taxes to Caesar?

20 ^RSo they watched *Him*, and sent spies who pretended to be righteous, that they might seize on His words, in order to deliver Him to the power and the authority of the governor.   Matt. 22:15

21 Then they asked Him, saying, ^R"Teacher, we know that You say and teach rightly, and You do not show personal favoritism, but teach the way of God in truth: Mark 12:14

22 "Is it lawful for us to pay taxes to Caesar or not?"

23 But He perceived their craftiness, and said to them, *"Why do you test Me?

24 "Show Me a ^Tdenarius. Whose image and inscription does it have?" They answered and said, "Caesar's."   1 day's wage, $32

25 And He said to them, ^T"Render therefore to Caesar the things that are Caesar's, and to God the things that are God's."   Pay

26 But they could not catch Him in His words in the presence of the people. And they marveled at His answer and kept silent.

The Sadducees: What About the Resurrection?

27 ^RThen some of the Sadducees, ^Rwho deny that there is a resurrection, came to *Him* and asked Him,   Mark 12:18–27 · Acts 23:6, 8

28 saying: "Teacher, Moses wrote to us *that* if a man's brother dies, having a wife, and he dies without children, his brother should take his wife and raise up offspring for his brother.

29 "Now there were seven brothers. And the first took a wife, and died without children.

30 "And the second *took her as wife, and he died childless.

31 "Then the third took her, and in like manner the seven *also; and they left no children, and died.

32 "Last of all the woman died also.

33 "Therefore, in the resurrection, whose wife does she become? For all seven had her as wife."

34 Jesus answered and said to them, "The sons of this age marry and are given in marriage.

35 "But those who are ^Rcounted worthy to attain that age, and the resurrection from the dead, neither marry nor are given in marriage;   Phil. 3:11

36 "nor can they die anymore, for ^Rthey are equal to the angels and are sons of God, being sons of the resurrection.   [1 John 3:2]

37 "But even Moses showed in the *burning* bush *passage* that the dead are raised, when he called the Lord * *the God of Abraham, the God of Isaac, and the God of Jacob.'*

38 "For He is not the God of the dead but of the living, for ^Rall live to Him."   [Rom. 6:10, 11]

39 Then some of the scribes answered and said, "Teacher, You have spoken well."

40 But after that they dared not question Him anymore.

Jesus: How Can David Call His Descendant Lord?

41 And He said to them, "How can they say that the Christ is the Son of David?

42 "Now David himself said in the Book of Psalms:

   ^R*The* LORD *said to my Lord,*
   "Sit at My right hand,   Ps. 110:1

43   *Till I make Your enemies Your*
       footstool."'

44 "Therefore David calls Him *'Lord'*; ^Rhow is He then his Son?"   Rom. 1:3; 9:4, 5

Beware of the Scribes

45 ^RThen, in the hearing of all the people, He said to His disciples,   Matt. 23:1–7

46 "Beware of the scribes, who desire to go around in long robes, love greetings in the marketplaces, the best seats in the synagogues, and the best places at feasts,

47 "who devour widows' houses, and for a ^Rpretense make long prayers. These will receive greater condemnation."   [Matt. 6:5, 6]

The Widow's Two Mites

21 And He looked up and saw the rich putting their gifts into the treasury,

2 and He saw also a certain ^Rpoor widow putting in ^Ttwo mites.   [2 Cor. 6:10] · $1

20:19 M *were afraid—for*
20:23 NU omits *Why do you test Me?*
20:30 NU omits the rest of v. 30.
20:31 NU, M *also left no children*
20:37 Ex. 3:1–6, 15; Acts 7:30–32

3 So He said, "Truly I say to you that this poor widow has put in more than all;

4 "for all these out of their abundance have put in offerings *for God, but she out of her poverty put in ᴿall the livelihood that she had."   [2 Cor. 8:12]

Jesus Predicts the Destruction of the Temple

5 ᴿThen, as some spoke of the temple, how it was ᵀadorned with beautiful stones and donations, He said,   Mark 13:1 · decorated

6 "These things which you see—the days will come in which ᴿnot one stone shall be left upon another that shall not be thrown down."   Luke 19:41-44

The Signs of the Times and the End of the Age

7 So they asked Him, saying, "Teacher, but when will these things be? And what sign will there be when these things are about to take place?"

8 And He said: "Take heed that you not be deceived. For many will come in My name, saying, 'I am He,' and, 'The time has drawn near.' *Therefore do not go after them.

9 "But when you hear of ᴿwars and commotions, do not be terrified; for these things must come to pass first, but the end will not come immediately."   Rev. 6:4

10 ᴿThen He said to them, "Nation will rise against nation, and kingdom against kingdom.   Matt. 24:7

11 "And there will be great ᴿearthquakes in various places, and famines and pestilences; and there will be fearful sights and great signs from heaven.   Rev. 6:12

12 "But before all these things, they will lay

21:4 NU omits for God
21:8 NU omits Therefore

their hands on you and persecute you, delivering you up to the synagogues and prisons. You will be brought before kings and rulers for My name's sake.

13 "But ᴿit will turn out for you as an occasion for testimony.   [Phil. 1:12-14, 28]

14 ᴿ"Therefore settle it in your hearts not to meditate beforehand on what you will ᵀanswer;   Luke 12:11 · say in defense

15 "for I will give you a mouth and wisdom ᴿwhich all your adversaries will not be able to contradict or ᵀresist.   Acts 6:10 · withstand

16 "You will be betrayed even by parents and brothers, relatives and friends; and they will put some of you to death.

17 "And ᴿyou will be hated by all for My name's sake.   Matt. 10:22

18 ᴿ"But not a hair of your head shall be lost.   Matt. 10:30

19 "By your patience possess your souls.

The Destruction of Jerusalem

34-E. From the Crucifixion to the Fall of ▼ Jerusalem

20 ᴿ"But when you see Jerusalem surrounded by armies, then know that its desolation is near.   Mark 13:14

21 "Then let those who are in Judea flee to the mountains, let those who are in the midst of her depart, and let not those who are in the country enter her.

22 "For these are the days of vengeance, that ᴿall things which are written may be fulfilled.   [Dan. 9:24-27]

23 ᴿ"But woe to those who are pregnant and to those who are nursing babies in those days! For there will be great distress in the land and wrath upon this people.   Matt. 24:19

24 "And they will fall by the edge of the sword, and be led away captive into all na-

---

34-E. From the Crucifixion to the Fall of Jerusalem (about 40 years) (Luke 21:20-24)—This prophecy was partially fulfilled in A.D. 70 when Titus led a Roman army in a siege against Jerusalem. They battered down its walls, sacked the city, destroyed the temple, and scattered the Hebrew people among all nations.

About fifteen hundred years before the fall of Jerusalem, under Titus, Moses prophesied the fall of Jerusalem, God's curse on the land, and the scattering of the Jews among all nations (Deut. 28:1-68, page 205). This unique prophecy falls into three detailed divisions:

(1) God promised to bless Israel above all nations if they would diligently obey the Lord their God (Deut. 28:1-14, page 205).

(2) God promised to curse them above all nations if they did not obey the Lord their God (Deut. 28:15-61, page 205).

(3) God promised to make them few in number and scatter them among all nations if they did not obey the Lord their God (Deut. 28:61-68, page 207).

From the Exodus to the fall of Jerusalem, we see the longsuffering of God toward Israel (about fifteen hundred years). In A.D. 70 they reached the end of God's forebearance when, just 40 years before the fall of Jerusalem and the destruction of the temple, they rejected and crucified their Messiah, crying, "His blood be on us and on our children" (Matt. 27:15-25, page 980). On the cross Christ prayed for His tormentors (both Jews and Gentiles), "Father, forgive them, for they do not know what they do" (Luke 23:34, page 1045). Surely all of us are obliged to be broken with shame by these words. It was our sins that put Jesus on the cross.

See Matthew 23:37—24:2, page 972, for **Point 34-F: From the Fall of Jerusalem to the Millennium.**

▽ tions. And Jerusalem will be trampled by
Gentiles ᴿuntil the times of the Gentiles are
▲ fulfilled.   [Dan. 9:27; 12:7]

The Coming of the Son of Man

25 ᴿ"And there will be signs in the sun, in
the moon, and in the stars; and on the earth
distress of nations, with perplexity, the sea
and the waves roaring;   [2 Pet. 3:10–12]
26 "men's hearts failing them from fear and
the expectation of those things which are
coming on the earth, ᴿfor the powers of the
heavens will be shaken.   Matt. 24:29
27 "Then they will see the Son of Man
ᴿcoming in a cloud with power and great
glory.   Rev. 1:7; 14:14
28 "Now when these things begin to happen, look up and lift up your heads, because
ᴿyour redemption draws near."   [Rom. 8:19, 23]

The Parable of the Fig Tree

29 Then He spoke to them a parable: "Look
at the fig tree, and all the trees.
30 "When they are already budding, you
see and know for yourselves that summer is
now near.
31 "So you also, when you see these things
happening, know that the kingdom of God is
near.
32 "Assuredly, I say to you, this generation
will by no means pass away till all things take
place.
33 "Heaven and earth will pass away, but
My words will by no means pass away.

The Importance of Watching

34 "But take heed to yourselves, lest your
hearts be weighed down with ᵀcarousing,
drunkenness, and cares of this life, and that
Day come on you unexpectedly.   *dissipation*
35 "For it will come as a snare on all those
who dwell on the face of the whole earth.
36 "Watch therefore, and pray always that
you may *be counted worthy to escape all
these things that will come to pass, and ᴿto
stand before the Son of Man."   [Eph. 6:13]
37 And in the daytime He was teaching in
the temple, but at night He went out and
stayed on the mountain called Olivet.
38 Then early in the morning all the people
came to Him in the temple to hear Him.

The Plot to Kill Jesus

22 Now the Feast of Unleavened Bread
drew near, which is called Passover.
2 And ᴿthe chief priests and the scribes
sought how they might kill Him, for they
feared the people.   John 11:47
3 ᴿThen Satan entered Judas, surnamed
Iscariot, who was numbered among the
ᴿtwelve.   Mark 14:10, 11 • Matt. 10:2–4

4 So he went his way and conferred with
the chief priests and captains, how he might
betray Him to them.
5 And they were glad, and ᴿagreed to give
him money.   Zech. 11:12
6 So he promised and sought opportunity
to ᴿbetray Him to them in the absence of the
multitude.   Ps. 41:9

Jesus and His Disciples Prepare the Passover

7 Then came the Day of Unleavened
Bread, when the Passover must be killed.
8 And He sent Peter and John, saying, "Go
and prepare the Passover for us, that we may
eat."
9 So they said to Him, "Where do You
want us to prepare?"
10 And He said to them, "Behold, when you
have entered the city, a man will meet you
carrying a pitcher of water; follow him into
the house which he enters.
11 "Then you shall say to the master of the
house, 'The Teacher says to you, "Where is
the guest room where I may eat the Passover
with My disciples?" '
12 "Then he will show you a large, furnished upper room; there make ready."
13 So they went and found it just as He had
said to them, and they prepared the Passover.

Jesus Institutes the Lord's Supper

14 When the hour had come, He sat down,
and the *twelve apostles with Him.
15 Then He said to them, "With *fervent*
desire I have desired to eat this Passover with
you before I suffer;
16 "for I say to you, I will no longer eat of it
until it is fulfilled in the kingdom of God."
17 Then He took the cup, and gave thanks,
and said, "Take this and divide *it* among
yourselves;
18 "for ᴿI say to you, *I will not drink of the
fruit of the vine until the kingdom of God
comes."   Mark 14:25
19 ᴿAnd He took bread, gave thanks and
broke *it*, and gave *it* to them, saying, "This is
My ᴿbody which is given for you; do this in
remembrance of Me."   Matt. 26:26 • [1 Pet. 2:24]
20 Likewise He also *took* the cup after
supper, saying, "This cup *is* the new covenant
in My blood, which is shed for you.
21 ᴿ"But behold, the hand of My betrayer *is*
with Me on the table.   Ps. 41:9
22 ᴿ"And truly the Son of Man goes ᴿas it
has been determined, but woe to that man by
whom He is betrayed!"   Matt. 26:24 • Acts 2:23
23 ᴿThen they began to question among
themselves, which of them it was who would
do this thing.   John 13:22, 25

22:14 NU omits *twelve*
22:18 NU adds *from now on*

21:36 NU *have strength to*

The Disciples Argue About Greatness

24 ᴿNow there was also a dispute among them, as to which of them should be considered the greatest.   Mark 9:34

25 ᴿAnd He said to them, "The kings of the Gentiles exercise lordship over them, and those who exercise authority over them are called 'benefactors.'   Mark 10:42-45

26 ᴿ"But not so *among* you; on the contrary, ᴿhe who is greatest among you, let him be as the younger, and he who governs as he who serves.   [1 Pet. 5:3] · Luke 9:48

27 ᴿ"For who *is* greater, he who sits at the table, or he who serves? *Is* it not he who sits at the table? Yet ᴿI am among you as the One who serves.   [Luke 12:37] · Phil. 2:7

28 "But you are those who have continued with Me in ᴿMy trials.   [Heb. 2:18; 4:15]

29 "And I bestow upon you a kingdom, just as My Father bestowed *one* upon Me,

30 "that you may eat and drink at My table *in My kingdom, ᴿand sit on thrones judging the twelve tribes of Israel."   [Rev. 3:21]

Jesus Predicts Peter's Denial

31 *And the Lord said, "Simon, Simon! Indeed, ᴿSatan has asked for you, that he may ᴿsift *you* as wheat.   1 Pet. 5:8 · Amos 9:9

32 "But I have prayed for you, that your faith should not fail; and when you have returned to *Me*, strengthen your brethren."

33 But he said to Him, "Lord, I am ready to go with You, both to prison and to death."

34 Then He said, "I tell you, Peter, the rooster shall not crow this day before you will deny three times that you know Me."

Supplies for the Road

35 And He said to them, "When I sent you without money bag, knapsack, and sandals, did you lack anything?" So they said, "Nothing."

36 Then He said to them, "But now, he who has a money bag, let him take *it*, and likewise a knapsack; and he who has no sword, let him sell his garment and buy one.

37 "For I say to you that this which is written must still be ᵀaccomplished in Me: ᴿ'And He was numbered with the transgressors.' For the things concerning Me have an end."   fulfilled · Is. 53:12; Luke 23:32; John 19:18

38 So they said, "Lord, look, here *are* two swords." And He said to them, "It is enough."

The Prayer in the Garden

39 ᴿComing out, ᴿHe went to the Mount of Olives, as He was accustomed, and His disciples also followed Him.   John 18:1 · Luke 21:37

40 ᴿWhen He came to the place, He said to them, "Pray that you may not enter into temptation."   Mark 14:32-42

41 ᴿAnd He was withdrawn from them about a stone's throw, and He knelt down and prayed,   Matt. 26:39

42 saying, "Father, if it is Your will, take this cup away from Me; nevertheless ᴿnot My will, but Yours, be done."   Is. 50:5

43 *Then ᴿan angel appeared to Him from heaven, strengthening Him.   Matt. 4:11

44 And being in agony, He prayed more earnestly. Then His sweat became like great drops of blood falling down to the ground.

45 When He rose up from prayer, and had come to His disciples, He found them sleeping from sorrow.

46 Then He said to them, "Why ᴿdo you sleep? Rise and ᴿpray, lest you enter into temptation."   Luke 9:32 · Luke 22:40

Betrayal and Arrest in Gethsemane

47 And while He was still speaking, behold, a multitude; and he who was called ᴿJudas, one of the twelve, went before them and drew near to Jesus to kiss Him.   Acts 1:16, 17

48 But Jesus said to him, "Judas, are you betraying the Son of Man with a kiss?"

49 When those around Him saw what was going to happen, they said to Him, "Lord, shall we strike with the sword?"

50 And one of them struck the servant of the high priest and cut off his right ear.

51 But Jesus answered and said, "Permit even this." And He touched his ear and healed him.

52 Then Jesus said to the chief priests, captains of the temple, and the elders who had come to Him, "Have you come out, as against a robber, with swords and clubs?

53 "When I was with you daily in the temple, you did not try to seize Me. But this is your hour, and the power of darkness."

Peter Denies Jesus, and Weeps Bitterly

54 Having arrested Him, they led *Him* and brought Him into the high priest's house. But Peter followed at a distance.

55 ᴿNow when they had kindled a fire in the midst of the courtyard and sat down together, Peter sat among them.   Mark 14:66-72

56 And a certain servant girl, seeing him as he sat by the fire, looked intently at him and said, "This man was also with Him."

57 But he denied *Him, saying, "Woman, I do not know Him."

58 ᴿAnd after a little while another saw him and said, "You also are of them." But Peter said, "Man, I am not!"   John 18:25

59 ᴿThen after about an hour had passed, another confidently affirmed, saying, "Surely

22:43 NU brackets vv. 43 and 44 as not in the original text.
22:57 NU *it*

22:30 M mss. omit *in My kingdom*
22:31 NU omits *And the Lord said*

this *fellow* also was with Him, for he is a
ᴿGalilean."　　　　　　Mark 14:70 · Acts 1:11; 2:7

60 But Peter said, "Man, I do not know
what you are saying!" Immediately, while he
was still speaking, *the rooster crowed.
61 And the Lord turned and looked at Peter. Then ᴿPeter remembered the word of the
Lord, how He had said to him, ᴿ"Before the
rooster *crows, you will deny Me three
times."　　　　　　　　Matt. 26:75 · John 13:38
62 So Peter went out and wept bitterly.

Jesus Mocked and Beaten

63 ᴿNow the men who held Jesus mocked
Him and beat Him.　　　Ps. 69:19; Is. 50:6; 52:14
64 And having blindfolded Him, they
ᴿstruck* Him on the face and asked Him,
saying, "Prophesy! Who is the one who
struck You?"　　　　　　　　　　Zech. 13:7
65 ᴿAnd many other things they blasphe-
mously spoke against Him.　　　　　Is. 53:3

Jesus Faces the Sanhedrin

66 ᴿAs soon as it was day, ᴿthe elders of the
people, both chief priests and scribes, came
together and led Him into their council,
saying,　　　　　　　　Matt. 27:1 · Acts 4:26
67 ᴿ"If You are the Christ, tell us." But He
said to them, "If I tell you, you will ᴿby no
means believe.　　Matt. 26:63-66 · Luke 20:5-7
68 "And if I *also ask *you*, you will by no
means answer *Me or let *Me* go.
69 "Hereafter the Son of Man will sit on the
right hand of the power of God."
70 Then they all said, "Are You then the
Son of God?" So He said to them, ᴿ"You
rightly say that I am."　　　　　　Luke 1:35
71 ᴿAnd they said, "What further testimony
do we need? For we have heard it ourselves
from His own mouth."　　　　　　Mark 14:63

Jesus Handed Over to Pontius Pilate

23 Then ᴿthe whole multitude of them
arose and led Him to Pilate.　Luke 18:32
2 And they began to accuse Him, saying,
"We found this *fellow* perverting *the nation,
and forbidding to pay taxes to Caesar, saying
that He Himself is Christ, a King."
3 ᴿThen Pilate asked Him, saying, "Are
You the King of the Jews?" And He answered
him and said, "It is *as* you say."　　1 Tim. 6:13
4 So Pilate said to the chief priests and the
crowd, "I find no fault in this Man."
5 But they were the more fierce, saying,
"He stirs up the people, teaching throughout
all Judea, beginning from ᴿGalilee to this
place."　　　　　　　　　　　　John 7:41

Jesus Faces Herod

6 When Pilate heard *of Galilee, he asked
if the Man were a Galilean.
7 And as soon as he knew that He belonged to ᴿHerod's jurisdiction, he sent Him
to Herod, who was also in Jerusalem at that
time.　　　　　　　　Luke 3:1; 9:7; 13:31
8 Now when Herod saw Jesus, ᴿhe was
exceedingly glad; for he had desired for a
long *time* to see Him, because ᴿhe had heard
many things about Him, and he hoped to see
some miracle done by Him.　Luke 9:9 · Matt. 14:1
9 Then he questioned Him with many
words, but He answered him nothing.
10 And the chief priests and scribes stood
and vehemently accused Him.
11 ᴿThen Herod, with his ᵀmen of war,
treated Him with contempt and mocked *Him*,
arrayed Him in a gorgeous robe, and sent
Him back to Pilate.　Ps. 69:19; Is. 53:3 · *troops*
12 That very day Pilate and Herod became
friends with each other, for previously they
had been at enmity with each other.

Taking the Place of Barabbas

13 ᴿThen Pilate, when he had called together the chief priests, the rulers, and the
people,　　　　　　　　　　　Mark 15:14
14 said to them, ᴿ"You have brought this
Man to me, as one who misleads the people.
And indeed, ᴿhaving examined *Him* in your
presence, I have found no fault in this Man
concerning those things of which you accuse
Him;　　　　　　　　Luke 23:1, 2 · Luke 23:4
15 "no, neither did Herod, for *I sent you
back to him; and indeed nothing deserving of
death has been done by Him.
16 ᴿ"I will therefore chastise Him and release *Him*"　　　　　　　　　　John 19:1
17 ᴿ(for* it was necessary for him to release
one to them at the feast).　　　　John 18:39
18 And ᴿthey all cried out at once, saying,
"Away with this *Man*, and release to us
Barabbas"—　　　　　　Is. 53:3; Acts 3:13-15
19 who had been thrown into prison for a
certain rebellion made in the city, and for
murder.
20 Pilate, therefore, wishing to release
Jesus, again called out to them.
21 But they shouted, saying, "Crucify *Him*,
crucify Him!"
22 Then he said to them the third time,
"Why, what evil has He done? I have found
no reason for death in Him. I will therefore
chastise Him and let *Him* go."
23 But they were insistent, demanding with
loud voices that He be crucified. And the
voices of these men *and of the chief priests
prevailed.

22:60 NU, M *a rooster*
22:61 NU adds *today*
22:64 NU *And having blindfolded Him, they asked Him*
22:68 NU omits *also* • NU omits the rest of v. 68.
23:2 NU *our*

23:6 NU omits *of Galilee*
23:15 NU *he sent Him back to us*
23:17 NU omits this verse.
23:23 NU omits *and of the chief priests*

24 So ^RPilate gave sentence that it should be as they requested. Mark 15:15

25 ^RAnd he released *to them the one they requested, who for rebellion and murder had been thrown into prison; but he delivered Jesus to their will. Is. 53:8

The King on a Cross

26 ^RNow as they led Him away, they laid hold of a certain man, Simon a Cyrenian, who was coming from the country, and on him they laid the cross that he might bear it after Jesus. Matt. 27:32

27 And a great multitude of the people followed Him, and women who also mourned and lamented Him.

28 But Jesus, turning to them, said, "Daughters of Jerusalem, do not weep for Me, but weep for yourselves and for your children.

29 ^R"For indeed the days are coming in which they will say, 'Blessed are the barren,

wombs that never bore, and breasts which never nursed!' Matt. 24:19

30 "Then they will begin ^R'to say to the mountains, "Fall on us!" and to the hills, "Cover us!"' Hos. 10:8; Rev. 6:16, 17; 9:6

31 ^R"For if they do these things in the green wood, what will be done in the dry?" [Jer. 25:29]

32 ^RThere were also two others, criminals, led with Him to be put to death. Is. 53:9, 12

33 And ^Rwhen they had come to the place called Calvary, there they ^Rcrucified Him, and the criminals, one on the right hand and the other on the left. John 19:17-24 • Ps. 22:16-18

33-E. The Barrier to Evangelism: ▼
Persecution of the Jewish People

34 *Then Jesus said, "Father, forgive them, for they do not know what they do." And ▲ they divided His garments and cast lots.

35 And ^Rthe people stood looking on. But even the rulers with them sneered, saying, "He saved others; let Him save Himself if He is the Christ, the chosen of God." Ps. 22:7, 8

23:25 NU, M omit to them

23:34 NU brackets the first sentence as a later addition.

33-E. The Barrier to Evangelism: Persecution of the Jewish People (Luke 23:34)—From the times of Moses until the present, Jewish people have been persecuted century after century and in country after country, even by professing Christians. (Remember that not all who *profess* actually *possess*—Matthew 7:21-23, page 946.) Such persecution has become an enormous barrier to Jewish evangelism. Let us review the pertinent Scriptures:

(1) Who are the Jewish people? They are the descendants of Abraham, Isaac, and Jacob. Today the terms Jewish person, Jew, or Israelite are usually used synonymously. Originally, a "Jew" was from Israel's royal tribe (David's tribe), Judah; but in later years a Jew might be any Israelite.

In 721 B.C. the Assyrians scattered the northern kingdom, called "Israel," and many mixed with the southern kingdom, "Judah." In 586 B.C. the Babylonians scattered Judah and Jerusalem. Since A.D. 70, when the Romans destroyed Jerusalem, the tribes have intermarried freely and Israelites and Jews have become one people.

Note that the apostle Paul, explaining his prayer for Israel (Rom. 10:1, page 1140), spoke of them collectively as the "Jew" (Rom. 10:12, page 1140). Likewise he referred to himself as "an Israelite" (Rom. 11:1, page 1141), a "Hebrew" (2 Cor. 11:22, page 1175), and a "Jew" (Acts 21:39, page 1117; 22:3, page 1118).

(2) The Bible prophesied that they would suffer persecution (Deut. 28:64-68, page 207). This is by no means an excuse for anyone who causes the Jewish people to suffer! Evil may befall them, but woe to those who cause it (Deut. 30:6, 7, page 208)!

(3) The Bible promises blessing to those who bless them and cursing to those who curse them (Gen. 12:3, page 17). Witness the nations of history who persecuted the Jew: Spain and Portugal, once great empires, promoted the Inquisition and are now third-rate powers, and Germany, which planned the Holocaust, is now divided into two nations.

(4) Christ prayed from the cross, "Father, forgive them, for they do not know what they do" (v. 34). "They" included the Jewish people. It is His everlasting wish that they be forgiven—not persecuted. Christ here met all of the conditions for answered prayer. His prayer will be answered, for those who repent will be pardoned.

(5) Paul desired the Jewish people to be saved, not persecuted (Rom. 9:3, 4, page 1139).

(6) Christ was a Jew, from the tribe of Judah (Rom. 9:5, page 1139; cf. Matt. 1:1, 2, page 930).

(7) Peter called himself a Jew (Acts 10:28, page 1103).

(8) Paul called himself a Jew (Acts 21:39, page 1117; 22:3, page 1118).

(9) Cornelius, the first Gentile convert to Christ and especially blessed of God, had a reputation for treating Jewish people well; God loved and honored him (Acts 10:22, page 1103).

(10) Wicked Haman is typical of people throughout the ages who have promoted anti-Semitism (Esth. 3:10, page 472). He was hanged, and the Bible praises this as justice to the wicked (Esth. 7:8-10, page 474).

(11) True Christians are the ambassadors of God's love to those of every nation and tribe. No race or national group today must ever be shunned or persecuted. Those filled with hate and persecution are not obedient to God's Word, and cannot please Him (Acts 10:28, page 1103).

See Isaiah 11:6-12, page 654, for **Point 33-F: The Peace That Someday Will Be Israel's.**

36 The soldiers also mocked Him, coming and offering Him ᴿsour wine,   Ps. 69:21
37 and saying, "If You are the King of the Jews, save Yourself."
38 ᴿAnd an inscription also was *written over Him in letters of Greek, Latin, and Hebrew: John 19:19

THIS IS THE KING OF THE JEWS.

39 Then one of the criminals who were hanged blasphemed Him, ᴿsaying, *"If You are the Christ, save Yourself and us."   Ps. 22:8
40 But the other, answering, rebuked him, saying, "Do you not even fear God, seeing you are under the same condemnation?
41 "And we indeed justly, for we receive the due reward of our deeds; but this Man has done ᴿnothing wrong."   [Heb. 7:26]
42 Then he said *to Jesus, "Lord, remember me when You come into Your kingdom."
43 And Jesus said to him, "Assuredly, I say to you, today you will be with Me in ᴿParadise."   [Rev. 2:7]

Jesus Dies on the Cross

44 ᴿNow it *was about the sixth hour, and there was darkness over all the earth until the ninth hour.   Amos 8:9
45 Then the sun was *darkened, and ᴿthe veil of the temple was torn in two.   Matt. 27:51
46 And when Jesus had cried out with a loud voice, He said, "Father, ᴿ'into Your hands I commit My spirit.'" ᴿHaving said this, He breathed His last.   Ps. 31:5 • Matt. 17:23
47 ᴿSo when the centurion saw what had happened, he glorified God, saying, "Certainly this was a righteous Man!"   Mark 15:39
48 And the whole crowd who came together to that sight, seeing what had been done, beat their breasts and returned.
49 ᴿBut all His acquaintances, and the women who followed Him from Galilee, stood at a distance, watching these things.   Ps. 38:11

Jesus Buried in Joseph's Tomb

50 ᴿNow behold, *there was* a man named Joseph, a council member, a good and just man.   Matt. 27:57-61
51 He had not consented to their decision and deed. *He was* from Arimathea, a city of the Jews, ᴿwho* himself was also waiting for the kingdom of God.   Luke 2:25, 38
52 ᴿThis man went to Pilate and asked for the body of Jesus.   Is. 53:9
53 ᴿThen he took it down, wrapped it in linen, and laid it in a tomb *that was* hewn out

of the rock, where no one had ever lain before.   Matt. 26:12; Mark 14:8
54 That day was ᴿthe Preparation, and the Sabbath drew near.   Matt. 27:62
55 And the women ᴿwho had come with Him from Galilee followed after, and ᴿthey observed the tomb and how His body was laid.   Luke 8:2 • Mark 15:47
56 Then they returned and prepared spices and fragrant oils. And they rested on the Sabbath according to the commandment.

He Is Risen

24 Now on the first *day* of the week, very early in the morning, they, *and certain *other women* with them, came to the tomb bringing the spices which they had prepared.
2 ᴿBut they found the stone rolled away from the tomb.   Mark 16:4
3 ᴿThen they went in and did not find the body of the Lord Jesus.   Mark 16:5
4 And it happened, as they were *greatly perplexed about this, that ᴿbehold, two men stood by them in shining garments.   John 20:12
5 Then, as they were afraid and bowed *their* faces to the earth, they said to them, "Why do you seek the living among the dead?
6 "He is not here, but is risen! ᴿRemember how He spoke to you when He was still in Galilee,   Matt. 16:21; Mark 8:31; Luke 9:22
7 "saying, 'The Son of Man must be delivered into the hands of sinful men, and be crucified, and the third day rise again.'"
8 And they remembered His words.
9 ᴿThen they returned from the tomb and told all these things to the eleven and to all the rest.   Mark 16:10
10 It was Mary Magdalene, ᴿJoanna, Mary *the mother* of James, and the other *women* with them, who told these things to the apostles.   Luke 8:3
11 And their words seemed to them like idle tales, and they did not believe them.
12 But Peter arose and ran to the tomb; and stooping down, he saw the linen cloths *lying by themselves; and he departed, marveling to himself at what had happened.

The Road to Emmaus

13 Now behold, two of them were traveling that same day to a village called Emmaus, which was seven miles from Jerusalem.
14 And they talked together of all these things which had happened.
15 So it was, while they conversed and reasoned, that ᴿJesus Himself drew near and went with them.   [Matt. 18:20]
16 But ᴿtheir eyes were restrained, so that they did not know Him.   John 20:14; 21:4

23:38 NU omits *written* and *in letters of Greek, Latin, and Hebrew*
23:39 NU *Are You not the Christ? Save*
23:42 NU *"Jesus, remember me*
23:44 NU adds *now*
23:45 NU *obscured*
23:51 NU *who was waiting*

24:1 NU omits *and certain other women with them*
24:4 NU omits *greatly*
24:12 NU omits *lying*

17 And He said to them, "What kind of conversation *is* this that you have with one another as you *walk and are sad?"

18 Then the one ᴿwhose name was Cleopas answered and said to Him, "Are You the only stranger in Jerusalem, and have You not known the things which happened there in these days?"   John 19:25

19 And He said to them, "What things?" So they said to Him, "The things concerning Jesus of Nazareth, ᴿwho was a Prophet ᴿmighty in deed and word before God and all the people,   Matt. 21:11 • Acts 7:22

20 ᴿ"and how the chief priests and our rulers delivered Him to be condemned to death, and crucified Him.   Acts 13:27, 28

21 "But we were hoping ᴿthat it was He who was going to redeem Israel. Indeed, besides all this, today is the third day since these things happened.   Luke 1:68; 2:38

22 "Yes, and ᴿcertain women of our company, who arrived at the tomb early, astonished us.   Mark 16:10

23 "When they did not find His body, they came saying that they had also seen a vision of angels who said He was alive.

24 "And certain of those *who were* with us went to the tomb and found *it* just as the women had said; but Him they did not see."

25 Then He said to them, "O foolish ones, and slow of heart to believe in all that the prophets have spoken!

26 "Ought not the Christ to have suffered these things and to enter into His glory?"

27 And beginning at Moses and all the Prophets, He expounded to them in all the Scriptures the things concerning Himself.

The Disciples' Eyes Opened

28 Then they drew near to the village where they were going, and ᴿHe indicated that He would have gone farther.   Mark 6:48

29 But ᴿthey constrained Him, saying, ᴿ"Abide with us, for it is toward evening, and the day is far spent." And He went in to stay with them.   Gen. 19:2, 3 • [John 14:23]

30 Now it came to pass, as ᴿHe sat at the table with them, that He took bread, blessed and broke *it*, and gave it to them.   Matt. 14:19

31 Then their eyes were opened and they knew Him; and He vanished from their sight.

32 And they said to one another, "Did not our heart burn within us while He talked with us on the road, and while He opened the Scriptures to us?"

33 So they rose up that very hour and returned to Jerusalem, and found the eleven and those *who were* with them gathered together,

34 saying, "The Lord is risen indeed, and ᴿhas appeared to Simon!"   1 Cor. 15:5

24:17 NU *walk? And they stood still, looking sad.*

35 And they told about the things *that had happened* on the road, and how He was known to them in the breaking of bread.

Jesus Appears to His Disciples

36 ᴿNow as they said these things, Jesus Himself stood in the midst of them, and said to them, "Peace to you."   Mark 16:14

37 But they were terrified and frightened, and supposed they had seen ᴿa spirit. Mark 6:49

38 And He said to them, "Why are you troubled? And why do doubts arise in your hearts?

39 "Behold My hands and My feet, that it is I Myself. ᴿHandle Me and see, for a ᴿspirit does not have flesh and bones as you see I have."   John 20:20, 27 • [1 Cor. 15:50]

40 *When He had said this, He showed them His hands and His feet.

41 But while they still did not believe ᴿfor joy, and marveled, He said to them, ᴿ"Have you any food here?"   Gen. 45:26 • John 21:5

42 So they gave Him a piece of a broiled fish *and some honeycomb.

43 And He took *it* and ate in their presence.

The Scriptures Opened

44 Then He said to them, "These *are* the words which I spoke to you while I was still with you, that all things must be fulfilled which were written in the Law of Moses and *the* Prophets and *the* Psalms concerning Me."

45 And He opened their understanding, that they might comprehend the Scriptures.

46 Then He said to them, ᴿ"Thus it is written, *and thus it was necessary for the Christ to suffer and to rise from the dead the third day,   Hos. 6:1, 2; Acts 17:3

47 "and that repentance and remission of sins should be preached in His name ᴿto all nations, beginning at Jerusalem.   [Jer. 31:34]

48 "And you are witnesses of these things.

49 ᴿ"Behold, I send the Promise of My Father upon you; but tarry in the city *of Jerusalem until you are endued with power from on high."   Is. 44:3; Joel 2:28; Acts 2:4

The Ascension

50 And He led them out as far as Bethany, and He lifted up His hands and blessed them.

51 ᴿNow it came to pass, while He blessed them, that He was parted from them and carried up into heaven.   Ps. 68:18; 110:1

52 ᴿAnd they worshiped Him, and returned to Jerusalem with great joy,   Matt. 28:9

53 and were continually ᴿin the temple *praising and blessing God. *Amen. Acts 2:46

24:40 Some printed New Testaments omit v. 40. It is found in nearly all Gr. mss.
24:42 NU omits *and some honeycomb*
24:46 NU *that the Christ should suffer and rise*
24:49 NU omits *of Jerusalem*
24:53 NU omits *praising and* • NU omits *Amen*

THE GOSPEL ACCORDING TO

John

The Gospel of John is one of the most beloved books in the entire Bible, and rightly so. Not only does it have a strong evangelistic thrust that has led many to faith in Christ (who hasn't heard John 3:16, which Martin Luther called "the gospel in a nutshell"?), but also it is loved by the most advanced and devout Christians. Who, for example, has not marveled at the devotional quality of the Upper Room Discourse (chs. 13—17)? It is not surprising that John is often the first book translated into languages that are beginning to open to Christianity. Even in the English-speaking world it is widely found in pocket editions that are given out freely by the millions.

How John Fits into the Bible. Of the four Gospels in the New Testament, the first three are *synoptic*, that is, they "view together" much the same events in Jesus' life in the same chronological order. Harmonies of the synoptic Gospels have been compiled, aligning parallel passages in Matthew, Mark, and Luke. Although some have sought to include a fourth column aligning the events in John's Gospel with those of the other three, such a chronological approach to John is successful only for the passion narratives. The Fourth Gospel is arranged by the Holy Spirit to be *theological* in approach, not chronological.

Authorship and Context. The traditional (and conservative) view is that John the beloved apostle, the son of Zebedee and an eyewitness of the events in the book, wrote this Gospel. He has been called "the disciple whom Jesus loved" by himself and by the church through the ages.

Liberal scholarship used to suggest that the book was the work of a second-century "religious genius" who was not an eyewitness but made up most of the speeches attributed to our Lord. However, when a fragment of the Gospel of John dating from about A.D. 130 (the Rylands Papyrus) was found deep in Egypt it became clear that the original, written in Asia Minor or Palestine, had to be dated some time before that, and the traditional late-first-century date was shown to be very logical. (Today some scholars, including very liberal ones, date John even earlier than the traditional date.)

Bishop Westcott's classic proof of the Johannine authorship has never been refuted, and we can read this book with confidence as the very work of the apostle who reclined on Jesus' bosom at the Last Supper.

Key Verse. The purpose of John's Gospel is to set forth a convincing theology of the person and work of Christ, which the Holy Spirit and Christian witnesses can use to persuade lost men and women that Jesus is who He claimed to be and accomplished what He set out to do. In other words, John's purpose is that stated in 20:30, 31—"These are written that you may believe that Jesus is the Christ, the Son of God, and that believing you may have life in His name." Thus the Gospel of John sets forth a Christology, a theology of Christ as the unique God and Savior of mankind.

Key Word. Many words are repeated in John, such as *world, life, light,* and *darkness,* but in view of the purpose of the book and the key verse, the *key* word is no doubt *believe.*

How John Fits Together. John's method is to present seven "signs" (Greek *semeia*) that build, one on the other, a heavy and persuasive proof of the deity and saving ability of Jesus Christ. Those seven signs are not necessarily in strict chronological order, although some scholars think they could be. An understanding of John's purpose and method as theological, rather than chronological, delivers us from the need to align these events with the others found in the first three Gospel accounts. The purpose of those accounts is to set forth a chronological record of Jesus' life and ministry, as Luke says in the prologue to his Gospel—they literally "set in order" those events in the life of Christ (Luke 1:1-4). John's purpose, however, is to build a theological case for the claims of Christ.

The seven signs are seven miracles that increase in might, power, and saving significance: (1) Turning water into wine (ch. 2); (2) Healing the nobleman's son (ch. 4); (3) Healing the lame man at Bethesda (ch. 5); (4) Feeding the five thousand (ch. 6); (5) Walking on the water (ch. 6); (6) Healing the man born blind (ch. 9); (7) Raising Lazarus from the dead (ch. 11).

From the occurrence of the last miracle (ch. 11) to the end of the book (ch. 21), the rest of the narrative traces through the betrayal, arrest, trial, scourging, crucifixion, and burial of Jesus Christ to the glorious account of His resurrection and post-resurrection appearances. One's heart cannot be but moved by the study of this Gospel to say with Thomas to Jesus, "My Lord and My God!" (20:28).

—J.W.B.

The Eternal Word

IN the beginning ᴿwas the Word, and the ᴿWord was ᴿwith God, and the Word was ᴿGod. 1 John 1:1 · Rev. 19:13 · [John 17:5] · [1 John 5:20]

2 He was in the beginning with God.

3 ᴿAll things were made through Him, and without Him nothing was made that was made.   [Col. 1:16, 17]

4 ᴿIn Him was life, and ᴿthe life was the light of men.   [1 John 5:11] · John 8:12; 9:5; 12:46

5 And the light shines in the darkness, and the darkness did not *comprehend it.

John's Witness: The True Light

6 There was a ᴿman sent from God, whose name *was* John.   Matt. 3:1-17

7 This man came for a ᴿwitness, to bear witness of the Light, that all through him might ᴿbelieve.   John 3:25-36; 5:33-35 · [John 3:16]

8 He was not that Light, but *was sent* to bear witness of that ᴿLight.   Is. 9:2; 49:6

9 That was the true Light which gives light to every man coming into the world.

10 He was in the world, and the world was made through Him, and ᴿthe world did not know Him.   Heb. 1:2

11 ᴿHe came to His *own, and His *own did not receive Him.   [Luke 19:14]

12 But as many as received Him, to them He gave the right to become children of God, to those who believe in His name:

13 ᴿwho were born, not of blood, nor of the will of the flesh, nor of the will of man, but of God.   [1 Pet. 1:23]

The Word Becomes Flesh

▼ 7-F. Jesus Is the God-Man

14 And the Word became flesh and dwelt among us, and ᴿwe beheld His glory, the glory

as of the only begotten of the Father, ᴿfull of grace and truth.   Is. 40:5 · [John 8:32; 14:6; 18:37] ▲

15 John bore witness of Him and cried out, saying, "This was He of whom I said, 'He who comes after me ᵀis preferred before me, for He was before me.' "   *ranks higher than I*

16 *And of His ᴿfullness we have all received, and grace for grace.   [Col. 1:19; 2:9]

17 For the law was given through Moses, *but* ᴿgrace and ᴿtruth came through Jesus Christ.   [Rom. 5:21; 6:14] · [John 8:32; 14:6; 18:37]

18 No one has seen God at any time. ᴿThe only begotten *Son, who is in the bosom of the Father, He has declared *Him.   Ps. 2:7

A Voice in the Wilderness

19 Now this is ᴿthe testimony of John, when the Jews sent priests and Levites from Jerusalem to ask him, "Who are you?" John 5:33

20 ᴿHe confessed, and did not deny, but confessed, "I am not the Christ."   Luke 3:15

21 And they asked him, "What then? Are you Elijah?" He said, "I am not." "Are you the Prophet?" And he answered, "No."

22 Then they said to him, "Who are you, that we may give an answer to those who sent us? What do you say about yourself?"

23 He said: "I *am*

ᴿ*The voice of one crying in the
    wilderness:*   Is. 40:3
"*Make straight the way of the* LORD," '

as the prophet Isaiah said."

24 Now those who were sent were from the Pharisees.

25 And they asked him, saying, "Why then do you baptize if you are not the Christ, nor Elijah, nor the Prophet?"

1:5 Or *overcome*
1:11 His own things or domain • His own people

1:16 NU *For*
1:18 NU *God*

7-F. Jesus Is the God-Man (John 1:14)—"And the Word became flesh" (v. 14). But who is the Word? John the Baptist provides the answer: "This was He of whom I said, 'He who comes after me is preferred before me, for He was before me'" (v. 15). Jesus Christ is the Word. The apostle John confirms this in the Revelation: "Now I saw heaven opened, and behold, a white horse. And He who sat on him was called Faithful and True . . . and His name is called The Word of God. . . . He Himself treads the winepress of the fierceness and wrath of Almighty God. And He has on His robe and on His thigh a name written: KING OF KINGS AND LORD OF LORDS" (Rev. 19:11-16, page 1312). In this Scripture Jesus is called "Faithful and True," "The Word of God," "Almighty God," and "KING OF KINGS AND LORD OF LORDS." The Word is the Lord Jesus Christ, the God-Man.

In John 1:1-18 (page 1049) we have eternal truth embodied in the Word. The Word is "God . . . manifested in the flesh" (1 Tim. 3:16, page 1220), a visible manifestation of the invisible God who cannot be seen in His essence, but was revealed to us when "the Word became flesh" (v. 14). John said four things about the Word:

(1) "In the beginning was the Word" (v. 1)—the fact of His timeless existence.
(2) "The Word was with God" (v. 1)—the fact of His timeless relationship with (literally "face to face with") God the Father and God the Holy Spirit.
(3) "The Word was God" (v. 1)—the fact of His absolute deity.
(4) "The Word became flesh" (v. 14)—the fact of His incarnation. When He became flesh, He did not begin as a new person, but continued His timeless existence, relationship, and deity. When "the Word became flesh" in human form, He revealed God to man. Jesus is the God-Man.

See Luke 4:31, 32, page 1017, for **Point 7-G: Jesus Is Sovereign.**

26 John answered them, saying, R"I baptize with water, Rbut there stands One among you whom you do not know.   Matt. 3:11 • Mal. 3:1
27 R"It is He who, coming after me, Tis preferred before me, whose sandal strap I am not worthy to loose."   Acts 19:4 • ranks higher than I
28 These things were done Rin *Bethabara beyond the Jordan, where John was baptizing.   Judg. 7:24

The Lamb of God

29 The next day John saw Jesus coming toward him, and said, "Behold! The Lamb of God who takes away the sin of the world!
30 "This is He of whom I said, 'After me comes a Man who Tis preferred before me, for He was before me.'   ranks higher than I
31 "I did not know Him; but that He should be revealed to Israel, Rtherefore I came baptizing with water."   Matt. 3:6
32 RAnd John bore witness, saying, "I saw the Spirit descending from heaven like a dove, and He remained upon Him.   Mark 1:10
33 "I did not know Him, but He who sent me to baptize with water said to me, 'Upon whom you see Rthe Spirit descending, and remaining on Him, this is He who baptizes with the Holy Spirit.'   Is. 42:1; 61:1
34 "And I have seen and testified that Rthis is the Son of God."   Ps. 2:7; Luke 1:35

The First Disciples

35 Again, the next day, John stood with two of his disciples.
36 And looking at Jesus as He walked, he said, R"Behold the Lamb of God!"   John 1:29
37 The two disciples heard him speak, and they Rfollowed Jesus.   Matt. 4:20, 22
38 Then Jesus turned, and seeing them following, said to them, "What do you seek?" They said to Him, "Rabbi" (which is to say, when translated, Teacher), "where are You staying?"
39 He said to them, "Come and see." They came and saw where He was staying, and remained with Him that day (now it was about the tenth hour).
40 One of the two who heard John speak,

1:28 NU, M Bethany

and followed Him, was RAndrew, Simon Peter's brother.   Matt. 4:18
41 He first found his own brother Simon, and said to him, "We have found the Messiah" (which is translated, the Christ).
42 And he brought him to Jesus. Now when Jesus looked at him, He said, "You are Simon the son of *Jonah. You shall be called Cephas" (which is translated, TA Stone).   Peter

Philip and Nathanael

43 The following day Jesus wanted to go to Galilee, and He found RPhilip and said to him, "Follow Me."   John 6:5; 12:21, 22; 14:8, 9
44 Now RPhilip was from Bethsaida, the city of Andrew and Peter.   John 12:21
45 Philip found Nathanael and said to him, "We have found Him of whom Moses in the law, and also the prophets, wrote—Jesus Rof Nazareth, the son of Joseph."   [Matt. 2:23]
46 And Nathanael said to him, R"Can anything good come out of Nazareth?" Philip said to him, "Come and see."   John 7:41, 42, 52
47 Jesus saw Nathanael coming toward Him, and said of him, "Behold, an Israelite indeed, in whom is no deceit!"
48 Nathanael said to Him, "How do You know me?" Jesus answered and said to him, "Before Philip called you, when you were under the fig tree, I saw you."
49 Nathanael answered and said to Him, "Rabbi, RYou are the Son of God! You are Rthe King of Israel!"   Ps. 2:7 • Matt. 21:5
50 Jesus answered and said to him, "Because I said to you, 'I saw you under the fig tree,' do you believe? You will see greater things than these."
51 And He said to him, "Most assuredly, I say to you, Rhereafter* you shall see heaven open, and the angels of God ascending and descending upon the Son of Man."   Gen. 28:12

Water Turned to Wine

8-A. Jesus Turned Water into Wine, ▼ **Proving His Deity in His Power to Create**

2 On the third day there was a Rwedding in RCana of Galilee, and the Rmother of Jesus was there.   [Heb. 13:4] • Josh. 19:28 • John 19:25

1:42 NU John
1:51 NU omits hereafter

8-A. Jesus Turned Water into Wine, Proving His Deity in His Power to Create (John 2:1–11)—Jesus chose a wedding in Cana of Galilee to present the first of seven signs that prove His deity.

In this first sign the Lord Jesus transcends the laws of nature that He established when He "created the heavens and the earth" (Gen. 1:1, page 2). Here He demonstrates His authority over creation, because He is the Creator. "For by Him all things were created" (Col. 1:16, page 1202).

Nature takes months to turn water into wine. The water, vitamins, and minerals are drawn up through the roots, stem, and branches of the grapevine, and through the complex process of photosynthesis they are turned into the fruit that ripens in the sun. The fruit is then harvested, pressed, and made into wine. Only God, who created all things and established the laws of nature, could, in an instant, duplicate the process of nature by turning water into wine. It was a perfect vintage, created by the omnipotent God.

It was the custom, at such a celebration, to serve the best wine at the beginning of the feast, and the

(Point 8-A continued on next page)

▽ 2 Now both Jesus and His disciples were invited to the wedding.

3 And when they ran out of wine, the mother of Jesus said to Him, "They have no wine."

4 Jesus said to her, ᴿ"Woman, ᴮwhat does your concern have to do with Me? My hour has not yet come." John 19:26 · 2 Sam. 16:10

5 His mother said to the servants, "Whatever He says to you, do *it*."

6 Now there were set there six waterpots of stone, ᴿaccording to the manner of purification of the Jews, containing twenty or thirty gallons apiece. [Mark 7:3]

7 Jesus said to them, "Fill the waterpots with water." And they filled them up to the brim.

8 And He said to them, "Draw *some* out now, and take *it* to the master of the feast." And they took *it*.

9 When the master of the feast had tasted ᴿthe water that was made wine, and did not know where it came from (but the servants who had drawn the water knew), the master of the feast called the bridegroom. John 4:46

10 And he said to him, "Every man at the beginning sets out the good wine, and when the *guests* have well drunk, then the inferior. You have kept the good wine until now!"

11 This beginning of signs Jesus did in Cana of Galilee, and ᵀmanifested His glory; and His
▲ disciples believed in Him. revealed

12 After this He went down to Capernaum, He, His mother, His brothers, and His disciples; and they did not stay there many days.

Jesus Cleanses the Temple

13 Now the Passover of the Jews was at hand, and Jesus went up to Jerusalem.

14 ᴿAnd He found in the temple those who sold oxen and sheep and doves, and the moneychangers doing business. Mal. 3:1

15 When He had made a whip of cords, He drove them all out of the temple, with the

sheep and the oxen, and poured out the changers' money and overturned the tables.

16 And He said to those who sold doves, "Take these things away! Do not make My Father's house a house of merchandise!"

17 Then His disciples remembered that it was written, ᴿ"*Zeal for Your house *has eaten Me up.*" Ps. 69:9

18 So the Jews answered and said to Him, ᴿ"What sign do You show to us, since You do these things?" Matt. 12:38

19 Jesus answered and said to them, ᴿ"Destroy this temple, and in three days I will raise it up." Matt. 26:61; 27:40; Acts 10:40

20 Then the Jews said, "It has taken forty-six years to build this temple, and will You raise it up in three days?"

21 But He was speaking ᴿof the temple of His body. [1 Cor. 3:16; 6:19]

22 Therefore, when He had risen from the dead, His disciples remembered that He had said this *to them; and they believed the Scripture and the word which Jesus had said.

The Discerner of Hearts

23 Now when He was in Jerusalem at the ᴿPassover, during the feast, many believed in His name when they saw the signs which He did. [Acts 2:22]

24 But Jesus did not commit Himself to them, because He ᴿknew all *men*, Rev. 2:23

25 and had no need that anyone should testify of man, for ᴿHe knew what was in man. Matt. 9:4

The New Birth

23-A. The Spiritual Birth

3 There was a man of the Pharisees named Nicodemus, a ruler of the Jews.

2 ᴿThis man came to Jesus by night and

2:17 NU, M *will eat*
2:22 NU, M omit *to them*

(Point 8-A continued from previous page)
poorest wine when all the guests were filled. When the servants served the newly created wine to the master of the feast, the master called the bridegroom and said, "You have kept the good wine until now!" (v. 10).

This is good news for those who are saved by faith in the Lord Jesus Christ—the best is yet to come. The Christian life, at its best in this world, is still inferior to that life enjoyed with Christ Jesus. When He comes for His bride, we will eat and drink with Him at the marriage supper of the Lamb (Rev. 19:7–9, page 1312). The best is yet to come, and it will never end. "Alleluia! For the Lord God Omnipotent reigns!" (Rev. 19:6, page 1312).

Jesus performed this sign to manifest His glory, and also to show His disciples that He is God (v. 11). If your faith cannot embrace the deity of Jesus Christ, it is not *saving faith* (John 20:28, 29, page 1083).

See John 4:46–54, page 1055, for **Point 8-B: Jesus Healed the Nobleman's Son, Proving His Deity in His Power to Prolong Life.**

23-A. The Spiritual Birth (John 3:1–8)—Birth was the subject of discourse between the Lord Jesus and Nicodemus, a Pharisee. Nicodemus began by saying, "Rabbi, we know that You are a teacher come from God; for no one can do these signs that You do unless God is with him" (v. 2). Now Jesus "knew all men . . . [and] what was in man" (John 2:24, 25), so His supernatural insight into the heart and life of this devoutly religious man prompted Jesus to raise the issue of spiritual birth. Ignoring Nicodemus's complimentary

(Point 23-A continued on next page)

▽ said to Him, "Rabbi, we know that You are a teacher come from God; for ᴿno one can do these signs that You do unless ᴿGod is with him."   John 7:50; 19:39 • John 9:16, 33 • [Acts 10:38]

3 Jesus answered and said to him, "Most assuredly, I say to you, unless one is born again, he cannot see the kingdom of God."

4 Nicodemus said to Him, "How can a man be born when he is old? Can he enter a second time into his mother's womb and be born?"

5 Jesus answered, "Most assuredly, I say to you, unless one is born of water and the Spirit, he cannot enter the kingdom of God.

6 "That which is born of the flesh is flesh, and that which is born of the Spirit is spirit.

7 "Do not marvel that I said to you, 'You must be born again.'

8 ᴿ"The wind blows where it wishes, and you hear the sound of it, but cannot tell where it comes from and where it goes. So is

▲ everyone who is born of the Spirit."   Eccl. 11:5

9 Nicodemus answered and said to Him, ᴿ"How can these things be?"   John 6:52, 60

10 Jesus answered and said to him, "Are you the teacher of Israel, and do not know these things?

11 "Most assuredly, I say to you, We speak what We know and testify what We have seen, and you do not receive Our witness.

12 "If I have told you earthly things and you do not believe, how will you believe if I tell you heavenly things?

13 ᴿ"No one has ascended to heaven but He who came down from heaven, *that is*, the Son of Man *who is in heaven.   Eph. 4:9

14 ᴿ"And as Moses lifted up the serpent in the wilderness, even so ᴿmust the Son of Man be lifted up,   Num. 21:9 • John 8:28; 12:34; 19:18

15 "that whoever believes in Him should *not perish but ᴿhave eternal life.   John 3:36

16 ᴿ"For God so loved the world that He gave His only begotten ᴿSon, that whoever believes in Him should not perish but have everlasting life.   Rom. 5:8 • [Is. 9:6]

3:13 NU omits *who is in heaven*

3:15 NU omits *not perish but*

(Point 23-A continued from previous page)

remarks, Jesus said, "Unless one is born again [from above], he cannot see the kingdom of God" (v. 3). Confused at this, his mind on the physical birth, Nicodemus asked a reasonable question: "How can a man be born when he is old? Can he enter a second time into his mother's womb and be born?" (v. 4).

Nicodemus received a supernatural answer to his natural question. Jesus replied, "Most assuredly, I say to you, unless one is born of water and the Spirit, he cannot enter the kingdom of God. That which is born of the flesh is flesh, and that which is born of the Spirit is spirit. Do not marvel that I said to you, 'You must be born again' " (vv. 5-7). The question is, what did Jesus mean by being "born of water"—what does water have to do with spiritual birth? To answer this question, we must see how the image of water is used in the Scriptures:

(1) *The Holy Spirit.* On the last day of the great feast, "Jesus stood and cried out, saying, 'If anyone thirsts, let him come to Me and drink. He who believes in Me, as the Scripture has said, out of his heart will flow rivers of living water.' But this He spoke concerning the Spirit . . . " (John 7:37-39, page 1061).

(2) *Everlasting life.* "But whoever drinks of the water that I shall give him will never thirst. But the water that I shall give him will become in him a fountain of water springing up into everlasting life" (John 4:14, page 1053).

(3) *The Word of God.* "That He might sanctify and cleanse her [the church] with the washing of water by the word" (Eph. 5:26, 27, page 1192). To fully understand the word "water" in verse 5, we must let Scripture interpret Scripture, for no Scripture is to be interpreted in isolation (2 Pet. 1:20, page 1273). Some commentators believe that "water" in this instance means water baptism. But if this is so then water baptism is essential to salvation; such an interpretation invalidates salvation by grace, ignoring the context of Ephesians 2:8, 9 (page 1187) and many, many other passages. Spiritual birth is a miracle of God's grace. It is "not by works of righteousness which we have done, but according to His mercy [that] He saved us, through the washing of regeneration and renewing of the Holy Spirit" (Titus 3:5, page 1231).

There is scriptural evidence that "water" in verse 5 is a metaphor for the Word of God:

(a) "Of His own will He brought us forth by the word of truth" (James 1:18, page 1256; 2 Cor. 5:17, page 1169).

(b) "So then faith [saving faith] comes by hearing, and hearing by the word of God" (Rom. 10:17, page 1140).

(c) "Having been born again [spiritual birth], not of corruptible seed [natural birth] but incorruptible [seed], through the word of God which lives and abides forever" (1 Pet. 1:23, page 1264).

In the light of these Scriptures, verse 5 can be paraphrased as follows: "Unless one is born of the Word of God and of the Holy Spirit of God, he cannot enter the kingdom of God." Both the Word of God and the Holy Spirit are essential to salvation. Water baptism is not a part of the new birth. At this juncture Jesus said to Nicodemus, "Do not marvel that I said to you, 'You must be born again.' The wind blows where it wishes, and you hear the sound of it, but cannot tell where it comes from and where it goes. So is everyone who is born of the Spirit" (vv. 7, 8).

See 1 Peter 1:23, page 1264, for **Point 23-B: The Spiritual Birth and the Natural Birth.**

17 "For God did not send His Son into the world to condemn the world, but ᴿthat the world through Him might be saved.   Matt. 1:21

18 ᴿ"He who believes in Him is not condemned; but he who does not believe is condemned already, because he has not believed in the name of the only begotten Son of God.   John 5:24; 6:40, 47; 20:31

19 "And this is the condemnation, ᴿthat the light has come into the world, and men loved darkness rather than light, because their deeds were evil.   [John 1:4, 9–11]

20 "For ᴿeveryone practicing evil hates the light and does not come to the light, lest his deeds should be exposed.   Eph. 5:11, 13

21 "But he who does the truth comes to the light, that his deeds may be clearly seen, that they have been ᴿdone in God."   1 Cor. 15:10

John the Baptist Exalts Christ

22 After these things Jesus and His disciples came into the land of Judea, and there He remained with them ᴿand baptized.   John 4:1, 2

23 Now John also was baptizing in Aenon near Salim, because there was much water there. And they came and were baptized.

24 For ᴿJohn had not yet been thrown into prison.   Matt. 4:12; 14:3

25 Then there arose a dispute between *some* of John's disciples and the Jews about purification.

26 And they came to John and said to him, "Rabbi, He who was with you beyond the Jordan, to whom you have testified—behold, He is baptizing, and all are coming to Him!"

27 John answered and said, ᴿ"A man can receive nothing unless it has been given to him from heaven.   1 Cor. 3:5, 6; 4:7

28 "You yourselves bear me witness, that I said, ᴿ'I am not the Christ,' but, ᴿ'I have been sent before Him.'   John 1:19–27 · Mal. 3:1

29 ᴿ"He who has the bride is the bridegroom; but ᴿthe friend of the bridegroom, who stands and hears him, rejoices greatly because of the bridegroom's voice. Therefore this joy of mine is fulfilled.   [2 Cor. 11:2] · Song 5:1

30 "He must increase, but I *must* decrease.

31 "He who comes from above is above all; ᴿhe who is of the earth is earthly and speaks of the earth. ᴿHe who comes from heaven is above all.   1 Cor. 15:47 · John 6:33

32 "And ᴿwhat He has seen and heard, that He testifies; ᴿand no one receives His testimony.   John 3:11; 15:15 · Is. 53:1, 3

33 "He who has received His testimony ᴿhas certified that God is true.   1 John 5:10

34 ᴿ"For He whom God has sent speaks the words of God, for God does not give the Spirit ᴿby measure.   Deut. 18:18 · John 1:16

35 ᴿ"The Father loves the Son, and has given all things into His hand.   [Heb. 2:8]

36 ᴿ"He who believes in the Son has everlasting life; and he who does not believe the Son shall not see life, but the ᴿwrath of God abides on him."   John 3:16, 17; 6:47 · Rom. 1:18

A Samaritan Woman Meets Her Messiah

4 Therefore, when the Lord knew that the Pharisees had heard that Jesus made and baptized more disciples than John

2 (though Jesus Himself did not baptize, but His disciples),

3 He left Judea and departed again to Galilee.

4 But He needed to go through Samaria.

5 So He came to a city of Samaria which is called Sychar, near the plot of ground that Jacob ᴿgave to his son Joseph.   Gen. 48:22

6 Now Jacob's well was there. Jesus therefore, being wearied from *His* journey, sat thus by the well. It was about the sixth hour.

7 A woman of Samaria came to draw water. Jesus said to her, "Give Me a drink."

8 For His disciples had gone away into the city to buy food.

9 Then the woman of Samaria said to Him, "How is it that You, being a Jew, ask a drink from me, a Samaritan woman?" For ᴿJews have no dealings with Samaritans.   Acts 10:28

10 Jesus answered and said to her, "If you knew the ᴿgift of God, and who it is who says to you, 'Give Me a drink,' you would have asked Him, and He would have given you ᴿliving water."   [Rom. 5:15] · Is. 12:3; 44:3

11 The woman said to Him, "Sir, You have nothing to draw with, and the well is deep. Where then do You get that living water?

12 "Are You greater than our father Jacob, who gave us the well, and drank from it himself, as well as his sons and his livestock?"

13 Jesus answered and said to her, "Whoever drinks of this water will thirst again,

14 "but ᴿwhoever drinks of the water that I shall give him will never thirst. But the water that I shall give him ᴿwill become in him a fountain of water springing up into everlasting life."   [John 6:35, 58] · John 7:37, 38

15 ᴿThe woman said to Him, "Sir, give me this water, that I may not thirst, nor come here to draw."   John 6:34, 35; 17:2, 3

16 Jesus said to her, "Go, call your husband, and come here."

17 The woman answered and said, "I have no husband." Jesus said to her, "You have well said, 'I have no husband,'

18 "for you have had five husbands, and the one whom you now have is not your husband; in that you spoke truly."

19 The woman said to Him, "Sir, ᴿI perceive that You are a prophet.   Luke 7:16, 39; 24:19

20 "Our fathers worshiped on this mountain, and you *Jews* say that in Jerusalem is the place where one ought to worship."

21 Jesus said to her, "Woman, believe Me, the hour is coming ᴿwhen you will neither on this mountain, nor in Jerusalem, worship the Father.   1 Tim. 2:8

22 "You worship ᴿwhat you do not know; we know what we worship, for ᴿsalvation is of the Jews.   [2 Kin. 17:28–41] • [Rom. 3:1; 9:4, 5]

▼ **28–C. Worship in the New Testament**

23 "But the hour is coming, and now is, when the true worshipers will worship the Father in spirit ᴿand truth; for the Father is seeking such to worship Him.   [John 1:17]

24 "God *is* Spirit, and those who worship
▲ Him must worship in spirit and truth."

25 The woman said to Him, "I know that Messiah is coming" (who is called Christ). "When He comes, He will tell us all things."

26 Jesus said to her, ᴿ"I who speak to you am He."   Dan. 9:25; Matt. 26:63, 64; Mark 14:61, 62

The Whitened Harvest

27 And at this *point* His disciples came, and they marveled that He talked with a woman;

yet no one said, "What do You seek?" or, "Why are You talking with her?"

28 The woman then left her waterpot, went her way into the city, and said to the men,

29 "Come, see a Man ᴿwho told me all things that I ever did. Could this be the Christ?"   John 4:25

30 Then they went out of the city and came to Him.

31 In the meantime His disciples urged Him, saying, "Rabbi, eat."

32 But He said to them, "I have food to eat of which you do not know."

33 Therefore the disciples said to one another, "Has anyone brought Him *anything* to eat?"

34 Jesus said to them, ᴿ"My food is to do the will of Him who sent Me, and to ᴿfinish His work.   Ps. 40:7, 8 • [John 6:38; 17:4; 19:30]

35 "Do you not say, 'There are still four months and *then* comes ᴿthe harvest'? Be-

---

28–C. Worship in the New Testament (John 4:23, 24)—The Old Testament ends four hundred years before the New Testament begins, with the temple having been rebuilt and the sacrificial worship system restored. As New Testament times began, this temple had been greatly beautified by Herod. With its gleaming white marble trimmed in real gold, it was one of the wonders of the age, its splendor visible from a distance as the people went up to Jerusalem to worship. This ornate, ritualistic worship continued throughout the New Testament era and only ceased with the destruction of Jerusalem in A.D. 70.

Two other forms of worship, however, are more pertinent to our study of this period:

(1) *Worship in the synagogue* (Acts 15:21, page 1109). The word *synagogue* is simply a Greek word for congregation. Local Jewish congregations had formed when the people of Israel were in exile and therefore had no temple. In the synagogue the Old Testament was taught, especially the Law, services of prayer were also conducted. A group of elders and the ruler or chief of the synagogue led the worship.

Scripture was read and expounded by men of the congregation; unlike today's modern synagogue in which a rabbi does most of the teaching and work, any man might read or speak in the ancient synagogue. Hence our Lord Himself, though unpopular with the religious leaders, could read and preach in the synagogue both in His home town, Nazareth (Luke 4:16–27, page 1016), and in His second home base, Capernaum (John 6:59, page 1060). Paul and his fellow missionaries were allowed to share their beliefs with the congregation because they were Jewish (Acts 13:14–52, page 1106).

Synagogue worship laid the foundation for Christian church worship, since many local synagogues in various countries were easily adapted to Christianity. Even the system of elders was retained (instructions for which may be found in Acts 20, page 1115; 1 and 2 Timothy, page 1218; and Titus, page 1230).

(2) *Worship in the church.* To the Samaritan woman, who was concerned about which temple of worship was the correct one—her Samaritan temple on Mount Gerizim or the Jewish temple in Jerusalem— our Lord foretold the then-future Christian dispensation, in which we worship in spirit and truth.

The Samaritans only accepted the Pentateuch (Genesis—Deuteronomy), rejecting all the rest of the Old Testament. Like cults of the present day, they did not worship in truth. Most of the Jews did possess the truth (except the liberal Sadducees who denied the supernatural and the resurrection), but the Pharisees were so legalistic they did not worship in spirit.

The major activities of the New Testament church are mentioned in Acts 2:42 (page 1090), such as the "breaking of bread" (the Lord's Supper), a ceremony especially suited to worship in spirit and truth (1 Cor. 11—14, page 1155). Its elements, reminding the believers of Christ's sacrificial death for them, are comparable to the actual sacrifice of Old Testament lambs and other animals. However, the book of Hebrews emphasizes that the Lord's Supper is not itself a sacrifice, since the ultimate sacrifice has already been made by the Lord Jesus Christ (Heb. 9:28, page 1245; 10:10, page 1246); rather it is a memorial to Calvary "in remembrance of Me" (1 Cor. 11:24, page 1156). It is not the Lord's Altar but the Lord's Table.

Since this service evolved from the yearly Passover, it was only natural that the church worship also continued the practice of hymns and prayers. And just as the Old Testament priest or worshiper sometimes actually ate bread and meat in communal worship, so the Christian believer partakes at the communion service as a sign of fellowship with other believers (1 Cor. 10:17, page 1155).

The earliest church (Acts 2:46, page 1090) broke bread daily, but by the end of the book of Acts, weekly communion (on the Lord's Day, to commemorate the Resurrection) seemed to be customary (Acts 20:7, page 1115).

See Luke 2:13, 14 page 1012, for **Point 28-D: Worship: Its Importance.**

hold, I say to you, lift up your eyes and look at the fields, ^Rfor they are already white for harvest!   Gen. 8:22 • Matt. 9:37

36 ^R"And he who reaps receives wages, and gathers fruit for eternal life, that ^Rboth he who sows and he who reaps may rejoice together.   Dan. 12:3 • 1 Thess. 2:19

37 "For in this the saying is true: ^R'One sows and another reaps.'   1 Cor. 3:5-9

38 "I sent you to reap that for which you have not labored; ^Rothers have labored, and you have entered into their labors."   [1 Pet. 1:12]

The Savior of the World

39 And many of the Samaritans of that city believed in Him ^Rbecause of the word of the woman who testified, "He told me all that I *ever* did."   John 4:29

40 So when the Samaritans had come to Him, they urged Him to stay with them; and He stayed there two days.

41 And many more believed because of His own ^Rword.   Luke 4:32

42 Then they said to the woman, "Now we believe, not because of what you said, for ^Rwe ourselves have heard *Him* and we know that this is indeed *the Christ, the Savior of the world."   1 John 4:14

Welcome at Galilee

43 Now after the two days He departed from there and went to Galilee.

44 For Jesus Himself testified that a prophet has no honor in his own country.

4:42 NU omits *the Christ*

45 So when He came to Galilee, the Galileans received Him, having seen all the things He did in Jerusalem at the feast; ^Rfor they also had gone to the feast.   Deut. 16:16

A Nobleman's Son Healed

8-B. Jesus Healed the Nobleman's Son, Proving His Deity in His Power to Prolong Life ▼

46 So Jesus came again to Cana of Galilee ^Rwhere He had made the water wine. And there was a certain ^Tnobleman whose son was sick at Capernaum.   John 2:1, 11 • *royal official*

47 When he heard that Jesus had come out of Judea into Galilee, he went to Him and implored Him to come down and heal his son, for he was at the point of death.

48 Then Jesus said to him, ^R"Unless you *people* see signs and wonders, you will by no means believe."   1 Cor. 1:22

49 The nobleman said to Him, "Sir, come down before my child dies!"

50 Jesus said to him, "Go your way; your son lives." So the man believed the word that Jesus spoke to him, and he went his way.

51 And as he was now going down, his servants met him and told *him*, saying, "Your son lives!"

52 Then he inquired of them the hour when he got better. And they said to him, "Yesterday at the seventh hour the fever left him."

53 So the father knew that *it was* at the same hour in which Jesus said to him, "Your son lives." And he himself believed, and his whole household.

8-B. Jesus Healed the Nobleman's Son, Proving His Deity in His Power to Prolong Life (John 4:46–54)—In the second of the seven signs recorded by John, Jesus demonstrated His power to prolong life. Later He would say, "Let not your heart be troubled . . . I am . . . the life" (John 14:1–6, page 1074). He is God of this life and of life eternal. He is the only source of all life, physical or spiritual (Gen. 2:7, page 4; 1 John 5:11, 12, page 1282).

After ministering in Judea and Samaria, Jesus had returned to Cana in Galilee, when a nobleman from Capernaum came to Him begging Him to "come down and heal his son, for he was at the point of death" (v. 47). His two words, "come down," revealed the limited measure of the nobleman's faith (Rom. 12:3, page 1142). It was a weak faith, requiring Jesus' actual presence. But just as Jesus knows all men and women (John 2:23–25, page 1051), He knew the nobleman completely. He knew the man's love for his son and his motive for coming, and also that he was looking for a sign to prop up his weak faith. Jesus rebuked the Jews for seeking signs: "Unless you people see signs and wonders, you will by no means believe" (v. 48). (Another time, when some of the scribes and Pharisees said, "Teacher, we want to see a sign from You" Jesus answered, "An evil and adulterous generation seeks after a sign, and no sign will be given to it except the sign of the prophet Jonah" [Matt. 12:38–42, page 954]. By then Jesus had demonstrated that He was the Christ by His life, by His words, and by sign-miracles aplenty.)

But Jesus graciously did not stop at rebuke. To strengthen the nobleman's faith, He gave him something much greater than a sign: He gave him His word. Jesus said, "Go your way; your son lives." These words of Jesus provided an opportunity for the nobleman to exercise his weak faith, and by so doing increase its measure. Faith will grow when we believe God's Word without having to see signs and wonders (Rom. 10:17, page 1140). The nobleman's faith no longer needed to see miracles. "Jesus said to him, 'Go your way; your son lives.' So the man believed the word that Jesus spoke to him, and he went his way" (v. 50).

Again Jesus transcended the natural laws of healing that God created in man, and healed the nobleman's son instantly, proving His deity in His power to prolong life. Only the Creator of life can extend life; therefore Jesus is God.

See John 5:1–18, page 1056, for **Point 8-C: Jesus Healed a Sick Man at the Pool of Bethesda, Proving His Deity in His Power to Give Life.**

▽ 54 This again *is* the second sign Jesus did
▲ when He had come out of Judea into Galilee.

A Man Healed at the Pool of Bethesda

▼ 8-C. Jesus Healed a Sick Man at the
Pool of Bethesda, Proving His Deity
in His Power to Give Life

5 After this there was a feast of the Jews,
and Jesus went up to Jerusalem.
2 Now there is in Jerusalem ᴿby the Sheep
Gate a pool, which is called in Hebrew, *Bethesda, having five porches.   Neh. 3:1, 32; 12:39
3 In these lay a great multitude of sick
people, blind, lame, ᵀparalyzed, *waiting for
the moving of the water.   *withered*
4 For an angel went down at a certain
time into the pool and stirred up the water;
then whoever stepped in first, after the stirring of the water, was made well of whatever
disease he had.
5 Now a certain man was there who had
an infirmity thirty-eight years.
6 When Jesus saw him lying there, and
knew that he already had been in *that condition* a long time, He said to him, "Do you
want to be made well?"
7 The sick man answered Him, "Sir, I have
no man to put me into the pool when the
water is stirred up; but while I am coming,
another steps down before me."
8 Jesus said to him, ᴿ"Rise, take up your
bed and walk."   Luke 5:24
9 And immediately the man was made

5:2 NU *Bethzatha*
5:3 NU omits the rest of v. 3 and all of v. 4.

well, took up his bed, and walked. And ᴿthat ▽
day was the Sabbath.   John 9:14
10 The Jews therefore said to him who was
cured, "It is the Sabbath; ᴿit is not lawful for
you to carry your bed."   Jer. 17:21, 22
11 He answered them, "He who made me
well said to me, 'Take up your bed and
walk.' "
12 Then they asked him, "Who is the Man
who said to you, 'Take up your bed and
walk'?"
13 But the one who was ᴿhealed did not
know who it was, for Jesus had withdrawn, a
multitude being in *that* place. Luke 13:14; 22:51
14 Afterward Jesus found him in the temple, and said to him, "See, you have been
made well. ᴿSin no more, lest a worse thing
come upon you."   John 8:11
15 The man departed and told the Jews that
it was Jesus who had made him well.

Honor the Father and the Son

16 For this reason the Jews persecuted
Jesus, *and sought to kill Him, because He
had done these things on the Sabbath.
17 But Jesus answered them, ᴿ"My Father
has been working until now, and I have been
working."   [John 9:4; 17:4]
18 Therefore the Jews sought all the more
to kill Him, because He not only broke the
Sabbath, but also said that God was His
Father, making Himself equal with God.   ▲
19 Then Jesus answered and said to them,
"Most assuredly, I say to you, ᴿthe Son can
do nothing of Himself, but what He sees the

5:16 NU omits *and sought to kill Him*

8-C. Jesus Healed a Sick Man at the Pool of Bethesda, Proving His Deity in His Power to Give Life (John
5:1–18)—The third of the seven signs proving the deity of Jesus Christ occurred in the city of Jerusalem at the
pool of Bethesda, near the Sheep Gate. Bethesda means "House of Mercy." Here one lame man out of a
multitude of ill people found grace in the eyes of the Lord Jesus, who said to the man, "Rise, take up your
bed and walk" (v. 8). This healing was pure grace—that is, it was unmerited and solely due to God's
kindness and mercy (Eph. 2:8, 9, page 1187). It was instantaneous and complete (Eccl. 3:14, page 628). The
man did not seek Jesus; Jesus sought him. The man did not ask to be healed; it was Jesus who asked, "Do
you want to be made well?" (v. 6). Even after Jesus healed him, he did not know who Jesus was. The Jews
asked him, "Who is the Man who said to you, 'Take up your bed and walk'? But the one who was healed did
not know who it was . . . Afterward Jesus found him in the temple" (vv. 12-14), and he finally learned who
had healed him. He then left the temple and told the Jews that it was Jesus.
   Now the last thing Jesus had said to him was, "See, you have been made well. Sin no more, lest a worse
thing come upon you" (v. 14). Of the seven signs, this was the most unusual. Only God has perfect, eternal
knowledge of all people and all events—past, present, and future. In this sign, when He revealed to the man
that his sins had caused his sickness, and warned him not to continue to practice sin, Jesus demonstrated
that He has all knowledge.
   Another question requires an answer: Why did Jesus heal only one man out of a multitude of sick and
lame people waiting to be healed? At other times "He . . . healed all who were sick" (Matt. 8:16, page 947),
and, "great multitudes followed Him, and He healed them all" (Matt. 12:15, page 952). In this sign we are
not told why He healed only one of a multitude. The answer is obvious—it was an act of His sovereign
will. Jesus said, "The Son gives life to whom He will" (John 5:21, page 1057).
   In this sign we see Jesus the Creator giving life to one of His creatures according to His sovereign will, by
bestowing grace upon a hopeless, helpless, sinful man who had suffered physical infirmity for thirty-eight
years. Thus did He prove that He is God.
   See John 6:1-14, page 1058, for **Point 8-D: Jesus Fed Five Thousand with a Lad's Lunch, Proving His
Deity in His Power to Supply the Necessities of Life.**

Father do; for whatever He does, the Son also does in like manner.   John 5:30; 6:38; 8:28; 12:49; 14:10

20 "For the Father loves the Son, and ᴿshows Him all things that He Himself does; and He will show Him greater works than these, that you may marvel.   [Matt. 11:27]

21 "For as the Father raises the dead and gives life to *them*, ᴿeven so the Son gives life to whom He will.   [John 11:25]

22 "For the Father judges no one, but ᴿhas committed all judgment to the Son, [Acts 17:31]

23 "that all should honor the Son just as they honor the Father. ᴿHe who does not honor the Son does not honor the Father who sent Him.   1 John 2:23

Life and Judgment Are Through the Son

▼ **18-A. The Judgment of the Believer's Sins**

24 "Most assuredly, I say to you, ᴿhe who hears My word and believes in Him who sent Me has everlasting life, and shall not come into judgment, ᴿbut has passed from death ▲ into life.   John 3:16, 18; 6:47 • [1 John 3:14]

25 "Most assuredly, I say to you, the hour is coming, and now is, when ᴿthe dead will hear the voice of the Son of God; and those who hear will live.   [Col. 2:13]

26 "For ᴿas the Father has life in Himself, so He has granted the Son to have ᴿlife in Himself,   Ps. 36:9 • 1 Cor. 15:45

27 "and ᴿhas given Him authority to execute judgment also, ᴿbecause He is the Son of Man.   [Acts 10:42; 17:31] • Dan. 7:13

28 "Do not marvel at this; for the hour is coming in which all who are in the graves will ᴿhear His voice   [1 Thess. 4:15-17]

29 ᴿ"and come forth—ᴿthose who have done good, to the resurrection of life, and those who have done evil, to the resurrection of condemnation.   Is. 26:19 • Dan. 12:2

30 ᴿ"I can of Myself do nothing. As I hear, I judge; and My judgment is righteous, be-

cause ᴿI do not seek My own will but the will of the Father who sent Me.   John 5:19 • Matt. 26:39

The Fourfold Witness

31 ᴿ"If I bear witness of Myself, My witness is not ᵀtrue.   John 8:14 • *valid* as testimony

32 ᴿ"There is another who bears witness of Me, and I know that the witness which He witnesses of Me is true.   [Matt. 3:17]

33 "You have sent to John, ᴿand he has borne witness to the truth.   [John 1:15, 19, 27, 32]

34 "Yet I do not receive testimony from man, but I say these things that you may be saved.

35 "He was the burning and ᴿshining lamp, and ᴿyou were willing for a time to rejoice in his light.   2 Pet. 1:19 • Mark 6:20

36 "But I have a greater witness than John's; for ᴿthe works which the Father has given Me to finish—the very ᴿworks that I do—bear witness of Me, that the Father has sent Me.   John 3:2; 10:25; 17:4 • John 9:16; 10:38

37 "And the Father Himself, who sent Me, has testified of Me. You have neither heard His voice at any time, nor seen His form.

38 "But you do not have His word abiding in you, because whom He sent, Him you do not believe.

39 "You search the Scriptures, for in them you think you have eternal life; and ᴿthese are they which testify of Me.   Luke 24:27

40 ᴿ"But you are not willing to come to Me that you may have life.   [John 1:11; 3:19]

41 "I do not receive honor from men.

42 "But I know you, that you do not have the love of God in you.

43 "I have come in My Father's name, and you do not receive Me; if another comes in his own name, him you will receive.

44 "How can you believe, who receive honor from one another, and do not seek the honor that *comes* from the only God?

45 "Do not think that I shall accuse you to the Father; ᴿthere is *one* who accuses you— Moses, in whom you trust.   Rom. 2:12

18-A. The Judgment of the Believer's Sins (John 5:24)—In the above verse, our Lord tells us that a believer "shall not come into judgment." Our sins were judged in Christ on Calvary, and every believer "has passed from death into life" (v. 24). This is present salvation. Christ paid for our sins. He was judged in the believer's stead. The believer will not come into judgment because

(1) Jesus Christ paid the penalty. On the grounds of His substitutionary death, the believer is separated from his sins forever (Ps. 103:12, page 570).

(2) The sins of the believer have been blotted out, and God has promised that He "will not remember your sins" (Is. 43:25, page 683).

(3) Our Lord suffered for our sins, "the just for the unjust," that we might be saved and never come into judgment as sinners (1 Pet. 3:18, page 1267).

(4) The believer will never be condemned with the world, because Christ was condemned in his place. "He made Him who knew no sin to be sin for us" (2 Cor. 5:21, page 1169). Christ was made a curse for us on the cross, and "has redeemed us from the curse of the law" (Gal. 3:13, page 1181). "He has appeared to put away sin by the sacrifice of Himself" (Heb. 9:26, page 1244). The believer will not come into judgment, because his sins have been purged (Heb. 1:3, page 1236).

See 1 Corinthians 11:31, 32, page 1157, for **Point 18-B: The Judgment of the Believer's Self.**

46 "For if you believed Moses, you would believe Me; for he wrote about Me.

47 "But if you ᴿdo not believe his writings, how will you believe My words?"   Luke 16:29, 31

Feeding the Five Thousand

▼ **8-D. Jesus Fed Five Thousand with a Lad's Lunch, Proving His Deity in His Power to Supply the Necessities of Life**

6 After ᴿthese things Jesus went over the Sea of Galilee, which is the Sea of ᴿTiberias.   Mark 6:32 · John 6:23; 21:1

2 Then a great multitude followed Him, because they saw His signs which He performed on those who were ᵀdiseased.   sick

3 And Jesus went up on a mountain, and there He sat with His disciples.

4 ᴿNow the Passover, a feast of the Jews, was near.   Deut. 16:1

5 ᴿThen Jesus lifted up His eyes, and seeing a great multitude coming toward Him, He said to ᴿPhilip, "Where shall we buy bread, that these may eat?"   Matt. 14:14 · John 1:43

6 But this He said to test him, for He Himself knew what He would do.

7 Philip answered Him, ᴿ"Two hundred denarii worth of bread is not sufficient for them, that every one of them may have a little."   Num. 11:21, 22

8 One of His disciples, ᴿAndrew, Simon Peter's brother, said to Him,   John 1:40

9 "There is a lad here who has five barley loaves and two small fish, ᴿbut what are they among so many?"   2 Kin. 4:43

10 Then Jesus said, "Make the people sit down." Now there was much grass in the place. So the men sat down, in number about five thousand.

11 And Jesus took the loaves, and when He had given thanks He distributed them *to the disciples, and the disciples to those sitting down; and likewise of the fish, as much as they wanted.

12 So when they were filled, He said to His disciples, "Gather up the fragments that remain, so that nothing is lost."

13 Therefore they gathered them up, and filled twelve baskets with the fragments of the five barley loaves which were left over by those who had eaten.

14 Then those men, when they had seen the sign that Jesus did, said, "This is truly the Prophet who is to come into the world."   ▲

6:11 NU omits to the disciples, and the disciples

8-D. Jesus Fed Five Thousand with a Lad's Lunch, Proving His Deity in His Power to Supply the Necessities of Life (John 6:1–14)—This fourth of the seven signs proving the deity of Christ is the only miracle recorded by all four of the Gospels. Because the Holy Spirit moved Matthew, Mark, Luke, and John to record this sign, it has unusual importance:

(1) It was a very public sign. Some of the miracles of Jesus were performed in the presence of a few. But in this instance, Matthew tells us, "those who had eaten were about five thousand men, besides women and children" (Matt. 14:21, page 959). The total might have numbered over fifteen thousand, since often such an occasion attracts more women and children than men. No other sign had as many witnesses.

(2) These witnesses not only saw the sign, they also participated in it, eating the bread and fish until they were satisfied.

(3) They not only saw Jesus create bread and fish, and ate of it themselves, but they also watched the disciples gather twelve baskets full of leftover food.

(4) Jesus worked with almost insignificant materials. The fish were small, and the five loaves were made of barley (only the poor ate barley bread). Jesus did not reject the loaves because they were not whole wheat, or the fish because they were not big. He took the little and blessed it, and the little became much!

(5) This is the only recorded time when Jesus asked anyone's advice. He asked Philip, "Where shall we buy bread, that these may eat?" (v. 5). Philip failed this test of faith. Jesus did not need his advice, for as in all matters, "He Himself knew what He would do" (v. 6).

(6) He used all twelve apostles to serve the multitude. God's plan is to use His servants to give His gospel to those who "hunger and thirst for righteousness" (Matt. 5:6, page 937).

(7) Afterward "they were about to come and take Him by force to make Him king" (v. 15). Because He could miraculously feed them, they were ready to crown Him king. But He knew their motives were wrong, and making Him king would be premature. When He returns to this earth He will come crowned as "KING OF KINGS AND LORD OF LORDS" (Rev. 19:16, page 1313).

In this fourth sign the Lord Jesus once again transcended the laws of nature, demonstrating His authority over His creation and proving His deity. In an instant He duplicated the process of nature, creating enough bread and fish to feed five thousand men, plus women and children. Only God can supply all the necessities of life.

See John 6:15–21, page 1059, for **Point 8-E: Jesus Walked on the Water, Proving His Deity in His Power to Protect Life.**

Jesus Walks on the Sea

▼ **8-E. Jesus Walked on the Water, Proving His Deity in His Power to Protect Life**

15 Therefore when Jesus perceived that they were about to come and take Him by force to make Him ᴿking, He departed again to a mountain by Himself alone.   [John 18:36]
16 ᴿNow when evening came, His disciples went down to the sea,   Matt. 14:23
17 got into the boat, and went over the sea toward Capernaum. And it was already dark, and Jesus had not come to them.
18 Then the sea arose because a great wind was blowing.
19 So when they had rowed about ᵀthree or four miles, they saw Jesus walking on the sea and drawing near the boat; and they were ᴿafraid.   Lit. *25 or 30 stadia* · Matt. 17:6
20 But He said to them, ᴿ"It is I; do not be afraid."   Is. 43:1, 2
21 Then they willingly received Him into the boat, and immediately the boat was at the
▲ land where they were going.

The Bread from Heaven

22 On the following day, when the people who were standing on the other side of the sea saw that there was no other boat there, except *that one *which His disciples had entered, and that Jesus had not entered the boat with His disciples, but His disciples had gone away alone—
23 however, other boats came from Tiberias, near the place where they ate bread after the Lord had given thanks—
24 when the people therefore saw that Jesus was not there, nor His disciples, they also got into boats and came to Capernaum, ᴿseeking Jesus.   Luke 4:42

6:22 NU omits *that* • NU omits *which His disciples had entered*

25 And when they found Him on the other side of the sea, they said to Him, "Rabbi, when did You come here?"
26 Jesus answered them and said, "Most assuredly, I say to you, you seek Me, not because you saw the signs, but because you ate of the loaves and were filled.
27 ᴿ"Do not labor for the food which perishes, but ᴿfor the food which endures to everlasting life, which the Son of Man will give you, ᴿbecause God the Father has set His seal on Him."   Matt. 6:19 · John 4:14 · Acts 2:22
28 Then they said to Him, "What shall we do, that we may work the works of God?"
29 Jesus answered and said to them, ᴿ"This is the work of God, that you believe in Him whom He sent."   [1 John 3:23]
30 Therefore they said to Him, "What sign will You perform then, that we may see it and believe You? What work will You do?
31 "Our fathers ate the manna in the desert; as it is written, ᴿ*He gave them bread from heaven to eat.'"   Ex. 16:4; Neh. 9:15; Ps. 78:24
32 Then Jesus said to them, "Most assuredly, I say to you, Moses did not give you the bread from heaven, but ᴿMy Father gives you the true bread from heaven.   John 3:13, 16
33 "For the bread of God is He who comes down from heaven and gives life to the world."
34 ᴿThen they said to Him, "Lord, give us this bread always."   John 4:15
35 And Jesus said to them, ᴿ"I am the bread of life. ᴿHe who comes to Me shall never hunger, and he who believes in Me shall never ᴿthirst.   John 6:48, 58 · John 4:14; 7:37 · Is. 55:1, 2
36 "But I said to you that you have seen Me and yet ᴿdo not believe.   John 10:26
37 "All that the Father gives Me will come to Me, and ᴿthe one who comes to Me I will ᵀby no means cast out.   2 Tim. 2:19 · *certainly not*
38 "For I have come down from heaven,

8-E. Jesus Walked on the Water, Proving His Deity in His Power to Protect Life (John 6:15-21)—This fifth of the seven signs proving the deity of Jesus Christ is recorded by Matthew, Mark, and John. John's account of this miracle is the most condensed of the three. Matthew and Mark give us more details than John. However, we must keep in mind that John is recording these signs for one purpose—to prove the deity of Jesus. Mark tells us that Jesus sent them into the storm because they did not understand the sign of the loaves and fish, "because their heart was hardened" (Mark 6:45–52, page 992):

(1) They were in the will of God, facing contrary winds, for "their heart was hardened" (cf. Heb. 3:7–15, page 1238).
(2) They made no progress, "because their heart was hardened."
(3) But they were in no danger because Jesus was on a mountain praying—just as now "He always lives to make intercession for them" (Heb. 7:25, page 1242). Again we are told, "We have an Advocate with the Father, Jesus Christ the righteous" (1 John 2:1, page 1278). An advocate pleads the cause of another. Knowing the hardness of their hearts, Jesus was pleading their cause before the Father.

Then Jesus came walking on the water. Here He transcended the law of gravity, as He walked upon the waters of Galilee in a storm to protect the lives of His own—proving His deity in His power over nature to protect life. He upholds all things by the word of His power (Heb. 1:3, page 1236). He speaks and all creation bows to His will. Only God has such authority over all powers in heaven and on earth.

See John 9:1–41, page 1065, for **Point 8-F: Jesus Gave Sight to a Blind Beggar, Proving His Deity in His Power to Illuminate Life.**

ᴿnot to do My own will, ᴿbut the will of Him who sent Me.   Matt. 26:39 • John 4:34

39 "This is the will of the Father who sent Me, that of all He has given Me I should lose nothing, but should raise it up at the last day.

40 "And this is the will of Him who sent Me, ᴿthat everyone who sees the Son and believes in Him may have everlasting life; and I will raise him up at the last day."   John 3:15, 16

Rejected by His Own

41 The Jews then ᵀcomplained against Him, because He said, "I am the bread which came down from heaven."   *grumbled*

42 And they said, ᴿ"Is not this Jesus, the son of Joseph, whose father and mother we know? How is it then that He says, 'I have come down from heaven'?"   Matt. 13:55

43 Jesus therefore answered and said to them, "Do not murmur among yourselves.

44 "No one can come to Me unless the Father who sent Me ᴿdraws him; and I will raise him up at the last day.   [Phil. 2:12, 13]

45 "It is written in the prophets, ᴿ*'And they shall all be taught by God.'* ᴿTherefore everyone who *has heard and learned from the Father comes to Me.   Is. 54:13 • John 6:37

46 ᴿ"Not that anyone has seen the Father, ᴿexcept He who is from God; He has seen the Father.   John 1:18 • Matt. 11:27

47 "Most assuredly, I say to you, he who believes *in Me has everlasting life.

48 ᴿ"I am the bread of life.   John 6:33, 35

49 ᴿ"Your fathers ate the manna in the wilderness, and are dead.   John 6:31, 58

50 ᴿ"This is the bread which comes down from heaven, that one may eat of it and not die.   John 6:51, 58

51 "I am the living bread ᴿwhich came down from heaven. If anyone eats of this bread, he will live forever; and ᴿthe bread that I shall give is My flesh, which I shall give for the life of the world."   John 3:13 • Heb. 10:5

52 The Jews therefore ᴿquarreled among themselves, saying, "How can this Man give us *His* flesh to eat?"   John 7:43; 9:16; 10:19

53 Then Jesus said to them, "Most assuredly, I say to you, unless ᴿyou eat the flesh of the Son of Man and drink His blood, you have no life in you.   Matt. 26:26

54 ᴿ"Whoever eats My flesh and drinks My blood has eternal life, and I will raise him up at the last day.   John 4:14; 6:27, 40

55 "For My flesh is *food indeed, and My blood is *drink indeed.

56 "He who eats My flesh and drinks My blood abides in Me, and I in him.

57 "As the living Father sent Me, and I live because of the Father, so he who feeds on Me will live because of Me.

58 ᴿ"This is the bread which came down from heaven—not ᴿas your fathers ate the manna, and are dead. He who eats this bread will live forever."   John 6:49-51 • Ex. 16:14-35

59 These things He said in the synagogue as He taught in Capernaum.

Many Disciples Turn Away

60 ᴿTherefore many of His disciples, when they heard *this*, said, "This is a ᵀhard saying; who can understand it?"   John 6:66 • *difficult*

61 When Jesus knew in Himself that His disciples complained about this, He said to them, "Does this ᵀoffend you?   *make you stumble*

62 ᴿ"*What* then if you should see the Son of Man ascend where He was before?   Acts 1:9

63 ᴿ"It is the Spirit who gives life; the flesh profits nothing. The words that I speak to you are spirit, and *they* are life.   2 Cor. 3:6

64 "But there are some of you who do not believe." For ᴿJesus knew from the beginning who they were who did not believe, and who would betray Him.   John 2:24, 25; 13:11

65 And He said, "Therefore I have said to you that no one can come to Me unless it has been granted to him by My Father."

66 From that *time* many of His disciples went back and walked with Him no more.

67 Then Jesus said to the twelve, "Do you also want to go away?"

68 But Simon Peter answered Him, "Lord, to whom shall we go? You have ᴿthe words of eternal life.   Acts 5:20

69 ᴿ"Also we have come to believe and know that You are the *Christ, the Son of the living God."   Luke 9:20

70 Jesus answered them, "Did I not choose you, the twelve, and one of you is a devil?"

71 He spoke of Judas Iscariot, *the son* of Simon, for it was he who would ᴿbetray Him, being one of the twelve.   Matt. 26:14-16

Jesus' Brothers Disbelieve

7 After these things Jesus walked in Galilee; for He did not want to walk in Judea, because the *Jews sought to kill Him.

2 ᴿNow the Jews' Feast of Tabernacles was at hand.   Lev. 23:34

3 ᴿHis brothers therefore said to Him, "Depart from here and go into Judea, that Your disciples also may see the works that You are doing.   Matt. 12:46

4 "For no one does anything in secret while he himself seeks to be known openly. If You do these things, show Yourself to the world."

5 For even His ᴿbrothers did not believe in Him.   Ps. 69:8; Mic. 7:6; Mark 3:21

6 Then Jesus said to them, "My time has not yet come, but your time is always ready.

6:45 M *hears and has learned*
6:47 NU omits *in Me*
6:55 NU *true food* • NU *true drink*

6:69 NU *Holy One of God.*
7:1 The ruling authorities

7 R"The world cannot hate you, but it hates Me Rbecause I testify of it that its works are evil.   [John 15:19] · John 3:19

8 "You go up to this feast. I am not *yet going up to this feast, Rfor My time has not yet fully come."   John 8:20

9 When He had said these things to them, He remained in Galilee.

The Heavenly Scholar

10 But when His brothers had gone up, then He also went up to the feast, not openly, but as it were in secret.

11 Then Rthe Jews sought Him at the feast, and said, "Where is He?"   John 11:56

12 And there was much complaining among the people concerning Him. RSome said, "He is good"; others said, "No, on the contrary, He deceives the people."   Luke 7:16

13 However, no one spoke openly of Him Rfor fear of the Jews.   [John 9:22; 12:42; 19:38]

14 Now about the middle of the feast RJesus went up into the temple and taught.   Ps. 22:22

15 RAnd the Jews marveled, saying, "How does this Man know letters, having never studied?"   Matt. 13:54

16 *Jesus answered them and said, "My doctrine is not Mine, but His who sent Me.

17 R"If anyone wills to do His will, he shall know concerning the doctrine, whether it is from God or *whether* I speak on My own authority.   John 3:21; 8:43

18 R"He who speaks from himself seeks his own glory; but He who Rseeks the glory of the One who sent Him is true, and Rno unrighteousness is in Him.   John 5:41 · John 8:50 · [2 Cor. 5:21]

19 R"Did not Moses give you the law, yet none of you keeps the law? RWhy do you seek to kill Me?"   Deut. 33:4 · Matt. 12:14

20 The people answered and said, "You have a demon. Who is seeking to kill You?"

21 Jesus answered and said to them, "I did one work, and you all marvel.

22 R"Moses therefore gave you circumcision (not that it is from Moses, Rbut from the fathers), and you circumcise a man on the Sabbath.   Lev. 12:3 · Gen. 17:9-14

23 "If a man receives circumcision on the Sabbath, so that the law of Moses should not be broken, are you angry with Me because I made a man completely well on the Sabbath?

24 "Do not judge according to appearance, but judge with righteous judgment."

Could This Be the Christ?

25 Now some of them from Jerusalem said, "Is this not He whom they seek to kill?

26 "But look! He speaks boldly, and they say nothing to Him. RDo the rulers know indeed that this is *truly the Christ?   John 7:48

27 R"However, we know where this Man is from; but when the Christ comes, no one knows where He is from."   Luke 4:22

28 Then Jesus cried out, as He taught in the temple, saying, "You both know Me, and you know where I am from; and RI have not come of Myself, but He who sent Me Ris true, whom you do not know."   John 5:43 · Rom. 3:4

29 *"But RI know Him, for I am from Him, and He sent Me."   Matt. 11:27

30 Therefore Rthey sought to take Him; but Rno one laid a hand on Him, because His hour had not yet come. Mark 11:18 · John 7:32, 44; 8:20; 10:39

31 And Rmany of the people believed in Him, and said, "When the Christ comes, will He do more signs than these which this *Man* has done?"   Matt. 12:23

Jesus and the Religious Leaders

32 The Pharisees heard the crowd murmuring these things concerning Him, and the Pharisees and the chief priests sent officers to take Him.

33 Then Jesus said *to them, R"I shall be with you a little while longer, and *then* I go to Him who sent Me.   Mark 16:19; Acts 1:9

34 "You will seek Me and not find *Me*, and where I am you Rcannot come."   [Matt. 5:20]

35 Then the Jews said among themselves, "Where does He intend to go that we shall not find Him? Does He intend to go to Rthe Dispersion among the Greeks and teach the Greeks?   James 1:1

36 "What is this thing that He said, 'You will seek Me and not find Me, and where I am you cannot come'?"

The Promise of the Holy Spirit

37 On the last day, that great *day* of the feast, Jesus stood and cried out, saying, "If anyone thirsts, let him come to Me and drink.

38 R"He who believes in Me, as the Scripture has said, Rout of his heart will flow rivers of living water."   Deut. 18:15 · Is. 12:3; 43:20; 44:3

39 RBut this He spoke concerning the Spirit, whom those *believing in Him would receive; for the *Holy Spirit was not yet *given*, because Jesus was not yet glorified.   Is. 44:3

Who Is He?

40 Therefore *many from the crowd, when they heard this saying, said, "Truly this is Rthe Prophet."   Deut. 18:15, 18

41 Others said, "This is Rthe Christ." But some said, "Will the Christ come out of Galilee?   John 4:42; 6:69

42 R"Has not the Scripture said that the Christ comes from the seed of David and

---

7:8 NU omits yet
7:16 NU, M So Jesus
7:26 NU omits truly

7:29 NU, M omit But
7:33 NU, M omit to them
7:39 NU who believed • NU omits Holy
7:40 NU some

from the town of Bethlehem, ^Rwhere David was?"   Mic. 5:2 • 1 Sam. 16:1, 4

43 So ^Rthere was a division among the people because of Him.   John 7:12

44 Now ^Rsome of them wanted to take Him, but no one laid hands on Him.   John 7:30

Rejected by the Authorities

45 Then the officers came to the chief priests and Pharisees, who said to them, "Why have you not brought Him?"

46 The officers answered, ^R"No man ever spoke like this Man!"   Luke 4:22

47 Then the Pharisees answered them, "Are you also deceived?

48 "Have any of the rulers or the Pharisees believed in Him?

49 "But this crowd that does not know the law is accursed."

50 Nicodemus (he who came to Jesus *by night, being one of them) said to them,

51 "Does our law judge a man before it hears him and knows what he is doing?"

52 They answered and said to him, "Are you also from Galilee? Search and look, for no prophet *has arisen out of Galilee."

An Adulteress Faces the Light of the World

53 *And everyone went to his own house.

8 But Jesus went to the Mount of Olives.
2 Now *early in the morning He came again into the temple, and all the people came to Him; and He sat down and taught them.

3 Then the scribes and Pharisees brought to Him a woman caught in adultery. And when they had set her in the midst,

4 they said to Him, "Teacher, *this woman was caught in adultery, in the very act.

5 ^R"Now *Moses, in the law, commanded us *that such should be stoned. But what do You *say?"   Lev. 20:10

6 This they said, testing Him, that they ^Rmight have something of which to accuse Him. But Jesus stooped down and wrote on the ground with His finger, *as though He did not hear.   Matt. 22:15

7 So when they continued asking Him, He *raised Himself up and said to them, ^R"He who is without sin among you, let him throw a stone at her first."   Deut. 17:7

7:50 NU before
7:52 NU is to rise
7:53 NU brackets 7:53 through 8:11 as not in the original text. They are present in over 900 mss. of John.
8:2 M very early
8:4 M we found this woman
8:5 M in our law Moses commanded • NU, M to stone such • M adds about her
8:6 NU, M omit as though He did not hear
8:7 M He looked up

8 And again He stooped down and wrote on the ground.

9 Then those who heard it, ^Rbeing* convicted by their conscience, went out one by one, beginning with the oldest even to the last. And Jesus was left alone, and the woman standing in the midst.   Rom. 2:22

10 When Jesus had raised Himself up *and *saw no one but the woman, He said to her, "Woman, where are those accusers *of yours? Has no one condemned you?"

11 She said, "No one, Lord." And Jesus said to her, ^R"Neither do I condemn you; go *and ^Rsin no more."   [John 3:17] • [John 5:14]

12 Then Jesus spoke to them again, saying, ^R"I am the light of the world. He who ^Rfollows Me shall not walk in darkness, but have the light of life."   John 1:4; 9:5; 12:35 • 1 Thess. 5:5

Jesus Defends His Self-Witness

13 The Pharisees therefore said to Him, ^R"You bear witness of Yourself; Your witness is not ^Ttrue."   John 5:31 • valid as testimony

14 Jesus answered and said to them, "Even if I bear witness of Myself, My witness is true, for I know where I came from and where I am going; but ^Ryou do not know where I come from and where I am going. John 7:28; 9:29

15 ^R"You judge according to the flesh; ^RI judge no one.   John 7:24 • [John 3:17; 12:47; 18:36]

16 "And yet if I do judge, My judgment is true; for ^RI am not alone, but I am with the Father who sent Me.   John 16:32

17 ^R"It is also written in your law that the testimony of two men is true.   Deut. 17:6; 19:15

18 "I am One who bears witness of Myself, and ^Rthe Father who sent Me bears witness of Me."   John 5:37

19 Then they said to Him, "Where is Your Father?" Jesus answered, "You know neither Me nor My Father. If you had known Me, you would have known My Father also."

20 These words Jesus spoke in ^Rthe treasury, as He taught in the temple; and ^Rno one laid hands on Him, for ^RHis hour had not yet come.   Mark 12:41, 43 • John 2:4; 7:30 • John 7:8

Jesus Predicts His Departure

21 Then Jesus said to them again, "I am going away, and ^Ryou will seek Me, and ^Rwill die in your sin. ^RWhere I go you cannot come."   John 7:34 • John 8:24 • Mark 16:19; Acts 1:9

22 So the Jews said, "Will He kill Himself, because He says, 'Where I go you cannot come'

23 And He said to them, ^R"You are from beneath; I am from above. ^RYou are of this world; I am not of this world. John 3:31 • 1 John 4:5

8:9 NU, M omit being convicted by their conscience
8:10 NU omits and saw no one but the woman • M He saw her and said, • NU, M omit of yours
8:11 NU, M add from now on

24 R"Therefore I said to you that you will die in your sins; for if you do not believe that I am He, you will die in your sins." John 8:21

25 Then they said to Him, "Who are You?" And Jesus said to them, "Just what I have been saying to you from the beginning.

26 "I have many things to say and to judge concerning you, but RHe who sent Me is true; and RI speak to the world those things which I heard from Him." John 7:28 • John 3:32; 15:15

27 They did not understand that He spoke to them of the Father.

28 Then Jesus said to them, "When you lift up the Son of Man, Rthen you will know that I am He, and Rthat I do nothing of Myself; but as My Father taught Me, I speak these things. [Rom. 1:4] • John 5:19, 30

29 "And RHe who sent Me is with Me. The Father has not left Me alone, for I always do those things that please Him." John 14:10

30 As He spoke these words, Rmany believed in Him. John 7:31; 10:42; 11:45

The Truth Shall Make You Free

31 Then Jesus said to those Jews who believed Him, "If you Rabide in My word, you are My disciples indeed. [John 14:15, 23]

32 "And you shall know the truth, and Rthe truth shall make you free." [Rom. 6:14, 18, 22]

33 They answered Him, R"We are Abraham's descendants, and have never been in bondage to anyone. How can you say, 'You will be made free'?" [Matt. 3:9]

34 Jesus answered them, "Most assuredly, I say to you, Rwhoever commits sin is a slave of sin. 2 Pet. 2:19

35 "And Ra slave does not abide in the house forever, but a son abides forever. Gal. 4:30

36 R"Therefore if the Son makes you free, you shall be free indeed. Gal. 5:1

Abraham's Seed and Satan's

37 "I know that you are Abraham's descendants, but Ryou seek to kill Me, because My word has no place in you. John 7:19

38 R"I speak what I have seen with My Father, and you do what you have *seen with your father." [John 3:32; 5:19, 30; 14:10, 24]

39 They answered and said to Him, R"Abraham is our father." Jesus said to them, R"If you were Abraham's children, you would do the works of Abraham. Matt. 3:9 • [Rom. 2:28]

40 "But now you seek to kill Me, a Man who has told you the truth which I heard from God. Abraham did not do this.

41 "You do the deeds of your father." Then they said to Him, "We were not born of fornication; we have one Father—God."

42 Jesus said to them, R"If God were your Father, you would love Me, for I proceeded forth and came from God; Rnor have I come of Myself, but He sent Me. 1 John 5:1 • Gal. 4:4

43 R"Why do you not understand My speech? Because you are not able to listen to My word. [John 7:17]

12-D. Satan: The Original Manslayer and ▼ Father of Lies

44 "You are of your father the devil, and the desires of your father you want to Rdo. He was a murderer from the beginning, and Rdoes not stand in the truth, because there is no truth in him. When he speaks a lie, he speaks from his own resources, for he is a liar and the father of it. [1 John 3:8–10, 15] • [Jude 6] ▲

45 "But because I tell the truth, you do not believe Me.

46 "Which of you convicts Me of sin? And if I tell the truth, why do you not believe Me?

47 R"He who is of God hears God's words; therefore you do not hear, because you are not of God." 1 John 4:6

Before Abraham Was, I AM

48 Then the Jews answered and said to Him, "Do we not say rightly that You are a Samaritan and Rhave a demon?" John 7:20; 10:20

8:38 NU heard from

12-D. Satan: The Original Manslayer and Father of Lies (John 8:44)—Jesus called Satan "a murderer from the beginning" (v. 44). He is the original manslayer.

God created Adam and Eve and placed them in Eden, in a perfect environment. They were sinless, but untested, until God warned them: "Of every tree of the garden you may freely eat; but of the tree of the knowledge of good and evil you shall not eat, for in the day that you eat of it you shall surely die" (Gen. 2:16, 17, page 5). But Eve was deceived by Satan and gave the forbidden fruit to Adam, who "was not deceived" (1 Tim. 2:13, 14, page 1219); he ate knowing that the penalty was death.

At that instant, when Satan instigated the fall of Adam and Eve in the Garden of Eden, he murdered the whole human race (Gen. 3:1–19, page 5). "Therefore, just as through one man sin entered the world, and death through sin [both spiritual and physical death], and thus death spread to all men, because all sinned" (Rom. 5:12, page 1133). That is, all humanity sinned in the person of Adam, the head of our race. We are all born in sin (Ps. 51:5, page 541), corrupted in our natures by Adam's initial sin; and consequently we live under a sentence of death (Rom. 5:12, page 1133).

Satan knows how much God loves mankind (John 3:16, page 1052), how He is longsuffering toward us, wanting no one to be lost in sin, longing for us all to repent and be saved (2 Pet. 3:9, page 1275). Satan knows that God takes no pleasure in the death of the wicked (Ezek. 33:11, page 811). Therefore, he works tirelessly to keep lost souls from believing in Christ as their personal Savior (John 3:36, page 1053).

(Point 12-D continued on next page)

49 Jesus answered, "I do not have a demon; but I honor My Father, and ᴿyou dishonor Me.   John 5:41

50 "And ᴿI do not seek My own glory; there is One who seeks and judges.   John 5:41; 7:18

51 "Most assuredly, I say to you, if anyone keeps My word he shall never see death."

52 Then the Jews said to Him, "Now we know that You ᴿhave a demon! ᴿAbraham is dead, and the prophets; and You say, 'If anyone keeps My word he shall never taste death.'   John 7:20; 10:20 · Zech. 1:5

53 "Are You greater than our father Abraham, who is dead? And the prophets are dead. Who do You make Yourself out to be?"

54 Jesus answered, ᴿ"If I honor Myself, My honor is nothing. ᴿIt is My Father who hon-

ors Me, of whom you say that He is *your God.   John 5:31, 32 · Acts 3:13

55 "Yet ᴿyou have not known Him, but I know Him. And if I say, 'I do not know Him,' I shall be a liar like you; but I do know Him and ᴿkeep His word.   John 7:28, 29 · [John 15:10]

7-B. Jesus Is the "I AM" of the New Testament   ▼

56 "Your father Abraham rejoiced to see My day, and he saw it and was glad."

57 Then the Jews said to Him, "You are not yet fifty years old, and have You seen Abraham?"

58 Jesus said to them, "Most assuredly, I say to you, before Abraham was, I AM."

59 Then ᴿthey took up stones to throw at Him; but Jesus hid Himself and went out of

8:54 NU, M our

(Point 12-D continued from previous page)

Satan is not only the original manslayer, he is also the father of lies. He is the great deceiver (Rev. 12:9, page 1305), aiming high to bring God's people down to his low, fallen level. Therefore, believers must always be on guard against his enticing power, for he has caused

    (1) Angels to fall in heaven. They will be cast out of heaven with him in the Great Tribulation (Rev. 12:9, page 1305);

    (2) Adam and Eve to fall in the Garden of Eden (Gen. 3:1–7, page 5);

    (3) King David to fall into sin, even though he was God's anointed king of Israel (2 Sam. 12:1–15, page 308);

    (4) Peter to fall into sin, even though he was an apostle (Matt. 26:69–75, page 979);

    (5) Judas to fall from the ministry and apostleship (Acts 1:25, page 1087);

    (6) Ananias and Sapphira to fall from the fellowship of the church. They dropped dead in the assembly, because the early church was so pure and strong that their lie could not live within its fellowship (Acts 5:1–11, page 1093).

    Remember that Satan, the original manslayer and father of lies, is powerful. Temptation is real, sin is attractive, and the flesh is weak; "therefore let him who thinks he stands take heed lest he fall" (1 Cor. 10:12, page 1155). Satan is thus the exact opposite of Jesus Christ, who is "the way, the truth, and the life" (John 14:6, page 1074).

    See Matthew 4:1–11, page 934, for **Point 12-E: Satan: The Tempter.**

7-B. Jesus Is the "I AM" of the New Testament (John 8:56–59)—Jesus fully disclosed His deity (i.e., that He was the God-Man) when He said, "Before Abraham was, I AM." In response, the Jews prepared to stone Him (vv. 58, 59). On another occasion Jesus said, "I and My Father are one." When the Jews again took up stones to stone Him, Jesus asked, "For which of those works do you stone Me?" They answered, "For a good work we do not stone You, but for blasphemy, and because You, being a Man, make Yourself God" (John 10:30–39, page 1068). Had they only known that He was indeed the God-Man, they would have believed in Him and worshiped Him. But they did not know, because the god of this age (Satan) had blinded their minds (2 Cor. 4:3, 4, page 1167). Satan continues to blind the minds of unbelievers to the glorious fact that Jesus is God.

    Now think on this awesome question. If Jesus is not God, then who is He? He is either the Deity or demonic! (Mark 3:22, page 987). Either He is the truth, or He is the chief of all liars (John 14:6, page 1074; cf. 8:44, page 1063). Either He is God, or He is the world's greatest blasphemer (Matt. 9:1–13, page 948). If Jesus is not the God-Man, He is not a good man: He is a hopelessly lost soul.

    Let us look at the "I AMs" in the Gospel of John, where He declared that He is Jehovah God.

    (1) "I AM the bread of life" (6:32–35, page 1059).
    (2) "I AM the light of the world" (8:12–20, page 1062).
    (3) "I AM the door of the sheep" (10:7–10, page 1067).
    (4) "I AM the good shepherd" (10:11–16, page 1067).
    (5) "I AM the resurrection and the life" (11:25–27, 38–44, page 1069).
    (6) "I AM the way, the truth, and the life" (14:6, page 1074).
    (7) "I AM the vine" (15:1–8, page 1076).

    See Isaiah 7:14–16, page 649, for **Point 7-C: Jesus Is Immanuel.**

▽ the temple, ᴿgoing* through the midst of
▲ them, and so passed by.   John 10:31 • Luke 4:30

A Man Born Blind Receives Sight

▼ 8-F. Jesus Gave Sight to a Blind Beggar,
Proving His Deity in His Power to
Illuminate Life

9 Now as *Jesus* passed by, He saw a man
who was blind from birth.

2 And His disciples asked Him, saying,
"Rabbi, ᴿwho sinned, this man or his parents,
that he was born blind?"   John 9:34

3 Jesus answered, "Neither this man nor
his parents sinned, ᴿbut that the works of
God should be revealed in him.   John 11:4

4 ᴿ'I* must work the works of Him who

8:59 NU omits the rest of v. 59.
9:4 NU *We*

sent Me while it is day; *the* night is coming ▽
when no one can work.   [John 4:34; 5:19, 36; 17:4]

5 "As long as I am in the world, ᴿI am the
light of the world."   [John 1:5, 9; 3:19; 8:12; 12:35, 46]

6 When He had said these things, ᴿHe spat
on the ground and made clay with the saliva;
and He anointed the eyes of the blind man
with the clay.   Mark 7:33; 8:23

7 And He said to him, "Go, wash ᴿin the
pool of Siloam" (which is translated, Sent).
So ᴿhe went and washed, and came back
seeing.   Neh. 3:15 • 2 Kin. 5:14

8 Therefore the neighbors and those who
previously had seen that he was *blind said,
"Is not this he who sat and begged?"

9 Some said, "This is he." Others *said*,
*"He is like him." He said, "I am *he*."

9:8 NU *a beggar*
9:9 NU *No, but he is like him*

8-F. Jesus Gave Sight to a Blind Beggar, Proving His Deity in His Power to Illuminate Life (John 9:1–41)—
The sixth of the seven signs that proves the deity of Jesus takes place in Jerusalem after His discourse in the
eighth chapter of John. Here Jesus gives self-witness to His deity. "Then they took up stones to throw at
Him; but Jesus hid Himself and went out of the temple, going through the midst of them, and so passed by"
(John 8:56–59, page 1064). Then chapter nine opens with these words, "Now as Jesus passed by, He saw a
man who was blind from birth." And Jesus had compassion on him.

(1) Let us look at *the blind beggar.* We are told that he was blind from birth. This is the only instance in
the Bible where the Lord healed someone with a *congenital* defect (although there may have been others).
Occurring on the Sabbath, when a great number of people must have been present in and near the temple,
this sign was immediately talked about. People asked, "Is not this he who sat and begged?" Some said, "This
is he," but others would only say, "He is like him." The beggar himself said, "I am he" (vv. 8, 9).

He was questioned by those Jews and Pharisees who were determined to put Jesus to death. The blind
beggar, his sight restored, was a faithful witness to the enemies of Jesus, saying, "One thing I know: that
though I was blind, now I see" (v. 25). Because of his bold testimony, the Jews and the Pharisees drove him
from the temple. Jesus found him and asked, "Do you believe in the Son of God?" (v. 35). The man
answered, "Who is He, Lord, that I may believe in Him?" (v. 36). Jesus then revealed Himself—and the man
believed in Jesus as the Son of God and worshiped Him (vv. 37, 38).

(2) Let us listen to *the words of the Lord Jesus.* The disciples asked Him, "Who sinned, this man or his
parents, that he was born blind?" (v. 2). This was a startling question. How could his physical defect be the
result of personal sin when he had been *born* blind? Can an unborn baby sin in the womb of its mother? Of
course not, though some rabbis taught prenatal sin. Or were the disciples thinking of reincarnation? Had the
man been born blind because he had sinned in another life? Or could his blindness be punishment for his
parents' sin? With seven well-chosen words, Jesus answered the question: "Neither this man nor his parents
sinned" (v. 3).

Now there is another question that needs an answer: Was it due to the fall of man that he was born
blind? In one sense the answer is yes, for all sickness, sufferings, congenital defects, sin, and death can be
charged to the fall of man (Gen. 3:1–24, page 5). It was not the will of God that this man be born blind, any
more than are the many other sorrows resulting from the ravages of sin.

But Jesus answered further, ". . . that the works of God should be revealed in him" (v. 3). God intended
to bring glory to Himself through this man, as Jesus opened his eyes. The miracle was a "sign" that God
desires to cure the cause and effect of universal suffering. He is in the business of opening eyes, not closing
them. As Jesus said, "I am the light of the world" (John 8:12, page 1062).

(3) Let us see *what Jesus did.* "He spat on the ground and made clay with the saliva; and He anointed the
eyes of the blind man with the clay. And He said to him, 'Go, wash in the pool of Siloam' " (vv. 6, 7). The
man obeyed the Lord Jesus—and he returned able to see. This reminds us of another time, in the book of
Genesis, when God took dust of the earth and formed man (Gen. 2:7, page 4).

Thus the same Creator who formed the first man, and breathed into him the breath of life, again used the
dust of the ground to anoint the blind eyes of one of His creation, illuminating his life. Again we see Jesus,
"the light of the world," transcending the laws of nature and opening the eyes of one born blind, proving His
deity. Only God can give instant sight to one born blind. Therefore Jesus is God.

See John 11:38–44, page 1070, for **Point 8-G: Jesus Raised Lazarus from the Dead, Proving His Deity in
His Power to Re-create Life.**

▽ 10 Therefore they said to him, "How were your eyes opened?"

11 He answered and said, ᴿ"A Man called Jesus made clay and anointed my eyes and said to me, 'Go to *the pool of Siloam and wash.' So I went and washed, and I received sight."   John 9:6, 7

12 Then they said to him, "Where is He?" He said, "I do not know."

The Pharisees Excommunicate the Healed Man

13 They brought him who formerly was blind to the Pharisees.

14 Now it was a Sabbath when Jesus made the clay and opened his eyes.

15 Then the Pharisees also asked him again how he had received his sight. He said to them, "He put clay on my eyes, and I washed, and I see."

16 Therefore some of the Pharisees said, "This Man is not from God, because He does not keep the Sabbath." Others said, "How can a man who is a sinner do such signs?" And there was a division among them.

17 They said to the blind man again, "What do you say about Him because He opened your eyes?" He said, "He is a prophet."

18 But the Jews did not believe concerning him, that he had been blind and received his sight, until they called the parents of him who had received his sight.

19 And they asked them, saying, "Is this your son, who you say was born blind? How then does he now see?"

20 His parents answered them and said, "We know that this is our son, and that he was born blind;

21 "but by what means he now sees we do not know, or who opened his eyes we do not know. He is of age; ask him. He will speak for himself."

22 His parents said these *things* because ᴿthey feared the Jews, for the Jews had agreed already that if anyone confessed *that* He *was* Christ, he ᴿwould be put out of the synagogue.   Acts 5:13 • John 16:2

23 Therefore his parents said, "He is of age; ask him."

24 So they again called the man who was blind, and said to him, "Give God the glory! We know that this Man is a sinner."

25 He answered and said, "Whether He is a sinner *or not* I do not know. One thing I know: that though I was blind, now I see."

26 Then they said to him again, "What did He do to you? How did He open your eyes?"

27 He answered them, "I told you already, ▽ and you did not listen. Why do you want to hear *it* again? Do you also want to become His disciples?"

28 Then they reviled him and said, "You are His disciple, but we are Moses' disciples.

29 "We know that God ᴿspoke to ᴿMoses; *as for* this *fellow*, ᴿwe do not know where He is from."   Num. 12:6–8 • [John 5:45–47] • John 7:27, 28; 8:14

30 The man answered and said to them, ᴿ"Why, this is a marvelous thing, that you do not know where He is from; yet He has opened my eyes!   John 3:10

31 "Now we know that ᴿGod does not hear sinners; but if anyone is a worshiper of God and does His will, He hears him.   Zech. 7:13

32 "Since the world began it has been unheard of that anyone opened the eyes of one who was born blind.

33 ᴿ"If this Man were not from God, He could do nothing."   John 3:2; 9:16

34 They answered and said to him, "You were completely born in sins, and are you teaching us?" And they cast him out.

True Vision and True Blindness

35 Jesus heard that they had cast him out; and when He had found him, He said to him, "Do you believe in the Son of *God?"

36 He answered and said, "Who is He, Lord, that I may believe in Him?"

37 And Jesus said to him, "You have both seen Him and ᴿit is He who is talking with you."   John 4:26

38 Then he said, "Lord, I believe!" And he ᴿworshiped Him.   Matt. 8:2

39 And Jesus said, ᴿ"For judgment I have come into this world, ᴿthat those who do not see may see, and that those who see may be made blind."   [John 3:17; 5:22, 27; 12:47] • Matt. 13:13

40 Then *some* of the Pharisees who were with Him heard these words, ᴿand said to Him, "Are we blind also?"   [Rom. 2:19]

41 Jesus said to them, ᴿ"If you were blind, you would have no sin; but now you say, 'We see.' Therefore your sin remains.   John 15:22, 24 ▲

Jesus the True Shepherd

10 "Most assuredly, I say to you, he who does not enter the sheepfold by the door, but climbs up some other way, the same is a thief and a robber.

2 "But he who enters by the door is the shepherd of the sheep.

3 "To him the doorkeeper opens, and the sheep hear his voice; and he calls his own sheep by ᴿname and leads them out.   John 20:16

▼ 2-C. Know That the Bible Stands Above All Human Opinions

4 "And when he brings out his own sheep, he goes before them; and the sheep follow him, for they know his voice.

5 "Yet they will by no means follow a stranger, but will flee from him, for they do

▲ not know the voice of strangers."

6 Jesus used this illustration, but they did not understand the things which He spoke to them.

Jesus the Good Shepherd

7 Then Jesus said to them again, "Most assuredly, I say to you, I am the door of the sheep.

8 "All who *ever* came *before Me are thieves and robbers, but the sheep did not hear them.

9 ᴿ"I am the door. If anyone enters by Me, he will be saved, and will go in and out and find pasture.   [Eph. 2:18]

10 "The thief does not come except to steal, and to kill, and to destroy. I have come that they may have life, and that they may have *it* more abundantly.

10:8 M omits *before Me*

11 ᴿ"I am the good shepherd. The good shepherd gives His life for the sheep.   Is. 40:11

12 "But a ᵀhireling, *he who is* not the shepherd, one who does not own the sheep, sees the wolf coming and ᴿleaves the sheep and flees; and the wolf catches the sheep and scatters them.   hired man • Zech. 11:16, 17

13 "The hireling flees because he is a hireling and does not care about the sheep.

14 "I am the good shepherd; and I know My *sheep*, and am known by My own.

15 ᴿ"As the Father knows Me, even so I know the Father; ᴿand I lay down My life for the sheep.   Matt. 11:27 • Matt. 27:50

16 "And ᴿother sheep I have which are not of this fold; them also I must bring, and they will hear My voice; ᴿand there will be one flock *and* one shepherd.   Is. 42:6; 56:8 • Eph. 2:13-18

17 "Therefore My Father ᴿloves Me, ᴿbecause I lay down My life that I may take it again.   John 5:20 • [Heb. 2:9]

18 "No one takes it from Me, but I lay it down of Myself. I have power to lay it down, and I have power to take it again. This command I have received from My Father."

19 Therefore there was a division again among the Jews because of these sayings.

20 And many of them said, ᴿ"He has a

2-C. Know That the Bible Stands Above All Human Opinions (John 10:4, 5)—"And when he brings out his own sheep, he goes before them; and the sheep follow him, for they know his voice. Yet they will by no means follow a stranger, but will flee from him" (vv. 4, 5).

It is said that in the Middle East, if you mingle several flocks of sheep, when their shepherds call to them they will separate and follow their own shepherd. Similarly, when we belong to Christ we recognize His "voice" in the Scriptures. The voice of God, throughout His entire Word, is distinctive and uniquely authoritative. Other voices will be heard in the world, but we are accountable to that voice of God as to no other.

Already we have seen that the Bible declares itself to be the inerrant Word of God (see Master Outline 1, "Inerrancy of the Scriptures," page 23). While some people dispute this truth, it will ultimately be God the Holy Spirit, in our hearts and minds, who infallibly attests the veracity of His Word. Human arguments, however plausible and persuasive, cannot do what only God Himself can do: convince us of the trustworthiness of His own written testimony. And once we are convinced by the Holy Spirit Himself, when we open the Bible we know we are in holy territory where no mere human ideas make any difference.

(1) The *written* Word of God saves us from the babel of human opinions. "And truly Jesus did many other signs . . . but these are written that you may believe that Jesus is the Christ" (John 20:30, 31, page 1084). Can you imagine the chaotic result if God's Word had been handed down merely by "word of mouth"? Of course He could have devised some other way to preserve the integrity of His Word. But He simply chose to inspire certain men who then committed His Word to writing (2 Tim. 3:16, page 1227; 2 Pet. 1:21, page 1264).

Since we have God's own verbally inspired record, we don't need to be confused by what others say and write. We may listen to people, sometimes to our great benefit, but we never need to be confused. Any time we are unsure of God's revealed Word on a subject, it is best that we postpone judgment until we have "searched the Scriptures . . . to find out whether these things were so" (Acts 17:11, page 1111). This is our daily responsibility and privilege as Christians.

(2) We must let the Word of God shape our opinions. "Your word I have hidden in my heart, that I might not sin against You" (Ps. 119:11, page 581). The Christian's great ambition should be to think God's thoughts after Him. As Paul states, we should aim at having "the mind of Christ" (1 Cor. 2:16, page 1149). Our minds must be renewed by the Word of God (Rom. 12:2, page 1142). The more you consistently study the Bible, the more you will share God's viewpoint on all matters. Of course you will never be infallible in this world, but your judgment will grow increasingly sharper, clearer, and more in line with God's revealed truth. "You shall know the truth, and the truth shall make you free" (John 8:32, page 1063).

See Colossians 2:8, page 1203, for **Point 2-D: Know That the Bible Deals in Facts.**

demon and is ᵀmad. Why do you listen to Him?"   John 7:20 • *insane*

21 Others said, "These are not the words of one who has a demon. ᴿCan a demon ᴿopen the eyes of the blind?"   [Ex. 4:11] • John 9:6, 7, 32, 33

The Shepherd Knows His Sheep

22 Now it was the Feast of Dedication in Jerusalem, and it was winter.

23 And Jesus walked in the temple, ᴿin Solomon's porch.   Acts 3:11; 5:12

24 Then the Jews surrounded Him and said to Him, "How long do You keep us in ᵀdoubt? If You are the Christ, tell us plainly."   *suspense*

25 Jesus answered them, "I told you, and you do not believe. The works that I do in My Father's name, they bear witness of Me.

26 "But you do not believe, because you are not of My sheep, *as I said to you.

27 ᴿ"My sheep hear My voice, and I know them, and they follow Me.   John 10:4, 14

28 "And I give them eternal life, and they shall never perish; neither shall anyone snatch them out of My hand.

29 "My Father, who has given *them* to Me, is greater than all; and no one is able to snatch *them* out of My Father's hand.

30 ᴿ"I and *My* Father are one."   John 17:11

10:26 NU omits *as I said to you*

Renewed Efforts to Stone Jesus

31 Then ᴿthe Jews took up stones again to stone Him.   John 8:59

32 Jesus answered them, "Many good works I have shown you from My Father. For which of those works do you stone Me?"

33 The Jews answered Him, saying, "For a good work we do not stone You, but for ᴿblasphemy, and because You, being a Man, ᴿmake Yourself God."   John 5:18 • Matt. 9:3

34 Jesus answered them, "Is it not written in your law, ᴿ'*I said, "You are gods"* '? Ps. 82:6

1-B. Christ Taught the Inerrancy of the Bible   ▼

35 "If He called them gods, ᴿto whom the word of God came (and the Scripture ᴿcannot be broken),   Matt. 5:17, 18 • 1 Pet. 1:25   ▲

36 "do you say of Him ᴿwhom the Father sanctified and ᴿsent into the world, 'You are blaspheming,' ᴿbecause I said, 'I am ᴿthe Son of God'?   John 6:27 • John 3:17 • John 5:17, 18 • Luke 1:35

37 ᴿ"If I do not do the works of My Father, do not believe Me;   John 10:25; 15:24

38 "but if I do, though you do not believe Me, ᴿbelieve the works, that you may know and *believe ᴿthat the Father *is* in Me, and I in Him."   John 5:36 • John 14:10, 11

10:38 NU *understand*

1-B. Christ Taught the Inerrancy of the Bible (John 10:35)—Christ, as the eternally preexistent member of the Trinity, now God incarnate, occupies a unique place in the Scriptures: He is the God-Man from heaven.

Note that when Christ said, "The Scripture cannot be broken" (v. 35), He declared categorically, without exception or limitation, that fault cannot be found in the Scriptures. He repeated this teaching in the following instances:

(1) "One jot or one tittle will by no means pass from the law" (Matt. 5:18, page 939). Jesus believed that the smallest letter of the Bible, a "jot" (equal in size to our apostrophe), and the smallest distinguishing part of a letter, a "tittle" (equivalent to our crossing the *t*), could not be dropped from the Scriptures or be found deficient. He preached inerrancy, even to the very *letters* of the words which composed God's Holy Word.

(2) "Heaven and earth will pass away, but My words will by no means pass away" (Matt. 24:35, page 974). Jesus further promised that the coming Helper, the Holy Spirit, would "bring to your [the apostles'] remembrance all things that I said to you" (John 14:26, page 1075). He attached an absolute importance to His words, and promised supernatural help to the apostles (the original twelve, plus Paul, whom He also personally sent forth), to help them recall these words. Thus He laid in advance the foundation for the New Testament Scriptures and their inerrancy (John 16:12-15, page 1077).

(3) "Have you not read that He who made [created] them at the beginning 'made them male and female' " (Matt. 19:4, 5, page 965; cf. Gen. 1:27, page 4; 2:21-25, page 5). He saw the Creation account of Genesis as inerrant, absolutely true.

(4) Jesus cited Old Testament miracle stories, teaching numerous authoritative lessons from their details, and thus certifying them as true, accurate, and inerrant. Jesus substantiated the truth and reality of the characters most often disputed by unbelievers, such as:

(a) Adam and Eve (Matt. 19:4-6, page 965; cf. Gen. 1:26, 27, page 4; 2:7, 18, page 4)
(b) Satan (Luke 11:18, page 1028; cf. Ezek. 28:11-19, page 805)
(c) Noah (Matt. 24:37, 38, page 974; cf. Gen. 6:1-14, page 11)
(d) Jonah (Matt. 12:39, 40, page 954; cf. Jon. 1:2, page 885)
(e) Lot's wife (Luke 17:32, page 1036; cf. Gen. 19:26, page 24)

Undeniably He took the Bible to be God's Word, true in every word, and entirely inerrant. This testimony of Christ should settle the matter finally for everyone who calls Him Lord.

See 2 Chronicles 36:20, 21, page 442, for **Point 1-C: The Prophets of the Old Testament Received the Scriptures as Inerrant.**

39 Therefore they sought again to seize Him, but He escaped out of their hand.

The Believers Beyond Jordan

40 And He went away again beyond the Jordan to the place ^Rwhere John was baptizing at first, and there He stayed. John 1:28

41 Then many came to Him and said, "John performed no sign, but all the things that John spoke about this Man were true."

42 And many believed in Him there.

The Death of Lazarus

11 Now a certain *man* was sick, Lazarus of Bethany, the town of ^RMary and her sister Martha. Luke 10:38, 39

2 It was *that* Mary who anointed the Lord with fragrant oil and wiped His feet with her hair, whose brother Lazarus was sick.

3 Therefore the sisters sent to Him, saying, "Lord, behold, he whom You love is sick."

4 When Jesus heard *that*, He said, "This sickness is not unto death, but for the glory of God, that the Son of God may be glorified through it."

5 Now Jesus loved Martha and her sister and Lazarus.

6 So, when He heard that he was sick, ^RHe stayed two more days in the place where He was. John 10:40

7 Then after this He said to *the* disciples, "Let us go to Judea again."

8 *The* disciples said to Him, "Rabbi, lately the Jews sought to ^Rstone You, and are You going there again?" John 8:59; 10:31

9 Jesus answered, "Are there not twelve hours in the day? ^RIf anyone walks in the day, he does not stumble, because he sees the ^Rlight of this world. John 9:4; 12:35 • Is. 9:2

10 "But ^Rif one walks in the night, he stumbles, because the light is not in him." John 12:35

11 These things He said, and after that He said to them, "Our friend Lazarus ^Rsleeps, but I go that I may wake him up." Matt. 9:24

12 Then His disciples said, "Lord, if he sleeps he will get well."

13 However, Jesus spoke of his death, but they thought that He was speaking about taking rest in sleep.

14 Then Jesus said to them plainly, "Lazarus is dead.

15 "And I am glad for your sakes that I was not there, that you may believe. Nevertheless let us go to him."

16 Then ^RThomas, who is called Didymus, said to his fellow disciples, "Let us also go, that we may die with Him." John 14:5; 20:26-28

I Am the Resurrection and the Life

17 So when Jesus came, He found that he had already been in the tomb four days.

18 Now Bethany was near Jerusalem, about ^Ttwo miles away. Lit. *15 stadia*

19 And many of the Jews had joined the women around Martha and Mary, to comfort them concerning their brother.

20 Then Martha, as soon as she heard that Jesus was coming, went and met Him, but Mary was sitting in the house.

21 Now Martha said to Jesus, "Lord, if You had been here, my brother would not have died.

22 "But even now I know that whatever You ask of God, God will give You."

23 Jesus said to her, "Your brother will rise again."

24 Martha said to Him, ^R"I know that he will rise again in the resurrection at the last day." [John 5:29]

25 Jesus said to her, "I am the resurrection and the life. He who believes in Me, though he may ^Rdie, he shall live. 1 Cor. 15:22

26 "And whoever lives and believes in Me shall never die. Do you believe this?"

27 She said to Him, "Yes, Lord, ^RI believe that You are the Christ, the Son of God, who is to come into the world." Matt. 16:16

Jesus and Death, the Last Enemy

28 And when she had said these things, she went her way and secretly called Mary her sister, saying, "The Teacher has come and is calling for you."

29 As soon as she heard *that*, she arose quickly and came to Him.

30 Now Jesus had not yet come into the town, but *was in the place where Martha met Him.

31 ^RThen the Jews who were with her in the house, and comforting her, when they saw that Mary rose up quickly and went out, followed her, *saying, "She is going to the tomb to weep there." John 11:19, 33

32 Then, when Mary came where Jesus was, and saw Him, she fell down at His feet, saying to Him, ^R"Lord, if You had been here, my brother would not have died." John 11:21

33 Therefore, when Jesus saw her weeping, and the Jews who came with her weeping, He groaned in the spirit and was troubled.

34 And He said, "Where have you laid him?" They said to Him, "Lord, come and see."

35 ^RJesus wept. Luke 19:41

36 Then the Jews said, "See how He loved him!"

37 And some of them said, "Could not this Man, ^Rwho opened the eyes of the blind, also have kept this man from dying?" John 9:6, 7

11:30 NU *was still*
11:31 NU *supposing that she was going*

Lazarus Raised from the Dead

▼ 8-G. **Jesus Raised Lazarus from the Dead, Proving His Deity in His Power to Re-create Life**

38 Then Jesus, again groaning in Himself, came to the tomb. It was a cave, and a ᴿstone lay against it.   Matt. 27:60, 66

39 Jesus said, "Take away the stone." Martha, the sister of him who was dead, said to Him, "Lord, by this time there is a stench, for he has been *dead* four days."

40 Jesus said to her, "Did I not say to you that if you would believe you would ᴿsee the glory of God?"   [John 11:4, 23]

41 Then they took away the stone *from* ▽ *the place* where the dead man was lying. And Jesus lifted up *His* eyes and said, "Father, I thank You that You have heard Me.

42 "And I know that You always hear Me, but ᴿbecause of the people who are standing by I said *this*, that they may believe that You sent Me."   John 12:30; 17:21

43 Now when He had said these things, He cried with a loud voice, "Lazarus, come forth!"

44 And he who had died came out bound hand and foot with graveclothes, and ᴿhis

11:41 NU omits *from the place where the dead man was lying*

8-G. Jesus Raised Lazarus from the Dead, Proving His Deity in His Power to Re-create Life (John 11:38–44)—The resurrection of Lazarus is the last of the seven signs recorded by John, as guided by the Holy Spirit (John 16:12–15, page 1077), giving many infallible proofs of the deity of Jesus Christ. Lazarus lived in Bethany with his sisters, Mary and Martha. Bethany was located on the road to Jericho, a few miles from Jerusalem, on the east slope of Mount Olivet. It is sometimes called the Judean home of Jesus; although most of His ministry in Judea was in Jerusalem, He preferred to lodge in Bethany. Some time after the resurrection of Lazarus, Bethany became known as Lazariyeh ("The Place of Lazarus"), which to this day reminds us of his resurrection.

The eleventh chapter of John opens with these words: "Now a certain man was sick, Lazarus of Bethany." Mary and Martha sent word to Jesus saying, "He whom You love is sick" (v. 3). But Jesus did not go to Bethany until Lazarus had been dead and in the tomb four days. When He came, but He came with all power and gave:

(1) *A divine command.* "Take away the stone" (v. 39). He could have commanded the stone to move, since He rules over all creation. He could have called for angels to roll it away, since He has all authority in heaven and on earth (Matt. 28:18, page 982). Jesus did neither: He commanded the people, "Take away the stone" (v. 39). The lesson here is simple and profound. Man is to do the possible and believe that God will do the humanly impossible.

(2) *A divine message.* "Did I not say to you that if you would believe you would see the glory of God?" We often hear that "seeing is believing." But Jesus said, "Believe" and "see the glory of God" (v. 40)—in that order. When we have done all that is humanly possible and the work is not finished, when we war against the demonic host of Satan and the battle is not won, there are two things we must do if we are to see the "impossible" achieved: We must work, and we must believe. We cannot see the glory of God by our works alone or by our faith alone (James 2:17–22, page 1257). First, Jesus said, "Take away the stone" (v. 39)—that is work. Second, He said, "Believe" and "see the glory of God" (v. 40)—that is faith.

(3) *A divine prayer.* "Father, I thank You that You have heard Me. And I know that You always hear Me, but because of the people who are standing by I said this, that they may believe that You sent Me" (vv. 41, 42). This prayer was *to* the Father, but *for* the benefit of the people gathered at the tomb. Jesus could have raised Lazarus without public prayer. Already He had turned water into wine, healed the nobleman's son, made the lame walk at the pool of Bethesda, walked on the water, and given sight to a blind beggar, all without public prayer. Why did He pray at the tomb of Lazarus? Because He wanted the people to believe that He was sent from God the Father (John 8:54–56, page 1064).

(4) *A divine call.* "He cried with a loud voice, 'Lazarus, come forth!'" (v. 43). Lazarus, who had been dead four days, heard the call of Jesus and came back from the dead. This is a *type*, or foreshadowing illustration, of the resurrection of the dead in Christ, who will hear His voice when He comes again "with a shout, with the voice of an archangel, and with the trumpet of God" (1 Thess. 4:16–18, page 1212).

(5) *A divine deliverance.* "Jesus said to them, 'Loose him, and let him go'" (v. 44). Lazarus came out of the tomb wearing grave clothes. He was alive, but his grave clothes identified him with death. Lazarus is a type of every living believer. Our mortal flesh identifies us with sin and death; we have been loosed from the power and penalty of sin, but not from the presence of sin. All believers who have experienced physical death have been loosed from their grave clothes (the flesh), but will not receive their glorified, immortal bodies until the rapture (taking up) of the church. All believers who are alive when He comes will have their grave clothes (the flesh) transformed, and be caught up to meet the Lord Jesus in the air (1 Thess. 4:16, 17, page 1212). Together we will receive our eternal and glorified bodies, like His resurrected body (1 John 3:2, page 1279). Jesus raised Lazarus from the dead, proving His deity by His power to re-create life.

The seven signs given to us by John, as he was guided by the Holy Spirit, are infallible, unerring evidence, proving that Jesus is God. Amen!

See Index, page 17, for your next study.

▽ face was wrapped with a cloth. Jesus said to
▲ them, "Loose him, and let him go."   John 20:7

The Plot to Kill Jesus

45 Then many of the Jews who had come to
Mary, ᴿand had seen the things Jesus did,
believed in Him.   John 2:23; 10:42; 12:11, 18
46 But some of them went away to the
Pharisees and told them the things Jesus did.
47 ᴿThen the chief priests and the Pharisees
gathered a council and said, "What shall we
do? For this Man works many signs.   Ps. 2:2
48 "If we let Him alone like this, everyone
will believe in Him, and the Romans will
come and take away both our place and
nation."
49 And one of them, ᴿCaiaphas, being high
priest that year, said to them, "You know
nothing at all,   Luke 3:2
50 ᴿ"nor do you consider that it is expedient
for *us that one man should die for the
people, and not that the whole nation should
perish."   John 18:14
51 Now this he did not say on his own
authority; but being high priest that year he
prophesied that Jesus would die for the nation,
52 and not for that nation only, but also
that He would gather together in one the
children of God who were scattered abroad.
53 Then, from that day on, they plotted to
ᴿput Him to death.   Matt. 26:4
54 ᴿTherefore Jesus no longer walked
openly among the Jews, but went from there
into the country near the wilderness, to a city
called ᴿEphraim, and there remained with His
disciples.   John 4:1, 3; 7:1 · 2 Chr. 13:19
55 ᴿAnd the Passover of the Jews was near,
and many went from the country up to
Jerusalem before the Passover, to ᴿpurify
themselves.   John 2:13; 5:1; 6:4 · Num. 9:10, 13; 31:19, 20
56 ᴿThen they sought Jesus, and spoke
among themselves as they stood in the temple, "What do you think—that He will not
come to the feast?"   John 7:11
57 Now both the chief priests and the
Pharisees had given a command, that if anyone knew where He was, he should report *it*,
that they might ᴿseize Him.   Matt. 26:14-16

The Anointing at Bethany

12 Then, six days before the Passover,
Jesus came to Bethany, ᴿwhere Lazarus was *who had been dead, whom He had
raised from the dead.   John 11:1, 43
2 ᴿThere they made Him a supper; and
Martha served, but Lazarus was one of those
who sat at the table with Him.   Mark 14:3
3 Then Mary took a pound of very costly
oil of spikenard, anointed the feet of Jesus,
and wiped His feet with her hair. And the
house was filled with the fragrance of the oil.
4 But one of His disciples, Judas Iscariot,
Simon's *son*, who would betray Him, said,
5 "Why was this fragrant oil not sold for
ᵀthree hundred denarii and given to the
poor?"   About 1 year's wages for a worker, or $9,600
6 This he said, not that he cared for the
poor, but because he was a thief, and ᴿhad
the money box; and he used to take what was
put in it.   John 13:29
7 But Jesus said, "Let her alone; *she has
kept this for the day of My burial.
8 "For the poor you have with you always,
but Me you do not have always."

The Plot to Kill Lazarus

9 Now a great many of the Jews knew that
He was there; and they came, not for Jesus'
sake only, but that they might also see Lazarus, whom He had raised from the dead.
10 But the chief priests plotted to put Lazarus to death also,
11 because on account of him many of the
Jews went away and believed in Jesus.

The Triumphal Entry

12 ᴿThe next day a great multitude that had
come to the feast, when they heard that
Jesus was coming to Jerusalem,   Matt. 21:4-9
13 took branches of palm trees and went
out to meet Him, and cried out:

"Hosanna!
ᴿ*'Blessed is He who comes in the name
    of the Lᴏʀᴅ!'*
The King of Israel!"   Ps. 118:26

14 Then Jesus, when He had found a young
donkey, sat on it; as it is written:

15 *"Fearᴿ not, daughter of Zion;
    Behold, your King is coming,
    Sitting on a donkey's colt."*   Zech. 9:9

16 His disciples did not understand these
things at first; but when Jesus was glorified,
ᴿthen they remembered that these things
were written about Him and *that* they had
done these things to Him.   [John 14:26]
17 Therefore the people, who were with
Him when He called Lazarus out of his tomb
and raised him from the dead, bore witness.
18 ᴿFor this reason the people also met
Him, because they heard that He had done
this sign.   John 12:11
19 The Pharisees therefore said among
themselves, ᴿ"You see that you are accomplishing nothing. Look, the world has gone
after Him!"   John 11:47, 48

The Fruitful Grain of Wheat

20 Now there were certain Greeks among
those who came up to worship at the feast.

11:50 NU *you*
12:1 NU omits *who had been dead*
12:7 NU *that she may keep*

21 Then they came to Philip, ᴿwho was from Bethsaida of Galilee, and asked him, saying, "Sir, we wish to see Jesus."   John 1:43
22 Philip came and told Andrew, and in turn Andrew and Philip told Jesus.
23 But Jesus answered them, saying, ᴿ"The hour has come ᴿthat the Son of Man should be glorified.   John 13:32 • Acts 3:13
24 "Most assuredly, I say to you, ᴿunless a grain of wheat falls into the ground and dies, it remains alone; but if it dies, it produces much ᵀgrain.   1 Cor. 15:36 • Lit. fruit
25 ᴿ"He who loves his life will lose it, and he who hates his life in this world will keep it for eternal life.   Mark 8:35
26 "If anyone serves Me, let him ᴿfollow Me; and ᴿwhere I am, there My servant will be also. If anyone serves Me, him My Father will honor.   [Matt. 16:24] • John 14:3; 17:24

Jesus Predicts His Death on the Cross

27 "Now My soul is troubled, and what shall I say? 'Father, save Me from this hour'? But for this purpose I came to this hour.
28 "Father, glorify Your name." Then a voice came from heaven, saying, "I have both glorified it and will glorify it again."
29 Therefore the people who stood by and heard it said that it had thundered. Others said, "An angel has spoken to Him."
30 Jesus answered and said, "This voice did not come because of Me, but for your sake.

▼ **12-H. Satan and the Death of Christ**

▲ 31 "Now is the judgment of this world; now the ruler of this world will be cast out.
32 "And I, if I am ᵀlifted up from the earth, will draw all peoples to Myself."   Crucified
33 ᴿThis He said, signifying by what death He would die.   John 18:32; 21:19
34 The people answered Him, ᴿ"We have heard from the law that the Christ remains forever; and how can You say, 'The Son of Man must be lifted up'? Who is this Son of Man?"   Mic. 4:7
35 Then Jesus said to them, "A little while longer the light is with you. ᴿWalk while you have the light, lest darkness overtake you; ᴿhe who walks in darkness does not know where he is going.   Eph. 5:8 • [1 John 2:9-11]
36 "While you have the light, believe in the light, that you may become ᴿsons of light."

These things Jesus spoke, and departed, and ᴿwas hidden from them.   Luke 16:8 • John 8:59

Who Has Believed Our Report?

37 But although He had done so many ᴿsigns before them, they did not believe in Him,   John 11:47
38 that the word of Isaiah the prophet might be fulfilled, which he spoke:

> ᴿ"Lord, who has believed our report?
> And to whom has the arm of the LORD
> been revealed?"   Is. 53:1

39 Therefore they could not believe, because Isaiah said again:

> 40 "Heᴿ has blinded their eyes and
> hardened their hearts,   Is. 6:9, 10
> ᴿLest they should see with their eyes,
> Lest they should understand with their
> hearts and turn,
> So that I should heal them."   Matt. 13:14

41 ᴿThese things Isaiah said *when he saw His glory and spoke of Him.   Is. 6:10

Walk in the Light

42 Nevertheless even among the rulers many believed in Him, but because of the Pharisees they did not confess Him, lest they should be put out of the synagogue;
43 ᴿfor they loved the praise of men more than the praise of God.   John 5:41, 44
44 Then Jesus cried out and said, "He who believes in Me, ᴿbelieves not in Me ᴿbut in Him who sent Me.   [John 3:16, 18, 36] • [John 5:24]
45 "And ᴿhe who sees Me sees Him who sent Me.   [John 14:9]
46 ᴿ"I have come as a light into the world, that whoever believes in Me should not abide in darkness.   John 1:4, 5; 8:12; 12:35, 36
47 "And if anyone hears My words and does not *believe, ᴿI do not judge him; for ᴿI did not come to judge the world but to save the world.   John 5:45 • John 3:17
48 ᴿ"He who rejects Me, and does not receive My words, has that which judges him— ᴿthe word that I have spoken will judge him in the last day.   [Luke 10:16] • Deut. 18:18, 19
49 "For ᴿI have not spoken on My own authority; but the Father who sent Me gave

12:41 NU because
12:47 NU keep them

12-H. Satan and the Death of Christ (John 12:31)—Referring to His impending crucifixion, Jesus said, "Now the ruler of this world will be cast out." This is the believer's Magna Carta of release: By His death Jesus, having defeated Satan, the believer's ancient foe, has released the believer from the bondage Satan had exercised since the time of Adam. Satan tempts and tries God's people, often discouraging them, just as he tormented Job (Job 1:11, page 479), but the "wicked one does not touch him [the believer]" (1 John 5:18, page 1283). Satan cannot destroy the believer or make the believer his slave (Job 42:10, page 507). At Calvary all the chains that might have bound the believer were shattered, and the accusations of "the slanderer [the Devil]" were exposed as the lies they really are (1 John 3:8, page 1280).

See Index, page 17, for your next study.

Me a command, ᴿwhat I should say and what I should speak.   John 8:38 • Deut. 18:18

50 "And I know that His command is everlasting life. Therefore, whatever I speak, just as the Father has told Me, so I speak."

Jesus Washes the Disciples' Feet

13 Now before the Feast of the Passover, when Jesus knew that His hour had come that He should depart from this world to the Father, having loved His own who were in the world, He loved them to the end.

2 And *supper being ended, the devil having already put it into the heart of Judas Iscariot, Simon's *son*, to betray Him,

3 Jesus, knowing that the Father had given all things into His hands, and that He had come from God and was going to God,

4 rose from supper and laid aside His garments, took a towel and girded Himself.

5 After that, He poured water into a basin and began to wash the disciples' feet, and to wipe *them* with the towel with which He was girded.

6 Then He came to Simon Peter. And *Peter* said to Him, ᴿ"Lord, are You washing my feet?"   Matt. 3:14

7 Jesus answered and said to him, "What I am doing you ᴿdo not understand now, ᴿbut you will know after this."   John 12:16 • John 13:19

8 Peter said to Him, "You shall never wash my feet!" Jesus answered him, "If I do not wash you, you have no part with Me."

9 Simon Peter said to Him, "Lord, not my feet only, but also *my* hands and *my* head!"

10 Jesus said to him, "He who is bathed needs only to wash *his* feet, but is completely clean; and you are clean, but not all of you."

11 For He knew who would betray Him; therefore He said, "You are not all clean."

12 So when He had washed their feet, taken His garments, and sat down again, He said to them, "Do you ᵀknow what I have done to you?   *understand*

13 ᴿ"You call Me Teacher and Lord, and you say well, for so I am.   Matt. 23:8, 10

14 ᴿ"If I then, *your* Lord and Teacher, have washed your feet, ᴿyou also ought to wash one another's feet.   Luke 22:27 • [Rom. 12:10]

15 "For I have given you an example, that you should do as I have done to you.

16 "Most assuredly, I say to you, a servant is not greater than his master; nor is he who is sent greater than he who sent him.

17 ᴿ"If you know these things, blessed are you if you do them.   [James 1:25]

Jesus Identifies His Betrayer

18 "I do not speak concerning all of you. I know whom I have chosen; but that the ᴿScripture may be fulfilled, ᴿ*He who eats*

bread with Me has lifted up his heel against Me.'   John 15:25; 17:12 • Ps. 41:9

19 ᴿ"Now I tell you before it comes, that when it does come to pass, you may believe that I am *He*.   John 14:29; 16:4

20 ᴿ"Most assuredly, I say to you, he who receives whomever I send receives Me; and he who receives Me receives Him who sent Me."   Matt. 10:40

21 ᴿWhen Jesus had said these things, ᴿHe was troubled in spirit, and testified and said, "Most assuredly, I say to you, ᴿone of you will betray Me."   Luke 22:21 • John 12:27 • John 18:2

22 Then the disciples looked at one another, perplexed about whom He spoke.

23 Now ᴿthere was ᵀleaning on Jesus' bosom one of His disciples, whom Jesus loved.   John 19:26; 20:2; 21:7, 20 • *reclining*

24 Simon Peter therefore motioned to him to ask who it was of whom He spoke.

25 Then, leaning *back on Jesus' breast, he said to Him, "Lord, who is it?"

26 Jesus answered, "It is he to whom I shall give a piece of bread when I have dipped *it*." And having dipped the bread, He gave *it* to ᴿJudas Iscariot, *the son* of Simon.   John 6:71

27 ᴿNow after the piece of bread, Satan entered him. Then Jesus said to him, "What you do, do quickly."   Luke 22:3

28 But no one at the table knew for what reason He said this to him.

29 For some thought, because Judas had the money box, that Jesus had said to him, "Buy *those things* we need for the feast," or that he should give something to the poor.

30 Having received the piece of bread, he then went out immediately. And it was night.

The New Commandment

31 So, when he had gone out, Jesus said, ᴿ"Now the Son of Man is glorified, and ᴿGod is glorified in Him.   John 12:23 • [1 Pet. 4:11]

32 "If God is glorified in Him, God will also glorify Him in Himself, and ᴿglorify Him immediately.   John 12:23

33 "Little children, I shall be with you a little while longer. You will seek Me; and as I said to the Jews, 'Where I am going, you cannot come,' so now I say to you.

34 ᴿ"A new commandment I give to you, that you love one another; as I have loved you, that you also love one another. 1 Thess. 4:9

35 "By this all will know that you are My disciples, if you have love for one another."

Jesus Predicts Peter's Denial

36 Simon Peter said to Him, "Lord, where are You going?" Jesus answered him, "Where I am going you cannot follow Me now, but you shall follow Me afterward."

13:18 NU *My bread has*
13:25 NU, M add *thus*

13:2 NU *during supper*

37 Peter said to Him, "Lord, why can I not follow You now? I will ᴿlay down my life for Your sake."   Mark 14:29-31

38 Jesus answered him, "Will you lay down your life for My sake? Most assuredly, I say to you, the rooster shall not ᴿcrow till you have denied Me three times.   John 18:25-27

The Way, the Truth, and the Life

▼ 17-A. Heaven Is a Place

14 "Let not your heart be troubled; you believe in God, believe also in Me.

2 "In My Father's house are many *mansions; if *it were* not *so*, *I would have told you. I go to prepare a place for you.

3 "And if I go and prepare a place for you, I will come again and receive you to Myself; that where I am, *there* you may be also.

4 "And where I go you know, and the way you know."

5 ᴿThomas said to Him, "Lord, we do not know where You are going, and how can we know the way?"   Matt. 10:3

14:2 Lit. *dwellings* • NU *would I have told you that I go* or *I would have told you; for I go*

6 Jesus said to him, "I am the way, the ▽ truth, and the life. No one comes to the Father ᴿexcept through Me.   [John 10:7-9] ▲

The Father Revealed

7 ᴿ"If you had known Me, you would have known My Father also; and from now on you know Him and have seen Him."   John 8:19

8 Philip said to Him, "Lord, show us the Father, and it is sufficient for us."

9 Jesus said to him, "Have I been with you so long, and yet you have not known Me, Philip? ᴿHe who has seen Me has seen the Father; so how can you say, 'Show us the Father'?   Col. 1:15

10 "Do you not believe that I am in the Father, and the Father in Me? The words that I speak to you ᴿI do not speak on My own *authority*; but the Father who dwells in Me does the works.   Deut. 18:18; John 5:19; 14:24

11 "Believe Me that I *am* in the Father and the Father in Me, ᴿor else believe Me for the sake of the works themselves.   John 5:36; 10:38

The Answered Prayer

12 ᴿ"Most assuredly, I say to you, he who believes in Me, the works that I do he will do

---

17-A. Heaven Is a Place (John 14:1-6)—It is a fact that heaven is an actual place. It is as real as the country in which you were born, as real as any place on earth. It is called a "city . . . whose builder and maker is God" (Heb. 11:10, page 1248), "a better, that is, a heavenly country" (Heb. 11:16, page 1249). It is above the earth (1 Kin. 8:23, page 335), and it is where God the Father dwells (Matt. 5:16, page 939). Heaven is called God the Father's throne (Matt. 5:34, page 941); the Lord Jesus Christ is there now, seated with God the Father upon the Father's eternal, heavenly throne (1 Pet. 3:22, page 1267; Rev. 3:21, page 1297).

(1) Heaven is a place, according to the Lord Jesus Christ. The words of the present text were spoken by our Lord to His troubled disciples the night before He was to die on the cross. They were, and are, words of comfort and hope to all true disciples. He said, "Let not your heart be troubled" (v. 1). He knew their hearts, their sorrows, and He also knew of the faith they had in God the Father. He called upon them to have the exact same faith in Him, God the Son, that they had in God the Father. "You believe in God [the Father], believe also in Me [God the Son]" (v. 1).

After His death, burial, and resurrection, the disciples gained this faith and lost their fearing, troubled hearts. The Scripture says, "Then the disciples were glad when they saw the [risen] Lord . . . [for now they believed] that Jesus is the Christ [the Messiah], the Son of God" (John 20:19-31, page 1083). To believe that heaven is a place requires faith in the deity of the Lord Jesus Christ. Asserting His deity, Jesus continued to encourage His disciples by saying, "Believe also in Me" (v. 1), and telling them about heaven. Paraphrased, He was saying, "Before you can believe what I am telling you about heaven, you must first believe in Me as you believe in God the Father." He went on to say:

(a) "In My Father's house are many mansions [habitable places]" (v. 2). Heaven is a place where we can live and make our eternal home.

(b) "I go to prepare a place for you" (v. 2). After His resurrection, the disciples saw Him ascend back into heaven whence He came (Acts 1:9-11, page 1087; cf. John 8:23, page 1062). Heaven is a prepared place for every born-again believer (John 3:36, page 1053).

(c) "I will come again and receive you to Myself; that where I am, there you may be also" (v. 3; cf. 1 Thess. 4:16-18, page 1212).

(d) "I am the way" to heaven, "the truth" about heaven, "and the life" of heaven for all believers (v. 6).

(e) "No one comes to the Father [in heaven] except through Me" (v. 6; cf. Acts 4:12, page 1091).

(2) Heaven is a place, according to the prophet Isaiah (Is. 6:1-8, page 647).

(3) Heaven is a place, according to the apostle Paul (2 Cor. 12:1-4, page 1175).

(4) Heaven is a place, according to the apostle John (Rev. 4:1-11, page 1297).

Our Lord called heaven a place twice in the present text, emphasizing that it is a real, eternal dwelling place with the Father, Son, and Holy Spirit (1 John 5:7, page 1282).

See Colossians 3:1-4, page 1205, for **Point 17-B: Heaven Is the Saint's Place.**

also; and greater *works* than these he will do, because I go to My Father. Luke 10:17

13 ᴿ"And whatever you ask in My name, that I will do, that the Father may be ᴿglorified in the Son. Matt. 7:7 · John 13:31

14 "If you ask anything in My name, I will do *it*.

Jesus Promises Another Helper

▼ **10-D. The Ministry of the Holy Spirit: The Helper**

15 ᴿ"If you love Me, *keep My commandments. 1 John 5:3

16 "And I will pray the Father, and ᴿHe will give you another ᵀHelper, that He may abide with you forever— Acts 2:4, 33 · *Comforter*

17 "the Spirit of truth, whom the world cannot receive, because it neither sees Him nor knows Him; but you know Him, for He ▲ dwells with you and will be in you.

18 ᴿ"I will not leave you orphans; ᴿI will come to you. [Matt. 28:20] · [John 14:3, 28]

14:15 NU *you will keep*

Indwelling of the Father and the Son

19 "A little while longer and the world will see Me no more, but you will see Me. ᴿBecause I live, you will live also. [1 Cor. 15:20]

20 "At that day you will know that I *am* in My Father, and you in Me, and I in you.

21 "He who has My commandments and keeps them, it is he who loves Me. And he who loves Me will be loved by My Father, and I will love him and manifest Myself to him."

22 ᴿJudas (not Iscariot) said to Him, "Lord, how is it that You will manifest Yourself to us, and not to the world?" Luke 6:16

23 Jesus answered and said to him, "If anyone loves Me, he will keep My word; and My Father will love him, and We will come to him and make Our home with him.

24 "He who does not love Me does not keep My words; and the word which you hear is not Mine but the Father's who sent Me.

The Gift of His Peace

25 "These things I have spoken to you while being present with you.

26 "But the Helper, the Holy Spirit, whom the Father will send in My name, He will

---

10-D. The Ministry of the Holy Spirit: The Helper (John 14:15-17)—"I will pray the Father, and He will give you another Helper" (v. 16). "Parakletos" is the Greek word used four times in the Gospel of John, and is translated "Helper." The word means, "one called alongside," i.e., to take the place of Jesus. The Lord Jesus was the first Helper sent by the Father; "He will give you another Helper" (v. 16). Now the Father would give the disciples the Holy Spirit (Paraclete) to "help" them and all believers, to be with them in the absence of Christ. The disciples were sorrowing because Jesus told them that He would go away, and they could not go with Him then. He said, "Let not your heart be troubled . . . I go to prepare a place for you . . . I will come again and receive you to Myself; that where I am, there you may be also" (John 14:1-3, page 1074).

(1) The Helper will "abide with you forever . . . and will be in you" (vv. 16, 17). Let this fact comfort you in these days of trials and tribulations. Paul said, "We also glory in tribulations . . . because the love of God has been poured out in our hearts by the Holy Spirit who was given to us" (Rom. 5:3-5, page 1133). The Helper has been given to all believers to fill our hearts with the love of God.

(2) The Helper was sent by the Father, in the name of Jesus, to take His place and continue to teach His disciples all things. He would also cause them to remember all that Jesus taught them, so that they could give us the complete Word of God (John 14:26, page 1075; cf. 2 Pet. 1:12, page 1272).

(3) The Helper, "whom I shall send to you from the Father," was sent to "testify of Me" (John 15:26, page 1076). For almost two thousand years the Holy Spirit has motivated believers to give testimony to the saving and keeping power of the Lord Jesus Christ (Acts 8:29-40, page 1099). And the Helper will continue to fill obedient believers with the power to share their faith with the lost (Acts 1:8, page 1086).

(4) "When He [the Helper] has come" (John 16:7-15, page 1077):

      (a) He will convict of sin, of righteousness, and of judgment;
      (b) He will guide you into all truth;
      (c) He will show you things to come;
      (d) He will glorify Christ;
      (e) He will take the things of Christ, and show it to you.

Jesus said that the Holy Spirit would take His doctrine and guide the apostles as they recorded what He taught. He would help them to remember, and show them things yet to come (Acts 1:1, 2, page 1086). On the Day of Pentecost the Helper began His ministry of evangelizing the world and guiding the apostles as they wrote the New Testament. He has continued to evangelize the world and to guide believers as they study God's Word, helping them to grow in the grace and knowledge of Jesus. He will continue His great ministry until Jesus comes to rapture the church (1 Thess. 4:13-18, page 1211).

See 1 Corinthians 12:1-31, page 1157, for **Point 10-E: The Ministry of the Holy Spirit: The Giver of Spiritual Gifts.**

teach you all things, and bring to your remembrance all things that I said to you.

27 ᴿ"Peace I leave with you, My peace I
give to you; not as the world gives do I give
to you. Let not your heart be troubled, neither let it be afraid.   Luke 1:79; [Phil. 4:7]

28 "You have heard Me ᴿsay to you, 'I am
going away and coming *back* to you.' If you
loved Me, you would rejoice because *I said,
ᴿ*I am going to the Father,' for ᴿMy Father is
greater than I.   John 14:3, 18 • John 16:16 • [Phil. 2:6]

29 "And ᴿnow I have told you before it
comes, that when it does come to pass, you
may believe.   John 13:19

30 "I will no longer talk much with you,
ᴿfor the ruler of this world is coming, and he
has ᴿnothing in Me.   [John 12:31] • [Heb. 4:15]

31 "But that the world may know that I
love the Father, and ᴿas the Father gave Me
commandment, so I do. Arise, let us go from
here.   Is. 50:5; John 10:18

The True Vine

15 "I am the true vine, and My Father is
the vinedresser.

2 ᴿ"Every branch in Me that does not bear
fruit He ᵀtakes away; and every *branch* that
bears fruit He prunes, that it may bear ᴿmore
fruit.   Matt. 15:13 • Or *lifts up* • [Matt. 13:12]

3 "You are already clean because of the
word which I have spoken to you.

4 ᴿ"Abide in Me, and I in you. As the
branch cannot bear fruit of itself, unless it
abides in the vine, neither can you, unless
you abide in Me.   [Col. 1:23]

5 "I am the vine, you *are* the branches. He
who abides in Me, and I in him, bears much
fruit; for without Me you can do nothing.

6 "If anyone does not abide in Me, ᴿhe is
cast out as a branch and is withered; and they
gather them and throw *them* into the fire,
and they are burned.   Matt. 3:10

7 "If you abide in Me, and My words abide
in you, ᴿyou* will ask what you desire, and it
shall be done for you.   John 14:13; 16:23

8 "By this My Father is glorified, that you
bear much fruit; so you will be My disciples.

Love and Joy Perfected

9 "As the Father ᴿloved Me, I also have
loved you; abide in My love.   John 5:20; 17:26

10 ᴿ"If you keep My commandments, you
will abide in My love, just as I have kept My
Father's commandments and abide in His
love.   John 14:15

11 "These things I have spoken to you, that
My joy may remain in you, and ᴿ*that* your
joy may be full.   1 John 1:4

12 "This is My commandment, that you
love one another as I have loved you.

13 ᴿ"Greater love has no one than this, than
to lay down one's life for his friends. 1 John 3:16

14 ᴿ"You are My friends if you do whatever
I command you.   [Matt. 12:50; 28:20]

15 "No longer do I call you servants, for a
servant does not know what his master is
doing; but I have called you friends, ᴿfor all
things that I heard from My Father I have
made known to you.   Gen. 18:17

16 "You did not choose Me, but I chose you
and ᴿappointed you that you should go and
bear fruit, and *that* your fruit should remain,
that whatever you ask the Father in My
name He may give you.   [Col. 1:6]

17 "These things I command you, that you
love one another.

The World's Hatred

18 ᴿ"If the world hates you, you know that
it hated Me before *it hated* you.   1 John 3:13

19 "If you were of the world, the world
would love its own. Yet because you are not
of the world, but I chose you out of the
world, therefore the world hates you.

20 "Remember the word that I said to you,
ᴿ'A servant is not greater than his master.' If
they persecuted Me, they will also persecute
you. ᴿIf they kept My word, they will keep
yours also.   John 13:16 • Ezek. 3:7

21 "But ᴿall these things they will do to you
for My name's sake, because they do not
know Him who sent Me.   Matt. 10:22; 24:9

22 ᴿ"If I had not come and spoken to them,
they would have no sin, ᴿbut now they have
no excuse for their sin. John 9:41; 15:24 • [James 4:17]

23 ᴿ"He who hates Me hates My Father
also.   1 John 2:23

24 "If I had not done among them ᴿthe
works which no one else did, they would
have no sin; but now they have seen and also
hated both Me and My Father.   John 3:2

25 "But *this happened* that the word might
be fulfilled which is written in their law,
ᴿ*'They hated Me without a cause.'*   Ps. 69:4

The Coming Rejection

26 "But when the ᵀHelper comes, whom I
shall send to you from the Father, the Spirit
of truth who proceeds from the Father, He
will testify of Me.   *Comforter*, Gr. *Parakletos*

27 "And ᴿyou also will bear witness, because ᴿyou have been with Me from the
beginning.   Luke 24:48 • Luke 1:2

16 "These things I have spoken to you,
that you ᴿshould not be made to
stumble.   Matt. 11:6

2 ᴿ"They will put you out of the synagogues; yes, the time is coming ᴿthat whoever kills you will think that he offers God
service.   John 9:22 • Acts 8:1

3 "And ᴿthese things they will do *to you

14:28 NU omits *I said*
15:7 NU omits *you will*   **16:3** NU, M omit *to you*

because they have not known the Father nor Me.   John 8:19; 15:21

4 "But these things I have told you, that when *the time comes, you may remember that I told you of them. And these things I did not say to you at the beginning, because I was with you.

The Work of the Holy Spirit

5 "But now I Rgo away to Him who sent Me, and none of you asks Me, 'Where are You going?'   John 7:33; 13:33; 14:28; 17:11

6 "But because I have said these things to you, sorrow has filled your heart.

7 "Nevertheless I tell you the truth. It is to your advantage that I go away; for if I do not go away, the Helper will not come to you; but Rif I depart, I will send Him to you.   Acts 2:33

8 "And when He has come, RHe will convict the world of sin, and of righteousness, and of judgment: Acts 1:8; 2:1-4, 37

9 R"of sin, because they do not believe in Me;   Acts 2:22

10 "of righteousness, Rbecause I go to My Father and you see Me no more;   John 5:32

11 R"of judgment, because Rthe ruler of this world is judged.   Acts 26:18 • [Luke 10:18]

12 "I still have many things to say to you, Rbut you cannot bear them now.   Mark 4:33

13 "However, when He, the Spirit of truth, has come, He will guide you into all truth; for He will not speak on His own authority, but whatever He hears He will speak; and RHe will tell you things to come.   Acts. 11:28; Rev. 1:19

14 R"He will glorify Me, for He will take of what is Mine and declare it to you.   John 15:26

15 R"All things that the Father has are Mine. Therefore I said that He *will take of Mine and declare it to you.   Matt. 11:27

Sorrow Will Turn to Joy

16 "A Rlittle while, and you will not see Me;

16:4 NU their
16:15 NU, M takes of Mine and will declare

and again a little while, and you will see Me, because I go to the Father."   John 19:42; 20:19

17 Then some of His disciples said among themselves, "What is this that He says to us, 'A little while, and you will not see Me; and again a little while, and you will see Me'; and, 'because I go to the Father'?"

18 They said therefore, "What is this that He says, 'A little while'? We do not Tknow what He is saying."   understand

19 Now Jesus knew that they desired to ask Him, and He said to them, "Are you inquiring among yourselves about what I said, 'A little while, and you will not see Me; and again a little while, and you will see Me'?

20 "Most assuredly, I say to you that you will weep and Rlament, but the world will rejoice; and you will be sorrowful, but your sorrow will be turned into joy.   John 20:20

21 R"A woman, when she is in labor, has sorrow because her hour has come; but as soon as she has given birth to the child, she no longer remembers the anguish, for joy that a human being has been born into the world.   Is. 13:8; 26:17; 42:14

22 "Therefore you now have sorrow; but I will see you again and Ryour heart will rejoice, and your joy no one will take from you.   John 20:20; Acts 2:46; 13:52; 1 Pet. 1:8

30-F. Pray in His Name   ▼

23 "And in that day you will ask Me nothing. RMost assuredly, I say to you, whatever you ask the Father in My name He will give you.   Matt. 7:7

24 "Until now you have asked nothing in My name. Ask, and you will receive, Rthat your joy may be Rfull.   John 17:13 • John 15:11 ▲

Jesus Christ Has Overcome the World

25 "These things I have spoken to you in figurative language; but the time is coming when I will no longer speak to you in figurative language, but I will tell you Rplainly about the Father.   John 7:13

26 "In that day you will ask in My name,

30-F. Pray in His Name (John 16:23, 24)—Christ teaches us to pray to the Father in His name. What a wonderful name to be able to use, what a great Friend to be our Mediator (1 Tim. 2:5, page 1219), what a mighty and holy Sovereign with which to storm the doors of heaven!

(1) Christ knows that we are sinners, but when we are robed in His righteousness we are dressed as children of the King (Rom. 10:1–10, page 1140). By ourselves, we deserve nothing from God. But when we ask in Christ's name, we can expect mountains to be moved (Matt. 17:20, page 964).

(2) Christ assures us that prayers in His name will be answered. He does this strongly by using the words, "Most assuredly," when He promises that the Father "will give you" the answer (v. 23).

(3) Christ teaches that we must ask in His will, for that is part of what it means to ask in His name. Those requests asked in His holy name must be asked by one who trusts in Him as Savior (1 John 5:14, 15, page 1283).

(4) Christ urges us to ask "in My name" that our "joy may be full" (v. 24). "He who did not spare His own Son, but delivered Him up for us all, how shall He not with Him also freely give us all things?" (Rom. 8:32, page 1138).

For the believer these lessons in prayer will yield peace and joy—now, and for eternity.
See Index, page 17, for your next study.

and I do not say to you that I shall pray the Father for you;

27 R"for the Father Himself loves you, because you have loved Me, and have believed that I came forth from God.　　　[John 14:21, 23]

28 R"I came forth from the Father and have come into the world. Again, I leave the world and go to the Father."　　　John 13:1, 3; 16:5, 10, 17

29 His disciples said to Him, "See, now You are speaking plainly, and using no figure of speech!

30 "Now we are sure that RYou know all things, and have no need that anyone should question You. By this Rwe believe that You came forth from God."　　　John 21:17 • John 17:8

31 Jesus answered them, "Do you now believe?

32 R"Indeed the hour is coming, yes, has now come, that you will be scattered, each to This own, and will leave Me alone. And yet I am not alone, because the Father is with Me.　　　Matt. 26:31, 56; Mark 14:50 • own things or place

33 "These things I have spoken to you, that in Me you may have peace. In the world you *will have tribulation; but be of good cheer, I have overcome the world."

Jesus Prays for Himself

17 Jesus spoke these words, lifted up His eyes to heaven, and said: "Father, Rthe hour has come. Glorify Your Son, that Your Son also may glorify You,　　　John 12:23

2 R"as You have given Him authority over all flesh, that He *should give eternal life to as many as You have given Him.　　　John 3:35

3 "And this is eternal life, that they may know You, the only true God, and Jesus Christ Rwhom You have sent.　　　John 3:34

4 R"I have glorified You on the earth. I have finished the work which You have given Me to do.　　　Is. 49:3; 50:5; John 13:31

5 "And now, O Father, glorify Me together Twith Yourself, with the glory which I had with You before the world was.　　　Lit. alongside

Jesus Prays for His Disciples

6 "I have Tmanifested Your name to the men whom You have given Me out of the world. They were Yours, You gave them to Me, and they have kept Your word.　　　revealed

7 "Now they have known that all things which You have given Me are from You.

8 "For RI have given to them the words which You have given Me; and they have received them, and have known surely that I came forth from You; and they have believed that You sent Me.　　　Deut. 18:18

9 "I pray for them. RI do not pray for the world but for those whom You have given Me, for they are Yours.　　　[1 John 5:19]

10 "And all Mine are Yours, and RYours are Mine, and I am glorified in them.　　　John 16:15

11 "Now I am no longer in the world, but these are in the world, and I come to You. Holy Father, Rkeep* through Your name those whom You have given Me, that they may be one Ras We are.　　　[1 Pet. 1:5] • John 10:30

12 "While I was with them *in the world, I kept them in *Your name. Those whom You gave Me I have kept; and none of them is lost except the son of Tperdition, that the Scripture might be fulfilled.　　　destruction

13 "But now I come to You, and these things I speak in the world, that they may have My joy fulfilled in themselves.

14 "I have given them Your word; and the world has hated them because they are not of the world, just as I am not of the world.

15 "I do not pray that You should take them out of the world, but Rthat You should keep them from the evil one.　　　1 John 5:18

16 "They are not of the world, just as I am not of the world.

17 R"SanctifyT them by Your truth. Your word is truth.　　　[Eph. 5:26] • Set them apart

18 R"As You sent Me into the world, I also have sent them into the world.　　　John 4:38; 20:21

19 "And for their sakes I sanctify Myself, that they also may be sanctified by the truth.

Jesus Prays for All Believers

20 "I do not pray for these alone, but also for those who *will believe in Me through their word;

21 R"that they all may be one, as RYou, Father, are in Me, and I in You; that they also may be one in Us, that the world may believe that You sent Me.　　　[Gal. 3:28] • John 10:38; 17:11, 23

22 "And the Rglory which You gave Me I have given them, Rthat they may be one just as We are one:　　　1 John 1:3 • [2 Cor. 3:18]

23 "I in them, and You in Me; that they may be made perfect in one, and that the world may know that You have sent Me, and have loved them as You have loved Me.

24 R"Father, I desire that they also whom You gave Me may be with Me where I am, that they may behold My glory which You have given Me; Rfor You loved Me before the foundation of the world.　　　[1 Thess. 4:17] • John 17:5

25 "O righteous Father! The world has not known You, but I have known You; and these have known that You sent Me.

26 R"And I have declared to them Your name, and will declare it, that the love Rwith which You loved Me may be in them, and I in them."　　　John 17:6 • John 15:9

17:11 NU, M keep them through Your name which You have given Me
17:12 NU omits in the world • NU Your name which You gave Me. And I guarded them (or it);
17:20 NU, M omit will

16:33 NU, M omit will
17:2 M shall

Betrayal and Arrest in Gethsemane

18 When Jesus had spoken these words, He went out with His disciples over the Brook Kidron, where there was a garden, which He and His disciples entered.

2 And Judas, who betrayed Him, also knew the place; ᴿfor Jesus often met there with His disciples.   Luke 21:37; 22:39

3 ᴿThen Judas, having received a detachment *of troops*, and officers from the chief priests and Pharisees, came there with lanterns, torches, and weapons.   Luke 22:47-53

4 Jesus therefore, knowing all things that would come upon Him, went forward and said to them, "Whom are you seeking?"

5 They answered Him, ᴿ"Jesus ᵀof Nazareth." Jesus said to them, "I am *He*." And Judas, who ᴿbetrayed Him, also stood with them.   Matt. 21:11 · Lit. *the Nazarene* · Ps. 41:9

6 Now when He said to them, "I am *He*," they drew back and fell to the ground.

7 Then He asked them again, "Whom are you seeking?" And they said, "Jesus of Nazareth."

8 Jesus answered, "I have told you that I am *He*. Therefore, if you seek Me, let these go their way,"

9 that the saying might be fulfilled which He spoke, ᴿ"Of those whom You gave Me I have lost none."   [John 6:39; 17:12]

10 ᴿThen Simon Peter, having a sword, drew it and struck the high priest's servant, and cut off his right ear. The servant's name was Malchus.   Matt. 26:51

11 So Jesus said to Peter, "Put your sword into the sheath. Shall I not drink the cup which My Father has given Me?"

Before the High Priest

12 Then the detachment *of troops* and the captain and the officers of the Jews arrested Jesus and bound Him.

13 And they led Him away to Annas first, for he was the father-in-law of ᴿCaiaphas who was high priest that year.   Matt. 26:3

14 Now it was Caiaphas who advised the Jews that it was ᵀexpedient that one man should die for the people.   *advantageous*

Peter Denies Jesus

15 And Simon Peter followed Jesus, and so did *another disciple. Now that disciple was known to the high priest, and went with Jesus into the courtyard of the high priest.

16 But Peter stood at the door outside. Then the other disciple, who was known to the high priest, went out and spoke to her who kept the door, and brought Peter in.

17 Then the servant girl who kept the door said to Peter, "You are not also *one* of this Man's disciples, are you?" He said, "I am ᴿnot."   Matt. 26:34

18 Now the servants and officers who had made a fire of coals stood there, for it was cold, and they warmed themselves. And Peter stood with them and warmed himself.

Jesus Questioned by the High Priest

19 The high priest then asked Jesus about His disciples and His doctrine.

20 Jesus answered him, "I spoke openly to the world. I always taught in synagogues and in the temple, where *the Jews always meet, and in secret I have said nothing.

21 "Why do you ask Me? Ask ᴿthose who have heard Me what I said to them. Indeed they know what I said."   Mark 12:37

22 And when He had said these things, one of the officers who stood by ᴿstruck Jesus with the palm of his hand, saying, "Do You answer the high priest like that?"   Lam. 3:30

23 Jesus answered him, "If I have spoken evil, bear witness of the evil; but if well, why do you strike Me?"

24 ᴿThen Annas sent Him bound to ᴿCaiaphas the high priest.   Matt. 26:57 · John 11:49

Peter Denies Twice More

25 Now Simon Peter stood and warmed himself. ᴿTherefore they said to him, "You are not also *one* of His disciples, are you?" He denied *it* and said, "I am not!"   Luke 22:58-62

26 One of the servants of the high priest, a relative *of him* whose ear Peter cut off, said, "Did I not see you in the garden with Him?"

27 ᴿPeter then denied again; and ᴿimmediately a rooster crowed.   Matt. 26:34 · John 13:38

In Pilate's Court

28 ᴿThen they led Jesus from Caiaphas to the Praetorium, and it was early morning. But they themselves did not go into the Praetorium, lest they should be defiled, but that they might eat the Passover.   John 18:32

29 ᴿPilate then went out to them and said, "What accusation do you bring against this Man?"   Matt. 27:11-14

30 They answered and said to him, "If He were not ᵀan evildoer, we would not have delivered Him up to you."   *a criminal*

31 Then Pilate said to them, "You take Him and judge Him according to your law." Therefore the Jews said to him, "It is not lawful for us to put anyone to death,"

32 that the saying of Jesus might be fulfilled which He spoke, ᴿsignifying by what death He would die.   John 3:14; 8:28; 12:32, 33

33 ᴿThen Pilate entered the Praetorium again, called Jesus, and said to Him, "Are You the King of the Jews?"   Matt. 27:11

34 Jesus answered him, "Are you speaking for yourself about this, or did others tell you this concerning Me?"

35 Pilate answered, "Am I a Jew? Your own nation and the chief priests have delivered You to me. What have You done?"

36 ᴿJesus answered, "My kingdom is not of this world. If My kingdom were of this world, My servants would fight, so that I should not be delivered to the Jews; but now My kingdom is not from here."   1 Tim. 6:13

37 Pilate therefore said to Him, "Are You a king then?" Jesus answered, "You say rightly that I am a king. For this cause I was born, and for this cause I have come into the world, ᴿthat I should bear ᴿwitness to the truth. Everyone who ᴿis of the truth hears My voice."   [Matt. 5:17; 20:28] • Is. 55:4 • [John 14:6]

38 Pilate said to Him, "What is truth?" And when he had said this, he went out again to the Jews, and said to them, ᴿ"I find no fault in Him at all.   John 19:4, 6

Taking the Place of Barabbas

39 ᴿ"But you have a custom that I should release someone to you at the Passover. Do you therefore want me to release to you the King of the Jews?"   Luke 23:17-25

40 ᴿThen they all cried again, saying, "Not this Man, but Barabbas!" ᴿNow Barabbas was a robber.   Is. 53:3; Acts 3:14 • Luke 23:19

The Soldiers Mock Jesus

19 So then ᴿPilate took Jesus and scourged Him.   Is. 50:6; Matt. 20:19; 27:26

2 And the soldiers twisted a crown of thorns and put it on His head, and they put on Him a purple robe.

3 *Then they said, "Hail, King of the Jews!" And they ᴿstruck Him with their hands.   Is. 50:6

4 Pilate then went out again, and said to them, "Behold, I am bringing Him out to you, ᴿthat you may know that I find no fault in Him."   John 18:33, 38

Pilate's Decision

5 Then Jesus came out, wearing the crown of thorns and the purple robe. And Pilate said to them, "Behold the Man!"

19:3 NU And they came up to Him and said

6 ᴿTherefore, when the chief priests and officers saw Him, they cried out, saying, "Crucify Him, crucify Him!" Pilate said to them, "You take Him and crucify Him, for I find no fault in Him."   Acts 3:13

7 The Jews answered him, ᴿ"We have a law, and according to *our law ᴿHe ought to die, because ᴿHe made Himself the Son of God."   Lev. 24:16 • Matt. 20:18 • Matt. 26:63-66

8 Therefore, when Pilate heard that saying, he was the more afraid,

9 and went again into the Praetorium, and said to Jesus, "Where are You from?" ᴿBut Jesus gave him no answer.   Ps. 38:13, 14; Is. 53:7

10 Then Pilate said to Him, "Are You not speaking to me? Do You not know that I have ᵀpower to crucify You, and ᵀpower to release You?"   authority

11 Jesus answered, "You could have no power at all against Me unless it had been given you from above. Therefore the one who delivered Me to you has the greater sin."

12 From then on Pilate sought to release Him, but the Jews cried out, saying, "If you let this Man go, you are not Caesar's friend. ᴿWhoever makes himself a king speaks against Caesar."   Luke 23:2

13 When Pilate therefore heard that saying, he brought Jesus out and sat down in the judgment seat in a place that is called The Pavement, but in Hebrew, Gabbatha.

14 Now it was the Preparation Day of the Passover, and about the sixth hour. And he said to the Jews, "Behold your King!"

15 ᴿBut they cried out, "Away with Him, away with Him! Crucify Him!" Pilate said to them, "Shall I crucify your King?" The chief priests answered, ᴿ"We have no king but Caesar!"   Is. 53:3 • [Gen. 49:10]

6-D. He Was Unique in His Death ▼

16 ᴿThen he delivered Him to them to be crucified. So they took Jesus *and led Him away.   Luke 23:24

19:7 NU the law
19:16 NU omits and led Him away

6-D. He Was Unique in His Death (John 19:16–30)—Though He underwent the greatest of public indignations as well as physical agonies, Christ's faultless behavior at His death has testified through the ages that "certainly this was a righteous Man!" (Luke 23:47, page 1046). Nowhere in history or literature is there a nobler account than that of Jesus facing the cross and then dying upon it.

(1) As Messiah He died for His people's sins, fulfilling David's detailed prophecy written a thousand years before (Ps. 22, page 522), and that of Isaiah seven hundred years before (Is. 52:13—53:12, page 693). Zechariah, about 450 B.C., foresaw His death as a death by piercing (Zech. 12:10, page 918).

(2) Jesus Himself prophesied that He would be put to death, and that His death would be for the sins of many (Mark 10:45, page 997; cf. Matt. 16:21, page 962).

(3) He died as the Passover Lamb, His innocent blood shed for the sins of mankind (John 1:29, page 1050). In the breaking of His body and in the outpouring of His blood, He saw the Passover Lamb's atonement at last fulfilled (1 Cor. 11:24, 25, page 1156).

(Point 6-D continued on next page)

▽ ## The King on a Cross

17 And He, bearing His cross, ᴿwent out to a place called *the Place* of a Skull, which is called in Hebrew, Golgotha,   Num. 15:36

18 where they ᴿcrucified Him, and two others with Him, one on either side, and Jesus in the center.   Ps. 22:16–18; Matt. 20:19; 26:2

19 ᴿNow Pilate wrote a title and put *it* on the cross. And the writing was: Matt. 27:37

JESUS OF NAZARETH, THE KING OF THE JEWS.

20 Then many of the Jews read this title, for the place where Jesus was crucified was near the city; and it was written in Hebrew, Greek, *and* Latin.

21 Therefore the chief priests of the Jews said to Pilate, "Do not write, 'The King of the Jews,' but, 'He said, "I am the King of the Jews." ' "

22 Pilate answered, "What I have written, I have written."

23 ᴿThen the soldiers, when they had crucified Jesus, took His garments and made four parts, to each soldier a part, and also the tunic. Now the tunic was without seam, woven from the top in one piece.   Luke 23:34

24 They said therefore among themselves, "Let us not tear it, but cast lots for it, whose it shall be," that the Scripture might be fulfilled which says:

> ᴿ*"They divided My garments among them,*   Ps. 22:18
> *And for My clothing they cast lots."*

Therefore the soldiers did these things.

Behold Your Mother

25 Now there stood by the cross of Jesus His mother, and His mother's sister, Mary the *wife* of Clopas, and Mary Magdalene.

26 When Jesus therefore saw His mother, and ᴿthe disciple whom He loved standing by, He said to His mother, ᴿ"Woman, behold your son!"   John 13:23; 20:2; 21:7, 20, 24 • John 2:4

27 Then He said to the disciple, "Behold your mother!" And from that hour that disciple took her to his own *home.*

It Is Finished

28 After this, Jesus, *knowing that all things were now accomplished, that the Scripture might be fulfilled, said, "I thirst!"

29 Now a vessel full of sour wine was sitting there; and ᴿthey filled a sponge with sour wine, put *it* on hyssop, and put *it* to His mouth.   Ps. 69:21; Matt. 27:48, 50

30 So when Jesus had received the sour wine, He said, ᴿ"It is finished!" And bowing His head, He gave up His spirit.   Zech. 11:10, 11 ▲

Jesus' Side Is Pierced

31 Therefore, because it was the Preparation *Day,* ᴿthat the bodies should not remain on the cross on the Sabbath (for that Sabbath was a ᴿhigh day), the Jews asked Pilate that their legs might be broken, and *that* they might be taken away.   Deut. 21:23 • Ex. 12:16

32 Then the soldiers came and broke the legs of the first and of the other who was crucified with Him.

33 But when they came to Jesus and saw that He was already dead, ᴿthey did not break His legs.   Ps. 34:20

34 But one of the soldiers pierced His side with a spear, and immediately ᴿblood and water came out.   [1 John 5:6, 8]

35 And he who has seen has testified, and his testimony is true; and he knows that he is telling the truth, so that you may believe.

36 For these things were done that the Scripture should be fulfilled, * *"Not one of His bones shall be broken."*

37 And again another Scripture says, ᴿ*"They shall look on Him whom they pierced."*   Zech. 12:10; 13:6

Jesus Buried in Joseph's Tomb

38 ᴿAfter this, Joseph of Arimathea, being a disciple of Jesus, but secretly, ᴿfor fear of the Jews, asked Pilate that he might take away the body of Jesus; and Pilate gave *him* permission. So he came and took the body of Jesus.   Is. 53:9; Luke 23:50–56 • [John 7:13; 9:22; 12:42]

19:28 M *seeing*
19:36 [Ex. 12:46; Num. 9:12]; Ps. 34:20

(Point 6-D continued from previous page)

(4) He died voluntarily, obeying the Father's will: "No one takes it from Me, but I lay it down of Myself" (John 10:17, 18, page 1067). Had He wished to resist His captors He could have summoned twelve legions of angels to fight for Him—but He did not (Matt. 26:52-54, page 978).

(5) God the Father hid His face from the Son at Calvary, for Jesus, though He had never sinned, was at that time bearing the sins of the world (Matt. 27:46, page 980; cf. 2 Cor. 5:21, page 1169).

(6) Even as He endured the agony of crucifixion He publicly asked forgiveness for His enemies: "Father, forgive them, for they do not know what they do" (Luke 23:34, page 1045).

(7) His upright and holy conduct at the cross even caused one of the two thieves crucified beside Him to accept Him as Savior and find eternal forgiveness. Such was the unique testimony and power of His dying (Luke 23:34-43, page 1045)!

See John 20:1–31, page 1082, for **Point 6-E: He Was Unique in His Resurrection.**

39 And Nicodemus, who at first came to Jesus by night, also came, bringing a mixture of myrrh and aloes, about a hundred pounds.

40 Then they took the body of Jesus, and ᴿbound it in strips of linen with the spices, as the custom of the Jews is to bury.   John 20:5, 7

41 Now in the place where He was crucified there was a garden, and in the garden a new tomb in which no one had yet been laid.

42 So ᴿthere they laid Jesus, ᴿbecause of the Jews' Preparation *Day*, for the tomb was nearby.   Is. 53:9; Matt. 26:12; Mark 14:8 · John 19:14, 31

The Empty Tomb

▼ 6-E. He Was Unique in His Resurrection

20 Now on the first *day* of the week Mary Magdalene went to the tomb early, while it was still dark, and saw *that* the stone had been taken away from the tomb.

2 Then she ran and came to Simon Peter, and to the ᴿother disciple, whom Jesus loved, and said to them, "They have taken away the Lord out of the tomb, and we do not know where they have laid Him."   John 21:23, 24

3 ᴿPeter therefore went out, and the other disciple, and were going to the tomb.   Luke 24:12

4 So they both ran together, and the other disciple outran Peter and came to the tomb first.

5 And he, stooping down and looking in, saw ᴿthe linen cloths lying *there*; yet he did not go in.   John 19:40

6 Then Simon Peter came, following him, and went into the tomb; and he saw the linen cloths lying *there*,

7 and the handkerchief that had been around His head, not lying with the linen cloths, but folded together in a place by itself.

8 Then the ᴿother disciple, who came to the tomb first, went in also; and he saw and believed.   John 21:23, 24

9 For as yet they did not know the Scripture, that He must rise again from the dead.

10 Then the disciples went away again to their own homes.

Mary Magdalene Sees the Risen Lord

11 ᴿBut Mary stood outside by the tomb weeping, and as she wept she stooped down *and looked* into the tomb.   Mark 16:5

12 And she saw two angels in white sitting, one at the head and the other at the feet, where the body of Jesus had lain.

13 Then they said to her, "Woman, why are you weeping?" She said to them, "Because they have taken away my Lord, and I do not know where they have laid Him."

14 Now when she had said this, she turned around and saw Jesus standing *there*, and ᴿdid not know that it was Jesus.   John 21:4

15 Jesus said to her, "Woman, why are you weeping? Whom are you seeking?" She, supposing Him to be the gardener, said to Him, "Sir, if You have carried Him away, tell me where You have laid Him, and I will take Him away."

6-E. He Was Unique in His Resurrection (John 20:1-31)—Jesus said, "I lay down My life that I may take it again" (John 10:17, page 1067). He stands alone among all the other so-called religious leaders of the ages: He alone was certified by God to be the Christ, by His resurrection from the dead (Rom. 1:4, page 1128).

(1) He rose according to the Old Testament prophecies that the Messiah would rise from the dead. "Nor will You allow Your Holy One to see corruption" (Ps. 16:10, page 518). The Crucifixion Psalm (Ps. 22, page 522), after describing the Messiah's death, speaks of His resurrection: "I [the resurrected Messiah] will declare Your name [the Father] to My brethren" (Ps. 22:22, page 523). The same is true in Isaiah's crucifixion passage (Is. 52:13—53:12, page 693). In the middle of Isaiah 53:10 (page 693), the subject changes from crucifixion to resurrection.

(2) He had prophesied His own resurrection: "From that time Jesus began to show to His disciples that He must . . . be killed, and be raised the third day" (Matt. 16:21, page 962).

(3) He rose from the dead, although His enemies had made sure that the tomb was sealed and that a guard had been posted against the possible theft of His body (Matt. 27:62-66, page 981).

(4) He appeared alive first to a woman. Perhaps He did this to honor those women who had wept and stood by Him, so faithfully and so alone, while the men forsook Him (vv. 11-19).

(5) His burial bandages were lying undisturbed in the tomb. His body had passed through the bandages that had bound it in death. Grave robbers, in fear of Roman arrest and their own death, would never have taken the time to unwrap a body; nor would His disciples have been so inclined, for fear of the normal putrefaction. Jesus had passed through His wrappings as He had passed through the bonds of death (vv. 6-9).

(6) He appeared over and over to His disciples, in various locations over a period of forty days. He displayed the energy of a person in excellent health—not of one resuscitated. He allowed them to examine His wounds, to see that it was He (vv. 27-29).

(7) He arose on the first day of the week (v. 1). Since that day the Christian church has worshiped on the first day of the week to commemorate God's rest from redeeming the world, just as the Old Testament saints observed the Sabbath to commemorate God's rest from creating the world (Ex. 20:8-11, page 79).

(8) By Christ's resurrection He became the firstfruits, the basis of our own resurrection (1 Cor. 15:20-24, page 1161).

See Acts 1:1-9, page 1086, for **Point 6-F: He Was Unique in His Ascension.**

▽ 16 Jesus said to her, ᴿ"Mary!" She turned and said to *Him, "Rabboni!" (which is to say, Teacher).   John 10:3

▼ **20-F. The Day of Atonement in the New Testament**

17 Jesus said to her, "Do not cling to Me, for I have not yet ascended to My Father; but go to My brethren and say to them, ᴿ'I am ascending to My Father and your Father, and ▲ to My God and your God.' "   Mark 16:19; Acts 1:9
18 Mary Magdalene came and told the *disciples that she had seen the Lord, and *that He had spoken these things to her.

The Apostles Commissioned

19 Then, the same day at evening, being the first *day* of the week, when the doors were shut where the disciples were *assembled, for ᴿfear of the Jews, ᴿJesus came and stood in the midst, and said to them, "Peace *be* with you."   John 9:22; 19:38 • John 16:16
20 When He had said this, He showed them *His* hands and His side. Then the disciples were glad when they saw the Lord.
21 So Jesus said to them again, "Peace to

20:16 NU adds *in Hebrew*
20:18 NU *disciples, " I have seen the Lord,"*
20:19 NU omits *assembled*

you! ᴿAs the Father has sent Me, I also send ▽ you."   John 17:18, 19
22 ᴿAnd when He had said this, He breathed on *them*, and said to them, "Receive the Holy Spirit.   John 16:20-22
23 ᴿ"If you forgive the sins of any, they are forgiven them; if you retain the *sins* of any, they are retained."   Matt. 16:19; 18:18

Seeing and Believing

24 Now Thomas, called the Twin, one of the twelve, was not with them when Jesus came.
25 The other disciples therefore said to him, "We have seen the Lord." So he said to them, "Unless I see in His hands the print of the nails, and put my finger into the print of the nails, and put my hand into His side, I will not believe."
26 And after eight days His disciples were again inside, and Thomas with them. Jesus came, the doors being shut, and stood in the midst, and said, "Peace to you!"
27 Then He said to Thomas, "Reach your finger here, and look at My hands; and reach your hand *here*, and put *it* into My side. Do not be unbelieving, but believing."
28 And Thomas answered and said to Him, "My Lord and my God!"

20-F. The Day of Atonement in the New Testament (John 20:17)—Mary Magdalene was the first person to see the risen Lord on that first Easter Sunday. God chose her for this honor—to show how great was the power of His atonement. At one time she had been lost, fallen, and even demon-possessed (Luke 8:2, page 1022). Through her tears she saw a man near the tomb, and thinking He was the gardener, said, "Sir, if You have carried Him away, tell me where You have laid Him, and I will take Him away." Jesus answered, "Mary!" (John 20:15, 16, page 1082).

Recognizing the risen Christ, she cried, "Rabboni!"—"Teacher!"—and reached out to touch Him. But Jesus said to her, "Do not cling to Me, for I have not yet ascended to My Father; but go to My brethren and say to them, 'I am ascending to My Father and your Father, and to My God and your God' " (vv. 16, 17).

As the first person to see Jesus alive after His resurrection, Mary was privileged to see Him before He entered the Most Holy Place in heaven as our High Priest. With the shedding of His own blood He made atonement for our sins, obtaining eternal redemption for us (Heb. 9:12, page 1243). Simon Peter said, "Knowing that you were not redeemed with corruptible things . . . but with the precious blood of Christ, as of a lamb without blemish and without spot" (1 Pet. 1:18, 19, page 1263). The sacrifice of God's Lamb was

(1) Volitional. Jesus Christ *willingly* chose to be God's sacrificial Lamb to take away the sins of the world (John 1:29, page 1050). None of the Old Testament sacrifices could bring eternal redemption. The high priest had to repeat the sacrifice and enter the Most Holy Place once every year to atone for the sins of the people (Lev. 16:12-16, page 124). All the animal sacrifices were imperfect types of Jesus Christ, our perfect blood sacrifice (Heb. 9:11-14, page 1243).

(2) Motivated by love. The love of the Holy Trinity (Father, Son, and Holy Spirit) for us is manifested in the vicarious death of Jesus Christ (John 3:16, page 1052).

(3) An act of rational obedience (Phil. 2:5-8, page 1197). In God's eternal economy He was "the Lamb slain from the foundation of the world" (Rev. 13:8, page 1306). Therefore, He knew beforehand every agonizing moment that He would endure on the cross, and the ignominious shame He would experience (Heb. 12:2, page 1250).

(4) The end of all animal sacrifices. "For if we [Hebrew believers in Christ] sin willfully after we have received the knowledge of the truth [that Christ died for our sins, was buried and rose from the dead], there no longer remains a sacrifice for sins" (Heb. 10:26-29, page 1246). "For Christ is the end of the [ceremonial] law for righteousness to everyone who believes" (Rom. 10:4, page 1140).

It was necessary for Christ, our High Priest, to enter the Most Holy Place in heaven after His resurrection and sprinkle His own blood upon the mercy seat to make atonement for the sins of Old and New Testament believers (Heb. 9:11, 12, page 1243).

See Hebrews 9:22, page 1244, for **Point 20-G: Without the Shedding of Blood.**

▽ 29 Jesus said to him, *"Thomas, because you have seen Me, you have believed. ᴿBlessed *are* those who have not seen and yet have believed."　　　　　　1 Pet. 1:8

That You May Believe

30 And ᴿtruly Jesus did many other signs in the presence of His disciples, which are not written in this book;　　　　　John 21:25

31 but these are written that ᴿyou may believe that Jesus ᴿis the Christ, the Son of God, ᴿand that believing you may have life in

▲ His name.　　　1 John 5:13 • Luke 2:11 • John 3:15, 16; 5:24

Breakfast by the Sea

21 After these things Jesus showed Himself again to the disciples at the Sea of Tiberias, and in this way He showed *Himself*:

2 Simon Peter, ᴿThomas called Didymus, ᴿNathanael of ᴿCana in Galilee, ᴿthe *sons of* Zebedee, and two others of His disciples were together.　　John 20:24 • John 1:45–51 • John 2:1 • Matt. 4:21

3 Simon Peter said to them, "I am going fishing." They said to him, "We are going with you also." They went out and *immediately got into the boat, and that night they caught nothing.

4 But when the morning had now come, Jesus stood on the shore; yet the disciples ᴿdid not know that it was Jesus.　　John 20:14

5 Then ᴿJesus said to them, "Children, have you any food?" They answered Him, "No."　　　　　　Luke 24:41

6 And He said to them, ᴿ"Cast the net on the right side of the boat, and you will find *some.*" So they cast, and now they were not able to draw it in because of the multitude of fish.　　　　　　Luke 5:4, 6, 7

7 Therefore that disciple whom Jesus loved said to Peter, "It is the Lord!" Now when Simon Peter heard that it was the Lord, he put on *his* outer garment (for he had removed it), and plunged into the sea.

8 But the other disciples came in the little boat (for they were not far from land, but about ᵀtwo hundred cubits), dragging the net with fish.　　　　　　300 ft.

9 Then, as soon as they had come to land, they saw a fire of coals there, and fish laid on it, and bread.

10 Jesus said to them, "Bring some of the fish which you have just caught."

11 Simon Peter went up and dragged the net to land, full of large fish, one hundred and fifty-three; and although there were so many, the net was not broken.

12 Jesus said to them, ᴿ"Come *and* eat breakfast." Yet none of the disciples dared ask Him, "Who are You?"—knowing that it was the Lord.　　　　　Acts 10:41

13 Jesus then came and took the bread and gave it to them, and likewise the fish.

14 This *is* now ᴿthe third time Jesus showed Himself to His disciples after He was raised from the dead.　　　John 20:19, 26

Jesus Restores Peter

15 So when they had eaten breakfast, Jesus said to Simon Peter, "Simon, *son of* *Jonah, do you love Me more than these?" He said to Him, "Yes, Lord; You know that I love You." He said to him, "Feed My lambs."

16 He said to him again a second time, "Simon, *son of* *Jonah, do you love Me?" He said to Him, "Yes, Lord; You know that I love You." He said to him, "Tend My sheep."

17 He said to him the third time, "Simon, *son of* *Jonah, do you love Me?" Peter was grieved because He said to him the third time, "Do you love Me?" And he said to Him, "Lord, ᴿYou know all things; You know that I ᵀlove You." Jesus said to him, "Feed My sheep.　　John 2:24, 25; 16:30 • *have affection for*

18 ᴿ"Most assuredly, I say to you, when you were younger, you girded yourself and walked where you wished; but when you are old, you will stretch out your hands, and another will gird you and carry *you* where you do not wish."　　　Acts 12:3, 4

19 This He spoke, signifying by what death he would glorify God. And when He had spoken this, He said to him, "Follow Me."

The Beloved Disciple and His Book

20 Then Peter, turning around, saw the disciple ᴿwhom Jesus loved following, ᴿwho also had leaned on His breast at the supper, and said, "Lord, who is the one who betrays You?"　　　John 13:23; 20:2 • John 13:25

21 Peter, seeing him, said to Jesus, "But Lord, what *about* this man?"

22 Jesus said to him, "If I ᵀwill that he remain ᴿtill I come, what *is that* to you? You follow Me."　　*desire* • [Rev. 2:25; 3:11; 22:7, 20]

23 Then this saying went out among the brethren that this disciple would not die. Yet Jesus did not say to him that he would not die, but, "If I will that he remain till I come, what *is that* to you?"

24 This is the disciple who ᴿtestifies of these things, and wrote these things; and we know that his testimony is true.　　　John 19:35

25 ᴿAnd there are also many other things that Jesus did, which if they were written one by one, ᴿI suppose that even the world itself could not contain the books that would be written. Amen.　　John 20:30 • Amos 7:10

20:29 NU, M omit *Thomas*
21:3 NU omits *immediately*

21:15 NU *John*
21:16 NU *John*
21:17 NU *John*

The Acts

OF THE APOSTLES

CONTEXT. This book could well be called the "Acts of the Holy Spirit," for it is certainly the unfolding narrative of the work of the Holy Spirit through the lives of God's people and God's churches in the first century after Christ. It is the story of the upsetting of the world (Acts 17:6). No movement has ever had so dramatic an impact on every level of society as has the propagation of the Christian gospel. This is the story of how God took little groups of simple, poor, and mostly uneducated folks and shook their world for Christ, turning the Roman empire upside down. It is the story of how they overcame great distances and inadequate transportation, language barriers, political alliances, and strong satanic opposition. Humanly speaking, you could write over their assignment, "Mission impossible," and yet the Holy Spirit accomplished through them what God had given them to do.

AUTHORSHIP. The author of the Acts was a companion of Paul, as we know from the so-called "we" sections, where the first person plural is used (Acts 16:10–17; 20:5—21:18; 27:1—28:16). The universal Christian tradition that this was "the beloved physician" Luke (Col. 4:14) is supported by the evidence. The author was clearly a cultured man, which is shown by his excellent Greek style, his use of quite a few medical terms (which fits in with Luke's profession), and the many characteristics suggesting a Gentile with a universal outlook. Luke probably wrote the book shortly after Paul's arrival at Rome, since subsequent events such as the great fire, Nero's persecution of Christians, and the beheading of Paul could scarcely have been left out if they had happened already. This would give a date in the very early 60s of the first century.

HOW ACTS FITS INTO THE BIBLE. If there were no book of Acts the gap in understanding the New Testament would be great. The Gospels tell us the story of Jesus and the Epistles address congregations scattered across the Roman empire and how they should live. Where did they come from? How did this teaching spread? The answer is in the Acts of the Apostles, the first church history ever written.

KEY VERSE: 1:8—"But you shall receive power when the Holy Spirit has come upon you; and you shall be witnesses to Me in Jerusalem, and in all Judea and Samaria, and to the end of the earth."

HOW ACTS FITS TOGETHER. Luke has divided his book into two main sections in keeping with the key verse. In chapters 1—12 the gospel is presented in Jerusalem, Judea, and Samaria. It is confined to Jerusalem in chapters 1—7, until Stephen and Philip dare to move out into Judea and Samaria in chapters 8—12. This section also contains the story of the Spirit's work in changing Simon the Weak into Peter the Rock. The radical transformation of this prejudiced, narrow-minded Jew to a flaming evangelist with a world-wide vision and a compassion for even the despised Gentile, is one of the great examples of the power of the Holy Spirit.

In the second main section of the book, chapters 13—28, the gospel moves to the end of the earth. Here is the moving story of the Holy Spirit's work in transforming Saul the slaughterer into Paul the dynamic first missionary of the Christian movement. This man's consuming passion for vexing and persecuting the church was transformed into a passion for souls that led him, during three missionary journeys, to share the gospel "to the uttermost."

The Spirit-filled men and women of the book of Acts went out as heralds from the high courts of heaven, proclaiming the good news of salvation. These witnesses were not sightseers but soul winners, not politicians but preachers. They stirred the synagogue, penetrated the palaces, and mastered the markets. They riled the Romans, altered Asia, and captured their cities for Christ.

The contents of the book of Acts cover a period of more than thirty years. This book is a classic textbook for missionary principles, the defense of the faith, the person and the work of the Holy Spirit, and the method and themes of Christian ministry and preaching. It is still, by far, the best manual for church growth ever written.

As the center of Christian activity moves from Jerusalem to Antioch and the chief personality is first Peter, and then Paul, we see the beginnings of a worldwide missionary program that is still going on today.

Dr. Luke wrote Volume I about the life of Jesus and Volume II on the life of the early church. Today, we are writing Volume III. God has given us, in the book of Acts, a pattern by which the church of our day is to be built. Acts is never finished. The book simply stops, but the "acts" are to be continued until Jesus comes for His church.

Acts 2:41–47 presents a portrait in microcosm of the spirit and activity of the first century church. It is expanded and illustrated throughout the book of Acts. It reveals the first century church to be a praying church, a powerful church, a preaching church, a persevering church, a pure church, a people's church, and a prepared church.

Perhaps the key to understanding the message of the book of Acts is to see it as a *continuation*. Luke refers to his "former account," his Gospel, as "all that Jesus began both to do and teach." As he ends his Gospel at our Lord's ascension, he here begins from it, so that his second account is a continuation of his first. The ascension of Jesus did not rob His followers of His presence. He was with them more after He had left them than He ever was before. This book is the amazing epic of what the crucified, risen, ascended Jesus *continued* to do by His Spirit through His chosen witnesses. What an encouragement this book becomes to us. We do not merely work *for* Jesus, it is He Himself, in us, working with us and through us. Remember— *we* are writing Volume III!

—R.H.

Prologue

▼ **6-F. He Was Unique in His Ascension**

THE former account I made, O [R]Theophilus, of all that Jesus began both to do and teach,   Luke 1:3

2 until the day in which [T]He was taken up, after He through the Holy Spirit [R]had given commandments to the apostles whom He had chosen,   He ascended into heaven. · Matt. 28:19

3 [R]to whom He also presented Himself alive after His suffering by many [T]infallible proofs, being seen by them during forty days and speaking of the things pertaining to the kingdom of God.   Mark 16:12, 14 · *unmistakable*

The Holy Spirit Promised

4 [R]And being assembled together with *them*, He commanded them not to depart from Jerusalem, but to wait for the Promise

of the Father, "which," He said, "you have ▽ [R]heard from Me;   Luke 24:49 · [John 14:16, 17, 26; 15:26]

5 "for John truly baptized with water, [R]but you shall be baptized with the Holy Spirit not many days from now."   [Joel 2:28]

6 Therefore, when they had come together, they asked Him, saying, "Lord, will You at this time restore the kingdom to Israel?"

7 And He said to them, "It is not for you to [R]know times or seasons which the Father has put in His own authority.   Matt. 24:36

8 [R]"But you shall receive power [R]when the Holy Spirit has come upon you; and [R]you shall be *witnesses to Me in Jerusalem, and in all Judea and [R]Samaria, and to the end of the earth."   [Acts 2:1, 4] · Luke 24:49 · Luke 24:48 · Acts 8:1

1:8 NU *My witnesses*

6-F. He Was Unique in His Ascension (Acts 1:1–9)—Enoch ascended into heaven but did not die. Elijah was taken to heaven in a whirlwind, but did not die. Jesus, after death, ascended into heaven by the power of His own word, having promised to return.

(1) The ascension of Jesus into heaven, like the taking up of Enoch (Gen. 5:24, page 10) and Elijah (2 Kin. 2:11, page 356), was a further acknowledgment of God the Father's approval of His teaching ministry and His atoning death on the cross (v. 9).

(2) The fact that He ascended on high supports the truth that He went to be with the Father, rather than that He merely vanished (v. 9).

(3) Christ made a promise, at His ascension, that the disciples would receive power to witness for Him after the Holy Spirit came upon them (v. 8).

(4) Christ expressed a command, at His ascension, that the disciples "shall be witnesses to Me in Jerusalem [home], and in all Judea [throughout their own nation] and Samaria [in adjoining nations, even though unfriendly], and to the end of the earth" (v. 8). Thus the Great Commission to evangelize was given (Matt. 28:16–20, page 982).

(5) Christ ascended into heaven, but night and day He manifests His concern for His own. He stood to receive Stephen, the first Christian martyr, in heaven (Acts 7:55, 56, page 1097). He stopped the hardened Saul on the Damascus road, and converted him into the apostle Paul (Acts 26:1, 12–18, page 1121). He appeared years later to the apostle John to reveal to him the contents of the book of Revelation (Rev. 1:9, 10, 18, page 1293). Now He walks daily among His churches (Rev. 1:20—2:1, page 1294).

(6) Christ ascended into heaven in order to become our High Priest who, as God the Son, would always answer the prayers of those who call upon Him in faith (Heb. 4:14–16, page 1239).

(7) Christ ascended into heaven to take His seat at the right hand of the Father and make continual intercession for believers (Heb. 7:25, page 1242; 8:1, page 1242).

See Matthew 16:27, page 963, for **Point 6-G: He Will Be Unique in His Second Coming.**

▽ *Jesus Ascends to Heaven*

9 Now when He had spoken these things, while they watched, He was taken up, and a
▲ cloud received Him out of their sight.
10 And while they looked steadfastly toward heaven as He went up, behold, two men stood by them ᴿin white apparel,   John 20:12
11 who also said, "Men of Galilee, why do you stand gazing up into heaven? This *same* Jesus, who was taken up from you into heaven, ᴿwill so come in like manner as you saw Him go into heaven."   Dan. 7:13

The Upper Room Prayer Meeting

12 ᴿThen they returned to Jerusalem from the mount called Olivet, which is near Jerusalem, a Sabbath day's journey.   Luke 24:52
13 And when they had entered, they went up into the upper room where they were staying: Peter, James, John, and Andrew; Philip and Thomas; Bartholomew and Matthew; James *the son* of Alphaeus and Simon the Zealot; and Judas *the son* of James.
14 These all continued with one ᵀaccord in prayer *and supplication, ᴿthe women and Mary the mother of Jesus, and with ᴿHis brothers.   *purpose* or *mind* · Luke 23:49, 55 · Matt. 13:55

Matthias Chosen

15 And in those days Peter stood up in the midst of the *disciples (altogether the number ᴿof names was about a hundred and twenty), and said,   Rev. 3:4
16 "Men *and* brethren, this Scripture had to be fulfilled, ᴿwhich the Holy Spirit spoke before by the mouth of David concerning

1:14 NU omits *and supplication*
1:15 NU *brethren*

Judas, ᴿwho became a guide to those who arrested Jesus;   Ps. 41:9 · Luke 22:47
17 "for he was numbered with us and obtained a part in ᴿthis ministry."   Acts 1:25
18 (Now this man purchased a field with the ᵀwages of iniquity; and falling headlong, he burst open in the middle and all his entrails gushed out.   *reward of unrighteousness*
19 And it became known to all those dwelling in Jerusalem; so that field is called in their own language, Akel Dama, that is, Field of Blood.)
20 "For it is written in the book of Psalms:

> ᴿ'Let his dwelling place be desolate,
>   And let no one live in it';   Ps. 69:25

and,

> ᴿ'Let another take his *office.'*   Ps. 109:8

21 "Therefore, of these men who have accompanied us all the time that the Lord Jesus went in and out among us,
22 "beginning from the baptism of John to that day when ᴿHe was taken up from us, one of these must ᴿbecome a witness with us of His resurrection."   Acts 1:9 · Acts 1:8; 2:32
23 And they proposed two: Joseph called ᴿBarsabas, who was surnamed Justus, and Matthias.   Acts 15:22
24 And they prayed and said, "You, O Lord, ᴿwho know the hearts of all, show which of these two You have chosen   1 Sam. 16:7

17-E. Hell Is the Sinner's Place   ▼

25 "to take part in this ministry and apostleship from which Judas by transgression fell, that he might go to his own place."   ▲

1:20 Gr. *episkopen*, position of overseer

17-E. Hell Is the Sinner's Place (Acts 1:25)—After Judas betrayed Jesus and saw that He was condemned to die on the cross, he "was remorseful." He returned to the chief priest and elders and tried to make restitution. Confessing his guilt, he said, "I have sinned by betraying innocent blood." Then he cast down the thirty pieces of silver in the temple, at the feet of the chief priest, "and went and hanged himself" (Matt. 27:3–8, page 979), "that he might go to his own place" (v. 25). Hell is the sinner's own place of torment (Luke 16:23, page 1035).

While the Upper Room congregation waited for Pentecost, they prayed that God would choose one to take the place of Judas. They prayed, "Show which of these two You have chosen to take part in this ministry and apostleship from which Judas by transgression fell, that he might go to his own place" (vv. 24, 25). The question is often asked, "Was Judas ever saved?" Keep in mind that Judas was one of the Twelve. He was an apostle. He sat at the feet of Jesus and was taught the Good News of salvation for three-and-a-half years. He saw Jesus heal the sick, raise the dead, open blind eyes, walk on the water, and feed five thousand with five barley loaves and two small fish. He was among the twelve disciples who were given power to cast out demons, heal all manner of sickness, cleanse the lepers, raise the dead, and preach the gospel of the kingdom (Matt. 10:1–8, page 949). Judas did all of this, but he was never saved (Matt. 7:21–23, page 946). Judas fell, but not from salvation. He fell from the ministry and from apostleship. Salvation is not in question in verse 25.

Jesus taught in Capernaum, saying, " 'Unless you eat the flesh of the Son of Man and drink His blood [symbolically], you have no life in you . . . ' From that time many of His disciples went back and walked with Him no more. Then Jesus said to the twelve, 'Do you also want to go away?' But Simon Peter answered Him, 'Lord, to whom shall we go? You have the words of eternal life. Also we have come to believe and know that You are the Christ, the Son of the living God.' Jesus answered them, 'Did I not choose you, the twelve, and

(Point 17-E continued on next page)

26 And they cast their lots, and the lot fell on Matthias. And he was numbered with the eleven apostles.

Coming of the Holy Spirit

▼ **10-B. The Ministry of the Holy Spirit on the Day of Pentecost and After**

2 When ᴿthe Day of Pentecost had fully come, ᴿthey were all *with one accord in one place.   Lev. 23:15 • Acts 1:14

2 And suddenly there came a sound from heaven, as of a rushing mighty wind, and ᴿit filled the whole house where they were sitting.   Acts 4:31

3 Then there appeared to them *divided

2:1 NU *together*
2:3 Or *tongues as of fire, distributed and resting on each*

tongues, as of fire, and *one* sat upon each of ▽ them.

4 And they were all filled with the Holy Spirit and began to speak with other tongues, as the Spirit gave them utterance.

The Crowd's Response

5 And there were dwelling in Jerusalem Jews, ᴿdevout men, from every nation under heaven.   Acts 8:2

6 And when this sound occurred, the ᴿmultitude came together, and were confused, because everyone heard them speak in his own language.   Acts 4:32

7 Then they were all amazed and marveled, saying to one another, "Look, are not all these who speak ᴿGalileans?   Acts 1:11

8 "And how *is it that* we hear, each in our own ⁷language in which we were born? *dialect*

(Point 17-E continued from previous page)

one of you is a devil?' He spoke of Judas Iscariot, the son of Simon, for it was he who would betray Him, being one of the twelve" (John 6:53–71, page 1060).

Jesus chose Judas even though He knew that this man would sell Him for the price of a slave and thus would fulfill prophecy (Zech. 11:12, 13, page 917). Judas is mentioned again in the Lord's prayer. "While I was with them in the world, I kept them in Your name. Those whom You gave Me I have kept; and none of them is lost except the son of perdition, that the Scripture might be fulfilled" (John 17:12, page 1078). He is called "the son of perdition" (utter destruction, the son of hell). Judas was never saved. After fulfilling prophecy, he went out and hanged himself, that he might go to his own place of torment.

See Matthew 25:41, page 976, for **Point 17-F: Hell Is an Eternal Place.**

10-B. The Ministry of the Holy Spirit on the Day of Pentecost and After (Acts 2:1–21)—When the Holy Spirit came on the Day of Pentecost, there were certain supernatural manifestations that marked the beginning of His ministry in the church age. The 120 disciples were in the Upper Room and in accord with one another.

(1) The first supernatural manifestation of the Holy Spirit on this occasion was for the ear—"There came a sound from heaven, as of a rushing mighty wind, and it filled the whole house where they were sitting" (v. 2). It was for the ear, not the eye. The Scriptures emphasize the importance of hearing God's Word (Rom. 10:17, page 1140). The risen Savior sent letters to the seven churches in Asia Minor and closed each message with the words, "He who has an ear, let him hear what the Spirit [the Holy Spirit] says to the churches" (Rev. 2 and 3, page 1294).

The sound was of hurricane force, without physical power. They could hear the wind, but did not feel its force. This lesson is simple but profound: The Holy Spirit is sovereign. He moves and does what He wills (John 3:8, page 1052). He does not conform to the will or expectations of man. Even though there was no physical power, however, this rushing mighty wind was filled with spiritual power. The Holy Spirit, with Pentecostal power, moved the Upper Room congregation from their place of worship into the city streets and into the temple, to witness and share their faith in holy boldness (Acts 4:13, page 1091).

(2) The second supernatural manifestation of the Holy Spirit was for the tongue—"Then there appeared to them divided tongues, as of fire, and one sat upon each of them" (v. 3). This was the cleansing of the tongue in preparation for witnessing (cf. Is. 6:5–8, page 648; James 3:5–10, page 1258). After the tongue was cleansed, each of them could say with Isaiah, "Here am I! Send me" (Is. 6:8, page 648).

(3) The third supernatural manifestation of the Holy Spirit was for witnessing power (Acts 1:8, page 1086)—"And they were all filled with the Holy Spirit and began to speak with other tongues, as the Spirit gave them utterance" (v. 4). All of the 120 disciples were chosen by the Holy Spirit to witness in languages unknown to them, but not unknown to the hearers (vv. 7, 8). They witnessed in the power of the Holy Spirit and prepared the people for Simon Peter's message. This was a great miracle. People from many nations heard the Upper Room congregation share their faith in the language of the hearers. Verse 6 implies that when Peter preached in his language, each one heard him in his own language (vv. 6–36). It is no wonder that about three thousand who heard the gospel in their own language believed it in their hearts, repented of their sins, and were baptized and added to the church (vv. 37–42).

Note that the Upper Room congregation, filled with the Spirit, went to the temple and there exalted Christ, not their Pentecostal experience. They were filled with the Holy Spirit to tell the lost how to be saved (Acts 1:8, page 1086).

See Acts 5:29–32, page 1094, for **Point 10-C: The Ministry of the Holy Spirit: The Evangelist.**

▽ 9 "Parthians and Medes and Elamites, those dwelling in Mesopotamia, Judea and ᴿCappadocia, Pontus and Asia,   1 Pet. 1:1

10 "Phrygia and Pamphylia, Egypt and the parts of Libya adjoining Cyrene, visitors from Rome, both Jews and proselytes,

11 "Cretans and ᵀArabs—we hear them speaking in our own tongues the wonderful works of God."   Arabians

12 So they were all amazed and perplexed, saying to one another, "Whatever could this mean?"

13 Others mocking said, "They are full of new wine."

Peter's Sermon

14 But Peter, standing up with the eleven, raised his voice and said to them, "Men of Judea and all who dwell in Jerusalem, let this be known to you, and heed my words.

15 "For these are not drunk, as you suppose, ᴿsince it is only ᵀthe third hour of the day.   1 Thess. 5:7 • 9 A.M.

16 "But this is what was spoken by the prophet Joel:

17 'Andᴿ it shall come to pass in the last
     days, says God,   Joel 2:28–32
   ᴿThat I will pour out of My Spirit on all
     flesh;   Acts 10:45
   Your sons and ᴿyour daughters shall
     prophesy,   Acts 21:9
   Your young men shall see visions,
   Your old men shall dream dreams.
18 And on My menservants and on My
     maidservants
   I will pour out My Spirit in those days;
   ᴿAnd they shall prophesy.   1 Cor. 12:10
19 ᴿI will show wonders in heaven above
   And signs in the earth beneath: Joel 2:30
   Blood and fire and vapor of smoke.
20 ᴿThe sun shall be turned into darkness,
   And the moon into blood,
   Before the coming of the great and
     awesome day of the LORD.   Matt. 24:29
21 And it shall come to pass
   That ᴿwhoever calls on the name of the
     LORD
▲   Shall be saved.'   Rom. 10:13

22 "Men of Israel, hear these words: Jesus of Nazareth, ᴿa Man attested by God to you ᴿby miracles, wonders, and signs which God did through Him in your midst, as you yourselves also know—   Is. 50:5 • John 3:2; 5:6

23 "Him, ᴿbeing delivered by the determined purpose and foreknowledge of God, ᴿyou *have taken by lawless hands, have crucified, and put to death;   Luke 22:22 • Acts 5:30

24 "whom God raised up, having ᵀloosed the pains of death, because it was not possible that He should be held by it.   destroyed

25 "For David says concerning Him:

ᴿ'I foresaw the LORD always before my
     face,
   For He is at my right hand, that I may
     not be shaken.   Ps. 16:8–11
26 Therefore my heart rejoiced, and my
     tongue was glad;
   Moreover my flesh also will rest in
     hope.
27 For You will not leave my soul in
     Hades,
   Nor will You allow Your Holy One to
     see ᴿcorruption.   Acts 13:30–37
28 You have made known to me the ways
     of life;
   You will make me full of joy in Your
     presence.'

29 "Men and brethren, let me speak freely to you ᴿof the patriarch David, that he is both dead and buried, and his tomb is with us to this day.   Acts 13:36

30 "Therefore, being a prophet, ᴿand knowing that God had sworn with an oath to him that of the fruit of his body, *according to the flesh, He would raise up the Christ to sit on his throne,   Ps. 132:11

31 "he, foreseeing this, spoke concerning the resurrection of the Christ, ᴿthat His soul was not left in Hades, nor did His flesh see corruption.   Ps. 16:10; Acts 13:35

32 ᴿ"This Jesus God has raised up, ᴿof which we are all witnesses. Ps. 68:18 • Acts 1:8; 3:15

33 "Therefore being exalted to the right hand of God, and having received from the Father the promise of the Holy Spirit, He poured out this which you now see and hear.

34 "For David did not ascend into the heavens, but he says himself:

ᴿ'The LORD said to my Lord,
   "Sit at My right hand,   Ps. 68:18; 110:1
35 Till I make Your enemies Your
     footstool." '

36 "Therefore let all the house of Israel know assuredly that God has made this Jesus, whom you crucified, both Lord and Christ."

37 Now when they heard this, ᴿthey were cut to the heart, and said to Peter and the rest of the apostles, "Men and brethren, what shall we do?"   John 16:8

38 Then Peter said to them, "Repent, and let every one of you be baptized in the name of Jesus Christ for the remission of sins; and you shall receive the gift of the Holy Spirit.

39 "For the promise is to you and to your children, and ᴿto all who are afar off, as many as the Lord our God will call."   Eph. 2:13

2:23 NU omits have taken   2:30 NU He would seat one on his throne,

A Vital Church Grows

40 And with many other words he testified and exhorted them, saying, "Be saved from this ᵀperverse generation."   *crooked*

▼ 39-C. The Baptism of the Believer

41 Then those who *gladly received his word were baptized; and that day about three thousand souls were added *to them.*

42 And they continued steadfastly in the apostles' ᵀdoctrine and fellowship, in the
▲ breaking of bread, and in prayers.   *teaching*

43 Then fear came upon every soul, and ᴿmany wonders and signs were done through the apostles.   Acts 2:22

44 Now all who believed were together, and ᴿhad all things in common,   Acts 4:32, 34, 37; 5:2

45 and ᵀsold their possessions and goods, and ᴿdividedᵀ them among all, as anyone had need.   *would sell* • Is. 58:7 • *distributed*

46 ᴿSo continuii g daily with one accord ᴿin the temple, and breaking bread from house to house, they ate their food with gladness and simplicity of heart,   Acts 1:14 • Luke 24:53

47 praising God and having favor with all the people. And the Lord added *to the church daily those who were being saved.

A Lame Man Healed

3 Now Peter and John went up together ᴿto the temple at the hour of prayer, ᴿthe ninth *hour.*   Acts 2:46 • Ps. 55:17

2:41 NU omits *gladly*
2:47 NU omits *to the church*

2 And ᴿa certain man lame from his mother's womb was carried, whom they laid daily at the gate of the temple which is called Beautiful, ᴿto ᵀask alms from those who entered the temple;   Acts 14:8 • John 9:8 • Beg

3 who, seeing Peter and John about to go into the temple, asked for alms.

4 And fixing his eyes on him, with John, Peter said, "Look at us."

5 So he gave them his attention, expecting to receive something from them.

6 Then Peter said, "Silver and gold I do not have, but what I do have I give you: ᴿIn the name of Jesus Christ of Nazareth, rise up and walk."   Acts 4:10

7 And he took him by the right hand and lifted *him* up, and immediately his feet and ankle bones received strength.

8 So he, ᴿleaping up, stood and walked and entered the temple with them—walking, leaping, and praising God.   Is. 35:6

9 ᴿAnd all the people saw him walking and praising God.   Acts 4:16, 21

10 Then they knew that it was he who sat begging alms at the Beautiful Gate of the temple; and they were filled with wonder and amazement at what had happened to him.

Preaching in Solomon's Portico

11 Now as the lame man who was healed held on to Peter and John, all the people ran together to them in the porch ᴿwhich is called Solomon's, greatly amazed.   John 10:23

39-C. The Baptism of the Believer (Acts 2:41, 42)—On the Day of Pentecost, three thousand believed in the Lord Jesus Christ, repented of their sins, and were obedient to follow their Lord in the ordinance of baptism. Water baptism does not cleanse us from our sins. Water baptism is an outward symbol of inward cleansing by the blood of Jesus Christ (1 Pet. 1:18, 19, page 1263). The apostle John said, "To Him [Jesus] who loved us and washed us from our sins in His own blood . . . be glory and dominion forever and ever. Amen" (Rev. 1:5, 6, page 1293).

(1) Baptism is the ordinance signifying public entrance into the church (v. 41). The words "were added" mean that those baptized were added to the assembly of believers, the church. Water baptism was open to all believers, giving them their first opportunity to obey their Lord and Savior Jesus Christ. Beginning on the Day of Pentecost, baptism took place immediately after their profession of faith in Christ as their personal Savior; "Then those who gladly received his word were baptized" (v. 41).

(2) Those baptized "continued steadfastly in the apostles' doctrine" (v. 42). Therefore they continued to "grow in the grace and knowledge of our Lord and Savior Jesus Christ" (2 Pet. 3:18, page 1276).

(3) Christ commanded His church to disciple those whom it baptized (Matt. 28:19, 20, page 982). Water baptism became the initiatory rite of the new faith. Those receiving baptism were to be discipled.

(4) Baptism is to be performed "in the name of the Father and of the Son and of the Holy Spirit" (Matt. 28:19, page 982). In this way the Christian becomes identified with the local church and Christ, who is the head of the church. The church is itself a microcosm (small model) of the total body of Christ.

(5) Baptism symbolizes our burial with Christ, and our newness of life with His resurrection (Rom. 6:4, 5, page 1134).

(6) The thief on the cross was saved, though never baptized. "Assuredly, I say to you, today you will be with Me in Paradise" (Luke 23:43, page 1046). This example of a person being saved without baptism explains how Paul could write, "For Christ did not send me to baptize, but to preach the gospel" (1 Cor. 1:11–17, page 1148).

(7) Water baptism was commanded to all who trust in Christ (Matt. 28:19, page 982). Note that it is Christ's command. He allowed Himself to be baptized by John "to fulfill all righteousness" (Matt. 3:15, page 934); likewise we are to obey and follow the Lord in baptism.

See Mark 14:12–26, page 1003, for **Point 39-D: The Lord's Supper.**

12 So when Peter saw *it*, he responded to the people: "Men of Israel, why do you marvel at this? Or why look so intently at us, as though by our own power or godliness we had made this man walk?

13 "The God of Abraham, Isaac, and Jacob, the God of our fathers, glorified His Servant Jesus, whom you ᴿdelivered up and ᴿdenied in the presence of Pilate, when he was determined to let *Him* go.   Matt. 27:2 • Matt. 27:20

14 "But you denied ᴿthe Holy One ᴿand the Just, and ᴿasked for a murderer to be granted to you,   Mark 1:24 • Acts 7:52 • John 18:40

15 "and killed the ᵀPrince of life, ᴿwhom God raised from the dead, ᴿof which we are witnesses.   Or *Originator* • Acts 2:24 • Acts 2:32

16 ᴿ"And His name, through faith in His name, has made this man strong, whom you see and know. Yes, the faith which *comes* through Him has given him this perfect soundness in the presence of you all. Matt. 9:22

17 "Yet now, brethren, I know that you did *it* in ignorance, as *did* also your rulers.

18 "But those things which God foretold by the mouth of all His prophets, that the Christ would suffer, He has thus fulfilled.

19 ᴿ"Repent therefore and be converted, that your sins may be blotted out, so that times of refreshing may come from the presence of the Lord,   [Acts 2:38; 26:20]

20 "and that He may send *Jesus Christ, ᴿwho was preached to you before,   Mal. 3:1

21 "whom heaven must receive until the times of restoration of all things, which God has spoken by the mouth of all His holy prophets since ᵀthe world began.   Or *time*

22 "For Moses truly said to the fathers, ᴿ'The Lᴏʀᴅ your God will raise up for you a Prophet like me from your brethren. Him you shall hear in all things, whatever He says to you.   Deut. 18:15, 18, 19

23 'And it shall be that every soul who will not hear that Prophet shall be utterly destroyed from among the people.'

24 "Yes, and all the prophets, from Samuel and those who follow, as many as have spoken, have also *foretold these days.

25 ᴿ"You are sons of the prophets, and of the covenant which God made with our fathers, saying to Abraham, ᴿ'And in your

seed all the families of the earth shall be blessed.'   [Rom. 9:4, 8] • Gen. 22:18; 26:4; 28:14

26 "To you ᴿfirst, God, having raised up His Servant Jesus, sent Him to bless you, ᴿin turning away every one of you from your iniquities."   [Rom. 1:16; 2:9] • Matt. 1:21

Peter and John Arrested

4 Now as they spoke to the people, the priests, the captain of the temple, and the ᴿSadducees came upon them,   Matt. 22:23

2 being greatly disturbed that they taught the people and preached in Jesus the resurrection from the dead.

3 And they laid hands on them, and put *them* in custody until the next day, for it was already evening.

4 However, many of those who heard the word believed; and the number of the men came to be about five thousand.

Addressing the Sanhedrin

5 And it came to pass, on the next day, that their rulers, elders, and scribes,

6 as well as ᴿAnnas the high priest, Caiaphas, John, and Alexander, and as many as were of the family of the high priest, were gathered together at Jerusalem.   Luke 3:2

7 And when they had set them in the midst, they asked, ᴿ"By what power or by what name have you done this?"   Matt. 21:23

8 ᴿThen Peter, filled with the Holy Spirit, said to them, "Rulers of the people and elders of Israel: Luke 12:11, 12

9 "If we this day are judged for a good deed *done* to *a* helpless man, by what means he has been made well,

10 "let it be known to you all, and to all the people of Israel, that by the name of Jesus Christ of Nazareth, whom you crucified, ᴿwhom God raised from the dead, by Him this man stands here before you whole.   Acts 2:24

11 "This is the ᴿ'stone which was rejected by you builders, which has become the chief cornerstone.'   Ps. 118:22; Is. 28:16

21-C. So Great in Power   ▼

12 "Nor is there salvation in any other, for there is no other name under heaven given among men by which we must be saved."   ▲

The Name of Jesus Forbidden

13 Now when they saw the boldness of Peter and John, ᴿand perceived that they

---

3:20 NU, M *Christ Jesus, who was ordained for you before*
3:24 NU, M *proclaimed*

21-C. So Great in Power (Acts 4:12)—The power of the gospel is concentrated in the death, burial, and resurrection of Christ. Paul says, "For the message of the cross is foolishness to those who are perishing, but to us who are being saved it is the power of God" (1 Cor. 1:18, page 1148). It is the most profound doctrine in the Bible. We often hear it called the "simple gospel." In one sense this is true, yet it is also profound. Peter said, "Knowing that you were not redeemed with corruptible things, like silver or gold, from your aimless conduct received by tradition from your fathers, but with the precious blood of Christ, as of a lamb without blemish and without spot" (1 Pet. 1:18, 19, page 1263). The gospel is incomprehensible to the

(Point 21-C continued on next page)

were uneducated and untrained men, they marveled. And they realized that they had been with Jesus.   [1 Cor. 1:27]

14 And seeing the man who had been healed ᴿstanding with them, they could say nothing against it.   Acts 3:11

15 But when they had commanded them to go aside out of the council, they conferred among themselves,

16 saying, "What shall we do to these men? For, indeed, that a notable miracle has been done through them *is* evident to all who dwell in Jerusalem, and we cannot deny *it.*

17 "But so that it spreads no further among the people, let us severely threaten them, that from now on they speak to no man in this name."

18 ᴿSo they called them and commanded them not to speak at all nor teach in the name of Jesus.   Acts 5:28, 40

19 But Peter and John answered and said to them, ᴿ"Whether it is right in the sight of God to listen to you more than to God, you judge.   Acts 5:29

20 "For we cannot but speak the things which we have seen and heard."

21 So when they had further threatened them, they let them go, finding no way of punishing them, ᴿbecause of the people, since they all ᴿglorified God for ᴿwhat had been done.   Acts 5:26 • Matt. 15:31 • Acts 3:7, 8

22 For the man was over forty years old on whom this miracle of healing had been performed.

Prayer for Boldness

23 And being let go, they went to their own *companions* and reported all that the chief priests and elders had said to them.

24 So when they heard that, they raised their voice to God with one accord and said: "Lord, You *are* God, who made heaven and earth and the sea, and all that is in them,

25 "who *by the mouth of Your servant David have said:

> ᴿ*Why did the nations rage,*   Ps. 2:1, 2
> *And the people plot vain things?*
>
> 26 *The kings of the earth took their stand,*
> *And the rulers were gathered together*
> *Against the* Lᴏʀᴅ *and against His* *Christ.'*

27 "For truly against Your holy Servant Jesus, whom You anointed, both Herod and Pontius Pilate, with the Gentiles and the people of Israel, were gathered together

28 "to do whatever Your hand and Your purpose determined before to be done.

29 "Now, Lord, look on their threats, and grant to Your servants ᴿthat with all boldness they may speak Your word,   Acts 4:13, 31; 9:27

30 "by stretching out Your hand to heal, ᴿand that signs and wonders may be done ᴿthrough the name of ᴿYour holy Servant Jesus."   Acts 2:43; 5:12 • Acts 3:6, 16 • Acts 4:27

31 And when they had prayed, ᴿthe place where they were assembled together was shaken; and they were all filled with the Holy

4:25 NU *through the Holy Spirit, by the mouth of our father, Your servant David,*

(Point 21-C continued from previous page)

unregenerate mind, because it came from the infallible mind of God and is beyond sinful man's fallible comprehension (1 Cor. 2:14–16, page 1149).

Paul said the following things about the gospel (Rom. 1:16–18, page 1128):

(1) "I am not ashamed of the gospel [Good News] of Christ." Paul was not ashamed of the gospel because he was not ashamed of Christ, his Messiah (cf. Mark 8:38, page 994). Death on the cross was so degrading and dishonorable that it was not spoken of in public. But Paul would go to Rome and preach the death of Christ on the ignominious cross.

(2) "For it [the gospel] is the power of God to salvation for everyone who believes." The gospel of Christ will not deliver you from sin until you believe "that Christ died for our sins according to the Scriptures, and that He was buried, and that He rose again the third day according to the Scriptures" (1 Cor. 15:3, 4, page 1161). This gospel, the principal doctrine of the Bible, is:

(a) Christ died on the cross bearing your sins in His own body (1 Pet. 2:24, page 1266);
(b) He was in the tomb three days and nights (Matt. 12:40, page 954);
(c) He rose from the dead on the third day in His glorified human body (John 20:24–31, page 1083).

(3) "For in it [the gospel of Christ] the righteousness of God is revealed from faith to faith." Christ is the righteousness of God; the believer is made righteous with the righteousness of God in Christ (2 Cor. 5:21, page 1169). Faith is the believer's principle of life: "as it is written, 'The just [those who have been declared by God to be righteous in Christ] shall live by faith.' "

(4) "For the wrath of God is revealed from heaven against all ungodliness and unrighteousness of men, who suppress [or, hold down] the truth in unrighteousness."

In these last days the human race is fast losing God-consciousness, because it is no longer sin-conscious. People are not conscious of the wrath of God that will be poured out on all ungodliness and unrighteousness of men. There is only one place that man can hide from the wrath of God; that place is in Christ.

See Ephesians 2:8, 9, page 1187, for **Point 21-D: So Great in Grace.**

Spirit, ^Rand they spoke the word of God with boldness. Acts 2:2, 4; 16:26 · Acts 4:29

Sharing in All Things

32 Now the multitude of those who believed ^Rwere of one heart and one soul; ^Rneither did anyone say that any of the things he possessed was his own, but they had all things in common. Rom. 15:5, 6 · Acts 2:44

33 And with great power the apostles gave witness to the resurrection of the Lord Jesus. And great grace was upon them all.

34 Nor was there anyone among them who lacked; ^Rfor all who were possessors of lands or houses sold them, and brought the proceeds of the things that were sold, Acts 2:45

35 and laid *them* at the apostles' feet; and they distributed to each as anyone had need.

36 And *Joses, who was also named Barnabas by the apostles (which is translated Son of ^TEncouragement), a Levite of the country of Cyprus, Or *Consolation*

37 having land, sold *it*, and brought the money and laid *it* at the apostles' feet.

Lying to the Holy Spirit

▼ **16-F. Consequences of Sin Committed by Ananias and Sapphira**

5 But a certain man named Ananias, with Sapphira his wife, sold a possession.

4:36 NU *Joseph*

2 And he kept back *part* of the proceeds, ▽ his wife also being aware *of it*, and brought a certain part and laid *it* at the apostles' feet.

3 ^RBut Peter said, "Ananias, why has ^RSatan filled your heart to lie to the Holy Spirit and keep back *part* of the price of the land for yourself? Deut. 23:21 · Luke 22:3

4 "While it remained, was it not your own? And after it was sold, was it not in your own control? Why have you conceived this thing in your heart? You have not lied to men but to God."

5 Then Ananias, hearing these words, fell down and breathed his last. So great fear came upon all those who heard these things.

6 And the young men arose and wrapped him up, carried *him* out, and buried *him*.

7 Now it was about three hours later when his wife came in, not knowing what had happened.

8 And Peter answered her, "Tell me whether you sold the land for so much?" She said, "Yes, for so much."

9 Then Peter said to her, "How is it that you have agreed together ^Rto test the Spirit of the Lord? Look, the feet of those who have buried your husband *are* at the door, and they will carry you out." Acts 5:3, 4

10 ^RThen immediately she fell down at his feet and breathed her last. And the young men came in and found her dead, and carrying *her* out, buried *her* by her husband. Acts 5:5

16-F. Consequences of Sin Committed by Ananias and Sapphira (Acts 5:1–11)—The fourth chapter of Acts closes with a beautiful picture of the young Jerusalem church. It was pure and powerful. "They had all things in common" (Acts 4:32–37). They had great power to witness and great grace to share in spiritual and material things.

The first word in the fifth chapter of Acts is "But," which suggests a contrast—a change within the congregation. Up to this chapter there was no major sin in the church. Barnabas owned some land, and out of love for Christ and His church he sold it and gave all the profits to the church. It must have been the talk of the congregation.

Ananias and Sapphira sold a possession and brought part of the profits to the Lord, *pretending* to bring all. This sin led to their premature deaths.

(1) The origin of their sin was Satan. Peter asked Ananias, "Why has Satan filled your heart to lie to the Holy Spirit?" (v. 3). This was Satan's first opportunity to bring sin into the church (but not his last). It is not sin *in the world* that defeats the church, but sin *within the congregation*. Before the church can clean up the world, it must first repent, confess, and forsake the sins within the assembly. See Revelation 3:14–22 (page 1296) for a true description of today's common local church. No wonder so many local churches are powerless!

(2) A sin within the fellowship of believers led to the death of Ananias and Sapphira. It consisted of:

(a) *Deception*. They pretended to give all when they gave only a part. They did not have to give any; they could have given any amount and pleased the Lord, had they been honest (Gal. 6:7, 8, page 1184).

(b) *Covetousness*. They wanted the glory that was showered upon Barnabas and others in the church, but they did not believe that God could take care of them.

(c) *Double-mindedness*. They had no stability (James 1:5–8, page 1255). They tried to get the best of two kingdoms—the kingdom of Satan (2 Cor. 4:4, page 1167) and the kingdom of God (Rom. 14:17, page 1144).

(d) *Hypocrisy* (Matt. 23:13–15, page 971). It has been said, "A hypocrite is a person who pretends outwardly to be what he never intends to be inwardly."

(e) *Lying*. They lied to God the Holy Spirit (vv. 3, 4).

The amazing part of this Scripture is that it shows us that the church was so pure that sin could not live in its holy atmosphere.

See 1 Corinthians 11:17–34, page 1156, for **Point 16-G: Consequences of Sin in the Corinthian Church.**

▽ 11 So great fear came upon all the church
▲ and upon all who heard these things.

Continuing Power in the Church

12 And through the hands of the apostles
many signs and wonders were done among
the people. ᴿAnd they were all with one
accord in Solomon's Porch.   Acts 3:11; 4:32

13 Yet none of the rest dared join them, but
the people esteemed them highly.

14 And believers were increasingly added to
the Lord, multitudes of both men and
women,

15 so that they brought the sick out into
the streets and laid *them* on beds and
couches, that at least the shadow of Peter
passing by might fall on some of them.

16 Also a multitude gathered from the surrounding cities to Jerusalem, bringing sick
people and those who were tormented by
unclean spirits, and they were all healed.

Imprisoned Apostles Freed

17 ᴿThen the high priest rose up, and all
those who *were* with him (which is the sect
of the Sadducees), and they were filled with
ᵀindignation,   Acts 4:1, 2, 6 • *jealousy*

18 ᴿand laid their hands on the apostles and
put them in the common prison.   Luke 21:12

19 But at night ᴿan angel of the Lord
opened the prison doors and brought them
out, and said,   Acts 12:7; 16:26

20 "Go, stand in the temple and speak to
the people all the words of this life."

21 And when they heard *that*, they entered
the temple early in the morning and taught.
But the high priest and those with him came
and called the ᵀcouncil together, with all the
elders of the children of Israel, and sent to
the prison to have them brought.   Sanhedrin

Apostles on Trial Again

22 But when the officers came and did not
find them in the prison, they returned and
reported,

23 saying, "Indeed we found the prison
shut securely, and the guards standing *outside before the doors; but when we opened
them, we found no one inside!"

24 Now when *the high priest, ᴿthe captain
of the temple, and the chief priests heard
these things, they wondered what the outcome would be.   Acts 4:1; 5:26

25 So one came and told them, *saying,
"Look, the men whom you put in prison are
standing in the temple and teaching the
people!"

26 Then the captain went with the officers
and brought them without violence, for they
feared the people, lest they should be stoned.

27 And when they had brought them, they
set *them* before the council. And the high
priest asked them,

28 saying, "Did we not strictly command
you not to teach in this name? And look, you
have filled Jerusalem with your doctrine, and
intend to bring this Man's blood on us!"

10-C. The Ministry of the Holy Spirit: ▼
The Evangelist

29 But Peter and the *other* apostles answered and said: ᴿ"We ought to obey God
rather than men.   Acts 4:19

30 "The God of our fathers raised up Jesus
whom you murdered by hanging on a tree.

31 "Him God has exalted to His right hand
to be Prince and Savior, ᴿto give repentance
to Israel and forgiveness of sins.   Luke 24:47

32 "And we are His witnesses to these
things, and *so* also *is* the Holy Spirit whom
God has given to those who obey Him."   ▲

Gamaliel's Advice

33 When they heard *this*, they were ᴿfurious and plotted to kill them.   Acts 7:54

5:23 NU, M omit *outside*
5:24 NU omits *the high priest*
5:25 NU, M omit *saying*

10-C. The Ministry of the Holy Spirit: The Evangelist (Acts 5:29–32)—The apostles were arrested and
brought before the Sanhedrin for evangelizing. They were accused of filling Jerusalem with the gospel—the
Good News that Jesus Christ was resurrected after having been crucified. In holy boldness Peter said, "The
God of our fathers raised up Jesus whom you murdered by hanging on a tree. . . . And we are His witnesses
to these things [the death, burial, and resurrection], and so also is the Holy Spirit whom God has given to
those who obey Him" (vv. 30–32). Paraphrased, Peter was saying, "We are witnesses [evangelists] and the
Holy Spirit is an evangelist also." We must live, that the lost may see Jesus in us; but even though they see
Jesus in us, they cannot know how to be saved until they hear the gospel.

Bearing similar witness in the book of Romans, Paul quoted the prophet Joel: "For 'whoever calls upon
the name of the LORD shall be saved' " (Rom. 10:13–17, page 1140; cf. Joel 2:32, page 870). In verses 14 and
15 Paul asks four questions which pertain to verse 13:

(1) "How then shall they call on Him in whom they have not believed?" They cannot call on Jesus and
be saved until they believe "that Christ died for our sins according to the Scriptures, and that He was buried,
and that He rose again the third day according to the Scriptures" (1 Cor. 15:1–4, page 1161).

(2) "How shall they believe in Him of whom they have not heard?" They cannot believe until they hear
the gospel, the Good News of salvation. Seeing Christ in the Christian is not enough; they must hear to
believe.

(Point 10-C continued on next page)

34 Then one in the council stood up, a Pharisee named ᴿGamaliel, a teacher of the law held in respect by all the people, and commanded them to put the apostles outside for a little while.   Acts 22:3

35 And he said to them: "Men of Israel, ᵀtake heed to yourselves what you intend to do regarding these men.   *be careful*

36 "For some time ago Theudas rose up, claiming to be somebody. A number of men, about four hundred, ᵀjoined him. He was slain, and all who obeyed him were scattered and came to nothing.   *followed*

37 "After this man, Judas of Galilee rose up in the days of the census, and drew away many people after him. He also perished, and all who obeyed him were dispersed.

38 "And now I say to you, keep away from these men and let them alone; for if this plan or this work is of men, it will come to nothing;

39 ᴿ"but if it is of God, you cannot overthrow it—lest you even be found ᴿto fight against God."   1 Cor. 1:25 • Acts 7:51; 9:5

40 And they agreed with him, and when they had called for the apostles and beaten *them*, they commanded that they should not speak in the name of Jesus, and let them go.

41 So they departed from the presence of the council, ᴿrejoicing that they were counted worthy to suffer shame for *His name.   [1 Pet. 4:13–16]

42 And daily in the temple, and in every house, ᴿthey did not cease teaching and preaching Jesus *as* the Christ.   Acts 4:20, 29

Seven Chosen to Serve

6 Now in those days, when *the number of* the disciples was multiplying, there arose a complaint against the Hebrews by the

5:41 NU *the name*, M *the name of Jesus*

*Hellenists, because their widows were neglected in the daily distribution.

2 Then the twelve summoned the multitude of the disciples and said, ᴿ"It is not desirable that we should leave the word of God and serve tables.   Ex. 18:17

3 "Therefore, brethren, ᴿseek out from among you seven men of good reputation, full of the Holy Spirit and wisdom, whom we may appoint over this business;   1 Tim. 3:7

4 "but we will give ourselves continually to prayer and to the ministry of the word."

5 And the saying pleased the whole multitude. And they chose Stephen, a man full of faith and the Holy Spirit, and Philip, Prochorus, Nicanor, Timon, Parmenas, and ᴿNicolas, a proselyte from Antioch,   Rev. 2:6, 15

6 whom they set before the apostles; and ᴿwhen they had prayed, ᴿthey laid hands on them.   Acts 1:24 • [2 Tim. 1:6]

7 Then ᴿthe word of God spread, and the number of the disciples multiplied greatly in Jerusalem, and a great many ᴿof the priests were obedient to the faith.   Acts 12:24 • John 12:42

Stephen Accused of Blasphemy

8 And Stephen, full of *faith and power, did great ᴿwonders and signs among the people.   Acts 2:43; 5:12; 8:15; 14:3

9 Then there arose some from what is called the Synagogue of the Freedmen (Cyrenians, Alexandrians, and those from Cilicia and Asia), disputing with Stephen.

10 And they were not able to resist the wisdom and the Spirit by which he spoke.

11 ᴿThen they secretly induced men to say, "We have heard him speak blasphemous words against Moses and God."   1 Kin. 21:10, 13

12 And they stirred up the people, the elders, and the scribes; and they came upon

6:1 Jews who had adopted Greek culture.
6:8 NU *grace*

(Point 10-C continued from previous page)

(3) "How shall they hear without a preacher [a witness]?" The lost must have a witness in order to hear; they must hear in order to believe; they must believe in order to call; and they must call in order to be saved.

(4) "And how shall they preach [witness, proclaim the gospel], unless they are sent?" The Holy Spirit came on the Day of Pentecost to baptize every born-again believer into the body of Christ (1 Cor. 12:13, page 1158), and empower the believer to witness, i.e., to evangelize (Acts 1:8, page 1086). The risen Christ instructed His disciples: "Tarry in the city of Jerusalem until you are endued with power from on high" (Luke 24:49, page 1047). Before His death, Jesus instructed His followers: "Therefore pray the Lord of the harvest to send out laborers into His harvest" (Matt. 9:38, page 949). The "Lord of the harvest" (the Holy Spirit) answered that prayer on the Day of Pentecost. The 120 were sent into the fields, "already white for harvest!" (John 4:35, page 1054). For almost two thousand years the Lord of the harvest (the Holy Spirit) has continued to send Holy Spirit-filled laborers into the fields, white already to harvest. When you enter the harvest to win souls to Christ, the Holy Spirit (the Lord of the harvest, the world's greatest evangelist) will go with you, indwell you, and fill you with power to evangelize.

Remember, the lost cannot be saved until they call on the Lord for salvation. But they cannot call until they believe, they cannot believe until they hear the gospel (Rom. 10:17, page 1140), and they cannot hear without a witness. The witness cannot witness unless he or she is sent by the Lord of the harvest, who will fill the witness with His power. He is waiting for you to say "Here am I! Send me" (Is. 6:8, page 648).

See John 14:15–17, page 1075, for **Point 10-D: The Ministry of the Holy Spirit: The Helper.**

him, seized him, and brought *him* to the council.

13 They also set up false witnesses who said, "This man does not cease to speak *blasphemous words against this holy place and the law;

14 ᴿ"for we have heard him say that this Jesus of Nazareth will destroy this place and change the customs which Moses delivered to us."   Acts 10:38; 25:8

15 And all who sat in the council, looking steadfastly at him, saw his face as the face of an angel.

Stephen's Address: The Call of Abraham

7 Then the high priest said, "Are these things so?"

2 And he said, "Brethren and fathers, listen: The ᴿGod of glory appeared to our father Abraham when he was in Mesopotamia, before he dwelt in Haran,   Ps. 29:3

3 "and said to him, ᴿ*'Get out of your country and from your relatives, and come to a land that I will show you.'*   Gen. 12:1

4 "Then he came out of the land of the Chaldeans and dwelt in Haran. And from there, when his father was dead, He moved him to this land in which you now dwell.

5 "And *God* gave him no inheritance in it, not even *enough* to set his foot on. But even when *Abraham* had no child, ᴿHe promised to give it to him for a possession, and to his descendants after him.   Gen. 12:7; 13:15; 15:3, 18

6 "But God spoke in this way: that his descendants would dwell in a foreign land, and that they would bring them into bondage and oppress *them* four hundred years.

7 ᴿ*'And the nation to whom they will be in bondage I will* ᴿ*judge,'* said God, ᴿ*'and after that they shall come out and serve Me in this place.'*   Gen. 15:14 · Ex. 14:13-31 · Ex. 3:12

8 "Then He gave him the covenant of circumcision; ᴿand so *Abraham* begot Isaac and circumcised him on the eighth day; ᴿand Isaac *begot* Jacob, and Jacob *begot* the twelve patriarchs.   Gen. 21:1-5 · Gen. 25:21-26

The Patriarchs in Egypt

9 ᴿ"And the patriarchs, becoming envious, ᴿsold Joseph into Egypt. ᴿBut God was with him   Gen. 37:4, 11, 28 · Gen. 37:28 · Gen. 39:2, 21, 23

10 "and delivered him out of all his troubles, ᴿand gave him favor and wisdom in the presence of Pharaoh, king of Egypt; and he made him governor over Egypt and all his house.   Gen. 41:38-44

11 "Now a famine and great ᵀtrouble came over all the land of Egypt and Canaan, and our fathers found no sustenance.   affliction

12 "But when Jacob heard that there was grain in Egypt, he sent out our fathers first.

13 "And the ᴿsecond *time* Joseph was made known to his brothers, and Joseph's family became known to the Pharaoh.   Gen. 45:4, 16

14 ᴿ"Then Joseph sent and called his father Jacob and ᴿall his relatives to *him*, *seventy-five people.   Gen. 45:9, 27 · Deut. 10:22

15 ᴿ"So Jacob went down to Egypt; ᴿand he died, he and our fathers.   Gen. 46:1-7 · Gen. 49:33

16 "And they were carried back to Shechem and laid in ᴿthe tomb that Abraham bought for a sum of money from the sons of Hamor, *the father* of Shechem.   Gen. 23:16

God Delivers Israel by Moses

17 "But when the time of the promise drew near which God had sworn to Abraham, the people grew and multiplied in Egypt

18 "till another king ᴿarose who did not know Joseph.   Ex. 1:8

19 "This man dealt treacherously with our people, and oppressed our forefathers, ᴿmaking them expose their babies, so that they might not live.   Ex. 1:22

20 "At this time Moses was born, and was well pleasing to God; and he was brought up in his father's house for three months.

21 "But ᴿwhen he was set out, ᴿPharaoh's daughter took him away and brought him up as her own son.   Ex. 2:3, 4 · Ex. 2:5-10

22 "And Moses was learned in all the wisdom of the Egyptians, and was ᴿmighty in words and deeds.   Luke 24:19

23 ᴿ"Now when he was forty years old, it came into his heart to visit his brethren, the children of Israel.   Ex. 2:11, 12

24 "And seeing one of *them* suffer wrong, he defended and avenged him who was oppressed, and struck down the Egyptian.

25 "For he supposed that his brethren would have understood that God would deliver them by his hand, but they did not understand.

26 "And the next day he appeared to two of them as they were fighting, and *tried to* reconcile them, saying, 'Men, you are brethren; why do you wrong one another?'

27 "But he who did his neighbor wrong pushed him away, saying, ᴿ*'Who made you a ruler and a judge over us?*   Ex. 2:14

28 *'Do you want to kill me as you did the Egyptian yesterday?'*

29 ᴿ"Then, at this saying, Moses fled and became a dweller in the land of Midian, where he had two sons.   Heb. 11:27

30 ᴿ"And when forty years had passed, an Angel *of the Lord appeared to him in a flame of fire in a bush, in the wilderness of Mount Sinai.   Ex. 3:1-10

31 "When Moses saw *it*, he marveled at the

7:14 Or *seventy*, Ex. 1:5
7:30 NU omits *of the Lord*

6:13 NU omits *blasphemous*

sight; and as he drew near to observe, the voice of the Lord came to him,

32 "saying, R'I am the God of your fathers—the God of Abraham, the God of Isaac, and the God of Jacob.' And Moses trembled and dared not look. Ex. 3:6, 15

33 R'Then the LORD said to him, "Take your sandals off your feet, for the place where you stand is holy ground. Ex. 3:5, 7, 8, 10

34 "I have surely Rseen the oppression of My people who are in Egypt; I have heard their groaning and have come down to deliver them. And now come, I will Rsend you to Egypt." ' Ex. 2:24, 25 • Ps. 105:26

35 "This Moses whom they rejected, saying, R'Who made you a ruler and a judge?' is the one God sent to be a ruler and a deliverer Rby the hand of the Angel who appeared to him in the bush. Ex. 2:14 • Ex. 14:21

36 "He brought them out, after he had shown wonders and signs in the land of Egypt, Rand in the Red Sea, Rand in the wilderness forty years. Ex. 14:21 • Ex. 16:1, 35

Israel Rebels Against God

37 "This is that Moses who said to the children of Israel, R'The LORD your God will raise up for you a Prophet like me from your brethren. RHim* you shall hear.' Deut. 18:15 • Matt. 17:5

38 "This is he who was in the Tcongregation in the wilderness with the Angel who spoke to him on Mount Sinai, and with our fathers, the one who received the living Toracles to give to us, assembly or church • sayings

39 "whom our fathers Rwould not obey, but rejected. And in their hearts they turned back to Egypt, Ps. 95:8-11

40 "saying to Aaron, R'Make us gods to go before us; as for this Moses who brought us out of the land of Egypt, we do not know what has become of him.' Ex. 32:1, 23

41 "And they made a calf in those days, offered sacrifices to the idol, and Rrejoiced in the works of their own hands. Ex. 32:6, 18, 19

42 "Then RGod turned and gave them up to worship the host of heaven, as it is written in the book of the Prophets: [2 Thess. 2:11]

R'Did you offer Me slaughtered animals and sacrifices during forty years in the wilderness, Amos 5:25-27 O house of Israel?

43 You also took up the tabernacle of Moloch, And the star of your god Remphan, Images which you made to worship; And RI will carry you away beyond Babylon.' Jer. 25:9-12

7:37 NU, M omit Him you shall hear

God's True Tabernacle

44 "Our fathers had the tabernacle of witness in the wilderness, as He appointed, instructing Moses Rto make it according to the pattern that he had seen, [Heb. 8:5]

45 R"which our fathers, having received it in turn, also brought with Joshua into the land possessed by the Gentiles, Rwhom God drove out before the face of our fathers until the Rdays of David, Josh. 3:14 • Ps. 44:2 • 2 Sam. 6:2-15

46 R"who found favor before God and Rasked to find a dwelling for the God of Jacob. 2 Sam. 7:1-13 • 1 Chr. 22:7

47 "But Solomon built Him a house.

48 "However, Rthe Most High does not dwell in temples made with hands, as the prophet says: 1 Kin. 8:27

49 'HeavenR is My throne, Is. 66:1, 2 And earth is My footstool. What house will you build for Me? says the LORD, Or what is the place of My rest?

50 Has My hand not Rmade all these things?' Ps. 102:25

Israel Resists the Holy Spirit

51 "You stiff-necked and uncircumcised in heart and ears! You always resist the Holy Spirit; as your fathers did, so do you.

52 R"Which of the prophets did your fathers not persecute? And they killed those who foretold the coming of Rthe Just One, of whom you now have become the betrayers and murderers, 2 Chr. 36:16 • Acts 3:14; 22:14

53 "who have received the law by the direction of angels and have not kept it."

Stephen the Martyr

54 RWhen they heard these things they were Tcut to the heart, and they gnashed at him with their teeth. Acts 5:33 • furious

55 But he, being full of the Holy Spirit, gazed into heaven and saw the glory of God, and Jesus standing at the right hand of God,

56 and said, "Look! RI see the heavens opened and the RSon of Man standing at the right hand of God!" Matt. 3:16 • Dan. 7:13

57 Then they cried out with a loud voice, stopped their ears, and ran at him with one accord;

58 and they cast him out of the city and stoned him. And Rthe witnesses laid down their clothes at the feet of a young man named Saul. Acts 22:20

59 And they stoned Stephen as he was calling on God and saying, "Lord Jesus, Rreceive my spirit." Ps. 31:5

60 Then he knelt down and cried out with a loud voice, R"Lord, do not charge them with this sin." And when he had said this, he fell asleep. Matt. 5:44

Saul Persecutes the Church

▼ **37-C. The Church: Its Beginning and Development**

8 Now Saul was consenting to his death. At that time a great persecution arose against the church which was at Jerusalem; and ᴿthey were all scattered throughout the regions of Judea and Samaria, except the apostles. Acts 8:4; 11:19

2 And devout men carried Stephen *to his burial*, and ᴿmade great lamentation over him. Gen. 23:2

3 As for Saul, ᴿhe made havoc of the church, entering every house, and dragging

off men and women, committing *them* to ▽ prison. Phil. 3:6

Christ Is Preached in Samaria

4 Therefore those who were scattered went everywhere preaching the word.

5 Then Philip went down to ᵀthe city of Samaria and preached Christ to them. Or *a*

6 And the multitudes with one accord heeded the things spoken by Philip, hearing and seeing the miracles which he did.

7 For ᴿunclean spirits, crying with a loud voice, came out of many who were possessed; and many who were paralyzed and lame were healed. Mark 16:17

8 And there was great joy in that city. ▲

37-C. The Church: Its Beginning and Development (Acts 8:1–8)—After the crucifixion and resurrection of Christ, His church was formed to take the gospel to the lost of all nations. The church went forward with the Good News, and the book of Acts records the two chief events: evangelizing the Jews (Acts 1—10, page 1086) and the Gentiles (Acts 11—28, page 1103).

(1) The church was established in Jerusalem and Israel through the following phases:

(a) *Commissioning.* Soon after Christ arose, He commanded that everyone be evangelized in Jerusalem, Samaria, and among all nations (Acts 1:8, page 1086).

(b) *Empowerment.* On the Day of Pentecost, the Holy Spirit came upon the Upper Room congregation of about 120 persons and filled them (Acts 1:15, page 1087) with power to go with the gospel and evangelize (Acts 1:8, page 1086). They shared their faith with the masses, resulting in approximately three thousand conversions (Acts 2:1–44, page 1088).

(c) *Witnessing.* The apostles preached, performed miracles, suffered persecution, united in prayer for Holy Spirit power, shared their faith and their worldly goods, and rejoiced that they were counted worthy to suffer shame for His name (Acts 3—5, page 1090).

(d) *Serving.* The first deacons were chosen by the apostles by the laying on of hands and prayer, and were commissioned to serve tables (Acts 6, page 1095).

(e) *Martyred.* Stephen was the first Christian martyred for preaching the gospel of the Lord Jesus Christ (Acts 7, page 1096).

(f) *The church persecuted and scattered.* As they went they evangelized, winning souls to Christ. Philip, the first evangelist, conducted a great soul-winning evangelistic crusade (Acts 8 and 9, page 1098).

(g) *Conversion of Paul.* Paul, who was then called Saul, was the chief persecutor of the church. He was miraculously converted as he was doing his destructive work (Acts 9, page 1100).

(h) *Opened doors.* The Gentiles were brought into the church—beginning a great new era of soul-winning and discipling of the Gentiles (Acts 10 and 11, page 1102).

(i) *Deliverance.* Simon Peter was imprisoned by Herod. That night the angel of the Lord led Peter out of prison and to his Christian friends who were assembled as a church in prayer for his deliverance (Acts 12, page 1104).

(2) The church was established among Gentiles:

(a) *By evangelism.* The church at Antioch was ministering to the Lord when the Holy Spirit said, "Now separate to Me Barnabas and Saul for the work to which I have called them" (Acts 13:2, page 1105). On their three missionary journeys, they were led by the Holy Spirit to evangelize in what is today Turkey and Greece (Acts 13—21, page 1105).

(b) *By deliverance from legalists.* Paul and Silas journeyed to the Jerusalem council to settle the question once and for all that the Gentiles who had been converted to Christ should not be expected to be burdened with the Jewish ceremonial laws (Acts 15, page 1108).

(c) *By continuing evangelism.* Paul and Silas took a second missionary journey in the Greek world (Acts 16—18, page 1110).

(d) *By strengthening.* The third missionary journey, again into Turkey and Greece, edified and strengthened the churches (Acts 19—21, page 1113).

(e) *By Paul's chains.* Though Paul was imprisoned in Caesarea, the gospel was not bound (Acts 22—26, page 1117).

(f) *By Paul's perilous voyage.* Paul was saved to evangelize on his hazardous voyage to Rome (Acts 27, page 1123).

(g) *By divinely opened doors.* Paul's imprisonment in Rome gave him the opportunity to witness and win those who were serving in Rome's palace guard (Acts 28, page 1124).

See Acts 13:1–3, page 1105, for **Point 37-D: The Evangelistic Missionary Journeys of Paul.**

The Sorcerer's Profession of Faith

9 But there was a certain man called Simon, who previously practiced sorcery in the city and astonished the people of Samaria, claiming that he was someone great,

10 to whom they all gave heed, from the least to the greatest, saying, "This man is the great power of God."

11 And they heeded him because he had astonished them with his ᵀsorceries for a long time.   *magic arts*

12 But when they believed Philip as he preached the things ᴿconcerning the kingdom of God and the name of Jesus Christ, both men and women were baptized.   Acts 1:3; 8:4

13 Then Simon himself also believed; and when he was baptized he continued with Philip, and was amazed, seeing the miracles and signs which were done.

The Sorcerer's Sin

14 Now when the ᴿapostles who were at Jerusalem heard that Samaria had received the word of God, they sent Peter and John to them,   Acts 5:12, 29, 40

15 who, when they had come down, prayed for them ᴿthat they might receive the Holy Spirit.   Acts 2:38; 19:2

16 For ᴿas yet He had fallen upon none of them. ᴿThey had only been baptized in the name of the Lord Jesus.   Acts 19:2 • Matt. 28:19

17 Then ᴿthey laid hands on them, and they received the Holy Spirit.   Acts 6:6; 19:6

18 And when Simon saw that through the laying on of the apostles' hands the Holy Spirit was given, he offered them money,

19 saying, "Give me this power also, that anyone on whom I lay hands may receive the Holy Spirit."

20 But Peter said to him, "Your money perish with you, because ᴿyou thought that ᴿthe gift of God could be purchased with money!   [Matt. 10:8] • [Acts 2:38; 10:45; 11:17]

21 "You have neither part nor portion in this matter, for your ᴿheart is not right in the sight of God.   Jer. 17:9

22 "Repent therefore of this your wickedness, and pray God ᴿif perhaps the thought of your heart may be forgiven you.   2 Tim. 2:25

23 "For I see that you are ᴿpoisoned by bitterness and bound by iniquity."   Heb. 12:15

24 Then Simon answered and said, "Pray to the Lord for me, that none of the things which you have spoken may come upon me."

25 So when they had testified and preached the word of the Lord, they returned to Jerusalem, preaching the gospel in many villages of the Samaritans.

Christ Is Preached to an Ethiopian

26 Now an angel of the Lord spoke to ᴿPhilip, saying, "Arise and go toward the south along the road which goes down from Jerusalem to Gaza." This is desert.   Acts 6:5

27 So he arose and went. And behold, a man of Ethiopia, a eunuch of great authority under Candace the queen of the Ethiopians, who had charge of all her treasury, and ᴿhad come to Jerusalem to worship,   John 12:20

28 was returning. And sitting in his chariot, he was reading Isaiah the prophet.

29 Then the Spirit said to Philip, "Go near and overtake this chariot."

30 So Philip ran to him, and heard him reading the prophet Isaiah, and said, "Do you understand what you are reading?"

31 And he said, "How can I, unless someone guides me?" And he asked Philip to come up and sit with him.

32 The place in the Scripture which he read was this:

> ᴿ"He was led as a sheep to the slaughter;
> And as a lamb before its shearer is
>   silent,
> So He opened not His mouth.   Is. 53:7, 8

33 In His humiliation His ᴿjustice was
>   taken away,   Luke 23:1-25
> And who will declare His generation?
> For His life is taken from the earth."

34 So the eunuch answered Philip and said, "I ask you, of whom does the prophet say this, of himself or of some other man?"

35 Then Philip opened his mouth, ᴿand beginning at this Scripture, preached Jesus to him.   Luke 24:27

36 Now as they went down the road, they came to some water. And the eunuch said, "See, *here is* water. ᴿWhat hinders me from being baptized?"   Acts 10:47; 16:33

37 *Then Philip said, ᴿ"If you believe with all your heart, you may." And he answered and said, ᴿ"I believe that Jesus Christ is the Son of God."   [Mark 16:16] • Matt. 16:16

38 So he commanded the chariot to stand still. And both Philip and the eunuch went down into the water, and he baptized him.

39 Now when they came up out of the water, ᴿthe Spirit of the Lord caught Philip away, so that the eunuch saw him no more; and he went on his way rejoicing.   Ezek. 3:12, 14

40 But Philip was found at ᵀAzotus. And passing through, he preached in all the cities till he came to Caesarea.   Same as Heb. *Ashdod*

8:37 NU, M omit v. 37. It is found in Western texts, including the Latin tradition.

The Damascus Road: Saul Converted

▼ 46-B. Paul's Conversion

9 Then ᴿSaul, still breathing threats and murder against the disciples of the Lord, went to the high priest   Acts 7:57; 8:1, 3; 26:10, 11

2 and asked ᴿletters from him to the synagogues of Damascus, so that if he found any who were of the Way, whether men or women, he might bring them bound to Jerusalem.   Acts 22:5

3 ᴿAs he journeyed he came near Damascus, and suddenly a light shone around him from heaven.   1 Cor. 15:8

4 Then he fell to the ground, and heard a voice saying to him, "Saul, Saul, ᴿwhy are you persecuting Me?"   [Matt. 25:40]

5 And he said, "Who are You, Lord?" Then the Lord said, "I am Jesus, whom you are persecuting. *It is hard for you to kick ▽ against the goads."

6 So he, trembling and astonished, said, "Lord, what do You want me to do?" Then the Lord said to him, "Arise and go into the city, and you will be told what you must do."

7 And ᴿthe men who journeyed with him stood speechless, hearing a voice but seeing no one.   [Acts 22:9; 26:13]

8 Then Saul arose from the ground, and when his eyes were opened he saw no one. But they led him by the hand and brought him into Damascus.

9 And he was three days without sight, and neither ate nor drank.

9:5 NU, M omit the rest of v. 5 and begin v. 6 with *But arise and go*

46-B. Paul's Conversion (Acts 9:1-18)—Entire volumes have been written on the subject of Paul's conversion, due to its unique and overwhelming circumstances, as a proof of the truth of Christianity. This conversion took place about A.D. 32.

(1) Paul originally had been a total unbeliever in Christ as the Messiah and Resurrected One, or that Christianity possessed any valid truth at all (1 Tim. 1:13, page 1218).

(2) Paul had demonstrated total rejection of Christianity by fervently persecuting Jews who had received the new faith (vv. 1, 2).

(3) While journeying to Damascus to persecute the Christians of that area, "a light shone around him from heaven" (v. 3). Being blinded by that light (Acts 22:11, page 1118), he "fell to the ground" (v. 4). The Lord Jesus then instructed Paul to go to Damascus where he would be told what to do (v. 6).

(4) Three days later, in Damascus, Ananias was sent to Saul (Paul), and Saul's blindness was lifted. Ananias instructed him further in Christ's will for his life, and then baptized him into the new faith (vv. 9–18).

(5) Ananias' vision confirmed the reality of Paul's. Ananias saw a vision to go to the church's number one enemy; at the same time Paul saw a vision of Christ, which converted him and told him to await further instructions at Damascus. The timing of the two visions defy human coincidence and confirm the supernatural origin of both (vv. 10–16).

(6) Note Christ's call to Paul: Christ instructed Ananias to go to Paul, which Ananias apparently communicated to Paul.

(a) Paul was "chosen" by Christ (v. 15), whereas he himself had not chosen Christ, but rejected Him.

(b) Paul was "to bear My [Christ's] name" (v. 15), whereas he had attempted to blot it out.

(c) Paul was to preach Christ "before Gentiles" (v. 15), whereas, being a Pharisee, he would have fled from the Gentiles.

(d) Paul was shown "how many things he must suffer for My name's sake" (v. 16), whereas he had sought only to bring pain to Christ and Christ's followers.

(7) Paul, for the rest of his life, unswervingly maintained that he personally had seen Christ, and had been sent into service by Him—the credential of an apostle (1 Cor. 15:5–9, page 1161).

(8) Paul, for the rest of his life, "labored more abundantly than they all" (1 Cor. 15:8–10, page 1161).

(9) Christ's appearance to Paul launched him upon a career which

(a) constantly proclaimed Christ for over three decades;

(b) took Paul fearlessly into martyrdom (2 Tim. 4:6–8, page 1228), according to the written testimony of the church fathers;

(c) took Paul, as originally promised, to preach to kings (v. 15);

(d) took Paul on three great missionary journeys and on a voyage to Rome, unparalleled in that age for endurance, singleness of purpose, and scope;

(e) caused Paul to endure continual perils and suffering, possibly unmatched in the annals of religion or mankind (2 Cor. 11:23–33, page 1175);

(f) made him the greatest of all time in establishing churches, year after year;

(g) produced the greatest religious teacher ever seen in the church or the world, aside from Christ.

Such a life could come only from a complete commitment in response to a true conversion call by Christ (Gal. 1:11, 12, page 1179).

See Acts 9:19–31, page 1101, for **Point 46-C: Paul's Early Ministry.**

▽   ▽

Ananias Baptizes Saul

10 Now there was a certain disciple at Damascus ᴿnamed Ananias; and to him the Lord said in a vision, "Ananias." And he said, "Here I am, Lord." *Acts 22:12*

11 So the Lord *said* to him, "Arise and go to the street called Straight, and inquire at the house of Judas for *one* called Saul ᴿof Tarsus, for behold, he is praying. *Acts 21:39; 22:3*

12 "And in a vision he has seen a man named Ananias coming in and putting *his* hand on him, so that he might receive his sight."

13 Then Ananias answered, "Lord, I have heard from many about this man, ᴿhow much ᵀharm he has done to Your saints in Jerusalem. *Acts 9:1 • bad things*

14 "And here he has authority from the chief priests to bind all ᴿwho call on Your name." *Acts 7:59; 9:2, 21*

15 But the Lord said to him, "Go, for he is a chosen vessel of Mine to bear My name before Gentiles, ᴿkings, and the ᴿchildrenᵀ of Israel. *Acts 25:22, 23; 26:1 • Rom. 1:16; 9:1-5 • Lit. sons*

16 "For I will show him how many things he must suffer for My name's sake."

17 And Ananias went his way and entered the house; and ᴿlaying his hands on him he said, "Brother Saul, the Lord *Jesus, who appeared to you on the road as you came, has sent me that you may receive your sight and be filled with the Holy Spirit." *Acts 8:17*

18 Immediately there fell from his eyes *something* like scales, and he received his

▲ sight at once; and he arose and was baptized.

▼ 46-C. Paul's Early Ministry

19 So when he had received food, he was strengthened. ᴿThen Saul spent some days with the disciples at Damascus. *Acts 26:20*

9:17 M omits Jesus

Saul Preaches Christ

20 Immediately he preached *the Christ in the synagogues, that He is the Son of God.

21 Then all who heard were amazed, and said, "Is this not he who destroyed those who called on this name in Jerusalem, and has come here for that purpose, so that he might bring them bound to the chief priests?"

22 But Saul increased all the more in strength, ᴿand confounded the Jews who dwelt in Damascus, proving that this *Jesus* is the Christ. *Acts 18:28*

Saul Escapes Death

23 Now after many days were past, ᴿthe Jews plotted to kill him. *2 Cor. 11:26*

24 ᴿBut their plot became known to Saul. And they watched the gates day and night, to kill him. *2 Cor. 11:32*

25 Then the disciples took him by night and ᴿlet *him* down through the wall in a large basket. *Josh. 2:15*

Saul at Jerusalem

26 And ᴿwhen Saul had come to Jerusalem, he tried to join the disciples; but they were all afraid of him, and did not believe that he was a disciple. *Acts 22:17-20; 26:20*

27 ᴿBut Barnabas took him and brought *him* to the apostles. And he declared to them how he had seen the Lord on the road, and that He had spoken to him, ᴿand how he had preached boldly at Damascus in the name of Jesus. *Acts 4:36; 13:2 • Acts 9:20, 22*

28 So ᴿhe was with them at Jerusalem, coming in and going out. *Gal. 1:18*

29 And he spoke boldly in the name of the Lord Jesus and disputed against the Hellenists, but they attempted to kill him.

9:20 NU Jesus

46-C. Paul's Early Ministry (Acts 9:19–31)—Now that Paul was called by Christ to preach the gospel, did he at once become the leader of the church? Was he recognized immediately as the chief apostle? The answers to these questions are most informative.

(1) After his sight returned and he was baptized, Paul bore witness to his new faith in Christ at the synagogues in Damascus (vv. 19–22).

(2) All saw his changed life (v. 21).

(3) He increased in spiritual wisdom (v. 22).

(4) He journeyed to Jerusalem and spent fifteen days with Peter (Gal. 1:18, page 1179).

(5) Some of his former friends were now his enemies (vv. 23–25).

(6) He now desired to fellowship with Christ's people (v. 26).

(7) God raised up a Christian friend for Paul (Barnabas), who introduced him to other believers (v. 27). New believers need Christian friends. God greatly used this friend in Paul's future life and ministry.

(8) His witness to his fellow Greek-speaking Jews caused such a furor that "the brethren . . . sent him out to Tarsus" (vv. 29, 30).

(9) His old friend Barnabas brought him to Antioch of Syria to serve as a co-worker in the Gentile church (Acts 11:25, 26, page 1104).

It is clearly seen from the above that although Paul was converted at the age of about thirty, he was not instantly rushed off to "stardom" by God. Rather, he was trained and nurtured step by step, combining witnessing in the present with solid preparation for the future.

See Galatians 2:7-10, page 1179, for **Point 46-D: Paul's Evangelistic Missionary Ministry to the Gentiles.**

▽ 30 When the brethren found out, they brought him down to Caesarea and sent him out to Tarsus.

The Church Prospers

31 Then the churches throughout all Judea, Galilee, and Samaria had peace and were ᴿedified.* And walking in the ᴿfear of the Lord and in the comfort of the Holy Spirit,
▲ they were multiplied.　　　[Eph. 4:16, 29] • Ps. 34:9

Aeneas Healed

32 Now it came to pass, as Peter went through all *parts of the country,* that he also came down to the saints who dwelt in Lydda.

33 There he found a certain man named Aeneas, who had been bedridden eight years and was paralyzed.

34 And Peter said to him, "Aeneas, ᴿJesus the Christ heals you. Arise and make your bed." Then he arose immediately.　　[Acts 4:10]

35 So all who dwelt at Lydda and Sharon saw him and ᴿturned to the Lord.　　Acts 11:21

Dorcas Restored to Life

36 At Joppa there was a certain disciple named Tabitha, which is translated ᵀDorcas. This woman was full of good works and charitable deeds which she did.　　*Gazelle*

37 But it happened in those days that she became sick and died. When they had washed her, they laid *her* in an upper room.

38 And since Lydda was near Joppa, and the disciples had heard that Peter was there, they sent two men to him, imploring *him* not to delay in coming to them.

39 Then Peter arose and went with them. When he had come, they brought *him* to the upper room. And all the widows stood by him weeping, showing the tunics and garments which Dorcas had made while she was with them.

40 But Peter put them all out, and knelt down and prayed. And turning to the body he said, "Tabitha, arise." And she opened her eyes, and when she saw Peter she sat up.

41 Then he gave her *his* hand and lifted her up; and when he had called the saints and widows, he presented her alive.

42 And it became known throughout all Joppa, and many believed on the Lord.

43 So it was that he stayed many days in Joppa with ᴿSimon, a tanner.　　Acts 10:6

Cornelius Sends a Delegation

10 There was a certain man in Caesarea called Cornelius, a centurion of what was called the Italian ᵀRegiment,　　*Cohort*

2 a devout *man* and one who ᴿfeared God with all his household, who gave ᵀalms generously to the people, and prayed to God always.　　[Acts 10:22, 35; 13:16, 26] • *charitable gifts*

3 About ᵀthe ninth hour of the day he saw clearly in a vision an angel of God coming in and saying to him, "Cornelius!"　　3 P.M.

4 And when he observed him, he was afraid, and said, "What is it, lord?" So he said to him, "Your prayers and your alms have come up for a memorial before God.

5 "Now ᴿsend men to Joppa, and send for Simon whose surname is Peter.　　Acts 11:13, 14

6 "He is lodging with ᴿSimon, a tanner, whose house is by the sea. ᴿHe* will tell you what you must do."　　Acts 9:43 • Acts 11:14

7 And when the angel who spoke to him had departed, Cornelius called two of his household servants and a devout soldier from among those who waited on him continually.

8 So when he had explained all *these* things to them, he sent them to Joppa.

Peter's Vision

9 The next day, as they went on their journey and drew near the city, ᴿPeter went up on the housetop to pray, about ᵀthe sixth hour.　　Acts 10:9–32; 11:5–14 • Noon

10 Then he became very hungry and wanted to eat; but while they made ready, he fell into a trance

11 and saw heaven opened and an object like a great sheet bound at the four corners, descending to him and let down to the earth.

12 In it were all kinds of four-footed animals of the earth, wild beasts, creeping things, and birds of the air.

13 And a voice came to him, "Rise, Peter; kill and eat."

14 But Peter said, "Not so, Lord! ᴿFor I have never eaten anything common or unclean."　　Deut. 14:3, 7

15 And a voice *spoke* to him again the second time, "What God has ᵀcleansed you must not call common."　　*declared clean*

16 This was done three times. And the object was taken up into heaven again.

Summoned to Caesarea

17 Now while Peter ᵀwondered within himself what this vision which he had seen meant, behold, the men who had been sent from Cornelius had made inquiry for Simon's house, and stood before the gate.　　*was perplexed*

18 And they called and asked whether Simon, whose surname was Peter, was lodging there.

19 While Peter thought about the vision, ᴿthe Spirit said to him, "Behold, three men are seeking you.　　Acts 11:12

20 ᴿ"Arise therefore, go down and go with them, doubting nothing; for I have sent them."　　Acts 15:7–9

21 Then Peter went down to the men *who

9:31 NU *church . . . was edified*

10:6 NU, M omit the rest of v. 6.

10:21 NU, M omit *who had been sent to him from Cornelius*

had been sent to him from Cornelius, and said, "Yes, I am he whom you seek. For what reason have you come?"

22 And they said, "Cornelius *the* centurion, a just man, one who fears God and ᴿhas a good reputation among all the nation of the Jews, was divinely instructed by a holy angel to summon you to his house, and to hear words from you."   Acts 22:12

23 Then he invited them in and lodged *them.* On the next day Peter went away with them, ᴿand some brethren from Joppa accompanied him.   Acts 10:45; 11:12

Peter Meets Cornelius

24 And the following day they entered Caesarea. Now Cornelius was waiting for them, and had called together his relatives and close friends.

25 As Peter was coming in, Cornelius met him and fell down at his feet and worshiped *him.*

26 But Peter lifted him up, saying, ᴿ"Stand up; I myself am also a man."   Acts 14:14, 15

27 And as he talked with him, he went in and found many who had come together.

28 Then he said to them, "You know how ᴿunlawful it is for a Jewish man to keep company with or go to one of another nation. But God has shown me that I should not call any man common or unclean.   John 4:9; 18:28

29 "Therefore I came without objection as soon as I was sent for. I ask, then, for what reason have you sent for me?"

30 So Cornelius said, *"Four days ago I was fasting until this hour; and at the ninth hour I prayed in my house, and behold, a man stood before me in bright clothing,

31 "and said, 'Cornelius, your prayer has been heard, and ᴿyour ᵀalms are remembered in the sight of God.   Heb. 6:10 • *charitable gifts*

32 'Send therefore to Joppa and call Simon here, whose surname is Peter. He is lodging in the house of Simon, a tanner, by the sea. *When he comes, he will speak to you.'

33 "So I sent to you immediately, and you have done well to come. Now therefore, we are all present before God, to hear all the things commanded you by God."

Preaching to Cornelius' Household

34 Then Peter opened *his* mouth and said: ᴿ"In truth I perceive that God shows no partiality.   Deut. 10:17

35 "But in every nation whoever fears Him and works righteousness is accepted by Him.

36 "The word which God sent to the ᵀchildren of Israel, preaching peace through Jesus Christ—He is Lord of all—   Lit. *sons*

37 "that word you know, which was pro-

claimed throughout all Judea, and ᴿbegan from Galilee after the baptism which John preached: Luke 4:14

38 "how ᴿGod anointed Jesus of Nazareth with the Holy Spirit and with power, who ᴿwent about doing good and healing all who were oppressed by the devil, ᴿfor God was with Him.   Luke 4:18 • Matt. 4:23 • John 3:2; 8:29

39 "And we are ᴿwitnesses of all things which He did both in the land of the Jews and in Jerusalem, whom *they ᴿkilled by hanging on a tree.   Acts 1:8 • Acts 2:23

40 "Him ᴿGod raised up on the third day, and showed Him openly,   Hos. 6:2; Matt. 12:39, 40

41 ᴿ"not to all the people, but to witnesses chosen before by God, *even* to us ᴿwho ate and drank with Him after He arose from the dead.   [John 14:17, 19, 22; 15:27] • Luke 24:30, 41–43

42 "And He commanded us to preach to the people, and to testify ᴿthat it is He who was ordained by God *to be* Judge ᴿof the living and the dead.   John 5:22, 27 • 1 Pet. 4:5

43 "To Him all the prophets witness that, through His name, whoever believes in Him will receive ᵀremission of sins."   *forgiveness*

The Holy Spirit Falls on the Gentiles

44 While Peter was still speaking these words, ᴿthe Holy Spirit fell upon all those who heard the word.   Acts 4:31

45 ᴿAnd ᵀthose of the circumcision who believed were astonished, as many as came with Peter, ᴿbecause the gift of the Holy Spirit had been poured out on the Gentiles also.   Acts 10:23 • The Jews • Acts 11:18

46 For they heard them speak with tongues and magnify God. Then Peter answered,

47 "Can anyone forbid water, that these should not be baptized who have received the Holy Spirit ᴿjust as we *have?*"   Acts 2:4; 10:44

48 And he commanded them to be baptized ᴿin the name of the Lord. Then they asked him to stay a few days.   Acts 2:38; 8:16; 19:5

Peter Defends God's Grace

11 Now the apostles and brethren who were in Judea heard that the Gentiles had also received the word of God.

2 And when Peter came up to Jerusalem, ᴿthose of the circumcision contended with him,   Acts 10:45

3 saying, ᴿ"You went in to uncircumcised men ᴿand ate with them!"   Acts 10:28 • Gal. 2:12

4 But Peter explained *it* to them ᴿin order from the beginning, saying: Luke 1:3

5 ᴿ"I was in the city of Joppa praying; and in a trance I saw a vision, an object descending like a great sheet, let down from heaven by four corners; and it came to me.   Acts 10:9

6 "When I observed it intently and considered, I saw four-footed animals of the earth,

wild beasts, creeping things, and birds of the air.

7 "And I heard a voice saying to me, 'Rise, Peter; kill and eat.'

8 "But I said, 'Not so, Lord! For nothing common or unclean has at any time entered my mouth.'

9 "But the voice answered me again from heaven, 'What God has cleansed you must not call common.'

10 "Now this was done three times, and all were drawn up again into heaven.

11 "At that very moment, three men stood before the house where I was, having been sent to me from Caesarea.

12 "Then ᴿthe Spirit told me to go with them, doubting nothing. Moreover ᴿthese six brethren accompanied me, and we entered the man's house. [John 16:13] • Acts 10:23

13 ᴿ"And he told us how he had seen an angel standing in his house, who said to him, 'Send men to Joppa, and call for Simon whose surname is Peter, Acts 10:30

14 'who will tell you words by which you and all your household will be saved.'

15 "And as I began to speak, the Holy Spirit fell upon them, as upon us at the beginning.

16 "Then I remembered the word of the Lord, how He said, ᴿ'John indeed baptized with water, but ᴿyou shall be baptized with the Holy Spirit.' John 1:26, 33 • Is. 44:3

17 ᴿ"If therefore God gave them the same gift as *He gave* us when we believed on the Lord Jesus Christ, ᴿwho was I that I could withstand God?" [Acts 15:8, 9] • Acts 10:47

18 When they heard these things they became silent; and they glorified God, saying, ᴿ"Then God has also granted to the Gentiles repentance to life." Rom. 10:12, 13; 15:9, 16

Barnabas and Saul at Antioch

19 ᴿNow those who were scattered after the persecution that arose over Stephen traveled as far as Phoenicia, Cyprus, and Antioch, preaching the word to no one but the Jews only. Acts 8:1, 4

20 But some of them were men from Cyprus and Cyrene, who, when they had come to Antioch, spoke to ᴿthe Hellenists, preaching the Lord Jesus. Acts 6:1; 9:29

21 And ᴿthe hand of the Lord was with them, and a great number believed and ᴿturned to the Lord. Luke 1:66 • Acts 9:35; 14:1

22 Then news of these things came to the ears of the church in Jerusalem, and they sent out Barnabas to go as far as Antioch.

23 When he came and had seen the grace of God, he was glad, and ᴿencouraged them all that with purpose of heart they should continue with the Lord. Acts 13:43; 14:22

24 For he was a good man, ᴿfull of the Holy Spirit and of faith. ᴿAnd a great many people were added to the Lord. Acts 6:5 • Acts 5:14; 11:21

25 Then Barnabas departed for ᴿTarsus to seek Saul. Acts 9:11, 30

26 And when he had found him, he brought him to Antioch. So it was that for a whole year they assembled with the church and taught a great many people. And the disciples were first called Christians in Antioch.

Relief to Judea

27 And in these days ᴿprophets came from Jerusalem to Antioch. 1 Cor. 12:28

28 Then one of them, named ᴿAgabus, stood up and showed by the Spirit that there was going to be a great famine throughout all the world, which also happened in the days of ᴿClaudius Caesar. Acts 21:10 • Acts 18:2

29 Then the disciples, each according to his ability, determined to send ᴿrelief to the brethren dwelling in Judea. 1 Cor. 16:1

30 This they also did, and sent it to the elders by the hands of Barnabas and Saul.

Herod's Violence to the Church

12 Now about that time Herod the king stretched out *his* hand to harass some from the church.

2 Then he killed James ᴿthe brother of John with the sword. Matt. 4:21; 20:23

3 And because he saw that it pleased the Jews, he proceeded further to seize Peter also. Now it was *during* ᴿthe Days of Unleavened Bread. Ex. 12:15; 23:15

4 So when he had arrested him, he put *him* in prison, and delivered *him* to four squads of soldiers to keep him, intending to bring him before the people after Passover.

Peter Freed from Prison

5 Peter was therefore kept in prison, but *constant prayer was offered to God for him by the church.

6 And when Herod was about to bring him out, that night Peter was sleeping, bound with two chains between two soldiers; and the guards before the door were ᵀkeeping the prison. *guarding*

7 Now behold, ᴿan angel of the Lord stood by *him*, and a light shone in the prison; and he struck Peter on the side and raised him up, saying, "Arise quickly!" And his chains fell off *his* hands. Acts 5:19

8 Then the angel said to him, "Gird yourself and tie on your sandals"; and so he did. And he said to him, "Put on your garment and follow me."

9 So he went out and followed him, and ᴿdid not know that what was done by the angel was real, but thought ᴿhe was seeing a vision. Ps. 126:1 • Acts 10:3, 17; 11:5

10 When they were past the first and the second guard posts, they came to the iron

12:5 NU *constantly* or *earnestly*

gate that leads to the city, ᴿwhich opened to them of its own accord; and they went out and went down one street, and immediately the angel departed from him.   Acts 5:19; 16:26

11 And when Peter had come to himself, he said, "Now I know for certain that ᴿthe Lord has sent His angel, and has delivered me from the hand of Herod and *from* all the expectation of the Jewish people."   [Ps. 34:7]

12 So, when he had considered *this*, he came to the house of Mary, the mother of John whose surname was Mark, where many were gathered together praying.

13 And as Peter knocked at the door of the gate, a girl named Rhoda came to answer.

14 When she recognized Peter's voice, because of *her* gladness she did not open the gate, but ran in and announced that Peter stood before the gate.

15 But they said to her, "You are beside yourself!" Yet she kept insisting that it was so. So they said, ᴿ"It is his angel."   [Matt. 18:10]

16 Now Peter continued knocking; and when they opened *the door* and saw him, they were astonished.

17 But ᴿmotioning to them with his hand to keep silent, he declared to them how the Lord had brought him out of the prison. And he said, "Go, tell these things to James and to the brethren." And he departed and went to another place.   Acts 13:16; 19:33; 21:40

18 Then, as soon as it was day, there was no small ᵀstir among the soldiers about what had become of Peter.   *disturbance*

19 But when Herod had searched for him and not found him, he examined the guards and commanded that *they* should be put to death. And he went down from Judea to Caesarea, and stayed *there*.

Herod's Violent Death

20 Now Herod had been very angry with the people of Tyre and Sidon; but they came to him with one accord, and having made Blastus ᵀthe king's personal aide their friend, they asked for peace, because their country was ᵀsupplied with food by the king's *country*.   *who was in charge of the king's chamber · Lit. nourished*

21 So on a set day Herod, arrayed in royal apparel, sat on his throne and gave an oration to them.

22 And the people kept shouting, "The voice of a god and not of a man!"

23 Then immediately an angel of the Lord struck him, because he did not give glory to God. And he was eaten by worms and died.

24 But ᴿthe word of God grew and multiplied.   Acts 6:7; 19:20

Barnabas and Saul Appointed

25 And ᴿBarnabas and Saul returned *from Jerusalem when they had fulfilled *their* ministry, and they also took with them John whose surname was Mark.   Acts 11:30

37-D. The Evangelistic Missionary ▼ Journeys of Paul

13 Now ᴿin the church that was at Antioch there were certain prophets and teachers: ᴿBarnabas, Simeon who was called Niger, ᴿLucius of Cyrene, Manaen who had been brought up with Herod the tetrarch, and Saul.   Acts 14:26 · Acts 11:22 · Rom. 16:21

2 As they ministered to the Lord and fasted, the Holy Spirit said, ᴿ"Now separate to Me Barnabas and Saul for the work ᴿto which I have called them."   Gal. 1:15; 2:9 · Heb. 5:4

12:25 NU, M *to*

37-D. The Evangelistic Missionary Journeys of Paul (Acts 13:1-3)—Missions is spreading the Good News that God forgives sinners who trust in Christ. The church sent forth Paul and Barnabas from Antioch of Syria (Rom. 10:15, page 1140). The first missionaries were sent out by their local church, and were undoubtedly supported by it, as they prayed together seeking God's will for these ministries (vv. 1-3). The apostle Paul and his associates endured extraordinary labors and poverty to give others the message (2 Cor. 11:23-29, page 1175). There may never have been another who labored so arduously, so long, and under such hardships, with such astonishing success as the brilliant apostle Paul.

(1) *Paul's calling and commission* (vv. 1-3). Paul and Barnabas were called to evangelize the Gentiles.

(2) *First missionary journey* (Acts 13 and 14).

(a) Cyprus—First they evangelized in Barnabas' native land. Saul became known by his Greek name, Paul. John Mark deserted them and returned to Jerusalem.

(b) Pisidia (Turkey)—Next they evangelized Paul's native land. They preached the gospel in Antioch, Iconium, Lystra, and Derbe. They were persecuted everywhere, but some believed.

(c) They returned to Antioch of Syria and reported to the church (Acts 14:24-28, page 1108).

(3) *Jerusalem council* (Acts 15, page 1108).

(a) Paul and Barnabas participated with the leaders of the church in seeking God's will regarding the relation of the ceremonial law to the Gentiles.

(b) The question of circumcision and ceremonial law was solved at the Jerusalem council, decreeing that it was God's will that Gentiles be fully and equally admitted into the church, without having the duty to obey the Jewish ceremonial laws (Acts 15:22-29, page 1109).

(Point 37-D continued on next page)

▽ 3 Then, having fasted and prayed, and laid
▲ hands on them, they sent *them* away.

Preaching in Cyprus

4 So, being sent out by the Holy Spirit,
they went down to Seleucia, and from there
they sailed to ᴿCyprus.   Acts 4:36
5 And when they arrived in Salamis, ᴿthey
preached the word of God in the synagogues
of the Jews. They also had ᴿJohn as *their*
assistant.   [Acts 13:46] • Acts 12:25; 15:37
6 Now when they had gone through *the
island to Paphos, they found ᴿa certain sorcerer, a false prophet, a Jew whose name *was*
Bar-Jesus,   Acts 8:9
7 who was with the proconsul, Sergius
Paulus, an intelligent man. This man called
for Barnabas and Saul and sought to hear the
word of God.
8 But Elymas the sorcerer (for so his name
is translated) withstood them, seeking to turn
the proconsul away from the faith.
9 Then Saul, who also *is called* Paul, filled
with the Holy Spirit, looked intently at him
10 and said, "O full of all deceit and all
fraud, ᴿyou son of the devil, *you* enemy of all
righteousness, will you not cease perverting
the straight ways of the Lord?   Matt. 13:38
11 "And now, indeed, the hand of the Lord
is upon you, and you shall be blind, not
seeing the sun for a time." And immediately a
dark mist fell on him, and he went around
seeking someone to lead him by the hand.
12 Then the proconsul believed, when he
saw what had been done, being astonished at
the teaching of the Lord.

13:6 NU *the whole island*

At Antioch in Pisidia

13 Now when Paul and his party set sail
from Paphos, they came to Perga in Pamphylia; and ᴿJohn, departing from them,
returned to Jerusalem.   Acts 15:38
14 But when they departed from Perga,
they came to Antioch in Pisidia, and ᴿwent
into the synagogue on the Sabbath day and
sat down.   Acts 16:13
15 And ᴿafter the reading of the Law and
the Prophets, the rulers of the synagogue
sent to them, saying, "Men *and* brethren, if
you have ᴿany word of ᵀexhortation for the
people, say on." Luke 4:16 • Heb. 13:22 • *encouragement*
16 Then Paul stood up, and motioning with
his hand said, "Men of Israel, and ᴿyou who
fear God, listen: Acts 10:35
17 "The God of this people *Israel chose
our fathers, and exalted the people ᴿwhen
they dwelt as strangers in the land of Egypt,
and with ᵀan uplifted arm He ᴿbrought them
out of it.   Acts 7:17 • Mighty power • Ex. 14:8
18 "Now for a time of about forty years He
put up with their ways in the wilderness.
19 "And when He had destroyed ᴿseven
nations in the land of Canaan, He distributed
their land to them by allotment.   Deut. 7:1
20 "After that ᴿHe gave *them* judges for
about four hundred and fifty years, ᴿuntil
Samuel the prophet.   Judg. 2:16 • 1 Sam. 3:20
21 "And afterward they asked for a king; so
God gave them Saul the son of Kish, a man of
the tribe of Benjamin, for forty years.
22 "And when He had removed him, He
raised up for them David as king, to whom

13:17 M omits *Israel*

(Point 37-D continued from previous page)
   (4) *Second missionary journey* (Acts 16:1—18:22, page 1110).

      (a) Paul and Barnabas separated, but the work continued. Paul took Silas on the second journey.
      (b) The churches started on the first journey were revisited (Acts 15:41, page 1110). This is our
example to nurture new converts.
      (c) In a vision, Paul was guided to enter Europe (Acts 16:9, 10, page 1110). Lydia was the first convert
in Europe (Acts 16:14, page 1110).
      (d) They witnessed in the great Greek cities of Philippi, Thessalonica, Athens, Corinth, and Ephesus.
      (e) They returned to Antioch of Syria and informed the church of their journeys.

   (5) *Third missionary journey* (Acts 18:23—21:16, page 1113).

      (a) The churches which had been started by Paul were revisited.
      (b) Paul taught in Ephesus for three years and displayed flexibility in staying at a location when
opportunity or need arose.
      (c) He revisited the various Greek cities as well as Jerusalem.

   (6) *Witnessed in Jerusalem* (Acts 21:17—23:32, page 1116). God gave Paul opportunity to witness to the
high priest and the Sanhedrin.
   (7) *Caesarean imprisonment* (Acts 23:31—26:32, page 1119). God gave Paul the opportunity to witness
to rulers of the land: the governors Felix and Festus, and King Agrippa II.
   (8) *Voyage to Rome* (Acts 27, page 1123). God preserved His servants to continue in their work.
   (9) *Roman imprisonment* (Acts 28:16—31, page 1124). God gave Paul opportunity to witness to the Jewish
community in Rome and to many great personages of the Roman Empire.
   (10) *Final travels* (Rom. 15:24, page 1145). Paul expressed his desire to witness in Spain.
   (11) *Second Roman imprisonment and martyrdom.* The writings of the earliest church fathers are
uniform in their testimony that Paul was martyred in Rome by Nero.

See Hebrews 3:12–19, page 1238, for **Point 37-E: The Fall of Jerusalem and the End of the First Century.**

also He gave testimony and said, *'I have found David* the son of Jesse, *a man after My own heart,* who will do all My will.'

23 R"From this man's seed, according Rto the promise, God raised up for Israel Ra* Savior—Jesus—   Is. 11:1 · Ps. 132:11 · [Matt. 1:21]

24 R"after John had first preached, before His coming, the baptism of repentance to all the people of Israel.   [Luke 3:3]

25 "And as John was finishing his course, he said, R'Who do you think I am? I am not He. But behold, Rthere comes One after me, the sandals of whose feet I am not worthy to loose.'   Mark 1:7 · John 1:20, 27

26 "Men and brethren, sons of the Tfamily of Abraham, and Rthose among you who fear God, Rto you the Tword of this salvation has been sent.   stock · Ps. 66:16 · Matt. 10:6 · message

27 "For those who dwell in Jerusalem, and their rulers, Rbecause they did not know Him, nor even the voices of the Prophets which are read every Sabbath, have fulfilled *them* in condemning *Him.*   Luke 23:34

28 R"And though they found no cause for death *in Him,* they asked Pilate that He should be put to death.   Matt. 27:22, 23

29 "Now when they had fulfilled all that was written concerning Him, they took *Him* down from the tree and laid *Him* in a tomb.

30 "But God raised Him from the dead.

31 "He was seen for many days by those who came up with Him from Galilee to Jerusalem, who are His witnesses to the people.

32 "And we declare to you glad tidings— that promise which was made to the fathers.

33 "God has fulfilled this for us their children, in that He has raised up Jesus. As it is also written in the second Psalm:

R'You are My Son,   Ps. 2:7; Heb. 1:5
    Today I have begotten You.'

34 "And that He raised Him from the dead, no more to return to Tcorruption, He has spoken thus: the state of decay

R'I will give you the sure Tmercies of
    David.'   Is. 55:3 · blessings

35 "Therefore He also says in another Psalm:

R'You will not allow Your Holy One to
    see corruption.'   Ps. 16:10

36 "For David, after he had served This own generation by the will of God, Rfell asleep, was buried with his fathers, and Tsaw corruption;   in his · Acts 2:29 · underwent decay

37 "but He whom God raised up Tsaw no corruption.   underwent no decay

38 "Therefore let it be known to you, breth-ren, that Rthrough this Man is preached to you the forgiveness of sins;   Jer. 31:34

39 "and by Him everyone who believes is justified from all things from which you could not be justified by the law of Moses.

40 "Beware therefore, lest what has been spoken in the prophets come upon you:

41 'Behold,R you despisers,
    Marvel and perish!
    For I work a work in your days,
    A work which you will by no means
        believe,   Hab. 1:5
    Though one were to declare it to
        you.'"

Blessing and Conflict at Antioch

42 *So when the Jews went out of the synagogue, the Gentiles begged that these words might be preached to them the next Sabbath.

43 Now when the congregation had broken up, many of the Jews and devout proselytes followed Paul and Barnabas, who, speaking to them, Rpersuaded them to continue in Rthe grace of God.   Acts 11:23 · Titus 2:11

44 On the next Sabbath almost the whole city came together to hear the word of God.

45 But when the Jews saw the multitudes, they were filled with envy; and contradicting and blaspheming, they Ropposed the things spoken by Paul.   1 Pet. 4:4

46 Then Paul and Barnabas grew bold and said, R"It was necessary that the word of God should be spoken to you first; but Rsince you reject it, and judge yourselves unworthy of everlasting life, behold, Rwe turn to the Gentiles.   Rom. 1:16 · Ex. 32:10 · Acts 18:6

47 "For so the Lord has commanded us:

R'I have set you as a light to the
    Gentiles,
    That you should be for salvation to the
        ends of the earth.'"   Is. 42:6; 49:6

48 Now when the Gentiles heard this, they were glad and glorified the word of the Lord. RAnd as many as had been appointed to eternal life believed.   [Acts 2:47]

49 And the word of the Lord was being spread throughout all the region.

50 But the Jews stirred up the devout and prominent women and the chief men of the city, Rraised up persecution against Paul and Barnabas, and expelled them from their region.   2 Tim. 3:11

51 But they shook off the dust from their feet against them, and came to Iconium.

52 And the disciples Rwere filled with joy and with the Holy Spirit.   John 16:22

13:42 Or And when they went out of the synagogue of the Jews; NU And when they went out of the synagogue, they begged

13:22 Ps. 89:20 · 1 Sam. 13:14
13:23 M salvation, after

At Iconium

14 Now it happened in Iconium that they went together to the synagogue of the Jews, and so spoke that a great multitude both of the Jews and of the Greeks believed.

2 But the unbelieving Jews stirred up the Gentiles and ᵀpoisoned their ᵀminds against the brethren.   embittered • Lit. *souls*

3 Therefore they stayed there a long time, speaking boldly in the Lord, who was bearing witness to the word of His grace, granting signs and wonders to be done by their hands.

4 But the multitude of the city was ᴿdivided: part sided with the Jews, and part with the ᴿapostles.   Luke 12:51 • Acts 13:2, 3

5 And when a violent attempt was made by both the Gentiles and Jews, with their rulers, ᴿto abuse and stone them,   2 Tim. 3:11

6 they became aware of it and ᴿfled to Lystra and Derbe, cities of Lycaonia, and to the surrounding region.   Matt. 10:23

7 And they were preaching the gospel there.

Idolatry at Lystra

8 And in Lystra a certain man without strength in his feet was sitting, a cripple from his mother's womb, who had never walked.

9 *This* man heard Paul speaking. ᵀPaul, observing him intently and seeing that he had faith to be healed,   Lit. *Who*

10 said with a loud voice, ᴿ"Stand up straight on your feet!" And he leaped and walked.   [Is. 35:6]

11 Now when the people saw what Paul had done, they raised their voices, saying in the Lycaonian *language*, "The gods have come down to us in the likeness of men!"

12 And Barnabas they called ᵀZeus, and Paul, ᵀHermes, because he was the chief speaker.   Or *Jupiter* • Or *Mercury*

13 Then the priest of Zeus, whose temple was in front of their city, brought oxen and garlands to the gates, ᴿintending to sacrifice with the multitudes.   Dan. 2:46

14 But when the apostles Barnabas and Paul heard this, they tore their clothes and ran in among the multitude, crying out

15 and saying, "Men, why are you doing these things? We also are men with the same nature as you, and preach to you that you should turn from these useless things to the living God, who made the heaven, the earth, the sea, and all things that are in them,

16 ᴿwho in bygone generations allowed all nations to walk in their own ways.   Ps. 81:12

17 "Nevertheless He did not leave Himself without witness, in that He did good, gave us rain from heaven and fruitful seasons, filling our hearts with food and gladness."

18 And with these sayings they could scarcely restrain the multitudes from sacrificing to them.

Stoning, Escape to Derbe

19 Then Jews from Antioch and Iconium came there; and having persuaded the multitudes, they stoned Paul *and* dragged *him* out of the city, supposing him to be dead.

20 However, when the disciples gathered around him, he rose up and went into the city. And the next day he departed with Barnabas to Derbe.

Strengthening the Converts

21 And when they had preached the gospel to that city and made many disciples, they returned to Lystra, Iconium, and Antioch,

22 strengthening the souls of the disciples, exhorting *them* to continue in the faith, and *saying,* ᴿ"We must through many tribulations enter the kingdom of God."   [2 Tim. 2:12; 3:12]

23 So when they had ᴿappointed elders in every church, and prayed with fasting, they commended them to the Lord in whom they had believed.   Titus 1:5

24 And after they had passed through Pisidia, they came to Pamphylia.

25 Now when they had preached the word in Perga, they went down to Attalia.

26 From there they sailed to Antioch, where they had been commended to the grace of God for the work which they had completed.

27 Now when they had come and gathered the church together, they reported all that God had done with them, and that He had opened the door of faith to the Gentiles.

28 So they stayed there a long time with the disciples.

Conflict over Circumcision

15 And certain *men* came down from Judea and taught the brethren, "Unless you are circumcised according to the custom of Moses, you cannot be saved."

2 Therefore, when Paul and Barnabas had no small dissension and dispute with them, they determined that ᴿPaul and Barnabas and certain others of them should go up to Jerusalem, to the apostles and elders, about this question.   Gal. 2:1

3 So, ᴿbeing sent on their way by the church, they passed through Phoenicia and Samaria, ᴿdescribing the conversion of the Gentiles; and they caused great joy to all the brethren.   Rom. 15:24 • Acts 14:27; 15:4, 12

4 And when they had come to Jerusalem, they were received by the church and the apostles and the elders; and they reported all things that God had done with them.

5 But some of the sect of the Pharisees who believed rose up, saying, "It is necessary to circumcise them, and to command *them* to keep the law of Moses."

The Jerusalem Council

6 Now the apostles and elders came together to consider this matter.

7 And when there had been much dispute, Peter rose up and said to them: R"Men and brethren, you know that a good while ago God chose among us, that by my mouth the Gentiles should hear the word of the gospel and believe.   Acts 10:20

8 "So God, who knows the heart, Tacknowledged them by giving them the Holy Spirit, just as He did to us,   *bore witness to*

9 "and made no distinction between us and them, purifying their hearts by faith.

10 "Now therefore, why do you test God Rby putting a yoke on the neck of the disciples which neither our fathers nor we were able to bear?   Matt. 23:4

11 "But Rwe believe that through the grace of the Lord Jesus *Christ we shall be saved in the same manner as they."   Rom. 3:4; 5:15

12 Then all the multitude kept silent and listened to Barnabas and Paul declaring how many miracles and wonders God had worked through them among the Gentiles.

13 And after they had Tbecome silent, RJames answered, saying, "Men *and* brethren, listen to me: *stopped speaking* · Acts 12:17

14 R"Simon has declared how God at the first visited the Gentiles to take out of them a people for His name.   Acts 15:7

15 "And with this the words of the prophets agree, just as it is written:

16 'AfterR this I will return
And will rebuild the tabernacle of
      David, which has fallen down;
I will rebuild its ruins,
And I will set it up;   Amos 9:11, 12

17 So that the rest of mankind may seek
      the LORD,
Even all the Gentiles who are called by
      My name,
Says the *LORD who does all these
      things.'

18 *"Known to God from eternity are all His works.

19 "Therefore RI judge that we should not trouble those from among the Gentiles who Rare turning to God,   Acts 15:28; 21:25 · 1 Thess. 1:9

20 "but that we write to them to abstain Rfrom things polluted by idols, Rfrom Tsexual immorality, *from* things strangled, and *from* blood.   [1 Cor. 8:1; 10:20, 28] · [1 Cor. 6:9] · Or *fornication*

21 "For Moses has had throughout many generations those who preach him in every city, Rbeing read in the synagogues every Sabbath."   Acts 13:15, 27

The Jerusalem Decree

22 Then it pleased the apostles and elders, with the whole church, to send chosen men of their own company to Antioch with Paul and Barnabas, *namely,* Judas who was also named RBarsabas,* and Silas, leading men among the brethren.   Acts 1:23

23 They wrote this *letter* by them:

The apostles, the elders, and the
brethren,
To the brethren who are of the Gentiles
in Antioch, Syria, and Cilicia:
Greetings.

24 Since we have heard that Rsome who
      went out from us have troubled you
      with words, unsettling your souls,
      *saying, "You must be circumcised and
      keep the law"—to whom we gave no
      such commandment—   Titus 1:10, 11

25 it seemed good to us, being assembled
      with one Taccord, to send chosen men
      to you with our beloved Barnabas and
      Paul,   *purpose* or *mind*

26 men who have risked their lives for the
      name of our Lord Jesus Christ.

27 We have therefore sent Judas and Silas,
      who will also report the same things by
      word of mouth.

28 For it seemed good to the Holy Spirit,
      and to us, to lay upon you no greater
      burden than these necessary things:

29 that you abstain from things offered to
      idols, Rfrom blood, from things
      strangled, and from RsexualT
      immorality. If you keep yourselves from
      these, you will do well.
Farewell.   Lev. 17:14 · Col. 3:5 · Or *fornication*

Continuing Ministry in Syria

30 So when they were sent off, they came to Antioch; and when they had gathered the multitude together, they delivered the letter.

31 When they had read it, they rejoiced over its encouragement.

32 Now Judas and Silas, themselves being Rprophets also, exhorted and strengthened the brethren with many words.   Eph. 4:11

33 And after they had stayed *there* for a time, they were Rsent back with greetings from the brethren to *the apostles.   Heb. 11:31

34 *However, it seemed good to Silas to remain there.

35 RPaul and Barnabas also remained in Antioch, teaching and preaching the word of the Lord, with many others also.   Acts 13:1

15:11 NU, M omit *Christ*
15:17 NU *Lord, who makes these things*
15:18 NU (continuing v. 17) *known from eternity (of old).'*

15:22 NU, M *Barsabbas*
15:24 NU omits *saying, "You must be circumcised and keep the law"*
15:33 NU *those who had sent them*
15:34 NU, M omit v. 34.

Division over John Mark

36 Then after some days Paul said to Barnabas, "Let us now go back and visit our brethren in every city where we have preached the word of the Lord, *and see* how they are doing."

37 Now Barnabas ᵀwas determined to take with them John called Mark.   *resolved*

38 But Paul insisted that they should not take with them ᴿthe one who had departed from them in Pamphylia, and had not gone with them to the work.   Acts 13:13

39 Then the contention became so sharp that they parted from one another. And so Barnabas took Mark and sailed to Cyprus;

40 but Paul chose Silas and departed, ᴿbeing ᵀcommended by the brethren to the grace of God.   Acts 11:23; 14:26 • *committed*

41 And he went through Syria and Cilicia, ᴿstrengthening the churches.   Acts 16:5

Timothy Joins Paul and Silas

16 Then he came to ᴿDerbe and Lystra. And behold, a certain disciple was there, ᴿnamed Timothy, ᴿ*the* son of a certain Jewish woman who believed, but his father *was* Greek.   Acts 14:6 • Rom. 16:21 • 2 Tim. 1:5; 3:15

2 He was well spoken of by the brethren who were at Lystra and Iconium.

3 Paul wanted to have him go on with him. And he took *him* and circumcised him because of the Jews who were in that region, for they all knew that his father was Greek.

4 And as they went through the cities, they delivered to them the ᴿdecrees to keep, ᴿwhich were determined by the apostles and elders at Jerusalem.   Acts 15:19-21 • Acts 15:28, 29

5 So the churches were strengthened in the faith, and increased in number daily.

The Macedonian Call

6 Now when they had gone through Phrygia and the region of ᴿGalatia, they were forbidden by the Holy Spirit to preach the word in ᵀAsia.   Gal. 1:1, 2 • The Roman province of Asia

7 After they had come to Mysia, they tried to go into Bithynia, but the *Spirit did not permit them.

8 So passing by Mysia, they ᴿcame down to Troas.   2 Cor. 2:12

9 And a vision appeared to Paul in the night. A ᴿman of Macedonia stood and pleaded with him, saying, "Come over to Macedonia and help us."   Acts 10:30

10 Now after he had seen the vision, immediately we sought to go ᴿto Macedonia, concluding that the Lord had called us to preach the gospel to them.   2 Cor. 2:13

16:7 NU adds *of Jesus*

Lydia Baptized at Philippi

11 Therefore, sailing from Troas, we ran a straight course to Samothrace, and the next *day* came to Neapolis,

12 and from there to ᴿPhilippi, which is the ᵀforemost city of that part of Macedonia, a colony. And we were staying in that city for some days.   Phil. 1:1 • Lit. *first*

13 And on the Sabbath day we went out of the city to the riverside, where prayer was customarily made; and we sat down and spoke to the women who met *there*.

14 Now a certain woman named Lydia heard *us*. She was a seller of purple from the city of ᴿThyatira, who worshiped God. ᴿThe Lord opened her heart to heed the things spoken by Paul.   Rev. 1:11; 2:18, 24 • Luke 24:45

15 And when she and her household were baptized, she begged *us*, saying, "If you have judged me to be faithful to the Lord, come to my house and stay." So ᴿshe persuaded us.   Judg. 19:21

Paul and Silas Imprisoned

16 Now it happened, as we went to prayer, that a certain slave girl possessed with a spirit of divination met us, who brought her masters much profit by fortune-telling.

17 This girl followed Paul and us, and cried out, saying, "These men are the servants of the Most High God, who proclaim to us the way of salvation."

18 And this she did for many days. But Paul, greatly ᵀannoyed, turned and said to the spirit, "I command you in the name of Jesus Christ to come out of her." ᴿAnd he came out that very hour.   *distressed* • Mark 16:17

19 But ᴿwhen her masters saw that their hope of profit was gone, they seized Paul and Silas and ᴿdragged *them* into the marketplace to the authorities.   Acts 16:16; 19:25, 26 • Matt. 10:18

20 And they brought them to the magistrates, and said, "These men, being Jews, ᴿexceedingly trouble our city;   Acts 17:8

21 "and they teach customs which are not lawful for us, being Romans, to receive or observe."

22 Then the multitude rose up together against them; and the magistrates tore off their clothes ᴿand commanded *them* to be beaten with rods.   1 Thess. 2:2

23 And when they had laid many stripes on them, they threw *them* into prison, commanding the jailer to keep them securely.

24 Having received such a charge, he put them into the inner prison and fastened their feet in the stocks.

The Philippian Jailer Saved

25 But at midnight Paul and Silas were praying and singing hymns to God, and the prisoners were listening to them.

26 Suddenly there was a great earthquake, so that the foundations of the prison were shaken; and immediately all the doors were opened and everyone's chains were loosed.

27 And the keeper of the prison, awaking from sleep and seeing the prison doors open, supposing the prisoners had fled, drew his sword and was about to kill himself.

28 But Paul called with a loud voice, saying, "Do yourself no harm, for we are all here."

29 Then he called for a light, ran in, and fell down trembling before Paul and Silas.

30 And he brought them out and said, "Sirs, what must I do to be saved?"

31 So they said, R"Believe on the Lord Jesus Christ, and you will be saved, you and your household."   [John 3:16, 36; 6:47]

32 Then they spoke the word of the Lord to him and to all who were in his house.

33 And he took them the same hour of the night and washed *their* stripes. And immediately he and all his family were baptized.

34 Now when he had brought them into his house, Rhe set food before them; and he rejoiced, having believed in God with all his household.   Luke 5:29; 19:6

Paul Refuses to Depart Secretly

35 And when it was day, the magistrates sent the officers, saying, "Let those men go."

36 So the keeper of the prison reported these words to Paul, saying, "The magistrates have sent to let you go. Now therefore depart, and go in peace."

37 But Paul said to them, "They have beaten us openly, uncondemned Romans, *and* have thrown *us* into prison. And now do they put us out secretly? No indeed! Let them come themselves and get us out."

38 And the officers told these words to the magistrates, and they were afraid when they heard that they were Romans.

39 Then they came and pleaded with them and brought *them* out, and Rasked *them* to depart from the city.   Matt. 8:34

40 So they went out of the prison Rand entered *the house* of Lydia; and when they had seen the brethren, they encouraged them and departed.   Acts 16:14

Preaching Christ at Thessalonica

17 Now when they had passed through Amphipolis and Apollonia, they came to RThessalonica, where there was a synagogue of the Jews.   1 Thess. 1:1

2 Then Paul, as his custom was, Rwent in to them, and for three Sabbaths reasoned with them from the Scriptures,   Luke 4:16

3 explaining and demonstrating Rthat the Christ had to suffer and rise again from the dead, and *saying*, "This Jesus whom I preach to you is the Christ."   Acts 18:5, 28

4 RAnd some of them were persuaded; and

a great multitude of the devout Greeks, and not a few of the leading women, joined Paul and RSilas.   Acts 28:24 • Acts 15:22, 27, 32, 40

Assault on Jason's House

5 But the Jews *who were not persuaded, *becoming envious, took some of the evil men from the marketplace, and gathering a mob, set all the city in an uproar and attacked the house of RJason, and sought to bring them out to the people.   Rom. 16:21

6 But when they did not find them, they dragged Jason and some brethren to the rulers of the city, crying out, R"These who have turned the world upside down have come here too.   [Acts 16:20]

7 "Jason has Tharbored them, and these are all acting contrary to the decrees of Caesar, Rsaying there is another king— Jesus."   *welcomed* • 1 Pet. 2:13

8 And they troubled the crowd and the rulers of the city when they heard these things.

9 So when they had taken security from Jason and the rest, they let them go.

Ministering at Berea

10 Then Rthe brethren immediately sent Paul and Silas away by night to Berea. When they arrived, they went into the synagogue of the Jews.   Acts 9:25; 17:14

11 These were more Tfair-minded than those in Thessalonica, in that they received the word with all readiness, and Rsearched the Scriptures daily *to find out* whether these things were so.   Lit. *noble* • John 5:39

12 Therefore many of them believed, and also not a few of the Greeks, prominent women as well as men.

13 But when the Jews from Thessalonica learned that the word of God was preached by Paul at Berea, they came there also and stirred up the crowds.

14 RThen immediately the brethren sent Paul away, to go to the sea; but both Silas and Timothy remained there.   Matt. 10:23

15 So those who conducted Paul brought him to Athens; and Rreceiving a command for Silas and Timothy to come to him with all speed, they departed.   Acts 18:5

The Philosophers at Athens

16 Now while Paul waited for them at Athens, Rhis spirit was provoked within him when he saw that the city was Tgiven over to idols.   2 Pet. 2:8 • *full of idols*

17 Therefore he reasoned in the synagogue with the Jews and with the *Gentile* worshipers, and in the marketplace daily with those who happened to be there.

17:5 NU omits *who were not persuaded* • M omits *becoming envious*

18 *Then certain Epicurean and Stoic philosophers encountered him. And some said, "What does this ᵀbabbler want to say?" Others said, "He seems to be a proclaimer of foreign gods," because he preached to them Jesus and the resurrection.   Lit. *seed picker*

19 And they took him and brought him to the Areopagus, saying, "May we know what this new doctrine *is* of which you speak?

20 "For you are bringing some strange things to our ears. Therefore we want to know what these things mean."

21 For all the Athenians and the foreigners who were there spent their time in nothing else but either to tell or to hear some new thing.

Addressing the Areopagus

22 Then Paul stood in the midst of the ᵀAreopagus and said, "Men of Athens, I perceive that in all things you are very religious;   Lit. *Hill of Ares, or Mars' Hill*

23 "for as I was passing through and considering the objects of your worship, I even found an altar with this inscription:

TO THE UNKNOWN GOD.

Therefore, the One whom you worship without knowing, Him I proclaim to you:

24 ᴿ"God, who made the world and everything in it, since He is ᴿLord of heaven and earth, ᴿdoes not dwell in temples made with hands.   Acts 14:15 • Matt. 11:25 • Acts 7:48-50

25 "Nor is He worshiped with men's hands, as though He needed anything, since He ᴿgives to all life, breath, and all things. Is. 42:5

26 "And He has made from one *blood every nation of men to dwell on all the face of the earth, and has determined their preappointed times and the boundaries of their dwellings,

27 ᴿ"so that they should seek the Lord, in the hope that they might grope for Him and find Him, ᴿthough He is not far from each one of us;   [Rom. 1:20] • Jer. 23:23, 24

28 "for in Him we live and move and have our being, as also some of your own poets have said, 'For we are also His offspring.'

29 "Therefore, since we are the offspring of God, we ought not to think that the Divine Nature is like gold or silver or stone, something shaped by art and man's devising.

22-F. Repentance: Its Importance ▼

30 "Truly, ᴿthese times of ignorance God overlooked, but ᴿnow commands all men everywhere to repent,   [Rom. 3:25] • [Titus 2:11, 12] ▲

31 "because He has appointed a day on which ᴿHe will judge the world in righteousness by the Man whom He has ordained. He has given assurance of this to all by ᴿraising Him from the dead."   Acts 10:42 • Acts 2:24

32 And when they heard of the resurrection of the dead, some mocked, while others said, "We will hear you again on this *matter*."

33 So Paul departed from among them.

34 However, some men joined him and believed, among them Dionysius the Areopa-

---

17:18 NU, M *Also then*   17:26 NU omits *blood*

22-F. Repentance: Its Importance (Acts 17:30)—Repentance is so important that God commands "all men everywhere to repent" (v. 30).

(1) The lost are to repent. Jesus said, "I did not come to call the righteous, but sinners, to repentance" (Matt. 9:13, page 948). Again He said, "Unless you repent you will all likewise perish" (Luke 13:3-5, page 1031).

(2) Backsliders are to repent. Paul said, "Now I rejoice, not that you were made sorry, but that your sorrow led to repentance" (2 Cor. 7:9, page 1170). There were carnal Christians in the church at Corinth. In Paul's first letter to them, he called upon the church to discipline the guilty. In his second letter he rejoices because the guilty repented.

(3) Local churches are to repent. In the book of Revelation, chapters 2 and 3 (page 1294), our Lord sent seven letters to seven local churches. He called upon five of the seven to repent:

(a) The church at Ephesus was to repent because she had left her first love.

(b) The church at Pergamos was to repent because she permitted the doctrine of Balaam to be taught, as well as allowing the people to eat things sacrificed to idols, and to commit fornication.

(c) The church at Thyatira was to repent because she allowed "Jezebel" to teach and seduce God's servants to commit fornication.

(d) The church at Sardis was to repent because she was a dead congregation.

(e) The church at Laodicea was to repent because she thought she was rich and needed nothing. In her opinion she was self-sufficient. She did not know that she was neither hot nor cold, but lukewarm, and God was ready to spit her out of His mouth.

The Lord called upon these five local churches to repent, or else He would remove their lampstands, and they would cease to be a light in darkness.

The lost are to repent or perish. The backslider is to repent, or be disciplined. The local church is to repent, or lose its effectiveness in a world lost in sin.

See Acts 26:19, 20, page 1122, for **Point 22-G: Repentance: The Evidence.**

gite, a woman named Damaris, and others with them.

Ministering at Corinth

18 After these things Paul departed from Athens and went to Corinth.

2 And he found a certain Jew named Aquila, born in Pontus, who had recently come from Italy with his wife Priscilla (because Claudius had commanded all the Jews to depart from Rome); and he came to them.

3 So, because he was of the same trade, he stayed with them ᴿand worked; for by occupation they were tentmakers.   Acts 20:34

4 ᴿAnd he reasoned in the synagogue every Sabbath, and persuaded both Jews and Greeks.   Acts 17:2

5 When Silas and Timothy had come from Macedonia, Paul was ᴿcompelled ᵀby the Spirit, and testified to the Jews *that Jesus is* the Christ.   Acts 18:28 · Or *in his spirit* or *in the Spirit*

6 But when they opposed him and blasphemed, ᴿhe shook *his* garments and said to them, ᴿ"Your blood *be* upon your *own* heads; ᴿI *am* clean. From now on I will go to the Gentiles."   Neh. 5:13 · 2 Sam. 1:16 · [Ezek. 3:18, 19]

7 And he departed from there and entered the house of a certain *man* named *Justus, one who worshiped God, whose house was next door to the synagogue.

8 ᴿThen Crispus, the ruler of the synagogue, believed on the Lord with all his household. And many of the Corinthians, hearing, believed and were baptized. 1 Cor. 1:14

9 Now ᴿthe Lord spoke to Paul in the night by a vision, "Do not be afraid, but speak, and do not keep silent;   Acts 23:11

10 ᴿ"for I am with you, and no one will attack you to hurt you; for I have many people in this city."   Jer. 1:18, 19

11 And he continued *there* a year and six months, teaching the word of God among them.

12 When Gallio was proconsul of Achaia, the Jews with one accord rose up against Paul and brought him to the judgment seat,

13 saying, "This *fellow* persuades men to worship God contrary to the law."

14 And when Paul was about to open *his* mouth, Gallio said to the Jews, "If it were a matter of wrongdoing or wicked crimes, O Jews, there would be reason why I should bear with you.

15 "But if it is a ᴿquestion of words and names and your own law, look *to it* yourselves; for I do not want to be a judge of such *matters."*   Acts 23:29; 25:19

16 And he drove them from the judgment seat.

17 Then *all the Greeks took ᴿSosthenes,

the ruler of the synagogue, and beat *him* before the judgment seat. But Gallio took no notice of these things.   1 Cor. 1:1

Paul Returns to Antioch

18 So Paul still remained ᵀa good while. Then he took leave of the brethren and sailed for Syria, and Priscilla and Aquila *were* with him. He had *his* hair cut off at Cenchrea, for he had taken a vow.   Lit. *many days*

19 And he came to Ephesus, and left them there; but he himself entered the synagogue and reasoned with the Jews.

20 When they asked *him* to stay a longer time with them, he did not consent,

21 but took leave of them, saying, *"I must by all means keep this coming feast in Jerusalem; but I will return again to you, God willing." And he sailed from Ephesus.

22 And when he had landed at ᴿCaesarea, and ᵀgone up and greeted the church, he went down to Antioch.   Acts 8:40 · To Jerusalem

23 After he had spent some time *there*, he departed and went over the region of ᴿGalatia and Phrygia ᵀin order, strengthening all the disciples.   Gal. 1:2 · *successively*

Ministry of Apollos

24 ᴿNow a certain Jew named Apollos, born at Alexandria, an eloquent man *and* mighty in the Scriptures, came to Ephesus. Titus 3:13

25 This man had been instructed in the way of the Lord; and being ᴿfervent in spirit, he spoke and taught accurately the things of the Lord, ᴿthough he knew only the baptism of John.   Rom. 12:11 · Acts 19:3

26 So he began to speak boldly in the synagogue. When Aquila and Priscilla heard him, they took him aside and explained to him the way of God more accurately.

27 And when he desired to cross to Achaia, the brethren wrote, exhorting the disciples to receive him; and when he arrived, ᴿhe greatly helped those who had believed through grace;   1 Cor. 3:6

28 for he vigorously refuted the Jews publicly, ᴿshowing from the Scriptures that Jesus is the Christ.   Acts 9:22; 17:3; 18:5

Paul at Ephesus

19 And it happened, while Apollos was at Corinth, that Paul, having passed through ᴿthe upper regions, came to Ephesus. And finding some disciples   Acts 18:23

2 he said to them, "Did you receive the Holy Spirit when you believed?" So they said to him, ᴿ"We have not so much as heard whether there is a Holy Spirit."   1 Sam. 3:7

3 And he said to them, "Into what then were you baptized?" So they said, ᴿ"Into John's baptism."   Acts 18:25

18:7 NU *Titius Justus*
18:17 NU *they all*

18:21 NU omits *I must by all means keep this coming feast in Jerusalem*

4 Then Paul said, [R]"John indeed baptized with a baptism of repentance, saying to the people that they should believe on Him who would come after him, that is, on Christ Jesus."   Matt. 3:11

5 When they heard *this*, they were baptized in the name of the Lord Jesus.

6 And when Paul had laid hands on them, the Holy Spirit came upon them, and [R]they spoke with tongues and prophesied.   Acts 2:4

7 Now the men were about twelve in all.

8 [R]And he went into the synagogue and spoke boldly for three months, reasoning and persuading [R]concerning the things of the kingdom of God.   Acts 17:2; 18:4 · Acts 1:3; 28:23

9 But when some were hardened and did not believe, but spoke evil [R]of the Way before the multitude, he departed from them and withdrew the disciples, reasoning daily in the school of Tyrannus.   Acts 9:2; 19:23; 22:4; 24:14

10 And this continued for two years, so that all who dwelt in Asia heard the word of the Lord Jesus, both Jews and Greeks.

Miracles Glorify Christ

11 Now [R]God worked unusual miracles by the hands of Paul,   Mark 16:20

12 [R]so that even handkerchiefs or aprons were brought from his body to the sick, and the diseases left them and the evil spirits went out of them.   Acts 5:15

13 Then some of the itinerant Jewish exorcists took it upon themselves to call the name of the Lord Jesus over those who had evil spirits, saying, *"We exorcise you by the Jesus whom Paul preaches."

14 Also there were seven sons of Sceva, a Jewish chief priest, who did so.

15 And the evil spirit answered and said, "Jesus I know, and Paul I know; but who are you?"

16 Then the man in whom the evil spirit was leaped on them, *overpowered them, and prevailed against *them, so that they fled out of that house naked and wounded.

17 This became known both to all Jews and Greeks dwelling in Ephesus; and [R]fear fell on them all, and the name of the Lord Jesus was magnified.   Luke 1:65; 7:16

18 And many who had believed came [R]confessing and telling their deeds.   Matt. 3:6

19 Also, many of those who had practiced magic brought their books together and burned *them* in the sight of all. And they counted up the value of them, and *it* totaled [T]fifty thousand *pieces* of silver. $6,400,000

20 [R]So the word of the Lord grew mightily and prevailed.   Acts 6:7; 12:24

The Riot at Ephesus

21 When these things were accomplished, Paul purposed in the Spirit, when he had passed through [R]Macedonia and Achaia, to go to Jerusalem, saying, "After I have been there, I must also see Rome."   Acts 20:1

22 So he sent into Macedonia two of those who ministered to him, Timothy and Erastus, but he himself stayed in Asia for a time.

23 And [R]about that time there arose a great commotion about [R]the Way.   2 Cor. 1:8 · Acts 9:2

24 For a certain man named Demetrius, a silversmith, who made silver shrines of [T]Diana, brought [R]no small profit to the craftsmen.   Gr. *Artemis* · Acts 16:16, 19

25 He called them together with the workers of similar occupation, and said: "Men, you know that we have our prosperity by this trade.

26 "Moreover you see and hear that not only at Ephesus, but throughout almost all Asia, this Paul has persuaded and turned away many people, saying that [R]they are not gods which are made with hands.   Is. 44:10-20

27 "So not only is this trade of ours in danger of falling into disrepute, but also the temple of the great goddess Diana may be despised and *her magnificence destroyed, whom all Asia and the world worship."

28 Now when they heard *this*, they were full of wrath and cried out, saying, "Great *is* Diana of the Ephesians!"

29 So the whole city was filled with confusion, and rushed into the theater with one accord, having seized [R]Gaius and [R]Aristarchus, Macedonians, Paul's travel companions.   Rom. 16:23 · Col. 4:10

30 And when Paul wanted to go in to the people, the disciples would not allow him.

31 Then some of the officials of Asia, who were his friends, sent to him pleading that he would not venture into the theater.

32 Some therefore cried one thing and some another, for the assembly was confused, and most of them did not know why they had come together.

33 And they drew Alexander out of the multitude, the Jews putting him forward. And [R]Alexander [R]motioned with his hand, and wanted to make his defense to the people.   2 Tim. 4:14 · Acts 12:17

34 But when they found out that he was a Jew, all with one voice cried out for about two hours, "Great *is* Diana of the Ephesians!"

35 And when the city clerk had quieted the crowd, he said: "Men of Ephesus, what man is there who does not know that the city of the Ephesians is temple guardian of the great goddess [T]Diana, and of the *image* which fell down from [T]Zeus?   Gr. *Artemis* · heaven

36 "Therefore, since these things cannot be

19:13 NU /

19:16 M *and they overpowered them* • NU *both of them*

19:27 NU *she be deposed from her magnificence*

denied, you ought to be quiet and do nothing rashly.

37 "For you have brought these men here who are neither robbers of temples nor blasphemers of *your goddess.

38 "Therefore, if Demetrius and his fellow craftsmen have a case against anyone, the courts are open and there are proconsuls. Let them bring charges against one another.

39 "But if you have any other inquiry to make, it shall be determined in the lawful assembly.

40 "For we are in danger of being ᵀcalled in question for today's uproar, there being no reason which we may give to account for this disorderly gathering."   Or charged with rebellion

41 And when he had said these things, he dismissed the assembly.

Journeys in Greece

20 After the uproar had ceased, Paul called the disciples to *himself,* embraced *them,* and ᴿdeparted to go to Macedonia.   1 Tim. 1:3

2 Now when he had gone over that region and encouraged them with many words, he came to ᴿGreece.   Acts 17:15; 18:1

3 and stayed three months. And ᴿwhen the Jews plotted against him as he was about to sail to Syria, he decided to return through Macedonia.   2 Cor. 11:26

4 And Sopater of Berea accompanied him to Asia—also Aristarchus and Secundus of the Thessalonians, and ᴿGaius of Derbe, and ᴿTimothy, and ᴿTychicus and ᴿTrophimus of Asia.   Acts 19:29 · Acts 16:1 · Eph. 6:21 · 2 Tim. 4:20

5 These men, going ahead, waited for us at ᴿTroas.   2 Tim. 4:13

6 But we sailed away from Philippi after ᴿthe Days of Unleavened Bread, and in five days joined them ᴿat Troas, where we stayed seven days.   Ex. 12:14, 15 · 2 Tim. 4:13

Ministering at Troas

7 Now on ᴿthe first *day* of the week, when the disciples came together ᴿto break bread, Paul, ready to depart the next day, spoke to them and continued his message until midnight.   1 Cor. 16:2 · Acts 2:42, 46; 20:11

8 There were many lamps in the upper room where *they were gathered together.

9 And in a window sat a certain young man named Eutychus, who was sinking into a deep sleep. He was overcome by sleep; and as Paul continued speaking, he fell down from the third story and was taken up dead.

10 But Paul went down, fell on him, and embracing *him* said, ᴿ"Do not trouble yourselves, for his life is in him."   Matt. 9:23, 24

11 Now when he had come up, had broken bread and eaten, and talked a long while, even till daybreak, he departed.

12 And they brought the young man in alive, and they were not a little comforted.

From Troas to Miletus

13 Then we went ahead to the ship and sailed to Assos, there intending to take Paul on board; for so he had ᵀgiven orders, intending himself to go on foot.   arranged it

14 And when he met us at Assos, we took him on board and came to Mitylene.

15 We sailed from there, and the next *day* came opposite Chios. The following *day* we arrived at Samos and stayed at Trogyllium. The next *day* we came to Miletus.

16 For Paul had decided to sail past Ephesus, so that he would not have to spend time in Asia; for he was hurrying to be at Jerusalem, if possible, on the Day of Pentecost.

The Ephesian Elders Exhorted

17 From Miletus he sent to Ephesus and called for the elders of the church.

18 And when they had come to him, he said to them: "You know, ᴿfrom the first day that I came to Asia, in what manner I always lived among you,   Acts 18:19; 19:1, 10; 20:4, 16

19 "serving the Lord with all humility, with many tears and trials which happened to me ᴿby the plotting of the Jews;   Acts 20:3

20 "how I kept back nothing that was helpful, but proclaimed it to you, and taught you publicly and from house to house,

21 ᴿ"testifying to Jews, and also to Greeks, ᴿrepentance toward God and faith toward our Lord Jesus Christ.   Acts 18:5; 19:10 · Mark 1:15

22 "And see, now ᴿI go bound in the spirit to Jerusalem, not knowing the things that will happen to me there,   Acts 19:21

23 "except that ᴿthe Holy Spirit testifies in every city, saying that chains and tribulations await me.   Acts 21:4, 11

24 *"But ᴿnone of these things move me; nor do I count my life dear to myself, ᴿso that I may finish my ᵀrace with joy, ᴿand the ministry ᴿwhich I received from the Lord Jesus, to testify to the gospel of the grace of God.   Acts 21:13 · 2 Tim. 4:7 · course · Acts 1:17 · Gal. 1:1

25 "And indeed, now I know that you all, among whom I have gone preaching the kingdom of God, will see my face no more.

26 "Therefore I testify to you this day that I *am* innocent of the blood of all *men.*

27 "For I have not ᵀshunned to declare to you the whole counsel of God.   avoided

28 "Therefore take heed to yourselves and to all the flock, among which the Holy Spirit ᴿhas made you overseers, to shepherd the

church *of God ^Rwhich He purchased ^Rwith His own blood.   1 Cor. 12:28 • Eph. 1:7, 14 • Heb. 9:14

29 "For I know this, that after my departure ^Rsavage wolves will come in among you, not sparing the flock.   Matt. 7:15

30 "Also from among yourselves men will rise up, speaking perverse things, to draw away the disciples after themselves.

31 "Therefore watch, and remember that ^Rfor three years I did not cease to warn everyone night and day with tears.   Acts 19:8

32 "So now, brethren, I commend you to God and to the word of His grace, which is able to build you up and give you an inheritance among all those who are sanctified.

33 "I have coveted no one's silver or gold or apparel.

34 *"Yes, you yourselves know ^Rthat these hands have provided for my necessities, and for those who were with me.   Acts 18:3

35 "I have shown you in every way, ^Rby laboring like this, that you must support the weak. And remember the words of the Lord Jesus, that He said, 'It is more blessed to give than to receive.' "   Rom. 15:1

36 And when he had said these things, he knelt down and prayed with them all.

37 Then they all wept ^Tfreely, and fell on Paul's neck and kissed him,   Lit. much

38 sorrowing most of all for the words which he spoke, that they would see his face no more. And they accompanied him to the ship.

Warnings on the Journey to Jerusalem

21 Now it came to pass, that when we had departed from them and set sail, running a straight course we came to Cos, the following day to Rhodes, and from there to Patara.

2 And finding a ship sailing over to Phoenicia, we went aboard and set sail.

3 When we had sighted Cyprus, we passed it on the left, sailed to Syria, and landed at Tyre; for there the ship was to unload her cargo.

4 And finding *disciples, we stayed there seven days. ^RThey told Paul through the Spirit not to go up to Jerusalem.   Acts 20:23

5 When we had come to the end of those days, we departed and went on our way; and they all accompanied us, with wives and children, till we were out of the city. And we knelt down on the shore and prayed.

6 When we had taken our leave of one another, we boarded the ship, and they returned ^Rhome.   John 1:11

7 And when we had finished our voyage from Tyre, we came to Ptolemais, greeted the brethren, and stayed with them one day.

8 On the next day we *who were Paul's companions departed and came to ^RCaesarea, and entered the house of Philip ^Rthe evangelist, ^Rwho was one of the seven, and stayed with him.   Acts 8:40; 21:16 • Eph. 4:11 • Acts 6:5

9 Now this man had four virgin daughters ^Rwho prophesied.   Joel 2:28

10 And as we stayed many days, a certain prophet named ^RAgabus came down from Judea.   Acts 11:28

11 When he had come to us, he took Paul's belt, bound his own hands and feet, and said, "Thus says the Holy Spirit, ^R'So shall the Jews at Jerusalem bind the man who owns this belt, and deliver him into the hands of the Gentiles.' "   Acts 20:23; 21:33; 22:25

12 Now when we heard these things, both we and those from that place pleaded with him not to go up to Jerusalem.

13 Then Paul answered, ^R"What do you mean by weeping and breaking my heart? For I am ready not only to be bound, but also to die at Jerusalem for the name of the Lord Jesus."   Acts 20:24, 37

14 So when he would not be persuaded, we ceased, saying, ^R"The will of the Lord be done."   Luke 11:2; 22:42

Paul Urged to Make Peace

15 And after those days we ^Tpacked and went up to Jerusalem.   made preparations

16 Also some of the disciples from Caesarea went with us and brought with them a certain Mnason of Cyprus, an early disciple, with whom we were to lodge.

17 ^RAnd when we had come to Jerusalem, the brethren received us gladly.   Acts 15:4

18 On the following day Paul went in with us to James, and all the elders were present.

19 When he had greeted them, he told in detail those things which God had done among the Gentiles through his ministry.

20 And when they heard it, they glorified the Lord. And they said to him, "You see, brother, how many myriads of Jews there are who have believed, and they are all ^Rzealous for the law;   Acts 15:1; 22:3

21 "but they have been informed about you that you teach all the Jews who are among the Gentiles to forsake Moses, saying that they ought not to circumcise their children nor to walk according to the customs.

22 *"What then? The assembly must certainly meet, for they will hear that you have come.

23 "Therefore do what we tell you: We have four men who have taken a vow.

24 "Take them and be purified with them, and pay their expenses so that they may

20:28 M of the Lord and God
20:34 NU, M omit Yes
21:4 NU the disciples

21:8 NU omits who were Paul's companions
21:22 NU What then is to be done? They will certainly hear

Rshave *their* heads, and that all may know that those things of which they were informed concerning you are nothing, but *that* you yourself also walk orderly and keep the law.   Acts 18:18

25 "But concerning the Gentiles who believe, we have written *and* decided *that they should observe no such thing, except that they should keep themselves from *things* offered to idols, from blood, from things strangled, and from sexual immorality."

Arrested in the Temple

26 Then Paul took the men, and the next day, having been purified with them, entered the temple to announce the expiration of the days of purification, at which time an offering should be made for each one of them.

27 Now when the seven days were almost ended, Rthe Jews from Asia, seeing him in the temple, stirred up the whole crowd and Rlaid hands on him,   Acts 20:19; 24:18 · Acts 26:21

28 crying out, "Men of Israel, help! This is the man who teaches all *men* everywhere against the people, the law, and this place; and furthermore he also brought Greeks into the temple and has defiled this holy place."

29 (For they had *previously seen RTrophimus the Ephesian with him in the city, whom they supposed that Paul had brought into the temple.)   Acts 20:4

30 And Rall the city was disturbed; and the people ran together, seized Paul, and dragged him out of the temple; and immediately the doors were shut.   Acts 16:19; 26:21

31 Now as they were seeking to kill him, news came to the commander of the garrison that all Jerusalem was in an uproar.

32 RHe immediately took soldiers and centurions, and ran down to them. And when

21:25 NU omits *that they should observe no such thing, except*
21:29 M omits *previously*

they saw the commander and the soldiers, they stopped beating Paul.   Acts 23:27; 24:7

33 Then the Rcommander came near and took him, and Rcommanded *him* to be bound with two chains; and he asked who he was and what he had done.   Acts 24:7 · Acts 20:23; 21:11

34 And some among the multitude cried one thing and some another. So when he could not ascertain the truth because of the tumult, he commanded him to be taken into the barracks.

35 When he reached the stairs, he had to be carried by the soldiers because of the violence of the mob.

36 For the multitude of the people followed after, crying out, R"Away with him!" John 19:15

Addressing the Jerusalem Mob

37 Then as Paul was about to be led into the barracks, he said to the commander, "May I speak to you?" He replied, "Can you speak Greek?

38 R"Are you not the Egyptian who some time ago stirred up a rebellion and led the four thousand assassins out into the wilderness?"   Acts 5:36

39 But Paul said, R"I am a Jew from Tarsus, in Cilicia, a citizen of no Tmean city; and I implore you, permit me to speak to the people."   Acts 9:11; 22:3 · *insignificant*

40 So when he had given him permission, Paul stood on the stairs and Rmotioned with his hand to the people. And when there was a great silence, he spoke to *them* in the RHebrew language, saying,   Acts 12:17 · Acts 22:2

46-A. Paul's Early Life   ▼

22 "BrethrenR and fathers, hear my defense before you now."   Acts 7:2

2 And when they heard that he spoke to them in the RHebrew language, they kept all the more silent. Then he said: Acts 21:40

46-A. Paul's Early Life (Acts 22:1–5)—From this passage and others, some facts concerning Paul's early life can be reconstructed.

(1) He was born about 1 B.C. He was raised in Tarsus (Acts 21:39, page 1117), a rich commercial center near the Mediterranean, and the capital city of the Roman province of Cilicia (today's southeast Turkey). Tarsus, along with Athens and Alexandria, was one of the three great eastern university cities.

(2) He had a strict Jewish upbringing. He was a Jew of the Dispersion, from the tribe of Benjamin. He was circumcised when he was eight days old. Later he went to Jerusalem for rabbinic studies, and apparently read and spoke Greek and Hebrew fluently (Phil. 3:5, page 1197; cf. Acts 21:37, 40, above).

(3) He studied under the famous Rabbi Gamaliel I, who was to become known as one of the seven great rabbins of Jewish history (v. 3). He became a strict Pharisee. He mastered rabbinic law, and became zealous for Pharisaic Judaism to the point that he, in the name of God, persecuted those whom he thought were abandoning the Jewish faith (Phil. 3:5, 6, page 1197; cf. Acts 22:3, 4, page 1118).

(4) He was a freeborn Roman citizen (Acts 22:25–29, page 1118). This status gave him many legal rights and privileges to travel more freely, which would be helpful during his later missionary journeys and legal hearings (Acts 16:37–39, page 1111).

(5) In the Bible he is first called Saul and later called Paul. The best explanation for the dual names of Saul and Paul is that the former was his Hebrew name, while the latter became his name to the Greco-Roman world (Acts 13:9, page 1106).

See Acts 9:1–18, page 1100, for **Point 46-B: Paul's Conversion.**

▽ 3 ᴿ"I am indeed a Jew, born in Tarsus of Cilicia, but brought up in this city at the feet of Gamaliel, taught according to the strictness of our fathers' law, and was zealous toward God as you all are today. 2 Cor. 11:22

4 ᴿ"I persecuted this Way to the death, binding and delivering into prisons both men and women, 1 Tim. 1:13

5 "as also the high priest bears me witness, and ᴿall the council of the elders, ᴿfrom whom I also received letters to the brethren, and went to Damascus ᴿto bring in chains even those who were there to Jerusalem to be ▲ punished. Acts 23:14 • Luke 22:66 • Acts 9:2

6 "Now ᴿit happened, as I journeyed and came near Damascus at about noon, suddenly a great light from heaven shone around me. Acts 9:3; 26:12, 13

7 "And I fell to the ground and heard a voice saying to me, 'Saul, Saul, why are you persecuting Me?'

8 "So I answered, 'Who are You, Lord?' And He said to me, 'I am Jesus of Nazareth, whom you are persecuting.'

9 "And those who were with me indeed saw the light *and were afraid, but they did not hear the voice of Him who spoke to me.

10 "So I said, 'What shall I do, Lord?' And the Lord said to me, 'Arise and go into Damascus, and there you will be told all things which are appointed for you to do.'

11 "And since I could not see for the glory of that light, being led by the hand of those who were with me, I came into Damascus.

12 "Then a certain Ananias, a devout man according to the law, having a good testimony with all the Jews who dwelt there,

13 "came to me; and he stood and said to me, 'Brother Saul, receive your sight.' And at that same hour I looked up at him.

14 "Then he said, ᴿ'The God of our fathers has chosen you that you should know His will, and see the Just One, ᴿand hear the voice of His mouth. Acts 3:13; 5:30 • Gal. 1:12

15 ᴿ'For you will be His witness to all men of what you have seen and heard. Acts 23:11

16 'And now why are you waiting? Arise and be baptized, ᴿand wash away your sins, calling on the name of the Lord.' Heb. 10:22

17 "Now ᴿit happened, when I returned to Jerusalem and was praying in the temple, that I was in a trance Acts 9:26; 26:20

18 "and ᴿsaw Him saying to me, ᴿ'Make haste and get out of Jerusalem quickly, for they will not receive your testimony concerning Me.' Acts 22:14 • Matt. 10:14

19 "So I said, 'Lord, ᴿthey know that in every synagogue I imprisoned and beat those who believe on You. Acts 8:3; 22:4

20 'And when the blood of Your martyr Stephen was shed, I also was standing by

consenting *to his death, and guarding the clothes of those who were killing him.'

21 "Then He said to me, 'Depart, for I will send you far from here to the Gentiles.' "

Paul's Roman Citizenship

22 And they listened to him until this word, and then they raised their voices and said, ᴿ"Away with such a *fellow* from the earth, for ᴿhe is not fit to live!" Acts 21:36 • Acts 25:24

23 Then, as they cried out and tore off *their* clothes and threw dust into the air,

24 the commander ordered him to be brought into the barracks, and said that he should be examined under scourging, so that he might know why they shouted so against him.

25 And as they bound him with thongs, Paul said to the centurion who stood by, ᴿ"Is it lawful for you to scourge a man who is a Roman, and uncondemned?" Acts 16:37

26 When the centurion heard *that*, he went and told the commander, saying, "Take care what you do, for this man is a Roman."

27 Then the commander came and said to him, "Tell me, are you a Roman?" He said, "Yes."

28 The commander answered, "With a large sum I obtained this citizenship." And Paul said, "But I was born *a citizen*."

29 Then immediately those who were about to examine him withdrew from him; and the commander was also afraid after he found out that he was a Roman, and because he had bound him.

The Sanhedrin Divided

30 The next day, because he wanted to know for certain why he was accused by the Jews, he released him from *his* bonds, and commanded the chief priests and all their council to appear, and brought Paul down and set him before them.

23 Then Paul, looking earnestly at the council, said, "Men *and* brethren, ᴿI have lived in all good conscience before God until this day." 2 Tim. 1:3

2 And the high priest Ananias commanded those who stood by him ᴿto strike him on the mouth. John 18:22

3 Then Paul said to him, "God will strike you, *you* whitewashed wall! For you sit to judge me according to the law, and ᴿdo you command me to be struck contrary to the law?" Deut. 25:1, 2

4 And those who stood by said, "Do you revile God's high priest?"

5 Then Paul said, ᴿ"I did not know, brethren, that he was the high priest; for it is written, ᴿ'You shall not speak evil of a ruler of your people.' " Lev. 5:17, 18 • Ex. 22:28

6 But when Paul perceived that one part were Sadducees and the other Pharisees, he cried out in the council, "Men *and* brethren, ᴿI am a Pharisee, the son of a Pharisee; ᴿconcerning the hope and resurrection of the dead I am being judged!" Phil. 3:5 • Acts 24:15, 21

7 And when he had said this, a dissension arose between the Pharisees and the Sadducees; and the assembly was divided.

8 ᴿFor Sadducees say that there is no resurrection—and no angel or spirit; but the Pharisees confess both. Matt. 22:23

9 Then there arose a loud outcry. And the scribes of the Pharisees' party arose and protested, saying, "We find no evil in this man; *but if a spirit or an angel has spoken to him, let us not fight against God."

10 Now when there arose a great dissension, the commander, fearing lest Paul might be pulled to pieces by them, commanded the soldiers to go down and take him by force from among them, and bring *him* into the barracks.

The Plot Against Paul

11 But the following night the Lord stood by him and said, "Be of good cheer, Paul; for as you have testified for Me in Jerusalem, so you must also bear witness at Rome."

12 And when it was day, ᴿsome of the Jews banded together and bound themselves under an oath, saying that they would neither eat nor drink till they had killed Paul. Acts 23:21, 30

13 Now there were more than forty who had formed this conspiracy.

14 They came to the chief priests and ᴿelders, and said, "We have bound ourselves under a great oath that we will eat nothing until we have killed Paul. Acts 4:5, 23; 6:12

15 "Now you, therefore, together with the council, suggest to the commander that he be brought down to you *tomorrow, as though you were going to make further inquiries concerning him; but we are ready to kill him before he comes near."

16 So when Paul's sister's son heard of their ambush, he went and entered the barracks and told Paul.

17 Then Paul called one of the centurions to *him* and said, "Take this young man to the commander, for he has something to tell him."

18 So he took him and brought *him* to the commander and said, "Paul the prisoner called me to *him* and asked *me* to bring this young man to you. He has something to say to you."

19 Then the commander took him by the hand, went aside, and asked privately, "What is it that you have to tell me?"

20 And he said, ᴿ"The Jews have agreed to ask that you bring Paul down to the council tomorrow, as though they were going to inquire more fully about him. Acts 23:12

21 "But do not yield to them, for more than forty of them lie in wait for him, men who have bound themselves by an oath that they will neither eat nor drink till they have killed him; and now they are ready, waiting for the promise from you."

22 So the commander let the young man depart, and commanded *him*, "Tell no one that you have revealed these things to me."

Sent to Felix

23 And he called for two centurions, saying, "Prepare two hundred soldiers, seventy horsemen, and two hundred spearmen to go to Caesarea at the third hour of the night;

24 "and provide mounts to set Paul on, and bring *him* safely to Felix the governor."

25 He wrote a letter in the following manner:

26 Claudius Lysias,
To the most excellent governor Felix:
Greetings.

27 This man was seized by the Jews and was about to be killed by them.
Coming with the troops I rescued him, having learned that he was a Roman.

28 ᴿAnd when I wanted to know the reason they accused him, I brought him before their council. Acts 22:30

29 I found out that he was accused ᴿconcerning questions of their law, but had nothing charged against him deserving of death or chains. Acts 18:15

30 And ᴿwhen it was told me that *the Jews lay in wait for the man, I sent him immediately to you, and ᴿalso commanded his accusers to state before you the charges against him.
Farewell. Acts 23:20 • Acts 24:8; 25:6

31 Then the soldiers, as they were commanded, took Paul and brought *him* by night to Antipatris.

32 The next day they left the horsemen to go on with him, and returned to the barracks.

33 When they came to ᴿCaesarea and had delivered the ᴿletter to the governor, they also presented Paul to him. Acts 8:40 • Acts 23:26-30

34 And when the governor had read *it*, he asked what province he was from. And when he understood that *he was* from Cilicia,

35 he said, ᴿ"I will hear you when your accusers also have come." And he commanded him to be kept in ᴿHerod's ᵀPraetorium. Acts 24:1, 10; 25:16 • Matt. 27:27 • Headquarters

Accused of Sedition

24 Now after five days Ananias the high priest came down with the elders and

23:9 NU *what if a spirit or an angel has spoken to him?* and omits the last clause
23:15 NU omits *tomorrow*
23:30 NU *there would be a plot against the man*

a certain orator *named* Tertullus. These gave evidence to the governor against Paul.

2 And when he was called upon, Tertullus began his accusation, saying: "Seeing that through you we enjoy great peace, and ᵀprosperity is being brought to this nation by your foresight,   *Or reforms are*

3 "we accept *it* always and in all places, most noble Felix, with all thankfulness.

4 "Nevertheless, not to be tedious to you any further, I beg you to hear, by your ᵀcourtesy, a few words from us.   *graciousness*

5 ᴿ"For we have found this man *a* plague, a creator of dissension among all the Jews throughout the world, and a ringleader of the sect of the Nazarenes.   1 Pet. 2:12, 15

6 ᴿ"He even tried to profane the temple, and we seized him, *and wanted ᴿto judge him according to our law.   Acts 21:28 • John 18:31

7 ᴿ"But the commander Lysias came by and with great violence took *him* out of our hands,   Acts 21:33; 23:10

8 ᴿ"commanding his accusers to come to you. By examining him yourself you may ascertain all these things of which we accuse him."   Acts 23:30

9 And the Jews also *assented, maintaining that these things were so.

The Defense Before Felix

10 Then Paul, after the governor had nodded to him to speak, answered: "Inasmuch as I know that you have been for many years a judge of this nation, I do the more cheerfully answer for myself,

11 "because you may ascertain that it is no more than twelve days since I went up to Jerusalem ᴿto worship.   Acts 21:15, 18, 26, 27; 24:17

12 ᴿ"And they neither found me in the temple disputing with anyone nor inciting the crowd, either in the synagogues or in the city.   Acts 25:8; 28:17

13 "Nor can they prove the things of which they now accuse me.

14 "But this I confess to you, that according to ᴿthe Way which they call a sect, so I worship the ᴿGod of my fathers, believing all things which are written in the Law and in the Prophets.   Acts 9:2; 24:22 • 2 Tim. 1:3

15 ᴿ"I have hope in God, which they themselves also accept, ᴿthat there will be a resurrection *of *the* dead, both of *the* just and *the* unjust.   Acts 23:6; 26:6, 7; 28:20 • [Dan. 12:2]

16 ᴿ"This *being* so, I myself always strive to have a conscience without offense toward God and men.   Acts 23:1

17 "Now after many years ᴿI came to bring alms and offerings to my nation,   Rom. 15:25-28

18 "in the midst of which some Jews from Asia found me ᴿpurified in the temple, neither with a mob nor with tumult.   Acts 21:26

19 ᴿ"They ought to have been here before you to object if they had anything against me.   [Acts 23:30; 25:16]

20 "Or else let those who are *here* themselves say *if they found any wrongdoing in me while I stood before the council,

21 "unless *it is* for this one statement which I cried out, standing among them, ᴿ'Concerning the resurrection of the dead I am being judged by you this day.'"   [Acts 23:6; 24:15; 28:20]

Felix Procrastinates

22 But when Felix heard these things, having more accurate knowledge of *the* Way, he adjourned the proceedings and said, "When ᴿLysias the commander comes down, I will make a decision on your case."   Acts 23:26; 24:7

23 So he commanded the centurion to keep Paul and to let *him* have liberty, and ᴿtold him not to forbid any of his friends to provide for or visit him.   Acts 23:16; 27:3; 28:16

24 And after some days, when Felix came with his wife Drusilla, who was Jewish, he sent for Paul and heard him concerning the ᴿfaith in Christ.   [Rom. 10:9]

25 Now as he reasoned about righteousness, self-control, and the judgment to come, Felix was afraid and answered, "Go away for now; when I have a convenient time I will call for you."

26 Meanwhile he also hoped that ᴿmoney would be given him by Paul, *that he might release him. Therefore he sent for him more often and conversed with him.   Ex. 23:8

27 But after two years Porcius Festus succeeded Felix; and Felix, ᴿwanting to do the Jews a favor, left Paul bound.   Acts 12:3; 23:35

Paul Appeals to Caesar

25 Now when Festus had come to the province, after three days he went up from ᴿCaesarea to Jerusalem.   Acts 8:40; 25:4, 6, 13

2 ᴿThen the *high priest and the chief men of the Jews informed him against Paul; and they petitioned him,   Acts 24:1; 25:15

3 asking a favor against him, that he would summon him to Jerusalem—while *they* lay in ambush along the road to kill him.

4 But Festus answered that Paul should be kept at Caesarea, and that he himself was going *there* shortly.

5 "Therefore," he said, "let those who have authority among you go down with *me* and accuse this man, to see ᴿif there is any fault in him."   Acts 18:14; 25:18

6 And when he had remained among them

24:6 NU ends the sentence here and omits the rest of v. 6, all of v. 7, and the first clause of v. 8.
24:9 NU, M *joined the attack*
24:15 NU omits *of the dead*

24:20 NU, M *what wrongdoing they found*
24:26 NU omits *that he might release him*
25:2 NU *chief priests*

more than ten days, he went down to Caesarea. And the next day, sitting on the judgment seat, he commanded Paul to be brought.

7 When he had come, the Jews who had come down from Jerusalem stood about ᴿand laid many serious complaints against Paul, which they could not prove,   Acts 24:5, 13

8 while he answered for himself, ᴿ"Neither against the law of the Jews, nor against the temple, nor against Caesar have I offended in anything at all."   Acts 6:13; 24:12; 28:17

9 But Festus, wanting to do the Jews a favor, answered Paul and said, "Are you willing to go up to Jerusalem and there be judged before me concerning these things?"

10 So Paul said, "I stand at Caesar's judgment seat, where I ought to be judged. To the Jews I have done no wrong, as you very well know.

11 ᴿ"For if I am an offender, or have committed anything deserving of death, I do not object to dying; but if there is nothing in these things of which these men accuse me, no one can deliver me to them. ᴿI appeal to Caesar."   Acts 18:14; 23:29; 25:25; 26:31 · Acts 26:32; 28:19

12 Then Festus, when he had conferred with the council, answered, "You have appealed to Caesar? To Caesar you shall go!"

Paul Before Agrippa

13 And after some days King Agrippa and Bernice came to Caesarea to greet Festus.

14 When they had been there many days, Festus laid Paul's case before the king, saying: ᴿ"There is a certain man left a prisoner by Felix,   Acts 24:27

15 ᴿ"about whom the chief priests and the elders of the Jews informed me, when I was in Jerusalem, asking for a judgment against him.   Acts 24:1; 25:2, 3

16 ᴿ"To them I answered, 'It is not the custom of the Romans to deliver any man *to destruction before the accused meets the accusers face to face, and has opportunity to answer for himself concerning the charge against him.'   Acts 25:4, 5

17 "Therefore when they had come together, ᴿwithout any delay, the next day I sat on the judgment seat and commanded the man to be brought in.   Acts 25:6, 10

18 "When the accusers stood up, they brought no accusation against him of such things as I ᵀsupposed,   suspected

19 ᴿ"but had some questions against him about their own religion and about a certain Jesus, who had died, whom Paul affirmed to be alive.   Acts 18:14, 15; 23:29

20 "And because I was uncertain of such questions, I asked whether he was willing to go to Jerusalem and there be judged concerning these matters.

25:16 NU omits to destruction

21 "But when Paul ᴿappealed to be reserved for the decision of Augustus, I commanded him to be kept till I could send him to Caesar."   Acts 25:11, 12

22 Then ᴿAgrippa said to Festus, "I also would like to hear the man myself." "Tomorrow," he said, "you shall hear him."   Acts 9:15

23 So the next day, when Agrippa and Bernice had come with great ᵀpomp, and had entered the auditorium with the commanders and the prominent men of the city, at Festus' command Paul was brought in.   pageantry

24 And Festus said: "King Agrippa and all the men who are here present with us, you see this man about whom ᴿthe whole assembly of the Jews petitioned me, both at Jerusalem and here, crying out that he was ᴿnot fit to live any longer.   Acts 25:2, 3, 7 · Acts 21:36; 22:22

25 "But when I found that ᴿhe had committed nothing deserving of death, ᴿand that he himself had appealed to Augustus, I decided to send him.   Acts 23:9, 29; 26:31 · Acts 25:11, 12

26 "I have nothing certain to write to my lord concerning him. Therefore I have brought him out before you, and especially before you, King Agrippa, so that after the examination has taken place I may have something to write.

27 "For it seems to me unreasonable to send a prisoner and not to specify the charges against him."

Paul's Early Life

26 Then Agrippa said to Paul, "You are permitted to speak for yourself." So Paul stretched out his hand and answered for himself:

2 "I think myself happy, King Agrippa, because today I shall answer ᴿfor myself before you concerning all the things of which I am accused by the Jews,   [1 Pet. 3:15, 16]

3 "especially because you are expert in all customs and questions which have to do with the Jews. Therefore I beg you to hear me patiently.

4 "My manner of life from my youth, which was spent from the beginning among my own nation at Jerusalem, all the Jews know.

5 "They knew me from the first, if they were willing to testify, that according to the strictest sect of our religion I lived a Pharisee.

6 ᴿ"And now I stand and am judged for the hope of ᴿthe promise made by God to our fathers.   Acts 23:6 · Acts 13:32

7 "To this promise ᴿour twelve tribes, earnestly serving God night and day, ᴿhope to attain. For this hope's sake, King Agrippa, I am accused by the Jews.   James 1:1 · Phil. 3:1

8 "Why should it be thought incredible by you that God raises the dead?

9 ᴿ"Indeed, I myself thought I must do

many things ᵀcontrary to the name of ᴿJesus of Nazareth.   1 Tim. 1:12, 13 • *against* • Acts 2:22; 10:38

10 ᴿ"This I also did in Jerusalem, and many of the saints I shut up in prison, having received authority ᴿfrom the chief priests; and when they were put to death, I cast my vote against *them.*   Acts 8:1-3; 9:13 • Acts 9:14

11 ᴿ"And I punished them often in every synagogue and compelled *them* to blaspheme; and being exceedingly enraged against them, I persecuted *them* even to foreign cities.   Acts 22:19

Paul Recounts His Conversion

12 ᴿ"While thus occupied, as I journeyed to Damascus with authority and commission from the chief priests,   Acts 9:3-8; 22:6-11; 26:12-18

13 "at midday, O king, along the road I saw a light from heaven, brighter than the sun, shining around me and those who journeyed with me.

14 "And when we all had fallen to the ground, I heard a voice speaking to me and saying in the Hebrew language, 'Saul, Saul, why are you persecuting Me? *It is* hard for you to kick against the goads.'

15 "So I said, 'Who are You, Lord?' And He said, 'I am Jesus, whom you are persecuting.

16 'But rise and stand on your feet; for I have appeared to you for this purpose, ᴿto make you a minister and a witness both of the things which you have seen and of the things which I will yet reveal to you. Acts 22:15

17 'I will ᵀdeliver you from the *Jewish* people, as well as *from* the Gentiles, ᴿto whom I *now send you,   rescue* • Acts 22:21

18 'to open their eyes, *in order* to turn *them* from darkness to light, and *from* the power of Satan to God, that they may receive forgive-

26:17 NU, M omit *now*

ness of sins and an inheritance among those who are ᵀsanctified by faith in Me.'   *set apart*

22-G. Repentance: The Evidence   ▼

Paul's Post-Conversion Life

19 "Therefore, King Agrippa, I was not disobedient to the heavenly vision,

20 "but declared first to those in Damascus and in Jerusalem, and throughout all the region of Judea, and *then* to the Gentiles, that they should repent, turn to God, and do ᴿworks befitting repentance.   Matt. 3:8 ▲

21 "For these reasons the Jews seized me in the temple and tried to kill *me.*

22 "Therefore, having obtained help from God, to this day I stand, witnessing both to small and great, saying no other things than those ᴿwhich the prophets and ᴿMoses said would come—   Rom. 3:21 • John 5:46

23 ᴿ"that the Christ would suffer, that He would be the first to rise from the dead, and ᴿwould proclaim light to the *Jewish* people and to the Gentiles."   Luke 24:26 • Luke 2:32

Agrippa Parries Paul's Challenge

24 Now as he thus made his defense, Festus said with a loud voice, "Paul, you are beside yourself! Much learning is driving you mad!"

25 But he said, "I am not ᵀmad, most noble Festus, but speak the words of truth and reason.   *out of my mind*

26 "For the king, before whom I also speak freely, ᴿknows these things; for I am convinced that none of these things escapes his attention, since this thing was not done in a corner.   Acts 26:3

27 "King Agrippa, do you believe the prophets? I know that you do believe."

28 Then Agrippa said to Paul, "You almost persuade me to become a Christian."

22-G. Repentance: The Evidence (Acts 26:19, 20)—The evidence of repentance toward God and faith in our Lord Jesus Christ is seen in many cases:

(1) Unbelieving Thomas repented (John 20:24–29, page 1083). Thomas would not believe that Christ had been raised from the dead until he saw the risen Savior, was given the opportunity to touch His nail-pierced hands, and thrust his hand into His wounded side. Thomas repented, believed, and made his confession of faith, "My Lord and my God!"

(2) Three thousand changed their minds, hearts, and wills on the Day of Pentecost, and immediately gave evidence of repentance (Acts 2:41–47, page 1090).

(3) Saul of Tarsus experienced repentance when he met Jesus on the Damascus road, and gave evidence of repentance (Acts 9:1–22, page 1100).

(4) Cornelius, his family, and his friends repented when they heard the gospel preached by Simon Peter, and evidence of repentance followed (Acts 10:24–48, page 1103).

(5) The Philippian jailer and his house repented when Paul and Silas witnessed to them; the evidence of repentance followed (Acts 16:26–34, page 1111). Repentance is a change of mind, heart, and will.

The proof of repentance is

(1) turning from sin (Ezek. 18:30, page 794);
(2) turning to God;
(3) good deeds following (v. 20).

See Index, page 17, for your next study.

29 And Paul said, "I would to God that not only you, but also all who hear me today, might become both almost and altogether such as I am, except for these chains."

30 When he had said these things, the king stood up, as well as the governor and Bernice and those who sat with them;

31 and when they had gone aside, they talked among themselves, saying, "This man is doing nothing deserving of death or chains."

32 Then Agrippa said to Festus, "This man might have been set Rfree Rif he had not appealed to Caesar."   Acts 28:18 • Acts 25:11

The Voyage to Rome Begins

27 And when it was decided that we should sail to Italy, they delivered Paul and some other prisoners to one named Julius, a centurion of the Augustan Regiment.

2 So, entering a ship of Adramyttium, we put to sea, meaning to sail along the coasts of Asia. RAristarchus, a Macedonian of Thessalonica, was with us.   Acts 19:29

3 And the next day we landed at Sidon. And Julius treated Paul kindly and gave him liberty to go to his friends and receive care.

4 When we had put to sea from there, we sailed under the shelter of Cyprus, because the winds were contrary.

5 And when we had sailed over the sea which is off Cilicia and Pamphylia, we came to Myra, a city of Lycia.

6 There the centurion found Ran Alexandrian ship sailing to Italy, and he put us on board.   Acts 28:11

7 When we had sailed slowly many days, and arrived with difficulty off Cnidus, the wind not permitting us to proceed, we sailed under the shelter of Crete off Salmone.

8 Passing it with difficulty, we came to a place called Fair Havens, near the city of Lasea.

Paul's Warning Ignored

9 Now when much time had been spent, and sailing was now dangerous because the Fast was already over, Paul advised them,

10 saying, "Men, I perceive that this voyage will end with disaster and much loss, not only of the cargo and ship, but also our lives."

11 Nevertheless the centurion was more persuaded by the helmsman and the owner of the ship than by the things spoken by Paul.

12 And because the harbor was not suitable to winter in, the majority advised to set sail from there also, if by any means they could reach Phoenix, a harbor of Crete opening toward the southwest and northwest, and winter there.

In the Tempest

13 When the south wind blew softly, supposing that they had obtained their desire, putting out to sea, they sailed close by Crete.

14 But not long after, a tempestuous head wind arose, called *Euroclydon.

15 So when the ship was caught, and could not head into the wind, we let her drive.

16 And running under the shelter of an island called *Clauda, we secured the skiff with difficulty.

17 When they had taken it on board, they used cables to undergird the ship; and fearing lest they should run aground on the *Syrtis Sands, they struck sail and so were driven.

18 And because we were exceedingly tempest-tossed, the next day they lightened the ship.

19 On the third day Rwe threw the ship's tackle overboard with our own hands.   Jon. 1:5

20 Now when neither sun nor stars appeared for many days, and no small tempest beat on us, all hope that we would be saved was finally given up.

21 But after long abstinence from food, then Paul stood in the midst of them and said, "Men, you should have listened to me, and not have sailed from Crete and incurred this disaster and loss.

22 "And now I urge you to take Theart, for there will be no loss of life among you, but only of the ship.   courage

23 R"For there stood by me this night an angel of the God to whom I belong and Rwhom I serve,   Acts 18:9; 23:11 • Dan. 6:16

24 "saying, 'Do not be afraid, Paul; you must be brought before Caesar; and indeed God has granted you all those who sail with you.'

25 "Therefore take heart, men, for I believe God that it will be just as it was told me.

26 "However, Rwe must run aground on a certain island."   Acts 28:1

27 Now when the fourteenth night had come, as we were driven up and down in the Adriatic Sea, about midnight the sailors sensed that they were drawing near some land.

28 And they took soundings and found it to be Ttwenty fathoms; and when they had gone a little farther, they took soundings again and found it to be Tfifteen fathoms.   120 ft. • 90 ft.

29 Then, fearing lest we should run aground on the rocks, they dropped four anchors from the stern, and prayed for day to come.

30 And as the sailors were seeking to escape from the ship, when they had let down the skiff into the sea, under pretense of putting out anchors from the prow,

31 Paul said to the centurion and the sol-

27:14 A southeast wind that stirs up broad waves; NU
Euraquilon, a northeaster
27:16 NU *Cauda*
27:17 M *Syrtes*

diers, "Unless these men stay in the ship, you cannot be saved."

32 Then the soldiers cut away the ropes of the skiff and let it fall off.

33 And as day was about to dawn, Paul implored *them* all to take food, saying, "Today is the fourteenth day you have waited and continued without food, and eaten nothing.

34 "Therefore I urge you to take nourishment, for this is for your survival, since not a hair will fall from the head of any of you."

35 And when he had said these things, he took bread and ᴿgave thanks to God in the presence of them all; and when he had broken *it* he began to eat.   [1 Tim. 4:3, 4]

36 Then they were all encouraged, and also took food themselves.

37 And in all we were two hundred and seventy-six ᴿpersons on the ship. Acts 2:41; 7:14

38 So when they had eaten enough, they lightened the ship and threw out the wheat into the sea.

Shipwrecked on Malta

39 When it was day, they did not recognize the land; but they observed a bay with a beach, onto which they planned to run the ship if possible.

40 And they ᵀlet go the anchors and left *them* in the sea, meanwhile loosing the rudder ropes; and they hoisted the mainsail to the wind and made for shore.   *cast off*

41 But striking ᵀa place where two seas met, ᴿthey ran the ship aground; and the prow stuck fast and remained immovable, but the stern was being broken up by the violence of the waves.   A reef · 2 Cor. 11:25

42 And the soldiers' plan was to kill the prisoners, lest any of them should swim away and escape.

43 But the centurion, wanting to save Paul, kept them from *their* purpose, and commanded that those who could swim should jump *overboard* first and get to land,

44 and the rest, some on boards and some on *parts* of the ship. And so it was that they all escaped safely to land.

Paul's Ministry on Malta

28 Now when they had escaped, they then found out that ᴿthe island was called Malta.   Acts 27:26

2 And the ᵀnatives showed us unusual kindness; for they kindled a fire and made us all welcome, because of the rain that was falling and because of the cold.   Lit. *barbarians*

3 But when Paul had gathered a bundle of sticks and laid *them* on the fire, a viper came out because of the heat, and fastened on his hand.

4 So when the natives saw the creature hanging from his hand, they said to one another, "No doubt this man is a murderer, whom, though he has escaped the sea, yet justice does not allow to live."

5 But he shook off the creature into the fire and ᴿsuffered no harm.   Mark 16:18

6 However, they were expecting that he would swell up or suddenly fall down dead. But after they had looked for a long time and saw no harm come to him, they changed their minds and said that he was a god.

7 In that region there was an estate of the ᵀleading citizen of the island, whose name was Publius, who received us and entertained us courteously for three days.   Magistrate

8 And it happened that the father of Publius lay sick of a fever and dysentery. Paul went in to him and ᴿprayed, and he laid his hands on him and healed him.   [James 5:14, 15]

9 So when this was done, the rest of those on the island who had diseases also came and were healed.

10 They also honored us in many ᴿways; and when we departed, they provided such things as were ᴿnecessary.   Matt. 15:6 · [Phil. 4:19]

Arrival at Rome

11 After three months we sailed in an Alexandrian ship whose figurehead was the ᵀTwin Brothers, which had wintered at the island.   Gr. *Dioskouroi,* Zeus's sons Castor and Pollux

12 And landing at Syracuse, we stayed three days.

13 From there we circled round and reached Rhegium. And after one day the south wind blew; and the next day we came to Puteoli,

14 where we found ᴿbrethren, and were invited to stay with them seven days. And so we went toward Rome.   Rom. 1:8

15 And from there, when the brethren heard about us, they came to meet us as far as Appii Forum and Three Inns. When Paul saw them, he thanked God and took courage.

16 Now when we came to Rome, the centurion delivered the prisoners to the captain of the guard; but ᴿPaul was permitted to dwell by himself with the soldier who guarded him.   Acts 23:11; 24:25; 27:3

Paul's Ministry at Rome

17 And it came to pass after three days that Paul called the leaders of the Jews together. So when they had come together, he said to them: "Men *and* brethren, ᴿthough I have done nothing against our people or the customs of our fathers, yet ᴿI was delivered as a prisoner from Jerusalem into the hands of the Romans,   Acts 23:29; 24:12, 13; 26:31 · Acts 21:33

18 "who, ᴿwhen they had examined me,

wanted to let *me* go, because there was no cause for putting me to death. Acts 22:24; 24:10

19 "But when the *Jews spoke against it, I was compelled to appeal to Caesar, not that I had anything of which to accuse my nation.

20 "For this reason therefore I have called for you, to see *you* and speak with *you*, because ᴿfor the hope of Israel I am bound with ᴿthis chain." Acts 26:6, 7 • Eph. 3:1; 4:1; 6:20

21 Then they said to him, "We neither received letters from Judea concerning you, nor have any of the brethren who came reported or spoken any evil of you.

22 "But we desire to hear from you what you think; for concerning this sect, we know that it is spoken against everywhere."

23 So when they had appointed him a day, many came to him at *his* lodging, to whom he explained and solemnly testified of the kingdom of God, persuading them concerning Jesus from both the Law of Moses and the Prophets, from morning till evening.

24 And some were persuaded by the things which were spoken, and some disbelieved.

25 So when they did not agree among themselves, they departed after Paul had said one word: "The Holy Spirit spoke rightly through Isaiah the prophet to *our fathers,

28:19 The ruling authorities
28:25 NU *your*

26 "saying,

ᴿ'Go to this people and say:
"Hearing you will hear, and shall not understand;
And seeing you will see, and not perceive; Is. 6:9, 10
27 For the hearts of this people have grown dull.
Their ears are hard of hearing,
And their eyes they have closed,
Lest they should see with their eyes and hear with their ears,
Lest they should understand with their hearts and turn,
So that I should heal them.' '

28 "Therefore let it be known to you that the salvation of God has been sent ᴿto the Gentiles, and they will hear it!" Is. 42:1; 49:6

29 *And when he had said these words, the Jews departed and had a great dispute among themselves.

30 Then Paul dwelt two whole years in his own rented house, and received all who came to him,

31 ᴿpreaching the kingdom of God and teaching the things which concern the Lord Jesus Christ with all confidence, no one forbidding him. Eph. 6:19

28:29 NU omits v. 29.

THE EPISTLE OF PAUL THE APOSTLE TO THE

Romans

To open the Letter to the Romans is all at once . . .
—To step into a diamond mine where gems of truth sparkle within immediate reach, and more await one's deeper probing;
—To sit down to a table where a rich combination of dietary basics is supplemented by gourmet delicacies providing both fundamental spiritual nourishment and the highest spiritual satisfaction;
—To plunge into a refreshing pond where the surface glistens in the sunlight with a warm welcome to godliness, and where the depths summon the diver to explore the splendor of the Almighty's grandest workings.

Writers exhaust hyperbole in attempting to describe Romans. But whatever else may be said, it is the believer's Magna Carta; it sets forth the pathway by which you and I can enter full understanding and live in full freedom. And it opens the way to our possessing the full dimensions of the spiritual real estate intended for us through the salvation Jesus Christ has purchased for us all.

AUTHORSHIP AND CONTEXT. The facts given us in the book of Acts join with specific statements in Romans to pinpoint precisely the time, place, and reason for its writing. It was written by Paul in the winter season which concluded A.D. 57, and continued into the New Year of 58. The time was during the three-month visit the apostle made to Corinth while waiting for the springtime shipping season to reopen, thereby allowing his trip to Jerusalem, at which time he would bring the corporate financial gift the Gentile churches had prepared to assist the needy, famine-stricken brethren in Judea (15:25, 26; cf. Acts 11:28–30).

KEY VERSE. The key verse 1:17, the verse the Holy Spirit used to usher in the great Protestant Reformation—"For in it the righteousness of God is revealed from faith to faith; as it is written, 'The just shall live by faith.' "

KEY WORDS. The key words are *justify*, *justification*, *righteous*, and *righteousness* (all the same root word in the original Greek).

HOW ROMANS FITS TOGETHER. Romans may be neatly divided into two parts, Doctrinal (chs. 1—11) and Dutiful (chs. 12—16). A more precise outline that does justice to the important section on God's unique dealings with Israel is as follows.
   (1) Chapters 1—8 are *Doctrinal:* Paul traces salvation from the depravity of man, through Christ's redemption, and the triumph in the Holy Spirit.
   (2) Chapters 9—11 are *Dispensational:* Paul traces God's special dealings with Israel, how they are only temporarily set aside and will have a wonderful future when they accept their Messiah.
   (3) Chapters 12—16 are *Dutiful:* Paul traces the duties of the Christian life, starting with presenting one's body to the Lord, and ultimately serving all those who are over us, our peers, and even those we may think beneath us.

The scope and profundity of the Roman Letter are such that an unfortunate human tendency plagues the common use of its contents. Scholars, revelling in its depths, often unintentionally intimidate the average simpler approach. Of course, it is unquestionable that Paul's intent in writing was filled with a sense of divine wonder and destiny which challenges the finest mind: "Oh, the depth of the riches both of the wisdom and knowledge of God! How unsearchable are His judgments and His ways past finding out! . . . For of Him and through Him and to Him are all things, to whom be glory forever. Amen" (11:33, 36). And yet it is equally certain that his focus, and the Holy Spirit's purpose, was to set forth truth which might be as easily grasped by the most ordinary reader as by the extraordinary student: "Paul . . . to all who are in Rome, beloved of God, called to be saints" (1:1, 7). The intensely practical, pastoral and personal features of the letter stand out with sufficient prominence to remove any notion that Romans is only a theologian's domain.

Paul's multifaceted ministry as an apostle, a preacher (evangelist), and a teacher to the nations (1 Tim. 2:7) shines forth in this epistle. Each aspect of his threefold ministry brings a distinct quality to Romans, all of which balance together to form this divinely inspired letter. We discover here (1) an *apostle* writing with a sense of infinity, (2) an *evangelist* writing with a sense of intensity, and (3) a *pastor* writing with a sense of integrity.

AN APOSTLE'S SENSE OF INFINITY. Understanding the strategy in the timing of this book's writing is essential to seeing the purpose in its content and structure. It is not the product of a man bent on impressing anyone with either philosophy or theology. It is an overflow of the heart of a man who sees the unfolding of a new hour for spiritual footings to provide a base from which he might seize that hour of possibility.

Paul's eyes are westward. Three missionary journeys throughout Asia Minor and Greece have been accomplished with much fruit. Special penetration to the East has emanated from his three years of ministry in Ephesus (Acts 19:20, 26). Now, the Holy Spirit, who first thrust him into Europe with the Macedonian vision years before, is prompting a desire to extend the impact of the kingdom of God to the westernmost regions of the Roman Empire, with the capital city as a new base for his outreach (Acts 19:21).

A strong group of believers already exists in Rome, and Paul's style is not to build on another man's foundation (Rom. 15:20). Therefore, he will not so much focus his ministry on those in Rome as to develop a relationship with them there. Then, he clearly hopes to enlist the help of these believers to assist in the fulfillment of his global vision (15:23, 24). This epistle, then, becomes a dual instrument: first, a means for blessing the Body in Rome (15:32) and second, a calling card, fully presenting the root system of the apostle's message ("my gospel," 2:16) and its practical applications. In a very real sense, Romans says, "This is my gospel as I preach and teach it. Let's partner together to spread it everywhere."

Thus, a sense of timelessness—of infinity—is woven into the spirit of this book. It reflects an eternal sense of destiny borne by a heart which sees the kingdom of God as intended to penetrate the central city of the Empire and as destined to reach its most distant perimeter. Timeless truth is presented to establish the basis of a relationship between the apostle and his potential supporters (15:28-32), while he declares the irresistible reality of that truth, fully expecting its power to manifest itself wherever this message is extended (1:13-17).

AN EVANGELIST'S SENSE OF INTENSITY. But the writer is not only a strategizing apostle, he is an impassioned preacher—an evangelist with unshakable convictions and unswerving confidence.

He is persuaded that the witness of God's person and power is in every human heart by reason of creation's testimony (1:19, 20); but that unless the clear message of the gospel of Christ is preached to them they cannot experience living faith (10:14, 15).

He is blunt in his assessment of the fruit of human sin, arrogance and perversion (1:21-32), but equally bold in describing the potential of God's forgiveness for any and all sins through the provision of the Lord Jesus Christ (3:9-26).

He is brutal in his denial to the Jew of any privileged position before God by reason of his religious tradition (2:17-24). Yet, in the interest of the same Jew, he requires priority be observed, that they should have the opportunity of a first hearing of the gospel (1:16, 17); and he declares his confidence that God's sovereign purposes shall ultimately triumph over, beyond, and through whatever rejection of the gospel the Jewish establishment has shown (chs. 9—11).

He declares that the grounds for the good news of man's full justification from sin and the possibility of total transformation by the Holy Spirit are God's grace (3:24), the blood of Jesus (3:25; 5:9), faith (3:26, 28), and the resurrection of Christ (4:24, 25).

The gospel resounds throughout this book, throbbing and pulsating from the heart of a man whose mission is to announce that a new era in human history has been introduced through Jesus Christ (5:12-21). What would eventually characterize the season of ministry he would conduct in their city (Acts 28:30, 31) is outlined here with passion and clarity.

A PASTOR'S SENSE OF INTEGRITY. As strategically apostolic or as passionately evangelistic as the epistle to the Romans may be, it is, above all, thoroughly pastoral. This is true in the sense that the truth unfolded is completely integrated into the practical details of daily living. The Gospel is not only held forth as truth in the sense of being correct, but as truth in the sense of bringing completeness.

Romans is doctrinal, but the mistake many people make about doctrine is supposing it is only ideological—just ideas to be believed. In fact, the Greek word didache ("doctrine," 6:17) means nothing more profound than teaching: truth to be learned so it may be lived. And throughout this letter, Paul the pastor, who planted so many churches and who stayed to shepherd two of them at length (Corinth and Ephesus), manifests an integrity with the truth. He insists that it be incarnated into practical life, not merely presented as a system of thought.

He presses for a life that appropriates what Christ's death and resurrection have accomplished, and with which the believer identifies (ch. 6).

He presents a solution to the frustrating sense of failure which so frequently besets sincere believers trying to cope with their old nature (ch. 7).

He proceeds to describe the Spirit-filled life in a way that moves from triumph over condemnation all the way to triumph over any and all adversity (ch. 8).

No epistle gives more explicit directives for the practical application of spiritual truth to the problems of daily life or the challenges of faithful service than this one (chs. 12—14). The heart of a pastor is manifestly faithful to show people what to do with what they believe.

Thus, the full-orbed ministry of Paul seems to be blended into one—the apostolic, the evangelistic, and the pastoral—and the Holy Spirit's inspirational breath and touch through the vessel of this gifted life present us with this masterpiece of doctrine coupled with a masterpiece of practical wisdom. Luther, speaking about Romans, said each believer should "not only know it word for word by heart but deal with it daily as with daily bread of the soul. For it can never be read or considered too much or too well, and the more it is handled, the more delightful it becomes, and the better it tastes."

—J.W.H.

Greeting

PAUL, a bondservant of Jesus Christ, Rcalled to be an apostle, Rseparated to the gospel of God   1 Tim. 1:11 • Acts 9:15; 13:2

2 which He promised before Rthrough His prophets in the Holy Scriptures,   Gal. 3:8

3 concerning His Son Jesus Christ our Lord, who Twas Rborn of the seed of David according to the flesh,   came • Is. 9:7; Gal. 4:4

4 and Rdeclared to be the Son of God with power according to the Spirit of holiness, by the resurrection from the dead. Ps. 2:7; 16:10, 11

5 Through Him we have received grace and apostleship for obedience to the faith among all nations Rfor His name,   Acts 9:15

6 among whom you also are the called of Jesus Christ;

7 To all who are in Rome, beloved of God, Rcalled to be saints: 1 Cor. 1:2, 24

RGrace to you and peace from God our Father and the Lord Jesus Christ.   1 Cor. 1:3

Desire to Visit Rome

8 First, I thank my God through Jesus Christ for you all, that Ryour faith is spoken of throughout the whole world.   Rom. 16:19

9 For God is my witness, whom I serve Twith my spirit in the gospel of His Son, that Rwithout ceasing I make mention of you always in my prayers,   Or in • 1 Thess. 3:10

10 making request if, by some means, now at last I may find a way in the will of God to come to you.

11 For I long to see you, that RI may impart to you some spiritual gift, so that you may be established—   Rom. 15:29

12 that is, that I may be encouraged together with you by Rthe mutual faith both of you and me.   Titus 1:4

13 Now I do not want you to be unaware, brethren, that I often planned to come to you (but Rwas hindered until now), that I might have some fruit among you also, just as among the other Gentiles.   [1 Thess. 2:18]

14 I am a debtor both to Greeks and to barbarians, both to wise and to unwise.

15 So, as much as is in me, I am ready to preach the gospel to you who are in Rome also.

The Just Live by Faith

16 For I am not ashamed of the gospel *of Christ, for Rit is the power of God to salvation for everyone who believes, Rfor the Jew first and also for the Greek.   1 Cor. 1:18, 24 • Acts 3:26

17 For in it the righteousness of God is revealed from faith to faith; as it is written, R"The just shall live by faith."   Hab. 2:4

19-B. The Nature of Man's Ruin   ▼

God's Wrath on Unrighteousness

18 RFor the wrath of God is revealed from heaven against all ungodliness and unrighteousness of men, who Tsuppress the truth in unrighteousness,   [Acts 17:30] • hold down

19 because Rwhat may be known of God is Tmanifest Tin them, for RGod has shown it to them.   [Acts 14:17; 17:24] • evident • among • [John 1:9]

20 For since the creation of the world RHis invisible attributes are clearly seen, being

1:16 NU omits of Christ

19-B. The Nature of Man's Ruin (Romans 1:18–32)—When Adam sinned he did not fall alone; the whole human race fell with him. He effected the ruin of all his seed (descendants). This is what David meant when he said, "Behold, I was brought forth in iniquity, and in sin my mother conceived me" (Ps. 51:5, page 541). David was not saying that conception in marriage is sinful; he was emphasizing the fact that he was born of the ruined descendants of Adam, i.e., ruined by Adam's original sin.

(Point 19-B continued on next page)

▽ understood by the things that are made, *even* His eternal power and ᵀGodhead, so that they are without excuse,   Ps. 19:1-6 • *divine nature*

21 because, although they knew God, they did not glorify *Him* as God, nor were thankful, but ᴿbecame futile in their thoughts, and their foolish hearts were darkened.   Jer. 2:5

22 ᴿProfessing to be wise, they became fools,   Jer. 10:14

23 and changed the glory of the incorruptible ᴿGod into an image made like ᵀcorruptible man—and birds and four-footed animals and creeping things.   Deut. 4:16-18 • *perishable*

24 Therefore God also gave them up to uncleanness, in the lusts of their hearts, to dishonor their bodies among themselves,

25 who exchanged ᴿthe truth of God ᴿfor the lie, and worshiped and served the creature rather than the Creator, who is blessed forever. Amen.   1 Thess. 1:9 • Is. 44:20

26 For this reason God gave them up to ᴿvile passions. For even their ᵀwomen exchanged the natural use for what is against nature.   Lev. 18:22 • Lit. *females*

27 Likewise also the ᵀmen, leaving the natural use of the ᵀwoman, burned in their lust for one another, ᵀmen with ᵀmen committing what is shameful, and receiving in themselves the penalty of their error which was due.   Lit. *males* • Lit. *female* • Lit. *males* • Lit. *males*

28 And even as they did not like to retain God in *their* knowledge, God gave them over to a debased mind, to do those things ᴿwhich are not fitting;   Eph. 5:4

29 being filled with all unrighteousness, *sexual immorality, wickedness, ᵀcovetousness, ᵀmaliciousness; full of envy, murder, strife, deceit, evil-mindedness; *they are* whisperers,   greed • *malice*

30 backbiters, haters of God, violent, proud, boasters, inventors of evil things, disobedient to parents,

31 ᵀundiscerning, untrustworthy, unloving, *unforgiving, unmerciful;   *without understanding*

32 who, ᴿknowing the righteous judgment of God, that those who practice such things

1:29 NU omits *sexual immorality*
1:31 NU omits *unforgiving*

ᴿare deserving of death, not only do the same but also ᴿapprove of those who practice them.   [Rom. 2:2] • [Rom. 6:21] • Hos. 7:3 ▲

God's Righteous Judgment

2 Therefore you are ᴿinexcusable, O man, whoever you are who judge, ᴿfor in whatever you judge another you condemn yourself; for you who judge practice the same things.   [Rom. 1:20] • [Matt. 7:1-5]

2 But we know that the judgment of God is according to truth against those who practice such things.

3 And do you think this, O man, you who judge those practicing such things, and doing the same, that you will escape the judgment of God?

4 Or do you despise ᴿthe riches of His goodness, ᴿforbearance, and longsuffering, not knowing that the goodness of God leads you to repentance?   [Eph. 1:7, 18; 2:7] • [Rom. 3:25]

5 But in accordance with your hardness and your ᵀimpenitent heart ᴿyou are ᵀtreasuring up for yourself wrath in the day of wrath and revelation of the righteous judgment of God,   *unrepentant* • [Deut. 32:34] • *storing*

6 who ᴿ*"will render to each one according to his deeds"*:   Ps. 62:12; Prov. 24:12

7 eternal life to those who by patient continuance in doing good seek for glory, honor, and immortality;

8 but to those who are self-seeking and ᴿdo not obey the truth, but obey unrighteousness—indignation and wrath,   [2 Thess. 1:8]

9 tribulation and anguish, on every soul of man who does evil, of the Jew ᴿfirst and also of the ᵀGreek;   1 Pet. 4:17 • *Gentile*

10 ᴿbut glory, honor, and peace to everyone who works what is good, to the Jew first and also to the Greek.   [1 Pet. 1:7]

11 For there is no partiality with God.

12 For as many as have sinned without law will also perish without law, and as many as have sinned in the law will be judged by the law

13 (for ᴿnot the hearers of the law *are* just in the sight of God, but the doers of the law will be justified;   [James 1:22, 25]

14 for when Gentiles, who do not have the

(Point 19-B continued from previous page)
There are two ways in which man demonstrates the nature of his ruin:

(1) *Spiritual depravity, which is spiritual wickedness.* They "suppress the truth in unrighteousness" (Rom. 1:18, page 1128) by preaching another gospel (Gal. 1:6–10, page 1178). Or they deny God's very existence. "Professing to be wise, they became fools" (v. 22). They are humanistic, i.e., they proclaim the supremacy of man and deny God in their religious philosophy; they make gods of themselves (vv. 18–23).

(2) *Moral depravity.* God is against all ungodliness, whether it be spiritual or moral, of which sexual promiscuity and homosexuality are most prominent as in the days of Sodom and Gomorrah. "For the wrath of God is revealed from heaven against all ungodliness and unrighteousness of men" (v. 18). "Therefore God also gave them up to uncleanness, in the lusts of their hearts, to dishonor their bodies among themselves" (vv. 24–32).

See 1 Corinthians 15:22, page 1161, for **Point 19-C: The Results of Man's Ruin.**

law, by nature do the things in the law, these, although not having the law, are a law to themselves,

15 who show the work of the law written in their hearts, their conscience also bearing witness, and between themselves *their* thoughts accusing or else excusing *them)*

16 ᴿin the day when God will judge the secrets of men ᴿby Jesus Christ, ᴿaccording to my gospel.   [Matt. 25:31] • Acts 10:42; 17:31 • 1 Tim. 1:11

The Jews Guilty as the Gentiles

17 *Indeed you are called a Jew, and rest on the law, and make your boast in God,

18 and ᴿknow *His* will, and ᴿapprove the things that are excellent, being instructed out of the law,   Deut. 4:8 • Phil. 1:10

19 and ᴿare confident that you yourself are a guide to the blind, a light to those who are in darkness,   Matt. 15:14

20 an instructor of the foolish, a teacher of babes, ᴿhaving the form of knowledge and truth in the law.   [2 Tim. 3:5]

21 You, therefore, who teach another, do you not teach yourself? You who preach that a man should not steal, do you steal?

22 You who say, "Do not commit adultery," do you commit adultery? You who abhor idols, ᴿdo you rob temples?   Mal. 3:8

23 You who make your boast in the law, do you dishonor God through breaking the law?

24 For ᴿ"the name of God is ᴿblasphemed among the Gentiles because of you," as it is written.   Is. 52:5; Ezek. 36:22 • Ezek. 16:27

Circumcision of No Avail

25 ᴿFor circumcision is indeed profitable if you keep the law; but if you are a breaker of the law, your circumcision has become uncircumcision.   [Gal. 5:3]

26 Therefore, ᴿif an uncircumcised man keeps the righteous requirements of the law, will not his uncircumcision be counted as circumcision?   [Acts 10:34]

27 And will not the physically uncircumcised, if he fulfills the law, judge you who, *even* with *your* written *code* and circumcision, *are* a transgressor of the law?

28 For ᴿhe is not a Jew who *is* one out-

wardly, nor *is* circumcision that which *is* outward in the flesh;   [Gal. 6:15]

29 but *he is* a Jew ᴿwho *is* one inwardly; and circumcision *is that* of the heart, in the Spirit, not in the letter; whose praise *is* not from men but from God.   [1 Pet. 3:4]

God's Judgment Defended

3 What advantage then has the Jew, or what *is* the profit of circumcision?

2 Much in every way! Chiefly because to them were committed the oracles of God.

3 For what if ᴿsome did not believe? ᴿWill their unbelief make the faithfulness of God without effect?   Heb. 4:2 • [2 Tim. 2:13]

4 Certainly not! Indeed, let ᴿGod be ᵀtrue but every man a liar. As it is written:

> ᴿ"That You may be justified in Your words,   John 3:33 • Found true • Ps. 51:4
> And may overcome when You are judged."

5 But if our unrighteousness demonstrates the righteousness of God, what shall we say? *Is* God unjust who inflicts wrath? ᴿ(I speak as a man.)   Gal. 3:15

6 Certainly not! For then ᴿhow will God judge the world?   [Gen. 18:25]

7 For if the truth of God has increased through my lie to His glory, why am I also still judged as a sinner?

8 And *why* not *say*, "Let us do evil that good may come"?—as we are slanderously reported and as some affirm that we say. Their ᵀcondemnation is just.   Lit. *judgment*

All Have Sinned

15-C. The Effects of Sin in Human Character   ▼

9 What then? Are we better *than they?* Not at all. For we have previously charged both Jews and Greeks that ᴿthey are all under sin.   Gal. 3:22

10 As it is written:

> "There* is none righteous, no, not one;
> 11 There is none who understands;
>   There is none who seeks after God.
> 12 They have all turned aside;

2:17 NU *But if*

3:10 Ps. 14:1–3; 53:1–3; Eccl. 7:20

15-C. The Effects of Sin in Human Character (Romans 3:9–18)—Christ said that "a bad tree bears bad fruit" (Matt. 7:17, page 946). Certainly this is proven true in the effects of the fall of Adam. Sin entered the human race and dominated it. The Bible vividly pictures what sinful men became as a result of the Fall:

(1) murderers (Gen. 4:8, page 8);
(2) indifferent to God and the welfare of others (v. 11; cf. Gen. 4:9, page 8);
(3) unrighteous (v. 10);
(4) evildoers, turning aside from God's paths and standards (v. 12);
(5) evil speakers, deceivers, gossips, and slanderers (v. 13);
(6) full of cursing and bitterness (v. 14);

(Point 15-C continued on next page)

▽ They have together become
  unprofitable;
  *There is none who does good, no, not
  one.*"
13 "*Their*ᴿ *throat is an open* ᵀ*tomb;
  With their tongues they have practiced
  deceit*";   Ps. 5:9 · *grave*
  "*The** *poison of asps is under their lips*";
14 "*Whose*ᴿ *mouth is full of cursing and
  bitterness.*"   Ps. 10:7
15 "*Their** *feet are swift to shed blood;
16 *Destruction and misery are in their
  ways;*
17 *And the way of peace they have not
  known.*"
18 "*There*ᴿ *is no fear of God before their
  eyes.*"   Ps. 36:1

19 Now we know that whatever the law
says, it says to those who are under the law,

3:13 Ps. 140:3
3:15 Prov. 1:16; Is. 59:7, 8

that every mouth may be stopped, and all the
world may become guilty before God.
20 Therefore ᴿby the deeds of the law no
flesh will be justified in His sight, for by the
law is the knowledge of sin.   [Gal. 2:16]

God's Righteousness Through Faith

21 But now the righteousness of God apart
from the law is revealed, being witnessed by
the Law ᴿand the Prophets,   1 Pet. 1:10
22 even the righteousness of God, through
faith in Jesus Christ, to all *and on all who
believe. For there is no difference;

14-B. How Did Mankind Fall, and What ▼
Were the Effects?

23 for ᴿall have sinned and fall short of the
glory of God,   Gal. 3:22 ▲
24 being justified ᵀfreely ᴿby His grace
ᴿthrough the redemption that is in Christ
Jesus,   *without any cost* · [Eph. 2:8] · [Heb. 9:12, 15]

3:22 NU omits *and on all*

(Point 15-C continued from previous page)
    (7) swift to shed blood (v. 15);
    (8) destructive and miserable in their ways (v. 16);
    (9) warlike and incapable of being appeased (v. 16);
    (10) immoral, prone to false religion and idols, and self-serving (Rom. 1:23–25, page 1129);
    (11) unrighteous, wicked, covetous, malicious, envious, deceitful, and injurious (Rom. 1:29, page 1129);
    (12) backbiters, haters of God, spiteful, proud and boastful, disobedient to parents, and inventors of evil
(Rom. 1:30, page 1129);
    (13) covenant breakers, unaffectionate, not understanding, implacable, and unmerciful (Rom. 1:31, page
1129);
    (14) rejoicing in evil (Rom. 1:32, page 1129);
    (15) kidnappers and slaveholders (Gen. 37:26–28, page 44);
    (16) rapists (2 Sam. 13:8–14, page 309);
    (17) harsh and selfish rulers (Ex. 5:6–8, page 63);
    (18) vengeful (Gen. 34:7–30, page 40);
    (19) thieves and cheats (1 Kin. 21:5–16, page 351).

    See James 4:1–5, page 1259, for **Point 15-D: The Effects of Sin in Human History.**

14-B. How Did Mankind Fall, and What Were the Effects? (Romans 3:23)—"For all have sinned and fall short
of the glory of God" (v. 23). All are born in sin because of Adam's fall (the first sin) in the Garden of Eden.
"Therefore, just as through one man sin entered the world, and death through sin, and thus death spread to
all men, because all sinned" (Rom. 5:12, page 1133).

    (1) God gave the first human couple freedom of will, and commanded them not to eat of the tree of the
knowledge of good and evil. The couple also had the gift of spoken language, which was a part of creation
(Gen. 2:16–20, page 5; cf. 3:8, page 6). It is debated whether this tree had special knowledge-giving
properties, or whether its use in the test alone gave it these qualities. This test was given amid an abundance
of trees good for food. It was simple and direct—a test of the will of humanity to submit, as grateful
subordinate creatures, to their all-wise, all-providing, caring Creator (Gen. 2:16, 17, page 5).
    (2) Satan, already a fallen angelic being, tempted Eve to disobey God (Gen. 3:1–5, page 5). Satan, as a
spirit, apparently had no physical body, and required one in this instance to communicate with Eve. He used
the body of an animal to speak with her.
    (3) Eve was lured by Satan through

        (a) her lingering near the forbidden place;
        (b) her talking with the tempter;
        (c) his quotation of half-truths, and misquotation of God's Word (Gen. 3:1–6, page 5).

    These ingredients of temptation are still available to Satan today.

(Point 14-B continued on next page)

25 whom God set forth [R]as a propitiation [R]by His blood, through faith, to demonstrate His righteousness, because in His forbearance God had passed over the sins that were previously committed,   Lev. 16:15 · Col. 1:20

26 to demonstrate at the present time His righteousness, that He might be just and the justifier of the one who has faith in Jesus.

Boasting Excluded

27 [R]Where is boasting then? It is excluded. By what law? Of works? No, but by the law of faith.   [1 Cor. 1:29]

28 Therefore we conclude [R]that a man is [T]justified by faith apart from the deeds of the law.   Gal. 2:16 · declared righteous

29 Or is He the God of the Jews only? Is He not also the God of the Gentiles? Yes, of the Gentiles also,

30 since [R]there is one God who will justify the circumcised by faith and the uncircumcised through faith.   [Gal. 3:8, 20]

31 Do we then make void the law through faith? Certainly not! On the contrary, we establish the law.

Abraham Justified by Faith

4 What then shall we say that Abraham our [T]father has found according to the flesh?   Or (fore)father according to the flesh has found

2 For if Abraham was [R]justified by works, he has something to boast about, but not before God.   Rom. 3:20, 27

3 For what does the Scripture say? [R]"Abraham believed God, and it was [T]accounted to him for righteousness."   Gen. 15:6 · imputed

4 Now [R]to him who works, the wages are not counted as grace but as debt.   Rom. 11:6

David Celebrates the Same Truth

5 But to him who does not work but believes on Him who justifies the ungodly, his faith is accounted for righteousness,

6 just as David also describes the blessedness of the man to whom God imputes righteousness apart from works:

7 "Blessed[R] are those whose lawless deeds
  are forgiven,   Ps. 32:1, 2
And whose sins are covered;
8 Blessed is the man to whom the LORD
  shall not impute sin."

Abraham Justified Before Circumcision

9 Does this blessedness then come upon the circumcised only, or upon the uncircumcised also? For we say that faith was accounted to Abraham for righteousness.

10 How then was it accounted? While he was circumcised, or uncircumcised? Not while circumcised, but while uncircumcised.

11 And he received the sign of circumcision, a seal of the righteousness of the faith which he had while still uncircumcised, that he might be the father of all those who believe, though they are uncircumcised, that righteousness might be imputed to them also,

12 and the father of circumcision to those who not only are of the circumcision, but who also walk in the steps of the faith which our father [R]Abraham had while still uncircumcised.   Rom. 4:18-22

The Promise Granted Through Faith

13 For the promise that he would be the [R]heir of the world was not to Abraham or to his seed through the law, but through the righteousness of faith.   Gen. 17:4-6; 22:17

14 For [R]if those who are of the law are heirs, faith is made void and the promise made of no effect,   Gal. 3:18

15 because [R]the law brings about wrath; for where there is no law there is no transgression.   Rom. 3:20

16 Therefore it is of faith that it might be [R]according to grace, [R]so that the promise might be sure to all the seed, not only to those who are of the law, but also to those

(Point 14-B continued from previous page)

(4) Adam fell with Eve. The Bible explains this as the fall of the human race, naming Adam as the head of the race. Neither Genesis 3:6 (page 5) nor any other verse in the entire Bible excuses Adam because he fell after Eve's fall (1 Tim. 2:14, page 1219).

(5) The sin of Adam and Eve brought down the future human race with them. Mankind fell in Adam (Rom. 5:12-19, page 1133). This is the uniform testimony of

   (a) the Genesis account (Gen. 3:16—4:9, page 7);
   (b) the Old Testament (Ps. 14:1-3, page 517);
   (c) the New Testament (1 Cor. 15:22, page 1161);
   (d) all human experience through ages of unremedied violence, misery, and suffering.

(6) With the entrance of sin into the human race came its companion, suffering (Gen. 3:15—4:8, page 7). Death, suffering, the will to do evil, and the inability to stop sinning, all came as a result of the Fall. The corruption of the earth—its vegetation with thorns and thistles, and the carnivorous nature of wild beasts—resulted from the Fall. The grief and suffering in the world was typified at once, by the first children of Adam and Eve, when Cain murdered Abel. Murder has continued unabated to the present day.

See Deuteronomy 6:5, page 187, for **Point 14-C: What Is God's Purpose for Mankind?**

who are of the faith of Abraham, ᴿwho is the father of us all [Rom. 3:24] • [Gal. 3:22] • Is. 51:2

17 (as it is written, ᴿ"*I have made you a father of many nations*") in the presence of Him whom he believed—God, who gives life to the dead and calls those things which do not exist as though they did; Gen. 17:5

18 who, contrary to hope, in hope believed, so that he became the father of many nations, according to what was spoken, ᴿ"*So shall your descendants be.*" Gen. 15:5

19 And not being weak in faith, ᴿhe did not consider his own body, already dead (since he was about a hundred years old), ᴿand the deadness of Sarah's womb. Gen. 17:17 • Heb. 11:11

20 He did not waver at the promise of God through unbelief, but was strengthened in faith, giving glory to God,

21 and being fully convinced that what He had promised He was also able to perform.

22 And therefore ᴿ"*it was accounted to him for righteousness.*" Gen. 15:6

23 Now ᴿit was not written for his sake alone that it was imputed to him, Rom. 15:4

24 but also for us. It shall be imputed to us who believe ᴿin Him who raised up Jesus our Lord from the dead, Acts 2:24

25 ᴿwho was delivered up because of our offenses, and ᴿwas raised because of our justification. Is. 53:4, 5 • [1 Cor. 15:17]

Faith Triumphs in Trouble

5 Therefore, ᴿhaving been justified by faith, *we have ᴿpeace with God through our Lord Jesus Christ, Is. 32:17 • [Eph. 2:14]

2 through whom also we have access by faith into this grace in which we stand, and rejoice in hope of the glory of God.

3 And not only *that*, but we also glory in

5:1 Some ancient mss. *let us have*

tribulations, ᴿknowing that tribulation produces ᵀperseverance; James 1:3 • *endurance*

4 ᴿand perseverance, ᵀcharacter; and character, hope. [James 1:12] • *approved character*

5 Now hope does not disappoint, because the love of God has been poured out in our hearts by the Holy Spirit who was given to us.

Christ in Our Place

6 For when we were still without strength, in due time Christ died for the ungodly.

7 For scarcely for a righteous man will one die; yet perhaps for a good man someone would even dare to die.

8 But ᴿGod demonstrates His own love toward us, in that while we were still sinners, Christ died for us. Is. 53:5; [John 3:16; 15:13]

9 Much more then, having now been justified ᴿby His blood, we shall be saved ᴿfrom wrath through Him. Eph. 2:13 • 1 Thess. 1:10

10 For ᴿif when we were enemies we were reconciled to God through the death of His Son, much more, having been reconciled, we shall be saved by His life. [Rom. 8:32]

11 And not only *that*, but we also ᴿrejoice in God through our Lord Jesus Christ, through whom we have now received the reconciliation. [Gal. 4:9]

Death in Adam, Life in Christ

19-A. The Ruin of Man ▼

12 Therefore, just as ᴿthrough one man sin entered the world, and ᴿdeath through sin, and thus death spread to all men, because all sinned— [1 Cor. 15:21] • Gen. 2:17

13 (For until the law sin was in the world, but sin is not imputed when there is no law.

14 Nevertheless death reigned from Adam to Moses, even over those who had not

19-A. The Ruin of Man (Romans 5:12-14)—The whole human race has one thing in common: death. Paul is saying that "all sinned" when Adam sinned; all fell when Adam fell; all were ruined when Adam was ruined. Though the law was not given until Moses, there were preachers of righteousness who lived by faith: Abel, Enoch, Noah, and Abraham, to mention a few (Heb. 11:1-29, page 1247). "Through one man [Adam] sin entered the world, and death [physical and spiritual] through sin, and thus death spread to all men, because all sinned" (v. 12; cf. Gen. 2:16, 17, page 5). When Adam fell in the Garden, the human race was ruined in him. Adam's sin was imputed judicially by God and transmitted by inheritance at birth to all of Adam's descendants. Only those who are born-again of God's incorruptible seed can escape eternal separation from God. This separation is called "the second death" (Rev. 20:14, page 1314). The rich and the poor, the educated and the uneducated, kings and peasants, bond or free, all participate in the ruin of Adam.

There are two Adams in the Bible (1 Cor. 15:45, page 1162). The first Adam was created; the last Adam was virgin-born (Luke 1:26-31, page 1010). The first Adam was tempted, and failed; the last Adam was tempted in all points as the first Adam, but was victorious over sin and Satan.

(1) Through the first Adam came the ruin of the race. Through the last Adam (Christ) came the righteousness of God for the redeemed (2 Cor. 5:21, page 1169).

(2) Through the first Adam came death. Through the last Adam came eternal life (John 3:36, page 1053).

(3) Through the first Adam came a ruined, sinful nature. Through the last Adam came an incorruptible nature (1 Pet. 1:23, page 1264). By faith we are made partakers of His divine nature (2 Pet. 1:4, page 1272).

Before people can know the righteousness of God in Jesus Christ, the last Adam, they must first recognize the ruin of the race in the first Adam.

See Romans 1:18-32, page 1128, for **Point 19-B: The Nature of Man's Ruin.**

▽ sinned according to the likeness of the transgression of Adam, ᴿwho is a type of Him who ▲ was to come.   [1 Cor. 15:21, 22]

15 But the free gift *is* not like the offense. For if by the one man's ᵀoffense many died, much more the grace of God and the gift by the grace of the one Man, Jesus Christ, abounded ᴿto many.   *trespass* or *false step* • [Is. 53:11]

16 And the gift *is* not like *that which came* through the one who sinned. For the judgment *which came* from one *offense resulted* in condemnation, but the free gift *which came* from many ᵀoffenses *resulted* in justification.   *trespasses*

17 For if by the one man's ᵀoffense death reigned through the one, much more those who receive abundance of grace and of the gift of righteousness will reign in life through the One, Jesus Christ.)   *trespass*

18 Therefore, as through one man's offense *judgment* came to all men, resulting in condemnation, even so ᴿthrough one Man's righteous act *the free gift came* to all men, resulting in justification of life.   Is. 53:11, 12

19 For as by one man's disobedience many were made sinners, so also by one Man's obedience many will be made righteous.

20 Moreover the law entered that the offense might abound. But where sin abounded, grace abounded much more,

21 so that as sin reigned in death, even so grace might reign through righteousness to eternal life through Jesus Christ our Lord.

Dead to Sin, Alive to God

6 What shall we say then? Shall we continue in sin that grace may abound?

2 Certainly not! How shall we who ᴿdied to sin live any longer in it?   [Gal. 2:19]

3 Or do you not know that ᴿas many of us as were baptized into Christ Jesus ᴿwere baptized into His death?   [Gal. 3:27] • [1 Cor. 15:29]

4 Therefore we were buried with Him through baptism into death, that ᴿjust as Christ was raised from the dead by ᴿthe glory of the Father, ᴿeven so we also should walk in newness of life.   1 Cor. 6:14 • John 2:11 • [Gal. 6:15]

5 For if we have been united together in the likeness of His death, certainly we also shall be *in the likeness* of *His* resurrection,

6 knowing this, that our old man was crucified with *Him*, that the body of sin might be ᵀdone away with, that we should no longer be slaves of sin.   *rendered inoperative*

7 For ᴿhe who has died has been ᵀfreed from sin.   1 Pet. 4:1 • *cleared*

8 Now ᴿif we died with Christ, we believe that we shall also live with Him,   2 Tim. 2:11

9 knowing that ᴿChrist, having been raised from the dead, dies no more. Death no longer has dominion over Him.   Rev. 1:18

10 For *the death* that He died, ᴿHe died to sin once for all; but *the life* that He lives, ᴿHe lives to God.   Heb. 9:27 • Luke 20:38

11 Likewise you also, ᵀreckon yourselves to be dead indeed to sin, but ᴿalive to God in Christ Jesus our Lord.   *consider* • [Gal. 2:19]

12 ᴿTherefore do not let sin reign in your mortal body, that you should obey it in its lusts.   Ps. 19:13

13 And do not present your members *as* ᵀinstruments of unrighteousness to sin, but present yourselves to God as being alive from the dead, and your members *as* ᵀinstruments of righteousness to God.   Or *weapons*

14 For ᴿsin shall not have dominion over you, for you are not under law but under grace.   [Gal. 5:18]

From Slaves of Sin to Slaves of God

15 What then? Shall we sin ᴿbecause we are not under law but under grace? Certainly not!   1 Cor. 9:21

16 Do you not know that ᴿto whom you present yourselves slaves to obey, you are that one's slaves whom you obey, whether of sin *leading* to death, or of obedience *leading* to righteousness?   2 Pet. 2:19

17 But God be thanked that *though* you were slaves of sin, yet you obeyed from the heart ᴿthat form of doctrine to which you were ᵀdelivered.   2 Tim. 1:13 • *entrusted*

18 And ᴿhaving been set free from sin, you became slaves of righteousness.   John 8:32

19 I speak in human *terms* because of the weakness of your flesh. For just as you presented your members *as* slaves of uncleanness, and of lawlessness *leading* to *more* lawlessness, so now present your members *as* slaves *of* righteousness for holiness.

20 For when you were ᴿslaves of sin, you were free in regard to righteousness.   John 8:34

21 What fruit did you have then in the things of which you are now ashamed? For ᴿthe end of those things *is* death.   Rom. 1:32

22 But now ᴿhaving been set free from sin, and having become slaves of God, you have your fruit ᵀto holiness, and the end, everlasting life.   Rom. 6:18; 8:2 • *unto sanctification*

25-A. The Christian Life Is an Eternal Life ▼

23 For ᴿthe wages of sin *is* death, but ᴿthe ᵀgift of God *is* eternal life in Christ Jesus our Lord.   Gen. 2:17 • 1 Pet. 1:4 • *free gift* ▲

25-A. The Christian Life Is an Eternal Life (Romans 6:23)—Christianity differs from all the religions of the world because it is infinitely more than mere religion. It is the very life of God's Son, made to live in every believer. If believers will commit themselves totally to Christ, He will live His life through them.

(Point 25-A continued on next page)

Freed from the Law

7 Or do you not know, brethren (for I speak to those who know the law), that the law [T]has dominion over a man as long as he lives?

2 For the woman who has a husband is bound by the law to *her* husband as long as he lives. But if the husband dies, she is released from the law of *her* husband.

3 So then if, while *her* husband lives, she marries another man, she will be called an adulteress; but if her husband dies, she is free from that law, so that she is no adulteress, though she has married another man.

4 Therefore, my brethren, you also have become dead to the law through the body of Christ, that you may be married to another— to Him who was raised from the dead, that we should [R]bear fruit to God.   Gal. 5:22

5 For when we were in the flesh, the sinful passions which were aroused by the law [R]were at work in our members [R]to bear fruit to death.   Rom. 6:13 • James 1:15

6 But now we have been delivered from the law, having died to what we were held by,

so that we should serve in the newness of the Spirit and not in the oldness of the letter.

Sin's Advantage in the Law

7 What shall we say then? *Is* the law sin? Certainly not! On the contrary, I would not have known sin except through the law. For I would not have known covetousness unless the law had said, *"You shall not covet."*

8 But sin, taking opportunity by the commandment, produced in me all *manner of evil* desire. For apart from the law sin *was* dead.

9 I was alive once without the law, but when the commandment came, sin revived and I died.

10 And the commandment, [R]which *was* to bring life, I found to *bring* death.   Lev. 18:5

11 For sin, taking occasion by the commandment, deceived me, and by it killed *me*.

12 Therefore [R]the law *is* holy, and the commandment holy and just and good.   Ps. 19:8

Law Cannot Save from Sin

13 Has then what is good become death to me? Certainly not! But sin, that it might

7:7 Ex. 20:17; Deut. 5:21; Acts 20:33

(Point 25-A continued from previous page)
    (1) "For the wages of sin is death." Sin pays wages, and those wages are eternal. They are more than just physical death; they are eternal separation from the very mercy, grace, and love of God.
    (2) "But the gift of God is eternal life in Christ Jesus our Lord." God gives man two choices:

        (a) To reject the Lord Jesus Christ as personal Savior and remain in sin;
        (b) To accept the Lord Jesus Christ by faith as personal Savior and receive everlasting life (John 3:36, page 1053; 10:27, 28, page 1068).

    If you say "no" to *God's* gracious *gift* of eternal life through His Son, you will collect *your wages* of sin— eternal separation from God. But thank God, you can accept His gift, which is eternal life. And when you do, the Lord Jesus Christ will come into your life, and His life within you will cancel the wages of sin, which is death.

    God has promised to

    (1) cast all our sins into the depths of the sea (Mic. 7:19, page 893);
    (2) remove our transgressions from us, as far as the east is from the west (Ps. 103:12, page 570);
    (3) cast all our sins behind His back (Is. 38:17, page 678);
    (4) blot out our transgressions like a thick cloud (Is. 44:22, page 684);
    (5) remember our sins no more (Jer. 31:34, page 746; cf. Heb. 8:12; 10:17, page 1243).

    God in His love offered His Son, the Messiah, to a nation Israel almost two thousand years ago. "He came to His own, and His own did not receive Him" (John 1:11, page 1049). They rejected their Messiah. But God has promised that Israel, as a nation, will one day receive His gift of eternal life through the Lord Jesus Christ—their Messiah (Rom. 11:25, 26, page 1141). The prophecy of Jeremiah will be fulfilled, "Behold, the days are coming, says the LORD, when I will make a new covenant with the house of Israel and with the house of Judah [that new covenant is through the Lord Jesus Christ] . . . For I will forgive their iniquity [their wages of sin], and their sin I will remember no more" (Jer. 31:31, 34, page 745). This is going to be a great day for God's people. But they don't have to wait individually. If they will come and receive the Lord Jesus Christ—God's gift—they can have that new covenant with God and know that all of their sins are cancelled; God will remember them no more—forever. When Jews or Gentiles accept God's wonderful gift, they have unending life.

    It is most difficult for us, being creatures of time, to understand an eternal God. Jesus Christ was with the Father from eternity; He has no beginning and no ending (Rev. 1:8, page 1293). He is with the Father now. God promises eternal life, and when we recognize that He is offering us the very life of Christ, it staggers our imagination. In the Gospel of John the Lord speaks of Himself as the Good Shepherd (John 10:11, 27-30, page 1067). He said:

    (1) "The good shepherd gives His life for the sheep." "He was wounded for our transgressions, He was
(Point 25-A continued on next page)

appear sin, was producing death in me through what is good, so that sin through the commandment might become exceedingly sinful.

14 For we know that the law is spiritual, but I am carnal, Rsold under sin.   2 Kin. 17:17

15 For what I am doing, I do not understand. RFor what I will to do, that I do not practice; but what I hate, that I do.   [Gal. 5:17]

16 If, then, I do what I will not to do, I agree with the law that *it is* good.

17 But now, *it is* no longer I who do it, but sin that dwells in me.

18 For I know that Rin me (that is, in my flesh) nothing good dwells; for to will is present with me, but *how* to perform what is good I do not find.   [Gen. 6:5; 8:21]

19 For the good that I will *to do*, I do not do; but the evil I will not *to do*, that I practice.

20 Now if I do what I will not *to do*, it is no longer I who do it, but sin that dwells in me.

21 I find then a law, that evil is present with me, the one who wills to do good.

22 For I Rdelight in the law of God according to Rthe inward man.   Ps. 1:2 • [2 Cor. 4:16]

23 But RI see another law in Rmy members,

warring against the law of my mind, and bringing me into captivity to the law of sin which is in my members.   [Gal. 5:17] • Rom. 6:13, 19

24 O wretched man that I am! Who will deliver me from this body of death?

25 RI thank God—through Jesus Christ our Lord! So then, with the mind I myself serve the law of God, but with the flesh the law of sin.   1 Cor. 15:57

Free from Indwelling Sin

8 *There is* therefore now no condemnation to those who are in Christ Jesus, Rwho* do not walk according to the flesh, but according to the Spirit.   Gal. 5:16

2 For Rthe law of the Spirit of life in Christ Jesus has made me free from Rthe law of sin and death.   Rom. 6:18, 22 • Rom. 7:24, 25

3 For Rwhat the law could not do in that it was weak through the flesh, RGod *did* by sending His own Son in the likeness of sinful flesh, on account of sin: He condemned sin in the flesh,   Acts 13:39 • [2 Cor. 5:21]

4 that the righteous requirement of the law might be fulfilled in us who Rdo not walk

8:1 NU omits the rest of v. 1.

(Point 25-A continued from previous page)

bruised for our iniquities; the chastisement for our peace was upon Him, and by His stripes we are healed" (Is. 53:5, page 693).

(2) "My sheep hear My voice." The Bible is the very Word of God. If you neglect to read God's Word, you will not hear the voice of the Shepherd, the Lord Jesus Christ (Heb. 3:7, 8, page 1238).

(3) "And I know them." If you are a sheep (born-again) you have eternal life. You will recognize the voice of God as you feed upon His Word.

(4) "And they follow Me." Are you a true follower of the Lord Jesus Christ? If you have eternal life you are one of His sheep, and when He speaks you follow. But remember, Jesus also said, "Not everyone who says to Me, 'Lord, Lord,' shall enter the kingdom of heaven" (Matt. 7:21, page 946). In other words, Jesus is saying that not everyone who *professes* to know Him as the Good Shepherd is one of His flock. If you have eternal life and know the Good Shepherd, you will want to follow Him and do His will.

(5) "And I give them eternal life." He gives this eternal life to all who will

     (a) recognize His deity;

     (b) recognize His voice;

     (c) take up their cross and follow Him (Mark 8:34–38, page 994).

(6) "And they shall never perish [be lost]; neither shall anyone snatch them out of My hand." Why? Because He is the all-powerful Good Shepherd.

(7) "My Father, who has given them to Me, is greater than all." He is their Good Shepherd to protect them from the wolves of this world. He is greater than

     (a) death or life;

     (b) angels or demons;

     (c) Satan;

     (d) things past, present, or future.

"Neither . . . height nor depth, nor any other created thing, shall be able to separate us from the love of God which is in Christ Jesus our Lord" (Rom. 8:38, 39, page 1138).

(8) "And no one is able to snatch them out of My Father's hand. I and My Father are one."

How safe are we in Christ? "The LORD [Jesus] is my shepherd; I shall not want" (Ps. 23:1, page 524). You can lie down in peace even though the world may hate you, because your Shepherd keeps you in the hollow of His hand.

Because one day you came to the Lord Jesus Christ by faith, and accepted Him (God's gift of eternal life) as your personal Savior, the Lord—Father, Son, and Holy Spirit—keeps you now, and will keep you forever.

See 1 Peter 5:5–9, page 1268, for **Point 25-B: The Christian Life Is a Faith Life.**

according to the flesh but according to the Spirit. Gal. 5:16, 25

5 For those who live according to the flesh set their minds on the things of the flesh, but those *who live* according to the Spirit, ᴿthe things of the Spirit. [Gal. 5:22–25]

6 For to be carnally minded is death, but to be spiritually minded is life and peace.

7 Because the ᵀcarnal mind is enmity against God; for it is not subject to the law of God, ᴿnor indeed can be. *fleshly* • 1 Cor. 2:14

8 So then, those who are in the flesh cannot please God.

9 But you are not in the flesh but in the Spirit, if indeed the Spirit of God dwells in you. Now if anyone does not have the Spirit of Christ, he is not His.

10 And if Christ is in you, the body is dead because of sin, but the Spirit is life because of righteousness.

11 But if the Spirit of ᴿHim who raised Jesus from the dead dwells in you, ᴿHe who raised Christ from the dead will also give life to your mortal bodies ᵀthrough His Spirit who dwells in you. Acts 2:24 • 1 Cor. 6:14 • Or *because of*

Sonship Through the Spirit

12 Therefore, brethren, we are debtors—not to the flesh, to live according to the flesh.

13 For if you live according to the flesh you will die; but if by the Spirit you put to death the deeds of the body, you will live.

14 For ᴿas many as are led by the Spirit of God, these are sons of God. [Gal. 5:18]

15 For you did not receive the spirit of bondage again to fear, but you received the ᴿSpirit of adoption by whom we cry out, "Abba,ᵀ Father." [Is. 56:5] • Lit., in Aram., *Father*

16 ᴿThe Spirit Himself bears witness with our spirit that we are children of God, Eph. 1:13

17 and if children, then ᴿheirs—heirs of God and joint heirs with Christ, ᴿif indeed we suffer with *Him*, that we may also be glorified together. Acts 26:18 • Phil. 1:29

From Suffering to Glory

18 For I consider that the sufferings of this present time are not worthy *to be compared* with the glory which shall be revealed in us.

19 For ᴿthe earnest expectation of the cre-

ation eagerly waits for the revealing of the sons of God. [2 Pet. 3:13]

20 For ᴿthe creation was subjected to futility, not willingly, but because of Him who subjected *it* in hope; Gen. 3:17-19

21 because the creation itself also will be delivered from the bondage of ᵀcorruption into the glorious ᴿliberty of the children of God. *decay* • [2 Cor. 3:17]

22 For we know that the whole creation ᴿgroans and labors with birth pangs together until now. Jer. 12:4, 11

23 Not only *that*, but we also who have the firstfruits of the Spirit, even we ourselves groan within ourselves, eagerly waiting for the adoption, the redemption of our body.

24 For we were saved in this hope, but ᴿhope that is seen is not hope; for why does one still hope for what he sees? Heb. 11:1

25 But if we hope for what we do not see, we eagerly wait for *it* with perseverance.

26 Likewise the Spirit also helps in our weaknesses. For we do not know what we should pray for as we ought, but ᴿthe Spirit Himself makes intercession *for us with groanings which cannot be uttered. Eph. 6:18

27 Now ᴿHe who searches the hearts knows what the mind of the Spirit is, because He makes intercession for the saints ᴿaccording to *the will of* God. 1 Chr. 28:9 • 1 John 5:14

28 And we know that all things work together for good to those who love God, to those ᴿwho are the called according to *His* purpose. 2 Tim. 1:9

5-D. The Sovereignty of God and Salvation ▼

29 For whom He foreknew, He also predestined ᴿ*to be* conformed to the image of His Son, ᴿthat He might be the firstborn among many brethren. [2 Cor. 3:18] • Heb. 1:6

30 Moreover whom He predestined, these He also ᴿcalled; whom He called, these He also ᴿjustified; and whom He justified, these He also glorified. [1 Pet. 2:9; 3:9] • [Gal. 2:16] ▲

God's Everlasting Love

31 What then shall we say to these things? If God is for us, who *can be* against us?

8:26 NU omits *for us*

5-D. The Sovereignty of God and Salvation (Romans 8:29, 30)—In this profound and difficult portion of Scripture we have five words that must be taken in the order given by the Holy Spirit if we are to understand the sovereignty of God in salvation.

(1) *Foreknow.* "For whom He foreknew" (v. 29). God's foreknowledge is not like our foreknowledge. Human foreknowledge means simply to know beforehand, i.e., to have foresight of things to come. Our "foreknowledge" is naturally very imperfect, very fallible. But with God the entire course of history, in every detail, is perfectly clear and settled. This is why history is sometimes referred to as "His story."

Actually, God's "knowledge" is even more active than this. The biblical Hebrew and Greek words for "know" and "foreknow" commonly have a more profound meaning. This is seen in God's remark concerning Abraham, as correctly translated, "For I have known him, in order that he may command his

(Point 5-D continued on next page)

32 He who did not spare His own Son, but delivered Him up for us all, how shall He not with Him also freely give us all things?

33 Who shall bring a charge against God's elect? ᴿIt is God who justifies.   Is. 50:8, 9

34 Who is he who condemns? It is Christ who died, and furthermore is also risen, who is even at the right hand of God, ᴿwho also makes intercession for us.   Heb. 7:25; 9:24

35 Who shall separate us from the love of Christ? Shall tribulation, or distress, or persecution, or famine, or nakedness, or peril, or sword?

36 As it is written:

ᴿ"For Your sake we are killed all day long;
We are accounted as sheep for the slaughter."   Ps. 44:22

37 Yet in all these things we are more than conquerors through Him who loved us.

38 For I am persuaded that neither death nor life, nor angels nor ᴿprincipalities nor powers, nor things present nor things to come,   [Eph. 1:21]

39 nor height nor depth, nor any other created thing, shall be able to separate us from the love of God which is in Christ Jesus our Lord.

(Point 5-D continued from previous page)
children and his household" (Gen. 18:19, page 23). As in similar cases where the word "know" is used, God here indicates a special relationship which He had established between Himself and Abraham. This special, personal, unmerited relationship was the basis of everything God had eternally decided to do with Abraham and Abraham's people. It is in this way that God also speaks to Jeremiah: "Before I formed you in the womb I knew you; before you were born I sanctified you" (Jer. 1:5, page 710). In this sense Paul also writes to the Romans, "For whom He foreknew, He also predestined to be conformed to the image of His Son" (v. 29). God saves us by grace (unmerited favor) because He "knew" us by grace—before we were born. To see how this truth relates to the truth of our responsibility before God, see Point 5-E, "The Sovereignty of God and the Responsibility of Mankind" (page 1139).

(2) *Predestinate.* "He also predestined" (v. 29). "Predestination," "election," and "being chosen" have similar meaning in God's Word. Therefore, predestination, election, or being chosen is always according to God's "foreknowledge," as in the case of Abraham and Jeremiah. Predestination is threefold:

(a) God predestines nations according to His foreknowledge. According to His foreknowledge, i.e., according to His previous and unmerited favor, He chose Israel to fulfill His sovereign purpose (Gen. 12:1-3, page 17; cf. Is. 41:8, 9, page 680; Matt. 24:21-24, page 973).

(b) God predestines individuals for service according to His foreknowledge. Thus He chose Moses to lead Israel, His chosen nation, out of Egypt (Ex. 3:1-14, page 60). When God has a work to do on planet earth, He chooses a man or woman to accomplish His sovereign purpose.

(c) He predestines individuals to eternal salvation by the same principle—according to His foreknowledge. This means that He intimately and eternally *knows* those who will believe on His Son, the Lord Jesus Christ (Acts 16:31, page 1111).

Predestination means that God, in His sovereign will, chooses to save those who, according to His eternal foreknowledge, will surely believe in Him (John 3:14-16, page 1052).

(3) *Called.* "He also called" (v. 30). Foreknowledge and predestination precede calling. God in eternity past called nations good and bad to fulfill His sovereign purpose on this earth. He calls individuals to serve Him in spiritual ministries, according to His sovereign will. He calls sinners to repentance and salvation according to His sovereign grace (Eph. 2:8-10, page 1187). "He chose us in Him before the foundation of the world" (Eph. 1:4, 5, page 1186). God has chosen us and called us to salvation by grace. Grace is unmerited favor. We are not called upon to decide whether God has chosen us. The responsibility is ours to respond affirmatively to His free offer of salvation in Christ.

(4) *Justified.* "He also justified" (v. 30). Foreknowledge, predestination, and calling precede justification. To be justified is to be judicially declared righteous by God through faith in the vicarious death, burial, and bodily resurrection of God's only begotten Son, the Lord Jesus Christ (1 Cor. 15:1-4, page 1161). God calls the sinner to salvation by His sovereign grace; the sinner answers the call by faith. Then God judicially declares the sinner righteous, whom He elected (chose) according to His foreknowledge.

(5) *Glorified.* "He also glorified" (v. 30). Foreknowledge, predestination, calling, and justification precede glorification. Glorification of the saved will complete the believer's redemption; Christ died to save the whole man, "spirit, soul, and body" (1 Thess. 5:23, page 1213). Our salvation will not be complete until Jesus returns to this earth, raptures the saved, and glorifies their bodies. John tells us, "We know that when He is revealed, we shall be like Him, for we shall see Him as He is" (1 John 3:1, 2, page 1279). All believers will be glorified when Jesus comes. When we see our God and Savior Jesus Christ in His glorified body, "we shall be like Him." Our new bodies will be like His eternal glorious body. But there will be one difference—His glorified body will bear the scars of Calvary forever; ours will not (Zech. 13:6, page 918).

See Romans 9:1-24, page 1139, for **Point 5-E: The Sovereignty of God and the Responsibility of Mankind.**

Israel's Rejection of Christ

▼ **5-E. The Sovereignty of God and the Responsibility of Mankind**

9 I ᴿtell the truth in Christ, I am not lying, my conscience also bearing me witness in the Holy Spirit,   2 Cor. 1:23

2 ᴿthat I have great sorrow and continual grief in my heart.   Rom. 10:1

3 For I could wish that I myself were accursed from Christ for my brethren, my ᵀcountrymen according to the flesh, Or *relatives*

4 who are Israelites, to whom pertain the adoption, the glory, ᴿthe covenants, ᴿthe giving of the law, ᴿthe service of God, and the promises;   Acts 3:25 • Ps. 147:19 • Heb. 9:1, 6

5 ᴿof whom *are* the fathers and from ᴿwhom, according to the flesh, Christ *came*, ᴿwho is over all, *the* eternally blessed God. Amen.   Deut. 10:15 • [Luke 1:34, 35; 3:23] • Jer. 23:6

Israel's Rejection and God's Purpose

6 ᴿBut it is not that the word of God has taken no effect. For ᴿthey *are* not all Israel who *are* of Israel,   Num. 23:19 • [Gal. 6:16]

7 ᴿnor *are they* all children because they are the seed of Abraham; but, ᴿ*"In Isaac your seed shall be called."*   [Gal. 4:23] • Gen. 21:12

8 That is, those who *are* the children of the flesh, these *are* not the children of God; but ᴿthe children of the promise are counted as the seed.   Gal. 4:28

9 For this *is* the word of promise: *"At this time I will come and Sarah shall have a son."*

10 And not only *this*, but when ᴿRebecca also had conceived by one man, *even* by our father Isaac   Gen. 25:21

11 (for *the children* not yet being born, nor

9:9 Gen. 18:10, 14; Heb. 11:11

having done any good or evil, that the pur- ▽
pose of God according to election might stand, not of works but of Him who calls),

12 it was said to her, ᴿ*"The older shall serve the younger."*   Gen. 25:23

13 As it is written, ᴿ*"Jacob I have loved, but Esau I have hated."*   Mal. 1:2, 3

Israel's Rejection and God's Justice

14 What shall we say then? *Is there* unrighteousness with God? Certainly not!

15 For He says to Moses, ᴿ*"I will have mercy on whomever I will have mercy, and I will have compassion on whomever I will have compassion."*   Ex. 33:19

16 So then *it is* not of him who wills, nor of him who runs, but of God who shows mercy.

17 For the Scripture says to the Pharaoh, *"For this very purpose I have raised you up, that I may show My power in you, and that My name may be declared in all the earth."*

18 Therefore He has mercy on whom He wills, and whom He wills He ᴿhardens. Ex. 4:21

19 You will say to me then, "Why does He still find fault? For ᴿwho has resisted His will?"   2 Chr. 20:6

20 But indeed, O man, who are you to reply against God? ᴿWill the thing formed say to him who formed *it*, "Why have you made me like this?"   Is. 29:16

21 Does not the potter have power over the clay, from the same lump to make one vessel for honor and another for dishonor?

22 *What* if God, wanting to show *His* wrath and to make His power known, endured with much longsuffering ᴿthe vessels of wrath ᴿprepared for destruction, [1 Thess. 5:9] • [1 Pet. 2:8]

23 and that He might make known ᴿthe riches of His glory on the vessels of mercy,

---

5-E. The Sovereignty of God and the Responsibility of Mankind (Romans 9:1–24)—The subject before us, which the apostle Paul addresses in a forthright way, has been very controversial in the experience of the Christian church throughout history. How can God be absolutely sovereign, while man is completely responsible for his own decisions and actions? We have elsewhere shown, and the Scriptures affirm, that there are mysteries in God's secret will and knowledge that necessarily defy human comprehension, just because these mysteries are understood completely by God alone. God is God, and man is man.

As humans—indeed, sinful humans—we dare not imagine that we will ever comprehend more than we have been gifted to understand, even in our finally glorified state in the presence of God. Thus, when Paul says, "It is not of him who wills, nor of him who runs, but of God who shows mercy" (v. 16), we bow before this truth, and acknowledge our inability to penetrate all that is said here. Similarly, when he says, "Therefore He has mercy on whom He wills, and whom He wills He hardens" (v. 18). However, at the same time, Paul makes clear that God holds us accountable for our response to His overtures of grace, love, and government: "Who are you to reply against God? Will the thing formed say to him who formed it, 'Why have you made me like this?'" (v. 20). So Paul makes clear that God is truly sovereign, and we are truly responsible. Further, he says, we have no reasonable basis for questioning these truths merely because they cannot humanly be understood—in the same way, for example, that the Trinity cannot humanly be understood. God has the right, grounded in His sovereignty, goodness, and trustworthiness, to expect and demand that we trust Him with all things—both the seemingly easy and the seemingly difficult matters of His self-revelation. Therefore, in reverence and obedience, let us resolve not to question the ways of God that surpass our understanding. Rather, let us humbly respond to His earnest invitation to become His adopted, compliant children through the finished work of Christ presented in the gospel.

See Index, page 17, for your next study.

▽ which He had ᴿprepared beforehand for glory,   [Col. 1:27] • [Rom. 8:28–30]

24 *even* us whom He called, not of the Jews
▲ only, but also of the Gentiles?

25 As He says also in Hosea:

> ᴿ*"I will call them My people, who were*
> *not My people,*
> *And her beloved, who was not*
> *beloved."*   Hos. 2:23

26 "And ᴿ it shall come to pass in the place
where it was said to them,
'You are not My people,'
There they shall be called sons of the
living God."   Hos. 1:10

27 Isaiah also cries out concerning Israel:

> *"Though ᴿ the number of the children of*
> *Israel be as the sand of the sea,*
> *The remnant will be saved.*   Is. 10:22, 23

28 *For He will finish the work and cut it*
short in righteousness,
ᴿ*Because the LORD will *make a short*
work upon the earth."   Is. 28:22

29 And as Isaiah said before:

> ᴿ*"Unless the LORD of ᵀSabaoth had left us*
> *a seed,*   Is. 1:9 • Lit., in Heb., *Hosts*
> ᴿ*We would have become like Sodom,*
> *And we would have been made like*
> *Gomorrah."*   Is. 13:19

Present Condition of Israel

30 What shall we say then? ᴿThat Gentiles,
who did not pursue righteousness, have attained to righteousness, ᴿeven the righteousness of faith;   Rom. 4:11 • Rom. 1:17; 3:21; 10:6

31 but Israel, ᴿpursuing the law of righteousness, ᴿhas not attained to the law *of
righteousness.   [Rom. 10:2–4] • [Gal. 5:4]

32 Why? Because *they* did not *seek* it by
faith, but as it were, *by the works of the law.
For they stumbled at that stumbling stone.

33 As it is written:

> ᴿ*"Behold, I lay in Zion a stumbling stone*
> *and rock of offense,*
> *And whoever believes on Him will not*
> *be put to shame."*   Is. 8:14; 28:16

Israel Needs the Gospel

10 Brethren, my heart's desire and prayer
to God for *Israel is that they may be
saved.

2 For I bear them witness ᴿthat they have
a zeal for God, but not according to knowledge.   Acts 21:20

3 For they being ignorant of ᴿGod's righteousness, and seeking to establish their own

ᴿrighteousness, have not submitted to the
righteousness of God.   [Rom. 1:17] • [Phil. 3:9]

4 For Christ *is* the end of the law for
righteousness to everyone who believes.

5 For Moses writes about the righteousness which is of the law, ᴿ*"The man who does*
those things shall live by them."   Lev. 18:5

6 But the righteousness of faith speaks in
this way, ᴿ*"Do not say in your heart, 'Who*
will ascend into heaven?' " (that is, to bring
Christ down *from above*)   Deut. 30:12–14

7 or, " 'Who will descend into the abyss?' "
(that is, to bring Christ up from the dead).

8 But what does it say? *"The word is near*
you, in your mouth and in your heart" (that
is, the word of faith which we preach):

9 that ᴿif you confess with your mouth the
Lord Jesus and believe in your heart that God
has raised Him from the dead, you will be
saved.   Luke 12:8

10 For with the heart one believes unto
righteousness, and with the mouth confession is made unto salvation.

11 For the Scripture says, * *"Whoever be-*
lieves on Him will not be put to shame."

12 For there is no distinction between Jew
and Greek, for ᴿthe same Lord over all ᴿis rich
to all who call upon Him.   Acts 10:36 • Eph. 1:7

13 For ᴿ*"whoever calls ᴿon the name of the*
LORD shall be saved."   Joel 2:32 • Acts 9:14

Israel Rejects the Gospel

14 How then shall they call on Him in
whom they have not believed? And how shall
they believe in Him of whom they have not
heard? And how shall they hear ᴿwithout a
preacher?   Titus 1:3

15 And how shall they preach unless they
are sent? As it is written:

> * *"How beautiful are the feet of those who*
> *preach the gospel of peace,*
> *Who bring glad tidings of good things!"*

16 But they have not all obeyed the gospel.
For Isaiah says, ᴿ*"Lord, who has believed our*
report?"   Is. 53:1; John 12:38

17 So then faith *comes* by hearing, and
hearing by the word of God.

18 But I say, have they not heard? Yes
indeed:

> ᴿ*"Their sound has gone out to all the*
> *earth,*
> ᴿ*And their words to the ends of the*
> *world."*   Ps. 19:4 • 1 Kin. 18:10

19 But I say, did Israel not know? First
Moses says:

> ᴿ*"I will provoke you to jealousy by those*
> *who are not a nation,*   Deut. 32:21

9:28 NU *finish the work and cut it short*
9:31 NU omits *of righteousness*
9:32 NU *by works,* omitting *of the law*
10:1 NU *them*

10:11 Is. 28:16; Jer. 17:7; Rom. 9:33
10:15 Is. 52:7; Nah. 1:15 • NU omits *preach the gospel*
of peace, Who

I will move you to anger by a foolish nation."

20 But Isaiah is very bold and says:

R*"I was found by those who did not seek Me;*
I was made manifest to those who did not ask for Me."   Is. 65:1

21 But to Israel he says:

R*"All day long I have stretched out My hands*   Is. 65:2
To a disobedient and contrary people."

Israel's Rejection Not Total

11 I say then, Rhas God cast away His people? RCertainly not! For RI also am an Israelite, of the seed of Abraham, *of* the tribe of Benjamin. Jer. 46:28 • 1 Sam. 12:22 • 2 Cor. 11:22

2 God has not cast away His people whom RHe foreknew. Or do you not know what the Scripture says of Elijah, how he pleads with God against Israel, saying,   [Rom. 8:29]

3 R*"Lord, they have killed Your prophets and torn down Your altars, and I alone am left, and they seek my life"*?   1 Kin. 19:10, 14

4 But what does the divine response say to him? R*"I have reserved for Myself seven thousand men who have not bowed the knee to Baal."*   1 Kin. 19:18

5 REven so then, at this present time there is a remnant according to the election of grace.   Rom. 9:27

6 And Rif by grace, then *it is* no longer of works; otherwise grace is no longer grace. *But if it is* of works, it is no longer grace; otherwise work is no longer work.   Rom. 4:4

7 What then? Israel has not obtained what it seeks; but the elect have obtained it, and the rest were Rblinded.   2 Cor. 3:14

8 Just as it is written:

R*"God has given them a spirit of stupor,*
R*Eyes that they should not see*
And ears that they should not hear,
To this very day."   Deut. 29:3, 4 • Is. 29:10, 13

9 And David says:

R*"Let their table become a snare and a trap,*
A stumbling block and a recompense to them.   Ps. 69:22, 23

10 *Let their eyes be darkened, so that they do not see,*
And bow down their back always."

Israel's Rejection Not Final

11 I say then, have they stumbled that they should fall? Certainly not! But through their Tfall, to provoke them to jealousy, salvation has come to the Gentiles.   trespass

12 Now if their fall *is* riches for the world,

and their failure Rriches for the Gentiles, how much more their fullness!   Hos. 1:10; 2:23

13 For I speak to you Gentiles; inasmuch as RI am an apostle to the Gentiles, I magnify my ministry,   Acts 9:15; 22:21

14 if by any means I may provoke to jealousy *those who are* my flesh and Rsave some of them.   1 Cor. 9:22

15 For if their being cast away *is* the reconciling of the world, what *will* their acceptance *be* Rbut life from the dead?   [Is. 26:16–19]

16 For if Rthe firstfruit *is* holy, the lump *is* also *holy;* and if the root *is* holy, so *are* the branches.   Lev. 23:10

17 And if Rsome of the branches were broken off, Rand you, being a wild olive tree, were grafted in among them, and with them became a partaker of the root and Tfatness of the olive tree,   Jer. 11:16 • [Eph. 2:12] • *richness*

18 do not boast against the branches. But if you do boast, *remember that* you do not support the root, but the root supports you.

19 You will say then, "Branches were broken off that I might be grafted in."

20 Well *said*. Because of Runbelief they were broken off, and you stand by faith. Do not be haughty, but fear.   Heb. 3:19

21 For if God did not spare the natural branches, He may not spare you either.

22 Therefore consider the goodness and severity of God: on those who fell, severity; but toward you, *goodness, Rif you continue in *His* goodness. Otherwise Ryou also will be cut off.   1 Cor. 15:2 • [John 15:2]

23 And they also, Rif they do not continue in unbelief, will be grafted in, for God is able to graft them in again.   [2 Cor. 3:16]

24 For if you were cut out of the olive tree which is wild by nature, and were grafted contrary to nature into a cultivated olive tree, how much more will these, who *are* natural *branches,* be grafted into their own olive tree?

25 For I do not desire, brethren, that you should be ignorant of this mystery, lest you should be Rwise in your own Topinion, that Rblindness in part has happened to Israel Runtil the fullness of the Gentiles has come in.   Rom. 12:16 • *estimation* • 2 Cor. 3:14 • Luke 21:24

26 And so all Israel will be *saved, as it is written:

R*"The Deliverer will come out of Zion,*
And He will turn away ungodliness from Jacob;   Is. 59:20, 21
27 For Rthis is My covenant with them,*
When I take away their sins."   Is. 27:9

28 Concerning the gospel *they are* enemies for your sake, but concerning the election *they are* beloved for the sake of the fathers.

11:6 NU omits the rest of v. 6.

11:22 NU adds *of God*
11:26 Or *delivered*

29 For the gifts and the calling of God *are* [R]irrevocable.   Num. 23:19

30 For as you [R]were once disobedient to God, yet have now obtained mercy through their disobedience,   [Eph. 2:2]

31 even so these also have now been disobedient, that through the mercy shown you they also may obtain mercy.

32 For God has [T]committed them [R]all to disobedience, that He might have mercy on all.   *shut them all up in* · [Gal. 3:22]

33 Oh, the depth of the riches both of the wisdom and knowledge of God! How unsearchable *are* His judgments and His ways past finding out!

34 "For who has known the [R]mind of the LORD?   Is. 40:13; Jer. 23:18
    Or who has become His counselor?"

35 "Or[R] who has first given to Him
    And it shall be repaid to him?"   Job 41:11

36 For [R]of Him and through Him and to Him *are* all things, [R]to whom *be* glory forever. Amen.   Heb. 2:10 · Heb. 13:21

29-C. God's Will Is Good, Acceptable, and Perfect   ▼

Living Sacrifices to God

12 I beseech you therefore, brethren, by the mercies of God, that you present your bodies a living sacrifice, holy, acceptable to God, *which is* your reasonable service.

2 And do not be conformed to this world, but be transformed by the renewing of your mind, that you may prove what *is* that good and acceptable and perfect will of God.   ▲

26-B. You Are What You Think   ▼

Serve God with Spiritual Gifts

3 For I say, through the grace given to me, to everyone who is among you, not to think

---

29-C. God's Will Is Good, Acceptable, and Perfect (Romans 12:1, 2)—Paul urges every believer to "prove [to yourself and others] what is that good and acceptable and perfect will of God" (v. 2). If you are a born-again believer and you do not know God's revealed will for your life, you are cheating yourself (living beneath your privilege) and grieving the Holy Spirit. God's revealed will is:

(1) *Good.* It is good in itself because it is God's will. It is good for you, and good to you. In the will of God, the believer can claim His promises, i.e., "For the LORD God is a sun and shield; the LORD will give grace and glory; no good thing will He withhold from those who walk uprightly" (Ps. 84:11, page 561). The key word in this promise is "give."

(a) "The LORD God" is the giver of every good and perfect gift (James 1:17, page 1256).
(b) This Giver is a "sun and shield." He is the light of the world to guide you each step of the way as you walk in His will (John 8:12, page 1062), and He is a shield to protect you (Ps. 3:2, 3, page 510).
(c) He gives "grace and glory." In the revealed will of God you know the grace of God that brings eternal riches. "For you know the grace of our Lord Jesus Christ, that though He was rich, yet for your sakes He became poor, that you through His poverty might become [eternally] rich" (2 Cor. 8:9, page 1171). His glory is also a gift; can you think of a greater reward? He will share His grace and glory with those who do His good will (Rom. 8:17, page 1137). Paul said, "hold fast what is good" (1 Thess. 5:21, page 1213).

(2) *Acceptable.* God's revealed will is the only will that is acceptable to Him. Man's natural will is rebellious, or carnal (Rom. 8:6–8, page 1137). Satan's will is totally evil (Is. 14:13, 14, page 657). Five times Satan said, "I will;" not once did he regard the will of God. The question is, to what degree does your will conform to God's will? You are either doing the will of Satan (which is evil), or the will of self (which is carnal), or the will of God (which is good, acceptable, and perfect). It is impossible to please God and walk in man's carnal way, or Satan's corrupt way (Eph. 2:1–3, page 1187).

(3) *Perfect.* Because God is perfect, His will is perfect. His will is pleasing to His perfect nature, in the most infinitesimal detail. The will of God can be discovered and obeyed by every believer. Because He has revealed to us the mystery of His will in His Word (Eph. 1:9, page 1186), God wants us to know and understand His revealed will, which is good, acceptable, and perfect (Eph. 5:17, page 1192).

See Hebrews 13:20, 21, page 1252, for **Point 29-D: God's Will Can Be Known.**

26-B. You Are What You Think (Romans 12:3)—You are not always what you think you are, you *are* what you *think.* As a child of God you must not think too *lowly* of yourself because you are a "new creation" in Christ, an ambassador for Christ. You have become "the righteousness of God in Him" (2 Cor. 5:17–21, page 1169). Don't you know that you belong to the aristocracy of heaven? So think like the spiritual aristocrat that you are. You are a part of God's nobility (1 John 3:2, page 1279).

However, you have an old sinful nature. Therefore, Paul tells us not to think of ourselves more *highly* than we ought to think (v. 3). He also said, "For I know that in me (that is, in my flesh) nothing good dwells" (Rom. 7:18, page 1136). Jesus said, "That which is born of the flesh is flesh" (John 3:6, page 1052). In other words, the New Birth in itself does not change or perfect the flesh. The flesh is carnal and there is no escaping it until death (Ps. 51:5, page 541), or until the rapture of the church, when we shall be changed "in the twinkling of an eye" (1 Cor. 15:52, page 1163). Therefore, if you are to be an effective child of God in this

(Point 26-B continued on next page)

▽ *of himself* more highly than he ought to think, but to think soberly, as God has dealt ▲ to each one a measure of faith.

4 For [R]as we have many members in one body, but all the members do not have the same function, 1 Cor. 12:12-14

5 so [R]we, *being* many, are one body in Christ, and individually members of one another. [1 Cor. 10:17]

6 Having then gifts differing according to the grace that is [R]given to us, *let us use them:* if prophecy, *let us* [R]prophesy in proportion to our faith; [John 3:27] • Acts 11:27

7 or ministry, *let us use it* in *our* ministering; [R]he who teaches, in teaching; Eph. 4:11

8 he who exhorts, in exhortation; [R]he who gives, with liberality; [R]he who leads, with diligence; he who shows mercy, [R]with cheerfulness. [Matt. 6:1-3] • [Acts 20:28] • 2 Cor. 9:7

Behave Like a Christian

9 *Let* love *be* without hypocrisy. [R]Abhor what is evil. Cling to what is good. Ps. 34:14

10 [R]*Be* kindly affectionate to one another with brotherly love, [R]in honor giving preference to one another; Heb. 13:1 • Phil. 2:3

11 not lagging in diligence, fervent in spirit, serving the Lord;

12 rejoicing in hope, patient in tribulation, continuing steadfastly in prayer;

13 distributing to the needs of the saints, [R]given[T] to hospitality. 1 Tim. 3:2 • Lit. *pursuing*

14 [R]Bless those who persecute you; bless and do not curse. [Matt. 5:44]

15 [R]Rejoice with those who rejoice, and weep with those who weep. [1 Cor. 12:26]

16 [R]Be of the same mind toward one another. [R]Do not set your mind on high things, but associate with the humble. Do not be wise in your own opinion. [Phil. 2:2; 4:2] • Jer. 45:5

17 Repay no one evil for evil. Have regard for good things in the sight of all men.

18 If it is possible, as much as depends on you, [R]live peaceably with all men. Heb. 12:14

19 Beloved, [R]do not avenge yourselves, but *rather* give place to wrath; for it is written, [R]"Vengeance is Mine, I will repay," says the Lord. Lev. 19:18 • Deut. 32:35

20 Therefore

[R]*"If your enemy hungers, feed him;*
If he thirsts, give him a drink;
For in so doing you will heap coals of
fire on his head." Prov. 25:21, 22

21 Do not be overcome by evil, but [R]overcome evil with good. [Rom. 12:1, 2]

Submit to Government

13 Let every soul be [R]subject to the governing authorities. For there is no authority except from God, and the authorities that exist are appointed by God. 1 Pet. 2:13

2 Therefore whoever resists the authority resists the ordinance of God, and those who resist will bring judgment on themselves.

3 For rulers are not a terror to good works, but to evil. Do you want to be unafraid of the authority? [R]Do what is good, and you will have praise from the same. 1 Pet. 2:14

(Point 26-B continued from previous page)
sin-cursed world, you must keep the fleshly nature under control and bring it into subjection to the will of God, or else be disqualified as Christ's ambassador (1 Cor. 9:27, page 1154).

One of the most important things you do is think. Your thinking can be profitable or futile. You are the master of your thoughts; you think by choice. You can think good or you can think evil—the choice is yours. You cannot think both good and evil simultaneously anymore than you can travel east and west at the same time. Every thought must be brought into subjection to the mind of Christ. Studying God's Word with the Spirit's illumination forms the mind of Christ in you.

How do you choose to think? You can think the following kind of thoughts (Phil. 4:8, page 1198):

(1) righteous or unrighteous
(2) clean or unclean
(3) moral or immoral
(4) honest or dishonest
(5) pure or impure
(6) true or untrue
(7) noble or ignoble
(8) just or unjust
(9) lovely or ugly
(10) good or bad
(11) virtuous or corrupt
(12) praiseworthy or unworthy

Accept God's great invitation: " 'Come now, and let us reason together,' says the LORD, 'Though your sins are like scarlet, they shall be as white as snow; though they are red like crimson, they shall be as wool'" (Is. 1:18, page 643). Think with the Lord, and hide God's Word in your heart, so that you do not sin against Him in thought, word, or deed (Ps. 119:11, page 581). You always sin in thought before you sin in word or deed. Remember, you are what you think.

See Isaiah 55:7–9, page 695, for **Point 26-C: Thinking Makes the Person.**

4 For he is God's minister to you for good. But if you do evil, be afraid; for he does not bear the sword in vain; for he is God's minister, an avenger to *execute* wrath on him who practices evil.

5 Therefore ᴿyou must be subject, not only because of wrath ᴿbut also for conscience' sake. Eccl. 8:2 • [1 Pet. 2:13, 19]

6 For because of this you also pay taxes, for they are God's ministers attending continually to this very thing.

7 ᴿRender therefore to all their due: taxes to whom taxes *are* due, customs to whom customs, fear to whom fear, honor to whom honor. Matt. 22:21

Love Your Neighbor

8 Owe no one anything except to love one another, for ᴿhe who loves another has fulfilled the law. [Gal. 5:13, 14]

9 For the commandments, * *"You shall not commit adultery," "You shall not murder," "You shall not steal,"* * *"You shall not bear false witness," "You shall not covet,"* and if there is any other commandment, are *all* summed up in this saying, namely, * *"You shall love your neighbor as yourself."*

10 Love does no harm to a neighbor; therefore love is the fulfillment of the law.

Put on Christ

11 And *do* this, knowing the time, that now it is high time ᴿto awake out of sleep; for now our salvation is nearer than when we *first* believed. [1 Cor. 15:34]

12 The night is far spent, the day is at hand. Therefore let us cast off the works of darkness, and let us put on the armor of light.

13 Let us walk properly, as in the day, not in revelry and drunkenness, not in lewdness and lust, ᴿnot in strife and envy. James 3:14

14 But ᴿput on the Lord Jesus Christ, and ᴿmake no provision for the flesh, to *fulfill its* lusts. Gal. 3:27 • [Gal. 5:16]

The Law of Liberty

14 Receive one who is weak in the faith, *but* not to disputes over doubtful things.

2 For one believes he may eat all things, but he who is weak eats *only* vegetables.

3 Let not him who eats despise him who does not eat, and ᴿlet not him who does not eat judge him who eats; for God has received him. [Col. 2:16]

4 ᴿWho are you to judge another's servant? To his own master he stands or falls. Indeed, he will be made to stand, for God is able to make him stand. James 4:11, 12

5 One person esteems *one* day above another; another esteems every day *alike.* Let each be fully convinced in his own mind.

6 He who observes the day, observes *it* to the Lord; *and he who does not observe the day, to the Lord he does not observe *it.* He who eats, eats to the Lord, for he gives God thanks; and he who does not eat, to the Lord he does not eat, and gives God thanks.

7 For ᴿnone of us lives to himself, and no one dies to himself. [Gal. 2:20]

8 For if we live, we live to the Lord; and if we die, we die to the Lord. Therefore, whether we live or die, we are the Lord's.

9 For to this end Christ died *and rose and lived again, that He might be ᴿLord of both the dead and the living. Acts 10:36

10 But why do you judge your brother? Or why do you show contempt for your brother? For ᴿwe shall all stand before the judgment seat of *Christ. 2 Cor. 5:10

11 For it is written:

> ᴿ*"As I live, says the LORD,*
> *Every knee shall bow to Me,*
> *And every tongue shall confess to God."* Is. 45:23

12 So then ᴿeach of us shall give account of himself to God. 1 Pet. 4:5

13 Therefore let us not judge one another ᵀanymore, but rather resolve this, ᴿnot to put a stumbling block or a cause to fall in *our* brother's way. *any longer* • 1 Cor. 8:9

The Law of Love

14 I know and am convinced by the Lord Jesus ᴿthat *there is* nothing unclean of itself; but to him who considers anything to be unclean, to him *it is* unclean. 1 Cor. 10:25

15 Yet if your brother is grieved because of *your* food, you are no longer walking in love. ᴿDo not destroy with your food the one for whom Christ died. 1 Cor. 8:11

16 ᴿTherefore do not let your good be spoken of as evil; [Rom. 12:17]

17 ᴿfor the kingdom of God is not eating and drinking, but righteousness and ᴿpeace and joy in the Holy Spirit. 1 Cor. 8:8 • [Rom. 8:6]

18 For he who serves Christ in *these things is acceptable to God and approved by men.

19 Therefore let us pursue the things *which make* for peace and the things by which one may ᵀedify another. *build up*

20 Do not destroy the work of God for the sake of food. All things indeed *are* pure, ᴿbut *it is* evil for the man who eats with ᵀoffense. 1 Cor. 8:9–12 • A feeling of giving offense

---

13:9 Ex. 20:13–17; Deut. 5:17–21; Matt. 19:18 • Lev. 19:18; Mark 12:31; James 2:8 • NU omits *"You shall not bear false witness,"*

14:6 NU omits the rest of this sentence.
14:9 NU omits *and rose*
14:10 NU God
14:18 NU *this thing*

21 *It is* good neither to eat meat nor drink wine nor *do anything* by which your brother stumbles *or is offended or is made weak.

22 *Do you have faith? Have *it* to yourself before God. Happy *is* he who does not condemn himself in what he approves.

23 But he who doubts is condemned if he eats, because *he does* not *eat* from faith; for Rwhatever *is* not from faith is sin.*   Titus 1:15

Bearing Others' Burdens

15 We Rthen who are strong ought to bear with the Tscruples of the weak, and not to please ourselves. [Gal. 6:1, 2] • *weaknesses*

2 Let each of us please *his* neighbor for *his* good, leading to Tedification.   *building up*

3 For even Christ did not please Himself; but as it is written, R*"The reproaches of those who reproached You fell on Me."* Ps. 69:7, 9, 20

4 For whatever things were written before were written for our learning, that we through the Tpatience and comfort of the Scriptures might have hope.   *perseverance*

5 RNow may the God of patience and comfort grant you to be like-minded toward one another, according to Christ Jesus,   1 Cor. 1:10

6 that you may Rwith one mind *and* one mouth glorify the God and Father of our Lord Jesus Christ.   Acts 4:24

Glorify God Together

7 Therefore receive one another, just as Christ also received *us, to the glory of God.

8 Now I say that RJesus Christ has become a Tservant to the circumcision for the truth of God, Rto confirm the promises *made* to the fathers,   Matt. 15:24 • *minister* • 2 Cor. 1:20

9 and Rthat the Gentiles might glorify God for *His* mercy, as it is written: John 10:16

R*"For this reason I will confess to You among the Gentiles,*   2 Sam. 22:50; Ps. 18:49
And sing to Your name."

10 And again he says:

"Rejoice, O Gentiles, with His people!"

11 And again:

R*"Praise the Lord, all you Gentiles! Laud Him, all you peoples!"*   Ps. 117:1

12 And again, Isaiah says:

R*"There shall be a root of Jesse; And He who shall rise to reign over the Gentiles,*   Is. 11:10
In Him the Gentiles shall hope."

13 Now may the God of hope fill you with all Rjoy and peace in believing, that you may abound in hope by the power of the Holy Spirit.   Rom. 12:12; 14:17

From Jerusalem to Illyricum

14 Now I myself am confident concerning you, my brethren, that you also are full of goodness, Rfilled with all knowledge, able also to admonish *one another.   1 Cor. 1:5; 8:1, 7, 10

15 Nevertheless, brethren, I have written more boldly to you on *some* points, as reminding you, Rbecause of the grace given to me by God,   Rom. 1:5; 12:3

16 that RI might be a minister of Jesus Christ to the Gentiles, ministering the gospel of God, that the Roffering Tof the Gentiles might be acceptable, sanctified by the Holy Spirit.   Rom. 11:13 • [Is. 66:20] • *Consisting of*

17 Therefore I have reason to glory in Christ Jesus Rin the things *which pertain* to God.   Heb. 2:17; 5:1

18 For I will not dare to speak of any of those things which Christ has not accomplished through me, in word and deed, Rto make the Gentiles obedient—   Rom. 1:5

19 in mighty signs and wonders, by the power of the Spirit of God, so that from Jerusalem and round about to Illyricum I have fully preached the gospel of Christ.

20 And so I have made it my aim to preach the gospel, not where Christ was named, lest I should build on another man's foundation,

21 but as it is written:

R*"To whom He was not announced, they shall see; *   Is. 52:15
And those who have not heard shall understand."

Plan to Visit Rome

22 For this reason RI also have been much hindered from coming to you.   Rom. 1:13

23 But now no longer having a place in these parts, and Rhaving a great desire these many years to come to you,   Acts 19:21; 23:11

24 whenever I journey to Spain, *I shall come to you. For I hope to see you on my journey, Rand to be helped on my way there by you, if first I may Renjoy your *company* for a while.   Acts 15:3 • Rom. 1:12

25 But now RI am going to Jerusalem to Tminister to the saints.   Acts 19:21 • *serve*

26 For Rit pleased those from Macedonia and Achaia to make a certain contribution for the poor among the saints who are in Jerusalem.   1 Cor. 16:1

27 It pleased them indeed, and they are their debtors. For if the Gentiles have been partakers of their spiritual things, their duty is also to minister to them in material things.

14:21 NU omits the rest of v. 21.
14:22 NU *The faith which you have—have*
14:23 M puts Rom. 16:25–27 here.
15:7 NU, M *you*
15:10 Deut. 32:43

15:14 M *others*
15:24 NU omits *I shall come to you* and joins *Spain* with the next sentence.

28 Therefore, when I have performed this and have sealed to them ᴿthis fruit, I shall go by way of you to Spain.   Phil. 4:17

29 ᴿBut I know that when I come to you, I shall come in the fullness of the blessing *of the gospel of Christ.   [Rom. 1:11]

30 Now I beg you, brethren, through the Lord Jesus Christ, and through the love of the Spirit, ᴿthat you strive together with me in prayers to God for me,   2 Cor. 1:11

31 ᴿthat I may be delivered from those in Judea who ᵀdo not believe, and that ᴿmy service for Jerusalem may be acceptable to the saints,   2 Tim. 3:11; 4:17 • *are disobedient* • 2 Cor. 8:4

32 ᴿthat I may come to you with joy ᴿby the will of God, and may ᴿbe refreshed together with you.   Rom. 1:10 • Acts 18:21 • 1 Cor. 16:18

33 Now ᴿthe God of peace *be* with you all. Amen.   1 Cor. 14:33

Sister Phoebe Commended

16 I commend to you Phoebe our sister, who is a servant of the church in Cenchrea,

2 ᴿthat you may receive her in the Lord ᴿin a manner worthy of the saints, and assist her in whatever business she has need of you; for indeed she has been a helper of many and of myself also.   Phil. 2:29 • Phil. 1:27

Greeting Roman Saints

3 Greet ᴿPriscilla and Aquila, my fellow workers in Christ Jesus,   Acts 18:2, 18, 26

4 who risked their own necks for my life, to whom not only I give thanks, but also all the churches of the Gentiles.

5 Likewise *greet* the church that is in their house. Greet my beloved Epaenetus, who is the firstfruits of *Achaia to Christ.

6 Greet Mary, who labored much for us.

7 Greet Andronicus and Junia, my countrymen and my fellow prisoners, who are of note among the ᴿapostles, who also ᴿwere in Christ before me.   Acts 1:13, 26 • Gal. 1:22

8 Greet Amplias, my beloved in the Lord.

9 Greet Urbanus, our fellow worker in Christ, and Stachys, my beloved.

10 Greet Apelles, approved in Christ. Greet those who are of the *household* of Aristobulus.

11 Greet Herodion, my ᵀcountryman. Greet those who are of the *household* of Narcissus who are in the Lord.   Or *relative*

12 Greet Tryphena and Tryphosa, who have labored in the Lord. Greet the beloved Persis, who labored much in the Lord.

13 Greet Rufus, ᴿchosen in the Lord, and his mother and mine.   2 John 1

14 Greet Asyncritus, Phlegon, Hermas, Patrobas, Hermes, and the brethren who are with them.

15 Greet Philologus and Julia, Nereus and his sister, and Olympas, and all the saints who are with them.

16 ᴿGreet one another with a holy kiss. *The churches of Christ greet you.   1 Cor. 16:20

Avoid Divisive Persons

17 Now I urge you, brethren, note those ᴿwho cause divisions and offenses, contrary to the doctrine which you learned, and ᴿavoid them.   [Acts 15:1] • [1 Cor. 5:9]

18 For those who are such do not serve our Lord *Jesus Christ, but their own belly, and ᴿby smooth words and flattering speech deceive the hearts of the simple.   Col. 2:4

19 For ᴿyour obedience has become known to all. Therefore I am glad on your behalf; but I want you to be wise in what is good, and ᵀsimple concerning evil.   Rom. 1:8 • *innocent*

20 And the God of peace will crush Satan under your feet shortly. The grace of our Lord Jesus Christ *be* with you. Amen.

Greetings from Paul's Friends

21 ᴿTimothy, my fellow worker, and ᴿLucius, ᴿJason, and ᴿSosipater, my countrymen, greet you.   Acts 16:1 • Acts 13:1 • Acts 17:5 • Acts 20:4

22 I, Tertius, who wrote *this* epistle, greet you in the Lord.

23 ᴿGaius, my host and *the* host of the whole church, greets you. ᴿErastus, the treasurer of the city, greets you, and Quartus, a brother.   1 Cor. 1:14 • Acts 19:22

24 ᴿThe* grace of our Lord Jesus Christ *be* with you all. Amen.   1 Thess. 5:28

Benediction

25 *Now ᴿto Him who is able to establish you ᴿaccording to my gospel and the preaching of Jesus Christ, according to the revelation of the mystery kept secret since the world began   [Eph. 3:20] • Rom. 2:16

26 but ᴿnow has been made manifest, and by the prophetic Scriptures has been made known to all nations, according to the commandment of the everlasting God, for ᴿobedience to the faith—   Eph. 1:9 • Rom. 1:5

27 to ᴿGod, alone wise, *be* glory through Jesus Christ forever. Amen.   Jude 25

15:29 NU omits *of the gospel*
16:5 NU *Asia*
16:16 NU *All the churches*
16:18 NU, M omit *Jesus*
16:24 NU omits v. 24.
16:25 M puts Rom. 16:25–27 after Rom. 14:23.

THE FIRST EPISTLE OF PAUL THE APOSTLE TO THE

Corinthians

AUTHORSHIP. The book of 1 Corinthians was written by the apostle Paul to a church that he had founded in the early part of his ministry. The Pauline authorship of the letter is scarcely doubted by anyone. Vocabulary, contents, and style all point to Paul. 1 Corinthians is also the first book to be credited specifically to Paul in the works of Clement of Rome (about A.D. 95).

HOW 1 CORINTHIANS FITS INTO THE BIBLE. This is a long, varied, and extremely important epistle. Because it deals with a church coming out of the darkness of paganism, it is most helpful on mission fields today. However, the church problems of Corinth also sound strangely familiar when one sees the things going on in many churches of the Western world today. Another benefit of this book is that it is so utterly practical and relates to common problems and real people in a very special way.

HOW 1 CORINTHIANS FITS TOGETHER. Because Paul is answering several questions asked by the Corinthians as well as commenting on other problems that he had heard about through "those of Chloe's household," a more detailed outline is needed than in some of the simpler epistles:

(1) Divisions in the Church (chs. 1—4)
(2) Immorality in the Church (ch. 5)
(3) The Law Courts and the Church (ch. 6)
(4) Christian Marriage (ch. 7)
(5) On Meat Offered to Idols (chs. 8—10)
(6) Head Coverings and the Lord's Supper (ch. 11)
(7) Spiritual Gifts in the Church (chs. 12—14)
(8) The Doctrine of Resurrection (ch. 15)
(9) The Collection and Personal Notes (ch. 16)

The Corinthian believers were richly blessed with spiritual gifts that would outfit this body of Christians to carry out the Great Commission, but because of immaturity, carnality, and lack of spiritual growth they were unable to accomplish God's will. There was internal confusion, strife, and division. Their immaturity and carnality produced the following problems:

—They were following human leadership instead of God.
—They were admiring human wisdom.
—They were judgmental of each other.
—They questioned authority.
—They permitted immorality in the church.
—Some were taking each other into the world's courts.
—They were not yielding the physical body to the Lord's service.
—They were confusing the marriage obligations.
—They were misusing their liberty in Christ.
—Some had become stumbling blocks to other believers.
—They were making no financial provision for Paul and were taking his services for granted.
—They were grumbling and complaining.
—They were selfish and greedy.
—Some were misusing the elements of the Lord's Supper and violating its order.
—They were magnifying the "showy" gifts of the Spirit and minimizing the others.
—They were guilty of not loving.
—They were misusing the gift of tongues.
—Some were questioning the resurrection of Christ.
—They were unfaithful in their regular giving.

Paul wrote this epistle to correct such problems within the church, and in each chapter you will read his stern rebuke and positive redirection. He admonished his readers to correct these things in the light of the judgment of Christ and the examining of their works (1 Cor. 3:11-15). His lessons need to be learned and applied, not just in the first century but also in the twentieth.

—G.G.

Greeting

PAUL, called *to be* an apostle of Jesus Christ ᴿthrough the will of God, and ᴿSosthenes *our* brother, 2 Cor. 1:1 • Acts 18:17

2 To the church of God which is at Corinth, to those who are ᵀsanctified in Christ Jesus, called *to be* saints, with all who in every place call on the name of Jesus Christ our Lord, both theirs and ours: *set apart*

3 ᴿGrace to you and peace from God our Father and the Lord Jesus Christ.   Rom. 1:7

Spiritual Gifts at Corinth

4 ᴿI thank my God always concerning you for the grace of God which was given to you by Christ Jesus,   Rom. 1:8

5 that you were enriched in everything by Him in all utterance and all knowledge,

6 even as ᴿthe testimony of Christ was confirmed ᵀin you,   2 Tim. 1:8 • Or *among*

7 so that you come short in no gift, eagerly ᴿwaiting for the revelation of our Lord Jesus Christ,   Phil. 3:20

8 ᴿwho will also confirm you to the end, ᴿ*that you may be* blameless in the day of our Lord Jesus Christ.   1 Thess. 3:13; 5:23 • Col. 1:22; 2:7

9 ᴿGod *is* faithful, by whom you were called into ᴿthe fellowship of His Son, Jesus Christ our Lord.   Is. 49:7 • [John 15:4]

Sectarianism Is Sin

10 Now I plead with you, brethren, by the name of our Lord Jesus Christ, that you all speak the same thing, and *that* there be no ᵀdivisions among you, but *that* you be perfectly joined together in the same mind and in the same judgment.   *schisms* or *dissensions*

11 For it has been declared to me concerning you, my brethren, by those of Chloe's *household*, that there are ᵀcontentions among you.   *quarrels*

12 Now I say this, that each of you says, "I am of Paul," or "I am of Apollos," or "I am of ᴿCephas," or "I am of Christ."   John 1:42

13 ᴿIs Christ divided? Was Paul crucified for you? Or were you baptized in the name of Paul?   2 Cor. 11:4

14 I thank God that I baptized ᴿnone of you except ᴿCrispus and Gaius,   John 4:2 • Acts 18:8

15 lest anyone should say that I had baptized in my own name.

16 Yes, I also baptized the household of ᴿStephanas. Besides, I do not know whether I baptized any other.   1 Cor. 16:15, 17

17 For Christ did not send me to baptize, but to preach the gospel, ᴿnot with wisdom of words, lest the cross of Christ should be made of no effect.   [1 Cor. 2:1, 4, 13]

Christ the Power and Wisdom of God

18 For the message of the cross is foolishness to those who are perishing, but to us who are being saved it is the power of God.

19 For it is written:

ᴿ"I *will destroy the wisdom of the wise,*
And bring to nothing the understanding
of the prudent."   Is. 29:14

20 Where *is* the wise? Where *is* the scribe? Where *is* the disputer of this age? Has not God made foolish the wisdom of this world?

21 For since, in the wisdom of God, the world through wisdom did not know God, it pleased God through the foolishness of the message preached to save those who believe.

22 For ᴿJews request a sign, and Greeks seek after wisdom;   Matt. 12:38

23 but we preach Christ crucified, to the Jews a ᵀstumbling block and to the *Greeks ᴿfoolishness,   Gr. *skandalon, offense* • [1 Cor. 2:14]

24 but to those who are called, both Jews and Greeks, Christ ᴿthe power of God and ᴿthe wisdom of God.   [Rom. 1:4] • Col. 2:3

25 Because the foolishness of God is wiser than men, and the weakness of God is stronger than men.

Glory Only in the Lord

26 For you see your calling, brethren, that not many wise according to the flesh, not many mighty, not many noble, *are called*.

27 But God has chosen the foolish things of the world to put to shame the wise, and God has chosen the weak things of the world to put to shame the things which are mighty;

28 and the ᵀbase things of the world and the things which are despised God has chosen, and the things which are not, to bring to nothing the things that are,   *insignificant* or *lowly*

29 that no flesh should glory in His presence.

30 But of Him you are in Christ Jesus, who became for us wisdom from God—and ᴿrighteousness and sanctification and redemption—   [2 Cor. 5:21]

31 that, as it is written, ᴿ"He who glories, let him glory in the Lᴏʀᴅ."   Jer. 9:23, 24

Christ Crucified

2 And I, brethren, when I came to you, did not come with excellence of speech or of wisdom declaring to you the *testimony of God.

2 For I determined not to know anything among you ᴿexcept Jesus Christ and Him crucified.   Gal. 6:14

3 ᴿI was with you ᴿin weakness, in fear, and in much trembling.   Acts 18:1 • [2 Cor. 4:7]

4 And my speech and my preaching ᴿ*were* not with persuasive words of *human wisdom, ᴿbut in demonstration of the Spirit and of power,   2 Pet. 1:16 • Rom. 15:19

1:23 NU *Gentiles*
2:1 NU *mystery*
2:4 NU omits *human*

5 that your faith should not be in the wisdom of men but in the power of God.

Spiritual Wisdom

6 However, we speak wisdom among those who are mature, yet not the wisdom of this age, nor of the rulers of this age, who are coming to nothing.

7 But we speak the wisdom of God in a mystery, the hidden *wisdom* which God ordained before the ages for our glory,

8 which none of the rulers of this age knew; for ᴿhad they known, they would not have crucified the Lord of glory.   Luke 23:34

9 But as it is written:

ᴿ"*Eye has not seen, nor ear heard,*
   Nor have entered into the heart of man
   The things which God has prepared for
      those who love Him."   [Is. 64:4; 65:17]

10 But God has revealed *them* to us through His Spirit. For the Spirit searches all things, yes, the deep things of God.

11 For what man knows the things of a man except the spirit of the man which is in him? ᴿEven so no one knows the things of God except the Spirit of God.   Rom. 11:33

12 Now we have received, not the spirit of the world, but ᴿthe Spirit who is from God, that we might know the things that have been freely given to us by God.   [Rom. 8:15]

13 These things we also speak, not in words which man's wisdom teaches but which the *Holy Spirit teaches, comparing spiritual things with spiritual.

14 But the natural man does not receive the things of the Spirit of God, for they are foolishness to him; nor can he know *them,* because they are spiritually discerned.

15 But he who is spiritual judges all things, yet he himself is *rightly* judged by no one.

16 For ᴿ"*who has known the mind of the* LORD *that he may instruct Him?"* ᴿBut we have the mind of Christ.   Is. 40:13 • [John 15:15]

Sectarianism Is Carnal

3 And I, brethren, could not speak to you as to spiritual *people* but as to carnal, as to ᴿbabes in Christ.   Heb. 5:13

2 I fed you with milk and not with solid food; for until now you were not able *to receive it,* and even now you are still not able;

3 for you are still carnal. For where *there are* envy, strife, and divisions among you, are you not carnal and behaving like *mere* men?

4 For when one says, "I am of Paul," and another, "I *am* of Apollos," are you not carnal?

Watering, Working, Warning

5 Who then is Paul, and who *is* Apollos, but ᴿministers through whom you believed, as the Lord gave to each one?   2 Cor. 3:3, 6

6 I planted, ᴿApollos watered, ᴿbut God gave the increase.   Acts 18:24-27 • [2 Cor. 3:5]

7 So then ᴿneither he who plants is anything, nor he who waters, but God who gives the increase.   [Gal. 6:3]

8 Now he who plants and he who waters are one, ᴿand each one will receive his own reward according to his own labor.   Ps. 62:12

9 For we are God's fellow workers; you are God's field, *you are* God's building.

10 ᴿAccording to the grace of God which was given to me, as a wise master builder I have laid ᴿthe foundation, and another builds on it. But let each one take heed how he builds on it.   Rom. 1:5 • 1 Cor. 4:15

11 For no other foundation can anyone lay than ᴿthat which is laid, ᴿwhich is Jesus Christ.   Is. 28:16 • Eph. 2:20

12 Now if anyone builds on this foundation *with* gold, silver, precious stones, wood, hay, straw,

13 each one's work will become clear; for the Day will declare it, because ᴿit will be revealed by fire; and the fire will test each one's work, of what sort it is.   Luke 2:35

14 If anyone's work which he has built on *it* endures, he will receive a reward.

15 If anyone's work is burned, he will suffer loss; but he himself will be saved, yet so as through fire.

16 ᴿDo you not know that you are the temple of God and *that* the Spirit of God dwells in you?   2 Cor. 6:16

17 If anyone ᵀdefiles the temple of God, God will destroy him. For the temple of God is holy, which *temple* you are.   destroys

Avoid Worldly Wisdom

18 Let no one deceive himself. If anyone among you seems to be wise in this age, let him become a fool that he may become wise.

19 For the wisdom of this world is foolishness with God. For it is written, ᴿ"*He catches the wise in their own craftiness";*   Job 5:13

20 and again, *"The LORD knows the thoughts of the wise, that they are futile."*

21 Therefore let no one boast in men. For ᴿall things are yours: [2 Cor. 4:5]

22 whether Paul or Apollos or Cephas, or the world or life or death, or things present or things to come—all are yours.

23 And ᴿyou *are* Christ's, and Christ *is* God's.   2 Cor. 10:7

Stewards of the Mysteries of God

4 Let a man so consider us, as ᴿservants of Christ ᴿand stewards of the mysteries of God.   Col. 1:25 • Titus 1:7

2 Moreover it is required in stewards that one be found faithful.

3 But with me it is a very small thing that

I should be judged by you or by a human *court. In fact, I do not even judge myself.

4 For I know of nothing against myself, yet I am not justified by this; but He who judges me is the Lord.

5 Therefore judge nothing before the time, until the Lord comes, who will both bring to light the hidden things of darkness and reveal the counsels of the hearts. Then each one's praise will come from God.

Fools for Christ's Sake

6 Now these things, brethren, I have figuratively transferred to myself and Apollos for your sakes, that you may learn in us not to think beyond what is written, that none of you may be ᵀpuffed up on behalf of one against the other.   *arrogant*

7 For who ᵀmakes you differ *from another*? And ᴿwhat do you have that you did not receive? Now if you did indeed receive *it*, why do you boast as if you had not received *it*?   *distinguishes you* · John 3:27

8 You are already full! ᴿYou are already rich! You have reigned as kings without us— and indeed I could wish you did reign, that we also might reign with you!   Rev. 3:17

9 For I think that God has displayed us, the apostles, last, as men condemned to death; for we have been made a spectacle to the world, both to angels and to men.

10 We *are* ᴿfools for Christ's sake, but you *are* wise in Christ! ᴿWe *are* weak, but you *are* strong! You *are* distinguished, but we *are* dishonored!   Acts 17:18; 26:24 · 2 Cor. 13:9

11 To the present hour we both hunger and thirst, and we are poorly clothed, and beaten, and homeless.

12 ᴿAnd we labor, working with our own hands. ᴿBeing reviled, we bless; being persecuted, we endure;   Acts 18:3; 20:34 · Matt. 5:44

13 being defamed, we ᵀentreat. We have been made as the filth of the world, the offscouring of all things until now.   *exhort*

Paul's Paternal Care

14 I do not write these things to shame you, but as my beloved children I warn *you*.

15 For though you might have ten thousand instructors in Christ, yet *you* do not *have* many fathers; for ᴿin Christ Jesus I have begotten you through the gospel.   Gal. 4:19

16 Therefore I urge you, imitate me.

17 For this reason I have sent ᴿTimothy to you, who is my beloved and faithful son in the Lord, who will ᴿremind you of my ways in Christ, as I ᴿteach everywhere ᴿin every church.   Acts 19:22 · 1 Cor. 11:2 · 1 Cor. 7:17 · 1 Cor. 14:33

18 ᴿNow some are ᵀpuffed up, as though I were not coming to you.   1 Cor. 5:2 · *arrogant*

19 But I will come to you shortly, if the Lord wills, and I will know, not the word of those who are puffed up, but the power.

20 For ᴿthe kingdom of God *is* not in word but in ᴿpower.   1 Thess. 1:5 · 1 Cor. 2:4

21 What do you want? ᴿShall I come to you with a rod, or in love and a spirit of gentleness?   2 Cor. 10:2

Immorality Defiles the Church

5 It is actually reported *that there is* sexual immorality among you, and such sexual immorality as is not even *named among the Gentiles—that a man has his father's wife!

2 And you are puffed up, and have not rather mourned, that he who has done this deed might be taken away from among you.

3 ᴿFor I indeed, as absent in body but present in spirit, have already judged (as though I were present) him who has so done this deed.   Col. 2:5

4 In the ᴿname of our Lord Jesus Christ, when you are gathered together, along with my spirit, ᴿwith the power of our Lord Jesus Christ,   [Matt. 18:20] · [John 20:23]

5 deliver such a one to Satan for the destruction of the flesh, that his spirit may be saved in the day of the Lord *Jesus.

6 ᴿYour glorying *is* not good. Do you not know that ᴿa little leaven leavens the whole lump?   1 Cor. 3:21 · Gal. 5:9

7 Therefore ᵀpurge out the old leaven, that you may be a new lump, since you truly are unleavened. For indeed ᴿChrist, our Passover, was sacrificed *for us.   *clean out* · Is. 53:7

8 Therefore let us keep the feast, not with old leaven, nor ᴿwith the leaven of malice and wickedness, but with the unleavened *bread* of sincerity and truth.   Matt. 16:6

Immorality Must Be Judged

9 I wrote to you in my epistle not to keep company with sexually immoral people.

10 Yet *I* certainly *did* not *mean* with the sexually immoral people of this world, or with the covetous, or extortioners, or idolaters, since then you would need to go ᴿout of the world.   John 17:15

11 But now I have written to you not to ᵀkeep company ᴿwith anyone named a brother, who is sexually immoral, or covetous, or an idolater, or a reviler, or a drunkard, or an extortioner—ᴿnot even to eat with such a person.   *associate* · Matt. 18:17 · Gal. 2:12

12 For what *have* I *to do* with judging those also who are outside? Do you not judge those who are inside?

13 But those who are outside God judges. Therefore ᴿ"put away from yourselves the *evil person.*"   Deut. 17:7; 19:19; 22:21, 24; 24:7

5:1 NU omits *named*
5:5 NU omits *Jesus*
5:7 NU omits *for us*

4:3 Lit. *day*

Do Not Sue the Brethren

6 Dare any of you, having a matter against another, go to law before the unrighteous, and not before the ᴿsaints?   Dan. 7:22

2 Do you not know that ᴿthe saints will judge the world? And if the world will be judged by you, are you unworthy to judge the smallest matters?   Ps. 49:14

▼ 13-E. Demons: Their Judgment

3 Do you not know that we shall ᴿjudge angels? How much more, things that pertain
▲ to this life?   2 Pet. 2:4

4 If then you have ᵀjudgments concerning things pertaining to this life, do you appoint those who are least esteemed by the church to judge?   courts

5 I say this to your shame. Is it so, that there is not a wise man among you, not even one, who will be able to judge between his brethren?

6 But brother goes to law against brother, and that before unbelievers!

7 Now therefore, it is already an utter failure for you that you go to law against one another. ᴿWhy do you not rather accept wrong? Why do you not rather *let yourselves* be cheated?   [Prov. 20:22]

8 No, you yourselves do wrong and cheat, and *you do* these things *to your* brethren!

9 Do you not know that the unrighteous will not inherit the kingdom of God? Do not be deceived. Neither fornicators, nor idolaters, nor adulterers, nor ᵀhomosexuals, nor sodomites,   Catamites, those submitting to homosexuals

10 nor thieves, nor covetous, nor drunkards, nor revilers, nor extortioners will inherit the kingdom of God.

11 And such were some of you. But you were washed, but you were ᵀsanctified, but you were justified in the name of the Lord Jesus and by the Spirit of our God.   set apart

Glorify God in Body and Spirit

12 ᴿAll things are lawful for me, but all things are not ᵀhelpful. All things are lawful for me, but I will not be brought under the power of ᵀany.   1 Cor. 10:23 • profitable • Or anything

13 ᴿFoods for the stomach and the stomach for foods, but God will destroy both it and them. Now the body *is* not for ᴿsexual immorality but ᴿfor the Lord, ᴿand the Lord for the body.   Matt. 15:17 • Gal. 5:19 • 1 Thess. 4:3 • [Eph. 5:23]

14 And God both raised up the Lord and will also raise us up ᴿby His power.   Eph. 1:19

15 Do you not know that ᴿyour bodies are members of Christ? Shall I then take the members of Christ and make *them* members of a harlot? Certainly not!   Rom. 12:5

16 Or do you not know that he who is joined to a harlot is one body *with her*? For

---

13-E. Demons: Their Judgment (1 Corinthians 6:3)—"Do you not know that we [the saved] shall judge angels?" (v. 3). Just think! God's Word says, "we shall judge angels." Truly, Satan and his angels have already been judged, and sentence has been passed. Some fallen angels are chained in darkness, awaiting execution of the judgment (Jude 6, page 1289). Others, including Satan, have been allowed to continue their evil work of accusing the brethren, buffeting the saints, and opposing the will of God (Job 1:6–11, page 479). Satan, also called Beelzebub, as the god of this world system, is master of the fallen angels; they do his will (Matt. 12:24, page 953). The Lord's final act, which will close the books on Satan and his demons, will be shared with His bride, the church. We will have a part in executing the sentence that has already been passed on the Devil and his angels (Matt. 25:41, page 976).

(1) When will we judge the fallen angels? Jude 6 (page 1289) tells us that the execution of the sentence will judicially be carried out at "the judgment of the great day." The "great day" is the day of the Lord (Is. 2:12–22, page 644).

(a) It will be a day of instituting peace and righteousness. "Then the King will say to those on His right hand, 'Come, you blessed of My Father, inherit the kingdom prepared for you from the foundation of the world'" (Matt. 25:31–40, page 976).

(b) It will also be a Day of Judgment. "Then He will also say to those on the left hand, 'Depart from Me, you cursed, into the everlasting fire prepared for the devil and his angels'" (Matt. 25:41–46, page 976). This is the beginning of "the judgment of the great day." The end will not come until the world has enjoyed righteous government for a thousand years. Simon Peter tells us "that with the Lord one day is as a thousand years, and a thousand years as one day" (2 Pet. 3:8, page 1275).

(c) For a thousand years Satan will be bound and cast into the bottomless pit. When the thousand years are finished, he will be released and will go out to deceive countless thousands who were born during the millennial (thousand-year) reign of Jesus Christ, but who were never born again (Rev. 20:1–3, 7–9, page 1313).

(2) The judgment of fallen angels will precede the Great White Throne judgment of the wicked dead, after the thousand years (Rev. 20:10, page 1313). Therefore, it is in harmony with the Scriptures to conclude that Satan and all evil angels will be judged by Christ and believers at the end of the thousand-year kingdom age, just before the Great White Throne judgment. Remember, Jesus said that hell was "prepared for the devil and his angels" (Matt. 25:41, page 976).

See Index, page 17, for your next study.

R "the two," He says, "shall become one flesh."   Gen. 2:24

17 RBut he who is joined to the Lord is one spirit with Him.   [John 17:21-23]

18 RFlee sexual immorality. Every sin that a man does is outside the body, but he who commits sexual immorality sins Ragainst his own body.   Heb. 13:4 • Rom. 1:24

19 Or Rdo you not know that your body is the temple of the Holy Spirit who is in you, whom you have from God, Rand you are not your own?   2 Cor. 6:16 • Rom. 14:7

20 For Ryou were bought at a price; therefore glorify God in your body *and in your spirit, which are God's.   2 Pet. 2:1

Principles of Marriage

7 Now concerning the things of which you wrote to me: RIt is good for a man not to touch a woman.   1 Cor. 7:8, 26

2 Nevertheless, because of sexual immorality, let each man have his own wife, and let each woman have her own husband.

3 RLet the husband render to his wife the affection due her, and likewise also the wife to her husband.   Ex. 21:10

4 The wife does not have authority over her own body, but the husband does. And likewise the husband does not have authority over his own body, but the wife does.

5 Do not deprive one another except with consent for a time, that you may give yourselves to fasting and prayer; and come together again so that Satan does not tempt you because of your lack of self-control.

6 But I say this as a concession, Rnot as a commandment.   2 Cor. 8:8

7 For I wish that all men were even as I myself. But each one has his own gift from God, one in this manner and another in that.

8 But I say to the unmarried and to the widows: RIt is good for them if they remain even as I am;   1 Cor. 7:1, 26

9 but Rif they cannot exercise self-control, let them marry. For it is better to marry than to burn with passion.   1 Tim. 5:14

Keep Your Marriage Vows

10 Now to the married I command, yet not I but the RLord: RA wife is not to depart from her husband.   Mark 10:6-10 • [Matt. 5:32]

11 But even if she does depart, let her remain unmarried or be reconciled to her husband. And a husband is not to divorce his wife.

12 But to the rest I, not the Lord, say: If any brother has a wife who does not believe, and she is willing to live with him, let him not divorce her.

13 And a woman who has a husband who does not believe, if he is willing to live with her, let her not divorce him.

14 For the unbelieving husband is sanctified by the wife, and the unbelieving wife is sanctified by the husband; otherwise Ryour children would be unclean, but now they are holy.   Mal. 2:15

15 But if the unbeliever departs, let him depart; a brother or a sister is not under bondage in such cases. But God has called us Rto peace.   Rom. 12:18

16 For how do you know, O wife, whether you will Rsave your husband? Or how do you know, O husband, whether you will save your wife?   1 Pet. 3:1

Live as You Are Called

17 But as God has distributed to each one, as the Lord has called each one, so let him walk. And so I ordain in all the churches.

18 Was anyone called while circumcised? Let him not become uncircumcised. Was anyone called while uncircumcised? RLet him not be circumcised.   Acts 15:1

19 Circumcision is nothing and uncircumcision is nothing, but Rkeeping the commandments of God is what matters.   [John 15:14]

20 Let each one remain in the same calling in which he was called.

21 Were you called while a slave? Do not be concerned about it; but if you can be made free, rather use it.

22 For he who is called in the Lord while a slave is the Lord's freedman. Likewise he who is called while free is Christ's slave.

23 RYou were bought at a price; do not become slaves of men.   1 Pet. 1:18, 19

24 Brethren, let each one remain with God in that state in which he was called.

To the Unmarried and Widows

25 Now concerning virgins: RI have no commandment from the Lord; yet I give judgment as one whom the Lord in His mercy has made Rtrustworthy.   2 Cor. 8:8 • 1 Tim. 1:12

26 I suppose therefore that this is good because of the present distress—Rthat it is good for a man to remain as he is: 1 Cor. 7:1, 8

27 Are you bound to a wife? Do not seek to be loosed. Are you loosed from a wife? Do not seek a wife.

28 But even if you do marry, you have not sinned; and if a virgin marries, she has not sinned. Nevertheless such will have trouble in the flesh, but I would spare you.

29 But Rthis I say, brethren, the time is short, so that from now on even those who have wives should be as though they had none,   1 Pet. 4:7

30 those who weep as though they did not weep, those who rejoice as though they did not rejoice, those who buy as though they did not possess,

31 and those who use this world as not

Rmisusing *it*. For Rthe form of this world is passing away.   1 Cor. 9:18 • [1 John 2:17]

32 But I want you to be without care. He who is unmarried cares for the things of the Lord—how he may please the Lord.

33 But he who is married cares about the things of the world—how he may please *his* wife.

34 There *is a difference between a wife and a virgin. The unmarried woman Rcares about the things of the Lord, that she may be holy both in body and in spirit. But she who is married cares about the things of the world—how she may please *her* husband.   Luke 10:40

35 And this I say for your own profit, not that I may put a leash on you, but for what is proper, and that you may serve the Lord without distraction.

36 But if any man thinks he is behaving improperly toward his Tvirgin, if she is past the flower of youth, and thus it must be, let him do what he wishes. He does not sin; let them marry.   Or *virgin daughter*

37 Nevertheless he who stands steadfast in his heart, having no necessity, but has power over his own will, and has so determined in his heart that he will keep his Tvirgin, does well.   Or *virgin daughter*

38 RSo then he who gives *her in marriage does well, but he who does not give *her* in marriage does better.   Heb. 13:4

39 RA wife is bound by law as long as her husband lives; but if her husband dies, she is at liberty to be married to whom she wishes, Ronly in the Lord.   Rom. 7:2 • 2 Cor. 6:14

40 But she is happier if she remains as she is, according to my judgment—and RI think I also have the Spirit of God.   1 Thess. 4:8

Be Sensitive to Conscience

8 Now concerning things offered to idols: We know that we all have knowledge. Knowledge puffs up, but love edifies.

2 And Rif anyone thinks that he knows anything, he knows nothing yet as he ought to know.   [1 Cor. 13:8-12]

3 But if anyone loves God, this one is known by Him.

4 Therefore concerning the eating of things offered to idols, we know that Ran idol *is* nothing in the world, Rand that *there is* no other God but one.   Is. 41:24 • Deut. 4:35, 39; 6:4

5 For even if there are Rso-called gods, whether in heaven or on earth (as there are many gods and many lords),   [John 10:34]

6 yet for us *there is* one God, the Father, of whom *are* all things, and we for Him; and one Lord Jesus Christ, through whom *are* all things, and through whom we *live*.

7 However, *there is* not in everyone that knowledge; for some, Rwith consciousness of the idol, until now eat *it* as a thing offered to an idol; and their conscience, being weak, is Rdefiled.   [1 Cor. 10:28] • Rom. 14:14, 22

8 But Rfood does not commend us to God; for neither if we eat are we the better, nor if we do not eat are we the worse.   [Rom. 14:17]

9 But beware lest somehow this liberty of yours become Ra Tstumbling block to those who are weak.   Rom. 12:13, 21 • *cause of offense*

10 For if anyone sees you who have knowledge eating in an idol's temple, will not the conscience of him who is weak be emboldened to eat those things offered to idols?

11 And Rbecause of your knowledge shall the weak brother perish, for whom Christ died?   Rom. 14:15, 20

12 But Rwhen you thus sin against the brethren, and wound their weak conscience, you sin against Christ.   Matt. 25:40

13 Therefore, Rif food makes my brother stumble, I will never again eat meat, lest I make my brother stumble.   Rom. 14:21

A Pattern of Self-Denial

9 Am RI not an apostle? Am I not free? Have I not seen Jesus Christ our Lord? Are you not my work in the Lord?   Acts 9:15

2 If I am not an apostle to others, yet doubtless I am to you. For you are the Tseal of my apostleship in the Lord.   *certification*

3 My defense to those who examine me is this:

4 Do we have no right to eat and drink?

5 Do we have no right to take along a believing wife, as *do* also the other apostles, the brothers of the Lord, and Cephas?

6 Or *is it* only Barnabas and I Rwho have no right to refrain from working?   Acts 4:36

7 Who ever goes to war at his own expense? Who plants a vineyard and does not eat of its fruit? Or who tends a flock and does not drink of the milk of the flock?

8 Do I say these things as a *mere* man? Or does not the law say the same also?

9 For it is written in the law of Moses, R*"You shall not muzzle an ox while it treads out the grain."* Is it oxen God is concerned about?   Deut. 25:4

10 Or does He say *it* altogether for our sakes? For our sakes, no doubt, *this* is written, that Rhe who plows should plow in hope, and he who threshes in hope should be partaker of his hope.   2 Tim. 2:6

11 RIf we have sown spiritual things for you, *is it* a great thing if we reap your material things?   Rom. 15:27

12 If others are partakers of *this* right over you, *are* we not even more? Nevertheless we have not used this right, but endure all things lest we hinder the gospel of Christ.

13 Do you not know that those who minister the holy things eat *of the things* of the

7:34 NU *is also*
7:38 NU *his own virgin*

temple, and those who serve at the altar partake of *the offerings of* the altar?

14 Even so ᴿthe Lord has commanded ᴿthat those who preach the gospel should live from the gospel.   Matt. 10:10 • Rom. 10:15

15 But ᴿI have used none of these things, nor have I written these things that it should be done so to me; for ᴿit *would be* better for me to die than that anyone should make my boasting void.   Acts 18:3; 20:33 • 2 Cor. 11:10

16 For if I preach the gospel, I have nothing to boast of, for necessity is laid upon me; yes, woe is me if I do not preach the gospel!

17 For if I do this willingly, I have a reward; but if against my will, ᴿI have been entrusted with a stewardship.   Gal. 2:7

18 What is my reward then? That ᴿwhen I preach the gospel, I may present the gospel *of Christ without charge, that I may not abuse my authority in the gospel.   1 Cor. 10:33

Serving All Men

19 For though I am free from all *men*, ᴿI have made myself a servant to all, ᴿthat I might win the more;   Gal. 5:13 • Matt. 18:15

20 and ᴿto the Jews I became as a Jew, that I might win Jews; to those *who are* under the law, as under the *law, that I might win those *who are* under the law;   Acts 16:3; 21:23-26

21 to those *who are* without law, as without law ᴿ(not being without *law toward God, but under *law toward Christ), that I might win those *who are* without law;   [1 Cor. 7:22]

22 ᴿto the weak I became *as weak, that I might win the weak. ᴿI have become all things to all *men*, ᴿthat I might by all means save some.   Rom. 14:1; 15:1 • 1 Cor. 10:33 • Rom. 11:14

9:18 NU omits *of Christ*
9:20 NU adds *though not being myself under the law*
9:21 NU *God's law* • NU *Christ's law*
9:22 NU omits *as*

---

23 Now this I do for the gospel's sake, that I may be partaker of it with *you.*

48-B. The Crown Imperishable   ▼

Striving for a Crown

24 Do you not know that those who run in a race all run, but one receives the prize? Run in such a way that you may obtain *it.*

25 And everyone who competes *for the prize* ᵀis temperate in all things. Now they *do it* to obtain a perishable crown, but we *for* ᴿan imperishable *crown.*   exercises self-control • James 1:12

26 Therefore I run thus: ᴿnot with uncertainty. Thus I fight: not as *one who* beats the air.   2 Tim. 2:5

27 But I discipline my body and bring *it* into subjection, lest, when I have preached to others, I myself should become disqualified. ▲

Old Testament Examples

10 Moreover, brethren, I do not want you to be unaware that all our fathers were under the cloud, all passed through the sea,

2 all were baptized into Moses in the cloud and in the sea,

3 all ate the same ᴿspiritual food,   Ex. 16:4

4 and all drank the same spiritual drink. For they drank of that spiritual Rock that followed them, and that Rock was Christ.

5 But with most of them God was not well pleased, for *their bodies* ᴿwere scattered in the wilderness.   Num. 14:29, 37; 26:65

6 Now these things became our examples, to the intent that we should not lust after evil things as ᴿthey also lusted.   Num. 11:4, 34

7 ᴿAnd do not become idolaters as *were* some of them. As it is written, ᴿ*"The people sat down to eat and drink, and rose up to play."*   1 Cor. 5:11; 10:14 • Ex. 32:6

8 Nor let us commit sexual immorality, as

48-B. The Crown Imperishable (1 Corinthians 9:24–27)—Paul uses the Greek games to illustrate the spiritual race of the believer. They ran to win a "perishable crown, but we for an imperishable crown" (v. 25). No young man could compete in the games unless he was a Greek citizen, born of Greek parents. No unsaved person can participate in the service of the Lord for rewards; only those born of God are eligible (John 3:3, page 1052).

Just as the athlete must deny himself many gratifications of the body, so the believer must "discipline [his] body and bring it into subjection" or he will be "disqualified" (v. 27). He will not lose his salvation, but he can lose his rewards.

The Greek games had rigid rules for all participants. The New Testament contains the rules for believers who would enter the spiritual race to win the "imperishable crown."

(1) The believer must deny himself anything that would weigh him down and hold him back (Heb. 12:1, page 1249).
(2) The believer must keep his eyes fixed on Christ, not looking to the right or left (Heb. 12:2, page 1250).
(3) The believer must find his strength in the Lord (Eph. 6:10–18, page 1192).
(4) The believer must place his all on the altar of the Lord (Rom. 12:1, 2, page 1142).
(5) The believer must, by faith, refuse anything that would impede spiritual progress (Heb. 11:24–29, page 1249).

Do not be a spiritual spectator. Enter the race and run to win the "imperishable crown."
See 1 Thessalonians 2:19, 20, page 1210, for **Point 48-C: The Crown of Rejoicing.**

^Rsome of them did, and ^Rin one day twenty-three thousand fell;   Num. 25:1-9 · Ps. 106:29

9 nor let us ^Ttempt Christ, as ^Rsome of them also tempted, and ^Rwere destroyed by serpents;   test · Ex. 17:2, 7 · Num. 21:6-9

10 nor complain, as ^Rsome of them also complained, and ^Rwere destroyed by ^Rthe destroyer.   Ex. 16:2 · Num. 14:37 · Ex. 12:23

11 Now *all these things happened to them as examples, and ^Rthey were written for our ^Tadmonition, ^Rupon whom the ends of the ages have come.   Rom. 15:4 · instruction · Phil. 4:5

12 Therefore ^Rlet him who thinks he stands take heed lest he fall.   Rom. 11:20

13 No temptation has overtaken you except such as is common to man; but God is faithful, who will not allow you to be tempted beyond what you are able, but with the temptation will also make the way of escape, that you may be able to bear it.

Flee from Idolatry

14 Therefore, my beloved, ^Rflee from idolatry.   2 Cor. 6:17

15 I speak as to ^Rwise men; judge for yourselves what I say.   1 Cor. 8:1

16 The cup of blessing which we bless, is it not the ^Tcommunion of the blood of Christ? The bread which we break, is it not the communion of the body of Christ?   sharing

17 For ^Rwe, though many, are one bread and one body; for we all partake of that one bread.   1 Cor. 12:12, 27

18 Observe Israel after the flesh: ^RAre not those who eat of the sacrifices ^Tpartakers of the altar?   Lev. 3:3; 7:6, 14 · fellowshippers or sharers

19 What am I saying then? ^RThat an idol is anything, or what is offered to idols is anything?   1 Cor. 8:4

20 Rather that the things which the Gentiles sacrifice ^Rthey sacrifice to demons and not to God, and I do not want you to have fellowship with demons.   Deut. 32:17

21 ^RYou cannot drink the cup of the Lord and ^Rthe cup of demons; you cannot partake of the ^RLord's table and of the table of demons.   2 Cor. 6:15, 16 · Deut. 32:38 · [1 Cor. 11:23-29]

22 Or do we provoke the Lord to jealousy? ^RAre we stronger than He?   Ezek. 22:14

All to the Glory of God

23 All things are lawful *for me, but not all things are helpful; all things are lawful for me, but not all things edify.

24 Let no one seek his own, but each one ^Rthe other's well-being.   Phil. 2:4

25 Eat whatever is sold in the meat market, asking no questions for conscience' sake;

26 for ^R"the earth is the Lord's, and all its fullness."   Ps. 24:1

27 If any of those who do not believe invites you to dinner, and you desire to go, ^Reat whatever is set before you, asking no question for conscience' sake.   Luke 10:7, 8

28 But if anyone says to you, "This was offered to idols," do not eat it ^Rfor the sake of the one who told you, and for conscience' sake; *for ^R"the earth is the Lord's, and all its fullness."   [1 Cor. 8:7, 10, 12] · Ps. 24:1

29 "Conscience," I say, not your own, but that of the other. For ^Rwhy is my liberty judged by another man's conscience?   Rom. 14:16

30 But if I partake with thanks, why am I evil spoken of for the food ^Rover which I give thanks?   Rom. 14:6

31 Therefore, whether you eat or drink, or whatever you do, do all to the glory of God.

32 ^RGive no offense, either to the Jews or to the Greeks or to the church of God,   Rom. 14:13

33 just ^Ras I also please all men in all things, not seeking my own profit, but the profit of many, that they may be saved.   Rom. 15:2

11 Imitate me, just as I also imitate Christ.

Head Coverings

2 Now I praise you, brethren, that you remember me in all things and keep the traditions as I delivered them to you.

3 But I want you to know that the head of every man is Christ, ^Rthe head of woman is man, and the head of Christ is God.   Gen. 3:16

4 Every man praying or prophesying, having his head covered, dishonors his head.

5 But every woman who prays or prophesies with her head uncovered dishonors her head, for that is one and the same as if her head were ^Rshaved.   Deut. 21:12

6 For if a woman is not covered, let her also be shorn. But if it is ^Rshameful for a woman to be shorn or shaved, let her be covered.   Num. 5:18

7 For a man indeed ought not to cover his head, since ^Rhe is the image and glory of God; but woman is the glory of man.   Gen. 1:26, 27

8 For man is not from woman, but woman ^Rfrom man.   Gen. 2:21-23

9 Nor was man created for the woman, but woman ^Rfor the man.   Gen. 2:18

10 For this reason the woman ought to have a symbol of authority on her head, because of the angels.

11 Nevertheless, ^Rneither is man independent of woman, nor woman independent of man, in the Lord.   [Gal. 3:28]

12 For as woman came from man, even so man also comes through woman; but all things are from God.

13 Judge among yourselves. Is it proper for a woman to pray to God with her head uncovered?

10:11 NU omits all
10:23 NU omits for me
10:28 NU omits the rest of v. 28.

14 Does not even nature itself teach you that if a man has long hair, it is a dishonor to him?

15 But if a woman has long hair, it is a glory to her; for *her* hair is given *to her for a covering.

16 But ᴿif anyone seems to be contentious, we have no such custom, ᴿnor *do the* churches of God.   1 Tim. 6:4 • 1 Cor. 7:17

▼ 16-G. Consequences of Sin in the Corinthian Church

Conduct at the Lord's Supper

17 Now in giving these instructions I do not praise *you*, since you come together not for the better but for the worse.

18 For first of all, when you come together as a church, I hear that there are divisions among you, and in part I believe it.

19 For there must also be factions among you, that those who are approved may be ᵀrecognized among you.   Lit. *evident, manifest*

20 Therefore when you come together in one place, it is not to eat the Lord's Supper.

21 For in eating, each one takes his own supper ahead of *others;* and one is hungry and ᴿanother is drunk.   Jude 12

22 What! Do you not have houses to eat and drink in? Or do you despise the church of God and ᴿshame ᵀthose who have nothing? What shall I say to you? Shall I praise you in this? I do not praise *you.*   James 2:6 • The poor

11:15 M omits *to her*

Institution of the Lord's Supper   ▽

23 For ᴿI received from the Lord that which I also delivered to you: ᴿthat the Lord Jesus on the *same* night in which He was betrayed took bread;   1 Cor. 15:3 • Matt. 26:26-28

24 and when He had given thanks, He broke *it* and said, *"Take, eat; this is My body which is *broken for you; do this in remembrance of Me."

25 In the same manner *He* also *took* the cup after supper, saying, "This cup is the new covenant in My blood. This do, as often as you drink *it,* in remembrance of Me."

26 For as often as you eat this bread and drink this cup, you proclaim the Lord's death ᴿtill He comes.   John 14:3

Examine Yourself

27 Therefore whoever eats ᴿthis bread or drinks *this* cup of the Lord in an unworthy manner will be guilty of the body and *blood of the Lord.   [John 6:51]

28 But let a man examine himself, and so let him eat of the bread and drink of the cup.

29 For he who eats and drinks *in an unworthy manner eats and drinks judgment to himself, not discerning the *Lord's body.

11:24 NU omits *Take, eat* • NU omits *broken*
11:27 NU, M *the blood*
11:29 NU omits *in an unworthy manner* • NU omits *Lord's*

16-G. Consequences of Sin in the Corinthian Church (1 Corinthians 11:17-34)—In this portion of Scripture the apostle Paul is correcting one of the errors of the Corinthian church—the manner in which they were observing the Lord's Supper. Some of the members had sinned, resulting in death. Paul warned the church, saying, "For this reason many are weak and sick among you, and many sleep," i.e., many sleep in death (vv. 30, 32). The sins that led to weakness, sickness, and death were

(1) *Division.* They were divided over personalities (1 Cor. 1:11–13, page 1148).

(2) *Dissension.* They tolerated heresies—wrong doctrine (vv. 18, 19) which caused divisions among the people. We are not told what the heresies were, but it is clear that there were factions and cliques held together by social function, or some theory or doctrine.

(3) *Drunkenness.* Some became drunk (v. 21).

(4) *Discrimination.* They shamed the poor among them, and showed no respect for the Lord and His church (v. 22).

(5) *Departure.* They left the proper observance of the Lord's Supper by failing to "proclaim the Lord's death till He comes" (vv. 26–30). The Lord's Supper is an illustrated sermon in two parts:

(a) It looks *back* to His vicarious death on the cross for our sins (1 Pet. 1:18, 19, page 1263).

(b) It looks *forward* to His Second Coming as King of kings and Lord of lords (Rev. 19:16, page 1313), when He will establish His kingdom on this earth and reign upon His kingdom throne (Matt. 25:31–46, page 976).

(6) *Defective Partaking.* They ate the bread and drank the cup of the Lord in an unworthy manner (v. 27). They must have thought themselves worthy to take the Lord's Supper; the only ones truly worthy to take the Lord's Supper are those who recognize their total unworthiness. It is the honest recognition of one's unworthiness that makes one worthy. If you *feel* worthy to partake, you are unworthy.

See Index, page 17, for your next study.

▽ 30 For this reason many *are* weak and sick among you, and many ᵀsleep.   Are dead

▼ **18-B. The Judgment of the Believer's Self**
31 For ᴿif we would judge ourselves, we would not be judged.   [1 John 1:9]
32 But when we are judged, ᴿwe are chastened by the Lord, that we may not be con-
▲ demned with the world.   Ps. 94:12
33 Therefore, my brethren, when you come together to eat, wait for one another.
34 But if anyone is hungry, let him eat at home, lest you come together for judgment.
▲ And the rest I will set in order when I come.

**10-E. The Ministry of the Holy Spirit: ▼
The Giver of Spiritual Gifts**

Spiritual Gifts: Unity in Diversity

12 Now concerning spiritual *gifts*, brethren, I do not want you to be ignorant:
2 You know ᴿthat* you were Gentiles, carried away to these ᴿdumbᵀ idols, however you were led.   Eph. 2:11 · Ps. 115:5 · *mute, silent*
3 Therefore I make known to you that no one speaking by the Spirit of God calls Jesus

12:2 NU, M *that when*

18-B. The Judgment of the Believer's Self (1 Corinthians 11:31, 32)—The believer's self-judgment means more than judging things in the believer's life. When the believer judges his life, the good and the bad in his life come to light; he confesses the bad (1 John 1:9, page 1278) and forsakes it (Is. 55:7, page 695). However, it is not enough just to judge sin in the believer; he must judge self.

(1) To judge self is to practice self-abnegation; for when the believer sees self as God sees him, he will renounce self. It is replacing the self-life with the Christ-life (Col. 3:4, page 1205). Christ is the believer's life.

(2) To judge self is to deny self. This is more than self-denial. Self-denial is denying one's self of fleshly gratifications. If we practice self-denial only, it is treating the symptom and not the illness. But when we deny self, we are attacking the root problem, for in self (i.e., in the flesh) "nothing good dwells" (Rom. 7:18, page 1136). To deny self is to take up our cross and follow Christ (Mark 8:34–38, page 994), to lose the self-life, and find the Christ-life (Gal. 2:20, page 1180).

(3) To judge self is to become less and less self-conscious, and more and more Christ-conscious (Matt. 28:20, page 982).

(4) To judge self is to become Christ-controlled (Acts 9:6, page 1100).

(5) To judge self is to esteem others better than self (Phil. 2:3, page 1197), to become selfless.

See 2 Corinthians 5:10, page 1168, for **Point 18-C: The Judgment of the Believer's Works.**

10-E. The Ministry of the Holy Spirit: The Giver of Spiritual Gifts (1 Corinthians 12:1–31)—We find the Holy Trinity working together from Genesis to Revelation. So it is no surprise to find the Father, Son, and Holy Spirit working together in the church, the body of Christ (vv. 12–31), so that the whole body of Christ may profit spiritually in every good thing (v. 7). The apostle Paul would not have us be ignorant of how the Trinity is involved in giving and using spiritual gifts for the edifying of the church:

(1) *The Holy Spirit.* "There are diversities [differences] of gifts, but the same Spirit" (v. 4). We are told to earnestly desire the best gifts (v. 31), especially the gift of prophecy (1 Cor. 14:1, page 1160). "He who speaks in a tongue edifies himself, but he who prophesies edifies the church" (1 Cor. 14:4, page 1160). You may choose a special gift and desire it, pray for it, and yet not receive it, because the Holy Spirit bestows spiritual gifts according to His sovereign will, and not always according to your wishes. "But one and the same Spirit works all these things [spiritual gifts], distributing to each one individually as He wills" (v. 11).

(2) *The Lord Jesus Christ.* "There are differences of ministries, but the same Lord" (v. 5). Paul says there are varieties of ministries in the church, and the Holy Spirit gives spiritual gifts according to His sovereign will, enabling all to perform their ministries in the power of the Holy Spirit, under the lordship of Christ, because Christ is the head of the church, the body of Christ (Col. 1:18, 19, page 1202).

(3) *God the Father.* "And there are diversities of activities, but it is the same God who works all in all" (v. 6). In the church there are varieties of operations; God the Father, working with God the Holy Spirit and God the Son, enables those who have been given spiritual gifts to exercise them to the honor and glory of the Father, Son, and Holy Spirit.

"But the manifestation of the Spirit is given to each one [in the body of Christ, the church] for the profit of all" (v. 7). Spiritual gifts, ministries, and operations are not bestowed on a person in order to attract attention to that person. They are given to attract sinners to Christ and to bless the whole body of Christ.

Every born-again child of God should have the attitude of John the Baptist. When asked, "Who are you?" he answered, "I am 'The voice of one crying in the wilderness: "Make straight the way of the LORD" ' " (John 1:22, 23, page 1049). In John's humble opinion he was not important, he was just the voice of one; he was one of many who helped prepare for the first coming of Christ. John also said of Jesus, "He must increase, but I must decrease" (John 3:30, page 1053).

Do you have a decreasing or expanding ego? The nearer you are to God, the smaller the ego; the farther you get from God, the bigger the ego. John delighted in exalting Christ, not himself. God the Father has

(Point 10-E continued on next page)

▽ ᵀaccursed, and no one can say that Jesus is Lord except by the Holy Spirit.   Gr. anathema

4 There are ᵀdiversities of gifts, but ᴿthe same Spirit.   allotments or various kinds · Eph. 4:4

5 ᴿThere are differences of ministries, but the same Lord.   Rom. 12:6

6 And there are diversities of activities, but it is the same God who works all in all.

7 But the manifestation of the Spirit is given to each one for the profit of all:

8 for to one is given the word of wisdom through the Spirit, to another ᴿthe word of knowledge through the same Spirit,   Rom. 15:14

9 to another faith by the same Spirit, to another gifts of healings by *the same Spirit,

12:9 NU one

10 to another the working of miracles, to ▽ another prophecy, to another discerning of spirits, to another different kinds of tongues, to another the interpretation of tongues.

11 But one and the same Spirit works all these things, ᴿdistributing to each one individually ᴿas He wills.   Rom. 12:6 · [John 3:8]

38-B. The Church: A Body   ▼

Unity and Diversity in One Body

12 For ᴿas the body is one and has many members, but all the members of that one body, being many, are one body, ᴿso also is Christ.   Rom. 12:4, 5 · [Gal. 3:16]

13 For ᴿby one Spirit we were all baptized

(Point 10-E continued from previous page)
exalted God the Son, and given Him a name above all names. At the name of the Son of God (not a servant of God), every knee in heaven, on earth, and in hell will bend; and every tongue will confess that Jesus Christ is Lord (Phil. 2:1–11, page 1197).

The apostle Paul lists nine spiritual gifts:

(1) the word of wisdom (v. 8)
(2) the word of knowledge (v. 8)
(3) faith (v. 9)
(4) gifts of healing (v. 9)
(5) the working of miracles (v. 10)
(6) prophecy (v. 10)
(7) discerning of spirits (v. 10)
(8) different kinds of tongues (languages) (v. 10)
(9) interpretations of tongues (v. 10)

Remember:

(1) They are gifts of the Spirit; you cannot earn them by keeping the law or doing good works. They are gifts of pure grace, not of works—just like salvation (Eph. 2:8, 9, page 1187).

(2) Are *all* spiritual gifts given to every member of the body of Christ? The answer is obvious—No (vv. 29, 30).

(3) Can the individual Christian choose the spiritual gift he or she would like to receive? You are to "desire spiritual gifts" (1 Cor. 14:1, page 1160); however, the gifts are given according to the sovereign will of the Holy Spirit (v. 11). You may desire the best gift; but you will not receive it unless it is the will of God.

(4) Are these spiritual gifts for the church today? Some say no—that God phased out some or all of the spiritual gifts, that they are not for the church today. It is true that these gifts are not apparent in *many* local churches, but that does not mean that they are not in *any* of the churches. Remember that God is sovereign, and does whatever pleases Him in heaven and on the earth (Ps. 135:6, page 588; Dan. 4:35, page 840).

At the close of chapter 12 Paul says, "But earnestly desire the best gifts. And yet I show you a more excellent way" (v. 31). In chapter 13 he reveals that love is the more excellent way to manifest spiritual gifts. It is surely the only effective way. "Though I speak with the tongues [languages] of men and of angels, but have not love, I have become sounding brass or a clanging cymbal" (1 Cor. 13:1, page 1159). There are two main Greek words for love:

(1) *Phileo*—this is love between friends (brotherly love); it is kindly feeling toward one another. This Greek word for love is found often in the Bible.

(2) *Agapao*, with the noun form *agape*—this is perfect love. God is *agape*—"God is love" (1 John 4:8, page 1281).

Paul was saying that you may be blessed with spiritual gifts, but if you do not have *agape* ("the love of God has been poured out in our hearts by the Holy Spirit who was given to us," Rom. 5:5, page 1133)—your spiritual gifts will be ineffective. You will become "sounding brass or a clanging cymbal" (1 Cor. 13:1, page 1159). In other words, you will be nothing but a religious noise.

See Index, page 17, for your next study.

38-B. The Church: A Body (1 Corinthians 12:12-31)—"For by one Spirit we were all baptized into one body. . . . For in fact the body is not one member but many" (vv. 13, 14). The apostle Paul sets forth the wonderful
(Point 38-B continued on next page)

▽ into one body—whether Jews or Greeks, whether slaves or free—and have all been made to drink *into one Spirit.   [Rom. 6:5]

14 For in fact the body is not one member but many.

15 If the foot should say, "Because I am not a hand, I am not of the body," is it therefore not of the body?

16 And if the ear should say, "Because I am not an eye, I am not of the body," is it therefore not of the body?

17 If the whole body were an eye, where would be the hearing? If the whole were hearing, where would be the smelling?

18 But now God has set the members, each one of them, in the body just as He pleased.

19 And if they were all one member, where would the body be?

20 But now indeed there are many members, yet one body.

21 And the eye cannot say to the hand, "I have no need of you"; nor again the head to the feet, "I have no need of you."

22 No, much rather, those members of the body which seem to be weaker are necessary.

23 And those members of the body which we think to be less honorable, on these we bestow greater honor; and our unpresentable parts have greater modesty,

24 but our presentable parts have no need. But God composed the body, having given greater honor to that part which lacks it,

25 that there should be no ᵀschism in the body, but that the members should have the same care for one another.   division

12:13 NU omits into

26 And if one member suffers, all the members suffer with it; or if one member is honored, all the members rejoice with it.

27 Now ᴿyou are the body of Christ, and ᴿmembers individually.   Rom. 12:5 • Eph. 5:30

28 And God has appointed these in the church: first ᴿapostles, second ᴿprophets, third teachers, after that miracles, then gifts of healings, helps, administrations, varieties of tongues.   [Eph. 2:20; 3:5] • Acts 13:1

29 Are all apostles? Are all prophets? Are all teachers? Are all workers of miracles?

30 Do all have gifts of healings? Do all speak with tongues? Do all interpret?

31 But earnestly desire the *best gifts. And yet I show you a more excellent way.   ▲

The Greatest Gift

13 Though I speak with the tongues of men and of angels, but have not love, I have become sounding brass or a clanging cymbal.

2 And though I have the gift of ᴿprophecy, and understand all mysteries and all knowledge, and though I have all faith, ᴿso that I could remove mountains, but have not love, I am nothing.   1 Cor. 12:8–10, 28; 14:1 • Matt. 17:20

3 And ᴿthough I bestow all my goods to feed the poor, and though I give my body *to be burned, but have not love, it profits me nothing.   Matt. 6:1, 2

4 Love suffers long and is ᴿkind; love ᴿdoes not envy; love does not parade itself, is not ᵀpuffed up;   Eph. 4:32 • Gal. 5:26 • arrogant

12:31 NU greater

13:3 NU so I may boast

(Point 38-B continued from previous page)
truth that the church (the body of believers) is, in a profound sense, Christ's body now on earth. Just as Christ used the hands of His disciples to give the food to the five thousand (John 6:11, page 1058), so today He uses the hands of His body, the church, to feed and care for His earthly children. "Now you are the body of Christ, and members individually" (v. 27). Based on this truth, Paul sets forth the following teachings concerning the church:

(1) God specifically commands that no member of His body think of himself as independently important (Rom. 12:3, page 1142). God warns us of this in a direct way because so many are prone to exalt themselves and lessen the worth of other believers.

(2) Each member of the body has his own function. Sometimes a person who has a gift or interest in one area may criticize others who serve God in different ways. One may see his own area as of supreme importance; however, other areas are also important and necessary (vv. 15–18).

(3) All members of the body belong to one another. All members, both prominent and obscure, are accepted servants of God; therefore all are to be honored (vv. 19–23).

(4) Each member has different abilities given to him by God. It is improper to expect everyone to function well in all areas. God has given different members different abilities, concerns, insights, and interests. He did not intend for all to have the same talents and tasks. Each has a duty to God to pursue his or her own gift for His glory (Rom. 12:6–8, page 1143). The apostle teaches that each member should concentrate on performing his own job well, and not worry about what other members are doing (John 21:20–22, page 1084).

(5) Members have a duty to God to care for one another in the body (vv. 25, 26). If the foot is cut, the mouth does not laugh, but rather calls for help. We must help one another, not rival one another like immature children. Jealousy among Christians is a vestige of the old nature, and should not be allowed in the body of Christ.

See Matthew 28:16–20, page 982, for **Point 38-C: The Church: Its Mission.**

5 does not behave rudely, does not seek its own, is not provoked, thinks no evil;

6 ᴿdoes not rejoice in iniquity, but ᴿrejoices in the truth;   Rom. 1:32 • 2 John 4

7 ᴿbears all things, believes all things, hopes all things, endures all things.   Gal. 6:2

8 Love never fails. But whether *there are* prophecies, they will fail; whether *there are* tongues, they will cease; whether *there is* knowledge, it will vanish away.

9 ᴿFor we know in part and we prophesy in part.   1 Cor. 8:2; 13:12

10 But when that which is ᵀperfect has come, then that which is in part will be done away.   complete

11 When I was a child, I spoke as a child, I understood as a child, I thought as a child; but when I became a man, I put away childish things.

12 For now we see in a mirror, dimly, but then face to face. Now I know in part, but then I shall know just as I also am known.

13 And now abide faith, hope, love, these three; but the greatest of these *is* love.

Prophecy and Tongues

14 Pursue love, and desire spiritual *gifts,* but especially that you may prophesy.

2 For he who ᴿspeaks in a tongue does not speak to men but to God, for no one understands *him;* however, in the spirit he speaks mysteries.   Acts 2:4; 10:46

3 But he who prophesies speaks edification and exhortation and comfort to men.

4 He who speaks in a tongue edifies himself, but he who prophesies edifies the church.

5 I wish you all spoke with tongues, but even more that you prophesied; *for he who prophesies *is* greater than he who speaks with tongues, unless indeed he interprets, that the church may receive edification.

Tongues Must Be Interpreted

6 But now, brethren, if I come to you speaking with tongues, what shall I profit you unless I speak to you either by ᴿrevelation, by knowledge, by prophesying, or by teaching?   1 Cor. 14:26

7 Even things without life, whether flute or harp, when they make a sound, unless they make a distinction in the sounds, how will it be known what is piped or played?

8 For if the trumpet makes an uncertain sound, who will prepare for battle?

9 So likewise you, unless you utter by the tongue words easy to understand, how will it be known what is spoken? For you will be speaking into the air.

10 There are, it may be, so many kinds of languages in the world, and none of them *is* without ᵀsignificance.   meaning

11 Therefore, if I do not know the meaning of the language, I shall be a ᵀforeigner to him who speaks, and he who speaks *will be* a foreigner to me.   Lit. *barbarian*

12 Even so you, since you are zealous for spiritual *gifts, let it be* for the edification of the church *that* you seek to excel.

13 Therefore let him who speaks in a tongue pray that he may ᴿinterpret. 1 Cor. 12:10

14 For if I pray in a tongue, my spirit prays, but my understanding is unfruitful.

15 What is *the conclusion* then? I will pray with the spirit, and I will also pray with the understanding. I will sing with the spirit, and I will also sing with the understanding.

16 Otherwise, if you bless with the spirit, how will he who occupies the place of the uninformed say "Amen" ᴿat your giving of thanks, since he does not understand what you say?   1 Cor. 11:24

17 For you indeed give thanks well, but the other is not edified.

18 I thank my God I speak with tongues more than you all;

19 yet in the church I would rather speak five words with my understanding, that I may teach others also, than ten thousand words in a tongue.

Tongues a Sign to Unbelievers

20 Brethren, ᴿdo not be children in understanding; however, in malice ᴿbe babes, but in understanding be mature.   Ps. 131:2 • [1 Pet. 2:2]

21 ᴿIn the law it is written: John 10:34

> ᴿ"With men of other tongues and other lips
> I will speak to this people;
> And yet, for all that, they will not hear Me,"   Is. 28:11, 12

says the Lord.

22 Therefore tongues are for a ᴿsign, not to those who believe but to unbelievers; but prophesying is not for unbelievers but for those who believe.   Mark 16:17

23 Therefore if the whole church comes together in one place, and all speak with tongues, and there come in *those who are* uninformed or unbelievers, ᴿwill they not say that you are ᵀout of your mind? Acts 2:13 • *insane*

24 But if all prophesy, and an unbeliever or an uninformed person comes in, he is convinced by all, he is convicted by all;

25 *And thus the secrets of his heart are revealed; and so, falling down on *his* face, he will worship God and report ᴿthat God is truly among you.   Is. 45:14

Order in Church Meetings

26 How is it then, brethren? Whenever you come together, each of you has a psalm, has a

teaching, has a tongue, has a revelation, has an interpretation. [R]Let all things be done for [T]edification. [2 Cor. 12:19] · *building up*

27 If anyone speaks in a tongue, *let there be* two or at the most three, *each* in turn, and let one interpret.

28 But if there is no interpreter, let him keep silent in church, and let him speak to himself and to God.

29 Let two or three prophets speak, and [R]let the others judge. 1 Cor. 12:10

30 But if *anything* is revealed to another who sits by, let the first keep silent.

31 For you can all prophesy one by one, that all may learn and all may be encouraged.

32 And [R]the spirits of the prophets are subject to the prophets. 1 John 4:1

33 For God is not *the author* of [T]confusion but of peace, [R]as in all the churches of the saints. *disorder* · 1 Cor. 11:16

34 [R]Let *your women keep silent in the churches, for they are not permitted to speak; but *they are* to be submissive, as the [R]law also says. 1 Tim. 2:11 · Gen. 3:16

35 And if they want to learn something, let them ask their own husbands at home; for it is shameful for women to speak in church.

36 Or did the word of God come *originally* from you? Or *was it* you only that it reached?

37 [R]If anyone thinks himself to be a prophet or spiritual, let him acknowledge that the things which I write to you are the commandments of the Lord. 2 Cor. 10:7

38 But *if anyone is ignorant, let him be ignorant.

39 Therefore, brethren, [R]desire earnestly to prophesy, and do not forbid to speak with tongues. 1 Cor. 12:31

40 [R]Let all things be done decently and in order. 1 Cor. 14:33

The Risen Christ, Faith's Reality

15 Moreover, brethren, I declare to you the gospel [R]which I preached to you, which also you received and [R]in which you stand, [Gal. 1:11] · [Rom. 5:2; 11:20]

2 [R]by which also you are saved, if you hold fast that word which I preached to you— unless [R]you believed in vain. Rom. 1:16 · Gal. 3:4

3 For I delivered to you first of all that which I also received: that Christ died for our sins according to the Scriptures,

4 and that He was buried, and that He rose

14:34 NU omits *your*
14:38 NU *if anyone does not recognize this, he is not recognized*

again the third day [R]according to the Scriptures, Ps. 16:10, 11; Is. 53:10; Luke 24:26; Acts 2:25

5 [R]and that He was seen by [T]Cephas, then [R]by the twelve. Luke 24:34 · Peter · Matt. 28:17

6 After that He was seen by over five hundred brethren at once, of whom the greater part remain to the present, but some have [T]fallen asleep. Died

7 After that He was seen by James, then [R]by all the apostles. Acts 1:3, 4

8 [R]Then last of all He was seen by me also, as by one born out of due time. Acts 9:3–8

9 For I am the least of the apostles, who am not worthy to be called an apostle, because I persecuted the church of God.

10 But by the grace of God I am what I am, and His grace toward me was not in vain; but I labored more abundantly than they all, yet not I, but the grace of God *which was* with me.

11 Therefore, whether *it was* I or they, so we preach and so you believed.

The Risen Christ, Our Hope

12 Now if Christ is preached that He has been raised from the dead, how do some among you say that there is no resurrection of the dead?

13 But if there is no resurrection of the dead, [R]then Christ is not risen. [1 Thess. 4:14]

14 And if Christ is not risen, then our preaching *is* empty and your faith *is* also empty.

15 Yes, and we are found false witnesses of God, because [R]we have testified of God that He raised up Christ, whom He did not raise up—if in fact the dead do not rise. Acts 2:24

16 For if *the* dead do not rise, then Christ is not risen.

17 And if Christ is not risen, your faith *is* futile; [R]you are still in your sins! [Rom. 4:25]

18 Then also those who have [T]fallen [R]asleep in Christ have perished. Died · Job 14:12

19 If in this life only we have hope in Christ, we are of all men the most pitiable.

The Last Enemy Destroyed

20 But now [R]Christ is risen from the dead, *and* has become [R]the firstfruits of those who have [T]fallen asleep. 1 Pet. 1:3 · Acts 26:23 · Died

21 For since by man *came* death, by Man also *came* the resurrection of the dead.

19-C. The Results of Man's Ruin   ▼

22 For as in Adam all die, even so in Christ all shall [R]be made alive. [John 5:28, 29] ▲

19-C. The Results of Man's Ruin (1 Corinthians 15:22)—"As in Adam all die" (v. 22). Adam was the head of the human race. By natural birth we are his descendants. When Adam sinned, death passed upon all because all sinned in Adam (Rom. 5:12, page 1133). When God created Adam and put him in the Garden of Eden, He gave him two commandments:

(Point 19-C continued on next page)

23 But ᴿeach one in his own order: Christ the firstfruits, afterward those *who are* Christ's at His coming.   [1 Thess. 4:15-17]

24 Then *comes* the end, when He delivers ᴿthe kingdom to God the Father, when He puts an end to all rule and all authority and power.   [Dan. 2:44; 7:14, 27]

25 For He must reign ᴿtill He has put all enemies under His feet.   Ps. 110:1; Acts 2:34, 35

26 ᴿThe last enemy *that* will be destroyed *is* death.   [2 Tim. 1:10; Rev. 20:14]

27 For ᴿ*"He has put all things under His feet."* But when He says "all things are put under *Him*," *it is* evident that He who put all things under Him is excepted.   Ps. 8:6

28 ᴿNow when all things are made subject to Him, then the Son Himself will also be subject to Him who put all things under Him, that God may be all in all.   [Phil. 3:21]

Effects of Denying the Resurrection

29 Otherwise, what will they do who are baptized for the dead, if the dead do not rise at all? Why then are they baptized for the dead?

30 And ᴿwhy do we stand in ᵀjeopardy every hour?   2 Cor. 11:26 · *danger*

31 I affirm, by the boasting in which I have in Christ Jesus our Lord, I die daily.

32 If, in the manner of men, I have fought with beasts at Ephesus, what advantage *is it* to me? If *the* dead do not rise, ᴿ*"Let us eat and drink, for tomorrow we die!"*   Is. 22:13

33 Do not be deceived: ᴿ"Evil company corrupts good habits."   [1 Cor. 5:6]

34 Awake to righteousness, and do not sin; ᴿfor some do not have the knowledge of God. I speak *this* to your shame.   [1 Thess. 4:5]

A Glorious Body

35 But someone will say, ᴿ"How are the dead raised up? And with what body do they come?"   Ezek. 37:3

36 Foolish one, ᴿwhat you sow is not made alive unless it dies.   John 12:24

37 And what you sow, you do not sow that body that shall be, but mere grain—perhaps wheat or some other *grain.*

38 But God gives it a body as He pleases, and to each seed its own body.

39 All flesh *is* not the same flesh, but *there is* one *kind* *of* flesh of men, another flesh of animals, another of fish, *and* another of birds.

40 *There are* also ᵀcelestial bodies and ᵀterrestrial bodies; but the glory of the celestial *is* one, and the glory of the terrestrial *is* another.   *heavenly · earthly*

41 *There is* one glory of the sun, another glory of the moon, and another glory of the stars; for *one* star differs from *another* star in glory.

42 ᴿSo also *is* the resurrection of the dead. *The body* is sown in corruption, it is raised in incorruption.   [Dan. 12:3]

43 ᴿIt is sown in dishonor, it is raised in glory. It is sown in weakness, it is raised in power.   [Phil. 3:21]

44 It is sown a natural body, it is raised a spiritual body. There is a natural body, and there is a spiritual body.

45 And so it is written, ᴿ*"The first man Adam became a living being."* The last Adam *became* a life-giving spirit.   Gen. 2:7

46 However, the spiritual is not first, but the natural, and afterward the spiritual.

47 ᴿThe first man *was* of the earth, ᴿmadeᵀ of dust; the second Man *is* *the Lord ᴿfrom heaven.*   John 3:31 · Gen. 2:7; 3:19 · *earthy* · John 3:13

48 As *was* the ᵀman of dust, so also *are* those *who are* ᵀmade of dust; ᴿand as *is* the heavenly Man, so also *are* those *who are* heavenly.   *earthy* · Phil. 3:20

49 And ᴿas we have borne the image of the *man* of dust, ᴿwe* shall also bear the image of the heavenly Man.   Gen. 5:3 · Rom. 8:29

15:39 NU, M omit *of flesh*
15:47 NU omits *the Lord*
15:49 M *let us also bear*

(Point 19-C continued from previous page)
  (1) Cultivate and tend the Garden;
  (2) Eat freely of every tree of the Garden; except "the tree of the knowledge of good and evil you shall not eat, for in the day that you eat of it you shall surely die" (Gen. 2:15-17, page 4).

  Adam ate the forbidden fruit; this was the ruin (fall) of mankind; the result of the ruin was death. Theologically, death is separation. According to the Scriptures there are three deaths:

  (1) When Adam sinned, he died spiritually; he was separated from God and the Garden of Eden (Gen. 3:22-24, page 7). This was the spiritual ruin of man (Eph. 2:1-5, page 1187).
  (2) In Genesis 4 we again see the results of the ruin. The first physical death was murder; Cain murdered his brother, Abel (Gen. 4:8, page 8). In Genesis 5 (page 9), from Adam to Noah, three little words are repeated: "and he died." The result of man's ruin is spiritual and physical death.
  (3) There is yet another death, called "the second death." This is separation from God and His mercies forever and ever: consignment to the lake of fire. Without salvation in Christ, all that mankind has to look forward to is eternal separation from God in the lake of fire (Rev. 20:14, 15, page 1314).

  See Mark 10:45, page 997, for **Point 19-D: God's Remedy for Man's Ruin.**

Our Final Victory

50 Now this I say, brethren, that flesh and blood cannot inherit the kingdom of God; nor does corruption inherit incorruption.

51 Behold, I tell you a mystery: We shall not all sleep, but we shall all be changed—

52 in a moment, in the twinkling of an eye, at the last trumpet. ᴿFor the trumpet will sound, and the dead will be raised incorruptible, and we shall be changed.   Matt. 24:31

53 For this corruptible must put on incorruption, and ᴿthis mortal *must* put on immortality.   2 Cor. 5:4

54 So when this corruptible has put on incorruption, and this mortal has put on immortality, then shall be brought to pass the saying that is written: ᴿ*"Death is swallowed up in victory."*   Is. 25:8

55 *"O* ᴿDeath, where is your sting?*   Hos. 13:14
    O Hades, where is your victory?"

56 The sting of death *is* sin, and ᴿthe strength of sin *is* the law.   [Rom. 3:20; 4:15; 7:8]

57 But thanks *be* to God, who gives us the victory through our Lord Jesus Christ.

58 Therefore, my beloved brethren, be steadfast, immovable, always abounding in the work of the Lord, knowing ᴿthat your labor is not in vain in the Lord.   [1 Cor. 3:8]

Collection for the Saints

16 Now concerning the collection for the saints, as I have given orders to the churches of Galatia, so you must do also:

2 ᴿOn the first *day* of the week let each one of you lay something aside, storing up as he may prosper, that there be no collections when I come.   Acts 20:7

3 And when I come, ᴿwhomever you approve by *your* letters I will send to bear your gift to Jerusalem.   2 Cor. 3:1; 8:18

4 ᴿBut if it is fitting that I go also, they will go with me.   2 Cor. 8:4, 19

Personal Plans

5 Now I will come to you ᴿwhen I pass through Macedonia (for I am passing through Macedonia).   2 Cor. 1:15, 16

6 And it may be that I will remain, or even spend the winter with you, that you may send me on my journey, wherever I go.

7 For I do not wish to see you now on the way; but I hope to stay a while with you, ᴿif the Lord permits.   James 4:15

8 But I will tarry in Ephesus until ᴿPentecost.   Lev. 23:15–22

9 For ᴿa great and effective door has opened to me, and ᴿ*there are* many adversaries.   Acts 14:27 • Acts 19:9

10 And ᴿif Timothy comes, see that he may be with you without fear; for he does the work of the Lord, as I also *do.*   Acts 19:22

11 ᴿTherefore let no one despise him. But send him on his journey ᴿin peace, that he may come to me; for I am waiting for him with the brethren.   1 Tim. 4:12 • Acts 15:33

12 Now concerning *our* brother ᴿApollos, I strongly urged him to come to you with the brethren, but he was quite unwilling to come at this time; however, he will come when he has a convenient time.   1 Cor. 1:12; 3:5

Final Exhortations

13 ᴿWatch, ᴿstand fast in the faith, be brave, be strong.   Matt. 24:42 • Phil. 1:27; 4:1

14 Let all *that* you *do* be done with love.

15 I urge you, brethren—you know the household of Stephanas, that it is the firstfruits of Achaia, and *that* they have devoted themselves to the ministry of the saints—

16 that you also submit to such, and to everyone who works and labors with *us.*

17 I am glad about the coming of Stephanas, Fortunatus, and Achaicus, for what was lacking on your part they supplied.

18 ᴿFor they refreshed my spirit and yours. Therefore acknowledge such men.   Col. 4:8

Greetings and a Solemn Farewell

19 The churches of Asia greet you. Aquila and Priscilla greet you heartily in the Lord, with the church that is in their house.

20 All the brethren greet you. ᴿGreet one another with a holy kiss.   Rom. 16:16

21 ᴿThe salutation with my own hand—Paul's.   Col. 4:18

22 If anyone does not love the Lord Jesus Christ, let him be *accursed. *O Lord, come!

23 ᴿThe grace of our Lord Jesus Christ *be* with you.   Rom. 16:20

24 My love *be* with you all in Christ Jesus. Amen.

15:55 NU *O Death, where is your victory? O Death, where is your sting?*

16:22 Gr. *anathema* • Aram. *Marana tha* or *Maranatha;* possibly *Maran atha, Our Lord has come*

THE SECOND EPISTLE OF PAUL THE APOSTLE TO THE

Corinthians

CONTEXT. The residents of Corinth must have been a frustrating people! They had the fortune to live in one of the most important centers of worship in Greece, if you can call the practice of perverted, idolatrous religion "worship." They were a people striving to express man's basic need to identify with the Supreme Being and yet perverting this need by the basest of conduct.

In this scene of religious debauchery and cosmopolitan corruption, the seasoned missionary Paul, on his second journey, established a New Testament church in Corinth and tried his best to instruct believers in true discipleship prior to continuing to Ephesus. (For the details of this first visit, see Acts 18:1-17.)

Looking back later, he penned his first epistle to the Corinthians in response to reports of ungodly conduct with regard to church discipline, actual unbelief within the church body, constant arguments, and an expressly divided spirit among the believers. How aware of their turmoil he must have been in his grief. With consolation and condemnation he expressed profound disappointment over the immorality in his struggling Corinthian church.

AUTHORSHIP. This particular book, Paul's second epistle to the "church of God at Corinth," apparently came as a result of the lackadaisical reception afforded his first letter. Paul practiced a simple philosophy: when the world doesn't listen the first time—repeat the message! This second epistle was written within a year of the first one and displays Paul's spiritual burden over the refusal of these frustrating friends to follow completely his apostolic authority.

HOW 2 CORINTHIANS FITS INTO THE BIBLE. Paul was not a defensive person, but when falsely attacked he did stand up for his position. Because of this we have a unique glimpse into the sufferings, ministry, and tender heart of the beloved apostle Paul. This book also gives us a very fine, detailed exposition of the Christian grace of giving. Because of its emotional style, 2 Corinthians is one of the more difficult books, and you will notice more italicized words— words that had to be supplied by the translators for smooth, clear English.

HOW 2 CORINTHIANS FITS TOGETHER. 2 Corinthians is analyzed by nearly everyone into three parts, with a section on giving at the center. (1) In chapters 1—7 Paul defends his change of plans in traveling to Macedonia instead of visiting them as he had intended. (2) In chapters 8 and 9 he encourages a generous collection for the poor Christians of Judea. (3) Lastly, in chapters 10—13 he presents his apostolic credentials, defending his ministry against others who sought to disparage him and so lead the Corinthians astray.

He begins his letter by defending both his character and conduct. By describing the very motives of his ministry, he appeals to the brethren to be set apart and cleansed like himself.

To understand this letter, a reader needs to empathize with the stress and anxiety Paul felt as he dealt with his spiritual babes concerning their Christian growth and the real joy of Christian living. He tried desperately to set a proper example in all areas of his personal life, even though constantly besieged by physical discomforts and persecution. On top of it all, there was the added hardship of having his authority questioned by his own converts. Yet despite all this he was able to instruct them (and us) from the overflow of a full life, both physically and spiritually. His instructions bring spiritual life to every reader willing to receive it. The unique effectiveness of Paul's overflow was certainly evident in his day and has not changed in content or process through the intervening years.

One cannot read this book from a detached perspective, because it focuses on some very personal matters in its heavily autobiographical presentation. Undoubtedly, the reader is given more insight into Paul's life from this book than from any other passage in the Bible. Readers become personally aware and acutely involved as Paul discusses his background before his conversion, his visions from God—especially the one that may be related to his stoning at Lystra (Acts 14:19)—and the persecutions he suffered as he traveled from each place of service.

The old "thorn in the flesh" that haunted Paul is also a widely discussed subject and is specifically mentioned in chapter 12. In case you have wondered about it, Paul confirms in 12:7 that it was given in order to control his pride and is certainly satanic in origin. Even though his requests for it to be removed were answered with a no, you can feel the fervor of his prayers. Any reader who has so dealt with God can identify with Paul's yearnings and also with the Lord's gentle answer, "My grace is sufficient for you, for My strength is made perfect in weakness" (12:9).

The letter ends with what amounts to a warning. Paul tells his readers that he is coming to visit them very shortly and hopes he won't need to scold or punish them when that time comes. He asks them to check up on themselves and see if they can really pass the test of a Christian. His warning holds concerns even for us today: "Examine yourselves as to whether you are in the faith. Test yourselves. Do you not know yourselves, that Jesus Christ is in you?—unless indeed you are disqualified" (13:5).

This letter is truly a lesson in living for every man and woman! As you read, look for comparisons between Israel's old covenant and your new one. Discover the ways you are a part of that comparison. Find promises of God that provide for your security as a believer. Learn about cheerful giving and God's abounding grace. Identify with Paul as he shows compassion and sincere love even to those who dislike and distrust him. And finally, be challenged as Paul exhorts us to "become complete," to "be of good comfort," and to "live in peace." Don't miss the blessing that can be yours from both reading and living the truths of this inspired epistle.

—D.E. and J.D.E.

Greeting

PAUL, ᴿan apostle of Jesus Christ by the will of God, and ᴿTimothy *our* brother,

To the church of God which is at Corinth, ᴿwith all the saints who are in all Achaia: 2 Tim. 1:1 • 1 Cor. 16:10 • Col. 1:2

2   ᴿGrace to you and peace from God our Father and the Lord Jesus Christ.   Rom. 1:7

Comfort in Suffering

3   ᴿBlessed *be* the God and Father of our Lord Jesus Christ, the Father of mercies and God of all comfort,   1 Pet. 1:3
4   who comforts us in all our tribulation, that we may be able to comfort those who are in ᴿany trouble, with the comfort with which we ourselves are comforted by God.
5   For as ᴿthe sufferings of Christ abound in us, so our ᵀconsolation also abounds through Christ.   [Acts 9:4] • *comfort*
6   Now if we are afflicted, ᴿ*it is* for your consolation and salvation, which is effective for enduring the same sufferings which we also suffer. Or if we are comforted, *it is* for your consolation and salvation.   2 Cor. 4:15; 12:15
7   And our hope for you *is* steadfast, because we know that ᴿas you are partakers of the sufferings, so also *you will partake* of the consolation.   [Rom. 8:17]

Delivered from Suffering

8   For we do not want you to be ignorant, brethren, of ᴿour ᵀtrouble which came to us in Asia: that we were burdened beyond measure, above strength, so that we despaired even of life.   Acts 19:23 • *tribulation*
9   Yes, we had the sentence of death in ourselves, that we should not trust in ourselves but in God who raises the dead,
10   ᴿwho delivered us from so great a death, and *does deliver us; in whom we trust that He will still deliver *us*,   [2 Pet. 2:9]

11   you also ᴿhelping together in prayer for us, that thanks may be given by many persons on *our behalf ᴿfor the gift *granted* to us through many.   Rom. 15:30 • 2 Cor. 4:15; 9:11

Paul's Sincerity

12   For our boasting is this: the testimony of our conscience that we conducted ourselves in the world in simplicity and godly sincerity, not with fleshly wisdom but by the grace of God, and more abundantly toward you.
13   For we are not writing any other things to you than what you read or understand. Now I trust you will understand, even to the end
14   (as also you have understood us in part), ᴿthat we are your boast as you also *are* ours, in the day of the Lord Jesus.   2 Cor. 5:12

Sparing the Church

15   And in this confidence ᴿI intended to come to you before, that you might have ᴿa second benefit—   1 Cor. 4:19 • Rom. 1:11; 15:29
16   to pass by way of you to Macedonia, to come again from Macedonia to you, and be helped by you on my way to Judea.
17   Therefore, when I was planning this, did I do it lightly? Or the things I plan, do I plan ᴿaccording to the flesh, that with me there should be Yes, Yes, and No, No?   2 Cor. 10:12
18   But *as* God *is* ᴿfaithful, our ᵀword to you was not Yes and No.   1 John 5:20 • *message*
19   For ᴿthe Son of God, Jesus Christ, who was preached among you by us—by me, Silvanus, and Timothy—was not Yes and No, ᴿbut in Him was Yes.   Mark 1:1 • [Heb. 13:8]
20   ᴿFor all the promises of God in Him *are* Yes, and in Him Amen, to the glory of God through us.   [Rom. 15:8, 9]
21   Now He who establishes us with you in Christ and ᴿhas anointed us *is* God, [1 John 2:20]
22   who ᴿalso has sealed us and given us the Spirit in our hearts as a guarantee.   [Eph. 4:30]

1:10 NU *shall*   1:11 NU *your behalf*

23 Moreover ᴿI call God as witness against my soul, ᴿthat to spare you I came no more to Corinth.   Gal. 1:20 · 1 Cor. 4:21

24 Not ᴿthat we ᵀhave dominion over your faith, but are fellow workers for your joy; for ᴿby faith you stand.   [1 Pet. 5:3] · *rule* · Rom. 11:20

2 But I determined this within myself, that I would not come again to you in sorrow.

2 For if I make you ᴿsorrowful, then who is he who makes me glad but the one who is made sorrowful by me?   2 Cor. 7:8

Forgive the Offender

3 And I wrote this very thing to you, lest, when I came, ᴿI should have sorrow over those from whom I ought to have joy, ᴿhaving confidence in you all that my joy is *the joy* of you all.   2 Cor. 12:21 · Gal. 5:10

4 For out of much ᵀaffliction and anguish of heart I wrote to you, with many tears, ᴿnot that you should be grieved, but that you might know the love which I have so abundantly for you.   *tribulation* · [2 Cor. 2:9; 7:8, 12]

5 But ᴿif anyone has caused grief, he has not grieved me, but all of you to some extent—not to be too severe.   [1 Cor. 5:1]

6 This punishment which *was inflicted* by the majority is sufficient for such a man,

7 ᴿso that, on the contrary, you *ought* rather to forgive and comfort *him*, lest perhaps such a one be swallowed up with too much sorrow.   Gal. 6:1

8 Therefore I urge you to reaffirm *your* love to him.

9 For to this end I also wrote, that I might put you to the test, whether you are ᴿobedient in all things.   2 Cor. 7:15; 10:6

10 Now whom you forgive anything, I also *forgive.* For *if indeed I have forgiven anything, I have forgiven that one for your sakes in the presence of Christ,

11 lest Satan should take advantage of us; for we are not ignorant of his devices.

Triumph in Christ

12 Furthermore, ᴿwhen I came to Troas to *preach* Christ's gospel, and a ᵀdoor was opened to me by the Lord,   Acts 16:8 · *Opportunity*

13 I had no rest in my spirit, because I did not find Titus my brother; but taking my leave of them, I departed for Macedonia.

14 Now thanks *be* to God who always leads us in triumph in Christ, and through us ᵀdiffuses the fragrance of His knowledge in every place.   *manifests*

15 For we are to God the fragrance of Christ among those who are being saved and ᴿamong those who are perishing.   [2 Cor. 4:3]

16 To the one *we are* the aroma of death *leading* to death, and to the other the aroma

of life *leading* to life. And who *is* sufficient for these things?

17 For we are not, as *so many, ᴿpeddlingᵀ the word of God; but as ᴿof sincerity, but as from God, we speak in the sight of God in Christ.   2 Pet. 2:3 · *adulterating for gain* · 2 Cor. 1:12

Christ's Epistle

3 Do ᴿwe begin again to commend ourselves? Or do we need, as some *others,* ᴿepistles of commendation to you or *letters* of commendation from you?   2 Cor. 5:12 · Acts 18:27

2 ᴿYou are our epistle written in our hearts, known and read by all men;   1 Cor. 9:2

3 clearly *you are* an epistle of Christ, ᴿministered by us, written not with ink but by the Spirit of the living God, not ᴿon tablets of stone but ᴿon tablets of flesh, *that is,* of the heart.   1 Cor. 3:5 · Ex. 24:12; 31:18; 32:15 · Ps. 40:8

The Spirit, Not the Letter

4 And we have such trust through Christ toward God.

5 ᴿNot that we are sufficient of ourselves to think of anything as *being* from ourselves, but our sufficiency *is* from God,   [John 15:5]

6 who also made us sufficient as ministers of the new covenant, not ᴿof the letter but of the ᵀSpirit; for ᴿthe letter kills, ᴿbut the Spirit gives life.   Rom. 2:27 · *Or spirit* · Gal. 3:10 · John 6:63

Glory of the New Covenant

7 But if ᴿthe ministry of death, ᴿwritten *and* engraved on stones, was glorious, ᴿso that the children of Israel could not look steadily at the face of Moses because of the glory of his countenance, which *glory* was passing away,   Rom. 7:10 · Ex. 34:1 · Ex. 34:29

8 how will ᴿthe ministry of the Spirit not be more glorious?   [Gal. 3:5]

9 For if the ministry of condemnation *had* glory, the ministry ᴿof righteousness exceeds much more in glory.   [Rom. 1:17; 3:21]

10 For even what was made glorious had no glory in this respect, because of the glory that excels.

11 For if what is passing away *was* glorious, what remains *is* much more glorious.

12 Therefore, since we have such hope, ᴿwe use great boldness of speech—   Eph. 6:19

13 unlike Moses, ᴿwho put a veil over his face so that the children of Israel could not look steadily at ᴿthe end of what was passing away.   Ex. 34:33–35 · [Gal. 3:23]

14 ᴿBut their minds were blinded. For until this day the same veil remains unlifted in the reading of the Old Testament, because the *veil* is taken away in Christ.   Is. 29:10

15 But even to this day, when Moses is read, a veil lies on their heart.

16 Nevertheless ᴿwhen one turns to the Lord, ᴿthe veil is taken away.   Rom. 11:23 · Is. 25:7

2:10 NU *indeed, what I have forgiven, if I have forgiven anything, I did it for your sakes*

2:17 M *the rest*

17 Now the Lord is the Spirit; and where the Spirit of the Lord *is*, there *is* liberty.

18 But we all, with unveiled face, beholding as in a mirror the glory of the Lord, ᴿare being transformed into the same image from glory to glory, just as ᵀby the Spirit of the Lord. [Rom. 8:29, 30] • Or *from the Lord, the Spirit*

The Light of Christ's Gospel

4 Therefore, since we have this ministry, ᴿas we have received mercy, we ᴿdo not lose heart. 1 Cor. 7:25 • 2 Cor. 4:16

2 But we have renounced the hidden things of shame, not walking in craftiness nor ᵀhandling the word of God deceitfully, but by manifestation of the truth ᴿcommending ourselves to every man's conscience in the sight of God. *adulterating the Word of God* • 2 Cor. 5:11

▼ 12-C. Satan: The God of This World

3 But even if our gospel is veiled, ᴿit is veiled to those who are perishing, [1 Cor. 1:18]

4 whose minds the god of this age has ▽ blinded, who do not believe, lest the light of the gospel of the glory of Christ, who is the image of God, should shine on them. ▲

5 ᴿFor we do not preach ourselves, but Christ Jesus the Lord, and ᴿourselves your bondservants for Jesus' sake. 1 Cor. 1:13 • 1 Cor. 9:19

6 For it is the God who commanded light to shine out of darkness, who has shone in our hearts to *give* the light of the knowledge of the glory of God in the face of Jesus Christ.

Cast Down but Unconquered

7 But we have this treasure in earthen vessels, ᴿthat the excellence of the power may be of God and not of us. 1 Cor. 2:5

8 *We are* ᴿhard pressed on every side, yet not crushed; *we are* perplexed, but not in despair; 2 Cor. 1:8; 7:5

9 persecuted, but not ᴿforsaken; ᴿstruck down, but not destroyed— Ps. 37:24 • [Heb. 13:5]

12-C. Satan: The God of This World (2 Corinthians 4:3, 4)—Many people underestimate the power of Satan, "the god of this age" (v. 4). God, in His sovereign will, has allowed Satan to exercise limited power over this world. We do not know why. This is one of God's secrets (Deut. 29:29, page 208). God has allowed him to roam about on this earth (Job 1:7, page 479), seeking whom he may devour (1 Pet. 5:8, page 1269).

(1) Satan has great power, but not all power. Only God is omnipotent (Matt. 28:18, page 982). God has all authority over His universe at all times.

(2) Satan has access to the presence of God, and he can roam this earth, but he is not omnipresent. He can only be in one place at one time. Only God is present in all places of the universe at all times (Ps. 139:7-10, page 590).

(3) Satan has great knowledge, but not all knowledge. Only God is omniscient (Ps. 147:5, page 594).

(4) As "the god of this age" (v. 4), Satan is worshiped. "So they worshiped the dragon" (Rev. 13:4, page 1306); the Dragon is Satan (Rev. 12:9, page 1305). Satan offered Jesus "all the kingdoms of the world and their glory . . . if you will fall down and worship me." And Jesus answered, "You shall worship the Lᴏʀᴅ your God, and Him only you shall serve" (Matt. 4:8-11, page 934). Only God is to be worshiped (Ex. 20:1-5, page 79).

(5) Satan has limited power to obstruct the gospel:

(a) He has power to hide (hinder, obscure) the gospel from "those who are perishing" (v. 3). If you are a child of God and you are not sharing the gospel with the lost, you are hiding it from them. To know the gospel and not tell it is to hide it. To hide the gospel from the lost is to assist Satan.

(b) He has power to blind the minds of those "who do not believe." But "the light of the gospel of the glory of Christ" (v. 4) has the power to illuminate their minds and set them free from spiritual darkness and eternal damnation. We must go with the gospel, and share it in the unlimited power of the indwelling Holy Spirit. We must always remember: "He [God the Holy Spirit] who is in you is greater than he [Satan, a supernatural, fallen angel] who is in the world" (1 John 4:4, page 1280).

(c) Satan has the power to steal the Word of God from the hearts of those who hear, but do not understand the gospel (Matt. 13:19, page 956). Therefore, we must take time to make very clear the Good News of salvation, because we are sharing with the "natural man" who does not have the spiritual capacity to understand the gospel (1 Cor. 2:14, page 1149).

(6) Satan has limited power over this world system:

(a) Three times in the Gospel of John the Lord Jesus Christ called Satan "the ruler of this world" (John 12:31, page 1072; 14:30, page 1076; 16:11, page 1077).

(b) Paul tells us that Satan is "the prince of the power of the air" (Eph. 2:1, 2, page 1187). "The air" is the abode of the disembodied evil spirits which are called demons. Believers are not completely immune to the power of Satan or the demons of the air (Acts 5:3, page 1093).

(c) Satan is also "the ruler of the demons" (Matt. 12:24, page 953). Satan is the chief devil, and all the disembodied evil spirits do his will.

(7) Satan has at least limited access to the presence of God, to accuse believers (Job 1:6-12, page 479; 2:1-8, page 480). He will be cast out of heaven permanently, however, by Michael the archangel (Rev. 12:7-9, page 1305).

See John 8:44, page 1063, for **Point 12-D: Satan: The Original Manslayer and Father of Lies.**

10 always carrying about in the body the dying of the Lord Jesus, that the life of Jesus also may be manifested in our body.

11 For we who live are always delivered to death for Jesus' sake, that the life of Jesus also may be manifested in our mortal flesh.

12 So then death is working in us, but life in you.

13 And since we have ᴿthe same spirit of faith, according to what is written, ᴿ"I believed and therefore I spoke," we also believe and therefore speak,   2 Pet. 1:1 • Ps. 116:10

14 knowing that ᴿHe who raised up the Lord Jesus will also raise us up with Jesus, and will present us with you.   [Rom. 8:11]

15 For ᴿall things are for your sakes, that ᴿgrace, having spread through the many, may cause thanksgiving to abound to the glory of God.   Col. 1:24 • 2 Cor. 1:11

Seeing the Invisible

16 Therefore we do not lose heart. Even though our outward man is perishing, yet the inward man is being renewed day by day.

17 For our light affliction, which is but for a moment, is working for us a far more exceeding and eternal weight of glory,

18 ᴿwhile we do not look at the things which are seen, but at the things which are not seen. For the things which are seen are temporary, but the things which are not seen are eternal.   [Heb. 11:1, 13]

Assurance of the Resurrection

5 For we know that if our earthly ᵀhouse, this tent, is destroyed, we have a building from God, a house ᴿnot made with hands, eternal in the heavens.   Physical body • Mark 14:58

2 For in this ᴿwe groan, earnestly desiring to be clothed with our ᵀhabitation which is from heaven,   Rom. 8:23 • dwelling

3 if indeed, ᴿhaving been clothed, we shall not be found naked.   Rev. 3:18

4 For we who are in this tent groan, being burdened, not because we want to be unclothed, ᴿbut further clothed, that mortality may be swallowed up by life.   1 Cor. 15:53

5 Now He who has prepared us for this very thing is God, who also has given us the Spirit as ᵀa guarantee.   down payment, earnest

6 So we are always confident, knowing that while we are at home in the body we are absent from the Lord.

7 For we walk by faith, not by sight.

8 We are confident, yes, ᴿwell pleased rather to be absent from the body and to be present with the Lord.   Phil. 1:23

The Judgment Seat of Christ

9 Therefore we make it our aim, whether present or absent, to be well pleasing to Him.

18-C. The Judgment of the Believer's Works   ▼

10 ᴿFor we must all appear before the judgment seat of Christ, ᴿthat each one may receive the things done in the body, according to what he has done, whether good or bad.   Rom. 2:16; 14:10, 12 • Gal. 6:7; Eph. 6:8 ▲

11 Knowing, therefore, ᴿthe terror of the Lord, we persuade men; but we are well known to God, and I also trust are well known in your consciences.   [Heb. 10:31; 12:29]

Be Reconciled to God

12 For ᴿwe do not commend ourselves again to you, but give you opportunity ᴿto boast on our behalf, that you may have an answer for those who boast in appearance and not in heart.   2 Cor. 3:1 • 2 Cor. 1:14

13 For if we are beside ourselves, it is for God; or if we are of sound mind, it is for you.

14 For the love of Christ compels us, because we judge thus: that ᴿif One died for all, then all died;   [Rom. 5:15; 6:6]

18-C. The Judgment of the Believer's Works (2 Corinthians 5:10)—The believer's works will be judged at the "judgment seat of Christ" (v. 10). The term "judgment seat of Christ" is found only twice in the Bible, but it is referred to many times. It is found in the above verse, and also in Romans 14:10 (page 1144). A careful reading of both verses in context reveals that only believers will appear at the judgment seat of Christ. Their works will be judged, not their sins; for we have already seen that the sins of the believer were judged in Christ on Calvary, and "there is therefore now no condemnation [judgment] to those who are in Christ Jesus" (Rom. 8:1, page 1136).

(1) This judgment will take place "in the air" following the first resurrection. "And the dead in Christ will rise first" (1 Thess. 4:14–18, page 1212). After the resurrection of the saved, a thousand years will pass before the resurrection of the unsaved (Rev. 20:4, 5, page 1313), and so there will be a thousand years between the judgment seat of Christ, where only saved will appear, and the judgment at the Great White Throne (Rev. 20:11, page 1313), where only unsaved will appear.

(2) At the judgment seat of Christ, the believer will give an account of himself to God. Therefore, we should look at our own works, and not judge the works of others (Rom. 14:10–13, page 1144).

(3) It is a most humbling thought to know that someday the believer will face all his works—good or bad. Some believers will be ashamed (1 John 2:28, page 1279) and "suffer loss"—not the loss of salvation, but the loss of rewards (1 Cor. 3:11–15, page 1149). So whatever you do, do it to the glory of God (Col. 3:17, page 1207).

See Matthew 25:31–46, page 976, for **Point 18-D: The Judgment of the Nations.**

15 and He died for all, that those who live should live no longer for themselves, but for Him who died for them and rose again.

16 Therefore, from now on, we regard no one according to the flesh. Even though we have known Christ according to the flesh, yet now we know Him thus no longer.

17 Therefore, if anyone is in Christ, he is a new creation; old things have passed away; behold, all things have become new.

18 Now all things are of God, ᴿwho has reconciled us to Himself through Jesus Christ, and has given us the ministry of reconciliation,   Rom. 5:10

19 that is, that ᴿGod was in Christ reconciling the world to Himself, not ᵀimputing their trespasses to them, and has committed to us the word of reconciliation.   [Rom. 3:24] · reckoning

20 Now then, we are ᴿambassadors for Christ, as though God were pleading through us: we implore you on Christ's behalf, be reconciled to God.   Eph. 6:20

21 For ᴿHe made Him who knew no sin to be sin for us, that we might become the righteousness of God in Him.   Is. 53:6, 9

Marks of the Ministry

6 We then, as ᴿworkers together with Him also ᴿplead with you not to receive the grace of God in vain.   1 Cor. 3:9 · 2 Cor. 5:20

2 For He says:

ᴿ"In an acceptable time I have heard you,
And in the day of salvation I have
    helped you."   Is. 49:8

Behold, now is the accepted time; behold, now is the day of salvation.

3 ᴿWe give no offense in anything, that our ministry may not be blamed.   Rom. 14:13

4 But in all things we commend ourselves as ministers of God: in much ᵀpatience, in tribulations, in needs, in distresses,   endurance

5 in stripes, in imprisonments, in tumults, in labors, in sleeplessness, in fastings;

6 by purity, by knowledge, by longsuffering, by kindness, by the Holy Spirit, by ᵀsincere love,   Lit. unhypocritical

7 by the word of truth, by the power of God, by ᴿthe armor of righteousness on the right hand and on the left,   2 Cor. 10:4

8 by honor and dishonor, by evil report and good report; as deceivers, and yet true;

9 as unknown, and yet well known; ᴿas dying, and behold we live; ᴿas chastened, and yet not killed;   1 Cor. 4:9, 11 · Ps. 118:18

10 as sorrowful, yet always rejoicing; as poor, yet making many rich; as having nothing, and yet possessing all things.

Be Holy

11 O Corinthians! We have spoken openly to you, ᴿour heart is wide open.   2 Cor. 7:3

12 You are not restricted by us, but you are restricted by your own affections.

13 Now in return for the same ᴿ(I speak as to children), you also be open.   1 Cor. 4:14

14 Do not be unequally yoked together with unbelievers. For what fellowship has righteousness with lawlessness? And what communion has light with darkness?

15 And what accord has Christ with Belial? Or what part has a believer with an unbeliever?

16 And what agreement has the temple of God with idols? For ᴿyou* are the temple of the living God. As God has said: [1 Cor. 6:19]

*"I will dwell in them
And walk among them.
I will be their God,
And they shall be My people."

17 Therefore

*"Come out from among them
And be separate, says the Lord.
Do not touch what is unclean,
And I will receive you."

18 "I will be a ᴿFather to you,   Jer. 31:1, 9
And you shall be My ᴿsons and
    daughters,   Rom. 8:14
Says the LORD Almighty."*

7 Therefore,ᴿ having these promises, beloved, let us cleanse ourselves from all filthiness of the flesh and spirit, perfecting holiness in the fear of God.   [1 John 3:3]

The Corinthians' Repentance

2 Open your hearts to us. We have wronged no one, we have corrupted no one, we have cheated no one.

3 I do not say this to condemn; for ᴿI have said before that you are in our hearts, to die together and to live together.   2 Cor. 6:11, 12

24-C. Faith Is Joyful in Tribulation   ▼

4 Great is my boldness of speech toward you, ᴿgreat is my boasting on your behalf. ᴿI

6:16 NU we • Ex. 29:45; Lev. 26:12; Jer. 31:33; 32:38; Zech. 8:8
6:17 Num. 33:51–56; Is. 52:11; Rev. 18:4
6:18 2 Sam. 7:14; Jer. 31:1, 9; [Rev. 21:7]

24-C. Faith Is Joyful in Tribulation (2 Corinthians 7:4, 5)—"I am exceedingly joyful in all our tribulation" (v. 4). The apostle Paul could truly say that his joy was overflowing, even in his afflictions. He did not merely submit to persecutions, neither did he overflow with joy *because* he was experiencing great tribulations; but he rejoiced *while* in afflictions, knowing by faith that this was part of God's perfect will for his life and ministry. This is commitment that remains strong, even in the face of overwhelming adversity (Rom. 8:28, page 1137).

(Point 24-C continued on next page)

▽ am filled with comfort. I am exceedingly joanful in all our tribulation.   1 Cor. 1:4 • Phil. 2:17

5 For indeed, when we came to Macedonia, our bodies had no rest, but ᴿwe were troubled on every side. ᴿOutside were conflicts, inside were fears.   2 Cor. 4:8 • Deut. 32:25

6 Nevertheless ᴿGod, who comforts the downcast, comforted us by ᴿthe coming of Titus,   2 Cor. 1:3, 4 • 2 Cor. 2:13; 7:13

7 and not only by his coming, but also by the ᵀconsolation with which he was comforted in you, when he told us of your earnest desire, your mourning, your zeal for me, so that I rejoiced even more.   comfort

8 For even if I made you sorry with my letter, I do not regret it; ᴿthough I did regret it. For I perceive that the same epistle made you sorry, though only for a while.   2 Cor. 2:4

9 Now I rejoice, not that you were made sorry, but that your sorrow led to repentance. For you were made sorry in a godly manner, that you might suffer loss from us in nothing.

10 For godly sorrow produces repentance leading to salvation, not to be regretted; but the sorrow of the world produces death.

11 For observe this very thing, that you sorrowed in a godly manner: What diligence it produced in you, what ᴿclearing of yourselves, what indignation, what fear, what vehement desire, what zeal, what vindication! In all things you proved yourselves to be ᴿclear in this matter.   Eph. 5:11 • 2 Cor. 2:5-11

12 Therefore, although I wrote to you, I did not do it for the sake of him who had done the wrong, nor for the sake of him who suffered wrong, but that our care for you in the sight of God might appear to you.

(Point 24-C continued from previous page)

When Paul and Silas were at Troas, the Holy Spirit told Paul in a vision at night to go to Macedonia. In the vision "A man of Macedonia stood and pleaded with him, saying, 'Come over to Macedonia and help us' " (Acts 16:8, 9, page 1110). Believing that the Lord had called them to preach the gospel in Macedonia, they set a straight course for Philippi, which was its chief city and a colony of Rome. There they were welcomed with a beating from the people, then cast into the Philippian prison where their feet were placed in stocks. "But at midnight Paul and Silas were praying and singing hymns to God, and the prisoners were listening to them" (Acts 16:16–25, page 1110). They sang because they were in the will of God; their faith produced overflowing joy in tribulation.

Paul never referred to himself as a prisoner of the Jews, or a prisoner of Rome. In every prison he spoke of himself as a "prisoner of Christ Jesus" (Eph. 3:1, page 1188). While in a Roman prison, he wrote to his friend and fellow laborer, Philemon, and referred to himself as "being such a one as Paul, the aged, and now also a prisoner of Jesus Christ" (Philem. 9, page 1234).

Paul did not allow outward circumstances to control his ministry for the Lord. To the Philippian believers he said, "I have learned in whatever state I am, to be content" (Phil. 4:11, page 1198). This is spiritual maturity. Paul had reached the place where he was content to be abased, humbled, or to abound (Phil. 4:12, page 1198). In plenty or poverty he had learned how to rejoice. By faith he could "glory in tribulations" (Rom. 5:1–5, page 1133). Having learned to be content in any external circumstance, he could shout, "I can do all things through Christ who strengthens me" (Phil. 4:13, page 1198). He believed that everything that happened to him was "for the furtherance of the gospel" (Phil. 1:12, page 1195).

(1) He said, "A thorn in the flesh was given to me, a messenger of Satan to buffet me . . . I pleaded with the Lord three times that it might depart from me. And He [the Lord] said to me, 'My grace is sufficient for you, for My strength is made perfect in weakness.' "

When Paul learned this, he said, "Therefore most gladly I will rather boast in my infirmities . . . Therefore I take pleasure

        (a) "In infirmities,
        (b) "In reproaches,
        (c) "In needs,
        (d) "In persecutions,
        (e) "In distresses, for Christ's sake. For when I am weak, then I am strong" (2 Cor. 12:7-10, page 1175).

(2) Again he wrote:

        (a) "we are hard pressed on every side, yet not crushed;
        (b) "we are perplexed, but not in despair;
        (c) "persecuted, but not forsaken;
        (d) "struck down, but not destroyed" (2 Cor. 4:8, 9, page 1167).

Paul's faith lifted him above outward circumstances (2 Cor. 11:21–33, page 1174), inward conflicts (Col. 2:1, page 1203), and fears. "And I, brethren, when I came to you . . . I was with you in weakness, in fear, and in much trembling. . . . that your faith should not be in the wisdom of men but in the power of God" (1 Cor. 2:1–5, page 1148). Paul wanted the church of Corinth to anchor its faith in God rather than in any servant of God, including himself.

See James 2:14–26, page 1257, for **Point 24-D: Faith Without Works Is Dead.**

The Joy of Titus

13 Therefore we have been comforted in your comfort. And we rejoiced exceedingly more for the joy of Titus, because his spirit ᴿhas been refreshed by you all.   Rom. 15:32

14 For if in anything I have boasted to him about you, I am not ashamed. But as we spoke all things to you in truth, even so our boasting to Titus was found true.

15 And his affections are greater for you as he remembers the obedience of you all, how with fear and trembling you received him.

16 Therefore I rejoice that ᴿI have confidence in you in everything.   2 Thess. 3:4

Excel in Giving

8 Moreover, brethren, we make known to you the grace of God bestowed on the churches of Macedonia:

2 that in a great trial of affliction the abundance of their joy and their deep poverty abounded in the riches of their liberality.

3 For I bear witness that according to *their* ability, yes, and beyond *their* ability, *they were* freely willing,

4 imploring us with much urgency *that we would receive the gift and the fellowship of the ministering to the saints.

5 And not *only* as we had hoped, but they first gave themselves to the Lord, and *then* to us by the ᴿwill of God.   [Eph. 6:6]

6 So ᴿwe urged Titus, that as he had begun, so he would also complete this grace in you as well.   2 Cor. 8:17; 12:18

7 But as ᴿyou abound in everything—in faith, in speech, in knowledge, in all diligence, and in your love for us—*see* that you abound in this grace also.   [1 Cor. 1:5; 12:13]

Christ Our Pattern

8 ᴿI speak not by commandment, but I am testing the sincerity of your love by the diligence of others.   1 Cor. 7:6

21-B. So Great in Giving   ▼

9 For you know the grace of our Lord Jesus Christ, that though He was rich, yet for your sakes He became poor, that you through His poverty might become rich.   ▲

8:4 NU, M omit *that we would receive,* thus changing text to *urgency for the favor and fellowship*

21-B. So Great in Giving (2 Corinthians 8:9)—The price for your salvation, paid by the Lord Jesus Christ, was the greatest ever paid for anything. "For you know the grace of our Lord Jesus Christ, that though He was rich, yet for your sakes He became poor, that you through His poverty might become rich" (v. 9). This verse reveals that "the grace of our Lord Jesus Christ" is the grace of giving:

(1) God the Father demonstrated the grace of giving when He "so loved the world that He gave His only begotten Son, that whoever believes in Him should not perish but have everlasting life" (John 3:16, page 1052).

(2) God the Son demonstrated the grace of giving when He gave His life on Calvary to redeem your lost soul and make you a child of God (John 1:12, page 1049).

(3) God the Holy Spirit demonstrated the grace of giving when, on the Day of Pentecost, He came to this earth in a special way to convict men:

(a) "Of sin, because they do not believe in Me" (John 16:9, page 1077).

(b) "Of righteousness, because I go to My Father and you see Me no more" (John 16:10, page 1077). He convicts us of our need of Christ's righteousness (Rom. 10:4, page 1140).

(c) "Of judgment, because the ruler of this world is judged" (John 16:11, page 1077). So are all unbelievers: "He who believes in Him is not condemned [judged]; but he who does not believe is condemned [judged] already, because he has not believed in the name of the only begotten Son of God" (John 3:18, page 1053).

You may know the grace of God *factually,* but you will never begin to comprehend God's grace of giving until you experientially accept His gift—salvation by grace, through faith in the Lord Jesus Christ. Only then will you begin to understand the great transformation taking place in your life. "Therefore, if anyone is in Christ, he is a new creation; old things have passed away; behold, all things have become new" (2 Cor. 5:17, page 1169).

To know the grace of the Lord Jesus Christ, you must know that, "though He was rich, yet for your sakes He became poor" (v. 9). He was rich in eternity past with God the Father; but He left the Father's side for this sinful world. He left the glory of heaven for the sorrow and gloom of this sin-cursed world. He was rich in the care and worship of all the angels of heaven. The Father said, "Let all the angels of God worship Him" (Heb. 1:6, page 1236). Yet, for your sake, He became poor, allowing sinful men to mock Him, curse Him, crucify Him, and put Him to shame. He, "despising the shame" (Heb. 12:2, page 1250), endured the agonies of hell on the cross that you might be rich with Him in glory forever and ever. Jesus Christ, the God-Man, suffered physically (Is. 52:14, page 693), spiritually (Is. 53:3–6, page 693), and emotionally (Matt. 27:46, page 980). He "Himself bore our sins in His own body on the tree" (1 Pet. 2:24, page 1266). Never did a man suffer like this Man. It was all for you, that you might be rich in this life and eternally rich in the life to come (John 20:30, 31, page 1084).

See Acts 4:12, page 1091, for **Point 21-C: So Great in Power.**

10 And in this I give advice: It is to your advantage not only to be doing what you began and were desiring to do a year ago;

11 but now you also must complete the doing *of it;* that as *there was* a readiness to desire *it,* so *there* also *may be* a completion out of what *you* have.

12 For if there is first a willing mind, *it is* accepted according to what one has, *and* not according to what he does not have.

13 For *I* do not *mean* that others should be eased and you burdened;

14 but by an equality, *that* now at this time your abundance *may supply* their lack, that their abundance also may supply your lack—that there may be equality.

15 As it is written, ᴿ*"He who gathered much had nothing left over, and he who gathered little had no lack."*   Ex. 16:18

Collection for the Judean Saints

16 But thanks *be* to God who *puts the same earnest care for you into the heart of Titus.

17 For he not only accepted the exhortation, but being more diligent, he went to you of his own accord.

18 And we have sent with him ᴿthe brother whose praise *is* in the gospel throughout all the churches,   2 Cor. 12:18

19 and not only *that,* but who was also ᴿchosen by the churches to travel with us with this gift, which is administered by us ᴿto the glory of the Lord Himself and *to show* your ready mind,   1 Cor. 16:3, 4 • 2 Cor. 4:15

20 avoiding this: that anyone should blame us in this lavish gift which is administered by us—

21 ᴿproviding honorable things, not only in the sight of the Lord, but also in the sight of men.   Rom. 12:17

22 And we have sent with them our brother whom we have often proved diligent in many things, but now much more diligent, because of the great confidence which *we have* in you.

23 If *anyone inquires* about Titus, *he is* my partner and fellow worker concerning you. Or if our brethren *are inquired about, they are* ᴿmessengersᵀ of the churches, the glory of Christ.   Phil. 2:25 • Lit. *apostles,* "sent ones"

24 Therefore show to them, *and before the churches, the proof of your love and of our ᴿboasting on your behalf.   2 Cor. 7:4, 14; 9:2

Administering the Gift

9 Now concerning ᴿthe ministering to the saints, it is superfluous for me to write to you;   Gal. 2:10

2 for I know your willingness, about which I boast of you to the Macedonians, that Achaia was ready a ᴿyear ago; and your zeal has stirred up the majority.   2 Cor. 8:10

3 Yet I have sent the brethren, lest our boasting of you should be in vain in this respect, that, as I said, you may be ready;

4 lest if *some* Macedonians come with me and find you unprepared, we (not to mention you!) should be ashamed of this *confident boasting.

5 Therefore I thought it necessary to exhort the brethren to go to you ahead of time, and prepare your generous gift beforehand, which *you had* previously promised, that it may be ready as *a matter of* generosity and not as a ᵀgrudging obligation.   Lit. *covetousness*

The Cheerful Giver

6 But this *I say:* He who sows sparingly will also reap sparingly, and he who sows bountifully will also reap bountifully.

7 *So let* each one *give* as he purposes in his heart, not grudgingly or of ᵀnecessity; for God loves a cheerful giver.   *compulsion*

8 ᴿAnd God *is* able to make all grace abound toward you, that you, always having all sufficiency in all *things,* may have an abundance for every good work.   [Prov. 11:24]

9 As it is written:

> ᴿ*"He has dispersed abroad,*   Ps. 112:9
> *He has given to the poor;*
> *His righteousness endures forever."*

10 Now *may He who ᴿsupplies seed to the sower, and bread for food, *supply and multiply the seed you have *sown* and increase the fruits of your ᴿrighteousness,   Is. 55:10 • Hos. 10:12

11 while *you are* enriched in everything for all liberality, ᴿwhich causes thanksgiving through us to God.   2 Cor. 1:11

12 For the administration of this service not only ᴿsupplies the needs of the saints, but also is abounding through many thanksgivings to God,   2 Cor. 8:14

13 while, through the proof of this ministry, they glorify God for the obedience of your confession to the gospel of Christ, and for *your* liberal sharing with them and all *men,*

14 and by their prayer for you, who long for you because of the exceeding ᴿgrace of God in you.   2 Cor. 8:1

15 Thanks *be* to God ᴿfor His indescribable gift!   [James 1:17]

The Spiritual War

10 Now I, Paul, myself am pleading with you by the meekness and gentleness of Christ—who in presence *am* lowly among you, but being absent am bold toward you.

2 But I beg *you* ᴿthat when I am present I

8:16 NU *has put*
8:24 NU, M omit *and*

9:4 NU *confidence.*
9:10 NU omits *may* • NU *will supply*

may not be bold with that confidence by which I intend to be bold against some, who think of us as if we walked according to the flesh.   1 Cor. 4:21

▼ **25-D. The Christian Life Is a Warring Life**

3 For though we walk in the flesh, we do not war according to the flesh.

4 ᴿFor the weapons of our warfare *are* not ᵀcarnal but ᴿmighty in God ᴿfor pulling down strongholds,   Eph. 6:13 • *of the flesh* • Acts 7:22 • Jer. 1:10

5 ᴿcasting down arguments and every high thing that exalts itself against the knowledge of God, bringing every thought into captivity to the obedience of Christ,   1 Cor. 1:19 ▲

6 and being ready to punish all disobedience when your obedience is fulfilled.

25-D. The Christian Life Is a Warring Life (2 Corinthians 10:3–5)—The Christian life is a spiritual warfare. Your enemy is Satan, the god of this humanistic world system (see Point 12-C, "Satan: The God of This World," page 1167). In his army are legions of demons, who perform his will (see Point 13-A, "Demons: Their Identity," page 1289). There are only two families in this world (1 John 3:10, page 1280):

(1) The family of Satan (John 8:44, page 1063).
(2) The family of God (1 John 3:1, 2, page 1279).

Every human being, from Adam to the last person to live upon this earth, is or will be a member of the family of Satan or the family of God.

Satan hates the Lord Jesus Christ and the family of God because the Lord came into the world to "destroy the works of the devil" (1 John 3:8, page 1280)—this Jesus did on Calvary when He spoke the word of victory saying, "It is finished!" (John 19:30, page 1081). Satan is a defeated foe and God will, at the end of the Millennium, cast him into hell—the eternal lake of fire (Rev. 20:10, page 1313).

"For the weapons of our warfare are not carnal" (v. 4). Even though we live and walk in a body of flesh, our weapons are not a product of man's ingenuity. We dare not war with Satan and his allies in the energy of our carnal nature, as Simon Peter attempted to do when the Roman soldiers came to arrest Jesus. Peter drew his sword and cut off the ear of Malchus, the servant of the high priest. Jesus reached out and healed his ear, then rebuked Peter by ordering him to put up his sword. When we war in the energy of the flesh we fail and stand to be rebuked as Peter was. Our warfare is not against flesh and blood, but against a satanic system that functions in the spiritual sphere of individuals, nations, cults, and false religions motivating them to rebel against God and His Word (Eph. 2:1–3, page 1187). Therefore, our weapons are not carnal, but spiritual.

The only way that we can defeat Satan and his legions of demons is to "be strong in the Lord and in the power of His might," and to "put on the whole armor of God, that you may be able to stand against the wiles of the devil" (Eph. 6:10–18, page 1192). There are seven spiritual parts to the armor of God. In their function, each one is just as important as the other. Each is a source of power and protection to all of the vital parts of the Christian. There are three parts of this spiritual armor that require special attention to prepare the Christian for a life of spiritual warfare:

(1) "The shield of faith with which you will be able to quench all the fiery darts of the wicked one" (Eph. 6:16, page 1192). Satan and his demons have power but our God, Jesus Christ, has all authority. In His resurrected body, Jesus said, "All authority has been given to Me in heaven and on earth" (Matt. 28:18, page 982). Our God has authority over all power. He is our shield of faith. When Abraham feared his enemies, God spoke to him saying, "Do not be afraid, Abram. I am your shield [defense], your exceedingly great reward" (Gen. 15:1, page 20). David said, "For You, O LORD, will bless the righteous; with favor You will surround him as with a shield" (Ps. 5:12, page 512; cf. 2 Sam. 22:2, 3, page 320). Our God is a shield to give us total protection in our spiritual warfare.

(2) "The sword of the Spirit, which is the word of God" (Eph. 6:17, page 1192). When Jesus was led by the Spirit into the wilderness to have personal combat with Satan, He was tempted (tested) in every point that we are, yet without sin (Heb. 4:15, page 1239; see Point 12-E, "Satan: The Tempter," page 934). In the wilderness, Jesus, the God-Man, defeated Satan in every temptation by using "the sword of the Spirit, which is the word of God." Three times He drew the all-powerful sword as He quoted from the book of Deuteronomy; He said, "It is written" (Matt. 4:4–11, page 934; cf. Deut. 6:13, 16, page 187; 8:3, page 189). He used the inerrant Word of God as the offensive weapon and defeated Satan.

(3) "Praying always with all prayer and supplication in the Spirit" (Eph. 6:18, page 1192). Unceasing prayer must always accompany the spiritual warrior as he engages Satan and his allies in spiritual conflict (1 Thess. 5:17, page 1213).

In the hour of our temptation, whether it be the "lust of the flesh, the lust of the eyes, and the pride of life" (1 John 2:15, 16, page 1279), God has promised that He "will also make the way of escape, that you may be able to bear it" (1 Cor. 10:13, page 1155). We have that way of escape with "the shield of faith" and "the sword of the Spirit, which is the word of God." Keep your armor polished with "all prayer and supplication in the Spirit" (Eph. 6:16–18, page 1192), and God has promised that we will be "more than conquerors through Him who loved us" (Rom. 8:37, page 1138). Another promise on which we can stand when tempted by the Devil or his demons is found in Isaiah. "No weapon formed against you shall prosper, and every tongue which rises against you in judgment you shall condemn. This is the heritage of the servants of the LORD" (Is. 54:17, page 695).

See Joshua 1:1–8, page 215, for **Point 25-E: The Christian Life Is a Successful Life.**

Reality of Paul's Authority

7 Do you look at things according to the outward appearance? If anyone is convinced in himself that he is Christ's, let him again consider this in himself, that just as he *is* Christ's, even *so we are* Christ's.

8 For even if I should boast somewhat more about our authority, which the Lord gave *us for edification and not for your destruction, I shall not be ashamed—

9 lest I seem to terrify you by letters.

10 "For *his* letters," they say, "*are* weighty and powerful, but ^Rhis bodily presence *is* weak, and *his* speech contemptible."   Gal. 4:13

11 Let such a person consider this, that what we are in word by letters when we are absent, such *we will* also *be* in deed when we are present.

Limits of Paul's Authority

12 ^RFor we dare not class ourselves or compare ourselves with those who commend themselves. But they, measuring themselves by themselves, and comparing themselves among themselves, are not wise.   2 Cor. 5:12

13 ^RWe, however, will not boast beyond measure, but within the limits of the sphere which God appointed us—a sphere which especially includes you.   2 Cor. 10:15

14 For we are not overextending ourselves (as though our authority did not extend to you), ^Rfor it was to you that we came with the gospel of Christ;   1 Cor. 3:5, 6

15 not boasting of things beyond measure, *that is,* in other men's labors, but having hope, *that* as your faith is increased, we shall be greatly enlarged by you in our sphere,

16 to preach the gospel in the *regions* beyond you, *and* not to boast in another man's sphere of accomplishment.

17 But ^R"he who glories, let him glory in the LORD."   Jer. 9:24

18 For not he who commends himself is approved, but whom the Lord commends.

Concern for Their Faithfulness

11 Oh, that you would bear with me in a little folly—and indeed you do bear with me.

2 For I am jealous for you with godly jealousy. For I have betrothed you to one husband, ^Rthat I may present *you* ^Ras a chaste virgin to Christ.   Col. 1:28 • Lev. 21:13

3 But I fear, lest somehow, as ^Rthe serpent deceived Eve by his craftiness, so your minds ^Rmay be corrupted from the *simplicity that is in Christ.   Gen. 3:4, 13 • Eph. 6:24

4 For if he who comes preaches another Jesus whom we have not preached, or *if* you receive a different spirit which you have not received, or a different gospel which you have not accepted—you may well put up with it!

Paul and False Apostles

5 For I consider that I am not at all inferior to the most eminent apostles.

6 Even though *I am* untrained in speech, yet *I am* not ^Rin knowledge. But ^Rwe have *been thoroughly manifested among you in all things.   [1 Cor. 1:17] • [Eph. 3:4] • [2 Cor. 12:12]

7 Did I commit sin in humbling myself that you might be exalted, because I preached the gospel of God to you free of charge?

8 I robbed other churches, taking wages *from them* to minister to you.

9 And when I was present with you, and in need, ^RI was a burden to no one, for what I lacked ^Rthe brethren who came from Macedonia supplied. And in everything I kept myself from being burdensome to you, and so I will keep *myself.*   Acts 20:33 • Phil. 4:10

10 ^RAs the truth of Christ is in me, ^Rno one shall stop me from this boasting in the regions of Achaia.   Rom. 1:9; 9:1 • 1 Cor. 9:15

11 Why? ^RBecause I do not love you? God knows!   2 Cor. 6:11; 12:15

12 But what I do, I will also continue to do, ^Rthat I may cut off the opportunity from those who desire an opportunity to be regarded just as we are in the things of which they boast.   1 Cor. 9:12

13 For such ^Rare false apostles, ^Rdeceitful workers, transforming themselves into apostles of Christ.   Phil. 1:15 • Phil. 3:2

14 And no wonder! For Satan himself transforms himself into an angel of light.

15 Therefore *it is* no great thing if his ministers also transform themselves into ministers of righteousness, ^Rwhose end will be according to their works.   [Phil. 3:19]

Reluctant Boasting

16 I say again, let no one think me a fool. If otherwise, at least receive me as a fool, that I also may boast a little.

17 What I speak, ^RI speak not according to the Lord, but as it were, foolishly, in this confidence of boasting.   1 Cor. 7:6

18 Seeing that many boast according to the flesh, I also will boast.

19 For you put up with fools gladly, ^Rsince you *yourselves* are wise!   1 Cor. 4:10

20 For you put up with it ^Rif one brings you into bondage, if one devours *you,* if one takes *from you,* if one exalts himself, if one strikes you on the face.   [Gal. 2:4; 4:3, 9; 5:1]

21 To *our* shame I say that we were too weak for that! But in whatever anyone is bold—I speak foolishly—I am bold also.

10:7 NU *as we are.*
10:8 NU omits *us*
11:3 NU adds *and purity*

11:6 NU omits *been*

Suffering for Christ

22 Are they [R]Hebrews? So *am* I. Are they Israelites? So *am* I. Are they the seed of Abraham? So *am* I. Phil. 3:4-6

23 Are they ministers of Christ?—I speak as a fool—I *am* more: in labors more abundant, in stripes above measure, in prisons more frequently, [R]in deaths often. 1 Cor. 15:30

24 From the Jews five times I received [R]forty [R]*stripes* minus one. Deut. 25:3 · 2 Cor. 6:5

25 Three times I was [R]beaten with rods; [R]once I was stoned; three times I [R]was shipwrecked; a night and a day I have been in the deep; Acts 16:22, 23; 21:32 · Acts 14:5, 19 · Acts 27:1-44

26 *in* journeys often, *in* perils of waters, *in* perils of robbers, *in* perils of *my own* countrymen, *in* perils of the Gentiles, *in* perils in the city, *in* perils in the wilderness, *in* perils in the sea, *in* perils among false brethren;

27 *in* weariness and toil, *in* sleeplessness often, [R]in hunger and thirst, *in* fastings often, *in* cold and nakedness— 1 Cor. 4:11

28 besides the other things, what comes upon me daily: [R]my deep concern for all the churches. Acts 20:18

29 [R]Who is weak, and I am not weak? Who is made to stumble, and I do not burn with indignation? [1 Cor. 8:9, 13; 9:22]

30 If I must boast, I will boast in the things which concern my [T]infirmity. *weakness*

31 [R]The God and Father of our Lord Jesus Christ, [R]who is blessed forever, knows that I am not lying. 1 Thess. 2:5 · Rom. 9:5

32 [R]In Damascus the governor, under Aretas the king, was guarding the city of the Damascenes with a garrison, desiring to arrest me; Acts 9:19-25

33 but I was let down in a basket through a window in the wall, and escaped from his hands.

The Vision of Paradise

12 It is *doubtless not profitable for me to boast. I will come to [R]visions and revelations of the Lord: Acts 16:9; 18:9

2 I know a man [R]in Christ who fourteen years ago—whether in the body I do not know, or whether out of the body I do not know, God knows—such a one [R]was caught up to the third heaven. Rom. 16:7 · Acts 22:17

3 And I know such a man—whether in the body or out of the body I do not know, God knows—

4 how he was caught up into [R]Paradise and heard inexpressible words, which it is not lawful for a man to utter. Luke 23:43

5 Of such a one I will boast; yet of myself I will not boast, except in my infirmities.

6 For though I might desire to boast, I will not be a fool; for I will speak the truth. But I refrain, lest anyone should think of me above what he sees me *to be* or hears from me.

13-C. Demons: Their Work   ▼

The Thorn in the Flesh

7 And lest I should be exalted above measure by the abundance of the revelations, a [R]thorn in the flesh was given to me, [R]a messenger of Satan to [T]buffet me, lest I be exalted above measure. Ezek. 28:24 · Job 2:7 · *beat*

8 [R]Concerning this thing I pleaded with the Lord three times that it might depart from me. Matt. 26:44

9 And He said to me, "My grace is sufficient for you, for My strength is made perfect in weakness." Therefore most gladly I will rather boast in my infirmities, that the power of Christ may rest upon me.

10 Therefore [R]I take pleasure in infirmities, in reproaches, in needs, in persecutions, in distresses, for Christ's sake. For when I am weak, then I am strong. [Rom. 5:3; 8:35] ▲

Signs of an Apostle

11 I have become a fool *in boasting; you have compelled me. For I ought to have been commended by you; for [R]in nothing was I behind the most eminent apostles, though [R]I am nothing. 2 Cor. 11:5 · 1 Cor. 3:7; 13:2; 15:9

12 Truly the signs of an apostle were accomplished among you with all perseverance, in signs and wonders and mighty deeds.

13 For what is it in which you were inferior to other churches, except that I myself was

---

12:1 NU *necessary, though not profitable, to boast*   **12:11** NU omits *in boasting*

13-C. Demons: Their Work (2 Corinthians 12:7-10)—"A thorn in the flesh was given to me, a messenger [angel] of Satan to buffet me" (v. 7). This is a startling statement. Paul is saying that God allowed Satan to assign one of his fallen angels to buffet this great apostle. Satan is the ruler of the demons, i.e., fallen angels (Matt. 12:24, page 953). They do the will of their master. Just as God assigns good angels to minister to "those who will inherit salvation" (Heb. 1:14, page 1237), so also Satan assigns demons to buffet born-again believers.

These evil spirits cannot enter a believer and possess his or her body; but they can influence the believer and make it difficult to do the will of God. God allows this for the believer's good and for the accomplishment of His purposes in our lives. Paul prayed three times that God would deliver him from this fallen angel, who was a "thorn in the flesh" (v. 7). God did not remove the demon, but said to Paul, "My grace is sufficient for you, for My strength is made perfect in weakness" (v. 9).

(Point 13-C continued on next page)

not burdensome to you? Forgive me this wrong!

Love for the Church

14 Now *for* the third time I am ready to come to you. And I will not be burdensome to you; for I do not seek yours, but you. For the children ought not to lay up for the parents, but the parents for the children.

15 And I will very gladly spend and be spent ᴿfor your souls; though the more abundantly I love you, the less I am loved.   [2 Tim. 2:10]

16 But be that *as it may,* ᴿI did not burden you. Nevertheless, being crafty, I caught you by cunning!   2 Cor. 11:9

17 Did I take advantage of you by any of those whom I sent to you?

18 I urged Titus, and sent our ᴿbrother with *him.* Did Titus take advantage of you? Did *we* not *walk* in the same spirit? Did *we* not *walk* in the same steps?   2 Cor. 8:18

19 *Again, do you think that we excuse ourselves to you? ᴿWe speak before God in Christ. ᴿBut *we do* all things, beloved, for your edification.   [Rom. 9:1, 2] • 1 Cor. 10:33

20 For I fear lest, when I come, I shall not find you such as I wish, and *that* ᴿI shall be found by you such as you do not wish; lest *there be* contentions, jealousies, outbursts of wrath, selfish ambitions, backbitings, whisperings, conceits, tumults;   1 Cor. 4:21

21 lest, when I come again, my God will humble me among you, and I shall mourn for many who have sinned before and have not

12:19 NU *You have been thinking for a long time that we*

repented of the uncleanness, fornication, and lewdness which they have practiced.

Coming with Authority

13 This *will be* the third *time* I am coming to you. * "*By the mouth of two or three witnesses every word shall be established.*"

2 I have told you before, and foretell as if I were present the second time, and now being absent *I write to those ᴿwho have sinned before, and to all the rest, that if I come again I will not spare—   2 Cor. 12:21

3 since you seek a proof of Christ ᴿspeaking in me, who is not weak toward you, but mighty ᴿin you.   Matt. 10:20 • [1 Cor. 9:2]

4 For though He was crucified in weakness, yet He lives by the power of God. For we also are weak in Him, but we shall live with Him by the power of God toward you.

5 Examine yourselves *as to* whether you are in the faith. Test yourselves. Do you not know yourselves, that Jesus Christ is in you?—unless indeed you are disqualified.

6 But I trust that you will know that we are not disqualified.

Paul Prefers Gentleness

7 Now *I pray to God that you do no evil, not that we should appear approved, but that you should do what is honorable, though ᴿwe may seem disqualified.   2 Cor. 6:9

13:1 Num. 35:30; Deut. 17:6; 19:15; Matt. 18:16; John 8:17; Heb. 10:28
13:2 NU omits *I write*
13:7 NU *we*

(Point 13-C continued from previous page)
In this experience, Paul learned a valuable lesson, the most difficult lesson for any believer to learn. He said, "I will rather boast in my infirmities, that the power of Christ may rest upon me. Therefore I take pleasure in infirmities, in reproaches, in needs, in persecutions, in distresses, for Christ's sake. For when I am weak, then I am strong" (vv. 9, 10).

Paul's thorn in the flesh, Satan's angel, was used by God as a help to Paul's ministry, not a hindrance. God knows how to take what Satan sends and turn it to good. Joseph was sold into slavery by his jealous brothers. But the Lord raised him to the highest office in Egypt. Pharaoh said, "Only in regard to the throne will I be greater than you" (Gen. 41:39, 40, page 47). In the time of famine Joseph's brothers came to Egypt for food. There they had to face him who had all authority over Egypt's wealth. When Joseph revealed his identity to his brothers, they feared for their lives. Then Joseph said to them, "You meant evil against me; but God meant it for good" (Gen. 50:20, page 56). Satan means evil against every saint, but God allows it for good (Phil. 1:12, page 1195).

Satan's evil angels not only buffet believers, they also:

(1) Afflict God's people. "There was a woman who had a spirit of infirmity eighteen years, and was bent over and could in no way raise herself up." Jesus loosed her from her infirmity, and the rulers of the synagogue were indignant because He healed on the Sabbath. Jesus asked, "Ought not this woman, being a daughter of Abraham, whom Satan has bound—think of it—for eighteen years, be loosed from this bond on the Sabbath?" (Luke 13:10–17, page 1031).

(2) Resist the servants of the Lord (Eph. 6:10–12, page 1192).

(3) Perform miracles (Rev. 16:13, 14, page 1309).

(4) Possess the bodies of humans and animals (Luke 8:26–39, page 1023).

If you love and serve the Lord, you can be sure that Satan will attempt to buffet you in every possible way.

See Mark 5:1–20, page 989, for **Point 13-D: Demons: Their Power.**

8 For we can do nothing against the truth, but for the truth.

9 For we are glad when we are weak and you are strong. And this also we pray, ^Rthat you may be made complete.   [1 Thess. 3:10]

10 ^RTherefore I write these things being absent, lest being present I should use sharpness, according to the ^Rauthority which the Lord has given me for edification and not for destruction.   1 Cor. 4:21 · 2 Cor. 10:8

Greetings and Benediction

11 Finally, brethren, farewell. Become complete. ^RBe of good comfort, be of one mind, live in peace; and the God of love ^Rand peace will be with you.   Rom. 12:16, 18 · Rom. 15:33

12 Greet one another with a holy kiss.

13 All the saints greet you.

14 The grace of the Lord Jesus Christ, and the love of God, and the ^Tcommunion of the Holy Spirit *be* with you all. Amen.   *fellowship*

THE EPISTLE OF PAUL THE APOSTLE TO THE

Galatians

AUTHORSHIP. Paul wrote Galatians to stem the wave of criticism begun by a team of Judaizers who dogged Paul's steps as he planted churches throughout Galatia. These false teachers, whose aim was to convince Paul's Gentile converts to adhere to the Mosaic law, spread two rumors about Paul: first, that he was not an apostle; second, that he did not preach the gospel.

HOW GALATIANS FITS TOGETHER. A simple outline of the book divides it by Paul's answer to the charges: (1) "I am an apostle" (chs. 1, 2) and (2) "I do preach the gospel" (chs. 3, 6).

A slightly more detailed outline divides the book into three sections of two chapters each: (1) Personal: Paul defends his gospel (chs. 1, 2); (2) Doctrinal: Paul refutes the legalistic Judaizers (chs. 3, 4); (3) Hortatory: Paul exhorts the Galatians to live in Christian freedom and spirituality (chs. 5, 6).

HOW GALATIANS FITS INTO THE BIBLE. Galatians is one of the earliest epistles of Paul, if not the earliest, and many have seen it as a sort of Romans in germ form. Galatians is a more emotional and brief treatment of the same topics handled in Romans; or we could say that Romans is a more developed and logical presentation of the message of Galatians. The great reformer Martin Luther was freed from his legalistic bondage through Romans and Galatians, and wrote a famous commentary on the latter. He even referred to Galatians as "my Katie von Bora," which was his beloved wife's name—high praise indeed, for both the woman and the book!

In spite of the fact that Galatians is a short book, it contains brilliant theological definition, classical development of thought, and able evangelical urgency. In it Paul clarifies the meaning of apostleship (1:1), faithful proclamation (1:8-10), the nature of revelation (1:11-12), personal testimony (1:13-24), the relation of the law to grace, the sinner's identity with Christ's crucifixion (2:20), the Spirit's role in the believer's continuation in the faith (3:1-5), the nature of righteousness (3:6-9), the teaching that brought the Reformation to the world (3:9-11), the connection between Abraham's faith and Christ's imputation of righteousness (3:12-18), how the Old Testament believer is saved (3:19-26), the universal, transracial nature of Christ (3:27-28), the Christian as the inheritor of all the promises to Abraham (3:29), the nature of redemption and adoption (4:1-7), the bondage of reverting to the law as a basis for salvation (4:8-20), the bondage of legalistic living and the freedom of living under grace (4:21-31), law-based salvation as impossible and far below salvation founded on grace (5:1-4), running the race in the liberty of love (5:5-15), the works of the flesh and the fruit of the Spirit (5:16-26), the practical expression of the fruit of the Spirit (6:1-6), sowing and reaping (6:7-10), and glorying in the Cross (6:11-17).

Perhaps no book, with the exception of Romans, covers the theological spectrum in so few words.

Galatians is the ringing of the Liberty Bell to all who are enslaved by sin.

—J.M.

Greeting

PAUL, an apostle (not from men nor through man, but ᴿthrough Jesus Christ and God the Father ᴿwho raised Him from the dead), Acts 9:6 · Acts 2:24

2 and all the brethren who are with me,

To the churches of Galatia:

3 Grace to you and peace from God the Father and our Lord Jesus Christ,

4 who gave Himself for our sins, that He might deliver us from this present evil age, according to the will of our God and Father,

5 to whom *be* glory forever and ever. Amen.

Only One Gospel

6 I marvel that you are turning away so soon ᴿfrom Him who called you in the grace of Christ, to a different gospel, Gal. 1:15; 5:8

7 ᴿwhich is not another; but there are some who trouble you and want to ᴿpervertᵀ the gospel of Christ. 2 Cor. 11:4 · 2 Cor. 2:17 · *distort*

8 But even if we, or an angel from heaven, preach any other gospel to you than what we have preached to you, let him be accursed.

9 As we have said before, so now I say again, if anyone preaches any other gospel to you ᴿthan what you have received, let him be accursed. Deut. 4:2

10 For ᴿdo I now ᴿpersuade men, or God? Or ᴿdo I seek to please men? For if I still

pleased men, I would not be a bondservant of Christ. 1 Thess. 2:4 • 1 Sam. 24:7 • 1 Thess. 2:4

Call to Apostleship

11 ᴿBut I make known to you, brethren, that the gospel which was preached by me is not according to man. 1 Cor. 15:1
12 For I neither received it from man, nor was I taught it, but it came ᴿthrough the revelation of Jesus Christ. [Eph. 3:3–5]
13 For you have heard of my former conduct in Judaism, how ᴿI persecuted the church of God beyond measure and ᴿtried to destroy it. Acts 9:1 • Acts 8:3; 22:4, 5
14 And I advanced in Judaism beyond many of my contemporaries in my own nation, ᴿbeing more exceedingly zealous ᴿfor the traditions of my fathers. Acts 26:9 • Jer. 9:14
15 But when it pleased God, ᴿwho separated me from my mother's womb and called me through His grace, Is. 49:1, 5
16 to reveal His Son in me, that I might preach Him among the Gentiles, I did not immediately confer with flesh and blood,
17 nor did I go up to Jerusalem to those who were apostles before me; but I went to Arabia, and returned again to Damascus.

Contacts at Jerusalem

18 Then after three years ᴿI went up to Jerusalem to see *Peter, and remained with him fifteen days. Acts 9:26
19 But I saw none of the other apostles except ᴿJames, the Lord's brother. Matt. 13:55
20 (Now concerning the things which I write to you, indeed, before God, I do not lie.)
21 ᴿAfterward I went into the regions of Syria and Cilicia. Acts 9:30
22 And I was unknown by face to the churches of Judea which were in Christ.
23 But they were hearing only, "He who formerly persecuted us now preaches the faith which he once tried to destroy."
24 And they ᴿglorified God in me. Acts 11:18

Defending the Gospel

2 Then after fourteen years ᴿI went up again to Jerusalem with Barnabas, and also took Titus with me. Acts 15:2

2 And I went up by revelation, and communicated to them that gospel which I preach among the Gentiles, but privately to those who were of reputation, lest by any means I might run, or had run, in vain.
3 Yet not even Titus who was with me, being a Greek, was compelled to be circumcised.
4 And this occurred because of ᴿfalse brethren secretly brought in (who came in by stealth to spy out our ᴿliberty which we have in Christ Jesus, ᴿthat they might bring us into bondage), Acts 15:1, 24 • Gal. 3:25; 5:1, 13 • Gal. 4:3, 9
5 to whom we did not yield submission even for an hour, that ᴿthe truth of the gospel might continue with you. [Gal. 1:6; 2:14; 3:1]
6 But from those who seemed to be something — whatever they were, it makes no difference to me; ᴿGod shows personal favoritism to no man—for those who seemed to be something added nothing to me. Acts 10:34

46-D. Paul's Evangelistic Missionary Ministry to the Gentiles ▼

7 But on the contrary, when they saw that the gospel for the uncircumcised ᴿhad been committed to me, as the gospel for the circumcised was to Peter 1 Thess. 2:4
8 (for He who worked effectively in Peter for the apostleship to the ᴿcircumcised ᴿalso ᴿworked effectively in me toward the Gentiles), 1 Pet. 1:1 • Acts 9:15 • [Gal. 3:5]
9 and when James, ᵀCephas, and John, who seemed to be pillars, perceived ᴿthe grace that had been given to me, they gave me and Barnabas the right hand of fellowship, ᴿthat we should go to the Gentiles and they to the circumcised. Peter • Rom. 1:5 • Acts 13:3
10 They desired only that we should remember the poor, ᴿthe very thing which I also was eager to do. Acts 11:30 ▲

No Return to the Law

11 ᴿNow when *Peter had come to Antioch, I ᵀwithstood him to his face, because he was to be blamed; Acts 15:35 • opposed
12 for before certain men came from James, ᴿhe would eat with the Gentiles; but when

1:18 NU Cephas   2:11 NU Cephas

46-D. Paul's Evangelistic Missionary Ministry to the Gentiles (Galatians 2:7–10)—The apostle Paul, while in a time of prayer, was called by the Holy Spirit to proclaim to those in other lands the gospel of salvation in Christ. The church at Antioch of Syria, after fasting, praying, and the laying on of hands, sent out Paul and Barnabas (Acts 13:1–3, page 1105). This era in Paul's life was to span about nine years. During this period he

(1) preached the gospel to Jews in synagogues (Acts 18:4, page 1113);
(2) preached the gospel to Gentiles (Acts 13:47, 48, page 1107);
(3) received gifts for his support (Phil. 4:14–17, page 1198);
(4) planted and established churches (Acts 14:23, page 1108);
(5) wrote letters to churches (2 Cor. 1:1, page 1165);
(6) wrote letters to individuals (Philem. 1, page 1234);
(7) made land journeys (Acts 13:14—14:6, page 1106);

(Point 46-D continued on next page)

they came, he withdrew and separated himself, fearing ᵀthose who were of the circumcision.   [Acts 10:28; 11:2, 3] · Jewish Christians

13 And the rest of the Jews also played the hypocrite with him, so that even Barnabas was carried away with their hypocrisy.

14 But when I saw that they were not straightforward about the truth of the gospel, I said to Peter before *them* all, "If you, being a Jew, live in the manner of Gentiles and not as the Jews, *why do you compel Gentiles to live as ᵀJews?   Some interpreters stop quotation here.

15 ᴿ"We *who are* Jews by nature, and not ᴿsinners of the Gentiles,   [Acts 15:10] · Matt. 9:11

16 "knowing that a man is not justified by the works of the law but by faith in Jesus Christ, even we have believed in Christ Jesus, that we might be justified by faith in Christ and not by the works of the law; for by the works of the law no flesh shall be justified.

17 "But if, while we seek to be justified by Christ, we ourselves also are found ᴿsinners, *is* Christ therefore a minister of sin? Certainly not!   [1 John 3:8]

18 "For if I build again those things which I destroyed, I make myself a transgressor.

19 "For I ᴿthrough the law died to the law that I might ᴿlive to God.   Rom. 8:2 · [Rom. 6:11]

20 "I have been crucified with Christ; it is no longer I who live, but Christ lives in me; and the *life* which I now live in the flesh I live by faith in the Son of God, who loved me and ᴿgave Himself for me.   Is. 53:12

21 "I do not set aside the grace of God; for ᴿif righteousness *comes* through the law, then Christ died ᵀin vain."   Heb. 7:11 · *for nothing*

Justification by Faith

3 O foolish Galatians! Who has bewitched you *that you should not obey the truth,

---

2:14 NU *how can you*

3:1 NU omits *that you should not obey the truth*

(Point 46-D continued from previous page)

    (8) made sea journeys (Acts 20:6, page 1115);
    (9) debated for the truth at a church council (Acts 15:6–22, page 1109);
    (10) performed miracles (Acts 19:11, 12, page 1114);
    (11) heard the voice of God (Acts 22:18, 21, page 1118);
    (12) was attacked by mobs (Acts 16:22, 23, page 1110);
    (13) was arrested by the Romans (Acts 21:32, 33, page 1117);
    (14) was put in chains, yet sang and rejoiced (Acts 16:24, 25, page 1110).

Paul's evangelistic ministry can be outlined by his various missionary journeys.

    (1) *First missionary journey* (Acts 13:1—14:28, page 1105). The first journey was launched at Antioch of Syria (Acts 13:1-3, page 1105) in company with Barnabas and John Mark. Eventually John Mark left Paul and Barnabas, and returned to Jerusalem before the party left for the regions of Pisidia and Cilicia. The first missionary journey ended at Antioch of Syria.

    (2) *The Jerusalem council* (Acts 15:1-35, page 1108). This meeting was an example of a Spirit-filled church seeking God's answer to a problem, and finding it in unity.

    (a) Legalists demanded that the Gentile converts observe the Mosaic laws (Acts 15:1, page 1108). Paul and Barnabas argued against this (Acts 15:12, page 1109).

    (b) James (the younger half-brother of Jesus), the spokesman and apparent chairman of the council, announced that God's will was that Gentiles be admitted into the church, and that they need not observe the Jewish ceremonial laws. The Gentiles were admonished, however, to avoid the appearance of condoning idolatry, immorality, and the drinking of blood (Acts 15:19–22, page 1109).

    (3) *Second missionary journey* (Acts 15:36, page 1110). The second journey started at Antioch.

    (a) Paul took Silas; Barnabas took John Mark, due to a disagreement between Paul and Barnabas (Acts 15:36-40, page 1110). Paul and Barnabas agreed to go separate ways; neither spoke ill of the other afterwards. God blessed both.

    (b) Paul and Silas visited the churches established on the first missionary journey (Acts 15:41—16:5, page 1110).

    (c) Then the vision of the needy Macedonian (Acts 16:9, page 1110) led them to take the gospel westward into Europe, rather than eastward. Thus, Christianity began its expansion through the world. In Europe they visited Philippi, Thessalonica, Berea, Athens, Corinth, and then Ephesus in Asia Minor (Acts 16:12—18:19, page 1110). The journey ended at Antioch of Syria.

    (4) *Third missionary journey* (Acts 18:23—21:17, page 1113).

    (a) The third journey began at Antioch of Syria, then on to Ephesus, Macedonia, Troas, Miletus, Tyre, Ptolemais, and Caesarea. It ended in Jerusalem.

    (b) Paul was arrested at Jerusalem by the Romans (Acts 21:32, 33, page 1117), when the Jewish crowd rioted against his preaching. In God's providence, his arrest and future trials proved to add evangelistic opportunities.

    See 2 Thessalonians 3:17, page 1216, for **Point 46-E: Paul's Letters.**

before whose eyes Jesus Christ was clearly portrayed *among you as crucified?

2 This only I want to learn from you: Did you receive the Spirit by the works of the law, ^Ror by the hearing of faith? Rom. 10:16, 17

3 Are you so foolish? ^RHaving begun in the Spirit, are you now being made perfect by ^Rthe flesh? [Gal. 4:9] • Heb. 7:16

4 Have you suffered so ^Tmany things in vain—if indeed it was in vain? Or great

5 Therefore He who supplies the Spirit to you and works miracles among you, does He do it by the works of the law, or by the hearing of faith?—

6 just as Abraham *"believed God, and it was accounted to him for righteousness."

7 Therefore know that only ^Rthose who are of faith are sons of Abraham. John 8:39

8 And the Scripture, foreseeing that God would justify the Gentiles by faith, preached the gospel to Abraham beforehand, saying, *"In you all the nations shall be blessed."

9 So then those who are of faith are blessed with believing Abraham.

3:1 NU omits among you
3:6 Gen. 15:6
3:8 Gen. 12:3; 18:18; 22:18; 26:4; 28:14

The Law Brings a Curse

10 For as many as are of the works of the law are under the curse; for it is written, ^R"Cursed is everyone who does not continue in all things which are written in the book of the law, to do them." Deut. 27:26

24-B. The Just Shall Live by Faith ▼

11 But that no one is ^Tjustified by the law in the sight of God is evident, for ^R"the just shall live by faith." declared righteous • Hab. 2:4 ▲

12 Yet the law is not of faith, but *"the man who does them shall live by them."

13 ^RChrist has redeemed us from the curse of the law, having become a curse for us (for it is written, ^R"Cursed is everyone who hangs on a tree"), [Rom. 8:3] • Deut. 21:23

14 ^Rthat the blessing of Abraham might come upon the Gentiles in Christ Jesus, that we might receive ^Rthe promise of the Spirit through faith. Is. 49:6; Rom. 4:9 • Is. 32:15

The Changeless Promise

15 Brethren, I speak in the manner of men: Though it is only a man's covenant, yet if it is confirmed, no one annuls or adds to it.

3:12 Lev. 18:5; Rom. 10:5

24-B. The Just Shall Live by Faith (Galatians 3:11)—The just, those who have been "justified by faith," are to live by faith (Rom. 5:1, page 1133; cf. Heb. 10:38, page 1247). Justification by faith in God the Son is more than acquittal; it is the judicial act of our Holy God, declaring the repentant sinner righteous with the righteousness of God in Christ (Rom. 10:3, 4, 9, 10, page 1140), because "he who believes in Him [Christ] is not condemned; but he who does not believe [in Christ] is condemned already, because he has not believed in the name of the only begotten Son of God" (John 3:18, page 1053). Therefore, by faith the just are eternally free from the guilt and penalty of sin; they are also declaratively invested with the righteousness of Christ (2 Cor. 5:21, page 1169).

Because Christians are justified by faith, they are to live their whole life by faith; "for whatever is not from faith is sin" (Rom. 14:23, page 1145; cf. Col. 3:17, page 1207). As a child of God:

(1) *Pray by faith*. When you ask anything from God in prayer, it must be by faith. There can be no doubting, for if you waver you will not receive anything from the Lord (James 1:5-7, page 1255).

(2) *Walk by faith*. "For we walk [live every day] by faith, not by sight" (2 Cor. 5:7, page 1168). In the Old Testament we are told that "Enoch walked with God" (Gen. 5:21-23, page 9). In the New Testament we are told that "by faith Enoch . . . pleased God. But without faith it is impossible to please Him" (Heb. 11:5, 6, page 1247). Therefore, his walk with God had to be by faith (John 8:12, page 1062). You can walk with God only by faith.

(3) *Understand by faith*. "By faith we understand that the worlds were framed by the word of God, so that the things which are seen were not made of things which are visible" (Heb. 11:3, page 1247). If you believe God's Word, you will not question any part of it from Genesis to Revelation. "In the beginning God created the heavens and the earth" (Gen. 1:1, page 2). You will have no problem with the theory of evolution when you believe that the Bible is the inerrant Word of God. But "he who does not believe God has made Him a liar, because he has not believed the testimony that God has given of His Son" (1 John 5:10, page 1282). Here is a part of the record that God the Father gave of God the Son. "For by Him [Christ] all things [not just some things] were created that are in heaven and that are on earth, visible and invisible, whether thrones or dominions or principalities or powers. All things were created through Him and for Him" (Col. 1:16, page 1202). Jesus Christ, God's Son, is the Creator and Sustainer of the universe (Heb. 1:2, 3, page 1236).

(4) *"Be filled with the Spirit" by faith*. This is a command—"And do not be drunk with wine, in which is dissipation; but be filled with the Spirit" (Eph. 5:18, page 1192)—and it is the only source of spiritual power for service. "But you shall receive power when the Holy Spirit has come upon you; and you shall be witnesses to Me in Jerusalem, and in all Judea and Samaria, and to the end of the earth" (Acts 1:8, page 1086). On the Day of Pentecost the Upper Room congregation (about 120) was filled with the Holy Spirit

(Point 24-B continued on next page)

16 Now ᴿto Abraham and his Seed were the promises made. He does not say, "And to seeds," as of many, but as of one, * "And to your Seed," who is Christ.   Gen. 12:3

17 And this I say, that the law, ᴿwhich was four hundred and thirty years later, cannot annul the covenant that was confirmed before by God *in Christ, ᴿthat it should make the promise of no effect.   Ex. 12:40 • [Rom. 4:13]

18 For if ᴿthe inheritance is of the law, ᴿit is no longer of promise; but God gave it to Abraham by promise.   [Rom. 8:17] • Rom. 4:14

Purpose of the Law

19 What purpose then does the law serve? It was added because of transgressions, till the Seed should come to whom the promise was made; and it was appointed through angels by the hand ᴿof a mediator.   Ex. 20:19

20 Now a mediator does not mediate for one only, ᴿbut God is one.   [Rom. 3:29]

21 Is the law then against the promises of God? Certainly not! For if there had been a law given which could have given life, truly righteousness would have been by the law.

22 But the Scripture has confined all under sin, that the promise by faith in Jesus Christ might be given to those who believe.

23 But before faith came, we were kept under guard by the law, ᵀkept for the faith which would afterward be revealed.   confined

3:16 Gen. 22:18
3:17 NU omits in Christ

24 Therefore the law was our tutor to bring us to Christ, that we might be justified by faith.

25 But after faith has come, we are no longer under a tutor.

Sons and Heirs

26 For you are all sons of God through faith in Christ Jesus.   John 1:12

27 For ᴿas many of you as were baptized into Christ have put on Christ.   [Rom. 6:3]

28 ᴿThere is neither Jew nor Greek, ᴿthere is neither slave nor free, there is neither male nor female; for you are all ᴿone in Christ Jesus.   Col. 3:11 • [1 Cor. 12:13] • [Eph. 2:15, 16]

29 And ᴿif you are Christ's, then you are Abraham's ᴿseed, and ᴿheirs according to the promise.   Gen. 12:3; Heb. 11:18 • Rom. 4:11 • Rom. 8:17

4 Now I say that the heir, as long as he is a child, does not differ at all from a slave, though he is master of all,

2 but is under guardians and stewards until the time appointed by the father.

3 Even so we, when we were children, ᴿwere in bondage under the elements of the world.   Col. 2:8, 20

4 But when the fullness of the time had come, God sent forth His Son, ᴿbornᵀ of a woman, born under the law,   Is. 7:14 • Or made

5 ᴿto redeem those who were under the law, ᴿthat we might receive the adoption as sons.   [Matt. 20:28] • [John 1:12]

6 And because you are sons, God has sent

(Point 24-B continued from previous page)
and began to serve the Lord immediately; the results were that approximately three thousand believed in the Lord Jesus Christ, repented, were baptized and added to the Jerusalem church.

Paul asked the Galatians if they had received the Holy Spirit by the works of the law, or by faith (Gal. 3:3, page 1181). Again he asked those who did miracles if they did it by the works of the law, or by faith (v. 5). Then Paul said to them, " 'The just shall live by faith.' Yet the law is not of faith . . . [for] Christ has redeemed us from the curse of the law, having become a curse for us . . . that we might receive the promise of the [Holy] Spirit through faith" (vv. 11–14). The just, who live by faith, are filled by faith with the Holy Spirit for service.

(5) Be healed by faith. The believer is warned, "Do not be carried about with various and strange doctrines" (Heb. 13:9, page 1252). The doctrine of divine healing is being attacked as never before. It is exploited by many and denied by others. It is abused by some for filthy lucre and worldly fame, while others declare that God no longer heals our sick bodies. It is time for those of us who are justified by faith to start living by faith. We must take our stand upon the Word of God and believe with all our heart, soul, and mind. By faith we resist the teachings of the cults and occult movements, who profess to perform miracles in the name of the Lord Jesus Christ. Our Lord warns us that many will deceitfully claim His power. But He will say to them, "I never knew you; depart from Me, you who practice lawlessness! " (Matt. 7:21–23, page 946).

The Lord Jesus still heals today because "Jesus Christ is the same yesterday, today, and forever" (Heb. 13:8, page 1252). If this verse is true, then Jesus Christ still heals. You can trust Him. When you ask Him to heal you, don't tell Him when or how to heal. He may choose to heal you instantly, or slowly over a period of time. He may use a human instrument, such as a doctor. All healing is from the Lord. A doctor can treat, but only God can heal. The psalmist said, "He sent His word and healed them" (Ps. 107:20, page 574). Again we read, "When evening had come, they brought to Him [Christ] many who were demon-possessed. And He cast out the spirits with a word, and healed all who were sick, that it might be fulfilled which was spoken by Isaiah the prophet, saying: 'He Himself took our infirmities and bore our sicknesses' " (Matt. 8:16, 17, page 947; cf. Is. 53:4, 5, page 693). The Lord Jesus Christ is Jehovah-Ropheka, "the LORD who heals you" (Ex. 15:26, page 75). He is "the same yesterday, today, and forever."

See 2 Corinthians 7:4, 5, page 1169, for **Point 24-C: Faith Is Joyful in Tribulation.**

forth the Spirit of His Son into your hearts, crying out, ᵀ"Abba, Father!"   Aram., *Father*

7 Therefore you are no longer a slave but a son, ᴿand if a son, then an heir *of God *through Christ.   [Rom. 8:16, 17]

Fears for the Church

8 But then, indeed, ᴿwhen you did not know God, ᴿyou served those which by nature are not gods.   Eph. 2:12 • Rom. 1:25

9 But now ᴿafter you have known God, or rather are known by God, ᴿhow *is it that* you turn again to ᴿthe weak and beggarly elements, to which you desire again to be in bondage?   [1 Cor. 8:3] • Col. 2:20 • Heb. 7:18

10 ᴿYou observe days and months and seasons and years.   Rom. 14:5

11 I am afraid for you, ᴿlest I have labored for you in vain.   1 Thess. 3:5

12 Brethren, I urge you to become like me, for I *became* like you. ᴿYou have not injured me at all.   2 Cor. 2:5

13 You know that ᴿbecause of physical infirmity I preached the gospel to you at the first.   1 Cor. 2:3

14 And my trial which was in my flesh you did not despise or reject, but you received me as an angel of God, *even* as Christ Jesus.

15 *What then was the blessing you *enjoyed?* For I bear you witness that, if possible, you would have plucked out your own eyes and given them to me.

16 Have I therefore become your enemy because I tell you the truth?

17 They ᴿzealously court you, *but* for no good; yes, they want to exclude you, that you may be zealous for them.   Rom. 10:2

18 But it is good to be zealous in a good thing always, and not only when I am present with you.

19 My little children, for whom I labor in birth again until Christ is formed in you,

20 I would like to be present with you now and to change my tone; for I have doubts about you.

Two Covenants

21 Tell me, you who desire to be under the law, do you not hear the law?

22 For it is written that Abraham had two sons: ᴿthe one by a bondwoman, ᴿthe other by a freewoman.   Gen. 16:15 • Gen. 21:2

23 But he *who was* of the bondwoman was born according to the flesh, ᴿand he of the freewoman through promise.   Heb. 11:11

24 which things are symbolic. For these are *the two covenants: the one from Mount ᴿSinai which gives birth to bondage, which is Hagar—   Deut. 33:2

25 for this Hagar is Mount Sinai in Arabia, and corresponds to Jerusalem which now is, and is in bondage with her children—

26 but the ᴿJerusalem above is free, which is the mother of us all.   [Is. 2:2]

27 For it is written:

> ᴿ"Rejoice, O barren,   Is. 54:1
> You who do not bear!
> Break forth and shout,
> You who are not in labor!
> For the desolate has many more
>   children
> Than she who has a husband."

28 Now ᴿwe, brethren, as Isaac *was,* are ᴿchildren of promise.   Gal. 3:29 • Acts 3:25

29 But, as he who was born according to the flesh then persecuted him *who was born* according to the Spirit, even so *it is* now.

30 Nevertheless what does the Scripture say? *"Cast out the bondwoman and her son, for the son of the bondwoman shall not be heir with the son of the freewoman."*

31 So then, brethren, we are not children of the bondwoman but of the free.

Christian Liberty

5 Stand* ᴿfast therefore in the liberty by which Christ has made us free, and do not be entangled again with a ᴿyoke of bondage.   Phil. 4:1 • Acts 15:10

2 Indeed I, Paul, say to you that ᴿif you become circumcised, Christ will profit you nothing.   Acts 15:1

3 And I testify again to every man who becomes circumcised ᴿthat he is ᵀa debtor to keep the whole law.   [Rom. 2:25] • *obligated*

4 ᴿYou have become estranged from Christ, you who *attempt* to be justified by law; you have fallen from grace.   [Rom. 9:31]

5 For we through the Spirit eagerly wait for the hope of righteousness by faith.

6 For ᴿin Christ Jesus neither circumcision nor uncircumcision avails anything, but faith working through love.   [Gal. 6:15]

Love Fulfills the Law

7 You ᴿran well. Who hindered you from obeying the truth?   1 Cor. 9:24

8 This persuasion does not *come* from Him who calls you.

9 A little leaven leavens the whole lump.

10 I have confidence in you, in the Lord, that you will have no other mind; but he who troubles you shall bear his judgment, whoever he is.

11 And I, brethren, if I still preach circumcision, why do I still suffer persecution? Then the offense of the cross has ceased.

4:7 NU *through God* • NU omits *through Christ*
4:15 NU *Where*
4:24 NU, M omit *the*

4:30 Gen. 21:10, 12
5:1 NU *For freedom Christ has made us free; stand fast therefore, and*

12 I could wish that those who trouble you would even cut themselves off!

13 For you, brethren, have been called to liberty; only ^Rdo not *use* liberty as an ^Ropportunity for the flesh, but ^Rthrough love serve one another.   1 Cor. 8:9 • 1 Pet. 2:16 • 1 Cor. 9:19

14 For ^Rall the law is fulfilled in one word, *even* in this: ^R*"You shall love your neighbor as yourself."*   Matt. 7:12; 22:40 • Lev. 19:18

15 But if you bite and devour one another, beware lest you be consumed by one another!

Walking in the Spirit

16 I say then: ^RWalk in the Spirit, and you shall not fulfill the lust of the flesh.   Rom. 6:12

17 For the flesh lusts against the Spirit, and the Spirit against the flesh; and these are contrary to one another, ^Rso that you do not do the things that you wish.   Rom. 7:15

18 But ^Rif you are led by the Spirit, you are not under the law.   [Rom. 6:14; 7:4; 8:14]

19 Now ^Rthe works of the flesh are evident, which are: *adultery, ^Tfornication, uncleanness, lewdness,   Eph. 5:3, 11 • sexual immorality

20 idolatry, sorcery, hatred, contentions, jealousies, outbursts of wrath, selfish ambitions, dissensions, heresies,

21 envy, *murders, drunkenness, revelries, and the like; of which I tell you beforehand, just as I also told *you* in time past, that ^Rthose who practice such things will not inherit the kingdom of God.   1 Cor. 6:9, 10

22 But ^Rthe fruit of the Spirit is ^Rlove, joy, peace, longsuffering, kindness, ^Rgoodness, faithfulness,   [John 15:2] • [Col. 3:12–15] • Rom. 15:14

23 ^Tgentleness, self-control. ^RAgainst such there is no law.   meekness • 1 Tim. 1:9

24 And those *who are* Christ's have crucified the flesh with its passions and desires.

25 ^RIf we live in the Spirit, let us also walk in the Spirit.   [Rom. 8:4, 5]

26 ^RLet us not become conceited, provoking one another, envying one another.   Phil. 2:3

Bear and Share the Burdens

6 Brethren, if a man is overtaken in any trespass, you who *are* spiritual restore such a one in a spirit of gentleness, considering yourself lest you also be tempted.

5:19 NU omits *adultery*
5:21 NU omits *murders*

2 ^RBear one another's burdens, and so fulfill ^Rthe law of Christ.   Rom. 15:1 • [James 2:8]

3 For ^Rif anyone thinks himself to be something, when ^Rhe is nothing, he deceives himself.   Rom. 12:3 • [2 Cor. 3:5]

4 But let each one examine his own work, and then he will have rejoicing in himself alone, and ^Rnot in another.   Luke 18:11

5 For each one shall bear his own load.

Be Generous and Do Good

6 Let him who is taught the word share in all good things with him who teaches.

7 Do not be deceived, God is not mocked; for ^Rwhatever a man sows, that he will also reap.   [Rom. 2:6]

8 For he who sows to his flesh will of the flesh reap corruption, but he who sows to the Spirit will of the Spirit reap everlasting life.

9 And ^Rlet us not grow weary while doing good, for in due season we shall reap ^Rif we do not lose heart.   1 Cor. 15:58 • [James 5:7, 8]

10 Therefore, as we have opportunity, ^Rlet us do good to all, ^Respecially to those who are of the household of faith.   Titus 3:8 • Rom. 12:13

Glory Only in the Cross

11 See with what large letters I have written to you with my own hand!

12 As many as desire to make a good showing in the flesh, these *would* compel you to be circumcised, ^Ronly that they may not suffer persecution for the cross of Christ.   Gal. 5:11

13 For not even those who are circumcised keep the law, but they desire to have you circumcised that they may boast in your flesh.

14 But God forbid that I should boast except in the cross of our Lord Jesus Christ, by ^Twhom the world has been crucified to me, and ^RI to the world.   Or which, the cross • Col. 2:20

15 For ^Rin Christ Jesus neither circumcision nor uncircumcision avails anything, but a new creation.   1 Cor. 7:19

Blessing and a Plea

16 And as many as walk according to this rule, peace and mercy *be* upon them, and upon the Israel of God.

17 From now on let no one trouble me, for I bear in my body the marks of the Lord Jesus.

18 Brethren, the grace of our Lord Jesus Christ *be* with your spirit. Amen.

THE EPISTLE OF PAUL THE APOSTLE TO THE
Ephesians

AUTHORSHIP. The first verse of Ephesians declares that Paul is the author of the epistle and only in modern times has his authorship been challenged. Some critics see elements in Ephesians that to them are inconsistent with Paul's other epistles. This alleged difference in content, style, and depth could be attributed to Paul's growing comprehension of the revelation of God. Hence there is no serious reason to doubt Paul's authorship of Ephesians, the first of his four "Prison Epistles."

HOW EPHESIANS FITS INTO THE BIBLE. Ephesians is important to the life of the church because of the totality of its scope. No basic elements of Christian truth have been omitted. Its scope includes the relationship between Jews and Gentiles, the comparison of earth and heaven, and a panoramic overview of all the ages—past, present, and future.

Most of the Pauline epistles focus on a specific church, individual, or need, but Ephesians is much broader in perspective. Most fittingly, the word *all* is found in the book over thirty times.

The theological discussions in Ephesians include such subjects as God's grace, predestination, what it means to become a Christian and to be a Christian, spiritual gifts, and the work of the Holy Spirit in the life of a believer. The practical discussion includes such subjects as how Christian unity should function, how a family should live, and how spiritual warfare is waged. Without the book of Ephesians, the New Testament canon would be sorely lacking. It ties up the loose ends and gives unity to the whole New Testament.

CONTEXT. Paul first visited the city of Ephesus near the end of his second missionary journey. The Ephesus of Paul's day has been called the "supreme metropolis of Asia," its population consisting of over 350,000 people. It was the home of the pagan fertility goddess, Diana (Artemis), which contributed a great deal to the moral degeneracy of the city. Ephesus was also recognized as a commercial and financial center. It was here that Paul established a church and later spent over three years ministering to it.

The church at Ephesus became very influential. Not only did Paul shepherd it, it was served later by Timothy and John the Apostle. It was also the home church of Apollos, the "silver-tongued" orator.

After leaving Ephesus and spending a few months in Greece, Paul set out for Syria, but stopped in Miletus for a farewell meeting with the Ephesian elders. He went on to Jerusalem, but was arrested there because of an uproar among the Jews. He appealed to Caesar and was sent to Rome. Paul arrived in Rome after a particularly hazardous journey, which included a shipwreck. He was put under house arrest and was permitted to see many of his friends and other Christians for the duration of his imprisonment. It was there during his first imprisonment that Paul wrote Ephesians, Philippians, Colossians, and Philemon, the so-called Prison Epistles.

Ephesians was written around A.D. 61 and sent by the hand of Tychicus along with Colossians and Philemon to their prescribed destinations.

There are some who believe that since the words "at Ephesus" are not included in three of the most ancient manuscripts (although they are included in the vast majority) that the letter to Ephesus was not to Ephesus alone, but to all the churches in the province of Asia. The other cities were Laodicea, Hierapolis and Colosse, and Ephesus was their capital. Another argument for the "encyclical theory" is that since Paul stayed in Ephesus as long as three years one would expect some personal references in the book, but there are none.

The other side argues that the books in which the most personal references are given (Colossians and Romans) were churches where Paul had had no personal contact. Also, since he knew so many in Ephesus, it might hurt some people's feelings if he mentioned only selected believers.

The fact remains that whether in the first or the present century, Ephesians is the Word of God, and is "profitable for doctrine, for reproof, for correction, for instruction in righteousness, that the man of God may be complete, thoroughly equipped for every good work" (2 Tim. 3:16, 17). Ephesians speaks to all churches in all generations.

THEME. Nearly every major commentary on Ephesians suggests a different main theme of the book. One of the favorite themes is that of *unity*—the unity *in* the church and the unity *of* the church. It is difficult, however, to establish a single theme for Ephesians because of the scope of its content. While unity of the Jews and Gentiles in the church is definitely a theme and certainly has application to the present generation, it is not the only theme. The book sets forth a high and

holy view of the church as the body of Christ. It also deals with the basic tenets of doctrine that help to establish believers in the faith. In addition, it encourages believers to move forward in their faith and not to fall back into a life-style reminiscent of their days in the flesh, before they had come to a saving knowledge of Jesus Christ.

It was written for the good of the church, for the good of the family, and ultimately for the good of society.

How Ephesians Fits Together. The book of Ephesians is basically divided into two equal parts. Chapters 1—3 form the doctrinal section of the book, while chapters 4—6 lean toward the practical side of the faith. The first section deals with a Christian's belief. The second section deals with the Christian's behavior. The first deals with the rudiments of grace and the second with the results of grace.

Key Words. *In Christ* (1:3, 10), or *in Him* (1:4, 7, 10, 11, 13) are key words because they form the base for both the doctrinal and the practical aspects of the book. The whole purpose of the book is to establish the Christian in his faith. This has its beginning, its continuation, and its culmination "in Him."

Key Verses. 2:8–10—"By grace you have been saved through faith, and that not of yourselves; it is the gift of God, not of works, lest anyone should boast. For we are His workmanship, created in Christ Jesus for good works, which God prepared beforehand that we should walk in them." These verses show how we get to be "in Him" and what effect it has on our life.

Key Passage: 4:7–16. This passage deals with spiritual gifts and how the body of Christ functions. If verses 11 and 12 are properly understood, they unlock the church for real growth. The apostles, prophets, evangelists, pastors, and teachers are given to equip the believers for the work of the ministry. This leads to a ministry of multiplication. One man cannot do all the work. All must be trained to minister, doing the work of the ministry; with such a work force the church cannot help but grow and be effective.

The overall message of Ephesians for today's world could be entitled "The Joy of Belonging." Modern man is burdened with insecurity and loneliness, and Ephesians brings stability into that scene. Being chosen in Christ before the foundation of the world provides loving relationships in the body of Christ, in the local church, in the family, and at work. Add to this the protection we are promised from the ravages of Satan, and we have believers who not only have a sense of security and worth, but who know the true joy of belonging to Him.

—J.M.L.

Greeting

PAUL, an apostle of Jesus Christ by the will of God,

To the saints who are in Ephesus, and faithful in Christ Jesus:

2 Grace to you and peace from God our Father and the Lord Jesus Christ.

Redemption in Christ

3 ᴿBlessed *be* the God and Father of our Lord Jesus Christ, who has blessed us with every spiritual blessing in the heavenly *places* in Christ,   2 Cor. 1:3

4 just as He chose us in Him before the foundation of the world, that we should be holy and without blame before Him in love,

5 having predestined us to adoption as sons by Jesus Christ to Himself, ᴿaccording to the good pleasure of His will,   [1 Cor. 1:21]

6 to the praise of the glory of His grace, ᴿby which He ᵀmade us accepted in the Beloved.   [Rom. 3:24] · Lit. *bestowed grace (favor) upon us*

7 In Him we have redemption through His blood, the forgiveness of sins, according to ᴿthe riches of His grace   [Rom. 3:24, 25]

8 which He made to abound toward us in all wisdom and ᵀprudence,   *understanding*

9 having made known to us the mystery of His will, according to His good pleasure ᴿwhich He purposed in Himself,   [2 Tim. 1:9]

10 that in the dispensation of the fullness of the times He might gather together in one all things in Christ, *both which are in heaven and which are on earth—in Him.

11 In Him also we have obtained an inheritance, being predestined according to ᴿthe purpose of Him who works all things according to the counsel of His will,   Is. 46:10

12 that we who first trusted in Christ should be to the praise of His glory.

13 In Him you also *trusted*, after you heard the word of truth, the gospel of your salvation; in whom also, having believed, you were sealed with the Holy Spirit of promise,

1:10 NU, M omit *both*

14 *who is the guarantee of our inheritance until the redemption of the purchased possession, to the praise of His glory.

Prayer for Spiritual Wisdom

15 Therefore I also, ᴿafter I heard of your faith in the Lord Jesus and your love for all the saints,   Col. 1:4
16 ᴿdo not cease to give thanks for you, making mention of you in my prayers: Rom. 1:9
17 that ᴿthe God of our Lord Jesus Christ, the Father of glory, ᴿmay give to you the spirit of wisdom and revelation in the knowledge of Him,   John 20:17 · Col. 1:9
18 the eyes of your *understanding being enlightened; that you may know what is the hope of His calling, what are the riches of the glory of His inheritance in the saints,
19 and what is the exceeding greatness of His power toward us who believe, ᴿaccording to the working of His mighty power   Col. 2:12
20 which He worked in Christ when He raised Him from the dead and seated Him at His right hand in the heavenly places,
21 far above all ᵀprincipality and ᵀpower and ᵀmight and dominion, and every name that is named, not only in this age but also in that which is to come.   rule · authority · power
22 And ᴿHe put all things under His feet, and gave Him ᴿto be head over all things to the church,   Dan. 7:13, 14; Matt. 28:18 · Heb. 2:7
23 ᴿwhich is His body, ᴿthe fullness of Him ᴿwho fills all in all.   Rom. 12:5 · Col. 2:9 · [1 Cor. 12:6]

By Grace Through Faith

2 And ᴿyou He made alive, ᴿwho were dead in trespasses and sins,   Col. 2:13 · Eph. 4:18
2 in which you once walked according to the course of this world, according to the prince of the power of the air, the spirit who now works in the sons of disobedience,
3 ᴿamong whom also we all once conducted ourselves in ᴿthe lusts of our flesh,

1:14 NU which
1:18 NU, M hearts

fulfilling the desires of the flesh and of the mind, and ᴿwere by nature children of wrath, just as the others.   1 Pet. 4:3 · Gal. 5:16 · [Ps. 51:5]
4 But God, who is rich in mercy, because of His great love with which He loved us,
5 ᴿeven when we were dead in trespasses, ᴿmade us alive together with Christ (by grace you have been saved),   Rom. 5:6, 8 · [Rom. 6:4, 5]
6 and raised us up together, and made us sit together ᴿin the heavenly places in Christ Jesus,   Eph. 1:20
7 that in the ages to come He might show the exceeding riches of His grace in ᴿHis kindness toward us in Christ Jesus.   Titus 3:4

21-D. So Great in Grace   ▼

8 ᴿFor by grace you have been saved through faith, and that not of yourselves; ᴿit is the gift of God,   [2 Tim. 1:9] · [John 1:12, 13]
9 not of works, lest anyone should boast. ▲
10 For we are ᴿHis workmanship, created in Christ Jesus for good works, which God prepared beforehand that we should walk in them.   Is. 19:25

Brought Near by His Blood

11 Therefore remember that you, once Gentiles in the flesh—who are called Uncircumcision by what is called ᴿthe Circumcision made in the flesh by hands—   [Col. 2:11]
12 that at that time you were without Christ, being aliens from the commonwealth of Israel and strangers from the covenants of promise, having no hope and without God in the world.
13 But now in Christ Jesus you who once were far off have been brought near by the blood of Christ.

Christ Our Peace

14 ᴿFor He Himself is our peace, who has made both one, and has broken down the middle wall of separation,   Is. 9:6
15 having abolished in His flesh the enmity, that is, the law of commandments contained in ordinances, so as to create in Himself one new man from the two, thus making peace,

---

21-D. So Great in Grace (Ephesians 2:8, 9)—Salvation by the grace of God rules out all human effort in accomplishing God's saving work. "For by grace you have been saved through faith, and that not of yourselves" (v. 8). Saving grace is not of yourself, "it is the gift of God." Even faith is not of yourself, it too is the gift of God. "So then faith comes by hearing, and hearing by the word of God" (Rom. 10:17, page 1140). Saving faith comes from God as the sinner hears the Word of God.

God's grace is inexhaustibly rich in saving and keeping power. Your sins may be great and many, but God's grace is greater. "But where sin abounded, grace abounded much more" (Rom. 5:20, page 1134). God's saving grace is limitless, inexhaustible, and eternal. Christ settled the question of sin on the cross; now you must settle the question concerning the Son—what will you do with Jesus? Will you accept Him by faith as your personal Savior, or reject Him? You will accept Him by faith or reject Him in unbelief, but you cannot ignore Him. When you are saved by grace through faith in the Lord Jesus Christ, you enter the state of eternal salvation, with all the rights of a born-again child of God. Describing the greatness of this grace, the apostle John says, "Behold what manner of love the Father has bestowed on us, that we should be called children of God! Therefore the world does not know us, because it did not know Him. Beloved, now we are children of God; and it has not yet been revealed what we shall be, but we know that when He is revealed, we shall be like Him, for we shall see Him as He is" (1 John 3:1, 2, page 1279).

See Revelation 22:17, page 1316, for **Point 21-E: So Great in Invitation.**

16 and that He might reconcile them both to God in one body through the cross, thereby putting to death the enmity.

17 And He came and preached peace to you who were afar off and to those who were near.

18 For through Him we both have access ᴿby one Spirit to the Father.   1 Cor. 12:13

▼ **38-A. The Church: A Holy Temple**

Christ Our Cornerstone

19 Now, therefore, you are no longer strangers and foreigners, but fellow citizens with the saints and members of the household of God,

20 having been built on the foundation of ▽ the apostles and prophets, Jesus Christ Himself being the chief cornerstone,

21 ᴿin whom the whole building, being fitted together, grows into ᴿa holy temple in the Lord,   Ps. 118:22 • 1 Cor. 3:16, 17

22 in whom you also are being built together for a dwelling place of God in the Spirit.   ▲

38-D. The Church: A Mystery   ▼

The Mystery Revealed

3 For this reason I, Paul, the prisoner of Christ Jesus for you Gentiles—

38-A. The Church: A Holy Temple (Ephesians 2:19–22)—Solomon's temple was built in 966 B.C. and stood in its glory for almost four centuries, until 586 B.C. when the Babylonians destroyed it. The second temple was dedicated and completed seventy years later, in 516 B.C., and it stood for almost six hundred years. In A.D. 70 the Romans conquered Jerusalem and destroyed the temple.

The temple of Jehovah in Jerusalem was a permanent building wherein God manifested His holy presence. There sacrifices to cover sin were offered, and there the priests and servants worshiped Him and prayed. It also provided a barrier which separated God's holiness from the world outside.

Paul calls the church at Ephesus "a holy temple" (v. 21). The pagan Greek world also had its white-stoned temples where the Greek gods were honored and sought after. The Ephesians understood Paul's figurative language. Note some striking lessons from this and other passages concerning the church as God's temple.

(1) In this age God's temple is His church; it is called "a dwelling place of God" (v. 22). "God is Spirit" (John 4:24, page 1054) and hence does not live in a house of stone; but He does live in the born-again believer's heart.

(2) God's Spirit indwells the church, His temple (v. 22). Paul wrote to the Corinthians, "your body is the temple of the Holy Spirit" (1 Cor. 6:19, page 1152). The Holy Spirit indwells every believer, and this indwelling converts the believer's body into a temple of God.

(3) Christ said that He would "build" His church upon Peter's confession that Jesus is "the Christ"—the Messiah (Matt. 16:16–18, page 962).

(4) At Pentecost the Comforter (the Holy Spirit) came to indwell all believers, as Christ had promised (John 16:7, page 1077). Pentecost was the celebration of the fullness of the harvest, fifty days after the "firstfruits" (Lev. 23:15–17, page 131). Christ was the "firstfruits" (1 Cor. 15:20, page 1161) from the dead, and then came the harvest of His church, fifty days after the Resurrection.

(5) The church, His temple, is now composed both of believing Jews and Gentiles. The Gentiles in Old Testament days were "strangers" and "foreigners"—now they are "fellow citizens" and family members "of the household of God" (v. 19).

(6) Jesus Christ is the chief cornerstone; the teachings of the apostles and prophets are the foundation of His temple (v. 20; cf. Is. 28:16, page 668). The psalmist saw the Messiah as the rejected, then the confirmed, cornerstone of God's temple (Ps. 118:22, page 580). His death for sin provided the theological basis for God to forgive believers. Jesus laid the foundation for the New Covenant teachings of the apostles whose New Testament writings are the infallible doctrines for the church.

(7) The church was planned as a harmonious temple structure, all parts "being fitted together" (v. 21). This was an echo of Christ's command to the church, "that you love one another" (John 13:34, 35, page 1073). Those who unlovingly disturb the fellowship and unity of the church deface God's temple.

(8) The church is to be a holy temple (v. 21). The original tabernacle and temple provided a place where God, upon the mercy seat, could meet with man and be worshiped, and yet retain a separation between His holy presence and sinful man. The church is to be holy, just as Israel in the Old Testament was to be holy (Lev. 20:7, page 128). This includes being separated from sin, and set apart for God's service.

(9) The church is to be a temple of prayer. Christ spoke of His earthly temple, and scolded the men of that age for making the temple "a den of thieves" (Matt. 21:13, page 968).

(10) The church is to be a temple of teaching. Christ daily taught the truth about God in the temple (Luke 22:53, page 1043). The early church continued to preach Christ in the temple as well as from house to house (Acts 2:46, page 1090).

See 1 Corinthians 12:12–31, page 1158, for **Point 38-B: The Church: A Body.**

38-D. The Church: A Mystery (Ephesians 3:1–11)—In the ancient world the word *mystery* denoted a special meaning, different from our modern understanding of the word. Today we define it as a riddle or unsolved

(Point 38-D continued on next page)

▽ 2 if indeed you have heard of the ᵀdispensation of the grace of God ᴿwhich was given to me for you,   *stewardship* · Acts 9:15

3 ᴿhow that by revelation ᴿHe made known to me the mystery (as I have briefly written already,   Acts 22:17, 21 · [Rom. 11:25; 16:25]

4 by which, when you read, you may understand my knowledge in the mystery of Christ),

5 which in other ages was not made known to the sons of men, as it has now been revealed by the Spirit to His holy apostles and prophets:

6 that the Gentiles ᴿshould be fellow heirs, of the same body, and partakers of His promise in Christ through the gospel,   Gal. 3:28, 29

7 of which I became a minister according to the gift of the grace of God given to me by the effective working of His power.

Purpose of the Mystery

8 To me, ᴿwho am less than the least of all the saints, this grace was given, that I should preach among the Gentiles ᴿthe unsearchable riches of Christ,   [1 Cor. 15:9] · [Col. 1:27; 2:2, 3]

9 and to make all see what is the *fellow- ▽ ship of the mystery, which from the beginning of the ages has been hidden in God who created all things *through Jesus Christ;

10 to the intent that now the ᵀmanifold wisdom of God might be made known by the church to the ᵀprincipalities and powers in the heavenly places,   *variegated* or *many-sided* · *rulers*

11 according to the eternal purpose which He accomplished in Christ Jesus our Lord, ▲

12 in whom we have boldness and access with confidence through faith in Him.

13 ᴿTherefore I ask that you do not lose heart at my tribulations for you, ᴿwhich is your glory.   Phil. 1:14 · 2 Cor. 1:6

Appreciation of the Mystery

14 For this reason I bow my knees to the ᴿFather *of our Lord Jesus Christ,   Eph. 1:3

15 from whom the whole family in heaven and earth is named,

16 that He would grant you, ᴿaccording to the riches of His glory, ᴿto be strengthened

3:9 NU, M *stewardship (dispensation)* • NU omits *through Jesus Christ*
3:14 NU omits *of our Lord Jesus Christ*

(Point 38-D continued from previous page)
puzzle; but in New Testament times it signified the secrets of a temple which only those who had been initiated were able to understand. With this orientation, the present passage suddenly becomes clear. Paul uses the word *mystery* three times (vv. 3, 4, 9). It is now clear that he is telling the secrets of God to those (the believers in Christ) who have now entered as full members into His holy temple. This newly revealed secret (the "mystery") is His church (v. 5).

(1) Isaiah, seven hundred years before Christ, saw that the Gentiles would find their rest in Israel's Messiah (Is. 11:10, page 654). That was not hidden. However, the following was hidden:

(a) The Gentiles would not have to become Jews (Acts 15:24, page 1109).

(b) The Gentiles and Jews together would form one body of God's children through faith in Christ (Rom. 1:16, page 1128).

The church was revealed to Paul and the other apostles by the Holy Spirit (vv. 3, 5). That the Gentiles and Jews would form this one holy, redeemed body in Christ was not explicitly revealed through Old Testament prophets—only the New Testament prophets understood this truth (John 10:16, page 1067).

(2) Through faith in Christ, Gentile believers are to become fellow-heirs of God's promises of eternal blessing (v. 6). Israel, at the close of the age, will be saved; God will not nullify His promises to the patriarchs (Rom. 11:26–28, page 1141).

(3) "The unsearchable riches" (v. 8) were to be the possession of those who become members of Christ's church. These undoubtedly include spiritual riches such as forgiveness, righteousness, and holiness, as well as eternal life and bliss with Christ forever (Rev. 2:7, 17, 26, 27, page 1294; cf. 3:5, 12, 21, page 1296).

(4) Loving fellowship exists in the church between Gentile and Jewish believers and Christ, as was never dreamed of by the ancient world (v. 9). The church will be Christ's loving "wife" throughout all eternity (Rev. 19:7–9, page 1312).

(5) The church was eternally planned (vv. 9, 11). Since the beginning of the world, God had determined to save penitent people through the death of Christ, and to combine both believing Jews and Gentiles into His church.

(6) The wisdom of God is made known by His wonderful plan of salvation, whereby Gentiles and Jews together are saved by grace, through faith in Christ (v. 10; Eph. 2:8, 9, page 1187).

(7) The gospel message of salvation is the means of enlarging the church, as more believe in Christ, are cleansed, and are baptized by the Holy Spirit into His eternal assembly. No wonder Paul saw himself as unworthy of bearing such Good News to the Gentiles (vv. 7, 8). Paul says triumphantly, "For I am not ashamed of the gospel of Christ, for it is the power of God to salvation for everyone who believes, for the Jew first and also for the Greek" (Rom. 1:16, page 1128).

See Matthew 16:13–20, page 961, for **Point 38-E: The Church: Its Builder.**

with might through His Spirit in ᴿthe inner man,   [Phil. 4:19] • Col. 1:11 • Rom. 7:22

17 ᴿthat Christ may dwell in your hearts through faith; that you, ᴿbeing rooted and grounded in love,   John 14:23 • Col. 1:23

18 ᴿmay be able to comprehend with all the saints ᴿwhat is the width and length and depth and height—   Eph. 1:18 • Rom. 8:39

19 to know the love of Christ which passes knowledge; that you may be filled ᴿwith all the fullness of God.   Eph. 1:23

▼ 26-E. Think Great Thoughts, Because You Serve a Great God

20 Now ᴿto Him who is able to do exceedingly abundantly ᴿabove all that we ask or think, ᴿaccording to the power that works in

▲ us,   Rom. 16:25 • 1 Cor. 2:9 • Col. 1:29

21 ᴿto Him be glory in the church by Christ Jesus to all generations, forever and ever. Amen.   Rom. 11:36

Walk in Unity

4 I, therefore, the prisoner of the Lord, ᵀbeseech you to walk worthy of the calling with which you were called,   *exhort*

2 with all lowliness and gentleness, with longsuffering, bearing with one another in love,

3 endeavoring to keep the unity of the Spirit ᴿin the bond of peace.   Col. 3:14

4 *There is* one body and one Spirit, just as you were called in one hope of your calling;

5 one Lord, one faith, one baptism;

6 one God and Father of all, who is above all, and through all, and in *you all.

Spiritual Gifts

7 But to each one of us grace was given according to the measure of Christ's gift.

8 Therefore He says:

ᴿ"When He ascended on high,
He led captivity captive,
And gave gifts to men."   Ps. 68:18

9 ᴿ(Now this, *"He ascended"*—what does it mean but that He also *first descended into the lower parts of the earth?   John 3:13; 20:17

4:6 M *us*; NU omits *you*
4:9 NU omits *first*

26-E. Think Great Thoughts, Because You Serve a Great God (Ephesians 3:20)—Our God "is able to do exceedingly abundantly above all that we ask or think, according to the power [of the Holy Spirit] that works in us" (v. 20). Because God is a great God, think great thoughts with confidence, knowing that your thoughts can never be greater than God. As we study the Bible and read of His mighty acts, we marvel at His greatness and claim to believe that He can do anything. But when it comes to a spiritual crisis, some believers (by thinking small thoughts) reduce Him in dignity and power and act as though God is no longer all-powerful. We forget that He has all authority in heaven and on earth (Matt. 28:18, page 982), that He created everything in this universe (Gen. 1:1, page 2), and sustains all things in His universe (Heb. 1:3, page 1236). We forget that He is "the same yesterday, today, and forever" (Heb. 13:8, page 1252). His universal authority and power have not diminished. Therefore, think great thoughts, because you serve a great God who does great things. He is immutable; i.e., He does not change (Mal. 3:6, page 924); He is infallible (James 1:13, page 1256).

How great is your God in your

(1) *Thinking?* Tell me what you think about your God and I will tell you how great He is in your thinking.
(2) *Vision?* (Prov. 29:18, page 622).
(3) *Faith?* No faith, no God. Small faith, a small God. Great faith, a great God.
(4) *Service?* Can you do all things through Christ? (Phil. 4:13, page 1198).

How great is your God? Is He greater than

(1) *Your personal problems?* If He is, why do you worry? (Phil. 1:12–14, page 1195).
(2) *All your enemies?* If He is, why live in fear? (Is. 54:17, page 695).
(3) *All the obstacles of your life?* If He is, why give up? (1 John 4:4, page 1280).

Don't be an unbelieving believer.

(1) Israel made their God look small at Kadesh Barnea, because they believed the evil report brought back by ten of the twelve spies. Only Joshua and Caleb believed their God was more powerful than the giants of Canaan. The people chose to follow the unbelieving spies, and God sent them back into the wilderness for thirty-eight additional years. Their unbelief made God look small. They said, "We saw the giants . . . and we were like grasshoppers in our own sight, and so we were in their sight" (Num. 13:33, page 153). Grasshopper Christians always make their God look small in the eyes of the world (Num. 13 and 14, page 152; cf. Deut. 1:1–46, page 181; cf. Heb. 3:7–12, page 1238).

(2) Israel's God was great in their eyes when they crossed Jordan thirty-eight years later; God caused the water to pile up and Israel crossed over on dry ground (Josh. 3:1–17, page 217). Their God was a great God to them at Jericho where, by faith, the walls came tumbling down (Josh. 6:1–20, page 220).

Pray that God will motivate a change in your attitude from fear to unlimited faith. Remember, our God is a great God; so think great thoughts with confidence to the glory of God (1 Cor. 1:31, page 1148; cf. Jer. 9:23, 24, page 721).

See Index, page 17, for your next study.

10 He who descended is also the One ᴿwho ascended far above all the heavens, that He might fill all things.)   John 20:17; Acts 1:9, 11

11 And He Himself gave some *to be* apostles, some prophets, some evangelists, and some pastors and teachers,

12 for the equipping of the saints for the work of ministry, ᴿfor the ᵀedifying of ᴿthe body of Christ,   1 Cor. 14:26 · *building up* · Col. 1:24

13 till we all come to the unity of the faith ᴿand of the knowledge of the Son of God, to ᴿa perfect man, to the measure of the stature of the fullness of Christ;   Col. 2:2 · 1 Cor. 14:20

14 that we should no longer be ᴿchildren, tossed to and fro and carried about with every wind of doctrine, by the trickery of men, in the cunning craftiness of ᴿdeceitful plotting,   1 Cor. 14:20 · Rom. 16:18

15 but, speaking the truth in love, may grow up in all things into Him who is the ᴿhead—Christ—   Eph. 1:22

16 from whom the whole body, joined and knit together by what every joint supplies, according to the effective working by which every part does its share, causes growth of the body for the edifying of itself in love.

The New Man

17 This I say, therefore, and testify in the Lord, that you should ᴿno longer walk as the *rest of the Gentiles walk, in the futility of their mind,   Eph. 2:2; 4:22

18 having their understanding darkened, being alienated from the life of God, because of the ignorance that is in them, because of the ᴿblindness of their heart;   Rom. 1:21

19 who, being past feeling, ᴿhave given themselves over to lewdness, to work all uncleanness with greediness.   1 Pet. 4:3

20 But you have not so learned Christ,

21 if indeed you have heard Him and have been taught by Him, as the truth is in Jesus:

22 that you ᴿput off, concerning your former conduct, the old man which grows corrupt according to the deceitful lusts,   Col. 3:8

23 and ᴿbe renewed in the spirit of your mind,   [Rom. 12:2]

24 and that you ᴿput on the new man which was created according to God, in true righteousness and holiness.   [Rom. 6:4; 7:6; 12:2]

Do Not Grieve the Spirit

25 Therefore, putting away lying, *"Let each one of you speak truth with his neighbor," for we are members of one another.

26 ᴿ*"Be angry, and do not sin"*: do not let the sun go down on your wrath,   Ps. 4:4; 37:8

27 nor give ᵀplace to the devil.   *opportunity*

28 Let him who stole steal no longer, but rather ᴿlet him labor, working with *his* hands

what is good, that he may have something ᴿto give him who has need.   Acts 20:35 · Luke 3:11

29 Let no corrupt word proceed out of your mouth, but what is good for necessary ᵀedification, ᴿthat it may impart grace to the hearers.   *building up* · Col. 3:16

30 And ᴿdo not grieve the Holy Spirit of God, by whom you were sealed for the day of redemption.   Is. 7:13

31 Let all bitterness, wrath, anger, ᵀclamor, and ᴿevil speaking be put away from you, ᴿwith all malice.   *loud quarreling* · James 4:11 · Titus 3:3

32 And be kind to one another, tenderhearted, ᴿforgiving one another, even as God in Christ forgave you.   [Mark 11:25]

Walk in Love

5 Thereforeᴿ be imitators of God as dear ᴿchildren.   Luke 6:36 · 1 Pet. 1:14–16

2 And ᴿwalk in love, ᴿas Christ also has loved us and given Himself for us, an offering and a sacrifice to God ᴿfor a sweet-smelling aroma.   1 Thess. 4:9 · Gal. 1:4 · 2 Cor. 2:14, 15

3 But fornication and all ᴿuncleanness or covetousness, let it not even be named among you, as is fitting for saints;   Col. 3:5–7

4 neither filthiness, nor foolish talking, nor coarse jesting, ᴿwhich are not fitting, but rather ᴿgiving of thanks.   Rom. 1:28 · Phil. 4:6

5 For *this you know, that no fornicator, unclean person, nor covetous man, who is an idolater, has any ᴿinheritance in the kingdom of Christ and God.   1 Cor. 6:9, 10

6 Let no one deceive you with empty words, for because of these things the wrath of God comes upon the sons of disobedience.

7 Therefore do not be ᴿpartakers with them.   1 Tim. 5:22

Walk in Light

8 For you were once darkness, but now *you are* ᴿlight in the Lord. Walk as children of light   1 Thess. 5:5

9 (for ᴿthe fruit of the *Spirit *is* in all goodness, righteousness, and truth),   Gal. 5:22

10 finding out what is acceptable to the Lord.

11 And have ᴿno fellowship with the unfruitful works of darkness, but rather ᵀexpose them.   2 Cor. 6:14 · *reprove*

12 For it is shameful even to speak of those things which are done by them in secret.

13 But ᴿall things that are ᵀexposed are made manifest by the light, for whatever makes manifest is light.   [John 3:20, 21] · *reproved*

14 Therefore He says:

ᴿ"Awake, you who sleep,   [Is. 26:19; 60:11]
    Arise from the dead,
    And Christ will give you light."

4:17 NU omits *the rest of*
4:25 Zech 8:16

5:5 NU *know this*
5:9 NU *light*

Walk in Wisdom

15 ᴿSee then that you walk ᵀcircumspectly, not as fools but as wise,   Col. 4:5 · *carefully*

16 ᴿredeeming the time, ᴿbecause the days are evil.   Col. 4:5 · Eccl. 11:2

17 ᴿTherefore do not be unwise, but understand what the will of the Lord *is*.   Col. 4:5

18 And ᴿdo not be drunk with wine, in which is dissipation; but be filled with the Spirit,   Prov. 20:1; 23:31

19 speaking to one another in psalms and hymns and spiritual songs, singing and making melody in your heart to the Lord,

20 ᴿgiving thanks always for all things to God the Father ᴿin the name of our Lord Jesus Christ,   Ps. 34:1 · [1 Pet. 2:5]

21 ᴿsubmitting to one another in the fear of *God.   [Phil. 2:3]

Marriage—Christ and the Church

22 Wives, ᴿsubmit to your own husbands, as to the Lord.   Col. 3:18—4:1

23 For ᴿthe husband is head of the wife, as also ᴿChrist is head of the church; and He is the Savior of the body.   [1 Cor. 11:3] · Col. 1:18

24 Therefore, just as the church is subject to Christ, so *let* the wives *be* to their own husbands ᴿin everything.   Titus 2:4, 5

25 ᴿHusbands, love your wives, just as Christ also loved the church and ᴿgave Himself for her,   Col. 3:19 · Acts 20:28

26 that He might sanctify and cleanse her with the washing of water by the word,

27 ᴿthat He might present her to Himself a glorious church, ᴿnot having spot or wrinkle or any such thing, but that she should be holy and without blemish.   Col. 1:22 · Song 4:7

28 So husbands ought to love their own wives as their own bodies; he who loves his wife loves himself.

29 For no one ever hated his own flesh, but nourishes and cherishes it, just as the Lord *does* the church.

30 For ᴿwe are members of His body, *of His flesh and of His bones.   Gen. 2:23

31 *"For this reason a man shall leave his father and mother and be joined to his wife, and the two shall become one flesh."*

32 This is a great mystery, but I speak concerning Christ and the church.

33 Nevertheless ᴿlet each one of you in particular so love his own wife as himself, and let the wife *see* that she ᴿrespects *her* husband.   Col. 3:19 · 1 Pet. 3:1, 6

Children and Parents

6 Children, ᴿobey your parents in the Lord, for this is right.   Col. 3:20

2 *"Honor your father and mother,"* which is the first commandment with promise:

3 *"that it may be well with you and you may live long on the earth."*

4 And you, fathers, do not provoke your children to wrath, but bring them up in the training and admonition of the Lord.

Bondservants and Masters

5 ᴿBondservants, be obedient to those who are your masters according to the flesh, ᴿwith fear and trembling, ᴿin sincerity of heart, as to Christ;   [1 Tim. 6:1] · 2 Cor. 7:15 · 1 Chr. 29:17

6 ᴿnot with eyeservice, as men-pleasers, but as bondservants of Christ, doing the will of God from the heart,   Col. 3:22

7 with good will doing service, as to the Lord, and not to men,

8 ᴿknowing that whatever good anyone does, he will receive the same from the Lord, whether *he is* a slave or free.   Rom. 2:6

9 And you, masters, do the same things to them, giving up threatening, knowing that *your own Master also is in heaven, and ᴿthere is no partiality with Him.   Rom. 2:11

The Whole Armor of God

10 Finally, my brethren, be strong in the Lord and in the power of His might.

11 ᴿPut on the whole armor of God, that you may be able to stand against the ᵀwiles of the devil.   [2 Cor. 6:7] · *schemings*

12 For we do not wrestle against flesh and blood, but against principalities, against powers, against ᴿthe rulers of *the darkness of this age, against spiritual *hosts* of wickedness in the heavenly *places*.   Luke 22:53

13 Therefore take up the whole armor of God, that you may be able to withstand in the evil day, and having done all, to stand.

14 Stand therefore, ᴿhaving girded your waist with truth, ᴿhaving put on the breastplate of righteousness,   Is. 11:5 · Is. 59:17

15 ᴿand having shod your feet with the preparation of the gospel of peace;   Is. 52:7

16 above all, taking ᴿthe shield of faith with which you will be able to quench all the fiery darts of the wicked one.   1 John 5:4

17 And ᴿtake the helmet of salvation, and ᴿthe sword of the Spirit, which is the word of God;   1 Thess. 5:8 · [Heb. 4:12]

18 praying always with all prayer and supplication in the Spirit, ᴿbeing watchful to this end with all perseverance and ᴿsupplication for all the saints—   [Matt. 26:41] · Phil. 1:4

19 and for me, that utterance may be given

5:21 NU *Christ*
5:30 NU omits the rest of v. 30.
5:31 Gen. 2:24; Matt. 19:5; Mark 10:7

6:2 Ex. 20:12; Deut. 5:16
6:9 NU *He who is both their Master and yours is*
6:12 NU *this darkness,*

to me, that I may open my mouth boldly to make known the mystery of the gospel,

20 for which ᴿI am an ambassador in chains; that in it I may speak boldly, as I ought to speak.   2 Cor. 5:20

A Gracious Greeting

21 But that you also may know my affairs and how I am doing, ᴿTychicus, a beloved brother and faithful minister in the Lord, will make all things known to you;   Acts 20:4

22 whom I have sent to you for this very purpose, that you may know our affairs, and that he may ᴿcomfort your hearts.   2 Cor. 1:6

23 Peace to the brethren, and love with faith, from God the Father and the Lord Jesus Christ.

24 Grace be with all those who love our Lord Jesus Christ in sincerity. Amen.

THE EPISTLE OF PAUL THE APOSTLE TO THE
Philippians

AUTHORSHIP. In the middle of the second century Polycarp reminded the Philippians that they had received letters from Paul. He was certainly referring to this epistle. The Philippians were generous to Paul, and in this beautiful thank-you letter he becomes more personal than in most of his church epistles.

CONTEXT. Paul was in custody waiting trial (1:7, 13, 16). In Roman times one was not put into prison for any length of time after his trial. He was either convicted and fined, beaten, exiled or executed, or he was acquitted and freed; but he was not put into prison as a sentence. So Paul was waiting trial, but not in a death cell just before the day of execution, nor even anticipating conviction. In fact he expected to be coming to see the Philippian Christians in the near future (2:24). Even now as Paul was writing, he had considerable freedom, though under guard. He could direct the activities of Timothy and Epaphroditus (2:19-30), write this epistle to the Philippians, and communicate with the palace guard (1:13). He was surrounded by companions (4:21). All of this fits well the house arrest in Rome, described at the close of the book of Acts (Acts 28:16ff.).

In his lifetime Paul was in prison on a number of occasions (2 Cor. 11:23). Clement of Rome specified seven times altogether but none of the known imprisonments fits so well as the first one in Rome. Paul was in prison in Caesarea, but he did not have the expectation of release reflected in this epistle (2:24). Paul had his troubles in Ephesus, but no imprisonment is explicitly noted. Any suggestion of an Ephesian or a Caesarean origin for the Philippian epistle has numerous objections at the outset. Rome is the most likely place of writing, and the time would be toward the close of Paul's first imprisonment there, about A.D. 63.

While in prison Paul had received a gift from the church at Philippi (4:10-19). This city was named after Philip of Macedon, the father of Alexander the Great, and was situated in northern Greece, seventy-five miles from Thessalonica, the capital of Macedonia. It was a Roman colony in the first of four Macedonian districts. Paul had established a church here on his second missionary journey (Acts 16:12-40). No doubt he had stopped here again as he passed through Macedonia on his way to Corinth at the close of his third missionary journey (Acts 20:1-3, 2 Cor. 7:5). After three months in Corinth, Paul returned through Macedonia and stopped at Philippi at Passover time (Acts 20:6). Then he went to Jerusalem, was arrested, kept in prison two years in Caesarea, and appealed for a trial before Caesar in Rome. Now, almost five years later, he is still under trial arrest as he writes to the Philippians.

HOW PHILIPPIANS FITS INTO THE BIBLE. Though not a doctrinal epistle, Philippians contains one of the most important passages on Christology in the New Testament, the famous passage on Christ's self-emptying, by which He laid aside the independent use of His divine attributes for a time (2:5-8). This letter also has a little autobiography of the apostle in 3:1-14, as well as many verses that are popular with Christians all over the world.

KEY WORDS. The key words in Philippians are *joy* and *rejoice.*

HOW PHILIPPIANS FITS TOGETHER. In this epistle Paul, who exhorts his readers to "join in following my example" (3:17), presents a model for our own rejoicing in Christ. Sometimes the model is Paul himself, sometimes it is the Philippian believers as Paul advises them.

The following is a helpful "handle" for the four chapters: Chapter 1 shows the Christian rejoicing in spite of suffering; chapter 2 shows the Christian rejoicing in service for the Lord; chapter 3 shows the Christian rejoicing in the excellence of Christ; and chapter 4 shows the Christian rejoicing through anxiety to find peace.

The church at Philippi was special to Paul. Not only was it the first church established on European soil, but this church alone supported him with gifts in the early days (4:15). More recently Epaphroditus had been sent with another gift, this time while Paul was in Rome (4:18). The trip involved both land and sea travel. The distance was less than a thousand miles and could possibly be completed in a month's time. Unfortunately Epaphroditus had become seriously ill after he had delivered both the gift and news of the church at Philippi.

When the Philippians learned of his condition, they were deeply concerned (2:25-30). It is not surprising that news went back and forth between Philippi and Rome so easily. Travel was common in that time and that part of the world. Furthermore, all roads led to Rome, and Philippi was a Roman colony, closely associated with the capital of the empire. Paul was in Rome for two whole years, thus allowing for a number of trips to have occurred. Now Paul was ready to send

the recovered Epaphroditus back to Philippi to provide complete assurance of his returned health (2:28).

PURPOSE. First, Paul wanted to say "thank you" for the gift he had received from the Philippians (4:10-18). Since Epaphroditus had delivered the contribution, this was an appropriate time to send an expression of appreciation with him as he returned.

Second, Paul wanted to share with them news about himself and express his feelings about the way things were turning out for him. This is an exceptionally personal epistle. Usually Paul spoke of himself only when he had been wrongfully criticized. Here, however, he wanted to open his heart and simply share his own problems (1:23-26). He wanted to tell them also of the possibility that he would come to see them soon (2:24).

Third, Paul wanted to encourage the Christians in Philippi, who were among Paul's favorites. Their particular needs can be deduced from his message to them. The bishops and deacons are specified in the greetings (1:1).

Fourth, Paul wanted, as always, to honor Christ and give Him as example and answer to whatever needs a person may have.

Finally, Paul wanted to give further instruction about the gospel. Whether Paul was writing his most polemic work (probably Galatians) or his least (probably Philippians), he always presented the heart of the gospel. The basic substance of the gospel is the very person of Jesus Christ (3:8-11).

Philippians begins as a message of gratitude to the Christians at Philippi in the first-century Roman Empire, but it does not end there; for it extends to Christians through the ages to our own lives. Paul teaches in his epistle by his example (3:17). All that he said of himself, he intends as exhortation to our Christian lives:

—Smiling through tears, rejoice (1:18; 2:17, 18, 28; 3:1; 4:4; 4:10).
—Holding on in Christ, be strong (3:14; 4:13).
—Following Jesus, help one another (1:24, 25; 2:4).
—Sharing the gospel, give thanks (1:3-6; 4:6, 17).

—L.F.

Greeting

PAUL and Timothy, bondservants of Jesus Christ,

To all the saints in Christ Jesus who are in Philippi, with the *bishops and deacons:

2 Grace to you and peace from God our Father and the Lord Jesus Christ.

Thankfulness and Prayer

3 ᴿI thank my God upon every remembrance of you,   1 Cor. 1:4

4 always in ᴿevery prayer of mine making request for you all with joy,   Eph. 1:16

5 ᴿfor your fellowship in the gospel from the first day until now,   [Rom. 12:13]

6 being confident of this very thing, that He who has begun a good work in you will complete it until the day of Jesus Christ;

7 just as it is right for me to think this of you all, because I have you in my heart,

1:1 Lit. *overseers*

inasmuch as both in my chains and in the defense and confirmation of the gospel, you all are partakers with me of grace.

8 For God is my witness, how greatly I long for you all with the affection of Jesus Christ.

9 And this I pray, that your love may abound still more and more in knowledge and all discernment,

10 that you may approve the things that are excellent, that you may be sincere and without offense till the day of Christ,

11 being filled with the fruits of righteousness ᴿwhich *are* by Jesus Christ, ᴿto the glory and praise of God.   Col. 1:6 · John 15:8

46-F. Paul's Imprisonments and Final Journeys   ▼

Christ Is Preached

12 But I want you to know, brethren, that the things *which happened* to me have actu-

---

46-F. Paul's Imprisonments and Final Journeys (Philippians 1:12-14)—This period of Paul's life covers the events from his arrest in Jerusalem to his martyrdom.

(1) *Arrest* (Acts 21:18—23:22, page 1116). Paul and Luke returned to Jerusalem from the third missionary journey. James asked Paul to make an appearance in the temple to show others that he, in his ministry to the

(Point 46-F continued on next page)

∇ ally turned out for the furtherance of the gospel,

13 so that it has become evident ᴿto the whole ᵀpalace guard, and to all the rest, that my chains are in Christ;   Phil. 4:22 · Or *praetorian*

14 and most of the brethren in the Lord, having become confident by my chains, are much more bold to speak the word without ▲ fear.

15 Some indeed preach Christ even from envy and strife, and some also from goodwill:

16 *The former preach Christ from selfish ambition, not sincerely, supposing to add affliction to my chains;

17 but the latter out of love, knowing that I am appointed for the defense of the gospel.

18 What then? Only *that* in every way, whether in pretense or in truth, Christ is preached; and in this I rejoice, yes, and will rejoice.

To Live Is Christ

19 For I know that ᴿthis will turn out for my deliverance through your prayer and the supply of the Spirit of Jesus Christ, Job 13:16, LXX

20 according to my earnest expectation and hope that in nothing I shall be ashamed, but ᴿwith all boldness, as always, so now also

Christ will be magnified in my body, whether by life ᴿor by death.   Eph. 6:19, 20 · [Rom. 14:8]

21 For to me, to live *is* Christ, and to die *is* gain.

22 But if *I* live on in the flesh, this *will mean* fruit from *my* labor; yet what I shall choose I ᵀcannot tell.   *do not know*

23 *For I am hard pressed between the two, having a ᴿdesire to depart and be with Christ, which is ᴿfar better.   [2 Cor. 5:2, 8] · [Ps. 16:11]

24 Nevertheless to remain in the flesh *is* more needful for you.

25 And being confident of this, I know that I shall remain and continue with you all for your progress and joy of faith,

26 that ᴿyour rejoicing for me may be more abundant in Jesus Christ by my coming to you again.   2 Cor. 1:14

Striving and Suffering for Christ

27 Only ᴿlet your conduct be worthy of the gospel of Christ, so that whether I come and see you or am absent, I may hear of your affairs, that you stand fast in one spirit, ᴿwith one mind ᴿstriving together for the faith of the gospel,   Eph. 4:1 · Eph. 4:3 · Jude 3

28 and not in any way terrified by your adversaries, which is to them a proof of

---

1:16 NU reverses vv. 16 and 17.   1:23 NU, M *But*

(Point 46-F continued from previous page)
Gentiles, still walked orderly and kept the law (Acts 21:24, page 1116). Paul was accused of bringing a Greek into the part of the temple forbidden to Gentiles. A riot ensued, and Paul testified of his conversion (Acts 21:40—22:22, page 1117). Another riot erupted, and Roman authorities brought him before the Sanhedrin (Acts 22:30—23:10, page 1118). After a third threat to Paul's life, the Romans finally moved Paul out of Jerusalem, for his own safety, to the Roman coastal city of Caesarea (Acts 23:23, page 1119).

(2) *Caesarean imprisonment* (Acts 23:23—26:32, page 1119). Caesarea was the Roman capital of Judea, where the governors lived and held court. Paul was tried there before Felix the governor for having incited a riot in a Roman province, for which he could be sentenced to death. Felix secretly wanted a bribe from Paul for his release. After two years of imprisonment, Festus arrived as the new governor. Felix, willing to please the Jews, left Paul bound (Acts 24:26, 27, page 1120). At a hearing before Festus, Paul appealed to Caesar on the grounds of his right as a Roman citizen (Acts 25:11, page 1121). Shortly thereafter, Festus discussed Paul's case with the Roman-appointed King Agrippa II. After the king heard Paul, it was determined that he should sail to Italy for his appeal before Caesar (Acts 27:1, page 1123).

(3) *Voyage to Rome* (Acts 27:1—28:15, page 1123). This is one of the great sea adventures of all time. The captain and crew did not want to spend their winter in dull Fair Havens (Acts 27:8, page 1123). Against Paul's advice they risked all to set out for Phoenix (Acts 27:12, page 1123), a better harbor and more of a playground city. A storm came up (Acts 27:14, page 1123), but, according to God's word to Paul, none of the 276 aboard lost their lives (Acts 27:22-25, 37, 44, page 1123). Acts 27:31 (page 1123) is a classic in the paradox of human means versus God's will. Paul told the centurion that if he allowed the sailors to abandon ship and save themselves, other lives would be lost. The ship foundered, but all landed safely on the island of Melita (today's Malta).

(4) *First Roman imprisonment* (Acts 28:16-31, page 1124). Paul spent the next two years in Rome, again awaiting trial. He preached Christ throughout this period (Acts 28:30, 31, page 1125), and some were saved, even among Caesar's household (Phil. 4:22, page 1199). During this time Paul wrote, among other letters, the three great Christological epistles: Ephesians, Colossians, and Philippians. Paul noted that his imprisonment had "turned out for the furtherance of the gospel" (vv. 12-14).

(5) *Persecution* (2 Tim. 1:8, 12, 16, 17, page 1224; 2:9, page 1225; 4:6-8, page 1228). When Rome burned, Nero blamed the Christians and began persecuting them. Our last glimpse of Paul finds him at the focus of this persecution, uttering these last, noble words of inspiration: "I have fought the good fight, I have finished the race, I have kept the faith" (2 Tim. 4:7, page 1228).

See Index, page 17, for your next study.

perdition, but *to you of salvation, and that from God.

29 For to you it has been granted on behalf of Christ, ᴿnot only to believe in Him, but also to ᴿsuffer for His sake,   Eph. 2:8 • [2 Tim. 3:12]

30 ᴿhaving the same conflict which you saw in me and now hear is in me.   Col. 1:29

Unity Through Humility

2 Therefore if there is any ᵀconsolation in Christ, if any comfort of love, if any fellowship of the Spirit, if any ᴿaffection and mercy,   Or encouragement • Col. 3:12

2 ᴿfulfill my joy ᴿby being like-minded, having the same love, being of ᴿone accord, of one mind.   John 3:29 • Rom. 12:16 • Phil. 4:2

3 Let nothing be done through selfish ambition or conceit, but in lowliness of mind let each esteem others better than himself.

4 ᴿLet each of you look out not only for his own interests, but also for the interests of ᴿothers.   1 Cor. 13:5 • Rom. 15:1, 2

The Humbled and Exalted Christ

5 ᴿLet this mind be in you which was also in Christ Jesus,   [Matt. 11:29]

6 who, being in the form of God, did not consider it robbery to be equal with God,

7 but made Himself of no reputation, taking the form of a bondservant, and coming in the likeness of men.

8 And being found in appearance as a man, He humbled Himself and ᴿbecame ᴿobedient to the point of death, even the death of the cross.   Matt. 26:39 • Heb. 5:8

9 ᴿTherefore God also ᴿhas highly exalted Him and ᴿgiven Him the name which is above every name,   Heb. 2:9 • Ps. 68:18; Acts 2:33 • Eph. 1:21

10 ᴿthat at the name of Jesus every knee should bow, of those in heaven, and of those on earth, and of those under the earth,   Is. 45:23

11 and ᴿthat every tongue should confess that Jesus Christ is Lord, to the glory of God the Father.   John 13:13

Light Bearers

12 Therefore, my beloved, ᴿas you have always obeyed, not as in my presence only, but now much more in my absence, ᴿwork out your own salvation with ᴿfear and trembling;   Phil. 1:5, 6; 4:15 • John 6:27, 29 • Eph. 6:5

13 for it is God who works in you both to will and to do for His good pleasure.

14 Do all things ᴿwithout ᵀcomplaining and ᴿdisputing,ᵀ   1 Pet. 4:9 • grumbling • Rom. 14:1 • arguing

15 that you may become blameless and ᵀharmless, children of God without fault in the midst of a crooked and perverse generation, among whom you shine as ᴿlights in the world,   innocent • Matt. 5:15, 16

16 holding fast the word of life, so that I

may rejoice in the day of Christ that ᴿI have not run in vain or labored in vain.   Gal. 2:2

17 Yes, and if ᴿI am being poured out as a drink offering on the sacrifice ᴿand service of your faith, ᴿI am glad and rejoice with you all.   2 Tim. 4:6 • Rom. 15:16 • 2 Cor. 7:4

18 For the same reason you also be glad and rejoice with me.

Timothy Commended

19 But I trust in the Lord Jesus to send Timothy to you shortly, that I also may be encouraged when I know your state.

20 For I have no one ᴿlike-minded, who will sincerely care for your state.   2 Tim. 3:10

21 For all seek their own, not the things which are of Christ Jesus.

22 But you know his proven character, ᴿthat as a son with his father he served with me in the gospel.   1 Cor. 4:17

23 Therefore I hope to send him at once, as soon as I see how it goes with me.

24 But I trust in the Lord that I myself shall also come shortly.

Epaphroditus Praised

25 Yet I considered it necessary to send to you ᴿEpaphroditus, my brother, fellow worker, and ᴿfellow soldier, ᴿbut your messenger and ᴿthe one who ministered to my need;   Phil. 4:18 • Philem. 2 • 2 Cor. 8:23 • 2 Cor. 11:9

26 ᴿsince he was longing for you all, and was distressed because you had heard that he was sick.   Phil. 1:8

27 For indeed he was sick almost unto death; but God had mercy on him, and not only on him but on me also, lest I should have sorrow upon sorrow.

28 Therefore I sent him the more eagerly, that when you see him again you may rejoice, and I may be less sorrowful.

29 Receive him therefore in the Lord with all gladness, and hold such men in esteem;

30 because for the work of Christ he came close to death, ᵀnot regarding his life, ᴿto supply what was lacking in your service toward me.   risking • 1 Cor. 16:17

All for Christ

3 Finally, my brethren, rejoice in the Lord. For me to write the same things to you is not tedious, but for you it is safe.

2 Beware of dogs, beware of evil workers, ᴿbeware of the mutilation!   Rom. 2:28

3 For we are the circumcision, who worship *God in the Spirit, rejoice in Christ Jesus, and have no confidence in the flesh,

4 though I also might have confidence in the flesh. If anyone else thinks he may have confidence in the flesh, I more so:

5 circumcised the eighth day, of the stock

of Israel, ᴿof the tribe of Benjamin, ᴿa Hebrew of the Hebrews; concerning the law, ᴿa Pharisee;   Rom. 11:1 • 2 Cor. 11:22 • Acts 23:6

6 concerning zeal, ᴿpersecuting the church; concerning the righteousness which is in the law, blameless.   Acts 8:3; 22:4, 5; 26:9-11

7 But ᴿwhat things were gain to me, these I have counted loss for Christ.   Matt. 13:44

8 Yet indeed I also count all things loss ᴿfor the excellence of the knowledge of Christ Jesus my Lord, for whom I have suffered the loss of all things, and count them as rubbish, that I may gain Christ   Jer. 9:23

9 and be found in Him, not having my own righteousness, which is from the law, but that which is through faith in Christ, the righteousness which is from God by faith;

10 that I may know Him and the power of His resurrection, and the fellowship of His sufferings, being conformed to His death,

11 if, by any means, I may ᵀattain to the resurrection from the dead.   Lit. arrive at

Pressing Toward the Goal

12 Not that I have already ᴿattained,ᵀ or am already perfected; but I press on, that I may lay hold of that for which Christ Jesus has also laid hold of me.   [1 Tim. 6:12, 19] • obtained it

13 Brethren, I do not count myself to have apprehended; but one thing I do, forgetting those things which are behind and reaching forward to those things which are ahead,

14 I press toward the goal for the prize of the upward call of God in Christ Jesus.

15 Therefore let us, as many as are mature, have this mind; and if in anything you think otherwise, God will reveal even this to you.

16 Nevertheless, to the degree that we have already ᵀattained, let us walk by the same *rule, let us be of the same mind.   arrived

Our Citizenship in Heaven

17 Brethren, ᴿjoin in following my example, and note those who so walk, as ᴿyou have us for a pattern.   [1 Cor. 4:16; 11:1] • Titus 2:7, 8

18 For many walk, of whom I have told you often, and now tell you even weeping, that they are the enemies of the cross of Christ:

19 ᴿwhose end is destruction, ᴿwhose god is their belly, and ᴿwhose glory is in their shame—ᴿwho set their mind on earthly things.   2 Cor. 11:15 • 1 Tim. 6:5 • Hos. 4:7 • Rom. 8:5

20 For our citizenship is in heaven, ᴿfrom which we also ᴿeagerly wait for the Savior, the Lord Jesus Christ,   Acts 1:11 • 1 Cor. 1:7

21 who will transform our lowly body that it may be conformed to His glorious body, according to the working by which He is able even to subdue all things to Himself.

4 Therefore, my beloved and longed-for brethren, ᴿmy joy and crown, so ᴿstand fast in the Lord, beloved.   2 Cor. 1:14 • Phil. 1:27

Be United, Joyful, and in Prayer

2 I implore Euodia and I implore Syntyche to be of the same mind in the Lord.

3 *And I urge you also, true companion, help these women who ᴿlabored with me in the gospel, with Clement also, and the rest of my fellow workers, whose names are in ᴿthe Book of Life.   Rom. 16:3 • Luke 10:20

4 ᴿRejoice in the Lord always. Again I will say, rejoice!   Rom. 12:12

5 Let your ᵀgentleness be known to all men. The Lord is at hand.   graciousness

6 ᴿBe anxious for nothing, but in everything by prayer and supplication, with ᴿthanksgiving, let your requests be made known to God;   Matt. 6:25 • [1 Thess. 5:17, 18]

7 and ᴿthe peace of God, which surpasses all understanding, will guard your hearts and minds through Christ Jesus.   [John 14:27]

Meditate on These Things

8 Finally, brethren, whatever things are true, whatever things are noble, whatever things are ᴿjust, ᴿwhatever things are pure, whatever things are ᴿlovely, whatever things are of good report, if there is any virtue and if there is anything praiseworthy—meditate on these things.   Deut. 16:20 • 1 Thess. 5:22 • 1 Cor. 13:4-7

9 The things which you learned and received and heard and saw in me, these do, and the God of peace will be with you.

Philippian Generosity

10 But I rejoiced in the Lord greatly that now at last your care for me has ᵀflourished again; though you surely did care, but you lacked opportunity.   you have revived your care

11 Not that I speak in regard to need, for I have learned in whatever state I am, ᴿto be content: 1 Tim. 6:6, 8

12 I know how to be abased, and I know how to abound. Everywhere and in all things I have learned both to be full and to be hungry, both to abound and to suffer need.

13 I can do all things ᴿthrough *Christ who strengthens me.   John 15:5

14 Nevertheless you have done well that ᴿyou shared in my distress.   Phil. 1:7

15 Now you Philippians know also that in the beginning of the gospel, when I departed from Macedonia, ᴿno church shared with me concerning giving and receiving but you only.   2 Cor. 11:8, 9

16 For even in Thessalonica you sent aid once and again for my necessities.

17 Not that I seek the gift, but I seek ᴿthe fruit that abounds to your account.   Titus 3:14

18 Indeed I ᵀhave all and abound. I am full,

3:16 NU omits rule and the rest of v. 16.

4:3 NU, M Yes
4:13 NU Him who

having received from Epaphroditus the things *sent* from you, a sweet-smelling aroma, ᴿan acceptable sacrifice, well pleasing to God. Or *have received all* • 2 Cor. 9:12

19 And my God ᴿshall supply all your need according to His riches in glory by Christ Jesus. Ps. 23:1

20 ᴿNow to our God and Father *be* glory forever and ever. Amen. Rom. 16:27

Greeting and Blessing

21 Greet every saint in Christ Jesus. The brethren ᴿwho are with me greet you. Gal. 1:2

22 All the saints greet you, but especially those who are of Caesar's household.

23 The grace of our Lord Jesus Christ be with *you all. Amen.

4:23 NU *your spirit*

THE EPISTLE OF PAUL THE APOSTLE TO THE
Colossians

AUTHORSHIP. While Paul awaited trial before Nero he wrote four letters that are traditionally called the "Prison Epistles." One of these is Colossians, in which book he mentions his imprisonment three times in the last chapter (4:3, 10, 18). The book was probably written at the same time as Ephesians, Philippians and Philemon, that is, in the early 60s.

HOW COLOSSIANS FITS INTO THE BIBLE. Though short, Colossians gives a necessary exposé of legalism, cultism and anything that would detract from the absolute deity and preeminence of our Lord Jesus Christ. Chapter 1, along with John 1 and Hebrews 1, is one of the strongest passages to refute the ancient Arian heresy that is still with us in many forms in its denial of the blessed Trinity.

KEY VERSE: 1:18—"And He is the head of the body, the church, who is the beginning, the firstborn from the dead, that in all things He may have the preeminence."

HOW COLOSSIANS FITS TOGETHER. The preeminence of the Lord Jesus Christ shows up in the general outline of the book:

(1) How Christ is Preeminent (1:1—2:7)
(2) Christ's Preeminence over All Teachings and Practices (2:8—3:4)
(3) Christ's Preeminence in the Believer's Life (3:5—4:6)
(4) Concluding Personal Notes (4:7-18)

The town of Colosse was located in what is today Turkey, several days' journey from the ancient city of Ephesus and less than a day's journey from Laodicea (the lukewarm church of the book of Revelation). The Colossian church was founded as a mission work out of Ephesus, under Epaphras, a student of the gospel under Paul. The inhabitants were a mixture of Greeks, Macedonians, descendants of native stock, and Jewish settlers, but primarily they were a Gentile community.

CONTEXT. Paul's knowledge of these people probably came from his early mission work in Galatia and Phrygia and from believers, such as Epaphras, Tychicus, and Onesimus, who brought Paul fresh news regarding the health of the body of Christ—plus bad news of false teachings troubling the Colossians. Thus Paul writes this letter from Rome, and from its content we know that he has not visited this congregation (2:1). Nevertheless, he feels burdened to write and tell them all that he knows about Jesus Christ, the Messiah of the Jews and Savior of the world.

Proceeding to reach out to the Colossians, Paul utilizes the Holy Spirit's insight into their needs, present and future, and grounds them in full revelation of Christ. He reveals Christ as the Savior and God incarnate, who paid the whole debt for sin for everyone, leaving no other work for repentant sinners to do except to trust His word and follow obediently. Then Paul says, since you are now free, let no one trick you Gentile believers into believing you must submit to circumcision, or other human teachings.

In 2:12 Paul suggests that the symbol of baptism says it all: being buried with Christ and raised with Christ means you are now to live as new, born-again people, seeking God's will, loving God's program, practicing God's will.

Thus, you must become Christlike in word and deed and go on to practice such mercy and love toward all others, especially in the home; between wives and husbands, parents and children, slaves and masters.

This letter includes many practical suggestions on how to survive when the apostles are not available for counsel and advice, rebuke or correction. Real believers are to practice love, meditate in the Word of God until filled and transformed, be thankful, be prayerful, and praise God . . . until their Christian walk and talk bear adequate witness to a genuine experience of faith.

Colossians appears to be a concise yet complete expansion of the Good News and is timeless in its practical application. It lifts up the majesty of God and the glory of Jesus Christ, who always was and always will be—"For by Him all things were created that are in heaven and that are on earth, visible and invisible" (1:16). Paul makes it quite clear that Jesus paid it all . . . all to Him we owe! Having nailed the sins of all who trust in Him to the cross, the Lord Jesus proclaims victory for every believer in the power of His resurrection.

—W.H.H.

Greeting

PAUL, an apostle of Jesus Christ by the will of God, and Timothy our brother,

2 To the saints ᴿand faithful brethren in Christ *who are* in Colosse: 1 Cor. 4:17

ᴿGrace to you and peace from God our Father *and the Lord Jesus Christ.   Gal. 1:3

Their Faith in Christ

3 ᴿWe give thanks to the God and Father of our Lord Jesus Christ, praying always for you,   Phil. 1:3
4 since we heard of your faith in Christ Jesus and of your love for all the saints;
5 because of the hope ᴿwhich is laid up for you in heaven, of which you heard before in the word of the truth of the gospel,   [1 Pet. 1:4]
6 which has come to you, as *it has* also in all the world, and is bringing forth *fruit, as *it is* also among you since the day you heard and knew the grace of God in truth;
7 as you also learned from ᴿEpaphras, our dear fellow servant, who is a faithful minister of Christ on your behalf,   Philem. 23

1:2 NU omits *and the Lord Jesus Christ*
1:6 NU, M add *and growing*

8 who also declared to us your ᴿlove in the Spirit.   Rom. 15:30

29-E. God's Will for Individuals   ▼

Preeminence of Christ

9 For this reason we also, since the day we heard it, do not cease to pray for you, and to ask that you may be filled with ᴿthe knowledge of His will ᴿin all wisdom and spiritual understanding;   [Rom. 12:2] • Eph. 1:8
10 that you may walk worthy of the Lord, fully pleasing *Him,* ᴿbeing fruitful in every good work and increasing in the ᴿknowledge of God;   Heb. 13:21 • 2 Pet. 3:18 ▲
11 strengthened with all might, according to His glorious power, ᴿfor all patience and longsuffering ᴿwith joy;   Eph. 4:2 • [Acts 5:41]
12 ᴿgiving thanks to the Father who has qualified us to be partakers of the inheritance of the saints in the light.   [Eph. 5:20]
13 He has delivered us from ᴿthe power of darkness and conveyed *us* into the kingdom of the Son of His love,   Eph. 6:12
14 ᴿin whom we have redemption *through His blood, the forgiveness of sins. Eph. 1:7

1:14 NU, M omit *through His blood*

29-E. God's Will for Individuals (Colossians 1:9, 10)—Are you filled with the knowledge of God's will for your life? Paul said he desired "that you may be filled with the knowledge of His will in all wisdom and spiritual understanding" (v. 9). This verse tells us God has a perfect plan for each believer, so that he or she can please Him and be fruitful in good works. Everyone can know God's will for his or her life in all spiritual wisdom and understanding. This spiritual wisdom does not come from within the natural (carnal) man (1 Cor. 2:14, page 1149); it comes from the throne of God by the prayer of faith.

James tells us that there are two kinds of wisdom. The first is earthly wisdom, born of carnal man. It is a superficial sort of wisdom, a part of this world system that says, "If there is a God, we do not need Him." "This wisdom does not descend from above [from God], but is earthly [beastly], sensual [lust of the flesh], demonic [demon-controlled]. For where envy [jealousy] and self-seeking exist, confusion and every evil thing are there" (James 3:13–16, page 1259). This earthly wisdom will never lead you into the perfect will of God.

The second kind is heavenly wisdom, and is a gift of God to all who meet the requirements in James 1:5–8 (page 1255). "But the wisdom that is from above is first pure, then peaceable, gentle, willing to yield, full of mercy and good fruits, without partiality and without hypocrisy" (James 3:17, page 1259). This heavenly wisdom will reveal God's perfect will for your life when you seek it with your whole heart through prayer and His Word.

Wisdom to know the perfect will of God for your life is a gift of God; spiritual understanding comes from a knowledge of God's revealed will in the Scriptures (2 Tim. 2:15, page 1226). "Therefore do not be unwise, but understand what the will of the Lord is" (Eph. 5:17, page 1192). Yes, God wants you to know His specific plan for your life and understand that in it "all things work together for good to those who love God, to those who are the called according to His purpose" (Rom. 8:28, page 1137).

We pray for spiritual wisdom to know the will of God. We pray for wisdom to read outward expressions of God's providence, to recognize open or closed doors, and always to be spiritually conscious of the indwelling Holy Spirit, who has promised to guide us into all truth. Remember that these outward and inward leadings never contradict the revealed will of God in His Word.

God has made known His perfect will to individuals in every biblical age, and the evidence is overwhelming.

(1) In the age before the Flood, God revealed His plan to the following persons:

(a) To Adam, when He placed him in the Garden of Eden (Gen. 2:15–17, page 4). When Adam and Eve sinned, God sent them out of the Garden and made known His will for them and their descendants, under the curse of sin (Gen. 3:1–24, page 5).

(b) To Enoch, who walked with God for three hundred years (Gen. 5:18–24, page 9).

(c) To Noah, who built the ark according to God's revealed instructions (Gen. 6:9–22, page 12).

(Point 29-E continued on next page)

15 He is the image of the invisible God, ᴿthe firstborn over all creation.   Rev. 3:14

▼ 11-A. Angels: Their Identity

16 For by Him all things were created that are in heaven and that are on earth, visible and invisible, whether thrones or dominions or ᵀprincipalities or powers. All things were ▲ created through Him and for Him.   rulers

17 ᴿAnd He is before all things, and in Him ᴿall things consist.   [John 17:5] • Heb. 1:3

18 And ᴿHe is the head of the body, the church, who is the beginning, ᴿthe firstborn

from the dead, that in all things He may have the preeminence.   Eph. 1:22 • Rev. 1:5

Reconciled in Christ

19 For it pleased the Father that ᴿin Him all the fullness should dwell,   John 1:16

20 and by Him to reconcile all things to Himself, by Him, whether things on earth or things in heaven, ᴿhaving made peace through the blood of His cross.   Eph. 1:10

21 And you, ᴿwho once were alienated and enemies in your mind ᴿby wicked works, yet now He has reconciled   [Eph. 2:1] • Titus 1:15

(Point 29-E continued from previous page)
(2) In the age of the patriarchs, from Abraham to Joshua, God revealed His plan to Abraham, whom He called and commissioned to walk in His will (Gen. 12:1-9, page 17). He failed in his first test and went down into Egypt (Gen. 12:10-20, page 17). He returned to Bethel, where he had built an altar, "And there Abram called on the name of the LORD" (Gen. 13:1-4, page 18). In Egypt he did not build an altar, nor did he call on the name of the Lord. He disobeyed the will of God when he chose his own course of action. No believer is capable of making the right decision merely on the basis of natural wisdom; Abraham was a wise man, but not that wise. When a believer has a decision to make, and he does not know the will of God, he can ask God for wisdom, "and it will be given to him. But let him ask in faith, with no doubting" (James 1:5-8, page 1255).

(3) God raised up the judges, from Othniel to Samuel, to do His will. Some failed the Lord, others walked in His will.

(4) In the kingdom period (from King Saul to King Zedekiah) God, through the prophets, revealed His plan to the kings of Israel and Judah. Some kings rebelled and did evil, but others walked in His will and were blessed by God.

(5) In the church age Jesus said, "For I have come down from heaven, not to do My own will, but the will of Him who sent Me" (John 6:38, page 1059). Jesus (the God-Man), whose will is as perfect as the Father's, united His will with the will of the Father. In this He is our great example. Therefore, we must seek to know and to do the will of God in everything (Col. 3:16, 17, page 1206). It would be difficult to mention all of the New Testament saints who walked in the will of God. Think of the millions of believers, since Jesus' day, who have walked in His will; add to that all the saints of the future who will know His plan for their lives and walk in it. Yes, God does have a perfect plan for your life; may you not rest until you know it, and learn how to walk in it.

See Index, page 17, for your next study.

11-A. Angels: Their Identity (Colossians 1:16)—"For by Him [Christ] all things were created that are in heaven and that are in earth" (v. 16). Angels are created spiritual beings with spiritual bodies: "And of the angels He says: 'Who makes His angels spirits and His ministers a flame of fire' " (Heb. 1:7, page 1236). They were created superior to man. The Lord made man "a little lower than the angels" (Ps. 8:3-5, page 514). However, in heaven we will be exalted above angels because we have been born into the family of God and are "joint heirs with Christ" (Rom. 8:17, page 1137). We have a relationship with Christ that no angel can ever know. Paul asked the church of Corinth, "Do you not know that we shall judge angels?" (1 Cor. 6:3, page 1151). In our glorified bodies we will judge the fallen angels.

(1) Angels are a part of all the things created by Christ, and for Him; they have been "made subject to Him" (1 Pet. 3:22, page 1267).

(2) Angels minister to Christ and His church. After Christ's temptation in the wilderness, "angels came and ministered to Him" (Matt. 4:11, page 935), and they will minister to Christ and His bride forever (Ps. 103:19-22, page 570).

(3) Angels, although spiritual, participate in human affairs at God's bidding. After the resurrection of Jesus, an angel came and rolled back the stone from the tomb to let the world behold the evidence of His bodily resurrection. Then the angel of the Lord sat on the stone. His face was as bright as flashing lightning, and his robe was pure white. The angel told the women to "go quickly and tell His disciples that He is risen from the dead" (Matt. 28:1-8, page 981).

(4) Angels, as part of the invisible spiritual world, will endure eternally. Our text tells us that Christ created all things visible and invisible. He created thrones, visible and invisible. He created dominions, visible and invisible. He created principalities or powers (angels), visible and invisible. The present visible creation will pass away, but the invisible will continue forever and ever, eternity without end (2 Cor. 4:18, page 1168). The things which are not seen are real and eternal; the things which are seen are real but temporal.

See Hebrews 12:22, page 1251, for **Point 11-B: Angels: Their Kinds and Ranks.**

22 in the body of His flesh through death, ^Rto present you holy, and blameless, and above reproach in His sight—   [Eph. 5:27]

23 if indeed you continue ^Rin the faith, grounded and steadfast, and are ^Rnot moved away from the hope of the gospel which you heard, ^Rwhich was preached to every creature under heaven, ^Rof which I, Paul, became a minister.   Eph. 3:17 • [John 15:6] • Col. 1:6 • Col. 1:25

Sacrificial Service for Christ

24 I now rejoice in my sufferings for you, and fill up in my flesh ^Rwhat is lacking in the afflictions of Christ, for ^Rthe sake of His body, which is the church,   [2 Cor. 1:5; 12:15] • Eph. 1:23

25 of which I became a minister according to ^Rthe ^Tstewardship from God which was given to me for you, to fulfill the word of God,   Gal. 2:7 • dispensation or administration

26 the ^Tmystery which has been hidden from ages and from generations, but now has been revealed to His saints.   hidden truth

27 To them God willed to make known what are ^Rthe riches of the glory of this mystery among the Gentiles: *which is Christ in you, the hope of glory.   Rom. 9:23

28 Him we preach, ^Rwarning every man and teaching every man in all wisdom, ^Rthat we may present every man perfect in Christ Jesus.   Acts 20:20 • Eph. 5:27

29 To this end I also labor, striving accord-

ing to His working which works in me ^Rmightily.   Eph. 3:7

Not Philosophy but Christ

2 For I want you to know what a great ^Rconflict^T I have for you and those in Laodicea, and for as many as have not seen my face in the flesh,   Phil. 1:30 • struggle

2 ^Rthat their hearts may be encouraged, being knit together in love, and attaining to all riches of the full assurance of understanding, to the knowledge of the mystery of God, *both of the Father and of Christ,   2 Cor. 1:6

3 ^Rin whom are hidden all the treasures of wisdom and knowledge.   1 Cor. 1:24, 30

4 Now this I say ^Rlest anyone should deceive you with persuasive words.   Rom. 16:18

5 For though I am absent in the flesh, yet I am with you in spirit, rejoicing ^Tto see your good order and the ^Rsteadfastness of your faith in Christ.   Lit. and seeing • 1 Pet. 5:9

6 ^RAs you therefore have received Christ Jesus the Lord, so walk in Him,   1 Thess. 4:1

7 ^Rrooted and built up in Him and established in the faith, as you have been taught, abounding *in it with thanksgiving.   Eph. 2:21

2-D. Know That the Bible Deals in Facts ▼

8 Beware lest anyone ^Tcheat you through philosophy and empty deceit, according to ^Rthe tradition of men, according to the basic

2:2 NU omits both of the Father and
2:7 NU omits in it

1:27 M who

2-D. Know That the Bible Deals in Facts (Colossians 2:8)—"Beware lest anyone cheat you through philosophy and empty deceit, according to the tradition of men . . . and not according to Christ" (v. 8).

Perhaps the greatest lie that has been broadcast by Satan, the arch-liar, is that there is no such thing as "truth"—but only illusions, opinions, and myths. So say humanist philosophers. So say the religions of the East, many of which are now clamoring for the attention of people of the Western world. Such a view is very comforting to many, because if there is no truth, we are all relieved of the responsibility for being right or wrong, true or false. After all, they say, there is no real difference in these "values" anyway—life is just a dream, and truth is all a matter of opinion.

The Bible says that the eternal God is the great, original fact, and that He created a lot of other facts. If nobody respected these facts, everybody would be doing entirely as he or she pleased. But then we would soon be begging to have the biblical view of truth back again, for we all would be reduced to anarchy, savagery, and starvation. So we see how crucial the Bible's world-view is for our very existence.

Thus, when we study the Bible, we need to be aware that although the Bible originated with God in heaven, most of its contents deal with the way we conduct our lives in this world (fact) and with all the other "facts" that God created. Dreamy fantasies about an invisible never-never-land are not biblical thoughts. In the Bible we are confronted with serious realities, whether in this world or in heaven, whether visible or invisible realities.

Here are a few guidelines to help us be more realistic and less fanciful in our Bible study:

(1) We need to pray for the Holy Spirit's illumination:

(a) To overrule a state of mind that prevents the truth from being understood as it is presented in the Word of God. The parable of the sower (Matt. 13:3–23, page 955) demonstrates the importance of this need. It is important that the seed of the Word should fall on prepared soil—minds and hearts made ready by the Holy Spirit. Otherwise the Word is wasted on us.

(b) In order that we may grow spiritually, and not merely in knowledge (1 Pet. 2:2, page 1264). It is possible for us to store up a lot of information from the Scriptures. But this information will not achieve its purpose of transforming our lives unless the Spirit of God enables us to mix the Word with faith.

(2) We need to have sanctified common sense. Studying the Bible in a purely mystical manner is

(Point 2-D continued on next page)

▽ principles of the world, and not according to
▲ Christt.   Lit. *plunder you* or *take you captive* • Gal. 1:14

9 For ᴿin Him dwells all the fullness of the Godhead ᵀbodily;   [John 1:14] • *in bodily form*

10 and you are complete in Him, who is the head of all principality and power.

Not Legalism but Christ

11 In Him you were also circumcised with the circumcision made without hands, by ᴿputting off the body *of the sins of the flesh, by the circumcision of Christ,   Rom. 6:6; 7:24

12 ᴿburied with Him in baptism, in which you also were raised with *Him* through ᴿfaith in the working of God, ᴿwho raised Him from the dead.   Rom. 6:4 • Eph. 1:19, 20 • Acts 2:24

13 And you, being dead in your trespasses and the uncircumcision of your flesh, He has made alive together with Him, having forgiven you all trespasses,

14 having wiped out the handwriting of requirements that was against us, which was contrary to us. And He has taken it out of the way, having nailed it to the cross.

15 ᴿHaving disarmed ᴿprincipalities and powers, He made a public spectacle of them, triumphing over them in it.   [Is. 53:12] • Eph. 6:12

2:11 NU omits *of the sins*

16 So let no one ᴿjudge you in food or in drink, or regarding a ᵀfestival or a new moon or sabbaths,   Rom. 14:3 • *feast day*

17 which are a shadow of things to come, but the ᵀsubstance is of Christ.   Lit. *body*

18 Let no one cheat you of your reward, taking delight in *false* humility and worship of angels, intruding into those things which he has *not seen, vainly puffed up by his fleshly mind,

19 and not holding fast to ᴿthe Head, from whom all the body, nourished and knit together by joints and ligaments, grows with the increase *that is* from God.   Eph. 4:15

20 *Therefore, if you ᴿdied with Christ from the basic principles of the world, why, as *though* living in the world, do you subject yourselves to regulations—   Rom. 6:2–5

21 ᴿ"Do not touch, do not taste, do not handle,"   1 Tim. 4:3

22 which all concern things which perish with the using—ᴿaccording to the commandments and doctrines of men?   Titus 1:14

23 These things indeed have an appearance of wisdom in self-imposed religion, *false* humility, and neglect of the body, *but are* of no value against the indulgence of the flesh.

2:18 NU omits *not*
2:20 NU, M omit *Therefore*

(Point 2-D continued from previous page)
dangerous: an example is closing your eyes and opening your Bible at random to seek an answer wherever your finger points. This procedure, and others like it, can be very injurious. God expects us to be adults in understanding: "In malice be babes, but in understanding be mature" (1 Cor. 14:20, page 1160). There is no understanding when the Bible is treated like a magic device. There is no substitute for careful, patient study, whether study in general or for the purpose of problem-solving.

(3) We need to have a serious respect for the revealed facts of the Bible. "The commandment of the LORD is pure, enlightening the eyes" (Ps. 19:8, page 520). Anybody who has thought about the use of language knows how the meanings of words can be twisted because of a perverse desire to avoid the truth. Sometimes this is done by "allegorizing." For example, the story of Adam and Eve and the fall of humankind is incorrectly treated by some people, not as a fact, but as a "spiritual" story about something that never actually happened, a story which they say is told to teach a general lesson about living. This is an improper method of reading Bible history.

History is about facts. Poetry may be about feelings and attitudes. Sometimes figures of speech are used, especially in biblical poetry, to express a spiritual idea. This is what Isaiah does when he says that "all the trees of the field shall clap their hands" (Is. 55:12, page 696). But such obvious and excellent figures of speech do not justify the mischief of allegorizing what the context plainly indicates as a matter of fact.

Reverence for God and His Word demands that we allegorize only where the context clearly compels us to see this intention in the language. God has no interest in confusing His seeking readers. He always gives us ample indication of His purpose. Here, again, the Holy Spirit must cleanse our thoughts.

(4) The context interprets the text of Scripture. This is a fixed principle in Bible study (and in all kinds of study). All words and statements of a speaker or writer must be understood by the *way* in which the speaker or writer indicates to us how he wishes to be understood—i.e., by the *context* in which the words are placed. Jesus tells us in the Sermon on the Mount that it was said by some that we should love our friends and hate our enemies. However, He goes on to contradict this idea of His contemporaries; He explains that we are indeed to love our enemies (Matt. 5:43, 44, page 942). *Out of context,* the first statement misrepresents the facts, which are properly understood by what follows. This is a common pitfall in Bible study—reading out of context. To avoid this error the Bible should be read primarily in longer *passages* rather than by *verses.* This matter will be discussed in the following point.

See 2 Timothy 2:15, page 1226, for **Point 2-E: Know the Correct Methods of Bible Study.**

▼ **17-B. Heaven Is the Saint's Place**

Not Carnality but Christ

3 If then you were raised with Christ, seek those things which are above, where Christ is, sitting at the right hand of God.

2 Set your mind on things above, not on things on the ᴿearth.   [Matt. 6:19-21]

3 ᴿFor you died, ᴿand your life is hidden ▽ with Christ in God.   [Rom. 6:2] • [2 Cor. 5:7]

4 When Christ *who is* our life appears, then you also will appear with Him in glory. ▲

5 ᴿTherefore put to death ᴿyour members which are on the earth: fornication, uncleanness, passion, evil desire, and covetousness, which is idolatry.   [Rom. 8:13] • [Rom. 6:13]

17-B. Heaven Is the Saint's Place (Colossians 3:1-4)—We have already seen that heaven is a place prepared for the saints of God. A saint is one who, by faith in the Lord Jesus Christ, has been spiritually born into the family of God. "For you are all sons of God through faith in Christ Jesus" (Gal. 3:26, page 1182). We become saints when "the blood of Jesus Christ His Son cleanses us from all sin" (1 John 1:7, page 1278); at the same time the blood of Jesus Christ sanctifies—sets the believer apart for His purpose (Heb. 13:12, page 1252).

(1) The Corinthian church had many doctrinal and moral imperfections. Both of Paul's letters to this church were written to correct their transgressions. He began both epistles reminding them that in spite of their spiritual inadequacies they were

(a) in "the church of God";
(b) "sanctified in Christ Jesus";
(c) "called to be saints" (1 Cor. 1:2, page 1148; cf. 2 Cor. 1:1, page 1165).

The Corinthian believers were saints by virtue of the fact that by faith they were, in Christ, sanctified—set apart for heaven.

(2) Writing to the Colossians, Paul said, "If then you were raised with Christ,

(a) "Seek those [heavenly] things which are above, where Christ is, sitting at the right hand of God" (v. 1). Christ, after His resurrection, entered into heaven itself, "now to appear in the presence of God for us" (Heb. 9:24, page 1244). Therefore, as saints, we have "boldness to enter into the holiest [heaven] by the blood of Jesus" (Heb. 10:19, page 1246), to seek heavenly things.

"For through Him [Christ] we both [Jew and Gentile] have access by one Spirit [the Holy Spirit] to the Father" (Eph. 2:18, page 1188). The least saint has access into the very presence of God in heaven, to seek every heavenly blessing that God offers to the greatest saint. We do not have to wait until after death to enjoy some of the heavenly benefits—they can be ours *now*.

(b) "Set your mind on things above, not on things on the earth" (v. 2). Earthly things are temporal, but heavenly things are eternal (2 Cor. 4:18, page 1168). James warns saints not to be double-minded. He said that a doubter is a "double-minded man, unstable in all his ways" (James 1:8, page 1255). Jesus declared, "No one can serve two masters . . . You cannot serve God and mammon [money]" (Matt. 6:24, page 943).

Before you were saved, your mind was set on earthly things. You had earthly goals and were in love with the things of this world. But now, as a saint, you are "not [to] love the world or the things in the world. If anyone loves the world, the love of the Father is not in him. For all that is in the world—the lust of the flesh, the lust of the eyes, and the pride of life—is not of the Father but is of the world. And the world is passing away, and the lust of it; but he who does the will of God abides forever" (1 John 2:15-17, page 1279). Set your mind on heavenly things.

In this, the Lord Jesus Christ is our perfect example. In Philippians 2:5-8 (page 1197) we have the doctrine of the *kenosis*, which means that when God the Son left heaven to be veiled "in the likeness of sinful flesh" (Rom. 8:3, page 1136), He did not empty Himself of His deity or attributes, "but made Himself of no reputation [He divested Himself of all outward appearance of deity and independent use of His divine attributes], taking the form of a bondservant, and coming in the likeness of men" (Phil. 2:7, page 1197).

In His mind, He was heavenly, holy, humble, and obedient to His undeserved, ignominious death on the cross (Heb. 12:2, page 1250). He took the form of a servant, to do the will of the Father that led Him to Calvary (Is. 53:4-6, page 693). He came down to this earth to please the Father, not Himself (Rom. 15:3, page 1145). His mind was a lowly mind. In Gethsemane He prayed, "O My Father, if this cup cannot pass away from Me unless I drink it, Your will be done" (Matt. 26:42, page 978).

Every saint can have the lowly, heavenly mind of Christ. Paul said, "Let this [lowly] mind be in you which was also in Christ Jesus" (Phil. 2:5, page 1197).

(c) "For you died, and your life is hidden with Christ in God" (v. 3). Before you became a saint, you were dead to God in sin (Is. 59:1, 2, page 698; Eph. 2:1-6, page 1187). Now you are a saint, dead to sin in God. As saints in God we are to regard ourselves as "dead indeed to sin, but alive to God in Christ Jesus our Lord" (Rom. 6:11, page 1134). Count it so, because it is so according to the Scriptures (Rom. 6:6, 7, page 1134; Gal. 2:20, page 1180).

Now we come to the saint's heavenly safety. First, the saint's life is "hidden with Christ"—this is

(Point 17-B continued on next page)

6 ᴿBecause of these things the wrath of God is coming upon ᴿthe sons of disobedience,   Rom. 1:18 · [Eph. 2:2]

7 ᴿin which you yourselves once walked when you lived in them.   1 Cor. 6:11

8 ᴿBut now you yourselves are to put off all these: anger, wrath, malice, blasphemy, filthy language out of your mouth.   Eph. 4:22

9 Do not lie to one another, since you have put off the old man with his deeds,

10 and have put on the new *man* who is renewed in knowledge according to the image of Him who ᴿcreated him,   [Eph. 2:10]

11 where there is neither ᴿGreek nor Jew, circumcised nor uncircumcised, barbarian, Scythian, slave *nor* free, ᴿbut Christ *is* all and in all.   Gal. 3:27, 28 · Eph. 1:23

Character of the New Man

12 Therefore, as *the* elect of God, holy and beloved, ᴿput on tender mercies, kindness, humility, meekness, longsuffering;   1 John 3:17

13 ᴿbearing with one another, and forgiving one another, if anyone has a complaint against another; even as Christ forgave you, so you also *must do.*   [Mark 11:25]

14 But above all these things ᴿput on love, which is the bond of perfection.   [1 Cor. 13]

15 And let the peace of God rule in your hearts, to which also you were called ᴿin one body; and ᴿbe thankful.   Eph. 4:4 · [1 Thess. 5:18]

25-C. The Christian Life Is a Service Life ▼

16 Let the word of Christ dwell in you richly in all wisdom, teaching and admonish-

---

(Point 17-B continued from previous page)
safety. Second, the saint's life is "hidden with Christ in God" (v. 3)—this is double safety. Third, the saint is "sealed with the Holy Spirit of promise" (Eph. 1:13, 14, page 1186)—this is triple safety. The believer is sealed by the Holy Spirit, hidden with Christ in God. This is heavenly safety in the Holy Trinity. To strengthen your faith in this heavenly fact see John 10:27-29 (page 1068) and Romans 8:35-39 (page 1138).

(d) "When Christ who is our life appears, then you also will appear with Him in glory" (v. 4). The saints will bask in the glory of God forever and ever. The following great prophetic events will occur after Christ's second coming, but before the new heaven, new earth, and New Jerusalem:

(i) The rapture of the church (1 Thess. 4:13-17, page 1211).

(ii) The seven years of Tribulation (Jer. 30:7, page 743; Dan. 9:27, page 851; Matt. 24:8-31, page 973; see also Point 51-C, "The Vision of the Seventy Weeks," page 848).

(iii) The conversion of Israel (Ezek. 20:34-38, page 796; 37:1-28, page 815). This is the *spiritual* resurrection of those from the twelve tribes who are alive and receive the gospel during the Great Tribulation (Zech. 12:10—13:1, page 918; Rom. 11:26, page 1141; Rev. 7:1-17, page 1300).

(iv) The judgment seat of Christ (2 Cor. 5:10, page 1168; see also Point 18-C, "The Judgment of the Believer's Works," page 1168).

(v) The marriage supper of the Lamb (Rev. 19:6-9, page 1312).

(vi) The second coming of Christ. At the end of the seven years of Tribulation, Christ will return to this earth with His bride to end the Battle of Armageddon (Rev. 16:13-16, page 1309; 19:17-19, page 1313; cf. Zech. 14:3, page 919; Matt. 24:21, 22, 29, 30, page 973).

(vii) The doom of the Beast and the False Prophet (Rev. 19:20, page 1313).

(viii) Satan bound and cast into the bottomless pit for a thousand years (Rev. 20:2, 3, page 1313).

(ix) The judgment of the nations. At the beginning of the Millennium, the Lord Jesus Christ will judge the living nations (Matt. 25:31-46, page 976; see also Point 18-D, "The Judgment of the Nations," page 976).

(x) The kingdom reign of the Lord Jesus Christ (Rev. 20:6, page 1313; cf. Is. 9:6, 7, page 651).

(xi) Satan released from the bottomless pit. At the end of the thousand years, Satan will be released from the bottomless pit to go out and deceive the unsaved of the kingdom, after which God will destroy them with fire from heaven (Rev. 20:7-9, page 1313).

(xii) Satan cast into the lake of fire. He, along with the Beast and the False Prophet, "will be tormented day and night forever and ever" (Rev. 20:10, page 1313).

(xiii) The Great White Throne judgment (Rev. 20:11-15, page 1313; see also Point 18-E, "The Judgment of the Wicked," page 1313).

(xiv) The destruction of the present heaven and earth by fire (2 Pet. 3:10-12, page 1276).

(xv) The new heaven, new earth, and New Jerusalem (2 Pet. 3:13, page 1276; Rev. 21:1, 2, page 1314). This is the end of the old world system and the beginning of the new—"Behold, I make all things new" (Rev. 21:5, page 1315).

See Isaiah 65:17, page 704, for **Point 17-C: Heaven Is an Eternal Place.**

25-C. The Christian Life Is a Service Life (Colossians 3:16, 17)—In verses 16 and 17, the Holy Spirit, through the apostle Paul, reveals four things that admonish and give direction to the Lord's servants:

(1) "Let the word of Christ dwell in you richly." The words of Christ are found in the Gospels, Acts, and Revelation, and are quoted in other New Testament books. The Word of Christ will make you rich in all spiritual wisdom and knowledge (Rom. 11:33, page 1142).

(Point 25-C continued on next page)

▽ ing one another ᴿin psalms and hymns and spiritual songs, singing with grace in your hearts to the Lord.   Eph. 5:19

17 And *whatever* you do in word or deed, *do* all in the name of the Lord Jesus, giving ▲ thanks to God the Father through Him.

The Christian Home

18 ᴿWives, submit to your own husbands, ᴿas is fitting in the Lord.   1 Pet. 3:1 • [Eph. 5:22—6:9]

19 ᴿHusbands, love your wives and do not be ᴿbitter toward them.   [Eph. 5:25] • Eph. 4:31

20 Children, obey your parents in all things, for this is well pleasing to the Lord.

21 ᴿFathers, do not provoke your children, lest they become discouraged.   Eph. 6:4

22 ᴿBondservants, obey in all things your masters according to the flesh, not with eyeservice, as men-pleasers, but in sincerity of heart, fearing God.   Eph. 6:5

23 ᴿAnd whatever you do, do it heartily, as to the Lord and not to men,   [Eccl. 9:10]

24 ᴿknowing that from the Lord you will receive the reward of the inheritance; ᴿfor* you serve the Lord Christ.   Eph. 6:8 • 1 Cor. 7:22

25 But he who does wrong will be repaid for what he has done, and there is no partiality.

4 Masters,ᴿ give your bondservants what is just and fair, knowing that you also have a Master in heaven.   Eph. 6:9

Christian Graces

2 ᴿContinue earnestly in prayer, being vigilant in it with thanksgiving;   Luke 18:1

3 ᴿmeanwhile praying also for us, that God would ᴿopen to us a door for the word, to speak the ᵀmystery of Christ, for which I am also in chains,   Eph. 6:19 • 1 Cor. 16:9 • *hidden truth*

3:24 NU omits *for*

(Point 25-C continued from previous page)

(2) "In all wisdom, teaching and admonishing one another." When the Holy Spirit makes you rich in the Word of Christ, you are to share it with others. The riches of His saving grace are to be shared with the lost (Matt. 28:19, page 982; cf. John 3:15, 18, page 1052). When the Holy Spirit gives us a greater understanding of any part of God's Word we are to pass it on to other servants of Christ.

(3) "In psalms and hymns and spiritual songs, singing with grace in your hearts to the Lord." This is worship. You are never qualified to serve until you first worship your Lord (see introduction to Master Outline 28, "Worship," page 44).

(4) "And *whatever* you do":

(a) "In word"—preach a sermon, teach a Sunday school lesson, read the Bible to the sick and pray with them, hand out a gospel tract, share God's plan of salvation with a lost soul.

(b) "Or deed"—clean the house, cook a meal, mow the lawn, run a business. Do whatever your lot in life is.

(c) "Do all in the name of the Lord Jesus"—regardless of how meager the task, if you will do it to the glory of God you will be blessed rather than frustrated.

(d) "Giving thanks to God the Father through Him" (vv. 16, 17). We often miss the greatest spiritual blessing when we do a good deed and then think, "This is beneath me, I am too big to have to perform such a small task." Jesus said, "For whoever gives you a cup of water to drink in My name, because you belong to Christ, assuredly, I say to you, he will by no means lose his reward" (Mark 9:41, page 996).

Every born-again Christian is to serve his Lord and Master, Jesus Christ. Paul called himself "a bondservant of Jesus Christ" (Rom. 1:1, page 1128). A bondservant was one sold into slavery for the rest of his life. Paul wrote to the church at Corinth reminding them of who they were in Christ (1 Cor. 6:19, 20, page 1152).

(1) "Do you not know that your body is the temple of the Holy Spirit who is in you?" Every believer has the indwelling Holy Spirit.

(2) "You are not your own." You belong to the Lord Jesus Christ, body, soul, and spirit.

(3) "For you were bought at a price." His holy, sinless life was the price He paid for you.

The life of service requires total commitment. "I beseech you therefore, brethren, by the mercies of God, that you present your bodies a living sacrifice, holy, acceptable to God, which is your reasonable [spiritual] service" (Rom. 12:1, page 1142). Christian services are of and by the Holy Spirit; therefore, they are spiritually discerned. If you are not a born-again child of God, this lesson to you is foolishness. Paul said, "For the message of the cross is foolishness to those who are perishing, but to us who are being saved it is the power of God" (1 Cor. 1:18, page 1148).

In the parable of the talents, the man who received five talents invested them and gained five more for His lord, who rewarded him saying, "Well done, good and faithful servant; you were faithful over a few things, I will make you ruler over many things. Enter into the joy of your lord" (Matt. 25:21, page 975). Likewise, the man with two talents was rewarded because he was faithful in the small things. Someone said, "There is nothing little about God and nothing great apart from Him." You cannot do a little thing for God if you will do it to His glory.

The Christian life is a life of service that will be rewarded here on earth and in heaven (see Master Outline 48, "Crowns for Christians," page 59).

See 2 Corinthians 10:3–5, page 1173, for **Point 25-D: The Christian Life Is a Warring Life.**

4 that I may make it manifest, as I ought to speak.

5 Walk in ᴿwisdom toward those who are outside, redeeming the time.   [Matt. 10:16]

6 Let your speech always be ᴿwith grace, seasoned with salt, that you may know how you ought to answer each one.   Eccl. 10:12

Final Greetings

7 Tychicus, a beloved brother, faithful minister, and fellow servant in the Lord, will tell you all the news about me.

8 ᴿI am sending him to you for this very purpose, that *he may know your circumstances and comfort your hearts,   Eph. 6:22

9 with ᴿOnesimus, a faithful and beloved brother, who is one of you. They will make known to you all things which are happening here.   Philem. 10

10 Aristarchus my fellow prisoner greets you, with ᴿMark the cousin of Barnabas (about whom you received instructions: if he comes to you, welcome him),   2 Tim. 4:11

11 and Jesus who is called Justus. These are my only fellow workers for the kingdom of God who are of the circumcision; they have proved to be a comfort to me.

4:8 NU you may know our circumstances and he may comfort

12 Epaphras, who is one of you, a bondservant of Christ, greets you, always laboring fervently for you in prayers, that you may stand perfect and *complete in all the will of God.

13 For I bear him witness that he has a great *zeal for you, and those who are in Laodicea, and those in Hierapolis.

14 ᴿLuke the beloved physician and ᴿDemas greet you.   2 Tim. 4:11 • 2 Tim. 4:10

15 Greet the brethren who are in Laodicea, and *Nymphas and ᴿthe church that is in *his house.   Rom. 16:5

Closing Exhortations and Blessing

16 Now when ᴿthis epistle is read among you, see that it is read also in the church of the Laodiceans, and that you likewise read the epistle from Laodicea.   1 Thess. 5:27

17 And say to ᴿArchippus, "Take heed to the ministry which you have received in the Lord, that you may fulfill it."   Philem. 2

18 ᴿThis salutation by my own hand—Paul. ᴿRemember my chains. Grace be with you. Amen.   1 Cor. 16:21 • Heb. 13:3

4:12 NU fully assured
4:13 NU concern
4:15 NU Nympha • NU her

THE FIRST EPISTLE OF PAUL THE APOSTLE TO THE
Thessalonians

AUTHORSHIP. 1 Thessalonians is considered one of Paul's earliest letters, written about A.D. 51. It reveals the apostle as a tender, affectionate man with a great concern for the spiritual welfare of his converts. This letter also shows the purity of Paul's motive, his compassion, and dedication. His innermost feelings are manifest in these pages.

CONTEXT. 1 Thessalonians interestingly shows the rich doctrine found even in the primitive evangelism of the early church. Apparently the apostle Paul had spent only one month teaching the Thessalonians basic Christian truths when he was in their city (Acts 17:2). In that time these people were enlightened from total heathenism to the Christian hope. A strong point in Paul's teaching throughout this epistle was to give them hope while living in anticipation of the Lord's return. He repeatedly challenges them to a practical Christian walk in preparation for this great event. The passage, 4:13—5:11, is one of the fullest New Testament developments of this crucial truth.

As Paul reflects on his personal experiences with this church, he points out several areas of weakness—laziness and sexual sins in particular. Paul also encourages the believer to live in faith, love, and hope as he anticipates the imminent return of our Lord and Savior Jesus Christ.

HOW 1 THESSALONIANS FITS INTO THE BIBLE. 1 Thessalonians has a unique contribution to the New Testament as a bridge between Paul's missionary work in Acts and the predictions of the future in Revelation. No other book tells us as much about the rapture of the church as 1 Thessalonians (4:13-18). It also has a great deal to say about the day of the Lord (5:1-11). The coming of Christ is so important in this book that every single chapter has something to say about it.

HOW 1 THESSALONIANS FITS TOGETHER. The two outstanding major sections of 1 Thessalonians are (1) Personal Experience (chs. 1—3) and (2) Practical Exhortation (chs. 4, 5).

Many models are pictured in this great book. Chapter 1 gives us a view of the model church and virtues of the Christian life. Chapter 2 gives a distinctive coverage of the model servant and his reward. The character traits of a model believer are clearly portrayed in chapter 3 in the feelings expressed toward the brethren within the church at Thessalonica. In chapters 4 and 5 we have an example of the model walk of santification and the ultimate hope of the believer while eagerly awaiting the Lord's return.

The final analysis of this book is the reflection of Christ as seen in the believer's hope of salvation both now and at His coming. When Christ returns, He will deliver (1:10; 5:4-11), reward (2:19), perfect (3:13), resurrect (4:13-18), and sanctify (5:23) all who trust Him. What a tremendous reward the believer has!

—M.R.B.

Greeting

PAUL, ᴿSilvanus, and Timothy,   1 Pet. 5:12

To the church of the ᴿThessalonians in God the Father and the Lord Jesus Christ:

Grace to you and peace *from God our Father and the Lord Jesus Christ.   1 Pet. 5:12

Their Good Example

2 We give thanks to God always for you all, making mention of you in our prayers,

3 remembering without ceasing ᴿyour work of faith, ᴿlabor of love, and patience of hope in our Lord Jesus Christ in the sight of our God and Father,   John 6:29 · Rom. 16:6

4 knowing, beloved brethren, ᴿyour election by God.   Col. 3:12

1:1 NU omits *from God our Father and the Lord Jesus Christ*

5 For ᴿour gospel did not come to you in word only, but also in power, ᴿand in the Holy Spirit ᴿand in much assurance, as you know what kind of men we were among you for your sake.   Mark 16:20 · 2 Cor. 6:6 · Heb. 2:3

6 And you became followers of us and of the Lord, having received the word in much affliction, with joy of the Holy Spirit,

7 so that you became examples to all in Macedonia and Achaia who believe.

8 For from you the word of the Lord ᴿhas sounded forth, not only in Macedonia and Achaia, but also ᴿin every place. Your faith toward God has gone out, so that we do not need to say anything.   Rom. 10:18 · Rom. 1:8; 16:19

9 For they themselves declare concerning us what manner of entry we had to you, ᴿand how you turned to God from idols to serve the living and true God,   1 Cor. 12:2

10 and to wait for His Son from heaven,

whom He raised from the dead, *even* Jesus who delivers us from the wrath to come.

Paul's Conduct

2 For you yourselves know, brethren, that our coming to you was not in vain.

2 But *even after we had suffered before and were spitefully treated at Philippi, as you know, we were bold in our God to speak to you the gospel of God in much conflict.

3 For our exhortation *did* not *come* from error or uncleanness, nor *was it* in deceit.

4 But as we have been approved by God ᴿto be entrusted with the gospel, even so we speak, ᴿnot as pleasing men, but God ᴿwho tests our hearts.   Titus 1:3 • Gal. 1:10 • Prov. 17:3

5 For neither at any time did we use flattering words, as you know, nor a ᵀcloak for covetousness—God *is* witness.   *pretext*

6 Nor did we seek glory from men, either from you or from others, when we might have made demands as apostles of Christ.

7 But we were gentle among you, just as a nursing *mother* cherishes her own children.

8 So, affectionately longing for you, we were well pleased to impart to you not only the gospel of God, but also our own lives, because you had become dear to us.

9 For you remember, brethren, our labor and toil; for laboring night and day, that we might not be a burden to any of you, we preached to you the gospel of God.

10 You *are* witnesses, and God *also*, how devoutly and justly and blamelessly we behaved ourselves among you who believe;

11 as you know how we exhorted, and comforted, and *charged every one of you, as a father *does* his own children,

2:2 NU, M omit *even*
2:11 NU, M *implored*

12 ᴿthat you would walk worthy of God ᴿwho calls you into His own kingdom and glory.   Eph. 4:1 • 1 Cor. 1:9

Their Conversion

13 For this reason we also thank God without ceasing, because when you received the word of God which you heard from us, you welcomed *it* not *as* the word of men, but as it is in truth, the word of God, which also effectively works in you who believe.

14 For you, brethren, became imitators ᴿof the churches of God which are in Judea in Christ Jesus. For ᴿyou also suffered the same things from your own countrymen, just as they *did* from the Judeans,   Gal. 1:22 • Acts 17:5

15 ᴿwho killed both the Lord Jesus and their own prophets, and have persecuted us; and they do not please God ᴿand are ᵀcontrary to all men,   Acts 2:23 • Esth. 3:8 • *hostile*

16 forbidding us to speak to the Gentiles that they may be saved, so as always to fill up *the measure of* their sins; ᴿbut wrath has come upon them to the uttermost.   Matt. 24:6

Longing to See Them

17 But we, brethren, having been taken away from you for a short time ᴿin presence, not in heart, endeavored more eagerly to see your face with great desire.   1 Cor. 5:3

18 Therefore we wanted to come to you— even I, Paul, time and again—but ᴿSatan hindered us.   Rom. 1:13; 15:22

48-C. The Crown of Rejoicing   ▼

19 For what *is* our hope, or joy, or crown of rejoicing? *Is it* not even you in the presence of our Lord Jesus Christ at His coming?

20 For you are our glory and joy.   ▲

48-C. The Crown of Rejoicing (1 Thessalonians 2:19, 20)—The "crown of rejoicing" (v. 19) is the soul winner's crown. The greatest work you are privileged to do for the Lord is to bring others to a knowledge of Christ as Savior. Much of your joy in heaven will be determined by the souls you have had a part in bringing to Christ. Paul tells the Thessalonian believers that they are his "glory and joy," now and when Jesus comes.

The Bible also gives these reasons for winning souls:

(1) It is wise to win souls to Christ (Prov. 11:30, page 606).
(2) It is an attack on sin to win souls to Christ (James 5:20, page 1261).
(3) It is a cause for joy in heaven to win souls to Christ (Luke 15:10, page 1034).
(4) Soul winners will shine as the stars forever (Dan. 12:3, page 856).

How you can win souls to Christ:

(1) Witness with your life—live so that others may see Christ in you (2 Cor. 3:2, page 1166; cf. Gal. 2:20, page 1180).
(2) Witness with your mouth, trusting the Holy Spirit to give power to the spoken word (Acts 1:8, page 1086).
(3) Witness by tithes and offerings, so that others may preach Christ, and you will have "fruit [reward] that abounds to your account" (Phil. 4:15–17, page 1198; cf. 2 Cor. 9:6, page 1172).

God has promised that your labor will not be in vain in the Lord (1 Cor. 15:58, page 1163). The soul winner will not rejoice alone—all of heaven will rejoice with him when he receives the "crown of rejoicing" (v. 19).

See 2 Timothy 4:5–8, page 1228, for **Point 48-D: The Crown of Righteousness.**

Concern for Their Faith

3 Therefore, when we could no longer endure it, we thought it good to be left in Athens alone,

2 and sent ᴿTimothy, our brother and minister of God, and our fellow laborer in the gospel of Christ, to establish you and encourage you concerning your faith,   Rom. 16:21

3 ᴿthat no one should be shaken by these afflictions; for you yourselves know that ᴿwe are appointed to this.   Eph. 3:13 • Acts 9:16; 14:22

4 For, in fact, we told you before when we were with you that we would suffer tribulation, just as it happened, and you know.

5 For this reason, when I could no longer endure it, I sent to know your faith, lest by some means the tempter had tempted you, and ᴿour labor might be in vain.   Gal. 2:2

Encouraged by Timothy

6 ᴿBut now that Timothy has come to us from you, and brought us good news of your faith and love, and that you always have good remembrance of us, greatly desiring to see us, ᴿas we also to see you—   Acts 18:5 • Phil. 1:8

7 therefore, brethren, in all our affliction and distress ᴿwe were comforted concerning you by your faith.   2 Cor. 1:4

8 For now we live, if you ᴿstand fast in the Lord.   Phil. 4:1

9 For what thanks can we render to God for you, for all the joy with which we rejoice for your sake before our God,

10 night and day praying exceedingly that we may see your face ᴿand perfect what is lacking in your faith?   2 Cor. 13:9

Prayer for the Church

11 Now may our God and Father Himself, and our Lord Jesus Christ, ᴿdirect our way to you.   Mark 1:3

12 And may the Lord make you increase and ᴿabound in love to one another and to all, just as we do to you,   Phil. 1:9

13 so that He may establish ᴿyour hearts blameless in holiness before our God and Father at the coming of our Lord Jesus Christ with all His saints.   2 Thess. 2:17

Plea for Purity

4 Finally then, brethren, we urge and exhort in the Lord Jesus ᴿthat you should abound more and more, ᴿjust as you received from us how you ought to walk and to please God;   1 Cor. 15:58 • Phil. 1:27

2 for you know what commandments we gave you through the Lord Jesus.

3 For this is ᴿthe will of God, ᴿyour sanctification: ᴿthat you should abstain from sexual immorality;   [Rom. 12:2] • Eph. 5:27 • [1 Cor. 6:15–20]

4 ᴿthat each of you should know how to possess his own vessel in sanctification and honor,   Rom. 6:19

5 ᴿnot in passion of lust, like the Gentiles ᴿwho do not know God;   Col. 3:5 • 1 Cor. 15:34

6 that no one should take advantage of and defraud his brother in this matter, because the Lord is the avenger of all such, as we also forewarned you and testified.

7 For God did not call us to uncleanness, ᴿbut in holiness.   Lev. 11:44

8 ᴿTherefore he who rejects this does not reject man, but God, ᴿwho* has also given us His Holy Spirit.   Luke 10:16 • 1 Cor. 2:10

A Brotherly and Orderly Life

9 But concerning brotherly love you have no need that I should write to you, for ᴿyou yourselves are taught by God ᴿto love one another;   [Jer. 31:33, 34] • Matt. 22:39

10 and indeed you do so toward all the brethren who are in all Macedonia. But we urge you, brethren, ᴿthat you increase more and more;   1 Thess. 3:12

11 that you also aspire to lead a quiet life, to mind your own business, and to work with your own hands, as we commanded you,

12 ᴿthat you may walk properly toward those who are outside, and that you may lack nothing.   Rom. 13:13

49-A. The Rapture of the Church   ▼

The Comfort of Christ's Coming

13 But I do not want you to be ignorant, brethren, concerning those who have fallen

4:8 NU who also gives

49-A. The Rapture of the Church (1 Thessalonians 4:13–18)—The word "rapture" (caught up physically and in ecstasy) has come into popular use today to refer to the Lord Jesus' coming for His bride (the church), to lift her up into the heavens (v. 17). It comes from the word *rapio* in the Latin Bible's translation of this verse. One raptured is "lifted up" in love.

The fact that the apostle refers to the believers who have died as those who "sleep in Jesus" (v. 14) is a powerful consolation to those who have buried Christian loved ones. They will be with Jesus when He returns a second time.

Note that here Christ comes *for* His church; at Armageddon Christ comes *with* His church (Rev. 19:14, page 1312).

(1) There will be a shout. "For the Lord Himself will descend from heaven with a shout, with the voice of an archangel" (v. 16). The archangel is believed to be Gabriel, God's messenger. His shout will awaken

(Point 49-A continued on next page)

▽ ᵀasleep, lest you sorrow ᴿas others ᴿwho have no hope.   Died • Lev. 19:28 • [Eph. 2:12]

14 For if we believe that Jesus died and rose again, even so God will bring with Him ᴿthose who *sleep in Jesus.   1 Cor. 15:20, 23

15 For this we say to you by the word of the Lord, that we who are alive *and* remain until the coming of the Lord will by no means precede those who are ᵀasleep.   Dead

16 For the Lord Himself will descend from heaven with a shout, with the voice of an archangel, and with the trumpet of God. And the dead in Christ will rise first.

17 Then we who are alive *and* remain shall be caught up together with them ᴿin the clouds to meet the Lord in the air. And thus we shall always be with the Lord.   Acts 1:9

18 ᴿTherefore comfort one another with ▲ these words.   1 Thess. 5:11

The Day of the Lord

5 But concerning ᴿthe times and the seasons, brethren, you have no need that I should write to you.   Matt. 24:3

2 For you yourselves know perfectly that ᴿthe day of the Lord so comes as a thief in the night.   [2 Pet. 3:10]

3 For when they say, "Peace and safety!" then ᴿsudden destruction comes upon them, ᴿas labor pains upon a pregnant woman. And they shall not escape.   Is. 13:6–9 • Hos. 13:13

4 ᴿBut you, brethren, are not in darkness,

4:14 Or *through Jesus sleep*

so that this Day should overtake you as a thief.   1 John 2:8

5 You are all sons of light and sons of the day. We are not of the night nor of darkness.

6 Therefore let us not sleep, as others *do*, but let us watch and be ᵀsober.   *self-controlled*

7 For those who sleep, sleep at night, and those who get drunk are drunk at night.

8 But let us who are of the day be sober, putting on the breastplate of faith and love, and *as* a helmet the hope of salvation.

9 For ᴿGod did not appoint us to wrath, ᴿbut to obtain salvation through our Lord Jesus Christ,   Rom. 9:22 • [2 Thess. 2:13]

10 who died for us, that whether we wake or sleep, we should live together with Him.

11 Therefore comfort each other and edify one another, just as you also are doing.

Various Exhortations

12 And we urge you, brethren, to recognize those who labor among you, and are over you in the Lord and ᵀadmonish you,   *warn*

13 and to esteem them very highly in love for their work's sake. ᴿBe at peace among yourselves.   Mark 9:50

14 Now we ᵀexhort you, brethren, warn those who are ᵀunruly, comfort the fainthearted, uphold the weak, ᴿbe patient with all.   *encourage • insubordinate* or *idle* • Gal. 5:22

15 See that no one renders evil for evil to anyone, but always ᴿpursue what is good both for yourselves and for all.   Gal. 6:10

16 ᴿRejoice always,   [2 Cor. 6:10]

(Point 49-A continued from previous page)
the dead in Christ. The sea and the earth will give up the bodies that will be raised and glorified (John 5:25, page 1057).

(2) "The trumpet of God" will sound (v. 16). This should not be coupled with the blowing of the trumpets of Revelation 8, 9, or 11 (page 1301). Paul calls this the "last trumpet" in 1 Corinthians 15:51, 52 (page 1163), referring to the Roman army's practice of leaving a camp by three trumpet calls. Figuratively speaking, the first signaled the "get ready;" the second, "load up;" and the "last trumpet" was "move out."

(3) "The dead in Christ will rise first" (v. 16).

(a) When He comes, Jesus will bring the souls and spirits of the dead in Christ with Him, and they will enter into their new "incorruptible," resurrected, glorified bodies (1 Cor. 15:52–54, page 1163).

(b) We who will be alive at Christ's coming, will not precede those who are asleep in Christ (v. 15).

(c) "The rest of the dead" (the lost unbelievers) are not raised until the thousand-year (millennial) period is over (Rev. 20:5, page 1313).

(4) Then the living believers will be "caught up"—raptured (v. 17).

(a) The believers who are alive at that time will be changed "in a moment, in the twinkling of an eye."

(b) Paul calls it a "mystery" (a secret revealed to believers) that there will be a generation of Christians yet alive when Christ comes for His bride. These fortunate ones will never die physically, but will be "changed" (1 Cor. 15:51, 52, page 1163).

(5) The transformed living believers will then join the "dead in Christ" who have been raised first (vv. 16, 17). If Christ could physically ascend into the clouds, as He did (Acts 1:9, page 1087), then believers can also; and they will, by the power of the Creator, who can override His own physical laws at will.

(6) Together His bride will "meet the Lord in the air" (v. 17). That they are caught up "in the clouds" (v. 17) may suggest that under cover of the earthly clouds, they will be transported as Jesus was at His ascension (Acts 1:9, page 1087) to that other dimension—heaven, where God dwells in the "many mansions" of which Jesus spoke (John 14:2, page 1074). Others believe these are clouds of angels or saints.

See Matthew 24:9–30, page 973, for **Point 49-B: The Tribulation on the Earth.**

▼ **30-D. Pray Without Ceasing**

17 ᴿpray without ceasing,   Eph. 6:18
18 in everything give thanks; for this is the
▲ will of God in Christ Jesus for you.
19 ᴿDo not quench the Spirit.   Eph. 4:30
20 ᴿDo not despise prophecies.   1 Cor. 14:1, 31
21 Test all things; hold fast what is good.
22 Abstain from every form of evil.

Blessing and Admonition

23 Now may the God of peace Himself
ᴿsanctifyᵀ you completely; and may your

whole spirit, soul, and body ᴿbe preserved
blameless at the coming of our Lord Jesus
Christ.   1 Thess. 3:13 • *set you apart* • 1 Cor. 1:8, 9
24 He who calls you *is* ᴿfaithful, who also
will ᴿdo *it*.   [1 Cor. 10:13] • Phil. 1:6
25 Brethren, pray for us.
26 Greet all the brethren with a holy kiss.
27 I charge you by the Lord that this epistle
be read to all the *holy brethren.
28 The grace of our Lord Jesus Christ *be*
with you. Amen.

5:27 NU omits *holy*

30-D. Pray Without Ceasing (1 Thessalonians 5:17, 18)—As Paul closed his first letter to the Christians at
Thessalonica, he stirred them with a series of brief exhortations (vv. 14–22). Among these we find the words,
"Pray without ceasing, in everything give thanks" (vv. 17, 18). Here are some life-long lessons for the believer
regarding his prayer life:

(1) Pray continually (v. 17). This command concerns the time of prayer. It urges the believer to a
continual life of prayer with God—morning, noon, and night (Dan. 6:10, page 843). It teaches the Christian
always to be in the attitude of prayer, and to be conscious of God's invisible presence.

(2) Pray continually, giving thanks in everything (v. 18). Prayer can wrongly become dominated by our
asking "things" of God. Although asking is indeed a definite, legitimate, and biblically commanded part of
prayer (Matt. 7:7, page 945), our prayers, like our attitudes in life, must be balanced. They should include
constant thanksgiving—for the many blessings God sends our way, as well as for the trials which He allows
us to face in order to mold us in Christ's image (Rom. 8:29, page 1137).

We must thank Him for mercies even in these difficult times, for "we know that all things work together
for good to those who love God" (Rom. 8:28, page 1137) and that "neither death nor life, nor angels nor
principalities nor powers, nor things present nor things to come, nor height nor depth, nor any other created
thing," shall be able to "separate us from the love of God which is in Christ Jesus our Lord" (Rom. 8:35–39,
page 1138; cf. James 1:2–4, page 1255).

(3) Pray continually, and don't faint. Christ urges us not to cease praying when we do not see our
problems disappear immediately. "Then He spoke a parable to them, that men always ought to pray and not
lose heart" (Luke 18:1, page 1037). Pray on, "pray without ceasing."

(4) Pray continually, "casting all your care upon Him, for He cares for you" (1 Pet. 5:7, page 1268).

(5) Pray continually, but "do not use vain repetitions" (Matt. 6:7, page 943).

(6) Pray continually, but not with an unforgiving heart (Matt. 6:14, 15, page 943).

(7) Pray continually, but not to be seen and admired by men (Matt. 6:5, page 942).

(8) Pray continually, including your enemies in your prayers (Matt. 5:44, page 942). This will help you to
see that they often face more severe problems than those difficulties they cause you to endure.

(9) Pray continually, "lest you enter into temptation" (Matt. 26:41, page 978).

These directions are God's will for you as a Christian. "The will of God . . . for you" (v. 18) signifies that
God both commands and desires continual prayer from His children. He desires your fellowship; He desires
you to have His forgiveness, peace, guidance, and the fullness of His Spirit; He longs for you to have His rest
in your soul; He longs to impart to you His good and perfect gifts (James 1:17, page 1256; Luke 11:9–13,
page 1028).

See Matthew 21:21, 22, page 968, for **Point 30-E: Pray Believing.**

THE SECOND EPISTLE OF PAUL THE APOSTLE TO THE
Thessalonians

AUTHORSHIP. There is general agreement among scholars that 2 Thessalonians was written only a few months after 1 Thessalonians. In all probability the epistle was written from Corinth while Paul was on his second missionary journey because, as noted in 2 Thessalonians 1:1, Silas and Timothy were still with him.

2 Thessalonians 1:1 and 3:17 plainly declare that Paul is the author of the epistle.

HOW 2 THESSALONIANS FITS INTO THE BIBLE. 2 Thessalonians is germane to the whole of New Testament truth, because it deals with three very specific problems which people still have trouble with today. In the first place, it deals with persecution, teaching that what the Thessalonians were going through was a normal part of being a Christian. Secondly, Paul dealt with the time of the Lord's return, a question that is still asked and often answered wrongly today. Thirdly, he encouraged all the believers to get busy until the Lord does return (3:6-11). Idleness has no part in God's economy.

CONTEXT. Paul went to Thessalonica on his second missionary journey. The account of this visit is recorded in Acts 17:1-9 and in 1 Thessalonians 1:7 and 2:2-18.

In Paul's day Thessalonica was a thriving commercial center on an important trade route. The city was established in 316 B.C. by King Cassandra of Macedonia. He named the city after his wife, Thessalonica, the half sister of Alexander the Great.

When Paul and Silas entered the city of Thessalonica to preach the gospel, it was the first time that the glorious message of salvation had ever been proclaimed there. The aforementioned Scripture references detail what a marvelous ministry God brought through them in less than a month. However, after three Sabbaths, the persecution was so bad that Paul, Silas, and Timothy fled by night to Berea. Persecution again arose in Berea over the preaching of God's Word, so Paul left for Athens. Timothy and Silas remained in Berea. Timothy then returned to Thessalonica and brought word to Paul again when the three of them were united in Corinth.

After preaching his famous Mars Hill sermon, Paul left Athens and went to Corinth. It was there that Silas and Timothy rejoined him, and it was also from there that Paul wrote 1 and 2 Thessalonians, only a few months apart. Most scholars believe that the year was about A.D. 51.

THEME. The book centers on a misunderstanding or a misrepresentation (2:2) concerning the coming day of the Lord. Apparently, someone had led the Thessalonian Christians to believe that the persecution that they were suffering was not normal. Therefore, they believed that this must be the terrible time of trouble which Old Testament prophets said would occur before the Messiah reigned in glory. Paul had himself instructed the Thessalonians concerning this terrible tribulation time in his first epistle. For the modern reader, who has access to the whole of the New Testament, this period is known as the Great Tribulation. In other words, they had been deceived into believing that they were living in the last days. Such false teaching had adverse effects on the heartbeat and life-style of the church. Paul dealt with the issue forthrightly and gave new revelation from God on the correct order of end-time events (2:1-12).

HOW 2 THESSALONIANS FITS TOGETHER. The structure of the epistle is typically Pauline and falls into a rather simple outline. The first four verses make up Paul's *introduction* to the letter. The main body of the letter, 1:5—3:15, contains his *instruction,* including words of consolation (1:5-12), explanation (2:1-12), and exhortation (2:13—3:15). Finally, 3:16-18 are his *conclusion* to his epistle.

KEY CHAPTER. Chapter 2:1-12 is the very heart of the epistle. It explains that the Thessalonians either had been misinformed or that they had misunderstood the sequence of events that would accompany the Lord's return. To alleviate their fear and misunderstanding, Paul explained the correct sequence of end-time events and showed them how this new knowledge, coupled with their present situation, could give them victory in Christ.

KEY VERSE: 2:3—"Let no one deceive you by any means; for that Day will not come unless the falling away comes first, and the man of sin is revealed, the son of perdition." If the mind is not shaken or confused it is easier to handle persecution by seeing it in the total scope of the Lord's plan for believers.

3:5—"Now may the Lord direct your hearts into the love of God and into the patience of Christ." Such controls lead to a life that honors God in all circumstances.

SUMMARY STATEMENT. Believers in every age must *look* for the Lord's return at any moment, but must *live* as if they had a lifetime to serve Him.

—J.M.L.

Greeting

PAUL, Silvanus, and Timothy,
To the church of the Thessalonians in God our Father and the Lord Jesus Christ:

2 ᴿGrace to you and peace from God our Father and the Lord Jesus Christ.   1 Cor. 1:3

God's Final Judgment and Glory

3 We are bound to thank God always for you, brethren, as it is fitting, because your faith grows exceedingly, and the love of every one of you all abounds toward each other,

4 so that we ourselves boast of you among the churches of God for your patience and faith in all your persecutions and ᵀtribulations that you endure,   *afflictions*

5 which is ᴿmanifestᵀ evidence of the righteous judgment of God, that you may be counted worthy of the kingdom of God, ᴿfor which you also suffer;   Phil. 1:28 • *plain* • 1 Thess. 2:14

6 ᴿsince *it is* a righteous thing with God to repay with ᵀtribulation those who trouble you,   Rev. 6:10 • *affliction*

7 and to *give* you who are troubled rest with us when ᴿthe Lord Jesus is revealed from heaven with His mighty angels,   Jude 14

8 in flaming fire taking vengeance on those who do not know God, and on those who do not obey the gospel of our Lord Jesus Christ.

9 These shall be punished with everlasting destruction from the presence of the Lord and ᴿfrom the glory of His power,   Deut. 33:2

10 when He comes, in that Day, to be glorified in His saints and to be admired among all those who *believe, because our testimony among you was believed.

11 Therefore we also pray always for you that our God would ᴿcount you worthy of *this* calling, and fulfill all the good pleasure of *His* goodness and ᴿthe work of faith with power,   Col. 1:12 • 1 Thess. 1:3

12 ᴿthat the name of our Lord Jesus Christ may be glorified in you, and you in Him, according to the grace of our God and the Lord Jesus Christ.   [Col. 3:17]

The Great Apostasy

2 Now, brethren, concerning the coming of our Lord Jesus Christ and our gathering together to Him, we ask you,

2 ᴿnot to be soon shaken in mind or troubled, either by spirit or by word or by letter, as if from us, as though the day of *Christ had come.   Matt. 24:4

3 Let no one deceive you by any means; for *that Day will not come* unless the falling away comes first, and the man of *sin is revealed, ᴿthe son of perdition,   John 17:12

4 who opposes and exalts himself ᴿabove all that is called God or that is worshiped, so that he sits *as God in the temple of God, showing himself that he is God.   1 Cor. 8:5

5 Do you not remember that when I was still with you I told you these things?

6 And now you know what is restraining, that he may be revealed in his own time.

7 For the mystery of lawlessness is already at work; only *He who now restrains *will do so* until He is taken out of the way.

8 And then the lawless one will be revealed, whom the Lord will consume with the breath of His mouth and destroy ᴿwith the brightness of His coming.   Heb. 10:27

9 The coming of the *lawless one* is according to the working of Satan, with all power, ᴿsigns, and lying wonders,   Deut. 13:1

10 and with all unrighteous deception among ᴿthose who perish, because they did not receive ᴿthe love of the truth, that they might be saved.   2 Cor. 2:15 • 1 Cor. 16:22

11 And for this reason God will send them strong delusion, that they should believe the lie,

12 that they all may be condemned who did not believe the truth but ᴿhad pleasure in unrighteousness.   Rom. 1:32

Stand Fast

13 But we are ᵀbound to give thanks to God always for you, brethren beloved by the Lord, because God from the beginning chose you for salvation through sanctification by the Spirit and belief in the truth,   *under obligation*

14 to which He called you by our gospel, for ᴿthe obtaining of the glory of our Lord Jesus Christ.   1 Pet. 5:10

15 Therefore, brethren, stand fast and hold the traditions which you were taught, whether by word or our ᵀepistle.   *letter*

16 Now may our Lord Jesus Christ Himself,

1:10 NU, M *have believed*

2:2 NU *the Lord*
2:3 NU *lawlessness*
2:4 NU omits *as God*
2:7 Or *he*

and our God and Father, ^Rwho has loved us and given *us* everlasting consolation and ^Rgood hope by grace,   [Rev. 1:5] • 1 Pet. 1:3

17 comfort your hearts and ^Testablish you in every good word and work.   *strengthen*

Pray for Us

3 Finally, brethren, pray for us, that the word of the Lord may run *swiftly* and be glorified, just as *it is* with you,

2 and ^Rthat we may be delivered from unreasonable and wicked men; ^Rfor not all have faith.   Rom. 15:31 • Acts 28:24

3 But the Lord is faithful, who will establish you and guard *you* from the evil one.

4 And ^Rwe have confidence in the Lord concerning you, both that you do and will do the things we command you.   2 Cor. 7:16

5 Now may ^Rthe Lord direct your hearts into the love of God and into the patience of Christ.   1 Chr. 29:18

Warning Against Idleness

6 But we command you, brethren, in the name of our Lord Jesus Christ, that you withdraw from every brother who walks ^Rdisorderly and not according to the tradition which *he received from us.   1 Thess. 4:11

7 For you yourselves know how you ought to follow us, for we were not disorderly among you;

8 nor did we eat anyone's bread ^Tfree of charge, but worked with ^Rlabor and toil night

3:6 NU, M *they*

and day, that we might not be a burden to any of you,   Lit. *for nothing* • 1 Thess. 2:9

9 not because we do not have ^Rauthority, but to make ourselves an example of how you should follow us.   1 Cor. 9:4, 6-14

10 For even when we were with you, we commanded you this: If anyone will not work, neither shall he eat.

11 For we hear that there are some who walk among you in a disorderly manner, not working at all, but are ^Rbusybodies.   1 Pet. 4:15

12 Now those who are such we command and ^Texhort through our Lord Jesus Christ ^Rthat they work in quietness and eat their own bread.   *encourage* • Eph. 4:28

13 But *as for* you, brethren, ^Rdo not grow weary *in* doing good.   Gal. 6:9

14 And if anyone does not obey our word in this ^Tepistle, note that person and ^Rdo not keep company with him, that he may be ashamed.   *letter* • Matt. 18:17

15 Yet do not count *him* as an enemy, ^Rbut ^Tadmonish *him* as a brother.   Titus 3:10 • *warn*

Benediction

16 Now may ^Rthe Lord of peace Himself give you peace always in every way. The Lord *be* with you all.   Rom. 15:33

46-E. Paul's Letters   ▼

17 ^RThe salutation of Paul with my own hand, which is a sign in every ^Tepistle; so I write.   1 Cor. 16:21 • *letter* ▲

18 ^RThe grace of our Lord Jesus Christ *be* with you all. Amen.   Rom. 16:20, 24

46-E. Paul's Letters (2 Thessalonians 3:17)—The apostle Paul has been called the world's unrivaled letter-writing genius of all time. In the present verse he explained that his personal signature certified the authenticity of each of his letters. The words, "not to be soon shaken . . . by letter, as if from us" (2 Thess. 2:2, page 1215), suggest that someone may have sent these Thessalonians a fraudulent letter, as if from Paul; or some may have misunderstood his first letter to them. During his evangelistic missionary journeys Paul wrote Romans, First and Second Corinthians, Galatians, Ephesians, Philippians, Colossians, First and Second Thessalonians, First and Second Timothy, Titus, and Philemon.

See Philippians 1:12–14, page 1195, for **Point 46-F: Paul's Imprisonments and Final Journeys.**

Timothy

AUTHORSHIP. 1 Timothy is one of the so-called Pastoral Epistles, written by the apostle Paul after his release from his first Roman imprisonment. Many feel that Titus was written at the same time.

To question the authorship of St. Paul would be to question the very Word of God, due to the evidence within the book which definitely reflects the temperament and character of the great apostle (1:1). The change in Paul's vocabulary is due to the new subject matter of the Pastoral Epistles.

Timothy, which means "Venerating God" or "Honoring to God," was a native of Lystra, a city in Asia Minor that Paul visited on his first (Acts 14:6) and second (Acts 16:1) missionary journeys. Timothy's father was a Greek (Acts 16:1), and his mother was Jewish. Though they were far removed from the larger colonies of Israelite families, he was still brought up with strong Old Testament training. However, he could not be called a Jewish boy because he had never been admitted by circumcision within the order of God's ancient covenant. The home he was raised in taught the hope of the Messiah (2 Tim. 1:5; 3:15). His mother, Eunice, and his grandmother, Lois, were full of tenderness and faith as they instructed him from the Scriptures. Even though no mention is made of Timothy until Paul's second missionary journey and visit to Lystra, it is thought that he was one of Paul's converts during his first visit there (1:2) and that at that time he was placed under the care of the elders of the church (Acts 14:23).

When Paul returned to Lystra on his second missionary journey, Timothy was so "well reported of by the brethren" that Paul desired to take him along on the second and then his third missionary journey (Acts 16:1-4). Those who spoke with a prophetic utterance and had the deepest insight into character acknowledged that Timothy was especially fit for missionary work (1 Tim. 1:18; 4:14); and because of this insight, he was set apart as an evangelist by the laying on of hands (4:14). Thus, he joined Paul and became one of his most constant and trusted companions. This is evidenced by the frequent mention of Timothy as he attended Paul by assisting and preaching the gospel to the many churches Paul established.

From the time Timothy joined Paul at Lystra (about A.D. 51), it appears they first journeyed to Troas, then to Philippi (Acts 16:6-12), then to Thessalonica and Berea where he tarried until Paul sent for him at Athens (Acts 17:14, 15). From there, Paul sent him back to Thessalonica (1 Thess. 3:1, 2). By the time he returned, Paul had gone to Corinth (Acts 18:5; 1 Thess. 3:6). There Timothy joined Paul in the writing of the Thessalonian letters.

The five following years of his life are somewhat uncertain. We know that Paul did send him from Ephesus to Corinth (1 Cor. 4:17). Paul later joined him in Macedonia where Timothy assisted in the writing of 2 Corinthians (Acts 19:22; 2 Cor. 1:1).

He accompanied Paul partway on his journey to Jerusalem (Acts 20:4). Whether Timothy went with Paul all the way to Jerusalem and then to Rome is not stated. However, Philippians 1:1; 2:19-22; Colossians 1:1; and Philemon 1 do indicate that he did spend time with Paul in Rome.

It follows from 1 Timothy 1:3 that Paul had been released from his first imprisonment and accompanied by Timothy. They revisited the province of Asia. Timothy then was instructed to stay at Ephesus to teach the church while the apostle Paul continued his journey into Macedonia. Here at Ephesus this first epistle from Paul to Timothy was received. Later he is urged by Paul to come to Rome during Paul's second imprisonment (2 Tim. 4:9). Whether he arrived in Rome before Paul's death or not is unknown.

CONTEXT. 1 Timothy was written between Paul's first and second imprisonment, which would place it in the year A.D. 64. Thus, 1 Timothy, along with some of the other Epistles, provides the only knowledge of Paul's movements in the closing years of his life. He is now aged, and the care of all the churches is a deep concern to him.

HOW 1 TIMOTHY FITS INTO THE BIBLE. Even though all the books of the New Testament were written within the first century after Christ, and even though two or three centuries passed before the canon was officially settled (A.D. 369), still each of these fits into a framework that enhances the entire Bible that is directed to the Jew, the Gentile, and the church.

The Gospels record the account of the pre-incarnate Christ becoming incarnate. His eternal being is emphasized as well as His virgin birth, life, earthly ministry, death, resurrection, and ascension. Jesus said in Matthew 16:18 that He would build His church.

Acts includes the ascension of Jesus and the account of the early work and ministry of the church. It is a bridge from the Gospels to the Epistles. Being the first book of church history, it gives us specific light into the life, ministry, and writings of the apostle Paul.

1 Timothy was written by Paul to Timothy, his son in the ministry. Timothy's work was primarily with the elders of the many small groups meeting in various homes. There were no church buildings or seminaries, yet there were many pastors needing direction.

At the start of the church, problems had been directed toward the apostles themselves; but now, with the spread of the gospel and the growth of the church, definite instructions applicable to all occasions and periods were necessary.

How 1 Timothy Fits Together. The following outline may prove helpful:

(1) Greetings and warning about those who warp the faith because of their unsound doctrine (1:1–11)
(2) Witness by Paul and charge to Timothy to wage a good warfare (1:12–20)
(3) Instructions in prayer and public worship (2:1–15)
(4) Requirements for church officers (3:1–16)
(5) Identifying apostates by their false teaching (4:1–5)
(6) Workable solutions to counter apostasy (4:6–16)
(7) Workable admonitions to individuals and groups in the church (5:1—6:10)
(8) Paul's charge to his son, Timothy, and concluding appeal (6:11–21)

Key Verse: 3:15—"But if I am delayed, I write so that you may know how you ought to conduct yourself in the house of God, which is the church of the living God, the pillar and ground of the truth."

Key Word: *Truth.*

Summary Sentence. A compassionate apostle writing a beloved son in the faith to warn and instruct the people to keep "the faith" by keeping sound doctrine (1 Tim. 1:2, 3, 10).

Paul's concluding appeal to his son in the faith was to keep that which was committed to his trust. The early traditional accounts relate that Timothy was martyred by stones and clubs in A.D. 97 while preaching near the temple of Diana.

He, like Paul, had a compassionate heart for those early Christians and especially the elders in the church.

What a challenge to pastors and Christian workers today, especially as we see the day approaching, to stay true to the Word of God and the God of the Word.

—R.B.

Greeting

PAUL, an apostle of Jesus Christ, by the commandment of God our Savior and the Lord Jesus Christ, our hope,

2 To Timothy, a true son in the faith:

ᴿGrace, mercy, *and* peace from God our Father and Jesus Christ our Lord.   Gal. 1:3

No Other Doctrine

3 As I urged you ᴿwhen I went into Macedonia—remain in Ephesus that you may ᵀcharge some ᴿthat they teach no other doctrine,   Acts 20:1, 3 · *command* · Gal. 1:6, 7

4 nor give heed to fables and endless genealogies, which cause disputes rather than godly edification which is in faith.

5 Now the purpose of the commandment is love ᴿfrom a pure heart, *from* a good conscience, and *from* sincere faith,   Eph. 6:24

6 from which some, having strayed, have turned aside to ᴿidle talk,   1 Tim. 6:4, 20

7 desiring to be teachers of the law, under-

standing neither what they say nor the things which they affirm.

8 But we know that the law *is* ᴿgood if one uses it lawfully,   Rom. 7:12, 16

9 knowing this: that the law is not made for a righteous person, but for *the* lawless and insubordinate, for *the* ungodly and for sinners, for *the* unholy and profane, for murderers of fathers and murderers of mothers, for manslayers,

10 for fornicators, for sodomites, for kidnappers, for liars, for perjurers, and if there is any other thing that is ᵀcontrary to sound doctrine,   *opposed*

11 according to the glorious gospel of the ᴿblessed God which was ᴿcommitted to my trust.   1 Tim. 6:15 · 1 Cor. 9:17

Glory to God for His Grace

12 And I thank Christ Jesus our Lord who has enabled me, because He counted me faithful, putting *me* into the ministry,

13 although ᴿI was formerly a blasphemer,

a persecutor, and an ᵀinsolent man; but I obtained mercy because ᴿI did it ignorantly in unbelief.   Acts 8:3 · violently arrogant · John 4:21

14 ᴿAnd the grace of our Lord was exceedingly abundant, ᴿwith faith and love which are in Christ Jesus.   Rom. 5:20 · 2 Tim. 1:13; 2:22

15 ᴿThis is a faithful saying and worthy of all acceptance, that ᴿChrist Jesus came into the world to save sinners, of whom I am chief.   2 Tim. 2:11 · Is. 53:5; Matt. 1:21; 9:13

16 However, for this reason I obtained mercy, that in me first Jesus Christ might show all longsuffering, as a pattern to those who are going to believe on Him for everlasting life.

17 Now to the King eternal, immortal, invisible, to *God who alone is wise, be honor and glory forever and ever. Amen.

Fight the Good Fight

18 This ᵀcharge I commit to you, son Timothy, according to the prophecies previously made concerning you, that by them you may wage the good warfare,   command

19 having faith and a good conscience, which some having rejected, concerning the faith have suffered shipwreck,

20 of whom are Hymenaeus and Alexander, whom I delivered to Satan that they may learn not to ᴿblaspheme.   Acts 13:45

Pray for All Men

2 Therefore I ᵀexhort first of all that supplications, prayers, intercessions, and giving of thanks be made for all men,   encourage

2 for kings and ᴿall who are in authority, that we may lead a quiet and peaceable life in all godliness and ᵀreverence.   [Rom. 13:1] · dignity

3 For this is ᴿgood and acceptable in the sight ᴿof God our Savior,   Rom. 12:2 · 2 Tim. 1:9

4 who desires all men to be saved and to come to the knowledge of the truth.

5 For there is one God and one Mediator between God and men, the Man Christ Jesus,

6 ᴿwho gave Himself a ransom for all, to be testified in due time,   Mark 10:45

7 ᴿfor which I was appointed a preacher and an apostle—I am speaking the truth *in Christ and not lying—ᴿa teacher of the Gentiles in faith and truth.   Eph. 3:7, 8 · [Gal. 1:15, 16]

Men and Women in the Church

8 I desire therefore that the men pray ᴿeverywhere, ᴿlifting up holy hands, without wrath and doubting.   Luke 23:34 · Ps. 134:2

1:17 NU the only God,
2:7 NU omits in Christ

9 in like manner also, that the women adorn themselves in modest apparel, with propriety and moderation, not with braided hair or gold or pearls or costly clothing,

10 ᴿbut, which is proper for women professing godliness, with good works.   1 Pet. 3:4

11 Let a woman learn in silence with all submission.

12 And ᴿI do not permit a woman to teach or to have authority over a man, but to be in silence.   1 Cor. 14:34

13 For Adam was formed first, then Eve.

14 And Adam was not deceived, but the woman being deceived, fell into transgression.

15 Nevertheless she will be saved in childbearing if they continue in faith, love, and holiness, with self-control.

Qualifications of Overseers

3 This is a faithful saying: If a man desires the position of a *bishop, he desires a good work.

2 A bishop then must be blameless, the husband of one wife, temperate, soberminded, of good behavior, hospitable, able to teach;

3 not ᵀgiven to wine, not violent, *not greedy for money, but gentle, not quarrelsome, not ᵀcovetous;   addicted · loving money

4 one who rules his own house well, having his children in submission with all reverence

5 (for if a man does not know how to rule his own house, how will he take care of the church of God?);

6 not a ᵀnovice, lest being puffed up with pride he fall into the same condemnation as the devil.   new convert

7 Moreover he must have a good testimony among those who are outside, lest he fall into reproach and the snare of the devil.

24-A. Faith Is a Mystery   ▼

Qualifications of Deacons

8 Likewise deacons must be reverent, not double-tongued, ᴿnot given to much wine, not greedy for money,   Ezek. 44:21

9 holding the ᵀmystery of the faith with a pure conscience.   hidden truth ▲

10 But let these also first be tested; then let them serve as deacons, being found blameless.

3:1 Lit. overseer
3:3 NU omits not greedy for money

24-A. Faith Is a Mystery (1 Timothy 3:8, 9)—"Likewise deacons must be reverent [having spiritual dignity], . . . holding the mystery of the faith with a pure [clear] conscience" (vv. 8, 9). A biblical mystery is a truth of God heretofore unrevealed to all, even though it has been known by some and preached for hundreds of years. Salvation by faith in the death, burial, and resurrection of the Lord Jesus Christ was such a "mystery"
(Point 24-A continued on next page)

11 Likewise, *their* wives *must be* reverent, not ᵀslanderers, temperate, faithful in all things.   *malicious gossips*

12 Let deacons be the husbands of one wife, ruling *their* children and their own houses well.

13 For those who have served well as deacons ᴿobtain for themselves a good standing and great boldness in the faith which is in Christ Jesus.   Matt. 25:21

The Great Mystery

14 These things I write to you, though I hope to come to you shortly;

15 but if I am delayed, *I write* so that you may know how you ought to conduct yourself in the house of God, which is the church of the living God, the pillar and ᵀground of the truth.   *foundation, mainstay*

16 And without controversy great is the ᵀmystery of godliness: *hidden truth*

ᴿGod* was manifested in the flesh,
ᴿJustified in the Spirit,   [John 1:14] • [Matt. 3:16]
ᴿSeen by angels,   Matt. 28:2

3:16 NU *Who*

ᴿPreached among the Gentiles,   Rom. 10:18
ᴿBelieved on in the world,   Col. 1:6, 23
ᴿReceived up in glory.   Luke 24:51

The Great Apostasy

4 Now the Spirit ᵀexpressly says that in latter times some will depart from the faith, giving heed ᴿto deceiving spirits and doctrines of demons,   *explicitly* • Rev. 16:14

2 speaking lies in hypocrisy, having their own conscience seared with a hot iron,

3 forbidding to marry, *and commanding* to abstain from foods which God created to be received with thanksgiving by those who believe and know the truth.

4 For every creature of God *is* good, and nothing is to be refused if it is received with thanksgiving;

5 for it is ᵀsanctified by the word of God and prayer.   *set apart*

A Good Servant of Jesus Christ

6 If you instruct the brethren in these things, you will be a good minister of Jesus Christ, ᴿnourished in the words of faith and

---

(Point 24-A continued from previous page)
until it was revealed to the world at the first coming of God the Son (1 Cor. 15:1-4, page 1161), and it remains a mystery to those who have never heard or received the gospel of the grace of God (Eph. 2:8, 9, page 1187). You are not born with saving faith. It is a mystery until it is perceived in the Scriptures or heard from one who has received the mystery of saving faith. Some believers, becoming so involved in church work and "the deeper Christian life," forget that the Good News of salvation is a mystery to the unsaved, and will remain so until it is shared with the unsaved.

(1) "If our gospel [the mystery of saving faith] is veiled, it is veiled to those who are perishing" (2 Cor. 4:3, page 1167), and they shall remain lost until they call upon Christ for salvation. "So then faith [saving faith] comes by hearing [the mystery of the faith], and hearing by the word of God" (Rom. 10:17, page 1140). The greatest mystery of all is the mystery of the gospel of grace. "In the beginning was the Word [God's only begotten Son], and the Word was with God, and the Word was God. . . . And the Word became flesh and dwelt among us, and we beheld His glory, the glory as of the only begotten of the Father, full of grace and truth" (John 1:1, 14, page 1049). In the womb of the Virgin Mary, God the Son was made flesh. Thirty-three years later the Son was made "to be sin for us, that we might become the righteousness of God in Him" (2 Cor. 5:21, page 1169). This is the mystery of the faith that we must share with the world (Matt. 28:19, page 982).

(2) "Now faith is the substance [assurance, confidence] of things hoped for, the evidence [proof] of things not seen" (Heb. 11:1, page 1247). We can be saved by grace through faith, that is, trust in Christ's saving work (Eph. 2:8, page 1187) and we can have the assurance of eternal life with Christ. Paul said, "I know whom I have believed and am persuaded that He is able to keep what [my body, soul, and spirit] I have committed [as an act of faith] to Him until that Day" (2 Tim. 1:12, page 1224).

(3) The Christian's assurance of eternal salvation is a twofold witness.

(a) God's Word witnesses to you. "He who believes in the Son has [present tense] everlasting life" (John 3:36, page 1053; cf. 6:35-40, page 1059). "Therefore, if anyone is in Christ [by faith], he is a new creation; old things have passed away; behold, all things have become new" (2 Cor. 5:17, page 1169). "This is the witness of God which He has testified of His Son" (1 John 5:9, page 1282). God's eternal, inerrant Word is our assurance of salvation by grace through faith in God the Son (Eph. 1:13, 14, page 1186).

(b) God the Holy Spirit witnesses with your spirit, assuring you that you are a child of God. "The Spirit Himself bears witness with our spirit that we are children of God" (Rom. 8:16, page 1137).

These two—God's inerrant Word, and God the indwelling Holy Spirit, witness as one—"that you may know that you have eternal life" (1 John 5:11, 13, page 1282). The Holy Spirit witnesses with your spirit in conjunction with the testimony of God's Word. The more you mix the Word of God with your faith, the deeper your relationship with Christ will become (Rom. 10:17, page 1140). The depth of such faith will also determine the extent of your spiritual effectiveness (Heb. 11:7, 33, page 1247).

See Galatians 3:11, page 1181, for **Point 24-B: The Just Shall Live by Faith.**

of the good doctrine which you have carefully followed.　　2 Tim. 3:14

7 But reject profane and old wives' fables, and exercise yourself toward godliness.

8 For ᴿbodily exercise profits a little, but godliness is profitable for all things, ᴿhaving promise of the life that now is and of that which is to come.　　1 Cor. 8:8 · Ps. 37:9

9 This is a faithful saying and worthy of all acceptance.

10 For to this end *we both labor and suffer reproach, because we trust in the living God, ᴿwho is the Savior of all men, especially of those who believe.　　Ps. 36:6

11 These things command and teach.

Take Heed to Your Ministry

12 Let no one despise your youth, but be an example to the believers in word, in conduct, in love, *in spirit, in faith, in purity.

13 Till I come, give attention to reading, to exhortation, to ᵀdoctrine.　　teaching

14 Do not neglect the gift that is in you, which was given to you by prophecy with the laying on of the hands of the eldership.

15 Meditate on these things; give yourself entirely to them, that your progress may be evident to all.

16 Take heed to yourself and to the doctrine. Continue in them, for in doing this you will save both yourself and those who hear you.

Treatment of Church Members

5 Do not rebuke an older man, but exhort him as a father, younger men as brothers,

2 older women as mothers, younger women as sisters, with all purity.

Honor True Widows

3 Honor widows who are really widows.

4 But if any widow has children or grandchildren, let them first learn to show piety at home and ᴿto repay their parents; for this is *good and acceptable before God.　　Gen. 45:10

5 Now she who is really a widow, and left alone, trusts in God and continues in supplications and prayers ᴿnight and day.　　Acts 26:7

6 But she who lives in ᵀpleasure is dead while she lives.　　indulgence

7 And these things command, that they may be blameless.

8 But if anyone does not provide for his own, ᴿand especially for those of his household, ᴿhe has denied the faith ᴿand is worse than an unbeliever.　　Is. 58:7 · 2 Tim. 3:5 · Matt. 18:17

9 Do not let a widow under sixty years old be taken into the number, and not unless she has been the wife of one man,

10 well reported for good works: if she has brought up children, if she has lodged strangers, if she has washed the saints' feet, if she has relieved the afflicted, if she has diligently followed every good work.

11 But refuse the younger widows; for when they have begun to grow wanton against Christ, they desire to marry,

12 having condemnation because they have cast off their first ᵀfaith.　　Or solemn promise

13 And besides they learn to be idle, wandering about from house to house, and not only idle but also gossips and busybodies, saying things which they ought not.

14 Therefore I desire that the younger widows marry, bear children, manage the house, give no opportunity to the adversary to speak reproachfully.

15 For some have already turned aside after Satan.

16 If any believing *man or woman has widows, let them ᵀrelieve them, and do not let the church be burdened, that it may relieve those who are really widows.　　give aid to

Honor the Elders

17 Let the elders who rule well be counted worthy of double honor, especially those who labor in the word and doctrine.

18 For the Scripture says, *"You shall not muzzle an ox while it treads out the grain," and, *"The laborer is worthy of his wages."

19 Do not receive an accusation against an elder except from two or three witnesses.

20 Those who are sinning rebuke in the presence of all, that the rest also may fear.

21 I charge you before God and the Lord Jesus Christ and the ᵀelect angels that you observe these things without ᴿprejudice, doing nothing with partiality.　　chosen · Deut. 1:17

22 Do not lay hands on anyone hastily, nor ᴿshare in other people's sins; keep yourself pure.　　Eph. 5:6, 7

23 No longer drink only water, but use a little wine for your stomach's sake and your frequent ᵀinfirmities.　　illnesses

24 Some men's sins are ᴿclearly evident, preceding them to judgment, but those of some men follow later.　　Gal. 5:19–21

25 Likewise, the good works of some are clearly evident, and those that are otherwise cannot be hidden.

Honor Masters

6 Let as many ᴿbondservants as are under the yoke count their own masters worthy of all honor, so that the name of God and His doctrine may not be blasphemed.　　Eph. 6:5

2 And those who have believing masters, let them not despise them because they are

---

4:10 NU we labor and strive,
4:12 NU omits in spirit
5:4 NU, M omit good and

5:16 NU omits man or
5:18 Deut. 25:4; 1 Cor. 9:7–9 • Lev. 19:13; Deut. 24:15;
Matt. 10:10; Luke 10:7; 1 Cor. 9:14

brethren, but rather serve *them* because those who are benefited are believers and beloved. Teach and exhort these things.

Error and Greed

3 If anyone teaches otherwise and does not consent to wholesome words, *even* the words of our Lord Jesus Christ, and to the doctrine which accords with godliness,

4 he is proud, knowing nothing, but is obsessed with disputes and arguments over words, from which come envy, strife, reviling, evil suspicions,

5 *useless wranglings of men of corrupt minds and destitute of the truth, who suppose that godliness is a *means of* gain. *From ᴿsuch withdraw yourself.   2 Tim. 3:5

6 Now godliness with ᴿcontentment is great gain.   Heb. 13:5

7 For we brought nothing into *this* world, *and it is* certain we can carry nothing out.

8 And having food and clothing, with these we shall be ᴿcontent.   Prov. 30:8, 9

9 But those who desire to be rich fall into temptation and a snare, and *into* many foolish and harmful lusts which drown men in destruction and perdition.

10 For the love of money is a root of all *kinds of* evil, for which some have strayed from the faith in their greediness, and pierced themselves through with many sorrows.

The Good Confession

11 But you, O man of God, flee these things and pursue righteousness, godliness, faith, love, patience, gentleness.

6:5 NU, M *constant friction* • NU omits the rest of v. 5.
6:7 NU omits *and it is certain*

12 Fight the good fight of faith, lay hold on eternal life, to which you were also called and have confessed the good confession in the presence of many witnesses.

13 I urge you in the sight of God who gives life to all things, and *before* Christ Jesus ᴿwho witnessed the good confession before Pontius Pilate,   John 18:36, 37

14 that you keep *this* commandment without spot, blameless until our Lord Jesus Christ's appearing,

15 which He will manifest in His own time, *He who is* the blessed and only ᵀPotentate, the King of kings and Lord of lords,   *Sovereign*

16 who alone has immortality, dwelling in ᴿunapproachable light, ᴿwhom no man has seen or can see, to whom *be* honor and everlasting power. Amen.   Dan. 2:22 • John 6:46

Instructions to the Rich

17 Command those who are rich in this present age not to be haughty, nor to trust in uncertain ᴿriches but in the living God, who gives us richly all things to enjoy.   Jer. 9:23

18 *Let them* do good, that they be rich in good works, ready to give, willing to share,

19 ᴿstoring up for themselves a good foundation for the time to come, that they may lay hold on eternal life.   [Matt. 6:20, 21; 19:21]

Guard the Faith

20 O Timothy! Guard what was committed to your trust, avoiding the profane *and* ᵀidle babble and contradictions of what is falsely called knowledge—   *empty chatter*

21 by professing it some have strayed concerning the faith. Grace *be* with you. Amen.

THE SECOND EPISTLE OF PAUL THE APOSTLE TO
Timothy

AUTHORSHIP. All the positive evidence says that the apostle Paul wrote 2 Timothy. So says the letter, so said the early church. Not until modern times has there been a dissenting voice, and Paul's authorship has never had any justifiable criticism. The evidence of the Epistles themselves shows Paul as the writer.

Paul's writings reveal the characteristics of a man of strong emotion. He could be very stern (Gal. 3:1-5; Acts 23:2, 3). But with profound tenderness he writes to Timothy, his "beloved son" (1:2; cf. Gal. 4:19, 20). As a warm and personal letter, it has much in common with 1 Timothy, Titus, and Philemon.

The most probable date is the spring of A.D. 68. Nero killed himself in early June of that year and Paul was surely put to death before that date.

In this letter Paul instructs Timothy how to carry on the work of God after the apostle's death. The emphasis is on the great apostasy and social corruptions which will exist in the latter days of the church. In this, Paul's last epistle, there is a mellow wisdom and a sereneness of purpose in the profound triumph of Paul's spirit over all opposition. Confident in the blessed hope of the Lord's return and his own reward (4:8), he exhorts and instructs the young pastor to be a good soldier, as faithful as Christ was and as Paul has been.

HOW 2 TIMOTHY FITS INTO THE BIBLE. 2 Timothy is Paul's farewell letter, not only to Timothy, but to all of the apostle's millions, and by now literally billions, of readers through the centuries. It is his last letter as he faces the Roman sword, but he is ready. He has finished his race and kept the faith.

KEY VERSE: 2:3—"You therefore must endure hardship as a good soldier of Jesus Christ."

HOW 2 TIMOTHY FITS TOGETHER. An outline based on the "good soldier" theme is:
(1) Greeting and Thanks for Timothy (1:1-7)
(2) The Good Soldier's Enlistment (1:8-18)
(3) The Good Soldier's Qualities (2:1-26)
(4) The Good Soldier's Apostate Enemies (ch. 3)
(5) The Good Soldier's Charge (4:1-5)
(6) The Good Soldier's Rewards (4:6-18)
(7) Final Greetings (4:19-22)

CONTEXT. In this letter Paul reveals something of his circumstances at the time of writing. As a religious outlaw, Paul had been brought to the Mamertine Prison at Rome. Arrested on a double charge, he was not this time the victim of Jewish hate or Judaizing jealousy, but rather of Gentile intervention in what Nero considered an assault on the worship of the old gods in general and emperor worship in particular. Moreover, blaming the Christians for the great conflagration that took place in Rome in A.D. 64, it was not difficult to accuse Paul of complicity in the burning of the city and so get him to Rome.

Charged with these capital crimes, Paul was not now allowed the liberty of his own hired house, as he was at his first arrest in Acts 28. Confined in the dungeon he was cold and lonely. He desired the cloak that he left with Carpus at Troas (4:13), and dreaded the prospect of another winter without it (4:21). He had already had his first court appearance and had escaped the mouths of the lions (4:16). Few of his friends dared to visit Paul, for now it was a crime to be a Christian, but Onesiphorus sought until he found him (1:16-18). Demas had forsaken him (4:10), and only Luke was with him.

We do not have a written account of Paul's death, but he was expecting to be led out soon to execution (4:6). Tradition tells us he was executed on the Ostian Road outside the city of Rome; so says Caius, quoted in Eusebius, *Ecclesiastical History*, 2:25. As a Roman citizen, he would be beheaded. Was Luke there? Let us hope so! Was Timothy there? He surely would be, unless he, too, were a prisoner. No matter! When all others failed, Jesus was with him (4:17). Christ had not failed Paul in all the years since He stopped him on the Damascus road, saved him and "revealed" to him the gospel of the Son of God (Gal. 1:11, 12).

—H.B.H.

Greeting

PAUL, an apostle of *Jesus Christ by the will of God, according to the ᴿpromise of life which is in Christ Jesus,   Titus 1:2

2 To Timothy, a ᴿbeloved son:

Grace, mercy, and peace from God the Father and Christ Jesus our Lord.   1 Tim. 1:2

Timothy's Faith and Heritage

3 I thank God, whom I serve with a pure conscience, as my ᴿforefathers did, as without ceasing I remember you in my prayers night and day,   Acts 24:14

4 greatly desiring to see you, being mindful of your tears, that I may be filled with joy,

5 when I call to remembrance the genuine faith that is in you, which dwelt first in your grandmother Lois and your mother Eunice, and I am persuaded is in you also.

6 Therefore I remind you ᴿto stir up the gift of God which is in you through the laying on of my hands.   1 Tim. 4:14

7 For ᴿGod has not given us a spirit of fear, ᴿbut of power and of love and of a sound mind.   Rom. 8:15 · [Acts 1:8]

Not Ashamed of the Gospel

8 Therefore do not be ashamed of the testimony of our Lord, nor of me His pris-

oner, but share with me in the sufferings for the gospel according to the power of God,

9 who has saved us and called us with a holy calling, ᴿnot according to our works, but ᴿaccording to His own purpose and grace which was given to us in Christ Jesus ᴿbefore time began,   [Rom. 3:20] · Rom. 8:28 · Rom. 16:25

10 but ᴿhas now been revealed by the appearing of our Savior Jesus Christ, who has abolished death and brought life and immortality to light through the gospel,   Eph. 1:9

11 to which I was appointed a preacher, an apostle, and a teacher *of the Gentiles.

21-F. So Great in Assurance   ▼

12 For this reason I also suffer these things; nevertheless I am not ashamed, ᴿfor I know whom I have believed and am persuaded that He is able to keep what I have committed to Him until that Day.   1 Pet. 4:19 ▲

Be Loyal to the Faith

13 Hold fast the pattern of ᴿsound words which you have heard from me, in faith and love which are in Christ Jesus.   1 Tim. 6:3

14 That good thing which was committed to you, keep by the Holy Spirit who dwells in us.

15 This you know, that all those in Asia

1:1 NU, M Christ Jesus

1:11 NU omits of the Gentiles

21-F. So Great in Assurance (2 Timothy 1:12)—The apostle Paul had a know-so salvation; he said, "for I know whom I have believed [his faith was in the risen Christ] and am persuaded that He is able to keep what I have committed to Him until that Day" (v. 12).

(1) Do you know in whom you believe? Is your faith in God the Son, or is it in church membership, baptism, the Lord's Supper, good works, the law, or a moral life? We are to observe all these things *because* we are saved by grace through faith in the Lord Jesus Christ, but never *in order to* be saved. If your faith is in anyone or anything other than Jesus Christ and Him alone, it is a vain faith (Acts 4:12, page 1091).

(2) Are you convinced that Christ is able—that He has the power to keep you saved? He said, "All authority has been given to Me in heaven and on earth" (Matt. 28:18, page 982). He has all power to save and all power to keep. He has all power over all other powers; His power is greater than the power of Satan, demons, sin, or this evil world system. Put your faith in the Lord Jesus Christ to save you and keep you saved. You are not trusting a weak or limited Savior. He has all authority in heaven and on earth, and He is able to do above all that we can ask or think, according to the power of God that works in the believer (Eph. 3:20, page 1190).

(3) The believer's assurance of salvation is based on the following witnesses:

(a) God's Word witnesses to you. "If we receive the witness of men [and we do—as, for example, the written witness of fallible historians], the witness of God is greater [because He is infallible]" (1 John 5:9, page 1282). If you believe the witness of fallible man, why can't you believe the witness of the infallible God? Let God witness to you out of His Word—"These things I have written to you who believe in the name of the Son of God, that you may know [not doubt] that you have eternal life" (1 John 5:13, page 1282). Yes, God wants you to be saved and know it.

(b) The Holy Spirit, who indwells all believers, witnesses with the believer's spirit, confirming his adoption as a child of God. "The Spirit Himself bears witness with our spirit that we are children of God" (Rom. 8:16, page 1137). God's Word and the Holy Spirit witness as one, that you may know that you have eternal salvation.

The Holy Spirit cannot witness with your spirit apart from your faith in God's Word. The better you know the Word of God, the greater your faith will become. The depth of your faith will determine the strength of your assurance. You can be saved and know it, because God, who cannot lie, tells you so in His infallible Word. When God says it, you can know it.

See Index, page 17, for your next study.

have turned away from me, among whom are Phygellus and Hermogenes.

16 The Lord grant mercy to the ᴿhousehold of Onesiphorus, for he often refreshed me, and was not ashamed of my chain;   2 Tim. 4:19

17 but when he arrived in Rome, he sought me out very zealously and found *me.*

18 The Lord grant to him that he may find mercy from the Lord ᴿin that Day—and you know very well how many ways he ᴿministered *to me* at Ephesus.   2 Thess. 1:10 • Heb. 6:10

Be Strong in Grace

2 You therefore, my son, ᴿbe strong in the grace that is in Christ Jesus.   Eph. 6:10

▼ 2-F. Know How to Use Bible Helps and Commentaries

2 And the things that you have heard from me among many witnesses, commit these to faithful men who will be able to teach others ▲ also.

3 You therefore must *endure hardship ᴿas a good soldier of Jesus Christ.   1 Tim. 1:18

4 No one engaged in warfare entangles himself with the affairs of *this* life, that he may please him who enlisted him as a soldier.

5 And also ᴿif anyone competes in athletics, he is not crowned unless he competes according to the rules.   [1 Cor. 9:25]

6 The hardworking farmer must be first to partake of the crops.

7 Consider what I say, and *may the Lord give you understanding in all things.

8 Remember that Jesus Christ, ᴿof the seed of David, ᴿwas raised from the dead ᴿaccording to my gospel,   Rom. 1:3, 4 • 1 Cor. 15:4 • Rom. 2:16

9 ᴿfor which I suffer trouble as an evildoer, ᴿ*even* to the point of chains; ᴿbut the word of God is not chained.   Acts 9:16 • Eph. 3:1 • Acts 28:31

10 Therefore ᴿI endure all things for the sake of the ᵀelect, ᴿthat they also may obtain the salvation which is in Christ Jesus with eternal glory.   Eph. 3:13 • *chosen ones* • 2 Cor. 1:6

11 *This is* a faithful saying:

For ᴿif we died with *Him,*
    We shall also live with *Him.*   Rom. 6:5, 8
12 ᴿIf we endure,   [Rom. 5:17; 8:17]
    We shall also reign with *Him.*
    ᴿIf we deny *Him,*
    He also will deny us.   Matt. 10:33
13 If we are faithless,
    He remains faithful;
    He ᴿcannot deny Himself.   Num. 23:19

2:3 NU *share*   2:7 NU *the Lord will give you*

2-F. Know How to Use Bible Helps and Commentaries (2 Timothy 2:2)—"And the things that you have heard from me among many witnesses, commit these to faithful men who will be able to teach others also" (v. 2).

We are not alone in our study of the Bible. First of all, we have the Holy Spirit to help us (see Point 2-C, "Know That the Bible Stands Above All Human Opinions," page 1067). In addition, we have the aid and encouragement of godly men who have spent their lives in deep study of the Scriptures and its original languages. These men are God's provision to help us along the road. Every "Timothy" needs a "Paul," and every "Elisha" needs an "Elijah." It is God's usual way of training His people.

The results of many studies have been committed to writing in the form of faithful Bible helps and commentaries. Your pastor, elder, or Sunday school teacher can give you good advice about where to seek and obtain these works. Thus, when you are puzzled about the intent of a particular text or passage, when your own resources fail, you can turn to the results of the labors of others for help. Here are some materials that will be useful to you:

(1) *An exhaustive concordance of the Bible.* Almost indispensable in finding texts whose locations you have forgotten. A concordance is also useful for making studies of words as they are used in different contexts of the Bible.

(2) *A Bible dictionary.* To assist in understanding Bible terms and names.

(3) *A Bible encyclopedia.* Immensely helpful in researching the background of the history, biography, geography, and text of the Bible.

(4) *A Bible commentary.* At least one good single-volume commentary, or better still, as many multiple-volume commentaries as you can afford. Commentaries won't solve *all* problems, but they will deal helpfully with difficult passages and texts of the Bible.

(5) *A biblical archaeology textbook.* At least one. Information about archaeological discoveries in Bible lands will be very encouraging and strengthening to your faith. Your usefulness as a witness to others also will be improved. People constantly have questions about events and places in the Bible, for which we now possess considerable information from archaeological exploration.

(6) *A biblical textbook of introduction to each of the books of the Old and New Testaments.* Useful for knowing how the Bible came to be written, as well as for knowing parallel historical events in biblical times. Another value of introductions to the Bible is the insight they give into how problems of the Bible text have been solved through the centuries, and how these problems are continually being resolved.

As your grasp of biblical studies grows, your faith will grow, and your usefulness as a servant of the Lord will be enhanced.

See Index, page 17, for your next study.

Approved and Disapproved Workers

14 Remind *them* of these things, charging *them* before the Lord not to strive about words to no profit, to the ruin of the hearers.

▼ **2-E. Know the Correct Methods of Bible Study**

15 Be diligent to present yourself approved to God, a worker who does not need to be ▲ ashamed, rightly dividing the word of truth.

16 But shun profane *and* idle babblings, for they will increase to more ungodliness.

17 And their message will spread like cancer. ᴿHymenaeus and Philetus are of this sort,   1 Tim. 1:20

18 who have strayed concerning the truth, saying that the resurrection is already past; and they overthrow the faith of some.

19 Nevertheless ᴿthe solid foundation of God stands, having this seal: "The Lord ᴿknows those who are His," and, "Let everyone who names the name of *Christ depart from iniquity."   [1 Cor. 3:11] • [Nah. 1:7]

20 But in a great house there are not only ᴿvessels of gold and silver, but also of wood and clay, some for honor and some for dishonor.   Rom. 9:21

21 Therefore if anyone cleanses himself from the latter, he will be a vessel for honor, ᵀsanctified and useful for the Master, ᴿprepared for every good work.   set apart • 2 Tim. 3:17

22 Flee also youthful lusts; but pursue righteousness, faith, love, peace with those who call on the Lord out of a pure heart.

23 But avoid foolish and ignorant disputes, knowing that they generate strife.

24 And ᴿa servant of the Lord must not quarrel but be gentle to all, ᴿable to teach, ᴿpatient,   Titus 3:2 • Titus 1:9 • 1 Tim. 3:3

2:19 NU, M *the Lord*

2-E. Know the Correct Methods of Bible Study (2 Timothy 2:15)—"Be diligent to present yourself approved to God, a worker who does not need to be ashamed, rightly dividing the word of truth" (v. 15). "Rightly dividing the word of truth" requires systematic methods of Bible study. Otherwise we will simply miss God's intention that we should understand "the whole counsel of God" (Acts 20:27, page 1115). Random, disjointed, undisciplined study may not be entirely fruitless, but it will also yield many worthless and even injurious results.

We have already seen that the Bible is not a magic box to be treated like a game of chance, which should be expected to render immediate answers to all problems at a glance. As our text shows, "diligence" is indispensable. Diligence dictates a *methodical* approach. Here are some useful methods:

(1) *Bible summary.* Determine the general varieties of literature in the Bible, their location, and how they relate to one another:

(a) *Law* principally occurs in the first five books of the Bible—Genesis through Deuteronomy. Understanding these books is fundamental to an understanding of all that follows.

(b) *History* is presented in the Old Testament from Joshua through Esther, and in the New Testament from Matthew through Acts. History is the record of the leading events in the divine/human drama of redemption, which is the great subject of the Bible.

(c) *Poetry* primarily comprises the books of Job through the Song of Solomon. This is the compendium of devotional and Wisdom Literature of the Bible. It has teaching as well as inspirational value. Much of the literature in the prophetic books also is poetry.

(d) *Prophecy* includes all the books from Isaiah through Malachi, as well as the Revelation in the New Testament and portions of the Gospels, such as the Olivet Discourse. Here we appreciate the ultimate purposes of God as they are revealed for the eternal future.

(e) *Teaching* is contained principally in the Gospels and Epistles of the New Testament, as well as in Wisdom Literature, i.e., Proverbs and Ecclesiastes in the Old Testament.

Each of these sections shares some of the values of all the others. But the *emphasis* of each section is distinctive.

(2) *Study by books.* This method consists of reading, organizing, and outlining each book of the Bible, preferably in the order in which the books occur in the Bible. The major purpose(s) and teaching(s) of each book should carefully be noted.

(3) *Study by chapter.* Each chapter is analyzed, and notes should be kept of its content and teachings.

(4) *Study by themes and doctrine.* By using a topical index, the leading thoughts and teachings of the Bible can be traced throughout the sixty-six books. Study of verses will be most meaningful by using this method. For example, to know what the Bible teaches about angels, ideally *all* verses concerning angels should be included in the study.

(5) *Devotional reading.* This method is at least as important as the others, and indeed may be combined with the others. The Bible is not merely a theological textbook, but is the chief means by which we draw near to God, because it is in the Bible that God draws near to us. If we do not come to know better the supreme Author of the Bible, then our study is in vain. The man of God must be "thoroughly equipped for every good work" (2 Tim. 3:16, 17, page 1227). Therefore, read selected books and passages for these benefits—knowing God, knowing ourselves, and knowing the will of God for our daily lives.

See 2 Timothy 2:2, page 1225, for **Point 2-F: Know How to Use Bible Helps and Commentaries.**

25 ᴿin humility correcting those who are in opposition, ᴿif God perhaps will grant them repentance, ᴿso that they may know the truth,   Gal. 6:1 • Acts 8:22 • 1 Tim. 2:4

26 and *that* they may come to their senses *and escape* the snare of the devil, having been taken captive by him to *do* his will.

Perilous Times and Perilous Men

3 But know this, that in the last days ᵀperilous times will come: *times of stress*

2 For men will be lovers of themselves, lovers of money, boasters, proud, blasphemers, disobedient to parents, unthankful, unholy,

3 unloving, unforgiving, slanderers, without self-control, brutal, despisers of good,

4 ᴿtraitors, headstrong, haughty, lovers of pleasure rather than lovers of God,   2 Pet. 2:10

5 having a form of godliness but denying its power. And from such people turn away!

6 For ᴿof this sort are those who creep into households and make captives of gullible women loaded down with sins, led away by various lusts,   Matt. 23:14

7 always learning and never able ᴿto come to the knowledge of the truth.   1 Tim. 2:4

8 ᴿNow as Jannes and Jambres resisted Moses, so do these also resist the truth: ᴿmen of corrupt minds, ᴿdisapproved concerning the faith;   Ex. 7:11, 12, 22; 8:7 • 1 Tim. 6:5 • Rom. 1:28

9 but they will progress no further, for their folly will be manifest to all, ᴿas theirs also was.   Ex. 7:11, 12; 8:18; 9:11

The Man of God and the Word of God

10 ᴿBut you have carefully followed my doctrine, manner of life, purpose, faith, long-suffering, love, perseverance,   1 Tim. 4:6

11 persecutions, afflictions, which happened to me at Antioch, at Iconium, at Lystra—what persecutions I endured. And out of *them* all the Lord delivered me.

12 Yes, and ᴿall who desire to live godly in Christ Jesus will suffer persecution.   [Ps. 34:19]

13 ᴿBut evil men and impostors will grow worse and worse, deceiving and being deceived.   2 Thess. 2:11

14 But you must continue in the things which you have learned and been assured of, knowing from whom you have learned *them,*

15 and that from childhood you have known ᴿthe Holy Scriptures, which are able to make you wise for salvation through faith which is in Christ Jesus.   John 5:39

1-A. The Bible Declares Itself to Be the Word of God ▼

16 ᴿAll Scripture *is* given by inspiration of God, ᴿand *is* profitable for doctrine, for reproof, for correction, for ᵀinstruction in righteousness,   [2 Pet. 1:20] • Rom. 15:4 • *training, discipline* ▲

1-A. The Bible Declares Itself to Be the Word of God (2 Timothy 3:16)—"All Scripture is given by inspiration of God" (v. 16). This great declaration explains and affirms why the Bible alone has been the final authority for the faith and practice of evangelical Christianity through the centuries. Note that:

(1) "All Scripture" refers to the entire Bible (Old and New Testaments), from the Creation account in Genesis to the new heaven and new earth in the book of Revelation.

(2) "All Scripture" refers to the written Word. The doctrine of biblical inerrancy asserts that God's Holy Spirit so guided "holy men of God" (2 Pet. 1:21, page 1273) so that the words they wrote, and which have been preserved as our Bible, were kept free from error, in fact or doctrine. It is not affirmed that Luke never erred as a person; rather, that when he penned his Gospel and the book of Acts, God's Spirit, by a special act of supernatural superintendance, so guided these particular writings that they

    (a) said what God wished to be said;
    (b) were written error-free in the autographs (original copies).

(3) "All Scripture" refers to the thirty-nine Old Testament books, which were received as the "Scripture" at the time the apostle Paul wrote these words, plus the twenty-seven New Testament works then being written, which already had been pre-authenticated by Christ (John 16:12, 13, page 1077). When Paul wrote to Timothy, in the first Christian century, the complete canon (official list) of the Old Testament Scriptures in Hebrew consisted of twenty-two books. Josephus, the Jewish historian, who lived in the first century A.D., wrote that the holy books of the Hebrews were twenty-two, the same as the number of letters in their alphabet. These twenty-two Old Testament books are identical to the thirty-nine books of our Old Testament, differing only in how they were divided (e.g., First and Second Samuel combined as one book). At the same time, the twenty-seven New Testament books (in Greek) were coming into existence and had the same authority for the church as the Old Testament.

(4) "By inspiration of God," *theopneustos* in Greek, literally means "God-breathed." The author of the Bible is declared to be God Himself, as He "breathed" the words through the mouths and pens of His chosen prophets (2 Pet. 1:21, page 1273).

(5) The Old Testament books claim to be God's Word numerous times. They were accepted by prophets and the faithful through the centuries as from God, hence inerrant (2 Kin. 22:8, 11, 13, page 378). In fact, in many cases the biblical words came directly as the speech of God: "I, the LORD, keep it, I water it every moment; lest any hurt it, I keep it night and day" (Is. 27:3, page 667).

(Point 1-A continued on next page)

17 that the man of God may be complete, thoroughly equipped for every good work.

Preach the Word

4 I ᴿcharge you *therefore before God and the Lord Jesus Christ, ᴿwho will judge the living and the dead *at His appearing and His kingdom: 1 Tim. 5:21 • Acts 10:42

2 Preach the word! Be ready in season *and* out of season. ᴿConvince, rebuke, exhort, with all longsuffering and teaching.   Titus 2:15

3 ᴿFor the time will come when they will not endure ᴿsound doctrine, ᴿbut according to their own desires, *because* they have itching ears, they will heap up for themselves teachers;   2 Tim. 3:1 • 1 Tim. 1:10 • 2 Tim. 3:6

4 and they will turn *their* ears away from the truth, and be turned aside to fables.

▼ 48-D. The Crown of Righteousness

5 But you be watchful in all things, ᴿendure afflictions, do the work of ᴿan evangelist, fulfill your ministry.   2 Tim. 1:8 • Acts 21:8

Paul's Valedictory

6 For ᴿI am already being poured out as a drink offering, and the time of ᴿmy departure is at hand.   Phil. 2:17 • [Phil. 1:23]

7 I have fought the good fight, I have finished the race, I have kept the faith.

8 Finally, there is laid up for me the crown of righteousness, which the Lord, the righ-

4:1 NU omits *therefore* • NU *and by*

teous ᴿJudge, will give to me ᴿon that Day, ▽ and not to me only but also to all who have loved His appearing.   John 5:22 • 2 Tim. 1:12 ▲

The Abandoned Apostle

9 Be diligent to come to me quickly;

10 for ᴿDemas has forsaken me, ᴿhaving loved this present world, and has departed for Thessalonica—Crescens for Galatia, Titus for Dalmatia.   Col. 4:14 • 1 John 2:15

11 Only Luke is with me. Get ᴿMark and bring him with you, for he is useful to me for ministry.   Acts 12:12, 25; 15:37-39

12 And Tychicus I have sent to Ephesus.

13 Bring the cloak that I left with Carpus at Troas when you come—and the books, especially the parchments.

14 ᴿAlexander the coppersmith did me much harm. May the Lord repay him according to his works.   1 Tim. 1:20

15 You also must beware of him, for he has greatly resisted our words.

16 At my first defense no one stood with me, but all forsook me. ᴿMay it not be charged against them.   Acts 7:60

The Lord Is Faithful

17 But the Lord stood with me and strengthened me, so that the message might be preached fully through me, and *that* all the Gentiles might hear. Also I was delivered ᴿout of the mouth of the lion.   1 Sam. 17:37

18 ᴿAnd the Lord will deliver me from every

(Point 1-A continued from previous page)
  (6) The New Testament books were accepted by the church as Scripture, even in the day of their writing; thus, Peter was already considering Paul's epistles as Scripture (2 Pet. 3:15, 16, page 1276). Likewise, the book of Revelation proclaims that God's judgment will befall anyone who dares to add to or subtract from "the words . . . of this prophecy" (Rev. 22:18, 19, page 1316). It labels itself as prophecy, a holy message from God. As part of Scripture it cannot be improved by additions or deletion; it is complete and inerrant.

  See John 10:35, page 1068, for **Point 1-B: Christ Taught the Inerrancy of the Bible.**

48-D. The Crown of Righteousness (2 Timothy 4:5-8)—The "crown of righteousness" (v. 8) is a reward. It is not to be confused with the "righteousness of God" which the believer receives when he becomes a Christian; for at that time, the believer is to "become the righteousness of God in Him" (2 Cor. 5:21, page 1169). This righteousness is imputed to *all* those saved by grace through faith. The "crown of righteousness" is a reward to be earned by the saved. If the believer looks for, and loves, the second coming of Christ, it will affect his whole life. Look at the dynamic impact this truth had on the life of the apostle Paul. He could say:

  (1) "I have fought the good fight" (v. 7; cf. 1 Cor. 15:32, page 1162). He fought a spiritual battle throughout his Christian life, and won. He never surrendered to the enemies of righteousness (Eph. 6:12, page 1192).

  (2) "I have finished the race" (v. 7). He had a course to travel, and he did not detour the hard places; neither did he look back (Luke 9:61, 62, page 1026). He finished his course with his eyes fixed on Christ (Phil. 1:6, page 1195).

  (3) "I have kept the faith" (v. 7). He preached the "whole counsel of God"—never betraying any of the great doctrines (Acts 20:24-31, page 1115). The apostle looked ahead to the "judgment seat of Christ" (2 Cor. 5:10, page 1168) where the "crown of righteousness" will be given to those who "have loved His appearing" (v. 8). How important it is for the believer to look with a heart of love for the second coming of our Lord and Savior Jesus Christ, that he may receive the "crown of righteousness" (v. 8).

  See 1 Peter 5:2-4, page 1268, for **Point 48-E: The Crown of Glory.**

evil work and preserve *me* for His heavenly kingdom. ᴿTo Him *be* glory forever and ever. Amen!   Ps. 121:7 • Rom. 11:36

Come Before Winter

19 Greet ᴿPrisca and Aquila, and the household of ᴿOnesiphorus.   Acts 18:2 • 2 Tim. 1:16
20 Erastus stayed in Corinth, but ᴿTrophimus I have left in Miletus sick.   Acts 20:4; 21:29

21 Do your utmost to come before winter. Eubulus greets you, as well as Pudens, Linus, Claudia, and all the brethren.

Farewell

22 The Lord *Jesus Christ be with your spirit. Grace be with you. Amen.

4:22 NU omits *Jesus Christ*

THE EPISTLE OF PAUL THE APOSTLE TO

Titus

AUTHORSHIP. The first verse of the letter identifies Paul as the author and this is confirmed by the contents as well as by church tradition from earliest days. Only in modern times have men attacked the Pauline authorship, and then largely through unbelief.

CONTEXT. The epistle appears to have been written from either Macedonia or Philippi during the period between Paul's first and second imprisonments, which would date it at approximately A.D. 63 or 64. According to 3:12 Paul was preparing to spend the winter in Nicopolis, on the west coast of Greece.

HOW TITUS FITS INTO THE BIBLE. Titus, along with 1 and 2 Timothy, makes up what we know as the Pastoral Epistles. The goals of Paul in writing this particular epistle included correcting false doctrine, motivating the recipients toward good works, and establishing order in the churches. He encourages Titus to do this by means of good, sound teaching (2:1).

SUMMARY STATEMENT. Titus is to speak the things which are proper for sound doctrine: correct false doctrines, do good works, and establish order in the churches.

HOW TITUS FITS TOGETHER. Sound doctrine, good works, and church order are the goals of Paul in this epistle and it may be divided to reflect them in this manner: (1) the first four verses establish Paul's authority; (2) the rest of chapter 1 consists of instruction for the appointment and selection of church leaders; (3) chapter 2 contains Paul's exhortation and instructions for sound doctrine among the saints; and (4) chapter 3 provides the conclusion to the epistle.

The epistle to Titus was written for the purpose of instructing him in how to deal with the issues that concerned Paul at that time. The fact that Titus had been successful as an emmisary of Paul in the past is reflected by his accomplishments at the church in Corinth. All records reveal him to be a man used by God to help overcome problems that had risen at a critical point in the growth of the early church.

—M.M.B.

Greeting

PAUL, a bondservant of God and an apostle of Jesus Christ, according to the faith of God's elect and the acknowledgment of the truth which accords with godliness,

2 in hope of eternal life which God, who cannot lie, promised before time began,

3 but has in due time manifested His word through preaching, which was committed to me according to the commandment of God our Savior;

4 To ᴿTitus, a true son in *our* common faith: 2 Cor. 2:13; 8:23

Grace, mercy, *and* peace from God the Father and *the Lord Jesus Christ our Savior.

Qualified Elders

5 For this reason I left you in Crete, that you should ᴿset in order the things that are lacking, and appoint elders in every city as I commanded you—   1 Cor. 11:34

6 if a man is blameless, the husband of one wife, having faithful children not accused of ᵀdissipation or insubordination.   *incorrigibility*

7 For a *bishop must be blameless, as a steward of God, not self-willed, not quick-tempered, ᴿnot given to wine, not violent, not greedy for money,   Lev. 10:9

8 but hospitable, a lover of what is good, sober-minded, just, holy, self-controlled,

9 holding fast the faithful word as he has been taught, that he may be able, by sound doctrine, both to exhort and convict those who contradict.

The Elders' Task

10 For there are many insubordinate, both idle ᴿtalkers and deceivers, especially those of the circumcision,   James 1:26

11 whose mouths must be stopped, who subvert whole households, teaching things which they ought not, ᴿfor the sake of dishonest gain.   1 Tim. 6:5

12 ᴿOne of them, a prophet of their own, said, "Cretans *are* always liars, evil beasts, lazy gluttons."   Acts 17:28

13 This testimony is true. ᴿTherefore rebuke them sharply, that they may be sound in the faith,   2 Cor. 13:10

14 not giving heed to Jewish fables and

^Rcommandments of men who turn from the truth.   Is. 29:13

15 ^RTo the pure all things are pure, but to those who are defiled and unbelieving nothing is pure; but even their mind and conscience are defiled.   1 Cor. 6:12

16 They profess to know God, but in works they deny Him, being abominable, disobedient, and disqualified for every good work.

Qualities of a Sound Church

2 But as for you, speak the things which are proper for sound doctrine:

2 that the older men be sober, reverent, temperate, sound in faith, in love, in patience;

3 the older women likewise, that they be reverent in behavior, not slanderers, not given to much wine, teachers of good things—

4 that they admonish the young women to love their husbands, to love their children,

5 to be discreet, chaste, homemakers, good, obedient to their own husbands, that the word of God may not be blasphemed.

6 Likewise, exhort the young men to be sober-minded,

7 in all things showing yourself *to be* a pattern of good works; in doctrine *showing* integrity, reverence, *incorruptibility,

8 sound speech that cannot be condemned, that one who is an opponent may be ashamed, having nothing evil to say of *you.

9 *Exhort* ^Rbondservants to be obedient to their own masters, to be well pleasing in all things, not answering back,   1 Tim. 6:1

2:7 NU omits *incorruptibility*
2:8 NU, M *us*

10 not ^Tpilfering, but showing all good ^Tfidelity, that they may adorn the doctrine of God our Savior in all things.   *thieving · honesty*

Trained by Saving Grace

11 For ^Rthe grace of God that brings salvation has appeared to all men,   [Rom. 5:15]

12 teaching us that, denying ungodliness and worldly lusts, we should live soberly, righteously, and godly in the present age,

13 ^Rlooking for the blessed ^Rhope and glorious appearing of our great God and Savior Jesus Christ,   1 Cor. 1:7 · [Col. 3:4]

14 who gave Himself for us, that He might redeem us from every lawless deed and purify for Himself *His* own special people, zealous for good works.   Is. 53:12; Gal. 1:4

15 Speak these things, exhort, and rebuke with all authority. Let no one despise you.

Graces of the Heirs of Grace

3 Remind them ^Rto be subject to rulers and authorities, to obey, ^Rto be ready for every good work,   1 Pet. 2:13 · Col. 1:10

2 to speak evil of no one, to be peaceable, gentle, showing all humility to all men.

3 For ^Rwe ourselves were also once foolish, disobedient, deceived, serving various lusts and pleasures, living in malice and envy, hateful and hating one another.   1 Cor. 6:11

4 But when the kindness and the love of God our Savior toward man appeared,

23-C. The Spiritual Birth Is the Washing   ▼   of Regeneration

5 not by works of righteousness which we have done, but according to His mercy He

---

23-C. The Spiritual Birth Is the Washing of Regeneration (Titus 3:5)—Regeneration is being born from above. It is the New Birth. It is partaking of the very nature of God—a new creation by a supernatural act of God. It does not reinforce, alter, or reform the old nature. It is a spiritual birth achieved by the power of God's Word and the regenerating work of the Holy Spirit.

(1) The Holy Spirit never works independently of the Scriptures. He does the washing with the Word and regenerates the believer by His power. In John 16:8–11 (page 1077), Jesus said, "And when He [the Holy Spirit] has come, He will convict the world of sin, and of righteousness, and of judgment:

(a) "Of *sin,* because they do not believe in Me." This sin of unbelief is the sin of condemnation (John 3:18, page 1053).

(b) "Of *righteousness,* because I go to My Father and you see Me no more." Jesus Christ is the righteousness of God. We are righteous because we are in Him (2 Cor. 5:21, page 1169).

(c) "Of *judgment,* because the ruler of this world [Satan] is judged." All unbelievers have already been judged, found guilty, and sentenced to eternal hell along with their father the Devil (John 8:44, page 1063; cf. 3:17, 18, page 1053). However, there is good news: any sinner who will repent and put his or her faith in the Lord Jesus Christ as personal Savior will be regenerated—born again.

On the Day of Pentecost the Upper Room congregation, filled with the Holy Spirit, shared their faith, each speaking in different languages that they themselves did not understand. Simon Peter, led by the Holy Spirit, preached that great Pentecostal sermon. The Scriptures say that "they were cut to the heart [convicted of sin], and said to Peter and the rest of the apostles, 'Men and brethren, what shall we do?'" (Acts 2:37, page 1089). The Scriptures tell us that about three thousand people were regenerated when they heard the gospel, and acted upon the Word of God as it was presented in the power of the Holy Spirit. A sinner cannot be saved without the convicting, regenerating power of the Holy Spirit, and the Word of God.

(2) Regeneration is a new creation. "Therefore, if anyone is in Christ, he is a new creation; old things

(Point 23-C continued on next page)

▽ saved us, through ᴿthe washing of regenera-
▲ tion and renewing of the Holy Spirit,　John 3:3

6 ᴿwhom He poured out on us abundantly through Jesus Christ our Savior,　Ezek. 36:25

7 that having been justified by His grace ᴿwe should become heirs according to the hope of eternal life.　[Rom. 8:17, 23, 24]

8 ᴿThis is a faithful saying, and these things I want you to affirm constantly, that those who have believed in God should be careful to maintain good works. These things are good and profitable to men.　1 Tim. 1:15

Avoid Dissension

9 But ᴿavoid foolish disputes, genealogies, contentions, and strivings about the law; for they are unprofitable and useless.　2 Tim. 2:23

10 ᴿReject a divisive man after the first and second ᵀadmonition,　Matt. 18:17 • warning

11 knowing that such a person is warped and sinning, being self-condemned.

Final Messages

12 When I send Artemas to you, or Tychicus, be diligent to come to me at Nicopolis, for I have decided to spend the winter there.

13 Send Zenas the lawyer and ᴿApollos on their journey with haste, that they may lack nothing.　Acts 18:24

14 And let our people also learn to maintain good works, to meet urgent needs, that they may not be unfruitful.

Farewell

15 All who are with me greet you. Greet those who love us in the faith. Grace be with you all. Amen.

(Point 23-C continued from previous page)
have passed away; behold, all things have become new" (2 Cor. 5:17, page 1169). A brief examination of this text will reveal four things:

(a) Anyone who is in Christ is regenerated—a child of God (Gal. 3:26, 29, page 1182).

(b) As a new creation he has all the privileges of God's family in heaven and earth (Eph. 3:14–21, page 1189).

(c) Old things have passed away, including old religious ceremonial laws (Rom. 10:1–4, page 1140), traditions from our fathers (1 Pet. 1:18, 19, page 1263), false gods (Ex. 20:3, page 79), and the guilt and penalty of all sins (Rom. 8:1–4, page 1136).

(d) All things have become new, including a new faith to live by (Rom. 1:17, page 1128), a new life to enjoy (John 10:10, page 1067), a new birth that relates us to God the Father (John 3:1–8, page 1051), a new family to rejoice in (Eph. 3:15, page 1189), a new name given to us by the Lord (Rev. 2:17, page 1295), a new hope (1 Pet. 1:3, page 1263), a new home to live in (John 14:1–3, page 1074), and a new power to serve God in this life and in the life to come (Acts 1:8, page 1086).

See 1 John 4:7–21, page 1280, for **Point 23-D: The Spiritual Birth: Its Evidence.**

Philemon

This brief letter is infinitely precious. It holds a unique place among the writings of Paul. Though others are included in the salutation, it is an intimate and private letter to Philemon, a lay member of the church at Colosse. Its content deals with an incident of domestic life without reference to any problem or question of general public interest.

In his other epistles Paul writes as teacher, preacher, missionary, theologian, or apostle to the Gentiles. Here we have a fascinating insight into the soul of Paul the man, the warm-hearted, practical Christian who wants to help a brother make things right. To do this he puts himself "on the line" for Onesimus, a runaway slave.

CONTEXT. Apparently Philemon was a wealthy slaveholder in Colosse. Paul had not yet visited there, so it is believed that Philemon had become a convert during Paul's long ministry at Ephesus (v. 19). He seems to have been a generous and hospitable man. He had offered his home as a meeting place for the church in Colosse. That Paul had deep affection and high esteem for "Philemon our beloved friend and fellow laborer," there can be no doubt (v. 1).

It is thought that Apphia was the wife of Philemon, and that Archippus may have been their son. Paul's references to Archippus (Col. 4:17 and Philem. 2) leave the impression that he was ministering in Colosse during the absence of Epaphras, who at the time was a fellow prisoner with Paul (v. 23).

Though the letter does not say so, it is believed that Onesimus was a runaway slave. He had apparently disappeared following an act of theft and, somehow had managed to get to Rome. In the providence of God he was led to faith in Christ as the result of Paul's ministry there. In Onesimus Paul found a faithful and devoted friend, one who was and might have continued to be very useful to him in Rome (vv. 11, 13).

Paul knew, however, that Onesimus had some unfinished business in Colosse. He needed to demonstrate his repentance by making restitution to his master, Philemon. Accordingly, Onesimus must return to Colosse and make things right. Since Greek and Roman slaves had no rights, this was a dangerous and courageous action. By going back Onesimus was placing himself entirely at the mercy of the master whom he had wronged. Roman law imposed few limitations to the power of a master over his slave.

But Paul took some precautions. He sent Tychicus along as mediator with the letters he had written to the churches at Laodicea and Colosse. Onesimus would be safer not to encounter Philemon alone. But Paul was not satisfied. He took pen in hand and wrote this eager entreaty, identifying himself with the plight of Onesimus. For Paul the conventional barrier between slave and free had vanished.

AUTHORSHIP. The epistle's existence and authenticity were acknowledged at an early date. Three times the writer of the letter calls himself Paul (vv. 1, 9, 19). Origen ascribes it to Paul, and Eusebius gave it a place on his list of acknowledged books, regarding it as "true, genuine, and recognized."

The evidence for Paul's authorship is overwhelming. Truly, in this brief letter we hear the pleading voice of the apostle himself.

It is believed that the letters of Philemon and Colossians were written in Rome (Acts 28:16-31) toward the end of Paul's two-year imprisonment (Col. 4:3, 10, 18; Philem. 9). This would place the date of writing at about A.D. 61 or 62. The belief is that Tychicus delivered the Colossian letter, and that he was accompanied by Onesimus (Col. 4:7, 9), who delivered Paul's epistle to Philemon.

The trip from Rome to Colosse was a long one in the first century A.D. (at least nine hundred fifty miles by air). Though Rome is in Europe, Colosse was in southwest Asia Minor (now Turkey), some one hundred miles east of Ephesus.

Paul becomes the advocate by pleading for reconciliation between Philemon and Onesimus. It was his purpose to persuade Philemon to forgive Onesimus, and to receive him, not as a slave, but as "a beloved brother, especially to me but how much more to you" (v. 16). It was the great apostle's hope that a broken relationship between two Christian brothers might be fully restored.

HOW PHILEMON FITS TOGETHER. This beautiful little letter can be analyzed as follows: (1) in verses 1-7 Paul greets Philemon's household and praises Philemon himself, (2) in verses 8-17 he intercedes for Onesimus, and (3) in verses 18-25 he gives his pledge and salutation.

How Philemon Fits into the Bible. In no other book are the social implications of the gospel more strikingly exerted. The nobility of Paul's character is nowhere more vividly portrayed. The Epistle to Philemon stands unrivaled as an expression of simple dignity and Christian courtesy. Its effect is due to the warm, loving spirit of the writer.

The world of the first century offered no understanding, hope, or sympathy to a slave who had violated Roman law. Paul's intercession brought the love of Christ to bear on slavery and other practices of society which violated the basic rights of persons.

There is reason to believe that the effects of what Paul wrote to Philemon had a significant influence on the abolishment of slavery many centuries later.

—J.R.S.

Greeting

PAUL, a ᴿprisoner of Christ Jesus, and Timothy *our* brother,

To Philemon our beloved *friend* and fellow laborer,   Eph. 3:1
2 to *the beloved Apphia, ᴿArchippus our fellow soldier, and to the church in your house: Col. 4:17

3 Grace to you and peace from God our Father and the Lord Jesus Christ.

Philemon's Love and Faith

4 ᴿI thank my God, making mention of you always in my prayers,   2 Thess. 1:3
5 ᴿhearing of your love and faith which you have toward the Lord Jesus and toward all the saints,   Col. 1:4
6 that the sharing of your faith may become effective ᴿby the acknowledgment of ᴿevery good thing which is in *you in Christ Jesus.   Phil. 1:9 • [1 Thess. 5:18]
7 For we *have great *joy and consolation in your love, because the hearts of the saints have been refreshed by you, brother.

The Plea for Onesimus

8 Therefore, though I might be very bold in Christ to command you what is fitting,
9 *yet* for love's sake I rather appeal *to you*—being such a one as Paul, the aged, and now also a prisoner of Jesus Christ—
10 I appeal to you for my son Onesimus, whom I have begotten *while* in my chains,
11 who once was unprofitable to you, but now is profitable to you and to me.

12 I am sending him *back. You therefore receive him, that is, my own heart,
13 whom I wished to keep with me, that on your behalf he might minister to me in my chains for the gospel.
14 But without your consent I wanted to do nothing, that your good deed might not be by compulsion, as it were, but voluntary.
15 For perhaps he departed for a while for this *purpose*, that you might receive him forever,
16 no longer as a slave but more than a slave—a beloved brother, especially to me but how much more to you, both in the ᴿflesh and in the Lord.   Col. 3:22

Philemon's Obedience Encouraged

17 If then you count me as a partner, receive him as *you would* me.
18 But if he has wronged you or owes anything, put that on my account.
19 I, Paul, am writing with my own ᴿhand. I will repay—not to mention to you that you owe me even your own self besides. 1 Cor. 16:21
20 Yes, brother, let me have joy from you in the Lord; refresh my heart in the Lord.
21 ᴿHaving confidence in your obedience, I write to you, knowing that you will do even more than I say.   2 Cor. 7:16
22 But, meanwhile, also prepare a guest room for me, for I trust that ᴿthrough your prayers I shall be granted to you.   2 Cor. 1:11

Farewell

23 ᴿEpaphras, my fellow prisoner in Christ Jesus, greets you,   Col. 1:7; 4:12
24 *as do* Mark, Aristarchus, ᴿDemas, ᴿLuke, my fellow laborers.   Col. 4:14 • 2 Tim. 4:11
25 ᴿThe grace of our Lord Jesus Christ *be* with your spirit. Amen.   2 Tim. 4:22

2 NU *our sister Apphia*
6 NU, M *us*
7 NU *had* • M *thanksgiving*

12 NU *back to you in person, that is, my own heart,*

THE EPISTLE TO THE
Hebrews

AUTHORSHIP. The writer of Hebrews is unknown. Paul has been advanced by many as the author, but the claim cannot be supported conclusively. However, it can be said with assurance that the author was thoroughly familiar with the Old Testament Scriptures; the book was written before the destruction of the temple in Jerusalem in A.D. 70 (10:11); and the masculine participle in 11:32 (in the original) indicates the author was a man. While the question of authorship remains unsettled, the genuineness of the book is unaffected. No book in the sacred canon presents a loftier portrait of the person and work of Jesus Christ.

CONTEXT. Hebrews was written to mid-first-century Christian Jews who were giving serious thought to renouncing their commitment to Jesus Christ by returning to the practice of Judaism. The author encourages these struggling believers not to give up their superior blessings and realities in Jesus Christ for the mere shadows and rituals of Judaism.

HOW HEBREWS FITS INTO THE BIBLE. The book of Hebrews addresses a very real problem—the problem of spiritual relevance. These Jewish Christians had begun to drift in their spiritual commitment. The persecution and pressures which they faced daily were robbing them of their inward joy and of the reality of their relationship with Jesus Christ. Doubts began to creep into their minds as they questioned the value of their commitment to Christ—perhaps they had been deceived, or perhaps one way to God was as good as another. So they began to let down and drift from their original commitment. The question was this: Is Jesus Christ relevant? Is a relationship with Him important?

SUMMARY STATEMENT. The Lord Jesus Christ is God's final word and man's only Savior.

KEY WORD: *Better.*

KEY VERSES: 2:1-4—"Therefore we must give the more earnest heed to the things we have heard lest we drift away. For if the word spoken through angels proved steadfast, and every transgression and disobedience received a just reward, how shall we escape if we neglect so great a salvation, which at the first began to be spoken by the Lord, and was confirmed to us by those who heard Him, God also bearing witness both with signs and wonders, with various miracles, and gifts of the Holy Spirit, according to His own will?"

HOW HEBREWS FITS TOGETHER. Hebrews divides itself very naturally around the theme of the superiority of Jesus Christ. (1) Chapters 1—4 display the superiority of the *person* of Christ, (2) 5:1—10:18 consider the superiority of His *work,* and (3) 10:19—13:25 proclaim the superiority of a *relationship* with Him.

The writer of Hebrews wrote to Christians of the first century who were tempted to return to Judaism. They had begun their journey in the Christian faith well, but as opposition and persecution arose around them, their commitment to Jesus Christ softened and they began to drift spiritually. The warnings found in this book trace the pattern of their spiritual drift.

Spiritual drift began with neglect. Believers didn't have time for worship, service, and fellowship. Other things crowded into their lives. Then, having stepped back a few paces from the mainstream of faith, they began to question their commitments and beliefs. Unbelief began to grow. Finally, they stood at the brink of apostasy, turning away from Jesus Christ altogether. These early Christians were at this crossroads in their spiritual lives. They could continue their spiritual drift or they could reaffirm their precious faith.

The writer to the Hebrews writes a word of exhortation to those struggling with the malady of spiritual drift (13:22). Using arguments from the Old Testament Scriptures with which they were familiar and which were applicable to their drift back into Judaism, he exhorts them to do certain things to arrest the process. The prescription is applicable today for those struggling with this spiritual virus.

What is the prescription? First, pay attention to the Word of God. There is no higher authority which man can seek or find (2:1; 12:25). Second, fix your thoughts on Jesus Christ (3:1; 12:2). What we think about will either feed our soul or it will consume us. Third, spend time in fellowship with Christians, engaged in encouraging one another (3:13; 10:24, 25; 13:1). Fourth, hold firmly to the faith which you have professed in Jesus Christ (4:14; 10:35; 12:7; 13:9). Finally, approach boldly and often the throne of grace in prayer (4:16; 10:22; 13:15).

Like these Hebrew Christians of the first century, we also sometimes lose our perspective. It is the Word of God that restores perspective. In the Word we see that our modern problems are very old, and the old spiritual prescriptions of reading the Bible, meditation, fellowship, perseverance, and prayer are still very effective. Why else would they be old?

—J.W.D.

God's Supreme Revelation

▼ 6-A. He Was Unique in His Person

GOD, who at various times and in various ways spoke in time past to the fathers by the prophets,

2 has in these last days spoken to us by His Son, whom He has appointed heir of all things, through whom also He made the ᵀworlds;   Or *ages,* Gr. *aiones,* aeons

3 who being the brightness of His glory and the express image of His person, and upholding all things by the word of His power, when He had *by Himself ᵀpurged *our sins, ᴿsat down at the right hand of the Majesty on high,   cleansed · Ps. 68:18; 110:1

4 having become so much better than the angels, as ᴿHe has by inheritance obtained a more excellent name than they.   [Phil. 2:9, 10]

The Son Exalted Above Angels

5 For to which of the angels did He ever say:

ᴿ*"You are My Son,*   Ps. 2:7
Today I have begotten You"?

1:3 NU omits *by Himself* • NU omits *our*

And again:

ᴿ*"I will be to Him a Father,*   2 Sam. 7:14
And He shall be to Me a Son"?

6 But when He again brings ᴿthe firstborn into the world, He says: [Rom. 8:29]

**"Let all the angels of God worship Him."*

7 And of the angels He says:

ᴿ*"Who makes His angels spirits*   Ps. 104:4
And His ministers a flame of fire."

8 But to the Son He says:

ᴿ*"Your throne, O God, is forever and*
ever;   Ps. 45:6, 7
A ᵀscepter of righteousness is the
scepter of Your kingdom.   A ruler's staff

9 *You have loved righteousness and*
hated lawlessness;
Therefore God, Your God, ᴿhas
anointed You   Ps. 45:7; Is. 61:3
With the oil of gladness more than
Your companions."

1:6 Deut. 32:43, LXX, DSS; Ps. 97:7; 1 Pet. 3:22; Rev. 5:11–13

6-A. He Was Unique in His Person (Hebrews 1:1–13)—These verses worshipfully proclaim the uniqueness of Jesus as the Son of God, the Christ, the God-Man, whose coming into the world was prophesied. They reveal the glory of His Godhead by proving through biblical citations His superiority over even the heavenly angels (vv. 4, 5, 7, 13). Christ is "so much better than the angels" (v. 4); therefore He stands uniquely above every man, prophet, or king who ever lived or will live.

(1) "God, who at various times and in various ways spoke in time past to the fathers by the prophets" (v. 1). God had already communicated frequently with mankind in various ways. But now, from Jesus the God-Man's birth to the coming of His kingdom, He stands as God's complete and final message to a lost world. On the Mount of Transfiguration God said, "This is My beloved Son, in whom I am well pleased. Hear Him!" (Matt. 17:5, page 963).

(2) "Whom He has appointed heir of all things" (v. 2). Jesus, the God-Man, is the heir to God's entire universe. All born-again believers are joint heirs with Him (Rom. 8:17, page 1137).

(3) "Through whom also He made the worlds" (v. 2). With the Father and the Spirit, Jesus was the co-Creator of all things (John 1:3, page 1049). He is the preexistent Creator, i.e., He is God. Paul tells us, "For by Him all things were created" (Col. 1:16, page 1202).

(4) "Who being the brightness of His glory and the express image of His person" (v. 3). Jesus is the out-flowing of the glory of the Father, and expresses the perfect character of God. He, the Father, and the Holy Spirit are one in essence (John 10:30, page 1068).

(5) "And upholding all things by the word of His power" (v. 3). Jesus, the God-Man, sustains the universe, exercising all power (authority) over the entire creation. He is sovereign (Matt. 28:18, page 982).

(6) "When He had by Himself purged our sins" (v. 3). Jesus, the God-Man, is the only Savior (Acts 4:12, page 1091), having suffered the penalty for all sinners (Is. 53:1–5, page 693).

(7) "Sat down at the right hand of the Majesty on high" (v. 3). Jesus, the God-Man, is the only mediator between God and man (1 Tim. 2:5, page 1219). As our High Priest He intercedes for us at the right hand of the Father (Heb. 4:14–16, page 1239).

See Luke 1:26–35, page 1010, for **Point 6-B: He Was Unique in His Birth.**

▽ 10 And:

R"You, LORD, in the beginning laid the
foundation of the earth,
And the heavens are the work of Your
hands.   Ps. 102:25-27
11 RThey will perish, but You remain;
And Rthey will all grow old like a
garment;   [Is. 34:4] • Is. 50:9; 51:6
12 Like a cloak You will fold them up,
And they will be changed.
But You are the Rsame,
And Your years will not fail."   Heb. 13:8

13 But to which of the angels has He ever
said:

R"Sit at My right hand,
Till I make Your enemies Your
▲   footstool"?   Ps. 110:1

14 RAre they not all ministering spirits sent
forth to minister for those who will Rinherit
salvation?   Ps. 103:20 • Rom. 8:17

Do Not Neglect Salvation

2 Therefore we must give Tthe more earnest heed to the things we have heard,
lest we drift away.   all the more careful attention
2 For if the word spoken through angels
proved steadfast, and every transgression and
disobedience received a just reward,
3 how shall we escape if we neglect so
great a salvation, which at the first began to
be spoken by the Lord, and was Rconfirmed to
us by those who heard Him,   Luke 1:2
4 RGod also bearing witness Rboth with
signs and wonders, with various miracles,
and Tgifts of the Holy Spirit, according to His
own will?   Mark 16:20 • Acts 2:22, 43 • distributions

The Son Made Lower than Angels

5 For He has not put the world to come, of
which we speak, in subjection to angels.
6 But one testified in a certain place, saying:

R"What is man that You are mindful of
him,
Or the son of man that You take care
of him?   Ps. 8:4-6
7 You have made him Ta little lower than
the angels;   Or for a little while
You have crowned him with glory and
honor,
*And set him over the works of Your
hands.
8 RYou have put all things in subjection
under his feet."   Matt. 28:18

For in that He put all in subjection under
him, He left nothing that is not put under
him. But now Rwe do not yet see all things
put under him.   1 Cor. 15:25, 27

9 But we see Jesus, who was made Ta little
lower than the angels, for the suffering of
death crowned with glory and honor, that He,
by the grace of God, might taste death Rfor
everyone.   Or for a little while • [John 3:16]

Bringing Many Sons to Glory

10 For it was fitting for Him, Rfor whom are
all things and by whom are all things, in
bringing many sons to glory, to make the
captain of their salvation Rperfect through
sufferings.   Col. 1:16 • Heb. 5:8, 9; 7:28
11 For Rboth He who Tsanctifies and those
who are being sanctified Rare all of one, for
which reason RHe is not ashamed to call them
brethren,   Heb. 10:10 • sets apart • Acts 17:26 • Matt. 28:10
12 saying:

R"I will declare Your name to My
brethren;
In the midst of the assembly I will sing
praise to You."   Ps. 22:22

13 And again:

*"I will put My trust in Him."

And again:

R"Here am I and the children whom God
has given Me."   Is. 8:18

14 Inasmuch then as the children have
partaken of flesh and blood, He Himself
likewise shared in the same, Rthat through
death He might destroy him who had the
power of death, that is, the devil,   Col. 2:15
15 and Rrelease those who Rthrough fear of
death were all their lifetime subject to bondage.   Is. 42:7; 49:9; 61:1 • [Luke 1:74]
16 For indeed He does not Tgive aid to
angels, but He does give aid to the seed of
Abraham.   Lit. take hold of
17 Therefore, in all things He had Rto be
made like His brethren, that He might be Ra
merciful and faithful High Priest in things
pertaining to God, to make propitiation for
the sins of the people.   Phil. 2:7 • [Heb. 4:15; 5:1-10]
18 RFor in that He Himself has suffered,
being Ttempted, He is able to aid those who
are tempted.   [Heb. 4:15, 16] • tested

The Son Was Faithful

3 Therefore, holy brethren, partakers of the
heavenly calling, consider the Apostle
and RHigh Priest of our confession, Christ
Jesus,   Ps. 110:4
2 who was faithful to Him who appointed
Him, as RMoses also was faithful in all His
house.   Num. 12:7
3 For this One has been counted worthy of
more glory than Moses, inasmuch as RHe who
built the house has more honor than the
house.   Zech. 6:12, 13

2:7 NU, M omit the rest of v. 7.

2:13 2 Sam. 22:3; Is. 8:17

4 For every house is built by someone, but ᴿHe who built all things *is* God.   [Eph. 2:10]

5 And Moses indeed *was* faithful in all His house as a servant, for a testimony of those things which would be spoken *afterward,*

6 but Christ as ᴿa Son over His own house, ᴿwhose house we are ᴿif we hold fast the confidence and the rejoicing of the hope *firm to the end.   Heb. 1:2 • [1 Cor. 3:16] • [Matt. 10:22]

▼ 26-D. Keep Your Thought Processes Active and Open to the Voice of God

Be Faithful

7 Therefore, as the Holy Spirit says:

▲ *"Today, if you will hear His voice,*
8 *Do not harden your hearts as in the rebellion,*
   In the day of trial in the wilderness,

3:6 NU omits *firm to the end*

9 *Where your fathers tested Me, tried Me,*
   And saw My works forty years.
10 *Therefore I was angry with that generation,*
   And said, 'They always go astray in their heart,
   And they have not known My ways.'
11 *So I swore in My wrath,*
   'They shall not enter My rest.' "

37-E. The Fall of Jerusalem and the End ▼ of the First Century

12 Beware, brethren, lest there be in any of you an evil heart of unbelief in departing from the living God;

13 but ᵀexhort one another daily, while it is called *"Today,"* lest any of you be hardened through the deceitfulness of sin.   *encourage*

14 For we have become partakers of Christ if we hold the beginning of our confidence steadfast to the end,

---

26-D. Keep Your Thought Processes Active and Open to the Voice of God (Hebrews 3:7)—"Today, if you will hear His voice" (v. 7). God continues to speak to man. Are you listening? If you will keep your thought processes active and open to the voice of God, you will grow in grace and knowledge of our Lord and Savior Jesus Christ. The Bible is filled with evidence that God does speak to man. He spoke to

(1) Adam and Eve (Gen. 3:8–19, page 6)
(2) Cain (Gen. 4:9–15, page 8)
(3) Abraham (Gen. 12:1–3, page 17)
(4) Hagar (Gen 16:7–13, page 21)
(5) Moses (Ex. 3:1–14, page 60)
(6) Joshua (Josh. 1:1–9, page 215)
(7) Samuel (1 Sam. 16:1–7, page 282)

There are many more to whom the Lord spoke in both the Old and New Testaments. Sometimes He speaks to man

(1) face to face; not in His essence, but by manifestation (Judg. 13:1–23, page 254);
(2) through His creation (Ps. 19:1–6, page 520);
(3) through His written Word (Ps. 19:7–14, page 520).

He is speaking today to the whole world through His Son, the Lord Jesus Christ (Heb. 1:1–3, page 1236), as revealed in the Scriptures.

Now when you think unhealthy or unrighteous thoughts, you need to repent and forsake your wicked thoughts, and return to the Lord. How should you do this?

(1) Repent (Is. 55:7, page 695), and "present your bodies a living sacrifice, holy, acceptable to God." This is a positive act.
(2) "And do not be conformed to this world." This is a negative act.
(3) "But be transformed by the renewing of your mind." This is a positive act.

It takes both the positive and negative to produce positive results. The positive results are "that you may prove what is that good and acceptable and perfect will of God" (Rom. 12:1, 2, page 1142). Heed the voice of God when He speaks to you through His Spirit, using His Word. Are your thought processes active and open to the voice of God? He is speaking; are you listening?

See Ephesians 3:20, page 1190, for **Point 26-E: Think Great Thoughts, Because You Serve a Great God.**

37-E. The Fall of Jerusalem and the End of the First Century (Hebrews 3:12–19)—This passage speaks of those who wandered forty years in the wilderness and, because of their lack of faith, never entered God's rest in Canaan. Similarly, after the Jerusalem religious leaders rejected Christ, God gave them forty years of apostolic preaching to change their minds and accept Him. When the majority did not believe, approximately forty years after the Crucifixion, the Romans destroyed Jerusalem (A.D. 70). Thus, Jesus told the women of Jerusalem who were weeping as He went to the cross, "Do not weep for Me, but weep for yourselves" (Luke 23:28, 29, page 1045). He went on to speak of the suffering which was ahead for this city, because it was cutting itself off from God's help by crucifying God the Son.

See Index, page 17, for your next study.

▽ 15 while it is said:

R *"Today, if you will hear His voice,*
Do not harden your hearts as in the
rebellion."   Ps. 95:7, 8

Failure of the Wilderness Wanderers

16 R For who, having heard, rebelled? Indeed, *was it* not all who came out of Egypt, led by Moses?   Num. 14:2, 11, 30

17 Now with whom was He angry forty years? *Was it* not with those who sinned, whose corpses fell in the wilderness?

18 And R to whom did He swear that they would not enter His rest, but to those who did not obey?   Num. 14:30

19 So we see that they could not enter in
▲ because of R unbelief.   1 Cor. 10:11, 12

The Promise of Rest

4 Therefore, since a promise remains of entering His rest, R let us fear lest any of you seem to have come short of it.   Heb. 12:15

2 For indeed the gospel was preached to us as well as to them; but the word which they heard did not profit them, *not being mixed with faith in those who heard *it.*

3 For we who have believed do enter that rest, as He has said:

R *"So I swore in My wrath,*
'They shall not enter My rest,' "   Ps. 95:11

although the works were finished from the foundation of the world.

4 For He has spoken in a certain place of the seventh *day* in this way: R *"And God rested on the seventh day from all His works";*   Gen. 2:2

5 and again in this *place:* R *"They shall not enter My rest."*   Ps. 95:11

6 Since therefore it remains that some *must* enter it, and those to whom it was first preached did not enter because of disobedience,

7 again He designates a certain day, saying in David, *"Today,"* after such a long time, as it has been said:

R *"Today, if you will hear His voice,*
Do not harden your hearts."   Ps. 95:7, 8

8 For if T Joshua had R given them rest, then He would not afterward have spoken of another day.   Gr. *Jesus,* same as Heb. *Joshua* • Josh. 22:4

9 There remains therefore a rest for the people of God.

10 For he who has entered His rest has himself also ceased from his works as God *did* from His.

4:2 NU, M *since they were not united by faith with those who heeded it.*

The Word Discovers Our Condition

11 R Let us therefore be diligent to enter that rest, lest anyone fall according to the same example of disobedience.   2 Pet. 1:10

12 For the word of God *is* R living and powerful, and R sharper than any R two-edged sword, piercing even to the division of soul and spirit, and of joints and marrow, and is R a discerner of the thoughts and intents of the heart.   Ps. 147:15 • Is. 49:2 • Eph. 6:17 • 1 Cor. 14:24, 25

13 R And there is no creature hidden from His sight, but all things *are* R naked and open to the eyes of Him to whom we *must* give account.   Ps. 33:13–15; 90:8 • Job 26:6

Our Compassionate High Priest

14 Seeing then that we have a great R High Priest who has passed through the heavens, Jesus the Son of God, R let us hold fast *our* confession.   Heb. 2:17; 7:26 • Heb. 10:23

15 For R we do not have a High Priest who cannot sympathize with our weaknesses, but R was in all *points* tempted as *we are,* R yet without sin.   Is. 53:3–5 • Luke 22:28 • 2 Cor. 5:21

16 Let us therefore come boldly to the throne of grace, that we may obtain mercy and find grace to help in time of need.

Qualifications for High Priesthood

5 For every high priest taken from among men R is appointed for men in things pertaining to God, that he may offer both gifts and sacrifices for sins.   Heb. 2:17; 8:3

2 He can have compassion on those who are ignorant and going astray, since he himself is also subject to weakness.

3 Because of this he is required as for the people, so also for himself, to offer *sacrifices* for sins.

4 And no man takes this honor to himself, but he who is called by God, just as R Aaron *was.*   Ex. 28:1

A Priest Forever

5 R So also Christ did not glorify Himself to become High Priest, *but it* was He who said to Him: John 8:54

R *"You are My Son,*
Today I have begotten You."   Ps. 2:7

6 As *He* also *says* in another *place:*

R *"You are a priest forever*
According to the order of
Melchizedek";   Ps. 110:4

7 who, in the days of His flesh, when He had offered up prayers and supplications, with vehement cries and tears to Him who was able to save Him from death, and was heard R because of His godly fear,   Matt. 26:37

8 though He was a Son, *yet* He learned obedience by the things which He suffered.

9 And ᴿhaving been perfected, He became the author of eternal salvation to all who obey Him,   Heb. 2:10

10 called by God as High Priest ᴿ"*according to the order of Melchizedek,*"   Ps. 110:4

11 of whom ᴿwe have much to say, and hard to explain, since you have become ᴿdull of hearing.   [John 16:12] • [Matt. 13:15]

Spiritual Immaturity

12 For though by this time you ought to be teachers, you need *someone* to teach you again the first principles of the ᵀoracles of God; and you have come to need ᴿmilk and not solid food.   *sayings,* Scriptures • 1 Cor. 3:1–3

13 For everyone who partakes *only* of milk *is* unskilled in the word of righteousness, for he is ᴿa babe.   Eph. 4:14

14 But solid food belongs to those who are ᵀof full age, *that is,* those who by reason of ᵀuse have their senses exercised ᴿto discern both good and evil.   *mature • practice •* Is. 7:15

The Peril of Not Progressing

22-C. Repentance from Dead Works   ▼

6 Therefore, leaving the discussion of the elementary *principles* of Christ, let us go on to ᵀperfection, not laying again the foundation of repentance from ᴿdead works and of faith toward God,   *maturity •* [Heb. 9:14] ▲

2 of the doctrine of baptisms, ᴿof laying on of hands, of resurrection of the dead, ᴿand of eternal judgment.   [Acts 8:17] • Acts 24:25

3 And this *we will do if God permits.

22-E. Repentance, Impossible to Renew   ▼
To

4 For *it is* impossible for those who were once enlightened, and have tasted ᴿthe heavenly gift, and ᴿhave become partakers of the Holy Spirit,   [John 4:10] • [Gal. 3:2, 5]

6:3 M *let us do*

22-C. Repentance from Dead Works (Hebrews 6:1)—What does the writer of Hebrews mean by "repentance from dead works" (v. 1)? First, we need to see two other categories of works:

(1) *Good works.* Only saved souls can do works that please God (Matt. 5:16, page 939). Of the lost He said, "There is none who does good, no, not one" (Ps. 14:1–3, page 517). The believer is not to hide his good works, but let them be seen to the glory of God.

Mary of Bethany anointed the head and feet of Jesus with precious ointment while He sat at the table of Simon the leper. Some of the disciples called her deed an extravagant waste. But Jesus said, "She has done a good work for Me. . . . She has done what she could" (Mark 14:3–9, page 1003). Like Mary, we are to do all we can to the glory of God, not in order to be saved but because we *are* saved. This is the way to do good works.

(2) *Wicked works* (Col. 1:20, 21, page 1202). These deeds are done by the unregenerated, natural man (1 Cor. 2:14, page 1149). He lives according to this world system. He is motivated by the "prince of the power of the air [Satan]." His talk is filled with the lust of the flesh, and he lives to gratify the desires of the flesh and the natural mind. He is a child of wrath, and his works are wicked because he is dead in sin (Eph. 2:1–3, page 1187).

Dead works (v. 1) could be called "religious" works. They are done for the purpose of meriting eternal life. They are legalistic efforts to keep the moral and ceremonial laws of God for the purpose of winning God's favor, and being saved by works (Eph. 2:8, 9, page 1187). Paul said, "Therefore by the deeds of the law no flesh will be justified in His sight" (Rom. 3:20, page 1131). Dead works are performed by the kind of religious people who, "ignorant of God's righteousness, and seeking to establish [by dead works] their own righteousness, have not submitted to the righteousness of God" (Rom. 10:1–4, page 1140).

Paul is a good illustration of repentance from dead works. He clearly stated that he had "no confidence in the flesh." Then he listed his dead works of which he had to repent (Phil. 3:1–9, page 1197). When he compared this righteousness which is by dead works of the law, with the righteousness of Christ which is by faith, he counted the former but rubbish. He knew the meaning of "repentance from dead works" (v. 1).

See Hebrews 7:21, page 1242, for **Point 22-D: Repentance and God.**

22-E. Repentance, Impossible to Renew To (Hebrews 6:4–6)—The key that unlocks the mystery of this difficult Scripture is the word "impossible" in verse four. The writer is saying that the person who so sins will find it impossible to repent again.

(1) Let us see what the writer does *not* mean. He does not mean a backslidden Christian. Simon Peter backslid (Matt. 26:69–75, page 979), repented (John 21:3–17, page 1084), and was restored to fellowship with the Lord. King David sinned (2 Sam. 11:1–27, page 307), repented (Ps. 51:1–19, page 541), and was restored to fellowship with the Lord (2 Sam. 12:13, page 308). Any backslidden Christian can repent and be restored to fellowship with God.

(2) Let us see what the writer *does* mean. Verses 4–6 are proof that being outwardly "religious" is not enough to save from sin. Some *professed,* but did not *possess* eternal life. In outward appearance they might be called Christians. But Jesus said, "Not everyone who says to Me, 'Lord, Lord,' shall enter the kingdom of heaven" (Matt. 7:21–23, page 946). Such persons cannot be restored because they have not first repented.

(Point 22-E continued on next page)

▽ 5 and have tasted the good word of God and the powers of the age to come,

6 *if they fall away, to renew them again to repentance, ᴿsince they crucify again for themselves the Son of God, and put *Him* to
▲ an open shame.   Heb. 10:29

7 For the earth which drinks in the rain that often comes upon it, and bears herbs useful for those by whom it is cultivated, ᴿreceives blessing from God;   Ps. 65:10

8 ᴿbut if it bears thorns and briers, *it is* rejected and near to being cursed, whose end *is* to be burned.   Is. 5:6

A Better Estimate

9 But, beloved, we are confident of better things concerning you, yes, things that accompany salvation, though we speak in this manner.

10 For God *is* not unjust to forget your work and *labor of love which you have shown toward His name, *in that* you have ministered to the saints, and do minister.

11 And we desire that each one of you show the same diligence ᴿto the full assurance of hope until the end,   Col. 2:2

12 that you do not become ᵀsluggish, but imitate those who through faith and patience ᴿinherit the promises.   *lazy* • Heb. 10:36

God's Infallible Purpose in Christ

13 For when God made a promise to Abraham, because He could swear by no one greater, ᴿHe swore by Himself,   Gen. 22:16, 17

14 saying, *"Surely blessing I will bless you, and multiplying I will multiply you."*

15 And so, after he had patiently endured, he obtained the ᴿpromise.   Gen. 12:4; 21:5

16 For men indeed swear by the greater, and ᴿan oath for confirmation *is* for them an end of all dispute.   Ex. 22:11

17 Thus God, determining to show more abundantly to the heirs of promise the ᵀimmutability of His counsel, ᵀconfirmed *it* by an oath,   *unchangeableness of His purpose* • *guaranteed*

18 that by two immutable things, in which it is impossible for God to lie, we *might have strong consolation, who have fled for refuge to lay hold of the hope set before *us*.

19 This *hope* we have as an anchor of the

6:6 Or *and have fallen away*
6:10 NU omits *labor of*
6:14 Gen. 22:16, 17
6:18 M omits *might*

soul, both sure and steadfast, ᴿand which enters the Presence *behind* the veil, Lev. 16:2, 15

20 where the forerunner has entered for us, *even* Jesus, having become High Priest forever according to the order of Melchizedek.

The King of Righteousness

7 For this ᴿMelchizedek, king of Salem, priest of the Most High God, who met Abraham returning from the slaughter of the kings and blessed him,   Gen. 14:18-20

2 to whom also Abraham gave a tenth part of all, first being translated "king of righteousness," and then also king of Salem, meaning "king of peace,"

3 without father, without mother, without genealogy, having neither beginning of days nor end of life, but made like the Son of God, remains a priest continually.

4 Now consider how great this man *was*, to whom even the patriarch Abraham gave a tenth of the ᵀspoils.   *plunder*

5 And indeed ᴿthose who are of the sons of Levi, who receive the priesthood, have a commandment to receive tithes from the people according to the law, that is, from their brethren, though they have come from the loins of Abraham;   Num. 18:21-26

6 but he whose genealogy is not derived from them received tithes from Abraham and blessed him who had the promises.

7 Now beyond all contradiction the lesser is blessed by the better.

8 Here mortal men receive tithes, but there he *receives them*, ᴿof whom it is witnessed that he lives.   Heb. 5:6; 6:20

9 Even Levi, who receives tithes, paid tithes through Abraham, so to speak,

10 for he was still in the loins of his father when Melchizedek met him.

Need for a New Priesthood

11 ᴿTherefore, if perfection were through the Levitical priesthood (for under it the people received the law), what further need *was there* that another priest should rise according to the order of Melchizedek, and not be called according to the order of Aaron?   Heb. 7:18; 8:7

12 For the priesthood being changed, of necessity there is also a change of the law.

13 For He of whom these things are spoken belongs to another tribe, from which no man has ᵀofficiated at the altar.   *served*

14 For *it is* evident that ᴿour Lord arose

(Point 22-E continued from previous page)
    Esau so sinned against the Lord when he sold his birthright to Jacob for a bowl of stew (Gen. 25:27–34, page 32). Later he tried to repent, but found it impossible to do so. The Scripture says, "He found no place for repentance, though he sought it diligently with tears" (Heb. 12:16, 17, page 1250).
    At the Great White Throne judgment, where only the wicked dead are judged (Rev. 20:11–15, page 1313), they too will try to repent but will find it impossible.
    See Acts 17:30, page 1112, for **Point 22-F: Repentance: Its Importance.**

from Judah, of which tribe Moses spoke nothing concerning *priesthood. Is. 1:1

15 And it is yet far more evident if, in the likeness of Melchizedek, there arises another priest

16 who has come, not according to the law of a fleshly commandment, but according to the power of an endless life.

17 For *He testifies:

R *"You are a priest forever
According to the order of
Melchizedek."* Ps. 110:4

18 For on the one hand there is an annulling of the former commandment because of Rits weakness and unprofitableness, [Rom. 8:3]

19 for Rthe law made nothing Tperfect; on the other hand, there is the bringing in of Ra better hope, through which Rwe draw near to God. [Acts 13:39] • complete • Heb. 6:18, 19 • Rom. 5:2

Greatness of the New Priest

20 And inasmuch as He was not made priest without an oath

▼ 22-D. Repentance and God

21 (for they have become priests without an oath, but He with an oath by Him who said to Him:

R *"The LORD has sworn* Ps. 110:4
And will not relent,
'*You are a priest *forever*
According to the order of
▲ *Melchizedek'* "),

22 by so much more Jesus has become a Tsurety of a Rbetter covenant. guarantee • Heb. 8:6

7:14 NU priests
7:17 NU it is testified
7:21 NU ends the quotation after forever.

23 Also there were many priests, because they were prevented by death from continuing.

24 But He, because He continues forever, has an unchangeable priesthood.

25 Therefore He is also Rable to save Tto the uttermost those who come to God through Him, since He always lives Rto make intercession for them. Jude 24 • completely or forever • Rom. 8:34

26 For such a High Priest was fitting for us, Rwho is holy, Tharmless, undefiled, separate from sinners, Rand has become higher than the heavens; Heb. 4:15 • innocent • Eph. 1:20

27 who does not need daily, as those high priests, to offer up sacrifices, first for His Rown sins and then for the people's, for this He did once for all when He offered up Himself. Lev. 9:7; 16:6

28 For the law appoints as high priests men who have weakness, but the word of the oath, which came after the law, appoints the Son who has been perfected forever.

The New Priestly Service

8 Now this is the main point of the things we are saying: We have such a High Priest, Rwho is seated at the right hand of the throne of the Majesty in the heavens, Col. 3:1

2 a Minister of Rthe Tsanctuary and of Rthe true tabernacle which the Lord erected, and not man. Heb. 9:8, 12 • Lit. holies • Heb. 9:11, 24

3 For Revery high priest is appointed to offer both gifts and sacrifices. Therefore it is necessary that this One also have something to offer. Heb. 5:1; 8:4 • [Eph. 5:2]

4 For if He were on earth, He would not be a priest, since there are priests who offer the gifts according to the law;

5 who serve the copy and Rshadow of the heavenly things, as Moses was divinely instructed when he was about to make the

---

22-D. Repentance and God (Hebrews 7:21)—"God is not a man, that He should lie, nor a son of man, that He should repent" (Num. 23:19, page 164). Yet the Bible tells us that He can be sorry (Gen. 6:5–7, page 12). This is not a contradiction. It is paradoxical, but not contradictory. In a man, a change is real; in God, however, a change of mind is only apparent (see Point 3-D, "God Is Immutable," page 164).

God makes two covenants with man:

(1) *Unconditional.* When He makes an unconditional covenant He never repents. He made such a covenant with Abraham (Gen. 12:1–3, page 17). It will stand forever because, "The LORD has sworn and will not relent" (Ps. 110:4, page 577). He made such a covenant with Israel (Rom. 11:25–36, page 1141).

(2) *Conditional.* "And the LORD said, 'My Spirit shall not strive with man forever, for he is indeed flesh; yet his days shall be one hundred and twenty years' " (Gen. 6:3, page 11). In the days of Noah, God gave the human race 120 years to repent. Only Noah and his family repented and "found grace in the eyes of the LORD" (Gen. 6:8, page 12). They met God's condition and were not judged with the rest of the human race who refused to repent. "The Lord is not slack concerning His promise, as some count slackness, but is longsuffering toward us, not willing that any should perish but that all should come to repentance" (2 Pet. 3:9, page 1275).

It is clear that God invites all lost souls to be saved; He is "not willing that any should perish." To be saved, the lost must meet His condition—"repentance toward God and faith toward our Lord Jesus Christ" (Acts 20:21, page 1115). Now if a man does not repent and believe in the Lord Jesus Christ, God will judge that man. In love He bestows grace; but if salvation by grace is rejected, in justice He terminates it. In this way God appears to change His attitude toward man.

See Hebrews 6:4–6, page 1240, for **Point 22-E: Repentance, Impossible to Renew To.**

tabernacle. For He said, [R]*"See that you make all things according to the pattern shown you on the mountain."*   Col. 2:17 • Ex. 25:40

6 But now [R]He has obtained a more excellent ministry, inasmuch as He is also Mediator of a [R]better covenant, which was established on better promises.   [2 Cor. 3:6–8] • Heb. 7:22

A New Covenant

7 For if that [R]first *covenant* had been faultless, then no place would have been sought for a second.   Ex. 3:8; 19:5

8 Because finding fault with them, He says: [R]*"Behold, the days are coming, says the* LORD, *when I will make a new covenant with the house of Israel and with the house of Judah—*   Jer. 31:31–34

9 *"not according to the covenant that I made with their fathers in the day when I took them by the hand to lead them out of the land of Egypt; because they did not continue in My covenant, and I disregarded them, says the* LORD.

10 *"For this is the covenant that I will make with the house of Israel after those days, says the* LORD: *I will put My laws in their mind and write them on their hearts; and I will be their God, and they shall be My people.*

11 *"None of them shall teach his neighbor, and none his brother, saying, 'Know the* LORD,' *for all shall know Me, from the least of them to the greatest of them.*

12 *"For I will be merciful to their unrighteousness,* [R]*and their sins* *and their lawless deeds I will remember no more."*   Rom. 11:27

13 [R]In that He says, *"A new covenant,"* He has made the first obsolete. Now what is becoming obsolete and growing old is ready to vanish away.   [2 Cor. 5:17]

The Earthly Sanctuary

9 Then indeed, even the first *covenant* had ordinances of divine service and [R]the earthly sanctuary.   Ex. 25:8

2 For a tabernacle was prepared: the first *part,* in which *was* the lampstand, the table, and the showbread, which is called the [T]sanctuary;   *holy place,* lit. *holies*

3 [R]and behind the second veil, the part of the tabernacle which is called the Holiest of All,   Ex. 26:31–35; 40:3

4 which had the golden censer and the ark of the covenant overlaid on all sides with gold, in which *were* the golden pot that had the manna, Aaron's rod that budded, and the tablets of the covenant;

5 and [R]above it were the cherubim of glory overshadowing the mercy seat. Of these things we cannot now speak in detail. Lev. 16:2

Limitations of the Earthly Service

6 Now when these things had been thus prepared, [R]the priests always went into the first part of the tabernacle, performing *the* services.   Num. 18:2–6; 28:3

7 But into the second part the high priest *went* alone once a year, not without blood, which he offered for himself and *for* the people's sins *committed* in ignorance;

8 the Holy Spirit indicating this, that [R]the way into the Holiest of All was not yet made manifest while the first tabernacle was still standing.   [John 14:6]

9 It *was* symbolic for the present time in which both gifts and sacrifices are offered which cannot make him who performed the service perfect in regard to the conscience—

10 *concerned* only with foods and drinks, various washings, and fleshly ordinances imposed until the time of reformation.

The Heavenly Sanctuary

11 But Christ came *as* High Priest of [R]the good things *to come, with the greater and more perfect tabernacle not made with hands, that is, not of this creation.   Heb. 10:1

12 Not with the blood of goats and calves, but with His own blood He entered the Most Holy Place [R]once for all, [R]having obtained eternal redemption.   Zech. 3:9 • [Dan. 9:24]

13 For if the blood of bulls and goats and the ashes of a heifer, sprinkling the unclean, sanctifies for the purifying of the flesh,

14 how much more shall the blood of Christ, who through the eternal Spirit [R]offered Himself without spot to God, cleanse your conscience from [R]dead works [R]to serve the living God?   Is. 53:12 • Heb. 6:1 • Luke 1:74

15 And for this reason [R]He is the Mediator of the new covenant, by means of death, for the redemption of the transgressions under the first covenant, that [R]those who are called may receive the promise of the eternal inheritance.   Rom. 3:25 • Heb. 3:1

The Mediator's Death Necessary

16 For where there is a testament, there must also of necessity be the death of the testator.

17 For [R]a testament is in force after men are dead, since it has no power at all while the testator lives.   Gal. 3:15

18 [R]Therefore not even the first *covenant* was dedicated without blood.   Ex. 24:6

19 For when Moses had spoken every precept to all the people according to the law, he took the blood of calves and goats, with water, scarlet wool, and hyssop, and sprinkled both the book itself and all the people,

20 saying, *"This is the blood of the covenant which God has commanded you."*

9:11 NU *that have come*
9:20 Ex. 24:3–8

8:12 NU omits *and their lawless deeds*

21 Then likewise ᴿhe sprinkled with blood both the tabernacle and all the vessels of the ministry.   Ex. 29:12, 36

▼ 20-G. Without the Shedding of Blood

22 And according to the law almost all things are purified with blood, and without ▲ shedding of blood there is no remission.

▼ 35-B. The Pattern of the Tabernacle

Greatness of Christ's Sacrifice

23 Therefore it was necessary that the copies of the things in the heavens should be purified with these, but the heavenly things ▽ themselves with better sacrifices than these.

24 For Christ has not entered the holy places made with hands, which are copies of the true, but into heaven itself, now to appear in the presence of God for us;   ▲

25 not that He should offer Himself often, as ᴿthe high priest enters the Most Holy Place every year with blood of another—   Heb. 9:7

26 He then would have had to suffer often since the foundation of the world; but now, once at the end of the ages, He has appeared to put away sin by the sacrifice of Himself.

27 ᴿAnd as it is appointed for men to die once, but after this the judgment,   Gen. 3:19

20-G. Without the Shedding of Blood (Hebrews 9:22)—"Without shedding of blood there is no remission" (v. 22). This is one of God's imperatives. Without the atoning blood of the Lord Jesus there is no remission of past, present, or future sins. Without His blood there is no remission of sins of action or neglect, nor is there remission of sins committed in ignorance, nor is there remission for the sin of doing the right thing in the wrong way. Unless the sinner is cleansed from sin by the blood of God the Son, there is no remission at all. Without shedding of blood there is:

(1) *No justification.* To be justified is to be declared judicially righteous because you have been washed and made white in the blood of the Lamb (Rom. 3:24–26, page 1131; cf. Rev. 1:5, page 1293).

(2) *No redemption.* To redeem is to buy back. God's only begotten Son shed His blood to redeem (buy back) sinful man (Eph. 1:7, page 1186).

(3) *No forgiveness.* "In whom we have redemption through His blood, the forgiveness of sins" (Col. 1:14, page 1201).

(4) *No cleansing.* The blood of Jesus continues to cleanse us from sin day after day (1 John 1:7, page 1278).

(5) *No atonement.* "For it is the blood that makes atonement for the soul" (Lev. 17:11, page 126).

(6) *No sanctification.* To sanctify means to set apart for God's use. The blood of Jesus sets every cleansed believer apart for salvation and service (Heb. 13:12, page 1252).

(7) *No victory.* The saints (all true believers) will overcome Satan, sin, and all the powers of darkness by the blood of Jesus Christ the Lamb (Rev. 12:11, page 1305). No wonder Peter calls it "the precious blood of Christ" (1 Pet. 1:18, 19, page 1263).

See Index, page 17, for your next study.

35-B. The Pattern of the Tabernacle (Hebrews 9:23, 24)—On Mt. Sinai, God showed Moses the complete and exact plan of the tabernacle (Ex. 25—27, page 83). This was a giant, life-sized, visible parable to Israel and the nations. It illustrated the truths surrounding sinful mankind's separation from God (Is. 59:2, page 699). It was also an object lesson of God's provision for the believer's salvation and daily cleansing through the sacrifice of Christ, which was typified during the Old Testament period by animal sacrifices. Let us first examine the general pattern and truths of the tabernacle. In subsequent outlines the details will be discussed.

(1) *The courtyard.* The courtyard was a rectangle, 100 by 50 cubits (150 x 75 ft.). Its length ran east and west, with its single gate opening on the east side. It was surrounded by a wall 5 cubits (7½ ft.) high of fine, white linen curtains, which in turn was supported every 5 cubits by a wooden pillar (or post) which had a brass socket at the base and a silver one at the top. The single gate was 20 cubits (30 ft.) wide, opening toward the east; it featured a screen of the same width, made of blue, purple, and scarlet thread and fine linen (Ex. 27:9–19, page 86). The single gate reminds us that Christ said, "I am the door. If anyone enters by Me, he will be saved" (John 10:9, page 1067). A barrier existed between the holiness of God's fellowship and fallen man on the outside.

(2) *The bronze altar.* This altar of sacrifice stood in the foreground of the court as the first item one would approach. It was 5 by 5 cubits (7½ x 7½ ft.) square, and 3 cubits (4½ ft.) high. It had an acacia-wood frame, overlaid with brass, with a brass grate to hold the fire. It also had four brass horns, one on each corner. Here the animal sacrifice died for the sins of the people (Ex. 27:1–8, page 86). The burnt offering was a male of the herd without blemish. Its blood was poured out and its skin flayed (stripped off). The animal was offered to God on the wood and brass of this altar which stood outside the tabernacle (Lev. 1:1–7, page 105). We see here a type of Christ, a male of the stock of mankind, without blemish, His blood poured out and His skin flayed, offered upon the wooden cross with metal nails (Mark 15:20–25, page 1006).

(3) *The laver.* This was a large brass vessel for holding water. It stood in the courtyard between the bronze altar and the tabernacle (Ex. 30:17–21, page 90). The priests had to wash their hands and feet with the

(Point 35-B continued on next page)

28 so ᴿChrist was offered once to bear the sins of many. To those who eagerly wait for Him He will appear a second time, apart from sin, for salvation.   Is. 53:12; Rom. 6:10

Animal Sacrifices Insufficient

10 For the law, having a shadow of the good things to come, *and* not the very image of the things, can never with these

(Point 35-B continued from previous page)
water before entering the tabernacle, "lest they die" (Ex. 30:20, 21, page 90). The priests could not touch the holy vessels in the Holy Place with dirty hands, nor track in dirt with soiled feet. This pictures the truth that the believer, after the sacrifice of the altar (Christ's death and our salvation), still needs daily cleansing to enter the presence of God (John 13:8–10, page 1073; cf. 1 John 1:9, page 1278).

(4) *The tabernacle* (Ex. 26:15–30, page 86). The tabernacle was composed of two basic parts:

(a) *The wooden structure.* This was a rectangle, running lengthwise east and west, and open at the east end. It was made of twenty upright boards on north and south, and six on the west side. The boards were each 10 cubits (15 ft.) high and 1½ cubits (27 in.) wide. They were connected by horizontal bars and loops which held the bars. Each board sat in two silver sockets, and its acacia wood was covered by gold (Ex. 26:15–30, page 86). Gold does not oxidize, even in a thousand years. It thus speaks to us of what never fades, that which remains pure through the centuries and through eternity.

(b) *The tents* (Ex. 26:1–14, page 85). The tabernacle, or tent, was in reality four tents or layers, one on top of the other.

(i) *The first tent* (Ex. 26:1–6, page 85). The tabernacle proper was the interior tent. It was made of 10 sections, each 28 by 4 cubits (42 x 6 ft.), which were attached to make a linen interior 28 by 40 cubits (42 x 60 ft.). The 4 cubit-wide (6 ft.) sections each were colored one color, and included white (plain linen), blue, purple, and scarlet. To this beautiful interior were added the gold-covered boards that composed the sides of the tabernacle. The colors were white, representing holiness; blue, representing heaven; purple, representing royalty; and scarlet, representing blood. All of this exactly fits the life and ministry of Christ who was to come.

(ii) *The second tent* (Ex. 26:7–13, page 85). This tent was made of goat's hair. It hung over the linen tabernacle for protection, and added strength. It was a goat that died for the nation's sins on the Day of Atonement (Lev. 16:7–10, 15–21, page 123), while a "scapegoat" took their sins into the wilderness.

(iii) *The third tent* (Ex. 26:14, page 86). This tent was made of ram skins, dyed red. It would be beautiful, and yet could only remind onlookers of the shed blood of sacrifice.

(iv) *The fourth tent* (Ex. 26:14, page 86). This tent was the storm tent, made of badger skins. The tent could represent heaven and, to us, symbolize the outer body of flesh which was taken on by Christ.

(5) *The Holy Place* (Ex. 26:35, page 86). This section was the longer first room of the tabernacle; it measured 12 by 6 cubits (18 x 9 ft.). Here, amid the gold-covered wooden boards and the linen curtains above, were placed

(a) the table for the showbread;
(b) the seven-lamped candelabra (Ex. 26:35, page 86);
(c) the altar of incense (Ex. 35:15, page 96).

These in turn represented the unity of God's people, God's eternal care, and the high-priestly intercession made daily by Christ for His people (Heb. 7:25, page 1242).

(6) *The veil and the Most Holy Place* (Ex. 26:31–34, page 86). The innermost room of the tabernacle was cubical, 6 cubits (9 ft.) to a side, and its entry was sealed off by the heavy veil (Ex. 26:31–35, page 86). This veil of white, blue, purple, and scarlet spoke of all that God stood for in holiness—His absolute separation from all that is sinful and defiling. Within this chamber stood the sacred ark of the covenant, made of wood overlaid with gold, 2½ by 1½ by 1½ cubits (45 x 27 x 27 in.) with the wings of the cherubim placed above it. It became the mercy seat, where God's sacred presence was manifested. The shekinah glory shone upon this place where the high priest, on the annual Day of Atonement, sprinkled the goat's blood for the covering of sin (Ex. 25:10–22, page 84).

Christ, by His death and shed blood, eternally paid the penalty for sin. For the believer the veil has now been opened to God and His presence, His forgiveness, and His manifold blessings (Matt. 27:51, page 981).

(7) *The cloud of glory over the tabernacle* (Ex. 40:34–38, page 103; Num. 9:15–23, page 149). Above the tent stood the cloud of God's glory. It moved before them and led them on the march in the wilderness, as a pillar of cloud by day and a pillar of fire by night. This manifestation of God's leading first occurred after the Exodus from Egypt, before the tabernacle was built (Ex. 13:21, 22, page 73). Once the tabernacle was set up, the cloud localized itself above it. God's shekinah glory apparently manifested itself in the tabernacle in an even more special way—perhaps by supernatural glowing of the cloud when God desired to speak with them (Num. 16:41–44, page 157). This leading of the cloud, above the tabernacle, is a figure of God's daily leading of the believer in his actions and in his resting.

See Exodus 35:30–35, page 96, for **Point 35-C: The Furniture of the Tabernacle.**

same sacrifices, which they offer continually year by year, make those who approach perfect.

2 For then would they not have ceased to be offered? For the worshipers, once ᵀpurified, would have had no more consciousness of sins.   cleansed

3 But in those *sacrifices there is* a reminder of sins every year.

4 For *it is* not possible that the blood of bulls and goats could take away sins.

Christ's Death Fulfills God's Will

5 Therefore, when He came into the world, He said:

> ᴿ*"Sacrifice and offering You did not*
> *   desire,*   Ps. 40:6–8
> *But a body You have prepared for Me.*
> 6 *In burnt offerings and sacrifices for sin*
> *   You had no pleasure.*
> 7 *Then I said, 'Behold, I have come—*
> *   In the volume of the book it is written*
> *   of Me—*
> *   To do Your will, O God.' "*

8 Previously saying, *"Sacrifice and offering, burnt offerings, and offerings for sin You did not desire, nor had pleasure in them"* (which are offered according to the law),

9 then He said, *"Behold, I have come to do Your will, *O God."* He takes away the first that He may establish the second.

10 ᴿBy that will we have been ᵀsanctified ᴿthrough the offering of the body of Jesus Christ once *for all.*   Is. 53:12 • *set apart* • [Heb. 9:12]

Christ's Death Perfects the Sanctified

11 And every priest stands ministering daily and offering repeatedly the same sacrifices, which can never take away sins.

12 ᴿBut this Man, after He had offered one sacrifice for sins forever, sat down ᴿat the right hand of God,   Ps. 68:18; Col. 3:1 • Ps. 110:1

13 from that time waiting ᴿtill His enemies are made His footstool.   Ps. 110:1

14 For by one offering He has perfected forever those who are being sanctified.

15 But the Holy Spirit also witnesses to us; for after He had said before,

16 ᴿ*"This is the covenant that I will make with them after those days, says the Lᴏʀᴅ: I will put My laws into their hearts, and in their minds I will write them,"*   Jer. 31:33, 34

17 then He adds, *"Their sins and their lawless deeds I will remember no more."*

18 Now where there is ᵀremission of these, *there is* no longer an offering for sin. forgiveness

Hold Fast Your Confession

19 Therefore, brethren, having boldness to enter the Holiest by the blood of Jesus,

20 by a new and ᴿliving way which He consecrated for us, through the veil, that is, His flesh,   John 14:6

21 and *having* a ᴿHigh Priest over the house of God,   Ps. 110:4

22 let us draw near with a true heart ᴿin full assurance of faith, having our hearts sprinkled from an evil conscience and our bodies washed with pure water.   Eph. 3:12

23 Let us hold fast the confession of *our* hope without wavering, for ᴿHe who promised *is* faithful.   1 Cor. 1:9; 10:13

24 And let us consider one another in order to stir up love and good works,

25 not forsaking the assembling of ourselves together, as *is* the manner of some, but exhorting *one another*, and so much the more as you see the Day approaching.

The Just Live by Faith

26 For if we sin willfully after we have received the knowledge of the truth, there no longer remains a sacrifice for sins,

27 but a certain fearful expectation of judgment, and ᴿfiery indignation which will devour the adversaries.   Zeph. 1:18

28 Anyone who has rejected Moses' law dies without mercy on the testimony of two or three ᴿwitnesses.   Deut. 17:2–6; 19:15

29 Of how much worse punishment, do you suppose, will he be thought worthy who has trampled the Son of God underfoot, counted the blood of the covenant by which he was sanctified a common thing, ᴿand insulted the Spirit of grace?   [Matt. 12:31]

30 For we know Him who said, ᴿ*"Vengeance is Mine, I will repay," *says* the Lord. And again, ᴿ*"The Lᴏʀᴅ will judge His people."*   Deut. 32:35 • Deut. 32:36

31 ᴿIt is a fearful thing to fall into the hands of the living God.   [Luke 12:5]

32 But recall the former days in which, after you were ᵀilluminated, you endured a great struggle with sufferings: enlightened

33 partly while you were made ᴿa spectacle both by reproaches and tribulations, and partly while ᴿyou became companions of those who were so treated;   1 Cor. 4:9 • Phil. 1:7

34 for you had compassion on *me in my chains, and ᴿjoyfully accepted the plundering of your ᵀgoods, knowing that ᴿyou have a better and an enduring possession for yourselves *in heaven. Matt. 5:12 • *possessions* • Matt. 6:20

35 Therefore do not cast away your confidence, ᴿwhich has great reward.   Matt. 5:12

36 ᴿFor you have need of endurance, so that after you have done the will of God, ᴿyou may receive the promise: Luke 21:19 • [Col. 3:24]

10:30 NU omits *says the Lord*
10:34 NU *the prisoners* instead of *me in my chains* • NU omits *in heaven*

37 *"For*[R] *yet a little while,*   Hab. 2:3, 4
   And [R]*He who is coming will come and*
      will not [T]*tarry.*   Luke 18:8 • delay
38 *Now* [R]*the* just shall live by faith;*
   But if anyone draws back,   Rom. 1:17
   My soul has no pleasure in him."

39 But we are not of those [R]who draw back
to [T]perdition, but of those who [R]believe to the
saving of the soul.   2 Pet. 2:20 • destruction • Acts 16:31

By Faith We Understand

11 Now faith is the [T]substance of things
   hoped for, the [T]evidence [R]of things not
seen.   realization • Or confidence • Rom. 8:24

2 For by it the elders obtained a *good*
testimony.

3 By faith we understand that the [T]worlds
were framed by the word of God, so that the
things which are seen were not made of
things which are visible.   Or *ages,* Gr. *aiones,* aeons

10:38 NU *my just one*

Faith at the Dawn of History

4 By faith [R]Abel offered to God a more
excellent sacrifice than Cain, through which
he obtained witness that he was righteous,
God testifying of his gifts; and through it he
being dead still [R]speaks.   Gen. 4:3-5 • Heb. 12:24

44-B. Enoch Walked by Faith with God   ▼

5 By faith Enoch was taken away so that
he did not see death, [R]*"and was not found,
because God had taken him"*; for before he
was taken he had this testimony, that he
pleased God.   Gen. 5:24

6 But without faith *it is* impossible to
please *Him,* for he who comes to God must
believe that He is, and *that* He is a rewarder
of those who diligently seek Him.   ▲

45-E. Noah: A Man of Faith   ▼

7 By faith Noah, being divinely warned of
things not yet seen, moved with godly fear,
[R]prepared an ark for the saving of his house-

44-B. Enoch Walked by Faith with God (Hebrews 11:5, 6)—God's Word reveals seven things that Enoch did by faith:

(1) By faith Enoch walked with God three hundred years. His faith must have been tested and tried many times. But there is no evidence that he ever lowered the "shield of faith," with which he was able to quench all of Satan's fiery darts (Eph. 6:16, page 1192).

(2) By faith Enoch was "taken away," that is, taken up to heaven—body, soul, and spirit. And his body of flesh was glorified because "flesh and blood cannot inherit the kingdom of God" (1 Cor. 15:50-55, page 1163).

(3) By faith Enoch "did not see death" (v. 5). Enoch is a type of all born-again believers who will be alive when Jesus comes back to this world. The dead in Christ will be resurrected, and the living will be caught up with the resurrected saints to meet the Lord in the air (1 Thess. 4:13-18, page 1211).

(4) By faith Enoch pleased God. Because Enoch walked with God by faith, all who knew him knew that he pleased God. "He had this testimony, that he pleased God" (v. 5). Enoch had faith that could be seen by all who knew him—by the way he talked, lived, and worked. Faith can be seen in our manner of life.

Jesus was teaching in a house in Capernaum, and four men brought a paralytic to Him. When they could not enter (because the house was filled with people), they went up on top of the house, removed a section of the roof, and let the man down on his bed before Jesus. And the Scripture says, "When Jesus saw their faith" He forgave the sins of the paralytic and healed him (Mark 2:1-5, page 986). Can your loved ones, friends, neighbors, and acquaintances see the proof of your faith?

(5) By faith Enoch believed that Almighty God did exist. "For he who comes to God must believe that He is" (v. 6). Where did Enoch get such great faith? He did not have the Bible or any books of the Bible. God must have manifested Himself to Enoch, as He did to others, before the Son, the Lord Jesus Christ, became a man. Enoch had an ever-present witness of God.

He also had God's creation: "The heavens declare the glory of God; and the firmament shows His handiwork. Day unto day utters speech, and night unto night reveals knowledge" (Ps. 19:1, 2, page 520). Creation reveals the glory of the Creator, day and night. When Enoch looked at God's creation, he saw more than the sun, moon, and stars. He saw more than mountains, valleys, rivers, lakes, streams, and seas. He saw more than trees, flowers, the birds of the air, the beast of the fields, the fish of the sea, or man who was created in the image of God. Enoch, by faith, saw the reflection of the Creator in His creation. He sought the Creator God, and found Him, because he sought Him with his whole heart (Ps. 119:2, page 580).

(6) By faith Enoch was rewarded. He was not rewarded with eternal life, because eternal life is God's gift; it cannot be earned (Eph. 2:8, 9, page 1187). God rewarded Enoch by allowing him to walk with Himself.

(7) By faith Enoch diligently sought God. We do not know how long he sought Him before God invited Enoch to walk with Him; it could have been sixty-five years. The years of seeking were years of growing. As he sought God one day, his growth in grace and knowledge was sufficient, and he walked by faith into the very heavenly presence of God.

See Micah 6:8, page 892, for **Point 44-C: Enoch Walked Humbly with God.**

45-E. Noah: A Man of Faith (Hebrews 11:7)—In this brief text the Holy Spirit reveals seven elements that embody faith. Noah had great faith. Noah "walked with God" (Gen. 6:9, page 12), lived, worked, and

(Point 45-E continued on next page)

▽ hold, by which he condemned the world and became heir of ᴿthe righteousness which is according to faith.   1 Pet. 3:20 · Rom. 3:22

▲

Faithful Abraham

8 By faith Abraham obeyed when he was called to go out to the place which he would receive as an inheritance. And he went out, not knowing where he was going.

9 By faith he dwelt in the land of promise as in a foreign country, dwelling in tents with Isaac and Jacob, ᴿthe heirs with him of the same promise;   Heb. 6:17

10 for he waited for ᴿthe city which has foundations, ᴿwhose builder and maker is God.   [Heb. 12:22; 13:14] · [Rev. 21:10]

11 By faith Sarah herself also received strength to conceive seed, and *she bore a child when she was past the age, because she judged Him faithful who had promised.

12 Therefore from one man, and him as good as dead, were born as many as the stars of the sky in multitude—innumerable as the sand which is by the seashore.

11:11 NU omits she bore a child

(Point 45-E continued from previous page)

preached righteousness for 120 years. The world was so corrupt that the Lord said "the wickedness of man was great in the earth, and that every intent of the thoughts of his heart was only evil continually" (Gen. 6:5, page 12). The seven parts of Noah's great faith are:

(1) *The foundation*—being warned by God. The only foundation for saving faith is the infallible Word of God. "So then faith comes by hearing, and hearing by the Word of God" (Rom. 10:17, page 1140). Faith not founded upon God's inerrant Word is vain belief (1 Cor. 15:1–4, page 1161). By faith Noah was triumphant over the evils of the people who lived before the Flood, which ended in the judgment of God (Gen. 7:20–24, page 13).

(2) *The measure*—he believed "things not yet seen." Paul tells us that "God has dealt to each one [believer] a measure of faith" (Rom. 12:3, page 1142). Real faith does not have to see to believe: "Did I not say to you that if you would believe you would see the glory of God?" (John 11:40, page 1070). For 120 years Noah believed "things not yet seen"; then he saw the prophecy of the Flood fulfilled. Noah did not look at visible things, but by faith he looked at invisible things, because they are eternal (2 Cor. 4:18, page 1168). By faith Noah and his family came through the judgment of the Flood, and saw God's glory.

(3) *The power*—he was "moved with godly fear." He was moved to act with godly fear in reverence that led to repentance, resulting in salvation by the grace of God. Noah not only believed God's promise of grace, but also His promise of judgment. Those who do not believe that God will punish sin in the impenitent sinner do not know saving faith. Noah, like all lost sinners, had a choice: he could accept the gift of God, which is eternal life, or he could choose to live in sin and collect its wages, which are eternal separation from the mercy of God (Rom. 6:23, page 1134). The power of Noah's faith moved him with holy fear to obey God and build the ark. He believed that God would judge man, as He promised, saying, "I will destroy man whom I have created from the face of the earth" (Gen. 6:7, page 12).

(4) *The proof*—he "prepared an ark." To those who lived before the Flood, Noah was a fool. He was building a huge ark of gopherwood on dry land, which seemed senseless. The ark was the evidence of Noah's faith; he had a living, working faith. His faith provided the working force that "prepared an ark." Faith that does not motivate works is dead (James 2:17, page 1257).

(5) *The fruits*—"for the saving of his household." Noah was a preacher of righteousness, and his labor was not in vain. He ministered to his wife, three sons, and three daughters-in-law. All seven believed, and were saved by the grace of God.

(6) *The function*—"by which he condemned the world." The gospel of the grace of God will do one of two things when proclaimed by faith:

(a) It will bring salvation, when believed (Acts 16:31, page 1111).

(b) It will bring condemnation when rejected in unbelief (John 3:36, page 1053). To illustrate, the sun will melt a hard chunk of ice, but also harden a soft lump of clay. The gospel preached in the power of the Holy Spirit will save or condemn.

(7) *The recompense*—and "became heir of the righteousness which is according to faith." When we were saved by faith in Christ, we were made righteous with the righteousness of Christ (2 Cor. 5:21, page 1169), even though we remain in this body of flesh which is under the curse of sin and death (Rom. 7:24, 25, page 1136). God sees us as righteous because we are in Christ by faith. However, there is a righteousness that we cannot know until we stand before Him in our resurrected, glorified bodies; then "we shall be like Him, for we shall see Him as He is" (1 John 3:2, page 1279).

The reward that God promised Noah was that he would become "heir of the righteousness which is according to faith." God tells us that we are "heirs of God and joint heirs with Christ" (Rom. 8:17, page 1137). None of the saved of the Old or New Testament have entered into their inheritance. Noah, along with all the saints, must wait until Jesus comes and resurrects the bodies of all believers before he can enter his full inheritance as an "heir of the righteousness which is according to faith."

How does your faith compare with Noah's?

See Index, page 17, for your next study.

The Heavenly Hope

13 These all died in faith, not having received the promises, but having seen them afar off *were assured of them, embraced *them* and ᴿconfessed that they were strangers and pilgrims on the earth. Ps. 39:12

14 For those who say such things ᴿdeclare plainly that they seek a homeland. Heb. 13:14

15 And truly if they had called to mind that *country* from which they had come out, they would have had opportunity to return.

16 But now they desire a better, that is, a heavenly *country*. Therefore God is not ashamed ᴿto be called their God, for He has ᴿprepared a city for them. Ex. 3:6 • [Rev. 21:2]

The Faith of the Patriarchs

17 By faith Abraham, when he was tested, offered up Isaac, and he who had received the promises offered up his only begotten *son,*

18 ᵀof whom it was said, ᴿ*"In Isaac your seed shall be called,"* to • Gen. 21:12

19 concluding that God *was* able to raise *him* up, even from the dead, from which he also received him in a figurative sense.

20 By faith ᴿIsaac blessed Jacob and Esau concerning things to come. Gen. 27:26–40

21 By faith Jacob, when he was dying, blessed each of the sons of Joseph, and worshiped, *leaning* on the top of his staff.

22 By faith ᴿJoseph, when he was dying, made mention of the departure of the children of Israel, and gave instructions concerning his bones. Gen. 50:24, 25

The Faith of Moses

23 By faith Moses, when he was born, was hidden three months by his parents, because they saw *he was* a beautiful child; and they were not afraid of the king's command.

24 By faith ᴿMoses, when he became of age, refused to be called the son of Pharaoh's daughter, Ex. 2:11–15

25 choosing rather to suffer affliction with the people of God than to enjoy the ᵀpassing pleasures of sin, temporary

26 esteeming the ᵀreproach of Christ greater riches than the treasures *in Egypt; for he looked to the reward. reviling because of

27 By faith ᴿhe forsook Egypt, not fearing the wrath of the king; for he endured as seeing Him who is invisible. Ex. 10:28

28 By faith ᴿhe kept the Passover and the sprinkling of blood, lest he who destroyed the firstborn should touch them. Ex. 12:21

29 By faith they passed through the Red Sea as by dry *land; whereas* the Egyptians, attempting *to do* so, were drowned.

By Faith They Overcame

30 By faith the walls of Jericho fell down after they were encircled for seven days.

31 By faith the harlot Rahab did not perish with those who did not believe, when ᴿshe had received the spies with peace. Josh. 2:1

32 And what more shall I say? For the time would fail me to tell of Gideon and ᴿBarak and Samson and Jephthah, also *of* David and Samuel and the prophets: Judg. 4:6–24

33 who through faith subdued kingdoms, worked righteousness, obtained promises, ᴿstopped the mouths of lions, Dan. 6:22

34 ᴿquenched the violence of fire, escaped the edge of the sword, out of weakness were made strong, became valiant in battle, turned to flight the armies of the aliens. Dan. 3:23–28

35 ᴿWomen received their dead raised to life again. Others were ᴿtortured, not accepting deliverance, that they might obtain a better resurrection. 1 Kin. 17:22 • Acts 22:25

36 Still others had trial of mockings and scourgings, yes, and ᴿof chains and imprisonment. Gen. 39:20

37 ᴿThey were stoned, they were sawn in two, *were tempted, were slain with the sword. ᴿThey wandered about ᴿin sheepskins and goatskins, being destitute, afflicted, tormented— 1 Kin. 21:13 • 2 Kin. 1:8 • Zech. 13:4

38 of whom the world was not worthy. They wandered in deserts and mountains, ᴿ*in* dens and caves of the earth. 1 Kin. 18:4, 13; 19:9

39 And all these, ᴿhaving obtained a good testimony through faith, did not receive the promise, Heb. 11:2, 13

40 God having provided something better for us, that they should not be ᴿmade ᵀperfect apart from us. Heb. 5:9 • complete

The Race of Faith

24-E. Saving Faith Is in Christ ▼

12 Therefore we also, since we are surrounded by so great a cloud of witnesses, let us lay aside every weight, and the

---

11:13 NU, M omit *were assured of them*

11:26 NU, M *of*

11:37 NU omits *were tempted*

24-E. Saving Faith Is in Christ (Hebrews 12:1, 2)—That person in whom we have saving faith is the God-Man, Christ, the promised Messiah. As His followers, we are to "run with endurance the race that is set before us" (v. 1). We are to be conscious of that great cloud, the host of heavenly witnesses, the Old and New Testament saints as represented in Hebrews 11 (page 1247), knowing that they are our heavenly spectators. We are to run the race by faith, looking to Jesus, who is:

(1) *The author of our faith* (v. 2). Christ is the leader of our faith. We are the sheep of His pasture, and
(Point 24-E continued on next page)

▽ sin which so easily ensnares us, and let us run with endurance the race that is set before us, 2 looking unto Jesus, the author and finisher of our faith, who for the joy that was set before Him ᴿendured the cross, despising the shame, and has sat down at the right hand of
▲ the throne of God.   Ps. 68:18; 69:7, 19

The Discipline of God

3 ᴿFor consider Him who endured such hostility from sinners against Himself, ᴿlest you become weary and discouraged in your souls.   Matt. 10:24 · Gal. 6:9
4 ᴿYou have not yet resisted to bloodshed, striving against sin.   [1 Cor. 10:13]
5 And you have forgotten the exhortation which speaks to you as to sons:

ᴿ*"My son, do not despise the* ᵀ*chastening
   of the LORD,
Nor be discouraged when you are
   rebuked by Him;*   Prov. 3:11, 12 · *discipline*
6 *For* ᴿ*whom the LORD loves He chastens,
And scourges every son whom He
   receives."*   Rev. 3:19

7 ᴿIf* you endure chastening, God deals with you as with sons; for what son is there whom a father does not chasten?   Deut. 8:5
8 But if you are without chastening, ᴿof which all have become partakers, then you are illegitimate and not sons.   1 Pet. 5:9
9 Furthermore, we have had human fathers who corrected us, and we paid them respect. Shall we not much more readily be in subjection to ᴿthe Father of spirits and live?   [Job 12:10]

10 For they indeed for a few days chastened us as seemed best to them, but He for our profit, ᴿthat we may be partakers of His holiness.   Lev. 11:44
11 Now no ᵀchastening seems to be joyful for the present, but painful; nevertheless, afterward it yields ᴿthe peaceable fruit of righteousness to those who have been trained by it.   discipline · James 3:17, 18

Renew Your Spiritual Vitality

12 Therefore ᴿstrengthen the hands which hang down, and the feeble knees,   Is. 35:3
13 and make straight paths for your feet, so that what is lame may not be *dislocated*, but rather be healed.
14 Pursue peace with all *people*, and holiness, without which no one will see the Lord:
15 looking carefully lest anyone ᴿfall short of the grace of God; lest any ᴿroot of bitterness springing up cause trouble, and by this many become defiled;   Heb. 4:1 · Deut. 29:18
16 lest there be any ᴿfornicator or ᵀprofane person like Esau, who for one morsel of food sold his birthright.   [1 Cor. 6:13–18] · *godless*
17 For you know that afterward, when he wanted to inherit the blessing, he was rejected, for he found no place for repentance, though he sought it diligently with tears.

The Glorious Company

18 For you have not come *to ᴿthe mountain that may be touched and that burned with fire, and to blackness and *darkness and tempest,   Deut. 4:11; 5:22
19 and the sound of a trumpet and the voice of words, so that those who heard it ᴿbegged

12:7 NU, M *It is for discipline that you endure; God*   12:18 NU *to that which* • NU *gloom*

(Point 24-E continued from previous page)
we hear and know His voice as He speaks to us out of the written Word (Rom. 10:17, page 1140). To know our spiritual Leader by faith is to take up our cross and follow Him (Mark 8:34–38, page 994).

(2) *The finisher of our faith* (v. 2). Christ is the perfecter of our faith. On the cross, He said, "It is finished! " (John 19:30, page 1081). These words were a shout of victory, a triumph of His faith. Paul said, "The life which I now live in the flesh I live by faith in the Son of God" (Gal. 2:20, page 1180). Paul did not live by faith in any patriarch or prophet. He learned and profited by their lives of faith, but he lived only by the faith he found in God the Son.

(3) *The object of our faith.* "Jesus Christ is the same yesterday, today, and forever" (Heb. 13:8, page 1252). His faith, like His human and divine nature, is immutable. He is the worthy object of our faith (Mal. 3:6, page 924).

(4) *The embodiment of our faith.* Our faith is certified as effective because He is the resurrected God-Man, who is seated at the right hand of the Father (v. 2).

(5) *The way of saving faith.* Jesus is our "way" of faith, our "truth" of faith, and our "life" of faith. "No one comes to the Father except through Me" (John 14:6, page 1074; cf. Acts 4:12, page 1091).

(6) *The forerunner of our faith.* The word "forerunner" means to scout, to go before us and experience every inch of the way. As we run the believer's race, looking unto Jesus who ran the course before us, understanding the race He ran, there should be no surprises; for He "was in all points tempted as we are, yet without sin" (Heb. 4:14–16, page 1239).

Saving faith is in a person. That person is God the Son, the Lord Jesus Christ. This saving faith is not your faith until you accept Him as your personal Savior, for He alone is your saving faith (Acts 4:12, page 1091).

See Index, page 17, for your next study.

that the word should not be spoken to them anymore.   Ex. 20:18-26

20 (For they could not endure what was commanded: R"And if so much as a beast touches the mountain, it shall be stoned *or shot with an arrow."   Ex. 19:12, 13

21 And so terrifying was the sight that Moses said, R"I am exceedingly afraid and trembling.")   Deut. 9:19

▼ 11-B. Angels: Their Kinds and Ranks

22 But you have come to Mount Zion and to the city of the living God, the heavenly Jerusalem, to an innumerable company of
▲ angels,

23 to the Tgeneral assembly and church of the firstborn who are registered in heaven, to God the Judge of all, to the spirits of just men Rmade Tperfect,   festal gathering · Phil. 3:12 · complete

24 to Jesus the Mediator of the new covenant, and to the blood of sprinkling that speaks better things than that of Abel.

Hear the Heavenly Voice

25 See that you do not refuse Him who speaks. For Rif they did not escape who

12:20 NU, M omit the rest of v. 20.

refused Him who spoke on earth, much more shall we not escape if we turn away from Him who speaks from heaven,   Heb. 2:2, 3

26 whose voice then shook the earth; but now He has promised, saying, R"Yet once more I *shake not only the earth, but also heaven."   Hag. 2:6

27 Now this, "Yet once more," indicates the removal of those things that are being shaken, as of things that are made, that the things which cannot be shaken may remain.

28 Therefore, since we are receiving Ra kingdom which cannot be shaken, let us have grace, by which we *may serve God acceptably with reverence and godly fear.   [Dan. 2:44]

29 For Rour God is a consuming fire. Ex. 24:17

Concluding Moral Directions

13 Let Rbrotherly love continue. Rom. 12:10
2 RDo not forget to entertain strangers, for by so doing Rsome have unwittingly entertained angels.   Matt. 25:35 · Gen. 18:1-22; 19:1

3 Remember the prisoners as if chained with them—those who are mistreated—since you yourselves are in the body also.

12:26 NU will shake
12:28 M omits may

11-B. Angels: Their Kinds and Ranks (Hebrews 12:22)—Not only are there various kinds and ranks of angels, they are also innumerable. All are created holy, intelligent, powerful spirit beings. It is reasonable to believe they differ from one another in kind, rank, personality, and power. There are no two human beings exactly alike; there are no two fingerprints alike; there are no two leaves alike on all the trees in the world. Creation tells us that our Creator is unlimited in all things in heaven and on earth. Yet, we often think that angels are all exactly alike, that God made them all from a single mold.

There are three angels whose names are made known in the Scriptures:

(1) *Michael, the archangel.* When he disputed with the Devil about the body of Moses, Michael dared not bring against him (Satan) a reviling accusation, but said, "The Lord rebuke you!" (Jude 9, page 1290). Michael is God's warring general, and seems especially related to Israel.

(2) *Gabriel.* This angel seems to be a special messenger of the Lord. He is mentioned three times in Scripture:

(a) In Daniel 8 and 9 (page 846), God delivered messages to Daniel pertaining to Israel in the Great Tribulation (Dan. 8:15-27, page 848; 9:20-27, page 851).

(b) He announced the birth of John the Baptist to his father, Zacharias the priest (Luke 1:8-19, page 1009).

(c) In Luke, he told the Virgin Mary that she would be the mother of the Messiah (Luke 1:26-38, page 1010).

(3) *Lucifer, son of the morning (Satan).* This is a fallen angel, who was created a perfect and powerful angel. He was given power and a place in God's kingdom, greater than any other created being (see Master Outline 12, "Satan," page 31).

The seraphim (from the Hebrew word for "burn") are found only once in the Bible. They are in the presence of the throne of God, and they cry one to another: "Holy, holy, holy, is the LORD of hosts." They have six wings—two to cover their faces, two to cover their feet, and two to fly. One of the seraphim, with a coal from the altar of God, touched the lips of Isaiah and pronounced him purged of his sin (Is. 6:1-8, page 647).

"Cherubim" is the plural of "cherub," from the Hebrew word for "draw near." Cherubim were placed in the Garden of Eden to guard the Tree of Life, after the fall of Adam and Eve (Gen. 3:24, page 7). They are *near* the throne of God; they cover and protect it (Ezek. 28:14, page 806). Moses made golden images of cherubim to overshadow the mercy seat in the Most Holy Place (Ex. 25:17-22, page 85). Satan was the "anointed cherub" (Ezek. 28:14, page 806). It appears that he was the head of the cherubim. Some of the cherubim, along with the fallen angels, may have fallen with him (Rev. 12:4, page 1305).

See Psalms 103:19-21, page 570, for **Point 11-C: Angels: Their Nature.**

4 ᴿMarriage *is* honorable among all, and the bed undefiled; ᴿbut fornicators and adulterers God will judge.   Prov. 5:18, 19 • 1 Cor. 6:9

5 *Let your* conduct *be* without covetousness; *be* content with such things as you have. For He Himself has said, ᴿ*"I will never leave you nor forsake you."*   Deut. 31:6, 8; Josh. 1:5

6 So we may boldly say:

ᴿ*"The* LORD *is my helper;*   Ps. 27:1; 118:6
I will not fear.
What can man do to me?"

Concluding Religious Directions

7 Remember those who ᵀrule over you, who have spoken the word of God to you, whose faith follow, considering the outcome of *their* conduct.   *lead*

8 Jesus Christ *is* ᴿthe same yesterday, today, and forever.   Heb. 1:12

9 Do not be carried *about with various and strange doctrines. For *it is* good that the heart be established by grace, not with foods which have not profited those who have been occupied with them.

10 We have an altar from which those who serve the tabernacle have no right to eat.

11 For the bodies of those animals, whose blood is brought into the sanctuary by the high priest for sin, are burned outside the camp.

13:9 NU, M *away*

12 Therefore Jesus also, that He might ᵀsanctify the people with His own blood, suffered outside the gate.   *set apart*

13 Therefore let us go forth to Him, outside the camp, bearing ᴿHis reproach.   1 Pet. 4:14

14 For here we have no continuing city, but we seek the one to come.

15 ᴿTherefore by Him let us continually offer ᴿthe sacrifice of praise to God, that is, ᴿthe fruit of *our* lips, ᵀgiving thanks to His name.   Eph. 5:20 • Lev. 7:12 • Hos. 14:2 • Lit. *confessing*

16 ᴿBut do not forget to do good and to share, for ᴿwith such sacrifices God is well pleased.   Rom. 12:13 • Phil. 4:18

17 Obey those who ᵀrule over you, and be submissive, for they watch out for your souls, as those who must give account. Let them do so with joy and not with grief, for that would be unprofitable for you.   *lead*

Prayer Requested

18 ᴿPray for us; for we are confident that we have ᴿa good conscience, in all things desiring to live honorably.   Eph. 6:19 • Acts 23:1

19 But I especially urge *you* to do this, that I may be restored to you the sooner.

29-D. God's Will Can Be Known   ▼

Benediction, Final Exhortation, Farewell

20 Now may the God of peace ᴿwho brought up our Lord Jesus from the dead,

---

29-D. God's Will Can Be Known (Hebrews 13:20, 21)—In the old Adamic nature, we are not capable of knowing and doing the perfect will of God. To the unsaved, spiritual things are foolishness (1 Cor. 1:18, page 1148). The unsaved may be religious, but they do not possess the spiritual capacity to discern spiritual things (1 Cor. 2:14, page 1149). If you are a born-again, Spirit-filled believer who desires to know and do the perfect will of God, God will take control of your life and "make you complete in every good work to do His will" (v. 21).

God does have a plan for your life. He did not save you to let you go your way and make your own decisions, according to your carnal nature. God gives the believer a new nature to combat the ways of his old nature (2 Pet. 1:4, page 1272). We have already seen that man's natural way is carnal, and that Satan's way is totally evil. But, God's way is perfect, and is the only way that pleases Him. It is impossible for a carnal, or rebellious, Christian to please God (Rom. 8:5–9, page 1137). Therefore, it is imperative that you know the will of God for your life and do it.

The question is, how can I know the perfect will of God for my life?

(1) You must sincerely desire to do His will. This is an act of faith. "The just shall live by faith" (Heb. 10:38, page 1247).

(2) You must search the Scriptures if you are going to know the will of God for your life. The apostle Paul tells us that the Bereans "were more fair-minded than those in Thessalonica, in that they received the word with all readiness, and searched the Scriptures daily to find out whether these things were so" (Acts 17:11, page 1111). The Berean believers did two things—they heard and accepted the Word of God as it was preached, and they "searched the Scriptures daily to find out whether these things were so." The best way for believers to know the will of God for their lives is to search the Scriptures, which continually point to Christ (John 5:39, page 1057; 8:31, 32, page 1063). If you choose to "grow in the grace and knowledge of . . . Christ" (2 Pet 3:18, page 1276) through the study of His Word, God will equip you to know and live out His perfect plan for your life.

(3) If you sincerely desire to know God's will, you must recognize the ministry of the indwelling Holy Spirit.

(a) He communicates with our spirit, always in harmony with the Scriptures, assuring us that we are the children of God (Rom. 8:16, page 1137). When we are not sure of God's will in our daily decisions, we

(Point 29-D continued on next page)

▽ that great Shepherd of the sheep, through the
blood of the everlasting covenant,   Hos. 6:2
21 make you complete in every good work
to do His will, working in *you what is well
pleasing in His sight, through Jesus Christ, to
▲ whom *be* glory forever and ever. Amen.

13:21 NU, M *us*

22 And I appeal to you, brethren, bear with
the word of exhortation, for I have written to
you in few words.
23 Know that *our* brother Timothy has
been set free, with whom I shall see you if he
comes shortly.
24 Greet all those who ᵀrule over you, and
all the saints. Those from Italy greet you.   *lead*
25 Grace *be* with you all. Amen.

(Point 29-D continued from previous page)
can trust the indwelling Holy Spirit to reveal His perfect will, because He always intercedes for the believer
"according to the will of God" (Rom. 8:27, page 1137).

(b) Jesus promised the apostles that the Holy Spirit would guide them into all truth (John 16:13,
page 1077). Through the Scriptures the Holy Spirit also leads us into all the truth we need to know about
God's will for our lives. The Holy Spirit will guide us day after day, as we walk according to the will of God
revealed in the Scriptures (Eph. 1:9, page 1186).

(4) You must read outward signs of God's providence. Jesus said to the Philadelphia church, "I know
your works. See, I have set before you an open door, and no one can shut it" (Rev. 3:7, 8, page 1296). When
a church or an individual is living in God's perfect plan, God will open doors of service that no one can close
(2 Cor. 2:12, page 1166), or He will close doors that no one can open. You must be fully committed to Christ
and His will before the Lord can show you His open doors. When you are seeking the will of God and there
is before you an open door, wait upon the Lord (Is. 40:31, page 680). Pray as you wait—pray that the Lord
will close the door to you if you should not enter. Yes, God does use outward circumstances to reveal His
will to us. If you have a desire to serve the Lord in a special ministry and the door is closed, don't try to force
it open. Learn to wait on the Lord, and He will direct your path (Prov. 3:5, 6, page 599).

(5) Seek the counsel of godly leaders such as pastors, teachers, elders, deacons, and also parents and
spiritually mature Christians (Prov. 11:14, page 605; 13:10, page 607).

God has a purpose—a perfect plan for every born-again child of God who desires to know and do His
pleasure. If you sincerely desire God's will, He will cause everything to work together for your spiritual good
(Rom. 8:28, 29, page 1137).

See Colossians 1:9, 10, page 1201, for **Point 29-E: God's Will for Individuals.**

THE EPISTLE OF
James

AUTHORSHIP. The author of the book introduces himself as "James, a bondservant of God and of the Lord Jesus Christ" (1:1). This presents a problem since the New Testament speaks of five men whose name was James. These are: James the son of Cleophas, James the father of the apostle Judas, James the son of Zebedee, James the Less, and James the half-brother of Jesus.

For the most part evangelical scholarship is in agreement that James, our Lord's half-brother, was the author. There are three theories, however, as to the meaning of the word "brother."

First, the Hieronymian theory states that the word "brother" actually means "cousin." This would make James, the son of Cleophas, the author of the book. This is in error, however. The Greek word used is *adelphos,* which refers to boys in the same family. Jesus and the author of the epistle were not cousins: they were in the same family.

Second is the Epiphanian theory, suggested in A.D. 370. This is based on a legend of an elderly couple who had only one daughter, Mary, who became the virgin mother of Christ. When Mary was twelve, the high priest arranged for her to marry Joseph, who was an old widower. The two of them never engaged in sexual relations. Joseph simply provided for Mary and Jesus.

These first two theories were developed to protect the dogma that Mary was perpetually a virgin. Scripture teaches otherwise. Matthew 1:25 informs us that Joseph did not know Mary *until* after the birth of Jesus. This implies that following this blessed event Mary and Joseph had normal marital relations. Jesus is called a "firstborn Son," which indicates that there were other children in the home. Their names are given in Matthew 13:55 and Mark 6:3.

The third theory, known as the Helvidian theory, is the correct one. It simply states that after Mary as a virgin gave birth to Jesus, she and Joseph had other sons and daughters by natural procreation. One of these was James, the author of the epistle that bears his name.

While they were growing up together in the same family James was hostile to Jesus (John 7:1–5). He evidently felt that his elder brother was suffering from illusions of grandeur. This all changed as the result of Jesus' appearing to James personally following the Resurrection (1 Cor. 15:7). From that moment on he became an avid disciple of his brother.

CONTEXT. In order to get a clear picture of those to whom James was writing, it is necessary to consider verses 1 and 2 of the first chapter. In verse 1 James addresses "the twelve tribes which are scattered abroad." A literal translation of this would be "the twelve tribes of the Diaspora" (a technical term referring to all the Jews living outside Palestine). In commenting on the magnitude of this group, Strabo, the Greek geographer, wrote, "It is hard to find a spot in the whole world which is not occupied and dominated by Jews." Josephus, the Jewish historian, put it this way: "There is no city, no tribe, whether Greek or barbarian, in which Jewish law and Jewish customs have not taken root."

In the first part of verse 2 James speaks to "My brethren"; this definitely indicates that he was addressing fellow Christians who were a part of the Diaspora. Evidently James was privy to a number of problems that had arisen in their lives as they sought to maintain a good testimony for the Savior. This letter was written in part at least to furnish guidance for them in the solution of their problems. It is down-to-earth and most practical.

Bible students are generally agreed that, with the possible exception of Mark, James was the first New Testament book to be written. The date of its writing falls somewhere between A.D. 45 and 50, or in other words just a short time before the Jerusalem conference in which it was clarified that salvation is by grace alone (Acts 15:1–35). James, the most prominent leader of the Jerusalem church, presided over this conference and articulated its findings.

James 5:1–6 indicates that the author was writing this letter with a heavy heart because of the way the rich were oppressing the poor in Israel. He warned them that God's judgment for this was inevitable. Just twenty years later, in A.D. 70, that judgment fell as the Roman legions came into Jerusalem and sacked the city.

HOW JAMES FITS INTO THE BIBLE. Even though James was written in the form of a letter, it belongs to what is known as the "Wisdom Literature" of the Scriptures. This type of writing was prevalent in the Near East. It deals with instructions for successful living and contemplations of the problems facing mankind. It is to the New Testament what Job, Proverbs, and Ecclesiastes are to the Old.

A careful reading of the book reveals in the teaching of James a remarkable similarity to that of Jesus. For example, the Sermon on the Mount is generally reflected in the epistle. Even though James does not quote Jesus directly, he does make twenty-six allusions to His words.

SUMMARY STATEMENT. James is the most practical book in the New Testament. It teaches that the articulation of our lips should be matched by the activity of our lives. It is not so much what a person says as what he does that is important. Both God and man prefer to see a sermon than to hear one.

KEY VERSES: 2:17-20—"Thus also faith by itself, if it does not have works, is dead. But someone will say, 'You have faith, and I have works.' Show me your faith without your works and I will show you my faith by my works. You believe that there is one God. You do well. Even the demons believe—and tremble! But do you want to know, O foolish man, that faith without works is dead?"

HOW JAMES FITS TOGETHER. James deals with twelve important subjects:
  (1) Two types of temptation (1:2-18)
  (2) Not only hearing but doing the Word of God (1:19-27)
  (3) Treating everyone the same (2:1-13)
  (4) Faith demonstrated by works (2:14-26)
  (5) The need to tame the tongue (3:1-12)
  (6) True and false wisdom (3:13-18)
  (7) The need to follow God rather than Satan (4:1-12)
  (8) The folly of presumption (4:13-17)
  (9) The need for social justice (5:1-6)
  (10) Practical preparation for the coming of the Lord (5:7-12)
  (11) God's formula for healing (5:13-18)
  (12) The restoration of backsliders (5:19, 20)

While these subjects appear to be miscellaneous in nature, they are tied together in the sense that the believer who practices them will have a life-style pleasing to God.

—H.L.F.

Greeting to the Twelve Tribes

J AMES, ᴿa bondservant of God and of the Lord Jesus Christ,   Acts 12:17
    To the twelve tribes which are scattered abroad:

Greetings.

Profiting from Trials

2 My brethren, ᴿcount it all joy ᴿwhen you fall into various trials,   Acts 5:41 · 2 Pet. 1:6
3 knowing that the testing of your faith produces ᵀpatience.   *endurance or perseverance*
4 But let patience have *its* perfect work, that you may be ᵀperfect and complete, lacking nothing.   *mature*
5 If any of you lacks wisdom, let him ask of God, who gives to all liberally and without reproach, and it will be given to him.
6 But let him ask in faith, with no doubting, for he who doubts is like a wave of the sea driven and tossed by the wind.

7 For let not that man suppose that he will receive anything from the Lord;
8 he is ᴿa double-minded man, unstable in all his ways.   James 4:8

The Perspective of Rich and Poor

9 Let the lowly brother glory in his exaltation,
10 but the rich in his humiliation, because as a flower of the field he will pass away.
11 For no sooner has the sun risen with a burning heat than it withers the grass; its flower falls, and its beautiful appearance perishes. So the rich man also will fade away in his pursuits.

48-A. The Crown of Life   ▼

Loving God under Trials

12 Blessed *is* the man who endures temptation; for when he has been approved, he will

---

48-A. The Crown of Life (James 1:12)—This reward could be called the crown of those who love God. Upon examination of the above verse, we discover that through his love for God the believer finds strength to overcome temptation and endure trials. Paul said, "We also glory in tribulations." Do we today glory in tribulations? We can do so only if the "love of God has been poured out in our hearts by the Holy Spirit"

(Point 48-A continued on next page)

▽ receive the crown of life ᴿwhich the Lord has
▲ promised to those who love Him.   Matt. 10:22
13 Let no one say when he is tempted, "I
am tempted by God"; for God cannot be
tempted by evil, nor does He Himself tempt
anyone.
14 But each one is tempted when he is
drawn away by his own desires and enticed.
15 Then, when desire has conceived, it
gives birth to sin; and sin, when it is full-
grown, ᴿbrings forth death.   [Rom. 5:12; 6:23]
16 Do not be deceived, my beloved brethren.
17 ᴿEvery good gift and every perfect gift is
from above, and comes down from the Father
of lights, ᴿwith whom there is no variation or
shadow of turning.   John 3:27 • Num. 23:19
18 Of His own will He brought us forth by
the word of truth, ᴿthat we might be a kind of
firstfruits of His creatures.   [Eph. 1:12, 13]

Qualities Needed in Trials

19 *So then, my beloved brethren, let every
man be swift to hear, ᴿslow to speak, ᴿslow to
wrath;   Prov. 10:19; 17:27 • Prov. 14:17; 16:32
20 for the wrath of man does not produce
the righteousness of God.

Doers—Not Hearers

21 Therefore ᴿlay aside all filthiness and
ᵀoverflow of wickedness, and receive with
meekness the implanted word, ᴿwhich is able
to save your souls.   Col. 3:8 • abundance • Acts 13:26
22 But ᴿbe doers of the word, and not hear-
ers only, deceiving yourselves.   Matt. 7:21-28
23 For ᴿif anyone is a hearer of the word
and not a doer, he is like a man observing his
natural face in a mirror;   Luke 6:47
24 for he observes himself, goes away, and
immediately forgets what kind of man he
was.
25 But he who looks into the perfect law of
liberty and continues in it, and is not a
forgetful hearer but a doer of the work, this
one will be blessed in what he does.
26 If anyone *among you thinks he is religious, and ᴿdoes not bridle his tongue but
deceives his own heart, this one's religion is
useless.   Ps. 34:13

1:19 NU Know this or This you know
1:26 NU omits among you

27 Pure and undefiled religion before God
and the Father is this: ᴿto visit orphans and
widows in their trouble, ᴿand to keep oneself
unspotted from the world.   Is. 1:17 • [Rom. 12:2]

Beware of Personal Favoritism

2 My brethren, do not hold the faith of our
Lord Jesus Christ, ᴿthe Lord of glory,
with ᴿpartiality.   1 Cor. 2:8 • Lev. 19:15
2 For if there should come into your assembly a man with gold rings, in ᵀfine apparel, and there should also come in a poor
man in ᵀfilthy clothes,   bright • vile
3 and you ᵀpay attention to the one wearing the fine clothes and say to him, "You sit
here in a good place," and say to the poor
man, "You stand there," or, "Sit here at my
footstool,"   Lit. look upon
4 have you not ᵀshown partiality among
yourselves, and become judges with evil
thoughts?   differentiated
5 Listen, my beloved brethren: Has God
not chosen the poor of this world to be rich in
faith and heirs of the kingdom ᴿwhich He
promised to those who love Him?   Ex. 20:6
6 But ᴿyou have dishonored the poor man.
Do not the rich oppress you ᴿand drag you
into the courts?   1 Cor. 11:22 • Acts 13:50
7 Do they not blaspheme that noble name
by which you are ᴿcalled?   1 Pet. 4:16
8 If you really fulfill the royal law according to the Scripture, ᴿ"You shall love your
neighbor as yourself," you do well;   Lev. 19:18
9 but if you ᵀshow partiality, you commit
sin, and are convicted by the law as ᴿtrans-
gressors.   Lit. to receive the face • Deut. 1:17
10 For whoever shall keep the whole law,
and yet ᴿstumble in one point, ᴿhe is guilty of
all.   Gal. 3:10 • Deut. 27:26
11 For He who said, *"Do not commit adultery," also said, "Do not murder." Now if you
do not commit adultery, but you do murder,
you have become a transgressor of the law.
12 So speak and so do as those who will be
judged by ᴿthe law of liberty.   James 1:25
13 For judgment is without mercy to the
one who has shown no ᴿmercy. ᴿMercy triumphs over judgment.   Mic. 7:18 • Rom. 12:8

2:11 Ex. 20:13, 14; Deut. 5:17, 18

(Point 48-A continued from previous page)
(Rom. 5:3-5, page 1133). Without love for God in the heart of the believer, trials can cause him to become
bitter and critical; he may lose the "crown of life" (v. 12).
   All believers have eternal life (John 3:15, 16, page 1052), but not all believers will be rewarded with the
"crown of life." This crown will be given to those who are "faithful until death" (Rev. 2:10, page 1295). To
receive the "crown of life," the believer must love the Lord more than his own life. "For whoever desires to
save his life [live for self] will lose it, but whoever loses his life for My sake and the gospel's [live for Christ
at all cost] will save it" (Mark 8:35, page 994). This reward will be given to those who live for Christ, and
endure temptations, in the power of the love of God (1 Cor. 10:13, page 1155).
   See 1 Corinthians 9:24-27, page 1154, for **Point 48-B: The Crown Imperishable.**

▼ 24-D. Faith Without Works Is Dead

Faith Without Works Is Dead

14 ᴿWhat *does it* profit, my brethren, if someone says he has faith but does not have works? Can faith save him?   Matt. 7:21-23, 26

15 ᴿIf a brother or sister is naked and destitute of daily food,   Luke 3:11

16 and ᴿone of you says to them, "Depart in peace, be warmed and filled," but you do not give them the things which are needed for the body, what *does it* profit?   [1 John 3:17, 18]

17 Thus also faith by itself, if it does not have works, is dead.

18 But someone will say, "You have faith, and I have works." ᴿShow me your faith without *your works, ᴿand I will show you my faith by *my works.   Heb. 6:10 · James 3:13

19 You believe that there is one God. You do well. Even the demons believe—and tremble! ▽

20 But do you want to know, O foolish man, that faith without works is *dead?

21 Was not Abraham our father justified by works ᴿwhen he offered Isaac his son on the altar?   Gen. 22:9, 10, 12, 16-18

22 Do you see ᴿthat faith was working together with his works, and by ᴿworks faith was made ᵀperfect?   Heb. 11:17 · John 8:39 · *complete*

23 And the Scripture was fulfilled which says, ᴿ*"Abraham believed God, and it was accounted to him for righteousness."* And he was called the friend of God.   Gen. 15:6

24 You see then that a man is justified by works, and not by faith only.

25 Likewise, was not Rahab the harlot also justified by works when she received the messengers and sent *them* out another way?

26 For as the body without the spirit is dead, so faith without works is dead also. ▲

2:18 NU omits *your* • NU omits *my*   2:20 NU *useless*

24-D. Faith Without Works Is Dead (James 2:14–26)—There are those who wrongly believe that James and Paul had a doctrinal disagreement regarding justification by faith or by works. Are people saved by works, or by faith? James is exposing dead faith (v. 17), while Paul uncovers dead works (Heb. 6:1, page 1240; see also Point 22-C, "Repentance from Dead Works," page 1240). They both agree that dead faith always produces dead works, and neither can justify sinners. Faith that does not work is not the faith of the Bible, and therefore is not valid faith. "But do you want to know, O foolish man, that faith without works is dead?" (v. 20).

James asked, "Was not Abraham our father justified by works when he offered Isaac his son on the altar?" (v. 21). The faith of Abraham resulted in his works. Offering Isaac on the altar was an act of works by faith that, in turn, perfected his faith (v. 22). "And the Scripture was fulfilled which says, 'Abraham believed God [he believed God with faith that resulted in deeds], and it [his faith] was accounted to him for righteousness' " (v. 23). James is saying that Abraham was saved by a living faith that brought forth living fruit.

What is dead faith? First, everyone has faith of some kind. There are hundreds of religions in this world, and they all require faith; but they do not all require the faith that justifies. How can I know that my faith is the faith that justifies the sinner? There is only one faith that saves, that is, faith in the saving life and work of Christ, the God-Man (Gal. 2:20, page 1180). All other faith is empty and dead.

Paul taught "that a man is justified by faith apart from the deeds of the law" (Rom. 3:28, page 1132). Again he said, "By the works of the law no flesh shall be justified. . . . For I through the law [by faith] died to the law that I might live to God. I have been crucified with Christ . . . [therefore] the life which I now live in the flesh I live by faith in the Son of God, who loved me and gave Himself for me. I do not set aside the grace of God [by adding the works of the law to God's grace]; for if righteousness comes through the law, then Christ died in vain" (Gal. 2:15–21, page 1180).

Furthermore, Paul taught that *saving* faith is also *serving* faith, faith that produces works—not in order to be saved, but *because* the doer is saved. Every sinner who is justified by faith will stand before the Lord Jesus at the judgment seat of Christ: "For we must all appear before the judgment seat of Christ, that each one may receive the things done in the body, according to what he has done, whether good or bad. Knowing, therefore, the terror of the Lord, we persuade men; but we are well known to God, and I also trust are well known in your consciences" (2 Cor. 5:10, 11, page 1168). He said, "We make it our aim" (2 Cor. 5:9, page 1168).

Paul labored for Christ more than most believers. Why? Because he knew that he, along with all who are justified or will be justified by faith, will stand before Christ where our works will be judged; not our sins, for they were judged on Calvary in the body of Christ, our Savior (Rom. 8:1, page 1136; 2 Cor. 5:21, page 1169). For details of this judgment, where only our works will be judged, see 1 Corinthians 3:8–15 (page 1149) and the introduction to Master Outline 48, "Crowns for Christians" (page 59).

Paul wrote of a living faith, given by God. We do not live by faith that we ourselves generate; that is always dead, empty faith. The faith that justifies is the gift of God. "For by grace you have been saved through faith, and that not of yourselves; it [faith] is the gift of God, not of works, lest anyone should boast" (Eph. 2:8, 9, page 1187). This faith, God's gift, can only be found through the infallible Word of God (Rom. 10:17, page 1140).

(Point 24-D continued on next page)

The Untamable Tongue

3 My brethren, ᴿlet not many of you become teachers, knowing that we shall receive a stricter judgment.　　[Matt. 23:8]

2 For ᴿwe all stumble in many things. ᴿIf anyone does not stumble in word, ᴿhe *is* a ᵀperfect man, able also to bridle the whole body.　　1 Kin. 8:46 • Ps. 34:13 • [Matt. 12:34–37] • *mature*

3 *Indeed, ᴿwe put bits in horses' mouths that they may obey us, and we turn their whole body.　　Ps. 32:9

4 Look also at ships: although they are so large and are driven by fierce winds, they are turned by a very small rudder wherever the pilot desires.

5 Even so the tongue is a little member and ᴿboasts great things. See how great a forest a little fire kindles!　　Ps. 12:3; 73:8

6 And the tongue *is* a fire, a world of ᵀiniquity. The tongue is so set among our members that it defiles the whole body, and sets on fire the course of ᵀnature; and it is set on fire by ᵀhell.　　*unrighteousness • existence • Gr. Gehenna*

7 For every kind of beast and bird, of reptile and creature of the sea, is tamed and has been tamed by mankind.

8 But no man can tame the tongue. *It is* an unruly evil, ᴿfull of deadly poison.　　Ps. 140:3

9 With it we bless our God and Father, and with it we curse men, who have been made ᴿin the ᵀsimilitude of God.　　Gen. 1:26; 5:1 • *likeness*

10 Out of the same mouth proceed blessing and cursing. My brethren, these things ought not to be so.

11 Does a spring send forth fresh *water* and bitter from the same opening?

12 Can a ᴿfig tree, my brethren, bear olives, or a grapevine bear figs? *Thus no spring yields both salt water and fresh.　　Matt. 7:16–20

3:3 NU *Now if*

3:12 NU *Neither can a salty spring produce fresh water.*

(Point 24-D continued from previous page)

　　"The life which I now live in the flesh I live by faith in the Son of God" (Gal. 2:20, page 1180). Paul had religious faith and zeal before he came to know Christ as his Savior. His life was filled with dead, religious works which were the fruits of his dead, religious faith (Acts 9:1, 2, page 1100; 26:9–11, page 1121).

　　Saving faith results in a changed life. "Therefore, if anyone is in Christ [by faith], he is a new creation; old things have passed away; behold, all things have become new"—new faith, new life, new hope, new love (2 Cor. 5:17, page 1169). For example, in Philippians 3:3–9 (page 1197) Paul says, "We . . . have no confidence in the flesh, though I also might have confidence in the flesh. If anyone else thinks he may have confidence in the flesh, I more so:

　　(1) "Circumcised the eighth day" (Lev. 12:3, page 117);
　　(2) "Of the stock [nation] of Israel" (Ex. 4:22, 23, page 62);
　　(3) "Of the tribe of Benjamin" (the youngest son of Jacob—Gen. 35:16–19, page 42);
　　(4) "A Hebrew of the Hebrews" (2 Cor. 11:22, page 1175);
　　(5) "Concerning the law, a Pharisee" (they were separatists);
　　(6) "Concerning zeal, persecuting the church" (Acts 7:54—8:4, page 1097);
　　(7) "Concerning the righteousness which is in the law, blameless" (Rom. 10:1–4, page 1140). The righteousness of the law had blinded him to the righteousness of God in Christ; under that law Paul was blind.

　　"But what things were gain to me [under the law], these I have counted loss for Christ . . . and count them as rubbish . . . not having my own righteousness, which is from the law, but that which is through faith in Christ, the righteousness which is from God by faith." This is the great change that came into the life of Paul when he came to know Christ as his Savior, through "faith in the Son of God."

　　James and Paul are looking at the same truth—justification. Like a coin it has two sides: one side is faith, the other side is works.

　　Paul teaches that faith justifies the sinner before God, entirely apart from works. "Abraham believed God, and it was accounted [imputed] to him for righteousness" (Rom. 4:3, page 1132). *This is faith as God sees it,* one side of the truth.

　　James sees works as *evidence* of the faith that justifies; if there are no works, there is no evidence of saving faith. He said, "Show me your faith without your works, and I will show you my faith by my works" (v. 18). James concludes that faith without works is dead, and cannot justify the sinner. *This is faith as man sees it,* the other side of the truth.

　　As we look at both sides of the truth, we see that the faith that justifies is the faith that produces works. There is no doctrinal disagreement between James and Paul. James said, "Abraham believed God, and it was accounted [imputed] to him for righteousness" (v. 23). Paul said, "Abraham believed God, and it was accounted to him for righteousness" (Rom. 4:3, page 1132). Both James and Paul believed in a living faith that bears living fruit; all other faith is dead, useless faith (1 Cor. 15:1–4, page 1161). Faith in Christ's vicarious death on Calvary, His physical burial for three days and nights, and His bodily resurrection from the dead is the only faith that will justify sinners in the sight of God. "For the LORD does not see as man sees; for man looks at the outward appearance, but the LORD looks at the heart" (1 Sam. 16:7, page 283).

　　See Hebrews 12:1, 2, page 1249, for **Point 24-E: Saving Faith Is in Christ.**

Heavenly Versus Demonic Wisdom

13 Who *is* wise and understanding among you? Let him show by good conduct *that* his works *are done* in the meekness of wisdom.

14 But if you have bitter envy and [T]self-seeking in your hearts, [R]do not boast and lie against the truth.   *selfish ambition* · Rom. 2:17

15 This wisdom does not descend from above, but *is* earthly, sensual, demonic.

16 For where envy and self-seeking *exist*, confusion and every evil thing *are* there.

17 But the wisdom that is from above is first pure, then peaceable, gentle, willing to yield, full of mercy and good fruits, without partiality [R]and without hypocrisy.   Rom. 12:9

18 [R]Now the fruit of righteousness is sown in peace by those who make peace.   Prov. 11:18

▼ 15-D. The Effects of Sin in Human History

Pride Promotes Strife

4 Where do [T]wars and fights *come* from among you? Do *they* not *come* from your desires for pleasure [R]that war in your members?   *battles* · Rom. 7:23

2 You lust and do not have. You murder and covet and cannot obtain. You fight and [T]war. *Yet you do not have because you do not ask.   battle

3 [R]You ask and do not receive, [R]because you ask amiss, that you may spend *it* on your pleasures.   Job 27:8, 9 · [Ps. 66:18]

4 *Adulterers and adulteresses! Do you not know that [R]friendship with the world is enmity with God? [R]Whoever therefore wants to be a friend of the world makes himself an enemy of God.   1 John 2:15 · Gal. 1:4

5 Or do you think that the Scripture says in vain, [R]"The Spirit who dwells in us yearns jealously"?   Gen. 6:5 ▲

6 But He gives more grace. Therefore He says:

> [R]"God resists the proud,   Prov. 3:34
> But gives grace to the humble."

Humility Cures Worldliness

7 Therefore submit to God. [R]Resist the devil and he will flee from you.   [Eph. 4:27; 6:11]

8 [R]Draw near to God and He will draw near to you. [R]Cleanse *your* hands, *you* sinners; and [R]purify *your* hearts, *you* double-minded.   2 Chr. 15:2 · Is. 1:16 · 1 Pet. 1:22

9 [R]Lament and mourn and weep! Let your

4:2 NU, M omit *Yet*
4:4 NU omits *Adulterers and*

15-D. The Effects of Sin in Human History (James 4:1–5)—James made it clear that wars on earth historically stem from sinful desires within our hearts and bodies, "desires for pleasure that war in your members" (vv. 1, 2). Christians, on the other hand, should seek God in prayer to have their needs met, rather than having unchecked desires within their hearts or resorting to violence to obtain these desires.

The following points of human history are illustrative of the history of sin upon the planet:

(1) Adam and Eve disobeyed God and plunged the race into sin (Gen. 3:1–24, page 5).

(2) Cain killed Abel, and murder among humans began (Gen. 4:8–12, page 8).

(3) Mankind, before the Flood, became so universally wicked that "the LORD was sorry that He had made man," and God sent the Flood to destroy humanity, except for the family of righteous Noah (Gen. 6:5–8, page 12).

(4) Mankind's lifespan began dropping dramatically after the Flood (Gen. 11:10, 11, 24, 25, page 16; cf. 5:27, page 10).

(5) By 2700 B.C. Egypt had fallen into idolatry, and three lone Pharaohs caused an entire nation to labor for a century to build their burial tombs.

(6) By about 2000 B.C. two entire cities, Sodom and Gomorrah, had become so evil that God destroyed them by fire and brimstone (Gen. 19:1–29, page 23).

(7) By 1450 B.C. the Hebrew nation as a whole was under the cruel bondage of slavery to Pharaoh (Ex. 3:7, page 60).

(8) By 1400 B.C. the Canaanite tribes had become so perverted by evil that God ordered their total destruction (Lev. 18:21–25, page 126; cf. Josh. 6:21–24, page 221).

(9) By 1000 B.C. Israel's first king had become so evil that God ordered him replaced (1 Sam. 15:11, 26, page 282).

(10) By 721 B.C. the northern kingdom, Israel, was scattered by the fierce and cruel Assyrians (2 Kin. 17:5–9, page 372).

(11) By 586 B.C. the southern kingdom, Judah, was destroyed and taken captive by the wicked Babylonians (2 Chr. 36:17–20, page 441).

(12) By A.D. 30 Christ predicted "wars and rumors of wars" for the world (Matt. 24:6–8, 21, page 973).

(13) By A.D. 30 the human race crucified the Christ, who came to save it (Luke 23:13–33, page 1044).

(14) In A.D. 70 the Romans destroyed Jerusalem and the temple.

(15) In the second and third centuries the Roman Empire persecuted and killed Christians.

(16) In the fourth and fifth centuries the barbarian invader, Attila the Hun, invaded Europe and slaughtered thousands.

(Point 15-D continued on next page)

laughter be turned to mourning and your joy to gloom.   Matt. 5:4

10 [R]Humble yourselves in the sight of the Lord, and He will lift you up.   Job 22:29

Do Not Judge a Brother

11 Do not speak evil of one another, brethren. He who speaks evil of a brother and judges his brother, speaks evil of the law and judges the law. But if you judge the law, you are not a doer of the law but a judge.

12 There is one *Lawgiver, [R]who is able to save and to destroy. [R]Who* are you to judge *another?   [Matt. 10:28] • Rom. 14:4

Do Not Boast about Tomorrow

13 Come now, you who say, "Today or tomorrow *we will go to such and such a city, spend a year there, buy and sell, and make a profit";

14 whereas you do not know what will happen tomorrow. For what is your life? [R]It is even a vapor that appears for a little time and then vanishes away.   Job 7:7

15 Instead you ought to say, "If the Lord wills, we shall live and do this or that."

16 But now you boast in your arrogance. [R]All such boasting is evil.   1 Cor. 5:6

17 Therefore, to him who knows to do good and does not do it, to him it is sin.

Rich Oppressors Will Be Judged

5 Come now, you rich, weep and howl for your miseries that are coming upon you!

2 Your riches [T]are corrupted, and [R]your garments are moth-eaten.   have rotted • Job 13:28

3 Your gold and silver are corroded, and their corrosion will be a witness against you and will eat your flesh like fire. [R]You have heaped up treasure in the last days.   Rom. 2:5

4 Indeed the wages of the laborers who mowed your fields, which you kept back by fraud, cry out; and the cries of the reapers have reached the ears of the Lord of *Sabaoth.

5 You have lived on the earth in pleasure and [T]luxury; you have [T]fattened your hearts *as in a day of slaughter.   indulgence • nourished

6 You have condemned, you have murdered the just; he does not resist you.

Be Patient and Persevering

7 Therefore be patient, brethren, until the coming of the Lord. See how the farmer waits for the precious fruit of the earth, waiting patiently for it until it receives the early and latter rain.

8 You also be patient. Establish your hearts, for the coming of the Lord is at hand.

9 Do not [T]grumble against one another, brethren, lest you be *condemned. Behold, the Judge is standing at the door!   Lit. groan

---

4:12 NU adds and Judge • NU, M But who • NU a neighbor
4:13 M let us

5:4 Lit., in Heb., Hosts
5:5 NU omits as
5:9 NU, M judged

(Point 15-D continued from previous page)

(17) In the seventh and eighth centuries the Muslims conquered the Middle East and southern Europe.

(18) In the twelfth and thirteenth centuries the Crusaders and Muslims warred against one another.

(19) In the twelfth through the eighteenth centuries the Inquisitors burned countless Jews and alleged "heretics."

(20) In the thirteenth century Genghis Khan rode to slaughter great numbers.

(21) In the sixteenth and seventeenth centuries the Protestants and Catholics engaged in bloody religious wars.

(22) In the eighteenth century the French Revolution's guillotine killed thousands in the Reign of Terror.

(23) In the twentieth century World War I and World War II claimed almost one hundred million lives, including those of six million European Jews.

(24) In the twentieth century the satanic Communists rose to slaughter thousands, and revolution reigned for the supposed "good of the masses" in Russia, China, Africa, Central and South America, Korea, Cambodia, Afghanistan, and Vietnam.

(25) In Iran's revolution of the twentieth century, thousands were killed.

(26) In twentieth-century Ireland, Central America, Africa, and Israel, struggles continue in "wars and rumors of wars" (Matt. 24:6, page 973).

(27) In the future a satanic world leader will arise and lead another slaughter (2 Thess. 2:3–10, page 1215), as world armies gather at Armageddon (Matt. 24:21, page 973; cf. Rev. 16:16, page 1310).

Every age has had its advocates of the false philosophy of "the basic goodness of man," and its prophets have said that man would end war and live in peace. Each age has also had its saviors with their humanistic remedies for world disorder and misery. Hitler's remedy was built on the totalitarian state and racism, and Marx and Lenin's on economic theory, atheism, and revolution. Some have looked to education to deliver this world. All these have failed. The Bible, through the centuries, has correctly identified the cause as the sin of man, and cited only Christ's death (for the peace of the individual) and His second coming (for the peace of the nations) as the answers to this planet's dilemma.

See Revelation 14:13, page 1307, for **Point 15-E: The End of Sin.**

10 ᴿMy brethren, take the prophets, who spoke in the name of the Lord, as an example of suffering and ᴿpatience.   Matt. 5:12 • Heb. 10:36

11 Indeed ᴿwe count them blessed who ᴿendure. You have heard of ᴿthe perseverance of Job and seen the end *intended by* the Lord—that the Lord is very compassionate and merciful.   [Ps. 94:12] • [James 1:12] • Job 1:22; 2:10

12 But above all, my brethren, ᴿdo not swear, either by heaven or by earth or with any other oath. But let your "Yes" be "Yes," and *your* "No," "No," lest you fall into *judgment.   Matt. 5:34-37

Meeting Specific Needs

13 Is anyone among you suffering? Let him ᴿpray. Is anyone cheerful? ᴿLet him sing psalms.   Ps. 50:14, 15 • Eph. 5:19

14 Is anyone among you sick? Let him call for the elders of the church, and let them pray over him, ᴿanointing him with oil in the name of the Lord.   Mark 6:13; 16:18

5:12 M *hypocrisy*

15 And the prayer of faith will save the sick, and the Lord will raise him up. ᴿAnd if he has committed sins, he will be forgiven.   Is. 33:24

16 *Confess *your* trespasses to one another, and pray for one another, that you may be healed. The effective, ᵀfervent prayer of a righteous man avails much.   *supplication*

17 Elijah was a man with a nature like ours, and ᴿhe prayed earnestly that it would not rain; and it did not rain on the land for three years and six months.   1 Kin. 17:1; 18:1

18 And he prayed again, and the heaven gave rain, and the earth produced its fruit.

Bring Back the Erring One

19 Brethren, if anyone among you wanders from the truth, and someone ᴿturns him back,   Gal. 6:1

20 let him know that he who turns a sinner from the error of his way will save *a soul from death and cover a multitude of sins.

5:16 NU *Therefore confess your sins*
5:20 NU *his soul*

THE FIRST EPISTLE OF

Peter

AUTHORSHIP. Simon Peter, brother of Andrew, son of Jonah, is the author. He was called by Jesus while engaged in his fisherman trade in Bethsaida on the Sea of Galilee. Through the instruction of Jesus' three-year earthly ministry, the crystalization of his commitment during the forty days of Jesus' post-resurrection appearances and through the coming of the Holy Spirit at Pentecost, he became Peter (*Petros,* a rock), a pillar of the New Testament church.

CONTEXT. 1 Peter is set against a backdrop of impending trial and persecution. Nero would use Christians as a scapegoat for the fire of Rome in A.D. 64. Through his satanically inspired attack on Christianity, both Peter and Paul would lose their lives. Jesus foretold Peter's death by martyrdom (John 21:18, 19). The most satisfactory date for the writing of 1 Peter is A.D. 63 or early 64, a little before the outbreak of the Neronian persecution.

The place of writing of 1 Peter is identified as Babylon (5:13). Some scholars interpret this literally as the ancient city of Mesopotamia. At this time in history it was a center of uncompromising Judaism, which might conceivably give it a claim on Peter, the apostle to the circumcised (Gal. 2:7, 8). It is thought that this part of the eastern world is where Peter lived and did his work. Other interpreters have designated "Babylon" as symbolic of Rome, because of the intrinsic evil of the ancient capital of the Roman empire. In this case Rome would be the place of writing of 1 Peter. The definite place of writing is still an open question.

HOW 1 PETER FITS INTO THE BIBLE. 1 Peter is a masterpiece of encouragement for Christians. It deals with the question of the suffering of the people of God. The letter is addressed to Christians of Pontus, Galatia, Cappadocia, Asia and Bithynia. They are called "pilgrims," aliens living among the unsaved. They are citizens of heaven on a mission for Jesus in a hostile world (2:9–12). They are called "the Dispersion" (Greek *Diaspora*). This term was used for sowing of seed (from *dia,* "through," and *spora,* "seed"). The people of God are scattered like seed through the present trials. They are planted in death through fiery trial and martyrdom. Everywhere the seed of life is planted, fruit comes forth to eternal life. The scattered seed produces an eventual harvest for our Lord.

Suffering Christians are purified through the trial of fire. Through suffering they identify with Jesus in His sufferings.

SUMMARY STATEMENT. 1 Peter is a message of hope and encouragement for Christians facing the "fiery trials" of persecution and opposition. They are purified and matured, becoming like the Savior in His fellowship of suffering.

KEY VERSES: 4:12, 13—"Beloved, do not think it strange concerning the fiery trial which is to try you, as though some strange thing happened to you; but rejoice to the extent that you partake of Christ's sufferings, that when His glory is revealed, you may also be glad with exceeding joy."

HOW 1 PETER FITS TOGETHER. The letter has four main divisions: (1) The believer's security in the light of their heritage in Christ (1:3–12); (2) encouragement based on the Christian's heritage (1:13—2:10); (3) encouragement based on the Christian's relationships (2:11—4:11); and (4) encouragement based on the Christian's trials (4:7—5:14).

1 Peter sets forth the action of the triune God (1:2). He brought these whose faith is under fire into a position of grace. They abide in peace because of:

The Purpose of the Father—"Elect according to the foreknowledge of God the Father."
The Provision of the Son—"For obedience and sprinkling of the blood of Jesus Christ."
The Perfecting of the Spirit—"In sanctification of the Spirit."

God has acted to give victory through suffering. The concluding prophetic prayer of Peter for these who will suffer for a little while is that the result will be maturity as they are established, strengthened and settled.

This, indeed, is *triumph over trouble.*

—D.W.R.

Greeting to the Elect Pilgrims

PETER, an apostle of Jesus Christ,

To the pilgrims of the Dispersion in Pontus, Galatia, Cappadocia, Asia, and Bithynia, 2 elect ᴿaccording to the foreknowledge of God the Father, in sanctification of the Spirit, for obedience and ᴿsprinkling of the blood of Jesus Christ: [Rom. 8:29] • Is. 52:15

Grace to you and peace be multiplied.

A Heavenly Inheritance

3 Blessed *be* the God and Father of our Lord Jesus Christ, who according to His abundant mercy ᴿhas begotten us again to a living hope through the resurrection of Jesus Christ from the dead,   [John 3:3, 5]
4 to an inheritance ᵀincorruptible and undefiled and that does not fade away, ᴿreserved in heaven for you,   *imperishable* • Col. 1:5
5 ᴿwho are kept by the power of God through faith for salvation ready to be revealed in the last time.   John 10:28
6 In this you greatly rejoice, though now for a little while, if need be, ᴿyou have been ᵀgrieved by various trials,   James 1:2 • *distressed*
7 that the genuineness of your faith, *being* much more precious than gold that perishes, though ᴿit is tested by fire, ᴿmay be found to praise, honor, and glory at the revelation of Jesus Christ,   Job 23:10 • [Rom. 2:7]
8 ᴿwhom having not *seen you love. ᴿThough now you do not see *Him*, yet believing, you rejoice with joy inexpressible and full of glory,   1 John 4:20 • John 20:29
9 receiving the end of your faith—the salvation of *your* souls.
10 Of this salvation the prophets have in-

quired and searched carefully, who prophesied of the grace *that would come* to you,
11 searching what, or what manner of time, ᴿthe Spirit of Christ who was in them was indicating when He testified beforehand the sufferings of Christ and the glories that would follow.   2 Pet. 1:21
12 To them it was revealed that, not to themselves, but to *us they were ministering the things which now have been reported to you through those who have preached the gospel to you by the Holy Spirit sent from heaven—things which ᴿangels desire to look into.   Eph. 3:10

Living Before God Our Father

13 Therefore gird up the loins of your mind, be sober, and rest *your* hope fully upon the grace that is to be brought to you at the revelation of Jesus Christ;
14 as obedient children, not ᴿconforming yourselves to the former lusts, *as* in your ignorance;   [Rom. 12:2]
15 ᴿbut as He who called you *is* holy, you also be holy in all *your* conduct,   [2 Cor. 7:1]
16 because it is written, ᴿ*"Be holy, for I am holy."*   Lev. 11:44, 45; 19:2; 20:7
17 And if you call on the Father, who ᴿwithout partiality judges according to each one's work, conduct yourselves throughout the time of your stay *here* in fear;   Acts 10:34

19-E. The Results of God's Remedy for Man's Ruin   ▼

18 knowing that you were not ᴿredeemed with ᵀcorruptible things, *like* silver or gold, from your aimless conduct *received* by tradition from your fathers,   Is. 52:3 • *perishable*
19 but ᴿwith the precious blood of Christ,

1:8 M *known*   1:12 NU, M *you*

19-E. The Results of God's Remedy for Man's Ruin (1 Peter 1:18, 19)—The effects of God's remedy for man's ruin are:

(1) Redemption through the precious blood of Jesus. God did not redeem us with corruptible things, silver and gold, that we may become His slaves. Neither are we redeemed by our good works, that we may have grounds to boast; nor did He send angels to redeem us, that we may become angels. He sent His only begotten Son to redeem us "with the precious blood of Christ, as of a lamb without blemish and without spot" (v. 19), so that we might become sons of God. This is accomplished through believing that "Christ died for our sins according to the Scriptures, and that He was buried, and that He rose again the third day according to the Scriptures" (1 Cor. 15:3, 4, page 1161).

Christ is our Redeemer. His blood was the price He paid for our redemption. Jesus paid the price required by God the Father for the forgiveness of our sins. "The Lord [God the Father] has laid on Him [God the Son] the iniquity of us all" (Is. 53:6, page 693). "Without shedding of blood there is no remission," that is, no forgiveness of sin (Heb. 9:22, page 1244). The precious blood of Jesus is upon the mercy seat in heaven's tabernacle, which was not made with hands, and is not of this earth. "With His own blood [after His resurrection] He entered the Most Holy Place once for all." Jesus, our High Priest, sprinkled His own blood upon the mercy seat, "having obtained eternal redemption" (Heb. 9:11–15, page 1243). Jesus paid sin's debt in full on Calvary when He came the first time to put away sin by the sacrifice of Himself on the cross (Heb. 9:25–28, page 1244). It is no wonder that Peter called the blood of Jesus "precious blood" (v. 19).

(2) A new creation in Christ Jesus. "Old things have passed away; behold, all things have become new"

(Point 19-E continued on next page)

▽ ᴿas of a lamb without blemish and without
▲ spot.   Acts 20:28 · Ex. 12:5; Is. 53:7
  20 ᴿHe indeed was foreordained before the
foundation of the world, but was manifest ᴿin
these last times for you   Rom. 3:25 · Gal. 4:4
  21 who through Him believe in God, ᴿwho
raised Him from the dead and ᴿgave Him
glory, so that your faith and hope are in
God.   Acts 2:24 · Acts 2:33

The Enduring Word

  22 Since you ᴿhave purified your souls in
obeying the truth *through the Spirit in
sincere love of the brethren, love one another
fervently with a pure heart,   Acts 15:9

▼ 23-B. The Spiritual Birth and the Natural
       Birth

  23 having been born again, not of corruptible seed but incorruptible, through the word
▲ of God which lives and abides *forever,

  1:22 NU omits *through the Spirit*
  1:23 NU omits *forever*

24 because
  ᴿ"All flesh is as grass,   Is. 40:6-8
    And all *the glory of man as the flower
      of the grass.
    The grass withers,
      And its flower falls away,
25 ᴿBut the word of the Lᴏʀᴅ endures
      forever."   Is. 40:8
ᴿNow this is the word which by the gospel
was preached to you.   [John 1:1]
2 Therefore, ᴿlaying aside all malice, all
   deceit, hypocrisy, envy, and all evil
speaking,   Heb. 12:1
  2 as newborn babes, desire the pure milk
of the word, that you may grow *thereby,
  3 if indeed you have ᴿtasted that the Lord
is gracious.   Heb. 6:5

The Chosen Stone and His Chosen
    People

  4 Coming to Him *as to* a living stone,

  1:24 NU *its glory as*
  2:2 NU adds *up to salvation*

(Point 19-E continued from previous page)
(2 Cor. 5:17, page 1169; cf. 2 Pet. 1:4, page 1272). Because believers are now partakers of the divine nature
of God, they are born-again children of God (v. 23). Because they born again of the incorruptible seed
of God, they will never be the same.
    All who have been redeemed by the precious blood of Jesus (who are new creations in Christ) will join
the four living creatures and the twenty-four elders around the throne of God to sing the new theme song
of heaven: redeemed by the blood of the Lamb. It will be the theme song on earth during the kingdom, and
forever in the new heaven and the new earth (Rev. 5:8-14, page 1297).
    Without faith in the precious blood of Jesus that cleanses us from all sin (1 John 1:7, page 1278), there is
no remedy for your ruin by sin.
    See Index, page 17, for your next study.

23-B. The Spiritual Birth and the Natural Birth (1 Peter 1:23)—As you study the two births, keep in mind that
the first birth is natural and the second birth is supernatural. The natural birth produces a mortal body of
flesh, under the sentence of death. The spiritual birth ultimately produces an immortal body that will never
die.
    (1) If you have been *born* only *once*, you will *die twice*. The first death will be physical, that is, the spirit
and the soul will be separated from your body of flesh. The second death will take place at the Great White
Throne judgment, where all of the "once-born" will be cast into the lake of fire. "This is the second death"
(Rev. 20:11-15, page 1313).
    (2) If you have been *born twice* (of the flesh and also of the spirit), you will *die* only *once*—physically.
At this death your spirit and soul will go to be with the Lord Jesus Christ in heaven (Phil. 1:21-23, page 1196)
to await the first resurrection, when your natural body will be raised a spiritual body.
    "There is a natural body, and there is a spiritual body" (1 Cor. 15:44, page 1162). "And as we have borne
the image of the man of dust [Adam], we shall also bear the image of the heavenly Man [Christ]" (1 Cor.
15:49, page 1162; cf. 1 John 3:2, page 1279). We will have spiritual, glorified bodies like the resurrected body
of our Lord and Savior Jesus Christ (1 John 3:2, page 1279). This is why Jesus said, "That which is born of
the flesh is flesh [the first birth], and that which is born of the Spirit is spirit [the second birth]" (John 3:6,
page 1052). Born once, you will die twice; born twice, you will die once.
    You will never in this life comprehend spiritual birth. Jesus said, "The wind blows where it wishes, and
you hear the sound of it, but cannot tell where it comes from and where it goes. So is everyone who is born
of the Spirit" (John 3:8, page 1052). The spiritual birth is a mystery you cannot understand, but you can
believe it and be born from above (John 3:14-18, page 1052).
    In verse 23 we have:
    (1) *Two seeds.*
    (a) *The corruptible seed.* This is the depraved seed of Adam. "In Adam all die" (1 Cor. 15:22, page
1161) because all are born in sin (Ps. 51:5, page 541; Rom. 3:23, page 1131).
(Point 23-B continued on next page)

R rejected indeed by men, but chosen by God
and precious,   Ps. 118:22

5 you also, as living stones, are being built
up a spiritual house, a holy priesthood, to
offer up spiritual sacrifices acceptable to God
through Jesus Christ.

6 Therefore it is also contained in the
Scripture,

R "Behold, I lay in Zion
   A chief cornerstone, elect, precious,
   And he who believes on Him will by no
      means be put to shame."   Is. 28:16

7 Therefore, to you who believe, He is
precious; but to those who *are disobedient,

* "The stone which the builders rejected
   Has become the chief cornerstone,"

8 and

R "A stone of stumbling
   And a rock of offense."   Is. 8:14

They stumble, being disobedient to the word,
to which they also were appointed.

9 But you are a chosen generation, a royal
priesthood, a holy nation, His own special

2:7 NU disbelieve • Ps. 118:22; Matt. 21:42; Luke 2:34

(Point 23-B continued from previous page)

(b) *The incorruptible seed.* This is the holy seed of God. "So in Christ all [believers] shall be made alive" (1 Cor. 15:22, page 1161). By the spiritual birth we are partakers of the holy nature of God (2 Pet. 1:4, page 1274).

(2) *Two births.*

(a) *The corruptible birth.* This birth is of the flesh. "That which is born of the flesh is flesh" (John 3:6, page 1052). The flesh will never, in this life, be anything but sinful.

(b) *The incorruptible birth.* This birth is of God. "That which is born of the Spirit is spirit" (John 3:6, page 1052). It will always be sinless because it is born of God, and that which is born of God *cannot* sin (1 John 3:9, page 1280).

(3) *Two natures.*

(a) *The corruptible nature.* This nature (pattern of capabilities and tendencies) is "carnal, sold under sin" (Rom. 7:14, page 1136).

(b) *The incorruptible nature.* This nature is divine because it is born from above (1 Pet. 1:3–5, page 1263).

"That which is born of the flesh is flesh, and that which is born of the Spirit is spirit. Do not marvel that I said to you, 'You must be born again'" (John 3:6, 7, page 1052). Every born-again believer has two natures—the old nature born in sin, and the new nature born in righteousness. These two natures are not compatible; they war against each other. Paul said, "In me (that is, in my flesh [old nature]) nothing good dwells . . . I find then a law, that evil is present with me, the one who wills to do good" (Rom. 7:18, 21, page 1136). If you are a born-again believer, your two natures will war within your body until death (Gal. 5:16, 17, page 1184). Throughout your life, when you obey the old nature, the new nature will object; or, when you obey your new nature, your old nature will rebel. Paul found the spiritual power to gain victory over this problem. He said, "Put on the whole armor of God." If we would emulate the victorious life of this great apostle, then we must put on the whole armor of God revealed to us in Ephesians 6:10–18 (page 1192). Each part of this armor is the Lord Jesus Christ.

(1) *The girdle of truth.* Jesus is the truth (John 8:31, 32, page 1063; 14:6, page 1074).
(2) *The breastplate of righteousness.* Christ is our righteousness (2 Cor. 5:21, page 1169).
(3) *The gospel shoes.* The Good News of salvation is Jesus Christ (Rom. 1:16, page 1128).
(4) *The shield of faith.* Paul said, "I live by faith in the Son of God" (Gal. 2:20, page 1180).
(5) *The helmet of salvation.* Christ is our eternal salvation. There is no other (Acts 4:12, page 1091).
(6) *The sword of the Spirit.* This sword is the Word of God:

(a) Jesus Christ is the *living* Word of God (John 1:14, page 1049).
(b) The Bible is the *written* Word of God that reveals to us the living Word of God—the Lord Jesus Christ (Heb. 4:12, page 1239).

(7) *Praying always.* Keep the armor of God polished with prayer so that you may share the Lord Jesus Christ with this world that is in spiritual darkness (1 Thess. 5:17, page 1213).

Further Paul said, "I discipline my body [his fleshly nature] and bring it into subjection [to his spiritual nature], lest, when I have preached to others, I myself should become disqualified [disapproved of God and without reward]" (1 Cor. 9:27, page 1154). The flesh is a personal problem for every born-again believer, and it will be your problem from the cradle to the grave. Nevertheless, you can be victorious over the old nature through the power of the indwelling Holy Spirit; for "He who is in you [the Holy Spirit] is greater than he who is in the world [Satan and his demons, who will test you by tempting the old nature to rebel against all that is good and righteous]" (1 John 4:4, page 1280).

See Titus 3:5, page 1231, for **Point 23-C: The Spiritual Birth Is the Washing of Regeneration.**

people, that you may proclaim the praises of Him who called you out of ᴿdarkness into His marvelous light;   [Acts 26:18]

10 who once *were* not a people but *are* now the people of God, who had not obtained mercy but now have obtained mercy.

Living Before the World

11 Beloved, I beg *you* as sojourners and pilgrims, abstain from fleshly lusts ᴿwhich war against the soul,   James 4:1

12 ᴿhaving your conduct honorable among the Gentiles, that when they speak against you as evildoers, ᴿthey may, by *your* good works which they observe, glorify God in the day of visitation.   Phil. 2:15 • Matt. 5:16; 9:8

Submission to Government

13 Therefore submit yourselves to every ᵀordinance of man for the Lord's sake, whether to the king as supreme,   *institution*

14 or to governors, as to those who are sent by him for the punishment of evildoers and *for* the praise of those who do good.

15 For this is the will of God, that by doing good you may put to silence the ignorance of foolish men—

16 as free, yet not using liberty as a cloak for vice, but as bondservants of God.

17 Honor all *people*. Love the brotherhood. Fear ᴿGod. Honor the king.   Prov. 24:21

Submission to Masters

18 ᴿServants, *be* submissive to *your* masters with all fear, not only to the good and gentle, but also to the harsh.   Eph. 6:5–8

19 For this *is* ᴿcommendable, if because of conscience toward God one endures grief, suffering wrongfully.   Matt. 5:10

20 For what credit *is it* if, when you are beaten for your faults, you take it patiently? But when you do good and suffer, if you take it patiently, this *is* commendable before God.

21 For to this you were called, because Christ also suffered for *us, leaving *us an example, that you should follow His steps:

22 "Whoᴿ committed no sin,   Is. 53:9
    Nor was deceit found in His mouth";

23 ᴿwho, when He was reviled, did not revile in return; when He suffered, He did not threaten, but ᴿcommitted *Himself* to Him who judges righteously;   Is. 53:7 • Luke 23:46

24 who Himself bore our sins in His own body on the tree, that we, having died to sins, might live for righteousness—ᴿby whose ᵀstripes you were healed.   Is. 53:5 • *wounds*

25 For you were like sheep going astray, but have now returned ᴿto the Shepherd and *Overseer of your souls.   [Ezek. 34:23]; Zech. 13:7

Submission to Husbands

3 Wives, likewise, *be* submissive to your own husbands, that even if some do not obey the word, they, without a word, may be won by the conduct of their wives,

2 ᴿwhen they observe your chaste conduct *accompanied* by fear.   1 Pet. 2:12; 3:6

3 Do not let your adornment be *merely* outward—arranging the hair, wearing gold, or putting on *fine* apparel—

4 rather *let it be *ᴿthe hidden person of the heart, with the ᵀincorruptible *beauty* of a gentle and quiet spirit, which is very precious in the sight of God.   Rom. 2:29 • *imperishable*

5 For in this manner, in former times, the holy women who trusted in God also adorned themselves, being submissive to their own husbands,

6 as Sarah obeyed Abraham, ᴿcalling him lord, whose daughters you are if you do good and are not afraid with any terror.   Gen. 18:12

A Word to Husbands

7 ᴿHusbands, likewise, dwell with *them* with understanding, giving honor to the wife, as to the weaker vessel, and as *being* heirs together of the grace of life, that your prayers may not be hindered.   [Eph. 5:25]

Called to Blessing

8 Finally, all *of you be *of one mind, having compassion for one another; love as brothers, *be* tenderhearted, *be* *courteous;

9 ᴿnot returning evil for evil or reviling for reviling, but on the contrary ᴿblessing, knowing that you were called to this, that you may inherit a blessing.   [Prov. 17:13] • Matt. 5:44

10 For

      ᴿ"He who would love life   Ps. 34:12–16
      And see good days,
      Let him refrain his tongue from evil,
      And his lips from speaking deceit.

11 Let him ᴿturn away from evil and do
      good;   Ps. 37:27
      Let him seek peace and pursue it.

12 For the eyes of the LORD are on the
      righteous,
      ᴿAnd His ears are open to their prayers;
      But the face of the LORD is against
      those who do evil."   John 9:31

Suffering for Right and Wrong

13 ᴿAnd who *is* he who will harm you if you become followers of what is good?   Prov. 16:7

14 ᴿBut even if you should suffer for righteousness' sake, *you are* blessed. ᴿ*"And do not be afraid of their threats, nor be troubled."*   James 1:12 • Is. 8:12

2:21 NU *you* • NU, M *you*
2:25 Gr. *Episkopos*   3:8 NU *humble*

15 But sanctify *the Lord God in your hearts, and always *be* ready to *give* a defense to everyone who asks you a reason for the hope that is in you, with meekness and fear;

16 ᴿhaving a good conscience, that when they defame you as evildoers, those who revile your good conduct in Christ may be ashamed.   Heb. 13:18

17 For *it is* better, if it is the will of God, to suffer for doing good than for doing evil.

Christ's Suffering and Ours

18 For Christ also suffered once for sins, the just for the unjust, that He might bring *us to God, being put to death in the flesh but made alive by the Spirit,

19 by whom also He went and preached to the spirits in prison,

20 who formerly were disobedient, *when once the Divine longsuffering waited in the days of Noah, while *the* ark was being prepared, in which a few, that is, eight souls, were saved through water.

21 There is also an antitype which now saves us—baptism (not the removal of the filth of the flesh, ᴿbut the answer of a good conscience toward God), through the resurrection of Jesus Christ,   [Rom. 10:10]

22 who has gone into heaven and ᴿis at the right hand of God, ᴿangels and authorities and powers having been made subject to Him.   Ps. 110:1 • Rom. 8:38

4 Therefore, since Christ suffered *for us in the flesh, arm yourselves also with the same mind, for he who has suffered in the flesh has ceased from sin,

2 that he no longer should live the rest of *his* time in the flesh for the lusts of men, ᴿbut for the will of God.   John 1:13

3 For we *have spent* enough of our past *lifetime in doing the will of the Gentiles— when we walked in lewdness, lusts, drunkenness, revelries, drinking parties, and abominable idolatries.

4 In regard to these, they think it strange that you do not run with *them* in the same flood of dissipation, speaking evil of *you*.

5 They will give an account to Him who is ready to judge the living and the dead.

6 For this reason the gospel was preached also to those who are dead, that they might be judged according to men in the flesh, but ᴿlive according to God in the spirit. [Rom. 8:9,13]

Serving for God's Glory

7 But ᴿthe end of all things is at hand; therefore be serious and watchful in your prayers.   Rom. 13:11

8 And above all things have fervent love for one another, for ᴿ*"love will cover a multitude of sins."*   [Prov. 10:12]

9 ᴿBe hospitable to one another ᴿwithout grumbling.   Heb. 13:2 • 2 Cor. 9:7

10 ᴿAs each one has received a gift, minister it to one another, as good stewards of ᴿthe manifold grace of God.   Rom. 12:6–8 • [1 Cor. 12:4]

11 ᴿIf anyone speaks, *let him speak* as ᵀthe oracles of God. If anyone ministers, *let him do it* as with the ability which God supplies, that in all things God may be glorified through Jesus Christ, to whom belong the glory and the ᵀdominion forever and ever. Amen.   Eph. 4:29 • *utterances* • *sovereignty*

Suffering for God's Glory

12 Beloved, do not think it strange concerning the fiery trial which is to try you, as though some strange thing happened to you;

13 but rejoice ᴿto the extent that you partake of Christ's sufferings, that ᴿwhen His glory is revealed, you may also be glad with exceeding joy.   James 1:2 • 2 Tim. 2:12

14 If you are ᵀreproached for the name of Christ, ᴿblessed *are you*, for the Spirit of glory and of God rests upon you. *On their part He is blasphemed, ᴿbut on your part He is glorified.   *insulted* or *reviled* • Matt. 5:11 • Matt. 5:16

15 But let none of you suffer as a murderer, a thief, an evildoer, or as a ᵀbusybody in other people's matters.   *meddler*

16 Yet if *anyone suffers* as a Christian, let him not be ashamed, but let him glorify God in this *matter.

17 For the time *has come* ᴿfor judgment to begin at the house of God; and if *it begins* with us first, what will *be* the end of those who do not obey the gospel of God?   Is. 10:12

18 Now

> ᴿ*"If the righteous one is scarcely saved,*
> *Where will the ungodly and the sinner*
> *appear?"*   Prov. 11:31

19 Therefore let those who suffer according to the will of God commit their souls *to Him* in doing good, as to a faithful Creator.

Shepherd the Flock

5 The elders who are among you I exhort, I who am a fellow elder and a ᴿwitness of the sufferings of Christ, and also a partaker of the glory that will be revealed: Matt. 26:37

3:15 NU *Christ as Lord*
3:18 NU, M *you*
3:20 NU, M *when the longsuffering of God waited patiently*
4:1 NU omits *for us*
4:3 NU *time*

4:14 NU omits the rest of v. 14.
4:16 NU *name*

▼ 48-E. The Crown of Glory

2 ᴿShepherd the flock of God which is among you, serving as overseers, ᴿnot by compulsion but *willingly, not for dishonest gain but eagerly;   Acts 20:28 • 1 Cor. 9:17

3 nor as ᴿbeing ᵀlords over ᴿthose entrusted to you, but ᴿbeing examples to the flock;   Ezek. 34:4 • *masters* • Ps. 33:12 • Phil. 3:17

4 and when ᴿthe Chief Shepherd appears, you will receive ᴿthe crown of glory that does ▲ not fade away.   Heb. 13:20 • 2 Tim. 4:8

5:2 NU adds *according to God*

25-B. The Christian Life Is a Faith Life ▼

Submit to God, Resist the Devil

5 Likewise you younger people, submit yourselves to your elders. Yes, ᴿall of you be submissive to one another, and be clothed with humility, for   Eph. 5:21

ᴿ*"God resists the proud,*   Prov. 3:34
But ᴿ*gives grace to the humble."* Is. 57:15

6 Therefore humble yourselves under the mighty hand of God, that He may exalt you in due time,

7 casting all your care upon Him, for He cares for you.

48-E. The Crown of Glory (1 Peter 5:2–4)—The "crown of glory" (v. 4) is a special reward for faithful, obedient, God-called pastors. They will receive this reward when the "Chief Shepherd appears." It is eternal; it "does not fade away" (v. 4). Every believer may share in the pastor's "crown of glory." "He who receives a prophet in the name of a prophet shall receive a prophet's reward" (Matt. 10:41, page 951). Support your faithful, God-called pastor by praying for him and encouraging him in the work of the Lord. Undergird his ministry with your tithes and offerings (Mal. 3:10, page 925), giving freely of your time to the Lord's service. God will reward you for supporting His chosen servant by allowing you to share in your pastor's reward.

The pastor will earn this "crown of glory" by:

(1) *Feeding the church.* He is to proclaim the Word of God without fear or favor, and when necessary, to "convince, rebuke, exhort, with all longsuffering and teaching" (2 Tim. 4:1–5, page 1228).

(2) *Taking the spiritual oversight of the church.* A pastor is responsible to God for the message preached to his people. No pastor should preach to please the people; he is to please his Lord (Gal. 1:10, page 1178).

(3) *Being an example to the church.* He is not to serve for the reward of money. However, the church is responsible to care for his material needs (1 Tim. 5:18, page 1221). He is to be a spiritual leader, and not a dictator. He is to walk with God by faith. "And when the Chief Shepherd appears, [He] will receive the crown of glory that does not fade away" (v. 4).

See Index, page 17, for your next study.

25-B. The Christian Life Is a Faith Life (1 Peter 5:5–9)—Faith is a gift of God. Faith comes by hearing, and hearing by the Word of God (Rom. 10:17, page 1140).

(1) We are saved by faith (Eph. 2:8, page 1187).

(2) Faith helps us to steadfastly resist our adversary the Devil, who like a roaring lion walks around seeking to devour us (v. 8).

(3) We live by faith (Rom. 1:17, page 1128; Gal. 3:11, page 1181; Heb. 10:38, page 1247).

(4) We walk by faith (Rom. 4:12, page 1132).

(5) Faith moves mountains (Matt. 21:21, page 968).

(6) Faith builds us up (Jude 20, page 1290).

(7) Faith quenches all the fiery darts of the wicked (Eph. 6:16, page 1192).

(8) Faith helps us to overcome the world (1 John 5:4, page 1282).

There are two things that the Bible requires of the Christian's faith (Heb. 11:6, page 1247):

(1) The Christian must believe that God *is.* None of the writers of the Bible argued for the existence of God; it was assumed. Even the Lord Jesus Christ, who came down from the Father, never tried to prove that He exists. To believe that there is a Creator is the first part of Christian faith. Only a fool says, "There is no God" (Ps. 14:1, page 517).

(2) The Christian must believe that God is a "rewarder of those who diligently seek Him." The Christian faith is believing that God does exist, and that He rewards faith in this life and the life to come (Rev. 22:12, 13, page 1316).

The Christian's faith:

(1) Keeps the Christian saved by the power of God and ready for heaven anytime (1 Pet. 1:5, page 1263).

(2) Is of greater value than gold refined with fire. Your faith will be tested many times and in many ways, but it is more precious than gold that perishes. For the more it is tested the stronger it becomes (1 Pet. 1:6, 7, page 1263).

Because you have Christian faith, you are sometimes "grieved by various trials . . . yet believing, you rejoice with joy inexpressible and full of glory" (1 Pet. 1:6, 8, page 1263; cf. James 1:2–4, page 1255).

Job's faith was tested to the fullest. Then he took his case directly to God, and cried out, "Though He

(Point 25-B continued on next page)

▼ **12-F. Satan: His Work**

8 Be sober, be ᵀvigilant; *because your adversary the devil walks about like a roaring
▲ lion, seeking whom he may devour.   *watchful*

9 Resist him, steadfast in the faith, knowing that the same sufferings are experienced
▲ by your brotherhood in the world.

5:8 NU, M omit *because*
5:10 NU *the God of all grace,* • NU, M *you* • NU *will perfect*

10 *But may the God of all grace, ᴿwho called *us to His eternal glory by Christ Jesus, after you have suffered a while, *perfect, establish, strengthen, and settle you.   1 Cor. 1:9

11 ᴿTo Him be the glory and the dominion forever and ever. Amen.   Rev. 1:6

Farewell and Peace

12 By Silvanus, our faithful brother as I consider him, I have written to you briefly, exhorting and testifying ᴿthat this is the true grace of God in which you stand.   Acts 20:24

(Point 25-B continued from previous page)
slay me, yet will I trust Him." Then in unswerving faith he declared, "I know that I shall be vindicated" (Job 13:1-18, page 487). That is faith!

"Now faith is the substance of things hoped for, the evidence of things not seen" (Heb. 11:1, page 1247). In this abstract definition of faith, there are two spheres of operation:

(1) *"Things hoped for."* This is the realm of the material and the physical. When the Christian has a need in the material or the physical, faith can hope for it. If it is a need that will glorify God, you can claim it by faith, standing upon promises found in the Word of God, such as:

(a) "My God shall supply all your need according to His riches in glory by Christ Jesus" (Phil. 4:19, page 1199).

(b) "The LORD is my shepherd; I shall not want" (Ps. 23:1, page 524).

(c) "Call upon Me in the day of trouble; I will deliver you, and you shall glorify Me" (Ps. 50:15, page 541).

(d) "I can do all things through Christ who strengthens me" (Phil. 4:13, page 1198).

(e) "God is faithful, who will not allow you to be tempted beyond what you are able, but with the temptation will also make the way of escape, that you may be able to bear it" (1 Cor. 10:13, page 1155).

(2) *"Things not seen."* This is the realm of the spiritual, the invisible. We do not usually need faith to believe in things we can see. Faith believes in things that cannot be seen. It was reported of Moses, "By faith he forsook Egypt, not fearing the wrath of the king; for he endured as seeing Him [God] who is invisible" (Heb. 11:27, page 1249). By faith Moses was conscious of the presence of God whom he could not see. That is faith!

"But without faith it is impossible to please Him" (Heb. 11:6, page 1247).

See Colossians 3:16, 17, page 1206, for **Point 25-C: The Christian Life Is a Service Life.**

12-F. Satan: His Work (1 Peter 5:8)—Satan is an untiring, cruel, and crafty worker, and he is a powerful adversary of the human race. He began his work on earth against God and man in the Garden of Eden, and will continue "seeking whom he may devour" (v. 8) until he is cast into the lake of fire (Rev. 20:10, page 1313). So, to withstand the "wiles of the devil" (Eph. 6:11, page 1192), you must put on the whole armor of God:

(1) the girdle of truth (John 14:6, page 1074)
(2) the breastplate of righteousness (Rom. 10:1-4, page 1140)
(3) the gospel sandals (1 Cor. 15:3, 4, page 1161)
(4) the shield of faith (Heb. 11:5, 6, page 1247)
(5) the helmet of salvation (Heb. 5:9, page 1240)
(6) the sword of the Spirit, which is the Word of God (Heb. 4:12, page 1239)
(7) praying always (1 Thess. 5:17, page 1213)

This armor is found in Ephesians 6:10-18 (page 1192), and without it you will live a defeated Christian life.

You need to be aware of some of Satan's works:

(1) He snares the unbeliever and takes him captive to do his will (2 Tim. 2:26, page 1227; cf. Eph. 2:1-3, page 1187).

(2) He entices men to commit evil (1 Thess. 3:5, page 1211).

(3) He has the power of death (Heb. 2:14, page 1237). He is the slayer of men (John 8:44, page 1063).

(4) He motivates professing believers to betray Christ (John 13:2, page 1073).

(5) He inspires believers to lie to God in the church (Acts 5:1-11, page 1093).

(6) He enters into people and causes them to do his will (John 13:21-27, page 1073).

(7) He has the power to steal the Word of God from the hearts of those who hear the Word of God, but do not understand it (Matt. 13:19, page 956).

(Point 12-F continued on next page)

13 She who is in Babylon, elect together with *you*, greets you; and *so does* ᴿMark my son.   Acts 12:12, 25; 15:37, 39

14 Greet one another with a kiss of love. Peace to you all who are in Christ Jesus. Amen.

(Point 12-F continued from previous page)
   (8) He blinds the minds of unbelievers to keep them from being saved (2 Cor. 4:4, page 1167).
   (9) He has access to the throne of God and accuses the brethren before God (Rev. 12:10, page 1305).
   (10) He sifts the believer to bring out the chaff in his life (Luke 22:31, 32, page 1043).
   (11) He will work through the Antichrist in the Great Tribulation (2 Thess. 2:8–12, page 1215).

For thousands of years Satan did everything in his power to block the first coming of Christ and to keep Him from fulfilling the Old Testament types and prophecies of His atoning death on Calvary (Is. 53:1–12, page 693).

See Job 1:6–12, page 479, for **Point 12-G: Satan: His Present and Eternal Abodes.**

THE SECOND EPISTLE OF

Peter

AUTHORSHIP. The Second Epistle of Peter was written by "Simon Peter, a bondservant and apostle of Jesus Christ" (1:1).

Because of a difference in vocabulary, Greek usage, and content, some critics have thought that this epistle must have been written by someone other than Peter. Others have felt that the polished language of 1 Peter is attributable to his use of an amanuensis, or secretary (1 Pet. 5:12), and that 2 Peter represents either Peter's own style and vocabulary or that of a different amanuensis. Some have noted that Peter is called "uneducated and untrained" in Acts 4:13 and as such would probably not even be able to write Greek in the relatively simple style of 2 Peter, let alone the polished turns of 1 Peter.

All such arguments against Petrine authorship of 2 Peter assume that every author must always use the same content, vocabulary, and literary style. These arguments force the author into a sterile straitjacket that would never allow him to modify his style, use different vocabulary, or write on any other subject. The alternatives to Petrine authorship are either pseudonymous authorship (use of "Peter" as an assumed name by another writer) or fraudulent authorship. If one accepts either of these alternatives one should be prepared to include all pseudepigraphic books in the canon of Scripture!

Actually, 2 Peter contains many revealing Petrine biographical citations: the apostle's presence at the Transfiguration (1:17–18), his impending death (1:14), his reference to 1 Peter (3:1), and his association with Paul (3:15).

Peter's ability with Greek, when Aramaic was probably his native language, should not be an insurmountable objection. The Pharisees in Acts who noted that Peter and John were "uneducated and untrained" were not commenting on their intelligence, but were observing that they were not products of the rabbinical schools of the day and hence presuming that they were not properly trained to proclaim God's truth. It was common for people of the day to be not only bilingual but trilingual, speaking Aramaic (their native language), Greek (their cultural language), and Latin (their commercial language). In addition, those who were versed in the Scriptures knew Hebrew. The common Scripture of Peter's day was the Septuagint (the Greek translation of the Old Testament), which the New Testament writers, including Peter, quoted freely.

With all the objections and evidence considered there is no reason why the claim of Petrine authorship in 1:1 should not be received at face value. It is heightened and made more personal by the inclusion of "Simon," Peter's Aramaic name.

CONTEXT. 2 Peter was written in the mid-sixties of the first century, shortly after 1 Peter. It was probably written before Jude, because the false teachers that Peter says *will* come (2:1ff.) already *had* come when Jude wrote (Jude 4). It is the approaching danger of false teachers that makes Peter take his pen in hand and write to the same people he had addressed in his first letter (1 Pet. 1:1). His emotional involvement with the peril facing his readers adequately accounts for the difference in style, vocabulary, and grammar between 1 and 2 Peter. 1 Peter is more carefully thought out and logical; 2 Peter is more emotional and topical. The error against which Peter warned was incipient Gnosticism, a forerunner of modern rational humanism which plagues the theological thought and churches of today.

HOW 2 PETER FITS INTO THE BIBLE. The Gospels, Acts, and Revelation supply the historical framework for our understanding of God's work on earth—past, present, and future. The Pauline Epistles provide the theological framework so necessary for the doctrine of the church. When Paul laid down his pen, Peter took up his (3:15, 16) and wrote two epistles, 1 and 2 Peter. In the first epistle he amplifies the salvation about which Paul wrote and shows how it should impact every area of the lives of believers on every level of life. In 2 Peter he instructs his readers about the cycle of growth in which they should be continuously involved (1:4–9) and thus escape the false teachers who are coming (2:1ff.), who will give rise to questioning the coming of the Lord (3:1ff.). 2 Peter, then, provides the growth cycle necessary after initial conversion in order to live a life pleasing to God and not fall prey to heresy.

HOW 2 PETER FITS TOGETHER. It has been said that there are three reasons why the destructive critic does not like 2 Peter: chapter 1, chapter 2, and chapter 3! The critic can find no rhyme or reason to 2 Peter because he does not see the organizing principle which gives the epistle

meaning. This principle is found in 3:1, in which Peter states that his purpose in writing is to stir up his readers' minds by way of remembrance.

This purpose provides the key for unifying the epistle: Chapter 1 is a reminder of faith in Christ and the divinely appointed means of spiritual growth. Chapter 2 is a reminder of the coming of false teachers who will seek to draw believers away from their salvation. Chapter 3 is a reminder of the certain coming of the Lord.

KEY VERSE: 3:1—"Beloved, I now write to you this second epistle (in both of which I stir up your pure minds by way of reminder)."

KEY WORD: *Remember.*

SUMMARY STATEMENT. Remember the growth cycle which you as a believer are to follow always, lest the coming false teachers lead you into heresy; and do not let them make you lose sight of Christ's coming, despite His apparent delay.

Remember the growth cycle (1:5–7) in which you are to be involved from the day of your conversion (ch. 1). Remember that false teachers are coming (ch. 2) and you will be a candidate to fall into their doctrinal traps if you are not growing spiritually. Finally, remember that Christ is coming just as He promised (ch. 3). He has not forgotten His promise, as the false teachers would have you believe. He is keeping time by a different clock, and by that clock it has not even been a day since He left (3:8). He has not forgotten His coming; He is in a different phase of His eternal plan, calling out a people for His own name (3:9) and when that last person has been added to His Body, the church, He will return.

Far from being the illogical and meaningless book negative critics would make it, 2 Peter remains an anvil of God that has worn out many a blacksmith's hammer. The more the critic seeks to destroy it, the firmer it stands, pointing out to believers today that they have been brought to a saving faith in Christ. That faith, however, is not the end. It is the beginning and the foundation on which they are to build all their life long, adding to that faith the virtues of the growth cycle of 1:5–7 so that they will not be swayed by false teachers but will continue in the certain hope that Jesus will indeed come and establish His eternal kingdom on this earth, bringing to completion all that God purposed in eternity past.

—P.R.F.

Greeting the Faithful

SIMON PETER, a bondservant and ᴿapostle of Jesus Christ,   Gal. 2:8

To those who have ᵀobtained like precious faith with us by the righteousness of our God and Savior Jesus Christ: received

2 Grace and peace be multiplied to you in the knowledge of God and of Jesus our Lord,

3 as His ᴿdivine power has given to us all things that *pertain* to life and godliness, through the knowledge of Him ᴿwho called us by glory and virtue,   1 Pet. 1:5 • 1 Thess. 2:12

4 by which have been given to us exceedingly great and precious promises, that through these you may be partakers of the divine nature, having escaped the ᵀcorruption *that is* in the world through lust.   depravity

Fruitful Growth in the Faith

5 But also for this very reason, ᴿgiving all diligence, add to your faith virtue, to virtue ᴿknowledge,   2 Pet. 3:18 • 1 Pet. 3:7

6 to knowledge self-control, to self-control perseverance, to perseverance godliness,

7 to godliness brotherly kindness, and ᴿto brotherly kindness love.   Gal. 6:10

8 For if these things are yours and abound,

you will be neither barren nor unfruitful in the knowledge of our Lord Jesus Christ.

9 For he who lacks these things is shortsighted, even to blindness, and has forgotten that he was cleansed from his old sins.

10 Therefore, brethren, be even more diligent to make your call and election sure, for if you do these things you will never stumble;

11 for so an entrance will be supplied to you abundantly into the everlasting kingdom of our Lord and Savior Jesus Christ.

Peter's Approaching Death

12 For this reason ᴿI will not be negligent to remind you always of these things, ᴿthough you know and are established in the present truth.   Phil. 3:1 • 1 Pet. 5:12

13 Yes, I think it is right, as long as I am in this tent, to stir you up by reminding *you*,

14 ᴿknowing that shortly I *must* ᵀput off my tent, just as our Lord Jesus Christ showed me.   [2 Tim. 4:6] • Die and leave this body

15 Moreover I will be careful to ensure that you always have a reminder of these things after my ᵀdecease.   Lit. *exodus, departure*

The Trustworthy Prophetic Word

16 For we did not follow cunningly devised fables when we made known to you the

power and coming of our Lord Jesus Christ, but were eyewitnesses of His majesty.

17 For He received from God the Father honor and glory when such a voice came to Him from the Excellent Glory: "This is My beloved Son, in whom I am well pleased."

18 And we heard this voice which came from heaven when we were with Him on ᴿthe holy mountain.   Matt. 17:1

19 *And so we have the prophetic word confirmed, which you do well to heed as a ᴿlight that shines in a dark place, until the day dawns and the morning star rises in your hearts;   [John 1:4, 5, 9]

20 knowing this first, that no prophecy of Scripture is of any private *interpretation,

1:19 Or *We also have the more sure prophetic word*
1:20 Or *origin*

1-D. Christ and the Apostles Authenticated the New Testament as Inerrant   ▼

21 for ᴿprophecy never came by the will of man, but *holy men of God spoke *as they were* moved by the Holy Spirit.   [2 Tim. 3:16] ▲

Destructive Doctrines

2 But there were also false prophets among the people, even as there will be ᴿfalse teachers among you, who will secretly bring in destructive heresies, even denying the Lord who bought them, *and* bring on themselves swift destruction.   1 Tim. 4:1, 2

2 And many will follow their destructive ways, because of whom the way of truth will be blasphemed.

1:21 NU *men spoke from God*

1-D. Christ and the Apostles Authenticated the New Testament as Inerrant (2 Peter 1:21)—In addition to both the Old Testament prophets and Christ, the New Testament apostles and writers agreed that the Scriptures were truly from God, hence inerrant.

(1) Peter denied that "prophecy" (speaking for God), during and after the Old Testament period, ever "came by the will of man" (v. 21)—that is, no group of theologians decided to make up or fabricate the Bible accounts. No, the Scriptures did not originate in man's mind as some have supposed. "Holy men of God [the writers of the Scriptures] spoke as they were moved by the Holy Spirit." It was the Spirit of God who initiated the Scriptures by communicating with the biblical authors, by moving them to speak and write God's message.

(2) Peter further denied that, during the New Testament period, the apostles had followed "cunningly devised fables" (vv. 16–18). He emphasized that they did not invent the accounts circulating in already-written Gospels about the miracle-working of Christ. Rather, he asserted, "we . . . were eyewitnesses of His majesty." He assured us that he and the other apostles had personally seen "the power" displayed by Christ, and had even personally heard God's voice commend Christ on the Mount of Transfiguration (Matt. 17:1–9, page 963). Thus the apostle placed his approval on the Gospel accounts.

(3) Peter recognized the apostle Paul's epistles (letters) as being Scripture (2 Pet. 3:15, 16, page 1276).

(4) John the apostle was shown the vision of the book of Revelation when he was exiled by the Romans to the Isle of Patmos (Rev. 1:9, page 1293). He acknowledged that his book of Revelation is Scripture by announcing a God-appointed curse on all who would add to or subtract from any words written in this last New Testament book (Rev. 22:18, 19, page 1316).

(5) Christ pre-authenticated the coming New Testament as inerrant Scripture and equal in authority to the Old Testament. He said:

(a) "I still have many things to say to you" (John 16:12, page 1077). Here, at the close of His earthly ministry, Christ made it clear that God had more to communicate to man. This further communication came in the New Testament.

(b) "The Holy Spirit . . . will teach you all things" (John 14:26, page 1075). He thus established for us that the author of the coming New Testament would be the Holy Spirit, who would use the apostles to proclaim God's scriptural message.

(c) "The Holy Spirit . . . will . . . bring to your remembrance all things that I said to you" (John 14:26, page 1075). Here Christ pre-authenticated the gospels.

(d) "He [the Spirit] will guide you into all truth" (John 16:13, page 1077). "I still have many things to say to you" (John 16:12, page 1077). By these statements Christ pre-authenticated the epistles—which record the teachings of God on many topics.

(e) "He [the Spirit] will tell you things to come" (John 16:13, page 1077). Here Christ pre-authenticated the book of Revelation, as well as other New Testament prophecy.

(6) All New Testament books (the New Testament canon) were written either by an apostle or by an associate (traveling companion) of an apostle (one especially commissioned by the Lord Himself). The New Testament which we possess was pre-authenticated by Christ, given by the Holy Spirit, and recognized as Scripture by the apostles, just as it was written. It has been so received by the true church universal. It is thus part of the Scriptures and entirely inerrant, our only rule of faith and practice.

See Matthew 19:4, page 965, for **Point 1-E: Christ and the Apostles Accepted Genesis as a Factual Account.**

3 By covetousness they will exploit you with deceptive words; for a long time their judgment has not been idle, and their destruction *does not slumber.

Doom of False Teachers

4 For if God did not spare the angels who sinned, but cast *them* down to ᵀhell and delivered *them* into chains of darkness, to be reserved for judgment;   Lit. *Tartarus*

▼ **45-C. Noah: A Preacher of Righteousness**

5 and did not spare the ancient world, but saved Noah, *one of* eight *people*, a preacher of righteousness, bringing in the flood on the

▲ world of the ungodly;

6 and turning the cities of Sodom and Gomorrah into ashes, condemned *them* to destruction, making *them* an example to those who afterward would live ungodly;

7 and delivered righteous Lot, *who was* oppressed by the filthy conduct of the wicked

8 (for that righteous man, dwelling among them, ᴿtormented *his* righteous soul from day to day by seeing and hearing *their* lawless deeds)—   Ps. 119:139

9 *then* ᴿthe Lord knows how to deliver the godly out of temptations and to reserve the unjust under punishment for the day of judgment,   Ps. 34:15-19

10 and especially ᴿthose who walk according to the flesh in the lust of uncleanness and despise authority. They *are* presumptuous, self-willed. They are not afraid to speak evil of ᵀdignitaries,   Jude 4, 7, 8 • *glorious ones*, lit. *glories*

11 whereas angels, who are greater in power and might, do not bring a reviling accusation against them before the Lord.

2:3 M *will not*

Depravity of False Teachers

12 But these, ᴿlike natural brute beasts made to be caught and destroyed, speak evil of the things they do not understand, and will utterly perish in their own corruption,   Jude 10

13 *and* will receive the wages of unrighteousness, *as* those who count it pleasure to ᵀcarouse in the daytime. *They are* spots and blemishes, ᵀcarousing in their own deceptions while they feast with you,   *revel • reveling*

14 having eyes full of adultery and that cannot cease from sin, enticing unstable souls. *They have* a heart trained in covetous practices, *and are* accursed children.

15 They have forsaken the right way and gone astray, following the way of ᴿBalaam the *son* of Beor, who loved the wages of unrighteousness;   Num. 22:5, 7

16 but he was rebuked for his iniquity: a dumb donkey speaking with a man's voice restrained the madness of the prophet.

17 ᴿThese are wells without water, *clouds carried by a tempest, for whom is reserved the blackness of darkness *forever.   Jude 12, 13

Deceptions of False Teachers

18 For when they speak great swelling *words* of emptiness, they allure through the lusts of the flesh, through lewdness, the ones who *have actually escaped from those who live in error.

19 While they promise them liberty, they themselves are slaves of ᵀcorruption; ᴿfor by whom a person is overcome, by him also he is brought into ᵀbondage.   *depravity • John 8:34 • slavery*

20 For if, after they ᴿhave escaped the pollutions of the world through the knowledge of the Lord and Savior Jesus Christ, they are ᴿagain entangled in them and over-

2:17 NU *and mists* • NU omits *forever*
2:18 NU *are barely escaping*

45-C. Noah: A Preacher of Righteousness (2 Peter 2:5)—The Scriptures tell us that Noah was "a preacher of righteousness" (v. 5). He heralded the righteousness of God.

The righteousness and justice of God are revealed in two ways:

(1) By punishing the wicked for rejecting the righteousness of God in Christ (Ps. 11:5, 6, page 516);
(2) By rewarding the righteous who were made the righteousness of God through Christ (2 Cor. 5:20, 21, page 1169).

The righteousness of God is that attribute which assures man that God is just and will always do what is right. The righteousness and justice of God are manifestations of His holiness. To say that God is holy is to say that He is wholly pure and separate from sin. In eternity past, present, and future, He is pure. He is the same yesterday, today, and forever (Heb. 13:8, page 1252).

Noah was a preacher of righteousness and justice. It is not possible to declare the righteousness and holiness of God and not proclaim His justice (Jer. 23:5, 6, page 735). This preacher of righteousness warned the wicked of their ways for 120 years (Ezek. 33:7-9, page 811). It has been said that Noah never had a convert, but this is not true. He preached the righteousness of God; his wife and his three sons and daughters-in-law were saved by grace through faith. During the 120 years that Noah preached the righteousness of God, the Holy Spirit was striving with the lost (Gen. 6:3, page 11). Some could have been saved and died before the Flood. However, he certainly won seven souls to faith in "THE LORD OUR RIGHTEOUSNESS" (Jer. 23:6, page 735).

See Genesis 6:22, page 12, for **Point 45-D: Noah: A Man of Action.**

come, the latter end is worse for them than the beginning.   Matt. 12:45 · [Heb. 6:4-6]

21 For Rit would have been better for them not to have known the way of righteousness, than having known it, to turn from the holy commandment delivered to them.   Luke 12:47

22 But it has happened to them according to the true proverb: R"*A dog returns to his own vomit,*" and, "a sow, having washed, to her wallowing in the mire."   Prov. 26:11

God's Promise Is Not Slack

3 Beloved, I now write to you this second epistle (in *both* of which RI stir up your pure minds by way of reminder),   2 Pet. 1:13

2 that you may be mindful of the words which were spoken before by the holy prophets, Rand of the commandment of *us, the apostles of the Lord and Savior,   Jude 17

3 knowing this first: that scoffers will come in the last days, Rwalking according to their own lusts,   2 Pet. 2:10

3:2 NU, M *the apostles of your Lord and Savior* or *your apostles of the Lord and Savior*

4 and saying, "Where is the promise of His coming? For since the fathers fell asleep, all things continue as *they were* from the beginning of Rcreation."   Gen. 6:1-7

5 For this they willfully forget: that by the word of God the heavens were of old, and the earth standing out of water and in the water,

6 Rby which the world *that* then existed perished, being flooded with water.   Gen. 7:11

7 But the heavens and the earth *which* now *exist* are kept in store by the same word, reserved for fire until the day of judgment and Tperdition of ungodly men.   destruction

8 But, beloved, do not forget this one thing, that with the Lord one day *is* as a thousand years, and Ra thousand years as one day.   Ps. 90:4

22-A. Repentance Defined   ▼

9 The Lord is not slack concerning *His* promise, as some count slackness, but Ris longsuffering toward *us, Rnot willing that

3:9 NU *you*

22-A. Repentance Defined (2 Peter 3:9)—First, let us see that repentance is *not:*

(1) Merely sorrow—"godly sorrow produces repentance leading to salvation" (2 Cor. 7:9, 10, page 1170). Godly sorrow is a guilty feeling that leads to repentance, but it is not repentance.

(2) Penance—an act on the part of the guilty to render payment for sin, an effort to atone for wrongs done against God or man. God calls all men to repentance, not to do penance.

(a) Jesus did not say, "Do penance and believe in the gospel." He said, "Repent, and believe in the gospel" (Mark 1:15, page 984).

(b) Peter did not say, "Do penance and let every one of you be baptized in the name of Jesus Christ." He said, "Repent, and let every one of you be baptized in the name of Jesus Christ for the remission of sins" (Acts 2:38, page 1089).

(c) Paul did not say, "God . . . commands all men everywhere to do penance." He said, "God . . . commands all men everywhere to repent" (Acts 17:30, page 1112). If penance is repentance, then salvation is not the gift of God, and we are not saved by grace through faith (Eph. 2:8, 9, page 1187).

(3) Reformation—a change brought about by the efforts of man for self-glorification (Matt. 12:43-45, page 954), such as:

(a) turning away from known sin
(b) giving up a bad habit
(c) trying to refine the old nature
(d) turning over a new leaf
(e) making restitution

Second, let us see that repentance *is:*

(1) A change, always evidenced in three elements:

(a) the intellectual element—a change of mind
(b) the emotional element—a change of heart
(c) the volitional element—a change of will

(2) The parable of the prodigal is a perfect illustration of repentance. He had a change of mind, a change of heart, and a change of will (Luke 15:11-32, page 1034):

(a) the intellectual element—"He came to himself"
(b) the emotional element—"I have sinned"
(c) the volitional element—"I will arise and go to my father"

Repentance is a change. The prodigal son had a change of mind; his change of mind caused a change of heart, and his change of heart effected a change of will. No one is ever saved until he wills to be (Rev. 22:17, page 1316). Repentance is a change of mind, of heart, and of will.

See Mark 1:1-4, page 983, for **Point 22-B: Repentance Preached.**

▽ any should perish but ᴿthat all should come
▲ to repentance.   Is. 30:18 • Ezek. 33:11 • [Rom. 2:4]

The Day of the Lord

10 But ᴿthe day of the Lord will come as a
thief in the night, in which ᴿthe heavens will
pass away with a great noise, and the elements will melt with fervent heat; both the
earth and the works that are in it will be
*burned up.   Matt. 24:43 • Ps. 102:25, 26

11 Therefore, since all these things will be
dissolved, what manner *of persons* ought you
to be ᴿin holy conduct and godliness, 1 Pet. 1:15

12 looking for and hastening the coming of
the day of God, because of which the heavens
will be dissolved, being on fire, and the elements will melt with fervent heat?

13 Nevertheless we, according to His promise, look for new heavens and a ᴿnew earth in
which righteousness dwells.   Rev. 21:1

3:10 NU *laid bare*, lit. *found*

Be Steadfast

14 Therefore, beloved, looking forward to
these things, be diligent to be found by Him
in peace, without spot and blameless;

15 and consider *that* ᴿthe longsuffering of
our Lord *is* salvation—as also our beloved
brother Paul, according to the wisdom given
to him, has written to you,   Rom. 2:4

16 as also in all his ᴿepistles, speaking in
them of these things, in which are some
things hard to understand, which untaught
and unstable *people* twist to their own destruction, as *they do* also the ᴿrest of the
Scriptures.   1 Cor. 15:24 • 2 Tim. 3:16

17 You therefore, beloved, since you know
this beforehand, beware lest you also fall
from your own steadfastness, being led away
with the error of the wicked;

18 but grow in the grace and knowledge of
our Lord and Savior Jesus Christ. To Him *be*
the glory both now and forever. Amen.

THE FIRST EPISTLE OF

John

The First Epistle of John is one of the latest biblical writings given to us by the Spirit of God. The epistle is not addressed to any particular church, but is thought of as a "circular letter" sent to several churches. It is a family epistle or letter—and may be designated as "the joy book" or "salvation letter." The epistle is a letter of fellowship, and can be rightly called a family letter because the believers are viewed as the family of God. This is attested to by the repeated use of the word *children*.

KEY WORDS: *know, believe, love,* and *fellowship.*

AUTHORSHIP. The apostle John was probably the only one of the twelve apostles who did not suffer a martyr's death. After his imprisonment on the island of Patmos, his last years were spent in Ephesus, where he died and was buried. It would be supposed, then, that the epistle was written there in about A.D. 90.

The epistle is addressed to the believers or "born ones," so that they might distinguish between truth and error that was creeping into the churches of that day.

HOW 1 JOHN FITS INTO THE BIBLE. 1 John is one of the most profound and spiritual books in the New Testament. Though the language is very simple and the vocabulary is small, making it one of the first books that students of Greek study in the original, the concepts are worthy of lifelong meditation. The young fisherman of Galilee whom Jesus called a "Son of Thunder" (Mark 3:17) is now the aged apostle of love and addresses Christians throughout the province of Asia, and ultimately the entire world. Tradition tells us that in his extreme old age when he could no longer minister the word, John was carried into the church and when asked for a word of wisdom, would invariably say, "Little children, love one another."

HOW 1 JOHN FITS TOGETHER. Letters as personal as 1 John will be variously divided by different scholars. Most outlines stress the theme of "fellowship" in some way or another and the following is a handy beginning for grasping this epistle:

(1) Conditions of Fellowship (1:1—2:2)
(2) Conduct of Fellowship (2:3–11)
(3) Enemies of Fellowship (2:12–27)
(4) Tests of Fellowship (2:28—3:24)
(5) Cautions of Fellowship (ch. 4)
(6) Results of Fellowship (ch. 5)

CONTEXT. John wrote the epistle to refute a form of the heresy of Gnosticism. This philosophy denied Christ's incarnation. It taught that Jesus was just a natural man, and the Divine Spirit came upon Him at His baptism, but left Him at the cross. This heresy also taught that all material substance was evil, and that only the spirit was good. They believed that man was lost because of being imprisoned in a material body. His only hope of salvation, they taught, was through self-knowledge.

John wrote the epistle as a restatement of the gospel. The message is that he who is born of God accepts the incarnation of Jesus Christ the Son of God. He lives a life of righteousness, and this is evidenced by love for his brothers in Christ.

The apostle dwells on the spiritual and moral elements in Christianity rather than on external forms. He has very little to say about the church, church ordinances, church officers, or conduct of public worship. He emphasizes the union of believers with Christ. He thus dwells on faith, love, prayer, and eternal verities.

The epistle reveals the deep, abiding interest and intimacy the author has toward his dear children. Their interest is his interest; their joy is his joy; their struggle is his struggle.

John "the Elder" writing to his "little children" knew what the true gospel was. He was there when it began. He had seen, heard, and touched the incarnate Word of Life.

—D.W.

What Was Heard, Seen, and Touched

THAT which was from the beginning, which we have heard, which we have seen with our eyes, which we have looked upon, and ^Rour hands have handled, concerning the Word of life—   Luke 24:39

2 the life was manifested, and we have seen, and bear witness, and declare to you that eternal life which was ^Rwith the Father and was manifested to us—   [John 1:1, 18; 16:28]

3 that which we have seen and heard we declare to you, that you also may have fellowship with us; and truly our fellowship *is* ^Rwith the Father and with His Son Jesus Christ.   1 Cor. 1:9

4 And these things we write to you ^Rthat *your joy may be full.   John 15:11; 16:24

▼ 3-C. God Is Light

Fellowship with Him and One Another

5 This is the message which we have heard from Him and declare to you, that God is ▲ light and in Him is no darkness at all.

1:4 NU, M *our*

6 ^RIf we say that we have fellowship with Him, and walk in darkness, we lie and do not practice the truth.   [1 John 2:9-11]

7 But if we ^Rwalk in the light as He is in the light, we have fellowship with one another, and ^Rthe blood of Jesus Christ His Son cleanses us from all sin.   Is. 2:5 • [1 Cor. 6:11]

8 If we say that we have no sin, we deceive ourselves, and the truth is not in us.

9 If we confess our sins, He is ^Rfaithful and just to forgive us *our* sins and to cleanse us from all unrighteousness.   [Rom. 3:24-26]

10 If we say that we have not sinned, we make Him a liar, and His word is not in us.

2 My little children, these things I write to you, so that you may not sin. And if anyone sins, ^Rwe have an Advocate with the Father, Jesus Christ the righteous.   Heb. 7:25

2 And ^RHe Himself is the propitiation for our sins, and not for ours only but ^Ralso for the whole world.   [Rom. 3:25] • John 1:29

The Test of Knowing Him

3 Now by this we know that we know Him, if we keep His commandments.

3-C. God Is Light (1 John 1:5)—The Scriptures contain four definitions of the nature of God. They do not fully define His infinite, spiritual nature; however, they do give believers reason to stand in reverential awe as, by faith, they touch the hem of His holy nature. The four definitions are:

(1) *"God is light"* (v. 5). "In Him was life [eternal life], and the life was the light of men" (John 1:4, page 1049). There is life in light (even the house plant will lean toward the window to feed upon God's created light). "Light [Jesus] has come into the world" (John 3:19–21, page 1053). Those who hate the light (Jesus) seek darkness, but those who love the truth will come to the light by faith and feast on eternal life that comes from God the Son, who is pure light. Jesus is "the light of the world" (John 8:12, page 1062). He is the spiritual life of all who come to the light (John 9:5, page 1065).

(2) *"God is Spirit"* (John 4:24, page 1054). God, in His spiritual nature, is without material substance, and therefore invisible to the world of matter. The things of this material world are temporal, while the things of the spiritual world are eternal (2 Cor. 4:18, page 1168). Some theologians teach that when God said, "Let Us make man in Our image, according to Our likeness" (Gen. 1:26, page 4), He did not mean that man's physical likeness would be in the image and likeness of God's spiritual essence but rather in the image and likeness of the Trinity of God. Man is a trinity, not three persons in one man, but three elements—spirit, soul, and body—in one person (1 Thess. 5:23, page 1213). Other theologians believe that the image and likeness of God in man consisted of the moral and intellectual likeness rather than the physical. God is an infinite Spirit and is limited only by His own intrinsic character—His unchangeable wisdom, power, justice, goodness, and truth.

(3) *"God is a consuming fire"* (Heb. 12:28, 29, page 1251). We are to worship and serve God in reverential awe because He is the Holy God, and His holiness demands justice and judgment. As the lost of all ages stand before Him at the Great White Throne judgment (Rev. 20:11-15, page 1313), they will know that "our God is a consuming fire."

(4) *"God is love"* (1 John 4:8, page 1281). It is God's nature to love. The love of God is more than an attribute. It is the essence of His invisible, unchangeable nature. God expresses His love in that:

(a) He is "longsuffering toward us, not willing that any should perish but that all should come to repentance" (2 Pet. 3:9, page 1275; cf. Ex. 34:6–9, page 95).

(b) "He first loved us" (1 John 4:19, page 1282). God loved us before we were born. "I have loved you with an everlasting love; therefore with lovingkindness I have drawn you" (Jer. 31:3, page 744; cf. 1:4, 5, page 710).

(c) He "so loved the world that He gave His only begotten Son, that whoever believes in Him should not perish but have everlasting life. For God did not send His Son into the world to condemn the world, but that the world through Him might be saved" (John 3:16, 17, page 1052).

(d) He sent the Holy Spirit to fill our hearts and lives with His love (Rom. 5:5, page 1133).

(e) There is no separation of the saints "from the love of God" (Rom. 8:38, 39, page 1138).

Thus "light," "Spirit," "fire," and "love" describe His eternal, immutable, and holy nature.
See Numbers 23:19, page 164, for **Point 3-D: God Is Immutable.**

4 He who says, "I know Him," and does not keep His commandments, is a Rliar, and the truth is not in him.   Rom. 3:4

5 But whoever keeps His word, truly the love of God Tis perfected in him. By this we know that we are in Him.   *has been completed*

6 He who says he abides in Him ought himself also to walk just as He walked.

7 *Brethren, I write no new commandment to you, but an old commandment which you have had Rfrom the beginning. The old commandment is the word which you heard *from the beginning.   1 John 3:11, 23; 4:21

8 Again, a new commandment I write to you, which thing is true in Him and in you, Rbecause the darkness is passing away, and the true light is already shining.   Rom. 13:12

9 RHe who says he is in the light, and hates his brother, is in darkness until now. [1 Cor. 13:2]

10 RHe who loves his brother abides in the light, and Rthere is no cause for stumbling in him.   [1 John 3:14] • 2 Pet. 1:10

11 But he who Rhates his brother is in darkness and walks in darkness, and does not know where he is going, because the darkness has blinded his eyes.   [1 John 2:9; 3:15; 4:20]

Their Spiritual State

12 I write to you, little children,
   Because Ryour sins are forgiven you
      for His name's sake.   [1 Cor. 6:11]

13 I write to you, fathers,
   Because you have known Him *who is*
      Rfrom the beginning.   John 1:1
   I write to you, young men,
   Because you have overcome the
      wicked one.
   I write to you, little children,
   Because you have known the Father.

14 I have written to you, fathers,
   Because you have known Him *who is*
      from the beginning.
   I have written to you, young men,
   Because Ryou are strong, and the
      word of God abides in you,   Eph. 6:10
   And you have overcome the wicked
      one.

Do Not Love the World

15 RDo not love the world or the things in the world. If anyone loves the world, the love of the Father is not in him.   [Rom. 12:2]

16 For all that *is* in the world—the lust of the flesh, Rthe lust of the eyes, and the pride of life—is not of the Father but is of the world.   [Eccl. 5:10, 11]

17 And Rthe world is passing away, and the lust of it; but he who does the will of God abides forever.   1 Cor. 7:31

Deceptions of the Last Hour

18 RLittle children, Rit is the last hour; and as you have heard that Rthe* Antichrist is coming, Reven now many antichrists have come, by which we know that it is the last hour.   John 21:5 • 1 Pet. 4:7 • 2 Thess. 2:3 • 2 John 7

19 RThey went out from us, but they were not of us; for Rif they had been of us, they would have continued with us; but *they went out* that they might be made manifest, that none of them were of us.   Deut. 13:13 • Matt. 24:24

20 But you have an anointing Rfrom the Holy One, and *you know all things.   Acts 3:14

21 I have not written to you because you do not know the truth, but because you know it, and that no lie is of the truth.

22 Who is a liar but he who denies that RJesus is the Christ? He is antichrist who denies the Father and the Son.   1 John 4:3

23 RWhoever denies the Son does not have the RFather either; he who acknowledges the Son has the Father also.   John 15:23 • John 5:23

Let Truth Abide in You

24 Therefore let that abide in you which you heard from the beginning. If what you heard from the beginning abides in you, you also will abide in the Son and in the Father.

25 RAnd this is the promise that He has promised us—eternal life.   John 3:14-16; 6:40; 17:2, 3

26 These things I have written to you concerning those who *try to* deceive you.

27 But the anointing which you have received from Him abides in you, and you do not need that anyone teach you; but as the same anointing teaches you concerning all things, and is true, and is not a lie, and just as it has taught you, you *will abide in Him.

The Children of God

28 And now, little children, abide in Him, that *when He appears, we may have Rconfidence and not be ashamed before Him at His coming.   1 John 3:21; 4:17; 5:14

29 RIf you know that He is righteous, you know that Reveryone who practices righteousness is born of Him.   Acts 22:14 • 1 John 3:7, 10

3 Behold Rwhat manner of love the Father has bestowed on us, that Rwe should be called children of *God! Therefore the world does not know *us, Rbecause it did not know Him.   [1 John 4:10] • [John 1:12] • John 15:18, 21; 16:3

2 Beloved, now we are children of God; and Rit has not yet been revealed what we shall be, but we know that when He is revealed, we shall be like Him, for Rwe shall see Him as He is.   [Rom. 8:18, 19, 23] • [Ps. 16:11]

2:7 NU *Beloved* • NU omits *from the beginning*
2:18 NU omits *the*
2:20 NU *you all know.*
2:27 NU omits *will*
2:28 NU *if*
3:1 NU adds *And we are* • M *you*

3 ᴿAnd everyone who has this hope in Him purifies himself, just as He is pure. 1 John 4:17

Sin and the Child of God

4 Whoever commits sin also commits lawlessness, and ᴿsin is lawlessness. Rom. 4:15

5 And you know ᴿthat He was manifested ᴿto take away our sins, and ᴿin Him there is no sin. 1 John 1:2; 3:8 • John 1:29 • [2 Cor. 5:21]

6 Whoever abides in Him does not sin. Whoever sins has neither seen Him nor known Him.

7 Little children, let no one deceive you. He who practices righteousness is righteous, just as He is righteous.

8 He who sins is of the devil, for the devil has sinned from the beginning. For this purpose the Son of God was manifested, that He might destroy the works of the devil.

9 Whoever has been born of God does not sin, for His seed remains in him; and he cannot sin, because he has been born of God.

The Imperative of Love

10 In this the children of God and the children of the devil are manifest: Whoever does not practice righteousness is not of God, nor *is* he who does not love his brother.

11 For this is the message that you heard from the beginning, ᴿthat we should love one another, [John 13:34; 15:12]

12 not as ᴿCain *who* was of the wicked one and murdered his brother. And why did he murder him? Because his works were evil and his brother's righteous. Gen. 4:4, 8

13 Do not marvel, my brethren, if ᴿthe world hates you. [John 15:18; 17:14]

14 We know that we have passed from death to life, because we love the brethren. He who does not love *his brother abides in death.

15 Whoever hates his brother is a murderer, and you know that ᴿno murderer has eternal life abiding in him. [Gal. 5:20, 21]

The Outworking of Love

16 By this we know love, because He laid down His life for us. And we also ought to lay down *our* lives for the brethren.

17 But ᴿwhoever has this world's goods, and sees his brother in need, and shuts up his heart from him, how does the love of God abide in him? Deut. 15:7

18 My little children, let us not love in word or in tongue, but in deed and in truth.

3:14 NU omits *his brother*

19 And by this we *know ᴿthat we are of the truth, and shall ᵀassure our hearts before Him. John 18:37 • *persuade, set at rest*

20 For if our heart condemns us, God is greater than our heart, and knows all things.

21 Beloved, if our heart does not condemn us, we have confidence toward God.

22 And ᴿwhatever we ask we receive from Him, because we keep His commandments ᴿand do those things that are pleasing in His sight. Ps. 34:15 • John 8:29

23 And this is His commandment: that we should believe on the name of His Son Jesus Christ ᴿand love one another, as He gave *us commandment. Matt. 22:39

The Spirit of Truth and the Spirit of Error

24 Now ᴿhe who keeps His commandments abides in Him, and He in him. And ᴿby this we know that He abides in us, by the Spirit whom He has given us. John 14:23 • Rom. 8:9, 14, 16

4 Beloved, do not believe every spirit, but ᴿtest the spirits, whether they are of God; because ᴿmany false prophets have gone out into the world. 1 Cor. 14:29 • Matt. 24:5

2 By this you know the Spirit of God: ᴿEvery spirit that confesses that Jesus Christ has come in the flesh is of God, 1 Cor. 12:3

3 and every spirit that does not confess *that Jesus *Christ has come in the flesh is not of God. And this is the *spirit* of the Antichrist, which you have heard was coming, and is now already in the world.

4 You are of God, little children, and have overcome them, because He who is in you is greater than he who is in the world.

5 ᴿThey are of the world. Therefore they speak *as* of the world, and ᴿthe world hears them. John 3:31 • John 15:19; 17:14

6 We are of God. He who knows God hears us; he who is not of God does not hear us. ᴿBy this we know the spirit of truth and the spirit of error. [1 Cor. 2:12–16]

23-D. The Spiritual Birth: Its Evidence ▼

Knowing God Through Love

7 Beloved, let us love one another, for love is of God; and everyone who ᴿloves is born of God and knows God. 1 Thess. 4:9

3:19 NU *shall know*
3:23 M omits *us*
4:3 NU omits *that* • NU omits *Christ has come in the flesh*

23-D. The Spiritual Birth: Its Evidence (1 John 4:7–21)—Evidence of spiritual birth is set forth in this portion of Scripture in a most powerful, edifying way. One of the four definitions of God in the Bible is, "God is love" (vv. 8, 16). Love is not merely an attribute of God, it is the very essence of His holy, unchangeable nature. God loves because it is His nature. His is not an ordinary love. He manifested this great love when
(Point 23-D continued on next page)

▼ **21-A. So Great in Love**

▽   8 He who does not love does not know
▲ God, for God is love.

9 ᴿIn this the love of God was manifested
toward us, that God has sent His only begotten ᴿSon into the world, that we might live ▽
through Him.   Rom. 5:8 • John 3:16

10 In this is love, ᴿnot that we loved God,
but that He loved us and sent His Son ᴿto be
the propitiation for our sins.   Titus 3:5 • 1 John 2:2

11 Beloved, ᴿif God so loved us, we also
ought to love one another.   Matt. 18:33

(Point 23-D continued from previous page)
He sent His only begotten Son into this world to go to Calvary, where He suffered death and the agonies of
hell in our place, that we might be made the righteousness of God in Him (2 Cor. 5:21, page 1169). John said,
"For God so loved the world that He gave His only begotten Son [love always gives, expecting nothing in
return], that whoever believes in Him should not perish but have everlasting life. For God did not send His
Son into the world to condemn the world, but that the world through Him [His gift of love] might be saved"
(John 3:16, 17, page 1052).

God manifested His love toward us when He so loved the world that He gave His only begotten Son to
die in our place. We who are born from above are to *manifest* our love to God and to our fellow man by our
daily walk, and the keeping of two commandments. When the Lord Jesus Christ was asked, "Which is the
great commandment in the law?" He answered, " 'You shall love the Lᴏʀᴅ your God with all your heart, with
all your soul, and with all your mind.' This is the first and great commandment. And the second is like it: 'You
shall love your neighbor as yourself' " (Matt. 22:36-40, page 970). There is only one love capable of
observing these two great commandments, and that is the love of God. This love is put in our hearts by the
Holy Spirit when we are spiritually born into the family of God (Gal. 3:26, page 1182). Only those who have
been born from above are capable of loving God with all their heart, soul, and mind, and loving their
neighbor as themselves.

Keep in mind that the spiritual birth is the work of God the Holy Spirit. Therefore, "Beloved, let us love
one another, for love is of God; and everyone who loves is born of God" (v. 7).

(1) Everyone born of God:

(a) Has the love of God shed abroad in his or her heart by the Holy Spirit, who "birthed" him or her
into the family of God (Rom. 5:5, page 1133). It is impossible to be born of the Holy Spirit and not have the
love of God in your heart. Remember, His love is the essence of His nature, and every born-again believer
is a partaker of God's nature (2 Pet. 1:4, page 1272). "Everyone who loves is born of God and knows God.
He who does not love does not know God, for God is love" (vv. 7, 8).

(b) Will bear the fruit of the Spirit. "But the fruit of the Spirit is love, [and love is demonstrated in]
joy, peace, longsuffering, kindness, goodness, faithfulness, gentleness, self-control. Against such there is no
law [no restraints]" (Gal. 5:22, 23, page 1184).

(c) Is commanded to love his brother (vv. 20, 21).

(d) Will have no fear (vv. 17, 18). We will have no fear because we have the perfect love of God, and
in that love there is reverential fear, but no fear of God in judgment. "There is therefore now no
condemnation [judgment] to those who are in Christ Jesus, who do not walk according to the flesh [the old
nature], but according to the Spirit [the new nature]" (Rom. 8:1, page 1136). As we walk in the Spirit, God's
love is perfected in us.

(2) Further evidence of the New Birth is found in the fact that you are able to comprehend the four
dimensions of God's love. These dimensions are found in Ephesians 3:14-19 (page 1189):

(a) *The breadth of God's love.* This love extends to all people of all nations, of all ages, at all times.

(b) *The length of God's love.* This love is from eternity to eternity. To His nation Israel He said, "Yes,
I have loved you with an everlasting love" (Jer. 31:3, page 744).

(c) *The depth of God's love.* On Calvary God sent His Son to the very depths of man's sin and
misery, in order that He might manifest His love to a lost sinful world. "And the Lᴏʀᴅ has laid on Him [Jesus
Christ] the iniquity of us all" (Is. 53:6, page 693). "For He [God the Father] made Him [God the Son] who
knew no sin to be sin for us, that we [lost sinners] might become the righteousness of God in Him" (2 Cor.
5:21, page 1169). On the cross, God's Son endured the iniquities of us all. Despising the shame He unveiled
the depths of God's love. "Beloved, if God so loved us, we also ought to love one another" (v. 11).

(d) *The height of God's love.* This love is as high as the third heaven, where Christ is seated at the
right hand of God the Father (Col. 3:1, page 1205; Rev. 3:21, page 1297). "God is love, and he who abides in
love abides in God, and God in him" (v. 16).

The love of God, manifested in our hearts and lives, is evidence of the New Birth. Have you been born
again?

See Index, page 17, for your next study.

21-A. So Great in Love (1 John 4:8)—Salvation is so great in love because "God is love" (v. 8). Love is the
essence of God's eternal and holy nature. God does not love you because you are worthy of His salvation;
He loves you because He is God. Being eternal God, He loves you with an everlasting love and draws you
(Point 21-A continued on next page)

▽ ## Seeing God Through Love

12 ᴿNo one has seen God at any time. If we love one another, God abides in us, and His love has been perfected in us.   John 1:18

13 ᴿBy this we know that we abide in Him, and He in us, because He has given us of His Spirit.   John 14:20

14 And ᴿwe have seen and testify that ᴿthe Father has sent the Son *as* Savior of the world.   John 1:14 • John 3:17; 4:42; 1 John 2:2

15 Whoever confesses that Jesus is the Son of God, God abides in him, and he in God.

16 And we have known and believed the love that God has for us. God is love, and ᴿhe who abides in love abides in God, and God ᴿin him.   [1 John 3:24] • [John 14:23]

The Consummation of Love

17 Love has been perfected among us in this: that ᴿwe may have boldness in the day of judgment; because as He is, so are we in this world.   1 John 2:28

18 There is no fear in love; but perfect love casts out fear, because fear involves torment. But he who fears has not been made perfect in love.

19 We love *Him because He first loved us.

Obedience by Faith

20 If someone says, "I love God," and hates his brother, he is a liar; for he who does not love his brother whom he has seen, *how can he love God whom he has not seen?

21 And ᴿthis commandment we have from Him: that he who loves God *must* love his
▲ brother also.   [Matt. 5:43, 44; 22:37]

5 Whoever believes that ᴿJesus is the Christ is ᴿborn of God, and everyone who loves Him who begot also loves Him who is begotten of Him.   1 John 2:22; 4:2, 15 • John 1:13

2 By this we know that we love the children of God, when we love God and ᴿkeep His commandments.   John 15:10

3 ᴿFor this is the love of God, that we keep

His commandments. And His commandments are not burdensome.   John 14:15

4 For ᴿwhatever is born of God overcomes the world. And this is the victory that has overcome the world—*our faith.   John 16:33

5 Who is he who overcomes the world, but ᴿhe who believes that Jesus is the Son of God?   1 Cor. 15:57

The Certainty of God's Witness

6 This is He who came by water and blood—Jesus Christ; not only by water, but by water and blood. And it is the Spirit who bears witness, because the Spirit is truth.

7 For there are three that bear *witness in heaven: the Father, ᴿthe Word, and the Holy Spirit; and these three are one.   [John 1:1]

8 And there are three that bear witness on earth: ᴿthe Spirit, the water, and the blood; and these three agree as one.   John 15:26

9 If we receive ᴿthe witness of men, the witness of God is greater; ᴿfor this is the witness of *God which He has testified of His Son.   John 5:34, 37; 8:17, 18 • [Matt. 3:16, 17]

10 He who believes in the Son of God ᴿhas the witness in himself; he who does not believe God ᴿhas made Him a liar, because he has not believed the testimony that God has given of His Son.   [Rom. 8:16] • John 3:18, 33

11 And this is the testimony: that God has given us eternal life, and this life is in His Son.

12 ᴿHe who has the Son has ᵀlife; he who does not have the Son of God does not have ᵀlife.   [John 3:15, 36; 6:47; 17:2, 3] • Or *the life*

13 These things I have written to you who believe in the name of the Son of God, that you may know that you have eternal life, *and that you may *continue to* believe in the name of the Son of God.

5:4 M *your*
5:7 NU, M omit the words from *in heaven* (v. 7) through *on earth* (v. 8).
5:9 NU, *God, that*
5:13 NU omits the rest of v. 13.

4:19 NU omits *Him*
4:20 NU *he cannot*

(Point 21-A continued from previous page)
to Himself with lovingkindness (Jer. 31:3, page 744). The love of God draws the lost to Christ for salvation. Jesus said, "No one can come to Me unless the Father who sent Me draws him; and I will raise him up at the last day" (John 6:44, page 1060). Again Jesus said, "And I, if I am lifted up [on the cross] from the earth, will draw all peoples to Myself" (John 12:32, page 1072). God in His everlasting love is drawing you to Himself with the cords of eternal compassion. "For God so loved the world that He gave His only begotten Son, that whoever [including you] believes in Him should not perish but have everlasting life" (John 3:16, page 1052).

Again, in this verse, we have that little word *so* that reveals the degree of God's love. God does not just love you, He *so* loves you that He gave His only begotten Son to bear your sins in His own body on the cross, so that you, by faith in Christ, may have eternal salvation. God the Father did not send His Son into the world to condemn you, but to save you, because He loves you with eternal love (John 3:17, 18, page 1053). There is no greater love!

See 2 Corinthians 8:9, page 1171, for **Point 21-B: So Great in Giving.**

▼ 30-C. Pray According to God's Will

Confidence and Compassion in Prayer

14 Now this is the confidence that we have in Him, that ᴿif we ask anything according to His will, He hears us.   [1 John 2:28; 3:21, 22]

15 And if we know that He hears us, whatever we ask, we know that we have the ▲ petitions that we have asked of Him.

16 If anyone sees his brother sinning a sin *which does* not *lead* to death, he will ask, and ᴿHe will give him life for those who commit sin not *leading* to death. ᴿThere is sin *leading* to death. ᴿI do not say that he should pray about that.   Job 42:8 • [Matt. 12:31] • Jer. 7:16; 14:11

17 ᴿAll unrighteousness is sin, and there is sin not *leading* to death.   1 John 3:4

Knowing the True—Rejecting the False

18 We know that ᴿwhoever is born of God does not sin; but he who has been born of God ᵀkeeps *himself, and the wicked one does not touch him.   [1 Pet. 1:23] • guards

19 We know that we are of God, and ᴿthe whole world lies *under the sway of* the wicked one.   Gal. 1:4

20 And we know that the Son of God has come and has given us an understanding, that we may know Him who is true; and we are in Him who is true, in His Son Jesus Christ. This is the true God and eternal life.

21 Little children, keep yourselves from idols. Amen.

5:18 NU *him*

30-C. Pray According to God's Will (1 John 5:14, 15)—God's will for the Christian is good, acceptable, and perfect (Rom. 12:2, page 1142).

(1) *The object of God's will.* God's will includes holiness and His eternal plan (often called the decree of God).

(2) *Knowing God's will.* We learn His will first from:

    (a) the Scriptures
    (b) the leading of the Spirit within us
    (c) the circumstances which He allows to occur in our lives (providence)

(3) *Christ put God the Father's will first.* The ultimate example of praying for God's will was Christ's going to the cross with the words, "Not as I will, but as You will" (Matt. 26:39, page 978). This agony unto death paid the penalty of sin for every believer (1 Pet. 3:18, page 1267).

(4) *Untrue perception of God's will.* When Christ clearly told the Twelve that He was to be killed in Jerusalem, Peter declared, "Far be it from You, Lord; this shall not happen to You" (Matt. 16:21, 22, page 962). Suppose Peter began to pray that Jesus would not be allowed to die? Peter would have been praying contrary to the will of God. Thus, we too must be guided by the Scriptures and the Spirit to pray, not necessarily for the most comfortable, immediate, apparent good, but rather for that holy, lasting, eternal, more important good, *according to the will of God* (Heb. 12:2, page 1250).

(5) *Praying in God's will produces confidence.* According to verses 14 and 15, "if we ask anything according to His will," we have confidence that God hears us and that our petitions will be granted.

(6) *The Lord's Prayer—"Your will be done"* (Matt. 6:10, page 943). It is no accident that, in the Lord's model prayer for us, the sentence before the beginning of our own personal requests is the prayer, "Your will be done." To be effective, our requests must consider His holy purposes before all other things. God's way is always best.

See 1 Thessalonians 5:17, 18, page 1213, for **Point 30-D: Pray Without Ceasing.**

THE SECOND EPISTLE OF

John

AUTHORSHIP. The author of 2 John simply identifies himself as "the elder" (v. 1). While some have held that John the apostle and John the elder are different people, it is generally believed that the elder is the apostle John. Both internal and external evidence support this position.

(1) *Internal Evidence.* John's Gospel and 1 John were recognized by early church fathers as having been written by the apostle. When the similarities between 2 John and 1 John are compared, it is obvious the author of the two epistles is the same.

(2) *External Evidence.* 2 John was not referred to as often as 1 John by early church fathers since it is so brief. Among the church fathers who did attribute portions of the second letter to the apostle John, however, is Irenaeus, who died A.D. 202. He quotes 2 John 7, 8 almost word for word and attributes the writing to John "the disciple of the Lord."

At a later date, Cyprian, in describing the Council at Carthage (A.D. 256) noted that Bishop Curelius of Chullabi referred to 2 John 10, 11 and stated, "John the apostle laid it down in his Epistle."

Thus, while some suggested that two different men by the name of John wrote the books now attributed to John, there is evidence the apostle John was the human author of all these books.

The authority expressed in 2 John indicates the writer was in an official position. The use of the expression "little children" in 1 John indicated he was advanced in age. Thus the title "elder" was appropriate both from the standpoint of age and church position.

CONTEXT. 2 John was probably written as late as A.D. 95 to 98, while the apostle was living in Ephesus. According to early church fathers he had moved to Ephesus prior to the destruction of Jerusalem in A.D. 70. The letter was written after 1 John, because unlike that epistle it presupposes knowledge concerning those referred to as antichrists.

The letter is addressed to "the elect lady." Some hold the recipient is an individual, while others hold it is a community of believers.

If an individual is in view she must have been a person so well known that she would have been loved by "all those who have known the truth" (v. 1).

If a local congregation is intended there is precedent for referring to a church with the feminine form. The church is referred to as a bride in Revelation 21:2, 9. Paul in speaking of the husband-wife relationship wrote, "I speak concerning Christ and the church" (Eph. 5:31, 32). If "elect lady" is the personification of a church the "children of the elect lady" would then be members of the local congregation. The "elect sister" would have been a sister congregation.

HOW 2 JOHN FITS INTO THE BIBLE. 2 John deals primarily with the problem of incipient Gnosticism. Scholars have shown this heresy is referred to or dealt with in other books of the New Testament, such as John's Gospel, Acts, Corinthians, Ephesians, Colossians, Timothy, Titus, John's epistles, and Revelation.

Gnosticism was based on the belief that all matter is evil. Some went so far as to teach there are two eternal independent principles from which all good and all evil come. Others held creation was produced by someone at the end of a long series of "emanations" from God.

Because Gnostics believed the spiritual or intellectual part of man was imprisoned in an evil body, their concern was more with redemption from *matter* than from *sin.* According to them salvation was achieved by some kind of mystical enlightenment which was received in a secret initiation ceremony. The enlightened prided themselves in this nebulous knowledge and considered themselves an elite class.

The belief by the initiated that all matter is evil led to two extremes in morality. Some held the body was evil and needed to be punished. Paul dealt with this form of error in Colossians 2:22, 23 and 1 Timothy 4:1-5, among other passages. Others held that sin could not effect the enlightened spirit. Consequently they indulged in every conceivable form of evil. Paul dealt with the influence of this error in Romans 6:1, 2. John also dealt with it by pointing out that anyone who is born of God does not practice sinning (1 John 3:9).

2 John deals primarily with the Christological heresy of Gnosticism. Other New Testament books, including 1 John, deal at greater length with both the moral and Christological aberrations.

How 2 John Fits Together. 2 John has been described as a condensation of 1 John because it deals with similar issues:

(1) A greeting in which the writer mentions truth and love, key emphases of the letter (vv. 1–3)
(2) Exhortation to love one another and walk according to God's commandments (vv. 4–6)
(3) A warning concerning those who do not teach that Jesus Christ came in the flesh (vv. 7–9)
(4) Instruction not to grant hospitality to false teachers (vv. 10, 11)
(5) Conclusion in which future plans are mentioned and greetings extended (vv. 12, 13)

Key Word: *Truth.*

Summary Statements. John emphasizes the importance of loving one another and walking according to God's commandments, but especially stresses the importance of not encouraging heresy by granting hospitality to deceivers.

In New Testament times inns were often places of ill repute. For this reason, hospitality was frequently extended to travelers in private homes. Believers were especially generous in entertaining fellow Christians traveling through their area. Such fellowship generally inspired and strengthened the faith of both host and guest. Heretics, however, took advantage of hospitality and tried to subvert the faith of their hosts. For a Christian to extend hospitality to those John described as deceivers and antichrists would produce two negative effects: it would result in loss of the things for which the church had worked (v. 8), and the Christian would be encouraging heresy by sharing in the evil deeds of the deceivers (vv. 10, 11).

—T.F.Z.

Greeting the Elect Lady

THE ELDER,

To the ᵀelect lady and her children, whom I love in truth, and not only I, but also all those who have known the truth,   *chosen*
2 because of the truth which abides in us and will be with us forever:

3 ᴿGrace, mercy, *and* peace will be with *you from God the Father and from the Lord Jesus Christ, the Son of the Father, in truth and love.   1 Tim. 1:2

Walk in Christ's Commandments

4 I rejoiced greatly that I have found *some* of your children walking in truth, as we received commandment from the Father.
5 And now I plead with you, lady, not as though I wrote a new commandment to you, but that which we have had from the beginning: ᴿthat we love one another.   John 13:34
6 This is love, that we walk according to His commandments. This is the commandment, that ᴿas you have heard from the beginning, you should walk in it.   1 John 2:24

3 NU, M *us*

Beware of Antichrist Deceivers

7 For ᴿmany deceivers have gone out into the world ᴿwho do not confess Jesus Christ *as* coming in the flesh. ᴿThis is a deceiver and an antichrist.   1 John 2:19; 4:1 • 1 John 4:2 • 1 John 2:22
8 ᴿLook to yourselves, ᴿthat *we* do not lose those things we worked for, but *that* we may receive a full reward.   Mark 13:9 • Gal. 3:4
9 ᴿWhoever *transgresses and does not abide in the doctrine of Christ does not have God. He who abides in the doctrine of Christ has both the Father and the Son.   John 7:16
10 If anyone comes to you and ᴿdoes not bring this doctrine, do not receive him into your house nor greet him;   Rom. 16:17
11 for he who greets him shares in his evil deeds.

John's Farewell Greeting

12 ᴿHaving many things to write to you, I did not wish *to do so* with paper and ink; but I hope to come to you and speak face to face, ᴿthat our joy may be full.   3 John 13, 14 • John 17:13
13 ᴿThe children of your elect sister greet you. Amen.   1 Pet. 5:13

8 NU *you*
9 NU *goes ahead*

THE THIRD EPISTLE OF
John

3 John is a unique gold mine. Though marked by its brevity, this book deals with the biggest of problems—power struggles in the church. The secret of the greatest joy is found in its words. John's third epistle tells us plainly whom Christians should support. The book deals with a quest of all men—assurance of salvation. The teacher finds in 3 John a helpful message on "Three Typical Church Members": Gaius, the beloved believer; Diotrephes, the domineering disciple; and Demetrius, the complimented Christian.

AUTHORSHIP. Like 1 and 2 John, John's third epistle was penned by the apostle of love when he was an old man, probably between A.D. 85-95.

HOW 3 JOHN FITS INTO THE BIBLE. Though very short, this epistle would be missed if it were not here. It gives a colorful glimpse into the life and problems of the late first century church. Its warning against church dictators is much needed today in some circles.

HOW 3 JOHN FITS TOGETHER. The outline of the book follows the three main characters:
(1) Greetings to the Godly and Generous Gaius (vv. 1-8)
(2) Denunciation of the Dictatorial Diotrephes (vv. 9-11)
(3) Commendation of Demetrius and Complementary Close (vv. 12-14)

KEY WORD. As with 2 John, the key word in 3 John is *truth*. It appears six times in the book's 296 words. The word *true* is also found once, giving seven mentions of truth in this single chapter work. 3 John underscores Martin Luther's resolve, "Peace if possible, but truth at any rate." Truth is the foundation of love in a Christian fellowship: "Gaius, whom I love in truth" (v. 1). Truth, in our heart, liberates us from the enslaving passions of life: "the truth that is in you, just as you walk in the truth" (v. 3). Verse 4 says, "I have no greater joy than to hear that my children walk in truth"; the greatest joy a Christian worker can ever experience is winning another person and leading them to "walk in truth."

A power struggle within the church resulted from Diotrephes' violation of the truth. He sought "to have the preeminence" (v. 9). The high-handed methods of some men in modern church life were present in this early church. Diotrephes, like Lucifer, asserted his authority above the authority of the truth. He expelled members from the church on the basis of whom they associated with.

By contrast, Demetrius is held up as an ideal disciple, having a good testimony from men and "from the truth itself" (v. 12). Such a man, who obeys the truth, has assurance he is of God. The man who disobeys the truth proves he has not seen God (v. 11). Horace Mann said, "Keep one thing forever in view—the truth; and if you do this, though it may seem to lead you away from the opinion of men, it will assuredly conduct you to the throne of God."

Pilate once considered John's "truth," asking, "What is truth?" But his mind wandered to other matters, and he arose and left before he found the answer. Emerson said, "God offers to every mind its choice between truth and repose. Take which you please—you can never have both."

Dig deep in the truth of 3 John. The hard work will bring a rich reward.

—M.A.

Greeting to Gaius

THE ELDER,

To the beloved Gaius, ᴿwhom I love in truth: 2 John 1

2 Beloved, I pray that you may prosper in all things and be in health, just as your soul prospers.

3 For I ᴿrejoiced greatly when brethren came and testified of the truth *that is* in you, just as you walk in the truth.   2 John 4

4 I have no greater joy than to hear that ᴿmy children walk in *truth.   [1 Cor. 4:15]

Gaius Commended for Generosity

5 Beloved, you do faithfully whatever you do for the brethren *and for strangers,

6 who have borne witness of your love before the church. *If* you send them forward on their journey in a manner worthy of God, you will do well,

4 NU *the truth*
5 NU *and especially for*

7 because they went forth for His name's sake, taking nothing from the Gentiles.

8 We therefore ought to ᴿreceive* such, that we may become fellow workers for the truth.   Matt. 10:40

Diotrephes and Demetrius

9 I wrote to the church, but Diotrephes, who loves to have the preeminence among them, does not receive us.

10 Therefore, if I come, I will call to mind his deeds which he does, ᵀprating against us with malicious words. And not content with that, he himself does not receive the breth-ren, and forbids those who wish to, putting *them* out of the church.   *talking nonsense*

11 Beloved, do not imitate what is evil, but what is good. He who does good is of God, *but he who does evil has not seen God.

12 Demetrius ᴿhas a *good* testimony from all, and from the truth itself. And we also ᵀbear witness, ᴿand you know that our testimony is true.   1 Tim. 3:7 • *testify* • John 19:35; 21:24

Farewell Greeting

13 ᴿI had many things to write, but I do not wish to write to you with pen and ink;   2 John 12

14 but I hope to see you shortly, and we shall speak face to face. Peace to you. Our friends greet you. Greet the friends by name.

---

8 NU *support*   11 NU, M omit *but*

THE EPISTLE OF
Jude

AUTHORSHIP. The author of this brief but significant New Testament letter refers to himself as "Jude, a bondservant of Jesus Christ, and brother of James" (v. 1). The reference to "James" without any additional identifiers makes it virtually certain that James, leader of the Jerusalem congregation and brother of Jesus, is the man referred to. The author, Jude, then, would be the brother of Jesus; he is so specified in Matthew 13:55 ("Judas").

The writer's sincerity and humility are evidenced by the fact that he did not capitalize on his status as a brother of Jesus, instead describing himself as a "bondservant of Jesus Christ." It is remarkable, and indeed inspiring, to realize that one who once wanted to "put Jesus away," thinking Him to be beside Himself, later became a bondservant of that same Jesus, and was employed as an instrument in expressing the divine word to man!

CONTEXT. While the specific time of the writing of Jude cannot be ascertained from the book itself, many scholars suggest a time period of about A.D. 60–80 for its origin—within a decade either way of the destruction of Jerusalem and the temple in 70. The question of date is definitely influenced by the relationship between Jude and 2 Peter. Jude 4–18 and 2 Peter 2:1–19 and 3:1–3 are nearly identical at several points. If Jude were written first, as some scholars believe, then it would have had to be issued before the writing of 2 Peter and his probable death under Nero about A.D. 64. In this case, a date somewhat earlier than 60 would become likely. On the other hand, the apostates that Peter predicted are seen in Jude as having already "crept in" (v. 4), so many believe Jude was written after 2 Peter.

Due to early written tradition and other factors, it is widely believed that the letter of Jude was written at Rome.

HOW JUDE FITS INTO THE BIBLE. The book of Jude takes its place along with the other "General Letters" (Hebrews, James 1 and 2 Peter, and the Johannine letters) as a part of God's inspired guidance for the church after the first few decades of its existence. As Christianity expanded, and the apostles began to pass on, questions and circumstances arose which required Spirit-directed teaching and writing. Heretics with their errors began to make inroads into the fellowship and its life. Some of the most common problems, and some of the most severe ones, were generated by teachings known as "Gnostic," relating particularly to the nature of God and Christ and to specific standards of living. The author of Jude had apparently received word of such developments in the church; some had departed from and were causing others to depart from the faith.

At such a crucial time in the life of the church, Jude expressed in no uncertain terms God's continuing condemnation of all evil men and their practices, and at the same time His warning and encouragement to those who would remain faithful. Jude's denunciation of evil, and of those who practice it, is one of the strongest in the New Testament—indeed, in the entire Bible.

KEY VERSE: 3—"Beloved, while I was very diligent to write to you concerning our common salvation, I found it necessary to write to you exhorting you to contend earnestly for the faith which was once for all delivered to the saints."

SUMMARY STATEMENT. Jude's message is clear, and rings like that of a threefold trumpet blast: Divine condemnation is, has always been, and will always be on evil and those who practice it; the only sure foundation is the "most holy faith," as represented by the teachings of Christ and the apostles; and those who live by this faith shall endure to eternal life.

These key emphases in Jude are well-expressed in verses 14, 15, "Behold, the Lord comes with ten thousands of His saints, to execute judgment on all, to convict all who are ungodly among them," and verses 20, 21, "But you, beloved, building yourselves up on your most holy faith, praying in the Holy Spirit, keep yourselves in the love of God, looking for the mercy of our Lord Jesus Christ unto eternal life."

HOW JUDE FITS TOGETHER. Although Jude is not lengthy or complex in structure, this brief outline may help in making an organized study, and in keeping the major themes of the book in mind:

(1) Greeting and Occasion for the Letter (vv. 1–4)
(2) Character and Fate of Heretical Intruders (vv. 5–16)
(3) The Apostolic Faith: The True Foundation (vv. 17–23)
(4) Doxology (vv. 24, 25)

Jude's brief book contains one of the most graphic and colorful descriptions or characterizations of evil men and their practices in all of religious literature. Also notable is his use of Old Testament events. Israel and some of the Canaanite cities serve as examples of God's action regarding evil in the past; the vile perverters of the faith are likened to Cain, Balaam, and Korah. The doxology (statement of praise and glory to God) at the close of Jude is like the writing as a whole—brief, but powerful and profound. Surely if God's people "build themselves up on their most holy faith" and "keep themselves in the love of God," they may expect to be presented "faultless before the presence of His glory with exceeding joy"!

—G.M.

Greeting to the Called

JUDE, a bondservant of Jesus Christ, and ᴿbrother of James,

To those who are ᴿcalled, *sanctified by God the Father, and ᴿpreserved in Jesus Christ: Acts 1:13 • Rom. 1:7 • John 17:1

2 Mercy, ᴿpeace, and love be multiplied to you.   1 Pet. 1:2

Contend for the Faith

3 Beloved, while I was very diligent to write to you ᴿconcerning our common salvation, I found it necessary to write to you exhorting ᴿyou to contend earnestly for the faith which was once for all delivered to the saints.   Titus 1:4 • Phil. 1:27

4 For certain men have crept in unnoticed, who long ago were marked out for this con-demnation, ungodly men, who turn the grace of our God into lewdness and deny the only Lord *God and our Lord Jesus Christ.

Old and New Apostates

5 But I want to remind you, though you once knew this, that the Lord, having saved the people out of the land of Egypt, afterward destroyed those who did not believe.

13-A. Demons: Their Identity ▼

6 And the angels who did not keep their proper domain, but left their own abode, He has reserved in everlasting chains under darkness for the judgment of the great day; ▲

7 as ᴿSodom and Gomorrah, and the cities around them in a similar manner to these, having given themselves over to sexual im-morality and gone after strange flesh, are set

1 NU beloved   4 NU omits God

13-A. Demons: Their Identity (Jude 6)—Demons are fallen angels, "who did not keep their proper domain, but left their own abode" (v. 6). When created, they were perfect and were given the power of choice. Demons are angels who chose to disobey God and do the will of Satan.

There are two divisions of fallen angels:

First, those who sinned and are now imprisoned in "chains of darkness" (2 Pet. 2:4, page 1274) waiting for the judgment of angels (1 Cor. 6:3, page 1151).

Second, those who fell, and whom God has allowed to continue to serve Satan and his kingdom. The reason for this is one of God's secrets (Deut. 29:29, page 208). Satan is not omnipresent, but he has a multitude of demons or disembodied spirits, who do his will so thoroughly that it seems as though he is present everywhere.

(1) Demons are unclean spirits. Some are more wicked than others. They can "possess" a person. They can also invite other demons to enter and dwell with them (Matt. 12:43–45, page 954).

(2) Demons are intelligent beings. They spoke to Jesus from a possessed man and said, "Let us alone! What have we to do with You, Jesus of Nazareth? Did You come to destroy us? I know who You are—the Holy One of God!" (Luke 4:31-37, page 1017). This demon

(a) talked to Jesus;
(b) knew Jesus;
(c) knew that Jesus had the power to destroy him;
(d) knew that Jesus was the "Holy One of God."

(3) Demons have supernatural strength. In the country of the Gadarenes, Jesus met a man with an unclean spirit, who was so strong that no chains or shackles could hold him (Mark 5:1-4, page 989).

In human strength we are no match for Satan or his demons. Our protection is "the sword of the Spirit, which is the word of God" (Eph. 6:17, page 1192), and the indwelling Holy Spirit. Let the Holy Spirit possess every part of your being, and present your body to the Lord as "a living sacrifice, holy, acceptable to God" (Rom. 12:1, 2, page 1142).

(Point 13-A continued on next page)

forth as an example, suffering the ᵀvengeance of eternal fire.   Gen. 19:24 • *punishment*
8 Likewise also these dreamers defile the flesh, reject authority, and ᴿspeak evil of ᵀdignitaries.   Ex. 22:28 • *glorious ones, lit. glories*
9 Yet Michael the archangel, in ᵀcontending with the devil, when he disputed about the body of Moses, dared not bring against him a reviling accusation, but said, ᴿ"The Lord rebuke you!"   *arguing* • Zech. 3:2
10 ᴿBut these speak evil of whatever they do not know; and whatever they know naturally, like brute beasts, in these things they corrupt themselves.   2 Pet. 2:12
11 Woe to them! For they have gone in the way of Cain, ᴿhave run greedily in the error of Balaam for profit, and perished ᴿin the rebellion of Korah.   2 Pet. 2:15 • Num. 16:1-3, 31-35

Apostates Depraved and Doomed

12 These are ᵀspots in your love feasts, while they feast with you without fear, serving *only* themselves. *They are* clouds without water, carried *about by the winds; late autumn trees without fruit, twice dead, pulled up by the roots;   *hidden reefs or stains*
13 raging waves of the sea, foaming up their own shame; wandering stars for whom is reserved the blackness of darkness forever.
14 ᴿNow Enoch, the seventh from Adam,

12 NU, M *along*

prophesied about these men also, saying, "Behold, the Lord comes with ten thousands of His saints,   Gen. 5:18; Dan. 7:10; Zech. 14:5
15 ᴿ"to execute judgment on all, to convict all who are ungodly among them of all their ungodly deeds which they have committed in an ungodly way, and of all the ᴿharsh things which ungodly sinners have spoken against Him."   2 Pet. 2:6 • 1 Sam. 2:3

Apostates Predicted

16 These are grumblers, complainers, walking according to their own lusts; and they ᴿmouth great swelling *words,* ᴿflattering people to gain advantage.   2 Pet. 2:18 • Prov. 28:21
17 ᴿBut you, beloved, remember the words which were spoken before by the apostles of our Lord Jesus Christ: 2 Pet. 3:2
18 how they told you that there would be mockers in the last time who would walk according to their own ungodly lusts.
19 These are ᵀsensual persons, who cause divisions, not having the Spirit. *soulish* or *worldly*

30-B. Pray in the Spirit   ▼

Maintain Your Life with God

20 But you, beloved, ᴿbuilding yourselves up on your most holy faith, ᴿpraying in the Holy Spirit,   Col. 2:7 • [Rom. 8:26] ▲
21 keep yourselves in the love of God, ᴿlooking for the mercy of our Lord Jesus Christ unto eternal life.   Titus 2:13

(Point 13-A continued from previous page)
Remember, "He who is in you is greater than he who is in the world" (1 John 4:4, page 1280). James tells us:

(a) "Therefore submit to God."
(b) "Resist the devil [Satan], and he will flee from you."
(c) "Draw near to God and He will draw near to you" (James 4:6-8, page 1259).

See Matthew 12:24, page 953, for **Point 13-B: Demons: Servants of Satan.**

30-B. Pray in the Spirit (Jude 20)—Jude tells us that we are to pray in the Holy Spirit. The Spirit especially assists in prayer; so we are to pray in the Spirit. That is, we are to be guided and controlled by the One who dwells within us. However, Scripture states that God will neither hear us nor look upon us as we pray, if we are regarding iniquity in our hearts or retaining any known and unconfessed sins (Is. 59:1, 2, page 698). "If I regard iniquity in my heart, the Lord will not hear" (Ps. 66:18, page 548). We must first confess by name all known sin (1 John 1:9, page 1278).
Paul reveals some of the benefits of praying in the Holy Spirit (Rom. 8:26, 27, page 1137):
(1) We need the Spirit's guidance to know what to pray for. Just as a child tends to ask the parent for useless gifts, neglecting to ask for the necessities of life, we also need the Holy Spirit to guide us to pray more with eternity in mind. We do not know the future, but the Holy Spirit does. He alone knows what we will need and what our requests should be.
(2) We need the Spirit's intercession to speak to the Father for us. Just as a street beggar may not know the proper wording to petition a king, so we need the Holy Spirit to make "intercession for us with groanings which cannot be uttered" (Rom. 8:26, page 1137).
(3) We need the Spirit's mind to pray unselfishly, purely, and correctly. God searches hearts, and He sees when our prayers have an aspect of selfishness in them. The mind of the Holy Spirit, however, does not lead us to present petitions to the Father that His searching holiness could not grant. We need the mind of the Holy Spirit to pray in the Spirit (Rom. 8:27, page 1137; cf. Phil. 2:5, page 1197).
(4) We need the Spirit's intercession so that we may pray according to the will of God. Well-meaning Christians often pray apart from God's will for the world, for others, or for themselves. It is the Holy Spirit within the believer who guides each person so that he or she does not ask contrary to God's will (James 4:3,
(Point 30-B continued on next page)

22 And on some have compassion, *making a distinction;
23 but others save *with fear, ᴿpulling *them* out of the *fire, hating even ᴿthe garment defiled by the flesh.   Amos 4:11 • [Zech. 3:4, 5]

Glory to God

24 ᴿNow to Him who is able to keep *you from stumbling,

And ᴿto present *you* faultless
Before the presence of His glory with
    exceeding joy,   [Eph. 3:20] • Col. 1:22
25 To *God our Savior,
*Who alone is wise,
Be glory and majesty,
Dominion and *power,
Both now and forever.
Amen.

22 NU who are doubting (or making distinctions)
23 NU omits with fear • NU adds and on some have mercy with fear
24 M them

25 NU the only God our • NU Through Jesus Christ our Lord, Be glory • NU adds Before all time,

---

(Point 30-B continued from previous page)
page 1259). Thus Christ, who was always filled with the Holy Spirit, prayed, "Nevertheless not My will, but Yours, be done" (Luke 22:42, page 1043). The Spirit must lead us to seek His will. We may pray fearlessly for His will because "we know that all things work together for good to those who love God" (Rom. 8:28, page 1137).

See 1 John 5:14, 15, page 1283, for **Point 30-C: Pray According to God's Will.**

The Revelation
OF JESUS CHRIST

Revelation is the only largely prophetic book of the New Testament. In this intensely interesting book, the veil is pulled aside and the future disclosed in a series of panoramic visions beheld by the apocalyptic seer.

AUTHORSHIP. Four times in the book itself a man named John is identified as the author. Early Christian tradition, including the specific remark by Irenaeus that John the son of Zebedee wrote Revelation, centered on the last living apostle as the author. John was exiled by the anti-Christian emperor Domitian to the rock quarries on the island of Patmos, due west from the coast of Miletus. It has been pointed out that the style of Revelation is different from that of John's Gospel or epistles. This can be accounted for by the fact that it is a vision and that he would not have had an amanuensis on the island, and by the very varied subject matter in these Johannine writings. There are also many similarities between the Gospel, the epistles and Revelation. There is, for example, John's fondness for the titles "Word" and "Lamb of God," and the expression "he who has an ear." There is no strong reason to reject the traditional Christian view that John the son of Zebedee is the author.

HOW REVELATION FITS INTO THE BIBLE. Revelation is the "Grand Central Station" of the Bible, where all the "trains" come in. The trains of thought that started in Genesis and wended their way through sixty-four books come to a conclusion in this remarkable book. While many people underrate Revelation (some go to the other extreme!) it is the most fitting finale to the Word of God imaginable. It places the capstone on all the revelations in God's Word with the final Revelation of Jesus Christ, looking forward to the future when He will be indisputably King of Kings and Lord of Lords.

HOW REVELATION FITS TOGETHER. Revelation is one of those books that has the key (the outline) right inside the door, in 1:19. In that verse "the things which you have seen" refer to the past, namely the vision of the glorified Christ that John saw in chapter 1; "the things which are" refer to the present church age which is detailed in chapters 2 and 3; and "the things which will take place after this" refer to the prophecies of chapters 4 through 22, having to do with the Great Tribulation, the judgment, and the eternal state. The last and largest division consists of five sevens: seven seals (4:1—8:1), seven trumpets (8:2—11:19), seven bowls (15:1—16:21), seven dooms (17:1—20:15) and seven new things (21:1—22:21). There are also a number of parenthetical sections breaking up this long series of judgments, including some very beautiful passages of worship, such as chapters 4 and 5.

God, Christ, and Satan; men, saved and unsaved; and angels, holy and unholy, are the actors in this marvelous book of plan and purpose. Light and darkness, good and evil are the moral forces in opposition. The scenes shift and change, now time, then eternity. Heaven, earth, the abyss, and the lake of fire form the platform and theater of display. There is the song of the victor and the wail of the vanquished.

Revelation reveals God's triumphs, the millennial and eternal glories of Christ shining forth in undiminished and undying splendor. Then shall be brought to pass the saying of the Hebrew prophet, "He shall see the labor of His soul, and be satisifed" (Is. 53:11).

The new heaven, the new city, and the new earth become the eternal abodes of all that is holy and good; while the lake of fire becomes the eternal home of all the wicked and ungodly of all the ages.

For nearly two thousand years this last book in the Bible has been both an inspiration and a mystery to the people of God. It is also one of the most misunderstood and neglected books. There is widespread prejudice against the study of this wonderful book. Yet a special blessing is upon all who read and hear the words of this prophecy (1:3). There is also a terrible curse and plague placed upon everyone who tries to add or take away from the words of the book of these prophecies (22:18, 19).

In times of darkness and persecution it has given courage to its readers, enabling them to endure hardship and death for the sake of Christ. In periods of ease and prosperity it has been the battleground of exegetes who have endeavored to fashion the strange pageant into a consistent eschatology.

Man has attempted to do with this book the very thing that God, in the book, told him not to do; namely, "Do not seal the words of the prophecy of this book, for the time is at hand" (22:10).

The book of Revelation is both literal and figurative. It is to be taken as literal wherever possible. To treat this book as a mystery or to spiritualize it is to deny what it professes to be. Every truth and every scene is clearly explained in the book itself. This last book in the Bible is in perfect harmony with all preceding prophecies and is the logical and harmonious completion of them.

The structure of Revelation declares the progress of the thought; the imagery has to be interpreted in terms of the concepts and literature familiar to the early saints; and the phenomenon of the contemporary social, political, and religious scene which is reflected in allusions and prophecies.

This wonderfully inspired book is exactly what its name implies: it is a *revelation,* an unveiling (the title of the book is not plural). It is the one great manifestation of the Lord Jesus Christ as He is, as He was, and as He ever shall be. One learns as the study of the book progresses that Jesus is seated in majesty, crowned with glory, and clothed with all authority. In this last book in the Bible we see Jesus, God's Son, as the consummation of all things and the Lion of the tribe of Judah.

Genesis is the seedbed out of which all revealed truth has grown. This last book in the Bible, Revelation, is the full flower and fruit of these truths seen in the finished work of our Lord.

—J.H.S.

Introduction and Benediction

THE Revelation of Jesus Christ, ᴿwhich God gave Him to show His servants—things which must ᵀshortly take place. And ᴿHe sent and signified *it* by His angel to His servant John, John 3:32 · *quickly or swiftly* · Rev. 22:6

2 ᴿwho bore witness to the word of God, and to the testimony of Jesus Christ, to all things ᴿthat he saw. 1 Cor. 1:6 · 1 John 1:1

3 ᴿBlessed *is* he who reads and those who hear the words of this prophecy, and keep those things which are written in it; for ᴿthe time *is* near. Luke 11:28 · James 5:8

Greeting the Seven Churches

4 John, to the seven churches which are in Asia:

Grace to you and peace from Him ᴿwho is and ᴿwho was and who is to come, ᴿand from the seven Spirits who are before His throne, Ex. 3:14 · John 1:1 · [Is. 11:2]

5 and from Jesus Christ, ᴿthe faithful ᴿwitness, the firstborn from the dead, and ᴿthe ruler over the kings of the earth. To Him who *loved us and washed us from our sins in His own blood, John 8:14 · Is. 55:4 · Ps. 89:27

6 and has made us *kings and priests to His God and Father, ᴿto Him *be glory and dominion forever and ever. Amen. 1 Tim. 6:16

7 Behold, He is coming with clouds, and every eye will see Him, even they who pierced Him. And all the tribes of the earth will mourn because of Him. Even so, Amen.

8 ᴿ"I am the Alpha and the Omega, *the Beginning and the End," says the *Lord,

ᴿ"who is and who was and who is to come, the ᴿAlmighty." Is. 41:4 · Rev. 4:8; 11:17 · Is. 9:6

Vision of the Son of Man

9 I, John, *both your brother and companion in the tribulation and ᴿkingdom and patience of Jesus Christ, was on the island that is called Patmos for the word of God and for the testimony of Jesus Christ. [2 Tim. 2:12]

10 ᴿI was in the Spirit on ᴿthe Lord's Day, and I heard behind me ᴿa loud voice, as of a trumpet, Acts 10:10 · Acts 20:7 · Rev. 4:1

11 saying,*"I am the Alpha and the Omega, the First and the Last," and, "What you see, write in a book and send *it* to the seven churches *which are in Asia: to Ephesus, to Smyrna, to Pergamos, to Thyatira, to Sardis, to Philadelphia, and to Laodicea."

12 Then I turned to see the voice that spoke with me. And having turned ᴿI saw seven golden lampstands, Ex. 25:37; 37:23

13 ᴿand in the midst of the seven lampstands *One* like the Son of Man, clothed with a garment down to the feet and girded about the chest with a golden band. Rev. 2:1

14 His head and ᴿhair *were* white like wool, as white as snow, and ᴿHis eyes like a flame of fire; Dan. 7:9 · Dan. 7:9; 10:6

15 ᴿHis feet *were* like fine brass, as if refined in a furnace, and ᴿHis voice as the sound of many waters; Ezek. 1:7 · Ezek. 1:24; 43:2

16 He had in His right hand seven stars, ᴿout of His mouth went a sharp two-edged sword, and His countenance *was* like the sun shining in its strength. Is. 49:2

17 And ᴿwhen I saw Him, I fell at His feet as dead. But He laid His right hand on me,

1:5 NU, M *loves us and freed*
1:6 NU, M *a kingdom*
1:8 NU, M omit *the Beginning and the End* • NU, M *Lord God*
1:9 NU, M omit *both*
1:11 NU, M omit *"I am the Alpha and Omega, the First and the Last," and* • NU, M omit *which are in Asia*

saying *to me, "Do not be afraid; ᴿI am the
First and the Last.   Ezek. 1:28 • Is. 41:4; 44:6; 48:12
18 "I *am* He who lives, and was dead, and
behold, I am alive forevermore. Amen. And I
have the keys of Hades and of Death.
19 *"Write the things which you have seen,
and the things which are, and the things
which will take place after this.
20 "The ᵀmystery of the seven stars which
you saw in My right hand, and the seven
golden lampstands: The seven stars are the
ᵀangels of the seven churches, and ᴿthe seven
lampstands *which you saw are the seven
churches.   hidden truth • Or messengers • Zech. 4:2

▼ 52-A. The Seven Churches

The Loveless Church

2 "To the ᵀangel of the church of Ephesus
write,   Or messenger
'These things says He who holds the
seven stars in His right hand, who walks in
the midst of the seven golden lampstands:
2 "I know your works, your labor, your
ᵀpatience, and that you cannot ᵀbear those

1:17 NU, M omit to me
1:19 NU, M Therefore, write
1:20 NU, M omit which you saw

who are evil. And you have tested those who ▽
say they are apostles and are not, and have
found them liars;   perseverance • endure
3 "and you have persevered and have
patience, and have labored for My name's
sake and have ᴿnot become weary.   Gal. 6:9
4 "Nevertheless I have *this* against you,
that you have left your first love.
5 "Remember therefore from where you
have fallen; repent and do the first works, ᴿor
else I will come to you quickly and remove
your lampstand from its place—unless you
repent.   Matt. 21:41
6 "But this you have, that you hate the
deeds of the Nicolaitans, which I also hate.
7 ᴿ"He who has an ear, let him hear what
the Spirit says to the churches. To him who
overcomes I will give ᴿto eat from ᴿthe tree of
life, which is in the midst of the Paradise of
God." '   Matt. 11:15 • [Rev. 22:2, 14] • [Gen. 2:9; 3:22]

The Persecuted Church

8 "And to the ᵀangel of the church in
Smyrna write,   Or messenger
'These things says ᴿthe First and the
Last, who was dead, and came to life: Rev. 1:8
9 "I know your works, tribulation, and
poverty (but you are rich); and I *know* the

52-A. The Seven Churches (Revelation 2:1—3:22)—

(1) "To the angel [or messenger] of the church of Ephesus" (2:1-7). This local congregation had left its
first love; Christ therefore warned that He would remove its lampstand, its distinction as a local church,
unless it repented (2:4, 5). Christ is apparently unwilling to have a church continue to exist without love.
Leaving their love was fatal unless they repented. The love which they left was their first love—love for the
Savior. To this assembly of believers, Christ came as the One who held the church's life in His hand (2:1).
Christ promised, "To him who overcomes I will give to eat from the tree of life, which is in the midst of the
Paradise of God" (2:7).

(2) "And to the angel [or messenger] of the church in Smyrna" (2:8-11). This local congregation was to
face persecution (2:10). Christ came to the church as the persecuted one who "was dead, and came to life"
(2:8). He admonished them to "not fear any of those things" (2:10), and held forth to the overcomer the
promise that he "shall not be hurt by the second death." The second death is eternal separation from the
mercy and grace of God (2:11; 20:14, page 1314). Note that Smyrna and Philadelphia are the only churches
not rebuked or called to repent.

(3) "And to the angel [or messenger] of the church in Pergamos" (2:12-17). This local assembly tolerated
certain evils:

(a) "The doctrine of Balaam" (2:14). Balaam was a mercenary prophet who "put a stumbling block
before the children of Israel" (2:14) and advised Balak (Num. 22:2, page 163), the king of Midian, to lead the
children of Israel in eating things sacrificed to idols (Num. 25:1-3, page 166; cf. 2 Pet. 2:15, page 1274), as
well as having the Midianite women seduce the men of Israel's army, causing them to "trespass [in adultery]
against the Lᴏʀᴅ" (Num. 31:16, page 173).

(b) "The doctrine of the Nicolaitans, which thing I hate" (2:15). We do not know definitely what the
Nicolaitans taught; we do know that Jesus hated it. The name itself means "conqueror of the laity" (people).

Thus, Christ comes to the church with "the sharp two-edged sword"—the Word of God (2:12, 16; cf.
Heb. 4:12, page 1239) which separates the good from evil (Ps. 119:11, page 581). To the overcomer Christ
gives "the hidden manna" (spiritual nourishment) and a new name—every born-again child of God will
receive a new name in glory (2:17).

(4) "And to the angel [or messenger] of the church in Thyatira" (2:18-29). This local congregation was
dominated by "Jezebel," a false teacher, who was allowed to corrupt the church with her evil doctrine
(2:20). She apparently was a carbon copy of Queen Jezebel during the time of Elijah. Thus, to this church,
Christ comes with "[His] eyes like a flame of fire, and His feet like fine brass," ready to stamp in judgment
(2:18; 2 Kin. 9:30-37, page 365). The overcomers are promised power to rule over the nations (2:26, 27). All

(Point 52-A continued on next page)

▽ blasphemy of those who say they are Jews and are not, but *are* a synagogue of Satan.

10 "Do not fear any of those things which you are about to suffer. Indeed, the devil is about to throw *some* of you into prison, that you may be tested, and you will have tribulation ten days. Be faithful until death, and I will give you ᴿthe crown of life.   James 1:12

11 ᴿ"He who has an ear, let him hear what the Spirit says to the churches. He who overcomes shall not be hurt by ᴿthe second death." '   Rev. 13:9 • [Rev. 20:6, 14; 21:8]

The Compromising Church

12 "And to the ᵀangel of the church in Pergamos write,   Or *messenger*

'These things says ᴿHe who has the sharp two-edged sword: Is. 49:2

13 "I know your works, and where you dwell, where Satan's throne *is*. And you hold fast to My name, and did not deny My faith even in the days in which Antipas *was* My faithful martyr, who was killed among you, where Satan dwells.

14 "But I have a few things against you, because you have there those who hold the doctrine of Balaam, who taught Balak to put a stumbling block before the children of ▽ Israel, to eat things sacrificed to idols, ᴿand to commit sexual immorality.   1 Cor. 6:13

15 "Thus you also have those who hold the doctrine of the Nicolaitans, *which thing I hate.

16 "Repent, or else I will come to you quickly and ᴿwill fight against them with the sword of My mouth.   2 Thess. 2:8

17 "He who has an ear, let him hear what the Spirit says to the churches. To him who overcomes I will give some of the hidden ᴿmanna to eat. And I will give him a white stone, and on the stone ᴿa new name written which no one knows except him who receives *it*." '   Ex. 16:33, 34 • Rev. 3:12

The Corrupt Church

18 "And to the ᵀangel of the church in Thyatira write,   Or *messenger*

'These things says the Son of God, ᴿwho has eyes like a flame of fire, and His feet like fine brass: Rev. 1:14, 15

19 "I know your works, love, *service, faith,

2:15 NU, M *likewise*.
2:19 NU, M *faith, service*

(*Point 52-A continued from previous page*)

who refuse to follow the teachings of that Jezebel, in Thyatira and all the other churches, will be rewarded in the Millennium with power to rule the nations with Christ (3:21).

(5) "And to the angel [or messenger] of the church in Sardis" (3:1-6). This local assembly had a good outward reputation, but was spiritually dead (3:1). Christ tells them to "remember therefore how you have received and heard; hold fast and repent" (3:3). To the overcomer Christ promises a glorious, outward robe of white, reflecting a true, inward holy life that will never be blotted out (3:5).

(6) "And to the angel [or messenger] of the church in Philadelphia" (3:7-13). This local congregation has much in common with Smyrna in that after Jesus identified Himself as the writer of this epistle, He commended the Philadelphian assembly, reminding them that He set before them "an open door, and no one can shut it" (3:8). The message here is for any church that will be faithful in teaching and preaching the whole counsel of God, that will keep the Word of God, that will not allow false teachers to come into their midst and "deny My name" (3:7, 8). The Philadelphia church has no room for liars. They know the love of God that passes all understanding (3:9). Jesus promised, "I also will keep you from [Greek *ek*, "out of"] the hour of trial [the Great Tribulation] which shall come upon the whole world" (3:10). He reminds the church that His coming will be quick, instant, without warning, and "in the twinkling of an eye" (1 Cor. 15:52, page 1163). He urges Philadelphia to hold fast to His Word lest they lose their crown (reward) (3:11; cf. 2 Tim. 4:8, page 1228). The Lord describes the rewards for the overcomer (3:12):

(a) He will be a pillar in the temple;

(b) Upon him will be written the name of God the Father, the name of the New Jerusalem, and Christ's "new name."

(7) "And to the angel [or messenger] of the church of the Laodiceans" (3:14-22). This is obviously not a Spirit-filled, Christ-honoring church. Laodicea is being judged by its works. Jesus said, "I know your works." They were neither "cold nor hot" (3:15). They were satisfied with their outward profession. Jesus knew their works, but they did not. The most difficult person to reach with the gospel is the one who is self-satisfied and lukewarm. Paraphrased, Jesus said, "You make Me sick at My stomach, therefore I will vomit you out of My mouth. You claim to be rich, but you are spiritually poverty-stricken. You think you do not need anything, when you need everything. You think you know it all, and you do not know that you are wretched, miserable, poor, blind, and spiritually naked" (3:16, 17). Our Lord implores them to repent (3:18, 19). The Lord Jesus stands at the door of the Laodicean church, knocking, waiting for someone to open the door of the church, that He may enter and revive that person (3:20). Whoever overcomes will be rewarded in Christ's kingdom.

"Come out from among them and be separate" (2 Cor. 6:14-18, page 1169). You cannot fellowship with an unrighteous apostate church and fellowship with the Lord Jesus.

See Revelation 6:1-17; 8:1, page 1299, for **Point 52-B: The Seven Seals.**

▽ and your ᵀpatience; and *as* for your works, the last *are* more than the first.   *perseverance*

20 "Nevertheless *I have a few things against you, because you allow *that woman ᴿJezebel, who calls herself a prophetess, *to teach and seduce My servants ᴿto commit sexual immorality and eat things sacrificed to idols.   1 Kin. 16:31; 21:25 • Ex. 34:15

21 "And I gave her time to *repent of her sexual immorality, and she did not repent.

22 "Indeed I will cast her into a sickbed, and those who commit adultery with her into great tribulation, unless they repent of *their deeds.

23 "I will kill her children with death, and all the churches shall know that I am He who ᴿsearchesᵀ the minds and hearts. And I will give to each one of you according to your works.   Jer. 11:20; 17:10 • *examines*

24 "Now to you I say, *and to the rest in Thyatira, as many as do not have this doctrine, and who have not known the ᴿdepths of Satan, as they say, ᴿI *will put on you no other burden.   2 Tim. 3:1–9 • Acts 15:28

25 "But hold fast ᴿwhat you have till I come.   Rev. 3:11

26 "And he who overcomes, and keeps ᴿMy works until the end, ᴿto him I will give power over the nations—   [John 6:29] • [Matt. 19:28]

27 '*Heᴿ shall rule them with a rod of iron;*
They shall be dashed to pieces like the
potter's vessels'—   Ps. 2:9

as I also have received from My Father;

28 "and I will give him the morning star.

29 "He who has an ear, let him hear what the Spirit says to the churches." '

The Dead Church

3 "And to the ᵀangel of the church in Sardis write,   Or *messenger*
'These things says He who ᴿhas the seven Spirits of God and the seven stars: "I know your works, that you have a name that you are alive, but you are dead.   Rev. 1:4, 16

2 "Be watchful, and strengthen the things which remain, that are ready to die, for I have not found your works perfect before *God.

3 "Remember therefore how you have received and heard; hold fast and repent. Therefore if you will not watch, I will come upon you ᴿas a thief, and you will not know what hour I will come upon you.   [Rev. 16:15]

4 *"You have ᴿa few names *even in Sar-

dis who have not ᴿdefiled their garments; and ▽ they shall walk with Me ᴿin white, for they are worthy.   Acts 1:15 • [Jude 23] • Rev. 4:4; 6:11

5 "He who overcomes ᴿshall be clothed in white garments, and I will not ᴿblot out his name from the ᴿBook of Life; but I will confess his name before My Father and before His angels.   [Rev. 19:8] • Ex. 32:32 • Phil. 4:3

6 ᴿ"He who has an ear, let him hear what the Spirit says to the churches." '   Rev. 2:7

The Faithful Church

7 "And to the ᵀangel of the church in Philadelphia write,   Or *messenger*
'These things says He who is holy, He who is true, ᴿ*"He who has ᴿthe key of David,* ᴿ*He who opens and no one shuts, and shuts and no one opens"*:   Is. 22:22 • Is. 9:7 • [Matt. 16:19]

8 ᴿ"I know your works. See, I have set before you ᴿan open door, *and no one can shut it; for you have a little strength, have kept My word, and have not denied My name.   Rev. 3:1 • 1 Cor. 16:9

9 "Indeed I will make ᴿthose of the synagogue of Satan, who say they are Jews and are not, but lie—indeed I will make them come and worship before your feet, and to know that I have loved you.   Rev. 2:9

10 "Because you have kept ᵀMy command to persevere, I also will keep you from the hour of trial which shall come upon ᴿthe whole world, to test those who dwell ᴿon the earth.   Lit. *the word of My patience* • Luke 2:1 • Is. 24:17

11 *"Behold, ᴿI am coming quickly! ᴿHold fast what you have, that no one may take ᴿyour crown.   Phil. 4:5 • Rev. 2:25 • [Rev. 2:10]

12 "He who overcomes, I will make him a pillar in the temple of My God, and he shall go out no more. I will write on him the name of My God and the name of the city of My God, the New Jerusalem, which ᴿcomes down out of heaven from My God. And *I will write on him* My new name.   Rev. 21:2

13 ᴿ"He who has an ear, let him hear what the Spirit says to the churches." '   Rev. 2:7

The Lukewarm Church

14 "And to the ᵀangel of the church *of the Laodiceans write,   Or *messenger*
'These things says the Amen, ᴿthe Faithful and True Witness, ᴿthe Beginning of the creation of God: Rev. 1:5; 3:7; 19:11 • [Col. 1:15]

15 ᴿ"I know your works, that you are neither cold nor hot. I could wish you were cold or hot.   Rev. 3:1

16 "So then, because you are lukewarm, and neither *cold nor hot, I will vomit you out of My mouth.

2:20 NU, M *against you that you tolerate* • M *your wife Jezebel* • NU, M *and teaches and seduces*
2:21 NU, M *repent, and she does not want to repent of her sexual immorality.*
2:22 NU, M *her*
2:24 NU, M omit *and* • NU, M omit *will*
3:2 NU, M *My God*
3:4 NU, M *Nevertheless you* • NU, M omit *even*

3:8 NU, M *which no one can shut*
3:11 NU, M omit *Behold*
3:14 NU, M *in Laodicea*
3:16 NU, M *hot nor cold*

▽ 17 "Because you say, ᴿ'I am rich, have become wealthy, and have need of nothing'— and do not know that you are wretched, miserable, poor, blind, and naked—   Hos. 12:8

18 "I counsel you ᴿto buy from Me gold refined in the fire, that you may be rich; and ᴿwhite garments, that you may be clothed, *that* the shame of your nakedness may not be revealed; and anoint your eyes with eye salve, that you may see.   Is. 55:1 • 2 Cor. 5:3

19 "As many as I love, I rebuke and chasten. Therefore be zealous and repent.

20 "Behold, I stand at the door and knock. ᴿIf anyone hears My voice and opens the door, ᴿI will come in to him and dine with him, and he with Me.   Luke 12:36, 37 • [John 14:23]

21 "To him who overcomes I will grant to sit with Me on My throne, as I also overcame and sat down with My Father on His throne.

▲ 22 ᴿ"He who has an ear, let him hear what the Spirit says to the churches."' "   Rev. 2:7

The Throne Room of Heaven

4 After these things I looked, and behold, a door *standing* ᴿopen in heaven. And the first voice which I heard *was* like a ᴿtrumpet speaking with me, saying, "Come up here, and I will show you things which must take place after this."   Ezek. 1:1 • Rev. 1:10

2 Immediately ᴿI was in the Spirit; and behold, ᴿa throne set in heaven, and *One* sat on the throne.   Rev. 1:10 • Is. 6:1

3 *And He who sat there was like a jasper and a sardius stone in appearance; ᴿand *there was* a rainbow around the throne, in appearance like an emerald.   Ezek. 1:28

4 Around the throne *were* twenty-four thrones, and on the thrones I saw twenty-four elders sitting, clothed in white *robes; and they had crowns of gold on their heads.

5 And from the throne proceeded lightnings, *thunderings, and voices. Seven lamps of fire *were* burning before the throne, which are *the seven Spirits of God.

6 Before the throne *there* *was ᴿa sea of glass, like crystal. ᴿAnd in the midst of the throne, and around the throne, *were* four living creatures full of eyes in front and in back.   Rev. 15:2 • Ezek. 1:5

7 ᴿThe first living creature *was* like a lion, the second living creature like a calf, the third living creature had a face like a man, and the fourth living creature *was* like a flying eagle.   Ezek. 1:10; 10:14

8 *The* four living creatures, each having ᴿsix wings, were full of eyes around and within. And they do not rest day or night, saying: Is. 6:2

ᴿ"Holy,* holy, holy,   Is. 6:3
  ᴿLord God Almighty,   Rev. 1:8
  ᴿWho was and is and is to come!"   Rev. 1:4

9 Whenever the living creatures give glory and honor and thanks to Him who sits on the throne, ᴿwho lives forever and ever,   Rev. 1:18

10 ᴿThe twenty-four elders fall down before Him who sits on the throne and worship Him who lives forever and ever, and cast their crowns before the throne, saying: Rev. 5:8, 14

11 "YouᴿR are worthy, *O Lord,   Rev. 1:6; 5:12
  To receive glory and honor and power;
  ᴿFor You created all things,   Gen. 1:1
  And by ᴿYour will they *exist and were created."   Col. 1:16

The Lamb Takes the Scroll

5 And I saw in the right *hand* of Him who sat on the throne a scroll written inside and on the back, sealed with seven seals.

2 Then I saw a strong angel proclaiming with a loud voice, ᴿ"Who is worthy to open the scroll and to loose its seals?"   Rev. 4:11; 5:9

3 And no one in heaven or on the earth or under the earth was able to open the scroll, or to look at it.

4 So I wept much, because no one was found worthy to open *and read the scroll, or to look at it.

5 But one of the elders said to me, "Do not weep. Behold, the Lion of the tribe of Judah, the Root of David, has prevailed to open the scroll and *to loose its seven seals."

6 And I looked, *and behold, in the midst of the throne and of the four living creatures, and in the midst of the elders, stood a Lamb as though it had been slain, having seven horns and seven eyes, which are the seven Spirits of God sent out into all the earth.

7 Then He came and took the scroll out of the right hand of Him who sat on the throne.

Worthy Is the Lamb

8 Now when He had taken the scroll, the four living creatures and the twenty-four elders fell down before the Lamb, each having a harp, and golden bowls full of incense, which are the ᴿprayers of the saints.   Rev. 8:3

9 And ᴿthey sang a new song, saying:

ᴿ"You are worthy to take the scroll,
  And to open its seals;
  For You were slain,   Rev. 14:3 • Rev. 4:11
  And ᴿhave redeemed us to God ᴿby
    Your blood   John 1:29 • [Heb. 9:12]
  Out of every tribe and tongue and
    people and nation,

4:3 M omits *And He who sat there was*, making the following a description of the throne.
4:4 NU, M *robes, with crowns*
4:5 NU, M *voices, and thunderings.* • M omits *the*
4:6 NU, M add *something like*

4:8 M has *holy* nine times.
4:11 NU, M *Our Lord and God* • NU, M *existed*
5:4 NU, M omit *and read*
5:5 NU, M omit *to loose*
5:6 NU, M *saw,* omitting *and behold*

10　And have made *us ᴿkings* and ᴿpriests
　　to our God;　　　　　　　　Ex. 19:6 • Is. 61:6
　　And *we shall reign on the earth."

▼ 11-D. Angels: Their Ministry in Heaven and on Earth

11　Then I looked, and I heard the voice of
many angels around the throne, the living
creatures, and the elders; and the number of
them was ten thousand times ten thousand,
and thousands of thousands,
　12　saying with a loud voice:

"Worthy is the ᴿLamb who was slain
To receive power and riches and
　wisdom,

5:10 NU, M *them* • NU *a kingdom* • NU, M *they*

And strength and honor and glory and　▽
　blessing!"　　　　　　　　　　　Is. 53:7

13　And ᴿevery creature which is in heaven
and on the earth and under the earth and
such as are in the sea, and all that are in
them, I heard saying:　　　　　　Phil. 2:10

"Blessing and honor and glory and
　power
Be to Him who sits on the throne,
And to the Lamb, forever and *ever!"

14　Then the four living creatures said,
"Amen!" And the *twenty-four elders fell
down and worshiped *Him who lives forever
and ever.　　　　　　　　　　　　　▲

5:13 M adds *Amen*
5:14 NU, M omit *twenty-four* • NU, M omit *Him who lives forever and ever*

11-D. Angels: Their Ministry in Heaven and on Earth (Revelation 5:11–14)—

(1) The heavenly ministry of angels:

(a) John said, "I heard the voice of many angels around the throne" (v. 11). He also saw "living creatures." These living creatures are cherubim; they guard the throne of God (Ezek. 1:5–12, page 780; 10:15–22, page 786).

(b) The number of the angels was "ten thousand times ten thousand, and thousands of thousands" (v. 11). They were an innumerable host, along with the elders, praising and worshiping Christ the Lamb (vv. 11–14; cf. Is. 6:1–9, page 647). When God the Father brings His Son, the Lord Jesus Christ, back into this world, He says, "Let all the angels of God worship Him" (Heb. 1:6, page 1236). Angels were created to worship, praise, and serve God the Father, God the Son, and God the Holy Spirit.

(2) The earthly ministry of angels:

(a) "Are they [angels] not all ministering spirits, sent forth to minister for them who shall be heirs of salvation?" (Heb. 1:13, 14, page 1237). Angels minister to all believers, all who are saved by faith in Christ. If you belong to Christ, you have angels ministering to you in many ways. Believers are seldom aware of their presence. "Do not forget to entertain strangers, for by so doing some have unwittingly entertained angels" (Heb. 13:2, page 1251). Lot entertained angels who came to deliver him from the wrath of God, even though he was not living in complete harmony with the will of God (Gen. 19:1–29, page 23). Abraham entertained the same two angels before they visited Lot in Sodom. However, there were three men who called on Abraham. This was a *theophany,* or manifestation of God, and doubtless included a pre-New Testament revelation of Christ, called a *Christophany* (Gen. 18:1–33, page 22).

(b) Angels assist the servants of the Lord. "Now an angel of the Lord spoke to Philip, saying, 'Arise and go toward the south along the road which goes down from Jerusalem to Gaza.' " When Philip saw a chariot on the road, the angel told him to "go near and overtake this chariot" (Acts 8:26–40, page 1099). In the chariot was a man from Ethiopia. He was to be one of the heirs of salvation (Heb. 1:13, 14, page 1237). Angels minister to those who are to be saved even before they are converted. God is omniscient; He knows beforehand who will believe and be saved, and sends His angels to minister to them. Another example of an angel assisting in the salvation of those who were to be heirs of salvation is found in Acts 10 (page 1102). Cornelius was praying when an angel of God came and told him to summon Simon Peter from Joppa, and bring him to his house. Peter would tell him how to be saved (Acts 10:1–48, page 1102).

(c) An angel of the Lord delivered Peter from prison, even though he was chained between two guards. The next morning, when the guards could not find him, "there was no small stir among the soldiers about what had become of Peter" (Acts 12:1–19, page 1104). Now Herod had planned to put Peter to death, but God had other plans and sent an angel to rescue him.

(d) Another angel helped to save the lives of Paul and all on the ship that was taking him to Rome as a prisoner. Paul said to all on board the endangered ship, "For there stood by me this night an angel of the God to whom I belong and whom I serve, saying, 'Do not be afraid, Paul; you must be brought before Caesar; and indeed God has granted you all those who sail with you' " (Acts 27:21–25, page 1123).

Have you ever stopped to thank God for your ministering angel or angels?
See Mark 13:26, 27, page 1002, for **Point 11-E: Angels: Their Part in the Second Coming of Christ.**

▼ **52-B. The Seven Seals**

First Seal: The Conqueror

6 Now ᴿI saw when the Lamb opened one of the *seals; and I heard one of the four living creatures saying with a voice like thunder, "Come and see."   [Rev. 5:5-7, 12; 13:8]

2 And I looked, and behold, a white horse.

6:1 NU, M *seven seals*

He who sat on it had a bow; and a crown was ▽ given to him, and he went out ᴿconquering and to conquer.   Matt. 24:5

Second Seal: Conflict on Earth

3 When He opened the second seal, ᴿI heard the second living creature saying, "Come *and see."   Rev. 4:7

6:3 NU, M omit *and see*

52-B. The Seven Seals (Revelation 6:1–17; 8:1)—Chapters 4 and 5 feature a scene in heaven, in which God the Father holds a scroll closed by seven seals. A search revealed that no one in heaven or earth was worthy to open it (Rev. 5:2–4, page 1297). Then it was proclaimed that the Lion of Judah, who had "prevailed" over sin at the cross, was worthy; and all heaven broke into an anthem of praise to Him (Rev. 5:5, 9–14, page 1297). As Christ removed the seals from the book, events of judgment began to take place on the earth.

(1) *The first seal: a white horse* (6:2). The rider on the white horse is the Antichrist. The apostle Paul gives us a vivid picture of the coming of this rider. Before he comes, two things will happen:

(a) "The falling away." This spiritual falling away will take place during the church age and will be intensified in the end time.

(b) "The man of sin [Antichrist] is revealed, the son of perdition" (utter destruction). He will appear on the political scene, using his demonic psychology, with a solution to all the problems of the nations. He will exalt himself "above all that is called God." He will be worshiped by unbelievers, "so that he sits as God in the temple of God, showing himself that he is God" (2 Thess. 2:3, 4, page 1215; cf. Matt. 24:15–22, page 973; Dan. 9:27, page 851).

Note: The rider of the white horse is not the Lord Jesus Christ, who later rides into history as seen in Revelation (19:11–16, page 1312). Here, Jesus is the One who opens the seal, revealing the false christ who rides rampant for the seven-year Tribulation period prior to Christ's second coming.

(2) *The second seal: a red horse* (6:4). The world, for thousands of years, has had "wars and rumors of wars" (Matt. 24:4–7, page 973). Many great battles have been fought, but none can compare with the wars that will be fought in the last three-and-one-half years of the Tribulation. The rider of the red horse will do the will of the Antichrist and lead the nations of the world into the Battle of Armageddon. Because the first three-and-one-half years of the Antichrist's rule will be an era of world peace, people will think that he has ushered in permanent peace, until the rider of the red horse comes with the sword of warfare to do battle with the Lord Jesus Christ and His army (Rev. 19:11–19, page 1312).

(3) *The third seal: a black horse* (6:5, 6). The rider of the black horse, with scales in hand, is death by famine. He portrays an initial period of plenty for all; but afterward the average man's daily wage will be the price of a quart of wheat or three quarts of barley. Only the powerful and rich will enjoy the oil and the wine. At the end of the church age, famines, pestilences, and earthquakes will increase (Matt. 24:7, page 973), but this cannot be compared with the latter part of the Tribulation period, portrayed by the rider of the black horse.

(4) *The fourth seal: a pale horse* (6:7, 8). The rider of the pale horse is called "Death, and Hades followed with him." Hades is the place of lost souls (Luke 16:19–31, page 1035). "Then Death and Hades were cast into the lake of fire. This is the second death"—eternal separation from God (Rev. 20:14, page 1314).

(5) *The fifth seal: souls under the altar* (6:9–11). Among the events of this period, the Tribulation saints who will turn to Christ (Matt. 24:21, 22, page 973) will face martyrdom. They overcome by the blood of the Lamb. These martyred saints include all those who lose their lives by preaching the Word of God during the Tribulation (Rev. 12:11, page 1305). They are the 144,000 of the twelve tribes of Israel, along with an innumerable host of Gentiles (7:1–17).

(6) *The sixth seal: earthquakes and signs in the heavens* (6:12–17). When the Lamb opens the sixth seal, great judgment falls upon the earth. Earthquakes move mountains and islands out of their places. The sun becomes black as sackcloth of hair. The earth is in total darkness. There are catastrophes in the heavens. The moon becomes like blood. The "stars of heaven" (6:13), great meteors, fall to the earth (Luke 21:25–27, page 1042). All rebels against the Lord will try to hide from the Lamb and escape the judgment of the nations at the end of the Tribulation (Matt. 25:31, page 976), as well as the Great White Throne judgment (at the end of the Millennium) where all the wicked dead stand before Christ to be judged and cast into the lake of fire. They fill the dens and caves of the world, and pray for the mountains to cover them from the Lamb of God who died on Calvary. "For the great day of His [the Lamb's] wrath has come, and who is able to stand?" (6:17).

(7) *The seventh seal: seven trumpets* (8:1). Chapter 7 is a parenthesis amid the judgments of the book which shows the salvation of two saved multitudes, one Jewish and the other much larger, from every kindred and nation. Then the seventh seal is opened, out of which seven more judgments appear—the trumpet judgments of chapters 8 and 9.

See Revelation 8:2—9:21; 11:15–19, page 1301, for **Point 52-C: The Seven Trumpets.**

▽ 4 ᴿAnother horse, fiery red, went out. And it was granted to the one who sat on it to ᴿtake peace from the earth, and that *people* should kill one another; and there was given to him a great sword.   Zech. 1:8; 6:2 • Matt. 24:6, 7

Third Seal: Scarcity on Earth

5 When He opened the third seal, ᴿI heard the third living creature say, "Come and see." So I looked, and behold, ᴿa black horse, and he who sat on it had a pair of ᴿscalesᵀ in his hand.   Rev. 4:7 • Zech. 6:2, 6 • Matt. 24:7 • *balances*

6 And I heard a voice in the midst of the four living creatures saying, "A *quart of wheat for a *denarius, and three quarts of barley for a denarius; and ᴿdo not harm the oil and the wine."   Rev. 7:3; 9:4

Fourth Seal: Widespread Death on Earth

7 When He opened the fourth seal, ᴿI heard the voice of the fourth living creature saying, "Come and see."   Rev. 4:7

8 So I looked, and behold, a pale horse. And the name of him who sat on it was Death, and Hades followed with him. And power was given to them over a fourth of the earth, to kill with sword, with hunger, with death, and by the beasts of the earth.

Fifth Seal: The Cry of the Martyrs

9 When He opened the fifth seal, I saw under ᴿthe altar ᴿthe souls of those who had been slain for the word of God and for the testimony which they held.   Rev. 8:3 • [Rev. 20:4]

10 And they cried with a loud voice, saying, "How long, O Lord, ᴿholy and true, ᴿuntil You judge and avenge our blood on those who dwell on the earth?"   Rev. 3:7 • Rev. 11:18

11 Then a ᴿwhite robe was given to each of them; and it was said to them ᴿthat they should rest a little while longer, until both *the number of* their fellow servants and their brethren, who would be killed as they *were*, was completed.   Rev. 3:4, 5; 7:9 • Heb. 11:40

Sixth Seal: Cosmic Disturbances

12 I looked when He opened the sixth seal, and *behold, there was a great earthquake; and the sun became black as sackcloth of hair, and the *moon became like blood.

13 ᴿAnd the stars of heaven fell to the earth, as a fig tree drops its late figs when it is shaken by a mighty wind.   Rev. 8:10; 9:1

14 Then the sky ᵀreceded as a scroll when it is rolled up, and every mountain and island was moved out of its place.   *split apart*

15 And the ᴿkings of the earth, the great men, *the rich men, the commanders, the

mighty men, every slave and every free man, ▽ ᴿhid themselves in the caves and in the rocks of the mountains,   Ps. 2:2-4 • Is. 2:10, 19, 21; 24:21

16 ᴿand said to the mountains and rocks, "Fall on us and hide us from the face of Him who ᴿsits on the throne and from the wrath of the Lamb!   Luke 23:29, 30 • Rev. 20:11

17 "For the great day of His wrath has come, ᴿand who is able to stand?"   Zeph. 1:14 ▲

The Sealed of Israel

7 After these things I saw four angels standing at the four corners of the earth, holding the four winds of the earth, ᴿthat the wind should not blow on the earth, on the sea, or on any tree.   Rev. 7:3; 8:7; 9:4

2 Then I saw another angel ascending from the east, having the seal of the living God. And he cried with a loud voice to the four angels to whom it was granted to harm the earth and the sea,

3 saying, ᴿ"Do not harm the earth, the sea, or the trees till we have sealed the servants of our God ᴿon their foreheads."   Rev. 6:6 • Rev. 22:4

4 And I heard the number of those who were sealed. ᴿOne hundred *and* forty-four thousand ᴿof all the tribes of the children of Israel *were* sealed: Rev. 14:1, 3 • Gen. 49:1-27

5 of the tribe of Judah
    twelve thousand *were* sealed;
  of the tribe of Reuben
    twelve thousand *were* *sealed;
  of the tribe of Gad
    twelve thousand *were* sealed;
6 of the tribe of Asher
    twelve thousand *were* sealed;
  of the tribe of Naphtali
    twelve thousand *were* sealed;
  of the tribe of Manasseh
    twelve thousand *were* sealed;
7 of the tribe of Simeon
    twelve thousand *were* sealed;
  of the tribe of Levi
    twelve thousand *were* sealed;
  of the tribe of Issachar
    twelve thousand *were* sealed;
8 of the tribe of Zebulun
    twelve thousand *were* sealed;
  of the tribe of Joseph
    twelve thousand *were* sealed;
  of the tribe of Benjamin
    twelve thousand *were* sealed.

A Multitude from the Great Tribulation

9 After these things I looked, and behold, a great multitude which no one could number, ᴿof all nations, tribes, peoples, and tongues, standing before the throne and before the Lamb, clothed with white robes, with palm branches in their hands,   Rev. 5:9

6:6 Gr. *choinix*, about 1 quart • About 1 day's wage for a worker
6:12 NU, M omit *behold* • NU, M *whole moon*
6:15 NU, M *the commanders, the rich men,*

7:5 NU, M omit *sealed* in vv. 5b–8b.

10 and crying out with a loud voice, saying, R"Salvation *belongs* to our God Rwho sits on the throne, and to the Lamb!"   Ps. 3:8 · Rev. 5:13

11 RAll the angels stood around the throne and the elders and the four living creatures, and fell on their faces before the throne and Rworshiped God,   Rev. 4:6 · Rev. 4:11

12 Rsaying:

"Amen! Blessing and glory and wisdom,
Thanksgiving and honor and power and
    might,
Be to our God forever and ever.
Amen."   Rev. 5:13, 14

13 Then one of the elders answered, saying to me, "Who are these arrayed in white robes, and where did they come from?"

14 And I said to him, *"Sir, you know." So he said to me, R"These are the ones who come out of the great tribulation, and Rwashed their robes and made them white in the blood of the Lamb.   Rev. 6:9 · [Heb. 9:14]

15 "Therefore they are before the throne of

God, and serve Him day and night in His temple. And He who sits on the throne will Rdwell among them.   Is. 4:5, 6

16 R"They shall neither hunger anymore nor thirst anymore; Rthe sun shall not strike them, nor any heat;   Is. 49:10 · Ps. 121:6

17 "for the Lamb who is in the midst of the throne will shepherd them and lead them to *living fountains of waters. And God will wipe away every tear from their eyes."

Seventh Seal: Prelude to the Seven Trumpets

8 WhenR He opened the seventh seal, there was silence in heaven for about half an hour.   Rev. 6:1 ▲

52-C. The Seven Trumpets   ▼

2 RAnd I saw the seven angels who stand before God, Rand to them were given seven trumpets.   [Matt. 18:10] · 2 Chr. 29:25–28

3 Then another angel, having a golden censer, came and stood at the altar. He was

---

7:14 NU, M *My lord*

7:17 NU, M *fountains of the waters of life*

52-C. The Seven Trumpets (Revelation 8:2—9:21; 11:15–19)—At the opening of the seventh seal, a silence will fill heaven (8:1). This silence is not itself the content of the seventh seal, but a reaction in heaven to its awesome contents.

The trumpets sound the battle cry of impending holy judgment. This judgment against the wicked is required by God's holiness, and is also a long-awaited answer to the prayers of the saints (8:3) who have cried for God to clear the earth of wickedness (Rev. 6:9, 10, page 1300). As the trumpets sound, one after another, God's might is unleashed against the impenitent of the earth who still spurn Him. Notice that God does not permit these evils to fall until His 144,000 witnesses are first sealed (Rev. 7:2, 3, page 1300).

(1) *The first trumpet: hail and fire* (8:7). A third part of the trees and all green grass are destroyed by hail and fire. The greenery of the earth gives us oxygen and food that grows. Humanists and other rebels will want no part of God; thus God removes a portion of the earth's vital nourishment which He had provided for man on the third day of Creation.

(2) *The second trumpet: bloody waters* (8:8, 9). According to the Scriptures, it is not a mountain, but something as great as a mountain, that is burning with fire and cast into the sea. A third of the sea becomes blood, which is not an entirely new occurrence (Ex. 7:19–25, page 65). A third of the sea creatures die, and a third of the ships are destroyed. This is a great miracle of judgment on the Antichrist and his government.

(3) *The third trumpet: bitter waters* (8:10, 11). A third part of the rivers are suddenly and violently polluted by what appears to be a giant, burning meteorite. It affects the water table and underground reservoirs. Upon contact it causes a part of the water to become wormwood—very bitter (Jer. 9:13–15, page 721), and many die because of the toxic chemicals in the water.

(4) *The fourth trumpet: restricted light* (8:12). A third part of the sun, moon, and stars are blotted out of sight (Luke 21:25–28, page 1042), perhaps the direct result of the meteor of the third trumpet having caused enormous clouds of dust to fill the atmosphere.

The fifth, sixth, and seventh trumpets are called "woes" (8:13), showing the steadily increasing severity of God's judgments.

(5) *The fifth trumpet, the first woe: locusts from the pit* (9:1–11). The star (angel) from heaven comes down to earth and is given a key to the bottomless pit (Rev. 20:1–3, page 1313). When he unlocks the bottomless pit, there arises a smoke that darkens the sun. Out of the smoke come locusts such as the world has never known. The description that John gives us is beyond anything that man could imagine. They go out and torment the ungodly for five months. Their sting is like that of a scorpion. Men pray to die, but death eludes them. According to verse 11, they must be demonized locusts, for their king is Apollyon (Satan).

(6) *The sixth trumpet, the second woe: invasion of the two hundred million* (9:13–21). Horsemen, two hundred million of them, come from the East and cross the Euphrates River into the Middle East (9:14, 16). This fits the description of Revelation 16:12 (page 1309), which pictures eastern armed forces pouring into Armageddon (Rev. 16:16, page 1310). They kill a third of mankind (9:15, 18), not worldwide, but in the area of their assault. Some Bible students see this vast cavalry as totally supernatural, demons (or demon-

(Point 52-C continued on next page)

▽ given much incense, that he should offer *it* with the prayers of all the saints upon the golden altar which was before the throne.

4 And ᴿthe smoke of the incense, with the prayers of the saints, ascended before God from the angel's hand.   Ps. 141:2

5 Then the angel took the censer, filled it with fire from the altar, and threw *it* to the earth. And there were noises, thunderings, lightnings, ᴿand an earthquake.   2 Sam. 22:8

6 So the seven angels who had the seven trumpets prepared themselves to sound.

First Trumpet: Vegetation Struck

7 The first angel sounded: ᴿAnd hail and fire followed, mingled with blood, and they were thrown ᴿto the *earth. And a third of the trees were burned up, and all green grass was burned up.   Ezek. 38:22 • Rev. 16:2

Second Trumpet: The Seas Struck

8 Then the second angel sounded: And *something* like a great mountain burning with fire was thrown into the sea, and a third of the sea ᴿbecame blood.   Ezek. 14:19

9 ᴿAnd a third of the living creatures in the sea died, and a third of the ships were destroyed.   Rev. 16:3

Third Trumpet: The Waters Struck

10 Then the third angel sounded: ᴿAnd a great star fell from heaven, burning like a torch, ᴿand it fell on a third of the rivers and on the springs of water.   Is. 14:12 • Rev. 14:7; 16:4

11 ᴿThe name of the star is Wormwood. ᴿA third of the waters became wormwood, and many men died from the water, because it was made bitter.   Ruth 1:20 • Ex. 15:23

Fourth Trumpet: The Heavens Struck

12 Then the fourth angel sounded: And a third of the sun was struck, a third of the moon, and a third of the stars, so that a third of them were darkened. A third of the day did not shine, and likewise the night.

13 And I looked, ᴿand I heard an *angel ▽ flying through the midst of heaven, saying with a loud voice, "Woe, woe, woe to the inhabitants of the earth, because of the remaining blasts of the trumpet of the three angels who are about to sound!"   Rev. 14:6

Fifth Trumpet: The Locusts from the Bottomless Pit

9 Then the fifth angel sounded: ᴿAnd I saw a star fallen from heaven to the earth. To him was given the key to ᴿthe ᵀbottomless pit.   Rev. 8:10 • Luke 8:31 • Lit. *shaft of the abyss*

2 And he opened the bottomless pit, and smoke arose out of the pit like the smoke of a great furnace. So the sun and the air were darkened because of the smoke of the pit.

3 Then out of the smoke locusts came upon the earth. And to them was given power, ᴿas the scorpions of the earth have power.   Judg. 7:12

4 They were commanded not to harm the grass of the earth, or any green thing, or any tree, but only those men who do not have the seal of God on their foreheads.

5 And they were not given *authority* to kill them, but to torment them *for* five months. Their torment *was* like the torment of a scorpion when it strikes a man.

6 In those days ᴿmen will seek death and will not find it; they will desire to die, and death will flee from them.   Jer. 8:3

7 The shape of the locusts was like horses prepared for battle. On their heads were crowns of something like gold, and their faces *were* like the faces of men.

8 They had hair like women's hair, and ᴿtheir teeth were like lions' *teeth*.   Joel 1:6

9 And they had breastplates like breastplates of iron, and the sound of their wings *was* ᴿlike the sound of chariots with many horses running into battle.   Joel 2:5-7

10 They had tails like scorpions, and there were stings in their tails. Their power *was* to hurt men five months.

8:7 NU, M add *and a third of the earth was burned up*   8:13 NU, M *eagle*

(Point 52-C continued from previous page)
possessed men) going out in the power of Satan, who are completely destroyed by the power of the Lord Jesus Christ, who personally ends the Battle of Armageddon and establishes His kingdom (Zech. 14:1-4, page 919; cf. Matt. 24:21, 22, page 973).

(7) *The seventh trumpet, the third woe: the end of Satan's dominion* (11:15-19). There is great joy in heaven, because the kingdom of this world (Satan's kingdom) comes to an eternal end, and God's kingdom is restored to earth. At the fall of man in Eden, Satan became the false god of this world system (2 Cor. 4:4, page 1167), "the ruler of the demons" (Matt. 12:24, page 953), and ruler of all who disobey God (Eph. 2:2, page 1187). At the end of Satan's kingdom, the host of heaven rejoices in worship because creation is once again the kingdom of God and His Son, Jesus Christ, who will reign forever and ever. By this trumpet we are given a glimpse of God's eternal temple (11:19).

The seven bowls of God's wrath remain to be poured out on the wicked. The nations of this world unknowingly are preparing themselves for the final holocaust.

See Revelation 11:3—13:8, page 1303, for **Point 52-D: The Seven Personages**.

▽ 11 And they had as king over them the angel of the bottomless pit, whose name in Hebrew is ᵀAbaddon, but in Greek he has the name ᵀApollyon.   Lit. *Destruction* · Lit. *Destroyer*

12 ᴿOne woe is past. Behold, still two more woes are coming after these things.   Rev. 8:13

Sixth Trumpet: The Angels from the Euphrates

13 Then the sixth angel sounded: And I heard a voice from the four horns of the ᴿgolden altar which is before God,   Rev. 8:3

14 saying to the sixth angel who had the trumpet, "Release the four angels who are bound at the great river Euphrates."

15 So the four angels, who had been prepared for the hour and day and month and year, were released to kill a ᴿthird of mankind.   Rev. 8:7-9; 9:18

16 Now the number of the army ᴿof the horsemen *was* two hundred million; ᴿI heard the number of them.   Ezek. 38:4 · Rev. 7:4

17 And thus I saw the horses in the vision: those who sat on them had breastplates of fiery red, hyacinth blue, and sulfur yellow; ᴿand the heads of the horses *were* like the heads of lions; and out of their mouths came fire, smoke, and brimstone.   Is. 5:28, 29

18 By these three *plagues* a third of mankind was killed—by the fire and the smoke and the brimstone which came out of their mouths.

19 For *their power is in their mouth and in their tails; for their tails *are* like serpents, having heads; and with them they do harm.

20 But the rest of mankind, who were not killed by these plagues, did not repent of the works of their hands, that they should not worship ᴿdemons, ᴿand idols of gold, silver, brass, stone, and wood, which can neither see nor hear nor walk.   1 Cor. 10:20 · Dan. 5:23

21 And they did not repent of their murders ᴿor their *sorceries or their sexual immorality ▲ or their thefts.   Rev. 21:8; 22:15

The Mighty Angel with the Little Book

10 I saw still another mighty angel coming down from heaven, clothed with a cloud. ᴿAnd a rainbow *was* on ᴿhis head, his face *was* like the sun, and ᴿhis feet like pillars of fire.   Rev. 4:3 · Rev. 1:16 · Rev. 1:15

2 He had a little book open in his hand. ᴿAnd he set his right foot on the sea and *his* left foot on the land,   Matt. 28:18

3 and cried with a loud voice, as *when* a

9:19 NU, M *the power of the horses*
9:21 NU, M *drugs*

lion roars. When he cried out, ᴿseven thunders uttered their voices.   Ps. 29:3-9

4 Now when the seven thunders *uttered their voices, I was about to write; but I heard a voice from heaven saying *to me, ᴿ"Seal up the things which the seven thunders uttered, and do not write them."   Dan. 8:26; 12:4, 9

5 The angel whom I saw standing on the sea and on the land ᴿraised up his *hand to heaven   Dan. 12:7

6 and swore by Him who lives forever and ever, who created heaven and the things that are in it, the earth and the things that are in it, and the sea and the things that are in it, that there should be delay no longer,

7 but in the days of the sounding of the seventh angel, when he is about to sound, the mystery of God would be finished, as He declared to His servants the prophets.

John Eats the Little Book

8 Then the voice which I heard from heaven spoke to me again and said, "Go, take the little book which is open in the hand of the angel who stands on the sea and on the earth."

9 So I went to the angel and said to him, "Give me the little book." And he said to me, ᴿ"Take and eat it; and it will make your stomach bitter, but it will be as sweet as honey in your mouth."   Jer. 15:16

10 Then I took the little book out of the angel's hand and ate it, and it was as sweet as honey in my mouth. But when I had eaten it, ᴿmy stomach became bitter.   Ezek. 2:10

11 And *he said to me, "You must prophesy again about many peoples, nations, tongues, and kings."

The Two Witnesses

11 Then I was given a reed like a measuring rod. *And the angel stood, saying, "Rise and measure the temple of God, the altar, and those who worship there.

2 "But leave out the court which is outside the temple, and do not measure it, ᴿfor it has been given to the Gentiles. And they will ᴿtread the holy city underfoot *for* ᴿforty-two months.   Ps. 79:1 · Dan. 8:10 · Rev. 12:6; 13:5

52-D. The Seven Personages   ▼

3 "And I will give *power* to my two ᴿwitnesses, ᴿand they will prophesy ᴿone thou-

10:4 NU, M *sounded,* • NU, M omit *to me*
10:5 NU, M *right hand*
10:11 NU, M *they*
11:1 NU, M omit *And the angel stood*

52-D. The Seven Personages (Revelation 11:3—13:18)—There are seven key personages whose identities are essential for understanding the visions of chapters 11—13. These three chapters show the height of Satan's kingdom and prepare us for the necessity of God's judgments which must follow as described in chapters 15—20.

(Point 52-D continued on next page)

▽ sand two hundred and sixty days, clothed in
sackcloth."   Rev. 20:4 • Rev. 19:10 • Rev. 12:6

4 These are the ᴿtwo olive trees and the
two lampstands standing before the *God of
the earth.   Zech. 4:2, 3, 11, 14

5 And if anyone wants to harm them, fire
proceeds from their mouth and devours their
enemies. And if anyone wants to harm them,
he must be killed in this manner.

6 These ᴿhave power to shut heaven, so
that no rain falls in the days of their prophecy; and they have power over waters to turn
them to blood, and to strike the earth with all
plagues, as often as they desire.   1 Kin. 17:1

The Witnesses Killed

7 When they finish their testimony, the
beast that ascends ᴿout of the bottomless pit
ᴿwill make war against them, overcome
them, and kill them.   Rev. 9:1, 2 • Dan. 7:21

8 And their dead bodies *will lie* in the
street of ᴿthe great city which spiritually is
called Sodom and Egypt, ᴿwhere also *our
Lord was crucified.   Rev. 14:8 • Heb. 13:12

9 Then *those* from the peoples, tribes, ▽
tongues, and nations *will see their dead
bodies three-and-a-half days, and not allow
their dead bodies to be put into graves.

10 ᴿAnd those who dwell on the earth will
rejoice over them, make merry, ᴿand send
gifts to one another, ᴿbecause these two
prophets tormented those who dwell on the
earth.   Rev. 12:12 • Esth. 9:19, 22 • Rev. 16:10

The Witnesses Resurrected

11 Now after the three-and-a-half days ᴿthe
breath of life from God entered them, and
they stood on their feet, and great fear fell on
those who saw them.   Ezek. 37:5, 9, 10

12 And *they heard a loud voice from
heaven saying to them, "Come up here."
ᴿAnd they ascended to heaven ᴿin a cloud,
and their enemies saw them.   Is. 14:13 • Acts 1:9

13 In the same hour there was a great
earthquake, ᴿand a tenth of the city fell. In
the earthquake seven thousand people were
killed, and the rest were afraid and gave glory
to the God of heaven.   Rev. 16:19

11:4 NU, M *Lord*

11:8 NU, M *their*

11:9 NU, M *see . . . and will not allow*

11:12 M *I*

(Point 52-D continued from previous page)

(1) *The witnesses* (11:3–12). These are God's two end-time prophets who preach against the world's sin
during the first period of the Great Tribulation—the Seventieth Week of years of Daniel 9:27 (page 851)
which close this era. They come in the power of Moses and Elijah and are slain by the Beast (see (6) below),
but are raised from the dead by God.

(2) *The woman* (12:1, 2, 13–17). She is the nation of Israel, the Old Testament wife of Jehovah, as shown
by the sun, moon, and twelve stars matching Joseph's dream of Israel in Genesis 37:9, 10 (page 43). This
chapter teaches us that at the close of the age, and in the Tribulation period, Satan persecutes Israel, but
God delivers and rescues her as her people turn to Christ (Zech. 12:10, page 918; Rom. 11:26, page 1141).

(3) *The Dragon* (12:3, 4). This figure is clearly Satan, as Revelation 12:9 declares, that "serpent of old"
who deceived Eve (1 Tim. 2:14, page 1219), the one who through Herod sought to kill the Christ child in
Bethlehem (Jer. 31:15, page 745; cf. Matt. 2:16–18, page 932). The "dragon" is the ruler of the fallen angels
(Matt. 12:24, page 953), the persecutor of Israel and of the saints of the ages, and the false father of the
counterfeit trinity who gives power to his false son, the Beast (13:2). He is bound during the Millennium
(Rev. 20:2, page 1313) and finally cast into the lake of fire (Rev. 20:10, page 1313).

(4) *The Child* (12:4). The Child is Christ, born of the woman, Israel (12:1, 2; cf. Rom. 1:3, page 1128).
Satan, the Dragon, sought to slay Him with the infants in Bethlehem "as soon as it [He] was born." It is the
Christ who will rule the nations "with a rod of iron" (Ps. 2:9, page 510) during His thousand-year reign, which
He will establish at His second coming. The enemy of Israel, Satan, has always been the enemy of Christ.

(5) *Michael, the archangel* (12:7). Michael defends Israel during "the time of Jacob's trouble" (Jer. 30:7,
page 743; cf. Dan. 12:1, page 856). Christ called this a time of "great tribulation" (Matt. 24:21, page 973).
Amid Satan's final attack on the woman (Israel), Michael is seen doing heavenly battle with Satan and his
hosts.

(6) *The Beast* (13:1). The Beast corresponds to the Roman Empire (the fourth beast of Daniel) and to its
leader Antichrist (Dan. 7:7, page 844; cf. 8:19–27, page 848). This beast (the Antichrist) rises up out of the
revived Roman Empire. Christ is the stone, cut out without hands, who falls upon the feet (the kingdom of
the Antichrist, the revived Roman Empire) and grinds it to powder (Dan. 2:31–35, page 835). The Beast is the
counterfeit "son" who receives his power from Satan (13:2) and will be wounded and healed (13:14). He is
"cast alive into the lake of fire burning with brimstone" (Rev. 19:20, page 1313) at Christ's second coming,
following Armageddon (Rev. 16:16, page 1310).

(7) *The second beast*. This is the False Prophet (13:11–18), the third member of the counterfeit "trinity"
(Rev. 16:13, page 1309), who arises after the Beast is healed and causes all to worship the first Beast (13:12),
and who marks his own with the mark of the Beast (13:17, 18). See Romans 8:9 (page 1137) and Ephesians
1:13 (page 1186). Note how this false spirit copies and counterfeits the work of the true Trinity. Satan's
kingdom, however, is destroyed at the coming of Christ.

See Revelation 16:1–21, page 1308, for **Point 52-E: The Seven Bowls.**

▽ 14 ᴿThe second woe is past. Behold, the third woe is coming quickly.   Rev. 8:13; 9:12

Seventh Trumpet: The Kingdom Proclaimed

▼ 15 Then the seventh angel sounded: And there were loud voices in heaven, saying, "The *kingdoms of this world have become *the kingdoms* of our Lord and of His Christ, and He shall reign forever and ever!"

16 And the twenty-four elders who sat before God on their thrones fell on their faces and ᴿworshiped God,   Rev. 4:11; 5:9, 12, 14; 7:11

17 saying:

"We give You thanks, O Lord God Almighty,
   The One ᴿwho is and who was *and who is to come,
   Because You have taken Your great power ᴿand reigned.   Rev. 16:5 • Rev. 19:6
18 The nations were ᴿangry, and Your ᵀwrath has come,
   And the time of the ᴿdead, that they should be judged,
   And that You should reward Your servants the prophets and the saints,
   And those who fear Your name, small and great,
   And should destroy those who destroy the earth."   Ps. 2:1 • anger • Dan. 7:10

19 Then ᴿthe temple of God was opened in heaven, and the ark of *His covenant was seen in His temple. And ᴿthere were lightnings, noises, thunderings, an earthquake,
▲ ᴿand great hail.   Rev. 4:1; 15:5, 8 • Rev. 8:5 • Rev. 16:21

The Woman, the Child, and the Dragon

12 Now a great sign appeared in heaven: a woman clothed with the sun, with the moon under her feet, and on her head a garland of twelve stars.

2 Then being with child, she cried out ᴿin labor and in pain to give birth.   Is. 26:17; 66:6–9

3 And another sign appeared in heaven: behold, ᴿa great, fiery red dragon having seven heads and ten horns, and seven diadems on his heads.   Rev. 13:1; 17:3, 7, 9

4 His tail drew a third of the stars of heaven and threw them to the earth. And the dragon stood ᴿbefore the woman who was ready to give birth, ᴿto devour her Child as soon as it was born.   Rev. 12:2 • Matt. 2:16

5 She bore a male Child who was to rule all nations with a rod of iron. And her Child was caught up to God and His throne.

6 Then ᴿthe woman fled into the wilderness, where she has a place prepared by God, that they should feed her there one thousand two hundred and sixty days.   Rev. 12:4

Satan Thrown Out of Heaven   ▽

7 And war broke out in heaven: Michael and his angels fought with the dragon; and the dragon and his angels fought,

8 but they did not prevail, nor was a place found for *them in heaven any longer.

9 So ᴿthe great dragon was cast out, ᴿthat serpent of old, called the Devil and Satan, ᴿwho deceives the whole world; ᴿhe was cast to the earth, and his angels were cast out with him.   John 12:31 • Gen. 3:1, 4 • Rev. 20:3 • Rev. 9:1

10 Then I heard a loud voice saying in heaven, "Now salvation, and strength, and the kingdom of our God, and the power of His Christ have come, for the accuser of our brethren, ᴿwho accused them before our God day and night, has been cast down.   Zech. 3:1

11 "And ᴿthey overcame him by the blood of the Lamb and by the word of their testimony, ᴿand they did not love their lives to the death.   Rom. 16:20 • Luke 14:26

12 "Therefore rejoice, O heavens, and you who dwell in them! Woe to the inhabitants of the earth and the sea! For the devil has come down to you, having great wrath, because he knows that he has a short time."

The Woman Persecuted

13 Now when the dragon saw that he had been cast to the earth, he persecuted the woman who gave birth to the male *Child*.

14 But the woman was given two wings of a great eagle, that she might fly ᴿinto the wilderness to her place, where she is nourished for a time and times and half a time, from the presence of the serpent.   Rev. 17:3

15 So the serpent ᴿspewed water out of his mouth like a flood after the woman, that he might cause her to be carried away by the flood.   Is. 59:19

16 But the earth helped the woman, and the earth opened its mouth and swallowed up the flood which the dragon had spewed out of his mouth.

17 And the dragon was enraged with the woman, and he went to make war with the rest of her offspring, who keep the commandments of God and have the testimony of Jesus *Christ.

The Beast from the Sea

13 Then *I stood on the sand of the sea. And I saw a beast rising up out of the sea, ᴿhaving *seven heads and ten horns, and on his horns ten crowns, and on his heads a ᴿblasphemous name.   Rev. 12:3 • Rev. 17:3

2 Now the beast which I saw was like a leopard, his feet were like *the feet of* a bear, and his mouth like the mouth of a lion. The

11:15 NU, M kingdom . . . has become the kingdom
11:17 NU, M omit and who is to come
11:19 M the covenant of the Lord

12:8 M him
12:17 NU, M omit Christ
13:1 NU he • NU, M ten horns and seven heads

▽ ᴿdragon gave him his power, his throne, and great authority.   Rev. 12:3, 9; 13:4, 12

3 And *I saw* one of his heads as if it had been mortally wounded, and his deadly wound was healed. And ᴿall the world marveled and followed the beast.   Rev. 17:8

4 So they worshiped the dragon who gave authority to the beast; and they worshiped the beast, saying, ᴿ"Who *is* like the beast? Who is able to make war with him?" Rev. 18:18

5 And he was given ᴿa mouth speaking great things and blasphemies, and he was given authority to *continue for ᴿforty-two months.   Dan. 7:8, 11, 20, 25; 11:36 • Rev. 11:2

6 Then he opened his mouth in blasphemy against God, to blaspheme His name, His tabernacle, and those who dwell in heaven.

7 It was granted to him ᴿto make war with the saints and to overcome them. And ᴿauthority was given him over every ᴿtribe, tongue, and nation.   Dan. 7:21 • Rev. 11:18

8 All who dwell on the earth will worship him, whose names have not been written in the Book of Life of the Lamb slain ᴿfrom the foundation of the world.   Rev. 17:8

9 If anyone has an ear, let him hear.

10 He who leads into captivity shall go into captivity; he who kills with the sword must be killed with the sword. Here is the patience and the faith of the saints.

The Beast from the Earth

11 Then I saw another beast ᴿcoming up out of the earth, and he had two horns like a lamb and spoke like a dragon.   Rev. 11:7

12 And he exercises all the authority of the first beast in his presence, and causes the earth and those who dwell in it to worship the first beast, ᴿwhose deadly wound was healed.   Rev. 13:3, 4

13 He performs great signs, ᴿso that he even makes fire come down from heaven on the earth in the sight of men.   1 Kin. 18:38

14 ᴿAnd he deceives *those who dwell on the earth ᴿby those signs which he was granted to do in the sight of the beast, telling those who dwell on the earth to make an image to the beast who was wounded by the sword ᴿand lived.   Rev. 12:9 • 2 Thess. 2:9 • 2 Kin. 20:7

15 He was granted *power* to give breath to the image of the beast, that the image of the beast should both speak ᴿand cause as many as would not worship the image of the beast to be killed.   Rev. 16:2

16 He causes all, both small and great, rich and poor, free and slave, to receive a mark on their right hand or on their foreheads,

17 and that no one may buy or sell except one who has the mark *or the name of the ▽ beast, ᴿor the number of his name.   Rev. 15:2

18 Here is wisdom. Let him who has ᴿunderstanding calculate ᴿthe number of the beast, ᴿfor it is the number of a man: His number *is* 666.   [1 Cor. 2:14] • Rev. 15:2 • Rev. 21:17 ▲

The Lamb and the 144,000

14 Then I looked, and behold, *a ᴿLamb standing on Mount Zion, and with Him ᴿone hundred *and* forty-four thousand, *having His Father's name ᴿwritten on their foreheads.   Rev. 5:6 • Rev. 7:4; 14:3 • Rev. 7:3; 22:4

2 And I heard a voice from heaven, like the voice of many waters, and like the voice of loud thunder. And I heard the sound of ᴿharpists playing their harps.   Rev. 5:8

3 They sang as it were a new song before the throne, before the four living creatures, and the elders; and no one could learn that song except the hundred *and* forty-four thousand who were redeemed from the earth.

4 These are the ones who were not defiled with women, ᴿfor they are virgins. These are the ones ᴿwho follow the Lamb wherever He goes. These ᴿwere *redeemed *from *among* men, ᴿ*being* firstfruits to God and to the Lamb.   [2 Cor. 11:2] • Rev. 3:4; 7:17 • Rev. 5:9 • James 1:18

5 And ᴿin their mouth was found no deceit,* for ᴿthey are without fault *before the throne of God.   Ps. 32:2 • Eph. 5:27

The Proclamations of Three Angels

6 Then I saw another angel ᴿflying in the midst of heaven, ᴿhaving the everlasting gospel to preach to those who dwell on the earth—ᴿto every nation, tribe, tongue, and people—   Rev. 8:13 • Eph. 3:9 • Rev. 13:7

7 saying with a loud voice, ᴿ"Fear God and give glory to Him, for the hour of His judgment has come; ᴿand worship Him who made heaven and earth, the sea and springs of water."   Rev. 11:18 • Neh. 9:6

8 And another angel followed, saying, *"Babylon is fallen, is fallen, that great city, because she has made all nations drink of the wine of the wrath of her fornication."

9 Then a third angel followed them, saying with a loud voice, "If anyone worships the beast and his image, and receives *his* ᴿmark on his forehead or on his hand,   Rev. 13:16

10 "he himself shall also drink of the wine of the wrath of God, which is poured out full strength into the cup of His indignation. He shall be tormented with ᴿfire and brimstone in the presence of the holy angels and in the presence of the Lamb.   2 Thess. 1:7

13:5 M *make war*
13:7 NU, M add *and people*
13:14 M *my own people*

14:1 NU, M *the* • NU, M add *His name and*
14:4 M adds *by Jesus*
14:5 NU, M *falsehood* • NU, M omit the rest of v. 5.
14:8 NU, M *Babylon the great is fallen, because*

11 "And ᴿthe smoke of their torment ascends forever and ever; and they have no rest day or night, who worship the beast and his image, and whoever receives the mark of his name."   Is. 34:8-10

12 Here is the patience of the saints; *here are those who keep the commandments of God and the faith of Jesus.

▼ 15-E. The End of Sin

13 Then I heard a voice from heaven saying *to me, "Write: 'Blessed are the dead who die in the Lord from now on.'" "Yes," says the Spirit, "that they may rest from their labors, ▲ and their works follow them."

Reaping the Earth's Harvest

14 Then I looked, and behold, a white cloud, and on the cloud One like the Son of Man, having on His head a golden crown, and in His hand a sharp sickle.

15 And another angel came out of the temple, crying with a loud voice to Him who sat

14:12 NU, M omit here are those
14:13 NU, M omit to me

on the cloud, "Thrust in Your sickle and reap, for the time has come *for You to reap, for the harvest of the earth is ripe."

16 So He who sat on the cloud thrust in His sickle on the earth, and the earth was reaped.

Reaping the Grapes of Wrath

17 Then another angel came out of the temple which is in heaven, he also having a sharp sickle.

18 And another angel came out from the altar, who had power over fire, and he cried with a loud cry to him who had the sharp sickle, saying, ᴿ"Thrust in your sharp sickle and gather the clusters of the vine of the earth, for her grapes are fully ripe."   Joel 3:13

19 So the angel thrust his sickle into the earth and gathered the vine of the earth, and threw it into ᴿthe great winepress of the wrath of God.   Rev. 19:15

20 And the winepress was trampled outside the city, and blood came out of the winepress, ᴿup to the horses' bridles, for ᵀone thousand six hundred furlongs.   Is. 34:3 • 184 mi.

14:15 NU, M omit for You

15-E. The End of Sin (Revelation 14:13)—

(1) Christ is the "end of sin" for all believers, both living and dead:

(a) Those who "die in the Lord . . . may rest from their labors and their works follow them" (v. 13).

(b) Those believers who are alive at the second coming of Christ for His church (called the Rapture) will "always be with the Lord" (1 Thess. 4:17, page 1212).

(c) Believers who are alive at Christ's judgment of the nations will enter into eternal life (Matt. 25:34, 46, page 976).

(d) All believers have eternal life and cannot be touched by the second death (Rev. 20:6, page 1313).

(e) All believers will appear before the judgment seat of Christ to receive their eternal rewards (2 Cor. 5:10, page 1168).

(f) The church will be united to Christ forever at the marriage of the Lamb (Rev. 19:7, 8, page 1312).

(2) At Christ's second coming, all evildoers will be eliminated:

(a) The Beast and his False Prophet will be cast into the lake of fire (Rev. 19:20, page 1313).

(b) Satan will be bound during the Millennium (a thousand years) and then be cast forever into the lake of fire (Rev. 20:10, page 1313).

(c) The unbelievers who are alive when Christ judges the nations will be cast out of His kingdom forever (Matt. 25:45, 46, page 977).

(d) After the judgment of the Great White Throne, the lost of the ages (from Old and New Testament eras) will be cast into the lake of fire (Rev. 20:11-15, page 1313).

(e) The fallen angels will be judged and cast out forever (Jude 6, page 1289).

(3) The world of the new heaven, new earth, and New Jerusalem will be completely free forever from the effects or traces of sin:

(a) This present world, with its marks of sin, will be burned and dissolved, and the new heaven and earth will be brought forth (2 Pet. 3:10-13, page 1276).

(b) The new heaven and earth will be marked by "righteousness" (2 Pet. 3:13, page 1276).

(c) The New Jerusalem will not be man-made but will be God-made, descending from heaven (Rev. 21:2, page 1315).

(d) God will again dwell with man, as in the Garden of Eden, in eternal, unbroken fellowship (Rev. 21:3, 22, page 1315).

Believers will "reign forever and ever" (Rev. 22:5, page 1316). All are invited to enter this everlasting bliss, by faith in Christ: "And let him who thirsts come. Whoever desires, let him take the water of life freely" (Rev. 22:17, page 1316). "Believe on the Lord Jesus Christ, and you will be saved" (Acts 16:31, page 1111; see also Master Outline 21, "So Great Salvation," page 38).

See Index, page 17, for your next study.

Prelude to the Bowl Judgments

15 Then I saw another sign in heaven, great and marvelous: seven angels having the seven last plagues, ᴿfor in them the wrath of God is complete.   Rev. 14:10

2 And I saw *something* like ᴿa sea of glass ᴿmingled with fire, and those who have the victory over the beast, ᴿover his image and *over his mark *and* over the number of his name, standing on the sea of glass, having harps of God.   Rev. 4:6 • [Matt. 3:11] • Rev. 13:14, 15

3 They sing ᴿthe song of Moses, the servant of God, and the song of the ᴿLamb, saying: Ex. 15:1-21 • Rev. 15:3

> ᴿ"Great and marvelous *are* Your works,
>   Lord God Almighty!   Deut. 32:3, 4
> ᴿJust and true *are* Your ways,
>   O King of the *saints!   Ps. 145:17
> 4 ᴿWho shall not fear You, O Lord, and
>   glorify Your name?
> For *You* alone *are* ᴿholy.
> For ᴿall nations shall come and worship
>   before You,
> For Your judgments have been
>   manifested."   Ex. 15:14 • Lev. 11:44 • Is. 66:23

5 After these things I looked, and *behold, the ᵀtemple of the tabernacle of the testimony in heaven was opened.   The inner shrine

15:2 NU, M omit *over his mark*
15:3 NU, M *nations*
15:5 NU, M omit *behold*

6 And out of the ᵀtemple came the seven angels having the seven plagues, clothed in pure bright linen, and having their chests girded with golden bands.   The inner shrine

7 ᴿThen one of the four living creatures gave to the seven angels seven golden bowls full of the wrath of God ᴿwho lives forever and ever.   Rev. 4:6 • 1 Thess. 1:9

8 The temple was filled with smoke from the glory of God and from His power, and no one was able to enter the temple till the seven plagues of the seven angels were completed.

52-E. The Seven Bowls   ▼

16 Then I heard a loud voice from the temple saying ᴿto the seven angels, "Go and pour out the *bowls ᴿof the wrath of God on the earth."   Rev. 15:1 • Rev. 14:10

First Bowl: Loathsome Sores

2 So the first went and poured out his bowl ᴿupon the earth, and a ᵀfoul and ᴿloathsome sore came upon the men who had the mark of the beast and those who worshiped his image.   Rev. 8:7 • Lit. *bad and evil* • Ex. 9:9-11

Second Bowl: The Sea Turns to Blood

3 Then the second angel poured out his bowl ᴿon the sea, and ᴿit became blood as of a dead *man;* ᴿand every living creature in the sea died.   Rev. 8:8; 11:6 • Ex. 7:17-21 • Rev. 8:9

16:1 NU, M *seven bowls*

52-E. The Seven Bowls (Revelation 16:1–21)—The term, "the seven last plagues" (Rev. 15:1, above), indicates that they are the last series of God's judgments (following the seals of chapter 6 and the trumpets of chapters 8 and 9) before Christ returns to destroy the wicked at Armageddon (v. 16; cf. Rev. 19:11–20, page 1312).

(1) *The first bowl: sores.* This bowl is a loathsome sore (v. 2) with a noxious odor, which falls upon those who have the mark of the Beast (666) and upon those who worship his image. A similar curse was placed upon the Egyptians by the Lord (Ex. 9:8–11, page 67), and Moses warned the children of Israel of physical plagues that would come upon them if they disobeyed the Lord (Deut. 28:27, 35, page 206).

(2) *The second bowl: the bloody sea.* The oceans become like the "blood as of a dead man; and every living creature in the sea died" (v. 3). In the trumpet judgment, the third part of the sea is turned to blood. God also turned water into blood to plague the Egyptians in the days of Moses (Ex. 7:15-25, page 65).

(3) *The third bowl: the bloody rivers.* God will judge the mass of murderers who flood the earth with men's blood by causing the rivers to become blood (vv. 4–7).

(4) *The fourth bowl: the solar furnace.* The sun burns (vv. 8, 9). Solar energy will scorch mankind, who reject the Creator of all light, heat, and energy which makes life on earth possible. Still they do not repent.

(5) *The fifth bowl: darkness.* The seat (throne) of the Beast is darkened (vv. 10, 11). The Beast (Antichrist), and all those who worship him as God, are thrown into total darkness. They go mad, and gnaw their tongues for pain. Still they do not repent.

(6) *The sixth bowl: the Euphrates dries up.* By drying up the great river (v. 12), God creates a land route for the vast armies of the east as they march to their destruction at Armageddon in northern Israel (Rev. 19:19-21, page 1313).

(7) *The seventh bowl: Babylon destroyed.* The capital city of the Antichrist is destroyed, and a heavenly voice fittingly declares, "It is done!" (v. 17). This destruction is the subject of Revelation 18 (page 1311), and with it comes cosmic and geological disruption of the earth and its islands (vv. 18–21). The capital of the Antichrist is called "Babylon" because of its gross immorality, its religious confusion, and its souls belonging to Satan. Some Bible students believe a literal city will be rebuilt on the ancient site of Babylon in the last times.

See Revelation 17:1—20:15, page 1310, for **Point 52-F: The Seven Dooms.**

▽ *Third Bowl: The Waters Turn to Blood*

4 Then the third angel poured out his bowl
ᴿon the rivers and springs of water, ᴿand they
became blood.   Rev. 8:10 • Ex. 7:17-20

5 And I heard the angel of the waters
saying:

ᴿ"You are righteous, *O Lord,
The One ᴿwho is and *who was and
   who is to be,   Rev. 15:3, 4 • Rev. 1:4, 8
Because You have judged these things.
6 For ᴿthey have shed the blood ᴿof saints
   and prophets,
ᴿAnd You have given them blood to
   drink.   Matt. 23:34 • Rev. 11:18 • Is. 49:26
*For it is their just due."

7 And I heard *another from the altar
saying, "Even so, ᴿLord God Almighty, true
and righteous *are* Your judgments."   Rev. 15:3

Fourth Bowl: Men Are Scorched

8 Then the fourth angel poured out his
bowl on the sun, ᴿand power was given to
him to scorch men with fire.   Rev. 9:17, 18

9 And men were scorched with great heat,
and they blasphemed the name of God who
has power over these plagues; and they did
not repent ᴿand give Him glory.   Rev. 11:13

16:5 NU, M omit *O Lord* • NU, M *was, the Holy One*
16:6 NU, M omit *For*
16:7 NU, M omit *another from*

Fifth Bowl: Darkness and Pain   ▽

10 Then the fifth angel poured out his bowl
on the throne of the beast, and his kingdom
became full of darkness; ᴿand they gnawed
their tongues because of the pain.   Rev. 11:10

11 They blasphemed the God of heaven
because of their pains and their sores, and did
not repent of their deeds.

Sixth Bowl: Euphrates Dried Up

12 Then the sixth angel poured out his bowl
ᴿon the great river Euphrates, and its water
was dried up, so that the way of the kings
from the east might be prepared.   Rev. 9:14

49-C. The Battle of Armageddon   ▼

13 And I saw three unclean spirits like frogs
coming out of the mouth of the dragon, out
of the mouth of the beast, and out of the
mouth of the false prophet.

14 For they are spirits of demons, ᴿperform-
ing signs, *which* go out to the kings *of the
earth ᴿand of the whole world, to gather
them to ᴿthe battle of that great day of God
Almighty.   2 Thess. 2:9 • Luke 2:1 • Rev. 17:14; 19:19; 20:8

15 ᴿ"Behold, I am coming as a thief. Blessed
is he who watches, and keeps his garments, lest he walk naked and they see his
shame."   Matt. 24:43

16:14 NU, M omit *of the earth and*

49-C. The Battle of Armageddon (Revelation 16:13-16)—Armageddon, we are told in this verse, represents
the Hebrew name *Har-Magedon* ("Mount Megiddo"). It denotes the flat open valley in northern Israel (in
Galilee) that sits quietly at the break of the north-south chain of the Anti-Lebanon Mountains. The field is
about twenty by forty miles, beside the great north seaport of Haifa, and was labeled by no less than
Napoleon as one of the world's great natural battlefields. Note the following about the place and the battle:

(1) It is a real geographical site in northern Israel. We speak not of a mythical war ground, but of the flat
open miles which have often been a battleground for Israel. Saul and Jonathan died there at Gilboa, on its
south-central edge. There, in World War I, Allenby marched through to conquer Palestine. It presents the
ideal rallying ground for large forces to mount a northwest to southeast valley attack against Jerusalem. It
also touches Haifa's port which could allow munition and troopships by the hundreds to dock and unload.

(2) God named this as the scene of the final battle of this age (v. 16). It is also called "the battle of that
great day of God Almighty" where the kings of the earth are gathered together (v. 14).

(3) The armies that gather at Armageddon will come at the call of Satan (vv. 13, 14).

(4) The armies of the kings of the east will come (v. 12). "Two hundred million" will march to the battle
(Rev. 9:16, page 1303). It is a satanic crusade.

(5) The aim will be to destroy Israel once and for all (Zech. 12:2, 3, page 918).

(6) God, however, will appear and rescue Israel (Rev. 14:14-20, page 1307). Israel will at last look in faith
at her long-awaited Messiah (Zech. 12:10, 11, page 918). Christ's own feet will stand on the Mount of Olives
(Zech. 14:4, page 919).

(7) At this time Christ will come with His church (Rev. 19:14, page 1312). The armies "clothed in fine
linen, white and clean" are the redeemed saints.

(8) Christ will subdue and destroy the forces of evil at His Revelation—His coming with His church to
reign:

  (a) The Antichrist (beast), and the False Prophet will be cast into the lake of fire (Rev. 19:20, page
1313).

  (b) The armies following the Antichrist will be destroyed by the Lord Jesus and His heavenly army
(Rev. 19:11-21, page 1312; cf. Zech. 14:3, page 919; Matt. 24:21, 22, page 973).

  (c) Satan will be taken out of the picture, sealed in the bottomless pit for a period of a thousand years
(Rev. 20:1-3, page 1313).

See Joel 3:11-17, page 871, for **Point 49-D: The Establishment of the Millennial Kingdom.**

▽ 16 And they gathered them together to the
▲ place called in Hebrew, *Armageddon.

Seventh Bowl: The Earth Utterly Shaken

17 Then the seventh angel poured out his
bowl into the air, and a loud voice came out
of the temple of heaven, from the throne,
saying, ᴿ"It is done!"   Rev. 10:6; 21:6
18 And ᴿthere were noises and thunderings
and lightnings; ᴿand there was a great earthquake, such a mighty and great earthquake
ᴿas had not occurred since men were on the
earth.   Rev. 4:5 • Rev. 11:13 • Dan. 12:1
19 Now the great city was divided into
three parts, and the cities of the nations fell.
And great Babylon ᴿwas remembered before
God, ᴿto give her the cup of the wine of the
fierceness of His wrath.   Rev. 14:8; 18:5 • Is. 51:17
20 Then ᴿevery island fled away, and the
mountains were not found.   Rev. 6:14; 20:11
21 And great hail from heaven fell upon
men, *each hailstone* about the weight of a
ᵀtalent. Men blasphemed God because of the

plague of the hail, since that plague was ▽
exceedingly great.   75 lb. ▲

The Scarlet Woman and the Scarlet Beast

52-F. The Seven Dooms   ▼

17 Then one of the seven angels who had
the seven bowls came and talked with
me, saying *to me, "Come, ᴿI will show you
the judgment of ᴿthe great harlot ᴿwho sits
on many waters,   Rev. 16:19 • Nah. 3:4 • Jer. 51:13
2 ᴿ"with whom the kings of the earth
committed fornication, and ᴿthe inhabitants
of the earth were made drunk with the wine
of her fornication."   Rev. 2:22; 18:3, 9 • Jer. 51:7
3 So he carried me away in the Spirit ᴿinto
the wilderness. And I saw a woman sitting
ᴿon a scarlet beast *which was* full of ᴿnames
of blasphemy, having seven heads and ten
horns.   Rev. 12:6, 14; 21:10 • Rev. 12:3 • Rev. 13:1
4 The woman was arrayed in purple and
scarlet, and adorned with gold and precious
stones and pearls, having in her hand a

16:16 Lit. *Mount Megiddo*, M *Megiddo*   17:1 NU, M omit *to me*

52-F. The Seven Dooms (Revelation 17:1—20:15)—The heavenly throng now shouts "Alleluia!" for God's
judgments (19:1). Previously the heavenly martyrs anxiously cried to God, "How long, O Lord, holy and true,
until You judge and avenge our blood?" (Rev. 6:10, page 1300). These judgments are just, and necessary to
save life on the planet (Matt. 24:22, page 973).

(1) *The first doom: the harlot.* The false, harlot church will be totally corrupt (17:1–18; cf. Matt. 7:21–23,
page 946). She deceives the world (17:2), slays God's saints (17:6), and rises with Antichrist as he climbs to
power (17:3). The Antichrist's own coalition of rulers finally turns against this false church and destroys it
(17:12, 16, 17).

(2) *The second doom: Babylon.* The Antichrist builds a coastal city somewhere in the Middle East—
Babylon the Great (18:1–24, page 1311). This port city will be the center of commerce, wealth, and
wickedness (18:16–19). This city of power and persecution of the Tribulation saints is totally destroyed by
the power of God in one hour (18:17–24).

(3) *The third doom: soldiers at Armageddon and Jerusalem.* Not all the world is destroyed at
Armageddon (19:17–19, 21). The soldiers are destroyed who are enlisted from armies coming to destroy
Israel at the Antichrist's command (Zech. 14:12, 16, page 919; cf. Ezek. 39:1–12, 17, page 817).

(4) *The fourth doom: the first and second Beasts.* The Antichrist, posing as Christ, and the False Prophet
deceive the nations of the world until these two partners are cast into the eternal lake of fire (19:19, 20).

(5) *The fifth doom: Gog and Magog* (20:7–9). When Satan is released, at the end of the thousand years
of righteous government under Christ, he goes out to all the nations of the earth, gathering together all of
those who were born during the Millennium, but were never saved. They follow Satan into battle and try to
overthrow God. In this we see the influence of sin and the great power of Satan over lost humanity, as well
as the omnipotence of God to deal with the last vestige of evil on the face of planet earth.

(6) *The sixth doom: the Dragon, Satan* (20:1–3, 10). At Christ's glorious coming with His church at the
close of the seven years of this age, the Tribulation (Dan. 9:27, page 851), all three members of the false
"trinity" are captured, so that the Millennium of peace may begin. The Beast (or Antichrist) and his False
Prophet are both cast into the lake of fire; Satan is cast into a bottomless pit at the same time. Hence, he will
"deceive the nations no more till the thousand years were finished. But after these things he must be
released for a little while" (20:3) and then cast into the lake of fire where the Beast and the False Prophet are.

(7) *The seventh doom: the unsaved at the Great White Throne judgment* (20:11–15). The final doom of
all lost humanity will be the lake of fire. Here death and hell produce the lost souls for judgment. "Hell" in
Greek is *Hades,* literally "Unseen," and refers to the unseen location of the unseen dead. The believing dead go
to be "with the Lord" (2 Cor. 5:8, page 1168). That this throne is white reflects the holy, perfect, spotless
truth of God's law against sin.

Let no reader despair, however; Christ Himself invites you to live eternally (Rev. 3:20, page 1297; 22:17,
page 1316). Believe that He died for your sins, and so be saved today (see Master Outline 21, "So Great
Salvation," page 38).

See Revelation 21:1—22:7, page 1314, for **Point 52-G: The Seven New Wonders.**

▽ golden cup ᴿfull of abominations and the filthiness of *her fornication.   Rev. 14:8

5 And on her forehead a name *was* written:

ᴿMYSTERY,   2 Thess. 2:7
BABYLON THE GREAT,
THE MOTHER OF HARLOTS AND OF THE
ABOMINATIONS OF THE EARTH.

6 I saw the woman, drunk with the blood of the saints and with the blood of ᴿthe martyrs of Jesus. And when I saw her, I marveled with great amazement.   Rev. 6:9, 10

The Meaning of the Woman and the Beast

7 But the angel said to me, "Why did you marvel? I will tell you the mystery of the woman and of the beast that carries her, which has the seven heads and the ten horns.

8 "The beast that you saw was, and is not, and will ascend out of the bottomless pit and go to perdition. And those who dwell on the earth ᴿwill marvel, whose names are not written in the Book of Life from the foundation of the world, when they see the beast that was, and is not, and *yet is.   Rev. 13:3

9 ᴿ"Here *is* the mind which has wisdom: ᴿThe seven heads are seven mountains on which the woman sits.   Rev. 13:18 · Rev. 13:1

10 There are also seven kings. Five have fallen, one is, *and* the other has not yet come. And when he comes, he must ᴿcontinue a short time.   Rev. 13:5

11 "The ᴿbeast that was, and is not, is himself also the eighth, and is of the seven, and is going to ᵀperdition.   Rev. 13:3 · destruction

12 "ᴿThe ten horns which you saw are ten kings who have received no kingdom as yet, but they receive authority for one hour as kings with the beast.   Dan. 7:20

13 "These are of one mind, and they will give their power and authority to the beast.

14 ᴿ"These will make war with the Lamb, and the Lamb will ᴿovercome them, ᴿfor He is Lord of lords and King of kings; and those *who are* with Him *are* called, chosen, and faithful."   Rev. 16:14; 19:19 · Rev. 19:20 · 1 Tim. 6:15

15 Then he said to me, "The waters which you saw, where the harlot sits, ᴿare peoples, multitudes, nations, and tongues.   Rev. 13:7

16 "And the ten horns which you *saw on the beast, these will hate the harlot, make her desolate ᴿand naked, eat her flesh and ᴿburn her with fire.   Ezek. 16:37, 39 · Rev. 18:8

17 ᴿ"For God has put it into their hearts to fulfill His purpose, to be of one mind, and to give their kingdom to the beast, ᴿuntil the words of God are fulfilled.   2 Thess. 2:11 · Rev. 10:7

18 "And the woman whom you saw ᴿis that ▽ great city ᴿwhich reigns over the kings of the earth."   Rev. 11:8; 16:19 · Rev. 12:4

The Fall of Babylon the Great

18 Afterᴿ these things I saw another angel coming down from heaven, having great authority, ᴿand the earth was illuminated with his glory.   Rev. 17:1, 7 · Ezek. 43:2

2 And he cried *mightily with a loud voice, saying, "Babylon the great is fallen, is fallen, and has become a dwelling place of demons, a prison for every foul spirit, and ᴿa cage for every unclean and hated bird!   Is. 14:23

3 "For all the nations have drunk of the wine of the wrath of her fornication, the kings of the earth have committed fornication with her, ᴿand the merchants of the earth have become rich through the ᵀabundance of her luxury."   Is. 47:15 · Lit. strengths

4 And I heard another voice from heaven saying, ᴿ"Come out of her, my people, lest you share in her sins, and lest you receive of her plagues.   Is. 48:20

5 "For her sins have reached to heaven, and God has remembered her iniquities.

6 ᴿ"Render to her just as she rendered *to you, and repay her double according to her works; ᴿin the cup which she has mixed, ᴿmix double for her.   Ps. 137:8 · Rev. 14:10 · Rev. 16:19

7 "In the measure that she glorified herself and lived ᵀluxuriously, in the same measure give her torment and sorrow; for she says in her heart, 'I sit *as* queen, and am no widow, and will not see sorrow.'   sensually

8 "Therefore her plagues will come ᴿin one day—death and mourning and famine. And she will be utterly burned with fire, for strong *is* the Lord God who *judges her.   Rev. 18:10

The World Mourns Babylon's Fall

9 "The kings of the earth who committed fornication and lived luxuriously with her will weep and lament for her, ᴿwhen they see the smoke of her burning,   Rev. 19:3

10 "standing at a distance for fear of her torment, saying, ᴿ'Alas, alas, that great city Babylon, that mighty city! ᴿFor in one hour your judgment has come.'   Is. 21:9 · Rev. 18:17, 19

11 "And ᴿthe merchants of the earth will weep and mourn over her, for no one buys their merchandise anymore: Ezek. 27:27-34

12 ᴿ"merchandise of gold and silver, precious stones and pearls, fine linen and purple, silk and scarlet, every kind of citron wood, every kind of object of ivory, every kind of object of most precious wood, bronze, iron, and marble;   Rev. 17:4

17:4 M *the fornication of the earth*
17:8 NU, M *shall be present*
17:16 NU, M *saw, and the beast*

18:2 NU, M omit *mightily*
18:6 NU, M omit *to you*
18:8 NU, M *has judged*

▽ 13 "and cinnamon and incense, fragrant oil and frankincense, wine and oil, fine flour and wheat, cattle and sheep, horses and chariots, and bodies and ᴿsouls of men.   Ezek. 27:13

14 "The fruit that your soul longed for has gone from you, and all the things which are rich and splendid have *gone from you, and you shall find them no more at all.

15 "The merchants of these things, who became rich by her, will stand at a distance for fear of her torment, weeping and wailing,

16 "and saying, 'Alas, alas, ᴿthat great city ᴿthat was clothed in fine linen, purple, and scarlet, and adorned with gold and precious stones and pearls!   Rev. 17:18 • Rev. 17:4

17 'For in one hour such great riches came to nothing.' ᴿEvery shipmaster, all who travel by ship, sailors, and as many as trade on the sea, stood at a distance   Is. 23:14

18 ᴿ"and cried out when they saw the smoke of her burning, saying, ᴿ'What is like this great city?'   Ezek. 27:30 • Rev. 13:4

19 "ᴿThey threw dust on their heads and cried out, weeping and wailing, and saying, 'Alas, alas, that great city, in which all who had ships on the sea became rich by her wealth! ᴿFor in one hour she ᵀis made desolate.'   Josh. 7:6 • Rev. 18:8 • has been laid waste

20 ᴿ"Rejoice over her, O heaven, and you *holy apostles and prophets, for ᴿGod has avenged you on her!"   Jer. 51:48 • Luke 11:49

Finality of Babylon's Fall

21 Then a mighty angel took up a stone like a great millstone and threw it into the sea, saying, ᴿ"Thus with violence the great city Babylon shall be thrown down, and ᴿshall not be found anymore.   Jer. 51:63, 64 • Rev. 12:8; 16:20

22 "The sound of harpists, musicians, flutists, and trumpeters shall not be heard in you anymore. No craftsman of any craft shall be found in you anymore, and the sound of a millstone shall not be heard in you anymore.

23 "And the light of a lamp shall not shine in you anymore, and the voice of bridegroom and bride shall not be heard in you anymore. For your merchants were the great men of the earth, ᴿfor by your sorcery all the nations were deceived.   2 Kin. 9:22

24 "And ᴿin her was found the blood of prophets and saints, and of all who ᴿwere slain on the earth."   Rev. 16:6; 17:6 • Jer. 51:49

Heaven Exults over Babylon

19 After these things I *heard a loud voice of a great multitude in heaven, saying, "Alleluia! ᴿSalvation and glory and honor and power belong to *the Lord our God!   Rev. 4:11

2 "For true and righteous are His judgments, because He has judged the great harlot who corrupted the earth with her fornication; and He has avenged on her the blood of His servants shed by her."

3 Again they said, "Alleluia! ᴿHer smoke rises up forever and ever!"   Is. 34:10

4 And ᴿthe twenty-four elders and the four living creatures fell down and worshiped God who sat on the throne, saying, ᴿ"Amen! Alleluia!"   Rev. 4:4, 6, 10 • 1 Chr. 16:36

5 Then a voice came from the throne, saying, ᴿ"Praise our God, all you His servants and those who fear Him, ᴿboth* small and great!"   Ps. 134:1 • Rev. 11:18

6 ᴿAnd I heard, as it were, the voice of a great multitude, as the sound of many waters and as the sound of mighty thunderings, saying, "Alleluia! For ᴿthe* Lord God Omnipotent reigns!   Ezek. 1:24 • Rev. 11:15

7 "Let us be glad and rejoice and give Him glory, for the marriage of the Lamb has come, and His wife has made herself ready."

8 And to her it was granted to be arrayed in fine linen, clean and bright, for the fine linen is the righteous acts of the saints.

9 Then he said to me, "Write: 'Blessed are those who are called to the marriage supper of the Lamb!' " And he said to me, ᴿ"These are the true sayings of God."   Rev. 22:6

10 And I fell at his feet to worship him. But he said to me, "See that you do not do that! I am your ᴿfellow servant, and of your brethren ᴿwho have the testimony of Jesus. Worship God! For the testimony of Jesus is the spirit of prophecy."   [Heb. 1:14] • 1 John 5:10

Christ on a White Horse

11 Now I saw heaven opened, and behold, a white horse. And He who sat on him was called Faithful and True, and ᴿin righteousness He judges and makes war.   Is. 11:4

12 ᴿHis eyes were like a flame of fire, and on His head were many crowns. ᴿHe *had a name written that no one knew except Himself.   Rev. 1:14 • Rev. 2:17; 19:16

13 ᴿHe was clothed with a robe dipped in blood, and His name is called ᴿThe Word of God.   Is. 63:2, 3 • [John 1:1, 14]

14 ᴿAnd the armies in heaven, ᴿclothed in *fine linen, white and clean, followed Him on white horses.   Rev. 14:20 • Matt. 28:3

15 Now ᴿout of His mouth goes a *sharp sword, that with it He should strike the nations. And ᴿHe will rule them with a rod of iron. ᴿHe Himself treads the winepress of the fierceness and wrath of Almighty God.   Is. 11:4 • Ps. 2:8, 9 • Is. 63:3–6

18:14 NU, M been lost to you
18:20 NU, M saints and apostles
19:1 NU, M add something like • NU, M omit the Lord
19:5 NU, M omit both
19:6 NU, M our
19:12 M adds names written, and
19:14 NU, M clean white linen
19:15 M sharp two-edged

▽ 16 And ᴿHe has on *His* robe and on His thigh a name ᴿwritten: Rev. 2:17 • Dan. 2:47

KING OF KINGS
AND LORD OF LORDS.

The Beast and His Armies Defeated

17 Then I saw an angel standing in the sun; and he cried with a loud voice, saying to all the birds that fly in the midst of heaven, ᴿ"Come and gather together for the *supper of the great God,   Ezek. 39:17

18 ᴿ"that you may eat the flesh of kings, the flesh of captains, the flesh of mighty men, the flesh of horses and of those who sit on them, and the flesh of all *people,* *free and slave, both small and great."   Ezek. 39:18-20

19 ᴿAnd I saw the beast, the kings of the earth, and their armies, gathered together to make war against Him who sat on the horse and against His army.   Rev. 16:13-16

20 Then the beast was captured, and with him the false prophet who worked signs in his presence, by which he deceived those who received the mark of the beast and ᴿthose who worshiped his image. ᴿThese two were cast alive into the lake of fire ᴿburning with brimstone.   Rev. 13:8, 12, 13 • Dan. 7:11 • Rev. 14:10

21 And the rest were killed with the sword which proceeded from the mouth of Him who sat on the horse. ᴿAnd all the birds ᴿwere filled with their flesh.   Rev. 19:17, 18 • Rev. 17:16

Satan Bound 1000 Years

20 Then I saw an angel coming down from heaven, having the key to the bottomless pit and a great chain in his hand.

2 He laid hold of ᴿthe dragon, that serpent of old, who is *the* Devil and Satan, and bound him for a thousand years;   2 Pet. 2:4

3 and he cast him into the bottomless pit, and shut him up, and ᴿset a seal on him, ᴿso that he should deceive the nations no more till the thousand years were finished. But after these things he must be released for a little while.   Dan. 6:17 • Rev. 12:9; 20:8, 10

The Saints Reign with Christ 1000 Years ▽

4 And I saw ᴿthrones, and they sat on them, and ᴿjudgment was committed to them. Then *I saw* ᴿthe souls of those who had been beheaded for their witness to Jesus and for the word of God, who had not worshiped the beast or his image, and had not received *his* mark on their foreheads or on their hands. And they lived and reigned with Christ for *a thousand years.   Dan. 7:9 • [1 Cor. 6:2, 3] • Rev. 6:9

5 But the rest of the dead did not live again until the thousand years were finished. This *is* the first resurrection.

6 Blessed and holy *is* he who has part in the first resurrection. Over such ᴿthe second death has no power, but they shall be ᴿpriests of God and of Christ, and shall reign with Him a thousand years.   [Rev. 2:11; 20:14] • Is. 61:6

Satanic Rebellion Crushed

7 Now when the thousand years have expired, Satan will be released from his prison

8 and will go out ᴿto deceive the nations which are in the four corners of the earth, ᴿGog and Magog, ᴿto gather them together to battle, whose number *is* as the sand of the sea.   Rev. 12:9; 20:3, 10 • Ezek. 38:2; 39:1, 6 • Rev. 16:14

9 They went up on the breadth of the earth and surrounded the camp of the saints and the beloved city. And fire came down from God out of heaven and devoured them.

10 The devil, who deceived them, was cast into the lake of fire and brimstone ᴿwhere* the beast and the false prophet *are.* And they ᴿwill be tormented day and night forever and ever.   Rev. 19:20; 20:14, 15 • Rev. 14:10

The Great White Throne Judgment

18-E. The Judgment of the Wicked ▼

11 Then I saw a great white throne and Him who sat on it, from whose face ᴿthe earth and the heaven fled away. ᴿAnd there was found no place for them. 2 Pet. 3:7 • Dan. 2:35

12 And I saw the dead, small and great, standing before *God, and books were opened. And another book was opened,

19:17 NU, M *great supper of God*
19:18 NU, M *both free*

20:4 M *the*
20:10 NU, M *where also*
20:12 NU, M *the throne*

18-E. The Judgment of the Wicked (Revelation 20:11-15)—The Great White Throne judgment will follow the thousand-year reign of Christ. This is the final judgment, and only the wicked dead are to be judged. According to Revelation 20:5 (above), believers were resurrected a thousand years before this judgment, and their works were judged at the "judgment seat of Christ" (2 Cor. 5:10, page 1168).

(1) At this judgment the wicked dead will seek a hiding place from the face of the Lord Jesus Christ, the Judge. But there is no hiding place.

(2) At this judgment the "dead, small and great" (v. 12), will stand before God. But the greatness of the great will be of no value. "There is none who does good, no, not one" (Rom. 3:12, page 1130).

(3) At this judgment the "Book of Life" (v. 12) will be opened to show conclusively that these people are not in the Lamb's Book of Life.

(Point 18-E continued on next page)

▽ which is *the Book* of Life. And the dead were judged according to their works, by the things which were written in the books.

13 The sea gave up the dead who were in it, and Death and Hades delivered up the dead who were in them. ᴿAnd they were judged, each one according to his works.   Rev. 2:23

14 Then Death and Hades were cast into the lake of fire. This is the second *death.

20:14 NU, M *death, the lake of fire.*

15 And anyone not found written in the ▽ Book of Life was cast into the lake of fire. ▲

All Things Made New

52-G. The Seven New Wonders   ▼

21 Now ᴿI saw a new heaven and a new earth, ᴿfor the first heaven and the first earth had passed away. Also there was no more sea.   [2 Pet. 3:13] • Rev. 20:11

(Point 18-E continued from previous page)

(4) At this judgment the dead will be judged "each one according to his works" (v. 13). God is a just God, and since there are degrees of punishment in hell, some will be punished more than others (Luke 12:42–48, page 1031).

(5) At this judgment there will be no acquittal, no higher court to which the lost may appeal. They are lost, and lost forever; they are damned to all eternity, without hope. In hell there is no hope, no sympathy, no love. Even the love of God does not extend into the portals of hell.

See Index, page 17, for your next study.

52-G. The Seven New Wonders (Revelation 21:1—22:7)—We now come to that wonderful, glorious, and exciting close of this great book of the Revelation of Jesus Christ—the seven new wonders. Keep in mind that these seven new wonders will be new throughout eternity. This is the end of the Millennium and the beginning of a perfect, glorious, and holy existence with our Lord and Savior Jesus Christ in our new glorified bodies.

(1) *The new heaven* (21:1). When man sinned in the Garden of Eden, the earth and the atmospheric heaven came under the curse of sin. Satan became the "god of this age"—this world system (2 Cor. 4:4, page 1167). He also became "the prince of the power of the air"—the atmospheric heaven (Eph. 2:2, page 1187). When Satan is cast into the lake of fire, along with the Antichrist and the False Prophet, then Christ the Creator will recreate the atmospheric heaven, as well as the earth. This will be the end of destructive storms of all kinds, as well as polluted air. We do not know just how far in space the curse extends; but God's new heaven will cover the total curse. All will be new (2 Pet. 3:12, 13, page 1276).

(2) *The new earth* (21:1). "The elements will melt with fervent heat" (2 Pet. 3:10, page 1276). All traces of sin that once existed are gone forever. The earth becomes a total Garden of Eden, and there is no more sea.

(3) *The New Jerusalem* (21:2). The new Holy City comes down from God out of heaven (21:9–23). Some Bible students get confused when they read that the Holy City is the wife of the Lamb. The marriage supper is over and the Lord Jesus brings down from heaven the bride's future eternal home. This eternal home for the church, the bride, was "prepared as a bride adorned for her husband" (21:2). This magnificent city is not the wife of the Lamb until the Lamb brings his bride over the threshold into this eternal city of gold. "I go to prepare a place for you" (John 14:1–3, page 1074). This is the New Jerusalem that Jesus, after His resurrection, promised He would prepare for His bride.

(4) *The new nations* (21:24). These nations are the twelve tribes of the children of Israel, plus the saved from the antediluvian period, as well as all the saved Jews and Gentiles from the Tribulation and millennial kingdom. These inherit the earth. There is no need for sun or moon, because the presence of God's glory is the light of the new world. Everyone comes to the New Jerusalem to worship and serve the Lamb (22:3–5).

(5) *The new river* (22:1). There is no way to compare this "river of water of life" with the rivers and streams of this sin-cursed world. Fallen man has polluted the water of this world. We have nothing to compare with this crystal-clear, pure river of life that flows out to the nations of the world.

(6) *The new Tree of Life* (22:2). This tree bears twelve kinds of fruit twelve times a year, and grows on each side of the river of life. The bride of Christ and the nations of the world drink from this river and eat the fruit of the Tree of Life. This is the same tree that God planted in the Garden of Eden. When man sinned, God placed "cherubim . . . and a flaming sword" (Gen. 3:24, page 7) to keep Adam and Eve from eating from the Tree of Life and living forever in their fallen nature. But in the new Eden all the nations and the bride have access to the life-giving waters, as well as the Tree of Life which produces fruit beyond anything that man can imagine. The leaves are for the healing of the nations. There will be no sin or sickness in heaven.

(7) *The new throne* (22:3–7). There is no new temple because God reigns upon His new throne in the New Jerusalem, to be worshiped and served by the nations and the angelic host that are in His presence continually. The bride and the nations never get tired.

We may close the seven sevens of Revelation with John's prayer, "Even so, come, Lord Jesus!" (22:20). See Index, page 17, for your next study.

▽ 2 Then I, *John, saw ᴿthe holy city, New Jerusalem, coming down out of heaven from God, prepared ᴿas a bride adorned for her husband.   Is. 52:1 • 2 Cor. 11:2

3 And I heard a loud voice from heaven saying, "Behold, ᴿthe tabernacle of God *is* with men, and He will dwell with them, and they shall be His people. God Himself will be with them *and be* their God.   Lev. 26:11

4 ᴿ"And God will wipe away every tear from their eyes; there shall be no more death, ᴿnor sorrow, nor crying. There shall be no more pain, for the former things have passed away."   Is. 25:8 • Is. 35:10

5 Then ᴿHe who sat on the throne said, ᴿ"Behold, I make all things new." And He said *to me, "Write, for ᴿthese words are true and faithful."   Rev. 20:11 • Is. 43:19 • Rev. 19:9; 22:6

6 And He said to me, *"It is done! I am the Alpha and the Omega, the Beginning and the End. I will give of the fountain of the water of life freely to him who thirsts.

7 "He who overcomes *shall inherit all things, and ᴿI will be his God and he shall be My son.   Zech. 8:8

8 "But the cowardly, *unbelieving, abominable, murderers, sexually immoral, sorcerers, idolaters, and all liars shall have their part in the lake which burns with fire and brimstone, which is the second death."

The New Jerusalem

9 Then one of ᴿthe seven angels who had the seven bowls filled with the seven last plagues came *to me and talked with me, saying, "Come, I will show you ᴿthe *bride, the Lamb's wife."   Rev. 15:1 • Rev. 19:7; 21:2

10 And he carried me away ᴿin the Spirit to a great and high mountain, and showed me the *great city, the holy Jerusalem, descending out of heaven from God,   Rev. 1:10

11 ᴿhaving the glory of God. Her light *was* like a most precious stone, like a jasper stone, clear as crystal.   Rev. 15:8; 21:23; 22:5

12 Also she had a great and high wall with ᴿtwelve gates, and twelve angels at the gates, and names written on them, which are *the names* of the twelve tribes of the children of Israel: Ezek. 48:31–34

13 ᴿthree gates on the east, three gates on the north, three gates on the south, and three gates on the west.   Ezek. 48:31–34

14 Now the wall of the city had twelve foundations, and ᴿon them were the *names of the twelve apostles of the Lamb.   Eph. 2:20

15 And he who talked with me ᴿhad a gold ᵀreed to measure the city, its gates, and its wall.   Ezek. 40:3 • 10.5 ft.

16 The city is laid out as a square; its length is as great as its breadth. And he measured the city with the reed: twelve thousand ᵀfurlongs. Its length, breadth, and height are equal.   1377 mi.

17 Then he measured its wall: ᵀone hundred *and* forty-four cubits, *according to* the measure of a man, that is, of an angel.   216 ft.

18 The construction of its wall was *of* jasper; and the city *was* pure gold, like clear glass.

19 ᴿThe foundations of the wall of the city *were* adorned with all kinds of precious stones: the first foundation *was* jasper, the second sapphire, the third chalcedony, the fourth emerald,   Is. 54:11

20 the fifth sardonyx, the sixth sardius, the seventh chrysolite, the eighth beryl, the ninth topaz, the tenth chrysoprase, the eleventh jacinth, and the twelfth amethyst.

21 The twelve gates *were* twelve ᴿpearls: each individual gate was of one pearl. ᴿAnd the street of the city *was* pure gold, like transparent glass.   Matt. 13:45, 46 • Rev. 22:2

The Glory of the New Jerusalem

22 But I saw no temple in it, for the Lord God Almighty and the Lamb are its temple.

23 The city had no need of the sun or of the moon to shine *in it, for the *glory of God illuminated it. The Lamb *is* its light.

24 And the nations *of those who are saved shall walk in its light, and the kings of the earth bring *their glory and honor into it.

25 Its gates shall not be shut at all by day ᴿ(there shall be no night there).   Is. 60:20

26 ᴿAnd they shall bring the glory and honor of the nations into *it.   Rev. 21:24

27 But ᴿthere shall by no means enter it anything *that defiles, or causes an abomination or a lie, but only those who are written in the Lamb's ᴿBook of Life.   Joel 3:17 • Phil. 4:3

The River of Life

22 And he showed me a *pure river of water of life, clear as crystal, proceeding from the throne of God and of the Lamb.

2 ᴿIn the middle of its street, and on either side of the river, *was* the tree of life, which bore twelve fruits, each *tree* yielding its fruit every month. The leaves of the tree *were* for the healing of the nations.   Ezek. 47:12

▽ 3 And there shall be no more curse, but the throne of God and of the Lamb shall be in it, and His servants shall serve Him.

4 ᴿThey shall see His face, and ᴿHis name *shall be* on their foreheads.   [Matt. 5:8] • Rev. 14:1

5 There shall be no night there: They need no lamp nor light of the sun, for ᴿthe Lord God gives them light. ᴿAnd they shall reign forever and ever.   Ps. 36:9 • Dan. 7:18, 27

The Time Is Near

6 Then he said to me, ᴿ"These words *are* faithful and true." And the Lord God of the *holy prophets ᴿsent His angel to show His servants the things which must ᴿshortly take place.   Rev. 19:9 • Rev. 1:1 • Heb. 10:37

7 ᴿ"Behold, I am coming quickly! ᴿBlessed *is* he who keeps the words of the prophecy of ▲ this book."   [Rev. 3:11] • Rev. 1:3

8 Now I, John, *saw and heard these things. And when I heard and saw, ᴿI fell down to worship before the feet of the angel who showed me these things.   Rev. 19:10

9 Then he said to me, ᴿ"See *that you do* not *do that.* *For I am your fellow servant, and of your brethren the prophets, and of those who keep the words of this book. Worship God."   Rev. 19:10

10 ᴿAnd he said to me, "Do not seal the words of the prophecy of this book, ᴿfor the time is at hand.   Dan. 8:26 • Rev. 1:3

11 "He who is unjust, let him be unjust still; he who is filthy, let him be filthy still; he who

is righteous, let him *be righteous still; he who is holy, let him be holy still."

Jesus Testifies to the Churches

12 "And behold, I am coming quickly, and ᴿMy reward *is* with Me, ᴿto give to every one according to his work.   Is. 40:10 • Rev. 20:12

13 ᴿ"I am the Alpha and the Omega, *the* *Beginning and *the* End, the First and the Last."   Is. 41:4

14 Blessed *are* those *who *do His commandments, that they may have the right ᴿto the tree of life, ᴿand may enter through the gates into the city.   [Prov. 11:30] • Rev. 21:27

15 *But outside *are* dogs and sorcerers and sexually immoral and murderers and idolaters, and whoever loves and practices a lie.

16 "I, Jesus, have sent My angel to testify to you these things in the churches. ᴿI am the Root and the Offspring of David, ᴿthe Bright and Morning Star."   Rev. 5:5 • Num. 24:17

21-E. So Great in Invitation   ▼

17 And the Spirit and ᴿthe bride say, "Come!" And let him who hears say, "Come!" ᴿAnd let him who thirsts come. Whoever desires, let him take the water of life freely.   [Rev. 21:2, 9] • Is. 55:1 ▲

A Warning

18 *For I testify to everyone who hears the words of the prophecy of this book: If anyone

22:11 NU, M *do right*
22:13 NU, M *First and the Last, the Beginning and the End.*
22:14 NU *wash their robes,*
22:15 NU, M omit *But*
22:18 NU, M omit *For*

22:6 NU, M *spirits of the prophets*
22:8 NU, M *am the one who heard and saw*
22:9 NU, M omit *For*

21-E. So Great in Invitation (Revelation 22:17)—The time is coming when God, in love, will extend the last invitation for the lost to come and be saved by His grace. Before John closed the last book of the Bible (The Revelation of Jesus Christ), it is as though God said, "John, give the invitation one more time for the lost to come and be saved," for in verse 17 John wrote:

(1) *"And the Spirit and the bride say, 'Come!' "* The Holy Spirit, who indwells the bride (the church), will invite the lost to come and receive Christ and be saved.

(2) *"And let him who hears say, 'Come!' "* All who are saved at the time of the last invitation will join the Spirit and the bride by inviting others to come and be saved.

(3) *"And let him who thirsts come."* Jesus gave the same invitation in the temple almost two thousand years ago. He said, "If anyone thirsts, let him come to Me and drink" (John 7:37, page 1061). At Jacob's well Jesus said to the Samaritan woman, "Whoever drinks of this water will thirst again, but whoever drinks of the water that I shall give him will never thirst. But the water that I shall give him will become in him a fountain of water springing up into everlasting life" (John 4:13, 14, page 1053). When you accept God's invitation to come to Christ by faith, and drink the Water of Life, God's promise is that you "will never thirst." In other words, salvation through Jesus Christ satisfies forever. "Whoever desires, let him take the water of life freely" (v. 17). Salvation is free, but not cheap. It cost the Lord Jesus Christ His life's blood.

The apostle Peter tells us that we are "not redeemed [bought back from Satan and sin] with corruptible things, like silver or gold, . . . but with the precious blood of Christ, as of a lamb without blemish and without spot" (1 Pet. 1:18, 19, page 1263). The blood of Jesus is precious because

(1) it cleanses you from all your sins—not some, but all—past, present, and future (1 John 1:7, page 1278);

(2) without the shed blood of Jesus, there is no remission (forgiveness) of sin (Heb. 9:22, page 1244);

(3) Jesus loved us and washed us from all our sins in His own blood (Rev. 1:5, page 1293).

(Point 21-E continued on next page)

adds to these things, *God will add to him the plagues that are written in this book;

19 and if anyone takes away from the words of the book of this prophecy, ᴿGod* shall take away his part from the *Book of Life, from the holy city, and *from the things which are written in this book.   Ex. 32:33

22:18 M *may God add*
22:19 M *may God take away* • NU, M *tree of life*

I Am Coming Quickly

20 He who testifies to these things says, "Surely I am coming quickly." Amen. Even so, come, Lord Jesus!

21 The grace of our Lord Jesus Christ *be* *with you all. Amen.

22:21 NU *with all;* M *with all the saints*

(Point 21-E continued from previous page)

The Philippian jailer brought Paul and Silas out of prison into the outer court of the jail and said, "Sirs, what must I do to be saved?" His question revealed to them that this man was ready to accept Christ by faith as his personal Savior. Their answer to his question was simple, to the point, and yet profound: "Believe on the Lord Jesus Christ, and you will be saved, you and your household." So the jailer and his family believed on the Lord Jesus Christ and were given eternal salvation (Acts 16:25–34, page 1110).

When you believe on the Lord Jesus Christ and accept Him as your personal Savior, you will be saved immediately and eternally. "He who believes in the Son [Jesus Christ] has [present tense] everlasting life; and he who does not believe the Son shall not see life, but the wrath of God abides on him" (John 3:36, page 1053).

See 2 Timothy 1:12, page 1224, for **Point 21-F: So Great in Assurance.**

SUBJECT INDEX

The Subject Index is a guide to topics found in the Christian Life Master Outlines and Study Notes and to the introductions to each book of the Bible. Page numbers refer to the pages on which the cited outline points or book introductions begin.

THE INTERTESTAMENTAL PERIOD

When God delivered His final message through Malachi, He paused in His communications through man for nearly four hundred years. A deafening silence in divine revelation resulted.

No doubt the silence of God gave rise to many theories about His nature. Some might have demanded that He act as He had always acted. Others might have surmised that man was too sinful to hear from God (this is always an absurdity since *any* sin is an affront to God and apart from grace He would not have communed with any person or generation *before* Malachi's time, let alone after). Still others might have suggested, and quite strongly so, that man's lack of faith was the cause of God's silence and apparent inactivity.

None of these theories would have taken into account the omniscience and sovereignty of Jehovah God. His determined, covenantal love (Hebrew *hesed*) had already set His course. This long silence was part of His eternal plan. He had spoken on numerous occasions and through various people, but He was now preparing to speak His greatest and most powerful Word to mankind: Jesus. A pause—a long and distinct pause—would add emphasis to that monumental revelation.

The ways of God are certainly beyond the complete grasp of man. "For as the heavens are higher than the earth, so are My ways higher than your ways, and My thoughts than your thoughts" (Is. 55:9). But the Architect of this universe is not without order and symmetry in His work, even in His dealings with finite, fickle human beings. Occasionally that order may be discerned.

A brief review of the way God ministered to man during the years chronicled in the Old Testament is very instructive. A consistent pattern of action emerges from the accounts recorded through the Holy Spirit's inspiration. Such consistency in the past sheds light upon the workings of God during what may be called the Intertestamental Period.

Two things stand out. First, God generally designed or allowed a *desperate situation* to arise before presenting His message or providing His deliverance. Secondly, He always called upon a *faithful servant* to "stand in the gap," making intercession to Him on behalf of the people (Ezek. 22:30), and to be His agent through whom He performed His work.

Consider the terrible conditions that prevailed in antediluvian society. God expressed regret that He had even created man (Gen. 6:6). Against the backdrop of this dark, dismal scene, the Bible declares: "But Noah found grace in the eyes of the LORD" (Gen. 6:8). Thus we have a desperate situation, and God's faithful servant.

This pattern was repeated with Abraham in God's calling of a chosen people out of a human race enmeshed in pride and idolatry. It appeared again with Joseph in the sparing of Israel from famine. Moses was another deliverer, who came just in time to rescue God's people from apparently impossible circumstances. The same theme runs through the book of Judges, and continues to appear in such lives as Esther and Nehemiah.

In each of these examples, and others like them, the efforts of man had to be frustrated before divine intervention ensued. The recorded history of the Intertestamental Period points to a similar experience. It seems that God allowed His people to exhaust their resources and to be reduced to another desperate situation before He brought to the scene His most faithful and only perfect Servant, His Son Jesus Christ.

THE PERIOD IN QUESTION

If the book of Malachi was completed in 397 B.C., then the period under consideration begins at that point and continues until the angel's announcement of the birth of John the Baptist (Luke 1:11–17). Throughout this four-hundred-year span of time there were no prophets and no inspired writers of divine revelation.

Six historical divisions are observable. The Persian Era, which actually dates all the way back to 536 B.C. but coincides with the Intertestamental Period from 397 to 336 B.C.; the Greek Era (336–323 B.C.); the Egyptian Era (323–198 B.C.); the Syrian Era (198–165 B.C.); the Maccabean Era

(165–63 B.C.); and the Roman Era (63–4 B.C.). This study will be presented chronologically according to these six divisions. Attention will be given to the historical situation and the religious developments within each segment.

THE PERSIAN ERA (397–336 B.C.)

Historical Situation

As has already been noted, the Persians were the dominating power in the Middle East as far back as 536 B.C. God had used the Persians to deliver Israel from the Babylonian captivity (Dan. 5:30, 31).

Persia's attitude was tolerant toward the Jewish remnant in Palestine, until internal rivalry over the politically powerful office of high priest resulted in partial destruction of Jerusalem by the Persian governor. Otherwise the Jewish people were left undisturbed during this period.

Religious Developments

The Babylonian captivity was used by God to purge idolatry from His people. They returned to Jerusalem with a new reverence for the Scriptures, especially the law of Moses. They also had a firm grasp on the theological concept of monotheism. These two influences carried over into the Intertestamental Period.

The rise of the *synagogue* as the local center of worship can be traced back to this period. *Scribes* became very important for the interpretation of the Scriptures in the synagogue services. By the time Jesus was born, the synagogue was well developed in organization and was widely spread throughout the Jewish communities of the world.

Another development that affected the spread of the gospel during New Testament times had its origin toward the end of the Persian rule. A temple was founded in Samaria, establishing a form of worship that rivaled Judaism. That event encouraged the ultimate social and religious separation between Jew and Samaritan.

THE GREEK ERA (336–323 B.C.)

Historical Situation

Alexander the Great, in many respects the greatest conqueror of all time, was the central figure of this brief period. He conquered Persia, Babylon, Palestine, Syria, Egypt, and western India. Although he died at the age of thirty-three, having reigned over Greece only thirteen years, his influence lived long after him.

Religious Developments

The cherished desire of Alexander was to found a worldwide empire united by language, custom, and civilization. Under his influence the world began to speak and study the Greek language. This process, called Hellenization, included the adoption of Greek culture and religion in all parts of the world. Hellenism became so popular that it persisted and was encouraged even into New Testament times by the Romans.

The struggle that developed between the Jews and Hellenism's influence upon their culture and religion was long and bitter. Although the Greek language was sufficiently widespread by 270 B.C. to bring about a Greek translation of the Old Testament (the Septuagint), faithful Jews staunchly resisted pagan polytheism.

THE EGYPTIAN ERA (323–198 B.C.)

Historical Situation

With the death of Alexander in 323 B.C., the Greek empire became divided into four segments under as many generals: Ptolemy, Lysimachus, Cassander, and Selenus. These were Daniel's "four kingdoms" which took the place of the "large horn" (Dan. 8:21, 22).

Ptolemy Soter, the first of the Ptolemaic dynasty, received Egypt and soon dominated nearby Israel. He dealt severely with the Jews at first, but toward the end of his reign and on into the rule of Ptolemy Philadelphus, his successor, the Jews were treated favorably. It was during this time that the Septuagint was authorized.

The Jews prospered until near the end of the Ptolemaic dynasty when conflicts between Egypt and Syria escalated. Israel was again caught in the middle. When the Syrians defeated Egypt in the Battle of Panion in 198 B.C., Judea was annexed to Syria.

Religious Developments

The policy of toleration followed by the Ptolemies, by which Judaism and Hellenism coexisted peacefully, was very dan-

gerous for the Jewish faith. A gradual infiltration of Greek influence and an almost unnoticed assimilation of the Greek way of life took place.

Hellenism's emphasis on beauty, shape, and movement encouraged Jews to neglect Jewish religious rites which were aesthetically unappealing. Thus worship was influenced to become more external than internal, a notion that had a lasting impact upon Judaism.

Two religious parties emerged: the Hellenizing party, which was pro-Syrian, and the orthodox Jews, in particular the Hasidim or "Pious Ones" (predecessors of the Pharisees). A struggle for power between these two groups resulted in a polarization of the Jews along political, cultural, and religious lines. It was this same conflict that brought about the attack of Antiochus Epiphanes in 168 B.C.

THE SYRIAN ERA (198-165 B.C.)

Historical Situation

Under the rule of Antiochus the Great and his successor Seleucus Philopater, the Jews, though treated harshly, were nonetheless allowed to maintain local rule under their high priest. All went well until the Hellenizing party decided to have their favorite, Jason, appointed to replace Onias III, the high priest favored by the orthodox Jews, and to bring this about by bribing Seleucus's successor, Antiochus Epiphanes. This set off a political conflict that finally brought Antiochus to Jerusalem in a fit of rage.

In 168 B.C. Antiochus set about destroying every distinctive characteristic of the Jewish faith. He forbade all sacrifices, outlawed the rite of circumcision, and canceled observance of the Sabbath and feast days. The Scriptures were mutilated or destroyed. Jews were forced to eat pork and to sacrifice to idols. His final act of sacrilege, and the one that spelled his ultimate ruin, was to desecrate the Most Holy Place by building an altar and offering a sacrifice to the god Zeus. Many Jews died in the ensuing persecutions.

Perhaps a reminder of God's way of working with man is needed at this point. He creates or allows a desperate situation, then calls upon a special, faithful servant.

However, man often attempts to rescue himself and seems to be almost at the point of success only to wind up in worse shape than before. This was about to happen in the life of God's people the Jews. God was simply setting the stage for the coming of the true Deliverer.

Religious Developments

As can be seen by the historical developments of this period, the Jewish religion was divided over the issue of Hellenism. The groundwork was laid for an orthodox party, generally led by the scribes and later called the Pharisees, and for what we may call a more pragmatic faction of Jews which became more or less associated with the office of high priest. The pattern of thinking upon which the latter group was based fostered the rise of the Sadducees at a later date.

THE MACCABEAN ERA (165-63 B.C.)

Historical Situation

An elderly priest named Mattathias, of the house of Hasmon, lived with his five sons in the village of Modein, northwest of Jerusalem. When a Syrian official tried to enforce heathen sacrifice in Modein, Mattathias revolted, killed a renegade Jew who did offer sacrifice, slew the Syrian official, and fled to the mountains with his family. Thousands of faithful Jews joined him, and history records one of the most noble demonstrations of holy jealousy for the honor of God.

After the death of Mattathias three of his sons carried on the revolt in succession: Judas surnamed Maccabaeus (166-160 B.C.), Jonathan (160-142 B.C.), and Simon (143-134 B.C.). These men had such success that by December 25, 165 B.C., they had retaken Jerusalem, cleansed the temple, and restored worship. This event is commemorated even today as the Feast of Hanukkah (Dedication).

Fighting continued in the outlying areas of Judea with several futile attempts by Syria to defeat the Maccabeans. Finally, under the leadership of Simon, the Jews received their independence (142 B.C.). They experienced almost seventy years of independence under the reign of the Hasmonaean dynasty, the most notable leaders of

which were John Hyrcanus (134–104 B.C.) and Alexander Jannaeus (102–76 B.C.).

Religious Developments

The most significant religious development of this period resulted from a strong difference of opinion concerning the kingship and high priesthood of Judea. For hundreds of years the position of high priest had taken on some very obvious political overtones. Emphasis had not been upon the Aaronite line but upon political strength. Orthodox Jews resented and resisted this development. When John Hyrcanus became governor and high priest of Israel, he conquered Transjordan and Idumaea and destroyed the Samaritan temple. His power and popularity led him to refer to himself as a king. This flew in the face of the orthodox Jews, who by this time were called Pharisees. They recognized no king unless he was of the lineage of David, and the Hasmonaeans were not.

Those who opposed the Pharisees and supported the Hasmonaeans were called Sadducees. These names appeared for the first time during the reign of John Hyrcanus who himself became a Sadducee.

THE ROMAN ERA (63–4 B.C.)

Historical Situation

The independence of the Jews ended in 63 B.C., when Pompey of Rome took Syria and entered Israel. Aristobulus II, claiming to be the king of Israel, locked Pompey out of Jerusalem. The Roman leader in anger took the city by force and reduced the size of Judea. Israel's attempt at freedom from oppression had paid off for a while, but now all hope seemed to be lost.

Antipater the Idumaean was appointed procurator of Judea by Julius Caesar in 47 B.C. Herod, the son of Antipater, eventually became the king of the Jews around 40 B.C.

Although Herod the Great, as he was called, planned and carried out the building of the new temple in Jerusalem, he was a devoted Hellenist and hated the Hasmonaean family. He killed every descendant of the Hasmonaeans, even his own wife Marianne, the granddaughter of John Hyrcanus. Then he proceeded to murder his own two sons by Marianne, Aristobulus and Alexander. This is the man on the throne when Jesus was born in Bethlehem. What a dark and desperate situation for God's people!

Religious Developments

The rise of the Pharisees and Sadducees has already been mentioned. Before moving on to a discussion of three other important parties, some attention needs to be given to these two major groups.

(1) *The Pharisees* were so named early in the reign of John Hyrcanus. The name means "Separatists." They depended heavily upon the scribes and were loyal to the law and religion of Jehovah. Their emphasis upon the strict adherence to the Scriptures led to a strong attachment to the "oral law," or Mishnah, which sought to apply the written law to everyday life.

During the earthly ministry of Jesus, the "oral law" was so rigid with legalistic expansions that it usually had little to do with the original intent of Scripture. What started out to be a very wholesome and much-needed dependence on the Word of God deteriorated to a formalism and legalism that denied the spirit of the Word.

(2) *The Sadducees* derived their name from the word *Zadokites* or maybe from the Hebrew word *tsaddik*, meaning "righteous." Whereas the Pharisees were strongly connected with the scribes, the Sadducees were related to the high priest. The priests seem to have tended toward the more social, political, and earthly aspects of their position. This pattern of thinking was attractive to many of the more socially minded Jewish leaders.

Numerically a much smaller party than the Pharisees, the Sadducees belonged mostly to the wealthy influential priestly families who formed the social aristocracy of the Jewish nation. They felt that God's law and a nation's politics were totally separate. In other words, they saw no relationship between the need for holiness and the destiny of their nation. Religion was religion; politics was politics. They were therefore very skeptical of the Pharisees and seemingly concluded that the latter were old-fashioned, irrelevant, and fanatical.

(3) *The Herodians* emerged during the Roman Era (Matt. 22:16). This was a politi-

cal party whose major aim was to further the cause of Herod's government. They were perhaps motivated by a fear of the Roman government and the possibility of total destruction that could result from an act of rebellion on the part of the Jews. They were strongly inclined toward Hellenism and were opposed to the Pharisees and their constant emphasis on separation.

(4) *The Zealots* (or "Cananaeans," from the Aramaic *kanna'ah*, "zealous"—"Canaanites" in the NKJV New Testament) were also a political party but were in direct opposition to the Herodians. They would not conform to Roman rule, and they did not believe in waiting submissively like the Pharisees until Israel's Messiah would come and overthrow the Romans. In their opinion God only helped those who helped themselves. The Jews must be ready to fight for independence.

To a Pharisee-like fanaticism for the letter of the law, the Zealots added a fiery nationalistic spirit. The teachings of this group stressed a type of man-made, military deliverance rather than divine intervention.

(5) *The Essenes* were also a product of the Roman Era. They are not mentioned in the New Testament but have received considerable attention since the discovery of the Dead Sea Scrolls.

This group of people was religious, not political. They were a type of pseudospiritual cult which felt that they must withdraw from ordinary human society and practice a monastic kind of life and a mystical kind of Judaism.

With a passion for the spirit of the law and a separation to God, the Essenes lost all consciousness of the evangelistic mission of Israel. They were content to lock out the world, ignore its problems, and let it die without hope.

CONCLUSION

The stage was set. Man's futile attempts to deal with the shifting tide of political power and religious belief had produced very little. Israel was in a kind of spiritual bondage that was even worse than her political bondage. The rise of the various parties and movements discussed above was evidence of a sincere search for some final solution to her problem. All seemed to have failed. The stage of history was dark. The situation was indeed desperate.

Amid this setting God broke four hundred years of silence with the announcement of the coming of Christ, the faithful Servant of the Lord, and the Intertestamental Period came to an end.

—J.E.J.

BACKSLIDING:
ITS CAUSE AND CURE

"Oh, where is the joy I knew when first I found the Lord?" This is the question that is on the hearts of many Christians today. "If only I could feel the way I felt right after I was saved!" "I want to see people saved, but I am not fruitful so far as my own personal witness is concerned." "I don't have the desire for prayer and fellowship with God that I once had." "My life and ministry is no longer one of peace, joy, and faith, as it once was."

These statements, and others like them too numerous to mention, are the honest confessions of many in the church today. Many others in the church feel this way but are not honest enough to admit it. They go on wearing themselves out in the service of the Lord, trying to make up in zeal what they lack in the Spirit. All these have ceased to progress in their growth as Christians, and have instead fallen back to a lower level of maturity, if not back to the bottom of the ladder. In a word, they have become *backsliders*.

Many have given up on the Christian life and are now back in the world. Were these truly saved? Possibly they were not. Before you can backslide, you must have something to backslide *from*. A backslider is one who has known the real thing. He has been born again. He has walked in the Spirit. He has received Christ as Savior and Lord. A backslider loses his fellowship with God, but not his salvation.

Many think of a backslider as one who commits murder, adultery, fornication, blasphemy, or some other gross sin. These and other sins, however, are but the results or evidence of a backslidden condition. Backsliding begins in the heart, although if it is not confessed and forsaken it will be noticeable in our lives in a very short time.

Giving in to self-interest—the center of our lives before we are saved—and to Satan's enticements sends us back in the direction of the old life. Old friends, old habits, old excuses begin to come back. We no longer have the desire we once had for fellowship with other Christians. We once lived our lives in and around the church, but now it is easy to find something that is

more "important" than fellowship with others who love the Lord Jesus Christ. We once read the Bible personally, and with our families, but we no longer make this a priority. We are no longer sensitive to the little sins over which God once broke our hearts. Our burden for people who are lost is gone, or, if we are interested in others, we no longer have the compassion that once marked our lives and our ministry.

How is it with you? Do you see yourself in some of these questions and observations? If so, you need not despair. There is indeed a way back to fellowship with God. Before we look at the way back, however, let us examine:

THE CAUSE OF BACKSLIDING

In Luke 22:31–34 we see the spirit of Simon Peter before the death, burial and resurrection of our Lord:

> And the Lord said, "Simon, Simon! Indeed, Satan has asked for you, that he may sift you as wheat. But I have prayed for you, that your faith should not fail; and when you have returned to Me, strengthen your brethren."
> But he said to Him, "Lord, I am ready to go with You, both to prison and to death."
> Then He said, "I tell you, Peter, the rooster shall not crow this day before you will deny three times that you know Me."

What did Peter say after Jesus warned and encouraged him? He simply said what the flesh always says: "Lord Jesus, *I* have what it takes. Within myself, because I am Your loyal friend and follower, I am prepared to follow You to prison and even to the grave—to die with You—if that is what You want. I love You, Lord Jesus; I'm behind You all the way." Jesus was not impressed; He told Peter exactly what would happen.

Simon Peter is the typical picture of the attitude and resulting behavior of those who are about to backslide. When self is on the throne of our lives, when Jesus is not allowed to be Lord of every circumstance,

backsliding always results. Let us look at the account of Peter during his time of crisis, and let us see if we are not looking at ourselves as we are motivated by our old nature instead of the "new nature" (the very nature of Christ Himself) which we received when we were born again. In this account we will find *seven ways to backslide.*

The First Way: Boast of Loyalty to Christ

Peter answered and said to Him, "Even if all are made to stumble because of You, I will never be made to stumble."

Jesus said to him, "Assuredly, I say to you that this night, before the rooster crows, you will deny Me three times."

Peter said to Him, "Even if I have to die with You, I will not deny You!"

And so said all the disciples.

—Matthew 26:33-35

Proverbs 27:1 says: "Do not boast about tomorrow, for you do not know what a day may bring forth." Even as Peter was boasting he forgot this admonition, and Jesus reminded him that before the rooster crowed to announce the dawn he would have denied the very One to whom he now proclaimed his loyalty. *Pride and boasting go together like twins.* Consider these four prides:

(1) *Pride of race.* Study the tenth chapter of Acts (especially Acts 10:28) and see how God had to send a vision to take the racial prejudice out of Peter the Jew before He could use him to preach Christ to Cornelius the Gentile and his company.

(2) *Pride of place.* Luke 18:9-14 gives us the parable of the Pharisee and the tax collector. Because of his self-righteousness the Pharisee could not get his prayer answered. He had held an exalted place in the temple for so long that he had forgotten the attitude necessary to approach God in prayer. A friend of mine once said, "A lot of people would not look so small if they were not so highly placed." A real servant of God can serve the Lord in any role, at any time, to the glory of God—with no need or desire for the applause of men.

(3) *Pride of face.* Proverbs 6:16-19 tells us seven things God hates, and at the top of the list is "a proud look." The look of pride can make the most beautiful face ugly, and the look of humility can make the ugliest face beautiful. Be thankful for the face God gave you, because it is the exact one He wanted you to have—but make sure you adorn it with humility. Pray that all may see the peace and contentment of Christ Himself on your face in all of life's circumstances.

(4) *Pride of grace.* This is the worst of the four prides: to be haughty because of what God has done in you through Christ. Paul demanded of the argumentative Corinthians, "Who makes you differ from another? And what do you have that you did not receive? Now if you did indeed receive it, why do you boast as if you had not received it?" (1 Cor. 4:7).

Never have an inflated religious ego that looks askance at a weaker brother or sister. If anyone had anything to glory in or brag about, then certainly Paul did. Yet to his followers he said, "By the grace of God I am what I am, and His grace toward me was not in vain; but I labored more abundantly than they all, yet not I, but the grace of God which was with me" (1 Cor. 15:10). To Timothy his son in the ministry he wrote, "[God] has saved us and called us with a holy calling, not according to our works, but according to His own purpose and grace which was given to us in Christ Jesus before time began (2 Tim. 1:9).

If Paul bragged about anything, it was his weaknesses! "And He said to me, 'My grace is sufficient for you, for My strength is made perfect in weakness.' Therefore most gladly I will rather boast in my infirmities, that the power of Christ may rest upon me. Therefore I take pleasure in infirmities, in reproaches, in needs, in persecutions, in distresses, for Christ's sake. For when I am weak, then I am strong" (2 Cor. 12:9, 10).

There is no room at all for pride and boasting about anything we have done, will do, or ever dream of doing. Even our faith is a gift of God, made available when we repent and receive Christ as our Lord and Savior. Ephesians 2:8-10 says it all: "For by grace you have been saved through faith, and that not of yourselves; it is the gift of God, not of works, lest anyone should boast. For we are His workmanship, created in Christ Jesus for good

works, which God prepared beforehand that we should walk in them."

The Second Way: Always Seek the Easy Way Out in the Christian Life

> Then He came to the disciples and found them sleeping, and said to Peter, "What! Could you not watch with Me one hour?"
> ...And He came and found them asleep again, for their eyes were heavy.
>
> —Matthew 26:40, 43

Peter had been instructed to "watch" with Jesus while He prayed concerning the death He was about to die. But three times our Lord went away to pray and came back to find them asleep. This was a time to be alert, for He had warned them of the coming arrest and trial, and they needed to be with Him in this time of crisis. But they chose instead to give in to their weariness and slept.

How many of us take the easy way out in our lives and ministry? When your doctor tells you to slow down, this gives the excuse you have been looking for to give up your Sunday School class. I have had people tell me that the reason they don't attend church anymore is that their doctor told them to avoid crowds. And yet I have watched the same people get excited and wear themselves out with hobbies, sporting events, or whatever else they like to do.

I can't be too hard on Peter and the rest of the disciples at this point in their lives. They didn't have the facts that we have today. They didn't understand that Jesus had to die that they might live. They were living on the other side of the Resurrection. Pentecost had not yet come. They had been walking with Jesus, but they didn't know the power of having Jesus alive within them, as we know Him today. We, on the other hand, do not have this excuse.

In light of all that we know and have experienced as born-again believers, how can we seek the easy way out in the Christian life? How can we become insensitive to the needs of others? How can we allow the sharp edge of commitment to Christ and obedience to the Word of God to become dulled by selfishness and unconfessed sin in our lives?

The Lord Jesus does promise us rest, if we pursue it in the right way. In Matthew 11:28-30 He says, "Come to Me, all you who labor and are heavy laden, and I will give you rest. Take My yoke upon you and learn from Me, for I am gentle and lowly in heart, and you will find rest for your souls. For My yoke is easy and My burden is light." Living in the will of God, enjoying the salvation that comes to us apart from works, is rest indeed. (Learn more about it by studying Hebrews 4.) What a blessing it is to know the "rest" that is ours as we allow Christ to control our lives.

Satan knows how and when to attack us in this regard. Many of us are easygoing by nature and find it easy to relate to people and go along with the crowd. We don't want to hurt anyone's feelings, so we compromise our convictions. Some of us are headstrong and impulsive by nature. Others are moody and quiet. I know people who are perfectionists in all they do. Satan seeks to use these natural strengths and weaknesses to his advantage. Call the roll of the Old Testament and you will find that many of the great men of God gave in to their weakness and suffered the consequences in their life and walk with God. This brings us to the reason for Peter's failure.

The Third Way: Live a Prayerless Christian Life

> Then He came to His disciples and said to them, "Are you still sleeping and resting? Behold, the hour is at hand, and the Son of Man is being betrayed into the hands of sinners."
>
> —Matthew 26:45

Since they had been sleeping and taking it easy when they could have been praying, it was now too late to make a difference. In verse 41 Jesus had told them to "watch and pray, lest you enter into temptation. The spirit indeed is willing, but the flesh is weak."

Those who meet life prayerless find themselves powerless in the hour of temptation. The backsliding Christian takes his first step toward defeat when he starts leaving off prayer and Bible study on a personal, daily basis. Jesus himself found it necessary to slip away and pray on a regular basis. He instructed his disciples, "But

you, when you pray, go into your room, and when you have shut your door, pray to your Father who is in the secret place; and your Father who sees in secret will reward you openly" (Matt. 6:6).

Attending prayer meetings and church services and doing Christian work are never substitutes for prayer. Many so-called great Christian workers have worn themselves out in the flesh doing the Lord's work and have confessed that the weariness all started when they became lax in their prayer life.

Prayer is the only avenue we have to communicate with God. More has been written about prayer than nearly any subject in the Bible, and yet many seem to have this attitude: "Why spend time in prayer, when God knows what you are going to ask for and He knows how He is going to answer before you pray?" In other words, what is to be will be whether you pray or not. Thus they betray their ignorance of the place given to prayer in the Scriptures and in the history of the church. God earnestly desires our prayers, and acts in response to them. What is more, He desires for us to pray because in doing so we keep ourselves open to His voice and the leading of His Spirit. What a difference it would make if we taught our children to pray! There is not enough emphasis put on prayer and Bible study in our homes. A person with a healthy prayer life cannot stay backslidden very long.

What place did prayer occupy in the life of Jesus? What place did prayer occupy in the early church? The answer, of course, is *first place*. What place does prayer occupy in your life?

The following illustration has meant a lot to me through the years. Supposing someone were to come to you representing a syndicate that had enough money to do anything they wanted to do—to purchase anything in the world—and this person said to you, "I'm buying up prayer rights. How much would you take for your right to pray for the next year?" Most of us would be insulted that anyone would even suggest such a horrible transaction. Let's be honest with ourselves, though. How many of us have used our right to pray unselfishly and decisively this past year, this past month, this past week, or even today?

The right of access to God in prayer is priceless. Those who have learned to "pray without ceasing" and to pray in light of the Scriptures and the promises of God are the ones who know what real fellowship with Him is all about.

The Fourth Way: Serve the Lord in the Energy of the Flesh

> Then Simon Peter, having a sword, drew it and struck the high priest's servant, and cut off his right ear. The servant's name was Malchus.
>
> —John 18:10

Most carnal, backslidden Christians would be like Peter—they would feel that Jesus needs help. Peter saw Jesus in danger, drew his sword, and cut off the ear of one named Malchus. Many scholars believe his intent was to cut off Malchus's head.

There is no doubt in my mind that Simon Peter thought he was meeting the need of the hour. He had said he was prepared to die with Jesus, and this is proof as far as he is concerned. But Jesus didn't need Peter's help; it was Peter who needed the help of Jesus. Jesus will not call on many of us to die for Him, but all are called upon to live His resurrection life on a moment-by-moment basis. What a liberating truth it is that *it's not what I do that pleases God, it's what I allow Him to do through me that really counts.*

What are my resources as I serve God? Am I living and working after His leading and with His resources? Or am I acting "in the flesh"—on my own initiative, using my own ideas and methods?

Satan's big lie is that *we* have what it takes to live the Christian life. But listen to Proverbs 3:5: "Trust in the LORD with all your heart, and do not lean on your own understanding." The Christian life is a supernatural life that cannot be explained in terms of human wisdom and understanding. Simon Peter acted by drawing a sword because he saw men coming with swords. Our human understanding says that we need to "fight fire with fire." If force were needed, however, Jesus could have called thousands of angels to come and defend Him. But He was sent from God to be totally available to all that God had in mind

for His life. For us to live the quality of life that God has in mind, we must be totally available to all that Christ is in our daily lives.

The only person who ever lived and served in a way that was acceptable to God is Jesus the Son of God. The only person ever to live the Christian life is Jesus the Christ. Jesus wants to live His resurrection life in us and through us to the glory of God. As this begins to happen we no longer have any need to get glory for what we do. God gets the glory for everything that we will do in *His* way and for *His* glory. All else is wood, hay, and straw, and will be burned up at the judgment seat of Christ (1 Cor. 3:12-15).

Many are backslidden and do not know it. They have been preaching in the flesh, teaching in the flesh, attempting to win souls in the flesh, and running the church in the flesh for so long that if there were no God they would never know the difference. What has happened in your life lately that can only be accounted for by the resurrection power of the indwelling Christ? The all-powerful Son of God does not need defending with the sword or any other weapon of the flesh. Jesus wants to clothe our humanity with His divinity in such a way that mere humans cannot explain our lives in any other way except to say that we have been born again, that we have become new creatures in Christ Jesus. But by contrast, many are applying merely human devices to the church, using Madison Avenue techniques to insure the success of the work of the Lord.

Let's refresh ourselves with the Word of God. "Are you so foolish? Having begun in the Spirit, are you now being made perfect by the flesh?" (Gal. 3:3). "For the flesh lusts against the Spirit, and the Spirit against the flesh; and these are contrary to one another, so that you do not do the things that you wish" (Gal. 5:17). No matter what God wants us to do, or how He wants it done, the flesh always has a "better way." Anything that derives from the lower nature and the self-directed life, no matter how outstanding its results may be, is *fleshly*—and abhorrent to God.

Most of the world's religions tell men to *do something* (perform rituals, recite formulas, do good works, etc.) and God will be pleased. This attitude has crept into the thinking of men who call themselves Christians. But neither salvation and service are by human means. Both are from the Lord, that God might be glorified and that Christ might have preeminence.

Many have backslidden because no one bothered to teach them how to be filled with the Spirit, how to walk in the Spirit, and how to serve God from a standpoint of spiritual rest. "I say then: Walk in the Spirit, and you shall not fulfill the lust of the flesh" (Gal. 5:16). People who serve God in the flesh eventually wear out, get discouraged, and finally drop by the wayside. If they stay in the church they become more addicted to doing God's work in the flesh, and as a result wear everyone else out.

If you find that you are working from human motivations, with human methods, seeking human glory, or otherwise doing the work of the Lord in the flesh, take a moment right now to confess this sin for what it is, and by faith ask God to fill you with His Spirit to His glory. "Do not be drunk with wine, in which is dissipation; but be filled with the Spirit" (Eph. 5:18). When God fills you, there is no room for the ways of the flesh.

The Fifth Way: Follow the Lord, but Don't Walk Too Close

> But Peter followed Him at a distance to the high priest's courtyard. And he went in and sat with the servants to see the end.
> —Matthew 26:58

As Jesus was being led away to be tried, "Peter followed Him." Wouldn't it be great if we could stop there? But we cannot: "Peter followed Him *at a distance.*" The manner in which Peter follows Jesus on this occasion will never be forgotten. He brought up the rear. He kept his distance and stayed out of harm's way. I can understand Peter doing this in light of the setting and his lack of knowledge concerning what Jesus is doing. But what about the distant disciples of our day?

The old song says well what our goal should be:

> I am weak, but Thou art strong;
> Jesus, keep me from all wrong;
> I'll be satisfied as long

As I walk, let me walk close to
Thee.

Just a closer walk with Thee,
Grant it, Jesus, is my plea;
Daily walking close to Thee,
Let it be, dear Lord, let it be.

Simon Peter found out after the resurrection of Jesus what it meant to be a close follower of Jesus. Peter, full of the Holy Spirit, preached on the Day of Pentecost and three thousand souls were added to the church. Under the control of the Holy Spirit, the early church turned the known world upside down.

Writing about our relationship to Christ, Paul speaks of "Christ in you, the hope of glory" (Col. 1:27). How much closer a relationship could you want with Christ? A few verses earlier Paul writes, "For by Him all things were created that are in heaven and that are on earth, visible and invisible, whether thrones or dominions or principalities or powers. All things were created through Him and for Him. And He is before all things, and in Him all things consist. And He is the head of the body, the church, who is the beginning, the firstborn from the dead, that in all things He may have the preeminence. For it pleased the Father that in Him all the fullness should dwell" (Col. 1:16-19). Since all things were made by Him and for Him, since He holds everything together, and since all fullness is in Him, then, as Major Ian Thomas has said, *"All of Christ in all of you is all it takes."*

To walk under His control is a life of faith and excitement at its best. Paul continues, "As you therefore have received Christ Jesus the Lord, so walk in Him" (Col. 2:6). How did we receive Him? By faith. How then are we to walk? By faith!

Many have not backslidden from this kind of walk; they have never known nor have they discovered who they are in Christ. When we fully understand this relationship, backsliding for any length of time is almost out of the question. Paul sums it up in Galatians 2:20: "I have been crucified with Christ; it is no longer I who live, but Christ lives in me; and the life which I now live in the flesh I live by faith in the Son of God, who loved me and gave Himself for me." Paul is simply saying that when Christ died on the cross he, Paul, died with Him, and the life that he now lives is in reality not his own, but it is the life of Christ who by faith has been given complete control. Study this Scripture, for it is one of the most liberating verses in all the Bible.

The Sixth Way: Seek Fellowship with the Lord's Enemies

Having arrested Him, they led Him and brought Him into the high priest's house. But Peter followed at a distance. Now when they had kindled a fire in the midst of the courtyard and sat down together, Peter sat among them.
—Luke 22:54, 55

Peter not only dissociated himself from Jesus but he "sat down among" those who had arrested Him. In 2 Corinthians 6:17 we read, "Come out from among them and be separate, says the Lord. Do not touch what is unclean, and I will receive you." Christians who find themselves enjoying the social life of the world are on their way to losing their fellowship with Christ.

John says, "Do not love the world or the things in the world. If anyone loves the world, the love of the Father is not in him. For all that is in the world—the lust of the flesh, the lust of the eyes, and the pride of life—is not of the Father but is of the world. And the world is passing away, and the lust of it; but he who does the will of God abides forever" (1 John 2:15-17). Why waste your time loving something that is going to pass away?

One day everything the world counts dear will melt with fervent heat and be reduced to ashes, and yet so many professed Christians are so engrossed in these *things* that they don't have time to fellowship with God's people. Can you imagine looking down on the earth a few minutes after it has been reduced to ashes? You can look at all the things that you possessed—or that possessed you—and you will be able to exclaim, "Look, my pile of ashes is bigger than your pile of ashes!"

The crowd that Peter sat down with soon crucified his best friend. The world today walks in darkness, and by their rejection, still cries, "Crucify Him, crucify Him!" Peter was not comfortable with this crowd and neither are we if we really know the

Lord. We can't stay camped out with the things of the world and enjoy our fellowship with Him. Where are you seated at this moment?

The Seventh Way: Deny that You Know Him

Now Peter sat outside in the courtyard. And a servant girl came to him, saying, "You also were with Jesus of Galilee."

But he denied it before them all, saying, "I do not know what you are saying."

And when he had gone out to the gateway, another girl saw him and said to those who were there, "This fellow also was with Jesus of Nazareth."

But again he denied with an oath, "I do not know the Man!"

And a little later those who stood by came up and said to Peter, "Surely you also are one of them, for your speech betrays you."

Then he began to curse and swear, saying, "I do not know the Man!"

Immediately a rooster crowed. And Peter remembered the word of Jesus who had said to him, "Before the rooster crows, you will deny Me three times." So he went out and wept bitterly.
—Matthew 26:69-75

This is the final stage of backsliding. The story is a familiar and tragic one. What a testimony Peter could have given to these people, whose uppermost thoughts were of Jesus of Nazareth! He had walked with Jesus for nearly three years. He could attest to the feeding of the five thousand, to the raising of Lazarus, to the salvation of the woman at the well, to all the miracles. He could have said, "Yes, I know Him, I love Him, and I will stand with Him to the end." Like many of us, he had already bragged about what he would do if he had the chance. But at the crucial moment, just as this crowd recognized him as one of the followers of Jesus and confronted him, his words and his actions said, "No!"

Listen to this Scripture: "They profess to know God, but in works they deny Him, being abominable, disobedient, and disqualified for every good work" (Titus 1:16).

This is a warning about rebellious *unbelievers*—and yet it describes well those who have backslidden to the point of denying Christ. How tragic it is when one who has been born again is outwardly no different from one who has never known the Savior! "If we endure, we shall also reign with Him. If we deny Him, He also will deny us" (2 Tim. 2:12; cf. Matt. 10:33; Mark 8:38).

THE CURE FOR BACKSLIDING

How can the backslidden believer be restored to fellowship with God? Look at Revelation 2:4: "Nevertheless I have this against you, that you have left your first love." This is what Simon Peter did, and this is what we do when we backslide, regardless of the extent of shame that is brought upon us because of our desertion. The solution is given in the next verse, Revelation 2:5: "Remember therefore from where you have fallen; repent and do the first works, or else I will come to you quickly and remove your lampstand from its place—unless you repent." In these verses we see *three steps to restoration*: "remember," "repent," and "do the first works."

Step One: Remember How It Was When You Were Walking in Fellowship with the Lord

Remember the joy you had when you witnessed to lost people and saw them come to Christ. Remember how clean and pure life was as you knew the joy of cleansing and the unbroken fellowship with God. Remember how good it felt to be accepted by God with nothing to stand in the way of getting your prayers answered. Remember how good it was to sing the great songs of faith with other believers and sense the presence of God in worship and fellowship with them. Remember what it was like to hear a good sermon and have your faith built up by the Word of God. Remember the answered prayers and the worry-free life that was yours because everything was completely surrendered to Him. Just remembering the sweet fellowship you once had with God and fellow members of His church will point you in the direction of complete restoration.

Step Two: Repent of the Unconfessed Sins That Have Piled Up in Your Life

The word *repent* means "change one's mind." The word *confess* means "say what God says." Instead of making excuses as to why you chose to become a backslidden Christian, simply see yourself as God sees you. Don't indulge yourself a minute longer in self-pity and guilt. Don't believe the devil when he tries (as he will) to convince you that God doesn't love you and that others in the church don't care. Neither is true. You may shed tears of remorse as did Simon Peter, "for godly sorrow produces repentance" (2 Cor. 7:10). Real repentance is always produced by godly sorrow. In this attitude of repentance, change your mind about your sin and say what God says about it: that it is *not* good and worthwhile, but rather is abhorrent to Him and grieves Him. Let it grieve you also.

Why not find a quiet place and make a list of all of the unconfessed sins in your life? List only those sins that the Holy Spirit brings to your mind. After doing this, copy 1 John 1:9 across the list—"If we confess our sins, He is faithful and just to forgive us our sins and to cleanse us from all unrighteousness"—and tear the list up. Then, as an act of faith, thank God for His perfect cleansing and forgiveness. These sins are forgiven and forgotten because you have obeyed God. All of this is possible because of the blood of Christ that keeps on cleansing us from all sin (1 John 1:7).

Now that all sin is confessed, cleansed, and forgiven, you can know in your heart that everything is just as it used to be in your walk with God. Anytime one of these past sins comes before you and points an accusing finger of guilt in your direction, remember what God has done. This accusation is the only way Satan has of defeating us in our walk with God. Satan is the accuser of the brethren (Rev. 12:10). Recognize him as the liar that he is. Never live another moment in defeat because of sin. When in weakness you do sin, immediately repent and confess it and keep on walking with God.

Step Three: Go Back to the First Works

This is what spiritual renewal is all about. By faith, ask God to fill you with His Spirit. On the basis of God's Word, believe that you are filled with the very life of Christ Himself. "Now this is the confidence that we have in Him, that if we ask anything according to His will, He hears us. And if we know that He hears us, whatever we ask, we know that we have the petitions that we have asked of Him" (1 John 5:14, 15). Is it God's will that you be filled with His Spirit? Indeed it is, because God *commanded* every Christian to be filled with the Spirit in Ephesians 5:18. If there is no unconfessed sin in our lives and if we have sincerely asked Him to fill us with His Spirit, then by faith we know we are filled with His presence and power.

Now you are back where you once were in your walk of faith with God. You will enjoy the fellowship of fellow believers in worship. You will once again experience His power in witnessing (Acts 1:8). Bible study and prayer will take on a new meaning in your life. Your body is once again "a living sacrifice, holy, acceptable to God" (Rom. 12:1). As a result you will be more and more conformed to the image of Jesus Christ, as God once again produces the fruit of the Spirit in your life (Gal. 5:22, 23). All these are "the first works"—the works of Christ who controlled your life as by faith you allowed Him to live His resurrection life in and through you. They are yours again to do. Do them with joy!

If you have never received Christ as your personal Lord and Savior, I urge you to do it now. If you are backslidden, God will chasten you as His child (Heb. 12:5-11); His chastening can involve intense anguish of soul (Ps. 32:3, 4) or—if you let your backslidden state continue too long—even death (1 Cor. 11:30). I urge you to "remember," "repent," and "do the first works."

Simon Peter returned to the Lord confessing and forsaking his sin. He learned a valuable lesson that was to remain with him for the rest of his life: In himself he did *not* have what it takes to stay with Jesus. He lacked the resurrection power to live the Christian life. But when he humbly returned to Christ and drew upon His resources, God used him mightily as a spokesman and, as his Lord had com-

manded him, to strengthen his brethren (Luke 22:32).

Tradition has it that Simon Peter came to his own death by crucifixion, and that he asked to be crucified upside down because he was not worthy to die in the same manner that Jesus died. Whether this is true or not, one thing we do know: his example shows us that God can and will forgive the person who has turned his back on the truth, if he will turn to Him in confession and repentance. Not only will God forgive but He will use him, perhaps in a way that he has never been used before.

—J.J.M.

NEW TESTAMENT EVANGELISM

New Testament evangelism is not simply an act or a program, it is a life-style. It is part of the new life that begins when one comes to know Jesus Christ as Savior and Lord. From that moment the believer's entire outlook is changed: heaven is now his home, Jesus is now his Lord, and he discovers that His grace is all-sufficient and His love unbounded. Christians have the privilege of living out this limitless, measureless love as they introduce the unsaved world to Jesus Christ as Savior, saying to all, as He once said to Nicodemus, "You must be born again" (John 3:7).

Living evangelistically is not only a privilege, it is rewarding. Fulfilling experiences will come to those who will become "fishers of men." "He who wins souls is wise," says Proverbs 11:30—and every Christian who learns this wisdom finds that "she is more precious than rubies, and all the things you may desire cannot compare with her" (Prov. 3:15).

THE MESSAGE OF NEW TESTAMENT EVANGELISM

The Gospel Itself

Jesus Christ came to do for humanity what humanity could never do for itself. Mankind was caught in a trap of its own making, by its own choice; a rescue was needed that none but God could provide.

When Adam disobeyed God and sinned in the Garden of Eden, humanity died. The corruption of a sinful nature came upon Adam, Eve, and all their descendants. As a result, not only did men and women begin to die physically, but from that time onward spiritual death separated God from man and man from God, ultimately consigning man to the condemnation of hell (Gen. 2:17; Rom. 5:12; 1 Cor. 15:21, 22; Rev. 20:15). All this was and is humanly inescapable; men cannot change their sinful nature any more than a leopard can change its own spots (Jer. 13:23), and even if they could they cannot annul the sins of the past.

"For this purpose I came to this hour," Jesus said (John 12:27). From the beginning (Gen. 3:15), God had foretold the coming of a divine Savior, or Rescuer, who would make atonement for humanity's sins. In Jesus Christ, the incarnate Son of God, that Rescuer had arrived. As He explained, "God so loved the world that He gave His only begotten Son, that whoever believes in Him should not perish but have everlasting life. For God did not send His Son into the world to condemn the world, but that the world through Him might be saved" (John 3:16, 17).

When Jesus on the cross said, "It is finished!" and gave up His spirit (John 19:30), He completed man's salvation. That day shook the world: the daylight became darkness for three hours, the earth quaked, and the veil of the temple was torn in two from top to bottom. During that time He died physically, just as all men and women have done beginning with Adam. But not only did He die man's physical death, He also died man's spiritual death, as on the cross God the Father cut Him off from fellowship, leaving Him to the agonies of hell.

Jesus did all this as a substitute for mankind—a substitution that is fully accomplished for everyone who believes in Him, and He proved that His work was accepted by rising again from the grave (Rom. 4:25). Truly He can say, "I am the resurrection and the life. He who believes in Me, though he may die, he shall live. And whoever lives and believes in Me shall never die" (John 11:25, 26).

This is just cause for praise and adoration of our blessed Savior who gave to us salvation. His salvation has delivered us from the power and penalty of sin, and in the future will deliver us from the very presence of sin. It is with great privilege that the church can gather in worship and sing, "Praise God from whom all blessings flow!"

The Restlessness of Mankind

It is evident that people are born with a sense of lostness, incompleteness, and unfulfillment. Man was created a spiritual being, made to have fellowship with God. Without this fellowship, the unrighteous person is unsettled and without peace. Augustine knew this in his own life: "You made us for yourself," he said to God, "and

our heart is restless until it find rest in you."

The Jewish ruler and teacher Nicodemus, naturally well equipped and established in life, was yet lacking and knew it. His sense of need drove him to come to Jesus by night, in secret, to seek answers from God. The Savior identified his need immediately: "You must be born again" (John 3:3, 7).

Nicodemus's later actions show that he willingly received Christ and was indeed born again. With Joseph of Arimathea, he presented himself publicly before Pilate—not secretly this time!—to take the body of Jesus for preparation and burial. He had known of his need, and in God's providence someone (the Savior Himself) had shown him the One whom he needed and he had accepted Him.

Becoming a Child of God

Mankind's greatest privilege is to become a child of the living God. Experiencing this transformation has one simple requirement: faith. Acknowledging that as a sinner you can do nothing to earn salvation, believe that Jesus is the only Savior and that He died as your substitute, bearing your sins. Trust Him to be not only the Savior of mankind, but *your* Savior personally. As you believe, it will help you if you talk to Him, asking Him to save you. The Bible prescribes no specific words; God hears the simplest prayer as well as the most complex.

After you have become a child of God, two things necessarily follow, both in obedience to the Scriptures. The first is *confession*—not confessing sins before God (that has already been done) but confessing Christ before others. Be ready to say openly that you are trusting Christ as your Savior. This does not mean that every believer is to become a dynamic speaker; a quiet statement can be just as effective as a loud one. The point is how you respond when asked your opinion of God and Christ—whether you confess Him, like Paul before Agrippa, or deny Him, like Peter during his Master's trial. "Whoever confesses Me before men," He said, "him I will also confess before My Father who is in heaven" (Matt. 10:32).

The second thing that follows belief in Christ is *baptism*. This is not an elective; Matthew 28:19 makes it clear that every believer is to be baptized. Peter in his Pentecost sermon insisted on it: "Repent, and let every one of you be baptized in the name of Jesus Christ" (Acts 2:38). It was the logical desire of the Ethiopian eunuch; when Philip had told him about salvation in Christ and they then spotted water, he said, "What hinders me from being baptized?" Philip baptized him, and "he went on his way rejoicing" (Acts 8:36, 39). This same rejoicing and willingness to obey the Word of God will become a very real part of life in Christ Jesus the Lord.

THE PRACTICE OF NEW TESTAMENT EVANGELISM

New Testament Evangelism Is for Every Believer

To his protege Timothy the apostle Paul said, "Be watchful in all things, endure afflictions, do the work of an evangelist, fulfill your ministry" (2 Tim. 4:5). The word *ministry* does not refer to a special class of worker, professional or otherwise; it means "service," and all believers are called to a ministry of some kind (Eph. 4:12). Part of the believer's ministry is to "do the work of an evangelist." The Scriptures do not say that you *are* an evangelist necessarily, but that as a believer you are to *do the work of* an evangelist. This is a work given to all.

New Testament Evangelism Is Personal Evangelism

New Testament evangelism is simply following Jesus Christ's example in unfolding the Word. Jesus went everywhere preaching repentance. Probably His most outstanding converts were found and ministered to individually.

For example, Jesus saw Zacchaeus in a sycamore tree and said to him, "Zacchaeus, make haste and come down, for today I must stay at your house." Zacchaeus gave clear indications of his new life in Christ: first, he joyfully and publicly welcomed Christ into his house; second, he determined to give half his wealth to the poor and to restore, four times over, taxes he had collected dishonestly. Jesus emphatically declared at that moment, "For the

Son of Man has come to seek and to save that which was lost" (Luke 19:1-9).

Jesus was the master soul winner. He witnessed to and won John and Andrew (John 1:35-40), Nicodemus (John 3:1-21), and the Samaritan woman (John 4:5-25). Though He did not win all to whom He witnessed—the rich young ruler was one who went away grieved after Jesus spoke to him (Mark 10:17-22)—Jesus practiced person-to-person evangelism. And to us, as to His disciples, He gives the call: "Follow Me, and I will make you fishers of men" (Matt. 4:19).

Personal Evangelism Is More Important than Mass Evangelism

In today's society there is a place for church evangelism meetings, revivals, and other forms of mass evangelism, and indeed much of the church's initial growth was through mass evangelism. But the most effective work in changing lives and the eternal destiny of men and women is done through *personal* evangelism—by believers who get involved in the lives of others and show them how the Good News applies specifically to them. There is a line that is so true: "They will not come, they must be brought; they will not study, they must be taught." A great present-day evangelist said, "No one is coming to a saving knowledge of Jesus Christ by my preaching alone; they come because someone cared, ministered to them in their need, and brought them to the meeting."

New Testament Evangelism Produces Disciples

Jesus' commission to the church was not, "Go therefore and make converts of all the nations." Rather, it was, "Go therefore and *make disciples* of all the nations... teaching them to observe all things that I have commanded you" (Matt. 28:19, 20). God's desire is to produce disciples, believers who will live out their commitment to Him by studying and obeying His Word.

At Pentecost the infant church made disciples, as those who were saved "continued steadfastly in the apostles' doctrine and fellowship, in the breaking of bread, and in prayers" (Acts 2:42). The goal of Paul's missionary work was to make disciples and to strengthen them (Acts 14:21, 22; 18:23).

And the purpose of God's gifts to the church, the body of Christ, is that it may grow both in numbers and in maturity—that is, that the number of mature disciples may increase (Eph. 4:11-16). God desires that men and women be born again, and much more besides—He desires that they be obedient, growing followers of the Lord Jesus Christ.

New Testament Evangelism Produces Soul Winners

The work and ministry of New Testament evangelism is not complete in the life of a convert to Christ until the convert in turn becomes a soul winner. When Jesus told some rugged, professional fishermen, "I will make you fishers of men," they not only responded, they went out and brought others. Philip brought Nathanael to Jesus (John 1:44-51). Andrew brought his brother Simon (John 1:40-42), who became Peter, the first chief spokesman for the young church. The woman at the well, accepting Jesus' gift of "living water," went immediately to her friends and men of previous marriages with the invitation, "Come, see a Man who told me all things that I ever did," and many believed (John 4:28-30, 39-42). She simply shared her experience with the Savior—simply, but with profound results.

The Power of New Testament Evangelism: The Holy Spirit

Many Christians allow timidity or fear to dominate their lives and prevent them from speaking to anyone about Christ. Some excuse themselves, believing not everyone is a soul winner. Not so: if you are genuinely saved, you can share that salvation experience. The Holy Spirit is your enabler.

" 'Not by might nor by power, but by My Spirit,' says the LORD of hosts" (Zech. 4:6). The Holy Spirit is our Helper (John 14:16), and He will enable and empower. He will draw the unbeliever to desire new birth. He will convict the unbelieving mind and bring it to personal faith in Jesus Christ (John 16:8-10).

The ministry of the Holy Spirit is well demonstrated in Acts 8:26-40. It was God, speaking through His angel, who told Philip to go to the Jerusalem-Gaza road,

and it was the Spirit of God who directed him to the passing chariot of the Ethiopian eunuch while the eunuch was studying a prophecy of Christ. As Philip spoke to the eunuch the Spirit was convicting and teaching, and the man's salvation was assured. Afterward, the Spirit caught Philip away, taking him to other duties, and the Ethiopian returned home rejoicing. Clearly, the Spirit was at work throughout the entire episode, from beginning to end.

This same blessed Holy Spirit, the third person of the Trinity, enables every obedient child of God in personal soul-winning ministry, touching the lives of men and women around the world. Through the ages this promise has stood firm: "You shall receive power when the Holy Spirit has come upon you; and you shall be witnesses to Me in Jerusalem, and in all Judea and Samaria, and to the end of the earth" (Acts 1:8).

The Key to New Testament Evangelism: Prayer

Prayer is the very life of evangelism. Well has it been said, "No prayer, no power; little prayer, little power; great prayer, great power." If Jesus Christ, the very Son of God, found it necessary to pray to His Father during His life of service, how can we mortals expect to reach this world for the Savior without prayer?

Firmly He told His disciples concerning salvation: "With men it is impossible, but not with God; for with God all things are possible" (Mark 10:27). Men cannot save themselves, nor will they come to Christ for salvation apart from a special work of God (John 6:44). But God's work is available through the prayers of His people, who pray according to His will in submissive faith (Matt. 21:22; 1 John 5:14, 15).

The Church and New Testament Evangelism

The church is charged with the responsibility of New Testament evangelism. Many segments of ministry can be accomplished effectively by a group of believers in fellowship with one another. When a body of believers is abiding in the will of the Father, ministering to spiritual needs, and accepting the many and varied challenges around

the world, it is powerful. When it undertakes the task of personal evangelism, obeying the Word of God and the Spirit of God, it is a mighty army indeed.

The leadership of the church must be especially sensitive to this evangelistic responsibility. A pastor's attitude soon spreads to his people. If his spiritual ardor dims, the hearts of the people will grow cold. If he loses the passion for lost souls, it will likely soon die out in the congregation. But if that passion burns in him, it will be kindled in them as well.

A burning heart is essential in evangelism. Only the vigorous will impress the world. Peter burned with this passion on the Day of Pentecost, and ignited a revival that blazed for over four hundred years. Paul had this passion kindled in his heart when he declared, "Woe is me if I do not preach the gospel!" (1 Cor. 9:16). The spirit of evangelism in the church, which is basic in soul winning, cannot endure apart from the presence and power of the Holy Spirit—but with continual dependence upon Him, it will burn ever brighter day by day.

The church today would do well to study the early church as it lived in the presence and power of the Holy Spirit. At first the believers on the Day of Pentecost numbered about 120 (Acts 1:15), but that day they increased by about three thousand—twenty-five times the original number (Acts 2:41). Soon they were five thousand strong, and eventually they grew beyond counting and were simply called "the multitude of those who believed" (Acts 4:32). Their unity and the apostles' preaching were such powerful testimonies to the resurrection of the Lord Jesus that the Jewish leadership complained, "You have filled Jerusalem with your doctrine!" (Acts 5:28). This New Testament evangelism explosion saw an entire city taken by the power of God—without today's communications media. Even with every advantage available to the modern church, this kind of church growth has not yet been equaled.

Would that every Christian man and woman today also truly understood the *nature* of the church! A stranger once asked me the natural question, "Where is your church in this city?" I responded, "I'm not sure." Noticing his growing puzzlement, I

quickly added, "The building is downtown"—I gave the location and address—"but, you see, that is where we worship and from there we go out to serve the living Lord." Still he went on assuming that the building was the church. This is the general assumption today; people who hear the word *church* think of a building, when they should be thinking of the *people* who meet in the building.

The church is a congregation, a body of believers. "The body of Christ," it is called—and yet that body is made up of individual members (1 Cor. 12:27). Each believer, throughout the world, is a unique part of that body with a special function and special significance. When the Bible says,

— "You are the salt of the earth" (Matt. 5:13),

— "You are the light of the world" (Matt. 5:14),

— "Let your light so shine among men" (Matt. 5:16),

— "Go therefore and make disciples of all the nations" (Matt. 28:19),

— "Be an example to the believers" (1 Tim. 4:12), and

— "Do the work of an evangelist" (2 Tim. 4:5),

it has in view not only the church as a whole but each individual believer. The saying is true: "If it's going to be, it's up to me." If we as believers do not do the work, the church will not have done it.

New Testament evangelism is alive in the world today. Simply, and gloriously, it is the individual members of the church—in obedience to the Word and example of Jesus Christ, and energized by the Holy Spirit through prayer—telling the people of the world, "God loves you," and leading them to new life as disciples of the Savior, the Lord Jesus Christ, who was crucified and who rose again on their behalf. It thrives where the church (following the pattern of Acts 2:41-47) gladly receives and preaches the Word of God, and continues steadfastly in the apostles' doctrine and fellowship, in the breaking of bread, and in prayers. And the Lord—now as then—adds to the church daily those who are being saved.

—J.H.G.

CONCORDANCE

A

ABASED
I know how to be *a* ......Phil 4:12

ABBA
And He said, "*A* ......Mark 14:36
whom we cry out, "*A* ....Rom 8:15
crying out, "*A* ....Gal 4:6

ABHOR
My soul shall not *a*......Lev 26:11
Therefore I *a* myself......Job 42:6
nations will *a* him ......Prov 24:24
a the pride of Jacob .....Amos 6:8
A what is evil ....Rom 12:9

ABHORRED
a own inheritance.....Ps 106:40
he who is *a* by the......Prov 22:14
and their soul also *a* .....Zech 11:8

ABHORRENCE
They shall be an *a*........Is 66:24

ABHORRENT
you have made us *a*.......Ex 5:21

ABHORS
So that his life *a*........Job 33:20

ABIDE
nor *a* in its paths ......Job 24:13
LORD, who may *a* ....Ps 15:1
He shall *a* before God......Ps 61:7
the Most High shall ......Ps 91:1
Him, "If you *a*........John 8:31
And a slave does not *a*...John 8:35
Helper, that He may *a*...John 14:16
"*A* in Me ....John 15:4
"If you *a* in Me........John 15:7
a in My love............John 15:9
And now *a* faith ......1 Cor 13:13
does the love of God *a* .1 John 3:17
this we know that we *a*..1 John 4:13

ABIDES
them, even He who *a*.....Ps 55:19
He who *a* in Me ....John 15:5
lives and *a* forever ......1 Pet 1:23
will of God *a* forever ....1 John 2:17

ABIDING
do not have His word *a*..John 5:38
has eternal life *a* ......1 John 3:15

ABILITY
understand, who had *a* ....Dan 1:4
according to his own *a*...Matt 25:15
and beyond their *a*........2 Cor 8:3
a which God supplies.....1 Pet 4:11

ABLE
you are *a* to number......Gen 15:5
shall give as he is *a* .....Deut 16:17
For who is *a* to judge ....1 Kin 3:9
"The LORD is *a* ....2 Chr 25:9
Who then is *a* to stand...Job 41:10
God whom we serve is *a*...Dan 3:17
God is *a* to raise up ......Matt 3:9
believe that I am *a*......Matt 9:28
fear Him who is *a*......Matt 10:28
Are you *a* to drink the...Matt 20:22
beyond what you are *a* .1 Cor 10:13
And God is *a* to make.....2 Cor 9:8

may be *a* to comprehend...Eph 3:18
persuaded that He is *a*..2 Tim 1:12
learning and never *a* ......2 Tim 3:7
being tempted, He is *a* ...Heb 2:18
that God was *a* to ......Heb 11:19
to Him who is *a* ....Jude 24
has come, and who is *a*...Rev 6:17

ABODE
but left their own *a* ....Jude 6

ABOLISHED
your works may be *a* .....Ezek 6:6
having *a* in His flesh......Eph 2:15
Christ, who has *a* ......2 Tim 1:10

ABOMINABLE
not make yourselves *a* ...Lev 11:43
They have done *a* ....Ps 14:1
your grave like an *a*........Is 14:19
Oh, do not do this *a* ......Jer 44:4
they deny Him, being *a*...Titus 1:16
and *a* idolatries...........1 Pet 4:3
unbelieving, *a* ....Rev 21:8

ABOMINATION
every shepherd is an *a*...Gen 46:34
If we sacrifice the *a*........Ex 8:26
You have made me an *a*...Ps 88:8
yes, seven are an *a* .....Prov 6:16
wickedness is an *a*........Prov 8:7
Dishonest scales are an *a*..Prov 11:1
the scoffer is an *a* ......Prov 24:9
prayer shall be an *a*......Prov 28:9
An unjust man is an *a*..Prov 29:27
incense is an *a* ....Is 1:13
and place there the *a*.....Dan 11:31
the *a* of desolation......Dan 12:11
the '*a* of desolation,'....Matt 24:15
among men is an *a* .....Luke 16:15

ABOMINATIONS
to follow the *a*...........Deut 18:9
delights in their *a* ....Is 66:3
will put away your *a* ......Jer 4:1
your harlotry, your *a* .....Jer 13:27
you will see greater *a* ...Ezek 8:6
a which they commit ...Ezek 8:17
you, throw away the *a* ...Ezek 20:7
show her all her *a* ......Ezek 22:2
a golden cup full of *a* .....Rev 17:4
harlots and of the *a* ......Rev 17:5

ABOUND
lawlessness will *a* ....Matt 24:12
the offense might *a*......Rom 5:20
sin that grace may *a* ......Rom 6:1
thanksgiving to *a* ....2 Cor 4:15
to make all grace *a*.......2 Cor 9:8
and I know how to *a* .....Phil 4:12
that you should *a* ......1 Thess 4:1
things are yours and *a*...2 Pet 1:8

ABOUNDED
But where sin *a*..........Rom 5:20

ABOUNDING
and *a* in mercy ....Ps 103:8
immovable, always *a* ....1 Cor 15:58

ABOVE
that is in heaven *a*........Ex 20:4
"He sent from *a* ....2 Sam 22:17
A it stood seraphim..........Is 6:2
nor a servant *a* ....Matt 10:24

"He who comes from *a*....John 3:31
I am from *a* ....John 8:23
been given you from *a* ...John 19:11
of all, who is *a* ....Eph 4:6
the name which is *a* ....Phil 2:9
things which are *a* ....Col 3:1
perfect gift is from *a* ....James 1:17

ABSENT
For I indeed, as *a*........1 Cor 5:3
in the body we are *a* ......2 Cor 5:6

ABSTAIN
we write to them to *a*....Acts 15:20
A from every form.....1 Thess 5:22
and commanding to *a*....1 Tim 4:3
and pilgrims, *a*...........1 Pet 2:11

ABUNDANCE
is the sound of *a* ......1 Kin 18:41
workmen with you in *a*..1 Chr 22:15
shall flourish, and *a* ......Ps 72:7
eyes bulge with *a* ....Ps 73:7
nor he who loves *a*......Eccl 5:10
delight itself in *a* ....Is 55:2
For out of the *a*........Matt 12:34
put in out of their *a*....Mark 12:44
not consist in the *a*.....Luke 12:15
of affliction the *a* ....2 Cor 8:2
above measure by the *a*..2 Cor 12:7
rich through the *a*........Rev 18:3

ABUNDANT
Longsuffering and *a*.......Ps 86:15
slow to anger and *a*........Jon 4:2
in labors more *a*........2 Cor 11:23
Lord was exceedingly *a* .1 Tim 1:14
a mercy has begotten......1 Pet 1:3

ABUNDANTLY
a satisfied with the........Ps 36:8
may have it more *a* ......John 10:10
to do exceedingly *a* ......Eph 3:20
to show more *a* to the ...Heb 6:17

ACCEPT
For I will *a* him ....Job 42:8
a your burnt ....Ps 20:3
offering, I will not *a* ....Jer 14:12
Should I *a* this from......Mal 1:13

ACCEPTABLE
sought to find *a* ....Eccl 12:10
a time I have heard........Is 49:8
proclaim the *a* year ....Is 61:2
proclaim the *a* year ......Luke 4:19
is that good and *a* ....Rom 12:2
finding out what is *a* .....Eph 5:10
For this is good and *a* ....1 Tim 2:3
spiritual sacrifices *a*......1 Pet 2:5

ACCEPTABLY
we may serve God *a*......Heb 12:28

ACCEPTED
Behold, now is the *a* ....2 Cor 6:2
which He made us *a* ......Eph 1:6

ACCESS
whom also we have *a* .....Rom 5:2
we have boldness and *a*...Eph 3:12

ACCOMPLISHED
today the LORD has *a*...1 Sam 11:13
A desire *a* is sweet to ....Prov 13:19

ACCORD (continued)

must still be *a* . . . . Luke 22:37
all things were now *a* . . . . John 19:28

ACCORD

and Israel with one *a* . . . . . Josh 9:2
serve Him with one *a* . . . . . . Zeph 3:9
continued with one *a* . . . . . Acts 1:14
daily with one *a* . . . . Acts 2:46
a has Christ with . . . . 2 Cor 6:15
love, being of one *a* . . . . Phil 2:2

ACCOUNT

they will give *a* . . . . Matt 12:36
The former *a* I made . . . . . . Acts 1:1
of us shall give *a* . . . . Rom 14:12
put that on my *a* . . . . Philem 18
those who must give *a* . . Heb 13:17

ACCOUNTED

in the LORD, and He *a* . . . . Gen 15:6
And that was *a* to him . . . Ps 106:31
his faith is *a* . . . . Rom 4:5
a as sheep for the . . . . Rom 8:36
God, and it was *a* . . . . Gal 3:6
God, and it was *a* . . . . . . James 2:23

ACCURSED

he who is hanged is *a* . . . . Deut 21:23
regarding the *a* . . . . Josh 7:1
years old shall be *a* . . . . . . Is 65:20
not know the law is *a* . . . . John 7:49
that I myself were *a* . . . . . . Rom 9:3
of God calls Jesus *a* . . . . . 1 Cor 12:3
to you, let him be *a* . . . . Gal 1:8

ACCUSATION

reign, they wrote an *a* . . . . . Ezra 4:6
over His head the *a* . . . . Matt 27:37
they might find an *a* . . . . . Luke 6:7
Do not receive an *a* . . . . . 1 Tim 5:19
not bring a reviling *a* . . . . 2 Pet 2:11

ACCUSE

anyone or *a* falsely . . . . Luke 3:14
they began to *a* Him . . . . Luke 23:2
think that I shall *a* . . . . . . John 5:45

ACCUSED

forward and *a* the Jews . . . . Dan 3:8
while He was being *a* . . . . Matt 27:12

ACCUSER

a of our brethren . . . . Rev 12:10

ACCUSING

their thoughts *a* . . . . Rom 2:15

ACKNOWLEDGE

did he *a* his brothers . . . . . Deut 33:9
a my transgressions . . . . Ps 51:3
in all your ways *a* . . . . Prov 3:6
and Israel does not *a* . . . . . . Is 63:16
a your iniquity . . . . Jer 3:13
spiritual, let him *a* . . . 1 Cor 14:37

ACKNOWLEDGED

of Israel, and God *a* . . . . Ex 2:25
a my sin to You . . . . Ps 32:5

ACKNOWLEDGES

there is no one who *a* . . . . . Ps 142:4
a the Son has the . . . . . . 1 John 2:23

ACQUAINT

a yourself with Him . . . . . Job 22:21

ACQUAINTANCES

You have put away my *a* . . . Ps 88:8
All my *a* watched for . . . . . Jer 20:10
But all His *a* . . . . Luke 23:49

ACQUAINTED

lying down, and are *a* . . . . . Ps 139:3
a Man of sorrows and *a* . . . . . Is 53:3

ACQUIT

at all *a* the wicked . . . . Nah 1:3

ACT

seen every great *a* . . . . Deut 11:7
is time for You to *a* . . . . . Ps 119:126
His *a*, His unusual *a* . . . . . . Is 28:21
in the very *a* . . . . John 8:4

ACTIONS

by Him *a* are weighed . . . . 1 Sam 2:3

ACTS

LORD, the righteous *a* . . . . . Judg 5:11
to Moses, His *a* . . . . Ps 103:7
declare Your mighty *a* . . . . Ps 145:4
of Your awesome *a* . . . . Ps 145:6

ADD

"You shall not *a* . . . . Deut 4:2
Do not *a* to His words . . . . Prov 30:6

ADDED

things shall be *a* . . . . Matt 6:33
And the Lord *a* to the . . . . Acts 2:47
many people were *a* . . . . . Acts 11:24
It was *a* because of . . . . Gal 3:19

ADMINISTERS

a justice for the . . . . Deut 10:18

ADMONISH

also to *a* one another . . . . . Rom 15:14
a him as a . . . . 2 Thess 3:15

ADMONISHED

further, my son, be *a* . . . . . Eccl 12:12
Angel of the LORD *a* . . . . . . Zech 3:6

ADMONISHING

a one another in . . . . Col 3:16

ADMONITION

were written for our *a* . . . 1 Cor 10:11
in the training and *a* . . . . . . Eph 6:4

ADOPTION

the Spirit of *a* . . . . Rom 8:15
waiting for the *a* . . . . Rom 8:23
to whom pertain the *a* . . . . . Rom 9:4
we might receive the *a* . . . . . Gal 4:5
a as sons by Jesus . . . . Eph 1:5

ADORN

a the monuments . . . . . . Matt 23:29
also, that the women *a* . . . . 1 Tim 2:9

ADORNED

By His Spirit He *a* . . . . . . Job 26:13
You shall again be *a* . . . . . . Jer 31:4
temple, how it was *a* . . . . . Luke 21:5
God also *a* themselves . . . . 1 Pet 3:5
prepared as a bride *a* . . . . . Rev 21:2

ADRIFT

a among the dead . . . . Ps 88:5

ADULTERER

neighbor's wife, the *a* . . . . Lev 20:10
The eye of the *a* . . . . Job 24:15

ADULTERERS

the land is full of *a* . . . . . . Jer 23:10
nor idolaters, nor *a* . . . . . . 1 Cor 6:9
a God will judge . . . . Heb 13:4
A and adulteresses . . . . . James 4:4

ADULTERIES

I have seen your *a* . . . . Jer 13:27
her sight, and her *a* . . . . Hos 2:2
evil thoughts, *a* . . . . Mark 7:21

ADULTEROUS

a generation . . . . Matt 12:39

ADULTERY

You shall not commit *a* . . . Ex 20:14
Whoever commits *a* . . . . . Prov 6:32
Israel had committed *a* . . . . . Jer 3:8
already committed *a* . . . . . Matt 5:28
is divorced commits *a* . . . . Matt 5:32
another commits *a* . . . . . . Mark 10:11
a woman caught in *a* . . . . . John 8:3
and those who commit *a* . . Rev 2:22

ADVANTAGE

a will it be to You . . . . Job 35:3
man has no *a* over . . . . Eccl 3:19
a that I go away . . . . John 16:7
What *a* then has the . . . . . . Rom 3:1
Satan should take *a* . . . . . 2 Cor 2:11
no one should take *a* . . . . 1 Thess 4:6
people to gain *a* . . . . Jude 16

ADVERSARIES

The *a* of the LORD . . . . . . 1 Sam 2:10
rid Myself of My *a* . . . . Is 1:24
a will not be able . . . . Luke 21:15
and there are many *a* . . . . 1 Cor 16:9
terrified by your *a* . . . . Phil 1:28
will devour the *a* . . . . Heb 10:27

ADVERSARY

in the way as an *a* . . . . . . Num 22:22
battle he become our *a* . . 1 Sam 29:4
how long will the *a* . . . . . . Ps 74:10
a has spread his hand . . . . Lam 1:10
"Agree with your *a* . . . . . . Matt 5:25
justice for me from *a* . . . . . Luke 18:3
opportunity to the *a* . . . . . 1 Tim 5:14
a the devil walks . . . . 1 Pet 5:8

ADVERSITIES

you from all your *a* . . . . . 1 Sam 10:19
known my soul in *a* . . . . Ps 31:7

ADVERSITY

them with every *a* . . . . . . 2 Chr 15:6
I shall never be in *a* . . . . Ps 10:6
from the days of *a* . . . . Ps 94:13
brother is born for *a* . . . . . Prov 17:17
faint in the day of *a* . . . . . Prov 24:10
the day of *a* consider . . . . . Eccl 7:14
you the bread of *a* . . . . Is 30:20

ADVICE

And blessed is your *a* . . 1 Sam 25:33
in this I give my *a* . . . . . . 2 Cor 8:10

ADVOCATE

sins, we have an *A* . . . . . . 1 John 2:1

AFAR

and worship from *a* . . . . Ex 24:1
sons shall come from *a* . . . . . Is 60:4
and not a God *a* . . . . Jer 23:23
and saw Abraham *a* . . . . Luke 16:23
to all who are *a* . . . . Acts 2:39
to you who were *a* . . . . Eph 2:17
but having seen them *a* . . Heb 11:13

AFFAIRS

he will guide his *a* . . . . Ps 112:5
I may hear of your *a* . . . . . Phil 1:27
himself with the *a* . . . . 2 Tim 2:4

AFFECTION

to his wife the *a* . . . . .1 Cor 7:3
for you all with the *a* . . . . . . .Phil 1:8
the Spirit, if any *a* . . . . .Phil 2:1

AFFECTIONATE

Be kindly *a* to one. . . . . . .Rom 12:10

AFFIRM

you to *a* constantly . . . . . . .Titus 3:8

AFFLICT

a them with their . . . . .Ex 1:11
oath to *a* her soul . . . . . .Num 30:13
may be bound to *a* you . . .Judg 16:6
a the descendants . . . . .1 Kin 11:39
will hear, and *a* them . . . . . .Ps 55:19
a Your heritage . . . . .Ps 94:5
a man to *a* his soul . . . . .Is 58:5
to destroy, and to *a* . . . . .Jer 31:28
For He does not *a* . . . . . . .Lam 3:33
deal with all who *a* . . . . .Zeph 3:19

AFFLICTED

"Why have You *a* . . . . . .Num 11:11
and the Almighty has *a*. .Ruth 1:21
To him who is *a*. . . . . .Job 6:14
hears the cry of the *a* . . . .Job 34:28
You *a* the peoples . . . . .Ps 44:2
a I went astray . . . . .Ps 119:67
I am *a* very much . . . . .Ps 119:107
a time they have *a* . . . . . .Ps 129:1
the cause of the *a* . . . . .Ps 140:12
days of the *a* are evil. . . .Prov 15:15
smitten by God, and *a* . . . .Is 53:4
oppressed and He was *a*. . . .Is 53:7
"O you *a* one . . . . .Is 54:11
Why have we *a* our . . . . . . .Is 58:3
and satisfy the *a* . . . . .Is 58:10
her virgins are *a*. . . . . .Lam 1:4
she has relieved the *a* . . .1 Tim 5:10
being destitute, *a* . . . . . . .Heb 11:37

AFFLICTING

a the just and taking . . . .Amos 5:12

AFFLICTION

in the land of my *a*. . . . . .Gen 41:52
is, the bread of *a* . . . . . . .Deut 16:3
indeed look on the *a*. . . . .1 Sam 1:11
LORD saw that the *a* . . .2 Kin 14:26
a take hold of me . . . . . . .Job 30:16
days of *a* confront me. . . .Job 30:27
held in the cords of *a*. . . . .Job 36:8
of death, bound in *a* . . . . .Ps 107:10
is my comfort in my *a* . . . .Ps 119:50
and it is an evil *a* . . . . .Eccl 6:2
a He was afflicted . . . . .Is 63:9
refuge in the day of *a* . . . .Jer 16:19
"O LORD, behold my *a* . . . .Lam 1:9
not grieved for the *a* . . . . .Amos 6:6
For our light *a* . . . . .2 Cor 4:17
supposing to add *a*. . . . . . .Phil 1:16
the word in much *a* . . . .1 Thess 1:6

AFRAID

garden, and I was *a* . . . . . .Gen 3:10
saying, "Do not be *a* . . . . .Gen 15:1
his face, for he was *a* . . . . . .Ex 3:6
none will make you *a* . . . . .Lev 26:6
of whom you are *a* . . . . . .Deut 7:19
I will not be *a* . . . . .Ps 3:6
ungodliness made me *a* . . .Ps 18:4
Do not be *a* when one. . . . .Ps 49:16
Whenever I am *a*. . . . . .Ps 56:3
farthest parts are *a*. . . . . . .Ps 65:8
a conspiracy, nor be *a* . . . . .Is 8:12
one will make them *a* . . . . .Is 17:2
that you should be *a* . . . . .Is 51:12

dream which made me *a* . . . .Dan 4:5
do not be *a* . . . . .Matt 14:27
if you do evil, be *a*. . . . . . .Rom 13:4
do good and are not *a* . . . .1 Pet 3:6

AFTERWARD

A he will let you go . . . . .Ex 11:1
a we will speak . . . . .Job 18:2
a receive me to glory . . . . .Ps 73:24
you shall follow Me *a* . . .John 13:36
the firstfruits, *a* . . . . .1 Cor 15:23

AGAIN

day He will rise *a* . . . . . .Matt 20:19
'You must be born *a* . . . . . .John 3:7
to renew them *a* . . . . .Heb 6:6
having been born *a*. . . . . . .1 Pet 1:23

AGAINST

his hand shall be *a*. . . . . . .Gen 16:12
'I will set My face *a* . . . . . .Lev 20:3
come to 'set a man *a* . . . .Matt 10:35
or house divided *a* . . . . .Matt 12:25
Me is *a* Me . . . . .Matt 12:30
a the Spirit will not . . . . .Matt 12:31
For nation will rise *a* . . . .Matt 24:7
out, as *a* a robber . . . . . .Matt 26:55
I have sinned *a* . . . . .Luke 15:18
lifted up his heel *a* . . . . . .John 13:18
LORD and *a* His Christ . . . .Acts 4:26
to kick *a* the goads . . . . . . .Acts 9:5
all men everywhere *a* . . . .Acts 21:28
let us not fight *a* . . . . .Acts 23:9
a the promises of God . . . . .Gal 3:21
we do not wrestle *a* . . . . . .Eph 6:12
I have a few things *a* . . . . .Rev 2:20

AGE

well advanced in *a* . . . . . .Gen 18:11
Israel were dim with *a* . . .Gen 48:10
the flower of their *a* . . . .1 Sam 2:33
the grave at a full *a* . . . . . .Job 5:26
a is as nothing. . . . . .Ps 39:5
and in the *a* to come . . . .Mark 10:30
"The sons of this *a* . . . . .Luke 20:34
He is of *a*. . . . . .John 9:21
who are of full *a* . . . . .Heb 5:14
the powers of the *a* . . . . . . .Heb 6:5

AGED

Wisdom is with *a* . . . . . . .Job 12:12
a one as Paul, the *a* . . . . . .Philem 9

AGES

ordained before the *a*. . . . .1 Cor 2:7
a was not made known . . . .Eph 3:5
at the end of the *a* . . . . . . .Heb 9:26

AGONY

And being in *a* . . . . .Luke 22:44

AGREE

A with your adversary. . .Matt 5:25
that if two of you *a* . . . . .Matt 18:19
testimonies did not *a*. . . .Mark 14:56
and these three *a* . . . . . . .1 John 5:8

AGREED

unless they are *a* . . . . . . .Amos 3:3
they were glad, and *a*. . . .Luke 22:5

AGREEMENT

with Sheol we are in *a*. . . . .Is 28:15
the North to make an *a*. . . .Dan 11:6
what *a* has the temple. . . .2 Cor 6:16

AIDE

the king's personal *a*. . . . .Acts 12:20

AIR

the birds of the *a* . . . . .Gen 1:26

of the *a* have nests . . . . . .Luke 9:58
as one who beats the *a* . . .1 Cor 9:26
be speaking into the *a* . . .1 Cor 14:9
of the power of the *a* . . . . . .Eph 2:2
meet the Lord in the *a*. .1 Thess 4:17
his bowl into the *a* . . . . . .Rev 16:17

ALARM

to sound the *a* against . .2 Chr 13:12
and *a* against the fortified Zeph 1:16

ALIEN

because you were an *a* . . .Deut 23:7
I am an *a* in their . . . . .Job 19:15
who turn away an *a* . . . . . . .Mal 3:5

ALIENATED

a herself from them . . . .Ezek 23:17
darkened, being *a*. . . . . . . .Eph 4:18
you, who once were *a*. . . . . .Col 1:21

ALIENS

For we are *a* and . . . . . . .1 Chr 29:15
For I have loved *a* . . . . .Jer 2:25
A have devoured his. . . . . . .Hos 7:9
Christ, being *a* . . . . .Eph 2:12
the armies of the *a*. . . . . . .Heb 11:34

ALIKE

All things come *a*. . . . . .Eccl 9:2
esteems every day *a* . . . . . .Rom 14:5

ALIVE

in the ark remained *a*. . . . . .Gen 7:23
with them went down *a* . .Num 16:33
LORD your God are *a* . . . . .Deut 4:4
I kill and I make *a*. . . . . .Deut 32:39
Let them go down *a* . . . . . .Ps 55:15
he preserves himself *a* . .Ezek 18:27
heard that He was *a* . . . .Mark 16:11
son was dead and is *a* . .Luke 15:24
presented Himself *a* . . . . . .Acts 1:3
indeed to sin, but *a* . . . . . .Rom 6:11
I was *a* once without. . . . . .Rom 7:9
all shall be made *a* . . . . .1 Cor 15:22
trespasses, made us *a* . . . . .Eph 2:5
flesh, He has made *a* . . . . .Col 2:13
that we who are *a*. . . . . .1 Thess 4:15
the flesh but made *a* . . . . .1 Pet 3:18
and behold, I am *a*. . . . . . . .Rev 1:18
a name that you are *a* . . . . .Rev 3:1
These two were cast *a* . . . .Rev 19:20

ALL

for this is man's *a* . . . . . . .Eccl 12:13

ALLELUIA

Again they said, "*A* . . . . . .Rev 19:3

ALLOW

a Your Holy One. . . . . .Ps 16:10
a My faithfulness . . . . .Ps 89:33
a those who are. . . . . .Matt 23:13
a Your Holy One . . . . .Acts 2:27
who will not *a*. . . . . .1 Cor 10:13

ALLOWED

bygone generations *a* . . . .Acts 14:16

ALLURE

behold, I will *a* . . . . .Hos 2:14
of emptiness, they *a*. . . . . .2 Pet 2:18

ALMOND

a blossoms on one . . . . .Ex 25:33
a tree blossoms . . . . .Eccl 12:5

ALMOST

for me, my feet had *a* . . . . . .Ps 73:2
a persuade me to. . . . . . . .Acts 26:28
a all things are . . . . .Heb 9:22

ALMS

But rather give *a* . . . . . . Luke 11:41
you have and give *a* . . . . Luke 12:33
I came to bring *a* . . . . Acts 24:17

ALOES

with myrrh and *a* . . . . Ps 45:8
my bed with myrrh, *a* . . . . Prov 7:17
mixture of myrrh and *a* . . John 19:39

ALPHA

"I am the *A* and the. . . . . . . Rev 1:8
"I am the *A* and the. . . . . Rev 22:13

ALTAR

Then Noah built an *a*. . . . Gen 8:20
'An *a* of earth you . . . . Ex 20:24
a shall be kept. . . . . Lev 6:9
it to you upon the *a* . . . . . Lev 17:11
offering for the *a*. . . . . . . Num 7:84
of Gad called the *a*. . . . . Josh 22:34
and tear down the *a*. . . . . Judg 6:25
"Go up, erect an *a* . . . . 2 Sam 24:18
out against the *a*. . . . . 1 Kin 13:2
I will go to the *a*. . . . . Ps 43:4
day there will be an *a* . . . . . Is 19:19
Lord has spurned His *a* . . . Lam 2:7
you cover the *a* . . . . Mal 2:13
your gift to the *a* . . . . . . Matt 5:23
swears by the *a*. . . . . . . Matt 23:18
I even found an *a* . . . . . . Acts 17:23
the offerings of the *a* . . . 1 Cor 9:13
partakers of the *a* . . . . . 1 Cor 10:18
We have an *a* from . . . . . . Heb 13:10
Isaac his son on the *a* . . James 2:21
and stood at the *a*. . . . . Rev 8:3

ALTARS

a Hezekiah has taken . . . 2 Kin 18:22
Even Your *a*, O Lord . . . . . . Ps 84:3
on the horns of your *a* . . . . Jer 17:1
a shall be broken. . . . . Ezek 6:4
has made many *a* . . . . Hos 8:11
a shall be heaps . . . . Hos 12:11
destruction on the *a* . . . . Amos 3:14
and torn down Your *a* . . . . Rom 11:3

ALTERED

of His face was *a* . . . . Luke 9:29

ALWAYS

delight, rejoicing *a* . . . . . . Prov 8:30
the poor with you *a* . . . . Matt 26:11
Me you do not have *a* . . Matt 26:11
lo, I am with you *a* . . . . . Matt 28:20
'Son, you are *a* . . . . Luke 15:31
to them, that men *a* . . . . Luke 18:1
immovable, *a* . . . . 1 Cor 15:58
Rejoice in the Lord *a* . . . . . Phil 4:4
thus we shall *a* . . . . 1 Thess 4:17
a be ready to give *a* . . . . . 1 Pet 3:15

AM

to Moses, "I *A* WHO I *A* . . Ex 3:14
First and I *a* the Last. . . . . . Is 44:6
in My name, I *a* . . . . . . Matt 18:20
a the bread of life . . . . . . John 6:35
a the light of the. . . . . . . John 8:12
I *a* from above. . . . . John 8:23
Abraham was, I *A* . . . . . John 8:58
"I *a* the door. . . . . John 10:9
a the good shepherd . . . . John 10:11
a the resurrection . . . . . John 11:25
to him, "I *a* the way. . . . John 14:6
of God I *a* what I *a* . . . 1 Cor 15:10

AMAZED

trembled and were *a* . . . . . Mark 16:8

AMBASSADOR

but a faithful *a* . . . . Prov 13:17
for which I am an *a* . . . . . . Eph 6:20

AMBASSADORS

which sends *a* by sea. . . . . . Is 18:2
cry outside, the *a* . . . . Is 33:7
we are *a* for Christ . . . . . 2 Cor 5:20

AMBITION

Christ from selfish *a* . . . . . Phil 1:16
through selfish *a*. . . . . Phil 2:3

AMEN

uninformed say "*A* . . . . 1 Cor 14:16
are Yes, and in Him *A* . . . 2 Cor 1:20
creatures said, "*A*. . . . . . . Rev 5:14

AMEND

A your ways and your. . . . . . Jer 7:3
from his evil way, *a* . . . . . Jer 35:15

ANCHOR

hope we have as an *a* . . . . . Heb 6:19

ANCIENT

Do not remove the *a* . . . . Prov 23:10
a times that I. . . . . Is 37:26
"until the *A* of Days . . . . . Dan 7:22

ANGEL

Now the *A* of the Lord . . . Gen 16:7
A who has redeemed me . . Gen 48:16
"Behold, I send an *A* . . . . . Ex 23:20
the donkey saw the *A* . . . Num 22:23
For I have seen the *A* . . . Judg 6:22
Manoah said to the *A* . . . Judg 13:17
in my sight as an *a* . . . . . 1 Sam 29:9
a who was destroying. . 2 Sam 24:16
night that the *a* . . . . 2 Kin 19:35
the *A* of His Presence . . . . . Is 63:9
struggled with the *A* . . . . Hos 12:4
standing before the *A* . . . . Zech 3:3
like God, like the *A*. . . . . . Zech 12:8
things, behold, an *a* . . . . . Matt 1:20
for an *a* of the Lord . . . . Matt 28:2
Then an *a* of the Lord . . . Luke 1:11
And behold, an *a* . . . . Luke 2:9
a appeared to Him from. . Luke 22:43
For an *a* went down at . . . . John 5:4
a has spoken to Him . . . John 12:29
But at night an *a* . . . . Acts 5:19
A who appeared to him . . . Acts 7:35
Then immediately an *a* . . Acts 12:23
and no *a* or spirit. . . . . Acts 23:8
a has spoken to him . . . . . Acts 23:9
by me this night an *a* . . . . Acts 27:23
himself into an *a* . . . . . . 2 Cor 11:14
even if we, or an *a*. . . . . Gal 1:8
Then I saw a strong *a* . . . . . Rev 5:2
over them the *a* . . . . Rev 9:11
Then I saw an *a* . . . . Rev 19:17
Jesus, have sent My *a* . . . Rev 22:16

ANGELS

if He charges His *a* . . . . Job 4:18
lower than the *a* . . . . Ps 8:5
He shall give His *a* . . . . . . Ps 91:11
Praise Him, all His *a* . . . . . Ps 148:2
He shall give His *a* . . . . . . Matt 4:6
a will come forth. . . . . . . Matt 13:49
a always see the face . . . . Matt 18:10
but are like *a* . . . . Matt 22:30
not even the *a* . . . . Matt 24:36
and all the holy *a* . . . . . . Matt 25:31
twelve legions of *a* . . . . . Matt 26:53
the presence of the *a* . . . . Luke 15:10
was carried by the *a*. . . . Luke 16:22
are equal to the *a* . . . . . Luke 20:36
And she saw two *a*. . . . . . John 20:12

that we shall judge *a*. . . . . 1 Cor 6:3
head, because of the *a*. . . 1 Cor 11:10
and worship of *a* . . . . Col 2:18
with His mighty *a* . . . . . 2 Thess 1:7
the Spirit, seen by *a* . . . . . 1 Tim 3:16
much better than the *a* . . . . Heb 1:4
does not give aid to *a* . . . . Heb 2:16
company of *a* . . . . Heb 12:22
entertained *a*. . . . . Heb 13:2
things which *a* desire. . . . 1 Pet 1:12
did not spare the *a* . . . . . . 2 Pet 2:4
a who did not keep. . . . . Jude 6
Michael and his *a* . . . . Rev 12:7

ANGER

Cursed be their *a* . . . . Gen 49:7
sun, that the fierce *a* . . . . Num 25:4
fierceness of His *a* . . . . . . Deut 13:17
of this great *a* . . . . Deut 29:24
So the *a* of the Lord . . . . Judg 10:7
to provoke Me to *a* . . . . . 1 Kin 16:2
For His *a* is but for a . . . . . Ps 30:5
let Your wrathful *a* . . . . . . Ps 69:24
a time He turned His *a* . . . . Ps 78:38
made a path for His *a* . . . . Ps 78:50
You prolong Your *a* . . . . . . Ps 85:5
the power of Your *a*. . . . . . Ps 90:11
gracious, slow to *a* . . . . . . Ps 103:8
Nor will He keep His *a* . . . Ps 103:9
harsh word stirs up *a* . . . . Prov 15:1
a sins against his own . . . . Prov 20:2
a rests in the bosom . . . . . Eccl 7:9
a the Holy One of . . . . Is 1:4
a is not turned away . . . . . . Is 5:25
a is turned away. . . . . Is 12:1
'I will not cause My *a* . . . . . Jer 3:12
For great is the *a* . . . . Jer 36:7
and I will send My *a* . . . . Ezek 7:3
does not retain His *a* . . . . . Mic 7:18
fierceness of His *a* . . . . . . Nah 1:6
a is kindled against. . . . . Zech 10:3
around at them with *a*. . . . Mark 3:5
bitterness, wrath, *a* . . . . . . Eph 4:31

ANGRY

Cain, "Why are you *a*. . . . . Gen 4:6
"Let not the Lord be *a* . . Gen 18:30
the Son, lest He be *a* . . . . . Ps 2:12
judge, and God is *a* . . . . Ps 7:11
When once You are *a* . . . . . Ps 76:7
Will You be *a* forever . . . . . Ps 79:5
friendship with an *a* . . . . Prov 22:24
backbiting tongue an *a*. . . Prov 25:23
a man stirs up strife. . . . Prov 29:22
in your spirit to be *a* . . . . . Eccl 7:9
I was *a* with My people . . . . Is 47:6
nor will I always be *a* . . . . Is 57:16
covetousness I was *a*. . . . . Is 57:17
right for you to be *a* . . . . . Jon 4:4
Lord has been very *a* . . . . Zech 1:2
I am exceedingly *a* . . . . . Zech 1:15
you that whoever is *a*. . . . Matt 5:22
"Be *a*, and do not. . . . . Eph 4:26
Therefore I was *a* . . . . Heb 3:10
with whom was He *a*. . . . . Heb 3:17
The nations were *a* . . . . . . Rev 11:18

ANGUISH

a has come upon me. . . . . 2 Sam 1:9
a make him afraid. . . . . . . Job 15:24
I will be in *a* over my . . . . . Ps 38:18
a have overtaken . . . . . . Ps 119:143
longer remembers the *a* . John 16:21
tribulation and *a* . . . . Rom 2:9
much affliction and *a*. . . . . 2 Cor 2:4

ANIMAL

of every clean *a*. . . . . Gen 7:2
'Whoever kills an *a* . . . . . Lev 24:18

the life of his *a*.........Prov 12:10
set him on his own *a* ....Luke 10:34

ANIMALS

of *a* after their kind ......Gen 6:20
sacrifices of fat *a*.........Ps 66:15
of four-footed *a* ....Acts 10:12
and four-footed *a* ....Rom 1:23

ANISE

tithe of mint and *a*......Matt 23:23

ANNUL

and who will *a* ....Is 14:27
years later, cannot *a* ....Gal 3:17

ANNULLING

one hand there is an *a* .....Heb 7:18

ANNULS

is confirmed, no one *a*......Gal 3:15

ANOINT

You shall *a* them.........Ex 28:41
but you shall not *a*......Deut 28:40
you shall *a* for Me the ...1 Sam 16:3
a yourself with oil.......2 Sam 14:2
a my head with oil ....Ps 23:5
Arise, you princes, *a* ....Is 21:5
a the Most Holy.........Dan 9:24
when you fast, *a* ....Matt 6:17
a My body for burial.....Mark 14:8
they might come and *a* ...Mark 16:1
a your eyes with eye.......Rev 3:18

ANOINTED

the priest, who is *a*.......Lev 16:32
"Surely the LORD's *a* ....1 Sam 16:6
destroy the LORD's *a* ...2 Sam 1:14
he cursed the LORD's *a* 2 Sam 19:21
shows mercy to His *a* ..2 Sam 22:51
"Do not touch My *a* ...1 Chr 16:22
the LORD saves His *a* ....Ps 20:6
because the LORD has *a* .....Is 61:1
"These are the two *a* ....Zech 4:14
because He has *a* ....Luke 4:18
but this woman has *a*....Luke 7:46
a the eyes of the ....John 9:6
It was that Mary who *a*..John 11:2
Jesus, whom You *a*.......Acts 4:27
and has *a* us is God......2 Cor 1:21

ANOINTING

also made the holy *a* .....Ex 37:29
them pray over him, *a* ..James 5:14
But you have an *a* ......1 John 2:20
but as the same *a* ......1 John 2:27

ANOTHER

that you love one *a*.....John 13:34
and He will give you *a* ..John 14:16
'Let *a* take his ....Acts 1:20

ANSWER

will give Pharaoh an *a*...Gen 41:16
a I should take back ..2 Sam 24:13
Him, he could not *a* ....Job 9:3
call, and I will *a* ....Job 13:22
how shall I *a* Him.......Job 31:14
and you shall *a* ....Job 40:7
the day that I call, *a*......Ps 102:2
In Your faithfulness *a*.....Ps 143:1
a turns away wrath......Prov 15:1
A man has joy by the *a* ..Prov 15:23
He who gives a right *a* ...Prov 24:26
a a fool according ......Prov 26:4
was there none to *a* ....Is 50:2
for there is no *a*........Mic 3:7
or what you should *a* ...Luke 12:11
that you may have an *a*..2 Cor 5:12

ought to *a* each one........Col 4:6

ANSWERS

a a matter before he .....Prov 18:13
but the rich *a*...........Prov 18:23
money *a* everything......Eccl 10:19

ANT

Go to the *a*..............Prov 6:6

ANTICHRIST

have heard that the *A*...1 John 2:18
a who denies the ....1 John 2:22
is the spirit of the *A* .....1 John 4:3
is a deceiver and an *a*.....2 John 7

ANTITYPE

a which now saves us.....1 Pet 3:21

ANXIETIES

the multitude of my *a* .....Ps 94:19
Try me, and know my *a* ..Ps 139:23

ANXIETY

A in the heart of man....Prov 12:25
eat their bread with *a*....Ezek 12:19

ANXIOUS

drink, nor have an *a* .....Luke 12:29
Be *a* for nothing...........Phil 4:6

APART

that you shall set *a* ......Ex 13:12
she shall be set *a* ....Lev 15:19
the LORD has set *a* ....Ps 4:3
justified by faith *a* ......Rom 3:28

APOSTLE

called to be an *a* ....Rom 1:1
inasmuch as I am an *a*...Rom 11:13
Am I not an *a* ....1 Cor 9:1
the signs of an *a* were ...2 Cor 12:12
a preacher and an *a*......1 Tim 2:7
consider the *A* ....Heb 3:1

APOSTLES

of the twelve *a* ....Matt 10:2
whom He also named *a* ...Luke 6:13
displayed us, the *a*.......1 Cor 4:9
am the least of the *a* .....1 Cor 15:9
to the most eminent *a* ...2 Cor 11:5
themselves into *a*.......2 Cor 11:13
none of the other *a* ....Gal 1:19
gave some to be *a*........Eph 4:11
who say they are *a* ....Rev 2:2
heaven, and you holy *a*...Rev 18:20

APOSTLESHIP

in this ministry and *a*....Acts 1:25
received grace and *a* ....Rom 1:5
are the seal of my *a*......1 Cor 9:2
in Peter for the *a*.........Gal 2:8

APPAREL

is glorious in His *a* ....Is 63:1
clothed with foreign *a*....Zeph 1:8
by them in white *a* ......Acts 1:10
themselves in modest *a* ...1 Tim 2:9
gold rings, in fine *a* ......James 2:2
or putting on fine *a* ....1 Pet 3:3

APPEAL

I *a* to Caesar ....Acts 25:11
love's sake I rather *a* .....Philem 9

APPEAR

and let the dry land *a* .....Gen 1:9
all your males shall *a*.....Ex 23:17
all Israel comes to *a* ....Deut 31:11
shall I come and *a* ....Ps 42:2
Let Your work *a* ....Ps 90:16

He shall *a* in His.........Ps 102:16
doings your sins *a* .....Ezek 21:24
faces that they may *a* ....Matt 6:16
also outwardly *a* ....Matt 23:28
kingdom of God would *a* Luke 19:11
For we must all *a* ....2 Cor 5:10
for Him He will *a*........Heb 9:28
and the sinner *a* ....1 Pet 4:18

APPEARANCE

Do not look at his *a*.....1 Sam 16:7
a is blacker than soot .....Lam 4:8
As He prayed, the *a*.....Luke 9:29
judge according to *a*.....John 7:24
those who boast in *a* ....2 Cor 5:12
to the outward *a*.......2 Cor 10:7
found in *a* as a man........Phil 2:8
indeed have an *a* ....Col 2:23

APPEARED

an angel of the Lord *a* ...Luke 1:11
who *a* in glory and ......Luke 9:31
brings salvation has *a*....Titus 2:11
of the ages, He has *a*......Heb 9:26

APPEARING

Lord Jesus Christ's *a* ....1 Tim 6:14
been revealed by the *a*....2 Tim 1:10
and the dead at His *a* ....2 Tim 4:1
who have loved His *a* ....2 Tim 4:8
hope and glorious *a*.......Titus 2:13

APPEARS

can stand when He *a*......Mal 3:2
who is our life *a*...........Col 3:4
the Chief Shepherd *a*....1 Pet 5:4
in Him, that when He *a* 1 John 2:28

APPETITE

or satisfy the *a* ....Job 38:39
are a man given to *a*.....Prov 23:2

APPLE

He kept him as the *a* ...Deut 32:10
and my law as the *a* ......Prov 7:2
Like an *a* tree among......Song 2:3
you touches the *a* ....Zech 2:8

APPLES

fitly spoken is like *a* .....Prov 25:11
refresh me with *a* ....Song 2:5

APPLIED

a my heart to know ......Eccl 7:25

APPOINT

I will even *a* terror ....Lev 26:16
a each of them to his .....Num 4:19
a me ruler over the......2 Sam 6:21
a salvation for walls ......Is 26:1
For God did not *a* ......1 Thess 5:9
a elders in every city ......Titus 1:5

APPOINTED

You have *a* his limits ......Job 14:5
To release those *a* ....Ps 102:20
And as it is *a* for men ....Heb 9:27

APPROACH

a anyone who is near .....Lev 18:6
And cause to *a* You.........Ps 65:4
year, make those who *a*...Heb 10:1

APPROACHING

take delight in *a* God ......Is 58:2
as you see the Day *a* .....Heb 10:25

APPROVE

their posterity who *a* .....Ps 49:13
do the same but also *a* ....Rom 1:32
a the things that........Rom 2:18

a the things that are ......Phil 1:10

APPROVED
to God and *a* by men ....Rom 14:18
to present yourself *a* ....2 Tim 2:15
when he has been *a* .....James 1:12

ARBITRATOR
Me a judge or an *a* ......Luke 12:14

ARCHANGEL
with the voice of an *a* .1 Thess 4:16
Yet Michael the *a* ....Jude 9

ARGUMENTS
fill my mouth with *a* ......Job 23:4
casting down *a* and .....2 Cor 10:5

ARISE
needy, now I will *a* ....Ps 12:5
A for our help ....Ps 44:26
Let God *a* ....Ps 68:1
A, shine...................Is 60:1
but the LORD will *a* ....Is 60:2
Righteousness shall *a*......Mal 4:2
'I will *a* and go to......Luke 15:18
you who sleep, *a*..........Eph 5:14

ARK
"Make yourself an *a*......Gen 6:14
him, she took an *a*.........Ex 2:3
Bezalel made the *a*........Ex 37:1
seat which is on the *a*.....Lev 16:2
Let us bring the *a* ....1 Sam 4:3
golden censer and the *a*....Heb 9:4
of Noah, while the *a*...1 Pet 3:20
in heaven, and the *a*......Rev 11:19

ARM
with an outstretched *a*......Ex 6:6
"Has the LORD's *a* .....Num 11:23
"With him is an *a* ....2 Chr 32:8
a that has no strength ....Job 26:2
Have you an *a* like God ...Job 40:9
Break the *a* of the .....Ps 10:15
You have a mighty *a*......Ps 89:13
a have gained Him the......Ps 98:1
a shall rule for Him........Is 40:10
therefore His own *a*.......Is 59:16
strength with His *a* ....Luke 1:51
with an uplifted *a* ......Acts 13:17
a yourselves also with .....1 Pet 4:1

ARMED
You have a me with ....2 Sam 22:40
a strong man, fully *a* ....Luke 11:21

ARMIES
make captains of the *a*....Deut 20:9
"I defy the *a* ....1 Sam 17:10
any number to His *a*.......Job 25:3
not go out with our *a*.....Ps 60:10
And he sent out his *a* ....Matt 22:7
surrounded by *a* ....Luke 21:20
And the *a* in heaven......Rev 19:14
the earth, and their *a*....Rev 19:19

ARMOR
but he put his *a* ......1 Sam 17:54
spears, put on the *a*.......Jer 46:4
let us put on the *a* ......Rom 13:12
Put on the whole *a*.......Eph 6:11

ARMS
are the everlasting *a*....Deut 33:27
into the clash of *a*......Job 39:21
It is God who *a*...........Ps 18:32
a will judge the ....Is 51:5
wounds between your *a* ..Zech 13:6
took them up in His *a*..Mark 10:16

took Him up in his *a* ....Luke 2:28

ARMY
the multitude of an *a* ......Ps 33:16
an exceedingly great *a* ...Ezek 37:10
the number of the *a* ......Rev 9:16

AROMA
smelled a soothing *a* .....Gen 8:21
the one we are the *a*......2 Cor 2:16
for a sweet-smelling *a* ...Eph 5:2
a sweet-smelling *a* ....Phil 4:18

AROUSED
the LORD was greatly *a* ..Num 11:10
his wrath was *a*..........Job 32:2
Then Joseph, being *a*.....Matt 1:24

ARRAYED
his glory was not *a*......Matt 6:29
"Who are these *a* ....Rev 7:13
The woman was *a*........Rev 17:4

ARROGANCE
pride and *a* and the......Prov 8:13
I will halt the *a* ....Is 13:11

ARROGANT
the fruit of the *a* ....Is 10:12
My sanctuary, your *a*....Ezek 24:21

ARROW
deliverance and the *a*....2 Kin 13:17
a cannot make him flee ...Job 41:28
make ready their *a* ....Ps 11:2
a that flies by day..........Ps 91:5
a sword, and a sharp *a* ...Prov 25:18
Their tongue is an *a* ....Jer 9:8
as a target for the *a* .....Lam 3:12

ARROWS
He sent out *a* and.....2 Sam 22:15
a pierce me deeply ....Ps 38:2
There He broke the *a* .....Ps 76:3
Like *a* in the hand of .....Ps 127:4
He has caused the *a* .....Lam 3:13
were sworn over Your *a*....Hab 3:9

ASCEND
Who may *a* into the ....Ps 24:3
If I *a* into heaven ....Ps 139:8
'I will *a* into heaven........Is 14:13
a as high as the eagle......Obad 4
see the Son of Man *a* ....John 6:62

ASCENDED
You have *a* on high........Ps 68:18
Who has *a* into heaven ....Prov 30:4
"No one has *a* ....John 3:13
"When He *a* on high ......Eph 4:8
also the One who *a* ......Eph 4:10
And they *a* to heaven.....Rev 11:12

ASCENDING
angels of God were *a* .....Gen 28:12
the angels of God *a* ......John 1:51

ASCRIBE
a greatness to our God....Deut 32:3
a righteousness ....Job 36:3
A strength to God ....Ps 68:34

ASHAMED
I am too a and...........Ezra 9:6
all my enemies be *a* ....Ps 6:10
Let me not be *a*...........Ps 25:2
who waits on You be *a* ....Ps 25:3
The wise men are *a* ......Jer 8:9
forsake You shall be *a* ....Jer 17:13
and Israel shall be *a*......Hos 10:6
For whoever is *a*........Mark 8:38

am not *a* of the gospel ....Rom 1:16
nothing I shall be *a* ......Phil 1:20
Therefore God is not *a*....Heb 11:16
in Christ may be *a* ......1 Pet 3:16
let him not be *a* ....1 Pet 4:16
and not be *a* before ....1 John 2:28

ASHES
are proverbs of *a* ....Job 13:12
become like dust and *a*....Job 30:19
For I have eaten *a*.........Ps 102:9
He feeds on *a*.............Is 44:20
sackcloth and sat in *a* ....Jon 3:6
in sackcloth and *a*......Luke 10:13
and goats and the *a*......Heb 9:13

ASIDE
of you lay something *a* ...1 Cor 16:2
lay *a* all filthiness.......James 1:21
Therefore, laying *a* ....1 Pet 2:1

ASK
"Why is it that you *a* ....Gen 32:29
when your children *a*......Josh 4:6
"*A* a sign for yourself ......Is 7:11
They shall *a* the way......Jer 50:5
the young children *a* ......Lam 4:4
A the LORD for rain in ...Zech 10:1
whatever things you *a* ...Matt 21:22
a, and it will be.........Luke 11:9
that whatever You *a* .....John 11:22
a anything in My name ...John 14:14
in that day you will *a* .....John 16:23
something, let them *a* ...1 Cor 14:35
above all that we *a*.......Eph 3:20
wisdom, let him *a*........James 1:5
But let him *a* in faith....James 1:6
because you do not *a* .....James 4:2
us, whatever we *a* ......1 John 5:15

ASKS
For everyone who *a* ......Matt 7:8
you who, if his son *a* .....Matt 7:9
Or if he *a* for a fish......Luke 11:11

ASLEEP
down, and was fast *a* ......Jon 1:5
But He was *a* ....Matt 8:24
but some have fallen *a*....1 Cor 15:6
those who are *a* ....1 Thess 4:15
the fathers fell *a*..........2 Pet 3:4

ASSEMBLED
of the God of Israel *a*.....Ezra 9:4
behold, the kings *a*........Ps 48:4

ASSEMBLING
not forsaking the *a* ......Heb 10:25

ASSEMBLY
to kill this whole *a*........Ex 16:3
It is a sacred *a* ....Lev 23:36
a I will praise You.........Ps 22:22
I have hated the *a*........Ps 26:5
also in the *a* of the ....Ps 89:5
to be feared in the *a*......Ps 89:7
will rest in the *a* of the...Prov 21:16
fast, call a sacred *a* ......Joel 1:14
people, sanctify the *a*....Joel 2:16
a I will sing praise......Heb 2:12
to the general *a* ....Heb 12:23
come into your *a*........James 2:2

ASSURANCE
night, and have no *a*.....Deut 28:66
riches of the full *a*.........Col 2:2
Spirit and in much *a* ....1 Thess 1:5
to the full *a* of hope .....Heb 6:11
a true heart in full *a* .....Heb 10:22

ASSURE

a our hearts before .....1 John 3:19

ASSURED

but I will give you *a* ..... Jer 14:13
learned and been *a* ......2 Tim 3:14

ASTONISHED

Just as many were *a* .... Is 52:14
that the people were *a* ....Matt 7:28
who heard Him were *a* ....Luke 2:47

ASTONISHMENT

you shall become an *a* ...Deut 28:37
a has taken hold...........Jer 8:21

ASTRAY

is a people who go *a* ....Ps 95:10
a fool, shall not go *a* ....Is 35:8
Their lies lead them *a* ....Amos 2:4
and one of them goes *a* ..Matt 18:12
They always go *a* ....Heb 3:10
like sheep going *a*........1 Pet 2:25

ATONEMENT

a year he shall make *a*.....Ex 30:10
priest shall make *a* ......Lev 16:30
the blood that makes *a* ..Lev 17:11
for it is the Day of *A* ....Lev 23:28
what shall I make *a*.....2 Sam 21:3
offerings to make *a* ......Neh 10:33
a is provided for ....Prov 16:6
there will be no *a*.........Is 22:14
I provide you an *a* .....Ezek 16:63

ATTAIN

It is high, I cannot *a* .....Ps 139:6
understanding will *a* ....Prov 1:5
How long until they *a* ...Hos 8:5
worthy to a that age....Luke 20:35
by any means, I may *a* ...Phil 3:11

ATTEND

just cause, O LORD,.......Ps 17:1
And *a* to the voice of ......Ps 86:6
Behold, I will *a* ....Jer 23:2

ATTENTION

My son, give *a* to my ....Prov 4:20
Till I come, give *a* ....1 Tim 4:13
and you pay *a* to the .....James 2:3

ATTENTIVE

Let Your ears be *a*........Ps 130:2
the people were very *a* ..Luke 19:48

ATTESTED

a Man *a* by God to you....Acts 2:22

AUSTERE

because you are an *a* ....Luke 19:21

AUTHOR

For God is not the *a* ....1 Cor 14:33
He became the *a* ....Heb 5:9
unto Jesus, the *a* ....Heb 12:2

AUTHORITIES

a that exist are ....Rom 13:1
of God, angels and *a* .....1 Pet 3:22

AUTHORITY

Jew, wrote with full *a*.....Esth 9:29
the righteous are in *a* .....Prov 29:2
them as one having *a*....Matt 7:29
are great exercise *a*......Matt 20:25
"All *a* has been given....Matt 28:18
a I will give You ....Luke 4:6
and has given Him *a* ....John 5:27
You have given Him *a* ...John 17:2
has put in His own *a*......Acts 1:7

For there is no *a* ....Rom 13:1
to have a symbol of *a* ...1 Cor 11:10
and all who are in *a*.......1 Tim 2:2
and rebuke with all *a*.....Titus 2:15
the flesh, reject *a* ....Jude 8

AUTUMN

a trees without fruit ....Jude 12

AVAILS

nor uncircumcision *a*........Gal 5:6
of a righteous man *a* ...James 5:16

AVENGE

for He will *a* the ....Deut 32:43
you that He will *a*.......Luke 18:8
Beloved, do not *a*.......Rom 12:19
a our blood on those......Rev 6:10

AVENGER

'The *a* of blood ....Num 35:19
the enemy and the *a*........Ps 8:2
God's minister, an *a* ......Rom 13:4
the Lord is the *a* ....1 Thess 4:6

AVENGES

It is God who *a* ......2 Sam 22:48
When He *a* blood ....Ps 9:12

AWAKE

be satisfied when I *a* ......Ps 17:15
I lie *a* ....Ps 102:7
A, lute and harp ....Ps 108:2
My eyes are *a* through...Ps 119:148
A, O north wind ....Song 4:16
but my heart is *a* ....Song 5:2
of the earth shall *a*........Dan 12:2
it is high time to *a* ......Rom 13:11
A to righteousness......1 Cor 15:34
"*A*, you who sleep ....Eph 5:14

AWAY

the wind drives *a* ....Ps 1:4
Do not cast me *a* ....Ps 51:11
a time to cast *a* ....Eccl 3:5
fair one, and come *a*....Song 2:10
and the shadows flee *a*...Song 2:17
minded to put her *a* .....Matt 1:19
and earth will pass *a* ....Matt 24:35
and steal Him *a* ....Matt 27:64
the rich He has sent *a* ...Luke 1:53
of God who takes *a* ......John 1:29
"I am going *a* ....John 8:21
they cried out, "*A*......John 19:15
"They have taken *a* .....John 20:2
crying out, "*A*..........Acts 21:36
the veil is taken *a*......2 Cor 3:14
Barnabas was carried *a* ...Gal 2:13
unless the falling *a*......2 Thess 2:3
in Asia have turned *a* ....2 Tim 1:15
heard, lest we drift *a* ......Heb 2:1
if they fall *a* ....Heb 6:6
which can never take *a*...Heb 10:11
that does not fade *a* ....1 Pet 5:4
the world is passing *a*...1 John 2:17
and the heaven fled *a*....Rev 20:11
if anyone takes *a*........Rev 22:19
God shall take *a* ....Rev 22:19

AWE

the world stand in *a*.......Ps 33:8
my heart stands in *a* ....Ps 119:161

AWESOME

a is this place ....Gen 28:17
a thing that I will do......Ex 34:10
God, the great and *a* ....Deut 7:21
God, mighty and *a* ......Deut 10:17
Angel of God, very *a*....Judg 13:6
a deeds for Your land....2 Sam 7:23

heaven, O great and *a* ......Neh 1:5
hand shall teach You *a*.....Ps 45:4
By *a* deeds in..............Ps 65:5
a are Your works...........Ps 66:3
He is *a* in His doing.......Ps 66:5
O God, You are more *a*....Ps 68:35
He is *a* to the kings ......Ps 76:12
Your great and *a* name......Ps 99:3
of the might of Your *a* ...Ps 145:6
When You did *a* things .....Is 64:3
with me as a mighty, *a* ...Jer 20:11
her collapse was *a* ....Lam 1:9
"O Lord, great and *a* ......Dan 9:4

AWL

his ear with an *a*...........Ex 21:6
you shall take an *a* .....Deut 15:17

AX

a stroke with the *a* ......Deut 19:5
Abimelech took an *a* ....Judg 9:48
a tree, the iron *a*..........2 Kin 6:5
If the *a* is dull ....Eccl 10:10
a boast itself against.......Is 10:15
And even now the *a* .....Matt 3:10

B

BABBLER

b is no different ....Eccl 10:11
"What does this *b*.......Acts 17:18

BABBLINGS

the profane and idle *b*....1 Tim 6:20

BABE

the *b* leaped in my ......Luke 1:44
You will find a *B*........Luke 2:12
for he is a *b*..............Heb 5:13

BABES

Out of the mouth of *b* ....Ps 8:2
b shall rule over them........Is 3:4
revealed them to *b* ......Matt 11:25
'Out of the mouth of *b*...Matt 21:16
a teacher of *b*............Rom 2:20
as to carnal, as to *b*......1 Cor 3:1
as newborn *b*.............1 Pet 2:2

BACK

Jordan turned *b* ....Ps 114:3
but a rod is for the *b*....Prov 10:13
for the fool's *b* ....Prov 26:3
I gave My *b* to those.......Is 50:6
cast Me behind your *b*...Ezek 23:35
found Him, bring *b*.......Matt 2:8
plow, and looking *b*......Luke 9:62
they drew *b* and fell .....John 18:6
I am sending him *b* ....Philem 12
of those who draw *b* ....Heb 10:39
someone turns him *b* ...James 5:19
inside and on the *b*........Rev 5:1

BACKBITERS

b, haters of God..........Rom 1:30

BACKBITING

b tongue an angry.......Prov 25:23

BACKSLIDER

The *b* in heart will be ....Prov 14:14

BACKSLIDINGS

b will rebuke you ....Jer 2:19
and I will heal your *b* .....Jer 3:22
b have increased...........Jer 5:6
for our *b* are many.........Jer 14:7

BACKWARD

fell off the seat *b* ......1 Sam 4:18

BAD

shadow ten degrees *b* . . .2 Kin 20:11

BAD

speak to you either *b* . . . . .Gen 24:50
it, good for *b* or *b* . . . . . . .Lev 27:10
b tree bears *b* fruit . . . . . . .Matt 7:17

BAG

is sealed up in a *b* . . . . . . .Job 14:17
wages to put into a *b* . . . . . .Hag 1:6
"nor *b* for your . . . . .Matt 10:10

BAKE

b twelve cakes with it. . . . . .Lev 24:5

BAKED

b unleavened cakes. . . . . . .Ex 12:39
b unleavened . . . . .1 Sam 28:24

BAKER

the butler and the *b* . . . . . .Gen 40:1

BAKERS

of bread from the *b* . . . . . .Jer 37:21

BAKES

kindles it and *b* bread . . . . .Is 44:15

BALANCE

b is an abomination . . . . . .Prov 11:1
small dust on the *b* . . . . . . .Is 40:15

BALANCES

falsifying the *b* . . . . .Amos 8:5

BALD

shall not make any *b* . . . . . .Lev 21:5
every head shall be *b* . . . . . .Jer 48:37
completely *b* because . . . .Ezek 27:31

BALDHEAD

Go up, you *b*. . . . . .2 Kin 2:23

BALM

a little *b* and a . . . . .Gen 43:11
no *b* in Gilead. . . . . .Jer 8:22

BAND

A *b* of robbers takes . . . . . .Hos 7:1
with a golden *b* . . . . .Rev 1:13

BANDAGED

him and *b* his wounds . . .Luke 10:34

BANKERS

my money with the *b* . . . .Matt 25:27

BANNERS

we will set up our *b* . . . . . . .Ps 20:5
They set up their *b* . . . . . . .Ps 74:4
as an army with *b*. . . . . . . .Song 6:4

BANQUET

b that I have prepared . . . .Esth 5:4
companions make a *b* . . . . .Job 41:6
lords, came to the *b* . . . . . .Dan 5:10

BANQUETING

He brought me to the *b* . . . .Song 2:4

BANQUETS

b shall be removed . . . . . .Amos 6:7

BAPTISM

coming to his *b* . . . . .Matt 3:7
b that I am baptized . . . .Matt 20:22
" The *b* of John. . . . . .Matt 21:25
"But I have a *b* . . . . .Luke 12:50
said, "Into John's *b* . . . . . .Acts 19:3
with Him through *b* . . . . . .Rom 6:4
Lord, one faith, one *b* . . . . .Eph 4:5
buried with Him in *b* . . . . . .Col 2:12

now saves us—*b* . . . . .1 Pet 3:21

BAPTISMS

of the doctrine of *b* . . . . . . .Heb 6:2

BAPTIZE

"I indeed *b* you with . . . . .Matt 3:11
"Why then do you *b* . . . . . .John 1:25
Himself did not *b* . . . . .John 4:2
did not send me to *b* . . . . .1 Cor 1:17

BAPTIZED

"I need to be *b* . . . . .Matt 3:14
b will be saved . . . . .Mark 16:16
b more disciples . . . . .John 4:1
every one of you be *b* . . . . .Acts 2:38
all his family were *b* . . . .Acts 16:33
believed and were *b* . . . . . .Acts 18:8
Arise and be *b* . . . . .Acts 22:16
I thank God that I *b* . . . . .1 Cor 1:14
b the household . . . . .1 Cor 1:16
all were *b* into Moses. . . . .1 Cor 10:2
Spirit we were all *b* . . .1 Cor 12:13
who are *b* for the dead . .1 Cor 15:29
of you as were *b* . . . . .Gal 3:27

BAPTIZING

b them in the name of . . .Matt 28:19
therefore I came *b*. . . . . . .John 1:31

BARBARIAN

nor uncircumcised, *b* . . . . . .Col 3:11

BARE

make yourselves *b* . . . . . . .Is 32:11
The LORD has made *b* . . . . .Is 52:10

BARLEY

a land of wheat and *b*. . . . .Deut 8:8
b bread tumbled . . . . .Judg 7:13
beginning of *b* harvest. . . . .Ruth 1:22
here who has five *b* . . . . . .John 6:9
and three quarts of *b* . . . . . .Rev 6:6

BARN

seed still in the *b* . . . . .Hag 2:19
the wheat into my *b* . . . .Matt 13:30
storehouse nor *b* . . . . . . .Luke 12:24

BARNS

b will be filled . . . . .Prov 3:10
b are broken down . . . . . . .Joel 1:17
reap nor gather into *b* . . . .Matt 6:26
I will pull down my *b* . . . .Luke 12:18

BARREN

But Sarai was *b* . . . . .Gen 11:30
b has borne seven. . . . . . . .1 Sam 2:5
He grants the *b*. . . . . .Ps 113:9
"Sing, O *b*. . . . . .Is 54:1
'Blessed are the *b* . . . . . .Luke 23:29
"Rejoice, O *b* . . . . .Gal 4:27
you will be neither *b* . . . . .2 Pet 1:8

BARRENNESS

A fruitful land into *b* . . . . .Ps 107:34

BARS

has strengthened the *b*. . . .Ps 147:13
bronze and cut the *b* . . . . . . .Is 45:2
the earth with its *b* . . . . . . .Jon 2:6

BASE

the elder, and the *b* . . . . .Is 3:5
and the *b* things of . . . . . .1 Cor 1:28

BASIN

poured water into a *b* . . . . .John 13:5

BASKET

Cursed shall be your *b* . . .Deut 28:17
b had very good figs . . . . . .Jer 24:2
and put it under a *b*. . . . . .Matt 5:15
I was let down in a *b* . . . .2 Cor 11:33

BASKETS

there were three white *b* . .Gen 40:16
and there were two *b* . . . . . .Jer 24:1
they took up twelve *b* . . .Matt 14:20
up seven large *b* . . . . . . .Matt 15:37

BATHED

My sword shall be *b* . . . . . . .Is 34:5
to him, "He who is *b* . . . .John 13:10

BATS

to the moles and *b*. . . . . . . .Is 2:20

BATTLE

b is the LORD'S . . . . .1 Sam 17:47
out to God in the *b* . . . . . .1 Chr 5:20
strength for the *b* . . . . .Ps 18:39
for the day of *b* . . . . .Prov 21:31
the *b* to the strong. . . . . . .Eccl 9:11
who turn back the *b* . . . . . . .Is 28:6
A sound of *b* is in the . . . .Jer 50:22
prepare for *b* . . . . .1 Cor 14:8
became valiant in *b* . . . . . .Heb 11:34
gather them to the *b* . . . . .Rev 16:14

BEAR

greater than I can *b* . . . . . .Gen 4:13
whom Sarah shall *b* . . . . .Gen 17:21
not *b* false witness. . . . . . . .Ex 20:16
from the paw of the *b* . .1 Sam 17:37
they shall *b* you up in. . . . .Ps 91:12
b a broken spirit . . . . . . .Prov 18:14
be clean, you who *b* . . . . . .Is 52:11
b their iniquities . . . . .Is 53:11
LORD could no longer *b* . . . .Jer 44:22
b deprived of her cubs. . . . .Hos 13:8
lion, and a *b* met him . . . .Amos 5:19
He shall *b* the glory . . . . .Zech 6:13
child, and *b* a Son. . . . . . .Matt 1:23
A good tree cannot *b* . . . . .Matt 7:18
how long shall I *b*. . . . . . .Matt 17:17
by, to *b* His cross. . . . . . .Mark 15:21
wife Elizabeth will *b*. . . . .Luke 1:13
And whoever does not *b* .Luke 14:27
in Me that does not *b*. . . . .John 15:2
for he does not *b* . . . . .Rom 13:4
are strong ought to *b* . . . . .Rom 15:1
you may be able to *b* . . . .1 Cor 10:13
B one another's . . . . .Gal 6:2
I *b* in my body the . . . . .Gal 6:17
b the sins of many . . . . . . .Heb 9:28
like the feet of a *b*. . . . . . . .Rev 13:2

BEARD

the edges of your *b* . . . . . .Lev 19:27
I caught it by its *b* . . . . .1 Sam 17:35
took Amasa by the *b* . . . .2 Sam 20:9
running down on the *b* . . . .Ps 133:2

BEARING

goes forth weeping, *b* . . . . .Ps 126:6
And He, *b* His cross. . . . . .John 19:17
b with one another . . . . . . .Col 3:13
the camp, *b* His reproach Heb 13:13

BEARS

Every branch that *b*. . . . . .John 15:2
b all things . . . . .1 Cor 13:7
it is the Spirit who *b*. . . . .1 John 5:6

BEAST

b has devoured him . . . . . .Gen 37:20
You preserve man and *b*. . . .Ps 36:6
I was like a *b* before . . . . . .Ps 73:22

to the *b* its food . . . . .Ps 147:9
b touches the mountain. . .Heb 12:20
And I saw a *b* rising . . . . .Rev 13:1
Then I saw another *b*. . . .Rev 13:11
the mark of the *b* . . . . . . .Rev 19:20

BEASTS

are we counted as *b* . . . . . .Job 18:3
The *b* go into dens . . . . . . .Job 37:8
like the *b* that perish . . . . .Ps 49:12
I have fought with *b* . . . .1 Cor 15:32
like brute *b* . . . . .Jude 10

BEAT

I will *b* down his foes . . . . . .Ps 89:23
You shall *b* him with a . .Prov 23:14
b their swords into. . . . . .Is 2:4
you shall *b* in pieces . . . . . .Mic 4:13
spat in His face and *b* . .Matt 26:67
but *b* his breast. . . . . . . .Luke 18:13

BEATEN

and you will be *b* . . . . .Mark 13:9
his will, shall be *b* . . . . . .Luke 12:47
Three times I was *b* . . . .2 Cor 11:25
it if, when you are *b* . . . . .1 Pet 2:20

BEAUTIFUL

but Rachel was *b* . . . . .Gen 29:17
B in elevation . . . . .Ps 48:2
has made everything *b* . . .Eccl 3:11
my love, you are as *b* . . . .Song 6:4
of the LORD shall be *b*. . . . . .Is 4:2
How *b* upon the. . . . . .Is 52:7
indeed appear *b* . . . . . . .Matt 23:27
begging alms at the *B* . . . .Acts 3:10
they saw he was a *b*. . . . .Heb 11:23

BEAUTIFY

b the humble with. . . . . . . .Ps 149:4
b the place of My. . . . . .Is 60:13

BEAUTY

for glory and for *b* . . . . .Ex 28:2
"The *b* of Israel is . . . . . .2 Sam 1:19
to behold the *b* . . . . .Ps 27:4
and *b* is passing . . . . .Prov 31:30
see the King in His *b*. . . . .Is 33:17
no *b* that we should. . . . . . . .Is 53:2
the one I called *B* . . . . . .Zech 11:7
Do not let your *b* . . . . .1 Pet 3:3
the incorruptible *b* . . . . . . .1 Pet 3:4

BECAME

b a living being. . . . . .Gen 2:7
to the Jews I *b*. . . . . .1 Cor 9:20
for I *b* like you. . . . . .Gal 4:12

BED

house, if I make my *b*. . . .Job 17:13
I remember You on my *b* . . . .Ps 63:6
if I make my *b* in hell. . . . . .Ps 139:8
Also our *b* is green . . . . . . .Song 1:16
b is too short to stretch . . . .Is 28:20
you have set your *b*. . . . . . . .Is 57:7
"Arise, take up your *b*. . . .Matt 9:6
be two men in one *b*. . . . .Luke 17:34
and the *b* undefiled . . . . . .Heb 13:4

BEDS

sing aloud on their *b* . . . . . .Ps 149:5
shall rest in their *b* . . . . .Is 57:2
who lie on *b* of ivory. . . . . .Amos 6:4

BEE

Egypt, and for the *b* . . . . . . .Is 7:18

BEFOREHAND

up, do not worry *b*. . . . . .Mark 13:11
told you all things *b* . . . .Mark 13:23

not to meditate *b* . . . . . .Luke 21:14
when He testified *b* . . . . . .1 Pet 1:11

BEG

I would *b* mercy of my. . . . .Job 9:15
I am ashamed to *b* . . . . . . .Luke 16:3
b you as sojourners . . . . . .1 Pet 2:11

BEGAN

Then men *b* to call on . . . . .Gen 4:26
since the world *b*. . . . . . . .Luke 1:70

BEGETS

b a scoffer does . . . . .Prov 17:21
b a wise child will . . . . . . .Prov 23:24
b a hundred children . . . . . .Eccl 6:3

BEGGAR

and lifts the *b* . . . . .1 Sam 2:8
there was a certain *b* . . . .Luke 16:20

BEGGARLY

weak and *b* elements. . . . . . .Gal 4:9

BEGINNING

b God created the. . . . . .Gen 1:1
Though your *b* was. . . . . . . .Job 8:7
of the LORD is the *b* . . . . .Ps 111:10
that God does from *b* . . . . .Eccl 3:11
who made them at the *b* . .Matt 19:4
In the *b* was the Word . . . . .John 1:1
This *b* of signs Jesus . . . . .John 2:11
a murderer from the *b* . . . .John 8:44
with Me from the *b* . . . . .John 15:27
the *b*, the firstborn . . . . .Col 1:18
having neither *b*. . . . . .Heb 7:3
True Witness, the *B* . . . . . .Rev 3:14
and the Omega, the *B* . . . .Rev 21:6

BEGOTTEN

I have *b* You . . . . .Ps 2:7
heart, 'Who has *b* . . . . .Is 49:21
glory as of the only *b*. . . .John 1:14
Christ Jesus I have *b* . . . .1 Cor 4:15
abundant mercy has *b*. . . .1 Pet 1:3
loves him who is *b*. . . . . . .1 John 5:1

BEGUILING

b unstable souls . . . . .2 Pet 2:14

BEGUN

Having *b* in the Spirit . . . . . .Gal 3:3
that He who has *b*. . . . . .Phil 1:6

BEHALF

to speak on God's *b* . . . . . .Job 36:2
you on Christ's *b* . . . . . .2 Cor 5:20
has been granted on *b* . . . .Phil 1:29

BEHAVE

I will *b* wisely in a . . . . .Ps 101:2
does not *b* rudely . . . . .1 Cor 13:5

BEHAVED

sent him, and *b* wisely. . .1 Sam 18:5
and blamelessly we *b*. .1 Thess 2:10

BEHAVIOR

of good *b*, hospitable. . . . . .1 Tim 3:2
they be reverent in *b* . . . . . .Titus 2:3

BEHEADED

he sent and had John *b*. .Matt 14:10
those who had been *b*. . . . .Rev 20:4

BEHOLD

the eyes to *b* the sun. . . . . .Eccl 11:7
B, you are fair. . . . . .Song 1:15
the virgin shall . . . . .Is 7:14
Judah, "*B* your God . . . . . . .Is 40:9
B the Lamb of God . . . . .John 1:36

I am, that they may *b* . .John 17:24
to them, "*B* the Man . . . .John 19:5
B what manner of love . . .1 John 3:1

BEHOLDING

with unveiled face, *b* . . . . .2 Cor 3:18

BEING

man became a living *b*. . . . . .Gen 2:7
God while I have my *b*. . . .Ps 104:33
move and have our *b*. . . . .Acts 17:28
who, *b* in the form of . . . . . . .Phil 2:6

BELIEF

by the Spirit and *b* . . . .2 Thess 2:13

BELIEVE

B in the LORD your God .2 Chr 20:20
tears, "Lord, I *b*. . . . . .Mark 9:24
b that you receive . . . . . . .Mark 11:24
because they did not *b* . .Mark 16:14
have no root, who *b* . . . . .Luke 8:13
and slow of heart to *b* . .Luke 24:25
to those who *b*. . . . . .John 1:12
how will you *b*. . . . . .John 3:12
sent, Him you do not *b* . .John 5:38
we may see it and *b* . . . . .John 6:30
to him, "Do you *b*. . . . . . .John 9:35
this, that they may *b* . . .John 11:42
you *b* in God . . . . .John 14:1
written that you may *b* . .John 20:31
King Agrippa, do you *b* . .Acts 26:27
the Lord Jesus and *b* . . . . .Rom 10:9
And how shall they *b* . . . .Rom 10:14
a wife who does not *b* . . .1 Cor 7:12
I spoke," we also *b*. . . . . .2 Cor 4:13
given to those who *b* . . . . . .Gal 3:22
Christ, not only to *b* . . . . . .Phil 1:29
comes to God must *b* . . . . .Heb 11:6
b that there is one . . . . .James 2:19
Even the demons *b* . . . .James 2:19
Beloved, do not *b*. . . . . . .1 John 4:1

BELIEVED

And he *b* in the LORD . . . . .Gen 15:6
b that I would see the . . . .Ps 27:13
Who has *b* our report . . . . . .Is 53:1
of that city *b* in Him . . . . .John 4:39
seen Me, you have *b*. . . . .John 20:29
who heard the word *b* . . . . .Acts 4:4
of those who *b* were of . . . .Acts 4:32
Holy Spirit when you *b* . . . .Acts 19:2
"Abraham *b* God. . . . . .Rom 4:3
I know whom I have *b* . . .2 Tim 1:12

BELIEVERS

be an example to the *b*. . .1 Tim 4:12
are benefited are *b*. . . . . . . .1 Tim 6:2

BELIEVES

The simple *b* every . . . . . .Prov 14:15
"He who *b* and is. . . . . . .Mark 16:16
that whoever *b* in Him . . .John 3:16
"He who *b* in the Son. . . .John 3:36
with the heart one *b* . . . . .Rom 10:10
b all things . . . . .1 Cor 13:7

BELIEVING

you ask in prayer, *b* . . . . .Matt 21:22
blessed with *b* Abraham. . . . .Gal 3:9

BELLY

on your *b* you shall go. . . . .Gen 3:14
And Jonah was in the *b*. . . .Jon 1:17
three nights in the *b* . . . .Matt 12:40
whose god is their *b* . . . . . .Phil 3:19

BELONG

To the Lord our God *b*. . . . .Dan 9:9
My name, because you *b*. .Mark 9:41

BELOVED

"The *b* of the LORD . . . . . Deut 33:12
so He gives His *b* . . . . Ps 127:2
of myrrh is my *b* . . . . Song 1:13
My *b* is mine . . . . Song 2:16
b more than another . . . . . . Song 5:9
Where has your *b* . . . . Song 6:1
leaning upon her *b* . . . . Song 8:5
a song of my *B* . . . . Is 5:1
for you are greatly *b* . . . . . Dan 9:23
"This is My *b* . . . . Matt 3:17
election they are *b* . . . . Rom 11:28
us accepted in the *B* . . . . . . Eph 1:6
b physician and Demas . . . . . Col 4:14
than a slave as a *b* . . . . Philem 16
"This is My *b* . . . . 2 Pet 1:17
our *b* brother Paul . . . . . . 2 Pet 3:15
the saints and the *b* . . . . . . Rev 20:9

BELT

with a leather *b* . . . . Matt 3:4
us, he took Paul's *b* . . . . . . Acts 21:11

BEMOAN

Or who will *b* you . . . . Jer 15:5
for the dead, nor *b* . . . . Jer 22:10

BEND

The wicked *b* their bow . . . . . Ps 11:2

BENEATH

and on the earth *b* . . . . . . Deut 4:39
"You are from *b* . . . . John 8:23

BENEFACTORS

them are called '*b* . . . . . . Luke 22:25

BENEFIT

That I may see the *b* . . . . . Ps 106:5
people who could not *b* . . . . . Is 30:5
might have a second *b* . . . . 2 Cor 1:15

BENT

behold, this vine *b* . . . . . . Ezek 17:7

BEREAVE

I will *b* them of . . . . Jer 15:7
no more shall you *b* . . . . Ezek 36:12
children, yet I will *b* . . . . . . Hos 9:12

BESEECH

Return, we *b* You . . . . Ps 80:14
b you therefore . . . . Rom 12:1
of the Lord, *b* you to . . . . . . Eph 4:1

BESIDE

He leads me *b* the . . . . Ps 23:2
"Paul, you are *b* . . . . Acts 26:24
For if we are *b* . . . . 2 Cor 5:13

BEST

with the *b* ointments . . . . . Amos 6:6
'Bring out the *b* . . . . Luke 15:22
earnestly desire the *b* . . . 1 Cor 12:31

BESTOW

LORD, that He may *b* . . . . . Ex 32:29
b greater honor . . . . 1 Cor 12:23

BESTOWED

love the Father has *b* . . . . 1 John 3:1

BETRAY

the outcasts, do not *b* . . . . . . Is 16:3
you, one of you will *b* . . . . Matt 26:21
"Now brother will *b* . . . . . Mark 13:12

BETRAYED

Man is about to be *b* . . . . Matt 17:22
in which He was *b* . . . . . . 1 Cor 11:23

BETRAYER

See, My *b* is at . . . . Matt 26:46

BETRAYING

"Judas, are you *b* . . . . . . Luke 22:48

BETRAYS

who is the one who *b* . . . . John 21:20

BETROTH

"You shall *b* a wife . . . . . Deut 28:30
"I will *b* you to Me . . . . . . Hos 2:19

BETROTHED

to a virgin *b* to a man . . . . Luke 1:27
For I have *b* you to . . . . . . 2 Cor 11:2

BETTER

b than sacrifice . . . . 1 Sam 15:22
It is *b* to trust in . . . . Ps 118:8
B is a little with the . . . . . Prov 15:16
B is a dry morsel . . . . Prov 17:1
B is the poor who . . . . Prov 19:1
B to dwell in . . . . Prov 21:19
b is a neighbor . . . . Prov 27:10
B a handful with . . . . Eccl 4:6
Two are *b* than one . . . . Eccl 4:9
B a poor and wise . . . . Eccl 4:13
were the former days *b* . . . Eccl 7:10
features appeared *b* . . . . . . Dan 1:15
For it is *b* to marry . . . . . . 1 Cor 7:9
Christ, which is far *b* . . . . . Phil 1:23
b than the angels . . . . Heb 1:4
b things concerning . . . . . . Heb 6:9
b things than that . . . . . . Heb 12:24

BEWARE

"*B* of false prophets . . . . . Matt 7:15
b of evil workers . . . . Phil 3:2
B lest anyone cheat . . . . Col 2:8

BEWITCHED

b you that you should . . . . . . Gal 3:1

BEYOND

b what is written . . . . 1 Cor 4:6
b their ability . . . . 2 Cor 8:3
advanced in Judaism *b* . . . . . Gal 1:14

BILLOWS

b have gone over me . . . . . . Ps 42:7
all Your *b* and Your . . . . Jon 2:3

BIND

b the cluster of the . . . . . . Job 38:31
b the wild ox in the . . . . . Job 39:10
b them around your . . . . . . Prov 3:3
B them on your fingers . . . Prov 7:3
B up the testimony . . . . Is 8:16
but He will *b* us up . . . . Hos 6:1
and whatever you *b* . . . . . . Matt 16:19
B him hand and foot . . . . Matt 22:13
b heavy burdens . . . . Matt 23:4

BIRD

the blood of the *b* . . . . Lev 14:52
with him as with a *b* . . . . . Job 41:5
soul, "Flee as a *b* . . . . Ps 11:1
has escaped as a *b* . . . . . . Ps 124:7
b hastens to the snare . . . Prov 7:23
for a *b* of the air may . . . Eccl 10:20
fly away like a *b* . . . . Hos 9:11
unclean and hated *b* . . . . . Rev 18:2

BIRDS

b will eat your flesh . . . . . Gen 40:19
b make their nests . . . . . . Ps 104:17
b caught in a snare . . . . . . Eccl 9:12
"Look at the *b* . . . . Matt 6:26
"Foxes have holes and *b* . . Matt 8:20

BIRTH

heaven, who gives it *b* . . . Job 38:29
makes the deer give *b* . . . . . Ps 29:9
the day of one's *b* . . . . Eccl 7:1
bring to the time of *b* . . . . . . Is 66:9
the deer also gave *b* . . . . . . Jer 14:5
Now the *b* of Jesus . . . . . . Matt 1:18
will rejoice at his *b* . . . . . . Luke 1:14
who was blind from *b* . . . . . . John 9:1
conceived, it gives *b* . . . . James 1:15

BIRTHDAY

which was Pharaoh's *b* . . . Gen 40:20
b gave a feast for his . . . . . Mark 6:21

BIRTHRIGHT

"Sell me your *b* . . . . Gen 25:31
Esau despised his *b* . . . . . Gen 25:34
according to his *b* . . . . Gen 43:33
of food sold his *b* . . . . Heb 12:16

BISHOP

the position of a *b* . . . . 1 Tim 3:1
b must be blameless . . . . . . Titus 1:7

BIT

and they *b* the people . . . . Num 21:6
be harnessed with *b* . . . . . . Ps 32:9

BITE

A serpent may *b* . . . . Eccl 10:11
But if you *b* and . . . . Gal 5:15

BITS

the great house into *b* . . . Amos 6:11
Indeed, we put *b* . . . . James 3:3

BITTER

made their lives *b* . . . . Ex 1:14
b herbs they . . . . Ex 12:8
to those who are *b* . . . . . . Prov 31:6
who put *b* for sweet . . . . . . Is 5:20
and do not be *b* . . . . Col 3:19
But if you have *b* . . . . . . James 3:14
make your stomach *b* . . . . Rev 10:9

BITTERLY

has dealt very *b* . . . . Ruth 1:20
And Hezekiah wept *b* . . . 2 Kin 20:3
he went out and wept *b* . . Matt 26:75

BITTERNESS

man dies in the *b* . . . . Job 21:25
heart knows its own *b* . . . Prov 14:10
all my years in the *b* . . . . . Is 38:15
you are poisoned by *b* . . . . Acts 8:23
b springing up cause . . . . Heb 12:15

BLACK

My skin grows *b* . . . . Job 30:30
wavy, and *b* as a raven . . . Song 5:11
one hair white or *b* . . . . . Matt 5:36
a *b* horse . . . . Rev 6:5
and the sun became *b* . . . . Rev 6:12

BLACKNESS

the heavens with *b* . . . . Is 50:3
whom is reserved the *b* . . . Jude 13

BLACKSMITH

The *b* with the tongs . . . . . . Is 44:12
I have created the *b* . . . . . . Is 54:16

BLADE

went in after the *b* . . . . . . Judg 3:22
first the *b* . . . . Mark 4:28

BLAME

that anyone should *b* . . . . 2 Cor 8:20
be holy and without *b* . . . . . Eph 1:4

BLAMELESS

"You shall be *b* . . . . Deut 18:13
and that man was *b* . . . . Job 1:1
when You speak, and *b* . . . . . . Ps 51:4
Let my heart be *b* . . . . Ps 119:80
end, that you may be *b* . . . . 1 Cor 1:8
which is in the law, *b* . . . . . . Phil 3:6
you holy, and *b* . . . . Col 1:22
your hearts *b* in . . . . 1 Thess 3:13
body be preserved *b* . . 1 Thess 5:23
bishop then must be *b* . . 1 Tim 3:2
deacons, being found *b* . . 1 Tim 3:10
without spot and *b* . . . . . . 2 Pet 3:14

BLAMELESSLY

b we behaved . . . . 1 Thess 2:10

BLASPHEME

b Your name forever . . . . Ps 74:10
compelled them to *b* . . . . . Acts 26:11
may learn not to *b* . . . . . . 1 Tim 1:20
b that noble name . . . . James 2:7
God, to *b* His name . . . . . . Rev 13:6

BLASPHEMED

a foolish people has *b* . . . . . Ps 74:18
b continually every . . . . . . Is 52:5
who passed by *b* Him . . . Matt 27:39
who were hanged *b* . . . Luke 23:39
The name of God is *b* . . . Rom 2:24
doctrine may not be *b* . . . . 1 Tim 6:1
On their part He is *b* . . . . 1 Pet 4:14
great heat, and they *b* . . . . Rev 16:9

BLASPHEMER

I was formerly a *b* . . . . 1 Tim 1:13

BLASPHEMERS

boasters, proud, *b* . . . . . . 2 Tim 3:2

BLASPHEMES

b the name of the LORD . . . Lev 24:16
"This Man *b* . . . . Matt 9:3

BLASPHEMIES

false witness, *b* . . . . Matt 15:19
is this who speaks *b* . . . . . Luke 5:21
great things and *b* . . . . Rev 13:5

BLASPHEMY

men, but the *b* against . . Matt 12:31
"He has spoken *b* . . . . . Matt 26:65
was full of names of *b* . . . . Rev 17:3

BLAST

By the *b* of God they . . . . . . Job 4:9
for the *b* of the . . . . Is 25:4

BLASTED

"I *b* you with blight . . . . . . Amos 4:9

BLEATING

"What then is this *b* . . 1 Sam 15:14

BLEMISH

shall be without *b* . . . . Ex 12:5
LORD, a ram without *b* . . . . Lev 6:6
be holy and without *b* . . . . Eph 5:27
as of a lamb without *b* . . . 1 Pet 1:19

BLEMISHED

to the Lord what is *b* . . . . . Mal 1:14

BLESS

b those who *b* you . . . . . . Gen 12:3
You go unless You *b* . . . Gen 32:26
"The LORD *b* you and . . . . Num 6:24
b the LORD at all . . . . Ps 34:1
b You while I live . . . . Ps 63:4
b His holy name . . . . Ps 103:1
b the house of Israel . . . . . Ps 115:12

b those who fear the . . . . . . Ps 115:13
b you in the name of . . . . . . Ps 129:8
I will abundantly *b* . . . . . . Ps 132:15
b those who curse . . . . Luke 6:28
B those who persecute . . . Rom 12:14
Being reviled, we *b* . . . . . . 1 Cor 4:12
With it we *b* our God . . . . James 3:9

BLESSED

And God *b* them . . . . Gen 1:22
the earth shall be *b* . . . . . . Gen 12:3
b be those who . . . . Gen 27:29
indeed he shall be *b* . . . . . Gen 27:33
B is he who . . . . Num 24:9
B shall be the . . . . Deut 28:4
You have *b* the work of . . . . Job 1:10
B is the man who walks . . . . Ps 1:1
B is the man to whom . . . . . Ps 32:2
B is the nation whose . . . . . Ps 33:12
B is he who considers . . . . . Ps 41:1
B are those who keep . . . . . Ps 106:3
B is he who comes . . . . . . Ps 118:26
b who fears the LORD . . . . . Ps 128:4
rise up and call her *b* . . . Prov 31:28
will call you *b* . . . . Mal 3:12
B are the poor in . . . . Matt 5:3
B are those who mourn . . . Matt 5:4
B are the meek . . . . Matt 5:5
B are those who hunger . . . Matt 5:6
B are the merciful . . . . Matt 5:7
B are the pure in . . . . Matt 5:8
B are the peacemakers . . . . Matt 5:9
B are those who are . . . . . Matt 5:10
B are you when they . . . . . Matt 5:11
b is he who is . . . . Matt 11:6
b are your eyes . . . . Matt 13:16
B is He who comes . . . . . . Matt 21:9
hand, 'Come, you *b* . . . . . Matt 25:34
Jesus took bread, *b* . . . . . Matt 26:26
b are you among women . Luke 1:28
know these things, *b* . . . . John 13:17
B are those who have . . . John 20:29
'It is more *b* to give . . . . . Acts 20:35
the Creator, who is *b* . . . . Rom 1:25
all, the eternally *b* . . . . Rom 9:5
B be the God and . . . . Eph 1:3
b God which was . . . . 1 Tim 1:11
the lesser is *b* . . . . Heb 7:7
this one will be *b* . . . . . . James 1:25
B is he who reads . . . . Rev 1:3
B are the dead who . . . . . Rev 14:13
B is he who watches . . . . . Rev 16:15
B are those who are . . . . . Rev 19:9
B and holy is he who . . . . Rev 20:6
B is he who keeps the . . . . Rev 22:7
B are those who do His . . Rev 22:14

BLESSING

and you shall be a *b* . . . . . . Gen 12:2
I will command My *b* . . . . Lev 25:21
before you today a *b* . . . . Deut 11:26
The *b* of a perishing . . . . . Job 29:13
Your *b* is upon Your . . . . . . Ps 3:8
The *b* of the LORD . . . . . . Prov 10:22
shall be showers of *b* . . . Ezek 34:26
relent, and leave a *b* . . . . . Joel 2:14
and you shall be a *b* . . . . . Zech 8:13
the fullness of the *b* . . . . . Rom 15:29
b which we bless . . . . . . 1 Cor 10:16
that the *b* of Abraham . . . . Gal 3:14
with every spiritual *b* . . . . . Eph 1:3
cultivated, receives *b* . . . . . Heb 6:7
to inherit the *b* . . . . Heb 12:17
honor and glory and *b* . . . . Rev 5:12

BLESSINGS

of the law, the *b* . . . . Josh 8:34
B are on the head of . . . . Prov 10:6

BLIGHT

I blasted you with *b* . . . . . Amos 4:9
'I struck you with *b* . . . . . Hag 2:17

BLIND

I was eyes to the *b* . . . . . . Job 29:15
B yourselves and be . . . . . . Is 29:9
To open *b* eyes . . . . Is 42:7
I will bring the *b* . . . . Is 42:16
b people who have eyes . . . . Is 43:8
His watchmen are *b* . . . . . . Is 56:10
They wandered *b* . . . . Lam 4:14
when you offer the *b* . . . . . . Mal 1:8
The *b* see . . . . Matt 11:5
b leads the *b* . . . . Matt 15:14
of sight to the *b* . . . . Luke 4:18
to Him, "Are we *b* . . . . . . John 9:40
miserable, poor, *b* . . . . Rev 3:17

BLINDED

b their eyes and . . . . John 12:40
and the rest were *b* . . . . . Rom 11:7
of this age has *b* . . . . 2 Cor 4:4
the darkness has *b* . . . . 1 John 2:11

BLINDS

a bribe, for a bribe *b* . . . . Deut 16:19

BLOOD

of your brother's *b* . . . . . . Gen 4:10
b shall be shed . . . . Gen 9:6
you are a husband of *b* . . . . Ex 4:25
b that makes atonement . Lev 17:11
b sustains its life . . . . Lev 17:14
do not cover my *b* . . . . . . Job 16:18
is there in my *b* . . . . Ps 30:9
And condemn innocent *b* . . . Ps 94:21
hands are full of *b* . . . . Is 1:15
also disclose her *b* . . . . . . Is 26:21
and the moon into *b* . . . . . Joel 2:31
For this is My *b* . . . . . . Matt 26:28
called the Field of *B* . . . . . Matt 27:8
His *b* be on us and . . . . . Matt 27:25
new covenant in My *b* . . Luke 22:20
were born, not of *b* . . . . . . John 1:13
b has eternal life . . . . John 6:54
b every nation of men . . . Acts 17:26
with His own *b* . . . . Acts 20:28
propitiation by His *b* . . . . Rom 3:25
justified by His *b* . . . . Rom 5:9
through His *b* . . . . Eph 1:7
brought near by the *b* . . . . Eph 2:13
against flesh and *b* . . . . . . Eph 6:12
peace through the *b* . . . . . Col 1:20
" This is the *b* . . . . Heb 9:20
are purified with *b* . . . . . . Heb 9:22
of *b* there is no . . . . Heb 9:22
the Holiest by the *b* . . . . Heb 10:19
sprinkling of the *b* . . . . . . 1 Pet 1:2
with the precious *b* . . . . . 1 Pet 1:19
b of Jesus Christ His . . . 1 John 1:7
our sins in His own *b* . . . . . Rev 1:5
us to God by Your *b* . . . . . Rev 5:9
them white in the *b* . . . . . . Rev 7:14
overcame him by the *b* . . . Rev 12:11
a robe dipped in *b* . . . . . . Rev 19:13

BLOODSHED

me from the guilt of *b* . . . . Ps 51:14
the land is full of *b* . . . . . Ezek 9:9
build up Zion with *b* . . . . . Mic 3:10

BLOODTHIRSTY

The LORD abhors the *b* . . . . . Ps 5:6
B and deceitful men . . . . . Ps 55:23

BLOSSOM

Israel shall *b* and bud . . . . . . Is 27:6
and *b* as the rose . . . . Is 35:1
the fig tree may not *b* . . . . Hab 3:17

BLOT

say that He would *b* . . . .2 Kin 14:27
from my sins, and *b* . . . . . . .Ps 51:9
and I will not *b* . . . . .Rev 3:5

BLOTTED

Let them be *b* out of . . . . .Ps 69:28
I have *b* out . . . . .Is 44:22
your sins may be *b* . . . . . . .Acts 3:19

BLOW

an east wind to *b* . . . . .Ps 78:26
B upon my garden . . . . . .Song 4:16
with a very severe *b* . . . . . .Jer 14:17

BLOWS

B that hurt cleanse . . . . . .Prov 20:30
breath of the LORD *b* . . . . .Is 40:7
" The wind *b* where it . . . . . John 3:8

BOAST

puts on his armor *b* . . . . .1 Kin 20:11
soul shall make its *b* . . . . .Ps 34:2
God we *b* all day long . . . . . . .Ps 44:8
and make your *b* . . . . Rom 2:17
that we are your *b* . . . .2 Cor 1:14
you, and not to *b* . . . . . .2 Cor 10:16
that I also may *b* . . . . . .2 Cor 11:16
lest anyone should *b* . . . . . . .Eph 2:9
your hearts, do not *b* . . .James 3:14

BOASTERS

God, violent, proud, *b* . . . . .Rom 1:30
lovers of money, *b* . . . . . . .2 Tim 3:2

BOASTFUL

b shall not stand . . . . .Ps 5:5
I was envious of the *b* . . . . . .Ps 73:3

BOASTING

Where is *b* then . . . . .Rom 3:27
should make my *b* . . . . . .1 Cor 9:15
you, great is my *b* . . . . . .2 Cor 7:4
All such *b* is evil . . . . . . .James 4:16

BOASTS

Whoever falsely *b* . . . . . .Prov 25:14

BODIES

valley of the dead *b* . . . . . .Jer 31:40
b a living sacrifice . . . . . . .Rom 12:1
not know that your *b* . . . .1 Cor 6:15
also celestial *b* . . . . .1 Cor 15:40
wives as their own *b* . . . . .Eph 5:28
and chariots, and *b* . . . . . .Rev 18:13

BODILY

b form like a dove . . . . . . .Luke 3:22
b presence is weak . . . . . .2 Cor 10:10
of the Godhead *b* . . . . .Col 2:9
b exercise . . . . .1 Tim 4:8

BODY

b clings to the ground . . . . .Ps 44:25
b is carved ivory . . . . .Song 5:14
b was wet with the dew . . . .Dan 4:33
of the *b* is the eye . . . . . . .Matt 6:22
those who kill the *b* . . . . .Matt 10:28
this is My *b* . . . . .Matt 26:26
and asked for the *b* . . . . .Matt 27:58
around his naked *b* . . . . .Mark 14:51
of the temple of His *b* . . . .John 2:21
deliver me from this *b* . . . .Rom 7:24
redemption of our *b* . . . . .Rom 8:23
many members in one *b* . . .Rom 12:4

and the Lord for the *b* . . . .1 Cor 6:13
against his own *b* . . . . .1 Cor 6:18
not know that your *b* . . . .1 Cor 6:19
glorify God in your *b* . . . . .1 Cor 6:20
But I discipline my *b* . . . .1 Cor 9:27
one bread and one *b* . . . .1 Cor 10:17
b which is broken . . . . . .1 Cor 11:24
be guilty of the *b* . . . . . . .1 Cor 11:27
For as the *b* is one . . . . . .1 Cor 12:12
baptized into one *b* . . . . .1 Cor 12:13
b is not one member . . . .1 Cor 12:14
are the *b* of Christ . . . . . .1 Cor 12:27
though I give my *b* . . . . . .1 Cor 13:3
It is sown a natural *b* . . .1 Cor 15:44
both to God in one *b* . . . . .Eph 2:16
be magnified in my *b* . . . . .Phil 1:20
in the *b* of His flesh . . . . . .Col 1:22
by putting off the *b* . . . . . . .Col 2:11
and neglect of the *b* . . . . . . .Col 2:23
were called in one *b* . . . . . . .Col 3:15
b You have prepared . . . . . .Heb 10:5
the offering of the *b* . . . . .Heb 10:10
For as the *b* without . . . .James 2:26
our sins in His own *b* . . . .1 Pet 2:24

BOILS

Job with painful *b* . . . . .Job 2:7

BOLD

the righteous are *b* . . . . . .Prov 28:1
whatever anyone is *b* . . .2 Cor 11:21
are much more *b* . . . . .Phil 1:14

BOLDLY

I may open my mouth *b* . . .Eph 6:19
therefore come *b* . . . . .Heb 4:16
So we may *b* say . . . . .Heb 13:6

BOLDNESS

Great is my *b* of . . . . .2 Cor 7:4
in whom we have *b* . . . . . .Eph 3:12
but with all *b* . . . . .Phil 1:20
standing and great *b* . . . . .1 Tim 3:13
brethren, having *b* . . . . . . .Heb 10:19
that we may have *b* . . . .1 John 4:17

BOND

bring you into the *b* . . . . .Ezek 20:37
of the Spirit in the *b* . . . . . .Eph 4:3
love, which is the *b* . . . . . . .Col 3:14

BONDAGE

because of the *b* . . . . .Ex 2:23
out of the house of *b* . . . . .Ex 13:14
the spirit of *b* . . . . .Rom 8:15
might bring us into *b* . . . . . .Gal 2:4
which gives birth to *b* . . . . .Gal 4:24
again with a yoke of *b* . . . . .Gal 5:1
lifetime subject to *b* . . . . . .Heb 2:15
he is brought into *b* . . . . . .2 Pet 2:19

BONDS

" Let us break Their *b* . . . . . .Ps 2:3

BONDSERVANTS

B, be obedient to . . . . .Eph 6:5
Masters, give your *b* . . . . . . .Col 4:1
for vice, but as *b* . . . . .1 Pet 2:16

BONDWOMAN

"Cast out this *b* . . . . .Gen 21:10
the one by a *b* . . . . .Gal 4:22

BONE

" This is now *b* . . . . .Gen 2:23
b clings to my skin . . . . . . .Job 19:20
bones came together, *b* . . . .Ezek 37:7

BONES

shall carry up my *b* . . . . . .Gen 50:25

which made all my *b* . . . . . .Job 4:14
His *b* are like beams . . . . . .Job 40:18
I can count all My *b* . . . . . . .Ps 22:17
and my *b* waste away . . . . . .Ps 31:10
I kept silent, my *b* . . . . .Ps 32:3
the wind, or how the *b* . . . .Eccl 11:5
say to them, 'O dry *b* . . . .Ezek 37:4
b are the whole house . . . .Ezek 37:11
of dead men's *b* . . . . .Matt 23:27
b shall be broken . . . . . . .John 19:36
concerning his *b* . . . . .Heb 11:22

BOOK

you will find in the *b* . . . .Ezra 4:15
distinctly from the *b* . . . . . .Neh 8:8
were inscribed in a *b* . . . . .Job 19:23
"Search from the *b* . . . . . .Is 34:16
'Write in a *b* for . . . . .Jer 30:2
found written in the *b* . . . . .Dan 12:1
so a *b* of remembrance . . . .Mal 3:16
are written in the *b* . . . . . . .Gal 3:10
sprinkled both the *b* . . . . . .Heb 9:19
in the Lamb's *B* . . . . .Rev 21:27
the prophecy of this *b* . . . .Rev 22:18
the words of the *b* . . . . . . .Rev 22:19

BOOKS

b there is no end . . . . .Eccl 12:12
not contain the *b* . . . . . . .John 21:25
magic brought their *b* . . . .Acts 19:19
God, and *b* were opened . . .Rev 20:12

BOOTH

b which a watchman . . . . . .Job 27:18
of Zion is left as a *b* . . . . .Is 1:8

BORDERS

and enlarge your *b* . . . . .Ex 34:24
makes peace in your *b* . . .Ps 147:14
and enlarge the *b* . . . . . . .Matt 23:5

BORE

conceived and *b* Cain . . . . . .Gen 4:1
and to Sarah who *b* . . . . .Is 51:2
b the sin of many . . . . .Is 53:12
and He *b* them and . . . . .Is 63:9
b our sicknesses . . . . .Matt 8:17
who Himself *b* our sins . . .1 Pet 2:24
b a male Child who was . . . .Rev 12:5

BORN

"Every son who is *b* . . . .Ex 1:20
yet man is *b* to . . . . .Job 5:7
"Man who is *b* . . . . .Job 14:1
'This one was *b* . . . . .Ps 87:4
A time to be *b* . . . . .Eccl 3:2
unto us a Child is *b* . . . . .Is 9:6
Or shall a nation be *b* . . . . . .Is 66:8
b Jesus who is called . . . .Matt 1:16
"For there is *b* . . . . .Luke 2:11
unless one is *b* again . . . . .John 3:3
"That which is *b* . . . . . . .John 3:6
For this cause I was *b* . .John 18:37
me also, as by one *b* . . . .1 Cor 15:8
of the bondwoman was *b* . . .Gal 4:23
having been *b* again . . . . . .1 Pet 1:23
who loves is *b* of God . . . .1 John 4:7
is the Christ is *b* . . . . . . .1 John 5:1
know that whoever is *b* . .1 John 5:18

BORNE

And as we have *b* . . . . . .1 Cor 15:49

BORROWER

b is servant to the . . . . . . .Prov 22:7
lender, so with the *b* . . . . . . .Is 24:2

BORROWS

The wicked *b* and does . . . . .Ps 37:21

BOSOM

man take fire to his *b* . . . . . Prov 6:27
consolation of her *b* . . . . Is 66:11
angels to Abraham's *b* . . . Luke 16:22
Son, who is in the *b* . . . . . . John 1:18
leaning on Jesus' *b* . . . . . John 13:23

BOTTLE

b shall be filled. . . . . Jer 13:12

BOTTOMLESS

given the key to the *b* . . . . . Rev 9:1
ascend out of the *b* . . . . Rev 17:8
the key to the *b*. . . . . Rev 20:1

BOUGHS

cedars with its *b* . . . . Ps 80:10
She sent out her *b* . . . . Ps 80:11

BOUGHT

the hand of him who *b* . . . . Lev 25:28
not your Father, who *b* . . . . Deut 32:6
b the threshing floor . . . 2 Sam 24:24
b the field from . . . . Jer 32:9
all that he had and *b* . . . Matt 13:46
For you were *b* at a . . . . . . 1 Cor 6:20
denying the Lord who *b* . . . 2 Pet 2:1

BOUND

of the wicked have *b* . . . . . . Ps 119:61
b the waters in a . . . . Prov 30:4
not been closed or *b* . . . . Is 1:6
on earth will be *b* . . . . . . Matt 16:19
b hand and foot with . . . John 11:44
And see, now I go *b* . . . . . Acts 20:22
of Israel I am *b* . . . . Acts 28:20
who has a husband is *b* . . . Rom 7:2
Are you *b* to a wife . . . . . . 1 Cor 7:27
Devil and Satan, and *b*. . . . Rev 20:2

BOUNDARY

b that they may not . . . . . . Ps 104:9

BOUNTIFUL

the miser said to be *b* . . . . . . Is 32:5
you into a *b* country . . . . Jer 2:7

BOUNTIFULLY

Because He has dealt *b* . . . . . Ps 13:6
and he who sows *b* . . . . 2 Cor 9:6

BOW

b remained in strength . . . Gen 49:24
"You shall not *b* . . . . Ex 23:24
to serve them and *b* . . . . . . Judg 2:19
b is renewed in my . . . . . . Job 29:20
will not trust in my *b* . . . . . . Ps 44:6
He breaks the *b*. . . . . Ps 46:9
like a deceitful *b* . . . . Ps 78:57
let us worship and *b* . . . . . . Ps 95:6
B down Your heavens . . . . . . Ps 144:5
not save them by *b* . . . . Hos 1:7
who sat on it had a *b* . . . . . . Rev 6:2

BOWED

stood all around and *b*. . . . Gen 37:7
b the heavens also . . . . 2 Sam 22:10
whose knees have not *b* . 1 Kin 19:18
They have *b* down and . . . . . Ps 20:8
And they *b* the knee . . . Matt 27:29
men who have not *b* . . . . . Rom 11:4

BOWL

his hand in the *b* . . . . Prov 19:24
or the golden *b* . . . . Eccl 12:6
and poured out his *b* . . . . . Rev 16:2

BOWLS

who drink wine from *b* . . . . Amos 6:6
a harp, and golden *b*. . . . . . Rev 5:8

Go and pour out the *b* . . . . Rev 16:1
who had the seven *b*. . . . . . Rev 21:9

BOWS

"The *b* of the mighty . . . . 1 Sam 2:4

BOX

Judas had the money *b* . . John 13:29

BOYS

shall be full of *b* . . . . Zech 8:5

BRAIDED

not with *b* hair or . . . . 1 Tim 2:9

BRAMBLE

gather grapes from a *b*. . . Luke 6:44

BRANCH

blossoms on one *b* . . . . Ex 25:33
b will not be green . . . . . . Job 15:32
from Israel, palm *b* . . . . Is 9:14
B shall grow out of . . . . Is 11:1
raise to David a *B* . . . . Jer 23:5
grow up to David a *B* . . . . Jer 33:15
forth My Servant the *B* . . . Zech 3:8
whose name is the *B*. . . . . Zech 6:12
b has already become. . . . Matt 24:32
b that bears fruit He . . . . John 15:2
b cannot bear fruit . . . . . . John 15:4
he is cast out as a *b* . . . . . John 15:6

BRANCHES

in the sun, and his *b*. . . . . . Job 8:16
and bring forth *b* . . . . Job 14:9
and cut down the *b* . . . . Is 18:5
and its *b* are broken. . . . . . Jer 11:16
His *b* shall spread . . . . Hos 14:6
vine, you are the *b* . . . . . . John 15:5
b were broken off. . . . . . . Rom 11:17

BRASS

become sounding *b* . . . . . 1 Cor 13:1
feet were like fine *b*. . . . . . . Rev 1:15

BRAVE

in the faith, be *b* . . . . . . 1 Cor 16:13

BREACHES

heal its *b* . . . . Ps 60:2

BREAD

face you shall eat *b* . . . . . . Gen 3:19
of Salem brought out *b* . . Gen 14:18
"Behold, I will rain *b* . . . . . . Ex 16:4
shall eat unleavened *b* . . . . Ex 23:15
not live by *b* alone . . . . . . Deut 8:3
lives, I do not have *b* . . . 1 Kin 17:12
new wine, a land of *b*. . . 2 Kin 18:32
that his life abhors *b* . . . . Job 33:20
people as they eat *b* . . . . . . Ps 14:4
Can He give *b* also . . . . . . Ps 78:20
up late, to eat the *b* . . . . . Ps 127:2
her poor with *b* . . . . Ps 132:15
For they eat the *b* . . . . . . Prov 4:17
b eaten in secret is . . . . . . Prov 9:17
B gained by deceit is . . . Prov 20:17
Go, eat your *b* with . . . . . . Eccl 9:7
Cast your *b* upon the. . . . . Eccl 11:1
b will be given him . . . . Is 33:16
for what is not *b* . . . . Is 55:2
to share your *b* . . . . Is 58:7
We get our *b* at the . . . . . . Lam 5:9
who give me my *b* . . . . Hos 2:5
For their *b* shall be. . . . . . . Hos 9:4
And lack of *b* in all. . . . . . Amos 4:6
these stones become *b* . . . Matt 4:3
not live by *b* alone . . . . Matt 4:4
this day our daily *b* . . . . . Matt 6:11
eating, Jesus took *b*. . . . . Matt 26:26

no bag, no *b* . . . . Mark 6:8
is he who shall eat *b*. . . . Luke 14:15
gives you the true *b* . . . . . John 6:32
"I am the *b* of life. . . . . . . John 6:48
having dipped the *b* . . . . John 13:26
b which we break . . . . . . 1 Cor 10:16
He was betrayed took *b* 1 Cor 11:23
as you eat this *b* . . . . . . 1 Cor 11:26
did we eat anyone's *b*. . . 2 Thess 3:8
and eat their own *b* . . . 2 Thess 3:12

BREADTH

is as great as its *b* . . . . . . Rev 21:16

BREAK

b their bones and . . . . Num 24:8
torment my soul, and *b* . . . Job 19:2
They *b* up my path. . . . . . Job 30:13
B their teeth in their . . . . . . Ps 58:6
And now they *b* down . . . . Ps 74:6
b My statutes and do. . . . . Ps 89:31
covenant I will not *b* . . . . . Ps 89:34
Remember, do not *b* . . . . . Jer 14:21
together to *b* bread . . . . . . Acts 20:7

BREAKING

in the *b* of bread . . . . Acts 2:42
b bread from house to . . . . Acts 2:46
weeping and *b* my heart. . Acts 21:13
dishonor God through *b*. . . Rom 2:23

BREAKS

He *b* in pieces mighty . . . Job 34:24
My soul *b* with longing . . . Ps 119:20
Until the day *b* . . . . Song 2:17
"Whoever therefore *b*. . . . Matt 5:19

BREAST

back on Jesus' *b* . . . . John 13:25

BREASTPLATE

a *b*, an ephod . . . . Ex 28:4
righteousness as a *b* . . . . . . Is 59:17
having put on the *b*. . . . . . Eph 6:14

BREASTS

blessings of the *b*. . . . . . . Gen 49:25
on My mother's *b* . . . . Ps 22:9
doe, let her *b* satisfy. . . . . Prov 5:19
Your two *b* are like . . . . . . Song 4:5
b which nursed You . . . . Luke 11:27
done, beat their *b* . . . . . . Luke 23:48

BREATH

nostrils the *b* of life . . . . . . Gen 2:7
at the blast of the *b*. . . 2 Sam 22:16
that there was no *b* . . . . 1 Kin 17:17
perish, and by the *b* . . . . . . Job 4:9
as long as my *b* . . . . Job 27:3
has made me, and the *b*. . . Job 33:4
You take away their *b*. . . . Ps 104:29
Man is like a *b* . . . . Ps 144:4
everything that has *b* . . . . . Ps 150:6
they all have one *b*. . . . . . . Eccl 3:19
from it, who gives *b*. . . . . . . Is 42:5
Surely I will cause *b*. . . . . Ezek 37:5
God who holds your *b* . . . . Dan 5:23
gives to all life, *b*. . . . . . Acts 17:25
consume with the *b* . . . . 2 Thess 2:8
power to give *b* . . . . Rev 13:15

BREATHE

me, and such as *b*. . . . . Ps 27:12
winds, O breath, and *b*. . . Ezek 37:9

BREATHES

indeed he *b* his last. . . . . . Job 14:10

BRETHREN

presence of all his *b* . . . . . Gen 16:12

be lifted above his *b* . . . .Deut 17:20
and you are all *b* . . . . .Matt 23:8
least of these My *b* . . . . .Matt 25:40
Go and tell My *b* . . . . . .Matt 28:10
firstborn among many *b*. . .Rom 8:29
to judge between his *b* . . . .1 Cor 6:5
thus sin against the *b* . . . .1 Cor 8:12
over five hundred *b* . . . . .1 Cor 15:6
perils among false *b*. . . .2 Cor 11:26
b secretly brought. . . . . .Gal 2:4
to be made like His *b* . . . . .Heb 2:17
sincere love of the *b* . . . . .1 Pet 1:22
because we love the *b* . . .1 John 3:14
our lives for the *b* . . . . . .1 John 3:16
does not receive the *b* . . .3 John 10
of your *b* the prophets . . . .Rev 22:9

BRIBE

you shall take no *b*. . . . . . . .Ex 23:8
b blinds the eyes. . . . . . .Deut 16:19
b debases the heart . . . . .Eccl 7:7

BRIBERY

consume the tents of *b*. . . .Job 15:34

BRIBES

hand is full of *b*. . . . . .Ps 26:10
but he who hates *b* . . . . . .Prov 15:27
but he who receives *b* . . . . .Prov 29:4
everyone loves *b*. . . . . .Is 1:23
the just and taking *b* . . . .Amos 5:12

BRICK

people straw to make *b* . . . .Ex 5:7
incense on altars of *b* . . . . . . .Is 65:3
Make strong the *b* . . . . .Nah 3:14

BRICKS

"Come, let us make *b*. . . . . .Gen 11:3
b which they made. . . . . .Ex 5:8
deliver the quota of *b*. . . . . . .Ex 5:18
b have fallen down. . . . . .Is 9:10

BRIDE

them on you as a *b* . . . . .Is 49:18
"He who has the *b* . . . . . . .John 3:29
I will show you the *b* . . . . .Rev 21:9
the Spirit and the *b* . . . . .Rev 22:17

BRIDEGROOM

righteousness, as a *b*. . . . . . .Is 61:10
and as the *b* rejoices . . . . . . .Is 62:5
mourn as long as the *b* . . .Matt 9:15
b will be taken away. . . . . . .Matt 9:15
went out to meet the *b* . . .Matt 25:1
b fast while the . . . . .Mark 2:19
the friend of the *b*. . . . . . .John 3:29

BRIDLE

with bit and *b*. . . . . .Ps 32:9
b the whole body . . . . . . .James 3:2

BRIER

b shall come up the. . . . . . . .Is 55:13
longer be a pricking *b* . .Ezek 28:24
of them is like a *b*. . . . . .Mic 7:4

BRIERS

there shall come up *b* . . . . . . .Is 5:6
their words, though *b*. . . . .Ezek 2:6

BRIGHTER

Her Nazirites were *b*. . . . . .Lam 4:7
a light from heaven, *b*. . .Acts 26:13

BRIGHTNESS

From the *b* before Him 2 Sam 22:13
and kings to the *b*. . . . . .Is 60:3
goes forth as *b* . . . . .Is 62:1
very dark, with no *b*. . . . .Amos 5:20
who being the *b* . . . . .Heb 1:3

BRIMSTONE

Then the LORD rained *b*. . .Gen 19:24
b is scattered on his . . . . . .Job 18:15
fire, smoke, and *b* . . . . . . .Rev 9:17
the lake of fire and *b* . . . .Rev 20:10

BRING

LORD your God will *b*. . . .Deut 30:3
b back his soul . . . . .Job 33:30
for they *b* down. . . . . .Ps 55:3
Lord said, "I will *b*. . . . . . .Ps 68:22
B forth your. . . . . .Is 41:21
b forth justice . . . . .Is 42:3
b My righteousness. . . . . . .Is 46:13
Though they *b* up their . . .Hos 9:12
"And she will *b*. . . . . .Matt 1:21
b no fruit to maturity . . .Luke 8:14
b this Man's blood . . . . . .Acts 5:28
Who shall *b* a charge . . . .Rom 8:33
b Christ down from. . . . . .Rom 10:6
b Christ up from the. . . . .Rom 10:7
even so God will *b* . . . .1 Thess 4:14

BROAD

set me in a *b* place . . . . . . .Ps 118:5
b is the way that . . . . . . .Matt 7:13
their phylacteries *b*. . . . . .Matt 23:5

BROKE

b them at the foot of . . . . . .Ex 32:19
b open the fountain. . . . . . .Ps 74:15
covenant which they *b* . . .Jer 31:32
He blessed and *b* . . . . . .Matt 14:19
b the flask and poured . . .Mark 14:3
b the legs of the . . . . . . .John 19:32

BROKEN

he has *b* My covenant . . . .Gen 17:14
I am like a *b* vessel. . . . . . .Ps 31:12
their bows shall be *b* . . . . .Ps 37:15
He has *b* his covenant . . . .Ps 55:20
heart the spirit is *b*. . . . . .Prov 15:13
b spirit dries the . . . . . . .Prov 17:22
but who can bear a *b* . . . .Prov 18:14
in the staff of this *b* . . . . . .Is 36:6
heart within me is *b* . . . . .Jer 23:9
is oppressed and *b*. . . . . . . .Hos 5:11
this stone will be *b*. . . . . .Matt 21:44
Scripture cannot be *b*. . .John 10:35
is My body which is *b*. . .1 Cor 11:24

BROKENHEARTED

He heals the *b* and . . . . .Ps 147:3

BRONZE

So Moses made a *b*. . . . . .Num 21:9
your head shall be *b*. . . . .Deut 28:23
b serpent that Moses . . . .2 Kin 18:4
Or is my flesh *b* . . . . .Job 6:12
b as rotten wood . . . . .Job 41:27
broken the gates of *b* . . . .Ps 107:16
b I will bring . . . . .Is 60:17
b walls against the. . . . . . . .Jer 1:18
people a fortified *b*. . . . . . .Jer 15:20
a third kingdom of *b* . . . . .Dan 2:39
make your hooves *b* . . . . . .Mic 4:13
were mountains of *b* . . . . .Zech 6:1

BROOD

The *b* of evildoers . . . . .Is 14:20
"*B* of vipers. . . . . .Matt 12:34
as a hen gathers her *b* . . .Luke 13:34

BROOK

stones from the *b* . . . . . .1 Sam 17:40
shall drink of the . . . . .Ps 110:7
disciples over the *B* . . . . .John 18:1

BROOKS

good land, a land of *b*. . . . . .Deut 8:7

b that pass away. . . . . .Job 6:15
for the water *b*. . . . . .Ps 42:1

BROTHER

"Where is Abel your *b*. . . . .Gen 4:9
he were my friend or *b*. . . .Ps 35:14
speak against your *b* . . . . .Ps 50:20
and a *b* is born for. . . . . . .Prov 17:17
b offended is harder . . . . .Prov 18:19
has neither son nor *b*. . . . . .Eccl 4:8
and do not trust any *b* . . . . .Jer 9:4
he pursued his *b* . . . . .Amos 1:11
"Was not Esau Jacob's *b*. . .Mal 1:2
b will deliver up . . . . .Matt 10:21
how often shall my *b* . . .Matt 18:21
"Teacher, tell my *b*. . . . . .Luke 12:13
b will rise again. . . . . . . .John 11:23
do you judge your *b* . . . . .Rom 14:10
b goes to law against. . . . .1 Cor 6:6
shall the weak *b*. . . . . .1 Cor 8:11
slave–a beloved *b* . . . . . . .Philem 16
He who loves his *b* . . . .1 John 2:10
and murdered his *b* . . . .1 John 3:12
Whoever hates his *b* . . .1 John 3:15
b sinning a sin which . . .1 John 5:16
I, John, both your *b*. . . . . . .Rev 1:9

BROTHER'S

Am I my *b* keeper . . . . .Gen 4:9
at the speck in your *b* . . . . .Matt 7:3

BROTHERHOOD

the covenant of *b*. . . . . . . .Amos 1:9
I might break the *b* . . . . .Zech 11:14
Love the *b*. . . . . .1 Pet 2:17
experienced by your *b* . . . .1 Pet 5:9

BROTHERLY

to one another with *b* . . . .Rom 12:10
b love continue . . . . .Heb 13:1

BROTHERS

My *b* have dealt . . . . .Job 6:15
a stranger to my *b* . . . . .Ps 69:8
is My mother, or My *b* . . .Mark 3:33
b are these who hear . . . .Luke 8:21
b did not believe . . . . .John 7:5
love as *b* . . . . .1 Pet 3:8

BROUGHT

He *b* out His people. . . . . .Ps 105:43
The king has *b* me into . . .Song 1:4
to heaven, will be *b*. . . . .Luke 10:15

BRUISE

He shall *b* your head . . . . .Gen 3:15
LORD binds up the *b* . . . . . .Is 30:26
the LORD to *b* Him . . . . .Is 53:10

BRUISED

b reed He will not . . . . .Is 42:3
He was *b* for our . . . . .Is 53:5
b reed He will not. . . . . . .Matt 12:20

BRUTAL

b men who are. . . . . .Ezek 21:31

BUCKLER

be your shield and *b*. . . . . . .Ps 91:4

BUD

it bring forth and *b*. . . . . . . .Is 55:10

BUFFET

of Satan to *b* me . . . . . . .2 Cor 12:7

BUILD

b ourselves a city. . . . . . . .Gen 11:4
"Would you a house . . . .2 Sam 7:5
b a temple for the name . .1 Kin 8:17
that the LORD will *b* . . . .1 Chr 17:10

Solomon who shall *b* . . . . .1 Chr 28:6
able to *b* Him a temple . . . .2 Chr 2:6
labor in vain who *b* . . . . . . .Ps 127:1
down, and a time to *b* . . . . . .Eccl 3:3
house that you will *b* . . . . . . .Is 66:1
I will *b* them and not . . . . . .Jer 24:6
Who *b* up Zion with . . . . . .Mic 3:10
b the desolate . . . . .Mal 1:4
'This man began to *b* . . . .Luke 14:30
What house will you give . . . .Acts 7:49
b you up and give you . . .Acts 20:32
named, lest I should *b* . . .Rom 15:20
"For if I *b* again . . . . .Gal 2:18

BUILDER

me, as a wise master *b* . . .1 Cor 3:10
foundations, whose *b* . . . . .Heb 11:10

BUILDING

field, you are God's *b* . . . . . .1 Cor 3:9
destroyed, we have a *b* . . . .2 Cor 5:1
in whom the whole *b* . . . . . .Eph 2:21
But you, beloved, *b* . . . . . . .Jude 20

BUILDS

The LORD *b* up . . . . .Ps 147:2
The wise woman *b* . . . . . . .Prov 14:1
one take heed how he *b* . . .1 Cor 3:10

BUILT

Wisdom has *b* her house . . .Prov 9:1
my works great, I *b* . . . . . . .Eccl 2:4
Babylon, that I have *b* . . . .Dan 4:30
to a wise man who *b* . . . . .Matt 7:24
a foolish man who *b* . . . . . .Matt 7:26
work which he has *b* . . . . .1 Cor 3:14
having been *b* on the . . . . . .Eph 2:20
rooted and *b* up in Him . . . .Col 2:7
For every house is *b* . . . . . . .Heb 3:4
stones, are being *b* . . . . . . .1 Pet 2:5

BULL

I will not take a *b* . . . . .Ps 50:9
like an untrained *b* . . . . . . .Jer 31:18

BULLS

in the blood of *b* . . . . .Is 1:11
For if the blood of *b* . . . . . . .Heb 9:13

BULWARKS

Mark well her *b* . . . . .Ps 48:13
for walls and *b* . . . . .Is 26:1

BUNDLE

each man's *b* of money . . .Gen 42:35
A *b* of myrrh is my . . . . . .Song 1:13

BURDEN

You have laid the *b* . . . . . .Num 11:11
one knows his own *b* . . . . .2 Chr 6:29
so that I am a *b* . . . . .Job 7:20
Cast your *b* on the . . . . . . .Ps 55:22
the grasshopper is a *b* . . . . .Eccl 12:5
in that day that his *b* . . . . . .Is 10:27
its reproach is a *b* . . . . . . .Zeph 3:18
easy and My *b* is light . . .Matt 11:30
as it may, I did not *b* . . . .2 Cor 12:16
we might not be a *b* . . . . .1 Thess 2:9
on you no other *b* . . . . .Rev 2:24

BURDENED

but you have *b* Me with . . . .Is 43:24

BURDENS

and looked at their *b* . . . . . . .Ex 2:11
For they bind heavy *b* . . . .Matt 23:4
Bear one another's *b* . . . . . . .Gal 6:2

BURDENSOME

b task God has given . . . . .Eccl 1:13
his life will be *b* . . . . .Is 15:4

I myself was not *b* . . . . . .2 Cor 12:13
commandments are not *b* .1 John 5:3

BURIAL

indeed he has no *b* . . . . .Eccl 6:3
she did it for My *b* . . . . . .Matt 26:12
for the day of My *b* . . . . .John 12:7
Stephen to his *b* . . . . .Acts 8:2

BURIED

and there will I be *b* . . . . . .Ruth 1:17
I saw the wicked *b* . . . . .Eccl 8:10
away the body and *b* . . . .Matt 14:12
also died and was *b* . . . .Luke 16:22
Therefore we were *b* . . . . . . .Rom 6:4
and that He was *b* . . . . . . .1 Cor 15:4
b with Him in baptism . . . .Col 2:12

BURN

the bush does not *b* . . . . .Ex 3:3
that My wrath may *b* . . . .Ex 32:10
b their chariots . . . . .Josh 11:6
both will *b* together . . . . .Is 1:31
"Did not our heart *b* . . .Luke 24:32
eat her flesh and *b* . . . . . .Rev 17:16

BURNED

If anyone's work is *b* . . . . .1 Cor 3:15
I give my body to be *b* . . .1 Cor 13:3
whose end is to be *b* . . . . . .Heb 6:8
be touched and that *b* . . . .Heb 12:18
are *b* outside the camp . .Heb 13:11
in it will be *b* . . . . .2 Pet 3:10
all green grass was *b* . . . . . .Rev 8:7

BURNING

b torch that passed . . . . . .Gen 15:17
with severe *b* fever . . . . .Deut 28:22
on his lips like a *b* . . . . . .Prov 16:27
b fire shut up in my . . . . . . .Jer 20:9
b jealousy against the . . . .Ezek 36:5
plucked from the *b* . . . . . .Amos 4:11
a great mountain *b* . . . . . . .Rev 8:8
fell from heaven, *b* . . . . . . .Rev 8:10

BURNT

lamb for a *b* offering . . . . .Gen 22:7
delight in *b* offering . . . . . .Ps 51:16
b offerings are not . . . . .Jer 6:20
Though you offer Me *b* . .Amos 5:22

BURST

it is ready to *b* . . . . .Job 32:19
with doors, when it *b* . . . . .Job 38:8
the new wine will *b* . . . . .Luke 5:37
falling headlong, he *b* . . . .Acts 1:18

BURY

b your dead in the . . . . . . .Gen 23:6
was no one to *b* them . . . . . .Ps 79:3
go and *b* my father . . . . . .Matt 8:21
and let the dead *b* . . . . . . .Matt 8:22

BUSH

from the midst of a *b* . . . . . . .Ex 3:2
Him who dwelt in the *b* . .Deut 33:16
to him in the *b* . . . . .Acts 7:35

BUSINESS

in ships, who do *b* . . . . . .Ps 107:23
farm, another to his *b* . . . .Matt 22:5
about My Father's *b* . . . . .Luke 2:49

BUSYBODIES

at all, but are *b* . . . . .2 Thess 3:11
but also gossips and *b* . . .1 Tim 5:13

BUTLER

b did not remember . . . . . .Gen 40:23

BUTTER

So he took *b* and milk . . . . .Gen 18:8
were smoother than *b* . . . . . .Ps 55:21
of milk produces *b* . . . . . . .Prov 30:33

BUY

in Egypt to *b* grain . . . . . .Gen 41:57
B the truth . . . . .Prov 23:23
Yes, come, *b* wine and . . . . . .Is 55:1
that we may *b* the poor . . .Amos 8:6
b food for all these . . . . . .Luke 9:13
"*B* those things we . . . . . .John 13:29
rejoice, those who *b* . . . . .1 Cor 7:30
spend a year there, *b* . . . .James 4:13
"I counsel you to *b* . . . . .Rev 3:18
and that no one may *b* . . . .Rev 13:17

BUYER

nothing," cries the *b* . . . . .Prov 20:14
as with the *b* . . . . .Is 24:2
'Let not the *b* . . . . .Ezek 7:12

BUYS

a field and *b* it . . . . .Prov 31:16
has and *b* that field . . . . .Matt 13:44
b their merchandise . . . . . .Rev 18:11

BYGONE

b generations . . . . .Acts 14:16

BYWORD

But He has made me a *b* . . .Job 17:6
You make us a *b* . . . . .Ps 44:14

C

CAGE

c is full of birds . . . . .Jer 5:27
foul spirit, and a *c* . . . . .Rev 18:2

CAKE

Ephraim is a *c* . . . . .Hos 7:8

CAKES

Sustain me with *c* . . . . .Song 2:5
and love the raisin *c* . . . . . . .Hos 3:1

CALAMITIES

refuge, until these *c* . . . . . . .Ps 57:1

CALAMITY

for the day of their *c* . . . .Deut 32:35
will laugh at your *c* . . . . . .Prov 1:26
c shall come suddenly . . . .Prov 6:15
If there is *c* in a . . . . .Amos 3:6

CALCULATED

c the dust of the . . . . .Is 40:12

CALDRON

this city is the *c* . . . . .Ezek 11:3

CALF

and made a molded *c* . . . . . .Ex 32:4
They made a *c* in Horeb . .Ps 106:19
is, than a fatted *c* . . . . . . .Prov 15:17
like a stubborn *c* . . . . .Hos 4:16
Your *c* is rejected . . . . .Hos 8:5
And bring the fatted *c* . . .Luke 15:23
creature like a *c* . . . . .Rev 4:7

CALL

I will *c* to the LORD . . . .1 Sam 12:17
c their lands after . . . . .Ps 49:11
To you, O men, I *c* . . . . . . .Prov 8:4
c upon Him while He . . . . . .Is 55:6
'*C* to Me . . . . .Jer 33:3
Arise, and *c* on your God . .Jon 1:6
They will *c* on My name . .Zech 13:9
c His name JESUS . . . . . . .Matt 1:21

CALLED

c the righteous ....Matt 9:13
Lord our God will c......Acts 2:39
c them My people.......Rom 9:25
then shall they c ....Rom 10:14
For God did not c ....1 Thess 4:7
to make your c and .....2 Pet 1:10

CALLED

c the light Day...........Gen 1:5
c his wife's name Eve ....Gen 3:20
"I, the LORD, have c......Is 42:6
I have c you by your.......Is 43:1
The LORD has c Me from ....Is 49:1
and out of Egypt I c ....Hos 11:1
"Out of Egypt I c.......Matt 2:15
a city c Nazareth ....Matt 2:23
For many are c ....Matt 20:16
to those who are the c....Rom 8:28
these He also c ....Rom 8:30
But God has c us to .....1 Cor 7:15
praises of Him who c....1 Pet 2:9
knowledge of Him who c...2 Pet 1:3
c Children of God ......1 John 3:1

CALLING

the gifts and the c......Rom 11:29
For you see your c.....1 Cor 1:26
remain in the same c.....1 Cor 7:20
to walk worthy of the c....Eph 4:1
in one hope of your c......Eph 4:4
us with a holy c.........2 Tim 1:9
of the heavenly c ....Heb 3:1

CALLS

c them all by name.......Ps 147:4
there is no one who c........Is 64:7
David himself c ....Mark 12:37
c his own sheep.........John 10:3
For "whoever c ....Rom 10:13

CALM

the sea will become c .....Jon 1:12
there was a great c......Matt 8:26

CALMED

Surely I have c ....Ps 131:2

CALVES

advice made two c......1 Kin 12:28
their cow c without......Job 21:10
like stall-fed c ....Mal 4:2
blood of goats and c ......Heb 9:12
he took the blood of c .....Heb 9:19

CAMEL

it is easier for a c ....Matt 19:24
and swallow a c........Matt 23:24

CAMP

"This is God's c..........Gen 32:2
who went before the c .....Ex 14:19
to Him, outside the c.....Heb 13:13

CAN

I c do all things ....Phil 4:13

CANCER

will spread like c ....2 Tim 2:17

CANE

bought Me no sweet c.....Is 43:24
Sheba, and sweet c ....Jer 6:20

CANOPIES

He made darkness c....2 Sam 22:12

CANOPY

His c around Him was .....Ps 18:11

CAPSTONE

bring forth the c ....Zech 4:7

CAPTAIN

which, having no c ....Prov 6:7

CAPTIVE

have led captivity c ......Ps 68:18
of your neck, O c........Is 52:2
they shall now go c.......Amos 6:7
and be led away c......Luke 21:24
He led captivity c ....Eph 4:8

CAPTIVES

will bring back the c.....Amos 9:14
and return their c........Zeph 2:7
households and make c....2 Tim 3:6

CAPTIVITY

bring you back from c ....Deut 30:3
high, You have led c ......Ps 68:18
Judah has gone into c......Lam 1:3
from David until the c....Matt 1:17
and bringing me into c....Rom 7:23
every thought into c ....2 Cor 10:5
on high, He led c ....Eph 4:8
shall go into c ....Rev 13:10

CARCASS

honey were in the c.......Judg 14:8
For wherever the c .....Matt 24:28

CARE

"Lord, do You not c .....Luke 10:40
you to be without c ....1 Cor 7:32
who will sincerely c ......Phil 2:20
how will he take c ....1 Tim 3:5
casting all your c ....1 Pet 5:7

CARED

he said, not that he c ....John 12:6

CAREFULLY

c keep all these ....Deut 11:22
I shall walk c all my ....Is 38:15

CARELESS

but he who is c ....Prov 19:16

CARES

no one c for my soul......Ps 142:4
and are choked with c ....Luke 8:14
He who is unmarried c ...1 Cor 7:32
for He c for you ....1 Pet 5:7

CARNAL

spiritual, but I am c......Rom 7:14
c mind is enmity ....Rom 8:7
for you are still c ....1 Cor 3:3
our warfare are not c ....2 Cor 10:4

CARNALLY

we may know them c......Gen 19:5
that we may know him c ..Judg 19:22
c minded is death ....Rom 8:6

CAROUSE

count it pleasure to c....2 Pet 2:13

CAROUSING

be weighed down with c..Luke 21:34

CARPENTER

"Is this not the c........Mark 6:3

CARRIED

the LORD your God c ....Deut 1:31
and c our sorrows ....Is 53:4
parted from them and c..Luke 24:51
c me away in the.........Rev 17:3

CARRY

their hands cannot c.......Job 5:12
c them away like a ....Ps 90:5

I am not worthy to c .....Matt 3:11
for you to c your bed ....John 5:10
it is certain we can c......1 Tim 6:7

CARRYING

a man will meet you c...Mark 14:13
always c about in the ....2 Cor 4:10

CASE

c that is too hard ....Deut 1:17
I have prepared my c ....Job 13:18
I would present my c .....Job 23:4
"Present your c ....Is 41:21
Festus laid Paul's c.....Acts 25:14

CASSIA

myrrh and aloes and c .....Ps 45:8

CAST

When they c you down....Job 22:29
c away Their ....Ps 2:3
Why are you c down........Ps 42:5
But You have c off........Ps 44:9
c me away from Your ......Ps 51:11
He c on them the ....Ps 78:49
the LORD will not c.......Ps 94:14
me up and c me away......Ps 102:10
and the earth shall c......Is 26:19
My sight, as I have c .....Jer 7:15
C away from you all.....Ezek 18:31
brought Daniel and c.....Dan 6:16
c all our sins into ....Mic 7:19
whole body to be c......Matt 5:29
the kingdom will be c.....Matt 8:12
spirits, to c them out....Matt 10:1
In My name they will c..Mark 16:17
by no means c out ....John 6:37
c away His people ....Rom 11:1
c away your confidence ...Heb 10:35
c their crowns before ....Rev 4:10
the great dragon was c....Rev 12:9

CASTING

nation which I am c.....Lev 20:23
Andrew his brother, c....Matt 4:18
c down arguments ....2 Cor 10:5
c all your care............1 Pet 5:7

CASTS

"If Satan c ....Matt 12:26
perfect love c out.......1 John 4:18

CATCH

in wait to c the poor........Ps 10:9
c Him in His words.....Mark 12:13
down your nets for a c....Luke 5:4
From now on you will c ..Luke 5:10

CATCHES

and the wolf c the.......John 10:12
c the wise in their ....1 Cor 3:19

CATERPILLAR

their crops to the c.......Ps 78:46

CATTLE

c you shall take as........Josh 8:2
does not let their c ......Ps 107:38

CAUGHT

behind him was a ram c...Gen 22:13
and that night they c.....John 21:3
Spirit of the Lord c ......Acts 8:39
her Child was c up ....Rev 12:5

CAUSE

I would commit my c.....Job 5:8
my enemy without c........Ps 7:4
hate me without a c......Ps 35:19
c His face to shine ....Ps 67:1
C me to know the way ....Ps 143:8

CAVES

one to plead his *c* . . . . . . .Prov 18:17
God, Who pleads the *c* . . . .Is 51:22
He judged the *c* . . . . .Jer 22:16
brother without a *c* . . . . . .Matt 5:22
hated Me without a *c* . . . .John 15:25
For this *c* I was born . . . .John 18:37

CAVES

the people hid in *c* . . . . . .1 Sam 13:6
rocks, and into the *c* . . . . .Is 2:19
in dens and *c* of the . . . . . .Heb 11:38

CEASE

and night shall not *c* . . . . .Gen 8:22
Why should the work *c* . . . . .Neh 6:3
There the wicked *c* . . . . . . .Job 3:17
He makes wars *c* . . . . .Ps 46:9
C listening to . . . . .Prov 19:27
C to do evil . . . . .Is 1:16
tongues, they will *c* . . . . .1 Cor 13:8
do not *c* to give . . . . .Eph 1:16
do not *c* to pray for . . . . .Col 1:9

CEASED

c building the city . . . . .Gen 11:8
the sea, and the sea *c* . . . . .Jon 1:15

CEASES

for the godly man *c* . . . . .Ps 12:1

CEASING

c your work of faith . . . . .1 Thess 1:3
thank God without *c* . . .1 Thess 2:13
pray without *c* . . . . .1 Thess 5:17

CEDAR

dwell in a house of *c* . . . . . .2 Sam 7:2
He shall grow like a *c* . . . . .Ps 92:12
of our houses are *c* . . . . .Song 1:17
it, paneling it with *c* . . . . .Jer 22:14
Indeed Assyria was a *c* . .Ezek 31:3

CEDARS

the LORD breaks the *c* . . . . .Ps 29:5
c of Lebanon which He . . .Ps 104:16

CELESTIAL

but the glory of the *c* . . .1 Cor 15:40

CENSER

Aaron, each took his *c* . . . .Lev 10:1
Each man had a *c* . . . . . . .Ezek 8:11
which had the golden *c* . . . .Heb 9:4
the angel took the *c* . . . . . . .Rev 8:5

CERTAINTY

make you know the *c* . . . .Prov 22:21
you may know the *c* . . . . . .Luke 1:4

CERTIFICATE

a man to write a *c* . . . . . .Mark 10:4

CERTIFIED

His testimony has *c* . . . . .John 3:33

CHAFF

c that a storm . . . . .Job 21:18
c which the wind . . . . .Ps 1:4
Let them be like *c* . . . . . . .Ps 35:5
be chased like the *c* . . . . . . .Is 17:13
You shall conceive *c* . . . . . .Is 33:11
the day passes like *c* . . . . .Zeph 2:2
He will burn up the *c* . . . . .Matt 3:12

CHAIN

He has made my *c* . . . . .Lam 3:7
pit and a great *c* . . . . .Rev 20:1

CHAINED

of God is not *c* . . . . .2 Tim 2:9
the prisoners as if *c* . . . . . .Heb 13:3

CHAINS

their kings with *c* . . . . .Ps 149:8
your neck with *c* . . . . .Song 1:10
And his *c* fell off . . . . .Acts 12:7
am, except for these *c* . . . .Acts 26:29
Remember my *c* . . . . .Col 4:18
minister to me in my *c* . . . .Philem 13
delivered them into *c* . . . . .2 Pet 2:4

CHAMBERS

and the *c* of the south . . . . .Job 9:9
brought me into his *c* . . . . .Song 1:4
and his *c* by injustice . . . .Jer 22:13

CHAMPION

And a *c* went out from. . .1 Sam 17:4

CHANGE

c his countenance . . . . . . .Job 14:20
c the night into day . . . . .Job 17:12
and who can make Him *c* .Job 23:13
Because they do not *c* . . . . .Ps 55:19
a cloak You will *c* . . . . . . .Ps 102:26
with those given to *c* . . . .Prov 24:21
Can the Ethiopian *c* . . . . .Jer 13:23
c times and law . . . . .Dan 7:25
c their glory into . . . . .Hos 4:7
the LORD, I do not *c* . . . . . . .Mal 3:6
now and to *c* my tone . . . . . .Gal 4:20
there is also a *c* . . . . .Heb 7:12

CHANGED

But My people have *c* . . . . .Jer 2:11
c the glory of the . . . . . . .Rom 1:23
but we shall all be *c* . . . . .1 Cor 15:51
the priesthood being *c* . . . .Heb 7:12

CHANGERS'

and poured out the *c* . . . .John 2:15

CHANGES

c the times and the . . . . . .Dan 2:21

CHANNELS

c of the sea were seen . . . . . .Ps 18:15

CHARACTER

and *c*, hope . . . . .Rom 5:4

CHARGED

May it not be *c* . . . . .2 Tim 4:16

CHARIOT

He took off their *c* . . . . . . .Ex 14:25
that suddenly a *c* . . . . . . .2 Kin 2:11
makes the clouds His *c* . . . .Ps 104:3
and overtake this *c* . . . . . .Acts 8:29

CHARIOTS

the clatter of his *c* . . . . . .Judg 5:28
Some trust in *c* . . . . .Ps 20:7
The *c* of God are . . . . .Ps 68:17

CHARITABLE

you do not do your *c* . . . . .Matt 6:1
"that your *c* deed . . . . .Matt 6:4
c deeds which she . . . . . . .Acts 9:36

CHARM

C is deceitful and . . . . . . .Prov 31:30

CHARMERS

heed the voice of *c* . . . . .Ps 58:5

CHARMS

women who sew magic *c* .Ezek 13:18

CHASE

Five of you shall *c* . . . . . . .Lev 26:8
How could one *c* . . . . . .Deut 32:30
angel of the LORD *c* . . . . . . .Ps 35:5

CHASTE

may present you as a *c* . . .2 Cor 11:2
to be discreet, *c* . . . . .Titus 2:5
c conduct accompanied . . . .1 Pet 3:2

CHASTEN

C your son while there . . .Prov 19:18
is My desire, I will *c* . . . . .Hos 10:10
a father does not *c* . . . . .Heb 12:7
I love, I rebuke and *c* . . . . . .Rev 3:19

CHASTENED

c my soul with fasting . . . . .Ps 69:10
c every morning . . . . .Ps 73:14
The LORD has *c* me . . . . . . .Ps 118:18
In vain I have *c* . . . . .Jer 2:30
c us as seemed best . . . . . .Heb 12:10

CHASTENING

have not seen the *c* . . . . . . .Deut 11:2
do not despise the *c* . . . . . .Job 5:17
'I have borne *c* . . . . .Job 34:31
a prayer when Your *c* . . . . . .Is 26:16
if you are without *c* . . . . . . .Heb 12:8
Now no *c* seems to be . . . .Heb 12:11

CHASTENS

the LORD loves He *c* . . . . . . .Heb 12:6

CHASTISE

and I, even I, will *c* . . . . . .Lev 26:28
c them according . . . . .Hos 7:12
I will therefore *c* . . . . . . .Luke 23:22

CHASTISEMENT

the *c* for our peace . . . . .Is 53:5

CHATTER

c leads only to . . . . .Prov 14:23

CHEAT

'You shall not *c* . . . . .Lev 19:13
Beware lest anyone *c* . . . . . . .Col 2:8

CHEATED

let yourselves be *c* . . . . .1 Cor 6:7
we have *c* no one . . . . .2 Cor 7:2

CHEEK

Let him give his *c* . . . . . . .Lam 3:30
with a rod on the *c* . . . . . . .Mic 5:1
on your right *c* . . . . .Matt 5:39

CHEEKBONE

my enemies on the *c* . . . . .Ps 3:7

CHEEKS

c are lovely with . . . . .Song 1:10
His *c* are like a bed . . . . . .Song 5:13
struck Me, and My *c* . . . . . . .Is 50:6

CHEER

and let your heart *c* . . . . . .Eccl 11:9
"Son, be of good *c* . . . . . . .Matt 9:2

CHEERFUL

for God loves a *c* . . . . .2 Cor 9:7
Is anyone *c* . . . . .James 5:13

CHEERFULNESS

shows mercy, with *c* . . . . .Rom 12:8

CHEESE

and curdle me like *c* . . . . .Job 10:10

CHERISHES

but nourishes and *c* . . . . . . .Eph 5:29
as a nursing mother *c* . . .1 Thess 2:7

CHERUB

He rode upon a *c* . . . . . .2 Sam 22:11

CHERUBIM

and He placed *c* ....Gen 3:24
dwell between the *c* ......Ps 80:1
fire from among the *c* ....Ezek 10:2
above it were the *c* ....Heb 9:5

CHIEF

is white and ruddy, *c* ....Song 5:10
of whom I am *c* ....1 Tim 1:15
Zion a *c* cornerstone......1 Pet 2:6
has become the *c* ....1 Pet 2:7
C Shepherd appears......1 Pet 5:4

CHILD

Like a weaned *c*..........Ps 131:2
c is known by his.......Prov 20:11
Train up a *c* in the......Prov 22:6
For unto us a *C* ....Is 9:6
c shall lead them ....Is 11:6
When Israel was a *c*......Hos 11:1
virgin shall be with *c*.....Matt 1:23
He took a little *c* ....Mark 9:36
of God as a little *c*.....Mark 10:15
kind of *c* will this be......Luke 1:66
So the *c* grew and......Luke 1:80
When I was a *c* ....1 Cor 13:11
She bore a male *C*........Rev 12:5

CHILDBEARING

she will be saved in *c* ....1 Tim 2:15

CHILDBIRTH

pain as a woman in *c*........Is 13:8

CHILDHOOD

from your flesh, for *c*....Eccl 11:10
And he said, "From *c* ...Mark 9:21
c you have known ......2 Tim 3:15

CHILDLESS

give me, seeing I go *c* .....Gen 15:2
this man down as *c* ......Jer 22:30

CHILDREN

she bore Jacob no *c* ......Gen 30:1
and all of you are *c*.........Ps 82:6
c are a heritage ....Ps 127:3
He has blessed your *c* ....Ps 147:13
let the *c* of Zion be ....Ps 149:2
c are blessed after.......Prov 20:7
c rise up and call her ....Prov 31:28
c are their oppressors ....Is 3:12
c whom the LORD has .....Is 8:18
be the peace of your *c*......Is 54:13
they are My people, ...Is 63:8
the hearts of the *c* ....Mal 4:6
c will rise up against ....Matt 10:21
and become as little *c* ....Matt 18:3
c were brought to Him...Matt 19:13
"Let the little *c*.........Matt 19:14
the right to become *c*....John 1:12
you were Abraham's *c* ...John 8:39
spirit that we are *c* ......Rom 8:16
but as my beloved *c*.....1 Cor 4:14
Brethren, do not be *c*...1 Cor 14:20
c ought not to lay up....2 Cor 12:14
and were by nature *c* ......Eph 2:3
should no longer be *c*.....Eph 4:14
Walk as *c* of light........Eph 5:8
and harmless, *c*..........Phil 2:15
now we are *c* of God ....1 John 3:2
that we love the *c* ......1 John 5:2
to hear that my *c* ....3 John 4

CHOICE

rather than *c* gold ....Prov 8:10

CHOOSE

therefore *c* life..........Deut 30:19
c none of his ways.......Prov 3:31

evil and *c* the good ....Is 7:15
will still *c* Israel...........Is 14:1
will again *c* Jerusalem ...Zech 1:17
"You did not *c*..........John 15:16
yet what I shall *c* ....Phil 1:22

CHOOSES

in the way He *c*..........Ps 25:12

CHOSE

a good while ago God *c* ...Acts 15:7
just as He *c* us in Him .....Eph 1:4
from the beginning *c* ..2 Thess 2:13

CHOSEN

of Jacob, His *c*.........1 Chr 16:13
people He has *c*..........Ps 33:12
a covenant with My *c*......Ps 89:3
c the way of truth.......Ps 119:30
servant whom I have *c* .....Is 43:10
c that good part ......Luke 10:42
I know whom I have *c* ...John 13:18
c you that you should....Acts 22:14
c the foolish things ......1 Cor 1:27
Has God not *c* the poor....James 2:5
But you are a *c*..........1 Pet 2:9

CHRIST

genealogy of Jesus *C*....Matt 1:1
Jesus who is called *C*.....Matt 1:16
"You are the *C* ....Matt 16:16
if You are the *C*.........Matt 26:63
a Savior, who is *C*.......Luke 2:11
that He Himself is *C* ....Luke 23:2
the law that the *C*.......John 12:34
he preached the *C* ......Acts 9:20
have the Spirit of *C*.......Rom 8:9
It is *C* who died.........Rom 8:34
C did not please.........Rom 15:3
Is *C* divided ....1 Cor 1:13
Him you are in *C* Jesus...1 Cor 1:30
to be justified by *C*........Gal 2:17
been crucified with *C* ....Gal 2:20
but *C* lives in me.........Gal 2:20
your Seed," who is *C*.....Gal 3:16
before by God in *C*.......Gal 3:17
C may dwell in your.......Eph 3:17
C will give you ....Eph 5:14
C is head of the ....Eph 5:23
to me, to live is *C*.......Phil 1:21
confess that Jesus *C*.....Phil 2:11
C who strengthens ....Phil 4:13
which is *C* in you........Col 1:27
C who is our..............Col 3:4
C is all and in all ....Col 3:11
and men, the Man *C*.....1 Tim 2:5
Jesus *C* is the same......Heb 13:8
C His Son cleanses us...1 John 1:7
that Jesus is the *C* ......1 John 5:1
of His *C* have come......Rev 12:10
and reigned with *C*......Rev 20:4

CHRISTIAN

me to become a *C* ......Acts 26:28
anyone suffers as a *C*.....1 Pet 4:16

CHRISTIANS

were first called *C* ......Acts 11:26

CHRISTS

"For false *c* and ....Matt 24:24

CHURCH

rock I will build My *c*....Matt 16:18
them, tell it to the *c*.....Matt 18:17
c daily those who were ...Acts 2:47
elders in every *c*........Acts 14:23
do you despise the *c* ....1 Cor 11:22
be made known by the *c*..Eph 3:10
also loved the *c*..........Eph 5:25

Himself a glorious *c*......Eph 5:27
as the Lord does the *c*.....Eph 5:29
body, which is the *c*.......Col 1:24
and do not let the *c*......1 Tim 5:16
general assembly and *c*...Heb 12:23
To the angel of the *c*.......Rev 2:1

CHURCHES

strengthening the *c*......Acts 15:41
The *c* of Christ greet.....Rom 16:16
imitators of the *c*......1 Thess 2:14
John, to the seven *c* ....Rev 1:4
angels of the seven *c* .....Rev 1:20
these things in the *c*......Rev 22:16

CHURNING

For as the *c* of milk......Prov 30:33

CHURNS

My heart *c* within Me ....Hos 11:8

CIRCLE

He walks above the *c*.....Job 22:14
when He drew a *c* ......Prov 8:27
who sits above the *c* ......Is 40:22

CIRCUIT

of heaven, and its *c*........Ps 19:6
comes again on its *c* ....Eccl 1:6

CIRCUMCISE

c the foreskin of your....Deut 10:16
LORD your God will *c*....Deut 30:6
C yourselves to the ....Jer 4:4
is necessary to *c* them ....Acts 15:5

CIRCUMCISED

among you shall be *c*.....Gen 17:10
who will justify the *c* ....Rom 3:30
While he was *c*.........Rom 4:10
the gospel for the *c*........Gal 2:7
if you become *c* ....Gal 5:2
c the eighth day ....Phil 3:5
In Him you were also *c*....Col 2:11

CIRCUMCISION

him the covenant of *c* .....Acts 7:8
c that which is outward ...Rom 2:28
c is that of the heart.....Rom 2:29
a servant to the *c* ....Rom 15:8
C is nothing and ....1 Cor 7:19
Christ Jesus neither *c*......Gal 5:6
For we are the *c* ....Phil 3:3
circumcised with the *c* ....Col 2:11
those of the *c* ....Titus 1:10

CIRCUMSPECTLY

then that you walk *c*......Eph 5:15

CISTERN

waters of his own *c* .....2 Kin 18:31
from your own *c* ....Prov 5:15

CITIES

He overthrew those *c*.....Gen 19:25
repair the ruined *c*........Is 61:4
c are a wilderness ....Is 64:10
c will be laid waste ....Jer 4:7
three parts, and the *c*.....Rev 16:19

CITIZEN

But I was born a *c* ......Acts 22:28

CITIZENS

"But his *c* hated him ....Luke 19:14
but fellow *c* with the ......Eph 2:19

CITIZENSHIP

sum I obtained this *c* ....Acts 22:28
For our *c* is in heaven .....Phil 3:20

CITY

And he built a c . . . . Gen 4:17
shall make glad the c . . . . . . Ps 46:4
c shall flourish . . . . Ps 72:16
They found no c . . . . Ps 107:4
c that is compact . . . . Ps 122:3
the LORD guards the c . . . . . Ps 127:1
at the entry of the c . . . . . . Prov 8:3
c has become a harlot . . . . . . Is 1:21
upon Zion, the c . . . . Is 33:20
after the holy c . . . . Is 48:2
How lonely sits the c . . . . . . Lam 1:1
Nineveh, that great c . . . . . Jon 4:11
c that dwelt securely . . . . Zeph 2:15
to the oppressing c . . . . Zeph 3:1
c called Nazareth . . . . Matt 2:23
c that is set on a . . . . Matt 5:14
He has prepared a c . . . . . . Heb 11:16
Zion and to the c . . . . Heb 12:22
have no continuing c . . . . . Heb 13:14
will tread the holy c . . . . . . Rev 11:2
fallen, that great c . . . . Rev 14:8
and the beloved c . . . . Rev 20:9
John, saw the holy c . . . . . Rev 21:2
c was pure gold . . . . Rev 21:18
c had no need of the . . . . . Rev 21:23
the gates into the c . . . . . . Rev 22:14

CLAMOROUS

A foolish woman is c . . . . . . Prov 9:13

CLAP

c their hands at him . . . . . . Job 27:23
Oh, c your hands . . . . Ps 47:1
let the rivers c . . . . Ps 98:8
of the field shall c . . . . Is 55:12

CLAY

dwell in houses of c . . . . . . Job 4:19
have made me like c . . . . . . Job 10:9
are defenses of c . . . . Job 13:12
been formed out of c . . . . . Job 33:6
takes on form like c . . . . . . Job 38:14
pit, out of the miry c . . . . . . Ps 40:2
be esteemed as the c . . . . . . Is 29:16
Shall the c say to him . . . . . . Is 45:9
we are the c . . . . Is 64:8
"Look, as the c . . . . Jer 18:6
iron and partly of c . . . . . . Dan 2:33
blind man with the c . . . . . John 9:6
have power over the c . . . . . Rom 9:21

CLEAN

seven each of every c . . . . . . Gen 7:2
between unclean and c . . . . Lev 10:10
wash in them and be c . . . 2 Kin 5:12
Who can bring a c . . . . Job 14:4
He who has c hands and . . . Ps 24:4
make yourselves c . . . . Is 1:16
Then I will sprinkle c . . . . Ezek 36:25
c out His threshing floor . Matt 3:12
You can make me c . . . . . . Matt 8:2
all things are c . . . . Luke 11:41
but is completely c . . . . . . John 13:10
"You are not all c . . . . John 13:11
"You are already c . . . . John 15:3
in fine linen, c . . . . Rev 19:8

CLEANSE

You shall c the altar . . . . . . Ex 29:36
C me from secret . . . . Ps 19:12
and c me from my sin . . . . . . Ps 51:2
How can a young man c . . . Ps 119:9
I will c you from all . . . . . Ezek 36:25
c the lepers, raise . . . . Matt 10:8
might sanctify and c . . . . . . Eph 5:26
c your conscience . . . . Heb 9:14
C your hands . . . . James 4:8
us our sins and to c . . . . . . 1 John 1:9

CLEANSED

Surely I have c . . . . Ps 73:13
and you were not c . . . . . Ezek 24:13
the lepers are c . . . . Matt 11:5
Were there not ten c . . . . Luke 17:17

CLEANSES

Therefore if anyone c . . . . . 2 Tim 2:21
Jesus Christ His Son c . . . 1 John 1:7

CLEAR

c shining after rain . . . . . 2 Sam 23:4
fair as the moon, c . . . . . . Song 6:10
yourselves to be c . . . . 2 Cor 7:11
like a jasper stone, c . . . . . Rev 21:11
of life, c as crystal . . . . Rev 22:1

CLEFTS

to go into the c . . . . Is 2:21
valleys and in the c . . . . Is 7:19
you who dwell in the c . . . Jer 49:16

CLERK

c had quieted the . . . . Acts 19:35

CLIFF

secret places of the c . . . . . Song 2:14

CLIMB

go into thickets and c . . . . . Jer 4:29
mighty men, they c . . . . . . Joel 2:7
though they c up to . . . . . . Amos 9:2

CLIMBS

c up some other way . . . . . John 10:1

CLING

and that you may c . . . . . Deut 30:20
to her, "Do not c . . . . John 20:17
C to what is good . . . . Rom 12:9

CLINGS

and My tongue c . . . . Ps 22:15
My soul c to the dust . . . . Ps 119:25

CLOAK

c You will change them . . Ps 102:26
let him have your c . . . . . . Matt 5:40
c You will fold them . . . . . . Heb 1:12
using liberty as a c . . . . . . 1 Pet 2:16

CLODS

The c of the valley . . . . . . Job 21:33

CLOSE

c friends abhor me . . . . . . Job 19:19
of Christ he came c . . . . . . Phil 2:30

CLOSED

and has c your eyes . . . . Is 29:10
for the words are c . . . . . . Dan 12:9
the deep c around me . . . . . Jon 2:5

CLOTH

a piece of unshrunk c . . . . Matt 9:16
in a clean linen c . . . . Matt 27:59

CLOTHE

c them with tunics . . . . Ex 40:14
c me with skin and . . . . . . Job 10:11
c her priests with . . . . Ps 132:16
His enemies I will c . . . . . Ps 132:18
Though you c yourself . . . . Jer 4:30
He not much more c . . . . . Matt 6:30

CLOTHED

of skin, and c them . . . . . . Gen 3:21
Have you c his neck . . . . . Job 39:19
off my sackcloth and c . . . . . Ps 30:11
The pastures are c . . . . Ps 65:13
the LORD is c . . . . Ps 93:1

You are c with honor . . . . . . Ps 104:1
c himself with cursing . . . . Ps 109:18
Let Your priests be c . . . . Ps 132:9
all her household is c . . . Prov 31:21
c you with fine linen . . . . Ezek 16:10
A man c in soft . . . . Matt 11:8
I was naked and you c . . . Matt 25:36
legion, sitting and c . . . . . Mark 5:15
And they c Him with . . . . Mark 15:17
rich man who was c . . . . . Luke 16:19
desiring to be c . . . . 2 Cor 5:2
that you may be c . . . . Rev 3:18
a woman c with the sun . . . Rev 12:1
He was c with a robe . . . . Rev 19:13

CLOTHES

c will abhor me . . . . Job 9:31
c became shining . . . . Mark 9:3
many spread their c . . . Luke 19:36
laid down their c . . . . Acts 7:58
and tore off their c . . . . . Acts 22:23
a poor man in filthy c . . . James 2:2

CLOTHING

c they cast lots . . . . Ps 22:18
c is woven with gold . . . . . Ps 45:13
will provide your c . . . . . Prov 27:26
and honor are her c . . . . . Prov 31:25
of vengeance for c . . . . Is 59:17
the body more than c . . . . Matt 6:25
do you worry about c . . . . Matt 6:28
to you in sheep's c . . . . . . Matt 7:15
those who wear soft c . . . . Matt 11:8
c as white as snow . . . . . . Matt 28:3
c they cast lots . . . . John 19:24
before me in bright c . . . . Acts 10:30

CLOTHS

wrapped in swaddling c . . Luke 2:12
in, saw the linen c . . . . . . John 20:5

CLOUD

My rainbow in the c . . . . . Gen 9:13
day in a pillar of c . . . . . . Ex 13:21
c covered the mountain . . . Ex 24:15
c descended and stood . . . Ex 33:9
c did not depart . . . . Neh 9:19
He led them with the c . . Ps 78:14
his favor is like a c . . . . . Prov 16:15
these who fly like a c . . . . . Is 60:8
like a morning c . . . . Hos 6:4
behold, a bright c . . . . . . Matt 17:5
of Man coming in a c . . . . Luke 21:27
c received Him out of . . . . . Acts 1:9
were under the c . . . . 1 Cor 10:1
by so great a c . . . . Heb 12:1

CLOUDS

a morning without c . . . . 2 Sam 23:4
c poured out water . . . . Ps 77:17
and hail, snow and c . . . . . Ps 148:8
c drop down the dew . . . . Prov 3:20
he who regards the c . . . . Eccl 11:4
of Man coming on the c . . Matt 24:30
with them in the c . . . 1 Thess 4:17
are c without water . . . . . . Jude 12
He is coming with c . . . . . Rev 1:7

CLOUDY

them by day with a c . . . . Neh 9:12
spoke to them in the c . . . . Ps 99:7

CLOVEN

the hoof, having c . . . . Lev 11:3
chew the cud or have c . . Deut 14:7

CLUSTER

beloved is to me a c . . . . . Song 1:14
wine is found in the c . . . . . Is 65:8

COAL

in his hand a live *c* ....Is 6:6
it shall not be a *c*......... Is 47:14

COALS

wicked He will rain *c*.....Ps 11:6
c were kindled by it ....Ps 18:8
let burning *c* fall........Ps 140:10
Can one walk on hot *c* ....Prov 6:28
so you will heap *c* .....Prov 25:22
doing you will heap *c* ....Rom 12:20

COBRA

it becomes *c* venom ......Job 20:14
c that stops its ear.........Ps 58:4
the lion and the *c* ....Ps 91:13

COBRA'S

shall play by the *c*.........Is 11:8

COFFIN

and he was put in a *c*.....Gen 50:26
David followed the *c*....2 Sam 3:31
and touched the open *c* ...Luke 7:14

COIN

sold for a copper *c* ......Matt 10:29
if she loses one *c*........Luke 15:8

COLD

and harvest, *c* and ....Gen 8:22
can stand before His *c* ....Ps 147:17
Like the *c* of snow in ....Prov 25:13
c water to a weary......Prov 25:25
c water in the name of . .Matt 10:42
of many will grow *c* ....Matt 24:12
that you are neither *c*.....Rev 3:15

COLLECTED

coming I might have *c*...Luke 19:23

COLLECTION

from Jerusalem the *c*....2 Chr 24:6
concerning the *c*........1 Cor 16:1

COLT

and his donkey's *c* ......Gen 49:11
on a donkey, a *c*...........Zech 9:9
on a donkey, a *c* ....Matt 21:5
own clothes on the *c*.....Luke 19:35

COME

then does wisdom *c* .....Job 28:20
of glory shall *c* ....Ps 24:7
Our God shall *c*...........Ps 50:3
You all flesh will *c*.......Ps 65:2
C with me from Lebanon. .Song 4:8
He will *c* and save you .....Is 35:4
who have no money, *c* .....Is 55:1
Your kingdom *c*........Matt 6:10
"*C* to Me ....Matt 11:28
For many will *c* ....Matt 24:5
Israel, let Him now *c* ....Matt 27:42
If anyone desires to *c* ....Luke 9:23
kingdom of God has *c* ....Luke 10:9
"I have *c* in My........John 5:43
and I have not *c* ....John 7:28
thirsts, let him *c* ....John 7:37
c that they may have ....John 10:10
c as a light into the ....John 12:46
I will *c* to you ....John 14:18
"If I had not *c* ....John 15:22
savage wolves will *c* ....Acts 20:29
O Lord, *c*...............1 Cor 16:22
the door, I will *c* ....Rev 3:20
the bride say, "*C*........Rev 22:17

COMELINESS

He has no form or *c* ....Is 53:2

COMES

Who is this who *c* ....Is 63:1
'Come,' and he *c*........Matt 8:9
Lord's death till He *c* ..1 Cor 11:26
Then *c* the end........1 Cor 15:24

COMFORT

with him, and to *c* him...Job 2:11
and Your staff, they *c*......Ps 23:4
When will You *c* ....Ps 119:82
yes, *c* My people ....Is 40:1
For the LORD will *c* ......Is 51:3
c all who mourn...........Is 61:2
she has none to *c* her .....Lam 1:2
the LORD will again *c* ....Zech 1:17
and God of all *c* ....2 Cor 1:3
trouble, with the *c*.......2 Cor 1:4
in Christ, if any *c*........Phil 2:1
c each other and edify .1 Thess 5:11

COMFORTED

So Isaac was *c* after......Gen 24:67
soul refused to be *c*.........Ps 77:2
For the LORD has *c* ....Is 49:13
refusing to be *c* ....Jer 31:15
but now he is *c*........Luke 16:25

COMFORTER

she had no *c* ....Lam 1:9

COMFORTS

the army, as one who *c*...Job 29:25
I, even I, am He who *c*.....Is 51:12
him, and restore *c* ....Is 57:18
one whom his mother *c*....Is 66:13
who *c* us in all our ....2 Cor 1:4
who *c* the downcast .....2 Cor 7:6

COMING

your salvation is *c*........Is 62:11
behold, the day is *c* ....Mal 4:1
but He who is *c* ....Matt 3:11
"Are You the *C*.........Matt 11:3
be the sign of Your *c* .....Matt 24:3
is delaying his *c*........Matt 24:48
see the Son of Man *c*....Mark 13:26
mightier than I is *c* ......Luke 3:16
are Christ's at His *c* ....1 Cor 15:23
to you the power and *c* ..2 Pet 1:16
the promise of His *c*......2 Pet 3:4
Behold, I am *c*............Rev 3:11
"Behold, I am *c*..........Rev 22:7
"Surely I am *c*..........Rev 22:20

COMMAND

in order that he may *c*...Gen 18:19
" The LORD will *c* ....Deut 28:8
"in that I *c* you.........Deut 30:16
c His lovingkindness ....Ps 42:8
c victories for Jacob.......Ps 44:4
to all that I *c* ....Jer 11:4
if it is You, *c* ....Matt 14:28
c fire to come down .....Luke 9:54
c I have received........John 10:18
And I know that His *c*..John 12:50
if you do whatever I *c* ...John 15:14
do the things we *c* ......2 Thess 3:4

COMMANDED

"Have you *c* the ....Job 38:12
c His covenant forever....Ps 111:9
For there the LORD *c* ....Ps 133:3
it is the God who *c* ......2 Cor 4:6
not endure what was *c*....Heb 12:20

COMMANDMENT

c of the LORD is pure ....Ps 19:8
c is exceedingly broad ...Ps 119:96
For the *c* is a lamp ......Prov 6:23
Me is taught by the *c* .....Is 29:13

COMMANDMENT

which is the great *c* .....Matt 22:36
"A new *c* I give to .....John 13:34
the Father gave Me *c* ...John 14:31
law, but when the *c*.......Rom 7:9
the *c* might become......Rom 7:13
which is the first *c*........Eph 6:2
c is the word which .....1 John 2:7
And this is His *c*.......1 John 3:23
as we received *c* ....2 John 4
This is the *c* ....2 John 6

COMMANDMENTS

covenant, the Ten *C*......Ex 34:28
to observe all these *c* ....Deut 6:25
who remember His *c*......Ps 103:18
do not hide Your *c*......Ps 119:19
myself in Your *c*........Ps 119:47
for I believe Your *c*......Ps 119:66
Your *c* are faithful.......Ps 119:86
c more than gold........Ps 119:127
as doctrines the *c*........Matt 15:9
c hang all the Law ......Matt 22:40
"He who has My *c* .....John 14:21
according to the *c*.........Col 2:22
Now he who keeps His *c*.1 John 3:24

COMMANDS

with authority He *c*......Mark 1:27

COMMEND

But food does not *c*.......1 Cor 8:8

COMMENDABLE

For this is *c*..............1 Pet 2:19
patiently, this is *c*........1 Pet 2:20

COMMENDED

A man will be *c* ....Prov 12:8
c the unjust steward......Luke 16:8
where they had been *c* ...Acts 14:26

COMMENDING

of the truth *c* ....2 Cor 4:2

COMMENDS

but whom the Lord *c*....2 Cor 10:18

COMMIT

"You shall not *c* ....Ex 20:14
C your works to the .....Prov 16:3
mammon, who will *c* ...Luke 16:11
into Your hands I *c*.....Luke 23:46
But Jesus did not *c* ......John 2:24
c sexual immorality......1 Cor 10:8
c these to faithful ....2 Tim 2:2
c their souls to Him......1 Pet 4:19
c sin not leading ....1 John 5:16

COMMITS

to you, whoever *c*.......John 8:34
sin also *c* lawlessness ....1 John 3:4

COMMITTED

For My people have *c* .....Jer 2:13
c things deserving .....Luke 12:48
For God has *c* them all...Rom 11:32
Guard what was *c* ......1 Tim 6:20
"Who *c* no sin...........1 Pet 2:22
c Himself to Him who....1 Pet 2:23

COMMON

of the *c* people sins.......Lev 4:27
poor have this in *c*.......Prov 22:2
c people heard Him ....Mark 12:37
had all things in *c*.......Acts 2:44
never eaten anything *c*...Acts 10:14
not call any man *c*......Acts 10:28
a true son in our *c* ....Titus 1:4
concerning our *c*...........Jude 3

COMMOTION
there arose a great c . . . . .Acts 19:23

COMMUNED
I c with my heart. . . . . .Eccl 1:16

COMMUNION
bless, is it not the c . . . . .1 Cor 10:16
c has light with . . . . .2 Cor 6:14
c of the Holy Spirit . . . . .2 Cor 13:14

COMPANION
a man my equal, My c . . . . .Ps 55:13
I am a c of all who . . . . . . .Ps 119:63
the Man who is My C. . . . .Zech 13:7
urge you also, true c. . . . . .Phil 4:3
your brother and c . . . . .Rev 1:9

COMPANIONS
are rebellious, and c. . . . . . . .Is 1:23
and calling to their c . . . .Matt 11:16
more than Your c . . . . .Heb 1:9
while you became c . . . . .Heb 10:33

COMPANY
great was the c . . . . .Ps 68:11
epistle not to keep c . . . . . .1 Cor 5:9
c corrupts good habits . .1 Cor 15:33
and do not keep c. . . . . .2 Thess 3:14
to an innumerable c. . . . .Heb 12:22

COMPARE
may desire cannot c . . . . .Prov 3:15
c ourselves with those. . .2 Cor 10:12

COMPARED
the heavens can be c. . . . . . .Ps 89:6
may desire cannot be c . . . .Prov 8:11
are not worthy to be c. . . . .Rom 8:18

COMPASSION
show you mercy, have c . .Deut 13:17
His people and have c . . .Deut 32:36
He, being full of c. . . . . . . .Ps 78:38
are a God full of c . . . . .Ps 86:15
will return and have c . . . .Jer 12:15
yet He will show c . . . . . . .Lam 3:32
c everyone to his . . . . .Zech 7:9
He was moved with c. . . . .Matt 9:36
also have had c . . . . .Matt 18:33
"I have c on the. . . . . .Mark 8:2
whomever I will have c . . . .Rom 9:15
He can have c on those . . . .Heb 5:2
of one mind, having c . . . . .1 Pet 3:8
And on some have c. . . . . . .Jude 22

COMPASSIONATE
c women have cooked . . . .Lam 4:10
the Lord is very c . . . . . . .James 5:11

COMPASSIONS
because His c fail not . . . .Lam 3:22

COMPEL
c them to come in. . . . . .Luke 14:23

COMPELLED
Macedonia, Paul was c . . . .Acts 18:5

COMPELS
the spirit within me c. . . . .Job 32:18
"And whoever c . . . . .Matt 5:41
the love of Christ c . . . . . .2 Cor 5:14

COMPLACENCY
slay them, and the c. . . . . .Prov 1:32
who are settled in c . . . . . .Zeph 1:12

COMPLAIN
should a living man c . . . . .Lam 3:39

COMPLAINED
and you c in your . . . . . . .Deut 1:27
but c in their tents . . . . . .Ps 106:25
as some of them also c . .1 Cor 10:10

COMPLAINERS
These are grumblers, c . . . .Jude 16

COMPLAINING
all things without c . . . . . . .Phil 2:14

COMPLAINT
"Even today my c. . . . . . . .Job 23:2
I pour out my c. . . . . .Ps 142:2
for the LORD has a c. . . . . . .Mic 6:2
if anyone has a c . . . . .Col 3:13

COMPLAINTS
Who has c . . . . .Prov 23:29
laid many serious c . . . . . .Acts 25:7

COMPLETE
that you may be made c . .2 Cor 13:9
work in you will c. . . . . .Phil 1:6
and you are c in Him. . . . . .Col 2:10
of God may be c . . . . .2 Tim 3:17
make you c in every. . . . . .Heb 13:21
the wrath of God is c . . . . . .Rev 15:1

COMPLETELY
I made a man c well. . . . .John 7:23
Himself sanctify you c .1 Thess 5:23

COMPOSED
But God c the body. . . . .1 Cor 12:24

COMPREHEND
which we cannot c. . . . . . . .Job 37:5
c my path and my lying. . .Ps 139:3
the darkness did not c . . . .John 1:5
may be able to c . . . . .Eph 3:18

CONCEAL
Almighty I will not c. . . . . .Job 27:11
c pride from man. . . . . . . .Job 33:17
of God to c a matter. . . . .Prov 25:2

CONCEALED
c Your lovingkindness. . . . . .Ps 40:10
than love carefully c . . . . .Prov 27:5

CONCEIT
selfish ambition or c. . . . . . .Phil 2:3

CONCEITED
Let us not become c . . . . . . .Gal 5:26

CONCEIVE
the virgin shall c . . . . .Is 7:14
And behold, you will c . . .Luke 1:31

CONCEIVED
in sin my mother c . . . . . . .Ps 51:5
when desire has c . . . . . .James 1:15

CONCERN
Neither do I c myself . . . . .Ps 131:1
the things which c. . . . . .Acts 28:31
my deep c for all the . . . .2 Cor 11:28

CONCERNED
Is it oxen God is c. . . . . . . .1 Cor 9:9

CONCESSION
But I say this as a c . . . . . .1 Cor 7:6

CONCILIATION
c pacifies great. . . . . .Eccl 10:4

CONCLUSION
Let us hear the c . . . . .Eccl 12:13

CONDEMN
say to God, 'Do not c . . . . . .Job 10:2
world to c the world . . . . .John 3:17
her, "Neither do I c . . . . . .John 8:11
judge another you c . . . . . .Rom 2:1
our heart does not c . . . .1 John 3:21

CONDEMNATION
will receive greater c. . . . .Matt 23:14
can you escape the c . . . .Matt 23:33
subject to eternal c. . . . . .Mark 3:29
And this is the c. . . . . . . .John 3:19
the resurrection of c . . . . .John 5:29
Their c is just . . . . .Rom 3:8
therefore now no c. . . . . . . .Rom 8:1
of c had glory. . . . . .2 Cor 3:9
having c because they. . . .1 Tim 5:12
marked out for this c. . . . . . .Jude 4

CONDEMNED
words you will be c. . . . . .Matt 12:37
does not believe is c . . . . .John 3:18
c sin in the flesh . . . . .Rom 8:3

CONDEMNS
Who is he who c . . . . .Rom 8:34
For if our heart c. . . . . . .1 John 3:20

CONDUCT
c yourselves like men. . . . .1 Sam 4:9
who are of upright c . . . . . . .Ps 37:14
c yourself in the. . . . . .1 Tim 3:15
c that his works are . . . .James 3:13
to each one's work, c . . . . .1 Pet 1:17
from your aimless c . . . . . .1 Pet 1:18
may be won by the c . . . . . .1 Pet 3:1

CONFESS
c my transgressions . . . . .Ps 32:5
that if you c with . . . . . . .Rom 10:9
every tongue shall c . . . . .Rom 14:11
C your trespasses. . . . . . . .James 5:16
If we c our sins . . . . .1 John 1:9
but I will c his name . . . . . .Rev 3:5

CONFESSED
c that He was Christ . . . .John 9:22
c the good confession . . . .1 Tim 6:12

CONFESSES
prosper, but whoever c . . .Prov 28:13
c that Jesus is the. . . . . .1 John 4:15

CONFESSION
of Israel, and make c . . . . .Josh 7:19
with the mouth c. . . . . . . .Rom 10:10
confessed the good c . . . . .1 Tim 6:12
witnessed the good c . . . .1 Tim 6:13
High Priest of our c. . . . . . .Heb 3:1
let us hold fast our c . . . . . .Heb 4:14

CONFIDENCE
You who are the c . . . . .Ps 65:5
the LORD than to put c. . . .Ps 118:8
c shall be your . . . . .Is 30:15
Jesus, and have no c . . . . . .Phil 3:3
if we hold fast the c . . . . . . .Heb 3:6
appears, we may have c .1 John 2:28

CONFINED
saying, "I am c . . . . .Jer 36:5
the Scripture has c . . . . . . .Gal 3:22

CONFIRM
c the promises . . . . .Rom 15:8
who will also c . . . . .1 Cor 1:8

CONFIRMED
covenant that was c . . . . . . .Gal 3:17
by the Lord, and was c . . . .Heb 2:3

CONFIRMING

c it by an oath .... Heb 6:17
prophetic word c .... 2 Pet 1:19

CONFIRMING

c the word through the .. Mark 16:20

CONFLICT

having the same c .... Phil 1:30
to know what a great c ..... Col 2:1

CONFLICTS

Outside were c .... 2 Cor 7:5

CONFORMED

predestined to be c .... Rom 8:29
And do not be c .... Rom 12:2
sufferings, being c .... Phil 3:10
body that it may be c .... Phil 3:21

CONFOUNDED

who seek You be c .... Ps 69:6

CONFUSE

c their language .... Gen 11:7

CONFUSED

there the LORD c .... Gen 11:9
for the assembly was c ... Acts 19:32

CONFUSION

c who plot my hurt .... Ps 35:4
us drink the wine of c ...... Ps 60:3

CONGREGATION

nor sinners in the c .... Ps 1:5
the c of the wicked .... Ps 22:16
God stands in the c .... Ps 82:1

CONQUER

conquering and to c .... Rev 6:2

CONQUERORS

we are more than c ...... Rom 8:37

CONSCIENCE

convicted by their c ...... John 8:9
strive to have a c .... Acts 24:16
I am not lying, my c ...... Rom 9:1
wrath but also for c ...... Rom 13:5
no questions for c ...... 1 Cor 10:25
faith with a pure c .... 1 Tim 3:9
having their own c ...... 1 Tim 4:2
to God, cleanse your c .... Heb 9:14
from an evil c and our .... Heb 10:22
having a good c .... 1 Pet 3:16

CONSECRATE

'C to Me all the .... Ex 13:2
c himself this day .... 1 Chr 29:5
the trumpet in Zion, c .... Joel 2:15
c their gain to the .... Mic 4:13

CONSECRATED

c this house which you .... 1 Kin 9:3

CONSENT

entice you, do not c ...... Prov 1:10
and does not c to .... 1 Tim 6:3

CONSENTED

you saw a thief, you c ..... Ps 50:18
He had not c to their .... Luke 23:51

CONSENTING

Now Saul was c to his ...... Acts 8:1

CONSIDER

When I c Your heavens ...... Ps 8:3
c her palaces .... Ps 48:13
c carefully what is .... Prov 23:1
C the work of God .... Eccl 7:13
My people do not c .... Is 1:3

c the operation .... Is 5:12
your God will c .... Jon 1:6
"C your ways .... Hag 1:5
C the lilies of the .... Matt 6:28
"C the ravens .... Luke 12:24
Let a man so c us .... 1 Cor 4:1
c how great this man ...... Heb 7:4
c one another in order .... Heb 10:24
c Him who endured ...... Heb 12:3

CONSIDERS

c all their works .... Ps 33:15

CONSIST

in Him all things c .... Col 1:17

CONSOLATION

waiting for the C .... Luke 2:25
have received your c ..... Luke 6:24
abound in us, so our c ..... 2 Cor 1:5
if there is any c .... Phil 2:1
given us everlasting c .. 2 Thess 2:16
we might have strong c.... Heb 6:18

CONSOLATIONS

Are the c of God too..... Job 15:11

CONSOLE

c those who mourn .... Is 61:3

CONSPIRE

What do you c against ..... Nah 1:9

CONSTANT

c prayer was............. Acts 12:5

CONSULT

They only c to cast........ Ps 62:4

CONSULTED

c together against.......... Ps 83:3

CONSUME

your midst, lest I c .... Ex 33:3
this great fire will c ..... Deut 5:25
C them in wrath .... Ps 59:13
whom the Lord will c, .. 2 Thess 2:8

CONSUMED

but the bush was not c ..... Ex 3:2
c the burnt .... 1 Kin 18:38
For we have been c ...... Ps 90:7
mercies we are not c ..... Lam 3:22
beware lest you be c ...... Gal 5:15

CONSUMING

the LORD was like a c ..... Ex 24:17
before you as a c .... Deut 9:3
our God is a c fire ...... Heb 12:29

CONSUMMATION

I have seen the c .... Ps 119:96

CONSUMPTION

will strike you with c .... Deut 28:22

CONTAIN

of heavens cannot c .... 2 Chr 6:6
c the books that would.. John 21:25

CONTEMPT

He pours c on princes.... Job 12:21
wicked comes, c comes.... Prov 18:3
and everlasting c .... Dan 12:2
and be treated with c.... Mark 9:12

CONTEMPTIBLE

of the LORD is c .... Mal 1:7
also have made you c ...... Mal 2:9
and his speech c........ 2 Cor 10:10

CONTEND

show me why You c ...... Job 10:2
Will you c for God .... Job 13:8
let us c together........... Is 43:26
for I will c with him ...... Is 49:25
then how can you c ...... Jer 12:5
c earnestly for the .... Jude 3

CONTENDED

Therefore the people c ..... Ex 17:2

CONTENT

state I am, to be c .... Phil 4:11
these we shall be c .... 1 Tim 6:8
covetousness; be c .... Heb 13:5

CONTENTION

lips enter into c .... Prov 18:6
and c will leave .... Prov 22:10
strife and a man of c ..... Jer 15:10

CONTENTIONS

Casting lots causes c .... Prov 18:18
sorcery, hatred, c .... Gal 5:20
genealogies, c .... Titus 3:9

CONTENTIOUS

than with a c and .... Prov 21:19
shared with a c woman... Prov 25:24
anyone seems to be c.... 1 Cor 11:16

CONTENTMENT

c is great gain .... 1 Tim 6:6

CONTINUAL

a merry heart has a c .... Prov 15:15
in wrath with a c .... Is 14:6
c coming she weary me .. Luke 18:5
c grief in my heart........ Rom 9:2

CONTINUALLY

heart was only evil c ...... Gen 6:5
His praise shall c .... Ps 34:1
and Your truth c .... Ps 40:11
of God endures c.......... Ps 52:1
I keep Your law c .... Ps 119:44
Before Me c are grief...... Jer 6:7
and wait on your God c... Hos 12:6
will give ourselves c ...... Acts 6:4
remains a priest c......... Heb 7:3
c offer the sacrifice ...... Heb 13:15

CONTINUE

tells lies shall not c ...... Ps 101:7
persuaded them to c .... Acts 13:43
Shall we c in sin that ..... Rom 6:1
who does not c in all..... Gal 3:10
C earnestly in prayer....... Col 4:2
because they did not c.... Heb 8:9
Let brotherly love c ...... Heb 13:1
asleep, all things c .... 2 Pet 3:4

CONTINUED

c steadfastly in the ...... Acts 2:42
us, they would have c ... 1 John 2:19

CONTINUES

But He, because He c ..... Heb 7:24
law of liberty and c ..... James 1:25

CONTRADICTIONS

idle babble and c........ 1 Tim 6:20

CONTRARY

to worship God c........ Acts 18:13
and these are c .... Gal 5:17
please God and are c .. 1 Thess 2:15
other thing that is c .... 1 Tim 1:10

CONTRIBUTION

to make a certain c ...... Rom 15:26

CONTRITE

saves such as have a c . . . . . Ps 34:18
a broken and a c . . . . Ps 51:17
with him who has a c . . . . . . Is 57:15
poor and of a c spirit . . . . Is 66:2

CONTROVERSY

another, matters of c . . . . . Deut 17:8
for the LORD has a c . . . . . Jer 25:31
c great is . . . . 1 Tim 3:16

CONVERSION

describing the c . . . . Acts 15:3

CONVERTED

unless you are c . . . . Matt 18:3

CONVEYED

of darkness and c . . . . Col 1:13

CONVICT

He has come, He will c . . John 16:8
c those who . . . . Titus 1:9
c all who are ungodly . . . . . . Jude 15

CONVICTS

"Which of you c . . . . John 8:46

CONVINCED

Let each be fully c . . . . Rom 14:5

COOKED

c their own children . . . . . . Lam 4:10

COOL

in the garden in the c . . . . . Gen 3:8
water and c my tongue . Luke 16:24

COPIES

necessary that the c . . . . . . Heb 9:23
hands, which are c . . . . Heb 9:24

COPPER

hills you can dig c . . . . Deut 8:9
of cups, pitchers, c . . . . Mark 7:4
sold for two c coins . . . . . . Luke 12:6

COPPERSMITH

c did me much harm . . . . 2 Tim 4:14

COPY

who serve the c . . . . Heb 8:5

CORD

this line of scarlet c . . . . . Josh 2:18
And a threefold c . . . . Eccl 4:12
before the silver c . . . . Eccl 12:6

CORDS

in pieces the c . . . . Ps 129:4
he is caught in the c . . . . . Prov 5:22
draw iniquity with c . . . . . . Is 5:18
them with gentle c . . . . . . Hos 11:4
had made a whip of c . . . . John 2:15

CORNER

was not done in a c . . . . . Acts 26:26

CORNERSTONE

Or who laid its c . . . . Job 38:6
has become the chief c . . . Ps 118:22
stone, a precious c . . . . Is 28:16

become the chief c . . . . . Matt 21:42
in Zion a chief c . . . . 1 Pet 2:6

CORPSE

c was thrown on the . . . 1 Kin 13:24
c trodden underfoot . . . . Is 14:19

CORRECT

with rebukes You c . . . . . . Ps 39:11
C your son . . . . Prov 29:17
But I will c you in . . . . Jer 30:11

CORRECTED

human fathers who c . . . . . Heb 12:9

CORRECTION

nor detest His c . . . . Prov 3:11
but he who refuses c . . . . Prov 10:17
but he who hates c . . . . . . Prov 12:1
c will drive it . . . . Prov 22:15
Do not withhold c . . . . . . Prov 23:13
they received no c . . . . Jer 2:30
for reproof, for c . . . . 2 Tim 3:16

CORRECTS

is the man whom God c . . . Job 5:17
the LORD loves He c . . . . . Prov 3:12

CORRODED

and silver are c . . . . James 5:3

CORRUPT

have together become c . . . . Ps 14:3
have together become c . . . . Ps 53:3
old man which grows c . . . Eph 4:22
men of c minds . . . . 2 Tim 3:8
in these things they c . . . . . Jude 10

CORRUPTED

for all flesh had c . . . . Gen 6:12
we have c no one . . . . 2 Cor 7:2
so your minds may be c . . 2 Cor 11:3
Your riches are c . . . . James 5:2
the great harlot who c . . . . . Rev 19:2

CORRUPTIBLE

For this c must put on . . 1 Cor 15:53
redeemed with c things . . . 1 Pet 1:18

CORRUPTION

Your Holy One to see c . . . . Ps 16:10
God raised up saw no c . Acts 13:37
from the bondage of c . . . . . Rom 8:21
The body is sown in c . . . 1 Cor 15:42
c inherit incorruption . . . 1 Cor 15:50
of the flesh reap c . . . . Gal 6:8
having escaped the c . . . . . 2 Pet 1:4
perish in their own c . . . . . 2 Pet 2:12

COST

and count the c . . . . Luke 14:28

COULD

has done what she c . . . . . Mark 14:8
c remove mountains . . . . . 1 Cor 13:2
which no one c number . . . . Rev 7:9

COUNCILS

deliver you up to c . . . . . . Mark 13:9

COUNSEL

and strength, He has c . . . Job 12:13
the c of the wicked is . . . . Job 21:16
when the friendly c . . . . . . Job 29:4
is this who darkens c . . . . Job 38:2
who walks not in the c . . . . . Ps 1:1
We took sweet c . . . . Ps 55:14
guide me with Your c . . . . Ps 73:24
you disdained all my c . . . . Prov 1:25
have none of my c . . . . . . Prov 1:30
Where there is no c . . . . . Prov 11:14

C in the heart of man . . . . Prov 20:5
by wise c wage war . . . . . Prov 20:18
whom did He take c . . . . . Is 40:14
'You are great in c . . . . Jer 32:19
according to the c . . . . Eph 1:11
immutability of His c . . . . Heb 6:17
"I c you to buy from . . . . . Rev 3:18

COUNSELOR

be called Wonderful, C . . . . . Is 9:6
but there was no c . . . . Is 41:28
Has your c perished . . . . . . Mic 4:9
who has become His c . . Rom 11:34

COUNSELORS

c there is safety . . . . Prov 11:14

COUNT

c the people of Israel . . . . 2 Sam 24:4
c my life dear to . . . . Acts 20:24
c me as a partner . . . . Philem 17
His promise, as some c . . . 2 Pet 3:9

COUNTED

Even a fool is c . . . . Prov 17:28
c as the small dust . . . . Is 40:15
the wages are not c . . . . Rom 4:4
He c me faithful . . . . 1 Tim 1:12
who rule well be c . . . . . . 1 Tim 5:17

COUNTENANCE

the LORD lift up His c . . . . Num 6:26
c they did not cast . . . . . . Job 29:24
up the light of Your c . . . . Ps 4:6
His c is like Lebanon . . . . Song 5:15
with a sad c . . . . Matt 6:16
His c was like . . . . Matt 28:3
of the glory of his c . . . . . . 2 Cor 3:7
sword, and His c . . . . Rev 1:16

COUNTRY

"Get out of your c . . . . Gen 12:1
good news from a far c . . Prov 25:25
and went into a far c . . . Matt 21:33
as in a foreign c . . . . Heb 11:9
that is, a heavenly c . . . . . Heb 11:16

COURAGE

strong and of good c . . . . . Deut 31:6
thanked God and took c . Acts 28:15

COURSE

and sets on fire the c . . . . James 3:6

COURT

appoint my day in c . . . . . . Job 9:19
by you or by a human c . . . 1 Cor 4:3
They zealously c . . . . Gal 4:17

COURTEOUS

be tenderhearted, be c . . . . 1 Pet 3:8

COURTS

he may dwell in Your c . . . . . Ps 65:4
even faints for the c . . . . . . Ps 84:2
flourish in the c . . . . Ps 92:13
and into His c . . . . Ps 100:4
drink it in My holy c . . . . . . Is 62:9

COVENANT

I will establish My c . . . . . Gen 6:18
day the LORD made a c . . Gen 15:18
for Me, behold, My c . . . . Gen 17:4
as a perpetual c . . . . Ex 31:16
it is a c of salt . . . . Num 18:19
Remember His c forever . 1 Chr 16:15
"I have made a c . . . . Job 31:1
will show them His c . . . . Ps 25:14
c shall stand firm . . . . Ps 89:28
sons will keep My c . . . . Ps 132:12
and give You as a c . . . . Is 42:6

the words of this *c* . . . . Jer 11:2
I will make a new *c* . . . . . . Jer 31:31
'I made a *c* with your . . . . Jer 34:13
I might break the *c* . . . . Zech 11:10
the Messenger of the *c* . . . . . Mal 3:1
This cup is the new *c* . . . Luke 22:20
c that was confirmed . . . . . Gal 3:17
Mediator of a better *c* . . . . . Heb 8:6
c had been faultless . . . . Heb 8:7
He says, "A new *c* . . . . Heb 8:13
Mediator of the new *c* . . . Heb 12:24
of the everlasting *c* . . . . . Heb 13:20

COVENANTED

your kingdom, as I *c* . . . 2 Chr 7:18
to the word that I *c* . . . . Hag 2:5

COVENANTS

the glory, the *c* . . . . Rom 9:4
these are the two *c* . . . . . . Gal 4:24

COVER

the rock, and will *c* . . . . Ex 33:22
He shall *c* you with . . . . Ps 91:4
c Yourself with light . . . . . . Ps 104:2
LORD as the waters *c* . . . . . . Is 11:9
and will no more *c* . . . . Is 26:21
from the wind, and a *c* . . . . . Is 32:2
not to *c* his head . . . . 1 Cor 11:7
c a multitude of sins . . . James 5:20

COVERED

The depths have *c* . . . . Ex 15:5
c my transgressions as . . . Job 31:33
whose sin is *c* . . . . Ps 32:1
the wings of a dove *c* . . . . Ps 68:13
c all their sin . . . . Ps 85:2
You *c* me in my . . . . Ps 139:13
with two he *c* his face . . . . . . Is 6:2
of Jacob will be *c* . . . . Is 27:9
You have *c* Yourself . . . . . Lam 3:44
For there is nothing *c* . . Matt 10:26

COVERING

spread a cloud for a *c* . . . . Ps 105:39
make sackcloth their *c* . . . . . Is 50:3
given to her for a *c* . . . . 1 Cor 11:15

COVERINGS

and made themselves *c* . . . . Gen 3:7

COVET

"You shall not *c* . . . . Ex 20:17
c fields and take them . . . . . Mic 2:2
You murder and *c* . . . . . . James 4:2

COVETED

c no one's silver . . . . Acts 20:33

COVETOUS

nor thieves, nor *c* . . . . 1 Cor 6:10
trained in *c* practices . . . . 2 Pet 2:14

COVETOUSNESS

but he who hates *c* . . . . . Prov 28:16
for nothing but your *c* . . . . Jer 22:17
heed and beware of *c* . . . Luke 12:15
would not have known *c* . . . Rom 7:7
all uncleanness or *c* . . . . Eph 5:3
conduct be without *c* . . . . . Heb 13:5

COWARDLY

the *c*, unbelieving . . . . Rev 21:8

CRAFTILY

His people, to deal *c* . . . . . Ps 105:25

CRAFTINESS

wise in their own *c* . . . . Job 5:13
not walking in *c* . . . . 2 Cor 4:2
deceived Eve by his *c* . . . . 2 Cor 11:3

in the cunning *c* . . . . Eph 4:14

CRAFTSMAN

instructor of every *c* . . . . . . Gen 4:22
c encouraged the . . . . Is 41:7
c stretches out his . . . . Is 44:13

CRAFTY

Jonadab was a very *c* . . . . 2 Sam 13:3
the devices of the *c* . . . . Job 5:12
They have taken *c* . . . . Ps 83:3
of a harlot, and a *c* . . . . . . Prov 7:10
Nevertheless, being *c* . . . 2 Cor 12:16

CRANE

Like a *c* or a swallow . . . . . . Is 38:14

CRAVES

and his soul still *c* . . . . Is 29:8

CREAM

she brought out *c* . . . . Judg 5:25
were bathed with *c* . . . . Job 29:6

CREATE

peace and *c* calamity . . . . . . Is 45:7
For behold, I *c* . . . . Is 65:17

CREATED

So God *c* man in His . . . . . . Gen 1:27
Spirit, they are *c* . . . . Ps 104:30
and they were *c* . . . . Ps 148:5
and see who has *c* . . . . Is 40:26
of Israel has *c* . . . . Is 41:20
For the LORD has *c* . . . . . . Jer 31:22
Has not one God *c* . . . . . . Mal 2:10
Nor was man *c* for the . . . 1 Cor 11:9
c in Christ Jesus . . . . Eph 2:10
hidden in God who *c* . . . . . . Eph 3:9
new man which was *c* . . . . . Eph 4:24
Him all things were *c* . . . . . Col 1:16
from foods which God *c* . . . 1 Tim 4:3
for You *c* all things . . . . Rev 4:11

CREATION

c which God . . . . Mark 13:19
c was subjected . . . . Rom 8:20
know that the whole *c* . . . . Rom 8:22
Christ, he is a new *c* . . . . 2 Cor 5:17
anything, but a new *c* . . . . . Gal 6:15
firstborn over all *c* . . . . Col 1:15

CREATOR

Remember now your *C* . . . Eccl 12:1
God, the LORD, the *C* . . . . . Is 40:28
rather than the *C* . . . . Rom 1:25
to a faithful *C* . . . . 1 Pet 4:19

CREATURE

the gospel to every *c* . . . . Mark 16:15
For every *c* of God is . . . . 1 Tim 4:4
And there is no *c* . . . . Heb 4:13
And every *c* which is . . . . . . Rev 5:13
and every living *c* . . . . Rev 16:3

CREATURES

created great sea *c* . . . . Gen 1:21
firstfruits of His *c* . . . . . James 1:18
were four living *c* . . . . Rev 4:6

CREDIT

who love you, what *c* . . . . Luke 6:32
For what *c* is it if . . . . 1 Pet 2:20

CREDITOR

Every *c* who has lent . . . . Deut 15:2
c is coming to take my . . . 2 Kin 4:1
c seize all that he . . . . Ps 109:11
There was a certain *c* . . . . Luke 7:41

CREEP

of the forest *c* . . . . Ps 104:20
sort are those who *c* . . . . . 2 Tim 3:6

CREEPING

c thing and beast of . . . . . . Gen 1:24
every sort of *c* thing . . . . . Ezek 8:10

CREPT

For certain men have *c* . . . . Jude 4

CRIB

donkey its master's *c* . . . . Is 1:3

CRIED

the poor who *c* out . . . . . . Job 29:12
They *c* to You . . . . Ps 22:5
of the depths I have *c* . . . . Ps 130:1

CRIES

your brother's blood *c* . . . . Gen 4:10
with vehement *c* . . . . Heb 5:7

CRIMES

land is filled with *c* . . . . . Ezek 7:23

CRIMINALS

also two others, *c* . . . . . . Luke 23:32

CROOKED

turn aside to their *c* . . . . . Ps 125:5
whose ways are *c* . . . . Prov 2:15
c places shall be made . . . . . . Is 40:4
c places straight . . . . Is 45:2
c places shall be made . . . . Luke 3:5
in the midst of a *c* . . . . Phil 2:15

CROSS

does not take his *c* . . . . Matt 10:38
to bear His *c* . . . . Matt 27:32
come down from the *c* . . . Matt 27:40
lest the *c* of Christ . . . . 1 Cor 1:17
persecution for the *c* . . . . . . Gal 6:12
boast except in the *c* . . . . . . Gal 6:14
one body through the *c* . . . . Eph 2:16
the enemies of the *c* . . . . . Phil 3:18
Him endured the *c* . . . . . . Heb 12:2

CROWD

shall not follow a *c* . . . . . . Ex 23:2

CROWN

You set a *c* of pure . . . . Ps 21:3
c the year with Your . . . . . Ps 65:11
have profaned his *c* . . . . . . Ps 89:39
upon Himself His *c* . . . . . Ps 132:18
The *c* of the wise is . . . . . Prov 14:24
head is a *c* of glory . . . . . Prov 16:31
Woe to the *c* of pride . . . . . . Is 28:1
hosts will be for a *c* . . . . . . Is 28:5
c has fallen from our . . . . . Lam 5:16
they had twisted a *c* . . . . Matt 27:29
obtain a perishable *c* . . . . 1 Cor 9:25
brethren, my joy and *c* . . . . Phil 4:1
laid up for me the *c* . . . . . 2 Tim 4:8
he will receive the *c* . . . . James 1:12
no one may take your *c* . . . Rev 3:11
on His head a golden *c* . . . Rev 14:14

CROWNED

angels, and You have *c* . . . . . Ps 8:5
but the prudent are *c* . . . . Prov 14:18
athletics, he is not *c* . . . . . 2 Tim 2:5
You have *c* him with glory . . Heb 2:7

CROWNS

and they had *c* of gold . . . . Rev 4:4
on his horns ten *c* . . . . Rev 13:1
His head were many *c* . . . . Rev 19:12

CRUCIFIED

"Let Him be *c*.........Matt 27:22
Calvary, there they *c* ...Luke 23:33
lawless hands, have *c* .....Acts 2:23
that our old man was *c*....Rom 6:6
Was Paul *c* for you.......1 Cor 1:13
Jesus Christ and Him *c* ..1 Cor 2:2
they would not have *c* .....1 Cor 2:8
though He was *c* ....2 Cor 13:4
"I have been *c* ....Gal 2:20

CRUCIFY

out again, "*C* Him......Mark 15:13
I have power to *c* You....John 19:10
since they *c* again.........Heb 6:6

CRUEL

wrath, for it is *c* ....Gen 49:7
spirit and *c* bondage ....Ex 6:9
hate me with *c* hatred .....Ps 25:19
of the wicked are *c* .....Prov 12:10

CRUELTY

of *c* are in their...........Gen 49:5
the haunts of *c* ....Ps 74:20
c you have ruled ....Ezek 34:4

CRUSH

that a foot may *c* ....Job 39:15
that your foot may *c*......Ps 68:23
the poor, who *c* ....Amos 4:1
of peace will *c* ....Rom 16:20

CRUSHED

in the dust, who are *c*.....Job 4:19
c my life to the ....Ps 143:3
every side, yet not *c*......2 Cor 4:8

COUNTRYMEN

for my brethren, my *c*.....Rom 9:3

CRUST

man is reduced to a *c* .....Prov 6:26

CRY

and their *c* came up to......Ex 2:23
of oppressions they *c* ....Job 35:9
heart and my flesh *c*.......Ps 84:2
I *c* out with my whole ...Ps 119:145
Does not wisdom *c* ....Prov 8:1
"What shall I *c* ....Is 40:6
nor lift up a *c* ....Jer 7:16
c mightily to God ....Jon 3:8
at midnight a *c* ....Matt 25:6
His own elect who *c*......Luke 18:7

CRYING

" The voice of one *c* ......Matt 3:3
nor sorrow, nor *c*.........Rev 21:4

CRYSTAL

nor *c* can equal it ....Job 28:17
your gates of *c* ....Is 54:12
of an awesome *c* ....Ezek 1:22
a sea of glass, like *c* ....Rev 4:6

CUBIT

shall finish it to a *c* ......Gen 6:16
worrying can add one *c* ...Matt 6:27

CUCUMBERS

in Egypt, the *c* ....Num 11:5
a hut in a garden of *c* ....Is 1:8

CUNNING

the serpent was more *c* .....Gen 3:1
c comes quickly...........Job 5:13
c craftiness of deceitful ...Eph 4:14

CUP

my *c* runs over ....Ps 23:5

c are drained by them......Ps 73:10
the LORD there is a *c* ......Ps 75:8
I will take up the *c*.......Ps 116:13
the dregs of the *c*.........Is 51:17
men give them the *c* ......Jer 16:7
" Take this wine *c* ....Jer 25:15
The *c* of the LORD's.......Hab 2:16
make Jerusalem a *c* ....Zech 12:2
little ones only a *c* .....Matt 10:42
Then He took the *c* .....Matt 26:27
possible, let this *c*.......Matt 26:39
c is the new covenant....Luke 22:20
You cannot drink the *c* ..1 Cor 10:21
c is the new covenant ...1 Cor 11:25
to give her the *c* ....Rev 16:19

CURE

but they could not *c*.....Matt 17:16
and to *c* diseases..........Luke 9:1

CURES

demons and perform *c* ...Luke 13:32

CURSE

c the ground for man's.....Gen 8:21
c a ruler of your ....Ex 22:28
'You shall not *c* ....Lev 19:14
c this people for me .....Num 22:6
Balaam, "Neither *c*.......Num 23:25
your God turned the *c* ...Deut 23:5
said to him, '*C* David...2 Sam 16:10
C God and die ....Job 2:9
mouth, but they *c*.........Ps 62:4
The *c* of the LORD is.......Prov 3:33
Do not *c* the king.......Eccl 10:20
do not *c* the rich ....Eccl 10:20
"I will send a *c* ....Mal 2:2
are cursed with a *c*.......Mal 3:9
law are under the *c* ....Gal 3:10

CURSED

"*c* more than all cattle.....Gen 3:14
C is the man who.........Jer 17:5
c is he who keeps..........Jer 48:10
'Depart from Me, you *c* ..Matt 25:41
and near to being *c* ....Heb 6:8

CURSES

I will curse him who *c* .....Gen 12:3
'For everyone who *c* .....Lev 20:9
c his father or his ......Prov 20:20

CURSINGS

by the sword for the *c* ....Hos 7:16

CURTAIN

of each *c* shall be ....Ex 26:2
the heavens like a *c* ......Ps 104:2

CUSTOM

to me, as Your *c* ....Ps 119:132
according to the *c* ....Acts 15:1
we have no such *c* .....1 Cor 11:16

CUT

confidence shall be *c*......Job 8:14
evildoers shall be *c* ....Ps 37:9
the wicked will be *c*......Prov 2:22
causes you to sin, *c* .....Matt 5:30
and will *c* him in.......Matt 24:51
him whose ear Peter *c* ..John 18:26
He had his hair *c*.......Acts 18:18

CYMBAL

or a clanging *c* ....1 Cor 13:1

D

DAILY

much as they gather *d*.....Ex 16:5

d He shall be.............Ps 72:15
to me, watching *d* ....Prov 8:34
Yet they seek Me *d* ....Is 58:2
Give us this day our *d* ...Matt 6:11
I sat *d* with you ....Matt 26:55
take up his cross *d* ......Luke 9:23
the Scriptures *d*..........Acts 17:11
our Lord, I die *d* ....1 Cor 15:31
stands ministering *d* .....Heb 10:11

DANCE

and their children *d* .....Job 21:11
His name with the *d*.....Ps 149:3
mourn, and a time to *d*....Eccl 3:4
d has turned into........Lam 5:15
and you did not *d*.......Matt 11:17

DANCED

Then David *d* before ....2 Sam 6:14
daughter of Herodias *d* ..Matt 14:6

DANCING

saw the calf and the *d*.....Ex 32:19
me my mourning into *d* ...Ps 30:11
he heard music and *d*...Luke 15:25

DARE

someone would even *d* .....Rom 5:7
D any of you.............1 Cor 6:1

DARK

dwell in the *d* cloud.....1 Kin 8:12
I am *d* ....Song 1:5
d place of the earth........Is 45:19
d places like the dead .....Lam 3:6
and makes the day *d*.....Amos 5:8
and the day shall be *d* .....Mic 3:6
I tell you in the *d*.......Matt 10:27
while it was still *d* ....John 20:1
shines in a *d* place ....2 Pet 1:19

DARKENED

so that the land was *d*.....Ex 10:15
Let their eyes be *d*.......Ps 69:23
their understanding *d* .....Eph 4:18

DARKNESS

d He called Night..........Gen 1:5
shall enlighten my *d*...2 Sam 22:29
through the deep *d*......Job 22:13
Those who sat in *d*......Ps 107:10
d shall not hide..........Ps 139:12
d have seen a ....Is 9:2
I will make *d* light........Is 42:16
and deep *d* the people......Is 60:2
Israel, or a land of *d* ....Jer 2:31
body will be full of *d* ....Matt 6:23
cast out into outer *d* ....Matt 8:12
and the power of *d* ....Luke 22:53
d rather than light ......John 3:19
d does not know ....John 12:35
For you were once *d*.......Eph 5:8
the rulers of the *d* ......Eph 6:12
us from the power of *d* ....Col 1:13
of the night nor of *d* ...1 Thess 5:5
and to blackness and *d*...Heb 12:18
called you out of *d*......1 Pet 2:9
d is reserved ....2 Pet 2:17
and in Him is no *d* ......1 John 1:5
Him, and walk in *d* ......1 John 1:6
d is passing away ....1 John 2:8
blackness of *d* forever .....Jude 13

DARTS

quench all the fiery *d*......Eph 6:16

DASH

You shall *d* them to.........Ps 2:9
lest you *d* your foot ....Matt 4:6

DASHED

hand, O LORD, has d . . . . . . .Ex 15:6
also will be d to . . . . .Is 13:16
infants shall be d . . . . . . .Hos 13:16

DAUGHTER

had neither son nor d . . . .Judg 11:34
Rejoice greatly, O d . . . . . . .Zech 9:9
"Fear not, d of Zion . . . . .John 12:15
the son of Pharaoh's d . . . .Heb 11:24

DAUGHTERS

he had sons and d . . . . .Gen 5:4
of God saw the d . . . . .Gen 6:2
a bird, and all the d . . . . . .Eccl 12:4
d shall prophesy . . . . .Acts 2:17
man had four virgin d . . . .Acts 21:9
shall be My sons and d . . .2 Cor 6:18

DAY

God called the light D . . . . .Gen 1:5
and d and night . . . . .Gen 8:22
shall observe this d . . . . . .Ex 12:17
"Remember the Sabbath d . .Ex 20:8
and cursed the d . . . . .Job 3:1
d utters speech . . . . .Ps 19:2
For a d in Your courts . . . . .Ps 84:10
d the LORD has . . . . .Ps 118:24
not strike you by d . . . . . . .Ps 121:6
night shines as the d . . . . .Ps 139:12
do not know what a d . . . .Prov 27:1
For the d of the LORD . . . .Joel 2:11
who put far off the d . . . . . .Amos 6:3
for the d of the LORD . . . . .Zeph 1:7
who has despised the d . .Zech 4:10
who can endure the d . . . . . .Mal 3:2
d our daily bread . . . . . . .Matt 6:11
and Gomorrah in the d .Matt 10:15
sent Me while it is d . . . . . .John 9:4
great and awesome d . . . . .Acts 2:20
person esteems one d . . . . .Rom 14:5
D will declare it . . . . .1 Cor 3:13
again the third d . . . . . . .1 Cor 15:4
perfectly that the d . . .1 Thess 5:2
and sons of the d . . . . . .1 Thess 5:5
with the Lord one d . . . . . .2 Pet 3:8

DAYS

d are swifter than a . . . . . . .Job 7:6
Let me alone, for my d . . . .Job 7:16
of woman is of few d . . . . . .Job 14:1
blessed the latter d . . . . . .Job 42:12
The d of our lives are . . . . .Ps 90:10
for length of d . . . . .Prov 3:2
"Why were the former d . .Eccl 7:10
before the difficult d . . . . . .Eccl 12:1
and tested them ten d . . . .Dan 1:14
had shortened those d . .Mark 13:20
raise it up in three d . . . . . .John 2:20
You observe d and . . . . .Gal 4:10
life and see good d . . . . . .1 Pet 3:10

DAYSPRING

with which the D . . . . .Luke 1:78

DEACONS

with the bishops and d . . . .Phil 1:1
d must be reverent . . . . . . .1 Tim 3:8
d be the husbands. . . . . . .1 Tim 3:12

DEAD

"We shall all be d . . . . .Ex 12:33
he stood between the d . .Num 16:48
work wonders for the d . . .Ps 88:10
who have long been d . . . . .Ps 143:3
but the d know nothing . .Eccl 9:5
shall cast out the d . . . . . . .Is 26:19
d bury their own d . . . . . .Matt 8:22
d are raised up and. . . . . . .Matt 11:5

not the God of the d . . . .Matt 22:32
for this my son was d. . . .Luke 15:24
d will hear the voice . . . . .John 5:25
was raised from the d . . . . .Rom 6:4
yourselves to be d . . . . . . .Rom 6:11
from the law sin was d . . . . .Rom 7:8
be Lord of both the d . . . .Rom 14:9
resurrection of the d . . . .1 Cor 15:12
baptized for the d . . . . . .1 Cor 15:29
made alive, who were d . . . .Eph 2:1
And the d in Christ . . . .1 Thess 4:16
d while she lives . . . . .1 Tim 5:6
without works is d . . . . .James 2:26
d did not live again. . . . . . .Rev 20:5
And the d were judged. . . .Rev 20:12

DEADLY

they drink anything d . .Mark 16:18
evil, full of d poison . . . . . .James 3:8
d wound was healed . . . . . .Rev 13:3

DEADNESS

the d of Sarah's womb . . . .Rom 4:19

DEAF

makes the mute, the d . . . . .Ex 4:11
d shall hear the words. . . . .Is 29:18
d shall be unstopped. . . . . . .Is 35:5
d as My messenger . . . . .Is 42:19
d who have ears . . . . .Is 43:8
their ears shall be d . . . . . .Mic 7:16
are cleansed and the d . . . .Matt 11:5

DEAL

Do you thus d with the . . .Deut 32:6
My Servant shall d . . . . . . .Is 52:13

DEATH

Let me die the d . . . . . . .Num 23:10
d parts you and me . . . . .Ruth 1:17
and the shadow of d . . . . .Job 10:21
You will bring me to d . . .Job 30:23
For in d there is no . . . . .Ps 6:5
I sleep the sleep of d . . . . . .Ps 13:3
of the shadow of d . . . . . . .Ps 23:4
my soul from d . . . . .Ps 56:13
can live and not see d. . . . .Ps 89:48
house leads down to d . . . .Prov 2:18
who hate me love d . . . . . .Prov 8:36
D and life are in the . . . . .Prov 18:21
swallow up d forever . . . . . . .Is 25:8
no pleasure in the d . . . . .Ezek 18:32
redeem them from d. . . . . .Hos 13:14
turns the shadow of d . . . .Amos 5:8
who shall not taste d . . . .Matt 16:28
but has passed from d . . . .John 5:24
he shall never see d . . . . . .John 8:51
Nevertheless d reigned . . .Rom 5:14
as sin reigned in d . . . . . . .Rom 5:21
D no longer has. . . . . .Rom 6:9
the wages of sin is d . . . . . .Rom 6:23
to bear fruit to d . . . . .Rom 7:5
proclaim the Lord's d . . .1 Cor 11:26
since by man came d . . . .1 Cor 15:21
D is swallowed up in . . . .1 Cor 15:54
The sting of d is sin . . . .1 Cor 15:56
we are the aroma of d . . . .2 Cor 2:16
d is working in us . . . . . . .2 Cor 4:12
the world produces d . . . . .2 Cor 7:10
to the point of d . . . . .Phil 2:8
d crowned with glory. . . . . .Heb 2:9
who had the power of d . . .Heb 2:14
that he did not see d . . . . . .Heb 11:5
brings forth d . . . . .James 1:15
to God, being put to d . . .1 Pet 3:18
is sin leading to d . . . . . .1 John 5:16
Be faithful until d . . . . .Rev 2:10
Over such the second d . . . .Rev 20:6
shall be no more d . . . . . . .Rev 21:4

which is the second d . . . . . .Rev 21:8

DEBTOR

I am a d both to . . . . .Rom 1:14
that he is a d to keep . . . . . . .Gal 5:3

DEBTORS

as we forgive our d . . . . . . .Matt 6:12
of his master's d . . . . .Luke 16:5
brethren, we are d . . . . . . .Rom 8:12
and they are their d . . . . .Rom 15:27

DECEIT

spirit there is no d . . . . .Ps 32:2
from speaking d . . . . .Ps 34:13
d shall not dwell . . . . .Ps 101:7
D is in the heart of . . . . .Prov 12:20
nor was any d in His. . . . . . .Is 53:9
They hold fast to d . . . . . . .Jer 8:5
in whom is no d . . . . .John 1:47
"O full of all d . . . . .Acts 13:10
philosophy and empty d . . . .Col 2:8
no sin, nor was d . . . . .1 Pet 2:22
mouth was found no d . . . .Rev 14:5

DECEITFUL

deliver me from the d . . . . . .Ps 43:1
d men shall not. . . . . .Ps 55:23
of the wicked are d . . . . . .Prov 12:5
of an enemy are d . . . . . .Prov 27:6
"The heart is d . . . . .Jer 17:9
are false apostles, d . . . .2 Cor 11:13

DECEITFULLY

an idol, nor sworn d . . . . . . .Ps 24:4
the word of God d . . . . . . .2 Cor 4:2

DECEITFULNESS

this world and the d. . . . .Matt 13:22
hardened through the d. . . .Heb 3:13

DECEIVE

'Do not d yourselves . . . . . .Jer 37:9
rise up and d many . . . . .Matt 24:11
wonders to d . . . . .Matt 24:24
Let no one d himself . . . . .1 Cor 3:18
Let no one d you with . . . . .Eph 5:6
we have no sin, we d . . . . .1 John 1:8

DECEIVED

"The serpent d. . . . . .Gen 3:13
d heart has turned him . . . .Is 44:20
by the commandment, d. . .Rom 7:11
as the serpent d . . . . .2 Cor 11:3
but the woman being d. . .1 Tim 2:14
deceiving and being d. . . .2 Tim 3:13

DECEIVER

"But cursed be the d . . . . . .Mal 1:14
how that d said. . . . . . . .Matt 27:63
This is a d and an. . . . . . .2 John 7

DECEIVES

heed that no one d . . . . . .Matt 24:4
d his own heart. . . . . . . .James 1:26

DECENTLY

all things be done d . . . . .1 Cor 14:40

DECEPTION

d all the day long . . . . .Ps 38:12

DECEPTIVE

you with d words . . . . .2 Pet 2:3

DECISION

but its every d . . . . .Prov 16:33
in the valley of d . . . . .Joel 3:14

DECLARE

The heavens d the. . . . . . . .Ps 19:1

DECLARED

d Your name to My........Ps 22:22
d what He has done.......Ps 66:16
d that the LORD is ....Ps 92:15
d His generation ....Is 53:8
"I will *d* Your name......Heb 2:12
seen and heard we *d* .....1 John 1:3

DECLARED

the Father, He has *d*.....John 1:18
and *d* to be the Son of .....Rom 1:4

DECREE

"I will declare the *d* ....Ps 2:7
d which shall not pass .....Ps 148:6
in those days that a *d* .....Luke 2:1

DEDICATED

house and has not *d*.....Deut 20:5
every *d* thing in ....Ezek 44:29
first covenant was *d* .....Heb 9:18

DEDICATION

sacrifices at the *d* ....Ezra 6:17
it was the Feast of *D* ....John 10:22

DEED

d has been done ....Judg 19:30
you do a charitable *d* .....Matt 6:2
you do in word or *d*........Col 3:17

DEEDS

Declare His *d* among ....Ps 9:11
vengeance on their *d*.......Ps 99:8
harlot by their own *d*.....Ps 106:39
declare His *d* among ....Is 12:4
they surpass the *d*........Jer 5:28
because their *d* ....John 3:19
"You do the *d* ....John 8:41
one according to his *d*.....Rom 2:6
you put to death the *d* ....Rom 8:13
shares in his evil *d* ....2 John 11

DEEP

LORD God caused a *d*.....Gen 2:21
He lays up the *d* ....Ps 33:7
D calls unto *d* ....Ps 42:7
In His hand are the *d*......Ps 95:4
His wonders in the *d*.....Ps 107:24
put out in *d* darkness....Prov 20:20
led them through the *d*....Is 63:13
d closed around me........Jon 2:5
d uttered its voice ....Hab 3:10
"Launch out into the *d* ....Luke 5:4
I have been in the *d*.....2 Cor 11:25

DEEPER

D than Sheol ....Job 11:8

DEEPLY

Drink, yes, drink *d*........Song 5:1
But He sighed *d*........Mark 8:12

DEER

"Naphtali is a *d* ....Gen 49:21
As the *d* pants for the ......Ps 42:1
shall leap like a *d*..........Is 35:6

DEFEATED

and Israel was *d*........1 Sam 4:10

DEFECT

who has any *d*..........Lev 21:17

DEFEND

'For I will *d* this ....2 Kin 19:34
d my own ways before ....Job 13:15
D the poor and ....Ps 82:3
d the fatherless ....Is 1:17
of hosts *d* Jerusalem........Is 31:5

DEFENDER

a *d* of widows ....Ps 68:5

DEFENSE

For wisdom is a *d* ....Eccl 7:12
d will be the ....Is 33:16
am appointed for the *d* ....Phil 1:17
d no one stood with me ..2 Tim 4:16
be ready to give a *d*......1 Pet 3:15

DEFILE

the heart, and they *d*....Matt 15:18
also these dreamers *d* ......Jude 8

DEFILED

d the dwelling place ....Ps 74:7
For your hands are *d*.......Is 59:3
lest they should be *d* ...John 18:28
to those who are *d* ....Titus 1:15
and conscience are *d* .....Titus 1:15
even the garment *d* ....Jude 23

DEFILES

mouth, this *d* a man.....Matt 15:11
d the temple of God......1 Cor 3:17
it anything that *d*........Rev 21:27

DEFRAUD

d his brother in this.....1 Thess 4:6

DEGENERATE

before Me into the *d* ......Jer 2:21
d is your heart ....Ezek 16:30

DEGREES

go forward ten *d*........2 Kin 20:9

DELICACIES

let me eat of their *d* ......Ps 141:4
Do not desire his *d* ......Prov 23:3
of the king's *d* ....Dan 1:5

DELICATE

be called tender and *d*.......Is 47:1
a lovely and *d* woman ....Jer 6:2

DELIGHT

the LORD as great *d*....1 Sam 15:22
And his heart took *d*.....2 Chr 17:6
Will he *d* himself in .....Job 27:10
But his *d* is in the..........Ps 1:2
D yourself also in the.......Ps 37:4
I *d* to do Your will.........Ps 40:8
Your law had been my *d*..Ps 119:92
d ourselves with love ....Prov 7:18
and I was daily His *d*.....Prov 8:30
truthfully are His *d*.....Prov 12:22
and let your soul *d*........Is 55:2
call the Sabbath a *d* ....Is 58:13
For I *d* in the law of .....Rom 7:22

DELIGHTED

The LORD *d* only in......Deut 10:15

DELIGHTS

O love, with your *d*........Song 7:6
for the LORD *d* in you ......Is 62:4
forever, because He *d*......Mic 7:18

DELIVER

d them out of the hand .....Ex 3:8
He shall *d* you in six .....Job 5:19
is no one who can *d* .....Job 10:7
'*D* him from going down . .Job 33:24
Let Him *d* Him............Ps 22:8
d their soul from........Ps 33:19
I will *d* him and honor ....Ps 91:15
d you from the immoral . .Prov 2:16
wickedness will not *d* ....Eccl 8:8
have I no power to *d* ....Is 50:2

DEFENDER

we serve is able to *d* .....Dan 3:17
into temptation, but *d* . . .Matt 6:13
let Him *d* Him now if. . . .Matt 27:43
d such a one to Satan .....1 Cor 5:5
And the Lord will *d* ....2 Tim 4:18
d the godly out of........2 Pet 2:9

DELIVERANCE

d He gives to His king.....Ps 18:50
but *d* is of the LORD .....Prov 21:31
not accepting *d*.........Heb 11:35

DELIVERED

d the poor who cried......Job 29:12
for You have *d* my soul.....Ps 56:13
For He has *d* the life.....Jer 20:13
All things have been *d*. .Matt 11:27
who was *d* up because .....Rom 4:25
But now we have been *d*....Rom 7:6
who *d* us from so great ..2 Cor 1:10
was once for all *d*..........Jude 3

DELIVERER

the LORD raised up a *d*.....Judg 3:9
LORD gave Israel a *d*.....2 Kin 13:5
D will come out of.......Rom 11:26

DELIVERERS

d who saved them ....Neh 9:27

DELIVERS

d the kingdom to God...1 Cor 15:24
dead, even Jesus who *d*.1 Thess 1:10

DELUSION

send them strong *d* ...2 Thess 2:11

DEMON

Jesus rebuked the *d*.....Matt 17:18
you say, 'He has a *d*.....Luke 7:33
Samaritan and have a *d*. .John 8:48

DEMONIC

is earthly, sensual, *d*.....James 3:15

DEMONS

They sacrificed to *d* .....Deut 32:17
their daughters to *d* ......Ps 106:37
authority over all *d*........Luke 9:1
even the *d* are subject ..Luke 10:17
Lord and the cup of *d* . .1 Cor 10:21
Even the *d* believe .....James 2:19
a dwelling place of *d*......Rev 18:2

DEMONSTRATE

faith, to *d* His ....Rom 3:25

DEMONSTRATES

d His own love toward .....Rom 5:8

DEN

in the viper's *d*............Is 11:8
by My name, become a *d* . .Jer 7:11
cast him into the *d*........Dan 6:16
it a '*d* of thieves ....Matt 21:13

DENARIUS

the laborers for a *d*.......Matt 20:2
they brought Him a *d* ...Matt 22:19
quart of wheat for a *d* .....Rev 6:6

DENIED

before men will be *d*......Luke 12:9
Peter then *d* again ......John 18:27
d the Holy One and the ...Acts 3:14
things cannot be *d* ......Acts 19:36
household, he has *d*.......1 Tim 5:8
word, and have not *d* .....Rev 3:8

DENIES

But whoever *d*.........Matt 10:33

d that Jesus is the...... 1 John 2:22

DENS

lie down in their *d*....... Ps 104:22
and mountains, in *d*..... Heb 11:38

DENY

lest I be full and *d* ...... Prov 30:9
let him *d* himself....... Matt 16:24
He cannot *d* Himself ....2 Tim 2:13
in works they *d*........... Titus 1:16
d the only Lord .... Jude 4
d My faith even.......... Rev 2:13

DENYING

but *d* its power .... 2 Tim 3:5
d ungodliness and .... Titus 2:12
d the Lord who bought ....2 Pet 2:1

DEPART

scepter shall not *d*....... Gen 49:10
they say to God, '*D* ..... Job 21:14
D from evil............... Ps 34:14
fear the Lord and *d* ...... Prov 3:7
the mountains shall *d*..... Is 54:10
on the left hand, '*D* .... Matt 25:41
will *d* from the faith ..... 1 Tim 4:1

DEPARTED

the day that you *d* ...... Deut 9:7

DEPARTING

heart of unbelief in *d*..... Heb 3:12

DEPARTURE

d savage wolves will .... Acts 20:29
and the time of my *d* .... 2 Tim 4:6

DEPRESSION

of man causes *d*........ Prov 12:25

DEPRIVE

d myself of good .... Eccl 4:8
d one another except..... 1 Cor 7:5

DEPTH

because they had no *d*.... Matt 13:5
nor height nor *d*....... Rom 8:39
Oh, the *d* of the........ Rom 11:33
width and length and *d*... Eph 3:18

DEPTHS

d have covered them ...... Ex 15:5
The *d* also trembled ...... Ps 77:16
my soul from the *d*....... Ps 86:13
led them through the *d* ... Ps 106:9
go down again to the *d*... Ps 107:26
d I was brought forth.... Prov 8:24
our sins into the *d* .... Mic 7:19
have not known the *d*..... Rev 2:24

DERANGED

the nations are *d* .... Jer 51:7

DERISION

shall hold them in *d*........ Ps 2:4
I am in *d* daily........... Jer 20:7

DESCEND

His glory shall not *d* ..... Ps 49:17
d now from the cross.... Mark 15:32
Lord Himself will *d* ...1 Thess 4:16
This wisdom does not *d*. James 3:15

DESCENDANTS

All you *d* of Jacob .... Ps 22:23
d shall inherit the....... Ps 25:13
In the Lord all the *d*...... Is 45:25
"We are Abraham's *d*..... John 8:33

DESCENDED

because the Lord *d* .... Ex 19:18
that He also first *d* .... Eph 4:9
He who *d* is also the ..... Eph 4:10

DESCENDING

were ascending and *d*..... Gen 28:12
"I saw the Spirit *d*....... John 1:32
of God ascending and *d*.. John 1:51
the holy Jerusalem, *d*..... Rev 21:10

DESERT

d shall rejoice.............. Is 35:1
and rivers in the *d*....... Is 43:19
'Look, He is in the *d* ... Matt 24:26

DESERTED

d place by Himself...... Matt 14:13

DESERTS

led them through the *d*..... Is 48:21
They wandered in *d*...... Heb 11:38

DESERVE

to them what they *d*....... Ps 28:4
d I will judge them....... Ezek 7:27

DESIGN

with an artistic *d*......... Ex 26:31
may keep its whole *d*.... Ezek 43:11

DESIRABLE

the eyes, and a tree *d*...... Gen 3:6
d that we should leave ..... Acts 6:2

DESIRE

d shall be for your .... Gen 3:16
for we do not *d*......... Job 21:14
him his heart's *d*......... Ps 21:2
Behold, You *d* truth in ..... Ps 51:6
upon earth that I *d*....... Ps 73:25
the *d* of the wicked...... Ps 112:10
and satisfy the *d*........ Ps 145:16
The *d* of the lazy........ Prov 21:25
a burden, and *d* fails ..... Eccl 12:5
d of our soul is .... Is 26:8
d I have desired .... Luke 22:15
"Father, I *d* that....... John 17:24
all manner of evil *d*....... Rom 7:8
Brethren, my heart's *d* .... Rom 10:1
the best gifts........... 1 Cor 12:31
d spiritual gifts .... 1 Cor 14:1
the two, having a *d* ...... Phil 1:23
passion, evil *d* .... Col 3:5
d has conceived........ James 1:15

DESIRED

d are they than gold....... Ps 19:10
One thing I have *d*....... Ps 27:4
guides them to their *d* ... Ps 107:30
What is *d* in a man is... Prov 19:22
Whatever my eyes *d* ..... Eccl 2:10
desire I have *d* .... Luke 22:15

DESIRES

Who is the man who *d*.... Ps 34:12
shall give you the *d* ...... Ps 37:4
the devil, and the *d*...... John 8:44
fulfilling the *d*............ Eph 2:3
not come from your *d* ... James 4:1

DESOLATE

on me, for I am *d* .... Ps 25:16
the wilderness in a *d* ..... Ps 107:4
my children and am *d*..... Is 49:21
any more be termed *D*...... Is 62:4
to make your land *d* ...... Jer 4:7
house is left to you *d*... Matt 23:38
one hour she is made *d*..Rev 18:19

DESOLATION

the 'abomination of *d*.... Matt 24:15
then know that its *d*..... Luke 21:20

DESOLATIONS

Lord, who has made *d*..... Ps 46:8

DESPAIRED

turned my heart and *d* ....Eccl 2:20
strength, so that we *d*..... 2 Cor 1:8

DESPERATELY

he flees *d* from its........ Job 27:22

DESPISE

if you *d* My statutes...... Lev 26:15
d Me shall be lightly ....1 Sam 2:30
d your mother when she. .Prov 23:22
d your feast days........ Amos 5:21
to you priests who *d*....... Mal 1:6
one and *d* the other ..... Matt 6:24
d the riches of His....... Rom 2:4
d the church of God..... 1 Cor 11:22
and *d* authority .... 2 Pet 2:10

DESPISED

poor man's wisdom is *d* ...Eccl 9:16
d the word of the Holy ...... Is 5:24
He is *d* and rejected .... Is 53:3
the things which are *d*.... 1 Cor 1:28

DESPISES

wisdom *d* his neighbor ...Prov 11:12
d the word will be ...... Prov 13:13
d his neighbor sins ...... Prov 14:21
but a foolish man *d*...... Prov 15:20
d the scepter of My ..... Ezek 21:10

DESPISING

the cross, *d* the shame..... Heb 12:2

DESTINY

did not consider her *d*..... Lam 1:9

DESTITUTE

the prayer of the *d* ...... Ps 102:17
of corrupt minds and *d*....1 Tim 6:5
sister is naked and *d* ....James 2:15

DESTROY

d the righteous.......... Gen 18:23
d all the wicked.......... Ps 101:8
of the Lord I will *d* ...... Ps 118:10
the wicked He will *d*..... Ps 145:20
why should you *d*....... Eccl 7:16
shall not hurt nor *d*......... Is 11:9
have mercy, but will *d*.... Jer 13:14
d them with double...... Jer 17:18
I did not come to *d* ..... Matt 5:17
Him who is able to *d*... Matt 10:28
Barabbas and *d* Jesus .. Matt 27:20
d this temple .... Mark 14:58
to save life or to *d*...... Luke 6:9
d men's lives but to ..... Luke 9:56
d the work of God for.... Rom 14:20
d the wisdom of the..... 1 Cor 1:19
foods, but God will *d*.... 1 Cor 6:13
able to save and to *d* ....James 4:12

DESTROYED

d all living things......... Gen 7:23
d those who hated me .. 2 Sam 22:41
My people are *d* .... Hos 4:6
"O Israel, you are *d*..... Hos 13:9
house, this tent, is *d* ..... 2 Cor 5:1

DESTROYER

the paths of the *d*......... Ps 17:4
him who is a great *d*..... Prov 18:9
destroyed by the *d*..... 1 Cor 10:10

DESTRUCTION

not be afraid of d ....Job 5:21
D has no covering........Job 26:6
d come upon him...........Ps 35:8
cast them down to d......Ps 73:18
You turn man to d ....Ps 90:3
d that lays waste..........Ps 91:6
your life from d...........Ps 103:4
d will come to the.......Prov 10:29
Pride goes before d.....Prov 16:18
d the heart of a man....Prov 18:12
called the City of D.......Is 19:18
neither wasting nor d .....Is 60:18
heifer, but d comes .....Jer 46:20
wrath prepared for d.....Rom 9:22
one to Satan for the d....1 Cor 5:5
whose end is d ....Phil 3:19
then sudden d..........1 Thess 5:3
with everlasting d .....2 Thess 1:9
which drown men in d ...1 Tim 6:9
twist to their own d.....2 Pet 3:16

DESTRUCTIVE

bring in d heresies ....2 Pet 2:1

DETERMINED

Since his days are d ......Job 14:5
of hosts will make a d.....Is 10:23
"Seventy weeks are d ....Dan 9:24
d their preappointed ....Acts 17:26
For I d not to know.......1 Cor 2:2

DETESTABLE

shall not eat any d ......Deut 14:3

DEVICE

there is no work or d.....Eccl 9:10

DEVICES

not ignorant of his d .....2 Cor 2:11

DEVIL

to be tempted by the d ...Matt 4:1
prepared for the d......Matt 25:41
forty days by the d......Luke 4:2
then the d comes and....Luke 8:12
and one of you is a d .....John 6:70
of your father the d ......John 8:44
d having already put ....John 13:2
give place to the d ....Eph 4:27
the wiles of the d........Eph 6:11
the snare of the d ......2 Tim 2:26
Resist the d and he ......James 4:7
the works of the d.......1 John 3:8
contending with the d.......Jude 9
Indeed, the d is about ....Rev 2:10

DEVIOUS

crooked, and who are d....Prov 2:15

DEVISE

Do not d evil against .....Prov 3:29
Woe to those who d ....Mic 2:1

DEVISES

d wickedness on his ....Ps 36:4
he d evil continually .....Prov 6:14
d wicked plans to.........Is 32:7
But a generous man d......Is 32:8

DEVOID

He who is d of wisdom...Prov 11:12

DEVOTED

d offering is most ....Lev 27:28
"Every d thing in......Num 18:14
Your servant, who is d...Ps 119:38

DEVOUR

A fire shall d before ....Ps 50:3

For you d widows' ......Matt 23:14
bite and d one another ....Gal 5:15
seeking whom he may d ...1 Pet 5:8
d her Child as ....Rev 12:4

DEVOURED

Some wild beast has d....Gen 37:20
rebel, you shall be d.........Is 1:20
the curse has d............Is 24:6
Your sword has d ....Jer 2:30
For shame has d ....Jer 3:24
have d their judges ....Hos 7:7
trees, the locust d ....Amos 4:9
birds came and d them ...Matt 13:4
of heaven and d them.....Rev 20:9

DEVOURER

I will rebuke the d ....Mal 3:11

DEVOURING

You love all d words ....Ps 52:4
the flame of d fire ....Is 29:6

DEVOUT

man was just and d .....Luke 2:25
d men carried...........Acts 8:2
d soldier from among ....Acts 10:7
d proselytes ....Acts 13:43

DEW

God give you of the d ....Gen 27:28
shall also drop d ....Deut 33:28
his favor is like d.......Prov 19:12
your d is like the d ....Is 26:19
like the early d ....Hos 6:4
many peoples, like d.......Mic 5:7

DIADEM

LORD, and a royal d.........Is 62:3

DIADEMS

ten horns, and seven d ....Rev 12:3

DIAMOND

d it is engraved ....Jer 17:1

DICTATES

according to the d ....Jer 23:17

DIE

it you shall surely d ......Gen 2:17
but a person shall d.......2 Chr 25:4
sees wise men d ....Ps 49:10
I shall not d ....Ps 118:17
who are appointed to d...Prov 31:8
how does a wise man d...Eccl 2:16
born, and a time to d.......Eccl 3:2
why should you d........Eccl 7:17
wicked way, he shall d ...Ezek 3:19
"Even if I have to d ....Matt 26:35
nor can they d.........Luke 20:36
eat of it and not d.......John 6:50
to you that you will d....John 8:24
though he may d.......John 11:25
that one man should d ...John 11:50
that Jesus would d.....John 11:51
our law He ought to d ...John 19:7
the flesh you will d ......Rom 8:13
For as in Adam all d ...1 Cor 15:22
and to d is gain.........Phil 1:21
for men to d once......Heb 9:27
are the dead who ......Rev 14:13

DIED

And all flesh d ....Gen 7:21
"Oh, that we had d ....Ex 16:3
was that the beggar d ...Luke 16:22
in due time Christ d ......Rom 5:6
Christ d for us...........Rom 5:8
For he who has d........Rom 6:7

Now if we d with.........Rom 6:8
sin revived and I d ....Rom 7:9
that if One d for all .....2 Cor 5:14
and He d for all ....2 Cor 5:15
through the law d........Gal 2:19
who d for us ....1 Thess 5:10
for if we d with Him.....2 Tim 2:11
These all d in faith.......Heb 11:13
having d to sins ....1 Pet 2:24

DIES

made alive unless it d ...1 Cor 15:36

DIFFERS

for one star d from......1 Cor 15:41

DIFFUSED

By what way is light d....Job 38:24

DILIGENCE

d is man's..............Prov 12:27
d it produced in you .....2 Cor 7:11
of your love by the d.....2 Cor 8:8

DILIGENT

and my spirit makes d.....Ps 77:6
d makes rich ....Prov 10:4
of the d will rule ....Prov 12:24
d shall be made rich .....Prov 13:4
Let us therefore be d.....Heb 4:11

DILIGENTLY

d followed every good ....1 Tim 5:10
d lest anyone fall ....Heb 12:15

DIM

His eyes were not d .....Deut 34:7
the windows grow d......Eccl 12:3
the gold has become d ....Lam 4:1

DIMLY

we see in a mirror, d ....1 Cor 13:12

DINE

asked Him to d with ....Luke 11:37
come in to him and d.....Rev 3:20

DINNER

I have prepared my d....Matt 22:4
invites you to d ....1 Cor 10:27

DIP

d your piece of bread ....Ruth 2:14

DIPPED

d his finger in the..........Lev 9:9
of bread when I have d .John 13:26
clothed with a robe d ....Rev 19:13

DIRECT

the morning I will d........Ps 5:3
d their work in truth.......Is 61:8
Now may the Lord d....2 Thess 3:5

DIRT

I cast them out like d.....Ps 18:42
cast up mire and d.........Is 57:20

DISAPPEARS

As water d from the......Job 14:11

DISARMED

d principalities...........Col 2:15

DISARMS

and d the mighty ....Job 12:21

DISASTER

D will come upon ....Ezek 7:26
you shall see d..........Zeph 3:15
voyage will end with d ...Acts 27:10

DISCERN

Can I *d* between the....2 Sam 19:35
Then you shall again *d*....Mal 3:18
d the face of the sky ....Matt 16:3
senses exercised to *d*....Heb 5:14

DISCERNED

they are spiritually *d*....1 Cor 2:14

DISCERNER

d of the thoughts........Heb 4:12

DISCERNMENT

and takes away the *d*....Job 12:20

DISCERNS

a wise man's heart *d*......Eccl 8:5

DISCIPLE

d is not above his......Matt 10:24
in the name of a *d*....Matt 10:42
he cannot be My *d*....Luke 14:26
d whom Jesus loved....John 21:7

DISCIPLES

but Your *d* do not fast....Matt 9:14
d transgress the........Matt 15:2
took the twelve *d*......Matt 20:17
My word, you are My *d*..John 8:31
to become His *d*........John 9:27
but we are Moses' *d*....John 9:28
so you will be My *d*....John 15:8

DISCIPLINE

Harsh *d* is for him who ..Prov 15:10

DISCIPLINES

but he who loves him *d* ..Prov 13:24

DISCLOSE

d my dark saying........Ps 49:4

DISCORD

and one who sows *d*....Prov 6:19

DISCOURAGED

will not fail nor be *d*......Is 42:4
lest they become *d*........Col 3:21
you become weary and *d*..Heb 12:3

DISCRETION

d will preserve you ....Prov 2:11
out knowledge and *d*....Prov 8:12
woman who lacks *d*....Prov 11:22
The *d* of a man makes ...Prov 19:11
the heavens at His *d*....Jer 10:12

DISFIGURE

d their faces that......Matt 6:16

DISGUISES

and he *d* his face........Job 24:15
He who hates, *d*......Prov 26:24

DISHONOR

d who wish me evil......Ps 40:14
d the pride of all ......Is 23:9
My Father, and you *d* Me .John 8:49
d their bodies among....Rom 24
and another for *d*......Rom 9:21
It is sown in *d*........1 Cor 15:43
honor and some for *d*...2 Tim 2:20

DISHONORED

But you have *d* the......James 2:6

DISHONORS

For son *d* father........Mic 7:6
covered, *d* his head ....1 Cor 11:4

DISOBEDIENCE

d many were made ......Rom 5:19
works in the sons of *d*....Eph 2:2
d received a just........Heb 2:2

DISOBEDIENT

out My hands to a *d*....Rom 10:21
d, deceived, serving......Titus 3:3
They stumble, being *d*....1 Pet 2:8
who formerly were *d* ....1 Pet 3:20

DISORDERLY

for this *d* gathering......Acts 19:40
brother who walks *d* ....2 Thess 3:6

DISPENSATION

d of the fullness of........Eph 1:10
d of the grace of God......Eph 3:2

DISPERSE

d them throughout the...Ezek 20:23

DISPERSION

intend to go to the *D*....John 7:35
the pilgrims of the *D*......1 Pet 1:1

DISPLEASE

LORD see it, and it *d*....Prov 24:18

DISPLEASED

that David had done *d*..2 Sam 11:27
You have been *d*........Ps 60:1
they were greatly *d*......Matt 20:24
it, He was greatly *d*....Mark 10:14

DISPUTE

Now there was also a *d* .Luke 22:24

DISPUTER

Where is the *d* of this ....1 Cor 1:20

DISPUTES

d rather than godly........1 Tim 1:4
but is obsessed with *d* ....1 Tim 6:4
foolish and ignorant *d*...2 Tim 2:23
But avoid foolish *d*........Titus 3:9

DISQUALIFIED

myself should become *d* .1 Cor 9:27
indeed you are *d*........2 Cor 13:5
though we may seem *d* ..2 Cor 13:7

DISQUIETED

And why are you *d*......Ps 42:5

DISSENSION

had no small *d* and......Acts 15:2

DISSENSIONS

selfish ambitions, *d*......Gal 5:20

DISSIPATION

not accused of *d*........Titus 1:6
in the same flood of *d* ....1 Pet 4:4

DISSOLVED

of heaven shall be *d*......Is 34:4
the heavens will be *d*....2 Pet 3:12

DISTINCTION

and made no *d*........Acts 15:9
For there is no *d*......Rom 10:12

compassion, making a *d* ....Jude 22

DISTRESS

me in the day of my *d*....Gen 35:3
"When you are in *d*.....Deut 4:30
my life from every *d*.....1 Kin 1:29
you out of dire *d*........Job 36:16
keep you from *d*........Job 36:19
d them in His deep........Ps 2:5
on the LORD in *d*........Ps 118:5
a whirlwind, when *d*.....Prov 1:27
and on the earth *d*......Luke 21:25
tribulation, or *d*........Rom 8:35
of the present *d*........1 Cor 7:26

DISTRESSED

heart within me is *d*......Ps 143:4
troubled and deeply *d*...Mark 14:33

DISTRESSES

bring me out of my *d*......Ps 25:17

DISTRIBUTE

that you have and *d*....Luke 18:22

DISTRIBUTED

and they *d* to each as ....Acts 4:35
But as God has *d*........1 Cor 7:17

DISTRIBUTING

d to the needs of the.....Rom 12:13

DITCH

will fall into a *d*........Matt 15:14

DIVERSITIES

There are *d*............1 Cor 12:4

DIVIDE

D the living child........1 Kin 3:25
d their tongues............Ps 55:9
d the spoil with the.....Prov 16:19
d the inheritance........Luke 12:13
"Take this and *d* ......Luke 22:17

DIVIDED

and the waters were *d*....Ex 14:21
death they were not *d* ...2 Sam 1:23
And You *d* the sea......Neh 9:11
"Who has *d* a channel ...Job 38:25
shall they ever be *d* ....Ezek 37:22
kingdom has been *d*......Dan 5:28
your land shall be *d* ....Amos 7:17
"Every kingdom *d*......Matt 12:25
and a house against ..Luke 11:17
in one house will be *d*...Luke 12:52
So he *d* to them his ....Luke 15:12
appeared to them *d*......Acts 2:3
d them among all ....Acts 2:45
Is Christ *d* ....1 Cor 1:13
the great city was *d*.....Rev 16:19

DIVIDES

at home the spoil........Ps 68:12

DIVIDING

rightly *d* the word of.....2 Tim 2:15

DIVINATION

shall you practice *d*......Lev 19:26
D is on................Prov 16:10
darkness without *d*........Mic 3:6
a spirit of *d* met us......Acts 16:16

DIVINE

futility and who *d*........Ezek 13:9
and her prophets *d*.......Mic 3:11
d service and the........Heb 9:1
d power has given........2 Pet 1:3

DIVINERS

your prophets, your d . . . . .Jer 27:9

DIVISION

So there was a d . . . . .John 7:43
piercing even to the d . . . . .Heb 4:12

DIVISIONS

note those who cause d. . .Rom 16:17
and that there be no d. . . .1 Cor 1:10
envy, strife, and d . . . . . .1 Cor 3:3
hear that there are d . . . .1 Cor 11:18
persons, who cause d. . . . . .Jude 19

DIVISIVE

Reject a d man after . . . . .Titus 3:10

DIVORCE

her a certificate of d. . . . . .Deut 24:1
of your mother's d. . . . . .Is 50:1
a certificate of d. . . . . . . .Mark 10:4

DO

set in them to d evil . . . . . .Eccl 8:11
I will also d it. . . . . .Is 46:11
men to d to you, a . . . . . .Matt 7:12
d this and you will . . . . .Luke 10:28
He sees the Father d . . . .John 5:19
without Me you can d . . . .John 15:5
"Sirs, what must I d. . . . .Acts 16:30
d evil that good may. . . . . .Rom 3:8
For what I will to d . . . . . .Rom 7:15
good that I will to d . . . . .Rom 7:19
or whatever you d, d . . . .1 Cor 10:31
d all things through. . . . . . .Phil 4:13
d in word or deed, d. . . . . . .Col 3:17
d good and to share. . . . . .Heb 13:16
and d this or that. . . . . .James 4:15

DOCTRINE

said, 'My d is pure . . . . . . .Job 11:4
for I give you good d . . . . . .Prov 4:2
idol is a worthless d. . . . . .Jer 10:8
of bread, but of the d. . . .Matt 16:12
What new d is this . . . . . .Mark 1:27
"My d is not Mine . . . .John 7:16
Jerusalem with your d. . . .Acts 5:28
heart that form of d . . . . .Rom 6:17
with every wind of d . . . . .Eph 4:14
is contrary to sound d . . .1 Tim 1:10
followed my d. . . . . .2 Tim 3:10
is profitable for d. . . . . . .2 Tim 3:16
not endure sound d. . . . . .2 Tim 4:3
in d showing. . . . . .Titus 2:7
they may adorn the d . . . .Titus 2:10
not abide in the d. . . . . . . .2 John 9

DOCTRINES

the commandments and d . .Col 2:22
spirits and d of . . . . .1 Tim 4:1
various and strange d . . . . .Heb 13:9

DOERS

of God, but the d. . . . . . . .Rom 2:13
But be d of the word . . . .James 1:22

DOG

to David, "Am I a d. . . .1 Sam 17:43
they growl like a d . . . . . . .Ps 59:6
d returns to his own . . . . .Prov 26:11
d is better than a. . . . . .Eccl 9:4
d returns to his own. . . . . .2 Pet 2:22

DOGS

Yes, they are greedy d. . . . . .Is 56:11
what is holy to the d . . . . .Matt 7:6
d eat the crumbs which. .Matt 15:27
Moreover the d came . . . .Luke 16:21
But outside are d . . . . . . .Rev 22:15

DOMINION

let them have d. . . . . .Gen 1:26
"D and fear belong. . . . . . .Job 25:2
made him to have d . . . . . . .Ps 8:6
let them not have d . . . . . .Ps 19:13
besides You have had d. . . . .Is 26:13
d is an everlasting . . . . . . .Dan 4:34
sin shall not have d. . . . . . .Rom 6:14
Not that we have d . . . . . .2 Cor 1:24
glory and majesty, d . . . . . .Jude 25

DONKEY

d saw the Angel . . . . . . .Num 22:23
Does the wild d . . . . .Job 6:5
d its master's crib . . . . .Is 1:3
and riding on a d. . . . . . . .Zech 9:9
colt, the foal of a d . . . . . .Matt 21:5
He had found a young d John 12:14
d speaking with a. . . . . . . .2 Pet 2:16

DONKEY'S

d colt is born a man . . . . .Job 11:12

DONKEYS

d quench their thirst . . . . .Ps 104:11
a chariot of d . . . . .Is 21:7
And the wild d stood. . . . . .Jer 14:6

DOOM

for the day of d . . . . .Prov 16:4

DOOR

sin lies at the d. . . . . .Gen 4:7
keep watch over the d . . . .Ps 141:3
d turns on its hinges. . . . .Prov 26:14
stone against the d. . . . . .Matt 27:60
to you, I am the d. . . . . . . .John 10:7
and effective d . . . . .1 Cor 16:9
d was opened to me by . .2 Cor 2:12
would open to us a . . . . .Col 4:3
is standing at the d . . . . .James 5:9
before you an open d . . . . . .Rev 3:8
I stand at the d. . . . . .Rev 3:20
and behold, a d . . . . .Rev 4:1

DOORKEEPER

I would rather be a d . . . . .Ps 84:10
"To him the d. . . . . .John 10:3

DOORPOSTS

write them on the d . . . . . .Deut 6:9
"Strike the d . . . . .Amos 9:1

DOORS

up, you everlasting d . . . . . .Ps 24:7
the entrance of the d. . . . . .Prov 8:3
when the d are shut in . . .Eccl 12:4
who would shut the d. . . . . .Mal 1:10

DOUBLE

from the LORD's hand d . . . . .Is 40:2
first I will repay d. . . . . . . .Jer 16:18
worthy of d honor . . . . . . .1 Tim 5:17
and repay her d . . . . .Rev 18:6

DOUBLE-MINDED

I hate the d . . . . .Ps 119:113
he is a d man . . . . .James 1:8
your hearts, you d . . . . . . .James 4:8

DOUBT

life shall hang in d . . . . .Deut 28:66
faith, why did you d. . . . .Matt 14:31

DOUBTING

without wrath and d. . . . . .1 Tim 2:8
in faith, with no d . . . . . .James 1:6

DOUBTS

And why do d arise in . . .Luke 24:38

for I have d about you . . . . .Gal 4:20
doubting, for he who d . . .James 1:6

DOVE

d found no resting . . . . .Gen 8:9
I had wings like a d . . . . . .Ps 55:6
I mourned like a d. . . . . . . .Is 38:14
also is like a silly d. . . . . . .Hos 7:11
descending like a d . . . . . .Matt 3:16

DOVES

and moan sadly like d. . . . . .Is 59:11
and harmless as d . . . . . .Matt 10:16
of those who sold d . . . . .Matt 21:12

DOWNCAST

who comforts the d . . . . . .2 Cor 7:6

DRAGNET

gather them in their d. . . . . .Hab 1:15
d that was cast. . . . . . . .Matt 13:47

DRAGON

a great, fiery red d . . . . . . .Rev 12:3
fought with the d . . . . .Rev 12:7
they worshiped the d . . . . .Rev 13:4
He laid hold of the d . . . . .Rev 20:2

DRAIN

wicked of the earth d . . . . . .Ps 75:8

DRAINED

all faces are d . . . . .Joel 2:6

DRANK

them, and they all d . . .Mark 14:23
d the same spiritual. . . . . .1 Cor 10:4

DRAW

d honey from the rock . . .Deut 32:13
me to d near to God . . . . . .Ps 73:28
and the years d . . . . .Eccl 12:1
D me away. . . . . .Song 1:4
Woe to those who d. . . . . . . .Is 5:18
with joy you will d. . . . . . . .Is 12:3
"D some out now . . . . . . .John 2:8
You have nothing to d . . . .John 4:11
will d all peoples . . . . . . .John 12:32
let us d near with a . . . . . .Heb 10:22
D near to God and He . . .James 4:8

DRAWN

The wicked have d . . . . .Ps 37:14
tempted when he is d. . . .James 1:14

DRAWS

and my life d near to . . . . . .Ps 88:3
your redemption d . . . . .Luke 21:28

DREAD

fear of you and the d . . . . . .Gen 9:2
begin to put the d. . . . . . .Deut 2:25

DREADFUL

of the great and d. . . . . .Mal 4:5

DREAM

Now Joseph had a d . . . . . .Gen 37:5
I speak to him in a d . . . . .Num 12:6
will fly away like a d. . . . . .Job 20:8
As a d when one awakes . . .Ps 73:20
like those who d . . . . .Ps 126:1
For a d comes through . . . . .Eccl 5:3
her, shall be as a d. . . . . .Is 29:7
prophet who has a d . . . . . .Jer 23:28
do not let the d. . . . . .Dan 4:19
your old men shall d . . . . . .Joel 2:28
to Joseph in a d . . . . .Matt 2:13
things today in a d. . . . . . .Matt 27:19
your old men shall d. . . . . .Acts 2:17

DREAMERS

d defile the flesh. . . . . .Jude 8

DREAMS

in the multitude of *d* . . . . . .Eccl 5:7
when a hungry man *d* . . . . . .Is 29:8
Nebuchadnezzar had *d* . . . .Dan 2:1

DREGS

d shall all the wicked . . . . . . .Ps 75:8
has settled on his *d* . . . . . .Jer 48:11

DRIED

My strength is *d*. . . . . .Ps 22:15
of her blood was *d* . . . . . .Mark 5:29
saw the fig tree *d* . . . . . .Mark 11:20
and its water was *d* . . . . . .Rev 16:12

DRIFT

have heard, lest we *d* . . . . . .Heb 2:1

DRINK

"What shall we *d* . . . . .Ex 15:24
"Do not *d* wine or. . . . . . . .Lev 10:9
and let him *d* of the . . . . .Job 21:20
gave me vinegar to *d* . . . . . .Ps 69:21
D water from your own. . . .Prov 5:15
mocker, strong *d* . . . . .Prov 20:1
lest they *d* and forget . . . . .Prov 31:5
Give strong *d* to him. . . . . .Prov 31:6
Let him *d* and forget. . . . . .Prov 31:7
d your wine with a. . . . . . .Eccl 9:7
follow intoxicating *d* . . . . . . .Is 5:11
mixing intoxicating *d* . . . . . .Is 5:22
d the milk of the . . . . .Is 60:16
My servants shall *d*. . . . . . . .Is 65:13
bosom, that you may *d*. . . . .Is 66:11
d water by measure . . . . .Ezek 4:11
"Bring wine, let us *d* . . . . .Amos 4:1
to you of wine and *d*. . . . . .Mic 2:11
and you gave Me no *d* . .Matt 25:42
that day when I *d*. . . . . . .Matt 26:29
mingled with gall to *d* . .Matt 27:34
with myrrh to *d* . . . . . . .Mark 15:23
to her, "Give Me a *d*. . . . . .John 4:7
him come to Me and *d*. . . .John 7:37
d wine nor do anything. . .Rom 14:21
do, as often as you *d*. . .1 Cor 11:25
all been made to *d* . . . . .1 Cor 12:13
No longer *d* only water. . .1 Tim 5:23
has made all nations *d* . . . .Rev 14:8

DRINKS

to her, "Whoever *d* . . . . . .John 4:13
d My blood has. . . . . .John 6:54
For he who eats and *d*. . .1 Cor 11:29
For the earth which *d* . . . . .Heb 6:7

DRIPPING

wife are a continual *d* . . . .Prov 19:13
His lips are lilies, *d*. . . . . .Song 5:13

DRIVE

of the wicked *d* . . . . .Ps 36:11
They shall *d* you from . . . . .Dan 4:25
temple and began to *d*. . .Mark 11:15

DRIVEN

They were *d* out from . . . . . .Job 30:5
Let them be *d* backward . . .Ps 40:14
sail and so were *d* . . . . . .Acts 27:17
a wave of the sea *d*. . . . . .James 1:6

DROP

They *d* on the pastures . . . .Ps 65:12
the nations are as a *d* . . . . . .Is 40:15

DROSS

of the earth like *d*. . . . . .Ps 119:119
Take away the *d*. . . . . .Prov 25:4

purge away your *d*. . . . . .Is 1:25
of Israel has become *d*. . .Ezek 22:18

DROUGHT

through a land of *d* . . . . .Jer 2:6
in the year of *d*. . . . . .Jer 17:8
For I called for a *d*. . . . . . .Hag 1:11

DROVE

So He *d* out the man . . . . .Gen 3:24
temple of God and *d* . . .Matt 21:12
a whip of cords, He *d*. . . .John 2:15

DROWN

nor can the floods *d* . . . . . .Song 8:7
harmful lusts which *d*. . . . .1 Tim 6:9

DROWSINESS

d will clothe a . . . . .Prov 23:21

DRUNK

of the wine and was *d* . . . . .Gen 9:21
d my wine with my milk . .Song 5:1
you afflicted, and *d* . . . . . . .Is 51:21
My anger, made them *d*. . . .Is 63:6
be satiated and made *d*. . . .Jer 46:10
the guests have well *d*. . . . .John 2:10
For these are not *d* . . . . . .Acts 2:15
and another is *d*. . . . . . . .1 Cor 11:21
And do not be *d*. . . . . .Eph 5:18
and those who get *d* . . .1 Thess 5:7
the earth were made *d*. . . . .Rev 17:2
I saw the woman, *d* . . . . . .Rev 17:6

DRUNKARD

d could be included. . . . .Deut 29:19
d is a proverb in the . . . . . .Prov 26:9
to and fro like a *d* . . . . .Is 24:20
or a reviler, or a *d*. . . . . . .1 Cor 5:11

DRUNKEN

I am like a *d* man . . . . .Jer 23:9

DRUNKENNESS

will be filled with *d*. . . . .Ezek 23:33
Jerusalem a cup of *d*. . . . .Zech 12:2
with carousing, *d* . . . . . . .Luke 21:34
not in revelry and *d*. . . . . .Rom 13:13
envy, murders, *d* . . . . .Gal 5:21
lusts, *d*. . . . . .1 Pet 4:3

DRY

place, and let the *d*. . . . . . . .Gen 1:9
made the sea into *d* . . . . . .Ex 14:21
It was *d* on the fleece. . . . .Judg 6:40
I will *d* up her sea . . . . . . .Jer 51:36
d tree flourish . . . . .Ezek 17:24
will make the rivers *d* . . .Ezek 30:12
will be done in the *d*. . . . .Luke 23:31

DUE

because it is your *d* . . . . . .Lev 10:13
their food in *d* season. . . . .Ps 104:27
pay all that was *d* . . . . . .Matt 18:34
d time Christ died. . . . . . . .Rom 5:6
to whom taxes are *d* . . . . .Rom 13:7
d season we shall. . . . . .Gal 6:9
exalt you in *d* time. . . . . . .1 Pet 5:6

DULL

heart of this people *d* . . . . . .Is 6:10
people have grown *d*. . . .Matt 13:15
you have become *d*. . . . . . .Heb 5:11

DUMB

the tongue of the *d* . . . . . . .Is 35:6
"Deaf and *d* spirit . . . . . .Mark 9:25

DUNGHILL

the land nor for the *d*. . . .Luke 14:35

DUST

formed man of the *d* . . . . . .Gen 2:7
d you shall return. . . . . .Gen 3:19
descendants as the *d* . . . . .Gen 13:16
now, I who am but *d* . . . . .Gen 18:27
"Who can count the *d* . . .Num 23:10
lay your gold in the *d*. . . . .Job 22:24
and repent in *d* . . . . .Job 42:6
Will the *d* praise You . . . . . .Ps 30:9
like the whirling *d*. . . . . . . .Ps 83:13
show favor to her *d* . . . . . .Ps 102:14
that we are *d* . . . . .Ps 103:14
or the primal *d*. . . . . .Prov 8:26
all are from the *d*. . . . . . . .Eccl 3:20
counted as the small *d* . . . . .Is 40:15
They shall lick the *d*. . . . . .Mic 7:17
city, shake off the *d* . . . . .Matt 10:14
image of the man of *d*. . .1 Cor 15:49

DUTY

done what was our *d* . . . .Luke 17:10

DWELL

O LORD, make me *d* . . . . . . .Ps 4:8
Who may *d* in Your holy . . . .Ps 15:1
He himself shall *d*. . . . . . . .Ps 25:13
d in the land . . . . .Ps 37:3
the LORD God might *d*. . . . .Ps 68:18
of my God than *d* . . . . .Ps 84:10
Him, that glory may *d* . . . . .Ps 85:9
Woe is me, that I *d* . . . . . .Ps 120:5
he will *d* on high . . . . .Is 33:16
into Egypt to *d* there . . . . . .Is 52:4
"I *d* in the high and . . . . . .Is 57:15
"They shall no longer *d*. . .Lam 4:15
they enter and *d* there . . .Matt 12:45
of Judea and all who *d*. . .Acts 2:14
"I will *d* in them . . . . .2 Cor 6:16
that Christ may *d*. . . . . . . .Eph 3:17
the fullness should *d* . . . . . .Col 1:19
the word of Christ *d* . . . . . .Col 3:16
men, and He will *d*. . . . . . .Rev 21:3

DWELLER

fled and became a *d* . . . . .Acts 7:29

DWELLING

A people *d* alone . . . . .Num 23:9
is the way to the *d* . . . . . .Job 38:19
built together for a *d*. . . . . .Eph 2:22
a foreign country, *d* . . . . . .Heb 11:9

DWELLS

He who *d* in the secret. . . . . .Ps 91:1
but the Father who *d*. . . .John 14:10
do it, but sin that *d* . . . . . .Rom 7:17
the Spirit of God *d* . . . . . . .Rom 8:9
from the dead *d*. . . . . .Rom 8:11
the Spirit of God *d* . . . . .1 Cor 3:16
d all the fullness . . . . .Col 2:9
which righteousness *d* . . . .2 Pet 3:13
you, where Satan *d* . . . . . . .Rev 2:13

DWELT

Egypt, and Jacob *d* . . . . . .Ps 105:23
became flesh and *d* . . . . . .John 1:14
By faith he *d* in the. . . . . . .Heb 11:9

DYING

I do not object to *d*. . . . . .Acts 25:11
in the body the *d* . . . . .2 Cor 4:10
Jacob, when he was *d* . . . .Heb 11:21

E

EAGLE

As an *e* stirs up its. . . . . .Deut 32:11
e swooping on its prey . . . . .Job 9:26
fly away like an *e*. . . . . . . .Prov 23:5

EAGLES

the way of an *e* ....Prov 30:19
nest as high as the *e* .....Jer 49:16
had the face of an *e* .....Ezek 1:10
like a flying *e*..............Rev 4:7
two wings of a great *e* ....Rev 12:14

EAGLES

up with wings like *e* ......Is 40:31
are swifter than *e*.........Jer 4:13
e will be gathered......Matt 24:28

EAGLES'

how I bore you on *e* ....Ex 19:4

EAR

shall pierce his *e*..........Ex 21:6
Does not the *e* test......Job 12:11
Bow down Your *e* ....Ps 31:2
and the *e* of the wise.....Prov 18:15
He awakens My *e* ....Is 50:4
e is uncircumcised ....Jer 6:10
what you hear in the *e*...Matt 10:27
cut off his right *e* ......John 18:10
not seen, nor *e* heard .....1 Cor 2:9
if the *e* should say .....1 Cor 12:16
"He who has an *e* ....Rev 2:7

EARLY

Very *e* in the morning ...Mark 16:2
arrived at the tomb *e*....Luke 24:22

EARNEST

must give the more *e*.......Heb 2:1

EARNESTLY

if you *e* obey My.......Deut 11:13
He prayed more *e*......Luke 22:44
in this we groan, *e* ....2 Cor 5:2
e that it would not.....James 5:17
you to contend *e*...........Jude 3

EARS

both his *e* will tingle ....2 Kin 21:12
Whoever shuts his *e* .....Prov 21:13
and hear with their *e*.......Is 6:10
"He who has *e* ....Matt 11:15
e are hard of hearing ....Matt 13:15
they had itching *e* ....2 Tim 4:3
e are open to their ....1 Pet 3:12

EARTH

e which is under you ....Deut 28:23
e are the LORD'S ....1 Sam 2:8
coming to judge the *e*...1 Chr 16:33
service for man on *e*........Job 7:1
He hangs the *e* on........Job 26:7
foundations of the *e* ......Job 38:4
e is the LORD'S..............Ps 24:1
the shields of the *e* ....Ps 47:9
You visit the *e*.............Ps 65:9
You had formed the *e* ......Ps 90:2
let the *e* be moved........Ps 99:1
glory is above the *e*.....Ps 148:13
wisdom founded the *e*....Prov 3:19
there was ever an *e* .....Prov 8:23
For three things the *e*...Prov 30:21
e abides forever ....Eccl 1:4
for the meek of the *e*.......Is 11:4
e is My footstool ....Is 66:1
and the *e* shone with ....Ezek 43:2
I will darken the *e*........Amos 8:9
e will be filled...........Hab 2:14
shall inherit the *e*........Matt 5:5
heaven and *e* pass away....Matt 5:18
e as it is in heaven ....Matt 6:10
treasures on *e* ....Matt 6:19
then shook the *e*........Heb 12:26
"Do not harm the *e*........Rev 7:3
from whose face the *e*....Rev 20:11
new heaven and a new *e*....Rev 21:1

EARTHLY

If I have told you *e*......John 3:12
if our *e* house ....2 Cor 5:1
their mind on *e* things....Phil 3:19
from above, but is *e*....James 3:15

EARTHQUAKE

after the wind an *e* ....1 Kin 19:11
as you fled from the *e*....Zech 14:5
there was a great *e*......Matt 28:2
there was a great *e*.......Rev 6:12

EARTHQUAKES

And there will be *e* ......Mark 13:8

EASE

I was at *e*................Job 16:12
you women who are at *e* .....Is 32:9
to you who are at *e*.......Amos 6:1
take your *e*.............Luke 12:19

EASIER

"Which is *e*, to say ......Mark 2:9
"It is *e* for a camel......Mark 10:25

EAST

goes toward the *e*.........Gen 2:14
the LORD brought an *e*....Ex 10:13
e wind scattered ....Job 38:24
As far as the *e*...........Ps 103:12
descendants from the *e*....Is 43:5
wise men from the *E* .....Matt 2:1
many will come from *e*....Matt 8:11
will come from the *e*....Luke 13:29
e might be prepared .....Rev 16:12

EAT

you may freely *e*.........Gen 2:16
'You shall not *e*..........Gen 3:17
my people as they *e* ....Ps 53:4
good to *e* much honey...Prov 25:27
e this scroll ....Ezek 3:1
on your couches, *e*.......Amos 6:4
e the flesh of My.........Mic 3:3
life, what you will *e* .....Matt 6:25
You to *e* the Passover....Matt 26:17
give us His flesh to *e*....John 6:52
one believes he may *e* ....Rom 14:2
e meat nor drink wine...Rom 14:21
I will never again *e* ......1 Cor 8:13
neither shall he *e* .....2 Thess 3:10
e your flesh like fire ....James 5:3

EATEN

Have you *e* from the ......Gen 3:11
e my honeycomb with my ..Song 5:1
e the fruit of lies.......Hos 10:13
And he was *e* by worms ..Acts 12:23

EATS

The righteous *e* ....Prov 13:25
receives sinners and *e*....Luke 15:2
"Whoever *e* My flesh ....John 6:54
e this bread will live ....John 6:58
e despise him who does ...Rom 14:3
He who *e*, *e* to the........Rom 14:6
an unworthy manner *e*....1 Cor 11:29

EDIFICATION

his good, leading to *e* .....Rom 15:2
prophesies speaks *e*......1 Cor 14:3
things be done for *e* .....1 Cor 14:26
the Lord gave us for *e*....2 Cor 10:8
has given me for *e* ......2 Cor 13:10
rather than godly *e*........1 Tim 1:4

EDIFIES

puffs up, but love *e* ......1 Cor 8:1
he who prophesies *e*......1 Cor 14:4

EDIFY

but not all things *e* .....1 Cor 10:23
and *e* one another .....1 Thess 5:11

EDIFYING

of the body for the *e* ......Eph 4:16

EFFECTIVELY

for He who worked *e*.......Gal 2:8
e works in you who ....1 Thess 2:13

EGG

in the white of an *e*........Job 6:6
Or if he asks for an *e*...Luke 11:12

EIGHT

a few, that is, *e*..........1 Pet 3:20

ELDER

The *e* and honorable ....Is 9:15
against an *e* except......1 Tim 5:19
I who am a fellow *e* ......1 Pet 5:1

ELDERS

and seventy of the *e*.......Ex 24:1
And teach his *e*..........Ps 105:22
and counsel from the *e*...Ezek 7:26
the tradition of the *e* ....Matt 15:2
be rejected by the *e* .....Luke 9:22
they had appointed *e* ....Acts 14:23
and called for the *e*.....Acts 20:17
e who rule well be ......1 Tim 5:17
lacking, and appoint *e*....Titus 1:5
e obtained a good.........Heb 11:2
Let him call for the *e*....James 5:14
e who are among you I ....1 Pet 5:1
I saw twenty-four *e* ....Rev 4:4

ELDERSHIP

of the hands of the *e*.....1 Tim 4:14

ELECT

whom I uphold, My *E*.......Is 42:1
and Israel My *e* ....Is 45:4
e shall long enjoy the .....Is 65:22
gather together His *e*...Matt 24:31
e have obtained it ....Rom 11:7
e according to the.........1 Pet 1:2
a chief cornerstone, *e*.....1 Pet 2:6
e sister greet you ....2 John 13

ELECTION

e they are beloved ......Rom 11:28
call and *e* sure..........2 Pet 1:10

ELEMENTS

weak and beggarly *e*.......Gal 4:9
e will melt with.........2 Pet 3:10

ELEVEN

and his *e* sons...........Gen 32:22
e disciples went away....Matt 28:16
numbered with the *e*......Acts 1:26

ELOQUENT

"O my Lord, I am not *e* ....Ex 4:10
an *e* man and mighty in...Acts 18:24

EMBALM

to *e* his father...........Gen 50:2

EMBANKMENT

will build an *e*.........Luke 19:43

EMERALDS

for your wares *e* ....Ezek 27:16

EMPTY

appear before Me *e*........Ex 23:15
e things which ....1 Sam 12:21
not listen to *e* talk ......Job 35:13

EMPTY-HEADED (cont.)

Lord makes the earth *e* . . . . . Is 24:1
comes, he finds it *e* . . . . . Matt 12:44
He has sent away *e* . . . . . . Luke 1:53
you with *e* words . . . . Eph 5:6

EMPTY-HEADED

e man will be wise. . . . . . . Job 11:12

ENABLED

our Lord who has *e* . . . . . . 1 Tim 1:12

ENCHANTER

and the expert *e* . . . . Is 3:3

ENCOURAGED

is, that I may be *e* . . . . Rom 1:12
and all may be *e* . . . . 1 Cor 14:31
their hearts may be *e* . . . . . . Col 2:2

END

yet your latter *e* . . . . Job 8:7
make me to know my *e* . . . . . Ps 39:4
shall keep it to the *e* . . . . . . Ps 119:33
e is the way of death. . . . Prov 14:12
There was no *e* of all . . . . . Eccl 4:16
Declaring the *e* . . . . Is 46:10
Our *e* was near. . . . . Lam 4:18
whose iniquity shall *e* . . . Ezek 21:25
what shall be the *e* . . . . Dan 12:8
e has come upon my . . . . . . Amos 8:2
the harvest is the *e* . . . . . Matt 13:39
to pass, but the *e* . . . . Matt 24:6
always, even to the *e* . . . . Matt 28:20
He loved them to the *e* . . . John 13:1
For Christ is the *e* . . . . Rom 10:4
the hope firm to the *e* . . . . . Heb 3:6
but now, once at the *e* . . . . Heb 9:26
of Job and seen the *e* . . . James 5:11
But the *e* of all . . . . 1 Pet 4:7
what will be the *e* . . . . 1 Pet 4:17
the latter *e* is worse . . . . . 2 Pet 2:20
My works until the *e* . . . . . Rev 2:26
Beginning and the *E* . . . . . Rev 22:13

ENDEAVORING

e to keep the unity. . . . . Eph 4:3

ENDLESS

and *e* genealogies . . . . 1 Tim 1:4
to the power of an *e* . . . . . . Heb 7:16

ENDS

All the *e* of the world . . . . . Ps 22:27
established all the *e* . . . . . Prov 30:4
she came from the *e* . . . . Matt 12:42
to the *e* of the . . . . Acts 13:47
their words to the *e* . . . . . Rom 10:18

ENDURANCE

For you have need of *e* . . . Heb 10:36
e the race that . . . . Heb 12:1

ENDURE

But the Lord shall *e* . . . . . . Ps 9:7
as the sun and moon *e* . . . . . Ps 72:5
His name shall *e* . . . . Ps 72:17
nor does a crown *e* . . . . . . Prov 27:24
"Can your heart *e* . . . . . Ezek 22:14
being persecuted, we . . . 1 Cor 4:12
Therefore I *e* all. . . . . 2 Tim 2:10
them blessed who *e* . . . . James 5:11

ENDURED

what persecutions I *e* . . . 2 Tim 3:11
he had patiently *e* . . . . . . Heb 6:15
e as seeing Him who is . . Heb 11:27
For consider Him who *e* . . Heb 12:3

ENDURES

And His truth *e* . . . . Ps 100:5
For His mercy *e* . . . . Ps 136:1

But he who *e* to the . . . . Matt 10:22
e only for a while . . . . . . Matt 13:21
for the food which *e* . . . . John 6:27
he has built on it *e*. . . . . 1 Cor 3:14
hopes all things, *e* . . . . . 1 Cor 13:7
is the man who *e* . . . . . James 1:12
the word of the Lord *e* . . . 1 Pet 1:25

ENDURING

the Lord is clean, *e* . . . . . . Ps 19:9
e possession for . . . . Heb 10:34

ENEMIES

Your *e* be scattered . . . . . Num 10:35
delivers me from my *e* . . . . Ps 18:48
the presence of my *e* . . . . . Ps 23:5
Let not my *e* triumph. . . . . Ps 25:2
But my *e* are vigorous . . . . Ps 38:19
e will lick the dust . . . . Ps 72:9
me wiser than my *e* . . . . . Ps 119:98
I count them my *e* . . . . . Ps 139:22
e are the men of his . . . . . . Mic 7:6
to you, love your *e* . . . . . . Matt 5:44
e will be those. . . . . Matt 10:36
be saved from our *e* . . . . . Luke 1:71
e we were reconciled . . . . Rom 5:10
the gospel they are *e* . . . Rom 11:28
till He has put all *e* . . . 1 Cor 15:25
were alienated and *e* . . . . . Col 1:21
His *e* are made His . . . . . Heb 10:13
and devours their *e*. . . . . . Rev 11:5

ENEMY

then I will be an *e* . . . . . . Ex 23:22
regard me as Your *e* . . . . Job 13:24
He counts me as His *e* . . . Job 33:10
or have plundered my *e* . . . . Ps 7:4
You may silence the *e* . . . . . Ps 8:2
e does not triumph. . . . . . . Ps 41:11
e who reproaches my . . . . Ps 55:12
e has persecuted my . . . . Ps 143:3
If your *e* is hungry . . . . . Prov 25:21
e are deceitful . . . . Prov 27:6
with the wound of an *e* . . . Jer 30:14
rejoice over me, my *e* . . . . . Mic 7:8
and hate your *e* . . . . Matt 5:43
last *e* that will be. . . . . . 1 Cor 15:26
become your *e* because . . . . Gal 4:16
not count him as an *e* . . 2 Thess 3:15
makes himself an *e* . . . . . James 4:4

ENGRAVE

two onyx stones and *e* . . . . Ex 28:9
e its inscription . . . . Zech 3:9

ENJOY

e its sabbaths as long . . . Lev 26:34
therefore *e* pleasure . . . . . Eccl 2:1
richly all things to *e* . . . . 1 Tim 6:17
than to *e* the passing. . . . Heb 11:25

ENJOYMENT

So I commended *e* . . . . . . Eccl 8:15

ENLARGES

He *e* nations . . . . Job 12:23
e his desire as hell . . . . . . Hab 2:5

ENLIGHTEN

E my eyes . . . . Ps 13:3
the Lord my God will *e* . . . Ps 18:28

ENLIGHTENED

those who were once *e* . . . . Heb 6:4

ENMITY

And I will put *e* . . . . Gen 3:15
the carnal mind is *e* . . . . . . Rom 8:7
in His flesh the *e* . . . . . . Eph 2:15
putting to death the *e* . . . . Eph 2:16

with the world is *e* . . . . . James 4:4

ENOUGH

never say, "*E* . . . . Prov 30:15
It is *e*. . . . . Mark 14:41
servants have bread *e*. . . . Luke 15:17

ENRAGED

being exceedingly *e* . . . . . Acts 26:11
And the dragon was *e* . . . . Rev 12:17

ENRAPTURED

and always be *e* . . . . Prov 5:19

ENRICHED

that you were *e*. . . . . 1 Cor 1:5
while you are *e* . . . . 2 Cor 9:11

ENSNARED

The wicked is *e* . . . . Prov 12:13

ENSNARES

sin which so easily *e* . . . . . Heb 12:1

ENTANGLE

how they might *e* . . . . . . Matt 22:15

ENTANGLES

engaged in warfare *e* . . . . . 2 Tim 2:4

ENTER

E into His gates . . . . Ps 100:4
Do not *e* into judgment . . . Ps 143:2
E into the rock. . . . . Is 2:10
He shall *e* into peace. . . . . . . Is 57:2
you will by no means *e* . . . Matt 5:20
"*E* by the narrow . . . . Matt 7:13
e the kingdom of God . . Matt 19:24
E into the joy of your . . . Matt 25:21
and pray, lest you *e* . . . . Matt 26:41
"Strive to *e* through. . . . . Luke 13:24
you, he who does not *e* . . . John 10:1
who have believed do *e* . . . Heb 4:3
e the Holiest by the . . . . . Heb 10:19
e the temple till the . . . . . Rev 15:8
e through the gates . . . . . Rev 22:14

ENTERED

Then Satan *e* Judas . . . . . Luke 22:3
through one man sin *e* . . . Rom 5:12
ear heard, nor have *e* . . . . 1 Cor 2:9
the forerunner has *e* . . . . . Heb 6:20
e the Most Holy Place. . . . Heb 9:12

ENTERS

If anyone *e* by Me. . . . . . John 10:9
e the Presence behind . . . . Heb 6:19

ENTHRONED

You are holy, *e* in. . . . . Ps 22:3

ENTICED

his own desires and *e* . . . . James 1:14

ENTICING

e speech she caused . . . . . Prov 7:21

ENTIRELY

give yourself *e* . . . . 1 Tim 4:15

ENTRANCE

The *e* of Your words . . . . Ps 119:130
e will be supplied . . . . . . 2 Pet 1:11

ENTREAT

"*E* me not to leave you . . . Ruth 1:16
"But now *e* God's favor . . . Mal 1:9
being defamed, we *e* . . . . 1 Cor 4:13

ENTREATED

man of God *e* the Lord. . . 1 Kin 13:6
e our God for this . . . . . . Ezra 8:23

ENVIOUS

For I was e of the..........Ps 73:3
Do not be e of evil........Prov 24:1
patriarchs, becoming e ....Acts 7:9

ENVY

e slays a simple............Job 5:2
e the oppressor.........Prov 3:31
e is rottenness.........Prov 14:30
not let your heart e......Prov 23:17
e have now perished.......Eccl 9:6
full of e.................Rom 1:29
not in strife and e......Rom 13:13
love does not e..........1 Cor 13:4
e, murders...............Gal 5:21
living in malice and e.....Titus 3:3
For where e and ....James 3:16
deceit, hypocrisy, e........1 Pet 2:1

EPISTLE

You are our e written......2 Cor 3:2
you are an e ....2 Cor 3:3
by word or our e.......2 Thess 2:15
our word in this e.....2 Thess 3:14
is a sign in every e.....2 Thess 3:17

EPISTLES

e of commendation to .....2 Cor 3:1
as also in all his e........2 Pet 3:16

EQUAL

it was you, a man my e ....Ps 55:13
and you made them e...Matt 20:12
making Himself e........John 5:18
it robbery to be e.........Phil 2:6

EQUALITY

that there may be e......2 Cor 8:14

EQUITY

You have established e.....Ps 99:4
judgment, and e ....Prov 1:3
and e cannot enter........Is 59:14
and pervert all e ....Mic 3:9
with Me in peace and e ...Mal 2:6

ERR

you cause you to e.........Is 3:12
My people Israel to e .....Jer 23:13

ERROR

God that it was an e ......Eccl 5:6
e which was due.........Rom 1:27
a sinner from the e.......James 5:20
led away with the e .....2 Pet 3:17
and the spirit of e ....1 John 4:6
run greedily in the e ......Jude 11

ERRORS

can understand his e ......Ps 19:12

ESCAPE

E to the mountains .....Gen 19:17
and they shall not e .....Job 11:20
Shall they e by ....Ps 56:7
speaks lies will not e.....Prov 19:5
and how shall we e.........Is 20:6
e all these things .....Luke 21:36
same, that you will e......Rom 2:3
also make the way of e ..1 Cor 10:13
how shall we e if we......Heb 2:3
e who refused Him who..Heb 12:25

ESCAPED

my flesh, and I have e ....Job 19:20
Our soul has e as a........Ps 124:7
after they have e........2 Pet 2:20

ESTABLISH

to e them forever ....2 Chr 9:8

'Your seed I will e..........Ps 89:4
e the work of our..........Ps 90:17
E Your word to Your......Ps 119:38
e an everlasting........Ezek 16:60
e justice in the gate .....Amos 5:15
seeking to e their own.....Rom 10:3
faithful, who will e........2 Thess 3:3
E your hearts ....James 5:8
a while, perfect, e........1 Pet 5:10

ESTABLISHED

also is firmly e.........1 Chr 16:30
David my father be e......2 Chr 1:9
a rock, and e my steps......Ps 40:2
e a testimony in Jacob......Ps 78:5
Your throne is e..........Ps 93:2
let all your ways be e ....Prov 4:26
e the clouds above.......Prov 8:28
lip shall be e forever ....Prov 12:19
house shall be e...........Is 2:2
by His power, He has e....Jer 10:12
built up in Him and e......Col 2:7
covenant, which was e.....Heb 8:6
that the heart be e........Heb 13:9

ESTABLISHES

The king e the land by ....Prov 29:4
Now He who e us with ..2 Cor 1:21

ESTEEM

high wall in his own e....Prov 18:11
and we did not e ....Is 53:3
e others better than.......Phil 2:3
and hold such men in e ....Phil 2:29
e them very highly.....1 Thess 5:13

ESTEEMED

For what is highly e.....Luke 16:15
those who are least e......1 Cor 6:4

ESTEEMS

One person e one day .....Rom 14:5

ESTRANGED

The wicked are e...........Ps 58:3
because they are all e....Ezek 14:5
You have become e ....Gal 5:4

ETERNAL

e God is your refuge....Deut 33:27
For man goes to his e .....Eccl 12:5
I do that I may have e..Matt 19:16
and inherit e life........Matt 19:29
in the age to come, e ....Mark 10:30
not perish but have e ....John 3:15
you think you have e .....John 5:39
And I give them e life...John 10:28
that He should give e....John 17:2
"And this is e life.......John 17:3
e life to those who by .....Rom 2:7
the gift of God is e ......Rom 6:23
e weight of glory ....2 Cor 4:17
are not seen are e ....2 Cor 4:18
not made with hands, e....2 Cor 5:1
lay hold on e life ....1 Tim 6:12
e life which God ....Titus 1:2
and of e judgment ....Heb 6:2
e life which was ....1 John 1:2
that no murderer has e ..1 John 3:15
God has given us e .....1 John 5:11
that you have e life ......1 John 5:13
Jesus Christ unto e ......Jude 21

ETERNITY

Also He has put e ....Eccl 3:11
One who inhabits e ....Is 57:15

EUNUCH

of Ethiopia, a e ....Acts 8:27

EUNUCHS

have made themselves e Matt 19:12

EVANGELIST

of Philip the e ....Acts 21:8
do the work of an e.......2 Tim 4:5

EVANGELISTS

some prophets, some e ....Eph 4:11

EVEN

E in laughter the........Prov 14:13
E a child is known ......Prov 20:11
e nature itself teach.....1 Cor 11:14
e denying the Lord who....2 Pet 2:1

EVENING

At e they return ....Ps 59:6
e it is cut down and ....Ps 90:6
of my hands as the e.....Ps 141:2
e do not withhold your ....Eccl 11:6
and more fierce than e.....Hab 1:8

EVERLASTING

God of Israel from e ....1 Chr 16:36
of the LORD is from e ....Ps 103:17
righteousness is an e ...Ps 119:142
Your kingdom is an e ....Ps 145:13
in YAH, the LORD, is e......Is 26:4
will be to you an e ....Is 60:19
from E is Your name ....Is 63:16
awake, some to e life .....Dan 12:2
not perish but have e .....John 3:16
Him who sent Me has e....John 5:24
endures to e life..........John 6:27
in Him may have e........John 6:40
believes in Me has e.....John 6:47
unworthy of e life ....Acts 13:46
of the Spirit reap e ....Gal 6:8
e destruction from the...2 Thess 1:9

EVERYONE

said, 'Repent now e ....Jer 25:5
e who is born of the ......John 3:8
E who is of the truth ....John 18:37

EVIDENCE

e of things not seen.......Heb 11:1

EVIDENT

the sight of God is e........Gal 3:11
of some are clearly e.....1 Tim 5:25
e that our Lord arose.....Heb 7:14

EVIL

of good and e ....Gen 2:9
knowing good and e........Gen 3:5
his heart was only e.......Gen 6:5
e have been the.........Gen 47:9
rebellious and e city .....Ezra 4:12
e shall touch you........Job 5:19
I looked for good, e......Job 30:26
nor shall e dwell ....Ps 5:4
I will fear no e............Ps 23:4
E shall slay the..........Ps 34:21
he does not abhor e ....Ps 36:4
e more than good ....Ps 52:3
e shall befall you.........Ps 91:10
To do e is like sport......Prov 10:23
shall be filled with e.....Prov 12:21
e will bow before the....Prov 14:19
keeping watch on the e...Prov 15:3
Whoever rewards e ....Prov 17:13
e will not depart ....Prov 17:13
e all the days of her ....Prov 31:12
There is a severe e ....Eccl 5:13
of men are full of e......Eccl 9:3
to those who call e.........Is 5:20
is taken away from e ......Is 57:1
of peace and not of e.....Jer 29:11

commit this great *e* . . . . . . .Jer 44:7
Seek good and not *e* . . . . .Amos 5:14
deliver us from the *e* . . . . .Matt 6:13
If you then, being *e* . . . . .Matt 7:11
"Why do you think *e* . . . . .Matt 9:4
e treasure brings. . . . . . .Matt 12:35
everyone practicing *e* . . . .John 3:20
bear witness of the *e* . . . .John 18:23
e I will not to do . . . . .Rom 7:19
then a law, that *e* . . . . .Rom 7:21
done any good or *e* . . . . . .Rom 9:11
Abhor what is *e* . . . . .Rom 12:9
Repay no one *e* for . . . . . .Rom 12:17
not be overcome by *e* . . . .Rom 12:21
simple concerning *e*. . . . .Rom 16:19
provoked, thinks no *e* . . . .1 Cor 13:5
from every form of *e* . .1 Thess 5:22

EVIL-MINDEDNESS

strife, deceit, *e*. . . . . .Rom 1:29

EVILDOER

"If He were not an *e* . . .John 18:30
suffer trouble as an *e* . . . .2 Tim 2:9
a thief, an *e*. . . . . .1 Pet 4:15

EVILDOERS

e shall be cut off. . . . . .Ps 37:9
Depart from me, you *e* . .Ps 119:115
iniquity, a brood of *e*. . . . . . . .Is 1:4
e shall never be . . . . .Is 14:20
against you as *e* . . . . .1 Pet 2:12

EVILS

e have surrounded me. . . . . .Ps 40:12
have committed two *e*. . . . .Jer 2:13

EXALT

God, and I will *e* . . . . .Ex 15:2
e the horn of His . . . . . . .1 Sam 2:10
e His name together. . . . . . . .Ps 34:3
E the LORD our God. . . . . .Ps 99:5
are my God, I will *e* . . . . . .Ps 118:28
if I do not *e* . . . . .Ps 137:6
into heaven, I will *e*. . . . . . .Is 14:13
E the humble . . . . .Ezek 21:26
and he shall *e* himself . . . .Dan 8:25

EXALTATION

e comes neither from . . . . . . .Ps 75:6
who rejoice in My *e*. . . . . . . .Is 13:3
brother glory in his *e* . . . .James 1:9

EXALTED

Let God be *e* . . . . .2 Sam 22:47
built You an *e*. . . . . .2 Chr 6:2
name, which is *e*. . . . . .Neh 9:5
when vileness is *e*. . . . . .Ps 12:8
I will be *e* among the . . . . .Ps 46:10
righteous shall be *e*. . . . . . .Ps 75:10
favor our horn is *e*. . . . . . . .Ps 89:17
You are *e* far above. . . . . . . .Ps 97:9
His name alone is *e* . . . . .Ps 148:13
upright the city is *e* . . . . .Prov 11:11
LORD alone shall be *e* . . . . . .Is 2:11
valley shall be *e* . . . . .Is 40:4
"Him God has *e* . . . . .Acts 5:31
And lest I should be *e* . . .2 Cor 12:7
also has highly *e*. . . . . .Phil 2:9

EXALTS

Righteousness *e*. . . . . . . .Prov 14:34
high thing that *e* . . . . . . .2 Cor 10:5
e himself above all . . . . . .2 Thess 2:4

EXAMINE

E me, O LORD . . . . .Ps 26:2
But let a man *e* . . . . .1 Cor 11:28
But let each one *e*. . . . . .Gal 6:4

EXAMPLE

to make her a public *e* . . . .Matt 1:19
I have given you an *e*. . . .John 13:15
in following my *e* . . . . .Phil 3:17
to make ourselves an *e* . .2 Thess 3:9
youth, but be an *e*. . . . . . .1 Tim 4:12
us, leaving us an *e*. . . . . . .1 Pet 2:21
making them an *e* . . . . . . .2 Pet 2:6
are set forth as an *e*. . . . . . .Jude 7

EXAMPLES

happened to them as *e* . .1 Cor 10:11
so that you became *e*. . . .1 Thess 1:7
to you, but being *e*. . . . . . . .1 Pet 5:3

EXCEEDING

He might show the *e*. . . . . . .Eph 2:7

EXCEEDINGLY

for the LORD must be *e*. . .1 Chr 22:5
You have made him *e* . . . . . .Ps 21:6
is far off and *e* deep. . . . . .Eccl 7:24
e high mountain . . . . .Matt 4:8
"Rejoice and be *e* . . . . . . .Matt 5:12

EXCEEDS

your righteousness *e* . . . . .Matt 5:20

EXCEL

you His angels, who *e* . . . .Ps 103:20
but you *e* them all. . . . . . .Prov 31:29
that you seek to *e* . . . . . .1 Cor 14:12

EXCELLENCE

e You have overthrown. . . . . .Ex 15:7
did not come with *e*. . . . . . .1 Cor 2:1

EXCELLENT

He is *e* in power . . . . .Job 37:23
It shall be as *e* . . . . .Ps 141:5
will speak of *e* things . . . . .Prov 8:6
like Lebanon, *e* . . . . .Song 5:15
for He has done *e* . . . . .Is 12:5
in counsel and *e* . . . . .Is 28:29
"Inasmuch as an *e*. . . . . . .Dan 5:12
the things that are *e*. . . . . .Rom 2:18
the things that are *e*. . . . . . .Phil 1:10
e sacrifice than Cain . . . . .Heb 11:4
came to Him from the *E* . .2 Pet 1:17

EXCELS

Do you see a man who *e*. .Prov 22:29
I saw that wisdom *e* . . . . .Eccl 2:13
of the glory that *e* . . . . . .2 Cor 3:10

EXCHANGE

man give in *e* for his soul Matt 16:26

EXCHANGED

nor can it be *e*. . . . . .Job 28:17
e the truth of God for. . . . .Rom 1:25
For even their women *e* . . .Rom 1:26

EXCLUDE

you, and when they *e*. . . . .Luke 6:22
they want to *e* you . . . . .Gal 4:17

EXCUSE

God be angry at your *e*. . . .Eccl 5:6
but now they have no *e* . .John 15:22
they are without *e*. . . . . . . .Rom 1:20
do you think that we *e* . .2 Cor 12:19

EXCUSES

accord began to make *e* . .Luke 14:18

EXECUTE

e vengeance on the. . . . . . .Ps 149:7
if you thoroughly *e* . . . . . . .Jer 7:5
e the fierceness. . . . . .Hos 11:9
e judgment also . . . . .John 5:27

e wrath on him who . . . . . .Rom 13:4

EXECUTES

by the judgment He *e* . . . . . .Ps 9:16
e righteousness . . . . .Ps 103:6
e justice for the. . . . . .Ps 146:7
e justice for me. . . . . .Mic 7:9

EXERCISE

those who are great *e*. . . .Matt 20:25
e yourself toward. . . . . . . .1 Tim 4:7
e profits a little . . . . .1 Tim 4:8

EXERCISED

have their senses *e*. . . . . . .Heb 5:14

EXHORT

we command and *e* . . . .2 Thess 3:12
e him as a father . . . . .1 Tim 5:1
and *e* these things. . . . . . . .1 Tim 6:2
doctrine, both to *e* . . . . . . .Titus 1:9
Speak these things, *e*. . . . .Titus 2:15
e one another . . . . .Heb 3:13

EXHORTATION

you have any word of *e*. . .Acts 13:15
he who exhorts, in *e* . . . . . .Rom 12:8
to reading, to *e* . . . . .1 Tim 4:13
with the word of *e* . . . . . . .Heb 13:22

EXHORTED

For I earnestly *e* . . . . .Jer 11:7
e and strengthened . . . . .Acts 15:32
as you know how we *e*. .1 Thess 2:11

EXILE

and also an *e* from . . . . .2 Sam 15:19
The captive *e* hastens . . . . . .Is 51:14

EXIST

things which do not *e*. . . . . .Rom 4:17
by Your will they *e* . . . . . . .Rev 4:11

EXPECT

an hour you do not *e* . . . .Luke 12:40

EXPECTATION

The *e* of the poor. . . . . .Ps 9:18
God alone, for my *e* . . . . . .Ps 62:5
the people were in *e* . . . . .Luke 3:15
a certain fearful *e*. . . . . . .Heb 10:27

EXPERT

and the *e* enchanter. . . . . .Is 3:3
those of an *e* warrior. . . . . .Jer 50:9
because you are *e* . . . . . . .Acts 26:3

EXPLAIN

was no one who could *e*. . .Gen 41:24
days they could not *e*. . . .Judg 14:14
"*E* this parable to us . . . .Matt 15:15
to say, and hard to *e* . . . . .Heb 5:11

EXPLAINED

He *e* all things to His . . . .Mark 4:34

EXPLOIT

e all your. . . . . .Is 58:3
against those who *e*. . . . . . .Mal 3:5
they will *e* you with . . . . . .2 Pet 2:3

EXPOSED

his deeds should be *e*. . . . .John 3:20
all things that are *e*. . . . . . .Eph 5:13

EXPOUNDED

He *e* to them in all . . . . .Luke 24:27

EXPRESS

man cannot *e* it . . . . .Eccl 1:8
of His glory and the *e*. . . . .Heb 1:3

EXPRESSLY

of the LORD came e....... Ezek 1:3
Now the Spirit e .... 1 Tim 4:1

EXTEND

none to e mercy to him ...Ps 109:12
"Behold, I will e........... Is 66:12
did not e to you .... 2 Cor 10:14

EXTINGUISHED

broken, my days are e..... Job 17:1
they are e .... Is 43:17

EXTOL

I will e You .... Ps 30:1
e Him who rides .... Ps 68:4

EXTOLLED

shall be exalted and e ..... Is 52:13

EXTORTION

e gathers it for him...... Prov 28:8
your neighbors by e .... Ezek 22:12
they are full of e .... Matt 23:25

EXTORTIONERS

e will inherit .... 1 Cor 6:10

EXULT

in anguish I would e...... Job 6:10

EYE

"e for e .... Ex 21:24
the ear, but now my e.... Job 42:5
guide you with My e ...... Ps 32:8
Behold, the e of the ...... Ps 33:18
He who formed the e ...... Ps 94:9
and the seeing e........ Prov 20:12
who has a generous e ... Prov 22:9
A man with an evil e .... Prov 28:22
e that mocks his .... Prov 30:17
e is not satisfied....... Eccl 1:8
labors, nor is his e........ Eccl 4:8
for they shall see e.......... Is 52:8
e seen any God besides...... Is 64:4
the apple of His e .... Zech 2:8
if your right e .... Matt 5:29
it was said, 'An e .... Matt 5:38
plank in your own e ...... Matt 7:3
e causes you to sin...... Matt 18:9
Or is your e evil .... Matt 20:15
e causes you sin...... Mark 9:47
the e of a needle .... Luke 18:25
"Because I am not an e .1 Cor 12:16
whole body were an e ....1 Cor 12:17
the twinkling of an e....1 Cor 15:52
every e will see Him....... Rev 1:7
your eyes with e salve .... Rev 3:18

EYELIDS

His eyes behold, His e...... Ps 11:4
e look right before....... Prov 4:25

EYES

e will be opened .... Gen 3:5
and you can be our e ....Num 10:31
she put paint on her e....2 Kin 9:30
"For the e of the ....2 Chr 16:9
Do You have e of flesh .... Job 10:4
and my e shall behold....Job 19:27
I was e to the blind ..... Job 29:15
e observe from afar...... Job 39:29
e are secretly fixed ...... Ps 10:8
e are ever toward the ..... Ps 25:15
The e of the LORD are..... Ps 34:15
e fail while I wait .... Ps 69:3
e shall you look........... Ps 91:8
I will lift up my e .... Ps 121:1
not give sleep to my e ... Ps 132:4
e saw my substance ..... Ps 139:16

e look straight ahead .... Prov 4:25
but the e of a fool ...... Prov 17:24
Will you set your e ...... Prov 23:5
Who has redness of e .... Prov 23:29
be wise in his own e ..... Prov 26:5
so the e of man are ..... Prov 27:20
The wise man's e .... Eccl 2:14
e than the wandering...... Eccl 6:9
You have dove's e ...... Song 1:15
e have seen the King........ Is 6:5
of the book, and the e .... Is 29:18
e fail from looking........ Is 38:14
O LORD, are not Your e ..... Jer 5:3
who have e and see .... Jer 5:21
e will weep bitterly ...... Jer 13:17
For I will set My e .... Jer 24:6
rims were full of e...... Ezek 1:18
full of e all around ..... Ezek 10:12
that horn which had e .... Dan 7:20
horn between his e........ Dan 8:5
You are of purer e....... Hab 1:13
But blessed are your e ... Matt 13:16
"He put clay on my e.... John 9:15
e they have closed...... Acts 28:27
e that they should not .... Rom 11:8
plucked out your own e ...Gal 4:15
have seen with our e ....1 John 1:1
the lust of the e........1 John 2:16
as snow, and His e .... Rev 1:14
and anoint your e .... Rev 3:18
creatures full of e .... Rev 4:6
horns and seven e....... Rev 5:6
tear from their e .... Rev 21:4

EYESERVICE

not with e .... Eph 6:6
the flesh, not with e ...... Col 3:22

EYEWITNESSES

the beginning were e ..... Luke 1:2
e of His majesty........ 2 Pet 1:16

F

FABLES

nor give heed to f ....1 Tim 1:4
be turned aside to f......2 Tim 4:4
cunningly devised f .....2 Pet 1:16

FACE

"For I have seen God f ...Gen 32:30
f shone while he .... Ex 34:29
he put a veil on his f ..... Ex 34:33
the LORD make His f .....Num 6:25
Then he turned his f ....2 Kin 20:2
curse You to Your f...... Job 1:11
me, I will see Your f ..... Ps 17:15
Why do You hide Your f... Ps 44:24
and cause His f .... Ps 67:1
of his f is changed .... Eccl 8:1
sins have hidden His f...... Is 59:2
I have made your f....... Ezek 3:8
but to us shame of f ...... Dan 9:7
before Your f who .... Matt 11:10
f shone like the sun ..... Matt 17:2
always before my f ...... Acts 2:25
dimly, but then f ....1 Cor 13:12
look steadily at the f.....2 Cor 3:7
with unveiled f ....2 Cor 3:18
withstood him to his f ....Gal 2:11
his natural f in a........ James 1:23
but the f of the LORD....1 Pet 3:12
They shall see His f ...... Rev 22:4

FACES

f were not ashamed........ Ps 34:5
hid, as it were, our f ...... Is 53:3
be afraid of their f ...... Jer 1:8
and all f turned pale ...... Jer 30:6

they disfigure their f ..... Matt 6:16

FACTIONS

there must also be f.....1 Cor 11:19

FADE

we all f as a leaf........... Is 64:6
and the leaf shall f........ Jer 8:13
rich man also will f..... James 1:11
and that does not f.......1 Pet 1:4

FADES

withers, the flower f .... Is 40:7

FAIL

eyes shall look and f.... Deut 28:32
flesh and my heart f...... Ps 73:26
of the thirsty to f........... Is 32:6
their tongues f............ Is 41:17
whose waters do not f..... Is 58:11
have caused wine to f .... Jer 48:33
of the olive may f........ Hab 3:17
nor shall the vine f...... Mal 3:11
that when you f....... Luke 16:9
tittle of the law to f .... Luke 16:17
faith should not f .... Luke 22:32
they will f.............. 1 Cor 13:8
Your years will not f ..... Heb 1:12
For the time would f ..... Heb 11:32

FAILED

Not a word f of any..... Josh 21:45
My relatives have f...... Job 19:14
refuge has f me........... Ps 142:4

FAILING

"men's hearts f........ Luke 21:26

FAILS

my strength f because .... Ps 31:10
my spirit f............... Ps 143:7
and every vision f...... Ezek 12:22
Love never f .... 1 Cor 13:8

FAINT

the youths shall f.......... Is 40:30
shall walk and not f....... Is 40:31
my heart is f in me ...... Jer 8:18
and the infants f .... Lam 2:11

FAINTED

thirsty, their soul f....... Ps 107:5

FAINTHEARTED

unruly, comfort the f...1 Thess 5:14

FAINTS

longs, yes, even f.......... Ps 84:2
My soul f for Your ..... Ps 119:81
and the whole heart f...... Is 1:5
the earth, neither f .... Is 40:28

FAIR

Behold, you are f......... Song 1:15
of the Lord is not f.....Ezek 18:25
to a place called F....... Acts 27:8
what is just and f .... Col 4:1

FAIR-MINDED

These were more f...... Acts 17:11

FAIRER

f than the sons .... Ps 45:2

FAIREST

another beloved, O f..... Song 5:9
your beloved gone, O f.... Song 6:1

FAITH

in whom is no f......... Deut 32:20
shall live by his f.......... Hab 2:4

you, O you of little *f*......Matt 6:30
not found such great *f*....Matt 8:10
f as a mustard seed.....Matt 17:20
it that you have no *f*....Mark 4:40
to them, "Have *f*......Mark 11:22
"Increase our *f*........Luke 17:5
will He really find *f*.....Luke 18:8
a man full of *f*.........Acts 6:5
are sanctified by *f*......Acts 26:18
for obedience to the *f*.....Rom 1:5
God is revealed from *f*....Rom 1:17
God, through *f*...........Rom 3:22
f apart from the deeds ....Rom 3:28
his *f* is accounted for......Rom 4:5
f is made void and the ....Rom 4:14
those who are of the *f*....Rom 4:16
f which we preach .....Rom 10:8
f comes by hearing .....Rom 10:17
and you stand by *f*.....Rom 11:20
in proportion to our *f*....Rom 12:6
Do you have *f*.........Rom 14:22
he does not eat from *f*....Rom 14:23
though I have all *f*.....1 Cor 13:2
And now abide *f*.......1 Cor 13:13
For we walk by *f*.......2 Cor 5:7
the flesh I live by *f*.......Gal 2:20
or by the hearing of *f*.....Gal 3:2
f are sons of Abraham .....Gal 3:7
the law is not of *f*........Gal 3:12
But after *f* has come......Gal 3:25
f working through love.....Gal 5:6
of the household of *f*......Gal 6:10
been saved through *f*......Eph 2:8
one Lord, one *f*...........Eph 4:5
to the unity of the *f*......Eph 4:13
taking the shield of *f*.....Eph 6:16
ceasing your work of *f*...1 Thess 1:3
for not all have *f*......2 Thess 3:2
having *f* and a good .....1 Tim 1:19
the mystery of the *f*......1 Tim 3:9
he has denied the *f*......1 Tim 5:8
I have kept the *f*........2 Tim 4:7
in our common *f*........Titus 1:4
not being mixed with *f*....Heb 4:2
f is the substance........Heb 11:1
f it is ....Heb 11:6
someone says he has *f*...James 2:14
Show me your *f*........James 2:18
and not by *f* only ......James 2:24
f will save the sick .....James 5:15
add to your *f* virtue .....2 Pet 1:5
on your most holy *f*.......Jude 20
the patience and the *f* ....Rev 13:10
of God and the *f*.........Rev 14:12

FAITHFUL

God, He is God, the *f*.....Deut 7:9
f disappear from among.....Ps 12:1
LORD preserves the *f*.....Ps 31:23
whose spirit was not *f*.....Ps 78:8
eyes shall be on the *f*.....Ps 101:6
f spirit conceals a ......Prov 11:13
but who can find a *f*......Prov 20:6
f witness between us......Jer 42:5
the Holy One who is *f*....Hos 11:12
"Who then is a *f*.......Matt 24:45
good and *f* servant .....Matt 25:23
"He who is *f* in what ....Luke 16:10
if you have not been *f*....Luke 16:12
have judged me to be *f*..Acts 16:15
God is *f*.................1 Cor 1:9
is my beloved and *f*.....1 Cor 4:17
But as God is *f*.........2 Cor 1:18
f brethren in Christ ....Col 1:2
He who calls you to *f*...1 Thess 5:24
This is a *f* saying and....1 Tim 1:15
f High Priest in ....Heb 2:17
as Moses also was *f*.....Heb 3:2
He who promised is *f*.....Heb 10:23

He is *f* and just to.......1 John 1:9
Be *f* until death..........Rev 2:10
words are true and *f*......Rev 21:5

FAITHFULNESS

I have declared Your *f*...Ps 40:10
f You shall establish ....Ps 89:2
Your *f* also surrounds .....Ps 89:8
and Your *f* every night.....Ps 92:2
f endures to all ....Ps 119:90
In Your *f* answer me.....Ps 143:1
counsels of old are *f*........Is 25:1
great is Your *f* ....Lam 3:23
unbelief make the *f*........Rom 3:3

FAITHLESS

"O *f* generation.........Mark 9:19
If we are *f*..............2 Tim 2:13

FALL

a deep sleep to *f*..........Gen 2:21
but do not let me *f*.....2 Sam 24:14
Let them *f* by their........Ps 5:10
For I am ready to *f*........Ps 38:17
Yes, all kings shall *f*......Ps 72:11
a righteous man may *f*...Prov 24:16
but the wicked shall *f*....Prov 24:16
digs a pit will *f*.........Prov 26:27
all their host shall *f*........Is 34:4
men shall utterly *f*.......Is 40:30
of music, you shall *f*.......Dan 3:5
And great was its *f*......Matt 7:27
the blind, both will *f*......Matt 15:14
the stars will *f*.........Matt 24:29
"I saw Satan *f*.........Luke 10:18
that they should *f*......Rom 11:11
take heed lest he *f*.....1 Cor 10:12
with pride he *f*..........1 Tim 3:6
if they *f* away ....Heb 6:6
lest anyone *f* short of.....Heb 12:15
it all joy when you *f*......James 1:2
and rocks, "F............Rev 6:16

FALLEN

"Babylon is *f* ....Is 21:9
you have *f* from grace......Gal 5:4
And I saw a star *f* ....Rev 9:1
"Babylon is *f*..............Rev 14:8

FALLING

great drops of blood *f*....Luke 22:44
f away comes first ......2 Thess 2:3

FALLS

who is alone when he *f*...Eccl 4:10
"And whoever *f*........Matt 21:44
master he stands or *f*....Rom 14:4
its flower *f*...............James 1:11
so that no rain *f* ....Rev 11:6

FALSE

"You shall not bear *f*.....Ex 20:16
I hate every *f* way.......Ps 119:104
gives heed to *f* lips ....Prov 17:4
f witness shall perish ....Prov 21:28
and do not love a *f*......Zech 8:17
"Beware of *f* prophets ....Matt 7:15
f christs and *f* ....Matt 24:24
and we are found *f*.....1 Cor 15:15
among *f* brethren ....2 Cor 11:26
of *f* brethren ....Gal 2:4
f prophets have gone.....1 John 4:1
mouth of the *f* prophet....Rev 16:13

FALSEHOOD

those who speak *f*........Ps 5:6
and brings forth *f*........Ps 7:14
for their deceit is *f*.....Ps 119:118
remove *f* and lies far .....Prov 30:8
f we have................Is 28:15

offspring of *f* ....Is 57:4

FALSELY

it, and swears *f*...........Lev 6:3
nor have we dealt *f*.......Ps 44:17
surely they swear *f*.........Jer 5:2
words, swearing *f*........Hos 10:4
of evil against you *f*.....Matt 5:11
f called knowledge.......1 Tim 6:20

FAME

Sheba heard of the *f*.....1 Kin 10:1
"Your *f* went out........Ezek 16:14
them for praise and *f*....Zeph 3:19
Then His *f* went ....Matt 4:24

FAMILIES

in you all the *f*...........Gen 12:3
and makes their *f*.......Ps 107:41
the God of all the *f*.......Jer 31:1
f which the LORD has ....Jer 33:24
in your seed all the *f*.....Acts 3:25

FAMILY

shall mourn, every *f*.....Zech 12:12
f were baptized ....Acts 16:33
from whom the whole *f*...Eph 3:15

FAMINE

Now there was a *f*.......Gen 12:10
keep them alive in *f*......Ps 33:19
He called for a *f*.........Ps 105:16
send the sword, the *f*.....Jer 24:10
of the fever of *f* ....Lam 5:10
I will increase the *f*......Ezek 5:16
there arose a severe *f*...Luke 15:14

FAMINES

And there will be *f*......Matt 24:7

FAMISH

righteous soul to *f*.......Prov 10:3

FAMISHED

honorable men are *f*.........Is 5:13

FAMOUS

and may his name be *f*...Ruth 4:14

FAN

not to *f* or to cleanse......Jer 4:11
"His winnowing *f*......Matt 3:12

FANCIES

with their own *f*.........Prov 1:31

FAR

removed my brothers *f*...Job 19:13
Your judgments are *f*.....Ps 10:5
Be not *f* from Me ....Ps 22:11
those who are *f*..........Ps 73:27
The LORD is *f* from the...Prov 15:29
but it was *f* from me .....Eccl 7:23
removed their hearts *f*.....Is 29:13
Those near and those *f*...Ezek 22:5
their heart is *f* from .....Matt 15:8
going to a *f* country.....Mark 13:34
though He is not *f*.......Acts 17:27
you who once were *f*......Eph 2:13

FARMER

The hard-working *f*.......2 Tim 2:6
See how the *f* waits .....James 5:7

FASHIONED

have made me and *f*......Job 10:8

FASHIONS

He *f* their hearts..........Ps 33:15

FAST

f as you do this day........Is 58:4
f that I have chosen ....Is 58:5
"Moreover, when you f....Matt 6:16
disciples do not f ....Matt 9:14
'I f twice a week........Luke 18:12

FASTED

'Why have we f ....Is 58:3
'When you f and ....Zech 7:5
And when He had f ......Matt 4:2

FASTENED

were its foundations f.....Job 38:6
'the peg that is f ....Is 22:25

FASTING

humbled myself with f.....Ps 35:13
are weak through f ......Ps 109:24
house on the day of f......Jer 36:6
except by prayer and f..Matt 17:21
give yourselves to f.......1 Cor 7:5

FASTINGS

in sleeplessness, in f ......2 Cor 6:5

FAT

and you will eat the f.....Gen 45:18
f is the LORD's............Lev 3:16
Now Eglon was a very f..Judg 3:17
have closed up their f......Ps 17:10

FATHER

man shall leave his f .....Gen 2:24
and you shall be a f......Gen 17:4
'You are my f...........Job 17:14
I was a f to the poor......Job 29:16
A f of the fatherless......Ps 68:5
f pities his children.......Ps 103:13
the instruction of a f......Prov 4:1
God, everlasting F..........Is 9:6
You, O LORD, are our F....Is 63:16
time cry to Me, 'My F .....Jer 3:4
for I am a F to Israel .....Jer 31:9
"A son honors his f ....Mal 1:6
Have we not all one F ....Mal 2:10
Our F in heaven ....Matt 6:9
"He who loves f ....Matt 10:37
does anyone know the F Matt 11:27
'He who curses f........Matt 15:4
for One is your F ......Matt 23:9
F will be divided.......Luke 12:53
F loves the Son.........John 3:35
F has been working .....John 5:17
F raises the dead ......John 5:21
F judges no one ....John 5:22
He has seen the F.......John 6:46
F who sent Me bears ....John 8:18
we have one F ....John 8:41
of your f the devil.......John 8:44
"I and My F are one ...John 10:30
and believe that the F....John 10:38
'I am going to the F....John 14:28
F is the vinedresser ....John 15:1
came forth from the F ...John 16:28
that he might be the f ...Rom 4:11
"I have made you a f .....Rom 4:17
"I will be a F ....2 Cor 6:18
one God and F of all .....Eph 4:6
but exhort him as a f.....1 Tim 5:1
"I will be to Him a F......Heb 1:5
without f................Heb 7:3
comes down from the F..James 1:17
if you call on the F.......1 Pet 1:17
and testify that the F...1 John 4:14

FATHER'S

you in My F kingdom ...Matt 26:29
I must be about My F...Luke 2:49
F house are many ....John 14:2
that a man has his f .....1 Cor 5:1

FATHERLESS

my hand against the f ...Job 31:21
the helper of the f......Ps 10:14
to do justice to the f......Ps 10:18
He relieves the f ....Ps 146:9
the fields of the f.......Prov 23:10
do not defend the f........Is 1:23
they may rob the f........Is 10:2
You the f finds mercy.....Hos 14:3

FATHERS

the LORD God of our f....Ezra 7:27
f trusted in You........Ps 22:4
our ears, O God, our f......Ps 44:1
have sinned with our f.....Ps 106:6
f ate the manna......John 6:31
of whom are the f ....Rom 9:5
you do not have many f..1 Cor 4:15
unaware that all our f ....1 Cor 10:1

FATLING

and the f together ....Is 11:6

FATNESS

as with marrow and f......Ps 63:5
of the root and f ....Rom 11:17

FATTED

f cattle are..............Matt 22:4
has killed the f ....Luke 15:27

FATTENED

f your hearts as ....James 5:5

FAULT

find no charge or f ....Dan 6:4
I have found no f ....Luke 23:14
does He still find f ......Rom 9:19
of God without f..........Phil 2:15
for they are without f.....Rev 14:5

FAULTLESS

covenant had been f......Heb 8:7
to present you f ....Jude 24

FAULTS

"I remember my f ....Gen 41:9
me from secret f ....Ps 19:12
are beaten for your f .....1 Pet 2:20

FAVOR

granted me life and f ....Job 10:12
f You will ....Ps 5:12
His f is for life.............Ps 30:5
A good man obtains f....Prov 12:2
but his f is like dew .....Prov 19:12
and seek the LORD's f....Jer 26:19
and stature, and in f.....Luke 2:52
God and having f........Acts 2:47
to do the Jews a f......Acts 24:27

FAVORABLE

And will He be f.........Ps 77:7
LORD, You have been f......Ps 85:1

FAVORED

because You f them........Ps 44:3
"Rejoice, highly f......Luke 1:28

FAVORITISM

do not show personal f..Luke 20:21
God shows personal f......Gal 2:6

FEAR

this and live, for I f God..Gen 42:18

f the people of the.......Num 14:9
to put the dread and f ...Deut 2:25
f Me all the days........Deut 4:10
f the LORD your God .....Deut 6:2
book, that you may f ...Deut 28:58
said, "Does Job f ....Job 1:9
Yes, you cast off f........Job 15:4
Surely no f of me will......Job 33:7
He mocks at f..........Job 39:22
they are in great f........Ps 14:5
The f of the LORD is ......Ps 19:9
of death, I will f ....Ps 23:4
whom shall I f..........Ps 27:1
Let all the earth f.........Ps 33:8
Oh, f the LORD...........Ps 34:9
there is no f of God........Ps 36:1
they are in great f........Ps 53:5
hear, all you who f......Ps 66:16
f You as long as the ......Ps 72:5
heart to f Your name .....Ps 86:11
The f of the LORD is .....Ps 111:10
f You will be glad ....Ps 119:74
f the LORD and depart ....Prov 3:7
The f of man brings a...Prov 29:25
it, that men should f......Eccl 3:14
F God and keep His .....Eccl 12:13
let Him be your f..........Is 8:13
"Be strong, do not f ....Is 35:4
Do you not f Me ....Jer 5:22
who would not f.........Jer 10:7
but I will put My f ......Jer 32:40
f My name the Sun ......Mal 4:2
f Him who is able......Matt 10:28
"Do not f ....Luke 12:32
a judge who did not f....Luke 18:2
"Do you not even f......Luke 23:40
And walking in the f......Acts 9:31
the rest also may f ......1 Tim 5:20
given us a spirit of f......2 Tim 1:7
those who through f......Heb 2:15
His rest, let us f..........Heb 4:1
because of His godly f.....Heb 5:7
F God ....1 Pet 2:17
love casts out f.........1 John 4:18
"Do not f any of ....Rev 2:10

FEARED

But the midwives f ....Ex 1:17
He is also to be f ......1 Chr 16:25
f God more than........Neh 7:2
Yourself, are to be f........Ps 76:7
Then those who f ....Mal 3:16

FEARFUL

f in praises, doing........Ex 15:11
them, "Why are you f ...Matt 8:26
It is a f thing to.........Heb 10:31

FEARFUL-HEARTED

to those who are f ....Is 35:4

FEARFULLY

f and wonderfully made ...Ps 139:14

FEARFULNESS

F and trembling have......Ps 55:5
f has seized the ....Is 33:14

FEARING

is devoted to f You ......Ps 119:38
sincerity of heart, f........Col 3:22
forsook Egypt, not f......Heb 11:27

FEARS

upright man, one who f....Job 1:8
Who is the man that f....Ps 25:12
me from all my f.........Ps 34:4
an oath as he who f........Eccl 9:2
every nation whoever f...Acts 10:35
f has not been made ....1 John 4:18

FEAST

Then he made them a *f*....Gen 19:3
and you shall keep a *f*...Num 29:12
f is made for laughter....Eccl 10:19
f day the terrors that.....Lam 2:22
hate, I despise your *f*....Amos 5:21
every year at the F......Luke 2:41
when you give a *f*......Luke 14:13
Now the Passover, a *f*.....John 6:4
great day of the *f*......John 7:37
let us keep the *f*.........1 Cor 5:8

FEASTING

go to the house of *f*.......Eccl 7:2

FEASTS

I will turn your *f*.......Amos 8:10
the best places at *f*.....Luke 20:46
spots in your love *f*.......Jude 12

FED

f me all my life long.....Gen 48:15
and *f* you with manna....Deut 8:3
but the shepherds *f*.....Ezek 34:8
f you with milk and.......1 Cor 3:2

FEEBLE

strengthened the *f*.......Job 4:4
and there was none *f*.....Ps 105:37
and my flesh is *f*........Ps 109:24
Every hand will be *f*.....Ezek 7:17
hang down, and the *f*....Heb 12:12

FEED

ravens to *f* you there.....1 Kin 17:4
death shall *f* on them......Ps 49:14
of the righteous.......Prov 10:21
and *f* your flocks..........Is 61:5
to him, "F My lambs...John 21:15
to him, "F My sheep...John 21:17
your enemy hungers, *f*...Rom 12:20
my goods to *f* the poor...1 Cor 13:3

FEEDS

"Ephraim *f* on the wind....Hos 12:1
your heavenly Father *f*...Matt 6:26

FEET

So she lay at his *f*.......Ruth 3:14
so my *f* did not slip...2 Sam 22:37
f they hang far..........Job 28:4
I was *f* to the lame......Job 29:15
all things under his *f*....Ps 8:6
He makes my *f* like the...Ps 18:33
You have set my *f*.........Ps 31:8
does not allow our *f*....Ps 66:9
f had almost stumbled.....Ps 73:2
f have been standing......Ps 122:2
for their *f* run to........Prov 1:16
Her *f* go down to death...Prov 5:5
sandals off your *f*.......Is 20:2
called him to His *f*.......Is 41:2
up the dust of your *f*....Is 49:23
mountains are the *f*....Is 52:7
place of My *f* glorious.....Is 60:13
are the dust of His *f*....Nah 1:3
in that day His *f*........Zech 14:4
two hands or two *f*....Matt 18:8
began to wash His *f*....Luke 7:38
also sat at Jesus' *f*.....Luke 10:39
wash the disciples' *f*....John 13:5
at the apostles' *f*......Acts 4:35
f are swift to shed.......Rom 3:15
beautiful are the *f*......Rom 10:15
all things under His *f*...1 Cor 15:27
and having shod your *f*...Eph 6:15
fell at His *f* as dead......Rev 1:17
And I fell at his *f*......Rev 19:10

FELLOW

f servants who owed.....Matt 18:28
begins to beat his *f*.....Matt 24:49
f worker concerning.....2 Cor 8:23
f citizens with the.......Eph 2:19
Gentiles should be *f*......Eph 3:6
rest of my *f* workers......Phil 4:3
These are my only *f*.......Col 4:11
that we may become *f*.....3 John 8
I am your *f* servant.....Rev 19:10

FELLOWSHIP

doctrine and *f*..........Acts 2:42
were called into the *f*....1 Cor 1:9
not want you to have *f*..1 Cor 10:20
f has righteousness.....2 Cor 6:14
the right hand of *f*......Gal 2:9
And have no *f* with the...Eph 5:11
for your *f* in the.........Phil 1:5
of love, if any *f*.........Phil 2:1
and the *f* of His.........Phil 3:10
also may have *f*.........1 John 1:3
we say that we have *f*...1 John 1:6
the light, we have *f*.....1 John 1:7

FENCE

and a tottering *f*.........Ps 62:3

FENCED

He has *f* up my way......Job 19:8

FERTILIZE

I dig around it and *f*.....Luke 13:8

FERVENT

and being *f* in spirit.....Acts 18:25
f prayer of a..........James 5:16
all things have *f*........1 Pet 4:8
will melt with *f*.........2 Pet 3:10

FERVENTLY

you, always laboring *f*.....Col 4:12
love one another *f*.......1 Pet 1:22

FESTIVAL

night when a holy *f*........Is 30:29
or regarding a *f*..........Col 2:16

FETCH

f my knowledge from.....Job 36:3

FETTERS

hurt his feet with *f*......Ps 105:18
their nobles with *f*.......Ps 149:8

FEVER

f which shall...........Lev 26:16
my bones burn with *f*....Job 30:30
and rebuked the *f*.......Luke 4:39

FEW

f and evil have been......Gen 47:9
f days and full of........Job 14:1
Let his days be *f*.........Ps 109:8
let your words be *f*.......Eccl 5:2
and there are *f*........Matt 7:14
but the laborers are *f*....Matt 9:37
called, but *f* chosen......Matt 20:16
"Lord, are there *f*.......Luke 13:23
prepared, in which a *f*...1 Pet 3:20
I have a *f* things..........Rev 2:20

FIDELITY

but showing all good *f*....Titus 2:10

FIELD

let the *f* be joyful.........Ps 96:12
to house; they add *f*.......Is 5:8
becomes a fruitful *f*.....Is 32:15
"The *f* is the world.....Matt 13:38

and buys that *f*........Matt 13:44
f has been called the.....Matt 27:8
you are God's *f*..........1 Cor 3:9

FIELDS

f yield no food..........Hab 3:17
living out in the *f*........Luke 2:8
eyes and look at the *f*....John 4:35

FIERCENESS

f has deceived you.......Jer 49:16
the winepress of the *f*....Rev 19:15

FIERY

the LORD sent *f* serpents..Num 21:6
right hand came a *f*......Deut 33:2
shall make them as a *f*.....Ps 21:9
offspring will be a *f*........Is 14:29
burning *f* furnace.........Dan 3:6
concerning the *f*.........1 Pet 4:12
f red dragon having.......Rev 12:3

FIG

f leaves together.........Gen 3:7
his vine and his *f*........1 Kin 4:25
fruit falling from a *f*......Is 34:4
f tree may not blossom....Hab 3:17
fruit on this *f*..........Luke 13:7
"Look at the *f*.........Luke 21:29
'I saw you under the *f*....John 1:50
Can a *f* tree...........James 3:12
f tree drops its late........Rev 6:13

FIGHT

"The LORD will *f*........Ex 14:14
you go with me to *f*......1 Kin 22:4
Our God will *f* for us......Neh 4:20
My servants would *f*....John 18:36
to him, let us not *f*......Acts 23:9
f the good *f*............1 Tim 6:12
have fought the good *f*...2 Tim 4:7
You *f* and war..........James 4:2

FIGHTS

your God is He who *f*....Josh 23:10
because my lord *f*......1 Sam 25:28
f come from among you...James 4:1

FIGS

puts forth her green *f*.....Song 2:13
f set before the...........Jer 24:1
from thornbushes or *f*.....Matt 7:16
men do not gather *f*......Luke 6:44
or a grapevine bear *f*....James 3:12

FIGURATIVELY

brethren, I have *f*.........1 Cor 4:6

FIGURE

and using no *f*.........John 16:29

FILL

f the earth and subdue....Gen 1:28
wealth, that I may *f*.....Prov 8:21
"do I not *f* heaven........Jer 23:24
f this temple with........Hag 2:7
"F the waterpots.........John 2:7
that He might *f*.........Eph 4:10
so as always to *f*.......1 Thess 2:16

FILLED

the whole earth be *f*......Ps 72:19
Then our mouth was *f*....Ps 126:2
for they shall be *f*.......Matt 5:6
let the children be *f*.....Mark 7:27
he would gladly have *f*...Luke 15:16
being *f* with all.........Rom 1:29
full of goodness, *f*......Rom 15:14
that you may be *f*.......Eph 3:19
but be *f* with the........Eph 5:18

FILTH (cont.)

being *f* with the ....Phil 1:11
peace, be warmed and *f* . .James 2:16

FILTH

has washed away the *f* ....Is 4:4
been made as the *f*......1 Cor 4:13
the removal of the *f*.....1 Pet 3:21

FILTHINESS

from all your *f*.........Ezek 36:25
ourselves from all *f* ....2 Cor 7:1
lay aside all *f*..........James 1:21
abominations and the *f* . . . .Rev 17:4

FILTHY

is abominable and *f*......Job 15:16
with *f* garments..........Zech 3:3
malice, blasphemy, *f* ....Col 3:8
poor man in *f* clothes.....James 2:2
oppressed by the *f* ....2 Pet 2:7
let him be *f* ....Rev 22:11

FIND

sure your sin will *f* .....Num 32:23
Almighty, we cannot *f* . . . .Job 37:23
life to those who *f* ....Prov 4:22
that no one can *f* ....Eccl 3:11
waters, for you will *f* .....Eccl 11:1
seek, and you will *f*........Matt 7:7
for My sake will *f*.......Matt 10:39
when he comes, will *f*. . . Matt 24:46
f a Babe wrapped ....Luke 2:12
f no fault in this Man....Luke 23:4
I *f* then a law...........Rom 7:21
f grace to help in ....Heb 4:16

FINDING

great things past *f* ....Job 9:10
and *f* none ....Luke 11:24
and His ways past *f* ....Rom 11:33

FINDS

f me *f* life ....Prov 8:35
f a wife *f* a good.........Prov 18:22
Whatever your hand *f*.....Eccl 9:10
and he who seeks *f*.......Matt 7:8
f his life will lose........Matt 10:39
and he who seeks *f*......Luke 11:10

FINE

Then I beat them as *f* . .2 Sam 22:43
gold, yea, than much *f*.....Ps 19:10
f gold is a wise..........Prov 25:12
set on bases of *f* gold....Song 5:15
more rare than *f*..........Is 13:12
and for *f* clothing........Is 23:18
how changed the *f*........Lam 4:1
rings, in *f* apparel.......James 2:2
for the *f* linen is the ....Rev 19:8

FINGER

written with the *f*........Ex 31:18
f shall be thicker ....1 Kin 12:10
the pointing of the *f* ....Is 58:9
dip the tip of his *f* .....Luke 16:24
the ground with His *f*.....John 8:6
"Reach your *f* ....John 20:27

FINGERS

the work of Your *f*..........Ps 8:3
he points with his *f*......Prov 6:13
that which their own *f*......Is 2:8
with one of their *f*.......Matt 23:4

FINISH

city, to *f* the ....Dan 9:24
he has enough to *f* ......Luke 14:28
has given Me to *f*.......John 5:36
so that I may *f* ....Acts 20:24

FINISHED

f the work which You ....John 17:4
He said, "It is *f*........John 19:30
I have *f* the race ....2 Tim 4:7
thousand years were *f* .....Rev 20:3

FIRE

rained brimstone and *f*....Gen 19:24
to him in a flame of *f*........Ex 3:2
by day, and *f* was over....Ex 40:38
God who answers by *f*. . .1 Kin 18:24
LORD was not in the *f*. . .1 Kin 19:12
I was musing, the *f*........Ps 39:3
we went through the *f*.....Ps 66:12
they have set *f*.............Ps 74:7
f goes before Him ....Ps 97:3
f and hail ....Ps 148:8
burns as the *f*.............Is 9:18
says the LORD, whose *f*....Is 31:9
you walk through the *f*.....Is 43:2
f that burns all the ....Is 65:5
on whose bodies the *f* ....Dan 3:27
He break out like *f* ......Amos 5:6
for conflict by *f*.........Amos 7:4
like a refiner's *f*............Mal 3:2
the Holy Spirit and *f*....Matt 3:11
f is not quenched ....Mark 9:44
"I came to send *f*......Luke 12:49
tongues, as of *f* ....Acts 2:3
f taking vengeance......2 Thess 1:8
and that burned with *f* . . .Heb 12:18
And the tongue is a *f*.....James 3:6
vengeance of eternal *f* ......Jude 7
f came down from God....Rev 20:9
into the lake of *f*........Rev 20:14

FIREBRAND

f plucked from the.......Amos 4:11

FIREBRANDS

a madman who throws *f*..Prov 26:18
two stubs of smoking *f*......Is 7:4

FIRM

their strength is *f*.........Ps 73:4
f the feeble knees..........Is 35:3
of the hope *f* to the ....Heb 3:6

FIRMAMENT

Thus God made the *f*......Gen 1:7
f shows His handiwork......Ps 19:1
in His mighty *f*..........Ps 150:1
brightness of the *f*.......Dan 12:3

FIRST

The *f* one to plead his....Prov 18:17
f father sinned ....Is 43:27
desires to be *f*........Matt 20:27
f shall be slave ....Mark 10:44
And the gospel must *f*. .Mark 13:10
evil, of the Jew *f*.........Rom 2:9
"Or who has *f* ....Rom 11:35
f man Adam became a...1 Cor 15:45
f a willing mind ....2 Cor 8:12
that we who *f* trusted ....Eph 1:12
For Adam was formed *f* . .1 Tim 2:13
f covenant had been........Heb 8:7
love Him because He *f* . .1 John 4:19
I am the *F* and the.......Rev 1:17
you have left your *f* ....Rev 2:4
is the *f* resurrection ......Rev 20:5

FIRST-RIPE

f fruit which my soul ......Mic 7:1

FIRSTBORN

LORD struck all the *f*......Ex 12:29
I will make him My *f*......Ps 89:27
Shall I give my *f*.........Mic 6:7
brought forth her *f*......Matt 1:25

FIRSTFRUIT

For if the *f* is holy.......Rom 11:16

FIRSTFRUITS

and with the *f* ....Prov 3:9
also who have the *f*......Rom 8:23
and has become the *f*. . .1 Cor 15:20
Christ the *f*...........1 Cor 15:23
might be a kind of *f*....James 1:18
among men, being *f* ......Rev 14:4

FISH

f taken in a cruel net......Eccl 9:12
had prepared a great *f* . . . .Jon 1:17
do You make men like *f*. . .Hab 1:14
Or if he asks for a *f*......Matt 7:10
belly of the great *f*......Matt 12:40
five loaves and two *f* . . . .Matt 14:17
and likewise the *f* ......John 21:13

FISHERMEN

The *f* also will mourn ....Is 19:8
I will send for many *f* . . . .Jer 16:16

FISHERS

and I will make you *f*.....Matt 4:19

FIT

and looking back, is *f*......Luke 9:62

FITTING

Is it *f* to say to a.........Job 34:18
Luxury is not *f* ....Prov 19:10
so honor is not *f* ....Prov 26:1
things which are not *f*......Rom 1:28
a High Priest was *f*.......Heb 7:26

FIVE

f smooth stones ....1 Sam 17:40
about *f* thousand men . . .Matt 14:21
and *f* were foolish ....Matt 25:2

FIXED

f My limit for it..........Job 38:10
is a great gulf *f*........Luke 16:26

FLAME

appeared to him in a *f*.....Ex 3:2
f will dry out his ....Job 15:30
f consumes the chaff........Is 5:24
and tempest and the *f*......Is 29:6
nor shall the *f*............Is 43:2
behind them a *f* ....Joel 2:3
am tormented in this *f*. . .Luke 16:24
and His ministers a *f*......Heb 1:7
and His eyes like a *f*......Rev 1:14

FLAMES

the LORD divides the *f*......Ps 29:7

FLAMING

f sword which turned.....Gen 3:24
f fire in their land ......Ps 105:32
in *f* fire taking ....2 Thess 1:8

FLATTER

I do not know how to *f*....Job 32:22
They *f* with their...........Ps 5:9

FLATTERED

Nevertheless they *f*........Ps 78:36

FLATTERING

f mouth works ruin.....Prov 26:28
f speech deceive.........Rom 16:18
any time did we use *f* . . .1 Thess 2:5

swelling words, f . . . . .Jude 16

FLATTERS

with one who f with . . . . .Prov 20:19
f his neighbor spreads. . . . . Prov 29:5

FLATTERY

shall corrupt with f . . . . . .Dan 11:32

FLAVOR

the salt loses its f . . . . . . .Matt 5:13

FLAVORLESS

f food be eaten. . . . . .Job 6:6

FLAX

f He will not quench . . . . .Is 42:3
f He will not quench. . . . .Matt 12:20

FLED

The sea saw it and f . . . . . .Ps 114:3
who have f for refuge. . . . . .Heb 6:18

FLEE

f away secretly . . . . .Gen 31:27
those who hate You f . . . .Num 10:35
such a man as I f . . . .:Neh 6:11
who see me outside f . . . . .Ps 31:11
Or where can I f . . . . .Ps 139:7
and the shadows f. . . . . . .Song 2:17
who are in Judea f . . . . . .Matt 24:16
F sexual immorality. . . . . .1 Cor 6:18
f these things and . . . . . . .1 Tim 6:11
devil and he will f . . . . . . .James 4:7

FLESH

bone of my bones and f. . . .Gen 2:23
shall become one f . . . . . . .Gen 2:24
f had corrupted their . . . . .Gen 6:12
f I shall see God . . . . .Job 19:26
my f also will rest in. . . . . .Ps 16:9
that they were but f . . . . . .Ps 78:39
my heart and my f . . . . .Ps 84:2
f shall bless His holy . . . .Ps 145:21
is wearisome to the f. . . . .Eccl 12:12
and all f shall see it. . . . . . . .Is 40:5
"All f is grass. . . . . .Is 40:6
out My Spirit on all f. . . . .Joel 2:28
Simon Bar-Jonah, for f .Matt 16:17
two shall become one f . . . .Matt 19:5
were shortened, no f. . . . .Matt 24:22
two shall become one f . . .Mark 10:8
f shall see the . . . . .Luke 3:6
And the Word became f. . .John 1:14
I shall give is My f . . . . . .John 6:51
unless you eat the f . . . . .John 6:53
f profits nothing . . . . .John 6:63
according to the f . . . . . . .John 8:15
when we were in the f. . . . .Rom 7:5
of God, but with the f . . . .Rom 7:25
on the things of the f . . . . .Rom 8:5
you are not in the f . . . . . . .Rom 8:9
to the f you will die. . . . . .Rom 8:13
f should glory in His . . . .1 Cor 1:29
"shall become one f . . . . .1 Cor 6:16
there is one kind of f . . . .1 Cor 15:39
For the f lusts . . . . .Gal 5:17
have crucified the f . . . . . .Gal 5:24
good showing in the f. . . . .Gal 6:12
may boast in your f . . . . . .Gal 6:13
f has ceased from sin . . . .1 Pet 4:1
of his time in the f. . . . . . .1 Pet 4:2
the lust of the f . . . . .1 John 2:16
has come in the f. . . . . . . .1 John 4:2
dreamers defile the f . . . . . . .Jude 8

FLESHLY

f wisdom but by the . . . .2 Cor 1:12
law of a f commandment. . .Heb 7:16
f lusts which . . . . .1 Pet 2:11

FLIES

will send swarms of f . . . . .Ex 8:21
He sent swarms of f . . . . . .Ps 78:45
Dead f putrefy the. . . . . . .Eccl 10:1

FLIGHT

f shall perish from . . . . . . .Amos 2:14
And pray that your f . . . .Matt 24:20

FLINT

will seem like f . . . . .Is 5:28
set My face like a f . . . . .Is 50:7

FLINTY

out of the f rock . . . . .Deut 8:15

FLOAT

and he made the iron f . . . .2 Kin 6:6

FLOCK

Your people like a f . . . . . .Ps 77:20
wilderness like a f. . . . . . . .Ps 78:52
lead Joseph like a f. . . . . . . .Ps 80:1
the footsteps of the f . . . . .Song 1:8
He will feed His f . . . . .Is 40:11
you do not feed the f . . . .Ezek 34:3
are My f, the f. . . . . .Ezek 34:31
though the f be cut . . . . . .Hab 3:17
my God, "Feed the f. . . . .Zech 11:4
sheep of the f . . . . .Matt 26:31
"Do not fear, little f . . . .Luke 12:32
there will be none f. . . . . .John 10:16
of the milk of the f. . . . . . .1 Cor 9:7
Shepherd the f of God . . . .1 Pet 5:2
examples to the f . . . . .1 Pet 5:3

FLOCKS

are clothed with f . . . . .Ps 65:13

FLOOD

the waters of the f . . . . . . .Gen 7:10
sat enthroned at the F . . . .Ps 29:10
them away like a f. . . . . . . .Ps 90:5
will you do in the f . . . . . .Jer 12:5
the days before the f . . .Matt 24:38
bringing in the f . . . . .2 Pet 2:5
of his mouth like a f. . . . .Rev 12:15

FLOODS

me, and the f of. . . . . .Ps 18:4
f on the dry ground . . . . .Is 44:3
rain descended, the f . . . .Matt 7:25

FLOURISH

the righteous shall f. . . . . . .Ps 72:7

FLOURISHED

your care for me has f . . . .Phil 4:10

FLOURISHES

In the morning it f. . . . . . . .Ps 90:6

FLOW

f away as waters which . . . . .Ps 58:7
and the waters f . . . . .Ps 147:18
that its spices may f . . . . .Song 4:16
all nations shall f. . . . . .Is 2:2
of his heart will f . . . . . . .John 7:38

FLOWER

comes forth like a f. . . . . . .Job 14:2
as a f of the field. . . . . . . .Ps 103:15
beauty is a fading f. . . . . .Is 28:4
is like the f of the . . . . .Is 40:6
grass withers, the f . . . . .Is 40:7
if she is past the f . . . . . .1 Cor 7:36
of man as the f . . . . .1 Pet 1:24

FLOWERS

f appear on the earth . . . .Song 2:12

FLOWING

'a land f with milk . . . . . . .Deut 6:3
of wisdom is a f. . . . . .Prov 18:4
the Gentiles like a f. . . . . . .Is 66:12

FLUTE

play the harp and f . . . . . .Gen 4:21
sound of the horn, f. . . . . . .Dan 3:5

FLUTES

instruments and f. . . . . . . .Ps 150:4

FLUTISTS

harpists, musicians, f. . . . .Rev 18:22

FLY

I would f . . . . .Ps 55:6
soon cut off, and we f. . . . .Ps 90:10
they f away like an . . . . . .Prov 23:5

FOE

and scattered the f . . . . . . .Ps 18:14

FOES

my enemies and f . . . . .Ps 27:2
I will beat down his f . . . . .Ps 89:23

FOLD

are not of this f . . . . .John 10:16
a cloak You will f . . . . .Heb 1:12

FOLDING

slumber, a little f. . . . . . . .Prov 6:10

FOLLOW

f what is altogether . . . . .Deut 16:20
to Me, you who f . . . . .Is 51:1
f You wherever You go . . . .Matt 8:19
He said to him, "F . . . . . . .Matt 9:9
up his cross, and f . . . . . .Mark 8:34
someone who does not f . .Mark 9:38
will by no means f . . . . . .John 10:5
serves Me, let him f . . . . .John 12:26
those of some men f . . . . .1 Tim 5:24
that you should f . . . . .1 Pet 2:21
f the Lamb wherever He . . .Rev 14:4
and their works f . . . . .Rev 14:13

FOLLOWED

f the Lord my God . . . . . .Josh 14:8
Lord took me as I f . . . . . .Amos 7:15
we have left all and f . . . .Mark 10:28

FOLLOWS

My soul f close behind . . . . . .Ps 63:8
f Me shall not walk. . . . . .John 8:12

FOLLY

taken much notice of f. . . .Job 35:15
not turn back to f . . . . .Ps 85:8
F is joy to him who is. . . . .Prov 15:21
of fools is f . . . . .Prov 16:22
f is set in great. . . . . .Eccl 10:6

FOOD

you it shall be for f . . . . . . .Gen 1:29
that lives shall be f . . . . . . .Gen 9:3
stranger, giving him f. . . .Deut 10:18
He gives f in . . . . .Job 36:31
he may bring forth f. . . . . .Ps 104:14
Who gives f to all . . . . . .Ps 136:25
Much f is in the. . . . . . . .Prov 13:23
night, and provides f. . . . .Prov 31:15
f which you eat shall . . . .Ezek 4:10
the fields yield no f . . . . . .Hab 3:17
that there may be f . . . . . .Mal 3:10
to give them f . . . . .Matt 24:45
and you gave Me f . . . . .Matt 25:35
and he who has f . . . . . . .Luke 3:11
have you any f. . . . . .John 21:5

they ate their *f*..........Acts 2:46
our hearts with *f*........Acts 14:17
destroy with your *f*.....Rom 14:15
f makes my brother......1 Cor 8:13
the same spiritual *f*.....1 Cor 10:3
sower, and bread for *f*...2 Cor 9:10
And having *f* and........1 Tim 6:8
and not solid *f*..........Heb 5:12
But solid *f* belongs to....Heb 5:14
of *f* sold his.............Heb 12:16
destitute of daily *f*.....James 2:15

FOODS

F for the stomach.......1 Cor 6:13
f which God.............1 Tim 4:3

FOOL

f has said in his..........Ps 14:1
is like sport to a *f*......Prov 10:23
f will be servant........Prov 11:29
f is right in his own......Prov 12:15
f lays open his folly.....Prov 13:16
is too lofty for a *f*.......Prov 24:7
whoever says, 'You *f*......Matt 5:22
I speak as a *f*..........2 Cor 11:23
I have become a *f*.......2 Cor 12:11

FOOLISH

of the *f* women speaks.....Job 2:10
I was so *f* and............Ps 73:22
f pulls it down with......Prov 14:1
f man squanders it......Prov 21:20
"For My people are......Jer 4:22
Has not God made *f*....1 Cor 1:20
O *f* Galatians...........Gal 3:1
were also once *f*.........Titus 3:3
But avoid *f* disputes.......Titus 3:9

FOOLISHLY

I speak *f*..............2 Cor 11:21

FOOLISHNESS

O God, You know my *f*.....Ps 69:5
Forsake *f* and live........Prov 9:6
of fools proclaims *f*......Prov 12:23
The *f* of a man twists....Prov 19:3
F is bound up in the.....Prov 22:15
devising of *f* is sin......Prov 24:9
person will speak *f*.........Is 32:6
of the cross is *f*..........1 Cor 1:18
Because the *f* of God.....1 Cor 1:25

FOOLS

f despise wisdom..........Prov 1:7
folly of *f* is deceit........Prov 14:8
F mock at sin............Prov 14:9
has no pleasure in *f*.......Eccl 5:4
We are *f* for Christ's......1 Cor 4:10

FOOT

will not allow your *f*.......Ps 121:3
f will not stumble.......Prov 3:23
From the sole of the *f*......Is 1:6
you turn away your *f*......Is 58:13
f causes you to sin......Matt 18:8
you dash your *f*........Luke 4:11
If the *f* should say......1 Cor 12:15

FOOTMEN

have run with the *f*........Jer 12:5

FOOTSTEPS

f were not known..........Ps 77:19
and shall make His *f*......Ps 85:13

FOOTSTOOL

Your enemies Your *f*.......Ps 110:1
Your enemies Your *f*.....Matt 22:44
"Sit here at my *f*........James 2:3

FORBID

said, "Do not *f*..........Mark 9:39
"Can anyone *f*..........Acts 10:47
prophesy, and do not *f*...1 Cor 14:39
f that I should boast......Gal 6:14

FORBIDDING

confidence, no one *f*......Acts 28:31
f us to speak to the....1 Thess 2:16
f to marry...............1 Tim 4:3

FORCE

violent take it by *f*......Matt 11:12
come and take Him by *f*.John 6:15
a testament is in *f*........Heb 9:17

FORCEFUL

f are right words..........Job 6:25

FORCES

Though they join *f*......Prov 11:21

FOREFATHERS

f who refused to hear......Jer 11:10
and oppressed our *f*......Acts 7:19
conscience, as my *f*......2 Tim 1:3

FOREHEADS

against their *f*............Ezek 3:8
put a mark on the *f*......Ezek 9:4
seal of God on their *f*.....Rev 9:4
his mark on their *f*........Rev 20:4

FOREIGNER

"I am a *f* and a..........Gen 23:4
of me, since I am a *f*......Ruth 2:10
to God except this *f*.....Luke 17:18
who speaks will be a *f*..1 Cor 14:11

FOREIGNERS

with the children of *f*........Is 2:6
f shall build up your.......Is 60:10
f who were there spent..Acts 17:21
longer strangers and *f*.....Eph 2:19

FOREKNEW

For whom He *f*..........Rom 8:29
His people whom He *f*....Rom 11:2

FOREKNOWLEDGE

purpose and *f* of God....Acts 2:23
according to the *f*.........1 Pet 1:2

FOREORDAINED

He indeed was *f*.........1 Pet 1:20

FORERUNNER

f has entered for us......Heb 6:20

FORESAW

'I *f* the LORD............Acts 2:25

FORESEEING

f that God would............Gal 3:8

FORESEES

A prudent man *f*........Prov 22:3

FOREST

beast of the *f* is Mine.....Ps 50:10
See how great a *f*.......James 3:5

FORESTS

and strips the *f*............Ps 29:9

FORETOLD

have also *f* these days.....Acts 3:24
killed those who *f*.......Acts 7:52

FOREVER

and eat, and live *f*........Gen 3:22
to our children *f*........Deut 29:29

has loved Israel *f*........1 Kin 10:9
I would not live *f*.........Job 7:16
from this generation *f*......Ps 12:7
LORD sits as King *f*.......Ps 29:10
Do not cast us off *f*.......Ps 44:23
throne, O God, is *f*........Ps 45:6
"You are a priest *f*.......Ps 110:4
His mercy endures *f*......Ps 136:1
will bless Your name *f*....Ps 145:1
who keeps truth *f*........Ps 146:6
The LORD shall reign *f*...Ps 146:10
for riches are not *f*......Prov 27:24
Trust in the LORD *f*.......Is 26:4
of our God stands *f*........Is 40:8
My salvation will be *f*......Is 51:6
will not cast off *f*........Lam 3:31
be the name of God *f*....Dan 2:20
like the stars *f*..........Dan 12:3
of the LORD our God *f*.....Mic 4:5
and the glory *f*..........Matt 6:13
the Christ remains *f*....John 12:34
who is blessed *f*........2 Cor 11:31
to whom be glory *f*........Gal 1:5
generation, *f* and ever....Eph 3:21
and Father be glory *f*.....Phil 4:20
throne, O God, is *f*........Heb 1:8
has been perfected *f*......Heb 7:28
lives and abides *f*.......1 Pet 1:23
of darkness *f*..........Jude 13
power, both now and *f*.....Jude 25
And they shall reign *f*....Rev 22:5

FOREVERMORE

Blessed be the LORD *f*.....Ps 89:52
this time forth and *f*......Ps 113:2
behold, I am alive *f*........Rev 1:18

FOREWARNED

all such, as we also *f*....1 Thess 4:6

FORGAVE

f the iniquity of my........Ps 32:5
to repay, he freely *f*.....Luke 7:42
God in Christ *f*..........Eph 4:32
even as Christ *f*..........Col 3:13

FORGED

The proud have *f*........Ps 119:69

FORGERS

But you *f* of lies..........Job 13:4

FORGET

"For God has made me *f*..Gen 41:51
yourselves, lest you *f*....Deut 4:23
f the covenant of your....Deut 4:31
f the LORD who brought....Deut 6:12
the paths of all who *f*.....Job 8:13
all the nations that *f*........Ps 9:17
this, you who *f*..........Ps 50:22
f the works of God........Ps 78:7
I will not *f* Your word....Ps 119:16
If I *f* you................Ps 137:5
My son, do not *f*.........Prov 3:1
f her nursing child........Is 49:15
f the LORD your Maker....Is 51:13
f her ornaments..........Jer 2:32
f your work and labor....Heb 6:10

FORGETFULNESS

in the land of *f*..........Ps 88:12

FORGETS

f the covenant of her.....Prov 2:17
and immediately *f*.....James 1:24

FORGETTING

f those things which.......Phil 3:13

FORGIVE

dwelling place, and *f* .....1 Kin 8:39
f their sin and heal ......2 Chr 7:14
good, and ready to *f* ....Ps 86:5
And *f* us our debts.......Matt 6:12
Father will also *f*.........Matt 6:14
f men their trespasses ....Matt 6:15
his heart, does not *f*.....Matt 18:35
Who can *f* sins but God ...Mark 2:7
f the sins of any ....John 20:23
you ought rather to *f*......2 Cor 2:7
anything, I also *f*.......2 Cor 2:10
F me this wrong.......2 Cor 12:13
f us our sins and to......1 John 1:9

FORGIVEN

transgression is *f*..........Ps 32:1
sins be *f* them...........Mark 4:12
to whom little is *f*........Luke 7:47
indeed I have *f*..........2 Cor 2:10
f you all trespasses ....Col 2:13
sins, he will be *f* ....James 5:15
your sins are *f* ....1 John 2:12

FORGIVENESS

But there is *f* with ....Ps 130:4
God belong mercy and *f* ...Dan 9:9
preached to you the *f* ...Acts 13:38
they may receive *f*......Acts 26:18
His blood, the *f* ....Eph 1:7

FORGIVES

f all your iniquities ....Ps 103:3
"Who is this who even *f*...Luke 7:49

FORGIVING

tenderhearted, *f* ....Eph 4:32
and *f* one another.........Col 3:13

FORGOT

remember Joseph, but *f*...Gen 40:23
f the LORD their God .....Judg 3:7
f His works and His.......Ps 78:11
They soon *f* His works....Ps 106:13

FORGOTTEN

f the God who fathered ..Deut 32:18
"Why have You *f*...........Ps 42:9
If we had *f* the name .....Ps 44:20
memory of them is *f* ......Eccl 9:5
you will not be *f*...........Is 44:21
and my Lord has *f*.........Is 49:14
I have *f* prosperity.......Lam 3:17
not one of them is *f*......Luke 12:6
f the exhortation ....Heb 12:5
f that he was cleansed.....2 Pet 1:9

FORM

earth was without *f*........Gen 1:2
Who would *f* a god or ......Is 44:10
f the light and create.......Is 45:7
descended in bodily *f*.....Luke 3:22
time, nor seen His *f*.......John 5:37
For the *f* of this ....1 Cor 7:31
who, being in the *f*......Phil 2:6
Abstain from every *f*...1 Thess 5:22
having a *f* of............2 Tim 3:5

FORMED

And the LORD God *f* ....Gen 2:7
And His hands *f*..........Ps 95:5
f my inward parts.......Ps 139:13
f everything gives the....Prov 26:10
say of him who *f* ....Is 29:16
Me there was no God *f*.....Is 43:10
This people I have *f*......Is 43:21
"Before I *f* you in..........Jer 1:5
Will the thing *f*.........Rom 9:20
say to him who *f*.........Rom 9:20
until Christ is *f*..........Gal 4:19

For Adam was *f* first ....1 Tim 2:13

FORMER

f lovingkindnesses.........Ps 89:49
f days better than ....Eccl 7:10
f rain to the earth.........Hos 6:3
f prophets preached.......Zech 1:4
f conduct in Judaism .....Gal 1:13
your *f* conduct ....Eph 4:22
f things have passed.......Rev 21:4

FORMS

clay say to him who *f* ....Is 45:9
f the spirit of man.......Zech 12:1

FORNICATION

We were not born of *f*....John 8:41
of the wrath of her *f*.......Rev 14:8

FORNICATOR

you know, that no *f* ....Eph 5:5
lest there be any *f* ......Heb 12:16

FORNICATORS

but *f* and adulterers.......Heb 13:4

FORSAKE

but if you *f* Him.........2 Chr 15:2
"If his sons *f*.............Ps 89:30
f His inheritance.........Ps 94:14
But I did not *f* ....Ps 119:87
father, and do not *f*.......Prov 1:8
worthless idols *f* ....Jon 2:8
of you does not *f*......Luke 14:33
never leave you nor *f*......Heb 13:5

FORSAKEN

My God, why have You *f*...Ps 22:1
seen the righteous *f* ......Ps 37:25
you dread will be *f*........Is 7:16
cities will be as a *f*.........Is 17:9
a mere moment I have *f*....Is 54:7
no longer be termed *F*......Is 62:4
they have *f* Me...........Jer 2:13
My God, why have You *f*.Matt 27:46
persecuted, but not *f*.....2 Cor 4:9
for Demas has *f*.........2 Tim 4:10
f the right way ....2 Pet 2:15

FORSAKING

f the assembling.........Heb 10:25

FORSOOK

f God who made him ....Deut 32:15
all the disciples *f*.......Matt 26:56
with me, but all *f*.......2 Tim 4:16
By faith he *f* Egypt......Heb 11:27

FORTRESS

LORD is my rock, my *f*...2 Sam 22:2
my rock of refuge, a *f*.......Ps 31:2

FOUL

My wounds are *f*.........Ps 38:5
f weather today.........Matt 16:3
a prison for every *f*.......Rev 18:2

FOUND

f a helper comparable......Gen 2:20
where can wisdom be *f*...Job 28:12
when You may be *f*......Ps 32:6
f My servant David ......Ps 89:20
a thousand I have *f*......Eccl 7:28
this only I have *f*......Eccl 7:29
f the one I love ....Song 3:4
LORD while He may be *f*....Is 55:6
your fruit is *f*..........Hos 14:8
fruit on it and *f* none ....Luke 13:6
he was lost and is *f*.....Luke 15:24
f the Messiah" (which ...John 1:41
I *f* to bring death ......Rom 7:10

and be *f* in Him ....Phil 3:9
be diligent to be *f*.......2 Pet 3:14

FOUNDATION

he shall lay its *f*.........Josh 6:26
His *f* is in the holy ....Ps 87:1
and justice are the *f*.......Ps 89:14
Of old You laid the *f*......Ps 102:25
has an everlasting *f*.....Prov 10:25
deep and laid the *f*......Luke 6:48
the earth without a *f* ....Luke 6:49
loved Me before the *f* ...John 17:24
I have laid the *f*.........1 Cor 3:10
f can anyone lay than ....1 Cor 3:11
us in Him before the *f*......Eph 1:4
the solid *f* of God ....2 Tim 2:19
not laying again the *f* ......Heb 6:1
Lamb slain from the *f* ....Rev 13:8
the first *f* was jasper ....Rev 21:19

FOUNDATIONS

when I laid the *f*..........Job 38:4
f are destroyed............Ps 11:3
You who laid the *f*.......Ps 104:5
shall raise up the *f*........Is 58:12
And the *f* of the wall ....Rev 21:19

FOUNDED

For He has *f* it upon.......Ps 24:2
shake it, for it was *f*.....Luke 6:48

FOUNTAIN

will become in him a *f*....John 4:14

FOUNTAINS

on that day all the *f*.......Gen 7:11
f be dispersed abroad ....Prov 5:16
when there were no *f*.....Prov 8:24
lead them to living *f*......Rev 7:17

FOX

build, if even a *f*..........Neh 4:3
"Go, tell that *f* ....Luke 13:32

FOXES

caught three hundred *f* ...Judg 15:4
f that spoil the vines ....Song 2:15
F have holes and birds....Luke 9:58

FRAGMENTS

f that remained.........Matt 14:20
of the leftover *f*.........Luke 9:17
baskets with the *f*.......John 6:13

FRAGRANCE

garments is like the *f*....Song 4:11
was filled with the *f*.....John 12:3
we are to God the *f* ......2 Cor 2:15

FRAIL

that I may know how *f*......Ps 39:4

FRAME

For He knows our *f* ......Ps 103:14
f was not hidden.........Ps 139:15

FRAMED

that the worlds were *f*.....Heb 11:3

FREE

and the servant is *f*.......Job 3:19
let the oppressed go *f* ......Is 58:6
'You will be made *f*......John 8:33
if the Son makes you *f*....John 8:36
And having been set *f*....Rom 6:18
now having been set *f*......Rom 6:22
Jesus has made me *f*.......Rom 8:2
Am I not *f*..............1 Cor 9:1
is neither slave nor *f*......Gal 3:28
Jerusalem above is *f*......Gal 4:26
Christ has made us *f*.......Gal 5:1

FREED

he is a slave or *f* . . . . .Eph 6:8
poor, *f* and slave . . . . .Rev 13:16

FREED

has died has been *f* . . . . .Rom 6:7

FREEDMAN

slave is the Lord's *f* . . . . . .1 Cor 7:22

FREELY

the garden you may *f* . . . . . .Gen 2:16
I will love them *f* . . . . .Hos 14:4
F you have received . . . . .Matt 10:8
f give us all . . . . .Rom 8:32
that have been *f* . . . . .1 Cor 2:12
the water of life *f* . . . . .Rev 22:17

FREEWOMAN

the other by a *f* . . . . .Gal 4:22
with the son of the *f* . . . . . .Gal 4:30

FRESH

My glory is *f* within . . . . .Job 29:20
They shall be *f* . . . . .Ps 92:14
both salt water and *f* . . .James 3:12

FRETS

and his heart *f* . . . . .Prov 19:3

FRIEND

a man speaks to his *f* . . . . . .Ex 33:11
of Abraham Your *f* . . . . . .2 Chr 20:7
though he were my *f* . . . . . . .Ps 35:14
f You have put . . . . .Ps 88:18
f loves at all times . . . . . . .Prov 17:17
f who sticks closer. . . . . . .Prov 18:24
not forsake your own *f* . . .Prov 27:10
a *f* of tax collectors. . . . . .Matt 11:19
of you shall have a *f* . . . . .Luke 11:5
f Lazarus sleeps . . . . . . .John 11:11
you are not Caesar's *f* . . . .John 19:12
Philemon our beloved *f* . . .Philem 1
he was called the *f* . . . . . .James 2:23
wants to be a *f* . . . . .James 4:4

FRIENDS

and hate your *f* . . . . .2 Sam 19:6
My *f* scorn me. . . . . .Job 16:20
f have forgotten me. . . . . .Job 19:14
the rich has many *f* . . . . .Prov 14:20
one's life for his *f* . . . . . .John 15:13
"You are My *f* . . . . .John 15:14
I have called you *f* . . . . . .John 15:15
to forbid any of his *f* . . . .Acts 24:23

FROGS

your territory with *f* . . . . . . .Ex 8:2
f coming out of the. . . . . .Rev 16:13

FRONTLETS

on your hand and as *f* . . . .Ex 13:16
and they shall be as *f* . . . . .Deut 6:8

FROZEN

the broad waters are *f* . . .Job 37:10

FRUIT

and showed them the *f* . . .Num 13:26
Blessed shall be the *f* . . . .Deut 28:4
brings forth its *f* . . . . .Ps 1:3
f is better than gold . . . . .Prov 8:19
The *f* of the righteous . . .Prov 11:30
with good by the *f* . . . . . .Prov 12:14
f was sweet to my. . . . . . .Song 2:3
they shall eat the *f* . . . . .Is 3:10
like the first *f* . . . . .Is 28:4
"I create the *f* . . . . .Is 57:19
f is found in Me . . . . .Hos 14:8
does not bear good *f* . . . .Matt 3:10
good tree bears good *f*. . .Matt 7:17
not drink of this *f*. . . . . .Matt 26:29

and blessed is the *f* . . . . . .Luke 1:42
life, and bring no *f* . . . . . .Luke 8:14
and he came seeking *f* . . . .Luke 13:6
'And if it bears *f* . . . . . . .Luke 13:9
branch that bears *f* . . . . . .John 15:2
that you bear much *f* . . . .John 15:8
should go and bear *f* . . . .John 15:16
f did you have then in. . . . .Rom 6:21
God, you have your *f* . . . . .Rom 6:22
that we should bear *f* . . . . . .Rom 7:4
But the *f* of the . . . . .Gal 5:22
but I seek the *f* . . . . .Phil 4:17
yields the peaceable *f* . . . .Heb 12:11
Now the *f* of . . . . .James 3:18
autumn trees without *f*. . . .Jude 12
tree yielding its *f* . . . . .Rev 22:2

FRUITFUL

them, saying, "Be *f* . . . . . .Gen 1:22
a *f* bough, a *f* . . . . .Gen 49:22
wife shall be like a *f* . . . . .Ps 128:3
heaven and *f* seasons . . .Acts 14:17
pleasing Him, being *f* . . . . .Col 1:10

FRUITS

Therefore bear *f* . . . . .Matt 3:8
know them by their *f* . . . . .Matt 7:16
and increase the *f*. . . . . . .2 Cor 9:10
of mercy and good *f*. . . . .James 3:17
which bore twelve *f*. . . . . . .Rev 22:2

FUEL

people shall be as *f* . . . . .Is 9:19
into the fire for *f* . . . . . . .Ezek 15:4

FULFILL

the Lord, to *f* his vow . . .Lev 22:21
And you shall *f* . . . . .1 Kin 8:15
f all your petitions . . . . .Ps 20:5
f the desire of those . . . . .Ps 145:19
for us to *f* all . . . . .Matt 3:15
f the law of Christ. . . . . .Gal 6:2
f my joy by being. . . . . . . .Phil 2:2
and *f* all the good. . . . . .2 Thess 1:11
If you really *f* . . . . .James 2:8

FULFILLED

the law till all is *f* . . . . . . .Matt 5:18
of the Gentiles are *f*. . . . .Luke 21:24
all things must be *f* . . . . .Luke 24:44
of the law might be *f* . . . . .Rom 8:4
loves another has *f* . . . . . .Rom 13:8
For all the law is *f* . . . . . . .Gal 5:14

FULFILLMENT

for there will be a *f* . . . . . .Luke 1:45
love is the *f* of the . . . . . .Rom 13:10

FULL

"I went out *f*. . . . . .Ruth 1:21
For I am *f* of words. . . . . .Job 32:18
of the Lord is *f*. . . . . .Ps 29:4
who has his quiver *f*. . . . . .Ps 127:5
Lest I be *f* and deny . . . . .Prov 30:9
yet the sea is not *f*. . . . . . . .Eccl 1:7
the whole earth is *f* . . . . .Is 6:3
and it was *f* of bones . . . .Ezek 37:1
But truly I am *f*. . . . . .Mic 3:8
whole body will be *f*. . . . .Matt 6:22
that your joy may be *f*. . . .John 15:11
chose Stephen, a man *f*. . . .Acts 6:5
You are already *f* . . . . . . .1 Cor 4:8
learned both to be *f* . . . . . .Phil 4:12
I am *f*. . . . . .Phil 4:18

FULL-GROWN

and sin, when it is *f* . . . .James 1:15

FULLNESS

satisfied with the *f* . . . . .Ps 36:8
f we have all received . . . . .John 1:16
to Israel until the *f* . . . . . .Rom 11:25
But when the *f* of the. . . . . . .Gal 4:4
dispensation of the *f* . . . . .Eph 1:10
filled with all the *f*. . . . . . .Eph 3:19
Him dwells all the *f* . . . . . . .Col 2:9

FUME

Why do you *f* with envy. . . .Ps 68:16

FUNCTION

do not have the same *f*. . . .Rom 12:4

FURIOUS

You have been *f*. . . . . .Ps 89:38
f man do not go. . . . . .Prov 22:24
fury and in *f* rebukes . . . .Ezek 5:15
Lord avenges and is *f*. . . . .Nah 1:2
this, they were *f*. . . . . .Acts 5:33

FURIOUSLY

for he drives *f*. . . . . .2 Kin 9:20

FURNACE

you out of the iron *f*. . . . .Deut 4:20
tested you in the *f*. . . . . . . .Is 48:10
of a burning fiery *f*. . . . . . .Dan 3:6
cast them into the *f* . . . .Matt 13:42
the smoke of a great *f* . . . .Rev 9:2

FURNISHED

also *f* her table. . . . . .Prov 9:2
a large upper room, *f*. . . .Mark 14:15

FURY

F is not in Me . . . . .Is 27:4
they are full of the *f* . . . . . .Is 51:20
f to His adversaries . . . . . . .Is 59:18
and My own *f*. . . . . .Is 63:5
even in anger and *f* . . . . . .Jer 21:5
and I will cause My *f*. . . .Ezek 5:13
Thus will I spend My *f* . . .Ezek 6:12
in anger and *f* on the . . . . . .Mic 5:15

FUTILE

For it is not a *f* . . . . .Deut 32:47
of the peoples are *f* . . . . . . .Jer 10:3
wise, that they are *f* . . . . .1 Cor 3:20
risen, your faith is *f* . . . . .1 Cor 15:17

FUTILITY

allotted months of *f* . . . . . . .Job 7:3
f have You created all . . . . .Ps 89:47
was subjected to *f*. . . . . . . .Rom 8:20

FUTURE

for the *f* of that man. . . . . .Ps 37:37
the *f* of the wicked . . . . . . .Ps 37:38
to give you a *f* . . . . .Jer 29:11

G

GAIN

g than fine gold. . . . . .Prov 3:14
will have no lack of *g* . . . .Prov 31:11
a time to *g* . . . . .Eccl 3:6
to get dishonest *g*. . . . . . .Ezek 22:27
him who covets evil *g* . . . . .Hab 2:9
and to die is *g*. . . . . .Phil 1:21
rubbish, that I may *g* . . . . .Phil 3:8
is a means of *g* . . . . .1 Tim 6:5
contentment is great *g* . . .1 Tim 6:6
for dishonest *g* . . . . .1 Pet 5:2

GAINED

g more wisdom than all. . . .Eccl 1:16
g five more talents . . . . . .Matt 25:20

GAINS

g the whole world......Matt 16:26

GALL

They also gave me *g*......Ps 69:21
the wormwood and the *g* ..Lam 3:19
turned justice into *g*....Amos 6:12
wine mingled with *g*....Matt 27:34

GAP

and stand in the *g* .....Ezek 22:30

GARDEN

LORD God planted a *g* .....Gen 2:8
g enclosed is my........Song 4:12
like a watered *g*.........Is 58:11
Eden, the *g* of God.....Ezek 28:13
raise up for them a *g* ...Ezek 34:29
where there was a *g*.....John 18:1
g a new tomb in which...John 19:41

GARDENER

Him to be the *g* ....John 20:15

GARDENS

I made myself *g*..........Eccl 2:5
plant *g* and eat their......Jer 29:5

GARLANDS

brought oxen and *g*.....Acts 14:13

GARMENT

beautiful Babylonian *g*...Josh 7:21
g that is moth-eaten....Job 13:28
made sackcloth my *g*......Ps 69:11
with light as with a *g*.....Ps 104:2
one who takes away a *g* ..Prov 25:20
the hem of His *g*........Matt 9:20
have on a wedding *g*....Matt 22:11
cloth on an old *g*.......Mark 2:21
all grow old like a *g*......Heb 1:11
hating even the *g*.........Jude 23

GARMENTS

g did not wear out on.....Deut 8:4
Why are your *g* hot .....Job 37:17
They divide My *g*.......Ps 22:18
g always be white ....Eccl 9:8
g rolled in blood............Is 9:5
from Edom, with dyed *g*....Is 63:1
Take away the filthy *g* ..Zech 3:4
man clothed in soft *g*....Matt 11:8
spread their *g* on the ...Matt 21:8
and divided His *g*......Matt 27:35
by them in shining *g*....Luke 24:4
g are moth-eaten.........James 5:2
be clothed in white *g* ......Rev 3:5

GARRISON

gathered the whole *g* ...Matt 27:27
Damascenes with a *g* ...2 Cor 11:32

GATE

This is the *g* of the.......Ps 118:20
by the narrow *g*.......Matt 7:13
by the Sheep *G* a pool .....John 5:2
laid daily at the *g* ....Acts 3:2
suffered outside the *g* ...Heb 13:12
each individual *g*........Rev 21:21

GATES

possess the *g* of those ....Gen 24:60
g are burned with fire ....Neh 1:3
they go down to the *g* ...Job 17:16
your heads, O you *g*......Ps 24:7
The LORD loves the *g* .....Ps 87:2
Open to me the *g* ......Ps 118:19
is known in the *g*......Prov 31:23
go through the *g* ....Is 62:10
and the *g* of Hades......Matt 16:18

wall with twelve *g*......Rev 21:12
g were twelve pearls.....Rev 21:21
g shall not be shut......Rev 21:25

GATHER

g my soul with sinners......Ps 26:9
G My saints ....Ps 50:5
and a time to *g* stones......Eccl 3:5
g the lambs with His .....Is 40:11
g His wheat into the ....Matt 3:12
sow nor reap nor *g*......Matt 6:26
Do men *g* grapes from....Matt 7:16
g where I have not.....Matt 25:26
g together His ....Mark 13:27

GATHERED

g little had no lack........Ex 16:18
And *g* out of the lands....Ps 107:3
g some of every kind....Matt 13:47
the nations will be *g*....Matt 25:32

GATHERING

g together of the.........Gen 1:10
g together to Him ......2 Thess 2:1

GATHERS

g the waters of the........Ps 33:7
His heart *g* iniquity......Ps 41:6
g her food in the ....Prov 6:8
The Lord GOD, who *g* ......Is 56:8
together, as a hen *g* ....Matt 23:37

GAVE

to be with me, she *g*....Gen 3:12
g You this authority....Matt 21:23
that He *g* His only......John 3:16
Those whom You *g*....John 17:12
but God *g* the increase ...1 Cor 3:6
g Himself for our sins....Gal 1:4
g Himself for me........Gal 2:20
g Himself for it ....Eph 5:25
The sea *g* up the dead ...Rev 20:13

GAZED

g into heaven and saw ...Acts 7:55

GAZING

why do you stand *g*......Acts 1:11

GENEALOGIES

fables and endless *g* .....1 Tim 1:4

GENEALOGY

The book of the *g*......Matt 1:1
mother, without *g* ....Heb 7:3

GENERATION

perverse and crooked *g* ..Deut 32:5
The *g* of the upright......Ps 112:2
g shall praise Your ......Ps 145:4
g that curses its ......Prov 30:11
g that is pure in its......Prov 30:12
One *g* passes away........Eccl 1:4
g it shall lie ....Is 34:10
who will declare His *g*....Is 53:8
and adulterous *g*........Matt 12:39
this *g* will by no ....Matt 24:34
from this perverse *g* .....Acts 2:40
But you are a chosen *g*...1 Pet 2:9

GENERATIONS

be remembered in all *g*.....Ps 45:17
Your praise to all *g*........Ps 79:13
for a thousand *g*........Ps 105:8
g will call me blessed....Luke 1:48

GENEROUS

g soul will be made......Prov 11:25
g eye will be blessed......Prov 22:9
no longer be called *g*.......Is 32:5
g man devises *g*........Is 32:8

GENTILES

G were separated ....Gen 10:5
as a light to the *G*.........Is 42:6
G shall come to your........Is 60:3
the riches of the *G*.........Is 61:6
all these things the *G* ....Matt 6:32
into the way of the *G*.....Matt 10:5
revelation to the *G* ......Luke 2:32
G are fulfilled ....Luke 21:24
bear My name before *G* ..Acts 9:15
poured out on the *G* ....Acts 10:45
a light to the *G*.........Acts 13:47
blasphemed among the *G*. .Rom 2:24
also the God of the *G*....Rom 3:29
even named among the *G*..1 Cor 5:1
mystery among the *G*.....Col 1:27
a teacher of the *G*.......1 Tim 2:7
nothing from the *G* ....3 John 7

GENTLE

g tongue breaks a bone ..Prov 25:15
from Me, for I am *g* ....Matt 11:29
But we were *g* among ...1 Thess 2:7
to be peaceable, *g*........Titus 3:2
only to the good and *g*....1 Pet 2:18
ornament of a *g*........1 Pet 3:4

GENTLENESS

g has made me great ......Ps 18:35
love and a spirit of *g* ....1 Cor 4:21
g, self-control.............Gal 5:23
all lowliness and *g* ....Eph 4:2
Let your *g* be known to....Phil 4:5
love, patience, *g*........1 Tim 6:11

GHOST

supposed it was a *g* .....Mark 6:49

GIFT

g makes room for him....Prov 18:16
A *g* in secret pacifies ...Prov 21:14
it is the *g* of God........Eccl 3:13
is Corban"-'(that is, a *g* ..Mark 7:11
If you knew the *g*......John 4:10
But the free *g* is not .....Rom 5:15
but the *g* of God is......Rom 6:23
each one has his own *g* ...1 Cor 7:7
though I have the *g*.....1 Cor 13:2
it is the *g* of God......Eph 2:8
Not that I seek the *g*....Phil 4:17
Do not neglect the *g*....1 Tim 4:14
you to stir up the *g*......2 Tim 1:6
tasted the heavenly *g* .....Heb 6:4
Every good *g* and every. .James 1:17
one has received a *g*.....1 Pet 4:10

GIFTED

the women who were *g* ...Ex 35:25
but good-looking, *g*......Dan 1:4

GIFTS

g you shall offer ....Num 18:29
You have received *g* ......Ps 68:18
and Seba will offer *g*......Ps 72:10
though you give many *g*...Prov 6:35
to one who gives *g* ......Prov 19:6
how to give good *g*......Matt 7:11
rich putting their *g*......Luke 21:1
g differing ....Rom 12:6
are diversities of *g*......1 Cor 12:4
and desire spiritual *g*....1 Cor 14:1
captive, and gave *g*......Eph 4:8

GIRD

G Your sword upon Your ....Ps 45:3
of wrath You shall *g*......Ps 76:10
I will *g* you................Is 45:5
and another will *g*......John 21:18
Therefore *g* up the ......1 Pet 1:13

GIRDED

a towel and *g* Himself ....John 13:4
down to the feet and *g* .....Rev 1:13

GIVE

g thanks to the LORD ....1 Chr 16:8
g me wisdom and........2 Chr 1:10
G ear to my prayer.........Ps 17:1
G to them according........Ps 28:4
g you the desires...........Ps 37:4
Yes, the LORD will *g* ......Ps 85:12
G me understanding........Ps 119:34
g me your heart.........Prov 23:26
You will *g* truth to........Mic 7:20
"*G* to him who asks.....Matt 5:42
G us this day our ....Matt 6:11
what you have and *g* ...Matt 19:21
authority I will *g* ....Luke 4:6
g them eternal life ....John 10:28
new commandment I *g* .John 13:34
but what I do have I *g* ....Acts 3:6
g us all things ....Rom 8:32
G no offense...........1 Cor 10:32
So let each one *g* ....2 Cor 9:7
g him who has need.......Eph 4:28
g thanks to God.......2 Thess 2:13
g yourself entirely.......1 Tim 4:15
good works, ready to *g* ..1 Tim 6:18

GIVEN

to him more will be *g* ....Matt 13:12
has, more will be *g* .....Matt 25:29
to whom much is *g* .....Luke 12:48
g Me I should lose ......John 6:39
Spirit was not yet *g* ......John 7:39
have been freely *g* ......1 Cor 2:12
not *g* to wine............1 Tim 3:3

GIVES

He who *g* to the poor ...Prov 28:27
For God *g* wisdom and ...Eccl 2:26
g life to the world.......John 6:33
All that the Father *g* .....John 6:37
The good shepherd *g* ...John 10:11
not as the world *g*......John 14:27
g us richly all things......1 Tim 6:17
who *g* to all liberally ....James 1:5
But He *g* more grace ....James 4:6
g grace to the humble ...James 4:6

GLAD

I will be *g* and.............Ps 9:2
my heart is *g*.............Ps 16:9
Be *g* in the LORD and......Ps 32:11
streams shall make *g* ....Ps 46:4
And wine that makes *g* ..Ps 104:15
I was *g* when they said ...Ps 122:1
make merry and be *g* ....Luke 15:32
he saw it and was *g* .....John 8:56

GLADNESS

in the day of your *g* .....Num 10:10
day of feasting and *g* .....Esth 9:17
You have put *g* in my.......Ps 4:7
me hear joy and *g*........Ps 51:8
Serve the LORD with *g* .....Ps 100:2
shall obtain joy and *g* .....Is 35:10
over you with *g*.........Zeph 3:17
receive it with *g* ....Mark 4:16

GLASS

there was a sea of *g* ....Rev 4:6
like transparent *g* ......Rev 21:21

GLORIFIED

the people I must be *g*....Lev 10:3
and they *g* the God of ...Matt 15:31
Jesus was not yet *g*......John 7:39
when Jesus was *g*......John 12:16

By this My Father is *g* ...John 15:8
"I have *g* You on the .....John 17:4
g His Servant Jesus......Acts 3:13
these He also *g* ....Rom 8:30
things God may be *g*.....1 Pet 4:11

GLORIFY

My altar, and I will *g* ....Is 60:7
g your Father in ....Matt 5:16
"Father, *g* Your name....John 12:28
"He will *g* Me..........John 16:14
And now, O Father, *g*....John 17:5
what death He would *g* ..John 21:19
God, they did not *g*......Rom 1:21
therefore *g* God in ......1 Cor 6:20
also Christ did not *g* ......Heb 5:5
ashamed, but let him *g* ..1 Pet 4:16

GLORIOUS

daughter is all *g* ....Ps 45:13
And blessed be His *g* .....Ps 72:19
G things are spoken ....Ps 87:3
is honorable and *g* ....Ps 111:3
g splendor of Your ......Ps 145:5
habitation, holy and *g*....Is 63:15
it to Himself a *g*.........Eph 5:27
be conformed to His *g*....Phil 3:21
g appearing of our ....Titus 2:13

GLORY

Please, show me Your *g*...Ex 33:18
g has departed from.....1 Sam 4:21
G in His holy name.....1 Chr 16:10
a shield for me, my *g* ....Ps 3:3
who have set Your *g* ......Ps 8:1
Who is this King of *g*......Ps 24:8
the place where Your *g*...Ps 26:8
Your power and Your *g*...Ps 63:2
shall speak of the *g* ......Ps 145:11
wise shall inherit *g* ......Prov 3:35
The *g* of young men is ...Prov 20:29
It is the *g* of God to ......Prov 25:2
"*G* to the righteous........Is 24:16
g I will not give............Is 42:8
g will be seen upon ....Is 60:2
then be likened in *g* .....Ezek 31:18
I will change their *g*.......Hos 4:7
and I will be the *g*........Zech 2:5
He shall bear the *g*.......Zech 6:13
that they may have *g*.....Matt 6:2
the power and the *g* .....Matt 6:13
g was not arrayed.......Matt 6:29
Man will come in the *g* .Matt 16:27
with power and great *g* ..Matt 24:30
"*G* to God in the........Luke 2:14
and we beheld His *g* .....John 1:14
and manifested His *g* ....John 2:11
I do not seek My own *g*...John 8:50
"Give God the *g*.........John 9:24
g which I had with You ..John 17:5
g which You gave Me I ..John 17:22
he did not give *g* ....Acts 12:23
doing good seek for *g* .....Rom 2:7
fall short of the *g* ....Rom 3:23
in faith, giving *g* ....Rom 4:20
the adoption, the *g* ......Rom 9:4
the riches of His *g* ....Rom 9:23
God, alone wise, be *g* ...Rom 16:27
who glories, let him *g* ....1 Cor 1:31
but woman is the *g* ......1 Cor 11:7
of the *g* that excels ......2 Cor 3:10
of the gospel of the *g*.....2 Cor 4:4
eternal weight of *g*......2 Cor 4:17
who glories, let him *g* ...2 Cor 10:17
to His riches in *g* ....Phil 4:19
appear with Him in *g* ......Col 3:4
For you are our *g* .....1 Thess 2:20
many sons to *g* ....Heb 2:10
grass, and all the *g*......1 Pet 1:24

---

to whom belong the *g* ....1 Pet 4:11
for the Spirit of *g*........1 Pet 4:14
the presence of His *g*......Jude 24
O Lord, to receive *g* ......Rev 4:11
g of God illuminated .....Rev 21:23

GLORYING

Your *g* is not good ....1 Cor 5:6

GLUTTON

g will come to poverty ...Prov 23:21
you say, 'Look, a *g* ......Luke 7:34

GLUTTONS

g shames his ....Prov 28:7
evil beasts, lazy *g*.......Titus 1:12

GNASHING

will be weeping and *g*....Matt 8:12

GO

He said, "Let Me *g* ......Gen 32:26
'Let My people *g* ....Ex 5:1
Presence does not *g* ......Ex 33:15
for wherever you *g*......Ruth 1:16
"Look, I *g* forward ....Job 23:8
For I used to *g* ....Ps 42:4
g astray as soon as........Ps 58:3
I will *g* in the ....Ps 71:16
Those who *g* down to ....Ps 107:23
Where can I *g* from ......Ps 139:7
G to the ant.............Prov 6:6
All *g* to one place........Eccl 3:20
of mourning than to *g* ....Eccl 7:2
of Zion shall *g* ....Is 2:3
You wherever You *g*......Matt 8:19
do not *g* out ....Matt 24:26
He said to them, "*G* ....Mark 16:15
And I say to one, '*G* .....Luke 7:8
also want to *g* away .....John 6:67
to whom shall we *g*......John 6:68
g you cannot come ......John 8:21
I *g* to prepare a place....John 14:2
will do, because I *g*......John 14:12
seek Me, let these *g* .....John 18:8
and he shall *g* out no more .Rev 3:12

GOADS

of the wise are like *g*....Eccl 12:11
to kick against the *g*......Acts 9:5

GOAL

I press toward the *g*......Phil 3:14

GOATS

drink the blood of *g* ......Ps 50:13
his sheep from the *g*....Matt 25:32
with the blood of *g* ......Heb 9:12
g could take away ....Heb 10:4

GOD

G created the heavens .....Gen 1:1
Abram of *G* Most High...Gen 14:19
and I will be their *G* .....Gen 17:8
of the Mighty *G*.........Gen 49:24
the *G* of Abraham ....Ex 3:6
He is my *G* ....Ex 15:2
Stand before *G* for the....Ex 18:19
I am the LORD your *G*......Ex 20:2
"This is your *g* ....Ex 32:4
"*G* is not a man ....Num 23:19
G is a consuming fire......Deut 4:24
great and awesome *G*....Deut 7:21
my people, and your *G*....Ruth 1:16
know that there is a *G*..1 Sam 17:46
a rock, except our *G*....2 Sam 22:32
If the LORD is *G* ....1 Kin 18:21
G is greater than all ......2 Chr 2:5
G is greater than.......Job 33:12
"Behold, *G* is mighty.....Job 36:5

GODDESS (continued)

"Behold, *G* is great......Job 36:26
You have been My *G* .....Ps 22:10
"Where is your *G* ....Ps 42:3
G is our refuge ....Ps 46:1
G is in the midst of ....Ps 46:5
G is the King of all.......Ps 47:7
The Mighty One, *G* ....Ps 50:1
I am *G* ....Ps 50:7
me a clean heart, O *G* ....Ps 51:10
Our *G* is the *G* ....Ps 68:20
Who is so great a *G* ....Ps 77:13
Restore us, O *G*...........Ps 80:7
You alone are *G*..........Ps 86:10
Exalt the LORD our *G* ....Ps 99:9
Yes, our *G* is merciful.....Ps 116:5
give thanks to the *G* .....Ps 136:26
For *G* is in heaven........Eccl 5:2
Counselor, Mighty *G*.......Is 9:6
G is my salvation.........Is 12:2
Behold, this is our *G*.......Is 25:9
"Behold your *G* ....Is 40:9
Is there a *G* besides ......Is 44:8
to Zion, "Your *G* ....Is 52:7
stricken, smitten by *G* .....Is 53:4
and I will be their *G* .....Jer 31:33
and I saw visions of *G*.....Ezek 1:1
Who is a *G* like You ......Mic 7:18
"*G* with us.............Matt 1:23
in *G* my Savior.........Luke 1:47
the Word was with *G* .....John 1:1
enter the kingdom of *G* ...John 3:5
"For *G* so loved the ......John 3:16
has certified that *G* ......John 3:33
"*G* is Spirit ....John 4:24
"My Lord and my *G* ....John 20:28
Christ is the Son of *G*....Acts 8:37
to the unknown *G*.......Acts 17:23
Indeed, let *G* be true......Rom 3:4
If *G* is for us ....Rom 8:31
G is faithful ....1 Cor 1:9
us there is one *G* ....1 Cor 8:6
G shall supply all........Phil 4:19
and I will be their *G* .....Heb 8:10
G is a consuming fire ....Heb 12:29
G is greater than our ...1 John 3:20
for *G* is love ....1 John 4:8
No one has seen *G*.....1 John 4:12
in the temple of My *G* ....Rev 3:12
gave glory to the *G* ......Rev 11:13
G Himself will be ....Rev 21:3
and I will be his *G* ....Rev 21:7

GODDESS

after Ashtoreth the *g* ....1 Kin 11:5
of the great *g* Diana .....Acts 19:35

GODHEAD

eternal power and *G* ......Rom 1:20
the fullness of the *G* ....Col 2:9

GODLINESS

is the mystery of *g* ......1 Tim 3:16
g is profitable............1 Tim 4:8
Now *g* with contentment ..1 Tim 6:6
having a form of *g* ....2 Tim 3:5
pertain to life and *g* ......2 Pet 1:3
to perseverance *g* ....2 Pet 1:6

GODLY

Himself him who is *g*......Ps 4:3
everyone who is *g*.........Ps 32:6
who desire to live *g* ......2 Tim 3:12
righteously, and *g*.......Titus 2:12
reverence and *g* fear.....Heb 12:28
to deliver the *g*...........2 Pet 2:9

GODS

your God is God of *g* ....Deut 10:17
the household *g* ....2 Kin 23:24

He judges among the *g* .....Ps 82:1
I said, "You are *g* ....Ps 82:6
yourselves with *g*..........Is 57:5
If He called them *g* ....John 10:35
g have come down to us ..Acts 14:11

GOLD

And the *g* of that land ...Gen 2:12
a mercy seat of pure *g*....Ex 25:17
multiply silver and *g* ...Deut 17:17
"If I have made *g*.......Job 31:24
yea, than much fine *g*....Ps 19:10
is like apples of *g* ......Prov 25:11
is Mine, and the *g* ......Hag 2:8
g I do not have ....Acts 3:6
with braided hair or *g*....1 Tim 2:9
a man with *g* rings......James 2:2
Your *g* and silver are ....James 5:3
more precious than *g*.....1 Pet 1:7
like silver or *g*..........1 Pet 1:18
of the city was pure *g* ...Rev 21:21

GONE

I am *g* like a shadow .....Ps 109:23
I have *g* astray like a ....Ps 119:176
the word has *g* out of ......Is 45:23
like sheep have *g* ....Is 53:6

GOOD

God saw that it was *g*....Gen 1:10
but God meant it for *g* ...Gen 50:20
LORD has promised *g* .....Num 10:29
you have spoken is *g*...2 Kin 20:19
seeking the *g* of his .....Esth 10:3
indeed accept *g*........Job 2:10
"Who will show us any *g*....Ps 4:6
is none who does *g*.........Ps 14:1
G and upright is the......Ps 25:8
that he may see *g*........Ps 34:12
Truly God is *g* to ....Ps 73:1
g man deals graciously....Ps 112:5
Your Spirit is *g* ....Ps 143:10
g man obtains favor .....Prov 12:2
g word makes it glad ....Prov 12:25
on the evil and the *g*.....Prov 15:3
A merry heart does *g* ...Prov 17:22
who knows what is *g*.....Eccl 6:12
learn to do *g*.............Is 1:17
Zion, you who bring *g*......Is 40:9
tidings of *g* things.........Is 52:7
talked to me, with *g* .....Zech 1:13
they may see your *g*.....Matt 5:16
said, "Be of *g* cheer .....Matt 9:22
"A *g* man out of the.....Matt 12:35
"*G* Teacher, what *g*....Matt 19:16
No one is *g* but One.....Matt 19:17
For she has done a *g* ...Matt 26:10
behold, I bring you *g*.....Luke 2:10
on earth peace, *g*.......Luke 2:14
"Can anything *g*........John 1:46
Some said, "He is *g* .....John 7:12
g works I have shown ..John 10:32
who went about doing *g*..Acts 10:38
For he was a *g* man......Acts 11:24
in that He did *g*........Acts 14:17
g man someone would......Rom 5:7
in my flesh) nothing *g*....Rom 7:18
overcome evil with *g*.....Rom 12:21
Jesus for *g* works........Eph 2:10
fruitful in every *g* ....Col 1:10
know that the law is a ...1 Tim 1:8
For this is *g* and ....1 Tim 2:3
bishop, he desires a *g*....1 Tim 3:1
for this is *g* and..........1 Tim 5:4
be rich in *g* works ....1 Tim 6:18
prepared for every *g* .....2 Tim 2:21
and have tasted the *g* ....Heb 6:5
Every *g* gift and every...James 1:17
g works which they ......1 Pet 2:12

to suffer for doing *g*......1 Pet 3:17

GOODNESS

"I will make all My *g* ....Ex 33:19
and abounding in *g* ......Ex 34:6
"You are my Lord, my *g*....Ps 16:2
Surely *g* and mercy........Ps 23:6
that I would see the *g* ....Ps 27:13
how great is Your *g*.......Ps 31:19
The *g* of God endures......Ps 52:1
how great is its *g* ......Zech 9:17
the riches of His *g*........Rom 2:4
consider the *g* and......Rom 11:22
kindness, *g*...............Gal 5:22

GOODS

When *g* increase.........Eccl 5:11
and plunder his *g* ......Matt 12:29
ruler over all his *g* ....Matt 24:47
"Soul, you have many *g*..Luke 12:19
man was wasting his *g*...Luke 16:1
I give half of my *g*......Luke 19:8
has this world's *g* .....1 John 3:17

GOSPEL

The beginning of the *g* ....Mark 1:1
and believe in the *g* .....Mark 1:15
g must first be........Mark 13:10
to testify to the *g* ....Acts 20:24
separated to the *g*.......Rom 1:1
not ashamed of the *g* ....Rom 1:16
should live from the *g* ...1 Cor 9:14
if our *g* is veiled.........2 Cor 4:3
to a different *g*............Gal 1:6
of truth, the *g*...........Eph 1:13
the mystery of the *g* .....Eph 6:19
g which you heard........Col 1:23
the everlasting *g*.........Rev 14:6

GOSSIPS

only idle but also *g*......1 Tim 5:13

GOVERNMENT

and the *g* will be upon ....Is 9:6

GRACE

But Noah found *g* ....Gen 6:8
g is poured upon Your ......Ps 45:2
The LORD will give *g* .....Ps 84:11
the Spirit of *g* ....Zech 12:10
and the *g* of God was....Luke 2:40
g and truth came ....John 1:17
And great *g* was upon ...Acts 4:33
G to you and peace.......Rom 1:7
receive abundance of *g* ...Rom 5:17
g is no longer *g* ....Rom 11:6
The *g* of our Lord ....Rom 16:20
For you know the *g* ......2 Cor 8:9
g is sufficient ....2 Cor 12:9
The *g* of the Lord......2 Cor 13:14
you have fallen from *g* .....Gal 5:4
to the riches of His *g*......Eph 1:7
g you have been ....Eph 2:8
dispensation of the *g*......Eph 3:2
g was given according.....Eph 4:7
G be with all those ......Eph 6:24
shaken, let us have *g*.....Heb 12:28
But He gives more *g* ....James 4:6
this is the true *g*.........1 Pet 5:12
but grow in the *g* ....2 Pet 3:18

GRACIOUS

he said, "God be *g*......Gen 43:29
I will be *g* to whom I.....Ex 33:19
then He is *g* to him ......Job 33:24
wise man's mouth are *g* ..Eccl 10:12
of hosts will be *g*.......Amos 5:15
know that You are a *g* ....Jon 4:2
that He may be *g*........Mal 1:9
at the *g* words which ....Luke 4:22

GRAFTED

that the Lord is *g* ....1 Pet 2:3

GRAFTED

in unbelief, will be *g* .....Rom 11:23

GRAIN

Israel went to buy *g*.....Gen 42:5
it treads out the *g*.......Deut 25:4
You provide their *g*........Ps 65:9
be an abundance of *g* .....Ps 72:16
him who withholds *g* ...Prov 11:26
be revived like *g* ....Hos 14:7
G shall make the young ..Zech 9:17
to pluck heads of *g*......Matt 12:1
unless a *g* of wheat.....John 12:24
it treads out the *g* ....1 Cor 9:9

GRANT

and *g* us Your ....Ps 85:7
G that these two.......Matt 20:21
who overcomes I will *g*....Rev 3:21

GRAPES

in the blood of *g*........Gen 49:11
their *g* are *g*...........Deut 32:32
g give a good smell.......Song 2:13
vines have tender *g* .....Song 2:15
brought forth wild *g* ....Is 5:2
Yet gleaning *g* will be ......Is 17:6
"No *g* shall be ....Jer 8:13
have eaten sour *g* ....Ezek 18:2
Do men gather *g* ....Matt 7:16
g are fully ripe...........Rev 14:18

GRASPING

all is vanity and *g* ....Eccl 1:14

GRASS

they were as the *g* .....2 Kin 19:26
offspring like the *g* ....Job 5:25
g which grows up ....Ps 90:5
his days are like *g*.......Ps 103:15
The *g* withers.............Is 40:7
so clothes the *g*........Matt 6:30
to sit down on the *g*...Matt 14:19
"All flesh is as *g*........1 Pet 1:24

GRASSHOPPERS

inhabitants are like *g* .....Is 40:22
generals like great *g*......Nah 3:17

GRAVE

g does not come ....Job 7:9
for the *g* as my house....Job 17:13
my soul up from the *g* .....Ps 30:3
the power of the *g*........Ps 49:15
or wisdom in the *g*......Eccl 9:10
And they made His *g* ......Is 53:9
the power of the *g* ......Hos 13:14

GRAVES

there were no *g*...........Ex 14:11
and the *g* were opened ..Matt 27:52
g which are not........Luke 11:44
g will hear His voice.....John 5:28

GRAY

would bring down my *g*...Gen 42:38
the man of *g* hairs .....Deut 32:25
of old men is their *g* ...Prov 20:29

GREAT

and make your name *g* ...Gen 12:2
He has done us this *g* ...1 Sam 6:9
For the Lord is *g* ......1 Chr 16:25
I build will be *g* ....2 Chr 2:5
"The work is *g*..........Neh 4:19
Who does *g* things ....Job 5:9
G men are not always....Job 32:9
in the *g* assembly ....Ps 22:25

g are Your works..........Ps 92:5
my God, You are very *g* ...Ps 104:1
"the Lord has done *g*.....Ps 126:2
g is the sum of them .....Ps 139:17
in the place of the *g*......Prov 25:6
g is the Holy One ....Is 12:6
And do you seek *g*.........Jer 45:5
g is Your faithfulness ....Lam 3:23
The *g* day of the Lord....Zeph 1:14
he shall be called *g*.....Matt 5:19
one pearl of *g* price....Matt 13:46
desires to become *g* .....Matt 20:26
g drops of blood ....Luke 22:44
that he was someone *g*....Acts 8:9
"*G* is Diana of the.......Acts 19:28
that I have *g* sorrow....Rom 9:2
without controversy *g*...1 Tim 3:16
with contentment is *g*....1 Tim 6:6
But in a *g* house ....2 Tim 2:20
appearing of our *g* ......Titus 2:13
See how a *g* forest ......James 3:5
g men, the rich men ......Rev 6:15
BABYLON THE *G* ......Rev 17:5
Then I saw a *g* white....Rev 20:11
the dead, small and *g*....Rev 20:12

GREATER

the throne will I be *g*.....Gen 41:40
g than all the gods......Ex 18:11
whose appearance was *g*...Dan 7:20
kingdom of heaven is *g* ..Matt 11:11
place there is One *g*.....Matt 12:6
g than Jonah is here ...Matt 12:41
g than Solomon is here ..Matt 12:42
g things than these .....John 1:50
g than our father ....John 4:12
a servant is not *g* .....John 13:16
g than he who sent him .John 13:16
G love has no one ....John 15:13
'A servant is not *g*.....John 15:20
parts have *g* modesty ..1 Cor 12:23
he who prophesies is *g* ..1 Cor 14:5
swear by no one *g*......Heb 6:13
condemns us, God is *g* ..1 John 3:20
witness of God is *g*.....1 John 5:9

GREATEST

little child is the *g* ......Matt 18:4
be considered the *g*......Luke 22:24
but the *g* of these is ...1 Cor 13:13

GREATNESS

And in the *g* of Your ....Ex 15:7
According to the *g* ....Ps 79:11
g is unsearchable ....Ps 145:3
I will declare Your *g* ......Ps 145:6
I have attained *g* ....Eccl 1:16
traveling in the *g* ....Is 63:1
is the exceeding *g* ....Eph 1:19

GREED

part is full of *g* ....Luke 11:39

GREEDINESS

all uncleanness with *g*.....Eph 4:19
the faith in their *g*......1 Tim 6:10

GREEDY

of everyone who is *g* .....Prov 1:19
not violent, not *g*......1 Tim 3:3
not violent, not *g* ....Titus 1:7

GREEK

written in Hebrew, *G* ....John 19:20
and also for the *G*......Rom 1:16
with me, being a *G*........Gal 2:3
is neither Jew nor *G*......Gal 3:28

GREEN

lie down in *g* pastures ......Ps 23:2

GREET

g your brethren only .....Matt 5:47
G one another with a....1 Cor 16:20
into your house nor *g* ..2 John 1:10
G the friends by name....3 John 14

GREETED

and *g* Elizabeth.........Luke 1:40

GREW

And the Child *g* ....Luke 2:40
But the word of God *g* ..Acts 12:24
the word of the Lord *g* ..Acts 19:20

GRIEF

burden and his own *g* ....2 Chr 6:29
g were fully weighed.......Job 6:2
Though I speak, my *g* ....Job 16:6
observe trouble and *g*.....Ps 10:14
of mirth may be *g*.....Prov 14:13
much wisdom is much *g*...Eccl 1:18
and acquainted with *g*......Is 53:3
joy and not with *g*......Heb 13:17

GRIEVE

g the children of men ....Lam 3:33
g the Holy Spirit ....Eph 4:30

GRIEVED

earth, and He was *g*.......Gen 6:6
Has not my soul *g* .....Job 30:25
forty years I was *g*......Ps 95:10
a woman forsaken and *g*....Is 54:6
g His Holy Spirit........Is 63:10
with anger, being *g* .....Mark 3:5
Peter was *g* because ....John 21:17

GRINDERS

when the *g* cease ....Eccl 12:3

GRINDING

the sound of *g* is low.....Eccl 12:4
g the faces of the...........Is 3:15
"Two women will be *g*...Matt 24:41

GROAN

The dying *g* in the ......Job 24:12
even we ourselves *g*......Rom 8:23
who are in this tent *g* ....2 Cor 5:4

GROANING

So God heard their *g*......Ex 2:24
I am weary with my *g* ....Ps 6:6
Then Jesus, again *g* ....John 11:38

GROANINGS

g which cannot ....Rom 8:26

GROPE

And you shall *g* ....Deut 28:29
They *g* in the dark ......Job 12:25
We *g* for the wall like .....Is 59:10
hope that they might *g* ..Acts 17:27

GROUND

"Cursed is the *g* ....Gen 3:17
you stand is holy *g* ....Ex 3:5
up your fallow *g* ....Jer 4:3
give its fruit, the *g* ......Zech 8:12
others fell on good *g* .....Matt 13:8
bought a piece of *g*.....Luke 14:18
God, the pillar and *g* ....1 Tim 3:15

GROUNDED

being rooted and *g*.......Eph 3:17

GROW

they will all *g* ....Ps 102:26
the horn of David *g* .....Ps 132:17
the earth will *g*............Is 51:6
you shall go out and *g* .....Mal 4:2

GRUDGINGLY

truth in love, may g ......Eph 4:15
and they will all g ....Heb 1:11
but g in the grace and ....2 Pet 3:18

GRUDGINGLY

in his heart, not g ....2 Cor 9:7

GRUMBLERS

These are g ....Jude 16

GUARANTEE

in our hearts as a g ......2 Cor 1:22
us the Spirit as a g ......2 Cor 5:5
who is the g of our.......Eph 1:14

GUARD

g the way to the tree ......Gen 3:24
will be your rear g ....Is 52:12
g the doors of your........Mic 7:5
we were kept under g ......Gal 3:23
G what was committed ..1 Tim 6:20

GUARDIANS

but is under g and.........Gal 4:2

GUARDS

Unless the Lord g ....Ps 127:1
And the g shook for......Matt 28:4

GUIDANCE

and excellent in g ....Is 28:29

GUIDE

He will be our g ....Ps 48:14
Father, You are the g.......Jer 3:4
g our feet into the.......Luke 1:79
has come, He will g ....John 16:13
Judas, who became a g...Acts 1:16
you yourself are a g......Rom 2:19

GUIDES

to you, blind g.........Matt 23:16
unless someone g.........Acts 8:31

GUILT

they accept their g ......Lev 26:41
g has grown up to the.....Ezra 9:6
of your fathers' g ......Matt 23:32

GUILTLESS

g who takes His name......Ex 20:7
have condemned the g ....Matt 12:7

GUILTY

"We are truly g.........Gen 42:21
we have been very g ......Ezra 9:7
the world may become g..Rom 3:19
in one point, he is g ....James 2:10

GULF

you there is a great g...Luke 16:26

H

HABITATION

to Your holy h............Ex 15:13
your rightful h............Job 8:6
Is God in His holy h ......Ps 68:5
their h be desolate .....Ps 69:25
the Most High, your h....Ps 91:9
go to a city for h.........Ps 107:7
establish a city for h......Ps 107:36
but He blesses the h......Prov 3:33
in a peaceful h ....Is 32:18
Jerusalem, a quiet h ......Is 33:20
from His holy h.........Zech 2:13
'Let his h be.............Acts 1:20
be clothed with our h ....2 Cor 5:2

HADES

be brought down to H ...Matt 11:23

H shall not ....Matt 16:18
being in torments in H ..Luke 16:23
not leave my soul in H ...Acts 2:27
I have the keys of H.......Rev 1:18
H were cast into the.....Rev 20:14

HAIL

cause very heavy h.........Ex 9:18
seen the treasury of h......Job 38:22
He casts out His h.......Ps 147:17
h will sweep away the ......Is 28:17
of the plague of the h.....Rev 16:21

HAILSTONES

clouds passed with h ......Ps 18:12

HAIR

bring down my gray h ....Gen 42:38
the h on my body stood....Job 4:15
Your h is like a flock......Song 4:1
you cannot make one h ..Matt 5:36
"But not a h of your ...Luke 21:18
if a woman has long h...1 Cor 11:15
not with braided h.......1 Tim 2:9
h like women's h ....Rev 9:8

HAIRS

are more than the h ......Ps 40:12
h I will carry you.......Is 46:4
yes, gray h are here ....Hos 7:9
"But the very h ....Matt 10:30

HAIRY

h garment all over ....Gen 25:25
him, "A h man..........2 Kin 1:8

HALLOW

hosts, Him you shall h ......Is 8:13
h the Holy One of ....Is 29:23
h the Sabbath day.......Jer 17:24

HALLOWED

the Sabbath day and h ...Ex 20:11
but I will be h...........Lev 22:32
who is holy shall be h ......Is 5:16
heaven, h be Your name...Matt 6:9

HAMMER

h that breaks the rock....Jer 23:29
How the h of the whole...Jer 50:23

HAND

h shall be against........Gen 16:12
tooth for tooth, h ....Ex 21:24
the h of God was very ...1 Sam 5:11
and strengthened his h 1 Sam 23:16
Uzzah put out his h ......2 Sam 6:6
let us fall into the h ....2 Sam 24:14
Then, by the good h .....Ezra 8:18
He would loose His h.......Job 6:9
he stretches out his h....Job 15:25
that your own right h......Job 40:14
h has held me up.........Ps 18:35
My times are in Your h ...Ps 31:15
and night Your h.........Ps 32:4
Your right h is full ....Ps 48:10
Let Your h be upon the ...Ps 80:17
h shall be established......Ps 89:21
"Sit at My right h ....Ps 110:1
days is in her right h......Prov 3:16
heart is in the h.........Prov 21:1
Whatever your h ....Eccl 9:10
is at his right h ....Eccl 10:2
do not withhold your h....Eccl 11:6
His left h is under my ....Song 8:3
My h has laid the ....Is 48:13
Behold, the Lord's h.......Is 59:1
are the work of Your h ....Is 64:8
Am I a God near at h.....Jer 23:23
of heaven is at h ....Matt 3:2

if your right h...........Matt 5:30
do not let your left h ......Matt 6:3
h causes you to sin ......Mark 9:43
sitting at the right h....Mark 14:62
delivered from the h......Luke 1:74
at the right h of God .....Acts 7:55
is even at the right h .....Rom 8:34
with my own h.........1 Cor 16:21
to you with my own h.......Gal 6:11
The Lord is at h..........Phil 4:5
"Sit at My right h.......Heb 1:13
down at the right h ......Heb 10:12
stars in His right h.........Rev 2:1

HANDIWORK

firmament shows His h .....Ps 19:1

HANDLE

h the law did not know.....Jer 2:8
H Me and see ....Luke 24:39
do not taste, do not h ......Col 2:21

HANDLED

and our hands have h ....1 John 1:1

HANDS

the h are the h ....Gen 27:22
here we are, in your h.....Josh 9:25
took his life in his h.....1 Sam 19:5
put my life in my h ....1 Sam 28:21
but His h make whole ......Job 5:18
and cleanse my h ....Job 9:30
h have made me and........Job 10:8
They pierced My h ......Ps 22:16
h formed the dry land ......Ps 95:5
stretches out her h ......Prov 31:19
say, 'He has no h ....Is 45:9
than having two h ......Matt 18:8
"Behold My h and My...Luke 24:39
only, but also my h.......John 13:9
h the print of the ......John 20:25
know that these h.......Acts 20:34
his h what is good ....Eph 4:28
lifting up holy h ....1 Tim 2:8
the laying on of the h....1 Tim 4:14
to fall into the h........Heb 10:31

HANDWRITING

having wiped out the h.....Col 2:14

HANGED

for he who is h ....Deut 21:23
and went and h himself ...Matt 27:5

HANGS

h the earth on nothing....Job 26:7
is everyone who h ....Gal 3:13

HAPPEN

show us what will h.......Is 41:22
understand what will h ..Dan 10:14
not know what will h....James 4:14

HAPPINESS

one year, and bring h .....Deut 24:5

HAPPY

H is the man who has .....Ps 127:5
H are the people who......Ps 144:15
H is the man who finds ...Prov 3:13
mercy on the poor, h....Prov 14:21
trusts in the Lord, h ....Prov 16:20
h is he who keeps ....Prov 29:18
H is he who does not ....Rom 14:22

HARASS

and Judah shall not h......Is 11:13
h some from the church ...Acts 12:1

HARD

"Is anything too h.......Gen 18:14

HARDEN

His heart is as *h* . . . . .Job 41:24
shown Your people *h* . . . . .Ps 60:3
I knew you to be a *h* . . .Matt 25:24
This is a *h* saying . . . . . . .John 6:60
are some things *h* . . . . .2 Pet 3:16

HARDEN

But I will *h* his heart . . . . . .Ex 4:21
Do not *h* your hearts . . . . . .Ps 95:8
h your hearts as . . . . .Heb 3:8

HARDENED

But Pharaoh *h* his . . . . .Ex 8:32
Who has *h* himself . . . . .Job 9:4
their heart was *h* . . . . . . .Mark 6:52
eyes and *h* their hearts. . .John 12:40
lest any of you be *h* . . . . . .Heb 3:13

HARDENS

A wicked man *h* his . . . . .Prov 21:29
h his heart will fall . . . . .Prov 28:14
and whom He wills He *h* . .Rom 9:18

HARDSHIP

h that has befallen us. . . .Num 20:14
h as a good soldier . . . . . . .2 Tim 2:3

HARLOT

of a *h* named Rahab . . . . . .Josh 2:1
h is a deep pit . . . . .Prov 23:27
h is one body with her. . . .1 Cor 6:16
h Rahab did not perish . . .Heb 11:31
of the great *h* who . . . . . . .Rev 17:1

HARLOTRIES

the land with your *h* . . . . . . .Jer 3:2
Let her put away her *h* . . . .Hos 2:2

HARLOTRY

through her casual *h* . . . . . . .Jer 3:9
the lewdness of your *h* . . .Jer 13:27
let them put their *h* . . . . .Ezek 43:9
are the children of *h* . . . . . .Hos 2:4
Ephraim, you commit *h* . . . .Hos 5:3
for the spirit of *h* . . . . .Hos 5:4

HARLOTS

his blood while the *h*. . .1 Kin 22:38
h enter the. . . . . .Matt 21:31
THE MOTHER OF *H*. . . .Rev 17:5

HARM

do My prophets no *h*. . . .1 Chr 16:22
and I will not *h* . . . . .Jer 25:6
and do not *h* the oil . . . . . . .Rev 6:6

HARMLESS

become blameless and *h* . .Phil 2:15
for us, who is holy, *h* . . . . .Heb 7:26

HARMONIOUS

the harp, with *h* sound. . . . .Ps 92:3

HARP

those who play the *h* . . . . .Gen 4:21
with the lute and *h* . . . . . . .Ps 150:3
Lamb, each having a *h* . . . . .Rev 5:8

HARPS

We hung our *h* upon the . . .Ps 137:2
playing their *h*. . . . . .Rev 14:2

HARSH

"Your words have been *h*. . .Mal 3:13
but also to the *h*. . . . . . . .1 Pet 2:18

HARVEST

seedtime and *h* . . . . .Gen 8:22
to the joy of *h* . . . . .Is 9:3
shall eat up your *h*. . . . . . .Jer 5:17
"The *h* is past . . . . .Jer 8:20

HASTE

you shall eat it in *h* . . . . . .Ex 12:11
For I said in my *h*. . . . . . .Ps 31:22
And they came with *h* . . .Luke 2:16
"Zacchaeus, make *h* . . . . .Luke 19:5

HASTEN

be multiplied who *h* . . . . . .Ps 16:4
Do not *h* in your . . . . .Eccl 7:9
I, the LORD, will *h*. . . . . . . .Is 60:22

HASTENING

h the coming of the . . . . .2 Pet 3:12

HASTENS

and he sins who *h* . . . . . . .Prov 19:2
with an evil eye *h* . . . . . .Prov 28:22
is near and *h* quickly . . . . .Zeph 1:14

HASTILY

heart utter anything *h* . . . .Eccl 5:2
lay hands on anyone *h* . . .1 Tim 5:22

HASTY

Do you see a man *h* . . . . .Prov 29:20

HATE

"You shall not *h* . . . . .Lev 19:17
h all workers of . . . . .Ps 5:5
h the righteous shall. . . . . .Ps 34:21
love the LORD, *h* evil. . . . . .Ps 97:10
h every false way . . . . . .Ps 119:104
h the double-minded. . . . .Ps 119:113
I *h* and abhor lying . . . . .Ps 119:163
love, and a time to *h* . . . . .Eccl 3:8
h robbery for burnt . . . . . . .Is 61:8
You who *h* good and. . . . . . .Mic 3:2
either he will *h* . . . . .Matt 6:24

HATED

Therefore I *h* life . . . . .Eccl 2:17
h all my labor in. . . . . .Eccl 2:18
but Esau I have *h*. . . . . .Mal 1:3
And you will be *h*. . . . . . .Matt 10:22
have seen and also *h* . . . .John 15:24
but Esau I have *h* . . . . . . .Rom 9:13
For no one ever *h* . . . . . . .Eph 5:29
and *h* lawlessness. . . . . .Heb 1:9

HATEFUL

h woman when she is . . .Prov 30:23
in malice and envy, *h* . . . . .Titus 3:3

HATERS

The *h* of the LORD. . . . . . . .Ps 81:15
backbiters, *h* of God . . . . .Rom 1:30

HATES

six things the LORD *h*. . . . .Prov 6:16
lose it, and he who *h* . . . .John 12:25
"If the world *h* . . . . .John 15:18
h his brother is . . . . .1 John 2:11

HAUGHTY

Your eyes are on the *h* . .2 Sam 22:28
bring down *h* looks. . . . . . .Ps 18:27
my heart is not *h* . . . . . . .Ps 131:1
h spirit before a fall. . . . .Prov 16:18
A proud and *h* man. . . . . .Prov 21:24
Do not be *h* . . . . .Rom 11:20
age not to be *h* . . . . .1 Tim 6:17

HAUNTS

are full of the *h*. . . . . .Ps 74:20

HAVEN

shall dwell by the *h* . . . . .Gen 49:13
to their desired *h*. . . . . . . .Ps 107:30

HAVOC

for Saul, he made *h*. . . . . . . .Acts 8:3

HEAD

He shall bruise your *h*. . . . .Gen 3:15
my skin, and laid my *h*. . . .Job 16:15
return upon his own *h* . . . . .Ps 7:16
h is covered with dew. . . . .Song 5:2
The whole *h* is sick . . . . .Is 1:5
it to bow down his *h* . . . . . . .Is 58:5
could lift up his *h* . . . . . . .Zech 1:21
you swear by your *h*. . . . . .Matt 5:36
having his *h* covered . . . .1 Cor 11:4
and gave Him to be *h* . . . . .Eph 1:22
For the husband is *h* . . . . . .Eph 5:23
His *h* and his hair. . . . . . . .Rev 1:14

HEADS

men to ride over our *h* . . . . .Ps 66:12
Him, wagging their *h*. . . .Matt 27:39
dragon having seven *h* . . . . .Rev 12:3

HEAL

I wound and I *h* . . . . .Deut 32:39
O LORD, *h* me . . . . .Ps 6:2
sent Me to *h* the . . . . .Is 61:1
h your backslidings . . . . . . .Jer 3:22
who can *h* you . . . . .Lam 2:13
torn, but He will *h* . . . . .Hos 6:1
"*H* the sick . . . . .Matt 10:8
so that I should *h*. . . . . . .Matt 13:15
sent Me to *h* the. . . . . . . .Luke 4:18
Physician, *h* yourself . . . .Luke 4:23

HEALED

His word and *h* them . . . .Ps 107:20
and return and be *h*. . . . . . .Is 6:10
His stripes we are *h*. . . . . . .Is 53:5
h the hurt of My . . . . .Jer 6:14
When I would have *h*. . . . . .Hos 7:1
and He *h* them . . . . .Matt 4:24
he had faith to be *h*. . . . . .Acts 14:9
that you may be *h* . . . . . .James 5:16
his deadly wound was *h*. . . .Rev 13:3

HEALING

h shall spring forth . . . . .Is 58:8
so that there is no *h* . . . . .Jer 14:19
Your injury has no *h* . . . . .Nah 3:19
shall arise with *h* . . . . .Mal 4:2
and *h* all kinds of . . . . . . .Matt 4:23
tree were for the *h* . . . . . . .Rev 22:2

HEALINGS

to another gifts of *h* . . . . .1 Cor 12:9
Do all have gifts of *h*. . . .1 Cor 12:30

HEALS

h all your diseases . . . . .Ps 103:3
h the stroke of their . . . . . .Is 30:26
Jesus the Christ *h*. . . . . . . .Acts 9:34

HEALTH

to the soul and *h* . . . . . . .Prov 16:24
and for a time of *h*. . . . . . . .Jer 8:15
no recovery for the *h*. . . . . .Jer 8:22
all things and be in *h*. . . . .3 John 2

HEAP

I could *h* up words . . . . . . .Job 16:4
sea together as a *h* . . . . . . .Ps 33:7
ears, they will *h*. . . . . .2 Tim 4:3

HEAPS

Though he *h* up silver . . . .Job 27:16

HEAR

"H, O Israel.............Deut 6:4
Him you shall h ....Deut 18:15
H me when I call ....Ps 4:1
O You who h prayer ....Ps 65:2
h what God the Lord.......Ps 85:8
ear, shall He not h ....Ps 94:9
h the words of the.......Prov 22:17
h rather than to give.......Eccl 5:1
H, O heavens ....Is 1:2
H, you who are afar.......Is 33:13
Let the earth h...........Is 34:1
I spoke, you did not h......Is 65:12
'Hearing you will h.....Matt 13:14
if he will not h.........Matt 18:16
"Take heed what you h...Mark 4:24
ears, do you not h ....Mark 8:18
h the sound of it.........John 3:8
that God does not h......John 9:31
And how shall they h ....Rom 10:14
man be swift to h.......James 1:19
h what the Spirit says ......Rev 2:7

HEARD

h the sound of the ....Gen 3:8
h their cry because of ....Ex 3:7
you only h a voice........Deut 4:12
certainly God has h ....Ps 66:19
quietly, should be h ......Eccl 9:17
Have you not h ....Is 40:21
world men have not h ....Is 64:4
Who has h such a thing ...Is 66:8
h Ephraim bemoaning....Jer 31:18
that they will be h ....Matt 6:7
h the word believed........Acts 4:4
I say, have they not h....Rom 10:18
not seen, nor ear h........1 Cor 2:9
h inexpressible ....2 Cor 12:4
things that you have h....2 Tim 2:2
the things we have h.......Heb 2:1
the word which they h......Heb 4:2
from death, and was h.......Heb 5:7
which we have h........1 John 1:1
Lord's Day, and I h......Rev 1:10

HEARER

if anyone is a h........James 1:23
is not a forgetful h.....James 1:25

HEARERS

for not the h of the ....Rom 2:13
impart grace to the h......Eph 4:29
of the word, and not h...James 1:22

HEARING

and read in the h ....Ex 24:7
Book of Moses in the h....Neh 13:1
Do not speak in the h.....Prov 23:9
'Keep on h ....Is 6:9
h they do not..........Matt 13:13
h they may hear.......Mark 4:12
If the whole were h ....1 Cor 12:17
or by the h of faith........Gal 3:2
have become dull of h .....Heb 5:11

HEARS

for Your servant h ....1 Sam 3:9
out, and the Lord h......Ps 34:17
He who hears My Me....Luke 10:16
of God h God's words....John 8:47
"And if anyone h ......John 12:47
who is of the truth h ...John 18:37
He who knows God h ...1 John 4:6
And let him who h.......Rev 22:17

HEART

h was only evil ....Gen 6:5
for you know the h........Ex 23:9
great searchings of h ....Judg 5:16

h rejoices in the Lord ....1 Sam 2:1
God gave him another h 1 Sam 10:9
Lord looks at the h .....1 Sam 16:7
his wives turned his h....1 Kin 11:4
He pierces my h ....Job 16:13
How my h yearns within ..Job 19:27
For God made my h.....Job 23:16
My h is in turmoil and....Job 30:27
My h also instructs me ....Ps 16:7
your h live forever........Ps 22:26
h is overflowing...........Ps 45:1
My h is steadfast ....Ps 57:7
Thus my h was grieved ....Ps 73:21
my h and my flesh cry......Ps 84:2
h shall depart from me....Ps 101:4
look and a proud h........Ps 101:5
with my whole h ....Ps 111:1
h is not haughty.........Ps 131:1
h makes a cheerful ......Prov 15:13
The king's h is in the ....Prov 21:1
as he thinks in his h .....Prov 23:7
with a wicked h.........Prov 26:23
h reveals the man ......Prov 27:19
trusts in his own h ......Prov 28:26
The h of the wise is......Eccl 7:4
and a wise man's h ....Eccl 8:5
h yearned for him ....Song 5:4
and the whole h ....Is 1:5
h shall resound..........Is 16:11
the yearning of Your h ....Is 63:15
the mind and the h ......Jer 11:20
h is deceitful above ....Jer 17:9
I will give them a h ......Jer 24:7
therefore My h yearns....Jer 31:20
and take the stony h ...Ezek 11:19
get yourselves a new h ...Ezek 18:31
uncircumcised in h ......Ezek 44:7
are the pure in h ....Matt 5:8
is, there your h ....Matt 6:21
of the h proceed evil....Matt 15:19
h will flow rivers......John 7:38
"Let not your h.........John 14:1
believed were of one h......Acts 4:32
Satan filled your h.......Acts 5:3
h is not right in the......Acts 8:21
h that God has raised....Rom 10:9
in sincerity of h ....Eph 6:5
refresh my h in the.......Philem 20
and shuts up his h.....1 John 3:17
if our h condemns us....1 John 3:20

HEARTILY

you do, do it h ....Col 3:23

HEARTS

God tests the h.............Ps 7:9
who seek God, your h......Ps 69:32
let the h of those.........Ps 105:3
And he will turn the h......Mal 4:6
h failing them from ....Luke 21:26
purifying their h ....Acts 15:9
will guard your h ....Phil 4:7
of God rule in your h......Col 3:15

HEATHEN

repetitions as the h.......Matt 6:7
him be to you like a h ...Matt 18:17

HEAVEN

called the firmament H .....Gen 1:8
precious things of h ....Deut 33:13
Lord looks down from h ...Ps 14:2
word is settled in h......Ps 119:89
For God is in h..........Eccl 5:2
"H is My throne ....Is 66:1
"If h above can be........Jer 31:37
and the birds of the ....Dan 2:38
come to know that H.....Dan 4:26
for the kingdom of h ......Matt 3:2

your Father in h.........Matt 5:16
on earth as it is in h......Matt 6:10
"H and earth will......Matt 24:35
from Him a sign from h ..Mark 8:11
have sinned against h....Luke 15:18
you shall see h..........John 1:51
one has ascended to h ....John 3:13
the true bread from h ....John 6:32
a voice came from h.....John 12:28
sheet, let down from h ....Acts 11:5
the whole family in h......Eph 3:15
laid up for you in h ....Col 1:5
and the h gave rain ....James 5:18
there was silence in h.......Rev 8:1
sign appeared in h ....Rev 12:1
Now I saw a new h.......Rev 21:1

HEAVENLY

your h Father will.......Matt 6:14
h host praising God .....Luke 2:13
if I tell you h things......John 3:12
are those who are h ....1 Cor 15:48
blessing in the h..........Eph 1:3
and have tasted the h......Heb 6:4
h things themselves......Heb 9:23
a better, that is, a h.....Heb 11:16
the living God, the h ....Heb 12:22

HEAVENS

I will make your h ......Lev 26:19
and the highest h ....Deut 10:14
h cannot contain ....1 Kin 8:27
the Lord made the h....1 Chr 16:26
Till the h are no more....Job 14:12
in the h shall laugh.........Ps 2:4
h declare the glory ......Ps 19:1
Let the h declare His ....Ps 50:6
h can be compared ....Ps 89:6
The h are Yours...........Ps 89:11
For as the h are high ....Ps 103:11
When He prepared the h ..Prov 8:27
h are higher than the.......Is 55:9
behold, I create new h......Is 65:17
and behold, the h ....Matt 3:16
h will be shaken ....Matt 24:29
h are the work of Your.....Heb 1:10
h will pass away ....2 Pet 3:10

HEAVINESS

and I am full of h ....Ps 69:20
My soul melts from h.....Ps 119:28

HEAVY

the bondage was h........Neh 5:18

HEDGE

behold, I will h............Hos 2:6
sharper than a thorn h.....Mic 7:4
a vineyard and set a h....Mark 12:1

HEDGED

and whom God has h ......Job 3:23
You have h me behind .....Ps 139:5
He has h me in so that....Lam 3:7

HEED

By taking h according ....Ps 119:9
if you h Me...........Jer 17:24
and let us not give h ....Jer 18:18
nor give h to fables.......1 Tim 1:4
the more earnest h........Heb 2:1

HEEDS

h counsel is wise ....Prov 12:15

HEEL

you shall bruise His h....Gen 3:15
took hold of Esau's h.....Gen 25:26
has lifted up his h.........Ps 41:9
Me has lifted up his h ...John 13:18

HEIGHT

"Is not God in the *h*......Job 22:12
looked down from the *h*...Ps 102:19
nor *h* nor depth..........Rom 8:39
length and depth and *h*....Eph 3:18

HEIR

Has he no *h*..............Jer 49:1
Now I say that the *h*......Gal 4:1
if a son, then an *h*........Gal 4:7
He has appointed *h*........Heb 1:2
the world and became *h*...Heb 11:7

HEIRS

if children, then *h*........Rom 8:17
of God and joint *h*.......Rom 8:17
should be fellow *h*........Eph 3:6
be rich in faith and *h*....James 2:5
vessel, and as being *h*.....1 Pet 3:7

HELL

shall be turned into *h*.......Ps 9:17
go down alive into *h*......Ps 55:15
house is the way to *h*.....Prov 7:27
his soul from *h*..........Prov 23:14
H and Destruction are...Prov 27:20
"*H* from beneath is.........Is 14:9
be in danger of *h* fire....Matt 5:22
to be cast into *h*.........Matt 18:9
the condemnation of *h*..Matt 23:33
power to cast into *h*.....Luke 12:5
it is set on fire by *h*....James 3:6

HELMET

a breastplate, and a *h*......Is 59:17
And take the *h* of........Eph 6:17
and love, and as a *h*....1 Thess 5:8

HELP

the shield of your *h*.....Deut 33:29
Is my *h* not within me....Job 6:13
"There is no *h*..........Ps 3:2
May He send you *h*.......Ps 20:2
He is our *h* and our......Ps 33:20
yet praise Him, the *h*.....Ps 42:11
A very present *h*..........Ps 46:1
Give us *h* from trouble....Ps 60:11
God, make haste to *h*.....Ps 71:12
"I have given *h*..........Ps 89:19
the LORD had been my *h*...Ps 94:17
there was none to *h*.....Ps 107:12
He is their *h* and.........Ps 115:9
Our *h* is in the name......Ps 124:8
let no one *h* him........Prov 28:17
h my unbelief..........Mark 9:24
tell her to *h* me........Luke 10:40
and find grace to *h*.......Heb 4:16

HELPED

far the LORD has *h*....1 Sam 7:12
fall, but the LORD *h*....Ps 118:13
of salvation I have *h*......Is 49:8
h His servant Israel.....Luke 1:54

HELPER

I will make him a *h*......Gen 2:18
Behold, God is my *h*.......Ps 54:4
give you another *H*.....John 14:16
"But when the *H*......John 15:26
she has been a *h*........Rom 16:2
"The LORD is my *h*......Heb 13:6

HELPFUL

all things are not *h*.....1 Cor 6:12

HELPS

the Spirit also *h*..........Rom 8:26
gifts of healings, *h*......1 Cor 12:28

HEM

and touched the *h*.......Matt 9:20
might only touch the *h*..Matt 14:36

HERE

Then I said, "*H* am I........Is 6:8

HERESIES

dissensions, *h*............Gal 5:20
in destructive *h*..........2 Pet 2:1

HERITAGE

give it to you as a *h*........Ex 6:8
have given me the *h*......Ps 61:5
for that is his *h*.........Eccl 3:22
for it is his *h*..........Eccl 5:18
This is the *h* of the.......Is 54:17
of My people, My *h*.......Joel 3:2
the flock of Your *h*.......Mic 7:14

HEWN

in a tomb that was *h*...Luke 23:53

HID

and I *h* myself...........Gen 3:10

HIDDEN

and the LORD has *h*......2 Kin 4:27
It is *h* from the eyes.....Job 28:21
h Your righteousness....Ps 40:10
and my sins are not *h*......Ps 69:5
Your word I have *h*.....Ps 119:11
h riches of secret..........Is 45:3
there His power was *h*.....Hab 3:4
h that will not..........Matt 10:26
the *h* wisdom which God..1 Cor 2:7
bring to light the *h*......1 Cor 4:5
have renounced the *h*.....2 Cor 4:2
rather let it be the *h*.....1 Pet 3:4
give some of the *h*........Rev 2:17

HIDE

H me under the shadow....Ps 17:8
You shall *h* them in........Ps 31:20
O God, and do not *h*......Ps 55:1
You *h* Your face..........Ps 104:29
darkness shall not *h*.....Ps 139:12
You are God, who *h*......Is 45:15
h yourself from your.......Is 58:7
"Fall on us and *h*.......Rev 6:16

HIDES

He *h* His face............Ps 10:11

HIDING

You are my *h* place......Ps 32:7
A man will be as a *h*......Is 32:2

HIGH

priest of God Most *H*...Gen 14:18
For the LORD Most *H*......Ps 47:2
h is Your right...........Ps 89:13
are on *h* forevermore......Ps 92:8
the LORD is on *h*.........Ps 138:6
"I dwell in the *h*..........Is 57:15
know that the Most *H*....Dan 4:17
whose habitation is *h*.....Obad 3
up on a *h* mountain by...Matt 17:1
your mind on *h* things...Rom 12:16
h thing that exalts.......2 Cor 10:5
and faithful *H* Priest......Heb 2:17

HIGHER

They are *h* than heaven...Job 11:8
you, 'Friend, go up *h*...Luke 14:10
h than the heavens.......Heb 7:26

HIGHWAY

of the upright is a *h*.....Prov 15:19
in the desert a *h*..........Is 40:3

up, build up the *h*........Is 62:10

HIGHWAYS

h shall be elevated........Is 49:11
go into the *h*...........Matt 22:9

HILL

My King on My holy *h*.....Ps 2:6
h cannot be hidden......Matt 5:14
and *h* brought low.......Luke 3:5
to the brow of the *h*.....Luke 4:29

HILLS

of the everlasting *h*.....Gen 49:26
possess is a land of *h*...Deut 11:11
of the *h* are His also.....Ps 95:4
up my eyes to the *h*......Ps 121:1
settled, before the *h*....Prov 8:25

HINDER

takes away, who can *h*....Job 9:12
all things lest we *h*......1 Cor 9:12

HINDERED

come to you (but was *h*...Rom 1:13
Who *h* you from obeying....Gal 5:7
prayers may not be *h*......1 Pet 3:7

HIP

socket of Jacob's *h*......Gen 32:25

HIRE

h laborers for his........Matt 20:1

HIRED

h man who eagerly........Job 7:2
h servants have bread...Luke 15:17

HIRELING

"The *h* flees because....John 10:13

HOLD

h my eyelids open........Ps 77:4
right hand shall *h*........Ps 139:10
LORD your God, will *h*....Is 41:13
I cannot *h* my peace......Jer 4:19
h fast that word which...1 Cor 15:2
h fast our confession.....Heb 4:14
h fast and repent.........Rev 3:3

HOLES

"Foxes have *h*..........Matt 8:20

HOLIER

near me, for I am *h*........Is 65:5

HOLIEST

the way into the *H*........Heb 9:8
to enter the *H* by the....Heb 10:19

HOLINESS

You, glorious in *h*........Ex 15:11
has spoken in His *h*......Ps 60:6
I have sworn by My *h*.....Ps 89:35
h adorns Your house.......Ps 93:5
the Highway of *H*.........Is 35:8
to the Spirit of *h*........Rom 1:4
spirit, perfecting *h*.......2 Cor 7:1
uncleanness, but in *h*....1 Thess 4:7
be partakers of His *h*.....Heb 12:10

HOLY

where you stand is *h*......Ex 3:5
priests and a *h* nation.....Ex 19:6
day, to keep it *h*.........Ex 20:8
distinguish between *h*...Lev 10:10
the LORD your God am *h*...Lev 19:2
"No one is *h*...........1 Sam 2:2
h seed is mixed..........Ezra 9:2
h ones will you turn......Job 5:1
God sits on His *h*.........Ps 47:8

God, in His *h* mountain . . . . .Ps 48:1
my life, for I am *h*. . . . . .Ps 86:2
"H, *h*, *h*. . . . . .Is 6:3
child of the *H* Spirit. . . . .Matt 1:18
baptize you with the *H* . . . .Mark 1:8
who speak, but the *H* . . .Mark 13:11
H Spirit will come . . . . . .Luke 1:35
H Spirit descended. . . . . .Luke 3:22
Father give the *H*. . . . . . .Luke 11:13
H Spirit will teach . . . . . .Luke 12:12
H Spirit was not. . . . . . . .John 7:39
H Spirit has come. . . . . . . .Acts 1:8
all filled with the *H*. . . . . . .Acts 2:4
apostles' hands the *H*. . . . .Acts 8:18
to speak, the *H* Spirit. . . .Acts 11:15
good to the *H* Spirit. . . . . .Acts 15:28
receive the *H* Spirit. . . . . . .Acts 19:2
if the firstfruit is *h* . . . . .Rom 11:16
peace and joy in the *H* . . .Rom 14:17
one another with a *h*. . . . .Rom 16:16
H Spirit teaches. . . . . .1 Cor 2:13
that we should be *h*. . . . . . .Eph 1:4
were sealed with the *H* . . .Eph 1:13
partakers of the *H*. . . . . . . .Heb 6:4
has not entered the *h*. . . . .Heb 9:24
H Spirit sent from . . . . . .1 Pet 1:12
He who called you is *h* . . .1 Pet 1:15
it is written, "Be *h*. . . . . . .1 Pet 1:16
moved by the *H* Spirit. . . .2 Pet 1:21
anointing from the *H* . . .1 John 2:20
says He who is *h*. . . . . .Rev 3:7
For You alone are *h*. . . . . . .Rev 15:4
is *h*, let him be *h*. . . . . . . .Rev 22:11

HOME

LORD has brought me *h*. . .Ruth 1:21
sparrow has found a *h* . . . . .Ps 84:3
the stork has her *h*. . . . . .Ps 104:17
to his eternal *h*. . . . . .Eccl 12:5
said to him, "Go *h*. . . . . .Mark 5:19
into an everlasting *h*. . . . .Luke 16:9
to him and make Our *h* .John 14:23
took her to his own *h* . . .John 19:27
let him eat at *h* . . . . . . .1 Cor 11:34
own husbands at *h*. . . . . .1 Cor 14:35
that while we are at *h* . . . .2 Cor 5:6
to show piety at *h*. . . . . . .1 Tim 5:4

HOMELESS

and beaten, and *h* . . . . . .1 Cor 4:11

HOMEMAKERS

be discreet, chaste, *h* . . . . .Titus 2:5

HONEST

we are *h* men. . . . . .Gen 42:11

HONEY

"What is sweeter than *h* .Judg 14:18
and with *h* from the . . . . . . .Ps 81:16
My son, eat *h* because . . .Prov 24:13
not good to eat much *h* . .Prov 25:27
h and milk are under . . . .Song 4:11
was locusts and wild *h*. . . .Matt 3:4

HONEYCOMB

than honey and the *h*. . . . .Ps 19:10
words are like a *h* . . . . . .Prov 16:24
fish and some *h*. . . . . . . .Luke 24:42

HONOR

H your father and your . . . .Ex 20:12
both riches and *h*. . . . . . . .1 Kin 3:13
the king delights to *h*. . . . .Esth 6:6
earth, and lay my *h* . . . . .Ps 7:5
A man who is in *h*. . . . . . . .Ps 49:20
Sing out the *h* of His . . . . . .Ps 66:2
will deliver him and *h*. . . . .Ps 91:15
H and majesty are . . . . .Ps 96:6
h have all His saints. . . . . . .Ps 149:9

H the LORD with your. . . . . .Prov 3:9
before *h* is humility. . . . . .Prov 15:33
h is not fitting. . . . . .Prov 26:1
spirit will retain *h* . . . . . .Prov 29:23
Father, where is My *h* . . . . .Mal 1:6
is not without *h* . . . . .Matt 13:57
H your father and your . .Matt 15:4
h the Son just as they . . .John 5:23
"I do not receive *h*. . . . . . .John 5:41
but I *h* My Father . . . . . .John 8:49
"If I *h* Myself. . . . . .John 8:54
him My Father will *h*. . .John 12:26
make one vessel for *h* . . . .Rom 9:21
to whom fear, *h*. . . . . .Rom 13:7
we bestow greater *h*. . . . .1 Cor 12:23
sanctification and *h*. . . . .1 Thess 4:4
alone is wise, be *h*. . . . . . .1 Tim 1:17
worthy of double *h* . . . . . .1 Tim 5:17
and clay, some for *h* . . . . .2 Tim 2:20
no man takes this *h*. . . . . . .Heb 5:4
H the king. . . . . .1 Pet 2:17
from God the Father *h* . .2 Pet 1:17
give glory and *h* . . . . .Rev 4:9

HONORABLE

of God, and he is an *h*. . . .1 Sam 9:6
His work is *h* and. . . . . . . .Ps 111:3
It is *h* for a man to. . . . . . .Prov 20:3
traders are the *h* . . . . .Is 23:8
holy day of the LORD *h*. . . .Is 58:13
providing *h* things. . . . . . .2 Cor 8:21
Marriage is *h* among. . . . .Heb 13:4
having your conduct *h*. . . .1 Pet 2:12

HONORABLY

desiring to live *h* . . . . . . .Heb 13:18

HONORS

h those who fear the. . . . . . .Ps 15:4
"This people *h* Me . . . . . .Mark 7:6
It is My Father who *h* . . .John 8:54

HOOKS

will lament who cast *h* . . . . .Is 19:8
spears into pruning *h*. . . . . .Mic 4:3

HOPE

I should say I have *h*. . . . .Ruth 1:12
are spent without *h*. . . . . . . .Job 7:6
so You destroy the *h*. . . . .Job 14:19
where then is my *h*. . . . . . .Job 17:15
h He has uprooted . . . . . . .Job 19:10
also will rest in *h* . . . . .Ps 16:9
heart, all you who *h* . . . . .Ps 31:24
My *h* is in You. . . . . .Ps 39:7
For You are my *h* . . . . .Ps 71:5
I *h* in Your word . . . . . . .Ps 119:147
O Israel, *h* in the. . . . . . . .Ps 130:7
h will not be cut . . . . . . .Prov 23:18
There is more *h* . . . . .Prov 26:12
the living there is *h*. . . . . . .Eccl 9:4
O the *H* of Israel. . . . . . . .Jer 14:8
good that one should *h*. . . .Lam 3:26
Achor as a door of *h*. . . . . .Hos 2:15
you prisoners of *h*. . . . . . .Zech 9:12
"I have *h* in God . . . . . . .Acts 24:15
to *h*, in *h* believed . . . . . . .Rom 4:18
and rejoice in *h* . . . . .Rom 5:2
h does not disappoint . . . . .Rom 5:5
were saved in this *h* . . . . . .Rom 8:24
h that is seen is. . . . . .Rom 8:24
But if we *h* for what . . . . . .Rom 8:25
And now abide faith, *h* . .1 Cor 13:13
life only we have *h*. . . . . .1 Cor 15:19
may know what is the *h* . . .Eph 1:18
were called in one *h* . . . . . .Eph 4:4
h which is laid . . . . .Col 1:5
Christ in you, the *h*. . . . . . . .Col 1:27
For what is our *h* . . . . . .1 Thess 2:19

others who have no *h*. . .1 Thess 4:13
and as a helmet the *h* . . .1 Thess 5:8
Jesus Christ, our *h* . . . . . . .1 Tim 1:1
in *h* of eternal life. . . . . . . .Titus 1:2
for the blessed *h*. . . . . .Titus 2:13
to lay hold of the *h* . . . . . . .Heb 6:18
in of a better *h* . . . . .Heb 7:19
us again to a living *h*. . . . . .1 Pet 1:3
you a reason for the *h* . . . .1 Pet 3:15
who has this *h* in Him . . .1 John 3:3

HOPED

substance of things *h* . . . .Heb 11:1

HORN

my shield and the *h* . . . . . . .Ps 18:2
h will be exalted . . . . .Ps 112:9
goat had a notable *h* . . . . . .Dan 8:5
and has raised up a *h*. . . . .Luke 1:69

HORRIBLE

h thing has been . . . . .Jer 5:30
I have seen a *h* . . . . .Hos 6:10

HORROR

and behold, *h* and. . . . . . .Gen 15:12
sorrow, the cup of *h* . . . .Ezek 23:33
you will become a *h* . . . .Ezek 27:36

HORSE

The *h* and its rider He. . . . .Ex 15:1
Have you given the *h*. . . . .Job 39:19
h is a vain hope. . . . . .Ps 33:17
the strength of the *h* . . . . .Ps 147:10
h is prepared for the. . . . .Prov 21:31
and behold, a white *h*. . . . . .Rev 6:2
and behold, a black *h*. . . . . .Rev 6:5
and behold, a pale *h* . . . . . .Rev 6:8
and behold, a white *h*. . . .Rev 19:11

HORSES

seen servants on *h*. . . . . . .Eccl 10:7
h are swifter than . . . . .Jer 4:13
Do *h* run on rocks. . . . . . .Amos 6:12
we put bits in *h* . . . . .James 3:3

HOSANNA

H in the highest . . . . .Matt 21:9

HOSPITABLE

of good behavior, *h* . . . . . .1 Tim 3:2
Be *h* to one another . . . . . .1 Pet 4:9

HOST

who brings out their *h* . . . .Is 40:26
of the heavenly *h* . . . . . . .Luke 2:13

HOSTILITY

Him who endured such *h* . .Heb 12:3

HOSTS

name of the LORD of *h*. . .1 Sam 17:45
As the LORD of *h* lives . .1 Kin 18:15
The LORD of *h* is with. . . . . .Ps 46:7
LORD, all you His *h*. . . . . .Ps 103:21
praise Him, all His *h* . . . . .Ps 148:2
word of the LORD of *h* . . . . .Is 39:5
LORD of *h* is His name . . . . .Is 47:4
against spiritual *h*. . . . . . . .Eph 6:12

HOT

of the LORD was *h* . . . . . . .Judg 2:14
My heart was *h* within. . . . . .Ps 39:3
are neither cold nor *h*. . . . .Rev 3:15

HOUND

My enemies would *h*. . . . . . .Ps 56:2

HOUR

h what you should . . . . . .Matt 10:19
day and *h* no one knows .Matt 24:36

HOURS

Man is coming at an *h*...Matt 24:44
Behold, the *h* is at ......Matt 26:45
But this is your *h*......Luke 22:53
h has not yet come.......John 2:4
"But the *h* is coming ....John 4:23
h has come that the ....John 12:23
save Me from this *h* .....John 12:27
"Father, the *h* ....John 17:1
will not know what *h* ......Rev 3:3
keep you from the *h* ......Rev 3:10

HOURS

Are there not twelve *h*...John 11:9

HOUSE

from your father's *h*......Gen 12:1
But as for me and my *h*..Josh 24:15
h appointed for all.......Job 30:23
with them to the *h* ....Ps 42:4
the goodness of Your *h*.....Ps 65:4
For her *h* leads down .....Prov 2:18
Through wisdom a *h*.....Prov 24:3
better to go to the *h* ......Eccl 7:2
of the *h* tremble..........Eccl 12:3
to the *h* of the God of ......Is 2:3
to those who join *h* ....Is 5:8
h was filled with ....Is 6:4
'Set your *h* in order ....Is 38:1
h shall be called a ....Is 56:7
and beat on that *h* ......Matt 7:25
h divided against ....Matt 12:25
h shall be called a .....Matt 21:13
h may be filled ....Luke 14:23
not make My Father's *h* ..John 2:16
h are many mansions ....John 14:2
publicly and from *h*......Acts 20:20
in his own rented *h* ......Acts 28:30
who rules his own *h* .....1 Tim 3:4
the church in your *h*......Philem 2
For every *h* is built ....Heb 3:4
His own, *h*, whose *h* ....Heb 3:6
him into your *h* ....2 John 1:10

HOUSEHOLD

over the ways of her *h*....Prov 31:27
"If the *h* is worthy......Matt 10:13
be those of his own *h* ....Matt 10:36
h were baptized ....Acts 16:15
saved, you and your *h*....Acts 16:31
also baptized the *h* ......1 Cor 1:16
those who are of the *h* ...Gal 6:10
who are of Caesar's *h*....Phil 4:22

HOUSEHOLDER

h who brings out of ....Matt 13:52

HOUSES

h are safe from fear.......Job 21:9
Yet He filled their *h* .....Job 22:18
is that their *h* ....Ps 49:11
H and riches are an......Prov 19:14
who has left *h* or.......Matt 19:29
you devour widows' *h*....Matt 23:14
Do you not have *h* ......1 Cor 11:22

HOVERING

Spirit of God was *h* ......Gen 1:2

HOW

"*H* can this be ....Luke 1:34
H long do You keep ....John 10:24
h you turned to God ....1 Thess 1:9

HUMAN

we have had *h* fathers ....Heb 12:9

HUMBLE

man Moses was very *h*...Num 12:3
h you and test you ....Deut 8:2
who is proud, and *h* .....Job 40:11

the cry of the *h* ....Ps 9:12
Do not forget the *h*.......Ps 10:12
the desire of the *h*.......Ps 10:17
h He guides in justice ....Ps 25:9
h shall hear of it and .....Ps 34:2
LORD lifts up the *h*.......Ps 147:6
h spirit with the ....Prov 16:19
contrite and *h* spirit ....Is 57:15
a meek and *h* people.....Zeph 3:12
associate with the *h* .....Rom 12:16
gives grace to the *h* ......James 4:6
H yourselves in the ....James 4:10
gives grace to the *h* ......1 Pet 5:5
h yourselves under the.....1 Pet 5:6

HUMBLED

h himself greatly ....2 Chr 33:12
as a man, He *h* Himself.....Phil 2:8

HUMBLES

h Himself to behold ....Ps 113:6

HUMILIATION

to plunder, and to *h*.......Ezra 9:7
h His justice was.........Acts 8:33
but the rich in his *h*.....James 1:10

HUMILITY

By *h* and the fear of .....Prov 22:4
righteousness, seek *h* .....Zeph 2:3
the Lord with all *h* .....Acts 20:19
delight in false *h* ....Col 2:18
mercies, kindness, *h* ......Col 3:12
h correcting those ....2 Tim 2:25
gentle, showing all *h* ......Titus 3:2
and be clothed with *h* .....1 Pet 5:5

HUNGER

you, allowed you to *h*.....Deut 8:3
lack and suffer *h*.........Ps 34:10
They shall neither *h* .....Is 49:10
likely to die from *h* ....Jer 38:9
are those who *h*.........Matt 5:6
for you shall *h*..........Luke 6:25
to Me shall never *h*......John 6:35
present hour we both *h*...1 Cor 4:11
They shall neither *h* ......Rev 7:16

HUNGRY

bread from the *h* ....Job 22:7
and fills the *h* ....Ps 107:9
gives food to the *h* ....Ps 146:7
h soul every bitter.......Prov 27:7
your soul to the *h* ....Is 58:10
'for I was *h* and you.....Matt 25:35
when did we see You *h*...Matt 25:37
and one is *h* and........1 Cor 11:21
But if anyone is *h* ......1 Cor 11:34
to be full and to be *h*.....Phil 4:12

HUNT

Yet you *h* my life to ....1 Sam 24:11
h the violent man ....Ps 140:11
h the souls of My ......Ezek 13:18

HUNTER

Nimrod the mighty *h*.....Gen 10:9
Esau was a skillful *h* ....Gen 25:27

HURT

h a woman with child ....Ex 21:22
who plot my *h* ....Ps 35:4
but I was not *h* ....Prov 23:35
another to his own *h* .....Eccl 8:9
They shall not *h*...........Is 11:9
of my people I am *h*.......Jer 8:21
Woe is me for my *h*.......Jer 10:19
it will by no means *h*.....Mark 16:18
shall not be *h* by the .....Rev 2:11

HUSBAND

She also gave to her *h* ......Gen 3:6
"Surely you are a *h* ......Ex 4:25
h safely trusts her......Prov 31:11
your Maker is your *h*......Is 54:5
though I was a *h* ....Jer 31:32
now have is not your *h*...John 4:18
woman have her own *h* ....1 Cor 7:2
For the unbelieving *h* .....1 Cor 7:14
you will save your *h*.....1 Cor 7:16
betrothed you to one *h* ...2 Cor 11:2
For the *h* is head of ......Eph 5:23
the *h* of one wife ....1 Tim 3:2

HUSBANDS

them ask their own *h* ...1 Cor 14:35
H, love your wives ....Eph 5:25
Let deacons be the *h*.....1 Tim 3:12

HYMN

when they had sung a *h* Matt 26:30

HYMNS

praying and singing *h*....Acts 16:25
in psalms and *h* ....Eph 5:19

HYPOCRISY

you are full of *h* ....Matt 23:28
Pharisees, which is *h* ....Luke 12:1
Let love be without *h* .....Rom 12:9
away with their *h* ....Gal 2:13
and without *h*, ...James 3:17
malice, all deceit, *h*......1 Pet 2:1

HYPOCRITE

of the *h* shall perish .....Job 8:13
and the joy of the *h* ......Job 20:5
is the hope of the *h*.......Job 27:8
for everyone is a *h* ....Is 9:17
also played the *h* ....Gal 2:13

HYPOCRITES

"But the *h* in heart.......Job 36:13
will I go in with *h*.........Ps 26:4
"For you were *h* ....Jer 42:20
not be like the *h* ....Matt 6:5
do you test Me, you *h* ...Matt 22:18
and Pharisees, *h* ......Matt 23:13

HYSSOP

Purge me with *h* ....Ps 51:7
sour wine, put it on *h*....John 19:29

I

ICE

dark because of the *i* ......Job 6:16

IDLE

For they are *i* ....Ex 5:8
i person will suffer ......Prov 19:15
i word men may speak ...Matt 12:36
saw others standing *i*.....Matt 20:3
they learn to be *i* ....1 Tim 5:13
both *i* talkers and........Titus 1:10

IDOL

if he blesses an *i* ....Is 66:3
thing offered to an *i*......1 Cor 8:7
That an *i* is anything....1 Cor 10:19

IDOLATER

or covetous, or an *i* .....1 Cor 5:11
man, who is an *i*..........Eph 5:5

IDOLATERS

fornicators, nor *i* ....1 Cor 6:9
immoral, sorcerers, *i*......Rev 21:8
and murderers and *i*.....Rev 22:15

IDOLATRIES
and abominable *i* ....1 Pet 4:3

IDOLATRY
beloved, flee from *i*......1 Cor 10:14
i, sorcery................Gal 5:20

IDOLS
stolen the household *i* ....Gen 31:19
of the peoples are *i*.........Ps 96:5
i are silver and gold ......Ps 115:4
land is also full of *i* ....Is 2:8
insane with their *i* ....Jer 50:38
in the room of his *i*......Ezek 8:12
from their wooden *i* ......Hos 4:12
who regard worthless *i* .....Jon 2:8
i speak delusion.........Zech 10:2
things polluted by *i*.......Acts 15:20
You who abhor *i* ....Rom 2:22
This was offered to *i* ...1 Cor 10:28
keep yourselves from *i* ..1 John 5:21
worship demons, and *i* .....Rev 9:20

IGNORANCE
that you did it in *i*........Acts 3:17
i God overlooked ....Acts 17:30
sins committed in *i* ....Heb 9:7
to silence the *i* ....1 Pet 2:15

IGNORANT
I was so foolish and *i* ......Ps 73:22
though Abraham was *i* .....Is 63:16
not want you to be *i* ....1 Cor 12:1
But if anyone is *i* ......1 Cor 14:38
on those who are *i* ....Heb 5:2

IGNORANTLY
because I did it *i*........1 Tim 1:13

ILLEGITIMATE
then you are *i* ....Heb 12:8

ILLUMINATED
after you were *i* ....Heb 10:32
and the earth was *i*........Rev 18:1
for the glory of God *i*....Rev 21:23

IMAGE
Us make man in Our *i*.....Gen 1:26
yourselves a carved *i* ....Deut 4:16
shall despise their *i*........Ps 73:20
the king made an *i*.........Dan 3:1
to them, "Whose *i*......Matt 22:20
since he is the *i* ....1 Cor 11:7
He is the *i* of the.........Col 1:15
and not the very *i* ....Heb 10:1
the beast and his *i* ....Rev 14:9
who worshiped his *i* .....Rev 19:20

IMAGINATION
the proud in the *i* ....Luke 1:51

IMITATE
I urge you, *i* me ....1 Cor 4:16
as I also *i* Christ ....1 Cor 11:1
i those who through......Heb 6:12

IMMANUEL
shall call His name *I*........Is 7:14
shall call His name *I* .....Matt 1:23

IMMEDIATELY
i the Spirit ....Mark 1:12
hear, Satan comes *i* .....Mark 4:15
i forgets what ....James 1:24
I I was in the Spirit ....Rev 4:2

IMMORAL
i woman is a deep pit ....Prov 22:14
murderers, sexually *i* .....Rev 21:8

IMMORALITY
except sexual *i* ....Matt 5:32
i as is not even named.....1 Cor 5:1
abstain from sexual *i*....1 Thess 4:3

IMMORTAL
to the King eternal, *i* ....1 Tim 1:17

IMMORTALITY
glory, honor, and *i* ....Rom 2:7
mortal must put on *i* .....1 Cor 15:53
who alone has *i* ....1 Tim 6:16
and brought life and *i*...2 Tim 1:10

IMMOVABLE
be steadfast, *i*..........1 Cor 15:58

IMMUTABLE
that by two *i* things.......Heb 6:18

IMPART
see you, that I may *i*......Rom 1:11
that it may *i* grace.......Eph 4:29

IMPENITENT
i heart you are ....Rom 2:5

IMPLANTED
with meekness the *i*.....James 1:21

IMPOSSIBLE
and nothing will be *i* ....Matt 17:20
"With men this is *i*......Matt 19:26
God nothing will be *i*......Luke 1:37
without faith it is *i*......Heb 11:6

IMPOSTORS
i will grow worse.......2 Tim 3:13

IMPRISONMENT
and of chains and *i* ......Heb 11:36

IMPRISONMENTS
in stripes, in *i*...........2 Cor 6:5

IMPULSIVE
but he who is *i*.........Prov 14:29

IMPURITY
a woman during her *i*...Ezek 18:6

IMPUTE
"Do not let my lord *i* ..2 Sam 19:19
the LORD does not *i* ....Ps 32:2
the LORD shall not *i* ......Rom 4:8

IMPUTED
bloodshed shall be *i* ......Lev 17:4
might be *i* to them ......Rom 4:11
alone that it was *i*.......Rom 4:23
but sin is not *i*...........Rom 5:13

IMPUTES
i righteousness apart ......Rom 4:6

INCENSE
golden bowls full of *i* ....Rev 5:8

INCLINE
i your heart to the......Josh 24:23
i my heart to any evil......Ps 141:4

INCORRUPTIBLE
the glory of the *i* ....Rom 1:23
dead will be raised *i* ....1 Cor 15:52
to an inheritance *i* ....1 Pet 1:4
corruptible seed but *i*....1 Pet 1:23

INCORRUPTION
it is raised in *i* ....1 Cor 15:42
corruption inherit *i* .....1 Cor 15:50
must put on *i*..........1 Cor 15:53

INCREASE
if riches *i* ....Ps 62:10
the LORD give you *i* .....Ps 115:14
hear and *i* learning ....Prov 1:5
When goods *i* ....Eccl 5:11
Of the *i* of His ....Is 9:7
and knowledge shall *i* .....Dan 12:4
Lord, "*I* our faith ....Luke 17:5
"He must *i*............John 3:30
but God gave the *i*.......1 Cor 3:6
grows with the *i*..........Col 2:19
for they will *i* ....2 Tim 2:16

INCREASED
The waters *i* and.........Gen 7:17
i your mercy which you...Gen 19:19
nation and *i* its joy ....Is 9:3
And Jesus *i* in wisdom....Luke 2:52

INCREASES
i knowledge *i* ....Eccl 1:18
who have no might He *i*....Is 40:29

INCREDIBLE
should it be thought *i*.....Acts 26:8

INCURABLE
My wound is *i*...........Job 34:6
'Your affliction is *i*......Jer 30:12
Your sorrow is *i* ....Jer 30:15

INDEBTED
everyone who is *i* ....Luke 11:4

INDEED
i it was very ....Gen 1:31
"But will God *i* ....1 Kin 8:27
"Behold, an Israelite *i* ....John 1:47

INDICATING
the Holy Spirit *i*.........Heb 9:8
who was in them was *i* ...1 Pet 1:11

INDIGNANT
saw it, they were *i* ......Matt 26:8

INDIGNATION
of His anger, wrath, *i*......Ps 78:49
I has taken hold ....Ps 119:53
in whose hand is My *i*......Is 10:5
For the *i* of the LORD.......Is 34:2
have filled me with *i* .....Jer 15:17
can stand before His *i*......Nah 1:6
i which will devour......Heb 10:27
into the cup of His *i*......Rev 14:10

INDUCED
O LORD, You *i* me.........Jer 20:7
if the prophet is *i* ....Ezek 14:9
I the LORD have *i* ....Ezek 14:9

INDULGENCE
no value against the *i* ......Col 2:23

INEXCUSABLE
Therefore you are *i* ....Rom 2:1

INEXPRESSIBLE
Paradise and heard *i* .....2 Cor 12:4
you rejoice with joy *i*......1 Pet 1:8

INFALLIBLE
suffering by many *i*........Acts 1:3

INFANTS
i who never saw..........Job 3:16
they also brought *i*......Luke 18:15

INFERIOR
another kingdom *i*.......Dan 2:39
that I am not at all *i*.....2 Cor 11:5

INFIRMITIES

"He Himself took our *i* . . .Matt 8:17
boast, except in my *i* . . . . .2 Cor 12:5
and your frequent *i* . . . . . .1 Tim 5:23

INFLAMING

i yourselves with gods. . . . . .Is 57:5

INHABIT

the wicked will not *i* . . . .Prov 10:30
cities and *i* them . . . . .Amos 9:14

INHABITANT

Cry out and shout, O *i* . . . . . .Is 12:6
And the *i* will not say . . . . . .Is 33:24

INHABITANTS

He looks on all the *i* . . . . . .Ps 33:14
give ear, all *i* . . . . .Ps 49:1
Let the *i* of Sela sing. . . . . .Is 42:11
Woe to the *i* of the . . . . . .Rev 12:12

INHABITED

rejoicing in His *i* . . . . .Prov 8:31
'You shall be *i*. . . . . .Is 44:26
who formed it to be *i*. . . . . .Is 45:18

INHERIT

i the iniquities. . . . . .Job 13:26
descendants shall *i* . . . . . .Ps 25:13
The righteous shall *i*. . . . . .Ps 37:29
The wise shall *i* . . . . .Prov 3:35
love me to *i* wealth . . . . . .Prov 8:21
The simple *i* folly . . . . . .Prov 14:18
the blameless will *i* . . . . . .Prov 28:10
i the kingdom prepared . .Matt 25:34
I do that I may *i* . . . . . . .Mark 10:17
unrighteous will not *i* . . . . .1 Cor 6:9
you may *i* a blessing . . . . . .1 Pet 3:9
who overcomes shall *i*. . . . . .Rev 21:7

INHERITANCE

"You shall have no *i* . . . . .Num 18:20
is the place of His *i* . . . . .Deut 32:9
the portion of my *i* . . . . . .Ps 16:5
yes, I have a good *i*. . . . . . .Ps 16:6
i shall be forever. . . . . . . .Ps 37:18
He will choose our *i* . . . . . .Ps 47:4
You confirmed Your *i* . . . . . .Ps 68:9
the tribe of Your *i* . . . . . . .Ps 74:2
i gained hastily . . . . .Prov 20:21
right of *i* is yours. . . . . . .Jer 32:8
i has been turned. . . . . . . .Lam 5:2
will arise to your *i* . . . . . .Dan 12:13
And God gave him no *i* . . . . .Acts 7:5
and give you an *i*. . . . . . . .Acts 20:32
For if the *i* is of the. . . . . .Gal 3:18
we have obtained an *i* . . . .Eph 1:11
be partakers of the *i* . . . . . .Col 1:12
receive as an *i*. . . . . .Heb 11:8
i incorruptible. . . . . .1 Pet 1:4

INIQUITIES

How many are my *i* . . . . .Job 13:23
i have overtaken me . . . . . .Ps 40:12
I prevail against me . . . . . .Ps 65:3
forgives all your *i* . . . . . . .Ps 103:3
LORD, should mark *i* . . . . . .Ps 130:3
was bruised for our *i* . . . . . .Is 53:5
He shall bear their *i* . . . . . .Is 53:11
i have separated you . . . . .Is 59:2

INIQUITY

God, visiting the *i* of the. . .Ex 20:5
He has not observed *i* . . .Num 23:21
wicked brings forth *i* . . . . . .Ps 7:14
O LORD, pardon my *i* . . . . . .Ps 25:11
i I have not hidden. . . . . . . .Ps 32:5
was brought forth in *i* . . . . .Ps 51:5
If I regard *i* in my. . . . . . . .Ps 66:18

INJUSTICE

of truth and without *i* . . . .Deut 32:4
i shuts her mouth. . . . . . . .Job 5:16
i have your fathers. . . . . . . .Jer 2:5

INK

us, written not with *i* . . . . .2 Cor 3:3
do so with paper and *i* . .2 John 1:12

INN

room for them in the *i* . . .Luke 2:7
brought him to an *i* . . . . .Luke 10:34

INNOCENCE

of my heart and *i* . . . . .Gen 20:5
washed my hands in *i*. . . . . .Ps 73:13

INNOCENT

do not kill the *i*. . . . . .Ex 23:7
a bribe to slay an *i* . . . . .Deut 27:25
i will divide the . . . . .Job 27:17
a bribe against the *i*. . . . . . .Ps 15:5
because I was found *i* . . . .Dan 6:22
saying, "I am *i* . . . . .Matt 27:24
this day that I am *i* . . . . .Acts 20:26

INNUMERABLE

i as the sand which is . . . .Heb 11:12
i company of angels. . . . . .Heb 12:22

INQUIRED

children of Israel *i* . . . . . .Judg 20:27
Therefore David *i* . . . . . . .1 Sam 23:2
the LORD, nor *i* of Him. . . . .Zeph 1:6
the prophets have *i* . . . . . .1 Pet 1:10

INQUIRY

shall make careful *i*. . . . . .Deut 19:18

INSANE

images, and they are *i* . . . . .Jer 50:38
the spiritual man is *i* . . . . . .Hos 9:7

INSCRIBED

Oh, that they were *i* . . . . . .Job 19:23
See, I have *i* you on. . . . . . .Is 49:16

INSPIRATION

is given by *i* of God . . . .2 Tim 3:16

INSTRUCT

good Spirit to *i* them . . . . . .Neh 9:20
I will *i* you and teach . . . . . .Ps 32:8
the LORD that he may *i*. . .1 Cor 2:16

INSTRUCTED

Surely you have *i* . . . . .Job 4:3
counsel, and who *i*. . . . . . . .Is 40:14
This man had been *i* . . . . .Acts 18:25
are excellent, being *i*. . . . . .Rom 2:18
Moses was divinely *i* . . . . . .Heb 8:5

INSTRUCTION

seeing you hate *i*. . . . . . . .Ps 50:17
despise wisdom and *i* . . . . . .Prov 1:7
Take firm hold of *i*. . . . . . .Prov 4:13

Hear *i* and be wise . . . . . .Prov 8:33
Give *i* to a wise man. . . . . .Prov 9:9
i loves knowledge. . . . . . . .Prov 12:1
Cease listening to *i* . . . . . .Prov 19:27
Apply your heart to *i* . . . .Prov 23:12
for correction, for *i* . . . . . .2 Tim 3:16

INSTRUCTORS

have ten thousand *i*. . . . . .1 Cor 4:15

INSTRUCTS

My heart also *i* . . . . .Ps 16:7
He who *i* the nations . . . . . .Ps 94:10

INSTRUMENT

to Him with an *i*. . . . . .Ps 33:2
on an *i* of ten strings . . . . . . .Ps 92:3

INSTRUMENTS

i of cruelty are in . . . . .Gen 49:5
with stringed *i*. . . . . .Ps 150:4
your members as *i*. . . . . . . .Rom 6:13
and your members as *i* . . . .Rom 6:13

INSUBORDINATE

for the lawless and *i* . . . . . .1 Tim 1:9
For there are many *i* . . . . .Titus 1:10

INSUBORDINATION

of dissipation or *i*. . . . . . . .Titus 1:6

INSULTED

will be mocked and *i* . . . .Luke 18:32
i the Spirit of grace . . . . . .Heb 10:29

INSULTS

nor be afraid of their *i*. . . . . .Is 51:7

INTEGRITY

In the *i* of my heart. . . . . . .Gen 20:5
he holds fast to his *i*. . . . . . . .Job 2:3
that God may know my *i*. . .Job 31:6
I have walked in my *i*. . . . . .Ps 26:1
You uphold me in my *i* . . . . .Ps 41:12
The *i* of the upright . . . . . .Prov 11:3
in doctrine showing *i* . . . . .Titus 2:7

INTELLIGENT

Sergius Paulus, an *i* . . . . . .Acts 13:7

INTERCEDE

the LORD, who will *i*. . . . .1 Sam 2:25

INTERCESSION

of many, and made *i* . . . . . .Is 53:12
Spirit Himself makes *i* . . . .Rom 8:26
always lives to make *i* . . . . .Heb 7:25

INTERCESSOR

that there was no *i* . . . . . . .Is 59:16

INTEREST

shall not charge him *i* . . . .Ex 22:25
men lent to me for *i*. . . . . .Jer 15:10
collected it with *i* . . . . . . .Luke 19:23

INTERPRET

Do all *i*?. . . . . .1 Cor 12:30
pray that he may *i*. . . . . .1 Cor 14:13
in turn, and let one *i* . . . .1 Cor 14:27

INTERPRETATION

"This is the *i* . . . . .Gen 40:12
to another the *i* . . . . .1 Cor 12:10
a revelation, has an *i* . . . .1 Cor 14:26
of any private *i*. . . . . .2 Pet 1:20

INTERPRETATIONS

Do not *i* belong to God . . .Gen 40:8
that you can give *i*. . . . . . .Dan 5:16

INTRIGUE

seize the kingdom by *i* . . .Dan 11:21
join with them by *i* . . . . . .Dan 11:34

INVISIBLE

of the world His *i* . . . . . . .Rom 1:20
is the image of the *i* . . . . . .Col 1:15
eternal, immortal, *i* . . . . . .1 Tim 1:17
as seeing Him who is *i* . . .Heb 11:27

INWARD

i part is destruction . . . . .Ps 5:9
Both the *i* thought . . . . .Ps 64:6
You have formed my *i*. . . . .Ps 139:13
God according to the *i* . . . .Rom 7:22
i man is being renewed . . .2 Cor 4:16

INWARDLY

i they are . . . . .Matt 7:15
is a Jew who is one *i*. . . . . .Rom 2:29

IRON

He regards *i* as straw . . . . .Job 41:27
i sharpens *i* . . . . .Prov 27:17
and your neck was an *i*. . . . . .Is 48:4
its feet partly of *i*. . . . . . . .Dan 2:33

ISRAEL

be called Jacob, but *I* . . . .Gen 32:28
"Hear, O *I* . . . . .Deut 6:4
shepherd My people *I* . . .2 Sam 7:7
Truly God is good to *I* . . . . . .Ps 73:1
helped His servant *I* . . . . .Luke 1:54
For they are not all *I* . . . . . .Rom 9:6
and upon the *I* of God . . . . .Gal 6:16

ITCHING

they have *i* ears . . . . .2 Tim 4:3

ITINERANT

i Jewish exorcists . . . . . . .Acts 19:13

J

JEALOUS

God, am a *j* God. . . . . .Ex 20:5
LORD, whose name is *J* . . .Ex 34:14
a consuming fire, a *j*. . . . .Deut 4:24
For I am *j* for you . . . . . . .2 Cor 11:2

JEALOUSY

They provoked Him to *j*. .Deut 32:16
Will Your *j* burn like. . . . . . . .Ps 79:5
j is a husband's . . . . .Prov 6:34
as strong as death, *j*. . . . . .Song 8:6
will provoke you to *j*. . . . .Rom 10:19
for you with godly *j*. . . . . .2 Cor 11:2

JEOPARDY

stand in *j* every hour . . . .1 Cor 15:30

JESTING

talking, nor coarse *j*. . . . . . .Eph 5:4

JESUS

J Christ was as. . . . . .Matt 1:18
shall call His name *J* . . . . .Matt 1:21
J was led up by the . . . . . .Matt 4:1
These twelve *J* sent . . . . . .Matt 10:5
and laid hands on *J* . . . .Matt 26:50
Barabbas and destroy *J*. .Matt 27:20

we to do with You, *J* . . . .Mark 1:24
J withdrew with His . . . . . .Mark 3:7
J went into Jerusalem. . .Mark 11:11
as they were eating, *J* . . .Mark 14:22
and he delivered *J* . . . . .Mark 15:15
J rebuked the . . . . .Luke 9:42
truth came through *J*. . . .John 1:17
J lifted up His eyes. . . . . . .John 6:5
J wept . . . . .John 11:35
J was crucified . . . . .John 19:20
This *J* God has raised. . . . .Acts 2:32
of Your holy Servant *J* . . .Acts 4:30
believed on the Lord *J* . .Acts 11:17
baptized into Christ *J*. . . . .Rom 6:3
your mouth the Lord *J*. . .Rom 10:9
among you except *J*. . . . . .1 Cor 2:2
the day of the Lord *J* . . . .1 Cor 5:5
perfect in Christ *J*. . . . . . . .Col 1:28
J who is called . . . . .Col 4:11
exhort in the Lord *J* . . . .1 Thess 4:1
But we see *J*. . . . . .Heb 2:9
looking unto *J* . . . . .Heb 12:2
J Christ the righteous. . .1 John 2:1
Revelation of *J* Christ . . . . . .Rev 1:1
so, come, Lord *J* . . . . .Rev 22:20

JEWELS

your thighs are like *j* . . . . .Song 7:1
that I make them My *j* . . . .Mal 3:17

JOIN

Woe to those who *j* . . . . .Is 5:8
'Come and let us *j* . . . . .Jer 50:5
of the rest dared *j* . . . . . . .Acts 5:13

JOINED

and mother and be *j*. . . . . .Gen 2:24
for him who is *j* . . . . .Eccl 9:4
"Ephraim is *j* . . . . .Hos 4:17
what God has *j*. . . . . .Matt 19:6
you be perfectly *j*. . . . . . . .1 Cor 1:10
But he who is *j*. . . . . .1 Cor 6:17
whom the whole body, *j*. . .Eph 4:16

JOINT

j as He wrestled . . . . .Gen 32:25
My bones are out of *j*. . . . .Ps 22:14
j heirs with Christ. . . . . . .Rom 8:17
by what every *j* . . . . .Eph 4:16

JOINTS

and knit together by *j*. . . . .Col 2:19
and spirit, and of *j*. . . . . . .Heb 4:12

JOT

one *j* or one tittle . . . . . . .Matt 5:18

JOURNEY

us go three days' *j* . . . . .Ex 3:18
busy, or he is on a *j*. . . .1 Kin 18:27
Nevertheless I must *j*. . . .Luke 13:33
wearied from His *j* . . . . . . .John 4:6

JOY

LORD your God with *j* . .Deut 28:47
heart to sing for *j* . . . . . . .Job 29:13
is fullness of *j* . . . . .Ps 16:11
j comes in the morning . . . .Ps 30:5
To God my exceeding *j*. . . . .Ps 43:4
You according to the *j*. . . . . .Is 9:3
j you will draw . . . . .Is 12:3
ashes, the oil of *j*. . . . . .Is 61:3
j shall be theirs . . . . .Is 61:7
shall sing for *j* . . . . .Is 65:14
word was to me the *j*. . . . .Jer 15:16
receives it with *j* . . . . .Matt 13:20
Enter into the *j*. . . . . .Matt 25:21
in my womb for *j* . . . . . . .Luke 1:44
there will be more *j*. . . . . .Luke 15:7
did not believe for *j* . . . .Luke 24:41

My *j* may remain in you. .John 15:11
they may have My *j*. . . . .John 17:13
fill you with all *j* . . . . .Rom 15:13
that my *j* is the *j* . . . . . . .2 Cor 2:3
the Spirit is love, *j* . . . . . . .Gal 5:22
brethren, my *j* and . . . . . . .Phil 4:1
longsuffering with *j*. . . . . . .Col 1:11
are our glory and *j*. . . .1 Thess 2:20
j that was set before . . . . .Heb 12:2
count it all *j* . . . . .James 1:2
j inexpressible. . . . . .1 Pet 4:13
with exceeding *j*. . . . . .1 Pet 4:13
I have no greater *j* . . . . . . .3 John 4

JOYFUL

And my soul shall be *j*. . . . . .Ps 35:9
Make a *j* shout to the. . . . . .Ps 100:1
of prosperity be *j*. . . . . . . .Eccl 7:14
and make them *j* . . . . .Is 56:7
I am exceedingly *j*. . . . . . .2 Cor 7:4

JUDAISM

And I advanced in *J*. . . . . . .Gal 1:14

JUDGE

The LORD *j* between you . . .Gen 16:5
For the LORD will *j* . . . . . .Deut 32:36
coming to *j* the earth. . . .1 Chr 16:33
Rise up, O *J* of the . . . . .Ps 94:2
sword the LORD will *j* . . . . . .Is 66:16
deliver you to the *j* . . . . . .Matt 5:25
"*J* not. . . . . .Matt 7:1
"Man, who made Me a *j* .Luke 12:14
j who did not fear God. . . .Luke 18:2
As I hear, I *j*. . . . . .John 5:30
"Do not *j* according . . . . .John 7:24
I *j* no one. . . . . .John 8:15
j the world but to . . . . . . .John 12:47
this, O man, you who *j*. . . . .Rom 2:3
then how will God *j*. . . . . . .Rom 3:6
Therefore let us not *j* . . . .Rom 14:13
Christ, who will *j*. . . . . .2 Tim 4:1
Lord, the righteous *J* . . . . .2 Tim 4:8
heaven, to God the *J* . . . . .Heb 12:23
But if you *j* the law . . . .James 4:11
are you to *j* another . . . . .James 4:12

JUDGES

j who delivered . . . . .Judg 2:16
in the days when the *j* . . . . .Ruth 1:1
Surely He is God who *j* . . .Ps 58:11
He *j* among the gods . . . . . .Ps 82:1
He makes the *j* of the . . . . .Is 40:23
j are evening wolves . . . . . .Zeph 3:3
For the Father *j* . . . . .John 5:22
he who is spiritual *j*. . . . . .1 Cor 2:15
j me is the Lord . . . . .1 Cor 4:4
Him who *j* righteously. . . .1 Pet 2:23

JUDGMENT

show partiality in *j*. . . . . . .Deut 1:17
Teach me good *j* . . . . .Ps 119:66
him in right *j* . . . . .Is 28:26
from prison and from *j* . . . . .Is 53:8
I will also speak *j* . . . . .Jer 4:12
j was made in favor of. . . . .Dan 7:22
be in danger of the *j*. . . . . .Matt 5:21
will rise up in the *j*. . . . . .Matt 12:42
shall not come into *j*. . . . . .John 5:24
and My *j* is righteous. . . . .John 5:30
if I do judge, My *j* . . . . . . .John 8:16
"Now is the *j*. . . . . .John 12:31
the righteous *j*. . . . . .Rom 1:32
j which came from one . . . .Rom 5:16
all stand before the *j*. . . . .Rom 14:10
eats and drinks *j* . . . . . . .1 Cor 11:29
appear before the *j*. . . . . .2 Cor 5:10
after this the *j* . . . . .Heb 9:27
For *j* is without mercy. . .James 2:13

JUDGMENTS

receive a stricter *j* . . . . .James 3:1
time has come for *j* . . . . . .1 Pet 4:17
a long time their *j* . . . . .2 Pet 2:3
darkness for the *j*. . . . . .Jude 6

JUDGMENTS

The *j* of the LORD are . . . . . . .Ps 19:9
j are a great deep . . . . .Ps 36:6
I dread, for Your *j*. . . . . . . .Ps 119:39
unsearchable are His *j* . . .Rom 11:33
righteous are His *j* . . . . . . .Rev 19:2

JUST

Noah was a *j* man . . . . .Gen 6:9
Hear a *j* cause. . . . . .Ps 17:1
It is a joy for the *j* . . . . . .Prov 21:15
j man who perishes . . . . . . .Eccl 7:15
For there is not a *j*. . . . . . .Eccl 7:20
j is uprightness . . . . .Is 26:7
the blood of the *j*. . . . . . . .Lam 4:13
j shall live by his . . . . .Hab 2:4
He is *j* and having. . . . . . . .Zech 9:9
her husband, being a *j* . . . .Matt 1:19
resurrection of the *j* . . . . .Luke 14:14
j persons who need no . . . .Luke 15:7
the Holy One and the *J* . . .Acts 3:14
dead, both of the *j* . . . . .Acts 24:15
j shall live by faith . . . . . .Rom 1:17
that He might be *j* . . . . . . .Rom 3:26
whatever things are *j* . . . . . .Phil 4:8
j men made perfect . . . . .Heb 12:23
have murdered the *j*. . . . . .James 5:6
He is faithful and *j* . . . . . .1 John 1:9
J and true are Your. . . . . . . .Rev 15:3

JUSTICE

for all His ways are *j* . . . . .Deut 32:4
the Almighty pervert *j*. . . . . .Job 8:3
j as the noonday . . . . .Ps 37:6
and Your poor with *j*. . . . . . .Ps 72:2
He will bring *j*. . . . . .Ps 72:4
Do *j* to the afflicted . . . . . . .Ps 82:3
and *j* are the . . . . .Ps 89:14
revenues without *j*. . . . . . .Prov 16:8
do not understand *j* . . . . . .Prov 28:5
j the measuring line. . . . . . .Is 28:17
the LORD is a God of *j*. . . . .Is 30:18
He will bring forth *j* . . . . . . .Is 42:1
No one calls for *j* . . . . .Is 59:4
J is turned back. . . . . .Is 59:14
I, the LORD, love *j* . . . . .Is 61:8
you, O home of *j* . . . . . . .Jer 31:23
plundering, execute *j* . . . .Ezek 45:9
truth, and His ways *j* . . . . .Dan 4:37
observe mercy and *j*. . . . . .Hos 12:6
'Execute true *j*. . . . . .Zech 7:9
"Where is the God of *j*. . . . .Mal 2:17
and He will declare *j* . . . .Matt 12:18
His humiliation His *j* . . . . .Acts 8:33

JUSTIFICATION

because of our *j*. . . . . .Rom 4:25
offenses resulted in *j*. . . . . .Rom 5:16
men, resulting in *j*. . . . . . . .Rom 5:18

JUSTIFIED

Me that you may be *j*. . . . .Job 40:8
of Israel shall be *j* . . . . .Is 45:25
words you will be *j*. . . . . . .Matt 12:37
But wisdom is *j* . . . . .Luke 7:35
j rather than the. . . . . . .Luke 18:14
who believes is *j* . . . . . . .Acts 13:39
"That You may be *j* . . . . . . .Rom 3:4
law no flesh will be *j* . . . . . .Rom 3:20
j freely by His grace . . . . . .Rom 3:24
having been *j* by . . . . .Rom 5:1
these He also *j*. . . . . .Rom 8:30
but you were *j* . . . . .1 Cor 6:11
that we might be *j* . . . . . . .Gal 2:16

no flesh shall be *j* . . . . .Gal 2:16
who attempt to be *j* . . . . . . .Gal 5:4
j in the Spirit. . . . . .1 Tim 3:16
then that a man is *j*. . . .James 2:24
the harlot also *j* . . . . . . .James 2:25

JUSTIFIER

be just and the *j* . . . . .Rom 3:26

JUSTIFIES

He who *j* the wicked . . . . .Prov 17:15
It is God who *j* . . . . .Rom 8:33

JUSTIFY

j the wicked for a. . . . . .Is 5:23
wanting to *j* himself . . . .Luke 10:29
"You are those who *j* . . . .Luke 16:15
is one God who will *j* . . . . .Rom 3:30
that God would *j*. . . . . .Gal 3:8

JUSTLY

of you but to do *j* . . . . .Mic 6:8
"And we indeed *j* . . . . . .Luke 23:41
how devoutly and *j* . . . .1 Thess 2:10

K

KEEP

k you wherever you go. . . .Gen 28:15
day, to *k* it holy . . . . .Ex 20:8
and *k* My judgments . . . .Lev 18:26
k all My commandments 1 Kin 6:12
and that You would *k* . . . .1 Chr 4:10
Even he who cannot *k* . . . . .Ps 22:29
K my soul . . . . .Ps 25:20
do not *k* silence. . . . . .Ps 35:22
k Your righteous . . . . . .Ps 119:106
k them in the midst of . . . .Prov 4:21
K your heart with all . . . . .Prov 4:23
a time to *k* silence . . . . . . .Eccl 3:7
Let all the earth *k* . . . . .Hab 2:20
k the commandments. . . . .Matt 19:17
If you love Me, *k* . . . . . . .John 14:15
k through Your name . . . . .John 17:11
orderly and *k* the law . . . .Acts 21:24
Let your women *k* . . . . . .1 Cor 14:34
k the unity of the. . . . . .Eph 4:3
k yourself pure. . . . . .1 Tim 5:22
k His commandments. . . .1 John 2:3
k yourselves in the. . . . . . . .Jude 21
k you from stumbling . . . . .Jude 24
k those things . . . . .Rev 1:3

KEEPER

Am I my brother's *k* . . . . . .Gen 4:9
The LORD is your *k*. . . . . . .Ps 121:5

KEEPERS

in the day when the *k* . . . .Eccl 12:3

KEEPS

the faithful God who *k*. . . . .Deut 7:9
k truth forever. . . . . .Ps 146:6
k his way preserves. . . . . .Prov 16:17
k the commandment . . . . .Prov 19:16
Whoever *k* the law is a . . .Prov 28:7
none of you *k* the law. . . .John 7:19
born of God *k* himself. . .1 John 5:18
and *k* his garments. . . . . . .Rev 16:15

KEPT

For I have *k* the ways . .2 Sam 22:22
vineyard I have not *k*. . . . .Song 1:6
these things I have *k*. . . . .Matt 19:20
all these things I have *k* Mark 10:20
k all these things . . . . . . .Luke 2:19
love, just as I have *k* . . .John 15:10
k back part of the . . . . .Acts 5:2
I have *k* the faith . . . . .2 Tim 4:7
who are *k* by the power . . . .1 Pet 1:5

which now exist are *k* . . . . .2 Pet 3:7

KEY

The *k* of the house of . . . . . .Is 22:22
have taken away the *k* . . .Luke 11:52
"He who has the *k* . . . . .Rev 3:7
heaven, having the *k* . . . . .Rev 20:1

KEYS

I will give you the *k*. . . . .Matt 16:19
And I have the *k* . . . . .Rev 1:18

KICK

is hard for you to *k* . . . . . . .Acts 9:5

KIDNAPPERS

for sodomites, for *k*. . . . . .1 Tim 1:10

KIDNAPS

"He who *k* a man and . . . .Ex 21:16

KILL

who finds me will *k* . . . . . .Gen 4:14
k the Passover . . . . .Ex 12:21
I *k* and I make alive. . . . .Deut 32:39
"Am I God, to *k* . . . . .2 Kin 5:7
a time to *k* . . . . .Eccl 3:3
to save life or to *k* . . . . . . .Mark 3:4
of them they will *k*. . . . . .Luke 11:49
afraid of those who *k* . . . .Luke 12:4
Why do you seek to *k* . . . .John 7:19
k and eat . . . . .Acts 10:13

KILLED

Abel his brother and *k*. . . . . .Gen 4:8
For I have *k* a man for . . . .Gen 4:23
LORD *k* all the. . . . . .Ex 13:15
"Your servant has *k* . . . .1 Sam 17:36
for Your sake we are *k* . . . .Ps 44:22
and scribes, and be *k*. . . .Matt 16:21
Siloam fell and *k* them. . . .Luke 13:4
k the Prince of life. . . . . . .Acts 3:15
me, and by it *k* . . . . .Rom 7:11
"For Your sake we are *k* . . .Rom 8:36
who *k* both the Lord . . .1 Thess 2:15
martyr, who was *k* . . . . . . .Rev 2:13

KILLS

"The LORD *k* and. . . . . . . .1 Sam 2:6
the one who *k* the. . . . . . .Matt 23:37
for the letter *k* . . . . .2 Cor 3:6

KIND

animals after their *k* . . . . .Gen 6:20
k can come out by . . . . . .Mark 9:29
For He is *k* to the. . . . . . . .Luke 6:35
suffers long and is *k* . . . . .1 Cor 13:4
And be *k* to one . . . . .Eph 4:32

KINDLED

When His wrath is *k* . . . . . . .Ps 2:12
I, the LORD, have *k*. . . . .Ezek 20:48
wish it were already *k* . . .Luke 12:49

KINDLY

The LORD deal *k*. . . . . . . .Ruth 1:8
Julius treated Paul *k*. . . . .Acts 27:3
k affectionate to one . . . . .Rom 12:10

KINDNESS

may the LORD show *k* . . . .2 Sam 2:6
anger, abundant in *k* . . . . .Neh 9:17
me His marvelous *k* . . . . . .Ps 31:21
For His merciful *k* . . . . . . .Ps 117:2
tongue is the law of *k* . . . .Prov 31:26
k shall not depart . . . . .Is 54:10
I remember you, the *k*. . . . .Jer 2:2
by longsuffering, by *k* . . . .2 Cor 6:6
longsuffering, *k* . . . . .Gal 5:22
But when the *k* and the . . .Titus 3:4
and to brotherly *k* . . . . . . .2 Pet 1:7

KING

Then Melchizedek k......Gen 14:18
days there was no k.....Judg 17:6
said, "Give us a k.......1 Sam 8:6
"Long live the k.......1 Sam 10:24
they anointed David k....2 Sam 2:4
Yet I have set My K.......Ps 2:6
The LORD is K forever.....Ps 10:16
K answer us when we......Ps 20:9
And the K of glory........Ps 24:7
k is saved by the..........Ps 33:16
k Your judgments......Ps 72:1
For God is my K.........Ps 74:12
do who succeeds the k ...Eccl 2:12
out of prison to be k.....Eccl 4:14
when your k is a child...Eccl 10:16
In the year that K...........Is 6:1
k will reign in.............Is 32:1
the LORD is our K.........Is 33:22
Is not her K in her......Jer 8:19
and the everlasting K....Jer 10:10
k of Babylon, k..........Ezek 26:7
I gave you a k in My....Hos 13:11
the LORD shall be K.....Zech 14:9
He who has been born K...Matt 2:2
This Is Jesus the K....Matt 27:37
by force to make Him k...John 6:15
"Behold your K........John 19:14
there is another k.......Acts 17:7
Now to the K eternal....1 Tim 1:17
only Potentate, the K....1 Tim 6:15
this Melchizedek, k.......Heb 7:1
Honor the k............1 Pet 2:17
k of kings and lord of.....Rev 19:16

KINGDOM

you shall be to Me a k......Ex 19:6
LORD has torn the k....1 Sam 15:28
Yours is the k..........1 Chr 29:11
k is the LORD's..........Ps 22:28
the scepter of Your k......Ps 45:6
in heaven, and His k.....Ps 103:19
is an everlasting k........Ps 145:13
k which shall never be.....Dan 2:44
High rules in the k.......Dan 4:17
k shall be the LORD's.....Obad 21
"Repent, for the k........Matt 3:2
for Yours is the k.......Matt 6:13
But seek first the k.....Matt 6:33
the mysteries of the k..Matt 13:11
are the sons of the k....Matt 13:38
of such is the k........Matt 19:14
up to half of my k......Mark 6:23
are not far from the k...Mark 12:34
back, is fit for the k.....Luke 9:62
against nation, and k....Luke 21:10
he cannot see the k......John 3:3
he cannot enter the k.....John 3:5
If My k were of this....John 18:36
for the k of God is......Rom 14:17
when He delivers the k..1 Cor 15:24
will not inherit the k......Gal 5:21
the scepter of Your k.....Heb 1:8
we are receiving a k....Heb 12:28
into the everlasting k.....2 Pet 1:11

KINGDOMS

the k were moved.........Ps 46:6
tremble, who shook k....Is 14:16
showed Him all the k......Matt 4:8
have become the k......Rev 11:15

KINGS

The k of the earth set........Ps 2:2
k shall fall down.......Ps 72:11
He is awesome to the k...Ps 76:12
By me k reign........Prov 8:15
He will stand before k...Prov 22:29
k is unsearchable........Prov 25:3

that which destroys k.....Prov 31:3
it is not for k...........Prov 31:4
K shall be your foster.....Is 49:23
"They set up k...........Hos 8:4
before governors and k...Matt 10:18
k have desired to see....Luke 10:24
You have reigned as k....1 Cor 4:8
and has made us k........Rev 1:6
that the way of the k....Rev 16:12
may eat the flesh of k....Rev 19:18

KISS

K the Son................Ps 2:12
Let him k me with the....Song 1:2
"You gave Me no k.......Luke 7:45
another with a holy k....Rom 16:16
one another with a k.....1 Pet 5:14

KISSED

And they k one another 1 Sam 20:41
and k Him............Matt 26:49
and she k His feet and...Luke 7:38

KNEE

that to Me every k........Is 45:23
And they bowed the k...Matt 27:29
have not bowed the k....Rom 11:4
every k shall bow to....Rom 14:11
of Jesus every k.........Phil 2:10

KNEES

make firm the feeble k......Is 35:3
be dandled on her k........Is 66:12
this reason I bow my k...Eph 3:14
and the feeble k.........Heb 12:12

KNEW

Adam k Eve his wife......Gen 4:1
in the womb I k..........Jer 1:5
to them, 'I never k......Matt 7:23
k what was in man......John 2:25
For He made Him who k.2 Cor 5:21

KNIT

of Jonathan was k.....1 Sam 18:1
k me together with......Job 10:11
be encouraged, being k.....Col 2:2

KNOCK

k, and it will be..........Matt 7:7
at the door and k........Rev 3:20

KNOW

k good and evil...........Gen 3:22
and I did not k..........Gen 28:16
k that I am the LORD......Ex 6:7
k that there is no God....2 Kin 5:15
you, my son Solomon, k..1 Chr 28:9
Hear it, and k for........Job 5:27
and k nothing...........Job 8:9
k that my Redeemer.....Job 19:25
'What does God k........Job 22:13
k Your name will put......Ps 9:10
k that I am God.........Ps 46:10
make me to k wisdom....Ps 51:6
Who can k it..............Jer 17:9
saying, 'K the LORD.....Jer 31:34
for you to k justice........Mic 3:1
k what hour your Lord...Matt 24:42
an oath, "I do not k.....Matt 26:72
the world did not k......John 1:10
We speak what We k....John 3:11
k what we worship......John 4:22
k that You are..........John 6:69
hear My voice, then k...John 10:27
If you k these things...John 13:17
k whom I have chosen...John 13:18
we are sure that You k...John 16:30
k that I love You.......John 21:15
k times or seasons........Acts 1:7

and said, "Jesus I k.....Acts 19:15
wisdom did not k........1 Cor 1:21
nor can he k them.......1 Cor 2:14
For we k in part and.....1 Cor 13:9
k a man in Christ who....2 Cor 12:2
k the love of Christ.......Eph 3:19
k whom I have believed..2 Tim 1:12
so that they may k.......2 Tim 2:25
this we k that we k Him..1 John 2:3
He who says, "I k.......1 John 2:4
and you k all things.....1 John 2:20
By this we k love......1 John 3:16
k that we are of the....1 John 3:19
k that He abides.......1 John 3:24
k that we are of God....1 John 5:19
"I k your works...........Rev 2:2

KNOWLEDGE

and the tree of the k.......Gen 2:9
LORD is the God of k.....1 Sam 2:3
Can anyone teach God k.Job 21:22
who is perfect in k........Job 36:4
unto night reveals k.......Ps 19:2
k is too wonderful.........Ps 139:6
k the depths were.......Prov 3:20
k rather than............Prov 8:10
Wise people store up k...Prov 10:14
k is easy to him who......Prov 14:6
k spares his words.......Prov 17:27
a soul to be without k....Prov 19:2
and he who increases k....Eccl 1:18
k is that wisdom......Eccl 7:12
no work or device or k....Eccl 9:10
Whom will he teach k.....Is 28:9
k shall increase.........Dan 12:4
you have rejected k.......Hos 4:6
having more accurate k.. Acts 24:22
having the form of k.......Rom 2:20
by the law is the k of sin..Rom 3:20
K puffs up ....1 Cor 8:1
whether there is k.......1 Cor 13:8
Christ which passes k....Eph 3:19
is falsely called k........1 Tim 6:20
in the grace and k.......2 Pet 3:18

KNOWN

In Judah God is k.........Ps 76:1
my mouth will I make k....Ps 89:1
If you had k Me......John 8:19
My sheep, and am k.....John 10:14
The world has not k....John 17:25
peace they have not k....Rom 3:17
I would not have k.......Rom 7:7
"For who has k.........Rom 11:34
after you have k.........Gal 4:9
requests be made k.......Phil 4:6
k the Holy Scriptures....2 Tim 3:15

KNOWS

"For God k that in........Gen 3:5
k the secrets of the......Ps 44:21
he understands and k....Jer 9:24
k what is in the........Dan 2:22
k those who trust.........Nah 1:7
k the things you have....Matt 6:8
and hour no one k......Matt 24:36
k who the Son is.......Luke 10:22
but God k your hearts...Luke 16:15
searches the hearts k....Rom 8:27
k the things of God.....1 Cor 2:11
k those who are His....2 Tim 2:19
to him who k to do....James 4:17
and k all things........1 John 3:20
written which no one k....Rev 2:17

L

LABOR

Six days you shall l........Ex 20:9

why then do I *l* . . . . .Job 9:29
their boast is only *l* . . . . . . .Ps 90:10
The *l* of the righteous . . . .Prov 10:16
l will increase . . . . .Prov 13:11
l there is profit. . . . . .Prov 14:23
things are full of *l* . . . . .Eccl 1:8
has man for all his *l* . . . . . .Eccl 2:22
He shall see the *l* . . . . .Is 53:11
"Before she was in *l* . . . . .Is 66:7
from the womb to see *l* . . . .Jer 20:18
to Me, all you who *l* . . . . .Matt 11:28
"Do not *l* for the . . . . .John 6:27
knowing that your *l* . . . . .1 Cor 15:58
but rather let him *l* . . . . . .Eph 4:28
mean fruit from my *l* . . . . . .Phil 1:22
your work of faith, *l* . . . .1 Thess 1:3
forget your work and *l* . . . .Heb 6:10
your works, your *l* . . . . .Rev 2:2

LABORED

l more abundantly than .1 Cor 15:10
for you, lest I have *l* . . . . . .Gal 4:11

LABORERS

but the *l* are few . . . . .Matt 9:37

LABORING

of a *l* man is sweet . . . . . . .Eccl 5:12
l night and day . . . . .1 Thess 2:9

LABORS

The person who *l* . . . . . .Prov 16:26
is no end to all his *l* . . . . . . .Eccl 4:8
entered into their *l* . . . . . .John 4:38
creation groans and *l* . . . . .Rom 8:22
l more abundant . . . . . . .2 Cor 11:23
may rest from their *l* . . . . .Rev 14:13

LACK

anyone perish for *l* . . . . . .Job 31:19
the LORD shall not *l* . . . . . .Ps 34:10
to the poor will not *l* . . . .Prov 28:27
What do I still *l* . . . . . . .Matt 19:20
"One thing you *l* . . . . . .Mark 10:21

LACKED

among them who *l* . . . . . .Acts 4:34

LACKING

the things that are *l* . . . . . . .Titus 1:5

LADDER

and behold, a *l* . . . . .Gen 28:12

LADEN

nation, a people *l* . . . . .Is 1:4
and are heavy *l* . . . . .Matt 11:28

LADIES

wisest *l* answered her . . . .Judg 5:29
very day the noble *l* . . . . .Esth 1:18

LADY

'I shall be a *l* . . . . .Is 47:7
Elder, To the elect *l* . . . . .2 John 1:1

LAGGING

not *l* in diligence . . . . . . .Rom 12:11

LAID

But man dies and is *l* . . . .Job 14:10
the place where they *l* . . .Mark 16:6
Where have you *l* . . . . . .John 11:34

LAKE

cast alive into the *l* . . . . . .Rev 19:20

LAMB

but where is the *l* . . . . . .Gen 22:7
took the poor man's *l* . . . .2 Sam 12:4
shall dwell with the *l* . . . . . . .Is 11:6

He was led as a *l* . . . . .Is 53:7
l shall feed together . . . . .Is 65:25
The *L* of God who takes . .John 1:29
of Christ, as of a *l* . . . . . .1 Pet 1:19
the elders, stood a *L* . . . . . . .Rev 5:6
"Worthy is the *L* . . . . .Rev 5:12
by the blood of the *L* . . . . .Rev 12:11
Book of Life of the *L* . . . . .Rev 13:8
supper of the *L* . . . . .Rev 19:9

LAME

l take the prey . . . . .Is 33:23
l shall leap like a . . . . .Is 35:6
when you offer the *l* . . . . . .Mal 1:8
blind see and the *l* . . . . . .Matt 11:5
And a certain man *l* . . . . . .Acts 3:2
so that what is *l* . . . . .Heb 12:13

LAMENTATION

was heard in Ramah, *l* . . . .Jer 31:15
was heard in Ramah, *l* . . . .Matt 2:18
and made great *l* . . . . .Acts 8:2

LAMP

For You are my *l* . . . . . . .2 Sam 22:29
"How often is the *l* . . . . . .Job 21:17
You will light my *l* . . . . . . .Ps 18:28
Your word is a *l* . . . . .Ps 119:105
l of the wicked . . . . .Prov 13:9
his *l* will be put out . . . . . .Prov 20:20
Nor do they light a *l* . . . . .Matt 5:15
"The *l* of the body . . . . . .Matt 6:22
when he has lit a *l* . . . . . .Luke 8:16
l gives you light . . . . . . .Luke 11:36
does not light a *l* . . . . . . .Luke 15:8
burning and shining *l* . . . .John 5:35
l shall not shine . . . . .Rev 18:23
They need no *l* nor . . . . . . .Rev 22:5

LAMPS

he made its seven *l* . . . . . . .Ex 37:23
Jerusalem with *l* . . . . . . .Zeph 1:12
and trimmed their *l* . . . . .Matt 25:7
Seven *l* of fire . . . . .Rev 4:5

LAMPSTAND

branches of the *l* . . . . .Ex 25:32
and there is a *l* . . . . .Zech 4:2
a basket, but on a *l* . . . . .Matt 5:15
in which was the *l* . . . . .Heb 9:2
and remove your *l* . . . . .Rev 2:5

LAND

l that I will show you . . . .Gen 12:1
l flowing with milk . . . . . . .Ex 3:8
l which I am giving . . . . . .Josh 1:2
is heard in our *l* . . . . .Song 2:12
they will see the *l* . . . . .Is 33:17
Bethlehem, in the *l* . . . . . . .Matt 2:6

LANDMARK

your neighbor's *l* . . . . . . .Deut 19:14
remove the ancient *l* . . . .Prov 22:28
those who remove a *l* . . . . .Hos 5:10

LANGUAGE

whole earth had one *l* . . . . .Gen 11:1
is no speech nor *l* . . . . .Ps 19:3
a people of strange *l* . . . . . .Ps 114:1
the peoples a pure *l* . . . . .Zeph 3:9
speak in his own *l* . . . . . . .Acts 2:6
blasphemy, filthy *l* . . . . .Col 3:8

LANGUAGES

according to their *l* . . . . . .Gen 10:20
be, so many kinds of *l* . .1 Cor 14:10

LAST

He shall stand at *l* . . . . . .Job 19:25
First and I am the *L* . . . . . .Is 44:6

l man the same as . . . . .Matt 20:14
l will be first . . . . .Matt 20:16
children, it is the *l* . . . . .1 John 2:18
the First and the *L* . . . . . . .Rev 1:11

LATTER

former rain, and the *l* . . . . .Joel 2:23
l times some will . . . . .1 Tim 4:1

LATTICE

I looked through my *l* . . . . .Prov 7:6
gazing through the *l* . . . . . .Song 2:9

LAUGH

Why did Sarah *l* . . . . .Gen 18:13
"God has made me *l* . . . . . .Gen 21:6
You, O LORD, shall *l* . . . . . . .Ps 59:8
Woe to you who *l* . . . . . .Luke 6:25

LAUGHS

he *l* at the threat of . . . . . .Job 41:29
The Lord *l* at him . . . . .Ps 37:13

LAUGHTER

was filled with *l* . . . . .Ps 126:2
your *l* be turned to . . . . . .James 4:9

LAW

stones a copy of the *l* . . . .Josh 8:32
When He made a *l* . . . . . .Job 28:26
The *l* of the LORD is . . . . . . .Ps 19:7
The *l* of his God is in . . . . .Ps 37:31
I delight in Your *l* . . . . . .Ps 119:70
The *l* of Your mouth is . . .Ps 119:72
l is my delight . . . . .Ps 119:77
Oh, how I love Your *l* . . . . .Ps 119:97
And Your *l* is truth . . . . .Ps 119:142
and the *l* is a light . . . . . . .Prov 6:23
shall go forth the *l* . . . . .Is 2:3
l will proceed from Me . . . .Is 51:4
in whose heart is My *l* . . . . .Is 51:7
the *L* is no more . . . . .Lam 2:9
The *l* of truth was in . . . . . .Mal 2:6
to destroy the *L* . . . . .Matt 5:17
for this is the *L* . . . . .Matt 7:12
hang all the *L* and the . .Matt 22:40
"The *l* and the . . . . .Luke 16:16
l was given through . . . . . .John 1:17
"Does our *l* judge a . . . . .John 7:51
l is the knowledge . . . . . . .Rom 3:20
because the *l* brings . . . . .Rom 4:15
when there is no *l* . . . . . . .Rom 5:13
you are not under *l* . . . . . .Rom 6:14
Is the *l* sin . . . . .Rom 7:7
For we know that the *l* . . . .Rom 7:14
warring against the *l* . . . . .Rom 7:23
For what the *l* could . . . . . .Rom 8:3
who are without *l* . . . . . .1 Cor 9:21
l that I might live . . . . .Gal 2:19
under guard by the *l* . . . . .Gal 3:23
born under the *l* . . . . .Gal 4:4
l is fulfilled in one . . . . .Gal 5:14
l is not made for a . . . . . . .1 Tim 1:9
into the perfect *l* . . . . . . .James 1:25
fulfill the royal *l* . . . . .James 2:8

LAWFUL

doing what is not *l* . . . . . .Matt 12:2
Is it *l* to pay taxes . . . . . .Matt 22:17
All things are *l* . . . . .1 Cor 6:12

LAWGIVER

Judah is My *l* . . . . .Ps 60:7
the LORD is our *L* . . . . .Is 33:22
There is one *L* . . . . .James 4:12

LAWLESS

l one will be revealed . . . .2 Thess 2:8
and hearing their *l* . . . . . . .2 Pet 2:8

LAWLESSNESS

Me, you who practice *l*. . . .Matt 7:23
l is already at work . . . . .2 Thess 2:7
and hated *l* . . . . .Heb 1:9
and sin is *l* . . . . .1 John 3:4

LAWYERS

l rejected the will of . . . . .Luke 7:30
Woe to you also, *l* . . . . . . .Luke 11:46

LAY

nowhere to *l* His head . . . .Matt 8:20
l hands may receive. . . . . . .Acts 8:19
Do not *l* hands on . . . . . . .1 Tim 5:22
l aside all. . . . . .James 1:21

LAZINESS

L casts one into a . . . . . . .Prov 19:15
l the building decays . . . . .Eccl 10:18

LAZY

l man will be put to . . . . .Prov 12:24
l man does not roast . . . . .Prov 12:27
soul of a *l* man desires . . .Prov 13:4
l man buries his hand . . .Prov 19:24
by the field of the *l* . . . . .Prov 24:30
l man is wiser in his . . . .Prov 26:16
wicked and *l* servant . . . .Matt 25:26
liars, evil beasts, *l* . . . . . .Titus 1:12

LEAD

they sank like *l*. . . . . .Ex 15:10
L me in Your truth and . . . . .Ps 25:5
L me and guide me. . . . . . . .Ps 31:3
Your hand shall *l*. . . . . .Ps 139:10
And do not *l* us into. . . . .Matt 6:13
"Can the blind *l* . . . . .Luke 6:39

LEADS

He *l* me beside the . . . . .Ps 23:2
He *l* me in the paths. . . . . .Ps 23:3
And if the blind *l* . . . . . .Matt 15:14
by name and *l* them out. .John 10:3
the goodness of God *l*. . . . .Rom 2:4

LEAF

plucked olive *l*. . . . . .Gen 8:11
Will You frighten a *l*. . . . .Job 13:25
l will be green. . . . . .Jer 17:8

LEAN

all your heart, and *l* . . . . .Prov 3:5
Yet they *l* on the LORD. . . . .Mic 3:11

LEANING

Then, *l* back on Jesus' . .John 13:25
l on the top of his. . . . . . .Heb 11:21

LEANNESS

request, but sent *l*. . . . . . .Ps 106:15
of hosts, will send *l*. . . . . . .Is 10:16

LEAP

by my God I can *l*. . . . . . . .Ps 18:29
Then the lame shall *l*. . . . . .Is 35:6

LEARN

it, may hear and *l*. . . . . . .Deut 31:13
l Your statutes. . . . . .Ps 119:71
lest you *l* his ways. . . . . . .Prov 22:25
l to do good . . . . .Is 1:17
neither shall they *l*. . . . . .Is 2:4
My yoke upon you and *l* Matt 11:29
Let a woman *l* in . . . . .1 Tim 2:11
let our people also *l* . . . . .Titus 3:14

LEARNED

Me the tongue of the *l* . . .Is 50:4
who has heard and *l*. . . . .John 6:45
have not so *l* Christ. . . . . .Eph 4:20

in all things I have *l*. . . . . .Phil 4:12
l obedience by the . . . . .Heb 5:8

LEARNING

hear and increase *l* . . . . .Prov 1:5
l is driving you mad . . . .Acts 26:24
were written for our *l* . . . . .Rom 15:4

LEAST

Judah, are not the *l* . . . . . .Matt 2:6
so, shall be called *l*. . . . . .Matt 5:19
For I am the *l* of the . . . . .1 Cor 15:9

LEAVE

a man shall *l* his. . . . . .Gen 2:24
He will not *l* you nor . . . .Deut 31:6
For You will not *l* . . . . .Ps 16:10
do not *l* me nor . . . . .Ps 27:9
"I will never *l* . . . . .Heb 13:5

LEAVEN

day you shall remove *l*. . . .Ex 12:15
of heaven is like *l* . . . . . .Matt 13:33
and beware of the *l*. . . . . .Matt 16:6
know that a little *l*. . . . . . .1 Cor 5:6
l leavens the whole . . . . .Gal 5:9

LEAVES

and they sewed fig *l*. . . . . . .Gen 3:7
nothing on it but *l* . . . . . .Matt 21:19
l the sheep and flees. . . . .John 10:12
The *l* of the tree . . . . .Rev 22:2

LED

l the people around by. . . . .Ex 13:18
so the LORD alone *l* . . . . . .Deut 32:12
l them forth by the . . . . . . .Ps 107:7
l them by the right . . . . . . .Is 63:12
For as many as are *l* . . . . .Rom 8:14
l captivity captive . . . . .Eph 4:8
l away by various . . . . .2 Tim 3:6

LEFT

l hand know what your . . . .Matt 6:3
"See, we have *l* . . . . .Matt 19:27
And everyone who has *l*. .Matt 19:29

LEGACY

shame shall be the *l* . . . . .Prov 3:35

LEGS

Like the *l* of the lame . . . .Prov 26:7
l are pillars of . . . . .Song 5:15
did not break His *l*. . . . . .John 19:33

LEND

"If you *l* money to . . . . . . .Ex 22:25
l him sufficient . . . . .Deut 15:8
"And if you *l*. . . . . .Luke 6:34
l me three loaves. . . . . . . .Luke 11:5

LENDER

is servant to the *l* . . . . . . .Prov 22:7
as with the *l*. . . . . .Is 24:2

LENDING

and my servants, am *l*. . . . .Neh 5:10

LENDS

ever merciful, and *l*. . . . . . .Ps 37:26
deals graciously and *l*. . . . .Ps 112:5
has pity on the poor *l*. . . .Prov 19:17

LENGTH

The *l* of the ark shall . . . . .Gen 6:15
is your life and the *l*. . . .Deut 30:20
L of days is in her. . . . . . .Prov 3:16
l is as great as its. . . . . . .Rev 21:16

LENGTHENS

a shadow when it *l*. . . . . . .Ps 109:23

LEOPARD

the *l* shall lie down. . . . . .Is 11:6
or the *l* its spots . . . . .Jer 13:23

LEPERS

And when these *l*. . . . . . . .2 Kin 7:8
"And many *l* were in . . . .Luke 4:27

LET

"*L* there be light". . . . . .Gen 1:3
L the little. . . . . .Matt 19:14

LETTER

the oldness of the *l* . . . . . . .Rom 7:6
for the *l* kills. . . . . .2 Cor 3:6
you sorry with my *l*. . . . . .2 Cor 7:8
or by word or by *l* . . . . . .2 Thess 2:2

LETTERS

does this Man know *l*. . . .John 7:15
to you or I of. . . . . .2 Cor 3:1
"For his *l*. . . . . .2 Cor 10:10
with what large *l*. . . . . .Gal 6:11

LEVIATHAN

"Can you draw out *L* . . . . .Job 41:1
L Which You have made . .Ps 104:26

LEVITE

"Is not Aaron the *L*. . . . . . . .Ex 4:14
"Likewise a *L* . . . . .Luke 10:32
a *L* of the country of. . . . .Acts 4:36

LEVITICAL

were through the *L* . . . . . . .Heb 7:11

LEWDNESS

wickedness, deceit, *l* . . . . .Mark 7:22
drunkenness, not in *l* . . . .Rom 13:13
themselves over to *l*. . . . . . .Eph 4:19
when we walked in *l*. . . . . .1 Pet 4:3

LIAR

for he is a *l* and the . . . . .John 8:44
but every man a *l* . . . . .Rom 3:4
we make Him a *l* . . . . . . .1 John 1:10
Who is a *l* but he who. . .1 John 2:22
his brother, he is a *l*. . . . .1 John 4:20
God has made Him a *l* . .1 John 5:10

LIARS

"All men are *l* . . . . .Ps 116:11
Cretans are always *l*. . . . . .Titus 1:12
and have found them *l*. . . . .Rev 2:2
l shall have their. . . . . .Rev 21:8

LIBERALITY

he who gives, with *l* . . . . . .Rom 12:8
the riches of their *l* . . . . . .2 Cor 8:2

LIBERALLY

who gives to all *l* . . . . . .James 1:5

LIBERTY

year, and proclaim *l* . . . . .Lev 25:10
And I will walk at *l* . . . . . .Ps 119:45
to proclaim *l* to the . . . . .Is 61:1
to proclaim *l* to the. . . . . .Luke 4:18
into the glorious *l* . . . . . . .Rom 8:21
For why is my *l* . . . . .1 Cor 10:29
Lord is, there is *l* . . . . . . .2 Cor 3:17
therefore in the *l* . . . . .Gal 5:1
l as an opportunity . . . . .Gal 5:13
the perfect law of *l*. . . . . .James 1:25
yet not using *l* . . . . .1 Pet 2:16

LIE

man, that He should *l* . .Num 23:19
For now I will *l* . . . . .Job 7:21
I will not *l* to David . . . . . .Ps 89:35
Do not *l* to one. . . . . .Col 3:9

LIED

God, who cannot *l* ....Titus 1:2
do not boast and *l* .....James 3:14
know it, and that no *l* ...1 John 2:21
an abomination or a *l* .....Rev 21:27

LIED

They have *l* about the ......Jer 5:12
You have not *l* to men.....Acts 5:4

LIES

sin *l* at the door ....Gen 4:7
and he who speaks *l* .....Prov 19:5
speaking *l* in ....1 Tim 4:2
and the whole world *l* ..1 John 5:19

LIFE

the breath of *l* ....Gen 2:7
l was also in the ....Gen 2:9
then you shall give *l* ......Ex 21:23
'For the *l* of the.........Lev 17:11
before you today *l*......Deut 30:15
You have granted me *l* ...Job 10:12
in whose hand is the *l* ...Job 12:10
God takes away his *l* ....Job 27:8
with the light of *l* ....Job 33:30
He will redeem their *l*.....Ps 72:14
word has given me *l*.....Ps 119:50
regain the paths of *l*......Prov 2:19
She is a tree of *l* ....Prov 3:18
so they will be *l*.........Prov 3:22
finds me finds *l*.........Prov 8:35
l winds upward for the ..Prov 15:24
thief hates his own *l*.....Prov 29:24
is that wisdom gives *l*.....Eccl 7:12
I have cut off my *l* ....Is 38:12
you the way of *l*.........Jer 21:8
l shall be as a prize ......Jer 39:18
not worry about your *l*....Matt 6:25
l does not consist ......Luke 12:15
L is more than ....Luke 12:23
l was the light ....John 1:4
so the Son gives *l* ....John 5:21
as the Father has *l*......John 5:26
spirit, and they are *l*......John 6:63
have the light of *l*......John 8:12
and I lay down My *l*.....John 10:15
resurrection and the *l*...John 11:25
you lay down your *l* ....John 13:38
God, who gives *l* ....Rom 4:17
that pertain to this *l* ......1 Cor 6:3
Lord Jesus, that the *l* ...2 Cor 4:10
l which I now live ......Gal 2:20
l is hidden with ....Col 3:3
of God who gives *l* ......1 Tim 6:13
For what is your *l*......James 4:14
that pertain to *l* ....2 Pet 1:3
l was manifested ......1 John 1:2
and the pride of *l*.....1 John 2:16
has given us eternal *l* ...1 John 5:11
who has the Son has *l*...1 John 5:12
the Lamb's Book of L ....Rev 21:27
right to the tree of *l* ......Rev 22:14
the water of *l* freely .....Rev 22:17
from the Book of L......Rev 22:19

LIFT

I will *l* up my hands ......Ps 63:4
I will *l* up my eyes to .....Ps 121:1
l our hearts and hands ...Lam 3:41
Lord, and He will *l*.....James 4:10

LIFTED

O Lord, for You have *l*....Ps 30:1
your heart is ....Ezek 28:2
in Hades, he *l* up his ...Luke 16:23
the Son of Man be *l*.....John 3:14
"And I, if I am *l*........John 12:32
of Man must be *l* ......John 12:34

LIGHT

"Let there be *l* ....Gen 1:3
" The *l* of the wicked .....Job 18:5
l will shine on your ......Job 22:28
the wicked their *l* ....Job 38:15
to the dwelling of *l* ......Job 38:19
Lord, lift up the *l*........Ps 4:6
The Lord is my *l* ....Ps 27:1
Oh, send out Your *l*......Ps 43:3
L is sown for the.........Ps 97:11
and He has given us *l* ...Ps 118:27
and a *l* to my path .....Ps 119:105
The *l* of the righteous.....Prov 13:9
The *l* of the eyes ....Prov 15:30
The Lord gives *l*.......Prov 29:13
Truly the *l* is sweet ......Eccl 11:7
let us walk in the *l*.........Is 2:5
l is darkened by the.........Is 5:30
because there is no *l* ....Is 8:20
moon will be as the *l*......Is 30:26
l shall break forth ....Is 58:8
for your *l* has come ....Is 60:1
be your everlasting *l* ......Is 60:20
gives the sun for a *l*......Jer 31:35
l that goes................Hos 6:5
"You are the *l* ....Matt 5:14
"Let your *l* so shine .....Matt 5:16
body will be full of *l*.....Matt 6:22
than the sons of *l*.......Luke 16:8
and the life was the *l* .....John 1:4
That was the true L ....John 1:9
darkness rather than *l* ....John 3:19
evil hates the *l*..........John 3:20
truth comes to the *l*......John 3:21
saying, "I am the *l*.......John 8:12
believe in the *l*.........John 12:36
"I have come as a *l*.....John 12:46
l the hidden..............1 Cor 4:5
God who commanded *l* ....2 Cor 4:6
Walk as children of *l* ......Eph 5:8
You are all sons of *l* ...1 Thess 5:5
and immortality to *l* ......2 Tim 1:10
into His marvelous *l*......1 Pet 2:9
do well to heed as a *l*....2 Pet 1:19
to you, that God is *l*.....1 John 1:5
l as He is in the..........1 John 1:7
says he is in the *l*.......1 John 2:9
The Lamb is its *l* ....Rev 21:23
Lord God gives them *l*....Rev 22:5

LIGHTEN

L the yoke which........1 Kin 12:9
the sea, to *l* the load.......Jon 1:5

LIGHTLY

this, did I do it *l* ....2 Cor 1:17

LIGHTNING

"For as the *l* ....Matt 24:27
countenance was like *l*...Matt 28:3
saw Satan fall like *l* .....Luke 10:18

LIGHTNINGS

were thunderings and *l* ...Ex 19:16
the *l* lit up the world ......Ps 77:18
l light the world ....Ps 97:4
the throne proceeded *l* .....Rev 4:5

LIGHTS

"Let there be *l* ....Gen 1:14
Him who made great *l*....Ps 136:7
whom you shine as *l*......Phil 2:15
from the Father of *l*....James 1:17

LIKE

"Who is *l* You ....Ex 15:11
L a lily among thorns ....Song 2:2
be made *l* His brethren ..Heb 2:17

LIKE-MINDED

grant you to be *l* ....Rom 15:5
For I have no one *l*.......Phil 2:20

LIKENESS

according to Our *l* ....Gen 1:26
carved image-or any *l* .....Ex 20:4
when I awake in Your *l*....Ps 17:15
His own Son in the *l*......Rom 8:3
and coming in the *l* ......Phil 2:7

LILY

the *l* of the valleys ......Song 2:1
Like a *l* among thorns .....Song 2:2
shall grow like the *l* ......Hos 14:5

LIMIT

Do you *l* wisdom to.......Job 15:8
to the sea its *l* ....Prov 8:29

LIMITED

l the Holy One of ....Ps 78:41

LINE

l has gone out through......Ps 19:4
upon precept, *l* upon......Is 28:10
I am setting a plumb *l* ....Amos 7:8

LINEAGE

was of the house and *l* ....Luke 2:4

LINEN

her clothing is fine *l* ....Prov 31:22
wrapped Him in the *l* ...Mark 15:46
l is the righteous.........Rev 19:8

LINGER

Those who *l* long at ....Prov 23:30
salvation shall not *l*.......Is 46:13

LION

he lies down as a *l* ......Gen 49:9
like a fierce *l* ....Job 10:16
l shall eat straw.........Is 11:7
For I will be like a *l*......Hos 5:14

LIONS

My soul is among *l*.......Ps 57:4
the mouths of *l*.........Heb 11:33

LIPS

of uncircumcised *l* ....Ex 6:12
off all flattering *l* ....Ps 12:3
Let the lying *l*...........Ps 31:18
The *l* of the righteous....Prov 10:21
but the *l* of knowledge ...Prov 20:15
am a man of unclean *l*......Is 6:5
asps is under their *l* .....Rom 3:13
other *l* I will speak......1 Cor 14:21
from evil, and his *l*......1 Pet 3:10

LISTEN

L carefully to Me..........Is 55:2
O Lord, *l* and act ......Dan 9:19
you are not able to *l* .....John 8:43
Why do you *l* to Him ...John 10:20
you who fear God, *l*.....Acts 13:16

LISTENS

but whoever *l* to me .....Prov 1:33

LITTLE

l foxes that spoil the ....Song 2:15
We have a *l* sister ....Song 8:8
upon line, here a *l* ....Is 28:10
though you are *l* ....Mic 5:2
indeed it came to *l*......Hag 1:9
for I was a *l* angry ......Zech 1:15
l ones only a cup........Matt 10:42
"O you of *l* faith ......Matt 14:31
Whoever receives one *l*...Matt 18:5

LIVE

to whom *l* is forgiven . . . . .Luke 7:47
faithful in a very *l*. . . . . . .Luke 19:17
exercise profits a *l*. . . . . . . .1 Tim 4:8

LIVE

eat, and *l* forever. . . . . .Gen 3:22
a man does, he shall *l*. . . .Lev 18:5
I would not *l* forever. . . . . .Job 7:16
L joyfully with the . . . . .Eccl 9:9
by these things men *l* . . . . .Is 38:16
sin, he shall surely *l* . . . . . .Ezek 3:21
"Seek Me and *l* . . . . .Amos 5:4
but the just shall *l*. . . . . . . .Hab 2:4
l by bread alone . . . . .Matt 4:4
who feeds on Me will *l*. . . .John 6:57
"for in Him we *l* . . . . . . .Acts 17:28
l peaceably with all . . . . .Rom 12:18
the life which I now *l* . . . . .Gal 2:20
If we *l* in the Spirit. . . . . . .Gal 5:25
to me, to *l* is Christ . . . . . .Phil 1:21
l godly in Christ . . . . . . .2 Tim 3:12
to *l* honorably. . . . . .Heb 13:18
l according to God in . . . . .1 Pet 4:6

LIVED

died and rose and *l* . . . . . .Rom 14:9
And they *l* and reigned . . . .Rev 20:4

LIVES

but man *l* by every . . . . . . .Deut 8:3
have risked their *l*. . . . . . .Acts 15:26
He *l* to God . . . . .Rom 6:10
For none of us *l* . . . . .Rom 14:7
but Christ *l* in me . . . . .Gal 2:20
to lay down our *l* . . . .1 John 3:16
"I am He who *l*. . . . . .Rev 1:18

LIVING

and man became a *l*. . . . . . .Gen 2:7
in the light of the *l*. . . . . . .Ps 56:13
l will take it to . . . . .Eccl 7:2
l know that they will . . . . . .Eccl 9:5
Why should a *l* man . . . . . .Lam 3:39
the dead, but of the *l*. . .Matt 22:32
Why do you seek the *l*. . . .Luke 24:5
to be Judge of the *l*. . . . .Acts 10:42
who will judge the *l* . . . . .2 Tim 4:1
the word of God is *l*. . . . . .Heb 4:12
ready to judge the *l* . . . . . .1 Pet 4:5
l creature was like a . . . . .Rev 4:7

LOAD

shall bear his own *l*. . . . . . . .Gal 6:5

LOATHE

I *l* my life. . . . . .Job 7:16
l themselves for the . . . . . .Ezek 6:9

LOATHSOME

but a wicked man is *l* . . . . .Prov 13:5

LOAVES

have here only five *l*. . . . .Matt 14:17
He took the seven *l* . . . .Matt 15:36
lend me three *l* . . . . .Luke 11:5
you ate of the *l* . . . . .John 6:26

LOCUST

What the chewing *l* . . . . . . .Joel 1:4
left, the swarming *l* . . . . . . .Joel 1:4

LOCUSTS

as numerous as *l*. . . . . .Judg 7:12
He spoke, and *l* came. . . . .Ps 105:34
the *l* have no king . . . . . .Prov 30:27
and his food was *l*. . . . . . .Matt 3:4
waist, and he ate *l*. . . . . . .Mark 1:6
out of the smoke *l*. . . . . . . .Rev 9:3

LODGED

them in and *l* them . . . . .Acts 10:23
children, if she has *l* . . . . .1 Tim 5:10

LOFTILY

they speak *l*. . . . . .Ps 73:8

LOFTY

haughty, nor my eyes *l*. . . . .Ps 131:1
Wisdom is too *l* . . . . .Prov 24:7
l are their eyes . . . . .Prov 30:13
and *L* One who. . . . . .Is 57:15

LOINS

gird up the *l* of your. . . . . .1 Pet 1:13

LONG

your days may be *l*. . . . . . .Deut 5:16
who *l* for death . . . . .Job 3:21
me the thing that I *l* . . . . . .Job 6:8
I *l* for Your salvation . . . .Ps 119:174
go around in *l* robes. . . . .Mark 12:38
how greatly I *l* . . . . .Phil 1:8

LONGSUFFERING

and gracious, *l*. . . . . .Ps 86:15
is love, joy, peace, *l* . . . . . .Gal 5:22
and gentleness, with *l* . . . . . .Eph 4:2
for all patience and *l* . . . . . .Col 1:11
might show all *l*. . . . . .1 Tim 1:16
when once the Divine *l* . . .1 Pet 3:20
and consider that the *l* . . .2 Pet 3:15

LOOK

Do not *l* behind you. . . . . .Gen 19:17
who has a haughty *l*. . . . . . .Ps 101:5
A proud *l* . . . . .Prov 6:17
that day a man will *l*. . . . . . .Is 17:7
L upon Zion . . . . .Is 33:20
"*L* to Me. . . . . .Is 45:22
we *l* for light. . . . . .Is 59:9
we *l* for justice. . . . . .Is 59:11
l on Me whom they. . . . . .Zech 12:10
say to you, '*L* here . . . . .Luke 17:23
of Israel could not *l* . . . . . .2 Cor 3:7
while we do not *l* . . . . . . .2 Cor 4:18
Let each of you *l*. . . . . .Phil 2:4
L to yourselves . . . . .2 John 1:8

LOOKED

But when I *l* for good. . . .Job 30:26
They *l* to Him and were. . . . .Ps 34:5
For He *l* down from the. . .Ps 102:19
He *l* for justice. . . . . .Is 5:7
"We *l* for peace. . . . . .Jer 8:15
"You *l* for much . . . . .Hag 1:9
the Lord turned and *l*. . . .Luke 22:61
for he *l* to the reward. . . .Heb 11:26

LOOKING

the plow, and *l* back . . . . .Luke 9:62
l for the blessed hope. . . . .Titus 2:13
l unto Jesus . . . . .Heb 12:2
l carefully lest. . . . . .Heb 12:15
l for the mercy of . . . . .Jude 21

LOOKS

Absalom for his good *l* 2 Sam 14:25
Then he *l* at men and . . . . .Job 33:27
God *l* down from heaven . . . .Ps 53:2
The lofty *l* of man . . . . .Is 2:11
to you that whoever *l*. . . .Matt 5:28

LOOM

and the web from the *l*. .Judg 16:14
cuts me off from the *l*. . . . .Is 38:12

LOOSE

l the armor of kings. . . . . . . .Is 45:1
and whatever you *l*. . . . . .Matt 16:19

LORD

said to them, "*L* him . . . .John 11:44

LOOSED

You have *l* my bonds . . . . .Ps 116:16
the silver cord is *l* . . . . . . .Eccl 12:6

LORD

L is my strength . . . . .Ex 15:2
L is a man of war. . . . . .Ex 15:3
L our God, the *L*. . . . . .Deut 6:4
L your God a bull. . . . . . . .Deut 17:1
may know that the *L* . . .1 Kin 8:60
If the *L* is God. . . . . .1 Kin 18:21
You alone are the *L* . . . . . . .Neh 9:6
The *L* of hosts. . . . . .Ps 24:10
belongs to the *L* . . . . .Ps 89:18
let us sing to the *L*. . . . . . . .Ps 95:1
L is the great God . . . . .Ps 95:3
Gracious is the *L* . . . . .Ps 116:5
L surrounds His people . . . .Ps 125:2
The *L* is righteous . . . . . . .Ps 129:4
L is near to all who. . . . . . .Ps 145:18
L is a God of justice . . . . . . .Is 30:18
L OUR RIGHTEOUSNESS Jer 23:6
L has done marvelous . . . .Joel 2:21
L God is my strength . . . .Hab 3:19
"the *L* is one . . . . .Zech 14:9
shall not tempt the *L*. . . . .Matt 4:7
shall worship the *L*. . . . . . .Matt 4:10
Son of Man is also *L*. . . . .Mark 2:28
who is Christ the *L* . . . . .Luke 2:11
why do you call Me '*L*. . . .Luke 6:46
L is risen indeed. . . . . . . .Luke 24:34
call me Teacher and *L* . .John 13:13
He is *L* of all . . . . .Acts 10:36
'Who are You, *L*. . . . . . . .Acts 26:15
with your mouth the *L*. . .Rom 10:9
Greek, for the same *L*. . . .Rom 10:12
say that Jesus is *L* . . . . .1 Cor 12:3
second Man is the *L* . . . .1 Cor 15:47
the Spirit of the *L*. . . . . . .2 Cor 3:17
that Jesus Christ is *L* . . . .Phil 2:11
and deny the only *L*. . . . . . . .Jude 4
L God Omnipotent. . . . . . .Rev 19:6

LORDS

many gods and many *l* . . .1 Cor 8:5
nor as being *l* over . . . . . . .1 Pet 5:3
for He is Lord of *l*. . . . . . .Rev 17:14

LORDSHIP

Gentiles exercise *l*. . . . . .Luke 22:25

LOSE

gain, and a time to *l* . . . . . .Eccl 3:6
save his life will *l* . . . . . . .Matt 16:25
reap if we do not *l*. . . . . . . .Gal 6:9
that we do not *l* . . . . .2 John 8

LOSES

but if the salt *l*. . . . . .Matt 5:13
and *l* his own soul. . . . . . .Matt 16:26
if she *l* one coin. . . . . . . .Luke 15:8
l his life will. . . . . .Luke 17:33

LOSS

he will suffer *l* . . . . .1 Cor 3:15
count all things *l* . . . . .Phil 3:8

LOST

are dry, our hope is *l*. . . . .Ezek 37:11
save that which was *l*. . . .Matt 18:11
the one which is *l* . . . . . . .Luke 15:4
my sheep which was *l* . . .Luke 15:6
the piece which I *l* . . . . . .Luke 15:9
and none of them is *l* . . . .John 17:12
You gave Me I have *l* . . . .John 18:9

LOT

shall be divided by *l*. . . . . .Num 26:55

LOTS

You maintain my *l*..........Ps 16:5
cast in your *l* among......Prov 1:14
l is cast into the lap.....Prov 16:33
delivered righteous *L*......2 Pet 2:7

LOTS

l causes contentions.....Prov 18:18
garments, casting *l*.....Mark 15:24
And they cast their *l*......Acts 1:26

LOUD

I cried out with a *l*......Gen 39:14
Him with *l* cymbals.......Ps 150:5
cried out with a *l*......Matt 27:46
I heard behind me a *l*......Rev 1:10

LOVE

l your neighbor as.......Lev 19:18
l the LORD your God.....Deut 6:5
your *l* to me was........2 Sam 1:26
How long will you *l*.........Ps 4:2
Oh, *l* the LORD.............Ps 31:23
l righteousness...........Ps 45:7
he has set his *l*.........Ps 91:14
Oh, how I *l* Your law.....Ps 119:97
peace have those who *l*..Ps 119:165
preserves all who *l*......Ps 145:20
us take our fill of *l*.......Prov 7:18
l covers all sins.........Prov 10:12
a time to *l*.............Eccl 3:8
People know neither *l*.....Eccl 9:1
l is better than wine......Song 1:2
banner over me was *l*......Song 2:4
stir up nor awaken *l*.......Song 3:5
I will give you my *l*......Song 7:12
l is as strong as..........Song 8:6
waters cannot quench *l*...Song 8:7
time was the time of *l*...Ezek 16:8
backsliding, I will *l*......Hos 14:4
do justly, to *l* mercy.......Mic 6:8
to you, *l* your enemies...Matt 5:44
l those who *l* you........Matt 5:46
which of them will *l*.....Luke 7:42
you do not have the *l*....John 5:42
if you have *l* for one....John 13:35
"If you *l* Me..........John 14:15
and My Father will *l*...John 14:23
l one another as I.......John 15:12
l has no one than this...John 15:13
I Me more than these...John 21:15
of Jonah, do you *l*......John 21:16
You know that I *l*......John 21:16
because the *l* of God.....Rom 5:5
Let *l* be without........Rom 12:9
to *l* one another.........Rom 13:8
L does no harm to a.....Rom 13:10
up, but *l* edifies..........1 Cor 8:1
L suffers long and is....1 Cor 13:4
l does not envy........1 Cor 13:4
l does not parade.......1 Cor 13:4
L never fails.........1 Cor 13:8
greatest of these is *l*....1 Cor 13:13
For the *l* of Christ......2 Cor 5:14
and the God of *l*.......2 Cor 13:11
of the Spirit is *l*..........Gal 5:22
Husbands, *l* your wives...Eph 5:25
of the Son of His *l*........Col 1:13
l your wives and do.......Col 3:19
the commandment is *l*......1 Tim 1:5
continue in faith, *l*......1 Tim 2:15
word, in conduct, in *l*....1 Tim 4:12
For the *l* of money is....1 Tim 6:10
l their husbands.........Titus 2:4
Let brotherly *l*.........Heb 13:1
having not seen you *l*.....1 Pet 1:8
L the brotherhood.......1 Pet 2:17
for "*l* will cover a.........1 Pet 4:8
with a kiss of *l*..........1 Pet 5:14
brotherly kindness *l*......2 Pet 1:7

loves the world, the *l*...1 John 2:15
we *l* the brethren.......1 John 3:14
By this we know *l*......1 John 3:16
him, how does the *l*...1 John 3:17
Beloved, let us *l*.........1 John 4:7
know God, for God is *l*...1 John 4:8
In this is *l*..............1 John 4:10
If we *l* one another.....1 John 4:12
L has been perfected...1 John 4:17
There is no fear in *l*.....1 John 4:18
l Him because He first...1 John 4:19
who loves God must *l*...1 John 4:21
For this is the *l*.........1 John 5:3
have left your first *l*........Rev 2:4
and they did not *l*.......Rev 12:11

LOVED

Because the LORD has *l*...1 Kin 10:9
L one and friend You......Ps 88:18
"I have *l* you............Mal 1:2
Yet Jacob I have *l*........Mal 1:2
forgiven, for she *l*........Luke 7:47
so *l* the world that.........John 3:16
"See how He *l*.........John 11:36
whom Jesus *l*..........John 13:23
"As the Father *l*.........John 15:9
l them as You have.....John 17:23
"Jacob I have *l*..........Rom 9:13
the Son of God, who *l*....Gal 2:20
l the church and gave.....Eph 5:25
l righteousness...........Heb 1:9
God, but that He *l*.....1 John 4:10
Beloved, if God so *l*.....1 John 4:11
To Him who *l* us and......Rev 1:5

LOVELY

l is Your tabernacle........Ps 84:1
l woman who lacks.....Prov 11:22
he is altogether *l*.........Song 5:16
whatever things are *l*.......Phil 4:8

LOVER

a *l* of what is good.......Titus 1:8

LOVERS

For men will be *l*........2 Tim 3:2

LOVES

l righteousness...........Ps 33:5
life, and *l* many days.....Ps 34:12
A friend *l* at all........Prov 17:17
"He who *l* father or.....Matt 10:37
l his life will lose.......John 12:25
l Me will be loved......John 14:21
l a cheerful giver.......2 Cor 9:7
who *l* his wife *l*..........Eph 5:28
If anyone *l* the world....1 John 2:15
l God must love his....1 John 4:21
l him who is............1 John 5:1

LOVESICK

apples, for I am *l*.........Song 2:5
you tell him I am *l*........Song 5:8

LOVINGKINDNESS

not concealed Your *l*......Ps 40:10
l is better than life.........Ps 63:3
to declare Your *l*.........Ps 92:2
l I have drawn..........Jer 31:3

LOW

He brings *l* and lifts......1 Sam 2:7
both *l* and high........Ps 49:2
it *l*, He lays it *l*...........Is 26:5
and hill brought *l*........Luke 3:5

LOWER

made him a little *l*........Ps 8:5
shall go into the *l*.........Ps 63:9
made him a little *l*........Heb 2:7

LOWEST

and sets over it the *l*......Dan 4:17

LOWLINESS

with all *l* and.............Eph 4:2
or conceit, but in *l*........Phil 2:3

LOWLY

yet He regards the *l*.......Ps 138:6
for I am gentle and *l*....Matt 11:29
He has regarded the *l*....Luke 1:48
and exalted the *l*........Luke 1:52
in presence am I.........2 Cor 10:1
l body that it may be.......Phil 3:21
l brother glory..........James 1:9

LOYAL

or else he will be *l*.......Matt 6:24

LUKEWARM

because you are *l*.........Rev 3:16

LUMP

from the same *l*.........Rom 9:21
you may be a new *l*......1 Cor 5:7

LUST

Do not *l* after her.......Prov 6:25
caught by their *l*.......Prov 11:6
looks at a woman to *l*....Matt 5:28
not fulfill the *l*..........Gal 5:16
not in passion of *l*.....1 Thess 4:5
You *l* and do not have...James 4:2
the *l* of the flesh......1 John 2:16

LUSTS

to fulfill its *l*...........Rom 13:14
l which drown men......1 Tim 6:9
also youthful *l*..........2 Tim 2:22
and worldly *l*..........Titus 2:12
to the former *l*.........1 Pet 1:14
abstain from fleshly *l*....1 Pet 2:11
to their own ungodly *l*.....Jude 18

LUTE

Awake, *l* and harp.........Ps 57:8
l I will praise You.........Ps 71:22
harp with the *l*............Ps 81:2
ten strings, on the *l*.......Ps 92:3
Awake, *l* and harp.......Ps 108:2
Praise Him with the *l*....Ps 150:3

LUXURY

L is not fitting.........Prov 19:10
l are in kings' courts....Luke 7:25
in pleasure and *l*........James 5:5
the abundance of her *l*....Rev 18:3

LYING

I hate and abhor *l*......Ps 119:163
righteous man hates *l*.....Prov 13:5
not trust in those.........Jer 7:4
in swaddling cloths, *l*....Luke 2:12
saw the linen cloths *l*....John 20:5
putting away *l*..........Eph 4:25
signs, and *l* wonders....2 Thess 2:9

M

MAD

has a demon and is *m*...John 10:20
he said, "I am not *m*.....Acts 26:25

MADE

m the stars also..........Gen 1:16
wife the LORD God *m*......Gen 3:21
hear long ago how I *m*....Is 37:26
things My hand has *m*.....Is 66:2
All things were *m*........John 1:3

MADNESS

before them, *m* . . . . .1 Sam 21:13
wisdom and to know *m* . . . .Eccl 1:17
m is in their hearts . . . . .Eccl 9:3

MAGIC

women who sew *m* . . . . . .Ezek 13:18
m brought their books . . .Acts 19:19

MAGNIFICENCE

m I cannot endure . . . . . . .Job 31:23

MAGNIFIED

So let Your name be *m*. . .2 Sam 7:26
"Let the LORD be *m* . . . . . . .Ps 35:27
for You have *m* Your. . . . . . .Ps 138:2
the Lord Jesus was *m*. . . .Acts 19:17
also Christ will be *m* . . . . .Phil 1:20

MAGNIFIES

"My soul *m* the Lord. . . . .Luke 1:46

MAGNIFY

m the LORD with me. . . . . . . .Ps 34:3
m himself above every. . . .Dan 11:36

MAIDENS

Both young men and *m* . . .Ps 148:12
She has sent out her *m*. . . . .Prov 9:3

MAIDSERVANT

"I am Ruth, your *m* . . . . . . .Ruth 3:9
save the son of Your *m*. . . . .Ps 86:16
"Behold the *m*. . . . . .Luke 1:38
lowly state of His *m* . . . . .Luke 1:48

MAIDSERVANTS

m shall lead her as. . . . . .Nah 2:7
m I will pour out My . . . . .Acts 2:18

MAIMED

to enter into life *m*. . . . . . .Mark 9:43
the poor and the *m*. . . . . .Luke 14:21

MAINTAIN

and *m* their cause . . . . . . .1 Kin 8:45

MAINTAINED

For You have *m* my. . . . . .Ps 9:4

MAJESTY

with God is awesome *m*. . .Job 37:22
splendor of Your *m*. . . . . . .Ps 145:5
right hand of the *M*. . . . . . . .Heb 1:3
eyewitnesses of His *m*. . . .2 Pet 1:16
wise, be glory and *m*. . . . . . .Jude 25

MAKE

Let Us make *m* in Our . . . . .Gen 1:26
let us *m* a name for . . . . . .Gen 11:4
m you a great nation . . . . . .Gen 12:2
"You shall not *m* . . . . .Ex 20:4
m Our home with him . . .John 14:23

MAKER

where is God my *M* . . . . .Job 35:10
man will look to his *M* . . . . .Is 17:7
who strives with his *M*. . . . .Is 45:9
M is your husband . . . . .Is 54:5
has forgotten his *M* . . . . . .Hos 8:14
builder and *m* is God. . . . .Heb 11:10

MALICE

however, in *m* be babes . .1 Cor 14:20
pleasures, living in *m*. . . . . .Titus 3:3
laying aside all *m* . . . . .1 Pet 2:1

MALICIOUSNESS

covetousness, *m*. . . . . .Rom 1:29

MALIGN

m a servant to his. . . . . . .Prov 30:10

MAN

"Let Us make *m*. . . . . .Gen 1:26
"You are the *m* . . . . .2 Sam 12:7
"What is *m* . . . . .Job 7:17
For an empty-headed *m*. . .Job 11:12
"Are you the first *m*. . . . . .Job 15:7
m that You are mindful . . . . .Ps 8:4
What can *m* do to me. . . . . .Ps 118:6
coming of the Son of *M*. .Matt 24:27
"Behold the *M* . . . . .John 19:5
m is not from woman . . . .1 Cor 11:8
since by *m* came death . .1 Cor 15:21
though our outward *m* . . .2 Cor 4:16
in Himself one new *m* . . . .Eph 2:15
that the *m* of God may. . .2 Tim 3:17
is the number of a *m* . . . . .Rev 13:18

MANGER

Will he bed by your *m* . . . .Job 39:9
and laid Him in a *m*. . . . . . .Luke 2:7
the Babe lying in a *m* . . . .Luke 2:16

MANIFEST

m Myself to him. . . . . . . .John 14:21
is it that You will *m* . . . .John 14:22

MANIFESTATION

But the *m* of the . . . . .1 Cor 12:7
deceitfully, but by *m* . . . . .2 Cor 4:2

MANIFESTED

"I have *m* Your name. . . .John 17:6
God was *m* in the flesh. . .1 Tim 3:16
the life was *m*. . . . . .1 John 1:2
the love of God was *m* . .1 John 4:9

MANIFOLD

m are Your works . . . . . . .Ps 104:24
the *m* wisdom of God . . . . .Eph 3:10
good stewards of the *m* . . .1 Pet 4:10

MANNA

of Israel ate *m* . . . . .Ex 16:35
had rained down *m*. . . . . . .Ps 78:24
Our fathers ate the *m*. . . . .John 6:31
of the hidden *m*. . . . . .Rev 2:17

MANNER

Is this the *m* of man . . . .2 Sam 7:19
in an unworthy *m*. . . . . . .1 Cor 11:27
sorrowed in a godly *m*. . . .2 Cor 7:11
as is the *m* of some . . . . .Heb 10:25
what *m* of persons . . . . . .2 Pet 3:11
Behold what *m* of love . .1 John 3:1
m worthy of God . . . . .3 John 6

MANSIONS

house are many *m*. . . . . . .John 14:2

MANTLE

Then he took the *m*. . . . . .2 Kin 2:14

MARCHED

people, when You *m* . . . . . .Ps 68:7

MARK

And the LORD set a *m*. . . . .Gen 4:15
M the blameless man . . . .Ps 37:37
slave, to receive a *m*. . . . .Rev 13:16
whoever receives the *m* . . .Rev 14:11

MARKET

is sold in the meat *m*. . . .1 Cor 10:25

MARRED

so His visage was *m* . . . . . .Is 52:14
he made of clay was *m* . . . .Jer 18:4

MARRIAGE

nor are given in *m* . . . . .Matt 22:30
her in *m* does well . . . . . . .1 Cor 7:38
M is honorable among. . . . .Heb 13:4
the *m* of the Lamb has. . . . .Rev 19:7

MARRIED

"for I am *m* to you . . . . . . .Jer 3:14
But he who is *m*. . . . . . . .1 Cor 7:33
But she who is *m*. . . . . . .1 Cor 7:34

MARROW

and of joints and *m*. . . . . . .Heb 4:12

MARRY

it is better not to *m*. . . . .Matt 19:10
they neither *m* nor are. . .Matt 22:30
let them *m* . . . . .1 Cor 7:9
forbidding to *m* . . . . .1 Tim 4:3
the younger widows *m* . . .1 Tim 5:14

MARRYING

and drinking, *m* . . . . . . .Matt 24:38

MARTYR

m Stephen was shed . . . . .Acts 22:20
was My faithful *m* . . . . . . .Rev 2:13

MARTYRS

the blood of the *m* . . . . . . .Rev 17:6

MARVEL

"Do not *m* at this. . . . . . .John 5:28

MARVELED

Jesus heard it, He *m* . . . .Matt 8:10
And the multitudes *m* . . . .Matt 9:33
so that Pilate *m*. . . . . . . .Mark 15:5
And all the world *m* . . . . . .Rev 13:3
when I saw her, I *m* . . . . . .Rev 17:6

MARVELOUS

m things He did . . . . .Ps 78:12
It is *m* in our eyes . . . . . . .Ps 118:23
M are Your works. . . . . . .Ps 139:14
of darkness into His *m* . . .1 Pet 2:9

MARVELS

people I will do *m* . . . . . . .Ex 34:10

MASTER

of Abraham his *m* . . . . . . .Gen 24:9
a servant like his *m* . . . . .Matt 10:25
not greater than his *m*. . .John 15:20
m builder I have laid . . . .1 Cor 3:10
and useful for the *M*. . . . .2 Tim 2:21

MASTERS

m besides You have . . . . . .Is 26:13
can serve two *m* . . . . . . .Luke 16:13
M, give your bondservants. . .Col 4:1
who have believing *m* . . . . .1 Tim 6:2

MATTER

m is found in me. . . . . . . .Job 19:28
He who answers a *m*. . . . .Prov 18:13

MATTERS

the weightier *m*. . . . . .Matt 23:23
judge the smallest *m*. . . . . .1 Cor 6:2

MATURE

among those who are *m* . .1 Cor 2:6
in understanding be *m* . .1 Cor 14:20
us, as many as are *m* . . . . . .Phil 3:15

MEAN

"What do you *m* . . . . .Ex 12:26

MEANING

"What is the *m* . . . . .Deut 6:20

MEANT

if I do not know the m . . 1 Cor 14:11

MEANT

but God m it for good . . . . Gen 50:20

MEASURE

a perfect and just m . . . . Deut 25:15
apportion the waters by m Job 28:25
and the short m . . . . Mic 6:10
give the Spirit by m . . . . . John 3:34
to each one a m . . . . Rom 12:3
m the temple of God . . . . . . Rev 11:1

MEASURED

m the waters in the . . . . Is 40:12
you use, it will be m . . . . . . Matt 7:2
Then he m its wall . . . . . . Rev 21:17

MEASURES

your house differing m . . Deut 25:14
weights and diverse m . . . Prov 20:10

MEASURING

the man's hand was a m . . Ezek 40:5
behold, a man with a m . . . . Zech 2:1
m themselves by . . . . 2 Cor 10:12
given a reed like a m . . . . . . Rev 11:1

MEAT

Can He provide m . . . . Ps 78:20
He also rained m . . . . Ps 78:27
good neither to eat m . . . . Rom 14:21
will never again eat m . . . . 1 Cor 8:13
is sold in the m . . . . 1 Cor 10:25

MEDDLE

why should you m . . . . . 2 Kin 14:10

MEDIATE

a mediator does not m . . . . . Gal 3:20

MEDIATOR

Nor is there any m . . . . Job 9:33
by the hand of a m . . . . Gal 3:19
is one God and one M . . . . 1 Tim 2:5
as He is also M . . . . Heb 8:6
to Jesus the M of the . . . . Heb 12:24

MEDICINE

does good, like m . . . . Prov 17:22

MEDICINES

you will use many m . . . . . . Jer 46:11

MEDITATE

Isaac went out to m . . . . . . Gen 24:63
but you shall m . . . . Josh 1:8
M within your heart on . . . . Ps 4:4
I m within my heart . . . . Ps 77:6
I will m on Your . . . . Ps 119:15
Your heart will m . . . . Is 33:18
m beforehand on what . . Luke 21:14
m on these things . . . . Phil 4:8

MEDITATES

in His law he m . . . . Ps 1:2

MEDITATION

of my mouth and the m . . . . Ps 19:14
m be sweet to Him . . . . Ps 104:34
It is my m all the day . . . . Ps 119:97

MEDIUM

or a woman who is a m . . Lev 20:27
me a woman who is a m 1 Sam 28:7

MEDIUM'S

shall be like a m . . . . Is 29:4

MEDIUMS

Seek those who are m . . . . . . Is 8:19

MEEK

with equity for the m . . . . Is 11:4
Blessed are the m . . . . Matt 5:5

MEEKNESS

with you by the m . . . . 2 Cor 10:1
are done in the m . . . . James 3:13

MEET

For You m him with the . . . . . Ps 21:3
prepare to m your God . . Amos 4:12
go out to m him . . . . Matt 25:6
m the Lord in the air . . 1 Thess 4:17

MEETING

In the tabernacle of m . . . . . Ex 27:21
burned up all the m . . . . Ps 74:8

MELODY

make sweet m . . . . Is 23:16
singing and making m . . . . Eph 5:19

MELT

You make his beauty m . . . . Ps 39:11
man's heart will m . . . . Is 13:7
the elements will m . . . . . . 2 Pet 3:10

MEMBER

the body is not one m . . . 1 Cor 12:14
tongue is a little m . . . . . . James 3:5

MEMBERS

you that one of your m . . . Matt 5:29
do not present your m . . . . Rom 6:13
that your bodies are m . . . 1 Cor 6:15
neighbor, for we are m . . . . Eph 4:25

MEMORIAL

and this is My m . . . . Ex 3:15
also be told as a m . . . . . Matt 26:13
be told of as a m . . . . Mark 14:9

MEMORY

The m of him perishes . . . . Job 18:17
He may cut off the m . . . . . Ps 109:15
The m of the righteous . . . . Prov 10:7

MEN

m began to call on the . . . . Gen 4:26
saw the daughters of m . . . . . Gen 6:2
you shall die like m . . . . Ps 82:7
the Egyptians are m . . . . Is 31:3
make you fishers of m . . . Matt 4:19
good will toward m . . . . . . Luke 2:14
from heaven or from m . . . Luke 20:4
Likewise also the m . . . . . . Rom 1:27
let no one boast in m . . . . 1 Cor 3:21
the Lord, and not to m . . . . Eph 6:7
between God and m . . . . . 1 Tim 2:5

MENSERVANTS

And also on My m . . . . Joel 2:29
And on My m and on My . Acts 2:18

MENTION

I will make m of Your . . . . . Ps 71:16
by You only we make m . . . Is 26:13
You who make m of the . . . Is 62:6
he was dying, made m . . . Heb 11:22

MERCHANDISE

perceives that her m . . . . Prov 31:18
house a house of m . . . . . John 2:16

MERCHANTS

set it in a city of m . . . . . Ezek 17:4
have multiplied your m . . . Nah 3:16
m were the great men . . . Rev 18:23

MERCIES

for His m are great . . . . 2 Sam 24:14

and His tender m . . . . Ps 145:9
give you the sure m . . . . . Acts 13:34
the Father of m . . . . 2 Cor 1:3

MERCIFUL

LORD, the LORD God, m . . . . Ex 34:6
He is ever m . . . . Ps 37:26
God be m to us and . . . . Ps 67:1
Blessed are the m . . . . Matt 5:7
saying, 'God be m . . . . . . Luke 18:13
For I will be m . . . . Heb 8:12
compassionate and m . . . . James 5:11

MERCY

but showing m to . . . . Ex 20:6
and abundant in m . . . . . Num 14:18
m endures forever . . . . . 1 Chr 16:34
to Your m remember me . . . . Ps 25:7
I trust in the m . . . . Ps 52:8
shall send forth His m . . . . . Ps 57:3
You, O Lord, belongs m . . . . Ps 62:12
m ceased forever . . . . Ps 77:8
M and truth have met . . . . Ps 85:10
M shall be built . . . . Ps 89:2
m and truth go before . . . . . Ps 89:14
m is everlasting . . . . Ps 100:5
I will sing of m . . . . Ps 101:1
For Your m is great . . . . . . Ps 108:4
is full of Your m . . . . Ps 119:64
the LORD there is m . . . . . . Ps 130:7
Let not m and truth . . . . Prov 3:3
who honors Him has m . . Prov 14:31
cruel and have no m . . . . . . Jer 6:23
Lord our God belong m . . . . Dan 9:9
For I desire m and not . . . . Hos 6:6
do justly, to love m . . . . Mic 6:8
'I desire m and not . . . . . . Matt 9:13
And His m is on those . . . Luke 1:50
"I will have m . . . . Rom 9:15
of God who shows m . . . . Rom 9:16
that He might have m . . . Rom 11:32
m has made trustworthy . 1 Cor 7:25
as we have received m . . . . 2 Cor 4:1
God, who is rich in m . . . . . Eph 2:4
but I obtained m . . . . 1 Tim 1:13
him that he may find m . . 2 Tim 1:18
to His m He saved us . . . . Titus 3:5
that we may obtain m . . . . Heb 4:16
judgment is without m . James 2:13
God, looking for the m . . . . Jude 21

MERRY

m heart makes a . . . . Prov 15:13
eat, drink, and be m . . . . . Eccl 8:15
that we should make m . Luke 15:32

MESSAGE

I have heard a m . . . . Jer 49:14
For the m of the cross . . . 1 Cor 1:18

MESSENGER

is a faithful m . . . . Prov 25:13
"Behold, I send My m . . . . . Mal 3:1
'Behold, I send My m . . . Matt 11:10

MESSIAH

until M the Prince . . . . Dan 9:25
"We have found the M . . . John 1:41

MIDST

God is in the m . . . . Ps 46:5
that I am in the m . . . . Joel 2:27
I am there in the m . . . . . Matt 18:20

MIGHT

'My power and the m . . . . Deut 8:17
shall speak of the m . . . . . . Ps 145:6
the greatness of His m . . . . Is 40:26
man glory in his m . . . . Jer 9:23
their m has failed . . . . Jer 51:30

'Not by *m* nor by.........Zech 4:6
in the power of His *m* .....Eph 6:10
greater in power and *m* . . .2 Pet 2:11
honor and power and *m* ....Rev 7:12

MIGHTIER

coming after me is *m* .....Matt 3:11

MIGHTILY

to shake the earth *m*........Is 2:19
which works in me *m* ......Col 1:29

MIGHTY

He was a *m* hunter.......Gen 10:9
for they are too *m*.......Num 22:6
How the *m* have fallen...2 Sam 1:19
is wise in heart and *m* .....Job 9:4
the LORD *m* in battle ....Ps 24:8
their Redeemer is *m* ....Prov 23:11
Woe to men *m* at...........Is 5:22
great in counsel and *m* ...Jer 32:19
m men are made red ......Nah 2:3
m has done great ....Luke 1:49
He has put down the *m*...Luke 1:52
the flesh, not many *m* ....1 Cor 1:26
the working of His *m* .....Eph 1:19
from heaven with His *m* 2 Thess 1:7

MILK

for water, she gave *m* ....Judg 5:25
honey and *m* are under . . .Song 4:11
come, buy wine and *m* .....Is 55:1
and whiter than *m*........Lam 4:7
shall flow with *m* ....Joel 3:18
have come to need *m* .....Heb 5:12
m is unskilled in the .....Heb 5:13
desire the pure *m* ....1 Pet 2:2

MILL

be grinding at the *m* ....Matt 24:41

MILLSTONE

m were hung around his . .Matt 18:6
a stone like a great *m*.....Rev 18:21

MIND

put wisdom in the *m* ....Job 38:36
perfect peace, whose *m*.....Is 26:3
nor have an anxious *m*. . .Luke 12:29
m I myself serve the......Rom 7:25
who has known the *m*....Rom 11:34
Be of the same *m* ......Rom 12:16
convinced in his own *m* . . .Rom 14:5
"Who has known the *m* ..1 Cor 2:16
you are out of your *m* ...1 Cor 14:23
Let this *m* be in you ......Phil 2:5
to *m* your own ....1 Thess 4:11
love and of a sound *m*.....2 Tim 1:7

MINDFUL

is man that You are *m* ....Ps 8:4
The LORD has been *m*.....Ps 115:12
for you are not *m*.......Matt 16:23
is man that You are *m*.....Heb 2:6

MINDS

people change their *m* ....Ex 13:17
put My law in their *m*.....Jer 31:33
I stir up your pure *m*.....2 Pet 3:1
He who searches the *m* ....Rev 2:23

MINISTER

to make you a *m* ....Acts 26:16
for he is God's *m*.........Rom 13:4
you will be a good *m*......1 Tim 4:6
a *M* of the sanctuary.......Heb 8:2

MINISTERED

But the child *m* ....1 Sam 2:11
a thousand thousands *m*. . .Dan 7:10

As they *m* to the Lord ....Acts 13:2

MINISTERS

angels spirits, His *m* ......Ps 104:4
for they are God's *m*.....Rom 13:6
commend ourselves as *m* . .2 Cor 6:4
Are they *m* of Christ....2 Cor 11:23
If anyone *m*............1 Pet 4:11

MINISTRIES

are differences of *m* ......1 Cor 12:5

MINISTRY

I magnify my *m* ....Rom 11:13
But if the *m* of death .....2 Cor 3:7
since we have this *m* .....2 Cor 4:1
and has given us the *m*...2 Cor 5:18
for the work of *m*.........Eph 4:12
m which you have ....Col 4:17
fulfill your *m* ....2 Tim 4:5
a more excellent *m*.........Heb 8:6

MINT

For you pay tithe of *m*...Matt 23:23

MIRACLE

saying, 'Show a *m* ....Ex 7:9
no one who works a *m*....Mark 9:39
that a notable *m* ....Acts 4:16

MIRACLES

God worked unusual *m*...Acts 19:11
the working of *m* ....1 Cor 12:10
Are all workers of *m* ....1 Cor 12:29
with various *m* ....Heb 2:4

MIRTH

I will test you with *m* ......Eccl 2:1
is in the house of *m*.......Eccl 7:4
joy is darkened, the *m* .....Is 24:11

MISER

eat the bread of a *m* .....Prov 23:6

MISERIES

m that are coming ......James 5:1

MISERY

would forget your *m*.....Job 11:16
and remember his *m*......Prov 31:7

MISTREATED

But the Egyptians *m*.....Deut 26:6
those who are *m*..........Heb 13:3

MISTREATS

m his father and ....Prov 19:26

MITES

widow putting in two *m*. . .Luke 21:2

MOAN

m sadly like doves.........Is 59:11

MOCK

I will *m* when your ....Prov 1:26
Fools *m* at sin ....Prov 14:9
to the Gentiles to *m*.....Matt 20:19

MOCKED

at noon, that Elijah *m* ..1 Kin 18:27
"I am one *m* by his.......Job 12:4
knee before Him and *m*..Matt 27:29
deceived, God is not *m*......Gal 6:7

MOCKER

Wine is a *m* ....Prov 20:1

MOCKERS

that there would be *m*......Jude 18

MOCKINGS

others had trial of *m* .....Heb 11:36

MOCKS

He who *m* the poor.......Prov 17:5

MODERATION

with propriety and *m* .....1 Tim 2:9

MOMENT

consume them in a *m*....Num 16:21
In a *m* they die.........Job 34:20
face from you for a *m* ......Is 54:8
in a *m*, in the ....1 Cor 15:52
which is but for a *m* .....2 Cor 4:17

MONEY

does not put out his *m*.....Ps 15:5
m answers every ....Eccl 10:19
be redeemed without *m*.....Is 52:3
and you who have no *m* .....Is 55:1
and hid his lord's *m* ....Matt 25:18
promised to give him *m* Mark 14:11
"Carry neither *m* ....Luke 10:4
I sent you without *m* ....Luke 22:35
be purchased with *m*.....Acts 8:20
not greedy for *m* ....1 Tim 3:3
m is a root of all ....1 Tim 6:10
not greedy for *m*.........Titus 1:7

MONEYCHANGERS

the tables of the *m*.....Matt 21:12
m doing business ....John 2:14

MONSTER

me up like a *m*..........Jer 51:34
of Egypt, O great *m*.....Ezek 29:3

MOON

until the *m* is no more ......Ps 72:7
morning, fair as the *m*....Song 6:10
sun and *m* grow dark......Joel 2:10
m will not give its .....Mark 13:24

MORNING

the eyelids of the *m* .....Job 41:18
Evening and *m* and at.....Ps 55:17
the wings of the *m* ....Ps 139:9
looks forth as the *m*......Song 6:10
Lucifer, son of the *m*.......Is 14:12
established as the *m* ....Hos 6:3
very early in the *m*......Luke 24:1
the Bright and *M* Star...Rev 22:16

MORSEL

or eaten my *m* by ....Job 31:17
Better is a dry *m*........Prov 17:1
Esau, who for one *m* .....Heb 12:16

MORTAL

sin reign in your *m* ....Rom 6:12
and this *m* must put....1 Cor 15:53

MORTALITY

m may be swallowed ......2 Cor 5:4

MORTALS

with idolatrous *m* ....Ps 26:4

MOST

His mouth is *m* sweet ....Song 5:16
on your *m* holy faith ....Jude 20

MOTH

m will eat them ....Is 50:9
where *m* and rust........Matt 6:19

MOTHER

because she was the *m* ....Gen 3:20
like a joyful *m*............Ps 113:9
the only one of her *m*.....Song 6:9

MOUNT

m might have been my . . . .Jer 20:17
leave his father and *m* . . . .Matt 19:5
"Behold your *m*. . . . . . . .John 19:27
free, which is the *m*. . . . . . .Gal 4:26
THE *M* OF HARLOTS. . . .Rev 17:5

MOUNT

come up to *M* Sinai . . . . . . .Ex 19:23
you like *M* Carmel . . . .Song 7:5
they shall *m* up with . . . . . .Is 40:31
for this Hagar is *M*. . . . . . .Gal 4:25

MOUNTAIN

to Horeb, the *m* . . . . .Ex 3:1
"But as a *m* falls. . . . . . . .Job 14:18
You have made my *m* . . . . .Ps 30:7
of many peaks is the *m* . . . .Ps 68:15
let us go up to the *m*. . . . . . . .Is 2:3
image became a great *m* . .Dan 2:35
Who are you, O great *m*. . .Zech 4:7
you will say to this *m* . . .Matt 17:20
with Him on the holy *m* . .2 Pet 1:18

MOUNTAINS

He removes the *m*. . . . . .Job 9:5
Surely the *m* yield. . . . . . .Job 40:20
m will bring peace. . . . . . . .Ps 72:3
excellent than the *m*. . . . . . .Ps 76:4
m were brought forth . . . . . . .Ps 90:2
m melt like wax at the . . . . . .Ps 97:5
m skipped like rams . . . . . .Ps 114:4
m surround Jerusalem . . . . .Ps 125:2
m shall depart and the . . . . .Is 54:10
in Judea flee to the *m* . .Matt 24:16
that I could remove *m*. . . .1 Cor 13:2
m were not found . . . . .Rev 16:20

MOURN

and you *m* at last . . . . .Prov 5:11
a time to *m*. . . . . .Eccl 3:4
are those who *m* . . . . .Matt 5:4
Lament and *m* and weep . .James 4:9
of the earth will *m* . . . . . . .Rev 1:7

MOURNED

we *m* to you. . . . . .Matt 11:17
and have not rather *m*. . . . .1 Cor 5:2

MOURNING

This is a deep *m*. . . . . .Gen 50:11
m all the day long. . . . . .Ps 38:6
m shall be ended . . . . .Is 60:20
men break bread in *m* . . . . . .Jer 16:7
I will turn their *m* . . . . .Jer 31:13
shall be a great *m* . . . . . . .Zech 12:11
be turned to *m* and . . . . . .James 4:9

MOURNS

heavily, as one who *m*. . . . .Ps 35:14
The earth *m* and fades . . . . .Is 24:4
for Him as one *m* . . . . . .Zech 12:10

MOUTH

"Who has made man's *m* . .Ex 4:11
Out of the *m* of babes . . . . . .Ps 8:2
The *m* of the righteous. . . . . .Ps 37:30
m shall speak wisdom . . . . .Ps 49:3
iniquity stops its *m* . . . . . .Ps 107:42
knowledge, but the *m*. . . . .Prov 10:14
m preserves his life . . . . . .Prov 13:3
The *m* of an immoral . . .Prov 22:14
and a flattering *m*. . . . . .Prov 26:28
m speaking pompous. . . . . .Dan 7:8
the doors of your *m* . . . . . .Mic 7:5
m defiles a man . . . . . . .Matt 15:11
m I will judge you . . . . .Luke 19:22
I will give you a *m* . . . . .Luke 21:15
m confession is made . . . .Rom 10:10
m great swelling words . . . . .Jude 16
vomit you out of My *m* . . . .Rev 3:16

MOVE

and the earth will *m* . . . . . . .Is 13:13
the mountain shall *m* . . . . .Zech 14:4
in Him we live and *m* . . . .Acts 17:28

MOVED

shall never be *m* . . . . .Ps 15:5
she shall not be *m*. . . . . .Ps 46:5
spoke as they were *m*. . . . .2 Pet 1:21

MUCH

m study is. . . . . .Eccl 12:12
m better than wine is. . . . .Song 4:10
to whom *m* is given . . . . .Luke 12:48
M more then . . . . .Rom 5:9

MULTIPLIED

sorrows shall be *m* . . . . .Ps 16:4
of the disciples *m* . . . . .Acts 6:7
word of God grew and *m* Acts 12:24

MULTIPLY

"Be fruitful and *m*. . . . . . .Gen 1:22
m your descendants. . . . . .Gen 16:10
m my days as the . . . . . . .Job 29:18
m the descendants. . . . . . . .Jer 33:22

MULTITUDE

stars of heaven in *m*. . . . . .Deut 1:10
Your house in the *m* . . . . . . .Ps 5:7
m that kept a pilgrim. . . . . . .Ps 42:4
In the *m* of words sin. . . .Prov 10:19
In a *m* of people is a. . . . .Prov 14:28
compassion on the *m* . . .Matt 15:32
with the angel a *m* . . . . . .Luke 2:13
"love will cover a *m* . . . . . .1 Pet 4:8
and behold, a great *m* . . . . .Rev 7:9

MURDER

"You shall not *m* . . . . .Ex 20:13
'You shall not *m* . . . . .Matt 5:21
threats and *m* against. . . . . .Acts 9:1
You *m* and covet and . . . . .James 4:2

MURDERED

sons of those who *m* . . . .Matt 23:31
up Jesus whom you *m* . . .Acts 5:30
one and *m* his brother. . .1 John 3:12

MURDERER

He was a *m* from the . . . . .John 8:44
and asked for a *m* . . . . . . .Acts 3:14
of you suffer as a *m*. . . . . .1 Pet 4:15
his brother is a *m* . . . . . .1 John 3:15

MURDERERS

in it, but now *m*. . . . . .Is 1:21
and profane, for *m*. . . . . . .1 Tim 1:9
abominable, for *m*. . . . . .Rev 21:8

MURDERS

evil thoughts, *m* . . . . .Matt 15:19
envy, *m*. . . . . .Gal 5:21

MUSIC

So David played *m*. . . . .1 Sam 18:10
m are brought low . . . . . . .Eccl 12:4
the house, he heard *m* . .Luke 15:25

MUSING

while I was *m*. . . . . .Ps 39:3

MUTE

Or who makes the *m*. . . . . .Ex 4:11
m who does not open . . . . .Ps 38:13
I was *m* with silence. . . . . . .Ps 39:2
I was *m*. . . . . .Ps 39:9

MUTILATION

beware of the *m* . . . . .Phil 3:2

MUTUAL

by the *m* faith both. . . . . . .Rom 1:12

MUZZLE

"You shall not *m*. . . . . . . .Deut 25:4
"You shall not *m* . . . . . . .1 Tim 5:18

MYSTERIES

to you to know the *m*. . . .Matt 13:11
and understand all *m* . . . .1 Cor 13:2
the spirit he speaks *m*. . . .1 Cor 14:2

MYSTERIOUS

today is not too *m* . . . . . .Deut 30:11

MYSTERY

given to know the *m* . . . . .Mark 4:11
wisdom of God in a *m*. . . .1 Cor 2:7
Behold, I tell you a *m*. . .1 Cor 15:51
made known to us the *m*. . . .Eph 1:9
This is a great *m* . . . . .Eph 5:32
m which has been . . . . .Col 1:26
the *m* of godliness. . . . . . .1 Tim 3:16

N

NAILED

n it to the cross . . . . .Col 2:14

NAKED

And they were both *n* . . . . .Gen 2:25
knew that they were *n* . . . . .Gen 3:7
N I came from my . . . . .Job 1:21
Isaiah has walked *n*. . . . . .Is 20:3
'I was *n* and you. . . . . . . .Matt 25:36
and fled from them *n*. . . .Mark 14:52
shall not be found *n*. . . . . . .2 Cor 5:3
but all things are *n* . . . . . . .Heb 4:13
brother or sister is *n* . . . .James 2:15
poor, blind, and *n* . . . . .Rev 3:17

NAKEDNESS

of Canaan, saw the *n*. . . . .Gen 9:22
or famine, or *n*. . . . . .Rom 8:35
often, in cold and *n* . . . . .2 Cor 11:27
n may not be revealed . . . .Rev 3:18

NAME

Abram called on the *n*. . . . .Gen 13:4
Israel shall be your *n*. . . . .Gen 35:10
This is My *n* forever . . . . . .Ex 3:15
shall not take the *n* . . . . . . .Ex 20:7
are called by the *n*. . . . . . .Deut 28:10
glorious and awesome *n*. .Deut 28:58
by My *n* will humble. . . . .2 Chr 7:14
and he has no *n*. . . . . .Job 18:17
excellent is Your *n*. . . . . .Ps 8:1
n will put their trust . . . . . . .Ps 9:10
be His glorious *n* . . . . .Ps 72:19
n is great in Israel . . . . .Ps 76:1
do not call on Your *n* . . . . . .Ps 79:6
to Your *n* give glory . . . . . .Ps 115:1
above all Your *n* . . . . .Ps 138:2
He calls them all by *n* . . . .Ps 147:4
The *n* of the LORD is a . . .Prov 18:10
A good *n* is to be. . . . . . . .Prov 22:1
what is His Son's *n*. . . . . .Prov 30:4
make mention of Your *n* . . . .Is 26:13
the LORD, that is My *n*. . . . .Is 42:8
be to the LORD for a *n*. . . . . .Is 55:13
be called by a new *n* . . . . . .Is 62:2
Everlasting is Your *n* . . . . . .Is 63:16
who calls on Your *n* . . . . .Is 64:7
it shall be to Me a *n* . . . . . .Jer 33:9
and made Yourself a *n*. . . .Dan 9:15
we will walk in the *n* . . . . . .Mic 4:5
They will call on My *n* . . .Zech 13:9
n shall be great. . . . . .Mal 1:11
to you who fear My *n*. . . . . .Mal 4:2

you shall call His n......Matt 1:21
hallowed be Your n.......Matt 6:9
prophesied in Your n ....Matt 7:22
righteous man in the n...Matt 10:41
n Gentiles will trust......Matt 12:21
together in My n ....Matt 18:20
many will come in My n .Matt 24:5
"My n is Legion.......Mark 5:9
The virgin's n was ......Luke 1:27
"His n is John..........Luke 1:63
and cast out your n .....Luke 6:22
who believe in His n.....John 1:12
comes in the n ......John 5:43
his own sheep by n......John 10:3
through faith in His n....Acts 3:16
there is no other n.......Acts 4:12
suffer shame for His n ...Acts 5:41
which is above every n....Phil 2:9
deed, do all in the n......Col 3:17
a more excellent n ......Heb 1:4
blaspheme that noble n...James 2:7
reproached for the n.....1 Pet 4:14
you hold fast to My n ....Rev 2:13
n that you are alive........Rev 3:1
having His Father's n .....Rev 14:1
and glorify Your n........Rev 15:4
n written that no one....Rev 19:12

NAME'S

saved them for His n.....Ps 106:8
forgiven you for His n...1 John 2:12

NAMED

let my name be n........Gen 48:16
I have n you..............Is 45:4

NARROW

"Enter by the n gate ....Matt 7:13
n is the gate and........Matt 7:14

NATION

make you a great n ......Gen 12:2
You slay a righteous n....Gen 20:4
priests and a holy n......Ex 19:6
dealt thus with any n....Ps 147:20
exalts a n..............Prov 14:34
up sword against n ......Is 2:4
that the righteous n ......Is 26:2
a small one a strong n....Is 60:22
n that was not called.....Is 65:1
n changed its gods........Jer 2:11
I will make them one n ..Ezek 37:22
since there was a n........Dan 12:1
n will rise against.......Matt 24:7
for he loves our n ....Luke 7:5
those who are not a n...Rom 10:19
tribe, tongue, and n .....Rev 13:7

NATIONS

itself among the n.......Num 23:9
Why do the n rage ....Ps 2:1
I will give You the n......Ps 2:8
n shall serve Him ....Ps 72:11
n shall call Him..........Ps 72:17
n shall fear the name ....Ps 102:15
is high above all n.......Ps 113:4
All n before Him are ......Is 40:17
n who do not know ....Is 55:5
the wise men of the n ....Jer 10:7
n shall be joined ....Zech 2:11
disciples of all the n.....Matt 28:19
who was to rule all n .....Rev 12:5
the healing of the n ......Rev 22:2

NATURAL

women exchanged the n...Rom 1:26
the men, leaving the n ...Rom 1:27
did not spare the n......Rom 11:21
n man does not receive ...1 Cor 2:14
It is sown a n body .....1 Cor 15:44

not first, but the n......1 Cor 15:46

NATURE

for what is against n......Rom 1:26
n itself teach you.......1 Cor 11:14
We who are Jews by n ....Gal 2:15
by n children of wrath.....Eph 2:3
of the divine n ....2 Pet 1:4

NEAR

that has God so n........Deut 4:7
But the word is very n...Deut 30:14
The Lord is n to all .....Ps 145:18
upon Him while He is n....Is 55:6
know that it is n.......Matt 24:33
kingdom of God is n ...Luke 21:31
"The word is n.........Rom 10:8
to those who were n......Eph 2:17
for the time is n ....Rev 1:3

NEARER

now our salvation is n....Rom 13:11

NECESSARY

mouth more than my n ..Job 23:12
and thus it was n ......Luke 24:46
burden than these n .....Acts 15:28
I found it n to write........Jude 3

NECESSITIES

have provided for my n...Acts 20:34
and again for my n.......Phil 4:16

NECESSITY

n is laid upon me ....1 Cor 9:16
not grudgingly or of n....2 Cor 9:7

NECK

smooth part of his n .....Gen 27:16
and grace to your n.......Prov 3:22
n was an iron sinew.......Is 48:4
were hung around his n ..Matt 18:6
ran and fell on his n.....Luke 15:20

NECKS

stiffened their n ....Neh 9:29
with outstretched n........Is 3:16
who risked their own n....Rom 16:4

NEED

in nakedness, and in n ..Deut 28:48
a prowler, and your n ...Prov 24:34
the things you have n ....Matt 6:8
The Lord has n........Matt 21:3
each as anyone had n ....Acts 4:35
hand, "I have no n...1 Cor 12:21
who ministered to my n...Phil 2:25
supply all your n ....Phil 4:19
to help in time of n......Heb 4:16
sees his brother in n ....1 John 3:17
The city had no n ....Rev 21:23

NEEDY

your poor and your n ....Deut 15:11
They push the n ....Job 24:4
n shall not always be ......Ps 9:18
He will deliver the n......Ps 72:12
and lifts the n............Ps 113:7
to rob the n of ....Is 10:2
n will lie down in ....Is 14:30
a strength to the n ....Is 25:4

NEGLECT

n the gift that is ....1 Tim 4:14
if we n so great a........Heb 2:3

NEGLECTED

n the weightier ....Matt 23:23
their widows were n ......Acts 6:1

NEIGHBOR

you shall love your n ....Lev 19:18
for better is a n........Prov 27:10
every man teach his n....Jer 31:34
gives drink to his n ......Hab 2:15
You shall love your n ....Matt 5:43
"And who is my n......Luke 10:29
You shall love your n.....Rom 13:9

NEST

and make its n ....Job 39:27
n is a man who wanders...Prov 27:8
though you set your n .....Obad 4
that he may set his n ......Hab 2:9

NET

me with His n............Job 19:6
have hidden their n........Ps 35:7
They have prepared a n ....Ps 57:6
an antelope in a n ....Is 51:20
catch them in their n......Hab 1:15
I will let down the n......Luke 5:5
to them, "Cast the n.....John 21:6

NEVER

in Me shall n thirst......John 6:35
in Me shall n die........John 11:26
Love n fails.............1 Cor 13:8
n take away sins........Heb 10:11
"I will n leave you........Heb 13:5
for prophecy n came by...2 Pet 1:21

NEW

Now there arose a n........Ex 1:8
the Lord creates a n.....Num 16:30
They chose n gods ......Judg 5:8
and there is nothing n.....Eccl 1:9
Behold, I will do a n......Is 43:19
For behold, I create n.....Is 65:17
when I will make a n.....Jer 31:31
n every morning.........Lam 3:23
wine into n wineskins....Matt 9:17
of the n covenant......Matt 26:28
n commandment I give .John 13:34
tell or to hear some n...Acts 17:21
he is a n creation ....2 Cor 5:17
n man who is renewed....Col 3:10
when I will make a n.....Heb 8:8
n heavens and a n........2 Pet 3:13
n name written which......Rev 2:17
And they sang a n ....Rev 5:9
And I saw a n heaven ....Rev 21:1
I make all things n.......Rev 21:5

NEWNESS

also should walk in n ....Rom 6:4
should serve in the n......Rom 7:6

NEWS

heard this bad n..........Ex 33:4
soul, so is good n........Prov 25:25
him who brings good n......Is 52:7

NIGHT

darkness He called N.......Gen 1:5
It is a n of solemn ....Ex 12:42
pillar of fire by n ....Ex 13:22
and the n be ended........Job 7:4
gives songs in the n......Job 35:10
n reveals..................Ps 19:2
awake through the n......Ps 119:148
and stars to rule by n ....Ps 136:9
desired You in the n.......Is 26:9
and perished in a n.......Jon 4:10
and continued all n.......Luke 6:12
man came to Jesus by n ..John 3:2
n is coming when no......John 9:4
came to Jesus by n.......John 19:39
The n is far spent ......Rom 13:12

NINE

as a thief in the *n*.......1 Thess 5:2
We are not of the *n* .....1 Thess 5:5
there shall be no *n* ......Rev 21:25
there shall be no *n* ....Rev 22:5

NINE

where are the *n* ....Luke 17:17

NINETY-NINE

he not leave the *n*.......Matt 18:12
n just persons...........Luke 15:7

NOBLE

whatever things are *n* ......Phil 4:8
not blaspheme that *n*....James 2:7

NOBLES

voice of *n* was hushed....Job 29:10
king is the son of *n* ......Eccl 10:17
n have sent their lads .....Jer 14:3
your *n* rest in the.........Nah 3:18

NOISE

The *n* of a multitude........Is 13:4
people who make a *n*.......Is 17:12
of Egypt, is but a *n*......Jer 46:17
They have made a *n* ......Lam 2:7
away with a great *n*.....2 Pet 3:10

NOSTRILS

n the breath of life.........Gen 2:7
breath of God in my *n* ....Job 27:3
breath is in his *n* ....Is 2:22

NOTE

urge you, brethren, *n*.....Rom 16:17
n those who so walk......Phil 3:17

NOTHING

For now you are *n*........Job 6:21
rich, yet has *n* ....Prov 13:7
"It is good for *n* ....Prov 20:14
before Him are as *n*.......Is 40:17
their works are *n*.......Is 41:29
I can of Myself do *n*.....John 5:30
Me you can do *n* ....John 15:5
men, it will come to *n*....Acts 5:38
bring to the things.....1 Cor 1:28
For I know of *n* against ..1 Cor 4:4
have not love, I am *n*.....1 Cor 13:2
love, it profits me *n* ...1 Cor 13:3
Be anxious for *n*.........Phil 4:6
For we brought *n*.......1 Tim 6:7
complete, lacking *n* .....James 1:4
name's sake, taking *n*......3 John 7

NOTORIOUS

n prisoner called.......Matt 27:16

NOURISHED

"I have *n* and..............Is 1:2
n and knit together........Col 2:19
n in the words of.........1 Tim 4:6

NOURISHES

n and cherishes it........Eph 5:29

NOVICE

not a *n* ....1 Tim 3:6

NUMBER

if a man could *n* ....Gen 13:16
that I may know the *n*...2 Sam 24:2
things without *n* ....Job 5:9
For now You in my steps...Job 14:16
n the clouds by wisdom ...Job 38:37
teach us to *n* our days .....Ps 90:12
He counts the *n*.........Ps 147:4
which no one could *n* ......Rev 7:9
His *n* is 666..............Rev 13:18

NUMBERED

are more than can be *n*......Ps 40:5
God has *n* your kingdom...Dan 5:26
'And He was *n* with....Luke 22:37

O

OAKS

Wail, O *o* of Bashan .....Zech 11:2

OARSMEN

o brought you into ......Ezek 27:26

OATH

people feared the *o*.....1 Sam 14:26
for the sake of your *o* .....Eccl 8:2
I may establish the *o* .....Jer 11:5
And you shall be an *o*....Jer 42:18
he denied with an *o* ....Matt 26:72
o which He swore.......Luke 1:73
themselves under an *o* ..Acts 23:12

OATHS

shall perform your *o*.....Matt 5:33
because of the *o* ....Matt 14:9

OBEDIENCE

and apostleship for *o*......Rom 1:5
o many will be made......Rom 5:19
captivity to the *o*........2 Cor 10:5
confidence in your *o*.....Philem 21
yet He learned *o*..........Heb 5:8
for *o* and sprinkling ....1 Pet 1:2

OBEDIENT

you are willing and *o*.......Is 1:19
of the priests were *o* .....Acts 6:7
to make the Gentiles *o* ..Rom 15:18
bondservants, be *o* ......Eph 6:5
Himself and became *o*.....Phil 2:8
homemakers, good, *o* .....Titus 2:5
as *o* children ....1 Pet 1:14

OBEY

LORD, that I should *o* ......Ex 5:2
God and *o* His voice.....Deut 4:30
o the commandments...Deut 11:27
His voice we will *o* .....Josh 24:24
o is better than........1 Sam 15:22
they hear of me they *o* ....Ps 18:44
if you diligently *o* ....Zech 6:15
o God rather than men....Acts 5:29
and do not *o* the truth .....Rom 2:8
yourselves slaves to *o* ....Rom 6:16
o your parents in all ......Col 3:20
Bondservants, *o* in all ....Col 3:22
on those who do not *o* ..2 Thess 1:8
O those who rule ....Heb 13:17
if some do not *o* ....1 Pet 3:1

OBEYED

of sin, yet you *o*.........Rom 6:17
they have not all *o*.....Rom 10:16
By faith Abraham *o*......Heb 11:8
as Sarah *o* Abraham .....1 Pet 3:6

OBEYING

o the truth through ......1 Pet 1:22

OBSCURITY

shall see out of *o* ....Is 29:18

OBSERVANCE

the LORD, a solemn *o* .....Ex 12:42

OBSERVATION

does not come with *o* ...Luke 17:20

OBSERVE

man, and *o* the upright ....Ps 37:37

and let your eyes *o* .....Prov 23:26
o mercy and justice ....Hos 12:6
teaching them to *o* all ...Matt 28:20
o days and months and ....Gal 4:10
o your chaste conduct .....1 Pet 3:2

OBSERVES

o the wind will not........Eccl 11:4
He who *o* the day ....Rom 14:6

OBSERVING

o his natural face ......James 1:23

OBSESSED

nothing, but is *o* ....1 Tim 6:4

OBSOLETE

Now what is becoming *o*...Heb 8:13

OBSTINATE

and made his heart *o* .....Deut 2:30
I knew that you were *o*....Is 48:4

OBTAIN

They shall *o* joy and .....Is 35:10
they also may *o* mercy ..Rom 11:31
o salvation through .....1 Thess 5:9
and covet and cannot *o* ..James 4:2

OBTAINED

o a part in this..........Acts 1:17
yet have now *o* mercy....Rom 11:30
endured, he *o* the.........Heb 6:15
To those who have *o*.....2 Pet 1:1

OBTAINS

o favor from the LORD.....Prov 8:35

OFFEND

I will *o* no more.........Job 34:31
that devour him will *o*.....Jer 2:3
lest we *o* them.........Matt 17:27
than that he should *o*....Luke 17:2
them, "Does this *o*.....John 6:61

OFFENDED

So they were *o* at Him...Matt 13:57
stumbles or is *o*.........Rom 14:21

OFFENDER

who make a man an *o*....Is 29:21
"For if I am an *o*.......Acts 25:11

OFFENSE

and a rock of *o*..........Is 8:14
You are an *o* to Me.....Matt 16:23
by the one man's *o* ......Rom 5:17
Give no *o*..............1 Cor 10:32
the *o* of the cross.........Gal 5:11
sincere and without *o*.....Phil 1:10
and a rock of *o* ....1 Pet 2:8

OFFENSES

For *o* must come........Matt 18:7
impossible that no *o*.....Luke 17:1
up because of our *o*......Rom 4:25

OFFER

o the blind as a ....Mal 1:8
come and *o* your gift ....Matt 5:24
let us continually *o* ......Heb 13:15

OFFERED

to eat those things *o* .....1 Cor 8:10
the eternal Spirit *o*.......Heb 9:14
so Christ was *o*.........Heb 9:28
o one sacrifice..........Heb 10:12
By faith Abel *o* ....Heb 11:4

OFFERING

you shall bring your *o* ......Lev 1:2

OFFERINGS

o You did not require . . . . . . .Ps 40:6
You make His soul an o . . . .Is 53:10
to the LORD an o . . . . .Mal 3:3
Himself for us, an o . . . . . . .Eph 5:2
out as a drink o . . . . .Phil 2:17
o You did not . . . . .Heb 10:5
o He has perfected. . . . . . .Heb 10:14
is no longer an o. . . . . .Heb 10:18

OFFERINGS

and offered burnt o . . . . . . .Gen 8:20
He remember all your o . . . . .Ps 20:3
In burnt o and . . . . .Heb 10:6

OFFICE

let another take his o . . . . . .Ps 109:8
sitting at the tax o . . . . . . .Matt 9:9

OFFICERS

also make your o . . . . .Is 60:17

OFFSCOURING

You have made us an o . . . .Lam 3:45
the o of all things. . . . . . .1 Cor 4:13

OFFSPRING

My blessing on your o . . . . . .Is 44:3
He seeks godly o . . . . .Mal 2:15
wife and raise up o . . . . . .Matt 22:24
For we are also His o . . . .Acts 17:28
am the Root and the O . . .Rev 22:16

OFTEN

o I wanted to gather . . . .Luke 13:34
as o as you eat this . . . . .1 Cor 11:26
in sleeplessness o. . . . . . .2 Cor 11:27
should offer Himself o. . . . .Heb 9:25

OIL

for the anointing o . . . . .Ex 25:6
I cease giving my o . . . . . . .Judg 9:9
a bin, and a little o . . . .1 Kin 17:12
poured out rivers of o . . . . .Job 29:6
anointed with fresh o . . . . .Ps 92:10
the heart of man, o. . . . . .Ps 104:15
like the precious o. . . . . . .Ps 133:2
be as excellent o . . . . .Ps 141:5
thousand rivers of o . . . . . .Mic 6:7
very costly fragrant o . . . .Matt 26:7
o might have been sold . .Matt 26:9
anointing him with o . . . .James 5:14
and do not harm the o . . . . . .Rev 6:6

OINTMENT

O and perfume delight . . . .Prov 27:9
your name is o . . . . .Song 1:3

OLD

young, and now am o . . . . .Ps 37:25
all manner, new and o . . . .Song 7:13
was said to those of o . . . .Matt 5:21
yet fifty years o . . . . .John 8:57
but when you are o. . . . . .John 21:18
your o men shall dream . . .Acts 2:17
o man was crucified . . . . .Rom 6:6
of the O Testament . . . . .2 Cor 3:14
o things have passed. . . . .2 Cor 5:17
have put off the o man . . . .Col 3:9
obsolete and growing o . . . .Heb 8:13
that serpent of o. . . . . .Rev 20:2

OLDER

o shall serve the. . . . . . . .Gen 25:23
o than your father. . . . . . .Job 15:10
"Now his o son was . . . .Luke 15:25
not rebuke an o man . . . . .1 Tim 5:1
o women as mothers . . . . . .1 Tim 5:2

OLDEST

beginning with the o . . . . . .John 8:9

OLIVE

a freshly plucked o . . . . . . .Gen 8:11
I am like a green o . . . . .Ps 52:8
of the o may fail. . . . . .Hab 3:17
o tree which is wild. . . . . .Rom 11:24

OMNIPOTENT

For the Lord God O . . . . . .Rev 19:6

ONCE

died, He died to sin o . . . . .Rom 6:10
for men to die o . . . . .Heb 9:27
also suffered o. . . . . .1 Pet 3:18

ONE

God may speak in o way . .Job 33:14
Two are better than o . . . . .Eccl 4:9
you will be gathered o. . . . . .Is 27:12
O thing you lack . . . . . .Mark 10:21
o thing is needed . . . . . .Luke 10:42
I and My Father are o . . .John 10:30
Me, that they may be o . .John 17:11
o accord in the temple . . .Acts 2:46
for you are all o . . . . .Gal 3:28
to create in Himself o . . . .Eph 2:15
o body and o Spirit . . . . . . .Eph 4:4
o hope of your calling . . . . .Eph 4:4
o Lord . . . . .Eph 4:5
o faith . . . . .Eph 4:5
o baptism . . . . .Eph 4:5
o God and Father of . . . . . .Eph 4:6
For there is o God and . . .1 Tim 2:5
o Mediator between God . .1 Tim 2:5
the husband of o wife . . . .1 Tim 3:2
a thousand years as o . . . .2 Pet 3:8
and these three are o. . . . .1 John 5:7

OPEN

o His lips against you . . . .Job 11:5
You o Your hand . . . . .Ps 104:28
O your mouth for the . . . .Prov 31:8
and no one shall o . . . . .Is 22:22
a lamb in country . . . . . .Hos 4:16
Can a demon o the eyes . .John 10:21
our heart is wide o. . . . . .2 Cor 6:11
things are naked and o . . .Heb 4:13
o the scroll and to. . . . . .Rev 5:2

OPENED

o not His mouth . . . . .Is 53:7
Then their eyes were o . .Luke 24:31
o the Scriptures . . . . . . .Luke 24:32
o their understanding. . . .Luke 24:45
effective door has o . . . . .1 Cor 16:9
when the Lamb o . . . . .Rev 6:1
Now I saw heaven o . . . . .Rev 19:11

OPENS

o the ears of men . . . . . . .Job 33:16
The LORD o the eyes of. . . .Ps 146:8
him the doorkeeper o . . . .John 10:3
and shuts and no one o . . . . .Rev 3:7

OPINION

dared not declare my o. . . .Job 32:6
be wise in your own o . . . .Rom 11:25

OPINIONS

falter between two o . . . .1 Kin 18:21

OPPORTUNITY

But sin, taking o . . . . .Rom 7:8
as we have o. . . . . .Gal 6:10
but you lacked o . . . . .Phil 4:10
they would have had o . . . .Heb 11:15

OPPOSES

who o and exalts . . . . . . .2 Thess 2:4

OPPRESS

you shall not o. . . . . .Lev 25:17
You that You should o . . . . .Job 10:3
He does not o . . . . .Job 37:23
he loves to o . . . . .Hos 12:7
o the widow or the . . . . . .Zech 7:10
Do not the rich o . . . . . . .James 2:6

OPPRESSED

Whom have I o. . . . . .1 Sam 12:3
For he has o and. . . . . . . .Job 20:19
fatherless and the o . . . . . .Ps 10:18
for all who are o . . . . .Ps 103:6
The tears of the o . . . . .Eccl 4:1
He was o and He was . . . . . .Is 53:7
her midst, and the o . . . . .Amos 5:12
healing all who were o . . .Acts 10:38
Lot, who was o by . . . . . . .2 Pet 2:7

OPPRESSES

o the poor reproaches . . . .Prov 14:31
o the poor to increase . . . .Prov 22:16
A poor man who o. . . . . . .Prov 28:3

OPPRESSION

have surely seen the o . . . . . .Ex 3:7
"For the o of the. . . . . .Ps 12:5
Do not trust in o. . . . . . . .Ps 62:10
their life from o . . . . .Ps 72:14
brought low through o . . .Ps 107:39
Redeem me from the o . . .Ps 119:134
considered all the o . . . . . . .Eccl 4:1
o destroys a wise . . . . .Eccl 7:7
justice, but behold, o. . . . . . .Is 5:7
surely seen the o . . . . . . .Acts 7:34

OPPRESSIONS

of o they cry out. . . . . . . .Job 35:9

OPPRESSOR

the voice of the o . . . . .Job 3:18
Do not envy the o . . . . . . .Prov 3:31
is a great o . . . . .Prov 28:16
of the fury of the o . . . . . . .Is 51:13
No more shall an o . . . . . .Zech 9:8

OPPRESSORS

not leave me to my o . . . .Ps 119:121
o there is power . . . . .Eccl 4:1

ORACLES

received the living o . . . . .Acts 7:38
were committed the o . . . . .Rom 3:2
principles of the o . . . . . . .Heb 5:12
let him speak as the o . . . .1 Pet 4:11

ORDAINED

infants You have o . . . . .Ps 8:2
o you a prophet . . . . .Jer 1:5
the Man whom He has o .Acts 17:31

ORDER

'Set your house in o. . . . . .2 Kin 20:1
set your words in o . . . . . .Job 33:5
you, and set them in o . . . .Ps 50:21
swept, and put in o . . . . .Matt 12:44
done decently and in o . .1 Cor 14:40
each one in his own o . . .1 Cor 15:23
to see your good o . . . . .Col 2:5
according to the o . . . . .Heb 5:6

ORDERS

o his conduct aright I. . . . .Ps 50:23

ORDINANCE

resists the o of God. . . . . .Rom 13:2
yourselves to every o . . . . .1 Pet 2:13

ORDINANCES

Do you know the o . . . . . .Job 38:33

73

ORNAMENT

"If those *o* depart . . . . . . .Jer 31:36
not appointed the *o* . . . . . .Jer 33:25
gone away from My *o* . . . . . .Mal 3:7
and fleshly *o* imposed . . . . .Heb 9:10

ORNAMENT

will be a graceful *o* . . . . . . .Prov 1:9
of gold and an *o* . . . . .Prov 25:12
with them all as an *o* . . . . . .Is 49:18

ORNAMENTS

a virgin forget her *o* . . . . . . .Jer 2:32

ORPHANS

We have become *o* . . . . .Lam 5:3
I will not leave you *o* . . . .John 14:18
to visit *o* and widows . . . .James 1:27

OSTRICHES

o will dwell there . . . . .Is 13:21
is cruel, like *o* . . . . .Lam 4:3
a mourning like the *o* . . . . . .Mic 1:8

OUGHT

what Israel *o* to do . . . . .1 Chr 12:32
These you *o* to have . . . . .Matt 23:23
pray for as we *o* . . . . .Rom 8:26
how you *o* to conduct . . . .1 Tim 3:15
which they *o* not . . . . .1 Tim 5:13
persons *o* you to be . . . . . .2 Pet 3:11

OUTCAST

they called you an *o* . . . . . .Jer 30:17

OUTCASTS

gathers together the *o* . . . . .Ps 147:2
will assemble the *o* . . . . . . .Is 11:12
hide the *o* . . . . .Is 16:3
Let My *o* dwell with . . . . . . .Is 16:4

OUTCRY

that there be no *o* . . . . .Ps 144:14

OUTGOINGS

You make the *o* of the . . . . . .Ps 65:8

OUTRAGE

lewdness and *o* in . . . . .Judg 20:6

OUTRAN

the other disciple *o* . . . . . .John 20:4

OUTSIDE

and dish, that the *o* . . . .Matt 23:26
Pharisees make the *o* . . .Luke 11:39
toward those who are *o* . . . . .Col 4:5
to Him, *o* the camp . . . . .Heb 13:13
But *o* are dogs and . . . . . .Rev 22:15

OUTSTRETCHED

and with an *o* arm . . . . . .Deut 26:8
against you with an *o* . . . . .Jer 21:5

OUTWARD

at the *o* appearance . . . .1 Sam 16:7
adornment be merely *o* . . . .1 Pet 3:3

OUTWARDLY

appear beautiful *o* . . . . . .Matt 23:27
not a Jew who is one *o* . . . .Rom 2:28

OUTWIT

The enemy shall not *o* . . . . .Ps 89:22

OVEN

make them as a fiery *o* . . . . .Ps 21:9
burning like an *o* . . . . .Mal 4:1
is thrown into the *o* . . . . . .Matt 6:30

OVERCAME

My throne, as I also *o* . . . . .Rev 3:21
"And they *o* him by . . . . . .Rev 12:11

OVERCOME

good cheer, I have *o* . . . .John 16:33
o evil with good . . . . .Rom 12:21
because you have *o* . . . . .1 John 2:13
and the Lamb will *o* . . . . .Rev 17:14

OVERCOMES

of God *o* the world . . . . . . .1 John 5:4
o I will give to eat . . . . .Rev 2:7
o shall not be hurt . . . . .Rev 2:11
o shall inherit all . . . . .Rev 21:7

OVERFLOWING

My heart is *o* with a . . . . . . .Ps 45:1

OVERSEER

Then he made him *o* . . . . . .Gen 39:4
having no captain, *o* . . . . . . .Prov 6:7
to the Shepherd and *O*. . . .1 Pet 2:25

OVERSEERS

Spirit has made you *o* . . . .Acts 20:28
you, serving as *o* . . . . .1 Pet 5:2

OVERSHADOW

of the Highest will *o* . . . .Luke 1:35

OVERTAKE

does righteousness *o* . . . . . . .Is 59:9
you feared shall *o* . . . . .Jer 42:16
and *o* this chariot . . . . . . .Acts 8:29
that this Day should *o* . .1 Thess 5:4

OVERTAKEN

No temptation has *o* . . . .1 Cor 10:13
if a man is *o* in any . . . . .Gal 6:1

OVERTHREW

So He *o* those cities . . . . . .Gen 19:25
will be as when God *o* . . . . .Is 13:19
As God *o* Sodom and . . . .Jer 50:40
"I *o* some of you . . . . . . .Amos 4:11

OVERTHROW

you shall utterly *o* . . . . . . .Ex 23:24
o the righteous in . . . . . . .Prov 18:5
o the throne of . . . . .Hag 2:22
o the faith of some . . . . . .2 Tim 2:18

OVERTHROWN

Their judges are *o* . . . . .Ps 141:6
of Sodom, which was *o* . . . .Lam 4:6
I will make it *o* . . . . .Ezek 21:27
and Nineveh shall be *o* . . . . .Jon 3:4

OVERTHROWS

and *o* the mighty . . . . . . .Job 12:19
o them in the night . . . . . .Job 34:25
o the words of the . . . . . . .Prov 22:12

OVERTURNED

my heart is *o* within . . . . .Lam 1:20
o the tables of the . . . . .Matt 21:12
money and the tables . .John 2:15

OVERWHELM

o the fatherless . . . . .Job 6:27
sends them out, they *o*. . . .Job 12:15

OVERWHELMED

when my heart is *o* . . . . . . .Ps 61:2
and my spirit was *o* . . . . . . .Ps 77:3
o their enemies . . . . .Ps 78:53
waters would have *o* . . . . .Ps 124:4
my spirit is *o* within . . . . . .Ps 143:4

OVERWORK

Do not *o* to be rich . . . . . .Prov 23:4

OWE

'How much do you *o* . . . . .Luke 16:5

OWED

o him ten thousand . . . .Matt 18:24
fellow servants who *o* . . . .Matt 18:28
o five hundred denarii . . .Luke 7:41

OWN

He came to His *o* . . . . .John 1:11
having loved His *o* . . . . . . .John 13:1
world would love its *o*. . . John 15:19
and you are not your *o* . . .1 Cor 6:19
But each one has his *o* . . . .1 Cor 7:7
For all seek their *o* . . . . .Phil 2:21
from our sins in His *o* . . . . .Rev 1:5

OX

shall not muzzle an *o* . . . .Deut 25:4
"Will the wild *o* . . . . .Job 39:9
you bind the wild *o* . . . . . .Job 39:10
like a young wild *o* . . . . .Ps 29:6
exalted like a wild *o* . . . . . .Ps 92:10
o knows its owner . . . . .Is 1:3
had the face of an *o* . . . . .Ezek 1:10
Sabbath loose his *o* . . . .Luke 13:15
shall not muzzle an *o* . . . . . .1 Cor 9:9

P

PACE

are majestic in *p* . . . . .Prov 30:29

PACIFIES

A gift in secret *p* . . . . .Prov 21:14
for conciliation *p* . . . . .Eccl 10:4

PAILS

p are full of milk . . . . .Job 21:24

PAIN

p you shall bring . . . . .Gen 3:16
p as a woman in . . . . .Is 13:8
are filled with *p* . . . . .Is 21:3
before her *p* came . . . . .Is 66:7
Why is my *p* perpetual . . . .Jer 15:18
shall be no more *p* . . . . .Rev 21:4

PAINED

My heart is severely *p* . . . . .Ps 55:4
I am *p* in my very . . . . .Jer 4:19

PAINFUL

this, it was too *p* . . . . .Ps 73:16
for the present, but *p* . . . .Heb 12:11

PAINS

The *p* of death . . . . .Ps 116:3
having loosed the *p* . . . . . .Acts 2:24
upon them, as labor *p* . . .1 Thess 5:3

PAINT

and she put *p* on her . . . .2 Kin 9:30
your eyes with *p* . . . . .Jer 4:30

PAINTING

it with cedar and *p* . . . . . .Jer 22:14

PALACE

enter the King's *p* . . . . .Ps 45:15
a *p* of foreigners . . . . .Is 25:2
guards his own *p* . . . . . .Luke 11:21
evident to the whole *p* . . . .Phil 1:13

PALACES

out of the ivory *p* . . . . .Ps 45:8
God is in her *p* . . . . .Ps 48:3
has entered our *p* . . . . .Jer 9:21

PALE

his face now grow *p* . . . . . . .Is 29:22

PALM

and all faces turned p . . . . . Jer 30:6
behold, a p horse . . . . Rev 6:8

PALM

of water and seventy p . . . . Ex 15:27
p trees and went out . . . . . John 12:13
p branches in their . . . . Rev 7:9

PALMS

struck Him with the p . . Matt 26:67

PAMPERS

p his servant from . . . . Prov 29:21

PANGS

The p of death . . . . Ps 18:4
P and sorrows will . . . . Is 13:8
labors with birth p . . . . Rom 8:22

PANICKED

the men of Benjamin p . . Judg 20:41

PANT

They p after the dust . . . . . Amos 2:7

PANTS

As the deer p for the . . . . Ps 42:1

PAPYRUS

"Can the p grow up . . . . Job 8:11

PARABLE

open my mouth in a p . . . . . . Ps 78:2
p He did not speak . . . . . . Matt 13:34
do You speak this p . . . . . Luke 12:41

PARABLES

'Does he not speak p . . . . Ezek 20:49
understand all the p . . . . . Mark 4:13
rest it is given in p . . . . Luke 8:10

PARADE

love does not p . . . . 1 Cor 13:4

PARADISE

will be with Me in P . . . . Luke 23:43
was caught up into P . . . . 2 Cor 12:4
in the midst of the P . . . . . . Rev 2:7

PARCHMENTS

especially the p . . . . 2 Tim 4:13

PARDON

p your transgressions . . . . . Ex 23:21
O LORD, p my iniquity . . . . Ps 25:11
He will abundantly p . . . . . . Is 55:7
p all their iniquities . . . . Jer 33:8

PARDONING

is a God like You, p . . . . Mic 7:18

PARENTS

will rise up against p . . . . Matt 10:21
has left house or p . . . . . . Luke 18:29
disobedient to p . . . . Rom 1:30
to lay up for the p . . . . . . 2 Cor 12:14

PART

You have no p in the . . . . . Josh 22:25
has chosen that good p . . Luke 10:42
you, you have no p . . . . . . John 13:8
For we know in p . . . . 1 Cor 13:9
p has a believer . . . . 2 Cor 6:15
shall take away his p . . . . . Rev 22:19

PARTAKE

for we all p of that . . . . . . 1 Cor 10:17
you cannot p of the . . . . 1 Cor 10:21

PARTAKER

and have been a p . . . . Ps 50:18
in hope should be p . . . . . . 1 Cor 9:10

Christ, and also a p . . . . 1 Pet 5:1

PARTAKERS

Gentiles have been p . . . . Rom 15:27
of the sacrifices p . . . . 1 Cor 10:18
know that as you are p . . . . 2 Cor 1:7
gospel, you all are p . . . . Phil 1:7
qualified us to be p . . . . Col 1:12
For we have become p . . . . . Heb 3:14

PARTED

them, that He was p . . . . Luke 24:51
so sharp that they p . . . . . Acts 15:39

PARTIAL

You shall not be p . . . . Lev 19:15

PARTIALITY

'You shall not show p . . . . Deut 1:17
unjustly, and show p . . . . . . Ps 82:2
is not good to show p . . . . . Prov 18:5
but have shown p . . . . Mal 2:9
that God shows no p . . . . Acts 10:34
For there is no p . . . . Rom 2:11
doing nothing with p . . . 1 Tim 5:21
but if you show p . . . . James 2:9
good fruits, without p . . . James 3:17

PARTIES

revelries, drinking p . . . . 1 Pet 4:3

PARTITION

the Testimony, and p . . . . . . Ex 40:3

PARTNER

Whoever is a p with a . . . . Prov 29:24
you count me as a p . . . . . . Philem 17

PARTRIDGE

when one hunts a p . . . . 1 Sam 26:20

PARTS

anything but death p . . . . . Ruth 1:17
in the inward p . . . . Ps 51:6
Shout, you lower p . . . . Is 44:23
but our presentable p . . . 1 Cor 12:24
into the lower p . . . . Eph 4:9

PASS

I will p over you . . . . Ex 12:13
of the sea that p . . . . Ps 8:8
When you p through the . . . . Is 43:2
"I will make you p . . . . . Ezek 20:37
I will not p by them . . . . . . Amos 7:8
and earth will p . . . . Matt 24:35

PASSED

And behold, the LORD p   1 Kin 19:11
forbearance God had p . . . . Rom 3:25
High Priest who has p . . . Heb 4:14
We know that we have p   1 John 3:14

PASSES

For the wind p over it . . . Ps 103:16
of Christ which p . . . . Eph 3:19

PASSION

than to burn with p . . . . . . 1 Cor 7:9
uncleanness, p . . . . Col 3:5

PASSIONS

gave them up to vile p . . . Rom 1:26

PASSOVER

It is the LORD's P . . . . Ex 12:11
of King Josiah this P . . 2 Kin 23:23
I will keep the P . . . . Matt 26:18
indeed Christ, our P . . . . 1 Cor 5:7
By faith he kept the P . . . . Heb 11:28

PAST

My days are p . . . . Job 17:11
lo, the winter is p . . . . Song 2:11
and His ways p finding . . Rom 11:33
ways spoke in time p . . . . . . Heb 1:1
p lifetime in doing . . . . 1 Pet 4:3

PASTORS

and some p and . . . . Eph 4:11

PASTURE

the sheep of Your p . . . . Ps 74:1
the people of His p . . . . Ps 95:7
feed them in good p . . . . Ezek 34:14
in and out and find p . . . . John 10:9

PASTURES

to lie down in green p . . . . . . Ps 23:2

PATH

p no bird knows . . . . Job 28:7
You will show me the p . . . . Ps 16:11
lead me in a smooth p . . . . . Ps 27:11
But the p of the just . . . . . . Prov 4:18
way in the sea and a p . . . . Is 43:16

PATHS

He leads me in the p . . . . . . Ps 23:3
Teach me Your p . . . . Ps 25:4
and all her p are . . . . Prov 3:17
p they have not . . . . Is 42:16
themselves crooked p . . . . . . Is 59:8
make His p straight . . . . . . Matt 3:3
and make straight p . . . . . Heb 12:13

PATIENCE

'Master, have p . . . . Matt 18:26
and bear fruit with p . . . . Luke 8:15
Now may the God of p . . . . Rom 15:5
labor of love, and p . . . . . 1 Thess 1:3
faith, love, p . . . . 1 Tim 6:11
your faith produces p . . . . . James 1:3
p have its perfect . . . . James 1:4
in the kingdom and p . . . . . . Rev 1:9
Here is the p and the . . . . Rev 13:10

PATIENT

rejoicing in hope, p . . . . . Rom 12:12
uphold the weak, be p . 1 Thess 5:14

PATIENTLY

the LORD, and wait p . . . . . Ps 37:7
if you take it p . . . . 1 Pet 2:20

PATRIARCHS

begot the twelve p . . . . Acts 7:8

PATTERN

p which you were shown . . Ex 26:30
as you have us for a p . . . . Phil 3:17
Hold fast the p . . . . 2 Tim 1:13
p shown you on the . . . . Heb 8:5

PAVILION

shall hide me in His p . . . . . Ps 27:5
them secretly in a p . . . . . . Ps 31:20

PAWS

He p in the valley . . . . Job 39:21

PAY

with which to p . . . . Prov 22:27
priests teach for p . . . . Mic 3:11
with me, and I will p . . . . Matt 18:26
p taxes to Caesar . . . . Matt 22:17
For you p tithe of . . . . Matt 23:23

PEACE

"These men are at p . . . . Gen 34:21
I will give p in the . . . . Lev 26:6
you, and give you p . . . . . . Num 6:26

'Make p with me by a . . .2 Kin 18:31
field shall be at p . . . . .Job 5:23
both lie down in p . . . . .Ps 4:8
seek p . . . . .Ps 34:14
for He will speak p . . . . .Ps 85:8
p have those who love . . .Ps 119:165
I am for p . . . . .Ps 120:7
for the p of Jerusalem . . . .Ps 122:6
P be within your walls . . . .Ps 122:7
P be upon Israel . . . . .Ps 125:5
war, and a time of p . . . . . . .Eccl 3:8
Father, Prince of P . . . . .Is 9:6
keep him in perfect p . . . . . .Is 26:3
p they have not . . . . .Is 59:8
slightly, saying, 'P . . . . .Jer 6:14
"We looked for p . . . . .Jer 8:15
give you assured p . . . . . . .Jer 14:13
they will seek p . . . . .Ezek 13:16
P be multiplied . . . . .Dan 4:1
this One shall be p . . . . .Mic 5:5
place I will give p . . . . .Hag 2:9
is worthy, let your p . . .Matt 10:13
that I came to bring p . . .Matt 10:34
and on earth p . . . . .Luke 2:14
if a son of p is there . . . . .Luke 10:6
that make for your p . . . .Luke 19:42
I leave with you, My p . . .John 14:27
in Me you may have p . . .John 16:33
Grace to you and p . . . . . . .Rom 1:7
by faith, we have p . . . . . . .Rom 5:1
God has called us to p . . . .1 Cor 7:15
p will be with you . . . . . .2 Cor 13:11
Spirit is love, joy, p . . . . . . .Gal 5:22
He Himself is our p . . . . . .Eph 2:14
and the p of God . . . . .Phil 4:7
heaven, having made p . . . .Col 1:20
And let the p of God . . . . . .Col 3:15
Be at p among . . . . .1 Thess 5:13
faith, love, p . . . . .2 Tim 2:22
meaning "king of p," . . . . . . .Heb 7:2
is sown in p by those . . . .James 3:18
p be multiplied . . . . .2 Pet 1:2

PEACEABLE
and p life in all . . . . .1 Tim 2:2
is first pure, then p . . . . .James 3:17

PEACEABLY
depends on you, live p . . .Rom 12:18

PEACEFUL
in a p habitation . . . . .Is 32:18

PEACEMAKERS
Blessed are the p . . . . .Matt 5:9

PEARL
he had found one p . . . . .Matt 13:46
gate was of one p . . . . . . .Rev 21:21

PEARLS
nor cast your p . . . . .Matt 7:6
hair or gold or p . . . . .1 Tim 2:9
gates were twelve p . . . . . .Rev 21:21

PEG
wife, took a tent p . . . . . . .Judg 4:21
will fasten him as a p . . . . . .Is 22:23

PEN
My tongue is the p . . . . .Ps 45:1
on it with a man's p . . . . .Is 8:1
to write to you with p . . . .3 John 13

PENNY
have paid the last p . . . . . .Matt 5:26

PENTECOST
P had fully come . . . . .Acts 2:1

PEOPLE
will take you as My p . . . . . . .Ex 6:7
Who is like you, a p . . . . .Deut 33:29
p shall be my p . . . . .Ruth 1:16
p who know the joyful . . . . .Ps 89:15
We are His p and the . . . . . .Ps 100:3
Happy are the p . . . . .Ps 144:15
Blessed is Egypt My p . . . . .Is 19:25
this is a rebellious p . . . . . .Is 30:9
p who provoke Me . . . . .Is 65:3
and they shall be My p . . . .Jer 24:7
for you are not My p . . . . . .Hos 1:9
like p, like priest. . . . . .Hos 4:9
to make ready a p . . . . . . .Luke 1:17
take out of them a p . . . . .Acts 15:14
who were not My p . . . . . . .Rom 9:25
and they shall be My p . . .2 Cor 6:16
His own special p . . . . . . .Titus 2:14
LORD will judge His p . . .Heb 10:30
but are now the p . . . . . . .1 Pet 2:10
tribe and tongue and p . . . . .Rev 5:9
they shall be His p . . . . . . .Rev 21:3

PERCEIVE
given you a heart to p . . . .Deut 29:4
but I cannot p . . . . .Job 23:8
seeing, but do not p . . . . .Is 6:9
they may see and not p . . . Mark 4:12

PERDITION
except the son of p . . . . . .John 17:12
to them a proof of p . . . . . . .Phil 1:28
revealed, the son of p . . .2 Thess 2:3
who draw back to p . . . . . .Heb 10:39
day of judgment and p . . . .2 Pet 3:7

PERFECT
Noah was a just man, p . . . . .Gen 6:9
one who is p in . . . . .Job 36:4
for God, His way is p . . . . .Ps 18:30
You were p in your . . . . . .Ezek 28:15
Father in heaven is p . . . . .Matt 5:48
"If you want to be p . . . . .Matt 19:21
they may be made p . . . . . .John 17:23
and p will of God. . . . . .Rom 12:2
when that which is p . . . .1 Cor 13:10
present every man p . . . . . .Col 1:28
the law made nothing p . . . .Heb 7:19
of just men made p . . . . . .Heb 12:23
good gift and every p . . . .James 1:17
in word, he is a p . . . . . . .James 3:2
p love casts out fear . . .1 John 4:18

PERFECTED
third day I shall be p . . . .Luke 13:32
or am already p . . . . .Phil 3:12
the Son who has been p . . .Heb 7:28
the love of God is p . . . . .1 John 2:5

PERFECTION
the p of beauty . . . . .Ps 50:2
consummation of all p . . .Ps 119:96
let us go on to p . . . . .Heb 6:1

PERFORM
p Your statutes . . . . .Ps 119:112
am ready to p My word . . .Jer 1:12
p what is good I . . . . .Rom 7:18

PERIL
or nakedness, or p . . . . . .Rom 8:35

PERILOUS
from the p pestilence . . . . . .Ps 91:3
in the last days p . . . . . . .2 Tim 3:1

PERILS
journeys often, in p . . . . .2 Cor 11:26

PERISH
"Surely we die, we p . . . . .Num 17:12
All flesh would p . . . . .Job 34:15
they p at the rebuke . . . . . .Ps 80:16
very day his plans p . . . . . .Ps 146:4
so that we may not p . . . . . . .Jon 1:6
little ones should p . . . . .Matt 18:14
will all likewise p . . . . . . .Luke 13:3
in Him should not p . . . . .John 3:16
and they shall never p . . .John 10:28
concern things which p . . . .Col 2:22
among those who p . . . .2 Thess 2:10
that any should p . . . . .2 Pet 3:9

PERISHABLE
do it to obtain a p . . . . . . .1 Cor 9:25

PERISHED
p being innocent . . . . .Job 4:7
Truth has p and has . . . . . .Jer 7:28
The faithful man has p . . . .Mic 7:2

PERISHING
We are p . . . . .Matt 8:25
to those who are p . . . . . . .2 Cor 4:3

PERJURER
p shall be expelled . . . . .Zech 5:3

PERMIT
the Spirit did not p . . . . . .Acts 16:7
And I do not p a woman 1 Tim 2:12

PERMITS
you, if the Lord p . . . . . . .1 Cor 16:7
we will do if God p . . . . .Heb 6:3

PERMITTED
p no one to do them . . . . . .Ps 105:14

PERPETUATED
Your name shall be p . . . . . .Nah 1:14

PERPLEXED
at one another, p . . . . . . .John 13:22
we are p . . . . .2 Cor 4:8

PERSECUTE
p me as God does . . . . . . .Job 19:22
p me wrongfully . . . . .Ps 119:86
when they revile and p . . .Matt 5:11
Bless those who p . . . . . . .Rom 12:14

PERSECUTED
p the poor and needy . . . .Ps 109:16
p the prophets who. . . . . . .Matt 5:12
If they p Me . . . . .John 15:20
p the church of God. . . . . .1 Cor 15:9
p, but not forsaken . . . . . . .2 Cor 4:9
p us now preaches the . . . . .Gal 1:23

PERSECUTES
wicked in his pride p . . . . . .Ps 10:2

PERSECUTION
p arises because of . . . . .Matt 13:21
At that time a great p . . . . .Acts 8:1
do I still suffer p . . . . .Gal 5:11

PERSECUTOR
a blasphemer, a p . . . . . . .1 Tim 1:13

PERSEVERANCE
tribulation produces p . . . . .Rom 5:3
to this end with all p . . . . . .Eph 6:18
longsuffering, love, p . . . .2 Tim 3:10
to self-control p . . . . .2 Pet 1:6

PERSEVERE
kept My command to p . . . .Rev 3:10

PERSISTENCE

p he will rise and . . . . .Luke 11:8

PERSON

In whose eyes a vile *p* . . . . . .Ps 15:4
p will suffer hunger. . . . . .Prov 19:15
do not regard the *p*. . . . .Matt 22:16
express image of His *p* . . . . .Heb 1:3
let it be the hidden *p* . . . . .1 Pet 3:4

PERSUADE

"You almost *p* me . . . . . .Acts 26:28
the Lord, we *p* men . . . . . .2 Cor 5:11
For do I now *p* men . . . . . . .Gal 1:10

PERSUADED

a ruler is *p* . . . . .Prov 25:15
neither will they be *p* . . . .Luke 16:31
p that He is able. . . . . . . .2 Tim 1:12

PERSUASIVE

p words of human . . . . .1 Cor 2:4
you with *p* words. . . . . .Col 2:4

PERTAINING

Priest in things *p*. . . . . . . .Heb 2:17
for men in things *p* . . . . .Heb 5:1

PERTURBED

things the earth is *p* . . . . .Prov 30:21

PERVERSE

because your way is *p* . . .Num 22:32
for the *p* person is an . . . . .Prov 3:32
p lips far from you . . . . . . .Prov 4:24
p heart will be . . . . .Prov 12:8
p man sows strife . . . . . .Prov 16:28
but he who is *p* . . . . .Prov 28:18
from this *p* generation . . . .Acts 2:40

PERVERSITY

in oppression and *p*. . . . . . .Is 30:12

PERVERT

"You shall not *p* justice . .Deut 16:19
and *p* all equity. . . . . .Mic 3:9
p the gospel of Christ. . . . . .Gal 1:7

PERVERTING

We found this fellow *p* . . .Luke 23:2
will you not cease *p*. . . . . .Acts 13:10

PERVERTS

p the words of the . . . . .Ex 23:8
p his ways will become. . . .Prov 10:9

PESTILENCE

from the perilous *p*. . . . . . . .Ps 91:3
p that walks in . . . . .Ps 91:6
Before Him went *p* . . . . . . .Hab 3:5

PESTILENCES

will be famines, *p* . . . . . .Matt 24:7

PETITION

of Israel grant your *p*. . . .1 Sam 1:17

PETITIONS

fulfill all your *p*. . . . . .Ps 20:5
p that we have asked . . .1 John 5:15

PHARISEE

to pray, one a *P*. . . . . . .Luke 18:10
and brethren, I am a *P*. . . .Acts 23:6

PHILOSOPHERS

p encountered him. . . . . . .Acts 17:18

PHILOSOPHY

cheat you through *p* . . . . .Col 2:8

PHYLACTERIES

They make their *p* . . . . . .Matt 23:5

PHYSICIAN

Gilead, is there no *p* . . . . . . .Jer 8:22
have no need of a *p* . . . . . .Matt 9:12
Luke the beloved . . . . .Col 4:14

PHYSICIANS

are all worthless *p*. . . . . . . .Job 13:4
her livelihood on *p* . . . . . .Luke 8:43

PIECES

for my wages thirty *p*. . .Zech 11:12
they took the thirty *p* . . . .Matt 27:9
shall be dashed to *p* . . . . . .Rev 2:27

PIERCE

and his master shall *p*. . . . .Ex 21:6
a sword will *p* . . . . .Luke 2:35

PIERCED

p My hands and My feet. . .Ps 22:16
on Me whom they have *p*.Zech 12:10
of the soldiers *p* . . . . . . .John 19:34
p themselves through. . . .1 Tim 6:10
and they also who *p* . . . . . . .Rev 1:7

PIERCING

p even to the division . . . . .Heb 4:12

PIETY

first learn to show *p* . . . . . .1 Tim 5:4

PILGRIMAGE

heart is set on *p* . . . . .Ps 84:5
In the house of my *p* . . . .Ps 119:54

PILGRIMS

we are aliens and *p* . . . . .1 Chr 29:15
were strangers and *p* . . . . .Heb 11:13

PILLAR

and she became a *p* . . . . . .Gen 19:26
and by night in a *p* . . . . . . .Ex 13:21
the living God, the *p*. . . . .1 Tim 3:15

PILLARS

break their sacred *p*. . . . . .Ex 34:13
I set up its *p* firmly . . . . . . .Ps 75:3
out her seven *p* . . . . .Prov 9:1
blood and fire and *p*. . . . . .Joel 2:30
and his feet like *p*. . . . . . . .Rev 10:1

PILOT

rudder wherever the *p* . . . .James 3:4

PINE

cypress tree and the *p*. . . . .Is 41:19
for these *p* away . . . . .Lam 4:9

PINNACLE

set Him on the *p*. . . . . .Luke 4:9

PIT

cast him into some *p* . . . . .Gen 37:20
soul draws near the *P*. . . .Job 33:22
who go down to the *p*. . . . . .Ps 28:1
woman is a deep *p*. . . . . .Prov 22:14
a harlot is a deep *p* . . . . .Prov 23:27
fall into his own *p* . . . . . .Prov 28:10
my life in the *p* . . . . .Lam 3:53
who descend into the *P* . .Ezek 31:16
up my life from the *p* . . . . . .Jon 2:6
from the waterless *p* . . . . . .Zech 9:11
if it falls into a *p*. . . . . . . .Matt 12:11
into the bottomless *p* . . . . .Rev 20:3

PITCHERS

hand, with empty *p* . . . . .Judg 7:16
the washing of cups, *p* . . . .Mark 7:4

PITIABLE

of all men the most *p* . . .1 Cor 15:19

PITS

The proud have dug *p* . . . .Ps 119:85

PITY

eye shall have no *p* . . . . . .Deut 7:16
"Have *p* on me . . . . .Job 19:21
for someone to take *p*. . . . . .Ps 69:20
He who has *p* on the. . . . .Prov 19:17
p He redeemed them. . . . . . .Is 63:9
land, and *p* His people. . . . .Joel 2:18
And should I not *p*. . . . . . . .Jon 4:11
just as I had *p* . . . . .Matt 18:33

PLACE

p know him anymore . . . . .Job 7:10
All go to one *p* . . . . .Eccl 3:20
return again to My *p*. . . . . .Hos 5:15
Come, see the *p*. . . . . . . .Matt 28:6
My word has no *p*. . . . . . .John 8:37
I go to prepare a *p* . . . . . .John 14:2
might go to his own *p*. . . . .Acts 1:25

PLACES

set them in slippery *p* . . . . .Ps 73:18
dark *p* of the earth . . . . . . .Ps 74:20
and the rough *p*. . . . . .Is 40:4
They love the best *p*. . . . .Matt 23:6
in the heavenly *p* . . . . .Eph 1:3

PLAGUE

bring yet one more *p* . . . . . .Ex 11:1
p come near your . . . . .Ps 91:10
and the *p* was stopped. . . .Ps 106:30

PLAGUES

I will send all My *p* . . . . . . .Ex 9:14
I will be your *p*. . . . . .Hos 13:14
p that are written. . . . . . . .Rev 22:18

PLAINLY

the Christ, tell us *p* . . . . .John 10:24
now You are speaking *p* . .John 16:29
such things declare *p*. . . . .Heb 11:14

PLAN

p evil things in their. . . . . . .Ps 140:2
Let none of you *p* . . . . . . .Zech 7:10

PLANK

First remove the *p* . . . . . . .Matt 7:5

PLANS

He makes the *p* of the . . . . .Ps 33:10
in that very day his *p* . . . . .Ps 146:4
that devises wicked *p* . . . .Prov 6:18
A man's heart *p*. . . . . .Prov 16:9
P are established. . . . . . .Prov 20:18

PLANT

a time to *p* . . . . .Eccl 3:2
Him as a tender *p* . . . . .Is 53:2
they shall *p* vineyards. . . . . .Is 65:21
p of an alien vine. . . . . . . .Jer 2:21
p which My heavenly. . . .Matt 15:13

PLANTED

shall be like a tree *p*. . . . . . .Ps 1:3
Your right hand has *p* . . . .Ps 80:15
shall they be *p* . . . . .Is 40:24
by the roots and be *p*. . . . .Luke 17:6
I *p*, Apollos watered . . . . .1 Cor 3:6

PLANTS

our sons may be as *p*. . . . .Ps 144:12
down its choice *p*. . . . . .Is 16:8
neither he who *p* . . . . .1 Cor 3:7

PLATFORM

scribe stood on a *p* . . . . Neh 8:4

PLATTER

head here on a *p* . . . . Matt 14:8

PLAY

and rose up to *p* . . . . Ex 32:6
p skillfully with a . . . . Ps 33:3
nursing child shall *p* . . . . Is 11:8
and rose up to *p* . . . . 1 Cor 10:7

PLEAD

the one who would *p* . . . . Judg 6:31
Oh, that one might *p* . . . . Job 16:21
p my cause against an . . . . . Ps 43:1
p with your friend . . . . Prov 6:3
Behold, I will *p* . . . . Jer 2:35
p His case with all . . . . Jer 25:31

PLEADED

Then Moses *p* with the . . . . Ex 32:11
this thing I *p* with . . . . . . 2 Cor 12:8

PLEADING

though God were *p* . . . . . . 2 Cor 5:20

PLEASANT

food, that it was *p* . . . . Gen 3:6
they despised the *p* . . . . . . Ps 106:24
how good and how *p* . . . . . . Ps 133:1
and knowledge is *p* . . . . . . Prov 2:10
P words are like a . . . . Prov 16:24
p places of the . . . . Jer 23:10
Is he a *p* child . . . . Jer 31:20
I ate no *p* food . . . . Dan 10:3

PLEASANTNESS

Her ways are ways of *p* . . . Prov 3:17

PLEASE

When a man's ways *p* . . . . . Prov 16:7
do those things that *p* . . . . John 8:29
in the flesh cannot *p* . . . . . . Rom 8:8
p his neighbor for his . . . . . Rom 15:2
how he may *p* the Lord . . 1 Cor 7:32
Or do I seek to *p* men . . . . . Gal 1:10
is impossible to *p* Him . . . . Heb 11:6

PLEASED

Then You shall be *p* . . . . Ps 51:19
The Lord is well *p* . . . . Is 42:21
Would he be *p* with you . . . . Mal 1:8
in whom I am well *p* . . . . . Matt 3:17
God was not well *p* . . . . . . 1 Cor 10:5
testimony, that he *p* . . . . . . Heb 11:5
in whom I am well *p* . . . . 2 Pet 1:17

PLEASES

He does whatever He *p* . . . Ps 115:3
Whatever the Lord *p* . . . . . . Ps 135:6

PLEASING

sacrifice, well *p* . . . . Phil 4:18
for this is well *p* . . . . Col 3:20
in you what is well *p* . . . . . Heb 13:21

PLEASURE

not a God who takes *p* . . . . . . Ps 5:4
Do good in Your good *p* . . . Ps 51:18
Your servants take *p* . . . . . Ps 102:14
p will be a poor man . . . . . Prov 21:17
for He has no *p* . . . . Eccl 5:4
shall perform all My *p* . . . . Is 44:28
your fast you find *p* . . . . Is 58:3
nor finding your own *p* . . . . Is 58:13
"Do I have any *p* . . . . . . Ezek 18:23
I have no *p* in you . . . . Mal 1:10
your Father's good *p* . . . Luke 12:32
to the good *p* of His . . . . Eph 1:5

fulfill all the good *p* . . . . 2 Thess 1:11
p is dead while . . . . 1 Tim 5:6
for sin You had no *p* . . . . . . Heb 10:6
back, My soul has no *p* . . Heb 10:38
p that war in your . . . . James 4:1
on the earth in *p* . . . . James 5:5

PLEASURES

Your right hand are *p* . . . . . . Ps 16:11
cares, riches, and *p* . . . . . . Luke 8:14
to enjoy the passing *p* . . . . Heb 11:25

PLEIADES

Bear, Orion, and the *P* . . . . . Job 9:9

PLENTIFUL

You, O God, sent a *p* . . . . Ps 68:9
The harvest truly is *p* . . . Matt 9:37

PLENTIFULLY

rich man yielded *p* . . . . . Luke 12:16

PLENTY

p which were in the . . . . . Gen 41:53
Lord will grant you *p* . . Deut 28:11
his land will have *p* . . . . . Prov 28:19

PLIGHT

He laughs at the *p* . . . . Job 9:23

PLOT

and the people *p* . . . . Ps 2:1
p became known to Saul . . Acts 9:24

PLOTS

The wicked *p* against . . . . . . Ps 37:12

PLOTTED

and *p* to take Jesus by . . . . Matt 26:4
chief priests *p* . . . . John 12:10

PLOW

lazy man will not *p* . . . . . . Prov 20:4
Does one *p* there with . . . . Amos 6:12
put his hand to the *p* . . . . . Luke 9:62
he who plows should *p* . . . 1 Cor 9:10

PLOWED

"Zion shall be *p* . . . . Jer 26:18
You have *p* wickedness . . . Hos 10:13
of you Zion shall be *p* . . . . . Mic 3:12

PLOWMAN

p shall overtake the . . . . . . Amos 9:13

PLUCK

grain, you may *p* . . . . Deut 23:25
who pass by the way *p* . . . . Ps 80:12
obey, I will utterly *p* . . . . . Jer 12:17
p the heads of grain . . . . . Mark 2:23

PLUCKED

p the victim from his . . . . Job 29:17
cheeks to those who *p* . . . . . Is 50:6
And His disciples *p* . . . . . . Luke 6:1
you would have *p* . . . . Gal 4:15

PLUMB

a *p* line, with a *p* . . . . Amos 7:7
rejoice to see the *p* . . . . . . Zech 4:10

PLUNDER

p the Egyptians . . . . Ex 3:22
who pass by the way *p* . . . . Ps 89:41
the *p* of the poor is . . . . Is 3:14
p you shall become . . . . . . Jer 30:16
house and *p* his goods . . . Matt 12:29

PLUNDERED

stouthearted were *p* . . . . Ps 76:5
a people robbed and *p* . . . . . Is 42:22

"And when you are *p* . . . . . Jer 4:30
Because you have *p* . . . . Hab 2:8

PLUNDERING

me because of the *p* . . . . Is 22:4
accepted the *p* of your . . . . Heb 10:34

POETS

some of your own *p* . . . . . Acts 17:28

POISON

the *p* of asps is under . . . . . . Ps 140:3
" The *p* of asps is . . . . Rom 3:13
evil, full of deadly *p* . . . . James 3:8

POISONED

p by bitterness . . . . Acts 8:23
p their minds against . . . . Acts 14:2

POLLUTIONS

have escaped the *p* . . . . . . 2 Pet 2:20

POMP

multitude and their *p* . . . . . . Is 5:14
p is brought down to . . . . . . Is 14:11
had come with great *p* . . Acts 25:23

POMPOUS

and a mouth speaking *p* . . . . Dan 7:8

PONDER

P the path of your . . . . Prov 4:26

PONDERED

p them in her heart . . . . . Luke 2:19

PONDERS

p all his paths . . . . Prov 5:21

POOL

the wilderness a *p* . . . . Is 41:18
by the Sheep Gate a *p* . . . . John 5:2

POOLS

also covers it with *p* . . . . . . Ps 84:6
a wilderness into *p* . . . . . . Ps 107:35
your eyes like the *p* . . . . . . Song 7:4

POOR

p shall not give less . . . . . . Ex 30:15
be partial to the *p* . . . . Lev 19:15
p will never cease . . . . . . Deut 15:11
So the *p* have hope . . . . Job 5:16
and forsaken the *p* . . . . . . Job 20:19
I delivered the *p* . . . . Job 29:12
soul grieved for the *p* . . . . Job 30:25
p shall eat and be . . . . Ps 22:26
p man cried out . . . . Ps 34:6
But I am *p* and needy . . . . Ps 40:17
goodness for the *p* . . . . Ps 68:10
Let the *p* and needy . . . . . . Ps 74:21
yet He sets the *p* . . . . Ps 107:41
He raises the *p* . . . . Ps 113:7
a slack hand becomes *p* . . Prov 10:4
p man is hated even . . . . . Prov 14:20
who has mercy on the *p* . . Prov 14:21
He who oppresses the *p* . . Prov 14:31
p reproaches his Maker . . Prov 17:5
p man is better than a . . . Prov 19:22
p have this in common . . . Prov 22:2
Do not rob the *p* . . . . Prov 22:22
p man who oppresses . . . . Prov 28:3
remembered that same *p* . . Eccl 9:15
for silver, and the *p* . . . . . Amos 2:6
the alien or the *p* . . . . Zech 7:10
in particular the *p* . . . . . . Zech 11:7
"Blessed are the *p* . . . . . . Matt 5:3
p have the gospel . . . . . . Matt 11:5
For you have the *p* . . . . . Matt 26:11
your sakes He became *p* . . 2 Cor 8:9
should remember the *p* . . . Gal 2:10

PORTION

God not chosen the *p*. . . .James 2:5
have dishonored the *p* . . . .James 2:6
wretched, miserable, *p* . . . . .Rev 3:17

PORTION

For the LORD's *p*. . . . . . . .Deut 32:9
This is the *p* from God. . . .Job 20:29
O LORD, You, are the *p*. . . . .Ps 16:5
heart and my *p* forever. . . . .Ps 73:26
You are my *p* . . . . .Ps 119:57
I will divide Him a *p*. . . . . .Is 53:12
rejoice in their *p*. . . . . .Is 61:7
The *P* of Jacob is not . . . .Jer 10:16
they have trodden My *p* . .Jer 12:10
"The LORD is my *p*. . . . . . .Lam 3:24
and appoint him his *p* . . .Matt 24:51
to give them their *p* . . . .Luke 12:42
Father, give me the *p*. . . .Luke 15:12

PORTRAYED

Christ was clearly *p* . . . . .Gal 3:1

POSITION

If a man desires the *p*. . . . .1 Tim 3:1

POSSESS

descendants shall *p* . . . . . .Gen 22:17
p the land which . . . . .Josh 1:11
By your patience *p*. . . . .Luke 21:19
p his own vessel. . . . . . .1 Thess 4:4

POSSESSED

much land yet to be *p*. . . .Josh 13:1
"The LORD *p* me at . . . . .Prov 8:22
of the things he *p* . . . . . . .Acts 4:32

POSSESSING

and yet *p* all things . . . . . .2 Cor 6:10

POSSESSION

as an everlasting *p*. . . . . .Gen 17:8
the rest of their *p* . . . . .Ps 17:14
they did not gain *p*. . . . . . .Ps 44:3
of the purchased *p*. . . . . . .Eph 1:14
and an enduring *p* . . . . . .Heb 10:34

POSSESSIONS

is full of Your *p* . . . . .Ps 104:24
kinds of precious *p* . . . . . .Prov 1:13
Yes, I had greater *p*. . . . . . .Eccl 2:7
for he had great *p* . . . . .Mark 10:22
and there wasted his *p*. . .Luke 15:13
and sold their *p* . . . . .Acts 2:45

POSSIBLE

God all things *p* . . . . .Matt 19:26
p that the blood . . . . .Heb 10:4

POSTERITY

to preserve a *p* . . . . .Gen 45:7
p shall serve Him . . . . .Ps 22:30
p who approve their . . . . . .Ps 49:13

POT

to Aaron, "Take a *p*. . . . . .Ex 16:33
from a boiling *p*. . . . . . . .Job 41:20
The refining *p* is for . . . . . .Prov 17:3
p that had the manna . . . . .Heb 9:4

POTENTATE

the blessed and only *P*. . .1 Tim 6:15

POTS

when we sat by the *p*. . . . . .Ex 16:3
also took away the *p* . . . . .Jer 52:18
are regarded as clay *p*. . . . .Lam 4:2

POTSHERD

for himself a *p*. . . . . .Job 2:8
is dried up like a *p* . . . . . . .Ps 22:15
Let the *p* strive with. . . . . . .Is 45:9

POUR

p out your heart . . . . .Ps 62:8
P out Your wrath . . . . .Ps 79:6
p My Spirit on your . . . . . . .Is 44:3
and let the skies *p*. . . . . .Is 45:8
P out Your fury . . . . .Jer 10:25
that I will *p* out My. . . . . .Joel 2:28
"And I will *p* . . . . .Zech 12:10
angels, "Go and *p*. . . . . . . .Rev 16:1

POURED

And now my soul is *p*. . . .Job 30:16
I am *p* out like water . . . . . .Ps 22:14
grace is *p* upon Your. . . . . . .Ps 45:2
name is ointment *p*. . . . . . .Song 1:3
visited You, they *p*. . . . . . . .Is 26:16
strong, because He *p*. . . . . .Is 53:12
and My fury will be *p* . . . .Jer 7:20
His fury is *p* out like. . . . . . .Nah 1:6
broke the flask and *p*. . . .Mark 14:3
of God has been *p* . . . . .Rom 5:5
if I am being *p* . . . . .Phil 2:17
I am already being *p*. . . . . .2 Tim 4:6
whom He *p* out on us . . . .Titus 3:6

POVERTY

of the poor is their *p*. . . . .Prov 10:15
but it leads to *p*. . . . . .Prov 11:24
P and shame will come. . .Prov 13:18
leads only to *p*. . . . . .Prov 14:23
lest you come to *p*. . . . . . .Prov 20:13
give me neither *p*. . . . . . . .Prov 30:8
p put in all the . . . . .Luke 21:4
and their deep *p*. . . . . .2 Cor 8:2
p might become rich . . . . .2 Cor 8:9
tribulation, and *p* . . . . .Rev 2:9

POWER

that I may show My *p* . . . .Ex 9:16
become glorious in *p* . . . . . .Ex 15:6
for God has *p* to help . . . .2 Chr 25:8
him who is without *p* . . . .Job 26:2
p who can understand . . . .Job 26:14
p belongs to God. . . . . .Ps 62:11
p Your enemies shall. . . . . . .Ps 66:3
gives strength and *p*. . . . . . .Ps 68:35
a king is, there is *p* . . . . . . .Eccl 8:4
No one has *p* over the . . . . .Eccl 8:8
the strength of His *p* . . . . . .Is 40:26
truly I am full of *p*. . . . . . . .Mic 3:8
anger and great in *p* . . . . . .Nah 1:3
Not by might nor by *p* . . . .Zech 4:6
the kingdom and the *p*. . . .Matt 6:13
the Son of Man has *p*. . . . .Matt 9:6
who had given such *p* . . . . .Matt 9:8
Scriptures nor the *p*. . . . . .Matt 22:29
And the *p* of the Lord . . . .Luke 5:17
p went out from Him. . . . .Luke 6:19
you are endued with *p* . . .Luke 24:49
I have *p* to lay it. . . . . . .John 10:18
not know that I have *p* . .John 19:10
"You could have no *p* . . .John 19:11
you shall receive *p*. . . . . . . .Acts 1:8
as though by our own *p* . .Acts 3:12
man is the great *p*. . . . . . . .Acts 8:10
"Give me this *p*. . . . . .Acts 8:19
for it is the *p* . . . . .Rom 1:16
even His eternal *p*. . . . . . . .Rom 1:20
saved it is the *p* . . . . .1 Cor 1:18
Greeks, Christ the *p* . . . . .1 Cor 1:24
be brought under the *p*. . .1 Cor 6:12
that the *p* of Christ . . . . . .2 Cor 12:9
greatness of His *p* . . . . .Eph 1:19
working of His *p* . . . . .Eph 3:7
the Lord and in the *p*. . . . . .Eph 6:10
to His glorious *p* . . . . .Col 1:11
the glory of His *p* . . . . .2 Thess 1:9
of fear, but of *p* . . . . .2 Tim 1:7
by the word of His *p* . . . . . .Heb 1:3

p of death, that . . . . .Heb 2:14
but according to the *p*. . . . .Heb 7:16
as His divine *p* . . . . .2 Pet 1:3
dominion and *p* . . . . .Jude 25
to him I will give *p*. . . . . . .Rev 2:26
glory and honor and *p* . . . .Rev 4:11
honor and glory and *p* . . . .Rev 5:13

POWERFUL

of the LORD is *p* . . . . .Ps 29:4
of God is living and *p* . . . .Heb 4:12

POWERS

principalities and *p* . . . . .Col 2:15
word of God and the *p*. . . . .Heb 6:5

PRAISE

your brothers shall *p* . . . . .Gen 49:8
"He is your *p* . . . . .Deut 10:21
I will sing *p* to the . . . . . . .Judg 5:3
p shall be of You in. . . . . . .Ps 22:25
For *p* from the upright. . . . . .Ps 33:1
p shall continually be. . . . . . .Ps 34:1
the people shall *p* . . . . .Ps 45:17
Whoever offers *p*. . . . . .Ps 50:23
P is awaiting You . . . . .Ps 65:1
make His *p* glorious . . . . . . .Ps 66:2
let all the peoples *p*. . . . . . . .Ps 67:3
Let heaven and earth *p* . . . .Ps 69:34
p shall be continually. . . . . . .Ps 71:6
And the heavens will *p*. . . . .Ps 89:5
silent, O God of my *p*. . . . .Ps 109:1
Seven times a day I *p* . . . .Ps 119:164
All Your works shall *p* . . . .Ps 145:10
shall speak the *p*. . . . . .Ps 145:21
P the LORD . . . . .Ps 148:1
that has breath *p* . . . . .Ps 150:6
Let another man *p* . . . . . . .Prov 27:2
let her own works *p*. . . . . .Prov 31:31
and your gates *P*. . . . . .Is 60:18
He makes Jerusalem a *p*. . . .Is 62:7
for You are my *p* . . . . .Jer 17:14
Me a name of joy, a *p* . . . . .Jer 33:9
give you fame and *p*. . . . . .Zeph 3:20
You have perfected *p* . . . .Matt 21:16
of men more than the *p* . .John 12:43
p is not from men but. . . . .Rom 2:29
Then each one's *p* . . . . . . .1 Cor 4:5
the brother whose *p*. . . . . .2 Cor 8:18
should be to the *p*. . . . . .Eph 1:12
to the glory and *p* . . . . .Phil 1:11
I will sing *p* to You . . . . . . .Heb 2:12
the sacrifice of *p*. . . . . .Heb 13:15
and for the *p* of those . . . .1 Pet 2:14
saying, "*P* our God. . . . . . . .Rev 19:5

PRAISED

who is worthy to be *p* . . .2 Sam 22:4
daily He shall be *p* . . . . .Ps 72:15
LORD's name is to be *p*. . . . .Ps 113:3
and greatly to be *p* . . . . . . .Ps 145:3
where our fathers *p* . . . . . . .Is 64:11
the Most High and *p*. . . . . .Dan 4:34

PRAISES

enthroned in the *p* . . . . .Ps 22:3
it is good to sing *p*. . . . . . . .Ps 147:1
husband also, and he *p*. . .Prov 31:28
shall proclaim the *p*. . . . . . . .Is 60:6
you may proclaim the *p*. . .1 Pet 2:9

PRAISEWORTHY

if there is anything *p* . . . . . .Phil 4:8

PRAISING

they will still be *p*. . . . . .Ps 84:4
of the heavenly host *p* . . .Luke 2:13
in the temple *p* . . . . .Luke 24:53

PRATING

p fool will fall............Prov 10:8

PRAY

LORD in ceasing to *p* ...1 Sam 12:23
at noon I will *p* ....Ps 55:17
who hate you, and *p* .....Matt 5:44
"And when you *p* ....Matt 6:5
"But you, when you *p* ....Matt 6:6
manner, therefore, *p* ......Matt 6:9
"Watch and *p* ....Matt 26:41
to the mountain to *p* ...Mark 6:46
"Lord, teach us to *p* .....Luke 11:1
men always ought to *p* ...Luke 18:1
"And I will *p* ....John 14:16
I do not *p* for the ....John 17:9
"I do not *p* for.........John 17:20
know what we should *p* ...Rom 8:26
I will *p* with the........1 Cor 14:15
p without ceasing......1 Thess 5:17
Brethren, *p* for us......1 Thess 5:25
therefore that the men *p* ..1 Tim 2:8
Let him *p* ....James 5:13
to one another, and *p*...James 5:16
say that he should *p*....1 John 5:16
p that you may prosper ....3 John 2

PRAYED

Pharisee stood and *p* ...Luke 18:11
p more earnestly.......Luke 22:44
p earnestly that it .....James 5:17

PRAYER

in heaven their *p* ....1 Kin 8:45
p made in this place ....2 Chr 7:15
fear, and restrain *p*.....Job 15:4
and my *p* is pure........Job 16:17
p would return to my ....Ps 35:13
a *p* to the God of my ......Ps 42:8
p also will be made.......Ps 72:15
Let my *p* come before......Ps 88:2
He shall regard the *p* ...Ps 102:17
but I give myself to *p* ....Ps 109:4
to the LORD, but the *p* ....Prov 15:8
not go out except by *p* ..Matt 17:21
all night in *p* to God......Luke 6:12
continually to *p*..........Acts 6:4
where *p* was............Acts 16:13
steadfastly in *p*.......Rom 12:12
to fasting and *p*.........1 Cor 7:5
always with all *p* ....Eph 6:18
but in everything by *p*.....Phil 4:6
the word of God and *p* ....1 Tim 4:5
And the *p* of faith .....James 5:15

PRAYERS

though you make many *p*....Is 1:15
a pretense make long *p* ..Matt 23:14
fervently for you in *p* ......Col 4:12
that supplications, *p*......1 Tim 2:1
p may not be hindered.....1 Pet 3:7
are open to their *p* ....1 Pet 3:12
and watchful in *p*....1 Pet 4:7
which are the *p* ....Rev 5:8

PREACH

that great city, and *p* ......Jon 3:2
time Jesus began to *p* ....Matt 4:17
you hear in the ear, *p*....Matt 10:27
p the gospel to the ......Luke 4:18
p the kingdom of God ....Luke 9:60
And how shall they *p* ....Rom 10:15
p Christ crucified........1 Cor 1:23
is me if I do not *p* ....1 Cor 9:16
was I or they, so we *p* ...1 Cor 15:11
For we do not *p* ....2 Cor 4:5
p Christ even from ....Phil 1:15
P the word.............2 Tim 4:2

PREACHED

p that people ....Mark 6:12
out and *p* everywhere ...Mark 16:20
of sins should be *p* ......Luke 24:47
p Christ to them ....Acts 8:5
through this Man is *p*....Acts 13:38
lest, when I have *p* .....1 Cor 9:27
whom we have not *p* .....2 Cor 11:4
than what we have *p*.......Gal 1:8
in truth, Christ is *p* ......Phil 1:18
the gospel was *p*..........Heb 4:2
also He went and *p* ......1 Pet 3:19

PREACHER

The words of the *P* ....Eccl 1:1
they hear without a *p* ...Rom 10:14
I was appointed a *p* .....1 Tim 2:7
of eight people, a *p*......2 Pet 2:5

PREACHES

the Jesus whom Paul *p*...Acts 19:13
p another Jesus whom ..2 Cor 11:4
p any other gospel.........Gal 1:9
p the faith which he ....Gal 1:23

PREACHING

p Jesus as the ....Acts 5:42
to my gospel and the *p*...Rom 16:25
not risen, then our *p* ...1 Cor 15:14

PRECEDE

p those who are asleep 1 Thess 4:15

PRECEPT

p must be upon *p* ....Is 28:10

PRECEPTS

and commanded them *p* ...Neh 9:14
all His *p* are sure.........Ps 111:7
us to keep Your *p* ....Ps 119:4
how I love Your *p* ......Ps 119:159
and kept all his *p*........Jer 35:18

PRECIOUS

because my life was *p* ..1 Sam 26:21
P in the sight of the......Ps 116:15
How *p* also are Your.....Ps 139:17
She is more *p* than ......Prov 3:15
Since you were *p* ....Is 43:4
p things shall not ....Is 44:9
if you take out the *p* ....Jer 15:19
The *p* sons of Zion........Lam 4:2
farmer waits for the *p* ...James 5:7
more *p* than gold ....1 Pet 1:7
who believe, He is *p* ....1 Pet 2:7
p in the sight of ....1 Pet 3:4

PREDESTINED

He foreknew, He also *p*....Rom 8:29
having *p* us to ....Eph 1:5
inheritance, being *p* ......Eph 1:11

PREEMINENCE

He may have the *p* ....Col 1:18
loves to have the *p* ......3 John 9

PREFERENCE

in honor giving *p*.......Rom 12:10

PREFERRED

comes after me is *p* ......John 1:15

PREJUDICE

these things without *p* ...1 Tim 5:21

PREMEDITATE

p what you will ....Mark 13:11

PREPARATION

Now it was the *P* ......John 19:14
your feet with the *p*......Eph 6:15

PREPARE

p your hearts for the .....1 Sam 7:3
p a table before me in......Ps 23:5
p mercy and truth.........Ps 61:7
P the way of the LORD ......Is 40:3
P the way for the.........Is 62:10
P the way of the LORD ....Mark 1:3
will, and did not *p* ....Luke 12:47
p a place for you........John 14:2

PREPARED

place which I have *p* ......Ex 23:20
You *p* room for it.........Ps 80:9
When He *p* the heavens ...Prov 8:27
for the LORD has *p* ....Zeph 1:7
for whom it is *p* ....Matt 20:23
which You have *p* ....Luke 2:31
mercy, which He had *p*....Rom 9:23
things which God has *p* ...1 Cor 2:9
Now He who has *p* ....2 Cor 5:5
p beforehand that we......Eph 2:10
God, for He has *p* ....Heb 11:16

PRESENCE

themselves from the *p* ......Gen 3:8
went out from the *p*......Gen 4:16
we die in your *p* ....Gen 47:15
P will go with you ....Ex 33:14
and honor the *p*.........Lev 19:32
afraid in any man's *p* ....Deut 1:17
am terrified at His *p*.....Job 23:15
p is fullness of joy ....Ps 16:11
shall dwell in Your *p*......Ps 140:13
not tremble at My *p* ......Jer 5:22
shall shake at My *p*.....Ezek 38:20
Be silent in the *p* ....Zeph 1:7
and drank in Your *p* ....Luke 13:26
full of joy in Your *p*......Acts 2:28
but his bodily *p* ....2 Cor 10:10
obeyed, not as in my *p*....Phil 2:12

PRESENT

we are all *p* before......Acts 10:33
evil is *p* with me ....Rom 7:21
p your bodies a living......Rom 12:1
or death, or things *p* .....1 Cor 3:22
absent in body but *p* .....1 Cor 5:3
not only when I am *p*......Gal 4:18
that He might *p*.........Eph 5:27
to *p* yourself............2 Tim 2:15
p you faultless ....Jude 24

PRESENTED

treasures, they *p*........Matt 2:11
For just as you *p*........Rom 6:19

PRESENTS

kings will bring *p* ....Ps 68:29

PRESERVE

before you to *p* life........Gen 45:5
You shall *p* me from ....Ps 32:7
O LORD, You *p* man and....Ps 36:6
He shall *p* your soul......Ps 121:7
The LORD shall *p*.........Ps 121:8
children, I will *p*.........Jer 49:11
pardon those whom I *p*...Jer 50:20
loses his life will *p* .....Luke 17:33
every evil work and *p* ...2 Tim 4:18

PRESERVED

and my life is *p*..........Gen 32:30
soul, and body be *p* ....1 Thess 5:23

PRESERVES

For the LORD *p* the........Ps 31:23
p the souls of His.........Ps 97:10
The LORD *p* the simple......Ps 116:6
who guards his mouth *p*...Prov 13:3
he who keeps his way *p* ..Prov 16:17

PRESS

I *p* toward the goal........Phil 3:14

PRESSED

p her virgin bosom.......Ezek 23:8
We are hard *p* on every ....2 Cor 4:8
For I am hard *p* ....Phil 1:23

PRESUMPTUOUS

servant also from *p*........Ps 19:13

PRETENDED

before them, *p* madness.1 Sam 21:13

PRETENSE

whole heart, but in *p*......Jer 3:10
p make long prayers.....Matt 23:14

PREVAIL

no man shall *p* ....1 Sam 2:9
our tongue we will *p*........Ps 12:4
but they shall not *p*......Jer 1:19
of Hades shall not *p*.....Matt 16:18

PREVAILED

hand, that Israel *p*........Ex 17:11
with the Angel and *p*......Hos 12:4
grew mightily and *p*.....Acts 19:20

PREY

the mountains of *p*........Ps 76:4
has not given us as *p*......Ps 124:6
Shall the *p* be taken ......Is 49:24
evil makes himself a *p*......Is 59:15
shall no longer be a *p*...Ezek 34:22
when he has no *p* ....Amos 3:4

PRICE

be weighed for its *p* .....Job 28:15
a fool the purchase *p*....Prov 17:16
one pearl of great *p* .....Matt 13:46
back part of the *p* ....Acts 5:3
you were bought at a *p*...1 Cor 6:20

PRIDE

p come against me ....Ps 36:11
p serves as...............Ps 73:6
p and arrogance and .....Prov 8:13
By *p* comes nothing ....Prov 13:10
P goes before...........Prov 16:18
p will bring him low ....Prov 29:23
and her daughter had *p* .Ezek 16:49
p He is able to put down...Dan 4:37
was hardened in *p* ....Dan 5:20
has sworn by the *p* ......Amos 8:7
For the *p* of the.........Zech 11:3
evil eye, blasphemy, *p* ...Mark 7:22
p he fall into the ....1 Tim 3:6
of the eyes, and the *p* ...1 John 2:16

PRIEST

he was the *p* of God.....Gen 14:18
Myself a faithful *p* .....1 Sam 2:35
p forever according........Ps 110:4
the *p* and the prophet......Is 28:7
so He shall be a *p* ....Zech 6:13
of a *p* should keep ....Mal 2:7
and faithful High *P*.......Heb 2:17
we have a great High *P*...Heb 4:14
p forever according........Heb 5:6
Christ came as High *P* ...Heb 9:11

PRIESTHOOD

be an everlasting *p*........Ex 40:15
have defiled the *p*........Neh 13:29
p being changed.........Heb 7:12
has an unchangeable *p* ...Heb 7:24
house, a holy *p* ....1 Pet 2:5
generation, a royal *p*.......1 Pet 2:9

PRIESTS

to Me a kingdom of *p* .....Ex 19:6
her *p* teach for pay........Mic 3:11
made us kings and *p* ......Rev 1:6
but they shall be *p*........Rev 20:6

PRINCE

"Who made you a *p*.......Ex 2:14
is the house of the *p*......Job 21:28
is the downfall of a *p* ...Prov 14:28
everlasting Father, *P*........Is 9:6
until Messiah the *P*......Dan 9:25
except Michael your *p*...Dan 10:21
days without king or *p* .....Hos 3:4
p asks for gifts ....Mic 7:3
and killed the *P*.........Acts 3:15
His right hand to be *P*...Acts 5:31
the *p* of the power ....Eph 2:2

PRINCES

He is not partial to *p*.....Job 34:19
to bind his *p* at his........Ps 105:22
He may seat him with *p* ...Ps 113:8
to put confidence in *p*......Ps 118:9
P also sit and speak........Ps 119:23
p and all judges of ....Ps 148:11
good, nor to strike *p*.....Prov 17:26
is a child, and your *p*....Eccl 10:16
of nobles, and your *p*.....Eccl 10:17
children to be their *p*.........Is 3:4
p will rule with.............Is 32:1
He brings the *p*...........Is 40:23

PRINCIPAL

Wisdom is the *p* ....Prov 4:7

PRINCIPALITY

far above all *p*...........Eph 1:21
is the head of all *p*........Col 2:10

PRINCIPLES

from the basic *p*..........Col 2:20
again the first *p*..........Heb 5:12

PRISON

and put him into the *p* ...Gen 39:20
Bring my soul out of *p*.....Ps 142:7
in darkness from the *p* ......Is 42:7
the opening of the *p*.......Is 61:1
should put him in *p*.......Jer 29:26
John had heard in *p*.....Matt 11:2
I was in *p* and you......Matt 25:36
to the spirits in *p*........1 Pet 3:19

PRISONER

the groaning of the *p* ......Ps 79:11
reason I, Paul, the *p* ......Eph 3:1
Lord, nor of me His *p*....2 Tim 1:8

PRISONERS

p rest together...........Job 3:18
does not despise His *p*....Ps 69:33
gives freedom to the *p*.....Ps 146:7
the stronghold, you *p*...Zech 9:12
Remember the *p* as if ....Heb 13:3

PRISONS

the synagogues and *p* ...Luke 21:12
p more frequently ......2 Cor 11:23

PRIZE

life shall be as a *p* ....Jer 21:9
but one receives the *p* ....1 Cor 9:24
the goal for the *p* ....Phil 3:14

PROCEED

For they *p* from evil........Jer 9:3
of the same mouth *p* ....James 3:10

PROCEEDED

for I *p* forth.............John 8:42

PROCEEDS

by every word that *p* .....Deut 8:3
by every word that *p*.....Matt 4:4
Spirit of truth who *p* ...John 15:26
back part of the *p*........Acts 5:2

PROCESSION

They have seen Your *p*.....Ps 68:24

PROCLAIM

you, and I will *p*.........Ex 33:19
p the name of the LORD...Deut 32:3
p it not in the ....2 Sam 1:20
and they shall *p*...........Is 60:6
began to *p* it freely ......Mark 1:45
knowing, Him I *p* ....Acts 17:23
drink this cup, you *p*....1 Cor 11:26

PROCLAIMED

p the good news ....Ps 40:9
company of those who *p* ...Ps 68:11
he went his way and *p*....Luke 8:39
inner rooms will be *p* ....Luke 12:3

PROCLAIMER

"He seems to be a *p* .....Acts 17:18

PROCLAIMS

good news, who *p* ....Is 52:7

PROCONSUL

seeking to turn the *p* .....Acts 13:8
When Gallio was *p* ......Acts 18:12

PRODIGAL

with *p* living ....Luke 15:13

PRODUCE

land shall yield its *p*......Lev 26:4
all kinds of *p*............Ps 144:13

PROFANE

and offered *p* fire.........Lev 10:1
and priest are *p*..........Jer 23:11
"But you *p* it ....Mal 1:12
tried to *p* the temple......Acts 24:6
But reject the old and .....1 Tim 4:7
p person like Esau.......Heb 12:16

PROFANED

p his crown by casting.....Ps 89:39
and *p* My Sabbaths .....Ezek 22:8
p the LORD's holy........Mal 2:11

PROFANENESS

of Jerusalem *p* has ....Jer 23:15

PROFANING

p the covenant of the......Mal 2:10

PROFESS

They *p* to know God .....Titus 1:16

PROFESSING

P to be wise.............Rom 1:22
is proper for women *p*....1 Tim 2:10

PROFIT

p is there in my blood ......Ps 30:9
p has a man from all......Eccl 1:3
There was no *p* under .....Eccl 2:11
for they will not *p* ....Is 57:12
words that cannot *p* ....Jer 7:8
p which you have made ..Ezek 22:13
p is it that we have.......Mal 3:14
For what *p* is it to ......Matt 16:26
For what will it *p*........Mark 8:36
"For what *p* is it to .....Luke 9:25

PROFITABLE (continued)

her masters much *p* . . . . .Acts 16:16
hope of *p* was gone . . . . . .Acts 16:19
brought no small *p* . . . . . .Acts 19:24
the *p* of circumcision? . . . . . .Rom 3:1
not seeking my own *p* . . .1 Cor 10:33
Christ will *p* you . . . . .Gal 5:2
about words to no *p* . . . .2 Tim 2:14
them, but He for our *p* . . .Heb 12:10
What does it *p* . . . . .James 2:14
and sell, and make a *p* . . .James 4:13

PROFITABLE

"Can a man be *p* . . . . .Job 22:2
It is doubtless not *p* . . . . .2 Cor 12:1
of God, and is *p* . . . . .2 Tim 3:16
things are good and *p* . . . . .Titus 3:8
to you, but now is *p* . . . . .Philem 11

PROFITS

p a man nothing that . . . . . .Job 34:9
have not love, it *p* . . . . . .1 Cor 13:3
exercise *p* a little . . . . .1 Tim 4:8

PROFOUND

with things too *p* . . . . .Ps 131:1

PROLONG

you will not *p* your . . . . . .Deut 4:26
p Your anger to all *p* . . . . . . .Ps 85:5
nor will he *p* his days . . . . .Eccl 8:13

PROLONGED

and his days are *p* . . . . . . .Eccl 8:12

PROLONGS

The fear of the LORD . . .Prov 10:27

PROMISE

of all His good *p* . . . . .1 Kin 8:56
Behold, I send the *P* . . . .Luke 24:49
but to wait for the *P* . . . . . .Acts 1:4
"For the *p* is to you . . . . . .Acts 2:39
p drew near which God . . . .Acts 7:17
for the hope of the *p* . . . . .Acts 26:6
is made void and no *p* . . . .Rom 4:14
p might be sure . . . . .Rom 4:16
it is no longer of *p* . . . . .Gal 3:18
Therefore, since a *p* . . . . . . .Heb 4:1
to the heirs of *p* . . . . .Heb 6:17
did not receive the *p* . . . . .Heb 11:39
they *p* them liberty . . . . . .2 Pet 2:19
p that He has promised 1 John 2:25

PROMISED

bless you as He has *p* . . . .Deut 1:11
Him faithful who had *p* . . .Heb 11:11

PROMISES

For all the *p* of God . . . . . .2 Cor 1:20
his Seed were the *p* . . . . . . .Gal 3:16
patience inherit the *p* . . . . .Heb 6:12
having received the *p* . . . . .Heb 11:13
great and precious *p* . . . . . .2 Pet 1:4

PROMPTLY

him disciplines him *p* . . . .Prov 13:24

PROOF

which is to them a *p* . . . . . .Phil 1:28

PROOFS

by many infallible *p* . . . . . . .Acts 1:3

PROPER

you, but for what is *p* . . . .1 Cor 7:35
Is it *p* for a woman to . .1 Cor 11:13
but, which is *p* . . . . .1 Tim 2:10

PROPERLY

Let us walk *p* . . . . .Rom 13:13

PROPHECY

miracles, to another *p* . . .1 Cor 12:10
for *p* never came by the . . .2 Pet 1:21
is the spirit of *p* . . . . .Rev 19:10
of the book of this *p* . . . . . .Rev 22:19

PROPHESIED

upon them, that they *p* . .Num 11:25
to them, yet they *p* . . . . . .Jer 23:21
Lord, have we not *p* . . . . . .Matt 7:22
prophets and the law *p* . .Matt 11:13
virgin daughters who *p* . . . .Acts 21:9
even more that you *p* . . . .1 Cor 14:5

PROPHESIES

for the prophet who *p* . . . . .Jer 28:9
woman who prays or *p* . . .1 Cor 11:5
p edifies the church . . . . . .1 Cor 14:4

PROPHESY

prophets, "Do not *p* . . . . . . .Is 30:10
the prophets *p* falsely . . . . .Jer 5:31
your daughters shall *p* . . . .Joel 2:28
Who can but *p* . . . . .Amos 3:8
saying, "*P* to us . . . . .Matt 26:68
your daughters shall *p* . . . .Acts 2:17
if prophecy, let us *p* . . . . . .Rom 12:6
know in part and we *p* . . .1 Cor 13:9
desire earnestly to *p* . . . .1 Cor 14:39

PROPHET

shall be your *p* . . . . .Ex 7:1
raise up for you a *P* . . . . .Deut 18:15
arisen in Israel a *P* . . . . .Deut 34:10
"I alone am left a *p* . . . .1 Kin 18:22
is no longer any *p* . . . . .Ps 74:9
I ordained you a *p* . . . . .Jer 1:5
p is induced to speak . . . .Ezek 14:9
The *p* is a fool. . . . . .Hos 9:7
nor was I a son of a *p* . . .Amos 7:14
send you Elijah the *p* . . . . . .Mal 4:5
p shall receive a . . . . . . .Matt 10:41
p is not without honor . .Matt 13:57
by Daniel the *p* . . . . .Mark 13:14
is not a greater *p* . . . . . . .Luke 7:28
it cannot be that a *p* . . .Luke 13:33
Nazareth, who was a *P* . .Luke 24:19
"Are you the *P* . . . . .John 1:21
"This is truly the *P* . . . . .John 6:14
with him the false *p* . . . . .Rev 19:20

PROPHETIC

p word confirmed . . . . .2 Pet 1:19

PROPHETS

LORD's people were *p* . . . .Num 11:29
Saul also among the *p* . .1 Sam 10:12
the mouth of all his *p* . . .1 Kin 22:22
Where now are your *p* . . . .Jer 37:19
prophesy against the *p* . . .Ezek 13:2
Her *p* are insolent . . . . .Zeph 3:4
the Law or the *P* . . . . .Matt 5:17
is the Law and the *P* . . . . .Matt 7:12
or one of the *p* . . . . .Matt 16:14
the tombs of the *p* . . . . . .Matt 23:29
indeed, I send you *p* . . . . .Matt 23:34
one who kills the *p* . . . . . .Matt 23:37
Then many false *p* . . . . . .Matt 24:11
have Moses and the *p* . . .Luke 16:29
You are sons of the *p* . . . .Acts 3:25
p did your fathers not . . . .Acts 7:52
To Him all the *p* . . . . . . .Acts 10:43
do you believe the *p* . . . .Acts 26:27
before through His *p* . . . . . .Rom 1:2
by the Law and the *P* . . . .Rom 3:21

PROUD (column header)

have killed Your *p* . . . . . . .Rom 11:3
p are subject to the . . . . .1 Cor 14:32
to be apostles, some *p* . . . . .Eph 4:11
brethren, take the *p* . . . .James 5:10
this salvation the *p* . . . . . .1 Pet 1:10
were also false *p* . . . . .2 Pet 2:1
because many false *p* . . . .1 John 4:1
blood of saints and *p* . . . . .Rev 16:6
found the blood of *p* . . . . . .Rev 18:24
of your brethren the *p* . . . . .Rev 22:9

PROPITIATION

set forth as a *p* . . . . .Rom 3:25
to God, to make *p* . . . . .Heb 2:17
He Himself is the *p* . . . . .1 John 2:2
His Son to be the *p* . . . . .1 John 4:10

PROPORTION

let us prophesy in *p* . . . . . .Rom 12:6

PROPRIETY

modest apparel, with *p* . . . .1 Tim 2:9

PROSECUTOR

answer me, that my *P* . . . .Job 31:35

PROSELYTE

and sea to win one *p* . . . .Matt 23:15

PROSELYTES

Rome, both Jews and *p* . . .Acts 2:10

PROSPER

made all he did to *p* . . . . . .Gen 39:3
you shall not *p* . . . . .Deut 28:29
LORD, God made him *p* . . .2 Chr 26:5
they *p* who love you . . . . . .Ps 122:6
his sins will not *p* . . . . . . .Prov 28:13
of the LORD shall *p* . . . . . . .Is 53:10
against you shall *p* . . . . .Is 54:17
please, and it shall *p* . . . . . .Is 55:11
of the wicked *p* . . . . .Jer 12:1
King shall reign and *p* . . . .Jer 23:5
storing up as he may *p* . . .1 Cor 16:2
I pray that you may *p* . . . .3 John 2

PROSPERED

since the LORD has *p* . . . . .Gen 24:56

PROSPERING

His ways are always *p* . . . . .Ps 10:5

PROSPERITY

p all your days . . . . .Deut 23:6
p exceed the fame . . . . . . .1 Kin 10:7
p the destroyer . . . . .Job 15:21
spend their days in *p* . . . .Job 36:11
Now in my *p* I said . . . . . . .Ps 30:6
has pleasure in the *p* . . . . .Ps 35:27
when I saw the *p* . . . . .Ps 73:3
I pray, send now *p* . . . . . .Ps 118:25
the day of *p* be joyful . . . .Eccl 7:14
that we have our *p* . . . . . .Acts 19:25

PROSPEROUS

had made his journey *p* . . .Gen 24:21
will make your way *p* . . . . . .Josh 1:8

PROSPERS

he turns, he *p* . . . . .Prov 17:8
just as your soul *p* . . . . . . .3 John 2

PROSTRATE

of the proud lie *p* . . . . .Job 9:13

PROUD

p waves must stop . . . . . .Job 38:11
tongue that speaks *p* . . . . . .Ps 12:3
and fully repays the *p* . . . . .Ps 31:23
does not respect the *p* . . . . .Ps 40:4
a haughty look and a *p* . . .Ps 101:5

PROVE

p He knows from afar .....Ps 138:6
the house of the *p*......Prov 15:25
Everyone *p*............Prov 16:5
p heart stirs up ....Prov 28:25
is better than the *p*.......Eccl 7:8
by wine, he is a *p*.........Hab 2:5
He has scattered the *p*...Luke 1:51
"God resists the *p*.......1 Pet 5:5

PROVE

p yourself a man ....1 Kin 2:2
does your arguing *p* ......Job 6:25
mind, that you may *p*.....Rom 12:2

PROVERB

an astonishment, a *p* ...Deut 28:37
incline my ear to a *p*........Ps 49:4
that hang limp is a *p* ....Prov 26:7
of a drunkard is a *p* ......Prov 26:9
one shall take up a *p* ......Mic 2:4
to the true *p* ....2 Pet 2:22

PROVERBS

spoke three thousand *p*...1 Kin 4:32
in order many *p* ....Eccl 12:9

PROVIDE

"My son, God will *p* .....Gen 22:8
Can He *p* meat for His...Ps 78:20
prosperity that I *p*.......Jer 33:9
"*P* neither gold nor......Matt 10:9
if anyone does not *p* ......1 Tim 5:8

PROVIDED

these hands have *p* ......Acts 20:34
p something better ......Heb 11:40

PROVIDES

p food for the raven ......Job 38:41
p her supplies in the.......Prov 6:8

PROVISION

abundantly bless her *p*...Ps 132:15
no *p* for the flesh........Rom 13:14

PROVOKE

do not *p* Him ....Ex 23:21
p God are secure ....Job 12:6
"Do they *p* Me to ....Jer 7:19
p them to jealousy ......Rom 11:11
you, fathers, do not *p* .....Eph 6:4

PROVOKED

How often they *p*........Ps 78:40
p the Most High..........Ps 78:56
Thus they *p* Him to......Ps 106:29
his spirit was *p* ....Acts 17:16
seek its own, is not *p*.....1 Cor 13:5

PRUDENCE

to give *p* to the ....Prov 1:4
wisdom, dwell with *p* ....Prov 8:12
us in all wisdom and *p* ....Eph 1:8

PRUDENT

p man covers shame ....Prov 12:16
A *p* man conceals ......Prov 12:23
The wisdom of the *p*.....Prov 14:8
p considers well........Prov 14:15
heart will be called *p*...Prov 16:21
p acquires knowledge ....Prov 18:15
p wife is from the ....Prov 19:14
p man foresees evil ......Prov 22:3
perished from the *p*......Jer 49:7
Therefore the *p* ....Amos 5:13
from the wise and *p*...Matt 11:25

PRUDENTLY

Servant shall deal *p*.......Is 52:13

PRUNES

that bears fruit He *p* ....John 15:2

PSALM

and the sound of a *p*......Ps 98:5
in the second *P* ....Acts 13:33
each of you has a *p* .....1 Cor 14:26

PSALMIST

and the sweet *p* ....2 Sam 23:1

PSALMS

Sing to Him, sing *p*......1 Chr 16:9
to one another in *p*.......Eph 5:19
Let him sing *p*.........James 5:13

PSALTERY

harp, lyre, and *p*.........Dan 3:10

PUBLISHED

to be proclaimed and *p*.....Jon 3:7

PUFFED

Now some are *p* up .....1 Cor 4:18
itself, is not *p*...........1 Cor 13:4
a novice, lest being *p* .....1 Tim 3:6

PUFFS

Knowledge *p* up..........1 Cor 8:1

PULL

P me out of the net ....Ps 31:4
I will *p* down my barns .Luke 12:18

PUNISH

take that man and *p*.....Deut 22:18
p the righteous is ....Prov 17:26
"I will *p* the world.........Is 13:11
Shall I not *p* them for......Jer 5:9
p all who oppress them....Jer 30:20
p your iniquity..........Lam 4:22
So I will *p* them for ....Hos 4:9

PUNISHED

You our God have *p* .....Ezra 9:13
because He has not *p*.....Job 35:15
p them often in every ....Acts 26:11
These shall be *p*........2 Thess 1:9

PUNISHES

will you say when He *p*...Jer 13:21

PUNISHMENT

p is greater than I ....Gen 4:13
you do in the day of *p*.....Is 10:3
p they shall be cast ......Jer 8:12
p they shall perish.......Jer 10:15
a man for the *p* ....Lam 3:39
The *p* of the iniquity......Lam 4:6
days of *p* have come.......Hos 9:7
not turn away its *p* ......Amos 1:3
into everlasting *p* ......Matt 25:46
p which was inflicted.....2 Cor 2:6
Of how much worse *p* ...Heb 10:29
sent by him for the *p*....1 Pet 2:14
the unjust under *p*.......2 Pet 2:9

PURCHASED

of God could be *p* ......Acts 8:20
of the *p* possession.......Eph 1:14

PURE

a mercy seat of *p* gold....Ex 25:17
Can a man be more *p*....Job 4:17
if you were *p* and..........Job 8:6
'My doctrine is *p*........Job 11:4
that he could be *p*.......Job 15:14
the heavens are not *p*....Job 15:15
the stars are not *p* ....Job 25:5
of the LORD are *p*........Ps 12:6
will show Yourself *p* ......Ps 18:26

To such as are *p* ....Ps 73:1
of the *p* are pleasant.....Prov 15:26
ways of a man are *p* ......Prov 16:2
my heart clean, I am *p*....Prov 20:9
but as for the *p*..........Prov 21:8
a generation that is *p* ....Prov 30:12
Shall I count *p* ....Mic 6:11
things indeed are *p*......Rom 14:20
whatever things are *p* ......Phil 4:8
keep yourself *p* ....1 Tim 5:22
p all things are *p* ....Titus 1:15
above is first *p* ....James 3:17
babes, desire the *p*.......1 Pet 2:2
just as He is *p*...........1 John 3:3

PURER

p eyes than to behold .....Hab 1:13

PURGE

P me with hyssop..........Ps 51:7
p them as gold and........Mal 3:3

PURGED

away, and your sin *p* ....Is 6:7
He had by Himself *p*......Heb 1:3

PURIFICATION

for the water of *p* ....Num 19:9
with the water of *p*......Num 31:23

PURIFIED

earth, *p* seven times ....Ps 12:6
all things are *p*..........Heb 9:22
Since you have *p*........1 Pet 1:22

PURIFIES

hope in Him *p* himself ...1 John 3:3

PURIFY

p the sons of Levi........Mal 3:3
and *p* your hearts.......James 4:8

PURIFYING

thus *p* all foods ....Mark 7:19
p their hearts by ....Acts 15:9
sanctifies for the *p*.......Heb 9:13

PURIM

called these days *P*......Esth 9:26

PURITY

be delivered by the *p* .....Job 22:30
He who loves *p* of ......Prov 22:11
by *p*, by knowledge ......2 Cor 6:6
spirit, in faith, in *p* ......1 Tim 4:12

PURPLE

who was clothed in *p* ...Luke 16:19
they put on Him a *p*.....John 19:2
She was a seller of *p*.....Acts 16:14

PURPOSE

and fulfill all your *p*.......Ps 20:4
a time for every *p* ....Eccl 3:1
p that is purposed.........Is 14:26
But for this *p* I came...John 12:27
by the determined *p* .....Acts 2:23
them all that with *p* .....Acts 11:23
to the eternal *p*...........Eph 3:11
Now the *p* of the ....1 Tim 1:5
to fulfill His *p* ....Rev 17:17

PURPOSED

For the LORD had *p* ...2 Sam 17:14
LORD of hosts has *p* ....Is 23:9
But Daniel *p* in his ......Dan 1:8
pleasure which He *p* ....Eph 1:9

PURPOSES

each one give as he *p*......2 Cor 9:7

PURSE

let us all have one *p* ......Prov 1:14

PURSES

p his lips and brings.....Prov 16:30

PURSUE

And will You *p* dry ......Job 13:25
p my honor as the wind ...Job 30:15
The sword shall *p*.........Jer 48:2
but their hearts *p*.......Ezek 33:31
Let us know, let us *p* ......Hos 6:3
p righteousness ....Rom 9:30
P love ....1 Cor 14:1
p righteousness ....1 Tim 6:11
him seek peace and *p*.....1 Pet 3:11

PURSUES

Evil *p* sinners ....Prov 13:21
flee when no one *p* ......Prov 28:1

PURSUING

but Israel, *p* the law ......Rom 9:31

PUT

Also He has *p* eternity ...Eccl 3:11
pride He is able to *p* down Dan 4:37
what you will *p* on ......Matt 6:25
p my hand into His ....John 20:25
But *p* on the Lord ......Rom 13:14

PUTREFYING

bruises and *p* sores ....Is 1:6

Q

QUAIL

and it brought *q* ......Num 11:31
and He brought *q* ......Ps 105:40

QUAKED

the whole mountain *q* ....Ex 19:18
and the earth *q*........Matt 27:51

QUAKES

The earth *q* before ....Joel 2:10

QUALIFIED

the Father who has *q* .....Col 1:12

QUARREL

see how he seeks a *q* .....2 Kin 5:7
any fool can start a *q* ....Prov 20:3
He will not *q* nor cry ....Matt 12:19
of the Lord must not *q* ...2 Tim 2:24

QUARRELSOME

but gentle, not *q* ....1 Tim 3:3

QUARTZ

be made of coral or *q* ....Job 28:18

QUEEN

Q Vashti also made a .....Esth 1:9
hand stands the *q*........Ps 45:9
burn incense to the *q* ....Jer 44:17
"The *q* of the South ....Matt 12:42
under Candace the *q*.....Acts 8:27
heart, 'I sit as *q* ....Rev 18:7

QUEENS

There are sixty *q* ....Song 6:8
q your nursing mothers ....Is 49:23

QUENCH

Many waters cannot *q* .....Song 8:7
so that no one can *q* ....Jer 4:4
flax He will not *q* ......Matt 12:20
q all the fiery ....Eph 6:16
Do not *q* the Spirit ....1 Thess 5:19

QUENCHED

LORD, the fire was *q* .....Num 11:2
they were *q* like a ....Ps 118:12
their fire is not *q* ....Is 66:24
that shall never be *q* .....Mark 9:43
and the fire is not *q*......Mark 9:44
q the violence of fire .....Heb 11:34

QUESTIONS

test him with hard *q* .....1 Kin 10:1
and asking them ......Luke 2:46
market, asking no *q*.....1 Cor 10:25

QUICK-TEMPERED

q man acts foolishly .....Prov 14:17
not self-willed, not *q* ......Titus 1:7

QUICKLY

have turned aside *q* ....Ex 32:8
with your adversary *q* ....Matt 5:25
"What you do, do *q* ....John 13:27
"Behold, I am coming *q*....Rev 3:11
Surely I am coming *q*.....Rev 22:20

QUIET

lain still and been *q* ......Job 3:13
'Take heed, and be *q* ....Is 7:4
earth is at rest and *q*........Is 14:7
gladness, He will *q*......Zeph 3:17
warned him to be *q* ....Mark 10:48
aspire to lead a *q* ......1 Thess 4:11
we may lead a *q* and.....1 Tim 2:2
a gentle and *q* spirit.......1 Pet 3:4

QUIETED

calmed and *q* my soul ....Ps 131:2
the city clerk had *q*.....Acts 19:35

QUIETNESS

will give peace and *q*.....1 Chr 22:9
When He gives *q* ....Job 34:29
a handful with *q*..........Eccl 4:6
in *q* and confidence ......Is 30:15
of righteousness, *q* ....Is 32:17
that they work in *q* ...2 Thess 3:12

QUIETS

q the earth by the.......Job 37:17

QUIVER

q rattles against him ....Job 39:23
the man who has his *q*.....Ps 127:5
q He has hidden Me ....Is 49:2
Their *q* is like an ....Jer 5:16

R

RABBI

be called by men, '*R*......Matt 23:7
do not be called '*R* ......Matt 23:8

RACA

to his brother, '*R* ....Matt 5:22

RACE

man to run its *r*...........Ps 19:5
r is not to the swift ....Eccl 9:11
who run in a *r* all run ...1 Cor 9:24
I have finished the *r* .....2 Tim 4:7
with endurance the *r* .....Heb 12:1

RADIANT

to Him and were *r*..........Ps 34:5

RAGE

Disperse the *r* of your ....Job 40:11
Why do the nations *r*........Ps 2:1
'Why did the nations *r*....Acts 4:25

RAGES

he *r* against all wise ......Prov 18:1

RAGS

clothe a man with *r*......Prov 23:21

RAIN

had not caused it to *r* ......Gen 2:5
And the *r* was on the......Gen 7:12
He gives *r* on the ....Job 5:10
to the gentle *r*...........Job 37:6
sent a plentiful *r*..........Ps 68:9
clouds, who prepares *r* ....Ps 147:8
snow in summer and *r* ....Prov 26:1
r which leaves no food ...Prov 28:3
not return after the *r*......Eccl 12:2
the *r* is over and gone ....Song 2:11
our God, who gives *r*.......Jer 5:24
I will *r* down on him.....Ezek 38:22
given you the former *r*.....Joel 2:23
there will be no *r*........Zech 14:17
the good, and sends *r*.....Matt 5:45
"and the *r* descended ....Matt 7:25
He did good, gave us *r*....Acts 14:17
r that often comes ....Heb 6:7
that it would not *r*......James 5:17
and the heaven gave *r* ...James 5:18

RAINBOW

"I set My *r* in the ....Gen 9:13
and there was a *r* ....Rev 4:3

RAINED

had *r* down manna on....Ps 78:24
r fire and brimstone .....Luke 17:29

RAINS

r righteousness..........Hos 10:12

RAISE

third day He will *r*........Hos 6:2
that God is able to *r*......Matt 3:9
in three days I will *r*.....John 2:19
and I will *r* him up at....John 6:40
Lord and will also *r*......1 Cor 6:14
and the Lord will *r*.....James 5:15

RAISED

this purpose I have *r*......Ex 9:16
be killed, and be *r*......Matt 16:21
"whom God *r* up ....Acts 2:24
just as Christ was *r*......Rom 6:4
Spirit of Him who *r*......Rom 8:11
And God both *r* up the ...1 Cor 6:14
"How are the dead *r* ...1 Cor 15:35
and the dead will be *r* ...1 Cor 15:52
and *r* us up together ......Eph 2:6
then you were *r* ....Col 3:1

RAISES

r the poor out of the......Ps 113:7
r those who are bowed ...Ps 146:8
For as the Father *r*......John 5:21
but in God who *r*........2 Cor 1:9

RAM

r which had two horns.....Dan 8:3

RAMS

the sweet aroma of *r*......Ps 66:15
r of Nebaioth shall.........Is 60:7

RAN

they both *r* together......John 20:4
You *r* well ....Gal 5:7

RANSOM

r would not help you......Job 36:18
nor give to God a *r*.......Ps 49:7
The *r* of a man's life .....Prov 13:8

RANSOMED

"I will *r* them from . . . . . .Hos 13:14
to give His life a *r* . . . . .Mark 10:45
who gave Himself a *r* . . . . .1 Tim 2:6

RANSOMED

and the *r* of the LORD . . . . . .Is 35:10
redeemed Jacob, and *r* . . . .Jer 31:11

RARE

of the LORD was *r* . . . . .1 Sam 3:1
make a mortal more *r* . . . . . .Is 13:12

RASH

Do not be *r* with your . . . . .Eccl 5:2

RASHLY

so that he spoke *r* . . . . . . .Ps 106:33
and do nothing *r* . . . . . .Acts 19:36

RAVEN

food for the *r* . . . . .Job 38:41
and black as a *r* . . . . .Song 5:11

RAVENOUS

inwardly they are *r* . . . . . .Matt 7:15

RAVENS

and to the young *r* . . . . . . .Ps 147:9
"Consider the *r* . . . . .Luke 12:24

RAVISHED

You have *r* my heart . . . . . .Song 4:9
r the women in Zion . . . . .Lam 5:11

RAZOR

like a sharp *r* . . . . .Ps 52:2

REACHED

earth, and its top *r* . . . . . .Gen 28:12
For her sins have *r* . . . . . .Rev 18:5

REACHING

r forward to those . . . . .Phil 3:13

READ

"Have you never *r* . . . . . .Matt 21:42
day, and stood up to *r* . . . .Luke 4:16
hearts, known and *r* . . . . . .2 Cor 3:2
when Moses is *r* . . . . .2 Cor 3:15
when this epistle is *r* . . . . . .Col 4:16

READER

let the *r* understand . . . .Mark 13:14

READINESS

the word with all *r* . . . . . .Acts 17:11
that as there was a *r* . . . .2 Cor 8:11

READING

r the prophet Isaiah . . . . . .Acts 8:30
give attention to *r* . . . . . .1 Tim 4:13

READS

that he may run who *r* . . . .Hab 2:2
Blessed is he who *r* . . . . .Rev 1:3

READY

" The LORD was *r* . . . . .Is 38:20
and those who were *r* . . . .Matt 25:10
"Lord, I am *r* . . . . .Luke 22:33
and being *r* to punish . . . .2 Cor 10:6
Be *r* in season and out . . . .2 Tim 4:2
and always be *r* . . . . .1 Pet 3:15

REAFFIRM

r your love to him . . . . . .2 Cor 2:8

REAP

in tears shall *r* . . . . .Ps 126:5
r the whirlwind . . . . .Hos 8:7
they neither sow nor *r* . . . .Matt 6:26
you knew that I *r* . . . . . . .Matt 25:26

that he will also *r* . . . . .Gal 6:7
due season we shall *r* . . . . . . .Gal 6:9

REAPED

wheat but *r* thorns . . . . . . .Jer 12:13
you have *r* iniquity . . . . . . .Hos 10:13

REAPER

r does not fill his . . . . .Ps 129:7

REAPERS

I will say to the *r* . . . . . .Matt 13:30
r are the angels . . . . .Matt 13:39

REAPING

r what I did not . . . . .Luke 19:22

REAPS

One sows and another *r* . . John 4:37

REASON

out wisdom and the *r* . . . .Eccl 7:25
Come now, and let us *r* . . . . .Is 1:18
faith, why do you *r* . . . . . .Matt 16:8
words of truth and *r* . . . . .Acts 26:25
who asks you a *r* . . . . .1 Pet 3:15

REASONED

for three Sabbaths *r* . . . . . .Acts 17:2
r about righteousness . . . .Acts 24:25

REBEL

"Only do not *r* . . . . .Num 14:9
Will you *r* against the . . . .Neh 2:19
There are those who *r* . . . .Job 24:13
and they did not *r* . . . . . .Ps 105:28
if you refuse and *r* . . . . .Is 1:20

REBELLING

more against Him by *r* . . . . .Ps 78:17

REBELLION

r is as the sin . . . . .1 Sam 15:23
For he adds *r* to his . . . . .Job 34:37
evil man seeks only *r* . . . .Prov 17:11
you have taught *r* . . . . . . .Jer 28:16
hearts as in the *r* . . . . .Heb 3:8
and perished in the *r* . . . . . .Jude 11

REBELLIOUS

r exalt themselves . . . . .Ps 66:7
but the *r* dwell in a . . . . . . .Ps 68:6
day long to a *r* people . . . . . .Is 65:2
a defiant and *r* heart . . . . . .Jer 5:23
their princes are *r* . . . . .Hos 9:15

REBELS

are all stubborn *r* . . . . .Jer 6:28

REBUILD

God, to *r* its ruins . . . . .Ezra 9:9
tombs, that I may *r* . . . . . . .Neh 2:5
r it as in the days of . . . .Amos 9:11

REBUKE

He will surely *r* . . . . .Job 13:10
astonished at His *r* . . . . . .Job 26:11
they perish at the *r* . . . . . .Ps 80:16
At Your *r* they fled . . . . . .Ps 104:7
And let him *r* me . . . . .Ps 141:5
Turn at my *r* . . . . .Prov 1:23
r a wise man . . . . .Prov 9:8
R is more effective . . . . . .Prov 17:10
r is better than love . . . . .Prov 27:5
better to hear the *r* . . . . . .Eccl 7:5
the *r* of the oppressor . . . . .Is 1:17
sake I have suffered *r* . . . .Jer 15:15
r strong nations . . . . .Mic 4:3
sins against you, *r* . . . . . .Luke 17:3
r Your disciples . . . . .Luke 19:39
Do not *r* an older man . . . .1 Tim 5:1

who are sinning *r* . . . . .1 Tim 5:20
r them sharply . . . . .Titus 1:13
The Lord *r* you . . . . .Jude 9
As many as I love, I *r* . . . . .Rev 3:19

REBUKED

r the winds and the . . . . . .Matt 8:26
r their unbelief . . . . .Mark 16:14
when you are *r* by Him . . . .Heb 12:5
but he was *r* for his . . . . . .2 Pet 2:16

REBUKES

with *r* You correct . . . . .Ps 39:11
r a wicked man . . . . .Prov 9:7
ear that hears the *r* . . . . . .Prov 15:31
r a man will find more . . .Prov 28:23

RECALL

r the former days . . . . . . .Heb 10:32

RECEIVE

He shall *r* blessing . . . . .Ps 24:5
r us graciously . . . . .Hos 14:2
you are willing to *r* . . . . .Matt 11:14
believing, you will *r* . . . . .Matt 21:22
and His own did not *r* . . . . .John 1:11
"I do not *r* honor . . . . . . .John 5:41
will come again and *r* . . . . .John 14:3
the world cannot *r* . . . . . .John 14:17
Ask, and you will *r* . . . . .John 16:24
R the Holy Spirit . . . . . . .John 20:22
"Lord Jesus, *r* . . . . .Acts 7:59
r the Holy Spirit . . . . .Acts 19:2
R one who is weak . . . . . .Rom 14:1
that each one may *r* . . . . . .2 Cor 5:10
r the grace of God in . . . . .2 Cor 6:1
r the Spirit by the . . . . .Gal 3:2
R him therefore in the . . . .Phil 2:29
suppose that he will *r* . . . .James 1:7
whatever we ask we *r* . . .1 John 3:22

RECEIVED

r your consolation . . . . . . .Luke 6:24
in your lifetime you *r* . . . .Luke 16:25
But as many as *r* . . . . . . .John 1:12
for God has *r* him . . . . . . .Rom 14:3
For I *r* from the Lord . . .1 Cor 11:23
r Christ . . . . .Col 2:6
r up in glory . . . . .1 Tim 3:16
For He *r* from God the . . .2 Pet 1:17

RECEIVES

r correction is prudent . . . .Prov 15:5
r you Me . . . . .Matt 10:40
r one little child . . . . .Matt 18:5
and whoever *r* Me . . . . . .Mark 9:37

RECEIVING

r a kingdom which . . . . . . .Heb 12:28

RECOMPENSE

He will accept no *r* . . . . . . .Prov 6:35
not say, "I will *r* . . . . . . .Prov 20:22
days of *r* have come . . . . .Hos 9:7

RECOMPENSED

of my hands He has *r* . .2 Sam 22:21
the LORD has *r* me . . . .2 Sam 22:25

RECONCILE

and that He might *r* . . . . . .Eph 2:16
r all things to . . . . .Col 1:20

RECONCILED

First be *r* to your . . . . . . .Matt 5:24
were enemies we were *r* . . . .Rom 5:10
Christ's behalf, be *r* . . . . . .2 Cor 5:20

RECONCILIATION

now received the *r* . . . . . . .Rom 5:11
to us the word of *r* . . . . . .2 Cor 5:19

RECONCILING

cast away is the r . . . . . . .Rom 11:15
God was in Christ r . . . . . .2 Cor 5:19

RECORD

r My name I will come . . . .Ex 20:24

RED

the first came out r . . . . . .Gen 25:25
though they are r . . . . .Is 1:18
Why is Your apparel r . . . . . . .Is 63:2
for the sky is r . . . . .Matt 16:2

REDEEM

man you shall surely r . . .Num 18:15
in our power to r them . . . . . .Neh 5:5
In famine He shall r . . . . . . .Job 5:20
R me from the hand of . . . .Job 6:23
can by any means r . . . . .Ps 49:7
But God will r my soul . . . .Ps 49:15
r their life from . . . . .Ps 72:14
And He shall r Israel . . . . . .Ps 130:8
all that it cannot r . . . . .Is 50:2
I will r them from . . . . . . .Hos 13:14
was going to r Israel . . .Luke 24:21
r those who were . . . . .Gal 4:5
us, that He might r . . . . .Titus 2:14

REDEEMED

people whom You have r . . .Ex 15:13
r them from the hand . . . . .Ps 106:10
Let the r of the LORD . . . . . .Ps 107:2
r shall walk there . . . . .Is 35:9
sea a road for the r . . . . . . .Is 51:10
and you shall be r . . . . .Is 52:3
and r His people . . . . .Luke 1:68
Christ has r us from . . . . . .Gal 3:13
that you were not r . . . . . .1 Pet 1:18
were slain, and have r . . . . .Rev 5:9
These were r from . . . . .Rev 14:4

REDEEMER

For I know that my R . . . .Job 19:25
Most High God their R . . . .Ps 78:35
for their R is mighty . . . .Prov 23:11
the LORD and your R . . . . . .Is 41:14
R will come to Zion . . . . . .Is 59:20
our R from Everlasting . . . . .Is 63:16
Their R is strong . . . . .Jer 50:34

REDEEMING

r the time . . . . .Eph 5:16

REDEMPTION

For the r of their . . . . .Ps 49:8
with Him is abundant . . . .Ps 130:7
r is yours to buy it . . . . .Jer 32:7
those who looked for r . . . .Luke 2:38
your r draws near . . . . . .Luke 21:28
grace through the r . . . . . .Rom 3:24
the adoption, the r . . . . . .Rom 8:23
sanctification and r . . . . .1 Cor 1:30
In Him we have r . . . . .Eph 1:7
for the day of r . . . . .Eph 4:30
obtained eternal r . . . . .Heb 9:12

REED

r He will not break . . . . .Is 42:3
r shaken by the wind . . . . .Matt 11:7
on the head with a r . . . .Mark 15:19

REEDS

r flourish without . . . . .Job 8:11
the beasts of the r . . . . . . .Ps 68:30

REFINED

where gold is r . . . . .Job 28:1
us as silver is r . . . . .Ps 66:10

REFINER

He will sit as a r . . . . .Mal 3:3

REFORMATION

until the time of r . . . . . . .Heb 9:10

REFRAIN

R from meddling with. . .2 Chr 35:21
who have no right to r . . . . .1 Cor 9:6
good days, let him r . . . . .1 Pet 3:10

REFRESH

bread, that you may r . . . . .Gen 18:5
r my heart in the Lord . . . .Philem 20

REFRESHED

of God, and may be r . . . .Rom 15:32
his spirit has been r . . . . . .2 Cor 7:13
for he often r . . . . .2 Tim 1:16

REFRESHES

r the soul of his . . . . .Prov 25:13

REFRESHING

r may come from the . . . . .Acts 3:19

REFUGE

six cities of r . . . . .Num 35:6
eternal God is your r . . . .Deut 33:27
you have come for r . . . . . .Ruth 2:12
but the LORD is his r . . . . . .Ps 14:6
God is our r and . . . . .Ps 46:1
wings I will make my r . . . . .Ps 57:1
God is a r for us . . . . .Ps 62:8
You are my strong r . . . . . . .Ps 71:7
who have fled for r . . . . . . .Heb 6:18

REFUSE

r the evil and choose . . . . .Is 7:15
through deceit they r . . . . . . .Jer 9:6
hear or whether they r . . . .Ezek 2:5
See that you do not r . . . . .Heb 12:25

REFUSED

They r to obey . . . . .Neh 9:17

REFUSES

My soul r to touch . . . . .Job 6:7
"And if he r to hear . . . . .Matt 18:17

REGARD

r the rich more than . . . . . .Job 34:19
r iniquity in my heart . . . . . .Ps 66:18
r the prayer of the . . . . . . .Ps 102:17
did not fear God nor r . . . .Luke 18:2

REGARDED

my hand and no one r . . . . .Prov 1:24
r the lowly state . . . . .Luke 1:48

REGARDS

r a rebuke will be . . . . . . .Prov 13:18
He no longer r them . . . . . .Lam 4:16

REGENERATION

to you, that in the r . . . .Matt 19:28
the washing of r . . . . .Titus 3:5

REGISTERED

So all went to be r . . . . . . .Luke 2:3
firstborn who are r . . . . . .Heb 12:23

REGRETTED

but afterward he r . . . . . .Matt 21:29

REGULATIONS

yourselves to r . . . . .Col 2:20

REIGN

but a king shall r . . . . . .1 Sam 12:12

hypocrite should not r . . . .Job 34:30
so the LORD will r . . . . .Mic 4:7
"And He will r . . . . .Luke 1:33
not have this man to r . . .Luke 19:14
righteousness will r . . . . . . .Rom 5:17
so grace might r . . . . .Rom 5:21
do not let sin r . . . . .Rom 6:12
For He must r till He . . .1 Cor 15:25
and we shall r on the . . . . .Rev 5:10
of Christ, and shall r . . . . . .Rev 20:6

REIGNED

so that as sin r . . . . .Rom 5:21
You have r as kings . . . . . . .1 Cor 4:8
And they lived and r . . . . . .Rev 20:4

REIGNS

God r over the nations . . . . . .Ps 47:8
The LORD r . . . . .Ps 93:1
to Zion, "Your God r . . . . . . .Is 52:7
Lord God Omnipotent r . . . .Rev 19:6

REJECT

will these people r . . . . . .Num 14:11
r all those who stray . . . .Ps 119:118
"All too well you r . . . . . .Mark 7:9
R a divisive man . . . . .Titus 3:10

REJECTED

r has become the chief . . . .Ps 118:22
He is despised and r . . . . . . .Is 53:3
Israel has r the . . . . .Hos 8:3
r has become the chief . .Matt 21:42
many things and be r . . . .Luke 17:25
This Moses whom they r . .Acts 7:35
to a living stone, r . . . . .1 Pet 2:4
r has become the chief . . . .1 Pet 2:7

REJECTION

you shall know My r . . . . .Num 14:34

REJECTS

he who r Me r . . . . .Luke 10:16
r this does not reject . . . .1 Thess 4:8

REJOICE

so the LORD will r . . . . . .Deut 28:63
let the field r . . . . .1 Chr 16:32
and let Your saints r . . . . .2 Chr 6:41
r who put their trust . . . . . . .Ps 5:11
people, let Jacob r . . . . .Ps 14:7
R in the LORD . . . . .Ps 33:1
mutual confusion who r . . . .Ps 35:26
The righteous shall r . . . . . .Ps 58:10
of Your wings I will r . . . . . . .Ps 63:7
But the king shall r . . . . . . .Ps 63:11
Let them r before God . . . . .Ps 68:3
In Your name they r . . . . . .Ps 89:16
Let the heavens r . . . . .Ps 96:11
Let the earth r . . . . .Ps 97:1
righteous see it and r . . . . .Ps 107:42
we will r and be glad . . . . .Ps 118:24
who r in doing evil . . . . . .Prov 2:14
be blessed, and r . . . . .Prov 5:18
she shall r in time to . . . .Prov 31:25
R, O young man . . . . .Eccl 11:9
We will be glad and r . . . . .Song 1:4
among men shall r . . . . .Is 29:19
I will greatly r . . . . .Is 61:10
My servants shall r . . . . .Is 65:13
your heart shall r . . . . .Is 66:14
'Yes, I will r . . . . .Jer 32:41
Do not r over me . . . . .Mic 7:8
He will r over you . . . . . . .Zeph 3:17
Nevertheless do not r . . . .Luke 10:20
loved Me, you would r . . .John 14:28
but the world will r . . . . . .John 16:20
and your heart will r . . . . .John 16:22
R with those who . . . . . . .Rom 12:15
and in this I r . . . . .Phil 1:18

REJOICED

faith, I am glad and *r* . . . . .Phil 2:17
R in the Lord always . . . . . . .Phil 4:4
R always . . . . .1 Thess 5:16
yet believing, you *r* . . . . .1 Pet 1:8

REJOICED

for good as He *r* . . . . .Deut 30:9
for my heart *r* . . . . .Eccl 2:10
and my spirit has *r* . . . . . .Luke 1:47
In that hour Jesus *r* . . . .Luke 10:21
Your father Abraham *r* . . . .John 8:56
But I *r* in the Lord . . . . . . .Phil 4:10

REJOICES

glad, and my glory *r* . . . . . . .Ps 16:9
but *r* in the truth . . . . .1 Cor 13:6

REJOICING

His works with *r* . . . . .Ps 107:22
The voice of *r* and . . . . . . .Ps 118:15
for they are the *r* . . . . . . .Ps 119:111
come again with *r* . . . . .Ps 126:6
r in His inhabited . . . . .Prov 8:31
he went on his way *r* . . . . .Acts 8:39
yet always *r* . . . . .2 Cor 6:10
or joy, or crown of *r* . . . .1 Thess 2:19
confidence and the *r* . . . . . . .Heb 3:6

RELATIVES

r stand afar off . . . . .Ps 38:11

RELEASE

do you want me to *r* . . . . .Matt 27:17
and power to *r* You . . . . .John 19:10
"*R* the four angels . . . . .Rev 9:14

RELENT

sworn and will not *r* . . . . . . .Ps 110:4
and will not *r* . . . . .Jer 4:28
then the Lord will *r* . . . . .Jer 26:13
if He will turn and *r* . . . . . .Joel 2:14
sworn and will not *r* . . . . . .Heb 7:21

RELENTED

So the Lord *r* from the . . . .Ex 32:14
the Lord looked and *r* . .1 Chr 21:15
and God *r* from the . . . . . . .Jon 3:10

RELENTING

I am weary of *r* . . . . .Jer 15:6

RELIEF

saw that there was *r* . . . . . . .Ex 8:15
that I may find *r* . . . . .Job 32:20

RELIEVE

of my lips would *r* . . . . .Job 16:5
r those who are really . . . .1 Tim 5:16

RELIEVED

You have *r* me when I . . . . . . .Ps 4:1

RELIEVES

r the fatherless . . . . .Ps 146:9

RELIGION

about their own *r* . . . . . . .Acts 25:19
in self-imposed *r* . . . . .Col 2:23
heart, this one's *r* . . . . . . .James 1:26
and undefiled *r* . . . . .James 1:27

RELIGIOUS

things you are very *r* . . . .Acts 17:22
you thinks he is *r* . . . . . . .James 1:26

RELY

name of the Lord and *r* . . . .Is 50:10
"You *r* on your sword . . . .Ezek 33:26

REMAIN

shall let none of it *r* . . . . . . .Ex 12:10

r angry forever . . . . .Jer 3:5
and this city shall *r* . . . . . . .Jer 17:25
that if ten men *r* . . . . .Amos 6:9
you, that My joy may *r* . .John 15:11
your fruit should *r* . . . . . .John 15:16
If I will that he *r* . . . . . .John 21:22
the greater part *r* . . . . . . .1 Cor 15:6
Nevertheless to *r* . . . . .Phil 1:24
we who are alive and *r* . .1 Thess 4:15
the things which *r* . . . . .Rev 3:2

REMAINDER

with the *r* of wrath . . . . .Ps 76:10
I am deprived of the *r* . . . . .Is 38:10

REMAINED

Also my wisdom *r* . . . . .Eccl 2:9
And Mary *r* with her . . . .Luke 1:56
like a dove, and He *r* . . . . .John 1:32

REMAINS

"While the earth *r* . . . . . . .Gen 8:22
Therefore your sin *r* . . . . .John 9:41
There *r* therefore a . . . . .Heb 4:9
sin, for His seed *r* . . . . . .1 John 3:9

REMEMBER

"But *r* me when it is . . . . .Gen 40:14
R the Sabbath day . . . . .Ex 20:8
r that you were a . . . . . . .Deut 15:15
R His marvelous works. .1 Chr 16:12
but we will *r* the name . . . .Ps 20:7
r the sins of my youth . . . . .Ps 25:7
r Your name in the . . . . . .Ps 119:55
R now your Creator . . . . . .Eccl 12:1
r your love more than . . . . . .Song 1:4
r the former things . . . . . . .Is 43:18
"*I r* you. . . . . .Jer 2:2
and their sin I will *r* . . . . .Jer 31:34
r the covenant of . . . . .Amos 1:9
in wrath *r* mercy . . . . .Hab 3:2
and to *r* His holy . . . . . . .Luke 1:72
"*R* Lot's wife. . . . . .Luke 17:32
r the words of the . . . . . . .Acts 20:35
R my chains. . . . . .Col 4:18
R that Jesus Christ . . . . . .2 Tim 2:8
R those who rule . . . . .Heb 13:7

REMEMBERED

Then God *r* Noah . . . . .Gen 8:1
r His covenant with . . . . . . .Ex 2:24
I *r* God. . . . . .Ps 77:3
r His covenant forever . . . . .Ps 105:8
r Your judgments . . . . . . .Ps 119:52
Who is in our lowly. . . . .Ps 136:23
yea, we wept when we *r* . . . . .Ps 137:1
r that same poor man . . . .Eccl 9:15
r the days of old. . . . . .Is 63:11
And Peter *r* the word . . . .Matt 26:75
r the word of the Lord . .Acts 11:16

REMEMBERS

My soul still *r* . . . . .Lam 3:20

REMEMBRANCE

in death there is no *r* . . . . . . .Ps 6:5
r my song in the night . . . . .Ps 77:6
There is no *r* of. . . . . .Eccl 1:11
Put Me in *r* . . . . .Is 43:26
do this in *r* of Me . . . . . . .Luke 22:19
do this in *r* of Me. . . . . . .1 Cor 11:24

REMIND

r you always of these . . . . .2 Pet 1:12
But I want to *r* you . . . . .Jude 5

REMINDER

there is a *r* of sins . . . . . . .Heb 10:3
you always have a *r* . . . . . .2 Pet 1:15
pure minds by way of *r* . . . .2 Pet 3:1

REMISSION

repentance for the *r* . . . . . .Mark 1:4
Jesus Christ for the *r* . . . .Acts 2:38
where there is *r* . . . . .Heb 10:18

REMNANT

to us a very small *r* . . . . .Is 1:9
The *r* will return. . . . . .Is 10:21
be well with your *r* . . . . . . .Jer 15:11
I will gather the *r* . . . . .Jer 23:3
and all the *r* of Judah . . . .Jer 44:28
Yet I will leave a *r* . . . . . . .Ezek 6:8
r whom the Lord calls. . . .Joel 2:32
I will not treat the *r* . . . . . .Zech 8:11
time there is a *r* . . . . .Rom 11:5

REMORSEFUL

been condemned, was *r* . . .Matt 27:3

REMOVE

R Your plague from me . . . .Ps 39:10
R Your gaze from me . . . . . .Ps 39:13
r your foot from evil . . . . . .Prov 4:27
r falsehood and lies . . . . . .Prov 30;8
Therefore *r* sorrow . . . . . . .Eccl 11:10
r this cup from Me . . . . . .Luke 22:42
r your lampstand . . . . .Rev 2:5

REMOVED

Though the earth be *r* . . . . . .Ps 46:2
r our transgressions . . . . . .Ps 103:12
will never be *r* . . . . .Prov 10:30
and the hills be *r* . . . . .Is 54:10
this mountain, 'Be *r* . . . . .Matt 21:21

REMOVES

r the mountains. . . . . .Job 9:5

REND

So *r* your heart . . . . .Joel 2:13

RENDER

What shall I *r* to the . . . . .Ps 116:12
who will *r* to him the . . . .Matt 21:41
R therefore to Caesar . . . .Matt 22:21

RENEW

r a steadfast . . . . .Ps 51:10
r the face of the. . . . . .Ps 104:30
on the Lord shall *r* . . . . . . .Is 40:31

RENEWED

that your youth is *r* . . . . . . .Ps 103:5
inward man is being *r* . . . .2 Cor 4:16
and be *r* in the spirit . . . . .Eph 4:23
the new man who is *r* . . . . .Col 3:10

RENEWING

transformed by the *r* . . . . .Rom 12:2
of regeneration and *r* . . . . .Titus 3:5

RENOUNCE

Why do the wicked *r* . . . . . .Ps 10:13

RENOUNCED

r the covenant of Your . . . . .Ps 89:39
r the hidden things . . . . . . .2 Cor 4:2

RENOUNCES

greedy and *r* the Lord . . . . . .Ps 10:3

RENOWN

were of old, men of *r* . . . . . .Gen 6:4

REPAID

done, so God has *r* . . . . .Judg 1:7
And he has *r* me evil . . .1 Sam 25:21
good shall be *r* . . . . .Prov 13:21
Shall evil be *r* . . . . .Jer 18:20

REPAIR

r the house of your ......2 Chr 24:5
r the ruined cities ....Is 61:4

REPAY

He will *r* him to his ......Deut 7:10
silence, but will *r* ....Is 65:6
He will surely *r* ....Jer 51:56
again, I will *r*..........Luke 10:35
because they cannot *r* ...Luke 14:14
R no one evil for evil.....Rom 12:17
is Mine, I will *r* ....Rom 12:19
r their parents ....1 Tim 5:4
I will *r* ....Philem 19

REPAYS

and who *r* him for what ...Job 21:31
r the proud person ....Ps 31:23
shall he be who *r*..........Ps 137:8
the Lord, Who fully *r*.......Is 66:6

REPEATS

r a matter separates ......Prov 17:9

REPENT

I abhor myself, and *r* .....Job 42:6
"*R*, for the kingdom......Matt 3:2
you *r* you will all.......Luke 13:3
said to them, "*R*......Acts 2:38
men everywhere to *r*.....Acts 17:30
be zealous and *r* ....Rev 3:19

REPENTANCE

you with water unto *r* ...Matt 3:11
a baptism of *r* for the ....Mark 1:4
persons who need no *r*...Luke 15:7
sorrow produces *r*......2 Cor 7:10
will grant them *r*........2 Tim 2:25
renew them again to *r*.....Heb 6:6
found no place for *r*.....Heb 12:17
all should come to *r*......2 Pet 3:9

REPENTED

No man *r* of his ....Jer 8:6
after my turning, I *r*......Jer 31:19
it, because they *r* ......Matt 12:41

REPETITIONS

r as the heathen do.......Matt 6:7

REPORT

circulate a false *r* ....Ex 23:1
For it is not a good *r* ...1 Sam 2:24
r makes the bones......Prov 15:30
Who has believed our *r*.....Is 53:1
who has believed our *r* ...Rom 10:16
things are of good *r* ....Phil 4:8

REPRIMANDED

And they *r* him sharply ...Judg 8:1

REPROACH

r me as long as I live ......Job 27:6
does he take up a *r*........Ps 15:3
You make us a *r* ....Ps 44:13
sake I have borne *r*.......Ps 69:7
R has broken my heart.....Ps 69:20
nation, but sin is a *r*.....Prov 14:34
with dishonor comes *r* ....Prov 18:3
do not fear the *r*...........Is 51:7
not remember the *r*.......Jer 15:15
bring an everlasting *r* .....Jer 23:40
because I bore the *r*......Jer 31:19
you shall bear the *r* ......Mic 6:16
these things You *r* ......Luke 11:45
lest he fall into *r* ....1 Tim 3:7
esteeming the *r*..........Heb 11:26
and without *r* ....James 1:5

REPROACHED

If you are *r* for the.......1 Pet 4:14

REPROACHES

is not an enemy who *r* .....Ps 55:12
oppresses the poor *r* ....Prov 14:31
curse, and Israel to *r*......Is 43:28
in infirmities, in *r*......2 Cor 12:10

REPROACHFULLY

they strike me *r*.........Job 16:10

REPROOF

for doctrine, for *r*......2 Tim 3:16

REPROOFS

r of instruction are ......Prov 6:23

REPUTATION

seven men of good *r* ......Acts 6:3
to those who were of *r* .....Gal 2:2
made Himself of no *r*.......Phil 2:7

REQUEST

not withheld the *r*..........Ps 21:2
He gave them their *r* ....Ps 106:15
the Lord God to make *r* ...Dan 9:3
For Jews *r* a sign........1 Cor 1:22
of mine making *r* ....Phil 1:4

REQUESTS

r be made known ....Phil 4:6

REQUIRE

the Lord your God *r* ....Deut 10:12
a foreigner you may *r*....Deut 15:3
"You will not *r*...........Ps 10:13
offering You did not *r*......Ps 40:6
what does the Lord *r*......Mic 6:8

REQUIRED

of the world may be *r*...Luke 11:50
your soul will be *r*......Luke 12:20
him much will be *r*......Luke 12:48
Moreover it is *r*..........1 Cor 4:2

REQUIREMENTS

keeps the righteous *r* .....Rom 2:26
r that was against us ......Col 2:14

RESCUE

R me from their ....Ps 35:17
and no one shall *r*........Hos 5:14

RESERVE

r the unjust under ....2 Pet 2:9

RESERVED

which I have *r* for the.....Job 38:23
"I have *r* for Myself ......Rom 11:4
r in heaven for you........1 Pet 1:4
of darkness, to be *r* .....2 Pet 2:4
habitation, He has *r*........Jude 6

RESIDUE

The *r* of My people.......Zeph 2:9

RESIST

r an evil person ....Matt 5:39
r the Holy Spirit ....Acts 7:51
R the devil and he ......James 4:7

RESISTED

For who has *r* His will ....Rom 9:19
Jannes and Jambres *r* ....2 Tim 3:8
for he has greatly *r*......2 Tim 4:15
You have not yet *r* ....Heb 12:4

RESISTS

"God *r* the proud ....James 4:6
for "God *r* the proud ......1 Pet 5:5

RESOLVED

'I have *r* what to do .....Luke 16:4

RESORT

to which I may *r*..........Ps 71:3

RESOUND

my heart shall *r*...........Is 16:11

RESPECT

Have *r* to the covenant.....Ps 74:20
his eyes will have *r* ....Is 17:7
saying, 'They will *r*.....Matt 21:37
of the law held in *r*......Acts 5:34
and we paid them *r* ......Heb 12:9

RESPECTED

And the Lord *r* Abel......Gen 4:4
little folly to one *r* ....Eccl 10:1

RESPONSE

in whose mouth is no *r*.....Ps 38:14

REST

is the Sabbath of *r*........Ex 31:15
you shall find no *r* ......Deut 28:65
to build a house of *r* .....1 Chr 28:2
I would have been at *r* ....Job 3:13
the weary are at *r* ....Job 3:17
R in the Lord ....Ps 37:7
fly away and be at *r* ....Ps 55:6
of the Lord shall ....Is 11:2
whole earth is at *r*.........Is 14:7
" This is the *r*............Is 28:12
sake I will not *r*..........Is 62:1
is the place of My *r*........Is 66:1
then you will find *r* ......Jer 6:16
and I will give you *r*.....Matt 11:28
and you will find *r* .....Matt 11:29
shall not enter My *r*.......Heb 3:11
remains therefore a *r* ......Heb 4:9
to enter that *r*...........Heb 4:11
And they do not *r*........Rev 4:8
that they should *r*........Rev 6:11
"that they may *r*........Rev 14:13
But the *r* of the dead .....Rev 20:5

RESTED

He had done, and He *r* .....Gen 2:2
glory of the Lord *r* ......Ex 24:16
when the Spirit *r*......Num 11:25
"And God *r* on the........Heb 4:4

RESTING

do not plunder his *r* .....Prov 24:15
r place shall be............Is 11:10
all the earth is *r*.........Zech 1:11
still sleeping and *r* .....Matt 26:45

RESTLESS

I am *r* in my complaint ....Ps 55:2

RESTORATION

until the times of *r* ....Acts 3:21

RESTORE

R to me the joy...........Ps 51:12
I still must *r* ....Ps 69:4
r your judges as...........Is 1:26
r them to this place......Jer 27:22
For I will *r* health to .....Jer 30:17
"So I will *r* to you ....Joel 2:25
declare that I will *r*.......Zech 9:12
and will *r* all things .....Matt 17:11
I *r* fourfold.............Luke 19:8
You at this time *r* ....Acts 1:6
who are spiritual *r*........Gal 6:1

RESTORER

may he be to you a *r* .....Ruth 4:15

RESTORES

with joy, for He r . . . . .Job 33:26
He r my soul . . . . .Ps 23:3

RESTRAIN

now r Your hand . . . . . . .2 Sam 24:16
Therefore I will not r . . . . . .Job 7:11
Will You r Yourself. . . . . . . .Is 64:12
no one can r His hand . . . . .Dan 4:35

RESTRAINED

r my feet from every. . . . .Ps 119:101
Are they r. . . . . .Is 63:15

RESTRAINS

For nothing r the LORD . .1 Sam 14:6
r his lips is wise. . . . . .Prov 10:19
only He who now r. . . . .2 Thess 2:7

RESTRAINT

they have cast off r . . . . . .Job 30:11
they break all r. . . . . .Hos 4:2

RESTS

r quietly in the heart . . . .Prov 14:33

RESURRECTION

who say there is no r . . . .Matt 22:23
"Therefore, in the r . . . .Matt 22:28
done good, to the r. . . . . .John 5:29
to her, "I am the r . . . . . .John 11:25
them Jesus and the r . . . .Acts 17:18
that there will be a r. . . . .Acts 24:15
the likeness of His r . . . . . .Rom 6:5
say that there is no r . . . .1 Cor 15:12
and the power of His r. . . .Phil 3:10
that the r is already . . . . .2 Tim 2:18
obtain a better r. . . . . . . .Heb 11:35
This is the first r . . . . . . .Rev 20:5

RETAIN

happy are all who r. . . . . .Prov 3:18
spirit to r the spirit . . . . . . .Eccl 8:8
r the sins of any . . . . . . .John 20:23
like to r God in their. . . . . .Rom 1:28

RETURN

So the LORD will r . . . . . .1 Kin 2:32
and r to our neighbors . . . . .Ps 79:12
R, O LORD . . . . .Ps 90:13
none who go to her r. . . . . .Prov 2:19
womb, naked shall he r. . . .Eccl 5:15
the clouds do not r . . . . . .Eccl 12:2
let him r to the LORD. . . . . . .Is 55:7
it shall not r to Me . . . . . . .Is 55:11
"If you will r . . . . .Jer 4:1
for they shall r . . . . .Jer 24:7
me, and I will r . . . . .Jer 31:18
say, 'I will go and r . . . . . . .Hos 2:7
help of your God, r. . . . . . .Hos 12:6
"R to Me . . . . .Zech 1:3
he says, 'I will r . . . . . . .Matt 12:44

RETURNED

and they r and sought . . . . .Ps 78:34
yet you have not r. . . . . . . .Amos 4:6
astray, but have now r . . . .1 Pet 2:25

RETURNING

"I am r to Jerusalem . . . .Zech 1:16
r evil for evil or. . . . . .1 Pet 3:9

RETURNS

spirit departs, he r . . . . .Ps 146:4
As a dog r to his own . . . .Prov 26:11
"A dog r to his own . . . . . .2 Pet 2:22

REVEAL

The heavens will r. . . . . . .Job 20:27
I will heal them and r . . . . .Jer 33:6

the Son wills to r Him . . .Matt 11:27
r His Son in me. . . . . .Gal 1:16
otherwise, God will r . . . . .Phil 3:15

REVEALED

things which are r. . . . . . .Deut 29:29
of the LORD shall be r . . . . . .Is 40:5
righteousness to be r. . . . . . .Is 56:1
Then the secret was r. . . . .Dan 2:19
the Son of Man is r . . . .Luke 17:30
the wrath of God is r . . . . .Rom 1:18
glory which shall be r . . . . .Rom 8:18
But God has r them to . .1 Cor 2:10
as it has now been r. . . . . . .Eph 3:5
but now has been r . . . . . . .Col 1:26
the Lord Jesus is r. . . . .2 Thess 1:7
lawless one will be r . . . .2 Thess 2:8
ready to be r in the . . . . . .1 Pet 1:5
when His glory is r . . . . .1 Pet 4:13
r what we shall be . . . . . .1 John 3:2

REVEALER

Lord of kings, and a r . . . .Dan 2:47

REVEALING

waits for the r . . . . .Rom 8:19

REVEALS

as a talebearer . . . . .Prov 20:19
r deep and secret . . . . .Dan 2:22
r secrets has made . . . . . . .Dan 2:29
r His secret to His . . . . . .Amos 3:7

REVELATION

Where there is no r . . . . .Prov 29:18
the day of wrath and r . . . . .Rom 2:5
has a tongue, has a r . . . .1 Cor 14:26
it came through the r . . . . .Gal 1:12
spirit of wisdom and r. . . . .Eph 1:17
r He made known to . . . . . .Eph 3:3
and glory at the r. . . . . . . .1 Pet 1:7

REVELATIONS

come to visions and r . . . .2 Cor 12:1

REVELRIES

drunkenness, r. . . . . .Gal 5:21
lusts, drunkenness, r . . . . .1 Pet 4:3

REVENGE

and we will take our r . . . .Jer 20:10

REVENUES

than vast r without. . . . . .Prov 16:8

REVERENCE

and r My sanctuary . . . . . .Lev 19:30
and to be held in r . . . . .Ps 89:7
Master, where is My r . . . . . .Mal 1:6
submission with all r. . . .1 Tim 3:4
God acceptably with r . . . .Heb 12:28

REVERENT

man who is always r . . . . .Prov 28:14
their wives must be r . . . .1 Tim 3:11
older men be sober, r . . . . .Titus 2:2

REVILE

are you when they r . . . . . .Matt 5:11
r God's high priest . . . . . .Acts 23:4
evildoers, those who r . . . .1 Pet 3:16

REVILED

crucified with Him r . . . .Mark 15:32
who, when He was r. . . . . .1 Pet 2:23

REVILER

or an idolater, or a r. . . . . .1 Cor 5:11

REVILERS

nor drunkards, nor r . . . . .1 Cor 6:10

REVILING

come envy, strife, r . . . . . . .1 Tim 6:4

REVIVAL

give us a measure of r. . . . .Ezra 9:8

REVIVE

troubles, shall r. . . . . .Ps 71:20
Will You not r us. . . . . .Ps 85:6
r me according to Your. . . .Ps 119:25
r the spirit of the. . . . . .Is 57:15
two days He will r . . . . . . .Hos 6:2
r Your work in the . . . . .Hab 3:2

REVIVED

they shall be r. . . . . .Hos 14:7
came, sin r and I died. . . . .Rom 7:9

REVOLT

You will r more and. . . . . . . .Is 1:5

REVOLTED

Israel have deeply r. . . . . . . .Is 31:6
they have r and . . . . .Jer 5:23

REVOLTERS

r are deeply involved . . . . . .Hos 5:2

REWARD

exceedingly great r. . . . . . .Gen 15:1
them there is great r. . . . . . .Ps 19:11
r me evil for good . . . . . . .Ps 35:12
"Surely there is a r . . . . . . .Ps 58:11
look, and see the r. . . . . . . .Ps 91:8
will a sure r . . . . .Prov 11:18
and the LORD will r . . . . .Prov 25:22
and this was my r . . . . . . .Eccl 2:10
behold, His r is with . . . . . .Is 40:10
r them for their deeds . . . . .Hos 4:9
You have loved for r . . . . . .Hos 9:1
for great is your r. . . . . . .Matt 5:12
you have no r from . . . . . . .Matt 6:1
you, they have their r. . . . .Matt 6:2
receive a prophet's r. . . . .Matt 10:41
by no means lose his r. . . .Matt 10:42
r will be great . . . . .Luke 6:35
we receive the due r . . . .Luke 23:41
will receive his own r . . . . . .1 Cor 3:8
cheat you of your r . . . . . . .Col 2:18
for he looked to the r. . . . .Heb 11:26
may receive a full r . . . .2 John 1:8
quickly, and My r . . . . . . .Rev 22:12

REWARDED

Thus they have r. . . . . .Ps 109:5

REWARDER

and that He is a r . . . . . . .Heb 11:6

REWARDS

Whoever r evil for . . . . . .Prov 17:13
and follows after r. . . . . .Is 1:23
and give your r. . . . . .Dan 5:17

RICH

Abram was very r . . . . . . .Gen 13:2
makes poor and makes r. .1 Sam 2:7
r man will lie down . . . . . .Job 27:19
the r among the people . . . .Ps 45:12
when one becomes r . . . . . .Ps 49:16
soul will be made r . . . . . .Prov 11:25
who makes himself r. . . . .Prov 13:7
r has many friends . . . . .Prov 14:20
The r and the poor . . . . . .Prov 22:2
r rules over the poor . . . . . .Prov 22:7
r man is wise in his. . . . . .Prov 28:11
do not curse the r . . . . . . .Eccl 10:20
it is hard for a r . . . . .Matt 19:23
to you who are r . . . . .Luke 6:24
from the r man's table . . .Luke 16:21

RICHES

for he was very *r*. . . . . . .Luke 18:23
Lord over all is *r* . . . . .Rom 10:12
You are already *r* . . . . .1 Cor 4:8
though He was *r* . . . . .2 Cor 8:9
who desire to be *r* . . . . . . .1 Tim 6:9
but the *r* in his . . . . .James 1:10
So the *r* man also will . .James 1:11
of this world to be *r* . . . . .James 2:5
you say, 'I am *r*. . . . . .Rev 3:17

RICHES

Both *r* and honor come . .1 Chr 29:12
He swallows down *r* . . . . .Job 20:15
he heaps up *r*. . . . . .Ps 39:6
the abundance of his *r* . . . . .Ps 52:7
if *r* increase . . . . .Ps 62:10
r will be in his house . . . . .Ps 112:3
in her left hand *r*. . . . . . . .Prov 3:16
R and honor are. . . . . .Prov 8:18
R do not profit. . . . . .Prov 11:4
in his *r* will fall . . . . .Prov 11:28
yet has great *r* . . . . .Prov 13:7
of the wise is their *r* . . . .Prov 14:24
and *r* are an . . . . .Prov 19:14
of the LORD are *r*. . . . . . . .Prov 22:4
r are not forever. . . . . . . .Prov 27:24
r kept for their owner . . . .Eccl 5:13
darkness and hidden *r*. . . . . .Is 45:3
you shall eat the *r* . . . . .Is 61:6
so is he who gets *r*. . . . . . .Jer 17:11
have increased your *r*. . . .Ezek 28:5
for those who have *r* . . . .Mark 10:23
do you despise the *r* . . . . . .Rom 2:4
might make known the *r* . .Rom 9:23
what are the *r*. . . . . .Eph 1:18
show the exceeding *r* . . . . .Eph 2:7
the unsearchable *r* . . . . . . .Eph 3:8
trust in uncertain *r* . . . . .1 Tim 6:17
r than the treasures . . . . . .Heb 11:26
r are corrupted . . . . .James 5:2
to receive power and *r* . . . .Rev 5:12

RICHLY

Christ dwell in you *r* . . . . . .Col 3:16
God, who gives us *r* . . . . .1 Tim 6:17

RIDDLE

"Let me pose a *r*. . . . . . .Judg 14:12

RIDDLES

the wise and their *r*. . . . . . .Prov 1:6

RIDE

wind and cause me to *r* . .Job 30:22
in Your majesty *r* . . . . .Ps 45:4
have caused men to *r* . . . . .Ps 66:12

RIDER

r He has thrown. . . . . .Ex 15:1
the horse and its *r* . . . . . .Job 39:18

RIDES

Behold, the LORD *r* . . . . .Is 19:1

RIDGES

You water its *r*. . . . . .Ps 65:10

RIDICULE

those who see Me *r* Me . . . .Ps 22:7
Whom do you *r* . . . . .Is 57:4

RIDICULED

they *r* Him. . . . . .Matt 9:24

RIGHT

you shall do what is *r*. . . . .Deut 6:18
the *r* of the firstborn . . . .Deut 21:17
did what was *r* in his . . . Judg 21:25
"Is your heart *r*. . . . . . . .2 Kin 10:15
them forth by the *r*. . . . . . .Ps 107:7

Lord, "Sit at My *r* . . . . .Ps 110:1
is a way which seems *r*. . .Prov 14:12
way of a man is *r*. . . . . . . .Prov 21:2
things that are *r* . . . . .Is 45:19
until He comes whose *r* . .Ezek 21:27
of the LORD are *r* . . . . .Hos 14:9
do not know to do *r* . . . . .Amos 3:10
and whatever is *r* . . . . . . .Matt 20:4
clothed and in his *r* . . . . .Mark 5:15
not judge what is *r*. . . . . .Luke 12:57
to them He gave the *r* . . . .John 1:12
your heart is not *r*. . . . . . .Acts 8:21
Do we have no *r*. . . . . .1 Cor 9:4
seven stars in His *r* . . . . . . .Rev 2:1

RIGHTEOUS

also destroy the *r*. . . . . . . .Gen 18:23
and they justify the *r*. . . . .Deut 25:1
"You are more *r*. . . . . . .1 Sam 24:17
that he could be *r* . . . . . . .Job 15:14
r will hold to his way . . . . .Job 17:9
"The *r* see it and . . . . . . .Job 22:19
knows the way of the *r*. . . . . .Ps 1:6
LORD, will bless the *r* . . . . . .Ps 5:12
r God tests the hearts . . . . . .Ps 7:9
what can the *r*. . . . . .Ps 11:3
The *r* cry out. . . . . .Ps 34:17
the LORD upholds the *r* . . . .Ps 37:17
r shows mercy and . . . . . . .Ps 37:21
I have not seen the *r* . . . . .Ps 37:25
the *r* will be in. . . . . .Ps 112:6
The LORD is *r* in all. . . . . .Ps 145:17
the LORD loves the *r* . . . . . .Ps 146:8
will not allow the *r* . . . . . .Prov 10:3
r is a well of life. . . . . .Prov 10:11
The labor of the *r* . . . . . . .Prov 10:16
r will be gladness . . . . . . .Prov 10:28
r is delivered from . . . . . . .Prov 11:8
r will be delivered . . . . . . .Prov 11:21
r will flourish. . . . . .Prov 11:28
r will be recompensed . . .Prov 11:31
r man regards the life . . . .Prov 12:10
r should choose his . . . . . .Prov 12:26
r there is much . . . . .Prov 15:6
the prayer of the *r*. . . . . . .Prov 15:29
the *r* run to it and. . . . . . . .Prov 18:10
r are bold as a lion . . . . . .Prov 28:1
When the *r* are in . . . . .Prov 29:2
r considers the cause. . . . . .Prov 29:7
Do not be overly *r* . . . . . . .Eccl 7:16
event happens to the *r* . . . .Eccl 9:2
r that it shall be. . . . . .Is 3:10
the gates, that the *r* . . . . . . .Is 26:2
with My *r* right hand . . . . .Is 41:10
By His knowledge My *r* . . .Is 53:11
The *r* perishes . . . . .Is 57:1
people shall be all *r* . . . . . .Is 60:21
R are You . . . . .Jer 12:1
your sins by being *r* . . . . . .Dan 4:27
they sell the *r*. . . . . .Amos 2:6
not come to call the *r*. . . . .Matt 9:13
r men desired to see . . . . .Matt 13:17
r will shine forth as . . . . .Matt 13:43
And they were both *r* . . . . .Luke 1:6
that they were *r* . . . . .Luke 18:9
"Certainly this was a *r*. . .Luke 23:47
"There is none *r* . . . . .Rom 3:10
r man will one die . . . . . . .Rom 5:7
witness that he was *r* . . . .Heb 11:4
Jesus Christ the *r*. . . . . . . .1 John 2:1
just as He is *r* . . . . .1 John 3:7
r are Your. . . . . .Rev 16:7
fine linen is the *r*. . . . . .Rev 19:8

RIGHTEOUSLY

judge the people *r*. . . . . .Ps 67:4
He who walks *r* and. . . . . . .Is 33:15
should live soberly, *r* . . . .Titus 2:12
to Him who judges *r* . . . . .1 Pet 2:23

RIGHTEOUSNESS

it to him for *r* . . . . .Gen 15:6
My *r* I hold fast . . . . .Job 27:6
I put on *r*. . . . . .Job 29:14
I will ascribe *r*. . . . . .Job 36:3
I call, O God of my *r* . . . . . . .Ps 4:1
righteous, He loves *r* . . . . . .Ps 11:7
from the LORD, and *r* . . . . . .Ps 24:5
shall speak of Your *r*. . . . . .Ps 35:28
the good news of *r* . . . . .Ps 40:9
You love *r* and hate. . . . . . . .Ps 45:7
heavens declare His *r* . . . . . .Ps 50:6
sing aloud of Your *r*. . . . . . .Ps 51:14
r and peace have. . . . . .Ps 85:10
R will go before Him . . . . . .Ps 85:13
r they are exalted . . . . .Ps 89:16
will return to *r*. . . . . .Ps 94:15
r and justice are the. . . . . . .Ps 97:2
and he who does *r*. . . . . . .Ps 106:3
r endures forever. . . . . .Ps 111:3
r is an everlasting. . . . . . .Ps 119:142
r delivers from death. . . . .Prov 10:2
The *r* of the blameless . . .Prov 11:5
The *r* of the upright . . . . .Prov 11:6
r leads to life . . . . .Prov 11:19
the way of *r* is life . . . . . .Prov 12:28
R guards him whose way . .Prov 13:6
R exalts a nation. . . . . . . .Prov 14:34
found in the way of *r* . . . .Prov 16:31
He who follows *r* . . . . . . .Prov 21:21
r lodged in it. . . . . .Is 1:21
r He shall judge. . . . . .Is 11:4
R shall be the belt. . . . . .Is 11:5
he will not learn *r* . . . . . . .Is 26:10
and *r* the plummet. . . . . . . .Is 28:17
r will be peace . . . . .Is 32:17
in the LORD I have *r* . . . . . .Is 45:24
who are far from *r* . . . . . . .Is 46:12
r will be forever . . . . .Is 51:8
I will declare my *r* . . . . . . .Is 57:12
and His own *r* . . . . .Is 59:16
r as a breastplate. . . . . .Is 59:17
be called trees of *r* . . . . . . .Is 61:3
r goes forth as . . . . .Is 62:1
THE LORD OUR *R* . . . . . .Jer 23:6
to David a Branch of *r* . . .Jer 33:15
has revealed our *r* . . . . . . .Jer 51:10
The *r* of the righteous . . .Ezek 18:20
"O Lord, *r* belongs. . . . . . .Dan 9:7
in everlasting *r*. . . . . .Dan 9:24
who turn many to *r* . . . . . .Dan 12:3
for yourselves. . . . . .Hos 10:12
to fulfill all *r* . . . . .Matt 3:15
exceeds the *r* of the . . . . .Matt 5:20
to you in the way of *r*. . . .Matt 21:32
in holiness and *r*. . . . . .Luke 1:75
For in it the *r*. . . . . .Rom 1:17
even the *r* of God. . . . . .Rom 3:22
a seal of the *r*. . . . . .Rom 4:11
accounted to him for *r* . . . .Rom 4:22
r will reign in life. . . . . . . .Rom 5:17
might reign through *r* . . . . .Rom 5:21
is life because of *r* . . . . .Rom 8:10
who did not pursue *r*. . . . . .Rom 9:30
pursuing the law of *r* . . . . .Rom 9:31
ignorant of God's *r* . . . . . .Rom 10:3
we might become the *r* . . .2 Cor 5:21
r comes through the . . . . . .Gal 2:21
the breastplate of *r* . . . . . .Eph 6:14
not having my own *r* . . . . . .Phil 3:9
things and pursue *r*. . . . . .1 Tim 6:11
r which we have . . . . .Titus 3:5
r which is according. . . . . . .Heb 11:7
does not produce the *r*. . .James 1:20
should suffer for *r* . . . . . . .1 Pet 3:14
a preacher of *r*. . . . . .2 Pet 2:5
a new earth in which *r*. . . .2 Pet 3:13

who practices r......... 1 John 2:29
He who practices r ...... 1 John 3:7
does not practice r...... 1 John 3:10

RIGHTLY

wise uses knowledge r.... Prov 15:2
R do they love you .... Song 1:4
"You have answered r.... Luke 10:28
r dividing the word ...... 2 Tim 2:15

RIGHTS

and her marriage r........ Ex 21:10

RINGLEADER

the world, and a r .... Acts 24:5

RINGS

a man with gold r........ James 2:2

RIPE

figs that are first r......... Jer 24:2

RISE

is vain for you to r .... Ps 127:2
"Now I will r .... Is 33:10
for He makes His sun r... Matt 5:45
of Nineveh will r........ Matt 12:41
third day He will r..... Matt 20:19
false prophets will r.... Matt 24:24
persuaded though one r.. Luke 16:31
third day He will r..... Luke 18:33
had to suffer and r .... Acts 17:3
be the first to r .... Acts 26:23
fact the dead do not r... 1 Cor 15:15
in Christ will r .... 1 Thess 4:16

RISEN

of the LORD is r .... Is 60:1
women there has not r... Matt 11:11
disciples that He is r..... Matt 28:7
"The Lord is r........... Luke 24:34
furthermore is also r...... Rom 8:34
then Christ is not r..... 1 Cor 15:13
if Christ is not r .... 1 Cor 15:17
But now Christ is r..... 1 Cor 15:20

RISES

shall I do when God r..... Job 31:14
every tongue which r....... Is 54:17

RISING

may know from the r... Is 45:6
questioning what the r... Mark 9:10
for the fall and r......... Luke 2:34

RIVER

Indeed the r may rage .... Job 40:23
them drink from the r ..... Ps 36:8
r whose streams shall...... Ps 46:4
the r of God is full ...... Ps 65:9
went through the r........ Ps 66:6
peace to her like a r...... Is 66:12
in the Jordan R .... Mark 1:5
he showed me a pure r..... Rev 22:1

RIVERS

He turns r into a........ Ps 107:33
R of water run down..... Ps 119:136
By the r of Babylon .... Ps 137:1
All the r run into the...... Eccl 1:7
us a place of broad r....... Is 33:21
the wilderness and r ...... Is 43:19
the sea, I make the r...... Is 50:2
his heart will flow r ..... John 7:38

ROAD

I will even make a r........ Is 43:19
depths of the sea a r....... Is 51:10
seen the Lord on the r ....Acts 9:27

ROAR

Let the sea r............ 1 Chr 16:32
though its waters r.........Ps 46:3
The young lions r .... Ps 104:21
The LORD will r......... Jer 25:30
He will r like a lion...... Hos 11:10
The LORD also will r....... Joel 3:16
Will a lion r in the........ Amos 3:4

ROARING

wrath is like the r .... Prov 19:12
Like a r lion and a....... Prov 28:15
and the waves r........ Luke 21:25
walks about like a r...... 1 Pet 5:8

ROARS

their voice r like the ...... Jer 6:23
" The LORD r from........ Amos 1:2
as when a lion r........... Rev 10:3

ROB

r the poor because he .... Prov 22:22
r the needy of justice .... Is 10:2
"Will a man r God .... Mal 3:8
do you r temples .... Rom 2:22

ROBBED

r their treasuries .... Is 10:13
But this is a people r...... Is 42:22
Yet you have r Me .... Mal 3:8
r other churches........ 2 Cor 11:8

ROBBER

a son who is a r........ Ezek 18:10
is a thief and a r....... John 10:1
Now Barabbas was a r... John 18:40

ROBBERS

and Israel to the r......... Is 42:24
also crucified two r..... Mark 15:27
Me are thieves and r..... John 10:8
here who are neither r.... Acts 19:37
waters, in perils of r.... 2 Cor 11:26

ROBBERY

nor vainly hope in r .... Ps 62:10
I hate r for burnt........... Is 61:8
did not consider it r........ Phil 2:6

ROBE

justice was like a r...... Job 29:14
instead of a rich r .... Is 3:24
covered me with the r...... Is 61:10
'Bring out the best r .... Luke 15:22
on Him a purple r....... John 19:2
Then a white r was....... Rev 6:11

ROBES

to the King in r........... Ps 45:14
have stained all My r ...... Is 63:3
clothe you with rich r...... Zech 3:4
to go around in long r... Luke 20:46
clothed with white r....... Rev 7:9

ROCK

you shall strike the r...... Ex 17:6
and struck the r .... Num 20:11
R who begot you....... Deut 32:18
For their r is not........ Deut 32:31
nor is there any r........ 1 Sam 2:2
" The LORD is my r....... 2 Sam 22:2
And who is a r .... 2 Sam 22:32
Blessed be my R....... 2 Sam 22:47
away, and as a r....... Job 14:18
set me high upon a r ...... Ps 27:5
For You are my r........... Ps 31:3
r that is higher than..... Ps 61:2
and my God the r........ Ps 94:22
who turned the r....... Ps 114:8
been mindful of the R...... Is 17:10

shadow of a great r .... Is 32:2
his house on the r....... Matt 7:24
r I will build My........ Matt 16:18
"Some fell on r .... Luke 8:6
stumbling stone and r.... Rom 9:33
R that followed them..... 1 Cor 10:4

ROCKS

and the r were split .... Matt 27:51
to the mountains and r ... Rev 6:16

ROD

And Moses took the r.... .Ex 4:20
chasten him with the r.. .2 Sam 7:14
Your r and Your staff ..... Ps 23:4
The r and rebuke give.... Prov 29:15
shall come forth a R....... Is 11:1
you pass under the r ... Ezek 20:37
I come to you with a r.... 1 Cor 4:21
rule them with a r........ Rev 2:27

ROLL

ruinous storm they r..... Job 30:14
r away the stone........ Mark 16:3

ROLLED

the heavens shall be r....... Is 34:4
the stone had been r ..... Mark 16:4

ROOM

You prepared r for it........ Ps 80:9
until no more r.......... Zech 10:10
you a large upper r ..... Mark 14:15
no r for them in the ...... Luke 2:7
still there is r........... Luke 14:22
into the upper r.......... Acts 1:13

ROOMS

make r in the ark .... Gen 6:14
He is in the inner r...... Matt 24:26

ROOSTER

him, "Before the r........ Matt 26:75

ROOT

r bearing bitterness ..... Deut 29:18
the foolish taking r........ Job 5:3
r may grow old in the...... Job 14:8
day there shall be a R...... Is 11:10
shall again take r.......... Is 37:31
because they had no r .... Matt 13:6
and if the r is holy...... Rom 11:16
of money is a r........... 1 Tim 6:10
lest any r of .... Heb 12:15
I am the R and the...... Rev 22:16

ROOTED

that you, being r .... Eph 3:17
r and built up in Him .... Col 2:7

ROOTS

because its r reached .... Ezek 31:7
and lengthen his r .... Hos 14:5
dried up from the r..... Mark 11:20
pulled up by the r .... Jude 12

ROSE

I am the r of Sharon ...... Song 2:1
and blossom as the r....... Is 35:1
end Christ died and r..... Rom 14:9
buried, and that He r .... 1 Cor 15:4
that Jesus died and r.. 1 Thess 4:14

RUBIES

of wisdom is above r..... Job 28:18
more precious than r..... Prov 3:15
is better than r .... Prov 8:11
worth is far above r...... Prov 31:10
your pinnacles of r........ Is 54:12
ruddy in body than r...... Lam 4:7

RUDDY

Now he was *r* ....1 Sam 16:12
beloved is white and *r* ....Song 5:10

RUIN

r those two can bring ....Prov 24:22
have made a city a *r* ....Is 25:2
will not be your *r* ......Ezek 18:30
And the *r* of that ....Luke 6:49
to no profit, to the *r* ....2 Tim 2:14

RUINED

shall be utterly *r* ....Is 60:12
the mighty trees are *r* ....Zech 11:2
wineskins will be *r* ......Luke 5:37

RUINS

rebuild the old *r* ....Is 61:4

RULE

and he shall *r* ....Gen 3:16
r the raging of the. ....Ps 89:9
A wise servant will *r* .....Prov 17:2
Yet he will *r* over all.......Eccl 2:19
puts an end to all *r* .....1 Cor 15:24
us walk by the same *r* ....Phil 3:16
let the peace of God *r* ....Col 3:15
let the elders who *r* .....1 Tim 5:17
Remember those who *r* ....Heb 13:7

RULER

the sheep, to be *r* .....2 Sam 7:8
down to eat with a *r* .....Prov 23:1
bear is a wicked *r* ......Prov 28:15
r pays attention ....Prov 29:12
to Me the One to be *r* ......Mic 5:2
by Beelzebub, the *r* ....Matt 12:24
I will make you *r* .....Matt 25:21
the *r* of this world......John 12:31
because the *r* of this....John 16:11
'Who made you a *r* ....Acts 7:27
speak evil of a *r* ....Acts 23:5

RULERS

and the *r* take counsel ....Ps 2:2
r decree justice ....Prov 8:15
"You know that the *r* ....Matt 20:25
"Have any of the *r* .....John 7:48
r are not a...............Rom 13:3
which none of the *r* ......1 Cor 2:8
powers, against the *r* ......Eph 6:12
to be subject to *r* ....Titus 3:1

RULES

'He who *r* over men .....2 Sam 23:3
them know that God *r* .....Ps 59:13
He *r* by His power ....Ps 66:7
r his spirit than he ......Prov 16:32
that the Most High *r*......Dan 4:17
that the Most High *r*.....Dan 4:32
r his own house well ......1 Tim 3:4
according to the *r* ......2 Tim 2:5

RULING

r their children..........1 Tim 3:12

RUMOR

r will be upon *r*.........Ezek 7:26

RUMORS

hear of wars and *r* .....Matt 24:6
you hear of wars and *r* ...Mark 13:7

RUN

I will *r* the course of......Ps 119:32
r and not be weary ......Is 40:31
many shall *r* to and ......Dan 12:4
Therefore I *r* thus ......1 Cor 9:26
I might *r*, or had *r*.........Gal 2:2
that I have not *r*.........Phil 2:16

us, and let us *r*...........Heb 12:1
that you do not *r* ....1 Pet 4:4

RUNNER

are swifter than a *r*.......Job 9:25
r will run to meet........Jer 51:31

RUNS

word *r* very swiftly.......Ps 147:15
nor of him who *r* ....Rom 9:16

RUSH

The nations will *r*..........Is 17:13

S

SABAOTH

S had left us a...........Rom 9:29
ears of the Lord of *S* ....James 5:4

SABBATH

'Tomorrow is a *S*.........Ex 16:23
"Remember the *S*.........Ex 20:8
S was made for man .....Mark 2:27
is also Lord of the *S* ....Mark 2:28
not only broke the *S*......John 5:18

SABBATHS

S you shall keep ....Ex 31:13
The New Moons, the *S* .....Is 1:13
also gave them My *S* ...Ezek 20:12

SACKCLOTH

You have put off my *s* .....Ps 30:11
and remove the *s* ....Is 20:2

SACRED

iniquity and the *s* ....Is 1:13

SACRIFICE

do you kick at My *s*.....1 Sam 2:29
S and offering You did ......Ps 40:6
offer to You the *s* ......Ps 116:17
to the Lord than *s* ......Prov 21:3
For the Lord has a *s*.......Is 34:6
who will bring the *s*......Jer 33:11
of My offerings they *s*....Hos 8:13
But I will *s* to You ......Jon 2:9
Lord has prepared a *s* ....Zeph 1:7
offer the blind as a *s* .....Mal 1:8
desire mercy and not *s*....Matt 9:13
s will be seasoned ......Mark 9:49
an offering and a *s*........Eph 5:2
aroma, an acceptable *s*....Phil 4:18
put away sin by the *s* .....Heb 9:26
He had offered one *s* .....Heb 10:12
no longer remains a *s*.....Heb 10:26
God a more excellent *s* ...Heb 11:4
offer the *s* of praise .....Heb 13:15

SACRIFICED

s their sons and their.....Ps 106:37
to eat things *s*...........Rev 2:14

SACRIFICES

The *s* of God are a ....Ps 51:17
multitude of your *s* ....Is 1:11
Bring no more futile *s*......Is 1:13
he who *s* a lamb ....Is 66:3
acceptable, nor your *s* .....Jer 6:20
by him the daily *s* ....Dan 8:11
burnt offerings and *s*....Mark 12:33
priests, to offer up *s* .....Heb 7:27
s God is well pleased ....Heb 13:16
offer up spiritual *s* ....1 Pet 2:5

SAD

"Why is your face *s* ....Neh 2:2
s countenance in ....Eccl 7:3
whom I have not made *s* .Ezek 13:22

as you walk and are *s*....Luke 24:17

SAFE

and I shall be *s* ....Ps 119:117
in the Lord shall be *s*....Prov 29:25
he has received him *s*....Luke 15:27

SAFELY

And He led them on *s* .....Ps 78:53
make them lie down *s* .....Hos 2:18

SAFETY

sons are far from *s* ....Job 5:4
take your rest in *s*........Job 11:18
will set him in the *s* ....Ps 12:5
say, "Peace and *s* ....1 Thess 5:3

SAFETY'S

by you for *s* sake........Prov 3:29

SAINTS

ten thousands of *s* ......Deut 33:2
the feet of His *s* ....1 Sam 2:9
puts no trust in His *s*....Job 15:15
s who are on the earth.....Ps 16:3
does not forsake His *s*....Ps 37:28
"Gather My *s* ....Ps 50:5
the souls of His *s* ....Ps 97:10
is the death of His *s* ....Ps 116:15
the way of His *s* ....Prov 2:8
war against the *s* ....Dan 7:21
shall persecute the *s* .....Dan 7:25
Jesus, called to be *s*.......1 Cor 1:2
the least of all the *s* ......Eph 3:8
Christ with all His *s* ...1 Thess 3:13
be glorified in His *s* ...2 Thess 1:10
all delivered to the *s* ....Jude 3
ways, O King of the *s*....Rev 15:3
shed the blood of *s*........Rev 16:6
the camp of the *s* ....Rev 20:9

SALT

shall season with *s* ....Lev 2:13
"You are the *s* ....Matt 5:13
s loses its flavor........Mark 9:50

SALVATION

still, and see the *s* ......Ex 14:13
For this is all my *s*......2 Sam 23:5
the good news of His *s* ..1 Chr 16:23
S belongs to the Lord ......Ps 3:8
is my light and my *s* ......Ps 27:1
on earth, Your *s*..........Ps 67:2
God is the God of *s* .....Ps 68:20
and Your *s* all the day .....Ps 71:15
Surely His *s* is near ......Ps 85:9
and He has become my *s*..Ps 118:14
S is far from the......Ps 119:155
God will appoint *s*.........Is 26:1
with an everlasting *s*....Is 45:17
for My *s* is about to ....Is 56:1
call your walls *S*........Is 60:18
s as a lamp that burns ....Is 62:1
Lord our God is the *s*....Jer 3:23
joy in the God of my *s* ....Hab 3:18
is just and having *s* .....Zech 9:9
raised up a horn of *s* ....Luke 1:69
eyes have seen Your *s* ....Luke 2:30
to him, "Today *s* ......Luke 19:9
what we worship, for *s*....John 4:22
"Nor is there *s*..........Acts 4:12
you should be for *s* .....Acts 13:47
the power of God to *s*....Rom 1:16
s is nearer than ....Rom 13:11
and is the day of *s*........2 Cor 6:2
work out your own *s* ......Phil 2:12
wrath, but to obtain *s*...1 Thess 5:9
chose you for *s* ....2 Thess 2:13
also may obtain the *s* ....2 Tim 2:10
of God that brings *s*.....Titus 2:11

SAMARITAN

neglect so great a s . . . . .Heb 2:3
s the prophets have . . . . . .1 Pet 1:10

SAMARITAN

But a certain S . . . . .Luke 10:33
a drink from me, a S. . . . . . .John 4:9

SANCTIFICATION

righteousness and s . . . . . .1 Cor 1:30
will of God, your s . . . . . .1 Thess 4:3
salvation through s . . . .2 Thess 2:13

SANCTIFIED

I have commanded My s . . . .Is 13:3
you were born I s . . . . .Jer 1:5
Him whom the Father s . .John 10:36
they also may be s . . . . .John 17:19
might be acceptable, s . .Rom 15:16
to those who are s . . . . .1 Cor 1:2
washed, but you were s . .1 Cor 6:11
husband is s by the . . . . . .1 Cor 7:14
for it is s by the. . . . . .1 Tim 4:5
those who are being s . . . . .Heb 2:11
will we have been s . . . . . .Heb 10:10
who are called, s. . . . . .Jude 1

SANCTIFIES

or the temple that s . . . . .Matt 23:17
For both He who s. . . . . . . .Heb 2:11

SANCTIFY

would send and s them. . . . . .Job 1:5
s My great name. . . . . . .Ezek 36:23
that I, the LORD, s . . . . .Ezek 37:28
Myself and s Myself. . . . .Ezek 38:23
S them by Your truth. . .John 17:17
for their sakes I s . . . . . .John 17:19
that He might s . . . . .Eph 5:26

SANCTUARY

let them make Me a s . . . . .Ex 25:8
I went into the s . . . . .Ps 73:17
set fire to Your s . . . . .Ps 74:7
O God, is in the s . . . . .Ps 77:13
He will be as a s . . . . .Is 8:14
He has abandoned His s . . . .Lam 2:7
I shall be a little s . . . . . .Ezek 11:16
to shine on Your s . . . . . . .Dan 9:17
and the earthly s . . . . .Heb 9:1

SAND

descendants as the s . . . . .Gen 32:12
be heavier than the s . . . . . . .Job 6:3
in number than the s . . . . .Ps 139:18
O Israel, be as the s . . . . . . .Is 10:22
innumerable as the s . . . . .Heb 11:12

SAPPHIRES

are the source of s. . . . . . . .Job 28:6

SAT

of Babylon, there we s . . . . .Ps 137:1
I s down in his shade. . . . .Song 2:3
s alone because of . . . . . . .Jer 15:17
up into heaven, and s . . .Mark 16:19
And He who s there was . . . .Rev 4:3

SATAN

S stood up against. . . . . . .1 Chr 21:1
before the LORD, and S. . . . .Job 1:6
And the LORD said to S. . . .Zech 3:2
"Away with you, S . . . . . .Matt 4:10
"Get behind Me, S. . . . . .Matt 16:23
"How can S cast out . . . .Mark 3:23
to them, "I saw S. . . . . .Luke 10:18
S has asked for you . . . .Luke 22:31
S filled your heart. . . . . . . .Acts 5:3
such a one to S. . . . . .1 Cor 5:5
For S himself . . . . .2 Cor 11:14
to the working of S . . . .2 Thess 2:9

are a synagogue of S . . . . . .Rev 2:9
you, where S dwells . . . . . .Rev 2:13
known the depths of S. . . .Rev 2:24
called the Devil and S . . . .Rev 12:9
years have expired, S . . . . .Rev 20:7

SATIATED

s the weary soul. . . . . .Jer 31:25
It shall be s and made . . . .Jer 46:10

SATISFIED

I shall be s when I . . . . .Ps 17:15
his land will be s . . . . . . .Prov 12:11
a good man will be s . . . .Prov 14:14
s soul loathes the . . . . . . .Prov 27:7
that are never s . . . . .Prov 30:15
silver will not be s . . . . .Eccl 5:10
left hand and not be s. . . . . .Is 9:20
of His soul, and be s . . . . . .Is 53:11
My people shall be s . . . . .Jer 31:14
still were not s. . . . . .Ezek 16:28
but they were not s. . . . . . .Amos 4:8
and cannot be s . . . . .Hab 2:5

SATISFIES

s your mouth with good. . . .Ps 103:5
s the longing soul . . . . .Ps 107:9

SATISFY

s us early with Your . . . . . .Ps 90:14
long life I will s . . . . .Ps 91:16
s her poor with bread. . . .Ps 132:15
for what does not s . . . . .Is 55:2

SATISFYING

eats to the s of his . . . . . .Prov 13:25

SAVE

the LORD does not s. . . .1 Sam 17:47
there was none to s . . . .2 Sam 22:42
s the humble person. . . . .Job 22:29
Oh, s me for Your . . . . .Ps 6:4
S Your people . . . . .Ps 28:9
send from heaven and s. . . .Ps 57:3
s the children of the . . . . . .Ps 72:4
s the souls of the . . . . .Ps 72:13
LORD, and He will s . . . .Prov 20:22
He will come and s . . . . . . .Is 35:4
LORD was ready to s . . . . . .Is 38:20
s your children. . . . . .Is 49:25
that it cannot s . . . . .Is 59:1
mighty to s. . . . . .Is 63:1
one who cannot s . . . . .Jer 14:9
s you and deliver you . . . .Jer 15:20
s me. . . . . .Jer 17:14
O LORD, s Your people. . . .Jer 31:7
other, that he may s . . . . .Hos 13:10
Assyria shall not s. . . . . . .Hos 14:3
the Mighty One, will s. . . .Zeph 3:17
JESUS, for He will s . . . . .Matt 1:21
s his life will . . . . .Matt 16:25
s that which was. . . . . . .Matt 18:11
s life or to kill. . . . . .Mark 3:4
let Him s Himself if. . . .Luke 23:35
You are the Christ, s. . . .Luke 23:39
'Father, s Me from . . . . .John 12:27
but to s the world. . . . . .John 12:47
and s some of them. . . . . .Rom 11:14
the world to s sinners. . . .1 Tim 1:15
doing this you will s . . . .1 Tim 4:16
able to s your souls . . . .James 1:21
Can faith s him. . . . . . . .James 2:14

SAVED

like you, a people s. . . . . .Deut 33:29
But You have s us from . . . . .Ps 44:7
and we are not s . . . . .Jer 8:20
"Who then can be s . . . . .Matt 19:25
"He s others . . . . .Matt 27:42
that we should be s . . . . . .Luke 1:71

"Your faith has s. . . . . . . .Luke 7:50
through Him might be s . .John 3:17
them, saying, "Be s. . . . . .Acts 2:40
what must I do to be s. . .Acts 16:30
For we were s in this. . . . .Rom 8:24
is that they may be s . . . . .Rom 10:1
all Israel will be s . . . . . .Rom 11:26
his spirit may be s. . . . . . .1 Cor 5:5
which also you are s . . . . .1 Cor 15:2
those who are being s . . . .2 Cor 2:15
grace you have been s . . . . .Eph 2:8
all men to be s . . . . .1 Tim 2:4
she will be s in. . . . . .1 Tim 2:15
to His mercy He s . . . . .Titus 3:5
eight souls, were s . . . . . . .1 Pet 3:20
of those who are s. . . . . . .Rev 21:24

SAVES

s the needy from the. . . . . .Job 5:15
s such as have a . . . . .Ps 34:18
antitype which now s. . . . .1 Pet 3:21

SAVIOR

forgot God their S . . . . . . .Ps 106:21
He will send them a S. . . . . .Is 19:20
of Israel, your S. . . . . .Is 43:3
Me, a just God and a S. . . . .Is 45:21
I, the LORD, am your S. . . . . .Is 60:16
So He became their S . . . . . .Is 63:8
for there is no s . . . . .Hos 13:4
rejoiced in God my S . . . . .Luke 1:47
the city of David a S . . . . .Luke 2:11
the Christ, the S. . . . . .John 4:42
to be Prince and S. . . . . . .Acts 5:31
up for Israel a S . . . . .Acts 13:23
and He is the S . . . . .Eph 5:23
of God our S and the . . . .1 Tim 1:1
God, who is the S . . . . . . .1 Tim 4:10
of our S Jesus Christ . . . .2 Tim 1:10
God and S Jesus Christ. . .Titus 2:13

SAVIORS

s shall come to Mount . . . . .Obad 21

SAVOR

days, and I do not s . . . . .Amos 5:21

SAWN

stoned, they were s . . . . . .Heb 11:37

SAY

"But I s to you that. . . . . .Matt 5:22
"But who do you s . . . . . .Matt 16:15
s that we have no sin . . . .1 John 1:8

SAYING

disclose my dark s . . . . .Ps 49:4
cannot accept this s . . . . .Matt 19:11
"This is a hard s. . . . . . . .John 6:60
This is a faithful s. . . . . . .1 Tim 1:15

SAYINGS

I will utter dark s . . . . .Ps 78:2
whoever hears these s . . . .Matt 7:24

SCALES

You shall have honest s . . .Lev 19:36
be weighed on honest s . . . .Job 31:6
deceitful s are in his. . . . . .Hos 12:7
on it had a pair of s . . . . .Rev 6:5

SCARLET

s cord in the window. . . . . .Josh 2:18
are like a strand of s. . . . . . .Song 4:3
your sins are like s. . . . . .Is 1:18
s beast which was full . . . . .Rev 17:3

SCATTER

I will s you among the. . . .Lev 26:33
S the peoples who. . . . . . . .Ps 68:30

SCATTERED

s the sheep of My . . . . .Jer 23:1
I will *s* to all winds . . . . . .Jer 49:32

SCATTERED

lest we be *s* abroad. . . . . . . .Gen 11:4
of iniquity shall be *s*. . . . . . .Ps 92:9
"You have *s* My flock . . . . .Jer 23:2
s Israel will gather. . . . . . .Jer 31:10
Israel is like a sheep . . . . . .Jer 50:17
they were weary and *s* . . . .Matt 9:36
the sheep will be *s*. . . . . . .Mark 14:27
that you will be *s* . . . . . . .John 16:32

SCATTERS

s the frost like ashes . . . . .Ps 147:16
There is one who *s* . . . . . .Prov 11:24
throne of judgment *s* . . . .Prov 20:8
not gather with Me *s* . . . .Matt 12:30

SCEPTER

s shall not depart. . . . . . .Gen 49:10
S shall rise out of . . . . . .Num 24:17
a *s* of righteousness . . . . . . .Ps 45:6
a *s* of righteousness. . . . . . .Heb 1:8

SCHEME

perfected a shrewd *s*. . . . . . .Ps 64:6

SCHEMER

will be called a *s* . . . . .Prov 24:8

SCHEMES

who brings wicked *s*. . . . . . .Ps 37:7
have sought out many *s* . . .Eccl 7:29

SCHISM

there should be no *s* . . .1 Cor 12:25

SCHOOL

daily in the *s* of . . . . .Acts 19:9

SCOFF

They *s* and speak . . . . .Ps 73:8
They *s* at kings . . . . .Hab 1:10

SCOFFER

"He who corrects a *s* . . . . . .Prov 9:7
s does not listen . . . . .Prov 13:1
s seeks wisdom and . . . . . .Prov 14:6
s is an abomination. . . . . . .Prov 24:9

SCOFFERS

S ensnare a city. . . . . .Prov 29:8
s will come in the. . . . . . . .2 Pet 3:3

SCORCHED

sun was up they were *s* . . .Matt 13:6
And men were *s* with . . . . . .Rev 16:9

SCORN

My friends *s* me . . . . .Job 16:20
to our neighbors, a *s*. . . . . .Ps 44:13

SCORNED

consider, for I am *s*. . . . . .Lam 1:11
and princes are *s* . . . . .Hab 1:10

SCORNS

He *s* the scornful. . . . . . . .Prov 3:34
s obedience to his . . . . . . .Prov 30:17

SCORPIONS

and you dwell among *s*. . . .Ezek 2:6
on serpents and *s* . . . . .Luke 10:19
They had tails like *s* . . . . . .Rev 9:10

SCOURGE

hosts will stir up a *s* . . . . . .Is 10:26
up to councils and *s*. . . . . .Matt 10:17
will mock Him, and *s* . . .Mark 10:34

SCOURGES

s every son whom. . . . . . . .Heb 12:6

SCRIBE

"Where is the *s* . . . . .Is 33:18

SCRIBES

and not as the *s* . . . . .Matt 7:29
"But woe to you, *s* . . . . . .Matt 23:13
"Beware of the *s* . . . . . . .Mark 12:38

SCRIPTURE

what is noted in the *S* . . . .Dan 10:21
S was fulfilled which . . . .Mark 15:28
"Today this *S* . . . . .Luke 4:21
S cannot be broken. . . . .John 10:35
For what does the *S* . . . . . .Rom 4:3
S has confined all . . . . . . .Gal 3:22
All *S* is given by . . . . .2 Tim 3:16
that no prophecy of *S* . . . .2 Pet 1:20

SCRIPTURES

not knowing the *S* . . . . . .Matt 22:29
S must be fulfilled. . . . . .Mark 14:49
and mighty in the *S* . . . . .Acts 18:24
have known the Holy *S* .2 Tim 3:15
also the rest of the *S* . . . . .2 Pet 3:16

SCROLL

in the *s* of the book . . . . . . .Ps 40:7
and note it on a *s*. . . . . .Is 30:8
eat this *s* . . . . .Ezek 3:1
saw there a flying *s*. . . . . . .Zech 5:1
on the throne a *s*. . . . . .Rev 5:1
was able to open the *s* . . . . .Rev 5:3
the sky receded as a *s* . . . . .Rev 6:14

SEA

drowned in the Red *S* . . . .Ex 15:4
this great and wide *s* . . . . .Ps 104:25
who go down to the *s*. . . . .Ps 107:23
to the *s* its limit . . . . .Prov 8:29
rebuke I dry up the *s* . . . . . .Is 50:2
the waters cover the *s*. . . . .Hab 2:14
and the *s* obey Him . . . . .Matt 8:27
throne there was a *s*. . . . . . .Rev 4:6
standing on the *s* . . . . . . .Rev 15:2
there was no more *s* . . . . . .Rev 21:1

SEAL

Set me as a *s* upon. . . . . . .Song 8:6
of circumcision, a *s* . . . . . . .Rom 4:11
stands, having this *s*. . . . .2 Tim 2:19
He opened the second *s* . . . . .Rev 6:3

SEALED

My transgression is *s*. . . . .Job 14:17
who also has *s* us and . . . .2 Cor 1:22
by whom you were *s* . . . . . .Eph 4:30
of those who were *s* . . . . . . .Rev 7:4

SEAM

tunic was without *s* . . . . .John 19:23

SEANCE

"Please conduct a *s* . . . .1 Sam 28:8

SEARCH

"Can you *s* out the . . . . . . .Job 11:7
would not God *s* . . . . .Ps 44:21
glory of kings is to *s*. . . . .Prov 25:2
found it by secret *s* . . . . . . .Jer 2:34
I, the LORD, *s* the. . . . . . . .Jer 17:10
s the Scriptures. . . . . .John 5:39

SEARCHED

O LORD, You have *s* . . . . . .Ps 139:1
s the Scriptures. . . . . . . .Acts 17:11
and *s* carefully . . . . .1 Pet 1:10

SEARCHES

for the LORD *s* all. . . . . . .1 Chr 28:9
s the hearts knows . . . . . .Rom 8:27
For the Spirit *s*. . . . . .1 Cor 2:10
that I am He who *s* . . . . . .Rev 2:23

SEASON

there is a *s* . . . . .Eccl 3:1
Be ready in *s* and out. . . . .2 Tim 4:2

SEASONED

how shall it be *s* . . . . . . .Matt 5:13
"For everyone will be *s* . . .Mark 9:49

SEASONS

days and months and *s* . . . .Gal 4:10
the times and the *s* . . . . .1 Thess 5:1

SEAT

shall make a mercy *s* . . . . . .Ex 25:17
I might come to His *s* . . . . .Job 23:3
that He may *s* him with. . . .Ps 113:8
sit in Moses' *s* . . . . .Matt 23:2
before the judgment *s* . . . .2 Cor 5:10
the mercy *s* . . . . .Heb 9:5

SEATS

at feasts, the best *s* . . . . . .Matt 23:6
you love the best *s* . . . . .Luke 11:43

SECRET

s things belong . . . . .Deut 29:29
The *s* of the LORD is. . . . . .Ps 25:14
in the *s* place of His . . . . . .Ps 27:5
when I was made in *s*. . . . .Ps 139:15
do not disclose the *s* . . . . .Prov 25:9
I have not spoken in *s*. . . . . .Is 45:19
Father who is in the *s* . . . .Matt 6:6
are done by them in *s* . . . .Eph 5:12

SECRETLY

"Now a word was *s*. . . . . . .Job 4:12
He lies in wait *s* . . . . .Ps 10:9

SECRETS

would show you the *s*. . . . .Job 11:6
For He knows the *s* . . . . . .Ps 44:21
A talebearer reveals *s* . . . .Prov 11:13
heaven who reveals *s* . . . .Dan 2:28
God will judge the *s* . . . . .Rom 2:16
And thus the *s* of his . . .1 Cor 14:25

SECT

him (which is the *s* . . . . . .Acts 5:17
to the strictest *s* . . . . .Acts 26:5

SECURELY

pleasures, who dwell *s*. . . . . .Is 47:8
nation that dwells *s*. . . . . .Jer 49:31

SEDUCED

flattering lips she *s*. . . . . .Prov 7:21
because they have *s* . . . . .Ezek 13:10

SEE

for no man shall *s* . . . . . . .Ex 33:20
the LORD does not *s*. . . . .1 Sam 16:7
in my flesh I shall *s* . . . . .Job 19:26
s the works of God. . . . . . . .Ps 66:5
lest they *s* with their. . . . . . .Is 6:10
for sin, He shall *s* . . . . .Is 53:10
for they shall *s* God . . . . .Matt 5:8
seeing they do not *s*. . . . .Matt 13:13
s greater things than . . . .John 1:50
rejoiced to *s* My day. . . . .John 8:56
we wish to *s* Jesus . . . . .John 12:21
and the world will *s* . . . .John 14:19
Him, for we shall *s* . . . . .1 John 3:2
They shall *s* His face . . . . .Rev 22:4

SEED

s shall be called . . . . Gen 21:12
s shall be its stump . . . . Is 6:13
He shall see His *s* . . . . Is 53:10
you a noble vine, a *s* . . . . . . Jer 2:21
s is the word of God . . . . . Luke 8:11
had left us a *s* . . . . Rom 9:29
to each *s* its own body . . 1 Cor 15:38
S were the promises . . . . . . Gal 3:16
you are Abraham's *s* . . . . . . .Gal 3:29
Jesus Christ, of the *s* . . . . . 2 Tim 2:8
of corruptible *s* . . . . 1 Pet 1:23
not sin, for His *s* . . . . 1 John 3:9

SEEDS

the good *s* are the . . . . Matt 13:38
not say, "And to *s* . . . . Gal 3:16

SEEK

will find Him if you *s* . . . . .Deut 4:29
and pray and *s* My face . .2 Chr 7:14
your heart to *s* God . . . . . .2 Chr 19:3
s your God as you do . . . . . Ezra 4:2
may God above not *s* . . . . . . Job 3:4
countenance does not *s* . . . .Ps 10:4
Lord, that will I *s* . . . . .Ps 27:4
You said, "*S* My face . . . . . . .Ps 27:8
early will I *s* You . . . . .Ps 63:1
s me diligently will . . . . . . Prov 8:17
s one's own glory . . . . .Prov 25:27
s justice . . . . .Is 1:17
Should they *s* the dead . . . . .Is 8:19
the Gentiles shall *s* . . . . . . .Is 11:10
Jacob, '*S* Me in vain . . . . . .Is 45:19
S the Lord while He . . . . . . .Is 55:6
Yet they *s* Me daily . . . . .Is 58:2
s great things for . . . . Jer 45:5
s what was lost . . . . Ezek 34:16
"*S* Me and live . . . . Amos 5:4
and people should *s* . . . . . . .Mal 2:7
things the Gentiles *s* . . . . Matt 6:32
s, and you will find . . . . . . .Matt 7:7
of Man has come to *s* . . . .Luke 19:10
because I do not *s* . . . . . . John 5:30
"You will *s* Me and . . . . . .John 7:34
in doing good *s* . . . . .Rom 2:7
Because they do not *s* . . . .Rom 9:32
Let no one *s* his own . . . .1 Cor 10:24
for I do not *s* yours . . . . .2 Cor 12:14
For all *s* their own . . . . . . .Phil 2:21
s those things that . . . . .Col 3:1
s the one to come . . . . . . .Heb 13:14

SEEKING

run to and fro, *s* . . . . .Amos 8:12
and he came *s* fruit. . . . . .Luke 13:6
for the Father is *s* . . . . . . John 4:23
like a roaring lion, *s* . . . . . .1 Pet 5:8

SEEKS

no one *s* her . . . . Jer 30:17
receives, and he who *s* . . . .Matt 7:8
there is none who *s* . . . . . .Rom 3:11

SEEMS

There is a way which *s* . .Prov 14:12
have, even what he *s* . . . .Luke 8:18
If anyone among you *s* . . .1 Cor 3:18

SEEN

s God face to face . . . . . . .Gen 32:30
All this I have *s* . . . . .Eccl 8:9
s the one I love . . . . Song 3:3
Who has *s* such things . . . . . Is 66:8
s strange things today . . . .Luke 5:26

No one has *s* God at . . . . . .John 1:18
time, nor *s* His form . . . . . .John 5:37
I speak what I have *s* . . . .John 8:38
s Me has *s* the . . . . .John 14:9
things which we have *s* . . .Acts 4:20
s Jesus Christ our . . . . .1 Cor 9:1
things which are not *s* . . .2 Cor 4:18
whom no man has *s* . . . . .1 Tim 6:16
heard, which we have *s* . . .1 John 1:1

SEES

here seen Him who *s* . . . . .Gen 16:13
s all the sons of men . . . . . .Ps 33:13
s his brother in need . . . .1 John 3:17
s his brother sinning . . . .1 John 5:16

SELF-CONFIDENT

a fool rages and is *s* . . . . .Prov 14:16

SELF-CONTROL

about righteousness, *s* . . .Acts 24:25
they cannot exercise *s* . . . .1 Cor 7:9
gentleness, *s* . . . . .Gal 5:23
slanderers, without *s* . . . . .2 Tim 3:3
to knowledge *s* . . . . .2 Pet 1:6

SELF-CONTROLLED

just, holy, *s* . . . . .Titus 1:8

SELF-SEEKING

where envy and *s* exist . .James 3:16

SELL

said, "*S* me your . . . . .Gen 25:31
s Your people for . . . . .Ps 44:12
s the righteous . . . . .Amos 2:6
s whatever you have . . . .Mark 10:21
no sword, let him *s* . . . . .Luke 22:36
no one may buy or *s* . . . . .Rev 13:17

SEND

He shall *s* from heaven . . . . .Ps 57:3
"Whom shall I *s* . . . . .Is 6:8
s them a Savior . . . . .Is 19:20
"Behold, I *s* you out . . . . .Matt 10:16
The Son of Man will *s* . . .Matt 13:41
s Lazarus that he . . . . . . .Luke 16:24
whom the Father will *s* . .John 14:26
has sent Me, I also *s* . . . .John 20:21

SENSELESS

Understand, you *s* . . . . .Ps 94:8

SENSES

of use have their *s* . . . . . . .Heb 5:14

SENSIBLY

men who can answer *s* . . .Prov 26:16

SENSUAL

but is earthly, *s* . . . . .James 3:15
These are *s* persons . . . . . . .Jude 19

SENT

and His Spirit have *s* . . . . . .Is 48:16
s these prophets . . . . .Jer 23:21
As the Father has *s* . . . . .John 20:21
unless they are *s* . . . . . . .Rom 10:15
s His Son to be the . . . . .1 John 4:10

SEPARATE

'he shall *s* himself . . . . .Num 6:3
s yourselves from the . . . .Ezra 10:11
let not man *s* . . . . .Matt 19:6
Who shall *s* us from . . . . .Rom 8:35
harmless, undefiled, *s* . . . .Heb 7:26

SEPARATED

but the poor is *s* . . . . .Prov 19:4
"The Lord has utterly *s* . . . .Is 56:3
to be an apostle, *s* . . . . . . .Rom 1:1

it pleased God, who *s* . . . . . .Gal 1:15

SEPARATES

who repeats a matter *s* . . . .Prov 17:9

SEPARATION

the middle wall of *s* . . . . . .Eph 2:14

SERAPHIM

Above it stood *s* . . . . .Is 6:2

SERIOUS

therefore be *s* and . . . . .1 Pet 4:7

SERPENT

s was more cunning . . . . .Gen 3:1
"The *s* deceived me . . . . . . .Gen 3:13
"Make a fiery *s* . . . . .Num 21:8
like the poison of a *s* . . . . . .Ps 58:4
s you shall trample . . . . . . .Ps 91:13
their tongues like a *s* . . . . .Ps 140:3
air, the way of a *s* . . . . . . .Prov 30:19
s may bite when it is . . . . .Eccl 10:11
be a fiery flying *s* . . . . .Is 14:29
and wounded the *s* . . . . .Is 51:9
will he give him a *s* . . . . .Matt 7:10
Moses lifted up the *s* . . . .John 3:14
was cast out, that *s* . . . . . . .Rev 12:9

SERPENTS

is the poison of *s* . . . . . . .Deut 32:33
Therefore be wise as *s* . . .Matt 10:16
to trample on *s* . . . . .Luke 10:19

SERVANT

a *s* of servants he . . . . .Gen 9:25
s who earnestly . . . . .Job 7:2
and the fool will be *s* . . . .Prov 11:29
s will rule over a son . . . . .Prov 17:2
A *s* will not be . . . . .Prov 29:19
Who is blind but My *s* . . . .Is 42:19
"Is Israel a *s* . . . . .Jer 2:14
and a *s* his master . . . . .Mal 1:6
you, let him be your *s* . . .Matt 20:26
good and faithful *s* . . . . . .Matt 25:21
"You wicked and lazy *s* . . .Matt 25:26
the unprofitable *s* . . . . . . .Matt 25:30
that *s* who knew his . . . . .Luke 12:47
s does not know what . . . .John 15:15
against Your holy *S* . . . . . .Acts 4:27

SERVANTS

puts no trust in His *s* . . . . . .Job 4:18
for all are Your *s* . . . . .Ps 119:91
on the ground like *s* . . . . . .Eccl 10:7
shall call you the *s* . . . . .Is 61:6
S rule over us . . . . .Lam 5:8
"We are unprofitable *s* . . .Luke 17:10
longer do I call you *s* . . . .John 15:15
so consider us, as *s* . . . . . .1 Cor 4:1

SERVE

Lord your God are . . . . . .Deut 6:13
land, so you shall *s* aliens . . .Jer 5:19
s Him with one accord . . . .Zeph 3:9
You cannot *s* God and . . . .Matt 6:24
to be served, but to *s* . . . .Matt 20:28
the mind I myself *s* . . . . . .Rom 7:25
but through love *s* . . . . . . .Gal 5:13
s the Lord Christ . . . . .Col 3:24
s the living God . . . . .Heb 9:14
s Him day and night in . . . .Rev 7:15

SERVES

"If anyone *s* Me . . . . .John 12:26

SERVICE

do you mean by this *s* . . . .Ex 12:26
that he offers God *s* . . . . .John 16:2
is your reasonable *s* . . . . . .Rom 12:1

with good will doing s . . . . . Eph 6:7
your works, love, s . . . . Rev 2:19
SERVING
years I have been s . . . . . Luke 15:29
s the Lord with all. . . . . . Acts 20:19
fervent in spirit, s . . . . . . Rom 12:11
you, s as overseers . . . . 1 Pet 5:2
SET
"See, I have s . . . . Deut 30:15
s the Lord always. . . . . Ps 16:8
I will s him on high . . . . . . Ps 91:14
s aside the grace . . . . Gal 2:21
SETTLE
"Therefore s it in . . . . . . Luke 21:14
SETTLED
and my speech s . . . . Job 29:22
O Lord, Your word is s . . Ps 119:89
the mountains were s . . . . . Prov 8:25
s accounts with them. . . . Matt 25:19
SEVEN
S times a day I praise . . Ps 119:164
s other spirits more . . . . Luke 11:26
s times in a day . . . . Luke 17:4
out from among you s . . . . . Acts 6:3
s churches which are . . . . Rev 1:4
SEVENTY
S weeks are. . . . . Dan 9:24
up to s times seven. . . . . Matt 18:22
Then the s returned . . . . . Luke 10:17
SEVERE
My wound is s . . . . Jer 10:19
not to be too s . . . . 2 Cor 2:5
SEVERITY
the goodness and s . . . . . Rom 11:22
SHADE
I sat down in his s . . . . Song 2:3
be a tabernacle for s . . . . Is 4:6
may nest under its s . . . . Mark 4:32
SHADOW
May darkness and the s . . . . Job 3:5
He flees like a s. . . . . Job 14:2
hide me under the s . . . . . . Ps 17:8
walks about like a s . . . . . . Ps 39:6
like a passing s . . . . Ps 144:4
he passes like a s . . . . Eccl 6:12
and to trust in the s . . . . . . Is 30:2
in the s of His hand . . . . . . Is 49:2
which are a s of . . . . Col 2:17
the law, having a s . . . . . . Heb 10:1
is no variation or s . . . . . James 1:17
SHADOWS
my members are like s . . . . Job 17:7
and the s flee away . . . . . . Song 2:17
SHAKE
Who is he who will s . . . . . Job 17:3
s the earth . . . . Is 2:19
S yourself from the . . . . Is 52:2
s their heads at the . . . . . Lam 2:15
and the knees s . . . . Nah 2:10
hiss and s my fist . . . . . . Zeph 2:15
I will s all nations . . . . . . Hag 2:7
s not only the earth. . . . . Heb 12:26
SHAKEN
he will never be s . . . . Ps 112:6
together was s . . . . Acts 4:31
not to be soon s . . . . 2 Thess 2:2

SHAKES
s the earth out of its. . . . . . Job 9:6
s the Wilderness . . . . Ps 29:8
SHAME
you turn my glory to s. . . . . Ps 4:2
let them be put to s . . . . . . Ps 83:17
s who serve carved . . . . Ps 97:7
hate Zion be put to s . . . . Ps 129:5
s shall be the . . . . Prov 3:35
is a son who causes s . . . . Prov 10:5
hide My face from s . . . . . . Is 50:6
S has covered our. . . . . . . Jer 51:51
their glory into s . . . . Hos 4:7
never be put to s . . . . Joel 2:26
the unjust knows no s . . . . Zeph 3:5
worthy to suffer s . . . . Acts 5:41
will not be put to s . . . . . . Rom 9:33
to put to s the wise . . . . . 1 Cor 1:27
I say this to your s . . . . . . 1 Cor 6:5
glory is in their s . . . . Phil 3:19
put Him to an open s . . . . . Heb 6:6
SHAMEFUL
committing what is s . . . . . Rom 1:27
for it is s for women . . . . 1 Cor 14:35
For it is s even to. . . . . Eph 5:12
SHARE
a stranger does not s . . . . Prov 14:10
s your bread with the . . . . . . Is 58:7
is taught the word s . . . . . . Gal 6:6
to give, willing to s . . . . . 1 Tim 6:18
to do good and to s . . . . . Heb 13:16
SHARING
for your liberal s. . . . . 2 Cor 9:13
SHARP
s as a two-edged sword. . . . Prov 5:4
SHARPEN
s their tongue like a . . . . . . Ps 64:3
and one does not s . . . . . . Eccl 10:10
SHARPENS
my adversary s His . . . . . . Job 16:9
SHARPNESS
present I should use s . . . 2 Cor 13:10
SHATTERED
at ease, but He has s . . . . Job 16:12
SHEATH
'Return it to its s . . . . . . Ezek 21:30
your sword into the s . . . . John 18:11
SHEAVES
bringing his s . . . . Ps 126:6
nor he who binds s . . . . . . Ps 129:7
gather them like s. . . . . . . Mic 4:12
SHED
which is s for many . . . . Matt 26:28
SHEDDING
blood, and without s . . . . . Heb 9:22
SHEEP
astray like a lost s . . . . . Ps 119:176
slaughter, and as a s . . . . . Is 53:7
Pull them out like s . . . . . Jer 12:3
have been lost s . . . . Jer 50:6
will search for My s . . . . Ezek 34:11
shall judge between s . . . Ezek 34:17
s will be scattered . . . . . . Zech 13:7
rather to the lost s . . . . . . Matt 10:6
I send you out as s . . . . . Matt 10:16
And He will set the s . . . Matt 25:33
having a hundred s. . . . . . Luke 15:4

and he calls his own s . . . John 10:3
and I know My s . . . . . John 10:14
s I have which are not . . John 10:16
"He was led as a s . . . . . Acts 8:32
like s going astray . . . . . 1 Pet 2:25
SHEEPFOLDS
lie down among the s . . . . Ps 68:13
SHEET
object like a great s. . . . . Acts 10:11
SHELTER
I will trust in the s . . . . Ps 61:4
in You I take s. . . . . Ps 143:9
the Lord will be a s . . . . . Joel 3:16
SHELTERS
s him all the day long . . Deut 33:12
be pastures, with s . . . . . . Zeph 2:6
SHEOL
down to the gates of S . . . Job 17:16
not leave my soul in S . . . . Ps 16:10
S laid hold of me. . . . . . . Ps 116:3
S cannot thank . . . . Is 38:18
the belly of S I cried. . . . . . Jon 2:2
SHEPHERD
s is an abomination . . . . . Gen 46:34
s My people Israel . . . . . 2 Sam 5:2
The Lord is my s . . . . Ps 23:1
s Jacob His people . . . . . . Ps 78:71
His flock like a s . . . . Is 40:11
of Cyrus, 'He is My s . . . . Is 44:28
s who follows You . . . . . . Jer 17:16
because there was no s . . . Ezek 34:5
I will establish one s . . . Ezek 34:23
"As a s takes from . . . . . Amos 3:12
to the worthless s . . . . . . Zech 11:17
'I will strike the S . . . . . Matt 26:31
"I am the good s. . . . . . . John 10:11
s the church of God . . . . Acts 20:28
the dead, that great S. . . . Heb 13:20
S the flock of God . . . . 1 Pet 5:2
when the Chief S . . . . 1 Pet 5:4
of the throne will s . . . . . . Rev 7:17
SHEPHERDS
your sons shall be s . . . . Num 14:33
And they are s who. . . . . . . Is 56:11
And I will give you s. . . . . Jer 3:15
s who destroy and . . . . . . Jer 23:1
s who feed My people . . . . Jer 23:2
s have led them astray . . . Jer 50:6
s fed themselves . . . . . . Ezek 34:8
in the same country s . . . . Luke 2:8
SHIELD
I am your s . . . . Gen 15:1
He is a s to all who . . . 2 Sam 22:31
my s and the horn of . . . . . Ps 18:2
God is a sun and s . . . . . . Ps 84:11
truth shall be your s . . . . . . Ps 91:4
all, taking the s . . . . Eph 6:16
SHINE
Lord make His face s . . . Num 6:25
cause His face to s . . . . . . Ps 67:1
the cherubim, s . . . . Ps 80:1
Make Your face s . . . . . Ps 119:135
who are wise shall s. . . . . Dan 12:3
the righteous will s. . . . . Matt 13:43
among whom you s . . . . . Phil 2:15
SHINED
them a light has s . . . . Is 9:2
SHINES
And the light s . . . . John 1:5

SHINING

heed as a light that s . . . . .2 Pet 1:19

SHINING

the earth, by clear s . . . . .2 Sam 23:4
His clothes became s . . . . .Mark 9:3
light is already s . . . . .1 John 2:8
was like the sun s . . . . .Rev 1:16

SHIPS

pass by like swift s . . . . . . .Job 9:26
down to the sea in s . . . . .Ps 107:23
like the merchant s . . . . . .Prov 31:14
Look also at s . . . . .James 3:4

SHIPWRECK

faith have suffered s . . . . .1 Tim 1:19

SHOOT

they s out the lip . . . . .Ps 22:7
But God shall s . . . . .Ps 64:7

SHORT

have sinned and fall s . . . . .Rom 3:23
the work and cut it s . . . . .Rom 9:28

SHORTENED

his youth You have s . . . . . .Ps 89:45
the wicked will be s . . . . . .Prov 10:27
those days were s . . . . . . .Matt 24:22

SHOT

shall be stoned or s . . . . . .Heb 12:20

SHOUT

s joyfully to the Rock . . . . . . .Ps 95:1
S joyfully to the LORD . . . . . .Ps 98:4
Make a joyful s . . . . .Ps 100:1
from heaven with a s . . .1 Thess 4:16

SHOW

a land that I will s . . . . . . .Gen 12:1
S me Your ways . . . . .Ps 25:4
s yourselves men . . . . .Is 46:8
s Him greater works . . . . .John 5:20
s us the Father . . . . .John 14:8

SHOWBREAD

you shall set the s . . . . . . .Ex 25:30
s which had been taken . .1 Sam 21:6
s which was not lawful . . .Matt 12:4

SHOWERS

make it soft with s . . . . . . .Ps 65:10
s have been withheld . . . . . . .Jer 3:3
can the heavens give s . . . .Jer 14:22
from the LORD, like s . . . . . .Mic 5:7

SHREWDLY

because he had dealt s . . . .Luke 16:8

SHRINES

who made silver s . . . . . .Acts 19:24

SHRIVELED

You have s me up . . . . .Job 16:8

SHUFFLES

with his eyes, he s . . . . . . .Prov 6:13

SHUNNED

feared God and s evil . . . . . .Job 1:1

SHUT

"Or who s in the sea . . . . . .Job 38:8
Has He in anger s . . . . .Ps 77:9
For you s up the . . . . . . .Matt 23:13

SHUTS

s his ears to the cry . . . . .Prov 21:13
s his eyes from seeing . . . . . .Is 33:15
brother in need, and s . . .1 John 3:17
who opens and no one s . . . .Rev 3:7

SICK

have made him s . . . . .Hos 7:5
I was s and you . . . . . . .Matt 25:36
he whom You love is s . . . .John 11:3
many are weak and s . . . .1 Cor 11:30
have left in Miletus s . . . .2 Tim 4:20
faith will save the s . . . . .James 5:15

SICKLE

Put in the s . . . . .Joel 3:13
"Thrust in Your s . . . . .Rev 14:15

SICKNESS

will sustain him in s . . . . .Prov 18:14
"This s is not unto . . . . . .John 11:4

SICKNESSES

and bore our s . . . . .Matt 8:17

SIDE

The LORD is on my s . . .' . .Ps 118:6
the net on the right s . . . .John 21:6

SIFT

s the nations with the . . . . . .Is 30:28
s the house of Israel . . . . .Amos 9:9
for you, that he may s . .Luke 22:31

SIFTS

A wise king s out the . . . .Prov 20:26

SIGH

our years like a s . . . . .Ps 90:9
the merry-hearted s . . . . .Is 24:7
of the men who s . . . . .Ezek 9:4

SIGHING

For my s comes before . . . . .Job 3:24
s is not hidden . . . . .Ps 38:9

SIGHT

and see this great s . . . . .Ex 3:3
seemed good in Your s . . .Matt 11:26
by faith, not by s . . . . .2 Cor 5:7

SIGN

Show me a s for good . . . . . .Ps 86:17
will give you a s . . . . .Is 7:14
for an everlasting s . . . . .Is 55:13
we want to see a s . . . . .Matt 12:38
seeks after a s . . . . .Matt 12:39
And what will be the s . . . .Matt 24:3
s which will be spoken . . .Luke 2:34
again is the second s . . . .John 4:54
For Jews request a s . . . . .1 Cor 1:22
Now a great s appeared . . .Rev 12:1

SIGNS

and let them be for s . . . . . .Gen 1:14
you not know their s . . . . . .Job 21:29
They performed His s . . . . .Ps 105:27
We are for s and . . . . .Is 8:18
How great are His s . . . . . . .Dan 4:3
cannot discern the s . . . . .Matt 16:3
the accompanying s . . . .Mark 16:20
s Jesus did in Cana of . . . .John 2:11
no one can do these s . . . . .John 3:2
you people see s . . . . .John 4:48
because you saw the s . . . .John 6:26
is a sinner do such s . . . . .John 9:16
this Man works many s . .John 11:47
Jesus did many other s . .John 20:30
demons, performing s . . . .Rev 16:14

SILENCE

that You may s . . . . .Ps 8:2
I was mute with s . . . . .Ps 39:2
soon have settled in s . . . . . .Ps 94:17
"Sit in s . . . . .Is 47:5
seal, there was s . . . . .Rev 8:1

SILENT

the wicked shall be s . . . .1 Sam 2:9
season, and am not s . . . . . .Ps 22:2
Do not be s to me . . . . .Ps 28:1
Let them be s in the . . . . . .Ps 31:17
Be s in the presence . . . . . .Zeph 1:7
Let your women keep s . .1 Cor 14:34

SILK

and covered you with s . .Ezek 16:10

SILLY

They are s children . . . . . . .Jer 4:22

SILVER

and your precious s . . . . . .Job 22:25
Though he heaps up s . . . .Job 27:16
s tried in a furnace . . . . .Ps 12:6
have refined us as s . . . . . . .Ps 66:10
than the profits of s . . . . . .Prov 3:14
chosen rather than s . . . .Prov 16:16
refining pot is for s . . . . . .Prov 17:3
He who loves s will . . . . . .Eccl 5:10
s has become dross . . . . .Is 1:22
call them rejected s . . . . . . .Jer 6:30
may buy the poor for s . . . .Amos 8:6
him thirty pieces of s . . . .Matt 26:15

SIMILITUDE

been made in the s . . . . . .James 3:9

SIMPLE

making wise the s . . . . .Ps 19:7
LORD preserves the s . . . . . .Ps 116:6
understanding to the s . . .Ps 119:130
s believes every word . . . .Prov 14:15
the hearts of the s . . . . . . .Rom 16:18

SIMPLICITY

ones, will you love s . . . . . .Prov 1:22
in the world in s . . . . .2 Cor 1:12
corrupted from the s . . . . .2 Cor 11:3

SIN

committed a great s . . . . . . .Ex 32:20
he died in his own s . . . . . .Num 27:3
and be sure your s . . . . .Num 32:23
to death for his own s . . . .Deut 24:16
all this Job did not s . . . . . .Job 2:10
and search out my s . . . . . .Job 10:6
Be angry, and do not s . . . . . .Ps 4:4
my ways, lest I s . . . . .Ps 39:1
s is always before me . . . . . .Ps 51:3
in s my mother . . . . .Ps 51:5
s is a reproach . . . . .Prov 14:34
good and does not s . . . . . .Eccl 7:20
soul an offering for s . . . . . .Is 53:10
and He bore the s . . . . .Is 53:12
s I will remember no . . . . . .Jer 31:34
They eat up the s . . . . .Hos 4:8
Now they s more and . . . . .Hos 13:2
who believe in Me to s . . . .Matt 18:6
who takes away the s . . . .John 1:29
S no more . . . . .John 5:14
"He who is without s . . . . .John 8:7
convict the world of s . . . . .John 16:8
they are all under s . . . . . . .Rom 3:9
s entered the world . . . . . . .Rom 5:12
s is not imputed . . . . .Rom 5:13
s that grace may . . . . .Rom 6:1
died to s once for all . . . . . .Rom 6:10
s shall not have . . . . .Rom 6:14
Shall we s because we . . . . .Rom 6:15
s that dwells in me . . . . . . .Rom 7:17
Him who knew no s . . . . . .2 Cor 5:21
man of s is revealed . . . . . .2 Thess 2:3
we are, yet without s . . . . . .Heb 4:15
appeared to put away s . . . .Heb 9:26
s willfully after we . . . . . .Heb 10:26

SINCERE

it gives birth to s . . . . . . .James 1:15
do it, to him it is s . . . . .James 4:17
"Who committed no s . . . .1 Pet 2:22
say that we have no s . . . .1 John 1:8
that you may not s . . . . .1 John 2:1
s is lawlessness . . . . .1 John 3:4
in Him there is no s . . . .1 John 3:5
and he cannot s . . . . .1 John 3:9
for those who commit s 1 John 5:16
unrighteousness is s . . . .1 John 5:17

SINCERE

Holy Spirit, by s love . . . . .2 Cor 6:6
and from s faith. . . . . .1 Tim 1:5
s love of the brethren. . . . .1 Pet 1:22

SINCERITY

LORD, serve Him in s . . . .Josh 24:14
unleavened bread of s . . . . .1 Cor 5:8
simplicity and godly s . . . .2 Cor 1:12
men-pleasers, but in s . . . . . .Col 3:22

SINFUL

Alas, s nation. . . . . .Is 1:4
and s generation. . . . . . .Mark 8:38
from me, for I am a s. . . . .Luke 5:8
the hands of s men. . . . . .Luke 24:7
become exceedingly s . . . . .Rom 7:13
likeness of s flesh . . . . .Rom 8:3

SING

"S to the LORD . . . . .Ex 15:21
the widow's heart to s . . . .Job 29:13
S out the honor. . . . . .Ps 66:2
I will s of mercy and . . . . .Ps 101:1
"S us one of the songs. . . . .Ps 137:3
My servants shall s. . . . . . .Is 65:14
I will s with the. . . . . . . .1 Cor 14:15
assembly I will s . . . . .Heb 2:12
Let him s psalms . . . . . .James 5:13

SINGERS

The s went before . . . . .Ps 68:25
male and female s . . . . .Eccl 2:8

SINGING

His presence with s . . . . . .Ps 100:2
and our tongue with s . . . .Ps 126:2
the time of s has come. . .Song 2:12
break forth into s. . . . . .Is 14:7
even with joy and . . . . .Is 35:2
come to Zion with s. . . . . . .Is 35:10
and spiritual songs, s . . . .Eph 5:19

SINISTER

who understands s. . . . . . .Dan 8:23

SINK

I s in deep mire. . . . . .Ps 69:2
to s he cried out . . . . . . .Matt 14:30

SINNED

You only, have I s . . . . . . .Ps 51:4
Jerusalem has s. . . . . .Lam 1:8
Our fathers s and are . . . . .Lam 5:7
"Father, I have s. . . . . . .Luke 15:18
"Rabbi, who s . . . . .John 9:2
For as many as have s . . .Rom 2:12
for all have s and. . . . . . . .Rom 3:23
marries, she has not s . . .1 Cor 7:28
say that we have not s .1 John 1:10
for the devil has s . . . . . .1 John 3:8

SINNER

s He gives the work. . . . . .Eccl 2:26
s does evil a hundred. . . . .Eccl 8:12
s destroys much good . . . .Eccl 9:18
the city who was a s. . . . . .Luke 7:37
s who repents than. . . . . . .Luke 15:7
can a man who is a s . . . .John 9:16

the ungodly and the s . . . .1 Pet 4:18

SINNERS

in the path of s . . . . .Ps 1:1
therefore He teaches s . . . . . .Ps 25:8
soul with s . . . . .Ps 26:9
s be consumed from the. . .Ps 104:35
son, if s entice you . . . . . . .Prov 1:10
The s in Zion are . . . . .Is 33:14
the righteous, but s . . . . .Matt 9:13
tax collectors and s . . . . .Matt 11:19
s love those who love . . . . .Luke 6:32
Galileans were worse s . . . .Luke 13:2
God does not hear s . . . . . .John 9:31
while we were still s . . . . . .Rom 5:8
many were made s. . . . . . .Rom 5:19
the ungodly and for s. . . . .1 Tim 1:9
the world to save s . . . .1 Tim 1:15
separate from s. . . . . .Heb 7:26
such hostility from s . . . . .Heb 12:3
things which ungodly s. . . . .Jude 15

SINS

my iniquities and s . . . . . .Job 13:23
from presumptuous s . . . . . .Ps 19:13
You, our secret s . . . . .Ps 90:8
but he who s against . . . .Prov 8:36
s have hidden His face . . . . .Is 59:2
the soul who s shall . . . . .Ezek 18:4
to make an end of s . . . . . .Dan 9:24
if your brother s . . . . . . .Matt 18:15
I take away their s . . . . .Rom 11:27
s according to the . . . . . .1 Cor 15:3
are still in your s . . . . . .1 Cor 15:17
the forgiveness of s . . . . . . .Eph 1:7
s are clearly evident . . . .1 Tim 5:24
once to bear the s. . . . . . . .Heb 9:28
If we confess our s . . . . .1 John 1:9
propitiation for our s . . . .1 John 2:2
s are forgiven you . . . . . .1 John 2:12
Whoever s has neither. . .1 John 3:6
you share in her s . . . . . .Rev 18:4

SISTER

are my mother and my s .Job 17:14
We have a little s . . . . .Song 8:8
is My brother and s . . . .Matt 12:50
to you Phoebe our s . . . . . .Rom 16:1
s is not under bondage . . .1 Cor 7:15

SIT

Those who s in the . . . . . . .Ps 69:12
"Come down and s. . . . . .Is 47:1
"Why do we s still . . . . . . .Jer 8:14
but to s on My right . . . .Matt 20:23
and the Pharisees . . . . . . .Matt 23:2
"S at My right hand . . . . .Heb 1:13
say to him, "You s . . . . . .James 2:3
I will grant to s. . . . . .Rev 3:21
heart, 'I s as queen. . . . . . .Rev 18:7

SITS

God s on His holy. . . . . .Ps 47:8
It is He who s above. . . . . .Is 40:22
so that he s as God . . . .2 Thess 2:4
where the harlot s. . . . . . .Rev 17:15

SITTING

You know my s down and . .Ps 139:2
see the Son of Man s. . . .Mark 14:62
where Christ is, s. . . . . .Col 3:1

SKILL

hand forget its s . . . . .Ps 137:5
nor favor to men of s. . . . . .Eccl 9:11
them knowledge and s. . . .Dan 1:17
forth to give you s . . . . . . .Dan 9:22

SKILLFULNESS

guided them by the s . . . . .Ps 78:72

SKIN

God made tunics of s. . . . . .Gen 3:21
LORD and said, "S. . . . . .Job 2:4
have escaped by the s. . . .Job 19:20
Ethiopian change his s . . . .Jer 13:23
s is hot as an oven. . . . . . .Lam 5:10

SKIP

He makes them also s . . . . .Ps 29:6

SKIPPING

upon the mountains, s . . . .Song 2:8

SKULL

to say, Place of a S. . . . . .Matt 27:33

SKY

s receded as a scroll . . . . . .Rev 6:14

SLACK

He will not be s. . . . . .Deut 7:10
s hand becomes poor. . . . . .Prov 10:4
The Lord is not s . . . . .2 Pet 3:9

SLAIN

s his thousands. . . . . .1 Sam 18:7
beauty of Israel is s . . . .2 Sam 1:19
the dead, like the s . . . . . . .Ps 88:5
and all who were s. . . . . . .Prov 7:26
I shall be s in the . . . . . . .Prov 22:13
s men are not s . . . . .Is 22:2
no more cover her s . . . . . . .Is 26:21
and the s of the LORD . . . . .Is 66:16
and night for the s. . . . . .Jer 9:1
Those s by the sword . . . . .Lam 4:9
the prophets, I have s . . . . .Hos 6:5
is the Lamb who was s . . . .Rev 5:12

SLANDER

s your own mother's. . . . . . .Ps 50:20
and whoever spreads s . . .Prov 10:18

SLANDERERS

be reverent, not s. . . . . . . .1 Tim 3:11
unforgiving, s. . . . . .2 Tim 3:3
in behavior, not s . . . . .Titus 2:3

SLANDEROUSLY

as we are s reported . . . . . .Rom 3:8

SLAUGHTER

as sheep for the s . . . . .Ps 44:22
led as a lamb to the s . . . . . .Is 53:7
but the Valley of S. . . . . . . .Jer 7:32
"Feed the flock for s. . . . .Zech 11:4
as sheep for the s . . . . . . .Rom 8:36

SLAVE

that you were a s . . . . . . .Deut 15:15
commits sin is a s. . . . . . . .John 8:34
you called while a s . . . . .1 Cor 7:21
you are no longer a s. . . . . . .Gal 4:7

SLAVES

should no longer be s . . . . .Rom 6:6
though you were s. . . . . . . .Rom 6:17
your members as s . . . . . . .Rom 6:19
do not become s. . . . . .1 Cor 7:23

SLAY

s the righteous . . . . .Gen 18:25
s a righteous nation. . . . . .Gen 20:4
Evil shall s the . . . . .Ps 34:21
Oh, that You would s . . . . .Ps 139:19
s them before me . . . . . . .Luke 19:27

SLEEP

God caused a deep s . . . . . .Gen 2:21
the night, when deep s . . . .Job 4:13
my eyes, lest I s . . . . .Ps 13:3
Why do You s . . . . .Ps 44:23

SLEEPERS (cont.)

have sunk into their s .... Ps 76:5
they are like a s .... Ps 90:5
neither slumber nor s ...... Ps 121:4
He gives His beloved s .... Ps 127:2
I will not give s .... Ps 132:4
s will be sweet .... Prov 3:24
For they do not s .... Prov 4:16
A little s .... Prov 6:10
Do not love s .... Prov 20:13
The s of a laboring ...... Eccl 5:12
the spirit of deep s .... Is 29:10
Also his s went from ..... Dan 6:18
me, I was in a deep s .... Dan 8:18
them, "Why do you s ... Luke 22:46
among you, and many s 1 Cor 11:30
We shall not all s ...... 1 Cor 15:51
"Awake, you who s ...... Eph 5:14
with Him those who s ..1 Thess 4:14
Therefore let us not s .... 1 Thess 5:6

SLEEPERS

gently the lips of s .... Song 7:9

SLEEPING

is not dead, but s .... Matt 9:24
"Are you still s .... Matt 26:45
that night Peter was s ... Acts 12:6

SLEEPLESSNESS

in labors, in s .... 2 Cor 6:5
and toil, in s often ...... 2 Cor 11:27

SLEEPS

wise son; he who s .... Prov 10:5
"Our friend Lazarus s .. John 11:11

SLEPT

I lay down and s .... Ps 3:5
but while men s .... Matt 13:25

SLIGHTED

is the one who is s .... Prov 12:9

SLING

he had, and his s ...... 1 Sam 17:40
s is he who gives .... Prov 26:8

SLIP

their foot shall s .... Deut 32:35
my footsteps may not s ..... Ps 17:5

SLIPPERY

way be dark and s .... Ps 35:6
set them in s places ...... Ps 73:18
be to them like s .... Jer 23:12

SLOOPS

all the beautiful s .... Is 2:16

SLOW

but I am s of speech ...... Ex 4:10
He who is s to wrath .... Prov 14:29
hear, s to speak, s ...... James 1:19

SLUGGARD

will you slumber, O s ...... Prov 6:9

SLUMBERED

delayed, they all s .... Matt 25:5

SLUMBERING

upon men, while s ...... Job 33:15

SMALL

'The place is too s .... Is 49:20
I will make you s .... Jer 49:15
may stand, for he is s ... Amos 7:2
I will make you s .... Obad 2
the day of s things ...... Zech 4:10
And I saw the dead, s ... Rev 20:12

SMELL

and he smelled the s ..... Gen 27:27
s there will be a .... Is 3:24

SMELLS

s the battle from afar .... Job 39:25

SMITTEN

Him stricken, s .... Is 53:4

SMOKE

went up like the s ...... Gen 19:28
s is driven away .... Ps 68:2
are consumed like s ...... Ps 102:3
like a wineskin in s ...... Ps 119:83
like pillars of s .... Song 3:6
s shall ascend forever ...... Is 34:10
vanish away like s .... Is 51:6
fire and vapor of s .... Acts 2:19
s arose out of the pit ...... Rev 9:2
was filled with s .... Rev 15:8
Her s rises up .... Rev 19:3

SMOOTH

speak to us s things ...... Is 30:10
and the rough places ...... Is 40:4
though they speak s ...... Jer 12:6
the rough ways s .... Luke 3:5

SMOOTH-SKINNED

man, and I am a s ...... Gen 27:11

SNAIL

s which melts away as ...... Ps 58:8

SNARE

it will surely be a s ...... Ex 23:33
It became a s to .... Judg 8:27
that she may be a s .. 1 Sam 18:21
s snatches their .... Job 5:5
and he walks into a s ... Job 18:8
their table become a s ... Ps 69:22
as a bird from the s ...... Ps 124:7
birds caught in a s .... Eccl 9:12
and the pit and the s ..... Is 24:17
I have laid a s .... Jer 50:23
s have come upon us ..... Lam 3:47
is a fowler's s .... Hos 9:8
a bird fall into a s .... Amos 3:5
it will come as a s ...... Luke 21:35
temptation and a s ...... 1 Tim 6:9
and escape the s .... 2 Tim 2:26

SNARED

The wicked is s .... Ps 9:16
and be broken, be s .... Is 8:15
all of them are s .... Is 42:22

SNARES

the s of death .... Ps 18:5
who seek my life lay s ..... Ps 38:12
and built great s .... Eccl 9:14
wait as one who sets s ..... Jer 5:26

SNATCH

s the fatherless .... Job 24:9
neither shall anyone s ... John 10:28

SNATCHES

s away what was .... Matt 13:19

SNEER

and you s at it .... Mal 1:13

SNIFFED

they s at the wind .... Jer 14:6

SNORTING

s strikes terror .... Job 39:20

SNOW

and heat consume the s ... Job 24:19
For He says to the s ...... Job 37:6
the treasury of s .... Job 38:22
shall be whiter than s ...... Ps 51:7
He gives s like wool ..... Ps 147:16
As s in summer and ...... Prov 26:1
She is not afraid of s .... Prov 31:21
shall be as white as s ...... Is 1:18
garment was white as s ... Dan 7:9
clothing as white as s ... Matt 28:3
wool, as white as s .... Rev 1:14

SOAKED

their land shall be s .... Is 34:7

SOAP

lye, and use much s .... Jer 2:22

SOBER

of the day be s .... 1 Thess 5:8
the older men be s .... Titus 2:2

SOBERLY

think, but to think s ...... Rom 12:3
we should live s .... Titus 2:12

SODA

and like vinegar on s ..... Prov 25:20

SODOMITES

nor homosexuals, nor s .... 1 Cor 6:9
for fornicators, for s ...... 1 Tim 1:10

SOFTER

his words were s .... Ps 55:21

SOJOURNER

But no s had to lodge.... Job 31:32

SOJOURNERS

are strangers and s ...... Lev 25:23
I beg you as s .... 1 Pet 2:11

SOLD

s his birthright .... Gen 25:33
the house that was s ..... Lev 25:33
their Rock had .... Deut 32:30
and He s them into the .. Judg 2:14
s themselves to do...... 2 Kin 17:17
Had we been s as male..... Esth 7:4
who was s as a slave..... Ps 105:17
s all that he had .... Matt 13:46
they bought, they s ..... Luke 17:28
s their possessions ...... Acts 2:45
but I am carnal, s .... Rom 7:14
Eat whatever is s....... 1 Cor 10:25

SOLDIER

hardship as a good s...... 2 Tim 2:3
enlisted him as a s .... 2 Tim 2:4

SOLDIERS

sum of money to the s ... Matt 28:12
The s also mocked ..... Luke 23:36
s twisted a crown .... John 19:2

SOLEMNLY

saying, "The man s...... Gen 43:3
s testified of the ...... Acts 28:23

SOLITARILY

heritage, who dwell s ...... Mic 7:14

SOLITARY

God sets the s in........ Ps 68:6

SOMEBODY

up, claiming to be s...... Acts 5:36

SOMETHING

"Simon, I have s........Luke 7:40
thinks himself to be s.......Gal 6:3

SON

Me, 'You are My S ....Ps 2:7
I was my father's s.......Prov 4:3
s makes a glad father....Prov 10:1
s is a grief to his.......Prov 17:25
And what, s of my womb. .Prov 31:2
is born, unto us a S..........Is 9:6
heaven, O Lucifer, s........Is 14:12
fourth is like the S.......Dan 3:25
He is an unwise s.......Hos 13:13
prophet, nor was I a s....Amos 7:14
s honors his father........Mal 1:6
will bring forth a S........Matt 1:21
" This is My beloved S ..Matt 3:17
Jesus, You S of God.....Matt 8:29
not the carpenter's s ...Matt 13:55
You are the S of God ....Matt 14:33
are the Christ, the S....Matt 16:16
of all he sent his s .....Matt 21:37
Whose S is He ....Matt 22:42
'Lord,' how is He his S..Matt 22:45
him twice as much a s ..Matt 23:15
coming of the S of Man..Matt 24:37
'I am the S of God......Matt 27:43
" Truly this was the S ..Matt 27:54
of Jesus Christ, the S .....Mark 1:1
called the S of the.......Luke 1:32
out, the only s...........Luke 7:12
"And if a s of peace.....Luke 10:6
to be called your s ....Luke 15:19
because he also is a s ....Luke 19:9
The only begotten S.....John 1:14
that this is the S........John 1:34
of the only begotten S ...John 3:18
S can do nothing.......John 5:19
s abides forever.........John 8:35
you believe in the S......John 9:35
I said, 'I am the S .....John 10:36
"Woman, behold your s ..John 19:26
Jesus Christ is the S.....Acts 8:37
declared to be the S ......Rom 1:4
in the gospel of His S.....Rom 1:9
by sending His own S.....Rom 8:3
not spare His own S .....Rom 8:32
S Himself will also be ...1 Cor 15:28
live by faith in the S......Gal 2:20
God sent forth His S......Gal 4:4
longer a slave but a s.....Gal 4:7
the knowledge of the S ....Eph 4:13
you for my s Onesimus ...Philem 10
"You are My S ....Heb 1:5
but Christ as a S over His .Heb 3:6
though He was a S......Heb 5:8
but made like the S.......Heb 7:3
to be called the s ....Heb 11:24
" This is My beloved S ..2 Pet 1:17
Whoever denies the S ..1 John 2:23
God has given of His S ..1 John 5:11
One like the S of Man ....Rev 1:13

SONG

is my strength and s ....Ex 15:2
Sing to Him a new s........Ps 33:3
He has put a new s........Ps 40:3
in the night His s ....Ps 42:8
me, and I am the s.........Ps 69:12
asked of us a s ....Ps 137:3
I will sing a new s ....Ps 144:9
to my Well-beloved a s........Is 5:1
their taunting s ....Lam 3:14
I am their taunting s .....Lam 3:63
as a very lovely s ......Ezek 33:32
They sang a new s ....Rev 5:9
And they sing the s ....Rev 15:3

SONGS

my Maker, who gives s....Job 35:10
surround me with s........Ps 32:7
have been my s In the ....Ps 119:54
Sing us one of the s ......Ps 137:3
is one who sings s ....Prov 25:20
and spiritual s ....Eph 5:19

SONS

s come to honor.........Job 14:21
shall be Your s.........Ps 45:16
my beloved among the s ..Song 2:3
s shall come from afar......Is 60:4
"Has Israel no s..........Jer 49:1
The precious s of Zion.....Lam 4:2
'You are the s ....Hos 1:10
He will purify the s ......Mal 3:3
to him, " Then the s....Matt 17:26
and you will be s.........Luke 6:35
that you may become s ..John 12:36
"You are s of the ....Acts 3:25
of God, these are s ......Rom 8:14
who are of faith are s ......Gal 3:7
the adoption as s...........Gal 4:5
because you are s ....Gal 4:6
You are all s of light ...1 Thess 5:5
in bringing many s........Heb 2:10
speaks to you as to s.....Heb 12:5
illegitimate and not s.....Heb 12:8

SOON

for it is s cut off ....Ps 90:10
s forgot His works ......Ps 106:13

SOOTHED

or bound up, or s...........Is 1:6

SORCERER

omens, or a s.........Deut 18:10
But Elymas the s ......Acts 13:8

SORCERERS

soothsayers, or your s.....Jer 27:9
outside are dogs and s ...Rev 22:15

SORCERESS

shall not permit a s ......Ex 22:18

SORCERY

For there is no s ....Num 23:23
idolatry, s ....Gal 5:20

SORES

and putrefying s ....Is 1:6
Lazarus, full of s.......Luke 16:20

SORROW

multiply your s...........Gen 3:16
s dances before him ......Job 41:22
in my soul, having s......Ps 13:2
s is continually ....Ps 38:17
I found trouble and s.....Ps 116:3
and He adds no s ....Prov 10:22
the heart may s ....Prov 14:13
S is better than ....Eccl 7:3
Therefore remove s.....Eccl 11:10
and desperate s ....Is 17:11
you shall cry for s ....Is 65:14
to see labor and s.......Jer 20:18
Your s is incurable ....Jer 30:15
added grief to my s ....Jer 45:3
gather those who s ....Zeph 3:18
them sleeping from s ...Luke 22:45
s has filled your ....John 16:6
s will be turned..........John 16:20
that I have great s ....Rom 9:2
s produces repentance ...2 Cor 7:10
lest I should have s ......Phil 2:27
s as others who have ..1 Thess 4:13
no more death, nor s.......Rev 21:4

SORROWFUL

am a woman of s spirit ..1 Sam 1:15
But I am poor and s.......Ps 69:29
For all his days are s .....Eccl 2:23
replenished every s ......Jer 31:25
were exceedingly s .....Matt 17:23
saying, he went away s .Matt 19:22
soul is exceedingly s....Matt 26:38
and went away s.......Mark 10:22
and you will be s.......John 16:20
if I make you s...........2 Cor 2:2
and I may be less s.......Phil 2:28

SORROWS

the s of Sheol ....2 Sam 22:6
s God distributes ....Job 21:17
s shall be multiplied.......Ps 16:4
by men, a Man of s......Is 53:3
are the beginning of s ....Matt 24:8
through with many s ...1 Tim 6:10

SORRY

s that He had made man....Gen 6:6
who will be s for you......Is 51:19
And the king was s .....Matt 14:9
For you were made s .....2 Cor 7:9

SOUGHT

I s the LORD ....Ps 34:4
whole heart I have s.....Ps 119:10
s the one I love..........Song 3:1
you shall be called S ......Is 62:12
"So I s for a man ....Ezek 22:30
s what was lost.........Ezek 34:4
s favor from Him ......Hos 12:4
LORD, and have not s .....Zeph 1:6
s it diligently ....Heb 12:17

SOUL

s enter their council......Gen 49:6
with all your s...........Deut 6:5
was knit to the s........1 Sam 18:1
your heart and your s ..1 Chr 22:19
"My s loathes life......Job 10:1
as you do, if your s.......Job 16:4
s draws near the Pit......Job 33:22
will not leave my s ....Ps 16:10
converting the s ....Ps 19:7
He restores my s ....Ps 23:3
s shall make its boast......Ps 34:2
s shall be joyful..........Ps 35:9
you cast down, O my s.....Ps 42:5
s silently waits ....Ps 62:1
He has done for my s .....Ps 66:16
Let my s live...........Ps 119:175
s knows very well ....Ps 139:14
no one cares for my s ....Ps 142:4
so destroys his own s ....Prov 6:32
me wrongs his own s ....Prov 8:36
it is not good for a s .....Prov 19:2
A satisfied s loathes .....Prov 27:7
When You make His s.....Is 53:10
s delight itself ....Is 55:2
and your s shall live .....Is 55:3
you have heard, O my s .....Jer 4:19
the s of the father as ....Ezek 18:4
the proud, his s ....Hab 2:4
able to destroy both s ...Matt 10:28
and loses his own s......Matt 16:26
with all your s........Matt 22:37
Now My s is troubled....John 12:27
of one heart and one s ...Acts 4:32
your whole spirit, s ...1 Thess 5:23
to the saving of the s.....Heb 10:39
his way will save a s ...James 5:20
his righteous s ....2 Pet 2:8
health, just as your s......3 John 2

SOULS

and will save the *s* . . . . .Ps 72:13
and he who wins *s* . . . . . .Prov 11:30
s shall be like a . . . . .Jer 31:12
who made our very *s* . . . . .Jer 38:16
unsettling your *s* . . . . .Acts 15:24
is able to save your *s* . . . .James 1:21

SOUND

s heart is life . . . . .Prov 14:30
one rises up at the *s* . . . . . .Eccl 12:4
voice was like the *s* . . . . . .Ezek 43:2
s an alarm in My holy . . . . .Joel 2:1
do not *s* a trumpet . . . . .Matt 6:2
s words which you . . . . . . .2 Tim 1:13
that they may be *s* . . . . . . .Titus 1:13

SOUNDNESS

There is no *s* in my . . . . .Ps 38:3
him this perfect *s* . . . . . . .Acts 3:16

SOUNDS

Dreadful *s* are in his . . . . . .Job 15:21
a distinction in the *s* . . . . .1 Cor 14:7

SOW

s trouble reap. . . . . .Job 4:8
then let me *s* . . . . .Job 31:8
s fields and plant . . . . .Ps 107:37
Those who *s* in tears . . . . . .Ps 126:5
the wind will not *s* . . . . .Eccl 11:4
Blessed are you who *s* . . . . . .Is 32:20
ground, and do not *s* . . . . . . .Jer 4:3
"They *s* the wind. . . . . .Hos 8:7
S for yourselves . . . . .Hos 10:12
s is not made alive . . . . . .1 Cor 15:36

SOWER

may give seed to the *s* . . . .Is 55:10
"Behold, a *s* went . . . . .Matt 13:3

SOWN

shall they be *s* . . . . .Is 40:24
a land not *s*. . . . . .Jer 2:2
"You have *s* much . . . . . . .Hag 1:6
s spiritual things . . . . .1 Cor 9:11
It is *s* in weakness . . . . . .1 Cor 15:43
of righteousness is *s* . . .James 3:18

SOWS

s righteousness will . . . . . .Prov 11:18
s the good seed is the . . .Matt 13:37
'One *s* and another . . . . . .John 4:37
s sparingly will. . . . . .2 Cor 9:6
for whatever a man *s* . . . . . .Gal 6:7

SPARE

The LORD would not *s* . . .Deut 29:20
hand, but *s* his life . . . . .Job 2:6
s the poor and needy . . . . . .Ps 72:13
I will not pity nor *s* . . . . . .Jer 13:14
say, "*S* Your people . . . . . .Joel 2:17
s them as a man spares . . .Mal 3:17
He who did not *s* . . . . .Rom 8:32
s the natural branches . .Rom 11:21
branches, He may not *s* . .Rom 11:21
flesh, but I would *s* . . . . . .1 Cor 7:28
if God did not *s* . . . . .2 Pet 2:4

SPARES

s his rod hates his . . . . . . .Prov 13:24

SPARK

the work of it as a *s* . . . . .Is 1:31

SPARKLES

it is red, when it *s* . . . . . .Prov 23:31

SPARKS

to trouble, as the *s* . . . . .Job 5:7

s you have kindled . . . . .Is 50:11

SPARROW

s has found a home . . . . .Ps 84:3
awake, and am like a *s* . . . . .Ps 102:7

SPARROWS

more value than many *s* Matt 10:31

SPAT

Then they *s* on Him . . . . .Matt 27:30
in his ears, and He *s* . . . . .Mark 7:33

SPEAK

only the word that I *s* . .Num 22:35
s just once more . . . . .Judg 6:39
s good words to them . . . .1 Kin 12:7
oh, that God would *s* . . . . .Job 11:5
Will you *s* wickedly . . . . . . .Job 13:7
For God may *s* in one . . . .Job 33:14
Will he *s* softly to . . . . .Job 41:3
Do not *s* in the . . . . .Prov 23:9
and a time to *s* . . . . .Eccl 3:7
If they do not *s* . . . . .Is 8:20
tongue He will *s*. . . . . .Is 28:11
s anymore in His name . . . .Jer 20:9
at the end it will *s* . . . . . . .Hab 2:3
s each man the truth . . . .Zech 8:16
or what you should *s* . . . .Matt 10:19
it is not you who *s* . . . . . .Matt 10:20
to you when all men *s* . . .Luke 6:26
s what We know and . . . . .John 3:11
s what I have seen . . . . . .John 8:38
He hears He will *s* . . . . . .John 16:13
Spirit and began to *s* . . . .Acts 2:4
Do all *s* with tongues . . .1 Cor 12:30
I would rather *s* . . . . .1 Cor 14:19
So *s* and so do as . . . . . .James 2:12

SPEAKING

s your own words . . . . .Is 58:13
while they are still *s* . . . . . . .Is 65:24
a proof of Christ *s* . . . . . .2 Cor 13:3
envy, and all evil *s* . . . . . . .1 Pet 2:1

SPEAKS

to face, as a man *s* . . . . . . .Ex 33:11
this day that God *s* . . . . . .Deut 5:24
day that I am He who *s* . . . . .Is 52:6
He whom God has sent *s* . .John 3:34
When he *s* a lie . . . . .John 8:44
he being dead still *s* . . . . . .Heb 11:4
of sprinkling that *s* . . . . . .Heb 12:24

SPEAR

lay hold on bow and *s* . . . . .Jer 6:23
His side with a *s*. . . . . . . .John 19:34

SPEARS

whose teeth are *s* . . . . .Ps 57:4
and their *s* into . . . . .Is 2:4
pruninghooks into *s* . . . . . . .Joel 3:10

SPECK

do you look at the *s* . . . . . .Matt 7:3

SPECTACLE

and make you a *s* . . . . .Nah 3:6
we have been made a *s* . . . .1 Cor 4:9
He made a public *s* . . . . .Col 2:15
you were made a *s* . . . . . . .Heb 10:33

SPEECH

one language and one *s* . . . .Gen 11:1
drop as the rain, my *s* . . . .Deut 32:2
s settled on them as . . . . . .Job 29:22
There is no *s* nor. . . . . .Ps 19:3
s is not becoming . . . . . . .Prov 17:7
your *s* shall be low. . . . . . . .Is 29:4
a people of obscure *s* . . . . . .Is 33:19

not understand My *s* . . . .John 8:43
s deceive the hearts . . . . .Rom 16:18
and his *s* contemptible . .2 Cor 10:10
I am untrained in *s* . . . . . .2 Cor 11:6
s always be with grace . . . . .Col 4:6

SPEECHLESS

your mouth for the *s* . . . . . .Prov 31:8
And he was *s* . . . . .Matt 22:12

SPEED

they shall come with *s* . . . . . .Is 5:26

SPEEDILY

judgment be executed *s* . .Ezra 7:26
to me, deliver me *s* . . . . .Ps 31:2
I call, answer me *s* . . . . .Ps 102:2

SPEND

Why do you *s* money for . . . . .Is 55:2
whatever more you *s* . . . .Luke 10:35
I will very gladly *s* . . . . .2 Cor 12:15
amiss, that you may *s* . . .James 4:3

SPENT

strength shall be *s* . . . . . .Lev 26:20
For my life is *s* . . . . .Ps 31:10
in vain, I have *s* . . . . .Is 49:4
"But when he had *s* . . . .Luke 15:14

SPEW

nor hot, I will *s* . . . . .Rev 3:16

SPIDER

s skillfully grasps . . . . . . .Prov 30:28

SPIES

to them, "You are *s* . . . . . . .Gen 42:9
men who had been *s* . . . . .Josh 6:23
s who pretended . . . . . . .Luke 20:20

SPIN

neither toil nor *s* . . . . .Matt 6:28

SPINDLE

her hand holds the *s* . . . . .Prov 31:19

SPIRIT

And the *S* of God was . . . . . .Gen 1:2
S shall not strive . . . . .Gen 6:3
in whom is the *S* . . . . .Gen 41:38
and everyone whose *s* . . . .Ex 35:21
S that is upon you and . .Num 11:17
And the *S* rested upon . . .Num 11:26
LORD would put His *S* . .Num 11:29
he has a different *s* . . . . . .Num 14:24
in whom is the *S* . . . . .Num 27:18
portion of your *s* . . . . .2 Kin 2:9
there was no more *s* . . . . . .2 Chr 9:4
s came forward and . . . . .2 Chr 18:20
also gave Your good *S* . . . .Neh 9:20
against them by Your *S* . . . .Neh 9:30
Then a *s* passed before . . . .Job 4:15
And whose *s* came from . . . .Job 26:4
The *S* of God has made . . .Job 33:4
hand I commit my *s* . . . . . .Ps 31:5
s was not faithful . . . . .Ps 78:8
You send forth Your *S* . . .Ps 104:30
Your *S* is good. . . . . .Ps 143:10
The *s* of a man is the . . . .Prov 20:27
Who knows the *s* . . . . .Eccl 3:21
s will return to God . . . . . .Eccl 12:7
night, yes, by my *s* . . . . .Is 26:9
out on you the *s* . . . . .Is 29:10
are flesh, and not *s* . . . . .Is 31:3
S has gathered them . . . . . .Is 34:16
is the life of my *s* . . . . .Is 38:16
I have put My *S* . . . . .Is 42:1
and His *S* have sent Me . . . .Is 48:16
s would fail before Me . . . . . .Is 57:16

SPIRITS

" The *S* of the Lord . . . . Is 61:1
S entered me when He . . . . Ezek 2:2
the *S* lifted me up . . . . Ezek 3:12
who follow their own *s* . . . . Ezek 13:3
new heart and a new *s* . . . Ezek 18:31
be feeble, every *s* . . . . Ezek 21:7
"I will put My *S* . . . . Ezek 36:27
in him is the *S* . . . . Dan 4:8
as an excellent *s* . . . . Dan 5:12
walk in a false *s* . . . . Mic 2:11
and forms the *s* . . . . Zech 12:1
and He saw the *S* . . . . Matt 3:16
I will put My *S* . . . . Matt 12:18
S descending upon Him . Mark 1:10
Immediately the *S* . . . . . . Mark 1:12
s indeed is willing . . . . . Mark 14:38
go before Him in the *s* . . . . Luke 1:17
in the power of the *S* . . . . Luke 4:14
manner of *s* you are of . . . . Luke 9:55
hands I commit My *s* . . Luke 23:46
they had seen a *s* . . . . . . Luke 24:37
s does not have flesh . . . . Luke 24:39
"God is *S* . . . . John 4:24
I speak to you are *s* . . . . . John 6:63
He was troubled in *s* . . . . John 13:21
"the *S* of truth . . . . John 14:17
when He, the *S* . . . . John 16:13
but if a *s* or an angel . . . . . . Acts 23:9
whom I serve with my *s* . . . Rom 1:9
according to the *s* . . . . Rom 8:5
the flesh but in the *S* . . . . . Rom 8:9
does not have the *S* . . . . . . Rom 8:9
s that we are children . . . . . Rom 8:16
what the mind of the *S*. . . . Rom 8:27
to us through His *S* . . . . . 1 Cor 2:10
also have the *S* . . . . 1 Cor 7:40
gifts, but the same *S* . . . . 1 Cor 12:4
in a tongue, my *s* . . . . . . 1 Cor 14:14
but the *S* gives life. . . . . . . 2 Cor 3:6
Now the Lord is the *S* . . . 2 Cor 3:17
we have the same *s* . . . . . 2 Cor 4:13
Having begun in the *S* . . . . . Gal 3:3
has sent forth the *S* . . . . Gal 4:6
he who sows to the *S* . . . . . Gal 6:8
with the Holy *S* . . . . Eph 1:13
may give to you the *s* . . . . Eph 1:17
the unity of the *S*. . . . . Eph 4:3
is one body and one *S* . . . . . Eph 4:4
stand fast in one *s* . . . . . . Phil 1:27
yet I am with you in *s* . . . . . Col 2:5
and may your whole *s* . 1 Thess 5:23
S expressly says that . . . . . 1 Tim 4:1
division of soul and *s* . . . . . Heb 4:12
through the eternal *S* . . . . Heb 9:14
S who dwells in us . . . . . James 4:5
made alive by the *S* . . . . . 1 Pet 3:18
S whom He has given . . . 1 John 3:24
do not believe every *s* . . . 1 John 4:1
By this you know the *S* . . 1 John 4:2
By this we know the *S* . . 1 John 4:6
has given us of His *S* . . 1 John 4:13
S who bears witness . . . . 1 John 5:6
not having the *S* . . . . Jude 19
I was in the *S* on the . . . . . Rev 1:10
him hear what the *S*. . . . . . Rev 2:7
And the *S* and the . . . . . . Rev 22:17

SPIRITS

God, the God of the *s* . . . Num 16:22
who makes His angels . . . . Ps 104:4
the Lord weighs the *s* . . . Prov 16:2
power over unclean *s* . . . . Matt 10:1
heed to deceiving *s* . . . . . 1 Tim 4:1
not all ministering *s* . . . . . . Heb 1:14
to the Father of *s* . . . . Heb 12:9
and preached to the *s* . . . . 1 Pet 3:19
spirit, but test the *s* . . . . 1 John 4:1

SPIRITUAL

s judges all things . . . . 1 Cor 2:15
s people but as to. . . . . 1 Cor 3:1
to be a prophet or *s* . . . . . 1 Cor 14:37
However, the *s* is not. . . . 1 Cor 15:46
s restore such a one. . . . . Gal 6:1

SPIRITUALLY

s minded is life . . . . Rom 8:6
because they are *s* . . . . . . 1 Cor 2:14

SPITEFULLY

for those who *s* . . . . Matt 5:44

SPITTING

face from shame and *s* . . . . . Is 50:6

SPLENDOR

on the glorious *s* . . . . Ps 145:5
of Zion all her *s* . . . . Lam 1:6

SPOIL

hate us have taken *s* . . . . . . Ps 44:10
when they divide the *s* . . . . . Is 9:3
He shall divide the *s* . . . . . . Is 53:12
Take *s* of silver . . . . Nah 2:9
s will be divided . . . . Zech 14:1

SPOILER

I have created the *s* . . . . Is 54:16

SPOKE

s they did not hear . . . . Is 66:4
who feared the Lord *s* . . . . Mal 3:16
"No man ever *s* . . . . John 7:46
"We know that God *s* . . . John 9:29
I was a child, I *s* . . . . . . 1 Cor 13:11
in various ways *s* . . . . Heb 1:1
s as they were moved. . . . 2 Pet 1:21

SPOKEN

'just as you have *s* . . . . . . Num 14:28
God has *s* once . . . . Ps 62:11
commandment in secret. . . . . Is 45:19
'What have we *s* . . . . Mal 3:13
why am I evil *s* . . . . 1 Cor 10:30

SPOKESMAN

So he shall be your *s* . . . . . . Ex 4:16

SPONGE

them ran and took a *s* . . . Matt 27:48

SPOT

and there is no *s* . . . . Song 4:7
church, not having *s* . . . . . . Eph 5:27
commandment without *s* 1 Tim 6:14
Himself without *s* . . . . Heb 9:14

SPOTS

They are *s* and . . . . 2 Pet 2:13
These are *s* in your . . . . Jude 12

SPREAD

fell on my knees and *s* . . . . Ezra 9:5
they have a net by . . . . Ps 140:5
Then He *s* it before me . . . Ezek 2:10
Then the word of God *s* . . . Acts 6:7
the Lord was being *s* . . . Acts 13:49
their message will *s* . . . . 2 Tim 2:17

SPREADS

He alone *s* out the . . . . Job 9:8
s them out like a tent . . . . . Is 40:22
Zion *s* out her hands . . . . . . Lam 1:17

SPRING

Truth shall *s* out of. . . . . . . Ps 85:11
is like a murky *s* . . . . . . Prov 25:26
sister, my spouse, a *s* . . . Song 4:12
s forth I tell you . . . . Is 42:9

SPRINGING

a fountain of water *s* . . . . John 4:14
of bitterness *s*. . . . . Heb 12:15

SPRINGS

"Have you entered the *s* . . Job 38:16
He sends the *s* into. . . . . . Ps 104:10
and the thirsty land *s* . . . . . . Is 35:7
and the dry land *s* . . . . Is 41:18

SPRINKLE

He *s* many nations . . . . Is 52:15
"Then I will *s*. . . . . Ezek 36:25

SPRINKLED

s dust on his head. . . . . Job 2:12
and hyssop, and *s* . . . . Heb 9:19
having our hearts *s* . . . . . Heb 10:22

SPRINKLING

s that speaks . . . . Heb 12:24
for obedience and *s* . . . . . 1 Pet 1:2

SPROUT

down, that it will *s* . . . . . . Job 14:7
and the seed should *s* . . . Mark 4:27

SQUARES

voice in the open *s* . . . . . . Prov 1:20
s I will seek the one . . . . . . Song 3:2

STABILITY

will be the *s* of your. . . . . . . Is 33:6

STAFF

this Jordan with my *s* . . . . Gen 32:10
your feet, and your *s* . . . . . Ex 12:11
Your rod and Your *s* . . . . . . Ps 23:4
Lord has broken the *s* . . . . . Is 14:5
'How the strong *s* . . . . . . Jer 48:17
they have been a *s* . . . . . Ezek 29:6
on the top of his *s* . . . . . . Heb 11:21

STAGGER

and He makes them *s*. . . Job 12:25
they will drink and *s* . . . . Jer 25:16

STAGGERS

as a drunken man *s*. . . . . . . Is 19:14

STAKES

s will ever be removed. . . . . . Is 33:20

STALLS

be no herd in the *s*. . . . . . . Hab 3:17

STAMMERERS

s will be ready . . . . Is 32:4

STAMMERING

For with *s* lips and . . . . Is 28:11
s tongue that you . . . . Is 33:19

STAMPING

At the noise of the *s* . . . . . Jer 47:3

STAND

one shall be able to *s* . . . . Deut 7:24
"Who is able to *s* . . . . . . 1 Sam 6:20
but it does not *s* . . . . Job 8:15
lives, and He shall *s*. . . . . Job 19:25
ungodly shall not *s* . . . . Ps 1:5
Why do You *s* afar off . . . . Ps 10:1
Or who may *s* in His . . . . . Ps 24:3
Who will *s* up for me . . . . Ps 94:16
and let an accuser *s* . . . . . Ps 109:6
he will not *s* before . . . . Prov 22:29

STANDARD (cont.)

Do not take your s........Eccl 8:3
"It shall not s ....Is 7:7
"S in the ways and ......Jer 6:16
not lack a man to s ....Jer 35:19
whose words will s.......Jer 44:28
and it shall s.............Dan 2:44
but she shall not s......Dan 11:17
Who can s before His .....Nah 1:6
And who can s when He ....Mal 3:2
that kingdom cannot s ..Mark 3:24
he will be made to s ......Rom 14:4
Watch, s fast in the.....1 Cor 16:13
for by faith you s........2 Cor 1:24
having done all, to s .....Eph 6:13
S therefore................Eph 6:14
s fast in the Lord..........Phil 4:1
now we live, if you s ...1 Thess 3:8
of God in which you s ....1 Pet 5:12
"Behold, I s at the.......Rev 3:20

STANDARD

LORD will lift up a s........Is 59:19
Set up the s toward........Jer 4:6

STANDING

the LORD, and Satan s ....Zech 3:1
they love to pray s ......Matt 6:5
and the Son of Man s ....Acts 7:56
Then I saw an angel s ...Rev 19:17

STANDS

The LORD s up to plead.....Is 3:13
him who thinks he s ....1 Cor 10:12

STAR

S shall come out of......Num 24:17
For we have seen His s ....Matt 2:2
for one s differs from....1 Cor 15:41
give him the morning s ...Rev 2:28
And a great s fell.........Rev 8:10
Bright and Morning S ...Rev 22:16

STARS

He made the s also ....Gen 1:16
s are not pure in His......Job 25:5
when the morning s ......Job 38:7
the moon and the s.........Ps 8:3
praise Him, all you s .....Ps 148:3
born as many as the s.....Heb 11:12
wandering s for whom.....Jude 13
a garland of twelve s .....Rev 12:1

STARVED

His strength is s........Job 18:12

STATE

man at his best s ....Ps 39:5
us in our lowly s ....Ps 136:23
and the last of that....Matt 12:45
learned in whatever s.....Phil 4:11

STATURE

add one cubit to his s ....Matt 6:27
in wisdom and s ....Luke 2:52
the measure of the s .....Eph 4:13

STATUTE

shall be a perpetual ......Lev 3:17

STATUTES

the s of the LORD are .....Ps 19:8
Teach me Your s.......Ps 119:12
s have been my songs....Ps 119:54
not walked in My s.......Ezek 5:6

STAY

her feet would not s .....Prov 7:11
S here and watch with..Matt 26:38
for today I must s ......Luke 19:5
the time of your s.......1 Pet 1:17

STEADFAST

yes, you could be s ......Job 11:15
O God, my heart is s ......Ps 57:7
their heart was not s .....Ps 78:37
his heart is s ....Ps 112:7
God, and s forever ....Dan 6:26
beloved brethren, be s ..1 Cor 15:58
faith, grounded and s .....Col 1:23
angels proved s............Heb 2:2
of our confidence s.......Heb 3:14
soul, both sure and s ......Heb 6:19
Resist him, s in the ......1 Pet 5:9

STEADFASTLY

s set His face to go......Luke 9:51
And they continued s ....Acts 2:42
continuing s in..........Rom 12:12

STEADFASTNESS

good order and the s ......Col 2:5
from your own s ....2 Pet 3:17

STEADILY

could not look s ....2 Cor 3:13

STEADY

and his hands were s ......Ex 17:12

STEAL

"You shall not s ....Ex 20:15
"Will you s ....Jer 7:9
s My words every one.....Jer 23:30
thieves break in and s ..Matt 6:19
night and s Him away ..Matt 27:64
murder, 'Do not s........Mark 10:19
not come except to s ...John 10:10
a man should not s ......Rom 2:21
Let him who stole s......Eph 4:28

STEEP

s places shall fall.......Ezek 38:20
waters poured down a s .....Mic 1:4
violently down the s......Matt 8:32

STEM

forth a Rod from the s ......Is 11:1

STENCH

there will be a s ....Is 3:24
this time there is a s ...John 11:39

STEP

there is but a s ....1 Sam 20:3
s has turned from the.....Job 31:7

STEPS

has held fast to His s....Job 23:11
and count all my s ....Job 31:4
and He sees all his s.....Job 34:21
Uphold my s in Your ....Ps 17:5
The s of a good man ......Ps 37:23
of his s shall slide........Ps 37:31
and established my s ......Ps 40:2
hide, they mark my s ......Ps 56:6
s had nearly slipped ......Ps 73:2
Direct my s by You.....Ps 119:133
s will not be hindered ....Prov 4:12
the LORD directs his s.....Prov 16:9
A man's s are of the ....Prov 20:24
to direct his own s.......Jer 10:23
should follow His s......1 Pet 2:21

STEWARD

faithful and wise s .....Luke 12:42
you can no longer be s ....Luke 16:2
commended the unjust s ..Luke 16:8
be blameless, as a s ....Titus 1:7

STEWARDS

of Christ and s ....1 Cor 4:1

one another, as good s ....1 Pet 4:10

STEWARDSHIP

entrusted with a s ....1 Cor 9:17

STICK

and his bones s ....Job 33:21
'For Joseph, the s......Ezek 37:16

STICKS

a man gathering s......Num 15:32
"And the s on which ....Ezek 37:20

STIFF

rebellion and your s ....Deut 31:27
do not speak with a s.......Ps 75:5

STIFF-NECKED

"Now do not be s........2 Chr 30:8
"You s and ....Acts 7:51

STILL

on your bed, and be s.....Ps 4:4
s the noise of the ....Ps 65:7
earth feared and was s.....Ps 76:8
that its waves are s.....Ps 107:29
When I awake, I am s ....Ps 139:18
time, I have been s ....Is 42:14
rest and be s.............Jer 47:6
sea, "Peace, be s........Mark 4:39
let him be holy s.........Rev 22:11

STILLBORN

I not hidden like a s......Job 3:16
as it goes, like a s.........Ps 58:8
burial, I say that a s......Eccl 6:3

STINGS

like a serpent, and s .....Prov 23:32

STIR

that he would dare s......Job 41:10
S up Yourself.............Ps 35:23
I remind you to s........2 Tim 1:6
another in order to s .....Heb 10:24

STIRRED

fulfilled, the LORD s.....2 Chr 36:22
and my sorrow was s ....Ps 39:2
So the LORD s up the.....Hag 1:14

STIRS

and the innocent s ....Job 17:8
it s up the dead for ....Is 14:9
on Your name, who s.......Is 64:7

STOCKS

put my feet in the s ......Job 13:27
s that were in the.........Jer 20:2

STOIC

and S philosophers ......Acts 17:18

STOMACH

mouth goes into the s ...Matt 15:17
his heart but his s ......Mark 7:19
Foods for the s..........1 Cor 6:13

STOMACH'S

little wine for your s .....1 Tim 5:23

STONE

him, a pillar of s........Gen 35:14
to the bottom like a s ......Ex 15:5
s shall be a witness.....Josh 24:27
heart is as hard as s .....Job 41:24
s which the builders.....Ps 118:22
s is heavy and sand is.....Prov 27:3
I lay in Zion a s...........Is 28:16
foundation, a tried s......Is 28:16
take the heart of s .....Ezek 36:26

STONED

You watched while a s . . . . .Dan 2:34
s will cry out from . . . . .Hab 2:11
to silent s . . . . .Hab 2:19
will give him a s . . . . .Matt 7:9
s will be broken . . . . .Matt 21:44
secure, sealing the s . . . .Matt 27:66
s which the builders . . . .Luke 20:17
you, let him throw a s . . . .John 8:7
those works do you s . . .John 10:32
Jews sought to s You . . . .John 11:8
not on tablets of s . . . . . .2 Cor 3:3
Him as to a living s . . . . . .1 Pet 2:4
give him a white s . . . . . .Rev 2:17
angel took up a s . . . . . . .Rev 18:21
like a jasper s . . . . .Rev 21:11

STONED

s Stephen as he was . . . . . .Acts 7:59
once I was s . . . . .2 Cor 11:25
They were s . . . . .Heb 11:37

STONES

I will lay your s . . . . .Is 54:11
Among the smooth s . . . . . . .Is 57:6
Abraham from these s . . . .Matt 3:9
command that these s . . . .Matt 4:3
see what manner of s . . . . .Mark 13:1
also, as living s . . . . .1 Pet 2:5
kinds of precious s . . . . . .Rev 21:19

STONY

them, and take the s . . . .Ezek 11:19
Some fell on s ground . . . .Mark 4:5

STOOPED

And again He s down . . . . . .John 8:8

STOPPED

speak lies shall be s . . . . . . .Ps 63:11
her flow of blood s . . . . . .Luke 8:44

STORE

no room to s my crops . . .Luke 12:17
exist are kept in s . . . . .2 Pet 3:7

STORK

s has her home in the . . . . .Ps 104:17
"Even the s in the . . . . .Jer 8:7

STORM

from the windy s . . . . .Ps 55:8
He calms the s . . . . .Ps 107:29
terror comes like a s . . . . .Prov 1:27
for a shelter from s . . . . . . .Is 4:6
a refuge from the s . . . . . . .Is 25:4
and a destroying s . . . . .Is 28:2
coming like a s . . . . .Ezek 38:9
whirlwind and in the s . . . . . .Nah 1:3

STOUTHEARTED

s were plundered . . . . .Ps 76:5

STRAIGHT

make Your way s . . . . .Ps 5:8
for who can make s . . . . . .Eccl 7:13
make s in the desert a . . . . . .Is 40:3
Their legs were s . . . . .Ezek 1:7
LORD, make His paths s . .Luke 3:4
to the street called S . . . . .Acts 9:11
and make s paths for . . . .Heb 12:13

STRAIGHTFORWARD

that they were not s . . . . . . .Gal 2:14

STRAIN

"Blind guides, who s . . . .Matt 23:24

STRAITS

and desperate s . . . . .Deut 28:53

STRANGE

were considered a s . . . . . . .Hos 8:12
"We have seen s . . . . .Luke 5:26
are bringing some s . . . . .Acts 17:20
these, they think it s . . . . . .1 Pet 4:4
s thing happened . . . . .1 Pet 4:12

STRANGER

but he acted as a s . . . . . . .Gen 42:7
"I have been a s . . . . .Ex 2:22
neither mistreat a s . . . . . . .Ex 22:21
and loves the s . . . . .Deut 10:18
I have become a s . . . . .Ps 69:8
s will suffer for it . . . . . . .Prov 11:15
s does not share its . . . . . .Prov 14:10
should You be like a s . . . . .Jer 14:8
I was a s and you took . .Matt 25:35
"Are You the only s . . . .Luke 24:18

STRANGERS

descendants will be s . . . . .Gen 15:13
s plunder his labor . . . . . . .Ps 109:11
watches over the s . . . . . . .Ps 146:9
s devour your land . . . . .Is 1:7
S shall stand and feed . . . . .Is 61:5
know the voice of s . . . . .John 10:5
of Israel and s . . . . .Eph 2:12
you are no longer s . . . . . . .Eph 2:19
if she has lodged s . . . . . .1 Tim 5:10
that they were s . . . . .Heb 11:13
forget to entertain s . . . . . .Heb 13:2
the brethren and for s . . . .3 John 5

STRANGLING

that my soul chooses s . . . .Job 7:15

STRAP

than I, whose sandal s . . . .Mark 1:7

STRAW

They are like s . . . . .Job 21:18
stones, wood, hay, s . . . . . .1 Cor 3:12

STRAY

the cursed, who s . . . . . . .Ps 119:21
who make my people s . . . .Mic 3:5

STRAYED

yet I have not s . . . . .Ps 119:110
for which some have s . . .1 Tim 6:10
who have s concerning . . .2 Tim 2:18

STREAM

like an overflowing s . . . . . . .Is 30:28
of the LORD, like a s . . . . . .Is 30:33
like a flowing s . . . . .Is 66:12

STREAMS

He dams up the s . . . . . . .Job 28:11
He also brought s . . . . .Ps 78:16
O LORD, as the s . . . . .Ps 126:4

STREET

to be heard in the s . . . . . . .Is 42:2
s called Straight . . . . .Acts 9:11
And the s of the city . . . . .Rev 21:21
In the middle of its s . . . . .Rev 22:2

STREETS

the corners of the s . . . . . .Matt 6:5
You taught in our s . . . . .Luke 13:26
out quickly into the s . . . .Luke 14:21

STRENGTH

for by s of hand the . . . . . . .Ex 13:3
just as my s was then . . . .Josh 14:11
my soul, march on in s . . . .Judg 5:21
a man is, so is his s . . . . . .Judg 8:21
s no man shall . . . . .1 Sam 2:9
the God of my s . . . . .2 Sam 22:3

have armed me with s . .2 Sam 22:40
the LORD glory and s . . . .1 Chr 16:28
Is my s the s . . . . .Job 6:12
Him are wisdom and s . . . .Job 12:13
him because his s . . . . .Job 39:11
You have ordained s . . . . .Ps 8:2
love You, O LORD, my s . . . . .Ps 18:1
The LORD is the s . . . . .Ps 27:1
The LORD is their s . . . . .Ps 28:8
The LORD will give s . . . . . .Ps 29:11
delivered by great s . . . . . .Ps 33:16
He is their s in the . . . . .Ps 37:39
are the God of my s . . . . . . .Ps 43:2
is our refuge and s . . . . .Ps 46:1
is He who gives s . . . . .Ps 68:35
I will go in the s . . . . .Ps 71:16
but God is the s . . . . .Ps 73:26
They go from s to . . . . .Ps 84:7
the glory of their s . . . . . . .Ps 89:17
s and beauty are in . . . . . . .Ps 96:6
made me bold with s . . . . .Ps 138:3
of the LORD is s . . . . .Prov 10:29
knowledge increases s . . . .Prov 24:5
S and honor are her . . . . .Prov 31:25
is better than s . . . . .Eccl 9:16
for s and not for . . . . .Eccl 10:17
For You have been a s . . . . .Is 25:4
him take hold of My s . . . . .Is 27:5
of His might and the s . . . . .Is 40:26
might He increases s . . . . . .Is 40:29
works it with the s . . . . . . .Is 44:12
righteousness and s . . . . . . .Is 45:24
Put on your s . . . . .Is 52:1
O LORD, my s and my . . . .Jer 16:19
I will destroy the s . . . . . .Hag 2:22
He has shown s with . . . .Luke 1:51
were still without s . . . . . . .Rom 5:6
s is made perfect . . . . . . .2 Cor 12:9
you have a little s . . . . .Rev 3:8

STRENGTHEN

and He shall s . . . . .Ps 27:14
S the weak hands . . . . .Is 35:3
"So I will s them in . . . . .Zech 10:12
s your brethren . . . . .Luke 22:32
s the hands . . . . .Heb 12:12
s the things . . . . .Rev 3:2

STRENGTHENED

weak you have not s . . . . . .Ezek 34:4
unbelief, but was s . . . . . . .Rom 4:20
of His glory, to be s . . . . . .Eph 3:16
stood with me and s . . . . .2 Tim 4:17

STRENGTHENING

s the souls of the . . . . . . .Acts 14:22

STRENGTHENS

s the wise more than . . . . . .Eccl 7:19
through Christ who s . . . . . .Phil 4:13

STRETCH

will quickly s out her . . . . . .Ps 68:31
said to the man, "S . . . .Matt 12:13
are old, you will s . . . . . .John 21:18

STRETCHED

I have s out my hands . . . . .Ps 88:9
His wisdom, and has s . . . .Jer 10:12
"All day long I have s . . .Rom 10:21

STRETCHES

For he s out his hand . . . . .Job 15:25

STRICKEN

My heart is s and . . . . .Ps 102:4
yet we esteemed Him s . . . .Is 53:4
of My people He was s . . . . .Is 53:8
You have s them . . . . .Jer 5:3
He has s . . . . .Hos 6:1

STRIFE

let there be no s ....Gen 13:8
You have made us a s ......Ps 80:6
at the waters of s ....Ps 106:32
Hatred stirs up s.......Prov 10:12
comes nothing but s ....Prov 13:10
man stirs up s ....Prov 15:18
transgression loves s....Prov 17:19
borne me, a man of s.....Jer 15:10
and lust, not in s........Rom 13:13
even from envy and s.....Phil 1:15
which come envy, s ......1 Tim 6:4

STRIKE

said, "S this people .....2 Kin 6:18
The sun shall not s........Ps 121:6
Let the righteous s ....Ps 141:5
S a scoffer ....Prov 19:25
s your hands ....Ezek 21:14
s the waves of the sea...Zech 10:11
"S the Shepherd ....Zech 13:7
s the earth with a.........Mal 4:6
'I will s the Shepherd...Matt 26:31
if well, why do you s....John 18:23
the sun shall not s ....Rev 7:16
s the earth with all.......Rev 11:6

STRINGED

of your s instruments .....Is 14:11
of your s instruments....Amos 5:23

STRIP

s yourselves ....Is 32:11
s her naked and expose....Hos 2:3

STRIPES

their iniquity with s ......Ps 89:32
s we are healed...........Is 53:5
be beaten with many s...Luke 12:47
I received from s ....2 Cor 11:24
s you were healed.......1 Pet 2:24

STRIVE

My Spirit shall not s ......Gen 6:3
He will not always s......Ps 103:9
Do not s with a man.....Prov 3:30
Let the potsherd s.........Is 45:9
"S to enter through .....Luke 13:24
the Lord not to s.......2 Tim 2:14

STRIVING

for a man to stop s ......Prov 20:3

STROKE

with a mighty s ....Jer 14:17

STRONG

"Be s and conduct ....1 Sam 4:9
indeed He is s ....Job 9:19
The LORD is so mighty....Ps 24:8
bring me to the s ....Ps 60:9
s is Your hand...........Ps 89:13
A wise man s ....Prov 24:5
s shall be as tinder ....Is 1:31
"We have a s city..........Is 26:1
the weak say, 'I am s....Joel 3:10
"When a s man ....Luke 11:21
We then who are s.......Rom 15:1
I am weak, then I am s..2 Cor 12:10
are weak and you are s ..2 Cor 13:9
my brethren, be s.......Eph 6:10
weakness were made s....Heb 11:34
s is the Lord God ....Rev 18:8

STRONGHOLD

of my salvation, my s......Ps 18:2
down the trusted s .....Prov 21:22

STRUCK

s the rock twice........Num 20:11

the hand of God has s ....Job 19:21
s all my enemies ....Ps 3:7
Behold, He s the rock.....Ps 78:20
I was angry and s ....Is 57:17
in My wrath I s...........Is 60:10
s the head from the ......Hab 3:13
'I s you with blight......Hag 2:17
took the reed and s.....Matt 27:30
Him, they s Him on the..Luke 22:64

STUBBLE

shall bring forth s ....Is 33:11
his sword, as driven s......Is 41:2
they shall be as s.........Is 47:14
s that passes ....Jer 13:24
do wickedly will be s......Mal 4:1

STUBBORN

If a man has a s ....Deut 21:18
and s children ....Ezek 2:4

STUBBORN-HEARTED

"Listen to Me, you s......Is 46:12

STUBBORNNESS

do not look on the s .....Deut 9:27

STUDIED

having never s..........John 7:15

STUMBLE

causes them to s.......Ps 119:165
to make my steps s......Ps 140:4
your foot will not s ......Prov 3:23
know what makes them s..Prov 4:19
one will be weary or s ......Is 5:27
among them shall s ....Is 8:15
we s at noonday as at.....Is 59:10
that they might not s.....Is 63:13
before your feet s.......Jer 13:16
they will s and fall........Jer 46:6
have caused many to s.....Mal 2:8
you will be made to s...Matt 26:31
if all are made to s .....Matt 26:33
immediately they s .....Mark 4:17
who believe in Me to s...Mark 9:42
the day, he does not s....John 11:9
Who is made to s .....2 Cor 11:29
whole law, and yet s....James 2:10
For we all s in many.....James 3:2

STUMBLED

and those who s ....1 Sam 2:4
God, for you have s .....Hos 14:1
s that they should.......Rom 11:11

STUMBLES

word, immediately he s ..Matt 13:21

STUMBLING

but a stone of s ....Is 8:14
Behold, I will lay s .....Jer 6:21
watched for my s ......Jer 20:10
it became their s........Ezek 7:19
stumbled at that s........Rom 9:32
I lay in Zion a s.........Rom 9:33
this, not to put a s .....Rom 14:13
to the Jews a s ....1 Cor 1:23
of yours become a s ....1 Cor 8:9
and "A stone of s........1 Pet 2:8
is no cause for s........1 John 2:10
to keep you from s........Jude 24

STUMBLINGBLOCK

the deaf, nor put a s....Lev 19:14

STUPID

and regarded as s ....Job 18:3
who hates correction is s ..Prov 12:1
Surely I am more s ......Prov 30:2

SUBDUE

s the peoples under us ......Ps 47:3
shall s three kings ....Dan 7:24
s our iniquities ....Mic 7:19
s all things to ....Phil 3:21

SUBJECT

for it is not s ....Rom 8:7
Let every soul be s ....Rom 13:1
all things are made s....1 Cor 15:28
Himself will also be s ...1 Cor 15:28
Remind them to be s......Titus 3:1
all their lifetime s.........Heb 2:15
having been made s ......1 Pet 3:22

SUBJECTED

because of Him who s.....Rom 8:20

SUBJECTION

put all things in s.........Heb 2:8
more readily be in s ....Heb 12:9

SUBMISSION

in silence with all s ......1 Tim 2:11
his children in s..........1 Tim 3:4

SUBMISSIVE

Wives, likewise, be s ......1 Pet 3:1
Yes, all of you be s ....1 Pet 5:5

SUBMIT

Your enemies shall s........Ps 66:3
Wives, s to your own.....Eph 5:22
Therefore s to God ....James 4:7
s yourselves to every ....1 Pet 2:13
you younger people, s .....1 Pet 5:5

SUBSIDED

and the waters s..........Gen 8:1
the king's wrath s.......Esth 7:10

SUBSTANCE

Bless his s ....Deut 33:11
the LORD, and their s .....Mic 4:13

SUCCEED

For this will not s ....Num 14:41
you shall not s ....Jer 32:5

SUCCESS

please give me s ....Gen 24:12
You spoil my s ....Job 30:22
but wisdom brings s ....Eccl 10:10

SUCCESSFUL

Joseph, and he was a s ....Gen 39:2

SUDDENLY

whom you seek, will s ....Mal 3:1
s there was with the......Luke 2:13

SUE

s you and take away.....Matt 5:40

SUFFER

for a stranger will s.....Prov 11:15
for the Christ to s.....Luke 24:46
Christ, if indeed we s ....Rom 8:17
all the members s.......1 Cor 12:26
that they may not s......Gal 6:12
in Him, but also to s....Phil 1:29
s trouble as an..........2 Tim 2:9
when you do good and s ..1 Pet 2:20
the will of God, to s.....1 Pet 3:17
s as a murderer.........1 Pet 4:15
you are about to s........Rev 2:10

SUFFERED

s these things and to....Luke 24:26
Have you s so many ......Gal 3:4
for whom I have s ....Phil 3:8

with His own blood, s . . . .Heb 13:12
because Christ also s . . . . .1 Pet 2:21
For Christ also s . . . . .1 Pet 3:18
since Christ s . . . . .1 Pet 4:1
after you have s . . . . .1 Pet 5:10

SUFFERING

My eyes bring s . . . . .Lam 3:51
Is anyone among you s . .James 5:13
forth as an example, s . . . . . .Jude 7

SUFFERINGS

I consider that the s . . . . . .Rom 8:18
share with me in the s . . . .2 Tim 1:8
perfect through s . . . . .Heb 2:10
great struggle with s . . . . .Heb 10:32
beforehand the s . . . . .1 Pet 1:11

SUFFERS

Love s long and is . . . . . . .1 Cor 13:4

SUFFICIENCY

but our s is from God . . . . .2 Cor 3:5
always having all s . . . . . . .2 Cor 9:8

SUFFICIENT

S for the day is its . . . . . . .Matt 6:34
by the majority is s . . . . . . .2 Cor 2:6
Not that we are s . . . . .2 Cor 3:5

SUITABLE

by the hand of a s . . . . . . .Lev 16:21

SUM

How great is the s . . . . . . .Ps 139:17
s I obtained this . . . . .Acts 22:28

SUMMED

commandment, are all s . . .Rom 13:9

SUMMER

and heat, winter and s . . . . .Gen 8:22
into the drought of s . . . . . .Ps 32:4
You have made s . . . . .Ps 74:17
you know that s . . . . . . .Matt 24:32

SUMPTUOUSLY

fine linen and fared s . . . .Luke 16:19

SUN

So the s stood still . . . . .Josh 10:13
love Him be like the s . . . .Judg 5:31
grows green in the s . . . . . .Job 8:16
a tabernacle for the s . . . . . .Ps 19:4
the LORD God is a s . . . . . . .Ps 84:11
s shall not strike you . . . . .Ps 121:6
the s to rule by day . . . . . .Ps 136:8
to behold the s . . . . .Eccl 11:7
while the s and the . . . . . .Eccl 12:2
moon, clear as the s . . . . . .Song 6:10
s will be sevenfold . . . . . . .Is 30:26
s returned ten degrees. . . . . .Is 38:8
s shall no longer be . . . . . . .Is 60:19
s has gone down while. . . . . .Jer 15:9
LORD, who gives the s. . . . .Jer 31:35
the s and moon grow . . . . .Joel 2:10
s shall be turned. . . . . .Joel 2:31
s shall go down on the . . . . .Mic 3:6
The s and moon stood. . . .Hab 3:11
for He makes His s . . . . . .Matt 5:45
the s was darkened. . . . .Luke 23:45
is one glory of the s . . . .1 Cor 15:41
do not let the s. . . . . .Eph 4:26
s became black as. . . . . . . .Rev 6:12
s shall not strike. . . . . .Rev 7:16
had no need of the s . . . . .Rev 21:23

SUPPER

man gave a great s . . . . . .Luke 14:16
to eat the Lord's S. . . . . .1 Cor 11:20
took the cup after s . . . . .1 Cor 11:25

together for the s . . . . . . .Rev 19:17

SUPPLICATION

s that you have made . . . . .1 Kin 9:3
and make your s . . . . .Job 8:5
LORD has heard my s . . . . . . .Ps 6:9
to the LORD I made s . . . . . .Ps 30:8
Yourself from my s . . . . . . .Ps 55:1
Let my s come before. . . .Ps 119:170
They will make s . . . . .Is 45:14
with all prayer and s . . . . .Eph 6:18
by prayer and s . . . . .Phil 4:6

SUPPLIES

Now may He who s . . . .2 Cor 9:10
Therefore He who s. . . . . . .Gal 3:5
by what every joint s. . . . .Eph 4:16

SUPPLY

s what was lacking. . . . . . .Phil 2:30
And my God shall s. . . . . .Phil 4:19

SUPPORT

but the LORD was my s 2 Sam 22:19
this, that you must s . . . .Acts 20:35

SUPREME

to the king as s. . . . . .1 Pet 2:13

SURE

s your sin will find . . . . .Num 32:23
but no man is s . . . . .Job 24:22
call and election s. . . . . . .2 Pet 1:10

SURETY

Be s for Your servant. . . .Ps 119:122
one who hates being s . . .Prov 11:15
Jesus has become a s . . . . .Heb 7:22

SURROUND

But you shall s. . . . . .2 Kin 11:8
LORD, mercy shall s . . . . . .Ps 32:10

SURROUNDED

the waves of death s . . .2 Sam 22:5
The pangs of death s . . . . . .Ps 18:4
The pains of death s . . . . .Ps 116:3
All nations s me. . . . . . . .Ps 118:10
their own deeds have s. . . . .Hos 7:2
and the floods s. . . . . .Jon 2:3
also, since we are s. . . . . . .Heb 12:1

SURVIVOR

was no refugee or s . . . . .Lam 2:22

SUSPICIONS

reviling, evil s . . . . .1 Tim 6:4

SUSTAIN

You will s him on his . . . . . .Ps 41:3
of a man will s. . . . . .Prov 18:14
S me with cakes of . . . . . . .Song 2:5

SWADDLING

thick darkness its s . . . . . .Job 38:9
Him in s cloths. . . . . .Luke 2:7

SWALLOW

like a flying s. . . . . .Prov 26:2
Like a crane or a s. . . . . . .Is 38:14
s observe the time. . . . . .Jer 8:7
great fish to s Jonah . . . . . .Jon 1:17
a gnat and s a camel . . .Matt 23:24

SWEAR

shall I make you s. . . . . .1 Kin 22:16
in the earth shall s. . . . . . .Is 45:16
s oaths by the LORD. . . . . .Zeph 1:5
'You shall not s. . . . . .Matt 5:33
began to curse and s . . . .Matt 26:74
because He could s . . . . . .Heb 6:13

my brethren, do not s . . .James 5:12

SWEARING

By s and lying . . . . .Hos 4:2

SWEARS

he who s to his own . . . . .Ps 15:4
everyone who s by Him . . . .Ps 63:11
but whoever s by the . . . .Matt 23:18

SWEAT

In the s of your face . . . . .Gen 3:19
Then His s became like . .Luke 22:44

SWEET

Though evil is s. . . . . .Job 20:12
s are Your words. . . . . . . .Ps 119:103
His mouth is most s. . . . . .Song 5:16
but it will be as s . . . . .Rev 10:9

SWEETNESS

'Should I cease my s . . . . .Judg 9:11
called prudent, and s . . . .Prov 16:21
mouth like honey in s. . . . . .Ezek 3:3

SWELLING

they speak great s . . . . . .2 Pet 2:18

SWIFT

s as the eagle flies . . . . . .Deut 28:49
pass by like s ships. . . . . . . .Job 9:26
handles the bow, the s . . .Amos 2:15
let every man be s . . . . . .James 1:19

SWIFTLY

His word runs very s . . . . .Ps 147:15

SWIM

night I make my bed s. . . . . . .Ps 6:6

SWOON

as they s like the. . . . . . . .Lam 2:12

SWORD

s which turned every . . . . . .Gen 3:24
but not with your s. . . . . .Josh 24:12
the wicked with Your s. . . . .Ps 17:13
land by their own s. . . . . . .Ps 44:3
my bow, nor shall my s . . . . .Ps 44:6
their tongue a sharp s . . . . .Ps 57:4
shall not lift up s. . . . . .Is 2:4
s shall be bathed. . . . . .Is 34:5
The s of the LORD is . . . . . . .Is 34:6
And I will send a s . . . . . . .Jer 9:16
will die by the s . . . . .Ezek 7:15
'A s. . . . . .Ezek 21:9
a s is sharpened . . . . .Ezek 21:9
'A s, a s is. . . . . .Ezek 21:28
Bow and s of battle I. . . . . .Hos 2:18
"Awake, O s. . . . . .Zech 13:7
to bring peace but a s . . .Matt 10:34
for all who take the s. . . . .Matt 26:52
s will pierce through. . . . .Luke 2:35
he does not bear the s. . . . .Rom 13:4
the s of the Spirit. . . . . . . .Eph 6:17
than any two-edged s. . . . . .Heb 4:12
a sharp two-edged s . . . . .Rev 1:16
mouth goes a sharp s. . . . .Rev 19:15

SWORDS

yet they were drawn s . . . . .Ps 55:21
shall beat their s . . . . .Is 2:4
look, here are two s . . . .Luke 22:38

SWORE

So I s in My wrath. . . . . . .Ps 95:11
So I s in My wrath . . . . . . .Heb 3:11
and s by Him who lives. . . .Rev 10:6

SWORN

By Myself I have s . . . . . .Gen 22:16

SYMBOLIC

The LORD has s in....... .Ps 132:11
I have s by Myself........ .Is 45:23
"The LORD has s........ .Heb 7:21

SYMBOLIC

which things are s........ .Gal 4:24
It was s for the.......... .Heb 9:9

SYMBOLS

I have given s through . . .Hos 12:10

SYMPATHIZE

Priest who cannot s...... .Heb 4:15

SYMPATHY

My s is stirred .... .Hos 11:8

SYNAGOGUE

He went into the s ...... .Luke 4:16
but are a s of Satan .... .Rev 2:9

T

TABERNACLE

you shall make the t ...... .Ex 26:1
t He shall hide me .... .Ps 27:5
I will abide in Your t ...... .Ps 61:4
In Salem also is His t...... .Ps 76:2
How lovely is Your t...... .Ps 84:1
quiet home, a t........... .Is 33:20
You also took up the t..... .Acts 7:43
and will rebuild the t ...... .Acts 15:16
and more perfect t....... .Heb 9:11
"Behold, the t........... .Rev 21:3

TABERNACLES

us make here three t..... .Matt 17:4
Feast of T was at hand . . . .John 7:2

TABLE

shall also make a t....... .Ex 25:23
prepare a t before me ...... .Ps 23:5
t become a snare........ .Ps 69:22
dogs under the t........ .Mark 7:28
t become a snare .... .Rom 11:9
of the Lord's t .... .1 Cor 10:21

TABLES

t are full of vomit.......... .Is 28:8
and overturned the t .... .Matt 21:12
of God and serve t........ .Acts 6:2

TABLET

write them on the t....... .Prov 3:3
is engraved on the t....... .Jer 17:1

TAIL

the head and not the t . . .Deut 28:13
t drew a third of the...... .Rev 12:4

TAKE

T your sandal off your . . . .Josh 5:15
t Your Holy Spirit........ .Ps 51:11
t not the word of......... .Ps 119:43
in You I t shelter......... .Ps 143:9
t words with you .... .Hos 14:2
T My yoke upon you .... .Matt 11:29
T what is yours and..... .Matt 20:14
and t up his cross ..... .Mark 8:34
T this cup away .... .Mark 14:36
My life that I may t..... .John 10:17
I urge you to t heart..... .Acts 27:22

TAKEN

you are t by the words .... .Prov 6:2
He was t from prison ...... .Is 53:8
one will be t and the .... .Matt 24:40
what he has will be t.... .Mark 4:25
He was t up............. .Acts 1:9
until He is t out of..... .2 Thess 2:7

By faith Enoch was t away.Heb 11:5

TALEBEARER

not go about as a t...... .Lev 19:16
t reveals secrets........ .Prov 11:13

TALENT

went and hid your t..... .Matt 25:25

TALK

shall t of them when...... .Deut 6:7
t be vindicated .... .Job 11:2
with unprofitable t .... .Job 15:3
My tongue also shall t..... .Ps 71:24
entangle Him in His t . .Matt 22:15
"I will no longer t........ .John 14:30
turned aside to idle t...... .1 Tim 1:6

TALKED

within us while He t..... .Luke 24:32

TALKERS

both idle t and .... .Titus 1:10

TALL

to a nation t and .... .Is 18:2

TAMBOURINE

They sing to the t........ .Job 21:12
The mirth of the t.......... .Is 24:8

TARES

the t also appeared..... .Matt 13:26

TARGET

You set me as Your t...... .Job 7:20
and set me up as a t..... .Lam 3:12

TARRY

who turns aside to t ..... .Jer 14:8
come and will not t ...... .Heb 10:37

TASK

this burdensome t .... .Eccl 1:13

TASTE

and its t was like the ..... .Num 11:8
Oh, t and see that the ..... .Ps 34:8
are Your words to my t.... .Ps 119:103
was sweet to my t........ .Song 2:3
Do not touch, do not t .....Col 2:21
might t death for .... .Heb 2:9

TASTED

But when He had t ..... .Matt 27:34
t the heavenly gift .... .Heb 6:4
t the good word .... .Heb 6:5
t that the Lord is .... .1 Pet 2:3

TAUGHT

O God, You have t........ .Ps 71:17
as His counselor has t...... .Is 40:13
presence, and You t ..... .Luke 13:26
they shall all be t .... .John 6:45
but as My Father t....... .John 8:28
from man, nor was I t...... .Gal 1:12

TAUNT

and a byword, a t.......... .Jer 24:9

TAX

t collectors do the....... .Matt 5:46
received the temple t ... .Matt 17:24
I say to you that t....... .Matt 21:31
"Show Me the t .... .Matt 22:19

TAXES

take customs or t....... .Matt 17:25
Is it lawful to pay t .... .Matt 22:17
forbidding to pay t....... .Luke 23:2
t to whom t .... .Rom 13:7

TEACH

t them diligently......... .Deut 6:7
t Jacob Your judgments. .Deut 33:10
t you the good and the .1 Sam 12:23
"Can anyone t........... .Job 21:22
"I will t you about ...... .Job 27:11
t me what I do not see... .Job 34:32
t me Your paths .... .Ps 25:4
T me Your way .... .Ps 27:11
t you the fear of the ...... .Ps 34:11
t You awesome things...... .Ps 45:4
t transgressors Your ...... .Ps 51:13
So t us to number our ..... .Ps 90:12
He will t us His ways .... .Is 2:3
"Whom will he t .... .Is 28:9
a bribe, her priests t...... .Mic 3:11
t the way of God in .... .Matt 22:16
in My name, He will t . .John 14:26
even nature itself t...... .1 Cor 11:14
permit a woman to t..... .1 Tim 2:12
things command and t ...1 Tim 4:11
T and exhort these .... .1 Tim 6:2
t you again the first...... .Heb 5:12

TEACHER

for One is your T .... .Matt 23:8
asked Him, "Good T..." .Mark 10:17
know that You are a t..... .John 3:2
"You call me T .... .John 13:13
named Gamaliel, a t ..... .Acts 5:34
a t of babes, having....... .Rom 2:20
a t of the Gentiles in...... .1 Tim 2:7

TEACHERS

than all my t .... .Ps 119:99
t will not be moved .... .Is 30:20
prophets, third t........ .1 Cor 12:28
and some pastors and t... .Eph 4:11
desiring to be t .... .1 Tim 1:7
time you ought to be t.... .Heb 5:12
of you become t .... .James 3:1
there will be false t....... .2 Pet 2:1

TEACHES

therefore He t sinners...... .Ps 25:8
the Holy Spirit t .... .1 Cor 2:13
If anyone t otherwise .....1 Tim 6:3
the same anointing t....1 John 2:27

TEACHING

t them to observe all ....Matt 28:20
they did not cease t...... .Acts 5:42
he who teaches, in t...... .Rom 12:7
t every man in all......... .Col 1:28
t things which they ..... .Titus 1:11
t us that .... .Titus 2:12

TEAR

t yourself in anger........ .Job 18:4
lest they t me like a .... .Ps 7:2
I, even I, will t .... .Hos 5:14
feet, and turn and t .... .Matt 7:6
will wipe away every t ..... .Rev 21:4

TEARS

I have seen your t .... .2 Kin 20:5
my couch with my t....... .Ps 6:6
t have been my food .... .Ps 42:3
with the bread of t .... .Ps 80:5
drench you with my t ...... .Is 16:9
GOD will wipe away t....... .Is 25:8
eyes may run with t....... .Jer 9:18
My eyes fail with t ...... .Lam 2:11
His feet with her t ...... .Luke 7:38
night and day with t..... .Acts 20:31

TEETH

mindful of your *t*........2 Tim 1:4
vehement cries and *t*.......Heb 5:7
it diligently with *t*.......Heb 12:17

TEETH

t whiter than milk ....Gen 49:12
by the skin of my *t*......Job 19:20
You have broken the *t*.......Ps 3:7
As vinegar to the *t*......Prov 10:26
you cleanness of *t*........Amos 4:6

TELL

that you may *t* it to ....Ps 48:13
the message that I *t*........Jon 3:2
"Who can *t* if God ....Jon 3:9
t him his fault..........Matt 18:15
whatever they *t*..........Matt 23:3
He comes, He will *t*......John 4:25

TEMPERATE

for the prize is *t* in all ....1 Cor 9:25
husband of one wife, *t* ....1 Tim 3:2

TEMPEST

the windy storm and *t*......Ps 55:8
one, tossed with *t* ....Is 54:11
And suddenly a great *t* ...Matt 8:24

TEMPLE

So Solomon built the *t* ...1 Kin 6:14
Lord is in His holy *t* ....Ps 11:4
to inquire in His *t*........Ps 27:4
suddenly come to His *t*......Mal 3:1
One greater than the *t*...Matt 12:6
murdered between the *t*..Matt 23:35
found Him in the *t*.......Luke 2:46
"Destroy this *t*........John 2:19
was speaking of the *t*......John 2:21
one accord in the *t*........Acts 2:46
that you are the *t*.......1 Cor 3:16
your body is the *t*........1 Cor 6:19
grows into a holy *t*.......Eph 2:21
sits as God in the *t*......2 Thess 2:4
Then the *t* of God was...Rev 11:19
But I saw no *t* in it ......Rev 21:22
and the Lamb are its *t*...Rev 21:22

TEMPLES

t made with hands ....Acts 7:48

TEMPORARY

which are seen are *t*......2 Cor 4:18

TEMPT

Why do you *t* the Lord.....Ex 17:2
they even *t* God ....Mal 3:15
t the Lord your God .....Matt 4:7
that Satan does not *t* .....1 Cor 7:5
nor let us *t* Christ ....1 Cor 10:9
nor does He Himself *t*.. James 1:13

TEMPTATION

do not lead us into *t*......Matt 6:13
lest you enter into *t* ....Matt 26:41
in time of *t* fall away .....Luke 8:13
t has overtaken you ....1 Cor 10:13
to be rich fall into *t*......1 Tim 6:9
the man who endures *t* ..James 1:12

TEMPTED

forty days, *t* by Satan....Mark 1:13
not allow you to be *t*....1 Cor 10:13
lest you also be *t*..........Gal 6:1
has suffered, being *t* ......Heb 2:18
in all points *t* ....Heb 4:15
But each one is *t* ......James 1:14

TEMPTER

Now when the *t* came to ...Matt 4:3

TENDER

your heart was *t*........2 Kin 22:19
t shoots will not ....Job 14:7
no more be called *t* ....Is 47:1
through the *t* mercy of....Luke 1:78
put on *t* mercies...........Col 3:12

TENDERHEARTED

to one another, *t*..........Eph 4:32
love as brothers, be *t* ......1 Pet 3:8

TENDS

t a flock and does not .....1 Cor 9:7

TENT

shall know that your *t* .....Job 5:24
like a shepherd's *t*........Is 38:12
the place of your *t*........Is 54:2
My *t* is plundered ....Jer 10:20
earthly house, this *t* ......2 Cor 5:1
long as I am in this *t*....2 Pet 1:13
I must put off my *t*......2 Pet 1:14

TENTMAKERS

occupation they were *t* ....Acts 18:3

TENTS

those who dwell in *t*......Gen 4:20
"How lovely are your *t*....Num 24:5
The *t* of robbers ....Job 12:6
than dwell in the *t* ....Ps 84:10
I dwell among the *t*........Ps 120:5
Lord will save the *t*......Zech 12:7

TERRESTRIAL

bodies and *t* bodies .....1 Cor 15:40

TERRIBLE

t wilderness..............Deut 1:19
haughtiness of the *t* ....Is 13:11
is great and very *t* ....Joel 2:11

TERRIFIED

to you, 'Do not be *t* ......Deut 1:29
But they were *t*........Luke 24:37
and not in any way *t* ......Phil 1:28

TERRIFIES

and the Almighty *t*.......Job 23:16

TERRIFY

me with dreams and *t*......Job 7:14
not let dread of Him *t* ....Job 9:34
are coming to *t* them ....Zech 1:21

TERRIFYING

t was the sight.........Heb 12:21

TERROR

there shall be *t* ....Deut 32:25
are nothing, you see *t*.....Job 6:21
from God is a *t* ....Job 31:23
not be afraid of the *t* ......Ps 91:5
I will make you a *t* ......Jer 20:4
but a great *t* fell.........Dan 10:7

TERRORS

the *t* of God are...........Job 6:4
T frighten him on ....Job 18:11
before the king of *t*......Job 18:14
T overtake him like a ....Job 27:20
consumed with *t*..........Ps 73:19

TEST

God has come to *t* you ....Ex 20:20
t him with hard ....1 Kin 10:1
behold, His eyelids *t*......Ps 11:4
t them as gold is ....Zech 13:9
said, "Why do you *t*....Matt 22:18
t the Spirit of the ....Acts 5:9
why do you *t* God by ....Acts 15:10

and the fire will *t*........1 Cor 3:13
T yourselves...........2 Cor 13:5
T all things...........1 Thess 5:21
but *t* the spirits.........1 John 4:1

TESTAMENT

where there is a *t*........Heb 9:16
For a *t* is in force ....Heb 9:17

TESTATOR

be the death of the *t* ......Heb 9:16

TESTED

that God *t* Abraham ......Gen 22:1
You have *t* my heart........Ps 17:3
And they *t* God in ....Ps 78:18
t you at the waters of.......Ps 81:7
When your fathers *t* ....Ps 95:9
t them ten days ....Dan 1:14
also first be *t*...........1 Tim 3:10
where your fathers *t* ......Heb 3:9
though it is *t* by fire.......1 Pet 1:7
t those who say they ......Rev 2:2

TESTIFIED

Yet the Lord *t* against ..2 Kin 17:13
he who has seen has *t* ..John 19:35
for as you have *t* ....Acts 23:11
t beforehand the ....1 Pet 1:11
of God which He has *t*...1 John 5:9

TESTIFIES

and heard, that He *t*......John 3:32
that the Holy Spirit *t*....Acts 20:23

TESTIFY

yes, your own lips *t*........Job 15:6
You, and our sins *t* ....Is 59:12
T against Me..............Mic 6:3
t what We have..........John 3:11
these are they which *t* ....John 5:39
t that the Father ....1 John 4:14
sent My angel to *t* ......Rev 22:16

TESTIFYING

was righteous, God *t*......Heb 11:4
t that this is ....1 Pet 5:12

TESTIMONIES

those who keep His *t*......Ps 119:2
for I have kept Your *t*.....Ps 119:22
t are my meditation ......Ps 119:99
I love Your *t* ....Ps 119:119
t are wonderful ....Ps 119:129

TESTIMONY

two tablets of the *T*.......Ex 31:18
For He established a *t*......Ps 78:5
that I may keep the *t*.....Ps 119:88
Bind up the *t* ....Is 8:16
under your feet as a *t* ...Mark 6:11
Now this is the *t*........John 1:19
no one receives His *t* .....John 3:32
who has received His *t*...John 3:33
in your law that the *t* ...John 8:17
and we know that his *t* ..John 21:24
declaring to you the *t* .....1 Cor 2:1
obtained a good *t*........Heb 11:2
he had this *t* ....Heb 11:5
has not believed the *t* ...1 John 5:10
And this is the *t* ....1 John 5:11
For the *t* of Jesus is ......Rev 19:10

TESTING

came to Him, *t* Him......Matt 19:3
knowing that the *t*........James 1:3

TESTS

the righteous God *t* ....Ps 7:9
gold, but the Lord *t*......Prov 17:3

THANK

men, but God who *t*.....1 Thess 2:4

THANK

"I *t* You and praise ....Dan 2:23
"I *t* You, Father ....Matt 11:25
t that servant because....Luke 17:9
t You that I am not.....Luke 18:11
First, I *t* my God ....Rom 1:8
t Christ Jesus our.......1 Tim 1:12

THANKFUL

Be *t* to Him..............Ps 100:4
Him as God, nor were *t* ..Rom 1:21

THANKFULNESS

Felix, with all *t* ....Acts 24:3

THANKS

the cup, and gave *t*.....Matt 26:27
t He distributed them ...John 6:11
for he gives God *t*.......Rom 14:6
T be to God for His.....2 Cor 9:15
giving *t* always for.......Eph 5:20
t can we render........1 Thess 3:9

THANKSGIVING

with the voice of *t*.........Ps 26:7
Offer to God *t*..........Ps 50:14
His presence with *t*........Ps 95:2
into His gates with *t* ....Ps 100:4
the sacrifices of *t*.......Ps 107:22
supplication, with *t* ....Phil 4:6
vigilant in it with *t* ....Col 4:2
to be received with *t*......1 Tim 4:3

THEATER

and rushed into the *t* ....Acts 19:29

THIEF

When you saw a *t*........Ps 50:18
do not despise a *t*.......Prov 6:30
t hates his own life .....Prov 29:24
t is ashamed when he ....Jer 2:26
the windows like a *t*.......Joel 2:9
t shall be expelled ....Zech 5:3
known what hour the *t* ..Matt 24:43
t approaches nor moth...Luke 12:33
way, the same is a *t* .....John 10:1
because he was a *t*.......John 12:6
Lord will come as a *t*.....2 Pet 3:10
upon you as a *t*...........Rev 3:3

THIEVES

and companions of *t* ....Is 1:23
destroy and where *t* .....Matt 6:19
before Me are *t* ....John 10:8

THIGH

them hip and *t* with a ....Judg 15:8
good piece, the *t* ....Ezek 24:4

THINGS

in heaven give good *t*....Matt 7:11
evil, speak good *t* ......Matt 12:34
kept all these *t* ....Luke 2:51
Lazarus evil *t* ....Luke 16:25
the Scriptures the *t* ....Luke 24:27
share in all good *t*..........Gal 6:6

THINK

nor does his heart *t*........Is 10:7
t that they will be.......Matt 6:7
t you have eternal.......John 5:39
not to *t* of himself.......Rom 12:3
of ourselves to *t*.......2 Cor 3:5
all that we ask or *t* ....Eph 3:20

THINKS

yet the Lord *t* upon me....Ps 40:17
for as he *t* in his ....Prov 23:7
t that he knows ....1 Cor 8:2

t he stands take heed ...1 Cor 10:12
For if anyone *t*............Gal 6:3
t he is religious........James 1:26

THIRST

tongues fail for *t* ....Is 41:17
those who hunger and *t*....Matt 5:6
in Me shall never *t* ......John 6:35
said, "I *t*!",............John 19:28
we both hunger and *t* ...1 Cor 4:11
anymore nor *t* anymore ....Rev 7:16

THIRSTS

My soul *t* for God.........Ps 42:2
saying, "If anyone *t*.....John 7:37
if he *t* ....Rom 12:20
freely to him who *t*.......Rev 21:6
And let him who *t* ....Rev 22:17

THIRSTY

and if he is *t*...........Prov 25:21
as when a *t* man dreams.....Is 29:8
the drink of the *t*..........Is 32:6
t land springs of ....Is 35:7
on him who is *t* ....Is 44:3
but you shall be *t* ....Is 65:13
I was *t* and you gave ....Matt 25:35
we see You hungry or *t* ..Matt 25:44

THISTLES

t grow instead of........Job 31:40
or figs from *t*...........Matt 7:16

THORN

t that goes into the......Prov 26:9
t shall come up the ....Is 55:13
a *t* in the flesh was .....2 Cor 12:7

THORNBUSHES

gather grapes from *t* .....Matt 7:16

THORNS

Both *t* and thistles it......Gen 3:18
T and snares are ....Prov 22:5
all overgrown with *t* ....Prov 24:31
the crackling of *t* ....Eccl 7:6
Like a lily among *t*.......Song 2:2
and do not sow among *t* ....Jer 4:3
wheat but reaped *t* ......Jer 12:13
And some fell among *t*....Matt 13:7
wearing the crown of *t* ...John 19:5

THOUGHT

t is that their houses .....Ps 49:11
You *t* that I was ....Ps 50:21
Both the inward *t* ....Ps 64:6
I *t* about my ways ......Ps 119:59
You understand my *t*....Ps 139:2
"Surely, as I have *t* ......Is 14:24
to man what his *t* ......Amos 4:13
perceiving the *t*.........Luke 9:47
"And he *t* within ......Luke 12:17
I *t* as a child...........1 Cor 13:11

THOUGHTS

the intent of the *t* ......1 Chr 28:9
is in none of his *t* ....Ps 10:4
t toward us................Ps 40:5
t are very deep ....Ps 92:5
The Lord knows the *t* .....Ps 94:11
t will be established .....Prov 16:3
unrighteous man his *t* .....Is 55:7
"For My *t* are not your.....Is 55:8
long shall your evil *t*.......Jer 4:14
they do not know the *t*.....Mic 4:12
Jesus, knowing their *t*.....Matt 9:4
heart proceed evil *t*.....Matt 15:19
futile in their *t*...........Rom 1:21
" The Lord knows the *t* ..1 Cor 3:20

THREAT

shall flee at the *t*.........Is 30:17

THREATEN

suffered, He did not *t* ....1 Pet 2:23

THREATENING

to them, giving up *t*.......Eph 6:9

THREATS

Lord, look on their *t* ......Acts 4:29
still breathing *t* ....Acts 9:1

THREE

you will deny Me *t* .....Matt 26:34
hope, love, these *t* ....1 Cor 13:13
and these *t* are one .....1 John 5:7

THRESH

he does not *t* it............Is 28:28
t the mountains...........Is 41:15
it is time to *t* her........Jer 51:33
"Arise and *t* ....Mic 4:13

THRESHING

t shall last till the........Lev 26:5
like the dust at *t* ....2 Kin 13:7
Oh, my *t* and the grain.....Is 21:10

THROAT

t is an open tomb ....Ps 5:9
put a knife to your *t* .....Prov 23:2
unshod, and your *t* ....Jer 2:25
t is an open tomb ....Rom 3:13

THRONE

Lord sitting on His *t* ..1 Kin 22:19
He has prepared His *t* ....Ps 9:7
temple, the Lord's *t*.......Ps 11:4
Your *t*, O God, is..........Ps 45:6
has established His *t* ....Ps 103:19
he upholds his *t*........Prov 20:28
Lord sitting on a *t*..........Is 6:1
"Heaven is My *t*.........Is 66:1
shall be called The *T*......Jer 3:17
do not disgrace the *t*.....Jer 14:21
A glorious high *t*........Jer 17:12
t was a fiery flame........Dan 7:9
sit and rule on His *t*.....Zech 6:13
for it is God's *t*.........Matt 5:34
will give Him the *t*......Luke 1:32
"Your *t*, O God, is ....Heb 1:8
come boldly to the *t*......Heb 4:16
where Satan's *t* ....Rev 2:13
My Father on His *t*.......Rev 3:21
I saw a great white *t* .....Rev 20:11

THRONES

t are set there ....Ps 122:5
also sit on twelve *t*.....Matt 19:28
mighty from their *t* ......Luke 1:52
invisible, whether *t* ......Col 1:16
t I saw twenty-four........Rev 4:4

THRONG

house of God in the *t*......Ps 55:14

THROW

of your land and *t*.........Mic 5:11
t Yourself down..........Matt 4:6
children's bread and *t*....Matt 15:26

THROWN

their slain shall be *t* ....Is 34:3
neck, and he were *t* .....Mark 9:42

THRUST

and rose up and *t*.......Luke 4:29

THUNDER

But the *t* of His power....Job 26:14

THUNDERED

The voice of Your *t* ....Ps 77:18
the secret place of *t* ....Ps 81:7
t they hastened away ......Ps 104:7
that is, "Sons of T".......Mark 3:17
the voice of loud *t* ....Rev 14:2

THUNDERED

" The LORD *t* from .....2 Sam 22:14
The LORD *t*. ....Ps 18:13

THUNDERINGS

people witnessed the *t* .....Ex 20:18
the sound of mighty *t* .....Rev 19:6

THUNDERS

t marvelously with His.....Job 37:5
the God of glory *t* ....Ps 29:3

TIDINGS

be afraid of evil *t*. ....Ps 112:7
I bring you good *t* ....Luke 2:10
who bring glad *t* ....Rom 10:15

TILL

no man to *t* the ground .....Gen 2:5

TILLER

but Cain was a *t*...........Gen 4:2

TILLS

t his land will be ....Prov 12:11
t his land will have .....Prov 28:19

TIME

pray to You in a *t* ....Ps 32:6
ashamed in the evil *t* ......Ps 37:19
how short my *t* is ....Ps 89:47
A *t* to be born ....Eccl 3:2
but *t* and chance ....Eccl 9:11
your *t* was the *t* ....Ezek 16:8
you did not know the *t*..Luke 19:44
t has not yet come ....John 7:6
I have a convenient *t* ...Acts 24:25
for the *t* is near...........Rev 1:3

TIMES

understanding of the *t* ..1 Chr 12:32
t are not hidden..........Job 24:1
t are in Your hand........Ps 31:15
the signs of the *t* ....Matt 16:3
Gentiles until the *t*......Luke 21:24
not for you to know *t* .....Acts 1:7
their preappointed *t* ....Acts 17:26
last days perilous *t* ....2 Tim 3:1
God, who at various *t* ......Heb 1:1

TITHE

And he gave him a *t* .....Gen 14:20
LORD, a tenth of the *t* ...Num 18:26
"You shall truly *t* ....Deut 14:22
shall bring out the *t*....Deut 14:28
laying aside all the *t*....Deut 26:12
in abundantly the *t* ......2 Chr 31:5
Judah brought the *t*.....Neh 13:12
For you pay *t* of mint...Matt 23:23

TITHES

to redeem any of his *t* ...Lev 27:31
t which you receive.....Num 18:28
and to bring the *t*.......Neh 10:37
firstfruits, and the *t*.....Neh 12:44
the articles, the *t* ....Neh 13:5
Bring all the *t* ....Mal 3:10
I give *t* of all that I ....Luke 18:12
to receive *t* from the ......Heb 7:5
mortal men receive *t* ....Heb 7:8
Levi, who receives *t*.......Heb 7:9

TITHING

the year of *t*............Deut 26:12

TITLE

Now Pilate wrote a *t*.....John 19:19

TITTLE

away, one jot or one *t*.....Matt 5:18

TODAY

t I have begotten You........Ps 2:7
of the field, which *t* ......Matt 6:30
the grass, which *t*.......Luke 12:28
t you will be with Me....Luke 23:43
t I have begotten You .....Heb 1:5
"T, if you will hear.........Heb 3:7
the same yesterday, *t*......Heb 13:8

TOIL

t you shall eat of ....Gen 3:17
they neither *t* nor ....Matt 6:28
our labor and *t* ....1 Thess 2:9

TOILED

"Master, we have *t*.......Luke 5:5

TOLD

Behold, I have *t* ....Matt 28:7
things which were *t* ......Luke 2:18
t me all things that I .....John 4:29
t you the truth which.....John 8:40
so, I would have *t* ....John 14:2
"And now I have *t* .....John 14:29

TOLERABLE

you, it will be more *t* ....Matt 10:15

TOMB

throat is an open *t* ....Ps 5:9
in the garden a new *t* ...John 19:41
throat is an open *t*........Rom 3:13

TOMBS

like whitewashed *t* .....Matt 23:27
you build the *t* ....Matt 23:29
For you build the *t*.....Luke 11:47

TOMORROW

drink, for *t* we die ....Is 22:13
t will be as today..........Is 56:12
t is thrown into the .....Matt 6:30
do not worry about *t* .....Matt 6:34
drink, for *t* we die ......1 Cor 15:32
what will happen *t* .....James 4:14

TONGUE

the scourge of the *t*.......Job 5:21
hides it under his *t* ....Job 20:12
Keep your *t* from evil .....Ps 34:13
t shall speak of Your.......Ps 35:28
lest I sin with my *t* ....Ps 39:1
to you, you false *t*........Ps 120:3
laughter, and our *t* ....Ps 126:2
remember you, let my *t* ....Ps 137:6
is not a word on my *t*......Ps 139:4
but the perverse *t* ....Prov 10:31
forever, but a lying *t*.....Prov 12:19
A wholesome *t* is a ....Prov 15:4
t keeps his soul ....Prov 21:23
t breaks a bone ....Prov 25:15
t shall take an oath ....Is 45:23
GOD has given Me the *t* .....Is 50:4
t should confess that .....Phil 2:11
does not bridle his *t*....James 1:26
t is a little member.....James 3:5
And the *t* is a ....James 3:6
no man can tame the *t*....James 3:8
love in word or in *t* .....1 John 3:18
every nation, tribe, *t*......Rev 14:6

TONGUES

from the strife of *t* ....Ps 31:20
will speak with new *t*....Mark 16:17

TITLE (column 3)

to them divided *t*, as of fire..Acts 2:3
and they spoke with *t*.....Acts 19:6
I speak with the *t* ....1 Cor 13:1
Therefore *t* are for a.....1 Cor 14:22

TOOTH

"eye for eye, *t* ....Ex 21:24
is like a bad *t*...........Prov 25:19
eye for an eye and a *t*.....Matt 5:38

TOPHET

T was established ....Is 30:33
the high places of *T*.......Jer 7:31
make this city like *T* .....Jer 19:12
like the place of *T* ....Jer 19:13

TORCH

and like a fiery *t* ....Zech 12:6

TORCHES

When he had set the *t* ....Judg 15:5
his eyes like *t* ....Dan 10:6
come with flaming *t*.......Nah 2:3

TORMENT

"How long will you *t* ......Job 19:2
shall lie down in *t* ....Is 50:11
You come here to *t* ......Matt 8:29
to this place of *t* ....Luke 16:28
fear involves *t* ....1 John 4:18
t ascends forever........Rev 14:11

TORMENTED

for I am *t* in this........Luke 16:24
And they will be *t*.......Rev 20:10

TORMENTS

"And being in *t*........Luke 16:23

TORN

aside my ways and *t*......Lam 3:11
for He has *t*..............Hos 6:1
of the temple was *t*.....Matt 27:51

TORTURED

Others were *t* ....Heb 11:35

TOSSED

t with tempest...........Is 54:11
t to and fro and ....Eph 4:14

TOTTER

drunkard, and shall *t*......Is 24:20

TOUCH

seven no evil shall *t* .....Job 5:19
t no unclean thing ....Is 52:11
If only I may *t* ....Matt 9:21
that they might only *t*..Matt 14:36
a man not to *t* a woman ..1 Cor 7:1
wicked one does not *t*...1 John 5:18

TOUCHED

whose hearts God had *t*.1 Sam 10:26
t my mouth with it ....Is 6:7
hand and *t* my mouth......Jer 1:9
mountain that may be *t* ..Heb 12:18

TOUCHES

He *t* the hills............Ps 104:32
t you *t* the ....Zech 2:8

TOWER

t whose top is in the ......Gen 11:4
for me, a strong *t* ....Ps 61:3
my fortress, my high *t*....Ps 144:2
like an ivory *t* ....Song 7:4
a watchman in the *t* ....Is 21:5
in it and built a *t* ......Matt 21:33

TRACKED

t our steps so that we . . . . .Lam 4:18

TRADERS

are princes, whose *t*. . . . . .Is 23:8

TRADITION

transgress the *t*. . . . . .Matt 15:2
of no effect by your *t* . . . . .Matt 15:6
according to the *t* . . . . .Col 2:8
t which he received . . . . .2 Thess 3:6
conduct received by *t*. . . . .1 Pet 1:18

TRADITIONS

zealous for the *t*. . . . . .Gal 1:14
t which you were . . . . . .2 Thess 2:15

TRAIN

T up a child in the. . . . . . .Prov 22:6
t of His robe filled. . . . . .Is 6:1

TRAINED

who is perfectly *t* . . . . . . .Luke 6:40
those who have been *t*. . . .Heb 12:11

TRAINING

bring them up in the *t*. . . . . .Eph 6:4

TRAITOR

also became a *t*. . . . . .Luke 6:16

TRAITORS

t, headstrong . . . . .2 Tim 3:4

TRAMPLE

Your name we will *t* . . . . . . .Ps 44:5
serpent you shall *t* . . . . .Ps 91:13
hand, to *t* My courts. . . . . . .Is 1:12
You shall *t* the wicked . . . . .Mal 4:3
swine, lest they *t* . . . . .Matt 7:6
you the authority to *t* . . .Luke 10:19

TRAMPLED

t them in My fury. . . . . .Is 63:3
now she will be *t*. . . . . .Mic 7:10
t the nations in anger . . . .Hab 3:12
Jerusalem will be *t*. . . . .Luke 21:24
worthy who has *t*. . . . . . .Heb 10:29
the winepress was *t* . . . . .Rev 14:20

TRANCE

he fell into a *t* . . . . .Acts 10:10
t I saw a vision . . . . .Acts 11:5

TRANSFIGURED

and was *t* before them . . . .Matt 17:2

TRANSFORMED

this world, but be *t*. . . . . . .Rom 12:2
the Lord, are being *t* . . . . .2 Cor 3:18

TRANSGRESS

t the command of the. . . .Num 14:41
the LORD's people *t* . . . . .1 Sam 2:24
my mouth shall not *t*. . . . . .Ps 17:3
his mouth must not *t*. . . . .Prov 16:10
of bread a man will *t*. . . . .Prov 28:21
do Your disciples *t* . . . . . .Matt 15:2

TRANSGRESSED

t My covenant. . . . . .Josh 7:11
your mediators have *t*. . . . . .Is 43:27
the rulers also *t* . . . . .Jer 2:8
their fathers have *t* . . . . . .Ezek 2:3
Yes, all Israel has *t* . . . . . .Dan 9:11
t your commandment. . . .Luke 15:29

TRANSGRESSES

"Indeed, because he *t* . . . . .Hab 2:5
Whoever *t* and does not. . . .2 John 9

TRANSGRESSION

iniquity and *t* and sin . . . . .Ex 34:7
Make me know my *t*. . . . .Job 13:23
t is sealed up in a . . . . .Job 14:17
be innocent of great *t*. . . . .Ps 19:13
because of their *t* . . . . . . .Ps 107:17
He who covers a *t* . . . . . . .Prov 17:9
He who loves *t* loves. . . . .Prov 17:19
tell My people their *t* . . . . . .Is 58:1
at Gilgal multiply *t*. . . . . . .Amos 4:4
my firstborn for my *t*. . . . . .Mic 6:7
and passing over the *t* . . . . .Mic 7:18
no law there is no *t* . . . . . .Rom 4:15
deceived, fell into *t* . . . . . .1 Tim 2:14
steadfast, and every *t* . . . . .Heb 2:2

TRANSGRESSIONS

if I have covered my *t*. . . . .Job 31:33
"I will confess my *t* . . . . . . .Ps 32:5
me from all my *t* . . . . .Ps 39:8
mercies, blot out my *t* . . . . .Ps 51:1
For I acknowledge my *t* . . . .Ps 51:3
has He removed our *t*. . . . .Ps 103:12
who blots out your *t* . . . . . .Is 43:25
was wounded for our *t*. . . . . .Is 53:5
for the *t* of My people. . . . . .Is 53:8
from you all the *t* . . . . . .Ezek 18:31
was added because of *t*. . . . .Gal 3:19
redemption of the *t* . . . . . .Heb 9:15

TRANSGRESSOR

and were called a *t*. . . . . .Is 48:8
I make myself a *t* . . . . .Gal 2:18

TRANSGRESSORS

Then I will teach *t* . . . . . . .Ps 51:13
to any wicked *t* . . . . .Ps 59:5
numbered with the *t* . . . . . .Is 53:12
numbered with the *t* . . .Mark 15:28

TRAP

of Israel, as a *t*. . . . . .Is 8:14
where there is no *t*. . . . . . .Amos 3:5

TRAPS

they have set *t* . . . . .Ps 140:5
for me, and from the *t* . . . .Ps 141:9

TRAVEL

For you *t* land and sea. . .Matt 23:15

TRAVELER

t who turns aside. . . . . .Jer 14:8

TRAVELING

lie waste, the *t* . . . . .Is 33:8

TREACHEROUS

the *t* dealer deals. . . . . .Is 21:2
an assembly of *t* men . . . . . .Jer 9:2
are insolent, *t* . . . . .Zeph 3:4

TREACHEROUSLY

and you who deal *t* . . . . . . .Is 33:1
happy who deal so *t* . . . . . .Jer 12:1
even they have dealt *t* . . . . .Jer 12:6
They have dealt *t* . . . . .Hos 5:7
Why do we deal *t* . . . . . . .Mal 2:10
that you do not deal *t* . . . .Mal 2:16
" This man dealt *t*. . . . . . .Acts 7:19

TREAD

t down the wicked in . . . .Job 40:12
it is He who shall *t*. . . . . . .Ps 60:12
You shall *t* upon the. . . . . . .Ps 91:13
shout, as those who *t* . . . .Jer 25:30
will come down and *t*. . . . . .Mic 1:3
And they will *t* . . . . .Rev 11:2

TREADS

like one who *t* in the . . . . .Is 63:2
t the high places . . . . . . .Amos 4:13
an ox while it *t* . . . . .1 Tim 5:18
t the winepress . . . . .Rev 19:15

TREASURE

to you His good *t* . . . . . .Deut 28:12
one who finds great *t* . . . .Ps 119:162
for His special *t* . . . . .Ps 135:4
there is much *t* . . . . .Prov 15:6
There is desirable *t* . . . . .Prov 21:20
of the LORD is His *t*. . . . . . . .Is 33:6
"For where your *t*. . . . . . . .Matt 6:21
t brings forth evil. . . . . . .Matt 12:35
t things new and old . . . .Matt 13:52
and you will have *t*. . . . . .Matt 19:21
"So is he who lays up *t* . .Luke 12:21
But we have this *t* . . . . . . .2 Cor 4:7
You have heaped up *t*. . . .James 5:3

TREASURED

t the words of His. . . . . . . .Job 23:12

TREASURER

Erastus, the *t* of the . . . . .Rom 16:23

TREASURES

sealed up among My *t* . . .Deut 32:34
it more than hidden *t* . . . . .Job 3:21
her as for hidden *t*. . . . . . .Prov 2:4
t of wickedness profit. . . . .Prov 10:2
Getting *t* by a lying . . . . . .Prov 21:6
is no end to their *t*. . . . . .Is 2:7
I will give you the *t*. . . . . . . .Is 45:3
Are there yet the *t* . . . . . . .Mic 6:10
for yourselves *t*. . . . . .Matt 6:19
are hidden all the *t* . . . . . . .Col 2:3
riches than the *t*. . . . . . . .Heb 11:26

TREATY

Now Solomon made a *t*. . . .1 Kin 3:1

TREE

"but of the *t*. . . . . .Gen 2:17
you eaten from the *t* . . . . .Gen 3:11
there is hope for a *t* . . . . . .Job 14:7
t planted by the . . . . .Ps 1:3
like a native green *t* . . . . . .Ps 37:35
t falls to the south. . . . . . .Eccl 11:3
Like an apple *t* . . . . .Song 2:3
for as the days of a *t*. . . . . .Is 65:22
t planted by the. . . . . .Jer 17:8
t bears good fruit. . . . . . . .Matt 7:17
His own body on the *t*. . . .1 Pet 2:24
give to eat from the *t*. . . . . .Rev 2:7
the river, was the *t* . . . . . . .Rev 22:2

TREES

t once went forth . . . . .Judg 9:8
Also he spoke of *t* . . . . . .1 Kin 4:33
Then all the *t* of the. . . . . .Ps 96:12
The *t* of the LORD are. . . . .Ps 104:16
all kinds of fruit *t* . . . . . . .Eccl 2:5
they may be called *t* . . . . . . .Is 61:3
and on beast, on the *t* . . . . .Jer 7:20
so that all the *t*. . . . . .Ezek 31:9
"I see men like *t* . . . . . . .Mark 8:24
late autumn *t* without. . . . .Jude 12
the sea, or the *t*. . . . . .Rev 7:3

TREMBLE

T before Him . . . . .1 Chr 16:30
have made the earth *t* . . . . .Ps 60:2
let the peoples *t* . . . . .Ps 99:1
who made the earth *t* . . . . .Is 14:16
that the nations may *t* . . . . .Is 64:2
'Will you not *t* . . . . .Jer 5:22
wrath the earth will *t* . . . . .Jer 10:10
they shall fear and *t* . . . . . .Jer 33:9

my kingdom men must *t*...Dan 6:26

TREMBLED

of Edom, the earth *t* ......Judg 5:4
for his heart *t* ....1 Sam 4:13
Then everyone who *t*......Ezra 9:4
the earth shook and *t*......Ps 18:7
and indeed they *t*.........Jer 4:24

TREMBLES

the earth sees and *t* ......Ps 97:4

TREMBLING

it was a very great *t*...1 Sam 14:15
your water with *t* ......Ezek 12:18
in fear, and in much *t* ....1 Cor 2:3
t you received...........2 Cor 7:15
flesh, with fear and *t*......Eph 6:5
with fear and *t* ....Phil 2:12

TRENCH

and he made a *t*........1 Kin 18:32

TRESPASSES

still goes on in his *t* ......Ps 68:21
forgive men their *t*......Matt 6:14
not imputing their *t*....2 Cor 5:19
who were dead in *t*........Eph 2:1
forgiven you all *t* ....Col 2:13

TRIAL

as in the day of *t*...........Ps 95:8
in the day of *t*............Heb 3:8
concerning the fiery *t* ....1 Pet 4:12
t which shall come ....Rev 3:10

TRIBE

of old, the *t* of Your ....Ps 74:2
belongs to another *t*......Heb 7:13
the Lion of the *t* ....Rev 5:5
blood out of every *t* ....Rev 5:9

TRIBES

where the *t* go up ....Ps 122:4
to raise up the *t*...........Is 49:6
promise our twelve *t* .....Acts 26:7
t which are scattered .....James 1:1

TRIBULATION

there will be great *t* ......Matt 24:21
world you will have *t* .....John 16:33
in hope, patient in *t* .....Rom 12:12
joyful in all our *t* ....2 Cor 7:4
that we would suffer *t*...1 Thess 3:4
and you will have *t*.........2 Thess 1:6
with her into great *t* ......Rev 2:22
out of the great *t* ....Rev 7:14

TRIBULATIONS

t enter the kingdom .....Acts 14:22
but we also glory in *t* .....Rom 5:3
not lose heart at my *t* ....Eph 3:13
t that you endure.......2 Thess 1:4

TRIED

You have *t* me and have.....Ps 17:3
a *t* stone, a precious ....Is 28:16

TRIMMED

and *t* their lamps ....Matt 25:7

TRIUMPH

Let not my enemies *t*.......Ps 25:2
I will *t* in the works ....Ps 92:4
always leads us in *t*......2 Cor 2:14

TRIUMPHED

the Lord, for He has *t*......Ex 15:1

TRODDEN

t the winepress alone........Is 63:3

TROUBLE

that they were in *t*........Ex 5:19
no rest, for *t* comes.......Job 3:26
few days and full of *t* .....Job 14:1
for the time of *t*.........Job 38:23
have increased who *t* ....Ps 3:1
under his tongue is *t* ....Ps 10:7
from Me, for *t* is near......Ps 22:11
t He shall hide me ....Ps 27:5
O Lord, for I am in *t*.......Ps 31:9
not in *t* as other men ......Ps 73:5
will be with him in *t*......Ps 91:15
walk in the midst of *t*.....Ps 138:7
is delivered from *t*.......Prov 11:8
of the wicked is *t*........Prov 15:6
t they have ....Is 26:16
also in the time of *t*.......Is 33:2
and there was *t* ....Jer 8:15
Savior in time of *t* ....Jer 14:8
such will have *t* ....1 Cor 7:28
there are some who *t*........Gal 1:7

TROUBLED

Your face, and I was *t* ......Ps 30:7
Your face, they are *t* .....Ps 104:29
wicked are like the *t* ......Is 57:20
you are worried and *t*...Luke 10:41
to give you who are *t*...2 Thess 1:7
shaken in mind or *t*.....2 Thess 2:2

TROUBLES

"What *t* the people.....1 Sam 11:5
deliver you in six *t* ....Job 5:19
The *t* of my heart have.....Ps 25:17
out of all their *t*..........Ps 25:22
my soul is full of *t* ....Ps 88:3
because the former *t*......Is 65:16
will be famines and *t*.....Mark 13:8
him out of all his *t* ......Acts 7:10

TROUBLING

spirit from God is *t* ....1 Sam 16:15
wicked cease from *t* ....Job 3:17

TRUE

and Your words are *t* ....2 Sam 7:28
But the Lord is the *t* ....Jer 10:10
"Let the Lord be *t* ......Rom 3:4
we know that You are *t* ..Matt 22:16
He who sent Me is *t* .....John 7:28
about this Man were *t* ...John 10:41
Indeed, let God be *t* ......Rom 3:4
whatever things are *t*......Phil 4:8
may know Him who is *t* .1 John 5:20
is holy, He who is *t*........Rev 3:7
" These are the *t* ....Rev 19:9
for these words are *t*......Rev 21:5

TRUMPET

Blow the *t* at the time .....Ps 81:3
"Blow the *t* in the ....Jer 4:5
deed, do not sound a *t*....Matt 6:2
t makes an uncertain.....1 Cor 14:8
For the *t* will sound......1 Cor 15:52
loud voice, as of a *t* ......Rev 1:10

TRUST

t is a spider's web.........Job 8:14
If God puts no *t* ....Job 15:15
T in the Lord ....Ps 37:3
You are my *t* from my .....Ps 71:5
T in the Lord with all .....Prov 3:5
my salvation, I will *t*......Is 12:2
Let him *t* in the name.....Is 50:10
"Do not *t* in these ....Jer 7:4
Do not *t* in a friend ....Mic 7:5

TRUSTED

for those who *t*........Mark 10:24
committed to your *t* .....1 Tim 6:20

TRUSTED

"He *t* in the Lord.........Ps 22:8
"He *t* in God...........Matt 27:43
that we who first *t*.......Eph 1:12
the holy women who *t*....1 Pet 3:5

TRUSTS

but he who *t* in the........Ps 32:10
He who *t* in his own .....Prov 28:26

TRUTH

led me in the way of *t* ....Gen 24:48
justice, a God of *t*........Deut 32:4
and speaks the *t* ....Ps 15:2
t continually preserve......Ps 40:11
Behold, You desire *t*.......Ps 51:6
T shall spring out of......Ps 85:11
t shall be your shield ......Ps 91:4
t utterly out of my ......Ps 119:43
and Your law is *t*.......Ps 119:142
of Your word is *t* ....Ps 119:160
t is fallen in the ....Is 59:14
not valiant for the *t*........Jer 9:3
" There is no *t*............Hos 4:1
called the City of *T*.......Zech 8:3
speak each man the *t* .....Zech 8:16
t was in his mouth ....Mal 2:6
you shall know the *t*.......John 8:32
"I am the way, the *t*......John 14:6
He, the Spirit of *t*......John 16:13
to Him, "What is *t*.......John 18:38
speak the words of *t* .....Acts 26:25
who suppress the *t*........Rom 1:18
of sincerity and *t*.........1 Cor 5:8
but, speaking the *t*........Eph 4:15
your waist with *t* ....Eph 6:14
in the word of the *t*........Col 1:5
the love of the *t* ....2 Thess 2:10
I am speaking the *t* ....1 Tim 2:7
they may know the *t*.....2 Tim 2:25
the knowledge of the *t* ....2 Tim 3:7
in the present *t* ....2 Pet 1:12
way of *t* will be...........2 Pet 2:2
that we are of the *t* .....1 John 3:19
the Spirit is *t* ....1 John 5:6
t that is in you ....3 John 3

TRY

t my mind and my heart ....Ps 26:2
refine them and *t* them.....Jer 9:7
*t*Me now in this ....Mal 3:10
which is to *t* you.........1 Pet 4:12

TUMULT

their waves, and the *t*......Ps 65:7
Your enemies make a *t*......Ps 83:2

TUNIC

Also he made him a *t*......Gen 37:3
and take away your *t* ....Matt 5:40

TUNICS

the Lord God made *t* ......Gen 3:21
not to put on two *t* ......Mark 6:9
weeping, showing the *t*....Acts 9:39

TURBAN

like a robe and a *t*........Job 29:14
"Remove the *t*..........Ezek 21:26

TURN

you shall not *t* ....Deut 17:11
Then we will not *t*.........Ps 80:18
but let them not *t*.........Ps 85:8
yet I do not *t* ....Ps 119:51
T at my rebuke ....Prov 1:23
not let your heart *t*......Prov 7:25

'T now everyone from . . . . .Jer 35:15
"Repent, *t* away from. . . . .Ezek 14:6
yes, let every one *t* . . . . .Jon 3:8
"*T* now from your evil . . . . .Zech 1:4
on your right cheek, *t* . . . .Matt 5:39
t the hearts of the . . . . . . .Luke 1:17
you that you should *t* . . . .Acts 14:15
t them from darkness . . . .Acts 26:18
Let him *t* away from . . . . .1 Pet 3:11

TURNED

kept His way and not *t* . . .Job 23:11
The wicked shall be *t* . . . . . . .Ps 9:17
let them be *t* back and. . . . . .Ps 70:2
t my feet to Your. . . . . . . .Ps 119:59
of Israel, they have *t* . . . . . . .Is 1:4
number believed and *t* . . .Acts 11:21
to you, and how you *t* . . .1 Thess 1:9

TURNING

marvel that you are *t* . . . . . . .Gal 1:6
or shadow of *t*. . . . . .James 1:17

TURNS

of the wicked He *t* . . . . .Ps 146:9
A soft answer *t* . . . . .Prov 15:1
but no one *t* back. . . . . .Nah 2:8
him know that he who *t* .James 5:20

TURTLEDOVE

the life of Your *t* . . . . .Ps 74:19
t is heard in our land . . . .Song 2:12

TUTOR

the law was our *t*. . . . . . . .Gal 3:24
no longer under a *t* . . . . . . .Gal 3:25

TWIST

All day they *t* my . . . . .Ps 56:5
and unstable people *t* to . .2 Pet 3:16

TWO

the ark to Noah, *t* . . . . .Gen 7:15
t young pigeons. . . . . .Lev 12:8
T are better than one . . . . .Eccl 4:9
t he covered his . . . . .Is 6:2
t shall become one . . . . . .Matt 19:5
t young pigeons . . . . .Luke 2:24
one new man from the *t* . . .Eph 2:15

TYPE

of Adam, who is a *t*. . . . . .Rom 5:14

U

UNAFRAID

Do you want to be *u* . . . . . .Rom 13:3

UNBELIEF

because of their *u* . . . . . .Matt 13:58
help my *u* . . . . .Mark 9:24
and He rebuked their *u*. .Mark 16:14
did it ignorantly in *u* . .1 Tim 1:13
you an evil heart of *u* . . . . .Heb 3:12
enter in because of *u* . . . . .Heb 3:19

UNBELIEVERS

who believe but to *u* . . . .1 Cor 14:22
are uninformed or *u* . . . . .1 Cor 14:23
yoked together with *u* . . . .2 Cor 6:14

UNBELIEVING

Do not be *u* . . . . .John 20:27
u Jews stirred up the . . . . .Acts 14:2
For the *u* husband is . . . . .1 Cor 7:14
u nothing is pure . . . . .Titus 1:15
But the cowardly, *u* . . . . . . .Rev 21:8

UNCIRCUMCISED

You stiff-necked and *u* . . . .Acts 7:51

---

not the physically *u* . . . . . .Rom 2:27
by faith and the *u* . . . . .Rom 3:30
had been committed . . . . .Gal 2:7

UNCLEAN

of animals that are *u* . . . . . . .Gen 7:2
who touches any *u* . . . . .Lev 7:21
I am a man of *u* lips . . . . .Is 6:5
u shall no longer come . . . . . .Is 52:1
He commands even the *u* .Mark 1:27
He rebuked the *u* . . . . .Mark 9:25
any man common or *u* . . .Acts 10:28
there is nothing *u* . . . . . . .Rom 14:14
Do not touch what is *u* . . .2 Cor 6:17
that no fornicator, *u*. . . . . . . .Eph 5:5

UNCLEANNESS

men's bones and all *u*. . . .Matt 23:27
members as slaves of *u*. . . .Rom 6:19
did not call us to *u*. . . . . .1 Thess 4:7
flesh in the lust of *u*. . . . . .2 Pet 2:10

UNCLEANNESSES

from all your *u* . . . . .Ezek 36:29

UNCLOTHED

we want to be *u* . . . . .2 Cor 5:4

UNCOVER

skirt, *u* the thigh. . . . . .Is 47:2

UNCOVERS

u deep things out of . . . . .Job 12:22

UNDEFILED

Blessed are the *u* . . . . .Ps 119:1
all, and the bed *u*. . . . . . . .Heb 13:4
incorruptible and *u*. . . . . . . .1 Pet 1:4

UNDERMINE

and you *u* your friend. . . . . .Job 6:27

UNDERSTAND

u one another's speech. . . . .Gen 11:7
if there are any who *u* . . . . .Ps 14:2
in Egypt did not *u* . . . . . . .Ps 106:7
is to *u* his way . . . . .Prov 14:8
Evil men do not *u* . . . . . . .Prov 28:5
hearing, but do not *u* . . . . . . .Is 6:9
and quick to *u* . . . . .Dan 1:4
set your heart to *u*. . . . . .Dan 10:12
u shall instruct many . . . .Dan 11:33
of the wicked shall *u* . . . .Dan 12:10
people who do not *u* . . . . . .Hos 4:14
Let him *u* these things . . . . .Hos 14:9
Why do you not *u* . . . . . . .John 8:43
u what you are reading. . . .Acts 8:30
lest they should *u* . . . . . .Acts 28:27
u all mysteries . . . . .1 Cor 13:2
some things hard to *u* . . .2 Pet 3:16

UNDERSTANDING

asked for yourself *u*. . . . . .1 Kin 3:11
He has counsel and *u*. . . .Job 12:13
is the place of *u*. . . . . .Job 28:12
depart from evil is *u*. . . . . .Job 28:28
Almighty gives him *u*. . . . .Job 32:8
not endow her with *u* . . . .Job 39:17
my heart shall give *u* . . . . . .Ps 49:3
Give me *u* . . . . .Ps 119:34
Your precepts I get *u* . . . .Ps 119:104
His *u* is infinite. . . . . .Ps 147:5
apply your heart to *u* . . . . . .Prov 2:2
lean not on your own *u*. . . . .Prov 3:5
u He established . . . . .Prov 3:19
and go in the way of *u* . . . . .Prov 9:6
of the Holy One is *u*. . . . . .Prov 9:10
a man of *u* has wisdom. . .Prov 10:23
U is a wellspring . . . . .Prov 16:22
u will find good . . . . .Prov 19:8

---

and instruction and *u* . . . .Prov 23:23
but the poor who has *u* . .Prov 28:11
Spirit of wisdom and *u* . . . . .Is 11:2
His *u* is unsearchable . . . . . .Is 40:28
also still without *u* . . . . . .Matt 15:16
And He opened their *u* .Luke 24:45
also pray with the *u*. . . . .1 Cor 14:15
five words with my *u*. . . .1 Cor 14:19
and spiritual *u* . . . . .Col 1:9
the Lord give you *u*. . . . . . .2 Tim 2:7
Who is wise and *u* . . . . . .James 3:13
and has given us an *u* . . .1 John 5:20

UNDERSTANDS

all plain to him who *u*. . . . . .Prov 8:9
is easy to him who *u*. . . . . .Prov 14:6
there is none who *u*. . . . . . .Rom 3:11

UNDERSTOOD

Then I *u* their end . . . . .Ps 73:17
My heart has *u* great . . . .Eccl 1:16
Have you not *u* from. . . . . .Is 40:21
u all these things . . . . . . .Matt 13:51
clearly seen, being *u* . . . . .Rom 1:20

UNDESIRABLE

gather together, O *u* . . . . . .Zeph 2:1

UNDIGNIFIED

I will be even more *u* . . . .2 Sam 6:22

UNDISCERNING

u, untrustworthy . . . . .Rom 1:31

UNDONE

"Woe is me, for I am *u* . . . . . .Is 6:5
leaving the others *u* . . . .Matt 23:23

UNEDUCATED

that they were *u* . . . . .Acts 4:13

UNFAITHFUL

u will be uprooted . . . . . . .Prov 2:22
way of the *u* is hard . . . . .Prov 13:15

UNFAITHFULLY

back and acted *u*. . . . . .Ps 78:57

UNFORGIVING

unloving, *u*. . . . . .Rom 1:31

UNFORMED

substance, being yet *u* . . . .Ps 139:16

UNFRUITFUL

and it becomes *u* . . . . . . .Mark 4:19
that they may not be *u* . . .Titus 3:14

UNGODLINESS

u made me afraid . . . . .Ps 18:4
heaven against all *u* . . . . .Rom 1:18
He will turn away *u* . . . . .Rom 11:26

UNGODLY

delivered me to the *u* . . . . .Job 16:11
u shall not stand. . . . . .Ps 1:5
of the *u* shall perish . . . . .Ps 1:6
my cause against an *u* . . . . .Ps 43:1
u man digs up evil. . . . . . .Prov 16:27
who justifies the *u* . . . . . . .Rom 4:5
Christ died for the *u* . . . . . .Rom 5:6
and perdition of *u* men . . . .2 Pet 3:7
convict all who are *u* . . . . . . .Jude 15

UNHOLY

between the holy and *u* . .Ezek 22:26
for sinners, for the *u* . . . . . .1 Tim 1:9

UNINFORMED

the place of the *u*. . . . . . .1 Cor 14:16

UNINTENTIONALLY
kills his neighbor u . . . . . . .Deut 4:42

UNITE
u my heart to fear . . . . .Ps 86:11

UNITY
to dwell together in u . . . . . .Ps 133:1
to keep the u of the . . . . . . .Eph 4:3
we all come to the u . . . . . . .Eph 4:13

UNJUST
hope of the u perishes . . . . .Prov 11:7
u knows no shame . . . . .Zeph 3:5
master commended the u . .Luke 16:8
extortioners, u . . . . .Luke 18:11
of the just and the u . . . . .Acts 24:15
u who inflicts wrath . . . . . .Rom 3:5
For God is not u . . . . .Heb 6:10
the just for the u . . . . .1 Pet 3:18
let him be u still . . . . .Rev 22:11

UNJUSTLY
long will you judge u . . . . . . .Ps 82:2
he will deal u . . . . .Is 26:10

UNKNOWN
not stand before u . . . . . .Prov 22:29
TO THE U GOD . . . . . . .Acts 17:23
And I was u by face to . . . . .Gal 1:22

UNLEAVENED
the Feast of U Bread . . . . . .Ex 12:17
the Feast of U Bread . . . . .Mark 14:1
since you truly are u . . . . . .1 Cor 5:7

UNLOVING
untrustworthy, u . . . . .Rom 1:31

UNMERCIFUL
unforgiving, u . . . . .Rom 1:31

UNPREPARED
with me and find you u . . . .2 Cor 9:4

UNPRESENTABLE
u parts have greater . . . .1 Cor 12:23

UNPROFITABLE
'And cast the u . . . . .Matt 25:30
'We are u servants . . . . .Luke 17:10
have together become u . .Rom 3:12
who once was u to you . . .Philem 11
for that would be u . . . . .Heb 13:17

UNPROFITABLENESS
of its weakness and u . . . . .Heb 7:18

UNPUNISHED
wicked will not go u . . . . .Prov 11:21
be rich will not go u . . . . .Prov 28:20

UNQUENCHABLE
up the chaff with u . . . . . .Matt 3:12
He will burn with u . . . . . .Luke 3:17

UNRESTRAINED
that the people were u . . . . .Ex 32:25

UNRIGHTEOUS
u man his thoughts . . . . .Is 55:7
been faithful in the u . . . .Luke 16:11
u will not inherit the . . . . . .1 Cor 6:9

UNRIGHTEOUSNESS
and there is no u . . . . .Ps 92:15
builds his house by u . . . . .Jer 22:13
Him is true, and no u . . . . .John 7:18
all ungodliness and u . . . . .Rom 1:18
the truth, but obey u . . . . . .Rom 2:8
Is there u with God . . . . . .Rom 9:14

cleanse us from all u . . . . .1 John 1:9
All u is sin . . . . .1 John 5:17

UNRULY
warn those who are u . .1 Thess 5:14
It is an u evil . . . . .James 3:8

UNSEARCHABLE
heart of kings is u . . . . . . .Prov 25:3
u are His judgments . . . . .Rom 11:33

UNSKILLED
only of milk is u . . . . .Heb 5:13

UNSPOTTED
to keep oneself u . . . . . . .James 1:27

UNSTABLE
U as water . . . . .Gen 49:4

UNSTOPPED
of the deaf shall be u . . . . .Is 35:5

UNTAUGHT
which u and unstable . . . . .2 Pet 3:16

UNTRUSTWORTHY
undiscerning, u . . . . .Rom 1:31

UNWASHED
eat bread with u hands . . . .Mark 7:5

UNWISE
He is an u son . . . . .Hos 13:13
Therefore do not be u . . . . .Eph 5:17

UNWORTHY
and judge yourselves u . .Acts 13:46
u manner will be . . . . . . .1 Cor 11:27

UPHOLD
u the evildoers . . . . .Job 8:20
U me according to Your . .Ps 119:116
My Servant whom I . . . . . . .Is 42:1
there was no one to u . . . . . .Is 63:5

UPHOLDING
u all things by the . . . . .Heb 1:3

UPHOLDS
Your right hand u . . . . .Ps 63:8
LORD u all who fall . . . . . .Ps 145:14

UPPER
show you a large u . . . . . .Mark 14:15
went up into the u . . . . . . .Acts 1:13
many lamps in the u . . . . . .Acts 20:8

UPRIGHT
righteous and u is He . . . . .Deut 32:4
where were the u . . . . .Job 4:7
Good and u is the LORD . . . .Ps 25:8
u shall have dominion . . . . . .Ps 49:14
u will be blessed . . . . .Ps 112:2
u there arises light . . . . .Ps 112:4
is strength for the u . . . . .Prov 10:29
u will guide them . . . . .Prov 11:3
u will deliver them . . . . . . .Prov 11:6
u will flourish . . . . .Prov 14:11
u is His delight . . . . .Prov 15:8
of the u is a highway . . . .Prov 15:19
that God made man u . . . . .Eccl 7:29
and there is no one u . . . . . .Mic 7:2
his soul is not u . . . . .Hab 2:4

UPRIGHTNESS
to show man His u . . . . .Job 33:23
me in the land of u . . . . . .Ps 143:10
princes for their u . . . . . . .Prov 17:26
of the just is u . . . . .Is 26:7
land of u he will deal . . . . . .Is 26:10

UPROOT
"then I will u . . . . .2 Chr 7:20
u you from the land . . . . . . .Ps 52:5
u the wheat with them . . .Matt 13:29

URIM
of judgment the U . . . . . . .Ex 28:30
Thummim and Your U . . . .Deut 33:8

US
"God with u, ...Matt 1:23
who is not against u . . . .Mark 9:40
If God is for u . . . . .Rom 8:31
They went out from u . .1 John 2:19
none of them were of u . .1 John 2:19

USE
who spitefully u you . . . . . .Matt 5:44
leaving the natural u . . . . . .Rom 1:27
u this world as not . . . . . . .1 Cor 7:31
u liberty as an . . . . .Gal 5:13
u a little wine . . . . .1 Tim 5:23
u have their . . . . .Heb 5:14

USELESS
all of them are u . . . . .Is 44:9
are unprofitable and u . . . .Titus 3:9
one's religion is u . . . . . . .James 1:26

USES
if one u it lawfully . . . . .1 Tim 1:8

USING
u no figure of speech . . .John 16:29
perish with the u . . . . .Col 2:22
u liberty as a . . . . .1 Pet 2:16

USURY
Take no u or . . . . .Lev 25:36
put out his money at u . . . . . .Ps 15:5

UTTER
u pure knowledge . . . . .Job 33:3
u dark sayings of old . . . . . .Ps 78:2
let not your heart u . . . . . . .Eccl 5:2
lawful for a man to u . . . .2 Cor 12:4

UTTERANCE
the Spirit gave them u . . . . .Acts 2:4
u may be given to me . . . . .Eph 6:19

UTTERED
The deep u its voice . . . . . .Hab 3:10
which cannot be u . . . . . . .Rom 8:26
the seven thunders u . . . . . .Rev 10:4

UTTERMOST
upon them to the u . . . .1 Thess 2:16
u those who come . . . . . . .Heb 7:25

UTTERS
Day unto day u speech . . . . .Ps 19:2
u His voice from . . . . .Amos 1:2
and the great man u . . . . . . .Mic 7:3

V

VAGABOND
v you shall be on the . . . . . .Gen 4:12

VAIN
the people plot a v . . . . .Ps 2:1
v life which he passes . . . .Eccl 6:12
'I have labored in v . . . . .Is 49:4
you believed in v . . . . .1 Cor 15:2

VALIANT
Only be v for me . . . . . .1 Sam 18:17
They are not v for the . . . . . .Jer 9:3
v men swept away . . . . . . .Jer 46:15

VALIANTLY

while Israel does *v* ......Num 24:18
God we will do *v* ....Ps 60:12
of the LORD does *v* ....Ps 118:15

VALLEY

I walk through the *v* ....Ps 23:4
pass through the *V* ....Ps 84:6
the verdure of the *v* ......Song 6:11
v shall be exalted..........Is 40:4
in the midst of the *v* .....Ezek 37:1
v shall be filled ....Luke 3:5

VALOR

a mighty man of *v* .....1 Sam 16:18

VALUE

does not know its *v* ......Job 28:13
of more *v* than they ......Matt 6:26
they counted up the *v*....Acts 19:19

VALUED

It cannot be *v* in the .....Job 28:16

VANISH

when it is hot, they *v* .....Job 6:17
For the heavens will *v*.......Is 51:6
knowledge, it will *v* ......1 Cor 13:8
old is ready to *v* away .....Heb 8:13

VANISHED

and He *v* from their ....Luke 24:31

VANITY

of vanities, all is *v* ....Eccl 1:2

VAPOR

best state is but *v*..........Ps 39:5
surely every man is *v*......Ps 39:11
It is even a *v* that .....James 4:14

VARIATION

whom there is no *v*.....James 1:17

VEGETABLES

and let them give us *v*....Dan 1:12
is weak eats only *v* ....Rom 14:2

VEHEMENT

of fire, a most *v* ....Song 8:6

VEIL

he put a *v* on his face .....Ex 34:33
v of the temple was ....Matt 27:51
Moses, who put a *v* ......2 Cor 3:13
Presence behind the *v* ....Heb 6:19

VENGEANCE

'You shall not take *v*......Lev 19:18
V is Mine..............Deut 32:35
spare in the day of *v*......Prov 6:34
God will come with *v* ....Is 35:4
on the garments of *v*......Is 59:17
let me see Your *v* ....Jer 11:20
are the days of *v*......Luke 21:22
written, "*V* is Mine......Rom 12:19
flaming fire taking *v* ...2 Thess 1:8
suffering the *v* ....Jude 7

VENOM

it becomes cobra *v* ....Job 20:14

VESSEL

like a potter's *v* ....Ps 2:9
v that he made of clay .....Jer 18:4
like a precious *v*.........Jer 25:34
been emptied from *v* .....Jer 48:11
for he is a chosen *v*......Acts 9:15
lump to make one *v* ......Rom 9:21
to possess his own *v* ....1 Thess 4:4
to the weaker *v*..........1 Pet 3:7

VESSELS

longsuffering the *v* ....Rom 9:22
treasure in earthen *v*......2 Cor 4:7
like the potter's *v* ....Rev 2:27

VEXED

grieved, and I was *v*.......Ps 73:21

VICE

as a cloak for *v*..........1 Pet 2:16

VICTIM

and plucked the *v*.......Job 29:17

VICTORY

who gives us the *v*......1 Cor 15:57
v that has overcome .....1 John 5:4

VIEW

"Go, *v* the land ....Josh 2:1

VIGILANT

in prayer, being *v*...........Col 4:2
Be sober, be *v* ....1 Pet 5:8

VIGOR

nor his natural *v*........Deut 34:7

VILE

sons made themselves *v* .1 Sam 3:13
"Behold, I am *v* ....Job 40:4
them up to *v* passions ....Rom 1:26

VINDICATED

know that I shall be *v* ....Job 13:18

VINDICATION

Let my *v* come from........Ps 17:2

VINE

to the choice *v* ....Gen 49:11
their *v* is of the *v* ......Deut 32:32
You have brought a *v*......Ps 80:8
planted you a noble *v* ....Jer 2:21
grapes shall be on the *v* ..Jer 8:13
Israel empties his *v* ......Hos 10:1
shall sit under his *v* ......Mic 4:4
of this fruit of the *v*......Matt 26:29
"I am the true *v*........John 15:1

VINEDRESSER

and My Father is the *v* ..John 15:1

VINEGAR

As *v* to the teeth and ....Prov 10:26
weather, and like *v* ......Prov 25:20

VINES

foxes that spoil the *v*....Song 2:15
nor fruit be on the *v* .....Hab 3:17

VINEYARD

v which Your right ....Ps 80:15
laborers for his *v* ....Matt 20:1
Who plants a *v* and.......1 Cor 9:7

VIOLENCE

was filled with *v*..........Gen 6:11
You save me from *v* ....2 Sam 22:3
the one who loves *v* ....Ps 11:5
such as breathe out *v*......Ps 27:12
from oppression and *v*.....Ps 72:14
v covers the ....Prov 10:6
He had done no *v* ....Is 53:9
and *v* in the land ....Jer 51:46
cause the seat of *v* ....Amos 6:3
way and from the *v*.......Jon 3:8
rich men are full of *v* .....Mic 6:12
For plundering and *v*......Hab 1:3
one's garment with *v* .....Mal 2:16
of heaven suffers *v*......Matt 11:12

VIOLENT

me from the *v* man........Ps 18:48
let evil hunt the *v*......Ps 140:11
violence, and the *v*......Matt 11:12
haters of God, *v*.........Rom 1:30
given to wine, not *v* ......1 Tim 3:3

VIPER

and stings like a *v*......Prov 23:32
will come forth a *v*........Is 14:29
which is crushed a *v* ....Is 59:5

VIPERS

to them, "Brood of *v* .....Matt 3:7

VIRGIN

v shall conceive ....Is 7:14
O you oppressed *v*........Is 23:12
v daughter of my........Jer 14:17
The *v* of Israel has ......Amos 5:2
"Behold, the *v* shall .....Matt 1:23
between a wife and a *v* ...1 Cor 7:34
you as a chaste *v*........2 Cor 11:2

VIRGINS

v who took their lamps ...Matt 25:1
women, for they are *v*......Rev 14:4

VIRTUE

if there is any *v* ....Phil 4:8
us by glory and *v*........2 Pet 1:3
to your faith *v* ....2 Pet 1:5

VISAGE

v was marred more than....Is 52:14

VISIBLE

that are on earth, *v*........Col 1:16
of things which are *v*......Heb 11:3

VISION

chased away like a *v*......Job 20:8
Then You spoke in a *v* .....Ps 89:19
the Valley of *V*...........Is 22:1
a dream of a night *v* ......Is 29:7
her prophets find no *v* ....Lam 2:9
have night without *v* ......Mic 3:6
they had also seen a *v* ...Luke 24:23
in a trance I saw a *v*......Acts 11:5
v appeared to Paul in ....Acts 16:9
to the heavenly *v*........Acts 26:19

VISIONS

thoughts from the *v* ....Job 4:13
young men shall see *v* .....Joel 2:28
I will come to *v* ....2 Cor 12:1

VISIT

but God will surely *v*.....Gen 50:24
in the day when I *v* ......Ex 32:34
v the earth and water......Ps 65:9
Oh, *v* me with Your ....Ps 106:4
v orphans and widows...James 1:27

VISITATION

the time of your *v*......Luke 19:44
God in the day of *v*.....1 Pet 2:12

VISITED

he will not be *v* ....Prov 19:23
Israel, for He has *v* .....Luke 1:68
how God at the first *v* ...Acts 15:14

VISITING

v the iniquity of the fathers .Ex 20:5

VISITOR

am a foreigner and a *v*.....Gen 23:4

VITALITY

v was turned into the.......Ps 32:4

VOICE

"I heard Your *v* . . . . .Gen 3:10
v is Jacob's *v* . . . . .Gen 27:22
I should obey His *v* . . . . .Ex 5:2
fire a still small *v*. . . . . . .1 Kin 19:12
and my flute to the *v* . . . . .Job 30:31
you thunder with a *v* . . . . . .Job 40:9
He uttered His *v*. . . . . .Ps 46:6
He sends out His *v*. . . . . . .Ps 68:33
have lifted up their *v* . . . . . .Ps 93:3
if you will hear His *v* . . . . . .Ps 95:7
word, heeding the *v* . . . . . .Ps 103:20
for your *v* is sweet . . . . . .Song 2:14
The *v* of one crying in. . . . . .Is 40:3
the *v* of weeping shall . . . . . .Is 65:19
A *v* from the temple . . . . .Is 66:6
v was heard in Ramah. . . .Jer 31:15
who has a pleasant *v*. . .Ezek 33:32
v was heard in Ramah . . .Matt 2:18
"The *v* of one crying. . . . .Matt 3:3
And suddenly a *v*. . . . . . .Matt 3:17
will anyone hear His *v*. . .Matt 12:19
and suddenly a *v* . . . . . .Matt 17:5
for they know his *v*. . . . . .John 10:4
v did not come because . .John 12:30
the truth hears My *v*. . . .John 18:37
the *v* of an archangel. . .1 Thess 4:16
whose *v* then shook the. . .Heb 12:26
glory when such a *v*. . . . .2 Pet 1:17
If anyone hears My *v*. . . . .Rev 3:20

VOICES

shall lift up their *v* . . . . . .Is 52:8
and there were loud *v*. . . .Rev 11:15

VOID

they are a nation *v*. . . . .Deut 32:28
the Lord had made a *v* . .Judg 21:15
regarded Your law as *v*. . .Ps 119:126
Do we then make *v*. . . . . .Rom 3:31
heirs, faith is made *v* . . . .Rom 4:14
make my boasting *v* . . . .1 Cor 9:15

VOLUME

in the *v* of the book . . . . . . .Heb 10:7

VOLUNTEERS

Your people shall be *v* . . . . .Ps 110:3

VOMIT

'lest the land *v* . . . . .Lev 18:28
man staggers in his *v* . . . . .Is 19:14
returns to his own *v*. . . . .2 Pet 2:22

VOW

Then Jacob made a *v*. . . . .Gen 28:20
And Jephthah made a *v* . .Judg 11:30
he carried out his *v* . . . . .Judg 11:39
v shall be performed. . . . . . .Ps 65:1
When you make a *v*. . . . . .Eccl 5:4
not to *v* than to *v* . . . . . . .Eccl 5:5
for he had taken a *v* . . . . .Acts 18:18
men who have taken a *v*. .Acts 21:23

VOWS

you will pay your *v* . . . . . .Job 22:27
I will pay My *v*. . . . . .Ps 22:25
V made to You are . . . . . . .Ps 56:12
Make *v* to the Lord . . . . . .Ps 76:11
today I have paid my *v* . . .Prov 7:14
to reconsider his *v*. . . . . .Prov 20:25
And what, son of my *v*. . .Prov 31:2
to the Lord and took *v* . . . .Jon 1:16

W

WAGE

those who exploit *w*. . . . . . .Mal 3:5

w the good warfare . . . . . .1 Tim 1:18

WAGES

I will give you your *w* . . . . . .Ex 2:9
the *w* of the wicked. . . . .Prov 10:16
w will be troubled . . . . .Is 19:10
and he who earns *w*. . . . . .Hag 1:6
to you, give me my *w* . . . .Zech 11:12
and give them their *w* . . . .Matt 20:8
be content with your *w* . . .Luke 3:14
is worthy of his *w*. . . . . . .Luke 10:7
him who works, the *w*. . . . .Rom 4:4
For the *w* of sin is . . . . . . .Rom 6:23
is worthy of his *w* . . . . . .1 Tim 5:18
Indeed the *w* of the . . . . .James 5:4

WAIL

My heart shall *w* . . . . .Jer 48:36
"Son of man, *w*. . . . . . . .Ezek 32:18

WAILING

w is heard from Zion . . . . . .Jer 9:19
of heart and bitter *w* . . . .Ezek 27:31
There will be *w* . . . . .Matt 13:42

WAIT

hard service I will *w*. . . . . .Job 14:14
If I *w* for the grave. . . . . . .Job 17:13
W on the Lord . . . . .Ps 27:14
w patiently for Him . . . . . . .Ps 37:7
my eyes fail while I *w* . . . . .Ps 69:3
These all *w* for You. . . . . .Ps 104:27
And I will *w* on the. . . . . . .Is 8:17
the Lord will *w* . . . . .Is 30:18
those who *w* on the. . . . . .Is 40:31
not be ashamed who *w*. . . .Is 49:23
w quietly for the . . . . .Lam 3:26
I will *w* for the God . . . . . .Mic 7:7
be like men who *w* . . . . .Luke 12:36
see, we eagerly *w*. . . . . . .Rom 8:25
w for one another. . . . . .1 Cor 11:33
the Spirit eagerly *w* . . . . . .Gal 5:5
we also eagerly *w* . . . . . . .Phil 3:20
and to *w* for His Son. . .1 Thess 1:10
To those who eagerly *w*. . . .Heb 9:28

WAITED

and when I *w* for light. . .Job 30:26
w patiently for the . . . . . . .Ps 40:1
we have *w* for Him . . . . . . .Is 25:9
And the people *w* . . . . . . .Luke 1:21
day you have *w* and . . . .Acts 27:33
Divine, longsuffering *w*. . .1 Pet 3:20

WAITING

w at the posts of my. . . . . .Prov 8:34
w for the Consolation. . . . .Luke 2:25
who himself was also *w* . .Luke 23:51
ourselves, eagerly *w* . . . . .Rom 8:23
from that time *w* . . . . . . .Heb 10:13

WAITS

of the adulterer *w* . . . . . . .Job 24:15
my soul silently . . . . .Ps 62:1
My soul *w* for the Lord . . .Ps 130:6
for the one who *w* . . . . .Is 64:4
the creation eagerly *w*. . . .Rom 8:19

WAKE

us, that whether we *w*. .1 Thess 5:10

WALK

w before Me and be . . . . . .Gen 17:1
in which they must *w* . . . .Ex 18:20
"You shall *w* in all . . . . .Deut 5:33
Yea, though I *w*. . . . . .Ps 23:4
W about Zion . . . . .Ps 48:12
that Israel would *w* . . . . . .Ps 81:13

I will *w* within my . . . . . . .Ps 101:2
I will *w* before the. . . . . . .Ps 116:9
Though I *w* in the. . . . . . .Ps 138:7
W prudently when you . . . .Eccl 5:1
w in the ways of your . . . .Eccl 11:9
come and let us *w* . . . . .Is 2:5
"This is the way, *w*. . . . . . .Is 30:21
be weary, they shall *w*. . . . .Is 40:31
w in the light of your . . . . .Is 50:11
people, who *w* in a way. . . .Is 65:2
commit adultery and *w*. . .Jer 23:14
the righteous *w*. . . . . .Hos 14:9
w humbly with your God. . .Mic 6:8
take up your bed and *w*. . .John 5:8
W while you have the. . .John 12:35
so we also should *w*. . . . . .Rom 6:4
Let us *w* properly . . . . . .Rom 13:13
For we *w* by faith. . . . . . .2 Cor 5:7
W in the Spirit . . . . .Gal 5:16
that we should *w* . . . . . . .Eph 2:10
And *w* in love. . . . . .Eph 5:2
W as children of light . . . . .Eph 5:8
attained, let us *w* . . . . . . .Phil 3:16
note those who so *w*. . . . . .Phil 3:17
that you may *w* worthy . . . .Col 1:10
Jesus the Lord, so *w*. . . . . .Col 2:6
us how you ought to *w* .1 Thess 4:1
w just as He. . . . . .1 John 2:6
and they shall *w* . . . . .Rev 3:4

WALKED

Methuselah, Enoch *w* . . . .Gen 5:22
by His light I *w* . . . . .Job 29:3
The people who *w* . . . . .Is 9:2
He *w* with Me in peace . . . .Mal 2:6
Jesus no longer *w*. . . . . . .John 11:54
w according to the. . . . . .2 Cor 10:2
in which you once *w* . . . . .Eph 2:2
to walk just as He *w*. . . .1 John 2:6

WALKING

of the Lord God *w*. . . . . . . .Gen 3:8
see four men loose, *w*. . . . .Dan 3:25
before God, *w* in all . . . . .Luke 1:6
they saw Jesus *w* . . . . . . .John 6:19
And *w* in the fear of . . . . .Acts 9:31
you are no longer *w*. . . . . .Rom 14:15
not *w* in craftiness. . . . . . .2 Cor 4:2
of your children *w* . . . . . .2 John 1:4

WALKS

the Lord your God *w*. . . .Deut 23:14
is the man who *w* . . . . .Ps 1:1
He who *w* uprightly . . . . . . .Ps 15:2
He who *w* with . . . . .Prov 10:9
He who *w* with wise men .Prov 13:20
w blamelessly will be . . .Prov 28:18
w wisely will be . . . . . . .Prov 28:26
Whoever *w* the road . . . . . . .Is 35:8
Who *w* in darkness and . . . .Is 50:10
it is not in man who *w* . . . .Jer 10:23
do good to him who *w* . . . . .Mic 2:7
If anyone *w* in the day. . . .John 11:9
he who *w* in darkness. . .John 12:35
adversary the devil *w* . . . .1 Pet 5:8
is in darkness and *w* . . .1 John 2:11

WALL

then the *w* of the city . . . . .Josh 6:5
his face toward the *w* . . . .2 Kin 20:2
like a leaning *w*. . . . . .Ps 62:3
and like a high *w*. . . . . . .Prov 18:11
If she is a *w* . . . . .Song 8:9
We grope for the *w* . . . . . . .Is 59:10
you, you whitewashed *w*. . .Acts 23:3
a window in the *w* . . . . . .2 Cor 11:33
down the middle *w*. . . . . . .Eph 2:14
Now the *w* of the city . . . .Rev 21:14

WALLS

broken down, without w . .Prov 25:28
salvation for w . . . . .Is 26:1
you shall call your w . . . . . .Is 60:18
By faith the w of . . . . . . .Heb 11:30

WANDER

and makes them w . . . . . . .Job 12:24
ones cry to God, and w . . .Job 38:41
Indeed, I would w . . . . .Ps 55:7
Oh, let me not w . . . . .Ps 119:10
they have loved to w . . . . . .Jer 14:10

WANDERED

w blind in the streets . . . . .Lam 4:14
"My sheep w through . . . .Ezek 34:6
They w in deserts and. . . .Heb 11:38

WANDERERS

and they shall be w . . . . . . .Hos 9:17

WANDERING

learn to be idle, w . . . . . . .1 Tim 5:13
w stars for whom is. . . . . . . .Jude 13

WANDERS

He w about for bread . . . .Job 15:23
Like a bird that w . . . . . . .Prov 27:8
if anyone among you w . .James 5:19

WANT

I shall not w . . . . .Ps 23:1
he began to be in w . . . . .Luke 15:14

WANTING

balances, and found w . . . . .Dan 5:27

WANTON

necks and w eyes. . . . . .Is 3:16
have begun to grow w. . . .1 Tim 5:11

WAR

There is a noise of w . . . . . .Ex 32:17
the LORD for the w . . . . . .Num 32:20
my hands to make w . .2 Sam 22:35
day of battle and w. . . . . .Job 38:23
w may rise against. . . . . .Ps 27:3
speak, they are for w . . . . .Ps 120:7
by wise counsel wage w . .Prov 20:18
will wage your own w . . . .Prov 24:6
shall they learn w . . . . .Is 2:4
from the distress of w. . . . . .Is 21:15
we shall see no w . . . . .Jer 42:14
same horn was making w . .Dan 7:21
men returned from w . . . . . .Mic 2:8
king, going to make w . .Luke 14:31
Who ever goes to w . . . . .1 Cor 9:7
for pleasure that w. . . . . . .James 4:1
You fight and w . . . . .James 4:2
fleshly lusts which w . . . . .1 Pet 2:11
w broke out in heaven . . . .Rev 12:7
He judges and makes w. . .Rev 19:11

WARFARE

to her, that her w. . . . . .Is 40:2
w are not carnal. . . . . . . .2 Cor 10:4
may wage the good w . . . .1 Tim 1:18
w entangles . . . . .2 Tim 2:4

WARM

they will keep w . . . . .Eccl 4:11
but no one is w. . . . . .Hag 1:6

WARMED

w himself at the fire . . .Mark 14:54
Depart in peace, be w . . .James 2:16

WARMING

when she saw Peter w . . .Mark 14:67

WARMS

w them in the dust. . . . . . .Job 39:14
He even w himself and . . . . .Is 44:16

WARN

w the wicked from his . . .Ezek 3:18
w everyone night. . . . . . . .Acts 20:31
beloved children I w . . . .1 Cor 4:14
w those who are unruly.1 Thess 5:14

WARNED

"The man solemnly w. . . . .Gen 43:3
them Your servant is w . . . .Ps 19:11
Then, being divinely w. . .Matt 2:12
Who w you to flee . . . . . . .Matt 3:7
Noah, being divinely w . . . .Heb 11:7

WARNING

w every man and. . . . . .Col 1:28

WARPED

such a person is w . . . . . . .Titus 3:11

WARRING

w against the law of . . . . . .Rom 7:23

WARRIOR

He runs at me like a w. . . .Job 16:14

WARS

He makes w cease to . . . . . . .Ps 46:9
And you will hear of w . .Matt 24:6
Where do w and fights . .James 4:1

WASH

w myself with snow . . . . . .Job 9:30
I will w my hands in . . . . . .Ps 26:6
W me thoroughly . . . . .Ps 51:2
he shall w his feet in . . . . .Ps 58:10
"W yourselves . . . . .Is 1:16
O Jerusalem, w your . . . . . .Jer 4:14
head and w your face. . .Matt 6:17
For they do not w. . . . . . . .Matt 15:2
not eat unless they w . . . . .Mark 7:3
w His feet with her . . . . .Luke 7:38
said to him, "Go, w . . . . . .John 9:7
w the disciples'. . . . . .John 13:5
"You shall never w . . . . . .John 13:8
w one another's. . . . . . . .John 13:14
w away your sins. . . . . . .Acts 22:16

WASHED

and w my hands in. . . . . . . .Ps 73:13
When the Lord has w . . . . . .Is 4:4
cut, nor were you w . . . . .Ezek 16:4
w his hands before the. . .Matt 27:24
My feet, but she has w . .Luke 7:44
So when He had w . . . . . .John 13:12
w their stripes. . . . . .Acts 16:33
But you were w . . . . .1 Cor 6:11
if she has w the. . . . . . . .1 Tim 5:10
Him who loved us and w . . .Rev 1:5
w their robes and made . .Rev 7:14

WASHING

cleanse her with the w. . . .Eph 5:26
us, through the w. . . . . .Titus 3:5

WASHINGS

and drinks, various w . . . . .Heb 9:10

WASTE

who are left shall w . . . . .Lev 26:39
the cities are laid w . . . . . . .Is 6:11
empty and makes it w . . . . .Is 24:1
w the mountains . . . . .Is 42:15
"Why this w . . . . .Matt 26:8

WASTED

The field is w . . . . .Joel 1:10

this fragrant oil w . . . . . .Mark 14:4
w his possessions . . . . . . .Luke 15:13

WASTELAND

w shall be glad. . . . . .Is 35:1

WASTING

w and destruction are . . . . . .Is 59:7
that this man was w . . . .Luke 16:1

WATCH

of them we set a w. . . . . . . .Neh 4:9
my steps, but do not w . .Job 14:16
is past, and like a w . . . . . .Ps 90:4
keep w over the door . . . . . .Ps 141:3
and all who w for. . . . . .Is 29:20
W the road . . . . .Nah 2:1
"W therefore . . . . .Matt 24:42
"What! Could you not w .Matt 26:40
"W and pray . . . . .Matt 26:41
W, stand fast in the. . . . .1 Cor 16:13
submissive, for they w. . . .Heb 13:17

WATCHED

in the days when God w . .Job 29:2
come, he would have w . .Matt 24:43

WATCHES

w the righteous. . . . . .Ps 37:32
She w over the ways of. . .Prov 31:27
Blessed is he who w. . . . . .Rev 16:15

WATCHFUL

But you be w in all. . . . . . .2 Tim 4:5
be serious and w. . . . . .1 Pet 4:7

WATCHING

who listens to me, w. . . . . .Prov 8:34
the flock, who were w. . . .Zech 11:11
he comes, will find w . . .Luke 12:37

WATCHMAN

guards the city, the w. . . . . .Ps 127:1
W, what of the night. . . . . . .Is 21:11
I have made you a w . . . .Ezek 3:17
the day of your w . . . . .Mic 7:4

WATCHMEN

w who go about the . . . . . .Song 3:3
w shall lift up their . . . . .Is 52:8
His w are blind . . . . .Is 56:10
I have set w on your . . . . . . .Is 62:6
Also, I set w over you. . . . .Jer 6:17
strong, set up the w . . . . .Jer 51:12

WATER

Eden to w the garden . . . . .Gen 2:10
Unstable as w . . . . .Gen 49:4
your bread and your w . . .Ex 23:25
of affliction and w . . . . . .1 Kin 22:27
w disappears from the . . . .Job 14:11
w wears away stones . . . .Job 14:19
drinks iniquity like w . . . .Job 15:16
not given the weary w . . . .Job 22:7
He binds up the w . . . . . . .Job 26:8
I am poured out like w. . . .Ps 22:14
where there is no w. . . . . . . .Ps 63:1
they have shed like w. . . . . .Ps 79:3
Drink w from your own . .Prov 5:15
"Stolen w is sweet. . . . . . .Prov 9:17
the whole supply of w. . . . . . .Is 3:1
and needy seek w . . . . .Is 41:17
For I will pour w . . . . .Is 44:3
silence and given us w . . . .Jer 8:14
eye overflows with w. . . . .Lam 1:16
will be as weak as w. . . . .Ezek 7:17
w the land with the . . . .Ezek 32:6
you gave Me no w. . . . . . .Luke 7:44
there was much w. . . . . . .John 3:23
given you living w . . . . . .John 4:10

WATERED (continued)

rivers of living *w*........John 7:38
blood and *w* came out ...John 19:34
"Can anyone forbid *w*....Acts 10:47
with the washing of *w*.....Eph 5:26
can yield both salt *w*...James 3:12
were saved through *w* ....1 Pet 3:20
is He who came by *w* ....1 John 5:6
the Spirit, the *w* ....1 John 5:8
are clouds without *w* ....Jude 12
let him take the *w* ....Rev 22:17

WATERED

w the whole face..........Gen 2:6
that it was well *w*........Gen 13:10
I planted, Apollos *w* .....1 Cor 3:6

WATERS

and struck the *w* ....Ex 7:20
If He withholds the *w*....Job 12:15
me beside the still *w*.......Ps 23:2
though its *w* roar and......Ps 46:3
w have come up to my ....Ps 69:1
then the *w* would have....Ps 124:4
rich, and He who *w* .....Prov 11:25
Who has bound the *w* .....Prov 30:4
your bread upon the *w* ....Eccl 11:1
a well of living *w* ....Song 4:15
w cannot quench love.....Song 8:7
of the LORD as the *w*........Is 11:9
w will fail from the ....Is 19:5
because I give *w* ....Is 43:20
have sworn that the *w* .....Is 54:9
thirsts, come to the *w* ......Is 55:1
fountain of living *w*.......Jer 2:13
w flowed over my head ...Lam 3:54
the sound of many *w* ....Ezek 43:2
w surrounded me ....Jon 2:5
shall be that living *w* ....Zech 14:8
often, in perils of *w* ....2 Cor 11:26
living fountains of *w* ......Rev 7:17
w became wormwood .....Rev 8:11

WAVE

its fruit shall *w*..........Ps 72:16

WAVER

He did not *w* at the .....Rom 4:20

WAVERING

of our hope without *w*....Heb 10:23

WAVES

and here your proud *w*....Job 38:11
all Your *w* and billows .....Ps 42:7
the noise of their *w*.......Ps 65:7
the multitude of its *w*....Jer 51:42
was covered with the *w*...Matt 8:24
sea, tossed by the *w*....Matt 14:24
raging *w* of the sea ....Jude 13

WAX

My heart is like *w*.........Ps 22:14
w melts before the ....Ps 68:2
mountains melt like *w* .....Ps 97:5

WAY

and show them the *w* ....Ex 18:20
day I am going the *w* ....Josh 23:14
and the right *w*........1 Sam 12:23
As for God, His *w* .....2 Sam 22:31
to a man whose *w* ....Job 3:23
But He knows the *w* ....Job 23:10
"Where is the *w* ....Job 38:19
the LORD knows the *w* ....Ps 1:6
you perish in the *w*.......Ps 2:12
Teach me Your *w*.........Ps 27:11
This is the *w* of those...Ps 49:13
w may be known on ....Ps 67:2
Your *w* was in the sea.....Ps 77:19
where there is no *w*.......Ps 107:40

I have chosen the *w* ......Ps 119:30
I hate every false *w* ....Ps 119:104
in the *w* everlasting .....Ps 139:24
and preserves the *w* ......Prov 2:8
The *w* of the wicked is ....Prov 4:19
instruction are the *w*......Prov 6:23
w that seems right .....Prov 14:12
not know what is the *w* ..Eccl 11:5
of terrors in the *w* ......Eccl 12:5
The *w* of the just is.........Is 26:7
" This is the *w*............Is 30:21
LORD, who makes a *w*......Is 43:16
wicked forsake his *w*........Is 55:7
O LORD, I know the *w*......Jer 10:23
one heart and one *w* ......Jer 32:39
Israel, is it not My *w*....Ezek 18:25
w which is not fair ......Ezek 33:17
and pervert the *w* ....Amos 2:7
the LORD has His *w*.......Nah 1:3
he will prepare the *w* ......Mal 3:1
and broad is the *w* ......Matt 7:13
and difficult is the *w* ....Matt 7:14
will prepare Your *w*......Matt 11:10
and teach the *w* ....Matt 22:16
and the *w* you know......John 14:4
to him, "I am the *w* .....John 14:6
proclaim to us the *w*....Acts 16:17
explained to him the *w*...Acts 18:26
you a more excellent *w* .1 Cor 12:31
w which He consecrated ..Heb 10:20
forsaken the right *w* .....2 Pet 2:15
to have known the *w* ....2 Pet 2:21
have gone in the *w*........Jude 11

WAYS

for all His *w* are ....Deut 32:4
they do not know its *w* ..Job 24:13
is the first of the *w*......Job 40:19
Show me Your *w*..........Ps 25:4
transgressors Your *w* ......Ps 51:13
would walk in My *w*......Ps 81:13
w were directed..........Ps 119:5
I thought about my *w* ...Ps 119:59
righteous in all His *w*...Ps 145:17
For the *w* of man are ....Prov 5:21
w please the LORD.......Prov 16:7
He will teach us His *w* ......Is 2:3
nor are your *w* ....Is 55:8
"Stand in the *w* ....Jer 6:16
"Amend your *w* ....Jer 7:3
and examine our *w* ......Lam 3:40
and owns all your *w*......Dan 5:23
w are everlasting ....Hab 3:6
misery are in their *w*......Rom 3:16
judgments and His *w*....Rom 11:33
unstable in all his *w*.....James 1:8
their destructive *w* ......2 Pet 2:2
and true are Your *w*......Rev 15:3

WEAK

then I shall become *w* ....Judg 16:7
"And I am *w* today .....2 Sam 3:39
me, O LORD, for I am *w*.....Ps 6:2
gives power to the *w*......Is 40:29
knee will be as *w* ......Ezek 7:17
let the *w* say............Joel 3:10
not your hands be *w*......Zeph 3:16
but the flesh is *w* .....Matt 26:41
And not being *w* ....Rom 4:19
Receive one who is *w* ......Rom 14:1
God has chosen the *w*....1 Cor 1:27
We are *w* ....1 Cor 4:10
w I became as *w* .....1 Cor 9:22
this reason many are *w* .1 Cor 11:30
For when I am *w* ....2 Cor 12:10

WEAKENED

w my strength in the .....Ps 102:23
the ground, you who *w* .....Is 14:12

WEAKENS

w the hands of the men ....Jer 38:4

WEAKER

house of Saul grew *w*.....2 Sam 3:1
the wife, as to the *w* ......1 Pet 3:7

WEAKNESS

than men, and the *w* .....1 Cor 1:25
I was with you in *w*.......1 Cor 2:3
It is sown in *w* ....1 Cor 15:43
is also subject to *w*........Heb 5:2
w were made strong......Heb 11:34

WEAKNESSES

also helps in our *w* ......Rom 8:26
sympathize with our *w* ....Heb 4:15

WEALTH

have gained me this *w* ....Deut 8:17
a man of great *w* ....Ruth 2:1
not asked riches or *w* ....2 Chr 1:11
who trust in their *w*........Ps 49:6
w is his strong city......Prov 10:15
W gained by dishonesty. .Prov 13:11
W makes many friends....Prov 19:4
may bring to you the *w* ....Is 60:11

WEALTHY

w nation that dwells .....Jer 49:31
am rich, have become *w*....Rev 3:17

WEANED

w child shall put his ....Is 11:8
Those just *w* from milk.....Is 28:9

WEAPON

w formed against you ......Is 54:17
with a deadly *w* ....Ezek 9:1

WEAPONS

is better than *w*..........Eccl 9:18
the LORD and His *w* ....Is 13:5
For the *w* of our........2 Cor 10:4

WEAR

but the just will *w* ....Job 27:17
'What shall we *w* ....Matt 6:31

WEARIED

you have *w* Me with ......Is 43:24
You are *w* in the.........Is 57:10
and they have *w*..........Jer 12:5
You have *w* the LORD.....Mal 2:17
therefore, being *w* ....John 4:6

WEARINESS

say, 'Oh, what a *w* ....Mal 1:13
in *w* and toil...........2 Cor 11:27

WEARISOME

and much study is *w*.....Eccl 12:12

WEARY

to Isaac, "I am *w*.......Gen 27:46
lest he become *w*.......Prov 25:17
As cold water to a *w*.....Prov 25:25
No one will be *w* ....Is 5:27
you may cause the *w*......Is 28:12
shall run and not be *w* ....Is 40:31
to him who is *w*...........Is 50:4
I am *w* of holding it ....Jer 6:11
w themselves to commit...Jer 9:5
I was *w* of holding it......Jer 20:9
continual coming she *w*...Luke 18:5
And let us not grow *w* .....Gal 6:9
do not grow *w* in ......2 Thess 3:13
lest you become *w*........Heb 12:3

WEATHER

a garment in cold *w* .....Prov 25:20

WEDDING

'It will be fair w ....Matt 16:2

WEDDING

were invited to the w .....Matt 22:3
Come to the w...........Matt 22:4
find, invite to the w ......Matt 22:9
in with him to the w ....Matt 25:10
day there was a w ....John 2:1

WEEK

with many for one w .....Dan 9:27
the first day of the w.....Matt 28:1
the first day of the w.....Acts 20:7
the first day of the w ....1 Cor 16:2

WEEKS

w are determined.........Dan 9:24
w Messiah shall be cut ....Dan 9:26

WEEP

"Hannah, why do you w ..1 Sam 1:8
a time to w...............Eccl 3:4
you shall w no more ....Is 30:19
it, my soul will w.........Jer 13:17
W not for the dead ....Jer 22:10
to the LORD, w between...Joel 2:17
this commotion and w...Mark 5:39
Blessed are you who w...Luke 6:21
to her, "Do not w ....Luke 7:13
and you did not w ......Luke 7:32
of Jerusalem, do not w .Luke 23:28
to the tomb to w there...John 11:31
w with those who w ...Rom 12:15
those who w as though...1 Cor 7:30

WEEPING

of Israel, who were w .....Num 25:6
w as they went up .....2 Sam 15:30
the noise of the w ....Ezra 3:13
face is flushed from w ...Job 16:16
the voice of my w..........Ps 6:8
my drink with w..........Ps 102:9
of hosts called for w ....Is 22:12
w shall no longer..........Is 65:19
They shall come with w ...Jer 31:9
w they shall come ....Jer 50:4
were sitting there w .....Ezek 8:14
with fasting, with w......Joel 2:13
with tears, with w......Mal 2:13
There will be w ....Matt 8:12
outside by the tomb w ..John 20:11
"Woman, why are you w John 20:13
"What do you mean by w Acts 21:13

WEIGH

You w out the violence......Ps 58:2
O Most Upright, You w .....Is 26:7

WEIGHED

nor can silver be w ......Job 28:15
W the mountains..........Is 40:12
You have been w..........Dan 5:27
lest your hearts be w ...Luke 21:34

WEIGHS

eyes, but the LORD w .....Prov 16:2
Where is he who w ....Is 33:18

WEIGHT

a perfect and just w .....Deut 25:15
w is His delight..........Prov 11:1
and eternal w of glory ...2 Cor 4:17
us lay aside every w......Heb 12:1

WEIGHTIER

have neglected the w ....Matt 23:23

WELFARE

does not seek the w......Jer 38:4

WELL

"If you do w ....Gen 4:7
that it may go w........Deut 4:40
you when you do w.......Ps 49:18
daughters have done w..Prov 31:29
know that it will be w....Eccl 8:12
wheel broken at the w.....Eccl 12:6
that it shall be w..........Is 3:10
"Those who are w ......Matt 9:12
said to him, 'W done ...Matt 25:21
faith has made you w ...Mark 5:34
Now Jacob's w was.......John 4:6
the elders who rule w ....1 Tim 5:17

WELL-BEING

them, and their w.........Ps 69:22
each one the other's w...1 Cor 10:24

WELLS

draw water from the w ......Is 12:3
These are w without .....2 Pet 2:17

WENT

They w out from us.....1 John 2:19

WEPT

and the man of God w ...2 Kin 8:11
for the people w...........Ezra 10:1
that I sat down and w......Neh 1:4
Have I not w for him ....Job 30:25
down, yea, we w ....Ps 137:1
out and w bitterly .....Matt 26:75
He saw the city and w...Luke 19:41
Jesus w ....John 11:35
So I w much ....Rev 5:4

WET

They are w with the ......Job 24:8
his body was w with .....Dan 4:33

WHEAT

with the finest of w ......Ps 81:16
we may trade w..........Amos 8:5
even sell the bad w......Amos 8:6
but gather the w.......Matt 13:30
w falls into the ....John 12:24
perhaps w or some.....1 Cor 15:37
oil, fine flour and w .....Rev 18:13

WHEEL

brings the threshing w ..Prov 20:26
the fountain, or the w....Eccl 12:6
in the middle of a w......Ezek 1:16

WHEELS

off their chariot w ....Ex 14:25
the rumbling of his w .....Jer 47:3
appearance of the w .....Ezek 1:16
noise of rattling w ....Nah 3:2

WHERE

not knowing w he was.....Heb 11:8

WHIP

A w for the horse ....Prov 26:3
The noise of a w...........Nah 3:2

WHIRLWIND

Elijah went up by a w....2 Kin 2:11
Job out of the w ....Job 38:1
them away as with a w ....Ps 58:9
w will take them away .....Is 40:24
w shall scatter them ......Is 41:16
w shall be raised ....Jer 25:32
has His way in the w......Nah 1:3

WHISPER

my ear received a w ....Job 4:12
and wizards, who w.........Is 8:19

WHISPERER

w separates the best.....Prov 16:28

WHISPERERS

they are w ....Rom 1:29

WHISPERINGS

backbitings, w ....2 Cor 12:20

WHITE

My beloved is w ....Song 5:10
and make them w.......Dan 11:35
be purified, made w......Dan 12:10
for they are already w ...John 4:35
walk with Me in w ....Rev 3:4
clothed in w garments .....Rev 3:5
behold, a w horse ....Rev 6:2
and made them w.........Rev 7:14
Then I saw a great w.....Rev 20:11

WHOLE

w body were an eye ....1 Cor 12:17

WHOLESOME

w tongue is a tree ....Prov 15:4
not consent to w words ...1 Tim 6:3

WHOLLY

w followed the LORD......Deut 1:36
I will not leave you w ....Jer 46:28

WICKED

w shall be silent ....1 Sam 2:9
Should you help the w ...2 Chr 19:2
Why do the w live and ....Job 21:7
w are reserved for the.....Job 21:30
to nobles, 'You are w ....Job 34:18
with the w every day ......Ps 7:11
w is snared in the ....Ps 9:16
w shall be turned ....Ps 9:17
do the w renounce God ...Ps 10:13
w bend their bow ....Ps 11:2
w He will rain coals ....Ps 11:6
Evil shall slay the w.......Ps 34:21
w shall be no more ....Ps 37:10
The w watches the ....Ps 37:32
how long will the w........Ps 94:3
and the w be no more.....Ps 104:35
is far from the w.......Ps 119:155
if there is any w ....Ps 139:24
w will be cut off from ....Prov 2:22
w will fall by his own ....Prov 11:5
LORD is far from the w ..Prov 15:29
w flee when no one ......Prov 28:1
Do not be overly w ....Eccl 7:17
not be well with the w....Eccl 8:13
w forsake his way ....Is 55:7
But the w are like the.....Is 57:20
and desperately w ....Jer 17:9
w shall do wickedly .....Dan 12:10
at all acquit the w ....Nah 1:3
w one does not touch ...1 John 5:18
the sway of the w ......1 John 5:19

WICKEDLY

Will you speak w..........Job 13:7
God will never do w ......Job 34:12
"Those who do w ......Dan 11:32
yes, all who do w ....Mal 4:1

WICKEDNESS

LORD saw that the w ......Gen 6:5
can I do this great w......Gen 39:9
'W proceeds from the...1 Sam 24:13
w oppress them ....2 Sam 7:10
Is not your w great........Job 22:5
Oh, let the w of the ....Ps 7:9
alive into hell, for w ....Ps 55:15
in the tents of w ....Ps 84:10
I will not know w ....Ps 101:4

WIDE

eat the bread of *w* . . . . .Prov 4:17
w is an abomination . . . . . .Prov 8:7
w will not . . . . .Eccl 8:8
w burns as the. . . . . .Is 9:18
have trusted in your *w* . . . .Is 47:10
w will correct you . . . . .Jer 2:19
wells up with her *w* . . . . .Jer 6:7
man repented of his *w* . . . . . .Jer 8:6
not turn from his *w* . . . . .Ezek 3:19
You have plowed *w* . . . . . .Hos 10:13
and cannot look on *w* . . . . .Hab 1:13
for those who do *w* . . . . . . .Mal 3:15
is full of greed and *w* . . . .Luke 11:39
sexual immorality, *w* . . . . . .Rom 1:29
spiritual hosts of *w* . . . . . .Eph 6:12
and overflow of *w* . . . . . .James 1:21

WIDE

shall open your hand *w* . . .Deut 15:8
opened their mouth *w* . . . .Job 29:23
w his lips shall have . . . . .Prov 13:3
will build myself a *w* . . . . .Jer 22:14
w is the gate and . . . . . . .Matt 7:13
to you, our heart is *w* . . . .2 Cor 6:11

WIDOW

does no good for the *w*. . . .Job 24:21
They slay the *w*. . . . . .Ps 94:6
and his wife a *w* . . . . .Ps 109:9
the fatherless and *w* . . . . . .Ps 146:9
plead for the *w*. . . . . .Is 1:17
How like a *w* is she. . . . . . . .Lam 1:1
Then one poor *w* . . . . . .Mark 12:42
w has children or. . . . . . . .1 Tim 5:4
Do not let a *w* under. . . . . .1 Tim 5:9

WIDOW'S

and I caused the *w* . . . . . .Job 29:13

WIDOWS

a defender of *w* . . . . .Ps 68:5
and let your *w* trust . . . . .Jer 49:11
w were neglected. . . . . .Acts 6:1
that the younger *w* . . . . . .1 Tim 5:14
to visit orphans and *w*. . .James 1:27

WIFE

and be joined to his *w* . . . . .Gen 2:24
an excellent *w* is the . . . . .Prov 12:4
w finds a good thing. . . . . .Prov 18:22
but a prudent *w* . . . . . . .Prov 19:14
w whom you love all . . . . . .Eccl 9:9
like a youthful *w* . . . . .Is 54:6
"Go, take yourself a *w*. . . . . .Hos 1:2
w he tended sheep . . . . . .Hos 12:12
with the *w* of his . . . . .Mal 2:15
"Whoever divorces his *w*.Mark 10:11
'I have married a *w* . . . . .Luke 14:20
"Remember Lot's *w* . . . . .Luke 17:32
all seven had her as *w* . . .Luke 20:33
so love his own *w*. . . . . . . .Eph 5:33
the husband of one *w* . . . . .Titus 1:6
giving honor to the *w* . . . . .1 Pet 3:7
bride, the Lamb's *w* . . . . . .Rev 21:9

WILD

locusts and *w* honey. . . . . .Matt 3:4
olive tree which is *w* . . . . .Rom 11:24

WILDERNESS

wasteland, a howling *w* .Deut 32:10
w yields food for them . . . . .Job 24:5
coming out of the *w*. . . . . . .Song 3:6
made the world as a *w* . . . . .Is 14:17
I will make the *w*. . . . . .Is 41:18
Let the *w* and its. . . . . .Is 42:11
Have I been a *w*. . . . . .Jer 2:31
of one crying in the *w* . . . . .Matt 3:3
the serpent in the *w*. . . . . .John 3:14
congregation in the *w* . . . .Acts 7:38

WILES

to stand against the *w* . . . .Eph 6:11

WILL

w be done on earth as . . . .Matt 6:10
but he who does the *w* . . . .Matt 7:21
of the two did the *w*. . . . .Matt 21:31
on earth peace, good *w* . .Luke 2:14
nevertheless not My *w*. . .Luke 22:42
flesh, nor of the *w*. . . . . . .John 1:13
I do not seek My own *w* . .John 5:30
not to do My own *w*. . . . . .John 6:38
"This is the *w* . . . . .John 6:39
wills to do His *w*. . . . . . . .John 7:17
w is present with me. . . . . .Rom 7:18
and perfect *w* of God . . . . .Rom 12:2
works in you both to *w* . . . .Phil 2:13
the knowledge of His *w* . . . .Col 1:9
according to His own *w*. . . .Heb 2:4
come to do Your *w*. . . . . . .Heb 10:9
good work to do His *w* . . .Heb 13:21
but he who does the *w* .1 John 2:17

WILLFULLY

For if we sin *w*. . . . . .Heb 10:26
For this they *w*. . . . . .2 Pet 3:5

WILLING

is of a *w* heart . . . . .Ex 35:5
If you are *w* and . . . . .Is 1:19
him, saying, "I am *w*. . . . . .Matt 8:3
The spirit indeed is *w* . .Matt 26:41
The spirit indeed is *w* . .Mark 14:38
if there is first a *w*. . . . . . .2 Cor 8:12
w that any should . . . . .2 Pet 3:9

WILLINGLY

to futility, not *w* . . . . .Rom 8:20
For if I do this *w*. . . . . . . .1 Cor 9:17
by compulsion but *w*. . . . . .1 Pet 5:2

WILLOWS

our harps upon the *w*. . . . . .Ps 137:2

WILLS

to whom the Son *w* . . . . .Matt 11:27
it is not of him who *w* . . . . .Rom 9:16
say, "If the Lord *w*. . . . . .James 4:15

WIN

w one proselyte. . . . . . . .Matt 23:15
to all, that I might *w* . . . . .1 Cor 9:19

WIND

LORD was not in the *w* .1 Kin 19:11
w carries him away. . . . . . .Job 27:21
the chaff which the *w*. . . . . . .Ps 1:4
He causes His *w*. . . . . . . .Ps 147:18
will inherit the *w*. . . . . . .Prov 11:29
He who observes the *w*. . .Eccl 11:4
is the way of the *w* . . . . . .Eccl 11:5
Awake, O north *w*. . . . . . .Song 4:16
the prophets become *w*. . . .Jer 5:13
He brings the *w*. . . . . .Jer 51:16
Ephraim feeds on the *w* . .Hos 12:1
and creates the *w* . . . . . . .Amos 4:13
A reed shaken by the *w*. . .Matt 11:7
And the *w* ceased and. . . .Mark 4:39
and rebuked the *w* . . . . . .Luke 8:24
"The *w* blows where . . . . .John 3:8
of a rushing mighty *w* . . . .Acts 2:2
about with every *w* . . . . . .Eph 4:14

WINDOWS

looking through the *w* . . . .Song 2:9
has come through our *w* . . .Jer 9:21
upper room, with his *w*. . . .Dan 6:10
not open for you the *w*. . . . .Mal 3:10

WINDS

from the four *w*. . . . . .Ezek 37:9
be, that even the *w*. . . . . . .Matt 8:27
holding the four *w* . . . . .Rev 7:1

WINDSTORM

And a great *w* arose . . . . .Mark 4:37

WINE

Noah awoke from his *w* . . . .Gen 9:24
w that makes glad . . . . . . .Ps 104:15
W is a mocker . . . . .Prov 20:1
Do not look on the *w* . . . .Prov 23:31
love is better than *w* . . . . .Song 1:2
w inflames them . . . . .Is 5:11
Yes, come, buy *w* . . . . .Is 55:1
they gave Him sour *w* . . .Matt 27:34
when they ran out of *w* . . . .John 2:3
do not be drunk with *w*. . . .Eph 5:18
but use a little *w*. . . . . . . .1 Tim 5:23
not given to much *w* . . . . . .Titus 2:3
her the cup of the *w*. . . . . .Rev 16:19

WINEBIBBERS

Do not mix with *w* . . . . . .Prov 23:20

WINEPRESS

"I have trodden the *w*. . . . . .Is 63:3
for the *w* is full. . . . . .Joel 3:13
into the great *w* . . . . .Rev 14:19
Himself treads the *w* . . . . .Rev 19:15

WINESKIN

I have become like a *w*. . . .Ps 119:83

WINESKINS

new wine into old *w* . . . . .Matt 9:17

WING

One *w* of the cherub . . . .1 Kin 6:24
so I spread My *w* . . . . . . .Ezek 16:8

WINGS

w you have come . . . . . . .Ruth 2:12
He flew upon the *w* . . . . . .Ps 18:10
the shadow of Your *w*. . . . . .Ps 36:7
If I take the *w*. . . . . .Ps 139:9
each one had six *w* . . . . .Is 6:2
with healing in His *w*. . . . . .Mal 4:2
woman was given two *w* . .Rev 12:14

WINNOW

You shall *w* them. . . . . .Is 41:16

WINS

w souls is wise. . . . . .Prov 11:30

WINTER

have made summer and *w* .Ps 74:17
For lo, the *w* is past. . . . . .Song 2:11
w it shall occur . . . . .Zech 14:8
flight may not be in *w*. . .Matt 24:20

WIPE

the Lord GOD will *w* . . . . .Is 25:8
w them with the towel . . . .John 13:5
w away every tear. . . . . . . .Rev 21:4

WISDOM

for this is your *w* . . . . . . .Deut 4:6
w will die with you . . . . . . .Job 12:2
will make me to know *w* . . . .Ps 51:6
is the man who finds *w* . .Prov 3:13
Get *w* . . . . .Prov 4:5
W is the principal . . . . .Prov 4:7
is the beginning of *w* . . . . .Prov 9:10
to get *w* than gold. . . . . .Prov 16:16
w loves his own soul . . . . .Prov 19:8
W is too lofty for a . . . . . .Prov 24:7
w is much grief . . . . .Eccl 1:18

WISE

W is better than.........Eccl 9:16
w is justified by her....Matt 11:19
Jesus increased in *w*......Luke 2:52
riches both of the *w* ....Rom 11:33
the gospel, not with *w*...1 Cor 1:17
Greeks seek after *w*.......1 Cor 1:22
For the *w* of this world...1 Cor 3:19
not with fleshly *w* ....2 Cor 1:12
now the manifold *w*.......Eph 3:10
all the treasures of *w*.......Col 2:3
Walk in *w* toward those......Col 4:5
If any of you lacks *w*....James 1:5
power and riches and *w*...Rev 5:12
and glory and *w* ....Rev 7:12

WISE

great nation is a *w*.......Deut 4:6
He catches the *w* ....Job 5:13
God is *w* in heart and......Job 9:4
men are not always *w*......Job 32:9
when will you be *w*.........Ps 94:8
w will observe these......Ps 107:43
Do not be *w* in your ......Prov 3:7
he who wins souls is *w*...Prov 11:30
The *w* in heart will be...Prov 16:21
folly, lest he be *w*.......Prov 26:5
they are exceedingly *w*...Prov 30:24
The words of the *w* .....Eccl 12:11
They are *w* to do evil......Jer 4:22
Therefore be *w* as ......Matt 10:16
five of them were *w*.....Matt 25:2
barbarians, both to *w*......Rom 1:14
to God, alone *w* ....Rom 16:27
Where is the *w*..........1 Cor 1:20
sake, but you are *w*.....1 Cor 4:10
not as fools but as *w*......Eph 5:15
are able to make you *w*...2 Tim 3:15

WISELY

I will behave *w* ....Ps 101:2
who heeds the word *w* ...Prov 16:20
you do not inquire *w* .....Eccl 7:10

WISER

he was *w* than all men ...1 Kin 4:31
w than the birds ....Job 35:11
w than my enemies......Ps 119:98
of God is *w* than men ...1 Cor 1:25

WISH

for me to do what I *w* ...Matt 20:15
w it were already ......Luke 12:49

WISHED

Then he *w* death for ....Jon 4:8

WITCHCRAFT

is as the sin of *w* ......1 Sam 15:23

WITHDRAW

God will not *w* His........Job 9:13
He does not *w* His eyes ....Job 36:7
From such *w* yourself.....1 Tim 6:5

WITHER

also shall not *w*............Ps 1:3
w as the green............Ps 37:2
leaves will not *w*......Ezek 47:12
How did the fig tree *w*...Matt 21:20

WITHERS

The grass *w* ....Is 40:7
burning heat than it *w* ..James 1:11
The grass *w* ....1 Pet 1:24

WITHHELD

and your sins have *w*......Jer 5:25

WITHHOLD

w Your tender mercies .....Ps 40:11

good thing will He *w* ......Ps 84:11
Do not *w* good from ......Prov 3:27
your cloak, do not *w*......Luke 6:29

WITHOUT

having no hope and *w* ....Eph 2:12
pray *w* ceasing........1 Thess 5:17
w controversy ....1 Tim 3:16
w works is dead ....James 2:26

WITHSTAND

was I that I could *w*.....Acts 11:17
you may be able to *w* .....Eph 6:13

WITHSTOOD

I *w* him to his face ....Gal 2:11

WITNESS

see, God is *w* between ....Gen 31:50
Surely even now my *w* ....Job 16:19
like the faithful *w* ....Ps 89:37
w does not lie...........Prov 14:5
have given him as a *w*......Is 55:4
a true and faithful *w* .....Jer 42:5
I will be a swift *w* ....Mal 3:5
all the world as a *w* .....Matt 24:14
This man came for a *w*.....John 1:7
do not receive Our *w* ....John 3:11
"If I bear *w* of.........John 5:31
is another who bears *w* ...John 5:32
But I have a greater *w*....John 5:36
who was bearing *w* ......Acts 14:3
For you will be His *w*....Acts 22:15
For God is my *w*.........Phil 1:8
are three who bear *w*.....1 John 5:7
If we receive the *w* ......1 John 5:9
who bore *w* to the word ....Rev 1:2
Christ, the faithful *w* ......Rev 1:5
beheaded for their *w*......Rev 20:4

WITNESSED

is revealed, being *w*.......Rom 3:21
w the good confession....1 Tim 6:13

WITNESSES

of two or three *w* ....Deut 17:6
for Myself faithful *w*.........Is 8:2
"You are My *w*............Is 43:10
the presence of many *w* .1 Tim 6:12
the Holy Spirit also *w*....Heb 10:15
so great a cloud of *w*......Heb 12:1
give power to my two *w*....Rev 11:3

WIVES

Husbands, love your *w* ....Eph 5:25
w must be reverent......1 Tim 3:11

WIZARDS

who are mediums and *w*.....Is 8:19

WOLF

The *w* and the lamb ....Is 65:25
the sheep, sees the *w* ...John 10:12

WOLVES

they are ravenous *w*......Matt 7:15
out as lambs among *w*....Luke 10:3
my departure savage *w*...Acts 20:29

WOMAN

she shall be called *W*......Gen 2:23
w builds her house ......Prov 14:1
w who fears the LORD....Prov 31:30
w shall encompass a .....Jer 31:22
whoever looks at a *w* .....Matt 5:28
"Do you see this *w*......Luke 7:44
Then the *w* of Samaria....John 4:9
brought to Him a *w* ....John 8:3
"*W*, behold your ....John 19:26
w was full of good.......Acts 9:36

natural use of the *w* .....Rom 1:27
a man not to touch a *w*....1 Cor 7:1
w is the glory of man ....1 Cor 11:7
His Son, born of a *w*........Gal 4:4
Let a *w* learn in.........1 Tim 2:11
I do not permit a *w*.......1 Tim 2:12
w being deceived........1 Tim 2:14
w clothed with the sun.....Rev 12:1
the earth helped the *w*....Rev 12:16

WOMB

nations are in your *w*.....Gen 25:23
LORD had closed her *w*....1 Sam 1:5
took Me out of the *w* ......Ps 22:9
formed you from the *w* .....Is 44:2
called Me from the *w* ....Is 49:1
in the *w* I knew you ....Jer 1:5
is the fruit of your *w* ....Luke 1:42
"Blessed is the *w* ......Luke 11:27

WOMEN

blessed is she among *w* ..Judg 5:24
among Your honorable *w* ...Ps 45:9
O fairest among *w* ....Song 1:8
w rule over them ....Is 3:12
new wine the young *w* ...Zech 9:17
w will be grinding......Matt 24:41
are you among *w* ....Luke 1:28
w keep silent in the.....1 Cor 14:34
admonish the young *w* .....Titus 2:4
times, the holy *w* ....1 Pet 3:5
not defiled with *w*.........Rev 14:4

WONDER

I have become as a *w*......Ps 71:7
marvelous work and a *w*....Is 29:14

WONDERFUL

name, seeing it is *w* ....Judg 13:18
Your love to me was *w*...2 Sam 1:26
things too *w* for me ......Job 42:3
Your testimonies are *w*...Ps 119:129
name will be called *W*......Is 9:6
of hosts, who is *w* ....Is 28:29
and scribes saw the *w* ...Matt 21:15
our own tongues the *w* ....Acts 2:11

WONDERFULLY

fearfully and *w* made .....Ps 139:14

WONDERS

w which I will do ....Ex 3:20
are the God who does *w*....Ps 77:14
Shall Your *w* be known....Ps 88:12
who alone does great *w* ..Ps 136:4
Egypt with signs and *w* ..Jer 32:21
and how mighty His *w* ....Dan 4:3
He works signs and *w*....Dan 6:27
"And I will show *w* ......Joel 2:30
and done many *w*.......Matt 7:22
signs, and lying *w* ....2 Thess 2:9
both with signs and *w*....Heb 2:4

WONDROUS

and tell of all Your *w* ......Ps 26:7
w works declare that ....Ps 75:1
w works in the land of ....Ps 106:22
for they are a *w*..........Zech 3:8

WONDROUSLY

God, who has dealt *w* .....Joel 2:26

WOOD

precious stones, *w*.......1 Cor 3:12

WOODCUTTERS

but let them be *w* ....Josh 9:21

WOOL

they shall be as *w* ....Is 1:18

head was like pure *w* . . . . . . .Dan 7:9
hair were white like *w* . . . . .Rev 1:14

WORD

w that proceeds. . . . . .Deut 8:3
w is very near you . . . . . . .Deut 30:14
w I have hidden . . . . .Ps 119:11
w has given me life. . . . . . .Ps 119:50
w is a lamp to my feet . . .Ps 119:105
w makes it glad. . . . . . . .Prov 12:25
w spoken in due season . .Prov 15:23
w fitly spoken is . . . . . . .Prov 25:11
Every *w* of God is pure . . .Prov 30:5
The LORD sent a *w* . . . . .Is 9:8
the *w* of our God . . . . .Is 40:8
w has gone out of My . . . . .Is 45:23
w be that goes forth . . . . . .Is 55:11
But His *w* was in my . . . . .Jer 20:9
w will be his oracle . . . . . .Jer 23:36
w which I speak will . . . .Ezek 12:28
But only speak a *w* . . . . . .Matt 8:8
for every idle *w* . . . . .Matt 12:36
The seed is the *w* . . . . . . .Luke 8:11
mighty in deed and *w* . . .Luke 24:19
beginning was the *W* . . . .John 1:1
W became flesh and . . . . .John 1:14
if anyone keeps My *w* . . .John 8:51
w which you hear is . . . .John 14:24
Your *w* is truth . . . . .John 17:17
and glorified the *w* . . . . .Acts 13:48
to one is given the *w* . . . .1 Cor 12:8
of water by the *w*. . . . . . . .Eph 5:26
holding fast the *w* . . . . . . .Phil 2:16
Let the *w* of Christ . . . . . . .Col 3:16
come to you in only . . .1 Thess 1:5
in every good *w* . . . . . .2 Thess 2:17
by the *w* of His power. . . . . .Heb 1:3
w which they heard did. . . .Heb 4:2
For the *w* of God is . . . . . .Heb 4:12
the implanted *w* . . . . . . .James 1:21
does not stumble in *w* . . .James 3:2
through the *w* of God . . . .1 Pet 1:23
that by the *w* of God. . . . . .2 Pet 3:5
whoever keeps His *w*. . . .1 John 2:5
let us not love in *w* . . . . .1 John 3:18
the Father, the *W* . . . . . .1 John 5:7
name is called The *W*. . . .Rev 19:13

WORDS

Give ear to my *w* . . . . .Ps 5:1
Let the *w* of my mouth . . . .Ps 19:14
How sweet are Your *w* . . .Ps 119:103
pay attention to the *w* . . . .Prov 7:24
The *w* of the wise are . . . .Eccl 12:11
And I have put My *w* . . . . . .Is 51:16
Take *w* with you. . . . . .Hos 14:2
Do not My *w* do good to . . .Mic 2:7
pass away, but My *w* . . . .Matt 24:35
at the gracious *w* . . . . . . .Luke 4:22
w that I speak to you. . . .John 6:63
You have the *w* of. . . . . . .John 6:68
And remember the *w* . . . .Acts 20:35
not with wisdom of *w* . . . .1 Cor 1:17
those who hear the *w*. . . . . .Rev 1:3
is he who keeps the *w*. . . . .Rev 22:7

WORK

day God ended His *w* . . . . . .Gen 2:2
Moses finished the *w*. . . . . .Ex 40:33
people had a mind to *w*. . . . .Neh 4:6
You shall desire the *w*. . . . .Job 14:15
for they are all the *w*. . . . .Job 34:19
the *w* of Your fingers . . . . . .Ps 8:3
I hate the *w* of those . . . . .Ps 101:3
the heavens are the *w*. . . .Ps 102:25
Man goes out to his *w* . . .Ps 104:23
w is honorable and . . . . .Ps 111:3
man does deceptive *w*. . . .Prov 11:18

then I saw all the *w*. . . . . .Eccl 8:17
for there is no *w*. . . . . .Eccl 9:10
God will bring every *w* . . .Eccl 12:14
that He may do His *w* . . . . .Is 28:21
and all we are the *w* . . . . . .Is 64:8
him nothing for his *w* . . . . .Jer 22:13
and mighty in *w* . . . . .Jer 32:19
For I will *w* a *w*. . . . . .Hab 1:5
and said, 'Son, go, *w* . . . .Matt 21:28
could do no mighty *w* . . . .Mark 6:5
we do, that we may *w* . . . .John 6:29
This is the *w* of God. . . . . .John 6:29
"I must *w* the works . . . . . .John 9:4
w which You have given. . .John 17:4
know that all things *w* . . .Rom 8:28
He will finish the *w*. . . . . .Rom 9:28
w is no longer *w* . . . . .Rom 11:6
Do not destroy the *w* . . . .Rom 14:20
w will become manifest. . .1 Cor 3:13
Are you not my *w* . . . . .1 Cor 9:1
abounding in the *w* . . . . .1 Cor 15:58
without ceasing your *w*. .1 Thess 1:3
every good word and *w* .2 Thess 2:17
If anyone will not *w*. . . .2 Thess 3:10
but a doer of the *w* . . . . .James 1:25

WORKED

with one hand they *w* . . . . .Neh 4:17
and wonders God had *w*. .Acts 15:12
which He *w* in Christ . . . .Eph 1:20

WORKER

w is worthy of his. . . . . . .Matt 10:10
Timothy, my fellow *w* . . . .Rom 16:21
w who does not need . . . .2 Tim 2:15

WORKERS

You hate all *w* of. . . . . .Ps 5:5
we are God's fellow *w* . . . .1 Cor 3:9
dogs, beware of evil *w* . . . . .Phil 3:2

WORKING

everywhere, the Lord *w*. .Mark 16:20
My Father has been *w* . . . .John 5:17
according to the *w*. . . . . . . .Eph 1:19
through faith in the *w*. . . . .Col 2:12
manner, not *w* at all. . . .2 Thess 3:11

WORKMANSHIP

For we are His *w* . . . . .Eph 2:10

WORKS

the wondrous *w* of God . . .Job 37:14
are Your wonderful *w* . . . . .Ps 40:5
Come and see the *w* . . . . . .Ps 66:5
how great are Your *w* . . . . .Ps 92:5
manifold are Your *w* . . . . .Ps 104:24
The *w* of the LORD are . . . . .Ps 111:2
w shall praise You. . . . . . . .Ps 145:10
and let her own *w* . . . . . . .Prov 31:31
For I know their *w* . . . . . . .Is 66:18
of whose *w* are truth. . . . .Dan 4:37
show Him greater *w*. . . . .John 5:20
w that I do in My. . . . . . .John 10:25
w that I do he will do. . . .John 14:12
w righteousness. . . . . .Acts 10:35
might stand, not of *w*. . . . .Rom 9:11
let us cast off the *w* . . . . .Rom 13:12
is the same God who *w*. .1 Cor 12:6
not justified by *w*. . . . . .Gal 2:16
Now the *w* of the flesh. . . . .Gal 5:19
the spirit who now *w*. . . . . .Eph 2:2
not of *w*, lest anyone . . . . . .Eph 2:9
with the unfruitful *w*. . . . . . .Eph 5:11
for it is God who *w* . . . . . .Phil 2:13
w they deny Him . . . . .Titus 1:16
zealous for good *w* . . . . . .Titus 2:14
repentance from dead *w* . . . .Heb 6:1
but does not have *w* . . . .James 2:14
also justified by *w* . . . . .James 2:25

He might destroy the *w* . .1 John 3:8
"I know your *w*. . . . . .Rev 2:2
their *w* follow them . . . . .Rev 14:13
according to their *w* . . . . .Rev 20:12

WORLD

He shall judge the *w* . . . . . . .Ps 9:8
For the *w* is Mine. . . . . . . .Ps 50:12
w is established. . . . . .Ps 93:1
"The field is the *w*. . . . . .Matt 13:38
w are more shrewd . . . . . .Luke 16:8
He was in the *w* . . . . .John 1:10
For God so loved the *w* . . .John 3:16
His Son into the *w* . . . . . .John 3:17
the Savior of the *w* . . . . . .John 4:42
w cannot hate you . . . . . . .John 7:7
You are of this *w*. . . . . . . .John 8:23
Look, the *w* has gone. . .John 12:19
w will see Me no more . .John 14:19
"If the *w* hates you . . . .John 15:18
If you were of the *w* . . . .John 15:19
I have overcome the *w* . .John 16:33
do not pray for the *w*. . . . .John 17:9
w has not known You. . . .John 17:25
w may become guilty . . . .Rom 3:19
be conformed to this *w*. . .Rom 12:2
things of the *w*. . . . . .1 Cor 1:27
w is foolishness . . . . .1 Cor 3:19
w has been crucified . . . . . .Gal 6:14
without God in the *w* . . . . .Eph 2:12
loved this present *w* . . . . .2 Tim 4:10
He has not put the *w* . . . . . .Heb 2:5
unspotted from the *w* . . .James 1:27
w is enmity with God . . .James 4:4
Do not love the *w* . . . . . .1 John 2:15
all that is in the *w*. . . . . .1 John 2:16
w is passing away . . . . .1 John 2:17
w does not know us. . . . .1 John 3:1
They are of the *w* . . . . . .1 John 4:5
so are we in this *w*. . . . .1 John 4:17
And all the *w* marveled . . . .Rev 13:3

WORLDS

also He made the *w*. . . . . . .Heb 1:2

WORM

w should feed sweetly . . .Job 24:20
But I am a *w*. . . . . .Ps 22:6
"Fear not, you *w* . . . . .Is 41:14
their *w* does not die. . . . . . .Is 66:24
w does not die and the . . .Mark 9:44

WORMS

flesh is caked with *w* . . . . . .Job 7:5
you, and *w* cover you. . . . . .Is 14:11
And he was eaten by *w* . .Acts 12:23

WORMWOOD

end she is bitter as *w* . . . . .Prov 5:4
who turn justice to *w* . . . .Amos 5:7
of the star is *W*. . . . . .Rev 8:11

WORRY

to you, do not *w* . . . . .Matt 6:25
Therefore do not *w* . . . . . .Matt 6:31

WORRYING

w can add one. . . . . .Matt 6:27

WORSE

w than their fathers . . . . . . .Jer 7:26

WORSHIP

I will go yonder and *w*. . . . .Gen 22:5
He is your Lord, *w* . . . . . . .Ps 45:11
Oh come, let us *w* . . . . .Ps 95:6
and have come to *w* Him. .Matt 2:2
will fall down and *w*. . . . . .Matt 4:9
And in vain they *w*. . . . . . .Matt 15:9
w what you do not know . .John 4:22

WORSHIPED

true worshipers will *w* ....John 4:23
the One whom you *w* ....Acts 17:23
w the God of my ....Acts 24:14
false humility and *w* ......Col 2:18
the angels of God *w*........Heb 1:6
make them come and *w* ....Rev 3:9
w Him who lives.........Rev 4:10
w Him who made........Rev 14:7

WORSHIPED

"Our fathers *w* ....John 4:20
w Him who lives.........Rev 5:14
on their faces and *w*......Rev 11:16
w God who sat on the .....Rev 19:4

WORSHIPER

if anyone is a *w*.........John 9:31

WORTH

and make my speech *w* ...Job 24:25
of the wicked is *w*.......Prov 10:20

WORTHLESS

looking at *w* things.......Ps 119:37
A *w* person..............Prov 6:12
Indeed they are all *w*.......Is 41:29

WORTHLESSNESS

long will you love *w* ....Ps 4:2

WORTHY

"I am not *w* of the......Gen 32:10
sandals I am not *w* .....Matt 3:11
inquire who in it is *w*....Matt 10:11
invited were not *w* ......Matt 22:8
should do this was *w* .....Luke 7:4
and I am no longer *w*....Luke 15:19
present time are not *w* ....Rom 8:18
apostles, who am not *w*. .1 Cor 15:9
to walk *w* ....Eph 4:1
"The laborer is *w* ....1 Tim 5:18
the world was not *w* ....Heb 11:38
white, for they are *w* ......Rev 3:4
"You are *w*..............Rev 4:11
W is the Lamb who ....Rev 5:12

WOUND

I *w* and I heal.........Deut 32:39
My *w* is incurable........Job 34:6
But God will *w* the.......Ps 68:21
and my *w* incurable......Jer 15:18
and *w* their weak ....1 Cor 8:12
and his deadly *w*.........Rev 13:3

WOUNDED

and my heart is *w*........Ps 109:22
and *w* the serpent ....Is 51:9
But He was *w* for our......Is 53:5
there remained only *w*....Jer 37:10
with which I was *w*......Zech 13:6
to the beast who was *w* ..Rev 13:14

WOUNDING

killed a man for *w* ....Gen 4:23

WOUNDS

and binds up their *w* ......Ps 147:3
Faithful are the *w* ....Prov 27:6
and bandaged his *w* ....Luke 10:34

WRANGLINGS

useless *w* of men of.......1 Tim 6:5

WRATH

w has gone out from.....Num 16:46
provoked the LORD to *w*...Deut 9:22
Had I not feared the *w* ..Deut 32:27
w kills a foolish...........Job 5:2
speak to them in His *w* ......Ps 2:5
living and burning *w* ......Ps 58:9
Surely the *w* of man.......Ps 76:10

Your fierce *w* has gone .....Ps 88:16
Will Your *w* burn like......Ps 89:46
w we are terrified ....Ps 90:7
So I swore in My *w* ....Ps 95:11
in the day of His *w*........Ps 110:5
death is the king's *w*....Prov 16:14
The king's *w* is like.....Prov 19:12
of great *w* will suffer....Prov 19:19
w is heavier than.........Prov 27:3
W is cruel and anger a ...Prov 27:4
w I will give him ....Is 10:6
With a little *w* ....Is 54:8
in My *w* I struck you ......Is 60:10
I will pour out my *w* ....Hos 5:10
w remember mercy ....Hab 3:2
you to flee from the *w* .....Matt 3:7
see life, but the *w* ....John 3:36
For the *w* of God is.......Rom 1:18
up for yourself *w*..........Rom 2:5
the law brings about *w*....Rom 4:15
wanting to show His *w*....Rom 9:22
rather give place to *w*....Rom 12:19
not only because of *w*....Rom 13:5
outbursts of *w* ....2 Cor 12:20
nature children of *w*.......Eph 2:3
sun go down on your *w* ...Eph 4:26
Let all bitterness, *w* ......Eph 4:31
delivers us from the *w*. .1 Thess 1:10
w has come upon them .1 Thess 2:16
holy hands, without *w* ....1 Tim 2:8
So I swore in My *w*.......Heb 3:11
not fearing the *w* ....Heb 11:27
for the *w* of man does . .James 1:20
throne and from the *w* ....Rev 6:16
to you, having great *w* ...Rev 12:12
of the wine of the *w*......Rev 14:8
winepress of the *w* ......Rev 14:19
for in them the *w* ....Rev 15:1
fierceness of His *w* ......Rev 16:19

WRATHFUL

w man stirs up strife ....Prov 15:18

WRESTLE

For we do not *w*.........Eph 6:12

WRETCHED

w man that I am........Rom 7:24
know that you are *w*......Rev 3:17

WRETCHEDNESS

do not let me see my *w* ..Num 11:15

WRINGING

w the nose produces .....Prov 30:33

WRINKLE

not having spot or *w*......Eph 5:27

WRITE

"*W* these words ....Ex 34:27
w bitter things ....Job 13:26
w them on the tablet ......Prov 7:3
'*W* this man down as .....Jer 22:30
w them on their hearts ....Heb 8:10
their minds I will *w*.......Heb 10:16
I had many things to *w*. . .3 John 13

WRITING

the *w* was the *w*.........Ex 32:16

WRITINGS

do not believe his *w* ....John 5:47

WRITTEN

tablets of stone, *w* ....Ex 31:18
Have I not *w* to you .....Prov 22:20
your names are *w*.......Luke 10:20
"What I have *w* ....John 19:22
ministered by us, *w* ......2 Cor 3:3

the stone a new name *w*....Rev 2:17
the plagues that are *w*....Rev 22:18

WRONG

sinned, we have done *w*...2 Chr 6:37
I cry out concerning *w*....Job 19:7
not charge them with *w*..Job 24:12
no one to do them *w*......Ps 105:14
Do no *w* and do no ......Jer 22:3
I am doing you no *w* ...Matt 20:13
Man has done nothing *w*.Luke 23:41
of them suffer *w* ......Acts 7:24
Jews I have done no *w*...Acts 25:10
Forgive me this *w* .....2 Cor 12:13
But he who does *w* ....Col 3:25

WRONGED

then that God has *w* .....Job 19:6
We have *w* no one ....2 Cor 7:2
But if he has *w*.........Philem 18

WRONGS

me *w* his own soul.......Prov 8:36

WROTE

of the hand that *w*.......Dan 5:5
stooped down and *w*......John 8:6

WROUGHT

And skillfully *w* ....Ps 139:15

Y

YEAR

first month of the *y*........Ex 12:2
'In the *Y* of Jubilee ......Lev 27:24
the acceptable *y*...........Is 61:2
be his until the *y* ......Ezek 46:17
to Jerusalem every *y* ....Luke 2:41
went alone once a *y*.......Heb 9:7
of sins every *y* ....Heb 10:3

YEARS

and for days and *y*........Gen 1:14
Are Your *y* like the ......Job 10:5
y should teach............Job 32:7
I will remember the *y*......Ps 77:10
For a thousand *y*..........Ps 90:4
lives are seventy *y* ....Ps 90:10
Your *y* are throughout ....Ps 102:24
y will have no end.......Ps 102:27
when He was twelve *y* ...Luke 2:42
are not yet fifty *y*.......John 8:57
y will not fail ....Heb 1:12
for a thousand *y* ....Rev 20:2
with Him a thousand *y* ...Rev 20:6

YES

"But let your '*Y*.........Matt 5:37
No, but in Him was *Y*....2 Cor 1:19

YESTERDAY

for we are but of *y* ....Job 8:9

YOKE

you shall break his *y* .....Gen 27:40
and He will put a *y* .....Deut 28:48
Your father made our *y*...1 Kin 12:4
You have broken the *y*......Is 9:4
a man to bear the *y* .....Lam 3:27
"Take My *y* upon you...Matt 11:29
y count their own ....1 Tim 6:1

YOKED

Do not be unequally *y*....2 Cor 6:14

YOUNG

His flesh shall be *y*.......Job 33:25
I have been *y*.............Ps 37:25
she may lay her *y*.........Ps 84:3

YOUNGER

y ones shall lie . . . . .Is 11:7
dream dreams, your y . . . . .Joel 2:28
y man followed Him . . . .Mark 14:51
they admonish the y . . . . .Titus 2:4
I write to you, y. . . . . . . .1 John 2:13

YOUNGER

they mock at me, men y. . . .Job 30:1
y son gathered all. . . . . . .Luke 15:13
let him be as the y . . . . . .Luke 22:26
y women as sisters . . . . . . .1 Tim 5:2
Likewise you y people . . . . .1 Pet 5:5

YOURS

all that I have are y. . . . . .1 Kin 20:4
the battle is not y . . . . . .2 Chr 20:15
I am Y . . . . .Ps 119:94
Y is the kingdom . . . . . . .Matt 6:13
"Take what is y . . . . .Matt 20:14
y is the kingdom. . . . . . . .Luke 6:20
And all Mine are Y . . . . .John 17:10
For all things are y . . . . . .1 Cor 3:21

for I do not seek y . . . . . .2 Cor 12:14

YOUTH

for he was only a y . . . . .1 Sam 17:42
the LORD from my y . . . .1 Kin 18:12
the sins of my y . . . . .Ps 25:7
the companion of her y. . . .Prov 2:17
in the days of your y . . . . .Eccl 11:9
and y are vanity. . . . . . . .Eccl 11:10
the shame of your y . . . . . . .Is 54:4
speak, for I am a y . . . . .Jer 1:6
the kindness of your y . . . . .Jer 2:2
I have kept from my y. . .Matt 19:20
the flower of her y . . . . . . .1 Cor 7:36
no one despise your y. . . .1 Tim 4:12

YOUTHFUL

Flee also y lusts . . . . .2 Tim 2:22

YOUTHS

perceived among the y . . . . .Prov 7:7
y shall faint and be . . . . .Is 40:30

Z

ZEAL

The z of the LORD of . . . .2 Kin 19:31
z has consumed me. . . . . .Ps 119:139
He shall stir up His z . . . . . .Is 42:13
have spoken it in My z. . . .Ezek 5:13
for Zion with great z . . . . . .Zech 8:2
"Z for Your house has . . . .John 2:17
that they have a z . . . . .Rom 10:2
z has stirred up the . . . . . . .2 Cor 9:2

ZEALOUS

"I have been very z . . . . .1 Kin 19:10
'I am z for Zion with. . . . . .Zech 8:2
since you are z . . . . .1 Cor 14:12
But it is good to be z . . . . . .Gal 4:18
z for good works. . . . . .Titus 2:14